ARCTIC OCEAN

Barents Sea
Kara Sea
Laptev Sea
East Siberian Sea
Novaya Zemlya
Severnaya Zemlya
New Siberian Is.
Wrangel I.
Arctic Circle

RUSSIA
Murmansk
Arkhangel
ST. PETERSBURG
MOSCOW
Perm
Yekaterinburg
Kazan
Samara
Saratov
Volgograd
Astrakhan
Salekhard
Norilsk
Verkhoyansk
Yakutsk
Magadan
Okhotsk
Tomsk
Krasnoyarsk
Omsk
Novosibirsk
Barnaul
Chelyabinsk
Irkutsk
Ulan Ude
Komsomolsk
Khabarovsk
Vladivostok
Petropavlovsk-Kamchatskiy
Sakhalin
Sea of Okhotsk
Bering Sea
International Date Line
Kuril Is.

FINLAND
SWEDEN
NORWAY
Oslo
Stockholm
Helsinki
Copenhagen
ESTONIA
LATVIA
LITH.
Minsk
BELARUS
Berlin
Prague
Warsaw
POLAND
Kiev
UKRAINE
Odessa
Brussels
PARIS
Vienna
Budapest
ROMANIA
Bucharest
Belgrade
BULGARIA
Sofia
ITALY
Rome
Naples
Milan
GREECE
Athens
ISTANBUL
Ankara
TURKEY
Izmir
Black Sea
Caspian Sea
GEORGIA
Tbilisi
Yerevan
AZER.
Baku
Mediterranean Sea
Tunis
TUNISIA
MALTA
Crete
CYPRUS
Tripoli
Benghazi

KAZAKSTAN
Astana
Karaganda
L. Balkhash
Almaty
UZBEKISTAN
KYRGYZSTAN
Bishkek
Samarkand
Tashkent
Dushanbe
TAJIKISTAN
TURKMENISTAN
Ashkhabad
Tabriz
TEHRAN
Mashhad
IRAN
Shiraz
Kabul
AFGHANISTAN
SYRIA
Damascus
Beirut
Baghdad
IRAQ
Jerusalem
Amman
JORDAN
KUWAIT
The Gulf
BAHRAIN
QATAR
Riyadh
SAUDI ARABIA
Mecca
Abu Dhabi
U.A.E.
Muscat
OMAN
Sana
YEMEN
Aden
G. of Aden
Red Sea

MONGOLIA
Ulan Bator
Ürümqi
CHINA
Harbin
Changchun
SHENYANG
BEIJING
TIANJIN
Dalian
Taiyuan
Lanzhou
Xi'an
Nanjing
Wuhan
SHANGHAI
Chengdu
CHONGQING
Lhasa
TIBET
Kunming
GUANGZHOU
Fuzhou
Macau
HONG KONG
Taipei
TAIWAN
Hainan
East China Sea
Ryukyu Is.
NORTH KOREA
Pyongyang
SEOUL
SOUTH KOREA
JAPAN
Sapporo
TŌKYŌ
Ōsaka
Kitakyushu

PAKISTAN
Islamabad
Lahore
KARACHI
DELHI
New Delhi
Kanpur
NEPAL
Katmandu
INDIA
Ahmadabad
MUMBAI (Bombay)
Nagpur
CALCUTTA
BANGLADESH
DHAKA
Hyderabad
Bangalore
CHENNAI (Madras)
Arabian Sea
Bay of Bengal
SRI LANKA
Colombo
Lakshadweep Is. (India)
Andaman Is. (India)
Nicobar Is. (India)
MALDIVES

BURMA MYANMAR
Rangoon
THAILAND
BANGKOK
Vientiane
Hanoi
VIETNAM
CAMBODIA
Phnom Penh
Ho Chi Minh City
South China Sea
MANILA
PHILIPPINES
MALAYSIA
Kuala Lumpur
PEN. MALAYSIA
SINGAPORE
SABAH
SARAWAK
BRUNEI
Medan
Sumatra
Borneo
Palembang
Banjarmasin
INDONESIA
JAKARTA
Bandung
Java
Surabaya
Ujung Pandang
IRIAN JAYA
Timor
Arafura Sea

PACIFIC OCEAN
Bonin Is. (Japan)
Volcano Is. (Japan)
Marcus I. (Japan)
Tropic of Cancer
Wake I. (U.S.A.)
NORTHERN MARIANAS (U.S.A.)
GUAM (U.S.A.)
Yap
PALAU
FEDERATED STATES OF MICRONESIA
Caroline Is.
Truk
Pohnpei
MARSHALL IS.
Gilbert Is.
NAURU
KIRIBATI
PAPUA NEW GUINEA
Port Moresby
New Ireland
New Britain
SOLOMON IS.
Santa Cruz I.
TUVALU
VANUATU
NEW CALEDONIA (Fr.)
FIJI
Suva

LIBYA
EGYPT
CAIRO
Alexandria
Aswân
NIGER
CHAD
L. Chad
Niamey
Kano
NIGERIA
Abuja
Ibadan
Lagos
Ndjamena
SUDAN
Khartoum
Omdurman
Asmara
ERITREA
DJIBOUTI
Addis Ababa
ETHIOPIA
SOMALI REP.
Mogadishu
CAMEROON
Douala
Yaoundé
CENTRAL AFRICAN REP.
Bangui
EQUATORIAL GUINEA
GABON
Libreville
CONGO
Brazzaville
CONGO (DEM. REP. OF THE)
Kinshasa
Kisangani
Kigali
RWANDA
BURUNDI
Bujumbura
UGANDA
Kampala
KENYA
L. Turkana
Nairobi
Mombasa
Dodoma
Zanzibar
Dar es Salaam
TANZANIA
L. Tanganyika
Kananga
CABINDA (Angola)
Luanda
ANGOLA
Benguela
Lubumbashi
ZAMBIA
Lusaka
Lilongwe
MALAWI
Harare
ZIMBABWE
MOZAMBIQUE
Bulawayo
NAMIBIA
Windhoek
BOTSWANA
Gaborone
Pretoria
Johannesburg
Maputo
SWAZILAND
LESOTHO
SOUTH AFRICA
Durban
Cape Town
C. of Good Hope
Port Elizabeth
Mozambique Channel
MADAGASCAR
Antananarivo
COMOROS
Mayotte (Fr.)
SEYCHELLES
Amirante Is.
Aldabra Is.
Agalega Is.
Cargados Carajos
Rodriguez
MAURITIUS
RÉUNION (Fr.)
Socotra (Yemen)

INDIAN OCEAN
Equator
Chagos Arch. (U.K.)
Diego Garcia
Cocos Is. (Austral.)
Christmas I. (Austral.)
Tropic of Capricorn
Amsterdam I. (Fr.)
St. Paul (Fr.)
Prince Edward Is. (S.Africa)
Crozet Is. (Fr.)
Kerguelen (Fr.)
McDonald Is. (Austral.)
Heard I. (Austral.)
Bouvet I. (Norw.)

AUSTRALIA
Darwin
Cairns
Townsville
Port Hedland
Alice Springs
Rockhampton
Geraldton
Brisbane
Perth
Fremantle
Kalgoorlie-Boulder
Great Australian Bight
Adelaide
Darling
Newcastle
Sydney
Canberra
Melbourne
Tasmania
Hobart
Lord Howe I. (Austral.)
Norfolk I. (Austral.)
Tasman Sea
NEW ZEALAND
North I.
Auckland
Wellington
South I.
Christchurch
Dunedin
Stewart I.
Bounty Is. (N.Z.)
Antipodes Is.
Auckland Is. (N.Z.)
Campbell I. (N.Z.)
Macquarie Is. (Austral.)

ANTARCTIC OCEAN
Antarctic Circle
Antarctica
Ross Sea

East from Greenwich
Capital Cities

PHILIP'S

# Millennium ENCYCLOPEDIA & World Atlas

PHILIP'S

# Millennium ENCYCLOPEDIA & World Atlas

First published in Great Britain as
*The Philip's World Atlas and Encyclopedia by*

George Philip Limited,
an imprint of Octopus Publishing Group
2–4 Heron Quays
Docklands
London
E14 4JP



This edition produced for Borders, 1999

EDITOR Steve Luck

ART EDITOR Mike Brown

TEXT EDITORS Chris Humphries
Frances Adlington

CARTOGRAPHY BY Philip's

PRODUCTION Gudrun Hughes
Sally Banner

Reproduction by Colourpath Ltd, London

ISBN 0 540 07828 X



Library of Congress Cataloging-in-Publication Data available

Printed by Cayfosa, Spain

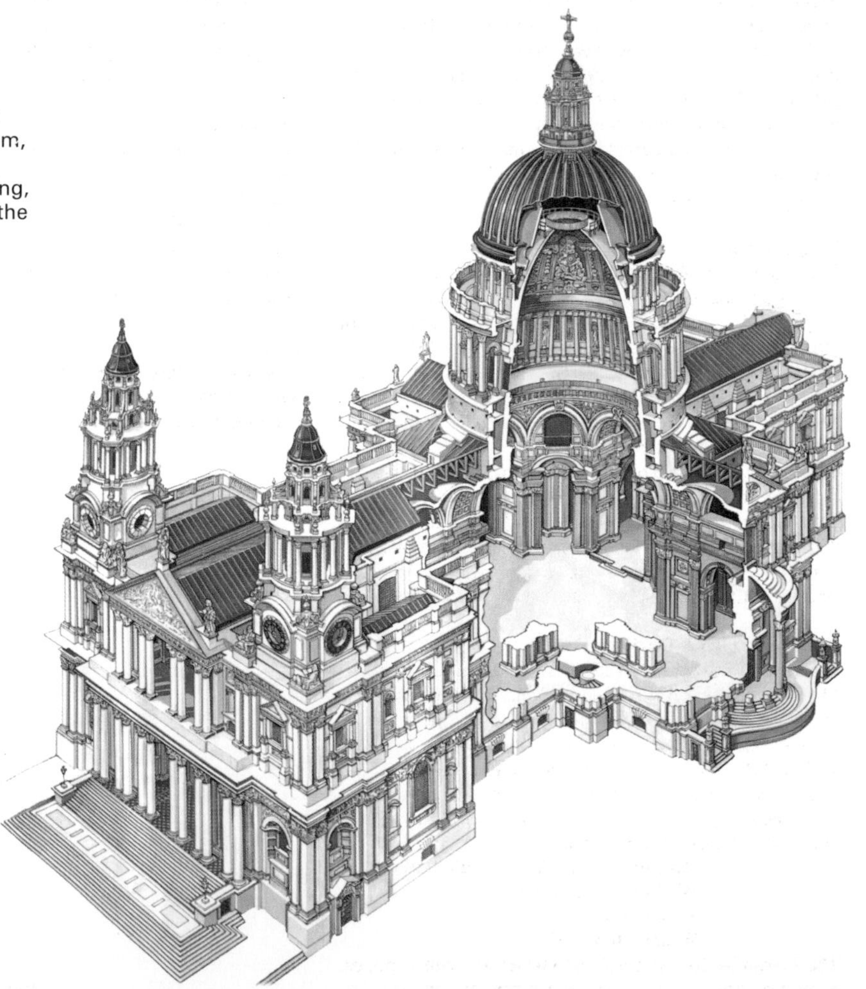

► **St Paul's Cathedral**

# PREFACE

The *Philip's Millennium Encyclopedia & World Atlas* is a unique concept in reference publishing, combining a comprehensive 96-page world atlas and 35,000 place name index with a detailed and colorful reference encyclopedia. Together they create an authoritative but stimulating reference source for everyday family use – as a study aid for school students, a first stop for general enquiries and puzzle answers, and a treasure-trove for browsers. The alphabetically organized Encyclopedia entries provide clear, essential information on a vast variety of subjects, from world affairs to science and the arts. The wealth of color illustrations, including maps, photographs, technological "cutaways" and artwork conveys visual information far beyond the descriptive power of many thousands of words.

When choosing a single-volume encyclopedia, the most important consideration for the user is the criteria by which the articles have been selected. The *Millennium Encyclopedia & World Atlas* has been created with school and college students particularly in mind. Core subjects (science and technology, English, history, contemporary politics, and the humanities) have been given the greatest attention. The articles, compatible with and complementary to what is learned in the classroom, are as up-to-date as possible, and have been written with exceptional clarity so that even complex concepts can be understood by readers as young as thirteen or fourteen.

An encyclopedia, however, must contain more than just a comprehensive coverage of core subjects. Equally full in their treatment are the articles that cover leisure interests, such as sports and popular music, animals and plants, movies, and current affairs, making this encyclopedia ideal for home reference as well as an important resource at school or college.

**World Atlas**

Created by Philip's renowned cartographers, the 96-page atlas section features up-to-date, newly digitized mapping that provides a stunning visual impression of the Earth's surface. Place names for which there is an article in the Encyclopedia section appear in bold within the 35,000 entry index.

## Cross References

The Encyclopedia also has more than 35,000 individual cross references, indicated by SMALL CAPITAL letters, that take readers from the primary article to all other articles that provide useful related information. For example, contained within the "pancreas" article are cross-references to small intestine, amylase, trypsin, insulin, and diabetes.

## Alphabetical Order

The order of articles is strictly alphabetical, except that Mc is treated as if it were spelled Mac, and abbreviations as if spelled out in full, thus St is treated as Saint. Articles that have more than one word in the heading, such as "Panama Canal", are ordered as if there were no space between the words. Articles that share the same main heading follow the basic hierarchy of people, places and things – for example:

Washington, Booker T. (Taliaferro)
Washington, George
Washington
Washington, D.C.

The hierarchy for biographical entries is: saints, popes, emperors, kings and queens, other royalty, non-royalty. However, when popes, emperors, and monarchs share the same name, they are collected together by country and then follow in chronological order. Thus Henry I, Henry II, Henry III, etc. (of England) are grouped together, followed by Henry II, Henry III, Henry IV (of France).

Places that share a name are ordered by the alphabetical order of the country. Within the US places with the same name are ordered by State. Foreign place names have been anglicized, with the local spelling in parenthesis, for example, Florence (Firenze); Moscow (Moskva).

## Alternative Spellings

For Chinese spellings the Pinyin system of transliteration is generally preferred, with cross-references to the Wade-Giles system where appropriate; for example, Peking *See* Beijing. Wade-Giles transliterations have also been retained where they remain in common use; for example, Chiang Kai-shek.

Alternative spellings and names of article titles follow the article title in parenthesis; for example, Dalai Lama (Grand Lama).

## International Coverage

The importance of cultures beyond the English-speaking world is deliberately emphasized. In an age when international barriers are being steadily removed, the *Millennium Encyclopedia & World Atlas* provides a greater proportion of entries on peoples, cultures, religions, and beliefs than any other single-volume encyclopedia.

## Science

In keeping with the conventions used in schools and colleges, modern scientific names have been used. For example, information on "acetaldehyde" will be found under "ethanal". Where the modern name used in the article title is less well known than the old name, a cross reference will be found under the old name directing readers to the article; for example, readers looking up formic acid will be directed to the article with the title methanoic acid.

American measurement units have been used throughout with corresponding metric measurements following in parenthesis.

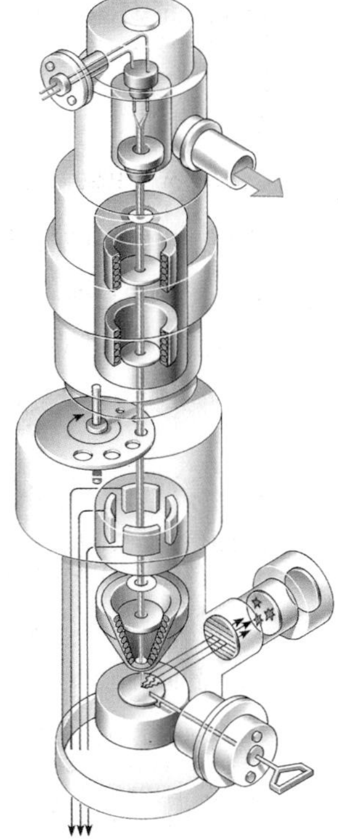

▲ electron microscope

► Toco toucan

# CONSULTANTS

**Anatomy/ Dentistry**
Prof. A.E. Walsby *University of Bristol*
**Animals and Agriculture**
Prof. K. Simkiss *University of Reading*
**Archaeology**
David Miles *Director of The Oxford Archaeological Unit*
**Art**
Prof. Martin Pitts *Middlesex University*
**Aviation**
Dr I. Hall *Victoria University of Manchester*
**Biology**
Prof. T. Halliday *Open University*
**Botany**
Prof. A.E. Walsby *University of Bristol*
**Chemistry**
Dr A.S. Bailey *University of Oxford*
**Earth Sciences/ Atmospheric Sciences/ Geology**
Prof. Michael Tooley *University of St Andrews*
**Economics**
Prof. A. Thirlwall
*University of Kent at Canterbury*
**Education**
Dr Charles Beresford *(Institute of Education) University College London*
**History (to 1300)**
Dr P.J. Heather *University College London*
**History (1301 to present)**
Dr Rick Halpern *University College London*
Dr Jonathan Morris *University College London*
**Language**
Prof. Richard Coates *University of Sussex*
**Literature/ Drama**
Dr Mary Peace
*Roehampton Institute, London*
**Mathematics**
Dr Jan Brandts *University of Bristol*
**Medicine**
Prof. S.L. Lightman *University of Bristol*
**Motion Pictures/ Media and Publishing/ Television and Radio/ Communications**
Uma Dinsmore *Goldsmiths College, London*
**Music**
Dr Derrick Puffett *University of Cambridge*
**Mythology**
Dr Allan Griffiths *University College London*
**Philosophy/ Computing**
Prof. Ron Chrisley *University of Sussex*
**Physics**
Prof. John Gribbin *University of Sussex*
**Politics**
Prof. Brian Barry *London School of Economics and Political Science*
**Psychology/ Psychiatry**
Prof. Margaret Boden *University of Sussex*
**Religion**
Prof. Colin Gunton *Kings College London*
**Sport**
Bob Peach *The Sports Council*
**Technology and Industrial Processes/ Engineering/ Material Science**
Dr P.L. Domone *University College London*

# EDITORIAL CREDITS

Jane Alden
Peter Astley
Jill Bailey
John Bailie
Richard Bird
Richard Brzezinski
Ian Chilvers
Roy Carr
John O.E. Clark
Sean Connolly
Peter Cowie
Mike Darton
Stephanie Driver
Harry Drost
Roger Few
William Gould
Neil Grant
Miles Gregory
Clare Haworth-Maden
Tony Holmes
William Houston
Elisabeth Ingles
Caroline Juler
Louise B. Lang
Jacqueline Lewis
Keith Lye
Angela Mackworth-Young
Judith Millidge
Eddie Mizzi
Paulette Pratt
Jenny Roberts
A.T.H. Rowland-Entwistle
Tom Ruppel
Jennifer Story
Clint Twist
Neil Wenborn
Keith Wicks
Richard Widdows
John D. Wright
Richard Wright
Iain Zaczek

**Curriculum consultants**
Duncan Hawley
David J. McHugh
Silvia Newton
Brian Speed
Jane Wheatley

# PICTURE CREDITS

**Bridgeman Art Library** /Belvoir Castle, Leicestershire 315, /British Museum, London 513 top right, /Christie's, London 699 bottom, /Crown Estate, Institute of Directors, London 216 bottom right, /Fitzwilliam Museum, University of Cambridge 643, 715 top, /Giraudon /Louvre, Paris 156 top, /Glasgow Art Gallery and Museum 201, /Guildhall Art Gallery, Corporation of London 472 bottom right, /Guildhall Library, Corporation of London 468, /Historisches Museum der Stadt, Vienna 75, /Index /Prado, Madrid 96 bottom right, 219 /Index /Private Collection / © Demart Pro Arte BV/DACS 1997, 196 bottom right, /Kunsthistorisches Museum,Vienna 125, /Art Institute of Chicago, USA 21, /Philip Mould, Historical Portraits Ltd, London 231 bottom right, 651 top right, /Musee d'Orsay, Paris 565 right, /Musee de la Tapisserie, Bayeux, with special authorisation of the city of Bayeux /Giraudon 72, /Nasjonalgalleriet, Oslo/The Munch Museum/The Munch-Ellingsen Group/DACS 1997 463 bottom, /National Museum of Wales, Cardiff 142, /National Palace, Mexico City 571 bottom right, /Novosti 393 top right, /Palazzo Medici-Riccardi, Florence 437, /Private Collection/ARS, NY and DACS, London 1997 2, 306, 452 top left, /Rafael Valls Gallery, London 531 right, /Schloss Immendorf, Austria 375, /Solomon R Guggenheim Museum, New York/ADAGP, Paris and DACS, London 1997 367, /Tate Gallery, London 577, /The Trustees of the Weston Park Foundation 321, /Vatican Museums and Galleries, Rome 443, /Wilhelm Lehmbruck Museum, Duisburg 484 bottom left.
**Hulton Getty Picture Collection** 79, 89, 92, 130, 144,145 bottom right, 158, 180 bottom right, 193 top right, 203 top left, 211 top right, 220 top left, 227 top right, 234, 238, 249 top right, 269, 275, 293 top right, 301 top right, 314 top left, 328 top left, 334 bottom left, 364, 369, 373 bottom right, 382, 383, 400 left of centre, 431 top right, 439 top right, 440 top left, 457 bottom right, 480 top left, 495 bottom right, 502 top left, 509 top right, 514, 542 left, 548 top left, 550 top left, 552 top left, 582, 587 bottom right, 591, 598 top left, 608, 641 bottom, 673 top right, 724, 725, 730, 735 top, 744.
**Picture Bank** 4, 16 bottom, 26 bottom, 256 bottom left, 460, 479 top right, 479 bottom right, 503 bottom left, 552 bottom left, 638 top left, 641 top, 655 top right, 675.
**Rex Features** 24, 26 top right, 73, 80, 154, 168 right of centre, 181, 184 top left, 203 bottom right, 207, 247, 255 bottom right, 263 bottom, 273 right of centre, 277, 284 top left, 291, 307, 311 bottom, 311 top right, 312 top left, 314 bottom, 319, 320 bottom, 355 right of centre, 360, 370, 385 top left, 390, 395 bottom, 419 bottom right, 420 left of centre, 433, 456, 522 top right, 527 left, 562 top right, 569 bottom right, 573 top right, 579 bottom right, 601, 605, 609 top right, 613 bottom right, 634 top left, 638 bottom, 648 bottom left, 659 bottom right, 663 bottom right, 700, 714 bottom, 735 bottom, /Action Press 519 top right, /Stephen Barker 18, /Michel Boudin 112 top, /Mark Brewer 305 top right, /Peter Brooker 261 bottom left, /Paul Brown 322 top, /Julian Calder 666, /David Cole 200, /Frederick de Klerk 425 right of centre, /Delahaye 138, /Demulder 34, /Doc Pele 392 top left, /Farnood 557 bottom right, /Fotex /Zone 5 199 top right, /Richard Gardner 217, /Gilson 489, /Grande 276 top left, /Chris Harris 685 bottom right, /David Hartley 164 top, /Percy Hatchman 719, /Peter Heimsath 39 bottom right, /Nils Jorgensen 88 bottom, /JSU/Sutton-Hibert 543, /Charles Knight 621 bottom right, /Dave Lewis 297, 479 centre right, /Miladinovic 310 left of centre, /NASA 327, /Rangefinders 350, /Larry Reider 135 bottom right, /Lehtikuva Oy 629/Tim Rooke 292 above centre, 588, /Setboun 330 top left, /Sichov 374 bottom, 623, /Sipa Press 57 top right, 143, 157 top, 170, 177 bottom right, 203 top right, 222 top left, 259 bottom, 330 bottom left, 344, 409, 469 bottom right, 491, 570 bottom left, /Stills 406, /SUU/Joffet 103 top, /Today 386, /Trippett 556, 561 bottom right, /Scott Wachter 362, /Gerry Whitmont 245, /Geoff Wilkinson 596, /Richard Young 417, 696 bottom.
**Science Photo Library** 732, /CERN, P. Loiex 110.
**Front Jacket**: bottom right: Rex Features/David Hartley
**Technology Illustrations** Ted McCausland

# WORLD MAPS

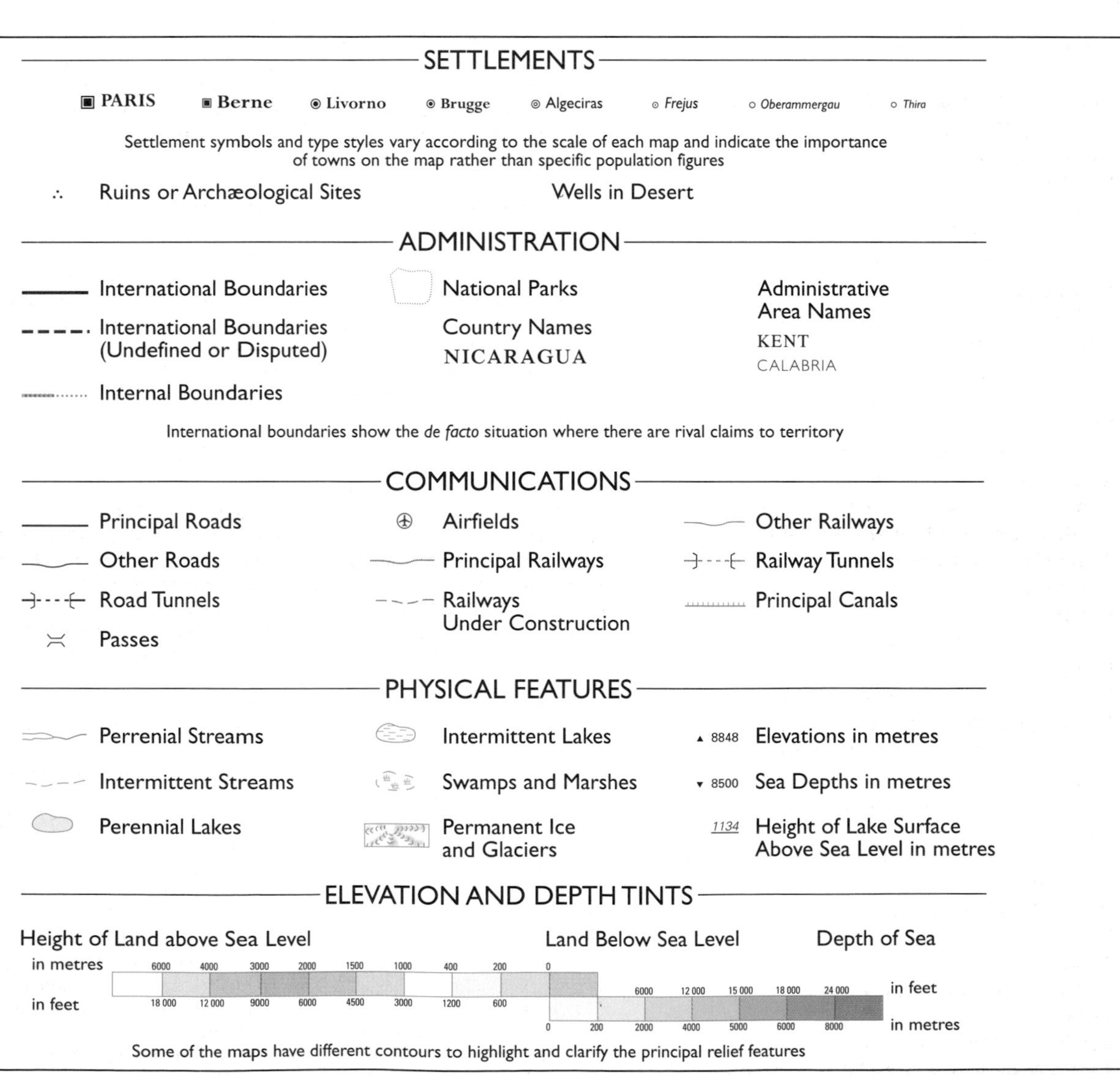
SETTLEMENTS
PARIS
Berne
Livorno
Brugge
Algeciras
Frejus
Oberammergau
Thira
Settlement symbols and type styles vary according to the scale of each map and indicate the importance of towns on the map rather than specific population figures
Ruins or Archæological Sites
Wells in Desert
ADMINISTRATION
International Boundaries
International Boundaries (Undefined or Disputed)
Internal Boundaries
National Parks
Country Names
NICARAGUA
Administrative Area Names
KENT
CALABRIA
International boundaries show the de facto situation where there are rival claims to territory
COMMUNICATIONS
Principal Roads
Other Roads
Road Tunnels
Passes
Airfields
Principal Railways
Railways Under Construction
Other Railways
Railway Tunnels
Principal Canals
PHYSICAL FEATURES
Perrenial Streams
Intermittent Streams
Perennial Lakes
Intermittent Lakes
Swamps and Marshes
Permanent Ice and Glaciers
8848 Elevations in metres
8500 Sea Depths in metres
1134 Height of Lake Surface Above Sea Level in metres
ELEVATION AND DEPTH TINTS
Height of Land above Sea Level
in metres
6000
4000
3000
2000
1500
1000
400
200
0
in feet
18 000
12 000
9000
6000
4500
3000
1200
600
Land Below Sea Level
Depth of Sea
in feet
6000
12 000
15 000
18 000
24 000
in metres
0
200
2000
4000
5000
6000
8000
Some of the maps have different contours to highlight and clarify the principal relief features

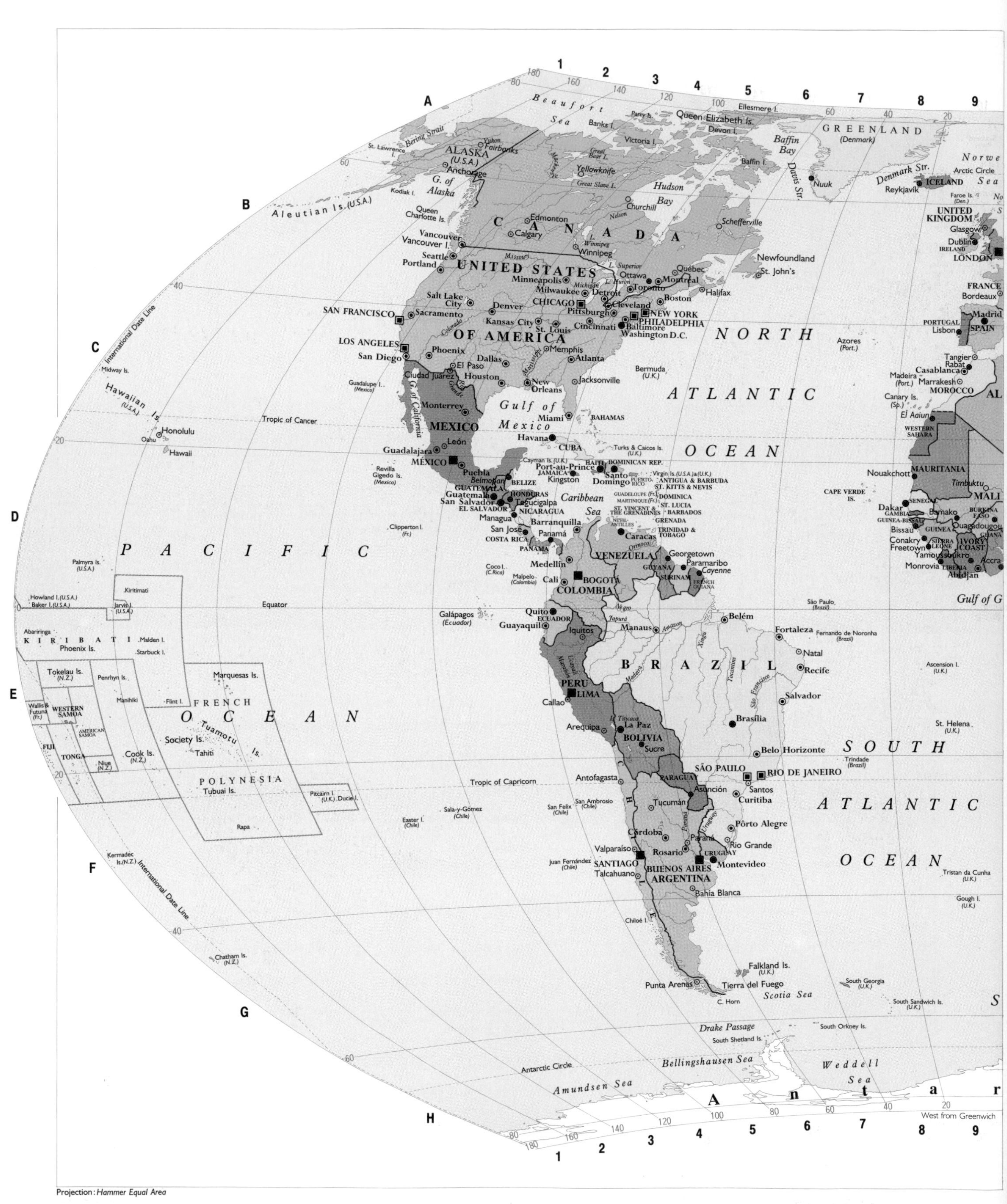


Projection: *Hammer Equal Area*

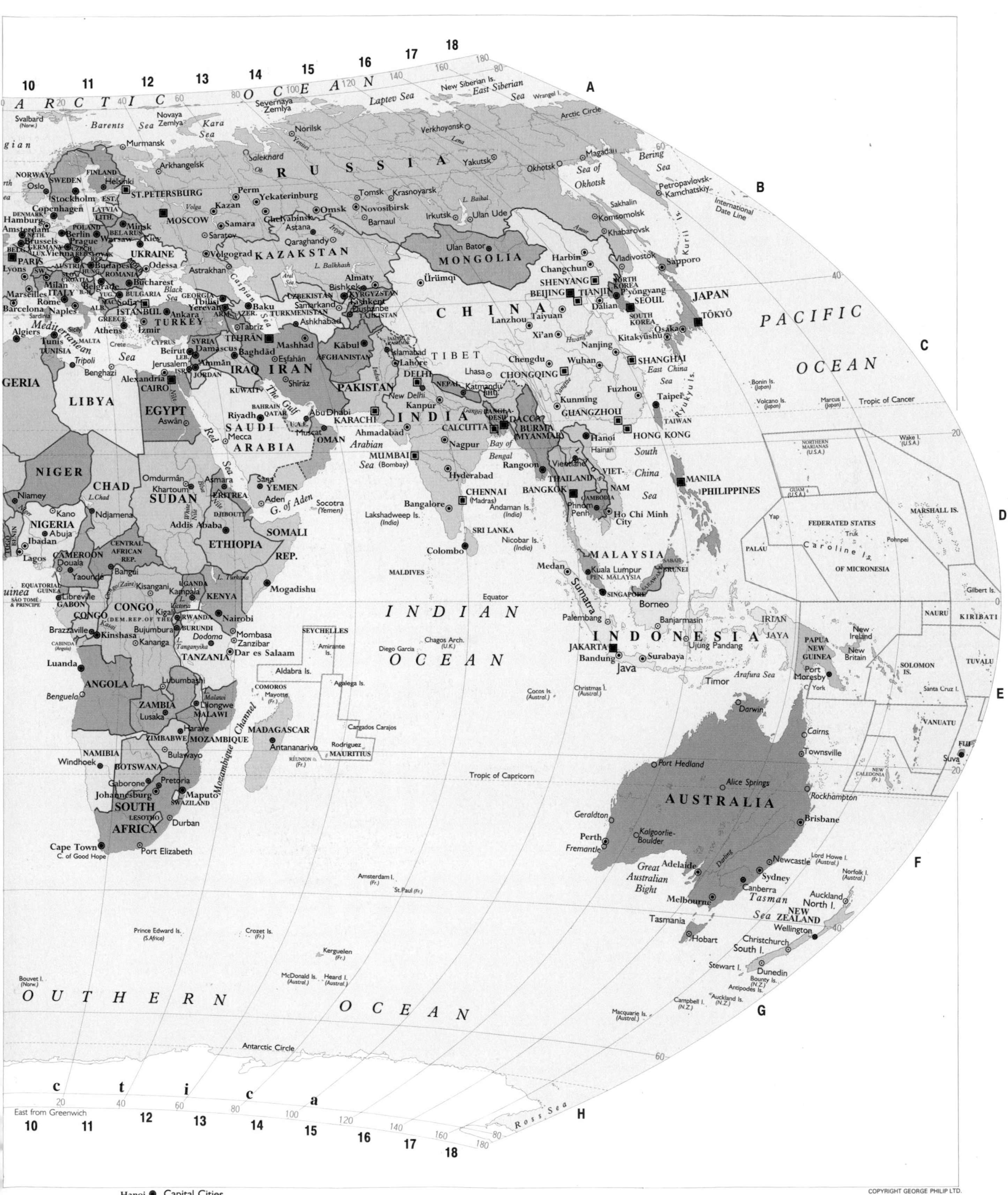


Hanoi ● Capital Cities

100 0 200 400 600 800 1000 1200 1400 km
100 0 200 400 600 800 1000 miles
PACIFIC OCEAN
Aleutian Islands (U.S.A.)
Near Is. (U.S.A.)
JAPAN
Hokkaidō
Kurilskiye Ostrova (Russia)
La Perouse Str.
Mys Lopatka
Dutch Harbor
Unimak I.
Bering Sea
Komandorskiye Ostrova
Petropavlovsk Kamchatskiy
Gora Klyuchevskaya 4850
Poluostrov Kamchatka
Sakhalin (Russia)
Sakhalinskiy Zaliv
Vanino
Sea of Okhotsk
Pribilof Is. (U.S.A.)
Bristol Bay
Alaska Pen.
Kodiak I.
St. Matthew (U.S.A.)
Mys Olyutorskiy
Ostrov Karaginskiy
Mys Navarin
Nunivak
St. Lawrence I. (U.S.A.)
Anadyrskiy Zaliv
Anadyr
Penzhino
Penzhinskaya G.
Gizhiginskaya Guba
Amur
Khabarovsk
Nikolayevsk
Ulbanskiy Zaliv
Udskaya Guba
Tauiskaya Guba
G. of Alaska
Seward
Prince William Sd.
Cook Inlet
Anchorage
Cordova
Mt. McKinley 6194
Mt. St. Elias 5489
Mt. Logan 6050
Prince Rupert
Skeena
Skagway
Whitehorse
Fairbanks
ALASKA (U.S.A.)
Yukon
Kuskokwim
Norton Sd.
Nome
Bering Str.
C. Prince of Wales
Kotzebue Sd.
Mys Dezhneva
Chukotskoye Nagorye
Kolymskoye Nagorye
Okhotsk
Stanovoy Khrebet
Aldan
Noatak
Koyukuk
Pt. Hope
C. Lisburne
Proliv Longa
Chukchi Sea
Ostrov Vrangelya (Russia)
Chaunskaya G.
Nizhne Kolymsk
Omolon
Kolyma
Srednekolymsk
Indigirka
Zashiversk
Yakutsk
Lena
Olekma
Verkhoyansk
Verkhoyanskiy Khrebet
Rocky Mountains
Dawson Creek
Dawson
Fort Yukon
Porcupine
Stewart
Peel
Prudhoe Bay
Pt. Barrow
C. Halkett
Harrison Bay
Fort McPherson
Herschel I.
Fort Simpson
Liard
Mackenzie
Fort Good Hope
Mackenzie Bay
Beaufort Sea
Russkoye Ustie
Novosibirskiye Ostrova
Lyakhovskiye Ostrova
Kazachye
Yana
Zhigansk
Vilyuy
Fort Vermilion
Peace
Tulita
Great Bear Lake
NORTH AMERICA
Athabasca
Athabasca Lake
Yellowknife
Great Slave Lake
Coppermine
Kugluktuk
C. Bathurst
Canada Basin
ARCTIC OCEAN
Mendeleyev Ridge
O. Bennetta (Russia)
O. Kotelnyy
Bulun
Tiksi
Olenek
C. Kellett
Banks I.
C. Prince Alfred
Dolphin & Union Sd.
Prince Albert Pen.
Wollaston Pen.
Coronation G.
Victoria Island
M'Clure Str.
Prince Patrick I.
Melville I.
Viscount Melville Sd.
Laptev Sea
Anabar
Nordvik
Ostrova Petra
Poluostrov Taymyr
Khatanga
Kotuy
Ozero Taymyr
Gory Putorana
Nizhnyaya Tunguska
Podkamennaya Tunguska
Parry Is.
Borden I.
M'Clintock Chan.
King William I.
Chesterfield Inlet
Back
Prince of Wales I.
Bathurst I.
North Magnetic Pole 1990
Ellef Ringnes I.
Sverdrup Is.
Boothia Pen.
Somerset I.
Barrow Str.
Alpha Cordillera
Makarov Basin
Lomonosov Ridge
NORTH POLE
Fram Basin
Nansen Cordillera
Severnaya Zemlya
O. Oktyabrskoy Revolyutsii
Hudson Bay
Roes Welcome Sd.
Gulf of Boothia
Prince Regent Inlet
Lancaster Sd.
Devon I.
Jones Sound
Axel Heiberg I.
Nansen Sd.
Eureka
Ellesmere I. (Canada)
C. Columbia
Lincoln Sea
Pyasina
Norilsk
Dudinka
Igarka
Yenisey
O. Uedineniya
O. Vise
O. Ushakova
Golchikha
Southampton I.
Coats I.
Melville Pen.
Foxe Chan.
Foxe Basin
Fury & Hecla Str.
Bylot I.
Smith Sund
Qaanaaq
Kane Basin
Robeson Chan.
Alert
Nansen Basin
Zemlya Frantsa Iosifa
O. Graham Bell
Z. Vilcheka
O. Belyy
Urengoy
Taz
Mansel I.
Prince Charles I.
Uummannaq
K. York
Sermersuaq
Knud Rasmussen Land
Peary Land
K. Morris Jesup
McKinley Sea
Z. Aleksandry (Russia)
Poluostrov Yamal
Novyy Port
Nadym
C. Wolstenholme
Nettilling L.
Baffin I.
Baffin Bay
Independence Fjord
Kong Frederik VIII.s Land
Nordkapp
Nordaustlandet
Novaya Zemlya
Kara Sea
Baydaratskaya Guba
Surgut
Hudson Str.
Feuilles
Iqaluit
Frobisher B.
Cumberland Sd.
Ungava Bay
C. Dyer
Upernavik
Vestspitsbergen
Svalbard (Norway)
Longyearbyen
Edgeøya
Barents Sea
Vorkuta
Salekhard
Khabarovo
Ob
Berezovo
Tobolsk
Narodnaya 1894
Resolution I.
Davis Str.
Qeqertarsuaq
GREENLAND (Denmark)
KALAALLIT NUNAAT
Kong Frederik IX.s Land
Kong Christian X.s Land
Greenland Sea
O. Kolguyev
Mys Kanin Nos
Pechora
Uralskie Gory
YEKATERINBURG
PERM
Labrador
Chidley
Nuuk
Bjørnøya
Vardø
Varangerfjorden
Kong Franz Joseph Fd.
Kong Oscar Fjord
Ittoqqortoormiit
Paamiut
Mt. Forel 3360
Kong Christian IX.s Land
Gunnbjørn Fjeld 3700
Kap Brewster
Jan Mayen (Norway)
Nordkapp
Hammerfest
Murmansk
Kolskiy Poluostrov
Mezen
Beloye More
Arkhangelsk
Hamilton Inlet
Qaqortoq
Alluitsup Paa
Kong Frederik VI.s Kyst
Ammassalik
Iceland Plateau
Tromsø
Lofoten
Sev. Dvina
UFA
Kap Farvel (Nunap Isua)
Denmark Str.
Horn
Breiðafjörður
Fontur
Norwegian Sea
Arctic Circle
Tornio
Onega
Onezhskoye Ozero
SAMARA
Reykjavík
ICELAND
Öræfajökull 2119
FINLAND
Gulf of Bothnia
Ladozhskoye Ozero
Volga
Mid-Atlantic Ridge
Trondheim
Helsinki
ST. PETERBURG
Gulf of Finland
Tallinn
EST.
MOSKVA
Saratov
Føroyar (Den.)
NORWAY
SWEDEN
STOCKHOLM
Chudskoye Ozero
VOLGOGRAD
Shetland Is. (U.K.)
Bergen
Oslo
Baltic Sea
LAT.
Riga
LITH.
Vilnius
BELARUS
RUSSIA
ATLANTIC OCEAN
Rockall (U.K.)
Hebrides (U.K.)
Orkney Is. (U.K.)
Skagerrak
Kaliningrad
KYYIV
ROSTOV
UNITED KINGDOM
SCOTLAND
Edinburgh
North Sea
KØBENHAVN
DENMARK
Wisla
WARSZAWA
UKRAINE
Belfast
Dublin
IRELAND
ENGLAND
WALES
HAMBURG
Elbe
BERLIN
POLAND
EUROPE
ODESA
Black Sea
C. Clear
AMSTERDAM
NETH.
GERMANY
LONDON
PRAHA
Maximum extent of sea ice
Summer extent of sea ice
Ice caps and permanent ice shelf
Projection : Zenithal Equidistant
West from Greenwich
East from Greenwich
COPYRIGHT GEORGE PHILIP LTD

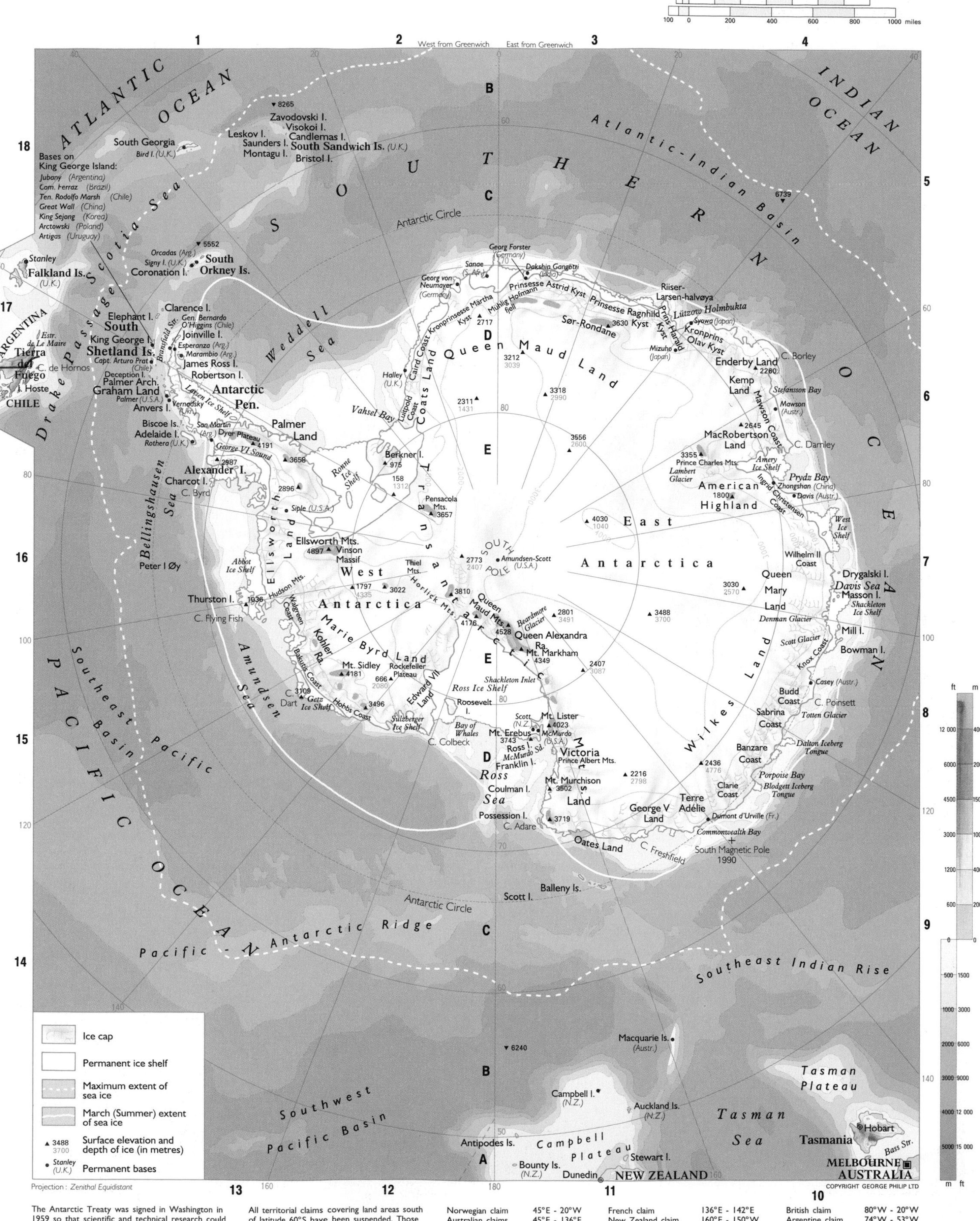




The Antarctic Treaty was signed in Washington in 1959 so that scientific and technical research could continue unhampered by international politics.

All territorial claims covering land areas south of latitude 60°S have been suspended. Those claims were:

| | | | | | |
|---|---|---|---|---|---|
| Norwegian claim | 45°E - 20°W | French claim | 136°E - 142°E | British claim | 80°W - 20°W |
| Australian claims | 45°E - 136°E | New Zealand claim | 160°E - 150°W | Argentine claim | 74°W - 53°W |
| | 142°E - 160°E | Chilean claim | 90°W - 53°W | | |

# EUROPE : Physical

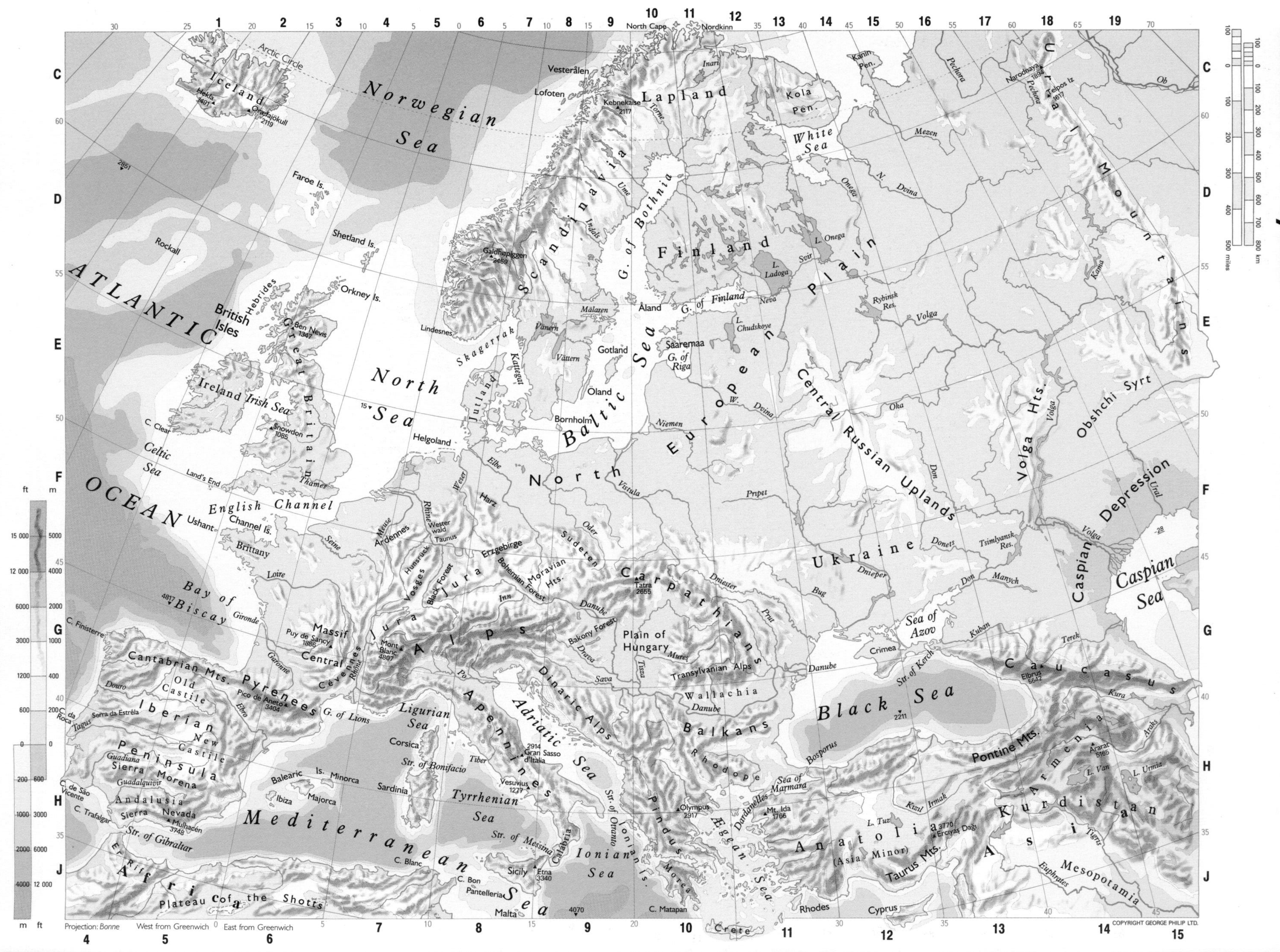

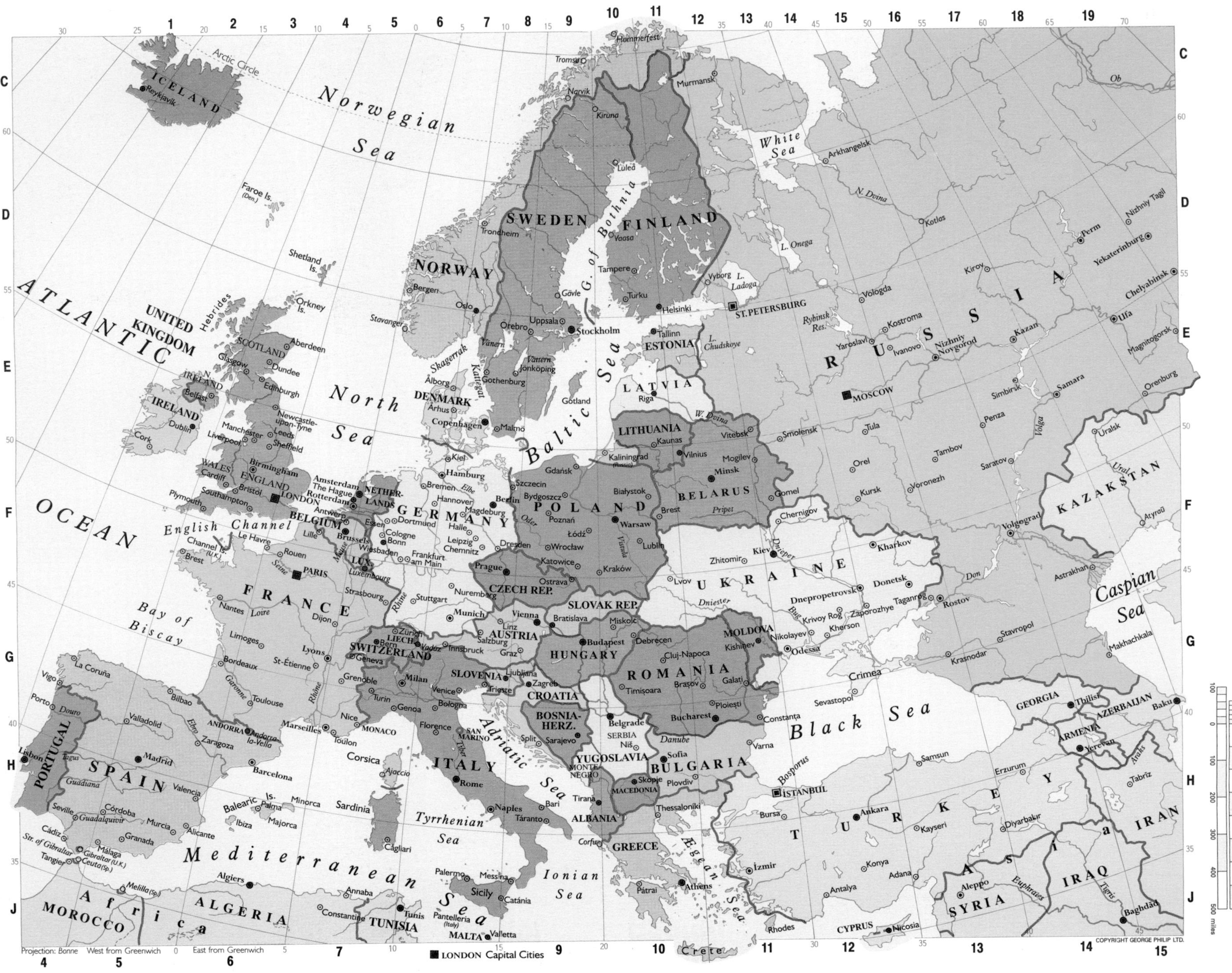

100 0 100 200 300 400 500 600 700 800 km
100 0 100 200 300 400 500 miles
Norwegian Sea
North Sea
Baltic Sea
G. of Bothnia
White Sea
ATLANTIC OCEAN
Bay of Biscay
English Channel
Mediterranean Sea
Tyrrhenian Sea
Adriatic Sea
Ionian Sea
Ægean Sea
Black Sea
Caspian Sea
ICELAND
UNITED KINGDOM
IRELAND
NORWAY
SWEDEN
FINLAND
DENMARK
ESTONIA
LATVIA
LITHUANIA
BELARUS
POLAND
GERMANY
NETHER-LANDS
BELGIUM
LUX.
FRANCE
SWITZERLAND
LIECH.
AUSTRIA
CZECH REP.
SLOVAK REP.
HUNGARY
SLOVENIA
CROATIA
BOSNIA-HERZ.
YUGOSLAVIA
SERBIA
MONTENEGRO
ALBANIA
MACEDONIA
GREECE
BULGARIA
ROMANIA
MOLDOVA
UKRAINE
RUSSIA
KAZAKSTAN
GEORGIA
ARMENIA
AZERBAIJAN
TURKEY
CYPRUS
SYRIA
IRAQ
IRAN
ITALY
SAN MARINO
MALTA
SPAIN
PORTUGAL
ANDORRA
MONACO
MOROCCO
ALGERIA
TUNISIA
Africa
LONDON
PARIS
MOSCOW
ST. PETERSBURG
ISTANBUL
■ LONDON Capital Cities
Projection: Bonne
West from Greenwich
East from Greenwich
COPYRIGHT GEORGE PHILIP LTD.

# SCANDINAVIA

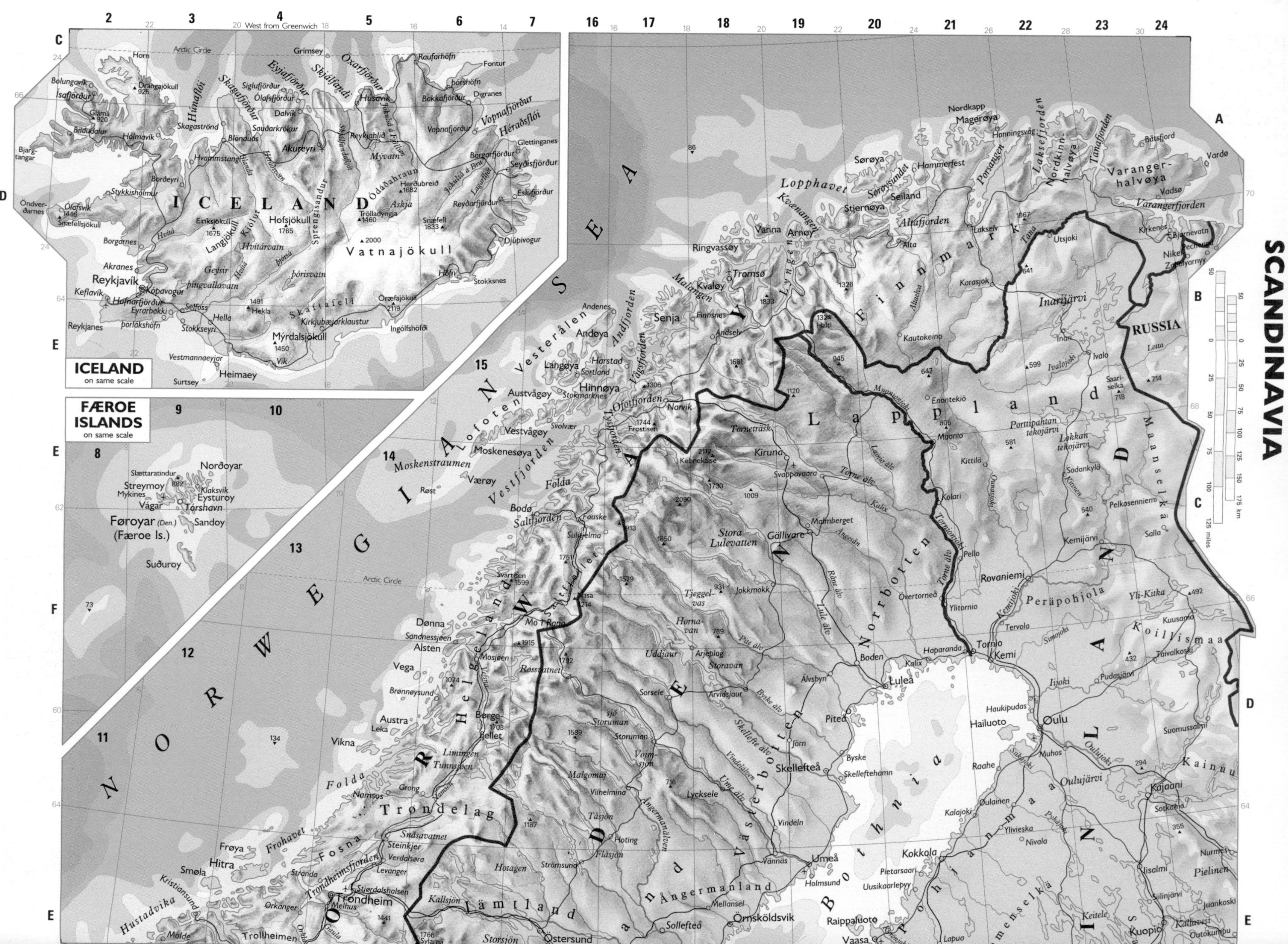

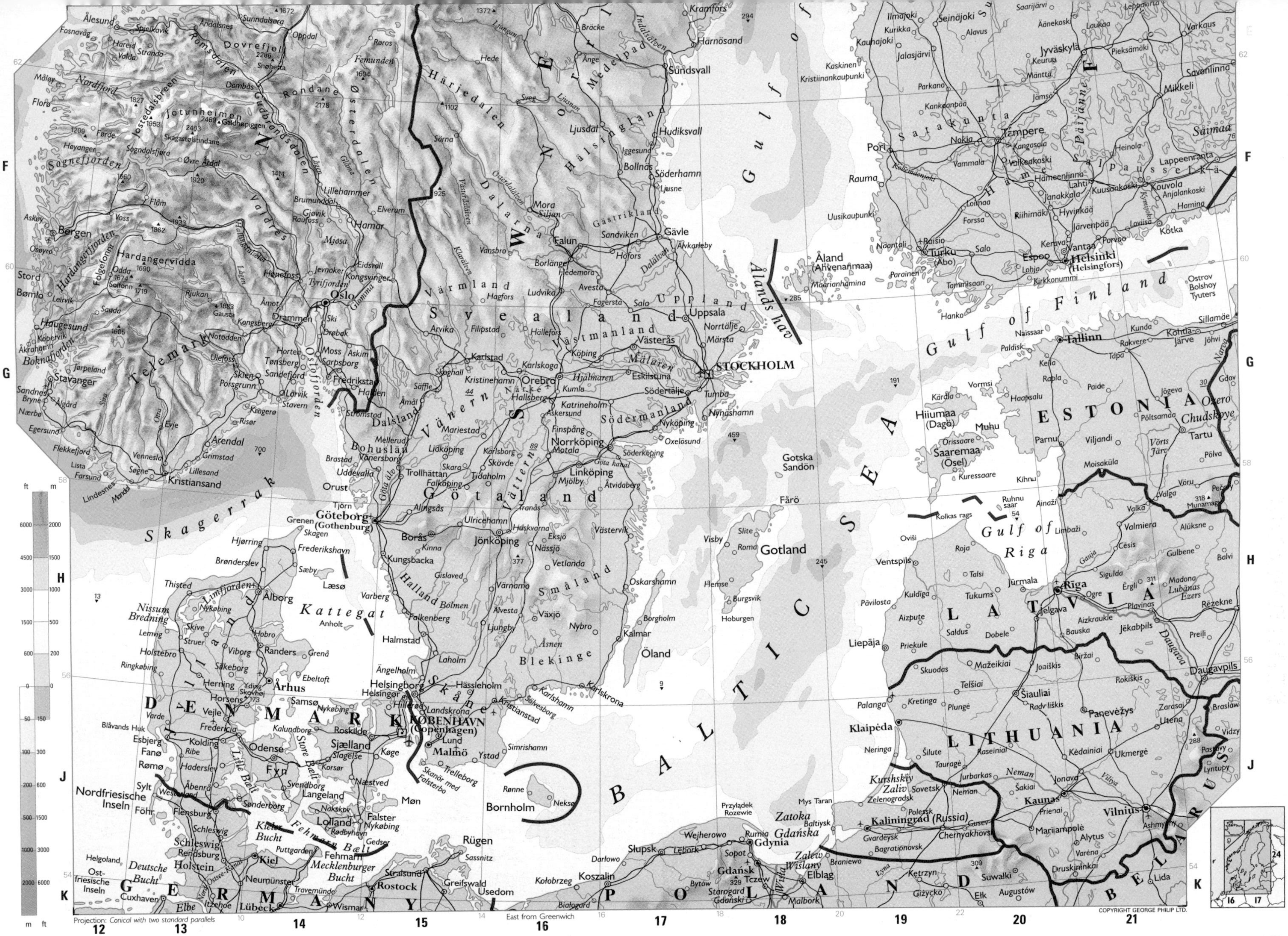

Skagerrak
Kattegat
BALTIC SEA
Gulf of Bothnia
Gulf of Finland
Gulf of Riga
Ålands hav
NORWAY
SWEDEN
FINLAND
ESTONIA
LATVIA
LITHUANIA
DENMARK
GERMANY
POLAND
BELARUS
STOCKHOLM
Oslo
KØBENHAVN (Copenhagen)
Helsinki (Helsingfors)
Tallinn
Riga
Vilnius
Kaliningrad (Russia)
Göteborg (Gothenburg)
Gotland
Öland
Bornholm

m ft
2000 6000
1000 3000
500 1500
200 600
100 300
50 150
0 0
200 600
500 1500
1000 3000
2000 6000
ft m

Projection: Conical with two standard parallels

East from Greenwich

COPYRIGHT GEORGE PHILIP LTD.

Key to English unitary authorities on map.
25. HARTLEPOOL
26. DARLINGTON
27. STOCKTON-ON-TEES
28. MIDDLESBROUGH
29. REDCAR AND CLEVELAND
30. BLACKPOOL
31. BLACKBURN WITH DARWEN
32. HALTON
33. WARRINGTON
34. KINGSTON UPON HULL
35. NORTH EAST LINCOLNSHIRE
36. STOKE-ON-TRENT
37. TELFORD AND WREKIN
38. DERBY CITY
39. CITY OF NOTTINGHAM
40. LEICESTER CITY
41. RUTLAND
42. PETERBOROUGH
43. MILTON KEYNES
44. LUTON
45. NORTH SOMERSET
46. CITY OF BRISTOL
47. BATH AND NORTH EAST SOMERSET
48. SWINDON
49. READING
50. WOKINGHAM
51. WINDSOR AND MAIDENHEAD
52. SLOUGH
53. BRACKNELL FOREST
54. THURROCK
55. SOUTHEND-ON-SEA
56. MEDWAY TOWNS
57. PLYMOUTH
58. TORBAY
59. POOLE
60. BOURNEMOUTH
61. SOUTHAMPTON
62. PORTSMOUTH
63. BRIGHTON AND HOVE
Key to Welsh unitary authorities on map.
15. SWANSEA
16. NEATH PORT TALBOT
17. BRIDGEND
18. RHONDDA CYNON TAFF
19. MERTHYR TYDFIL
20. CAERPHILLY
21. BLAENAU GWENT
22. TORFAEN
23. CARDIFF
24. NEWPORT
NORTH SEA
IRISH SEA
North Channel
SCOTLAND
NORTHERN IRELAND
ISLE OF MAN
Edinburgh
Glasgow
Newcastle-upon-Tyne
Sunderland
Middlesbrough
Leeds
Bradford
Manchester
Liverpool
Sheffield
Kingston upon Hull
Nottingham
Derby
Stoke-on-Trent
Blackpool
Preston
York
Belfast

| ft | m |
| --- | --- |
| 3000 | 1000 |
| 1500 | 500 |
| 600 | 200 |
| 300 | 100 |
| 0 | 0 |
| 50 | 150 |
| 100 | 300 |
| 200 | 600 |
| m | ft |

WALES

ENGLAND

FRANCE

ENGLISH CHANNEL

Bristol Channel

Cardigan Bay

Carmarthen Bay

Lyme Bay

Thames Estuary

Strait of Dover

Baie de la Seine

Baie de la Somme

CHANNEL ISLANDS (U.K.)

Alderney

Guernsey

St. Peter Port

Herm

Sark

Jersey

St. Helier

ISLE OF WIGHT

CORNWALL

DEVON

DORSET

SOMERSET

WILTSHIRE

HANTS

SURREY

WEST SUSSEX

EAST SUSSEX

KENT

ESSEX

SUFFOLK

NORFOLK

CAMBRIDGE

NORTHAMPTON

BEDFORD

BUCKS

HERTS

OXFORD

WEST BERKSHIRE

GLOUCS

HEREFORD

WORCESTER

WARWICK

LEICESTER

SHROPSHIRE

POWYS

CEREDIGION

PEMBROKESHIRE

CARMARTHENSHIRE

VALE OF GLAMORGAN

MONMOUTHSHIRE

SEINE-MARITIME

HAUTE-NORMANDIE

CALVADOS

MANCHE

Cotentin

Bessin

Pays de Caux

LONDON

BIRMINGHAM

Bristol

Cardiff

Swansea

Plymouth

Southampton

Portsmouth

Bournemouth

Brighton

Oxford

Cambridge

Northampton

Leicester

Coventry

Peterborough

Ipswich

Reading

Le Havre

Rouen

Caen

Cherbourg

Dieppe

Calais

Boulogne-sur-Mer

## Isles of Scilly

On same scale

Tresco

Isles of Scilly

St. Mary's

Penzance

Newlyn

Land's End

St. Ives

Hayle

Camborne

Projection : Lambert's Conformal Conic

West from Greenwich

East from Greenwich

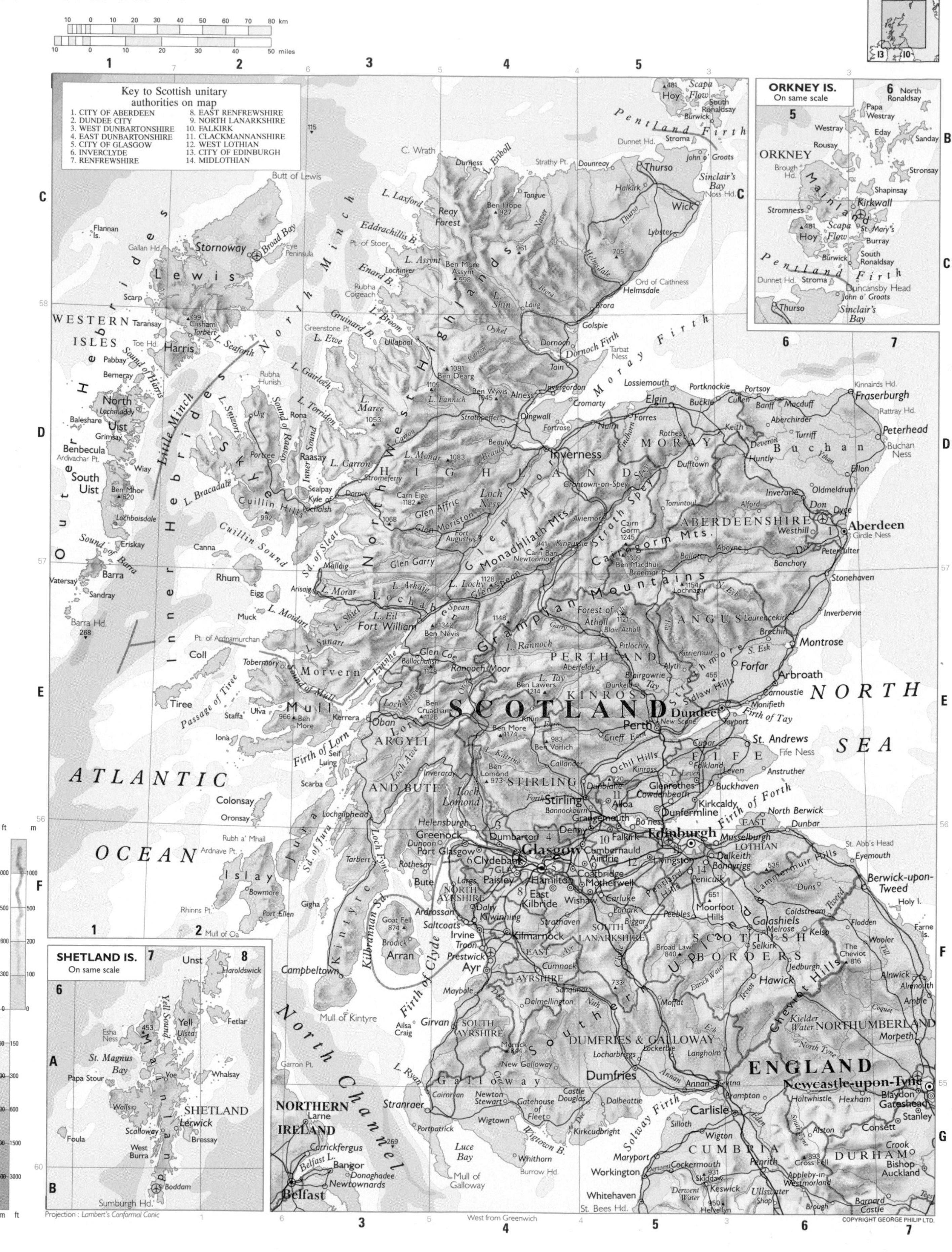
Key to Scottish unitary authorities on map
1. CITY OF ABERDEEN
2. DUNDEE CITY
3. WEST DUNBARTONSHIRE
4. EAST DUNBARTONSHIRE
5. CITY OF GLASGOW
6. INVERCLYDE
7. RENFREWSHIRE
8. EAST RENFREWSHIRE
9. NORTH LANARKSHIRE
10. FALKIRK
11. CLACKMANNANSHIRE
12. WEST LOTHIAN
13. CITY OF EDINBURGH
14. MIDLOTHIAN
ORKNEY IS.
On same scale
SHETLAND IS.
On same scale
SCOTLAND
ATLANTIC
OCEAN
NORTH SEA
ENGLAND
NORTHERN IRELAND
North Channel
Pentland Firth
Moray Firth
Firth of Forth
Firth of Clyde
Firth of Tay
Solway Firth
Firth of Lorn
North Minch
Little Minch
Outer Hebrides
Inner Hebrides
WESTERN ISLES
HIGHLAND
North West Highlands
Grampian Mountains
Cairngorm Mts.
Monadhliath Mts.
Glen More
MORAY
ABERDEENSHIRE
ANGUS
PERTH AND KINROSS
FIFE
STIRLING
ARGYLL AND BUTE
SCOTTISH BORDERS
DUMFRIES & GALLOWAY
SOUTH LANARKSHIRE
SOUTH AYRSHIRE
EAST AYRSHIRE
NORTH AYRSHIRE
EAST LOTHIAN
Southern Uplands
Cheviot Hills
NORTHUMBERLAND
CUMBRIA
DURHAM
Lewis
Harris
Skye
Mull
Islay
Jura
Arran
Kintyre
Orkney
Mainland
Hoy
Shetland
Edinburgh
Glasgow
Aberdeen
Dundee
Inverness
Perth
Stirling
Fort William
Stornoway
Kirkwall
Lerwick
Newcastle-upon-Tyne
Carlisle
Belfast
Projection : Lambert's Conformal Conic
West from Greenwich
COPYRIGHT GEORGE PHILIP LTD.

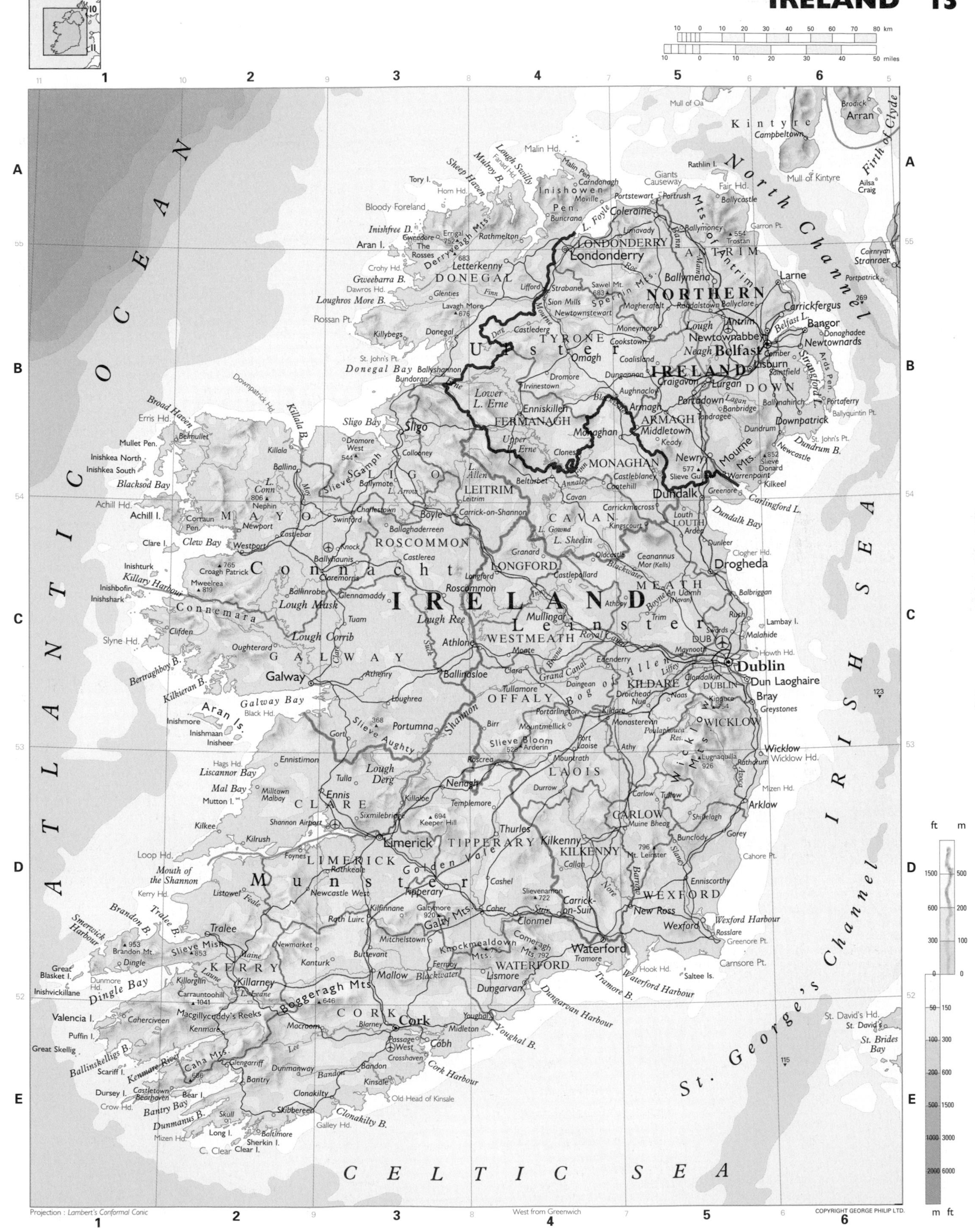

10 0 10 20 30 40 50 60 70 80 km
10 0 10 20 30 40 50 miles
1 2 3 4 5 6
A B C D E
ATLANTIC OCEAN
CELTIC SEA
IRISH SEA
North Channel
St. George's Channel
Mull of Oa
Kintyre
Campbeltown
Brodick
Arran
Firth of Clyde
Mull of Kintyre
Ailsa Craig
Rathlin I.
Fair Hd.
Ballycastle
Giants Causeway
Portrush
Portstewart
Coleraine
Malin Hd.
Malin Pen.
Carndonagh
Inishowen Pen.
Moville
Buncrana
L. Foyle
Lough Swilly
Fanad Hd.
Mulroy B.
Sheep Haven
Tory I.
Horn Hd.
Bloody Foreland
Inishfree B.
Gweedore
Errigal 752
Derryveagh Mts.
Rathmelton
Aran I.
The Rosses
683
Letterkenny
Crohy Hd.
Gweebarra B.
Dawros Hd.
DONEGAL
Glenties
Loughros More B.
Lavagh More 676
Rossan Pt.
Killybegs
Donegal
St. John's Pt.
Donegal Bay
Ballyshannon
Bundoran
Limavady
LONDONDERRY
Londonderry
Ballymoney
554 Trostan
Garron Pt.
ANTRIM
Mts. of Antrim
Ballymena
Larne
Cairnryan
Stranraer
Portpatrick
Lifford
Strabane
Sawel Mt. 683
Sperrin Mts.
Sion Mills
Newtownstewart
Magherafelt
Randalstown
Ballyclare
NORTHERN IRELAND
Carrickfergus
Antrim
Belfast L.
Bangor
Donaghadee
Newtownards
Newtownabbey
Belfast
Lough Neagh
Castlederg
TYRONE
Ulster
Omagh
Cookstown
Moneymore
Coalisland
Dungannon
Comber
Lisburn
Saintfield
Strangford L.
Ards Pen.
Dromore
Irvinestown
Lower L. Erne
Enniskillen
FERMANAGH
Upper L. Erne
Craigavon
Lurgan
Portadown
Aughnacloy
Armagh
ARMAGH
Banbridge
Tandragee
DOWN
Ballynahinch
Portaferry
Ballyquintin Pt.
Downpatrick
Dundrum
Dundrum B.
St. John's Pt.
Middletown
Keady
Monaghan
Clones
MONAGHAN
Newry
Mourne Mts.
852 Slieve Donard
Newcastle
577 Slieve Gullion
Warrenpoint
Kilkeel
Castleblaney
Cootehill
Dundalk
Greenore
Carlingford L.
Dundalk Bay
Downpatrick Hd.
Broad Haven
Erris Hd.
Belmullet
Killala B.
Killala
Mullet Pen.
Inishkea North
Inishkea South
Blacksod Bay
Ballina
L. Conn
806 Nephin
Achill Hd.
Achill I.
Corraun Pen.
MAYO
Newport
Castlebar
Clew Bay
Westport
Clare I.
Inishturk
765 Croagh Patrick
Killary Harbour
Mweelrea 819
Inishbofin
Inishshark
Connemara
Clifden
Slyne Hd.
Sligo Bay
Sligo
Dromore West 544
Collooney
Slieve Gamph
SLIGO
Ballymote
L. Arrow
Charlestown
Swinford
Boyle
Ballaghaderreen
Knock
Ballyhaunis
ROSCOMMON
Castlerea
Claremorris
Connacht
Ballinrobe
Glennamaddy
Lough Mask
Tuam
Lough Corrib
Oughterard
GALWAY
Galway
Athenry
Bertraghboy B.
Kilkieran B.
Galway Bay
Black Hd.
Aran Is.
Inishmore
Inishmaan
Inisheer
L. Allen
LEITRIM
Leitrim
Carrick-on-Shannon
Belturbet
Cavan
CAVAN
L. Gowna
L. Sheelin
Kingscourt
Carrickmacross
Louth
LOUTH
Ardee
Dunleer
Clogher Hd.
Drogheda
Granard
LONGFORD
Longford
Oldcastle
Castlepollard
Ceanannus Mor (Kells)
MEATH
An Uaimh (Navan)
Balbriggan
Roscommon
IRELAND
Athboy
Boyne
Trim
Rush
Lambay I.
Lough Ree
Mullingar
Leinster
WESTMEATH
Royal Canal
Athlone
Moate
Swords
Malahide
Maynooth
DUBLIN
Howth Hd.
Dublin
Dun Laoghaire
Edenderry
Liffey
Grand Canal
Clara
Ballinasloe
Tullamore
Daingean
Bog of Allen
KILDARE
Clondalkin
Bray
Droichead Nua
Naas
Kippure 754
Greystones
123
Loughrea
OFFALY
Kildare
Portarlington
Monasterevin
Poulaphouca Res.
WICKLOW
Wicklow Mts.
Birr
Mountmellick
Portumna
368
Slieve Aughty
Gort
Shannon
Slieve Bloom
528 Arderin
Port Laoise
Athy
Wicklow
Wicklow Hd.
Lugnaquilla 926
Rathdrum
Mountrath
Roscrea
Lough Derg
LAOIS
Durrow
Nenagh
Templemore
Carlow
Tullow
CARLOW
Muine Bheag
Shillelagh
Arklow
Mizen Hd.
Gorey
Bunclody
796 Mt. Leinster
Slaney
Ennistimon
Hags Hd.
Liscannor Bay
Mal Bay
Milltown Malbay
Mutton I.
Tulla
Ennis
CLARE
Killaloe
Sixmilebridge
694 Keeper Hill
Kilkee
Shannon Airport
Kilrush
Limerick
TIPPERARY
Thurles
Kilkenny
KILKENNY
Callan
Loop Hd.
Mouth of the Shannon
Foynes
LIMERICK
Rathkeale
Golden Vale
Cashel
Munster
Kerry Hd.
Listowel
Feale
Newcastle West
Tipperary
Slievenamon 722
Carrick-on-Suir
Nore
Barrow
WEXFORD
Enniscorthy
Cahore Pt.
New Ross
Wexford
Wexford Harbour
Rosslare
Greenore Pt.
Carnsore Pt.
Smerwick Harbour
Brandon B.
Tralee B.
953 Brandon Mt.
Tralee
Slieve Mish 853
Dingle
Maine
Great Blasket I.
KERRY
Dunmore Hd.
Dingle Bay
Killorglin
Killarney
Laune
Inishvickillane
Carrauntoohill 1041
L. Leane
Valencia I.
Cahirciveen
Macgillycuddy's Reeks
Puffin I.
Kenmare
Great Skellig
Ballinskelligs B.
Kenmare River
Caha Mts.
686
Scariff I.
Dursey I.
Castletown Bearhaven
Bear I.
Crow Hd.
Bantry Bay
Dunmanus B.
Mizen Hd.
Long I.
Skull
Baltimore
Sherkin I.
C. Clear
Clear I.
Kilfinnane
Rath Luirc
Galtymore 920
Galty Mts.
Caher
Clonmel
Suir
Comeragh Mts. 792
Waterford
Tramore
Tramore B.
Waterford Harbour
Hook Hd.
Saltee Is.
Mitchelstown
Newmarket
Kanturk
Buttevant
Knockmealdown Mts. 795
Fermoy
Mallow
Blackwater
Lismore
WATERFORD
Dungarvan
Dungarvan Harbour
Boggeragh Mts.
646
CORK
Cork
Youghal
Youghal B.
Macroom
Blarney
Midleton
Passage West
Cobh
Lee
Crosshaven
Cork Harbour
Dunmanway
Bandon
Bantry
Kinsale
Old Head of Kinsale
Clonakilty
Skibbereen
Clonakilty B.
Galley Hd.
115
St. David's Hd.
St. David's
St. Brides Bay
ft m
1500 500
600 200
300 100
0 0
50 150
100 300
200 600
500 1500
1000 3000
2000 6000
m ft
Projection : Lambert's Conformal Conic
West from Greenwich
COPYRIGHT GEORGE PHILIP LTD.

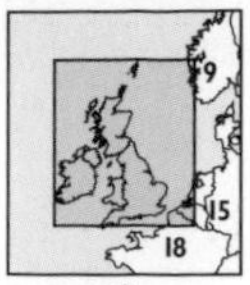
9
15
18

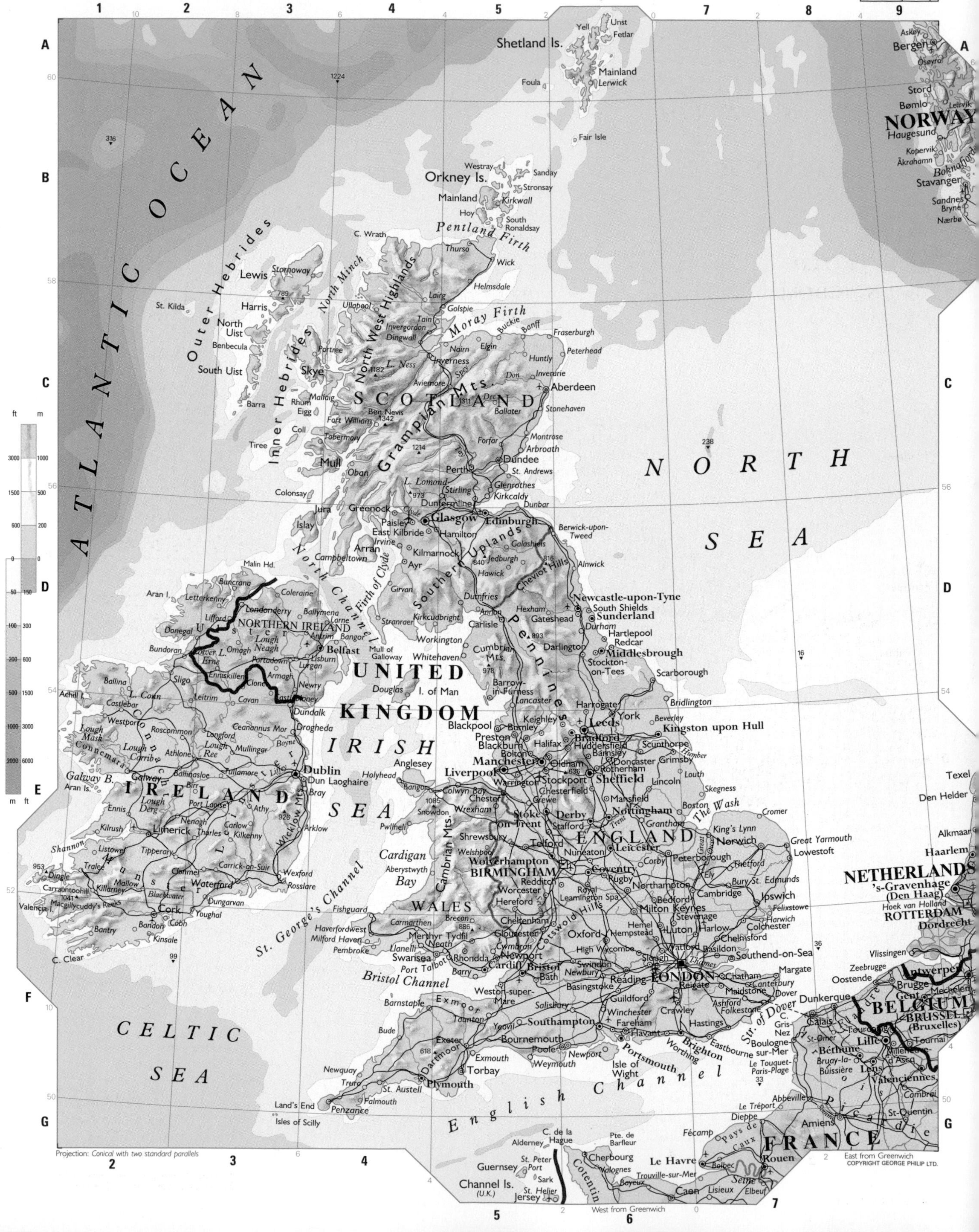
50 0 25 50 75 100 125 150 175 km
50 0 25 50 75 100 125 miles
ATLANTIC OCEAN
NORTH SEA
IRISH SEA
CELTIC SEA
English Channel
UNITED KINGDOM
IRELAND
SCOTLAND
ENGLAND
WALES
NORTHERN IRELAND
NORWAY
NETHERLANDS
BELGIUM
FRANCE
Shetland Is.
Yell
Unst
Fetlar
Mainland
Lerwick
Foula
Fair Isle
Orkney Is.
Westray
Sanday
Stronsay
Kirkwall
Hoy
South Ronaldsay
Pentland Firth
C. Wrath
Thurso
Wick
Helmsdale
Outer Hebrides
Lewis
Stornoway
Harris
St. Kilda
North Uist
Benbecula
South Uist
Barra
North Minch
Ullapool
North West Highlands
Lairg
Golspie
Tain
Invergordon
Dingwall
Moray Firth
Buckie
Banff
Fraserburgh
Peterhead
Nairn
Elgin
Huntly
Inverness
L. Ness
Inner Hebrides
Portree
Skye
Mallaig
Rhum
Eigg
Aviemore
Inverurie
Aberdeen
Ben Nevis
Fort William
Grampian Mts.
Ballater
Stonehaven
Coll
Tiree
Tobermory
Mull
Oban
Forfar
Montrose
Arbroath
Dundee
Perth
St. Andrews
Glenrothes
Kirkcaldy
L. Lomond
Stirling
Dunfermline
Dunbar
Colonsay
Jura
Islay
Greenock
Glasgow
Edinburgh
Paisley
East Kilbride
Hamilton
Irvine
Kilmarnock
Ayr
Arran
Campbeltown
Southern Uplands
Galashiels
Jedburgh
Hawick
Berwick-upon-Tweed
Cheviot Hills
Alnwick
Firth of Clyde
North Channel
Girvan
Stranraer
Kirkcudbright
Dumfries
Annan
Carlisle
Mull of Galloway
Newcastle-upon-Tyne
South Shields
Sunderland
Hexham
Gateshead
Durham
Hartlepool
Redcar
Middlesbrough
Stockton-on-Tees
Darlington
Workington
Whitehaven
Cumbrian Mts.
Pennines
Scarborough
Douglas
I. of Man
Barrow-in-Furness
Lancaster
Harrogate
York
Bridlington
Beverley
Kingston upon Hull
Blackpool
Keighley
Leeds
Burnley
Preston
Bradford
Blackburn
Halifax
Huddersfield
Bolton
Barnsley
Scunthorpe
Humber
Grimsby
Manchester
Oldham
Doncaster
Liverpool
Rotherham
Sheffield
Warrington
Stockport
Chesterfield
Lincoln
Louth
Skegness
Anglesey
Holyhead
Bangor
Colwyn Bay
Chester
Crewe
Mansfield
Boston
The Wash
Cromer
Snowdon
Wrexham
Stoke-on-Trent
Derby
Nottingham
Trent
Grantham
King's Lynn
Norwich
Great Yarmouth
Lowestoft
Pwllheli
Stafford
Shrewsbury
Telford
Nuneaton
Leicester
Cardigan Bay
Aberystwyth
Cambrian Mts.
Welshpool
Wolverhampton
BIRMINGHAM
Coventry
Corby
Peterborough
Thetford
Ely
Bury St. Edmunds
Redditch
Rugby
Northampton
Bedford
Cambridge
Ipswich
Worcester
Royal Leamington Spa
Milton Keynes
Felixstowe
Hereford
Stevenage
Harwich
Colchester
Cheltenham
Cotswold Hills
Luton
Harlow
Hemel Hempstead
Chelmsford
Gloucester
Oxford
Watford
Basildon
Fishguard
Carmarthen
Brecon
Haverfordwest
Milford Haven
Pembroke
Merthyr Tydfil
Neath
Llanelli
Swansea
Port Talbot
Rhondda
Cwmbran
Newport
Cardiff
Barry
Bristol
Bath
High Wycombe
Swindon
Slough
LONDON
Thames
Southend-on-Sea
Newbury
Reading
Chatham
Margate
Bristol Channel
Basingstoke
Maidstone
Canterbury
Dover
Weston-super-Mare
Guildford
Reigate
Crawley
Ashford
Folkestone
Str. of Dover
Barnstaple
Exmoor
Taunton
Salisbury
Winchester
Fareham
Havant
Hastings
Brighton
Worthing
Eastbourne
Bude
Yeovil
Southampton
Portsmouth
Isle of Wight
Newport
Exeter
Bournemouth
Poole
Weymouth
Dartmoor
Exmouth
Torbay
Newquay
Truro
St. Austell
Plymouth
Falmouth
Land's End
Penzance
Isles of Scilly
St. George's Channel
Malin Hd.
Buncrana
Aran I.
Letterkenny
Londonderry
Coleraine
Ballymena
Larne
Antrim
Lough Neagh
Bangor
Belfast
Lifford
Donegal
Omagh
Lisburn
Lurgan
Portadown
Armagh
Newry
Bundoran
Lower L. Erne
Enniskillen
Clones
Sligo
Ballina
Achill I.
L. Conn
Castlebar
Leitrim
Cavan
Dundalk
Westport
Lough Mask
Connacht
Roscommon
Longford
Ceanannus Mor
Drogheda
Boyne
Connemara
Lough Corrib
Athlone
Lough Ree
Mullingar
Galway
Galway B.
Aran Is.
Ballinasloe
Tullamore
Liffey
Dublin
Dun Laoghaire
Bray
Birr
Port Laoise
Leinster
Athy
Wicklow Mts.
Ennis
Lough Derg
Nenagh
Carlow
Kilkenny
Arklow
Kilrush
Limerick
Thurles
Shannon
Listowel
Tipperary
Munster
Tralee
Clonmel
Carrick-on-Suir
Wexford
Dingle
Carrauntoohill
Killarney
Mallow
Waterford
Rosslare
Blackwater
Valencia I.
Macgillycuddy's Reeks
Dungarvan
Cork
Youghal
Cobh
Bantry
Bandon
Kinsale
C. Clear
Bergen
Askøy
Osøyro
Stord
Bømlo
Leirvik
Haugesund
Kopervik
Åkrahamn
Boknafjorden
Stavanger
Sandnes
Bryne
Nærbø
Texel
Den Helder
Alkmaar
Haarlem
's-Gravenhage (Den Haag)
Hoek van Holland
ROTTERDAM
Dordrecht
Vlissingen
Antwerpen
Zeebrugge
Oostende
Brugge
Gent
Mechelen
BRUSSEL (Bruxelles)
Dunkerque
Calais
C. Gris-Nez
Boulogne-sur-Mer
Le Touquet-Paris-Plage
St-Omer
Béthune
Bruay-la-Buissière
Lille
Tourcoing
Tournai
Lens
Valenciennes
Cambrai
Abbeville
Le Tréport
Picardie
Amiens
St-Quentin
Dieppe
Fécamp
Pays de Caux
Le Havre
Bolbec
Rouen
Seine
Elbeuf
Trouville-sur-Mer
Lisieux
Caen
Bayeux
Cherbourg
Valognes
Cotentin
Pte. de Barfleur
C. de la Hague
Alderney
Guernsey
St. Peter Port
Sark
Channel Is. (U.K.)
St. Helier
Jersey
1224
316
789
1182
1311
1342
1214
973
840
816
893
978
636
1085
926
886
618
953
1041
238
16
36
33
99
ft m
3000 1000
1500 500
600 200
0 0
50 150
100 300
200 600
500 1500
1000 3000
2000 6000
m ft
Projection: Conical with two standard parallels
East from Greenwich
West from Greenwich
COPYRIGHT GEORGE PHILIP LTD.

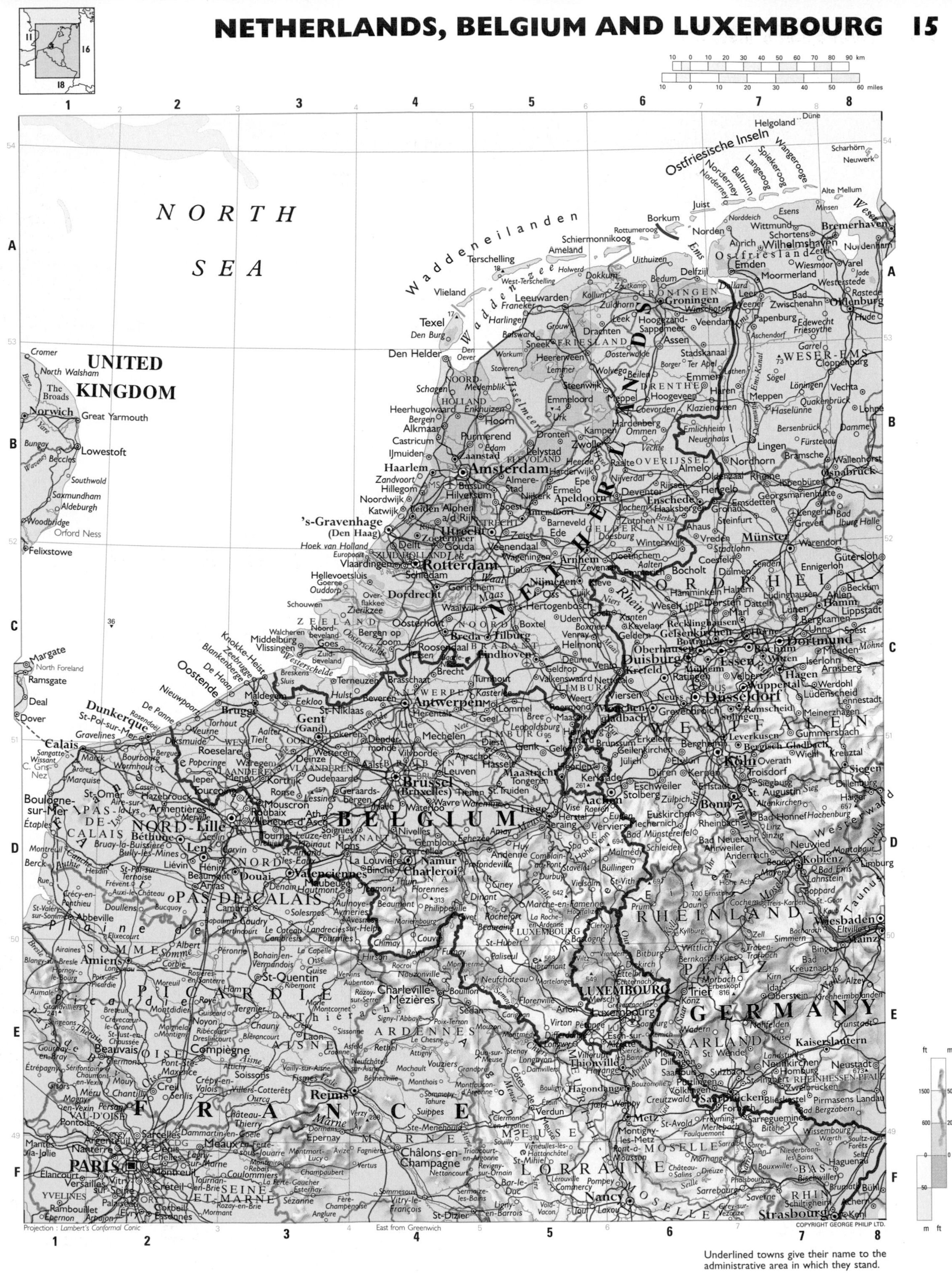


Underlined towns give their name to the administrative area in which they stand.

50 0 25 50 75 100 125 150 175 km
50 0 25 50 75 100 125 miles
NORTH SEA
BALTIC SEA
UNITED KINGDOM
DENMARK
NETHERLANDS
BELGIUM
LUXEMBOURG
GERMANY
FRANCE
SWITZERLAND
LIECHTENSTEIN
AUSTRIA
CZECH REP.
SLOVENIA
ITALY
MONACO
SAN MARINO
ADRIATIC SEA
Golfo di Génova
Golfo di Venézia
Nordfriesische Inseln
Ost-friesische Inseln
Deutsche Bucht
Kieler Bucht
Mecklenburger Bucht
Fehmarn Bælt
Rügen
Usedom
Stettiner Haff
HAMBURG
BERLIN
AMSTERDAM
ROTTERDAM
'S-Gravenhage (Den Haag)
BRUSSEL (Bruxelles)
LUXEMBOURG
PARIS
PRAHA (Prague)
MÜNCHEN (Munich)
MILANO
TORINO (Turin)
ZÜRICH
Bern
Genève
LYON
MARSEILLE
Frankfurt
Köln (Cologne)
Bonn
Düsseldorf
Dortmund
Essen
Hannover
Bremen
Leipzig
Dresden
Nürnberg
Stuttgart
Strasbourg
Venézia (Venice)
Firenze (Florence)
Génova
Ljubljana
Zagreb
Salzburg
Innsbruck
Linz
Niedersachsen
Nordrhein-Westfalen
Hessen
Rheinland-Pfalz
Bayern
Sachsen
Sachsen-Anhalt
Brandenburg
Mecklenburg
Thüringer Wald
Erzgebirge
Böhmerwald
Schwarzwald
Alpes Maritimes
Massif Central
Jura
Dolomiti
Tirol
Steiermark
Kärnten
Lombardia
Piemonte
Liguria
Provence
Bourgogne
Champagne
Lorraine
Picardie
Île-de-France
Projection: Conical with two standard parallels

LITHUANIA
BELARUS
POLAND
UKRAINE
SLOVAK REP.
CZECH REP.
HUNGARY
ROMANIA
MOLDOVA
YUGOSLAVIA
BOSNIA-HERZEGOVINA
BULGARIA
Zatoka Gdańska
Kaliningrad (Russia)
Vilnius
Minsk
Gdańsk
Gdynia
Olsztyn
Białystok
Hrodna
Bydgoszcz
Toruń
Poznań
Warszawa (Warsaw)
Łódź
Wrocław
Kraków
Katowice
Lublin
Radom
Kielce
Brest
Pinsk
Homyel
Babruysk
Mahilyow
Pripet Marshes
Kyyiv (Kiev)
Zhytomyr
Rivne
Lutsk
Lviv (Lvov)
Ternopil
Khmelnytskyy
Vinnytsya
Ivano-Frankivsk
Chernivtsi
Chişinău
Tiraspol
Bratislava
Košice
Budapest
Debrecen
Miskolc
Szeged
Iaşi
Cluj-Napoca
Braşov
Constanţa
Galaţi
Bucureşti (Bucharest)
Ruse
Varna
Beograd (Belgrade)
Novi Sad
Timişoara
Craiova
Sarajevo
Carpaţii Meridionali
Transilvania
Walachia
Vychodné Beskydy
Podolska Vysochyna
Dobruja
East from Greenwich

km
miles
FRANCE
UNITED KINGDOM
BELGIUM
LUXEMBOURG
GERMANY
SWITZERLAND
AUSTRIA
ITALY
SPAIN
ANDORRA
MONACO
English Channel
Bay of Biscay
Golfe de Gascogne
Golfe du Lion
MEDITERRANEAN SEA
Massif Central
PARIS
Corse (Corsica)
Projection: Conical with two standard parallels
West from Greenwich
East from Greenwich
COPYRIGHT GEORGE PHILIP LTD

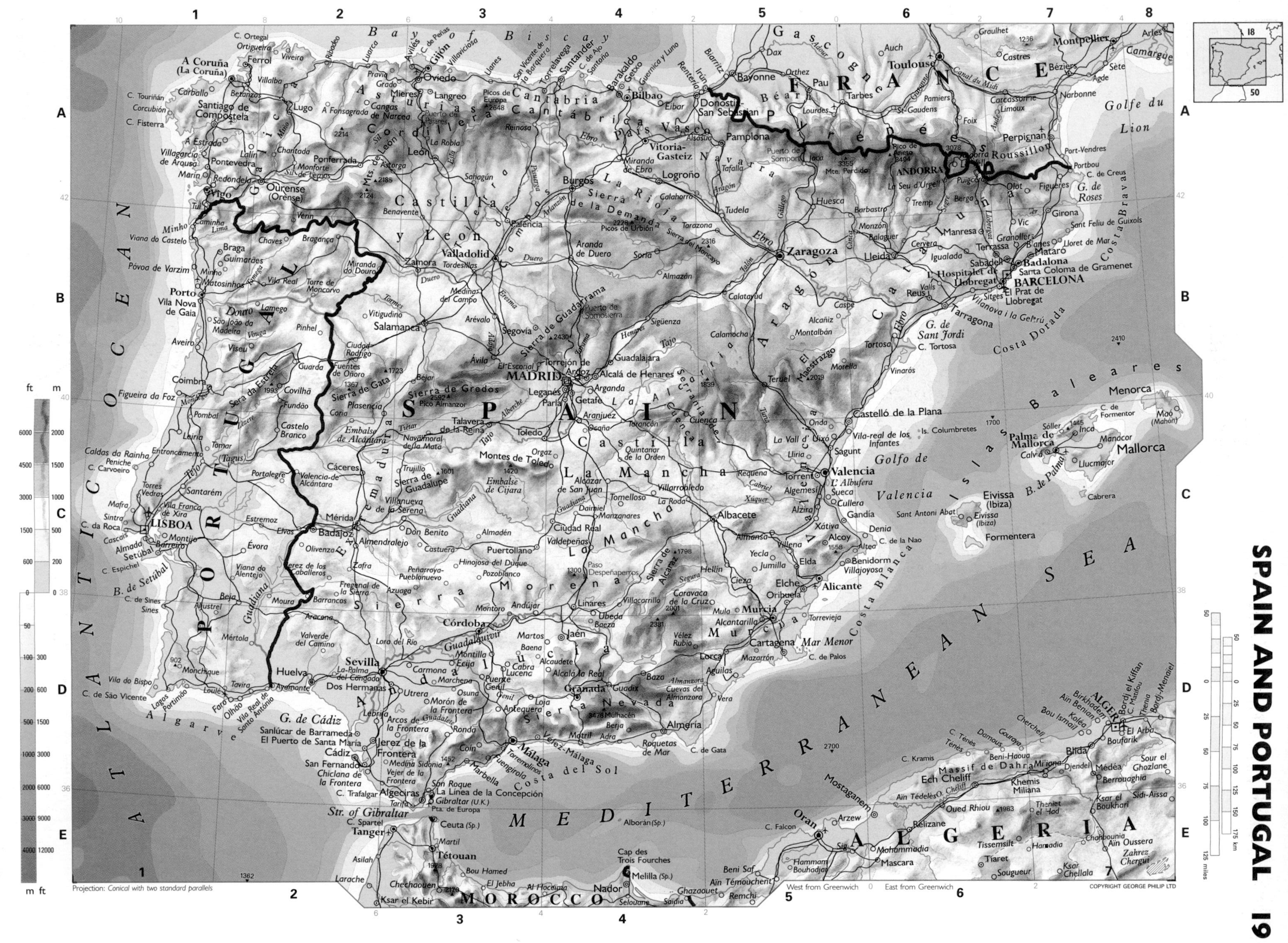
SPAIN
PORTUGAL
FRANCE
ALGERIA
MOROCCO
MADRID
LISBOA
BARCELONA
ANDORRA
ATLANTIC OCEAN
MEDITERRANEAN SEA
Bay of Biscay
Golfe du Lion
Islas Baleares
Mallorca
Menorca
Eivissa (Ibiza)
Formentera
Pyrénées
Sierra Nevada
Sierra Morena
Str. of Gibraltar
G. de Cádiz
Golfo de Valencia
Projection: Conical with two standard parallels
COPYRIGHT GEORGE PHILIP LTD
West from Greenwich
East from Greenwich
km
miles
m
ft

50 0 25 50 75 100 125 150 175 km
50 0 25 50 75 100 125 miles
SWITZERLAND
AUSTRIA
SLOVENIA
CROAT
FRANCE
MONACO
SAN MARINO
VATICAN CITY
ALGERIA
TUNISIA
MALTA
ITALY
LIGURIAN SEA
TYRRHENIAN SEA
ADRIATIC SEA
MEDITER
Golfo di Génova
Golfo di Venézia
Golfo di Táranto
Golfe de Tunis
Golfe de Hammamet
Bouches de Bonifacio
Str. di Messina
Corse
Sardegna
Sicilia
Ísole Eólie
Ísole Égadi
Ísole Ponziane
Ísole Pelagie (Italy)
Pantelleria (Italy)
Ústica (Italy)
Is. de la Galite (Tunisia)
Elba
Capri
Ìschia
Lampedusa
Linosa
Lampione
Gozo
Alpes Maritimes
Dolomiti
Lombardia
Piemonte
Liguria
Toscana
Lazio
Campania
Calabria
Dalmacija
Istra
Côte d'Azur
Riviera di Ponente
Riviera di Levante
MILANO
TORINO (Turin)
ROMA
NÁPOLI
Firenze (Florence)
Venézia (Venice)
Génova
Bologna
Palermo
Catánia
Messina
Bari
Táranto
Cágliari
Sássari
Ajaccio
Bastia
Trieste
Ljubljana
Zagreb
Graz
Klagenfurt
Split
Rijeka
Zadar
Banja Luka
MARSEILLE
LYON
Grenoble
Toulon
Nice
Cannes
Avignon
Tunis
Bizerte
Annaba
Constantine
Sousse
Kairouan
Valletta
Verona
Pádova
Brescia
Bérgamo
Parma
Módena
Ravenna
Rímini
Ancona
Perúgia
Pescara
Foggia
Salerno
Reggio di Calábria
Siracusa
Agrigento
Trápani
Marsala
Livorno
Pisa
Lucca
Siena
Arezzo
Terni
Viterbo
Latina
Caserta
Potenza
Cosenza
Catanzaro
Crotone
Projection: Conical with two standard parallels

HUNGARY
ROMANIA
UKRAINE
YUGOSLAVIA
BOSNIA-HERZEGOVINA
SERBIA
MONTENEGRO
MACEDONIA
ALBANIA
BULGARIA
GREECE
TURKEY
BLACK SEA
ÆGEAN SEA
IONIAN SEA
MEDITERRANEAN SEA
Str. of Otranto
Transilvania
Carpaţii Meridionali
Walahia
Dobrogea
Vojvodina
Stara Planina
Rhodopi Planina
Pirin Planina
Kosovo
Kopaonik
Makedhonia
Thrace
Mysia
Lydia
Caria
Pindhos Oros
Pelopónnisos
Kikládhes
Dhodhekánisos
Kríti
BUCUREŞTI (Bucharest)
BEOGRAD (Belgrade)
SOFIYA
Skopje
Tiranë
Sarajevo
Podgorica
ATHÍNAI (Athens)
İSTANBUL
İZMIR (Smyrna)
Thessaloníki
Constanţa
Varna
Burgas
Plovdiv
Ruse
Craiova
Ploieşti
Braşov
Galaţi
Brăila
Timişoara
Szeged
Pécs
Novi Sad
Niš
Priština
Bitola
Durrës
Shkodër
Vlorë
Korçë
Kérkira (Corfu)
Pátrai
Lárisa
Vólos
Edirne
Bursa
Balıkesir
Manisa
Çanakkale
Marmara Denizi (Sea of Marmara)
İstanbul Boğazı (Bosporus)
Çanakkale Boğazı (Dardanelles)
Saros Körfezi
Thermaïkós Kólpos
Korinthiakós Kólpos
Saronikós Kólpos
Lésvos
Límnos
Khíos
Sámos
Évvoia
Náxos
Ródhos (Rhodes)
Kárpathos
Kíthira
Iráklion
Khania
Kefallinía
Zákinthos
Levkás
East from Greenwich
COPYRIGHT GEORGE PHILIP LTD.

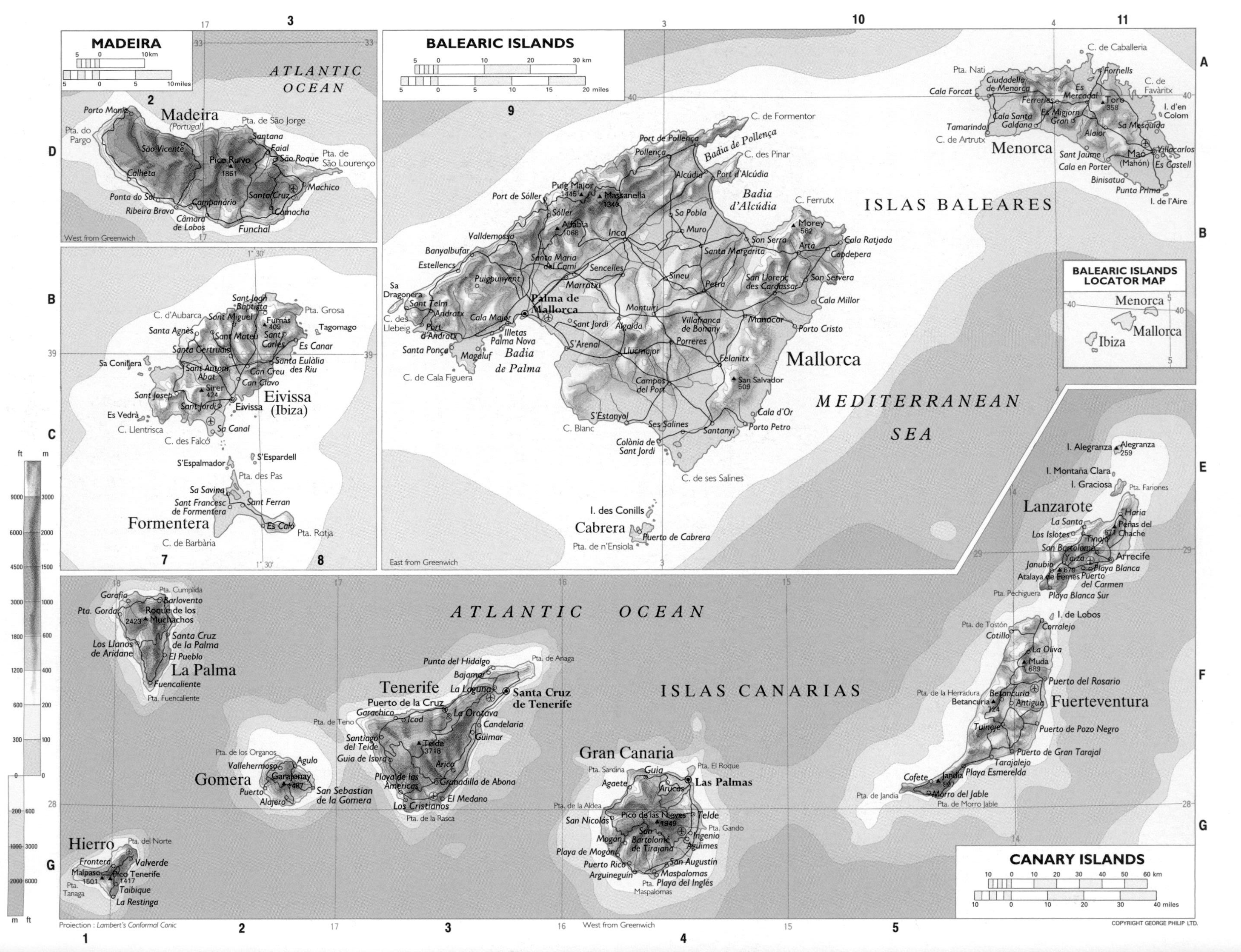

MADEIRA
ATLANTIC OCEAN
Madeira (Portugal)
Porto Moniz
Pta. do Pargo
São Vicente
Pico Ruivo 1861
Pta. de São Jorge
Santana
Faial
São Roque
Pta. de São Lourenço
Machico
Calheta
Ponta do Sol
Campanário
Santa Cruz
Ribeira Brava
Câmara de Lobos
Camacha
Funchal
West from Greenwich
BALEARIC ISLANDS
C. de Formentor
Port de Pollença
Pollença
Badia de Pollença
C. des Pinar
Alcúdia
Port d'Alcúdia
Badia d'Alcúdia
C. Ferrutx
Port de Sóller
Puig Major 1445
Massanella 1348
Sóller
Alfabia 1068
Sa Pobla
Muro
Inca
Valldemossa
Banyalbufar
Estellencs
Sa Dragonera
Sant Telm
C. des Llebeig
Andratx
Port d'Andratx
Santa Ponça
Magaluf
Puigpunyent
Santa Maria del Camí
Sencelles
Marratxí
Palma de Mallorca
Cala Major
Illetas
Palma Nova
Badia de Palma
C. de Cala Figuera
Sant Jordi
S'Arenal
Algaida
Montuïri
Sineu
Petra
Santa Margarita
Son Serra
Morey 562
Artà
Cala Ratjada
Capdepera
Son Servera
San Llorenç des Cardassar
Cala Millor
Manacor
Porto Cristo
Villafranca de Bonany
Porreres
Llucmajor
Felanitx
San Salvador 509
Campos del Port
Mallorca
Cala d'Or
Porto Petro
Santanyí
Ses Salines
S'Estanyol
C. Blanc
Colònia de Sant Jordi
C. de ses Salines
I. des Conills
Cabrera
Puerto de Cabrera
Pta. de n'Ensiola
ISLAS BALEARES
MEDITERRANEAN SEA
East from Greenwich
Menorca
Pta. Nati
Cala Forcat
Ciudadella de Menorca
Ferreries
Es Mercadal
Fornells
C. de Caballeria
C. de Favàritx
Toro 358
Es Migjorn Gran
Cala Santa Galdana
Tamarinda
C. de Artrutx
Alaior
Sa Mesquida
I. d'en Colom
Sant Jaume
Cala en Porter
Binisatua
Maó (Mahón)
Villacarlos
Es Castell
Punta Prima
I. de l'Aire
BALEARIC ISLANDS LOCATOR MAP
Menorca
Mallorca
Ibiza
Sant Joan Baptista
Pta. Grosa
Tagomago
C. d'Aubarca
Sant Miquel
Furnás 409
Santa Agnès
Sant Mateu
Sant Carles
Es Canar
Santa Gertrudis
Santa Eulàlia des Riu
Sa Conillera
Sant Antoni Abat
Can Creu
Can Clavo
Sant Josep
Sirer 424
Eivissa (Ibiza)
Sant Jordi
Eivissa
Es Vedrà
C. Llentrisca
Sa Canal
C. des Falcó
S'Espalmador
S'Espardell
Pta. des Pas
Sa Savina
Sant Francesc de Formentera
Sant Ferran
Formentera
Es Caló
Pta. Rotja
C. de Barbària
ATLANTIC OCEAN
ISLAS CANARIAS
I. Alegranza
Alegranza 259
I. Montaña Clara
I. Graciosa
Pta. Fariones
Lanzarote
Haria
La Santa
Peñas del Chache 671
Los Islotes
Tinajo
San Bartolomé
Arrecife
Janubio
Yaiza
Playa Blanca
Atalaya de Femes
Puerto del Carmen
Pta. Pechiguera
Playa Blanca Sur
I. de Lobos
Pta. de Tostón
Corralejo
Cotillo
La Oliva
Muda 689
Puerto del Rosario
Pta. de la Herradura
Betancuria
Antigua
Fuerteventura
Tuineje
Puerto de Pozo Negro
Puerto de Gran Tarajal
Tarajalejo
Cofete
Jandía
Playa Esmerelda
Pta. de Jandía
Morro del Jable
Pta. de Morro Jable
Garafía
Pta. Cumplida
Barlovento
Pta. Gorda
Roque de los Muchachos 2423
Santa Cruz de la Palma
Los Llanos de Aridane
El Pueblo
La Palma
Fuencaliente
Pta. Fuencaliente
Hierro
Pta. del Norte
Frontera
Valverde
Malpaso 1501
Pico Tenerife 1417
Pta. Tanaga
Taibique
La Restinga
Pta. de los Organos
Agulo
Vallehermoso
Garajonay 1487
Gomera
Puerto
Alajero
San Sebastian de la Gomera
Tenerife
Punta del Hidalgo
Pta. de Anaga
Bajamar
La Laguna
Santa Cruz de Tenerife
Puerto de la Cruz
Garachico
Icod
La Orotava
Candelaria
Pta. de Teno
Santiago del Teide
Teide 3718
Güimar
Guia de Isora
Arico
Playa de las Americas
Granadilla de Abona
El Medano
Los Cristianos
Pta. de la Rasca
Gran Canaria
Pta. Sardina
Guia
Pta. El Roque
Agaete
Arucas
Las Palmas
Pta. de la Aldea
San Nicolás
Pico de las Nieves 1949
Telde
Pta. Gando
Mogán
San Bartolomé de Tirajana
Ingenio
Agüimes
Playa de Mogán
Puerto Rico
San Augustín
Arguineguin
Maspalomas
Pta. Playa del Inglés
Maspalomas
CANARY ISLANDS
West from Greenwich
Projection : Lambert's Conformal Conic
COPYRIGHT GEORGE PHILIP LTD.

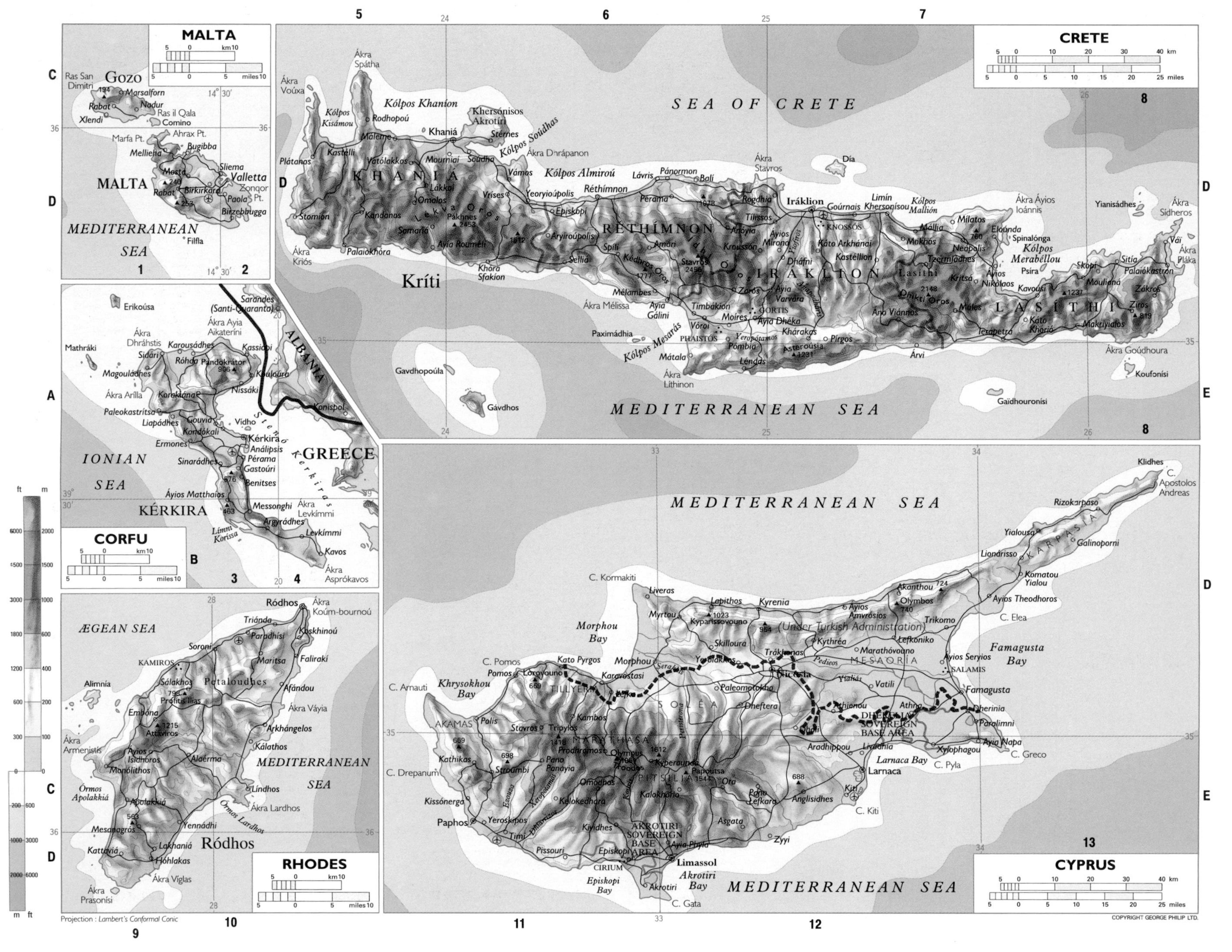
MALTA
Gozo
Comino
MALTA
Valletta
MEDITERRANEAN SEA
CRETE
SEA OF CRETE
Kríti
Khaniá
Réthimnon
Iráklion
Gávdhos
MEDITERRANEAN SEA
CORFU
ALBANIA
GREECE
IONIAN SEA
KÉRKIRA
Kérkira
RHODES
ÆGEAN SEA
Ródhos
Ródhos
MEDITERRANEAN SEA
CYPRUS
MEDITERRANEAN SEA
Nicosia
Kyrenia
Famagusta
Larnaca
Limassol
Paphos
Morphou Bay
Khrysokhou Bay
Famagusta Bay
Larnaca Bay
Akrotiri Bay
Episkopi Bay
(Under Turkish Administration)
DHEKELIA SOVEREIGN BASE AREA
AKROTIRI SOVEREIGN BASE AREA
MEDITERRANEAN SEA
Projection : Lambert's Conformal Conic
COPYRIGHT GEORGE PHILIP LTD.

50 0 100 200 300 400 km
50 0 50 100 150 200 250 miles
BARENTS SEA
BALTIC SEA
Gulf of Bothnia
Gulf of Finland
Gulf of Riga
Beloye More
FINLAND
SWEDEN
NORWAY
ESTONIA
LATVIA
LITHUANIA
BELARUS
POLAND
RUSSIA
KARELIA
KOMI
UDMURTIA
TATARSTAN
BASHKORTOSTAN
CHUVASHIA
MARI EL
MORDVINIA
Lappland
Uralskie Gory
Timanskiy Kryazh
Severnyye Uvaly
Kolskiy Poluostrov
Poluostrov Kanin
Ostrov Kolguyev
Ladozhskoye Ozero
Onezhskoye Ozero
MOSKVA
SANKT-PETERBURG
Helsinki
Tallinn
Riga
Vilnius
MINSK
WARSZAWA
Kaliningrad (Russia)
Arkhangelsk
Murmansk
KAZAN
PERM
SAMARA
UFA
Orenburg
Syktyvkar
Vorkuta

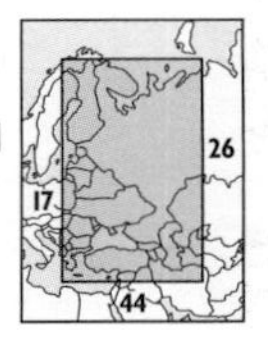

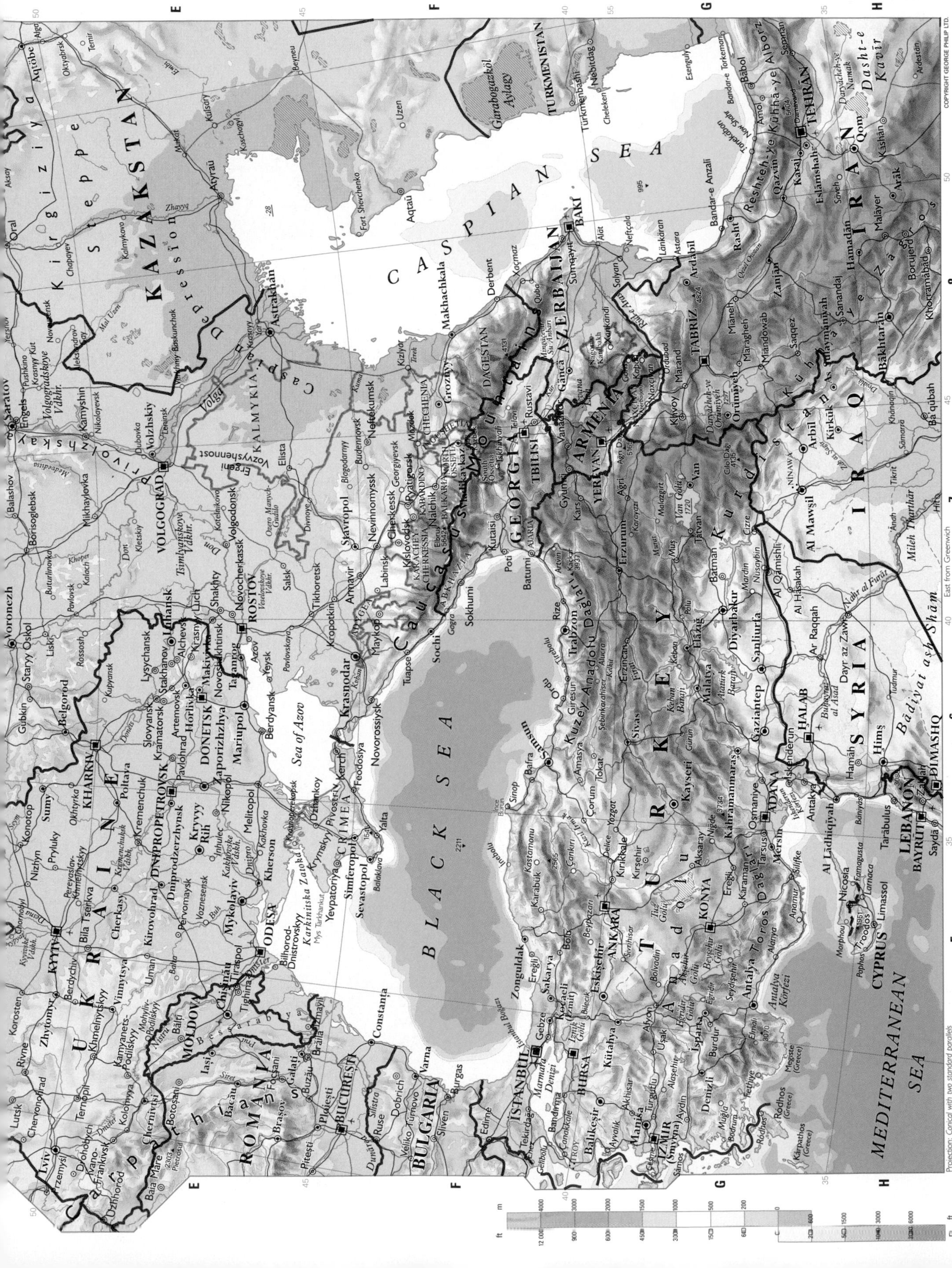

UKRAINE
MOLDOVA
ROMANIA
BULGARIA
TURKEY
GEORGIA
ARMENIA
AZERBAIJAN
KAZAKSTAN
TURKMENISTAN
IRAN
IRAQ
SYRIA
LEBANON
CYPRUS

BLACK SEA
CASPIAN SEA
MEDITERRANEAN SEA
Sea of Azov

Caspian Depression
Kirgiziya Steppe
Caucasus Mountains
Anadolu
Kurdistan
Zagros
Reshteh-ye Kuhha-ye Alborz
Dasht-e Kavir
Badiyat ash Sham

KYYIV
ODESA
KHARKIV
DNIPROPETROVSK
DONETSK
ROSTOV
VOLGOGRAD
BUCURESTI
ISTANBUL
ANKARA
IZMIR
BURSA
KONYA
ADANA
TBILISI
YEREVAN
BAKI
TABRIZ
TEHRAN
HALAB
DIMASHQ
BAYRUT

East from Greenwich

Projection: Conical with two standard parallels

| ft | m |
|---|---|
| 12 000 | 4000 |
| 9000 | 3000 |
| 6000 | 2000 |
| 4500 | 1500 |
| 3000 | 1000 |
| 1500 | 500 |
| 600 | 200 |
| 0 | 0 |
| 600 | 200 |
| 1500 | 500 |
| 3000 | 1000 |
| 6000 | 2000 |
| ft | m |

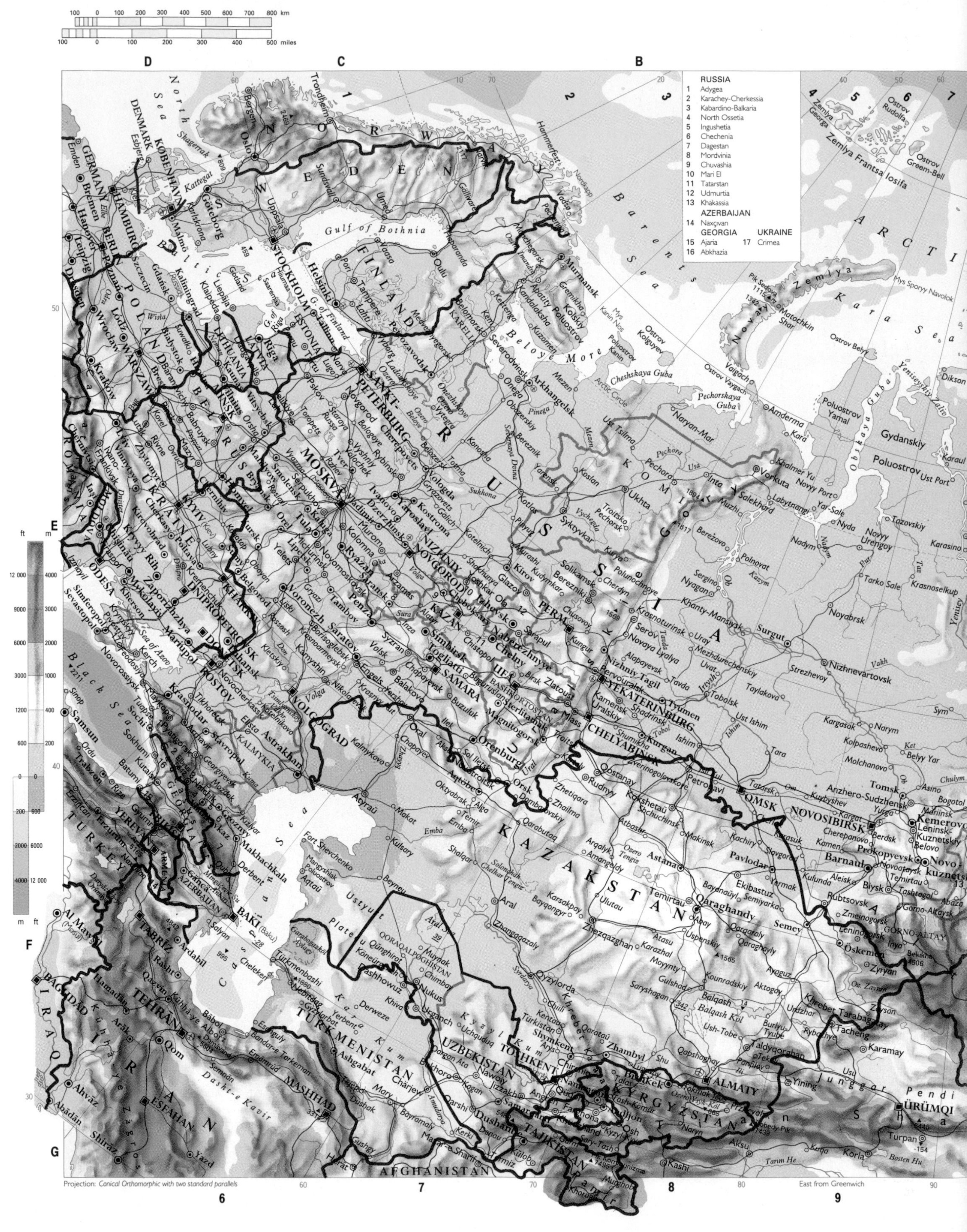
100 0 100 200 300 400 500 600 700 800 km
100 0 100 200 300 400 500 miles
RUSSIA
1 Adygea
2 Karachey-Cherkessia
3 Kabardino-Balkaria
4 North Ossetia
5 Ingushetia
6 Chechenia
7 Dagestan
8 Mordvinia
9 Chuvashia
10 Mari El
11 Tatarstan
12 Udmurtia
13 Khakassia
AZERBAIJAN
14 Naxçıvan
GEORGIA
15 Ajaria
16 Abkhazia
UKRAINE
17 Crimea
Projection: Conical Orthomorphic with two standard parallels
East from Greenwich
RUSSIA
KAZAKSTAN
UZBEKISTAN
TURKMENISTAN
KYRGYZSTAN
TAJIKISTAN
AFGHANISTAN
IRAN
IRAQ
TURKEY
GEORGIA
ARMENIA
AZERBAIJAN
UKRAINE
BELARUS
POLAND
FINLAND
SWEDEN
NORWAY
ESTONIA
LATVIA
LITHUANIA
DENMARK
GERMANY
ROMANIA
MOLDOVA
Barents Sea
Kara Sea
Black Sea
Caspian Sea
Aral Sea
Baltic Sea
North Sea
Gulf of Bothnia
MOSKVA
SANKT-PETERBURG
NIZHNIY NOVGOROD
YEKATERINBURG
NOVOSIBIRSK
OMSK
CHELYABINSK
VOLGOGRAD
SAMARA
KAZAN
PERM
UFA
ROSTOV
KYYIV
KHARKIV
DNIPROPETROVSK
ODESA
ALMATY
TOSHKENT
BAKI
TEHRAN
ÜRÜMQI

Severnaya Zemlya
Ostrov Oktyabrskoy Revolyutsii
Ostrov Bolshevik
Ostrov Komsomolets
Ostrov Shmidta
Ostrov Pioner
Mys Arkticheskiy
Mys Chelyuskin
Proliv Vilkitskogo
Poluostrov Taymyr
Gory Byrranga
Oz. Taymyr
O C E A N
Laptev Sea
Novosibirskiye Ostrova
Ostrov Kotelnyy
Ostrov Belkovskiy
Ostrov Stolbovoy
Ostrov Faddeyevskiy
Ostrov Novaya Sibir
Ostrova Delonga
Ostrov Bennetta
Lyakhovskiye Ostrova
Proliv Dmitriya Lapteva
East Siberian Sea
Ostrov Vrangelya
Ostrova Medvezhi
Chukchi Sea
Mys Dezhneva (East C.)
St. Lawrence I. (U.S.A.)
Chukotskoye Nagorye
Anadyrskiy Zaliv
Koryakskoye Nagorye
Bering Sea
Kolymskoye Nagorye
Sredinnyy Khrebet
Poluostrov Kamchatka
Petropavlovsk-Kamchatskiy
Sea of Okhotsk
Khrebet Cherskogo
Verkhoyanskiy Khrebet
Khrebet Dzhugdzur
Stanovoy Khrebet
Yablonovyy Khrebet
R U S S I A
Arctic Circle
Sakhalin
Kurilskiye Ostrova
Hokkaidō
SAPPORO
Sikhote Alin
Khabarovsk
Komsomolsk
Vladivostok
Nakhodka
Magadan
Yakutsk
Lena
Tiksi
Norilsk
Dudinka
Khatanga
Krasnoyarsk
Bratsk
Irkutsk
Angarsk
Ulan Ude
Chita
Blagoveshchensk
Vostochnyy Sayan
Ozero Baykal
Ulaanbaatar
M O N G O L I A
Hangayn Nuruu
Hentiyn Nuruu
Gobi
C H I N A
Da Hinggan Ling
Dongbei
QIQIHAR
HARBIN
CHANGCHUN
JILIN
SHENYANG
FUSHUN
ANSHAN
DALIAN
BEIJING
Baotou
Hohhot
Zhangjiakou
Hami
NORTH KOREA
PYONGYANG
SOUTH KOREA
SŎUL
INCH'ŎN
TAEJŎN
TAEGU
PUSAN
Sea of Japan
Honshū
JAPAN
ŌSAKA
Hakodate
Aomori
Niigata
Kanazawa
Fuji-San 3776
COPYRIGHT GEORGE PHILIP LTD.

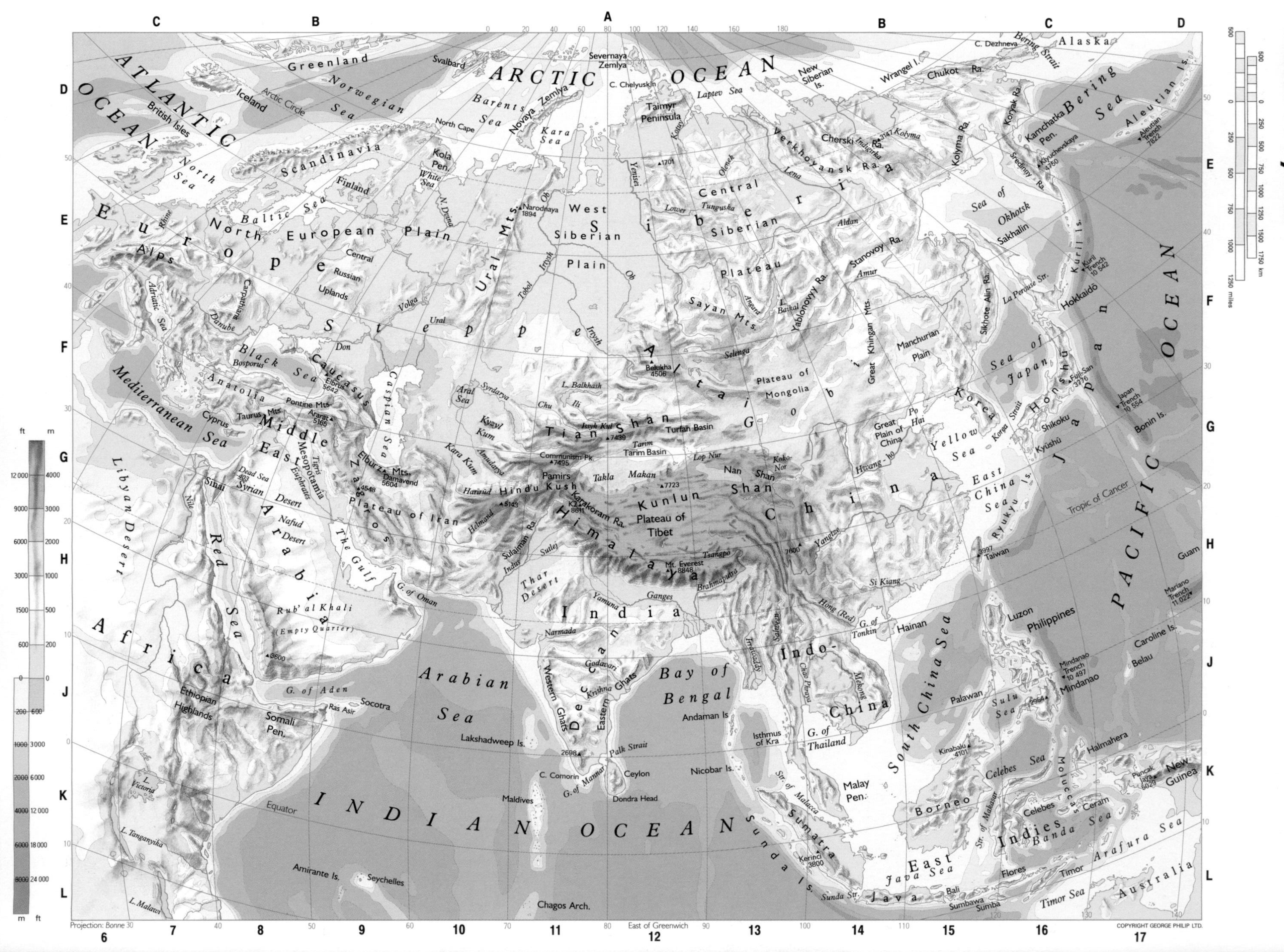

500 0 250 500 750 1000 1250 1500 1750 km
500 0 250 500 750 1000 1250 miles
ARCTIC OCEAN
PACIFIC OCEAN
INDIAN OCEAN
ATLANTIC OCEAN
Europe
Siberia
China
India
Arabia
Africa
Australia
Alaska
Greenland
Iceland
British Isles
Scandinavia
Svalbard
Severnaya Zemlya
Novaya Zemlya
Taimyr Peninsula
C. Chelyuskin
New Siberian Is.
Wrangel I.
C. Dezhneva
Bering Strait
Bering Sea
Aleutian Is.
Kamchatka Pen.
Sea of Okhotsk
Sakhalin
Kuril Is.
Hokkaido
Honshu
Shikoku
Kyūshū
Sea of Japan
Korea
Yellow Sea
East China Sea
Ryukyu Is.
Taiwan
Tropic of Cancer
Philippines
Luzon
Mindanao
South China Sea
Hainan
Indo-China
Malay Pen.
Sumatra
Java
Borneo
Celebes
New Guinea
Timor Sea
Arafura Sea
Banda Sea
Java Sea
East Indies
Bay of Bengal
Arabian Sea
Red Sea
The Gulf
Caspian Sea
Black Sea
Mediterranean Sea
Aral Sea
Barents Sea
Kara Sea
Laptev Sea
Norwegian Sea
North Sea
Baltic Sea
North European Plain
Central Russian Uplands
Ural Mts.
West Siberian Plain
Central Siberian Plateau
Verkhoyansk Ra.
Cherski Ra.
Kolyma Ra.
Stanovoy Ra.
Yablonovyy Ra.
Sayan Mts.
Altai
Gobi
Plateau of Mongolia
Great Khingan Mts.
Manchurian Plain
Great Plain of China
Tian Shan
Tarim Basin
Turfan Basin
Takla Makan
Kunlun Shan
Nan Shan
Plateau of Tibet
Himalaya
Mt. Everest 8848
Karakoram Ra.
Hindu Kush
Pamirs
Plateau of Iran
Elburz Mts.
Caucasus
Anatolia
Mesopotamia
Syrian Desert
Rub' al Khali (Empty Quarter)
Thar Desert
Deccan
Western Ghats
Eastern Ghats
Ceylon
Libyan Desert
Ethiopian Highlands
Somali Pen.
Equator
Ob
Yenisei
Lena
Amur
Irtysh
Volga
Ganges
Indus
Yangtze
Hwang-ho
Mekong
Irrawaddy
Projection: Bonne
East of Greenwich
COPYRIGHT GEORGE PHILIP LTD.
ft m

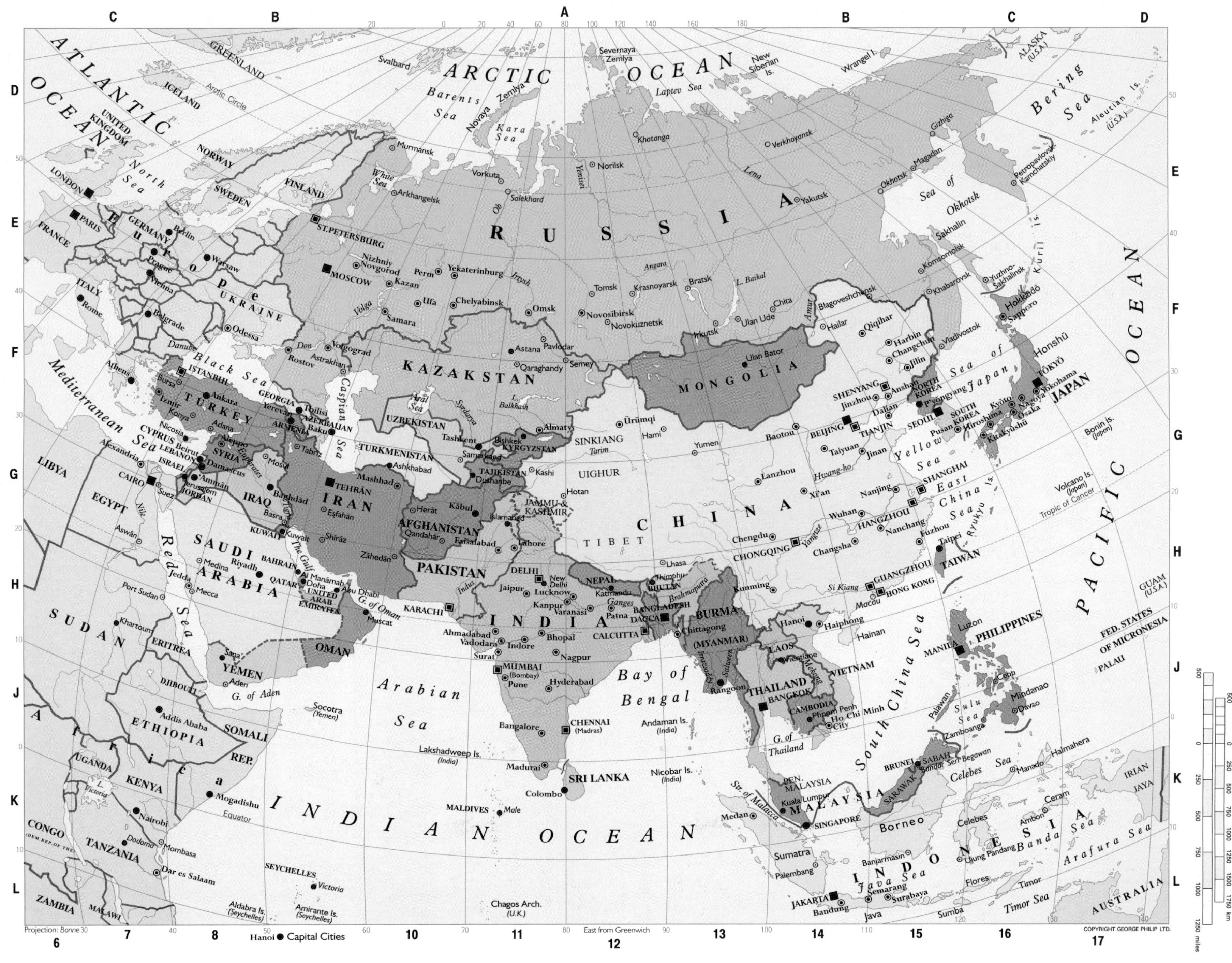

500 0 250 500 750 1000 1250 1500 1750 km
500 0 250 500 750 1000 1250 miles
ARCTIC OCEAN
ATLANTIC OCEAN
PACIFIC OCEAN
INDIAN OCEAN
R U S S I A
C H I N A
MONGOLIA
KAZAKSTAN
JAPAN
INDIA
PAKISTAN
AFGHANISTAN
IRAN
IRAQ
SAUDI ARABIA
TURKEY
SYRIA
OMAN
YEMEN
UZBEKISTAN
TURKMENISTAN
TAJIKISTAN
KYRGYZSTAN
NEPAL
BHUTAN
BANGLADESH
BURMA (MYANMAR)
THAILAND
LAOS
VIETNAM
CAMBODIA
MALAYSIA
SINGAPORE
PHILIPPINES
TAIWAN
SRI LANKA
I N D O N E S I A
E u r o p e
A f r i c a
EGYPT
SUDAN
ETHIOPIA
KENYA
TANZANIA
SOMALI REP.
Bay of Bengal
Arabian Sea
South China Sea
Caspian Sea
Black Sea
Red Sea
Mediterranean Sea
Sea of Japan
Sea of Okhotsk
Bering Sea
Yellow Sea
East China Sea
Hanoi ● Capital Cities
Projection: Bonne
East from Greenwich
COPYRIGHT GEORGE PHILIP LTD.

# JAPAN

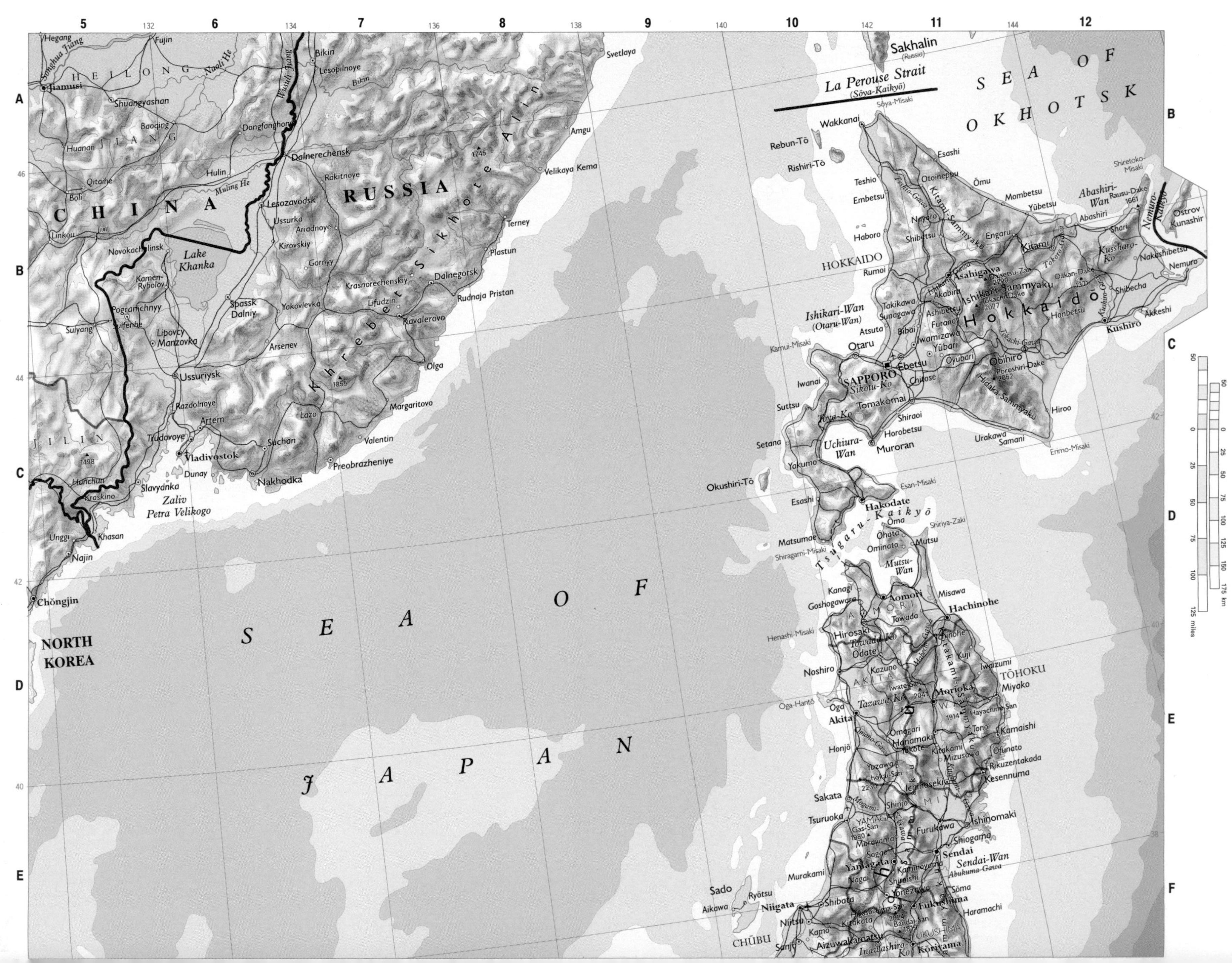
SEA OF OKHOTSK
SEA OF JAPAN
RUSSIA
CHINA
NORTH KOREA
HOKKAIDO
Hokkaidō
TŌHOKU
CHŪBU
HEILONGJIANG
JILIN
Sakhalin (Russia)
La Perouse Strait (Sōya-Kaikyō)
Tsugaru-Kaikyō
Ishikari-Wan (Otaru-Wan)
Uchiura-Wan
Mutsu-Wan
Sendai-Wan
Abashiri-Wan
Nemuro-Kaikyō
Ostrov Kunashir
Khrebet Sikhote Alin
Lake Khanka
Zaliv Petra Velikogo
SAPPORO
Hakodate
Asahigawa
Obihiro
Kushiro
Muroran
Otaru
Ebetsu
Tomakomai
Wakkanai
Nemuro
Hiroo
Abashiri
Kitami
Aomori
Hachinohe
Morioka
Akita
Sendai
Yamagata
Fukushima
Niigata
Sado
Okushiri-Tō
Rishiri-Tō
Rebun-Tō
Vladivostok
Nakhodka
Ussuriysk
Lesozavodsk
Dalnerechensk
Chŏngjin
Najin
Jiamusi
Olga
Terney
Svetlaya
Amgu
Preobrazheniye
Esashi
Matsumae
Sakata
Hirosaki
Noshiro
Kamaishi
Ishinomaki
Miyako
A
B
C
D
E
F
5
6
7
8
9
10
11
12
50 0 25 50 75 100 125 150 175 km
50 0 25 50 75 100 125 miles

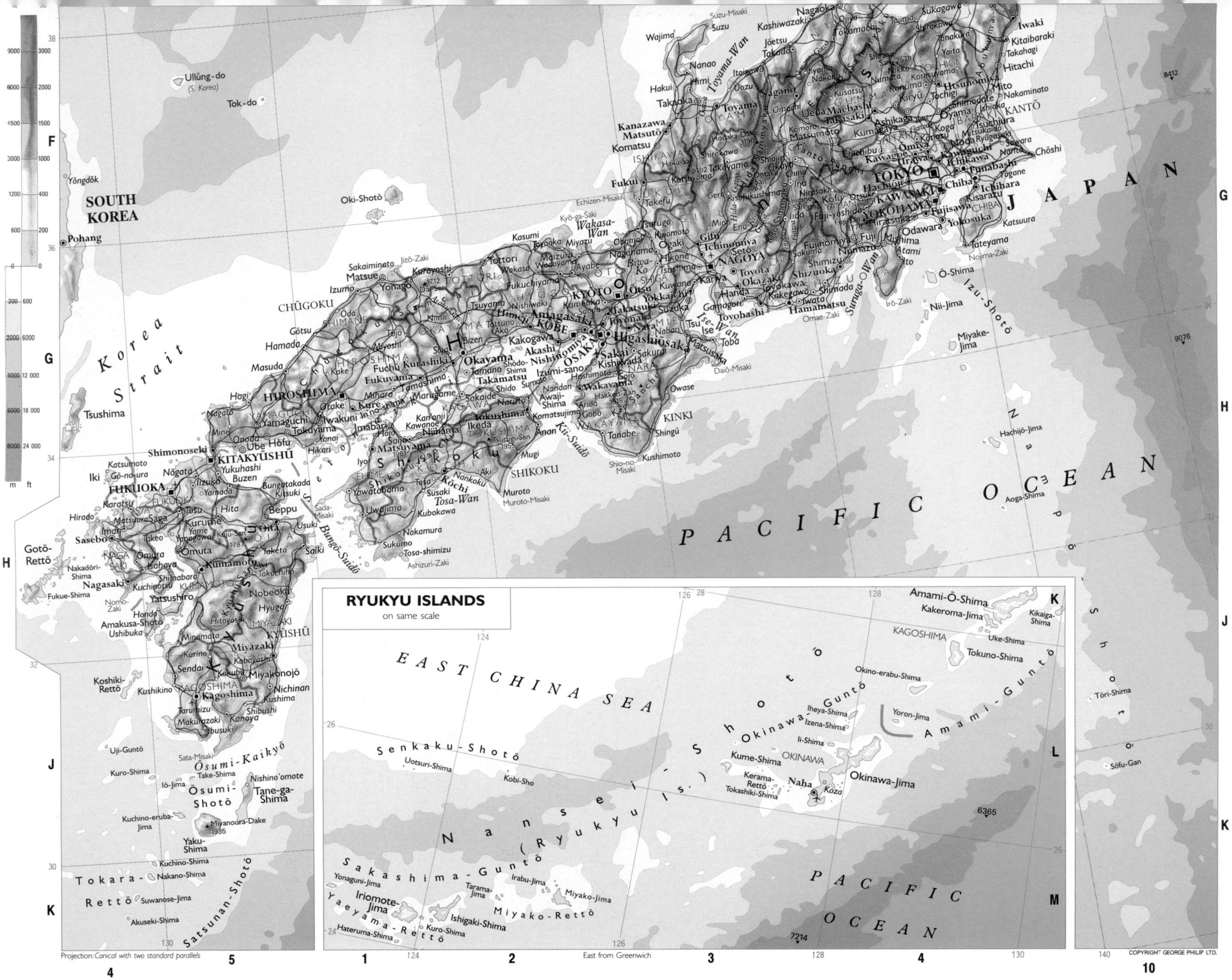

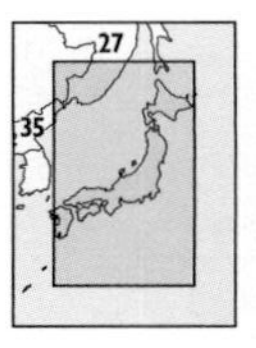


## RYUKYU ISLANDS

on same scale

Projection: Conical with two standard parallels

East from Greenwich

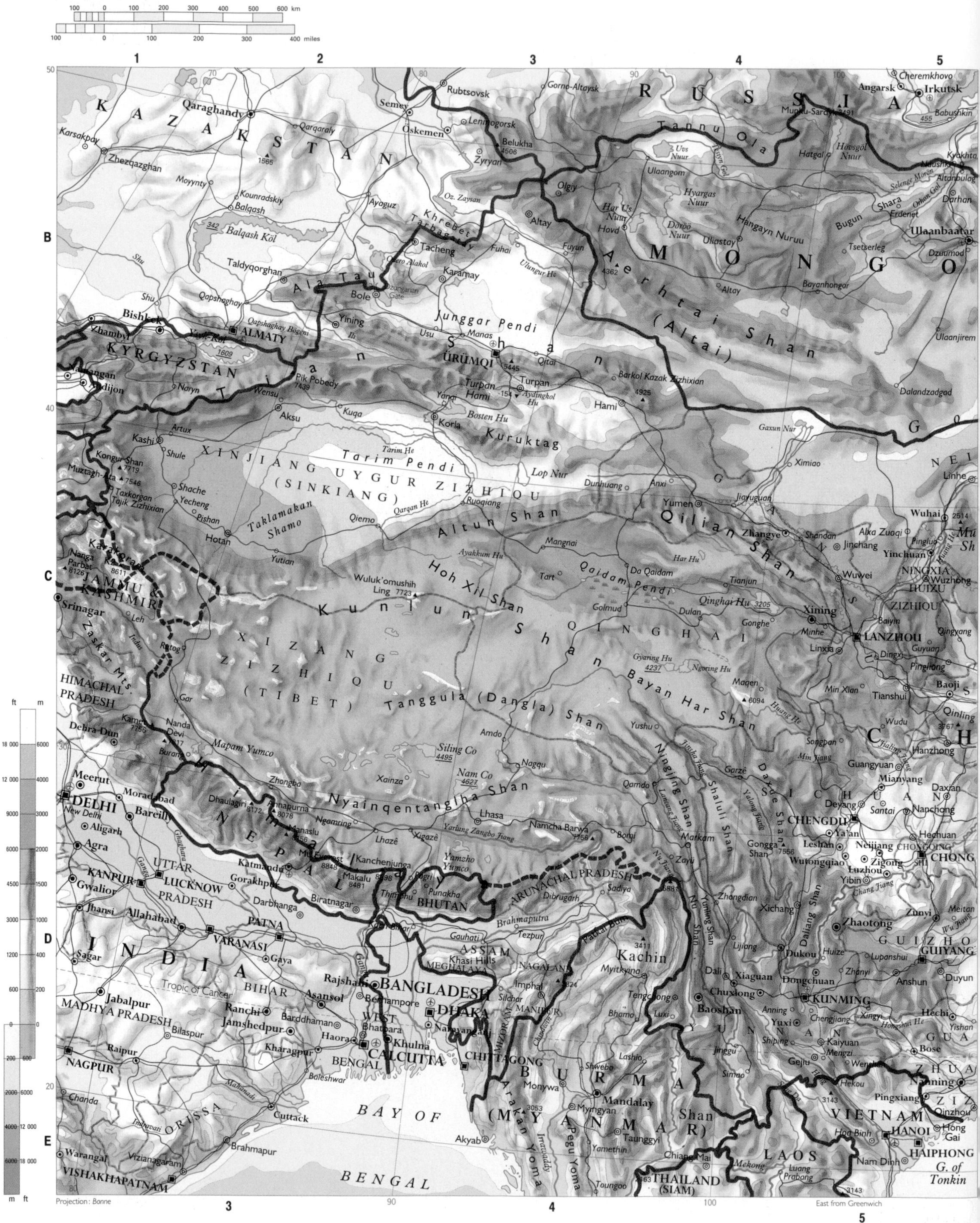
100 0 100 200 300 400 500 600 km
100 0 100 200 300 400 miles
RUSSIA
KAZAKSTAN
MONGOLIA
KYRGYZSTAN
XINJIANG UYGUR ZIZHIQU (SINKIANG)
XIZANG ZIZHIQU (TIBET)
QINGHAI
NINGXIA HUIZU ZIZHIQU
SICHUAN
GUIZHOU
YUNNAN
JAMMU & KASHMIR
HIMACHAL PRADESH
UTTAR PRADESH
MADHYA PRADESH
BIHAR
WEST BENGAL
ORISSA
ASSAM
MEGHALAYA
NAGALAND
MANIPUR
MIZORAM
ARUNACHAL PRADESH
INDIA
NEPAL
BHUTAN
BANGLADESH
BURMA (MYANMAR)
THAILAND (SIAM)
LAOS
VIETNAM
Tannu Ola
Aerhtai Shan (Altai)
Hangayn Nuruu
Tian Shan
Junggar Pendi
Tarim Pendi
Taklamakan Shamo
Kuruktag
Altun Shan
Qilian Shan
Qaidam Pendi
Hoh Xil Shan
Kunlun Shan
Bayan Har Shan
Tanggula (Dangla) Shan
Nyainqentanglha Shan
Himalaya
Karakoram
Zaskar Mts.
Ningjing Shan
Shaluli Shan
Daxue Shan
Daliang Shan
Khasi Hills
Patkai Bum
Kachin
Arakan Yoma
Pegu Yoma
Shan
Balqash Köl
Lop Nur
Qinghai Hu 3205
Gyaring Hu 4237
Ngoring Hu
Siling Co 4495
Nam Co 4627
Mapam Yumco
Yamzho Yumco
Bosten Hu
Gaxun Nur
Uvs Nuur
Hövsgöl Nuur
Hyargas Nuur
Har Us Nuur
Dörgön Nuur
Oz. Zaysan
Tarim He
Qarqan He
Ili
Indus
Ganga
Brahmaputra
Yarlung Zangbo Jiang
Nu Jiang
Lancang Jiang
Jinsha Jiang
Yalong Jiang
Min Jiang
Chang Jiang
Huang He
Mekong
Irrawaddy
Mahanadi
BAY OF BENGAL
G. of Tonkin
Tropic of Cancer
Mt. Everest 8848
Kanchenjunga 8598
Makalu 8481
Annapurna 8078
Dhaulagiri 8172
Manaslu 8156
Nanda Devi 7817
Kamet 7756
Nanga Parbat 8126
K2 8611
Kongur Shan 7719
Muztagh Ata 7546
Pik Pobedy 7439
Gongga Shan 7556
Namcha Barwa 7756
Wuluk'omushih Ling 7723
Belukha 4506
Qaraghandy
Semey
Oskemen
Rubtsovsk
Almaty
Bishkek
Zhambyl
Andijon
Namangan
Kashi
Ürümqi
Turpan
Hami
Korla
Aksu
Yining
Karamay
Altay
Hotan
Yecheng
Shache
Qiemo
Ruoqiang
Dunhuang
Yumen
Jiayuguan
Zhangye
Golmud
Xining
Lanzhou
Yinchuan
Wuhai
Baoji
Tianshui
Hanzhong
Lhasa
Xigazê
Nagqu
Qamdo
Chengdu
Chongqing
Leshan
Zigong
Yibin
Xichang
Kunming
Guiyang
Dali
Baoshan
Nanning
Hanoi
Haiphong
Ulaanbaatar
Irkutsk
Angarsk
Darhan
Ölgiy
Hovd
Uliastay
Delhi
New Delhi
Meerut
Agra
Aligarh
Kanpur
Lucknow
Allahabad
Varanasi
Patna
Gaya
Gwalior
Jhansi
Jabalpur
Nagpur
Raipur
Ranchi
Jamshedpur
Calcutta
Dhaka
Chittagong
Khulna
Rajshahi
Katmandu
Thimphu
Srinagar
Mandalay
Akyab
Chiang Mai
Vishakhapatnam
Projection: Bonne
East from Greenwich

Oz. Baykal
Bukachacha
Chita
Sretensk
Ulan Ude
Nerchinsk
Gulian
Shimanovsk
Svobodnyy
Chegdomyn
Amur
Aleksandrovsk-Sakhalinskiy
Komsomolsk
Poronaysk
Mys Terpeniya
Sakhalin
Petrovsk-Zabaykalskiy
Olovyannaya
Borzya
Priargunsk
Yilehuli Shan
Blagoveshchensk
Aihui
Bureya
Ozero Bolon
Vanino
Oroqen Zizhiqi
Birobidzhan
Manzhouli
Hulun Nur
Hailar
Nenjiang
Obluchye
Khabarovsk
Tartarskiy Proliv
Yuzhno-Sakhalinsk
Hentiyn Nuruu
Bei'an
Xiao Hinggan Ling
Amur
Qianjin
Kholmsk
Hegang
Yichun
Jiamusi
Shuangyashan
Bikin
Khrebet Sikhote Alin
La Perouse Str.
Kerulen
Choybalsan
Buir Nur
Butha Qi
QIQIHAR
Wakkanai
L I A
Solon
Daqing
Anda
Suihua
Hulin
Tamsagbulag
Horqin Youyi Qianqi
HARBIN
Jixi
Mishan
Kitami
Asahigawa
Shuangcheng
Baicheng
Tao'an
Fuyu
Da Hinggan Ling
Dongbei (Manchuria)
L. Khanka
2290
Hokkaidō
Otaru
SAPPORO
Kushiro
Saynshand
Huolin Gol
Mudanjiang
Ussuriysk
1855
Xilinhot
1949
CHANGCHUN
JILIN
Dunhua
Vladivostok
Artem
Partizansk
Muroran
Erimo-misaki
Borhoyn Tal
Erenhot
Shuangliao
Songhua Hu
Nakhodka
Hunchun
Linxi
Sonid Youqi
Tongliao
Siping
Liaoyuan
Changbai Shan
Yanji
Hakodate
Tsugaru-Kaikyō
MONGGOL ZIZHIQU (INNER MONGOLIA)
Duolun
Tieling
2744
Chŏngjin
Aomori
Hachinohe
Bayan Obo
Chifeng
Fuxin
FUSHUN
SHENYANG
Morioka
Chaoyang
Liaoyang
Benxi
SEA OF
Akita
Jining
Chengde
Jinzhou
LIAONING
Kimchaek
Hohhot
Zhangjiakou
ANSHAN
Yalu Jiang
Sakata
Ishinomaki
Yingkou
NORTH
Hŭngnam
Baotou
Datong
Xuanhua
Qinhuangdao
Dandong
Hamhung
KOREA
JAPAN
Yamagata
Sendai
Sado
BEIJING
(PEKING)
BEIJING SHI
Liaodong Wan
Liaodong Bandao
Korea Bay
Wŏnsan
Niigata
Fukushima
Us amo
TANGSHAN
TIANJINN SHI
P'YŎNGYANG
Kŏriyama
Baoding
Anci
TIANJIN
DALIAN
Namp'o
Ch'unch'ŏn
Kangnŭng
Wajima
Jōetsu
Utsunomiya
Yuanping
3058
HEBEI
Cangzhou
Haeju
Kaesŏng
Takaoka
Toyama
Mito
GREAT WALL
TAIYUAN
SHIJIAZHUANG
Bo Hai
SŎUL (SEOUL)
Kanazawa
TOKYO
KAWASAKI
Yantai
Weihai
INCH'ŎN
SOUTH
Komatsu
YOKOHAMA
Yangquan
Yuci
Dezhou
Huang He
Ye Xian
Shandong Bandao
KOREA
Matsue
NAGOYA
Fuji-San
3776
Fenyang
JINAN
Weifang
YELLOW
TAEJŎN
TAEGU
KYOTO
ŌSAKA
Shizuoka
Hamamatsu
Yan'an
Handan
ZIBO
QINGDAO
Kunsan
PUSAN
Chŏnju
Masan
Okayama
Changzhi
Anyang
Tai'an
SHANDONG
SEA
KWANGJU
1915
KŌBE
Sakai
Nampō-Shotō
Linfen
Jincheng
Xinxiang
Rizhao
Mokp'o
Tsushima
HIROSHIMA
Kure
Shikoku
Wakayama
Tongchuan
Luoyang
Kaifeng
Jining
Zaozhuang
Shimonoseki
Kōchi
Sanmenxia
Grand Canal
Lianyungang
KITAKYUSHU
Matsuyama
Xianyang
ZHENGZHOU
FUKUOKA
XI'AN
Shangqiu
Xuzhou
Qingjiang
Cheju-do
1950
Sasebo
Kumamoto
Shandi
Pingdingshan
Huaibei
Yancheng
Korea Strait
Nagasaki
Nanyang
Shangshui
HENAN
Hongze Hu
JIANGSU
Kyūshū
Fuyang
Bengbu
Miyazaki
Han Shui
Zhumadian
Huainan
Yangzhou
Taizhou
Kagoshima
Ankang
Shiyan
HEFEI
NANJING
Changzhou
Nantong
Daba Shan
Xiangfan
Xinyang
Huai He
Wuxi
SHANGHAI SHI
Dabie Shan
ANHUI
Ma'anshan
Suzhou
SHANGHAI
Tane-ga-Shima
Zhongxiang
Wuhu
Fengjie
HUBEI
Tongling
Wuxing
Jiaxing
Yaku-Shima
Wanxian
Yichang
WUHAN
Anqing
HANGZHOU
Hangzhou Wan
Enshi
Shashi
Huangshi
Chang Jiang (Yangtse)
Tunxi
Shaoxing
NINGBO
EAST CHINA
QING
Yueyang
Jiujiang
ZHEJIANG
Amami-Ō-Shima
Changde
Dongting Hu
Poyang Hu
Jingdezhen
Jinhua
LINHAI
Tokuno-Shima
Jishou
NANCHANG
Shangrao
Quzhou
SEA
Yuan Jiang
Yiyang
CHANGSHA
HUNAN
Xiangtan
JIANGXI
Wenzhou
2683
Huaihua
Pingxiang
Fuzhou
Wuyi Shan
2120
Okinawa-Jima
Shaoyang
Ji'an
Min Jiang
Nanping
Ryūkyū-rettō
Naha
Hongjiang
Hengyang
Gan Jiang
Sanming
FUZHOU
7507
PACIFIC
Ganzhou
Yong'an
FUJIAN
Taiwan Strait
Xing'an
Ruijin
Chilung
Nan Ling
Longyan
Putian
T'AIPEI
Sakishima-Guntō
Miyako-Jima
Guilin
Shaoguan
Quanzhou
Hsinchu
T'aichung
Ishigaki-Shima
Iriomote-Jima
Zhangzhou
Changhua
Tropic of Cancer
Liuzhou
Mei Xian
Xiamen
Chiai
Yu Shan
3997
GUANGDONG
Chaozhou
TAIWAN (FORMOSA)
Wuzhou
GUANGZHOU (CANTON)
Shantou
T'ainan
T'aitung
Zhaoqing
Foshan
Huizhou
P'ingtung
Jiangmen
KAOHSIUNG
Yangjiang
Macau
HONG KONG
OCEAN
Beihai
Maoming
Zhanjiang
Batan Is.
Leizhou Bandao
SOUTH CHINA
Qiongzhou Haixia
PHILIPPINES
Haikou
SEA
Babuyan Is.
Hainan Dao
1879
Yacheng
HAINAN
6
7
8
9
B
C
D
E
50
40
30
20
110
120
130
140

# NORTHERN CHINA AND KOREA

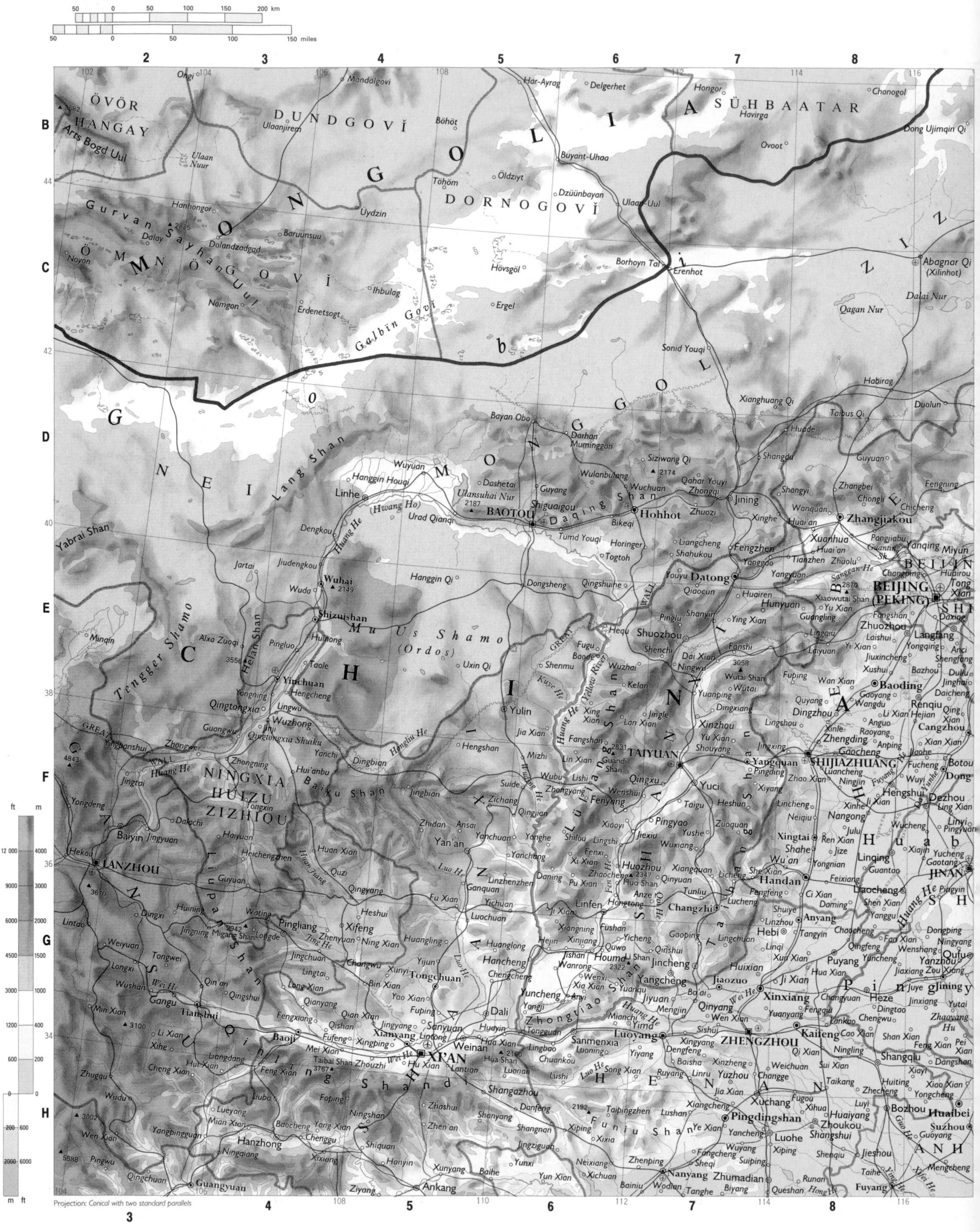

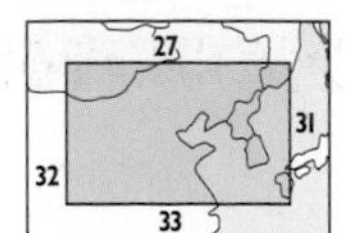

9 10 11 12 13 14 15 16

B C D E F G H

HARBIN
CHANGCHUN
JILIN
SHENYANG
FUSHUN
ANSHAN
DALIAN
TANGSHAN
TIANJIN SHI
TIANJIN
P'YŎNGYANG
SŎUL
INCH'ŎN
TAEJŎN
TAEGU
KWANGJU
PUSAN
ZIBO
QINGDAO
Vladivostok
Ussuriysk
Qiqihar
Mudanjiang
Jixi
Baicheng
Tongliao
Chifeng
Siping
Jinzhou
Huludao
Yingkou
Dandong
Benxi
Liaoyang
Qinhuangdao
Yantai
Weihai
Weifang
Linyi
Xuzhou
Huai'an
Yancheng
Hamhung
Ch'ŏngjin
Wŏnsan
Nampo
Kaesŏng
Kunsan
Chŏnju
Mokp'o
Ulsan
P'ohang
Cheju
Cheju-do
JAPAN
Sasebo
Nagasaki
Tsushima

H E I L O N G J I A N G
J I L I N
L I A O N I N G
S H A N D O N G
J I A N G S U
RUSSIA
NORTH KOREA
SOUTH KOREA
Dongbei (Manchuria)
Changbai Shan
Zhangguangcai Ling
Liaodong Bandao
Shandong Bandao
Liaodong Wan
Bo Hai
Korea Bay
Laizhou Wan
Tongjosŏn Man
SEA OF JAPAN
HUANG HAI (Yellow Sea)
Korea Strait
Paektu-san
Halla-san

East from Greenwich



9 10 11 12 13 14 15

100 0 100 200 300 400 500 km
100 0 50 100 150 200 250 300 350 miles
BURMA
(MYANMAR)
RANGOON
(YANGON)
G. of Martaban
THAILAND
LAOS
VIETNAM
CAMBODIA
BANGKOK
Phnom Penh
(Phnum Penh)
PHANH BHO HO CHI MINH
Gulf of Thailand
ANDAMAN SEA
SOUTH CHINA SEA
Paracel Is.
Spratly Is.
MALAYSIA
PENINSULAR MALAYSIA
KUALA LUMPUR
SINGAPORE
Johor Baharu
Strait of Malacca
BRUNEI
Bandar Seri Begawan
SARAWAK
SABAH
Kota Kinabalu
Borneo
KALIMANTAN
INDONESIA
MEDAN
PALEMBANG
JAKARTA
BANDUNG
SEMARANG
SURABAYA
Greater Sunda Islands
JAVA SEA
Java
Java Trench
INDIAN OCEAN
Kepulauan Natuna
Kepulauan Anambas
Kepulauan Riau
Bangka
Belitung
Siberut
Nias
Kepulauan Mentawai
Selat Karimata
BALI
Lombok
NUSA TENGGARA BARAT
Lesser
Da Nang
Hue
Dong Hoi
Vientiane
(Viangchan)
Nha Trang
Cam Ranh
Da Lat
Vung Tau
Can Tho
Ca Mau
Con Son
Phuket
Songkhla
Hat Yai
George Town
Kuala Terengganu
Kuantan
Pontianak
Kuching
Banjarmasin
Balikpapan
Samarinda
Padang
Pekanbaru
Jambi
Bengkulu
Tanjungkarang
Telukbetung
Bogor
Cirebon
Yogyakarta
Surakarta
Malang
Madura
Denpasar
Mataram
Projection: Mercator
East from Greenwich

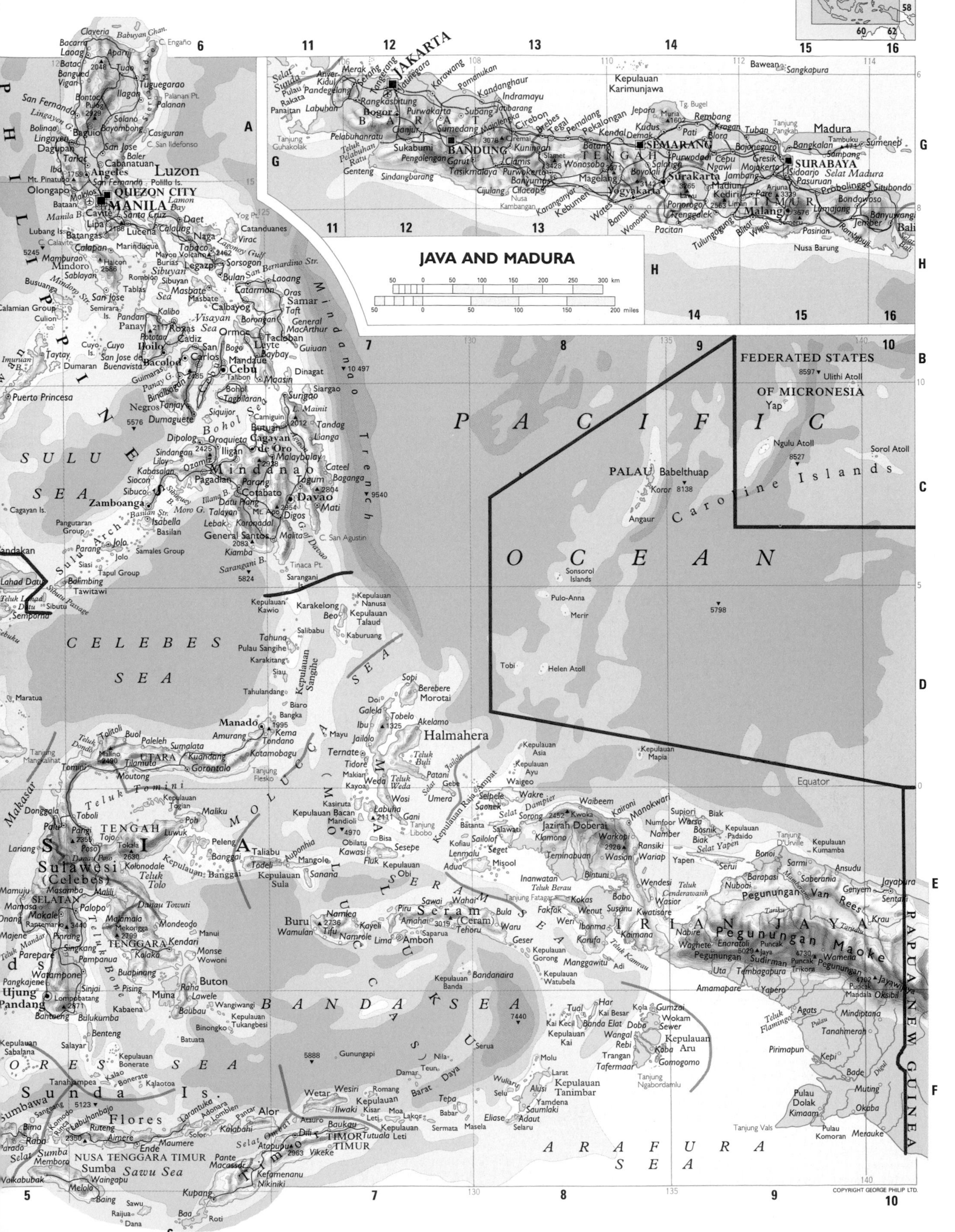

JAVA AND MADURA
PHILIPPINES
Luzon
QUEZON CITY
MANILA
Mindoro
Panay
Negros
Cebu
Samar
Leyte
Bohol
Mindanao
Davao
Zamboanga
Cagayan de Oro
Iligan
General Santos
SULU SEA
CELEBES SEA
Sulu Arch.
Mindanao Trench
PACIFIC OCEAN
FEDERATED STATES OF MICRONESIA
Yap
Ulithi Atoll
Ngulu Atoll
Sorol Atoll
Caroline Islands
PALAU
Babelthuap
Koror
Angaur
Sonsorol Islands
Pulo-Anna
Merir
Tobi
Helen Atoll
Kepulauan Talaud
Kepulauan Sangihe
Manado
Halmahera
Ternate
Tidore
Morotai
MOLUCCA SEA
Sulawesi (Celebes)
Teluk Tomini
Gorontalo
Palu
Poso
Kendari
Ujung Pandang
Buton
Kepulauan Sula
Kepulauan Banggai
Buru
Seram (Ceram)
Ambon
SERAM SEA
BANDA SEA
Kepulauan Aru
Kepulauan Tanimbar
Kepulauan Kai
Jazirah Doberai
Manokwari
Sorong
Biak
Yapen
IRIAN JAYA
Pegunungan Maoke
Pegunungan Van Rees
Jayapura
Puncak Jaya
PAPUA NEW GUINEA
ARAFURA SEA
Equator
Flores
Sumbawa
Sumba
Timor
Alor
Kupang
Dili
Sunda Is.
FLORES SEA
Sawu Sea
NUSA TENGGARA TIMUR
TIMOR TIMUR
JAKARTA
BANDUNG
SEMARANG
SURABAYA
Yogyakarta
Surakarta
Bogor
Cirebon
Madura
Malang
Kepulauan Karimunjawa
Bawean
Bali
Nusa Barung

# MAINLAND SOUTH-EAST ASIA

Gulf of Thailand
SOUTH CHINA SEA
MALAYSIA
PENINSULAR MALAYSIA
INDONESIA
Strait of Malacca
Myeik Kyunzu
Malay Peninsula
Sumatera
Cochin China
Borneo
SARAWAK (Malaysia)
Kepulauan Anambas (Indonesia)
Kepulauan Natuna Besar (Indonesia)
Kepulauan Natuna Selatan
Phnom Penh
THANH BHO HO CHI MINH (SAIGON)
Kuala Lumpur
SINGAPORE
George Town
Medan
Kuching
Mekong
Chuor Phnum Damrei
Phnum Kravanh
Cameron Highlands
Nha Trang
Songkhla
Hat Yai
Nakhon Si Thammarat
Surat Thani
Ipoh
Kota Baharu
Kuala Terengganu
Kuantan
Johor Baharu
Melaka
Phuket
Ko Samui
Con Son
Projection: Conical with two standard parallels
East from Greenwich
COPYRIGHT GEORGE PHILIP LTD.

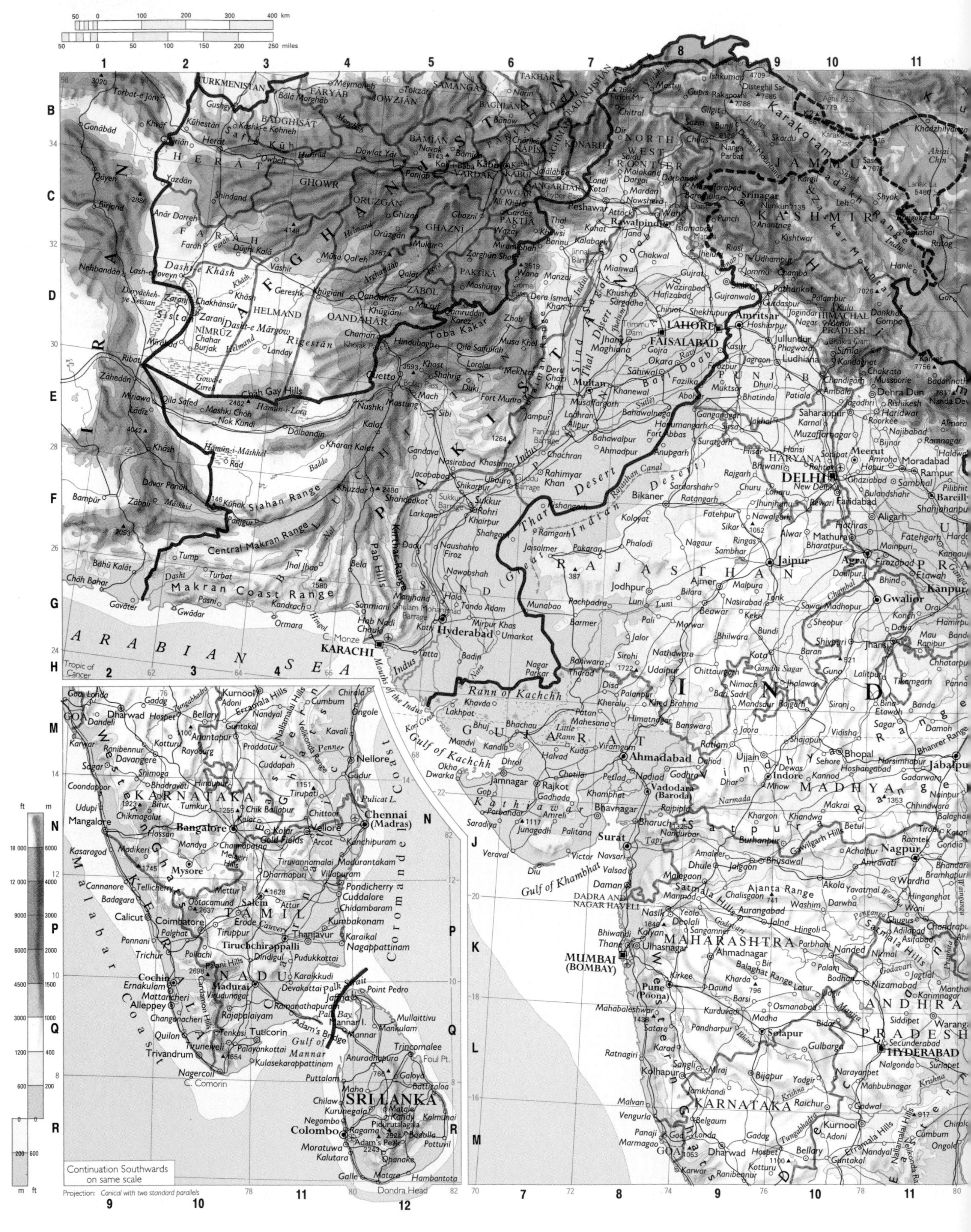

50 0 100 200 300 400 km
50 0 50 100 150 200 250 miles
TURKMENISTAN
AFGHANISTAN
PAKISTAN
IRAN
INDIA
KASHMIR
JAMMU
NORTH WEST FRONTIER
PUNJAB
HARYANA
RAJASTHAN
GUJARAT
SIND
MADHYA PRADESH
MAHARASHTRA
ANDHRA PRADESH
KARNATAKA
KERALA
TAMIL NADU
HIMACHAL PRADESH
DADRA AND NAGAR HAVELI
SRI LANKA
HERĀT
FARĀH
NĪMRŪZ
HELMAND
QANDAHĀR
GHOWR
ORUZGĀN
GHAZNĪ
PAKTĪKĀ
ZĀBOL
BĀMIĀN
BADGHĪSĀT
FĀRYĀB
JOWZJĀN
SAMANGĀN
BAGHLĀN
TAKHĀR
BADAKHSHAN
KONARHĀ
BALUCHISTAN
Karakoram
Hindu Kush
Safīd Kūh
Rīgestān
Dasht-e Khāsh
Dasht-e Mārgow
Chāh Gay Hills
Toba Kakar
Siahan Range
Central Makran Range
Makran Coast Range
Kirthar Range
Thar Desert
Great Indian Desert
Rann of Kachchh
Gulf of Kachchh
Gulf of Khambhat
Kathiawar
Western Ghats
Satpura Range
Ajanta Range
Malabar Coast
Coromandel Coast
Gulf of Mannar
Palk Strait
Palk Bay
Adam's Bridge
ARABIAN SEA
Tropic of Cancer
Mouths of the Indus
Indus
Kabul
Peshawar
Rawalpindi
Islamabad
Srinagar
LAHORE
FAISALABAD
Amritsar
Multan
Quetta
Sukkur
Hyderabad
KARACHI
DELHI
New Delhi
Meerut
Agra
Jaipur
Gwalior
Kanpur
Ahmadabad
Vadodara (Baroda)
Surat
MUMBAI (BOMBAY)
Pune (Poona)
Nagpur
Jabalpur
Bhopal
Indore
HYDERABAD
Secunderabad
Solapur
Chennai (Madras)
Bangalore
Mysore
Coimbatore
Madurai
Tiruchchirappalli
Cochin
Trivandrum
Colombo
Jaffna
Kandy
Trincomalee
C. Comorin
Dondra Head
Continuation Southwards on same scale
Projection: Conical with two standard parallels

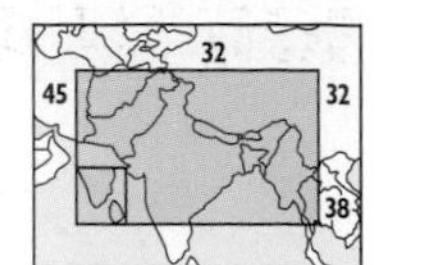


12 13 14 15 16 17 18 19 20 21 22

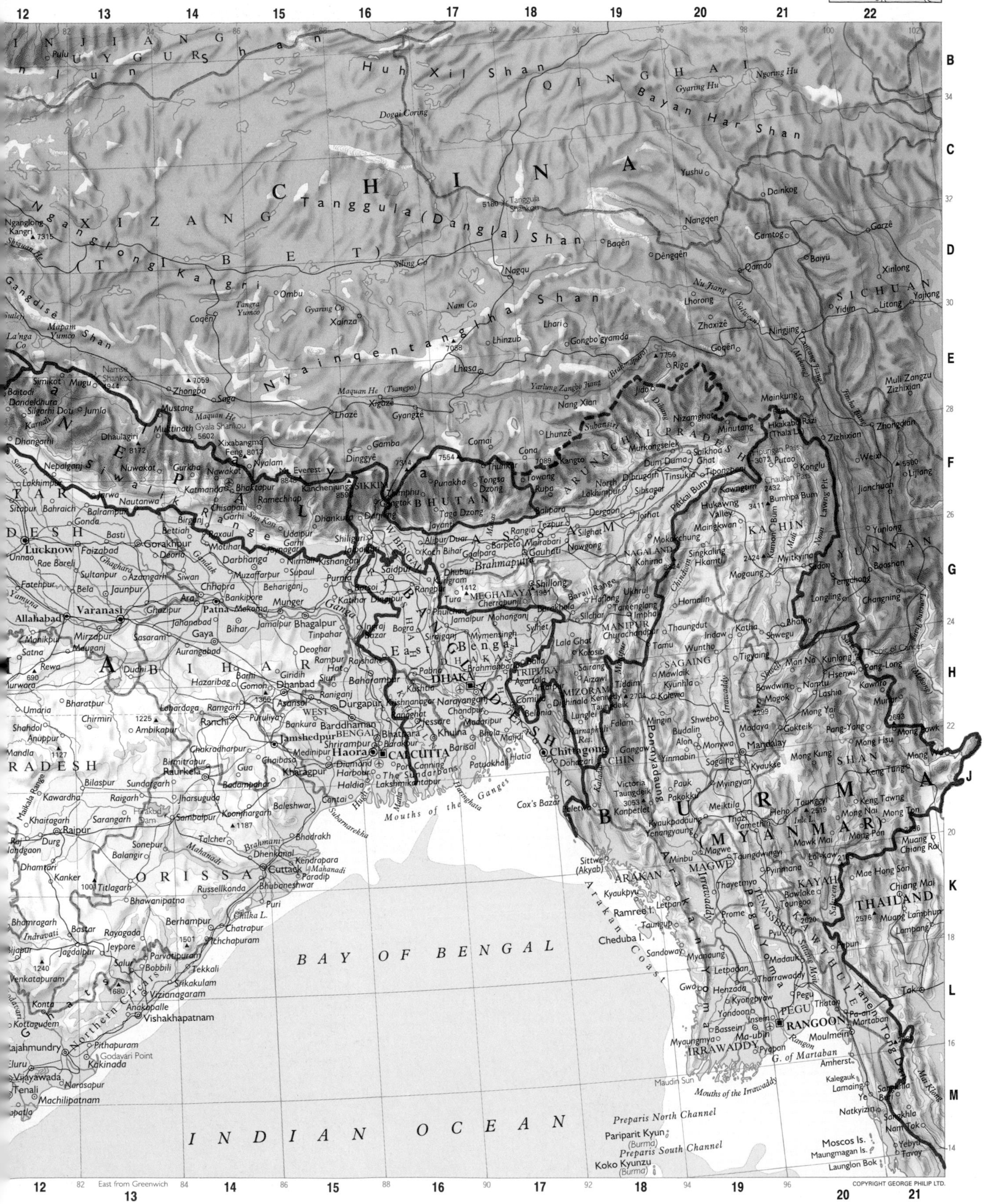

B C D E F G H J K L M

CHINA

XIZANG (TIBET)

QINGHAI

SICHUAN

YUNNAN

NEPAL

BHUTAN

SIKKIM

BANGLADESH

ARUNACHAL PRADESH

ASSAM

MEGHALAYA

NAGALAND

MANIPUR

MIZORAM

TRIPURA

W. BENGAL

WEST BENGAL

BIHAR

ORISSA

BURMA (MYANMAR)

KACHIN

SAGAING

CHIN

MAGWE

ARAKAN

PEGU

IRRAWADDY

KAYAH

KAWTHULE

TENASSERIM

SHAN

THAILAND

Huh Xil Shan

Bayan Har Shan

Tanggula (Dangla) Shan

Nyainqentanglha Shan

Nganglong Kangri

Gangdisê Shan

Siwalik Range

Arakan Yoma

Pegu Yoma

Ponnyadaung

Arakan Coast

Mouths of the Ganges

Mouths of the Irrawaddy

The Sundarbans

BAY OF BENGAL

INDIAN OCEAN

G. of Martaban

Preparis North Channel

Preparis South Channel

Lhasa

Xigazê

Gyangzê

Nagqu

Qamdo

Yushu

Mt. Everest 8848

Kanchenjunga 8598

Katmandu

Thimphu

Gangtok

Darjeeling

Lucknow

Varanasi

Allahabad

Patna

Gaya

Dhanbad

Jamshedpur

Ranchi

Haora

CALCUTTA

DHAKA

Chittagong

Khulna

Barisal

Mymensingh

Sylhet

Shillong

Gauhati

Imphal

Agartala

Aizawl

Cuttack

Bhubaneshwar

Puri

Berhampur

Vishakhapatnam

Rajahmundry

Kakinada

Vijayawada

Raipur

Mandalay

Myitkyina

Bhamo

Lashio

Sagaing

Magwe

Pegu

RANGOON

Bassein

Moulmein

Sittwe (Akyab)

Cheduba I.

Ramree I.

Cox's Bazar

Chiang Mai

Lampang

Tak

Tavoy

Moscos Is.

Paripari Kyun (Burma)

Koko Kyunzu (Burma)

Brahmaputra

Ganga

Irrawaddy

Chindwin

Salween

Mekong

East from Greenwich

12 13 14 15 16 17 18 19 20 21

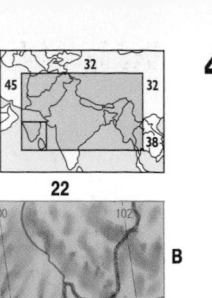

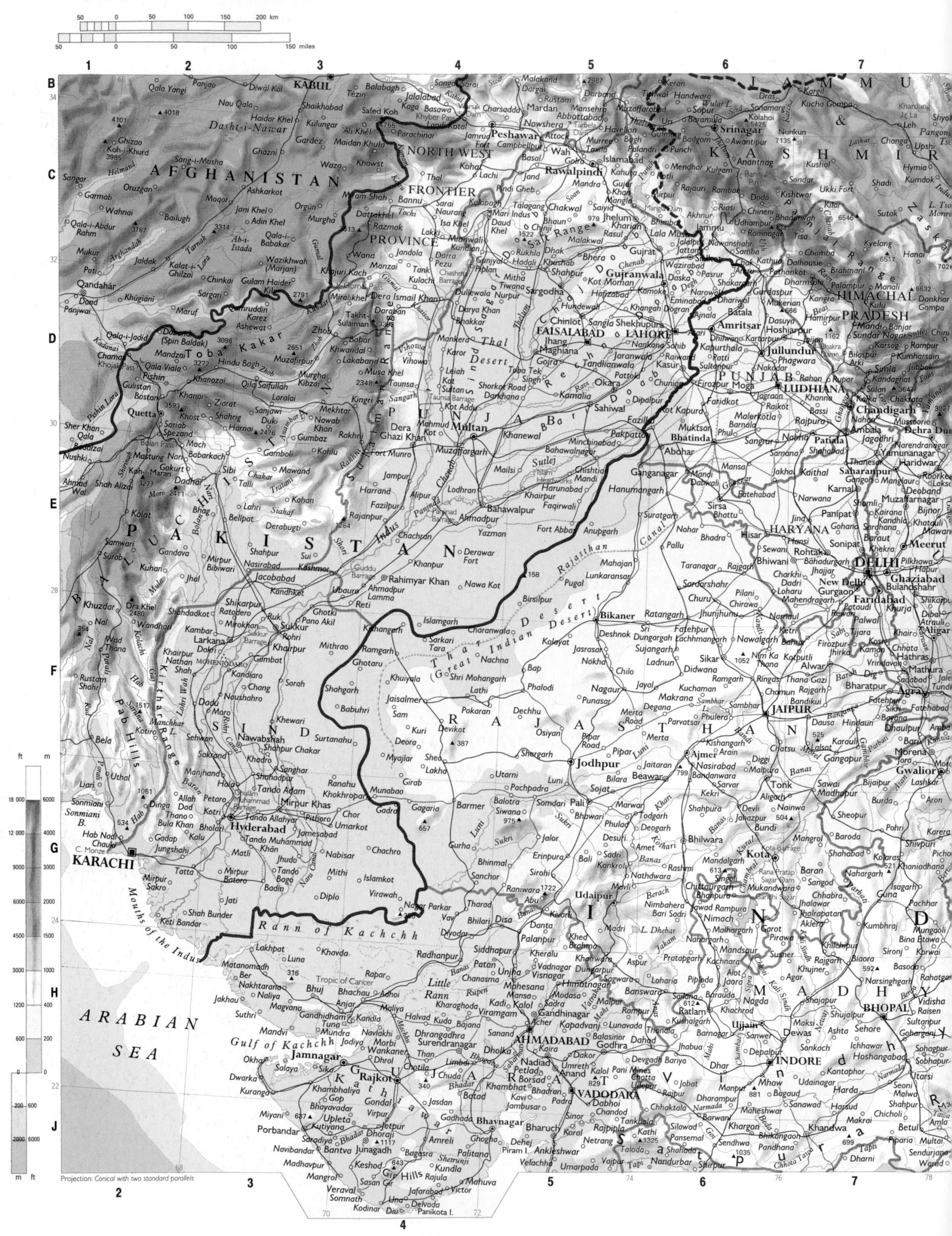

50 0 50 100 150 200 km
50 0 50 100 150 miles
AFGHANISTAN
PAKISTAN
NORTH WEST FRONTIER PROVINCE
BALUCHISTAN
PUNJAB
SIND
RAJASTHAN
HARYANA
HIMACHAL PRADESH
JAMMU & KASHMIR
MADHYA PRADESH
GUJARAT
INDIA
ARABIAN SEA
Gulf of Kachchh
Rann of Kachchh
Little Rann
Mouths of the Indus
Thar Desert (Great Indian Desert)
Thal Desert
Salt Range
Toba Kakar
Kirthar Range
Pab Hills
Dasht-i-Nawar
Indus
Tropic of Cancer
KABUL
Peshawar
Islamabad
Rawalpindi
Srinagar
Jammu
LAHORE
FAISALABAD
Gujranwala
Amritsar
Jullundur
LUDHIANA
Chandigarh
DELHI
New Delhi
Meerut
Agra
JAIPUR
Ajmer
Jodhpur
Bikaner
Multan
Bahawalpur
Quetta
Qandahar
Sukkur
Hyderabad
KARACHI
Udaipur
Kota
Gwalior
BHOPAL
Ujjain
INDORE
AHMADABAD
VADODARA
Rajkot
Jamnagar
Bhavnagar
Junagadh
Projection: Conical with two standard parallels
ft m
18 000 6000
12 000 4000
9000 3000
6000 2000
4500 1500
3000 1000
1200 400
600 200
0 0
200 600
2000 6000
m ft

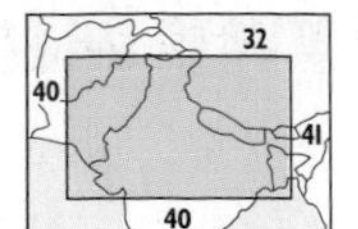

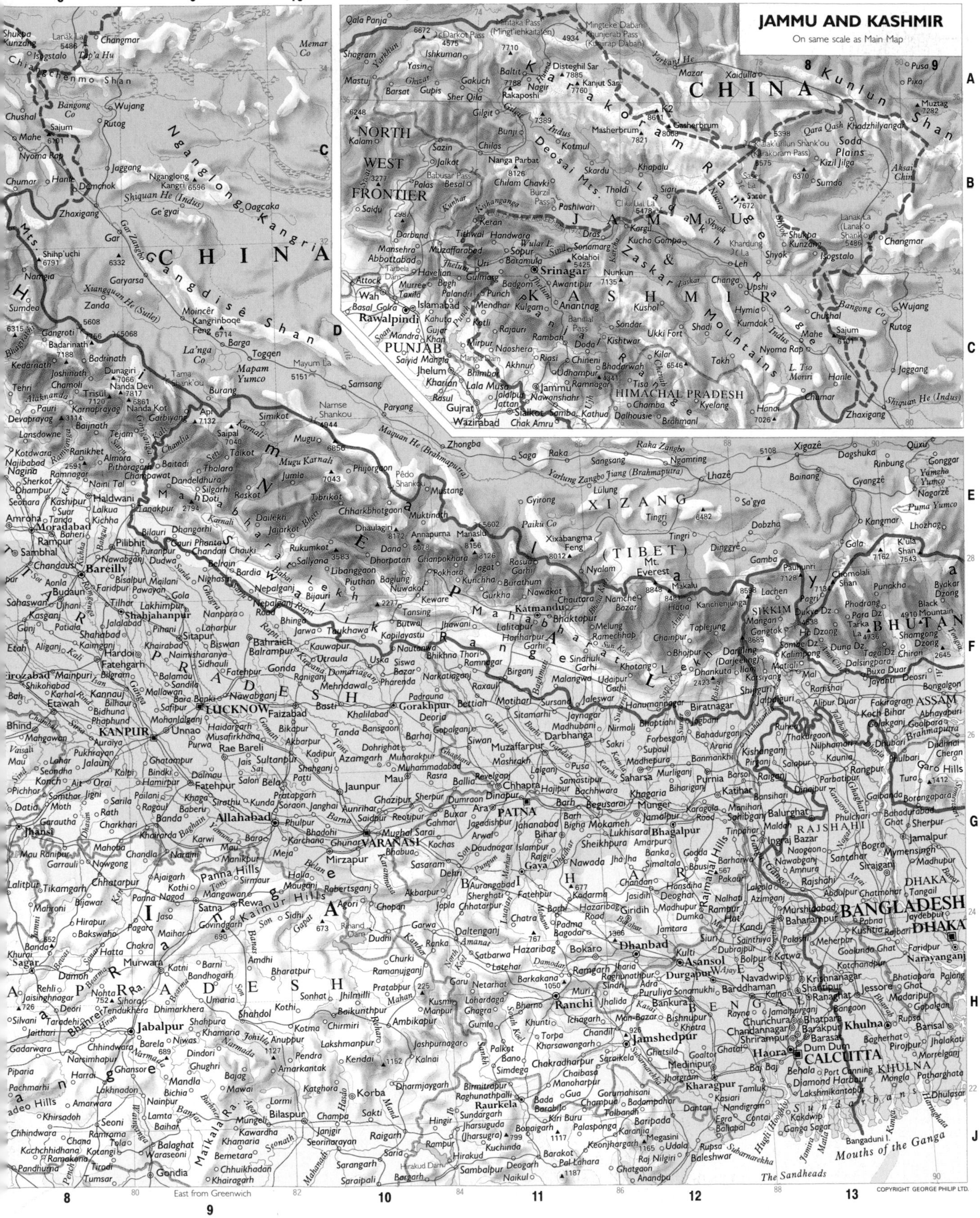

## JAMMU AND KASHMIR

On same scale as Main Map

East from Greenwich

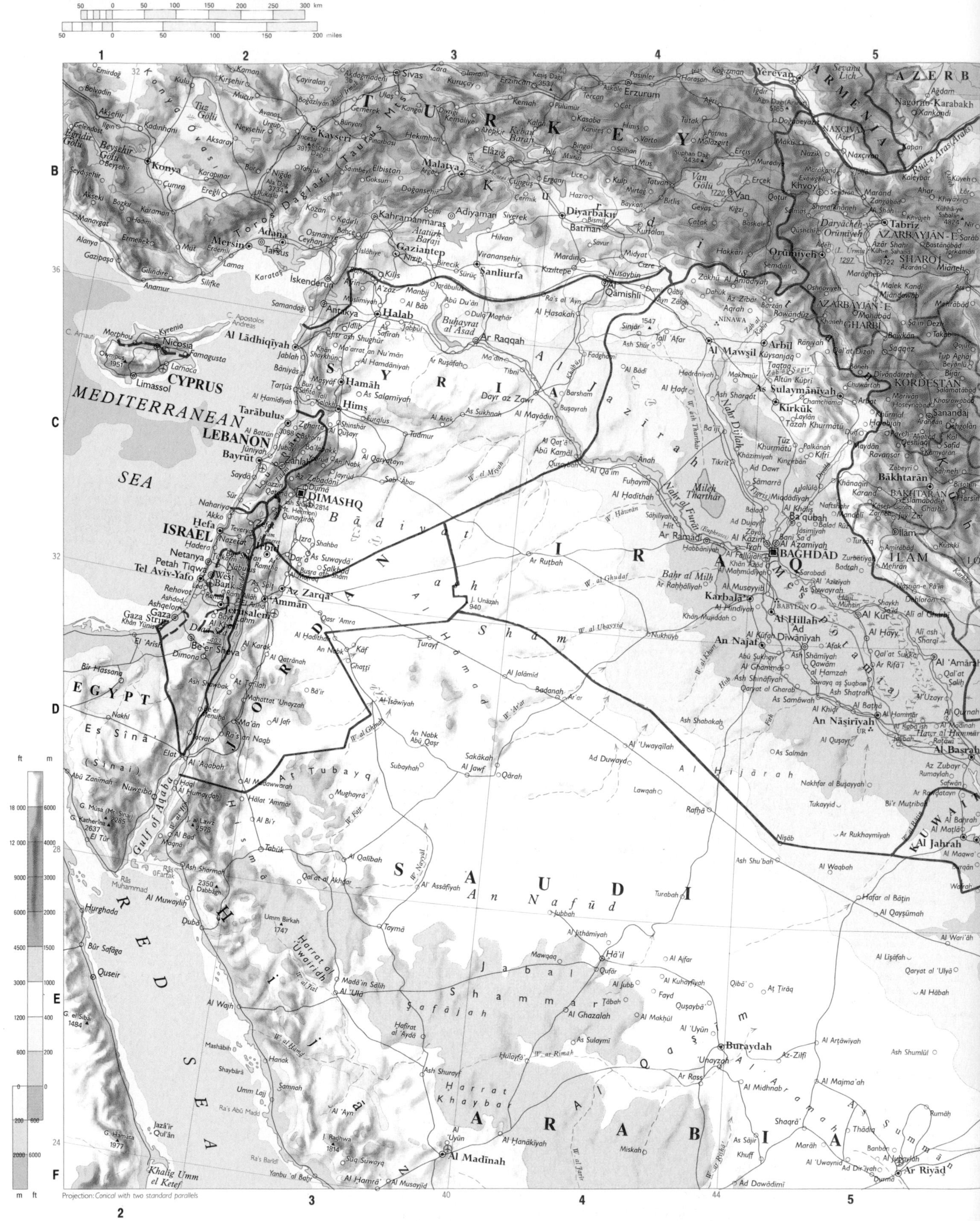
MEDITERRANEAN SEA
CYPRUS
LEBANON
ISRAEL
JORDAN
SYRIA
IRAQ
TURKEY
EGYPT
SAUDI ARABIA
RED SEA
DIMASHQ
BAGHDĀD
Projection: Conical with two standard parallels

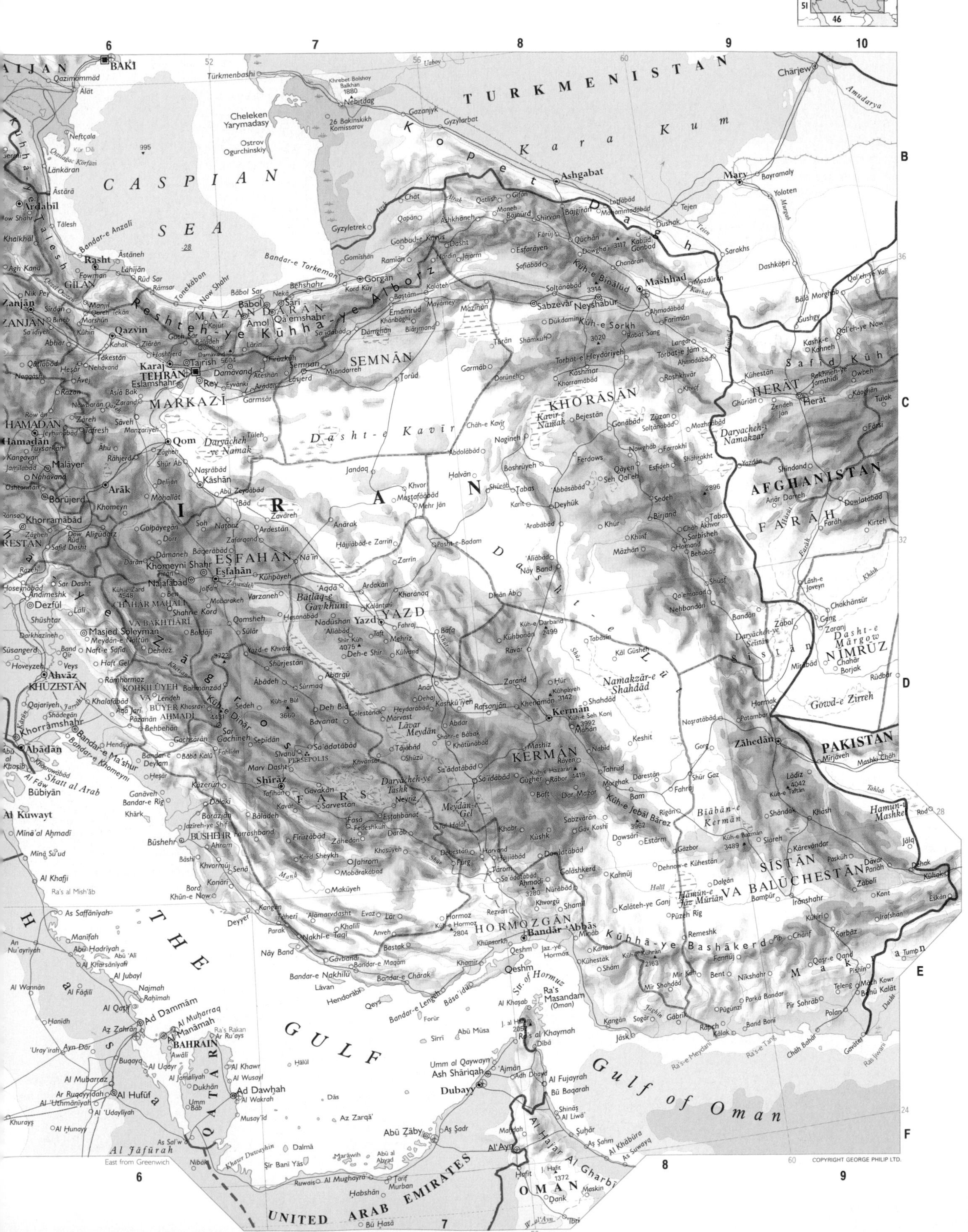

TURKMENISTAN
Kara Kum
Kopet Dag
CASPIAN SEA
IRAN
Dasht-e Kavir
Dasht-e Lut
AFGHANISTAN
PAKISTAN
THE GULF
Gulf of Oman
UNITED ARAB EMIRATES
OMAN
QATAR
BAHRAIN
Reshteh-ye Kuhha-ye Alborz
Zagros
TEHRAN
Baki
Ashgabat
Mashhad
Herat
Qom
Esfahan
Yazd
Kerman
Shiraz
Zahedan
Bandar-e 'Abbas
Ad Dawhah
Dubayy
Abu Zaby
Al Kuwayt
Ad Dammam
Al Manamah
Mary
Chärjew
Tabas
Ahvaz
Abadan
Bushehr
Hamadan
Kashan
Arak
Semnan
Rasht
Gorgan
Sari
Qazvin
Zanjan
Ardabil
SEMNAN
KHORASAN
MARKAZI
ESFAHAN
YAZD
KERMAN
FARS
HORMOZGAN
SISTAN VA BALUCHESTAN
KHUZESTAN
BUSHEHR
HAMADAN
MAZANDARAN
GILAN
ZANJAN
HERAT
FARAH
NIMRUZ
Daryacheh-ye Namak
Daryacheh-ye Namakzar
Daryacheh-ye Sistan
Dasht-e Margow
Gowd-e Zirreh
Namakzar-e Shahdad
Kuh-e Dinar
Kuh-e Binalud
Kuhha-ye Bashakerd
Safid Kuh
Str. of Hormuz
Shatt al Arab
Amudarya
Makran
East from Greenwich
COPYRIGHT GEORGE PHILIP LTD.

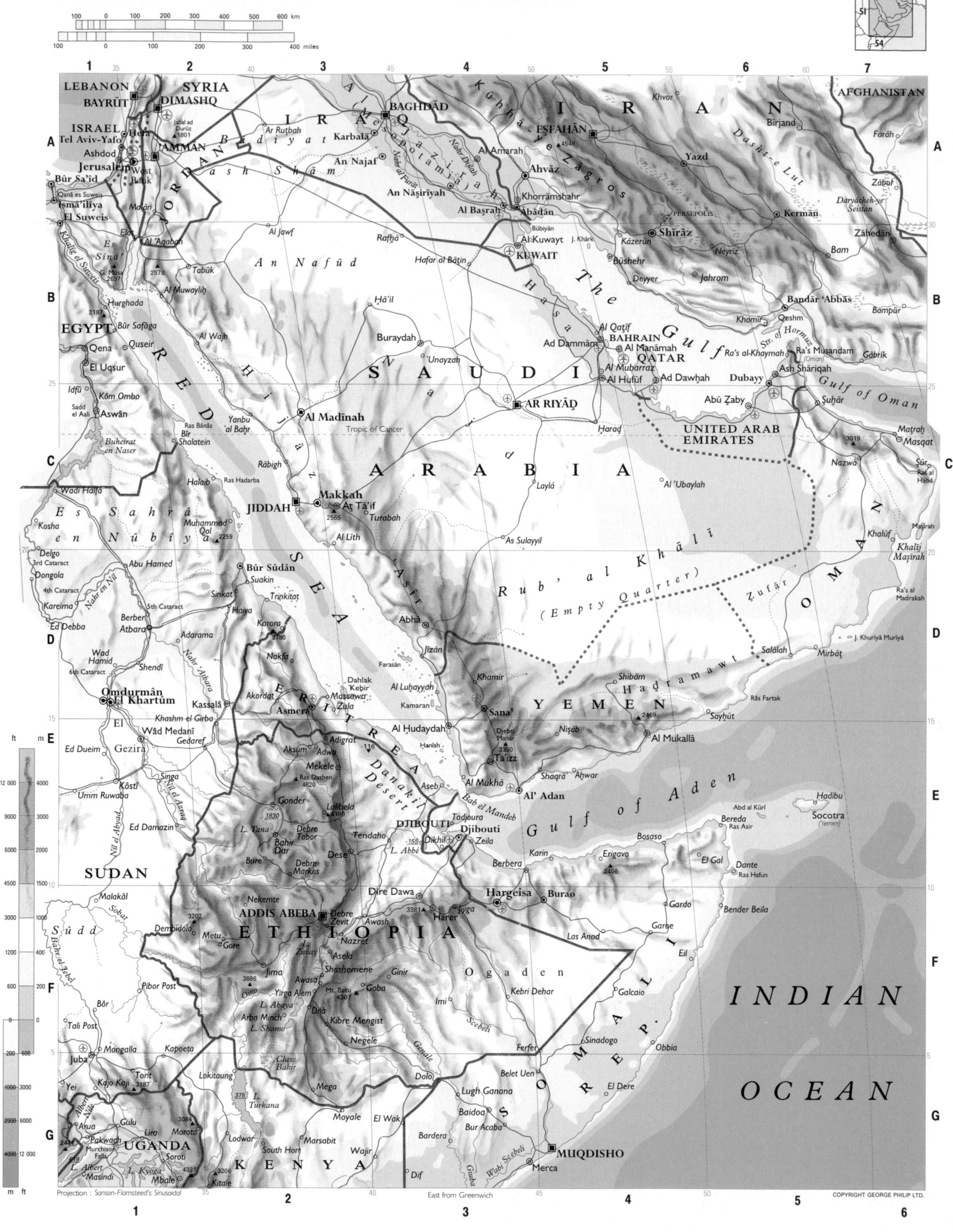

km 100 0 100 200 300 400 500 600
miles 100 0 100 200 300 400
LEBANON
BAYRŪT
SYRIA
DIMASHQ
ISRAEL
Tel Aviv-Yafo
Ashdod
Jerusalem
West Bank
AMMAN
JORDAN
Bûr Sa'îd
Ismâ'iliya
El Suweis
Ma'ān
Elat
Al 'Aqabah
Es Sînâ'
G. Mûsa 2637
Tabūk
2578
IRAQ
BAGHDĀD
Ar Rutbah
Karbalā
An Najaf
Bādiyat ash Shām
Al Jazīrah (Mesopotamia)
Nahr Dijlah
Nahr al Furāt
Al Amarah
An Nāşirīyah
Al Başrah
Ābādān
Khorramshahr
Ahvāz
IRAN
EŞFAHĀN
Kūhhā-ye Zāgros
4548
Khvor
Bīrjand
Yazd
Dasht-e Lut
PERSEPOLIS
Shīrāz
Kermān
Kāzerūn
Būshehr
Deyyer
Jahrom
Neyrīz
Bam
Zāhedān
Zābol
Daryācheh-ye Sīstan
AFGHANISTAN
Farāh
Bandar 'Abbās
Bampūr
Qeshm
Khamīr
Str. of Hormuz
Būbiyān
Al Kuwayt
KUWAIT
J. Khārk
Al Jawf
Rafhā
An Nafūd
Hafar al Bāţin
Hā'il
Buraydah
'Unayzah
The Gulf
Hasa
Al Qaţīf
BAHRAIN
Ad Dammām
Al Manāmah
QATAR
Al Mubarraz
Al Hufūf
Ad Dawhah
Ra's al-Khaymah
Ra's Musandam (Oman)
Gābrīk
Ash Shāriqah
Dubayy
Abū Zaby
Şuhār
Gulf of Oman
UNITED ARAB EMIRATES
Maţraḩ
Masqat
3019
Nazwā
Şūr
Ra's al Hadd
SAUDI ARABIA
Najd
AR RIYĀD
Haraḑ
Al Madīnah
Tropic of Cancer
Yanbu 'al Baḩr
Ḩijāz
Al Wajh
Al Muwaylih
Hurghada
2187
EGYPT
Bûr Safâga
Qena
Quseir
El Uqsur
Idfû
Kôm Ombo
Sadd el Aali
Aswân
Buheirat en Naser
Ras Bânâs
Bîr Shalatein
RED SEA
Rābigh
Makkah
Aţ Ţā'if
JIDDAH
2565
Turabah
Al Līth
Laylá
Al 'Ubaylah
As Sulayyil
Rub' al Khālī (Empty Quarter)
Zufār
OMAN
Khalūf
Maşīrah
Khalīj Maşīrah
Ra's al Madrakah
J. Khurīyā Murīyā
Mirbāţ
Şalālah
Wadi Halfa
Halaib
Ras Hadarba
Es Sahrâ en Nûbîya
Muhammad Qol
2259
Kosha
Delgo
3rd Cataract
Dongola
4th Cataract
Kareima
Abu Hamed
Nahr en Nîl
5th Cataract
Bûr Sûdân
Suakin
Sinkat
Trinkitat
Haiya
Berber
Atbara
Ed Debba
Adarama
Nahr 'Atbara
Wad Hamid
6th Cataract
Shendi
Omdurmân
El Khartûm
Kassala
Karora
2180
Nakfa
'Asīr
Abhā
Jīzān
Farasān
Dahlak Kebir
Massawa
Zula
Al Luḩayyah
Kamaran
Khamir
Akordat
Asmera
ERITREA
Şan'ā
Shibām
Ḩaḑramawt
YEMEN
2469
Sayḩūt
Rās Fartak
Al Ḩudaydah
Hanīsh
Djebel Manar 3350
Ta'izz
Nişāb
Al Mukallā
Khashm el Girba
Wâd Medanî
El Gezira
Gedaref
Ed Dueim
Adigrat
Aksum
Adwa
-116
Mekele
Ras Dashen 4620
Danakil Desert
Gonder
Lalibela
4190
1830
L. Tana
Bahir Dar
Debre Tabor
Shaqrā'
Aḩwar
Al Mukhā
Aseb
Bab el Mandeb
Al' Adan
Gulf of Aden
Hadibu
Abd al Kūrī
Socotra (Yemen)
Kôstî
Singa
Umm Ruwaba
Nil el Azraq
Ed Damazin
Nil el Abyad
Tendaho
DJIBOUTI
Tadjoura
Djibouti
-155
Dikhil
L. Abbé
Zeila
Dese
Bure
Debre Markos
Berbera
Karin
Erigavo
2406
Bosaso
El Gal
Bereda
Ras Asir
Dante
Ras Hafun
SUDAN
Malakâl
Sobat
Nekemte
ADDIS ABEBA
Debre Zevit
Dire Dawa
3381
Harer
Jijiga
Hargeisa
Burao
Gardo
Bender Beila
Garoe
Las Anod
Sudd
Dembidolo
3202
Metu
Gore
ETHIOPIA
Awash
Nazret
L. Zaway
Asela
Shashemene
Ginir
Eil
Ogaden
Bahr el Jebel
Pibor Post
3686
Jima
Omo
Awasa
Mt. Batu 4307
Goba
Yirga Alem
L. Abaya
Dila
Arba Minch
L. Shamo
Kibre Mengist
Imi
Kebri Dehar
Galcaio
INDIAN OCEAN
Bôr
Tali Post
Negele
Genale
Sceberi
Ferfer
Sinadogo
Obbia
SOMALI REP.
Juba
Mongalla
Kapoeta
Torit
Chew Bahir
Lokitaung
Dolo
Belet Uen
El Dere
Yei
Kajo Kaji
3187
375
L. Turkana
Mega
Lugh Ganana
Albert Nile
Arua
Gulu
Lira
Moroto
3084
Moyale
El Wak
Baidoa
Bur Acaba
2484
Pakwach
UGANDA
Murchison Falls
619
Soroti
Lodwar
South Horr
Marsabit
Wajir
Bardera
L. Albert
Masindi
L. Kyoga
Mbale
4321
3206
Kitale
KENYA
Dif
Giuba
Wabi Scebeli
MUQDISHO
Merca
Projection : Sanson-Flamsteed's Sinusoidal
East from Greenwich
COPYRIGHT GEORGE PHILIP LTD.

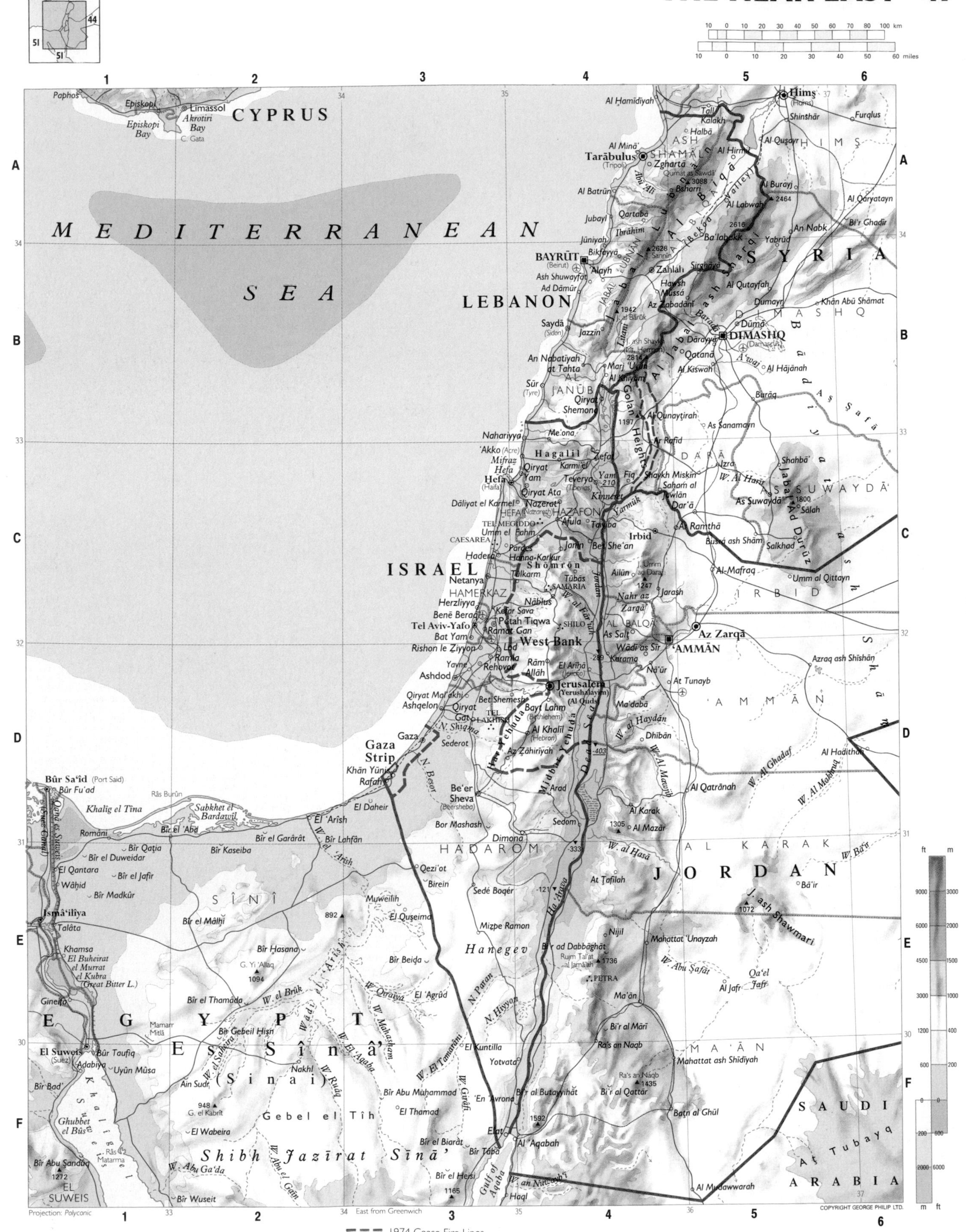


ﾟ 1974 Cease Fire Lines

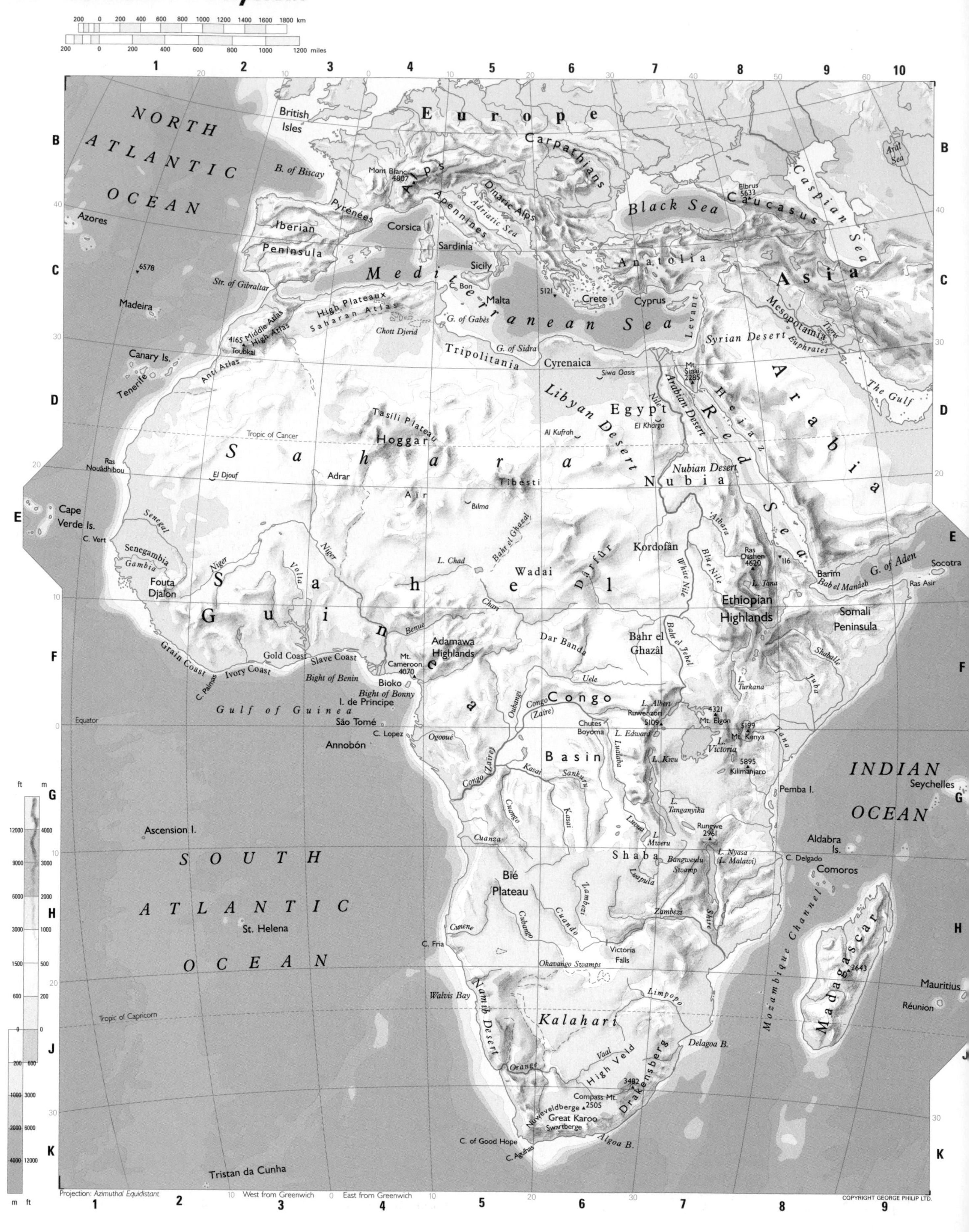
NORTH ATLANTIC OCEAN
Europe
British Isles
B. of Biscay
Mont Blanc 4807
Alps
Carpathians
Pyrénées
Dinaric Alps
Apennines
Adriatic Sea
Black Sea
Caucasus
Elbrus 5633
Caspian Sea
Aral Sea
Azores
Iberian Peninsula
Corsica
Sardinia
Sicily
Anatolia
Asia
Mediterranean Sea
Madeira
Str. of Gibraltar
High Plateaux
Saharan Atlas
Middle Atlas
High Atlas
4165 Toubkal
Chott Djerid
G. of Gabès
Malta
Crete
Cyprus
Levant
Mesopotamia
Tigris
Euphrates
Syrian Desert
Canary Is.
Tenerife
Anti Atlas
Tripolitania
G. of Sidra
Cyrenaica
Siwa Oasis
Mt. Sinai 2285
Arabia
The Gulf
Libyan Desert
Egypt
Nile
Arabian Desert
Hejaz
Red Sea
El Kharga
Al Kufrah
Tasili Plateau
Hoggar
Tropic of Cancer
Sahara
Ras Nouâdhibou
El Djouf
Adrar
Tibesti
Nubian Desert
Nubia
Aïr
Bilma
Cape Verde Is.
C. Vert
Senegal
Senegambia
Gambia
Niger
Volta
L. Chad
Bahr el Ghazal
Wadai
Darfûr
Kordofân
White Nile
Blue Nile
Atbara
Ras Dashen 4620
L. Tana
Barim
Bab el Mandeb
G. of Aden
Socotra
Ras Asir
Sahel
Fouta Djalon
Ethiopian Highlands
Somali Peninsula
Guinea
Chari
Benue
Adamawa Highlands
Dar Banda
Bahr el Ghazâl
Bahr el Jebel
Shaballe
Grain Coast
Gold Coast
Slave Coast
Ivory Coast
C. Palmas
Mt. Cameroon 4070
Bight of Benin
Bioko
Bight of Bonny
I. de Principe
Gulf of Guinea
São Tomé
Equator
C. Lopez
Annobón
Ogooué
Oubangi
Uele
Congo (Zaïre)
Congo Basin
L. Albert
Ruwenzori 5109
Chutes Boyoma
L. Edward
4321 Mt. Elgon
5199 Mt. Kenya
Tana
Turkana
Juba
L. Victoria
L. Kivu
5895 Kilimanjaro
Lualaba
Kasai
Sankuru
INDIAN OCEAN
Seychelles
Pemba I.
Cuango
L. Tanganyika
Rungwe 2961
Luvua
L. Mweru
Ascension I.
Cuanza
Shaba
Bangweulu Swamp
L. Nyasa (L. Malawi)
Aldabra Is.
C. Delgado
Comoros
SOUTH ATLANTIC OCEAN
Bié Plateau
Luapula
Lambezi
Zambezi
Shire
Mozambique Channel
Madagascar
2643
Cunene
Cubango
Cuando
St. Helena
C. Fria
Victoria Falls
Okavango Swamps
Walvis Bay
Namib Desert
Limpopo
Mauritius
Réunion
Tropic of Capricorn
Kalahari
Delagoa B.
Vaal
High Veld
Orange
Drakensberg
3482
Compass Mt. 2505
Nuweveldberge
Great Karoo
Swartberge
C. of Good Hope
C. Agulhas
Algoa B.
Tristan da Cunha
Projection: Azimuthal Equidistant
West from Greenwich
East from Greenwich
COPYRIGHT GEORGE PHILIP LTD.
6578
5121
116
Bon
km
miles
ft
m

200 0 200 400 600 800 1000 1200 1400 1600 1800 km
200 0 200 400 600 800 1000 1200 miles
NORTH ATLANTIC OCEAN
Azores (Port.)
Madeira (Port.)
Canary Is. (Sp.)
CAPE VERDE IS.
Praia
UNITED KINGDOM
LONDON
NETH.
BELG.
GERMANY
POLAND
Warsaw
RUSSIA
KAZAKSTAN
Aral Sea
Prague
CZECH REP.
PARIS
FRANCE
Vienna
SLOVAK REP.
AUSTRIA
HUNGARY
SWITZ.
Kiev
UKRAINE
Volgograd
B. of Biscay
CROATIA
BOS.-HERZ.
YUG.
ROMANIA
Odessa
Caspian Sea
Black Sea
BULGARIA
MAC.
ALB.
ITALY
Adriatic Sea
Rome
Corsica
Sardinia
Sicily
PORTUGAL
SPAIN
Madrid
Lisbon
GEORGIA
ARM.
AZER.
Baku
TURKMEN.
Ankara
TURKEY
GREECE
Athens
Crete
CYPRUS
Aleppo
SYRIA
Mosul
TEHRĀN
IRAN
Eşfahān
Tigris
Euphrates
Baghdād
IRAQ
LEB.
Damascus
Tel Aviv-Jaffa
Jerusalem
ISRAEL
JORDAN
Syrian Desert
Basra
KUWAIT
The Gulf
BAHRAIN
QATAR
Mediterranean Sea
Algiers
Annaba
Constantine
Tunis
Sfax
TUNISIA
MALTA
Chott Djerid
Tripoli
Misrātah
Benghazi
Alexandria
Port Said
CAIRO
Suez
El Faiyûm
Rabat
Tétouan
Casablanca
Fès
MOROCCO
Marrakesh
ALGERIA
In Salah
LIBYA
Marzūq
Al Jawf
EGYPT
Asyût
Nile
Aswān
Red Sea
SAUDI ARABIA
Riyadh
Medina
Jedda
Mecca
El Aaiún
WESTERN SAHARA
Dakhla
Fdérik
Tropic of Cancer
Sahara
Ras Nouâdhibou
MAURITANIA
Nouakchott
St-Louis
C. Vert
Dakar
SENEGAL
Senegal
GAMBIA
Banjul
GUINEA-BISSAU
Bissau
GUINEA
Conakry
Freetown
SIERRA LEONE
Monrovia
LIBERIA
Tombouctou
MALI
Bamako
Niger
NIGER
Agadès
Niamey
BURKINA FASO
Ouagadougou
Bobo-Dioulasso
IVORY COAST
Bouaké
Yamoussoukro
Abidjan
GHANA
Kumasi
Accra
Sekondi-Takoradi
TOGO
Lomé
BENIN
Porto Novo
NIGERIA
Abuja
Kano
Maiduguri
Ibadan
Lagos
Benue
Enugu
Port Harcourt
Bight of Benin
Gulf of Guinea
CHAD
L. Chad
Abéché
Ndjamena
Chari
Wadi Halfa
Port Sudan
Atbara
'Atbara
Omdurmân
Khartoum
Wad Medani
SUDAN
El Fâsher
El Obeid
White Nile
Blue Nile
Malakâl
Wau
Bahr el Jebel
ERITREA
Mesewa
Asmera
YEMEN
Socotra (Yemen)
G. of Aden
DJIBOUTI
Djibouti
Ras Asir
Berbera
L. Tana
Addis Ababa
Harer
ETHIOPIA
SOMALI REP.
Shaballe
Mogadishu
Juba
CENTRAL AFRICAN REP.
Bangui
CAMEROON
Douala
Yaoundé
Malabo
EQUATORIAL GUINEA
SÃO TOMÉ & PRINCIPE
Libreville
GABON
C. Lopez
Annobón
Equator
CONGO
Oubangi
Congo (Zaïre)
Mbandaka
Kisangani
L. Albert
UGANDA
Kampala
KENYA
Kisumu
Nairobi
Tana
Kismayu
L. Turkana
L. Edward
Lualaba
CONGO (DEM. REP. OF THE)
RWANDA
Kigali
L. Kivu
L. Victoria
BURUNDI
Bujumbura
Kasai
Brazzaville
Kinshasa
Pointe-Noire
CABINDA (Angola)
Matadi
Kananga
TANZANIA
Dodoma
Zanzibar
Dar es Salaam
Mombasa
L. Tanganyika
INDIAN OCEAN
SEYCHELLES
Aldabra Is.
C. Delgado
Moroni
COMOROS
Antsiranana
Mayotte (Fr.)
Luanda
Cuanza
ANGOLA
Lobito
Huambo
Namibe
Cunene
Cubango
L. Mweru
Likasi
Lubumbashi
L. Malawi
MALAWI
Ndola
Lilongwe
ZAMBIA
Lusaka
Zambezi
Blantyre
MOZAMBIQUE
Moçambique
Mozambique Channel
Mahajanga
Toamasina
Antananarivo
MADAGASCAR
Fianarantsoa
MAURITIUS
Port Louis
Réunion (Fr.)
Livingstone
Harare
ZIMBABWE
Bulawayo
Beira
C. Fria
NAMIBIA
Windhoek
BOTSWANA
Limpopo
Gaborone
Pretoria
Johannesburg
Maputo
Mbabane
SWAZ.
Vaal
Orange
Kimberley
Maseru
LESOTHO
Durban
SOUTH AFRICA
East London
Port Elizabeth
Cape Town
C. of Good Hope
C. Agulhas
Tropic of Capricorn
Ascension I. (U.K.)
SOUTH ATLANTIC OCEAN
St. Helena (U.K.)
Tristan da Cunha (U.K.)
Projection: Azimuthal Equidistant
West from Greenwich
East from Greenwich
Dakar Capital Cities

ATLANTIC OCEAN
Azores (Port.)
Madeira (Port.)
Porto Santo
Funchal
Islas Canarias (Sp.)
La Palma
Santa Cruz de Tenerife
Tenerife
Gomera
Hierro
Las Palmas
Gran Canaria
Lanzarote
Arrecife
Fuerteventura
SPAIN
Cádiz
Málaga
Almeria
Str. of Gibraltar
Gibraltar (U.K.)
Tanger
Ceuta (Sp.)
Tétouan
Al Hoceïma
Melilla (Sp.)
Nador
MOROCCO
Rabat
Salé
Kenitra
Fès
Meknès
Taza
Oujda
CASABLANCA
Mohammedia
El Jadida
Khouribga
Settat
Safi
Marrakech
Essaouira
Agadir
Taroudannt
Ouarzazate
Ifni
Goulimine
Tan-tan
Tarfaya
El Aaiún
Smara
Bu Craa
C. Bojador
WESTERN SAHARA
Dakhla
Bir Mogreïn
Tindouf
ALGERIA
ALGER
Oran
Mostaganem
Tlemcen
Sidi-bel-Abbès
Blida
Médéa
Sétif
Bejaia
Annaba
Skikda
Constantine
Batna
Biskra
Laghouat
Touggourt
El Oued
Ghardaïa
Ouargla
Hassi Messaoud
Béchar
El Goléa
Timimoun
In Salah
Illizi
Djanet
Tamanrasset
Grand Erg Occidental
Grand Erg Oriental
Plateau du Tademaït
Tassili n Ajjer
Ahaggar
Tanezrouft
Erg Iguidi
Erg Chech
El Djouf
Tropic of Cancer
MAURITANIA
Nouâdhibou
Zouîrât
Fdérik
Atâr
Chinguetti
Akjoujt
Nouakchott
Rosso
Kaédi
Kiffa
Aleg
Tidjikja
Néma
'Ayoûn el 'Atroûs
Aoukâr
MALI
Taoudenni
Tessalit
Adrar des Iforas
Kidal
Tombouctou
Gao
Bourem
Ménaka
Hombori
Mopti
Ségou
Bamako
Kayes
Sikasso
Nioro du Sahel
Niger
NIGER
Agadez
Arlit
Aïr
Ténéré
Tahoua
Zinder
Niamey
Dosso
SENEGAL
DAKAR
Thiès
St. Louis
Kaolack
Tambacounda
GAMBIA
Banjul
Ziguinchor
GUINEA-BISSAU
Bissau
Arq. dos Bijagós
GUINEA
Fouta Djalon
Conakry
Kankan
Labé
SIERRA LEONE
Freetown
LIBERIA
Monrovia
Buchanan
Harper
IVORY COAST
ABIDJAN
Yamoussoukro
Bouaké
Korhogo
San Pédro
BURKINA FASO
Ouagadougou
Bobo-Dioulasso
GHANA
Kumasi
Tamale
Accra
Sekondi-Takoradi
Lake Volta
Black Volta
TOGO
Lomé
BENIN
Cotonou
Porto-Novo
Parakou
NIGERIA
LAGOS
IBADAN
Abeokuta
Ogbomosho
Ilorin
Oshogbo
Kano
Zaria
Kaduna
Sokoto
Abuja
Minna
Jos
Enugu
Onitsha
Benin City
Port Harcourt
Calabar
Makurdi
Kainji Res.
Benue
Grain Coast
Ivory Coast
Gold Coast
Slave Coast
Bight of Benin
Bioko
Malabo
Projection : Sanson-Flamsteed's Sinusoidal
West from Greenwich
East from Greenwich

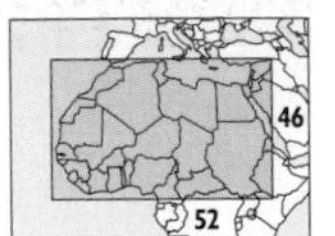

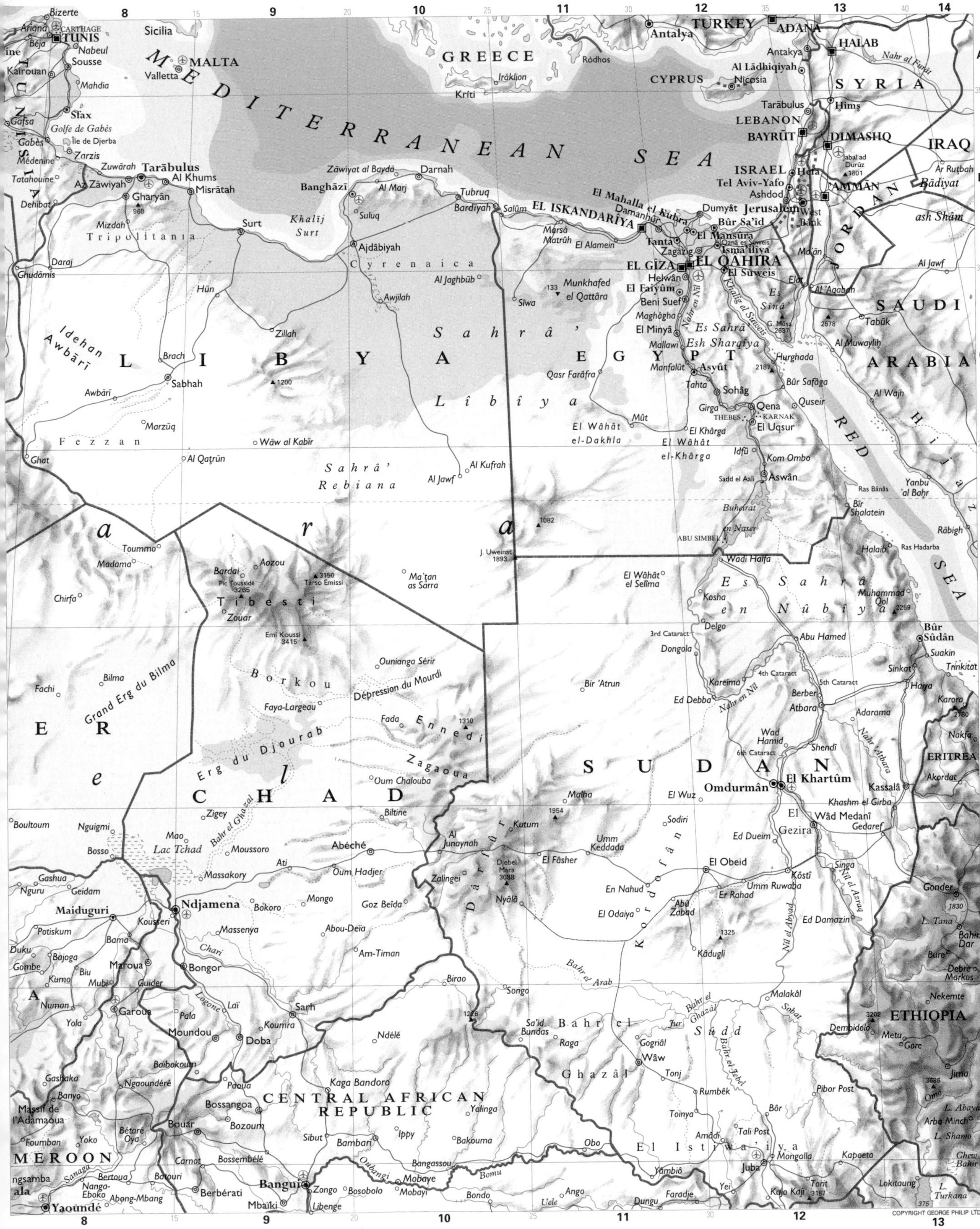

8 9 10 11 12 13 14

MEDITERRANEAN SEA

GREECE
Kríti
Iráklion
Ródhos
TURKEY
Antalya
ADANA
CYPRUS
Nicosia
SYRIA
HALAB
Antakya
Al Lādhiqīyah
Hims
Tarābulus
LEBANON
BAYRŪT
DIMASHQ
IRAQ
ISRAEL
Tel Aviv-Yafo
Ashdod
Jerusalem
West Bank
'AMMĀN
JORDAN
Bādiyat ash Shām
Ar Rutbah
Nahr al Furāt

Sicilia
MALTA
Valletta
Bizerte
CARTHAGE
TUNIS
Ariana
Béja
Nabeul
Sousse
Kairouan
Mahdia
TUNISIA
Sfax
Gafsa
Golfe de Gabès
Gabès
Île de Djerba
Medenine
Zarzis
Tatahouine
Dehibat

LIBYA
Zuwārah
Tarābulus
Al Khums
Az Zāwiyah
Gharyān
Misrātah
Mizdah
Tripolitania
Surt
Khalīj Surt
Banghāzī
Zāwiyat al Baydā
Darnah
Al Marj
Tubruq
Bardīyah
Sulūq
Ajdābiyah
Cyrenaica
Al Jaghbūb
Awjilah
Daraj
Ghudāmis
Hūn
Zillah
Idehan Awbārī
Brach
Sabhah
Awbārī
Marzūq
Fezzan
Wāw al Kabīr
Ghat
Al Qatrūn
Sahrâ' Libîya
Sahrâ' Rebiana
Al Jawf
Al Kufrah
Sahara

EGYPT
Salûm
EL ISKANDARÎYA
Marsâ Matrûh
El Alamein
Damanhûr
El Mahalla el Kubra
Tanta
Dumyât
Bûr Sa'îd
El Mansûra
Zagazig
Ismâ'ilîya
EL GÎZA
EL QÂHIRA
Helwân
El Suweis
El Faiyûm
Beni Suef
Maghâgha
El Minyâ
Mallawi
Manfalût
Asyût
Tahta
Sohâg
Girga
Qena
THEBES
KARNAK
El Uqsur
Idfû
Kom Ombo
Aswân
Sadd el Aali
Buheirat en Naser
ABU SIMBEL
Sîwa
Munkhafed el Qattâra
Qasr Farâfra
El Wâhât el-Dakhla
Mût
El Khârga
El Wâhât el-Khârga
Es Sahrâ Esh Sharqîya
Sînâ'
G. Mûsa 2637
Hurghada
Bûr Safâga
Quseir
Elat
Al 'Aqabah

SAUDI ARABIA
Tabūk
Al Muwaylih
Al Wajh
Hijaz
Yanbu 'al Bahr
Rābigh
Ras Bânâs
Bîr Shalatein
Halaib
Ras Hadarba
RED SEA

SUDAN
J. Uweinat 1893
Wadi Halfa
El Wâhât el Selîma
Es Sahrâ en Nûbîya
Kosha
Delgo
Muhammad Qol
3rd Cataract
Dongola
Abu Hamed
Bûr Sûdân
Suakin
Trinkitat
Kareima
4th Cataract
5th Cataract
Sinkat
Haiya
Bir 'Atrun
Ed Debba
Berber
Atbara
Nahr en Nîl
Adarama
Nahr Atbara
Wad Hamid
6th Cataract
Shendî
Omdurmân
El Khartûm
Kassalâ
Khashm el Girba
El Wuz
Malha
Wâd Medanî
Gedaref
El Gezira
Ed Dueim
Sodiri
Umm Keddada
El Fâsher
Kutum
Dârfûr
Djebel Mara 3088
Nyâlâ
Kordofân
El Obeid
En Nahud
El Odaiya
Abu Zabad
Umm Ruwaba
Er Rahad
Kôstî
Singa
Nîl el Azraq
Nîl el Abyad
Ed Damazin
Kâdugli
Bahr el Arab
Malakâl
Sobat
Bahr el Ghazâl
Sûdd
Bahr el Jebel
Jur
Gogriâl
Wâw
Tonj
Rumbêk
Pibor Post
Bôr
Toinya
Amadi
Tali Post
El Istwâ'iya
Mongalla
Kapoeta
Juba
Yambio
Yei
Kajo Kaji
Torit
Faradje

CHAD
Toummo
Madama
Chirfa
Bardai
Aozou
Pic Toussidé 3265
Tarso Emissi 3150
Tibesti
Zouar
Emi Koussi 3415
Ma'tan as Sarra
Ouniango Sérir
Borkou
Dépression du Mourdi
Faya-Largeau
Fada
Ennedi
Erg du Djourab
Zagaoua
Oum Chalouba
Biltine
Al Junaynah
Abéché
Zigey
Mao
Bahr el Ghazal
Moussoro
Lac Tchad
Ati
Oum Hadjer
Massakory
Zalingei
Ndjamena
Bokoro
Mongo
Goz Beïda
Massenya
Abou-Deïa
Am-Timan
Chari
Bongor
Sarh
Laï
Logone
Pala
Moundou
Doba
Koumra
Baïbokoum

NIGER
Fachi
Bilma
Grand Erg du Bilma
Boultoum
Nguigmi
Bosso

NIGERIA
Gashua
Geidam
Nguru
Maiduguri
Potiskum
Kousseri
Bama
Duku
Bajoga
Gombe
Biu
Kumo
Mubi
Numan
Yola

CAMEROON
Maroua
Guider
Garoua
Gashaka
Ngaoundéré
Banyo
Massif de l'Adamaoua
Foumban
Yoko
Bétaré Oya
Bouar
Bertoua
Batouri
Nkongsamba
Sanaga
Nanga-Eboko
Abong-Mbang
Yaoundé

CENTRAL AFRICAN REPUBLIC
Birao
Ndélé
Kaga Bandoro
Paoua
Bossangoa
Bozoum
Carnot
Bossembélé
Berbérati
Sibut
Bambari
Ippy
Yalinga
Bakouma
Bangassou
Mobaye
Oubangi
Bomu
Bangui
Zongo
Bosobolo
Mobayi
Mbaïki
Libenge
Bondo
Ango
Uele
Dungu
Obo
Songo
Sa'id Bundas
Raga
Bahr el Ghazâl

ERITREA
Karora
Nakfa
Akordat

ETHIOPIA
Gonder
L. Tana
Bahir Dar
Bure
Debre Markos
Nekemte
Dembidolo
Metu
Gore
Jima
Omo
L. Abaya
Arba Minch
L. Shamo
Chew Bahir
Lokitaung
L. Turkana

A B C D E F G H

8 9 10 11 12 13

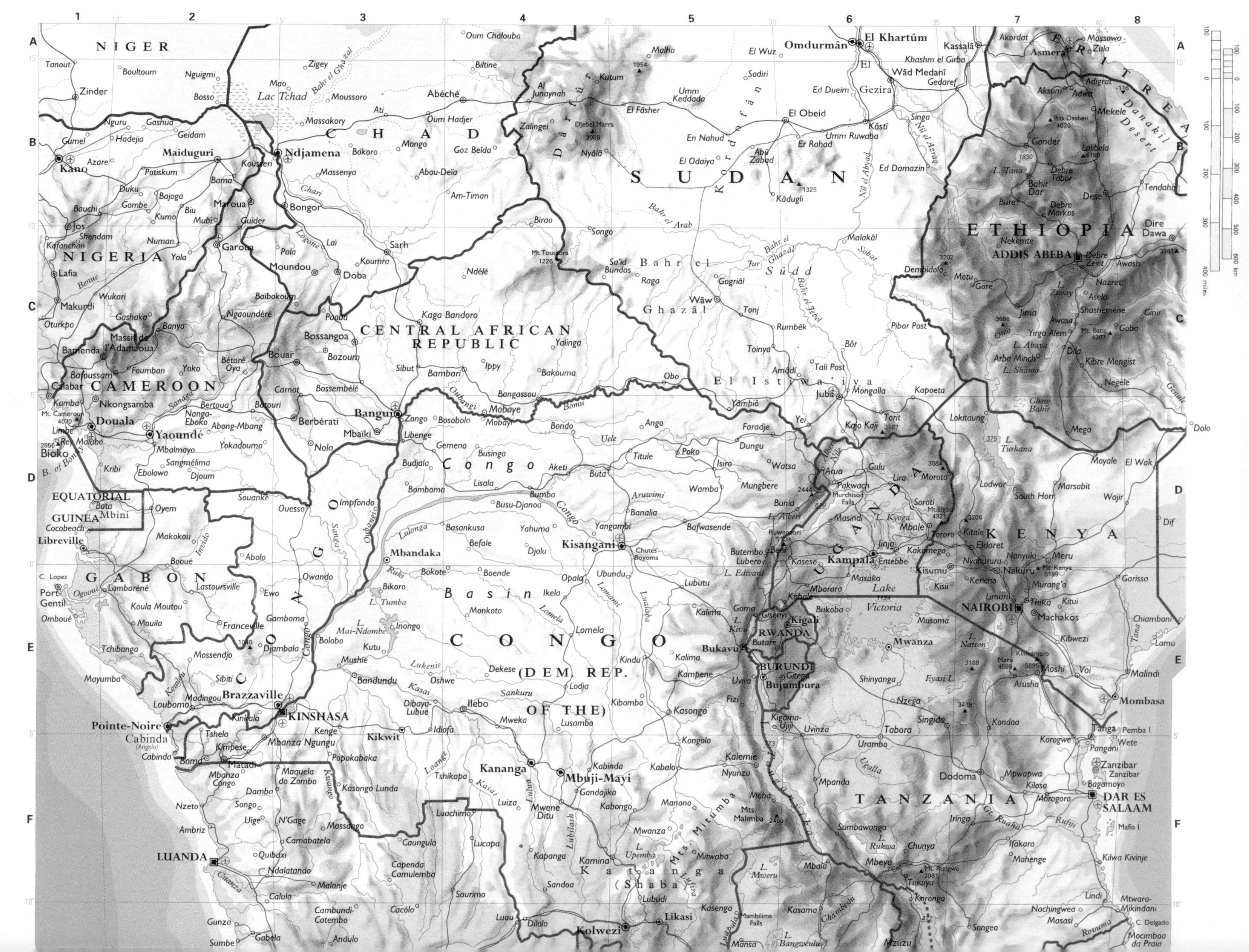
NIGER
Zinder
CHAD
Ndjamena
Lac Tchad
Abéché
SUDAN
Omdurmân
El Khartûm
El Obeid
ERITREA
Asmera
ETHIOPIA
ADDIS ABEBA
NIGERIA
Kano
Maiduguri
CAMEROON
Douala
Yaoundé
CENTRAL AFRICAN REPUBLIC
Bangui
EQUATORIAL GUINEA
Libreville
GABON
CONGO
Brazzaville
Pointe-Noire
Cabinda
KINSHASA
Congo Basin
CONGO (DEM. REP. OF THE)
Kisangani
Mbandaka
Kananga
Mbuji-Mayi
Kolwezi
Likasi
LUANDA
UGANDA
Kampala
Lake Victoria
KENYA
NAIROBI
Mombasa
RWANDA
Kigali
BURUNDI
Bujumbura
TANZANIA
DAR ES SALAAM

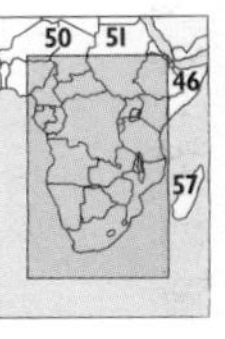

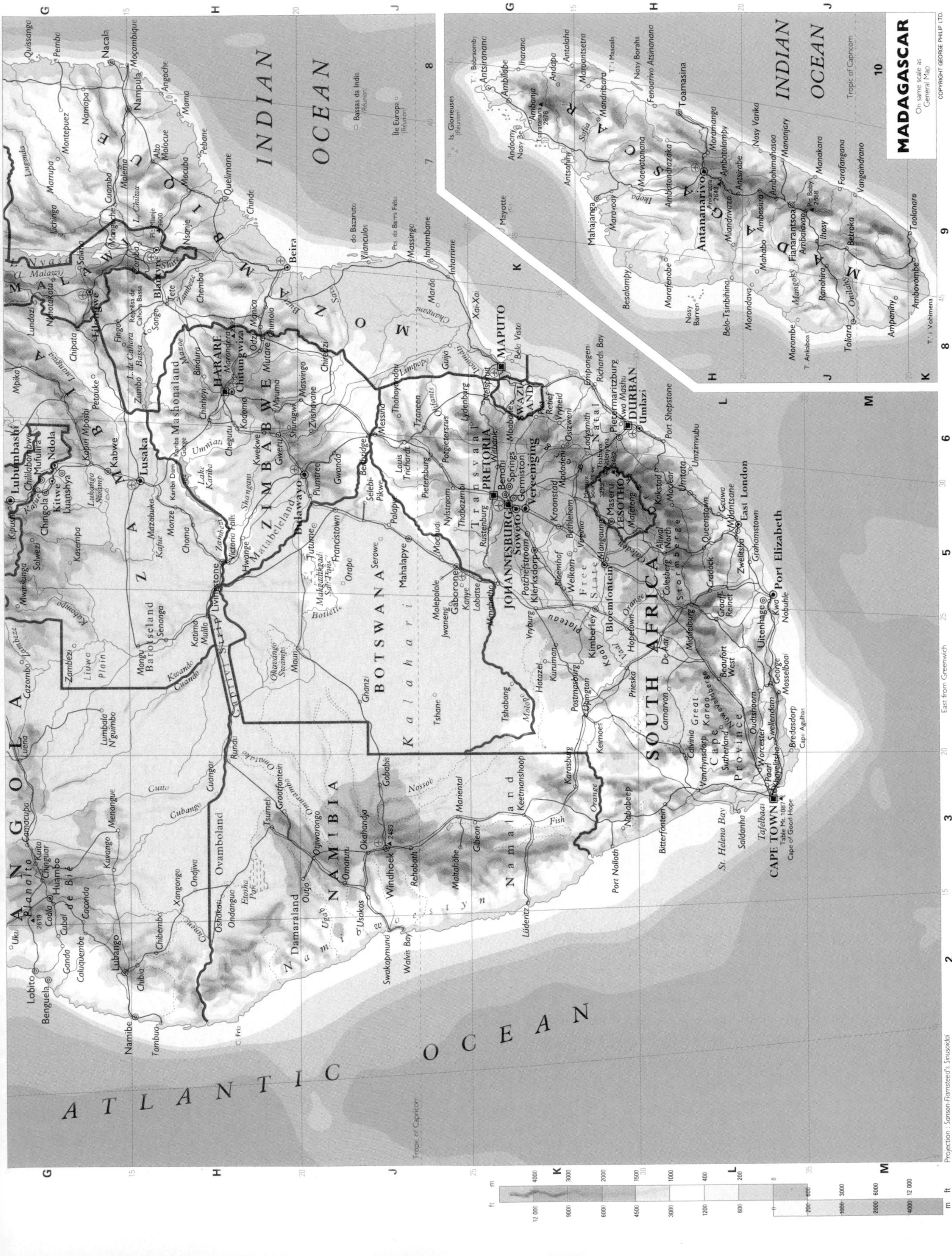

ATLANTIC OCEAN

INDIAN OCEAN

ANGOLA

ZAMBIA

MALAWI

MOZAMBIQUE

ZIMBABWE

NAMIBIA

BOTSWANA

SOUTH AFRICA

LESOTHO

SWAZILAND

Kalahari

Namib Desert

Transvaal

Natal

Orange Free State

Cape Province

Great Karoo

Stormberge

Nuweveldberge

Kaap Plateau

Ovamboland

Damaraland

Namaland

Barotseland

Mashonaland

Matabeleland

Caprivi Strip

Planalto de Bié

Liuwa Plain

Okavango Swamps

Makgadikgadi Salt Pans

Etosha Pan

Lubumbashi

Lusaka

HARARE

Bulawayo

PRETORIA

JOHANNESBURG

MAPUTO

Beira

DURBAN

CAPE TOWN

Port Elizabeth

East London

Bloemfontein

Windhoek

Gaborone

Maseru

Mbabane

Lilongwe

Blantyre

Nampula

Livingstone

Kimberley

Pietermaritzburg

Walvis Bay

Lüderitz

Table Mt. 1087

Cape of Good Hope

Cape Agulhas

Tropic of Capricorn

Projection : Sanson-Flamsteed's Sinusoidal

East from Greenwich

## MADAGASCAR

On same scale as General Map

Antananarivo

Toamasina

Mahajanga

Fianarantsoa

Toliara

Antsiranana

Taolanaro

Tsaratanana 2876

Ankaratra 2643

Pic Boby 2658

Is. Glorieuses (Réunion)

Mayotte (Fr.)

INDIAN OCEAN

Bassas da India (Réunion)

Île Europa (Réunion)

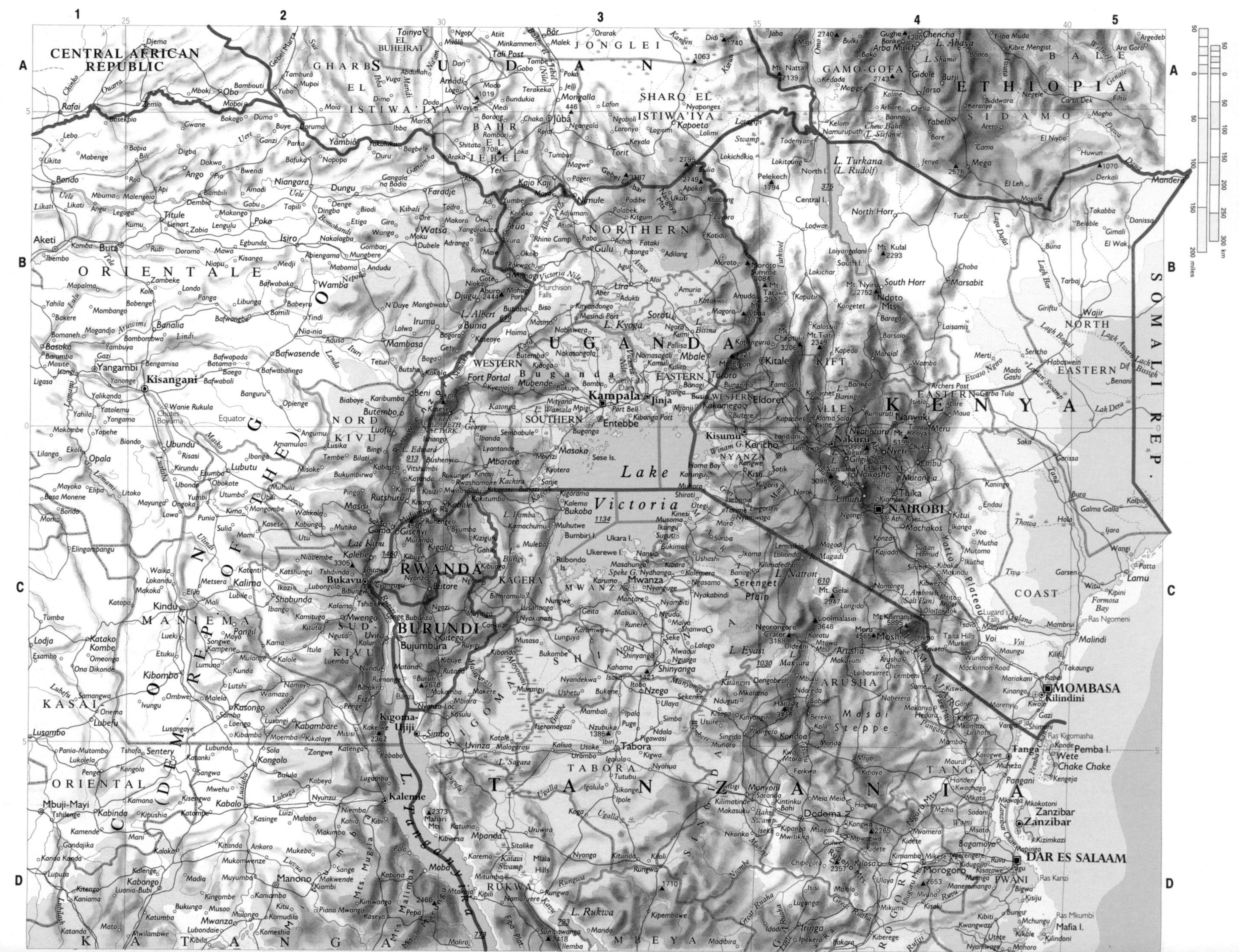
50 0 50 100 150 200 250 300 km
50 0 50 100 150 200 miles
CENTRAL AFRICAN REPUBLIC
SUDAN
ETHIOPIA
SOMALI REP.
KENYA
UGANDA
RWANDA
BURUNDI
TANZANIA
ORIENTALE
MANIEMA
KASAI
Lake Victoria
L. Tanganyika
L. Turkana (L. Rudolf)
NAIROBI
MOMBASA
DAR ES SALAAM
Kampala
Kisangani
Zanzibar

INDIAN OCEAN
L. Nyasa
Malawi
Lusaka
HARARE
Chitungwiza
BULAWAYO
Lilongwe
Blantyre
Zomba
Beira
Lubumbashi
Ndola
Kitwe
Mufulira
Chingola
Luanshya
Kabwe
Livingstone
Victoria Falls
L. Kariba
L. de Cahora Bassa
Lindi
Mtwara-Mikindani
Pemba
Moçambique
Nampula
Quelimane
Chinde
Angoche
Mutare
Gweru
Masvingo
Kadoma
Kwekwe
Messina
Serowe
Francistown
Makgadikgadi Salt Pans
Ile de Juan de Nova (Réunion)
I. do Bazaruto
I. Benguérua
SOUTH AFRICA
BOTSWANA
Caprivi Strip
NAMIBIA
ANGOLA
Projection: Lambert's Equivalent Azimuthal
East from Greenwich

Projection: Lambert's Equivalent Azimuthal
ATLANTIC OCEAN
ANGOLA
CUNENE
NAMIBE
CUANDO CUBANGO
ZAMBIA
WESTERN
SOUTHERN
NAMIBIA
BOTSWANA
SOUTH AFRICA
NORTH-WEST
FREE
NORTHERN CAPE
WESTERN CAPE
EASTERN CAPE
Ovamboland
Damaraland
Namaland
Namib Desert
Kaokoveld
Kalahari
Sandveld
Kaukauveld
Okavango Swamps
Caprivi Strip
Namaqualand
Great Karoo
Little Karoo
Etosha Pan
ETOSHA NAT. PARK
SKELETON COAST PARK
KALAHARI GEMSBOK NATIONAL PARK
CHOBE NATIONAL PARK
HWANGE NAT. PARK
Makgadikgadi Salt Pans
Ngami Depression
Tropic of Capricorn
Windhoek
Swakopmund
Walvisbaai
Lüderitz
Tsumeb
Grootfontein
Otjiwarongo
Outjo
Omaruru
Okahandja
Rehoboth
Mariental
Keetmanshoop
Gobabis
Oranjemund
Maun
Ghanzi
Serowe
Gaborone
Molepolole
Mochudi
Kanye
Lobatse
Livingstone
Victoria Falls
Upington
Kimberley
Bloemfontein
Welkom
Kroonstad
Vryburg
Springbok
Port Nolloth
Calvinia
De Aar
Beaufort West
Graaff-Reinet
Cradock
Queenstown
Grahamstown
Uitenhage
PORT ELIZABETH
CAPE TOWN
Parow
Paarl
Stellenbosch
Worcester
Saldanha
Vredenburg
Malmesbury
Oudtshoorn
George
Knysna
Mosselbaai
Swellendam
Hermanus
Simonstown
C. of Good Hope
C. Agulhas
Orange
Cunene
Kwando
Zambezi
Molopo
Nossob
Auob
Fish

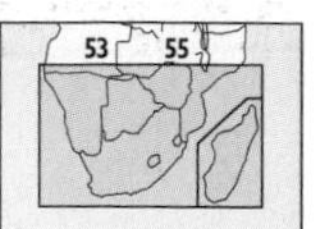

53
55

ZIMBABWE
MOZAMBIQUE
MADAGASCAR
SWAZILAND
LESOTHO
MALAWI
HARARE
Chitungwiza
BULAWAYO
Gweru
Masvingo
Mutare
Beira
Tete
Quelimane
Chinde
Angoche
Inhambane
Xai-Xai
Maputo
Mbabane
PRETORIA
JOHANNESBURG
Soweto
Vereeniging
Benoni
Springs
Pietersburg
Messina
Nelspruit
Pietermaritzburg
DURBAN
Umlazi
East London
Umtata
Antsiranana
Mahajanga
Toamasina
ANTANANARIVO
Antsirabe
Fianarantsoa
Toliara
Morondava
Taolanaro
MOZAMBIQUE CHANNEL
INDIAN OCEAN
Tropic of Capricorn
East from Greenwich
MADAGASCAR
On same scale as General Map
COPYRIGHT GEORGE PHILIP LTD.

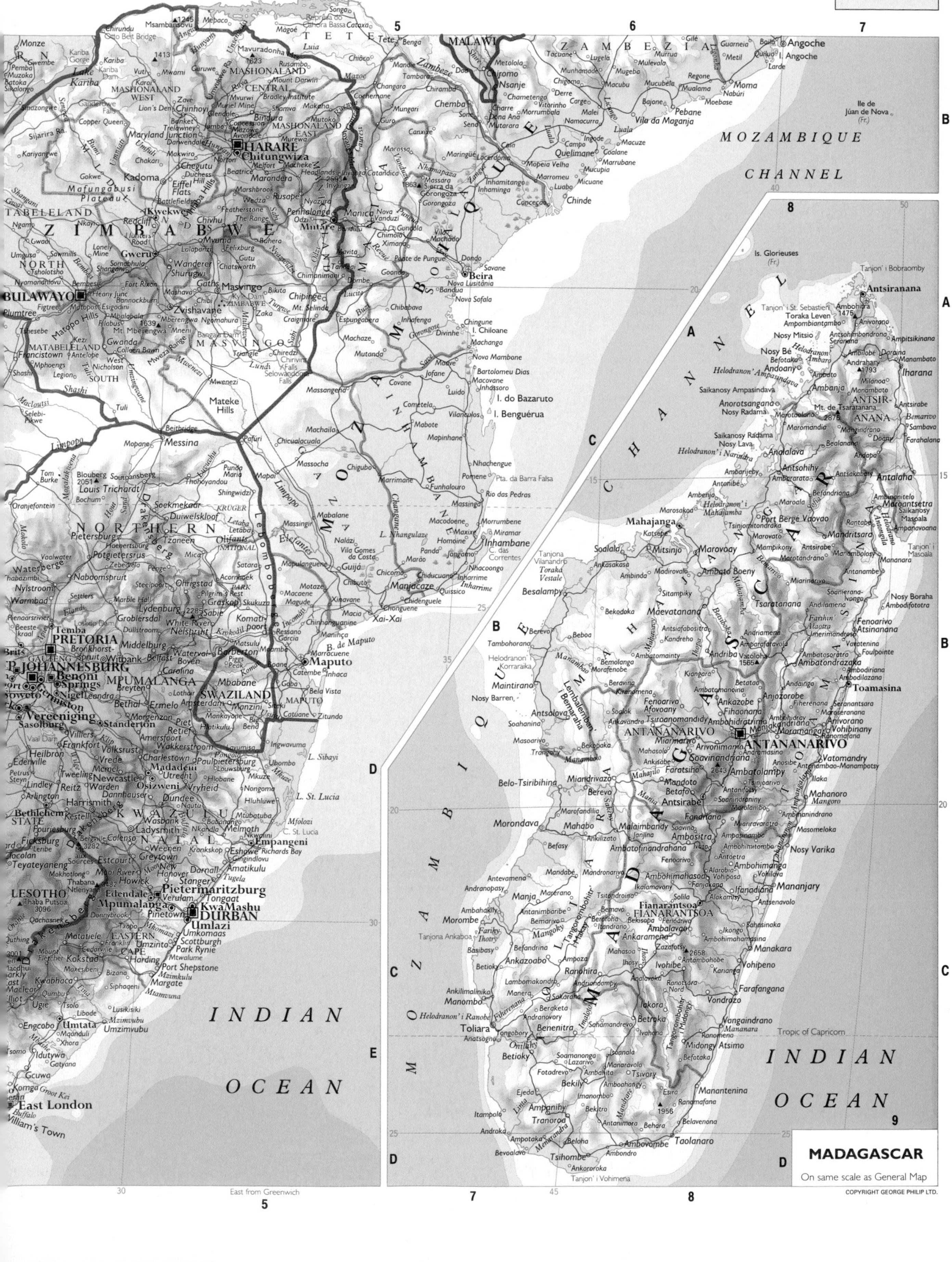

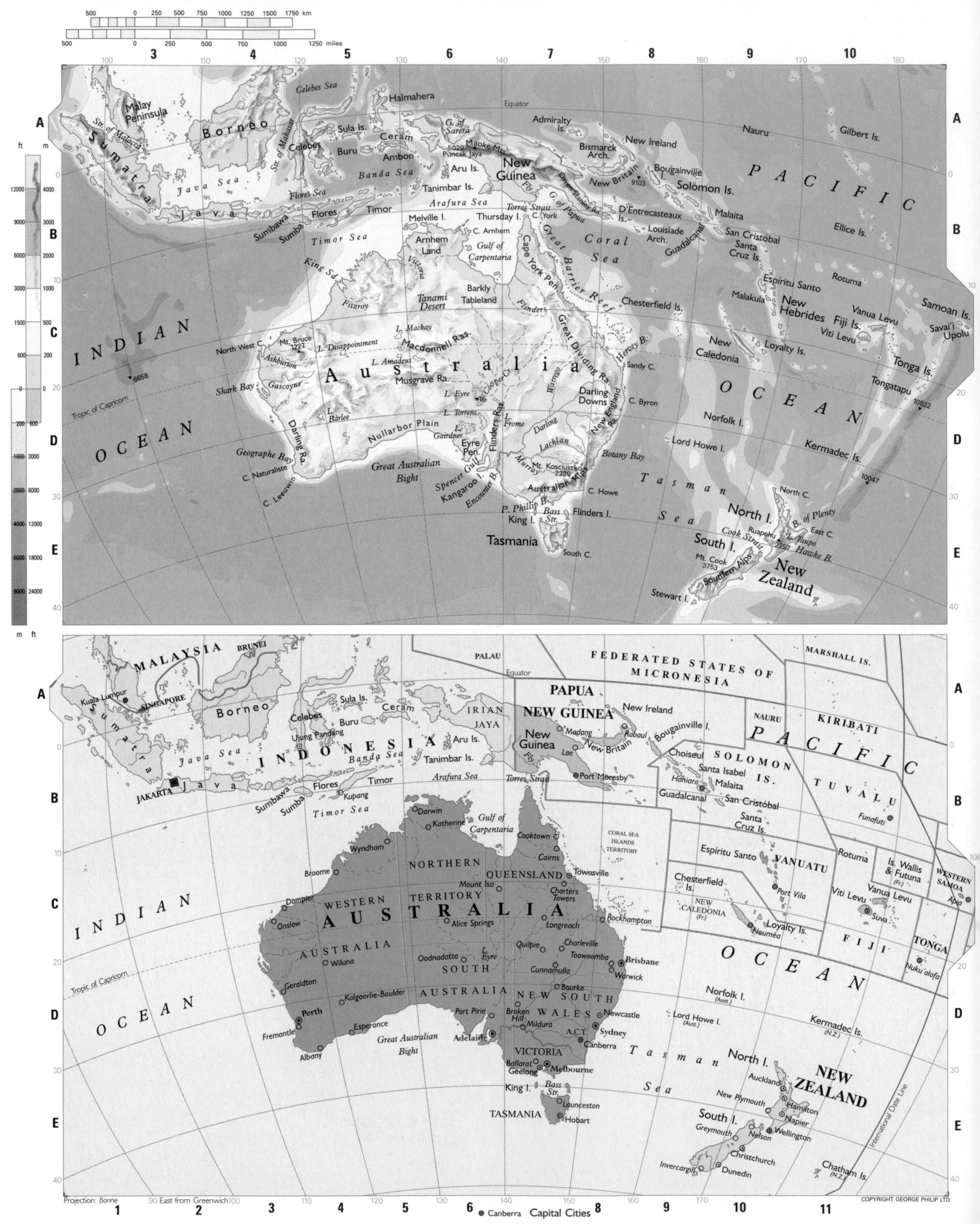

INDIAN OCEAN
PACIFIC OCEAN
Australia
New Guinea
Tasmania
New Zealand
North I.
South I.
Borneo
Sumatra
Java
Celebes
Malay Peninsula
Coral Sea
Tasman Sea
Arafura Sea
Timor Sea
Banda Sea
Java Sea
Gulf of Carpentaria
Great Australian Bight
Great Barrier Reef
Great Dividing Ra.
Nullarbor Plain
Macdonnell Ras.
Musgrave Ra.
L. Eyre
Tanami Desert
Barkly Tableland
Cape York Pen.
Mt. Kosciuszko 2230
Australian Alps
Mt. Cook 3753
Southern Alps
Solomon Is.
New Hebrides
New Caledonia
Fiji Is.
Tonga Is.
Samoan Is.
Kermadec Is.
Norfolk I.
Lord Howe I.
Tropic of Capricorn
Equator
MALAYSIA
BRUNEI
SINGAPORE
INDONESIA
JAKARTA
IRIAN JAYA
PAPUA NEW GUINEA
Port Moresby
PALAU
FEDERATED STATES OF MICRONESIA
MARSHALL IS.
NAURU
KIRIBATI
SOLOMON IS.
Honiara
TUVALU
Funafuti
VANUATU
Port Vila
NEW CALEDONIA (Fr.)
Nouméa
FIJI
Suva
TONGA
Nuku'alofa
WESTERN SAMOA
Apia
Is. Wallis & Futuna (Fr.)
CORAL SEA ISLANDS TERRITORY
AUSTRALIA
WESTERN AUSTRALIA
NORTHERN TERRITORY
QUEENSLAND
SOUTH AUSTRALIA
NEW SOUTH WALES
A.C.T.
VICTORIA
TASMANIA
Perth
Darwin
Brisbane
Sydney
Canberra
Melbourne
Adelaide
Hobart
Alice Springs
NEW ZEALAND
Auckland
Wellington
Christchurch
Dunedin
Chatham Is. (N.Z.)
International Date Line
Projection: Bonne
East from Greenwich
Canberra Capital Cities

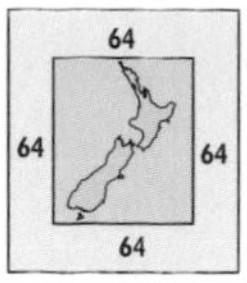

SAMOA ISLANDS

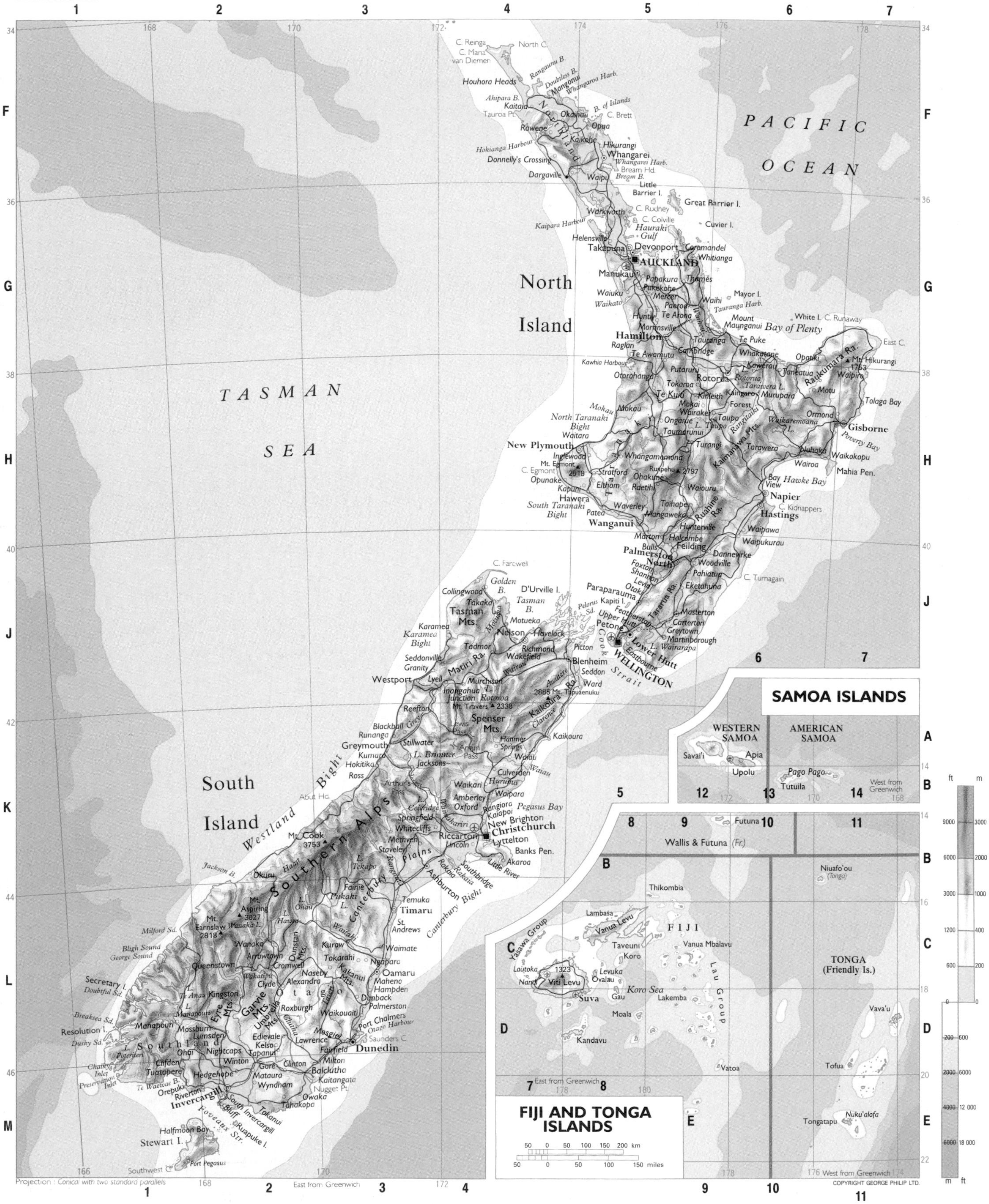

FIJI AND TONGA ISLANDS

Projection: Conical with two standard parallels

50 0 50 100 150 200 250 300 km
50 0 50 100 150 200 miles
INDONESIA
TIMOR SEA
INDIAN OCEAN
NORTHERN TERRITORY
Tanami Desert
Great Sandy Desert
Gibson Desert
Kimberley
King Leopold Ranges
Bonaparte Archipelago
Joseph Bonaparte Gulf
Hamersley Range
Pilbara
Eighty Mile Beach
Timor
Kupang
Sumba
Waingapu
Waikabubak
Sumbawa
Lombok
Bali
Roti
Sawu
Melville I.
Bathurst I.
Darwin
Katherine
Wyndham
Kununurra
Derby
Broome
Port Hedland
Karratha
Dampier
Onslow
Exmouth
Exmouth Gulf
Newman
Halls Creek
Fitzroy Crossing
Lake Mackay
Lake Disappointment
Rowley Shoals
Barrow I.
Monte Bello Is.
Tropic of Capricorn

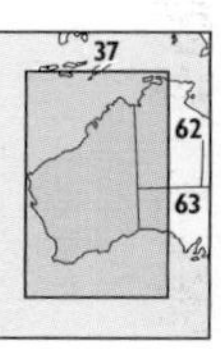


Projection: Bonne

East from Greenwich



ft m
3000 1000
1200 400
600 200
0 0
200 600
2000 6000
4000 12 000
m ft

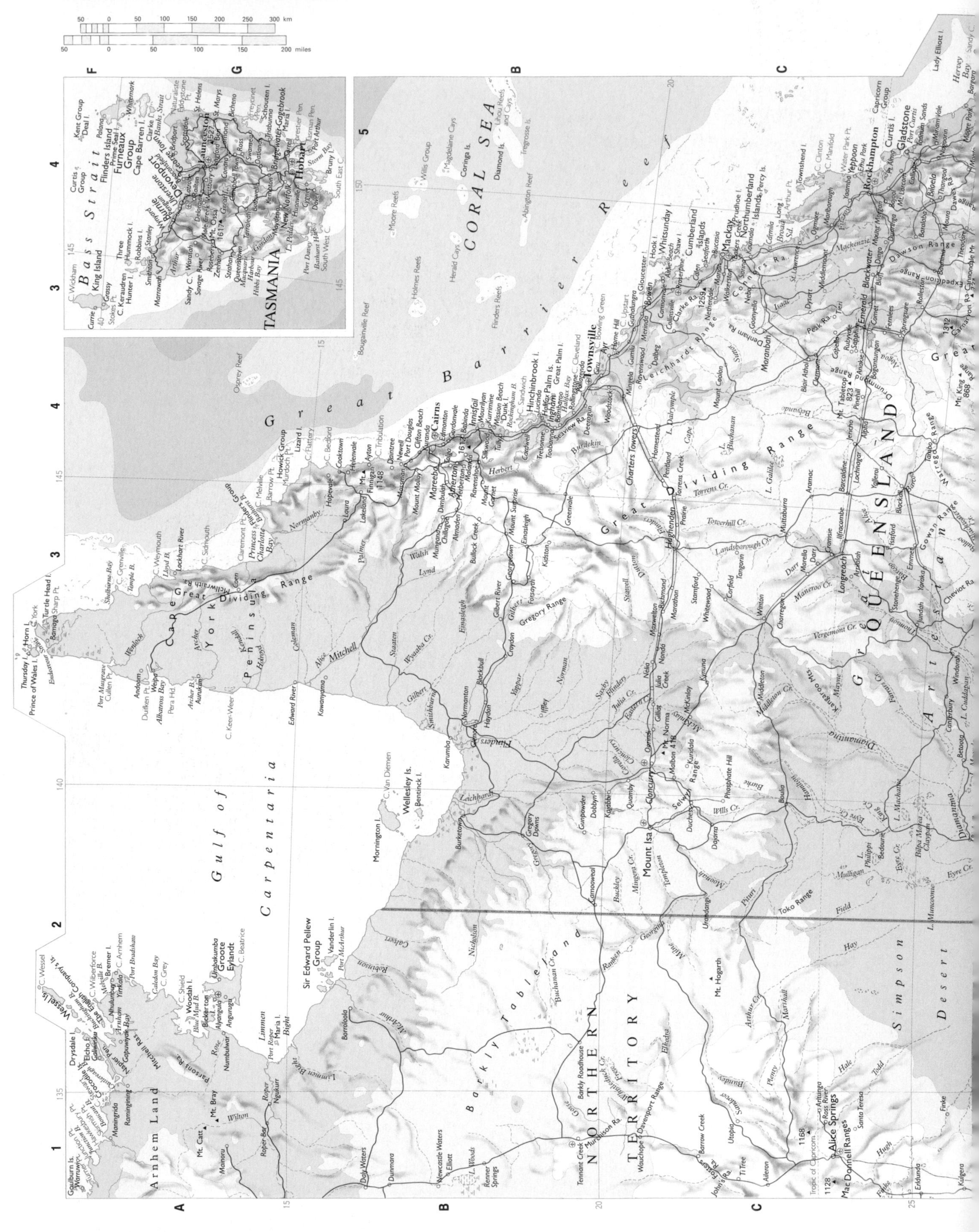

50 0 50 100 150 200 250 300 km
50 0 50 100 150 200 miles

SOUTH AUSTRALIA
NEW SOUTH WALES
V I C T O R I A
S O U T H E R N
O C E A N
T A S M A N
S E A
Bass Strait
SYDNEY
MELBOURNE
CANBERRA
ADELAIDE
BRISBANE
Gold Coast
Tweed Heads
Newcastle
Wollongong
Broken Hill
Mildura
Port Augusta
Port Pirie
Whyalla
Port Lincoln
Kangaroo I.
Spencer Gulf
Lake Eyre (North)
Lake Eyre (South)
Lake Torrens
Lake Gairdner
Lake Frome
Grey Range
Darling Downs
Toowoomba
Dubbo
Wagga Wagga
Albury-Wodonga
Bendigo
Ballarat
Geelong
Warrnambool
Mount Gambier
King Island
Flinders Island
Furneaux Group
Cape Barren I.
Bourke
Cobar
Orange
Bathurst
Tamworth
Armidale
Coffs Harbour
Port Macquarie
Lismore
Grafton
Maryborough
Bundaberg
Hervey Bay
Gympie
Ipswich
Charleville
Roma
St. George
Goulburn
Queanbeyan
Griffith
Shepparton
Projection: Bonne
East from Greenwich
COPYRIGHT, GEORGE PHILIP LTD.
m 1500 1000 400 200 0
ft 4500 3000 1200 600 0

 Equatorial Scale 1:60 000 000

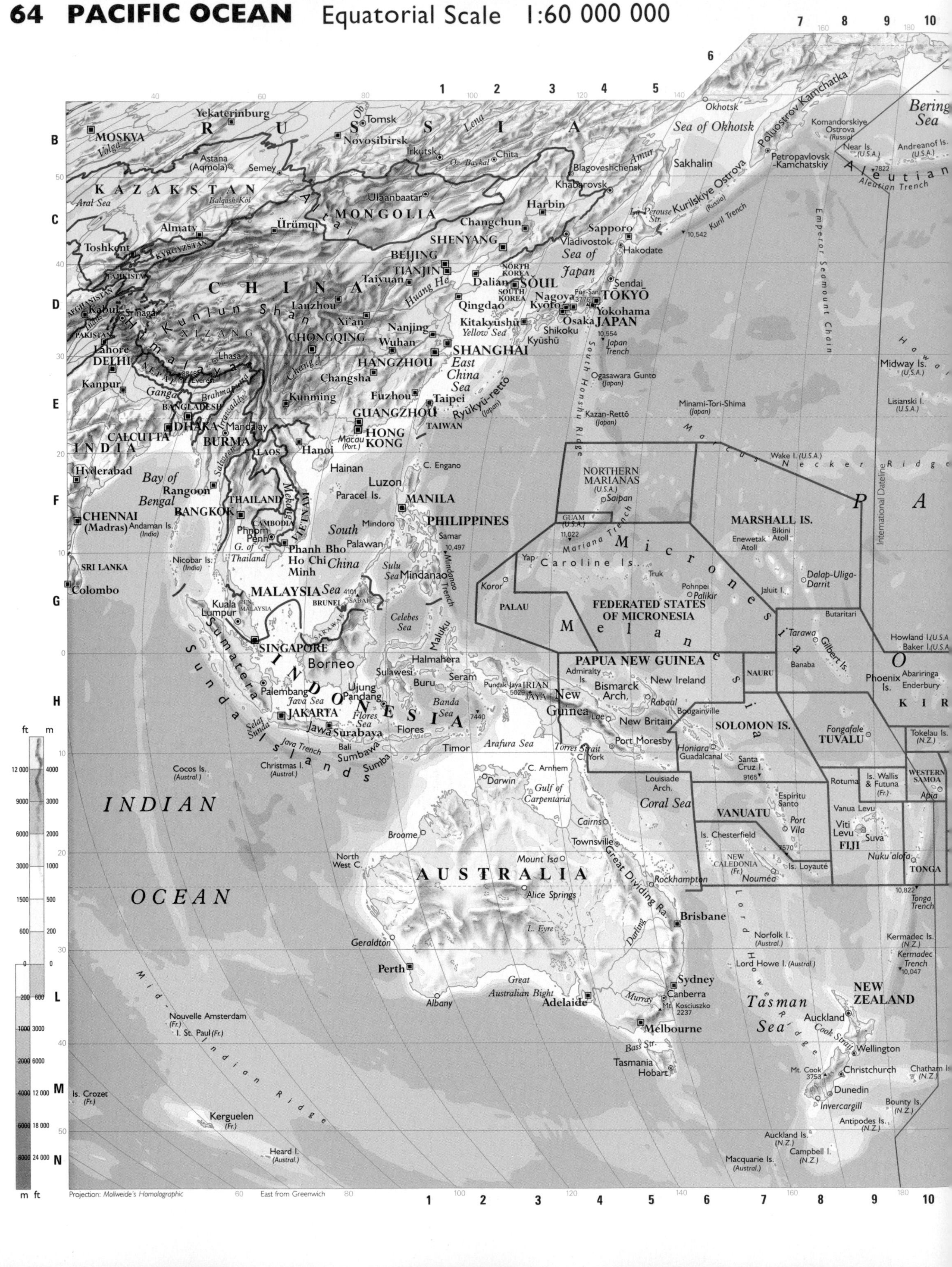

Projection: Mollweide's Homolographic

East from Greenwich

CANADA
ALASKA (U.S.A.)
Anchorage
Gulf of Alaska
Juneau
Bristol Bay
Prince of Wales I. (U.S.A.)
Prince Rupert
Queen Charlotte Is. (Canada)
Edmonton
Calgary
Regina
Winnipeg
L. Winnipeg
Newfoundland
St. Lawrence
St. John's
NORTH
Vancouver
Vancouver I.
Victoria
Seattle
Portland
Boise
Minneapolis
Missouri
L. Superior
Québec
Montréal
Ottawa
Toronto
L. Huron
L. Michigan
L. Ontario
Detroit
L. Erie
Buffalo
Boston
Salt Lake City
Denver
CHICAGO
Pittsburgh
NEW YORK CITY
PHILADELPHIA
Baltimore
Washington D.C.
C. Mendocino
Sacramento
SAN FRANCISCO
Kansas City
St. Louis
Cincinnati
UNITED STATES
ATLANTIC
Appalachian Mts.
Oklahoma City
Memphis
Atlanta
C. Hatteras
LOS ANGELES
San Diego
Phoenix
Dallas
Mississippi
Bermuda (U.K.)
Jacksonville
Ciudad Juárez
Houston
San Antonio
New Orleans
Guadalupe (Mex.)
Baja California
Golfo de California
Sargasso Sea
Gulf of Mexico
Miami
BAHAMAS
OCEAN
Monterrey
Florida Str.
Tropic of Cancer
C. San Lucas
La Habana
CUBA
West Indies
Canal de Yucatan
Honolulu
Oahu
HAWAIIAN IS. (U.S.A.)
Hawaii
Guadalajara
MEXICO
Mérida
Puebla
Acapulco
Is. Revilla Gigedo (Mex.)
HAITI
DOMINICAN REP.
JAMAICA
Kingston
PUERTO RICO (U.S.A.)
Leeward Is.
Johnston I. (U.S.A.)
BELIZE
HONDURAS
Caribbean Sea
GUATEMALA
Guatemala
San Salvador
EL SALVADOR
NICARAGUA
Managua
BARBADOS
Windward Is.
I. Clipperton (Fr.)
Barranquilla
Maracaibo
Caracas
San José
Colón
Panamá
COSTA RICA
PANAMA
Orinoco
VENEZUELA
North West Christmas Ridge
Palmyra Is. (U.S.A.)
Teraina
Tabuaeran
Kiritimati
I. del Coco (Costa Rica)
Medellín
Bogotá
I. de Malpelo (Colombia)
Cali
COLOMBIA
Equator
Galápagos (Ecuador)
Quito
ECUADOR
Jarvis I. (U.S.A.)
Malden I.
Starbuck I.
Guayaquil
Iquitos
Amazonas
C. Paliñas
BRAZIL
Tongareva
Caroline I.
Is. Marquises
Pukapuka
Manihiki
Vostok I.
Flint I.
Trujillo
PERU
LIMA
Suwarrow Is.
Is. de la Société
Tahiti
Papeete
Is. Tuamotu
Cuzco
L. Titicaca
Nevada Ancohuma
Arequipa
La Paz
BOLIVIA
Cook Is. (N.Z.)
FRENCH POLYNESIA
East Pacific Ridge
Peru-Chile Trench
Arica
Iquique
Rarotonga
Is. Tubuai
Mururoa
Tropic of Capricorn
Antofagasta
PARAGUAY
Asunción
Austral Seamount Chain
Ducie I.
Pitcairn I. (U.K.)
San Felix (Chile)
San Ambrosio (Chile)
San Miguel de Tucumán
Rapa
Sala-y-Gómez (Chile)
I. de Pascua (Chile)
Porto Alegre
Córdoba
Aconcagua
Arch. de Juan Fernández (Chile)
Valparaíso
Rosario
SANTIAGO
BUENOS AIRES
URUGUAY
Montevideo
Río de la Plata
Concepción
ARGENTINA
Chile Rise
SOUTH ATLANTIC OCEAN
Patagonia
Pacific-Antarctic Ridge
Falkland Is. (U.K.)
Punta Arenas
Est. de Magallanes
Tierra del Fuego
South Georgia (U.K.)
C. de Hornos
West from Greenwich
COPYRIGHT GEORGE PHILIP LTD.

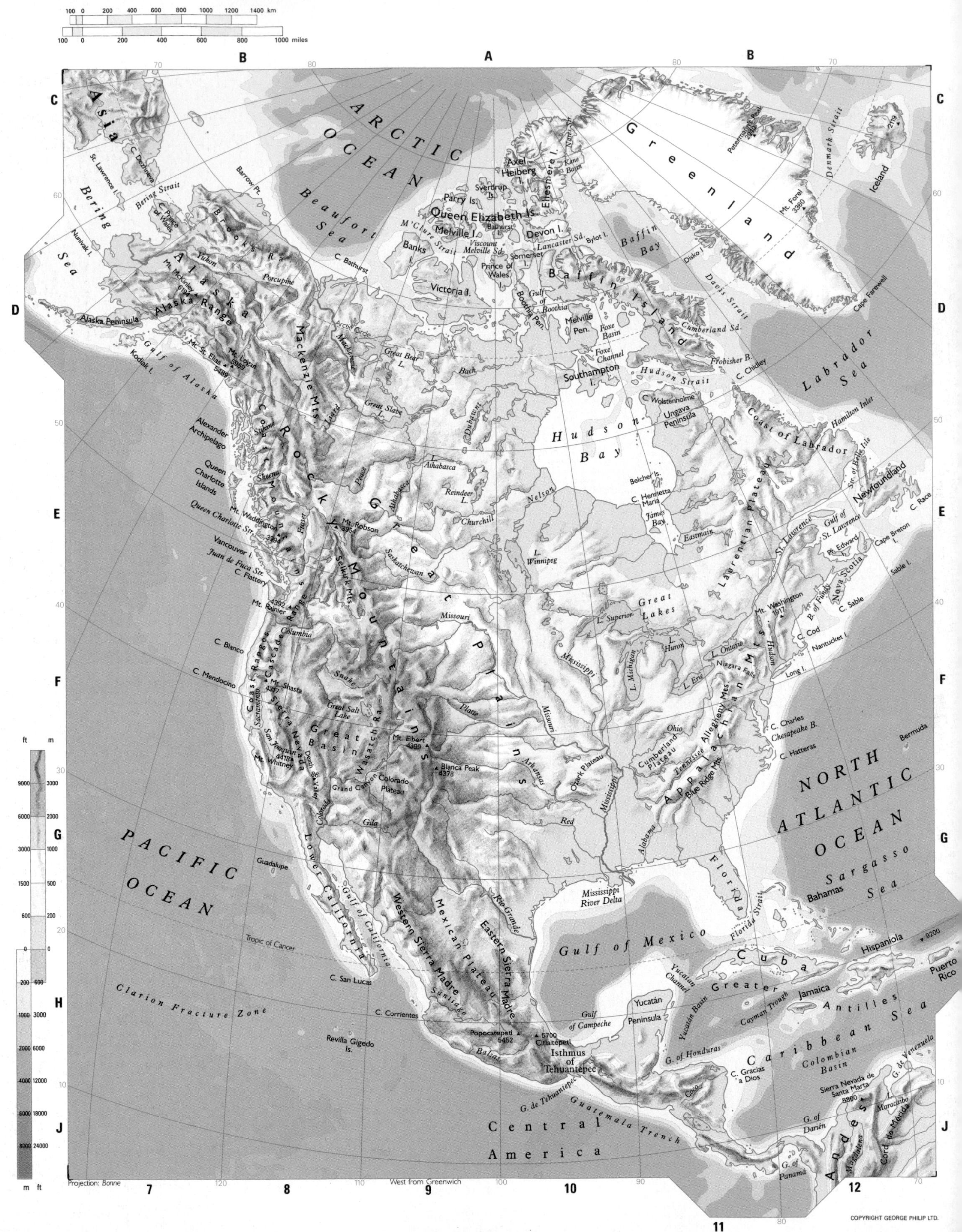

ARCTIC OCEAN
Beaufort Sea
Greenland
Queen Elizabeth Is.
Baffin Bay
Baffin Island
Hudson Bay
Labrador Sea
Bering Sea
Bering Strait
Asia
Alaska
Alaska Range
Alaska Peninsula
Gulf of Alaska
Brooks Ra.
Mackenzie Mts
Rocky Mountains
Great Plains
Coast Mountains
Great Lakes
Great Basin
Appalachian Mts
PACIFIC OCEAN
NORTH ATLANTIC OCEAN
Gulf of Mexico
Caribbean Sea
Sargasso Sea
Central America
Andes
Victoria I.
Banks I.
Melville I.
Devon I.
Axel Heiberg I.
Ellesmere I.
Iceland
Newfoundland
Cuba
Hispaniola
Jamaica
Puerto Rico
Bahamas
Bermuda
Mt. McKinley
Mt. Logan 5959
Mt. St. Elias 5489
Mt. Robson 3954
Mt. Rainier 4392
Mt. Shasta 4317
Mt. Whitney 4418
Mt. Elbert 4399
Blanca Peak 4378
Mt. Washington 1917
Popocatepetl 5452
Citlaltepetl 5700
Mt. Forel 3360
Sierra Nevada de Santa Marta 5800
Projection: Bonne
West from Greenwich

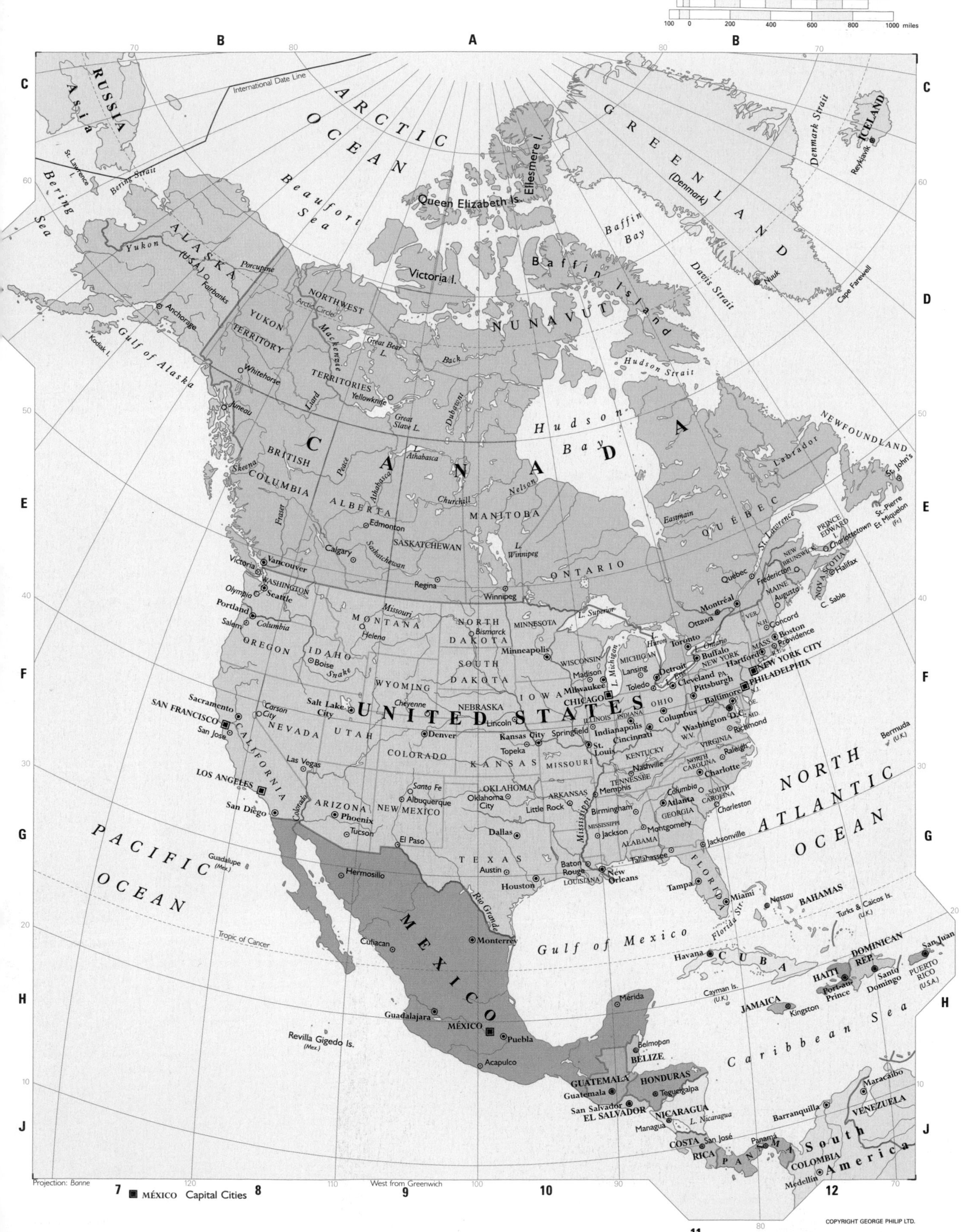
100 0 200 400 600 800 1000 1200 1400 km
100 0 200 400 600 800 1000 miles
A
B
C
D
E
F
G
H
J
7
8
9
10
11
12
RUSSIA
Asia
International Date Line
ARCTIC OCEAN
Beaufort Sea
Bering Strait
Bering Sea
St. Lawrence I.
GREENLAND (Denmark)
ICELAND
Reykjavík
Denmark Strait
Nuuk
Cape Farewell
Davis Strait
Baffin Bay
Baffin Island
Ellesmere I.
Queen Elizabeth Is.
Victoria I.
NUNAVUT
Hudson Strait
Hudson Bay
ALASKA (U.S.A.)
Yukon
Porcupine
Fairbanks
Anchorage
Kodiak I.
Gulf of Alaska
Juneau
YUKON TERRITORY
Whitehorse
NORTHWEST TERRITORIES
Arctic Circle
Mackenzie
Great Bear L.
Back
Yellowknife
Great Slave L.
Liard
Dubawnt
CANADA
BRITISH COLUMBIA
Skeena
Fraser
Peace
Athabasca
L. Athabasca
Churchill
Nelson
ALBERTA
Edmonton
Calgary
SASKATCHEWAN
Saskatchewan
Regina
MANITOBA
L. Winnipeg
Winnipeg
ONTARIO
QUÉBEC
Eastmain
Labrador
NEWFOUNDLAND
St. John's
St. Lawrence
PRINCE EDWARD I.
Charlottetown
St-Pierre Et Miquelon (Fr.)
NEW BRUNSWICK
Fredericton
NOVA SCOTIA
Halifax
C. Sable
Quebec
Montréal
Ottawa
Toronto
Victoria
Vancouver
WASHINGTON
Olympia
Seattle
Portland
Salem
Columbia
OREGON
IDAHO
Boise
Snake
MONTANA
Missouri
Helena
NORTH DAKOTA
Bismarck
SOUTH DAKOTA
MINNESOTA
Minneapolis
L. Superior
WISCONSIN
Madison
Milwaukee
L. Michigan
MICHIGAN
Lansing
L. Huron
L. Ontario
L. Erie
Detroit
Toledo
Cleveland
Buffalo
NEW YORK
PA.
Pittsburgh
VER.
N.H.
MAINE
Augusta
Concord
MASS.
Boston
Providence
CT.
R.I.
Hartford
NEW YORK CITY
PHILADELPHIA
N.J.
DE.
MD.
Baltimore
Washington D.C.
Richmond
W.V.
VIRGINIA
WYOMING
Cheyenne
Salt Lake City
UNITED STATES
NEBRASKA
Lincoln
IOWA
CHICAGO
ILLINOIS
INDIANA
Indianapolis
OHIO
Columbus
Cincinnati
Springfield
St. Louis
Kansas City
Topeka
KANSAS
MISSOURI
KENTUCKY
Nashville
TENNESSEE
Memphis
NORTH CAROLINA
Raleigh
Charlotte
SOUTH CAROLINA
Columbia
Charleston
Atlanta
GEORGIA
Birmingham
ALABAMA
Montgomery
MISSISSIPPI
Jackson
Mississippi
ARKANSAS
Little Rock
OKLAHOMA
Oklahoma City
TEXAS
Dallas
Austin
Houston
El Paso
Baton Rouge
LOUISIANA
New Orleans
Tallahassee
Jacksonville
FLORIDA
Tampa
Miami
Sacramento
SAN FRANCISCO
San Jose
Carson City
NEVADA
CALIFORNIA
UTAH
Denver
COLORADO
Las Vegas
LOS ANGELES
San Diego
Colorado
ARIZONA
Phoenix
Tucson
NEW MEXICO
Santa Fe
Albuquerque
Bermuda (U.K.)
NORTH ATLANTIC OCEAN
PACIFIC OCEAN
Guadalupe (Mex.)
Tropic of Cancer
Hermosillo
Rio Grande
MEXICO
Culiacan
Monterrey
Guadalajara
MÉXICO
Puebla
Acapulco
Revilla Gigedo Is. (Mex.)
Gulf of Mexico
Florida Str.
Nassau
BAHAMAS
Turks & Caicos Is. (U.K.)
Havana
CUBA
DOMINICAN REP.
Santo Domingo
HAITI
Port-au-Prince
San Juan
PUERTO RICO (U.S.A.)
Cayman Is. (U.K.)
JAMAICA
Kingston
Caribbean Sea
Mérida
Belmopan
BELIZE
GUATEMALA
Guatemala
HONDURAS
Tegucigalpa
San Salvador
EL SALVADOR
NICARAGUA
Managua
L. Nicaragua
COSTA RICA
San José
Panamá
PANAMA
Barranquilla
Maracaibo
VENEZUELA
COLOMBIA
Medellín
South America
Projection: Bonne
West from Greenwich
MÉXICO Capital Cities

PACIFIC OCEAN
ALASKA
YUKON TERRITORY
NORTHWEST TERRITORIES
BRITISH COLUMBIA
ALBERTA
SASKATCHEWAN
MANITOBA
Victoria Island
Great Bear L.
Great Slave L.
Lake Athabasca
Lake Winnipeg
Edmonton
Calgary
VANCOUVER
Victoria
SEATTLE
Winnipeg
Regina
Saskatoon
Whitehorse
Yellowknife
NORTH DAKOTA
SOUTH DAKOTA
MINNESOTA
MONTANA
NEBRASKA
BERING SEA
GULF OF ALASKA
Projection : Bonne
West from Greenwich

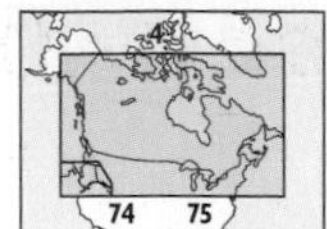

11 12 13 14 15 16

B
C
D
E

Devon I.
Lancaster Sound
Arctic Bay
Bylot I.
Borden Pen.
Brodeur Peninsula
Pond Inlet
Baffin Bay
C. Adair
Clyde River
Gulf of Boothia
Baffin Island
C. Raper
Home B.
Fury and Hecla Str.
Igloolik
Simpson Pen.
Pelly Bay
Committee B.
Melville Peninsula
Sanirajak
Prince Charles I.
Air Force I.
Foxe Basin
Qikiqtarjuaq
C. Dyer
Cumberland Peninsula
Pangnirtung
Hoare B.
Mercy C.
Cumberland Sd.
Nettilling L.
Rae Isthmus
Repulse Bay
Circle
NUNAVUT
C. Dorchester
Amadjuak L.
Foxe Pen.
Iqaluit
Hall Peninsula
Meta Incognita Peninsula
Kimmirut
Frobisher Bay
Resolution I.
Wager B.
Roes Welcome Sd.
Southampton I.
Salliq
Bell Pen.
Foxe Channel
Cape Dorset
Salisbury I.
Nottingham I.
Hudson Strait
Igluligaarjuk
Coats I.
Mansel I.
Ivujivik
Salluit
Kangiqsujuaq
Quaqtaq
Akpatok I.
C. Chidley
Davis Strait
Nunavik
Uummannaq
Qeqertarsuaq
Ilulissat
Qasigiannguit
Sisimiut
Kangerlussuaq
Maniitsoq
Nuuk
GREENLAND
(KALAALLIT NUNAAT)
(Denmark)
Kong Frederik VI's Kyst
Ammassalik
Qeqertarsuatsiaat
Paamiut
Arsuk
Qaqortoq
Nanortalik
Alluitsup Paa
Uummannarsuaq
2136
1890
2591
2850
3809
1652
257
1135
1190
814
6309
183
174
Labrador Sea
ATLANTIC OCEAN
Péninsule d'Ungava
Puvirnituq
L. Payne
Arnaud
Kangirsuk
Ungava Bay
Kangiqsualujjuaq
Hebron
Kuujjuaq
Feuilles
Koksoak
George
Baleine
Caniapiscau
Nain
Hopedale
C. Harrison
Rigolet
Cartwright
Hudson Bay
Ottawa Is.
Inukjuak
Sleeper Is.
King George Is.
Baker's Dozen Is.
L. Minto
Mélèzes
Smallwood Res.
NEWFOUNDLAND
Labrador
North West River
Happy Valley-Goose Bay
Churchill
Churchill Falls
Port Hope Simpson
Belle Isle
C. Bauld
St. Anthony
C. Tatnam
Belcher Is.
Kuujjuarapik
L. à l'Eau Claire
Grande Baleine
L. Bienville
Schefferville
Petitsikapau
Esker
Str. of Belle Isle
Notre Dame B.
Lewisporte
Gander
Bonavista
Trinity B.
Carbonear
St. John's
C. Henrietta Maria
Peawanuck
Winisk
Severn
Pte. Louis XIV
Kanaaupscow
La Grande
Rés. de Caniapiscau
Labrador City
Fermont
Ashuanipi
Natashquan
St-Augustin
Romaine
Baie Verte
Grand Falls
Deer Lake
Corner Brook
Newfoundland
Placentia
Placentia B.
C. Race
Marystown
Chisasibi
James Bay
Big Trout L.
Akimiski I.
Wemindji
Eastmain
Gagnon
Moisie
Rés. Manicouagan
Havre-St-Pierre
I. d'Anticosti
Stephenville
Channel-Port aux Basques
QUÉBEC
ONTARIO
Attawapiskat
Fort Albany
Charlton I.
Waskaganish
Rupert
L. Mistassini
L. Albanel
Péribonca
Manicouagan
Sept-Îles
Port-Cartier
Gulf of St. Lawrence
Cabot Str.
C. Ray
North C.
ST-PIERRE et MIQUELON (Fr.)
Albany
L. St. Joseph
Moosonee
Harricana
Nottaway
Chibougamau
Baie Comeau
St. Lawrence
Matane
Gaspé
Pén. de Gaspé
Îs. de la Madeleine
Cape Breton I.
Glace Bay
Sydney
Nakina
Kenogami
Missinaibi
Matagami
L. Matagami
Dolbeau
L. St-Jean
Chicoutimi
Rimouski
Campbellton
Bathurst
Miramichi
PR. EDWARD I.
Summerside
Charlottetown
Northumberland Str.
Port Hawkesbury
Antigonish
L. Nipigon
Nipigon
Geraldton
Hearst
Kapuskasing
Cochrane
Abitibi L.
Amos
Rés. Gouin
Roberval
Jonquière
Rivière-du-Loup
Edmundston
NEW BRUNSWICK
Moncton
NOVA SCOTIA
New Glasgow
Truro
Marathon
Oba
Timmins
Kirkland Lake
Rouyn-Noranda
Val-d'Or
La Tuque
Québec
Grand Falls
Woodstock
Amherst
Kentville
Dartmouth
Halifax
Sable I. (Nova Scotia)
Thunder Bay
Chapleau
New Liskeard
Lévis
Thetford Mines
Fredericton
Saint John
Digby
Bridgewater
Liverpool
Lake Superior
Wawa
Rés. Cabonga
Mont-Laurier
Shawinigan
Trois-Rivières
Joliette
St-Hyacinthe
MAINE
Bangor
B. of Fundy
Yarmouth
C. Sable
Houghton
Sault Ste. Marie
Elliot Lake
Sudbury
Ottawa
Ouatouais
MONTRÉAL
Sherbrooke
Augusta
Lewiston
Portland
Ironwood
Marquette
MICHIGAN
L. Nipissing
Parry Sound
North Bay
Pembroke
Hull
Granby
L. Champlain
Montpelier
Manistique
Manitoulin I.
Georgian Bay
Huntsville
Cornwall
Burlington
VERMONT
NEW HAMPSHIRE
Concord
Rhinelander
Escanaba
Menominee
Petoskey
Lake Huron
Barrie
Peterborough
Kingston
Manchester
Wausau
Green Bay
Traverse City
Owen Sound
Oshawa
Belleville
WISCONSIN
Appleton
Cadillac
TORONTO
L. Ontario
Syracuse
MASS.
BOSTON
C. Cod
Sheboygan
L. Michigan
Saginaw
Kitchener
Hamilton
Rochester
Albany
Springfield
Providence
MILWAUKEE
Grand Rapids
Flint
London
Niagara Falls
BUFFALO
NEW YORK
HARTFORD
CONN.
R.I.
Madison
Racine
Kenosha
Lansing
Sarnia
Elmira
Binghamton
New Haven
Rockford
CHICAGO
DETROIT
Windsor
L. Erie
Erie
Jamestown
Scranton
Bridgeport
NEW YORK
Gary
South Bend
Toledo
CLEVELAND
Newark
N.J.
Allentown
Trenton
ILLINOIS
INDIANA
OHIO
PENNSYLVANIA
CANADA
UNITED STATES

90 80 70 60 50 40 30

West from Greenwich

11 12 13 14

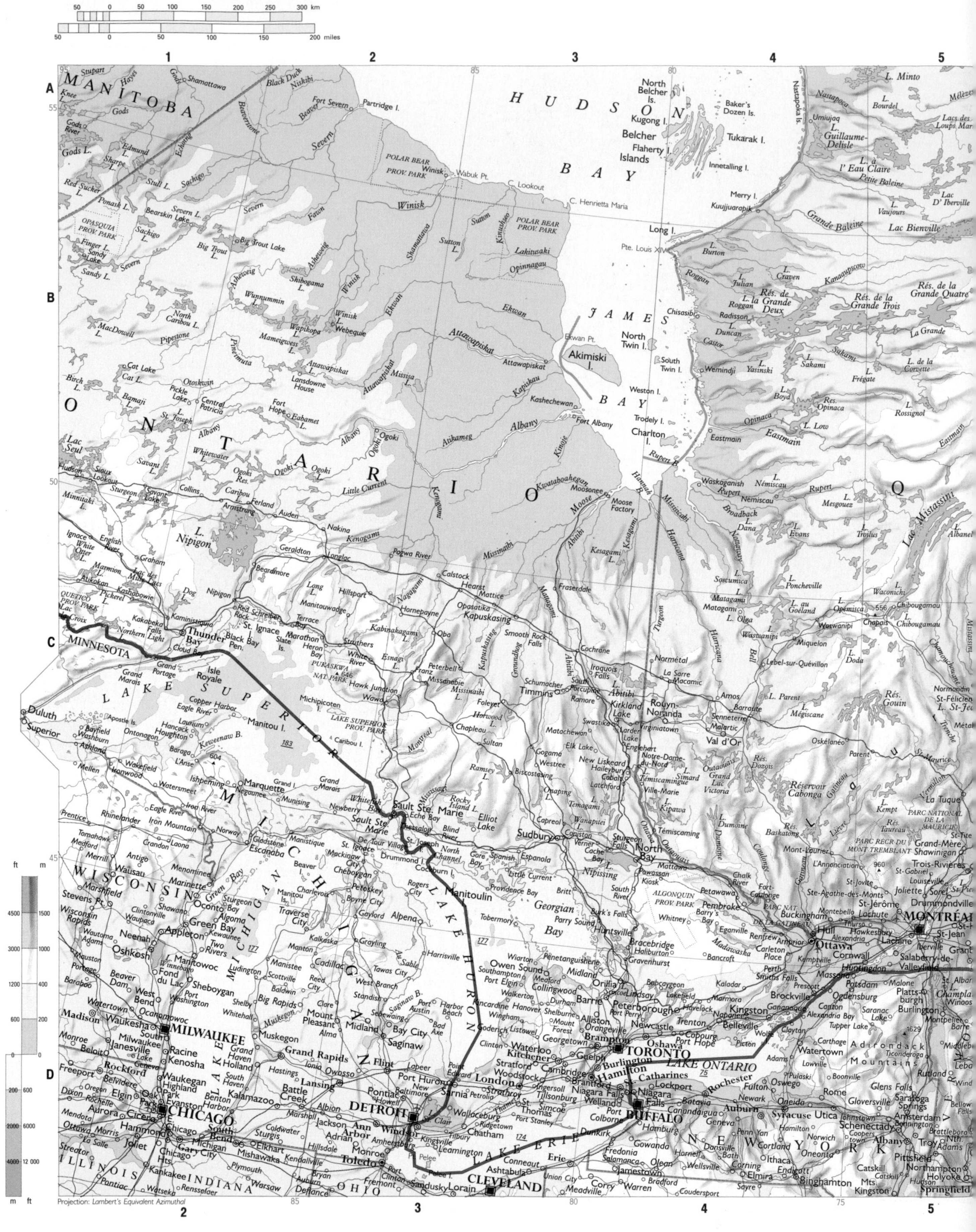
50 0 50 100 150 200 250 300 km
50 0 50 100 150 200 miles
1 2 3 4 5
A B C D
MANITOBA
ONTARIO
HUDSON BAY
JAMES BAY
Belcher Islands
Akimiski I.
POLAR BEAR PROV. PARK
L. Nipigon
LAKE SUPERIOR
MINNESOTA
WISCONSIN
MICHIGAN
LAKE MICHIGAN
LAKE HURON
Georgian Bay
LAKE ONTARIO
LAKE ERIE
ILLINOIS
INDIANA
OHIO
NEW YORK
Thunder Bay
Sault Ste. Marie
Sudbury
Timmins
North Bay
Ottawa
MONTRÉAL
TORONTO
Hamilton
BUFFALO
DETROIT
CLEVELAND
MILWAUKEE
CHICAGO
Duluth
Lac Mistassini
Réservoir Cabonga
Manitoulin
ALGONQUIN PROV. PARK
ft m
4500 1500
3000 1000
1200 400
600 200
0 0
200 600
2000 6000
4000 12 000
m ft
Projection: Lambert's Equivalent Azimuthal

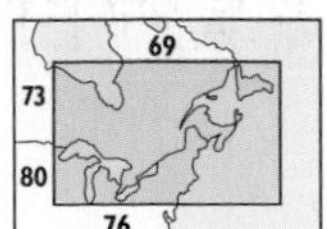

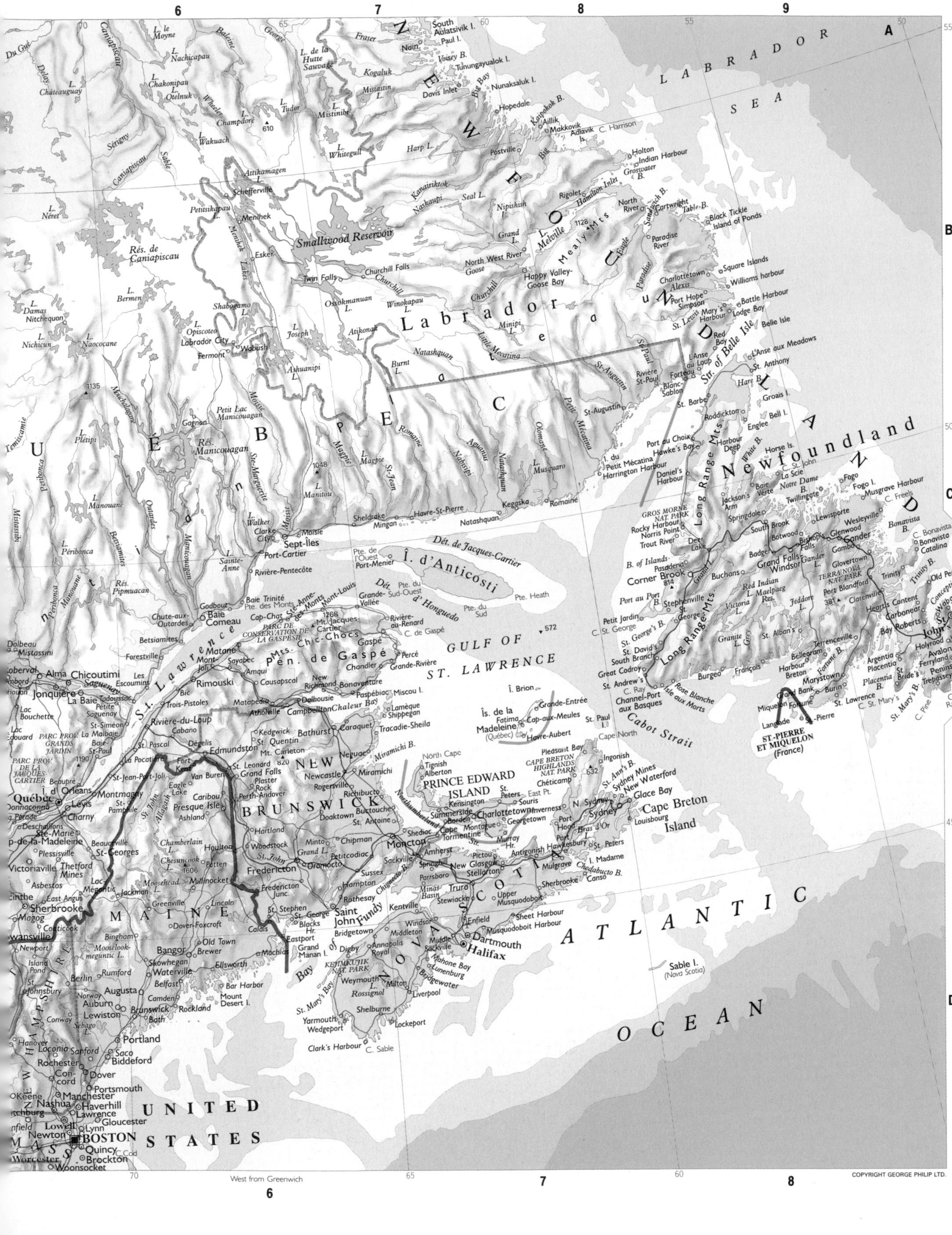

6 7 8 9

A B C D

LABRADOR SEA

NEWFOUNDLAND

Labrador

QUÉBEC

Newfoundland

GULF OF ST. LAWRENCE

Î. d'Anticosti

Pén. de Gaspé

NEW BRUNSWICK

PRINCE EDWARD ISLAND

NOVA SCOTIA

Cape Breton Island

Cabot Strait

ST-PIERRE ET MIQUELON (France)

MAINE

UNITED STATES

BOSTON

Halifax

Bay of Fundy

ATLANTIC OCEAN

Sable I. (Nova Scotia)

West from Greenwich

6 7 8

50 0 50 100 150 200 250 300 km
50 0 50 100 150 200 miles
YUKON TERRITORY
NORTHWEST TERRITORIES
BRITISH COLUMBIA
ALBERTA
ALASKA (U.S.A.)
WASHINGTON
IDAHO
UNITED STATES
PACIFIC OCEAN
GREAT SLAVE LAKE
WOOD BUFFALO NATIONAL PARK
Coast Mountains
Rocky Mountains
Skeena Mountains
Cariboo Mts.
Columbia Mts.
Monashee Mts.
Purcell Mts.
Birch Mountains
Caribou Mts.
Clear Hills
Swan Hills
Buffalo Head Hills
Whitehorse
Yellowknife
Juneau
Prince Rupert
Prince George
Fort St. John
Dawson Creek
Grande Prairie
Fort Nelson
Fort McMurray
Peace River
Edmonton
Red Deer
Calgary
Lethbridge
Kamloops
Kelowna
Penticton
Vernon
VANCOUVER
Victoria
Nanaimo
SEATTLE
Bellingham
Vancouver Island
Queen Charlotte Islands
Graham I.
Moresby I.
Queen Charlotte Sound
Hecate Strait
Dixon Entrance
Prince of Wales I.
Baranof I.
Chichagof I.
Admiralty I.
Alexander Arch.
Mt. Robson 3954
Mt. Waddington 3994
Mt. Columbia 3747
Mt. Fairweather 4663
BANFF NAT. PARK
JASPER NATIONAL PARK
TWEEDSMUIR PROV. PARK
Projection: Lambert's Equivalent Azimuthal
West from Greenwich

68
70
82
80

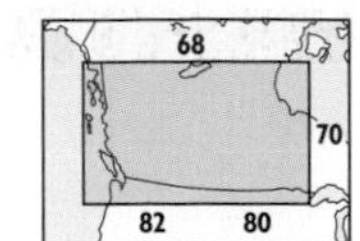

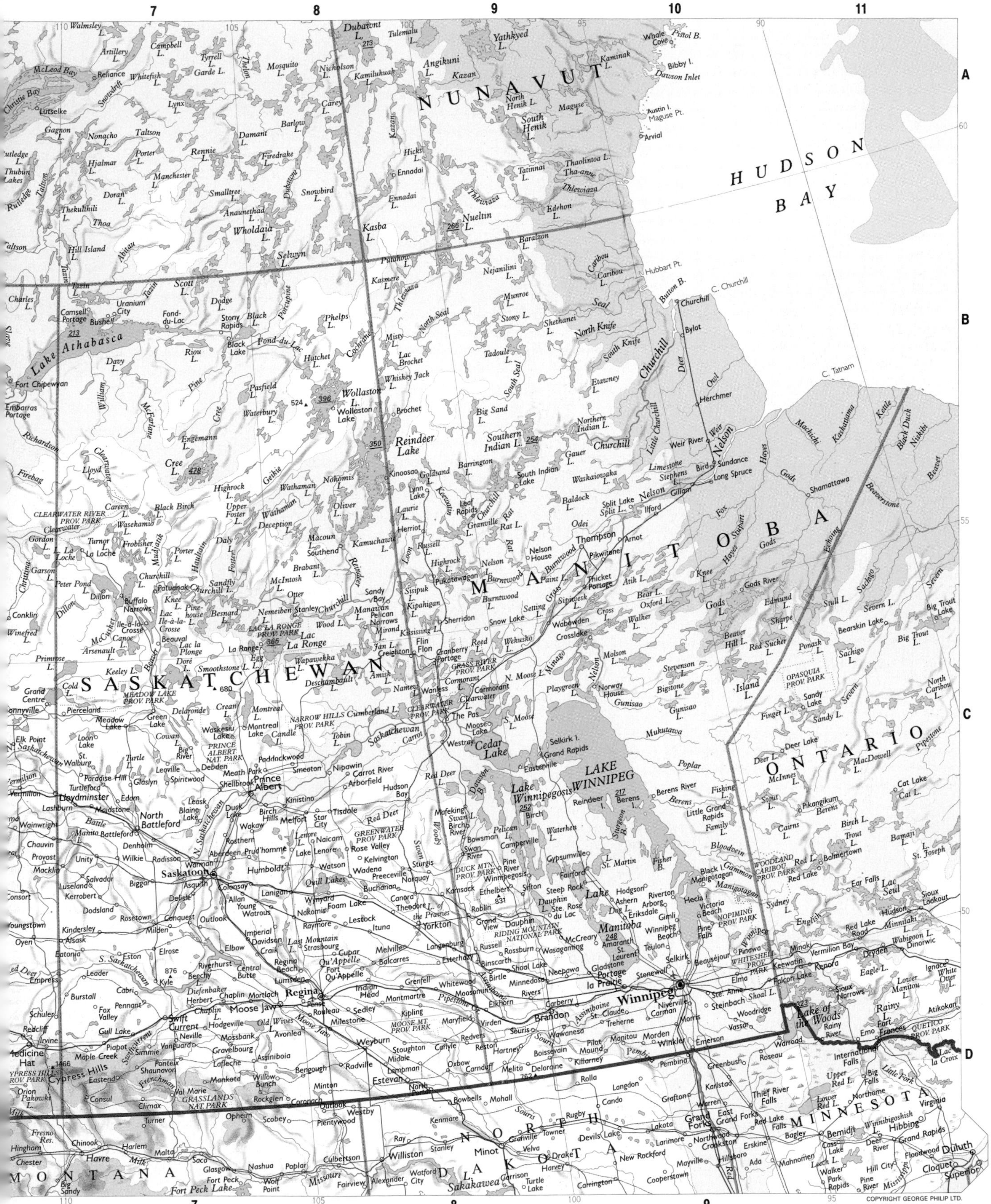

7
8
9
10
11
A
B
C
D
NUNAVUT
HUDSON BAY
SASKATCHEWAN
MANITOBA
ONTARIO
MONTANA
NORTH DAKOTA
MINNESOTA
Lake Athabasca
Wollaston L.
Reindeer Lake
Southern Indian L.
Cedar Lake
Lake Winnipegosis
LAKE WINNIPEG
Lake Manitoba
Lake of the Woods
Lac Seul
Dubawnt L.
Kasba L.
Nueltin L.
Yathkyed L.
Whale Cove
Arvial
Churchill
C. Churchill
C. Tatnam
Fort Chipewyan
Uranium City
Fond-du-Lac
Stony Rapids
Black Lake
Lynn Lake
Thompson
Flin Flon
The Pas
La Ronge
Lac La Ronge
Gillam
Split Lake
Norway House
Grand Rapids
Berens River
Red Lake
Sioux Lookout
Kenora
Dryden
Lloydminster
North Battleford
Prince Albert
Saskatoon
Regina
Moose Jaw
Swift Current
Yorkton
Melfort
Humboldt
Weyburn
Estevan
Medicine Hat
Brandon
Portage la Prairie
Winnipeg
Dauphin
Selkirk
Steinbach
Emerson
Grand Forks
Minot
Williston
Devils Lake
Havre
Bemidji
Hibbing
Grand Rapids
Duluth
Superior
Cloquet
International Falls
Fort Frances
Atikokan
Cypress Hills
Missouri
Lake Sakakawea
Fort Peck Lake
GRASSLANDS NAT. PARK
PRINCE ALBERT NAT. PARK
RIDING MOUNTAIN NATIONAL PARK
DUCK MTN. PROV. PARK
WHITESHELL PROV. PARK
NOPIMING PROV. PARK
WOODLAND CARIBOU PROV. PARK
QUETICO PROV. PARK
OPASQUIA PROV. PARK
CLEARWATER RIVER PROV. PARK
MEADOW LAKE PROV. PARK
NARROW HILLS PROV. PARK
GREENWATER PROV. PARK
MOOSE MT. PROV. PARK
GRASS RIVER PROV. PARK
CLEARWATER PROV. PARK
LAC LA RONGE PROV. PARK
110
105
100
95
90
60
55
50
COPYRIGHT GEORGE PHILIP LTD.

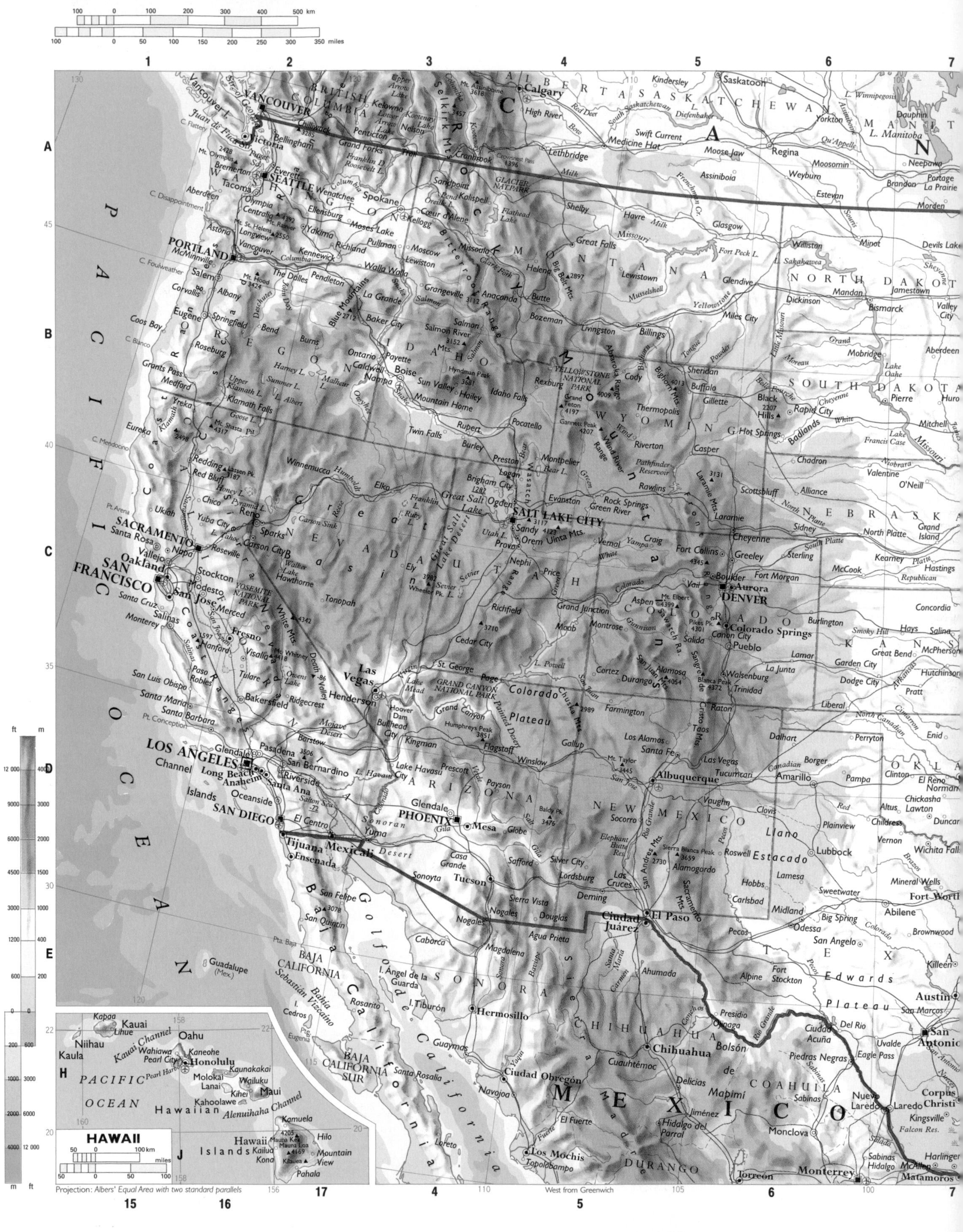

PACIFIC OCEAN
BRITISH COLUMBIA
ALBERTA
SASKATCHEWAN
MANITOBA
WASHINGTON
OREGON
CALIFORNIA
NEVADA
IDAHO
MONTANA
WYOMING
UTAH
COLORADO
ARIZONA
NEW MEXICO
NORTH DAKOTA
SOUTH DAKOTA
NEBRASKA
KANSAS
OKLAHOMA
TEXAS
MEXICO
SONORA
CHIHUAHUA
COAHUILA
DURANGO
BAJA CALIFORNIA
BAJA CALIFORNIA SUR
Golfo de California
Great Basin
Rocky Mountains
Colorado Plateau
Llano Estacado
Edwards Plateau
Bolsón de Mapimí
Sonoran Desert
Mojave Desert
Great Salt Lake
YELLOWSTONE NATIONAL PARK
GRAND CANYON NATIONAL PARK
YOSEMITE NATIONAL PARK
GLACIER NAT. PARK
VANCOUVER
SEATTLE
PORTLAND
SACRAMENTO
SAN FRANCISCO
LOS ANGELES
SAN DIEGO
PHOENIX
SALT LAKE CITY
DENVER
Calgary
Regina
Saskatoon
Spokane
Boise
Reno
Las Vegas
Tucson
Albuquerque
El Paso
Ciudad Juárez
Chihuahua
Hermosillo
Monterrey
San Antonio
Austin
HAWAII
Kauai
Oahu
Honolulu
Molokai
Lanai
Maui
Kahoolawe
Hawaii
Niihau
Kaula
Kauai Channel
Alenuihaha Channel
Hawaiian Islands
PACIFIC OCEAN
Mauna Kea 4205
Mauna Loa 4169
Hilo
Projection: Albers' Equal Area with two standard parallels
West from Greenwich

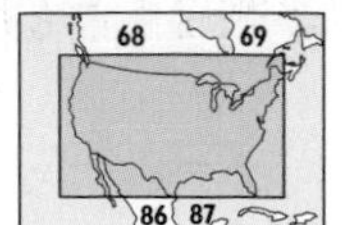
68
69
86
87

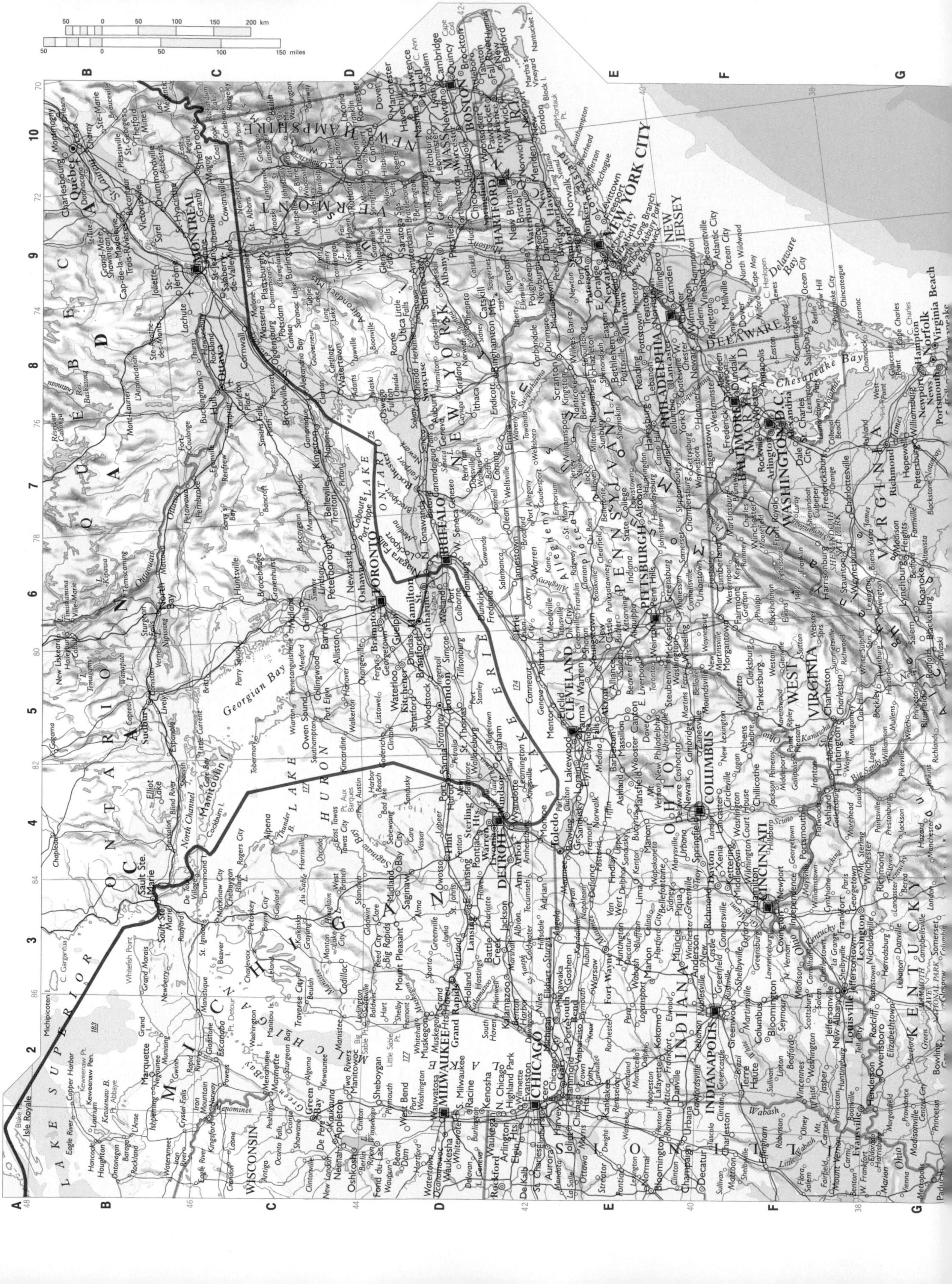
50 0 50 100 150 200 km
50 0 50 100 150 miles
NEW YORK CITY
BOSTON
HARTFORD
PHILADELPHIA
BALTIMORE
WASHINGTON D.C.
PITTSBURGH
BUFFALO
TORONTO
MONTREAL
Québec
Ottawa
CLEVELAND
COLUMBUS
CINCINNATI
INDIANAPOLIS
DETROIT
CHICAGO
MILWAUKEE
LAKE ONTARIO
LAKE ERIE
LAKE HURON
LAKE MICHIGAN
LAKE SUPERIOR
Georgian Bay
Chesapeake Bay
Delaware Bay
QUÉBEC
ONTARIO
NEW YORK
PENNSYLVANIA
NEW JERSEY
DELAWARE
MARYLAND
VIRGINIA
WEST VIRGINIA
OHIO
INDIANA
ILLINOIS
MICHIGAN
WISCONSIN
KENTUCKY
VERMONT
NEW HAMPSHIRE
MASS.
CONN.
R.I.

ATLANTIC OCEAN
GULF OF MEXICO
BAHAMAS
TENNESSEE
NORTH CAROLINA
SOUTH CAROLINA
GEORGIA
ALABAMA
MISSISSIPPI
FLORIDA
MAINE
NEW HAMPSHIRE
CANADA
Continuation Eastwards On same scale.
Nashville
Knoxville
Chattanooga
Asheville
CHARLOTTE
Raleigh
Durham
Greensboro
Winston-Salem
Wilmington
Columbia
Charleston
Savannah
ATLANTA
Macon
Augusta
Columbus
Birmingham
Montgomery
Mobile
Pensacola
Tallahassee
Jacksonville
Gainesville
Orlando
TAMPA
St. Petersburg
MIAMI
Fort Lauderdale
West Palm Beach
Daytona Beach
Panama City
Huntsville
Tuscaloosa
Portland
Augusta
Bangor
Grand Bahama
Great Abaco I.
Little Abaco I.
Freeport
Projection: Albers' Equal Area with two standard parallels
West from Greenwich
COPYRIGHT.GEORGE PHILIP LTD.

10 0 10 20 30 40 50 60 70 80 90 km
10 0 10 20 30 40 50 60 miles
Georgian Bay
Bruce Peninsula
LAKE HURON
LAKE ONTARIO
LAKE ERIE
MICHIGAN
CANADA
ONTARIO
NEW YORK
OHIO
PENNSYLVANIA
Allegheny Plateau
Allegheny Mountains
Tuscarora Mts.
TORONTO
Mississauga
Hamilton
Burlington
Oakville
Kitchener
Waterloo
Guelph
London
Brantford
St. Catharines
Niagara Falls
Sarnia
Port Huron
DETROIT
Windsor
Chatham
BUFFALO
Rochester
Erie
CLEVELAND
Akron
Youngstown
Canton
Mansfield
PITTSBURGH
Altoona
State College
Williamsport
Barrie
Peterborough
Belleville
Oshawa
Owen Sound
Thunder Bay
L. Simcoe
Long Point Bay
Pelee I.
Projection: Bonne

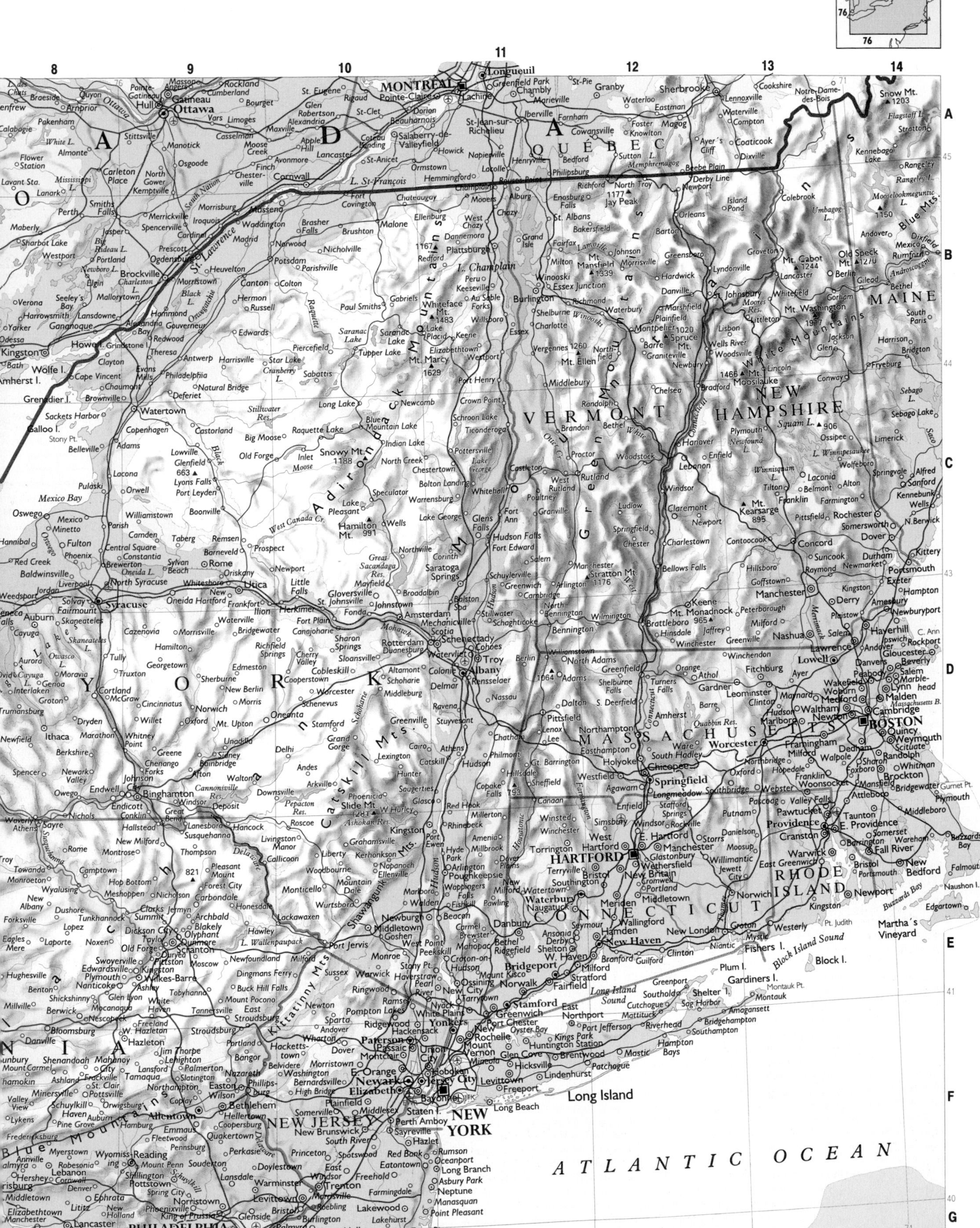
8
9
10
11
12
13
14
A
B
C
D
E
F
G
C A N A D A
Q U É B E C
N E W Y O R K
P E N N S Y L V A N I A
V E R M O N T
N E W H A M P S H I R E
M A I N E
M A S S A C H U S E T T S
C O N N E C T I C U T
R H O D E I S L A N D
NEW JERSEY
NEW YORK
A T L A N T I C O C E A N
Adirondack Mountains
Green Mountains
White Mountains
Catskill Mts.
Shawangunk Mts.
Kittatinny Mts.
Blue Mountains
Appalachian Mountains
Blue Mts.
Long Island
Long Island Sound
Block Island Sound
Buzzards Bay
Martha's Vineyard
Nantucket Sound
Block I.
Fishers I.
Gardiners I.
Plum I.
Shelter I.
Montauk Pt.
Pt. Judith
Elizabeth Is.
Naushon I.
Mexico Bay
Stony Pt.
L. Champlain
L. Memphremagog
L. Winnipesaukee
Squam L.
Sebago L.
Mooselookmeguntic L.
Umbagog L.
Rangeley L.
Quabbin Res.
L. Wallenpaupack
Cannonsville Res.
Pepacton Res.
Ashokan Res.
Great Sacandaga Res.
Stillwater Res.
L. George
Wolfe I.
Amherst I.
Galloo I.
Grenadier I.
Howe I.
Grindstone I.
St. Lawrence
L. St-François
Ottawa
Rideau L.
Mississippi L.
Hudson
Mohawk
Delaware
Susquehanna
Schuylkill
Connecticut
Housatonic
Merrimack
Androscoggin
Winooski
Lamoille
Otter Cr.
Black
Oswegatchie
Raquette
West Canada Cr.
Schoharie
Thames
Saco
Mt. Marcy 1629
Whiteface Mt. 1483
Snowy Mt. 1188
Hamilton Mt. 991
Slide Mt. 1281
Mt. Mansfield 1339
Jay Peak 1177
Spruce Mt. 1020
Mt. Ellen 1260
Stratton Mt. 1176
Mt. Washington 1917
Mt. Cabot 1244
Mt. Moosilauke 1466
Mt. Kearsarge 895
Mt. Monadnock 965
Old Speck Mt. 1270
Snow Mt. 1203
MONTREAL
Ottawa
Longueuil
Gatineau
Hull
BOSTON
HARTFORD
PHILADELPHIA
Providence
Albany
Syracuse
Utica
Binghamton
Scranton
Wilkes-Barre
Allentown
Bethlehem
Reading
Trenton
Camden
Newark
Jersey City
Paterson
Elizabeth
Yonkers
Stamford
Bridgeport
New Haven
Waterbury
Springfield
Worcester
Lowell
Lawrence
Manchester
Concord
Nashua
Portsmouth
Burlington
Montpelier
Rutland
Plattsburgh
Schenectady
Troy
Kingston
Poughkeepsie
Newburgh
Danbury
New London
Norwich
Pawtucket
Fall River
New Bedford
Brockton
Cambridge
Quincy
Lynn
Salem
Sherbrooke
Granby
Cornwall
Brockville
Watertown
Oswego
Ithaca
Cortland
Rome
Saratoga Springs
Glens Falls
Pittsfield
Keene
Brattleboro
Bennington
St. Johnsbury
Lewiston
Dover
Stroudsburg
Easton
Hazleton
Toms River
Long Branch
Asbury Park
Freeport
Long Beach
West from Greenwich
76
74
73
72
71
45
44
43
41
40
70

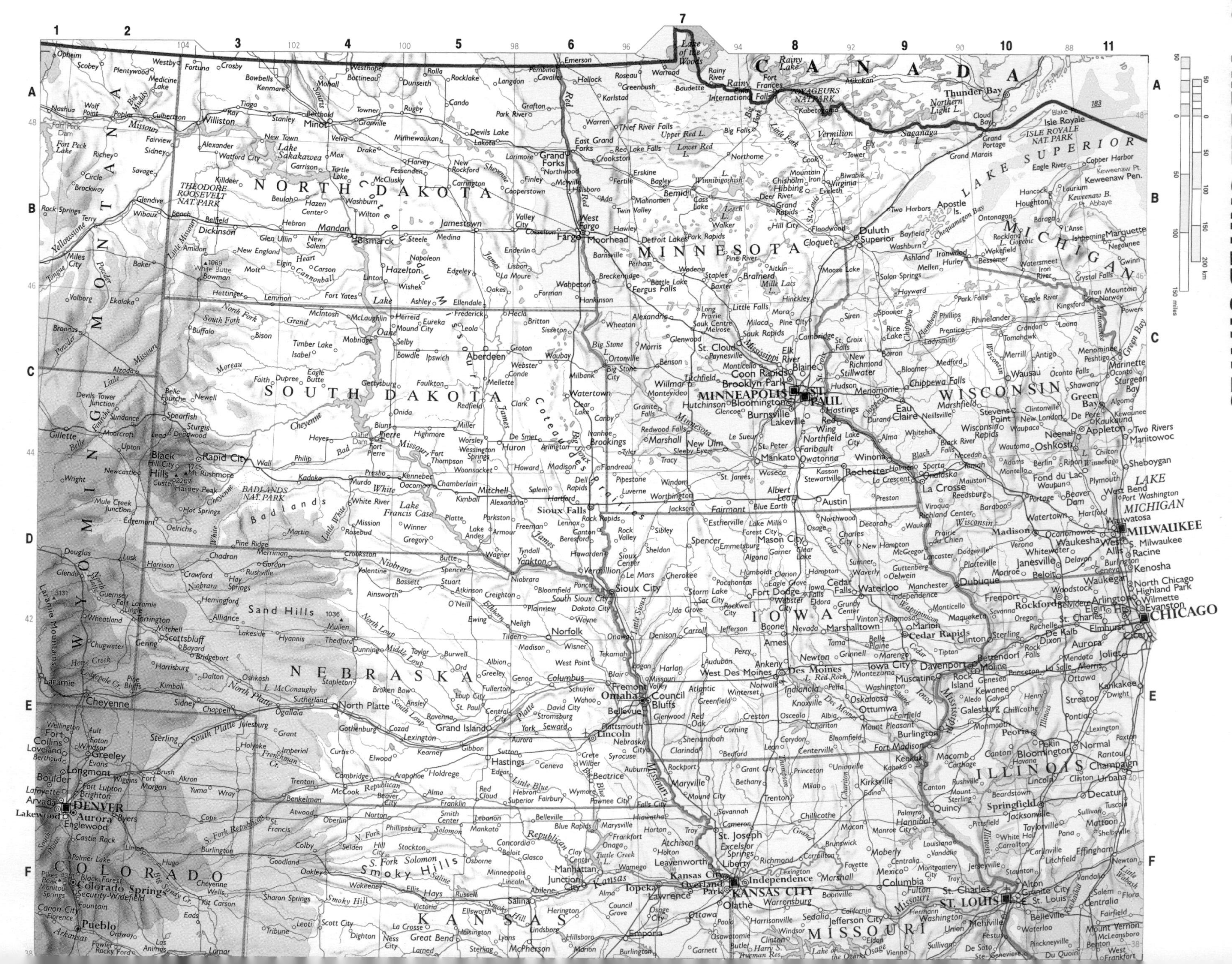
50 0 50 100 150 200 km
50 0 50 100 150 miles
CANADA
LAKE SUPERIOR
LAKE MICHIGAN
NORTH DAKOTA
SOUTH DAKOTA
MINNESOTA
WISCONSIN
MICHIGAN
IOWA
ILLINOIS
NEBRASKA
KANSAS
MISSOURI
MONTANA
WYOMING
COLORADO
MILWAUKEE
CHICAGO
MINNEAPOLIS
ST. PAUL
KANSAS CITY
ST. LOUIS
DENVER
ISLE ROYALE NAT. PARK
VOYAGEURS NAT. PARK
THEODORE ROOSEVELT NAT. PARK
BADLANDS NAT. PARK
Black Hills
Sand Hills
Smoky Hills
Laramie Mountains
Missouri
Mississippi

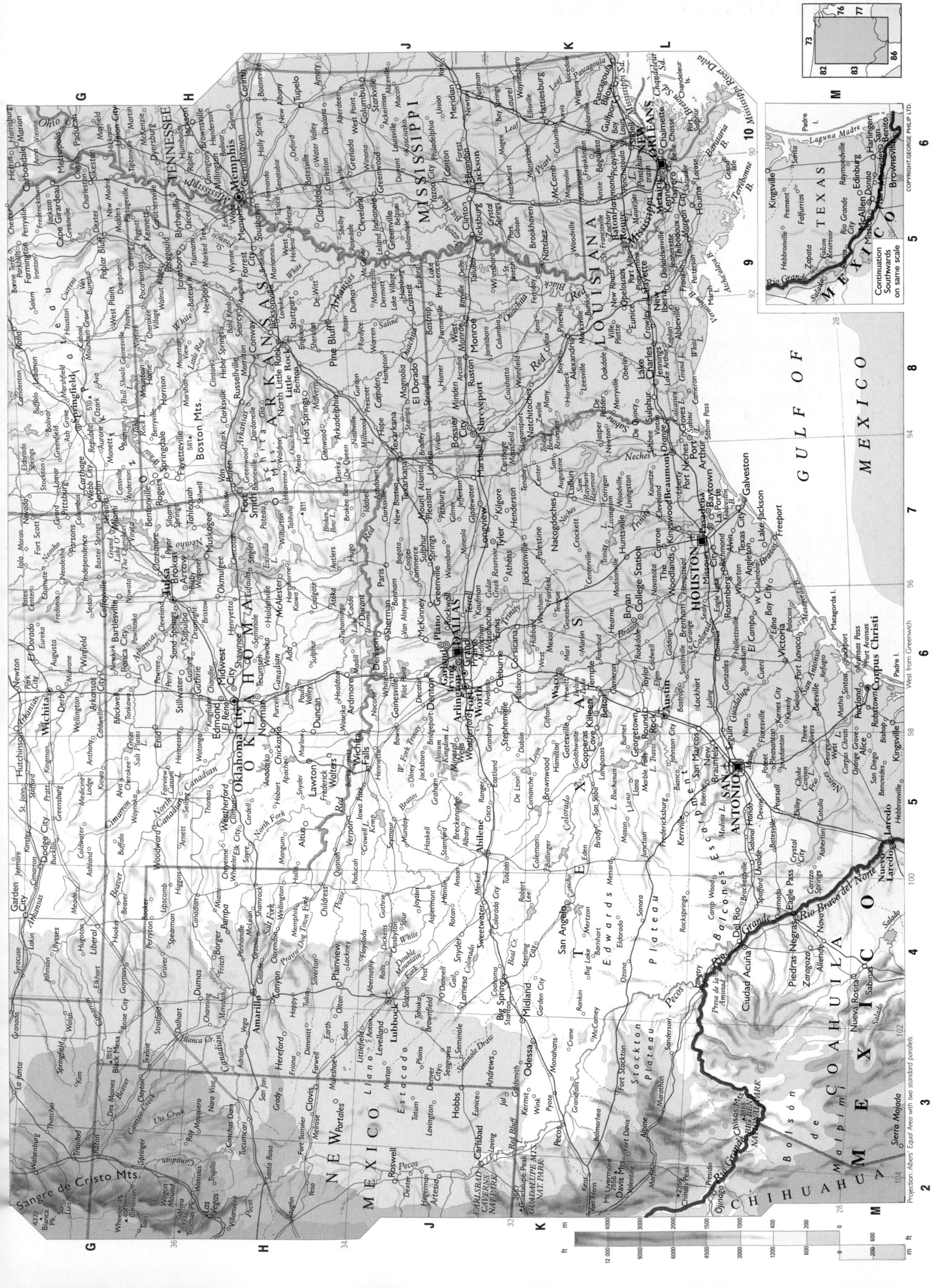

NEW MEXICO

OKLAHOMA

TEXAS

ARKANSAS

LOUISIANA

MISSISSIPPI

TENNESSEE

MEXICO

COAHUILA

CHIHUAHUA

GULF OF MEXICO

Sangre de Cristo Mts.

Llano Estacado

Edwards Plateau

Stockton Plateau

Balcones Escarpment

Ozark Plateau

Boston Mts.

Ouachita Mts.

Bolsón de Mapimí

Oklahoma City · Tulsa · Dallas · Fort Worth · Houston · San Antonio · Austin · Memphis · New Orleans · Little Rock · Shreveport · Jackson · Wichita · Amarillo · Lubbock · El Paso · Corpus Christi · Galveston · Beaumont · Baton Rouge · Waco · Abilene · Odessa · Midland · San Angelo · Laredo · Brownsville

Rio Grande · Pecos · Red · Arkansas · Canadian · Brazos · Colorado · Trinity · Sabine · Neches · Mississippi · Ouachita · White · Pearl

CARLSBAD CAVERNS NAT. PARK

GUADALUPE MTS. NAT. PARK

BIG BEND NATIONAL PARK

Continuation Southwards on same scale

Kingsville · Hebbronville · Zapata · Falcon Reservoir · Rio Grande City · McAllen · Edinburg · Harlingen · Brownsville · Laguna Madre · Padre I.

| ft | m |
|---|---|
| 12 000 | 4000 |
| 9000 | 3000 |
| 6000 | 2000 |
| 4500 | 1500 |
| 3000 | 1000 |
| 1200 | 400 |
| 600 | 200 |
| 0 | 0 |
| 200 | 600 |
| m | ft |

Projection: Albers' Equal Area with two standard parallels

West from Greenwich

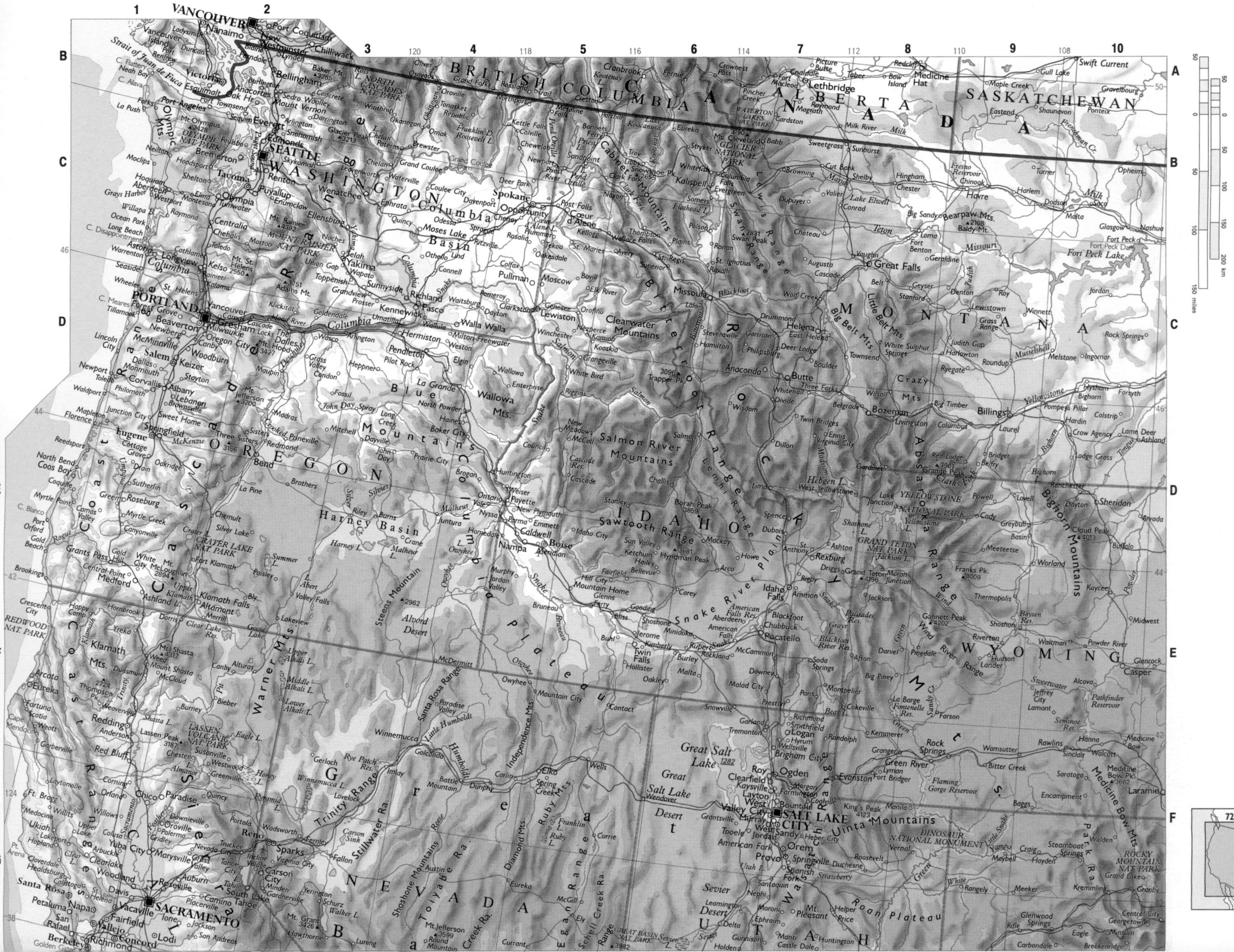
50 0 50 100 150 200 km
50 0 50 100 150 miles
72 80 81 86
BRITISH COLUMBIA
ALBERTA
SASKATCHEWAN
CANADA
WASHINGTON
OREGON
IDAHO
MONTANA
WYOMING
NEVADA
UTAH
VANCOUVER
SEATTLE
PORTLAND
SACRAMENTO
SALT LAKE CITY
Boise
Spokane
Helena
Great Falls
Billings
Missoula
Butte
Bozeman
Casper
Reno
Carson City
Ogden
Provo
Pocatello
Idaho Falls
Twin Falls
Eugene
Salem
Medford
Tacoma
Olympia
Yakima
Walla Walla
Lewiston
Coeur d'Alene
Kalispell
Lethbridge
Medicine Hat
Swift Current
Bighorn Mountains
Absaroka Range
Wind River Range
Salmon River Mountains
Sawtooth Range
Bitterroot Range
Lemhi Range
Clearwater Mountains
Blue Mountains
Cascade Range
Sierra Nevada
Uinta Mountains
Medicine Bow Mts.
Great Salt Lake
Great Salt Lake Desert
Great Basin
Columbia Basin
Snake River Plain
Columbia Plateau
Olympic Mts.
YELLOWSTONE NATIONAL PARK
GRAND TETON NAT. PARK
GLACIER NATIONAL PARK
CRATER LAKE NAT. PARK
LASSEN VOLCANIC NAT. PARK
REDWOOD NAT. PARK
Strait of Juan de Fuca
Puget Sound
Lake Tahoe

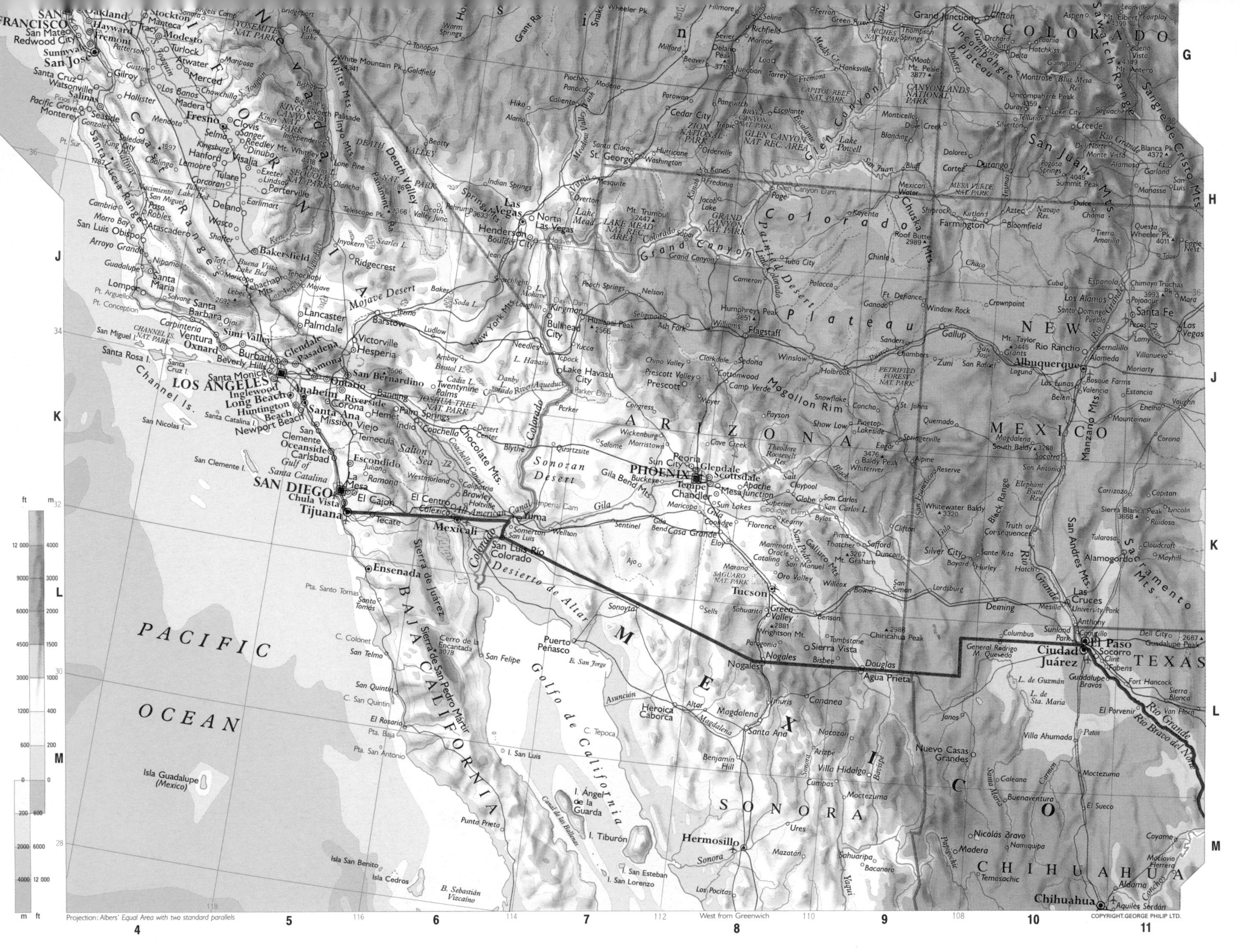
COLORADO
NEW MEXICO
ARIZONA
TEXAS
CHIHUAHUA
SONORA
BAJA CALIFORNIA
MEXICO
PACIFIC OCEAN
Golfo de California
Sierra Nevada
Coast Ranges
Sawatch Range
Sangre de Cristo Mts.
San Juan Mts.
Uncompahgre Plateau
Colorado Plateau
Painted Desert
Grand Canyon
Mogollon Rim
Sacramento Mts.
San Andres Mts.
Manzano Mts.
Black Range
Mojave Desert
Death Valley
Sonoran Desert
Desierto de Altar
Chocolate Mts.
White Mts.
Inyo Mts.
Sierra de Juárez
Sierra de San Pedro Mártir
Santa Lucia Range
Channel Is.
Salton Sea
Rio Grande
Rio Bravo del Norte
Colorado
Gila
LOS ANGELES
SAN DIEGO
PHOENIX
SAN FRANCISCO
San Jose
Oakland
Stockton
Modesto
Fresno
Bakersfield
Santa Barbara
Long Beach
Anaheim
San Bernardino
Riverside
Palm Springs
Las Vegas
Henderson
Tijuana
Mexicali
Ensenada
Yuma
Tucson
Nogales
Flagstaff
Prescott
Scottsdale
Mesa
Albuquerque
Santa Fe
Farmington
Gallup
Las Cruces
El Paso
Ciudad Juárez
Chihuahua
Hermosillo
Heroica Caborca
Puerto Peñasco
Agua Prieta
Nuevo Casas Grandes
Isla Guadalupe (Mexico)
Isla Cedros
I. Tiburón
I. Ángel de la Guarda
West from Greenwich
Projection: Albers' Equal Area with two standard parallels
COPYRIGHT GEORGE PHILIP LTD.

# CENTRAL AND SOUTHERN CALIFORNIA AND WESTERN WASHINGTON

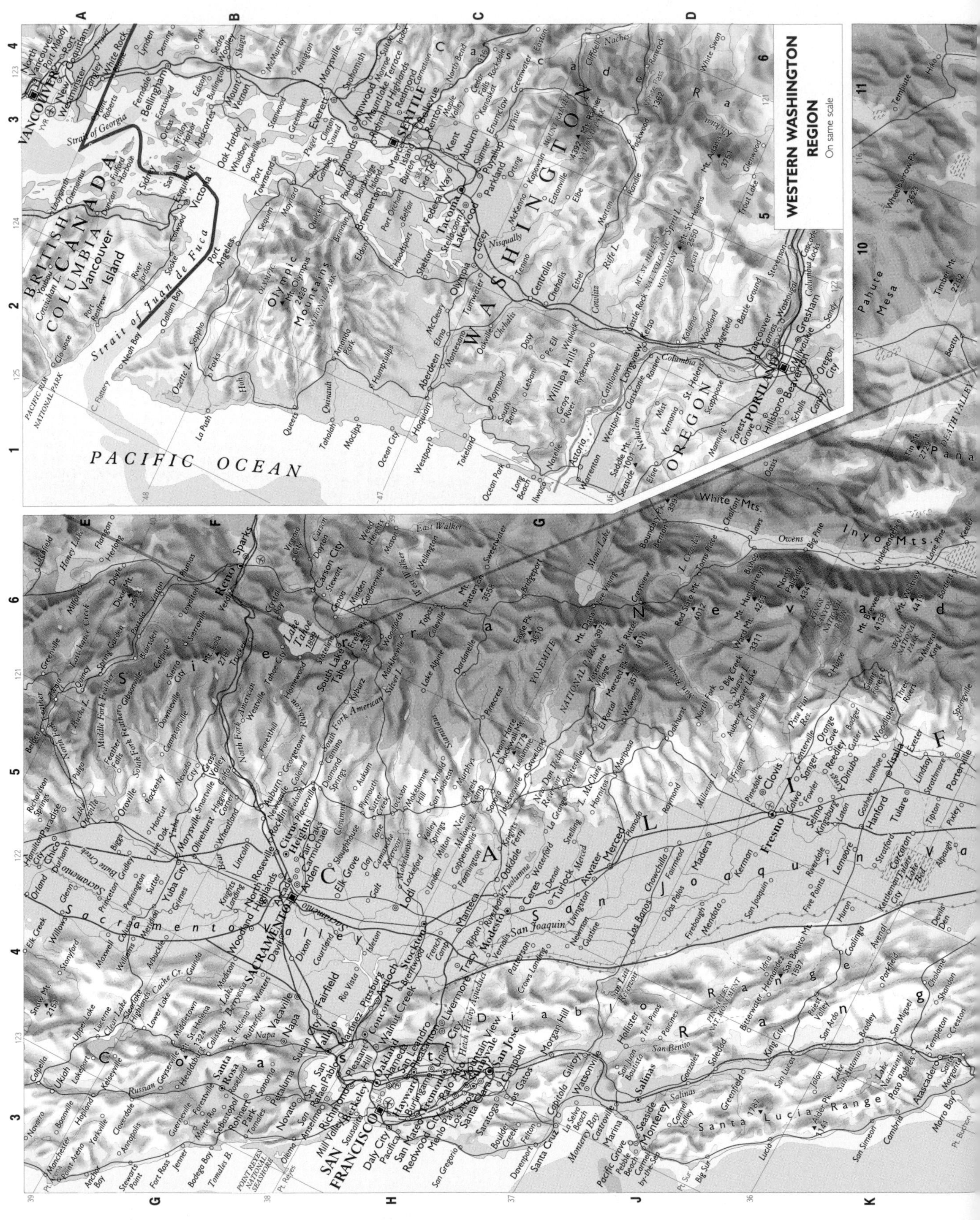

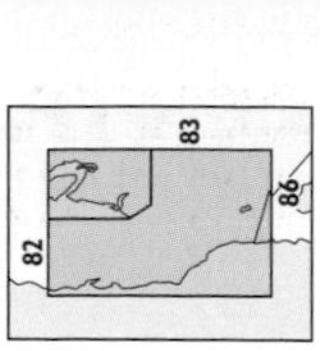

10 0 10 20 30 40 50 60 70 80 90 km

10 0 10 20 30 40 50 60 miles

NEVADA

ARIZONA

CALIFORNIA

MEXICO

BAJA CALIFORNIA

PACIFIC OCEAN

Mojave Desert

Sonoran Desert

LOS ANGELES

SAN DIEGO

Las Vegas

Tijuana

Mexicali

Channel Islands

Death Valley



West from Greenwich

Projection: Bonne

m 4000 3000 2000 1500 1000 400 200 0

ft 12 000 9000 6000 4500 3000 1200 600 0

0 200 2000 6000 m

0 600 6000 ft

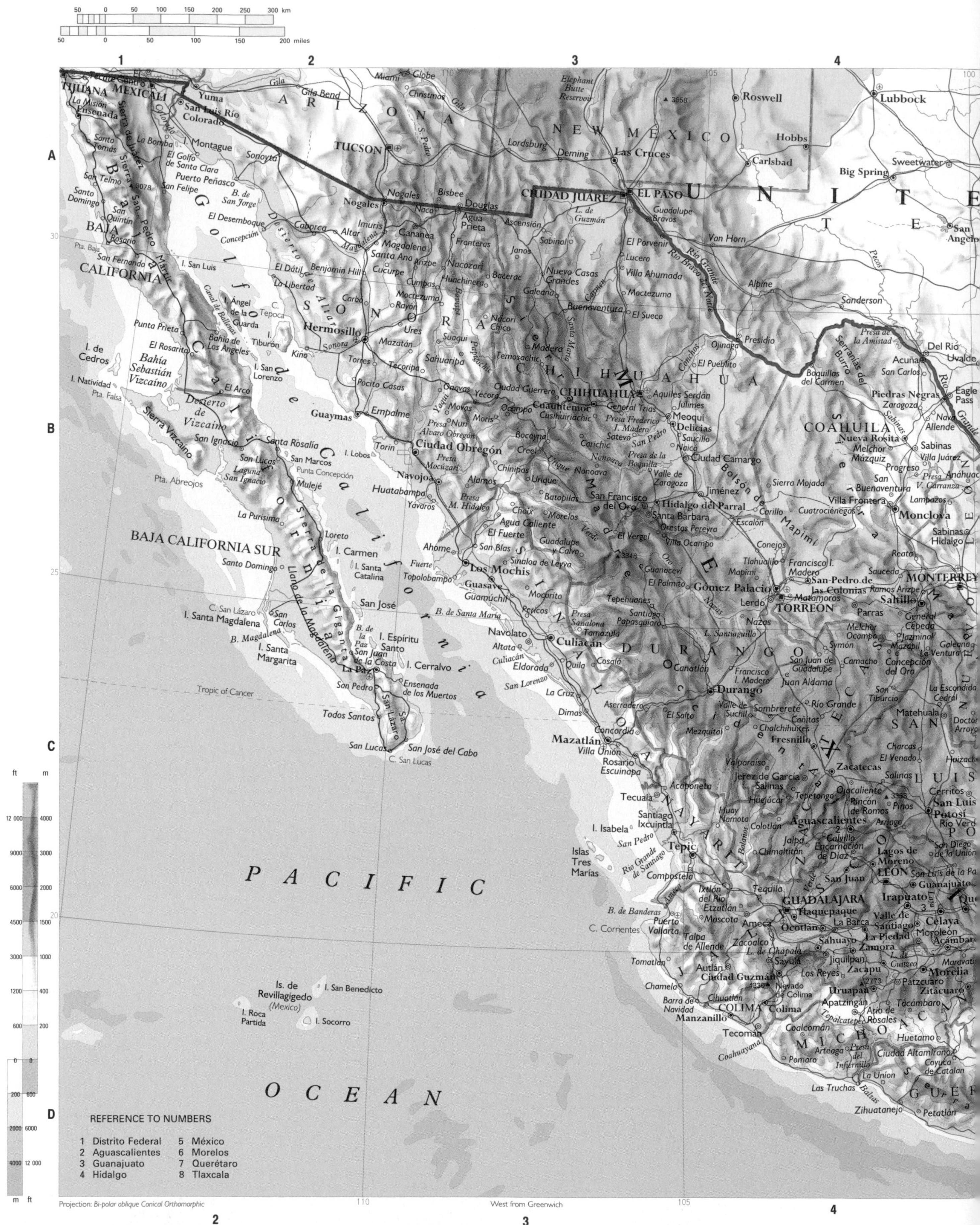
50 0 50 100 150 200 250 300 km
50 0 50 100 150 200 miles
REFERENCE TO NUMBERS
1 Distrito Federal
2 Aguascalientes
3 Guanajuato
4 Hidalgo
5 México
6 Morelos
7 Querétaro
8 Tlaxcala
PACIFIC OCEAN
Golfo de California
BAJA CALIFORNIA
BAJA CALIFORNIA SUR
SONORA
CHIHUAHUA
COAHUILA
SINALOA
DURANGO
NAYARIT
JALISCO
COLIMA
MICHOACÁN
ZACATECAS
ARIZONA
NEW MEXICO
Sierra Madre Occidental
TIJUANA
MEXICALI
Ensenada
Hermosillo
Guaymas
Ciudad Obregón
Los Mochis
Culiacán
Mazatlán
La Paz
CIUDAD JUÁREZ
EL PASO
TUCSON
CHIHUAHUA
TORREÓN
Durango
Zacatecas
Aguascalientes
GUADALAJARA
LEÓN
Morelia
Tepic
MONTERREY
Saltillo
Monclova
Tropic of Cancer
Is. de Revillagigedo (Mexico)
Islas Tres Marías
Projection: Bi-polar oblique Conical Orthomorphic
West from Greenwich

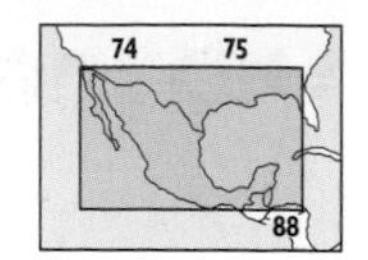

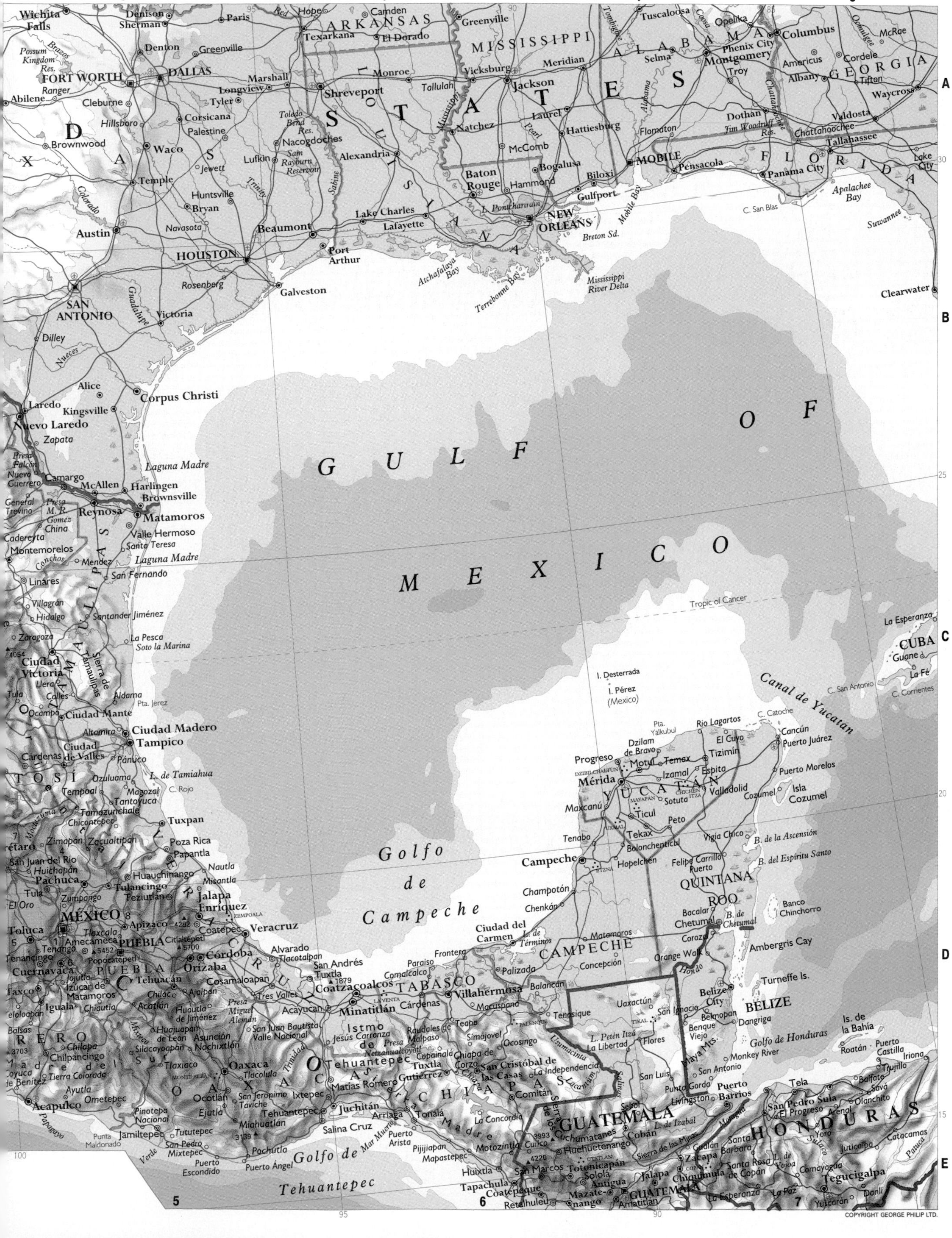

5 6 7 8

A B C D E

UNITED STATES

ARKANSAS
MISSISSIPPI
ALABAMA
GEORGIA
LOUISIANA
FLORIDA
TEXAS

Wichita Falls
Denison
Sherman
Paris
Hope
Camden
Texarkana
El Dorado
Greenville
Tuscaloosa
Opelika
Phenix City
Columbus
McRae
Denton
Greenville
Possum Kingdom Res.
FORT WORTH
DALLAS
Marshall
Monroe
Vicksburg
Meridian
Selma
Montgomery
Americus
Cordele
Tifton
Abilene
Ranger
Cleburne
Longview
Tyler
Shreveport
Tallulah
Jackson
Troy
Albany
Waycross
Corsicana
Palestine
Toledo Bend Res.
Natchez
Laurel
Hattiesburg
Dothan
Jim Woodruff Res.
Valdosta
Chattahoochee
Tallahassee
Hillsboro
Brownwood
Waco
Nacogdoches
Alexandria
McComb
Flomaton
Lufkin
Jewett
Sam Rayburn Reservoir
Baton Rouge
Bogalusa
Hammond
Biloxi
MOBILE
Pensacola
Panama City
Lake City
Temple
Huntsville
Bryan
Gulfport
Mobile Bay
Apalachee Bay
Colorado
Trinity
Sabine
Mississippi
Pearl
Alabama
Tombigbee
Coosa
Chattahoochee
Ocmulgee
Suwannee
Brazos
Lake Charles
Lafayette
L. Pontchartrain
NEW ORLEANS
C. San Blas
Austin
Navasota
Beaumont
Breton Sd.
HOUSTON
Port Arthur
Atchafalaya Bay
Terrebonne Bay
Mississippi River Delta
Rosenberg
Galveston
Clearwater
SAN ANTONIO
Guadalupe
Victoria
Dilley
Nueces
Alice
Corpus Christi
Laredo
Kingsville
Nuevo Laredo
Zapata
Presa Falcón
Laguna Madre
Nuevo Guerrero
Camargo
McAllen
Harlingen
Brownsville
General Treviño
Presa M. R. Gomez
China
Reynosa
Matamoros
Valle Hermoso
Cadereyta
Montemorelos
Santa Teresa
Conchos
Mendez
Laguna Madre
Linares
San Fernando
Villagrán
Hidalgo
Santander Jiménez
Zaragoza
La Pesca
Soto la Marina
4064
Ciudad Victoria
Sierra de Tamaulipas
Llera
Tula
Calles
Aldama
Pta. Jerez
Ocampo
Ciudad Mante
Altamira
Ciudad Madero
Tampico
Ciudad de Valles
Cardenas
Pánuco
Ozuluama
L. de Tamiahua
Tempoal
Magozal
C. Rojo
Tantoyuca
Tamazunchale
Chicontepec
Tuxpan
Zimapán
Zacualtipan
Poza Rica
Papantla
San Juan del Rio
Huichapan
Pachuca
Nautla
Misantla
Huauchinango
Tulancingo
Tula
Zumpango
Teziutlan
Jalapa Enríquez
El Oro
MÉXICO
ZEMPOALA
Toluca
Tlaxcala
Apizaco
4282
Coatepec
Veracruz
Amecameca
Citlaltépetl
Tenango
5452
PUEBLA
5700
Popocatepetl
Córdoba
Alvarado
Tlacotalpan
Cuernavaca
Orizaba
PUEBLA
San Andrés Tuxtla
Tehuacán
Cosamaloapan
1879
Coatzacoalcos
Jojutla
Izúcar de Matamoros
Taxco
Iguala
Chilac
Ajalpan
Tres Valles
Acatlán
Chiautla
Huautla de Jiménez
Presa Miguel Alemán
Acayucan
Minatitlán
Teloloapan
San Juan Bautista Valle Nacional
Jesús Carranza
Huajuapan de León
Asunción Nochixtlán
Balsas
3703
Chilpancingo
Silacayoapan
Istmo de Tehuantepec
Madre del Sur
Tierra Colorada
Tlaxiaco
Oaxaca
MONTE ALBÁN
Tlacolula
Coyuca de Benítez
Ayutla
Ometepec
OAXACA
Ocotlán
Ejutla
San Jerónimo Tavíche
Ixtepec
Matías Romero
Acapulco
Tehuantepec
Juchitán
Papagayo
Pinotepa Nacional
Miahuatlán
3139
Salina Cruz
Punta Maldonado
Jamiltepec
Tututepec
San Pedro Mixtepec
Pochutla
Puerto Escondido
Puerto Ángel
Verde
100
5
Golfo de Tehuantepec
Mar Muerto
Trinidad
Tonalá
Arriaga
Puerto Arista
Pijijiapan
Mapastepec
Huixtla
Tapachula
Coatepeque
Retalhuleu
6
95
Presa Netzahualcoyotl
Raudales de Malpaso
Copainalá
Tuxtla Gutiérrez
Chiapa de Corzo
San Cristóbal de las Casas
Simojovel
Ocosingo
Teapa
Macuspana
PALENQUE
Tenosique
La Independencia
Lacantún
Comitán
La Concordia
Sierra Madre
CHIAPAS
Motozintla
Cuilco
3993
4220
San Marcos
TABASCO
Villahermosa
Cárdenas
LA VENTA
Comalcalco
Paraiso
Frontera
Ciudad del Carmen
L. de Términos
Palizada
Balancán
Usumacinta
Chenkán
Champotón
Campeche
Tenabo
EDZNÁ
Hopelchén
Bolonchenticul
Tekax
UXMAL
Ticul
MAYAPÁN
Sotuta
Peto
Maxcanú
Mérida
DZIBILCHALTÚN
Progreso
Dzilam de Bravo
Motul
Temax
Izamal
Espita
CHICHÉN ITZÁ
Valladolid
Tizimín
Rio Lagartos
El Cuyo
Pta. Yalkubul
C. Catoche
Cancún
Puerto Juárez
Puerto Morelos
Cozumel
Isla Cozumel
YUCATÁN
Vigía Chico
B. de la Ascensión
Felipe Carrillo Puerto
B. del Espíritu Santo
QUINTANA ROO
Banco Chinchorro
Bacalar
Chetumal
B. de Chetumal
Corozal
Orange Walk
Hondo
Ambergris Cay
Matamoros
CAMPECHE
Concepción
Uaxactún
TIKAL
San Ignacio
Belize City
Belmopan
BELIZE
Turneffe Is.
Dangriga
Benque Viejo
L. Petén Itzá
La Libertad
Flores
Golfo de Honduras
Monkey River
Maya Mts.
San Antonio
San Luis
Punta Gorda
Livingston
Puerto Barrios
Is. de la Bahía
Roatán
Puerto Castilla
Iriona
Trujillo
Tela
Balfate
Savá
Olanchito
Arenal
San Pedro Sula
El Progreso
Yoro
Sulaco
HONDURAS
Juticalpa
Catacamas
Patuca
Seibal
Sierra de los Cuchumatanes
GUATEMALA
L. de Izabal
Cobán
Motagua
Sierra de las Minas
Gualán
Santa Barbara
Huehuetenango
UTATLÁN
Totonicapán
Sololá
Antigua
Mazatenango
Amatitlán
GUATEMALA
Jalapa
Zacapa
Chiquimula
Santa Rosa de Copán
COPÁN
L. de Yojoa
Comayagua
Tegucigalpa
Danlí
La Esperanza
La Paz
Yuscarán
7
90
Salinas

GULF OF MEXICO

Golfo de Campeche

Tropic of Cancer
I. Desterrada
I. Pérez (Mexico)
Canal de Yucatán
C. San Antonio
C. Corrientes
La Esperanza
CUBA
Guane
La Fé

30
25
20
15

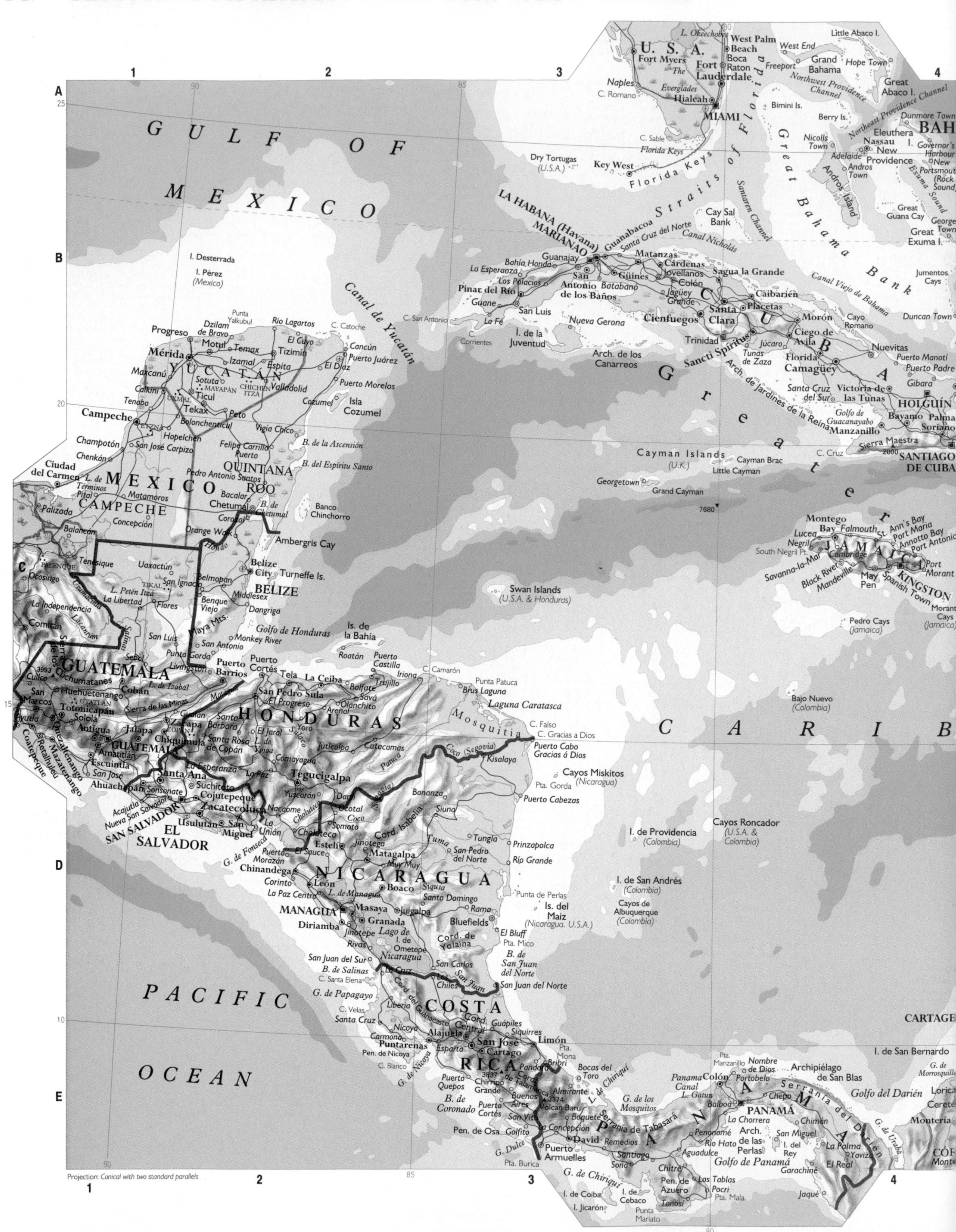


Projection: Conical with two standard parallels

50 0 50 100 150 200 250 300 km
50 0 50 100 150 200 miles

5 6 7 8

A B C D E

COPYRIGHT GEORGE PHILIP LTD

NORTH ATLANTIC OCEAN
Caribbean Sea
Greater Antilles
Lesser Antilles
Cuba
Turks & Caicos Is.
Hispaniola
Puerto Rico
Jamaica
Guadeloupe
Dominica
Martinique
St. Lucia
St. Vincent
Barbados
Grenada
Tobago
Trinidad
I. Margarita
Gulf of Campeche
Yucatán Peninsula
Yucatan Channel
Isthmus of Tehuantepec
G. de Honduras
C. Gracias a Dios
Guatemala Trench
L. Nicaragua
Panama Canal
G. of Darién
C. de la Aguja
Sierra Nevada de Santa Marta
L. Maracaibo
Orinoco
Llanos
Meta
Guiana Highlands
Mt. Roraima
Sierra Pacaraima
Serra Tumucumaque
C. Orange
Gulf of Panamá
Cordillera Occidental
Cordillera Central
Cordillera Oriental
Cord. de Mérida
Magdalena
Guaviare
C. de San Francisco
Caquetá
Negro
Branco
Cotopaxi
Chimborazo
Japurá
Putumayo
Napo
Amazon
Marajó I.
Equator
Galapagos Is.
G. of Guayaquil
Pta. Pariñas
Pta. Negra
Marañón
Juruá
Purus
Madeira
Tapajós
Xingu
Tocantins
Parnaíba
C. de São Roque
Selvas
Ucayali
Huascarán
Aripuanã
Roosevelt
Teles Pires
Araguaia
Plat. of Borborema
São Francisco
Madre de Dios
Arinos
Guaporé
Mamoré
Plateau of Mato Grosso
Brazilian Highlands
Chile Peru Trench
Chincha Alta
L. Titicaca
Nevada Ancohuma
Bolivian Plateau
L. de Poopó
PACIFIC OCEAN
Gran Chaco
Paraguay
Pilcomayo
Paraná
Abrolhos Bank
Serra da Mantiqueira
Pico da Bandeira
C. Frio
Tropic of Capricorn
Atacama Desert
Cerro Ojos del Salado
San Félix
San Ambrosio
Iguaçu Falls
Uruguay
Serra do Mar
Salado
Salinas Grandes
Entre Ríos
Sierra de Córdoba
L. Mar Chiquita
Mt. Aconcagua
L. dos Patos
Andes
Arch. de Juan Fernández
Pampas
Río de la Plata
Colorado
Bahía Blanca
Negro
G. San Matías
Valdés Peninsula
Chile Rise
Chiloé I.
Chubut
Chonos Archipelago
Mte. San Valentín
Taitao Peninsula
Gulf of Penas
Gulf of San Jorge
Patagonia
Argentine Basin
SOUTH ATLANTIC OCEAN
Wellington I.
Madre de Dios I.
Magellan's Str.
West Falkland
Falkland Is.
East Falkland
Santa Inés I.
Tierra del Fuego
Staten I.
Canal Cockburn
Canal Beagle
C. Horn
South Georgia
Tropic of Cancer
West from Greenwich
Projection: Lambert's Azimuthal Equal Area

NORTH ATLANTIC OCEAN
SOUTH ATLANTIC OCEAN
PACIFIC OCEAN
Caribbean Sea
Tropic of Cancer
Equator
Tropic of Capricorn
Havana
CUBA
BAHAMAS
Turks & Caicos Is. (U.K.)
HAITI
DOMINICAN REP.
Port-au-Prince
JAMAICA
Kingston
San Juan
PUERTO RICO (U.S.A.)
Virgin Is. (U.K.)
ST. KITTS & NEVIS
ANTIGUA & BARBUDA
Basse-Terre
GUADELOUPE (Fr.)
DOMINICA
Fort-de-France
MARTINIQUE (Fr.)
Castries
ST. LUCIA
ST. VINCENT
Kingstown
BARBADOS
Bridgetown
GRENADA
St. George's
Port of Spain
TRINIDAD & TOBAGO
Aruba
Curaçao
MEXICO
BELIZE
GUATEMALA
Guatemala
HONDURAS
Tegucigalpa
San Salvador
EL SALVADOR
NICARAGUA
Managua
COSTA RICA
San José
PANAMA
Panamá
G. of Darién
Gulf of Panamá
C. de la Aguja
Barranquilla
Cartagena
Maracaibo
Barquisimeto
Caracas
Valencia
Cúcuta
San Cristóbal
Bucaramanga
Medellín
Bogotá
Cali
Magdalena
COLOMBIA
VENEZUELA
Orinoco
Ciudad Guayana
Georgetown
GUYANA
Paramaribo
SURINAM
Cayenne
C. Orange
FRENCH GUIANA
Essequibo
RORAIMA
Branco
AMAPÁ
Galapagos Is. (Ecuador)
Quito
ECUADOR
Guayaquil
G. of Guayaquil
Napo
Putumayo
Japurá
Iquitos
Marañón
Amazon
Manaus
Santarém
Marajó I.
Belém
São Luís
AMAZONAS
PARÁ
Tapajós
Xingu
Tocantins
MARANHÃO
Teresina
Fortaleza
CEARÁ
C. de São Roque
RIO G. DO NORTE
Natal
PARAÍBA
Campina Grande
PERNAMBUCO
Recife
ALAGOAS
Maceió
SERGIPE
Aracaju
PIAUÍ
Parnaíba
Juruá
Purus
Madeira
Ucayali
Chiclayo
Trujillo
Chimbote
ACRE
Pôrto Velho
RONDÔNIA
PERU
Callao
LIMA
Madre de Dios
Cuzco
L. Titicaca
Arequipa
La Paz
BOLIVIA
Mamoré
Cochabamba
Santa Cruz
Sucre
BRAZIL
MATO GROSSO
TOCANTINS
Araguaia
BAHIA
Salvador
São Francisco
GOIÁS
DIS. FED.
Brasília
Cuiabá
Goiânia
MINAS GERAIS
Belo Horizonte
ESPIRITO SANTO
Vitória
MATO GROSSO DO SUL
Paraguay
Ribeirão Prêto
SÃO PAULO
Juiz de Fora
Campinas
R. DE J.
Niterói
Campos
SÃO PAULO
RIO DE JANEIRO
Paraná
PARANÁ
Curitiba
Iquique
PARAGUAY
Pilcomayo
Asunción
Antofagasta
Salta
San Félix (Chile)
San Ambrosio (Chile)
San Miguel de Tucumán
Resistencia
Corrientes
SANTA CATARINA
Uruguay
RIO GRANDE DO SUL
Pôrto Alegre
Salado
Córdoba
Santa Fe
Paraná
San Juan
Mendoza
Rosario
Pelotas
URUGUAY
Viña del Mar
Valparaíso
SANTIAGO
Arch. de Juan Fernández (Chile)
BUENOS AIRES
Montevideo
La Plata
Río de la Plata
Talca
Concepción
Bahía Blanca
Mar del Plata
Colorado
Valdivia
Negro
Viedma
Puerto Montt
Chubut
CHILE
ARGENTINA
Comodoro Rivadavia
Gulf of San Jorge
Gulf of Penas
West Falkland
FALKLAND IS. (U.K.)
Stanley
East Falkland
Magellan's Str.
Punta Arenas
Tierra del Fuego
C. Horn
South Georgia (U.K.)
West from Greenwich
Projection: Lambert's Azimuthal Equal Area
LIMA Capital Cities
COPYRIGHT GEORGE PHILIP LTD.

PACIFIC OCEAN
Peru-Chile Trench
Equator
COLOMBIA
VENEZUELA
ECUADOR
PERU
BOLIVIA
GUYANA
PANAMA
COSTA RICA
NICARAGUA
TRINIDAD & TOBAGO
GRENADA
CHILE
ARGENTINA
PARAGUAY
AMAZONAS
ACRE
RONDÔNIA
RORAIMA
Managua
San José
Panamá
BARRANQUILLA
Cartagena
Medellín
BOGOTÁ
Cali
MARACAIBO
Barquisimeto
VALENCIA
CARACAS
Barcelona
Ciudad Guayana
Maturín
Port of Spain
QUITO
GUAYAQUIL
Cuenca
Iquitos
Trujillo
Chiclayo
Piura
Chimbote
LIMA
Callao
Huancayo
Cuzco
Arequipa
Juliaca
LA PAZ
Cochabamba
Oruro
Sucre
Potosí
Santa Cruz
Arica
Iquique
MANAUS
Porto Velho
Rio Branco
Boa Vista
Amazonas
Sierra Pacaraima
Lago Titicaca
Projection: Sanson-Flamsteed's Sinusoidal

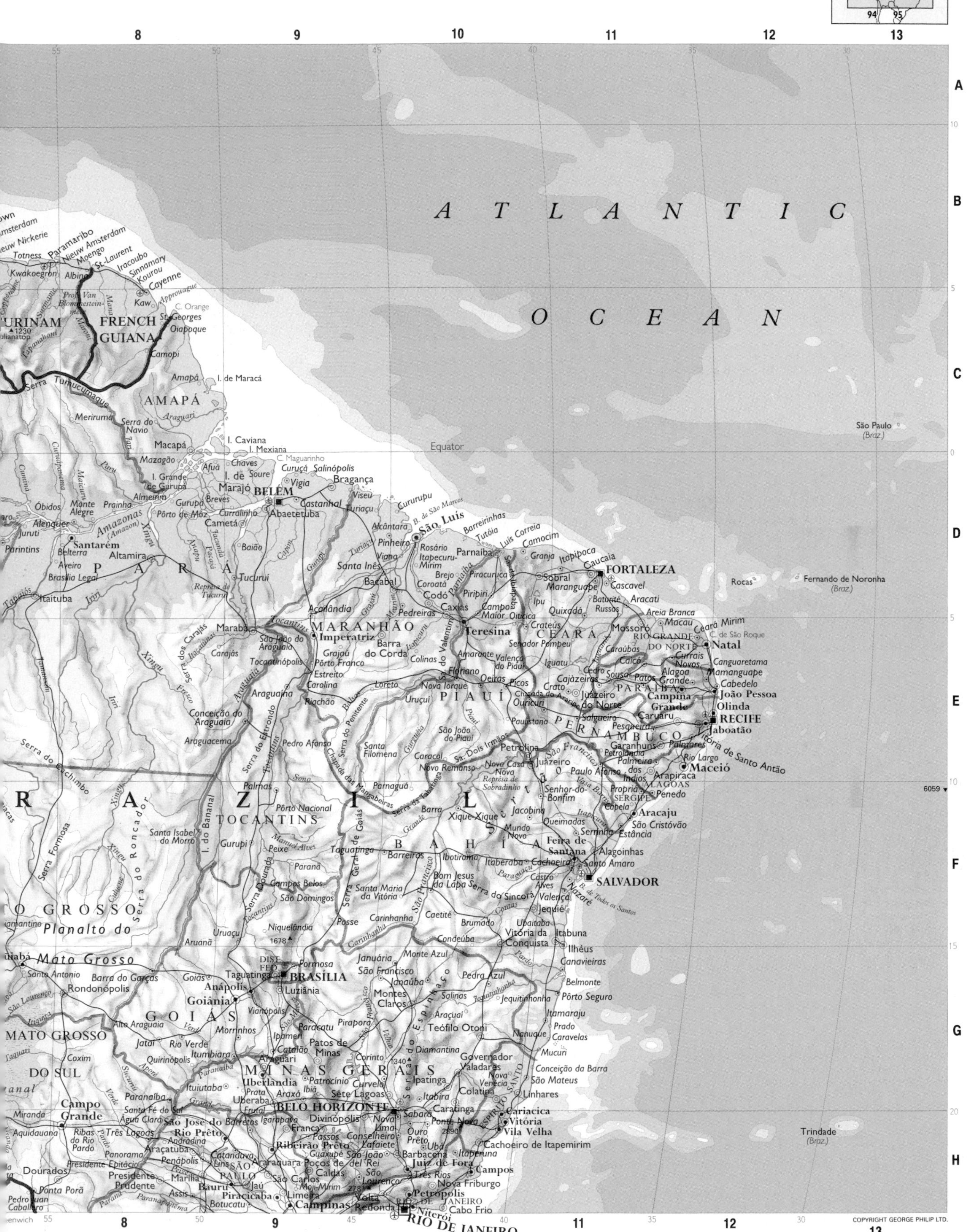

87
88
89
94
95
8
9
10
11
12
13
A
B
C
D
E
F
G
H
ATLANTIC
OCEAN
Equator
São Paulo (Braz.)
Rocas
Fernando de Noronha (Braz.)
Trindade (Braz.)
6059
SURINAM
FRENCH GUIANA
Paramaribo
Nieuw Amsterdam
Moengo
Nieuw Nickerie
Totness
Albina
St-Laurent
Iracoubo
Sinnamary
Kourou
Cayenne
Kaw
Approuague
C. Orange
St-Georges
Oiapoque
Camopi
Serra Tumucumaque
AMAPÁ
Amapá
I. de Maracá
Araguari
Merirumã
Serra do Navio
Macapá
I. Caviana
I. Mexiana
Mazagão
Afuá
Chaves
C. Maguarinho
Curuçá
Salinópolis
I. Grande de Gurupá
I. de Marajó
Soure
Vigia
Bragança
BELÉM
Castanhal
Viseu
Turiaçu
Cururupu
Almeirim
Gurupá
Breves
Monte Alegre
Prainha
Óbidos
Alenquer
Porto de Moz
Curralinho
Cametá
Abaetetuba
Amazonas (Amazon)
Xingu
Juruti
Santarém
Belterra
Parintins
Altamira
Aveiro
Baião
Brasília Legal
PARÁ
Tucuruí
Represa de Tucuruí
Itaituba
Tapajós
Iriri
B. de São Marcos
Alcântara
São Luís
Barreirinhas
Tutóia
Luís Correia
Camocim
Pinheiro
Viana
Rosário
Itapecuru-Mirim
Parnaíba
Granja
Itapipoca
Caucaia
FORTALEZA
Santa Inês
Brejo
Piracuruca
Sobral
Maranguape
Cascavel
Bacabal
Coroatá
Codó
Piripiri
Aracati
Açailândia
Pedreiras
Caxias
Campo Maior
Ipu
Quixadá
Baturité
Russas
Areia Branca
Macau
Ceará Mirim
C. de São Roque
Marabá
Tocantins
MARANHÃO
Teresina
Oiticica
Crateús
CEARÁ
Mossoró
RIO GRANDE DO NORTE
Natal
São João do Araguaia
Imperatriz
Barra do Corda
Senador Pompeu
Carajás
Serra dos Carajás
Grajaú
Porto Franco
Tocantinópolis
Estreito
Carolina
Colinas
Amarante
Valença do Piauí
Iguatu
Caraúbas
Caicó
Currais Novos
Canguaretama
Mamanguape
Cabedelo
João Pessoa
Floriano
Oeiras
Picos
Crato
Cajàzeiras
Sousa
Patos
Alagoa Grande
Campina Grande
PARAÍBA
Araguaína
Loreto
Nova Iorque
Uruçuí
PIAUÍ
Chapada do Araripe
Juàzeiro do Norte
Ouricuri
Salgueiro
Caruaru
Olinda
RECIFE
Jaboatão
Conceição do Araguaia
Riachão
Balsas
Paulistana
Pesqueira
PERNAMBUCO
Vitória de Santo Antão
Araguacema
Serra do Estrondo
Pedro Afonso
Serra do Penitente
São João do Piauí
Santa Filomena
Caracol
Petrolina
Juàzeiro
Garanhuns
Palmares
Petrolândia
Palmeira dos Índios
Rio Largo
Maceió
Serra do Cachimbo
Novo Remanso
Nova Casa Nova
Represa de Sobradinho
Paulo Afonso
Arapiraca
ALAGOAS
Penedo
Palmas
Paranaguá
Chapada das Mangabeiras
Serra da Tabatinga
Senhor-do-Bonfim
Propriá
SERGIPE
Capela
Aracaju
BRAZIL
Pôrto Nacional
TOCANTINS
Barra
Xique-Xique
Jacobina
Queimadas
Mundo Novo
São Cristóvão
Estância
Serrinha
Santa Isabel do Morro
I. do Bananal
Serra do Roncador
Serra Formosa
Gurupi
Peixe
Taguatinga
Barreiras
Ibotirama
BAHIA
Itaberaba
Cachoeira
Feira de Santana
Alagoinhas
Santo Amaro
SALVADOR
Paraná
Campos Belos
São Domingos
Serra Geral de Goiás
Santa Maria da Vitória
Bom Jesus da Lapa
Serra do Sincorá
Castro Alves
Valença
Nazaré
B. de Todos os Santos
Jequié
MATO GROSSO
Planalto do Mato Grosso
Serra Dourada
Uruaçu
Niquelândia
1678
Posse
Carinhanha
Caetité
Brumado
Vitória da Conquista
Itabuna
Ilhéus
Aruanã
Condeúba
Canavieiras
Januária
Monte Azul
Cuiabá
Santo Antônio
Barra do Garças
Goiás
DIST. FED.
Formosa
Taguatinga
BRASÍLIA
São Francisco
Pedra Azul
Rondonópolis
Anápolis
Luziânia
Janaúba
Belmonte
Pôrto Seguro
Goiânia
GOIÁS
Montes Claros
Salinas
Jequitinhonha
Serra do Espinhaço
Alto Araguaia
Vianópolis
Morrinhos
Paracatu
Pirapora
Araçuaí
Itamaraju
Teófilo Otoni
Prado
Caravelas
Nanuque
Mucuri
Jataí
Rio Verde
Quirinópolis
Itumbiara
Ipameri
Catalão
Araguari
Patos de Minas
Corinto
Diamantina
Governador Valadares
Conceição da Barra
São Mateus
Linhares
MATO GROSSO DO SUL
Coxim
Pantanal
MINAS GERAIS
Ituiutaba
Uberlândia
Prata
Araxá
Patrocínio
Ibiá
Curvelo
Ipatinga
Nova Venécia
Colatina
ESPÍRITO SANTO
Sete Lagoas
Itabira
Paranaíba
Uberaba
Frutal
Santa Fé do Sul
BELO HORIZONTE
Sabará
Caratinga
Ponte Nova
Cariacica
Vitória
Vila Velha
Campo Grande
Miranda
Aquidauana
Água Clara
São José do Rio Prêto
Igarapava
Franca
Divinópolis
Nova Lima
Ouro Prêto
2890
Cachoeiro de Itapemirim
Ribas do Rio Pardo
Três Lagoas
Andradina
Passos
Ribeirão Prêto
Conselheiro Lafaiete
Ubá
Araçatuba
Catanduva
Guaxupé
São João del Rei
Barbacena
Itaperuna
Panorama
Penápolis
Araraquara
Poços de Caldas
Juiz de Fora
Presidente Epitácio
Lins
SÃO PAULO
São Carlos
Três Rios
Campos
Dourados
Presidente Prudente
Marília
Bauru
Jaú
Mogi-Mirim
Lourenço
2787
Nova Friburgo
Ponta Porã
Assis
Piracicaba
Limeira
Petrópolis
Pedro Juan Caballero
Paranapanema
Botucatu
Campinas
Volta Redonda
RIO DE JANEIRO
Niterói
Cabo Frio
Greenwich
55
50
45
40
35
30
10
5
0
15
20
COPYRIGHT GEORGE PHILIP LTD.

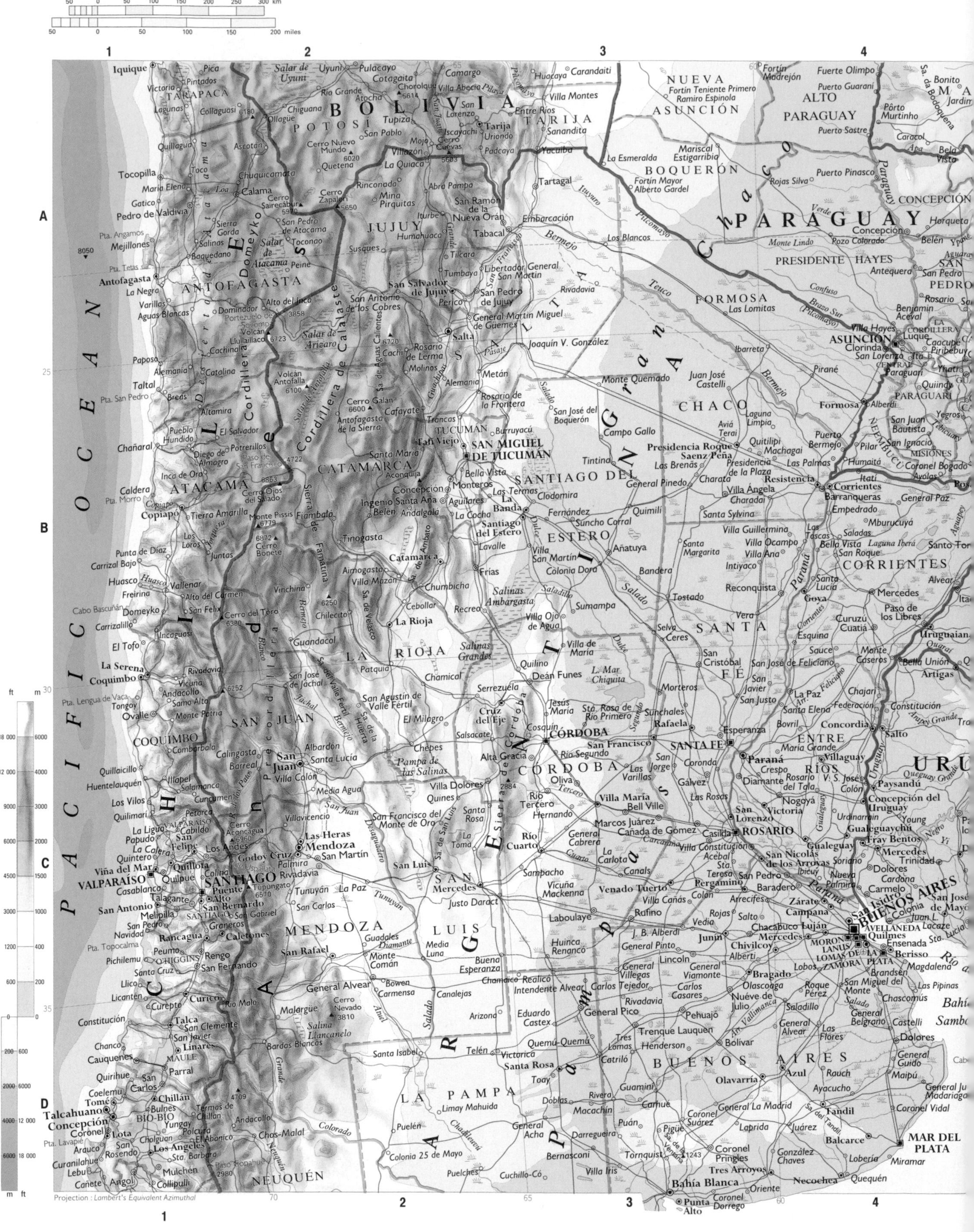

50 0 50 100 150 200 250 300 km
50 0 50 100 150 200 miles
PACIFIC OCEAN
BOLIVIA
POTOSÍ
TARIJA
NUEVA ASUNCIÓN
ALTO PARAGUAY
BOQUERÓN
PARAGUAY
PRESIDENTE HAYES
CONCEPCIÓN
Gran Chaco
FORMOSA
CHACO
SALTA
JUJUY
CATAMARCA
TUCUMAN
SANTIAGO DEL ESTERO
SANTA FE
CORRIENTES
ENTRE RIOS
LA RIOJA
SAN JUAN
CÓRDOBA
SAN LUIS
MENDOZA
LA PAMPA
NEUQUÉN
BUENOS AIRES
ARGENTINA
Pampas
CHILE
TARAPACA
ANTOFAGASTA
ATACAMA
COQUIMBO
VALPARAÍSO
SANTIAGO
O'HIGGINS
MAULE
BIO-BIO
Cordillera Domeyko
Desierto de Atacama
Andes
Iquique
Tocopilla
Antofagasta
Taltal
Chañaral
Copiapó
Vallenar
La Serena
Coquimbo
Ovalle
Valparaíso
Viña del Mar
SANTIAGO
Rancagua
Talca
Chillán
Concepción
Talcahuano
Los Angeles
Calama
Salta
San Salvador de Jujuy
SAN MIGUEL DE TUCUMÁN
Catamarca
La Rioja
Santiago del Estero
San Juan
Mendoza
San Rafael
San Luis
CÓRDOBA
Río Cuarto
Villa María
ROSARIO
SANTA FE
Paraná
Resistencia
Corrientes
Formosa
ASUNCIÓN
Concepción
Tarija
Yacuíba
Cerro Aconcagua 6960
BUENOS AIRES
La Plata
Mar del Plata
Bahía Blanca
Tandil
Azul
Olavarría
Santa Rosa
Projection : Lambert's Equivalent Azimuthal

ATLANTIC
OCEAN
BRAZIL
SÃO PAULO
PARANÁ
SANTA CATARINA
RIO GRANDE DO SUL
MATO GROSSO DO SUL
RIO DE JANEIRO
MISIONES
GUAY
BELO HORIZONTE
SÃO PAULO
RIO DE JANEIRO
CAMPINAS
SANTOS
SANTO ANDRÉ
NOVA IGUAÇU
DUQUE DE CAXIAS
SÃO GONÇALO
NITERÓI
CURITIBA
PÔRTO ALEGRE
MONTEVIDEO
CAMPOS
Vitória
Juiz de Fora
Volta Redonda
Londrina
Maringá
Ponta Grossa
Florianópolis
Joinville
Blumenau
Caxias do Sul
Pelotas
Rio Grande
Foz do Iguaçu
Ciudad del Este
Encarnación
Tropic of Capricorn
Ilha Grande
Ilha de São Sebastião
Ilha Comprida
Ilha do Cardoso
Ilha de Santa Catarina
Cabo Santa Marta Grande
Cabo Frio
Lagoa dos Patos
Lagoa Mirim
Lagoa Mangueira
Chuy
5304
West from Greenwich
COPYRIGHT GEORGE PHILIP LTD
A
B
C
D
5
6
7
25
30
35
55
50
45
40

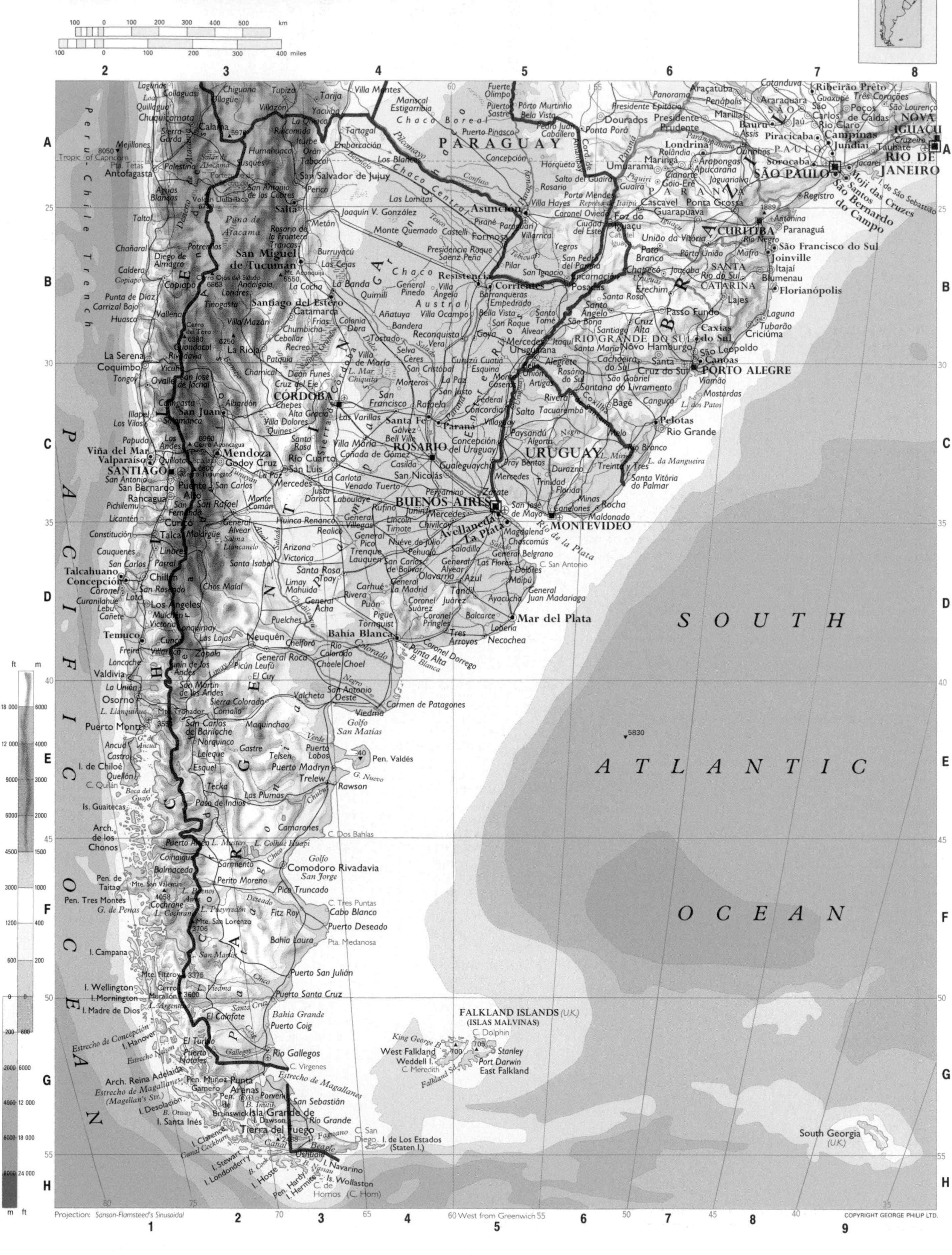

100 0 100 200 300 400 500 km
100 0 100 200 300 400 miles
94 95
SOUTH ATLANTIC OCEAN
PACIFIC OCEAN
Peru-Chile Trench
PARAGUAY
URUGUAY
Chaco Boreal
Chaco Central
Chaco Austral
Puna de Atacama
Tropic of Capricorn
Asunción
Corrientes
Resistencia
Posadas
Encarnación
Concepción
Salta
San Salvador de Jujuy
San Miguel de Tucumán
Santiago del Estero
Catamarca
La Rioja
Antofagasta
Calama
Copiapó
La Serena
Coquimbo
Ovalle
San Juan
Mendoza
Viña del Mar
Valparaíso
SANTIAGO
Rancagua
Curicó
Talca
Chillán
Talcahuano
Concepción
Los Angeles
Temuco
Valdivia
Osorno
Puerto Montt
I. de Chiloé
CÓRDOBA
Santa Fe
Paraná
ROSARIO
Río Cuarto
San Luis
San Nicolás
BUENOS AIRES
Avellaneda
La Plata
MONTEVIDEO
Río de la Plata
Mar del Plata
Bahía Blanca
Neuquén
Santa Rosa
Viedma
Carmen de Patagones
Golfo San Matías
San Carlos de Bariloche
Puerto Madryn
Trelew
Rawson
Pen. Valdés
Comodoro Rivadavia
Puerto Deseado
Puerto San Julián
Puerto Santa Cruz
Río Gallegos
Punta Arenas
Estrecho de Magallanes (Magellan's Str.)
Isla Grande de Tierra del Fuego
Ushuaia
Río Grande
I. de Los Estados (Staten I.)
C. de Hornos (C. Horn)
FALKLAND ISLANDS (U.K.) (ISLAS MALVINAS)
West Falkland
East Falkland
Stanley
South Georgia (U.K.)
SÃO PAULO
RIO DE JANEIRO
CURITIBA
PÔRTO ALEGRE
Florianópolis
Joinville
Pelotas
Rio Grande
Campinas
Santos
Londrina
Maringá
Foz do Iguaçu
Passo Fundo
Caxias do Sul
Santa Maria
RIO GRANDE DO SUL
SANTA CATARINA
PARANÁ
SÃO PAULO
Projection: Sanson-Flamsteed's Sinusoidal
60 West from Greenwich 55

# INDEX

The index contains the names of all the principal places and features shown on the World Maps. Names in bold type denote encyclopaedia entries. Each name is followed by an additional entry in italics giving the country or region within which it is located. The alphabetical order of names composed of two or more words is governed primarily by the first word and then by the second. This is an example of the rule:

| | | | |
|---|---|---|---|
| Mīr Kūh, *Iran* ............ | **45 E8** | 26 22N | 58 55 E |
| Mīr Shahdād, *Iran* ........ | **45 E8** | 26 15N | 58 29 E |
| Mira, *Italy* .............. | **20 B5** | 45 26N | 12 8 E |
| Mira por vos Cay, *Bahamas* . | **89 B5** | 22 9N | 74 30 W |
| Miraj, *India* ............. | **40 L9** | 16 50N | 74 45 E |

Physical features composed of a proper name (Erie) and a description (Lake) are positioned alphabetically by the proper name. The description is positioned after the proper name and is usually abbreviated:

| | | | |
|---|---|---|---|
| Erie, L., *N. Amer.* ......... | **78 D4** | 42 15N | 81 0 W |

Where a description forms part of a settlement or administrative name however, it is always written in full and put in its true alphabetic position:

| | | | |
|---|---|---|---|
| Mount Morris, *U.S.A.* ..... | **78 D7** | 42 44N | 77 52 W |

Names beginning with M' and Mc are indexed as if they were spelled Mac. Names beginning St. are alphabetised under Saint, but Sankt, Sint, Sant', Santa and San are all spelt in full and are alphabetised accordingly. If the same place name occurs two or more times in the index and all are in the same country, each is followed by the name of the administrative subdivision in which it is located. The names are placed in the alphabetical order of the subdivisions. For example:

| | | | |
|---|---|---|---|
| Jackson, *Ky., U.S.A.* ....... | **76 G4** | 37 33N | 83 23 W |
| Jackson, *Mich., U.S.A.* ..... | **76 D3** | 42 15N | 84 24 W |
| Jackson, *Minn., U.S.A.* ..... | **80 D7** | 43 37N | 95 1 W |

The number in bold type which follows each name in the index refers to the number of the map page where that feature or place will be found. This is usually the largest scale at which the place or feature appears.

The letter and figure which are in bold type immediately after the page number give the grid square on the map page, within which the feature is situated. The letter represents the latitude and the figure the longitude.

In some cases the feature itself may fall within the specified square, while the name is outside. This is usually the case only with features which are larger than a grid square.

For a more precise location the geographical coordinates which follow the letter/figure references give the latitude and the longitude of each place. The first set of figures represent the latitude which is the distance north or south of the Equator measured as an angle at the centre of the earth. The Equator is latitude 0°, the North Pole is 90°N, and the South Pole 90°S.

The second set of figures represent the longitude, which is the distance East or West of the prime meridian, which runs through Greenwich, England. Longitude is also measured as an angle at the centre of the earth and is given East or West of the prime meridian, from 0° to 180° in either direction.

The unit of measurement for latitude and longitude is the degree, which is subdivided into 60 minutes. Each index entry states the position of a place in degrees and minutes, a space being left between the degrees and the minutes.

The latitude is followed by N(orth) or S(outh) and the longitude by E(ast) or W(est).

Rivers are indexed to their mouths or confluences, and carry the symbol → after their names. A solid square ■ follows the name of a country, while an open square □ refers to a first order administrative area.

## Abbreviations used in the index

*A.C.T.* – Australian Capital Territory
*Afghan.* – Afghanistan
*Ala.* – Alabama
*Alta.* – Alberta
*Amer.* – America(n)
*Arch.* – Archipelago
*Ariz.* – Arizona
*Ark.* – Arkansas
*Atl. Oc.* – Atlantic Ocean
*B.* – Baie, Bahía, Bay, Bucht, Bugt
*B.C.* – British Columbia
*Bangla.* – Bangladesh
*Barr.* – Barrage
*Bos.-H.* – Bosnia-Herzegovina
*C.* – Cabo, Cap, Cape, Coast
*C.A.R.* – Central African Republic
*C. Prov.* – Cape Province
*Calif.* – California
*Cent.* – Central
*Chan.* – Channel
*Colo.* – Colorado
*Conn.* – Connecticut
*Cord.* – Cordillera
*Cr.* – Creek
*Czech.* – Czech Republic
*D.C.* – District of Columbia
*Del.* – Delaware
*Dep.* – Dependency
*Des.* – Desert
*Dist.* – District
*Dj.* – Djebel
*Domin.* – Dominica
*Dom. Rep.* – Dominican Republic
*E.* – East
*E. Salv.* – El Salvador
*Eq. Guin.* – Equatorial Guinea
*Fla.* – Florida
*Falk. Is.* – Falkland Is.
*G.* – Golfe, Golfo, Gulf, Guba, Gebel
*Ga.* – Georgia
*Gt.* – Great, Greater
*Guinea-Biss.* – Guinea-Bissau
*H.K.* – Hong Kong
*H.P.* – Himachal Pradesh
*Hants.* – Hampshire
*Harb.* – Harbor, Harbour
*Hd.* – Head
*Hts.* – Heights
*I.(s).* – Île, Ilha, Insel, Isla, Island, Isle
*Ill.* – Illinois
*Ind.* – Indiana
*Ind. Oc.* – Indian Ocean
*Ivory C.* – Ivory Coast
*J.* – Jabal, Jebel, Jazira
*Junc.* – Junction
*K.* – Kap, Kapp
*Kans.* – Kansas
*Kep.* – Kepulauan
*Ky.* – Kentucky
*L.* – Lac, Lacul, Lago, Lagoa, Lake, Limni, Loch, Lough
*La.* – Louisiana
*Liech.* – Liechtenstein
*Lux.* – Luxembourg
*Mad. P.* – Madhya Pradesh
*Madag.* – Madagascar
*Man.* – Manitoba
*Mass.* – Massachusetts
*Md.* – Maryland
*Me.* – Maine
*Medit. S.* – Mediterranean Sea
*Mich.* – Michigan
*Minn.* – Minnesota
*Miss.* – Mississippi
*Mo.* – Missouri
*Mont.* – Montana
*Mozam.* – Mozambique
*Mt.(e)* – Mont, Monte, Monti, Montaña, Mountain
*N.* – Nord, Norte, North, Northern, Nouveau
*N.B.* – New Brunswick
*N.C.* – North Carolina
*N. Cal.* – New Caledonia
*N. Dak.* – North Dakota
*N.H.* – New Hampshire
*N.I.* – North Island
*N.J.* – New Jersey
*N. Mex.* – New Mexico
*N.S.* – Nova Scotia
*N.S.W.* – New South Wales
*N.W.T.* – North West Territory
*N.Y.* – New York
*N.Z.* – New Zealand
*Nebr.* – Nebraska
*Neths.* – Netherlands
*Nev.* – Nevada
*Nfld.* – Newfoundland
*Nic.* – Nicaragua
*O.* – Oued, Ouadi
*Occ.* – Occidentale
*Okla.* – Oklahoma
*Ont.* – Ontario
*Or.* – Orientale
*Oreg.* – Oregon
*Os.* – Ostrov
*Oz.* – Ozero
*P.* – Pass, Passo, Pasul, Pulau
*P.E.I.* – Prince Edward Island
*Pa.* – Pennsylvania
*Pac. Oc.* – Pacific Ocean
*Papua N.G.* – Papua New Guinea
*Pass.* – Passage
*Pen.* – Peninsula, Péninsule
*Phil.* – Philippines
*Pk.* – Park, Peak
*Plat.* – Plateau
*Prov.* – Province, Provincial
*Pt.* – Point
*Pta.* – Ponta, Punta
*Pte.* – Pointe
*Qué.* – Québec
*Queens.* – Queensland
*R.* – Rio, River
*R.I.* – Rhode Island
*Ra.(s).* – Range(s)
*Raj.* – Rajasthan
*Reg.* – Region
*Rep.* – Republic
*Res.* – Reserve, Reservoir
*S.* – San, South, Sea
*Si. Arabia* – Saudi Arabia
*S.C.* – South Carolina
*S. Dak.* – South Dakota
*S.I.* – South Island
*S. Leone* – Sierra Leone
*Sa.* – Serra, Sierra
*Sask.* – Saskatchewan
*Scot.* – Scotland
*Sd.* – Sound
*Sev.* – Severnaya
*Sib.* – Siberia
*Sprs.* – Springs
*St.* – Saint
*Sta.* – Santa, Station
*Ste.* – Sainte
*Sto.* – Santo
*Str.* – Strait, Stretto
*Switz.* – Switzerland
*Tas.* – Tasmania
*Tenn.* – Tennessee
*Tex.* – Texas
*Tg.* – Tanjung
*Trin. & Tob.* – Trinidad & Tobago
*U.A.E.* – United Arab Emirates
*U.K.* – United Kingdom
*U.S.A.* – United States of America
*Ut. P.* – Uttar Pradesh
*Va.* – Virginia
*Vdkhr.* – Vodokhranilishche
*Vf.* – Vîrful
*Vic.* – Victoria
*Vol.* – Volcano
*Vt.* – Vermont
*W.* – Wadi, West
*W. Va.* – West Virginia
*Wash.* – Washington
*Wis.* – Wisconsin
*Wlkp.* – Wielkopolski
*Wyo.* – Wyoming
*Yorks.* – Yorkshire
*Yug.* – Yugoslavia

# A


A Coruña, *Spain* **19 A1** 43 20N 8 25W
A Estrada, *Spain* **19 A1** 42 43N 8 27W
A Fonsagrada, *Spain* **19 A2** 43 8N 7 4W
**Aachen**, *Germany* **16 C4** 50 45N 6 6 E
Aalborg = Ålborg, *Denmark* **9 H13** 57 2N 9 54 E
Aalen, *Germany* **16 D6** 48 51N 10 6 E
Aalst, *Belgium* **15 D4** 50 56N 4 2 E
Aalten, *Neths.* **15 C6** 51 56N 6 35 E
Aalter, *Belgium* **15 C3** 51 5N 3 28 E
Äänekoski, *Finland* **9 E21** 62 36N 25 44 E
Aarau, *Switz.* **18 C8** 47 23N 8 4 E
Aare →, *Switz.* **18 C8** 47 33N 8 14 E
**Aarhus** = Århus, *Denmark* **9 H14** 56 8N 10 11 E
Aarschot, *Belgium* **15 D4** 50 59N 4 49 E
Aba, *Dem. Rep. of the Congo* **54 B3** 3 58N 30 17 E
Aba, *Nigeria* **50 G7** 5 10N 7 19 E
Ābādān, *Iran* **45 D6** 30 22N 48 20 E
Ābādeh, *Iran* **45 D7** 31 8N 52 40 E
Abadla, *Algeria* **50 B5** 31 2N 2 45W
Abaetetuba, *Brazil* **93 D9** 1 40S 48 50W
Abagnar Qi, *China* **34 C9** 43 52N 116 2 E
Abai, *Paraguay* **95 B4** 25 58S 55 54W
Abakan, *Russia* **27 D10** 53 40N 91 10 E
Abancay, *Peru* **92 F4** 13 35S 72 55W
Abariringa, *Kiribati* **64 H10** 2 50S 171 40W
Abarqū, *Iran* **45 D7** 31 10N 53 20 E
Abashiri, *Japan* **30 C12** 44 0N 144 15 E
Abashiri-Wan, *Japan* **30 C12** 44 0N 144 30 E
Abay, *Kazakstan* **26 E8** 49 38N 72 53 E
Abaya, L., *Ethiopia* **46 F2** 6 30N 37 50 E
Abaza, *Russia* **26 D10** 52 39N 90 6 E
'Abbāsābād, *Iran* **45 C8** 33 34N 58 23 E
Abbay = Nîl el Azraq →, *Sudan* **51 E12** 15 38N 32 31 E
Abbaye, Pt., *U.S.A.* **76 B1** 46 58N 88 8W
Abbé, L., *Ethiopia* **46 E3** 11 8N 41 47 E
Abbeville, *France* **18 A4** 50 6N 1 49 E
Abbeville, *Ala., U.S.A.* **77 K3** 31 34N 85 15W
Abbeville, *La., U.S.A.* **81 L8** 29 58N 92 8W
Abbeville, *S.C., U.S.A.* **77 H4** 34 11N 82 23W
Abbot Ice Shelf, *Antarctica* **5 D16** 73 0S 92 0W
Abbottabad, *Pakistan* **42 B5** 34 10N 73 15 E
Abd al Kūrī, *Ind. Oc.* **46 E5** 12 5N 52 20 E
Ābdar, *Iran* **45 D7** 30 16N 55 19 E
'Abdolābād, *Iran* **45 C8** 34 12N 56 30 E
Abdulpur, *Bangla.* **43 G13** 24 15N 88 59 E
Abéché, *Chad* **51 F10** 13 50N 20 35 E
Abengourou, *Ivory C.* **50 G5** 6 42N 3 27W
Åbenrå, *Denmark* **9 J13** 55 3N 9 25 E
Abeokuta, *Nigeria* **50 G6** 7 3N 3 19 E
Aber, *Uganda* **54 B3** 2 12N 32 25 E
Aberaeron, *U.K.* **11 E3** 52 15N 4 15W
Aberayron = Aberaeron, *U.K.* **11 E3** 52 15N 4 15W
Aberchirder, *U.K.* **12 D6** 57 34N 2 37W
Abercorn = Mbala, *Zambia* **55 D3** 8 46S 31 24 E
Abercorn, *Australia* **63 D5** 25 12S 151 5 E
Aberdare, *U.K.* **11 F4** 51 43N 3 27W
Aberdare Ra., *Kenya* **54 C4** 0 15S 36 50 E
Aberdeen, *Australia* **63 E5** 32 9S 150 56 E
Aberdeen, *Canada* **73 C7** 52 20N 106 8W
Aberdeen, *S. Africa* **56 E3** 32 28S 24 2 E
**Aberdeen**, *U.K.* **12 D6** 57 9N 2 5W
Aberdeen, *Ala., U.S.A.* **77 J1** 33 49N 88 33W
Aberdeen, *Idaho, U.S.A.* **82 E7** 42 57N 112 50W
Aberdeen, *Md., U.S.A.* **76 F7** 39 31N 76 10W
Aberdeen, *S. Dak., U.S.A.* **80 C5** 45 28N 98 29W
Aberdeen, *Wash., U.S.A.* **84 D3** 46 59N 123 50W
Aberdeen, City of □, *U.K.* **12 D6** 57 10N 2 10W
Aberdeenshire □, *U.K.* **12 D6** 57 17N 2 36W
Aberdovey = Aberdyfi, *U.K.* **11 E3** 52 33N 4 3W
Aberdyfi, *U.K.* **11 E3** 52 33N 4 3W
Aberfeldy, *U.K.* **12 E5** 56 37N 3 51W
Abergavenny, *U.K.* **11 F4** 51 49N 3 1W
Abergele, *U.K.* **10 D4** 53 17N 3 35W
Abernathy, *U.S.A.* **81 J4** 33 50N 101 51W
Abert, L., *U.S.A.* **82 E3** 42 38N 120 14W
Aberystwyth, *U.K.* **11 E3** 52 25N 4 5W
Abhā, *Si. Arabia* **46 D3** 18 0N 42 34 E
Abhar, *Iran* **45 B6** 36 9N 49 13 E
Abhayapuri, *India* **43 F14** 26 24N 90 38 E
**Abidjan**, *Ivory C.* **50 G5** 5 26N 3 58W
Abilene, *Kans., U.S.A.* **80 F6** 38 55N 97 13W
Abilene, *Tex., U.S.A.* **81 J5** 32 28N 99 43W
Abingdon, *U.K.* **11 F6** 51 40N 1 17W
Abingdon, *U.S.A.* **77 G5** 36 43N 81 59W
Abington Reef, *Australia* **62 B4** 18 0S 149 35 E
Abitau →, *Canada* **73 B7** 59 53N 109 3W
Abitibi →, *Canada* **70 B3** 51 3N 80 55W
Abitibi, L., *Canada* **70 C4** 48 40N 79 40W
Abkhaz Republic = Abkhazia □, *Georgia* **25 F7** 43 12N 41 5 E
**Abkhazia** □, *Georgia* **25 F7** 43 12N 41 5 E
Abminga, *Australia* **63 D1** 26 8S 134 51 E
Åbo = Turku, *Finland* **9 F20** 60 30N 22 19 E
Abohar, *India* **42 D6** 30 10N 74 10 E
Abolo, *Congo* **52 D2** 0 8N 14 16 E
Abomey, *Benin* **50 G6** 7 10N 2 5 E
Abong-Mbang, *Cameroon* **52 D2** 4 0N 13 8 E
Abou-Deïa, *Chad* **51 F9** 11 20N 19 20 E
Aboyne, *U.K.* **12 D6** 57 4N 2 47W
Abra Pampa, *Argentina* **94 A2** 22 43S 65 42W
Abraham L., *Canada* **72 C5** 52 15N 116 35W
Abreojos, Pta., *Mexico* **86 B2** 26 50N 113 40W
Abrud, *Romania* **17 E12** 46 19N 23 5 E
Absaroka Range, *U.S.A.* **82 D9** 44 45N 109 50W
Abu, *India* **42 G5** 24 41N 72 50 E
Abu al Abyad, *U.A.E.* **45 E7** 24 11N 53 50 E
Abu al Khaşīb, *Iraq* **45 D6** 30 25N 48 0 E
Abū 'Alī, *Si. Arabia* **45 E6** 27 20N 49 27 E
Abū 'Alī →, *Lebanon* **47 A4** 34 25N 35 50 E
**Abu Dhabi** = Abū Ẓāby, *U.A.E.* **45 E7** 24 28N 54 22 E
Abū Du'ān, *Syria* **44 B3** 36 25N 38 15 E
Abu el Gairi, W. →, *Egypt* **47 F2** 29 35N 33 30 E
Abu Ga'da, W. →, *Egypt* **47 F1** 29 15N 32 53 E
Abū Ḥadrīyah, *Si. Arabia* **45 E6** 27 20N 48 58 E
Abu Hamed, *Sudan* **51 E12** 19 32N 33 13 E
Abū Kamāl, *Syria* **44 C4** 34 30N 41 0 E
Abū Madd, Ra's, *Si. Arabia* **44 E3** 24 50N 37 7 E
Abū Mūsā, *U.A.E.* **45 E7** 25 52N 55 3 E
Abu Şafāt, W. →, *Jordan* **47 E5** 30 24N 36 7 E
**Abu Simbel**, *Egypt* **51 D12** 22 18N 31 40 E
Abū Şukhayr, *Iraq* **44 D5** 31 54N 44 30 E
Abū Zabad, *Sudan* **51 F11** 12 25N 29 10 E
Abū Ẓāby, *U.A.E.* **45 E7** 24 28N 54 22 E
Abū Zeydābād, *Iran* **45 C6** 33 54N 51 45 E
**Abuja**, *Nigeria* **50 G7** 9 16N 7 2 E
Abukuma-Gawa →, *Japan* **30 E10** 38 6N 140 52 E
Abukuma-Sammyaku, *Japan* **30 F10** 37 30N 140 45 E
Abunã, *Brazil* **92 E5** 9 40S 65 20W
Abunã →, *Brazil* **92 E5** 9 41S 65 20W
Aburo, *Dem. Rep. of the Congo* **54 B3** 2 4N 30 53 E
Abut Hd., *N.Z.* **59 K3** 43 7S 170 15 E
Acadia National Park, *U.S.A.* **77 C11** 44 20N 68 13W
Açailândia, *Brazil* **93 D9** 4 57S 47 0W
Acajutla, *El Salv.* **88 D2** 13 36N 89 50W
Acámbaro, *Mexico* **86 D4** 20 0N 100 40W
Acaponeta, *Mexico* **86 C3** 22 30N 105 20W
**Acapulco**, *Mexico* **87 D5** 16 51N 99 56W
Acarai, Serra, *Brazil* **92 C7** 1 50N 57 50W
Acarigua, *Venezuela* **92 B5** 9 33N 69 12W
Acatlán, *Mexico* **87 D5** 18 10N 98 3W
Acayucan, *Mexico* **87 D6** 17 59N 94 58W
Accomac, *U.S.A.* **76 G8** 37 43N 75 40W
**Accra**, *Ghana* **50 G5** 5 35N 0 6W
Accrington, *U.K.* **10 D5** 53 45N 2 22W
Acebal, *Argentina* **94 C3** 33 20S 60 50W
Aceh □, *Indonesia* **36 D1** 4 15N 97 30 E
Achalpur, *India* **40 J10** 21 22N 77 32 E
Acheng, *China* **35 B14** 45 30N 126 58 E
Acher, *India* **42 H5** 23 10N 72 32 E
Achill Hd., *Ireland* **13 C1** 53 58N 10 15W
Achill I., *Ireland* **13 C1** 53 58N 10 1W
Achinsk, *Russia* **27 D10** 56 20N 90 20 E
Acireale, *Italy* **20 F6** 37 37N 15 10 E
Ackerman, *U.S.A.* **81 J10** 33 19N 89 11W
Acklins I., *Bahamas* **89 B5** 22 30N 74 0W
Acme, *Canada* **72 C6** 51 33N 113 30W
Acme, *U.S.A.* **78 F5** 40 8N 79 26W
**Aconcagua, Cerro**, *Argentina* **94 C2** 32 39S 70 0W
Aconquija, Mt., *Argentina* **94 B2** 27 0S 66 0W
Açores, Is. dos = Azores, *Atl. Oc.* **50 A1** 38 44N 29 0W
Acraman, L., *Australia* **63 E2** 32 2S 135 23 E
Acre = 'Akko, *Israel* **47 C4** 32 55N 35 4 E
Acre □, *Brazil* **92 E4** 9 1S 71 0W
Acre →, *Brazil* **92 E5** 8 45S 67 22W
Acton, *Canada* **78 C4** 43 38N 80 3W
Acuña, *Mexico* **86 B4** 29 18N 100 55W
Ad Dammām, *Si. Arabia* **45 E6** 26 20N 50 5 E
Ad Dāmūr, *Lebanon* **47 B4** 33 44N 35 27 E
Ad Dawādimī, *Si. Arabia* **44 E5** 24 35N 44 15 E
Ad Dawḥah, *Qatar* **45 E6** 25 15N 51 35 E
Ad Dawr, *Iraq* **44 C4** 34 27N 43 47 E
Ad Dir'īyah, *Si. Arabia* **44 E5** 24 44N 46 35 E
Ad Dīwānīyah, *Iraq* **44 D5** 32 0N 45 0 E
Ad Dujayl, *Iraq* **44 C5** 33 51N 44 14 E
Ad Duwayd, *Si. Arabia* **44 D4** 30 15N 42 17 E
Ada, *Minn., U.S.A.* **80 B6** 47 18N 96 31W
Ada, *Okla., U.S.A.* **81 H6** 34 46N 96 41W
Adabiya, *Egypt* **47 F1** 29 53N 32 28 E
Adair, C., *Canada* **69 A12** 71 31N 71 24W
Adaja →, *Spain* **19 B3** 41 32N 4 52W
Adak I., *U.S.A.* **68 C2** 51 45N 176 45W
Adamaoua, Massif de l', *Cameroon* **52 C2** 7 20N 12 20 E
Adamawa Highlands = Adamaoua, Massif de l', *Cameroon* **52 C2** 7 20N 12 20 E
Adamello, Mte., *Italy* **18 C9** 46 9N 10 30 E
Adaminaby, *Australia* **63 F4** 36 0S 148 45 E
Adams, *Mass., U.S.A.* **79 D11** 42 38N 73 7W
Adams, *N.Y., U.S.A.* **79 C8** 43 49N 76 1W
Adams, *Wis., U.S.A.* **80 D10** 43 57N 89 49W
Adam's Bridge, *Sri Lanka* **40 Q11** 9 15N 79 40 E
Adams L., *Canada* **72 C5** 51 10N 119 40W
Adams Mt., *U.S.A.* **84 D5** 46 12N 121 30W
Adam's Peak, *Sri Lanka* **40 R12** 6 48N 80 30 E
Adana, *Turkey* **25 G6** 37 0N 35 16 E
Adapazarı = Sakarya, *Turkey* **25 F5** 40 48N 30 25 E
Adarama, *Sudan* **51 E12** 17 10N 34 52 E
Adare, C., *Antarctica* **5 D11** 71 0S 171 0 E
Adaut, *Indonesia* **37 F8** 8 8S 131 7 E
Adavale, *Australia* **63 D3** 25 52S 144 32 E
Adda →, *Italy* **18 D8** 45 8N 9 53 E
**Addis Ababa** = Addis Abeba, *Ethiopia* **46 F2** 9 2N 38 42 E
Addis Abeba, *Ethiopia* **46 F2** 9 2N 38 42 E
Addison, *U.S.A.* **78 D7** 42 1N 77 14W
Addo, *S. Africa* **56 E4** 33 32S 25 45 E
Ādeh, *Iran* **44 B5** 37 42N 45 11 E
Adel, *U.S.A.* **77 K4** 31 8N 83 25W
**Adelaide**, *Australia* **63 E2** 34 52S 138 30 E
Adelaide, *Bahamas* **88 A4** 25 4N 77 31W
Adelaide, *S. Africa* **56 E4** 32 42S 26 20 E
Adelaide I., *Antarctica* **5 C17** 67 15S 68 30W
Adelaide Pen., *Canada* **68 B10** 68 15N 97 30W
Adelaide River, *Australia* **60 B5** 13 15S 131 7 E
Adelanto, *U.S.A.* **85 L9** 34 35N 117 22W
Adele I., *Australia* **60 C3** 15 32S 123 9 E
Adélie, Terre, *Antarctica* **5 C10** 68 0S 140 0 E
Adélie Land = Adélie, Terre, *Antarctica* **5 C10** 68 0S 140 0 E
**Aden** = Al 'Adan, *Yemen* **46 E4** 12 45N 45 0 E
Aden, G. of, *Asia* **46 E4** 12 30N 47 30 E
Adendorp, *S. Africa* **56 E3** 32 15S 24 30 E
Adh Dhayd, *U.A.E.* **45 E7** 25 17N 55 53 E
Adhoi, *India* **42 H4** 23 26N 70 32 E
Adi, *Indonesia* **37 E8** 4 15S 133 30 E
Adieu, C., *Australia* **61 F5** 32 0S 132 10 E
Adieu Pt., *Australia* **60 C3** 15 14S 124 35 E
Adige →, *Italy* **20 B5** 45 9N 12 20 E
Adigrat, *Ethiopia* **46 E2** 14 20N 39 26 E
Adilabad, *India* **40 K11** 19 33N 78 20 E
Adin Khel, *Afghan.* **40 C6** 32 45N 68 5 E
**Adirondack Mts.**, *U.S.A.* **79 C10** 44 0N 74 0W
Adjumani, *Uganda* **54 B3** 3 20N 31 50 E
Adlavik Is., *Canada* **71 A8** 55 2N 57 45W
Admiralty G., *Australia* **60 B4** 14 20S 125 55 E
Admiralty I., *U.S.A.* **72 B2** 57 30N 134 30W
Admiralty Is., *Papua N. G.* **64 H6** 2 0S 147 0 E
Adonara, *Indonesia* **37 F6** 8 15S 123 5 E
Adoni, *India* **40 M10** 15 33N 77 18 E
Adour →, *France* **18 E3** 43 32N 1 32W
Adra, *India* **43 H12** 23 30N 86 42 E
Adra, *Spain* **19 D4** 36 43N 3 3W
Adrano, *Italy* **20 F6** 37 40N 14 50 E
Adrar, *Algeria* **48 D4** 27 51N 0 11 E
Adrar, *Mauritania* **50 D3** 20 30N 7 30 E
Adrian, *Mich., U.S.A.* **76 E3** 41 54N 84 2W
Adrian, *Tex., U.S.A.* **81 H3** 35 16N 102 40W
**Adriatic Sea**, *Medit. S.* **20 C6** 43 0N 16 0 E
Adua, *Indonesia* **37 E7** 1 45S 129 50 E
Adwa, *Ethiopia* **46 E2** 14 15N 38 52 E
Adygea □, *Russia* **25 F7** 45 0N 40 0 E
Adzhar Republic = Ajaria □, *Georgia* **25 F7** 41 30N 42 0 E
Adzopé, *Ivory C.* **50 G5** 6 7N 3 49W
**Ægean Sea**, *Medit. S.* **21 E11** 38 30N 25 0 E
Aerhtai Shan, *Mongolia* **32 B4** 46 40N 92 45 E
'Afak, *Iraq* **44 C5** 32 4N 45 15 E
Afándou, *Greece* **23 C10** 36 18N 28 12 E
**Afghanistan** ■, *Asia* **40 C4** 33 0N 65 0 E
Aflou, *Algeria* **50 B6** 34 7N 2 3 E
**Africa** **48 E6** 10 0N 20 0 E
'Afrīn, *Syria* **44 B3** 36 32N 36 50 E
Afton, *N.Y., U.S.A.* **79 D9** 42 14N 75 32W
Afton, *Wyo., U.S.A.* **82 E8** 42 44N 110 56W
Afuá, *Brazil* **93 D8** 0 15S 50 20W
'Afula, *Israel* **47 C4** 32 37N 35 17 E
Afyon, *Turkey* **25 G5** 38 45N 30 33 E
Afyonkarahisar = Afyon, *Turkey* **25 G5** 38 45N 30 33 E
Agadès = Agadez, *Niger* **50 E7** 16 58N 7 59 E
Agadez, *Niger* **50 E7** 16 58N 7 59 E
**Agadir**, *Morocco* **50 B4** 30 28N 9 55W
Agaete, *Canary Is.* **22 F4** 28 6N 15 43W
Agar, *India* **42 H7** 23 40N 76 2 E
Agartala, *India* **41 H17** 23 50N 91 23 E
Agassiz, *Canada* **72 D4** 49 14N 121 46W
Agats, *Indonesia* **37 F9** 5 33S 138 0 E
Agawam, *U.S.A.* **79 D12** 42 5N 72 37W
Agboville, *Ivory C.* **50 G5** 5 55N 4 15W
Ağdam, *Azerbaijan* **44 B5** 40 0N 46 58 E
Agde, *France* **18 E5** 43 19N 3 28 E
Agen, *France* **18 D4** 44 12N 0 38 E
Āgh Kand, *Iran* **45 B6** 37 15N 48 4 E
Aginskoye, *Russia* **27 D12** 51 6N 114 32 E
Agnew, *Australia* **61 E3** 28 1S 120 31 E
Agori, *India* **43 G10** 24 33N 82 57 E
**Agra**, *India* **42 F7** 27 17N 77 58 E
Ağrı, *Turkey* **25 G7** 39 44N 43 3 E
Agri →, *Italy* **20 D7** 40 13N 16 44 E
Ağrı Dağı, *Turkey* **25 G7** 39 50N 44 15 E
Ağrı Karakose = Ağrı, *Turkey* **25 G7** 39 44N 43 3 E
Agrigento, *Italy* **20 F5** 37 19N 13 34 E
Agrínion, *Greece* **21 E9** 38 37N 21 27 E
Agua Caliente, *Baja Calif., Mexico* **85 N10** 32 29N 116 59W
Agua Caliente, *Sinaloa, Mexico* **86 B3** 26 30N 108 20W
Agua Caliente Springs, *U.S.A.* **85 N10** 32 56N 116 19W
Água Clara, *Brazil* **93 H8** 20 25S 52 45W
Agua Hechicero, *Mexico* **85 N10** 32 26N 116 14W
Agua Prieta, *Mexico* **86 A3** 31 20N 109 32W
Aguadilla, *Puerto Rico* **89 C6** 18 26N 67 10W
Aguadulce, *Panama* **88 E3** 8 15N 80 32W
Aguanga, *U.S.A.* **85 M10** 33 27N 116 51W
Aguanish, *Canada* **71 B7** 50 14N 62 2W
Aguanus →, *Canada* **71 B7** 50 13N 62 5W
Aguapey →, *Argentina* **94 B4** 29 7S 56 36W
Aguaray Guazú →, *Paraguay* **94 A4** 24 47S 57 19W
Aguarico →, *Ecuador* **92 D3** 0 59S 75 11W
Aguas Blancas, *Chile* **94 A2** 24 15S 69 55W
Aguas Calientes, Sierra de, *Argentina* **94 B2** 25 26S 66 40W
Aguascalientes, *Mexico* **86 C4** 21 53N 102 12W
Aguascalientes □, *Mexico* **86 C4** 22 0N 102 20W
Aguilares, *Argentina* **94 B2** 27 26S 65 35W
Aguilas, *Spain* **19 D5** 37 23N 1 35W
Agüimes, *Canary Is.* **22 G4** 27 58N 15 27W
Aguja, C. de la, *Colombia* **90 B3** 11 18N 74 12W
Agulhas, C., *S. Africa* **56 E3** 34 52S 20 0 E
Agulo, *Canary Is.* **22 F2** 28 11N 17 12W
Agung, *Indonesia* **36 F5** 8 20S 115 28 E
Agur, *Uganda* **54 B3** 2 28N 32 55 E
Agusan →, *Phil.* **37 C7** 9 0N 125 30 E
Aha Mts., *Botswana* **56 B3** 19 45S 21 0 E
Ahaggar, *Algeria* **50 D7** 23 0N 6 30 E
Ahar, *Iran* **44 B5** 38 35N 47 0 E
Ahipara B., *N.Z.* **59 F4** 35 5S 173 5 E
Ahiri, *India* **40 K12** 19 30N 80 0 E
Ahmad Wal, *Pakistan* **42 E1** 29 18N 65 58 E
**Ahmadabad**, *India* **42 H5** 23 0N 72 40 E
Aḥmadābād, *Khorāsān, Iran* **45 C9** 35 3N 60 50 E
Aḥmadābād, *Khorāsān, Iran* **45 C8** 35 49N 59 42 E
Aḥmadī, *Iran* **45 E8** 27 56N 56 42 E
Ahmadnagar, *India* **40 K9** 19 7N 74 46 E
Ahmadpur, *Pakistan* **42 E4** 29 12N 71 10 E
Ahmadpur Lamma, *Pakistan* **42 E4** 28 19N 70 3 E
Ahmedabad = Ahmadabad, *India* **42 H5** 23 0N 72 40 E
Ahmednagar = Ahmadnagar, *India* **40 K9** 19 7N 74 46 E
Ahome, *Mexico* **86 B3** 25 55N 109 11W
Ahoskie, *U.S.A.* **77 G7** 36 17N 76 59W
Ahram, *Iran* **45 D6** 28 52N 51 16 E
Ahrax Pt., *Malta* **23 D1** 35 59N 14 22 E
Āhū, *Iran* **45 C6** 34 33N 50 2 E
Ahuachapán, *El Salv.* **88 D2** 13 54N 89 52W
Ahvāz, *Iran* **45 D6** 31 20N 48 40 E
Ahvenanmaa = Åland, *Finland* **9 F19** 60 15N 20 0 E
Aḥwar, *Yemen* **46 E4** 13 30N 46 40 E
Ai →, *India* **43 F14** 26 26N 90 44 E
Aichi □, *Japan* **31 G8** 35 0N 137 15 E
Aigua, *Uruguay* **95 C5** 34 13S 54 46W
Aigues-Mortes, *France* **18 E6** 43 35N 4 12 E
Aihui, *China* **33 A7** 50 10N 127 30 E
Aija, *Peru* **92 E3** 9 50S 77 45W
Aikawa, *Japan* **30 E9** 38 2N 138 15 E
Aiken, *U.S.A.* **77 J5** 33 34N 81 43W
Aileron, *Australia* **62 C1** 22 39S 133 20 E
Aillik, *Canada* **71 A8** 55 11N 59 18W
Ailsa Craig, *U.K.* **12 F3** 55 15N 5 6W
'Ailūn, *Jordan* **47 C4** 32 18N 35 47 E
Aim, *Russia* **27 D14** 59 0N 133 55 E
Aimere, *Indonesia* **37 F6** 8 45S 121 3 E
Aimogasta, *Argentina* **94 B2** 28 33S 66 50W
Aïn Ben Tili, *Mauritania* **50 C4** 25 59N 9 27W
Aïn-Sefra, *Algeria* **50 B5** 32 47N 0 37W
'Ain Sudr, *Egypt* **47 F2** 29 50N 33 6 E
Ainaži, *Latvia* **9 H21** 57 50N 24 24 E
Ainsworth, *U.S.A.* **80 D5** 42 33N 99 52W
Aiquile, *Bolivia* **92 G5** 18 10S 65 10W
Aïr, *Niger* **50 E7** 18 30N 8 0 E
Air Force I., *Canada* **69 B12** 67 58N 74 5W
Air Hitam, *Malaysia* **39 M4** 1 55N 103 11 E
Airdrie, *Canada* **72 C6** 51 18N 114 2W
Airdrie, *U.K.* **12 F5** 55 52N 3 57W
Aire →, *U.K.* **10 D7** 53 43N 0 55W
Aire, I. de l', *Spain* **22 B11** 39 48N 4 16 E
Airlie Beach, *Australia* **62 C4** 20 16S 148 43 E
Aisne →, *France* **18 B5** 49 26N 2 50 E
Ait, *India* **43 G8** 25 54N 79 14 E
Aitkin, *U.S.A.* **80 B8** 46 32N 93 42W
Aiud, *Romania* **17 E12** 46 19N 23 44 E
**Aix-en-Provence**, *France* **18 E6** 43 32N 5 27 E
Aix-la-Chapelle = Aachen, *Germany* **16 C4** 50 45N 6 6 E
Aix-les-Bains, *France* **18 D6** 45 41N 5 53 E
Aíyion, *Greece* **21 E10** 38 15N 22 5 E
Aizawl, *India* **41 H18** 23 40N 92 44 E
Aizkraukle, *Latvia* **9 H21** 56 36N 25 11 E
Aizpute, *Latvia* **9 H19** 56 43N 21 40 E
Aizuwakamatsu, *Japan* **30 F9** 37 30N 139 56 E
Ajaccio, *France* **18 F8** 41 55N 8 40 E
Ajaigarh, *India* **43 G9** 24 52N 80 16 E
Ajalpan, *Mexico* **87 D5** 18 22N 97 15W
Ajanta Ra., *India* **40 J9** 20 28N 75 50 E
Ajari Rep. = Ajaria □, *Georgia* **25 F7** 41 30N 42 0 E
Ajaria □, *Georgia* **25 F7** 41 30N 42 0 E
Ajax, *Canada* **78 C5** 43 50N 79 1W
Ajdâbiyah, *Libya* **51 B10** 30 54N 20 4 E
Ajka, *Hungary* **17 E9** 47 4N 17 31 E
'Ajmān, *U.A.E.* **45 E7** 25 25N 55 30 E
Ajmer, *India* **42 F6** 26 28N 74 37 E
Ajnala, *India* **42 D6** 31 50N 74 48 E
Ajo, *U.S.A.* **83 K7** 32 22N 112 52W
Ajo, C. de, *Spain* **19 A4** 43 31N 3 35W
Akabira, *Japan* **30 C11** 43 33N 142 5 E
Akamas □, *Cyprus* **23 D11** 35 3N 32 18 E
Akanthou, *Cyprus* **23 D12** 35 22N 33 45 E
Akaroa, *N.Z.* **59 K4** 43 49S 172 59 E
Akashi, *Japan* **31 G7** 34 45N 134 58 E
Akbarpur, *Bihar, India* **43 G10** 24 39N 83 58 E
Akbarpur, *Ut. P., India* **43 F10** 26 25N 82 32 E
Akelamo, *Indonesia* **37 D7** 1 35N 129 40 E
Aketi, *Dem. Rep. of the Congo* **52 D4** 2 38N 23 47 E
Akharnaí, *Greece* **21 E10** 38 5N 23 44 E
Akhelóös →, *Greece* **21 E9** 38 19N 21 7 E
Akhisar, *Turkey* **21 E12** 38 56N 27 48 E
Akhnur, *India* **43 C6** 32 52N 74 45 E
Akhtyrka = Okhtyrka, *Ukraine* **25 D5** 50 25N 35 0 E
Aki, *Japan* **31 H6** 33 30N 133 54 E
Akimiski I., *Canada* **70 B3** 52 50N 81 30W
Akita, *Japan* **30 E10** 39 45N 140 7 E
Akita □, *Japan* **30 E10** 39 40N 140 30 E
Akjoujt, *Mauritania* **50 E3** 19 45N 14 15W
Akkeshi, *Japan* **30 C12** 43 2N 144 51 E
'Akko, *Israel* **47 C4** 32 55N 35 4 E
Aklavik, *Canada* **68 B6** 68 12N 135 0W
Aklera, *India* **42 G7** 24 26N 76 32 E
Akmolinsk = Astana, *Kazakstan* **26 D8** 51 10N 71 30 E
Akō, *Japan* **31 G7** 34 45N 134 24 E
Akola, *India* **40 J10** 20 42N 77 2 E
Akordat, *Eritrea* **46 D2** 15 30N 37 40 E
Akpatok I., *Canada* **69 B13** 60 25N 68 8W
Åkrahamn, *Norway* **9 G11** 59 15N 5 10 E
Akranes, *Iceland* **8 D2** 64 19N 22 5W
Akron, *Colo., U.S.A.* **80 E3** 40 10N 103 13W
**Akron**, *Ohio, U.S.A.* **78 E3** 41 5N 81 31W
Akrotiri, *Cyprus* **23 E11** 34 36N 32 57 E
Akrotiri Bay, *Cyprus* **23 E12** 34 35N 33 10 E
Aksai Chin, *India* **43 B8** 35 15N 79 55 E
Aksaray, *Turkey* **25 G5** 38 25N 34 2 E
Aksay, *Kazakstan* **25 D9** 51 11N 53 0 E
Akşehir, *Turkey* **44 B1** 38 18N 31 30 E
Akşehir Gölü, *Turkey* **25 G5** 38 30N 31 25 E
Aksu, *China* **32 B3** 41 5N 80 10 E
Aksum, *Ethiopia* **46 E2** 14 5N 38 40 E
Aktogay, *Kazakstan* **26 E8** 46 57N 79 40 E
Aktsyabrski, *Belarus* **17 B15** 52 38N 28 53 E
Aktyubinsk = Aqtöbe, *Kazakstan* **25 D10** 50 17N 57 10 E
Akure, *Nigeria* **50 G7** 7 15N 5 5 E
Akureyri, *Iceland* **8 D4** 65 40N 18 6W
Akuseki-Shima, *Japan* **31 K4** 29 27N 129 37 E
Akyab = Sittwe, *Burma* **41 J18** 20 18N 92 45 E
Al 'Adan, *Yemen* **46 E4** 12 45N 45 0 E
Al Aḥsā = Hasa □, *Si. Arabia* **45 E6** 25 50N 49 0 E
Al Ajfar, *Si. Arabia* **44 E4** 27 26N 43 0 E
Al Amādīyah, *Iraq* **44 B4** 37 5N 43 30 E
Al 'Amārah, *Iraq* **44 D5** 31 55N 47 15 E
Al 'Aqabah, *Jordan* **47 F4** 29 31N 35 0 E
Al Arak, *Syria* **44 C3** 34 38N 38 35 E
Al 'Aramah, *Si. Arabia* **44 E5** 25 30N 46 0 E
Al Arṭāwīyah, *Si. Arabia* **44 E5** 26 31N 45 20 E
Al 'Āṣimah = 'Ammān □, *Jordan* **47 D5** 31 40N 36 30 E
Al 'Assāfīyah, *Si. Arabia* **44 D3** 28 17N 38 59 E
Al 'Ayn, *Oman* **45 E7** 24 15N 55 45 E
Al 'Ayn, *Si. Arabia* **44 E3** 25 4N 38 6 E
Al 'Aẓamīyah, *Iraq* **44 C5** 33 22N 44 22 E
Al 'Azīzīyah, *Iraq* **44 C5** 32 54N 45 4 E
Al Bāb, *Syria* **44 B3** 36 23N 37 29 E
Al Bad', *Si. Arabia* **44 D2** 28 28N 35 1 E
Al Bādī, *Iraq* **44 C4** 35 56N 41 32 E
Al Baḥrah, *Kuwait* **44 D5** 29 40N 47 52 E
Al Baḥral Mayyit = Dead Sea, *Asia* **47 D4** 31 30N 35 30 E
Al Balqā' □, *Jordan* **47 C4** 32 5N 35 45 E
Al Bārūk, J., *Lebanon* **47 B4** 33 39N 35 40 E
Al Başrah, *Iraq* **44 D5** 30 30N 47 50 E
Al Baṭḥā, *Iraq* **44 D5** 31 6N 45 53 E
Al Batrūn, *Lebanon* **47 A4** 34 15N 35 40 E
Al Bayḍā, *Libya* **51 B10** 32 50N 21 44 E

Al Biqā, Lebanon 47 A5 34 10N 36 10 E
Al Bi'r, Si. Arabia 44 D3 28 51N 36 16 E
Al Burayj, Syria 47 A5 34 15N 36 46 E
Al Faḑilī, Si. Arabia 45 E6 26 58N 49 10 E
Al Fallūjah, Iraq 44 C4 33 20N 43 55 E
Al Fāw, Iraq 45 D6 30 0N 48 30 E
Al Fujayrah, U.A.E. 45 E8 25 7N 56 18 E
Al Ghadaf, W. ➝, Jordan 47 D5 31 26N 36 43 E
Al Ghammās, Iraq 44 D5 31 45N 44 37 E
Al Ghazālah, Si. Arabia 44 E4 26 48N 41 19 E
Al Hābah, Si. Arabia 44 E5 27 10N 47 0 E
Al Ḩadīthah, Iraq 44 C4 34 0N 41 13 E
Al Ḩadīthah, Si. Arabia 47 D6 31 28N 37 8 E
Al Ḩaḑr, Iraq 44 C4 35 35N 42 44 E
Al Hājānah, Syria 47 B5 33 20N 36 33 E
Al Hajar al Gharbi, Oman 45 E8 24 10N 56 15 E
Al Hāmad, Si. Arabia 44 D3 31 30N 39 30 E
Al Hamdānīyah, Syria 44 C3 35 25N 36 50 E
Al Ḩamīdīyah, Syria 47 A4 34 42N 35 57 E
Al Ḩammār, Iraq 44 D5 30 57N 46 51 E
Al Ḩamrā', Si. Arabia 44 E3 24 2N 38 55 E
Al Ḩanākīyah, Si. Arabia 44 E4 24 51N 40 31 E
Al Harīr, W. ➝, Syria 47 C4 32 44N 35 59 E
Al Ḩasā, W. ➝, Jordan 47 D4 31 4N 35 29 E
Al Ḩasakah, Syria 44 B4 36 35N 40 45 E
Al Haydān, W. ➝, Jordan 47 D4 31 29N 35 34 E
Al Ḩayy, Iraq 44 C5 32 5N 46 5 E
Al Ḩijarah, Asia 44 D4 30 0N 44 0 E
Al Ḩillah, Iraq 44 C5 32 30N 44 25 E
Al Hindīyah, Iraq 44 C5 32 30N 44 10 E
Al Hirmil, Lebanon 47 A5 34 26N 36 24 E
Al Hoceïma, Morocco 50 A5 35 8N 3 58W
Al Ḩudaydah, Yemen 46 E3 14 50N 43 0 E
Al Hufūf, Si. Arabia 45 E6 25 25N 49 45 E
Al Ḩumayḑah, Si. Arabia 44 D2 29 14N 34 56 E
Al Ḩunayy, Si. Arabia 45 E6 25 58N 48 45 E
Al Īsāwīyah, Si. Arabia 44 D3 30 43N 37 59 E
Al Jafr, Jordan 47 E5 30 18N 36 14 E
Al Jāfūrah, Si. Arabia 45 E7 25 0N 50 15 E
Al Jaghbūb, Libya 51 C10 29 42N 24 38 E
Al Jahrah, Kuwait 44 D5 29 25N 47 40 E
Al Jalāmīd, Si. Arabia 44 D3 31 20N 40 6 E
Al Jamalīyah, Qatar 45 E6 25 37N 51 5 E
Al Janūb □, Lebanon 47 B4 33 20N 35 20 E
Al Jawf, Libya 51 D10 24 10N 23 24 E
Al Jawf, Si. Arabia 44 D3 29 55N 39 40 E
Al Jazirah, Iraq 44 C5 33 30N 44 0 E
Al Jithāmīyah, Si. Arabia 44 E4 27 41N 41 43 E
Al Jubayl, Si. Arabia 45 E6 27 0N 49 50 E
Al Jubaylah, Si. Arabia 44 E5 24 55N 46 25 E
Al Jubb, Si. Arabia 44 E4 27 11N 42 17 E
Al Junaynah, Sudan 51 F10 13 27N 22 45 E
Al Kabā'ish, Iraq 44 D5 30 58N 47 0 E
Al Karak, Jordan 47 D4 31 11N 35 42 E
Al Karak □, Jordan 47 E5 31 0N 36 0 E
Al Kāzim Tyah, Iraq 44 C5 33 22N 44 12 E
Al Khābūra, Oman 45 F8 23 57N 57 5 E
Al Khafji, Si. Arabia 45 E6 28 24N 48 29 E
Al Khalīl, West Bank 47 D4 31 32N 35 6 E
Al Khāliş, Iraq 44 C5 33 49N 44 32 E
Al Kharsānīyah, Si. Arabia 45 E6 27 13N 49 18 E
Al Khaşab, Oman 45 E8 26 14N 56 15 E
Al Khawr, Qatar 45 E6 25 41N 51 30 E
Al Khiḑr, Iraq 44 D5 31 12N 45 33 E
Al Khiyām, Lebanon 47 B4 33 20N 35 36 E
Al Khums, Libya 51 B8 32 40N 14 17 E
Al Kiswah, Syria 47 B5 33 23N 36 14 E
Al Kūfah, Iraq 44 C5 32 2N 44 24 E
Al Kufrah, Libya 51 D10 24 17N 23 15 E
Al Kuhayfīyah, Si. Arabia 44 E4 27 12N 43 3 E
Al Kūt, Iraq 44 C5 32 30N 46 0 E
Al Kuwayt, Kuwait 44 D5 29 30N 48 0 E
Al Labwah, Lebanon 47 A5 34 11N 36 20 E
Al Lādhiqīyah, Syria 44 C2 35 30N 35 45 E
Al Līth, Si. Arabia 46 C3 20 9N 40 15 E
Al Liwā', Oman 45 E8 24 31N 56 36 E
Al Luḩayyah, Yemen 46 D3 15 45N 42 40 E
Al Madīnah, Iraq 44 D5 30 57N 47 16 E
Al Madīnah, Si. Arabia 46 C2 24 35N 39 52 E
Al Mafraq, Jordan 47 C5 32 17N 36 14 E
Al Maḩmūdīyah, Iraq 44 C5 33 3N 44 21 E
Al Majma'ah, Si. Arabia 44 E5 25 57N 45 22 E
Al Makhruq, W. ➝, Jordan 47 D6 31 28N 37 0 E
Al Makḩūl, Si. Arabia 44 E4 26 37N 42 39 E
Al Manāmah, Bahrain 45 E6 26 10N 50 30 E
Al Maqwa', Kuwait 44 D5 29 10N 47 59 E
Al Marj, Libya 51 B10 32 25N 20 30 E
Al Maţlā, Kuwait 44 D5 29 24N 47 40 E
Al Mawjib, W. ➝, Jordan 47 D4 31 28N 35 36 E
Al Mawşil, Iraq 44 B4 36 15N 43 5 E
Al Mayādin, Syria 44 C4 35 1N 40 27 E
Al Mazār, Jordan 47 D4 31 4N 35 41 E
Al Midhnab, Si. Arabia 44 E5 25 50N 44 18 E
Al Minā', Lebanon 47 A4 34 24N 35 49 E
Al Miqdādīyah, Iraq 44 C5 34 0N 45 0 E
Al Mubarraz, Si. Arabia 45 E6 25 30N 49 40 E
Al Mudawwarah, Jordan 47 F5 29 19N 36 0 E
Al Mughayrā', U.A.E. 45 E7 24 5N 53 32 E
Al Muḩarraq, Bahrain 45 E6 26 15N 50 40 E
Al Mukallā, Yemen 46 E4 14 33N 49 2 E
Al Mukhā, Yemen 46 E3 13 18N 43 15 E
Al Musayjīd, Si. Arabia 44 E3 24 5N 39 5 E
Al Musayyib, Iraq 44 C5 32 49N 44 20 E
Al Muwaylih, Si. Arabia 44 E2 27 40N 35 30 E
Al Qā'im, Iraq 44 C4 34 21N 41 7 E
Al Qalībah, Si. Arabia 44 D3 28 24N 37 42 E
Al Qāmishli, Syria 44 B4 37 10N 41 10 E
Al Qaryatayn, Syria 47 A6 34 12N 37 13 E
Al Qaşīm, Si. Arabia 44 E4 26 0N 43 0 E
Al Qaţ'ā, Syria 44 C4 34 40N 40 48 E
Al Qaţīf, Si. Arabia 45 E6 26 35N 50 0 E
Al Qatrānah, Jordan 47 D5 31 12N 36 6 E
Al Qaţrūn, Libya 51 D9 24 56N 15 3 E
Al Qayşūmah, Si. Arabia 44 D5 28 20N 46 7 E
Al Quds = Jerusalem, Israel 47 D4 31 47N 35 10 E
Al Qunayţirah, Syria 47 C4 32 55N 35 45 E
Al Qurnah, Iraq 44 D5 31 1N 47 25 E
Al Quşayr, Iraq 44 D5 30 39N 45 50 E
Al Quşayr, Syria 47 A5 34 31N 36 34 E
Al Qutayfah, Syria 47 B5 33 44N 36 36 E
Al 'Ubaylah, Si. Arabia 46 C5 21 59N 50 57 E
Al 'Uḑaylīyah, Si. Arabia 45 E6 25 8N 49 18 E
Al 'Ulā, Si. Arabia 44 E3 26 35N 38 0 E
Al 'Uqayr, Si. Arabia 45 E6 25 40N 50 15 E
Al 'Uthmānīyah, Si. Arabia 45 E6 25 5N 49 22 E
Al 'Uwaynid, Si. Arabia 44 E5 24 50N 46 0 E
Al 'Uwayqīlah, Si. Arabia 44 D4 30 30N 42 10 E
Al 'Uyūn, Ḩijāz, Si. Arabia 44 E3 24 33N 39 35 E
Al 'Uyūn, Najd, Si. Arabia 44 E4 26 30N 43 50 E
Al 'Uzayr, Iraq 44 D5 31 19N 47 25 E
Al Wajh, Si. Arabia 44 E3 26 10N 36 30 E
Al Wakrah, Qatar 45 E6 25 10N 51 40 E
Al Wannān, Si. Arabia 45 E6 26 55N 48 24 E
Al Waqbah, Si. Arabia 44 D5 28 48N 45 33 E
Al Wari'āh, Si. Arabia 44 E5 27 51N 47 25 E
Al Wusayl, Qatar 45 E6 25 29N 51 29 E
Ala Dağ, Turkey 44 B2 37 44N 35 9 E
Ala Tau Shankou = Dzungarian Gates, Kazakstan 32 B3 45 0N 82 0 E
**Alabama** □, U.S.A. 77 J2 33 0N 87 0W
Alabama ➝, U.S.A. 77 K2 31 8N 87 57W
Alabaster, U.S.A. 77 J2 33 15N 86 49W
Alaçam Dağları, Turkey 21 E13 39 18N 28 49 E
Alachua, U.S.A. 77 L4 29 47N 82 30W
Alaérma, Greece 23 C9 36 9N 27 57 E
Alagoa Grande, Brazil 93 E11 7 3S 35 35W
Alagoas □, Brazil 93 E11 9 0S 36 0W
Alagoinhas, Brazil 93 F11 12 7S 38 20W
Alaior, Spain 22 B11 39 57N 4 8 E
Alajero, Canary Is. 22 F2 28 3N 17 13W
Alajuela, Costa Rica 88 D3 10 2N 84 8W
Alakamisy, Madag. 57 C8 21 19S 47 14 E
Alaknanda ➝, India 43 D8 30 8N 78 36 E
Alakurtti, Russia 24 A5 67 0N 30 30 E
Alamarvdasht, Iran 45 E7 27 37N 52 59 E
Alameda, Calif., U.S.A. 84 H4 37 46N 122 15W
Alameda, N. Mex., U.S.A. 83 J10 35 11N 106 37W
Alamo, U.S.A. 85 J11 37 22N 115 10W
Alamo Crossing, U.S.A. 85 L13 34 16N 113 33W
Alamogordo, U.S.A. 83 K11 32 54N 105 57W
Alamos, Mexico 86 B3 27 0N 109 0W
Alamosa, U.S.A. 83 H11 37 28N 105 52W
**Åland**, Finland 9 F19 60 15N 20 0 E
Ålands hav, Sweden 9 F18 60 0N 19 30 E
Alandur, India 40 N12 13 0N 80 15 E
Alania = North Ossetia □, Russia 25 F7 43 30N 44 30 E
Alanya, Turkey 25 G5 36 38N 32 0 E
Alaotra, Farihin', Madag. 57 B8 17 30S 48 30 E
Alapayevsk, Russia 26 D7 57 52N 61 42 E
Alaşehir, Turkey 21 E13 38 23N 28 30 E
**Alaska** □, U.S.A. 68 B5 64 0N 154 0W
Alaska, G. of, Pac. Oc. 68 C5 58 0N 145 0W
Alaska Peninsula, U.S.A. 68 C4 56 0N 159 0W
Alaska Range, U.S.A. 68 B4 62 50N 151 0W
Älät, Azerbaijan 25 G8 39 58N 49 25 E
Alatyr, Russia 24 D8 54 55N 46 35 E
Alausi, Ecuador 92 D3 2 0S 78 50W
Alava, C., U.S.A. 82 B1 48 10N 124 44W
Alavus, Finland 9 E20 62 35N 23 36 E
Alawoona, Australia 63 E3 34 45S 140 30 E
'Alayh, Lebanon 47 B4 33 46N 35 33 E
Alba, Italy 20 B3 44 42N 8 2 E
Alba-Iulia, Romania 17 E12 46 8N 23 39 E
**Albacete**, Spain 19 C5 39 0N 1 50W
Albacutya, L., Australia 63 F3 35 45S 141 58 E
Albanel, L., Canada 70 B5 50 55N 73 12W
**Albania** ■, Europe 21 D9 41 0N 20 0 E
Albany, Australia 61 G2 35 1S 117 58 E
Albany, Ga., U.S.A. 77 K3 31 35N 84 10W
Albany, N.Y., U.S.A. 79 D11 42 39N 73 45W
Albany, Oreg., U.S.A. 82 D2 44 38N 123 6W
Albany, Tex., U.S.A. 81 J5 32 44N 99 18W
Albany ➝, Canada 70 B3 52 17N 81 31W
Albardón, Argentina 94 C2 31 20S 68 30W
Albatross B., Australia 62 A3 12 45S 141 30 E
Albemarle, U.S.A. 77 H5 35 21N 80 11W
Albemarle Sd., U.S.A. 77 H7 36 5N 76 0W
Alberche ➝, Spain 19 C3 39 58N 4 46W
Alberdi, Paraguay 94 B4 26 14S 58 20W
**Albert, L.**, Australia 63 F2 35 30S 139 10 E
Albert Edward Ra., Australia 60 C4 18 17S 127 57 E
Albert L., Africa 54 B3 1 30N 31 0 E
Albert Lea, U.S.A. 80 D8 43 39N 93 22W
Albert Nile ➝, Uganda 54 B3 3 36N 32 2 E
Albert Town, Bahamas 89 B5 22 37N 74 33W
**Alberta** □, Canada 72 C6 54 40N 115 0W
Alberti, Argentina 94 D3 35 1S 60 16W
Albertinia, S. Africa 56 E3 34 11S 21 34 E
Alberton, Canada 71 C7 46 50N 64 0W
Albertville = Kalemie, Dem. Rep. of the Congo 54 D2 5 55S 29 9 E
Albertville, France 18 D7 45 40N 6 22 E
Albertville, U.S.A. 77 H2 34 16N 86 13W
Albi, France 18 E5 43 56N 2 9 E
Albia, U.S.A. 80 E8 41 2N 92 48W
Albina, Surinam 93 B8 5 37N 54 15W
Albina, Ponta, Angola 56 B1 15 52S 11 44 E
Albion, Mich., U.S.A. 76 D3 42 15N 84 45W
Albion, Nebr., U.S.A. 80 E6 41 42N 98 0W
Albion, Pa., U.S.A. 78 E4 41 53N 80 22W
Alborán, Medit. S. 19 E4 35 57N 3 0W
Ålborg, Denmark 9 H13 57 2N 9 54 E
Alborz, Reshteh-ye Kūhhā-ye, Iran 45 C7 36 0N 52 0 E
**Albuquerque**, U.S.A. 83 J10 35 5N 106 39W
Albuquerque, Cayos de, Caribbean 88 D3 12 10N 81 50W
Alburg, U.S.A. 79 B11 44 59N 73 18W
Albury-Wodonga, Australia 63 F4 36 3S 146 56 E
Alcalá de Henares, Spain 19 B4 40 28N 3 22W
Alcalá la Real, Spain 19 D4 37 27N 3 57W
Álcamo, Italy 20 F5 37 59N 12 55 E
Alcañiz, Spain 19 B5 41 2N 0 8W
Alcântara, Brazil 93 D10 2 20S 44 30W
Alcántara, Embalse de, Spain 19 C2 39 44N 6 50W
Alcantarilla, Spain 19 D5 37 59N 1 12W
Alcaraz, Sierra de, Spain 19 C4 38 40N 2 20W
Alcaudete, Spain 19 D3 37 35N 4 5W
Alcázar de San Juan, Spain 19 C4 39 24N 3 12W
Alchevsk, Ukraine 25 E6 48 30N 38 45 E
Alcira = Alzira, Spain 19 C5 39 9N 0 30W
Alcova, U.S.A. 82 E10 42 34N 106 43W
Alcoy, Spain 19 C5 38 43N 0 30W
Alcúdia, Spain 22 B10 39 51N 3 7 E
Alcúdia, B. d', Spain 22 B10 39 47N 3 15 E
Aldabra Is., Seychelles 49 G8 9 22S 46 28 E
Aldama, Mexico 87 C5 23 0N 98 4W
Aldan, Russia 27 D13 58 40N 125 30 E
Aldan ➝, Russia 27 C13 63 28N 129 35 E
Aldea, Pta. de la, Canary Is. 22 G4 28 0N 15 50W
Aldeburgh, U.K. 11 E9 52 10N 1 37 E
Alder Pk., U.S.A. 84 K5 35 53N 121 22W
Alderney, U.K. 11 H5 49 42N 2 11W
Aldershot, U.K. 11 F7 51 15N 0 44W
Aledo, U.S.A. 80 E9 41 12N 90 45W
Aleg, Mauritania 50 E3 17 3N 13 55W
Alegranza, Canary Is. 22 E6 29 23N 13 32W
Alegranza, I., Canary Is. 22 E6 29 23N 13 32W
Alegre, Brazil 95 A7 20 50S 41 30W
Alegrete, Brazil 95 B4 29 40S 56 0W
Aleisk, Russia 26 D9 52 40N 83 0 E
Aleksandriya = Oleksandriya, Ukraine 17 C14 50 37N 26 19 E
Aleksandrov Gay, Russia 25 D8 50 9N 48 34 E
Aleksandrovsk-Sakhalinskiy, Russia 27 D15 50 50N 142 20 E
Além Paraíba, Brazil 95 A7 21 52S 42 41W
Alemania, Argentina 94 B2 25 40S 65 30W
Alemania, Chile 94 B2 25 10S 69 55W
Alençon, France 18 B4 48 27N 0 4 E
Alenquer, Brazil 93 D8 1 56S 54 46W
Alenuihaha Channel, U.S.A. 74 H17 20 30N 156 0W
**Aleppo** = Ḩalab, Syria 44 B3 36 10N 37 15 E
Alès, France 18 D6 44 9N 4 5 E
**Alessándria**, Italy 18 D8 44 54N 8 37 E
Ålesund, Norway 9 E12 62 28N 6 12 E
**Aleutian Is.**, Pac. Oc. 68 C2 52 0N 175 0W
Aleutian Trench, Pac. Oc. 64 C10 48 0N 180 0 E
Alexander, U.S.A. 80 B3 47 51N 103 39W
Alexander, Mt., Australia 61 E3 28 58S 120 16 E
Alexander Arch., U.S.A. 68 C6 56 0N 136 0W
Alexander Bay, S. Africa 56 D2 28 40S 16 30 E
Alexander City, U.S.A. 77 J3 32 56N 85 58W
Alexander I., Antarctica 5 C17 69 0S 70 0W
Alexandra, Australia 63 F4 37 8S 145 40 E
Alexandra, N.Z. 59 L2 45 14S 169 25 E
Alexandra Falls, Canada 72 A5 60 29N 116 18W
**Alexandria** = El Iskandarîya, Egypt 51 B11 31 13N 29 58 E
Alexandria, B.C., Canada 72 C4 52 35N 122 27W
Alexandria, Ont., Canada 79 A10 45 19N 74 38W
Alexandria, Romania 17 G13 43 57N 25 24 E
Alexandria, S. Africa 56 E4 33 38S 26 28 E
Alexandria, U.K. 12 F4 55 59N 4 35W
Alexandria, La., U.S.A. 81 K8 31 18N 92 27W
Alexandria, Minn., U.S.A. 80 C7 45 53N 95 22W
Alexandria, S. Dak., U.S.A. 80 D6 43 39N 97 47W
Alexandria, Va., U.S.A. 76 F7 38 48N 77 3W
Alexandria Bay, U.S.A. 79 B9 44 20N 75 55W
Alexandrina, L., Australia 63 F2 35 25S 139 10 E
Alexandroúpolis, Greece 21 D11 40 50N 25 54 E
Alexis ➝, Canada 71 B8 52 33N 56 8W
Alexis Creek, Canada 72 C4 52 10N 123 20W
Alfabia, Spain 22 B9 39 44N 2 44 E
Alfenas, Brazil 95 A6 21 20S 46 10W
Alford, Aberds., U.K. 12 D6 57 14N 2 41W
Alford, Lincs., U.K. 10 D8 53 15N 0 10 E
Alfred, Maine, U.S.A. 79 C14 43 29N 70 43W
Alfred, N.Y., U.S.A. 78 D7 42 16N 77 48W
Alfreton, U.K. 10 D6 53 6N 1 24W
Alga, Kazakstan 25 E10 49 53N 57 20 E
Algaida, Spain 22 B9 39 33N 2 53 E
Ålgård, Norway 9 G11 58 46N 5 53 E
Algarve, Portugal 19 D1 36 58N 8 20W
Algeciras, Spain 19 D3 36 9N 5 28W
Algemesí, Spain 19 C5 39 11N 0 27W
Alger, Algeria 50 A6 36 42N 3 8 E
**Algeria** ■, Africa 50 C6 28 30N 2 0 E
Alghero, Italy 20 D3 40 33N 8 19 E
**Algiers** = Alger, Algeria 50 A6 36 42N 3 8 E
Algoa B., S. Africa 56 E4 33 50S 25 45 E
Algoma, U.S.A. 76 C2 44 36N 87 26W
Algona, U.S.A. 80 D7 43 4N 94 14W
Algonac, U.S.A. 78 D2 42 37N 82 32W
Algonquin Prov. Park, Canada 70 C4 45 50N 78 30W
Algorta, Uruguay 96 C5 32 25S 57 23W
Alhambra, U.S.A. 85 L8 34 8N 118 6W
Alhucemas = Al Hoceïma, Morocco 50 A5 35 8N 3 58W
'Alī al Gharbī, Iraq 44 C5 32 30N 46 45 E
'Alī ash Sharqī, Iraq 44 C5 32 7N 46 44 E
'Alī Khēl, Afghan. 42 C3 33 57N 69 43 E
'Alī Shāh, Iran 44 B5 38 9N 45 50 E
'Alīābād, Khorāsān, Iran 45 C8 32 30N 57 30 E
'Alīābād, Kordestān, Iran 44 C5 35 4N 46 58 E
'Alīābād, Yazd, Iran 45 D7 31 41N 53 49 E
Aliağa, Turkey 21 E12 38 47N 26 59 E
Aliákmon ➝, Greece 21 D10 40 30N 22 36 E
Alicante, Spain 19 C5 38 23N 0 30W
Alice, S. Africa 56 E4 32 48S 26 55 E
Alice, U.S.A. 81 M5 27 45N 98 5W
Alice ➝, Queens., Australia 62 C3 24 2S 144 50 E
Alice ➝, Queens., Australia 62 B3 15 35S 142 20 E
Alice Arm, Canada 72 B3 55 29N 129 31W
Alice Springs, Australia 62 C1 23 40S 133 50 E
Alicedale, S. Africa 56 E4 33 15S 26 4 E
Aliceville, U.S.A. 77 J1 33 8N 88 9W
Aliganj, India 43 F8 27 30N 79 10 E
Aligarh, Raj., India 42 G7 25 55N 76 15 E
Aligarh, Ut. P., India 42 F8 27 55N 78 10 E
Alīgūdarz, Iran 45 C6 33 25N 49 45 E
Alimnía, Greece 23 C9 36 16N 27 43 E
Alingsås, Sweden 9 H15 57 56N 12 31 E
Alipur, Pakistan 42 E4 29 25N 70 55 E
Alipur Duar, India 41 F16 26 30N 89 35 E
Aliquippa, U.S.A. 78 F4 40 37N 80 15W
Alitus = Alytus, Lithuania 9 J21 54 24N 24 3 E
Aliwal North, S. Africa 56 E4 30 45S 26 45 E
Alix, Canada 72 C6 52 24N 113 11W
Aljustrel, Portugal 19 D1 37 55N 8 10W
Alkmaar, Neths. 15 B4 52 37N 4 45 E
All American Canal, U.S.A. 83 K6 32 45N 115 15W
Allagash ➝, U.S.A. 77 B11 47 5N 69 3W
Allah Dad, Pakistan 42 G2 25 38N 67 34 E
**Allahabad**, India 43 G9 25 25N 81 58 E
Allan, Canada 73 C7 51 53N 106 4W
Allanmyo, Burma 41 K19 19 30N 95 17 E
Allanridge, S. Africa 56 D4 27 45S 26 40 E
Allegany, U.S.A. 78 D6 42 6N 78 30W
Allegheny ➝, U.S.A. 78 F5 40 27N 80 1W
Allegheny Mts., U.S.A. 76 G6 38 15N 80 10W
Allegheny Reservoir, U.S.A. 78 E6 41 50N 79 0W
Allen, Bog of, Ireland 13 C5 53 15N 7 0W
Allen, L., Ireland 13 B3 54 8N 8 4W
Allendale, U.S.A. 77 J5 33 1N 81 18W
Allende, Mexico 86 B4 28 20N 100 50W
Allentown, U.S.A. 79 F9 40 37N 75 29W
Alleppey, India 40 Q10 9 30N 76 28 E
Aller ➝, Germany 16 B5 52 56N 9 12 E
Alliance, Nebr., U.S.A. 80 D3 42 6N 102 52W
Alliance, Ohio, U.S.A. 78 F3 40 55N 81 6W
Allier ➝, France 18 C5 46 57N 3 4 E
Alliford Bay, Canada 72 C2 53 12N 131 58W
Alliston, Canada 78 B5 44 9N 79 52W
Alloa, U.K. 12 E5 56 7N 3 47W
Allora, Australia 63 D5 28 2S 152 0 E
Alluitsup Paa = Sydprøven, Greenland 4 C5 60 30N 45 35W
Alma, Canada 71 C5 48 35N 71 40W
Alma, Ga., U.S.A. 77 K4 31 33N 82 28W
Alma, Kans., U.S.A. 80 F6 39 1N 96 17W
Alma, Mich., U.S.A. 76 D3 43 23N 84 39W
Alma, Nebr., U.S.A. 80 E5 40 6N 99 22W
Alma Ata = Almaty, Kazakstan 26 E8 43 15N 76 57 E
Almada, Portugal 19 C1 38 40N 9 9W
Almaden, Australia 62 B3 17 22S 144 40 E
Almadén, Spain 19 C3 38 49N 4 52W
Almanor, L., U.S.A. 82 F3 40 14N 121 9W
Almansa, Spain 19 C5 38 51N 1 5W
Almanzor, Pico, Spain 19 B3 40 15N 5 18W
Almanzora ➝, Spain 19 D5 37 14N 1 46W
**Almaty**, Kazakstan 26 E8 43 15N 76 57 E
Almazán, Spain 19 B4 41 30N 2 30W
Almeirim, Brazil 93 D8 1 30S 52 34W
Almelo, Neths. 15 B6 52 22N 6 42 E
Almendralejo, Spain 19 C2 38 41N 6 26W
Almere-Stad, Neths. 15 B5 52 20N 5 15 E
Almería, Spain 19 D4 36 52N 2 27W
Almirante, Panama 88 E3 9 10N 82 30W
Almiroú, Kólpos, Greece 23 D6 35 23N 24 20 E
Almond, U.S.A. 78 D7 42 19N 77 44W
Almont, U.S.A. 78 D1 42 55N 83 3W
Almonte, Canada 79 A8 45 14N 76 12W
Almora, India 43 E8 29 38N 79 40 E
Alness, U.K. 12 D4 57 41N 4 16W
Alnmouth, U.K. 10 B6 55 24N 1 37W
Alnwick, U.K. 10 B6 55 24N 1 42W
Aloi, Uganda 54 B3 2 16N 33 10 E
Alon, Burma 41 H19 22 12N 95 5 E
Alor, Indonesia 37 F6 8 15S 124 30 E
Alor Setar, Malaysia 39 J3 6 7N 100 22 E
Alot, India 42 H6 23 56N 75 40 E
Aloysius, Mt., Australia 61 E4 26 0S 128 38 E
Alpaugh, U.S.A. 84 K7 35 53N 119 29W
Alpena, U.S.A. 76 C4 45 4N 83 27W
Alpha, Australia 62 C4 23 39S 146 37 E
Alphen aan den Rijn, Neths. 15 B4 52 7N 4 40 E
Alpine, Ariz., U.S.A. 83 K9 33 51N 109 9W
Alpine, Calif., U.S.A. 85 N10 32 50N 116 46W
Alpine, Tex., U.S.A. 81 K3 30 22N 103 40W
**Alps**, Europe 18 C8 46 30N 9 30 E
**Alsace**, France 18 B7 48 15N 7 25 E
Alsask, Canada 73 C7 51 21N 109 59W
Alsasua, Spain 19 A4 42 54N 2 10W
Alsek ➝, U.S.A. 72 B1 59 10N 138 12W
Alsten, Norway 8 D15 65 58N 12 40 E
Alston, U.K. 10 C5 54 49N 2 25W
Alta, Norway 8 B20 69 57N 23 10 E
Alta Gracia, Argentina 94 C3 31 40S 64 30W
Alta Sierra, U.S.A. 85 K8 35 42N 118 33W
Altaelva ➝, Norway 8 B20 69 54N 23 17 E
Altafjorden, Norway 8 A20 70 5N 23 5 E
**Altai** = Aerhtai Shan, Mongolia 32 B4 46 40N 92 45 E
Altamaha ➝, U.S.A. 77 K5 31 20N 81 20W
Altamira, Brazil 93 D8 3 12S 52 10W
Altamira, Chile 94 B2 25 47S 69 51W
Altamira, Mexico 87 C5 22 24N 97 55W
Altamont, U.S.A. 79 D10 42 43N 74 3W
Altamura, Italy 20 D7 40 49N 16 33 E
Altanbulag, Mongolia 32 A5 50 16N 106 30 E
Altar, Mexico 86 A2 30 40N 111 50W
Altar, Desierto de, Mexico 86 B2 30 10N 112 0W
Altata, Mexico 86 C3 24 30N 108 0W
Altavista, U.S.A. 76 G6 37 6N 79 17W
Altay, China 32 B3 47 48N 88 10 E
Altea, Spain 19 C5 38 38N 0 2W
**Altiplano** = Bolivian Plateau, S. Amer. 90 E4 20 0S 67 30W
Alto Araguaia, Brazil 93 G8 17 15S 53 20W
Alto Cuchumatanes = Cuchumatanes, Sierra de los, Guatemala 88 C1 15 35N 91 25W
Alto del Carmen, Chile 94 B1 28 46S 70 30W
Alto del Inca, Chile 94 A2 24 10S 68 10W
Alto Ligonha, Mozam. 55 F4 15 30S 38 11 E
Alto Molocue, Mozam. 55 F4 15 50S 37 35 E
Alto Paraguay □, Paraguay 94 A4 21 0S 58 30W
Alto Paraná □, Paraguay 95 B5 25 30S 54 50W
Alton, Canada 78 C4 43 54N 80 5W
Alton, U.K. 11 F7 51 9N 0 59W
Alton, Ill., U.S.A. 80 F9 38 53N 90 11W
Alton, N.H., U.S.A. 79 C13 43 27N 71 13W
Altoona, U.S.A. 78 F6 40 31N 78 24W
Altūn Kūprī, Iraq 44 C5 35 45N 44 9 E
Altun Shan, China 32 C3 38 30N 88 0 E
Alturas, U.S.A. 82 F3 41 29N 120 32W
Altus, U.S.A. 81 H5 34 38N 99 20W
Alucra, Turkey 25 F6 40 22N 38 47 E
Alūksne, Latvia 9 H22 57 24N 27 3 E
Alunite, U.S.A. 85 K12 35 59N 114 55W
Alusi, Indonesia 37 F8 7 35S 131 40 E
Alva, U.S.A. 81 G5 36 48N 98 40W
Alvarado, Mexico 87 D5 18 40N 95 50W
Alvarado, U.S.A. 81 J6 32 24N 97 13W
Alvaro Obregón, Presa, Mexico 86 B3 27 55N 109 52W
Alvear, Argentina 94 B4 29 5S 56 30W
Alvesta, Sweden 9 H16 56 54N 14 35 E
Alvin, U.S.A. 81 L7 29 26N 95 15W
Alvinston, Canada 78 D3 42 49N 81 52W
Älvkarleby, Sweden 9 F17 60 34N 17 26 E
Alvord Desert, U.S.A. 82 E4 42 30N 118 25W
Älvsbyn, Sweden 8 D19 65 40N 21 0 E
Alwar, India 42 F7 27 38N 76 34 E
Alxa Zuoqi, China 34 E3 38 50N 105 40 E
Alyangula, Australia 62 A2 13 55S 136 30 E
Alyata = Älät, Azerbaijan 25 G8 39 58N 49 25 E
Alyth, U.K. 12 E5 56 38N 3 13W
Alytus, Lithuania 9 J21 54 24N 24 3 E
Alzada, U.S.A. 80 C2 45 2N 104 25W

Aomen = Macau, China 33 D6 22 16N 113 35 E
Aomori, Japan 30 D10 40 45N 140 45 E
Aomori □, Japan 30 D10 40 45N 140 40 E
Aonla, India 43 E8 28 16N 79 11 E
Aosta, Italy 18 D7 45 45N 7 20 E
Aouker, Mauritania 50 E4 17 40N 10 0W
Aozou, Chad 51 D9 21 45N 17 28 E
Apa →, S. Amer. 94 A4 22 6S 58 2W
Apache, U.S.A. 81 H5 34 54N 98 22W
Apache Junction, U.S.A. 83 K8 33 25N 111 33W
Apalachee B., U.S.A. 77 L4 30 0N 84 0W
Apalachicola, U.S.A. 77 L3 29 43N 84 59W
Apalachicola →, U.S.A. 77 L3 29 43N 84 58W
Apaporis →, Colombia 92 D5 1 23S 69 25W
Aparri, Phil. 37 A6 18 22N 121 38 E
Apatity, Russia 24 A5 67 34N 33 22 E
Apatzingán, Mexico 86 D4 19 0N 102 20W
Apeldoorn, Neths. 15 B5 52 13N 5 57 E
**Apennines** = Appennini, Italy 20 B4 44 0N 10 0 E
Apia, W. Samoa 59 A13 13 50S 171 50W
Apiacás, Serra dos, Brazil 92 E7 9 50S 57 0W
Apizaco, Mexico 87 D5 19 26N 98 9W
Aplao, Peru 92 G4 16 0S 72 40W
Apo, Mt., Phil. 37 C7 6 53N 125 14 E
Apolakkiá, Greece 23 C9 36 5N 27 48 E
Apolakkiá, Órmos, Greece 23 C9 36 5N 27 45 E
Apollo Bay, Australia 63 F3 38 45S 143 40 E
Apolo, Bolivia 92 F5 14 30S 68 30W
Aporé →, Brazil 93 G8 19 27S 50 57W
Apostle Is., U.S.A. 80 B9 47 0N 90 40W
Apóstoles, Argentina 95 B4 28 0S 56 0W
Apostolos Andreas, C., Cyprus 23 D13 35 42N 34 35 E
Apoteri, Guyana 92 C7 4 2N 58 32W
**Appalachian Mts.**, U.S.A. 76 G6 38 0N 80 0W
Appennini, Italy 20 B4 44 0N 10 0 E
Apple Hill, Canada 79 A10 45 13N 74 46W
Apple Valley, U.S.A. 85 L9 34 32N 117 14W
Appleby-in-Westmorland, U.K. 10 C5 54 35N 2 29W
Appleton, U.S.A. 76 C1 44 16N 88 25W
Approuague →, Fr. Guiana 93 C8 4 30N 51 57W
Aprília, Italy 20 D5 41 36N 12 39 E
Apsley, Canada 78 B6 44 45N 78 6W
Apucarana, Brazil 95 A5 23 55S 51 33W
Apure →, Venezuela 92 B5 7 37N 66 25W
Apurimac →, Peru 92 F4 12 17S 73 56W
Āqā Jarī, Iran 45 D6 30 42N 49 50 E
Aqaba = Al 'Aqabah, Jordan 47 F4 29 31N 35 0 E
**Aqaba, G. of**, Red Sea 44 D2 28 15N 33 20 E
'Aqabah, Khalīj al = Aqaba, G. of, Red Sea 44 D2 28 15N 33 20 E
'Aqdā, Iran 45 C7 32 26N 53 37 E
**Aqmola** = Astana, Kazakstan 26 D8 51 10N 71 30 E
Aqrah, Iraq 44 B4 36 46N 43 45 E
Aqtaū, Kazakstan 26 E6 43 39N 51 12 E
Aqtöbe, Kazakstan 25 D10 50 17N 57 10 E
Aquidauana, Brazil 93 H7 20 30S 55 50W
Aquiles Serdán, Mexico 86 B3 28 37N 105 54W
Aquin, Haiti 89 C5 18 16N 73 24W
Aquitain, Bassin, France 18 D3 44 0N 0 30W
Ar Rachidiya, Morocco 50 B5 31 58N 4 20W
Ar Rafid, Syria 47 C4 32 57N 35 52 E
Ar Raḩḩālīyah, Iraq 44 C4 32 44N 43 23 E
Ar Ramādī, Iraq 44 C4 33 25N 43 20 E
Ar Ramthā, Jordan 47 C5 32 34N 36 0 E
Ar Raqqah, Syria 44 C3 35 59N 39 8 E
Ar Rass, Si. Arabia 44 E4 25 50N 43 40 E
Ar Rifā'ī, Iraq 44 D5 31 50N 46 10 E
Ar Riyāḑ, Si. Arabia 46 C4 24 41N 46 42 E
Ar Ru'ays, Qatar 45 E6 26 8N 51 12 E
Ar Rukhaymīyah, Iraq 44 D5 29 22N 45 38 E
Ar Ruqayyidah, Si. Arabia 45 E6 25 21N 49 34 E
Ar Ruṣāfah, Syria 44 C3 35 45N 38 49 E
Ar Ruṭbah, Iraq 44 C4 33 0N 40 15 E
Ara, India 43 G11 25 35N 84 32 E
Arab, U.S.A. 77 H2 34 19N 86 30W
'Arab, Bahr el →, Sudan 51 G11 9 0N 29 30 E
'Arabābād, Iran 45 C8 33 2N 57 41 E
**Arabia**, Asia 28 G8 25 0N 45 0 E
Arabian Desert = Es Sahrâ' Esh Sharqîya, Egypt 51 C12 27 30N 32 30 E
Arabian Gulf = Gulf, The, Asia 45 E6 27 0N 50 0 E
Arabian Sea, Ind. Oc. 29 H10 16 0N 65 0 E
Aracaju, Brazil 93 F11 10 55S 37 4W
Aracati, Brazil 93 D11 4 30S 37 44W
Araçatuba, Brazil 95 A5 21 10S 50 30W
Aracena, Spain 19 D2 37 53N 6 38W
Araçuaí, Brazil 93 G10 16 52S 42 4W
'Arad, Israel 47 D4 31 15N 35 12 E
Arad, Romania 17 E11 46 10N 21 20 E
Arādān, Iran 45 C7 35 21N 52 30 E
Aradhippou, Cyprus 23 E12 34 57N 33 36 E
Arafura Sea, E. Indies 37 F9 9 0S 135 0 E
**Aragón** □, Spain 19 B5 41 25N 0 40W
Aragón →, Spain 19 A5 42 13N 1 44W
Araguacema, Brazil 93 E9 8 50S 49 20W
Araguaia →, Brazil 93 E9 5 21S 48 41W
Araguaína, Brazil 93 E9 7 12S 48 12W
Araguari, Brazil 93 G9 18 38S 48 11W
Araguari →, Brazil 93 C9 1 15N 49 55W
Arain, India 42 F6 26 27N 75 2 E
Arak, Algeria 50 C6 25 20N 3 45 E
Arāk, Iran 45 C6 34 0N 49 40 E
Arakan Coast, Burma 41 K19 19 0N 94 0 E
Arakan Yoma, Burma 41 K19 20 0N 94 40 E
Araks = Aras, Rūd-e →, Azerbaijan 44 B5 40 5N 48 29 E
Aral, Kazakstan 26 E7 46 41N 61 45 E
**Aral Sea**, Asia 26 E7 44 30N 60 0 E
Aral Tengizi = Aral Sea, Asia 26 E7 44 30N 60 0 E
Aralsk = Aral, Kazakstan 26 E7 46 41N 61 45 E
Aralskoye More = Aral Sea, Asia 26 E7 44 30N 60 0 E
Aramac, Australia 62 C4 22 58S 145 14 E
Aran I., Ireland 13 A3 55 0N 8 30W
Aran Is., Ireland 13 C2 53 6N 9 38W
Aranda de Duero, Spain 19 B4 41 39N 3 42W
Arandān, Iran 44 C5 35 23N 46 55 E
Aranjuez, Spain 19 B4 40 1N 3 40W
Aranos, Namibia 56 C2 24 9S 19 7 E
Aransas Pass, U.S.A. 81 M6 27 55N 97 9W
Aranyaprathet, Thailand 38 F4 13 41N 102 30 E
Arapahoe, U.S.A. 80 E5 40 18N 99 54W
Arapey Grande →, Uruguay 94 C4 30 55S 57 49W
Arapgir, Turkey 44 B3 39 5N 38 30 E
Arapiraca, Brazil 93 E11 9 45S 36 39W
Arapongas, Brazil 95 A5 23 29S 51 28W
Ar'ar, Si. Arabia 44 D4 30 59N 41 2 E
Araranguá, Brazil 95 B6 29 0S 49 30W
Araraquara, Brazil 93 H9 21 50S 48 0W
Ararás, Serra das, Brazil 95 B5 25 0S 53 10W
Ararat, Australia 63 F3 37 16S 143 0 E
**Ararat, Mt.** = Ağrı Dağı, Turkey 25 G7 39 50N 44 15 E
Araria, India 43 F12 26 9N 87 33 E
Araripe, Chapada do, Brazil 93 E11 7 20S 40 0W
Araruama, L. de, Brazil 95 A7 22 53S 42 12W
Aras, Rūd-e →, Azerbaijan 44 B5 40 5N 48 29 E
Arauca, Colombia 92 B4 7 0N 70 40W
Arauca →, Venezuela 92 B5 7 24N 66 35W
Arauco, Chile 94 D1 37 16S 73 25W
Araxá, Brazil 93 G9 19 35S 46 55W
Araya, Pen. de, Venezuela 92 A6 10 40N 64 0W
Arba Minch, Ethiopia 46 F2 6 0N 37 30 E
Arbat, Iraq 44 C5 35 26N 45 35 E
Árbatax, Italy 20 E3 39 56N 9 42 E
Arbīl, Iraq 44 B5 36 15N 44 5 E
Arborfield, Canada 73 C8 53 6N 103 39W
Arborg, Canada 73 C9 50 54N 97 13W
Arbroath, U.K. 12 E6 56 34N 2 35W
Arbuckle, U.S.A. 84 F4 39 1N 122 3W
Arcachon, France 18 D3 44 40N 1 10W
Arcade, Calif., U.S.A. 85 L8 34 2N 118 15W
Arcade, N.Y., U.S.A. 78 D6 42 32N 78 25W
Arcadia, Fla., U.S.A. 77 M5 27 13N 81 52W
Arcadia, La., U.S.A. 81 J8 32 33N 92 55W
Arcadia, Pa., U.S.A. 78 F6 40 47N 78 51W
Arcata, U.S.A. 82 F1 40 52N 124 5W
**Archangel** = Arkhangelsk, Russia 24 B7 64 38N 40 36 E
Archbald, U.S.A. 79 E9 41 30N 75 32W
Archer →, Australia 62 A3 13 28S 141 41 E
Archer B., Australia 62 A3 13 20S 141 30 E
Archers Post, Kenya 54 B4 0 35N 37 35 E
**Arches National Park**, U.S.A. 83 G9 38 45N 109 25W
Arckaringa Cr. →, Australia 63 D2 28 10S 135 22 E
Arco, U.S.A. 82 E7 43 38N 113 18W
Arcos de la Frontera, Spain 19 D3 36 45N 5 49W
Arcot, India 40 N11 12 53N 79 20 E
Arctic Bay, Canada 69 A11 73 1N 85 7W
**Arctic Ocean**, Arctic 4 B18 78 0N 160 0W
Arctic Red River = Tsiigehtchic, Canada 68 B6 67 15N 134 0W
Arda →, Bulgaria 21 D12 41 40N 26 30 E
Ardabīl, Iran 45 B6 38 15N 48 18 E
Ardakān = Sepīdān, Iran 45 D7 30 20N 52 5 E
Ardakān, Iran 45 C7 32 19N 53 59 E
Ardee, Ireland 13 C5 53 52N 6 33W
Arden, Canada 78 B8 44 43N 76 56W
Arden, Calif., U.S.A. 84 G5 38 36N 121 33W
Arden, Nev., U.S.A. 85 J11 36 1N 115 14W
Ardenne, Belgium 16 D3 49 50N 5 5 E
**Ardennes** = Ardenne, Belgium 16 D3 49 50N 5 5 E
Arderin, Ireland 13 C4 53 2N 7 39W
Ardestān, Iran 45 C7 33 20N 52 25 E
Ardivachar Pt., U.K. 12 D1 57 23N 7 26W
Ardlethan, Australia 63 E4 34 22S 146 53 E
Ardmore, Okla., U.S.A. 81 H6 34 10N 97 8W
Ardmore, Pa., U.S.A. 79 G9 39 58N 75 18W
Ardnamurchan, Pt. of, U.K. 12 E2 56 43N 6 14W
Ardnave Pt., U.K. 12 F2 55 53N 6 20W
Ardrossan, Australia 63 E2 34 26S 137 53 E
Ardrossan, U.K. 12 F4 55 39N 4 49W
Ards Pen., U.K. 13 B6 54 33N 5 34W
Arecibo, Puerto Rico 89 C6 18 29N 66 43W
Areia Branca, Brazil 93 E11 5 0S 37 0W
Arena, Pt., U.S.A. 84 G3 38 57N 123 44W
Arenal, Honduras 88 C2 15 21N 86 50W
Arendal, Norway 9 G13 58 28N 8 46 E
**Arequipa**, Peru 92 G4 16 20S 71 30W
Arévalo, Spain 19 B3 41 3N 4 43W
Arezzo, Italy 20 C4 43 25N 11 53 E
Arga, Turkey 44 B3 38 21N 37 59 E
Arganda, Spain 19 B4 40 19N 3 26W
Argenta, Canada 72 C5 50 11N 116 56W
Argentan, France 18 B3 48 45N 0 1W
Argentário, Mte., Italy 20 C4 42 24N 11 9 E
Argentia, Canada 71 C9 47 18N 53 58W
**Argentina** ■, S. Amer. 96 D3 35 0S 66 0W
Argentina Is., Antarctica 5 C17 66 0S 64 0W
Argentino, L., Argentina 96 G2 50 10S 73 0W
Argeș →, Romania 17 F14 44 5N 26 38 E
Arghandab →, Afghan. 42 D1 31 30N 64 15 E
Argolikós Kólpos, Greece 21 F10 37 20N 22 52 E
Árgos, Greece 21 F10 37 40N 22 43 E
Argostólion, Greece 21 E9 38 12N 20 33 E
Arguello, Pt., U.S.A. 85 L6 34 35N 120 39W
Arguineguín, Canary Is. 22 G4 27 46N 15 41W
Argun →, Russia 27 D13 53 20N 121 28 E
Argus Pk., U.S.A. 85 K9 35 52N 117 26W
Argyle, L., Australia 60 C4 16 20S 128 40 E
Argyll & Bute □, U.K. 12 E3 56 13N 5 28W
**Århus**, Denmark 9 H14 56 8N 10 11 E
Ariadnoye, Russia 30 B7 45 8N 134 25 E
Ariamsvlei, Namibia 56 D2 28 9S 19 51 E
Ariana, Tunisia 51 A7 36 52N 10 12 E
Arica, Chile 92 G4 18 32S 70 20W
Arica, Colombia 92 D4 2 0S 71 50W
Arico, Canary Is. 22 F3 28 9N 16 29W
Arid, C., Australia 61 F3 34 1S 123 10 E
Arida, Japan 31 G7 34 5N 135 8 E
Arílla, Ákra, Greece 23 A3 39 43N 19 39 E
Arima, Trin. & Tob. 89 D7 10 38N 61 17W
Arinos →, Brazil 92 F7 10 25S 58 20W
Ario de Rosales, Mexico 86 D4 19 12N 102 0W
Aripuanã, Brazil 92 E6 9 25S 60 30W
Aripuanã →, Brazil 92 E6 5 7S 60 25W
Ariquemes, Brazil 92 E6 9 55S 63 6W
Arisaig, U.K. 12 E3 56 55N 5 51W
Aristazabal I., Canada 72 C3 52 40N 129 10W
Arivonimamo, Madag. 57 B8 19 1S 47 11 E
Arizaro, Salar de, Argentina 94 A2 24 40S 67 50W
**Arizona**, Argentina 94 D2 35 45S 65 25W
Arizona □, U.S.A. 83 J8 34 0N 112 0W
Arizpe, Mexico 86 A2 30 20N 110 11W
Arjeplog, Sweden 8 D18 66 3N 18 2 E
Arjona, Colombia 92 A3 10 14N 75 22W
Arjuna, Indonesia 37 G15 7 49S 112 34 E
Arka, Russia 27 C15 60 15N 142 0 E
Arkadelphia, U.S.A. 81 H8 34 7N 93 4W
Arkaig, L., U.K. 12 E3 56 59N 5 10W
Arkalyk = Arqalyk, Kazakstan 26 D7 50 13N 66 50 E
**Arkansas** □, U.S.A. 81 H8 35 0N 92 30W
**Arkansas** →, U.S.A. 81 J9 33 47N 91 4W
Arkansas City, U.S.A. 81 G6 37 4N 97 2W
Arkaroola, Australia 63 E2 30 20S 139 22 E
Arkhángelos, Greece 23 C10 36 13N 28 7 E
Arkhangelsk, Russia 24 B7 64 38N 40 36 E
Arki, India 42 D7 31 9N 76 58 E
Arklow, Ireland 13 D5 52 48N 6 10W
Arkport, U.S.A. 78 D7 42 24N 77 42W
Arkticheskiy, Mys, Russia 27 A10 81 10N 95 0 E
Arkville, U.S.A. 79 D10 42 9N 74 37W
Arlanzón →, Spain 19 A3 42 3N 4 17W
Arlbergpass, Austria 16 E6 47 9N 10 12 E
Arles, France 18 E6 43 41N 4 40 E
Arlington, S. Africa 57 D4 28 1S 27 53 E
Arlington, N.Y., U.S.A. 79 E11 41 42N 73 54W
Arlington, Oreg., U.S.A. 82 D3 45 43N 120 12W
Arlington, S. Dak., U.S.A. 80 C6 44 22N 97 8W
Arlington, Tex., U.S.A. 81 J6 32 44N 97 7W
**Arlington**, Va., U.S.A. 76 F7 38 53N 77 7W
Arlington, Vt., U.S.A. 79 C11 43 5N 73 9W
Arlington, Wash., U.S.A. 84 B4 48 12N 122 8W
Arlington Heights, U.S.A. 76 D2 42 5N 87 59W
Arlit, Niger 50 E7 19 0N 7 38 E
Arlon, Belgium 15 E5 49 42N 5 49 E
Arltunga, Australia 62 C1 23 26S 134 41 E
**Armagh**, U.K. 13 B5 54 21N 6 39W
Armagh □, U.K. 13 B5 54 18N 6 37W
Armavir, Russia 25 E7 45 2N 41 7 E
**Armenia**, Colombia 92 C3 4 35N 75 45W
Armenia ■, Asia 25 F7 40 20N 45 0 E
Armenistís, Ákra, Greece 23 C9 36 8N 27 42 E
Armidale, Australia 63 E5 30 30S 151 40 E
Armour, U.S.A. 80 D5 43 19N 98 21W
Armstrong, B.C., Canada 72 C5 50 25N 119 10W
Armstrong, Ont., Canada 70 B2 50 18N 89 4W
Arnarfjörður, Iceland 8 D2 65 48N 23 40W
Arnaud →, Canada 69 C13 60 0N 70 0W
Arnauti, C., Cyprus 23 D11 35 6N 32 17 E
Arnett, U.S.A. 81 G5 36 8N 99 46W
**Arnhem**, Neths. 15 C5 51 58N 5 55 E
Arnhem, C., Australia 62 A2 12 20S 137 30 E
Arnhem B., Australia 62 A2 12 20S 136 10 E
Arnhem Land, Australia 62 A1 13 10S 134 30 E
Arno →, Italy 20 C4 43 41N 10 17 E
Arno Bay, Australia 63 E2 33 54S 136 34 E
Arnold, U.K. 10 D6 53 1N 1 7W
Arnold, U.S.A. 84 G6 38 15N 120 20W
Arnot, Canada 73 B9 55 56N 96 41W
Arnøy, Norway 8 A19 70 9N 20 40 E
Arnprior, Canada 79 A8 45 26N 76 21W
Arnsberg, Germany 16 C5 51 24N 8 5 E
Aroab, Namibia 56 D2 26 41S 19 39 E
Aron, India 42 G6 25 57N 77 56 E
Arqalyk, Kazakstan 26 D7 50 13N 66 50 E
Arrah = Ara, India 43 G11 25 35N 84 32 E
Arran, U.K. 12 F3 55 34N 5 12W
Arras, France 18 A5 50 17N 2 46 E
Arrecife, Canary Is. 22 F6 28 57N 13 37W
Arrecifes, Argentina 94 C3 34 6S 60 9W
Arrée, Mts. d', France 18 B2 48 26N 3 55W
Arriaga, Chiapas, Mexico 87 D6 16 15N 93 52W
Arriaga, San Luis Potosí, Mexico 86 C4 21 55N 101 23W
Arrilalah, Australia 62 C3 23 43S 143 54 E
Arrino, Australia 61 E2 29 30S 115 40 E
Arrow, L., Ireland 13 B3 54 3N 8 19W
Arrowhead, L., U.S.A. 85 L9 34 16N 117 10W
Arrowtown, N.Z. 59 L2 44 57S 168 50 E
Arroyo Grande, U.S.A. 85 K6 35 7N 120 35W
Ars, Iran 44 B5 37 9N 47 46 E
Arsenault L., Canada 73 B7 55 6N 108 32W
Arsenev, Russia 30 B6 44 10N 133 15 E
Árta, Greece 21 E9 39 8N 21 2 E
Artà, Spain 22 B10 39 41N 3 21 E
Arteaga, Mexico 86 D4 18 50N 102 20W
Artem, Russia 30 C6 43 22N 132 13 E
Artemovsk, Russia 27 D10 54 45N 93 35 E
Artemovsk, Ukraine 25 E6 48 35N 38 0 E
Artesia = Mosomane, Botswana 56 C4 24 2S 26 19 E
Artesia, U.S.A. 81 J2 32 51N 104 24W
Arthur, Canada 78 C4 43 50N 80 32W
Arthur →, Australia 62 G3 41 2S 144 40 E
Arthur Cr. →, Australia 62 C2 22 30S 136 25 E
Arthur Pt., Australia 62 C5 22 7S 150 3 E
Arthur River, Australia 61 F2 33 20S 117 2 E
Arthur's Pass, N.Z. 59 K3 42 54S 171 35 E
Arthur's Town, Bahamas 89 B4 24 38N 75 42W
Artigas, Uruguay 94 C4 30 20S 56 30W
Artillery L., Canada 73 A7 63 9N 107 52W
Artois, France 18 A5 50 20N 2 30 E
Artrutx, C. de, Spain 22 B10 39 55N 3 49 E
Artsyz, Ukraine 17 E15 46 4N 29 26 E
Artvin, Turkey 25 F7 41 14N 41 44 E
Aru, Kepulauan, Indonesia 37 F8 6 0S 134 30 E
Aru Is. = Aru, Kepulauan, Indonesia 37 F8 6 0S 134 30 E
Arua, Uganda 54 B3 3 1N 30 58 E
Aruanã, Brazil 93 F8 14 54S 51 10W
**Aruba** ■, W. Indies 89 D6 12 30N 70 0W
Arucas, Canary Is. 22 F4 28 7N 15 32W
Arun →, Nepal 43 F12 26 55N 87 10 E
Arun →, U.K. 11 G7 50 49N 0 33W
**Arunachal Pradesh** □, India 41 F19 28 0N 95 0 E
Arusha, Tanzania 54 C4 3 20S 36 40 E
Arusha □, Tanzania 54 C4 4 0S 36 30 E
Arusha Chini, Tanzania 54 C4 3 32S 37 20 E
Aruwimi →, Dem. Rep. of the Congo 54 B1 1 13N 23 36 E
Arvada, Colo., U.S.A. 80 F2 39 48N 105 5W
Arvada, Wyo., U.S.A. 82 D10 44 39N 106 8W
Árvi, Greece 23 E7 34 59N 25 28 E
Arviat, Canada 73 A10 61 6N 93 59W
Arvidsjaur, Sweden 8 D18 65 35N 19 10 E
Arvika, Sweden 9 G15 59 40N 12 36 E
Arvin, U.S.A. 85 K8 35 12N 118 50W
Arwal, India 43 G11 25 15N 84 41 E
Arxan, China 33 B6 47 11N 119 57 E
Aryirádhes, Greece 23 B3 39 27N 19 58 E
Aryiroúpolis, Greece 23 D6 35 17N 24 20 E
Arys, Kazakstan 26 E7 42 26N 68 48 E
Arzamas, Russia 24 C7 55 27N 43 55 E
Aş Şadr, U.A.E. 45 E7 24 40N 54 41 E
Aş Şafā, Syria 47 B6 33 10N 37 0 E
As Saffānīyah, Si. Arabia 45 E6 27 55N 48 50 E
As Safīrah, Syria 44 B3 36 5N 37 21 E
Aş Şahm, Oman 45 E8 24 10N 56 53 E
As Sājir, Si. Arabia 44 E5 25 11N 44 36 E
As Salamīyah, Syria 44 C3 35 1N 37 2 E
As Salmān, Iraq 44 D5 30 30N 44 32 E
As Salṭ, Jordan 47 C4 32 2N 35 43 E
As Sal'w'a, Qatar 45 E6 24 23N 50 50 E
As Samāwah, Iraq 44 D5 31 15N 45 15 E
As Sanamayn, Syria 47 B5 33 3N 36 10 E
As Sohar = Şuḩār, Oman 45 E8 24 20N 56 40 E
As Sukhnah, Syria 44 C3 34 52N 38 52 E
As Sulaymānīyah, Iraq 44 C5 35 35N 45 29 E
As Sulaymī, Si. Arabia 44 E4 26 17N 41 21 E
As Sulayyil, Si. Arabia 46 C4 20 27N 45 34 E
As Summān, Si. Arabia 44 E6 25 0N 47 0 E
As Suwaydā', Syria 47 C5 32 40N 36 30 E
As Suwaydā' □, Syria 47 C5 32 45N 36 45 E
As Suwayq, Oman 45 F8 23 51N 57 26 E
Aş Şuwayrah, Iraq 44 C5 32 55N 45 0 E
Asab, Namibia 56 D2 25 30S 18 0 E
Asad, Buḩayrat al, Syria 44 C3 36 0N 38 15 E
Asahi-Gawa →, Japan 31 G6 34 36N 133 58 E
Asahigawa, Japan 30 C11 43 46N 142 22 E
Asamankese, Ghana 50 G5 5 50N 0 40W
Asan →, India 43 F8 26 37N 78 24 E
Asansol, India 43 H12 23 40N 87 1 E
Asbesberge, S. Africa 56 D3 29 0S 23 0 E
Asbestos, Canada 71 C5 45 47N 71 58W
Asbury Park, U.S.A. 79 F10 40 13N 74 1W
**Ascensión**, Mexico 86 A3 31 6N 107 59W
Ascensión, B. de la, Mexico 87 D7 19 50N 87 20W
Ascension I., Atl. Oc. 49 G2 8 0S 14 15W
Aschaffenburg, Germany 16 D5 49 58N 9 6 E
Aschersleben, Germany 16 C6 51 45N 11 29 E
Áscoli Piceno, Italy 20 C5 42 51N 13 34 E
Ascope, Peru 92 E3 7 46S 79 8W
Ascotán, Chile 94 A2 21 45S 68 17W
Aseb, Eritrea 46 E3 13 0N 42 40 E
Asela, Ethiopia 46 F2 8 0N 39 0 E
Asenovgrad, Bulgaria 21 C11 42 1N 24 51 E
Aserradero, Mexico 86 C3 23 40N 105 43W
Asgata, Cyprus 23 E12 34 46N 33 15 E
Ash Fork, U.S.A. 83 J7 35 13N 112 29W
Ash Grove, U.S.A. 81 G8 37 19N 93 35W
Ash Shabakah, Iraq 44 D4 30 49N 43 39 E
Ash Shamāl □, Lebanon 47 A5 34 25N 36 0 E
Ash Shāmīyah, Iraq 44 D5 31 55N 44 35 E
Ash Shāriqah, U.A.E. 45 E7 25 23N 55 26 E
Ash Sharmah, Si. Arabia 44 D2 28 1N 35 16 E
Ash Sharqāt, Iraq 44 C4 35 27N 43 16 E
Ash Sharqi, Al Jabal, Lebanon 47 B5 33 40N 36 10 E
Ash Shaṭrah, Iraq 44 D5 31 30N 46 10 E
Ash Shawbak, Jordan 44 D2 30 32N 35 34 E
Ash Shawmari, J., Jordan 47 E5 30 35N 36 35 E
Ash Shināfiyah, Iraq 44 D5 31 35N 44 39 E
Ash Shu'bah, Si. Arabia 44 D5 28 54N 44 44 E
Ash Shumlūl, Si. Arabia 44 E5 26 31N 47 20 E
Ash Shūr'a, Iraq 44 C4 35 58N 43 13 E
Ash Shurayf, Si. Arabia 44 E3 25 43N 39 14 E
Ash Shuwayfāt, Lebanon 47 B4 33 45N 35 30 E
Asha, Russia 24 D10 55 0N 57 16 E
Ashau, Vietnam 38 D6 16 6N 107 22 E
Ashbourne, U.K. 10 D6 53 2N 1 43W
Ashburn, U.S.A. 77 K4 31 43N 83 39W
Ashburton, N.Z. 59 K3 43 53S 171 48 E
Ashburton →, Australia 60 D1 21 40S 114 56 E
Ashcroft, Canada 72 C4 50 40N 121 20W
Ashdod, Israel 47 D3 31 49N 34 35 E
Ashdown, U.S.A. 81 J7 33 40N 94 8W
Asheboro, U.S.A. 77 H6 35 43N 79 49W
Ashern, Canada 73 C9 51 11N 98 21W
Asherton, U.S.A. 81 L5 28 27N 99 46W
Asheville, U.S.A. 77 H4 35 36N 82 33W
Ashewat, Pakistan 42 D3 31 22N 68 32 E
Asheweig →, Canada 70 B2 54 17N 87 12W
Ashford, Australia 63 D5 29 15S 151 3 E
Ashford, U.K. 11 F8 51 8N 0 53 E
**Ashgabat**, Turkmenistan 26 F6 38 0N 57 50 E
Ashibetsu, Japan 30 C11 43 31N 142 11 E
Ashikaga, Japan 31 F9 36 28N 139 29 E
Ashington, U.K. 10 B6 55 11N 1 33W
Ashizuri-Zaki, Japan 31 H6 32 44N 133 0 E
Ashkarkot, Afghan. 42 C2 33 3N 67 58 E
Ashkhabad = Ashgabat, Turkmenistan 26 F6 38 0N 57 50 E
Āshkhāneh, Iran 45 B8 37 26N 56 55 E
Ashland, Kans., U.S.A. 81 G5 37 11N 99 46W
Ashland, Ky., U.S.A. 76 F4 38 28N 82 38W
Ashland, Mont., U.S.A. 82 D10 45 36N 106 16W
Ashland, Ohio, U.S.A. 78 F2 40 52N 82 19W
Ashland, Oreg., U.S.A. 82 E2 42 12N 122 43W
Ashland, Pa., U.S.A. 79 F8 40 45N 76 22W
Ashland, Va., U.S.A. 76 G7 37 46N 77 29W
Ashland, Wis., U.S.A. 80 B9 46 35N 90 53W
Ashley, N. Dak., U.S.A. 80 B5 46 2N 99 22W
Ashley, Pa., U.S.A. 79 E9 41 12N 75 55W
Ashmore Reef, Australia 60 B3 12 14S 123 5 E
Ashmyany, Belarus 9 J21 54 26N 25 52 E
Ashokan Reservoir, U.S.A. 79 E10 41 56N 74 13W
Ashqelon, Israel 47 D3 31 42N 34 35 E
Ashta, India 42 H7 23 1N 76 43 E
Ashtabula, U.S.A. 78 E4 41 52N 80 47W
Ashton, S. Africa 56 E3 33 50S 20 5 E
Ashton, U.S.A. 82 D8 44 4N 111 27W
Ashuanipi, L., Canada 71 B6 52 45N 66 15W
Ashville, U.S.A. 78 F6 40 34N 78 33W
**Asia** 28 E11 45 0N 75 0 E
Asia, Kepulauan, Indonesia 37 D8 1 0N 131 13 E
Āsīā Bak, Iran 45 C6 35 19N 50 30 E
Asifabad, India 40 K11 19 20N 79 24 E
Asinara, Italy 20 D3 41 4N 8 16 E
Asinara, G. dell', Italy 20 D3 41 0N 8 30 E
Asino, Russia 26 D9 57 0N 86 0 E
Asipovichy, Belarus 17 B15 53 19N 28 33 E
'Asīr □, Si. Arabia 46 D3 18 40N 42 30 E
Asir, Ras, Somali Rep. 46 E5 11 55N 51 10 E
Askersund, Sweden 9 G16 58 53N 14 55 E
Askham, S. Africa 56 D3 26 59S 20 47 E

Askim, Norway 9 G14 59 35N 11 10 E
Askja, Iceland 8 D5 65 3N 16 48W
Askøy, Norway 9 F11 60 29N 5 10 E
**Asmara** = Asmera, Eritrea 46 D2 15 19N 38 55 E
Asmera, Eritrea 46 D2 15 19N 38 55 E
Åsnen, Sweden 9 H16 56 37N 14 45 E
Aspen, U.S.A. 83 G10 39 11N 106 49W
Aspermont, U.S.A. 81 J4 33 8N 100 14W
Aspiring, Mt., N.Z. 59 L2 44 23S 168 46 E
Asprókavos, Ákra, Greece 23 B4 39 21N 20 6 E
Aspur, India 42 H6 23 58N 74 7 E
Asquith, Canada 73 C7 52 8N 107 13W
**Assam** □, India 41 G18 26 0N 93 0 E
Asse, Belgium 15 D4 50 24N 4 10 E
Assen, Neths. 15 A6 53 0N 6 35 E
Assiniboia, Canada 73 D7 49 40N 105 59W
Assiniboine →, Canada 73 D9 49 53N 97 8W
Assiniboine, Mt., Canada 72 C5 50 52N 115 39W
Assis, Brazil 95 A5 22 40S 50 20W
Assisi, Italy 20 C5 43 4N 12 37 E
Assynt, L., U.K. 12 C3 58 10N 5 3W
Astana, Kazakstan 26 D8 51 10N 71 30 E
Āstāneh, Iran 45 B6 37 17N 49 59 E
Astara, Azerbaijan 25 G8 38 30N 48 50 E
Asteroúsia, Greece 23 E7 34 59N 25 3 E
Asti, Italy 18 D8 44 54N 8 12 E
Astipálaia, Greece 21 F12 36 32N 26 22 E
Astorga, Spain 19 A2 42 29N 6 8W
Astoria, U.S.A. 84 D3 46 11N 123 50W
**Astrakhan**, Russia 25 E8 46 25N 48 5 E
**Asturias** □, Spain 19 A3 43 15N 6 0W
**Asunción**, Paraguay 94 B4 25 10S 57 30W
Asunción Nochixtlán, Mexico 87 D5 17 28N 97 14W
Aswa →, Uganda 54 B3 3 43N 31 55 E
**Aswân**, Egypt 51 D12 24 4N 32 57 E
Aswân High Dam = Sadd el Aali, Egypt 51 D12 23 54N 32 54 E
Asyût, Egypt 51 C12 27 11N 31 4 E
At Ṭafilah, Jordan 47 E4 30 45N 35 30 E
Aṭ Ṭā'if, Si. Arabia 46 C3 21 5N 40 27 E
Aṭ Ṭirāq, Si. Arabia 44 E5 27 19N 44 33 E
Aṭ Tubayq, Si. Arabia 44 D3 29 30N 37 0 E
Atacama □, Chile 94 B2 27 30S 70 0W
**Atacama, Desierto de**, Chile 94 A2 24 0S 69 20W
Atacama, Salar de, Chile 94 A2 23 30S 68 20W
Atalaya, Peru 92 F4 10 45S 73 50W
Atalaya de Femes, Canary Is. 22 F6 28 56N 13 47W
Atami, Japan 31 G9 35 5N 139 4 E
Atapupu, Indonesia 37 F6 9 0S 124 51 E
Atâr, Mauritania 50 D3 20 30N 13 5W
Atari, Pakistan 42 D6 30 56N 74 2 E
Atascadero, U.S.A. 84 K6 35 29N 120 40W
Atasu, Kazakstan 26 E8 48 30N 71 0 E
Atatürk Barajı, Turkey 25 G6 37 28N 38 30 E
Atauro, Indonesia 37 F7 8 10S 125 30 E
Atbara, Sudan 51 E12 17 42N 33 59 E
'Atbara →, Sudan 51 E12 17 40N 33 56 E
Atbasar, Kazakstan 26 D7 51 48N 68 20 E
Atchafalaya B., U.S.A. 81 L9 29 25N 91 25W
Atchison, U.S.A. 80 F7 39 34N 95 7W
Āteshān, Iran 45 C7 35 35N 52 37 E
Ath, Belgium 15 D3 50 38N 3 47 E
Athabasca, Canada 72 C6 54 45N 113 20W
Athabasca →, Canada 73 B6 58 40N 110 50W
**Athabasca, L.**, Canada 73 B7 59 15N 109 15W
Athboy, Ireland 13 C5 53 37N 6 56W
Athenry, Ireland 13 C3 53 18N 8 44W
**Athens** = Athínai, Greece 21 F10 37 58N 23 46 E
Athens, Ala., U.S.A. 77 H2 34 48N 86 58W
Athens, Ga., U.S.A. 77 J4 33 57N 83 23W
Athens, N.Y., U.S.A. 79 D11 42 16N 73 49W
Athens, Ohio, U.S.A. 76 F4 39 20N 82 6W
Athens, Pa., U.S.A. 79 E8 41 57N 76 31W
Athens, Tenn., U.S.A. 77 H3 35 27N 84 36W
Athens, Tex., U.S.A. 81 J7 32 12N 95 51W
Atherley, Canada 78 B5 44 37N 79 20W
Atherton, Australia 62 B4 17 17S 145 30 E
Athienou, Cyprus 23 D12 35 3N 33 32 E
Athínai, Greece 21 F10 37 58N 23 46 E
Athlone, Ireland 13 C4 53 25N 7 56W
Athna, Cyprus 23 D12 35 3N 33 47 E
Athol, U.S.A. 79 D12 42 36N 72 14W
Atholl, Forest of, U.K. 12 E5 56 51N 3 50W
Atholville, Canada 71 C6 47 59N 66 43W
Áthos, Greece 21 D11 40 9N 24 22 E
Athy, Ireland 13 C5 53 0N 7 0W
Ati, Chad 51 F9 13 13N 18 20 E
Atiak, Uganda 54 B3 3 12N 32 2 E
Atik L., Canada 73 B9 55 15N 96 0W
Atikameg →, Canada 70 B3 52 30N 82 46W
Atikokan, Canada 70 C1 48 45N 91 37W
Atikonak L., Canada 71 B7 52 40N 64 32W
Atka, Russia 27 C16 60 50N 151 48 E
Atka I., U.S.A. 68 C2 52 7N 174 30W
Atkinson, U.S.A. 80 D5 42 32N 98 59W
**Atlanta**, Ga., U.S.A. 77 J3 33 45N 84 23W
Atlanta, Tex., U.S.A. 81 J7 33 7N 94 10W
Atlantic, U.S.A. 80 E7 41 24N 95 1W
**Atlantic City**, U.S.A. 76 F8 39 21N 74 27W
**Atlantic Ocean** 2 E9 0 0 20 0W
**Atlas Mts.** = Haut Atlas, Morocco 50 B4 32 30N 5 0W
Atlin, Canada 72 B2 59 31N 133 41W
Atlin, L., Canada 72 B2 59 26N 133 45W
Atlin Prov. Park, Canada 72 B2 59 10N 134 30W
Atmore, U.S.A. 77 K2 31 2N 87 29W
Atoka, U.S.A. 81 H6 34 23N 96 8W
Atolia, U.S.A. 85 K9 35 19N 117 37W
Atrai →, Bangla. 43 G13 24 7N 89 22 E
Atrak = Atrek →, Turkmenistan 45 B8 37 35N 53 58 E
Atrauli, India 42 E8 28 2N 78 20 E
Atrek →, Turkmenistan 45 B8 37 35N 53 58 E
Atsuta, Japan 30 C10 43 24N 141 26 E
Attalla, U.S.A. 77 H2 34 1N 86 6W
Attapu, Laos 38 E6 14 48N 106 50 E
Attáviros, Greece 23 C9 36 12N 27 50 E
Attawapiskat, Canada 70 B3 52 56N 82 24W
Attawapiskat →, Canada 70 B3 52 57N 82 18W
Attawapiskat L., Canada 70 B2 52 18N 87 54W
Attica, Ind., U.S.A. 76 E2 40 18N 87 15W
Attica, Ohio, U.S.A. 78 E2 41 4N 82 53W
Attikamagen L., Canada 71 B6 55 0N 66 30W
Attleboro, U.S.A. 79 E13 41 57N 71 17W
Attock, Pakistan 42 C5 33 52N 72 20 E
Attopeu = Attapu, Laos 38 E6 14 48N 106 50 E
Attu I., U.S.A. 68 C1 52 55N 172 55 E
Attur, India 40 P11 11 35N 78 30 E
Atuel →, Argentina 94 D2 36 17S 66 50W
Åtvidaberg, Sweden 9 G17 58 12N 16 0 E
Atwater, U.S.A. 84 H6 37 21N 120 37W
Atwood, Canada 78 C3 43 40N 81 1W
Atwood, U.S.A. 80 F4 39 48N 101 3W
Atyraū, Kazakstan 25 E9 47 5N 52 0 E
Au Sable, U.S.A. 78 B1 44 25N 83 20W
Au Sable →, U.S.A. 76 C4 44 25N 83 20W
Au Sable Forks, U.S.A. 79 B11 44 27N 73 41W
Au Sable Pt., U.S.A. 78 B1 44 20N 83 20W
Aubagne, France 18 E6 43 17N 5 37 E
Aubarca, C. d', Spain 22 B7 39 4N 1 22 E
Aube →, France 18 B5 48 34N 3 43 E
Auberry, U.S.A. 84 H7 37 7N 119 29W
Auburn, Ala., U.S.A. 77 J3 32 36N 85 29W
Auburn, Calif., U.S.A. 84 G5 38 54N 121 4W
Auburn, Ind., U.S.A. 76 E3 41 22N 85 4W
Auburn, Maine, U.S.A. 77 C10 44 6N 70 14W
Auburn, N.Y., U.S.A. 79 D8 42 56N 76 34W
Auburn, Nebr., U.S.A. 80 E7 40 23N 95 51W
Auburn, Pa., U.S.A. 79 F8 40 36N 76 6W
Auburn, Wash., U.S.A. 84 C4 47 18N 122 14W
Auburn Ra., Australia 63 D5 25 15S 150 30 E
Aubusson, France 18 D5 45 57N 2 11 E
Auch, France 18 E4 43 39N 0 36 E
**Auckland**, N.Z. 59 G5 36 52S 174 46 E
Auckland Is., Pac. Oc. 64 N8 50 40S 166 5 E
Aude →, France 18 E5 43 13N 3 14 E
Auden, Canada 70 B2 50 14N 87 53W
Audubon, U.S.A. 80 E7 41 43N 94 56W
Augathella, Australia 63 D4 25 48S 146 35 E
Aughnacloy, U.K. 13 B5 54 25N 6 59W
Augrabies Falls, S. Africa 56 D3 28 35S 20 20 E
**Augsburg**, Germany 16 D6 48 25N 10 52 E
Augusta, Australia 61 F2 34 19S 115 9 E
Augusta, Italy 20 F6 37 13N 15 13 E
Augusta, Ark., U.S.A. 81 H9 35 17N 91 22W
Augusta, Ga., U.S.A. 77 J5 33 28N 81 58W
Augusta, Kans., U.S.A. 81 G6 37 41N 96 59W
**Augusta**, Maine, U.S.A. 69 D13 44 19N 69 47W
Augusta, Mont., U.S.A. 82 C7 47 30N 112 24W
Augustów, Poland 17 B12 53 51N 23 0 E
Augustus, Mt., Australia 61 D2 24 20S 116 50 E
Augustus I., Australia 60 C3 15 20S 124 30 E
Aukum, U.S.A. 84 G6 38 34N 120 43W
Auld, L., Australia 60 D3 22 25S 123 50 E
Ault, U.S.A. 80 E2 40 35N 104 44W
Aunis, France 18 C3 46 5N 0 50W
Auponhia, Indonesia 37 E7 1 58S 125 27 E
Aur, Pulau, Malaysia 39 L5 2 35N 104 10 E
Auraiya, India 43 F8 26 28N 79 33 E
Aurangabad, Bihar, India 43 G11 24 45N 84 18 E
Aurangabad, Maharashtra, India 40 K9 19 50N 75 23 E
Aurich, Germany 16 B4 53 28N 7 28 E
Aurillac, France 18 D5 44 55N 2 26 E
Aurora, Canada 78 C5 44 0N 79 28W
Aurora, S. Africa 56 E2 32 40S 18 29 E
Aurora, Colo., U.S.A. 80 F2 39 44N 104 52W
Aurora, Ill., U.S.A. 76 E1 41 45N 88 19W
Aurora, Mo., U.S.A. 81 G8 36 58N 93 43W
Aurora, N.Y., U.S.A. 79 D8 42 45N 76 42W
Aurora, Nebr., U.S.A. 80 E6 40 52N 98 0W
Aurora, Ohio, U.S.A. 78 E3 41 21N 81 20W
Aurukun, Australia 62 A3 13 20S 141 45 E
Aus, Namibia 56 D2 26 35S 16 12 E
Ausable →, Canada 78 C3 43 19N 81 46W
**Auschwitz** = Oświęcim, Poland 17 C10 50 2N 19 11 E
Austin, Minn., U.S.A. 80 D8 43 40N 92 58W
Austin, Nev., U.S.A. 82 G5 39 30N 117 4W
Austin, Pa., U.S.A. 78 E6 41 38N 78 6W
**Austin**, Tex., U.S.A. 81 K6 30 17N 97 45W
Austin, L., Australia 61 E2 27 40S 118 0 E
Austin I., Canada 73 A10 61 10N 94 0W
Austra, Norway 8 D14 65 8N 11 55 E
Austral Is. = Tubuai Is., Pac. Oc. 65 K13 25 0S 150 0W
Austral Seamount Chain, Pac. Oc. 65 K13 24 0S 150 0W
**Australia** ■, Oceania 64 K5 23 0S 135 0 E
**Australian Capital Territory** □, Australia 63 F4 35 30S 149 0 E
Australind, Australia 61 F2 33 17S 115 42 E
**Austria** ■, Europe 16 E8 47 0N 14 0 E
Austvågøy, Norway 8 B16 68 20N 14 40 E
Autlán, Mexico 86 D4 19 40N 104 30W
Autun, France 18 C6 46 58N 4 17 E
**Auvergne**, France 18 D5 45 20N 3 15 E
Auvergne, Mts. d', France 18 D5 45 20N 2 55 E
Auxerre, France 18 C5 47 48N 3 32 E
Ava, U.S.A. 81 G8 36 57N 92 40W
Avallon, France 18 C5 47 30N 3 53 E
Avalon, U.S.A. 85 M8 33 21N 118 20W
Avalon Pen., Canada 71 C9 47 30N 53 20W
Avanos, Turkey 44 B2 38 43N 34 51 E
Avaré, Brazil 95 A6 23 4S 48 58W
Avawatz Mts., U.S.A. 85 K10 35 40N 116 30W
Aveiro, Brazil 93 D7 3 10S 55 5W
Aveiro, Portugal 19 B1 40 37N 8 38W
Āvej, Iran 45 C6 35 40N 49 15 E
Avellaneda, Argentina 94 C4 34 50S 58 10W
Avellino, Italy 20 D6 40 54N 14 47 E
Avenal, U.S.A. 84 K6 36 0N 120 8W
Aversa, Italy 20 D6 40 58N 14 12 E
Avery, U.S.A. 82 C6 47 15N 115 49W
Aves, Is. las, Venezuela 89 D6 12 0N 67 30W
Avesta, Sweden 9 F17 60 9N 16 10 E
Avezzano, Italy 20 C5 42 2N 13 25 E
Aviá Terai, Argentina 94 B3 26 45S 60 50W
Aviemore, U.K. 12 D5 57 12N 3 50W
**Avignon**, France 18 E6 43 57N 4 50 E
Ávila, Spain 19 B3 40 39N 4 43W
Avila Beach, U.S.A. 85 K6 35 11N 120 44W
Avilés, Spain 19 A3 43 35N 5 57W
Avis, U.S.A. 78 E7 41 11N 77 19W
Avoca, U.S.A. 78 D7 42 25N 77 25W
Avoca →, Australia 63 F3 35 40S 143 43 E
Avoca →, Ireland 13 D5 52 48N 6 10W
Avola, Canada 72 C5 51 45N 119 19W
Avola, Italy 20 F6 36 56N 15 7 E
Avon, U.S.A. 78 D7 42 55N 77 45W
Avon →, Australia 61 F2 31 40S 116 7 E
**Avon** →, Bristol, U.K. 11 F5 51 29N 2 41W
Avon →, Dorset, U.K. 11 G6 50 44N 1 46W
Avon →, Warks., U.K. 11 E5 52 0N 2 8W
Avon Park, U.S.A. 77 M5 27 36N 81 31W
Avondale, Zimbabwe 55 F3 17 43S 30 58 E
Avonlea, Canada 73 D8 50 0N 105 0W
Avonmore, Canada 79 A10 45 10N 74 58W
Avranches, France 18 B3 48 40N 1 20W
A'waj →, Syria 47 B5 33 23N 36 20 E
Awaji-Shima, Japan 31 G7 34 30N 134 50 E
'Awālī, Bahrain 45 E6 26 0N 50 30 E
Awantipur, India 43 C6 33 55N 75 3 E
Awasa, Ethiopia 46 F2 7 3N 38 28 E
Awash, Ethiopia 46 F3 9 1N 40 10 E
Awatere →, N.Z. 59 J5 41 37S 174 10 E
Awbārī, Libya 51 C8 26 46N 12 57 E
Awe, L., U.K. 12 E3 56 17N 5 16W
Awjilah, Libya 51 C10 29 8N 21 7 E
Axe →, U.K. 11 F5 50 42N 3 4W
Axel Heiberg I., Canada 4 B3 80 0N 90 0W
Axim, Ghana 50 H5 4 51N 2 15W
Axiós →, Greece 21 D10 40 57N 22 35 E
Axminster, U.K. 11 G4 50 46N 3 0W
Ayabaca, Peru 92 D3 4 40S 79 53W
Ayabe, Japan 31 G7 35 20N 135 20 E
Ayacucho, Argentina 94 D4 37 5S 58 20W
Ayacucho, Peru 92 F4 13 0S 74 0W
Ayaguz, Kazakstan 26 E9 48 10N 80 10 E
Ayamonte, Spain 19 D2 37 12N 7 24W
Ayan, Russia 27 D14 56 30N 138 16 E
Ayaviri, Peru 92 F4 14 50S 70 35W
Aydın, Turkey 21 F12 37 51N 27 51 E
Aydin □, Turkey 25 G4 37 50N 28 0 E
Ayer, U.S.A. 79 D13 42 34N 71 35W
Ayer's Cliff, Canada 79 A12 45 10N 72 3W
**Ayers Rock**, Australia 61 E5 25 23S 131 5 E
Ayia Aikateríni, Ákra, Greece 23 A3 39 50N 19 50 E
Ayia Dhéka, Greece 23 D6 35 3N 24 58 E
Ayia Gálini, Greece 23 D6 35 6N 24 41 E
Ayia Napa, Cyprus 23 E13 34 59N 34 0 E
Ayia Phyla, Cyprus 23 E12 34 43N 33 1 E
Ayia Varvára, Greece 23 D7 35 8N 25 1 E
Áyios Amvrósios, Cyprus 23 D12 35 20N 33 35 E
Áyios Evstrátios, Greece 21 E11 39 34N 24 58 E
Áyios Ioánnis, Ákra, Greece 23 D7 35 20N 25 40 E
Áyios Isídhoros, Greece 23 C9 36 9N 27 51 E
Áyios Matthaíos, Greece 23 B3 39 30N 19 47 E
Áyios Nikólaos, Greece 23 D7 35 11N 25 41 E
Áyios Seryios, Cyprus 23 D12 35 12N 33 53 E
Ayios Theodhoros, Cyprus 23 D13 35 22N 34 1 E
Aykino, Russia 24 B8 62 15N 49 56 E
Aylesbury, U.K. 11 F7 51 49N 0 49W
Aylmer, Canada 78 D4 42 46N 80 59W
Aylmer, L., Canada 68 B8 64 0N 110 8W
'Ayn, Wādī al, Oman 45 F7 22 15N 55 28 E
Ayn Dār, Si. Arabia 45 E7 25 55N 49 10 E
Ayn Zālah, Iraq 44 B4 36 45N 42 35 E
Ayolas, Paraguay 94 B4 27 10S 56 59W
Ayon, Ostrov, Russia 27 C17 69 50N 169 0 E
'Ayoûn el 'Atroûs, Mauritania 50 E4 16 40N 9 37W
Ayr, Australia 62 B4 19 35S 147 25 E
Ayr, Canada 78 C4 43 17N 80 27W
Ayr, U.K. 12 F4 55 28N 4 38W
Ayr →, U.K. 12 F4 55 28N 4 38W
Ayre, Pt. of, U.K. 10 C3 54 25N 4 21W
Ayton, Australia 62 B4 15 56S 145 22 E
Aytos, Bulgaria 21 C12 42 42N 27 16 E
Ayu, Kepulauan, Indonesia 37 D8 0 35N 131 5 E
Ayutla, Guatemala 88 D1 14 40N 92 10W
Ayutla, Mexico 87 D5 16 58N 99 17W
Ayvacık, Turkey 21 E12 39 36N 26 24 E
Ayvalık, Turkey 21 E12 39 20N 26 46 E
Az Zabadānī, Syria 47 B5 33 43N 36 5 E
Aẓ Ẓāhirīyah, West Bank 47 D3 31 25N 34 58 E
Aẓ Ẓahrān, Si. Arabia 45 E6 26 10N 50 7 E
Az Zarqā, Jordan 47 C5 32 5N 36 4 E
Az Zarqā', U.A.E. 45 E7 24 53N 53 4 E
Az Zāwiyah, Libya 51 B8 32 52N 12 56 E
Az Zībār, Iraq 44 B5 36 52N 44 4 E
Az-Zilfī, Si. Arabia 44 E5 26 12N 44 52 E
Az Zubayr, Iraq 44 D5 30 26N 47 40 E
Azamgarh, India 43 F10 26 5N 83 13 E
Azangaro, Peru 92 F4 14 55S 70 13W
Āzār Shahr, Iran 44 B5 37 45N 45 59 E
Azarān, Iran 44 B5 37 25N 47 16 E
Azärbayjan = Azerbaijan ■, Asia 25 F8 40 20N 48 0 E
Āzarbāyjān-e Gharbī □, Iran 44 B5 37 0N 44 30 E
Āzarbāyjān-e Sharqī □, Iran 44 B5 37 20N 47 0 E
Azare, Nigeria 50 F8 11 55N 10 10 E
A'zāz, Syria 44 B3 36 36N 37 4 E
Azbine = Aïr, Niger 50 E7 18 30N 8 0 E
**Azerbaijan** ■, Asia 25 F8 40 20N 48 0 E
Azerbaijchan = Azerbaijan ■, Asia 25 F8 40 20N 48 0 E
Azimganj, India 43 G13 24 14N 88 16 E
Azogues, Ecuador 92 D3 2 35S 78 0W
**Azores**, Atl. Oc. 50 A1 38 44N 29 0W
Azov, Russia 25 E6 47 3N 39 25 E
**Azov, Sea of**, Europe 25 E6 46 0N 36 30 E
Azovskoye More = Azov, Sea of, Europe 25 E6 46 0N 36 30 E
Azraq ash Shīshān, Jordan 47 D5 31 50N 36 49 E
Aztec, U.S.A. 83 H10 36 49N 107 59W
Azúa de Compostela, Dom. Rep. 89 C5 18 25N 70 44W
Azuaga, Spain 19 C3 38 16N 5 39W
Azuero, Pen. de, Panama 88 E3 7 30N 80 30W
Azul, Argentina 94 D4 36 42S 59 43W
Azusa, U.S.A. 85 L9 34 8N 117 52W


# B


Ba Don, Vietnam 38 D6 17 45N 106 26 E
Ba Dong, Vietnam 39 H6 9 40N 106 33 E
Ba Ngoi = Cam Lam, Vietnam 39 G7 11 54N 109 10 E
Ba Tri, Vietnam 39 G6 10 2N 106 36 E
Ba Xian = Bazhou, China 34 E9 39 8N 116 22 E
Baa, Indonesia 37 F6 10 50S 123 0 E
Baarle-Nassau, Belgium 15 C4 51 27N 4 56 E
Bab el Mandeb, Red Sea 46 E3 12 35N 43 25 E
Baba Burnu, Turkey 21 E12 39 29N 26 2 E
Bābā Kalū, Iran 45 D6 30 7N 50 49 E
Babadag, Romania 17 F15 44 53N 28 44 E
Babadayhan, Turkmenistan 26 F7 37 42N 60 23 E
Babaeski, Turkey 21 D12 41 26N 27 6 E
Babahoyo, Ecuador 92 D3 1 40S 79 30W
Babai = Sarju →, India 43 F9 27 21N 81 23 E
Babar, Indonesia 37 F7 8 0S 129 30 E
Babar, Pakistan 42 D3 31 7N 69 32 E
Babarkach, Pakistan 42 E3 29 45N 68 0 E
Babb, U.S.A. 82 B7 48 51N 113 27W
Babelthuap, Pac. Oc. 37 C8 7 30N 134 30 E
Baberu, India 43 G9 25 33N 80 43 E
Babi Besar, Pulau, Malaysia 39 L4 2 25N 103 59 E
Babinda, Australia 62 B4 17 20S 145 56 E
Babine, Canada 72 B3 55 22N 126 37W
Babine →, Canada 72 B3 55 45N 127 44W
Babine L., Canada 72 C3 54 48N 126 0W
Babo, Indonesia 37 E8 2 30S 133 30 E
Bābol, Iran 45 B7 36 40N 52 50 E
Bābol Sar, Iran 45 B7 36 45N 52 45 E
Babruysk, Belarus 17 B15 53 10N 29 15 E
Babuhri, India 42 F3 26 49N 69 43 E
Babusar Pass, Pakistan 43 B5 35 12N 73 59 E
Babuyan Chan., Phil. 37 A6 18 40N 121 30 E
Babylon, Iraq 44 C5 32 34N 44 22 E
Bac Lieu, Vietnam 39 H5 9 17N 105 43 E
Bac Phan, Vietnam 38 B5 22 0N 105 0 E
Bacabal, Brazil 93 D10 4 15S 44 45W
Bacalar, Mexico 87 D7 18 50N 87 27W
Bacan, Kepulauan, Indonesia 37 E7 0 35S 127 30 E
Bacarra, Phil. 37 A6 18 15N 120 37 E
Bacău, Romania 17 E14 46 35N 26 55 E
Bacerac, Mexico 86 A3 30 18N 108 50W
Bach Long Vi, Dao, Vietnam 38 B6 20 10N 107 40 E
Bachelina, Russia 26 D7 57 45N 67 20 E
Bachhwara, India 43 G11 25 35N 85 54 E
Back →, Canada 68 B9 65 10N 104 0W
Bacolod, Phil. 37 B6 10 40N 122 57 E
Bacuk, Malaysia 39 J4 6 4N 102 25 E
Bād, Iran 45 C7 33 41N 52 1 E
Bad →, U.S.A. 80 C4 44 21N 100 22W
Bad Axe, U.S.A. 78 C2 43 48N 83 0W
Bad Ischl, Austria 16 E7 47 44N 13 38 E
Bad Kissingen, Germany 16 C6 50 11N 10 4 E
Bad Lands, U.S.A. 80 D3 43 40N 102 10W
Bada Barabil, India 43 H11 22 7N 85 24 E
Badagara, India 40 P9 11 35N 75 40 E
Badajós, L., Brazil 92 D6 3 15S 62 50W
Badajoz, Spain 19 C2 38 50N 6 59W
Badalona, Spain 19 B7 41 26N 2 15 E
Badalzai, Afghan. 42 E1 29 50N 65 35 E
Badampahar, India 41 H15 22 10N 86 10 E
Badanah, Si. Arabia 44 D4 30 58N 41 30 E
Badarinath, India 43 D8 30 45N 79 30 E
Badas, Kepulauan, Indonesia 36 D3 0 45N 107 5 E
Baddo →, Pakistan 40 F4 28 0N 64 20 E
Bade, Indonesia 37 F9 7 10S 139 35 E
Baden, Austria 16 D9 48 1N 16 13 E
Baden, U.S.A. 78 F4 40 38N 80 14W
Baden-Baden, Germany 16 D5 48 44N 8 13 E
**Baden-Württemberg** □, Germany 16 D5 48 20N 8 40 E
Badgastein, Austria 16 E7 47 7N 13 9 E
Badger, Canada 71 C8 49 0N 56 4W
Badger, U.S.A. 84 J7 36 38N 119 1W
Bādghīsāt □, Afghan. 40 B3 35 0N 63 0 E
Badgom, India 43 B6 34 1N 74 45 E
Badin, Pakistan 42 G3 24 38N 68 54 E
Badlands National Park, U.S.A. 80 D3 43 38N 102 56W
Badrah, Iraq 44 C5 33 6N 45 58 E
Badrinath, India 43 D8 30 44N 79 29 E
Badulla, Sri Lanka 40 R12 7 1N 81 7 E
Baena, Spain 19 D3 37 37N 4 20W
Baeza, Spain 19 D4 37 57N 3 25W
Baffin B., Canada 4 B4 72 0N 64 0W
**Baffin I.**, Canada 69 B12 68 0N 75 0W
Bafing →, Mali 50 F3 13 49N 10 50W
Bafliyūn, Syria 44 B3 36 37N 36 59 E
Bafoulabé, Mali 50 F3 13 50N 10 55W
Bafoussam, Cameroon 52 C2 5 28N 10 25 E
Bāfq, Iran 45 D7 31 40N 55 25 E
Bafra, Turkey 25 F6 41 34N 35 54 E
Bāft, Iran 45 D8 29 15N 56 38 E
Bafwasende, Dem. Rep. of the Congo 54 B2 1 3N 27 5 E
Bagamoyo, Tanzania 54 D4 6 28S 38 55 E
Bagan Datoh, Malaysia 39 L3 3 59N 100 47 E
Bagan Serai, Malaysia 39 K3 5 1N 100 32 E
Baganga, Phil. 37 C7 7 34N 126 33 E
Bagani, Namibia 56 B3 18 7S 21 41 E
Bagansiapiapi, Indonesia 36 D2 2 12N 100 50 E
Bagasra, India 42 J4 21 30N 71 0 E
Bagaud, India 42 H6 22 19N 75 53 E
Bagdad, U.S.A. 85 L11 34 35N 115 53W
Bagdarin, Russia 27 D12 54 26N 113 36 E
Bagé, Brazil 95 C5 31 20S 54 15W
Bagenalstown = Muine Bheag, Ireland 13 D5 52 42N 6 58W
Baggs, U.S.A. 82 F10 41 2N 107 39W
Bagh, Pakistan 43 C5 33 59N 73 45 E
Baghain →, India 43 G9 25 32N 81 1 E
**Baghdād**, Iraq 44 C5 33 20N 44 30 E
Bagheria, Italy 20 E5 38 5N 13 30 E
Baghlān, Afghan. 40 A6 36 12N 69 0 E
Bagley, U.S.A. 80 B7 47 32N 95 24W
Bagodar, India 43 G11 24 5N 85 52 E
Bagrationovsk, Russia 9 J19 54 23N 20 39 E
Baguio, Phil. 37 A6 16 26N 120 34 E
Bah, India 43 F8 26 53N 78 36 E
Bahadurganj, India 43 F12 26 16N 87 49 E
Bahadurgarh, India 42 E7 28 40N 76 57 E
Bahama, Canal Viejo de, W. Indies 88 B4 22 10N 77 30W
**Bahamas** ■, N. Amer. 89 B5 24 0N 75 0W
Baharampur, India 43 G13 24 2N 88 27 E
Bahawalnagar, Pakistan 42 E5 30 0N 73 15 E
Bahawalpur, Pakistan 42 E4 29 24N 71 40 E
Baheri, India 43 E8 28 45N 79 34 E
Bahgul →, India 43 F8 27 45N 79 36 E
Bahi, Tanzania 54 D4 5 58S 35 21 E
Bahi Swamp, Tanzania 54 D4 6 10S 35 0 E
Bahía = Salvador, Brazil 93 F11 13 0S 38 30W
Bahía □, Brazil 93 F10 12 0S 42 0W
Bahía, Is. de la, Honduras 88 C2 16 45N 86 15W

Bahía Blanca, Argentina 94 D3 38 35S 62 13W
Bahía de Caráquez, Ecuador 92 D2 0 40S 80 27W
Bahía Honda, Cuba 88 B3 22 54N 83 10W
Bahía Laura, Argentina 96 F3 48 10S 66 30W
Bahía Negra, Paraguay 92 H7 20 5S 58 5W
Bahir Dar, Ethiopia 46 E2 11 37N 37 10 E
Bahmanzād, Iran 45 D6 31 15N 51 47 E
Bahr el Ghazâl □, Sudan 51 G11 7 0N 28 0 E
Bahraich, India 43 F9 27 38N 81 37 E
**Bahrain** ■, Asia 45 E6 26 0N 50 35 E
Bahror, India 42 F7 27 51N 76 20 E
Bāhū Kalāt, Iran 45 E9 25 43N 61 25 E
Bai Bung, Mui = Ca Mau, Mui, Vietnam 39 H5 8 38N 104 44 E
Bai Duc, Vietnam 38 C5 18 3N 105 49 E
Bai Thuong, Vietnam 38 C5 19 54N 105 23 E
Baia Mare, Romania 17 E12 47 40N 23 35 E
Baião, Brazil 93 D9 2 40S 49 40W
Baïbokoum, Chad 51 G9 7 46N 15 43 E
Baicheng, China 35 B12 45 38N 122 42 E
Baidoa, Somali Rep. 46 G3 3 8N 43 30 E
Baie Comeau, Canada 71 C6 49 12N 68 10W
Baie-St-Paul, Canada 71 C5 47 28N 70 32W
Baie Trinité, Canada 71 C6 49 25N 67 20W
Baie Verte, Canada 71 C8 49 55N 56 12W
Baihar, India 43 H9 22 6N 80 33 E
Baihe, China 34 H6 32 50N 110 5 E
Ba'ījī, Iraq 44 C4 35 0N 43 30 E
Baijnath, India 43 E8 29 55N 79 37 E
**Baikal, L.** = Baykal, Oz., Russia 27 D11 53 0N 108 0 E
Baikunthpur, India 43 H10 23 15N 82 33 E
Baile Atha Cliath = Dublin, Ireland 13 C5 53 21N 6 15W
Băileşti, Romania 17 F12 44 1N 23 20 E
Bainbridge, Ga., U.S.A. 77 K3 30 55N 84 35W
Bainbridge, N.Y., U.S.A. 79 D9 42 18N 75 29W
Baing, Indonesia 37 F6 10 14S 120 34 E
Bainiu, China 34 H7 32 50N 112 15 E
Bā'ir, Jordan 47 E5 30 45N 36 55 E
Bairin Youqi, China 35 C10 43 30N 118 35 E
Bairin Zuoqi, China 35 C10 43 58N 119 15 E
Bairnsdale, Australia 63 F4 37 48S 147 36 E
Baisha, China 34 G7 34 20N 112 32 E
Baitadi, Nepal 43 E9 29 35N 80 25 E
Baiyin, China 34 F3 36 45N 104 14 E
Baiyu Shan, China 34 F4 37 15N 107 30 E
Baj Baj, India 43 H13 22 30N 88 5 E
Baja, Hungary 17 E10 46 12N 18 59 E
Baja, Pta., Mexico 86 B1 29 50N 116 0W
Baja California, Mexico 86 A1 31 10N 115 12W
Baja California □, Mexico 86 B2 30 0N 115 0W
Baja California Sur □, Mexico 86 B2 25 50N 111 50W
Bajag, India 43 H9 22 40N 81 21 E
Bajamar, Canary Is. 22 F3 28 33N 16 20W
Bajana, India 42 H4 23 7N 71 49 E
Bājgīrān, Iran 45 B8 37 36N 58 24 E
Bajimba, Mt., Australia 63 D5 29 17S 152 6 E
Bajo Nuevo, Caribbean 88 C4 15 40N 78 50W
Bajoga, Nigeria 51 F8 10 57N 11 20 E
Bajool, Australia 62 C5 23 40S 150 35 E
Bakel, Senegal 50 F3 14 56N 12 20W
Baker, Calif., U.S.A. 85 K10 35 16N 116 4W
Baker, Mont., U.S.A. 80 B2 46 22N 104 17W
Baker, L., Canada 68 B10 64 0N 96 0W
Baker City, U.S.A. 82 D5 44 47N 117 50W
Baker I., Pac. Oc. 64 G10 0 10N 176 35W
Baker I., U.S.A. 72 B2 55 20N 133 40W
Baker L., Australia 61 E4 26 54S 126 5 E
Baker Lake, Canada 68 B10 64 20N 96 3W
Baker Mt., U.S.A. 82 B3 48 50N 121 49W
Bakers Creek, Australia 62 C4 21 13S 149 7 E
Baker's Dozen Is., Canada 70 A4 56 45N 78 45W
Bakersfield, Calif., U.S.A. 85 K8 35 23N 119 1W
Bakersfield, Vt., U.S.A. 79 B12 44 45N 72 48W
Bākhtarān, Iran 44 C5 34 23N 47 0 E
Bākhtarān □, Iran 44 C5 34 0N 46 30 E
Bakı, Azerbaijan 25 F8 40 29N 49 56 E
Bakkafjörður, Iceland 8 C6 66 2N 14 48W
Bakony, Hungary 17 E9 47 10N 17 30 E
Bakony Forest = Bakony, Hungary 17 E9 47 10N 17 30 E
Bakouma, C.A.R. 52 C4 5 40N 22 56 E
Bakswaho, India 43 G8 24 15N 79 18 E
**Baku** = Bakı, Azerbaijan 25 F8 40 29N 49 56 E
Bakutis Coast, Antarctica 5 D15 74 0S 120 0W
Baky = Bakı, Azerbaijan 25 F8 40 29N 49 56 E
Bala, Canada 78 A5 45 1N 79 37W
Bala, U.K. 10 E4 52 54N 3 36W
Bala, L., U.K. 10 E4 52 53N 3 37W
Balabac I., Phil. 36 C5 8 0N 117 0 E
Balabac Str., E. Indies 36 C5 7 53N 117 5 E
Balabagh, Afghan. 42 B4 34 25N 70 12 E
Ba'labakk, Lebanon 47 B5 34 0N 36 10 E
Balabalangan, Kepulauan, Indonesia 36 E5 2 20S 117 30 E
Balad, Iraq 44 C5 34 1N 44 9 E
Balad Rūz, Iraq 44 C5 33 42N 45 5 E
Bālādeh, Fārs, Iran 45 D6 29 17N 51 56 E
Bālādeh, Māzandaran, Iran 45 B6 36 12N 51 48 E
Balaghat, India 40 J12 21 49N 80 12 E
Balaghat Ra., India 40 K10 18 50N 76 30 E
Balaguer, Spain 19 B6 41 50N 0 50 E
Balaklava, Ukraine 25 F5 44 30N 33 30 E
Balakovo, Russia 24 D8 52 4N 47 55 E
Balamau, India 43 F9 27 10N 80 21 E
Balancán, Mexico 87 D6 17 48N 91 32W
Balashov, Russia 25 D7 51 30N 43 10 E
Balasinor, India 42 H5 22 57N 73 23 E
Balasore = Baleshwar, India 41 J15 21 35N 87 3 E
Balaton, Hungary 17 E9 46 50N 17 40 E
Balbina, Reprêsa de, Brazil 92 D7 2 0S 59 30W
Balboa, Panama 88 E4 8 57N 79 34W
Balbriggan, Ireland 13 C5 53 37N 6 11W
Balcarce, Argentina 94 D4 38 0S 58 10W
Balcarres, Canada 73 C8 50 50N 103 35W
Balchik, Bulgaria 21 C13 43 28N 28 11 E
Balclutha, N.Z. 59 M2 46 15S 169 45 E
Balcones Escarpment, U.S.A. 81 L5 29 30N 99 15W
Bald Hd., Australia 61 G2 35 6S 118 1 E
Bald I., Australia 61 F2 34 57S 118 27 E
Bald Knob, U.S.A. 81 H9 35 19N 91 34W
Baldock L., Canada 73 B9 56 33N 97 57W
Baldwin, Mich., U.S.A. 76 D3 43 54N 85 51W
Baldwin, Pa., U.S.A. 78 F5 40 23N 79 59W
Baldwinsville, U.S.A. 79 C8 43 10N 76 20W
Baldy Mt., U.S.A. 82 B9 48 9N 109 39W
Baldy Peak, U.S.A. 83 K9 33 54N 109 34W
Baleares, Is., Spain 22 B10 39 30N 3 0 E
**Balearic Is.** = Baleares, Is., Spain 22 B10 39 30N 3 0 E
Baleine = Whale →, Canada 71 A6 58 15N 67 40W
Baler, Phil. 37 A6 15 46N 121 34 E
Baleshare, U.K. 12 D1 57 31N 7 22W
Baleshwar, India 41 J15 21 35N 87 3 E
Balfate, Honduras 88 C2 15 48N 86 25W
Balí, Greece 23 D6 35 25N 24 47 E
Bali, India 42 G5 25 11N 73 17 E
**Bali** □, Indonesia 36 F5 8 20S 115 0 E
Bali, Selat, Indonesia 37 H16 8 18S 114 25 E
Baliapal, India 43 J12 21 40N 87 17 E
Balıkeşir, Turkey 21 E12 39 39N 27 53 E
Balikpapan, Indonesia 36 E5 1 10S 116 55 E
Balimbing, Phil. 37 C5 5 5N 119 58 E
Baling, Malaysia 39 K3 5 41N 100 55 E
Balipara, India 41 F18 26 50N 92 45 E
**Balkan Mts.** = Stara Planina, Bulgaria 21 C10 43 15N 23 0 E
**Balkhash** = Balqash, Kazakstan 26 E8 46 50N 74 50 E
Balkhash, Ozero = Balqash Köl, Kazakstan 26 E8 46 0N 74 50 E
Balla, Bangla. 41 G17 24 10N 91 35 E
Ballachulish, U.K. 12 E3 56 41N 5 8W
Balladonia, Australia 61 F3 32 27S 123 51 E
Ballaghaderreen, Ireland 13 C3 53 55N 8 34W
Ballarat, Australia 63 F3 37 33S 143 50 E
Ballard, L., Australia 61 E3 29 20S 120 40 E
Ballater, U.K. 12 D5 57 3N 3 3W
Ballenas, Canal de, Mexico 86 B2 29 10N 113 45W
Balleny Is., Antarctica 5 C11 66 30S 163 0 E
Ballia, India 43 G11 25 46N 84 12 E
Ballina, Australia 63 D5 28 50S 153 31 E
Ballina, Ireland 13 B2 54 7N 9 9W
Ballinasloe, Ireland 13 C3 53 20N 8 13W
Ballinger, U.S.A. 81 K5 31 45N 99 57W
Ballinrobe, Ireland 13 C2 53 38N 9 13W
Ballinskelligs B., Ireland 13 E1 51 48N 10 13W
Ballston Spa, U.S.A. 79 D11 43 0N 73 51W
Ballycastle, U.K. 13 A5 55 12N 6 15W
Ballyclare, U.K. 13 B5 54 46N 6 0W
Ballyhaunis, Ireland 13 C3 53 46N 8 46W
Ballymena, U.K. 13 B5 54 52N 6 17W
Ballymoney, U.K. 13 A5 55 5N 6 31W
Ballymote, Ireland 13 B3 54 5N 8 31W
Ballynahinch, U.K. 13 B6 54 24N 5 54W
Ballyquintin Pt., U.K. 13 B6 54 20N 5 30W
Ballyshannon, Ireland 13 B3 54 30N 8 11W
Balmaceda, Chile 96 F2 46 0S 71 50W
Balmertown, Canada 73 C10 51 4N 93 41W
Balmoral, Australia 63 F3 37 15S 141 48 E
Balmorhea, U.S.A. 81 K3 30 59N 103 45W
Balonne →, Australia 63 D4 28 47S 147 56 E
Balotra, India 42 G5 25 50N 72 14 E
Balqash, Kazakstan 26 E8 46 50N 74 50 E
Balqash Köl, Kazakstan 26 E8 46 0N 74 50 E
Balrampur, India 43 F10 27 30N 82 20 E
Balranald, Australia 63 E3 34 38S 143 33 E
Balsas, Mexico 87 D5 18 0N 99 40W
Balsas →, Brazil 93 E9 7 15S 44 35W
Balsas →, Mexico 86 D4 17 55N 102 10W
Balston Spa, U.S.A. 79 D11 43 0N 73 52W
Balta, Ukraine 17 D15 48 2N 29 45 E
Bălţi, Moldova 17 E14 47 48N 27 58 E
**Baltic Sea**, Europe 9 H18 57 0N 19 0 E
Baltimore, Ireland 13 E2 51 29N 9 22W
**Baltimore**, Md., U.S.A. 76 F7 39 17N 76 37W
Baltimore, Ohio, U.S.A. 78 G2 39 51N 82 36W
Baltit, Pakistan 43 A6 36 15N 74 40 E
Baltiysk, Russia 9 J18 54 41N 19 58 E
**Baluchistan** □, Pakistan 40 F4 27 30N 65 0 E
Balurghat, India 43 G13 25 15N 88 44 E
Balvi, Latvia 9 H22 57 8N 27 15 E
Balya, Turkey 21 E12 39 44N 27 35 E
Bam, Iran 45 D8 29 7N 58 14 E
Bama, Nigeria 51 F8 11 33N 13 41 E
Bamaga, Australia 62 A3 10 50S 142 25 E
Bamaji L., Canada 70 B1 51 9N 91 25W
**Bamako**, Mali 50 F4 12 34N 7 55W
Bambari, C.A.R. 52 C4 5 40N 20 35 E
Bambaroo, Australia 62 B4 18 50S 146 10 E
Bamberg, Germany 16 D6 49 54N 10 54 E
Bamberg, U.S.A. 77 J5 33 18N 81 2W
Bambili, Dem. Rep. of the Congo 54 B2 3 40N 26 0 E
Bamenda, Cameroon 52 C1 5 57N 10 11 E
Bamfield, Canada 72 D3 48 45N 125 10W
Bāmīān □, Afghan. 40 B5 35 0N 67 0 E
Bamiancheng, China 35 C13 43 15N 124 2 E
Bampūr, Iran 45 E9 27 15N 60 21 E
Ban Ban, Laos 38 C4 19 31N 103 30 E
Ban Bang Hin, Thailand 39 H2 9 32N 98 35 E
Ban Chiang Klang, Thailand 38 C3 19 25N 100 55 E
Ban Chik, Laos 38 D4 17 15N 102 22 E
Ban Choho, Thailand 38 E4 15 2N 102 9 E
Ban Dan Lan Hoi, Thailand 38 D2 17 0N 99 35 E
Ban Don = Surat Thani, Thailand 39 H2 9 6N 99 20 E
Ban Don, Vietnam 38 F6 12 53N 107 48 E
Ban Don, Ao →, Thailand 39 H2 9 20N 99 25 E
Ban Dong, Thailand 38 C3 19 30N 100 59 E
Ban Hong, Thailand 38 C2 18 18N 98 50 E
Ban Kaeng, Thailand 38 D3 17 29N 100 7 E
Ban Kantang, Thailand 39 J2 7 25N 99 31 E
Ban Keun, Laos 38 C4 18 22N 102 35 E
Ban Khai, Thailand 38 F3 12 46N 101 18 E
Ban Kheun, Laos 38 B3 20 13N 101 7 E
Ban Khlong Kua, Thailand 39 J3 6 57N 100 8 E
Ban Khuan Mao, Thailand 39 J2 7 50N 99 37 E
Ban Ko Yai Chim, Thailand 39 G2 11 17N 99 26 E
Ban Kok, Thailand 38 D4 16 40N 103 40 E
Ban Laem, Thailand 38 F2 13 13N 99 59 E
Ban Lao Ngam, Laos 38 E6 15 28N 106 10 E
Ban Le Kathe, Thailand 38 E2 15 49N 98 53 E
Ban Mae Chedi, Thailand 38 C2 19 11N 99 31 E
Ban Mae Laeng, Thailand 38 B2 20 1N 99 17 E
Ban Mae Sariang, Thailand 38 C1 18 10N 97 56 E
Ban Mê Thuôt = Buon Ma Thuot, Vietnam 38 F7 12 40N 108 3 E
Ban Mi, Thailand 38 E3 15 3N 100 32 E
Ban Muong Mo, Laos 38 C4 19 4N 103 58 E
Ban Na Mo, Laos 38 D5 17 7N 105 40 E
Ban Na San, Thailand 39 H2 8 53N 99 52 E
Ban Na Tong, Laos 38 B3 20 56N 101 47 E
Ban Nam Bac, Laos 38 B4 20 38N 102 20 E
Ban Nam Ma, Laos 38 A3 22 2N 101 37 E
Ban Ngang, Laos 38 E6 15 59N 106 11 E
Ban Nong Bok, Laos 38 D5 17 5N 104 48 E
Ban Nong Boua, Laos 38 E6 15 40N 106 33 E
Ban Nong Pling, Thailand 38 E3 15 40N 100 10 E
Ban Pak Chan, Thailand 39 G2 10 32N 98 51 E
Ban Phai, Thailand 38 D4 16 4N 102 44 E
Ban Pong, Thailand 38 F2 13 50N 99 55 E
Ban Ron Phibun, Thailand 39 H2 8 9N 99 51 E
Ban Sanam Chai, Thailand 39 J3 7 33N 100 25 E
Ban Sangkha, Thailand 38 E4 14 37N 103 52 E
Ban Tak, Thailand 38 D2 17 2N 99 4 E
Ban Tako, Thailand 38 E4 14 5N 102 40 E
Ban Tha Dua, Thailand 38 D2 17 59N 98 39 E
Ban Tha Li, Thailand 38 D3 17 37N 101 25 E
Ban Tha Nun, Thailand 39 H2 8 12N 98 18 E
Ban Thahine, Laos 38 E5 14 12N 105 33 E
Ban Xien Kok, Laos 38 B3 20 54N 100 39 E
Ban Yen Nhan, Vietnam 38 B6 20 57N 106 2 E
Banaba, Kiribati 64 H8 0 45S 169 50 E
Banalia, Dem. Rep. of the Congo 54 B2 1 32N 25 5 E
Banam, Cambodia 39 G5 11 20N 105 17 E
Bananal, I. do, Brazil 93 F8 11 30S 50 30W
Banaras = Varanasi, India 43 G10 25 22N 83 0 E
Banas →, Gujarat, India 42 H4 23 45N 71 25 E
Banas →, Mad. P., India 43 G9 24 15N 81 30 E
Bânâs, Ras, Egypt 51 D13 23 57N 35 59 E
Banbān, Si. Arabia 44 E5 25 1N 46 35 E
Banbridge, U.K. 13 B5 54 22N 6 16W
Banbury, U.K. 11 E6 52 4N 1 20W
Banchory, U.K. 12 D6 57 3N 2 29W
Bancroft, Canada 78 A7 45 3N 77 51W
Band Bonī, Iran 45 E8 25 30N 59 33 E
Band Qīr, Iran 45 D6 31 39N 48 53 E
Banda, India 43 G9 25 30N 80 26 E
Banda, Mad. P., India 43 G8 24 3N 78 57 E
Banda, Kepulauan, Indonesia 37 E7 4 37S 129 50 E
Banda Aceh, Indonesia 36 C1 5 35N 95 20 E
Banda Banda, Mt., Australia 63 E5 31 10S 152 28 E
Banda Elat, Indonesia 37 F8 5 40S 133 5 E
Banda Is. = Banda, Kepulauan, Indonesia 37 E7 4 37S 129 50 E
Banda Sea, Indonesia 37 F8 6 0S 130 0 E
Bandai-San, Japan 30 F10 37 36N 140 4 E
Bandān, Iran 45 D9 31 23N 60 44 E
Bandanaira, Indonesia 37 E7 4 32S 129 54 E
Bandanwara, India 42 F6 26 9N 74 38 E
Bandar = Machilipatnam, India 41 L12 16 12N 81 8 E
Bandār 'Abbās, Iran 45 E8 27 15N 56 15 E
Bandar-e Anzalī, Iran 45 B6 37 30N 49 30 E
Bandar-e Bushehr = Būshehr, Iran 45 D6 28 55N 50 55 E
Bandar-e Chārak, Iran 45 E7 26 45N 54 20 E
Bandar-e Deylam, Iran 45 D6 30 5N 50 10 E
Bandar-e Khomeynı, Iran 45 D6 30 30N 49 5 E
Bandar-e Lengeh, Iran 45 E7 26 35N 54 58 E
Bandar-e Maqām, Iran 45 E7 26 56N 53 29 E
Bandar-e Ma'shur, Iran 45 D6 30 35N 49 10 E
Bandar-e Nakhīlū, Iran 45 E7 26 58N 53 30 E
Bandar-e Rīg, Iran 45 D6 29 29N 50 38 E
Bandar-e Torkeman, Iran 45 B7 37 0N 54 10 E
Bandar Maharani = Muar, Malaysia 39 L4 2 3N 102 34 E
Bandar Penggaram = Batu Pahat, Malaysia 39 M4 1 50N 102 56 E
**Bandar Seri Begawan**, Brunei 36 D5 4 52N 115 0 E
Bandar Sri Aman, Malaysia 36 D4 1 15N 111 32 E
Bandawe, Malawi 55 E3 11 58S 34 5 E
Bandeira, Pico da, Brazil 95 A7 20 26S 41 47W
Bandera, Argentina 94 B3 28 55S 62 20W
Banderas, B. de, Mexico 86 C3 20 40N 105 30W
Bandhogarh, India 43 H9 23 40N 81 2 E
Bandi →, India 42 F6 26 12N 75 47 E
Bandikui, India 42 F7 27 3N 76 34 E
Bandırma, Turkey 21 D13 40 20N 28 0 E
Bandon, Ireland 13 E3 51 44N 8 44W
Bandon →, Ireland 13 E3 51 43N 8 37W
Bandula, Mozam. 55 F3 19 0S 33 7 E
Bandundu, Dem. Rep. of the Congo 52 E3 3 15S 17 22 E
**Bandung**, Indonesia 37 G12 6 54S 107 36 E
Bāneh, Iran 44 C5 35 59N 45 53 E
Banes, Cuba 89 B4 21 0N 75 42W
Banff, Canada 72 C5 51 10N 115 34W
Banff, U.K. 12 D6 57 40N 2 33W
Banff Nat. Park, Canada 72 C5 51 30N 116 15W
Bang Fai →, Laos 38 D5 16 57N 104 45 E
Bang Hieng →, Laos 38 D5 16 10N 105 10 E
Bang Krathum, Thailand 38 D3 16 34N 100 18 E
Bang Lamung, Thailand 38 F3 13 3N 100 56 E
Bang Mun Nak, Thailand 38 D3 16 2N 100 23 E
Bang Pa In, Thailand 38 E3 14 14N 100 35 E
Bang Rakam, Thailand 38 D3 16 45N 100 7 E
Bang Saphan, Thailand 39 G2 11 14N 99 28 E
Bangaduni I., India 43 J13 21 34N 88 52 E
Bangala Dam, Zimbabwe 55 G3 21 7S 31 25 E
**Bangalore**, India 40 N10 12 59N 77 40 E
Banganga →, India 42 F6 27 6N 77 25 E
Bangaon, India 43 H13 23 0N 88 47 E
Bangassou, C.A.R. 52 D4 4 55N 23 7 E
Banggai, Indonesia 37 E6 1 34S 123 30 E
Banggai, Kepulauan, Indonesia 37 E6 1 40S 123 30 E
Banggai Arch. = Banggai, Kepulauan, Indonesia 37 E6 1 40S 123 30 E
Banggi, Malaysia 36 C5 7 17N 117 12 E
Banghāzī, Libya 51 B10 32 11N 20 3 E
Bangka, Sulawesi, Indonesia 37 D7 1 50N 125 5 E
Bangka, Sumatera, Indonesia 36 E3 2 0S 105 50 E
Bangka, Selat, Indonesia 36 E3 2 30S 105 30 E
Bangkalan, Indonesia 37 G15 7 2S 112 46 E
Bangkinang, Indonesia 36 D2 0 18N 101 5 E
Bangko, Indonesia 36 E2 2 5S 102 9 E
**Bangkok**, Thailand 38 F3 13 45N 100 35 E
**Bangladesh** ■, Asia 41 H17 24 0N 90 0 E
Bangong Co, India 43 B8 35 50N 79 20 E
Bangor, Down, U.K. 13 B6 54 40N 5 40W
Bangor, Gwynedd, U.K. 10 D3 53 14N 4 8W
Bangor, Maine, U.S.A. 69 D13 44 48N 68 46W
Bangor, Pa., U.S.A. 79 F9 40 52N 75 13W
Bangued, Phil. 37 A6 17 40N 120 37 E
**Bangui**, C.A.R. 52 D3 4 23N 18 35 E
Banguru, Dem. Rep. of the Congo 54 B2 0 30N 27 10 E
Bangweulu, L., Zambia 55 E3 11 0S 30 0 E
Bangweulu Swamp, Zambia 55 E3 11 20S 30 15 E
Bani, Dom. Rep. 89 C5 18 16N 70 22W
Banī Sa'd, Iraq 44 C5 33 34N 44 32 E
Banihal Pass, India 43 C6 33 30N 75 12 E
Bāniyās, Syria 44 C3 35 10N 36 0 E
Banja Luka, Bos.-H. 20 B7 44 49N 17 11 E
Banjar, India 42 D7 31 38N 77 21 E
Banjar →, India 43 H9 22 36N 80 22 E
Banjarmasin, Indonesia 36 E4 3 20S 114 35 E
**Banjul**, Gambia 50 F2 13 28N 16 40W
Banka, India 43 G12 24 53N 86 55 E
Banket, Zimbabwe 55 F3 17 27S 30 19 E
Bankipore, India 41 G14 25 35N 85 10 E
Banks I., B.C., Canada 72 C3 53 20N 130 0W
Banks I., N.W.T., Canada 68 A7 73 15N 121 30W
Banks Pen., N.Z. 59 K4 43 45S 173 15 E
Banks Str., Australia 62 G4 40 40S 148 10 E
Bankura, India 43 H12 23 11N 87 18 E
Banmankhi, India 43 G12 25 53N 87 11 E
Bann →, Arm., U.K. 13 B5 54 30N 6 31W
Bann →, L'derry., U.K. 13 A5 55 8N 6 41W
Bannang Sata, Thailand 39 J3 6 16N 101 16 E
Banning, U.S.A. 85 M10 33 56N 116 53W
Banningville = Bandundu, Dem. Rep. of the Congo 52 E3 3 15S 17 22 E
Bannockburn, Canada 78 B7 44 39N 77 33W
Bannockburn, U.K. 12 E5 56 5N 3 55W
Bannockburn, Zimbabwe 55 G2 20 17S 29 48 E
Bannu, Pakistan 40 C7 33 0N 70 18 E
Bano, India 43 H11 22 40N 84 55 E
Bansgaon, India 43 F10 26 33N 83 21 E
Banská Bystrica, Slovak Rep. 17 D10 48 46N 19 14 E
Banswara, India 42 H6 23 32N 74 24 E
Bantaeng, Indonesia 37 F5 5 32S 119 56 E
Bantry, Ireland 13 E2 51 41N 9 27W
Bantry B., Ireland 13 E2 51 37N 9 44W
Bantul, Indonesia 37 G14 7 55S 110 19 E
Bantva, India 42 J4 21 29N 70 12 E
Banu, Afghan. 40 B6 35 35N 69 5 E
Banyak, Kepulauan, Indonesia 36 D1 2 10N 97 10 E
Banyalbufar, Spain 22 B9 39 42N 2 31 E
Banyo, Cameroon 52 C2 6 52N 11 45 E
Banyumas, Indonesia 37 G13 7 32S 109 18 E
Banyuwangi, Indonesia 37 H16 8 13S 114 21 E
Banzare Coast, Antarctica 5 C9 68 0S 125 0 E
Banzyville = Mobayi, Dem. Rep. of the Congo 52 D4 4 15N 21 8 E
Bao Lac, Vietnam 38 A5 22 57N 105 40 E
Bao Loc, Vietnam 39 G6 11 32N 107 48 E
Baocheng, China 34 H4 33 12N 106 56 E
Baode, China 34 E6 39 1N 111 5 E
Baodi, China 35 E9 39 38N 117 20 E
Baoding, China 34 E8 38 50N 115 28 E
Baoji, China 34 G4 34 20N 107 5 E
Baoshan, China 32 D4 25 10N 99 5 E
Baotou, China 34 D6 40 32N 110 2 E
Baoying, China 35 H10 33 17N 119 20 E
Bap, India 42 F5 27 23N 72 18 E
Bapatla, India 41 M12 15 55N 80 30 E
Bāqerābād, Iran 45 C6 33 2N 51 58 E
Ba'qūbah, Iraq 44 C5 33 45N 44 50 E
Baquedano, Chile 94 A2 23 20S 69 52W
Bar, Montenegro, Yug. 21 C8 42 8N 19 6 E
Bar, Ukraine 17 D14 49 4N 27 40 E
Bar Bigha, India 43 G11 25 21N 85 47 E
Bar Harbor, U.S.A. 77 C11 44 23N 68 13W
Bar-le-Duc, France 18 B6 48 47N 5 10 E
Bara, India 43 G9 25 16N 81 43 E
Bara Banki, India 43 F9 26 55N 81 12 E
Barabai, Indonesia 36 E5 2 32S 115 34 E
Baraboo, U.S.A. 80 D10 43 28N 89 45W
Baracoa, Cuba 89 B5 20 20N 74 30W
Baradā →, Syria 47 B5 33 33N 36 34 E
Baradero, Argentina 94 C4 33 52S 59 29W
Baradine, Australia 63 E4 30 56S 149 4 E
Baraga, U.S.A. 80 B10 46 47N 88 30W
Barah →, India 42 F6 27 42N 77 5 E
Barahona, Dom. Rep. 89 C5 18 13N 71 7W
Barail Range, India 41 G18 25 15N 93 20 E
Barakaldo, Spain 19 A4 43 18N 2 59W
Barakar →, India 43 G12 24 7N 86 14 E
Barakhola, India 41 G18 25 0N 92 45 E
Barakot, India 43 J11 21 33N 84 59 E
Barakpur, India 43 H13 22 44N 88 30 E
Baralaba, Australia 62 C4 24 13S 149 50 E
Baralzon L., Canada 73 B9 60 0N 98 3W
Baramula, India 43 B6 34 15N 74 20 E
Baran, India 42 G7 25 9N 76 40 E
Baran →, Pakistan 42 G3 25 13N 68 17 E
Baranavichy, Belarus 17 B14 53 10N 26 0 E
Baranof, U.S.A. 72 B2 57 5N 134 50W
Baranof I., U.S.A. 68 C6 57 0N 135 0W
Barapasi, Indonesia 37 E9 2 15S 137 5 E
Barasat, India 43 H13 22 46N 88 31 E
Barat Daya, Kepulauan, Indonesia 37 F7 7 30S 128 0 E
Barataria B., U.S.A. 81 L10 29 20N 89 55W
Barauda, India 42 H6 23 33N 75 15 E
Baraut, India 42 E7 29 13N 77 7 E
Barbacena, Brazil 95 A7 21 15S 43 56W
**Barbados** ■, W. Indies 89 D8 13 10N 59 30W
Barbària, C. de, Spain 22 C7 38 39N 1 24 E
Barbastro, Spain 19 A6 42 2N 0 5 E
Barberton, S. Africa 57 D5 25 42S 31 2 E
Barberton, U.S.A. 78 E3 41 0N 81 39W
Barbosa, Colombia 92 B4 5 57N 73 37W
Barbourville, U.S.A. 77 G4 36 52N 83 53W
Barbuda, W. Indies 89 C7 17 30N 61 40W
Barcaldine, Australia 62 C4 23 43S 145 6 E
Barcellona Pozzo di Gotto, Italy 20 E6 38 9N 15 13 E
**Barcelona**, Spain 19 B7 41 21N 2 10 E
Barcelona, Venezuela 92 A6 10 10N 64 40W
Barcelos, Brazil 92 D6 1 0S 63 0W
Barcoo →, Australia 62 D3 25 30S 142 50 E
Bardaï, Chad 51 D9 21 25N 17 0 E
Bardas Blancas, Argentina 94 D2 35 49S 69 45W
Barddhaman, India 43 H12 23 14N 87 39 E
Bardejov, Slovak Rep. 17 D11 49 18N 21 15 E

Bardera, *Somali Rep.* **46 G3** 2 20N 42 27 E
Bardīyah, *Libya* **51 B10** 31 45N 25 5 E
Bardsey I., *U.K.* **10 E3** 52 45N 4 47W
Bardstown, *U.S.A.* **76 G3** 37 49N 85 28W
Bareilly, *India* **43 E8** 28 22N 79 27 E
Barela, *India* **43 H9** 23 6N 80 3 E
Barents Sea, *Arctic* **4 B9** 73 0N 39 0 E
Barfleur, Pte. de, *France* **18 B3** 49 42N 1 16W
Bargara, *Australia* **62 C5** 24 50S 152 25 E
Barguzin, *Russia* **27 D11** 53 37N 109 37 E
Barh, *India* **43 G11** 25 29N 85 46 E
Barhaj, *India* **43 F10** 26 18N 83 44 E
Barham, *Australia* **63 F3** 35 36S 144 8 E
Barharwa, *India* **43 G12** 24 52N 87 47 E
Barhi, *India* **43 G11** 24 15N 85 25 E
Bari, *India* **42 F7** 26 39N 77 39 E
Bari, *Italy* **20 D7** 41 8N 16 51 E
Bari Doab, *Pakistan* **42 D5** 30 20N 73 0 E
Bari Sadri, *India* **42 G6** 24 28N 74 30 E
Barīdī, Ra's, *Si. Arabia* **44 E3** 24 17N 37 31 E
Barīm, *Yemen* **48 E8** 12 39N 43 25 E
Barinas, *Venezuela* **92 B4** 8 36N 70 15W
Baring, C., *Canada* **68 B8** 70 0N 117 30W
Baringo, *Kenya* **54 B4** 0 47N 36 16 E
Baringo, L., *Kenya* **54 B4** 0 47N 36 16 E
Barisal, *Bangla.* **41 H17** 22 45N 90 20 E
Barisan, Bukit, *Indonesia* **36 E2** 3 30S 102 15 E
Barito →, *Indonesia* **36 E4** 4 0S 114 50 E
Bark L., *Canada* **78 A7** 45 27N 77 51W
Barkakana, *India* **43 H11** 23 37N 85 29 E
Barker, *U.S.A.* **78 C6** 43 20N 78 33W
Barkley, L., *U.S.A.* **77 G2** 37 1N 88 14W
Barkley Sound, *Canada* **72 D3** 48 50N 125 10W
Barkly East, *S. Africa* **56 E4** 30 58S 27 33 E
Barkly Roadhouse, *Australia* **62 B2** 19 52S 135 50 E
Barkly Tableland, *Australia* **62 B2** 17 50S 136 40 E
Barkly West, *S. Africa* **56 D3** 28 5S 24 31 E
Barkol Kazak Zizhixian, *China* **32 B4** 43 37N 93 2 E
Bârlad, *Romania* **17 E14** 46 15N 27 38 E
Bârlad →, *Romania* **17 F14** 45 38N 27 32 E
Barlee, L., *Australia* **61 E2** 29 15S 119 30 E
Barlee, Mt., *Australia* **61 D4** 24 38S 128 13 E
Barletta, *Italy* **20 D7** 41 19N 16 17 E
Barlovento, *Canary Is.* **22 F2** 28 48N 17 48W
Barlow L., *Canada* **73 A8** 62 0N 103 0W
Barmedman, *Australia* **63 E4** 34 9S 147 21 E
Barmer, *India* **42 G4** 25 45N 71 20 E
Barmera, *Australia* **63 E3** 34 15S 140 28 E
Barmouth, *U.K.* **10 E3** 52 44N 4 4W
Barna →, *India* **43 G10** 25 21N 83 3 E
Barnagar, *India* **42 H6** 23 7N 75 19 E
Barnala, *India* **42 D6** 30 23N 75 33 E
Barnard Castle, *U.K.* **10 C6** 54 33N 1 55W
Barnaul, *Russia* **26 D9** 53 20N 83 40 E
Barnesville, *U.S.A.* **77 J3** 33 3N 84 9W
Barnet, *U.K.* **11 F7** 51 38N 0 9W
Barneveld, *Neths.* **15 B5** 52 7N 5 36 E
Barneveld, *U.S.A.* **79 C9** 43 16N 75 14W
Barnhart, *U.S.A.* **81 K4** 31 8N 101 10W
Barnsley, *U.K.* **10 D6** 53 34N 1 27W
Barnstaple, *U.K.* **11 F3** 51 5N 4 4W
Barnstaple Bay = Bideford Bay, *U.K.* **11 F3** 51 5N 4 20W
Barnsville, *U.S.A.* **80 B6** 46 43N 96 28W
Barnwell, *U.S.A.* **77 J5** 33 15N 81 23W
Baro, *Nigeria* **50 G7** 8 35N 6 18 E
Baroda = Vadodara, *India* **42 H5** 22 20N 73 10 E
Baroda, *India* **42 G7** 25 29N 76 35 E
Baroe, *S. Africa* **56 E3** 33 13S 24 33 E
Baron Ra., *Australia* **60 D4** 23 30S 127 45 E
Barotseland, *Zambia* **53 H4** 15 0S 24 0 E
Barpeta, *India* **41 F17** 26 20N 91 10 E
Barques, Pt. Aux, *U.S.A.* **78 B2** 44 4N 82 58W
Barquísimeto, *Venezuela* **92 A5** 10 4N 69 19W
Barr Smith Range, *Australia* **61 E3** 27 4S 120 20 E
Barra, *Brazil* **93 F10** 11 5S 43 10W
Barra, *U.K.* **12 E1** 57 0N 7 29W
Barra, Sd. of, *U.K.* **12 D1** 57 4N 7 25W
Barra de Navidad, *Mexico* **86 D4** 19 12N 104 41W
Barra do Corda, *Brazil* **93 E9** 5 30S 45 10W
Barra do Piraí, *Brazil* **95 A7** 22 30S 43 50W
Barra Falsa, Pta. da, *Mozam.* **57 C6** 22 58S 35 37 E
Barra Hd., *U.K.* **12 E1** 56 47N 7 40W
Barra Mansa, *Brazil* **95 A7** 22 35S 44 12W
Barraba, *Australia* **63 E5** 30 21S 150 35 E
Barrackpur = Barakpur, *India* **43 H13** 22 44N 88 30 E
Barradale Roadhouse, *Australia* **60 D1** 22 42S 114 58 E
Barraigh = Barra, *U.K.* **12 E1** 57 0N 7 29W
Barranca, *Lima, Peru* **92 F3** 10 45S 77 50W
Barranca, *Loreto, Peru* **92 D3** 4 50S 76 50W
Barrancabermeja, *Colombia* **92 B4** 7 0N 73 50W
Barrancas, *Venezuela* **92 B6** 8 55N 62 5W
Barrancos, *Portugal* **19 C2** 38 10N 6 58W
Barranqueras, *Argentina* **94 B4** 27 30S 59 0W
Barranquilla, *Colombia* **92 A4** 11 0N 74 50W
Barraute, *Canada* **70 C4** 48 26N 77 38W
Barre, *Mass., U.S.A.* **79 D12** 42 25N 72 6W
Barre, *Vt., U.S.A.* **79 B12** 44 12N 72 30W
Barreal, *Argentina* **94 C2** 31 33S 69 28W
Barreiras, *Brazil* **93 F10** 12 8S 45 0W
Barreirinhas, *Brazil* **93 D10** 2 30S 42 50W
Barreiro, *Portugal* **19 C1** 38 40N 9 6W
Barren, Nosy, *Madag.* **57 B7** 18 25S 43 40 E
Barretos, *Brazil* **93 H9** 20 30S 48 35W
Barrhead, *Canada* **72 C6** 54 10N 114 24W
Barrie, *Canada* **78 B5** 44 24N 79 40W
Barrier Ra., *Australia* **63 E3** 31 0S 141 30 E
Barrière, *Canada* **72 C4** 51 12N 120 7W
Barrington, *U.S.A.* **79 E13** 41 44N 71 18W
Barrington L., *Canada* **73 B8** 56 55N 100 15W
Barrington Tops, *Australia* **63 E5** 32 6S 151 28 E
Barringun, *Australia* **63 D4** 29 1S 145 41 E
Barro do Garças, *Brazil* **93 G8** 15 54S 52 16W
Barron, *U.S.A.* **80 C9** 45 24N 91 51W
**Barrow**, *U.S.A.* **68 A4** 71 18N 156 47W
Barrow →, *Ireland* **13 D5** 52 25N 6 58W
Barrow Creek, *Australia* **62 C1** 21 30S 133 55 E
Barrow I., *Australia* **60 D2** 20 45S 115 20 E
Barrow-in-Furness, *U.K.* **10 C4** 54 7N 3 14W
Barrow Pt., *Australia* **62 A3** 14 20S 144 40 E
Barrow Pt., *U.S.A.* **66 B4** 71 24N 156 29W
Barrow Ra., *Australia* **61 E4** 26 0S 127 40 E
Barrow Str., *Canada* **4 B3** 74 20N 95 0W
Barry, *U.K.* **11 F4** 51 24N 3 16W
Barry's Bay, *Canada* **78 A7** 45 29N 77 41W
Barsat, *Pakistan* **43 A5** 36 10N 72 45 E
Barsham, *Syria* **44 C4** 35 21N 40 33 E
Barsi, *India* **40 K9** 18 10N 75 50 E
Barsoi, *India* **41 G15** 25 48N 87 57 E
Barstow, *U.S.A.* **85 L9** 34 54N 117 1W
Barthélemy, Col, *Vietnam* **38 C5** 19 26N 104 6 E
Bartica, *Guyana* **92 B7** 6 25N 58 40W
Bartlesville, *U.S.A.* **81 G7** 36 45N 95 59W
Bartlett, *U.S.A.* **84 J8** 36 29N 118 2W
Bartlett, L., *Canada* **72 A5** 63 5N 118 20W
Bartolomeu Dias, *Mozam.* **55 G4** 21 10S 35 8 E
Barton, *U.S.A.* **79 B12** 44 45N 72 11W
Barton upon Humber, *U.K.* **10 D7** 53 41N 0 25W
Bartow, *U.S.A.* **77 M5** 27 54N 81 50W
Barú, Volcan, *Panama* **88 E3** 8 55N 82 35W
Barumba, *Dem. Rep. of the Congo* **54 B1** 1 3N 23 37 E
Baruunsuu, *Mongolia* **34 C3** 43 43N 105 35 E
Barwani, *India* **42 H6** 22 2N 74 57 E
Barysaw, *Belarus* **17 A15** 54 17N 28 28 E
Barzān, *Iraq* **44 B5** 36 55N 44 3 E
Bāsa'idū, *Iran* **45 E7** 26 35N 55 20 E
Basal, *Pakistan* **42 C5** 33 33N 72 13 E
Basankusa, *Dem. Rep. of the Congo* **52 D3** 1 5N 19 50 E
Basarabeasca, *Moldova* **17 E15** 46 21N 28 58 E
Basawa, *Afghan.* **42 B4** 34 15N 70 50 E
Bascuñán, C., *Chile* **94 B1** 28 52S 71 35W
**Basel**, *Switz.* **18 C7** 47 35N 7 35 E
Bashākerd, Kūhhā-ye, *Iran* **45 E8** 26 42N 58 35 E
Bashaw, *Canada* **72 C6** 52 35N 112 58W
Bāshī, *Iran* **45 D6** 28 41N 51 4 E
Bashkir Republic = Bashkortostan □, *Russia* **24 D10** 54 0N 57 0 E
Bashkortostan □, *Russia* **24 D10** 54 0N 57 0 E
Basilan, *Phil.* **37 C6** 6 35N 122 0 E
Basilan Str., *Phil.* **37 C6** 6 50N 122 0 E
Basildon, *U.K.* **11 F8** 51 34N 0 28 E
Basim = Washim, *India* **40 J10** 20 3N 77 0 E
Basin, *U.S.A.* **82 D9** 44 23N 108 2W
Basingstoke, *U.K.* **11 F6** 51 15N 1 5W
Baskatong, Rés., *Canada* **70 C4** 46 46N 75 50W
Basle = Basel, *Switz.* **18 C7** 47 35N 7 35 E
Basoda, *India* **42 H7** 23 52N 77 54 E
Basoka, *Dem. Rep. of the Congo* **54 B1** 1 16N 23 40 E
Basque Provinces = País Vasco □, *Spain* **19 A4** 42 50N 2 45W
**Basra** = Al Başrah, *Iraq* **44 D5** 30 30N 47 50 E
Bass Str., *Australia* **62 F4** 39 15S 146 30 E
Bassano, *Canada* **72 C6** 50 48N 112 20W
Bassano del Grappa, *Italy* **20 B4** 45 46N 11 44 E
Bassas da India, *Ind. Oc.* **53 J7** 22 0S 39 0 E
Basse-Terre, *Guadeloupe* **89 C7** 16 0N 61 44W
Bassein, *Burma* **41 L19** 16 45N 94 30 E
**Basseterre**, *St. Kitts & Nevis* **89 C7** 17 17N 62 43W
Bassett, *U.S.A.* **80 D5** 42 35N 99 32W
Bassi, *India* **42 D7** 30 44N 76 21 E
Bastak, *Iran* **45 E7** 27 15N 54 25 E
Baştām, *Iran* **45 B7** 36 29N 55 4 E
Bastar, *India* **41 K12** 19 15N 81 40 E
Basti, *India* **43 F10** 26 52N 82 55 E
Bastia, *France* **18 E8** 42 40N 9 30 E
Bastogne, *Belgium* **15 D5** 50 1N 5 43 E
Bastrop, *La., U.S.A.* **81 J9** 32 47N 91 55W
Bastrop, *Tex., U.S.A.* **81 K6** 30 7N 97 19W
Bat Yam, *Israel* **47 C3** 32 2N 34 44 E
Bata, *Eq. Guin.* **52 D1** 1 57N 9 50 E
**Bataan**, *Phil.* **37 B6** 14 40N 120 25 E
Batabanó, *Cuba* **88 B3** 22 40N 82 20W
Batabanó, G. de, *Cuba* **88 B3** 22 30N 82 30W
Batac, *Phil.* **37 A6** 18 3N 120 34 E
Batagai, *Russia* **27 C14** 67 38N 134 38 E
Batala, *India* **42 D6** 31 48N 75 12 E
Batama, *Dem. Rep. of the Congo* **54 B2** 0 58N 26 33 E
Batamay, *Russia* **27 C13** 63 30N 129 15 E
Batang, *Indonesia* **37 G13** 6 55S 109 45 E
Batangas, *Phil.* **37 B6** 13 35N 121 10 E
Batanta, *Indonesia* **37 E8** 0 55S 130 40 E
Batatais, *Brazil* **95 A6** 20 54S 47 37W
Batavia, *U.S.A.* **78 D6** 43 0N 78 11W
Batchelor, *Australia* **60 B5** 13 4S 131 1 E
Batdambang, *Cambodia* **38 F4** 13 7N 103 12 E
Bateman's B., *Australia* **63 F5** 35 40S 150 12 E
Batemans Bay, *Australia* **63 F5** 35 44S 150 11 E
Bates Ra., *Australia* **61 E3** 27 27S 121 5 E
Batesburg, *U.S.A.* **77 J5** 33 54N 81 33W
Batesville, *Ark., U.S.A.* **81 H9** 35 46N 91 39W
Batesville, *Miss., U.S.A.* **81 H10** 34 19N 89 57W
Batesville, *Tex., U.S.A.* **81 L5** 28 58N 99 37W
Bath, *Canada* **79 B8** 44 11N 76 47W
**Bath**, *U.K.* **11 F5** 51 23N 2 22W
Bath, *Maine, U.S.A.* **77 D11** 43 55N 69 49W
Bath, *N.Y., U.S.A.* **78 D7** 42 20N 77 19W
Bath & North East Somerset □, *U.K.* **11 F5** 51 21N 2 27W
Batheay, *Cambodia* **39 G5** 11 59N 104 57 E
Bathurst = Banjul, *Gambia* **50 F2** 13 28N 16 40W
Bathurst, *Australia* **63 E4** 33 25S 149 31 E
Bathurst, *Canada* **71 C6** 47 37N 65 43W
Bathurst, *S. Africa* **56 E4** 33 30S 26 50 E
Bathurst, C., *Canada* **68 A7** 70 34N 128 0W
Bathurst B., *Australia* **62 A3** 14 16S 144 25 E
Bathurst Harb., *Australia* **62 G4** 43 15S 146 10 E
Bathurst I., *Australia* **60 B5** 11 30S 130 10 E
Bathurst I., *Canada* **4 B2** 76 0N 100 30W
Bathurst Inlet, *Canada* **68 B9** 66 50N 108 1W
Batlow, *Australia* **63 F4** 35 31S 148 9 E
Batman, *Turkey* **25 G7** 37 55N 41 5 E
Baţn al Ghūl, *Jordan* **47 F4** 29 36N 35 56 E
Batna, *Algeria* **50 A7** 35 34N 6 15 E
Batoka, *Zambia* **55 F2** 16 45S 27 15 E
**Baton Rouge**, *U.S.A.* **81 K9** 30 27N 91 11W
Batong, Ko, *Thailand* **39 J2** 6 32N 99 12 E
Batopilas, *Mexico* **86 B3** 27 0N 107 45W
Batouri, *Cameroon* **52 D2** 4 30N 14 25 E
Båtsfjord, *Norway* **8 A23** 70 38N 29 39 E
Battambang = Batdambang, *Cambodia* **38 F4** 13 7N 103 12 E
Batticaloa, *Sri Lanka* **40 R12** 7 43N 81 45 E
Battipáglia, *Italy* **20 D6** 40 37N 14 58 E
Battle, *U.K.* **11 G8** 50 55N 0 30 E
Battle →, *Canada* **73 C7** 52 43N 108 15W
Battle Creek, *U.S.A.* **76 D3** 42 19N 85 11W
Battle Ground, *U.S.A.* **84 E4** 45 47N 122 32W
Battle Harbour, *Canada* **71 B8** 52 16N 55 35W
Battle Lake, *U.S.A.* **80 B7** 46 17N 95 43W
Battle Mountain, *U.S.A.* **82 F5** 40 38N 116 56W
Battlefields, *Zimbabwe* **55 F2** 18 37S 29 47 E
Battleford, *Canada* **73 C7** 52 45N 108 15W
Batu, Kepulauan, *Indonesia* **36 E1** 0 30S 98 25 E
Batu, Mt., *Ethiopia* **46 F2** 6 55N 39 45 E
Batu Caves, *Malaysia* **39 L3** 3 15N 101 40 E
Batu Gajah, *Malaysia* **39 K3** 4 28N 101 3 E
Batu Is. = Batu, Kepulauan, *Indonesia* **36 E1** 0 30S 98 25 E
Batu Pahat, *Malaysia* **39 M4** 1 50N 102 56 E
Batuata, *Indonesia* **37 F6** 6 12S 122 42 E
Batumi, *Georgia* **25 F7** 41 39N 41 44 E
Baturaja, *Indonesia* **36 E2** 4 11S 104 15 E
Baturité, *Brazil* **93 D11** 4 28S 38 45W
Bau, *Malaysia* **36 D4** 1 25N 110 9 E
Baubau, *Indonesia* **37 F6** 5 25S 122 38 E
Bauchi, *Nigeria* **50 F7** 10 22N 9 48 E
Baudette, *U.S.A.* **80 A7** 48 43N 94 36W
Bauer, C., *Australia* **63 E1** 32 44S 134 4 E
Bauhinia, *Australia* **62 C4** 24 35S 149 18 E
Baukau, *Indonesia* **37 F7** 8 27S 126 27 E
Bauld, C., *Canada* **69 C14** 51 38N 55 26W
Bauru, *Brazil* **95 A6** 22 10S 49 0W
Bausi, *India* **43 G12** 24 48N 87 1 E
Bauska, *Latvia* **9 H21** 56 24N 24 15 E
Bautzen, *Germany* **16 C8** 51 10N 14 26 E
Bavānāt, *Iran* **45 D7** 30 28N 53 27 E
**Bavaria** = Bayern □, *Germany* **16 D6** 48 50N 12 0 E
Bavispe →, *Mexico* **86 B3** 29 30N 109 11W
Bawdwin, *Burma* **41 H20** 23 5N 97 20 E
Bawean, *Indonesia* **36 F4** 5 46S 112 35 E
Bawku, *Ghana* **50 F5** 11 3N 0 19W
Bawlake, *Burma* **41 K20** 19 11N 97 21 E
Baxley, *U.S.A.* **77 K4** 31 47N 82 21W
Baxter, *U.S.A.* **80 B7** 46 21N 94 17W
Baxter Springs, *U.S.A.* **81 G7** 37 2N 94 44W
Bay City, *Mich., U.S.A.* **76 D4** 43 36N 83 54W
Bay City, *Tex., U.S.A.* **81 L7** 28 59N 95 58W
Bay Minette, *U.S.A.* **77 K2** 30 53N 87 46W
Bay Roberts, *Canada* **71 C9** 47 36N 53 16W
Bay St. Louis, *U.S.A.* **81 K10** 30 19N 89 20W
Bay Springs, *U.S.A.* **81 K10** 31 59N 89 17W
Bay View, *N.Z.* **59 H6** 39 25S 176 50 E
Baya, *Dem. Rep. of the Congo* **55 E2** 11 53S 27 25 E
Bayamo, *Cuba* **88 B4** 20 20N 76 40W
Bayamón, *Puerto Rico* **89 C6** 18 24N 66 10W
Bayan Har Shan, *China* **32 C4** 34 0N 98 0 E
Bayan Hot = Alxa Zuoqi, *China* **34 E3** 38 50N 105 40 E
Bayan Obo, *China* **34 D5** 41 52N 109 59 E
Bayan-Ovoo = Erdenetsogt, *Mongolia* **34 C4** 42 55N 106 5 E
Bayana, *India* **42 F7** 26 55N 77 18 E
Bayanaūyl, *Kazakstan* **26 D8** 50 45N 75 45 E
Bayandalay, *Mongolia* **34 C2** 43 30N 103 29 E
Bayanhongor, *Mongolia* **32 B5** 46 8N 102 43 E
Bayard, *N. Mex., U.S.A.* **83 K9** 32 46N 108 8W
Bayard, *Nebr., U.S.A.* **80 E3** 41 45N 103 20W
Baybay, *Phil.* **37 B6** 10 40N 124 55 E
Bayern □, *Germany* **16 D6** 48 50N 12 0 E
Bayeux, *France* **18 B3** 49 17N 0 42W
Bayfield, *Canada* **78 C3** 43 34N 81 42W
Bayfield, *U.S.A.* **80 B9** 46 49N 90 49W
Bayındır, *Turkey* **21 E12** 38 13N 27 39 E
Baykal, Oz., *Russia* **27 D11** 53 0N 108 0 E
Baykan, *Turkey* **44 B4** 38 7N 41 44 E
Baykonur = Bayqongyr, *Kazakstan* **26 E7** 47 48N 65 50 E
Baymak, *Russia* **24 D10** 52 36N 58 19 E
Baynes Mts., *Namibia* **56 B1** 17 15S 13 0 E
Bayombong, *Phil.* **37 A6** 16 30N 121 10 E
Bayonne, *France* **18 E3** 43 30N 1 28W
Bayonne, *U.S.A.* **79 F10** 40 40N 74 7W
Bayovar, *Peru* **92 E2** 5 50S 81 0W
Bayqongyr, *Kazakstan* **26 E7** 47 48N 65 50 E
Bayram-Ali = Bayramaly, *Turkmenistan* **26 F7** 37 37N 62 10 E
Bayramaly, *Turkmenistan* **26 F7** 37 37N 62 10 E
Bayramiç, *Turkey* **21 E12** 39 48N 26 36 E
Bayreuth, *Germany* **16 D6** 49 56N 11 35 E
Bayrūt, *Lebanon* **47 B4** 33 53N 35 31 E
Bays, L. of, *Canada* **78 A5** 45 15N 79 4W
Baysville, *Canada* **78 A5** 45 9N 79 7W
Bayt Lahm, *West Bank* **47 D4** 31 43N 35 12 E
Baytown, *U.S.A.* **81 L7** 29 43N 94 59W
Baza, *Spain* **19 D4** 37 30N 2 47W
Bazaruto, I. do, *Mozam.* **57 C6** 21 40S 35 28 E
Bazhou, *China* **34 E9** 39 8N 116 22 E
Bazmān, Kūh-e, *Iran* **45 D9** 28 4N 60 1 E
Beach, *U.S.A.* **80 B3** 46 58N 104 0W
Beach City, *U.S.A.* **78 F3** 40 39N 81 35W
Beachport, *Australia* **63 F3** 37 29S 140 0 E
Beachy Hd., *U.K.* **11 G8** 50 44N 0 15 E
Beacon, *Australia* **61 F2** 30 26S 117 52 E
Beacon, *U.S.A.* **79 E11** 41 30N 73 58W
Beaconsfield, *Australia* **62 G4** 41 11S 146 48 E
Beagle, Canal, *S. Amer.* **96 H3** 55 0S 68 30W
Beagle Bay, *Australia* **60 C3** 16 58S 122 40 E
Bealanana, *Madag.* **57 A8** 14 33S 48 44 E
Beals Cr. →, *U.S.A.* **81 J4** 32 10N 100 51W
Beamsville, *Canada* **78 C5** 43 12N 79 28W
Bear →, *Calif., U.S.A.* **84 G5** 38 56N 121 36W
Bear →, *Utah, U.S.A.* **74 B4** 41 30N 112 8W
Bear I., *Ireland* **13 E2** 51 38N 9 50W
Bear L., *Canada* **73 B9** 55 8N 96 0W
Bear L., *U.S.A.* **82 F8** 41 59N 111 21W
Beardmore, *Canada* **70 C2** 49 36N 87 57W
Beardmore Glacier, *Antarctica* **5 E11** 84 30S 170 0 E
Beardstown, *U.S.A.* **80 F9** 40 1N 90 26W
Bearma →, *India* **43 G8** 24 20N 79 51 E
Béarn, *France* **18 E3** 43 20N 0 30W
Bearpaw Mts., *U.S.A.* **82 B9** 48 12N 109 30W
Bearskin Lake, *Canada* **70 B1** 53 58N 91 2W
Beas →, *India* **42 D6** 31 10N 74 59 E
Beata, C., *Dom. Rep.* **89 C5** 17 40N 71 30W
Beata, I., *Dom. Rep.* **89 C5** 17 34N 71 31W
Beatrice, *U.S.A.* **80 E6** 40 16N 96 45W
Beatrice, *Zimbabwe* **55 F3** 18 15S 30 55 E
Beatrice, C., *Australia* **62 A2** 14 20S 136 55 E
Beatton →, *Canada* **72 B4** 56 15N 120 45W
Beatton River, *Canada* **72 B4** 57 26N 121 20W
Beatty, *U.S.A.* **84 J10** 36 54N 116 46W
Beauce, Plaine de la, *France* **18 B4** 48 10N 1 45 E
Beauceville, *Canada* **71 C5** 46 13N 70 46W
Beaudesert, *Australia* **63 D5** 27 59S 153 0 E
Beaufort, *Malaysia* **36 C5** 5 30N 115 40 E
Beaufort, *N.C., U.S.A.* **77 H7** 34 43N 76 40W
Beaufort, *S.C., U.S.A.* **77 J5** 32 26N 80 40W
Beaufort Sea, *Arctic* **4 B1** 72 0N 140 0W
Beaufort West, *S. Africa* **56 E3** 32 18S 22 36 E
Beauharnois, *Canada* **79 A11** 45 20N 73 52W
Beaulieu →, *Canada* **72 A6** 62 3N 113 11W
Beauly, *U.K.* **12 D4** 57 30N 4 28W
Beauly →, *U.K.* **12 D4** 57 29N 4 27W
Beaumaris, *U.K.* **10 D3** 53 16N 4 6W
Beaumont, *Belgium* **15 D4** 50 15N 4 14 E
Beaumont, *U.S.A.* **81 K7** 30 5N 94 6W
Beaune, *France* **18 C6** 47 2N 4 50 E
Beaupré, *Canada* **71 C5** 47 3N 70 54W
Beauraing, *Belgium* **15 D4** 50 7N 4 57 E
Beauséjour, *Canada* **73 C9** 50 5N 96 35W
Beauvais, *France* **18 B5** 49 25N 2 8 E
Beauval, *Canada* **73 B7** 55 9N 107 37W
Beaver, *Okla., U.S.A.* **81 G4** 36 49N 100 31W
Beaver, *Pa., U.S.A.* **78 F4** 40 42N 80 19W
Beaver, *Utah, U.S.A.* **83 G7** 38 17N 112 38W
Beaver →, *B.C., Canada* **72 B4** 59 52N 124 20W
Beaver →, *Ont., Canada* **70 A2** 55 55N 87 48W
Beaver →, *Sask., Canada* **73 B7** 55 26N 107 45W
Beaver →, *U.S.A.* **81 G5** 36 35N 99 30W
Beaver City, *U.S.A.* **80 E5** 40 8N 99 50W
Beaver Creek, *Canada* **68 B5** 63 0N 141 0W
Beaver Dam, *U.S.A.* **80 D10** 43 28N 88 50W
Beaver Falls, *U.S.A.* **78 F4** 40 46N 80 20W
Beaver Hill L., *Canada* **73 C10** 54 5N 94 50W
Beaver I., *U.S.A.* **76 C3** 45 40N 85 33W
Beaverhill L., *Canada* **72 C6** 53 27N 112 32W
Beaverlodge, *Canada* **72 B5** 55 11N 119 29W
Beaverstone →, *Canada* **70 B2** 54 59N 89 25W
Beaverton, *Canada* **78 B5** 44 26N 79 9W
Beaverton, *U.S.A.* **84 E4** 45 29N 122 48W
Beawar, *India* **42 F6** 26 3N 74 18 E
Bebedouro, *Brazil* **95 A6** 21 0S 48 25W
Beboa, *Madag.* **57 B7** 17 22S 44 33 E
Beccles, *U.K.* **11 E9** 52 27N 1 35 E
Bečej, *Serbia, Yug.* **21 B9** 45 36N 20 3 E
Béchar, *Algeria* **50 B5** 31 38N 2 18W
Beckley, *U.S.A.* **76 G5** 37 47N 81 11W
Beddouza, Ras, *Morocco* **50 B4** 32 33N 9 9W
Bedford, *Canada* **79 A12** 45 7N 72 59W
Bedford, *S. Africa* **56 E4** 32 40S 26 10 E
Bedford, *U.K.* **11 E7** 52 8N 0 28W
Bedford, *Ind., U.S.A.* **76 F2** 38 52N 86 29W
Bedford, *Iowa, U.S.A.* **80 E7** 40 40N 94 44W
Bedford, *Ohio, U.S.A.* **78 E3** 41 23N 81 32W
Bedford, *Pa., U.S.A.* **78 F6** 40 1N 78 30W
Bedford, *Va., U.S.A.* **76 G6** 37 20N 79 31W
Bedford, C., *Australia* **62 B4** 15 14S 145 21 E
**Bedfordshire** □, *U.K.* **11 E7** 52 4N 0 28W
Bedourie, *Australia* **62 C2** 24 30S 139 30 E
Bedum, *Neths.* **15 A6** 53 18N 6 36 E
Beebe Plain, *Canada* **79 A12** 45 1N 72 9W
Beech Creek, *U.S.A.* **78 E7** 41 5N 77 36W
Beenleigh, *Australia* **63 D5** 27 43S 153 10 E
Be'er Menuha, *Israel* **44 D2** 30 19N 35 8 E
Be'er Sheva, *Israel* **47 D3** 31 15N 34 48 E
**Beersheba** = Be'er Sheva, *Israel* **47 D3** 31 15N 34 48 E
Beeston, *U.K.* **10 E6** 52 56N 1 14W
Beeville, *U.S.A.* **81 L6** 28 24N 97 45W
Befale, *Dem. Rep. of the Congo* **52 D4** 0 25N 20 45 E
Befandriana, *Madag.* **57 C7** 21 55S 44 0 E
Befotaka, *Madag.* **57 C8** 23 49S 47 0 E
Bega, *Australia* **63 F4** 36 41S 149 51 E
Begusarai, *India* **43 G12** 25 24N 86 9 E
Behābād, *Iran* **45 C8** 32 24N 59 47 E
Behala, *India* **43 H13** 22 30N 88 20 E
Behara, *Madag.* **57 C8** 24 55S 46 20 E
Behbehān, *Iran* **45 D6** 30 30N 50 15 E
Behm Canal, *U.S.A.* **72 B2** 55 10N 131 0W
Behshahr, *Iran* **45 B7** 36 45N 53 35 E
Bei Jiang →, *China* **33 D6** 23 2N 112 58 E
Bei'an, *China* **33 B7** 48 10N 126 20 E
Beihai, *China* **33 D5** 21 28N 109 6 E
**Beijing**, *China* **34 E9** 39 55N 116 20 E
Beijing □, *China* **34 E9** 39 55N 116 20 E
Beilen, *Neths.* **15 B6** 52 52N 6 27 E
Beilpajah, *Australia* **63 E3** 32 54S 143 52 E
Beinn na Faoghla = Benbecula, *U.K.* **12 D1** 57 26N 7 21W
Beipiao, *China* **35 D11** 41 52N 120 32 E
Beira, *Mozam.* **55 F3** 19 50S 34 52 E
**Beirut** = Bayrūt, *Lebanon* **47 B4** 33 53N 35 31 E
Beiseker, *Canada* **72 C6** 51 23N 113 32W
Beitaolaizhao, *China* **35 B13** 44 58N 125 58 E
Beitbridge, *Zimbabwe* **55 G3** 22 12S 30 0 E
Beizhen = Binzhou, *China* **35 F10** 37 20N 118 2 E
Beizhen, *China* **35 D11** 41 38N 121 54 E
Beizhengzhen, *China* **35 B12** 44 31N 123 30 E
Beja, *Portugal* **19 C2** 38 2N 7 53W
Béja, *Tunisia* **51 A7** 36 43N 9 12 E
Bejaia, *Algeria* **50 A7** 36 42N 5 2 E
Béjar, *Spain* **19 B3** 40 23N 5 46W
Bejestān, *Iran* **45 C8** 34 30N 58 5 E
Békéscsaba, *Hungary* **17 E11** 46 40N 21 5 E
Bekily, *Madag.* **57 C8** 24 13S 45 19 E
Bekok, *Malaysia* **39 L4** 2 20N 103 7 E
Bela, *India* **43 G10** 25 50N 82 0 E
Bela, *Pakistan* **42 F2** 26 12N 66 20 E
Bela Crkva, *Serbia, Yug.* **21 B9** 44 55N 21 27 E
Bela Vista, *Brazil* **94 A4** 22 12S 56 20W
Bela Vista, *Mozam.* **57 D5** 26 10S 32 44 E
Belan →, *India* **43 G9** 24 2N 81 45 E
**Belarus** ■, *Europe* **17 B14** 53 30N 27 0 E
**Belau** = Palau ■, *Pac. Oc.* **28 J17** 7 30N 134 30 E
Belavenona, *Madag.* **57 C8** 24 50S 47 4 E
Belawan, *Indonesia* **36 D1** 3 33N 98 32 E
Belaya →, *Russia* **24 C9** 54 40N 56 0 E
Belaya Tserkov = Bila Tserkva, *Ukraine* **17 D16** 49 45N 30 10 E
Belcher Is., *Canada* **70 A3** 56 15N 78 45W
Belden, *U.S.A.* **84 E5** 40 2N 121 17W
Belebey, *Russia* **24 D9** 54 7N 54 7 E
Belém, *Brazil* **93 D9** 1 20S 48 30W
Belén, *Argentina* **94 B2** 27 40S 67 5W
Belén, *Paraguay* **94 A4** 23 30S 57 6W
Belen, *U.S.A.* **83 J10** 34 40N 106 46W

Belet Uen, *Somali Rep.* . . . **46 G4** 4 30N 45 5 E
Belev, *Russia* . . . . . . . . . **24 D6** 53 50N 36 5 E
Belfair, *U.S.A.* . . . . . . . . **84 C4** 47 27N 122 50W
Belfast, *S. Africa* . . . . . . **57 D5** 25 42S 30 2 E
**Belfast**, *U.K.* . . . . . . . . **13 B6** 54 37N 5 56W
Belfast, *Maine, U.S.A.* . . . . **77 C11** 44 26N 69 1W
Belfast, *N.Y., U.S.A.* . . . . **78 D6** 42 21N 78 7W
Belfast L., *U.K.* . . . . . . . **13 B6** 54 40N 5 50W
Belfield, *U.S.A.* . . . . . . . **80 B3** 46 53N 103 12W
Belfort, *France* . . . . . . . **18 C7** 47 38N 6 50 E
Belfry, *U.S.A.* . . . . . . . . **82 D9** 45 9N 109 1W
Belgaum, *India* . . . . . . . **40 M9** 15 55N 74 35 E
**Belgium** ■, *Europe* . . . . . **15 D4** 50 30N 5 0 E
Belgorod, *Russia* . . . . . . **25 D6** 50 35N 36 35 E
Belgorod-Dnestrovskiy = Bilhorod-Dnistrovskyy, *Ukraine* . . . . . . . . . **25 E5** 46 11N 30 23 E
**Belgrade** = Beograd, *Serbia, Yug.* . . . . . . . **21 B9** 44 50N 20 37 E
Belgrade, *U.S.A.* . . . . . . . **82 D8** 45 47N 111 11W
Belhaven, *U.S.A.* . . . . . . **77 H7** 35 33N 76 37W
Beli Drim →, *Europe* . . . . **21 C9** 42 6N 20 25 E
Belinyu, *Indonesia* . . . . . **36 E3** 1 35S 105 50 E
Beliton Is. = Belitung, *Indonesia* . . . . . . . . . **36 E3** 3 10S 107 50 E
Belitung, *Indonesia* . . . . . **36 E3** 3 10S 107 50 E
**Belize** ■, *Cent. Amer.* . . . . **87 D7** 17 0N 88 30W
Belize City, *Belize* . . . . . **87 D7** 17 25N 88 0W
Belkovskiy, Ostrov, *Russia* . **27 B14** 75 32N 135 44 E
Bell →, *Canada* . . . . . . . **70 C4** 49 48N 77 38W
Bell I., *Canada* . . . . . . . **71 B8** 50 46N 55 35W
Bell-Irving →, *Canada* . . . **72 B3** 56 12N 129 5W
Bell Peninsula, *Canada* . . . **69 B11** 63 50N 82 0W
Bell Ville, *Argentina* . . . . . **94 C3** 32 40S 62 40W
Bella Bella, *Canada* . . . . . **72 C3** 52 10N 128 10W
Bella Coola, *Canada* . . . . . **72 C3** 52 25N 126 40W
Bella Unión, *Uruguay* . . . . . **94 C4** 30 15S 57 40W
Bella Vista, *Corrientes, Argentina* . . . . . . . . . **94 B4** 28 33S 59 0W
Bella Vista, *Tucuman, Argentina* . . . . . . . . . **94 B2** 27 10S 65 25W
Bellaire, *U.S.A.* . . . . . . . **78 F4** 40 1N 80 45W
Bellary, *India* . . . . . . . . **40 M10** 15 10N 76 56 E
Bellata, *Australia* . . . . . . **63 D4** 29 53S 149 46 E
Belle-Chasse, *U.S.A.* . . . . . **81 L10** 29 51N 89 59W
Belle Fourche, *U.S.A.* . . . . **80 C3** 44 40N 103 51W
Belle Fourche →, *U.S.A.* . . **80 C3** 44 26N 102 18W
Belle Glade, *U.S.A.* . . . . . **77 M5** 26 41N 80 40W
Belle-Île, *France* . . . . . . . **18 C2** 47 20N 3 10W
Belle Isle, *Canada* . . . . . . **71 B8** 51 57N 55 25W
Belle Isle, Str. of, *Canada* . . **71 B8** 51 30N 56 30W
Belle Plaine, *U.S.A.* . . . . . **80 E8** 41 54N 92 17W
Bellefontaine, *U.S.A.* . . . . **76 E4** 40 22N 83 46W
Bellefonte, *U.S.A.* . . . . . . **78 F7** 40 55N 77 47W
Belleoram, *Canada* . . . . . . **71 C8** 47 31N 55 25W
Belleville, *Canada* . . . . . . **78 B7** 44 10N 77 23W
Belleville, *Ill., U.S.A.* . . . . **80 F10** 38 31N 89 59W
Belleville, *Kans., U.S.A.* . . **80 F6** 39 50N 97 38W
Belleville, *N.Y., U.S.A.* . . . **79 C8** 43 46N 76 10W
Bellevue, *Canada* . . . . . . . **72 D6** 49 35N 114 22W
Bellevue, *Idaho, U.S.A.* . . . **82 E6** 43 28N 114 16W
Bellevue, *Nebr., U.S.A.* . . . **80 E7** 41 8N 95 53W
Bellevue, *Ohio, U.S.A.* . . . **78 E2** 41 17N 82 51W
Bellevue, *Wash., U.S.A.* . . . **84 C4** 47 37N 122 12W
Bellin = Kangirsuk, *Canada* **69 C13** 60 0N 70 0W
Bellingen, *Australia* . . . . . **63 E5** 30 25S 152 50 E
Bellingham, *U.S.A.* . . . . . **68 D7** 48 46N 122 29W
Bellingshausen Sea, *Antarctica* . . . . . . . . . **5 C17** 66 0S 80 0W
Bellinzona, *Switz.* . . . . . . **18 C8** 46 11N 9 1 E
Bello, *Colombia* . . . . . . . **92 B3** 6 20N 75 33W
Bellows Falls, *U.S.A.* . . . . **79 C12** 43 8N 72 27W
Bellpat, *Pakistan* . . . . . . **42 E3** 29 0N 68 5 E
Belluno, *Italy* . . . . . . . . **20 A5** 46 9N 12 13 E
Bellwood, *U.S.A.* . . . . . . . **78 F6** 40 36N 78 20W
Belmont, *Canada* . . . . . . . **78 D3** 42 53N 81 5W
Belmont, *S. Africa* . . . . . . **56 D3** 29 28S 24 22 E
Belmont, *U.S.A.* . . . . . . . **78 D6** 42 14N 78 2W
Belmonte, *Brazil* . . . . . . . **93 G11** 16 0S 39 0W
**Belmopan**, *Belize* . . . . . . **87 D7** 17 18N 88 30W
Belmullet, *Ireland* . . . . . . **13 B2** 54 14N 9 58W
**Belo Horizonte**, *Brazil* . . . **93 G10** 19 55S 43 56W
Belo-sur-Mer, *Madag.* . . . . **57 C7** 20 42S 44 0 E
Belo-Tsiribihina, *Madag.* . . **57 B7** 19 40S 44 30 E
Belogorsk, *Russia* . . . . . . **27 D13** 51 0N 128 20 E
Beloha, *Madag.* . . . . . . . . **57 D8** 25 10S 45 3 E
Beloit, *Kans., U.S.A.* . . . . . **80 F5** 39 28N 98 6W
Beloit, *Wis., U.S.A.* . . . . . **80 D10** 42 31N 89 2W
Belokorovichi, *Ukraine* . . . . **17 C15** 51 7N 28 2 E
Belomorsk, *Russia* . . . . . . **24 B5** 64 35N 34 54 E
Belonia, *India* . . . . . . . . **41 H17** 23 15N 91 30 E
Beloretsk, *Russia* . . . . . . **24 D10** 53 58N 58 24 E
Belorussia = Belarus ■, *Europe* . . . . . . . . . **17 B14** 53 30N 27 0 E
Belovo, *Russia* . . . . . . . . **26 D9** 54 30N 86 0 E
Beloye, Ozero, *Russia* . . . . **24 B6** 60 10N 37 35 E
Beloye More, *Russia* . . . . . **24 A6** 66 30N 38 0 E
Belozersk, *Russia* . . . . . . **24 B6** 60 1N 37 45 E
Belpre, *U.S.A.* . . . . . . . . **76 F5** 39 17N 81 34W
Belrain, *India* . . . . . . . . **43 E9** 28 23N 80 55 E
Belt, *U.S.A.* . . . . . . . . . **82 C8** 47 23N 110 55W
Beltana, *Australia* . . . . . . **63 E2** 30 48S 138 25 E
Belterra, *Brazil* . . . . . . . **93 D8** 2 45S 55 0W
Belton, *U.S.A.* . . . . . . . . **81 K6** 31 3N 97 28W
Belton L., *U.S.A.* . . . . . . **81 K6** 31 8N 97 32W
Beltsy = Bălţi, *Moldova* . . . **17 E14** 47 48N 27 58 E
Belturbet, *Ireland* . . . . . . **13 B4** 54 6N 7 26W
Belukha, *Russia* . . . . . . . **26 E9** 49 50N 86 50 E
Beluran, *Malaysia* . . . . . . **36 C5** 5 48N 117 35 E
Belvidere, *Ill., U.S.A.* . . . . **80 D10** 42 15N 88 50W
Belvidere, *N.J., U.S.A.* . . . **79 F9** 40 50N 75 5W
Belyando →, *Australia* . . . **62 C4** 21 38S 146 50 E
Belyy, Ostrov, *Russia* . . . . **26 B8** 73 30N 71 0 E
Belyy Yar, *Russia* . . . . . . **26 D9** 58 26N 84 39 E
Belzoni, *U.S.A.* . . . . . . . . **81 J9** 33 11N 90 29W
Bemaraha, Lembalemban' i, *Madag.* . . . . . . . . . **57 B7** 18 40S 44 45 E
Bemarivo, *Madag.* . . . . . . . **57 C7** 21 45S 44 45 E
Bemarivo →, *Madag.* . . . . **57 B8** 15 27S 47 40 E
Bemavo, *Madag.* . . . . . . . . **57 C8** 21 33S 45 25 E
Bembéréke, *Benin* . . . . . . **50 F6** 10 11N 2 43 E
Bembesi, *Zimbabwe* . . . . . **55 G2** 20 0S 28 58 E
Bembesi →, *Zimbabwe* . . . **55 F2** 18 57S 27 47 E
Bemetara, *India* . . . . . . . **43 J9** 21 42N 81 32 E
Bemidji, *U.S.A.* . . . . . . . . **80 B7** 47 28N 94 53W
Ben, *Iran* . . . . . . . . . . . **45 C6** 32 32N 50 45 E
Ben Cruachan, *U.K.* . . . . . . **12 E3** 56 26N 5 8W
Ben Dearg, *U.K.* . . . . . . . . **12 D4** 57 47N 4 56W
Ben Hope, *U.K.* . . . . . . . . **12 C4** 58 25N 4 36W
Ben Lawers, *U.K.* . . . . . . . **12 E4** 56 32N 4 14W
Ben Lomond, *N.S.W., Australia* . . . . . . . . . **63 E5** 30 1S 151 43 E
Ben Lomond, *Tas., Australia* **62 G4** 41 38S 147 42 E
Ben Lomond, *U.K.* . . . . . . . **12 E4** 56 11N 4 38W
Ben Luc, *Vietnam* . . . . . . . **39 G6** 10 39N 106 29 E
Ben Macdhui, *U.K.* . . . . . . **12 D5** 57 4N 3 40W
Ben Mhor, *U.K.* . . . . . . . . **12 D1** 57 15N 7 18W
Ben More, *Arg. & Bute, U.K.* **12 E2** 56 26N 6 1W
Ben More, *Stirl., U.K.* . . . . **12 E4** 56 23N 4 32W
Ben More Assynt, *U.K.* . . . . **12 C4** 58 8N 4 52W
**Ben Nevis**, *U.K.* . . . . . . . **12 E3** 56 48N 5 1W
Ben Quang, *Vietnam* . . . . . **38 D6** 17 3N 106 55 E
Ben Vorlich, *U.K.* . . . . . . . **12 E4** 56 21N 4 14W
Ben Wyvis, *U.K.* . . . . . . . **12 D4** 57 40N 4 35W
Bena, *Nigeria* . . . . . . . . . **50 F7** 11 20N 5 50 E
Benalla, *Australia* . . . . . . **63 F4** 36 30S 146 0 E
**Benares** = Varanasi, *India* **43 G10** 25 22N 83 0 E
Benavente, *Spain* . . . . . . . **19 A3** 42 2N 5 43W
Benavides, *U.S.A.* . . . . . . **81 M5** 27 36N 98 25W
Benbecula, *U.K.* . . . . . . . **12 D1** 57 26N 7 21W
Benbonyathe, *Australia* . . . **63 E2** 30 25S 139 11 E
Bend, *U.S.A.* . . . . . . . . . **82 D3** 44 4N 121 19W
Bendemeer, *Australia* . . . . **63 E5** 30 53S 151 8 E
Bender Beila, *Somali Rep.* . . **46 F5** 9 30N 50 48 E
Bendery = Tighina, *Moldova* . . . . . . . . . . **17 E15** 46 50N 29 30 E
Bendigo, *Australia* . . . . . . **63 F3** 36 40S 144 15 E
Benē Beraq, *Israel* . . . . . . **47 C3** 32 6N 34 51 E
Benenitra, *Madag.* . . . . . . **57 C8** 23 27S 45 5 E
Benevento, *Italy* . . . . . . . **20 D6** 41 8N 14 45 E
Benga, *Mozam.* . . . . . . . . **55 F3** 16 11S 33 40 E
**Bengal, Bay of**, *Ind. Oc.* . . **41 M17** 15 0N 90 0 E
Bengbu, *China* . . . . . . . . **35 H9** 32 58N 117 20 E
**Benghazi** = Banghāzī, *Libya* . . . . . . . . . . . **51 B10** 32 11N 20 3 E
Bengkalis, *Indonesia* . . . . . **36 D2** 1 30N 102 10 E
Bengkulu, *Indonesia* . . . . . **36 E2** 3 50S 102 12 E
Bengkulu □, *Indonesia* . . . **36 E2** 3 48S 102 16 E
Bengough, *Canada* . . . . . . **73 D7** 49 25N 105 10W
Benguela, *Angola* . . . . . . . **53 G2** 12 37S 13 25 E
Benguérua, I., *Mozam.* . . . . **57 C6** 21 58S 35 28 E
Beni, *Dem. Rep. of the Congo* . **54 B2** 0 30N 29 27 E
Beni →, *Bolivia* . . . . . . . **92 F5** 10 23S 65 24W
Beni Mellal, *Morocco* . . . . . **50 B4** 32 21N 6 21W
Beni Suef, *Egypt* . . . . . . . **51 C12** 29 5N 31 6 E
Beniah L., *Canada* . . . . . . **72 A6** 63 23N 112 17W
Benicia, *U.S.A.* . . . . . . . . **84 G4** 38 3N 122 9W
Benidorm, *Spain* . . . . . . . **19 C5** 38 33N 0 9W
**Benin** ■, *Africa* . . . . . . . **50 G6** 10 0N 2 0 E
Benin, Bight of, *W. Afr.* . . . **50 H6** 5 0N 3 0 E
Benin City, *Nigeria* . . . . . . **50 G7** 6 20N 5 31 E
Benitses, *Greece* . . . . . . . **23 A3** 39 32N 19 55 E
Benjamin Aceval, *Paraguay* **94 A4** 24 58S 57 34W
Benjamin Constant, *Brazil* . **92 D4** 4 40S 70 15W
Benjamin Hill, *Mexico* . . . . **86 A2** 30 10N 111 10W
Benkelman, *U.S.A.* . . . . . . **80 E4** 40 3N 101 32W
Bennett, *Canada* . . . . . . . **72 B2** 59 56N 134 53W
Bennett, L., *Australia* . . . . **60 D5** 22 50S 131 2 E
Bennetta, Ostrov, *Russia* . . **27 B15** 76 21N 148 56 E
Bennettsville, *U.S.A.* . . . . . **77 H6** 34 37N 79 41W
Bennington, *N.H., U.S.A.* . . **79 D11** 43 0N 71 55W
Bennington, *Vt., U.S.A.* . . . **79 D11** 42 53N 73 12W
Benoni, *S. Africa* . . . . . . . **57 D4** 26 11S 28 18 E
Benque Viejo, *Belize* . . . . . **87 D7** 17 5N 89 8W
Benson, *Ariz., U.S.A.* . . . . **83 L8** 31 58N 110 18W
Benson, *Minn., U.S.A.* . . . . **80 C7** 45 19N 95 36W
Bent, *Iran* . . . . . . . . . . . **45 E8** 26 20N 59 31 E
Benteng, *Indonesia* . . . . . . **37 F6** 6 10S 120 30 E
Bentinck I., *Australia* . . . . **62 B2** 17 3S 139 35 E
Bento Gonçalves, *Brazil* . . . **95 B5** 29 10S 51 31W
Benton, *Ark., U.S.A.* . . . . . **81 H8** 34 34N 92 35W
Benton, *Calif., U.S.A.* . . . . **84 H8** 37 48N 118 32W
Benton, *Ill., U.S.A.* . . . . . **80 G10** 38 0N 88 55W
Benton, *Pa., U.S.A.* . . . . . **79 E8** 41 12N 76 23W
Benton Harbor, *U.S.A.* . . . . **76 D2** 42 6N 86 27W
Bentonville, *U.S.A.* . . . . . . **81 G7** 36 22N 94 13W
Bentung, *Malaysia* . . . . . . **39 L3** 3 31N 101 55 E
Benue →, *Nigeria* . . . . . . **50 G7** 7 48N 6 46 E
Benxi, *China* . . . . . . . . . **35 D12** 41 20N 123 48 E
Beo, *Indonesia* . . . . . . . . **37 D7** 4 25N 126 50 E
Beograd, *Serbia, Yug.* . . . . **21 B9** 44 50N 20 37 E
Beppu, *Japan* . . . . . . . . . **31 H5** 33 15N 131 30 E
Beqaa Valley = Al Biqā, *Lebanon* . . . . . . . . . **47 A5** 34 10N 36 10 E
Ber Mota, *India* . . . . . . . . **42 H3** 23 27N 68 34 E
Berach →, *India* . . . . . . . **42 G6** 25 15N 75 2 E
Berati, *Albania* . . . . . . . . **21 D8** 40 43N 19 59 E
Berau, Teluk, *Indonesia* . . . **37 E8** 2 30S 132 30 E
Berber, *Sudan* . . . . . . . . . **51 E12** 18 0N 34 0 E
Berbera, *Somali Rep.* . . . . . **46 E4** 10 30N 45 2 E
Berbérati, *C.A.R.* . . . . . . . **52 D3** 4 15N 15 40 E
Berbice →, *Guyana* . . . . . **92 B7** 6 20N 57 32W
Berdichev = Berdychiv, *Ukraine* . . . . . . . . . **17 D15** 49 57N 28 30 E
Berdsk, *Russia* . . . . . . . . **26 D9** 54 47N 83 2 E
Berdyansk, *Ukraine* . . . . . . **25 E6** 46 45N 36 50 E
Berdychiv, *Ukraine* . . . . . . **17 D15** 49 57N 28 30 E
Berea, *U.S.A.* . . . . . . . . . **76 G3** 37 34N 84 17W
Berebere, *Indonesia* . . . . . **37 D7** 2 25N 128 45 E
Bereda, *Somali Rep.* . . . . . **46 E5** 11 45N 51 0 E
Berehove, *Ukraine* . . . . . . **17 D12** 48 15N 22 35 E
Berekum, *Ghana* . . . . . . . . **50 G5** 7 29N 2 34W
Berens →, *Canada* . . . . . . **73 C9** 52 25N 97 2W
Berens I., *Canada* . . . . . . . **73 C9** 52 18N 97 18W
Berens River, *Canada* . . . . . **73 C9** 52 25N 97 0W
Beresford, *U.S.A.* . . . . . . . **80 D6** 43 5N 96 47W
Berestechko, *Ukraine* . . . . . **17 C13** 50 22N 25 5 E
Berevo, *Mahajanga, Madag.* **57 B7** 17 14S 44 17 E
Berevo, *Toliara, Madag.* . . . **57 B7** 19 44S 44 58 E
Bereza, *Belarus* . . . . . . . . **17 B13** 52 31N 24 51 E
Berezhany, *Ukraine* . . . . . . **17 D13** 49 26N 24 58 E
Berezina = Byarezina →, *Belarus* . . . . . . . . . **17 B16** 52 33N 30 14 E
Bereznik, *Russia* . . . . . . . **24 B7** 62 51N 42 40 E
Berezniki, *Russia* . . . . . . . **24 C10** 59 24N 56 46 E
Berezovo, *Russia* . . . . . . . **26 C7** 64 0N 65 0 E
Berga, *Spain* . . . . . . . . . **19 A6** 42 6N 1 48 E
Bergama, *Turkey* . . . . . . . **21 E12** 39 8N 27 11 E
Bérgamo, *Italy* . . . . . . . . **18 D8** 45 41N 9 43 E
Bergen, *Neths.* . . . . . . . . **15 B4** 52 40N 4 43 E
**Bergen**, *Norway* . . . . . . . **9 F11** 60 20N 5 20 E
Bergen, *U.S.A.* . . . . . . . . **78 C7** 43 5N 77 57W
Bergen op Zoom, *Neths.* . . . **15 C4** 51 28N 4 18 E
Bergerac, *France* . . . . . . . **18 D4** 44 51N 0 30 E
Bergholz, *U.S.A.* . . . . . . . **78 F4** 40 31N 80 53W
Bergisch Gladbach, *Germany* . . . . . . . . . **15 D7** 50 59N 7 8 E
Bergville, *S. Africa* . . . . . . **57 D4** 28 52S 29 18 E
Berhala, Selat, *Indonesia* . . **36 E2** 1 0S 104 15 E
Berhampore = Baharampur, *India* . . . . . . . . . **43 G13** 24 2N 88 27 E
Berhampur = Brahmapur, *India* . . . . . . . . . **41 K14** 19 15N 84 54 E
**Bering Sea**, *Pac. Oc.* . . . . **68 C1** 58 0N 171 0 E
**Bering Strait**, *Pac. Oc.* . . . **68 B3** 65 30N 169 0W
Beringovskiy, *Russia* . . . . . **27 C18** 63 3N 179 19 E
Berisso, *Argentina* . . . . . . **94 C4** 34 56S 57 50W
Berja, *Spain* . . . . . . . . . . **19 D4** 36 50N 2 56W
Berkeley, *U.S.A.* . . . . . . . **84 H4** 37 52N 122 16W
Berkner I., *Antarctica* . . . . **5 D18** 79 30S 50 0W
Berkshire, *U.S.A.* . . . . . . . **79 D8** 42 19N 76 11W
Berkshire Downs, *U.K.* . . . . **11 F6** 51 33N 1 29W
Berlin, *Germany* . . . . . . . . **16 B7** 52 30N 13 25 E
Berlin, *Md., U.S.A.* . . . . . . **76 F8** 38 20N 75 13W
Berlin, *N.H., U.S.A.* . . . . . **79 B13** 44 28N 71 11W
Berlin, *N.Y., U.S.A.* . . . . . **79 D11** 42 42N 73 23W
Berlin, *Wis., U.S.A.* . . . . . **76 D1** 43 58N 88 57W
Berlin L., *U.S.A.* . . . . . . . **78 E4** 41 3N 81 0W
Bermejo →, *Formosa, Argentina* . . . . . . . . . **94 B4** 26 51S 58 23W
Bermejo →, *San Juan, Argentina* . . . . . . . . . **94 C2** 32 30S 67 30W
Bermen, L., *Canada* . . . . . . **71 B6** 53 35N 68 55W
**Bermuda** ■, *Atl. Oc.* . . . . **66 F13** 32 45N 65 0W
**Bern**, *Switz.* . . . . . . . . . **18 C7** 46 57N 7 28 E
Bernalillo, *U.S.A.* . . . . . . . **83 J10** 35 18N 106 33W
Bernardo de Irigoyen, *Argentina* . . . . . . . . . **95 B5** 26 15S 53 40W
Bernardo O'Higgins □, *Chile* **94 C1** 34 15S 70 45W
Bernardsville, *U.S.A.* . . . . . **79 F10** 40 43N 74 34W
Bernasconi, *Argentina* . . . . **94 D3** 37 55S 63 44W
Bernburg, *Germany* . . . . . . **16 C6** 51 47N 11 44 E
Berne = Bern, *Switz.* . . . . . **18 C7** 46 57N 7 28 E
Berneray, *U.K.* . . . . . . . . . **12 D1** 57 43N 7 11W
Bernier I., *Australia* . . . . . **61 D1** 24 50S 113 12 E
Bernina, Piz, *Switz.* . . . . . . **18 C8** 46 20N 9 54 E
Beroroha, *Madag.* . . . . . . . **57 C8** 21 40S 45 10 E
Beroun, *Czech Rep.* . . . . . . **16 D8** 49 57N 14 5 E
Berri, *Australia* . . . . . . . . **63 E3** 34 14S 140 35 E
Berriane, *Algeria* . . . . . . . **50 B6** 32 50N 3 46 E
Berrigan, *Australia* . . . . . . **63 F4** 35 38S 145 49 E
Berry, *Australia* . . . . . . . . **63 E5** 34 46S 150 43 E
Berry, *France* . . . . . . . . . **18 C5** 46 50N 2 0 E
Berry Is., *Bahamas* . . . . . . **88 A4** 25 40N 77 50W
Berryessa L., *U.S.A.* . . . . . **84 G4** 38 31N 122 6W
Berryville, *U.S.A.* . . . . . . . **81 G8** 36 22N 93 34W
Bershad, *Ukraine* . . . . . . . **17 D15** 48 22N 29 31 E
Berthold, *U.S.A.* . . . . . . . . **80 A4** 48 19N 101 44W
Berthoud, *U.S.A.* . . . . . . . **80 E2** 40 19N 105 5W
Bertoua, *Cameroon* . . . . . . **52 D2** 4 30N 13 45 E
Bertraghboy B., *Ireland* . . . **13 C2** 53 22N 9 54W
Berwick, *U.S.A.* . . . . . . . . **79 E8** 41 3N 76 14W
Berwick-upon-Tweed, *U.K.* . . **10 B6** 55 46N 2 0W
Berwyn Mts., *U.K.* . . . . . . . **10 E4** 52 54N 3 26W
Besal, *Pakistan* . . . . . . . . **43 B5** 35 4N 73 56 E
Besalampy, *Madag.* . . . . . . **57 B7** 16 43S 44 29 E
Besançon, *France* . . . . . . . **18 C7** 47 15N 6 2 E
Besar, *Indonesia* . . . . . . . **36 E5** 2 40S 116 0 E
Besnard L., *Canada* . . . . . . **73 B7** 55 25N 106 0W
Besni, *Turkey* . . . . . . . . . **44 B3** 37 41N 37 52 E
Besor, N. →, *Egypt* . . . . . . **47 D3** 31 28N 34 22 E
Bessarabiya, *Moldova* . . . . **17 E15** 47 0N 28 10 E
Bessarabka = Basarabeasca, *Moldova* . . . . . . . . . **17 E15** 46 21N 28 58 E
Bessemer, *Ala., U.S.A.* . . . . **77 J2** 33 24N 86 58W
Bessemer, *Mich., U.S.A.* . . . **80 B9** 46 29N 90 3W
Bessemer, *Pa., U.S.A.* . . . . **78 F4** 40 59N 80 30W
Beswick, *Australia* . . . . . . **60 B5** 14 34S 132 53 E
Bet She'an, *Israel* . . . . . . . **47 C4** 32 30N 35 30 E
Bet Shemesh, *Israel* . . . . . **47 D4** 31 44N 35 0 E
Betafo, *Madag.* . . . . . . . . **57 B8** 19 50S 46 51 E
Betancuria, *Canary Is.* . . . . **22 F5** 28 25N 14 3W
Betanzos, *Spain* . . . . . . . . **19 A1** 43 15N 8 12W
Bétaré Oya, *Cameroon* . . . . **52 C2** 5 40N 14 5 E
Bethal, *S. Africa* . . . . . . . **57 D4** 26 27S 29 28 E
Bethanien, *Namibia* . . . . . . **56 D2** 26 31S 17 8 E
Bethany, *Canada* . . . . . . . **78 B6** 44 11N 78 34W
Bethany, *U.S.A.* . . . . . . . . **80 E7** 40 16N 94 2W
Bethel, *Alaska, U.S.A.* . . . . **68 B3** 60 48N 161 45W
Bethel, *Conn., U.S.A.* . . . . . **79 E11** 41 22N 73 25W
Bethel, *Maine, U.S.A.* . . . . **79 B14** 44 25N 70 47W
Bethel, *Vt., U.S.A.* . . . . . . **79 C12** 43 50N 72 38W
Bethel Park, *U.S.A.* . . . . . . **78 F4** 40 20N 80 1W
**Bethlehem** = Bayt Lahm, *West Bank* . . . . . . . . . **47 D4** 31 43N 35 12 E
Bethlehem, *S. Africa* . . . . . **57 D4** 28 14S 28 18 E
Bethlehem, *U.S.A.* . . . . . . **79 F9** 40 37N 75 23W
Bethulie, *S. Africa* . . . . . . **56 E4** 30 30S 25 59 E
Béthune, *France* . . . . . . . **18 A5** 50 30N 2 38 E
Betioky, *Madag.* . . . . . . . . **57 C7** 23 48S 44 20 E
Betong, *Thailand* . . . . . . . **39 K3** 5 45N 101 5 E
Betoota, *Australia* . . . . . . **62 D3** 25 45S 140 42 E
Betroka, *Madag.* . . . . . . . . **57 C8** 23 16S 46 0 E
Betsiamites, *Canada* . . . . . **71 C6** 48 56N 68 40W
Betsiamites →, *Canada* . . . **71 C6** 48 56N 68 38W
Betsiboka →, *Madag.* . . . . **57 B8** 16 3S 46 36 E
Bettendorf, *U.S.A.* . . . . . . **80 E9** 41 32N 90 30W
Bettiah, *India* . . . . . . . . . **43 F11** 26 48N 84 33 E
Betul, *India* . . . . . . . . . . **40 J10** 21 58N 77 59 E
Betung, *Malaysia* . . . . . . . **36 D4** 1 24N 111 31 E
Betws-y-Coed, *U.K.* . . . . . . **10 D4** 53 5N 3 48W
Beulah, *Mich., U.S.A.* . . . . . **76 C2** 44 38N 86 6W
Beulah, *N. Dak., U.S.A.* . . . **80 B4** 47 16N 101 47W
Beveren, *Belgium* . . . . . . . **15 C4** 51 12N 4 16 E
Beverley, *Australia* . . . . . . **61 F2** 32 9S 116 56 E
Beverley, *U.K.* . . . . . . . . **10 D7** 53 51N 0 26W
Beverley Hills, *U.S.A.* . . . . **77 L4** 28 56N 82 28W
Beverly, *U.S.A.* . . . . . . . . **79 D14** 42 33N 70 53W
Beverly Hills, *U.S.A.* . . . . . **85 L8** 34 4N 118 25W
Bewas →, *India* . . . . . . . **43 H8** 23 59N 79 21 E
Bexhill, *U.K.* . . . . . . . . . **11 G8** 50 51N 0 29 E
Beyānlū, *Iran* . . . . . . . . . **44 C5** 36 0N 47 51 E
Beyneu, *Kazakstan* . . . . . . **25 E10** 45 18N 55 9 E
Beypazarı, *Turkey* . . . . . . **25 F5** 40 10N 31 56 E
Beyşehir Gölü, *Turkey* . . . . **25 G5** 37 41N 31 33 E
Béziers, *France* . . . . . . . . **18 E5** 43 20N 3 12 E
Bezwada = Vijayawada, *India* . . . . . . . . . **41 L12** 16 31N 80 39 E
Bhabua, *India* . . . . . . . . . **43 G10** 25 3N 83 37 E
Bhachau, *India* . . . . . . . . **40 H7** 23 20N 70 16 E
Bhadar →, *Gujarat, India* . **42 H5** 22 17N 72 20 E
Bhadar →, *Gujarat, India* . **42 J3** 21 27N 69 47 E
Bhadarwah, *India* . . . . . . . **43 C6** 32 58N 75 46 E
Bhadohi, *India* . . . . . . . . **43 G10** 25 25N 82 34 E
Bhadra, *India* . . . . . . . . . **42 E6** 29 8N 75 14 E
Bhadrakh, *India* . . . . . . . **41 J15** 21 10N 86 30 E
Bhadran, *India* . . . . . . . . **42 H5** 22 19N 72 6 E
Bhadravati, *India* . . . . . . **40 N9** 13 49N 75 40 E
Bhag, *Pakistan* . . . . . . . . **42 E2** 29 2N 67 49 E
Bhagalpur, *India* . . . . . . . **43 G12** 25 10N 87 0 E
Bhagirathi →, *Ut. P., India* **43 D8** 30 8N 78 35 E
Bhagirathi →, *W. Bengal, India* . . . . . . . . . **43 H13** 23 25N 88 23 E
Bhakkar, *Pakistan* . . . . . . **42 D4** 31 40N 71 5 E
Bhakra Dam, *India* . . . . . . **42 D7** 31 30N 76 45 E
Bhamo, *Burma* . . . . . . . . . **41 G20** 24 15N 97 15 E
Bhandara, *India* . . . . . . . **40 J11** 21 5N 79 42 E
Bhanpura, *India* . . . . . . . **42 G6** 24 31N 75 44 E
Bhanrer Ra., *India* . . . . . . **43 H8** 23 40N 79 45 E
Bhaptiahi, *India* . . . . . . . **43 F12** 26 19N 86 44 E
Bharat = India ■, *Asia* . . . **40 K11** 20 0N 78 0 E
Bharatpur, *Mad. P., India* . . **43 H9** 23 44N 81 46 E
Bharatpur, *Raj., India* . . . . **42 F7** 27 15N 77 30 E
Bharno, *India* . . . . . . . . . **43 H11** 23 14N 84 53 E
Bhatinda, *India* . . . . . . . **42 D6** 30 15N 74 57 E
Bhatpara, *India* . . . . . . . **43 H13** 22 50N 88 25 E
Bhattu, *India* . . . . . . . . . **42 E6** 29 36N 75 19 E
Bhaun, *Pakistan* . . . . . . . **42 C5** 32 55N 72 40 E
Bhaunagar = Bhavnagar, *India* . . . . . . . . . **40 J8** 21 45N 72 10 E
Bhavnagar, *India* . . . . . . . **40 J8** 21 45N 72 10 E
Bhawanipatna, *India* . . . . . **41 K12** 19 55N 80 10 E
Bhawari, *India* . . . . . . . . **42 G5** 25 42N 73 4 E
Bhayavadar, *India* . . . . . . **42 J4** 21 51N 70 15 E
Bhera, *Pakistan* . . . . . . . **42 C5** 32 29N 72 57 E
Bhikangaon, *India* . . . . . . **42 J6** 21 52N 75 57 E
Bhilsa = Vidisha, *India* . . . **42 H7** 23 28N 77 53 E
Bhilwara, *India* . . . . . . . . **42 G6** 25 25N 74 38 E
Bhima →, *India* . . . . . . . **40 L10** 16 25N 77 17 E
Bhimavaram, *India* . . . . . . **41 L12** 16 30N 81 30 E
Bhimbar, *Pakistan* . . . . . . **43 C6** 32 59N 74 3 E
Bhind, *India* . . . . . . . . . **43 F8** 26 30N 78 46 E
Bhinga, *India* . . . . . . . . . **43 F9** 27 43N 81 56 E
Bhinmal, *India* . . . . . . . . **42 G5** 25 0N 72 15 E
Bhiwandi, *India* . . . . . . . **40 K8** 19 20N 73 0 E
Bhiwani, *India* . . . . . . . . **42 E7** 28 50N 76 9 E
Bhogava →, *India* . . . . . . **42 H5** 22 26N 72 20 E
Bhola, *Bangla.* . . . . . . . . **41 H17** 22 45N 90 35 E
Bholari, *Pakistan* . . . . . . **42 G3** 25 19N 68 13 E
**Bhopal**, *India* . . . . . . . . **42 H7** 23 20N 77 30 E
Bhubaneshwar, *India* . . . . . **41 J14** 20 15N 85 50 E
Bhuj, *India* . . . . . . . . . . **42 H3** 23 15N 69 49 E
Bhusaval, *India* . . . . . . . . **40 J9** 21 3N 75 46 E
**Bhutan** ■, *Asia* . . . . . . . **41 F17** 27 25N 90 30 E
Biafra, B. of = Bonny, Bight of, *Africa* . . . . . . . . . **52 D1** 3 30N 9 20 E
Biak, *Indonesia* . . . . . . . . **37 E9** 1 10S 136 6 E
Biała Podlaska, *Poland* . . . **17 B12** 52 4N 23 6 E
Białogard, *Poland* . . . . . . **16 A8** 54 2N 15 58 E
Białystok, *Poland* . . . . . . . **17 B12** 53 10N 23 10 E
Biaora, *India* . . . . . . . . . **42 H7** 23 56N 76 56 E
Bīārjmand, *Iran* . . . . . . . . **45 B7** 36 6N 55 53 E
Biaro, *Indonesia* . . . . . . . **37 D7** 2 5N 125 26 E
Biarritz, *France* . . . . . . . . **18 E3** 43 29N 1 33W
Bibai, *Japan* . . . . . . . . . . **30 C10** 43 19N 141 52 E
Bibby I., *Canada* . . . . . . . **73 A10** 61 55N 93 0W
Biberach, *Germany* . . . . . . **16 D5** 48 5N 9 47 E
Bibungwa, *Dem. Rep. of the Congo* . **54 C2** 2 40S 28 15 E
Bic, *Canada* . . . . . . . . . . **71 C6** 48 20N 68 41W
Bicester, *U.K.* . . . . . . . . . **11 F6** 51 54N 1 9W
Bicheno, *Australia* . . . . . . **62 G4** 41 52S 148 18 E
Bichia, *India* . . . . . . . . . **43 H9** 22 27N 80 42 E
Bickerton I., *Australia* . . . . **62 A2** 13 45S 136 10 E
Bida, *Nigeria* . . . . . . . . . **50 G7** 9 3N 5 58 E
Bidar, *India* . . . . . . . . . . **40 L10** 17 55N 77 35 E
Biddeford, *U.S.A.* . . . . . . . **77 D10** 43 30N 70 28W
Bideford, *U.K.* . . . . . . . . **11 F3** 51 1N 4 13W
Bideford Bay, *U.K.* . . . . . . **11 F3** 51 5N 4 20W
Bidhuna, *India* . . . . . . . . **43 F8** 26 49N 79 31 E
Bidor, *Malaysia* . . . . . . . . **39 K3** 4 6N 101 15 E
Bié, Planalto de, *Angola* . . . **53 G3** 12 0S 16 0 E
Bieber, *U.S.A.* . . . . . . . . . **82 F3** 41 7N 121 8W
Biel, *Switz.* . . . . . . . . . . **18 C7** 47 8N 7 14 E
Bielefeld, *Germany* . . . . . . **16 B5** 52 1N 8 33 E
Biella, *Italy* . . . . . . . . . . **18 D8** 45 34N 8 3 E
Bielsk Podlaski, *Poland* . . . **17 B12** 52 47N 23 12 E
Bielsko-Biała, *Poland* . . . . **17 D10** 49 50N 19 2 E
Bien Hoa, *Vietnam* . . . . . . **39 G6** 10 57N 106 49 E
Bienne = Biel, *Switz.* . . . . . **18 C7** 47 8N 7 14 E
Bienville, L., *Canada* . . . . . **70 A5** 55 5N 72 40W
Biesiesfontein, *S. Africa* . . . **56 E2** 30 57S 17 58 E
Big →, *Canada* . . . . . . . . **71 B8** 54 50N 58 55W
Big B., *Canada* . . . . . . . . **71 A7** 55 43N 60 35W
Big Bear City, *U.S.A.* . . . . . **85 L10** 34 16N 116 51W
Big Bear Lake, *U.S.A.* . . . . **85 L10** 34 15N 116 56W
Big Belt Mts., *U.S.A.* . . . . . **82 C8** 46 30N 111 25W
Big Bend, *Swaziland* . . . . . **57 D5** 26 50S 31 58 E
Big Bend National Park, *U.S.A.* . . . . . . . . . **81 L3** 29 20N 103 5W
Big Black →, *U.S.A.* . . . . . **81 K9** 32 3N 91 4W
Big Blue →, *U.S.A.* . . . . . **80 F6** 39 35N 96 34W
Big Creek, *U.S.A.* . . . . . . . **84 H7** 37 11N 119 14W
Big Cypress National Preserve, *U.S.A.* . . . . . . **77 M5** 26 0N 81 10W
Big Cypress Swamp, *U.S.A.* . **77 M5** 26 12N 81 10W
Big Falls, *U.S.A.* . . . . . . . **80 A8** 48 12N 93 48W
Big Fork →, *U.S.A.* . . . . . **80 A8** 48 31N 93 43W
Big Horn Mts. = Bighorn Mts., *U.S.A.* . . . . . . . . **82 D10** 44 30N 107 30W
Big I., *Canada* . . . . . . . . . **72 A5** 61 7N 116 45W
Big Lake, *U.S.A.* . . . . . . . **81 K4** 31 12N 101 28W
Big Moose, *U.S.A.* . . . . . . **79 C10** 43 49N 74 58W
Big Muddy Cr. →, *U.S.A.* . . **80 A2** 48 8N 104 36W
Big Pine, *U.S.A.* . . . . . . . . **84 H8** 37 10N 118 17W
Big Piney, *U.S.A.* . . . . . . . **82 E8** 42 32N 110 7W
Big Rapids, *U.S.A.* . . . . . . **76 D3** 43 42N 85 29W
Big Rideau L., *Canada* . . . . **79 B8** 44 40N 76 15W
Big River, *Canada* . . . . . . . **73 C7** 53 50N 107 0W
Big Run, *U.S.A.* . . . . . . . . **78 F6** 40 57N 78 55W
Big Sable Pt., *U.S.A.* . . . . . **76 C2** 44 3N 86 1W
Big Salmon →, *Canada* . . . **72 A2** 61 52N 134 55W
Big Sand L., *Canada* . . . . . **73 B9** 57 45N 99 45W
Big Sandy, *U.S.A.* . . . . . . . **82 B8** 48 11N 110 7W
Big Sandy →, *U.S.A.* . . . . **76 F4** 38 25N 82 36W
Big Sandy Cr. →, *U.S.A.* . . **80 F3** 38 7N 102 29W
Big Sioux →, *U.S.A.* . . . . . **80 D6** 42 29N 96 27W

Big Spring, U.S.A. 81 J4 32 15N 101 28W
Big Stone City, U.S.A. 80 C6 45 18N 96 28W
Big Stone Gap, U.S.A. 77 G4 36 52N 82 47W
Big Stone L., U.S.A. 80 C6 45 30N 96 35W
Big Sur, U.S.A. 84 J5 36 15N 121 48W
Big Timber, U.S.A. 82 D9 45 50N 109 57W
Big Trout L., Canada 70 B2 53 40N 90 0W
Big Trout Lake, Canada 70 B2 53 45N 90 0W
Biğa, Turkey 21 D12 40 13N 27 14 E
Bigadiç, Turkey 21 E13 39 22N 28 7 E
Biggar, Canada 73 C7 52 4N 108 0W
Biggar, U.K. 12 F5 55 38N 3 32W
Bigge I., Australia 60 B4 14 35S 125 10 E
Biggenden, Australia 63 D5 25 31S 152 4 E
Biggleswade, U.K. 11 E7 52 5N 0 14W
Biggs, U.S.A. 84 F5 39 25N 121 43W
Bighorn, U.S.A. 82 C10 46 10N 107 27W
Bighorn —►, U.S.A. 82 C10 46 10N 107 28W
Bighorn L., U.S.A. 82 D9 44 55N 108 15W
Bighorn Mts., U.S.A. 82 D10 44 30N 107 30W
Bigstone L., Canada 73 C9 53 42N 95 44W
Bigwa, Tanzania 54 D4 7 10S 39 10 E
Bihać, Bos.-H. 16 F8 44 49N 15 57 E
**Bihar**, India 43 G11 25 5N 85 40 E
Bihar □, India 43 G12 25 0N 86 0 E
Biharamulo, Tanzania 54 C3 2 25S 31 25 E
Bihariganj, India 43 G12 25 44N 86 59 E
Bihor, Munţii, Romania 17 E12 46 29N 22 47 E
Bijagós, Arquipélago dos, Guinea-Biss. 50 F2 11 15N 16 10W
Bijaipur, India 42 F7 26 2N 77 20 E
Bijapur, Karnataka, India 40 L9 16 50N 75 55 E
Bijapur, Mad. P., India 41 K12 18 50N 80 50 E
Bījār, Iran 44 C5 35 52N 47 35 E
Bijawar, India 43 G8 24 38N 79 30 E
Bijeljina, Bos.-H. 21 B8 44 46N 19 14 E
Bijnor, India 42 E8 29 27N 78 11 E
Bikaner, India 42 E5 28 2N 73 18 E
Bikapur, India 43 F10 26 30N 82 7 E
Bikeqi, China 34 D6 40 43N 111 20 E
Bikfayyā, Lebanon 47 B4 33 55N 35 41 E
Bikin, Russia 27 E14 46 50N 134 20 E
Bikin —►, Russia 30 A7 46 51N 134 2 E
**Bikini Atoll**, Marshall Is. 64 F8 12 0N 167 30 E
Bikoro, Dem. Rep. of the Congo 52 E3 0 48S 18 15 E
Bila Tserkva, Ukraine 17 D16 49 45N 30 10 E
Bilara, India 42 F5 26 14N 73 53 E
Bilaspur, Mad. P., India 43 H10 22 2N 82 15 E
Bilaspur, Punjab, India 42 D7 31 19N 76 50 E
Bilauk Taungdan, Thailand 38 F2 13 0N 99 0 E
**Bilbao**, Spain 19 A4 43 16N 2 56W
Bilbo = Bilbao, Spain 19 A4 43 16N 2 56W
Bildudalur, Iceland 8 D2 65 41N 23 36W
Bílé Karpaty, Europe 17 D9 49 5N 18 0 E
Bilecik, Turkey 25 F5 40 5N 30 5 E
Bilgram, India 43 F9 27 11N 80 2 E
Bilhaur, India 43 F9 26 51N 80 5 E
Bilhorod-Dnistrovskyy, Ukraine 25 E5 46 11N 30 23 E
Bilibino, Russia 27 C17 68 3N 166 20 E
Bilibiza, Mozam. 55 E5 12 30S 40 20 E
Billabalong Roadhouse, Australia 61 E2 27 25S 115 49 E
Billiluna, Australia 60 C4 19 37S 127 41 E
Billings, U.S.A. 82 D9 45 47N 108 30W
Billiton Is. = Belitung, Indonesia 36 E3 3 10S 107 50 E
Bilma, Niger 51 E8 18 50N 13 30 E
Biloela, Australia 62 C5 24 24S 150 31 E
Biloxi, U.S.A. 81 K10 30 24N 88 53W
Bilpa Morea Claypan, Australia 62 D3 25 0S 140 0 E
Biltine, Chad 51 F10 14 40N 20 50 E
Bima, Indonesia 37 F5 8 22S 118 49 E
Bimini Is., Bahamas 88 A4 25 42N 79 25W
Bin Xian, Heilongjiang, China 35 B14 45 42N 127 32 E
Bin Xian, Shaanxi, China 34 G5 35 2N 108 4 E
Bina-Etawah, India 42 G8 24 13N 78 14 E
Bīnāb, Iran 45 B6 36 35N 48 41 E
Binalbagan, Phil. 37 B6 10 12N 122 50 E
Binalong, Australia 63 E4 34 40S 148 39 E
Bīnālūd, Kūh-e, Iran 45 B8 36 30N 58 30 E
Binatang = Bintangor, Malaysia 36 D4 2 10N 111 40 E
Binche, Belgium 15 D4 50 26N 4 10 E
Bindki, India 43 F9 26 2N 80 36 E
Bindura, Zimbabwe 55 F3 17 18S 31 18 E
Bingara, Australia 63 D5 29 52S 150 36 E
Bingham, U.S.A. 77 C11 45 3N 69 53W
Binghamton, U.S.A. 79 D9 42 6N 75 55W
Bingöl, Turkey 44 B4 38 53N 40 29 E
Binh Dinh = An Nhon, Vietnam 38 F7 13 55N 109 7 E
Binh Khe, Vietnam 38 F7 13 57N 108 51 E
Binh Son, Vietnam 38 E7 15 20N 108 40 E
Binhai, China 35 G10 34 2N 119 49 E
Binisatua, Spain 22 B11 39 50N 4 11 E
Binjai, Indonesia 36 D1 3 20N 98 30 E
Binnaway, Australia 63 E4 31 28S 149 24 E
Binongko, Indonesia 37 F6 5 55S 123 55 E
Binscarth, Canada 73 C8 50 37N 101 17W
Bintan, Indonesia 36 D2 1 0N 104 0 E
Bintangor, Malaysia 36 D4 2 10N 111 40 E
Bintulu, Malaysia 36 D4 3 10N 113 0 E
Bintuni, Indonesia 37 E8 2 7S 133 32 E
Binzert = Bizerte, Tunisia 51 A7 37 15N 9 50 E
Binzhou, China 35 F10 37 20N 118 2 E
Bío Bío □, Chile 94 D1 37 35S 72 0W
Bioko, Eq. Guin. 52 D1 3 30N 8 40 E
Bir, India 40 K9 19 0N 75 54 E
Bîr Abu Muḩammad, Egypt 47 F3 29 44N 34 14 E
Bi'r ad Dabbāghāt, Jordan 47 E4 30 26N 35 32 E
Bi'r al Butayyihāt, Jordan 47 F4 29 47N 35 20 E
Bi'r al Mārī, Jordan 47 E4 30 4N 35 33 E
Bi'r al Qattār, Jordan 47 F4 29 47N 35 32 E
Bir 'Atrun, Sudan 51 E11 18 15N 26 40 E
Bîr Beida, Egypt 47 E3 30 25N 34 29 E
Bîr el 'Abd, Egypt 47 D2 31 2N 33 0 E
Bîr el Biarât, Egypt 47 F3 29 30N 34 43 E
Bîr el Duweidar, Egypt 47 E1 30 56N 32 32 E
Bîr el Garârât, Egypt 47 D2 31 3N 33 34 E
Bîr el Heisi, Egypt 47 F3 29 22N 34 36 E
Bîr el Jafir, Egypt 47 E1 30 50N 32 41 E
Bîr el Mâlḩi, Egypt 47 E2 30 38N 33 19 E
Bîr el Thamâda, Egypt 47 E2 30 12N 33 27 E
Bîr Gebeil Ḩişn, Egypt 47 E2 30 2N 33 18 E
Bi'r Ghadīr, Syria 47 A6 34 6N 37 3 E
Bîr Ḩasana, Egypt 47 E2 30 29N 33 46 E
Bîr Kaseiba, Egypt 47 E2 31 0N 33 17 E
Bîr Lahfân, Egypt 47 E2 31 0N 33 51 E
Bîr Madkûr, Egypt 47 E1 30 44N 32 33 E
Bir Mogreïn, Mauritania 50 C3 25 10N 11 25W
Bi'r Muţribah, Kuwait 44 D5 29 54N 47 17 E
Bîr Qaţia, Egypt 47 E1 30 58N 32 45 E
Bîr Shalatein, Egypt 51 D13 23 5N 35 25 E
Biratnagar, Nepal 43 F12 26 27N 87 17 E
Birawa, Dem. Rep. of the Congo 54 C2 2 20S 28 48 E
Birch —►, Canada 72 B6 58 28N 112 17W
Birch Hills, Canada 73 C7 52 59N 105 25W
Birch I., Canada 73 C9 52 26N 99 54W
Birch L., N.W.T., Canada 72 A5 62 4N 116 33W
Birch L., Ont., Canada 70 B1 51 23N 92 18W
Birch Mts., Canada 72 B6 57 30N 113 10W
Birch River, Canada 73 C8 52 24N 101 6W
Birchip, Australia 63 F3 35 56S 142 55 E
Bird, Canada 73 B10 56 30N 94 13W
Bird I. = Las Aves, Is., W. Indies 89 C7 15 45N 63 55W
Birdsville, Australia 62 D2 25 51S 139 20 E
Birdum Cr., Australia 60 C5 15 14S 133 0 E
Birecik, Turkey 44 B3 37 2N 38 0 E
Birein, Israel 47 E3 30 50N 34 28 E
Bireuen, Indonesia 36 C1 5 14N 96 39 E
Birigui, Brazil 95 A5 21 18S 50 16W
Birjand, Iran 45 C8 32 53N 59 13 E
Birkenhead, U.K. 10 D4 53 23N 3 2W
Bîrlad = Bârlad, Romania 17 E14 46 15N 27 38 E
**Birmingham**, U.K. 11 E6 52 29N 1 52W
**Birmingham**, U.S.A. 77 J2 33 31N 86 48W
Birmitrapur, India 41 H14 22 24N 84 46 E
Birni Nkonni, Niger 50 F7 13 55N 5 15 E
Birnin Kebbi, Nigeria 50 F6 12 32N 4 12 E
Birobidzhan, Russia 27 E14 48 50N 132 50 E
Birr, Ireland 13 C4 53 6N 7 54W
Birrie —►, Australia 63 D4 29 43S 146 37 E
Birsilpur, India 42 E5 28 11N 72 15 E
Birsk, Russia 24 C10 55 25N 55 30 E
Birtle, Canada 73 C8 50 30N 101 5W
Birur, India 40 N9 13 30N 75 55 E
Biržai, Lithuania 9 H21 56 11N 24 45 E
Birzebbugga, Malta 23 D2 35 49N 14 32 E
Bisa, Indonesia 37 E7 1 15S 127 28 E
Bisalpur, India 43 E8 28 14N 79 48 E
Bisbee, U.S.A. 83 L9 31 27N 109 55W
**Biscay, B. of**, Atl. Oc. 18 D1 45 0N 2 0W
Biscayne B., U.S.A. 77 N5 25 40N 80 12W
Biscoe Bay, Antarctica 5 D13 77 0S 152 0W
Biscoe Is., Antarctica 5 C17 66 0S 67 0W
Biscostasing, Canada 70 C3 47 18N 82 9W
**Bishkek**, Kyrgyzstan 26 E8 42 54N 74 46 E
Bishnupur, India 43 H12 23 8N 87 20 E
Bisho, S. Africa 57 E4 32 50S 27 23 E
Bishop, Calif., U.S.A. 84 H8 37 22N 118 24W
Bishop, Tex., U.S.A. 81 M6 27 35N 97 48W
Bishop Auckland, U.K. 10 C6 54 39N 1 40W
Bishop's Falls, Canada 71 C8 49 2N 55 30W
Bishop's Stortford, U.K. 11 F8 51 52N 0 10 E
Bisina, L., Uganda 54 B3 1 38N 33 56 E
Biskra, Algeria 50 B7 34 50N 5 44 E
**Bismarck**, U.S.A. 80 B4 46 48N 100 47W
Bismarck Arch., Papua N. G. 64 H7 2 30S 150 0 E
Biso, Uganda 54 B3 1 44N 31 26 E
Bison, U.S.A. 80 C3 45 31N 102 28W
Bīsotūn, Iran 44 C5 34 23N 47 26 E
Bissagos = Bijagós, Arquipélago dos, Guinea-Biss. 50 F2 11 15N 16 10W
**Bissau**, Guinea-Biss. 50 F2 11 45N 15 45W
Bistcho L., Canada 72 B5 59 45N 118 50W
Bistriţa, Romania 17 E13 47 9N 24 35 E
Bistriţa —►, Romania 17 E14 46 30N 26 57 E
Biswan, India 43 F9 27 29N 81 2 E
Bitola, Macedonia 21 D9 41 1N 21 20 E
Bitolj = Bitola, Macedonia 21 D9 41 1N 21 20 E
Bitter Creek, U.S.A. 82 F9 41 33N 108 33W
Bitterfontein, S. Africa 56 E2 31 1S 18 32 E
Bitterroot —►, U.S.A. 82 C6 46 52N 114 7W
Bitterroot Range, U.S.A. 82 D6 46 0N 114 20W
Bitterwater, U.S.A. 84 J6 36 23N 121 0W
Biu, Nigeria 51 F8 10 40N 12 3 E
**Biwa-Ko**, Japan 31 G8 35 15N 136 10 E
Biwabik, U.S.A. 80 B8 47 32N 92 21W
Bixby, U.S.A. 81 H7 35 57N 95 53W
Biyang, China 34 H7 32 38N 113 21 E
Biysk, Russia 26 D9 52 40N 85 0 E
Bizana, S. Africa 57 E4 30 50S 29 52 E
Bizen, Japan 31 G7 34 43N 134 8 E
Bizerte, Tunisia 51 A7 37 15N 9 50 E
Bjargtangar, Iceland 8 D1 65 30N 24 30W
Bjelovar, Croatia 20 B7 45 56N 16 49 E
Bjørnevatn, Norway 8 B23 69 40N 30 0 E
Bjørnøya, Arctic 4 B8 74 30N 19 0 E
Black —►, Canada 78 B5 44 42N 79 19W
Black —►, Ariz., U.S.A. 83 K8 33 44N 110 13W
Black —►, Ark., U.S.A. 81 H9 35 38N 91 20W
Black —►, Mich., U.S.A. 78 D2 42 59N 82 27W
Black —►, N.Y., U.S.A. 79 C8 43 59N 76 4W
Black —►, Wis., U.S.A. 80 D9 43 57N 91 22W
Black Bay Pen., Canada 70 C2 48 38N 88 21W
Black Birch L., Canada 73 B7 56 53N 107 45W
Black Diamond, Canada 72 C6 50 45N 114 14W
Black Duck —►, Canada 70 A2 56 51N 89 2W
**Black Forest** = Schwarzwald, Germany 16 D5 48 30N 8 20 E
Black Forest, U.S.A. 80 F2 39 0N 104 43W
Black Hd., Ireland 13 C2 53 9N 9 16W
Black Hills, U.S.A. 80 D3 44 0N 103 45W
Black I., Canada 73 C9 51 12N 96 30W
Black L., Canada 73 B7 59 12N 105 15W
Black L., Mich., U.S.A. 76 C3 45 28N 84 16W
Black L., N.Y., U.S.A. 79 B9 44 31N 75 36W
Black Lake, Canada 73 B7 59 11N 105 20W
Black Mesa, U.S.A. 81 G3 36 58N 102 58W
Black Mt. = Mynydd Du, U.K. 11 F4 51 52N 3 50W
Black Mts., U.K. 11 F4 51 55N 3 7W
Black Range, U.S.A. 83 K10 33 15N 107 50W
Black River, Jamaica 88 C4 18 0N 77 50W
Black River Falls, U.S.A. 80 C9 44 18N 90 51W
**Black Sea**, Eurasia 25 F6 43 30N 35 0 E
Black Tickle, Canada 71 B8 53 28N 55 45W
Black Volta —►, Africa 50 G5 8 41N 1 33W
Black Warrior —►, U.S.A. 77 J2 32 32N 87 51W
Blackall, Australia 62 C4 24 25S 145 45 E
Blackball, N.Z. 59 K3 42 22S 171 26 E
Blackbull, Australia 62 B3 17 55S 141 45 E
Blackburn, U.K. 10 D5 53 45N 2 29W
Blackburn with Darwen □, U.K. 10 D5 53 45N 2 29W
Blackfoot, U.S.A. 82 E7 43 11N 112 21W
Blackfoot —►, U.S.A. 82 C7 46 52N 113 53W
Blackfoot River Reservoir, U.S.A. 82 E8 43 0N 111 43W
Blackie, Canada 72 C6 50 36N 113 37W
**Blackpool**, U.K. 10 D4 53 49N 3 3W
Blackpool □, U.K. 10 D4 53 49N 3 3W
Blackriver, U.S.A. 78 B1 44 46N 83 17W
Blacks Harbour, Canada 71 C6 45 3N 66 49W
Blacksburg, U.S.A. 76 G5 37 14N 80 25W
Blacksod B., Ireland 13 B1 54 6N 10 0W
Blackstone, U.S.A. 76 G7 37 4N 78 0W
Blackstone Ra., Australia 61 E4 26 0S 128 30 E
Blackwater, Australia 62 C4 23 35S 148 53 E
Blackwater —►, Meath, Ireland 13 C4 53 39N 6 41W
Blackwater —►, Waterford, Ireland 13 D4 52 4N 7 52W
Blackwater —►, U.K. 13 B5 54 31N 6 35W
Blackwell, U.S.A. 81 G6 36 48N 97 17W
Blackwells Corner, U.S.A. 85 K7 35 37N 119 47W
Blaenau Ffestiniog, U.K. 10 E4 53 0N 3 56W
Blaenau Gwent □, U.K. 11 F4 51 48N 3 12W
Blagodarnoye = Blagodarnyy, Russia 25 E7 45 7N 43 37 E
Blagodarnyy, Russia 25 E7 45 7N 43 37 E
Blagoevgrad, Bulgaria 21 C10 42 2N 23 5 E
Blagoveshchensk, Russia 27 D13 50 20N 127 30 E
Blain, U.S.A. 78 F7 40 20N 77 31W
Blaine, Minn., U.S.A. 80 C8 45 10N 93 13W
Blaine, Wash., U.S.A. 84 B4 48 59N 122 45W
Blaine Lake, Canada 73 C7 52 51N 106 52W
Blair, U.S.A. 80 E6 41 33N 96 8W
Blair Athol, Australia 62 C4 22 42S 147 31 E
Blair Atholl, U.K. 12 E5 56 46N 3 50W
Blairgowrie, U.K. 12 E5 56 35N 3 21W
Blairsden, U.S.A. 84 F6 39 47N 120 37W
Blairsville, U.S.A. 78 F5 40 26N 79 16W
Blake Pt., U.S.A. 80 A10 48 11N 88 25W
Blakely, Ga., U.S.A. 77 K3 31 23N 84 56W
Blakely, Pa., U.S.A. 79 E9 41 28N 75 37W
Blanc, C., Spain 22 B9 39 21N 2 51 E
**Blanc, Mont**, Alps 18 D7 45 48N 6 50 E
Blanc-Sablon, Canada 71 B8 51 24N 57 12W
Blanca, B., Argentina 96 D4 39 10S 61 30W
Blanca Peak, U.S.A. 83 H11 37 35N 105 29W
Blanche, C., Australia 63 E1 33 1S 134 9 E
Blanche, L., S. Austral., Australia 63 D2 29 15S 139 40 E
Blanche, L., W. Austral., Australia 60 D3 22 25S 123 17 E
Blanco, S. Africa 56 E3 33 55S 22 23 E
Blanco, U.S.A. 81 K5 30 6N 98 25W
Blanco —►, Argentina 94 C2 30 20S 68 42W
Blanco, C., Costa Rica 88 E2 9 34N 85 8W
Blanco, C., U.S.A. 82 E1 42 51N 124 34W
Blanda —►, Iceland 8 D3 65 37N 20 9W
Blandford Forum, U.K. 11 G5 50 51N 2 9W
Blanding, U.S.A. 83 H9 37 37N 109 29W
Blanes, Spain 19 B7 41 40N 2 48 E
Blankenberge, Belgium 15 C3 51 20N 3 9 E
Blanquilla, I., Venezuela 89 D7 11 51N 64 37W
Blanquillo, Uruguay 95 C4 32 53S 55 37W
Blantyre, Malawi 55 F4 15 45S 35 0 E
Blarney, Ireland 13 E3 51 56N 8 33W
Blasdell, U.S.A. 78 D6 42 48N 78 50W
Blåvands Huk, Denmark 9 J13 55 33N 8 4 E
Blaydon, U.K. 10 C6 54 58N 1 42W
Blayney, Australia 63 E4 33 32S 149 14 E
Blaze, Pt., Australia 60 B5 12 56S 130 11 E
Blekinge, Sweden 9 H16 56 25N 15 20 E
Blenheim, Canada 78 D3 42 20N 82 0W
Blenheim, N.Z. 59 J4 41 38S 173 57 E
Bletchley, U.K. 11 F7 51 59N 0 44W
Blida, Algeria 50 A6 36 30N 2 49 E
Bligh Sound, N.Z. 59 L1 44 47S 167 32 E
Blind River, Canada 70 C3 46 10N 82 58W
Bliss, Idaho, U.S.A. 82 E6 42 56N 114 57W
Bliss, N.Y., U.S.A. 78 D6 42 34N 78 15W
Blissfield, U.S.A. 78 F3 40 24N 81 58W
Blitar, Indonesia 37 H15 8 5S 112 11 E
Block I., U.S.A. 79 E13 41 11N 71 35W
Block Island Sd., U.S.A. 79 E13 41 15N 71 40W
Blodgett Iceberg Tongue, Antarctica 5 C9 66 8S 130 35 E
**Bloemfontein**, S. Africa 56 D4 29 6S 26 7 E
Bloemhof, S. Africa 56 D4 27 38S 25 32 E
Blois, France 18 C4 47 35N 1 20 E
Blönduós, Iceland 8 D3 65 40N 20 12W
Bloodvein —►, Canada 73 C9 51 47N 96 43W
Bloody Foreland, Ireland 13 A3 55 10N 8 17W
Bloomer, U.S.A. 80 C9 45 6N 91 29W
Bloomfield, Canada 78 C7 43 59N 77 14W
Bloomfield, Iowa, U.S.A. 80 E8 40 45N 92 25W
Bloomfield, N. Mex., U.S.A. 83 H10 36 43N 107 59W
Bloomfield, Nebr., U.S.A. 80 D6 42 36N 97 39W
Bloomington, Ill., U.S.A. 80 E10 40 28N 89 0W
Bloomington, Ind., U.S.A. 76 F2 39 10N 86 32W
Bloomington, Minn., U.S.A. 80 C8 44 50N 93 17W
Bloomsburg, U.S.A. 79 F8 41 0N 76 27W
Blora, Indonesia 37 G14 6 57S 111 25 E
Blossburg, U.S.A. 78 E7 41 41N 77 4W
Blouberg, S. Africa 57 C4 23 8S 28 59 E
Blountstown, U.S.A. 77 K3 30 27N 85 3W
Blue Earth, U.S.A. 80 D8 43 38N 94 6W
Blue Mesa Reservoir, U.S.A. 83 G10 38 28N 107 20W
Blue Mountain Lake, U.S.A. 79 C10 43 52N 74 30W
Blue Mts., Maine, U.S.A. 79 B14 44 50N 70 35W
Blue Mts., Oreg., U.S.A. 82 D4 45 15N 119 0W
Blue Mts., Pa., U.S.A. 79 F8 40 30N 76 30W
Blue Mud B., Australia 62 A2 13 30S 136 0 E
Blue Nile = Nîl el Azraq —►, Sudan 51 E12 15 38N 32 31 E
Blue Rapids, U.S.A. 80 F6 39 41N 96 39W
Blue Ridge Mts., U.S.A. 77 G5 36 30N 80 15W
Blue River, Canada 72 C5 52 6N 119 18W
Bluefield, U.S.A. 76 G5 37 15N 81 17W
Bluefields, Nic. 88 D3 12 20N 83 50W
Bluff, Australia 62 C4 23 35S 149 4 E
Bluff, N.Z. 59 M2 46 37S 168 20 E
Bluff, U.S.A. 83 H9 37 17N 109 33W
Bluff Knoll, Australia 61 F2 34 24S 118 15 E
Bluff Pt., Australia 61 E1 27 50S 114 5 E
Bluffton, U.S.A. 76 E3 40 44N 85 11W
Blumenau, Brazil 95 B6 27 0S 49 0W
Blunt, U.S.A. 80 C5 44 31N 99 59W
Bly, U.S.A. 82 E3 42 24N 121 3W
Blyth, Canada 78 C3 43 44N 81 26W
Blyth, U.K. 10 B6 55 8N 1 31W
Blythe, U.S.A. 85 M12 33 37N 114 36W
Blytheville, U.S.A. 81 H10 35 56N 89 55W
Bo, S. Leone 50 G3 7 55N 11 50W
Bo Duc, Vietnam 39 G6 11 58N 106 50 E
Bo Hai, China 35 E10 39 0N 119 0 E
Bo Xian = Bozhou, China 34 H8 33 55N 115 41 E
Boa Vista, Brazil 92 C6 2 48N 60 30W
Boaco, Nic. 88 D2 12 29N 85 35W
Bo'ai, China 34 G7 35 10N 113 3 E
Boalsburg, U.S.A. 78 F7 40 46N 77 47W
Boardman, U.S.A. 78 E4 41 2N 80 40W
Bobadah, Australia 63 E4 32 19S 146 41 E
Bobbili, India 41 K13 18 35N 83 30 E
Bobcaygeon, Canada 78 B6 44 33N 78 33W
Bobo-Dioulasso, Burkina Faso 50 F5 11 8N 4 13W
Bóbr —►, Poland 16 B8 52 4N 15 4 E
Bobraomby, Tanjon' i, Madag. 57 A8 12 40S 49 10 E
Bobruysk = Babruysk, Belarus 17 B15 53 10N 29 15 E
Boby, Pic, Madag. 53 J9 22 12S 46 55 E
Bôca do Acre, Brazil 92 E5 8 50S 67 27W
Boca Raton, U.S.A. 77 M5 26 21N 80 5W
Bocas del Toro, Panama 88 E3 9 15N 82 20W
Bochnia, Poland 17 D11 49 58N 20 27 E
Bochum, Germany 16 C4 51 28N 7 13 E
Bocoyna, Mexico 86 B3 27 52N 107 35W
Bodaybo, Russia 27 D12 57 50N 114 0 E
Boddam, U.K. 12 B7 59 56N 1 17W
Boddington, Australia 61 F2 32 50S 116 30 E
Bodega Bay, U.S.A. 84 G3 38 20N 123 3W
Boden, Sweden 8 D19 65 50N 21 42 E
Bodensee, Europe 18 C8 47 35N 9 25 E
Bodhan, India 40 K10 18 40N 77 44 E
Bodmin, U.K. 11 G3 50 28N 4 43W
Bodmin Moor, U.K. 11 G3 50 33N 4 36W
Bodø, Norway 8 C16 67 17N 14 24 E
Bodrog —►, Hungary 17 D11 48 11N 21 22 E
Bodrum, Turkey 21 F12 37 3N 27 30 E
Boende, Dem. Rep. of the Congo 52 E4 0 24S 21 12 E
Boerne, U.S.A. 81 L5 29 47N 98 44W
Bogalusa, U.S.A. 81 K10 30 47N 89 52W
Bogan —►, Australia 63 D4 29 59S 146 17 E
Bogan Gate, Australia 63 E4 33 7S 147 49 E
Bogantungan, Australia 62 C4 23 41S 147 17 E
Bogata, U.S.A. 81 J7 33 28N 95 13W
Boggabilla, Australia 63 D5 28 36S 150 24 E
Boggabri, Australia 63 E5 30 45S 150 5 E
Boggeragh Mts., Ireland 13 D3 52 2N 8 55W
Boglan = Solhan, Turkey 44 B4 38 57N 41 3 E
Bognor Regis, U.K. 11 G7 50 47N 0 40W
Bogo, Phil. 37 B6 11 3N 124 0 E
Bogong, Mt., Australia 63 F4 36 47S 147 17 E
Bogor, Indonesia 37 G12 6 36S 106 48 E
**Bogotá**, Colombia 92 C4 4 34N 74 0W
Bogotol, Russia 26 D9 56 15N 89 50 E
Bogra, Bangla. 41 G16 24 51N 89 22 E
Boguchany, Russia 27 D10 58 40N 97 30 E
Bohemian Forest = Böhmerwald, Germany 16 D7 49 8N 13 14 E
Böhmerwald, Germany 16 D7 49 8N 13 14 E
Bohol, Phil. 37 C6 9 50N 124 10 E
Bohol Sea, Phil. 37 C6 9 0N 124 0 E
Bohuslän, Sweden 9 G14 58 25N 12 0 E
Boi, Pta. de, Brazil 95 A6 23 55S 45 15W
Boiaçu, Brazil 92 D6 0 27S 61 46W
Boileau, C., Australia 60 C3 17 40S 122 7 E
**Boise**, U.S.A. 82 E5 43 37N 116 13W
Boise City, U.S.A. 81 G3 36 44N 102 31W
Boissevain, Canada 73 D8 49 15N 100 5W
Bojador C., W. Sahara 50 C3 26 0N 14 30W
Bojana —►, Albania 21 D8 41 52N 19 22 E
Bojnūrd, Iran 45 B8 37 30N 57 20 E
Bojonegoro, Indonesia 37 G14 7 11S 111 54 E
Bokaro, India 43 H11 23 46N 85 55 E
Bokhara —►, Australia 63 D4 29 55S 146 42 E
Boknafjorden, Norway 9 G11 59 14N 5 40 E
Bokoro, Chad 51 F9 12 25N 17 14 E
Bokote, Dem. Rep. of the Congo 52 E4 0 12S 21 8 E
Bokpyin, Burma 39 G2 11 18N 98 42 E
Bolan —►, Pakistan 42 E2 28 38N 67 42 E
Bolan Pass, Pakistan 40 E5 29 50N 67 20 E
Bolaños —►, Mexico 86 C4 21 14N 104 8W
Bolbec, France 18 B4 49 30N 0 30 E
Boldājī, Iran 45 D6 31 56N 51 3 E
Bole, China 32 B3 45 11N 81 37 E
Bolekhiv, Ukraine 17 D12 49 0N 23 57 E
Bolesławiec, Poland 16 C8 51 17N 15 37 E
Bolgrad = Bolhrad, Ukraine 17 F15 45 40N 28 32 E
Bolhrad, Ukraine 17 F15 45 40N 28 32 E
Bolívar, Argentina 94 D3 36 15S 60 53W
Bolivar, Mo., U.S.A. 81 G8 37 37N 93 25W
Bolivar, N.Y., U.S.A. 78 D6 42 4N 78 10W
Bolivar, Tenn., U.S.A. 81 H10 35 12N 89 0W
**Bolivia** ■, S. Amer. 92 G6 17 6S 64 0W
Bolivian Plateau, S. Amer. 90 E4 20 0S 67 30W
Bollnäs, Sweden 9 F17 61 21N 16 24 E
Bollon, Australia 63 D4 28 2S 147 29 E
Bolmen, Sweden 9 H15 56 55N 13 40 E
Bolobo, Dem. Rep. of the Congo 52 E3 2 6S 16 20 E
**Bologna**, Italy 20 B4 44 29N 11 20 E
Bologoye, Russia 24 C5 57 55N 34 5 E
Bolonchenticul, Mexico 87 D7 20 0N 89 49W
Boloven, Cao Nguyen, Laos 38 E6 15 10N 106 30 E
Bolpur, India 43 H12 23 40N 87 45 E
Bolsena, L. di, Italy 20 C4 42 36N 11 56 E
Bolshevik, Ostrov, Russia 27 B11 78 30N 102 0 E
Bolshoi Kavkas = Caucasus Mountains, Eurasia 25 F7 42 50N 44 0 E
Bolshoy Anyuy —►, Russia 27 C17 68 30N 160 49 E
Bolshoy Begichev, Ostrov, Russia 27 B12 74 20N 112 30 E

Bolshoy Lyakhovskiy, Ostrov, Russia 27 B15 73 35N 142 0 E
Bolshoy Tyuters, Ostrov, Russia 9 G22 59 51N 27 13 E
Bolsward, Neths. 15 A5 53 3N 5 32 E
Bolt Head, U.K. 11 G4 50 12N 3 48W
Bolton, Canada 78 C5 43 54N 79 45W
Bolton, U.K. 10 D5 53 35N 2 26W
Bolton Landing, U.S.A. 79 C11 43 32N 73 35W
Bolu, Turkey 25 F5 40 45N 31 35 E
Bolungavík, Iceland 8 C2 66 9N 23 15W
Bolvadin, Turkey 25 G5 38 45N 31 4 E
Bolzano, Italy 20 A4 46 31N 11 22 E
Bom Jesus da Lapa, Brazil 93 F10 13 15S 43 25W
Boma, Dem. Rep. of the Congo 52 F2 5 50S 13 4 E
Bombala, Australia 63 F4 36 56S 149 15 E
**Bombay** = Mumbai, India 40 K8 18 55N 72 50 E
Bomboma, Dem. Rep. of the Congo 52 D3 2 25N 18 55 E
Bombombwa, Dem. Rep. of the Congo 54 B2 1 40N 25 40 E
Bomili, Dem. Rep. of the Congo 54 B2 1 45N 27 5 E
Bømlo, Norway 9 G11 59 37N 5 13 E
Bomokandi →, Dem. Rep. of the Congo 54 B2 3 39N 26 8 E
Bomu →, C.A.R. 52 D4 4 40N 22 30 E
Bon, C., Tunisia 48 C5 37 1N 11 2 E
Bon Sar Pa, Vietnam 38 F6 12 24N 107 35 E
Bonaigarh, India 43 J11 21 50N 84 57 E
Bonaire, Neth. Ant. 89 D6 12 10N 68 15W
Bonang, Australia 63 F4 37 11S 148 41 E
Bonanza, Nic. 88 D3 13 54N 84 35W
Bonaparte Arch., Australia 60 B3 14 0S 124 30 E
Bonaventure, Canada 71 C6 48 5N 65 32W
Bonavista, Canada 71 C9 48 40N 53 5W
Bonavista, C., Canada 71 C9 48 42N 53 5W
Bonavista B., Canada 71 C9 48 45N 53 25W
Bondo, Dem. Rep. of the Congo 54 B1 3 55N 23 53 E
Bondoukou, Ivory C. 50 G5 8 2N 2 47W
Bondowoso, Indonesia 37 G15 7 55S 113 49 E
Bone, Teluk, Indonesia 37 E6 4 10S 120 50 E
Bonerate, Indonesia 37 F6 7 25S 121 5 E
Bonerate, Kepulauan, Indonesia 37 F6 6 30S 121 10 E
Bo'ness, U.K. 12 E5 56 1N 3 37W
Bonete, Cerro, Argentina 94 B2 27 55S 68 40W
Bong Son = Hoai Nhon, Vietnam 38 E7 14 28N 109 1 E
Bongor, Chad 51 F9 10 35N 15 20 E
Bonham, U.S.A. 81 J6 33 35N 96 11W
Bonifacio, France 18 F8 41 24N 9 10 E
Bonifacio, Bouches de, Medit. S. 20 D3 41 12N 9 15 E
Bonin Is. = Ogasawara Gunto, Pac. Oc. 28 G18 27 0N 142 0 E
**Bonn**, Germany 16 C4 50 46N 7 6 E
Bonne Terre, U.S.A. 81 G9 37 55N 90 33W
Bonners Ferry, U.S.A. 82 B5 48 42N 116 19W
Bonney, L., Australia 63 F3 37 50S 140 20 E
Bonnie Rock, Australia 61 F2 30 29S 118 22 E
Bonny, Bight of, Africa 52 D1 3 30N 9 20 E
Bonnyrigg, U.K. 12 F5 55 53N 3 6W
Bonnyville, Canada 73 C6 54 20N 110 45W
Bonoi, Indonesia 37 E9 1 45S 137 41 E
Bonsall, U.S.A. 85 M9 33 16N 117 14W
Bontang, Indonesia 36 D5 0 10N 117 30 E
Bonthe, S. Leone 50 G3 7 30N 12 33W
Bontoc, Phil. 37 A6 17 7N 120 58 E
Bonython Ra., Australia 60 D4 23 40S 128 45 E
Bookabie, Australia 61 F5 31 50S 132 41 E
Booker, U.S.A. 81 G4 36 27N 100 32W
Booligal, Australia 63 E3 33 58S 144 53 E
Boonah, Australia 63 D5 27 58S 152 41 E
Boone, Iowa, U.S.A. 80 D8 42 4N 93 53W
Boone, N.C., U.S.A. 77 G5 36 13N 81 41W
Booneville, Ark., U.S.A. 81 H8 35 8N 93 55W
Booneville, Miss., U.S.A. 77 H1 34 39N 88 34W
Boonville, Calif., U.S.A. 84 F3 39 1N 123 22W
Boonville, Ind., U.S.A. 76 F2 38 3N 87 16W
Boonville, Mo., U.S.A. 80 F8 38 58N 92 44W
Boonville, N.Y., U.S.A. 79 C9 43 29N 75 20W
Boorindal, Australia 63 E4 30 22S 146 11 E
Boorowa, Australia 63 E4 34 28S 148 44 E
Boothia, Gulf of, Canada 69 A11 71 0N 90 0W
Boothia Pen., Canada 68 A10 71 0N 94 0W
Bootle, U.K. 10 D4 53 28N 3 1W
Booué, Gabon 52 E2 0 5S 11 55 E
Boquete, Panama 88 E3 8 46N 82 27W
Boquilla, Presa de la, Mexico 86 B3 27 40N 105 30W
Boquillas del Carmen, Mexico 86 B4 29 17N 102 53W
Bor, Serbia, Yug. 21 B10 44 5N 22 7 E
Bôr, Sudan 51 G12 6 10N 31 40 E
Bor Mashash, Israel 47 D3 31 7N 34 50 E
Borah Peak, U.S.A. 82 D7 44 8N 113 47W
Borås, Sweden 9 H15 57 43N 12 56 E
Borāzjān, Iran 45 D6 29 22N 51 10 E
Borba, Brazil 92 D7 4 12S 59 34W
Borborema, Planalto da, Brazil 90 D7 7 0S 37 0W
Bord Khūn-e Now, Iran 45 D6 28 3N 51 28 E
Borda, C., Australia 63 F2 35 45S 136 34 E
**Bordeaux**, France 18 D3 44 50N 0 36W
Borden, Australia 61 F2 34 3S 118 12 E
Borden, Canada 71 C7 46 18N 63 47W
Borden I., Canada 4 B2 78 30N 111 30W
Borden Pen., Canada 69 A11 73 0N 83 0W
**Borders** = Scottish Borders □, U.K. 12 F6 55 35N 2 50W
Bordertown, Australia 63 F3 36 19S 140 45 E
Borðeyri, Iceland 8 D3 65 12N 21 6W
Bordj Fly Ste. Marie, Algeria 50 C5 27 19N 2 32W
Bordj-in-Eker, Algeria 50 D7 24 9N 5 3 E
Bordj Omar Driss, Algeria 50 C7 28 10N 6 40 E
Borehamwood, U.K. 11 F7 51 40N 0 15W
Borgå = Porvoo, Finland 9 F21 60 24N 25 40 E
Borgarfjörður, Iceland 8 D7 65 31N 13 49W
Borgarnes, Iceland 8 D3 64 32N 21 55W
Børgefjellet, Norway 8 D15 65 20N 13 45 E
Borger, Neths. 15 B6 52 54N 6 44 E
Borger, U.S.A. 81 H4 35 39N 101 24W
Borgholm, Sweden 9 H17 56 52N 16 39 E
Borhoyn Tal, Mongolia 34 C6 43 50N 111 58 E
Borikhane, Laos 38 C4 18 33N 103 43 E
Borisoglebsk, Russia 25 D7 51 27N 42 5 E
Borisov = Barysaw, Belarus 17 A15 54 17N 28 28 E
Borja, Peru 92 D3 4 20S 77 40W
Borkou, Chad 51 E9 18 15N 18 50 E
Borkum, Germany 16 B4 53 34N 6 40 E
Borlänge, Sweden 9 F16 60 29N 15 26 E
Borley, C., Antarctica 5 C5 66 15S 52 30 E
**Borneo**, E. Indies 36 D5 1 0N 115 0 E
Bornholm, Denmark 9 J16 55 10N 15 0 E
Borogontsy, Russia 27 C14 62 42N 131 8 E
Boron, U.S.A. 85 L9 35 0N 117 39W
Borongan, Phil. 37 B7 11 37N 125 26 E
Borovichi, Russia 24 C5 58 25N 33 55 E
Borrego Springs, U.S.A. 85 M10 33 15N 116 23W
Borroloola, Australia 62 B2 16 4S 136 17 E
Borşa, Romania 17 E13 47 41N 24 50 E
Borsad, India 42 H5 22 25N 72 54 E
Borth, U.K. 11 E3 52 29N 4 2W
Borūjerd, Iran 45 C6 33 55N 48 50 E
Boryslav, Ukraine 17 D12 49 18N 23 28 E
Borzya, Russia 27 D12 50 24N 116 31 E
Bosa, Italy 20 D3 40 18N 8 30 E
Bosanska Gradiška, Bos.-H. 20 B7 45 10N 17 15 E
Bosaso, Somali Rep. 46 E4 11 12N 49 18 E
Boscastle, U.K. 11 G3 50 41N 4 42W
Boshan, China 35 F9 36 28N 117 49 E
Boshof, S. Africa 56 D4 28 31S 25 13 E
Boshrūyeh, Iran 45 C8 33 50N 57 30 E
Bosna →, Bos.-H. 21 B8 45 4N 18 29 E
Bosna i Hercegovina = Bosnia-Herzegovina ■, Europe 20 B7 44 0N 18 0 E
**Bosnia-Herzegovina** ■, Europe 20 B7 44 0N 18 0 E
Bosnik, Indonesia 37 E9 1 5S 136 10 E
Bosobolo, Dem. Rep. of the Congo 52 D3 4 15N 19 50 E
**Bosporus** = İstanbul Boğazı, Turkey 21 D13 41 10N 29 10 E
Bosque Farms, U.S.A. 83 J10 34 53N 106 40W
Bossangoa, C.A.R. 52 C3 6 35N 17 30 E
Bossier City, U.S.A. 81 J8 32 31N 93 44W
Bosso, Niger 51 F8 13 43N 13 19 E
Bostan, Pakistan 42 D2 30 26N 67 2 E
Bostānābād, Iran 44 B5 37 50N 46 50 E
Bosten Hu, China 32 B3 41 55N 87 40 E
Boston, U.K. 10 E7 52 59N 0 2W
**Boston**, U.S.A. 79 D13 42 22N 71 4W
Boston Bar, Canada 72 D4 49 52N 121 30W
Boston Mts., U.S.A. 81 H8 35 42N 93 15W
Boswell, Canada 72 D5 49 28N 116 45W
Boswell, U.S.A. 78 F5 40 10N 79 2W
Botad, India 42 H4 22 15N 71 40 E
Botene, Laos 38 D3 17 35N 101 12 E
Bothaville, S. Africa 56 D4 27 23S 26 34 E
Bothnia, G. of, Europe 8 E19 63 0N 20 15 E
Bothwell, Australia 62 G4 42 20S 147 1 E
Bothwell, Canada 78 D3 42 38N 81 52W
Botletle →, Botswana 56 C3 20 10S 23 15 E
Botoşani, Romania 17 E14 47 42N 26 41 E
Botou, Burkina Faso 50 F6 12 40N 2 3 E
**Botswana** ■, Africa 56 C3 22 0S 24 0 E
Bottineau, U.S.A. 80 A4 48 50N 100 27W
Bottrop, Germany 15 C6 51 31N 6 58 E
Botucatu, Brazil 95 A6 22 55S 48 30W
Botwood, Canada 71 C8 49 6N 55 23W
Bouaflé, Ivory C. 50 G4 7 1N 5 47W
Bouaké, Ivory C. 50 G4 7 40N 5 2W
Bouar, C.A.R. 52 C3 6 0N 15 40 E
Bouârfa, Morocco 50 B5 32 32N 1 58W
Boucaut B., Australia 62 A1 12 0S 134 25 E
Bougainville, C., Australia 60 B4 13 57S 126 4 E
**Bougainville I.**, Papua N. G. 64 H7 6 0S 155 0 E
Bougainville Reef, Australia 62 B4 15 30S 147 5 E
Bougie = Bejaia, Algeria 50 A7 36 42N 5 2 E
Bougouni, Mali 50 F4 11 30N 7 20W
Bouillon, Belgium 15 E5 49 44N 5 3 E
Boulder, Colo., U.S.A. 80 E2 40 1N 105 17W
Boulder, Mont., U.S.A. 82 C7 46 14N 112 7W
Boulder City, U.S.A. 85 K12 35 59N 114 50W
Boulder Creek, U.S.A. 84 H4 37 7N 122 7W
Boulder Dam = Hoover Dam, U.S.A. 85 K12 36 1N 114 44W
Boulia, Australia 62 C2 22 52S 139 51 E
Boulogne-sur-Mer, France 18 A4 50 42N 1 36 E
Boultoum, Niger 51 F8 14 45N 10 25 E
Boun Neua, Laos 38 B3 21 38N 101 54 E
Boun Tai, Laos 38 B3 21 23N 101 58 E
Bouna, Ivory C. 50 G5 9 10N 3 0W
Boundary Peak, U.S.A. 84 H8 37 51N 118 21W
Boundiali, Ivory C. 50 G4 9 30N 6 20W
Bountiful, U.S.A. 82 F8 40 53N 111 53W
Bounty Is., Pac. Oc. 64 M9 48 0S 178 30 E
Bourbonnais, France 18 C5 46 28N 3 0 E
Bourdel L., Canada 70 A5 56 43N 74 10W
Bourem, Mali 50 E5 17 0N 0 24W
Bourg-en-Bresse, France 18 C6 46 13N 5 12 E
Bourg-St-Maurice, France 18 D7 45 35N 6 46 E
Bourges, France 18 C5 47 9N 2 25 E
Bourget, Canada 79 A9 45 26N 75 9W
Bourgogne, France 18 C6 47 0N 4 50 E
Bourke, Australia 63 E4 30 8S 145 55 E
Bourne, U.K. 10 E7 52 47N 0 22W
Bournemouth, U.K. 11 G6 50 43N 1 52W
Bournemouth □, U.K. 11 G6 50 43N 1 52W
Bouse, U.S.A. 85 M13 33 56N 114 0W
Bouvet I. = Bouvetøya, Antarctica 3 G10 54 26S 3 24 E
Bouvetøya, Antarctica 3 G10 54 26S 3 24 E
Bovill, U.S.A. 82 C5 46 51N 116 24W
Bovril, Argentina 94 C4 31 21S 59 26W
Bow →, Canada 72 C6 49 57N 111 41W
Bow Island, Canada 72 D6 49 50N 111 23W
Bowbells, U.S.A. 80 A3 48 48N 102 15W
Bowdle, U.S.A. 80 C5 45 27N 99 39W
Bowelling, Australia 61 F2 33 25S 116 30 E
Bowen, Argentina 94 D2 35 0S 67 31W
Bowen, Australia 62 C4 20 0S 148 16 E
Bowen Mts., Australia 63 F4 37 0S 147 50 E
Bowie, Ariz., U.S.A. 83 K9 32 19N 109 29W
Bowie, Tex., U.S.A. 81 J6 33 34N 97 51W
Bowkān, Iran 44 B5 36 31N 46 12 E
Bowland, Forest of, U.K. 10 D5 54 0N 2 30W
Bowling Green, Ky., U.S.A. 76 G2 36 59N 86 27W
Bowling Green, Ohio, U.S.A. 76 E4 41 23N 83 39W
Bowling Green, C., Australia 62 B4 19 19S 147 25 E
Bowman, U.S.A. 80 B3 46 11N 103 24W
Bowman I., Antarctica 5 C8 65 0S 104 0 E
Bowmanville, Canada 78 C6 43 55N 78 41W
Bowmore, U.K. 12 F2 55 45N 6 17W
Bowral, Australia 63 E5 34 26S 150 27 E
Bowraville, Australia 63 E5 30 37S 152 52 E
Bowron →, Canada 72 C4 54 3N 121 50W
Bowron Lake Prov. Park, Canada 72 C4 53 10N 121 5W
Bowser L., Canada 72 B3 56 30N 129 30W
Bowsman, Canada 73 C8 52 14N 101 12W
Bowwood, Zambia 55 F2 17 5S 26 20 E
Box Cr. →, Australia 63 E3 34 10S 143 50 E
Boxmeer, Neths. 15 C5 51 38N 5 56 E
Boxtel, Neths. 15 C5 51 36N 5 20 E
Boyce, U.S.A. 81 K8 31 23N 92 40W
Boyd L., Canada 70 B4 52 46N 76 42W
Boyle, Canada 72 C6 54 35N 112 49W
Boyle, Ireland 13 C3 53 59N 8 18W
Boyne →, Ireland 13 C5 53 43N 6 15W
Boyne City, U.S.A. 76 C3 45 13N 85 1W
Boynton Beach, U.S.A. 77 M5 26 32N 80 4W
Boyolali, Indonesia 37 G14 7 32S 110 35 E
Boyoma, Chutes, Dem. Rep. of the Congo 54 B2 0 35N 25 23 E
Boysen Reservoir, U.S.A. 82 E9 43 25N 108 11W
Boyuibe, Bolivia 92 G6 20 25S 63 17W
Boyup Brook, Australia 61 F2 33 50S 116 23 E
Boz Dağları, Turkey 21 E13 38 20N 28 0 E
Bozburun, Turkey 21 F13 36 43N 28 4 E
Bozcaada, Turkey 21 E12 39 49N 26 3 E
Bozdoğan, Turkey 21 F13 37 40N 28 17 E
Bozeman, U.S.A. 82 D8 45 41N 111 2W
Bozen = Bolzano, Italy 20 A4 46 31N 11 22 E
Bozhou, China 34 H8 33 55N 115 41 E
Bozoum, C.A.R. 52 C3 6 25N 16 35 E
Bra, Italy 18 D7 44 42N 7 51 E
Brabant □, Belgium 15 D4 50 46N 4 30 E
Brabant L., Canada 73 B8 55 58N 103 43W
Brač, Croatia 20 C7 43 20N 16 40 E
Bracadale, L., U.K. 12 D2 57 20N 6 30W
Bracciano, L. di, Italy 20 C5 42 7N 12 14 E
Bracebridge, Canada 78 A5 45 2N 79 19W
Brach, Libya 51 C8 27 31N 14 20 E
Bräcke, Sweden 9 E16 62 45N 15 26 E
Brackettville, U.S.A. 81 L4 29 19N 100 25W
Bracknell, U.K. 11 F7 51 25N 0 43W
Bracknell Forest □, U.K. 11 F7 51 25N 0 44W
Brad, Romania 17 E12 46 10N 22 50 E
Bradenton, U.S.A. 77 M4 27 30N 82 34W
Bradford, Canada 78 B5 44 7N 79 34W
**Bradford**, U.K. 10 D6 53 47N 1 45W
Bradford, Pa., U.S.A. 78 E6 41 58N 78 38W
Bradford, Vt., U.S.A. 79 C12 43 59N 72 9W
Bradley, Ark., U.S.A. 81 J8 33 6N 93 39W
Bradley, Calif., U.S.A. 84 K6 35 52N 120 48W
Bradley Institute, Zimbabwe 55 F3 17 7S 31 25 E
Brady, U.S.A. 81 K5 31 9N 99 20W
Braemar, U.K. 12 D5 57 0N 3 23W
Braeside, Canada 79 A8 45 28N 76 24W
Braga, Portugal 19 B1 41 35N 8 25W
Bragado, Argentina 94 D3 35 2S 60 27W
Bragança, Brazil 93 D9 1 0S 47 2W
Bragança, Portugal 19 B2 41 48N 6 50W
Bragança Paulista, Brazil 95 A6 22 55S 46 32W
Brahmanbaria, Bangla. 41 H17 23 58N 91 15 E
Brahmani →, India 41 J15 20 39N 86 46 E
Brahmapur, India 41 K14 19 15N 84 54 E
**Brahmaputra** →, India 43 H13 23 58N 89 50 E
Braich-y-pwll, U.K. 10 E3 52 47N 4 46W
Braidwood, Australia 63 F4 35 27S 149 49 E
Brăila, Romania 17 F14 45 19N 27 59 E
Brainerd, U.S.A. 80 B7 46 22N 94 12W
Braintree, U.K. 11 F8 51 53N 0 34 E
Braintree, U.S.A. 79 D14 42 13N 71 0W
Brak →, S. Africa 56 D3 29 35S 22 55 E
Brakwater, Namibia 56 C2 22 28S 17 3 E
Brampton, Canada 78 C5 43 45N 79 45W
Brampton, U.K. 10 C5 54 57N 2 44W
Branco →, Brazil 92 D6 1 20S 61 50W
Brandenburg = Neubrandenburg, Germany 16 B7 53 33N 13 15 E
Brandenburg, Germany 16 B7 52 25N 12 33 E
Brandenburg □, Germany 16 B6 52 50N 13 0 E
Brandfort, S. Africa 56 D4 28 40S 26 30 E
Brandon, Canada 73 D9 49 50N 99 57W
Brandon, U.S.A. 79 C11 43 48N 73 4W
Brandon B., Ireland 13 D1 52 17N 10 8W
Brandon Mt., Ireland 13 D1 52 15N 10 15W
Brandsen, Argentina 94 D4 35 10S 58 15W
Brandvlei, S. Africa 56 E3 30 25S 20 30 E
Branford, U.S.A. 79 E12 41 17N 72 49W
Braniewo, Poland 17 A10 54 25N 19 50 E
Bransfield Str., Antarctica 5 C18 63 0S 59 0W
Branson, U.S.A. 81 G8 36 39N 93 13W
Brantford, Canada 78 C4 43 10N 80 15W
Bras d'Or L., Canada 71 C7 45 50N 60 50W
Brasher Falls, U.S.A. 79 B10 44 49N 74 47W
Brasil, Planalto, Brazil 90 E6 18 0S 46 30W
Brasiléia, Brazil 92 F5 11 0S 68 45W
**Brasília**, Brazil 93 G9 15 47S 47 55W
Brasília Legal, Brazil 93 D7 3 49S 55 36W
Braslaw, Belarus 9 J22 55 38N 27 0 E
Braşov, Romania 17 F13 45 38N 25 35 E
Brasschaat, Belgium 15 C4 51 19N 4 27 E
Brassey, Banjaran, Malaysia 36 D5 5 0N 117 15 E
Brassey Ra., Australia 61 E3 25 8S 122 15 E
Brasstown Bald, U.S.A. 77 H4 34 53N 83 49W
Brastad, Sweden 9 G14 58 23N 11 30 E
**Bratislava**, Slovak Rep. 17 D9 48 10N 17 7 E
Bratsk, Russia 27 D11 56 10N 101 30 E
Brattleboro, U.S.A. 79 D12 42 51N 72 34W
Braunau, Austria 16 D7 48 15N 13 3 E
Braunschweig, Germany 16 B6 52 15N 10 31 E
Braunton, U.K. 11 F3 51 7N 4 10W
Bravo del Norte, Rio = Grande, Rio →, U.S.A. 81 N6 25 58N 97 9W
Brawley, U.S.A. 85 N11 32 59N 115 31W
Bray, Ireland 13 C5 53 13N 6 7W
Bray, Mt., Australia 62 A1 14 0S 134 30 E
Bray, Pays de, France 18 B4 49 46N 1 26 E
Brazeau →, Canada 72 C5 52 55N 115 14W
Brazil, U.S.A. 76 F2 39 32N 87 8W
**Brazil** ■, S. Amer. 93 F9 12 0S 50 0W
Brazilian Highlands = Brasil, Planalto, Brazil 90 E6 18 0S 46 30W
Brazo Sur →, S. Amer. 94 B4 25 21S 57 42W
Brazos →, U.S.A. 81 L7 28 53N 95 23W
**Brazzaville**, Congo 52 E3 4 9S 15 12 E
Brčko, Bos.-H. 21 B8 44 54N 18 46 E
Breaden, L., Australia 61 E4 25 51S 125 28 E
Breaksea Sd., N.Z. 59 L1 45 35S 166 35 E
Bream B., N.Z. 59 F5 35 56S 174 28 E
Bream Hd., N.Z. 59 F5 35 51S 174 36 E
Breas, Chile 94 B1 25 29S 70 24W
Brebes, Indonesia 37 G13 6 52S 109 3 E
Brechin, Canada 78 B5 44 32N 79 10W
Brechin, U.K. 12 E6 56 44N 2 39W
Brecht, Belgium 15 C4 51 21N 4 38 E
Breckenridge, Colo., U.S.A. 82 G10 39 29N 106 3W
Breckenridge, Minn., U.S.A. 80 B6 46 16N 96 35W
Breckenridge, Tex., U.S.A. 81 J5 32 45N 98 54W
Breckland, U.K. 11 E8 52 30N 0 40 E
Brecon, U.K. 11 F4 51 57N 3 23W
Brecon Beacons, U.K. 11 F4 51 53N 3 26W
**Breda**, Neths. 15 C4 51 35N 4 45 E
Bredasdorp, S. Africa 56 E3 34 33S 20 2 E
Bree, Belgium 15 C5 51 8N 5 35 E
Bregenz, Austria 16 E5 47 30N 9 45 E
Breiðafjörður, Iceland 8 D2 65 15N 23 15W
Brejo, Brazil 93 D10 3 41S 42 47W
**Bremen**, Germany 16 B5 53 4N 8 47 E
Bremer Bay, Australia 61 F2 34 21S 119 20 E
Bremer I., Australia 62 A2 12 5S 136 45 E
Bremerhaven, Germany 16 B5 53 33N 8 36 E
Bremerton, U.S.A. 84 C4 47 34N 122 38W
Brenham, U.S.A. 81 K6 30 10N 96 24W
Brennerpass, Austria 16 E6 47 2N 11 30 E
Brent, U.S.A. 77 J2 32 56N 87 10W
Brentwood, U.K. 11 F8 51 37N 0 19 E
Brentwood, Calif., U.S.A. 84 H5 37 56N 121 42W
Brentwood, N.Y., U.S.A. 79 F11 40 47N 73 15W
Bréscia, Italy 18 D9 45 33N 10 15 E
Breskens, Neths. 15 C3 51 23N 3 33 E
Breslau = Wrocław, Poland 17 C9 51 5N 17 5 E
Bressanone, Italy 20 A4 46 43N 11 39 E
Bressay, U.K. 12 A7 60 9N 1 6W
**Brest**, Belarus 17 B12 52 10N 23 40 E
**Brest**, France 18 B1 48 24N 4 31W
Brest-Litovsk = Brest, Belarus 17 B12 52 10N 23 40 E
Bretagne, France 18 B2 48 10N 3 0W
Breton, Canada 72 C6 53 7N 114 28W
Breton Sd., U.S.A. 81 L10 29 35N 89 15W
Brett, C., N.Z. 59 F5 35 10S 174 20 E
Brevard, U.S.A. 77 H4 35 14N 82 44W
Breves, Brazil 93 D8 1 40S 50 29W
Brewarrina, Australia 63 E4 30 0S 146 51 E
Brewer, U.S.A. 77 C11 44 48N 68 46W
Brewer, Mt., U.S.A. 84 J8 36 44N 118 28W
Brewster, N.Y., U.S.A. 79 E11 41 23N 73 37W
Brewster, Ohio, U.S.A. 78 F3 40 43N 81 36W
Brewster, Wash., U.S.A. 82 B4 48 6N 119 47W
Brewster, Kap, Greenland 4 B6 70 7N 22 0W
Brewton, U.S.A. 77 K2 31 7N 87 4W
Breyten, S. Africa 57 D5 26 16S 30 0 E
Brezhnev = Naberezhnyye Chelny, Russia 24 C9 55 42N 52 19 E
Briançon, France 18 D7 44 54N 6 39 E
Bribie I., Australia 63 D5 27 0S 153 10 E
Bribri, Costa Rica 88 E3 9 38N 82 50W
Bridgehampton, U.S.A. 79 F12 40 56N 72 19W
Bridgend, U.K. 11 F4 51 30N 3 34W
Bridgend □, U.K. 11 F4 51 36N 3 36W
Bridgeport, Calif., U.S.A. 84 G7 38 15N 119 14W
**Bridgeport**, Conn., U.S.A. 79 E11 41 11N 73 12W
Bridgeport, Nebr., U.S.A. 80 E3 41 40N 103 6W
Bridgeport, Tex., U.S.A. 81 J6 33 13N 97 45W
Bridger, U.S.A. 82 D9 45 18N 108 55W
Bridgeton, U.S.A. 76 F8 39 26N 75 14W
Bridgetown, Australia 61 F2 33 58S 116 7 E
**Bridgetown**, Barbados 89 D8 13 5N 59 30W
Bridgetown, Canada 71 D6 44 55N 65 18W
Bridgewater, Canada 71 D7 44 25N 64 31W
Bridgewater, Mass., U.S.A. 79 E14 41 59N 70 58W
Bridgewater, N.Y., U.S.A. 79 D9 42 53N 75 15W
Bridgewater, C., Australia 63 F3 38 23S 141 23 E
Bridgewater-Gagebrook, Australia 62 G4 42 44S 147 14 E
Bridgnorth, U.K. 11 E5 52 32N 2 25W
Bridgton, U.S.A. 79 B14 44 3N 70 42W
Bridgwater, U.K. 11 F5 51 8N 2 59W
Bridgwater B., U.K. 11 F4 51 15N 3 15W
Bridlington, U.K. 10 C7 54 5N 0 12W
Bridlington B., U.K. 10 C7 54 4N 0 10W
Bridport, Australia 62 G4 40 59S 147 23 E
Bridport, U.K. 11 G5 50 44N 2 45W
Brig, Switz. 18 C7 46 18N 7 59 E
Brigg, U.K. 10 D7 53 34N 0 28W
Brigham City, U.S.A. 82 F7 41 31N 112 1W
Bright, Australia 63 F4 36 42S 146 56 E
Brighton, Australia 63 F2 35 5S 138 30 E
Brighton, Canada 78 B7 44 2N 77 44W
**Brighton**, U.K. 11 G7 50 49N 0 7W
Brighton, Colo., U.S.A. 80 F2 39 59N 104 49W
Brighton, N.Y., U.S.A. 78 C7 43 8N 77 34W
Brilliant, U.S.A. 78 F4 40 15N 80 39W
Brindisi, Italy 21 D7 40 39N 17 55 E
Brinkley, U.S.A. 81 H9 34 53N 91 12W
Brinnon, U.S.A. 84 C4 47 41N 122 54W
Brion, I., Canada 71 C7 47 46N 61 26W
**Brisbane**, Australia 63 D5 27 25S 153 2 E
Brisbane →, Australia 63 D5 27 24S 153 9 E
**Bristol**, U.K. 11 F5 51 26N 2 35W
Bristol, Conn., U.S.A. 79 E12 41 40N 72 57W
Bristol, Pa., U.S.A. 79 F10 40 6N 74 51W
Bristol, R.I., U.S.A. 79 E13 41 40N 71 16W
Bristol, Tenn., U.S.A. 77 G4 36 36N 82 11W
Bristol, City of □, U.K. 11 F5 51 27N 2 36W
Bristol B., U.S.A. 68 C4 58 0N 160 0W
Bristol Channel, U.K. 11 F3 51 18N 4 30W
Bristol I., Antarctica 5 B1 58 45S 28 0W
Bristol L., U.S.A. 83 J5 34 23N 116 50W
Bristow, U.S.A. 81 H6 35 50N 96 23W
**Britain** = Great Britain, Europe 6 E5 54 0N 2 15W
**British Columbia** □, Canada 72 C3 55 0N 125 15W
**British Indian Ocean Terr.** = Chagos Arch., Ind. Oc. 29 K11 6 0S 72 0 E
**British Isles**, Europe 6 E5 54 0N 4 0W

Brits, *S. Africa* 57 D4 25 37S 27 48 E
Britstown, *S. Africa* 56 E3 30 37S 23 30 E
Britt, *Canada* 70 C3 45 46N 80 34W
**Brittany** = Bretagne, *France* 18 B2 48 10N 3 0W
Britton, *U.S.A.* 80 C6 45 48N 97 45W
Brive-la-Gaillarde, *France* 18 D4 45 10N 1 32 E
Brixen = Bressanone, *Italy* 20 A4 46 43N 11 39 E
Brixham, *U.K.* 11 G4 50 23N 3 31W
**Brno**, *Czech Rep.* 17 D9 49 10N 16 35 E
Broad →, *U.S.A.* 77 J5 34 1N 81 4W
Broad Arrow, *Australia* 61 F3 30 23S 121 15 E
Broad B., *U.K.* 12 C2 58 14N 6 18W
Broad Haven, *Ireland* 13 B2 54 20N 9 55W
Broad Law, *U.K.* 12 F5 55 30N 3 21W
Broad Sd., *Australia* 62 C4 22 0S 149 45 E
Broadalbin, *U.S.A.* 79 C10 43 4N 74 12W
Broadback →, *Canada* 70 B4 51 21N 78 52W
Broadford, *Australia* 63 F4 37 14S 145 4 E
Broadhurst Ra., *Australia* 60 D3 22 30S 122 30 E
**Broads, The**, *U.K.* 10 E9 52 45N 1 30 E
Broadus, *U.S.A.* 80 C2 45 27N 105 25W
Brochet, *Canada* 73 B8 57 53N 101 40W
Brochet, L., *Canada* 73 B8 58 36N 101 35W
Brocken, *Germany* 16 C6 51 47N 10 37 E
Brockport, *U.S.A.* 78 C7 43 13N 77 56W
Brockton, *U.S.A.* 79 D13 42 5N 71 1W
Brockville, *Canada* 79 B9 44 35N 75 41W
Brockway, *Mont., U.S.A.* 80 B2 47 18N 105 45W
Brockway, *Pa., U.S.A.* 78 E6 41 15N 78 47W
Brocton, *U.S.A.* 78 D5 42 23N 79 26W
Brodeur Pen., *Canada* 69 A11 72 30N 88 10W
Brodhead, Mt., *U.S.A.* 78 E7 41 39N 77 47W
Brodick, *U.K.* 12 F3 55 35N 5 9W
Brodnica, *Poland* 17 B10 53 15N 19 25 E
Brody, *Ukraine* 17 C13 50 5N 25 10 E
Brogan, *U.S.A.* 82 D5 44 15N 117 31W
Broken Arrow, *U.S.A.* 81 G7 36 3N 95 48W
Broken Bow, *Nebr., U.S.A.* 80 E5 41 24N 99 38W
Broken Bow, *Okla., U.S.A.* 81 H7 34 2N 94 44W
Broken Bow Lake, *U.S.A.* 81 H7 34 9N 94 40W
Broken Hill = Kabwe, *Zambia* 55 E2 14 30S 28 29 E
Broken Hill, *Australia* 63 E3 31 58S 141 29 E
Bromley, *U.K.* 11 F8 51 24N 0 2 E
Bromsgrove, *U.K.* 11 E5 52 21N 2 2W
Brønderslev, *Denmark* 9 H13 57 16N 9 57 E
Bronkhorstspruit, *S. Africa* 57 D4 25 46S 28 45 E
Brønnøysund, *Norway* 8 D15 65 28N 12 14 E
Brook Park, *U.S.A.* 78 E4 41 24N 81 51W
Brookhaven, *U.S.A.* 81 K9 31 35N 90 26W
Brookings, *Oreg., U.S.A.* 82 E1 42 3N 124 17W
Brookings, *S. Dak., U.S.A.* 80 C6 44 19N 96 48W
Brooklin, *Canada* 78 C6 43 55N 78 55W
Brooklyn Park, *U.S.A.* 80 C8 45 6N 93 23W
Brooks, *Canada* 72 C6 50 35N 111 55W
Brooks Range, *U.S.A.* 68 B5 68 0N 152 0W
Brooksville, *U.S.A.* 77 L4 28 33N 82 23W
Brookton, *Australia* 61 F2 32 22S 117 0 E
Brookville, *U.S.A.* 78 E5 41 10N 79 5W
Broom, L., *U.K.* 12 D3 57 55N 5 15W
Broome, *Australia* 60 C3 18 0S 122 15 E
Brora, *U.K.* 12 C5 58 0N 3 52W
Brora →, *U.K.* 12 C5 58 0N 3 51W
Brosna →, *Ireland* 13 C4 53 14N 7 58W
Brothers, *U.S.A.* 82 E3 43 49N 120 36W
Brough, *U.K.* 10 C5 54 32N 2 18W
Brough Hd., *U.K.* 12 B5 59 8N 3 20W
Broughton Island = Qikiqtarjuaq, *Canada* 69 B13 67 33N 63 0W
Brown, L., *Australia* 61 F2 31 5S 118 15 E
Brown, Pt., *Australia* 63 E1 32 32S 133 50 E
Brown City, *U.S.A.* 78 C2 43 13N 82 59W
Brown Willy, *U.K.* 11 G3 50 35N 4 37W
Brownfield, *U.S.A.* 81 J3 33 11N 102 17W
Browning, *U.S.A.* 82 B7 48 34N 113 1W
Brownsville, *Oreg., U.S.A.* 82 D2 44 24N 122 59W
Brownsville, *Pa., U.S.A.* 78 F5 40 1N 79 53W
Brownsville, *Tenn., U.S.A.* 81 H10 35 36N 89 16W
Brownsville, *Tex., U.S.A.* 81 N6 25 54N 97 30W
Brownville, *U.S.A.* 79 C9 44 0N 75 59W
Brownwood, *U.S.A.* 81 K5 31 43N 98 59W
Browse I., *Australia* 60 B3 14 7S 123 33 E
Bruas, *Malaysia* 39 K3 4 30N 100 47 E
Bruay-la-Buissière, *France* 18 A5 50 29N 2 33 E
Bruce, Mt., *Australia* 60 D2 22 37S 118 8 E
Bruce Pen., *Canada* 78 B3 45 0N 81 30W
Bruce Rock, *Australia* 61 F2 31 52S 118 8 E
Bruck an der Leitha, *Austria* 17 D9 48 1N 16 47 E
Bruck an der Mur, *Austria* 16 E8 47 24N 15 16 E
Brue →, *U.K.* 11 F5 51 13N 2 59W
**Bruges** = Brugge, *Belgium* 15 C3 51 13N 3 13 E
Brugge, *Belgium* 15 C3 51 13N 3 13 E
Bruin, *U.S.A.* 78 E5 41 3N 79 43W
Brûlé, *Canada* 72 C5 53 15N 117 58W
Brumado, *Brazil* 93 F10 14 14S 41 40W
Brumunddal, *Norway* 9 F14 60 53N 10 56 E
Bruneau, *U.S.A.* 82 E6 42 53N 115 48W
Bruneau →, *U.S.A.* 82 E6 42 56N 115 57W
Brunei = Bandar Seri Begawan, *Brunei* 36 D5 4 52N 115 0 E
**Brunei** ■, *Asia* 36 D5 4 50N 115 0 E
Brunner, L., *N.Z.* 59 K3 42 37S 171 27 E
Brunssum, *Neths.* 15 D5 50 57N 5 59 E
Brunswick = Braunschweig, *Germany* 16 B6 52 15N 10 31 E
Brunswick, *Ga., U.S.A.* 77 K5 31 10N 81 30W
Brunswick, *Maine, U.S.A.* 77 D11 43 55N 69 58W
Brunswick, *Md., U.S.A.* 76 F7 39 19N 77 38W
Brunswick, *Mo., U.S.A.* 80 F8 39 26N 93 8W
Brunswick, *Ohio, U.S.A.* 78 E3 41 14N 81 51W
Brunswick, Pen. de, *Chile* 96 G2 53 30S 71 30W
Brunswick B., *Australia* 60 C3 15 15S 124 50 E
Brunswick Junction, *Australia* 61 F2 33 15S 115 50 E
Bruny I., *Australia* 62 G4 43 20S 147 15 E
Brus Laguna, *Honduras* 88 C3 15 47N 84 35W
Brush, *U.S.A.* 80 E3 40 15N 103 37W
Brushton, *U.S.A.* 79 B10 44 50N 74 31W
Brusque, *Brazil* 95 B6 27 5S 49 0W
Brussel, *Belgium* 15 D4 50 51N 4 21 E
**Brussels** = Brussel, *Belgium* 15 D4 50 51N 4 21 E
Brussels, *Canada* 78 C3 43 44N 81 15W
Bruthen, *Australia* 63 F4 37 42S 147 50 E
Bruxelles = Brussel, *Belgium* 15 D4 50 51N 4 21 E
Bryan, *Ohio, U.S.A.* 76 E3 41 28N 84 33W
Bryan, *Tex., U.S.A.* 81 K6 30 40N 96 22W
Bryan, Mt., *Australia* 63 E2 33 30S 139 0 E
Bryansk, *Russia* 24 D5 53 13N 34 25 E
Bryce Canyon National Park, *U.S.A.* 83 H7 37 30N 112 10W
Bryne, *Norway* 9 G11 58 44N 5 38 E
Bryson City, *U.S.A.* 77 H4 35 26N 83 27W
Bsharri, *Lebanon* 47 A5 34 15N 36 0 E
Bū Baqarah, *U.A.E.* 45 E8 25 35N 56 25 E
Bu Craa, *W. Sahara* 50 C3 26 45N 12 50W
Bū Ḥasā, *U.A.E.* 45 F7 23 30N 53 20 E
Bua Yai, *Thailand* 38 E4 15 33N 102 26 E
Buapinang, *Indonesia* 37 E6 4 40S 121 30 E
Bubanza, *Burundi* 54 C2 3 6S 29 23 E
Būbiyān, *Kuwait* 45 D6 29 45N 48 15 E
Bucaramanga, *Colombia* 92 B4 7 0N 73 0W
Bucasia, *Australia* 62 C4 21 2S 149 10 E
Buccaneer Arch., *Australia* 60 C3 16 7S 123 20 E
Buchach, *Ukraine* 17 D13 49 5N 25 25 E
Buchan, *U.K.* 12 D6 57 32N 2 21W
Buchan Ness, *U.K.* 12 D7 57 29N 1 46W
Buchanan, *Canada* 73 C8 51 40N 102 45W
Buchanan, *Liberia* 50 G3 5 57N 10 2W
Buchanan, L., *Queens., Australia* 62 C4 21 35S 145 52 E
Buchanan, L., *W. Austral., Australia* 61 E3 25 33S 123 2 E
Buchanan, L., *U.S.A.* 81 K5 30 45N 98 25W
Buchanan Cr. →, *Australia* 62 B2 19 13S 136 33 E
Buchans, *Canada* 71 C8 48 50N 56 52W
**Bucharest** = Bucureşti, *Romania* 17 F14 44 27N 26 10 E
Buchon, Pt., *U.S.A.* 84 K6 35 15N 120 54W
Buck Hill Falls, *U.S.A.* 79 E9 41 11N 75 16W
Buckeye, *U.S.A.* 83 K7 33 22N 112 35W
Buckeye Lake, *U.S.A.* 78 G2 39 55N 82 29W
Buckhannon, *U.S.A.* 76 F5 39 0N 80 8W
Buckhaven, *U.K.* 12 E5 56 11N 3 3W
Buckhorn L., *Canada* 78 B6 44 29N 78 23W
Buckie, *U.K.* 12 D6 57 41N 2 58W
Buckingham, *Canada* 70 C4 45 37N 75 24W
Buckingham, *U.K.* 11 F7 51 59N 0 57W
Buckingham B., *Australia* 62 A2 12 10S 135 40 E
**Buckinghamshire** □, *U.K.* 11 F7 51 53N 0 55W
Buckle Hd., *Australia* 60 B4 14 26S 127 52 E
Buckleboo, *Australia* 63 E2 32 54S 136 12 E
Buckley, *U.K.* 10 D4 53 10N 3 5W
Buckley →, *Australia* 62 C2 20 10S 138 49 E
Bucklin, *U.S.A.* 81 G5 37 33N 99 38W
Bucks L., *U.S.A.* 84 F5 39 54N 121 12W
Buctouche, *Canada* 71 C7 46 30N 64 45W
Bucureşti, *Romania* 17 F14 44 27N 26 10 E
Bucyrus, *U.S.A.* 76 E4 40 48N 82 59W
Budalin, *Burma* 41 H19 22 20N 95 10 E
**Budapest**, *Hungary* 17 E10 47 29N 19 5 E
Budaun, *India* 43 E8 28 5N 79 10 E
Budd Coast, *Antarctica* 5 C8 68 0S 112 0 E
Bude, *U.K.* 11 G3 50 49N 4 34W
Budennovsk, *Russia* 25 F7 44 50N 44 10 E
Budge Budge = Baj Baj, *India* 43 H13 22 30N 88 5 E
Budgewoi, *Australia* 63 E5 33 13S 151 34 E
Budjala, *Dem. Rep. of the Congo* 52 D3 2 50N 19 40 E
Buellton, *U.S.A.* 85 L6 34 37N 120 12W
Buena Esperanza, *Argentina* 94 C2 34 45S 65 15W
Buena Park, *U.S.A.* 85 M9 33 52N 117 59W
Buena Vista, *Colo., U.S.A.* 83 G10 38 51N 106 8W
Buena Vista, *Va., U.S.A.* 76 G6 37 44N 79 21W
Buena Vista Lake Bed, *U.S.A.* 85 K7 35 12N 119 18W
Buenaventura, *Colombia* 92 C3 3 53N 77 4W
Buenaventura, *Mexico* 86 B3 29 50N 107 30W
**Buenos Aires**, *Argentina* 94 C4 34 30S 58 20W
Buenos Aires, *Costa Rica* 88 E3 9 10N 83 20W
Buenos Aires □, *Argentina* 94 D4 36 30S 60 0W
Buenos Aires, L., *Chile* 96 F2 46 35S 72 30W
Buffalo, *Mo., U.S.A.* 81 G8 37 39N 93 6W
**Buffalo**, *N.Y., U.S.A.* 78 D6 42 53N 78 53W
Buffalo, *Okla., U.S.A.* 81 G5 36 50N 99 38W
Buffalo, *S. Dak., U.S.A.* 80 C3 45 35N 103 33W
Buffalo, *Wyo., U.S.A.* 82 D10 44 21N 106 42W
Buffalo →, *Canada* 72 A5 60 5N 115 5W
Buffalo Head Hills, *Canada* 72 B5 57 25N 115 55W
Buffalo L., *Canada* 72 A5 60 12N 115 25W
Buffalo L., *Alta., Canada* 72 C6 52 27N 112 54W
Buffalo Narrows, *Canada* 73 B7 55 51N 108 29W
Buffels →, *S. Africa* 56 D2 29 36S 17 3 E
Buford, *U.S.A.* 77 H4 34 10N 84 0W
Bug = Buh →, *Ukraine* 25 E5 46 59N 31 58 E
Bug →, *Poland* 17 B11 52 31N 21 5 E
Buga, *Colombia* 92 C3 4 0N 76 15W
Buganda, *Uganda* 54 C3 0 0 31 30 E
Buganga, *Uganda* 54 C3 0 3S 32 0 E
Bugel, Tanjung, *Indonesia* 37 G14 6 26S 111 3 E
Bugibba, *Malta* 23 D1 35 57N 14 25 E
Bugsuk, *Phil.* 36 C5 8 15N 117 15 E
Bugulma, *Russia* 24 D9 54 33N 52 48 E
Bugun Shara, *Mongolia* 32 B5 49 0N 104 0 E
Buguruslan, *Russia* 24 D9 53 39N 52 26 E
Buh →, *Ukraine* 25 E5 46 59N 31 58 E
Buhl, *U.S.A.* 82 E6 42 36N 114 46W
Builth Wells, *U.K.* 11 E4 52 9N 3 25W
Buir Nur, *Mongolia* 33 B6 47 50N 117 42 E
**Bujumbura**, *Burundi* 54 C2 3 16S 29 18 E
Bukachacha, *Russia* 27 D12 52 55N 116 50 E
Bukama, *Dem. Rep. of the Congo* 55 D2 9 10S 25 50 E
Bukavu, *Dem. Rep. of the Congo* 54 C2 2 20S 28 52 E
Bukene, *Tanzania* 54 C3 4 15S 32 48 E
Bukhara = Bukhoro, *Uzbekistan* 26 F7 39 48N 64 25 E
Bukhoro, *Uzbekistan* 26 F7 39 48N 64 25 E
Bukima, *Tanzania* 54 C3 1 50S 33 25 E
Bukit Mertajam, *Malaysia* 39 K3 5 22N 100 28 E
Bukittinggi, *Indonesia* 36 E2 0 20S 100 20 E
Bukoba, *Tanzania* 54 C3 1 20S 31 49 E
Bukuya, *Uganda* 54 B3 0 40N 31 52 E
Būl, Kuh-e, *Iran* 45 D7 30 48N 52 45 E
Bula, *Indonesia* 37 E8 3 6S 130 30 E
Bulahdelah, *Australia* 63 E5 32 23S 152 13 E
Bulan, *Phil.* 37 B6 12 40N 123 52 E
Bulandshahr, *India* 42 E7 28 28N 77 51 E
**Bulawayo**, *Zimbabwe* 55 G2 20 7S 28 32 E
Buldan, *Turkey* 21 E13 38 2N 28 50 E
Bulgar, *Russia* 24 D8 54 57N 49 4 E
**Bulgaria** ■, *Europe* 21 C11 42 35N 25 30 E
Buli, Teluk, *Indonesia* 37 D7 1 5N 128 25 E
Buliluyan, C., *Phil.* 36 C5 8 20N 117 15 E
Bulkley →, *Canada* 72 B3 55 15N 127 40W
Bull Shoals L., *U.S.A.* 81 G8 36 22N 92 35W
Bullhead City, *U.S.A.* 85 K12 35 8N 114 32W
Büllingen, *Belgium* 15 D6 50 25N 6 16 E
Bullock Creek, *Australia* 62 B3 17 43S 144 31 E
Bulloo →, *Australia* 63 D3 28 43S 142 30 E
Bulloo L., *Australia* 63 D3 28 43S 142 25 E
Bulls, *N.Z.* 59 J5 40 10S 175 24 E
Bulnes, *Chile* 94 D1 36 42S 72 19W
Bulsar = Valsad, *India* 40 J8 20 40N 72 58 E
Bultfontein, *S. Africa* 56 D4 28 18S 26 10 E
Bulukumba, *Indonesia* 37 F6 5 33S 120 11 E
Bulun, *Russia* 27 B13 70 37N 127 30 E
Bumba, *Dem. Rep. of the Congo* 52 D4 2 13N 22 30 E
Bumbiri I., *Tanzania* 54 C3 1 40S 31 55 E
Bumhpa Bum, *Burma* 41 F20 26 51N 97 14 E
Bumi →, *Zimbabwe* 55 F2 17 0S 28 20 E
Buna, *Kenya* 54 B4 2 58N 39 30 E
Bunazi, *Tanzania* 54 C3 1 3S 31 23 E
Bunbury, *Australia* 61 F2 33 20S 115 35 E
Bunclody, *Ireland* 13 D5 52 39N 6 40W
Buncrana, *Ireland* 13 A4 55 8N 7 27W
Bundaberg, *Australia* 63 C5 24 54S 152 22 E
Bundey →, *Australia* 62 C2 21 46S 135 37 E
Bundi, *India* 42 G6 25 30N 75 35 E
Bundoran, *Ireland* 13 B3 54 28N 8 16W
Bung Kan, *Thailand* 38 C4 18 23N 103 37 E
Bungatakada, *Japan* 31 H5 33 35N 131 25 E
Bungay, *U.K.* 11 E9 52 27N 1 28 E
Bungil Cr. →, *Australia* 63 D4 27 5S 149 5 E
Bungo-Suidō, *Japan* 31 H6 33 0N 132 15 E
Bungoma, *Kenya* 54 B3 0 34N 34 34 E
Bungu, *Tanzania* 54 D4 7 35S 39 0 E
Bunia, *Dem. Rep. of the Congo* 54 B3 1 35N 30 20 E
Bunji, *Pakistan* 43 B6 35 45N 74 40 E
Bunkie, *U.S.A.* 81 K8 30 57N 92 11W
Buntok, *Indonesia* 36 E4 1 40S 114 58 E
Bunyu, *Indonesia* 36 D5 3 35N 117 50 E
Buol, *Indonesia* 37 D6 1 15N 121 32 E
Buon Brieng, *Vietnam* 38 F7 13 9N 108 12 E
Buon Ma Thuot, *Vietnam* 38 F7 12 40N 108 3 E
Buong Long, *Cambodia* 38 F6 13 44N 106 59 E
Buorkhaya, Mys, *Russia* 27 B14 71 50N 132 40 E
Buqayq, *Si. Arabia* 45 E6 26 0N 49 45 E
Bur Acaba, *Somali Rep.* 46 G3 3 12N 44 20 E
Bûr Safâga, *Egypt* 44 E2 26 43N 33 57 E
Bûr Sa'îd, *Egypt* 51 B12 31 16N 32 18 E
Bûr Sûdân, *Sudan* 51 E13 19 32N 37 9 E
Bura, *Kenya* 54 C4 1 4S 39 58 E
Burakin, *Australia* 61 F2 30 31S 117 10 E
Burao, *Somali Rep.* 46 F4 9 32N 45 32 E
Burāq, *Syria* 47 B5 33 11N 36 29 E
Buraydah, *Si. Arabia* 44 E5 26 20N 44 8 E
Burbank, *U.S.A.* 85 L8 34 11N 118 19W
Burda, *India* 42 G6 25 50N 77 35 E
Burdekin →, *Australia* 62 B4 19 38S 147 25 E
Burdur, *Turkey* 25 G5 37 45N 30 17 E
Burdwan = Barddhaman, *India* 43 H12 23 14N 87 39 E
Bure, *Ethiopia* 46 E2 10 40N 37 4 E
Bure →, *U.K.* 10 E9 52 38N 1 43 E
Bureya →, *Russia* 27 E13 49 27N 129 30 E
Burford, *Canada* 78 C4 43 7N 80 27W
Burgas, *Bulgaria* 21 C12 42 33N 27 29 E
Burgeo, *Canada* 71 C8 47 37N 57 38W
Burgersdorp, *S. Africa* 56 E4 31 0S 26 20 E
Burges, Mt., *Australia* 61 F3 30 50S 121 5 E
**Burgos**, *Spain* 19 A4 42 21N 3 41W
Burgsvik, *Sweden* 9 H18 57 3N 18 19 E
**Burgundy** = Bourgogne, *France* 18 C6 47 0N 4 50 E
Burhaniye, *Turkey* 21 E12 39 30N 26 58 E
Burhanpur, *India* 40 J10 21 18N 76 14 E
Burhi Gandak →, *India* 43 G12 25 20N 86 37 E
Burhner →, *India* 43 H9 22 43N 80 31 E
Burias, *Phil.* 37 B6 12 55N 123 5 E
Burica, Pta., *Costa Rica* 88 E3 8 3N 82 51W
Burien, *U.S.A.* 84 C4 47 28N 122 21W
Burigi, L., *Tanzania* 54 C3 2 2S 31 22 E
Burin, *Canada* 71 C8 47 1N 55 14W
Buriram, *Thailand* 38 E4 15 0N 103 0 E
Burj Sāfitā, *Syria* 44 C3 34 48N 36 7 E
Burkburnett, *U.S.A.* 81 H5 34 6N 98 34W
Burke →, *Australia* 62 C2 23 12S 139 33 E
Burke Chan., *Canada* 72 C3 52 10N 127 30W
Burketown, *Australia* 62 B2 17 45S 139 33 E
**Burkina Faso** ■, *Africa* 50 F5 12 0N 1 0W
Burk's Falls, *Canada* 70 C4 45 37N 79 24W
Burleigh Falls, *Canada* 78 B6 44 33N 78 12W
Burley, *U.S.A.* 82 E7 42 32N 113 48W
Burlingame, *U.S.A.* 84 H4 37 35N 122 21W
Burlington, *Canada* 78 C5 43 18N 79 45W
Burlington, *Colo., U.S.A.* 80 F3 39 18N 102 16W
Burlington, *Iowa, U.S.A.* 80 E9 40 49N 91 14W
Burlington, *Kans., U.S.A.* 80 F7 38 12N 95 45W
Burlington, *N.C., U.S.A.* 77 G6 36 6N 79 26W
Burlington, *N.J., U.S.A.* 79 F10 40 4N 74 51W
**Burlington**, *Vt., U.S.A.* 79 B11 44 29N 73 12W
Burlington, *Wash., U.S.A.* 84 B4 48 28N 122 20W
Burlington, *Wis., U.S.A.* 76 D1 42 41N 88 17W
Burlyu-Tyube, *Kazakstan* 26 E8 46 30N 79 10 E
**Burma** ■, *Asia* 41 J20 21 0N 96 30 E
Burnaby I., *Canada* 72 C2 52 25N 131 19W
Burnet, *U.S.A.* 81 K5 30 45N 98 14W
Burney, *U.S.A.* 82 F3 40 53N 121 40W
Burnham, *U.S.A.* 78 F7 40 38N 77 34W
Burnham-on-Sea, *U.K.* 11 F5 51 14N 3 0W
Burnie, *Australia* 62 G4 41 4S 145 56 E
Burnley, *U.K.* 10 D5 53 47N 2 14W
Burns, *U.S.A.* 82 E4 43 35N 119 3W
Burns Lake, *Canada* 72 C3 54 20N 125 45W
Burnside →, *Canada* 68 B9 66 51N 108 4W
Burnside, L., *Australia* 61 E3 25 22S 123 0 E
Burnsville, *U.S.A.* 80 C8 44 47N 93 17W
Burnt L., *Canada* 71 B7 53 35N 64 4W
Burnt River, *Canada* 78 B6 44 41N 78 42W
Burntwood →, *Canada* 73 B9 56 8N 96 34W
Burntwood L., *Canada* 73 B8 55 22N 100 26W
Burqān, *Kuwait* 44 D5 29 0N 47 57 E
Burra, *Australia* 63 E2 33 40S 138 55 E
Burray, *U.K.* 12 C6 58 51N 2 54W
Burren Junction, *Australia* 63 E4 30 7S 148 59 E
Burrinjuck Res., *Australia* 63 F4 35 0S 148 36 E
Burro, Serranías del, *Mexico* 86 B4 29 0N 102 0W
Burrow Hd., *U.K.* 12 G4 54 41N 4 24W
Burruyacú, *Argentina* 94 B3 26 30S 64 40W
Burry Port, *U.K.* 11 F3 51 41N 4 15W
Bursa, *Turkey* 21 D13 40 15N 29 5 E
Burstall, *Canada* 73 C7 50 39N 109 54W
Burton, *Ohio, U.S.A.* 78 E3 41 28N 81 8W
Burton, *S.C., U.S.A.* 77 J5 32 25N 80 45W
Burton, L., *Canada* 70 B4 54 45N 78 20W
Burton upon Trent, *U.K.* 10 E6 52 48N 1 38W
Buru, *Indonesia* 37 E7 3 30S 126 30 E
Burûn, Râs, *Egypt* 47 D2 31 14N 33 7 E
**Burundi** ■, *Africa* 54 C3 3 15S 30 0 E
Bururi, *Burundi* 54 C2 3 57S 29 37 E
Burutu, *Nigeria* 50 G7 5 20N 5 29 E
Burwell, *U.S.A.* 80 E5 41 47N 99 8W
Burwick, *U.K.* 12 C5 58 45N 2 58W
Bury, *U.K.* 10 D5 53 35N 2 17W
Bury St. Edmunds, *U.K.* 11 E8 52 15N 0 43 E
Buryatia □, *Russia* 27 D12 53 0N 110 0 E
Busango Swamp, *Zambia* 55 E2 14 15S 25 45 E
Buşayrah, *Syria* 44 C4 35 9N 40 26 E
**Būshehr**, *Iran* 45 D6 28 55N 50 55 E
Būshehr □, *Iran* 45 D6 28 20N 51 45 E
Bushell, *Canada* 73 B7 59 31N 108 45W
Bushenyi, *Uganda* 54 C3 0 35S 30 10 E
Bushire = Būshehr, *Iran* 45 D6 28 55N 50 55 E
Businga, *Dem. Rep. of the Congo* 52 D4 3 16N 20 59 E
Buşra ash Shām, *Syria* 47 C5 32 30N 36 25 E
Busselton, *Australia* 61 F2 33 42S 115 15 E
Bussum, *Neths.* 15 B5 52 16N 5 10 E
Busto Arsizio, *Italy* 18 D8 45 37N 8 51 E
Busu-Djanoa, *Dem. Rep. of the Congo* 52 D4 1 43N 21 23 E
Busuanga, *Phil.* 37 B6 12 10N 120 0 E
Buta, *Dem. Rep. of the Congo* 54 B1 2 50N 24 53 E
Butare, *Rwanda* 54 C2 2 31S 29 52 E
Butaritari, *Kiribati* 64 G9 3 30N 174 0 E
Bute, *U.K.* 12 F3 55 48N 5 2W
Bute Inlet, *Canada* 72 C4 50 40N 124 53W
Butemba, *Uganda* 54 B3 1 9N 31 37 E
Butembo, *Dem. Rep. of the Congo* 54 B2 0 9N 29 18 E
Butha Qi, *China* 33 B7 48 0N 122 32 E
Butiaba, *Uganda* 54 B3 1 50N 31 20 E
Butler, *Mo., U.S.A.* 80 F7 38 16N 94 20W
Butler, *Pa., U.S.A.* 78 F5 40 52N 79 54W
Buton, *Indonesia* 37 F6 5 0S 122 45 E
Butte, *Mont., U.S.A.* 82 C7 46 0N 112 32W
Butte, *Nebr., U.S.A.* 80 D5 42 58N 98 51W
Butte Creek →, *U.S.A.* 84 F5 39 12N 121 56W
Butterworth = Gcuwa, *S. Africa* 57 E4 32 20S 28 11 E
Butterworth, *Malaysia* 39 K3 5 24N 100 23 E
Buttevant, *Ireland* 13 D3 52 14N 8 40W
Buttfield, Mt., *Australia* 61 D4 24 45S 128 9 E
Button B., *Canada* 73 B10 58 45N 94 23W
Buttonwillow, *U.S.A.* 85 K7 35 24N 119 28W
Butty Hd., *Australia* 61 F3 33 54S 121 39 E
Butuan, *Phil.* 37 C7 8 57N 125 33 E
Butung = Buton, *Indonesia* 37 F6 5 0S 122 45 E
Buturlinovka, *Russia* 25 D7 50 50N 40 35 E
Buxa Duar, *India* 43 F13 27 45N 89 35 E
Buxar, *India* 43 G10 25 34N 83 58 E
Buxtehude, *Germany* 16 B5 53 28N 9 39 E
Buxton, *U.K.* 10 D6 53 16N 1 54W
Buy, *Russia* 24 C7 58 28N 41 28 E
Büyük Menderes →, *Turkey* 21 F12 37 28N 27 11 E
Büyükçekmece, *Turkey* 21 D13 41 2N 28 35 E
Buzău, *Romania* 17 F14 45 10N 26 50 E
Buzău →, *Romania* 17 F14 45 26N 27 44 E
Buzen, *Japan* 31 H5 33 35N 131 5 E
Buzi →, *Mozam.* 55 F3 19 50S 34 43 E
Buzuluk, *Russia* 24 D9 52 48N 52 12 E
Buzzards B., *U.S.A.* 79 E14 41 45N 70 37W
Buzzards Bay, *U.S.A.* 79 E14 41 44N 70 37W
Bwana Mkubwe, *Dem. Rep. of the Congo* 55 E2 13 8S 28 38 E
Byarezina →, *Belarus* 17 B16 52 33N 30 14 E
Bydgoszcz, *Poland* 17 B9 53 10N 18 0 E
Byelarus = Belarus ■, *Europe* 17 B14 53 30N 27 0 E
Byelorussia = Belarus ■, *Europe* 17 B14 53 30N 27 0 E
Byers, *U.S.A.* 80 F2 39 43N 104 14W
Byesville, *U.S.A.* 78 G3 39 58N 81 32W
Byford, *Australia* 61 F2 32 15S 116 0 E
Bykhaw, *Belarus* 17 B16 53 31N 30 14 E
Bykhov = Bykhaw, *Belarus* 17 B16 53 31N 30 14 E
Bylas, *U.S.A.* 83 K8 33 8N 110 7W
Bylot, *Canada* 73 B10 58 25N 94 8W
Bylot I., *Canada* 69 A12 73 13N 78 34W
Byrd, C., *Antarctica* 5 C17 69 38S 76 7W
Byrock, *Australia* 63 E4 30 40S 146 27 E
Byron Bay, *Australia* 63 D5 28 43S 153 37 E
Byrranga, Gory, *Russia* 27 B11 75 0N 100 0 E
Byrranga Mts. = Byrranga, Gory, *Russia* 27 B11 75 0N 100 0 E
Byske, *Sweden* 8 D19 64 57N 21 11 E
Byske älv →, *Sweden* 8 D19 64 57N 21 13 E
Bytom, *Poland* 17 C10 50 25N 18 54 E
Bytów, *Poland* 17 A9 54 10N 17 30 E
Byumba, *Rwanda* 54 C3 1 35S 30 4 E


# C


Ca →, *Vietnam* 38 C5 18 45N 105 45 E
Ca Mau, *Vietnam* 39 H5 9 7N 105 8 E
Ca Mau, Mui, *Vietnam* 39 H5 8 38N 104 44 E
Ca Na, *Vietnam* 39 G7 11 20N 108 54 E
Caacupé, *Paraguay* 94 B4 25 23S 57 5W
Caála, *Angola* 53 G3 12 46S 15 30 E
Caamano Sd., *Canada* 72 C3 52 55N 129 25W
Caazapá, *Paraguay* 94 B4 26 8S 56 19W
Caazapá □, *Paraguay* 95 B4 26 10S 56 0W
Cabanatuan, *Phil.* 37 A6 15 30N 120 58 E
Cabano, *Canada* 71 C6 47 40N 68 56W
Cabazon, *U.S.A.* 85 M10 33 55N 116 47W
Cabedelo, *Brazil* 93 E12 7 0S 34 50W

Chamba, Tanzania 55 E4 11 37S 37 0 E
Chambal →, India 43 F8 26 29N 79 15 E
Chamberlain, U.S.A. 80 D5 43 49N 99 20W
Chamberlain →, Australia 60 C4 15 30S 127 54 E
Chamberlain L., U.S.A. 77 B11 46 14N 69 19W
Chambers, U.S.A. 83 J9 35 11N 109 26W
Chambersburg, U.S.A. 76 F7 39 56N 77 40W
Chambéry, France 18 D6 45 34N 5 55 E
Chambeshi →, Zambia 52 G6 11 53S 29 48 E
Chambly, Canada 79 A11 45 27N 73 17W
Chambord, Canada 71 C5 48 25N 72 6W
Chamchamal, Iraq 44 C5 35 32N 44 50 E
Chamela, Mexico 86 D3 19 32N 105 5W
Chamical, Argentina 94 C2 30 22S 66 27W
Chamkar Luong, Cambodia 39 G4 11 0N 103 45 E
Chamoli, India 43 D8 30 24N 79 21 E
Chamonix-Mont Blanc, France 18 D7 45 55N 6 51 E
Chamouchouane →, Canada 70 C5 48 37N 72 20W
Champa, India 43 H10 22 2N 82 43 E
Champagne, Canada 72 A1 60 49N 136 30W
**Champagne**, France 18 B6 48 40N 4 20 E
Champaign, U.S.A. 76 E1 40 7N 88 15W
Champassak, Laos 38 E6 14 53N 105 52 E
Champawat, India 43 E9 29 20N 80 6 E
Champdoré, L., Canada 71 A6 55 55N 65 49W
Champion, U.S.A. 78 E4 41 19N 80 51W
Champlain, U.S.A. 79 B11 44 59N 73 27W
**Champlain, L.**, U.S.A. 79 B11 44 40N 73 20W
Champotón, Mexico 87 D6 19 20N 90 50W
Champua, India 43 H11 22 5N 85 40 E
Chana, Thailand 39 J3 6 55N 100 44 E
Chañaral, Chile 94 B1 26 23S 70 40W
Chanārān, Iran 45 B8 36 39N 59 6 E
Chanasma, India 42 H5 23 44N 72 5 E
Chanco, Chile 94 D1 35 44S 72 32W
Chand, India 43 J8 21 57N 79 7 E
Chandan, India 43 G12 24 38N 86 40 E
Chandan Chauki, India 43 E9 28 33N 80 47 E
Chandannagar, India 43 H13 22 52N 88 24 E
Chandausi, India 43 E8 28 27N 78 49 E
Chandeleur Is., U.S.A. 81 L10 29 55N 88 57W
Chandeleur Sd., U.S.A. 81 L10 29 55N 89 0W
**Chandigarh**, India 42 D7 30 43N 76 47 E
Chandil, India 43 H12 22 58N 86 3 E
Chandler, Australia 63 D1 27 0S 133 19 E
Chandler, Canada 71 C7 48 18N 64 46W
Chandler, Ariz., U.S.A. 83 K8 33 18N 111 50W
Chandler, Okla., U.S.A. 81 H6 35 42N 96 53W
Chandod, India 42 J5 21 59N 73 28 E
Chandpur, Bangla. 41 H17 23 8N 90 45 E
Chandrapur, India 40 K11 19 57N 79 25 E
Chānf, Iran 45 E9 26 38N 60 29 E
Chang, Pakistan 42 F3 26 59N 68 30 E
Chang, Ko, Thailand 39 G4 12 0N 102 23 E
Ch'ang Chiang = Chang Jiang →, China 33 C7 31 48N 121 10 E
Chang Jiang →, China 33 C7 31 48N 121 10 E
Changa, India 43 C7 33 53N 77 35 E
Changanacheri, India 40 Q10 9 25N 76 31 E
Changane →, Mozam. 57 C5 24 30S 33 30 E
Changbai, China 35 D15 41 25N 128 5 E
Changbai Shan, China 35 C15 42 20N 129 0 E
Changchiak'ou = Zhangjiakou, China 34 D8 40 48N 114 55 E
Ch'angchou = Changzhou, China 33 C6 31 47N 119 58 E
**Changchun**, China 35 C13 43 57N 125 17 E
Changchunling, China 35 B13 45 18N 125 27 E
Changde, China 33 D6 29 4N 111 35 E
Changdo-ri, N. Korea 35 E14 38 30N 127 40 E
Changhai = Shanghai, China 33 C7 31 15N 121 26 E
Changhua, Taiwan 33 D7 24 2N 120 30 E
Changhŭng, S. Korea 35 G14 34 41N 126 52 E
Changhŭngni, N. Korea 35 D15 40 24N 128 19 E
Changjiang, China 38 C7 19 20N 108 55 E
Changjin, N. Korea 35 D14 40 23N 127 15 E
Changjin-chŏsuji, N. Korea 35 D14 40 30N 127 15 E
Changli, China 35 E10 39 40N 119 13 E
Changling, China 35 B12 44 20N 123 58 E
Changlun, Malaysia 39 J3 6 25N 100 26 E
Changping, China 34 D9 40 14N 116 12 E
Changsha, China 33 D6 28 12N 113 0 E
Changwu, China 34 G4 35 10N 107 45 E
Changyi, China 35 F10 36 40N 119 30 E
Changyŏn, N. Korea 35 E13 38 15N 125 6 E
Changyuan, China 34 G8 35 15N 114 42 E
Changzhi, China 34 F7 36 10N 113 6 E
Changzhou, China 33 C6 31 47N 119 58 E
Chanhanga, Angola 56 B1 16 0S 14 8 E
Channapatna, India 40 N10 12 40N 77 15 E
**Channel Is.**, U.K. 11 H5 49 19N 2 24W
Channel Is., U.S.A. 85 M7 33 40N 119 15W
Channel Islands National Park, U.S.A. 85 M8 33 30N 119 0W
Channel-Port aux Basques, Canada 71 C8 47 30N 59 9W
**Channel Tunnel**, Europe 11 F9 51 0N 1 30 E
Channing, U.S.A. 81 H3 35 41N 102 20W
Chantada, Spain 19 A2 42 36N 7 46W
Chanthaburi, Thailand 38 F4 12 38N 102 12 E
Chantrey Inlet, Canada 68 B10 67 48N 96 20W
Chanute, U.S.A. 81 G7 37 41N 95 27W
Chao Phraya →, Thailand 38 F3 13 32N 100 36 E
Chao Phraya Lowlands, Thailand 38 E3 15 30N 100 0 E
Chaocheng, China 34 F8 36 4N 115 37 E
Chaoyang, China 35 D11 41 35N 120 22 E
Chaozhou, China 33 D6 23 42N 116 32 E
Chapais, Canada 70 C5 49 47N 74 51W
Chapala, Mozam. 55 F4 15 50S 37 35 E
Chapala, L. de, Mexico 86 C4 20 10N 103 20W
Chapayev, Kazakstan 25 D9 50 25N 51 10 E
Chapayevsk, Russia 24 D8 53 0N 49 40 E
Chapecó, Brazil 95 B5 27 14S 52 41W
Chapel Hill, U.S.A. 77 H6 35 55N 79 4W
Chapleau, Canada 70 C3 47 50N 83 24W
Chaplin, Canada 73 C7 50 28N 106 40W
Chaplin L., Canada 73 C7 50 22N 106 36W
Chappell, U.S.A. 80 E3 41 6N 102 28W
Chapra = Chhapra, India 43 G11 25 48N 84 44 E
Chara, Russia 27 D12 56 54N 118 20 E
Charadai, Argentina 94 B4 27 35S 59 55W
Charagua, Bolivia 92 G6 19 45S 63 10W
Charambirá, Punta, Colombia 92 C3 4 16N 77 32W
Charaña, Bolivia 92 G5 17 30S 69 25W
Charanwala, India 42 F5 27 51N 72 10 E
Charata, Argentina 94 B3 27 13S 61 14W
Charcas, Mexico 86 C4 23 10N 101 20W
Chard, U.K. 11 G5 50 52N 2 58W
Chardon, U.S.A. 78 E3 41 35N 81 12W
Chardzhou = Chärjew, Turkmenistan 26 F7 39 6N 63 34 E
Charente →, France 18 D3 45 57N 1 5W
Chari →, Chad 51 F8 12 58N 14 31 E
Chārīkār, Afghan. 40 B6 35 0N 69 10 E
Chariton →, U.S.A. 80 F8 39 19N 92 58W
Chärjew, Turkmenistan 26 F7 39 6N 63 34 E
Charkhari, India 43 G8 25 24N 79 45 E
Charkhi Dadri, India 42 E7 28 37N 76 17 E
Charleroi, Belgium 15 D4 50 24N 4 27 E
Charleroi, U.S.A. 78 F5 40 9N 79 57W
Charles, C., U.S.A. 76 G8 37 7N 75 58W
Charles City, U.S.A. 80 D8 43 4N 92 41W
Charles L., Canada 73 B6 59 50N 110 33W
Charles Town, U.S.A. 76 F7 39 17N 77 52W
Charleston, Ill., U.S.A. 76 F1 39 30N 88 10W
Charleston, Miss., U.S.A. 81 H9 34 1N 90 4W
Charleston, Mo., U.S.A. 81 G10 36 55N 89 21W
**Charleston**, S.C., U.S.A. 77 J6 32 46N 79 56W
**Charleston**, W. Va., U.S.A. 76 F5 38 21N 81 38W
Charleston L., Canada 79 B9 44 32N 76 0W
Charleston Peak, U.S.A. 85 J11 36 16N 115 42W
Charlestown, Ireland 13 C3 53 58N 8 48W
Charlestown, S. Africa 57 D4 27 26S 29 53 E
Charlestown, Ind., U.S.A. 76 F3 38 27N 85 40W
Charlestown, N.H., U.S.A. 79 C12 43 14N 72 25W
Charleville = Rath Luirc, Ireland 13 D3 52 21N 8 40W
Charleville, Australia 63 D4 26 24S 146 15 E
Charleville-Mézières, France 18 B6 49 44N 4 40 E
Charlevoix, U.S.A. 76 C3 45 19N 85 16W
Charlotte, Mich., U.S.A. 76 D3 42 34N 84 50W
Charlotte, N.C., U.S.A. 77 H5 35 13N 80 51W
Charlotte, Vt., U.S.A. 79 B11 44 19N 73 14W
Charlotte Amalie, Virgin Is. 89 C7 18 21N 64 56W
Charlotte Harbor, U.S.A. 77 M4 26 50N 82 10W
Charlotte L., Canada 72 C3 52 12N 125 19W
Charlottesville, U.S.A. 76 F6 38 2N 78 30W
Charlottetown, Nfld., Canada 71 B8 52 46N 56 7W
Charlottetown, P.E.I., Canada 71 C7 46 14N 63 8W
Charlton, Australia 63 F3 36 16S 143 24 E
Charlton, U.S.A. 80 E8 40 59N 93 20W
Charlton I., Canada 70 B4 52 0N 79 20W
Charny, Canada 71 C5 46 43N 71 15W
Charolles, France 18 C6 46 27N 4 16 E
Charre, Mozam. 55 F4 17 13S 35 10 E
Charsadda, Pakistan 42 B4 34 7N 71 45 E
Charters Towers, Australia 62 C4 20 5S 146 13 E
**Chartres**, France 18 B4 48 29N 1 30 E
Chascomús, Argentina 94 D4 35 30S 58 0W
Chasefu, Zambia 55 E3 11 55S 33 8 E
Chashma Barrage, Pakistan 42 C4 32 27N 71 20 E
Chāt, Iran 45 B7 37 59N 55 16 E
Châteaubriant, France 18 C3 47 43N 1 23W
Chateaugay, U.S.A. 79 B10 44 56N 74 5W
Châteauguay, L., Canada 71 A5 56 26N 70 3W
Châteaulin, France 18 B1 48 11N 4 8W
Châteauroux, France 18 C4 46 50N 1 40 E
Châtellerault, France 18 C4 46 50N 0 30 E
Chatham = Miramichi, Canada 71 C6 47 2N 65 28W
Chatham, Canada 78 D2 42 24N 82 11W
Chatham, U.K. 11 F8 51 22N 0 32 E
Chatham, U.S.A. 79 D11 42 21N 73 36W
Chatham Is., Pac. Oc. 64 M10 44 0S 176 40W
Chatmohar, Bangla. 43 G13 24 15N 89 15 E
Chatra, India 43 G11 24 12N 84 56 E
Chatrapur, India 41 K14 19 22N 85 2 E
Chats, L. des, Canada 79 A8 45 30N 76 20W
Chatsu, India 42 F6 26 36N 75 57 E
Chatsworth, Canada 78 B4 44 27N 80 54W
Chatsworth, Zimbabwe 55 F3 19 38S 31 13 E
Chattahoochee, U.S.A. 77 K3 30 42N 84 51W
Chattahoochee →, U.S.A. 77 K3 30 54N 84 57W
**Chattanooga**, U.S.A. 77 H3 35 3N 85 19W
Chatteris, U.K. 11 E8 52 28N 0 2 E
Chaturat, Thailand 38 E3 15 40N 101 51 E
Chau Doc, Vietnam 39 G5 10 42N 105 7 E
Chauk, Burma 41 J19 20 53N 94 49 E
Chaukan La, Burma 41 F20 27 0N 97 15 E
Chaumont, France 18 B6 48 7N 5 8 E
Chaumont, U.S.A. 79 B8 44 4N 76 8W
Chautauqua L., U.S.A. 78 D5 42 10N 79 24W
Chauvin, Canada 73 C6 52 45N 110 10W
Chaves, Brazil 93 D9 0 15S 49 55W
Chaves, Portugal 19 B2 41 45N 7 32W
Chawang, Thailand 39 H2 8 25N 99 30 E
Chaykovskiy, Russia 24 C9 56 47N 54 9 E
Chazy, U.S.A. 79 B11 44 53N 73 26W
Cheb, Czech Rep. 16 C7 50 9N 12 28 E
Cheboksary, Russia 24 C8 56 8N 47 12 E
Cheboygan, U.S.A. 76 C3 45 39N 84 29W
Chech, Erg, Africa 50 D5 25 0N 2 15W
Chechenia □, Russia 25 F8 43 30N 45 29 E
Checheno-Ingush Republic = Chechenia □, Russia 25 F8 43 30N 45 29 E
**Chechnya** = Chechenia □, Russia 25 F8 43 30N 45 29 E
Chech'ŏn, S. Korea 35 F15 37 8N 128 12 E
Checotah, U.S.A. 81 H7 35 28N 95 31W
Chedabucto B., Canada 71 C7 45 25N 61 8W
Cheduba I., Burma 41 K18 18 45N 93 40 E
Cheepie, Australia 63 D4 26 33S 145 1 E
Chegdomyn, Russia 27 D14 51 7N 133 1 E
Chegga, Mauritania 50 C4 25 27N 5 40W
Chegutu, Zimbabwe 55 F3 18 10S 30 14 E
Chehalis, U.S.A. 84 D4 46 40N 122 58W
Chehalis →, U.S.A. 84 D3 46 57N 123 50W
Cheju do, S. Korea 35 H14 33 29N 126 34 E
Chekiang = Zhejiang □, China 33 D7 29 0N 120 0 E
Chela, Sa. da, Angola 56 B1 16 20S 13 20 E
Chelan, U.S.A. 82 C4 47 51N 120 1W
Chelan, L., U.S.A. 82 B3 48 11N 120 30W
Cheleken, Turkmenistan 25 G9 39 34N 53 16 E
Cheleken Yarymadasy, Turkmenistan 45 B7 39 30N 53 15 E
Chelforó, Argentina 96 D3 39 0S 66 33W
Chelkar = Shalqar, Kazakstan 26 E6 47 48N 59 39 E
Chelkar Tengiz, Solonchak, Kazakstan 26 E7 48 5N 63 7 E
Chełm, Poland 17 C12 51 8N 23 30 E
Chełmno, Poland 17 B10 53 20N 18 30 E
Chelmsford, U.K. 11 F8 51 44N 0 29 E
Chelsea, U.S.A. 79 C12 43 59N 72 27W
Cheltenham, U.K. 11 F5 51 54N 2 4W
Chelyabinsk, Russia 26 D7 55 10N 61 24 E
Chelyuskin, C., Russia 28 B14 77 30N 103 0 E
Chemainus, Canada 84 B3 48 55N 123 42W
Chemba, Mozam. 53 H6 17 9S 34 53 E
Chemnitz, Germany 16 C7 50 51N 12 54 E
Chemult, U.S.A. 82 E3 43 14N 121 47W
Chen, Gora, Russia 27 C15 65 16N 141 50 E
Chenab →, Pakistan 42 D4 30 23N 71 2 E
Chenango Forks, U.S.A. 79 D9 42 15N 75 51W
Cheney, U.S.A. 82 C5 47 30N 117 35W
Cheng Xian, China 34 H3 33 43N 105 42 E
Chengcheng, China 34 G5 35 8N 109 56 E
Chengchou = Zhengzhou, China 34 G7 34 45N 113 34 E
Chengde, China 35 D9 40 59N 117 58 E
Chengdu, China 32 C5 30 38N 104 2 E
Chenggu, China 34 H4 33 10N 107 21 E
Chengjiang, China 32 D5 24 39N 103 0 E
Ch'engmai, China 38 C7 19 50N 109 58 E
Ch'engtu = Chengdu, China 32 C5 30 38N 104 2 E
Chengwu, China 34 G8 34 58N 115 50 E
Chengyang, China 35 F11 36 18N 120 21 E
Chenjiagang, China 35 G10 34 23N 119 47 E
Chenkán, Mexico 87 D6 19 8N 90 58W
Chennai, India 40 N12 13 8N 80 19 E
Cheo Reo, Vietnam 36 B3 13 25N 108 28 E
Cheom Ksan, Cambodia 38 E5 14 13N 104 56 E
Chepén, Peru 92 E3 7 15S 79 23W
Chepes, Argentina 94 C2 31 20S 66 35W
Chepo, Panama 88 E4 9 10N 79 6W
Chepstow, U.K. 11 F5 51 38N 2 41W
Cheptulil, Mt., Kenya 54 B4 1 25N 35 35 E
Chequamegon B., U.S.A. 80 B9 46 40N 90 30W
Cher →, France 18 C4 47 21N 0 29 E
Cheraw, U.S.A. 77 H6 34 42N 79 53W
Cherbourg, France 18 B3 49 39N 1 40W
Cherdyn, Russia 24 B10 60 24N 56 29 E
Cheremkhovo, Russia 27 D11 53 8N 103 1 E
Cherepanovo, Russia 26 D9 54 15N 83 30 E
Cherepovets, Russia 24 C6 59 5N 37 55 E
Chergui, Chott ech, Algeria 50 B6 34 21N 0 25 E
Cherikov = Cherykaw, Belarus 17 B16 53 32N 31 20 E
Cherkasy, Ukraine 25 E5 49 27N 32 4 E
Cherkessk, Russia 25 F7 44 15N 42 5 E
Cherlak, Russia 26 D8 54 15N 74 55 E
Chernaya, Russia 27 B9 70 30N 89 10 E
Chernigov = Chernihiv, Ukraine 24 D5 51 28N 31 20 E
Chernihiv, Ukraine 24 D5 51 28N 31 20 E
Chernivtsi, Ukraine 17 D13 48 15N 25 52 E
Chernobyl = Chornobyl, Ukraine 17 C16 51 20N 30 15 E
Chernogorsk, Russia 27 D10 53 49N 91 18 E
Chernovtsy = Chernivtsi, Ukraine 17 D13 48 15N 25 52 E
Chernyakhovsk, Russia 9 J19 54 36N 21 48 E
Chernysheyskiy, Russia 27 C12 63 0N 112 30 E
Cherokee, Iowa, U.S.A. 80 D7 42 45N 95 33W
Cherokee, Okla., U.S.A. 81 G5 36 45N 98 21W
Cherokee Village, U.S.A. 81 G9 36 17N 91 30W
Cherokees, Grand Lake O' The, U.S.A. 81 G7 36 28N 95 2W
Cherrapunji, India 41 G17 25 17N 91 47 E
Cherry Valley, Calif., U.S.A. 85 M10 33 59N 116 57W
Cherry Valley, N.Y., U.S.A. 79 D10 42 48N 74 45W
Cherskiy, Russia 27 C17 68 45N 161 18 E
Cherskogo Khrebet, Russia 27 C15 65 0N 143 0 E
Cherven, Belarus 17 B15 53 45N 28 28 E
Chervonohrad, Ukraine 17 C13 50 25N 24 10 E
Cherwell →, U.K. 11 F6 51 44N 1 14W
Cherykaw, Belarus 17 B16 53 32N 31 20 E
Chesapeake, U.S.A. 76 G7 36 50N 76 17W
**Chesapeake B.**, U.S.A. 76 G7 38 0N 76 10W
**Cheshire □**, U.K. 10 D5 53 14N 2 30W
Cheshskaya Guba, Russia 24 A8 67 20N 47 0 E
Cheshunt, U.K. 11 F7 51 43N 0 1W
Chesil Beach, U.K. 11 G5 50 37N 2 33W
Chesley, Canada 78 B3 44 17N 81 5W
**Chester**, U.K. 10 D5 53 12N 2 53W
Chester, Calif., U.S.A. 82 F3 40 19N 121 14W
Chester, Ill., U.S.A. 81 G10 37 55N 89 49W
Chester, Mont., U.S.A. 82 B8 48 31N 110 58W
Chester, Pa., U.S.A. 76 F8 39 51N 75 22W
Chester, S.C., U.S.A. 77 H5 34 43N 81 12W
Chester, Vt., U.S.A. 79 C12 43 16N 72 36W
Chester, W. Va., U.S.A. 78 F4 40 37N 80 34W
Chester-le-Street, U.K. 10 C6 54 51N 1 34W
Chesterfield, U.K. 10 D6 53 15N 1 25W
Chesterfield, Is., N. Cal. 64 J7 19 52S 158 15 E
Chesterfield Inlet, Canada 68 B10 63 30N 90 45W
Chesterton Ra., Australia 63 D4 25 30S 147 27 E
Chestertown, U.S.A. 79 C11 43 40N 73 48W
Chesterville, Canada 79 A9 45 6N 75 14W
Chestnut Ridge, U.S.A. 78 F5 40 20N 79 10W
Chesuncook L., U.S.A. 77 C11 46 0N 69 21W
Chéticamp, Canada 71 C7 46 37N 60 59W
Chetumal, Mexico 87 D7 18 30N 88 20W
Chetumal, B. de, Mexico 87 D7 18 40N 88 10W
Chetwynd, Canada 72 B4 55 45N 121 36W
Cheviot, The, U.K. 10 B5 55 29N 2 9W
Cheviot Hills, U.K. 10 B5 55 20N 2 30W
Cheviot Ra., Australia 62 D3 25 20S 143 45 E
Chew Bahir, Ethiopia 46 G2 4 40N 36 50 E
Chewelah, U.S.A. 82 B5 48 17N 117 43W
Cheyenne, Okla., U.S.A. 81 H5 35 37N 99 40W
Cheyenne, Wyo., U.S.A. 80 E2 41 8N 104 49W
Cheyenne →, U.S.A. 80 C4 44 41N 101 18W
Cheyenne Wells, U.S.A. 80 F3 38 49N 102 21W
Cheyne B., Australia 61 F2 34 35S 118 50 E
Chhabra, India 42 G7 24 40N 76 54 E
Chhaktala, India 42 H6 22 6N 74 11 E
Chhapra, India 43 G11 25 48N 84 44 E
Chhata, India 42 F7 27 42N 77 30 E
Chhatarpur, Bihar, India 43 G11 24 23N 84 11 E
Chhatarpur, Mad. P., India 43 G8 24 55N 79 35 E
Chhep, Cambodia 38 F5 13 45N 105 24 E
Chhindwara, Mad. P., India 43 H8 23 3N 79 29 E
Chhindwara, Mad. P., India 43 H8 22 2N 78 59 E
Chhlong, Cambodia 39 F5 12 15N 105 58 E
Chhota Tawa →, India 42 H7 22 14N 76 36 E
Chhoti Kali Sindh →, India 42 G6 24 2N 75 31 E
Chhuikhadan, India 43 J9 21 32N 80 59 E
Chhuk, Cambodia 39 G5 10 46N 104 28 E
Chi →, Thailand 38 E5 15 11N 104 43 E
Chiai, Taiwan 33 D7 23 29N 120 25 E
Chiamboni, Somali Rep. 52 E8 1 39S 41 35 E
Chiamussu = Jiamusi, China 33 B8 46 40N 130 26 E
Chiang Dao, Thailand 38 C2 19 22N 98 58 E
Chiang Kham, Thailand 38 C3 19 32N 100 18 E
Chiang Khan, Thailand 38 D3 17 52N 101 36 E
**Chiang Mai**, Thailand 38 C2 18 47N 98 59 E
Chiang Rai, Thailand 38 C2 19 52N 99 50 E
Chiapa →, Mexico 87 D6 16 42N 93 0W
Chiapa de Corzo, Mexico 87 D6 16 42N 93 0W
Chiapas □, Mexico 87 D6 17 0N 92 45W
Chiautla, Mexico 87 D5 18 18N 98 34W
Chiávari, Italy 18 D8 44 19N 9 19 E
Chiavenna, Italy 18 C8 46 19N 9 24 E
**Chiba**, Japan 31 G10 35 30N 140 7 E
Chiba □, Japan 31 G10 35 30N 140 20 E
Chibabava, Mozam. 57 C5 20 17S 33 35 E
Chibemba, Cunene, Angola 53 H2 15 48S 14 8 E
Chibemba, Huila, Angola 56 B2 16 20S 15 20 E
Chibia, Angola 53 H2 15 10S 13 42 E
Chibougamau, Canada 70 C5 49 56N 74 24W
Chibougamau, L., Canada 70 C5 49 50N 74 20W
Chic-Chocs, Mts., Canada 71 C6 48 55N 66 0W
Chicacole = Srikakulam, India 41 K13 18 14N 83 58 E
**Chicago**, U.S.A. 76 E2 41 53N 87 38W
Chicago Heights, U.S.A. 76 E2 41 30N 87 38W
Chichagof I., U.S.A. 68 C6 57 30N 135 30W
Chichén-Itzá, Mexico 87 C7 20 40N 88 36W
Chicheng, China 34 D8 40 55N 115 55 E
Chichester, U.K. 11 G7 50 50N 0 47W
Chichester Ra., Australia 60 D2 22 12S 119 15 E
Chichibu, Japan 31 F9 36 5N 139 10 E
Ch'ich'ihaerh = Qiqihar, China 27 E13 47 26N 124 0 E
Chicholi, India 42 H8 22 1N 77 40 E
Chickasha, U.S.A. 81 H6 35 3N 97 58W
Chiclana de la Frontera, Spain 19 D2 36 26N 6 9W
Chiclayo, Peru 92 E3 6 42S 79 50W
Chico, U.S.A. 84 F5 39 44N 121 50W
Chico →, Chubut, Argentina 96 E3 44 0S 67 0W
Chico →, Santa Cruz, Argentina 96 G3 50 0S 68 30W
Chicomo, Mozam. 57 C5 24 31S 34 6 E
Chicontepec, Mexico 87 C5 20 58N 98 10W
Chicopee, U.S.A. 79 D12 42 9N 72 37W
Chicoutimi, Canada 71 C5 48 28N 71 5W
Chicualacuala, Mozam. 57 C5 22 6S 31 42 E
Chidambaram, India 40 P11 11 20N 79 45 E
Chidenguele, Mozam. 57 C5 24 55S 34 11 E
Chidley, C., Canada 69 B13 60 23N 64 26W
Chiede, Angola 56 B2 17 15S 16 22 E
Chiefs Pt., Canada 78 B3 44 41N 81 18W
Chiem Hoa, Vietnam 38 A5 22 12N 105 17 E
Chiemsee, Germany 16 E7 47 53N 12 28 E
Chiengi, Zambia 55 D2 8 45S 29 10 E
Chiengmai = Chiang Mai, Thailand 38 C2 18 47N 98 59 E
Chiese →, Italy 18 D9 45 8N 10 25 E
Chieti, Italy 20 C6 42 21N 14 10 E
Chifeng, China 35 C10 42 18N 118 58 E
Chignecto B., Canada 71 C7 45 30N 64 40W
Chiguana, Bolivia 94 A2 21 0S 67 58W
Chigwell, U.K. 11 F8 51 37N 0 5 E
Chiha-ri, N. Korea 35 E14 38 40N 126 30 E
Chihli, G. of = Bo Hai, China 35 E10 39 0N 119 0 E
**Chihuahua**, Mexico 86 B3 28 40N 106 3W
Chihuahua □, Mexico 86 B3 28 40N 106 3W
Chiili, Kazakstan 26 E7 44 20N 66 15 E
Chik Bollapur, India 40 N10 13 25N 77 45 E
Chikmagalur, India 40 N9 13 15N 75 45 E
Chikwawa, Malawi 55 F3 16 2S 34 50 E
Chilac, Mexico 87 D5 18 20N 97 24W
Chilam Chavki, Pakistan 43 B6 35 5N 75 5 E
Chilanga, Zambia 55 F2 15 33S 28 16 E
Chilapa, Mexico 87 D5 17 40N 99 11W
Chilas, Pakistan 43 B6 35 25N 74 5 E
Chilaw, Sri Lanka 40 R11 7 30N 79 50 E
Chilcotin →, Canada 72 C4 51 44N 122 23W
Childers, Australia 63 D5 25 15S 152 17 E
Childress, U.S.A. 81 H4 34 25N 100 13W
**Chile ■**, S. Amer. 96 D2 35 0S 72 0W
Chile Rise, Pac. Oc. 65 L18 38 0S 92 0W
Chilecito, Argentina 94 B2 29 10S 67 30W
Chilete, Peru 92 E3 7 10S 78 50W
Chililabombwe, Zambia 55 E2 12 18S 27 43 E
Chilin = Jilin, China 35 C14 43 44N 126 30 E
Chilka L., India 41 K14 19 40N 85 25 E
Chilko →, Canada 72 C4 52 0N 123 40W
Chilko L., Canada 72 C4 51 20N 124 10W
Chillagoe, Australia 62 B3 17 7S 144 33 E
Chillán, Chile 94 D1 36 40S 72 10W
Chillicothe, Ill., U.S.A. 80 E10 40 55N 89 29W
Chillicothe, Mo., U.S.A. 80 F8 39 48N 93 33W
Chillicothe, Ohio, U.S.A. 76 F4 39 20N 82 59W
Chilliwack, Canada 72 D4 49 10N 121 54W
Chilo, India 42 F5 27 25N 73 32 E
Chiloane, I., Mozam. 57 C5 20 40S 34 55 E
Chiloé, I. de, Chile 96 E2 42 30S 73 50W
Chilpancingo, Mexico 87 D5 17 30N 99 30W
Chiltern Hills, U.K. 11 F7 51 40N 0 53W
Chilton, U.S.A. 76 C1 44 2N 88 10W
Chilubi, Zambia 55 E2 11 5S 29 58 E
Chilubula, Zambia 55 E3 10 14S 30 51 E
Chilumba, Malawi 55 E3 10 28S 34 12 E
Chilung, Taiwan 33 D7 25 3N 121 45 E
Chilwa, L., Malawi 55 F4 15 15S 35 40 E
Chimaltitán, Mexico 86 C4 21 46N 103 50W
Chimán, Panama 88 E4 8 45N 78 40W
Chimay, Belgium 15 D4 50 3N 4 20 E
Chimayo, U.S.A. 83 H11 36 0N 105 56W
Chimbay, Uzbekistan 26 E6 42 57N 59 47 E
Chimborazo, Ecuador 92 D3 1 29S 78 55W
Chimbote, Peru 92 E3 9 0S 78 35W
Chimkent = Shymkent, Kazakstan 26 E7 42 18N 69 36 E

Coari, *Brazil* 92 D6 4 8S 63 7W
Coast □, *Kenya* 54 C4 2 40S 39 45 E
Coast Mts., *Canada* 72 C3 55 0N 129 20W
Coast Ranges, *U.S.A.* 84 G4 39 0N 123 0W
Coatbridge, *U.K.* 12 F4 55 52N 4 6W
Coatepec, *Mexico* 87 D5 19 27N 96 58W
Coatepeque, *Guatemala* 88 D1 14 46N 91 55W
Coatesville, *U.S.A.* 76 F8 39 59N 75 50W
Coaticook, *Canada* 79 A13 45 10N 71 46W
Coats I., *Canada* 69 B11 62 30N 83 0W
Coats Land, *Antarctica* 5 D1 77 0S 25 0W
Coatzacoalcos, *Mexico* 87 D6 18 7N 94 25W
Cobalt, *Canada* 70 C4 47 25N 79 42W
Cobán, *Guatemala* 88 C1 15 30N 90 21W
Cobar, *Australia* 63 E4 31 27S 145 48 E
Cobargo, *Australia* 63 F4 36 20S 149 55 E
Cóbh, *Ireland* 13 E3 51 51N 8 17W
Cobija, *Bolivia* 92 F5 11 0S 68 50W
Cobleskill, *U.S.A.* 79 D10 42 41N 74 29W
Coboconk, *Canada* 78 B6 44 39N 78 48W
Cobourg, *Canada* 78 C6 43 58N 78 10W
Cobourg Pen., *Australia* 60 B5 11 20S 132 15 E
Cobram, *Australia* 63 F4 35 54S 145 40 E
Cóbuè, *Mozam.* 55 E3 12 0S 34 58 E
Coburg, *Germany* 16 C6 50 15N 10 58 E
Cocanada = Kakinada, *India* 41 L13 16 57N 82 11 E
Cochabamba, *Bolivia* 92 G5 17 26S 66 10W
Cochemane, *Mozam.* 55 F3 17 0S 32 54 E
Cochin, *India* 40 Q10 9 59N 76 22 E
Cochin China, *Vietnam* 39 G6 10 30N 106 0 E
Cochran, *U.S.A.* 77 J4 32 23N 83 21W
Cochrane, *Alta., Canada* 72 C6 51 11N 114 30W
Cochrane, *Ont., Canada* 70 C3 49 0N 81 0W
Cochrane, *Chile* 96 F2 47 15S 72 33W
Cochrane →, *Canada* 73 B8 59 0N 103 40W
Cochrane, L., *Chile* 96 F2 47 10S 72 0W
Cochranton, *U.S.A.* 78 E4 41 31N 80 3W
Cockburn, *Australia* 63 E3 32 5S 141 0 E
Cockburn, Canal, *Chile* 96 G2 54 30S 72 0W
Cockburn I., *Canada* 70 C3 45 55N 83 22W
Cockburn Ra., *Australia* 60 C4 15 46S 128 0 E
Cockermouth, *U.K.* 10 C4 54 40N 3 22W
Cocklebiddy, *Australia* 61 F4 32 0S 126 3 E
Coco →, *Cent. Amer.* 88 D3 15 0N 83 8W
Coco, I. del, *Pac. Oc.* 65 G19 5 25N 87 55W
Cocoa, *U.S.A.* 77 L5 28 21N 80 44W
Cocobeach, *Gabon* 52 D1 0 59N 9 34 E
Cocos Is., *Ind. Oc.* 64 J1 12 10S 96 55 E
**Cod, C.**, *U.S.A.* 76 D10 42 5N 70 10W
Codajás, *Brazil* 92 D6 3 55S 62 0W
Codó, *Brazil* 93 D10 4 30S 43 55W
Cody, *U.S.A.* 82 D9 44 32N 109 3W
Coe Hill, *Canada* 78 B7 44 52N 77 50W
Coelemu, *Chile* 94 D1 36 30S 72 48W
Coen, *Australia* 62 A3 13 52S 143 12 E
Cœur d'Alene, *U.S.A.* 82 C5 47 45N 116 51W
Cœur d'Alene L., *U.S.A.* 82 C5 47 32N 116 48W
Coevorden, *Neths.* 15 B6 52 40N 6 44 E
Cofete, *Canary Is.* 22 F5 28 6N 14 23W
Coffeyville, *U.S.A.* 81 G7 37 2N 95 37W
Coffin B., *Australia* 63 E2 34 38S 135 28 E
Coffin Bay, *Australia* 63 E2 34 37S 135 29 E
Coffin Bay Peninsula, *Australia* 63 E2 34 32S 135 15 E
Coffs Harbour, *Australia* 63 E5 30 16S 153 5 E
Cognac, *France* 18 D3 45 41N 0 20W
Cohocton, *U.S.A.* 78 D7 42 30N 77 30W
Cohocton →, *U.S.A.* 78 D7 42 9N 77 6W
Cohoes, *U.S.A.* 79 D11 42 46N 73 42W
Cohuna, *Australia* 63 F3 35 45S 144 15 E
Coiba, I., *Panama* 88 E3 7 30N 81 40W
Coig →, *Argentina* 96 G3 51 0S 69 10W
Coigeach, Rubha, *U.K.* 12 C3 58 6N 5 26W
Coihaique, *Chile* 96 F2 45 30S 71 45W
Coimbatore, *India* 40 P10 11 2N 76 59 E
Coimbra, *Brazil* 92 G7 19 55S 57 48W
Coimbra, *Portugal* 19 B1 40 15N 8 27W
Coín, *Spain* 19 D3 36 40N 4 48W
Coipasa, Salar de, *Bolivia* 92 G5 19 26S 68 9W
Cojimies, *Ecuador* 92 C3 0 20N 80 0W
Cojutepeque, *El Salv.* 88 D2 13 41N 88 54W
Cokeville, *U.S.A.* 82 E8 42 5N 110 57W
Colac, *Australia* 63 F3 38 21S 143 35 E
Colatina, *Brazil* 93 G10 19 32S 40 37W
Colbeck, C., *Antarctica* 5 D13 77 6S 157 48W
Colborne, *Canada* 78 C7 44 0N 77 53W
Colby, *U.S.A.* 80 F4 39 24N 101 3W
Colchester, *U.K.* 11 F8 51 54N 0 55 E
Cold L., *Canada* 73 C7 54 33N 110 5W
Coldstream, *Canada* 72 C5 50 13N 119 11W
Coldstream, *U.K.* 12 F6 55 39N 2 15W
Coldwater, *Canada* 78 B5 44 42N 79 40W
Coldwater, *Kans., U.S.A.* 81 G5 37 16N 99 20W
Coldwater, *Mich., U.S.A.* 76 E3 41 57N 85 0W
Coleambally, *Australia* 63 E4 34 49S 145 52 E
Colebrook, *U.S.A.* 79 B13 44 54N 71 30W
Coleman, *U.S.A.* 81 K5 31 50N 99 26W
Coleman →, *Australia* 62 B3 15 6S 141 38 E
Colenso, *S. Africa* 57 D4 28 44S 29 50 E
Coleraine, *Australia* 63 F3 37 36S 141 40 E
Coleraine, *U.K.* 13 A5 55 8N 6 41W
Coleridge, L., *N.Z.* 59 K3 43 17S 171 30 E
Colesberg, *S. Africa* 56 E4 30 45S 25 5 E
Coleville, *U.S.A.* 84 G7 38 34N 119 30W
Colfax, *Calif., U.S.A.* 84 F6 39 6N 120 57W
Colfax, *La., U.S.A.* 81 K8 31 31N 92 42W
Colfax, *Wash., U.S.A.* 82 C5 46 53N 117 22W
Colhué Huapi, L., *Argentina* 96 F3 45 30S 69 0W
Coligny, *S. Africa* 57 D4 26 17S 26 15 E
Colima, *Mexico* 86 D4 19 14N 103 43W
Colima □, *Mexico* 86 D4 19 10N 103 40W
Colima, Nevado de, *Mexico* 86 D4 19 35N 103 45W
Colina, *Chile* 94 C1 33 13S 70 45W
Colinas, *Brazil* 93 E10 6 0S 44 10W
Coll, *U.K.* 12 E2 56 39N 6 34W
Collaguasi, *Chile* 94 A2 21 5S 68 45W
Collarenebri, *Australia* 63 D4 29 33S 148 34 E
Colleen Bawn, *Zimbabwe* 55 G2 21 0S 29 12 E
College Park, *U.S.A.* 77 J3 33 40N 84 27W
College Station, *U.S.A.* 81 K6 30 37N 96 21W
Collie, *Australia* 61 F2 33 22S 116 8 E
Collier B., *Australia* 60 C3 16 10S 124 15 E
Collier Ra., *Australia* 61 D2 24 45S 119 10 E
Collina, Passo di, *Italy* 20 B4 44 2N 10 56 E
Collingwood, *Canada* 78 B4 44 29N 80 13W
Collingwood, *N.Z.* 59 J4 40 41S 172 40 E
Collins, *Canada* 70 B2 50 17N 89 27W
Collinsville, *Australia* 62 C4 20 30S 147 56 E
Collipulli, *Chile* 94 D1 37 55S 72 30W
Collooney, *Ireland* 13 B3 54 11N 8 29W
Colmar, *France* 18 B7 48 5N 7 20 E
Colo →, *Australia* 63 E5 33 25S 150 52 E
**Cologne** = Köln, *Germany* 16 C4 50 56N 6 57 E
Colom, I. d'en, *Spain* 22 B11 39 58N 4 16 E
Coloma, *U.S.A.* 84 G6 38 48N 120 53W
Colomb-Béchar = Béchar, *Algeria* 50 B5 31 38N 2 18W
**Colombia ■**, *S. Amer.* 92 C4 3 45N 73 0W
Colombian Basin, *S. Amer.* 66 H12 14 0N 76 0W
**Colombo**, *Sri Lanka* 40 R11 6 56N 79 58 E
Colón, *Buenos Aires, Argentina* 94 C3 33 53S 61 7W
Colón, *Entre Ríos, Argentina* 94 C4 32 12S 58 10W
Colón, *Cuba* 88 B3 22 42N 80 54W
Colón, *Panama* 88 E4 9 20N 79 54W
Colonia de Sant Jordi, *Spain* 22 B9 39 19N 2 59 E
Colonia del Sacramento, *Uruguay* 94 C4 34 25S 57 50W
Colonia Dora, *Argentina* 94 B3 28 34S 62 59W
Colonial Beach, *U.S.A.* 76 F7 38 15N 76 58W
Colonie, *U.S.A.* 79 D11 42 43N 73 50W
Colonsay, *Canada* 73 C7 51 59N 105 52W
Colonsay, *U.K.* 12 E2 56 5N 6 12W
**Colorado □**, *U.S.A.* 83 G10 39 30N 105 30W
Colorado →, *Argentina* 96 D4 39 50S 62 8W
**Colorado →**, *N. Amer.* 83 L6 31 45N 114 40W
Colorado →, *U.S.A.* 81 L7 28 36N 95 59W
Colorado City, *U.S.A.* 81 J4 32 24N 100 52W
Colorado Desert, *U.S.A.* 74 D3 34 20N 116 0W
Colorado Plateau, *U.S.A.* 83 H8 37 0N 111 0W
Colorado River Aqueduct, *U.S.A.* 85 L12 34 17N 114 10W
Colorado Springs, *U.S.A.* 80 F2 38 50N 104 49W
Colotlán, *Mexico* 86 C4 22 6N 103 16W
Colstrip, *U.S.A.* 82 D10 45 53N 106 38W
Colton, *U.S.A.* 79 B10 44 33N 74 56W
Columbia, *Ky., U.S.A.* 76 G3 37 6N 85 18W
Columbia, *La., U.S.A.* 81 J8 32 6N 92 5W
Columbia, *Miss., U.S.A.* 81 K10 31 15N 89 50W
Columbia, *Mo., U.S.A.* 80 F8 38 57N 92 20W
Columbia, *Pa., U.S.A.* 79 F8 40 2N 76 30W
**Columbia**, *S.C., U.S.A.* 77 J5 34 0N 81 2W
Columbia, *Tenn., U.S.A.* 77 H2 35 37N 87 2W
**Columbia →**, *N. Amer.* 84 D2 46 15N 124 5W
Columbia, C., *Canada* 4 A4 83 0N 70 0W
**Columbia, District of □**, *U.S.A.* 76 F7 38 55N 77 0W
Columbia, Mt., *Canada* 72 C5 52 8N 117 20W
Columbia Basin, *U.S.A.* 82 C4 46 45N 119 5W
Columbia Falls, *U.S.A.* 82 B6 48 23N 114 11W
Columbia Mts., *Canada* 72 C5 52 0N 119 0W
Columbia Plateau, *U.S.A.* 82 D5 44 0N 117 30W
Columbiana, *U.S.A.* 78 F4 40 53N 80 42W
Columbretes, Is., *Spain* 19 C6 39 50N 0 50 E
**Columbus**, *Ga., U.S.A.* 77 J3 32 28N 84 59W
Columbus, *Ind., U.S.A.* 76 F3 39 13N 85 55W
Columbus, *Kans., U.S.A.* 81 G7 37 10N 94 50W
Columbus, *Miss., U.S.A.* 77 J1 33 30N 88 25W
Columbus, *Mont., U.S.A.* 82 D9 45 38N 109 15W
Columbus, *N. Mex., U.S.A.* 83 L10 31 50N 107 38W
Columbus, *Nebr., U.S.A.* 80 E6 41 26N 97 22W
**Columbus**, *Ohio, U.S.A.* 76 F4 39 58N 83 0W
Columbus, *Tex., U.S.A.* 81 L6 29 42N 96 33W
Colusa, *U.S.A.* 84 F4 39 13N 122 1W
Colville, *U.S.A.* 82 B5 48 33N 117 54W
Colville →, *U.S.A.* 68 A4 70 25N 150 30W
Colville, C., *N.Z.* 59 G5 36 29S 175 21 E
Colwood, *Canada* 84 B3 48 26N 123 29W
Colwyn Bay, *U.K.* 10 D4 53 18N 3 44W
Comácchio, *Italy* 20 B5 44 42N 12 11 E
Comalcalco, *Mexico* 87 D6 18 16N 93 13W
Comallo, *Argentina* 96 E2 41 0S 70 5W
Comanche, *U.S.A.* 81 K5 31 54N 98 36W
Comayagua, *Honduras* 88 D2 14 25N 87 37W
Combahee →, *U.S.A.* 77 J5 32 30N 80 31W
Combarbalá, *Chile* 94 C1 31 11S 71 2W
Comber, *Canada* 78 D2 42 14N 82 33W
Comber, *U.K.* 13 B6 54 33N 5 45W
Combermere, *Canada* 78 A7 45 22N 77 37W
Comblain-au-Pont, *Belgium* 15 D5 50 29N 5 35 E
Comeragh Mts., *Ireland* 13 D4 52 18N 7 34W
Comet, *Australia* 62 C4 23 36S 148 38 E
Comilla, *Bangla.* 41 H17 23 28N 91 10 E
Comino, *Malta* 23 C1 36 2N 14 20 E
Comino, C., *Italy* 20 D3 40 32N 9 49 E
Comitán, *Mexico* 87 D6 16 18N 92 9W
Commerce, *Ga., U.S.A.* 77 H4 34 12N 83 28W
Commerce, *Tex., U.S.A.* 81 J7 33 15N 95 54W
Committee B., *Canada* 69 B11 68 30N 86 30W
Commonwealth B., *Antarctica* 5 C10 67 0S 144 0 E
Commoron Cr. →, *Australia* 63 D5 28 22S 150 8 E
Communism Pk. = Kommunizma, Pik, *Tajikistan* 26 F8 39 0N 72 2 E
Como, *Italy* 18 D8 45 47N 9 5 E
Como, Lago di, *Italy* 18 D8 46 0N 9 11 E
Comodoro Rivadavia, *Argentina* 96 F3 45 50S 67 40W
Comorin, C., *India* 40 Q10 8 3N 77 40 E
Comoro Is. = Comoros ■, *Ind. Oc.* 49 H8 12 10S 44 15 E
**Comoros ■**, *Ind. Oc.* 49 H8 12 10S 44 15 E
Comox, *Canada* 72 D4 49 42N 124 55W
Compiègne, *France* 18 B5 49 24N 2 50 E
Compostela, *Mexico* 86 C4 21 15N 104 53W
Comprida, I., *Brazil* 95 A6 24 50S 47 42W
Compton, *Canada* 79 A13 45 14N 71 49W
Compton, *U.S.A.* 85 M8 33 54N 118 13W
Comrat, *Moldova* 17 E15 46 18N 28 40 E
Con Cuong, *Vietnam* 38 C5 19 2N 104 54 E
Con Son, *Vietnam* 39 H6 8 41N 106 37 E
**Conakry**, *Guinea* 50 G3 9 29N 13 49W
Conara, *Australia* 62 G4 41 50S 147 26 E
Concarneau, *France* 18 C2 47 52N 3 56W
Conceição, *Mozam.* 55 F4 18 47S 36 7 E
Conceição da Barra, *Brazil* 93 G11 18 35S 39 45W
Conceição do Araguaia, *Brazil* 93 E9 8 0S 49 2W
Concepción, *Argentina* 94 B2 27 20S 65 35W
Concepción, *Bolivia* 92 G6 16 15S 62 8W
Concepción, *Chile* 94 D1 36 50S 73 0W
Concepción, *Mexico* 87 D6 18 15N 90 5W
Concepción, *Paraguay* 94 A4 23 22S 57 26W
Concepción □, *Chile* 94 D1 37 0S 72 30W
Concepción →, *Mexico* 86 A2 30 32N 113 2W
Concepción, Est. de, *Chile* 96 G2 50 30S 74 55W
Concepción, L., *Bolivia* 92 G6 17 20S 61 20W
Concepción, Punta, *Mexico* 86 B2 26 55N 111 59W
Concepción del Oro, *Mexico* 86 C4 24 40N 101 30W
Concepción del Uruguay, *Argentina* 94 C4 32 35S 58 20W
Conception, Pt., *U.S.A.* 85 L6 34 27N 120 28W
Conception B., *Canada* 71 C9 47 45N 53 0W
Conception B., *Namibia* 56 C1 23 55S 14 22 E
Conception I., *Bahamas* 89 B4 23 52N 75 9W
Concession, *Zimbabwe* 55 F3 17 27S 30 56 E
Conchas Dam, *U.S.A.* 81 H2 35 22N 104 11W
Concho, *U.S.A.* 83 J9 34 28N 109 36W
Concho →, *U.S.A.* 81 K5 31 34N 99 43W
Conchos →, *Chihuahua, Mexico* 86 B4 29 32N 105 0W
Conchos →, *Tamaulipas, Mexico* 87 B5 25 9N 98 35W
Concord, *Calif., U.S.A.* 84 H4 37 59N 122 2W
Concord, *N.C., U.S.A.* 77 H5 35 25N 80 35W
Concord, *N.H., U.S.A.* 79 C13 43 12N 71 32W
Concordia, *Argentina* 94 C4 31 20S 58 2W
Concórdia, *Brazil* 92 D5 4 36S 66 36W
Concordia, *Mexico* 86 C3 23 18N 106 2W
Concordia, *U.S.A.* 80 F6 39 34N 97 40W
Concrete, *U.S.A.* 82 B3 48 32N 121 45W
Condamine, *Australia* 63 D5 26 56S 150 9 E
Conde, *U.S.A.* 80 C5 45 9N 98 6W
Condeúba, *Brazil* 93 F10 14 52S 42 0W
Condobolin, *Australia* 63 E4 33 4S 147 6 E
Condon, *U.S.A.* 82 D3 45 14N 120 11W
Conegliano, *Italy* 20 B5 45 53N 12 18 E
Conejera, I. = Conills, I. des, *Spain* 22 B9 39 11N 2 58 E
Conejos, *Mexico* 86 B4 26 14N 103 53W
Confuso →, *Paraguay* 94 B4 25 9S 57 34W
Congleton, *U.K.* 10 D5 53 10N 2 13W
Congo (Kinshasa) = Congo, Dem. Rep. of the ■, *Africa* 52 E4 3 0S 23 0 E
**Congo ■**, *Africa* 52 E3 1 0S 16 0 E
**Congo →**, *Africa* 52 F2 6 4S 12 24 E
**Congo, Dem. Rep. of the ■**, *Africa* 52 E4 3 0S 23 0 E
Congo Basin, *Africa* 52 E4 0 10S 24 30 E
Congonhas, *Brazil* 95 A7 20 30S 43 52W
Congress, *U.S.A.* 83 J7 34 9N 112 51W
Conills, I. des, *Spain* 22 B9 39 11N 2 58 E
Coniston, *Canada* 70 C3 46 29N 80 51W
Conjeeveram = Kanchipuram, *India* 40 N11 12 52N 79 45 E
Conklin, *Canada* 73 B6 55 38N 111 5W
Conklin, *U.S.A.* 79 D9 42 2N 75 49W
Conn, L., *Ireland* 13 B2 54 3N 9 15W
Connacht □, *Ireland* 13 C2 53 43N 9 12W
Conneaut, *U.S.A.* 78 E4 41 57N 80 34W
**Connecticut □**, *U.S.A.* 79 E12 41 30N 72 45W
Connecticut →, *U.S.A.* 79 E12 41 16N 72 20W
Connell, *U.S.A.* 82 C4 46 40N 118 52W
Connellsville, *U.S.A.* 78 F5 40 1N 79 35W
Connemara, *Ireland* 13 C2 53 29N 9 45W
Connemaugh →, *U.S.A.* 78 F5 40 28N 79 19W
Connersville, *U.S.A.* 76 F3 39 39N 85 8W
Connors Ra., *Australia* 62 C4 21 40S 149 10 E
Conquest, *Canada* 73 C7 51 32N 107 14W
Conrad, *U.S.A.* 82 B8 48 10N 111 57W
Conran, C., *Australia* 63 F4 37 49S 148 44 E
Conroe, *U.S.A.* 81 K7 30 19N 95 27W
Consecon, *Canada* 78 C7 44 0N 77 31W
Conselheiro Lafaiete, *Brazil* 95 A7 20 40S 43 48W
Consett, *U.K.* 10 C6 54 51N 1 50W
Consort, *Canada* 73 C6 52 1N 110 46W
**Constance** = Konstanz, *Germany* 16 E5 47 40N 9 10 E
Constance, L. = Bodensee, *Europe* 18 C8 47 35N 9 25 E
Constanța, *Romania* 17 F15 44 14N 28 38 E
Constantia, *U.S.A.* 79 C8 43 15N 76 1W
Constantine, *Algeria* 50 A7 36 25N 6 42 E
Constitución, *Chile* 94 D1 35 20S 72 30W
Constitución, *Uruguay* 94 C4 31 0S 57 50W
Consul, *Canada* 73 D7 49 20N 109 30W
Contact, *U.S.A.* 82 F6 41 46N 114 45W
Contai, *India* 43 J12 21 54N 87 46 E
Contamana, *Peru* 92 E4 7 19S 74 55W
Contas →, *Brazil* 93 F11 14 17S 39 1W
Contoocook, *U.S.A.* 79 C13 43 13N 71 45W
Contra Costa, *Mozam.* 57 D5 25 9S 33 30 E
Contwoyto L., *Canada* 68 B8 65 42N 110 50W
Conway = Conwy, *U.K.* 10 D4 53 17N 3 50W
Conway = Conwy →, *U.K.* 10 D4 53 17N 3 50W
Conway, *Ark., U.S.A.* 81 H8 35 5N 92 26W
Conway, *N.H., U.S.A.* 79 C13 43 59N 71 7W
Conway, *S.C., U.S.A.* 77 J6 33 51N 79 3W
Conway, L., *Australia* 63 D2 28 17S 135 35 E
Conwy, *U.K.* 10 D4 53 17N 3 50W
Conwy □, *U.K.* 10 D4 53 10N 3 44W
Conwy →, *U.K.* 10 D4 53 17N 3 50W
Coober Pedy, *Australia* 63 D1 29 1S 134 43 E
Cooch Behar = Koch Bihar, *India* 41 F16 26 22N 89 29 E
Cooinda, *Australia* 60 B5 13 15S 130 5 E
Cook, *Australia* 61 F5 30 37S 130 25 E
Cook, *U.S.A.* 80 B8 47 49N 92 39W
Cook, B., *Chile* 96 H3 55 10S 70 0W
Cook, C., *Canada* 72 C3 50 8N 127 55W
Cook, Mt., *N.Z.* 59 K3 43 36S 170 9 E
Cook Inlet, *U.S.A.* 68 C4 60 0N 152 0W
**Cook Is.**, *Pac. Oc.* 65 J12 17 0S 160 0W
Cook Strait, *N.Z.* 59 J5 41 15S 174 29 E
Cookeville, *U.S.A.* 77 G3 36 10N 85 30W
Cookhouse, *S. Africa* 56 E4 32 44S 25 47 E
Cookshire, *Canada* 79 A13 45 25N 71 38W
Cookstown, *U.K.* 13 B5 54 39N 6 45W
Cooksville, *Canada* 78 C5 43 36N 79 35W
Cooktown, *Australia* 62 B4 15 30S 145 16 E
Coolabah, *Australia* 63 E4 31 1S 146 43 E
Cooladdi, *Australia* 63 D4 26 37S 145 23 E
Coolah, *Australia* 63 E4 31 48S 149 41 E
Coolamon, *Australia* 63 E4 34 46S 147 8 E
Coolgardie, *Australia* 61 F3 30 55S 121 8 E
Coolidge, *U.S.A.* 83 K8 32 59N 111 31W
Coolidge Dam, *U.S.A.* 83 K8 33 0N 110 20W
Cooma, *Australia* 63 F4 36 12S 149 8 E
Coon Rapids, *U.S.A.* 80 C8 45 9N 93 19W
Coonabarabran, *Australia* 63 E4 31 14S 149 18 E
Coonalpyn, *Australia* 63 F2 35 43S 139 52 E
Coonamble, *Australia* 63 E4 30 56S 148 27 E
Coonana, *Australia* 61 F3 31 0S 123 0 E
Coondapoor, *India* 40 N9 13 42N 74 40 E
Cooninie, L., *Australia* 63 D2 26 4S 139 59 E
Cooper, *U.S.A.* 81 J7 33 23N 95 42W
Cooper Cr. →, *Australia* 63 D2 28 29S 137 46 E
Cooperstown, *N. Dak., U.S.A.* 80 B5 47 27N 98 8W
Cooperstown, *N.Y., U.S.A.* 79 D10 42 42N 74 56W
Coorabie, *Australia* 61 F5 31 54S 132 18 E
Coorow, *Australia* 61 E2 29 53S 116 2 E
Cooroy, *Australia* 63 D5 26 22S 152 54 E
Coos Bay, *U.S.A.* 82 E1 43 22N 124 13W
Coosa →, *U.S.A.* 77 J2 32 30N 86 16W
Cootamundra, *Australia* 63 E4 34 36S 148 1 E
Cootehill, *Ireland* 13 B4 54 4N 7 5W
Copahue Paso, *Argentina* 94 D1 37 49S 71 8W
Copainalá, *Mexico* 87 D6 17 8N 93 11W
Copake Falls, *U.S.A.* 79 D11 42 7N 73 31W
Copán, *Honduras* 88 D2 14 50N 89 9W
Cope, *U.S.A.* 80 F3 39 40N 102 51W
**Copenhagen** = København, *Denmark* 9 J15 55 41N 12 34 E
Copenhagen, *U.S.A.* 79 C9 43 54N 75 41W
Copiapó, *Chile* 94 B1 27 30S 70 20W
Copiapó →, *Chile* 94 B1 27 19S 70 56W
Coplay, *U.S.A.* 79 F9 40 44N 75 29W
Copp L., *Canada* 72 A6 60 14N 114 40W
Coppename →, *Surinam* 93 B7 5 48N 55 55W
Copper Harbor, *U.S.A.* 76 B2 47 28N 87 53W
Copper Queen, *Zimbabwe* 55 F2 17 29S 29 18 E
Copperas Cove, *U.S.A.* 81 K6 31 8N 97 54W
Copperbelt □, *Zambia* 55 E2 13 15S 27 30 E
Coppermine = Kugluktuk, *Canada* 68 B8 67 50N 115 5W
Coppermine →, *Canada* 68 B8 67 49N 116 4W
Copperopolis, *U.S.A.* 84 H6 37 58N 120 38W
Coquet →, *U.K.* 10 B6 55 20N 1 32W
Coquilhatville = Mbandaka, *Dem. Rep. of the Congo* 52 D3 0 1N 18 18 E
Coquille, *U.S.A.* 82 E1 43 11N 124 11W
Coquimbo, *Chile* 94 C1 30 0S 71 20W
Coquimbo □, *Chile* 94 C1 31 0S 71 0W
Corabia, *Romania* 17 G13 43 48N 24 30 E
Coracora, *Peru* 92 G4 15 5S 73 45W
Coraki, *Australia* 63 D5 28 59S 153 17 E
Coral, *U.S.A.* 78 F5 40 29N 79 10W
Coral Gables, *U.S.A.* 77 N5 25 45N 80 16W
Coral Harbour = Salliq, *Canada* 69 B11 64 8N 83 10W
**Coral Sea**, *Pac. Oc.* 64 J7 15 0S 150 0 E
Coral Springs, *U.S.A.* 77 M5 26 16N 80 13W
Coraopolis, *U.S.A.* 78 F4 40 31N 80 10W
Corato, *Italy* 20 D7 41 9N 16 25 E
Corbin, *U.S.A.* 76 G3 36 57N 84 6W
Corby, *U.K.* 11 E7 52 30N 0 41W
Corcaigh = Cork, *Ireland* 13 E3 51 54N 8 29W
Corcoran, *U.S.A.* 84 J7 36 6N 119 33W
Corcubión, *Spain* 19 A1 42 56N 9 12W
Cordele, *U.S.A.* 77 K4 31 58N 83 47W
Cordell, *U.S.A.* 81 H5 35 17N 98 59W
Córdoba, *Argentina* 94 C3 31 20S 64 10W
Córdoba, *Mexico* 87 D5 18 50N 97 0W
**Córdoba**, *Spain* 19 D3 37 50N 4 50W
Córdoba □, *Argentina* 94 C3 31 22S 64 15W
Córdoba, Sierra de, *Argentina* 94 C3 31 10S 64 25W
Cordova, *U.S.A.* 68 B5 60 33N 145 45W
Corella →, *Australia* 62 B3 19 34S 140 47 E
Corfield, *Australia* 62 C3 21 40S 143 21 E
**Corfu** = Kérkira, *Greece* 23 A3 39 38N 19 50 E
Corfu, Str. of, *Greece* 23 A4 39 34N 20 0 E
Coria, *Spain* 19 C2 39 58N 6 33W
Corigliano Cálabro, *Italy* 20 E7 39 36N 16 31 E
Coringa Is., *Australia* 62 B4 16 58S 149 58 E
**Corinth** = Kórinthos, *Greece* 21 F10 37 56N 22 55 E
Corinth, *Miss., U.S.A.* 77 H1 34 56N 88 31W
Corinth, *N.Y., U.S.A.* 79 C11 43 14N 73 49W
Corinth, *N.Y., U.S.A.* 79 C11 43 15N 73 49W
Corinth, G. of = Korinthiakós Kólpos, *Greece* 21 E10 38 16N 22 30 E
Corinto, *Brazil* 93 G10 18 20S 44 30W
Corinto, *Nic.* 88 D2 12 30N 87 10W
**Cork**, *Ireland* 13 E3 51 54N 8 29W
Cork □, *Ireland* 13 E3 51 57N 8 40W
Cork Harbour, *Ireland* 13 E3 51 47N 8 16W
Çorlu, *Turkey* 21 D12 41 11N 27 49 E
Cormack L., *Canada* 72 A4 60 56N 121 37W
Cormorant, *Canada* 73 C8 54 14N 100 35W
Cormorant L., *Canada* 73 C8 54 15N 100 50W
Corn Is. = Maiz, Is. del, *Nic.* 88 D3 12 15N 83 4W
Cornélio Procópio, *Brazil* 95 A5 23 7S 50 40W
Corner Brook, *Canada* 71 C8 48 57N 57 58W
Cornești, *Moldova* 17 E15 47 21N 28 1 E
Corning, *Ark., U.S.A.* 81 G9 36 25N 90 35W
Corning, *Calif., U.S.A.* 82 G2 39 56N 122 11W
Corning, *Iowa, U.S.A.* 80 E7 40 59N 94 44W
Corning, *N.Y., U.S.A.* 78 D7 42 9N 77 3W
Cornwall, *Canada* 79 A10 45 2N 74 44W
Cornwall, *U.S.A.* 79 F8 40 17N 76 25W
**Cornwall □**, *U.K.* 11 G3 50 26N 4 40W
Corny Pt., *Australia* 63 E2 34 55S 137 0 E
Coro, *Venezuela* 92 A5 11 25N 69 41W
Coroatá, *Brazil* 93 D10 4 8S 44 0W
Corocoro, *Bolivia* 92 G5 17 15S 68 28W
Coroico, *Bolivia* 92 G5 16 0S 67 50W
Coromandel, *N.Z.* 59 G5 36 45S 175 31 E
Coromandel Coast, *India* 40 N12 12 30N 81 0 E
Corona, *Calif., U.S.A.* 85 M9 33 53N 117 34W
Corona, *N. Mex., U.S.A.* 83 J11 34 15N 105 36W
Coronach, *Canada* 73 D7 49 7N 105 31W
Coronado, *U.S.A.* 85 N9 32 41N 117 11W
Coronado, B. de, *Costa Rica* 88 E3 9 0N 83 40W
Coronados, Is. los, *U.S.A.* 85 N9 32 25N 117 15W
Coronation, *Canada* 72 C6 52 5N 111 27W
Coronation Gulf, *Canada* 68 B9 68 25N 110 0W
Coronation I., *Antarctica* 5 C18 60 45S 46 0W
Coronation Is., *Australia* 60 B3 14 57S 124 55 E
Coronda, *Argentina* 94 C3 31 58S 60 56W
Coronel, *Chile* 94 D1 37 0S 73 10W
Coronel Bogado, *Paraguay* 94 B4 27 11S 56 18W
Coronel Dorrego, *Argentina* 94 D3 38 40S 61 10W
Coronel Oviedo, *Paraguay* 94 B4 25 24S 56 30W

Coronel Pringles, Argentina 94 D3 38 0S 61 30W
Coronel Suárez, Argentina 94 D3 37 30S 61 52W
Coronel Vidal, Argentina 94 D4 37 28S 57 45W
Coropuna, Nevado, Peru 92 G4 15 30S 72 41W
Corowa, Australia 63 F4 35 58S 146 21 E
Corozal, Belize 87 D7 18 23N 88 23W
Corpus, Argentina 95 B4 27 10S 55 30W
Corpus Christi, U.S.A. 81 M6 27 47N 97 24W
Corpus Christi, L., U.S.A. 81 L6 28 2N 97 52W
Corralejo, Canary Is. 22 F6 28 43N 13 53W
Corraun Pen., Ireland 13 C2 53 54N 9 54W
Correntes, C. das, Mozam. 57 C6 24 6S 35 34 E
Corrib, L., Ireland 13 C2 53 27N 9 16W
Corrientes, Argentina 94 B4 27 30S 58 45W
Corrientes □, Argentina 94 B4 28 0S 57 0W
Corrientes →, Argentina 94 C4 30 42S 59 38W
Corrientes →, Peru 92 D4 3 43S 74 35W
Corrientes, C., Colombia 92 B3 5 30N 77 34W
Corrientes, C., Cuba 88 B3 21 43N 84 30W
Corrientes, C., Mexico 86 C3 20 25N 105 42W
Corrigan, U.S.A. 81 K7 31 0N 94 52W
Corrigin, Australia 61 F2 32 20S 117 53 E
Corry, U.S.A. 78 E5 41 55N 79 39W
Corryong, Australia 63 F4 36 12S 147 53 E
Corse, France 18 F8 42 0N 9 0 E
Corse, C., France 18 E8 43 1N 9 25 E
**Corsica** = Corse, France 18 F8 42 0N 9 0 E
Corsicana, U.S.A. 81 J6 32 6N 96 28W
Corte, France 18 E8 42 19N 9 11 E
Cortez, U.S.A. 83 H9 37 21N 108 35W
Cortland, N.Y., U.S.A. 79 D8 42 36N 76 11W
Cortland, Ohio, U.S.A. 78 E4 41 20N 80 44W
Çorum, Turkey 25 F5 40 30N 34 57 E
Corumbá, Brazil 92 G7 19 0S 57 30W
Corunna = A Coruña, Spain 19 A1 43 20N 8 25W
Corvallis, U.S.A. 82 D2 44 34N 123 16W
Corvette, L. de la, Canada 70 B5 53 25N 74 3W
Corydon, U.S.A. 80 E8 40 46N 93 19W
Cosalá, Mexico 86 C3 24 28N 106 40W
Cosamaloapan, Mexico 87 D5 18 23N 95 50W
Cosenza, Italy 20 E7 39 18N 16 15 E
Coshocton, U.S.A. 78 F3 40 16N 81 51W
Cosmo Newberry, Australia 61 E3 28 0S 122 54 E
Coso Junction, U.S.A. 85 J9 36 3N 117 57W
Coso Pk., U.S.A. 85 J9 36 13N 117 44W
Cosquín, Argentina 94 C3 31 15S 64 30W
Costa Blanca, Spain 19 C5 38 25N 0 10W
Costa Brava, Spain 19 B7 41 30N 3 0 E
Costa del Sol, Spain 19 D3 36 30N 4 30W
Costa Dorada, Spain 19 B6 41 12N 1 15 E
Costa Mesa, U.S.A. 85 M9 33 38N 117 55W
**Costa Rica** ■, Cent. Amer. 88 E3 10 0N 84 0W
Cosumnes →, U.S.A. 84 G5 38 16N 121 26W
Cotabato, Phil. 37 C6 7 14N 124 15 E
Cotagaita, Bolivia 94 A2 20 45S 65 40W
Côte d'Azur, France 18 E7 43 25N 7 10 E
Côte-d'Ivoire = Ivory Coast ■, Africa 50 G4 7 30N 5 0W
Coteau des Prairies, U.S.A. 80 C6 45 20N 97 50W
Coteau du Missouri, U.S.A. 80 B4 47 0N 100 0W
Coteau Landing, Canada 79 A10 45 15N 74 13W
Cotentin, France 18 B3 49 15N 1 30W
Cotillo, Canary Is. 22 F5 28 41N 14 1W
**Cotonou**, Benin 50 G6 6 20N 2 25 E
**Cotopaxi**, Ecuador 92 D3 0 40S 78 30W
**Cotswold Hills**, U.K. 11 F5 51 42N 2 10W
Cottage Grove, U.S.A. 82 E2 43 48N 123 3W
Cottbus, Germany 16 C8 51 45N 14 20 E
Cottonwood, U.S.A. 83 J7 34 45N 112 1W
Cotulla, U.S.A. 81 L5 28 26N 99 14W
Coudersport, U.S.A. 78 E6 41 46N 78 1W
Couedic, C. du, Australia 63 F2 36 5S 136 40 E
Coulee City, U.S.A. 82 C4 47 37N 119 17W
Coulman I., Antarctica 5 D11 73 35S 170 0 E
Coulonge →, Canada 70 C4 45 52N 76 46W
Coulterville, U.S.A. 84 H6 37 43N 120 12W
Council, U.S.A. 82 D5 44 44N 116 26W
Council Bluffs, U.S.A. 80 E7 41 16N 95 52W
Council Grove, U.S.A. 80 F6 38 40N 96 29W
Coupeville, U.S.A. 84 B4 48 13N 122 41W
Courantyne →, S. Amer. 92 B7 5 55N 57 5W
Courcelles, Belgium 15 D4 50 28N 4 22 E
Courtenay, Canada 72 D4 49 45N 125 0W
Courtland, U.S.A. 84 G5 38 20N 121 34W
Courtrai = Kortrijk, Belgium 15 D3 50 50N 3 17 E
Courtright, Canada 78 D2 42 49N 82 28W
Coushatta, U.S.A. 81 J8 32 1N 93 21W
Coutts Crossing, Australia 63 D5 29 49S 152 55 E
Couvin, Belgium 15 D4 50 3N 4 29 E
Cove I., Canada 78 A3 45 17N 81 44W
**Coventry**, U.K. 11 E6 52 25N 1 28W
Covilhã, Portugal 19 B2 40 17N 7 31W
Covington, Ga., U.S.A. 77 J4 33 36N 83 51W
Covington, Ky., U.S.A. 76 F3 39 5N 84 31W
Covington, Okla., U.S.A. 81 G6 36 18N 97 35W
Covington, Tenn., U.S.A. 81 H10 35 34N 89 39W
Covington, Va., U.S.A. 76 G5 37 47N 79 59W
Cowal, L., Australia 63 E4 33 40S 147 25 E
Cowan, L., Australia 61 F3 31 45S 121 45 E
Cowan L., Canada 73 C7 54 0N 107 15W
Cowangie, Australia 63 F3 35 12S 141 26 E
Cowansville, Canada 79 A12 45 14N 72 46W
Coward Springs, Australia 63 D2 29 24S 136 49 E
Cowcowing Lakes, Australia 61 F2 30 55S 117 20 E
Cowdenbeath, U.K. 12 E5 56 7N 3 21W
Cowell, Australia 63 E2 33 39S 136 56 E
Cowes, U.K. 11 G6 50 45N 1 18W
Cowichan L., Canada 84 B2 48 53N 124 17W
Cowlitz →, U.S.A. 84 D4 46 6N 122 55W
Cowra, Australia 63 E4 33 49S 148 42 E
Coxilha Grande, Brazil 95 B5 28 18S 51 30W
Coxim, Brazil 93 G8 18 30S 54 55W
Cox's Bazar, Bangla. 41 J17 21 26N 91 59 E
Coyote Wells, U.S.A. 85 N11 32 44N 115 58W
Coyuca de Benítez, Mexico 87 D4 17 1N 100 8W
Coyuca de Catalan, Mexico 86 D4 18 18N 100 41W
Cozad, U.S.A. 80 E5 40 52N 99 59W
Cozumel, Mexico 87 C7 20 31N 86 55W
Cozumel, Isla, Mexico 87 C7 20 30N 86 40W
Cracow = Kraków, Poland 17 C10 50 4N 19 57 E
Cracow, Australia 63 D5 25 17S 150 17 E
Cradock, Australia 63 E2 32 6S 138 31 E
Cradock, S. Africa 56 E4 32 8S 25 36 E
Craig, U.S.A. 82 F10 40 31N 107 33W
Craigavon, U.K. 13 B5 54 27N 6 23W
Craigmore, Zimbabwe 55 G3 20 28S 32 50 E
Craik, Canada 73 C7 51 3N 105 49W
Crailsheim, Germany 16 D6 49 8N 10 5 E
Craiova, Romania 17 F12 44 21N 23 48 E
Cramsie, Australia 62 C3 23 20S 144 15 E
Cranberry L., U.S.A. 79 B10 44 11N 74 50W
Cranberry Portage, Canada 73 C8 54 35N 101 23W
Cranbrook, Australia 61 F2 34 18S 117 33 E
Cranbrook, Canada 72 D5 49 30N 115 46W
Crandon, U.S.A. 80 C10 45 34N 88 54W
Crane, Oreg., U.S.A. 82 E4 43 25N 118 35W
Crane, Tex., U.S.A. 81 K3 31 24N 102 21W
Cranston, U.S.A. 79 E13 41 47N 71 26W
Crater L., U.S.A. 82 E2 42 56N 122 6W
Crater Lake National Park, U.S.A. 82 E2 42 55N 122 10W
Crateús, Brazil 93 E10 5 10S 40 39W
Crato, Brazil 93 E11 7 10S 39 25W
Craven, L., Canada 70 B4 54 20N 76 56W
Crawford, U.S.A. 80 D3 42 41N 103 25W
Crawfordsville, U.S.A. 76 E2 40 2N 86 54W
Crawley, U.K. 11 F7 51 7N 0 11W
Crazy Mts., U.S.A. 82 C8 46 12N 110 20W
Crean L., Canada 73 C7 54 5N 106 9W
Crediton, Canada 78 C3 43 17N 81 33W
Cree →, Canada 73 B7 58 57N 105 47W
Cree →, U.K. 12 G4 54 55N 4 25W
Cree L., Canada 73 B7 57 30N 106 30W
Creede, U.S.A. 83 H10 37 51N 106 56W
Creekside, U.S.A. 78 F5 40 40N 79 11W
Creel, Mexico 86 B3 27 45N 107 38W
Creemore, Canada 78 B4 44 19N 80 6W
Creighton, Canada 73 C8 54 45N 101 54W
Creighton, U.S.A. 80 D6 42 28N 97 54W
Crema, Italy 18 D8 45 22N 9 41 E
Cremona, Italy 18 D9 45 7N 10 2 E
Cres, Croatia 16 F8 44 58N 14 25 E
Crescent City, U.S.A. 82 F1 41 45N 124 12W
Crespo, Argentina 94 C3 32 2S 60 19W
Cresson, U.S.A. 78 F6 40 28N 78 36W
Crestline, Calif., U.S.A. 85 L9 34 14N 117 18W
Crestline, Ohio, U.S.A. 78 F2 40 47N 82 44W
Creston, Canada 72 D5 49 10N 116 31W
Creston, Calif., U.S.A. 84 K6 35 32N 120 33W
Creston, Iowa, U.S.A. 80 E7 41 4N 94 22W
Crestview, Calif., U.S.A. 84 H8 37 46N 118 58W
Crestview, Fla., U.S.A. 77 K2 30 46N 86 34W
**Crete** = Kríti, Greece 23 D7 35 15N 25 0 E
Crete, U.S.A. 80 E6 40 38N 96 58W
Créteil, France 18 B5 48 47N 2 28 E
Creus, C. de, Spain 19 A7 42 20N 3 19 E
Creuse →, France 18 C4 47 0N 0 34 E
Crewe, U.K. 10 D5 53 6N 2 26W
Crewkerne, U.K. 11 G5 50 53N 2 48W
Criciúma, Brazil 95 B6 28 40S 49 23W
Crieff, U.K. 12 E5 56 22N 3 50W
**Crimea** □, Ukraine 25 E5 45 30N 33 10 E
Crimean Pen. = Krymskyy Pivostriv, Ukraine 25 F5 45 0N 34 0 E
Crişul Alb →, Romania 17 E11 46 42N 21 17 E
Crişul Negru →, Romania 17 E11 46 42N 21 16 E
Crna →, Macedonia 21 D9 41 33N 21 59 E
Crna Gora = Montenegro □, Yugoslavia 21 C8 42 40N 19 20 E
Crna Gora, Macedonia 21 C9 42 10N 21 30 E
Crna Reka = Crna →, Macedonia 21 D9 41 33N 21 59 E
Croagh Patrick, Ireland 13 C2 53 46N 9 40W
**Croatia** ■, Europe 16 F9 45 20N 16 0 E
Crocker, Banjaran, Malaysia 36 C5 5 40N 116 30 E
Crockett, U.S.A. 81 K7 31 19N 95 27W
Crocodile = Krokodil →, Mozam. 57 D5 25 14S 32 18 E
Crocodile Is., Australia 62 A1 12 3S 134 58 E
Crohy Hd., Ireland 13 B3 54 55N 8 26W
Croix, L. La, Canada 70 C1 48 20N 92 15W
Croker, C., Australia 60 B5 10 58S 132 35 E
Croker, C., Canada 78 B4 44 58N 80 59W
Croker I., Australia 60 B5 11 12S 132 32 E
Cromarty, U.K. 12 D4 57 40N 4 2W
Cromer, U.K. 10 E9 52 56N 1 17 E
Cromwell, N.Z. 59 L2 45 3S 169 14 E
Cromwell, U.S.A. 79 E12 41 36N 72 39W
Crook, U.K. 10 C6 54 43N 1 45W
Crooked →, Canada 72 C4 54 50N 122 54W
Crooked →, U.S.A. 82 D3 44 32N 121 16W
Crooked I., Bahamas 89 B5 22 50N 74 10W
Crooked Island Passage, Bahamas 89 B5 23 0N 74 30W
Crookston, Minn., U.S.A. 80 B6 47 47N 96 37W
Crookston, Nebr., U.S.A. 80 D4 42 56N 100 45W
Crookwell, Australia 63 E4 34 28S 149 24 E
Crosby, U.K. 10 D4 53 30N 3 3W
Crosby, U.S.A. 78 E6 41 45N 78 23W
Crosbyton, U.S.A. 81 J4 33 40N 101 14W
Cross City, U.S.A. 77 L4 29 38N 83 7W
Cross Fell, U.K. 10 C5 54 43N 2 28W
Cross L., Canada 73 C9 54 45N 97 30W
Cross Lake, Canada 73 C9 54 37N 97 47W
Cross Sound, U.S.A. 68 C6 58 0N 135 0W
Crossett, U.S.A. 81 J9 33 8N 91 58W
Crosshaven, Ireland 13 E3 51 47N 8 17W
Crossville, U.S.A. 77 G3 35 57N 85 2W
Croswell, U.S.A. 78 C2 43 16N 82 37W
Croton-on-Hudson, U.S.A. 79 E11 41 12N 73 55W
Crotone, Italy 20 E7 39 5N 17 8 E
Crow →, Canada 72 B4 59 41N 124 20W
Crow Agency, U.S.A. 82 D10 45 36N 107 28W
Crow Hd., Ireland 13 E1 51 35N 10 9W
Crowell, U.S.A. 81 J5 33 59N 99 43W
Crowley, U.S.A. 81 K8 30 13N 92 22W
Crowley, L., U.S.A. 84 H8 37 35N 118 42W
Crown Point, Ind., U.S.A. 76 E2 41 25N 87 22W
Crown Point, N.Y., U.S.A. 79 C11 43 57N 73 26W
Crownpoint, U.S.A. 83 J9 35 41N 108 9W
Crows Landing, U.S.A. 84 H5 37 23N 121 6W
Crows Nest, Australia 63 D5 27 16S 152 4 E
Crowsnest Pass, Canada 72 D6 49 40N 114 40W
Croydon, Australia 62 B3 18 13S 142 14 E
Croydon, U.K. 11 F7 51 22N 0 5W
Crozet Is., Ind. Oc. 3 G12 46 27S 52 0 E
Cruz, C., Cuba 88 C4 19 50N 77 50W
Cruz Alta, Brazil 95 B5 28 45S 53 40W
Cruz del Eje, Argentina 94 C3 30 45S 64 50W
Cruzeiro, Brazil 95 A7 22 33S 45 0W
Cruzeiro do Oeste, Brazil 95 A5 23 46S 53 4W
Cruzeiro do Sul, Brazil 92 E4 7 35S 72 35W
Cry L., Canada 72 B3 58 45N 129 0W
Crystal Bay, U.S.A. 84 F7 39 15N 120 0W
Crystal Brook, Australia 63 E2 33 21S 138 12 E
Crystal City, U.S.A. 81 L5 28 41N 99 50W
Crystal Falls, U.S.A. 76 B1 46 5N 88 20W
Crystal River, U.S.A. 77 L4 28 54N 82 35W
Crystal Springs, U.S.A. 81 K9 31 59N 90 21W
Csongrád, Hungary 17 E11 46 43N 20 12 E
Cu Lao Hon, Vietnam 39 G7 10 54N 108 18 E
Cua Rao, Vietnam 38 C5 19 16N 104 27 E
Cuácua →, Mozam. 55 F4 17 54S 37 0 E
Cuamato, Angola 56 B2 17 2S 15 7 E
Cuamba, Mozam. 55 E4 14 45S 36 22 E
Cuando →, Angola 53 H4 17 30S 23 15 E
Cuando Cubango □, Angola 56 B3 16 25S 20 0 E
Cuangar, Angola 56 B2 17 36S 18 39 E
Cuanza →, Angola 52 F2 9 2S 13 30 E
Cuarto →, Argentina 94 C3 33 25S 63 2W
Cuatrociénegas, Mexico 86 B4 26 59N 102 5W
Cuauhtémoc, Mexico 86 B3 28 25N 106 52W
Cuba, N. Mex., U.S.A. 83 J10 36 1N 107 4W
Cuba, N.Y., U.S.A. 78 D6 42 13N 78 17W
**Cuba** ■, W. Indies 88 B4 22 0N 79 0W
Cubal, Angola 53 G2 12 26S 14 3 E
Cubango →, Africa 56 B3 18 50S 22 25 E
Cuchumatanes, Sierra de los, Guatemala 88 C1 15 35N 91 25W
Cuckfield, U.K. 11 F7 51 1N 0 8W
Cucuí, Brazil 92 C5 1 12N 66 50W
Cucurpe, Mexico 86 A2 30 20N 110 43W
Cúcuta, Colombia 92 B4 7 54N 72 31W
Cuddalore, India 40 P11 11 46N 79 45 E
Cuddapah, India 40 M11 14 30N 78 47 E
Cuddapan, L., Australia 62 D3 25 45S 141 26 E
Cue, Australia 61 E2 27 25S 117 54 E
Cuenca, Ecuador 92 D3 2 50S 79 9W
Cuenca, Spain 19 B4 40 5N 2 10W
Cuenca, Serranía de, Spain 19 C5 39 55N 1 50W
Cuernavaca, Mexico 87 D5 18 55N 99 15W
Cuero, U.S.A. 81 L6 29 6N 97 17W
Cuevas del Almanzora, Spain 19 D5 37 18N 1 58W
Cuevo, Bolivia 92 H6 20 15S 63 30W
Cuiabá, Brazil 93 G7 15 30S 56 0W
Cuiabá →, Brazil 93 G7 17 5S 56 36W
Cuijk, Neths. 15 C5 51 44N 5 50 E
Cuilco, Guatemala 88 C1 15 24N 91 58W
Cuillin Hills, U.K. 12 D2 57 13N 6 15W
Cuillin Sd., U.K. 12 D2 57 4N 6 20W
Cuito →, Angola 56 B3 18 1S 20 48 E
Cuitzeo, L. de, Mexico 86 D4 19 55N 101 5W
Cukai, Malaysia 39 K4 4 13N 103 25 E
Culbertson, U.S.A. 80 A2 48 9N 104 31W
Culcairn, Australia 63 F4 35 41S 147 3 E
Culgoa →, Australia 63 D4 29 56S 146 20 E
Culiacán, Mexico 86 C3 24 50N 107 23W
Culiacán →, Mexico 86 C3 24 30N 107 42W
Culion, Phil. 37 B6 11 54N 119 58 E
Cullarin Ra., Australia 63 E4 34 30S 149 30 E
Cullen, U.K. 12 D6 57 42N 2 49W
Cullen Pt., Australia 62 A3 11 57S 141 54 E
Cullera, Spain 19 C5 39 9N 0 17W
Cullman, U.S.A. 77 H2 34 11N 86 51W
Culpeper, U.S.A. 76 F7 38 30N 78 0W
Culuene →, Brazil 93 F8 12 56S 52 51W
Culver, Pt., Australia 61 F3 32 54S 124 43 E
Culverden, N.Z. 59 K4 42 47S 172 49 E
Cumaná, Venezuela 92 A6 10 30N 64 5W
Cumberland, B.C., Canada 72 D4 49 40N 125 0W
Cumberland, Ont., Canada 79 A9 45 29N 75 24W
Cumberland, U.S.A. 76 F6 39 39N 78 46W
Cumberland →, U.S.A. 77 G2 36 15N 87 0W
Cumberland, L., U.S.A. 77 G3 36 57N 84 55W
Cumberland I., U.S.A. 77 K5 30 50N 81 25W
Cumberland Is., Australia 62 C4 20 35S 149 10 E
Cumberland L., Canada 73 C8 54 3N 102 18W
Cumberland Pen., Canada 69 B13 67 0N 64 0W
Cumberland Plateau, U.S.A. 77 H3 36 0N 85 0W
Cumberland Sd., Canada 69 B13 65 30N 66 0W
Cumbernauld, U.K. 12 F5 55 57N 3 58W
Cumborah, Australia 63 D4 29 40S 147 45 E
**Cumbria** □, U.K. 10 C5 54 42N 2 52W
Cumbrian Mts., U.K. 10 C5 54 30N 3 0W
Cumbum, India 40 M11 15 40N 79 10 E
Cuminá →, Brazil 93 D7 1 30S 56 0W
Cummings Mt., U.S.A. 85 K8 35 2N 118 34W
Cummins, Australia 63 E2 34 16S 135 43 E
Cumnock, Australia 63 E4 32 59S 148 46 E
Cumnock, U.K. 12 F4 55 28N 4 17W
Cumpas, Mexico 86 B3 30 0N 109 48W
Cumplida, Pta., Canary Is. 22 F2 28 50N 17 48W
Cunco, Chile 96 D2 38 55S 72 2W
Cuncumén, Chile 94 C1 31 53S 70 38W
Cunderdin, Australia 61 F2 31 37S 117 12 E
Cunene →, Angola 56 B1 17 20S 11 50 E
Cúneo, Italy 18 D7 44 23N 7 32 E
Çüngüş, Turkey 44 B3 38 13N 39 17 E
Cunillera, I. = Sa Conillera, Spain 22 C7 38 59N 1 13 E
Cunnamulla, Australia 63 D4 28 2S 145 38 E
Cupar, Canada 73 C8 50 57N 104 10W
Cupar, U.K. 12 E5 56 19N 3 1W
Cupica, G. de, Colombia 92 B3 6 25N 77 30W
**Curaçao**, Neth. Ant. 89 D6 12 10N 69 0W
Curanilahue, Chile 94 D1 37 29S 73 28W
Curaray →, Peru 92 D4 2 20S 74 5W
Curepto, Chile 94 D1 35 8S 72 1W
Curiapo, Venezuela 92 B6 8 33N 61 5W
Curicó, Chile 94 C1 34 55S 71 20W
Curitiba, Brazil 95 B6 25 20S 49 10W
Curitibanos, Brazil 95 B5 27 18S 50 36W
Currabubula, Australia 63 E5 31 16S 150 44 E
Currais Novos, Brazil 93 E11 6 13S 36 30W
Curralinho, Brazil 93 D9 1 45S 49 46W
Currant, U.S.A. 82 G6 38 51N 115 32W
Current →, U.S.A. 81 G9 36 15N 90 55W
Currie, Australia 62 F3 39 56S 143 53 E
Currie, U.S.A. 82 F6 40 16N 114 45W
Curtea de Argeş, Romania 17 F13 45 12N 24 42 E
Curtis, U.S.A. 80 E4 40 38N 100 31W
Curtis Group, Australia 62 F4 39 30S 146 37 E
Curtis I., Australia 62 C5 23 35S 151 10 E
Curuápanema →, Brazil 93 D7 2 25S 55 2W
Curuçá, Brazil 93 D9 0 43S 47 50W
Curuguaty, Paraguay 95 A4 24 31S 55 42W
Curup, Indonesia 36 E2 4 26S 102 13 E
Cururupu, Brazil 93 D10 1 50S 44 50W
Curuzú Cuatiá, Argentina 94 B4 29 50S 58 5W
Curvelo, Brazil 93 G10 18 45S 44 27W
Cushing, U.S.A. 81 H6 35 59N 96 46W
Cushing, Mt., Canada 72 B3 57 35N 126 57W
Cusihuiriáchic, Mexico 86 B3 28 10N 106 50W
Custer, U.S.A. 80 D3 43 46N 103 36W
Cut Bank, U.S.A. 82 B7 48 38N 112 20W
Cutchogue, U.S.A. 79 E12 41 1N 72 30W
Cuthbert, U.S.A. 77 K3 31 46N 84 48W
Cutler, U.S.A. 84 J7 36 31N 119 17W
Cuttaburra →, Australia 63 D3 29 43S 144 22 E
Cuttack, India 41 J14 20 25N 85 57 E
Cuvier, C., Australia 61 D1 23 14S 113 22 E
Cuvier I., N.Z. 59 G5 36 27S 175 50 E
Cuxhaven, Germany 16 B5 53 51N 8 41 E
Cuyahoga Falls, U.S.A. 78 E3 41 8N 81 29W
Cuyo, Phil. 37 B6 10 50N 121 5 E
Cuyuni →, Guyana 92 B7 6 23N 58 41W
Cuzco, Bolivia 92 H5 20 0S 66 50W
**Cuzco**, Peru 92 F4 13 32S 72 0W
Cwmbran, U.K. 11 F4 51 39N 3 2W
Cyangugu, Rwanda 54 C2 2 29S 28 54 E
Cyclades = Kikládhes, Greece 21 F11 37 0N 24 30 E
Cygnet, Australia 62 G4 43 8S 147 1 E
Cynthiana, U.S.A. 76 F3 38 23N 84 18W
Cypress Hills, Canada 73 D7 49 40N 109 30W
Cypress Hills Prov. Park, Canada 73 D7 49 40N 109 30W
**Cyprus** ■, Asia 23 E12 35 0N 33 0 E
Cyrenaica, Libya 51 C10 27 0N 23 0 E
Czar, Canada 73 C6 52 27N 110 50W
Czech Rep. ■, Europe 16 D8 50 0N 15 0 E
Częstochowa, Poland 17 C10 50 49N 19 7 E


# D


Da Hinggan Ling, China 33 B7 48 0N 121 0 E
Da Lat, Vietnam 39 G7 11 56N 108 25 E
Da Nang, Vietnam 38 D7 16 4N 108 13 E
Da Qaidam, China 32 C4 37 50N 95 15 E
Da Yunhe →, China 35 G11 34 25N 120 5 E
Da'an, China 35 B13 45 30N 124 7 E
Daba Shan, China 33 C5 32 0N 109 0 E
Dabbagh, Jabal, Si. Arabia 44 E2 27 52N 35 45 E
Dabhoi, India 42 H5 22 10N 73 20 E
Dabo = Pasirkuning, Indonesia 36 E2 0 30S 104 33 E
Dabola, Guinea 50 F3 10 50N 11 5W
Dabung, Malaysia 39 K4 5 23N 102 1 E
Dacca = Dhaka, Bangla. 43 H14 23 43N 90 26 E
Dacca = Dhaka □, Bangla. 43 G14 24 25N 90 25 E
Dachau, Germany 16 D6 48 15N 11 26 E
Dadanawa, Guyana 92 C7 2 50N 59 30W
Dade City, U.S.A. 77 L4 28 22N 82 11W
Dadhar, Pakistan 42 E2 29 28N 67 39 E
Dadra & Nagar Haveli □, India 40 J8 20 5N 73 0 E
Dadri = Charkhi Dadri, India 42 E7 28 37N 76 17 E
Dadu, Pakistan 42 F2 26 45N 67 45 E
Daet, Phil. 37 B6 14 2N 122 55 E
Dagana, Senegal 50 E2 16 30N 15 35W
**Dagestan** □, Russia 25 F8 42 30N 47 0 E
Daggett, U.S.A. 85 L10 34 52N 116 52W
Daghestan Republic = Dagestan □, Russia 25 F8 42 30N 47 0 E
Dağlıq Qarabağ = Nagorno-Karabakh, Azerbaijan 25 F8 39 55N 46 45 E
Dagö = Hiiumaa, Estonia 9 G20 58 50N 22 45 E
Dagu, China 35 E9 38 59N 117 40 E
Dagupan, Phil. 37 A6 16 3N 120 20 E
Daguragu, Australia 60 C5 17 33S 130 30 E
Dahlak Kebir, Eritrea 46 D3 15 50N 40 10 E
Dahlonega, U.S.A. 77 H4 34 32N 83 59W
Dahod, India 42 H6 22 50N 74 15 E
Dahomey = Benin ■, Africa 50 G6 10 0N 2 0 E
Dahūk, Iraq 44 B3 36 50N 43 1 E
Dai Hao, Vietnam 38 C6 18 1N 106 25 E
Dai-Sen, Japan 31 G6 35 22N 133 32 E
Dai Xian, China 34 E7 39 4N 112 58 E
Daicheng, China 34 E9 38 42N 116 38 E
Daingean, Ireland 13 C4 53 18N 7 17W
Daintree, Australia 62 B4 16 20S 145 20 E
Daiō-Misaki, Japan 31 G8 34 15N 136 45 E
Daisetsu-Zan, Japan 30 C11 43 30N 142 57 E
Dajarra, Australia 62 C2 21 42S 139 30 E
Dak Dam, Cambodia 38 F6 12 20N 107 21 E
Dak Nhe, Vietnam 38 E6 15 28N 107 48 E
Dak Pek, Vietnam 38 E6 15 4N 107 44 E
Dak Song, Vietnam 39 F6 12 19N 107 35 E
Dak Sui, Vietnam 38 E6 14 55N 107 43 E
**Dakar**, Senegal 50 F2 14 34N 17 29W
Dakhla, W. Sahara 50 D2 23 50N 15 53W
Dakhla, El Wâhât el-, Egypt 51 C11 25 30N 28 50 E
Dakor, India 42 H5 22 45N 73 11 E
Dakota City, U.S.A. 80 D6 42 25N 96 25W
Đakovica, Yugoslavia 21 C9 42 22N 20 26 E
Dalachi, China 34 F3 36 48N 105 0 E
Dalai Nur, China 34 C9 43 20N 116 45 E
Dālaki, Iran 45 D6 29 26N 51 17 E
Dalälven, Sweden 9 F17 60 12N 16 43 E
Dalaman →, Turkey 21 F13 36 41N 28 43 E
Dalandzadgad, Mongolia 34 C3 43 27N 104 30 E
Dalap-Uliga-Darrit, Marshall Is. 64 G9 7 7N 171 24 E
Dalarna, Sweden 9 F16 61 0N 14 0 E
Dālbandīn, Pakistan 40 E4 29 0N 64 23 E
Dalbeattie, U.K. 12 G5 54 56N 3 50W
Dalbeg, Australia 62 C4 20 16S 147 18 E
Dalby, Australia 63 D5 27 10S 151 17 E
Dale City, U.S.A. 76 F7 38 38N 77 18W
Dale Hollow L., U.S.A. 77 G3 36 32N 85 27W
Dalgān, Iran 45 E8 27 31N 59 19 E
Dalhart, U.S.A. 81 G3 36 4N 102 31W
Dalhousie, Canada 71 C6 48 5N 66 26W
Dalhousie, India 42 C6 32 38N 75 58 E
Dali, Shaanxi, China 34 G5 34 48N 109 58 E
Dali, Yunnan, China 32 D5 25 40N 100 10 E
Dalian, China 35 E11 38 50N 121 40 E
Daliang Shan, China 32 D5 28 0N 102 45 E
Daling He →, China 35 D11 40 55N 121 40 E
Dāliyat el Karmel, Israel 47 C4 32 43N 35 2 E
Dalkeith, U.K. 12 F5 55 54N 3 4W
Dallas, Oreg., U.S.A. 82 D2 44 55N 123 19W
**Dallas**, Tex., U.S.A. 81 J6 32 47N 96 49W
Dalmā, U.A.E. 45 E7 24 30N 52 20 E

**Des Moines**, Iowa, U.S.A. 80 E8 41 35N 93 37W
Des Moines, N. Mex., U.S.A. 81 G3 36 46N 103 50W
Des Moines →, U.S.A. 80 E9 40 23N 91 25W
Desaguadero →, Argentina 94 C2 34 30S 66 46W
Desaguadero →, Bolivia 92 G5 16 35S 69 5W
Descanso, Pta., Mexico 85 N9 32 21N 117 3W
Deschaillons, Canada 71 C5 46 32N 72 7W
Deschambault L., Canada 73 C8 54 50N 103 30W
Deschutes →, U.S.A. 82 D3 45 38N 120 55W
Dese, Ethiopia 46 E2 11 5N 39 40 E
Deseado →, Argentina 96 F3 47 45S 65 54W
Desert Center, U.S.A. 85 M11 33 43N 115 24W
Desert Hot Springs, U.S.A. 85 M10 33 58N 116 30W
Deshnok, India 42 F5 27 48N 73 21 E
Desna →, Ukraine 17 C16 50 33N 30 32 E
Desolación, I., Chile 96 G2 53 0S 74 0W
Despeñaperros, Paso, Spain 19 C4 38 24N 3 30W
Dessau, Germany 16 C7 51 51N 12 14 E
Dessye = Dese, Ethiopia 46 E2 11 5N 39 40 E
D'Estrees B., Australia 63 F2 35 55S 137 45 E
Desuri, India 42 G5 25 18N 73 35 E
Det Udom, Thailand 38 E5 14 54N 105 5 E
Dete, Zimbabwe 55 F2 18 38S 26 50 E
Detmold, Germany 16 C5 51 56N 8 52 E
Detour, Pt., U.S.A. 76 C2 45 40N 86 40W
**Detroit**, U.S.A. 78 D1 42 20N 83 3W
Detroit Lakes, U.S.A. 80 B7 46 49N 95 51W
Deurne, Neths. 15 C5 51 27N 5 49 E
Deutsche Bucht, Germany 16 A5 54 15N 8 0 E
Deva, Romania 17 F12 45 53N 22 55 E
Devakottai, India 40 Q11 9 55N 78 45 E
Devaprayag, India 43 D8 30 13N 78 35 E
Deventer, Neths. 15 B6 52 15N 6 10 E
Deveron →, U.K. 12 D6 57 41N 2 32W
Devgadh Bariya, India 42 H5 22 40N 73 55 E
Devikot, India 42 F4 26 42N 71 12 E
Devils Den, U.S.A. 84 K7 35 46N 119 58W
Devils Lake, U.S.A. 80 A5 48 7N 98 52W
Devils Paw, Canada 72 B2 58 47N 134 0W
Devils Tower Junction, U.S.A. 80 C2 44 31N 104 57W
Devine, U.S.A. 81 L5 29 8N 98 54W
Devizes, U.K. 11 F6 51 22N 1 58W
Devli, India 42 G6 25 50N 75 20 E
Devon, Canada 72 C6 53 24N 113 44W
**Devon □**, U.K. 11 G4 50 50N 3 40W
Devon I., Canada 4 B3 75 10N 85 0W
Devonport, Australia 62 G4 41 10S 146 22 E
Devonport, N.Z. 59 G5 36 49S 174 49 E
Dewas, India 42 H7 22 59N 76 3 E
Dewetsdorp, S. Africa 56 D4 29 33S 26 39 E
Dexter, Maine, U.S.A. 77 C11 45 1N 69 18W
Dexter, Mo., U.S.A. 81 G10 36 48N 89 57W
Dexter, N. Mex., U.S.A. 81 J2 33 12N 104 22W
Dey-Dey, L., Australia 61 E5 29 12S 131 4 E
Deyhūk, Iran 45 C8 33 15N 57 30 E
Deyyer, Iran 45 E6 27 55N 51 55 E
Dezadeash L., Canada 72 A1 60 28N 136 58W
Dezfūl, Iran 45 C6 32 20N 48 30 E
Dezhneva, Mys, Russia 27 C19 66 5N 169 40W
Dezhou, China 34 F9 37 26N 116 18 E
Dhadhar →, India 43 G11 24 56N 85 24 E
Dháfni, Greece 23 D7 35 13N 25 3 E
Dhahiriya = Az Zāhirīyah, West Bank 47 D3 31 25N 34 58 E
Dhahran = Az Zahrān, Si. Arabia 45 E6 26 10N 50 7 E
Dhak, Pakistan 42 C5 32 25N 72 33 E
**Dhaka**, Bangla. 43 H14 23 43N 90 26 E
Dhaka □, Bangla. 43 G14 24 25N 90 25 E
Dhali, Cyprus 23 D12 35 1N 33 25 E
Dhampur, India 43 E8 29 19N 78 33 E
Dhamtari, India 41 J12 20 42N 81 35 E
Dhanbad, India 43 H12 23 50N 86 30 E
Dhangarhi, Nepal 41 E12 28 55N 80 40 E
Dhankuta, Nepal 43 F12 26 55N 87 40 E
Dhar, India 42 H6 22 35N 75 26 E
Dharampur, India 42 H6 22 13N 75 18 E
Dharamsala = Dharmsala, India 42 C7 32 16N 76 23 E
Dhariwal, India 42 D6 31 57N 75 19 E
Dharla →, Bangla. 43 G13 25 46N 89 42 E
Dharmapuri, India 40 N11 12 10N 78 10 E
Dharmjaygarh, India 43 H10 22 28N 83 13 E
Dharmsala, India 42 C7 32 16N 76 23 E
Dharni, India 42 J7 21 33N 76 53 E
Dhasan →, India 43 G8 25 48N 79 24 E
Dhaulagiri, Nepal 43 E10 28 39N 83 28 E
Dhebar, L., India 42 G6 24 10N 74 0 E
Dheftera, Cyprus 23 D12 35 5N 33 16 E
Dhenkanal, India 41 J14 20 45N 85 35 E
Dherinia, Cyprus 23 D12 35 3N 33 57 E
Dhiarrizos →, Cyprus 23 E11 34 41N 32 34 E
Dhībān, Jordan 47 D4 31 30N 35 46 E
Dhíkti Óros, Greece 23 D7 35 8N 25 30 E
Dhilwan, India 42 D6 31 31N 75 21 E
Dhimarkhera, India 43 H9 23 28N 80 22 E
Dhírfis = Dhírfis Óros, Greece 21 E10 38 40N 23 54 E
Dhírfis Óros, Greece 21 E10 38 40N 23 54 E
Dhodhekánisos, Greece 21 F12 36 35N 27 0 E
Dholka, India 42 H5 22 44N 72 29 E
Dhoraji, India 42 J4 21 45N 70 37 E
Dhráhstis, Ákra, Greece 23 A3 39 48N 19 40 E
Dhrangadhra, India 42 H4 22 59N 71 31 E
Dhrápanon, Ákra, Greece 23 D6 35 28N 24 14 E
Dhrol, India 42 H4 22 33N 70 25 E
Dhuburi, India 41 F16 26 2N 89 59 E
Dhule, India 40 J9 20 58N 74 50 E
Di Linh, Vietnam 39 G7 11 35N 108 4 E
Di Linh, Cao Nguyen, Vietnam 39 G7 11 30N 108 0 E
Día, Greece 23 D7 35 28N 25 14 E
Diablo, Mt., U.S.A. 84 H5 37 53N 121 56W
Diablo Range, U.S.A. 84 J5 37 20N 121 25W
Diafarabé, Mali 50 F5 14 9N 4 57W
Diamante, Argentina 94 C3 32 5S 60 40W
Diamante →, Argentina 94 C2 34 30S 66 46W
Diamantina, Brazil 93 G10 18 17S 43 40W
Diamantina →, Australia 63 D2 26 45S 139 10 E
Diamantino, Brazil 93 F7 14 30S 56 30W
Diamond Bar, U.S.A. 85 L9 34 1N 117 48W
Diamond Harbour, India 43 H13 22 11N 88 14 E
Diamond Is., Australia 62 B5 17 25S 151 5 E
Diamond Mts., U.S.A. 82 G6 39 50N 115 30W
Diamond Springs, U.S.A. 84 G6 38 42N 120 49W
Dībā, Oman 45 E8 25 45N 56 16 E
Dibai, India 42 E8 28 13N 78 15 E
Dibaya-Lubue, Dem. Rep. of the Congo 52 E3 4 12S 19 54 E
Dibete, Botswana 56 C4 23 45S 26 32 E
Dibrugarh, India 41 F19 27 29N 94 55 E
Dickens, U.S.A. 81 J4 33 37N 100 50W
Dickinson, U.S.A. 80 B3 46 53N 102 47W
Dickson = Dikson, Russia 26 B9 73 40N 80 5 E
Dickson, U.S.A. 77 G2 36 5N 87 23W
Dickson City, U.S.A. 79 E9 41 29N 75 40W
Didiéni, Mali 50 F4 13 53N 8 6W
Didsbury, Canada 72 C6 51 35N 114 10W
Didwana, India 42 F6 27 23N 74 36 E
Diefenbaker, L., Canada 73 C7 51 0N 106 55W
Diego de Almagro, Chile 94 B1 26 22S 70 3W
Diego Garcia, Ind. Oc. 3 E13 7 50S 72 50 E
Diekirch, Lux. 15 E6 49 52N 6 10 E
Dien Ban, Vietnam 38 E7 15 53N 108 16 E
Dien Khanh, Vietnam 39 F7 12 15N 109 6 E
Dieppe, France 18 B4 49 54N 1 4 E
Dierks, U.S.A. 81 H8 34 7N 94 1W
Diest, Belgium 15 D5 50 58N 5 4 E
Dif, Somali Rep. 46 G3 0 59N 0 56 E
Differdange, Lux. 15 E5 49 31N 5 54 E
Dig, India 42 F7 27 28N 77 20 E
Digba, Dem. Rep. of the Congo 54 B2 4 25N 25 48 E
Digby, Canada 71 D6 44 38N 65 50W
Diggi, India 42 F6 26 22N 75 26 E
Dighinala, Bangla. 41 H18 23 15N 92 5 E
Dighton, U.S.A. 80 F4 38 29N 100 28W
Digne-les-Bains, France 18 D7 44 5N 6 12 E
Digos, Phil. 37 C7 6 45N 125 20 E
Digranes, Iceland 8 C6 66 4N 14 44W
Digul →, Indonesia 37 F9 7 7S 138 42 E
Dihang →, India 41 F19 27 48N 95 30 E
Dijlah, Nahr →, Asia 44 D5 31 0N 47 25 E
**Dijon**, France 18 C6 47 20N 5 3 E
Dikkil, Djibouti 46 E3 11 8N 42 20 E
Dikomu di Kai, Botswana 56 C3 24 58S 24 36 E
Diksmuide, Belgium 15 C2 51 2N 2 52 E
Dikson, Russia 26 B9 73 40N 80 5 E
Dila, Ethiopia 46 F2 6 21N 38 22 E
Dili, Indonesia 37 F7 8 39S 125 34 E
Dilley, U.S.A. 81 L5 28 40N 99 10W
Dillingham, U.S.A. 68 C4 59 3N 158 28W
Dillon, Canada 73 B7 55 56N 108 35W
Dillon, Mont., U.S.A. 82 D7 45 13N 112 38W
Dillon, S.C., U.S.A. 77 H6 34 25N 79 22W
Dillon →, Canada 73 B7 55 56N 108 56W
Dillsburg, U.S.A. 78 F7 40 7N 77 2W
Dilolo, Dem. Rep. of the Congo 52 G4 10 28S 22 18 E
Dimas, Mexico 86 C3 23 43N 106 47W
Dimashq, Syria 47 B5 33 30N 36 18 E
Dimashq □, Syria 47 B5 33 30N 36 30 E
Dimbaza, S. Africa 57 E4 32 50S 27 14 E
Dimboola, Australia 63 F3 36 28S 142 7 E
Dîmboviţa = Dâmboviţa →, Romania 17 F14 44 12N 26 26 E
Dimbulah, Australia 62 B4 17 8S 145 4 E
Dimitrovgrad, Bulgaria 21 C11 42 5N 25 35 E
Dimitrovgrad, Russia 24 D8 54 14N 49 39 E
Dimitrovo = Pernik, Bulgaria 21 C10 42 35N 23 2 E
Dimmitt, U.S.A. 81 H3 34 33N 102 19W
Dimona, Israel 47 D4 31 2N 35 1 E
Dinagat, Phil. 37 B7 10 10N 125 40 E
Dinajpur, Bangla. 41 G16 25 33N 88 43 E
Dinan, France 18 B2 48 28N 2 2W
Dīnān Āb, Iran 45 C8 32 4N 56 49 E
Dinant, Belgium 15 D4 50 16N 4 55 E
Dinapur, India 43 G11 25 38N 85 5 E
Dīnār, Kūh-e, Iran 45 D6 30 42N 51 46 E
Dinara Planina, Croatia 20 C7 44 0N 16 30 E
Dinard, France 18 B2 48 38N 2 6W
**Dinaric Alps** = Dinara Planina, Croatia 20 C7 44 0N 16 30 E
Dindigul, India 40 P11 10 25N 78 0 E
Dindori, India 43 H9 22 57N 81 5 E
Ding Xian = Dingzhou, China 34 E8 38 30N 114 59 E
Dinga, Pakistan 42 G2 25 26N 67 10 E
Dingbian, China 34 F4 37 35N 107 32 E
Dingle, Ireland 13 D1 52 9N 10 17W
Dingle B., Ireland 13 D1 52 3N 10 20W
Dingmans Ferry, U.S.A. 79 E10 41 13N 74 55W
Dingo, Australia 62 C4 23 38S 149 19 E
Dingtao, China 34 G8 35 5N 115 35 E
Dingwall, U.K. 12 D4 57 36N 4 26W
Dingxi, China 34 G3 35 30N 104 33 E
Dingxiang, China 34 E7 38 30N 112 58 E
Dingzhou, China 34 E8 38 30N 114 59 E
Dinh, Mui, Vietnam 39 G7 11 22N 109 1 E
Dinokwe, Botswana 56 C4 23 29S 26 37 E
Dinorwic, Canada 73 D10 49 41N 92 30W
Dinosaur National Monument, U.S.A. 82 F9 40 30N 108 45W
Dinosaur Prov. Park, Canada 72 C6 50 47N 111 30W
Dinuba, U.S.A. 84 J7 36 32N 119 23W
Dipalpur, Pakistan 42 D5 30 40N 73 39 E
Diplo, Pakistan 42 G3 24 35N 69 35 E
Dipolog, Phil. 37 C6 8 36N 123 20 E
Dir, Pakistan 40 B7 35 8N 71 59 E
Dire Dawa, Ethiopia 46 F3 9 35N 41 45 E
Diriamba, Nic. 88 D2 11 51N 86 19W
Dirk Hartog I., Australia 61 E1 25 50S 113 5 E
Dirranbandi, Australia 63 D4 28 33S 148 17 E
Disa, India 42 G5 24 18N 72 10 E
Disappointment, C., U.S.A. 82 C2 46 18N 124 5W
Disappointment, L., Australia 60 D3 23 20S 122 40 E
Disaster B., Australia 63 F4 37 15S 149 58 E
Discovery B., Australia 63 F3 38 10S 140 40 E
Disko, Greenland 4 C5 69 45N 53 30W
Disko Bugt, Greenland 4 C5 69 10N 52 0W
Diss, U.K. 11 E9 52 23N 1 7 E
Disteghil Sar, Pakistan 43 A6 36 20N 75 12 E
Distrito Federal □, Brazil 93 G9 15 45S 47 45W
Distrito Federal □, Mexico 87 D5 19 15N 99 10W
Diu, India 42 J4 20 45N 70 58 E
Dīvāndarreh, Iran 44 C5 35 55N 47 2 E
Divide, U.S.A. 82 D7 45 45N 112 45W
Dividing Ra., Australia 61 E2 27 45S 116 0 E
Divinópolis, Brazil 93 H10 20 10S 44 54W
Divnoye, Russia 25 E7 45 55N 43 21 E
Divo, Ivory C. 50 G4 5 48N 5 15W
Dīwāl Kol, Afghan. 42 B2 34 23N 67 52 E
Dixie Mt., U.S.A. 84 F6 39 55N 120 16W
Dixon, Calif., U.S.A. 84 G5 38 27N 121 49W
Dixon, Ill., U.S.A. 80 E10 41 50N 89 29W
Dixon Entrance, U.S.A. 68 C6 54 30N 132 0W
Dixville, Canada 79 A13 45 4N 71 46W
Diyālā →, Iraq 44 C5 33 14N 44 31 E
Diyarbakır, Turkey 25 G7 37 55N 40 18 E
Diyodar, India 42 G4 24 8N 71 50 E
Djakarta = Jakarta, Indonesia 37 G12 6 9S 106 49 E
Djamba, Angola 56 B1 16 45S 13 58 E
Djambala, Congo 52 E2 2 32S 14 30 E
Djanet, Algeria 50 D7 24 35N 9 32 E
Djawa = Jawa, Indonesia 37 G14 7 0S 110 0 E
Djelfa, Algeria 50 B6 34 40N 3 15 E
Djema, C.A.R. 54 A2 6 3N 25 15 E
Djerba, I. de, Tunisia 51 B8 33 50N 10 48 E
Djerid, Chott, Tunisia 50 B7 33 42N 8 30 E
Djibouti, Djibouti 46 E3 11 30N 43 5 E
**Djibouti ■**, Africa 46 E3 12 0N 43 0 E
Djolu, Dem. Rep. of the Congo 52 D4 0 35N 22 5 E
Djoum, Cameroon 52 D2 2 41N 12 35 E
Djourab, Erg du, Chad 51 E9 16 40N 18 50 E
Djugu, Dem. Rep. of the Congo 54 B3 1 55N 30 35 E
Djúpivogur, Iceland 8 D6 64 39N 14 17W
Dmitriya Lapteva, Proliv, Russia 27 B15 73 0N 140 0 E
Dnepr = Dnipro →, Ukraine 25 E5 46 30N 32 18 E
Dneprodzerzhinsk = Dniprodzerzhynsk, Ukraine 25 E5 48 32N 34 37 E
Dnepropetrovsk = Dnipropetrovsk, Ukraine 25 E6 48 30N 35 0 E
Dnestr = Dnister →, Europe 17 E16 46 18N 30 17 E
Dnestrovski = Belgorod, Russia 25 D6 50 35N 36 35 E
**Dnieper** = Dnipro →, Ukraine 25 E5 46 30N 32 18 E
Dniester = Dnister →, Europe 17 E16 46 18N 30 17 E
Dnipro →, Ukraine 25 E5 46 30N 32 18 E
Dniprodzerzhynsk, Ukraine 25 E5 48 32N 34 37 E
Dnipropetrovsk, Ukraine 25 E6 48 30N 35 0 E
Dnister →, Europe 17 E16 46 18N 30 17 E
Dnistrovskyy Lyman, Ukraine 17 E16 46 15N 30 17 E
Dno, Russia 24 C4 57 50N 29 58 E
Dnyapro = Dnipro →, Ukraine 25 E5 46 30N 32 18 E
Doaktown, Canada 71 C6 46 33N 66 8W
Doba, Chad 51 G9 8 40N 16 50 E
Dobandi, Pakistan 42 D2 31 13N 66 50 E
Dobbyn, Australia 62 B3 19 44S 140 2 E
Dobele, Latvia 9 H20 56 37N 23 16 E
Doberai, Jazirah, Indonesia 37 E8 1 25S 133 0 E
Doblas, Argentina 94 D3 37 5S 64 0W
Dobo, Indonesia 37 F8 5 45S 134 15 E
Doboj, Bos.-H. 21 B8 44 46N 18 4 E
Dobreta-Turnu Severin, Romania 17 F12 44 39N 22 41 E
Dobrich, Bulgaria 21 C12 43 37N 27 49 E
Dobruja, Europe 17 F15 44 30N 28 15 E
Dobrush, Belarus 17 B16 52 25N 31 22 E
Doc, Mui, Vietnam 38 D6 17 58N 106 30 E
Docker River, Australia 61 D4 24 52S 129 5 E
Doctor Arroyo, Mexico 86 C4 23 40N 100 11W
Doda, India 43 C6 33 10N 75 34 E
Doda, L., Canada 70 C4 49 25N 75 13W
**Dodecanese** = Dhodhekánisos, Greece 21 F12 36 35N 27 0 E
Dodge City, U.S.A. 81 G5 37 45N 100 1W
Dodge L., Canada 73 B7 59 50N 105 36W
Dodgeville, U.S.A. 80 D9 42 58N 90 8W
**Dodoma**, Tanzania 54 D4 6 8S 35 45 E
Dodoma □, Tanzania 54 D4 6 0S 36 0 E
Dodsland, Canada 73 C7 51 50N 108 45W
Dodson, U.S.A. 82 B9 48 24N 108 15W
Doesburg, Neths. 15 B6 52 1N 6 9 E
Doetinchem, Neths. 15 C6 51 59N 6 18 E
Dog Creek, Canada 72 C4 51 35N 122 14W
Dog L., Man., Canada 73 C9 51 2N 98 31W
Dog L., Ont., Canada 70 C2 48 48N 89 30W
Dogi, Afghan. 40 C3 32 20N 62 50 E
Dogran, Pakistan 42 D5 31 48N 73 35 E
Doğubayazıt, Turkey 44 B5 39 31N 44 5 E
**Doha** = Ad Dawḩah, Qatar 45 E6 25 15N 51 35 E
Dohazari, Bangla. 41 H18 22 10N 92 5 E
Dohrighat, India 43 F10 26 16N 83 31 E
Doi, Indonesia 37 D7 2 14N 127 49 E
Doi Luang, Thailand 38 C3 18 30N 101 0 E
Doi Saket, Thailand 38 C2 18 52N 99 9 E
Dois Irmãos, Sa., Brazil 93 E10 9 0S 42 30W
Dokkum, Neths. 15 A5 53 20N 5 59 E
Dokri, Pakistan 42 F3 27 25N 68 7 E
Dolak, Pulau, Indonesia 37 F9 8 0S 138 30 E
Dolbeau, Canada 71 C5 48 53N 72 18W
Dole, France 18 C6 47 7N 5 31 E
Dolgellau, U.K. 10 E4 52 45N 3 53W
Dolgelley = Dolgellau, U.K. 10 E4 52 45N 3 53W
Dollard, Neths. 15 A7 53 20N 7 10 E
Dolo, Ethiopia 46 G3 4 11N 42 3 E
**Dolomites** = Dolomiti, Italy 20 A4 46 23N 11 51 E
Dolomiti, Italy 20 A4 46 23N 11 51 E
Dolores, Argentina 94 D4 36 20S 57 40W
Dolores, Uruguay 94 C4 33 34S 58 15W
Dolores, U.S.A. 83 H9 37 28N 108 30W
Dolores →, U.S.A. 83 G9 38 49N 109 17W
Dolphin, C., Falk. Is. 96 G5 51 10S 59 0W
Dolphin and Union Str., Canada 68 B8 69 5N 114 45W
Dom Pedrito, Brazil 95 C5 31 0S 54 40W
Domariaganj →, India 43 F10 26 17N 83 44 E
Domasi, Malawi 55 F4 15 15S 35 22 E
Dombarovskiy, Russia 26 D6 50 46N 59 32 E
Dombås, Norway 9 E13 62 4N 9 8 E
Domel I. = Letsôk-aw Kyun, Burma 39 G2 11 30N 98 25 E
Domeyko, Chile 94 B1 29 0S 71 0W
Domeyko, Cordillera, Chile 94 A2 24 30S 69 0W
Dominador, Chile 94 A2 24 21S 69 20W
**Dominica ■**, W. Indies 89 C7 15 20N 61 20W
Dominica Passage, W. Indies 89 C7 15 10N 61 20W
**Dominican Rep. ■**, W. Indies 89 C5 19 0N 70 30W
Domodóssola, Italy 18 C8 46 7N 8 17 E
Domville, Mt., Australia 63 D5 28 1S 151 15 E
**Don →**, Russia 25 E6 47 4N 39 18 E
Don →, Aberds., U.K. 12 D6 57 11N 2 5W
Don →, S. Yorks., U.K. 10 D7 53 41N 0 52W
Don, C., Australia 60 B5 11 18S 131 46 E
Don Benito, Spain 19 C3 38 53N 5 51W
Dona Ana = Nhamaabué, Mozam. 55 F4 17 25S 35 5 E
Donaghadee, U.K. 13 B6 54 39N 5 33W
Donald, Australia 63 F3 36 23S 143 0 E
Donaldsonville, U.S.A. 81 K9 30 6N 90 59W
Donalsonville, U.S.A. 77 K3 31 3N 84 53W
Donau = Dunărea →, Europe 17 F15 45 20N 29 40 E
Donau →, Austria 15 D3 48 10N 17 0 E
Donauwörth, Germany 16 D6 48 43N 10 47 E
Doncaster, U.K. 10 D6 53 32N 1 6W
Dondo, Mozam. 55 F3 19 33S 34 46 E
Dondo, Teluk, Indonesia 37 D6 0 50N 120 30 E
Dondra Head, Sri Lanka 40 S12 5 55N 80 40 E
Donegal, Ireland 13 B3 54 39N 8 5W
**Donegal □**, Ireland 13 B4 54 53N 8 0W
Donegal B., Ireland 13 B3 54 31N 8 49W
Donets →, Russia 25 E7 47 33N 40 55 E
Donetsk, Ukraine 25 E6 48 0N 37 45 E
Dong Ba Thin, Vietnam 39 F7 12 8N 109 13 E
Dong Giam, Vietnam 38 C5 19 25N 105 31 E
Dong Ha, Vietnam 38 D6 16 55N 107 8 E
Dong Hene, Laos 38 D5 16 40N 105 18 E
Dong Hoi, Vietnam 38 D6 17 29N 106 36 E
Dong Khe, Vietnam 38 A6 22 26N 106 27 E
Dong Ujimqin Qi, China 34 B9 45 32N 116 55 E
Dong Van, Vietnam 38 A5 23 16N 105 22 E
Dong Xoai, Vietnam 39 G6 11 32N 106 55 E
Dongara, Australia 61 E1 29 14S 114 57 E
Dongbei, China 35 D13 45 0N 125 0 E
Dongchuan, China 32 D5 26 8N 103 1 E
Dongfang, China 38 C7 18 50N 108 33 E
Dongfeng, China 35 C13 42 40N 125 34 E
Donggala, Indonesia 37 E5 0 30S 119 40 E
Donggou, China 35 E13 39 52N 124 10 E
Dongguang, China 34 F9 37 50N 116 30 E
Dongjingcheng, China 35 B15 44 5N 129 10 E
Dongning, China 35 B16 44 2N 131 5 E
Dongola, Sudan 51 E12 19 9N 30 22 E
Dongping, China 34 G9 35 55N 116 20 E
Dongsheng, China 34 E6 39 50N 110 0 E
Dongtai, China 35 H11 32 51N 120 21 E
Dongting Hu, China 33 D6 29 18N 112 45 E
Donington, C., Australia 63 E2 34 45S 136 0 E
Doniphan, U.S.A. 81 G9 36 37N 90 50W
Dønna, Norway 8 C15 66 6N 12 30 E
Donna, U.S.A. 81 M5 26 9N 98 4W
Donnaconna, Canada 71 C5 46 41N 71 41W
Donnelly's Crossing, N.Z. 59 F4 35 42S 173 38 E
Donnybrook, Australia 61 F2 33 34S 115 48 E
Donnybrook, S. Africa 57 D4 29 59S 29 48 E
Donora, U.S.A. 78 F5 40 11N 79 52W
Donostia = Donostia-San Sebastián, Spain 19 A5 43 17N 1 58W
Donostia-San Sebastián, Spain 19 A5 43 17N 1 58W
Doon →, U.K. 12 F4 55 27N 4 39W
Dora, L., Australia 60 D3 22 0S 123 0 E
Dora Báltea →, Italy 18 D8 45 11N 8 3 E
Doran L., Canada 73 A7 61 13N 108 6W
Dorchester, U.K. 11 G5 50 42N 2 27W
Dorchester, C., Canada 69 B12 65 27N 77 27W
**Dordogne →**, France 18 D3 45 2N 0 36W
Dordrecht, Neths. 15 C4 51 48N 4 39 E
Dordrecht, S. Africa 56 E4 31 20S 27 3 E
Doré L., Canada 73 C7 54 46N 107 17W
Doré Lake, Canada 73 C7 54 38N 107 36W
Dori, Burkina Faso 50 F5 14 3N 0 2W
Doring →, S. Africa 56 E2 31 54S 18 39 E
Doringbos, S. Africa 56 E2 31 59S 19 16 E
Dorion, Canada 79 A10 45 23N 74 3W
Dornbirn, Austria 16 E5 47 25N 9 45 E
Dornie, U.K. 12 D3 57 17N 5 31W
Dornoch, U.K. 12 D4 57 53N 4 2W
Dornoch Firth, U.K. 12 D4 57 51N 4 4W
Dornogovĭ □, Mongolia 34 C6 44 0N 110 0 E
Dorohoi, Romania 17 E14 47 56N 26 23 E
Döröö Nuur, Mongolia 32 B4 48 0N 93 0 E
Dorr, Iran 45 C6 33 17N 50 38 E
Dorre I., Australia 61 E1 25 13S 113 12 E
Dorrigo, Australia 63 E5 30 20S 152 44 E
Dorris, U.S.A. 82 F3 41 58N 121 55W
Dorset, Canada 78 A6 45 14N 78 54W
Dorset, U.S.A. 78 E4 41 40N 80 40W
**Dorset □**, U.K. 11 G5 50 45N 2 26W
**Dortmund**, Germany 16 C4 51 30N 7 28 E
Doruma, Dem. Rep. of the Congo 54 B2 4 42N 27 33 E
Dorūneh, Iran 45 C8 35 10N 57 18 E
Dos Bahías, C., Argentina 96 E3 44 58S 65 32W
Dos Hermanas, Spain 19 D3 37 16N 5 55W
Dos Palos, U.S.A. 84 J6 36 59N 120 37W
Dosso, Niger 50 F6 13 0N 3 13 E
Dothan, U.S.A. 77 K3 31 13N 85 24W
Doty, U.S.A. 84 D3 46 38N 123 17W
Douai, France 18 A5 50 21N 3 4 E
**Douala**, Cameroon 52 D1 4 0N 9 45 E
Douarnenez, France 18 B1 48 6N 4 21W
Double Island Pt., Australia 63 D5 25 56S 153 11 E
Double Mountain Fork →, U.S.A. 81 J4 33 16N 100 0W
Doubs →, France 18 C6 46 53N 5 1 E
Doubtful Sd., N.Z. 59 L1 45 20S 166 49 E
Doubtless B., N.Z. 59 F4 34 55S 173 26 E
Douglas, S. Africa 56 D3 29 4S 23 46 E
**Douglas**, U.K. 10 C3 54 10N 4 28W
Douglas, Ariz., U.S.A. 83 L9 31 21N 109 33W
Douglas, Ga., U.S.A. 77 K4 31 31N 82 51W
Douglas, Wyo., U.S.A. 80 D2 42 45N 105 24W
Douglas Chan., Canada 72 C3 53 40N 129 20W
Douglas Pt., Canada 78 B3 44 19N 81 37W
Douglasville, U.S.A. 77 J3 33 45N 84 45W
Dounreay, U.K. 12 C5 58 35N 3 44W
Dourada, Serra, Brazil 93 F9 13 10S 48 45W
Dourados, Brazil 95 A5 22 9S 54 50W
Dourados →, Brazil 95 A5 21 58S 54 18W
Dourados, Serra dos, Brazil 95 A5 23 30S 53 30W
**Douro →**, Europe 19 B1 41 8N 8 40W

Dove →, U.K. 10 E6 52 51N 1 36W
Dove Creek, U.S.A. 83 H9 37 46N 108 54W
Dover, Australia 62 G4 43 18S 147 2 E
**Dover**, U.K. 11 F9 51 7N 1 19 E
**Dover**, Del., U.S.A. 76 F8 39 10N 75 32W
Dover, N.H., U.S.A. 79 C14 43 12N 70 56W
Dover, N.J., U.S.A. 79 F10 40 53N 74 34W
Dover, Ohio, U.S.A. 78 F3 40 32N 81 29W
Dover, Pt., Australia 61 F4 32 32S 125 32 E
Dover, Str. of, Europe 11 G9 51 0N 1 30 E
Dover-Foxcroft, U.S.A. 77 C11 45 11N 69 13W
Dover Plains, U.S.A. 79 E11 41 43N 73 35W
Dovey = Dyfi →, U.K. 11 E3 52 32N 4 3W
Dovrefjell, Norway 9 E13 62 15N 9 33 E
Dow Rūd, Iran 45 C6 33 28N 49 4 E
Dowa, Malawi 55 E3 13 38S 33 58 E
Dowagiac, U.S.A. 76 E2 41 59N 86 6W
Dowerin, Australia 61 F2 31 12S 117 2 E
Dowgha'i, Iran 45 B8 36 54N 58 32 E
Dowlatābād, Iran 45 D8 28 20N 56 40 E
**Down** □, U.K. 13 B5 54 23N 6 2W
Downey, Calif., U.S.A. 85 M8 33 56N 118 7W
Downey, Idaho, U.S.A. 82 E7 42 26N 112 7W
Downham Market, U.K. 11 E8 52 37N 0 23 E
Downieville, U.S.A. 84 F6 39 34N 120 50W
Downpatrick, U.K. 13 B6 54 20N 5 43W
Downpatrick Hd., Ireland 13 B2 54 20N 9 21W
Downsville, U.S.A. 79 D10 42 5N 74 50W
Downton, Mt., Canada 72 C4 52 42N 124 52W
Dowsārī, Iran 45 D8 28 25N 57 59 E
Doyle, U.S.A. 84 E6 40 2N 120 6W
Doylestown, U.S.A. 79 F9 40 21N 75 10W
Dozois, Rés., Canada 70 C4 47 30N 77 5W
Dra Khel, Pakistan 42 F2 27 58N 66 45 E
Drachten, Neths. 15 A6 53 7N 6 5 E
Drăgăşani, Romania 17 F13 44 39N 24 17 E
Dragichyn, Belarus 17 B13 52 15N 25 8 E
Dragoman, Prokhod, Bulgaria 21 C10 42 58N 22 53 E
Draguignan, France 18 E7 43 32N 6 27 E
Drain, U.S.A. 82 E2 43 40N 123 19W
Drake, U.S.A. 80 B4 47 55N 100 23W
Drake Passage, S. Ocean 5 B17 58 0S 68 0W
Drakensberg, S. Africa 57 E4 31 0S 28 0 E
Dráma, Greece 21 D11 41 9N 24 10 E
Drammen, Norway 9 G14 59 42N 10 12 E
Drangajökull, Iceland 8 C2 66 9N 22 15W
Dras, India 43 B6 34 25N 75 48 E
Drau = Drava →, Croatia 21 B8 45 33N 18 55 E
Drava →, Croatia 21 B8 45 33N 18 55 E
Drayton Valley, Canada 72 C6 53 12N 114 58W
Drenthe □, Neths. 15 B6 52 52N 6 40 E
Drepanum, C., Cyprus 23 E11 34 54N 32 19 E
Dresden, Canada 78 D2 42 35N 82 11W
**Dresden**, Germany 16 C7 51 3N 13 44 E
Dreux, France 18 B4 48 44N 1 23 E
Driffield, U.K. 10 C7 54 0N 0 26W
Driftwood, U.S.A. 78 E6 41 20N 78 8W
Driggs, U.S.A. 82 E8 43 44N 111 6W
Drina →, Bos.-H. 21 B8 44 53N 19 21 E
Drini →, Albania 21 C8 42 1N 19 38 E
Drøbak, Norway 9 G14 59 39N 10 39 E
Drochia, Moldova 17 D14 48 2N 27 48 E
Drogheda, Ireland 13 C5 53 43N 6 22W
Drogichin = Dragichyn, Belarus 17 B13 52 15N 25 8 E
Drogobych = Drohobych, Ukraine 17 D12 49 20N 23 30 E
Drohobych, Ukraine 17 D12 49 20N 23 30 E
Droichead Atha = Drogheda, Ireland 13 C5 53 43N 6 22W
Droichead Nua, Ireland 13 C5 53 11N 6 48W
Droitwich, U.K. 11 E5 52 16N 2 8W
Dromedary, C., Australia 63 F5 36 17S 150 10 E
Dromore, U.K. 13 B4 54 31N 7 28W
Dromore West, Ireland 13 B3 54 15N 8 52W
Dronfield, U.K. 10 D6 53 19N 1 27W
Dronten, Neths. 15 B5 52 32N 5 43 E
Drumbo, Canada 78 C4 43 16N 80 35W
Drumheller, Canada 72 C6 51 25N 112 40W
Drummond, U.S.A. 82 C7 46 40N 113 9W
Drummond I., U.S.A. 76 C4 46 1N 83 39W
Drummond Pt., Australia 63 E2 34 9S 135 16 E
Drummond Ra., Australia 62 C4 23 45S 147 10 E
Drummondville, Canada 70 C5 45 55N 72 25W
Drumright, U.S.A. 81 H6 35 59N 96 36W
Druskininkai, Lithuania 9 J20 54 3N 23 58 E
Drut →, Belarus 17 B16 53 8N 30 5 E
Druzhina, Russia 27 C15 68 14N 145 18 E
Dry Tortugas, U.S.A. 88 B3 24 38N 82 55W
Dryden, Canada 73 D10 49 47N 92 50W
Dryden, U.S.A. 79 D8 42 30N 76 18W
Drygalski I., Antarctica 5 C7 66 0S 92 0 E
Drysdale →, Australia 60 B4 13 59S 126 51 E
Drysdale I., Australia 62 A2 11 41S 136 0 E
Du Bois, U.S.A. 78 E6 41 8N 78 46W
Du Gué →, Canada 70 A5 57 21N 70 45W
Du Quoin, U.S.A. 80 G10 38 1N 89 14W
Duanesburg, U.S.A. 79 D10 42 45N 74 11W
Duaringa, Australia 62 C4 23 42S 149 42 E
Ḑubā, Si. Arabia 44 E2 27 10N 35 40 E
**Dubai** = Dubayy, U.A.E. 45 E7 25 18N 55 20 E
Dubăsari, Moldova 17 E15 47 15N 29 10 E
Dubăsari Vdkhr., Moldova 17 E15 47 30N 29 0 E
Dubawnt →, Canada 73 A8 64 33N 100 6W
Dubawnt, L., Canada 73 A8 63 4N 101 42W
Dubayy, U.A.E. 45 E7 25 18N 55 20 E
Dubbo, Australia 63 E4 32 11S 148 35 E
Dubele, Dem. Rep. of the Congo 54 B2 2 56N 29 35 E
**Dublin**, Ireland 13 C5 53 21N 6 15W
Dublin, Ga., U.S.A. 77 J4 32 32N 82 54W
Dublin, Tex., U.S.A. 81 J5 32 5N 98 21W
Dublin □, Ireland 13 C5 53 24N 6 20W
Dubno, Ukraine 17 C13 50 25N 25 45 E
Dubois, U.S.A. 82 D7 44 10N 112 14W
Dubossary = Dubăsari, Moldova 17 E15 47 15N 29 10 E
Dubossary Vdkhr. = Dubăsari Vdkhr., Moldova 17 E15 47 30N 29 0 E
Dubovka, Russia 25 E7 49 5N 44 50 E
Dubrajpur, India 43 H12 23 48N 87 25 E
Dubréka, Guinea 50 G3 9 46N 13 31W
Dubrovitsa = Dubrovytsya, Ukraine 17 C14 51 31N 26 35 E
**Dubrovnik**, Croatia 21 C8 42 39N 18 6 E
Dubrovytsya, Ukraine 17 C14 51 31N 26 35 E
Dubuque, U.S.A. 80 D9 42 30N 90 41W
Duchesne, U.S.A. 82 F8 40 10N 110 24W
Duchess, Australia 62 C2 21 20S 139 50 E
Ducie I., Pac. Oc. 65 K15 24 40S 124 48W
Duck →, U.S.A. 77 G2 36 2N 87 52W
Duck Cr. →, Australia 60 D2 22 37S 116 53 E
Duck Lake, Canada 73 C7 52 50N 106 16W
Duck Mountain Prov. Park, Canada 73 C8 51 45N 101 0W
Duckwall, Mt., U.S.A. 84 H6 37 58N 120 7W
Dudhi, India 41 G13 24 15N 83 10 E
Dudinka, Russia 27 C9 69 30N 86 13 E
Dudley, U.K. 11 E5 52 31N 2 5W
Dudwa, India 43 E9 28 30N 80 41 E
Duero = Douro →, Europe 19 B1 41 8N 8 40W
Dufftown, U.K. 12 D5 57 27N 3 8W
Dugi Otok, Croatia 16 G8 44 0N 15 3 E
Duifken Pt., Australia 62 A3 12 33S 141 38 E
**Duisburg**, Germany 16 C4 51 26N 6 45 E
Duiwelskloof, S. Africa 57 C5 23 42S 30 10 E
Dūkdamīn, Iran 45 C8 35 59N 57 43 E
Dukelský Průsmyk, Slovak Rep. 17 D11 49 25N 21 42 E
Dukhān, Qatar 45 E6 25 25N 50 50 E
Duki, Pakistan 40 D6 30 14N 68 25 E
Duku, Nigeria 51 F8 10 43N 10 43 E
Dulce, U.S.A. 83 H10 36 56N 107 0W
Dulce →, Argentina 94 C3 30 32S 62 33W
Dulce, G., Costa Rica 88 E3 8 40N 83 20W
Dulf, Iraq 44 C5 35 7N 45 51 E
Dulit, Banjaran, Malaysia 36 D4 3 15N 114 30 E
Duliu, China 34 E9 39 2N 116 55 E
Dullewala, Pakistan 42 D4 31 50N 71 25 E
Dulq Maghār, Syria 44 B3 36 22N 38 39 E
Duluth, U.S.A. 80 B8 46 47N 92 6W
Dum Dum, India 43 H13 22 39N 88 33 E
Dum Duma, India 41 F19 27 40N 95 40 E
Dūmā, Syria 47 B5 33 34N 36 24 E
Dumaguete, Phil. 37 C6 9 17N 123 15 E
Dumai, Indonesia 36 D2 1 35N 101 28 E
Dumaran, Phil. 37 B5 10 33N 119 50 E
Dumas, Ark., U.S.A. 81 J9 33 53N 91 29W
Dumas, Tex., U.S.A. 81 H4 35 52N 101 58W
Ḑumayr, Syria 47 B5 33 39N 36 42 E
Dumbarton, U.K. 12 F4 55 57N 4 33W
Dumbleyung, Australia 61 F2 33 17S 117 42 E
Dumfries, U.K. 12 F5 55 4N 3 37W
**Dumfries & Galloway** □, U.K. 12 F5 55 9N 3 58W
Dumka, India 43 G12 24 12N 87 15 E
Dumoine →, Canada 70 C4 46 13N 77 51W
Dumoine, L., Canada 70 C4 46 55N 77 55W
Dumraon, India 43 G11 25 33N 84 8 E
Dumyât, Egypt 51 B12 31 24N 31 48 E
Dún Dealgan = Dundalk, Ireland 13 B5 54 1N 6 24W
Dun Laoghaire, Ireland 13 C5 53 17N 6 8W
Duna = Dunărea →, Europe 17 F15 45 20N 29 40 E
Dunagiri, India 43 D8 30 31N 79 52 E
Dunaj = Dunărea →, Europe 17 F15 45 20N 29 40 E
Dunakeszi, Hungary 17 E10 47 37N 19 8 E
Dunărea →, Europe 17 F15 45 20N 29 40 E
Dunaújváros, Hungary 17 E10 46 58N 18 57 E
Dunav = Dunărea →, Europe 17 F15 45 20N 29 40 E
Dunay, Russia 30 C6 42 52N 132 22 E
Dunback, N.Z. 59 L3 45 23S 170 36 E
Dunbar, U.K. 12 E6 56 0N 2 31W
Dunblane, U.K. 12 E5 56 11N 3 58W
Duncan, Canada 72 D4 48 45N 123 40W
Duncan, Ariz., U.S.A. 83 K9 32 43N 109 6W
Duncan, Okla., U.S.A. 81 H6 34 30N 97 57W
Duncan, L., Canada 70 B4 53 29N 77 58W
Duncan L., Canada 72 A6 62 51N 113 58W
Duncan Town, Bahamas 88 B4 22 15N 75 45W
Duncannon, U.S.A. 78 F7 40 23N 77 2W
Duncansby Head, U.K. 12 C5 58 38N 3 1W
Duncansville, U.S.A. 78 F6 40 25N 78 26W
Dundalk, Canada 78 B4 44 10N 80 24W
Dundalk, Ireland 13 B5 54 1N 6 24W
Dundalk, U.S.A. 76 F7 39 16N 76 32W
Dundalk Bay, Ireland 13 C5 53 55N 6 15W
Dundas, Canada 78 C5 43 17N 79 59W
Dundas, L., Australia 61 F3 32 35S 121 50 E
Dundas I., Canada 72 C2 54 30N 130 50W
Dundas Str., Australia 60 B5 11 15S 131 35 E
Dundee, S. Africa 57 D5 28 11S 30 15 E
**Dundee**, U.K. 12 E6 56 28N 2 59W
Dundee, U.S.A. 78 D8 42 32N 76 59W
Dundee City □, U.K. 12 E6 56 30N 2 58W
Dundgovĭ □, Mongolia 34 B4 45 10N 106 0 E
Dundrum, U.K. 13 B6 54 16N 5 52W
Dundrum B., U.K. 13 B6 54 13N 5 47W
**Dunedin**, N.Z. 59 L3 45 50S 170 33 E
Dunedin, U.S.A. 77 L4 28 1N 82 47W
Dunedoo, Australia 63 E4 32 0S 149 25 E
Dunfermline, U.K. 12 E5 56 5N 3 27W
Dungannon, Canada 78 C3 43 51N 81 36W
Dungannon, U.K. 13 B5 54 31N 6 46W
Dungarpur, India 42 H5 23 52N 73 45 E
Dungarvan, Ireland 13 D4 52 5N 7 37W
Dungarvan Harbour, Ireland 13 D4 52 4N 7 35W
Dungeness, U.K. 11 G8 50 54N 0 59 E
Dungo, L. do, Angola 56 B2 17 15S 19 0 E
Dungog, Australia 63 E5 32 22S 151 46 E
Dungu, Dem. Rep. of the Congo 54 B2 3 40N 28 32 E
Dungun, Malaysia 39 K4 4 45N 103 25 E
Dunhua, China 35 C15 43 20N 128 14 E
Dunhuang, China 32 B4 40 8N 94 36 E
Dunk I., Australia 62 B4 17 59S 146 29 E
Dunkeld, Australia 63 E4 33 25S 149 29 E
Dunkeld, U.K. 12 E5 56 34N 3 35W
Dunkerque, France 18 A5 51 2N 2 20 E
Dunkery Beacon, U.K. 11 F4 51 9N 3 36W
**Dunkirk** = Dunkerque, France 18 A5 51 2N 2 20 E
Dunkirk, U.S.A. 78 D5 42 29N 79 20W
Dúnleary = Dun Laoghaire, Ireland 13 C5 53 17N 6 8W
Dunleer, Ireland 13 C5 53 50N 6 24W
Dunmanus B., Ireland 13 E2 51 31N 9 50W
Dunmanway, Ireland 13 E2 51 43N 9 6W
Dunmara, Australia 62 B1 16 42S 133 25 E
Dunmore, U.S.A. 79 E9 41 25N 75 38W
Dunmore Hd., Ireland 13 D1 52 10N 10 35W
Dunmore Town, Bahamas 88 A4 25 30N 76 39W
Dunn, U.S.A. 77 H6 35 19N 78 37W
Dunnet Hd., U.K. 12 C5 58 40N 3 21W
Dunning, U.S.A. 80 E4 41 50N 100 6W
Dunnville, Canada 78 D5 42 54N 79 36W
Dunolly, Australia 63 F3 36 51S 143 44 E
Dunoon, U.K. 12 F4 55 57N 4 56W
Dunphy, U.S.A. 82 F5 40 42N 116 31W
Duns, U.K. 12 F6 55 47N 2 20W
Dunseith, U.S.A. 80 A4 48 50N 100 3W
Dunsmuir, U.S.A. 82 F2 41 13N 122 16W
Dunstable, U.K. 11 F7 51 53N 0 32W
Dunstan Mts., N.Z. 59 L2 44 53S 169 35 E
Dunster, Canada 72 C5 53 8N 119 50W
Dunvegan L., Canada 73 A7 60 8N 107 10W
Duolun, China 34 C9 42 12N 116 28 E
Duong Dong, Vietnam 39 G4 10 13N 103 58 E
Dupree, U.S.A. 80 C4 45 4N 101 35W
Dupuyer, U.S.A. 82 B7 48 13N 112 30W
Duque de Caxias, Brazil 95 A7 22 45S 43 19W
Durack →, Australia 60 C4 15 33S 127 52 E
Durack Ra., Australia 60 C4 16 50S 127 40 E
Durance →, France 18 E6 43 55N 4 45 E
Durand, U.S.A. 80 C9 44 38N 91 58W
Durango, Mexico 86 C4 24 3N 104 39W
Durango, U.S.A. 83 H10 37 16N 107 53W
Durango □, Mexico 86 C4 25 0N 105 0W
Durant, Miss., U.S.A. 81 J10 33 4N 89 51W
Durant, Okla., U.S.A. 81 J6 33 59N 96 25W
Durazno, Uruguay 94 C4 33 25S 56 31W
Durazzo = Durrësi, Albania 21 D8 41 19N 19 28 E
**Durban**, S. Africa 57 D5 29 49S 31 1 E
Durbuy, Belgium 15 D5 50 21N 5 28 E
Düren, Germany 16 C4 50 48N 6 29 E
Durg, India 41 J12 21 15N 81 22 E
Durgapur, India 43 H12 23 30N 87 20 E
Durham, Canada 78 B4 44 10N 80 49W
**Durham**, U.K. 10 C6 54 47N 1 34W
Durham, Calif., U.S.A. 84 F5 39 39N 121 48W
Durham, N.C., U.S.A. 77 H6 35 59N 78 54W
Durham, N.H., U.S.A. 79 C14 43 8N 70 56W
Durham □, U.K. 10 C6 54 42N 1 45W
Ḑurmā, Si. Arabia 44 E5 24 37N 46 8 E
Durmitor, Montenegro, Yug. 21 C8 43 10N 19 0 E
Durness, U.K. 12 C4 58 34N 4 45W
**Durrësi**, Albania 21 D8 41 19N 19 28 E
Durrow, Ireland 13 D4 52 51N 7 24W
Dursey I., Ireland 13 E1 51 36N 10 12W
Dursunbey, Turkey 21 E13 39 35N 28 37 E
Duru, Dem. Rep. of the Congo 54 B2 4 14N 28 50 E
Durūz, Jabal ad, Jordan 47 C5 32 35N 36 40 E
D'Urville, Tanjung, Indonesia 37 E9 1 28S 137 54 E
D'Urville I., N.Z. 59 J4 40 50S 173 55 E
Duryea, U.S.A. 79 E9 41 20N 75 45W
Dushak, Turkmenistan 26 F7 37 13N 60 1 E
**Dushanbe**, Tajikistan 26 F7 38 33N 68 48 E
Dushore, U.S.A. 79 E8 41 31N 76 24W
Dusky Sd., N.Z. 59 L1 45 47S 166 30 E
Dussejour, C., Australia 60 B4 14 45S 128 13 E
**Düsseldorf**, Germany 16 C4 51 14N 6 47 E
Dutch Harbor, U.S.A. 68 C3 53 53N 166 32W
Dutlwe, Botswana 56 C3 23 58S 23 46 E
Dutton, Canada 78 D3 42 39N 81 30W
Dutton →, Australia 62 C3 20 44S 143 10 E
Duwayhin, Khawr, U.A.E. 45 E6 24 20N 51 25 E
Duyun, China 32 D5 26 18N 107 29 E
Duzdab = Zāhedān, Iran 45 D9 29 30N 60 50 E
Dvina, Severnaya →, Russia 24 B7 64 32N 40 30 E
Dvinsk = Daugavpils, Latvia 9 J22 55 53N 26 32 E
Dvinskaya Guba, Russia 24 B6 65 0N 39 0 E
Dwarka, India 42 H3 22 18N 69 8 E
Dwellingup, Australia 61 F2 32 43S 116 4 E
Dwight, Canada 78 A5 45 20N 79 1W
Dwight, U.S.A. 76 E1 41 5N 88 26W
Dyatlovo = Dzyatlava, Belarus 17 B13 53 28N 25 28 E
Dyce, U.K. 12 D6 57 13N 2 12W
Dyer, C., Canada 69 B13 66 40N 61 0W
Dyer Bay, Canada 78 A3 45 10N 81 20W
Dyer Plateau, Antarctica 5 D17 70 45S 65 30W
Dyersburg, U.S.A. 81 G10 36 3N 89 23W
Dyfi →, U.K. 11 E3 52 32N 4 3W
Dymer, Ukraine 17 C16 50 47N 30 18 E
Dysart, Australia 62 C4 22 32S 148 23 E
Dzamin Üüd = Borhoyn Tal, Mongolia 34 C6 43 50N 111 58 E
Dzerzhinsk, Russia 24 C7 56 14N 43 30 E
Dzhalinda, Russia 27 D13 53 26N 124 0 E
Dzhambul = Zhambyl, Kazakstan 26 E8 42 54N 71 22 E
Dzhankoy, Ukraine 25 E5 45 40N 34 20 E
Dzhezkazgan = Zhezqazghan, Kazakstan 26 E7 47 44N 67 40 E
Dzhizak = Jizzakh, Uzbekistan 26 E7 40 6N 67 50 E
Dzhugdzur, Khrebet, Russia 27 D14 57 30N 138 0 E
Dzhungarskiye Vorota = Dzungarian Gates, Kazakstan 32 B3 45 0N 82 0 E
Działdowo, Poland 17 B11 53 15N 20 15 E
Dzibilchaltun, Mexico 87 C7 21 5N 89 36W
Dzierżoniów, Poland 17 C9 50 45N 16 39 E
Dzilam de Bravo, Mexico 87 C7 21 24N 88 53W
Dzungaria = Junggar Pendi, China 32 B3 44 30N 86 0 E
Dzungarian Gates, Kazakstan 32 B3 45 0N 82 0 E
Dzuumod, Mongolia 32 B5 47 45N 106 58 E
Dzyarzhynsk, Belarus 17 B14 53 40N 27 1 E
Dzyatlava, Belarus 17 B13 53 28N 25 28 E


## E


Eabamet L., Canada 70 B2 51 30N 87 46W
Eads, U.S.A. 80 F3 38 29N 102 47W
Eagar, U.S.A. 83 J9 34 6N 109 17W
Eagle, Alaska, U.S.A. 68 B5 64 47N 141 12W
Eagle, Colo., U.S.A. 82 G10 39 39N 106 50W
Eagle →, Canada 71 B8 53 36N 57 26W
Eagle Butte, U.S.A. 80 C4 45 0N 101 10W
Eagle Grove, U.S.A. 80 D8 42 40N 93 54W
Eagle L., Canada 73 D10 49 42N 93 13W
Eagle L., Calif., U.S.A. 82 F3 40 39N 120 45W
Eagle L., Maine, U.S.A. 77 B11 46 20N 69 22W
Eagle Lake, Canada 78 A6 45 8N 78 29W
Eagle Lake, Maine, U.S.A. 77 B11 47 3N 68 36W
Eagle Lake, Tex., U.S.A. 81 L6 29 35N 96 20W
Eagle Mountain, U.S.A. 85 M11 33 49N 115 27W
Eagle Nest, U.S.A. 83 H11 36 33N 105 16W
Eagle Pass, U.S.A. 81 L4 28 43N 100 30W
Eagle Pk., U.S.A. 84 G7 38 10N 119 25W
Eagle Pt., Australia 60 C3 16 11S 124 23 E
Eagle River, Mich., U.S.A. 76 B1 47 24N 88 18W
Eagle River, Wis., U.S.A. 80 C10 45 55N 89 15W
Eaglehawk, Australia 63 F3 36 44S 144 15 E
Eagles Mere, U.S.A. 79 E8 41 25N 76 33W
Ealing, U.K. 11 F7 51 31N 0 20W
Ear Falls, Canada 73 C10 50 38N 93 13W
Earle, U.S.A. 81 H9 35 16N 90 28W
Earlimart, U.S.A. 85 K7 35 53N 119 16W
Earn →, U.K. 12 E5 56 21N 3 18W
Earn, L., U.K. 12 E4 56 23N 4 13W
Earnslaw, Mt., N.Z. 59 L2 44 32S 168 27 E
Earth, U.S.A. 81 H3 34 14N 102 24W
Easley, U.S.A. 77 H4 34 50N 82 36W
**East Anglia**, U.K. 10 E9 52 30N 1 0 E
East Angus, Canada 71 C5 45 30N 71 40W
East Aurora, U.S.A. 78 D6 42 46N 78 37W
East Ayrshire □, U.K. 12 F4 55 26N 4 11W
East Bengal, Bangla. 41 H17 24 0N 90 0 E
East Beskids = Vychodné Beskydy, Europe 17 D11 49 20N 22 0 E
East Brady, U.S.A. 78 F5 40 59N 79 36W
East C., N.Z. 59 G7 37 42S 178 35 E
East Chicago, U.S.A. 76 E2 41 38N 87 27W
**East China Sea**, Asia 33 D7 30 0N 126 0 E
East Coulee, Canada 72 C6 51 23N 112 27W
East Dereham, U.K. 11 E8 52 41N 0 57 E
East Dunbartonshire □, U.K. 12 F4 55 57N 4 13W
East Falkland, Falk. Is. 96 G5 51 30S 58 30W
East Grand Forks, U.S.A. 80 B6 47 56N 97 1W
East Greenwich, U.S.A. 79 E13 41 40N 71 27W
East Grinstead, U.K. 11 F8 51 7N 0 0 E
East Hartford, U.S.A. 79 E12 41 46N 72 39W
East Helena, U.S.A. 82 C8 46 35N 111 56W
East Indies, Asia 28 K15 0 0 120 0 E
East Kilbride, U.K. 12 F4 55 47N 4 11W
East Lansing, U.S.A. 76 D3 42 44N 84 29W
East Liverpool, U.S.A. 78 F4 40 37N 80 35W
East London, S. Africa 57 E4 33 0S 27 55 E
East Lothian □, U.K. 12 F6 55 58N 2 44W
East Main = Eastmain, Canada 70 B4 52 10N 78 30W
East Northport, U.S.A. 79 F11 40 53N 73 20W
East Orange, U.S.A. 79 F10 40 46N 74 13W
East Pacific Ridge, Pac. Oc. 65 J17 15 0S 110 0W
East Palestine, U.S.A. 78 F4 40 50N 80 33W
East Pine, Canada 72 B4 55 48N 120 12W
East Point, U.S.A. 77 J3 33 41N 84 27W
East Providence, U.S.A. 79 E13 41 49N 71 23W
East Pt., Canada 71 C7 46 27N 61 58W
East Renfrewshire □, U.K. 12 F4 55 46N 4 21W
East Retford = Retford, U.K. 10 D7 53 19N 0 56W
East Riding of Yorkshire □, U.K. 10 D7 53 55N 0 30W
East Rochester, U.S.A. 78 C7 43 7N 77 29W
East St. Louis, U.S.A. 80 F9 38 37N 90 9W
East Schelde = Oosterschelde →, Neths. 15 C4 51 33N 4 0 E
East Siberian Sea, Russia 27 B17 73 0N 160 0 E
East Stroudsburg, U.S.A. 79 E9 41 1N 75 11W
**East Sussex** □, U.K. 11 G8 50 56N 0 19 E
East Tawas, U.S.A. 76 C4 44 17N 83 29W
**East Timor** = Timor Timur □, Indonesia 37 F7 9 0S 125 0 E
East Toorale, Australia 63 E4 30 27S 145 28 E
East Walker →, U.S.A. 84 G7 38 52N 119 10W
East Windsor, U.S.A. 79 F10 40 17N 74 34W
Eastbourne, N.Z. 59 J5 41 19S 174 55 E
Eastbourne, U.K. 11 G8 50 46N 0 18 E
Eastend, Canada 73 D7 49 32N 108 50W
**Easter I.** = Pascua, I. de, Pac. Oc. 65 K17 27 0S 109 0W
Eastern □, Kenya 54 C4 0 0 38 30 E
Eastern □, Uganda 54 B3 1 50N 33 45 E
**Eastern Cape** □, S. Africa 56 E4 32 0S 26 0 E
Eastern Cr. →, Australia 62 C3 20 40S 141 35 E
Eastern Ghats, India 40 N11 14 0N 78 50 E
Eastern Group = Lau Group, Fiji 59 C9 17 0S 178 30W
Eastern Group, Australia 61 F3 33 30S 124 30 E
Eastern Transvaal = Mpumalanga □, S. Africa 57 B5 26 0S 30 0 E
Easterville, Canada 73 C9 53 8N 99 49W
Easthampton, U.S.A. 79 D12 42 16N 72 40W
Eastlake, U.S.A. 78 E3 41 40N 81 26W
Eastland, U.S.A. 81 J5 32 24N 98 49W
Eastleigh, U.K. 11 G6 50 58N 1 21W
Eastmain, Canada 70 B4 52 10N 78 30W
Eastmain →, Canada 70 B4 52 27N 78 26W
Eastman, Canada 79 A12 45 18N 72 19W
Eastman, U.S.A. 77 J4 32 12N 83 11W
Easton, Md., U.S.A. 76 F7 38 47N 76 5W
Easton, Pa., U.S.A. 79 F9 40 41N 75 13W
Easton, Wash., U.S.A. 84 C5 47 14N 121 11W
Eastpointe, U.S.A. 78 D2 42 27N 82 56W
Eastport, U.S.A. 77 C12 44 56N 67 0W
Eastsound, U.S.A. 84 B4 48 42N 122 55W
Eaton, U.S.A. 80 E2 40 32N 104 42W
Eatonia, Canada 73 C7 51 13N 109 25W
Eatonton, U.S.A. 77 J4 33 20N 83 23W
Eatontown, U.S.A. 79 F10 40 19N 74 4W
Eatonville, U.S.A. 84 D4 46 52N 122 16W
Eau Claire, U.S.A. 80 C9 44 49N 91 30W
Eau Claire, L. à l', Canada 70 A5 56 10N 74 25W
Ebbw Vale, U.K. 11 F4 51 46N 3 12W
Ebeltoft, Denmark 9 H14 56 12N 10 41 E
Ebensburg, U.S.A. 78 F6 40 29N 78 44W
Eberswalde-Finow, Germany 16 B7 52 50N 13 49 E
Ebetsu, Japan 30 C10 43 7N 141 34 E
Ebolowa, Cameroon 52 D2 2 55N 11 10 E
**Ebro** →, Spain 19 B6 40 43N 0 54 E
Eceabat, Turkey 21 D12 40 11N 26 21 E
Ech Cheliff, Algeria 50 A6 36 10N 1 20 E
Echigo-Sammyaku, Japan 31 F9 36 50N 139 50 E
Echizen-Misaki, Japan 31 G7 35 59N 135 57 E
Echo Bay, N.W.T., Canada 68 B8 66 5N 117 55W

Echo Bay, *Ont., Canada* 70 C3 46 29N 84 4W
Echoing →, *Canada* 70 B1 55 51N 92 5W
Echternach, *Lux.* 15 E6 49 49N 6 25 E
Echuca, *Australia* 63 F3 36 10S 144 20 E
Ecija, *Spain* 19 D3 37 30N 5 10W
Eclipse Is., *Australia* 60 B4 13 54S 126 19 E
Eclipse Sd., *Canada* 69 A11 72 38N 79 0W
**Ecuador** ■, *S. Amer.* 92 D3 2 0S 78 0W
Ed Damazin, *Sudan* 51 F12 11 46N 34 21 E
Ed Debba, *Sudan* 51 E12 18 0N 30 51 E
Ed Dueim, *Sudan* 51 F12 14 0N 32 10 E
Edam, *Canada* 73 C7 53 11N 108 46W
Edam, *Neths.* 15 B5 52 31N 5 3 E
Eday, *U.K.* 12 B6 59 11N 2 47W
Eddrachillis B., *U.K.* 12 C3 58 17N 5 14W
Eddystone Pt., *Australia* 62 G4 40 59S 148 20 E
Ede, *Neths.* 15 B5 52 4N 5 40 E
Edehon L., *Canada* 73 A9 60 25N 97 15W
Eden, *Australia* 63 F4 37 3S 149 55 E
Eden, *N.C., U.S.A.* 77 G6 36 29N 79 53W
Eden, *N.Y., U.S.A.* 78 D6 42 39N 78 55W
Eden, *Tex., U.S.A.* 81 K5 31 13N 99 51W
Eden →, *U.K.* 10 C4 54 57N 3 1W
Edenburg, *S. Africa* 56 D4 29 43S 25 58 E
Edendale, *S. Africa* 57 D5 29 39S 30 18 E
Edenderry, *Ireland* 13 C4 53 21N 7 4W
Edenhope, *Australia* 63 F3 37 4S 141 19 E
Edenton, *U.S.A.* 77 G7 36 4N 76 39W
Edenville, *S. Africa* 57 D4 27 37S 27 34 E
Eder →, *Germany* 16 C5 51 12N 9 28 E
Edgar, *U.S.A.* 80 E6 40 22N 97 58W
Edgartown, *U.S.A.* 79 E14 41 23N 70 31W
Edge Hill, *U.K.* 11 E6 52 8N 1 26W
Edgefield, *U.S.A.* 77 J5 33 47N 81 56W
Edgeley, *U.S.A.* 80 B5 46 22N 98 43W
Edgemont, *U.S.A.* 80 D3 43 18N 103 50W
Edgeøya, *Svalbard* 4 B9 77 45N 22 30 E
Édhessa, *Greece* 21 D10 40 48N 22 5 E
Edievale, *N.Z.* 59 L2 45 49S 169 22 E
Edina, *U.S.A.* 80 E8 40 10N 92 11W
Edinboro, *U.S.A.* 78 E4 41 52N 80 8W
Edinburg, *U.S.A.* 81 M5 26 18N 98 10W
**Edinburgh**, *U.K.* 12 F5 55 57N 3 13W
Edineţ, *Moldova* 17 D14 48 9N 27 18 E
**Edirne**, *Turkey* 21 D12 41 40N 26 34 E
Edison, *U.S.A.* 84 B4 48 33N 122 27W
Edithburgh, *Australia* 63 F2 35 5S 137 43 E
Edmeston, *U.S.A.* 79 D9 42 42N 75 15W
Edmond, *U.S.A.* 81 H6 35 39N 97 29W
Edmonds, *U.S.A.* 84 C4 47 49N 122 23W
Edmonton, *Australia* 62 B4 17 2S 145 46 E
**Edmonton**, *Canada* 72 C6 53 30N 113 30W
Edmund L., *Canada* 70 B1 54 45N 93 17W
Edmundston, *Canada* 71 C6 47 23N 68 20W
Edna, *U.S.A.* 81 L6 28 59N 96 39W
Edremit, *Turkey* 21 E12 39 34N 27 0 E
Edremit Körfezi, *Turkey* 21 E12 39 30N 26 45 E
Edson, *Canada* 72 C5 53 35N 116 28W
Eduardo Castex, *Argentina* 94 D3 35 50S 64 18W
Edward →, *Australia* 63 F3 35 5S 143 30 E
Edward, L., *Africa* 54 C2 0 25S 29 40 E
Edward River, *Australia* 62 A3 14 59S 141 26 E
Edward VII Land, *Antarctica* 5 E13 80 0S 150 0W
Edwards, *Calif., U.S.A.* 85 L9 34 55N 117 51W
Edwards, *N.Y., U.S.A.* 79 B9 44 20N 75 15W
Edwards Air Force Base, *U.S.A.* 85 L9 34 50N 117 40W
Edwards Plateau, *U.S.A.* 81 K4 30 45N 101 20W
Edwardsville, *U.S.A.* 79 E9 41 15N 75 56W
Edzo, *Canada* 72 A5 62 49N 116 4W
Eeklo, *Belgium* 15 C3 51 11N 3 33 E
Effingham, *U.S.A.* 76 F1 39 7N 88 33W
Égadi, Ísole, *Italy* 20 F5 37 55N 12 16 E
Egan Range, *U.S.A.* 82 G6 39 35N 114 55W
Eganville, *Canada* 78 A7 45 32N 77 5W
Eger = Cheb, *Czech Rep.* 16 C7 50 9N 12 28 E
Eger, *Hungary* 17 E11 47 53N 20 27 E
Egersund, *Norway* 9 G12 58 26N 6 1 E
Egg L., *Canada* 73 B7 55 5N 105 30W
Éghezée, *Belgium* 15 D4 50 35N 4 55 E
Egmont, *Canada* 72 D4 49 45N 123 56W
Egmont, C., *N.Z.* 59 H4 39 16S 173 45 E
Egmont, Mt., *N.Z.* 59 H5 39 17S 174 5 E
Egra, *India* 43 J12 21 54N 87 32 E
Eğridir, *Turkey* 25 G5 37 52N 30 51 E
Eğridir Gölü, *Turkey* 25 G5 37 53N 30 50 E
Egvekinot, *Russia* 27 C19 66 19N 179 50W
**Egypt** ■, *Africa* 51 C12 28 0N 31 0 E
Ehime □, *Japan* 31 H6 33 30N 132 40 E
Ehrenberg, *U.S.A.* 85 M12 33 36N 114 31W
Eibar, *Spain* 19 A4 43 11N 2 28W
Eidsvold, *Australia* 63 D5 25 25S 151 12 E
Eidsvoll, *Norway* 9 F14 60 19N 11 14 E
Eifel, *Germany* 16 C4 50 15N 6 50 E
Eiffel Flats, *Zimbabwe* 55 F3 18 20S 30 0 E
Eigg, *U.K.* 12 E2 56 54N 6 10W
Eighty Mile Beach, *Australia* 60 C3 19 30S 120 40 E
Eil, *Somali Rep.* 46 F4 8 0N 49 50 E
Eil, L., *U.K.* 12 E3 56 51N 5 16W
Eildon, *Australia* 63 F4 37 14S 145 55 E
Eildon, L., *Australia* 63 F4 37 10S 146 0 E
Einasleigh, *Australia* 62 B3 18 32S 144 5 E
Einasleigh →, *Australia* 62 B3 17 30S 142 17 E
Eindhoven, *Neths.* 15 C5 51 26N 5 28 E
**Eire** = Ireland ■, *Europe* 13 C4 53 50N 7 52W
Eiríksjökull, *Iceland* 8 D3 64 46N 20 24W
Eirunepé, *Brazil* 92 E5 6 35S 69 53W
Eisenach, *Germany* 16 C6 50 58N 10 19 E
Eisenerz, *Austria* 16 E8 47 32N 14 54 E
Eivissa, *Spain* 22 C7 38 54N 1 26 E
Ejutla, *Mexico* 87 D5 16 34N 96 44W
Ekalaka, *U.S.A.* 80 C2 45 53N 104 33W
Eketahuna, *N.Z.* 59 J5 40 38S 175 43 E
Ekibastuz, *Kazakstan* 26 D8 51 50N 75 10 E
Ekoli, *Dem. Rep. of the Congo* 54 C1 0 23S 24 13 E
Eksjö, *Sweden* 9 H16 57 40N 14 58 E
Ekwan →, *Canada* 70 B3 53 12N 82 15W
Ekwan Pt., *Canada* 70 B3 53 16N 82 7W
El Aaiún, *W. Sahara* 50 C3 27 9N 13 12W
El Abanico, *Chile* 94 D1 37 20S 71 31W
El 'Agrûd, *Egypt* 47 E3 30 14N 34 24 E
**El Alamein**, *Egypt* 51 B11 30 48N 28 58 E
El 'Aqaba, W. →, *Egypt* 47 E2 30 7N 33 54 E
El Arīḥā, *West Bank* 47 D4 31 52N 35 27 E
El 'Arîsh, *Egypt* 47 D2 31 8N 33 50 E
El 'Arîsh, W. →, *Egypt* 47 D2 31 8N 33 47 E
El Asnam = Ech Cheliff, *Algeria* 50 A6 36 10N 1 20 E
El Bayadh, *Algeria* 50 B6 33 40N 1 1 E
El Bluff, *Nic.* 88 D3 11 59N 83 40W
El Brûk, W. →, *Egypt* 47 E2 30 15N 33 50 E
El Cajon, *U.S.A.* 85 N10 32 48N 116 58W
El Campo, *U.S.A.* 81 L6 29 12N 96 16W
El Centro, *U.S.A.* 85 N11 32 48N 115 34W
El Cerro, *Bolivia* 92 G6 17 30S 61 40W
El Compadre, *Mexico* 85 N10 32 20N 116 14W
El Cuy, *Argentina* 96 D3 39 55S 68 25W
El Cuyo, *Mexico* 87 C7 21 30N 87 40W
El Daheir, *Egypt* 47 D3 31 13N 34 10 E
El Dátil, *Mexico* 86 B2 30 7N 112 15W
El Dere, *Somali Rep.* 46 G4 3 50N 47 8 E
El Descanso, *Mexico* 85 N10 32 12N 116 58W
El Desemboque, *Mexico* 86 A2 30 30N 112 57W
El Diviso, *Colombia* 92 C3 1 22N 78 14W
El Djouf, *Mauritania* 50 D4 20 0N 9 0W
El Dorado, *Ark., U.S.A.* 81 J8 33 12N 92 40W
El Dorado, *Kans., U.S.A.* 81 G6 37 49N 96 52W
El Dorado, *Venezuela* 92 B6 6 55N 61 37W
El Escorial, *Spain* 19 B3 40 35N 4 7W
El Faiyûm, *Egypt* 51 C12 29 19N 30 50 E
El Fâsher, *Sudan* 51 F11 13 33N 25 26 E
El Ferrol = Ferrol, *Spain* 19 A1 43 29N 8 15W
El Fuerte, *Mexico* 86 B3 26 30N 108 40W
El Gal, *Somali Rep.* 46 E5 10 58N 50 20 E
El Geneina = Al Junaynah, *Sudan* 51 F10 13 27N 22 45 E
El Gîza, *Egypt* 51 C12 30 0N 31 10 E
El Goléa, *Algeria* 50 B6 30 30N 2 50 E
El Iskandarîya, *Egypt* 51 B11 31 13N 29 58 E
El Istiwa'iya, *Sudan* 51 G11 5 0N 28 0 E
El Jadida, *Morocco* 50 B4 33 11N 8 17W
El Jardal, *Honduras* 88 D2 14 54N 88 50W
El Kabrît, G., *Egypt* 47 F2 29 42N 33 16 E
El Khârga, *Egypt* 51 C12 25 30N 30 33 E
El Khartûm, *Sudan* 51 E12 15 31N 32 35 E
El Kuntilla, *Egypt* 47 E3 30 1N 34 45 E
El Maestrazgo, *Spain* 19 B5 40 30N 0 25W
El Mahalla el Kubra, *Egypt* 51 B12 31 0N 31 0 E
El Mansûra, *Egypt* 51 B12 31 0N 31 19 E
El Medano, *Canary Is.* 22 F3 28 3N 16 32W
El Milagro, *Argentina* 94 C2 30 59S 65 59W
El Minyâ, *Egypt* 51 C12 28 7N 30 33 E
El Monte, *U.S.A.* 85 L8 34 4N 118 1W
El Obeid, *Sudan* 51 F12 13 8N 30 10 E
El Odaiya, *Sudan* 51 F11 12 8N 28 12 E
El Oro, *Mexico* 87 D4 19 48N 100 8W
El Oued, *Algeria* 50 B7 33 20N 6 58 E
El Palmito, Presa, *Mexico* 86 B3 25 40N 105 30W
El Paso, *U.S.A.* 83 L10 31 45N 106 29W
El Paso Robles, *U.S.A.* 84 K6 35 38N 120 41W
El Portal, *U.S.A.* 84 H7 37 41N 119 47W
El Porvenir, *Mexico* 86 A3 31 15N 105 51W
El Prat de Llobregat, *Spain* 19 B7 41 18N 2 3 E
El Progreso, *Honduras* 88 C2 15 26N 87 51W
El Pueblito, *Mexico* 86 B3 29 3N 105 4W
El Pueblo, *Canary Is.* 22 F2 28 36N 17 47W
El Puerto de Santa María, *Spain* 19 D2 36 36N 6 13W
El Qâhira, *Egypt* 51 B12 30 1N 31 14 E
El Qantara, *Egypt* 47 E1 30 51N 32 20 E
El Quseima, *Egypt* 47 E3 30 40N 34 15 E
El Real, *Panama* 92 B3 8 0N 77 40W
El Reno, *U.S.A.* 81 H6 35 32N 97 57W
El Rio, *U.S.A.* 85 L7 34 14N 119 10W
El Roque, Pta., *Canary Is.* 22 F4 28 10N 15 25W
El Rosarito, *Mexico* 86 B2 28 38N 114 4W
El Saheira, W. →, *Egypt* 47 E2 30 5N 33 25 E
El Salto, *Mexico* 86 C3 23 47N 105 22W
**El Salvador** ■, *Cent. Amer.* 88 D2 13 50N 89 0W
El Sauce, *Nic.* 88 D2 13 0N 86 40W
El Sueco, *Mexico* 86 B3 29 54N 106 24W
El Suweis, *Egypt* 51 C12 29 58N 32 31 E
El Tamarâni, W. →, *Egypt* 47 E3 30 7N 34 43 E
El Thamad, *Egypt* 47 F3 29 40N 34 28 E
El Tigre, *Venezuela* 92 B6 8 44N 64 15W
El Tîh, Gebal, *Egypt* 47 F2 29 40N 33 50 E
El Tîna, Khalîg, *Egypt* 47 D1 31 10N 32 40 E
El Tofo, *Chile* 94 B1 29 22S 71 18W
El Tránsito, *Chile* 94 B1 28 52S 70 17W
El Tûr, *Egypt* 44 D2 28 14N 33 36 E
El Turbio, *Argentina* 96 G2 51 45S 72 5W
El Uqsur, *Egypt* 51 C12 25 41N 32 38 E
El Venado, *Mexico* 86 C4 22 56N 101 10W
El Vergel, *Mexico* 86 B3 26 28N 106 22W
El Vigía, *Venezuela* 92 B4 8 38N 71 39W
El Wabeira, *Egypt* 47 F2 29 34N 33 6 E
El Wak, *Kenya* 54 B5 2 49N 40 56 E
El Wuz, *Sudan* 51 E12 15 5N 30 7 E
**Elat**, *Israel* 47 F3 29 30N 34 56 E
Elâzığ, *Turkey* 25 G6 38 37N 39 14 E
**Elba**, *Italy* 20 C4 42 46N 10 17 E
Elba, *U.S.A.* 77 K2 31 25N 86 4W
Elbasani, *Albania* 21 D9 41 9N 20 9 E
Elbe, *U.S.A.* 84 D4 46 45N 122 10W
**Elbe** →, *Europe* 16 B5 53 50N 9 0 E
**Elbert, Mt.**, *U.S.A.* 83 G10 39 7N 106 27W
Elberton, *U.S.A.* 77 H4 34 7N 82 52W
Elbeuf, *France* 18 B4 49 17N 1 2 E
Elbidtan, *Turkey* 44 B3 38 13N 37 12 E
Elbing = Elbląg, *Poland* 17 A10 54 10N 19 25 E
Elbląg, *Poland* 17 A10 54 10N 19 25 E
Elbow, *Canada* 73 C7 51 7N 106 35W
**Elbrus**, *Asia* 25 F7 43 21N 42 30 E
Elburz Mts. = Alborz, Reshteh-ye Kūhhā-ye, *Iran* 45 C7 36 0N 52 0 E
Elche, *Spain* 19 C5 38 15N 0 42W
Elcho I., *Australia* 62 A2 11 55S 135 45 E
Elda, *Spain* 19 C5 38 29N 0 47W
Elde →, *Germany* 16 B6 53 7N 11 15 E
Eldon, *Mo., U.S.A.* 80 F8 38 21N 92 35W
Eldon, *Wash., U.S.A.* 84 C3 47 33N 123 3W
Eldora, *U.S.A.* 80 D8 42 22N 93 5W
Eldorado, *Argentina* 95 B5 26 28S 54 43W
Eldorado, *Canada* 78 B7 44 35N 77 31W
Eldorado, *Mexico* 86 C3 24 20N 107 22W
Eldorado, *Ill., U.S.A.* 76 G1 37 49N 88 26W
Eldorado, *Tex., U.S.A.* 81 K4 30 52N 100 36W
Eldorado Springs, *U.S.A.* 81 G8 37 52N 94 1W
Eldoret, *Kenya* 54 B4 0 30N 35 17 E
Eldred, *U.S.A.* 78 E6 41 58N 78 23W
Elea, C., *Cyprus* 23 D13 35 19N 34 4 E
Eleanora, Pk., *Australia* 61 F3 32 57S 121 9 E
Electra, *U.S.A.* 74 D7 34 2N 98 55W
Elefantes →, *Mozam.* 57 C5 24 10S 32 40 E
Elektrostal, *Russia* 24 C6 55 41N 38 32 E
Elephant Butte Reservoir, *U.S.A.* 83 K10 33 9N 107 11W
Elephant I., *Antarctica* 5 C18 61 0S 55 0W
Eleuthera, *Bahamas* 88 B4 25 0N 76 20W
Elgin, *Canada* 79 B8 44 36N 76 13W
Elgin, *U.K.* 12 D5 57 39N 3 19W
Elgin, *Ill., U.S.A.* 76 D1 42 2N 88 17W
Elgin, *N. Dak., U.S.A.* 80 B4 46 24N 101 51W
Elgin, *Oreg., U.S.A.* 82 D5 45 34N 117 55W
Elgin, *Tex., U.S.A.* 81 K6 30 21N 97 22W
Elgon, Mt., *Africa* 54 B3 1 10N 34 30 E
Eliase, *Indonesia* 37 F8 8 21S 130 48 E
Elim, *S. Africa* 56 E2 34 35S 19 45 E
Elisabethville = Lubumbashi, *Dem. Rep. of the Congo* 55 E2 11 40S 27 28 E
Elista, *Russia* 25 E7 46 16N 44 14 E
Elizabeth, *Australia* 63 E2 34 42S 138 41 E
Elizabeth, *N.J., U.S.A.* 79 F10 40 39N 74 13W
Elizabeth, *N.J., U.S.A.* 79 F10 40 40N 74 13W
Elizabeth City, *U.S.A.* 77 G7 36 18N 76 14W
Elizabethton, *U.S.A.* 77 G4 36 21N 82 13W
Elizabethtown, *Ky., U.S.A.* 76 G3 37 42N 85 52W
Elizabethtown, *N.Y., U.S.A.* 79 B11 44 13N 73 36W
Elizabethtown, *Pa., U.S.A.* 79 F8 40 9N 76 36W
Ełk, *Poland* 17 B12 53 50N 22 21 E
Elk →, *Canada* 72 C5 49 11N 115 14W
Elk →, *U.S.A.* 77 H2 34 46N 87 16W
Elk City, *U.S.A.* 81 H5 35 25N 99 25W
Elk Creek, *U.S.A.* 84 F4 39 36N 122 32W
Elk Grove, *U.S.A.* 84 G5 38 25N 121 22W
Elk Island Nat. Park, *Canada* 72 C6 53 35N 112 59W
Elk Lake, *Canada* 70 C3 47 40N 80 25W
Elk Point, *Canada* 73 C6 53 54N 110 55W
Elk River, *Idaho, U.S.A.* 82 C5 46 47N 116 11W
Elk River, *Minn., U.S.A.* 80 C8 45 18N 93 35W
Elkedra →, *Australia* 62 C2 21 8S 136 22 E
Elkhart, *Ind., U.S.A.* 76 E3 41 41N 85 58W
Elkhart, *Kans., U.S.A.* 81 G4 37 0N 101 54W
Elkhorn, *Canada* 73 D8 49 59N 101 14W
Elkhorn →, *U.S.A.* 80 E6 41 8N 96 19W
Elkhovo, *Bulgaria* 21 C12 42 10N 26 35 E
Elkin, *U.S.A.* 77 G5 36 15N 80 51W
Elkins, *U.S.A.* 76 F6 38 55N 79 51W
Elkland, *U.S.A.* 78 E7 41 59N 77 19W
Elko, *Canada* 72 D5 49 20N 115 10W
Elko, *U.S.A.* 82 F6 40 50N 115 46W
Elkton, *U.S.A.* 78 C1 43 49N 83 11W
Ell, L., *Australia* 61 E4 29 13S 127 46 E
Ellef Ringnes I., *Canada* 4 B2 78 30N 102 2W
Ellen, Mt., *U.S.A.* 79 B12 44 9N 72 56W
Ellenburg, *U.S.A.* 79 B11 44 54N 73 48W
Ellendale, *U.S.A.* 80 B5 46 0N 98 32W
Ellensburg, *U.S.A.* 82 C3 46 59N 120 34W
Ellenville, *U.S.A.* 79 E10 41 43N 74 24W
Ellery, Mt., *Australia* 63 F4 37 28S 148 47 E
Ellesmere, L., *N.Z.* 59 M4 47 47S 172 28 E
**Ellesmere I.**, *Canada* 4 B4 79 30N 80 0W
Ellesmere Port, *U.K.* 10 D5 53 17N 2 54W
**Ellice Is.** = Tuvalu ■, *Pac. Oc.* 64 H9 8 0S 178 0 E
Ellicottville, *U.S.A.* 78 D6 42 17N 78 40W
Elliot, *Australia* 62 B1 17 33S 133 32 E
Elliot, *S. Africa* 57 E4 31 22S 27 48 E
Elliot Lake, *Canada* 70 C3 46 25N 82 35W
Elliotdale = Xhora, *S. Africa* 57 E4 31 55S 28 38 E
Ellis, *U.S.A.* 80 F5 38 56N 99 34W
Elliston, *Australia* 63 E1 33 39S 134 53 E
Ellisville, *U.S.A.* 81 K10 31 36N 89 12W
Ellon, *U.K.* 12 D6 57 22N 2 4W
Ellore = Eluru, *India* 41 L12 16 48N 81 8 E
Ellsworth, *Kans., U.S.A.* 80 F5 38 44N 98 14W
Ellsworth, *Maine, U.S.A.* 77 C11 44 33N 68 25W
Ellsworth Land, *Antarctica* 5 D16 76 0S 89 0W
Ellsworth Mts., *Antarctica* 5 D16 78 30S 85 0W
Ellwood City, *U.S.A.* 78 F4 40 52N 80 17W
Elma, *Canada* 73 D9 49 52N 95 55W
Elma, *U.S.A.* 84 D3 47 0N 123 25W
Elmalı, *Turkey* 25 G4 36 44N 29 56 E
Elmhurst, *U.S.A.* 76 E2 41 53N 87 56W
Elmira, *Canada* 78 C4 43 36N 80 33W
Elmira, *U.S.A.* 78 D8 42 6N 76 48W
Elmira Heights, *U.S.A.* 78 D8 42 8N 76 50W
Elmore, *Australia* 63 F3 36 30S 144 37 E
Elmore, *U.S.A.* 85 M11 33 7N 115 49W
Elmshorn, *Germany* 16 B5 53 43N 9 40 E
Elmvale, *Canada* 78 B5 44 35N 79 52W
Elora, *Canada* 78 C4 43 41N 80 26W
Eloúnda, *Greece* 23 D7 35 16N 25 42 E
Eloy, *U.S.A.* 83 K8 32 45N 111 33W
Elrose, *Canada* 73 C7 51 12N 108 0W
Elsie, *U.S.A.* 84 E3 45 52N 123 36W
Elsinore = Helsingør, *Denmark* 9 H15 56 2N 12 35 E
Eltham, *N.Z.* 59 H5 39 26S 174 19 E
Eluru, *India* 41 L12 16 48N 81 8 E
Elvas, *Portugal* 19 C2 38 50N 7 10W
Elverum, *Norway* 9 F14 60 53N 11 34 E
Elvire →, *Australia* 60 C4 17 51S 128 11 E
Elvire, Mt., *Australia* 61 E2 29 22S 119 36 E
Elwell, L., *U.S.A.* 82 B8 48 22N 111 17W
Elwood, *Ind., U.S.A.* 76 E3 40 17N 85 50W
Elwood, *Nebr., U.S.A.* 80 E5 40 36N 99 52W
Elx = Elche, *Spain* 19 C5 38 15N 0 42W
Ely, *U.K.* 11 E8 52 24N 0 16 E
Ely, *Minn., U.S.A.* 80 B9 47 55N 91 51W
Ely, *Nev., U.S.A.* 82 G6 39 15N 114 54W
Elyria, *U.S.A.* 78 E2 41 22N 82 7W
Emāmrūd, *Iran* 45 B7 36 30N 55 0 E
Emba, *Kazakstan* 26 E6 48 50N 58 8 E
Emba →, *Kazakstan* 25 E9 46 55N 53 28 E
Embarcación, *Argentina* 94 A3 23 10S 64 0W
Embarras Portage, *Canada* 73 B6 58 27N 111 28W
Embetsu, *Japan* 30 B10 44 44N 141 47 E
Embi = Emba, *Kazakstan* 26 E6 48 50N 58 8 E
Embi = Emba →, *Kazakstan* 25 E9 46 55N 53 28 E
Embóna, *Greece* 23 C9 36 13N 27 51 E
Embrun, *France* 18 D7 44 34N 6 30 E
Embu, *Kenya* 54 C4 0 32S 37 38 E
Emden, *Germany* 16 B4 53 21N 7 12 E
Emerald, *Australia* 62 C4 23 32S 148 10 E
Emerson, *Canada* 73 D9 49 0N 97 10W
Emet, *Turkey* 21 E13 39 20N 29 15 E
Emi Koussi, *Chad* 51 E9 19 45N 18 55 E
Eminabad, *Pakistan* 42 C6 32 2N 74 8 E
Emine, Nos, *Bulgaria* 21 C12 42 40N 27 56 E
Emlenton, *U.S.A.* 78 E5 41 11N 79 43W
Emmaus, *U.S.A.* 79 F9 40 32N 75 30W
Emmeloord, *Neths.* 15 B5 52 44N 5 46 E
Emmen, *Neths.* 15 B6 52 48N 6 57 E
Emmet, *Australia* 62 C3 24 45S 144 30 E
Emmetsburg, *U.S.A.* 80 D7 43 7N 94 41W
Emmett, *Idaho, U.S.A.* 82 E5 43 52N 116 30W
Emmett, *Mich., U.S.A.* 78 D2 42 59N 82 46W
Emmonak, *U.S.A.* 68 B3 62 46N 164 30W
Emo, *Canada* 73 D10 48 38N 93 50W
Empalme, *Mexico* 86 B2 28 1N 110 49W
Empangeni, *S. Africa* 57 D5 28 50S 31 52 E
Empedrado, *Argentina* 94 B4 28 0S 58 46W
Emperor Seamount Chain, *Pac. Oc.* 64 D9 40 0N 170 0 E
Emporia, *Kans., U.S.A.* 80 F6 38 25N 96 11W
Emporia, *Va., U.S.A.* 77 G7 36 42N 77 32W
Emporium, *U.S.A.* 78 E6 41 31N 78 14W
Empress, *Canada* 73 C7 50 57N 110 0W
Empty Quarter = Rub' al Khālī, *Si. Arabia* 46 D4 18 0N 48 0 E
Ems →, *Germany* 16 B4 53 20N 7 12 E
Emsdale, *Canada* 78 A5 45 32N 79 19W
Emu, *China* 35 C15 43 40N 128 6 E
Emu Park, *Australia* 62 C5 23 13S 150 50 E
'En 'Avrona, *Israel* 47 F4 29 43N 35 0 E
En Nahud, *Sudan* 51 F11 12 45N 28 25 E
Ena, *Japan* 31 G8 35 25N 137 25 E
Enana, *Namibia* 56 B2 17 30S 16 23 E
Enaratoli, *Indonesia* 37 E9 3 55S 136 21 E
Enard B., *U.K.* 12 C3 58 5N 5 20W
Enare = Inarijärvi, *Finland* 8 B22 69 0N 28 0 E
Encampment, *U.S.A.* 82 F10 41 12N 106 47W
Encantadas, Serra, *Brazil* 95 C5 30 40S 53 0W
Encarnación, *Paraguay* 95 B4 27 15S 55 50W
Encarnación de Diaz, *Mexico* 86 C4 21 30N 102 13W
Encinitas, *U.S.A.* 85 M9 33 3N 117 17W
Encino, *U.S.A.* 83 J11 34 39N 105 28W
Encounter B., *Australia* 63 F2 35 45S 138 45 E
Endako, *Canada* 72 C3 54 6N 125 2W
Ende, *Indonesia* 37 F6 8 45S 121 40 E
Endeavour Str., *Australia* 62 A3 10 45S 142 0 E
Enderbury I., *Kiribati* 64 H10 3 8S 171 5W
Enderby, *Canada* 72 C5 50 35N 119 10W
Enderby I., *Australia* 60 D2 20 35S 116 30 E
Enderby Land, *Antarctica* 5 C5 66 0S 53 0 E
Enderlin, *U.S.A.* 80 B6 46 38N 97 36W
Endicott, *U.S.A.* 79 D8 42 6N 76 4W
Endwell, *U.S.A.* 79 D8 42 6N 76 2W
Endyalgout I., *Australia* 60 B5 11 40S 132 35 E
Eneabba, *Australia* 61 E2 29 49S 115 16 E
Enewetak Atoll, *Marshall Is.* 64 F8 11 30N 162 15 E
Enez, *Turkey* 21 D12 40 45N 26 5 E
Enfield, *Canada* 71 D7 44 56N 63 32W
Enfield, *Conn., U.S.A.* 79 E12 41 58N 72 36W
Enfield, *N.H., U.S.A.* 79 C12 43 39N 72 9W
Engadin, *Switz.* 18 C9 46 45N 10 10 E
Engaño, C., *Dom. Rep.* 89 C6 18 30N 68 20W
Engaño, C., *Phil.* 37 A6 18 35N 122 23 E
Engaru, *Japan* 30 B11 44 3N 143 31 E
Engcobo, *S. Africa* 57 E4 31 37S 28 0 E
Engels, *Russia* 25 D8 51 28N 46 6 E
Engemann L., *Canada* 73 B7 58 0N 106 55W
Enggano, *Indonesia* 36 F2 5 20S 102 40 E
England, *U.S.A.* 81 H9 34 33N 91 58W
**England** □, *U.K.* 10 D7 53 0N 2 0W
Englee, *Canada* 71 B8 50 45N 56 5W
Englehart, *Canada* 70 C4 47 49N 79 52W
Englewood, *U.S.A.* 80 F2 39 39N 104 59W
English →, *Canada* 73 C10 50 35N 93 30W
English Bazar = Ingraj Bazar, *India* 43 G13 24 58N 88 10 E
English Channel, *Europe* 11 G6 50 0N 2 0W
English River, *Canada* 70 C1 49 14N 91 0W
Enid, *U.S.A.* 81 G6 36 24N 97 53W
Enkhuizen, *Neths.* 15 B5 52 42N 5 17 E
Enna, *Italy* 20 F6 37 34N 14 16 E
Ennadai, *Canada* 73 A8 61 8N 100 53W
Ennadai L., *Canada* 73 A8 61 0N 101 0W
Ennedi, *Chad* 51 E10 17 15N 22 0 E
Enngonia, *Australia* 63 D4 29 21S 145 50 E
Ennis, *Ireland* 13 D3 52 51N 8 59W
Ennis, *Mont., U.S.A.* 82 D8 45 21N 111 44W
Ennis, *Tex., U.S.A.* 81 J6 32 20N 96 38W
Enniscorthy, *Ireland* 13 D5 52 30N 6 34W
Enniskillen, *U.K.* 13 B4 54 21N 7 39W
Ennistimon, *Ireland* 13 D2 52 57N 9 17W
Enns →, *Austria* 16 D8 48 14N 14 32 E
Enontekiö, *Finland* 8 B20 68 23N 23 37 E
Enosburg Falls, *U.S.A.* 79 B12 44 55N 72 48W
Enriquillo, L., *Dom. Rep.* 89 C5 18 20N 72 5W
Enschede, *Neths.* 15 B6 52 13N 6 53 E
Ensenada, *Argentina* 94 C4 34 55S 57 55W
Ensenada, *Mexico* 86 A1 31 50N 116 50W
Ensenada de los Muertos, *Mexico* 86 C2 23 59N 109 50W
Ensiola, Pta. de n', *Spain* 22 B9 39 7N 2 55 E
**Entebbe**, *Uganda* 54 B3 0 4N 32 28 E
Enterprise, *Canada* 72 A5 60 47N 115 45W
Enterprise, *Ala., U.S.A.* 77 K3 31 19N 85 51W
Enterprise, *Oreg., U.S.A.* 82 D5 45 25N 117 17W
Entre Ríos, *Bolivia* 94 A3 21 30S 64 25W
Entre Ríos □, *Argentina* 94 C4 30 30S 58 30W
Entroncamento, *Portugal* 19 C1 39 28N 8 28W
Enugu, *Nigeria* 50 G7 6 20N 7 30 E
Enumclaw, *U.S.A.* 84 C5 47 12N 121 59W
Eólie, Ís., *Italy* 20 E6 38 30N 14 57 E
Epe, *Neths.* 15 B5 52 21N 5 59 E
Épernay, *France* 18 B5 49 3N 3 56 E
Ephesus, *Turkey* 21 F12 37 55N 27 22 E
Ephraim, *U.S.A.* 82 G8 39 22N 111 35W
Ephrata, *Pa., U.S.A.* 79 F8 40 11N 76 11W
Ephrata, *Wash., U.S.A.* 82 C4 47 19N 119 33W
Épinal, *France* 18 B7 48 10N 6 27 E
Episkopi, *Cyprus* 23 E11 34 40N 32 54 E
Episkopí, *Greece* 23 D6 35 20N 24 20 E
Episkopi Bay, *Cyprus* 23 E11 34 35N 32 50 E
Epsom, *U.K.* 11 F7 51 19N 0 16W
Epukiro, *Namibia* 56 C2 21 40S 19 9 E
**Equatorial Guinea** ■, *Africa* 52 D1 2 0N 8 0 E
Er Rahad, *Sudan* 51 F12 12 45N 30 32 E
Er Rif, *Morocco* 50 A5 35 1N 4 1W

## F

Fraile Muerto, Uruguay 95 C5 32 31S 54 32W
Framingham, U.S.A. 79 D13 42 17N 71 25W
Franca, Brazil 93 H9 20 33S 47 30W
Francavilla Fontana, Italy 21 D7 40 32N 17 35 E
**France** ■, Europe 18 C5 47 0N 3 0 E
Frances, Australia 63 F3 36 41S 140 55 E
Frances →, Canada 72 A3 60 16N 129 10W
Frances L., Canada 72 A3 61 23N 129 30W
Franceville, Gabon 52 E2 1 40S 13 32 E
Franche-Comté, France 18 C6 46 50N 5 55 E
Francis Case, L., U.S.A. 80 D5 43 4N 98 34W
Francisco Beltrão, Brazil 95 B5 26 5S 53 4W
Francisco I. Madero, Coahuila, Mexico 86 B4 25 48N 103 18W
Francisco I. Madero, Durango, Mexico 86 C4 24 32N 104 22W
Francistown, Botswana 57 C4 21 7S 27 33 E
François, Canada 71 C8 47 35N 56 45W
François L., Canada 72 C3 54 0N 125 30W
Franeker, Neths. 15 A5 53 12N 5 33 E
Frankford, Canada 78 B7 44 12N 77 36W
Frankfort, S. Africa 57 D4 27 17S 28 30 E
Frankfort, Ind., U.S.A. 76 E2 40 17N 86 31W
Frankfort, Kans., U.S.A. 80 F6 39 42N 96 25W
**Frankfort**, Ky., U.S.A. 76 F3 38 12N 84 52W
Frankfort, N.Y., U.S.A. 79 C9 43 2N 75 4W
Frankfurt, Brandenburg, Germany 16 B8 52 20N 14 32 E
**Frankfurt**, Hessen, Germany 16 C5 50 7N 8 41 E
Fränkische Alb, Germany 16 D6 49 10N 11 23 E
Frankland →, Australia 61 G2 35 0S 116 48 E
Franklin, Ky., U.S.A. 77 G2 36 43N 86 35W
Franklin, La., U.S.A. 81 L9 29 48N 91 30W
Franklin, Mass., U.S.A. 79 D13 42 5N 71 24W
Franklin, N.H., U.S.A. 79 C13 43 27N 71 39W
Franklin, Nebr., U.S.A. 80 E5 40 6N 98 57W
Franklin, Pa., U.S.A. 78 E5 41 24N 79 50W
Franklin, Va., U.S.A. 77 G7 36 41N 76 56W
Franklin, W. Va., U.S.A. 76 F6 38 39N 79 20W
Franklin B., Canada 68 B7 69 45N 126 0W
Franklin D. Roosevelt L., U.S.A. 82 B4 48 18N 118 9W
Franklin I., Antarctica 5 D11 76 10S 168 30 E
Franklin L., U.S.A. 82 F6 40 25N 115 22W
Franklin Mts., Canada 68 B7 65 0N 125 0W
Franklin Str., Canada 68 A10 72 0N 96 0W
Franklinton, U.S.A. 81 K9 30 51N 90 9W
Franklinville, U.S.A. 78 D6 42 20N 78 27W
Franks Pk., U.S.A. 82 E9 43 58N 109 18W
Frankston, Australia 63 F4 38 8S 145 8 E
Frantsa Iosifa, Zemlya, Russia 26 A6 82 0N 55 0 E
Franz, Canada 70 C3 48 25N 84 30W
**Franz Josef Land** = Frantsa Iosifa, Zemlya, Russia 26 A6 82 0N 55 0 E
Fraser, U.S.A. 78 D2 42 32N 82 57W
Fraser →, B.C., Canada 72 D4 49 7N 123 11W
Fraser →, Nfld., Canada 71 A7 56 39N 62 10W
Fraser, Mt., Australia 61 E2 25 35S 118 20 E
Fraser I., Australia 63 D5 25 15S 153 10 E
Fraser Lake, Canada 72 C4 54 0N 124 50W
Fraserburg, S. Africa 56 E3 31 55S 21 30 E
Fraserburgh, U.K. 12 D6 57 42N 2 1W
Fraserdale, Canada 70 C3 49 55N 81 37W
Fray Bentos, Uruguay 94 C4 33 10S 58 15W
Fredericia, Denmark 9 J13 55 34N 9 45 E
Frederick, Md., U.S.A. 76 F7 39 25N 77 25W
Frederick, Okla., U.S.A. 81 H5 34 23N 99 1W
Frederick, S. Dak., U.S.A. 80 C5 45 50N 98 31W
Fredericksburg, Pa., U.S.A. 79 F8 40 27N 76 26W
Fredericksburg, Tex., U.S.A. 81 K5 30 16N 98 52W
**Fredericksburg**, Va., U.S.A. 76 F7 38 18N 77 28W
Fredericktown, Mo., U.S.A. 81 G9 37 34N 90 18W
Fredericktown, Ohio, U.S.A. 78 F2 40 29N 82 33W
Frederico I. Madero, Presa, Mexico 86 B3 28 7N 105 40W
Frederico Westphalen, Brazil 95 B5 27 22S 53 24W
Fredericton, Canada 71 C6 45 57N 66 40W
Fredericton Junction, Canada 71 C6 45 41N 66 40W
Frederikshåb, Greenland 4 C5 62 0N 49 43W
Frederikshavn, Denmark 9 H14 57 28N 10 31 E
Frederiksted, Virgin Is. 89 C7 17 43N 64 53W
Fredonia, Ariz., U.S.A. 83 H7 36 57N 112 32W
Fredonia, Kans., U.S.A. 81 G7 37 32N 95 49W
Fredonia, N.Y., U.S.A. 78 D5 42 26N 79 20W
Fredrikstad, Norway 9 G14 59 13N 10 57 E
**Free State** □, S. Africa 56 D4 28 30S 27 0 E
Freehold, U.S.A. 79 F10 40 16N 74 17W
Freel Peak, U.S.A. 84 G7 38 52N 119 54W
Freeland, U.S.A. 79 E9 41 1N 75 54W
Freels, C., Canada 71 C9 49 15N 53 30W
Freeman, Calif., U.S.A. 85 K9 35 35N 117 53W
Freeman, S. Dak., U.S.A. 80 D6 43 21N 97 26W
Freeport, Bahamas 88 A4 26 30N 78 47W
Freeport, Ill., U.S.A. 80 D10 42 17N 89 36W
Freeport, N.Y., U.S.A. 79 F11 40 39N 73 35W
Freeport, Ohio, U.S.A. 78 F3 40 12N 81 15W
Freeport, Pa., U.S.A. 78 F5 40 41N 79 41W
Freeport, Tex., U.S.A. 81 L7 28 57N 95 21W
**Freetown**, S. Leone 50 G3 8 30N 13 17W
Frégate, L., Canada 70 B5 53 15N 74 45W
Fregenal de la Sierra, Spain 19 C2 38 10N 6 39W
Freibourg = Fribourg, Switz. 18 C7 46 49N 7 9 E
Freiburg, Germany 16 E4 47 59N 7 51 E
Freire, Chile 96 D2 38 54S 72 38W
Freirina, Chile 94 B1 28 30S 71 10W
Freising, Germany 16 D6 48 24N 11 45 E
Freistadt, Austria 16 D8 48 30N 14 30 E
Fréjus, France 18 E7 43 25N 6 44 E
Fremantle, Australia 61 F2 32 7S 115 47 E
Fremont, Calif., U.S.A. 84 H4 37 32N 121 57W
Fremont, Mich., U.S.A. 76 D3 43 28N 85 57W
Fremont, Nebr., U.S.A. 80 E6 41 26N 96 30W
Fremont, Ohio, U.S.A. 76 E4 41 21N 83 7W
Fremont →, U.S.A. 83 G8 38 24N 110 42W
French Camp, U.S.A. 84 H5 37 53N 121 16W
French Creek →, U.S.A. 78 E5 41 24N 79 50W
**French Guiana** ■, S. Amer. 93 C8 4 0N 53 0W
French Pass, N.Z. 59 J4 40 55S 173 55 E
**French Polynesia** ■, Pac. Oc. 65 K13 20 0S 145 0W
Frenchman Cr. →, N. Amer. 82 B10 48 31N 107 10W
Frenchman Cr. →, U.S.A. 80 E4 40 14N 100 50W
Fresco →, Brazil 93 E8 7 15S 51 30W
Freshfield, C., Antarctica 5 C10 68 25S 151 10 E
Fresnillo, Mexico 86 C4 23 10N 103 0W
Fresno, U.S.A. 84 J7 36 44N 119 47W
Fresno Reservoir, U.S.A. 82 B9 48 36N 109 57W
Frew →, Australia 62 C2 20 0S 135 38 E
Frewsburg, U.S.A. 78 D5 42 3N 79 10W
Freycinet Pen., Australia 62 G4 42 10S 148 25 E
Fria, C., Namibia 56 B1 18 0S 12 0 E
Friant, U.S.A. 84 J7 36 59N 119 43W
Frías, Argentina 94 B2 28 40S 65 5W
Fribourg, Switz. 18 C7 46 49N 7 9 E
Friday Harbor, U.S.A. 84 B3 48 32N 123 1W
Friedens, U.S.A. 78 F6 40 3N 78 59W
Friedrichshafen, Germany 16 E5 47 39N 9 30 E
Friendly Is. = Tonga ■, Pac. Oc. 59 D11 19 50S 174 30W
Friendship, U.S.A. 78 D6 42 12N 78 8W
Friesland □, Neths. 15 A5 53 5N 5 50 E
Frio →, U.S.A. 81 L5 28 26N 98 11W
Frio, C., Brazil 90 F6 22 50S 41 50W
Friona, U.S.A. 81 H3 34 38N 102 43W
Fritch, U.S.A. 81 H4 35 38N 101 36W
Frobisher B., Canada 69 B13 62 30N 66 0W
Frobisher Bay = Iqaluit, Canada 69 B13 63 44N 68 31W
Frobisher L., Canada 73 B7 56 20N 108 15W
Frohavet, Norway 8 E13 64 0N 9 30 E
Frome, U.K. 11 F5 51 14N 2 19W
Frome →, U.K. 11 G5 50 41N 2 6W
Frome, L., Australia 63 E2 30 45S 139 45 E
Front Range, U.S.A. 74 C5 40 25N 105 45W
Front Royal, U.S.A. 76 F6 38 55N 78 12W
Frontera, Canary Is. 22 G2 27 47N 17 59W
Frontera, Mexico 87 D6 18 30N 92 40W
Fronteras, Mexico 86 A3 30 56N 109 31W
Frosinone, Italy 20 D5 41 38N 13 19 E
Frostburg, U.S.A. 76 F6 39 39N 78 56W
Frostisen, Norway 8 B17 68 14N 17 10 E
Frøya, Norway 8 E13 63 43N 8 40 E
**Frunze** = Bishkek, Kyrgyzstan 26 E8 42 54N 74 46 E
Frutal, Brazil 93 H9 20 0S 49 0W
Frýdek-Místek, Czech Rep. 17 D10 49 40N 18 20 E
Fryeburg, U.S.A. 79 B14 44 1N 70 59W
Fu Xian = Wafangdian, China 35 E11 39 38N 121 58 E
Fu Xian, China 34 G5 36 0N 109 20 E
Fucheng, China 34 F9 37 50N 116 10 E
Fuchou = Fuzhou, China 33 D6 26 5N 119 16 E
Fuchū, Japan 31 G6 34 34N 133 14 E
Fuencaliente, Canary Is. 22 F2 28 28N 17 50W
Fuencaliente, Pta., Canary Is. 22 F2 28 27N 17 51W
Fuengirola, Spain 19 D3 36 32N 4 41W
Fuentes de Oñoro, Spain 19 B2 40 33N 6 52W
Fuerte →, Mexico 86 B3 25 50N 109 25W
Fuerte Olimpo, Paraguay 94 A4 21 0S 57 51W
Fuerteventura, Canary Is. 22 F6 28 30N 14 0W
Fufeng, China 34 G5 34 22N 108 0 E
Fugou, China 34 G8 34 3N 114 25 E
Fugu, China 34 E6 39 2N 111 3 E
Fuhai, China 32 B3 47 2N 87 25 E
Fuḩaymī, Iraq 44 C4 34 16N 42 10 E
Fuji, Japan 31 G9 35 9N 138 39 E
Fuji-San, Japan 31 G9 35 22N 138 44 E
Fuji-yoshida, Japan 31 G9 35 30N 138 46 E
Fujian □, China 33 D6 26 0N 118 0 E
Fujinomiya, Japan 31 G9 35 10N 138 40 E
Fujisawa, Japan 31 G9 35 22N 139 29 E
**Fujiyama, Mt.** = Fuji-San, Japan 31 G9 35 22N 138 44 E
Fukien = Fujian □, China 33 D6 26 0N 118 0 E
Fukuchiyama, Japan 31 G7 35 19N 135 9 E
Fukue-Shima, Japan 31 H4 32 40N 128 45 E
Fukui, Japan 31 F8 36 5N 136 10 E
Fukui □, Japan 31 G8 36 0N 136 12 E
**Fukuoka**, Japan 31 H5 33 39N 130 21 E
Fukuoka □, Japan 31 H5 33 30N 131 0 E
Fukushima, Japan 30 F10 37 44N 140 28 E
Fukushima □, Japan 30 F10 37 30N 140 15 E
Fukuyama, Japan 31 G6 34 35N 133 20 E
Fulda, Germany 16 C5 50 32N 9 40 E
Fulda →, Germany 16 C5 51 25N 9 39 E
Fulford Harbour, Canada 84 B3 48 47N 123 27W
Fullerton, Calif., U.S.A. 85 M9 33 53N 117 56W
Fullerton, Nebr., U.S.A. 80 E6 41 22N 97 58W
Fulongquan, China 35 B13 44 20N 124 42 E
Fulton, Mo., U.S.A. 80 F9 38 52N 91 57W
Fulton, N.Y., U.S.A. 79 C8 43 19N 76 25W
Funabashi, Japan 31 G10 35 45N 140 0 E
**Funchal**, Madeira 22 D3 32 38N 16 54W
Fundación, Colombia 92 A4 10 31N 74 11W
Fundão, Portugal 19 B2 40 8N 7 30W
Fundy, B. of, Canada 71 D6 45 0N 66 0W
Funing, Hebei, China 35 E10 39 53N 119 12 E
Funing, Jiangsu, China 35 H10 33 45N 119 50 E
Funiu Shan, China 34 H7 33 30N 112 20 E
Funtua, Nigeria 50 F7 11 30N 7 18 E
Fuping, Hebei, China 34 E8 38 48N 114 12 E
Fuping, Shaanxi, China 34 G5 34 42N 109 10 E
Furano, Japan 30 C11 43 21N 142 23 E
Furāt, Nahr al →, Asia 44 D5 31 0N 47 25 E
Fūrg, Iran 45 D7 28 18N 55 13 E
Furnás, Spain 22 B8 39 3N 1 32 E
Furnas, Représa de, Brazil 95 A6 20 50S 45 30W
Furneaux Group, Australia 62 G4 40 10S 147 50 E
Furqlus, Syria 47 A6 34 36N 37 8 E
Fürstenwalde, Germany 16 B8 52 22N 14 3 E
Fürth, Germany 16 D6 49 28N 10 59 E
Furukawa, Japan 30 E10 38 34N 140 58 E
Fury and Hecla Str., Canada 69 B11 69 56N 84 0W
Fusagasuga, Colombia 92 C4 4 21N 74 22W
Fushan, Shandong, China 35 F11 37 30N 121 15 E
Fushan, Shanxi, China 34 G6 35 58N 111 51 E
Fushun, China 35 D12 41 50N 123 56 E
Fusong, China 35 C14 42 20N 127 15 E
Futuna, Wall. & F. Is. 59 B8 14 25S 178 20 E
Fuxin, China 35 C11 42 5N 121 48 E
Fuyang, China 34 H8 33 0N 115 48 E
Fuyang He →, China 34 E9 38 12N 117 0 E
Fuyu, China 35 B13 45 12N 124 43 E
**Fuzhou**, China 33 D6 26 5N 119 16 E
Fylde, U.K. 10 D5 53 50N 2 58W
Fyn, Denmark 9 J14 55 20N 10 30 E
Fyne, L., U.K. 12 F3 55 59N 5 23W

# G

Gabela, Angola 52 G2 11 0S 14 24 E
Gabès, Tunisia 51 B8 33 53N 10 2 E
Gabès, G. de, Tunisia 51 B8 34 0N 10 30 E
**Gabon** ■, Africa 52 E2 0 10S 10 0 E
**Gaborone**, Botswana 56 C4 24 45S 25 57 E
Gabriels, U.S.A. 79 B10 44 26N 74 12W
Gābrīk, Iran 45 E8 25 44N 58 28 E
Gabrovo, Bulgaria 21 C11 42 52N 25 19 E
Gāch Sār, Iran 45 B6 36 7N 51 19 E
Gachsārān, Iran 45 D6 30 15N 50 45 E
Gadag, India 40 M9 15 30N 75 45 E
Gadap, Pakistan 42 G2 25 5N 67 28 E
Gadarwara, India 43 H8 22 50N 78 50 E
Gadhada, India 42 J4 22 0N 71 35 E
Gadra, Pakistan 42 G4 25 40N 70 38 E
Gadsden, U.S.A. 77 H3 34 1N 86 1W
Gadwal, India 40 L10 16 10N 77 50 E
Gaffney, U.S.A. 77 H5 35 5N 81 39W
Gafsa, Tunisia 50 B7 34 24N 8 43 E
Gagaria, India 42 G4 25 43N 70 46 E
Gagnoa, Ivory C. 50 G4 6 56N 5 16W
Gagnon, Canada 71 B6 51 50N 68 5W
Gagnon, L., Canada 73 A6 62 3N 110 27W
Gahini, Rwanda 54 C3 1 50S 30 30 E
Gahmar, India 43 G10 25 27N 83 49 E
Gai Xian = Gaizhou, China 35 D12 40 22N 122 20 E
Gaïdhouronísi, Greece 23 E7 34 53N 25 41 E
Gail, U.S.A. 81 J4 32 46N 101 27W
Gaillimh = Galway, Ireland 13 C2 53 17N 9 3W
Gaines, U.S.A. 78 E7 41 46N 77 35W
Gainesville, Fla., U.S.A. 77 L4 29 40N 82 20W
Gainesville, Ga., U.S.A. 77 H4 34 18N 83 50W
Gainesville, Mo., U.S.A. 81 G8 36 36N 92 26W
Gainesville, Tex., U.S.A. 81 J6 33 38N 97 8W
Gainsborough, U.K. 10 D7 53 24N 0 46W
Gairdner, L., Australia 63 E2 31 30S 136 0 E
Gairloch, L., U.K. 12 D3 57 43N 5 45W
Gaizhou, China 35 D12 40 22N 122 20 E
Gaj →, Pakistan 42 F2 26 26N 67 21 E
Gakuch, Pakistan 43 A5 36 7N 73 45 E
Galán, Cerro, Argentina 94 B2 25 55S 66 52W
Galana →, Kenya 54 C5 3 9S 40 8 E
**Galápagos**, Pac. Oc. 90 D1 0 0 91 0W
Galashiels, U.K. 12 F6 55 37N 2 49W
Galați, Romania 17 F15 45 27N 28 2 E
Galatina, Italy 21 D8 40 10N 18 10 E
Galax, U.S.A. 77 G5 36 40N 80 56W
Galcaio, Somali Rep. 46 F4 6 30N 47 30 E
Galdhøpiggen, Norway 9 F12 61 38N 8 18 E
Galeana, Mexico 86 C4 24 50N 100 4W
Galeana, Nuevo León, Mexico 86 A3 24 50N 100 4W
Galela, Indonesia 37 D7 1 50N 127 49 E
Galena, U.S.A. 68 B4 64 44N 156 56W
Galera Point, Trin. & Tob. 89 D7 10 8N 61 0W
Galesburg, U.S.A. 80 E9 40 57N 90 22W
Galeton, U.S.A. 78 E7 41 44N 77 39W
Galich, Russia 24 C7 58 22N 42 24 E
**Galicia** □, Spain 19 A2 42 43N 7 45W
Galilee = Hagalil, Israel 47 C4 32 53N 35 18 E
Galilee, L., Australia 62 C4 22 20S 145 50 E
**Galilee, Sea of** = Yam Kinneret, Israel 47 C4 32 45N 35 35 E
Galinoporni, Cyprus 23 D13 35 31N 34 18 E
Galion, U.S.A. 78 F2 40 44N 82 47W
Galiuro Mts., U.S.A. 83 K8 32 30N 110 20W
Galiwinku, Australia 62 A2 12 2S 135 34 E
Gallan Hd., U.K. 12 C1 58 15N 7 2W
Gallatin, U.S.A. 77 G2 36 24N 86 27W
Galle, Sri Lanka 40 R12 6 5N 80 10 E
Gállego →, Spain 19 B5 41 39N 0 51W
Gallegos →, Argentina 96 G3 51 35S 69 0W
Galley Hd., Ireland 13 E3 51 32N 8 55W
Gallinas, Pta., Colombia 92 A4 12 28N 71 40W
**Gallipoli** = Gelibolu, Turkey 21 D12 40 28N 26 43 E
Gallípoli, Italy 21 D8 40 3N 17 58 E
Gallipolis, U.S.A. 76 F4 38 49N 82 12W
Gällivare, Sweden 8 C19 67 9N 20 40 E
Galloo I., U.S.A. 79 C8 43 55N 76 25W
Galloway, U.K. 12 F4 55 1N 4 29W
Galloway, Mull of, U.K. 12 G4 54 39N 4 52W
Gallup, U.S.A. 83 J9 35 32N 108 45W
Galoya, Sri Lanka 40 Q12 8 10N 80 55 E
Galt, U.S.A. 84 G5 38 15N 121 18W
Galty Mts., Ireland 13 D3 52 22N 8 10W
Galtymore, Ireland 13 D3 52 21N 8 11W
Galva, U.S.A. 80 E9 41 10N 90 3W
Galveston, U.S.A. 81 L7 29 18N 94 48W
Galveston B., U.S.A. 81 L7 29 36N 94 50W
Gálvez, Argentina 94 C3 32 0S 61 14W
Galway, Ireland 13 C2 53 17N 9 3W
**Galway** □, Ireland 13 C2 53 22N 9 1W
Galway B., Ireland 13 C2 53 13N 9 10W
Gam →, Vietnam 38 B5 21 55N 105 12 E
Gamagori, Japan 31 G8 34 50N 137 14 E
Gambat, Pakistan 42 F3 27 17N 68 26 E
Gambhir →, India 42 F6 26 58N 77 27 E
**Gambia** ■, W. Afr. 50 F2 13 25N 16 0W
Gambia →, W. Afr. 50 F2 13 28N 16 34W
Gambier, U.S.A. 78 F2 40 22N 82 23W
Gambier, C., Australia 60 B5 11 56S 130 57 E
Gambier Is., Australia 63 F2 35 3S 136 30 E
Gambo, Canada 71 C9 48 47N 54 13W
Gamboli, Pakistan 42 E3 29 53N 68 24 E
Gamboma, Congo 52 E3 1 55S 15 52 E
Gamlakarleby = Kokkola, Finland 8 E20 63 50N 23 8 E
Gammon →, Canada 73 C9 51 24N 95 44W
Gan Jiang →, China 33 D6 29 15N 116 0 E
Ganado, U.S.A. 83 J9 35 43N 109 33W
Gananoque, Canada 79 B8 44 20N 76 10W
Ganāveh, Iran 45 D6 29 35N 50 35 E
Gäncä, Azerbaijan 25 F8 40 45N 46 20 E
Gancheng, China 38 C7 18 51N 108 37 E
Gand = Gent, Belgium 15 C3 51 2N 3 42 E
Ganda, Angola 53 G2 13 3S 14 35 E
Gandajika, Dem. Rep. of the Congo 52 F4 6 45S 23 57 E
Gandak →, India 43 G11 25 39N 85 13 E
Gandava, Pakistan 42 E2 28 32N 67 32 E
Gander, Canada 71 C9 48 58N 54 35W
Gander L., Canada 71 C9 48 58N 54 35W
Ganderowe Falls, Zimbabwe 55 F2 17 20S 29 10 E
Gandhi Sagar, India 42 G6 24 40N 75 40 E
Gandhinagar, India 42 H5 23 15N 72 45 E
Gandía, Spain 19 C5 38 58N 0 9W
Gando, Pta., Canary Is. 22 G4 27 55N 15 22W
Ganedidalem = Gani, Indonesia 37 E7 0 48S 128 14 E
Ganga →, India 43 H14 23 20N 90 30 E
Ganga Sagar, India 43 J13 21 38N 88 5 E
Gangan →, India 43 E8 28 38N 78 58 E
Ganganagar, India 42 E5 29 56N 73 56 E
Gangapur, India 42 F7 26 32N 76 49 E
Gangaw, Burma 41 H19 22 5N 94 5 E
Gangdisê Shan, China 41 D12 31 20N 81 0 E
**Ganges** = Ganga →, India 43 H14 23 20N 90 30 E
Ganges, Canada 72 D4 48 51N 123 31W
Ganges, Mouths of the, India 43 J14 21 30N 90 0 E
Gangoh, India 42 E7 29 46N 77 18 E
Gangroti, India 43 D8 30 50N 79 10 E
Gangtok, India 41 F16 27 20N 88 37 E
Gangu, China 34 G3 34 40N 105 15 E
Gangyao, China 35 B14 44 12N 126 37 E
Gani, Indonesia 37 E7 0 48S 128 14 E
Ganj, India 43 F8 27 45N 78 57 E
Gannett Peak, U.S.A. 82 E9 43 11N 109 39W
Ganquan, China 34 F5 36 20N 109 20 E
**Gansu** □, China 34 G3 36 0N 104 0 E
Ganta, Liberia 50 G4 7 15N 8 59W
Gantheaume, C., Australia 63 F2 36 4S 137 32 E
Gantheaume B., Australia 61 E1 27 40S 114 10 E
Gantsevichi = Hantsavichy, Belarus 17 B14 52 49N 26 30 E
Ganyem = Genyem, Indonesia 37 E10 2 46S 140 12 E
Ganyu, China 35 G10 34 50N 119 8 E
Ganzhou, China 33 D6 25 51N 114 56 E
Gao, Mali 50 E5 16 15N 0 5W
Gaomi, China 35 F10 36 20N 119 42 E
Gaoping, China 34 G7 35 45N 112 55 E
Gaotang, China 34 F9 36 50N 116 15 E
Gaoua, Burkina Faso 50 F5 10 20N 3 8W
Gaoual, Guinea 50 F3 11 45N 13 25W
Gaoxiong = Kaohsiung, Taiwan 33 D7 22 35N 120 16 E
Gaoyang, China 34 E8 38 40N 115 45 E
Gaoyou Hu, China 35 H10 32 45N 119 20 E
Gaoyuan, China 35 F9 37 8N 117 58 E
Gap, France 18 D7 44 33N 6 5 E
Gapat →, India 43 G10 24 30N 82 28 E
Gapuwiyak, Australia 62 A2 12 25S 135 43 E
Gar, China 32 C2 32 10N 79 58 E
Garabogazköl Aylagy, Turkmenistan 25 F9 41 0N 53 30 E
Garachico, Canary Is. 22 F3 28 22N 16 46W
Garachiné, Panama 88 E4 8 0N 78 12W
Garafia, Canary Is. 22 F2 28 48N 17 57W
Garah, Australia 63 D4 29 5S 149 38 E
Garajonay, Canary Is. 22 F2 28 7N 17 14W
Garanhuns, Brazil 93 E11 8 50S 36 30W
Garautha, India 43 G8 25 34N 79 18 E
Garba Tula, Kenya 54 B4 0 30N 38 32 E
Garberville, U.S.A. 82 F2 40 6N 123 48W
Garbiyang, India 43 D9 30 8N 80 54 E
**Garda, L. di**, Italy 20 B4 45 40N 10 41 E
Garde L., Canada 73 A7 62 50N 106 13W
Garden City, Ga., U.S.A. 77 J5 32 6N 81 9W
Garden City, Kans., U.S.A. 81 G4 37 58N 100 53W
Garden City, Tex., U.S.A. 81 K4 31 52N 101 29W
Garden Grove, U.S.A. 85 M9 33 47N 117 55W
Gardēz, Afghan. 42 C3 33 37N 69 9 E
Gardiner, Maine, U.S.A. 77 C11 44 14N 69 47W
Gardiner, Mont., U.S.A. 82 D8 45 2N 110 22W
Gardiners I., U.S.A. 79 E12 41 6N 72 6W
Gardner, U.S.A. 79 D13 42 34N 71 59W
Gardner Canal, Canada 72 C3 53 27N 128 8W
Gardnerville, U.S.A. 84 G7 38 56N 119 45W
Gardo, Somali Rep. 46 F4 9 30N 49 6 E
Garey, U.S.A. 85 L6 34 53N 120 19W
Garfield, U.S.A. 82 C5 47 1N 117 9W
Garforth, U.K. 10 D6 53 47N 1 24W
Gargano, Mte., Italy 20 D6 41 43N 15 43 E
Garibaldi Prov. Park, Canada 72 D4 49 50N 122 40W
Garies, S. Africa 56 E2 30 32S 17 59 E
Garigliano →, Italy 20 D5 41 13N 13 45 E
Garissa, Kenya 54 C4 0 25S 39 40 E
Garland, Tex., U.S.A. 81 J6 32 55N 96 38W
Garland, Utah, U.S.A. 82 F7 41 47N 112 10W
Garm, Tajikistan 26 F8 39 0N 70 20 E
Garmāb, Iran 45 C8 35 25N 56 45 E
Garmisch-Partenkirchen, Germany 16 E6 47 30N 11 6 E
Garmsār, Iran 45 C7 35 20N 52 25 E
Garner, U.S.A. 80 D8 43 6N 93 36W
Garnett, U.S.A. 80 F7 38 17N 95 14W
Garo Hills, India 43 G14 25 30N 90 30 E
Garoe, Somali Rep. 46 F4 8 25N 48 33 E
Garonne →, France 18 D3 45 2N 0 36W
Garot, India 42 G6 24 19N 75 41 E
Garoua, Cameroon 51 G8 9 19N 13 21 E
Garrauli, India 43 G8 25 5N 79 22 E
Garrison, Mont., U.S.A. 82 C7 46 31N 112 49W
Garrison, N. Dak., U.S.A. 80 B4 47 40N 101 25W
Garrison Res. = Sakakawea, L., U.S.A. 80 B4 47 30N 101 25W
Garron Pt., U.K. 13 A6 55 3N 5 59W
Garry →, U.K. 12 E5 56 44N 3 47W
Garry, L., Canada 68 B9 65 58N 100 18W
Garsen, Kenya 54 C5 2 20S 40 5 E
Garson L., Canada 73 B6 56 19N 110 2W
Garu, India 43 H11 23 40N 84 14 E
Garub, Namibia 56 D2 26 37S 16 0 E
Garut, Indonesia 37 G12 7 14S 107 53 E
Garvie Mts., N.Z. 59 L2 45 30S 168 50 E
Garwa = Garoua, Cameroon 51 G8 9 19N 13 21 E
Garwa, India 43 G10 24 11N 83 47 E
Gary, U.S.A. 76 E2 41 36N 87 20W
Garzê, China 32 C5 31 38N 100 1 E
Garzón, Colombia 92 C3 2 10N 75 40W
Gas-San, Japan 30 E10 38 32N 140 1 E
Gasan Kuli = Esenguly, Turkmenistan 26 F6 37 37N 53 59 E
Gascogne, France 18 E4 43 45N 0 20 E
Gascogne, G. de, Europe 18 D2 44 0N 2 0W
**Gascony** = Gascogne, France 18 E4 43 45N 0 20 E
Gascoyne →, Australia 61 D1 24 52S 113 37 E

Gascoyne Junction, *Australia* **61 E2** 25 2S 115 17 E
Gashaka, *Nigeria* **51 G8** 7 20N 11 29 E
Gasherbrum, *Pakistan* **43 B7** 35 40N 76 40 E
Gashua, *Nigeria* **51 F8** 12 54N 11 0 E
Gaspé, *Canada* **71 C7** 48 52N 64 30W
Gaspé, C. de, *Canada* **71 C7** 48 48N 64 7W
Gaspé, Pén. de, *Canada* **71 C6** 48 45N 65 40W
Gaspésie, Parc de Conservation de la, *Canada* **71 C6** 48 55N 65 50W
Gasteiz = Vitoria-Gasteiz, *Spain* **19 A4** 42 50N 2 41W
Gastonia, *U.S.A.* **77 H5** 35 16N 81 11W
Gastre, *Argentina* **96 E3** 42 20S 69 15W
Gata, C., *Cyprus* **23 E12** 34 34N 33 2 E
Gata, C. de, *Spain* **19 D4** 36 41N 2 13W
Gata, Sierra de, *Spain* **19 B2** 40 20N 6 45W
Gataga →, *Canada* **72 B3** 58 35N 126 59W
Gatehouse of Fleet, *U.K.* **12 G4** 54 53N 4 12W
Gates, *U.S.A.* **78 C7** 43 9N 77 42W
Gateshead, *U.K.* **10 C6** 54 57N 1 35W
Gatesville, *U.S.A.* **81 K6** 31 26N 97 45W
Gaths, *Zimbabwe* **55 G3** 20 2S 30 32 E
Gatico, *Chile* **94 A1** 22 29S 70 20W
Gatineau, *Canada* **79 A9** 45 29N 75 38W
Gatineau →, *Canada* **70 C4** 45 27N 75 42W
Gatineau, Parc Nat. de la, *Canada* **70 C4** 45 40N 76 0W
Gatton, *Australia* **63 D5** 27 32S 152 17 E
Gatun, L., *Panama* **88 E4** 9 7N 79 56W
Gatyana, *S. Africa* **57 E4** 32 16S 28 31 E
Gau, *Fiji* **59 D8** 18 2S 179 18 E
Gauer L., *Canada* **73 B9** 57 0N 97 50W
Gauhati, *India* **41 F17** 26 10N 91 45 E
Gauja →, *Latvia* **9 H21** 57 10N 24 16 E
Gaula →, *Norway* **8 E14** 63 21N 10 14 E
Gauri Phanta, *India* **43 E9** 28 41N 80 36 E
Gausta, *Norway* **9 G13** 59 48N 8 40 E
**Gauteng** □, *S. Africa* **57 D4** 26 0S 28 0 E
Gāv Koshī, *Iran* **45 D8** 28 38N 57 12 E
Gāvakān, *Iran* **45 D7** 29 37N 53 10 E
Gavāter, *Iran* **45 E9** 25 10N 61 31 E
Gāvbandī, *Iran* **45 E7** 27 12N 53 4 E
Gavdhopoúla, *Greece* **23 E6** 34 56N 24 0 E
Gávdhos, *Greece* **23 E6** 34 50N 24 5 E
Gaviota, *U.S.A.* **85 L6** 34 29N 120 13W
Gāvkhūnī, Bātlāq-e, *Iran* **45 C7** 32 6N 52 52 E
Gävle, *Sweden* **9 F17** 60 40N 17 9 E
Gawachab, *Namibia* **56 D2** 27 4S 17 55 E
Gawilgarh Hills, *India* **40 J10** 21 15N 76 45 E
Gawler, *Australia* **63 E2** 34 30S 138 42 E
Gaxun Nur, *China* **32 B5** 42 22N 100 30 E
Gay, *Russia* **24 D10** 51 27N 58 27 E
**Gaya**, *India* **43 G11** 24 47N 85 4 E
Gaya, *Niger* **50 F6** 11 52N 3 28 E
Gaylord, *U.S.A.* **76 C3** 45 2N 84 41W
Gayndah, *Australia* **63 D5** 25 35S 151 32 E
Gaysin = Haysyn, *Ukraine* **17 D15** 48 57N 29 25 E
Gayvoron = Hayvoron, *Ukraine* **17 D15** 48 22N 29 52 E
Gaza, *Gaza Strip* **47 D3** 31 30N 34 28 E
Gaza □, *Mozam.* **57 C5** 23 10S 32 45 E
**Gaza Strip** □, *Asia* **47 D3** 31 29N 34 25 E
Gazanjyk, *Turkmenistan* **45 B7** 39 16N 55 32 E
Gāzbor, *Iran* **45 D8** 28 5N 58 51 E
Gazi, *Dem. Rep. of the Congo* **54 B1** 1 3N 24 30 E
Gaziantep, *Turkey* **25 G6** 37 6N 37 23 E
Gcuwa, *S. Africa* **57 E4** 32 20S 28 11 E
**Gdańsk**, *Poland* **17 A10** 54 22N 18 40 E
Gdańska, Zatoka, *Poland* **17 A10** 54 30N 19 20 E
Gdov, *Russia* **9 G22** 58 48N 27 55 E
Gdynia, *Poland* **17 A10** 54 35N 18 33 E
Gebe, *Indonesia* **37 D7** 0 5N 129 25 E
Gebze, *Turkey* **21 D13** 40 47N 29 25 E
Gedaref, *Sudan* **51 F13** 14 2N 35 28 E
Gediz →, *Turkey* **21 E12** 38 35N 26 48 E
Gedser, *Denmark* **9 J14** 54 35N 11 55 E
Gegugly Cr. →, *Australia* **60 C3** 18 32S 123 41 E
Geel, *Belgium* **15 C4** 51 10N 4 59 E
Geelong, *Australia* **63 F3** 38 10S 144 22 E
Geelvink B. = Cenderwasih, Teluk, *Indonesia* **37 E9** 3 0S 135 20 E
Geelvink Chan., *Australia* **61 E1** 28 30S 114 0 E
Geesthacht, *Germany* **16 B6** 53 26N 10 22 E
Geidam, *Nigeria* **51 F8** 12 57N 11 57 E
Geikie →, *Canada* **73 B8** 57 45N 103 52W
Geistown, *U.S.A.* **78 F6** 40 18N 78 52W
Geita, *Tanzania* **54 C3** 2 48S 32 12 E
Gejiu, *China* **32 D5** 23 20N 103 10 E
Gel, Meydān-e, *Iran* **45 D7** 29 4N 54 50 E
Gela, *Italy* **20 F6** 37 4N 14 15 E
Gelderland □, *Neths.* **15 B6** 52 5N 6 10 E
Geldrop, *Neths.* **15 C5** 51 25N 5 32 E
Geleen, *Neths.* **15 D5** 50 57N 5 49 E
Gelibolu, *Turkey* **21 D12** 40 28N 26 43 E
Gelsenkirchen, *Germany* **16 C4** 51 32N 7 6 E
Gemas, *Malaysia* **39 L4** 2 37N 102 36 E
Gembloux, *Belgium* **15 D4** 50 34N 4 43 E
Gemena, *Dem. Rep. of the Congo* **52 D3** 3 13N 19 48 E
Gemerek, *Turkey* **44 B3** 39 15N 36 10 E
Gemlik, *Turkey* **21 D13** 40 26N 29 9 E
Genale, *Ethiopia* **46 F2** 6 0N 39 30 E
General Acha, *Argentina* **94 D3** 37 20S 64 38W
General Alvear, *Buenos Aires, Argentina* **94 D4** 36 0S 60 0W
General Alvear, *Mendoza, Argentina* **94 D2** 35 0S 67 40W
General Artigas, *Paraguay* **94 B4** 26 52S 56 16W
General Belgrano, *Argentina* **94 D4** 36 35S 58 47W
General Cabrera, *Argentina* **94 C3** 32 53S 63 52W
General Cepeda, *Mexico* **86 B4** 25 23N 101 27W
General Guido, *Argentina* **94 D4** 36 40S 57 50W
General Juan Madariaga, *Argentina* **94 D4** 37 0S 57 0W
General La Madrid, *Argentina* **94 D3** 37 17S 61 20W
General MacArthur, *Phil.* **37 B7** 11 18N 125 28 E
General Martin Miguel de Güemes, *Argentina* **94 A3** 24 50S 65 0W
General Paz, *Argentina* **94 B4** 27 45S 57 36W
General Pico, *Argentina* **94 D3** 35 45S 63 50W
General Pinedo, *Argentina* **94 B3** 27 15S 61 20W
General Pinto, *Argentina* **94 C3** 34 45S 61 50W
General Roca, *Argentina* **96 D3** 39 2S 67 35W
General Santos, *Phil.* **37 C7** 6 5N 125 14 E
General Trevino, *Mexico* **87 B5** 26 14N 99 29W
General Trías, *Mexico* **86 B3** 28 21N 106 22W
General Viamonte, *Argentina* **94 D3** 35 1S 61 3W
General Villegas, *Argentina* **94 D3** 35 5S 63 0W
Genesee, *Idaho, U.S.A.* **82 C5** 46 33N 116 56W
Genesee, *Pa., U.S.A.* **78 E7** 41 59N 77 54W
Genesee →, *U.S.A.* **78 C7** 43 16N 77 36W
Geneseo, *Ill., U.S.A.* **80 E9** 41 27N 90 9W
Geneseo, *N.Y., U.S.A.* **78 D7** 42 48N 77 49W
**Geneva** = Genève, *Switz.* **18 C7** 46 12N 6 9 E
Geneva, *Ala., U.S.A.* **77 K3** 31 2N 85 52W
Geneva, *N.Y., U.S.A.* **78 D8** 42 52N 76 59W
Geneva, *Nebr., U.S.A.* **80 E6** 40 32N 97 36W
Geneva, *Ohio, U.S.A.* **78 E4** 41 48N 80 57W
**Geneva, L.** = Léman, L., *Europe* **18 C7** 46 26N 6 30 E
Geneva, L., *U.S.A.* **76 D1** 42 38N 88 30W
Genève, *Switz.* **18 C7** 46 12N 6 9 E
Genil →, *Spain* **19 D3** 37 42N 5 19W
Genk, *Belgium* **15 D5** 50 58N 5 32 E
Gennargentu, Mti. del, *Italy* **20 D3** 40 1N 9 19 E
**Genoa** = Génova, *Italy* **18 D8** 44 25N 8 57 E
Genoa, *Australia* **63 F4** 37 29S 149 35 E
Genoa, *N.Y., U.S.A.* **79 D8** 42 40N 76 32W
Genoa, *Nebr., U.S.A.* **80 E6** 41 27N 97 44W
Genoa, *Nev., U.S.A.* **84 F7** 39 2N 119 50W
Génova, *Italy* **18 D8** 44 25N 8 57 E
Génova, G. di, *Italy* **20 C3** 44 0N 9 0 E
Genriyetty, Ostrov, *Russia* **27 B16** 77 6N 156 30 E
Gent, *Belgium* **15 C3** 51 2N 3 42 E
Genteng, *Indonesia* **37 G12** 7 22S 106 24 E
Genyem, *Indonesia* **37 E10** 2 46S 140 12 E
Geographe B., *Australia* **61 F2** 33 30S 115 15 E
Geographe Chan., *Australia* **61 D1** 24 30S 113 0 E
Georga, Zemlya, *Russia* **26 A5** 80 30N 49 0 E
George, *S. Africa* **56 E3** 33 58S 22 29 E
George →, *Canada* **71 A6** 58 49N 66 10W
George, L., *N.S.W., Australia* **63 F4** 35 10S 149 25 E
George, L., *S. Austral., Australia* **63 F3** 37 25S 140 0 E
George, L., *W. Austral., Australia* **60 D3** 22 45S 123 40 E
George, L., *Uganda* **54 B3** 0 5N 30 10 E
George, L., *Fla., U.S.A.* **77 L5** 29 17N 81 36W
George, L., *N.Y., U.S.A.* **79 C11** 43 37N 73 33W
George Gill Ra., *Australia* **60 D5** 24 22S 131 45 E
George River = Kangiqsualujjuaq, *Canada* **69 C13** 58 30N 65 59W
George Sound, *N.Z.* **59 L1** 44 52S 167 25 E
George Town, *Australia* **62 G4** 41 6S 146 49 E
George Town, *Bahamas* **88 B4** 23 33N 75 47W
**George Town**, *Malaysia* **39 K3** 5 25N 100 15 E
George V Land, *Antarctica* **5 C10** 69 0S 148 0 E
George VI Sound, *Antarctica* **5 D17** 71 0S 68 0W
George West, *U.S.A.* **81 L5** 28 20N 98 7W
Georgetown, *Australia* **62 B3** 18 17S 143 33 E
Georgetown, *Ont., Canada* **78 C5** 43 40N 79 56W
Georgetown, *P.E.I., Canada* **71 C7** 46 13N 62 24W
Georgetown, *Cayman Is.* **88 C3** 19 20N 81 24W
Georgetown, *Gambia* **50 F3** 13 30N 14 47W
**Georgetown**, *Guyana* **92 B7** 6 50N 58 12W
Georgetown, *Calif., U.S.A.* **84 G6** 38 54N 120 50W
Georgetown, *Colo., U.S.A.* **82 G11** 39 42N 105 42W
Georgetown, *Ky., U.S.A.* **76 F3** 38 13N 84 33W
Georgetown, *N.Y., U.S.A.* **79 D9** 42 46N 75 44W
Georgetown, *Ohio, U.S.A.* **76 F4** 38 52N 83 54W
Georgetown, *S.C., U.S.A.* **77 J6** 33 23N 79 17W
Georgetown, *Tex., U.S.A.* **81 K6** 30 38N 97 41W
**Georgia** □, *U.S.A.* **77 K5** 32 50N 83 15W
**Georgia** ■, *Asia* **25 F7** 42 0N 43 0 E
Georgia, Str. of, *Canada* **72 D4** 49 25N 124 0W
Georgian B., *Canada* **78 A4** 45 15N 81 0W
Georgina →, *Australia* **62 C2** 23 30S 139 47 E
Georgina I., *Canada* **78 B5** 44 22N 79 17W
Georgiu-Dezh = Liski, *Russia* **25 D6** 51 3N 39 30 E
Georgiyevsk, *Russia* **25 F7** 44 12N 43 28 E
Gera, *Germany* **16 C7** 50 53N 12 4 E
Geraardsbergen, *Belgium* **15 D3** 50 45N 3 53 E
Geral, Serra, *Brazil* **95 B6** 26 25S 50 0W
Geral de Goiás, Serra, *Brazil* **93 F9** 12 0S 46 0W
Geraldine, *U.S.A.* **82 C8** 47 36N 110 16W
Geraldton, *Australia* **61 E1** 28 48S 114 32 E
Geraldton, *Canada* **70 C2** 49 44N 86 59W
Gereshk, *Afghan.* **40 D4** 31 47N 64 35 E
Gerik, *Malaysia* **39 K3** 5 50N 101 15 E
Gering, *U.S.A.* **80 E3** 41 50N 103 40W
Gerlach, *U.S.A.* **82 F4** 40 39N 119 21W
Germansen Landing, *Canada* **72 B4** 55 43N 124 40W
Germantown, *U.S.A.* **81 M10** 35 5N 89 49W
**Germany** ■, *Europe* **16 C6** 51 0N 10 0 E
Germī, *Iran* **45 B6** 39 1N 48 3 E
Germiston, *S. Africa* **57 D4** 26 15S 28 10 E
Gernika-Lumo, *Spain* **19 A4** 43 19N 2 40W
Gero, *Japan* **31 G8** 35 48N 137 14 E
Gerona = Girona, *Spain* **19 B7** 41 58N 2 46 E
Gerrard, *Canada* **72 C5** 50 30N 117 17W
Geser, *Indonesia* **37 E8** 3 50S 130 54 E
Getafe, *Spain* **19 B4** 40 18N 3 44W
Gettysburg, *Pa., U.S.A.* **76 F7** 39 50N 77 14W
Gettysburg, *S. Dak., U.S.A.* **80 C5** 45 1N 99 57W
Getxo, *Spain* **19 A4** 43 21N 2 59W
Getz Ice Shelf, *Antarctica* **5 D14** 75 0S 130 0W
Geyser, *U.S.A.* **82 C8** 47 16N 110 30W
Geyserville, *U.S.A.* **84 G4** 38 42N 122 54W
Ghaggar →, *India* **42 E6** 29 30N 74 53 E
Ghaghara →, *India* **43 G11** 25 45N 84 40 E
Ghaghat →, *Bangla.* **43 G13** 25 19N 89 38 E
Ghagra, *India* **43 H11** 23 17N 84 33 E
Ghagra →, *India* **43 F9** 27 29N 81 9 E
**Ghana** ■, *W. Afr.* **50 G5** 8 0N 1 0W
Ghansor, *India* **43 H9** 22 39N 80 1 E
Ghanzi, *Botswana* **56 C3** 21 50S 21 34 E
Ghanzi □, *Botswana* **56 C3** 21 50S 21 45 E
Ghardaïa, *Algeria* **50 B6** 32 20N 3 37 E
Gharyān, *Libya* **51 B8** 32 10N 13 0 E
Ghat, *Libya* **51 D8** 24 59N 10 11 E
Ghatal, *India* **43 H12** 22 40N 87 46 E
Ghatampur, *India* **43 F9** 26 8N 80 13 E
Ghatsila, *India* **43 H12** 22 36N 86 29 E
Ghaţţī, *Si. Arabia* **44 D3** 31 16N 37 31 E
Ghawdex = Gozo, *Malta* **23 C1** 36 3N 14 13 E
Ghazal, Bahr el →, *Chad* **51 F9** 13 0N 15 47 E
Ghazâl, Bahr el →, *Sudan* **51 G12** 9 31N 30 25 E
Ghaziabad, *India* **42 E7** 28 42N 77 26 E
Ghazipur, *India* **43 G10** 25 38N 83 35 E
Ghaznī, *Afghan.* **42 C3** 33 30N 68 28 E
Ghaznī □, *Afghan.* **40 C6** 32 10N 68 20 E
**Ghent** = Gent, *Belgium* **15 C3** 51 2N 3 42 E
Ghīnah, Wādī al, *Si. Arabia* **44 D3** 30 27N 38 14 E
Ghizao, *Afghan.* **42 C1** 33 20N 65 44 E
Ghizar →, *Pakistan* **43 A5** 36 15N 73 43 E
Ghotaru, *India* **42 F4** 27 20N 70 1 E
Ghotki, *Pakistan* **42 E3** 28 5N 69 21 E
Ghowr □, *Afghan.* **40 C4** 34 0N 64 20 E
Ghudaf, W. al →, *Iraq* **44 C4** 32 56N 43 30 E
Ghudāmis, *Libya* **51 B7** 30 11N 9 29 E
Ghughri, *India* **43 H9** 22 39N 80 41 E
Ghugus, *India* **40 K11** 19 58N 79 12 E
Ghulam Mohammad Barrage, *Pakistan* **42 G3** 25 30N 68 20 E
Ghūrīān, *Afghan.* **40 B2** 34 17N 61 25 E
Gia Dinh, *Vietnam* **39 G6** 10 49N 106 42 E
Gia Lai = Plei Ku, *Vietnam* **38 F7** 13 57N 108 0 E
Gia Nghia, *Vietnam* **39 G6** 11 58N 107 42 E
Gia Ngoc, *Vietnam* **38 E7** 14 50N 108 58 E
Gia Vuc, *Vietnam* **38 E7** 14 42N 108 34 E
Giant Forest, *U.S.A.* **84 J8** 36 36N 118 43W
**Giants Causeway**, *U.K.* **13 A5** 55 16N 6 29W
Giarabub = Al Jaghbūb, *Libya* **51 C10** 29 42N 24 38 E
Giarre, *Italy* **20 F6** 37 43N 15 11 E
Gibara, *Cuba* **88 B4** 21 9N 76 11W
Gibb River, *Australia* **60 C4** 16 26S 126 26 E
Gibbon, *U.S.A.* **80 E5** 40 45N 98 51W
Gibeon, *Namibia* **56 D2** 25 7S 17 45 E
**Gibraltar** ■, *Europe* **19 D3** 36 7N 5 22W
Gibraltar, Str. of, *Medit. S.* **19 E3** 35 55N 5 40W
Gibson Desert, *Australia* **60 D4** 24 0S 126 0 E
Gibsons, *Canada* **72 D4** 49 24N 123 32W
Gibsonville, *U.S.A.* **84 F6** 39 46N 120 54W
Giddings, *U.S.A.* **81 K6** 30 11N 96 56W
Giessen, *Germany* **16 C5** 50 34N 8 41 E
Gīfān, *Iran* **45 B8** 37 54N 57 28 E
Gift Lake, *Canada* **72 B5** 55 53N 115 49W
Gifu, *Japan* **31 G8** 35 30N 136 45 E
Gifu □, *Japan* **31 G8** 35 40N 137 0 E
Giganta, Sa. de la, *Mexico* **86 B2** 25 30N 111 30W
Gigha, *U.K.* **12 F3** 55 42N 5 44W
Giglio, *Italy* **20 C4** 42 20N 10 52 E
Gijón, *Spain* **19 A3** 43 32N 5 42W
Gil I., *Canada* **72 C3** 53 12N 129 15W
Gila →, *U.S.A.* **83 K6** 32 43N 114 33W
Gila Bend, *U.S.A.* **83 K7** 32 57N 112 43W
Gila Bend Mts., *U.S.A.* **83 K7** 33 10N 113 0W
Gīlān □, *Iran* **45 B6** 37 0N 50 0 E
Gilbert →, *Australia* **62 B3** 16 35S 141 15 E
**Gilbert Is.**, *Kiribati* **64 G9** 1 0N 172 0 E
Gilbert River, *Australia* **62 B3** 18 9S 142 52 E
Gilead, *U.S.A.* **79 B14** 44 24N 70 59W
Gilford I., *Canada* **72 C3** 50 40N 126 30W
Gilgandra, *Australia* **63 E4** 31 43S 148 39 E
Gilgil, *Kenya* **54 C4** 0 30S 36 20 E
Gilgit, *India* **43 B6** 35 50N 74 15 E
Gilgit →, *Pakistan* **43 B6** 35 44N 74 37 E
Gilgunnia, *Australia* **63 E4** 32 26S 146 2 E
Gillam, *Canada* **73 B10** 56 20N 94 40W
Gillen, L., *Australia* **61 E3** 26 11S 124 38 E
Gilles, L., *Australia* **63 E2** 32 50S 136 45 E
Gillette, *U.S.A.* **80 C2** 44 18N 105 30W
Gilliat, *Australia* **62 C3** 20 40S 141 28 E
Gillingham, *U.K.* **11 F8** 51 23N 0 33 E
Gilmer, *U.S.A.* **81 J7** 32 44N 94 57W
Gilmore, L., *Australia* **61 F3** 32 29S 121 37 E
Gilroy, *U.S.A.* **84 H5** 37 1N 121 34W
Gimli, *Canada* **73 C9** 50 40N 97 0W
Gin Gin, *Australia* **63 D5** 25 0S 151 58 E
Gingin, *Australia* **61 F2** 31 22S 115 54 E
Ginir, *Ethiopia* **46 F3** 7 6N 40 40 E
Gióna, Óros, *Greece* **21 E10** 38 38N 22 14 E
Gippsland, *Australia* **63 F4** 37 52S 147 0 E
Gir Hills, *India* **42 J4** 21 0N 71 0 E
Girab, *India* **42 F4** 26 2N 70 38 E
Girâfi, W. →, *Egypt* **47 F3** 29 58N 34 39 E
Girard, *Kans., U.S.A.* **81 G7** 37 31N 94 51W
Girard, *Ohio, U.S.A.* **78 E4** 41 9N 80 42W
Girard, *Pa., U.S.A.* **78 D4** 42 0N 80 19W
Girard, *Pa., U.S.A.* **78 E4** 42 0N 80 19W
Girdle Ness, *U.K.* **12 D6** 57 9N 2 3W
Giresun, *Turkey* **25 F6** 40 55N 38 30 E
Girga, *Egypt* **51 C12** 26 17N 31 55 E
Giri →, *India* **42 D7** 30 28N 77 41 E
Giridih, *India* **43 G12** 24 10N 86 21 E
Girne = Kyrenia, *Cyprus* **23 D12** 35 20N 33 20 E
Girona, *Spain* **19 B7** 41 58N 2 46 E
Gironde →, *France* **18 D3** 45 32N 1 7W
Giru, *Australia* **62 B4** 19 30S 147 5 E
Girvan, *U.K.* **12 F4** 55 14N 4 51W
Gisborne, *N.Z.* **59 H7** 38 39S 178 5 E
Gisenyi, *Rwanda* **54 C2** 1 41S 29 15 E
Gislaved, *Sweden* **9 H15** 57 19N 13 32 E
Gitega, *Burundi* **54 C2** 3 26S 29 56 E
Giuba →, *Somali Rep.* **46 G3** 1 30N 42 35 E
Giurgiu, *Romania* **17 G13** 43 52N 25 57 E
**Giza** = El Gîza, *Egypt* **51 C12** 30 0N 31 10 E
Gizhiga, *Russia* **27 C17** 62 3N 160 30 E
Gizhiginskaya Guba, *Russia* **27 C16** 61 0N 158 0 E
Giżycko, *Poland* **17 A11** 54 2N 21 48 E
Gjirokastra, *Albania* **21 D9** 40 7N 20 10 E
Gjoa Haven, *Canada* **68 B10** 68 20N 96 8W
Gjøvik, *Norway* **9 F14** 60 47N 10 43 E
Glace Bay, *Canada* **71 C8** 46 11N 59 58W
Glacier Bay National Park and Preserve, *U.S.A.* **72 B1** 58 45N 136 30W
**Glacier National Park**, *Canada* **72 C5** 51 15N 117 30W
Glacier National Park, *U.S.A.* **82 B7** 48 30N 113 18W
Glacier Peak, *U.S.A.* **82 B3** 48 7N 121 7W
Gladewater, *U.S.A.* **81 J7** 32 33N 94 56W
Gladstone, *Queens., Australia* **62 C5** 23 52S 151 16 E
Gladstone, *S. Austral., Australia* **63 E2** 33 15S 138 22 E
Gladstone, *Canada* **73 C9** 50 13N 98 57W
Gladstone, *U.S.A.* **76 C2** 45 51N 87 1W
Gladwin, *U.S.A.* **76 D3** 43 59N 84 29W
Glåma = Glomma →, *Norway* **9 G14** 59 12N 10 57 E
Gláma, *Iceland* **8 D2** 65 48N 23 0W
Glamis, *U.S.A.* **85 N11** 32 55N 115 5W
Glasco, *Kans., U.S.A.* **80 F6** 39 22N 97 50W
Glasco, *N.Y., U.S.A.* **79 D11** 42 3N 73 57W
**Glasgow**, *U.K.* **12 F4** 55 51N 4 15W
Glasgow, *Ky., U.S.A.* **76 G3** 37 0N 85 55W
Glasgow, *Mont., U.S.A.* **82 B10** 48 12N 106 38W
Glaslyn, *Canada* **73 C7** 53 22N 108 21W
Glastonbury, *U.K.* **11 F5** 51 9N 2 43W
Glastonbury, *U.S.A.* **79 E12** 41 43N 72 37W
Glazov, *Russia* **24 C9** 58 9N 52 40 E
Gleichen, *Canada* **72 C6** 50 52N 113 3W
Gleiwitz = Gliwice, *Poland* **17 C10** 50 22N 18 41 E
Glen, *U.S.A.* **79 B13** 44 7N 71 11W
Glen Affric, *U.K.* **12 D3** 57 17N 5 1W
Glen Canyon, *U.S.A.* **83 H8** 37 30N 110 40W
Glen Canyon Dam, *U.S.A.* **83 H8** 36 57N 111 29W
Glen Canyon National Recreation Area, *U.S.A.* **83 H8** 37 15N 111 0W
Glen Coe, *U.K.* **12 E3** 56 40N 5 0W
Glen Cove, *U.S.A.* **79 F11** 40 52N 73 38W
Glen Garry, *U.K.* **12 D3** 57 3N 5 7W
Glen Innes, *Australia* **63 D5** 29 44S 151 44 E
Glen Lyon, *U.S.A.* **79 E8** 41 10N 76 5W
Glen Mor, *U.K.* **12 D4** 57 9N 4 37W
Glen Moriston, *U.K.* **12 D4** 57 11N 4 52W
Glen Robertson, *Canada* **79 A10** 45 22N 74 30W
Glen Spean, *U.K.* **12 E4** 56 53N 4 40W
Glen Ullin, *U.S.A.* **80 B4** 46 49N 101 50W
Glencoe, *Canada* **78 D3** 42 45N 81 43W
Glencoe, *S. Africa* **57 D5** 28 11S 30 11 E
Glencoe, *U.S.A.* **80 C7** 44 46N 94 9W
Glendale, *Ariz., U.S.A.* **83 K7** 33 32N 112 11W
Glendale, *Calif., U.S.A.* **85 L8** 34 9N 118 15W
Glendale, *Zimbabwe* **55 F3** 17 22S 31 5 E
Glendive, *U.S.A.* **80 B2** 47 7N 104 43W
Glendo, *U.S.A.* **80 D2** 42 30N 105 2W
Glenelg →, *Australia* **63 F3** 38 4S 140 59 E
Glenfield, *U.S.A.* **79 C9** 43 43N 75 24W
Glengarriff, *Ireland* **13 E2** 51 45N 9 34W
Glenmont, *U.S.A.* **78 F2** 40 31N 82 6W
Glenmorgan, *Australia* **63 D4** 27 14S 149 42 E
Glenn, *U.S.A.* **84 F4** 39 31N 122 1W
Glennallen, *U.S.A.* **68 B5** 62 0N 145 50W
Glennamaddy, *Ireland* **13 C3** 53 37N 8 33W
Glenns Ferry, *U.S.A.* **82 E6** 42 57N 115 18W
Glenore, *Australia* **62 B3** 17 50S 141 12 E
Glenreagh, *Australia* **63 E5** 30 2S 153 1 E
Glenrock, *U.S.A.* **82 E11** 42 52N 105 52W
Glenrothes, *U.K.* **12 E5** 56 12N 3 10W
Glens Falls, *U.S.A.* **79 C11** 43 19N 73 39W
Glenside, *U.S.A.* **79 F9** 40 6N 75 9W
Glenties, *Ireland* **13 B3** 54 49N 8 16W
Glenville, *U.S.A.* **76 F5** 38 56N 80 50W
Glenwood, *Canada* **71 C9** 49 0N 54 58W
Glenwood, *Ark., U.S.A.* **81 H8** 34 20N 93 33W
Glenwood, *Hawaii, U.S.A.* **74 J17** 19 29N 155 9W
Glenwood, *Iowa, U.S.A.* **80 E7** 41 3N 95 45W
Glenwood, *Minn., U.S.A.* **80 C7** 45 39N 95 23W
Glenwood, *Wash., U.S.A.* **84 D5** 46 1N 121 17W
Glenwood Springs, *U.S.A.* **82 G10** 39 33N 107 19W
Glettinganes, *Iceland* **8 D7** 65 30N 13 37W
Gliwice, *Poland* **17 C10** 50 22N 18 41 E
Globe, *U.S.A.* **83 K8** 33 24N 110 47W
Głogów, *Poland* **16 C9** 51 37N 16 5 E
Glomma →, *Norway* **9 G14** 59 12N 10 57 E
Glorieuses, Is., *Ind. Oc.* **57 A8** 11 30S 47 20 E
Glossop, *U.K.* **10 D6** 53 27N 1 56W
Gloucester, *Australia* **63 E5** 32 0S 151 59 E
**Gloucester**, *U.K.* **11 F5** 51 53N 2 15W
Gloucester, *U.S.A.* **79 D14** 42 37N 70 40W
Gloucester I., *Australia* **62 C4** 20 0S 148 30 E
Gloucester Point, *U.S.A.* **76 G7** 37 15N 76 29W
**Gloucestershire** □, *U.K.* **11 F5** 51 46N 2 15W
Gloversville, *U.S.A.* **79 C10** 43 3N 74 21W
Glovertown, *Canada* **71 C9** 48 40N 54 3W
Glusk, *Belarus* **17 B15** 52 53N 28 41 E
Gmünd, *Austria* **16 D8** 48 45N 15 0 E
Gmunden, *Austria* **16 E7** 47 55N 13 48 E
Gniezno, *Poland* **17 B9** 52 30N 17 35 E
Gnowangerup, *Australia* **61 F2** 33 58S 117 59 E
Go Cong, *Vietnam* **39 G6** 10 22N 106 40 E
Gō-no-ura, *Japan* **31 H4** 33 44N 129 40 E
**Goa**, *India* **40 M8** 15 33N 73 59 E
Goa □, *India* **40 M8** 15 33N 73 59 E
Goalen Hd., *Australia* **63 F5** 36 33S 150 4 E
Goalpara, *India* **41 F17** 26 10N 90 40 E
Goaltor, *India* **43 H12** 22 43N 87 10 E
Goalundo Ghat, *Bangla.* **43 H13** 23 50N 89 47 E
Goat Fell, *U.K.* **12 F3** 55 38N 5 11W
Goba, *Ethiopia* **46 F2** 7 1N 39 59 E
Goba, *Mozam.* **57 D5** 26 15S 32 13 E
Gobabis, *Namibia* **56 C2** 22 30S 19 0 E
**Gobi**, *Asia* **34 C6** 44 0N 110 0 E
Gobō, *Japan* **31 H7** 33 53N 135 10 E
Gochas, *Namibia* **56 C2** 24 59S 18 55 E
Godavari →, *India* **41 L13** 16 25N 82 18 E
Godavari Pt., *India* **41 L13** 17 0N 82 20 E
Godbout, *Canada* **71 C6** 49 20N 67 38W
Godda, *India* **43 G12** 24 50N 87 13 E
Goderich, *Canada* **78 C3** 43 45N 81 41W
Godfrey Ra., *Australia* **61 D2** 24 0S 117 0 E
Godhavn, *Greenland* **4 C5** 69 15N 53 38W
Godhra, *India* **42 H5** 22 49N 73 40 E
Godoy Cruz, *Argentina* **94 C2** 32 56S 68 52W
Gods →, *Canada* **70 A1** 56 22N 92 51W
Gods L., *Canada* **70 B1** 54 40N 94 15W
Gods River, *Canada* **73 C10** 54 50N 94 5W
**Godthåb** = Nuuk, *Greenland* **69 B14** 64 10N 51 35W
Godwin Austen = K2, *Pakistan* **43 B7** 35 58N 76 32 E
Goeie Hoop, Kaap die = Good Hope, C. of, *S. Africa* **56 E2** 34 24S 18 30 E
Goéland, L. au, *Canada* **70 C4** 49 50N 76 48W
Goeree, *Neths.* **15 C3** 51 50N 4 0 E
Goes, *Neths.* **15 C3** 51 30N 3 55 E
Goffstown, *U.S.A.* **79 C13** 43 1N 71 36W
Gogama, *Canada* **70 C3** 47 35N 81 43W
Gogebic, L., *U.S.A.* **80 B10** 46 30N 89 35W
Gogra = Ghaghara →, *India* **43 G11** 25 45N 84 40 E
Gogriâl, *Sudan* **51 G11** 8 30N 28 8 E
Gohana, *India* **42 E7** 29 8N 76 42 E
Goharganj, *India* **42 H7** 23 1N 77 41 E
Goi →, *India* **42 H6** 22 4N 74 46 E
Goiânia, *Brazil* **93 G9** 16 43S 49 20W
Goiás, *Brazil* **93 G8** 15 55S 50 10W
Goiás □, *Brazil* **93 F9** 12 10S 48 0W

Goio-Ere, *Brazil* **95 A5** 24 12S 53 1W
Gojō, *Japan* **31 G7** 34 21N 135 42 E
Gojra, *Pakistan* **42 D5** 31 10N 72 40 E
Gökçeada, *Turkey* **21 D11** 40 10N 25 50 E
Gökova Körfezi, *Turkey* **21 F12** 36 55N 27 50 E
Gokteik, *Burma* **41 H20** 22 26N 97 0 E
Gokurt, *Pakistan* **42 E2** 29 40N 67 26 E
Gol Gol, *Australia* **63 E3** 34 12S 142 14 E
Gola, *India* **43 E9** 28 3N 80 32 E
Golakganj, *India* **43 F13** 26 8N 89 52 E
**Golan Heights** = Hagolan, *Syria* **47 C4** 33 0N 35 45 E
Golāshkerd, *Iran* **45 E8** 27 59N 57 16 E
Golchikha, *Russia* **4 B12** 71 45N 83 30 E
Golconda, *U.S.A.* **82 F5** 40 58N 117 30W
Gold, *U.S.A.* **78 E7** 41 52N 77 50W
Gold Beach, *U.S.A.* **82 E1** 42 25N 124 25W
Gold Coast, *W. Afr.* **50 H5** 4 0N 1 40W
Gold Hill, *U.S.A.* **82 E2** 42 26N 123 3W
Gold River, *Canada* **72 D3** 49 46N 126 3W
Golden, *Canada* **72 C5** 51 20N 116 59W
Golden B., *N.Z.* **59 J4** 40 40S 172 50 E
**Golden Gate**, *U.S.A.* **82 H2** 37 54N 122 30W
Golden Hinde, *Canada* **72 D3** 49 40N 125 44W
Golden Lake, *Canada* **78 A7** 45 34N 77 21W
Golden Vale, *Ireland* **13 D3** 52 33N 8 17W
Goldendale, *U.S.A.* **82 D3** 45 49N 120 50W
Goldfield, *U.S.A.* **83 H5** 37 42N 117 14W
Goldsand L., *Canada* **73 B8** 57 2N 101 8W
Goldsboro, *U.S.A.* **77 H7** 35 23N 77 59W
Goldsmith, *U.S.A.* **81 K3** 31 59N 102 37W
Goldsworthy, *Australia* **60 D2** 20 21S 119 30 E
Goldthwaite, *U.S.A.* **81 K5** 31 27N 98 34W
Goleniów, *Poland* **16 B8** 53 35N 14 50 E
Golestānak, *Iran* **45 D7** 30 36N 54 14 E
Goleta, *U.S.A.* **85 L7** 34 27N 119 50W
Golfito, *Costa Rica* **88 E3** 8 41N 83 5W
Golfo Aranci, *Italy* **20 D3** 40 59N 9 38 E
Goliad, *U.S.A.* **81 L6** 28 40N 97 23W
Golpāyegān, *Iran* **45 C6** 33 27N 50 18 E
Golra, *Pakistan* **42 C5** 33 37N 72 56 E
Golspie, *U.K.* **12 D5** 57 58N 3 59W
Goma, *Dem. Rep. of the Congo* **54 C2** 1 37S 29 10 E
Gomal Pass, *Pakistan* **42 D3** 31 56N 69 20 E
Gomati →, *India* **43 G10** 25 32N 83 11 E
Gombari, *Dem. Rep. of the Congo* **54 B2** 2 45N 29 3 E
Gombe, *Nigeria* **51 F8** 10 19N 11 2 E
Gombe →, *Tanzania* **54 C3** 4 38S 31 40 E
Gomel = Homyel, *Belarus* **17 B16** 52 28N 31 0 E
Gomera, *Canary Is.* **22 F2** 28 7N 17 14W
Gómez Palacio, *Mexico* **86 B4** 25 40N 104 0W
Gomīshān, *Iran* **45 B7** 37 4N 54 6 E
Gomogomo, *Indonesia* **37 F8** 6 39S 134 43 E
Gomoh, *India* **41 H15** 23 52N 86 10 E
Gompa = Ganta, *Liberia* **50 G4** 7 15N 8 59W
Gonābād, *Iran* **45 C8** 34 15N 58 45 E
Gonaïves, *Haiti* **89 C5** 19 20N 72 42W
Gonâve, G. de la, *Haiti* **89 C5** 19 29N 72 42W
Gonâve, I. de la, *Haiti* **89 C5** 18 45N 73 0W
Gonbad-e Kāvūs, *Iran* **45 B7** 37 20N 55 25 E
Gonda, *India* **43 F9** 27 9N 81 58 E
Gondal, *India* **42 J4** 21 58N 70 52 E
Gonder, *Ethiopia* **46 E2** 12 39N 37 30 E
Gondia, *India* **40 J12** 21 23N 80 10 E
Gondola, *Mozam.* **55 F3** 19 10S 33 37 E
Gönen, *Turkey* **21 D12** 40 6N 27 39 E
Gonghe, *China* **32 C5** 36 18N 100 32 E
Gongolgon, *Australia* **63 E4** 30 21S 146 54 E
Gongzhuling, *China* **35 C13** 43 30N 124 40 E
Gonzales, *Calif., U.S.A.* **84 J5** 36 30N 121 26W
Gonzales, *Tex., U.S.A.* **81 L6** 29 30N 97 27W
González Chaves, *Argentina* **94 D3** 38 2S 60 5W
**Good Hope, C. of**, *S. Africa* **56 E2** 34 24S 18 30 E
Gooderham, *Canada* **78 B6** 44 54N 78 21W
Gooding, *U.S.A.* **82 E6** 42 56N 114 43W
Goodland, *U.S.A.* **80 F4** 39 21N 101 43W
Goodlow, *Canada* **72 B4** 56 20N 120 8W
Goodooga, *Australia* **63 D4** 29 3S 147 28 E
Goodsprings, *U.S.A.* **85 K11** 35 49N 115 27W
Goole, *U.K.* **10 D7** 53 42N 0 53W
Goolgowi, *Australia* **63 E4** 33 58S 145 41 E
Goolwa, *Australia* **63 F2** 35 30S 138 47 E
Goomalling, *Australia* **61 F2** 31 15S 116 49 E
Goomeri, *Australia* **63 D5** 26 12S 152 6 E
Goonda, *Mozam.* **55 F3** 19 48S 33 57 E
Goondiwindi, *Australia* **63 D5** 28 30S 150 21 E
Goongarrie, L., *Australia* **61 F3** 30 3S 121 9 E
Goonyella, *Australia* **62 C4** 21 47S 147 58 E
Goose →, *Canada* **71 B7** 53 20N 60 35W
Goose Creek, *U.S.A.* **77 J5** 32 59N 80 2W
Goose L., *U.S.A.* **82 F3** 41 56N 120 26W
Gop, *India* **40 H6** 22 5N 69 50 E
Gopalganj, *India* **43 F11** 26 28N 84 30 E
Göppingen, *Germany* **16 D5** 48 42N 9 39 E
Gorakhpur, *India* **43 F10** 26 47N 83 23 E
Goražde, *Bos.-H.* **21 C8** 43 38N 18 58 E
Gorda, *U.S.A.* **84 K5** 35 53N 121 26W
Gorda, Pta., *Canary Is.* **22 F2** 28 45N 18 0W
Gorda, Pta., *Nic.* **88 D3** 14 20N 83 10W
Gordan B., *Australia* **60 B5** 11 35S 130 10 E
Gordon, *U.S.A.* **80 D3** 42 48N 102 12W
Gordon →, *Australia* **62 G4** 42 27S 145 30 E
Gordon L., *Alta., Canada* **73 B6** 56 30N 110 25W
Gordon L., *N.W.T., Canada* **72 A6** 63 5N 113 11W
Gordonvale, *Australia* **62 B4** 17 5S 145 50 E
Gore, *Ethiopia* **46 F2** 8 12N 35 32 E
Gore, *N.Z.* **59 M2** 46 5S 168 58 E
Gore Bay, *Canada* **70 C3** 45 57N 82 28W
Gorey, *Ireland* **13 D5** 52 41N 6 18W
Gorg, *Iran* **45 D8** 29 29N 59 43 E
Gorgān, *Iran* **45 B7** 36 50N 54 29 E
Gorgona, I., *Colombia* **92 C3** 3 0N 78 10W
Gorham, *U.S.A.* **79 B13** 44 23N 71 10W
Goriganga →, *India* **43 E9** 29 45N 80 23 E
Gorinchem, *Neths.* **15 C4** 51 50N 4 59 E
Goris, *Armenia* **25 G8** 39 31N 46 22 E
Gorízia, *Italy* **20 B5** 45 56N 13 37 E
Gorki = Nizhniy Novgorod, *Russia* **24 C7** 56 20N 44 0 E
Gorkiy = Nizhniy Novgorod, *Russia* **24 C7** 56 20N 44 0 E
Gorkovskoye Vdkhr., *Russia* **24 C7** 57 2N 43 4 E
Görlitz, *Germany* **16 C8** 51 9N 14 58 E
Gorlovka = Horlivka, *Ukraine* **25 E6** 48 19N 38 5 E
Gorman, *U.S.A.* **85 L8** 34 47N 118 51W
Gorna Dzhumayo = Blagoevgrad, *Bulgaria* **21 C10** 42 2N 23 5 E
Gorna Oryakhovitsa, *Bulgaria* **21 C11** 43 7N 25 40 E
Gorno-Altay □, *Russia* **26 D9** 51 0N 86 0 E
Gorno-Altaysk, *Russia* **26 D9** 51 50N 86 5 E
Gornyatski, *Russia* **24 A11** 67 32N 64 3 E
Gornyy, *Russia* **30 B6** 44 57N 133 59 E
Gorodenka = Horodenka, *Ukraine* **17 D13** 48 41N 25 29 E
Gorodok = Horodok, *Ukraine* **17 D12** 49 46N 23 32 E
Gorokhov = Horokhiv, *Ukraine* **17 C13** 50 30N 24 45 E
Goromonzi, *Zimbabwe* **55 F3** 17 52S 31 22 E
Gorong, Kepulauan, *Indonesia* **37 E8** 3 59S 131 25 E
Gorongose →, *Mozam.* **57 C5** 20 30S 34 40 E
Gorongoza, *Mozam.* **55 F3** 18 44S 34 2 E
Gorongoza, Sa. da, *Mozam.* **55 F3** 18 27S 34 2 E
Gorontalo, *Indonesia* **37 D6** 0 35N 123 5 E
Gort, *Ireland* **13 C3** 53 3N 8 49W
Gortis, *Greece* **23 D6** 35 4N 24 58 E
Gorzów Wielkopolski, *Poland* **16 B8** 52 43N 15 15 E
Gosford, *Australia* **63 E5** 33 23S 151 18 E
Goshen, *Calif., U.S.A.* **84 J7** 36 21N 119 25W
Goshen, *Ind., U.S.A.* **76 E3** 41 35N 85 50W
Goshen, *N.Y., U.S.A.* **79 E10** 41 24N 74 20W
Goshogawara, *Japan* **30 D10** 40 48N 140 27 E
Goslar, *Germany* **16 C6** 51 54N 10 25 E
Gospič, *Croatia* **16 F8** 44 35N 15 23 E
Gosport, *U.K.* **11 G6** 50 48N 1 9W
Gosse →, *Australia* **62 B1** 19 32S 134 37 E
Göta älv →, *Sweden* **9 H14** 57 42N 11 54 E
Göta kanal, *Sweden* **9 G16** 58 30N 15 58 E
Götaland, *Sweden* **9 G15** 57 30N 14 30 E
Göteborg, *Sweden* **9 H14** 57 43N 11 59 E
Gotha, *Germany* **16 C6** 50 56N 10 42 E
**Gothenburg** = Göteborg, *Sweden* **9 H14** 57 43N 11 59 E
Gothenburg, *U.S.A.* **80 E4** 40 56N 100 10W
Gotland, *Sweden* **9 H18** 57 30N 18 33 E
Gotō-Rettō, *Japan* **31 H4** 32 55N 129 5 E
Gotska Sandön, *Sweden* **9 G18** 58 24N 19 15 E
Gōtsu, *Japan* **31 G6** 35 0N 132 14 E
Gott Pk., *Canada* **72 C4** 50 18N 122 16W
Göttingen, *Germany* **16 C5** 51 31N 9 55 E
Gottwaldov = Zlín, *Czech Rep.* **17 D9** 49 14N 17 40 E
Goubangzi, *China* **35 D11** 41 20N 121 52 E
Gouda, *Neths.* **15 B4** 52 1N 4 42 E
Goúdhoura, Ákra, *Greece* **23 E8** 34 59N 26 6 E
Gough I., *Atl. Oc.* **2 G9** 40 10S 9 45W
Gouin, Rés., *Canada* **70 C5** 48 35N 74 40W
Goulburn, *Australia* **63 E4** 34 44S 149 44 E
Goulburn Is., *Australia* **62 A1** 11 40S 133 20 E
Goulimine, *Morocco* **50 C3** 28 56N 10 0W
Gourits →, *S. Africa* **56 E3** 34 21S 21 52 E
Goúrnais, *Greece* **23 D7** 35 19N 25 16 E
Gouverneur, *U.S.A.* **79 B9** 44 20N 75 28W
Gouviá, *Greece* **23 A3** 39 39N 19 50 E
Governador Valadares, *Brazil* **93 G10** 18 15S 41 57W
Governor's Harbour, *Bahamas* **88 A4** 25 10N 76 14W
Govindgarh, *India* **43 G9** 24 23N 81 18 E
Gowan Ra., *Australia* **62 D4** 25 0S 145 0 E
Gowanda, *U.S.A.* **78 D6** 42 28N 78 56W
Gowd-e Zirreh, *Afghan.* **40 E3** 29 45N 62 0 E
Gower, *U.K.* **11 F3** 51 35N 4 10W
Gowna, L., *Ireland* **13 C4** 53 51N 7 34W
Goya, *Argentina* **94 B4** 29 10S 59 10W
Goyder Lagoon, *Australia* **63 D2** 27 3S 138 58 E
Goyllarisquisga, *Peru* **92 F3** 10 31S 76 24W
Goz Beïda, *Chad* **51 F10** 12 10N 21 20 E
Gozo, *Malta* **23 C1** 36 3N 14 13 E
Graaff-Reinet, *S. Africa* **56 E3** 32 13S 24 32 E
Gračac, *Croatia* **16 F8** 44 18N 15 57 E
Gracias a Dios, C., *Honduras* **88 D3** 15 0N 83 10W
Graciosa, I., *Canary Is.* **22 E6** 29 15N 13 32W
Grado, *Spain* **19 A2** 43 23N 6 4W
Grady, *U.S.A.* **81 H3** 34 49N 103 19W
Grafham Water, *U.K.* **11 E7** 52 19N 0 18W
Grafton, *Australia* **63 D5** 29 38S 152 58 E
Grafton, *N. Dak., U.S.A.* **80 A6** 48 25N 97 25W
Grafton, *W. Va., U.S.A.* **76 F5** 39 21N 80 2W
Graham, *Canada* **70 C1** 49 20N 90 30W
Graham, *U.S.A.* **81 J5** 33 6N 98 35W
Graham, Mt., *U.S.A.* **83 K9** 32 42N 109 52W
Graham Bell, Ostrov = Greem-Bell, Ostrov, *Russia* **26 A7** 81 0N 62 0 E
Graham I., *B.C., Canada* **72 C2** 53 40N 132 30W
Graham I., *N.W.T., Canada* **68 C6** 77 25N 90 30W
Graham Land, *Antarctica* **5 C17** 65 0S 64 0W
Grahamstown, *S. Africa* **56 E4** 33 19S 26 31 E
Grahamsville, *U.S.A.* **79 E10** 41 51N 74 33W
Grain Coast, *W. Afr.* **50 H3** 4 20N 10 0W
Grajaú, *Brazil* **93 E9** 5 50S 46 4W
Grajaú →, *Brazil* **93 D10** 3 41S 44 48W
Grampian, *U.S.A.* **78 F6** 40 58N 78 37W
Grampian Highlands = Grampian Mts., *U.K.* **12 E5** 56 50N 4 0W
**Grampian Mts.**, *U.K.* **12 E5** 56 50N 4 0W
Grampians, The, *Australia* **63 F3** 37 0S 142 20 E
Gran Canaria, *Canary Is.* **22 G4** 27 55N 15 35W
**Gran Chaco**, *S. Amer.* **94 B3** 25 0S 61 0W
Gran Paradiso, *Italy* **18 D7** 45 33N 7 17 E
Gran Sasso d'Itália, *Italy* **20 C5** 42 27N 13 42 E
Granada, *Nic.* **88 D2** 11 58N 86 0W
**Granada**, *Spain* **19 D4** 37 10N 3 35W
Granada, *U.S.A.* **81 F3** 38 4N 102 19W
Granadilla de Abona, *Canary Is.* **22 F3** 28 7N 16 33W
Granard, *Ireland* **13 C4** 53 47N 7 30W
Granbury, *U.S.A.* **81 J6** 32 27N 97 47W
Granby, *Canada* **79 A12** 45 25N 72 45W
Granby, *U.S.A.* **82 F11** 40 5N 105 56W
Grand →, *Canada* **78 D5** 42 51N 79 34W
Grand →, *Mo., U.S.A.* **80 F8** 39 23N 93 7W
Grand →, *S. Dak., U.S.A.* **80 C4** 45 40N 100 45W
Grand Bahama, *Bahamas* **88 A4** 26 40N 78 30W
Grand Bank, *Canada* **71 C8** 47 6N 55 48W
Grand Bassam, *Ivory C.* **50 G5** 5 10N 3 49W
Grand-Bourg, *Guadeloupe* **89 C7** 15 53N 61 19W
**Grand Canal** = Yun Ho →, *China* **35 E9** 39 10N 117 10 E
**Grand Canyon**, *U.S.A.* **83 H7** 36 3N 112 9W
Grand Canyon National Park, *U.S.A.* **83 H7** 36 15N 112 30W
Grand Cayman, *Cayman Is.* **88 C3** 19 20N 81 20W
Grand Centre, *Canada* **73 C6** 54 25N 110 13W
Grand Coulee, *U.S.A.* **82 C4** 47 57N 119 0W
Grand Coulee Dam, *U.S.A.* **82 C4** 47 57N 118 59W
Grand Erg du Bilma, *Niger* **51 E8** 18 30N 14 0 E
Grand Erg Occidental, *Algeria* **50 B6** 30 20N 1 0 E
Grand Erg Oriental, *Algeria* **50 B7** 30 0N 6 30 E
Grand Falls, *Canada* **71 C6** 47 3N 67 44W
Grand Falls-Windsor, *Canada* **71 C8** 48 56N 55 40W
Grand Forks, *Canada* **72 D5** 49 0N 118 30W
Grand Forks, *U.S.A.* **80 B6** 47 55N 97 3W
Grand Gorge, *U.S.A.* **79 D10** 42 21N 74 29W
Grand Haven, *U.S.A.* **76 D2** 43 4N 86 13W
Grand I., *Mich., U.S.A.* **76 B2** 46 31N 86 40W
Grand I., *N.Y., U.S.A.* **78 D6** 43 0N 78 58W
Grand Island, *U.S.A.* **80 E5** 40 55N 98 21W
Grand Isle, *La., U.S.A.* **81 L9** 29 14N 90 0W
Grand Isle, *Vt., U.S.A.* **79 B11** 44 43N 73 18W
Grand Junction, *U.S.A.* **83 G9** 39 4N 108 33W
Grand L., *N.B., Canada* **71 C6** 45 57N 66 7W
Grand L., *Nfld., Canada* **71 C8** 49 0N 57 30W
Grand L., *Nfld., Canada* **71 B7** 53 40N 60 30W
Grand L., *U.S.A.* **81 L8** 29 55N 92 47W
Grand Lake, *U.S.A.* **82 F11** 40 15N 105 49W
Grand Manan I., *Canada* **71 D6** 44 45N 66 52W
Grand Marais, *Canada* **80 B9** 47 45N 90 25W
Grand Marais, *U.S.A.* **76 B3** 46 40N 85 59W
Grand-Mère, *Canada* **70 C5** 46 36N 72 40W
Grand Prairie, *U.S.A.* **81 J6** 32 47N 97 0W
Grand Rapids, *Canada* **73 C9** 53 12N 99 19W
Grand Rapids, *Mich., U.S.A.* **76 D2** 42 58N 85 40W
Grand Rapids, *Minn., U.S.A.* **80 B8** 47 14N 93 31W
Grand St-Bernard, Col du, *Europe* **18 D7** 45 50N 7 10 E
Grand Teton, *U.S.A.* **82 E8** 43 54N 111 50W
Grand Teton National Park, *U.S.A.* **82 D8** 43 50N 110 50W
Grand Union Canal, *U.K.* **11 E7** 52 7N 0 53W
Grand View, *Canada* **73 C8** 51 10N 100 42W
Grande →, *Jujuy, Argentina* **94 A2** 24 20S 65 2W
Grande →, *Mendoza, Argentina* **94 D2** 36 52S 69 45W
Grande →, *Bolivia* **92 G6** 15 51S 64 39W
Grande →, *Bahia, Brazil* **93 F10** 11 30S 44 30W
Grande →, *Minas Gerais, Brazil* **93 H8** 20 6S 51 4W
Grande, B., *Argentina* **96 G3** 50 30S 68 20W
Grande, Rio →, *U.S.A.* **81 N6** 25 58N 97 9W
Grande Baleine, R. de la →, *Canada* **70 A4** 55 16N 77 47W
Grande Cache, *Canada* **72 C5** 53 53N 119 8W
Grande-Entrée, *Canada* **71 C7** 47 30N 61 40W
Grande Prairie, *Canada* **72 B5** 55 10N 118 50W
Grande-Rivière, *Canada* **71 C7** 48 26N 64 30W
Grande-Vallée, *Canada* **71 C6** 49 14N 65 8W
Grandfalls, *U.S.A.* **81 K3** 31 20N 102 51W
Grandview, *U.S.A.* **82 C4** 46 15N 119 54W
Graneros, *Chile* **94 C1** 34 5S 70 45W
Grangemouth, *U.K.* **12 E5** 56 1N 3 42W
Granger, *U.S.A.* **82 F9** 41 35N 109 58W
Grangeville, *U.S.A.* **82 D5** 45 56N 116 7W
Granisle, *Canada* **72 C3** 54 53N 126 13W
Granite City, *U.S.A.* **80 F9** 38 42N 90 9W
Granite Falls, *U.S.A.* **80 C7** 44 49N 95 33W
Granite L., *Canada* **71 C8** 48 8N 57 5W
Granite Mt., *U.S.A.* **85 M10** 33 5N 116 28W
Granite Pk., *U.S.A.* **82 D9** 45 10N 109 48W
Graniteville, *U.S.A.* **79 B12** 44 8N 72 29W
Granity, *N.Z.* **59 J3** 41 39S 171 51 E
Granja, *Brazil* **93 D10** 3 7S 40 50W
Granollers, *Spain* **19 B7** 41 39N 2 18 E
Grant, *U.S.A.* **80 E4** 40 53N 101 42W
Grant, Mt., *U.S.A.* **82 G4** 38 34N 118 48W
Grant City, *U.S.A.* **80 E7** 40 29N 94 25W
Grant I., *Australia* **60 B5** 11 10S 132 52 E
Grant Range, *U.S.A.* **83 G6** 38 30N 115 25W
Grantham, *U.K.* **10 E7** 52 55N 0 38W
Grantown-on-Spey, *U.K.* **12 D5** 57 20N 3 36W
Grants, *U.S.A.* **83 J10** 35 9N 107 52W
Grants Pass, *U.S.A.* **82 E2** 42 26N 123 19W
Grantsville, *U.S.A.* **82 F7** 40 36N 112 28W
Granville, *France* **18 B3** 48 50N 1 35W
Granville, *N. Dak., U.S.A.* **80 A4** 48 16N 100 47W
Granville, *N.Y., U.S.A.* **79 C11** 43 24N 73 16W
Granville, *Ohio, U.S.A.* **78 F2** 40 4N 82 31W
Granville L., *Canada* **73 B8** 56 18N 100 30W
Graskop, *S. Africa* **57 C5** 24 56S 30 49 E
Grass →, *Canada* **73 B9** 56 3N 96 33W
Grass Range, *U.S.A.* **82 C9** 47 0N 109 0W
Grass River Prov. Park, *Canada* **73 C8** 54 40N 100 50W
Grass Valley, *Calif., U.S.A.* **84 F6** 39 13N 121 4W
Grass Valley, *Oreg., U.S.A.* **82 D3** 45 22N 120 47W
Grasse, *France* **18 E7** 43 38N 6 56 E
Grassflat, *U.S.A.* **78 F6** 41 0N 78 6W
Grasslands Nat. Park, *Canada* **73 D7** 49 11N 107 38W
Grassy, *Australia* **62 G3** 40 3S 144 5 E
Graulhet, *France* **18 E4** 43 45N 1 59 E
Gravelbourg, *Canada* **73 D7** 49 50N 106 35W
's-Gravenhage, *Neths.* **15 B4** 52 7N 4 17 E
Gravenhurst, *Canada* **78 B5** 44 52N 79 20W
Gravesend, *Australia* **63 D5** 29 35S 150 20 E
Gravesend, *U.K.* **11 F8** 51 26N 0 22 E
Gravois, Pointe-à-, *Haiti* **89 C5** 18 15N 73 56W
Grayling, *U.S.A.* **76 C3** 44 40N 84 43W
Grays Harbor, *U.S.A.* **82 C1** 46 59N 124 1W
Grays L., *U.S.A.* **82 E8** 43 4N 111 26W
Grays River, *U.S.A.* **84 D3** 46 21N 123 37W
**Graz**, *Austria* **16 E8** 47 4N 15 27 E
Greasy L., *Canada* **72 A4** 62 55N 122 12W
Great Abaco I., *Bahamas* **88 A4** 26 25N 77 10W
Great Artesian Basin, *Australia* **62 C3** 23 0S 144 0 E
Great Australian Bight, *Australia* **61 F5** 33 30S 130 0 E
Great Bahama Bank, *Bahamas* **88 B4** 23 15N 78 0W
Great Barrier I., *N.Z.* **59 G5** 36 11S 175 25 E
**Great Barrier Reef**, *Australia* **62 B4** 18 0S 146 50 E
Great Barrington, *U.S.A.* **79 D11** 42 12N 73 22W
**Great Basin**, *U.S.A.* **82 G5** 40 0N 117 0W
Great Basin Nat. Park, *U.S.A.* **82 G6** 38 55N 114 14W
Great Bear →, *Canada* **68 B7** 65 0N 124 0W
**Great Bear L.**, *Canada* **68 B8** 65 30N 120 0W
Great Belt = Store Bælt, *Denmark* **9 J14** 55 20N 11 0 E
Great Bend, *Kans., U.S.A.* **80 F5** 38 22N 98 46W
Great Bend, *Pa., U.S.A.* **79 E9** 41 58N 75 45W
Great Blasket I., *Ireland* **13 D1** 52 6N 10 32W
**Great Britain**, *Europe* **6 E5** 54 0N 2 15W
Great Codroy, *Canada* **71 C8** 47 51N 59 16W
**Great Dividing Ra.**, *Australia* **62 C4** 23 0S 146 0 E
Great Driffield = Driffield, *U.K.* **10 C7** 54 0N 0 26W
Great Exuma I., *Bahamas* **88 B4** 23 30N 75 50W
Great Falls, *U.S.A.* **82 C8** 47 30N 111 17W
Great Fish = Groot Vis →, *S. Africa* **56 E4** 33 28S 27 5 E
Great Guana Cay, *Bahamas* **88 B4** 24 0N 76 20W
Great Inagua I., *Bahamas* **89 B5** 21 0N 73 20W
Great Indian Desert = Thar Desert, *India* **42 F5** 28 0N 72 0 E
Great Karoo, *S. Africa* **56 E3** 31 55S 21 0 E
Great Lake, *Australia* **62 G4** 41 50S 146 40 E
**Great Lakes**, *N. Amer.* **66 E11** 46 0N 84 0W
Great Malvern, *U.K.* **11 E5** 52 7N 2 18W
Great Miami →, *U.S.A.* **76 F3** 39 20N 84 40W
Great Ormes Head, *U.K.* **10 D4** 53 20N 3 52W
Great Ouse →, *U.K.* **10 E8** 52 48N 0 21 E
Great Palm I., *Australia* **62 B4** 18 45S 146 40 E
Great Plains, *N. Amer.* **74 A6** 47 0N 105 0W
Great Ruaha →, *Tanzania* **54 D4** 7 56S 37 52 E
Great Sacandaga Res., *U.S.A.* **79 C10** 43 6N 74 16W
Great Saint Bernard Pass = Grand St-Bernard, Col du, *Europe* **18 D7** 45 50N 7 10 E
**Great Salt L.**, *U.S.A.* **82 F7** 41 15N 112 40W
Great Salt Lake Desert, *U.S.A.* **82 F7** 40 50N 113 30W
Great Salt Plains L., *U.S.A.* **81 G5** 36 45N 98 8W
Great Sandy Desert, *Australia* **60 D3** 21 0S 124 0 E
Great Sangi = Sangihe, Pulau, *Indonesia* **37 D7** 3 45N 125 30 E
Great Skellig, *Ireland* **13 E1** 51 47N 10 33W
**Great Slave L.**, *Canada* **72 A5** 61 23N 115 38W
**Great Smoky Mts. Nat. Park**, *U.S.A.* **77 H4** 35 40N 83 40W
Great Snow Mt., *Canada* **72 B4** 57 26N 124 0W
Great Stour = Stour →, *U.K.* **11 F9** 51 18N 1 22 E
Great Victoria Desert, *Australia* **61 E4** 29 30S 126 30 E
**Great Wall**, *China* **34 E5** 38 30N 109 30 E
Great Whernside, *U.K.* **10 C6** 54 10N 1 58W
Great Yarmouth, *U.K.* **11 E9** 52 37N 1 44 E
**Greater Antilles**, *W. Indies* **89 C5** 17 40N 74 0W
Greater London □, *U.K.* **11 F7** 51 31N 0 6W
Greater Manchester □, *U.K.* **10 D5** 53 30N 2 15W
Greater Sunda Is., *Indonesia* **36 F4** 7 0S 112 0 E
Greco, C., *Cyprus* **23 E13** 34 57N 34 5 E
Gredos, Sierra de, *Spain* **19 B3** 40 20N 5 0W
Greece, *U.S.A.* **78 C7** 43 13N 77 41W
**Greece** ■, *Europe* **21 E9** 40 0N 23 0 E
Greeley, *Colo., U.S.A.* **80 E2** 40 25N 104 42W
Greeley, *Nebr., U.S.A.* **80 E5** 41 33N 98 32W
Greem-Bell, Ostrov, *Russia* **26 A7** 81 0N 62 0 E
Green, *U.S.A.* **82 E2** 43 9N 123 22W
Green →, *Ky., U.S.A.* **76 G2** 37 54N 87 30W
Green →, *Utah, U.S.A.* **83 G9** 38 11N 109 53W
Green B., *U.S.A.* **76 C2** 45 0N 87 30W
Green Bay, *U.S.A.* **76 C2** 44 31N 88 0W
Green C., *Australia* **63 F5** 37 13S 150 1 E
Green Cove Springs, *U.S.A.* **77 L5** 29 59N 81 42W
Green Lake, *Canada* **73 C7** 54 17N 107 47W
Green Mts., *U.S.A.* **79 C12** 43 45N 72 45W
Green River, *Utah, U.S.A.* **83 G8** 38 59N 110 10W
Green River, *Wyo., U.S.A.* **82 F9** 41 32N 109 28W
Green Valley, *U.S.A.* **83 L8** 31 52N 110 56W
Greenbank, *U.S.A.* **84 B4** 48 6N 122 34W
Greenbush, *Mich., U.S.A.* **78 B1** 44 35N 83 19W
Greenbush, *Minn., U.S.A.* **80 A6** 48 42N 96 11W
Greencastle, *U.S.A.* **76 F2** 39 38N 86 52W
Greene, *U.S.A.* **79 D9** 42 20N 75 46W
Greenfield, *Calif., U.S.A.* **84 J5** 36 19N 121 15W
Greenfield, *Calif., U.S.A.* **85 K8** 35 15N 119 0W
Greenfield, *Ind., U.S.A.* **76 F3** 39 47N 85 46W
Greenfield, *Iowa, U.S.A.* **80 E7** 41 18N 94 28W
Greenfield, *Mass., U.S.A.* **79 D12** 42 35N 72 36W
Greenfield, *Mo., U.S.A.* **81 G8** 37 25N 93 51W
Greenfield Park, *Canada* **79 A11** 45 29N 73 29W
**Greenland** ■, *N. Amer.* **4 C5** 66 0N 45 0W
Greenland Sea, *Arctic* **4 B7** 73 0N 10 0W
Greenock, *U.K.* **12 F4** 55 57N 4 46W
Greenore, *Ireland* **13 B5** 54 2N 6 8W
Greenore Pt., *Ireland* **13 D5** 52 14N 6 19W
Greenough, *Australia* **61 E1** 28 58S 114 43 E
Greenough →, *Australia* **61 E1** 28 51S 114 38 E
Greenough Pt., *Canada* **78 B3** 44 58N 81 26W
Greenport, *U.S.A.* **79 E12** 41 6N 72 22W
Greensboro, *Ga., U.S.A.* **77 J4** 33 35N 83 11W
Greensboro, *N.C., U.S.A.* **77 G6** 36 4N 79 48W
Greensboro, *Vt., U.S.A.* **79 B12** 44 36N 72 18W
Greensburg, *Ind., U.S.A.* **76 F3** 39 20N 85 29W
Greensburg, *Kans., U.S.A.* **81 G5** 37 36N 99 18W
Greensburg, *Pa., U.S.A.* **78 F5** 40 18N 79 33W
Greenstone Pt., *U.K.* **12 D3** 57 55N 5 37W
Greenvale, *Australia* **62 B4** 18 59S 145 7 E
Greenville, *Ala., U.S.A.* **77 K2** 31 50N 86 38W
Greenville, *Calif., U.S.A.* **84 E6** 40 8N 120 57W
Greenville, *Maine, U.S.A.* **77 C11** 45 28N 69 35W
Greenville, *Mich., U.S.A.* **76 D3** 43 11N 85 15W
Greenville, *Miss., U.S.A.* **81 J9** 33 24N 91 4W
Greenville, *Mo., U.S.A.* **81 G9** 37 8N 90 27W
Greenville, *N.C., U.S.A.* **77 H7** 35 37N 77 23W
Greenville, *N.H., U.S.A.* **79 D13** 42 46N 71 49W
Greenville, *N.Y., U.S.A.* **79 D10** 42 25N 74 1W

Helwân, Egypt 51 C12 29 50N 31 20 E
Hemel Hempstead, U.K. 11 F7 51 44N 0 28W
Hemet, U.S.A. 85 M10 33 45N 116 58W
Hemingford, U.S.A. 80 D3 42 19N 103 4W
Hemmingford, Canada 79 A11 45 3N 73 35W
Hempstead, U.S.A. 81 K6 30 6N 96 5W
Hemse, Sweden 9 H18 57 15N 18 22 E
Henan □, China 34 H8 34 0N 114 0 E
Henares →, Spain 19 B4 40 24N 3 30W
Henashi-Misaki, Japan 30 D9 40 37N 139 51 E
Henderson, Argentina 94 D3 36 18S 61 43W
Henderson, Ky., U.S.A. 76 G2 37 50N 87 35W
Henderson, N.C., U.S.A. 77 G6 36 20N 78 25W
Henderson, Nev., U.S.A. 85 J12 36 2N 114 59W
Henderson, Tenn., U.S.A. 77 H1 35 26N 88 38W
Henderson, Tex., U.S.A. 81 J7 32 9N 94 48W
Hendersonville, N.C., U.S.A. 77 H4 35 19N 82 28W
Hendersonville, Tenn., U.S.A. 77 G2 36 18N 86 37W
Hendījān, Iran 45 D6 30 14N 49 43 E
Hendorābī, Iran 45 E7 26 40N 53 37 E
Hengcheng, China 34 E4 38 18N 106 28 E
Hengdaohezi, China 35 B15 44 52N 129 0 E
Hengelo, Neths. 15 B6 52 16N 6 48 E
Hengshan, China 34 F5 37 58N 109 5 E
Hengshui, China 34 F8 37 41N 115 40 E
Hengyang, China 33 D6 26 52N 112 33 E
Henlopen, C., U.S.A. 76 F8 38 48N 75 6W
Hennenman, S. Africa 56 D4 27 59S 27 1 E
Hennessey, U.S.A. 81 G6 36 6N 97 54W
Henrietta, U.S.A. 81 J5 33 49N 98 12W
Henrietta, Ostrov = Genriyetty, Ostrov, Russia 27 B16 77 6N 156 30 E
Henrietta Maria, C., Canada 70 A3 55 9N 82 20W
Henry, U.S.A. 80 E10 41 7N 89 22W
Henryetta, U.S.A. 81 H7 35 27N 95 59W
Henryville, Canada 79 A11 45 8N 73 11W
Hensall, Canada 78 C3 43 26N 81 30W
Hentiyn Nuruu, Mongolia 33 B5 48 30N 108 30 E
Henty, Australia 63 F4 35 30S 147 0 E
Henzada, Burma 41 L19 17 38N 95 26 E
Heppner, U.S.A. 82 D4 45 21N 119 33W
Hepworth, Canada 78 B3 44 37N 81 9W
Hequ, China 34 E6 39 20N 111 15 E
Héraðsflói, Iceland 8 D6 65 42N 14 12W
Héraðsvötn →, Iceland 8 D4 65 45N 19 25W
Herald Cays, Australia 62 B4 16 58S 149 9 E
Herāt, Afghan. 40 B3 34 20N 62 7 E
Herāt □, Afghan. 40 B3 35 0N 62 0 E
Herbert →, Australia 62 B4 18 31S 146 17 E
Herberton, Australia 62 B4 17 20S 145 25 E
Herceg-Novi, Montenegro, Yug. 21 C8 42 30N 18 33 E
Herchmer, Canada 73 B10 57 22N 94 10W
Herðubreið, Iceland 8 D5 65 11N 16 21W
Hereford, U.K. 11 E5 52 4N 2 43W
Hereford, U.S.A. 81 H3 34 49N 102 24W
**Herefordshire** □, U.K. 11 E5 52 8N 2 40W
Herentals, Belgium 15 C4 51 12N 4 51 E
Herford, Germany 16 B5 52 7N 8 39 E
Herington, U.S.A. 80 F6 38 40N 96 57W
Herkimer, U.S.A. 79 D10 43 0N 74 59W
Herlong, U.S.A. 84 E6 40 8N 120 8W
Herm, U.K. 11 H5 49 30N 2 28W
Hermann, U.S.A. 80 F9 38 42N 91 27W
Hermannsburg, Australia 60 D5 23 57S 132 45 E
Hermanus, S. Africa 56 E2 34 27S 19 12 E
Hermidale, Australia 63 E4 31 30S 146 42 E
Hermiston, U.S.A. 82 D4 45 51N 119 17W
Hermitage, N.Z. 59 K3 43 44S 170 5 E
Hermite, I., Chile 96 H3 55 50S 68 0W
Hermon, U.S.A. 79 B9 44 28N 75 14W
Hermon, Mt. = Shaykh, J. ash, Lebanon 47 B4 33 25N 35 50 E
Hermosillo, Mexico 86 B2 29 10N 111 0W
Hernád →, Hungary 17 D11 47 56N 21 8 E
Hernandarias, Paraguay 95 B5 25 20S 54 40W
Hernandez, U.S.A. 84 J6 36 24N 120 46W
Hernando, Argentina 94 C3 32 28S 63 40W
Hernando, U.S.A. 81 H10 34 50N 90 0W
Herndon, U.S.A. 78 F8 40 43N 76 51W
Herne, Germany 15 C7 51 32N 7 14 E
Herne Bay, U.K. 11 F9 51 21N 1 8 E
Herning, Denmark 9 H13 56 8N 8 58 E
Heroica = Caborca, Mexico 86 A2 30 40N 112 10W
Heroica Nogales = Nogales, Mexico 86 A2 31 20N 110 56W
Heron Bay, Canada 70 C2 48 40N 86 25W
Herradura, Pta. de la, Canary Is. 22 F5 28 26N 14 8W
Herreid, U.S.A. 80 C4 45 50N 100 4W
Herrin, U.S.A. 81 G10 37 48N 89 2W
Herriot, Canada 73 B8 56 22N 101 16W
Hershey, U.S.A. 79 F8 40 17N 76 39W
Hersonissos, Greece 23 D7 35 18N 25 22 E
Herstal, Belgium 15 D5 50 40N 5 38 E
Hertford, U.K. 11 F7 51 48N 0 4W
**Hertfordshire** □, U.K. 11 F7 51 51N 0 5W
's-Hertogenbosch, Neths. 15 C5 51 42N 5 17 E
Hertzogville, S. Africa 56 D4 28 9S 25 30 E
Hervey B., Australia 62 C5 25 0S 152 52 E
Herzliyya, Israel 47 C3 32 10N 34 50 E
Ḥeṣār, Fārs, Iran 45 D6 29 52N 50 16 E
Ḥeṣār, Markazī, Iran 45 C6 35 50N 49 12 E
Heshui, China 34 G5 35 48N 108 0 E
Heshun, China 34 F7 37 22N 113 32 E
Hesperia, U.S.A. 85 L9 34 25N 117 18W
Hesse = Hessen □, Germany 16 C5 50 30N 9 0 E
Hessen □, Germany 16 C5 50 30N 9 0 E
Hetch Hetchy Aqueduct, U.S.A. 84 H5 37 29N 122 19W
Hettinger, U.S.A. 80 C3 46 0N 102 42W
Heuvelton, U.S.A. 79 B9 44 37N 75 25W
Hewitt, U.S.A. 81 K6 31 27N 97 11W
Hexham, U.K. 10 C5 54 58N 2 4W
Hexigten Qi, China 35 C9 43 18N 117 30 E
Ḥeydarābād, Iran 45 D7 30 33N 55 38 E
Heysham, U.K. 10 C5 54 3N 2 53W
Heywood, Australia 63 F3 38 8S 141 37 E
Heze, China 34 G8 35 14N 115 20 E
Hi Vista, U.S.A. 85 L9 34 45N 117 46W
Hialeah, U.S.A. 77 N5 25 50N 80 17W
Hiawatha, U.S.A. 80 F7 39 51N 95 32W
Hibbing, U.S.A. 80 B8 47 25N 92 56W
Hibbs B., Australia 62 G4 42 35S 145 15 E
Hibernia Reef, Australia 60 B3 12 0S 123 23 E
Hickman, U.S.A. 81 G10 36 34N 89 11W
Hickory, U.S.A. 77 H5 35 44N 81 21W
Hicks, Pt., Australia 63 F4 37 49S 149 17 E
Hicks L., Canada 73 A9 61 25N 100 0W
Hicksville, U.S.A. 79 F11 40 46N 73 32W
Hida-Gawa →, Japan 31 G8 35 26N 137 3 E
Hida-Sammyaku, Japan 31 F8 36 30N 137 40 E
Hidaka-Sammyaku, Japan 30 C11 42 35N 142 45 E
Hidalgo, Mexico 87 C5 24 15N 99 26W
Hidalgo □, Mexico 87 C5 20 30N 99 10W
Hidalgo, Presa M., Mexico 86 B3 26 30N 108 35W
Hidalgo, Pta. del, Canary Is. 22 F3 28 33N 16 19W
Hidalgo del Parral, Mexico 86 B3 26 58N 105 40W
Hierro, Canary Is. 22 G1 27 44N 18 0W
Higashiajima-San, Japan 30 F10 37 40N 140 10 E
**Higashiōsaka**, Japan 31 G7 34 40N 135 37 E
Higgins, U.S.A. 81 G4 36 7N 100 2W
Higgins Corner, U.S.A. 84 F5 39 2N 121 5W
High Atlas = Haut Atlas, Morocco 50 B4 32 30N 5 0W
High Bridge, U.S.A. 79 F10 40 40N 74 54W
High Level, Canada 72 B5 58 31N 117 8W
High Point, U.S.A. 77 H6 35 57N 80 0W
High Prairie, Canada 72 B5 55 30N 116 30W
High River, Canada 72 C6 50 30N 113 50W
High Tatra = Tatry, Slovak Rep. 17 D11 49 20N 20 0 E
High Veld, Africa 48 J6 27 0S 27 0 E
High Wycombe, U.K. 11 F7 51 37N 0 45W
Highland □, U.K. 12 D4 57 17N 4 21W
Highland Park, U.S.A. 76 D2 42 11N 87 48W
Highmore, U.S.A. 80 C5 44 31N 99 27W
Highrock L., Canada 73 B8 55 45N 100 30W
Highrock L., Sask., Canada 73 B7 57 5N 105 32W
Higüey, Dom. Rep. 89 C6 18 37N 68 42W
Hiiumaa, Estonia 9 G20 58 50N 22 45 E
Ḥijāz □, Si. Arabia 46 C3 24 0N 40 0 E
Hijo = Tagum, Phil. 37 C7 7 33N 125 53 E
Hikari, Japan 31 H5 33 58N 131 58 E
Hiko, U.S.A. 84 H11 37 32N 115 14W
Hikone, Japan 31 G8 35 15N 136 10 E
Hikurangi, N.Z. 59 F5 35 36S 174 17 E
Hikurangi, Mt., N.Z. 59 H6 38 21S 176 52 E
Hildesheim, Germany 16 B5 52 9N 9 56 E
Hill →, Australia 61 F2 30 23S 115 3 E
Hill City, Idaho, U.S.A. 82 E6 43 18N 115 3W
Hill City, Kans., U.S.A. 80 F5 39 22N 99 51W
Hill City, S. Dak., U.S.A. 80 D3 43 56N 103 35W
Hill Island L., Canada 73 A7 60 30N 109 50W
Hillcrest Center, U.S.A. 85 K8 35 23N 118 57W
Hillegom, Neths. 15 B4 52 18N 4 35 E
Hillerød, Denmark 9 J15 55 56N 12 19 E
Hillsboro, Kans., U.S.A. 80 F6 38 21N 97 12W
Hillsboro, N. Dak., U.S.A. 80 B6 47 26N 97 3W
Hillsboro, N.H., U.S.A. 79 C13 43 7N 71 54W
Hillsboro, Ohio, U.S.A. 76 F4 39 12N 83 37W
Hillsboro, Oreg., U.S.A. 84 E4 45 31N 122 59W
Hillsboro, Tex., U.S.A. 81 J6 32 1N 97 8W
Hillsborough, Grenada 89 D7 12 28N 61 28W
Hillsdale, Mich., U.S.A. 76 E3 41 56N 84 38W
Hillsdale, N.Y., U.S.A. 79 D11 42 11N 73 30W
Hillsport, Canada 70 C2 49 27N 85 34W
Hillston, Australia 63 E4 33 30S 145 31 E
Hilo, U.S.A. 74 J17 19 44N 155 5W
Hilton, U.S.A. 78 C7 43 17N 77 48W
Hilton Head Island, U.S.A. 77 J5 32 13N 80 45W
Hilversum, Neths. 15 B5 52 14N 5 10 E
**Himachal Pradesh** □, India 42 D7 31 30N 77 0 E
**Himalaya**, Asia 43 E11 29 0N 84 0 E
Himatnagar, India 40 H8 23 37N 72 57 E
Himeji, Japan 31 G7 34 50N 134 40 E
Himi, Japan 31 F8 36 50N 136 55 E
Ḥimṣ, Syria 47 A5 34 40N 36 45 E
Ḥimṣ □, Syria 47 A6 34 30N 37 0 E
Hinche, Haiti 89 C5 19 9N 72 1W
Hinchinbrook I., Australia 62 B4 18 20S 146 15 E
Hinckley, U.K. 11 E6 52 33N 1 22W
Hinckley, U.S.A. 80 B8 46 1N 92 56W
Hindaun, India 42 F7 26 44N 77 5 E
Hindmarsh, L., Australia 63 F3 36 5S 141 55 E
Hindu Bagh, Pakistan 42 D2 30 56N 67 50 E
**Hindu Kush**, Asia 40 B7 36 0N 71 0 E
Hindubagh, Pakistan 40 D5 30 56N 67 57 E
Hindupur, India 40 N10 13 49N 77 32 E
Hines Creek, Canada 72 B5 56 20N 118 40W
Hinesville, U.S.A. 77 K5 31 51N 81 36W
Hinganghat, India 40 J11 20 30N 78 52 E
Hingham, U.S.A. 82 B8 48 33N 110 25W
Hingir, India 43 J10 21 57N 83 41 E
Hingoli, India 40 K10 19 41N 77 15 E
Hinna = Imi, Ethiopia 46 F3 6 28N 42 10 E
Hinnøya, Norway 8 B16 68 35N 15 50 E
Hinojosa del Duque, Spain 19 C3 38 30N 5 9W
Hinsdale, U.S.A. 79 D12 42 47N 72 29W
Hinton, Canada 72 C5 53 26N 117 34W
Hinton, U.S.A. 76 G5 37 40N 80 54W
Hirado, Japan 31 H4 33 22N 129 33 E
Hirakud Dam, India 41 J13 21 32N 83 45 E
Hiran →, India 43 H8 23 6N 79 21 E
Hirapur, India 43 G8 24 22N 79 13 E
Hiratsuka, Japan 31 G9 35 19N 139 21 E
Hiroo, Japan 30 C11 42 17N 143 19 E
Hirosaki, Japan 30 D10 40 34N 140 28 E
**Hiroshima**, Japan 31 G6 34 24N 132 30 E
Hiroshima □, Japan 31 G6 34 50N 133 0 E
Hisar, India 42 E6 29 12N 75 45 E
Hisb →, Iraq 44 D5 31 45N 44 17 E
Ḥismá, Si. Arabia 44 D3 28 30N 36 0 E
**Hispaniola**, W. Indies 89 C5 19 0N 71 0W
Hīt, Iraq 44 C4 33 38N 42 49 E
Hita, Japan 31 H5 33 20N 130 58 E
Hitachi, Japan 31 F10 36 36N 140 39 E
Hitchin, U.K. 11 F7 51 58N 0 16W
Hitoyoshi, Japan 31 H5 32 13N 130 45 E
Hitra, Norway 8 E13 63 30N 8 45 E
Hixon, Canada 72 C4 53 25N 122 35W
Ḥiyyon, N. →, Israel 47 E4 30 25N 35 10 E
Hjalmar L., Canada 73 A7 61 33N 109 25W
Hjälmaren, Sweden 9 G16 59 18N 15 40 E
Hjørring, Denmark 9 H13 57 29N 9 59 E
Hluhluwe, S. Africa 57 D5 28 1S 32 15 E
Hlyboka, Ukraine 17 D13 48 5N 25 56 E
**Ho Chi Minh City** = Phanh Bho Ho Chi Minh, Vietnam 39 G6 10 58N 106 40 E
Ho Thuong, Vietnam 38 C5 19 32N 105 48 E
Hoa Da, Vietnam 39 G7 11 16N 108 40 E
Hoa Hiep, Vietnam 39 G5 11 34N 105 51 E
Hoai Nhon, Vietnam 38 E7 14 28N 109 1 E
Hoang Lien Son, Vietnam 38 A4 22 0N 104 0 E
Hoare B., Canada 69 B13 65 17N 62 30W
**Hobart**, Australia 62 G4 42 50S 147 21 E
Hobart, U.S.A. 81 H5 35 1N 99 6W
Hobbs, U.S.A. 81 J3 32 42N 103 8W
Hobbs Coast, Antarctica 5 D14 74 50S 131 0W
Hobe Sound, U.S.A. 77 M5 27 4N 80 8W
Hoboken, U.S.A. 79 F10 40 45N 74 4W
Hobro, Denmark 9 H13 56 39N 9 46 E
Hoburgen, Sweden 9 H18 56 55N 18 7 E
Hodaka-Dake, Japan 31 F8 36 17N 137 39 E
Hodgeville, Canada 73 C7 50 7N 106 58W
Hodgson, Canada 73 C9 51 13N 97 36W
Hódmezővásárhely, Hungary 17 E11 46 28N 20 22 E
Hodna, Chott el, Algeria 50 A6 35 26N 4 43 E
Hodonín, Czech Rep. 17 D9 48 50N 17 10 E
Hoeamdong, N. Korea 35 C16 42 30N 130 16 E
Hoek van Holland, Neths. 15 C4 52 0N 4 7 E
Hoengsŏng, S. Korea 35 F14 37 29N 127 59 E
Hoeryong, N. Korea 35 C15 42 30N 129 45 E
Hoeyang, N. Korea 35 E14 38 43N 127 36 E
Hof, Germany 16 C6 50 19N 11 55 E
Hofmeyr, S. Africa 56 E4 31 39S 25 50 E
Höfn, Iceland 8 D6 64 15N 15 13W
Hofors, Sweden 9 F17 60 31N 16 15 E
Hofsjökull, Iceland 8 D4 64 49N 18 48W
Hōfu, Japan 31 G5 34 3N 131 34 E
Hogan Group, Australia 63 F4 39 13S 147 1 E
Hogarth, Mt., Australia 62 C2 21 48S 136 58 E
Hoggar = Ahaggar, Algeria 50 D7 23 0N 6 30 E
Hogsty Reef, Bahamas 89 B5 21 41N 73 48W
Hoh →, U.S.A. 84 C2 47 45N 124 29W
Hohe Venn, Belgium 15 D6 50 30N 6 5 E
Hohenwald, U.S.A. 77 H2 35 33N 87 33W
Hohhot, China 34 D6 40 52N 111 40 E
Hóhlakas, Greece 23 D9 35 57N 27 53 E
Hoi An, Vietnam 38 E7 15 30N 108 19 E
Hoisington, U.S.A. 80 F5 38 31N 98 47W
Hōjō, Japan 31 H6 33 58N 132 46 E
Hokianga Harbour, N.Z. 59 F4 35 31S 173 22 E
Hokitika, N.Z. 59 K3 42 42S 171 0 E
**Hokkaidō** □, Japan 30 C11 43 30N 143 0 E
Holbrook, Australia 63 F4 35 42S 147 18 E
Holbrook, U.S.A. 83 J8 34 54N 110 10W
Holden, U.S.A. 82 G7 39 6N 112 16W
Holdenville, U.S.A. 81 H6 35 5N 96 24W
Holdrege, U.S.A. 80 E5 40 26N 99 23W
**Holguín**, Cuba 88 B4 20 50N 76 20W
Hollams Bird I., Namibia 56 C1 24 40S 14 30 E
Holland, Mich., U.S.A. 76 D2 42 47N 86 7W
Holland, N.Y., U.S.A. 78 D6 42 38N 78 32W
Hollandale, U.S.A. 81 J9 33 10N 90 51W
Hollandia = Jayapura, Indonesia 37 E10 2 28S 140 38 E
Holley, U.S.A. 78 C6 43 14N 78 2W
Hollidaysburg, U.S.A. 78 F6 40 26N 78 24W
Hollis, U.S.A. 81 H5 34 41N 99 55W
Hollister, Calif., U.S.A. 84 J5 36 51N 121 24W
Hollister, Idaho, U.S.A. 82 E6 42 21N 114 35W
Holly Hill, U.S.A. 77 L5 29 16N 81 3W
Holly Springs, U.S.A. 81 H10 34 46N 89 27W
**Hollywood**, Calif., U.S.A. 74 D3 34 7N 118 25W
Hollywood, Fla., U.S.A. 77 N5 26 1N 80 9W
Holman, Canada 68 A8 70 42N 117 41W
Holman, N.W.T., Canada 68 A8 70 44N 117 44W
Hólmavík, Iceland 8 D3 65 42N 21 40W
Holmen, U.S.A. 80 D9 43 58N 91 15W
Holmes Reefs, Australia 62 B4 16 27S 148 0 E
Holmsund, Sweden 8 E19 63 41N 20 20 E
Holroyd →, Australia 62 A3 14 10S 141 36 E
Holstebro, Denmark 9 H13 56 22N 8 37 E
Holsworthy, U.K. 11 G3 50 48N 4 22W
Holton, Canada 71 B8 54 31N 57 12W
Holton, U.S.A. 80 F7 39 28N 95 44W
Holtville, U.S.A. 85 N11 32 49N 115 23W
Holwerd, Neths. 15 A5 53 22N 5 54 E
Holy I., Angl., U.K. 10 D3 53 17N 4 37W
Holy I., Northumb., U.K. 10 B6 55 40N 1 47W
Holyhead, U.K. 10 D3 53 18N 4 38W
Holyoke, Colo., U.S.A. 80 E3 40 35N 102 18W
Holyoke, Mass., U.S.A. 79 D12 42 12N 72 37W
Holyrood, Canada 71 C9 47 27N 53 8W
Homa Bay, Kenya 54 C3 0 36S 34 30 E
Homalin, Burma 41 G19 24 55N 95 0 E
Homand, Iran 45 C8 32 28N 59 37 E
Homathko →, Canada 72 C4 51 0N 124 56W
Hombori, Mali 50 E5 15 20N 1 38W
Home B., Canada 69 B13 68 40N 67 10W
Home Hill, Australia 62 B4 19 43S 147 25 E
Homedale, U.S.A. 82 E5 43 37N 116 56W
Homer, Alaska, U.S.A. 68 C4 59 39N 151 33W
Homer, La., U.S.A. 81 J8 32 48N 93 4W
Homer City, U.S.A. 78 F5 40 32N 79 10W
Homestead, Australia 62 C4 20 20S 145 40 E
Homestead, U.S.A. 77 N5 25 28N 80 29W
Homewood, U.S.A. 84 F6 39 4N 120 8W
Homoine, Mozam. 57 C6 23 55S 35 8 E
Homs = Ḥimṣ, Syria 47 A5 34 40N 36 45 E
Homyel, Belarus 17 B16 52 28N 31 0 E
Hon Chong, Vietnam 39 G5 10 25N 104 30 E
Hon Me, Vietnam 38 C5 19 23N 105 56 E
Honan = Henan □, China 34 H8 34 0N 114 0 E
Honbetsu, Japan 30 C11 43 7N 143 37 E
Honcut, U.S.A. 84 F5 39 20N 121 32W
Hondeklipbaai, S. Africa 56 E2 30 19S 17 17 E
Hondo, Japan 31 H5 32 27N 130 12 E
Hondo, U.S.A. 81 L5 29 21N 99 9W
Hondo →, Belize 87 D7 18 25N 88 21W
**Honduras** ■, Cent. Amer. 88 D2 14 40N 86 30W
Honduras, G. de, Caribbean 88 C2 16 50N 87 0W
Hønefoss, Norway 9 F14 60 10N 10 18 E
Honesdale, U.S.A. 79 E9 41 34N 75 16W
Honey L., U.S.A. 84 E6 40 15N 120 19W
Honfleur, France 18 B4 49 25N 0 13 E
Hong →, Vietnam 32 D5 22 0N 104 0 E
Hong He →, China 34 H8 32 25N 115 35 E
**Hong Kong** □, China 33 D6 22 11N 114 14 E
Hongch'ŏn, S. Korea 35 F14 37 44N 127 53 E
Hongjiang, China 33 D5 27 7N 109 59 E
Hongliu He →, China 34 F5 38 0N 109 50 E
Hongor, Mongolia 34 B7 45 45N 112 50 E
Hongsa, Laos 38 C3 19 43N 101 20 E
Hongshui He →, China 33 D5 23 48N 109 30 E
Hongsŏng, S. Korea 35 F14 36 37N 126 38 E
Hongtong, China 34 F6 36 16N 111 40 E
Honguedo, Détroit d', Canada 71 C7 49 15N 64 0W
Hongwon, N. Korea 35 E14 40 0N 127 56 E
Hongze Hu, China 35 H10 33 15N 118 35 E
Honiara, Solomon Is. 64 H7 9 27S 159 57 E
Honiton, U.K. 11 G4 50 47N 3 11W
Honjō, Japan 30 E10 39 23N 140 3 E
Honningsvåg, Norway 8 A21 70 59N 25 59 E
**Honolulu**, U.S.A. 74 H16 21 19N 157 52W
**Honshū**, Japan 31 G9 36 0N 138 0 E
Hood, Mt., U.S.A. 82 D3 45 23N 121 42W
Hood, Pt., Australia 61 F2 34 23S 119 34 E
Hood River, U.S.A. 82 D3 45 43N 121 31W
Hoodsport, U.S.A. 84 C3 47 24N 123 9W
Hoogeveen, Neths. 15 B6 52 44N 6 28 E
Hoogezand-Sappemeer, Neths. 15 A6 53 9N 6 45 E
Hooghly = Hugli →, India 43 J13 21 56N 88 4 E
Hooghly-Chinsura = Chunchura, India 43 H13 22 53N 88 27 E
Hook Hd., Ireland 13 D5 52 7N 6 56W
Hook I., Australia 62 C4 20 4S 149 0 E
Hook of Holland = Hoek van Holland, Neths. 15 C4 52 0N 4 7 E
Hooker, U.S.A. 81 G4 36 52N 101 13W
Hooker Creek, Australia 60 C5 18 23S 130 38 E
Hoonah, U.S.A. 72 B1 58 7N 135 27W
Hooper Bay, U.S.A. 68 B3 61 32N 166 6W
Hoopeston, U.S.A. 76 E2 40 28N 87 40W
Hoopstad, S. Africa 56 D4 27 50S 25 55 E
Hoorn, Neths. 15 B5 52 38N 5 4 E
Hoover, U.S.A. 77 J2 33 20N 86 11W
Hoover Dam, U.S.A. 85 K12 36 1N 114 44W
Hooversville, U.S.A. 78 F6 40 9N 78 55W
Hop Bottom, U.S.A. 79 E9 41 42N 75 46W
Hope, Canada 72 D4 49 25N 121 25W
Hope, Ariz., U.S.A. 85 M13 33 43N 113 42W
Hope, Ark., U.S.A. 81 J8 33 40N 93 36W
Hope, L., S. Austral., Australia 63 D2 28 24S 139 18 E
Hope, L., W. Austral., Australia 61 F3 32 35S 120 15 E
Hope I., Canada 78 B4 44 55N 80 11W
Hope Town, Bahamas 88 A4 26 35N 76 57W
Hopedale, Canada 71 A7 55 28N 60 13W
Hopedale, U.S.A. 79 D13 42 8N 71 33W
Hopefield, S. Africa 56 E2 33 3S 18 22 E
Hopei = Hebei □, China 34 E9 39 0N 116 0 E
Hopelchén, Mexico 87 D7 19 46N 89 50W
Hopetoun, Vic., Australia 63 F3 35 42S 142 22 E
Hopetoun, W. Austral., Australia 61 F3 33 57S 120 7 E
Hopetown, S. Africa 56 D3 29 34S 24 3 E
Hopevale, Australia 62 B4 15 16S 145 20 E
Hopewell, U.S.A. 76 G7 37 18N 77 17W
Hopkins, L., Australia 60 D4 24 15S 128 35 E
Hopkinsville, U.S.A. 77 G2 36 52N 87 29W
Hopland, U.S.A. 84 G3 38 58N 123 7W
Hoquiam, U.S.A. 84 D3 46 59N 123 53W
Horden Hills, Australia 60 D5 20 15S 130 0 E
Horinger, China 34 D6 40 28N 111 48 E
Horlick Mts., Antarctica 5 E15 84 0S 102 0W
Horlivka, Ukraine 25 E6 48 19N 38 5 E
Hormak, Iran 45 D9 29 58N 60 51 E
Hormoz, Iran 45 E7 27 35N 55 0 E
Hormoz, Jaz.-ye, Iran 45 E8 27 8N 56 28 E
Hormozgān □, Iran 45 E8 27 30N 56 0 E
Hormuz, Kūh-e, Iran 45 E7 27 27N 55 10 E
Hormuz, Str. of, The Gulf 45 E8 26 30N 56 30 E
Horn, Austria 16 D8 48 39N 15 40 E
Horn, Iceland 8 C2 66 28N 22 28W
Horn →, Canada 72 A5 61 30N 118 1W
**Horn, Cape** = Hornos, C. de, Chile 96 H3 55 50S 67 30W
Horn Head, Ireland 13 A3 55 14N 8 0W
Horn I., Australia 62 A3 10 37S 142 17 E
Horn Mts., Canada 72 A5 62 15N 119 15W
Hornavan, Sweden 8 C17 66 15N 17 30 E
Hornbeck, U.S.A. 81 K8 31 20N 93 24W
Hornbrook, U.S.A. 82 F2 41 55N 122 33W
Horncastle, U.K. 10 D7 53 13N 0 7W
Hornell, U.S.A. 78 D7 42 20N 77 40W
Hornell L., Canada 72 A5 62 20N 119 25W
Hornepayne, Canada 70 C3 49 14N 84 48W
Hornings Mills, Canada 78 B4 44 9N 80 12W
Hornitos, U.S.A. 84 H6 37 30N 120 14W
Hornos, C. de, Chile 96 H3 55 50S 67 30W
Hornsea, U.K. 10 D7 53 55N 0 11W
Horobetsu, Japan 30 C10 42 24N 141 6 E
Horodenka, Ukraine 17 D13 48 41N 25 29 E
Horodok, Khmelnytskyy, Ukraine 17 D14 49 10N 26 34 E
Horodok, Lviv, Ukraine 17 D12 49 46N 23 32 E
Horokhiv, Ukraine 17 C13 50 30N 24 45 E
Horqin Youyi Qianqi, China 35 A12 46 5N 122 3 E
Horqueta, Paraguay 94 A4 23 15S 56 55W
Horse Creek, U.S.A. 80 E3 41 57N 105 10W
Horse Is., Canada 71 B8 50 15N 55 50W
Horsefly L., Canada 72 C4 52 25N 121 0W
Horseheads, U.S.A. 78 D8 42 10N 76 49W
Horsens, Denmark 9 J13 55 52N 9 51 E
Horsham, Australia 63 F3 36 44S 142 13 E
Horsham, U.K. 11 F7 51 4N 0 20W
Horten, Norway 9 G14 59 25N 10 32 E
Horton, U.S.A. 80 F7 39 40N 95 32W
Horton →, Canada 68 B7 69 56N 126 52W
Horwood L., Canada 70 C3 48 5N 82 20W
Hose, Gunung-Gunung, Malaysia 36 D4 2 5N 114 6 E
Ḥoseynābād, Khuzestān, Iran 45 C6 32 45N 48 20 E
Ḥoseynābād, Kordestān, Iran 44 C5 35 33N 47 8 E
Hoshangabad, India 42 H7 22 45N 77 45 E
Hoshiarpur, India 42 D6 31 30N 75 58 E
Hospet, India 40 M10 15 15N 76 20 E
Hoste, I., Chile 96 H3 55 0S 69 0W
Hot, Thailand 38 C2 18 8N 98 29 E
Hot Creek Range, U.S.A. 82 G6 38 40N 116 20W
Hot Springs, Ark., U.S.A. 81 H8 34 31N 93 3W
Hot Springs, S. Dak., U.S.A. 80 D3 43 26N 103 29W
Hotagen, Sweden 8 E16 63 50N 14 30 E
Hotan, China 32 C2 37 25N 79 55 E
Hotazel, S. Africa 56 D3 27 17S 22 58 E
Hotchkiss, U.S.A. 83 G10 38 48N 107 43W
Hotham, C., Australia 60 B5 12 2S 131 18 E
Hoting, Sweden 8 D17 64 8N 16 15 E

Hotte, Massif de la, Haiti .. 89 C5 18 30N 73 45W
Hottentotsbaai, Namibia .. 56 D1 26 8S 14 59 E
Houffalize, Belgium ....... 15 D5 50 8N 5 48 E
Houghton, Mich., U.S.A. .. 80 B10 47 7N 88 34W
Houghton, N.Y., U.S.A. .... 78 D6 42 25N 78 10W
Houghton L., U.S.A. ...... 76 C3 44 21N 84 44W
Houhora Heads, N.Z. ..... 59 F4 34 49S 173 9 E
Houlton, U.S.A. .......... 77 B12 46 8N 67 51W
Houma, U.S.A. ........... 81 L9 29 36N 90 43W
Housatonic →, U.S.A. ... 79 E11 41 10N 73 7W
Houston, Canada ......... 72 C3 54 25N 126 39W
Houston, Mo., U.S.A. ..... 81 G9 37 22N 91 58W
**Houston**, Tex., U.S.A. .... 81 L7 29 46N 95 22W
Houtman Abrolhos,
Australia .............. 61 E1 28 43S 113 48 E
Hovd, Mongolia .......... 32 B4 48 2N 91 37 E
Hove, U.K. .............. 11 G7 50 50N 0 10W
Hoveyzeh, Iran .......... 45 D6 31 27N 48 4 E
Hövsgöl, Mongolia ....... 34 C5 43 37N 109 39 E
Hövsgöl Nuur, Mongolia .. 32 A5 51 0N 100 30 E
Howard, Australia ........ 63 D5 25 16S 152 32 E
Howard, Pa., U.S.A. ...... 78 F7 41 1N 77 40W
Howard, S. Dak., U.S.A. ... 80 C6 44 1N 97 32W
Howe, U.S.A. ............ 82 E7 43 48N 113 0W
Howe, C., Australia ....... 63 F5 37 30S 150 0 E
Howe I., Canada ......... 79 B8 44 16N 76 17W
Howell, U.S.A. ........... 76 D4 42 36N 83 56W
Howick, Canada .......... 79 A11 45 11N 73 51W
Howick, S. Africa ......... 57 D5 29 28S 30 14 E
Howick Group, Australia .. 62 A4 14 20S 145 30 E
Howitt, L., Australia ...... 63 D2 27 40S 138 40 E
Howland I., Pac. Oc. ...... 64 G10 0 48N 176 38W
Howrah = Haora, India ... 43 H13 22 37N 88 20 E
Howth Hd., Ireland ....... 13 C5 53 22N 6 3W
Höxter, Germany ......... 16 C5 51 46N 9 22 E
Hoy, U.K. ............... 12 C5 58 50N 3 15W
Høyanger, Norway ....... 9 F12 61 13N 6 4 E
Hoyerswerda, Germany ... 16 C8 51 26N 14 14 E
Hoylake, U.K. ............ 10 D4 53 24N 3 10W
Hpungan Pass, Burma .... 41 F20 27 30N 96 55 E
Hradec Králové, Czech Rep. 16 C8 50 15N 15 50 E
Hrodna, Belarus ......... 17 B12 53 42N 23 52 E
Hrodzyanka, Belarus ...... 17 B15 53 31N 28 42 E
Hron →, Slovak Rep. ..... 17 E10 47 49N 18 45 E
Hrvatska = Croatia ■,
Europe ............... 16 F9 45 20N 16 0 E
Hrymayliv, Ukraine ....... 17 D14 49 20N 26 5 E
Hsenwi, Burma .......... 41 H20 23 22N 97 55 E
Hsiamen = Xiamen, China 33 D6 24 25N 118 4 E
Hsian = Xi'an, China ..... 34 G5 34 15N 109 0 E
Hsinchu, Taiwan ......... 33 D7 24 48N 120 58 E
Hsinhailien = Lianyungang,
China ................. 35 G10 34 40N 119 11 E
Hsüchou = Xuzhou, China . 35 G9 34 18N 117 10 E
Hu Xian, China .......... 34 G5 34 8N 108 42 E
Hua Hin, Thailand ........ 38 F2 12 34N 99 58 E
Hua Xian, Henan, China ... 34 G8 35 30N 114 30 E
Hua Xian, Shaanxi, China . 34 G5 34 30N 109 48 E
Huachinera, Mexico ...... 86 A3 30 9N 108 55W
Huacho, Peru ........... 92 F3 11 10S 77 35W
Huade, China ............ 34 D7 41 55N 113 59 E
Huadian, China .......... 35 C14 43 0N 126 40 E
Huai He →, China ....... 33 C6 33 0N 118 30 E
Huai Yot, Thailand ....... 39 J2 7 45N 99 37 E
Huai'an, Hebei, China ..... 34 D8 40 30N 114 20 E
Huai'an, Jiangsu, China ... 35 H10 33 30N 119 10 E
Huaibei, China ........... 34 G9 34 0N 116 48 E
Huaide = Gongzhuling,
China ................. 35 C13 43 30N 124 40 E
Huaidezhen, China ....... 35 C13 43 48N 124 50 E
Huainan, China .......... 33 C6 32 38N 116 58 E
Huairen, China ........... 34 E7 39 48N 113 20 E
Huairou, China .......... 34 D9 40 20N 116 35 E
Huaiyang, China ......... 34 H8 33 40N 114 52 E
Huaiyin, China ........... 35 H10 33 30N 119 2 E
Huaiyuan, China ......... 35 H9 32 55N 117 10 E
Huajianzi, China ......... 35 D13 41 23N 125 20 E
Huajuapan de Leon, Mexico 87 D5 17 50N 97 48W
Hualapai Peak, U.S.A. ..... 83 J7 35 5N 113 54W
Huallaga →, Peru ........ 92 E3 5 15S 75 30W
Huambo, Angola ......... 53 G3 12 42S 15 54 E
Huan Jiang →, China .... 34 G5 34 28N 109 0 E
Huan Xian, China ......... 34 F4 36 33N 107 7 E
Huancabamba, Peru ...... 92 E3 5 10S 79 15W
Huancane, Peru .......... 92 G5 15 10S 69 44W
Huancavelica, Peru ....... 92 F3 12 50S 75 5W
Huancayo, Peru .......... 92 F3 12 5S 75 12W
Huanchaca, Bolivia ....... 92 H5 20 15S 66 40W
**Huang Hai** = Yellow Sea,
China ................. 35 G12 35 0N 123 0 E
**Huang He** →, China ..... 35 F10 37 55N 118 50 E
Huang Xian, China ....... 35 F11 37 38N 120 30 E
Huangling, China ......... 34 G5 35 34N 109 15 E
Huanglong, China ........ 34 G5 35 30N 109 59 E
Huangshan, China ........ 33 D6 29 42N 118 25 E
Huangshi, China ......... 33 C6 30 10N 115 3 E
Huangsongdian, China .... 35 C14 43 45N 127 25 E
Huantai, China ........... 35 F9 36 58N 117 56 E
Huánuco, Peru .......... 92 E3 9 55S 76 15W
Huaraz, Peru ............ 92 E3 9 30S 77 32W
Huarmey, Peru ........... 92 F3 10 5S 78 5W
Huascarán, Peru ......... 92 E3 9 8S 77 36W
Huasco, Chile ........... 94 B1 28 30S 71 15W
Huasco →, Chile ........ 94 B1 28 27S 71 13W
Huasna, U.S.A. .......... 85 K6 35 6N 120 24W
Huatabampo, Mexico ..... 86 B3 26 50N 109 50W
Huauchinango, Mexico .... 87 C5 20 11N 98 3W
Huautla de Jiménez, Mexico 87 D5 18 8N 96 51W
Huay Namota, Mexico ..... 86 C4 21 56N 104 30W
Huayin, China ........... 34 G6 34 35N 110 5 E
Hubbard, Ohio, U.S.A. .... 78 E4 41 9N 80 34W
Hubbard, Tex., U.S.A. ..... 81 K6 31 51N 96 48W
Hubbart Pt., Canada ...... 73 B10 59 21N 94 41W
Hubei □, China .......... 33 C6 31 0N 112 0 E
Hubli, India ............. 40 M9 15 22N 75 15 E
Huch'ang, N. Korea ...... 35 D14 41 25N 127 2 E
Hucknall, U.K. ........... 10 D6 53 3N 1 13W
Huddersfield, U.K. ........ 10 D6 53 39N 1 47W
Hudiksvall, Sweden ....... 9 F17 61 43N 17 10 E
Hudson, Canada ......... 70 B1 50 6N 92 9W
Hudson, Mass., U.S.A. .... 79 D13 42 23N 71 34W
Hudson, N.Y., U.S.A. ..... 79 D11 42 15N 73 46W
Hudson, Wis., U.S.A. ..... 80 C8 44 58N 92 45W
Hudson, Wyo., U.S.A. ..... 82 E9 42 54N 108 35W
**Hudson** →, U.S.A. ...... 79 F10 40 42N 74 2W
**Hudson Bay**, N.W.T.,
Canada ................ 69 C11 60 0N 86 0W
Hudson Bay, Sask., Canada 73 C8 52 51N 102 23W
Hudson Falls, U.S.A. ...... 79 C11 43 18N 73 35W
Hudson Mts., Antarctica ... 5 D16 74 32S 99 20W
Hudson Str., Canada ...... 69 B13 62 0N 70 0W
Hudson's Hope, Canada ... 72 B4 56 0N 121 54W
Hue, Vietnam ............ 38 D6 16 30N 107 35 E
Huehuetenango, Guatemala 88 C1 15 20N 91 28W
Huejúcar, Mexico ........ 86 C4 22 21N 103 13W
Huelva, Spain ........... 19 D2 37 18N 6 57W
Huentelauquén, Chile ..... 94 C1 31 38S 71 33W
Huerta, Sa. de la, Argentina 94 C2 31 10S 67 30W
Huesca, Spain ........... 19 A5 42 8N 0 25W
Huetamo, Mexico ........ 86 D4 18 36N 100 54W
Hugh →, Australia ....... 62 D1 25 1S 134 1 E
Hughenden, Australia ..... 62 C3 20 52S 144 10 E
Hughes, Australia ........ 61 F4 30 42S 129 31 E
Hughesville, U.S.A. ....... 79 E8 41 14N 76 44W
Hugli →, India .......... 43 J13 21 56N 88 4 E
Hugo, Colo., U.S.A. ....... 80 F3 39 8N 103 28W
Hugo, Okla., U.S.A. ....... 81 H7 34 1N 95 31W
Hugoton, U.S.A. ......... 81 G4 37 11N 101 21W
Hui Xian = Huixian, China . 34 G7 35 27N 113 12 E
Hui Xian, China .......... 34 H4 33 50N 106 4 E
Hui'anbu, China .......... 34 F4 37 28N 106 38 E
Huichapán, Mexico ....... 87 C5 20 24N 99 40W
Huifa He →, China ...... 35 C14 43 0N 127 50 E
Huila, Nevado del, Colombia 92 C3 3 0N 76 0W
Huimin, China ........... 35 F9 37 27N 117 28 E
Huinan, China ........... 35 C14 42 40N 126 2 E
Huinca Renancó, Argentina 94 C3 34 51S 64 22W
Huining, China ........... 34 G3 35 38N 105 0 E
Huinong, China .......... 34 E4 39 5N 106 35 E
Huisache, Mexico ........ 86 C4 22 55N 100 25W
Huiting, China ........... 34 G9 34 5N 116 5 E
Huixian, China ........... 34 G7 35 27N 113 12 E
Huixtla, Mexico .......... 87 D6 15 9N 92 28W
Huize, China ............ 32 D5 26 24N 103 15 E
Hukawng Valley, Burma ... 41 F20 26 30N 96 30 E
Hukuntsi, Botswana ...... 56 C3 23 58S 21 45 E
Hulayfā', Si. Arabia ....... 44 E4 25 58N 40 45 E
Huld = Ulaanjirem,
Mongolia .............. 34 B3 45 5N 105 30 E
Hulin He →, China ...... 35 B12 45 0N 122 10 E
**Hull** = Kingston upon Hull,
U.K. ................. 10 D7 53 45N 0 21W
Hull, Canada ............ 79 A9 45 25N 75 44W
Hull →, U.K. ............ 10 D7 53 44N 0 20W
Hulst, Neths. ............ 15 C4 51 17N 4 2 E
Hulun Nur, China ........ 33 B6 49 0N 117 30 E
Humahuaca, Argentina .... 94 A2 23 10S 65 25W
Humaitá, Brazil .......... 92 E6 7 35S 63 1W
Humaitá, Paraguay ....... 94 B4 27 2S 58 31W
Humansdorp, S. Africa .... 56 E3 34 2S 24 46 E
Humbe, Angola .......... 56 B1 16 40S 14 55 E
Humber →, U.K. ........ 10 D7 53 42N 0 27W
Humboldt, Canada ....... 73 C7 52 15N 105 9W
Humboldt, Iowa, U.S.A. ... 80 D7 42 44N 94 13W
Humboldt, Tenn., U.S.A. .. 81 H10 35 50N 88 55W
Humboldt →, U.S.A. ..... 82 F4 39 59N 118 36W
Humboldt Gletscher,
Greenland ............. 4 B4 79 30N 62 0W
Hume, U.S.A. ............ 84 J8 36 48N 118 54W
Hume, L., Australia ....... 63 F4 36 0S 147 5 E
Humenné, Slovak Rep. .... 17 D11 48 55N 21 50 E
Humphreys, Mt., U.S.A. ... 84 H8 37 17N 118 40W
Humphreys Peak, U.S.A. .. 83 J8 35 21N 111 41W
Humptulips, U.S.A. ....... 84 C3 47 14N 123 57W
Hūn, Libya .............. 51 C9 29 2N 16 0 E
Hun Jiang →, China ..... 35 D13 40 50N 125 38 E
Húnaflói, Iceland ......... 8 D3 65 50N 20 50W
**Hunan** □, China ......... 33 D6 27 30N 112 0 E
Hunchun, China .......... 35 C16 42 52N 130 28 E
Hundewali, Pakistan ...... 42 D5 31 55N 72 38 E
Hundred Mile House,
Canada ................ 72 C4 51 38N 121 18W
Hunedoara, Romania ..... 17 F12 45 40N 22 50 E
**Hungary** ■, Europe ....... 17 E10 47 20N 19 20 E
Hungary, Plain of, Europe . 6 F10 47 0N 20 0 E
Hungerford, Australia ..... 63 D3 28 58S 144 24 E
Hŭngnam, N. Korea ...... 35 E14 39 49N 127 45 E
Hunsberge, Namibia ...... 56 D2 27 45S 17 12 E
Hunsrück, Germany ...... 16 D4 49 56N 7 27 E
Hunstanton, U.K. ......... 10 E8 52 56N 0 29 E
Hunter, U.S.A. ........... 79 D10 42 13N 74 13W
Hunter I., Australia ....... 62 G3 40 30S 144 45 E
Hunter I., Canada ........ 72 C3 51 55N 128 0W
Hunter Ra., Australia ..... 63 E5 32 45S 150 15 E
Hunters Road, Zimbabwe . 55 F2 19 9S 29 49 E
Hunterville, N.Z. ......... 59 H5 39 56S 175 35 E
Huntingburg, U.S.A. ...... 76 F2 38 18N 86 57W
Huntingdon, Canada ...... 70 C5 45 6N 74 10W
Huntingdon, U.K. ......... 11 E7 52 20N 0 11W
Huntingdon, U.S.A. ....... 78 F6 40 30N 78 1W
Huntington, Ind., U.S.A. ... 76 E3 40 53N 85 30W
Huntington, Oreg., U.S.A. . 82 D5 44 21N 117 16W
Huntington, Utah, U.S.A. .. 82 G8 39 20N 110 58W
Huntington, W. Va., U.S.A. 76 F4 38 25N 82 27W
Huntington Beach, U.S.A. . 85 M9 33 40N 118 5W
Huntington Station, U.S.A. 79 F11 40 52N 73 26W
Huntly, N.Z. ............. 59 G5 37 34S 175 11 E
Huntly, U.K. ............. 12 D6 57 27N 2 47W
Huntsville, Canada ....... 78 A5 45 20N 79 14W
Huntsville, Ala., U.S.A. .... 77 H2 34 44N 86 35W
Huntsville, Tex., U.S.A. ... 81 K7 30 43N 95 33W
Hunyani →, Zimbabwe .. 55 F3 15 57S 30 39 E
Hunyuan, China .......... 34 E7 39 42N 113 42 E
Hunza →, India ......... 43 B6 35 54N 74 20 E
Huo Xian = Huozhou, China 34 F6 36 36N 111 42 E
Huong Hoa, Vietnam ..... 38 D6 16 37N 106 45 E
Huong Khe, Vietnam ..... 38 C5 18 13N 105 41 E
Huonville, Australia ...... 62 G4 43 0S 147 5 E
Huozhou, China .......... 34 F6 36 36N 111 42 E
Hupeh = Hubei □, China ... 33 C6 31 0N 112 0 E
Hūr, Iran ............... 45 D8 30 50N 57 7 E
Hurd, C., Canada ......... 78 A3 45 13N 81 44W
Hure Qi, China .......... 35 C11 42 45N 121 45 E
Hurghada, Egypt ......... 51 C12 27 15N 33 50 E
Hurley, N. Mex., U.S.A. ... 83 K9 32 42N 108 8W
Hurley, Wis., U.S.A. ...... 80 B9 46 27N 90 11W
Huron, Calif., U.S.A. ...... 84 J6 36 12N 120 6W
Huron, Ohio, U.S.A. ...... 78 E2 41 24N 82 33W
Huron, S. Dak., U.S.A. .... 80 C5 44 22N 98 13W
**Huron, L.**, U.S.A. ........ 78 B2 44 30N 82 40W
Hurricane, U.S.A. ........ 83 H7 37 11N 113 17W
Hurunui →, N.Z. ........ 59 K4 42 54S 173 18 E
Húsavík, Iceland ......... 8 C5 66 3N 17 21W
Huşi, Romania ........... 17 E15 46 41N 28 7 E
Huskvarna, Sweden ...... 9 H16 57 47N 14 15 E
Hustadvika, Norway ...... 8 E12 63 0N 7 0 E
Hustontown, U.S.A. ...... 78 F6 40 3N 78 2W
Hutchinson, Kans., U.S.A. . 81 F6 38 5N 97 56W
Hutchinson, Minn., U.S.A. . 80 C7 44 54N 94 22W
Hutte Sauvage, L. de la,
Canada ............... 71 A7 56 15N 64 45W
Hutton, Mt., Australia ..... 63 D4 25 51S 148 20 E
Huy, Belgium ............ 15 D5 50 31N 5 15 E
Huzhou, China ........... 33 C7 30 51N 120 8 E
Hvammstangi, Iceland .... 8 D3 65 24N 20 57W
Hvar, Croatia ............ 20 C7 43 11N 16 28 E
Hvítá →, Iceland ........ 8 D3 64 30N 21 58W
Hwachŏn-chŏsuji, S. Korea 35 E14 38 5N 127 50 E
Hwang Ho = Huang He →,
China ................. 35 F10 37 55N 118 50 E
Hwange, Zimbabwe ...... 55 F2 18 18S 26 30 E
Hwange Nat. Park,
Zimbabwe ............. 56 B4 19 0S 26 30 E
Hyannis, Mass., U.S.A. .... 76 E10 41 39N 70 17W
Hyannis, Nebr., U.S.A. .... 80 E4 42 0N 101 46W
Hyargas Nuur, Mongolia .. 32 B4 49 0N 93 0 E
Hydaburg, U.S.A. ........ 72 B2 55 15N 132 50W
Hyde Park, U.S.A. ........ 79 E11 41 47N 73 56W
Hyden, Australia ......... 61 F2 32 24S 118 53 E
Hyder, U.S.A. ............ 72 B2 55 55N 130 5W
**Hyderabad**, India ........ 40 L11 17 22N 78 29 E
**Hyderabad**, Pakistan ..... 42 G3 25 23N 68 24 E
Hyères, France .......... 18 E7 43 8N 6 9 E
Hyères, Îs. d', France ..... 18 E7 43 0N 6 20 E
Hyesan, N. Korea ........ 35 D15 41 20N 128 10 E
Hyland →, Canada ....... 72 B3 59 52N 128 12W
Hymia, India ............ 43 C8 33 40N 78 2 E
Hyndman Peak, U.S.A. .... 82 E6 43 45N 114 8W
Hyōgo □, Japan ......... 31 G7 35 15N 134 50 E
Hyrum, U.S.A. ........... 82 F8 41 38N 111 51W
Hysham, U.S.A. .......... 82 C10 46 18N 107 14W
Hythe, U.K. .............. 11 F9 51 4N 1 5 E
Hyūga, Japan ............ 31 H5 32 25N 131 35 E
Hyvinge = Hyvinkää,
Finland ............... 9 F21 60 38N 24 50 E
Hyvinkää, Finland ........ 9 F21 60 38N 24 50 E


# I


I-n-Gall, Niger ........... 50 E7 16 51N 7 1 E
Iaco →, Brazil .......... 92 E5 9 3S 68 34W
Iakora, Madag. .......... 57 C8 23 6S 46 40 E
Ialomiţa →, Romania ..... 17 F14 44 42N 27 51 E
**Iaşi**, Romania .......... 17 E14 47 10N 27 40 E
Ib →, India ............. 43 J10 21 34N 83 48 E
Iba, Phil. ............... 37 A6 15 22N 120 0 E
**Ibadan**, Nigeria ......... 50 G6 7 22N 3 58 E
Ibagué, Colombia ........ 92 C3 4 20N 75 20W
Ibar →, Serbia, Yug. ..... 21 C9 43 43N 20 45 E
Ibaraki □, Japan ......... 31 F10 36 10N 140 10 E
Ibarra, Ecuador .......... 92 C3 0 21N 78 7W
Ibembo,
Dem. Rep. of the Congo . 54 B1 2 35N 23 35 E
Ibera, L., Argentina ...... 94 B4 28 30S 57 9W
**Iberian Peninsula**, Europe 6 H5 40 0N 5 0W
Iberville, Canada ......... 79 A11 45 19N 73 17W
Iberville, Lac d', Canada ... 70 A5 55 55N 73 15W
Ibiá, Brazil .............. 93 G9 19 30S 46 30W
Ibicuí →, Brazil ........ 95 B4 29 25S 56 47W
Ibicuy, Argentina ........ 94 C4 33 55S 59 10W
Ibioapaba, Sa. da, Brazil ... 93 D10 4 0S 41 30W
**Ibiza** = Eivissa, Spain .... 22 C7 38 54N 1 26 E
Ibo, Mozam. ............. 55 E5 12 22S 40 40 E
Ibonma, Indonesia ....... 37 E8 3 29S 133 31 E
Ibotirama, Brazil ......... 93 F10 12 13S 43 12W
Ibrāhīm →, Lebanon .... 47 A4 34 4N 35 38 E
'Ibrī, Oman ............. 45 F8 23 14N 56 30 E
Ibu, Indonesia ........... 37 D7 1 35N 127 33 E
Ibusuki, Japan ........... 31 J5 31 12N 130 40 E
Ica, Peru ............... 92 F3 14 0S 75 48W
Iça →, Brazil ........... 92 D5 2 55S 67 58W
Içana, Brazil ............ 92 C5 0 21N 67 19W
Içana →, Brazil ......... 92 C5 0 26N 67 19W
İçel = Mersin, Turkey ..... 25 G5 36 51N 34 36 E
**Iceland** ■, Europe ....... 8 D4 64 45N 19 0W
Ich'ang = Yichang, China . 33 C6 30 40N 111 20 E
Ichchapuram, India ...... 41 K14 19 10N 84 40 E
Ichhawar, India .......... 42 H7 23 1N 77 1 E
Ichihara, Japan .......... 31 G10 35 28N 140 5 E
Ichikawa, Japan ......... 31 G9 35 44N 139 55 E
Ichilo →, Bolivia ........ 92 G6 15 57S 64 50W
Ichinohe, Japan ......... 30 D10 40 13N 141 17 E
Ichinomiya, Japan ....... 31 G8 35 18N 136 48 E
Ichinoseki, Japan ........ 30 E10 38 55N 141 8 E
Ichŏn, S. Korea .......... 35 F14 37 17N 127 27 E
Icod, Canary Is. .......... 22 F3 28 22N 16 43W
Ida Grove, U.S.A. ........ 80 D7 42 21N 95 28W
Idabel, U.S.A. ........... 81 J7 33 54N 94 50W
**Idaho** □, U.S.A. ......... 82 D7 45 0N 115 0W
Idaho City, U.S.A. ........ 82 E6 43 50N 115 50W
Idaho Falls, U.S.A. ....... 82 E7 43 30N 112 2W
Idar-Oberstein, Germany .. 16 D4 49 43N 7 16 E
Idfû, Egypt ............. 51 D12 24 55N 32 49 E
Ídhi Óros, Greece ........ 23 D6 35 15N 24 45 E
Ídhra, Greece ........... 21 F10 37 20N 23 28 E
Idi, Indonesia ........... 36 C1 5 2N 97 37 E
Idiofa,
Dem. Rep. of the Congo . 52 E3 4 55S 19 42 E
Idlib, Syria .............. 44 C3 35 55N 36 36 E
Idria, U.S.A. ............. 84 J6 36 25N 120 41W
Idutywa, S. Africa ........ 57 E4 32 8S 28 18 E
Ieper, Belgium ........... 15 D2 50 51N 2 53 E
Ierápetra, Greece ........ 23 E7 35 1N 25 44 E
Iesi, Italy ............... 20 C5 43 31N 13 14 E
Ifakara, Tanzania ........ 52 F7 8 8S 36 41 E
'Ifāl, W. al →, Si. Arabia . 44 D2 28 7N 35 3 E
Ifanadiana, Madag. ...... 57 C8 21 19S 47 39 E
Ife, Nigeria ............. 50 G6 7 30N 4 31 E
Iférouâne, Niger ......... 50 E7 19 5N 8 24 E
Iffley, Australia .......... 62 B3 18 53S 141 12 E
Ifni, Morocco ........... 50 C3 29 29N 10 12W
Iforas, Adrar des, Mali ... 50 E6 19 40N 1 40 E
Ifould, L., Australia ....... 61 F5 30 52S 132 6 E
Iganga, Uganda ......... 54 B3 0 37N 33 28 E
Igarapava, Brazil ......... 93 H9 20 3S 47 47W
Igarka, Russia ........... 26 C9 67 30N 86 33 E
Igatimi, Paraguay ........ 95 A4 24 5S 55 40W
Iggesund, Sweden ....... 9 F17 61 39N 17 10 E
Iglésias, Italy ............ 20 E3 39 19N 8 32 E
Igloolik, Canada ......... 69 B11 69 20N 81 49W
Igluligaarjuk, Canada ..... 69 B10 63 21N 90 42W
Ignace, Canada .......... 70 C1 49 30N 91 40W
İğneada Burnu, Turkey ... 21 D13 41 53N 28 2 E
Igoumenítsa, Greece ..... 21 E9 39 32N 20 18 E
Iguaçu →, Brazil ....... 95 B5 25 36S 54 36W
Iguaçu, Cat. del, Brazil .... 95 B5 25 41S 54 26W
Iguaçu Falls = Iguaçu, Cat.
del, Brazil ............. 95 B5 25 41S 54 26W
Iguala, Mexico ........... 87 D5 18 20N 99 40W
Igualada, Spain .......... 19 B6 41 37N 1 37 E
Iguassu = Iguaçu →, Brazil 95 B5 25 36S 54 36W
Iguatu, Brazil ........... 93 E11 6 20S 39 18W
Iharana, Madag. ......... 57 A9 13 25S 50 0 E
Ihbulag, Mongolia ........ 34 C4 43 11N 107 10 E
Iheya-Shima, Japan ...... 31 L3 27 4N 127 58 E
Ihosy, Madag. ........... 57 C8 22 24S 46 8 E
Ihotry, L., Madag. ........ 57 C7 21 56S 43 41 E
Ii, Finland .............. 8 D21 65 19N 25 22 E
Ii-Shima, Japan .......... 31 L3 26 43N 127 47 E
Iida, Japan .............. 31 G8 35 35N 137 50 E
Iijoki →, Finland ........ 8 D21 65 20N 25 20 E
Iisalmi, Finland .......... 8 E22 63 32N 27 10 E
Iiyama, Japan ........... 31 F9 36 51N 138 22 E
Iizuka, Japan ............ 31 H5 33 38N 130 42 E
Ijebu-Ode, Nigeria ....... 50 G6 6 47N 3 58 E
IJmuiden, Neths. ......... 15 B4 52 28N 4 35 E
IJssel →, Neths. ........ 15 B5 52 35N 5 50 E
**IJsselmeer**, Neths. ...... 15 B5 52 45N 5 20 E
Ijuí, Brazil .............. 95 B5 28 23S 53 55W
Ijuí →, Brazil ........... 95 B4 27 58S 55 20W
Ikaluktutiak, Canada ...... 68 B9 69 10N 105 0W
Ikare, Nigeria ........... 50 G7 7 32N 5 40 E
Ikaría, Greece ........... 21 F12 37 35N 26 10 E
Ikeda, Japan ............ 31 G6 34 1N 133 48 E
Ikela,
Dem. Rep. of the Congo . 52 E4 1 6S 23 6 E
Iki, Japan ............... 31 H4 33 45N 129 42 E
Ikimba L., Tanzania ...... 54 C3 1 30S 31 20 E
Ikopa →, Madag. ........ 57 B8 16 45S 46 40 E
Ikungu, Tanzania ........ 54 C3 1 33S 33 42 E
Ilagan, Phil. ............. 37 A6 17 7N 121 53 E
Īlām, Iran ............... 44 C5 33 36N 46 36 E
Ilam, Nepal ............. 43 F12 26 58N 87 58 E
Ilam □, Iran ............. 44 C5 33 0N 47 0 E
Ilanskiy, Russia .......... 27 D10 56 14N 96 3 E
Iława, Poland ............ 17 B10 53 36N 19 34 E
Île-à-la-Crosse, Canada .... 73 B7 55 27N 107 53W
Île-à-la-Crosse, Lac, Canada 73 B7 55 40N 107 45W
**Île-de-France** □, France .. 18 B5 49 0N 2 20 E
Ilebo,
Dem. Rep. of the Congo . 52 E4 4 17S 20 55 E
Ilek, Russia ............. 26 D6 51 32N 53 21 E
Ilek →, Russia .......... 24 D9 51 30N 53 22 E
Ilesha, Nigeria .......... 50 G6 7 37N 4 40 E
Ilford, Canada ........... 73 B9 56 4N 95 35W
Ilfracombe, Australia ..... 62 C3 23 30S 144 30 E
Ilfracombe, U.K. ......... 11 F3 51 12N 4 8W
Ilhéus, Brazil ............ 93 F11 14 49S 39 2W
Ili →, Kazakstan ........ 26 E8 45 53N 77 10 E
Iliamna L., U.S.A. ........ 68 C4 59 30N 155 0W
Iligan, Phil. ............. 37 C6 8 12N 124 13 E
Ilion, U.S.A. ............. 79 D9 43 1N 75 2W
Ilkeston, U.K. ............ 10 E6 52 58N 1 19W
Ilkley, U.K. .............. 10 D6 53 56N 1 48W
Illampu = Ancohuma,
Nevada, Bolivia ........ 92 G5 16 0S 68 50W
Illana B., Phil. ........... 37 C6 7 35N 123 45 E
Illapel, Chile ............ 94 C1 32 0S 71 10W
Iller →, Germany ....... 16 D6 48 23N 9 58 E
Illetas, Spain ............ 22 B9 39 32N 2 35 E
Illimani, Nevado, Bolivia .. 92 G5 16 30S 67 50W
**Illinois** □, U.S.A. ........ 80 E10 40 15N 89 30W
Illinois →, U.S.A. ....... 75 C8 38 58N 90 28W
Illium = Troy, Turkey ..... 21 E12 39 57N 26 12 E
Illizi, Algeria ............ 50 C7 26 31N 8 32 E
Ilmajoki, Finland ......... 9 E20 62 44N 22 34 E
Ilmen, Ozero, Russia ..... 24 C5 58 15N 31 10 E
Ilo, Peru ............... 92 G4 17 40S 71 20W
Iloilo, Phil. .............. 37 B6 10 45N 122 33 E
Ilorin, Nigeria ........... 50 G6 8 30N 4 35 E
Ilwaco, U.S.A. ........... 84 D2 46 19N 124 3W
Ilwaki, Indonesia ........ 37 F7 7 55S 126 30 E
Imabari, Japan .......... 31 G6 34 4N 133 0 E
Imaloto →, Madag. ...... 57 C8 23 27S 45 13 E
Imandra, Ozero, Russia ... 24 A5 67 30N 33 0 E
Imari, Japan ............ 31 H4 33 15N 129 52 E
Imatra, Finland .......... 24 B4 61 12N 28 48 E
Imbil, Australia .......... 63 D5 26 22S 152 32 E
imeni 26 Bakinskikh
Komissarov = Neftçala,
Azerbaijan ............. 25 G8 39 19N 49 12 E
Imeri, Serra, Brazil ....... 92 C5 0 50N 65 25W
Imerimandroso, Madag. ... 57 B8 17 26S 48 35 E
Imi, Ethiopia ............ 46 F3 6 28N 42 10 E
Imlay, U.S.A. ............ 82 F4 40 40N 118 9W
Imlay City, U.S.A. ........ 78 D1 43 2N 83 5W
Immingham, U.K. ........ 10 D7 53 37N 0 13W
Immokalee, U.S.A. ....... 77 M5 26 25N 81 25W
Ímola, Italy ............. 20 B4 44 20N 11 42 E
Imperatriz, Brazil ........ 93 E9 5 30S 47 29W
Impéria, Italy ............ 18 E8 43 53N 8 3 E
Imperial, Canada ........ 73 C7 51 21N 105 28W
Imperial, Calif., U.S.A. .... 85 N11 32 51N 115 34W
Imperial, Nebr., U.S.A. .... 80 E4 40 31N 101 39W
Imperial Beach, U.S.A. .... 85 N9 32 35N 117 8W
Imperial Dam, U.S.A. ..... 85 N12 32 55N 114 25W
Imperial Reservoir, U.S.A. . 85 N12 32 53N 114 28W
Imperial Valley, U.S.A. .... 85 N11 33 0N 115 30W
Imperieuse Reef, Australia . 60 C2 17 36S 118 50 E
Impfondo, Congo ........ 52 D3 1 40N 18 0 E
Imphal, India ............ 41 G18 24 48N 93 56 E
İmroz = Gökçeada, Turkey 21 D11 40 10N 25 50 E
Imuris, Mexico .......... 86 A2 30 47N 110 52W
Imuruan B., Phil. ......... 37 B5 10 40N 119 10 E
In Salah, Algeria ......... 50 C6 27 10N 2 32 E
Ina, Japan .............. 31 G8 35 50N 137 55 E
Inangahua Junction, N.Z. . 59 J3 41 52S 171 59 E
Inanwatan, Indonesia ..... 37 E8 2 10S 132 14 E
Iñapari, Peru ............ 92 F5 11 0S 69 40W
Inari, Finland ............ 8 B22 68 54N 27 5 E
Inarijärvi, Finland ........ 8 B22 69 0N 28 0 E
Inawashiro-Ko, Japan .... 30 F10 37 29N 140 6 E
Inca, Spain ............. 22 B9 39 43N 2 54 E
Inca de Oro, Chile ....... 94 B2 26 45S 69 54W
Incaguasi, Chile ......... 94 B1 29 12S 71 5W

## J

**Jaipur**, *India* 42 F6 27 0N 75 50 E
Jais, *India* 43 F9 26 15N 81 32 E
Jaisalmer, *India* 42 F4 26 55N 70 54 E
Jaisinghnagar, *India* 43 H8 23 38N 78 34 E
Jaitaran, *India* 42 F5 26 12N 73 56 E
Jaithari, *India* 43 H8 23 14N 78 37 E
Jājarm, *Iran* 45 B8 36 58N 56 27 E
Jakam →, *India* 42 H6 23 54N 74 13 E
**Jakarta**, *Indonesia* 37 G12 6 9S 106 49 E
Jakhal, *India* 42 E6 29 48N 75 50 E
Jakhau, *India* 42 H3 23 13N 68 43 E
Jakobstad = Pietarsaari, *Finland* 8 E20 63 40N 22 43 E
Jal, *U.S.A.* 81 J3 32 7N 103 12W
Jalalabad, *Afghan.* 42 B4 34 30N 70 29 E
Jalalabad, *India* 43 F8 27 41N 79 42 E
Jalalpur Jattan, *Pakistan* 42 C6 32 38N 74 11 E
Jalama, *U.S.A.* 85 L6 34 29N 120 29W
Jalapa, *Guatemala* 88 D2 14 39N 89 59W
Jalapa Enríquez, *Mexico* 87 D5 19 32N 96 55W
Jalasjärvi, *Finland* 9 E20 62 29N 22 47 E
Jalaun, *India* 43 F8 26 8N 79 25 E
Jaldhaka →, *Bangla.* 43 F13 26 16N 89 16 E
Jalesar, *India* 42 F8 27 29N 78 19 E
Jaleswar, *Nepal* 43 F11 26 38N 85 48 E
Jalgaon, *Maharashtra, India* 40 J10 21 2N 76 31 E
Jalgaon, *Maharashtra, India* 40 J9 21 0N 75 42 E
Jalībah, *Iraq* 44 D5 30 35N 46 32 E
Jalisco □, *Mexico* 86 D4 20 0N 104 0W
Jalkot, *Pakistan* 43 B5 35 14N 73 24 E
Jalna, *India* 40 K9 19 48N 75 38 E
Jalón →, *Spain* 19 B5 41 47N 1 4W
Jalor, *India* 42 G5 25 21N 72 37 E
Jalpa, *Mexico* 86 C4 21 38N 102 58W
Jalpaiguri, *India* 41 F16 26 32N 88 46 E
Jaluit I., *Marshall Is.* 64 G8 6 0N 169 30 E
Jalūlā, *Iraq* 44 C5 34 16N 45 10 E
**Jamaica ■**, *W. Indies* 88 C4 18 10N 77 30W
Jamalpur, *Bangla.* 41 G16 24 52N 89 56 E
Jamalpur, *India* 43 G12 25 18N 86 28 E
Jamalpurganj, *India* 43 H13 23 2N 87 59 E
Jamanxim →, *Brazil* 93 D7 4 43S 56 18W
Jambi, *Indonesia* 36 E2 1 38S 103 30 E
Jambi □, *Indonesia* 36 E2 1 30S 102 30 E
Jambusar, *India* 42 H5 22 3N 72 51 E
James →, *S. Dak., U.S.A.* 80 D6 42 52N 97 18W
James →, *Va., U.S.A.* 76 G7 36 56N 76 27W
James B., *Canada* 70 B3 54 0N 80 0W
James Ranges, *Australia* 60 D5 24 10S 132 30 E
James Ross I., *Antarctica* 5 C18 63 58S 57 50W
Jamesabad, *Pakistan* 42 G3 25 17N 69 15 E
Jamestown, *Australia* 63 E2 33 10S 138 32 E
Jamestown, *S. Africa* 56 E4 31 6S 26 45 E
Jamestown, *N. Dak., U.S.A.* 80 B5 46 54N 98 42W
Jamestown, *N.Y., U.S.A.* 78 D5 42 6N 79 14W
Jamestown, *Pa., U.S.A.* 78 E4 41 29N 80 27W
Jamīlābād, *Iran* 45 C6 34 24N 48 28 E
Jamiltepec, *Mexico* 87 D5 16 17N 97 49W
Jamira →, *India* 43 J13 21 35N 88 28 E
Jamkhandi, *India* 40 L9 16 30N 75 15 E
Jammu, *India* 42 C6 32 43N 74 54 E
**Jammu & Kashmir □**, *India* 43 B7 34 25N 77 0 E
Jamnagar, *India* 42 H4 22 30N 70 6 E
Jamni →, *India* 43 G8 25 13N 78 35 E
Jampur, *Pakistan* 42 E4 29 39N 70 40 E
Jamrud, *Pakistan* 42 C4 33 59N 71 24 E
Jämsä, *Finland* 9 F21 61 53N 25 10 E
Jamshedpur, *India* 43 H12 22 44N 86 12 E
Jamtara, *India* 43 H12 23 59N 86 49 E
Jämtland, *Sweden* 8 E15 63 31N 14 0 E
Jan L., *Canada* 73 C8 54 56N 102 55W
Jan Mayen, *Arctic* 4 B7 71 0N 9 0W
Janakkala, *Finland* 9 F21 60 54N 24 36 E
Janaúba, *Brazil* 93 G10 15 48S 43 19W
Jand, *Pakistan* 42 C5 33 30N 72 6 E
Jandaq, *Iran* 45 C7 34 3N 54 22 E
Jandia, *Canary Is.* 22 F5 28 6N 14 21W
Jandia, Pta. de, *Canary Is.* 22 F5 28 3N 14 31W
Jandola, *Pakistan* 42 C4 32 20N 70 9 E
Jandowae, *Australia* 63 D5 26 45S 151 7 E
Janesville, *U.S.A.* 80 D10 42 41N 89 1W
Janghai, *India* 43 G10 25 33N 82 19 E
Janīn, *West Bank* 47 C4 32 28N 35 18 E
Janjgir, *India* 43 J10 22 1N 82 34 E
Janos, *Mexico* 86 A3 30 45N 108 10W
Januária, *Brazil* 93 G10 15 25S 44 25W
Janubio, *Canary Is.* 22 F6 28 56N 13 50W
Jaora, *India* 42 H6 23 40N 75 10 E
**Japan ■**, *Asia* 31 G8 36 0N 136 0 E
Japan, Sea of, *Asia* 30 E7 40 0N 135 0 E
Japan Trench, *Pac. Oc.* 28 F18 32 0N 142 0 E
Japen = Yapen, *Indonesia* 37 E9 1 50S 136 0 E
Japla, *India* 43 G11 24 33N 84 1 E
Japurá →, *Brazil* 92 D5 3 8S 65 46W
Jaquarão, *Brazil* 95 C5 32 34S 53 23W
Jaqué, *Panama* 88 E4 7 27N 78 8W
Jarābulus, *Syria* 44 B3 36 49N 38 1 E
Jarama →, *Spain* 19 B4 40 24N 3 32W
Jaranwala, *Pakistan* 42 D5 31 15N 73 26 E
Jarash, *Jordan* 47 C4 32 17N 35 54 E
Jardim, *Brazil* 94 A4 21 28S 56 2W
Jardines de la Reina, Arch. de los, *Cuba* 88 B4 20 50N 78 50W
Jargalang, *China* 35 C12 43 5N 122 55 E
Jargalant = Hovd, *Mongolia* 32 B4 48 2N 91 37 E
Jari →, *Brazil* 93 D8 1 9S 51 54W
Jarīr, W. al →, *Si. Arabia* 44 E4 25 38N 42 30 E
Jarosław, *Poland* 17 C12 50 2N 22 42 E
Jarrahdale, *Australia* 61 F2 32 24S 116 5 E
Jarrahi →, *Iran* 45 D6 30 49N 48 48 E
Jarres, Plaine des, *Laos* 38 C4 19 27N 103 10 E
Jartai, *China* 34 E3 39 45N 105 48 E
Jarud Qi, *China* 35 B11 44 28N 120 50 E
Järvenpää, *Finland* 9 F21 60 29N 25 5 E
Jarvis, *Canada* 78 D4 42 53N 80 6W
Jarvis I., *Pac. Oc.* 65 H12 0 15S 159 55W
Jarwa, *India* 43 F10 27 38N 82 30 E
Jasdan, *India* 42 H4 22 2N 71 12 E
Jashpurnagar, *India* 43 H11 22 54N 84 9 E
Jasidih, *India* 43 G12 24 31N 86 39 E
Jāsimīyah, *Iraq* 44 C5 33 45N 44 41 E
Jasin, *Malaysia* 39 L4 2 20N 102 26 E
Jāsk, *Iran* 45 E8 25 38N 57 45 E
Jasło, *Poland* 17 D11 49 45N 21 30 E
Jaso, *India* 43 G9 24 30N 80 29 E
Jasper, *Alta., Canada* 72 C5 52 55N 118 5W
Jasper, *Ont., Canada* 79 B9 44 52N 75 57W
Jasper, *Ala., U.S.A.* 77 J2 33 50N 87 17W
Jasper, *Fla., U.S.A.* 77 K4 30 31N 82 57W
Jasper, *Ind., U.S.A.* 76 F2 38 24N 86 56W
Jasper, *Tex., U.S.A.* 81 K8 30 56N 94 1W
Jasper Nat. Park, *Canada* 72 C5 52 50N 118 8W
Jasrasar, *India* 42 F5 27 43N 73 49 E
Jászberény, *Hungary* 17 E10 47 30N 19 55 E
Jataí, *Brazil* 93 G8 17 58S 51 48W
Jati, *Pakistan* 42 G3 24 20N 68 19 E
Jatibarang, *Indonesia* 37 G13 6 28S 108 18 E
Jatinegara, *Indonesia* 37 G12 6 13S 106 52 E
Játiva = Xátiva, *Spain* 19 C5 38 59N 0 32W
Jaú, *Brazil* 95 A6 22 10S 48 30W
Jauja, *Peru* 92 F3 11 45S 75 15W
Jaunpur, *India* 43 G10 25 46N 82 44 E
**Java** = Jawa, *Indonesia* 37 G14 7 0S 110 0 E
Java Barat □, *Indonesia* 37 G12 7 0S 107 0 E
Java Sea, *Indonesia* 36 E3 4 35S 107 15 E
Java Tengah □, *Indonesia* 37 G14 7 0S 110 0 E
Java Timur □, *Indonesia* 37 G15 8 0S 113 0 E
Java Trench, *Ind. Oc.* 36 F3 9 0S 105 0 E
Javhlant = Uliastay, *Mongolia* 32 B4 47 56N 97 28 E
Jawa, *Indonesia* 37 G14 7 0S 110 0 E
Jawad, *India* 42 G6 24 36N 74 51 E
Jay Peak, *U.S.A.* 79 B12 44 55N 72 32W
Jaya, Puncak, *Indonesia* 37 E9 3 57S 137 17 E
Jayanti, *India* 41 F16 26 45N 89 40 E
Jayapura, *Indonesia* 37 E10 2 28S 140 38 E
Jayawijaya, Pegunungan, *Indonesia* 37 F9 5 0S 139 0 E
Jaynagar, *India* 41 F15 26 43N 86 9 E
Jayrūd, *Syria* 44 C3 33 49N 36 44 E
Jayton, *U.S.A.* 81 J4 33 15N 100 34W
Jāz Mūrīān, Hāmūn-e, *Iran* 45 E8 27 20N 58 55 E
Jazīreh-ye Shīf, *Iran* 45 D6 29 4N 50 54 E
Jazminal, *Mexico* 86 C4 24 56N 101 25W
Jazzīn, *Lebanon* 47 B4 33 31N 35 35 E
Jean, *U.S.A.* 85 K11 35 47N 115 20W
Jean Marie River, *Canada* 72 A4 61 32N 120 38W
Jean Rabel, *Haiti* 89 C5 19 50N 73 5W
Jeanerette, *U.S.A.* 81 L9 29 55N 91 40W
Jeanette, Ostrov = Zhannetty, Ostrov, *Russia* 27 B16 76 43N 158 0 E
Jeannette, *U.S.A.* 78 F5 40 20N 79 36W
Jebāl Bārez, Kūh-e, *Iran* 45 D8 28 30N 58 20 E
Jebel, Bahr el →, *Sudan* 51 G12 9 30N 30 25 E
Jedburgh, *U.K.* 12 F6 55 29N 2 33W
**Jedda** = Jiddah, *Si. Arabia* 46 C2 21 29N 39 10 E
Jeddore L., *Canada* 71 C8 48 3N 55 55W
Jędrzejów, *Poland* 17 C11 50 35N 20 15 E
Jefferson, *Iowa, U.S.A.* 80 D7 42 1N 94 23W
Jefferson, *Ohio, U.S.A.* 78 E4 41 44N 80 46W
Jefferson, *Tex., U.S.A.* 81 J7 32 46N 94 21W
Jefferson, Mt., *Nev., U.S.A.* 82 G5 38 51N 117 0W
Jefferson, Mt., *Oreg., U.S.A.* 82 D3 44 41N 121 48W
**Jefferson City**, *Mo., U.S.A.* 80 F8 38 34N 92 10W
Jefferson City, *Tenn., U.S.A.* 77 G4 36 7N 83 30W
Jeffersontown, *U.S.A.* 76 F3 38 12N 85 35W
Jeffersonville, *U.S.A.* 76 F3 38 17N 85 44W
Jeffrey City, *U.S.A.* 82 E10 42 30N 107 49W
Jega, *Nigeria* 50 F6 12 15N 4 23 E
Jēkabpils, *Latvia* 9 H21 56 29N 25 57 E
Jekyll I., *U.S.A.* 77 K5 31 4N 81 25W
Jelenia Góra, *Poland* 16 C8 50 50N 15 45 E
Jelgava, *Latvia* 9 H20 56 41N 23 49 E
Jemaja, *Indonesia* 39 L5 3 5N 105 45 E
Jemaluang, *Malaysia* 39 L4 2 16N 103 52 E
Jember, *Indonesia* 37 H15 8 11S 113 41 E
Jembongan, *Malaysia* 36 C5 6 45N 117 20 E
Jena, *Germany* 16 C6 50 54N 11 35 E
Jena, *U.S.A.* 81 K8 31 41N 92 8W
Jenkins, *U.S.A.* 76 G4 37 10N 82 38W
Jenner, *U.S.A.* 84 G3 38 27N 123 7W
Jennings, *U.S.A.* 81 K8 30 13N 92 40W
Jepara, *Indonesia* 37 G14 7 40S 109 14 E
Jeparit, *Australia* 63 F3 36 8S 142 1 E
Jequié, *Brazil* 93 F10 13 51S 40 5W
Jequitinhonha, *Brazil* 93 G10 16 30S 41 0W
Jequitinhonha →, *Brazil* 93 G11 15 51S 38 53W
Jerantut, *Malaysia* 39 L4 3 56N 102 22 E
Jérémie, *Haiti* 89 C5 18 40N 74 10W
Jerez, Punta, *Mexico* 87 C5 22 58N 97 40W
Jerez de García Salinas, *Mexico* 86 C4 22 39N 103 0W
Jerez de la Frontera, *Spain* 19 D2 36 41N 6 7W
Jerez de los Caballeros, *Spain* 19 C2 38 20N 6 45W
**Jericho** = El Arīḥā, *West Bank* 47 D4 31 52N 35 27 E
Jericho, *Australia* 62 C4 23 38S 146 6 E
Jerilderie, *Australia* 63 F4 35 20S 145 41 E
Jermyn, *U.S.A.* 79 E9 41 31N 75 31W
Jerome, *U.S.A.* 82 E6 42 44N 114 31W
Jerramungup, *Australia* 61 F2 33 55S 118 55 E
**Jersey**, *U.K.* 11 H5 49 11N 2 7W
Jersey City, *U.S.A.* 79 F10 40 44N 74 4W
Jersey Shore, *U.S.A.* 78 E7 41 12N 77 15W
Jerseyville, *U.S.A.* 80 F9 39 7N 90 20W
**Jerusalem**, *Israel* 47 D4 31 47N 35 10 E
Jervis B., *Australia* 63 F5 35 8S 150 46 E
Jervis Inlet, *Canada* 72 C4 50 0N 123 57W
Jesselton = Kota Kinabalu, *Malaysia* 36 C5 6 0N 116 4 E
Jessore, *Bangla.* 41 H16 23 10N 89 10 E
Jesup, *U.S.A.* 77 K5 31 36N 81 53W
Jesús Carranza, *Mexico* 87 D5 17 28N 95 1W
Jesús María, *Argentina* 94 C3 30 59S 64 5W
Jetmore, *U.S.A.* 81 F5 38 4N 99 54W
Jetpur, *India* 42 J4 21 45N 70 10 E
Jevnaker, *Norway* 9 F14 60 15N 10 26 E
Jewett, *U.S.A.* 78 F3 40 22N 81 2W
Jewett City, *U.S.A.* 79 E13 41 36N 72 0W
Jeyhūnābād, *Iran* 45 C6 34 58N 48 59 E
Jeypore, *India* 41 K13 18 50N 82 38 E
Jha Jha, *India* 43 G12 24 46N 86 22 E
Jhabua, *India* 42 H6 22 46N 74 36 E
Jhajjar, *India* 42 E7 28 37N 76 42 E
Jhal, *Pakistan* 42 E2 28 17N 67 27 E
Jhal Jhao, *Pakistan* 40 F4 26 20N 65 35 E
Jhalawar, *India* 42 G7 24 40N 76 10 E
Jhalida, *India* 43 H11 23 22N 85 58 E
Jhalrapatan, *India* 42 G7 24 33N 76 10 E
Jhang Maghiana, *Pakistan* 42 D5 31 15N 72 22 E
Jhansi, *India* 43 G8 25 30N 78 36 E
Jhargram, *India* 43 H12 22 27N 86 59 E
Jharia, *India* 43 H12 23 45N 86 26 E
Jharsuguda, *India* 41 J14 21 56N 84 5 E
Jhelum, *Pakistan* 42 C5 33 0N 73 45 E
Jhelum →, *Pakistan* 42 D5 31 20N 72 10 E
Jhilmilli, *India* 43 H10 23 24N 82 51 E
Jhudo, *Pakistan* 42 G3 24 58N 69 18 E
Jhunjhunu, *India* 42 E6 28 10N 75 30 E
Ji-Paraná, *Brazil* 92 F6 10 52S 62 57W
Ji Xian, *Hebei, China* 34 F8 37 35N 115 30 E
Ji Xian, *Henan, China* 34 G8 35 22N 114 5 E
Ji Xian, *Shanxi, China* 34 F6 36 7N 110 40 E
Jia Xian, *Henan, China* 34 H7 33 59N 113 12 E
Jia Xian, *Shaanxi, China* 34 E6 38 12N 110 28 E
Jiamusi, *China* 33 B8 46 40N 130 26 E
Ji'an, *Jiangxi, China* 33 D6 27 6N 114 59 E
Ji'an, *Jilin, China* 35 D14 41 5N 126 10 E
Jianchang, *China* 35 D11 40 55N 120 35 E
Jianchangying, *China* 35 D10 40 10N 118 50 E
Jiangcheng, *China* 32 D5 22 36N 101 52 E
Jiangmen, *China* 33 D6 22 32N 113 0 E
**Jiangsu □**, *China* 35 H11 33 0N 120 0 E
Jiangxi □, *China* 33 D6 27 30N 116 0 E
Jiao Xian = Jiaozhou, *China* 35 F11 36 18N 120 1 E
Jiaohe, *Hebei, China* 34 E9 38 2N 116 20 E
Jiaohe, *Jilin, China* 35 C14 43 40N 127 22 E
Jiaozhou, *China* 35 F11 36 18N 120 1 E
Jiaozhou Wan, *China* 35 F11 36 5N 120 10 E
Jiaozuo, *China* 34 G7 35 16N 113 12 E
Jiawang, *China* 35 G9 34 28N 117 26 E
Jiaxiang, *China* 34 G9 35 25N 116 20 E
Jiaxing, *China* 33 C7 30 49N 120 45 E
Jiayi = Chiai, *Taiwan* 33 D7 23 29N 120 25 E
Jibuti = Djibouti ■, *Africa* 46 E3 12 0N 43 0 E
Jicarón, I., *Panama* 88 E3 7 10N 81 50W
**Jiddah**, *Si. Arabia* 46 C2 21 29N 39 10 E
Jido, *India* 41 E19 29 2N 94 58 E
Jieshou, *China* 34 H8 33 18N 115 22 E
Jiexiu, *China* 34 F6 37 2N 111 55 E
Jiggalong, *Australia* 60 D3 23 21S 120 47 E
Jigni, *India* 43 G8 25 45N 79 25 E
Jihlava, *Czech Rep.* 16 D8 49 28N 15 35 E
Jihlava →, *Czech Rep.* 17 D9 48 55N 16 36 E
Jijiga, *Ethiopia* 46 F3 9 20N 42 50 E
Jilin, *China* 35 C14 43 44N 126 30 E
Jilin □, *China* 35 C14 44 0N 127 0 E
Jilong = Chilung, *Taiwan* 33 D7 25 3N 121 45 E
Jim Thorpe, *U.S.A.* 79 F9 40 52N 75 44W
Jima, *Ethiopia* 46 F2 7 40N 36 47 E
Jiménez, *Mexico* 86 B4 27 10N 104 54W
Jimo, *China* 35 F11 36 23N 120 30 E
Jin Xian = Jinzhou, *China* 34 E8 38 2N 115 2 E
Jin Xian, *China* 35 E11 38 55N 121 42 E
Jinan, *China* 34 F9 36 38N 117 1 E
Jincheng, *China* 34 G7 35 29N 112 50 E
Jind, *India* 42 E7 29 19N 76 22 E
Jindabyne, *Australia* 63 F4 36 25S 148 35 E
Jindřichův Hradec, *Czech Rep.* 16 D8 49 10N 15 2 E
Jing He →, *China* 34 G5 34 27N 109 4 E
Jingbian, *China* 34 F5 37 20N 108 30 E
Jingchuan, *China* 34 G4 35 20N 107 20 E
Jingdezhen, *China* 33 D6 29 20N 117 11 E
Jinggu, *China* 32 D5 23 35N 100 41 E
Jinghai, *China* 34 E9 38 55N 116 55 E
Jingle, *China* 34 E6 38 20N 111 55 E
Jingning, *China* 34 G3 35 30N 105 43 E
Jingpo Hu, *China* 35 C15 43 55N 128 55 E
Jingtai, *China* 34 F3 37 10N 104 6 E
Jingxing, *China* 34 E8 38 2N 114 8 E
Jingyang, *China* 34 G5 34 30N 108 50 E
Jingyu, *China* 35 C14 42 25N 126 45 E
Jingyuan, *China* 34 F3 36 30N 104 40 E
Jingziguan, *China* 34 H6 33 15N 111 0 E
Jinhua, *China* 33 D6 29 8N 119 38 E
Jining, *Nei Mongol Zizhiqu, China* 34 D7 41 5N 113 0 E
Jining, *Shandong, China* 34 G9 35 22N 116 34 E
Jinja, *Uganda* 54 B3 0 25N 33 12 E
Jinjang, *Malaysia* 39 L3 3 13N 101 39 E
Jinji, *China* 34 F4 37 58N 106 8 E
Jinnah Barrage, *Pakistan* 40 C7 32 58N 71 33 E
Jinotega, *Nic.* 88 D2 13 6N 85 59W
Jinotepe, *Nic.* 88 D2 11 50N 86 10W
Jinsha Jiang →, *China* 32 D5 28 50N 104 36 E
Jinxi, *China* 35 D11 40 52N 120 50 E
Jinxiang, *China* 34 G9 35 5N 116 22 E
Jinzhou, *Hebei, China* 34 E8 38 2N 115 2 E
Jinzhou, *Liaoning, China* 35 D11 41 5N 121 3 E
Jiparaná →, *Brazil* 92 E6 8 3S 62 52W
Jipijapa, *Ecuador* 92 D2 1 0S 80 40W
Jiquilpan, *Mexico* 86 D4 19 57N 102 42W
Jishan, *China* 34 G6 35 34N 110 58 E
Jisr ash Shughūr, *Syria* 44 C3 35 49N 36 18 E
Jitarning, *Australia* 61 F2 32 48S 117 57 E
Jitra, *Malaysia* 39 J3 6 16N 100 25 E
Jiu →, *Romania* 17 F12 43 47N 23 48 E
Jiudengkou, *China* 34 E4 39 56N 106 40 E
Jiujiang, *China* 33 D6 29 42N 115 58 E
Jiutai, *China* 35 B13 44 10N 125 50 E
Jiuxiangcheng, *China* 34 H8 33 12N 114 50 E
Jiuxincheng, *China* 34 E8 39 17N 115 59 E
Jixi, *China* 35 B16 45 20N 130 50 E
Jiyang, *China* 35 F9 37 0N 117 12 E
Jiyuan, *China* 34 G7 35 7N 112 57 E
Jīzān, *Si. Arabia* 46 D3 17 0N 42 20 E
Jize, *China* 34 F8 36 54N 114 56 E
Jīzl, Wādī al, *Si. Arabia* 44 E3 25 39N 38 25 E
Jizō-Zaki, *Japan* 31 G6 35 34N 133 20 E
Jizzakh, *Uzbekistan* 26 E7 40 6N 67 50 E
Joaçaba, *Brazil* 95 B5 27 5S 51 31W
João Pessoa, *Brazil* 93 E12 7 10S 34 52W
Joaquín V. González, *Argentina* 94 B3 25 10S 64 0W
Jobat, *India* 42 H6 22 25N 74 34 E
**Jodhpur**, *India* 42 F5 26 23N 73 8 E
Jodiya, *India* 42 H4 22 42N 70 18 E
Joensuu, *Finland* 24 B4 62 37N 29 49 E
Jōetsu, *Japan* 31 F9 37 12N 138 10 E
Jofane, *Mozam.* 57 C5 21 15S 34 18 E
Jogbani, *India* 43 F12 26 25N 87 15 E
Jõgeva, *Estonia* 9 G22 58 45N 26 24 E
Jogjakarta = Yogyakarta, *Indonesia* 37 G14 7 49S 110 22 E
**Johannesburg**, *S. Africa* 57 D4 26 10S 28 2 E
Johannesburg, *U.S.A.* 85 K9 35 22N 117 38W
Johilla →, *India* 43 H9 23 37N 81 14 E
John Day, *U.S.A.* 82 D4 44 25N 118 57W
John Day →, *U.S.A.* 82 D3 45 44N 120 39W
John D'Or Prairie, *Canada* 72 B5 58 30N 115 8W
John H. Kerr Reservoir, *U.S.A.* 77 G6 36 36N 78 18W
John o' Groats, *U.K.* 12 C5 58 38N 3 4W
Johnnie, *U.S.A.* 85 J10 36 25N 116 5W
John's Ra., *Australia* 62 C1 21 55S 133 23 E
Johnson, *Kans., U.S.A.* 81 G4 37 34N 101 45W
Johnson, *Vt., U.S.A.* 79 B12 44 38N 72 41W
Johnson City, *N.Y., U.S.A.* 79 D9 42 7N 75 58W
Johnson City, *Tenn., U.S.A.* 77 G4 36 19N 82 21W
Johnson City, *Tex., U.S.A.* 81 K5 30 17N 98 25W
Johnsonburg, *U.S.A.* 78 E6 41 29N 78 41W
Johnsondale, *U.S.A.* 85 K8 35 58N 118 32W
Johnson's Crossing, *Canada* 72 A2 60 29N 133 18W
Johnston, L., *Australia* 61 F3 32 25S 120 30 E
Johnston Falls = Mambilima Falls, *Zambia* 55 E2 10 31S 28 45 E
Johnston I., *Pac. Oc.* 65 F11 17 10N 169 8W
Johnstone Str., *Canada* 72 C3 50 28N 126 0W
Johnstown, *N.Y., U.S.A.* 79 C10 43 0N 74 22W
Johnstown, *Ohio, U.S.A.* 78 F2 40 9N 82 41W
Johnstown, *Pa., U.S.A.* 78 F6 40 20N 78 55W
Johor Baharu, *Malaysia* 39 M4 1 28N 103 46 E
Jõhvi, *Estonia* 9 G22 59 22N 27 27 E
Joinville, *Brazil* 95 B6 26 15S 48 55W
Joinville I., *Antarctica* 5 C18 65 0S 55 30W
Jojutla, *Mexico* 87 D5 18 37N 99 11W
Jokkmokk, *Sweden* 8 C18 66 35N 19 50 E
Jökulsá á Bru →, *Iceland* 8 D6 65 40N 14 16W
Jökulsá á Fjöllum →, *Iceland* 8 C5 66 10N 16 30W
Jolfā, *Āzarbājān-e Sharqī, Iran* 44 B5 38 57N 45 38 E
Jolfā, *Eşfahan, Iran* 45 C6 32 58N 51 37 E
Joliet, *U.S.A.* 76 E1 41 32N 88 5W
Joliette, *Canada* 70 C5 46 3N 73 24W
Jolo, *Phil.* 37 C6 6 0N 121 0 E
Jolon, *U.S.A.* 84 K5 35 58N 121 9W
Jombang, *Indonesia* 37 G15 7 33S 112 14 E
Jonava, *Lithuania* 9 J21 55 8N 24 12 E
Jones Sound, *Canada* 4 B3 76 0N 85 0W
Jonesboro, *Ark., U.S.A.* 81 H9 35 50N 90 42W
Jonesboro, *La., U.S.A.* 81 J8 32 15N 92 43W
Joniškis, *Lithuania* 9 H20 56 13N 23 35 E
Jönköping, *Sweden* 9 H16 57 45N 14 8 E
Jonquière, *Canada* 71 C5 48 27N 71 14W
Joplin, *U.S.A.* 81 G7 37 6N 94 31W
Jora, *India* 42 F6 26 20N 77 49 E
Jordan, *Mont., U.S.A.* 82 C10 47 19N 106 55W
Jordan, *N.Y., U.S.A.* 79 C8 43 4N 76 29W
**Jordan ■**, *Asia* 47 E5 31 0N 36 0 E
**Jordan** →, *Asia* 47 D4 31 48N 35 32 E
Jordan Valley, *U.S.A.* 82 E5 42 59N 117 3W
Jorhat, *India* 41 F19 26 45N 94 12 E
Jörn, *Sweden* 8 D19 65 4N 20 1 E
Jorong, *Indonesia* 36 E4 3 58S 114 56 E
Jørpeland, *Norway* 9 G11 59 3N 6 1 E
Jorquera →, *Chile* 94 B2 28 3S 69 58W
Jos, *Nigeria* 50 G7 9 53N 8 51 E
José Batlle y Ordóñez, *Uruguay* 95 C4 33 20S 55 10W
Joseph, L., *Nfld., Canada* 71 B6 52 45N 65 18W
Joseph, L., *Ont., Canada* 78 A5 45 10N 79 44W
Joseph Bonaparte G., *Australia* 60 B4 14 35S 128 50 E
Joshinath, *India* 43 D8 30 34N 79 34 E
Joshua Tree, *U.S.A.* 85 L10 34 8N 116 19W
Joshua Tree National Park, *U.S.A.* 85 M10 33 55N 116 0W
Jostedalsbreen, *Norway* 9 F12 61 40N 6 59 E
Jotunheimen, *Norway* 9 F13 61 35N 8 25 E
Jourdanton, *U.S.A.* 81 L5 28 55N 98 33W
Jovellanos, *Cuba* 88 B3 22 40N 81 10W
Ju Xian, *China* 35 F10 36 35N 118 20 E
Juan Aldama, *Mexico* 86 C4 24 20N 103 23W
Juan Bautista Alberdi, *Argentina* 94 C3 34 26S 61 48W
Juan de Fuca Str., *Canada* 84 B3 48 15N 124 0W
Juan de Nova, *Ind. Oc.* 57 B7 17 3S 43 45 E
Juan Fernández, Arch. de, *Pac. Oc.* 90 G2 33 50S 80 0W
Juan José Castelli, *Argentina* 94 B3 25 27S 60 57W
Juan L. Lacaze, *Uruguay* 94 C4 34 26S 57 25W
Juankoski, *Finland* 8 E23 63 3N 28 19 E
Juárez, *Argentina* 94 D4 37 40S 59 43W
Juárez, *Mexico* 85 N11 32 20N 115 57W
Juárez, Sierra de, *Mexico* 86 A1 32 0N 116 0W
Juàzeiro, *Brazil* 93 E10 9 30S 40 30W
Juàzeiro do Norte, *Brazil* 93 E11 7 10S 39 18W
Juba, *Sudan* 51 H12 4 50N 31 35 E
Jubayl, *Lebanon* 47 A4 34 5N 35 39 E
Jubbah, *Si. Arabia* 44 D4 28 2N 40 56 E
Jubbal, *India* 42 D7 31 5N 77 40 E
Jubbulpore = Jabalpur, *India* 43 H8 23 9N 79 58 E
Jubilee L., *Australia* 61 E4 29 0S 126 50 E
Juby, C., *Morocco* 50 C3 28 0N 12 59W
Júcar = Xúquer →, *Spain* 19 C5 39 5N 0 10W
Júcaro, *Cuba* 88 B4 21 37N 78 51W
Juchitán, *Mexico* 87 D5 16 27N 95 5W
Judaea = Har Yehuda, *Israel* 47 D3 31 35N 34 57 E
Judith →, *U.S.A.* 82 C9 47 44N 109 39W
Judith, Pt., *U.S.A.* 79 E13 41 22N 71 29W
Judith Gap, *U.S.A.* 82 C9 46 41N 109 45W
Jugoslavia = Yugoslavia ■, *Europe* 21 B9 43 20N 20 0 E
Juigalpa, *Nic.* 88 D2 12 6N 85 26W
Juiz de Fora, *Brazil* 95 A7 21 43S 43 19W
Jujuy □, *Argentina* 94 A2 23 20S 65 40W
Julesburg, *U.S.A.* 80 E3 40 59N 102 16W
Juli, *Peru* 92 G5 16 10S 69 25W
Julia Cr. →, *Australia* 62 C3 20 0S 141 11 E
Julia Creek, *Australia* 62 C3 20 39S 141 44 E
Juliaca, *Peru* 92 G4 15 25S 70 10W
Julian, *U.S.A.* 85 M10 33 4N 116 38W
Julian L., *Canada* 70 B4 54 25N 77 57W
Julianatop, *Surinam* 93 C7 3 40N 56 30W
Julianehåb, *Greenland* 4 C5 60 43N 46 0W
Julimes, *Mexico* 86 B3 28 25N 105 27W
Jullundur, *India* 42 D6 31 20N 75 40 E
Julu, *China* 34 F8 37 15N 115 2 E
Jumbo, *Zimbabwe* 55 F3 17 30S 30 58 E
Jumbo Pk., *U.S.A.* 85 J12 36 12N 114 11W
Jumentos Cays, *Bahamas* 88 B4 23 0N 75 40W
Jumilla, *Spain* 19 C5 38 28N 1 19W

# K

Kingston, N.Y., U.S.A. 79 E11 41 56N 73 59W
Kingston, Pa., U.S.A. 79 E9 41 16N 75 54W
Kingston, R.I., U.S.A. 79 E13 41 29N 71 30W
Kingston Pk., U.S.A. 85 K11 35 45N 115 54W
Kingston South East, Australia 63 F2 36 51S 139 55 E
**Kingston upon Hull**, U.K. 10 D7 53 45N 0 21W
Kingston upon Hull □, U.K. 10 D7 53 45N 0 21W
Kingston-upon-Thames, U.K. 11 F7 51 24N 0 17W
**Kingstown**, St. Vincent 89 D7 13 10N 61 10W
Kingstree, U.S.A. 77 J6 33 40N 79 50W
Kingsville, Canada 78 D2 42 2N 82 45W
Kingsville, U.S.A. 81 M6 27 31N 97 52W
Kingussie, U.K. 12 D4 57 6N 4 2W
Kingwood, U.S.A. 81 K7 29 54N 95 18W
Kınık, Turkey 21 E12 39 6N 27 24 E
Kinistino, Canada 73 C7 52 57N 105 2W
Kinkala, Congo 52 E2 4 18S 14 49 E
Kinki □, Japan 31 H8 33 45N 136 0 E
Kinleith, N.Z. 59 H5 38 20S 175 56 E
Kinmount, Canada 78 B6 44 48N 78 45W
Kinna, Sweden 9 H15 57 32N 12 42 E
Kinnairds Hd., U.K. 12 D6 57 43N 2 1W
Kinnarodden, Norway 6 A11 71 8N 27 40 E
Kino, Mexico 86 B2 28 45N 111 59W
Kinoje →, Canada 70 B3 52 8N 81 25W
Kinomoto, Japan 31 G8 35 30N 136 13 E
Kinoni, Uganda 54 C3 0 41S 30 28 E
Kinoosao, Canada 73 B8 57 5N 102 1W
Kinross, U.K. 12 E5 56 13N 3 25W
Kinsale, Ireland 13 E3 51 42N 8 31W
Kinsale, Old Hd. of, Ireland 13 E3 51 37N 8 33W
Kinsha = Chang Jiang →, China 33 C7 31 48N 121 10 E
**Kinshasa**, Dem. Rep. of the Congo 52 E3 4 20S 15 15 E
Kinsley, U.S.A. 81 G5 37 55N 99 25W
Kinsman, U.S.A. 78 E4 41 26N 80 35W
Kinston, U.S.A. 77 H7 35 16N 77 35W
Kintore Ra., Australia 60 D4 23 15S 128 47 E
Kintyre, U.K. 12 F3 55 30N 5 35W
Kintyre, Mull of, U.K. 12 F3 55 17N 5 47W
Kinushseo →, Canada 70 A3 55 15N 83 45W
Kinuso, Canada 72 B5 55 20N 115 25W
Kinyangiri, Tanzania 54 C3 4 25S 34 37 E
Kinzua, U.S.A. 78 E6 41 52N 78 58W
Kinzua Dam, U.S.A. 78 E6 41 53N 79 0W
Kiosk, Canada 70 C4 46 6N 78 53W
Kiowa, Kans., U.S.A. 81 G5 37 1N 98 29W
Kiowa, Okla., U.S.A. 81 H7 34 43N 95 54W
Kipahigan L., Canada 73 B8 55 20N 101 55W
Kipanga, Tanzania 54 D4 6 15S 35 20 E
Kiparissía, Greece 21 F9 37 15N 21 40 E
Kiparissiakós Kólpos, Greece 21 F9 37 25N 21 25 E
Kipawa, L., Canada 70 C4 46 50N 79 0W
Kipembawe, Tanzania 54 D3 7 38S 33 27 E
Kipengere Ra., Tanzania 55 D3 9 12S 34 15 E
Kipili, Tanzania 54 D3 7 28S 30 32 E
Kipini, Kenya 54 C5 2 30S 40 32 E
Kipling, Canada 73 C8 50 6N 102 38W
Kippure, Ireland 13 C5 53 11N 6 21W
Kipushi, Dem. Rep. of the Congo 55 E2 11 48S 27 12 E
Kirensk, Russia 27 D11 57 50N 107 55 E
Kirghizia = Kyrgyzstan ■, Asia 26 E8 42 0N 75 0 E
Kirghizstan = Kyrgyzstan ■, Asia 26 E8 42 0N 75 0 E
Kirgiziya Steppe, Eurasia 25 E10 50 0N 55 0 E
**Kiribati** ■, Pac. Oc. 64 H10 5 0S 180 0 E
Kırıkkale, Turkey 25 G5 39 51N 33 32 E
Kirillov, Russia 24 C6 59 49N 38 24 E
Kirin = Jilin, China 35 C14 43 44N 126 30 E
Kiritimati, Kiribati 65 G12 1 58N 157 27W
Kirkby, U.K. 10 D5 53 30N 2 54W
Kirkby Lonsdale, U.K. 10 C5 54 12N 2 36W
Kirkcaldy, U.K. 12 E5 56 7N 3 9W
Kirkcudbright, U.K. 12 G4 54 50N 4 2W
Kirkee, India 40 K8 18 34N 73 56 E
Kirkenes, Norway 8 B23 69 40N 30 5 E
Kirkfield, Canada 78 B6 44 34N 78 59W
Kirkjubæjarklaustur, Iceland 8 E4 63 47N 18 4W
Kirkkonummi, Finland 9 F21 60 8N 24 26 E
Kirkland Lake, Canada 70 C3 48 9N 80 2W
Kırklareli, Turkey 21 D12 41 44N 27 15 E
Kirksville, U.S.A. 80 E8 40 12N 92 35W
Kirkūk, Iraq 44 C5 35 30N 44 21 E
Kirkwall, U.K. 12 C6 58 59N 2 58W
Kirkwood, S. Africa 56 E4 33 22S 25 15 E
**Kirov**, Russia 24 C8 58 35N 49 40 E
Kirovabad = Gäncä, Azerbaijan 25 F8 40 45N 46 20 E
Kirovakan = Vanadzor, Armenia 25 F7 40 48N 44 30 E
Kirovograd = Kirovohrad, Ukraine 25 E5 48 35N 32 20 E
Kirovohrad, Ukraine 25 E5 48 35N 32 20 E
Kirovsk = Babadayhan, Turkmenistan 26 F7 37 42N 60 23 E
Kirovsk, Russia 24 A5 67 32N 33 41 E
Kirovskiy, Kamchatka, Russia 27 D16 54 27N 155 42 E
Kirovskiy, Primorsk, Russia 30 B6 45 7N 133 30 E
Kirriemuir, U.K. 12 E5 56 41N 3 1W
Kirsanov, Russia 24 D7 52 35N 42 40 E
Kırşehir, Turkey 25 G5 39 14N 34 5 E
Kirthar Range, Pakistan 42 F2 27 0N 67 0 E
Kirtland, U.S.A. 83 H9 36 44N 108 21W
Kiruna, Sweden 8 C19 67 52N 20 15 E
Kirundu, Dem. Rep. of the Congo 54 C2 0 50S 25 35 E
Kiryū, Japan 31 F9 36 24N 139 20 E
Kisaga, Tanzania 54 C3 4 30S 34 23 E
Kisalaya, Nic. 88 D3 14 40N 84 3W
Kisámou, Kólpos, Greece 23 D5 35 30N 23 38 E
Kisanga, Dem. Rep. of the Congo 54 B2 2 30N 26 35 E
**Kisangani**, Dem. Rep. of the Congo 54 B2 0 35N 25 15 E
Kisar, Indonesia 37 F7 8 5S 127 10 E
Kisarawe, Tanzania 54 D4 6 53S 39 0 E
Kisarazu, Japan 31 G9 35 23N 139 55 E
Kishanganga →, Pakistan 43 B5 34 18N 73 28 E
Kishanganj, India 43 F13 26 3N 88 14 E
Kishangarh, Raj., India 42 F6 26 34N 74 52 E
Kishangarh, Raj., India 42 F4 27 50N 70 30 E
Kishinev = Chişinău, Moldova 17 E15 47 2N 28 50 E
Kishiwada, Japan 31 G7 34 28N 135 22 E
Kishtwar, India 43 C6 33 20N 75 48 E
Kisii, Kenya 54 C3 0 40S 34 45 E
Kisiju, Tanzania 54 D4 7 23S 39 19 E
Kisizi, Uganda 54 C2 1 0S 29 58 E
Kiskőrös, Hungary 17 E10 46 37N 19 20 E
Kiskunfélegyháza, Hungary 17 E10 46 42N 19 53 E
Kiskunhalas, Hungary 17 E10 46 28N 19 37 E
Kislovodsk, Russia 25 F7 43 50N 42 45 E
Kismayu = Chisimaio, Somali Rep. 49 G8 0 22S 42 32 E
Kiso-Gawa →, Japan 31 G8 35 20N 136 45 E
Kiso-Sammyaku, Japan 31 G8 35 45N 137 45 E
Kisofukushima, Japan 31 G8 35 52N 137 43 E
Kisoro, Uganda 54 C2 1 17S 29 48 E
Kissidougou, Guinea 50 G3 9 5N 10 5W
Kissimmee, U.S.A. 77 L5 28 18N 81 24W
Kissimmee →, U.S.A. 77 M5 27 9N 80 52W
Kississing L., Canada 73 B8 55 10N 101 20W
Kissónerga, Cyprus 23 E11 34 49N 32 24 E
Kisumu, Kenya 54 C3 0 3S 34 45 E
Kiswani, Tanzania 54 C4 4 5S 37 57 E
Kiswere, Tanzania 55 D4 9 27S 39 30 E
Kit Carson, U.S.A. 80 F3 38 46N 102 48W
Kita, Mali 50 F4 13 5N 9 25W
Kitaibaraki, Japan 31 F10 36 50N 140 45 E
Kitakami, Japan 30 E10 39 20N 141 10 E
Kitakami-Gawa →, Japan 30 E10 38 25N 141 19 E
Kitakami-Sammyaku, Japan 30 E10 39 30N 141 30 E
Kitakata, Japan 30 F9 37 39N 139 52 E
Kitakyūshū, Japan 31 H5 33 50N 130 50 E
Kitale, Kenya 54 B4 1 0N 35 0 E
Kitami, Japan 30 C11 43 48N 143 54 E
Kitami-Sammyaku, Japan 30 B11 44 22N 142 43 E
Kitangiri, L., Tanzania 54 C3 4 5S 34 20 E
Kitaya, Tanzania 55 E5 10 38S 40 8 E
Kitchener, Canada 78 C4 43 27N 80 29W
Kitega = Gitega, Burundi 54 C2 3 26S 29 56 E
Kitengo, Dem. Rep. of the Congo 54 D1 7 26S 24 8 E
Kitgum, Uganda 54 B3 3 17N 32 52 E
Kíthira, Greece 21 F10 36 8N 23 0 E
Kíthnos, Greece 21 F11 37 26N 24 27 E
Kiti, Cyprus 23 E12 34 50N 33 34 E
Kiti, C., Cyprus 23 E12 34 48N 33 36 E
Kitimat, Canada 72 C3 54 3N 128 38W
Kitinen →, Finland 8 C22 67 14N 27 27 E
Kitsuki, Japan 31 H5 33 25N 131 37 E
Kittakittaooloo, L., Australia 63 D2 28 3S 138 14 E
Kittanning, U.S.A. 78 F5 40 49N 79 31W
Kittatinny Mts., U.S.A. 79 F10 41 0N 75 0W
Kittery, U.S.A. 77 D10 43 5N 70 45W
Kittilä, Finland 8 C21 67 40N 24 51 E
Kitui, Kenya 54 C4 1 17S 38 0 E
Kitwanga, Canada 72 B3 55 6N 128 4W
Kitwe, Zambia 55 E2 12 54S 28 13 E
Kivarli, India 42 G5 24 33N 72 46 E
Kivertsi, Ukraine 17 C13 50 50N 25 28 E
Kividhes, Cyprus 23 E11 34 46N 32 51 E
Kivu, L., Dem. Rep. of the Congo 54 C2 1 48S 29 0 E
Kiyev = Kyyiv, Ukraine 17 C16 50 30N 30 28 E
Kiyevskoye Vdkhr. = Kyyivske Vdskh., Ukraine 17 C16 51 0N 30 25 E
Kizel, Russia 24 C10 59 3N 57 40 E
Kiziguru, Rwanda 54 C3 1 46S 30 23 E
Kızıl Irmak →, Turkey 25 F6 41 44N 35 58 E
Kizil Jilga, India 43 B8 35 26N 78 50 E
Kızıltepe, Turkey 44 B4 37 12N 40 35 E
Kizimkazi, Tanzania 54 D4 6 28S 39 30 E
Kizlyar, Russia 25 F8 43 51N 46 40 E
Kizyl-Arvat = Gyzylarbat, Turkmenistan 26 F6 39 4N 56 23 E
Kjölur, Iceland 8 D4 64 50N 19 25W
Kladno, Czech Rep. 16 C8 50 10N 14 7 E
Klaeng, Thailand 38 F3 12 47N 101 39 E
Klagenfurt, Austria 16 E8 46 38N 14 20 E
Klaipeda, Lithuania 9 J19 55 43N 21 10 E
Klaksvík, Færoe Is. 8 E9 62 14N 6 35W
Klamath →, U.S.A. 82 F1 41 33N 124 5W
Klamath Falls, U.S.A. 82 E3 42 13N 121 46W
Klamath Mts., U.S.A. 82 F2 41 20N 123 0W
Klamono, Indonesia 37 E8 1 8S 131 30 E
Klappan →, Canada 72 B3 58 0N 129 43W
Klarälven →, Sweden 9 G15 59 23N 13 32 E
Klatovy, Czech Rep. 16 D7 49 23N 13 18 E
Klawer, S. Africa 56 E2 31 44S 18 36 E
Klazienaveen, Neths. 15 B6 52 44N 7 0 E
Kleena Kleene, Canada 72 C4 52 0N 124 59W
Klein-Karas, Namibia 56 D2 27 33S 18 7 E
Klerksdorp, S. Africa 56 D4 26 53S 26 38 E
Kletsk = Klyetsk, Belarus 17 B14 53 5N 26 45 E
Kletskiy, Russia 25 E7 49 16N 43 11 E
Klickitat, U.S.A. 82 D3 45 49N 121 9W
Klickitat →, U.S.A. 84 E5 45 42N 121 17W
Klidhes, Cyprus 23 D13 35 42N 34 36 E
Klinaklini →, Canada 72 C3 51 21N 125 40W
Klipdale, S. Africa 56 E2 34 19S 19 57 E
Klipplaat, S. Africa 56 E3 33 1S 24 22 E
Kłodzko, Poland 17 C9 50 28N 16 38 E
Klouto, Togo 50 G6 6 57N 0 44 E
Kluane L., Canada 68 B6 61 15N 138 40W
Kluane Nat. Park, Canada 72 A1 60 45N 139 30W
Kluczbork, Poland 17 C10 50 58N 18 12 E
Klukwan, U.S.A. 72 B1 59 24N 135 54W
Klyetsk, Belarus 17 B14 53 5N 26 45 E
Klyuchevskaya, Gora, Russia 27 D17 55 50N 160 30 E
Knaresborough, U.K. 10 C6 54 1N 1 28W
Knee L., Man., Canada 70 A1 55 3N 94 45W
Knee L., Sask., Canada 73 B7 55 51N 107 0W
Knight Inlet, Canada 72 C3 50 45N 125 40W
Knighton, U.K. 11 E4 52 21N 3 3W
Knights Ferry, U.S.A. 84 H6 37 50N 120 40W
Knights Landing, U.S.A. 84 G5 38 48N 121 43W
Knob, C., Australia 61 F2 34 32S 119 16 E
Knock, Ireland 13 C3 53 48N 8 55W
Knockmealdown Mts., Ireland 13 D4 52 14N 7 56W
Knokke-Heist, Belgium 15 C3 51 21N 3 17 E
**Knossós**, Greece 23 D7 35 16N 25 10 E
Knowlton, Canada 79 A12 45 13N 72 31W
Knox, U.S.A. 76 E2 41 18N 86 37W
Knox Coast, Antarctica 5 C8 66 30S 108 0 E
Knoxville, Iowa, U.S.A. 80 E8 41 19N 93 6W
Knoxville, Pa., U.S.A. 78 E7 41 57N 77 27W
Knoxville, Tenn., U.S.A. 77 H4 35 58N 83 55W
Knysna, S. Africa 56 E3 34 2S 23 2 E
Ko Kha, Thailand 38 C2 18 11N 99 24 E
Koartac = Quaqtaq, Canada 69 B13 60 55N 69 40W
Koba, Indonesia 37 F8 6 37S 134 37 E
Kobarid, Slovenia 16 E7 46 15N 13 30 E
Kobayashi, Japan 31 J5 31 56N 130 59 E
Kobdo = Hovd, Mongolia 32 B4 48 2N 91 37 E
**Kōbe**, Japan 31 G7 34 45N 135 10 E
København, Denmark 9 J15 55 41N 12 34 E
Kōbi-Sho, Japan 31 M1 25 56N 123 41 E
Koblenz, Germany 16 C4 50 21N 7 36 E
Kobryn, Belarus 17 B13 52 15N 24 22 E
Kocaeli, Turkey 25 F4 40 45N 29 50 E
Kočani, Macedonia 21 D10 41 55N 22 25 E
Koch Bihar, India 41 F16 26 22N 89 29 E
Kochang, S. Korea 35 G14 35 41N 127 55 E
Kochas, India 43 G10 25 15N 83 56 E
Kōchi, Japan 31 H6 33 30N 133 35 E
Kōchi □, Japan 31 H6 33 40N 133 30 E
Kochiu = Gejiu, China 32 D5 23 20N 103 10 E
Kodarma, India 43 G11 24 28N 85 36 E
Kodiak, U.S.A. 68 C4 57 47N 152 24W
Kodiak I., U.S.A. 68 C4 57 30N 152 45W
Kodinar, India 42 J4 20 46N 70 46 E
Koes, Namibia 56 D2 26 0S 19 15 E
Koffiefontein, S. Africa 56 D4 29 30S 25 0 E
Kofiau, Indonesia 37 E7 1 11S 129 50 E
Koforidua, Ghana 50 G5 6 3N 0 17W
Kōfu, Japan 31 G9 35 40N 138 30 E
Koga, Japan 31 F9 36 11N 139 43 E
Kogaluk →, Canada 71 A7 56 12N 61 44W
Køge, Denmark 9 J15 55 27N 12 11 E
Koh-i-Bābā, Afghan. 40 B5 34 30N 67 0 E
Koh-i-Khurd, Afghan. 42 C1 33 30N 65 59 E
Koh-i-Maran, Pakistan 42 E2 29 18N 66 50 E
Kohat, Pakistan 42 C4 33 40N 71 29 E
Kohima, India 41 G19 25 35N 94 10 E
Kohkīlūyeh va Būyer Aḥmadi □, Iran 45 D6 31 30N 50 30 E
Kohler Ra., Antarctica 5 D15 77 0S 110 0W
Kohlu, Pakistan 42 E3 29 54N 69 15 E
Kohtla-Järve, Estonia 9 G22 59 20N 27 20 E
Koillismaa, Finland 8 D23 65 44N 28 36 E
Koin-dong, N. Korea 35 D14 40 28N 126 18 E
Kojō, N. Korea 35 E14 38 58N 127 58 E
Kojonup, Australia 61 F2 33 48S 117 10 E
Kojūr, Iran 45 B6 36 23N 51 43 E
Kokand = Qūqon, Uzbekistan 26 E8 40 30N 70 57 E
Kokas, Indonesia 37 E8 2 42S 132 26 E
Kokchetav = Kökshetaū, Kazakstan 26 D7 53 20N 69 25 E
Kokemäenjoki →, Finland 9 F19 61 32N 21 44 E
Kokkola, Finland 8 E20 63 50N 23 8 E
Koko Kyunzu, Burma 41 M18 14 10N 93 25 E
Kokomo, U.S.A. 76 E2 40 29N 86 8W
Koksan, N. Korea 35 E14 38 46N 126 40 E
Kökshetaū, Kazakstan 26 D7 53 20N 69 25 E
Koksoak →, Canada 69 C13 58 30N 68 10W
Kokstad, S. Africa 57 E4 30 32S 29 29 E
Kokubu, Japan 31 J5 31 44N 130 46 E
Kola, Indonesia 37 F8 5 35S 134 30 E
Kola, Russia 24 A5 68 45N 33 8 E
Kola Pen. = Kolskiy Poluostrov, Russia 24 A6 67 30N 38 0 E
Kolachi →, Pakistan 42 F2 27 8N 67 2 E
Kolahoi, India 43 B6 34 12N 75 22 E
Kolaka, Indonesia 37 E6 4 3S 121 46 E
Kolar, India 40 N11 13 12N 78 15 E
Kolar Gold Fields, India 40 N11 12 58N 78 16 E
Kolaras, India 42 G6 25 14N 77 36 E
Kolari, Finland 8 C20 67 20N 23 48 E
Kolayat, India 40 F8 27 50N 72 50 E
Kolchugino = Leninsk-Kuznetskiy, Russia 26 D9 54 44N 86 10 E
Kolding, Denmark 9 J13 55 30N 9 29 E
Kolepom = Dolak, Pulau, Indonesia 37 F9 8 0S 138 30 E
Kolguyev, Ostrov, Russia 24 A8 69 20N 48 30 E
Kolhapur, India 40 L9 16 43N 74 15 E
Kolín, Czech Rep. 16 C8 50 2N 15 9 E
Kolkas rags, Latvia 9 H20 57 46N 22 37 E
Kollum, Neths. 15 A6 53 17N 6 10 E
Kolmanskop, Namibia 56 D2 26 45S 15 14 E
**Köln**, Germany 16 C4 50 56N 6 57 E
Koło, Poland 17 B10 52 14N 18 40 E
Kołobrzeg, Poland 16 A8 54 10N 15 35 E
Kolomna, Russia 24 C6 55 8N 38 45 E
Kolomyya, Ukraine 17 D13 48 31N 25 2 E
Kolonodale, Indonesia 37 E6 2 3S 121 25 E
Kolosib, India 41 G18 24 15N 92 45 E
Kolpashevo, Russia 26 D9 58 20N 83 5 E
Kolpino, Russia 24 C5 59 44N 30 39 E
Kolskiy Poluostrov, Russia 24 A6 67 30N 38 0 E
Kolskiy Zaliv, Russia 24 A5 69 23N 34 0 E
Kolwezi, Dem. Rep. of the Congo 55 E2 10 40S 25 25 E
Kolyma →, Russia 27 C17 69 30N 161 0 E
Kolymskoye Nagorye, Russia 27 C16 63 0N 157 0 E
Kôm Ombo, Egypt 51 D12 24 25N 32 52 E
Komandorskiye Is. = Komandorskiye Ostrova, Russia 27 D17 55 0N 167 0 E
Komandorskiye Ostrova, Russia 27 D17 55 0N 167 0 E
Komárno, Slovak Rep. 17 E10 47 49N 18 5 E
Komatipoort, S. Africa 57 D5 25 25S 31 55 E
Komatou Yialou, Cyprus 23 D13 35 25N 34 8 E
Komatsu, Japan 31 F8 36 25N 136 30 E
Komatsujima, Japan 31 H7 34 0N 134 35 E
Komi □, Russia 24 B10 64 0N 55 0 E
Kommunarsk = Alchevsk, Ukraine 25 E6 48 30N 38 45 E
**Kommunizma, Pik**, Tajikistan 26 F8 39 0N 72 2 E
Komodo, Indonesia 37 F5 8 37S 119 20 E
Komoran, Pulau, Indonesia 37 F9 8 18S 138 45 E
Komoro, Japan 31 F9 36 19N 138 26 E
Komotini, Greece 21 D11 41 9N 25 26 E
Kompasberg, S. Africa 56 E3 31 45S 24 32 E
Kompong Bang, Cambodia 39 F5 12 24N 104 40 E
Kompong Cham, Cambodia 39 G5 12 0N 105 30 E
Kompong Chhnang = Kampang Chhnang, Cambodia 39 F5 12 20N 104 35 E
Kompong Chikreng, Cambodia 38 F5 13 5N 104 18 E
Kompong Kleang, Cambodia 38 F5 13 6N 104 8 E
Kompong Luong, Cambodia 39 G5 11 49N 104 48 E
Kompong Pranak, Cambodia 38 F5 13 35N 104 55 E
Kompong Som = Kampong Saom, Cambodia 39 G4 10 38N 103 30 E
Kompong Som, Chhung = Kampong Saom, Chaak, Cambodia 39 G4 10 50N 103 32 E
Kompong Speu, Cambodia 39 G5 11 26N 104 32 E
Kompong Sralao, Cambodia 38 E5 14 5N 105 46 E
Kompong Thom, Cambodia 38 F5 12 35N 104 51 E
Kompong Trabeck, Cambodia 38 F5 13 6N 105 14 E
Kompong Trabeck, Cambodia 39 G5 11 9N 105 28 E
Kompong Trach, Cambodia 39 G5 11 25N 105 48 E
Kompong Tralach, Cambodia 39 G5 11 54N 104 47 E
Komrat = Comrat, Moldova 17 E15 46 18N 28 40 E
Komsberg, S. Africa 56 E3 32 40S 20 45 E
Komsomolets, Ostrov, Russia 27 A10 80 30N 95 0 E
Komsomolsk, Russia 27 D14 50 30N 137 0 E
Kon Tum, Vietnam 38 E7 14 24N 108 0 E
Kon Tum, Plateau du, Vietnam 38 E7 14 30N 108 30 E
Konarhā □, Afghan. 40 B7 35 30N 71 3 E
Konārī, Iran 45 D6 28 13N 51 36 E
Konch, India 43 G8 26 0N 79 10 E
Konde, Tanzania 54 C4 4 57S 39 45 E
Kondinin, Australia 61 F2 32 34S 118 8 E
Kondoa, Tanzania 54 C4 4 55S 35 50 E
Kondókali, Greece 23 A3 39 38N 19 51 E
Kondopaga, Russia 24 B5 62 12N 34 17 E
Kondratyevo, Russia 27 D10 57 22N 98 15 E
Köneürgench, Turkmenistan 26 E6 42 19N 59 10 E
Konevo, Russia 24 B6 62 8N 39 20 E
Kong = Khong →, Cambodia 38 F5 13 32N 105 58 E
Kong, Ivory C. 50 G5 8 54N 4 36W
Kong, Koh, Cambodia 39 G4 11 20N 103 0 E
Kong Christian IX.s Land, Greenland 4 C6 68 0N 36 0W
Kong Christian X.s Land, Greenland 4 B6 74 0N 29 0W
Kong Franz Joseph Fd., Greenland 4 B6 73 30N 24 30W
Kong Frederik IX.s Land, Greenland 4 C5 67 0N 52 0W
Kong Frederik VI.s Kyst, Greenland 4 C5 63 0N 43 0W
Kong Frederik VIII.s Land, Greenland 4 B6 78 30N 26 0W
Kong Oscar Fjord, Greenland 4 B6 72 20N 24 0W
Kongju, S. Korea 35 F14 36 30N 127 0 E
Konglu, Burma 41 F20 27 13N 97 57 E
Kongolo, Kasai-Or., Dem. Rep. of the Congo 54 D1 5 26S 24 49 E
Kongolo, Katanga, Dem. Rep. of the Congo 54 D2 5 22S 27 0 E
Kongsberg, Norway 9 G13 59 39N 9 39 E
Kongsvinger, Norway 9 F15 60 12N 12 2 E
Kongwa, Tanzania 54 D4 6 11S 36 26 E
Koni, Dem. Rep. of the Congo 55 E2 10 40S 27 11 E
Koni, Mts., Dem. Rep. of the Congo 55 E2 10 36S 27 10 E
**Königsberg** = Kaliningrad, Russia 9 J19 54 42N 20 32 E
Konin, Poland 17 B10 52 12N 18 15 E
Konjic, Bos.-H. 21 C7 43 42N 17 58 E
Konkiep, Namibia 56 D2 26 49S 17 15 E
Konosha, Russia 24 B7 61 0N 40 5 E
Kōnosu, Japan 31 F9 36 3N 139 31 E
Konotop, Ukraine 25 D5 51 12N 33 7 E
Końskie, Poland 17 C11 51 15N 20 23 E
Konstanz, Germany 16 E5 47 40N 9 10 E
Kont, Iran 45 E9 26 55N 61 50 E
Kontagora, Nigeria 50 F7 10 23N 5 27 E
**Konya**, Turkey 25 G5 37 52N 32 35 E
Konza, Kenya 54 C4 1 45S 37 7 E
Koocanusa, L., Canada 82 B6 49 20N 115 15W
Kookynie, Australia 61 E3 29 17S 121 22 E
Koolyanobbing, Australia 61 F2 30 48S 119 36 E
Koonibba, Australia 63 E1 31 54S 133 25 E
Koorawatha, Australia 63 E4 34 2S 148 33 E
Koorda, Australia 61 F2 30 48S 117 35 E
Kooskia, U.S.A. 82 C6 46 9N 115 59W
Kootenay →, U.S.A. 72 D5 49 19N 117 39W
Kootenay L., Canada 72 D5 49 45N 116 50W
Kootenay Nat. Park, Canada 72 C5 51 0N 116 0W
Kootjieskolk, S. Africa 56 E3 31 15S 20 21 E
Kopaonik, Serbia, Yug. 21 C9 43 10N 20 50 E
Kópavogur, Iceland 8 D3 64 6N 21 55W
Koper, Slovenia 16 F7 45 31N 13 44 E
Kopervik, Norway 9 G11 59 17N 5 17 E
Kopet Dagh, Asia 45 B8 38 0N 58 0 E
Kopi, Australia 63 E2 33 24S 135 40 E
Köping, Sweden 9 G17 59 31N 16 3 E
Koppeh Dāgh = Kopet Dagh, Asia 45 B8 38 0N 58 0 E
Koppies, S. Africa 57 D4 27 20S 27 30 E
Koprivnica, Croatia 20 A7 46 12N 16 45 E
Kopychyntsi, Ukraine 17 D13 49 7N 25 58 E
Korab, Macedonia 21 D9 41 44N 20 40 E
Korakiána, Greece 23 A3 39 42N 19 45 E
Koral, India 42 J5 21 50N 73 12 E
Korba, India 43 H10 22 20N 82 45 E
Korbu, G., Malaysia 39 K3 4 41N 101 18 E
Korça, Albania 21 D9 40 37N 20 50 E
Korce = Korça, Albania 21 D9 40 37N 20 50 E
Korčula, Croatia 20 C7 42 56N 16 57 E
Kord Kūy, Iran 45 B7 36 48N 54 7 E
Kord Sheykh, Iran 45 D7 28 31N 52 53 E
Kordestān □, Iran 44 C5 36 0N 47 0 E
Kordofân, Sudan 51 F11 13 0N 29 0 E
**Korea, North** ■, Asia 35 E14 40 0N 127 0 E
**Korea, South** ■, Asia 35 G15 36 0N 128 0 E
Korea Bay, Korea 35 E13 39 0N 124 0 E
Korea Strait, Asia 35 H15 34 0N 129 30 E
Korets, Ukraine 17 C14 50 40N 27 5 E
Korhogo, Ivory C. 50 G4 9 29N 5 28W
Korinthiakós Kólpos, Greece 21 E10 38 16N 22 30 E
Kórinthos, Greece 21 F10 37 56N 22 55 E

Kyle of Lochalsh, U.K. 12 D3 57 17N 5 44W
Kymijoki →, Finland 9 F22 60 30N 26 55 E
Kyneton, Australia 63 F3 37 10S 144 29 E
Kynuna, Australia 62 C3 21 37S 141 55 E
Kyō-ga-Saki, Japan 31 G7 35 45N 135 15 E
Kyoga, L., Uganda 54 B3 1 35N 33 0 E
Kyogle, Australia 63 D5 28 40S 153 0 E
Kyongju, S. Korea 35 G15 35 51N 129 14 E
Kyongpyaw, Burma 41 L19 17 12N 95 10 E
Kyŏngsŏng, N. Korea 35 D15 41 35N 129 36 E
**Kyōto**, Japan 31 G7 35 0N 135 45 E
Kyōto □, Japan 31 G7 35 15N 135 45 E
Kyparissovouno, Cyprus 23 D12 35 19N 33 10 E
Kyperounda, Cyprus 23 E11 34 56N 32 58 E
Kyrenia, Cyprus 23 D12 35 20N 33 20 E
**Kyrgyzstan** ■, Asia 26 E8 42 0N 75 0 E
Kyrönjoki →, Finland 8 E19 63 14N 21 45 E
Kystatyam, Russia 27 C13 67 20N 123 10 E
Kythréa, Cyprus 23 D12 35 15N 33 29 E
Kyunhla, Burma 41 H19 23 25N 95 15 E
Kyuquot Sound, Canada 72 D3 50 2N 127 22W
Kyūshū, Japan 31 H5 33 0N 131 0 E
Kyūshū □, Japan 31 H5 33 0N 131 0 E
Kyūshū-Sanchi, Japan 31 H5 32 35N 131 17 E
Kyustendil, Bulgaria 21 C10 42 16N 22 41 E
Kyusyur, Russia 27 B13 70 19N 127 30 E
Kyyiv, Ukraine 17 C16 50 30N 30 28 E
Kyyivske Vdskh., Ukraine 17 C16 51 0N 30 25 E
Kyzyl, Russia 27 D10 51 50N 94 30 E
**Kyzyl Kum**, Uzbekistan 26 E7 42 30N 65 0 E
Kyzyl-Kyya, Kyrgyzstan 26 E8 40 16N 72 8 E
Kzyl-Orda = Qyzylorda, Kazakstan 26 E7 44 48N 65 28 E


# L


La Alcarria, Spain 19 B4 40 31N 2 45W
La Asunción, Venezuela 92 A6 11 2N 63 53W
La Baie, Canada 71 C5 48 19N 70 53W
La Banda, Argentina 94 B3 27 45S 64 10W
La Barca, Mexico 86 C4 20 20N 102 40W
La Barge, U.S.A. 82 E8 42 16N 110 12W
La Belle, U.S.A. 77 M5 26 46N 81 26W
La Biche →, Canada 72 B4 59 57N 123 50W
La Biche, L., Canada 72 C6 54 50N 112 5W
La Bomba, Mexico 86 A1 31 53N 115 2W
La Calera, Chile 94 C1 32 50S 71 10W
La Canal = Sa Canal, Spain 22 C7 38 51N 1 23 E
La Carlota, Argentina 94 C3 33 30S 63 20W
La Ceiba, Honduras 88 C2 15 40N 86 50W
La Chaux-de-Fonds, Switz. 18 C7 47 7N 6 50 E
La Chorrera, Panama 88 E4 8 53N 79 47W
La Cocha, Argentina 94 B2 27 50S 65 40W
La Concepción, Panama 88 E3 8 31N 82 37W
La Concordia, Mexico 87 D6 16 8N 92 38W
La Coruña = A Coruña, Spain 19 A1 43 20N 8 25W
La Crescent, U.S.A. 80 D9 43 50N 91 18W
La Crete, Canada 72 B5 58 11N 116 24W
La Crosse, Kans., U.S.A. 80 F5 38 32N 99 18W
La Crosse, Wis., U.S.A. 80 D9 43 48N 91 15W
La Cruz, Costa Rica 88 D2 11 4N 85 39W
La Cruz, Mexico 86 C3 23 55N 106 54W
La Désirade, Guadeloupe 89 C7 16 18N 61 3W
La Escondida, Mexico 86 C5 24 6N 99 55W
La Esmeralda, Paraguay 94 A3 22 16S 62 33W
La Esperanza, Cuba 88 B3 22 46N 83 44W
La Esperanza, Honduras 88 D2 14 15N 88 10W
La Estrada = A Estrada, Spain 19 A1 42 43N 8 27W
La Fayette, U.S.A. 77 H3 34 42N 85 17W
La Fé, Cuba 88 B3 22 2N 84 15W
La Follette, U.S.A. 77 G3 36 23N 84 7W
La Grande, U.S.A. 82 D4 45 20N 118 5W
La Grande →, Canada 70 B5 53 50N 79 0W
La Grande Deux, Rés., Canada 70 B4 53 40N 76 55W
La Grande Quatre, Rés., Canada 70 B5 54 0N 73 15W
La Grande Trois, Rés., Canada 70 B4 53 40N 75 10W
La Grange, Calif., U.S.A. 84 H6 37 42N 120 27W
La Grange, Ga., U.S.A. 77 J3 33 2N 85 2W
La Grange, Ky., U.S.A. 76 F3 38 25N 85 23W
La Grange, Tex., U.S.A. 81 L6 29 54N 96 52W
La Guaira, Venezuela 92 A5 10 36N 66 56W
La Habana, Cuba 88 B3 23 8N 82 22W
La Independencia, Mexico 87 D6 16 31N 91 47W
La Isabela, Dom. Rep. 89 C5 19 58N 71 2W
La Junta, U.S.A. 81 F3 37 59N 103 33W
La Laguna, Canary Is. 22 F3 28 28N 16 18W
La Libertad, Guatemala 88 C1 16 47N 90 7W
La Libertad, Mexico 86 B2 29 55N 112 41W
La Ligua, Chile 94 C1 32 30S 71 16W
La Línea de la Concepción, Spain 19 D3 36 15N 5 23W
La Loche, Canada 73 B7 56 29N 109 26W
La Louvière, Belgium 15 D4 50 27N 4 10 E
La Malbaie, Canada 71 C5 47 40N 70 10W
La Mancha, Spain 19 C4 39 10N 2 54W
La Martre, L., Canada 72 A5 63 15N 117 55W
La Mesa, U.S.A. 85 N9 32 46N 117 3W
La Misión, Mexico 86 A1 32 5N 116 50W
La Moure, U.S.A. 80 B5 46 21N 98 18W
La Negra, Chile 94 A1 23 46S 70 18W
La Oliva, Canary Is. 22 F6 28 36N 13 57W
La Orotava, Canary Is. 22 F3 28 22N 16 31W
La Oroya, Peru 92 11 32S 75 54W
La Palma, Canary Is. 22 F2 28 40N 17 50W
La Palma, Panama 88 E4 8 15N 78 0W
La Palma del Condado, Spain 19 D2 37 21N 6 38W
La Paloma, Chile 94 C1 30 35S 71 0W
La Pampa □, Argentina 94 D2 36 50S 66 0W
La Paragua, Venezuela 92 B6 6 50N 63 20W
La Paz, Entre Ríos, Argentina 94 C4 30 50S 59 45W
La Paz, San Luis, Argentina 94 C2 33 30S 67 20W
**La Paz**, Bolivia 92 G5 16 20S 68 10W
La Paz, Honduras 88 D2 14 20N 87 47W
La Paz, Mexico 86 C2 24 10N 110 20W
La Paz Centro, Nic. 88 D2 12 20N 86 41W
La Pedrera, Colombia 92 D5 1 18S 69 43W
La Pérade, Canada 71 C5 46 35N 72 12W
La Perouse Str., Asia 30 B11 45 40N 142 0 E
La Pesca, Mexico 87 C5 23 46N 97 47W
La Piedad, Mexico 86 C4 20 20N 102 1W
La Pine, U.S.A. 82 E3 43 40N 121 30W
**La Plata**, Argentina 94 D4 35 0S 57 55W
La Pocatière, Canada 71 C5 47 22N 70 2W
La Porte, Ind., U.S.A. 76 E2 41 36N 86 43W
La Porte, Tex., U.S.A. 81 L7 29 39N 95 1W
La Purísima, Mexico 86 B2 26 10N 112 4W
La Push, U.S.A. 84 C2 47 55N 124 38W
La Quiaca, Argentina 94 A2 22 5S 65 35W
La Restinga, Canary Is. 22 G2 27 38N 17 59W
La Rioja, Argentina 94 B2 29 20S 67 0W
La Rioja □, Argentina 94 B2 29 30S 67 0W
La Rioja □, Spain 19 A4 42 20N 2 20W
La Robla, Spain 19 A3 42 50N 5 41W
La Roche-en-Ardenne, Belgium 15 D5 50 11N 5 35 E
La Roche-sur-Yon, France 18 C3 46 40N 1 25W
**La Rochelle**, France 18 C3 46 10N 1 9W
La Roda, Spain 19 C4 39 13N 2 15W
La Romana, Dom. Rep. 89 C6 18 27N 68 57W
La Ronge, Canada 73 B7 55 5N 105 20W
La Rumorosa, Mexico 85 N10 32 33N 116 4W
La Sabina = Sa Savina, Spain 22 C7 38 44N 1 25 E
La Salle, U.S.A. 80 E10 41 20N 89 6W
La Santa, Canary Is. 22 E6 29 5N 13 40W
La Sarre, Canada 70 C4 48 45N 79 15W
La Scie, Canada 71 C8 49 57N 55 36W
La Selva Beach, U.S.A. 84 J5 36 56N 121 51W
La Serena, Chile 94 B1 29 55S 71 10W
La Seu d'Urgell, Spain 19 A6 42 22N 1 23 E
La Seyne-sur-Mer, France 18 E6 43 7N 5 52 E
La Soufrière, St. Vincent 89 D7 13 20N 61 11W
La Spézia, Italy 18 D8 44 7N 9 50 E
La Tagua, Colombia 92 C4 0 3N 74 40W
La Tortuga, Venezuela 89 D6 11 0N 65 22W
La Tuque, Canada 70 C5 47 30N 72 50W
La Unión, Chile 96 E2 40 10S 73 0W
La Unión, El Salv. 88 D2 13 20N 87 50W
La Unión, Mexico 86 D4 17 58N 101 49W
La Urbana, Venezuela 92 B5 7 8N 66 56W
La Vall d'Uixó, Spain 19 C5 39 49N 0 15W
La Vega, Dom. Rep. 89 C5 19 20N 70 30W
La Vela de Coro, Venezuela 92 A5 11 27N 69 34W
La Venta, Mexico 87 D6 18 8N 94 3W
La Ventura, Mexico 86 C4 24 38N 100 54W
Labe = Elbe →, Europe 16 B5 53 50N 9 0 E
Labé, Guinea 50 F3 11 24N 12 16W
Laberge, L., Canada 72 A1 61 11N 135 12W
Labinsk, Russia 25 F7 44 40N 40 48 E
Labis, Malaysia 39 L4 2 22N 103 2 E
Laboulaye, Argentina 94 C3 34 10S 63 30W
**Labrador**, Canada 71 B7 53 20N 61 0W
Labrador City, Canada 71 B6 52 57N 66 55W
**Labrador Sea**, Atl. Oc. 69 C14 57 0N 54 0W
Lábrea, Brazil 92 E6 7 15S 64 51W
Labuan, Malaysia 36 C5 5 20N 115 14 E
Labuan, Pulau, Malaysia 36 C5 5 21N 115 13 E
Labuha, Indonesia 37 E7 0 30S 127 30 E
Labuhan, Indonesia 37 G11 6 22S 105 50 E
Labuhanbajo, Indonesia 37 F6 8 28S 120 1 E
Labuk, Telok, Malaysia 36 C5 6 10N 117 50 E
Labyrinth, L., Australia 63 E2 30 40S 135 11 E
Labytnangi, Russia 26 C7 66 39N 66 21 E
Lac Bouchette, Canada 71 C5 48 16N 72 11W
Lac Édouard, Canada 70 C5 47 40N 72 16W
Lac La Biche, Canada 72 C6 54 45N 111 58W
Lac la Martre = Wha Ti, Canada 68 B8 63 8N 117 16W
Lac La Ronge Prov. Park, Canada 73 B7 55 9N 104 41W
Lac-Mégantic, Canada 71 C5 45 35N 70 53W
Lac Seul, Res., Canada 70 B1 50 25N 92 30W
Lac Thien, Vietnam 38 F7 12 25N 108 11 E
Lacanau, France 18 D3 44 58N 1 5W
Lacantúm →, Mexico 87 D6 16 36N 90 40W
Laccadive Is. = Lakshadweep Is., Ind. Oc. 28 H11 10 0N 72 30 E
Lacepede B., Australia 63 F2 36 40S 139 40 E
Lacepede Is., Australia 60 C3 16 55S 122 0 E
Lacerdónia, Mozam. 55 F4 18 3S 35 35 E
Lacey, U.S.A. 84 C4 47 7N 122 49W
Lachhmangarh, India 42 F6 27 50N 75 4 E
Lachi, Pakistan 42 C4 33 25N 71 20 E
Lachine, Canada 79 A11 45 30N 73 40W
Lachlan →, Australia 63 E3 34 22S 143 55 E
Lachute, Canada 70 C5 45 39N 74 21W
Lackawanna, U.S.A. 78 D6 42 50N 78 50W
Lackawaxen, U.S.A. 79 E10 41 29N 74 59W
Lacolle, Canada 79 A11 45 5N 73 22W
Lacombe, Canada 72 C6 52 30N 113 44W
Lacona, U.S.A. 79 C8 43 39N 76 10W
Laconia, U.S.A. 79 C13 43 32N 71 28W
Ladakh Ra., India 43 C8 34 0N 78 0 E
Ladismith, S. Africa 56 E3 33 28S 21 15 E
Ladnun, India 42 F6 27 38N 74 25 E
**Ladoga, L.** = Ladozhskoye Ozero, Russia 24 B5 61 15N 30 30 E
Ladozhskoye Ozero, Russia 24 B5 61 15N 30 30 E
Lady Elliott I., Australia 62 C5 24 7S 152 42 E
Lady Grey, S. Africa 56 E4 30 43S 27 13 E
Ladybrand, S. Africa 56 D4 29 9S 27 29 E
Ladysmith, Canada 72 D4 49 0N 123 49W
Ladysmith, S. Africa 57 D4 28 32S 29 46 E
Ladysmith, U.S.A. 80 C9 45 28N 91 12W
Lae, Papua N. G. 64 H6 6 40S 147 2 E
Laem Ngop, Thailand 39 F4 12 10N 102 26 E
Laem Pho, Thailand 39 J3 6 55N 101 19 E
Læsø, Denmark 9 H14 57 15N 11 5 E
Lafayette, Colo., U.S.A. 80 F2 39 58N 105 12W
Lafayette, Ind., U.S.A. 76 E2 40 25N 86 54W
Lafayette, La., U.S.A. 81 K9 30 14N 92 1W
Lafayette, Tenn., U.S.A. 77 G2 36 31N 86 2W
Laferte →, Canada 72 A5 61 53N 117 44W
Lafia, Nigeria 50 G7 8 30N 8 34 E
Lafleche, Canada 73 D7 49 45N 106 40W
Lagan →, U.K. 13 B6 54 36N 5 55W
Lagarfljót →, Iceland 8 D6 65 40N 14 18W
Lågen →, Oppland, Norway 9 F14 61 8N 10 25 E
Lågen →, Vestfold, Norway 9 G14 59 3N 10 3 E
Laghouat, Algeria 50 B6 33 50N 2 59 E
Lagoa Vermelha, Brazil 95 B5 28 13S 51 32W
Lagonoy G., Phil. 37 B6 13 50N 123 50 E
**Lagos**, Nigeria 50 G6 6 25N 3 27 E
Lagos, Portugal 19 D1 37 5N 8 41W
Lagos de Moreno, Mexico 86 C4 21 21N 101 55W
Lagrange, Australia 60 C3 18 45S 121 43 E
Lagrange B., Australia 60 C3 18 38S 121 42 E
Laguna, Brazil 95 B6 28 30S 48 50W
Laguna, U.S.A. 83 J10 35 2N 107 25W
Laguna Beach, U.S.A. 85 M9 33 33N 117 47W
Laguna Limpia, Argentina 94 B4 26 32S 59 45W
Laguna Madre, U.S.A. 87 B5 27 0N 97 20W
Lagunas, Chile 94 A2 21 0S 69 45W
Lagunas, Peru 92 E3 5 10S 75 35W
Lahad Datu, Malaysia 37 D5 5 0N 118 20 E
Lahad Datu, Teluk, Malaysia 37 D5 4 50N 118 20 E
Lahan Sai, Thailand 38 E4 14 25N 102 52 E
Lahanam, Laos 38 D5 16 16N 105 16 E
Lahar, India 43 F8 26 12N 78 57 E
Laharpur, India 43 F9 27 43N 80 56 E
Lahat, Indonesia 36 E2 3 45S 103 30 E
Lahewa, Indonesia 36 D1 1 22N 97 12 E
Lāhījān, Iran 45 B6 37 10N 50 6 E
Lahn →, Germany 16 C4 50 19N 7 37 E
Laholm, Sweden 9 H15 56 30N 13 2 E
**Lahore**, Pakistan 42 D6 31 32N 74 22 E
Lahri, Pakistan 42 E3 29 11N 68 13 E
Lahti, Finland 9 F21 60 58N 25 40 E
Lahtis = Lahti, Finland 9 F21 60 58N 25 40 E
Laï, Chad 51 G9 9 25N 16 18 E
Laila = Laylá, Si. Arabia 46 C4 22 10N 46 40 E
Laingsburg, S. Africa 56 E3 33 9S 20 52 E
Lainio älv →, Sweden 8 C20 67 35N 22 40 E
Lairg, U.K. 12 C4 58 2N 4 24W
Laishui, China 34 E8 39 23N 115 45 E
Laiwu, China 35 F9 36 15N 117 40 E
Laixi, China 35 F11 36 50N 120 31 E
Laiyang, China 35 F11 36 59N 120 45 E
Laiyuan, China 34 E8 39 20N 114 40 E
Laizhou, China 35 F10 37 8N 119 57 E
Laizhou Wan, China 35 F10 37 30N 119 30 E
Laja →, Mexico 86 C4 20 55N 100 46W
Lajes, Brazil 95 B5 27 48S 50 20W
Lak Sao, Laos 38 C5 18 11N 104 59 E
Lakaband, Pakistan 42 D3 31 2N 69 15 E
Lake Alpine, U.S.A. 84 G7 38 29N 120 0W
Lake Andes, U.S.A. 80 D5 43 9N 98 32W
Lake Arthur, U.S.A. 81 K8 30 5N 92 41W
Lake Cargelligo, Australia 63 E4 33 15S 146 22 E
Lake Charles, U.S.A. 81 K8 30 14N 93 13W
Lake City, Colo., U.S.A. 83 G10 38 2N 107 19W
Lake City, Fla., U.S.A. 77 K4 30 11N 82 38W
Lake City, Mich., U.S.A. 76 C3 44 20N 85 13W
Lake City, Minn., U.S.A. 80 C8 44 27N 92 16W
Lake City, Pa., U.S.A. 78 D4 42 1N 80 21W
Lake City, S.C., U.S.A. 77 J6 33 52N 79 45W
Lake Cowichan, Canada 72 D4 48 49N 124 3W
**Lake District**, U.K. 10 C4 54 35N 3 20 E
Lake Elsinore, U.S.A. 85 M9 33 38N 117 20W
Lake George, U.S.A. 79 C11 43 26N 73 43W
Lake Grace, Australia 61 F2 33 7S 118 28 E
Lake Harbour = Kimmirut, Canada 69 B13 62 50N 69 50W
Lake Havasu City, U.S.A. 85 L12 34 27N 114 22W
Lake Hughes, U.S.A. 85 L8 34 41N 118 26W
Lake Isabella, U.S.A. 85 K8 35 38N 118 28W
Lake Jackson, U.S.A. 81 L7 29 3N 95 27W
Lake Junction, U.S.A. 82 D8 44 35N 110 28W
Lake King, Australia 61 F2 33 5S 119 45 E
Lake Lenore, Canada 73 C8 52 24N 104 59W
Lake Louise, Canada 72 C5 51 30N 116 10W
Lake Mead National Recreation Area, U.S.A. 85 K12 36 15N 114 30W
Lake Mills, U.S.A. 80 D8 43 25N 93 32W
Lake Placid, U.S.A. 79 B11 44 17N 73 59W
Lake Pleasant, U.S.A. 79 C10 43 28N 74 25W
Lake Providence, U.S.A. 81 J9 32 48N 91 10W
Lake St. Peter, Canada 78 A6 45 18N 78 2W
Lake Superior Prov. Park, Canada 70 C3 47 45N 84 45W
Lake Village, U.S.A. 81 J9 33 20N 91 17W
Lake Wales, U.S.A. 77 M5 27 54N 81 35W
Lake Worth, U.S.A. 77 M5 26 37N 80 3W
Lakefield, Canada 78 B6 44 25N 78 16W
Lakehurst, U.S.A. 79 F10 40 1N 74 19W
Lakeland, Australia 62 B3 15 49S 144 57 E
Lakeland, U.S.A. 77 M5 28 3N 81 57W
Lakemba, Fiji 59 D9 18 13S 178 47W
Lakeport, Calif., U.S.A. 84 F4 39 3N 122 55W
Lakeport, Mich., U.S.A. 78 C2 43 7N 82 30W
Lakes Entrance, Australia 63 F4 37 50S 148 0 E
Lakeside, Ariz., U.S.A. 83 J9 34 9N 109 58W
Lakeside, Calif., U.S.A. 85 N10 32 52N 116 55W
Lakeside, Nebr., U.S.A. 80 D3 42 3N 102 26W
Lakeside, Ohio, U.S.A. 78 E2 41 32N 82 46W
Lakeview, U.S.A. 82 E3 42 11N 120 21W
Lakeville, U.S.A. 80 C8 44 39N 93 14W
Lakewood, Colo., U.S.A. 80 F2 39 44N 105 5W
Lakewood, N.J., U.S.A. 79 F10 40 6N 74 13W
Lakewood, N.Y., U.S.A. 78 D5 42 6N 79 19W
Lakewood, Ohio, U.S.A. 78 E3 41 29N 81 48W
Lakewood, Wash., U.S.A. 84 C4 47 11N 122 32W
Lakha, India 42 F4 26 9N 70 54 E
Lakhaniá, Greece 23 D9 35 58N 27 54 E
Lakhimpur, India 43 F9 27 57N 80 46 E
Lakhnadon, India 43 H8 22 36N 79 36 E
Lakhonpheng, Laos 38 E5 15 54N 105 34 E
Lakhpat, India 42 H3 23 48N 68 47 E
Lakin, U.S.A. 81 G4 37 57N 101 15W
Lakitusaki →, Canada 70 B3 54 21N 82 25W
Lakki, Pakistan 42 C4 32 36N 70 55 E
Lákkoi, Greece 23 D5 35 24N 23 57 E
Lakonikós Kólpos, Greece 21 F10 36 40N 22 40 E
Lakor, Indonesia 37 F7 8 15S 128 17 E
Lakota, Ivory C. 50 G4 5 50N 5 30W
Lakota, U.S.A. 80 A5 48 2N 98 21W
Laksar, India 42 E8 29 46N 78 3 E
Laksefjorden, Norway 8 A22 70 45N 26 50 E
Lakselv, Norway 8 A21 70 2N 25 0 E
Lakshadweep Is., Ind. Oc. 28 H11 10 0N 72 30 E
Lakshmanpur, India 43 H10 22 58N 83 3 E
Lakshmikantapur, India 43 H13 22 5N 88 20 E
Lala Ghat, India 41 G18 24 30N 92 40 E
Lala Musa, Pakistan 42 C5 32 40N 73 57 E
Lalago, Tanzania 54 C3 3 28S 33 58 E
Lalapanzi, Zimbabwe 55 F3 19 20S 30 15 E
L'Albufera, Spain 19 C5 39 20N 0 27W
Lalganj, India 43 G11 25 52N 85 13 E
Lalgola, India 43 G13 24 25N 88 15 E
Lālī, Iran 45 C6 32 21N 49 6 E
Lalibela, Ethiopia 46 E2 12 2N 39 2 E
Lalin, China 35 B14 45 12N 127 0 E
Lalín, Spain 19 A1 42 40N 8 5W
Lalin He →, China 35 B13 45 32N 125 40 E
Lalitapur = Patan, Nepal 41 F14 27 40N 85 20 E
Lalitpur, India 43 G8 24 42N 78 28 E
Lalkua, India 43 E8 29 5N 79 31 E
Lalsot, India 42 F7 26 34N 76 20 E
Lam, Vietnam 38 B6 21 21N 106 31 E
Lam Pao Res., Thailand 38 D4 16 50N 103 15 E
Lamaing, Burma 41 M20 15 25N 97 53 E
Lamar, Colo., U.S.A. 80 F3 38 5N 102 37W
Lamar, Mo., U.S.A. 81 G7 37 30N 94 16W
Lamas, Peru 92 E3 6 28S 76 31W
Lambaréné, Gabon 52 E2 0 41S 10 12 E
Lambasa, Fiji 59 C8 16 30S 179 10 E
Lambay I., Ireland 13 C5 53 29N 6 1W
Lambert Glacier, Antarctica 5 D6 71 0S 70 0 E
Lamberts Bay, S. Africa 56 E2 32 5S 18 17 E
Lambeth, Canada 78 D3 42 54N 81 18W
Lambi Kyun, Burma 39 G2 10 50N 98 20 E
Lame Deer, U.S.A. 82 D10 45 37N 106 40W
Lamego, Portugal 19 B2 41 5N 7 52W
Lamèque, Canada 71 C7 47 45N 64 38W
Lameroo, Australia 63 F3 35 19S 140 33 E
Lamesa, U.S.A. 81 J4 32 44N 101 58W
Lamía, Greece 21 E10 38 55N 22 26 E
Lammermuir Hills, U.K. 12 F6 55 50N 2 40W
Lamoille →, U.S.A. 79 B11 44 38N 73 13W
Lamon B., Phil. 37 B6 14 30N 122 20 E
Lamont, Canada 72 C6 53 46N 112 50W
Lamont, Calif., U.S.A. 85 K8 35 15N 118 55W
Lamont, Wyo., U.S.A. 82 E10 42 13N 107 29W
Lampa, Peru 92 G4 15 22S 70 22W
Lampang, Thailand 38 C2 18 16N 99 32 E
Lampasas, U.S.A. 81 K5 31 4N 98 11W
Lampazos de Naranjo, Mexico 86 B4 27 2N 100 32W
Lampedusa, Medit. S. 20 G5 35 36N 12 40 E
Lampeter, U.K. 11 E3 52 7N 4 4W
Lampione, Medit. S. 20 G5 35 33N 12 20 E
Lampman, Canada 73 D8 49 25N 102 50W
Lampung □, Indonesia 36 F2 5 30S 104 30 E
Lamta, India 43 H9 22 8N 80 7 E
Lamu, Kenya 54 C5 2 16S 40 55 E
Lamy, U.S.A. 83 J11 35 29N 105 53W
Lan Xian, China 34 E6 38 15N 111 35 E
Lanai, U.S.A. 74 H16 20 50N 156 55W
Lanak La, India 43 B8 34 27N 79 32 E
Lanak'o Shank'ou = Lanak La, India 43 B8 34 27N 79 32 E
Lanark, Canada 79 A8 45 1N 76 22W
Lanark, U.K. 12 F5 55 40N 3 47W
Lancang Jiang →, China 32 D5 21 40N 101 10 E
**Lancashire** □, U.K. 10 D5 53 50N 2 48W
Lancaster, Canada 79 A10 45 10N 74 30W
Lancaster, U.K. 10 C5 54 3N 2 48W
Lancaster, Calif., U.S.A. 85 L8 34 42N 118 8W
Lancaster, Ky., U.S.A. 76 G3 37 37N 84 35W
Lancaster, N.H., U.S.A. 79 B13 44 29N 71 34W
Lancaster, N.Y., U.S.A. 78 D6 42 54N 78 40W
Lancaster, Ohio, U.S.A. 76 F4 39 43N 82 36W
Lancaster, Pa., U.S.A. 79 F8 40 2N 76 19W
Lancaster, S.C., U.S.A. 77 H5 34 43N 80 46W
Lancaster, Wis., U.S.A. 80 D9 42 51N 90 43W
Lancaster Sd., Canada 69 A11 74 13N 84 0W
Lancelin, Australia 61 F2 31 0S 115 18 E
**Lanchow** = Lanzhou, China 34 F2 36 1N 103 52 E
Lanciano, Italy 20 C6 42 14N 14 23 E
Lancun, China 35 F11 36 25N 120 10 E
Landeck, Austria 16 E6 47 9N 10 34 E
Lander, U.S.A. 82 E9 42 50N 108 44W
Lander →, Australia 60 D5 22 0S 132 0 E
Landes, France 18 D3 44 0N 1 0W
Landi Kotal, Pakistan 42 B4 34 7N 71 6 E
Landisburg, U.S.A. 78 F7 40 21N 77 19W
Land's End, U.K. 11 G2 50 4N 5 44W
Landsborough Cr. →, Australia 62 C3 22 28S 144 35 E
Landshut, Germany 16 D7 48 34N 12 8 E
Landskrona, Sweden 9 J15 55 53N 12 50 E
Lanesboro, U.S.A. 79 E9 41 57N 75 34W
Lanett, U.S.A. 77 J3 32 52N 85 12W
Lang Qua, Vietnam 38 A5 22 16N 104 27 E
Lang Shan, China 34 D4 41 0N 106 30 E
Lang Suan, Thailand 39 H2 9 57N 99 4 E
La'nga Co, China 41 D12 30 45N 81 15 E
Langar, Iran 45 C9 35 23N 60 25 E
Langara I., Canada 72 C2 54 14N 133 1W
Langdon, U.S.A. 80 A5 48 45N 98 22W
Langeberg, S. Africa 56 E3 33 55S 21 0 E
Langeberge, S. Africa 56 D3 28 15S 22 33 E
Langeland, Denmark 9 J14 54 56N 10 48 E
Langenburg, Canada 73 C8 50 51N 101 43W
Langholm, U.K. 12 F5 55 9N 3 0W
Langjökull, Iceland 8 D3 64 39N 20 12W
Langkawi, Pulau, Malaysia 39 J2 6 25N 99 45 E
Langklip, S. Africa 56 D3 28 12S 20 20 E
Langkon, Malaysia 36 C5 6 30N 116 40 E
Langlade, St- P. & M. 71 C8 46 50N 56 20W
Langley, Canada 84 A4 49 7N 122 39W
Langøya, Norway 8 B16 68 45N 14 50 E
Langreo, Spain 19 A3 43 18N 5 40W
Langres, France 18 C6 47 52N 5 20 E
Langres, Plateau de, France 18 C6 47 45N 5 3 E
Langsa, Indonesia 36 D1 4 30N 97 57 E
Langtry, U.S.A. 81 L4 29 49N 101 34W
Langu, Thailand 39 J2 6 53N 99 47 E
**Languedoc**, France 18 E5 43 58N 3 55 E
Langxiangzhen, China 34 E9 39 43N 116 8 E
Lanigan, Canada 73 C7 51 51N 105 2W
Lankao, China 34 G8 34 48N 114 50 E
Länkäran, Azerbaijan 25 G8 38 48N 48 52 E
Lannion, France 18 B2 48 46N 3 29W
L'Annonciation, Canada 70 C5 46 25N 74 55W
Lansdale, U.S.A. 79 F9 40 14N 75 17W
Lansdowne, Australia 63 E5 31 48S 152 30 E
Lansdowne, Canada 79 B8 44 24N 76 1W
Lansdowne, India 43 E8 29 50N 78 41 E
Lansdowne House, Canada 70 B2 52 14N 87 53W
L'Anse, Mich., U.S.A. 76 B1 46 42N 88 25W
L'Anse, Mich., U.S.A. 80 B10 46 45N 88 27W
L'Anse au Loup, Canada 71 B8 51 32N 56 50W
L'Anse aux Meadows, Canada 71 B8 51 36N 55 32W
Lansford, U.S.A. 79 F9 40 50N 75 53W

Lida, Belarus 9 K21 53 53N 25 15 E
Lidköping, Sweden 9 G15 58 31N 13 7 E
Liebig, Mt., Australia 60 D5 23 18S 131 22 E
**Liechtenstein ■**, Europe 18 C8 47 8N 9 35 E
**Liège**, Belgium 15 D5 50 38N 5 35 E
Liège □, Belgium 15 D5 50 32N 5 35 E
Liegnitz = Legnica, Poland 16 C9 51 12N 16 10 E
Lienart, Dem. Rep. of the Congo 54 B2 3 3N 25 31 E
Lienyünchiangshih = Lianyungang, China 35 G10 34 40N 119 11 E
Lienz, Austria 16 E7 46 50N 12 46 E
Liepāja, Latvia 9 H19 56 30N 21 0 E
Lier, Belgium 15 C4 51 7N 4 34 E
Lièvre →, Canada 70 C4 45 31N 75 26W
Liffey →, Ireland 13 C5 53 21N 6 13W
Lifford, Ireland 13 B4 54 51N 7 29W
Lifudzin, Russia 30 B7 44 21N 134 58 E
Lightning Ridge, Australia 63 D4 29 22S 148 0 E
Ligonier, U.S.A. 78 F5 40 15N 79 14W
Liguria □, Italy 18 D8 44 30N 8 50 E
Ligurian Sea, Medit. S. 20 C3 43 20N 9 0 E
Lihou Reefs and Cays, Australia 62 B5 17 25S 151 40 E
Lihue, U.S.A. 74 H15 21 59N 159 23W
Lijiang, China 32 D5 26 55N 100 20 E
Likasi, Dem. Rep. of the Congo 55 E2 10 55S 26 48 E
Likoma I., Malawi 55 E3 12 3S 34 45 E
Likumburu, Tanzania 55 D4 9 43S 35 8 E
**Lille**, France 18 A5 50 38N 3 3 E
Lille Bælt, Denmark 9 J13 55 20N 9 45 E
Lillehammer, Norway 9 F14 61 8N 10 30 E
Lillesand, Norway 9 G13 58 15N 8 23 E
Lillian Pt., Australia 61 E4 27 40S 126 6 E
Lillooet, Canada 72 C4 50 44N 121 57W
Lillooet →, Canada 72 D4 49 15N 121 57W
**Lilongwe**, Malawi 55 E3 14 0S 33 48 E
Liloy, Phil. 37 C6 8 4N 122 39 E
Lim →, Bos.-H. 21 C8 43 45N 19 15 E
Lima, Indonesia 37 E7 3 37S 128 4 E
**Lima**, Peru 92 F3 12 0S 77 0W
Lima, Mont., U.S.A. 82 D7 44 38N 112 36W
Lima, Ohio, U.S.A. 76 E3 40 44N 84 6W
Lima →, Portugal 19 B1 41 41N 8 50W
Liman, Indonesia 37 G14 7 48S 111 45 E
Limassol, Cyprus 23 E12 34 42N 33 1 E
Limavady, U.K. 13 A5 55 3N 6 56W
Limay →, Argentina 96 D3 39 0S 68 0W
Limay Mahuida, Argentina 94 D2 37 10S 66 45W
Limbang, Brunei 36 D5 4 42N 115 6 E
Limbaži, Latvia 9 H21 57 31N 24 42 E
Limbdi, India 42 H4 22 34N 71 51 E
Limbe, Cameroon 52 D1 4 1N 9 10 E
Limburg, Germany 16 C5 50 22N 8 4 E
Limburg □, Belgium 15 C5 51 2N 5 25 E
Limburg □, Neths. 15 C5 51 20N 5 55 E
Limeira, Brazil 95 A6 22 35S 47 28W
Limerick, Ireland 13 D3 52 40N 8 37W
Limerick, U.S.A. 79 C14 43 41N 70 48W
**Limerick** □, Ireland 13 D3 52 30N 8 50W
Limestone, U.S.A. 78 D6 42 2N 78 38W
Limestone →, Canada 73 B10 56 31N 94 7W
Limfjorden, Denmark 9 H13 56 55N 9 0 E
Limia = Lima →, Portugal 19 B1 41 41N 8 50W
Limingen, Norway 8 D15 64 48N 13 35 E
Limmen Bight, Australia 62 A2 14 40S 135 35 E
Limmen Bight →, Australia 62 B2 15 7S 135 44 E
Límnos, Greece 21 E11 39 50N 25 5 E
Limoges, Canada 79 A9 45 20N 75 16W
**Limoges**, France 18 D4 45 50N 1 15 E
Limón, Costa Rica 88 E3 10 0N 83 2W
Limon, U.S.A. 80 F3 39 16N 103 41W
Limousin, France 18 D4 45 30N 1 30 E
Limoux, France 18 E5 43 4N 2 12 E
**Limpopo** →, Africa 57 D5 25 5S 33 30 E
Limuru, Kenya 54 C4 1 2S 36 35 E
Lin Xian, China 34 F6 37 57N 110 58 E
Linares, Chile 94 D1 35 50S 71 40W
Linares, Mexico 87 C5 24 50N 99 40W
Linares, Spain 19 C4 38 10N 3 40W
Lincheng, China 34 F8 37 25N 114 30 E
Lincoln, Argentina 94 C3 34 55S 61 30W
Lincoln, N.Z. 59 K4 43 38S 172 30 E
**Lincoln**, U.K. 10 D7 53 14N 0 32W
Lincoln, Calif., U.S.A. 84 G5 38 54N 121 17W
Lincoln, Ill., U.S.A. 80 E10 40 9N 89 22W
Lincoln, Kans., U.S.A. 80 F5 39 3N 98 9W
Lincoln, Maine, U.S.A. 77 C11 45 22N 68 30W
Lincoln, N.H., U.S.A. 79 B13 44 3N 71 40W
Lincoln, N. Mex., U.S.A. 83 K11 33 30N 105 23W
**Lincoln**, Nebr., U.S.A. 80 E6 40 49N 96 41W
Lincoln City, U.S.A. 82 D1 44 57N 124 1W
Lincoln Hav = Lincoln Sea, Arctic 4 A5 84 0N 55 0W
Lincoln Sea, Arctic 4 A5 84 0N 55 0W
**Lincolnshire** □, U.K. 10 D7 53 14N 0 32W
Lincolnshire Wolds, U.K. 10 D7 53 26N 0 13W
Lincolnton, U.S.A. 77 H5 35 29N 81 16W
Lind, U.S.A. 82 C4 46 58N 118 37W
Linda, U.S.A. 84 F5 39 8N 121 34W
Linden, Guyana 92 B7 6 0N 58 10W
Linden, Ala., U.S.A. 77 J2 32 18N 87 48W
Linden, Calif., U.S.A. 84 G5 38 1N 121 5W
Linden, Tex., U.S.A. 81 J7 33 1N 94 22W
Lindenhurst, U.S.A. 79 F11 40 41N 73 23W
Lindesnes, Norway 9 H12 57 58N 7 3 E
Líndhos, Greece 23 C10 36 6N 28 4 E
Líndhos, Ákra, Greece 23 C10 36 4N 28 10 E
Lindi, Tanzania 55 D4 9 58S 39 38 E
Lindi □, Tanzania 55 D4 9 40S 38 30 E
Lindi →, Dem. Rep. of the Congo 54 B2 0 33N 25 5 E
Lindsay, Canada 78 B6 44 22N 78 43W
Lindsay, Calif., U.S.A. 84 J7 36 12N 119 5W
Lindsay, Okla., U.S.A. 81 H6 34 50N 97 38W
Lindsborg, U.S.A. 80 F6 38 35N 97 40W
Linesville, U.S.A. 78 E4 41 39N 80 26W
Linfen, China 34 F6 36 3N 111 30 E
Ling Xian, China 34 F9 37 22N 116 30 E
Lingao, China 38 C7 19 56N 109 42 E
Lingayen, Phil. 37 A6 16 1N 120 14 E
Lingayen G., Phil. 37 A6 16 10N 120 15 E
Lingbi, China 35 H9 33 33N 117 33 E
Lingchuan, China 34 G7 35 45N 113 12 E
Lingen, Germany 16 B4 52 31N 7 19 E
Lingga, Indonesia 36 E2 0 12S 104 37 E
Lingga, Kepulauan, Indonesia 36 E2 0 10S 104 30 E
Lingga Arch. = Lingga, Kepulauan, Indonesia 36 E2 0 10S 104 30 E
Lingle, U.S.A. 80 D2 42 8N 104 21W
Lingqiu, China 34 E8 39 28N 114 22 E
Lingshi, China 34 F6 36 48N 111 48 E
Lingshou, China 34 E8 38 20N 114 20 E
Lingshui, China 38 C8 18 27N 110 0 E
Lingtai, China 34 G4 35 0N 107 40 E
Linguère, Senegal 50 E2 15 25N 15 5W
Lingwu, China 34 E4 38 6N 106 20 E
Lingyuan, China 35 D10 41 10N 119 15 E
Linhai, China 33 D7 28 50N 121 8 E
Linhares, Brazil 93 G10 19 25S 40 4W
Linhe, China 34 D4 40 48N 107 20 E
Linjiang, China 35 D14 41 50N 127 0 E
Linköping, Sweden 9 G16 58 28N 15 36 E
Linkou, China 35 B16 45 15N 130 18 E
Linnhe, L., U.K. 12 E3 56 36N 5 25W
Linosa, I., Medit. S. 20 G5 35 51N 12 50 E
Linqi, China 34 G7 35 45N 113 52 E
Linqing, China 34 F8 36 50N 115 42 E
Linqu, China 35 F10 36 25N 118 30 E
Linru, China 34 G7 34 11N 112 52 E
Lins, Brazil 95 A6 21 40S 49 44W
Linton, Ind., U.S.A. 76 F2 39 2N 87 10W
Linton, N. Dak., U.S.A. 80 B4 46 16N 100 14W
Lintong, China 34 G5 34 20N 109 10 E
Linwood, Canada 78 C4 43 35N 80 43W
Linxi, China 35 C10 43 36N 118 2 E
Linxia, China 32 C5 35 36N 103 10 E
Linyanti →, Africa 56 B4 17 50S 25 5 E
Linyi, China 35 G10 35 5N 118 21 E
**Linz**, Austria 16 D8 48 18N 14 18 E
Linzhenzhen, China 34 F5 36 30N 109 59 E
Linzi, China 35 F10 36 50N 118 20 E
Lion, G. du, France 18 E6 43 10N 4 0 E
Lionárisso, Cyprus 23 D13 35 28N 34 8 E
Lions, G. of = Lion, G. du, France 18 E6 43 10N 4 0 E
Lion's Den, Zimbabwe 55 F3 17 15S 30 5 E
Lion's Head, Canada 78 B3 44 58N 81 15W
Lipa, Phil. 37 B6 13 57N 121 10 E
Lipali, Mozam. 55 F4 15 50S 35 50 E
Lípari, Italy 20 E6 38 26N 14 58 E
Lípari, Is. = Eólie, Ís., Italy 20 E6 38 30N 14 57 E
Lipcani, Moldova 17 D14 48 14N 26 48 E
Lipetsk, Russia 24 D6 52 37N 39 35 E
Lipkany = Lipcani, Moldova 17 D14 48 14N 26 48 E
Lipovcy Manzovka, Russia 30 B6 44 12N 132 26 E
Lipovets, Ukraine 17 D15 49 12N 29 1 E
Lippe →, Germany 16 C4 51 39N 6 36 E
Lipscomb, U.S.A. 81 G4 36 14N 100 16W
Liptrap C., Australia 63 F4 38 50S 145 55 E
Lira, Uganda 54 B3 2 17N 32 57 E
Liria = Lliria, Spain 19 C5 39 37N 0 35W
Lisala, Dem. Rep. of the Congo 52 D4 2 12N 21 38 E
Lisboa, Portugal 19 C1 38 42N 9 10W
**Lisbon** = Lisboa, Portugal 19 C1 38 42N 9 10W
Lisbon, N. Dak., U.S.A. 80 B6 46 27N 97 41W
Lisbon, N.H., U.S.A. 79 B13 44 13N 71 55W
Lisbon, Ohio, U.S.A. 78 F4 40 46N 80 46W
Lisbon Falls, U.S.A. 77 D10 44 0N 70 4W
Lisburn, U.K. 13 B5 54 31N 6 3W
Liscannor B., Ireland 13 D2 52 55N 9 24W
Lishi, China 34 F6 37 31N 111 8 E
Lishu, China 35 C13 43 20N 124 18 E
Lisianski I., Pac. Oc. 64 E10 26 2N 174 0W
Lisichansk = Lysychansk, Ukraine 25 E6 48 55N 38 30 E
Lisieux, France 18 B4 49 10N 0 12 E
Liski, Russia 25 D6 51 3N 39 30 E
Lismore, Australia 63 D5 28 44S 153 21 E
Lismore, Ireland 13 D4 52 8N 7 55W
Lista, Norway 9 G12 58 7N 6 39 E
Lister, Mt., Antarctica 5 D11 78 0S 162 0 E
Liston, Australia 63 D5 28 39S 152 6 E
Listowel, Canada 78 C4 43 44N 80 58W
Listowel, Ireland 13 D2 52 27N 9 29W
Litani →, Lebanon 47 B4 33 20N 35 15 E
Litchfield, Calif., U.S.A. 84 E6 40 24N 120 23W
Litchfield, Conn., U.S.A. 79 E11 41 45N 73 11W
Litchfield, Ill., U.S.A. 80 F10 39 11N 89 39W
Litchfield, Minn., U.S.A. 80 C7 45 8N 94 32W
Lithgow, Australia 63 E5 33 25S 150 8 E
Líthinon, Ákra, Greece 23 E6 34 55N 24 44 E
**Lithuania ■**, Europe 9 J20 55 30N 24 0 E
Lititz, U.S.A. 79 F8 40 9N 76 18W
Litoměřice, Czech Rep. 16 C8 50 33N 14 10 E
Little Abaco I., Bahamas 88 A4 26 50N 77 30W
Little Barrier I., N.Z. 59 G5 36 12S 175 8 E
Little Belt Mts., U.S.A. 82 C8 46 40N 110 45W
Little Blue →, U.S.A. 80 F6 39 42N 96 41W
Little Buffalo →, Canada 72 A6 61 0N 113 46W
Little Cayman, I., Cayman Is. 88 C3 19 41N 80 3W
Little Churchill →, Canada 73 B9 57 30N 95 22W
Little Colorado →, U.S.A. 83 H8 36 12N 111 48W
Little Current, Canada 70 C3 45 55N 82 0W
Little Current →, Canada 70 B3 50 57N 84 36W
Little Falls, Minn., U.S.A. 80 C7 45 59N 94 22W
Little Falls, N.Y., U.S.A. 79 C10 43 3N 74 51W
Little Fork →, U.S.A. 80 A8 48 31N 93 35W
Little Grand Rapids, Canada 73 C9 52 0N 95 29W
Little Humboldt →, U.S.A. 82 F5 41 1N 117 43W
Little Inagua I., Bahamas 89 B5 21 40N 73 50W
Little Karoo, S. Africa 56 E3 33 45S 21 0 E
Little Lake, U.S.A. 85 K9 35 56N 117 55W
Little Laut Is. = Laut Kecil, Kepulauan, Indonesia 36 E5 4 45S 115 40 E
Little-Mecatina = Petit-Mécatina →, Canada 71 B8 50 40N 59 30W
Little Minch, U.K. 12 D2 57 35N 6 45W
Little Missouri →, U.S.A. 80 B3 47 36N 102 25W
Little Ouse →, U.K. 11 E9 52 22N 1 12 E
Little Rann, India 42 H4 23 25N 71 25 E
Little Red →, U.S.A. 81 H9 35 11N 91 27W
Little River, N.Z. 59 K4 43 45S 172 49 E
**Little Rock**, U.S.A. 81 H8 34 45N 92 17W
Little Ruaha →, Tanzania 54 D4 7 57S 37 53 E
Little Sable Pt., U.S.A. 76 D2 43 38N 86 33W
Little Sioux →, U.S.A. 80 E6 41 48N 96 4W
Little Smoky →, Canada 72 C5 54 44N 117 11W
Little Snake →, U.S.A. 82 F9 40 27N 108 26W
Little Valley, U.S.A. 78 D6 42 15N 78 48W
Little Wabash →, U.S.A. 76 G1 37 55N 88 5W
Little White →, U.S.A. 80 D4 43 40N 100 40W
Littlefield, U.S.A. 81 J3 33 55N 102 20W
Littlehampton, U.K. 11 G7 50 49N 0 32W
Littleton, U.S.A. 79 B13 44 18N 71 46W
Liu He →, China 35 D11 40 55N 121 35 E
Liuba, China 34 H4 33 38N 106 55 E
Liugou, China 35 D10 40 57N 118 15 E
Liuhe, China 35 C13 42 17N 125 43 E
Liukang Tenggaja = Sabalana, Kepulauan, Indonesia 37 F5 6 45S 118 50 E
Liuli, Tanzania 55 E3 11 3S 34 38 E
Liuwa Plain, Zambia 53 G4 14 20S 22 30 E
Liuzhou, China 33 D5 24 22N 109 22 E
Liuzhuang, China 35 H11 33 12N 120 18 E
Livadhia, Cyprus 23 E12 34 57N 33 38 E
Live Oak, Calif., U.S.A. 84 F5 39 17N 121 40W
Live Oak, Fla., U.S.A. 77 K4 30 18N 82 59W
Liveras, Cyprus 23 D11 35 23N 32 57 E
Livermore, U.S.A. 84 H5 37 41N 121 47W
Livermore, Mt., U.S.A. 81 K2 30 38N 104 11W
Livermore Falls, U.S.A. 77 C11 44 29N 70 11W
Liverpool, Canada 71 D7 44 5N 64 41W
**Liverpool**, U.K. 10 D4 53 25N 3 0W
Liverpool, U.S.A. 79 C8 43 6N 76 13W
Liverpool Bay, U.K. 10 D4 53 30N 3 20W
Liverpool Plains, Australia 63 E5 31 15S 150 15 E
Liverpool Ra., Australia 63 E5 31 50S 150 30 E
Livingston, Guatemala 88 C2 15 50N 88 50W
Livingston, U.K. 12 F5 55 54N 3 30W
Livingston, Ala., U.S.A. 77 J1 32 35N 88 11W
Livingston, Calif., U.S.A. 84 H6 37 23N 120 43W
Livingston, Mont., U.S.A. 82 D8 45 40N 110 34W
Livingston, S.C., U.S.A. 77 J5 33 32N 80 53W
Livingston, Tenn., U.S.A. 77 G3 36 23N 85 19W
Livingston, Tex., U.S.A. 81 K7 30 43N 94 56W
Livingston, L., U.S.A. 81 K7 30 50N 95 10W
Livingston Manor, U.S.A. 79 E10 41 54N 74 50W
Livingstone, Zambia 55 F2 17 46S 25 52 E
Livingstone Mts., Tanzania 55 D3 9 40S 34 20 E
Livingstonia, Malawi 55 E3 10 38S 34 5 E
Livny, Russia 24 D6 52 30N 37 30 E
Livonia, Mich., U.S.A. 76 D4 42 23N 83 23W
Livonia, N.Y., U.S.A. 78 D7 42 49N 77 40W
Livorno, Italy 20 C4 43 33N 10 19 E
Livramento, Brazil 95 C4 30 55S 55 30W
Liwale, Tanzania 55 D4 9 48S 37 58 E
Lizard I., Australia 62 A4 14 42S 145 30 E
Lizard Pt., U.K. 11 H2 49 57N 5 13W
**Ljubljana**, Slovenia 16 E8 46 4N 14 33 E
Ljungan →, Sweden 9 E17 62 18N 17 23 E
Ljungby, Sweden 9 H15 56 49N 13 55 E
Ljusdal, Sweden 9 F17 61 46N 16 3 E
Ljusnan →, Sweden 9 F17 61 12N 17 8 E
Ljusne, Sweden 9 F17 61 13N 17 7 E
Llancanelo, Salina, Argentina 94 D2 35 40S 69 8W
Llandeilo, U.K. 11 F4 51 53N 3 59W
Llandovery, U.K. 11 F4 51 59N 3 48W
Llandrindod Wells, U.K. 11 E4 52 14N 3 22W
Llandudno, U.K. 10 D4 53 19N 3 50W
Llanelli, U.K. 11 F3 51 41N 4 10W
Llanes, Spain 19 A3 43 25N 4 50W
Llangollen, U.K. 10 E4 52 58N 3 11W
Llanidloes, U.K. 11 E4 52 27N 3 31W
Llano, U.S.A. 81 K5 30 45N 98 41W
Llano →, U.S.A. 81 K5 30 39N 98 26W
Llano Estacado, U.S.A. 81 J3 33 30N 103 0W
Llanos, S. Amer. 92 C4 5 0N 71 35W
Llanquihue, L., Chile 96 E1 41 10S 75 50W
Llanwrtyd Wells, U.K. 11 E4 52 7N 3 38W
Llebeig, C. des, Spain 22 B9 39 33N 2 18 E
Lleida, Spain 19 B6 41 37N 0 39 E
Llentrisca, C., Spain 22 C7 38 52N 1 15 E
Llera, Mexico 87 C5 23 19N 99 1W
Lleyn Peninsula, U.K. 10 E3 52 51N 4 36W
Llico, Chile 94 C1 34 46S 72 5W
Lliria, Spain 19 C5 39 37N 0 35W
Llobregat →, Spain 19 B7 41 19N 2 9 E
Lloret de Mar, Spain 19 B7 41 41N 2 53 E
Lloyd B., Australia 62 A3 12 45S 143 27 E
Lloyd L., Canada 73 B7 57 22N 108 57W
Lloydminster, Canada 73 C7 53 17N 110 0W
Llucmajor, Spain 22 B9 39 29N 2 53 E
Llullaillaco, Volcán, S. Amer. 94 A2 24 43S 68 30W
Lo →, Vietnam 38 B5 21 18N 105 25 E
Loa, U.S.A. 83 G8 38 24N 111 39W
Loa →, Chile 94 A1 21 26S 70 41W
Loaita I., S. China Sea 36 B4 10 41N 114 25 E
Loange →, Dem. Rep. of the Congo 52 E4 4 17S 20 2 E
Lobatse, Botswana 56 D4 25 12S 25 40 E
Lobería, Argentina 94 D4 38 10S 58 40W
Lobito, Angola 53 G2 12 18S 13 35 E
Lobos, Argentina 94 D4 35 10S 59 0W
Lobos, I., Mexico 86 B2 27 15N 110 30W
Lobos, I. de, Canary Is. 22 F6 28 45N 13 50W
Loc Binh, Vietnam 38 B6 21 46N 106 54 E
Loc Ninh, Vietnam 39 G6 11 50N 106 34 E
Locarno, Switz. 18 C8 46 10N 8 47 E
Loch Baghasdail = Lochboisdale, U.K. 12 D1 57 9N 7 20W
Loch Garman = Wexford, Ireland 13 D5 52 20N 6 28W
Loch Nam Madadh = Lochmaddy, U.K. 12 D1 57 36N 7 10W
Lochaber, U.K. 12 E3 56 59N 5 1W
Locharbriggs, U.K. 12 F5 55 7N 3 35W
Lochboisdale, U.K. 12 D1 57 9N 7 20W
Loche, L. La, Canada 73 B7 56 30N 109 30W
Lochem, Neths. 15 B6 52 9N 6 26 E
Loches, France 18 C4 47 7N 1 0 E
Lochgilphead, U.K. 12 E3 56 2N 5 26W
Lochinver, U.K. 12 C3 58 9N 5 14W
Lochmaddy, U.K. 12 D1 57 36N 7 10W
Lochnagar, Australia 62 C4 23 33S 145 38 E
Lochnagar, U.K. 12 E5 56 57N 3 15W
Lochy, L., U.K. 12 E4 57 0N 4 53W
Lock, Australia 63 E2 33 34S 135 46 E
Lock Haven, U.S.A. 78 E7 41 8N 77 28W
Lockeford, U.S.A. 84 G5 38 10N 121 9W
Lockeport, Canada 71 D6 43 47N 65 4W
Lockerbie, U.K. 12 F5 55 7N 3 21W
Lockhart, Australia 63 F4 35 14S 146 40 E
Lockhart, U.S.A. 81 L6 29 53N 97 40W
Lockhart, L., Australia 61 F2 33 15S 119 3 E
Lockhart River, Australia 62 A3 12 58S 143 30 E
Lockney, U.S.A. 81 H4 34 7N 101 27W
Lockport, U.S.A. 78 C6 43 10N 78 42W
Lod, Israel 47 D3 31 57N 34 54 E
Lodeinoye Pole, Russia 24 B5 60 44N 33 33 E
Lodge Bay, Canada 71 B8 52 14N 55 51W
Lodge Grass, U.S.A. 82 D10 45 19N 107 22W
Lodgepole Cr. →, U.S.A. 80 E2 41 20N 104 30W
Lodhran, Pakistan 42 E4 29 32N 71 30 E
Lodi, Italy 18 D8 45 19N 9 30 E
Lodi, Calif., U.S.A. 84 G5 38 8N 121 16W
Lodi, Ohio, U.S.A. 78 E3 41 2N 82 0W
Lodja, Dem. Rep. of the Congo 54 C1 3 30S 23 23 E
Lodwar, Kenya 54 B4 3 10N 35 40 E
**Łódź**, Poland 17 C10 51 45N 19 27 E
Loei, Thailand 38 D3 17 29N 101 35 E
Loengo, Dem. Rep. of the Congo 54 C2 4 48S 26 30 E
Loeriesfontein, S. Africa 56 E2 31 0S 19 26 E
Lofoten, Norway 8 B15 68 30N 14 0 E
Logan, Iowa, U.S.A. 80 E7 41 39N 95 47W
Logan, Ohio, U.S.A. 76 F4 39 32N 82 25W
Logan, Utah, U.S.A. 82 F8 41 44N 111 50W
Logan, W. Va., U.S.A. 76 G5 37 51N 81 59W
**Logan, Mt.**, Canada 68 B5 60 31N 140 22W
Logandale, U.S.A. 85 J12 36 36N 114 29W
Logansport, Ind., U.S.A. 76 E2 40 45N 86 22W
Logansport, La., U.S.A. 81 K8 31 58N 94 0W
Logone →, Chad 51 F9 12 6N 15 2 E
Logroño, Spain 19 A4 42 28N 2 27W
Lohardaga, India 43 H11 23 27N 84 45 E
Loharia, India 42 H6 23 45N 74 14 E
Loharu, India 42 E6 28 27N 75 49 E
Lohja, Finland 9 F21 60 12N 24 5 E
Lohri Wah →, Pakistan 42 F2 27 27N 67 37 E
Loi-kaw, Burma 41 K20 19 40N 97 17 E
Loimaa, Finland 9 F20 60 50N 23 5 E
Loir →, France 18 C3 47 33N 0 32W
**Loire** →, France 18 C2 47 16N 2 10W
Loja, Ecuador 92 D3 3 59S 79 16W
Loja, Spain 19 D3 37 10N 4 10W
Loji = Kawasi, Indonesia 37 E7 1 38S 127 28 E
Lokandu, Dem. Rep. of the Congo 54 C2 2 30S 25 45 E
Lokeren, Belgium 15 C3 51 6N 3 59 E
Lokichokio, Kenya 54 B3 4 19N 34 13 E
Lokitaung, Kenya 54 B4 4 12N 35 48 E
Lokkan tekojärvi, Finland 8 C22 67 55N 27 35 E
Lokoja, Nigeria 50 G7 7 47N 6 45 E
Lola, Mt., U.S.A. 84 F6 39 26N 120 22W
Loliondo, Tanzania 54 C4 2 2S 35 39 E
Lolland, Denmark 9 J14 54 45N 11 30 E
Lolo, U.S.A. 82 C6 46 45N 114 5W
Lom, Bulgaria 21 C10 43 48N 23 12 E
Lom Kao, Thailand 38 D3 16 53N 101 14 E
Lom Sak, Thailand 38 D3 16 47N 101 15 E
Loma, U.S.A. 82 C8 47 56N 110 30W
Loma Linda, U.S.A. 85 L9 34 3N 117 16W
Lomami →, Dem. Rep. of the Congo 54 B1 0 46N 24 16 E
Lomas de Zamóra, Argentina 94 C4 34 45S 58 25W
Lombadina, Australia 60 C3 16 31S 122 54 E
Lombárdia □, Italy 18 D8 45 40N 9 30 E
**Lombardy** = Lombárdia □, Italy 18 D8 45 40N 9 30 E
Lomblen, Indonesia 37 F6 8 30S 123 32 E
Lombok, Indonesia 36 F5 8 45S 116 30 E
**Lomé**, Togo 50 G6 6 9N 1 20 E
Lomela, Dem. Rep. of the Congo 52 E4 2 19S 23 15 E
Lomela →, Dem. Rep. of the Congo 52 E4 0 15S 20 40 E
Lommel, Belgium 15 C5 51 14N 5 19 E
Lomond, Canada 72 C6 50 24N 112 36W
**Lomond, L.**, U.K. 12 E4 56 8N 4 38W
Lomphat, Cambodia 38 F6 13 30N 106 59 E
Lompobatang, Indonesia 37 F5 5 24S 119 56 E
Lompoc, U.S.A. 85 L6 34 38N 120 28W
Łomza, Poland 17 B12 53 10N 22 2 E
Loncoche, Chile 96 D2 39 20S 72 50W
Londa, India 40 M9 15 30N 74 30 E
Londiani, Kenya 54 C4 0 10S 35 33 E
London, Canada 78 D3 42 59N 81 15W
**London**, U.K. 11 F7 51 30N 0 3W
London, Ky., U.S.A. 76 G3 37 8N 84 5W
London, Ohio, U.S.A. 76 F4 39 53N 83 27W
London, Greater □, U.K. 11 F7 51 36N 0 5W
**Londonderry**, U.K. 13 B4 55 0N 7 20W
Londonderry □, U.K. 13 B4 55 0N 7 20W
Londonderry, C., Australia 60 B4 13 45S 126 55 E
Londonderry, I., Chile 96 H2 55 0S 71 0W
Londres, Argentina 96 B3 27 43S 67 7W
Londrina, Brazil 95 A5 23 18S 51 10W
Lone Pine, U.S.A. 84 J8 36 36N 118 4W
Long B., U.S.A. 77 J6 33 35N 78 45W
Long Beach, Calif., U.S.A. 85 M8 33 47N 118 11W
Long Beach, N.Y., U.S.A. 79 F11 40 35N 73 39W
Long Beach, Wash., U.S.A. 84 D2 46 21N 124 3W
Long Branch, U.S.A. 79 F11 40 18N 74 0W
Long Creek, U.S.A. 82 D4 44 43N 119 6W
Long Eaton, U.K. 10 E6 52 53N 1 15W
Long I., Australia 62 C4 22 8S 149 53 E
Long I., Bahamas 89 B4 23 20N 75 10W
Long I., Canada 70 B4 54 50N 79 20W
Long I., Ireland 13 E2 51 30N 9 34W
**Long I.**, U.S.A. 79 F11 40 45N 73 30W
Long Island Sd., U.S.A. 79 E12 41 10N 73 0W
Long L., Canada 70 C2 49 30N 86 50W
Long Lake, U.S.A. 79 C10 43 58N 74 25W
Long Point B., Canada 78 D4 42 40N 80 10W
Long Prairie →, U.S.A. 80 C7 46 20N 94 36W
Long Pt., Canada 78 D4 42 35N 80 2W
Long Range Mts., Canada 71 C8 49 30N 57 30W
Long Reef, Australia 60 B4 14 1S 125 48 E
Long Spruce, Canada 73 B10 56 24N 94 21W
Long Str. = Longa, Proliv, Russia 4 C16 70 0N 175 0 E
Long Thanh, Vietnam 39 G6 10 47N 106 57 E
Long Xian, China 34 G4 34 55N 106 55 E
Long Xuyen, Vietnam 39 G5 10 19N 105 28 E
Longa, Proliv, Russia 4 C16 70 0N 175 0 E
Longbenton, U.K. 10 B6 55 1N 1 31W
Longboat Key, U.S.A. 77 M4 27 23N 82 39W
Longde, China 34 G4 35 30N 106 20 E
Longford, Australia 62 G4 41 32S 147 3 E
Longford, Ireland 13 C4 53 43N 7 49W

# M

Malinyi, *Tanzania* **55 D4** 8 56S 36 0 E
Malita, *Phil.* **37 C7** 6 19N 125 39 E
Maliwun, *Burma* **36 B1** 10 17N 98 40 E
Maliya, *India* **42 H4** 23 5N 70 46 E
Malkara, *Turkey* **21 D12** 40 53N 26 53 E
Mallacoota Inlet, *Australia* **63 F4** 37 34S 149 40 E
Mallaig, *U.K.* **12 D3** 57 0N 5 50W
Mallawan, *India* **43 F9** 27 4N 80 12 E
Mallawi, *Egypt* **51 C12** 27 44N 30 44 E
Mállia, *Greece* **23 D7** 35 17N 25 32 E
Mallión, Kólpos, *Greece* **23 D7** 35 19N 25 27 E
Mallorca, *Spain* **22 B10** 39 30N 3 0 E
Mallorytown, *Canada* **79 B9** 44 29N 75 53W
Mallow, *Ireland* **13 D3** 52 8N 8 39W
Malmberget, *Sweden* **8 C19** 67 11N 20 40 E
Malmédy, *Belgium* **15 D6** 50 25N 6 2 E
Malmesbury, *S. Africa* **56 E2** 33 28S 18 41 E
Malmö, *Sweden* **9 J15** 55 36N 12 59 E
Malolos, *Phil.* **37 B6** 14 50N 120 49 E
Malombe L., *Malawi* **55 E4** 14 40S 35 15 E
Malone, *U.S.A.* **79 B10** 44 51N 74 18W
Måløy, *Norway* **9 F11** 61 57N 5 6 E
Malpaso, *Canary Is.* **22 G1** 27 43N 18 3W
Malpelo, I. de, *Colombia* **92 C2** 4 3N 81 35W
Malpur, *India* **42 H5** 23 21N 73 27 E
Malpura, *India* **42 F6** 26 17N 75 23 E
Malta, *Idaho, U.S.A.* **82 E7** 42 18N 113 22W
Malta, *Mont., U.S.A.* **82 B10** 48 21N 107 52W
**Malta ■**, *Europe* **23 D2** 35 50N 14 30 E
Maltahöhe, *Namibia* **56 C2** 24 55S 17 0 E
Malton, *Canada* **78 C5** 43 42N 79 38W
Malton, *U.K.* **10 C7** 54 8N 0 49W
Maluku, *Indonesia* **37 E7** 1 0S 127 0 E
Maluku □, *Indonesia* **37 E7** 3 0S 128 0 E
Maluku Sea = Molucca Sea, *Indonesia* **37 E6** 2 0S 124 0 E
Malvan, *India* **40 L8** 16 2N 73 30 E
Malvern, *U.S.A.* **81 H8** 34 22N 92 49W
Malvern Hills, *U.K.* **11 E5** 52 0N 2 19W
Malvinas, Is. = Falkland Is. □, *Atl. Oc.* **96 G5** 51 30S 59 0W
Malya, *Tanzania* **54 C3** 3 5S 33 38 E
Malyn, *Ukraine* **17 C15** 50 46N 29 3 E
Malyy Lyakhovskiy, Ostrov, *Russia* **27 B15** 74 7N 140 36 E
Mama, *Russia* **27 D12** 58 18N 112 54 E
Mamanguape, *Brazil* **93 E11** 6 50S 35 4W
Mamarr Mitlā, *Egypt* **47 E1** 30 2N 32 54 E
Mamasa, *Indonesia* **37 E5** 2 55S 119 20 E
Mambasa, *Dem. Rep. of the Congo* **54 B2** 1 22N 29 3 E
Mamberamo →, *Indonesia* **37 E9** 2 0S 137 50 E
Mambilima Falls, *Zambia* **55 E2** 10 31S 28 45 E
Mambirima, *Dem. Rep. of the Congo* **55 E2** 11 25S 27 33 E
Mambo, *Tanzania* **54 C4** 4 52S 38 22 E
Mambrui, *Kenya* **54 C5** 3 5S 40 5 E
Mamburao, *Phil.* **37 B6** 13 13N 120 39 E
Mameigwess L., *Canada* **70 B2** 52 35N 87 50W
Mammoth, *U.S.A.* **83 K8** 32 43N 110 39W
Mammoth Cave National Park, *U.S.A.* **76 G3** 37 8N 86 13W
Mamoré →, *Bolivia* **92 F5** 10 23S 65 53W
Mamou, *Guinea* **50 F3** 10 15N 12 0W
Mamuju, *Indonesia* **37 E5** 2 41S 118 50 E
Man, *Ivory C.* **50 G4** 7 30N 7 40W
**Man, I. of**, *U.K.* **10 C3** 54 15N 4 30W
Man-Bazar, *India* **43 H12** 23 4N 86 39 E
Man Na, *Burma* **41 H20** 23 27N 97 19 E
Mana →, *Fr. Guiana* **93 B8** 5 45N 53 55W
Manaar, G. of = Mannar, G. of, *Asia* **40 Q11** 8 30N 79 0 E
Manacapuru, *Brazil* **92 D6** 3 16S 60 37W
Manacor, *Spain* **22 B10** 39 34N 3 13 E
Manado, *Indonesia* **37 D6** 1 29N 124 51 E
**Managua**, *Nic.* **88 D2** 12 6N 86 20W
Managua, L. de, *Nic.* **88 D2** 12 20N 86 30W
Manakara, *Madag.* **57 C8** 22 8S 48 1 E
Manali, *India* **42 C7** 32 16N 77 10 E
**Manama** = Al Manāmah, *Bahrain* **45 E6** 26 10N 50 30 E
Manambao →, *Madag.* **57 B7** 17 35S 44 0 E
Manambato, *Madag.* **57 A8** 13 43S 49 7 E
Manambolo →, *Madag.* **57 B7** 19 18S 44 22 E
Manambolosy, *Madag.* **57 B8** 16 2S 49 40 E
Mananara, *Madag.* **57 B8** 16 10S 49 46 E
Mananara →, *Madag.* **57 C8** 23 21S 47 42 E
Mananjary, *Madag.* **57 C8** 21 13S 48 20 E
Manantenina, *Madag.* **57 C8** 24 17S 47 19 E
Manaos = Manaus, *Brazil* **92 D7** 3 0S 60 0W
Manapire →, *Venezuela* **92 B5** 7 42N 66 7W
Manapouri, *N.Z.* **59 L1** 45 34S 167 39 E
Manapouri, L., *N.Z.* **59 L1** 45 32S 167 32 E
Manār, Jabal, *Yemen* **46 E3** 14 2N 44 17 E
Manas, *China* **32 B3** 44 17N 85 56 E
Manas →, *India* **41 F17** 26 12N 90 40 E
Manaslu, *Nepal* **43 E11** 28 33N 84 33 E
Manasquan, *U.S.A.* **79 F10** 40 8N 74 3W
Manassa, *U.S.A.* **83 H11** 37 11N 105 56W
Manaung, *Burma* **41 K18** 18 45N 93 40 E
Manaus, *Brazil* **92 D7** 3 0S 60 0W
Manawan L., *Canada* **73 B8** 55 24N 103 14W
Manbij, *Syria* **44 B3** 36 31N 37 57 E
Manchegorsk, *Russia* **26 C4** 67 54N 32 58 E
**Manchester**, *U.K.* **10 D5** 53 29N 2 12W
Manchester, *Calif., U.S.A.* **84 G3** 38 58N 123 41W
Manchester, *Conn., U.S.A.* **79 E12** 41 47N 72 31W
Manchester, *Ga., U.S.A.* **77 J3** 32 51N 84 37W
Manchester, *Iowa, U.S.A.* **80 D9** 42 29N 91 27W
Manchester, *Ky., U.S.A.* **76 G4** 37 9N 83 46W
Manchester, *N.H., U.S.A.* **79 D13** 42 59N 71 28W
Manchester, *N.Y., U.S.A.* **78 D7** 42 56N 77 16W
Manchester, *Pa., U.S.A.* **79 F8** 40 4N 76 43W
Manchester, *Tenn., U.S.A.* **77 H2** 35 29N 86 5W
Manchester, *Vt., U.S.A.* **79 C11** 43 10N 73 5W
Manchester L., *Canada* **73 A7** 61 28N 107 29W
Manchhar L., *Pakistan* **42 F2** 26 25N 67 39 E
**Manchuria** = Dongbei, *China* **35 D13** 45 0N 125 0 E
Manchurian Plain, *China* **28 E16** 47 0N 124 0 E
Mand →, *India* **43 J10** 21 42N 83 15 E
Mand →, *Iran* **45 D7** 28 20N 52 30 E
Manda, *Chunya, Tanzania* **54 D3** 6 51S 32 29 E
Manda, *Ludewe, Tanzania* **55 E3** 10 30S 34 40 E
Mandabé, *Madag.* **57 C7** 21 0S 44 55 E
Mandaguari, *Brazil* **95 A5** 23 32S 51 42W
Mandah = Töhöm, *Mongolia* **34 B5** 44 27N 108 2 E
Mandal, *Norway* **9 G12** 58 2N 7 25 E
Mandala, Puncak, *Indonesia* **37 E10** 4 44S 140 20 E
**Mandalay**, *Burma* **41 J20** 22 0N 96 4 E
Mandale = Mandalay, *Burma* **41 J20** 22 0N 96 4 E
Mandalgarh, *India* **42 G6** 25 12N 75 6 E
Mandalgovi, *Mongolia* **34 B4** 45 45N 106 10 E
Mandalī, *Iraq* **44 C5** 33 43N 45 28 E
Mandan, *U.S.A.* **80 B4** 46 50N 100 54W
Mandar, Teluk, *Indonesia* **37 E5** 3 35S 119 15 E
Mandaue, *Phil.* **37 B6** 10 20N 123 56 E
Mandera, *Kenya* **54 B5** 3 55N 41 53 E
Mandi, *India* **42 D7** 31 39N 76 58 E
Mandi Dabwali, *India* **42 E6** 29 58N 74 42 E
Mandimba, *Mozam.* **55 E4** 14 20S 35 40 E
Mandioli, *Indonesia* **37 E7** 0 40S 127 20 E
Mandla, *India* **43 H9** 22 39N 80 30 E
Mandorah, *Australia* **60 B5** 12 32S 130 42 E
Mandoto, *Madag.* **57 B8** 19 34S 46 17 E
Mandra, *Pakistan* **42 C5** 33 23N 73 12 E
Mandrare →, *Madag.* **57 D8** 25 10S 46 30 E
Mandritsara, *Madag.* **57 B8** 15 50S 48 49 E
Mandsaur, *India* **42 G6** 24 3N 75 8 E
Mandurah, *Australia* **61 F2** 32 36S 115 48 E
Mandvi, *India* **42 H3** 22 51N 69 22 E
Mandya, *India* **40 N10** 12 30N 77 0 E
Mandzai, *Pakistan* **42 D2** 30 55N 67 6 E
Maneh, *Iran* **45 B8** 37 39N 57 7 E
Maneroo Cr. →, *Australia* **62 C3** 23 21S 143 53 E
Manfalût, *Egypt* **51 C12** 27 20N 30 52 E
Manfredónia, *Italy* **20 D6** 41 38N 15 55 E
Mangabeiras, Chapada das, *Brazil* **93 F9** 10 0S 46 30W
Mangalia, *Romania* **17 G15** 43 50N 28 35 E
Mangalore, *India* **40 N9** 12 55N 74 47 E
Mangan, *India* **43 F13** 27 31N 88 32 E
Mangaung, *S. Africa* **53 K5** 29 10S 26 25 E
Mangawan, *India* **43 G9** 24 41N 81 33 E
Mangaweka, *N.Z.* **59 H5** 39 48S 175 47 E
Manggar, *Indonesia* **36 E3** 2 50S 108 10 E
Manggawitu, *Indonesia* **37 E8** 4 8S 133 32 E
Mangkalihat, Tanjung, *Indonesia* **37 D5** 1 2N 118 59 E
Mangla, *Pakistan* **42 C5** 33 7N 73 39 E
Mangla Dam, *Pakistan* **43 C5** 33 9N 73 44 E
Manglaur, *India* **42 E7** 29 44N 77 49 E
Mangnai, *China* **32 C4** 37 52N 91 43 E
Mango, *Togo* **50 F6** 10 20N 0 30 E
Mangoche, *Malawi* **55 E4** 14 25S 35 16 E
Mangoky →, *Madag.* **57 C7** 21 29S 43 41 E
Mangole, *Indonesia* **37 E6** 1 50S 125 55 E
Mangombe, *Dem. Rep. of the Congo* **54 C2** 1 20S 26 48 E
Mangonui, *N.Z.* **59 F4** 35 1S 173 32 E
Mangrol, *Mad. P., India* **42 J4** 21 7N 70 7 E
Mangrol, *Raj., India* **42 G6** 25 20N 76 31 E
Mangueira, L. da, *Brazil* **95 C5** 33 0S 52 50W
Mangum, *U.S.A.* **81 H5** 34 53N 99 30W
Mangyshlak Poluostrov, *Kazakstan* **26 E6** 44 30N 52 30 E
Manhattan, *U.S.A.* **80 F6** 39 11N 96 35W
Manhiça, *Mozam.* **57 D5** 25 23S 32 49 E
Mania →, *Madag.* **57 B8** 19 42S 45 22 E
Manica, *Mozam.* **57 B5** 18 58S 32 59 E
Manica e Sofala □, *Mozam.* **57 B5** 19 10S 33 45 E
Manicaland □, *Zimbabwe* **55 F3** 19 0S 32 30 E
Manicoré, *Brazil* **92 E6** 5 48S 61 16W
Manicouagan →, *Canada* **71 C6** 49 30N 68 30W
Manicouagan, Rés., *Canada* **71 B6** 51 5N 68 40W
Maniema □, *Dem. Rep. of the Congo* **54 C2** 3 0S 26 0 E
Manīfah, *Si. Arabia* **45 E6** 27 44N 49 0 E
Manifold, C., *Australia* **62 C5** 22 41S 150 50 E
Manigotagan, *Canada* **73 C9** 51 6N 96 18W
Manigotagan →, *Canada* **73 C9** 51 7N 96 20W
Manihari, *India* **43 G12** 25 21N 87 38 E
Manihiki, *Cook Is.* **65 J11** 10 24S 161 1W
Manika, Plateau de la, *Dem. Rep. of the Congo* **55 E2** 10 0S 25 5 E
Manikpur, *India* **43 G9** 25 4N 81 7 E
**Manila**, *Phil.* **37 B6** 14 40N 121 3 E
Manila, *U.S.A.* **82 F9** 40 59N 109 43W
Manila B., *Phil.* **37 B6** 14 40N 120 35 E
Manilla, *Australia* **63 E5** 30 45S 150 43 E
Maningrida, *Australia* **62 A1** 12 3S 134 13 E
Manipur □, *India* **41 G19** 25 0N 94 0 E
Manipur →, *Burma* **41 H19** 23 45N 94 20 E
Manisa, *Turkey* **21 E12** 38 38N 27 30 E
Manistee, *U.S.A.* **76 C2** 44 15N 86 19W
Manistee →, *U.S.A.* **76 C2** 44 15N 86 21W
Manistique, *U.S.A.* **76 C2** 45 57N 86 15W
Manito L., *Canada* **73 C7** 52 43N 109 43W
**Manitoba** □, *Canada* **73 B9** 55 30N 97 0W
Manitoba, L., *Canada* **73 C9** 51 0N 98 45W
Manitou, *Canada* **73 D9** 49 15N 98 32W
Manitou, L., *Canada* **71 B6** 50 55N 65 17W
Manitou Is., *U.S.A.* **76 C3** 45 8N 86 0W
Manitou Springs, *U.S.A.* **80 F2** 38 52N 104 55W
Manitoulin I., *Canada* **70 C3** 45 40N 82 30W
Manitouwadge, *Canada* **70 C2** 49 8N 85 48W
Manitowoc, *U.S.A.* **76 C2** 44 5N 87 40W
Manizales, *Colombia* **92 B3** 5 5N 75 32W
Manja, *Madag.* **57 C7** 21 26S 44 20 E
Manjacaze, *Mozam.* **57 C5** 24 45S 34 0 E
Manjakandriana, *Madag.* **57 B8** 18 55S 47 47 E
Manjhand, *Pakistan* **42 G3** 25 50N 68 10 E
Manjīl, *Iran* **45 B6** 36 46N 49 30 E
Manjimup, *Australia* **61 F2** 34 15S 116 6 E
Manjra →, *India* **40 K10** 18 49N 77 52 E
Mankato, *Kans., U.S.A.* **80 F5** 39 47N 98 13W
Mankato, *Minn., U.S.A.* **80 C8** 44 10N 94 0W
Mankayane, *Swaziland* **57 D5** 26 40S 31 4 E
Mankera, *Pakistan* **42 D4** 31 23N 71 26 E
Mankota, *Canada* **73 D7** 49 25N 107 5W
Manlay = Üydzin, *Mongolia* **34 B4** 44 9N 107 0 E
Manmad, *India* **40 J9** 20 18N 74 28 E
Mann Ranges, *Australia* **61 E5** 26 6S 130 5 E
Manna, *Indonesia* **36 E2** 4 25S 102 55 E
Mannahill, *Australia* **63 E3** 32 25S 140 0 E
Mannar, *Sri Lanka* **40 Q11** 9 1N 79 54 E
Mannar, G. of, *Asia* **40 Q11** 8 30N 79 0 E
Mannar I., *Sri Lanka* **40 Q11** 9 5N 79 45 E
**Mannheim**, *Germany* **16 D5** 49 29N 8 29 E
Manning, *Canada* **72 B5** 56 53N 117 39W
Manning, *Oreg., U.S.A.* **84 E3** 45 45N 123 13W
Manning, *S.C., U.S.A.* **77 J5** 33 42N 80 13W
Manning Prov. Park, *Canada* **72 D4** 49 5N 120 45W
Mannum, *Australia* **63 E2** 34 50S 139 20 E
Manoharpur, *India* **43 H11** 22 23N 85 12 E
Manokwari, *Indonesia* **37 E8** 0 54S 134 0 E
Manombo, *Madag.* **57 C7** 22 57S 43 28 E
Manono, *Dem. Rep. of the Congo* **54 D2** 7 15S 27 25 E
Manosque, *France* **18 E6** 43 49N 5 47 E
Manotick, *Canada* **79 A9** 45 13N 75 41W
Manouane →, *Canada* **71 C5** 49 30N 71 10W
Manouane, L., *Canada* **71 B5** 50 45N 70 45W
Manp'o, *N. Korea* **35 D14** 41 6N 126 24 E
Manpojin = Manp'o, *N. Korea* **35 D14** 41 6N 126 24 E
Manpur, *Mad. P., India* **42 H6** 22 26N 75 37 E
Manpur, *Mad. P., India* **43 H10** 23 17N 83 35 E
Manresa, *Spain* **19 B6** 41 48N 1 50 E
Mansa, *Gujarat, India* **42 H5** 23 27N 72 45 E
Mansa, *Punjab, India* **42 E6** 30 0N 75 27 E
Mansa, *Zambia* **55 E2** 11 13S 28 55 E
Mansehra, *Pakistan* **42 B5** 34 20N 73 15 E
Mansel I., *Canada* **69 B12** 62 0N 80 0W
Mansfield, *Australia* **63 F4** 37 4S 146 6 E
Mansfield, *U.K.* **10 D6** 53 9N 1 11W
Mansfield, *La., U.S.A.* **81 J8** 32 2N 93 43W
Mansfield, *Mass., U.S.A.* **79 D13** 42 2N 71 13W
Mansfield, *Ohio, U.S.A.* **78 F2** 40 45N 82 31W
Mansfield, *Pa., U.S.A.* **78 E7** 41 48N 77 5W
Mansfield, Mt., *U.S.A.* **79 B12** 44 33N 72 49W
Manson Creek, *Canada* **72 B4** 55 37N 124 32W
Manta, *Ecuador* **92 D2** 1 0S 80 40W
Mantalingajan, Mt., *Phil.* **36 C5** 8 55N 117 45 E
Mantare, *Tanzania* **54 C3** 2 42S 33 13 E
Manteca, *U.S.A.* **84 H5** 37 48N 121 13W
Manteo, *U.S.A.* **77 H8** 35 55N 75 40W
Mantes-la-Jolie, *France* **18 B4** 48 58N 1 41 E
Manthani, *India* **40 K11** 18 40N 79 35 E
Manti, *U.S.A.* **82 G8** 39 16N 111 38W
Mantiqueira, Serra da, *Brazil* **95 A7** 22 0S 44 0W
Manton, *U.S.A.* **76 C3** 44 25N 85 24W
Mántova, *Italy* **20 B4** 45 9N 10 48 E
Mänttä, *Finland* **9 E21** 62 0N 24 40 E
Mantua = Mántova, *Italy* **20 B4** 45 9N 10 48 E
Manu, *Peru* **92 F4** 12 10S 70 51W
Manu →, *Peru* **92 F4** 12 16S 70 55W
Manua Is., *Amer. Samoa* **59 B14** 14 13S 169 35W
Manuel Alves →, *Brazil* **93 F9** 11 19S 48 28W
Manui, *Indonesia* **37 E6** 3 35S 123 5 E
Manuripi →, *Bolivia* **92 F5** 11 6S 67 36W
Many, *U.S.A.* **81 K8** 31 34N 93 29W
Manyara, L., *Tanzania* **54 C4** 3 40S 35 50 E
Manych-Gudilo, Ozero, *Russia* **25 E7** 46 24N 42 38 E
Manyonga →, *Tanzania* **54 C3** 4 10S 34 15 E
Manyoni, *Tanzania* **54 D3** 5 45S 34 55 E
Manzai, *Pakistan* **42 C4** 32 12N 70 15 E
Manzanares, *Spain* **19 C4** 39 2N 3 22W
Manzanillo, *Cuba* **88 B4** 20 20N 77 31W
Manzanillo, *Mexico* **86 D4** 19 0N 104 20W
Manzanillo, Pta., *Panama* **88 E4** 9 30N 79 40W
Manzano Mts., *U.S.A.* **83 J10** 34 40N 106 20W
Manzarīyeh, *Iran* **45 C6** 34 53N 50 50 E
Manzhouli, *China* **33 B6** 49 35N 117 25 E
Manzini, *Swaziland* **57 D5** 26 30S 31 25 E
Mao, *Chad* **51 F9** 14 4N 15 19 E
Maó, *Spain* **22 B11** 39 53N 4 16 E
Maoke, Pegunungan, *Indonesia* **37 E9** 3 40S 137 30 E
Maolin, *China* **35 C12** 43 58N 123 30 E
Maoming, *China* **33 D6** 21 50N 110 54 E
Maoxing, *China* **35 B13** 45 28N 124 40 E
Mapam Yumco, *China* **32 C3** 30 45N 81 28 E
Mapastepec, *Mexico* **87 D6** 15 26N 92 54W
Mapia, Kepulauan, *Indonesia* **37 D8** 0 50N 134 20 E
Mapimí, *Mexico* **86 B4** 25 50N 103 50W
Mapimí, Bolsón de, *Mexico* **86 B4** 27 30N 104 15W
Mapinga, *Tanzania* **54 D4** 6 40S 39 12 E
Mapinhane, *Mozam.* **57 C6** 22 20S 35 0 E
Maple Creek, *Canada* **73 D7** 49 55N 109 29W
Maple Valley, *U.S.A.* **84 C4** 47 25N 122 3W
Mapleton, *U.S.A.* **82 D2** 44 2N 123 52W
Mapuera →, *Brazil* **92 D7** 1 5S 57 2W
**Maputo**, *Mozam.* **57 D5** 25 58S 32 32 E
Maputo, B. de, *Mozam.* **57 D5** 25 50S 32 45 E
Maqiaohe, *China* **35 B16** 44 40N 130 30 E
Maqnā, *Si. Arabia* **44 D2** 28 25N 34 50 E
Maquela do Zombo, *Angola* **52 F3** 6 0S 15 15 E
Maquinchao, *Argentina* **96 E3** 41 15S 68 50W
Maquoketa, *U.S.A.* **80 D9** 42 4N 90 40W
Mar, Serra do, *Brazil* **95 B6** 25 30S 49 0W
Mar Chiquita, L., *Argentina* **94 C3** 30 40S 62 50W
Mar del Plata, *Argentina* **94 D4** 38 0S 57 30W
Mar Menor, *Spain* **19 D5** 37 40N 0 45W
Mara, *Tanzania* **54 C3** 1 30S 34 32 E
Mara □, *Tanzania* **54 C3** 1 45S 34 20 E
Maraã, *Brazil* **92 D5** 1 52S 65 25W
Marabá, *Brazil* **93 E9** 5 20S 49 5W
Maracá, I. de, *Brazil* **93 C8** 2 10N 50 30W
**Maracaibo**, *Venezuela* **92 A4** 10 40N 71 37W
Maracaibo, L. de, *Venezuela* **92 B4** 9 40N 71 30W
Maracaju, *Brazil* **95 A4** 21 38S 55 9W
Maracay, *Venezuela* **92 A5** 10 15N 67 28W
Maradi, *Niger* **50 F7** 13 29N 7 20 E
Marāgheh, *Iran* **44 B5** 37 30N 46 12 E
Marāh, *Si. Arabia* **44 E5** 25 0N 45 35 E
Marajó, I. de, *Brazil* **93 D9** 1 0S 49 30W
Marākand, *Iran* **44 B5** 38 51N 45 16 E
Maralal, *Kenya* **54 B4** 1 0N 36 38 E
Maralinga, *Australia* **61 F5** 30 13S 131 32 E
Maran, *Malaysia* **39 L4** 3 35N 102 45 E
Marana, *U.S.A.* **83 K8** 32 27N 111 13W
Maranboy, *Australia* **60 B5** 14 40S 132 39 E
Marand, *Iran* **44 B5** 38 30N 45 45 E
Marang, *Malaysia* **39 K4** 5 12N 103 13 E
Maranguape, *Brazil* **93 D11** 3 55S 38 50W
Maranhão = São Luís, *Brazil* **93 D10** 2 39S 44 15W
Maranhão □, *Brazil* **93 E9** 5 0S 46 0W
Maranoa →, *Australia* **63 D4** 27 50S 148 37 E
Marañón →, *Peru* **92 D4** 4 30S 73 35W
Marão, *Mozam.* **57 C5** 24 18S 34 2 E
Maraş = Kahramanmaraş, *Turkey* **25 G6** 37 37N 36 53 E
Marathasa □, *Cyprus* **23 E11** 34 59N 32 51 E
Marathon, *Australia* **62 C3** 20 51S 143 32 E
Marathon, *Canada* **70 C2** 48 44N 86 23W
Marathon, *N.Y., U.S.A.* **79 D8** 42 26N 76 2W
Marathon, *N.Y., U.S.A.* **79 D8** 42 27N 76 2W
Marathon, *Tex., U.S.A.* **81 K3** 30 12N 103 15W
Marathóvouno, *Cyprus* **23 D12** 35 13N 33 37 E
Maratua, *Indonesia* **37 D5** 2 10N 118 35 E
Maravatío, *Mexico* **86 D4** 19 51N 100 25W
Marāwih, *U.A.E.* **45 E7** 24 18N 53 18 E
Marbella, *Spain* **19 D3** 36 30N 4 57W
Marble Bar, *Australia* **60 D2** 21 9S 119 44 E
Marble Falls, *U.S.A.* **81 K5** 30 35N 98 16W
Marblehead, *U.S.A.* **79 D14** 42 30N 70 51W
Marburg, *Germany* **16 C5** 50 47N 8 46 E
March, *U.K.* **11 E8** 52 33N 0 5 E
**Marche**, *France* **18 C4** 46 5N 1 20 E
Marche-en-Famenne, *Belgium* **15 D5** 50 14N 5 19 E
Marchena, *Spain* **19 D3** 37 18N 5 23W
Marco, *U.S.A.* **77 N5** 25 58N 81 44W
Marcos Juárez, *Argentina* **94 C3** 32 42S 62 5W
Marcus I. = Minami-Tori-Shima, *Pac. Oc.* **64 E7** 24 20N 153 58 E
Marcus Necker Ridge, *Pac. Oc.* **64 F9** 20 0N 175 0 E
Marcy, Mt., *U.S.A.* **79 B11** 44 7N 73 56W
Mardan, *Pakistan* **42 B5** 34 20N 72 0 E
Mardin, *Turkey* **25 G7** 37 20N 40 43 E
Maree, L., *U.K.* **12 D3** 57 40N 5 26W
Mareeba, *Australia* **62 B4** 16 59S 145 28 E
Marek = Stanke Dimitrov, *Bulgaria* **21 C10** 42 17N 23 9 E
Marengo, *U.S.A.* **80 E8** 41 48N 92 4W
Marenyi, *Kenya* **54 C4** 4 22S 39 8 E
Marerano, *Madag.* **57 C7** 21 23S 44 52 E
Marfa, *U.S.A.* **81 K2** 30 19N 104 1W
Marfa Pt., *Malta* **23 D1** 35 59N 14 19 E
Margaret →, *Australia* **60 C4** 18 9S 125 41 E
Margaret Bay, *Canada* **72 C3** 51 20N 127 35W
Margaret L., *Canada* **72 B5** 58 56N 115 25W
Margaret River, *Australia* **61 F2** 33 57S 115 4 E
Margarita, I. de, *Venezuela* **92 A6** 11 0N 64 0W
Margaritovo, *Russia* **30 C7** 43 25N 134 45 E
Margate, *S. Africa* **57 E5** 30 50S 30 20 E
Margate, *U.K.* **11 F9** 51 23N 1 23 E
Marguerite, *Canada* **72 C4** 52 30N 122 25W
Mari El □, *Russia* **24 C8** 56 30N 48 0 E
Mari Indus, *Pakistan* **42 C4** 32 57N 71 34 E
Mari Republic = Mari El □, *Russia* **24 C8** 56 30N 48 0 E
María Elena, *Chile* **94 A2** 22 18S 69 40W
María Grande, *Argentina* **94 C4** 31 45S 59 55W
Maria I., *N. Terr., Australia* **62 A2** 14 52S 135 45 E
Maria I., *Tas., Australia* **62 G4** 42 35S 148 0 E
Maria van Diemen, C., *N.Z.* **59 F4** 34 29S 172 40 E
Mariakani, *Kenya* **54 C4** 3 50S 39 27 E
Marian, *Australia* **62 C4** 21 9S 148 57 E
Marian L., *Canada* **72 A5** 63 0N 116 15W
Mariana Trench, *Pac. Oc.* **28 H18** 13 0N 145 0 E
Marianao, *Cuba* **88 B3** 23 8N 82 24W
Marianna, *Ark., U.S.A.* **81 H9** 34 46N 90 46W
Marianna, *Fla., U.S.A.* **77 K3** 30 46N 85 14W
Marias →, *U.S.A.* **82 C8** 47 56N 110 30W
Mariato, Punta, *Panama* **88 E3** 7 12N 80 52W
Maribor, *Slovenia* **16 E8** 46 36N 15 40 E
Marico →, *Africa* **56 C4** 23 35S 26 57 E
Maricopa, *Ariz., U.S.A.* **83 K7** 33 4N 112 3W
Maricopa, *Calif., U.S.A.* **85 K7** 35 4N 119 24W
Marié →, *Brazil* **92 D5** 0 27S 66 26W
Marie Byrd Land, *Antarctica* **5 D14** 79 30S 125 0W
Marie-Galante, *Guadeloupe* **89 C7** 15 56N 61 16W
Mariecourt = Kangiqsujuaq, *Canada* **69 B12** 61 30N 72 0W
Mariembourg, *Belgium* **15 D4** 50 6N 4 31 E
Mariental, *Namibia* **56 C2** 24 36S 18 0 E
Marienville, *U.S.A.* **78 E5** 41 28N 79 8W
Mariestad, *Sweden* **9 G15** 58 43N 13 50 E
Marietta, *Ga., U.S.A.* **77 J3** 33 57N 84 33W
Marietta, *Ohio, U.S.A.* **76 F5** 39 25N 81 27W
Marieville, *Canada* **79 A11** 45 26N 73 10W
Mariinsk, *Russia* **26 D9** 56 10N 87 20 E
Marijampole, *Lithuania* **9 J20** 54 33N 23 19 E
Marília, *Brazil* **95 A6** 22 13S 50 0W
Marín, *Spain* **19 A1** 42 23N 8 42W
Marina, *U.S.A.* **84 J5** 36 41N 121 48W
Marinduque, *Phil.* **37 B6** 13 25N 122 0 E
Marinette, *U.S.A.* **76 C2** 45 6N 87 38W
Maringá, *Brazil* **95 A5** 23 26S 52 2W
Marion, *Ala., U.S.A.* **77 J2** 32 38N 87 19W
Marion, *Ill., U.S.A.* **81 G10** 37 44N 88 56W
Marion, *Ind., U.S.A.* **76 E3** 40 32N 85 40W
Marion, *Iowa, U.S.A.* **80 D9** 42 2N 91 36W
Marion, *Kans., U.S.A.* **80 F6** 38 21N 97 1W
Marion, *N.C., U.S.A.* **77 H5** 35 41N 82 1W
Marion, *Ohio, U.S.A.* **76 E4** 40 35N 83 8W
Marion, *S.C., U.S.A.* **77 H6** 34 11N 79 24W
Marion, *Va., U.S.A.* **77 G5** 36 50N 81 31W
Marion, L., *U.S.A.* **77 J5** 33 28N 80 10W
Mariposa, *U.S.A.* **84 H7** 37 29N 119 58W
Mariscal Estigarribia, *Paraguay* **94 A3** 22 3S 60 40W
Maritime Alps = Maritimes, Alpes, *Europe* **18 D7** 44 10N 7 10 E
Maritimes, Alpes, *Europe* **18 D7** 44 10N 7 10 E
Maritsa = Évros →, *Bulgaria* **21 D12** 41 40N 26 34 E
Maritsá, *Greece* **23 C10** 36 22N 28 8 E
Mariupol, *Ukraine* **25 E6** 47 5N 37 31 E
Marīvān, *Iran* **44 C5** 35 30N 46 25 E
Marj 'Uyūn, *Lebanon* **47 B4** 33 20N 35 35 E
Markazī □, *Iran* **45 C6** 35 0N 49 30 E
Markdale, *Canada* **78 B4** 44 19N 80 39W
Marked Tree, *U.S.A.* **81 H9** 35 32N 90 25W
Market Drayton, *U.K.* **10 E5** 52 54N 2 29W
Market Harborough, *U.K.* **11 E7** 52 29N 0 55W
Market Rasen, *U.K.* **10 D7** 53 24N 0 20W
Markham, *Canada* **78 C5** 43 52N 79 16W
Markham, Mt., *Antarctica* **5 E11** 83 0S 164 0 E
Markleeville, *U.S.A.* **84 G7** 38 42N 119 47W
Markovo, *Russia* **27 C17** 64 40N 170 24 E
Marks, *Russia* **24 D8** 51 45N 46 50 E
Marksville, *U.S.A.* **81 K8** 31 8N 92 4W
Marla, *Australia* **63 D1** 27 19S 133 33 E
Marlbank, *Canada* **78 B7** 44 26N 77 6W
Marlboro, *Mass., U.S.A.* **79 D13** 42 19N 71 33W
Marlboro, *N.Y., U.S.A.* **79 E11** 41 36N 73 59W
Marlborough, *Australia* **62 C4** 22 46S 149 52 E
Marlborough, *U.K.* **11 F6** 51 25N 1 43W
Marlborough Downs, *U.K.* **11 F6** 51 27N 1 53W

Marlin, *U.S.A.* 81 K6 31 18N 96 54W
Marlow, *U.S.A.* 81 H6 34 39N 97 58W
Marmagao, *India* 40 M8 15 25N 73 56 E
Marmara, *Turkey* 21 D12 40 35N 27 38 E
Marmara, Sea of = Marmara Denizi, *Turkey* 21 D13 40 45N 28 15 E
Marmara Denizi, *Turkey* 21 D13 40 45N 28 15 E
Marmaris, *Turkey* 21 F13 36 50N 28 14 E
Marmion, Mt., *Australia* 61 E2 29 16S 119 50 E
Marmion L., *Canada* 70 C1 48 55N 91 20W
Marmolada, Mte., *Italy* 20 A4 46 26N 11 51 E
Marmora, *Canada* 78 B7 44 28N 77 41W
Marne →, *France* 18 B5 48 48N 2 24 E
Maroala, *Madag.* 57 B8 15 23S 47 59 E
Maroantsetra, *Madag.* 57 B8 15 26S 49 44 E
Maromandia, *Madag.* 57 A8 14 13S 48 5 E
Marondera, *Zimbabwe* 55 F3 18 5S 31 42 E
Maroni →, *Fr. Guiana* 93 B8 5 30N 54 0W
Maroochydore, *Australia* 63 D5 26 29S 153 5 E
Maroona, *Australia* 63 F3 37 27S 142 54 E
Marosakoa, *Madag.* 57 B8 15 26S 46 38 E
Maroua, *Cameroon* 51 F8 10 40N 14 20 E
Marovoay, *Madag.* 57 B8 16 6S 46 39 E
Marquard, *S. Africa* 56 D4 28 40S 27 28 E
**Marquesas Is.** = Marquises, Is., *Pac. Oc.* 65 H14 9 30S 140 0W
Marquette, *U.S.A.* 76 B2 46 33N 87 24W
Marquises, Is., *Pac. Oc.* 65 H14 9 30S 140 0W
Marra, Djebel, *Sudan* 51 F10 13 10N 24 22 E
Marracuene, *Mozam.* 57 D5 25 45S 32 35 E
**Marrakech**, *Morocco* 50 B4 31 9N 8 0W
Marrawah, *Australia* 62 G3 40 55S 144 42 E
Marree, *Australia* 63 D2 29 39S 138 1 E
Marrero, *U.S.A.* 81 L9 29 54N 90 6W
Marrimane, *Mozam.* 57 C5 22 58S 33 34 E
Marromeu, *Mozam.* 57 B6 18 15S 36 25 E
Marrowie Cr. →, *Australia* 63 E4 33 23S 145 40 E
Marrubane, *Mozam.* 55 F4 18 0S 37 0 E
Marrupa, *Mozam.* 55 E4 13 8S 37 30 E
Mars Hill, *U.S.A.* 77 B12 46 31N 67 52W
Marsá Matrûh, *Egypt* 51 B11 31 19N 27 9 E
Marsabit, *Kenya* 54 B4 2 18N 38 0 E
Marsala, *Italy* 20 F5 37 48N 12 26 E
Marsalforn, *Malta* 23 C1 36 4N 14 15 E
Marsden, *Australia* 63 E4 33 47S 147 32 E
Marseille, *France* 18 E6 43 18N 5 23 E
**Marseilles** = Marseille, *France* 18 E6 43 18N 5 23 E
Marsh I., *U.S.A.* 81 L9 29 34N 91 53W
Marshall, *Ark., U.S.A.* 81 H8 35 55N 92 38W
Marshall, *Mich., U.S.A.* 76 D3 42 16N 84 58W
Marshall, *Minn., U.S.A.* 80 C7 44 25N 95 45W
Marshall, *Mo., U.S.A.* 80 F8 39 7N 93 12W
Marshall, *Tex., U.S.A.* 81 J7 32 33N 94 23W
Marshall →, *Australia* 62 C2 22 59S 136 59 E
**Marshall Is.** ■, *Pac. Oc.* 64 G9 9 0N 171 0 E
Marshalltown, *U.S.A.* 80 D8 42 3N 92 55W
Marshfield, *Mo., U.S.A.* 81 G8 37 15N 92 54W
Marshfield, *Vt., U.S.A.* 79 B12 44 20N 72 20W
Marshfield, *Wis., U.S.A.* 80 C9 44 40N 90 10W
Marshūn, *Iran* 45 B6 36 19N 49 23 E
Märsta, *Sweden* 9 G17 59 37N 17 52 E
Mart, *U.S.A.* 81 K6 31 33N 96 50W
Martaban, *Burma* 41 L20 16 30N 97 35 E
Martaban, G. of, *Burma* 41 L20 16 5N 96 30 E
Martapura, *Kalimantan, Indonesia* 36 E4 3 22S 114 47 E
Martapura, *Sumatera, Indonesia* 36 E2 4 19S 104 22 E
Martelange, *Belgium* 15 E5 49 49N 5 43 E
Martha's Vineyard, *U.S.A.* 79 E14 41 25N 70 38W
Martigny, *Switz.* 18 C7 46 6N 7 3 E
Martigues, *France* 18 E6 43 24N 5 4 E
Martin, *Slovak Rep.* 17 D10 49 6N 18 58 E
Martin, *S. Dak., U.S.A.* 80 D4 43 11N 101 44W
Martin, *Tenn., U.S.A.* 81 G10 36 21N 88 51W
Martin L., *U.S.A.* 77 J3 32 41N 85 55W
Martina Franca, *Italy* 20 D7 40 42N 17 20 E
Martinborough, *N.Z.* 59 J5 41 14S 175 29 E
Martinez, *Calif., U.S.A.* 84 G4 38 1N 122 8W
Martinez, *Ga., U.S.A.* 77 J4 33 31N 82 4W
**Martinique** ■, *W. Indies* 89 D7 14 40N 61 0W
Martinique Passage, *W. Indies* 89 C7 15 15N 61 0W
Martinópolis, *Brazil* 95 A5 22 11S 51 12W
Martins Ferry, *U.S.A.* 78 F4 40 6N 80 44W
Martinsburg, *Pa., U.S.A.* 78 F6 40 19N 78 20W
Martinsburg, *W. Va., U.S.A.* 76 F7 39 27N 77 58W
Martinsville, *Ind., U.S.A.* 76 F2 39 26N 86 25W
Martinsville, *Va., U.S.A.* 77 G6 36 41N 79 52W
Marton, *N.Z.* 59 J5 40 4S 175 23 E
Martos, *Spain* 19 D4 37 44N 3 58W
Marudi, *Malaysia* 36 D4 4 11N 114 19 E
Ma'ruf, *Afghan.* 40 D5 31 30N 67 6 E
Marugame, *Japan* 31 G6 34 15N 133 40 E
Marunga, *Angola* 56 B3 17 28S 20 2 E
Marungu, Mts., *Dem. Rep. of the Congo* 54 D3 7 30S 30 0 E
Marv Dasht, *Iran* 45 D7 29 50N 52 40 E
Marvast, *Iran* 45 D7 30 30N 54 15 E
Marvel Loch, *Australia* 61 F2 31 28S 119 29 E
Marwar, *India* 42 G5 25 43N 73 45 E
Mary, *Turkmenistan* 26 F7 37 40N 61 50 E
Maryborough = Port Laoise, *Ireland* 13 C4 53 2N 7 18W
Maryborough, *Queens., Australia* 63 D5 25 31S 152 37 E
Maryborough, *Vic., Australia* 63 F3 37 0S 143 44 E
Maryfield, *Canada* 73 D8 49 50N 101 35W
**Maryland** ▭, *U.S.A.* 76 F7 39 0N 76 30W
Maryland Junction, *Zimbabwe* 55 F3 17 45S 30 31 E
Maryport, *U.K.* 10 C4 54 44N 3 28W
Mary's Harbour, *Canada* 71 B8 52 18N 55 51W
Marystown, *Canada* 71 C8 47 10N 55 10W
Marysville, *Canada* 72 D5 49 35N 116 0W
Marysville, *Calif., U.S.A.* 84 F5 39 9N 121 35W
Marysville, *Kans., U.S.A.* 80 F6 39 51N 96 39W
Marysville, *Mich., U.S.A.* 78 D2 42 54N 82 29W
Marysville, *Ohio, U.S.A.* 76 E4 40 14N 83 22W
Marysville, *Wash., U.S.A.* 84 B4 48 3N 122 11W
Maryville, *Mo., U.S.A.* 80 E7 40 21N 94 52W
Maryville, *Tenn., U.S.A.* 77 H4 35 46N 83 58W
Marzūq, *Libya* 51 C8 25 53N 13 57 E
Masahunga, *Tanzania* 54 C3 2 6S 33 18 E
Masai Steppe, *Tanzania* 54 C4 4 30S 36 30 E
Masaka, *Uganda* 54 C3 0 21S 31 45 E
Masalembo, Kepulauan, *Indonesia* 36 F4 5 35S 114 30 E
Masalima, Kepulauan, *Indonesia* 36 F5 5 4S 117 5 E
Masamba, *Indonesia* 37 E6 2 30S 120 15 E
Masan, *S. Korea* 35 G15 35 11N 128 32 E
Masandam, Ra's, *Oman* 45 E8 26 30N 56 30 E
Masasi, *Tanzania* 55 E4 10 45S 38 52 E
Masaya, *Nic.* 88 D2 12 0N 86 7W
Masbate, *Phil.* 37 B6 12 21N 123 36 E
Mascara, *Algeria* 50 A6 35 26N 0 6 E
Mascota, *Mexico* 86 C4 20 30N 104 50W
Masela, *Indonesia* 37 F7 8 9S 129 51 E
**Maseru**, *Lesotho* 56 D4 29 18S 27 30 E
Mashaba, *Zimbabwe* 55 G3 20 2S 30 29 E
Mashābih, *Si. Arabia* 44 E3 25 35N 36 30 E
Masherbrum, *Pakistan* 43 B7 35 38N 76 18 E
**Mashhad**, *Iran* 45 B8 36 20N 59 35 E
Mashīz, *Iran* 45 D8 29 56N 56 37 E
Mashkel, Hamun-i, *Pakistan* 40 E3 28 20N 62 56 E
Mashki Chāh, *Pakistan* 40 E3 29 5N 62 30 E
Mashonaland, *Zimbabwe* 53 H6 16 30S 31 0 E
Mashonaland Central ▭, *Zimbabwe* 57 B5 17 30S 31 0 E
Mashonaland East ▭, *Zimbabwe* 57 B5 18 0S 32 0 E
Mashonaland West ▭, *Zimbabwe* 57 B4 17 30S 29 30 E
Mashrakh, *India* 43 F11 26 7N 84 48 E
Masindi, *Uganda* 54 B3 1 40N 31 43 E
Masindi Port, *Uganda* 54 B3 1 43N 32 2 E
Maşīrah, *Oman* 46 C6 21 0N 58 50 E
Maşīrah, Khalīj, *Oman* 46 C6 20 10N 58 10 E
Masisi, *Dem. Rep. of the Congo* 54 C2 1 23S 28 49 E
Masjed Soleyman, *Iran* 45 D6 31 55N 49 18 E
Mask, L., *Ireland* 13 C2 53 36N 9 22W
Maskin, *Oman* 45 F8 23 30N 56 50 E
Masoala, Tanjon' i, *Madag.* 57 B9 15 59S 50 13 E
Masoarivo, *Madag.* 57 B7 19 3S 44 19 E
Masohi = Amahai, *Indonesia* 37 E7 3 20S 128 55 E
Masomeloka, *Madag.* 57 C8 20 17S 48 37 E
Mason, *Nev., U.S.A.* 84 G7 38 56N 119 8W
Mason, *Tex., U.S.A.* 81 K5 30 45N 99 14W
Mason City, *U.S.A.* 80 D8 43 9N 93 12W
Maspalomas, *Canary Is.* 22 G4 27 46N 15 35W
Maspalomas, Pta., *Canary Is.* 22 G4 27 43N 15 36W
Masqat, *Oman* 46 C6 23 37N 58 36 E
Massa, *Italy* 18 D9 44 1N 10 9 E
**Massachusetts** ▭, *U.S.A.* 79 D13 42 30N 72 0W
Massachusetts B., *U.S.A.* 79 D14 42 20N 70 50W
Massakory, *Chad* 51 F9 13 0N 15 49 E
Massanella, *Spain* 22 B9 39 48N 2 51 E
Massangena, *Mozam.* 57 C5 21 34S 33 0 E
Massango, *Angola* 52 F3 8 2S 16 21 E
Massawa = Mitsiwa, *Eritrea* 46 D2 15 35N 39 25 E
Massena, *U.S.A.* 79 B10 44 56N 74 54W
Massénya, *Chad* 51 F9 11 21N 16 9 E
Masset, *Canada* 72 C2 54 2N 132 10W
**Massif Central**, *France* 18 D5 44 55N 3 0 E
Massillon, *U.S.A.* 78 F3 40 48N 81 32W
Massinga, *Mozam.* 57 C6 23 15S 35 22 E
Masson, *Canada* 79 A9 45 32N 75 25W
Masson I., *Antarctica* 5 C7 66 10S 93 20 E
Mastanli = Momchilgrad, *Bulgaria* 21 D11 41 33N 25 23 E
Masterton, *N.Z.* 59 J5 40 56S 175 39 E
Mastic, *U.S.A.* 79 F12 40 47N 72 54W
Mastuj, *Pakistan* 43 A5 36 20N 72 36 E
Mastung, *Pakistan* 40 E5 29 50N 66 56 E
Masty, *Belarus* 17 B13 53 27N 24 38 E
Masuda, *Japan* 31 G5 34 40N 131 51 E
Masvingo, *Zimbabwe* 55 G3 20 8S 30 49 E
Masvingo ▭, *Zimbabwe* 55 G3 21 0S 31 30 E
Maşyāf, *Syria* 44 C3 35 4N 36 20 E
Matabeleland, *Zimbabwe* 53 H5 18 0S 27 0 E
Matabeleland North ▭, *Zimbabwe* 55 F2 19 0S 28 0 E
Matabeleland South ▭, *Zimbabwe* 55 G2 21 0S 29 0 E
Matachewan, *Canada* 70 C3 47 56N 80 39W
Matadi, *Dem. Rep. of the Congo* 52 F2 5 52S 13 31 E
Matagalpa, *Nic.* 88 D2 13 0N 85 58W
Matagami, *Canada* 70 C4 49 45N 77 34W
Matagami, L., *Canada* 70 C4 49 50N 77 40W
Matagorda B., *U.S.A.* 81 L6 28 40N 96 0W
Matagorda I., *U.S.A.* 81 L6 28 15N 96 30W
Matak, *Indonesia* 39 L6 3 18N 106 16 E
Mátala, *Greece* 23 E6 34 59N 24 45 E
Matam, *Senegal* 50 E3 15 34N 13 17W
Matamoros, *Campeche, Mexico* 87 D6 18 50N 90 50W
Matamoros, *Coahuila, Mexico* 86 B4 25 33N 103 15W
Matamoros, *Tamaulipas, Mexico* 87 B5 25 50N 97 30W
Ma'tan as Sarra, *Libya* 51 D10 21 45N 22 0 E
Matandu →, *Tanzania* 55 D3 8 45S 34 19 E
Matane, *Canada* 71 C6 48 50N 67 33W
Matanomadh, *India* 42 H3 23 33N 68 57 E
Matanzas, *Cuba* 88 B3 23 0N 81 40W
Matapan, C. = Taínaron, Ákra, *Greece* 21 F10 36 22N 22 27 E
Matapédia, *Canada* 71 C6 48 0N 66 59W
Matara, *Sri Lanka* 40 S12 5 58N 80 30 E
Mataram, *Indonesia* 36 F5 8 41S 116 10 E
Matarani, *Peru* 92 G4 17 0S 72 10W
Mataranka, *Australia* 60 B5 14 55S 133 4 E
Matarma, Râs, *Egypt* 47 E1 30 27N 32 44 E
Mataró, *Spain* 19 B7 41 32N 2 29 E
Matatiele, *S. Africa* 57 E4 30 20S 28 49 E
Mataura, *N.Z.* 59 M2 46 11S 168 51 E
Matehuala, *Mexico* 86 C4 23 40N 100 40W
Mateke Hills, *Zimbabwe* 55 G3 21 48S 31 0 E
Matera, *Italy* 20 D7 40 40N 16 36 E
Matetsi, *Zimbabwe* 55 F2 18 12S 26 0 E
Mathis, *U.S.A.* 81 L6 28 6N 97 50W
Mathráki, *Greece* 23 A3 39 48N 19 31 E
Mathura, *India* 42 F7 27 30N 77 40 E
Mati, *Phil.* 37 C7 6 55N 126 15 E
Matiali, *India* 43 F13 26 56N 88 49 E
Matías Romero, *Mexico* 87 D5 16 53N 95 2W
Matibane, *Mozam.* 55 E5 14 49S 40 45 E
Matima, *Botswana* 56 C3 20 15S 24 26 E
Matiri Ra., *N.Z.* 59 J4 41 38S 172 20 E
Matla →, *India* 43 J13 21 40N 88 40 E
Matli, *Pakistan* 42 G3 25 2N 68 39 E
Matlock, *U.K.* 10 D6 53 9N 1 33W
**Mato Grosso** ▭, *Brazil* 93 F8 14 0S 55 0W
Mato Grosso, Planalto do, *Brazil* 93 G8 15 0S 55 0W
**Mato Grosso do Sul** ▭, *Brazil* 93 G8 18 0S 55 0W
Matochkin Shar, *Russia* 26 B6 73 10N 56 40 E
Matopo Hills, *Zimbabwe* 55 G2 20 36S 28 20 E
Matopos, *Zimbabwe* 55 G2 20 20S 28 29 E
Matosinhos, *Portugal* 19 B1 41 11N 8 42W
Maţraḩ, *Oman* 46 C6 23 37N 58 30 E
Matsue, *Japan* 31 G6 35 25N 133 10 E
Matsumae, *Japan* 30 D10 41 26N 140 7 E
Matsumoto, *Japan* 31 F9 36 15N 138 0 E
Matsusaka, *Japan* 31 G8 34 34N 136 32 E
Matsutō, *Japan* 31 F8 36 31N 136 34 E
Matsuura, *Japan* 31 H4 33 20N 129 49 E
Matsuyama, *Japan* 31 H6 33 45N 132 45 E
Mattagami →, *Canada* 70 B3 50 43N 81 29W
Mattancheri, *India* 40 Q10 9 50N 76 15 E
Mattawa, *Canada* 70 C4 46 20N 78 45W
**Matterhorn**, *Switz.* 18 D7 45 58N 7 39 E
Matthew Town, *Bahamas* 89 B5 20 57N 73 40W
Matthew's Ridge, *Guyana* 92 B6 7 37N 60 10W
Mattice, *Canada* 70 C3 49 40N 83 20W
Mattituck, *U.S.A.* 79 F12 40 59N 72 32W
Mattoon, *U.S.A.* 76 F1 39 29N 88 23W
Matuba, *Mozam.* 57 C5 24 28S 32 49 E
Matucana, *Peru* 92 F3 11 55S 76 25W
Matūn = Khowst, *Afghan.* 42 C3 33 22N 69 58 E
Maturín, *Venezuela* 92 B6 9 45N 63 11W
Mau, *India* 43 G10 25 56N 83 33 E
Mau, *Mad. P., India* 43 F8 26 17N 78 41 E
Mau, *Ut. P., India* 43 G9 25 17N 81 23 E
Mau Escarpment, *Kenya* 54 C4 0 40S 36 0 E
Mau Ranipur, *India* 43 G8 25 16N 79 8 E
Maubeuge, *France* 18 A6 50 17N 3 57 E
Maud, Pt., *Australia* 60 D1 23 6S 113 45 E
Maude, *Australia* 63 E3 34 29S 144 18 E
Maudin Sun, *Burma* 41 M19 16 0N 94 30 E
Maués, *Brazil* 92 D7 3 20S 57 45W
Mauganj, *India* 41 G12 24 50N 81 55 E
Maughold Hd., *U.K.* 10 C3 54 18N 4 18W
Maui, *U.S.A.* 74 H16 20 48N 156 20W
Maulamyaing = Moulmein, *Burma* 41 L20 16 30N 97 40 E
Maule ▭, *Chile* 94 D1 36 5S 72 30W
Maumee, *U.S.A.* 76 E4 41 34N 83 39W
Maumee →, *U.S.A.* 76 E4 41 42N 83 28W
Maumere, *Indonesia* 37 F6 8 38S 122 13 E
Maun, *Botswana* 56 C3 20 0S 23 26 E
**Mauna Kea**, *U.S.A.* 74 J17 19 50N 155 28W
**Mauna Loa**, *U.S.A.* 74 J17 19 30N 155 35W
Maungmagan Is., *Burma* 38 F1 14 0N 97 30 E
Maungmagan Kyunzu, *Burma* 41 N20 14 0N 97 48 E
Maupin, *U.S.A.* 82 D3 45 11N 121 5W
Maurepas, L., *U.S.A.* 81 K9 30 15N 90 30W
Maurice, L., *Australia* 61 E5 29 30S 131 0 E
Mauricie, Parc Nat. de la, *Canada* 70 C5 46 45N 73 0W
**Mauritania** ■, *Africa* 50 E3 20 50N 10 0W
**Mauritius** ■, *Ind. Oc.* 49 J9 20 0S 57 0 E
Mauston, *U.S.A.* 80 D9 43 48N 90 5W
Mavli, *India* 42 G5 24 45N 73 55 E
Mavuradonha Mts., *Zimbabwe* 55 F3 16 30S 31 30 E
Mawa, *Dem. Rep. of the Congo* 54 B2 2 45N 26 40 E
Mawai, *India* 43 H9 22 30N 81 4 E
Mawana, *India* 42 E7 29 6N 77 58 E
Mawand, *Pakistan* 42 E3 29 33N 68 38 E
Mawk Mai, *Burma* 41 J20 20 14N 97 37 E
Mawlaik, *Burma* 41 H19 23 40N 94 26 E
Mawqaq, *Si. Arabia* 44 E4 27 25N 41 8 E
Mawson Coast, *Antarctica* 5 C6 68 30S 63 0 E
Max, *U.S.A.* 80 B4 47 49N 101 18W
Maxcanú, *Mexico* 87 C6 20 40N 92 0W
Maxesibeni, *S. Africa* 57 E4 30 49S 29 23 E
Maxhamish L., *Canada* 72 B4 59 50N 123 17W
Maxixe, *Mozam.* 57 C6 23 54S 35 17 E
Maxville, *Canada* 79 A10 45 17N 74 51W
Maxwell, *U.S.A.* 84 F4 39 17N 122 11W
Maxwelton, *Australia* 62 C3 20 43S 142 41 E
May, C., *U.S.A.* 76 F8 38 56N 74 58W
May Pen, *Jamaica* 88 C4 17 58N 77 15W
Maya →, *Russia* 27 D14 60 28N 134 28 E
Maya Mts., *Belize* 87 D7 16 30N 89 0W
Mayaguana, *Bahamas* 89 B5 22 30N 72 44W
Mayagüez, *Puerto Rico* 89 C6 18 12N 67 9W
Mayāmey, *Iran* 45 B7 36 24N 55 42 E
Mayanup, *Australia* 61 F2 33 57S 116 27 E
Mayapan, *Mexico* 87 C7 20 30N 89 25W
Mayarí, *Cuba* 89 B4 20 40N 75 41W
Maybell, *U.S.A.* 82 F9 40 31N 108 5W
Maybole, *U.K.* 12 F4 55 21N 4 42W
Maydān, *Iraq* 44 C5 34 55N 45 37 E
Maydena, *Australia* 62 G4 42 45S 146 30 E
Mayenne →, *France* 18 C3 47 30N 0 32W
Mayer, *U.S.A.* 83 J7 34 24N 112 14W
Mayerthorpe, *Canada* 72 C5 53 57N 115 8W
Mayfield, *Ky., U.S.A.* 77 G1 36 44N 88 38W
Mayfield, *N.Y., U.S.A.* 79 C10 43 6N 74 16W
Mayhill, *U.S.A.* 83 K11 32 53N 105 29W
Maykop, *Russia* 25 F7 44 35N 40 10 E
Maymyo, *Burma* 38 A1 22 2N 96 28 E
Maynard, *Mass., U.S.A.* 79 D13 42 26N 71 27W
Maynard, *Wash., U.S.A.* 84 C4 47 59N 122 55W
Maynard Hills, *Australia* 61 E2 28 28S 119 49 E
Mayne →, *Australia* 62 C3 23 40S 141 55 E
Maynooth, *Ireland* 13 C5 53 23N 6 34W
Mayo, *Canada* 68 B6 63 38N 135 57W
**Mayo** ▭, *Ireland* 13 C2 53 53N 9 3W
Mayon Volcano, *Phil.* 37 B6 13 15N 123 41 E
Mayor I., *N.Z.* 59 G6 37 16S 176 17 E
**Mayotte, I.**, *Mayotte* 53 G9 12 50S 45 10 E
Maysville, *U.S.A.* 76 F4 38 39N 83 46W
Mayu, *Indonesia* 37 D7 1 30N 126 30 E
Mayumba, *Gabon* 52 E2 3 25S 10 39 E
Mayville, *N. Dak., U.S.A.* 80 B6 47 30N 97 20W
Mayville, *N.Y., U.S.A.* 78 D5 42 15N 79 30W
Mayya, *Russia* 27 C14 61 44N 130 18 E
Mazabuka, *Zambia* 55 F2 15 52S 27 44 E
Mazagán = El Jadida, *Morocco* 50 B4 33 11N 8 17W
Mazagão, *Brazil* 93 D8 0 7S 51 16W
Mazán, *Peru* 92 D4 3 30S 73 0W
Māzandarān ▭, *Iran* 45 B7 36 30N 52 0 E
Mazapil, *Mexico* 86 C4 24 38N 101 34W
Mazara del Vallo, *Italy* 20 F5 37 39N 12 35 E
Mazarrón, *Spain* 19 D5 37 38N 1 19W
Mazaruni →, *Guyana* 92 B7 6 25N 58 35W
Mazatán, *Mexico* 86 B2 29 0N 110 8W
Mazatenango, *Guatemala* 88 D1 14 35N 91 30W
Mazatlán, *Mexico* 86 C3 23 13N 106 25W
Mažeikiai, *Lithuania* 9 H20 56 20N 22 20 E
Māzhān, *Iran* 45 C8 32 30N 59 0 E
Mazinan, *Iran* 45 B8 36 19N 56 56 E
Mazoe, *Mozam.* 55 F3 16 42S 33 7 E
Mazoe →, *Mozam.* 55 F3 16 20S 33 30 E
Mazowe, *Zimbabwe* 55 F3 17 28S 30 58 E
Mazurian Lakes = Mazurski, Pojezierze, *Poland* 17 B11 53 50N 21 0 E
Mazurski, Pojezierze, *Poland* 17 B11 53 50N 21 0 E
Mazyr, *Belarus* 17 B15 51 59N 29 15 E
**Mbabane**, *Swaziland* 57 D5 26 18S 31 6 E
Mbaïki, *C.A.R.* 52 D3 3 53N 18 1 E
Mbala, *Zambia* 55 D3 8 46S 31 24 E
Mbale, *Uganda* 54 B3 1 8N 34 12 E
Mbalmayo, *Cameroon* 52 D2 3 33N 11 33 E
Mbamba Bay, *Tanzania* 55 E3 11 13S 34 49 E
Mbandaka, *Dem. Rep. of the Congo* 52 D3 0 1N 18 18 E
Mbanza Congo, *Angola* 52 F2 6 18S 14 16 E
Mbanza Ngungu, *Dem. Rep. of the Congo* 52 F2 5 12S 14 53 E
Mbarara, *Uganda* 54 C3 0 35S 30 40 E
Mbashe →, *S. Africa* 57 E4 32 15S 28 54 E
Mbenkuru →, *Tanzania* 55 D4 9 25S 39 50 E
Mberengwa, *Zimbabwe* 55 G2 20 29S 29 57 E
Mberengwa, Mt., *Zimbabwe* 55 G2 20 37S 29 55 E
Mbesuma, *Zambia* 55 E3 10 0S 32 2 E
Mbeya, *Tanzania* 55 D3 8 54S 33 29 E
Mbeya ▭, *Tanzania* 54 D3 8 15S 33 30 E
Mbinga, *Tanzania* 55 E4 10 50S 35 0 E
Mbini ▭, *Eq. Guin.* 52 D2 1 30N 10 0 E
Mbour, *Senegal* 50 F2 14 22N 16 54W
Mbuji-Mayi, *Dem. Rep. of the Congo* 54 D1 6 9S 23 40 E
Mbulu, *Tanzania* 54 C4 3 45S 35 30 E
Mburucuyá, *Argentina* 94 B4 28 1S 58 14W
Mchinja, *Tanzania* 55 D4 9 44S 39 45 E
Mchinji, *Malawi* 55 E3 13 47S 32 58 E
Mdantsane, *S. Africa* 53 L5 32 56S 27 46 E
Mead, L., *U.S.A.* 85 J12 36 1N 114 44W
Meade, *U.S.A.* 81 G4 37 17N 100 20W
Meadow Lake, *Canada* 73 C7 54 10N 108 26W
Meadow Lake Prov. Park, *Canada* 73 C7 54 27N 109 0W
Meadow Valley Wash →, *U.S.A.* 85 J12 36 40N 114 34W
Meadville, *U.S.A.* 78 E4 41 39N 80 9W
Meaford, *Canada* 78 B4 44 36N 80 35W
Mealy Mts., *Canada* 71 B8 53 10N 58 0W
Meander River, *Canada* 72 B5 59 2N 117 42W
Meares, C., *U.S.A.* 82 D2 45 37N 124 0W
Mearim →, *Brazil* 93 D10 3 4S 44 35W
Meath ▭, *Ireland* 13 C5 53 40N 6 57W
Meath Park, *Canada* 73 C7 53 27N 105 22W
Meaux, *France* 18 B5 48 58N 2 50 E
Mebechi-Gawa →, *Japan* 30 D10 40 31N 141 31 E
Mecanhelas, *Mozam.* 55 F4 15 12S 35 54 E
**Mecca** = Makkah, *Si. Arabia* 46 C2 21 30N 39 54 E
Mecca, *U.S.A.* 85 M10 33 34N 116 5W
Mechanicsburg, *U.S.A.* 78 F8 40 13N 77 1W
Mechanicville, *U.S.A.* 79 D11 42 54N 73 41W
Mechelen, *Belgium* 15 C4 51 2N 4 29 E
Mecheria, *Algeria* 50 B5 33 35N 0 18W
Mecklenburg, *Germany* 16 B6 53 33N 11 40 E
Mecklenburger Bucht, *Germany* 16 A6 54 20N 11 40 E
Meconta, *Mozam.* 55 E4 14 59S 39 50 E
Medan, *Indonesia* 36 D1 3 40N 98 38 E
Medanosa, Pta., *Argentina* 96 F3 48 8S 66 0W
Médéa, *Algeria* 50 A6 36 12N 2 50 E
**Medellín**, *Colombia* 92 B3 6 15N 75 35W
Medelpad, *Sweden* 9 E17 62 33N 16 30 E
Medemblik, *Neths.* 15 B5 52 46N 5 8 E
Medford, *Mass., U.S.A.* 79 D13 42 25N 71 7W
Medford, *Oreg., U.S.A.* 82 E2 42 19N 122 52W
Medford, *Wis., U.S.A.* 80 C9 45 9N 90 20W
Medgidia, *Romania* 17 F15 44 15N 28 19 E
Media Agua, *Argentina* 94 C2 31 58S 68 25W
Media Luna, *Argentina* 94 C2 34 45S 66 44W
Medianeira, *Brazil* 95 B5 25 17S 54 5W
Mediaş, *Romania* 17 E13 46 9N 24 22 E
Medicine Bow, *U.S.A.* 82 F10 41 54N 106 12W
Medicine Bow Pk., *U.S.A.* 82 F10 41 21N 106 19W
Medicine Bow Ra., *U.S.A.* 82 F10 41 10N 106 25W
Medicine Hat, *Canada* 73 D6 50 0N 110 45W
Medicine Lake, *U.S.A.* 80 A2 48 30N 104 30W
Medicine Lodge, *U.S.A.* 81 G5 37 17N 98 35W
**Medina** = Al Madīnah, *Si. Arabia* 46 C2 24 35N 39 52 E
Medina, *N. Dak., U.S.A.* 80 B5 46 54N 99 18W
Medina, *N.Y., U.S.A.* 78 C6 43 13N 78 23W
Medina, *Ohio, U.S.A.* 78 E3 41 8N 81 52W
Medina →, *U.S.A.* 81 L5 29 16N 98 29W
Medina del Campo, *Spain* 19 B3 41 18N 4 55W
Medina L., *U.S.A.* 81 L5 29 32N 98 56W
Medina Sidonia, *Spain* 19 D3 36 28N 5 57W
Medinipur, *India* 43 H12 22 25N 87 21 E
**Mediterranean Sea**, *Europe* 6 H7 35 0N 15 0 E
Médoc, *France* 18 D3 45 10N 0 50W
Medveditsa →, *Russia* 25 E7 49 35N 42 41 E
Medvezhi, Ostrava, *Russia* 27 B17 71 0N 161 0 E
Medvezhyegorsk, *Russia* 24 B5 63 0N 34 25 E
Medway →, *U.K.* 11 F8 51 27N 0 46 E
Medway Towns ▭, *U.K.* 11 F8 51 25N 0 32 E
Meekatharra, *Australia* 61 E2 26 32S 118 29 E
Meeker, *U.S.A.* 82 F10 40 2N 107 55W
Meelpaeg Res., *Canada* 71 C8 48 15N 56 33W
Meerut, *India* 42 E7 29 1N 77 42 E
Meeteetse, *U.S.A.* 82 D9 44 9N 108 52W
Mega, *Ethiopia* 46 G2 3 57N 38 19 E
Mégara, *Greece* 21 F10 37 58N 23 22 E
Megasini, *India* 43 J12 21 38N 86 21 E
Meghalaya ▭, *India* 41 G17 25 50N 91 0 E

Mégiscane, L., Canada 70 C4 48 35N 75 55W
Meharry, Mt., Australia 60 D2 22 59S 118 35 E
Mehlville, U.S.A. 80 F9 38 30N 90 19W
Mehndawal, India 43 F10 26 58N 83 5 E
Mehr Jān, Iran 45 C7 33 50N 55 6 E
Mehrābād, Iran 44 B5 36 53N 47 55 E
Mehrān, Iran 44 C5 33 7N 46 10 E
Mehrīz, Iran 45 D7 31 35N 54 28 E
Mei Xian, China 34 G4 34 18N 107 55 E
Meiktila, Burma 41 J19 20 53N 95 54 E
Meissen, Germany 16 C7 51 9N 13 29 E
Meizhou, China 33 D6 24 16N 116 6 E
Meja, India 43 G10 25 9N 82 7 E
Mejillones, Chile 94 A1 23 10S 70 30W
Mekele, Ethiopia 46 E2 13 33N 39 30 E
Mekhtar, Pakistan 40 D6 30 30N 69 15 E
Meknès, Morocco 50 B4 33 57N 5 33W
**Mekong** →, Asia 39 H6 9 30N 106 15 E
Mekongga, Indonesia 37 E6 3 39S 121 15 E
Mekvari = Kür →, Azerbaijan 25 G8 39 29N 49 15 E
Melagiri Hills, India 40 N10 12 20N 77 30 E
**Melaka**, Malaysia 39 L4 2 15N 102 15 E
Melalap, Malaysia 36 C5 5 10N 116 5 E
Mélambes, Greece 23 D6 35 8N 24 40 E
**Melanesia**, Pac. Oc. 64 H7 4 0S 155 0 E
**Melbourne**, Australia 63 F4 37 50S 145 0 E
Melbourne, U.S.A. 77 L5 28 5N 80 37W
Melchor Múzquiz, Mexico 86 B4 27 50N 101 30W
Melchor Ocampo, Mexico 86 C4 24 52N 101 40W
Mélèzes →, Canada 69 C12 57 30N 71 0W
Mélèzes →, Qué., Canada 70 A5 57 40N 69 29W
Melfort, Canada 73 C8 52 50N 104 37W
Melfort, Zimbabwe 55 F3 18 0S 31 25 E
Melhus, Norway 8 E14 63 17N 10 18 E
Melilla, N. Afr. 19 E4 35 21N 2 57W
Melipilla, Chile 94 C1 33 42S 71 15W
Mélissa, Ákra, Greece 23 D6 35 6N 24 33 E
Melita, Canada 73 D8 49 15N 101 0W
Melitopol, Ukraine 25 E6 46 50N 35 22 E
Melk, Austria 16 D8 48 13N 15 20 E
Mellansel, Sweden 8 E18 63 25N 18 17 E
Mellen, U.S.A. 80 B9 46 20N 90 40W
Mellerud, Sweden 9 G15 58 41N 12 28 E
Mellette, U.S.A. 80 C5 45 9N 98 30W
Mellieha, Malta 23 D1 35 57N 14 21 E
Melo, Uruguay 95 C5 32 20S 54 10W
Melolo, Indonesia 37 F6 9 53S 120 40 E
Melouprey, Cambodia 38 F5 13 48N 105 16 E
Melrose, Australia 63 E4 32 42S 146 57 E
Melrose, U.K. 12 F6 55 36N 2 43W
Melrose, Minn., U.S.A. 80 C7 45 40N 94 49W
Melrose, N. Mex., U.S.A. 81 H3 34 26N 103 38W
Melstone, U.S.A. 82 C10 46 36N 107 52W
Melton Mowbray, U.K. 10 E7 52 47N 0 54W
Melun, France 18 B5 48 32N 2 39 E
Melville, Canada 73 C8 50 55N 102 50W
Melville, C., Australia 62 A3 14 11S 144 30 E
Melville, L., Canada 71 B8 53 30N 60 0W
Melville B., Australia 62 A2 12 0S 136 45 E
Melville I., Australia 60 B5 11 30S 131 0 E
Melville I., Canada 4 B2 75 30N 112 0W
Melville Pen., Canada 69 B11 68 0N 84 0W
Memba, Mozam. 55 E5 14 11S 40 30 E
Memboro, Indonesia 37 F5 9 30S 119 30 E
Memel = Klaipėda, Lithuania 9 J19 55 43N 21 10 E
Memel, S. Africa 57 D4 27 38S 29 36 E
Memmingen, Germany 16 E6 47 58N 10 10 E
Mempawah, Indonesia 36 D3 0 30N 109 5 E
Memphis, Mich., U.S.A. 78 D2 42 54N 82 46W
**Memphis**, Tenn., U.S.A. 81 H10 35 8N 90 3W
Memphis, Tex., U.S.A. 81 H4 34 44N 100 33W
Memphremagog, L., U.S.A. 79 B12 45 0N 72 12W
Mena, U.S.A. 81 H7 34 35N 94 15W
Menai Strait, U.K. 10 D3 53 11N 4 13W
Ménaka, Mali 50 E6 15 59N 2 18 E
Menan = Chao Phraya →, Thailand 38 F3 13 32N 100 36 E
Menarandra →, Madag. 57 D7 25 17S 44 30 E
Menard, U.S.A. 81 K5 30 55N 99 47W
Mendawai →, Indonesia 36 E4 3 30S 113 0 E
Mende, France 18 D5 44 31N 3 30 E
Mendez, Mexico 87 B5 25 7N 98 34W
Mendhar, India 43 C6 33 35N 74 10 E
Mendip Hills, U.K. 11 F5 51 17N 2 40W
Mendocino, U.S.A. 82 G2 39 19N 123 48W
Mendocino, C., U.S.A. 82 F1 40 26N 124 25W
Mendooran, Australia 63 E4 31 50S 149 6 E
Mendota, Calif., U.S.A. 84 J6 36 45N 120 23W
Mendota, Ill., U.S.A. 80 E10 41 33N 89 7W
Mendoza, Argentina 94 C2 32 50S 68 52W
Mendoza □, Argentina 94 C2 33 0S 69 0W
Mene Grande, Venezuela 92 B4 9 49N 70 56W
Menemen, Turkey 21 E12 38 34N 27 3 E
Menen, Belgium 15 D3 50 47N 3 7 E
Menggala, Indonesia 36 E3 4 30S 105 15 E
Mengjin, China 34 G7 34 55N 112 45 E
Mengyin, China 35 G9 35 40N 117 58 E
Mengzi, China 32 D5 23 20N 103 22 E
Menihek, Canada 71 B6 54 28N 56 36W
Menihek L., Canada 71 B6 54 0N 67 0W
Menin = Menen, Belgium 15 D3 50 47N 3 7 E
Menindee, Australia 63 E3 32 20S 142 25 E
Menindee L., Australia 63 E3 32 20S 142 25 E
Meningie, Australia 63 F2 35 50S 139 18 E
Menlo Park, U.S.A. 84 H4 37 27N 122 12W
Menominee, U.S.A. 76 C2 45 6N 87 37W
Menominee →, U.S.A. 76 C2 45 6N 87 36W
Menomonie, U.S.A. 80 C9 44 53N 91 55W
Menongue, Angola 53 G3 14 48S 17 52 E
Menorca, Spain 22 B11 40 0N 4 0 E
Mentakab, Malaysia 39 L4 3 29N 102 21 E
Mentawai, Kepulauan, Indonesia 36 E1 2 0S 99 0 E
Menton, France 18 E7 43 50N 7 29 E
Mentor, U.S.A. 78 E3 41 40N 81 21W
Menzelinsk, Russia 24 C9 55 47N 53 11 E
Menzies, Australia 61 E3 29 40S 121 2 E
Me'ona, Israel 47 B4 33 1N 35 15 E
Meoqui, Mexico 86 B3 28 17N 105 29W
Mepaco, Mozam. 55 F3 15 57S 30 48 E
Meppel, Neths. 15 B6 52 42N 6 12 E
Merabéllou, Kólpos, Greece 23 D7 35 10N 25 50 E
Merak, Indonesia 37 F12 6 10N 106 26 E
Meramangye, L., Australia 61 E5 28 25S 132 13 E
Meran = Merano, Italy 20 A4 46 40N 11 9 E
Merano, Italy 20 A4 46 40N 11 9 E
Merauke, Indonesia 37 F10 8 29S 140 24 E
Merbein, Australia 63 E3 34 10S 142 2 E
Merca, Somali Rep. 46 G3 1 48N 44 50 E
Merced, U.S.A. 84 H6 37 18N 120 29W
Merced →, U.S.A. 84 H6 37 21N 120 59W
Merced Pk., U.S.A. 84 H7 37 36N 119 24W
Mercedes, Buenos Aires, Argentina 94 C4 34 40S 59 30W
Mercedes, Corrientes, Argentina 94 B4 29 10S 58 5W
Mercedes, San Luis, Argentina 94 C2 33 40S 65 21W
Mercedes, Uruguay 94 C4 33 12S 58 0W
Mercedes, U.S.A. 81 M6 26 9N 97 55W
Merceditas, Chile 94 B1 28 20S 70 35W
Mercer, N.Z. 59 G5 37 16S 175 5 E
Mercer, U.S.A. 78 E4 41 14N 80 15W
Mercer Island, U.S.A. 84 C4 47 35N 122 15W
Mercury, U.S.A. 85 J11 36 40N 115 58W
Mercy C., Canada 69 B13 65 0N 63 30W
Mere, U.K. 11 F5 51 6N 2 16W
Meredith, C., Falk. Is. 96 G4 52 15S 60 40W
Meredith, L., U.S.A. 81 H4 35 43N 101 33W
Mergui, Burma 38 F2 12 26N 98 34 E
Mergui Arch. = Myeik Kyunzu, Burma 39 G1 11 30N 97 30 E
Mérida, Mexico 87 C7 20 58N 89 37W
Mérida, Spain 19 C2 38 55N 6 25W
Mérida, Venezuela 92 B4 8 24N 71 8W
Mérida, Cord. de, Venezuela 90 C3 9 0N 71 0W
Meriden, U.K. 11 E6 52 26N 1 38W
Meriden, U.S.A. 79 E12 41 32N 72 48W
Meridian, Calif., U.S.A. 84 F5 39 9N 121 55W
Meridian, Idaho, U.S.A. 82 E5 43 37N 116 24W
Meridian, Miss., U.S.A. 77 J1 32 22N 88 42W
Merimbula, Australia 63 F4 36 53S 149 54 E
Merinda, Australia 62 C4 20 2S 148 11 E
Meringur, Australia 63 E3 34 20S 141 19 E
Merir, Pac. Oc. 37 D8 4 10N 132 30 E
Merirumã, Brazil 93 C8 1 15N 54 50W
Merkel, U.S.A. 81 J5 32 28N 100 1W
Mermaid Reef, Australia 60 C2 17 6S 119 36 E
Merredin, Australia 61 F2 31 28S 118 18 E
Merrick, U.K. 12 F4 55 8N 4 28W
Merrickville, Canada 79 B9 44 55N 75 50W
Merrill, Oreg., U.S.A. 82 E3 42 1N 121 36W
Merrill, Wis., U.S.A. 80 C10 45 11N 89 41W
Merrimack →, U.S.A. 79 D14 42 49N 70 49W
Merriman, U.S.A. 80 D4 42 55N 101 42W
Merritt, Canada 72 C4 50 10N 120 45W
Merritt Island, U.S.A. 77 L5 28 21N 80 42W
Merriwa, Australia 63 E5 32 6S 150 22 E
Merry I., Canada 70 A4 55 29N 77 31W
Merryville, U.S.A. 81 K8 30 45N 93 33W
Mersch, Lux. 15 E6 49 44N 6 7 E
Mersea I., U.K. 11 F8 51 47N 0 58 E
Merseburg, Germany 16 C6 51 22N 11 59 E
Mersey →, U.K. 10 D4 53 25N 3 1W
**Merseyside** □, U.K. 10 D4 53 31N 3 2W
Mersin, Turkey 25 G5 36 51N 34 36 E
Mersing, Malaysia 39 L4 2 25N 103 50 E
Merta, India 42 F6 26 39N 74 4 E
Merta Road, India 42 F5 26 43N 73 55 E
Merthyr Tydfil, U.K. 11 F4 51 45N 3 22W
Merthyr Tydfil □, U.K. 11 F4 51 46N 3 21W
Mértola, Portugal 19 D2 37 40N 7 40W
Mertzon, U.S.A. 81 K4 31 16N 100 49W
Meru, Kenya 54 B4 0 3N 37 40 E
Meru, Tanzania 54 C4 3 15S 36 46 E
Mesa, U.S.A. 83 K8 33 25N 111 50W
Mesa Verde National Park, U.S.A. 83 H9 37 11N 108 29W
Mesanagrós, Greece 23 C9 36 1N 27 49 E
Mesaoria □, Cyprus 23 D12 35 12N 33 14 E
Mesarás, Kólpos, Greece 23 D6 35 6N 24 47 E
Mesgouez, L., Canada 70 B5 51 20N 75 0W
Meshed = Mashhad, Iran 45 B8 36 20N 59 35 E
Meshoppen, U.S.A. 79 E8 41 36N 76 3W
Mesilinka →, Canada 72 B4 56 6N 124 30W
Mesilla, U.S.A. 83 K10 32 16N 106 48W
Mesolóngion, Greece 21 E9 38 21N 21 28 E
Mesopotamia = Al Jazirah, Iraq 44 C5 33 30N 44 0 E
Mesopotamia, U.S.A. 78 E4 41 27N 80 57W
Mesquite, U.S.A. 83 H6 36 47N 114 6W
Messad, Algeria 50 B6 34 8N 3 30 E
Messalo →, Mozam. 55 E4 12 25S 39 15 E
**Messina**, Italy 20 E6 38 11N 15 34 E
Messina, S. Africa 57 C5 22 20S 30 5 E
Messina, Str. di, Italy 20 F6 38 15N 15 35 E
Messíni, Greece 21 F10 37 4N 22 1 E
Messiniakós Kólpos, Greece 21 F10 36 45N 22 5 E
Messonghi, Greece 23 B3 39 29N 19 56 E
Mesta →, Bulgaria 21 D11 40 54N 24 49 E
Meta →, S. Amer. 92 B5 6 12N 67 28W
Meta Incognita Peninsula, Canada 69 B13 62 40N 68 0W
Metabetchouan, Canada 71 C5 48 26N 71 52W
Metairie, U.S.A. 81 L9 29 58N 90 10W
Metaline Falls, U.S.A. 82 B5 48 52N 117 22W
Metán, Argentina 94 B3 25 30S 65 0W
Metangula, Mozam. 55 E3 12 40S 34 50 E
Metengobalame, Mozam. 55 E3 14 49S 34 30 E
Methven, N.Z. 59 K3 43 38S 171 40 E
Metil, Mozam. 55 F4 16 24S 39 0 E
Metlakatla, U.S.A. 68 C6 55 8N 131 35W
Metropolis, U.S.A. 81 G10 37 9N 88 44W
Mettur Dam, India 40 P10 11 45N 77 45 E
Metu, Ethiopia 46 F2 8 18N 35 35 E
**Metz**, France 18 B7 49 8N 6 10 E
Meulaboh, Indonesia 36 D1 4 11N 96 3 E
Meureudu, Indonesia 36 C1 5 19N 96 10 E
Meuse →, Europe 18 A6 50 45N 5 41 E
Mexia, U.S.A. 81 K6 31 41N 96 29W
Mexiana, I., Brazil 93 D9 0 0 49 30W
Mexicali, Mexico 85 N11 32 40N 115 30W
Mexican Plateau, Mexico 66 G9 25 0N 104 0W
Mexican Water, U.S.A. 83 H9 36 57N 109 32W
**México**, Mexico 87 D5 19 20N 99 10W
Mexico, Maine, U.S.A. 79 B14 44 34N 70 33W
Mexico, Mo., U.S.A. 80 F9 39 10N 91 53W
Mexico, N.Y., U.S.A. 79 C8 43 28N 76 18W
México □, Mexico 87 D5 19 20N 99 10W
**Mexico** ■, Cent. Amer. 86 C4 25 0N 105 0W
Mexico, G. of, Cent. Amer. 87 C7 25 0N 90 0W
Mexico B., U.S.A. 79 C8 43 35N 76 20W
Meydān-e Naftūn, Iran 45 D6 31 56N 49 18 E
Meydani, Ra's-e, Iran 45 E8 25 24N 59 6 E
Meymaneh, Afghan. 40 B4 35 53N 64 38 E
Mezen, Russia 24 A7 65 50N 44 20 E
Mezen →, Russia 24 A7 65 44N 44 22 E
Mézenc, Mt., France 18 D6 44 54N 4 11 E
Mezhdurechenskiy, Russia 26 D7 59 36N 65 56 E
Mezőkövesd, Hungary 17 E11 47 49N 20 35 E
Mezőtúr, Hungary 17 E11 47 1N 20 41 E
Mezquital, Mexico 86 C4 23 29N 104 23W
Mgeta, Tanzania 55 D4 8 22S 36 6 E
Mhlaba Hills, Zimbabwe 55 F3 18 30S 30 30 E
Mhow, India 42 H6 22 33N 75 50 E
Miahuatlán, Mexico 87 D5 16 21N 96 36W
**Miami**, Fla., U.S.A. 77 N5 25 47N 80 11W
Miami, Okla., U.S.A. 81 G7 36 53N 94 53W
Miami, Tex., U.S.A. 81 H4 35 42N 100 38W
Miami Beach, U.S.A. 77 N5 25 47N 80 8W
Mian Xian, China 34 H4 33 10N 106 32 E
Mianchi, China 34 G6 34 48N 111 48 E
Mīāndarreh, Iran 45 C7 35 37N 53 39 E
Mīāndowāb, Iran 44 B5 37 0N 46 5 E
Miandrivazo, Madag. 57 B8 19 31S 45 29 E
Mīāneh, Iran 44 B5 37 30N 47 40 E
Mianwali, Pakistan 42 C4 32 38N 71 28 E
Miarinarivo, Madag. 57 B8 18 57S 46 55 E
Miass, Russia 24 D11 54 59N 60 6 E
Michalovce, Slovak Rep. 17 D11 48 47N 21 58 E
**Michigan** □, U.S.A. 76 C3 44 0N 85 0W
**Michigan, L.**, U.S.A. 76 D2 44 0N 87 0W
Michigan City, U.S.A. 76 E2 41 43N 86 54W
Michipicoten I., Canada 70 C2 47 40N 85 40W
Michoacan □, Mexico 86 D4 19 0N 102 0W
Michurin, Bulgaria 21 C12 42 9N 27 51 E
Michurinsk, Russia 24 D7 52 58N 40 27 E
Mico, Pta., Nic. 88 D3 12 0N 83 30W
Micronesia, Pac. Oc. 64 G7 11 0N 160 0 E
Micronesia, Federated States of ■, Pac. Oc. 64 G7 9 0N 150 0 E
Midai, Indonesia 39 L6 3 0N 107 47 E
Midale, Canada 73 D8 49 25N 103 20W
Middelburg, Neths. 15 C3 51 30N 3 36 E
Middelburg, Eastern Cape, S. Africa 56 E4 31 30S 25 0 E
Middelburg, Mpumalanga, S. Africa 57 D4 25 49S 29 28 E
Middelwit, S. Africa 56 C4 24 51S 27 3 E
Middle Alkali L., U.S.A. 82 F3 41 27N 120 5W
Middle Bass I., U.S.A. 78 E2 41 41N 82 49W
**Middle East**, Asia 28 F7 38 0N 40 0 E
Middle Fork Feather →, U.S.A. 84 F5 38 33N 121 30W
Middle I., Australia 61 F3 34 6S 123 11 E
Middle Loup →, U.S.A. 80 E5 41 17N 98 24W
Middle Sackville, Canada 71 D7 44 47N 63 42W
Middleboro, U.S.A. 79 E14 41 54N 70 55W
Middleburg, Fla., U.S.A. 77 K5 30 4N 81 52W
Middleburg, N.Y., U.S.A. 79 D10 42 36N 74 20W
Middleburg, Pa., U.S.A. 78 F7 40 47N 77 3W
Middlebury, U.S.A. 79 B11 44 1N 73 10W
Middlemount, Australia 62 C4 22 50S 148 40 E
Middleport, N.Y., U.S.A. 78 C6 43 13N 78 29W
Middleport, Ohio, U.S.A. 76 F4 39 0N 82 3W
Middlesboro, U.S.A. 77 G4 36 36N 83 43W
**Middlesbrough**, U.K. 10 C6 54 35N 1 13W
Middlesbrough □, U.K. 10 C6 54 28N 1 13W
Middlesex, Belize 88 C2 17 2N 88 31W
Middlesex, N.J., U.S.A. 79 F10 40 36N 74 30W
Middlesex, N.Y., U.S.A. 78 D7 42 42N 77 16W
Middleton, Australia 62 C3 22 22S 141 32 E
Middleton, Canada 71 D6 44 57N 65 4W
Middleton Cr. →, Australia 62 C3 22 35S 141 51 E
Middletown, U.K. 13 B5 54 17N 6 51W
Middletown, Calif., U.S.A. 84 G4 38 45N 122 37W
Middletown, Conn., U.S.A. 79 E12 41 34N 72 39W
Middletown, N.Y., U.S.A. 79 E10 41 27N 74 25W
Middletown, Ohio, U.S.A. 76 F3 39 31N 84 24W
Middletown, Pa., U.S.A. 79 F8 40 12N 76 44W
Midhurst, U.K. 11 G7 50 59N 0 44W
Midi, Canal du →, France 18 E4 43 45N 1 21 E
Midland, Canada 78 B5 44 45N 79 50W
Midland, Calif., U.S.A. 85 M12 33 52N 114 48W
Midland, Mich., U.S.A. 76 D3 43 37N 84 14W
Midland, Pa., U.S.A. 78 F4 40 39N 80 27W
Midland, Tex., U.S.A. 81 K3 32 0N 102 3W
Midlands □, Zimbabwe 55 F2 19 40S 29 0 E
Midleton, Ireland 13 E3 51 55N 8 10W
Midlothian, U.S.A. 81 J6 32 30N 97 0W
Midlothian □, U.K. 12 F5 55 51N 3 5W
Midongy, Tangorombohitr' i, Madag. 57 C8 23 30S 47 0 E
Midongy Atsimo, Madag. 57 C8 23 35S 47 1 E
**Midway Is.**, Pac. Oc. 64 E10 28 13N 177 22W
Midway Wells, U.S.A. 85 N11 32 41N 115 7W
**Midwest**, U.S.A. 75 B9 42 0N 90 0W
Midwest, Wyo., U.S.A. 82 E10 43 25N 106 16W
Midwest City, U.S.A. 81 H6 35 27N 97 24W
Midyat, Turkey 44 B4 37 25N 41 23 E
Midžor, Bulgaria 21 C10 43 24N 22 40 E
Mie □, Japan 31 G8 34 30N 136 10 E
Międzychód, Poland 16 B8 52 35N 15 53 E
Międzyrzec Podlaski, Poland 17 C12 51 58N 22 45 E
Mielec, Poland 17 C11 50 15N 21 25 E
Mienga, Angola 56 B2 17 12S 19 48 E
Miercurea-Ciuc, Romania 17 E13 46 21N 25 48 E
Mieres, Spain 19 A3 43 18N 5 48W
Mifflintown, U.S.A. 78 F7 40 34N 77 24W
Mifraz Hefa, Israel 47 C4 32 52N 35 0 E
Miguel Alemán, Presa, Mexico 87 D5 18 15N 96 40W
Mihara, Japan 31 G6 34 24N 133 5 E
Mikese, Tanzania 54 D4 6 48S 37 55 E
Mikhaylovgrad = Montana, Bulgaria 21 C10 43 27N 23 16 E
Mikhaylovka, Russia 25 D7 50 3N 43 5 E
Mikkeli, Finland 9 F22 61 43N 27 15 E
Mikkwa →, Canada 72 B6 58 25N 114 46W
Míkonos, Greece 21 F11 37 30N 25 25 E
Mikumi, Tanzania 54 D4 7 26S 37 0 E
Mikun, Russia 24 B9 62 20N 50 0 E
Milaca, U.S.A. 80 C8 45 45N 93 39W
Milagro, Ecuador 92 D3 2 11S 79 36W
**Milan** = Milano, Italy 18 D8 45 28N 9 12 E
Milan, Mo., U.S.A. 80 E8 40 12N 93 7W
Milan, Tenn., U.S.A. 77 H1 35 55N 88 46W
Milang, Australia 63 F2 35 24S 138 58 E
Milange, Mozam. 55 F4 16 3S 35 45 E
Milano, Italy 18 D8 45 28N 9 12 E
Milâs, Turkey 21 F12 37 20N 27 50 E
Mílatos, Greece 23 D7 35 18N 25 34 E
Milazzo, Italy 20 E6 38 13N 15 15 E
Milbank, U.S.A. 80 C6 45 13N 96 38W
Milbanke Sd., Canada 72 C3 52 15N 128 35W
Milden, Canada 73 C7 51 29N 107 32W
Mildenhall, U.K. 11 E8 52 21N 0 32 E
Mildmay, Canada 78 B3 44 3N 81 7W
Mildura, Australia 63 E3 34 13S 142 9 E
Miles, Australia 63 D5 26 40S 150 9 E
Miles City, U.S.A. 80 B2 46 25N 105 51W
Milestone, Canada 73 D8 49 59N 104 31W
Miletus, Turkey 21 F12 37 30N 27 18 E
Milford, Calif., U.S.A. 84 E6 40 10N 120 22W
Milford, Conn., U.S.A. 79 E11 41 14N 73 3W
Milford, Del., U.S.A. 76 F8 38 55N 75 26W
Milford, Mass., U.S.A. 79 D13 42 8N 71 31W
Milford, N.H., U.S.A. 79 D13 42 50N 71 39W
Milford, Pa., U.S.A. 79 E10 41 19N 74 48W
Milford, Utah, U.S.A. 83 G7 38 24N 113 1W
Milford Haven, U.K. 11 F2 51 42N 5 7W
Milford Sd., N.Z. 59 L1 44 41S 167 47 E
Milḥ, Baḥr al, Iraq 44 C4 32 40N 43 35 E
Milikapiti, Australia 60 B5 11 26S 130 40 E
Miling, Australia 61 F2 30 30S 116 17 E
Milk →, U.S.A. 82 B10 48 4N 106 19W
Milk River, Canada 72 D6 49 10N 112 5W
Mill I., Antarctica 5 C8 66 0S 101 30 E
Mill Valley, U.S.A. 84 H4 37 54N 122 32W
Millau, France 18 D5 44 8N 3 4 E
Millbridge, Canada 78 B7 44 41N 77 36W
Millbrook, Canada 78 B6 44 10N 78 29W
Millbrook, U.S.A. 79 E11 41 47N 73 42W
Mille Lacs, L. des, Canada 70 C1 48 45N 90 35W
Mille Lacs L., U.S.A. 80 B8 46 15N 93 39W
Milledgeville, U.S.A. 77 J4 33 5N 83 14W
Millen, U.S.A. 77 J5 32 48N 81 57W
Miller, U.S.A. 80 C5 44 31N 98 59W
Millersburg, Ohio, U.S.A. 78 F3 40 33N 81 55W
Millersburg, Pa., U.S.A. 78 F8 40 32N 76 58W
Millerton, U.S.A. 79 E11 41 57N 73 31W
Millerton L., U.S.A. 84 J7 37 1N 119 41W
Millheim, U.S.A. 78 F7 40 54N 77 29W
Millicent, Australia 63 F3 37 34S 140 21 E
Millington, U.S.A. 81 H10 35 20N 89 53W
Millinocket, U.S.A. 77 C11 45 39N 68 43W
Millmerran, Australia 63 D5 27 53S 151 16 E
Millom, U.K. 10 C4 54 13N 3 16W
Mills L., Canada 72 A5 61 30N 118 20W
Millsboro, U.S.A. 78 G5 40 0N 80 0W
Milltown Malbay, Ireland 13 D2 52 52N 9 24W
Millville, N.J., U.S.A. 76 F8 39 24N 75 2W
Millville, Pa., U.S.A. 79 E8 41 7N 76 32W
Millwood L., U.S.A. 81 J8 33 42N 93 58W
Milne →, Australia 62 C2 21 10S 137 33 E
Milo, U.S.A. 77 C11 45 15N 68 59W
Mílos, Greece 21 F11 36 44N 24 25 E
Milparinka, Australia 63 D3 29 46S 141 57 E
Milton, N.S., Canada 71 D7 44 4N 64 45W
Milton, Ont., Canada 78 C5 43 31N 79 53W
Milton, N.Z. 59 M2 46 7S 169 59 E
Milton, Calif., U.S.A. 84 G6 38 3N 120 51W
Milton, Fla., U.S.A. 77 K2 30 38N 87 3W
Milton, Pa., U.S.A. 78 F8 41 1N 76 51W
Milton, Vt., U.S.A. 79 B11 44 38N 73 7W
Milton-Freewater, U.S.A. 82 D4 45 56N 118 23W
Milton Keynes, U.K. 11 E7 52 1N 0 44W
Milton Keynes □, U.K. 11 E7 52 1N 0 44W
Milverton, Canada 78 C4 43 34N 80 55W
**Milwaukee**, U.S.A. 76 D2 43 2N 87 55W
Milwaukee Deep, Atl. Oc. 89 C6 19 50N 68 0W
Milwaukie, U.S.A. 84 E4 45 27N 122 38W
Min Jiang →, Fujian, China 33 D6 26 0N 119 35 E
Min Jiang →, Sichuan, China 32 D5 28 45N 104 40 E
Min Xian, China 34 G3 34 25N 104 5 E
Mina Pirquitas, Argentina 94 A2 22 40S 66 30W
Mīnā Su'ud, Si. Arabia 45 D6 28 45N 48 28 E
Mīnā'al Aḥmadī, Kuwait 45 D6 29 5N 48 10 E
Minago →, Canada 73 C9 54 33N 98 59W
Minaki, Canada 73 D10 49 59N 94 40W
Minamata, Japan 31 H5 32 10N 130 30 E
Minami-Tori-Shima, Pac. Oc. 64 E7 24 20N 153 58 E
Minas, Uruguay 95 C4 34 20S 55 10W
Minas, Sierra de las, Guatemala 88 C2 15 9N 89 31W
Minas Basin, Canada 71 C7 45 20N 64 12W
Minas Gerais □, Brazil 93 G9 18 50S 46 0W
Minatitlán, Mexico 87 D6 17 59N 94 31W
Minbu, Burma 41 J19 20 10N 94 52 E
Minchinabad, Pakistan 42 D5 30 10N 73 34 E
**Mindanao**, Phil. 37 C7 8 0N 125 0 E
Mindanao Sea = Bohol Sea, Phil. 37 C6 9 0N 124 0 E
Mindanao Trench, Pac. Oc. 37 B7 12 0N 126 6 E
Minden, Canada 78 B6 44 55N 78 43W
Minden, Germany 16 B5 52 17N 8 55 E
Minden, La., U.S.A. 81 J8 32 37N 93 17W
Minden, Nev., U.S.A. 84 G7 38 57N 119 46W
Mindiptana, Indonesia 37 F10 5 55S 140 22 E
Mindoro, Phil. 37 B6 13 0N 121 0 E
Mindoro Str., Phil. 37 B6 12 30N 120 30 E
Mine, Japan 31 G5 34 12N 131 7 E
Minehead, U.K. 11 F4 51 12N 3 29W
Mineola, N.Y., U.S.A. 79 F11 40 45N 73 39W
Mineola, Tex., U.S.A. 81 J7 32 40N 95 29W
Mineral King, U.S.A. 84 J8 36 27N 118 36W
Mineral Wells, U.S.A. 81 J5 32 48N 98 7W
Minersville, U.S.A. 79 F8 40 41N 76 16W
Minerva, U.S.A. 78 F3 40 44N 81 6W
Minetto, U.S.A. 79 C8 43 24N 76 28W
Mingäçevir Su Anban, Azerbaijan 25 F8 40 57N 46 50 E
Mingan, Canada 71 B7 50 20N 64 0W
Mingechaurskoye Vdkhr. = Mingäçevir Su Anban, Azerbaijan 25 F8 40 57N 46 50 E
Mingela, Australia 62 B4 19 52S 146 38 E
Mingenew, Australia 61 E2 29 12S 115 21 E
Mingera Cr. →, Australia 62 C2 20 38S 137 45 E
Mingin, Burma 41 H19 22 50N 94 30 E
Mingo Junction, U.S.A. 78 F4 40 19N 80 37W
Mingyuegue, China 35 C15 43 2N 128 50 E
Minho = Miño →, Spain 19 A2 41 52N 8 40W
Minho, Portugal 19 B1 41 25N 8 20W
Minidoka, U.S.A. 82 E7 42 45N 113 29W

Minigwal, L., *Australia* 61 E3 29 31S 123 14 E
Minilya →, *Australia* 61 D1 23 45S 114 0 E
Minilya Roadhouse, *Australia* 61 D1 23 55S 114 0 E
Minipi L., *Canada* 71 B7 52 25N 60 45W
Mink L., *Canada* 72 A5 61 54N 117 40W
Minna, *Nigeria* 50 G7 9 37N 6 30 E
Minneapolis, *Kans., U.S.A.* 80 F6 39 8N 97 42W
**Minneapolis**, *Minn., U.S.A.* 80 C8 44 59N 93 16W
Minnedosa, *Canada* 73 C9 50 14N 99 50W
**Minnesota** □, *U.S.A.* 80 B8 46 0N 94 15W
Minnesota →, *U.S.A.* 80 C8 44 54N 93 9W
Minnewaukan, *U.S.A.* 80 A5 48 4N 99 15W
Minnipa, *Australia* 63 E2 32 51S 135 9 E
Minnitaki L., *Canada* 70 C1 49 57N 92 10W
Mino, *Japan* 31 G8 35 32N 136 55 E
Miño →, *Spain* 19 A2 41 52N 8 40W
Minorca = Menorca, *Spain* 22 B11 40 0N 4 0 E
Minot, *U.S.A.* 80 A4 48 14N 101 18W
Minqin, *China* 34 E2 38 38N 103 20 E
**Minsk**, *Belarus* 17 B14 53 52N 27 30 E
Mińsk Mazowiecki, *Poland* 17 B11 52 10N 21 33 E
Mintabie, *Australia* 63 D1 27 15S 133 7 E
Mintaka Pass, *Pakistan* 43 A6 37 0N 74 58 E
Minteke Daban = Mintaka Pass, *Pakistan* 43 A6 37 0N 74 58 E
Minto, *Canada* 71 C6 46 5N 66 5W
Minto, L., *Canada* 70 A5 57 13N 75 0W
Minton, *Canada* 73 D8 49 10N 104 35W
Minturn, *U.S.A.* 82 G10 39 35N 106 26W
Minusinsk, *Russia* 27 D10 53 43N 91 20 E
Minutang, *India* 41 E20 28 15N 96 30 E
Miquelon, *Canada* 70 C4 49 25N 76 27W
Miquelon, *St- P. & M.* 71 C8 47 8N 56 22W
Mīr Kūh, *Iran* 45 E8 26 22N 58 55 E
Mīr Shahdād, *Iran* 45 E8 26 15N 58 29 E
Mira, *Italy* 20 B5 45 26N 12 8 E
Mira por vos Cay, *Bahamas* 89 B5 22 9N 74 30W
Miraj, *India* 40 L9 16 50N 74 45 E
Miram Shah, *Pakistan* 42 C4 33 0N 70 2 E
Miramar, *Argentina* 94 D4 38 15S 57 50W
Miramar, *Mozam.* 57 C6 23 50S 35 35 E
Miramichi, *Canada* 71 C6 47 2N 65 28W
Miramichi B., *Canada* 71 C7 47 15N 65 0W
Miranda, *Brazil* 93 H7 20 10S 56 15W
Miranda →, *Brazil* 92 G7 19 25S 57 20W
Miranda de Ebro, *Spain* 19 A4 42 41N 2 57W
Miranda do Douro, *Portugal* 19 B2 41 30N 6 16W
Mirandópolis, *Brazil* 95 A5 21 9S 51 6W
Mirango, *Malawi* 55 E3 13 32S 34 58 E
Mirassol, *Brazil* 95 A6 20 46S 49 28W
Mirbāţ, *Oman* 46 D5 17 0N 54 45 E
Miri, *Malaysia* 36 D4 4 23N 113 59 E
Miriam Vale, *Australia* 62 C5 24 20S 151 33 E
Mirim, L., *S. Amer.* 95 C5 32 45S 52 50W
Mirnyy, *Russia* 27 C12 62 33N 113 53 E
Mirokhan, *Pakistan* 42 F3 27 46N 68 6 E
Mirond L., *Canada* 73 B8 55 6N 102 47W
Mirpur, *Pakistan* 43 C5 33 32N 73 56 E
Mirpur Batoro, *Pakistan* 42 G3 24 44N 68 16 E
Mirpur Bibiwari, *Pakistan* 42 E2 28 33N 67 44 E
Mirpur Khas, *Pakistan* 42 G3 25 30N 69 0 E
Mirpur Sakro, *Pakistan* 42 G2 24 33N 67 41 E
Mirtağ, *Turkey* 44 B4 38 23N 41 56 E
Miryang, *S. Korea* 35 G15 35 31N 128 44 E
Mirzapur, *India* 43 G10 25 10N 82 34 E
Mirzapur-cum-Vindhyachal = Mirzapur, *India* 43 G10 25 10N 82 34 E
Misantla, *Mexico* 87 D5 19 56N 96 50W
Misawa, *Japan* 30 D10 40 41N 141 24 E
Miscou I., *Canada* 71 C7 47 57N 64 31W
Mish'āb, Ra's al, *Si. Arabia* 45 D6 28 15N 48 43 E
Mishan, *China* 33 B8 45 37N 131 48 E
Mishawaka, *U.S.A.* 76 E2 41 40N 86 11W
Mishima, *Japan* 31 G9 35 10N 138 52 E
Misión, *Mexico* 85 N10 32 6N 116 53W
Misiones □, *Argentina* 95 B5 27 0S 55 0W
Misiones □, *Paraguay* 94 B4 27 0S 56 0W
Miskah, *Si. Arabia* 44 E4 24 49N 42 56 E
Miskitos, Cayos, *Nic.* 88 D3 14 26N 82 50W
Miskolc, *Hungary* 17 D11 48 7N 20 50 E
Misoke, *Dem. Rep. of the Congo* 54 C2 0 42S 28 2 E
Misool, *Indonesia* 37 E8 1 52S 130 10 E
Misrātah, *Libya* 51 B9 32 24N 15 3 E
Missanabie, *Canada* 70 C3 48 20N 84 6W
Missinaibi →, *Canada* 70 B3 50 43N 81 29W
Missinaibi L., *Canada* 70 C3 48 23N 83 40W
Mission, *Canada* 72 D4 49 10N 122 15W
Mission, *S. Dak., U.S.A.* 80 D4 43 18N 100 39W
Mission, *Tex., U.S.A.* 81 M5 26 13N 98 20W
Mission Beach, *Australia* 62 B4 17 53S 146 6 E
Mission Viejo, *U.S.A.* 85 M9 33 36N 117 40W
Missisa L., *Canada* 70 B2 52 20N 85 7W
Missisicabi →, *Canada* 70 B4 51 14N 79 31W
Mississagi →, *Canada* 70 C3 46 15N 83 9W
Mississauga, *Canada* 78 C5 43 32N 79 35W
**Mississippi** □, *U.S.A.* 81 J10 33 0N 90 0W
**Mississippi** →, *U.S.A.* 81 L10 29 9N 89 15W
Mississippi L., *Canada* 79 A8 45 5N 76 10W
Mississippi River Delta, *U.S.A.* 81 L9 29 10N 89 15W
Mississippi Sd., *U.S.A.* 81 K10 30 20N 89 0W
Missoula, *U.S.A.* 82 C7 46 52N 114 1W
**Missouri** □, *U.S.A.* 80 F8 38 25N 92 30W
**Missouri** →, *U.S.A.* 80 F9 38 49N 90 7W
Missouri City, *U.S.A.* 81 L7 29 37N 95 32W
Missouri Valley, *U.S.A.* 80 E7 41 34N 95 53W
Mist, *U.S.A.* 84 E3 45 59N 123 15W
Mistassibi →, *Canada* 71 B5 48 53N 72 13W
Mistassini, *Canada* 71 C5 48 53N 72 12W
Mistassini →, *Canada* 71 C5 48 42N 72 20W
Mistassini, L., *Canada* 70 B5 51 0N 73 30W
Mistastin L., *Canada* 71 A7 55 57N 63 20W
Mistinibi, L., *Canada* 71 A7 55 56N 64 17W
Misty L., *Canada* 73 B8 58 53N 101 40W
Misurata = Misrātah, *Libya* 51 B9 32 24N 15 3 E
Mitchell, *Australia* 63 D4 26 29S 147 58 E
Mitchell, *Canada* 78 C3 43 28N 81 12W
Mitchell, *Nebr., U.S.A.* 80 E3 41 57N 103 49W
Mitchell, *Oreg., U.S.A.* 82 D3 44 34N 120 9W
Mitchell, *S. Dak., U.S.A.* 80 D6 43 43N 98 2W
Mitchell →, *Australia* 62 B3 15 12S 141 35 E
Mitchell, Mt., *U.S.A.* 77 H4 35 46N 82 16W
Mitchell Ranges, *Australia* 62 A2 12 49S 135 36 E
Mitchelstown, *Ireland* 13 D3 52 15N 8 16W
Mitha Tiwana, *Pakistan* 42 C5 32 13N 72 6 E
Mithi, *Pakistan* 42 G3 24 44N 69 48 E
Mithrao, *Pakistan* 42 F3 27 28N 69 40 E
Mitilíni, *Greece* 21 E12 39 6N 26 35 E
Mito, *Japan* 31 F10 36 20N 140 30 E
Mitrovica = Kosovska Mitrovica, *Serbia, Yug.* 21 C9 42 54N 20 52 E
Mitsinjo, *Madag.* 57 B8 16 1S 45 52 E
Mitsiwa, *Eritrea* 46 D2 15 35N 39 25 E
Mitsukaidō, *Japan* 31 F9 36 1N 139 59 E
Mittagong, *Australia* 63 E5 34 28S 150 29 E
Mitú, *Colombia* 92 C4 1 15N 70 13W
Mitumba, *Tanzania* 54 D3 7 8S 31 2 E
Mitumba, Mts., *Dem. Rep. of the Congo* 54 D2 7 0S 27 30 E
Mitwaba, *Dem. Rep. of the Congo* 55 D2 8 2S 27 17 E
Mityana, *Uganda* 54 B3 0 23N 32 2 E
Mixteco →, *Mexico* 87 D5 18 11N 98 30W
Miyagi □, *Japan* 30 E10 38 15N 140 45 E
Miyah, W. el →, *Syria* 44 C3 34 44N 39 57 E
Miyake-Jima, *Japan* 31 G9 34 5N 139 30 E
Miyako, *Japan* 30 E10 39 40N 141 59 E
Miyako-Jima, *Japan* 31 M2 24 45N 125 20 E
Miyako-Rettō, *Japan* 31 M2 24 24N 125 0 E
Miyakonojō, *Japan* 31 J5 31 40N 131 5 E
Miyani, *India* 42 J3 21 50N 69 26 E
Miyanoura-Dake, *Japan* 31 J5 30 20N 130 31 E
Miyazaki, *Japan* 31 J5 31 56N 131 30 E
Miyazaki □, *Japan* 31 H5 32 30N 131 30 E
Miyazu, *Japan* 31 G7 35 35N 135 10 E
Miyet, Bahr el = Dead Sea, *Asia* 47 D4 31 30N 35 30 E
Miyoshi, *Japan* 31 G6 34 48N 132 51 E
Miyun, *China* 34 D9 40 28N 116 50 E
Miyun Shuiku, *China* 35 D9 40 30N 117 0 E
Mizdah, *Libya* 51 B8 31 30N 13 0 E
Mizen Hd., *Cork, Ireland* 13 E2 51 27N 9 50W
Mizen Hd., *Wick., Ireland* 13 D5 52 51N 6 4W
Mizhi, *China* 34 F6 37 47N 110 12 E
Mizoram □, *India* 41 H18 23 30N 92 40 E
Mizpe Ramon, *Israel* 47 E3 30 34N 34 49 E
Mizusawa, *Japan* 30 E10 39 8N 141 8 E
Mjölby, *Sweden* 9 G16 58 20N 15 10 E
Mjøsa, *Norway* 9 F14 60 40N 11 0 E
Mkata, *Tanzania* 54 D4 5 45S 38 20 E
Mkokotoni, *Tanzania* 54 D4 5 55S 39 15 E
Mkomazi, *Tanzania* 54 C4 4 40S 38 7 E
Mkomazi →, *S. Africa* 57 E5 30 12S 30 50 E
Mkulwe, *Tanzania* 55 D3 8 37S 32 20 E
Mkumbi, Ras, *Tanzania* 54 D4 7 38S 39 55 E
Mkushi, *Zambia* 55 E2 14 25S 29 15 E
Mkushi River, *Zambia* 55 E2 13 32S 29 45 E
Mkuze, *S. Africa* 57 D5 27 10S 32 0 E
Mladá Boleslav, *Czech Rep.* 16 C8 50 27N 14 53 E
Mlala Hills, *Tanzania* 54 D3 6 50S 31 40 E
Mlange = Mulanje, *Malawi* 55 F4 16 2S 35 33 E
Mlanje, Pic, *Malawi* 53 H7 15 57S 35 38 E
Mława, *Poland* 17 B11 53 9N 20 25 E
Mljet, *Croatia* 20 C7 42 43N 17 30 E
Mmabatho, *S. Africa* 56 D4 25 49S 25 30 E
Mo i Rana, *Norway* 8 C16 66 20N 14 7 E
Moa, *Cuba* 89 B4 20 40N 74 56W
Moa, *Indonesia* 37 F7 8 0S 128 0 E
Moab, *U.S.A.* 83 G9 38 35N 109 33W
Moala, *Fiji* 59 D8 18 36S 179 53 E
Moama, *Australia* 63 F3 36 7S 144 46 E
Moapa, *U.S.A.* 85 J12 36 40N 114 37W
Moate, *Ireland* 13 C4 53 24N 7 44W
Moba, *Dem. Rep. of the Congo* 54 D2 7 0S 29 48 E
Mobārakābād, *Iran* 45 D7 28 24N 53 20 E
Mobaye, *C.A.R.* 52 D4 4 25N 21 5 E
Mobayi, *Dem. Rep. of the Congo* 52 D4 4 15N 21 8 E
Moberley Lake, *Canada* 72 B4 55 50N 121 44W
Moberly, *U.S.A.* 80 F8 39 25N 92 26W
**Mobile**, *U.S.A.* 77 K1 30 41N 88 3W
Mobile B., *U.S.A.* 77 K2 30 30N 88 0W
Mobridge, *U.S.A.* 80 C4 45 32N 100 26W
Mobutu Sese Seko, L. = Albert L., *Africa* 54 B3 1 30N 31 0 E
Moc Chau, *Vietnam* 38 B5 20 50N 104 38 E
Moc Hoa, *Vietnam* 39 G5 10 46N 105 56 E
Mocabe Kasari, *Dem. Rep. of the Congo* 55 D2 9 58S 26 12 E
Moçambique, *Mozam.* 55 F5 15 3S 40 42 E
Moçâmedes = Namibe, *Angola* 53 H2 15 7S 12 11 E
Mocanaqua, *U.S.A.* 79 E8 41 9N 76 8W
Mochudi, *Botswana* 56 C4 24 27S 26 7 E
Mocimboa da Praia, *Mozam.* 55 E5 11 25S 40 20 E
Moclips, *U.S.A.* 84 C2 47 14N 124 13W
Mocoa, *Colombia* 92 C3 1 7N 76 35W
Mococa, *Brazil* 95 A6 21 28S 47 0W
Mocorito, *Mexico* 86 B3 25 30N 107 53W
Moctezuma, *Mexico* 86 B3 29 50N 109 0W
Moctezuma →, *Mexico* 87 C5 21 59N 98 34W
Mocuba, *Mozam.* 55 F4 16 54S 36 57 E
Mocúzari, Presa, *Mexico* 86 B3 27 10N 109 10W
Modane, *France* 18 D7 45 12N 6 40 E
Modasa, *India* 42 H5 23 30N 73 21 E
Modder →, *S. Africa* 56 D3 29 2S 24 37 E
Modderrivier, *S. Africa* 56 D3 29 2S 24 38 E
Módena, *Italy* 20 B4 44 40N 10 55 E
Modena, *U.S.A.* 83 H7 37 48N 113 56W
Modesto, *U.S.A.* 84 H6 37 39N 121 0W
Módica, *Italy* 20 F6 36 52N 14 46 E
Moe, *Australia* 63 F4 38 12S 146 19 E
Moebase, *Mozam.* 55 F4 17 3S 38 41 E
Moengo, *Surinam* 93 B8 5 45N 54 20W
Moffat, *U.K.* 12 F5 55 21N 3 27W
Moga, *India* 42 D6 30 48N 75 8 E
**Mogadishu** = Muqdisho, *Somali Rep.* 46 G4 2 2N 45 25 E
Mogador = Essaouira, *Morocco* 50 B4 31 32N 9 42W
Mogalakwena →, *S. Africa* 57 C4 22 38S 28 40 E
Mogami-Gawa →, *Japan* 30 E10 38 45N 140 0 E
Mogán, *Canary Is.* 22 G4 27 53N 15 43W
Mogaung, *Burma* 41 G20 25 20N 97 0 E
Mogi das Cruzes, *Brazil* 95 A6 23 31S 46 11W
Mogi-Guaçu →, *Brazil* 95 A6 20 53S 48 10W
Mogi-Mirim, *Brazil* 95 A6 22 29S 47 0W
Mogilev = Mahilyow, *Belarus* 17 B16 53 55N 30 18 E
Mogilev-Podolskiy = Mohyliv-Podilskyy, *Ukraine* 17 D14 48 26N 27 48 E
Mogincual, *Mozam.* 55 F5 15 35S 40 25 E
Mogocha, *Russia* 27 D12 53 40N 119 50 E
Mogok, *Burma* 41 H20 23 0N 96 40 E
Mogollon Rim, *U.S.A.* 83 J8 34 10N 110 50W
Mogumber, *Australia* 61 F2 31 2S 116 3 E
Mohács, *Hungary* 17 F10 45 58N 18 41 E
Mohales Hoek, *Lesotho* 56 E4 30 7S 27 26 E
Mohall, *U.S.A.* 80 A4 48 46N 101 31W
Moḩammadābād, *Iran* 45 B8 37 52N 59 5 E
Mohammedia, *Morocco* 50 B4 33 44N 7 21W
Mohana →, *India* 43 G11 24 43N 85 0 E
Mohanlalganj, *India* 43 F9 26 41N 80 58 E
Mohave, L., *U.S.A.* 85 K12 35 12N 114 34W
Mohawk →, *U.S.A.* 79 D11 42 47N 73 41W
Mohenjodaro, *Pakistan* 42 F3 27 19N 68 7 E
Mohicanville Reservoir, *U.S.A.* 78 F3 40 45N 82 0W
Mohoro, *Tanzania* 54 D4 8 6S 39 8 E
Mohyliv-Podilskyy, *Ukraine* 17 D14 48 26N 27 48 E
Moidart, L., *U.K.* 12 E3 56 47N 5 52W
Moira →, *Canada* 78 B7 44 21N 77 24W
Moires, *Greece* 23 D6 35 4N 24 56 E
Moisaküla, *Estonia* 9 G21 58 3N 25 12 E
Moisie, *Canada* 71 B6 50 12N 66 1W
Moisie →, *Canada* 71 B6 50 14N 66 5W
Mojave, *U.S.A.* 85 K8 35 3N 118 10W
**Mojave Desert**, *U.S.A.* 85 L10 35 0N 116 30W
Mojo, *Bolivia* 94 A2 21 48S 65 33W
Mojokerto, *Indonesia* 37 G15 7 28S 112 26 E
Mokai, *N.Z.* 59 H5 38 32S 175 56 E
Mokambo, *Dem. Rep. of the Congo* 55 E2 12 25S 28 20 E
Mokameh, *India* 43 G11 25 24N 85 55 E
Mokelumne →, *U.S.A.* 84 G5 38 13N 121 28W
Mokelumne Hill, *U.S.A.* 84 G6 38 18N 120 43W
Mokhós, *Greece* 23 D7 35 16N 25 27 E
Mokhotlong, *Lesotho* 57 D4 29 22S 29 2 E
Mokokchung, *India* 41 F19 26 15N 94 30 E
Mokp'o, *S. Korea* 35 G14 34 50N 126 25 E
Mokra Gora, *Serbia, Yug.* 21 C9 42 50N 20 30 E
Mol, *Belgium* 15 C5 51 11N 5 5 E
Molchanovo, *Russia* 26 D9 57 40N 83 50 E
Mold, *U.K.* 10 D4 53 9N 3 8W
**Moldavia** = Moldova ■, *Europe* 17 E15 47 0N 28 0 E
Molde, *Norway* 8 E12 62 45N 7 9 E
Moldova ■, *Europe* 17 E15 47 0N 28 0 E
Moldoveana, Vf., *Romania* 17 F13 45 36N 24 45 E
Mole →, *U.K.* 11 F7 51 24N 0 21W
Mole Creek, *Australia* 62 G4 41 34S 146 24 E
Molepolole, *Botswana* 56 C4 24 28S 25 28 E
Molfetta, *Italy* 20 D7 41 12N 16 36 E
Moline, *U.S.A.* 80 E9 41 30N 90 31W
Molinos, *Argentina* 94 B2 25 28S 66 15W
Moliro, *Dem. Rep. of the Congo* 54 D3 8 12S 30 30 E
Mollendo, *Peru* 92 G4 17 0S 72 0W
Mollerin, L., *Australia* 61 F2 30 30S 117 35 E
Molodechno = Maladzyechna, *Belarus* 17 A14 54 20N 26 50 E
Molokai, *U.S.A.* 74 H16 21 8N 157 0W
Molong, *Australia* 63 E4 33 5S 148 54 E
Molopo →, *Africa* 56 D3 27 30S 20 13 E
Molotov = Perm, *Russia* 24 C10 58 0N 56 10 E
Molson L., *Canada* 73 C9 54 22N 96 40W
Molteno, *S. Africa* 56 E4 31 22S 26 22 E
Molu, *Indonesia* 37 F8 6 45S 131 40 E
Molucca Sea, *Indonesia* 37 E6 2 0S 124 0 E
**Moluccas** = Maluku, *Indonesia* 37 E7 1 0S 127 0 E
Moma, *Dem. Rep. of the Congo* 54 C1 1 35S 23 52 E
Moma, *Mozam.* 55 F4 16 47S 39 4 E
**Mombasa**, *Kenya* 54 C4 4 2S 39 43 E
Mombetsu, *Japan* 30 B11 44 21N 143 22 E
Momchilgrad, *Bulgaria* 21 D11 41 33N 25 23 E
Momi, *Dem. Rep. of the Congo* 54 C2 1 42S 27 0 E
Mompós, *Colombia* 92 B4 9 14N 74 26W
Møn, *Denmark* 9 J15 54 57N 12 20 E
Mon →, *Burma* 41 J19 20 25N 94 30 E
Mona, Canal de la, *W. Indies* 89 C6 18 30N 67 45W
Mona, Isla, *Puerto Rico* 89 C6 18 5N 67 54W
Mona, Pta., *Costa Rica* 88 E3 9 37N 82 36W
Monaca, *U.S.A.* 78 F4 40 41N 80 17W
**Monaco** ■, *Europe* 18 E7 43 46N 7 23 E
Monadhliath Mts., *U.K.* 12 D4 57 10N 4 4W
Monadnock, Mt., *U.S.A.* 79 D12 42 52N 72 7W
Monaghan, *Ireland* 13 B5 54 15N 6 57W
**Monaghan** □, *Ireland* 13 B5 54 11N 6 56W
Monahans, *U.S.A.* 81 K3 31 36N 102 54W
Monapo, *Mozam.* 55 E5 14 56S 40 19 E
Monar, L., *U.K.* 12 D3 57 26N 5 8W
Monarch Mt., *Canada* 72 C3 51 55N 125 57W
Monashee Mts., *Canada* 72 C5 51 0N 118 43W
Monasterevin, *Ireland* 13 C4 53 8N 7 4W
Monastir = Bitola, *Macedonia* 21 D9 41 1N 21 20 E
Moncayo, Sierra del, *Spain* 19 B5 41 48N 1 50W
Monchegorsk, *Russia* 24 A5 67 54N 32 58 E
Mönchengladbach, *Germany* 16 C4 51 11N 6 27 E
Monchique, *Portugal* 19 D1 37 19N 8 38W
Moncks Corner, *U.S.A.* 77 J5 33 12N 80 1W
Monclova, *Mexico* 86 B4 26 50N 101 30W
Moncton, *Canada* 71 C7 46 7N 64 51W
Mondego →, *Portugal* 19 B1 40 9N 8 52W
Mondeodo, *Indonesia* 37 E6 3 34S 122 9 E
Mondovì, *Italy* 18 D7 44 23N 7 49 E
Mondrain I., *Australia* 61 F3 34 9S 122 14 E
Monessen, *U.S.A.* 78 F5 40 9N 79 54W
Monett, *U.S.A.* 81 G8 36 55N 93 55W
Moneymore, *U.K.* 13 B5 54 41N 6 40W
Monforte de Lemos, *Spain* 19 A2 42 31N 7 33W
Mong Hsu, *Burma* 41 J21 21 54N 98 30 E
Mong Kung, *Burma* 41 J20 21 35N 97 35 E
Mong Nai, *Burma* 41 J20 20 32N 97 46 E
Mong Pawk, *Burma* 41 H21 22 4N 99 16 E
Mong Ton, *Burma* 41 J21 20 17N 98 45 E
Mong Wa, *Burma* 41 J22 21 26N 100 27 E
Mong Yai, *Burma* 41 H21 22 21N 98 3 E
Mongalla, *Sudan* 51 G12 5 8N 31 42 E
Mongers, L., *Australia* 61 E2 29 25S 117 5 E
Monghyr = Munger, *India* 43 G12 25 23N 86 30 E
Mongibello = Etna, *Italy* 20 F6 37 50N 14 55 E
Mongo, *Chad* 51 F9 12 14N 18 43 E
**Mongolia** ■, *Asia* 27 E10 47 0N 103 0 E
Mongu, *Zambia* 53 H4 15 16S 23 12 E
Mônguа, *Angola* 56 B2 16 43S 15 20 E
Monifieth, *U.K.* 12 E6 56 30N 2 48W
Monkey Bay, *Malawi* 55 E4 14 7S 35 1 E
Monkey Mia, *Australia* 61 E1 25 48S 113 43 E
Monkey River, *Belize* 87 D7 16 22N 88 29W
Monkoto, *Dem. Rep. of the Congo* 52 E4 1 38S 20 35 E
Monkton, *Canada* 78 C3 43 35N 81 5W
Monmouth, *U.K.* 11 F5 51 48N 2 42W
Monmouth, *Ill., U.S.A.* 80 E9 40 55N 90 39W
Monmouth, *Oreg., U.S.A.* 82 D2 44 51N 123 14W
Monmouthshire □, *U.K.* 11 F5 51 48N 2 54W
Mono L., *U.S.A.* 84 H7 38 1N 119 1W
Monolith, *U.S.A.* 85 K8 35 7N 118 22W
Monólithos, *Greece* 23 C9 36 7N 27 45 E
Monongahela, *U.S.A.* 78 F5 40 12N 79 56W
Monópoli, *Italy* 20 D7 40 57N 17 18 E
Monroe, *Ga., U.S.A.* 77 J4 33 47N 83 43W
Monroe, *La., U.S.A.* 81 J8 32 30N 92 7W
Monroe, *Mich., U.S.A.* 76 E4 41 55N 83 24W
Monroe, *N.C., U.S.A.* 77 H5 34 59N 80 33W
Monroe, *N.Y., U.S.A.* 79 E10 41 20N 74 11W
Monroe, *Utah, U.S.A.* 83 G7 38 38N 112 7W
Monroe, *Wash., U.S.A.* 84 C5 47 51N 121 58W
Monroe, *Wis., U.S.A.* 80 D10 42 36N 89 38W
Monroe City, *U.S.A.* 80 F9 39 39N 91 44W
Monroeton, *U.S.A.* 79 E8 41 43N 76 29W
Monroeville, *Ala., U.S.A.* 77 K2 31 31N 87 20W
Monroeville, *Pa., U.S.A.* 78 F5 40 26N 79 45W
**Monrovia**, *Liberia* 50 G3 6 18N 10 47W
Mons, *Belgium* 15 D3 50 27N 3 58 E
Monse, *Indonesia* 37 E6 4 0S 123 10 E
Mont-de-Marsan, *France* 18 E3 43 54N 0 31W
Mont-Joli, *Canada* 71 C6 48 37N 68 10W
Mont-Laurier, *Canada* 70 C4 46 35N 75 30W
Mont-Louis, *Canada* 71 C6 49 15N 65 44W
Mont-St-Michel, Le = Le Mont-St-Michel, *France* 18 B3 48 40N 1 30W
Mont Tremblant, Parc Recr. du, *Canada* 70 C5 46 30N 74 30W
Montagu, *S. Africa* 56 E3 33 45S 20 8 E
Montagu I., *Antarctica* 5 B1 58 25S 26 20W
Montague, *Canada* 71 C7 46 10N 62 39W
Montague, I., *Mexico* 86 A2 31 40N 114 56W
Montague Ra., *Australia* 61 E2 27 15S 119 30 E
Montague Sd., *Australia* 60 B4 14 28S 125 20 E
Montalbán, *Spain* 19 B5 40 50N 0 45W
Montalvo, *U.S.A.* 85 L7 34 15N 119 12W
Montana, *Bulgaria* 21 C10 43 27N 23 16 E
Montaña, *Peru* 92 E4 6 0S 73 0W
**Montana** □, *U.S.A.* 82 C9 47 0N 110 0W
Montaña Clara, I., *Canary Is.* 22 E6 29 17N 13 33W
Montargis, *France* 18 C5 47 59N 2 43 E
Montauban, *France* 18 D4 44 2N 1 21 E
Montauk, *U.S.A.* 79 E13 41 3N 71 57W
Montauk Pt., *U.S.A.* 79 E13 41 4N 71 52W
Montbéliard, *France* 18 C7 47 31N 6 48 E
Montceau-les-Mines, *France* 18 C6 46 40N 4 23 E
Montclair, *U.S.A.* 79 F10 40 49N 74 13W
Monte Albán, *Mexico* 87 D5 17 2N 96 45W
Monte Alegre, *Brazil* 93 D8 2 0S 54 0W
Monte Azul, *Brazil* 93 G10 15 9S 42 53W
Monte Bello Is., *Australia* 60 D2 20 30S 115 45 E
**Monte-Carlo**, *Monaco* 18 E7 43 46N 7 23 E
Monte Caseros, *Argentina* 94 C4 30 10S 57 50W
Monte Comán, *Argentina* 94 C2 34 40S 67 53W
Monte Cristi, *Dom. Rep.* 89 C5 19 52N 71 39W
Monte Lindo →, *Paraguay* 94 A4 23 56S 57 12W
Monte Patria, *Chile* 94 C1 30 42S 70 58W
Monte Quemado, *Argentina* 94 B3 25 53S 62 41W
Monte Rio, *U.S.A.* 84 G4 38 28N 123 0W
Monte Santu, C. di, *Italy* 20 D3 40 5N 9 44 E
Monte Vista, *U.S.A.* 83 H10 37 35N 106 9W
Monteagudo, *Argentina* 95 B5 27 14S 54 8W
Montebello, *Canada* 70 C5 45 40N 74 55W
Montecito, *U.S.A.* 85 L7 34 26N 119 40W
Montecristo, *Italy* 20 C4 42 20N 10 19 E
Montego Bay, *Jamaica* 88 C4 18 30N 78 0W
Montélimar, *France* 18 D6 44 33N 4 45 E
Montello, *U.S.A.* 80 D10 43 48N 89 20W
Montemorelos, *Mexico* 87 B5 25 11N 99 42W
Montenegro, *Brazil* 95 B5 29 39S 51 29W
**Montenegro** □, *Yugoslavia* 21 C8 42 40N 19 20 E
Montepuez, *Mozam.* 55 E4 13 8S 38 59 E
Montepuez →, *Mozam.* 55 E5 12 32S 40 27 E
Monterey, *U.S.A.* 84 J5 36 37N 121 55W
Monterey B., *U.S.A.* 84 J5 36 45N 122 0W
Montería, *Colombia* 92 B3 8 46N 75 53W
Monteros, *Argentina* 94 B2 27 11S 65 30W
Monterrey, *Mexico* 86 B4 25 40N 100 30W
Montes Claros, *Brazil* 93 G10 16 30S 43 50W
Montesano, *U.S.A.* 84 D3 46 59N 123 36W
Montesilvano, *Italy* 20 C6 42 29N 14 8 E
**Montevideo**, *Uruguay* 95 C4 34 50S 56 11W
Montevideo, *U.S.A.* 80 C7 44 57N 95 43W
Montezuma, *U.S.A.* 80 E8 41 35N 92 32W
Montgomery = Sahiwal, *Pakistan* 42 D5 30 45N 73 8 E
Montgomery, *U.K.* 11 E4 52 34N 3 8W
**Montgomery**, *Ala., U.S.A.* 77 J2 32 23N 86 19W
Montgomery, *Pa., U.S.A.* 78 E8 41 10N 76 53W
Montgomery, *W. Va., U.S.A.* 76 F5 38 11N 81 19W
Montgomery City, *U.S.A.* 80 F9 38 59N 91 30W
Monticello, *Ark., U.S.A.* 81 J9 33 38N 91 47W
Monticello, *Fla., U.S.A.* 77 K4 30 33N 83 52W
Monticello, *Ind., U.S.A.* 76 E2 40 45N 86 46W
Monticello, *Iowa, U.S.A.* 80 D9 42 15N 91 12W
Monticello, *Ky., U.S.A.* 77 G3 36 50N 84 51W
Monticello, *Minn., U.S.A.* 80 C8 45 18N 93 48W
Monticello, *Miss., U.S.A.* 81 K9 31 33N 90 7W
Monticello, *N.Y., U.S.A.* 79 E10 41 39N 74 42W
Monticello, *Utah, U.S.A.* 83 H9 37 52N 109 21W
Montijo, *Portugal* 19 C1 38 41N 8 54W
Montilla, *Spain* 19 D3 37 36N 4 40W
Montluçon, *France* 18 C5 46 22N 2 36 E
Montmagny, *Canada* 71 C5 46 58N 70 34W
Montmartre, *Canada* 73 C8 50 14N 103 27W
Montmorillon, *France* 18 C4 46 26N 0 50 E
Monto, *Australia* 62 C5 24 52S 151 6 E
Montoro, *Spain* 19 C3 38 1N 4 27W
Montour Falls, *U.S.A.* 78 D8 42 21N 76 51W
Montoursville, *U.S.A.* 78 E8 41 15N 76 55W
Montpelier, *Idaho, U.S.A.* 82 E8 42 19N 111 18W

**Montpelier**, Vt., U.S.A. 79 B12 44 16N 72 35W
**Montpellier**, France 18 E5 43 37N 3 52 E
**Montréal**, Canada 79 A11 45 31N 73 34W
Montreal →, Canada 70 C3 47 14N 84 39W
Montreal L., Canada 73 C7 54 20N 105 45W
Montreal Lake, Canada 73 C7 54 3N 105 46W
Montreux, Switz. 18 C7 46 26N 6 55 E
Montrose, U.K. 12 E6 56 44N 2 27W
Montrose, Colo., U.S.A. 83 G10 38 29N 107 53W
Montrose, Pa., U.S.A. 79 E9 41 50N 75 53W
Monts, Pte. des, Canada 71 C6 49 20N 67 12W
**Montserrat** ■, W. Indies 89 C7 16 40N 62 10W
Montuiri, Spain 22 B9 39 34N 2 59 E
Monywa, Burma 41 H19 22 7N 95 11 E
Monza, Italy 18 D8 45 35N 9 16 E
Monze, Zambia 55 F2 16 17S 27 29 E
Monze, C., Pakistan 42 G2 24 47N 66 37 E
Monzón, Spain 19 B6 41 52N 0 10 E
Mooers, U.S.A. 79 B11 44 58N 73 35W
Mooi River, S. Africa 57 D4 29 13S 29 50 E
Moonah →, Australia 62 C2 22 3S 138 33 E
Moonda, L., Australia 62 D3 25 52S 140 25 E
Moonie, Australia 63 D5 27 46S 150 20 E
Moonie →, Australia 63 D4 29 19S 148 43 E
Moonta, Australia 63 E2 34 6S 137 32 E
Moora, Australia 61 F2 30 37S 115 58 E
Moorcroft, U.S.A. 80 C2 44 16N 104 57W
Moore →, Australia 61 F2 31 22S 115 30 E
Moore, L., Australia 61 E2 29 50S 117 35 E
Moore Park, Australia 62 C5 24 43S 152 17 E
Moore Reefs, Australia 62 B4 16 0S 149 5 E
Moorefield, U.S.A. 76 F6 39 5N 78 59W
Moores Res., U.S.A. 79 B13 44 45N 71 50W
Moorfoot Hills, U.K. 12 F5 55 44N 3 8W
Moorhead, U.S.A. 80 B6 46 53N 96 45W
Moorpark, U.S.A. 85 L8 34 17N 118 53W
Moorreesburg, S. Africa 56 E2 33 6S 18 38 E
Moose →, Canada 70 B3 51 20N 80 25W
Moose →, U.S.A. 79 C9 43 38N 75 24W
Moose Creek, Canada 79 A10 45 15N 74 58W
Moose Factory, Canada 70 B3 51 16N 80 32W
Moose Jaw, Canada 73 C7 50 24N 105 30W
Moose Jaw →, Canada 73 C7 50 34N 105 18W
Moose Lake, Canada 73 C8 53 43N 100 20W
Moose Lake, U.S.A. 80 B8 46 27N 92 46W
Moose Mountain Prov. Park, Canada 73 D8 49 48N 102 25W
Moosehead L., U.S.A. 77 C11 45 38N 69 40W
Mooselookmeguntic L., U.S.A. 77 C10 44 55N 70 49W
Moosilauke, Mt., U.S.A. 79 B13 44 3N 71 40W
Moosomin, Canada 73 C8 50 9N 101 40W
Moosonee, Canada 70 B3 51 17N 80 39W
Moosup, U.S.A. 79 E13 41 43N 71 53W
Mopeia Velha, Mozam. 55 F4 17 30S 35 40 E
Mopipi, Botswana 56 C3 21 6S 24 55 E
Mopoi, C.A.R. 54 A2 5 6N 26 54 E
Mopti, Mali 50 F5 14 30N 4 0W
Moqor, Afghan. 42 C2 32 50N 67 42 E
Moquegua, Peru 92 G4 17 15S 70 46W
Mora, Sweden 9 F16 61 2N 14 38 E
Mora, Minn., U.S.A. 80 C8 45 53N 93 18W
Mora, N. Mex., U.S.A. 83 J11 35 58N 105 20W
Mora →, U.S.A. 81 H2 35 35N 104 25W
Moradabad, India 43 E8 28 50N 78 50 E
Morafenobe, Madag. 57 B7 17 50S 44 53 E
Moramanga, Madag. 57 B8 18 56S 48 12 E
Moran, Kans., U.S.A. 81 G7 37 55N 95 10W
Moran, Wyo., U.S.A. 82 E8 43 53N 110 37W
Moranbah, Australia 62 C4 22 1S 148 6 E
Morant Cays, Jamaica 88 C4 17 22N 76 0W
Morant Pt., Jamaica 88 C4 17 55N 76 12W
Morar, India 42 F8 26 14N 78 14 E
Morar, L., U.K. 12 E3 56 57N 5 40W
Moratuwa, Sri Lanka 40 R11 6 45N 79 55 E
Morava →, Serbia, Yug. 21 B9 44 36N 21 4 E
Morava →, Slovak Rep. 17 D9 48 10N 16 59 E
Moravia, U.S.A. 79 D8 42 43N 76 25W
Moravian Hts. = Českomoravská Vrchovina, Czech Rep. 16 D8 49 30N 15 40 E
Morawa, Australia 61 E2 29 13S 116 0 E
Morawhanna, Guyana 92 B7 8 30N 59 40W
Moray □, U.K. 12 D5 57 31N 3 18W
Moray Firth, U.K. 12 D5 57 40N 3 52W
Morbi, India 42 H4 22 50N 70 42 E
Morden, Canada 73 D9 49 15N 98 10W
Mordovian Republic = Mordvinia □, Russia 24 D7 54 20N 44 30 E
Mordvinia □, Russia 24 D7 54 20N 44 30 E
Morea, Greece 6 H10 37 45N 22 10 E
Moreau →, U.S.A. 80 C4 45 18N 100 43W
Morecambe, U.K. 10 C5 54 5N 2 52W
Morecambe B., U.K. 10 C5 54 7N 3 0W
Moree, Australia 63 D4 29 28S 149 54 E
Morehead, U.S.A. 76 F4 38 11N 83 26W
Morehead City, U.S.A. 77 H7 34 43N 76 43W
Morel →, India 42 F7 26 13N 76 36 E
Morelia, Mexico 86 D4 19 42N 101 7W
Morella, Australia 62 C3 23 0S 143 52 E
Morella, Spain 19 B5 40 35N 0 5W
Morelos, Mexico 86 B3 26 42N 107 40W
Morelos □, Mexico 87 D5 18 40N 99 10W
Morena, India 42 F8 26 30N 78 4 E
Morena, Sierra, Spain 19 C3 38 20N 4 0W
Moreno Valley, U.S.A. 85 M10 33 56N 117 15W
Moresby I., Canada 72 C2 52 30N 131 40W
Moreton I., Australia 63 D5 27 10S 153 25 E
Morey, Spain 22 B10 39 44N 3 20 E
Morgan, U.S.A. 82 F8 41 2N 111 41W
Morgan City, U.S.A. 81 L9 29 42N 91 12W
Morgan Hill, U.S.A. 84 H5 37 8N 121 39W
Morganfield, U.S.A. 76 G2 37 41N 87 55W
Morganton, U.S.A. 77 H5 35 45N 81 41W
Morgantown, U.S.A. 76 F6 39 38N 79 57W
Morgenzon, S. Africa 57 D4 26 45S 29 36 E
Morghak, Iran 45 D8 29 7N 57 54 E
Morhar →, India 43 G11 25 29N 85 11 E
Moriarty, U.S.A. 83 J10 34 59N 106 3W
Morice L., Canada 72 C3 53 50N 127 40W
Morinville, Canada 72 C6 53 49N 113 41W
Morioka, Japan 30 E10 39 45N 141 8 E
Moris, Mexico 86 B3 28 8N 108 32W
Morlaix, France 18 B2 48 36N 3 52W
Mornington, Australia 63 F4 38 15S 145 5 E
Mornington, I., Chile 96 F1 49 50S 75 30W
Mornington I., Australia 62 B2 16 30S 139 30 E
Moro, Pakistan 42 F2 26 40N 68 0 E
Moro →, Pakistan 42 E2 29 42N 67 22 E
Moro G., Phil. 37 C6 6 30N 123 0 E
**Morocco** ■, N. Afr. 50 B4 32 0N 5 50W
Morogoro, Tanzania 54 D4 6 50S 37 40 E
Morogoro □, Tanzania 54 D4 8 0S 37 0 E
Moroleón, Mexico 86 C4 20 8N 101 32W
Morombe, Madag. 57 C7 21 45S 43 22 E
Moron, Argentina 94 C4 34 39S 58 37W
Morón, Cuba 88 B4 22 8N 78 39W
Morón de la Frontera, Spain 19 D3 37 6N 5 28W
Morona →, Peru 92 D3 4 40S 77 10W
Morondava, Madag. 57 C7 20 17S 44 17 E
Morongo Valley, U.S.A. 85 L10 34 3N 116 37W
**Moroni**, Comoros Is. 49 H8 11 40S 43 16 E
Moroni, U.S.A. 82 G8 39 32N 111 35W
Morotai, Indonesia 37 D7 2 10N 128 30 E
Moroto, Uganda 54 B3 2 28N 34 42 E
Moroto Summit, Kenya 54 B3 2 30N 34 43 E
Morpeth, U.K. 10 B6 55 10N 1 41W
Morphou, Cyprus 23 D11 35 12N 32 59 E
Morphou Bay, Cyprus 23 D11 35 15N 32 50 E
Morrilton, U.S.A. 81 H8 35 9N 92 44W
Morrinhos, Brazil 93 G9 17 45S 49 10W
Morrinsville, N.Z. 59 G5 37 40S 175 32 E
Morris, Canada 73 D9 49 25N 97 22W
Morris, Minn., U.S.A. 80 C7 45 35N 95 55W
Morris, N.Y., U.S.A. 79 D9 42 33N 75 15W
Morris, Pa., U.S.A. 78 E7 41 35N 77 17W
Morris, Mt., Australia 61 E5 26 9S 131 4 E
Morrisburg, Canada 79 B9 44 55N 75 7W
Morristown, Ariz., U.S.A. 83 K7 33 51N 112 37W
Morristown, N.J., U.S.A. 79 F10 40 48N 74 29W
Morristown, N.Y., U.S.A. 79 B9 44 35N 75 39W
Morristown, Tenn., U.S.A. 77 G4 36 13N 83 18W
Morrisville, N.Y., U.S.A. 79 D9 42 53N 75 35W
Morrisville, Pa., U.S.A. 79 F10 40 13N 74 47W
Morrisville, Vt., U.S.A. 79 B12 44 34N 72 36W
Morro, Pta., Chile 94 B1 27 6S 71 0W
Morro Bay, U.S.A. 84 K6 35 22N 120 51W
Morro del Jable, Canary Is. 22 F5 28 3N 14 23W
Morro Jable, Pta. de, Canary Is. 22 F5 28 2N 14 20W
Morrosquillo, G. de, Colombia 88 E4 9 35N 75 40W
Morrumbene, Mozam. 57 C6 23 31S 35 16 E
Morshansk, Russia 24 D7 53 28N 41 50 E
Morteros, Argentina 94 C3 30 50S 62 0W
Mortlach, Canada 73 C7 50 27N 106 4W
Mortlake, Australia 63 F3 38 5S 142 50 E
Morton, Tex., U.S.A. 81 J3 33 44N 102 46W
Morton, Wash., U.S.A. 84 D4 46 34N 122 17W
Morundah, Australia 63 E4 34 57S 146 19 E
Moruya, Australia 63 F5 35 58S 150 3 E
Morvan, France 18 C6 47 5N 4 3 E
Morven, Australia 63 D4 26 22S 147 5 E
Morvern, U.K. 12 E3 56 38N 5 44W
Morwell, Australia 63 F4 38 10S 146 22 E
Morzhovets, Ostrov, Russia 24 A7 66 44N 42 35 E
Moscos Is. = Maungmagan Is., Burma 38 F1 14 0N 97 30 E
**Moscow** = Moskva, Russia 24 C6 55 45N 37 35 E
Moscow, Idaho, U.S.A. 82 C5 46 44N 117 0W
Moscow, Pa., U.S.A. 79 E9 41 20N 75 31W
Mosel →, Europe 18 A7 50 22N 7 36 E
Moselle = Mosel →, Europe 18 A7 50 22N 7 36 E
Moses Lake, U.S.A. 82 C4 47 8N 119 17W
Mosgiel, N.Z. 59 L3 45 53S 170 21 E
Moshi, Tanzania 54 C4 3 22S 37 18 E
Moshupa, Botswana 56 C4 24 46S 25 29 E
Mosjøen, Norway 8 D15 65 51N 13 12 E
Moskenesøya, Norway 8 C15 67 58N 13 0 E
Moskenstraumen, Norway 8 C15 67 47N 12 45 E
Moskva, Russia 24 C6 55 45N 37 35 E
Mosomane, Botswana 56 C4 24 2S 26 19 E
Moson-magyaróvár, Hungary 17 E9 47 52N 17 18 E
Mosquera, Colombia 92 C3 2 35N 78 24W
Mosquero, U.S.A. 81 H3 35 47N 103 58W
Mosquitia, Honduras 88 C3 15 20N 84 10W
**Mosquito Coast** = Mosquitia, Honduras 88 C3 15 20N 84 10W
Mosquito Creek L., U.S.A. 78 E4 41 18N 80 46W
Mosquito L., Canada 73 A8 62 35N 103 20W
Mosquitos, G. de los, Panama 88 E3 9 15N 81 10W
Moss, Norway 9 G14 59 27N 10 40 E
Moss Vale, Australia 63 E5 34 32S 150 25 E
Mossbank, Canada 73 D7 49 56N 105 56W
Mossburn, N.Z. 59 L2 45 41S 168 15 E
Mosselbaai, S. Africa 56 E3 34 11S 22 8 E
Mossendjo, Congo 52 E2 2 55S 12 42 E
Mossgiel, Australia 63 E3 33 15S 144 5 E
Mossman, Australia 62 B4 16 21S 145 15 E
Mossoró, Brazil 93 E11 5 10S 37 15W
Mossuril, Mozam. 55 E5 14 58S 40 42 E
Most, Czech Rep. 16 C7 50 31N 13 38 E
Mosta, Malta 23 D1 35 54N 14 24 E
Moşţafáābād, Iran 45 C7 33 39N 54 53 E
Mostaganem, Algeria 50 A6 35 54N 0 5 E
Mostar, Bos.-H. 21 C7 43 22N 17 50 E
Mostardas, Brazil 95 C5 31 2S 50 51W
Mostiska = Mostyska, Ukraine 17 D12 49 48N 23 4 E
Mosty = Masty, Belarus 17 B13 53 27N 24 38 E
Mostyska, Ukraine 17 D12 49 48N 23 4 E
Mosul = Al Mawşil, Iraq 44 B4 36 15N 43 5 E
Mosŭlpo, S. Korea 35 H14 33 20N 126 17 E
Motagua →, Guatemala 88 C2 15 44N 88 14W
Motala, Sweden 9 G16 58 32N 15 1 E
Moth, India 43 G8 25 43N 78 57 E
Motherwell, U.K. 12 F5 55 47N 3 58W
Motihari, India 43 F11 26 30N 84 55 E
Motozintla de Mendoza, Mexico 87 D6 15 21N 92 14W
Motril, Spain 19 D4 36 31N 3 37W
Mott, U.S.A. 80 B3 46 23N 102 20W
Motueka, N.Z. 59 J4 41 7S 173 1 E
Motueka →, N.Z. 59 J4 41 5S 173 1 E
Motul, Mexico 87 C7 21 0N 89 20W
Mouchalagane →, Canada 71 B6 50 56N 68 41W
Moúdhros, Greece 21 E11 39 50N 25 18 E
Mouila, Gabon 52 E2 1 50S 11 0 E
Moulamein, Australia 63 F3 35 3S 144 1 E
Moulianá, Greece 23 D7 35 10N 25 59 E
Moulins, France 18 C5 46 35N 3 19 E
Moulmein, Burma 41 L20 16 30N 97 40 E
Moulouya, O. →, Morocco 50 B5 35 5N 2 25W
Moultrie, U.S.A. 77 K4 31 11N 83 47W
Moultrie, L., U.S.A. 77 J5 33 20N 80 5W
Mound City, Mo., U.S.A. 80 E7 40 7N 95 14W
Mound City, S. Dak., U.S.A. 80 C4 45 44N 100 4W
Moundou, Chad 51 G9 8 40N 16 10 E
Moundsville, U.S.A. 78 G4 39 55N 80 44W
Moung, Cambodia 38 F4 12 46N 103 27 E
Mount Airy, U.S.A. 77 G5 36 31N 80 37W
Mount Albert, Canada 78 B5 44 8N 79 19W
Mount Barker, S. Austral., Australia 63 F2 35 5S 138 52 E
Mount Barker, W. Austral., Australia 61 F2 34 38S 117 40 E
Mount Beauty, Australia 63 F4 36 47S 147 10 E
Mount Brydges, Canada 78 D3 42 54N 81 29W
Mount Burr, Australia 63 F3 37 34S 140 26 E
Mount Carmel, Ill., U.S.A. 76 F2 38 25N 87 46W
Mount Carmel, Pa., U.S.A. 79 F8 40 47N 76 24W
Mount Charleston, U.S.A. 85 J11 36 16N 115 37W
Mount Clemens, U.S.A. 78 D2 42 35N 82 53W
Mount Coolon, Australia 62 C4 21 25S 147 25 E
Mount Darwin, Zimbabwe 55 F3 16 47S 31 38 E
Mount Desert I., U.S.A. 77 C11 44 21N 68 20W
Mount Dora, U.S.A. 77 L5 28 48N 81 38W
Mount Edziza Prov. Park, Canada 72 B2 57 30N 130 45W
Mount Fletcher, S. Africa 57 E4 30 40S 28 30 E
Mount Forest, Canada 78 C4 43 59N 80 43W
Mount Gambier, Australia 63 F3 37 50S 140 46 E
Mount Garnet, Australia 62 B4 17 37S 145 6 E
Mount Holly, U.S.A. 79 G10 39 59N 74 47W
Mount Holly Springs, U.S.A. 78 F7 40 7N 77 12W
Mount Hope, N.S.W., Australia 63 E4 32 51S 145 51 E
Mount Hope, S. Austral., Australia 63 E2 34 7S 135 23 E
Mount Isa, Australia 62 C2 20 42S 139 26 E
Mount Jewett, U.S.A. 78 E6 41 44N 78 39W
Mount Kisco, U.S.A. 79 E11 41 12N 73 44W
Mount Laguna, U.S.A. 85 N10 32 52N 116 25W
Mount Larcom, Australia 62 C5 23 48S 150 59 E
Mount Lofty Ra., Australia 63 E2 34 35S 139 5 E
Mount Magnet, Australia 61 E2 28 2S 117 47 E
Mount Maunganui, N.Z. 59 G6 37 40S 176 14 E
Mount Molloy, Australia 62 B4 16 42S 145 20 E
Mount Morgan, Australia 62 C5 23 40S 150 25 E
Mount Morris, U.S.A. 78 D7 42 44N 77 52W
Mount Pearl, Canada 71 C9 47 31N 52 47W
Mount Penn, U.S.A. 79 F9 40 20N 75 54W
Mount Perry, Australia 63 D5 25 13S 151 42 E
Mount Pleasant, Iowa, U.S.A. 80 E9 40 58N 91 33W
Mount Pleasant, Mich., U.S.A. 76 D3 43 36N 84 46W
Mount Pleasant, Pa., U.S.A. 78 F5 40 9N 79 33W
Mount Pleasant, S.C., U.S.A. 77 J6 32 47N 79 52W
Mount Pleasant, Tenn., U.S.A. 77 H2 35 32N 87 12W
Mount Pleasant, Tex., U.S.A. 81 J7 33 9N 94 58W
Mount Pleasant, Utah, U.S.A. 82 G8 39 33N 111 27W
Mount Pocono, U.S.A. 79 E9 41 7N 75 22W
Mount Rainier Nat. Park, U.S.A. 84 D5 46 55N 121 50W
Mount Revelstoke Nat. Park, Canada 72 C5 51 5N 118 30W
Mount Robson Prov. Park, Canada 72 C5 53 0N 119 0W
Mount Shasta, U.S.A. 82 F2 41 19N 122 19W
Mount Signal, U.S.A. 85 N11 32 39N 115 37W
Mount Sterling, Ill., U.S.A. 80 F9 39 59N 90 45W
Mount Sterling, Ky., U.S.A. 76 F4 38 4N 83 56W
Mount Surprise, Australia 62 B3 18 10S 144 17 E
Mount Union, U.S.A. 78 F7 40 23N 77 53W
Mount Upton, U.S.A. 79 D9 42 26N 75 23W
Mount Vernon, Ill., U.S.A. 76 F1 38 19N 88 55W
Mount Vernon, Ind., U.S.A. 80 F10 38 17N 88 57W
Mount Vernon, N.Y., U.S.A. 79 F11 40 55N 73 50W
Mount Vernon, Ohio, U.S.A. 78 F2 40 23N 82 29W
Mount Vernon, Wash., U.S.A. 84 B4 48 25N 122 20W
Mountain Ash, U.K. 11 F4 51 40N 3 23W
Mountain Center, U.S.A. 85 M10 33 42N 116 44W
Mountain City, Nev., U.S.A. 82 F6 41 50N 115 58W
Mountain City, Tenn., U.S.A. 77 G5 36 29N 81 48W
Mountain Dale, U.S.A. 79 E10 41 41N 74 32W
Mountain Grove, U.S.A. 81 G8 37 8N 92 16W
Mountain Home, Ark., U.S.A. 81 G8 36 20N 92 23W
Mountain Home, Idaho, U.S.A. 82 E6 43 8N 115 41W
Mountain Iron, U.S.A. 80 B8 47 32N 92 37W
Mountain Pass, U.S.A. 85 K11 35 29N 115 35W
Mountain View, Ark., U.S.A. 81 H8 35 52N 92 7W
Mountain View, Calif., U.S.A. 84 H4 37 23N 122 5W
Mountain View, Hawaii, U.S.A. 74 J17 19 33N 155 7W
Mountainair, U.S.A. 83 J10 34 31N 106 15W
Mountlake Terrace, U.S.A. 84 C4 47 47N 122 19W
Mountmellick, Ireland 13 C4 53 7N 7 20W
Mountrath, Ireland 13 D4 53 0N 7 28W
Moura, Australia 62 C4 24 35S 149 58 E
Moura, Brazil 92 D6 1 32S 61 38W
Moura, Portugal 19 C2 38 7N 7 30W
Mourdi, Dépression du, Chad 51 E10 18 10N 23 0 E
Mourilyan, Australia 62 B4 17 35S 146 3 E
Mourne →, U.K. 13 B4 54 52N 7 26W
Mourne Mts., U.K. 13 B5 54 10N 6 0W
Mourniaí, Greece 23 D6 35 29N 24 1 E
Mournies = Mourniaí, Greece 23 D6 35 29N 24 1 E
Mouscron, Belgium 15 D3 50 45N 3 12 E
Moussoro, Chad 51 F9 13 41N 16 35 E
Moutohara, N.Z. 59 H6 38 27S 177 32 E
Moutong, Indonesia 37 D6 0 28N 121 13 E
Movas, Mexico 86 B3 28 10N 109 25W
Moville, Ireland 13 A4 55 11N 7 3W
Mowandjum, Australia 60 C3 17 22S 123 40 E
Moy →, Ireland 13 B2 54 8N 9 8W
Moyale, Kenya 54 B4 3 30N 39 0 E
Moyen Atlas, Morocco 50 B4 33 0N 5 0W
Moyne, L. le, Canada 71 A6 56 45N 68 47W
Moyo, Indonesia 36 F5 8 10S 117 40 E
Moyobamba, Peru 92 E3 6 0S 77 0W
Moyyero →, Russia 27 C11 68 44N 103 42 E
Moyynty, Kazakstan 26 E8 47 10N 73 18 E
Mozambique = Moçambique, Mozam. 55 F5 15 3S 40 42 E
**Mozambique** ■, Africa 55 F4 19 0S 35 0 E
Mozambique Chan., Africa 57 B7 17 30S 42 30 E
Mozdok, Russia 25 F7 43 45N 44 48 E
Mozdūrān, Iran 45 B9 36 9N 60 35 E
Mozhnābād, Iran 45 C9 34 7N 60 6 E
Mozyr = Mazyr, Belarus 17 B15 51 59N 29 15 E
Mpanda, Tanzania 54 D3 6 23S 31 1 E
Mpika, Zambia 55 E3 11 51S 31 25 E
Mpulungu, Zambia 55 D3 8 51S 31 5 E
Mpumalanga, S. Africa 57 D5 29 50S 30 33 E
Mpumalanga □, S. Africa 57 B5 26 0S 30 0 E
Mpwapwa, Tanzania 54 D4 6 23S 36 30 E
Msambansovu, Zimbabwe 55 F3 15 50S 30 3 E
M'sila →, Algeria 50 A6 35 30N 4 29 E
Msoro, Zambia 55 E3 13 35S 31 50 E
Mstislavl = Mstsislaw, Belarus 17 A16 54 0N 31 50 E
Mstsislaw, Belarus 17 A16 54 0N 31 50 E
Mtama, Tanzania 55 E4 10 17S 39 21 E
Mtilikwe →, Zimbabwe 55 G3 21 9S 31 30 E
Mtubatuba, S. Africa 57 D5 28 30S 32 8 E
Mtwara-Mikindani, Tanzania 55 E5 10 20S 40 20 E
Mu Gia, Deo, Vietnam 38 D5 17 40N 105 47 E
Mu Us Shamo, China 34 E5 39 0N 109 0 E
Muang Chiang Rai = Chiang Rai, Thailand 38 C2 19 52N 99 50 E
Muang Khong, Laos 36 B3 14 5N 105 52 E
Muang Khong, Laos 38 E5 14 7N 105 51 E
Muang Lamphun, Thailand 38 C2 18 40N 99 2 E
Muar, Malaysia 39 L4 2 3N 102 34 E
Muarabungo, Indonesia 36 E2 1 28S 102 52 E
Muaraenim, Indonesia 36 E2 3 40S 103 50 E
Muarajuloi, Indonesia 36 E4 0 12S 114 3 E
Muarakaman, Indonesia 36 E5 0 2S 116 45 E
Muaratebo, Indonesia 36 E2 1 30S 102 26 E
Muaratembesi, Indonesia 36 E2 1 42S 103 8 E
Muaratewe, Indonesia 36 E4 0 58S 114 52 E
Mubarakpur, India 43 F10 26 6N 83 18 E
Mubarraz = Al Mubarraz, Si. Arabia 45 E6 25 30N 49 40 E
Mubende, Uganda 54 B3 0 33N 31 22 E
Mubi, Nigeria 51 F8 10 18N 13 16 E
Mubur, Pulau, Indonesia 39 L6 3 20N 106 12 E
Mucajaí →, Brazil 92 C6 2 25N 60 52W
Muchachos, Roque de los, Canary Is. 22 F2 28 44N 17 52W
Muchinga Mts., Zambia 55 E3 11 30S 31 30 E
Muck, U.K. 12 E2 56 50N 6 15W
Muckadilla, Australia 63 D4 26 35S 148 23 E
Mucuri, Brazil 93 G11 18 0S 39 36W
Mucusso, Angola 56 B3 18 1S 21 25 E
Muda, Canary Is. 22 F6 28 34N 13 57W
Mudanjiang, China 35 B15 44 38N 129 30 E
Mudanya, Turkey 21 D13 40 25N 28 50 E
Muddy Cr. →, U.S.A. 83 H8 38 24N 110 42W
Mudgee, Australia 63 E4 32 32S 149 31 E
Mudjatik →, Canada 73 B7 56 1N 107 36W
Muecate, Mozam. 55 E4 14 55S 39 40 E
Mueda, Mozam. 55 E4 11 36S 39 28 E
Mueller Ra., Australia 60 C4 18 18S 126 46 E
Muende, Mozam. 55 E3 14 28S 33 0 E
Muerto, Mar, Mexico 87 D6 16 10N 94 10W
Mufulira, Zambia 55 E2 12 32S 28 15 E
Mufumbiro Range, Africa 54 C2 1 25S 29 30 E
Mughal Sarai, India 43 G10 25 18N 83 7 E
Mughayrā', Si. Arabia 44 D3 29 17N 37 41 E
Mugi, Japan 31 H7 33 40N 134 25 E
Mugila, Mts., Dem. Rep. of the Congo 54 D2 7 0S 28 50 E
Muğla, Turkey 21 F13 37 15N 28 22 E
Mugu, Nepal 43 E10 29 45N 82 30 E
Muhammad, Râs, Egypt 44 E2 27 44N 34 16 E
Muhammad Qol, Sudan 51 D13 20 53N 37 9 E
Muhammadabad, India 43 F10 26 4N 83 25 E
Muhesi →, Tanzania 54 D4 7 0S 35 20 E
Mühlhausen, Germany 16 C6 51 12N 10 27 E
Mühlig Hofmann fjell, Antarctica 5 D3 72 30S 5 0 E
Muhos, Finland 8 D22 64 47N 25 59 E
Muhu, Estonia 9 G20 58 36N 23 11 E
Muhutwe, Tanzania 54 C3 1 35S 31 45 E
Muine Bheag, Ireland 13 D5 52 42N 6 58W
Muir, L., Australia 61 F2 34 30S 116 40 E
Mukacheve, Ukraine 17 D12 48 27N 22 45 E
Mukachevo = Mukacheve, Ukraine 17 D12 48 27N 22 45 E
Mukah, Malaysia 36 D4 2 55N 112 5 E
Mukandwara, India 42 G6 24 49N 75 59 E
Mukdahan, Thailand 38 D5 16 32N 104 43 E
Mukden = Shenyang, China 35 D12 41 48N 123 27 E
Mukerian, India 42 D6 31 57N 75 37 E
Mukhtuya = Lensk, Russia 27 C12 60 48N 114 55 E
Mukinbudin, Australia 61 F2 30 55S 118 5 E
Mukishi, Dem. Rep. of the Congo 55 D1 8 30S 24 44 E
Mukomuko, Indonesia 36 E2 2 30S 101 10 E
Mukomwenze, Dem. Rep. of the Congo 54 D2 6 49S 27 15 E
Muktsar, India 42 D6 30 30N 74 30 E
Mukur = Moqor, Afghan. 42 C2 32 50N 67 42 E
Mukutawa →, Canada 73 C9 53 10N 97 24W
Mukwela, Zambia 55 F2 17 0S 26 40 E
Mula, Spain 19 C5 38 3N 1 33W
Mula →, Pakistan 42 F2 27 57N 67 36 E
Mulange, Dem. Rep. of the Congo 54 C2 3 40S 27 10 E
Mulanje, Malawi 55 F4 16 2S 35 33 E
Mulchén, Chile 94 D1 37 45S 72 20W
Mulde →, Germany 16 C7 51 53N 12 15 E
Mule Creek Junction, U.S.A. 80 D2 43 19N 104 8W
Muleba, Tanzania 54 C3 1 50S 31 37 E
Mulejé, Mexico 86 B2 26 53N 112 1W
Muleshoe, U.S.A. 81 H3 34 13N 102 43W
Mulgrave, Canada 71 C7 45 38N 61 31W
Mulhacén, Spain 19 D4 37 4N 3 20W
Mülheim, Germany 33 C6 51 25N 6 54 E
Mulhouse, France 18 C7 47 40N 7 20 E
Muling, China 35 B16 44 35N 130 10 E
Mull, U.K. 12 E3 56 25N 5 56W
Mull, Sound of, U.K. 12 E3 56 30N 5 50W
Mullaittivu, Sri Lanka 40 Q12 9 15N 80 49 E
Mullen, U.S.A. 80 D4 42 3N 101 1W

## N

Newala, Tanzania 55 E4 10 58S 39 18 E
Newark, Del., U.S.A. 76 F8 39 41N 75 46W
**Newark**, N.J., U.S.A. 79 F10 40 44N 74 10W
Newark, N.Y., U.S.A. 78 C7 43 3N 77 6W
Newark, Ohio, U.S.A. 78 F2 40 3N 82 24W
Newark-on-Trent, U.K. 10 D7 53 5N 0 48W
Newark Valley, U.S.A. 79 D8 42 14N 76 11W
Newberg, U.S.A. 82 D2 45 18N 122 58W
Newberry, Mich., U.S.A. 76 B3 46 21N 85 30W
Newberry, S.C., U.S.A. 77 H5 34 17N 81 37W
Newberry Springs, U.S.A. 85 L10 34 50N 116 41W
Newboro L., Canada 79 B8 44 38N 76 20W
Newbridge = Droichead Nua, Ireland 13 C5 53 11N 6 48W
Newburgh, Canada 78 B8 44 19N 76 52W
Newburgh, U.S.A. 79 E10 41 30N 74 1W
Newbury, U.K. 11 F6 51 24N 1 20W
Newbury, N.H., U.S.A. 79 B12 43 19N 72 3W
Newbury, Vt., U.S.A. 79 B12 44 5N 72 4W
Newburyport, U.S.A. 77 D10 42 49N 70 53W
Newcastle, Australia 63 E5 33 0S 151 46 E
Newcastle, N.B., Canada 71 C6 47 1N 65 38W
Newcastle, Ont., Canada 70 D4 43 55N 78 35W
Newcastle, S. Africa 57 D4 27 45S 29 58 E
Newcastle, U.K. 13 B6 54 13N 5 54W
Newcastle, Calif., U.S.A. 84 G5 38 53N 121 8W
Newcastle, Wyo., U.S.A. 80 D2 43 50N 104 11W
Newcastle Emlyn, U.K. 11 E3 52 2N 4 28W
Newcastle Ra., Australia 60 C5 15 45S 130 15 E
Newcastle-under-Lyme, U.K. 10 D5 53 1N 2 14W
**Newcastle-upon-Tyne**, U.K. 10 C6 54 58N 1 36W
Newcastle Waters, Australia 62 B1 17 30S 133 28 E
Newcastle West, Ireland 13 D2 52 27N 9 3W
Newcomb, U.S.A. 79 C10 43 58N 74 10W
Newcomerstown, U.S.A. 78 F3 40 16N 81 36W
Newdegate, Australia 61 F2 33 6S 119 0 E
Newell, Australia 62 B4 16 20S 145 16 E
Newell, U.S.A. 80 C3 44 43N 103 25W
Newfane, U.S.A. 78 C6 43 17N 78 43W
Newfield, U.S.A. 79 D8 42 18N 76 33W
Newfound L., U.S.A. 79 C13 43 40N 71 47W
Newfoundland, N. Amer. 66 E14 49 0N 55 0W
Newfoundland, U.S.A. 79 E9 41 18N 75 19W
**Newfoundland** □, Canada 71 B8 53 0N 58 0W
Newhall, U.S.A. 85 L8 34 23N 118 32W
Newhaven, U.K. 11 G8 50 47N 0 3 E
Newkirk, U.S.A. 81 G6 36 53N 97 3W
Newlyn, U.K. 11 G2 50 6N 5 34W
Newman, Australia 60 D2 23 18S 119 45 E
Newman, U.S.A. 84 H5 37 19N 121 1W
Newmarket, Canada 78 B5 44 3N 79 28W
Newmarket, Ireland 13 D2 52 13N 9 0W
Newmarket, U.K. 11 E8 52 15N 0 25 E
Newmarket, N.H., U.S.A. 79 C14 43 4N 70 56W
Newmarket, N.H., U.S.A. 79 C14 43 5N 70 56W
Newnan, U.S.A. 77 J3 33 23N 84 48W
Newport, Ireland 13 C2 53 53N 9 33W
Newport, I. of W., U.K. 11 G6 50 42N 1 17W
Newport, Newp., U.K. 11 F5 51 35N 3 0W
Newport, Ark., U.S.A. 81 H9 35 37N 91 16W
Newport, Ky., U.S.A. 76 F3 39 5N 84 30W
Newport, N.H., U.S.A. 79 C12 43 22N 72 10W
Newport, N.Y., U.S.A. 79 C9 43 11N 75 1W
Newport, Oreg., U.S.A. 82 D1 44 39N 124 3W
Newport, Pa., U.S.A. 78 F7 40 29N 77 8W
**Newport**, R.I., U.S.A. 79 E13 41 29N 71 19W
Newport, Tenn., U.S.A. 77 H4 35 58N 83 11W
Newport, Vt., U.S.A. 79 B12 44 56N 72 13W
Newport, Wash., U.S.A. 82 B5 48 11N 117 3W
Newport □, U.K. 11 F4 51 33N 3 1W
Newport Beach, U.S.A. 85 M9 33 37N 117 56W
**Newport News**, U.S.A. 76 G7 36 59N 76 25W
Newport Pagnell, U.K. 11 E7 52 5N 0 43W
Newquay, U.K. 11 G2 50 25N 5 6W
Newry, U.K. 13 B5 54 11N 6 21W
Newton, Ill., U.S.A. 80 F10 38 59N 88 10W
Newton, Iowa, U.S.A. 80 E8 41 42N 93 3W
Newton, Kans., U.S.A. 81 F6 38 3N 97 21W
Newton, Mass., U.S.A. 79 D13 42 21N 71 12W
Newton, Miss., U.S.A. 81 J10 32 19N 89 10W
Newton, N.C., U.S.A. 77 H5 35 40N 81 13W
Newton, N.J., U.S.A. 79 E10 41 3N 74 45W
Newton, Tex., U.S.A. 81 K8 30 51N 93 46W
Newton Abbot, U.K. 11 G4 50 32N 3 37W
Newton Aycliffe, U.K. 10 C6 54 37N 1 34W
Newton Falls, U.S.A. 78 E4 41 11N 80 59W
Newton Stewart, U.K. 12 G4 54 57N 4 30W
Newtonmore, U.K. 12 D4 57 4N 4 8W
Newtown, U.K. 11 E4 52 31N 3 19W
Newtownabbey, U.K. 13 B6 54 40N 5 56W
Newtownards, U.K. 13 B6 54 36N 5 42W
Newtownbarry = Bunclody, Ireland 13 D5 52 39N 6 40W
Newtownstewart, U.K. 13 B4 54 43N 7 23W
Newville, U.S.A. 78 F7 40 10N 77 24W
Neya, Russia 24 C7 58 21N 43 49 E
Neyrīz, Iran 45 D7 29 15N 54 19 E
Neyshābūr, Iran 45 B8 36 10N 58 50 E
Nezhin = Nizhyn, Ukraine 25 D5 51 5N 31 55 E
Nezperce, U.S.A. 82 C5 46 14N 116 14W
Ngabang, Indonesia 36 D3 0 23N 109 55 E
Ngabordamlu, Tanjung, Indonesia 37 F8 6 56S 134 11 E
N'Gage, Angola 52 F3 7 46S 15 16 E
Ngami Depression, Botswana 56 C3 20 30S 22 46 E
Ngamo, Zimbabwe 55 F2 19 3S 27 32 E
Nganglong Kangri, China 41 C12 33 0N 81 0 E
Ngao, Thailand 38 C2 18 46N 99 59 E
Ngaoundéré, Cameroon 52 C2 7 15N 13 35 E
Ngapara, N.Z. 59 L3 44 57S 170 46 E
Ngara, Tanzania 54 C3 2 29S 30 40 E
Ngawi, Indonesia 37 G14 7 24S 111 26 E
Ngoma, Malawi 55 E3 13 8S 33 45 E
Ngomahura, Zimbabwe 55 G3 20 26S 30 43 E
Ngomba, Tanzania 55 D3 8 20S 32 53 E
Ngoring Hu, China 32 C4 34 55N 97 5 E
Ngorongoro, Tanzania 54 C4 3 11S 35 32 E
Ngozi, Burundi 54 C2 2 54S 29 50 E
Ngudu, Tanzania 54 C3 2 58S 33 25 E
Nguigmi, Niger 51 F8 14 20N 13 20 E
Nguiu, Australia 60 B5 11 46S 130 38 E
Ngukurr, Australia 62 A1 14 44S 134 44 E
Ngulu Atoll, Pac. Oc. 37 C9 8 0N 137 30 E
Ngunga, Tanzania 54 C3 3 37S 33 37 E
Nguru, Nigeria 51 F8 12 56N 10 29 E
Nguru Mts., Tanzania 54 D4 6 0S 37 30 E
Nha Trang, Vietnam 39 F7 12 16N 109 10 E
Nhacoongo, Mozam. 57 C6 24 18S 35 14 E
Nhamaabué, Mozam. 55 F4 17 25S 35 5 E
Nhamundá →, Brazil 93 D7 2 12S 56 41W
Nhangutazi, L., Mozam. 57 C5 24 0S 34 30 E
Nhill, Australia 63 F3 36 18S 141 40 E
Nhulunbuy, Australia 62 A2 12 10S 137 20 E
Nia-nia, Dem. Rep. of the Congo 54 B2 1 30N 27 40 E
Niagara Falls, Canada 78 C5 43 7N 79 5W
**Niagara Falls**, U.S.A. 78 C6 43 5N 79 4W
Niagara-on-the-Lake, Canada 78 C5 43 15N 79 4W
Niah, Malaysia 36 D4 3 58N 113 46 E
**Niamey**, Niger 50 F6 13 27N 2 6 E
Niangara, Dem. Rep. of the Congo 54 B2 3 42N 27 50 E
Niantic, U.S.A. 79 E12 41 20N 72 11W
Nias, Indonesia 36 D1 1 0N 97 30 E
Niassa □, Mozam. 55 E4 13 30S 36 0 E
Nibāk, Si. Arabia 45 E7 24 25N 50 50 E
**Nicaragua** ■, Cent. Amer. 88 D2 11 40N 85 30W
Nicaragua, L. de, Nic. 88 D2 12 0N 85 30W
Nicastro, Italy 20 E7 38 59N 16 19 E
**Nice**, France 18 E7 43 42N 7 14 E
Niceville, U.S.A. 77 K2 30 31N 86 30W
Nichicun, L., Canada 71 B5 53 5N 71 0W
Nichinan, Japan 31 J5 31 38N 131 23 E
Nicholás, Canal, W. Indies 88 B3 23 30N 80 5W
Nicholasville, U.S.A. 76 G3 37 53N 84 34W
Nichols, U.S.A. 79 D8 42 1N 76 22W
Nicholson, Australia 60 C4 18 2S 128 54 E
Nicholson, U.S.A. 79 E9 41 37N 75 47W
Nicholson →, Australia 62 B2 17 31S 139 36 E
Nicholson L., Canada 73 A8 62 40N 102 40W
Nicholson Ra., Australia 61 E2 27 15S 116 45 E
Nicholville, U.S.A. 79 B10 44 41N 74 39W
**Nicobar Is.**, Ind. Oc. 28 J13 9 0N 93 0 E
Nicola, Canada 72 C4 50 12N 120 40W
Nicolls Town, Bahamas 88 A4 25 8N 78 0W
**Nicosia**, Cyprus 23 D12 35 10N 33 25 E
Nicoya, Costa Rica 88 D2 10 9N 85 27W
Nicoya, G. de, Costa Rica 88 E3 10 0N 85 0W
Nicoya, Pen. de, Costa Rica 88 E2 9 45N 85 40W
Nidd →, U.K. 10 D6 53 59N 1 23W
Niedersachsen □, Germany 16 B5 52 50N 9 0 E
Niekerkshoop, S. Africa 56 D3 29 19S 22 51 E
Niemba, Dem. Rep. of the Congo 54 D2 5 58S 28 24 E
Niemen = Neman →, Lithuania 9 J20 55 25N 21 10 E
Nienburg, Germany 16 B5 52 39N 9 13 E
Nieu Bethesda, S. Africa 56 E3 31 51S 24 34 E
Nieuw Amsterdam, Surinam 93 B7 5 53N 55 5W
Nieuw Nickerie, Surinam 93 B7 6 0N 56 59W
Nieuwoudtville, S. Africa 56 E2 31 23S 19 7 E
Nieuwpoort, Belgium 15 C2 51 8N 2 45 E
Nieves, Pico de las, Canary Is. 22 G4 27 57N 15 35W
Niğde, Turkey 25 G5 37 58N 34 40 E
Nigel, S. Africa 57 D4 26 27S 28 25 E
**Niger** ■, W. Afr. 50 E7 17 30N 10 0 E
**Niger** →, W. Afr. 50 G7 5 33N 6 33 E
**Nigeria** ■, W. Afr. 50 G7 8 30N 8 0 E
Nighasin, India 43 E9 28 14N 80 52 E
Nightcaps, N.Z. 59 L2 45 57S 168 2 E
Nii-Jima, Japan 31 G9 34 20N 139 15 E
Niigata, Japan 30 F9 37 58N 139 0 E
Niigata □, Japan 31 F9 37 15N 138 45 E
Niihama, Japan 31 H6 33 55N 133 16 E
Niihau, U.S.A. 74 H14 21 54N 160 9W
Niimi, Japan 31 G6 34 59N 133 28 E
Niitsu, Japan 30 F9 37 48N 139 7 E
Nijil, Jordan 47 E4 30 32N 35 33 E
Nijkerk, Neths. 15 B5 52 13N 5 30 E
Nijmegen, Neths. 15 C5 51 50N 5 52 E
Nijverdal, Neths. 15 B6 52 22N 6 28 E
Nīk Pey, Iran 45 B6 36 50N 48 10 E
Nikiniki, Indonesia 37 F6 9 49S 124 30 E
Nikkō, Japan 31 F9 36 45N 139 35 E
Nikolayev = Mykolayiv, Ukraine 25 E5 46 58N 32 0 E
Nikolayevsk, Russia 25 E8 50 0N 45 35 E
Nikolayevsk-na-Amur, Russia 27 D15 53 8N 140 44 E
Nikolskoye, Russia 27 D17 55 12N 166 0 E
Nikopol, Ukraine 25 E5 47 35N 34 25 E
Nīkshahr, Iran 45 E9 26 15N 60 10 E
Nikšić, Montenegro, Yug. 21 C8 42 50N 18 57 E
Nîl, Nahr en →, Africa 51 B12 30 10N 31 6 E
Nîl el Abyad →, Sudan 51 E12 15 38N 32 31 E
Nîl el Azraq →, Sudan 51 E12 15 38N 32 31 E
Nila, Indonesia 37 F7 6 44S 129 31 E
Niland, U.S.A. 85 M11 33 14N 115 31W
**Nile** = Nîl, Nahr en →, Africa 51 B12 30 10N 31 6 E
Niles, Mich., U.S.A. 76 E2 41 50N 86 15W
Niles, Ohio, U.S.A. 78 E4 41 11N 80 46W
Nim Ka Thana, India 42 F6 27 44N 75 48 E
Nimach, India 42 G6 24 30N 74 56 E
Nimbahera, India 42 G6 24 37N 74 45 E
Nîmes, France 18 E6 43 50N 4 23 E
Nimfaíon, Ákra = Pinnes, Ákra, Greece 21 D11 40 5N 24 20 E
Nimmitabel, Australia 63 F4 36 29S 149 15 E
Nīnawá, Iraq 44 B4 36 25N 43 10 E
Nindigully, Australia 63 D4 28 21S 148 50 E
Nineveh = Nīnawá, Iraq 44 B4 36 25N 43 10 E
Ning Xian, China 34 G4 35 30N 107 58 E
Ning'an, China 35 B15 44 22N 129 20 E
Ningbo, China 33 D7 29 51N 121 28 E
Ningcheng, China 35 D10 41 32N 119 53 E
Ningjin, China 34 F8 37 35N 114 57 E
Ningjing Shan, China 32 D4 30 0N 98 20 E
Ningling, China 34 G8 34 25N 115 22 E
Ningpo = Ningbo, China 33 D7 29 51N 121 28 E
Ningqiang, China 34 H4 32 47N 106 15 E
Ningshan, China 34 H5 33 21N 108 21 E
Ningsia Hui A.R. = Ningxia Huizu Zizhiqu □, China 34 F4 38 0N 106 0 E
Ningwu, China 34 E7 39 0N 112 18 E
Ningxia Huizu Zizhiqu □, China 34 F4 38 0N 106 0 E
Ningyang, China 34 G9 35 47N 116 45 E
Ninh Giang, Vietnam 38 B6 20 44N 106 24 E
Ninh Hoa, Vietnam 38 F7 12 30N 109 7 E
Ninh Ma, Vietnam 38 F7 12 48N 109 21 E
Ninove, Belgium 15 D4 50 51N 4 2 E
Nioaque, Brazil 95 A4 21 5S 55 50W
Niobrara, U.S.A. 80 D6 42 45N 98 2W
Niobrara →, U.S.A. 80 D6 42 46N 98 3W
Nioro du Sahel, Mali 50 E4 15 15N 9 30W
Niort, France 18 C3 46 19N 0 29W
Nipawin, Canada 73 C8 53 20N 104 0W
Nipigon, Canada 70 C2 49 0N 88 17W
Nipigon, L., Canada 70 C2 49 50N 88 30W
Nipishish L., Canada 71 B7 54 12N 60 45W
Nipissing, L., Canada 70 C4 46 20N 80 0W
Nipomo, U.S.A. 85 K6 35 3N 120 29W
Nipton, U.S.A. 85 K11 35 28N 115 16W
Niquelândia, Brazil 93 F9 14 33S 48 23W
Nīr, Iran 44 B5 38 2N 47 59 E
Nirasaki, Japan 31 G9 35 42N 138 27 E
Nirmal, India 40 K11 19 3N 78 20 E
Nirmali, India 43 F12 26 20N 86 35 E
Niš, Serbia, Yug. 21 C9 43 19N 21 58 E
Nişāb, Si. Arabia 44 D5 29 11N 44 43 E
Nişāb, Yemen 46 E4 14 25N 46 29 E
Nishinomiya, Japan 31 G7 34 45N 135 20 E
Nishino'omote, Japan 31 J5 30 43N 130 59 E
Nishiwaki, Japan 31 G7 34 59N 134 58 E
Niskibi →, Canada 70 A2 56 29N 88 9W
Nisqually →, U.S.A. 84 C4 47 6N 122 42W
Nissáki, Greece 23 A3 39 43N 19 52 E
Nissum Bredning, Denmark 9 H13 56 40N 8 20 E
Nistru = Dnister →, Europe 17 E16 46 18N 30 17 E
Nisutlin →, Canada 72 A2 60 14N 132 34W
Nitchequon, Canada 71 B5 53 10N 70 58W
Niterói, Brazil 95 A7 22 52S 43 0W
Nith →, Canada 78 C4 43 12N 80 23W
Nith →, U.K. 12 F5 55 14N 3 33W
Nitra, Slovak Rep. 17 D10 48 19N 18 4 E
Nitra →, Slovak Rep. 17 E10 47 46N 18 10 E
Niuafo'ou, Tonga 59 B11 15 30S 175 58W
**Niue**, Cook Is. 65 J11 19 2S 169 54W
Niut, Indonesia 36 D4 0 55N 110 6 E
Niuzhuang, China 35 D12 40 58N 122 28 E
Nivala, Finland 8 E21 63 56N 24 57 E
Nivelles, Belgium 15 D4 50 35N 4 20 E
Nivernais, France 18 C5 47 15N 3 30 E
Niwas, India 43 H9 23 3N 80 26 E
Nixon, U.S.A. 81 L6 29 16N 97 46W
Nizamabad, India 40 K11 18 45N 78 7 E
Nizamghat, India 41 E19 28 20N 95 45 E
Nizhne Kolymsk, Russia 27 C17 68 34N 160 55 E
Nizhnekamsk, Russia 24 C9 55 38N 51 49 E
Nizhneudinsk, Russia 27 D10 54 54N 99 3 E
Nizhnevartovsk, Russia 26 C8 60 56N 76 38 E
Nizhniy Novgorod, Russia 24 C7 56 20N 44 0 E
Nizhniy Tagil, Russia 24 C10 57 55N 59 57 E
Nizhyn, Ukraine 25 D5 51 5N 31 55 E
Nizip, Turkey 44 B3 37 5N 37 50 E
Nízké Tatry, Slovak Rep. 17 D10 48 55N 19 30 E
Njakwa, Malawi 55 E3 11 1S 33 56 E
Njanji, Zambia 55 E3 14 25S 31 46 E
Njinjo, Tanzania 55 D4 8 48S 38 54 E
Njombe, Tanzania 55 D3 9 20S 34 50 E
Njombe →, Tanzania 54 D4 6 56S 35 6 E
Nkana, Zambia 55 E2 12 50S 28 8 E
Nkayi, Zimbabwe 55 F2 19 41S 29 20 E
Nkhotakota, Malawi 55 E3 12 56S 34 15 E
Nkongsamba, Cameroon 52 D1 4 55N 9 55 E
Nkurenkuru, Namibia 56 B2 17 42S 18 32 E
Nmai →, Burma 41 G20 25 30N 97 25 E
Noakhali = Maijdi, Bangla. 41 H17 22 48N 91 10 E
Nobel, Canada 78 A4 45 25N 80 6W
Nobeoka, Japan 31 H5 32 36N 131 41 E
Noblesville, U.S.A. 76 E3 40 3N 86 1W
Nocera Inferiore, Italy 20 D6 40 44N 14 38 E
Nocona, U.S.A. 81 J6 33 47N 97 44W
Noda, Japan 31 G9 35 56N 139 52 E
Nogales, Mexico 86 A2 31 20N 110 56W
Nogales, U.S.A. 83 L8 31 20N 110 56W
Nōgata, Japan 31 H5 33 48N 130 44 E
Noggerup, Australia 61 F2 33 32S 116 5 E
Noginsk, Russia 27 C10 64 30N 90 50 E
Nogoa →, Australia 62 C4 23 40S 147 55 E
Nogoyá, Argentina 94 C4 32 24S 59 48W
Nohar, India 42 E6 29 11N 74 49 E
Nohta, India 43 H8 23 40N 79 34 E
Noire, Mts., France 18 B2 48 7N 3 28W
Noirmoutier, Î. de, France 18 C2 46 58N 2 10W
Nojane, Botswana 56 C3 23 15S 20 14 E
Nojima-Zaki, Japan 31 G9 34 54N 139 53 E
Nok Kundi, Pakistan 40 E3 28 50N 62 45 E
Nokaneng, Botswana 56 B3 19 40S 22 17 E
Nokia, Finland 9 F20 61 30N 23 30 E
Nokomis, Canada 73 C8 51 35N 105 0W
Nokomis L., Canada 73 B8 57 0N 103 0W
Nola, C.A.R. 52 D3 3 35N 16 4 E
Noma Omuramba →, Namibia 56 B3 18 52S 20 53 E
Nombre de Dios, Panama 88 E4 9 34N 79 28W
Nome, U.S.A. 68 B3 64 30N 165 25W
Nomo-Zaki, Japan 31 H4 32 35N 129 44 E
Nonacho L., Canada 73 A7 61 42N 109 40W
Nonda, Australia 62 C3 20 40S 142 28 E
Nong Chang, Thailand 38 E2 15 23N 99 51 E
Nong Het, Laos 38 C4 19 29N 103 59 E
Nong Khai, Thailand 38 D4 17 50N 102 46 E
Nong'an, China 35 B13 44 25N 125 5 E
Nongoma, S. Africa 57 D5 27 58S 31 35 E
Nonoava, Mexico 86 B3 27 28N 106 44W
Nonoava →, Mexico 86 B3 27 29N 106 45W
Nonthaburi, Thailand 38 F3 13 51N 100 34 E
Noonamah, Australia 60 B5 12 40S 131 4 E
Noord Brabant □, Neths. 15 C5 51 40N 5 0 E
Noord Holland □, Neths. 15 B4 52 30N 4 45 E
Noordbeveland, Neths. 15 C3 51 35N 3 50 E
Noordoostpolder, Neths. 15 B5 52 45N 5 45 E
Noordwijk, Neths. 15 B4 52 14N 4 26 E
Nootka I., Canada 72 D3 49 32N 126 42W
Nopiming Prov. Park, Canada 73 C9 50 30N 95 37W
Noralee, Canada 72 C3 53 59N 126 26W
Noranda = Rouyn-Noranda, Canada 70 C4 48 20N 79 0W
Norco, U.S.A. 85 M9 33 56N 117 33W
Nord-Kivu □, Dem. Rep. of the Congo 54 C2 1 0S 29 0 E
Nord-Ostsee-Kanal, Germany 16 A5 54 12N 9 32 E
Nordaustlandet, Svalbard 4 B9 79 14N 23 0 E
Nordegg, Canada 72 C5 52 29N 116 5W
Norderney, Germany 16 B4 53 42N 7 9 E
Norderstedt, Germany 16 B5 53 42N 10 1 E
Nordfjord, Norway 9 F11 61 55N 5 30 E
Nordfriesische Inseln, Germany 16 A5 54 40N 8 20 E
Nordhausen, Germany 16 C6 51 30N 10 47 E
Norðoyar, Færoe Is. 8 E9 62 17N 6 35W
Nordkapp, Norway 8 A21 71 10N 25 50 E
Nordkapp, Svalbard 4 A9 80 31N 20 0 E
Nordkinn = Kinnarodden, Norway 6 A11 71 8N 27 40 E
Nordkinn-halvøya, Norway 8 A22 70 55N 27 40 E
Nordrhein-Westfalen □, Germany 16 C4 51 45N 7 30 E
Nordvik, Russia 27 B12 74 2N 111 32 E
Nore →, Ireland 13 D4 52 25N 6 58W
Norfolk, Nebr., U.S.A. 80 D6 42 2N 97 25W
**Norfolk**, Va., U.S.A. 76 G7 36 51N 76 17W
**Norfolk** □, U.K. 11 E8 52 39N 0 54 E
**Norfolk I.**, Pac. Oc. 64 K8 28 58S 168 3 E
Norfork L., U.S.A. 81 G8 36 15N 92 14W
Norilsk, Russia 27 C9 69 20N 88 6 E
Norma, Mt., Australia 62 C3 20 55S 140 42 E
Normal, U.S.A. 80 E10 40 31N 88 59W
Norman, U.S.A. 81 H6 35 13N 97 26W
Norman →, Australia 62 B3 19 18S 141 51 E
Norman Wells, Canada 68 B7 65 17N 126 51W
Normanby →, Australia 62 A3 14 23S 144 10 E
Normandie, France 18 B4 48 45N 0 10 E
Normandin, Canada 70 C5 48 49N 72 31W
**Normandy** = Normandie, France 18 B4 48 45N 0 10 E
Normanhurst, Mt., Australia 61 E3 25 4S 122 30 E
Normanton, Australia 62 B3 17 40S 141 10 E
Normétal, Canada 70 C4 49 0N 79 22W
Norquay, Canada 73 C8 51 53N 102 5W
Norquinco, Argentina 96 E2 41 51S 70 55W
Norrbotten □, Sweden 8 C19 66 30N 22 30 E
Norris Point, Canada 71 C8 49 31N 57 53W
Norristown, U.S.A. 79 F9 40 7N 75 21W
Norrköping, Sweden 9 G17 58 37N 16 11 E
Norrland, Sweden 9 E16 62 15N 15 45 E
Norrtälje, Sweden 9 G18 59 46N 18 42 E
Norseman, Australia 61 F3 32 8S 121 43 E
Norsk, Russia 27 D14 52 30N 130 5 E
Norte, Pta. del, Canary Is. 22 G2 27 51N 17 57W
Norte, Serra do, Brazil 92 11 20S 59 0W
North, C., Canada 71 C7 47 2N 60 20W
North Adams, U.S.A. 79 D11 42 42N 73 7W
North Arm, Canada 72 A5 62 0N 114 30W
North Augusta, U.S.A. 77 J5 33 30N 81 59W
North Ayrshire □, U.K. 12 F4 55 45N 4 44W
North Bass I., U.S.A. 78 E2 41 43N 82 49W
North Battleford, Canada 73 C7 52 50N 108 17W
North Bay, Canada 70 C4 46 20N 79 30W
North Belcher Is., Canada 70 A4 56 50N 79 50W
North Bend, Oreg., U.S.A. 82 E1 43 24N 124 14W
North Bend, Pa., U.S.A. 78 E7 41 20N 77 42W
North Bend, Wash., U.S.A. 84 C5 47 30N 121 47W
North Bennington, U.S.A. 79 D11 42 56N 73 15W
North Berwick, U.K. 12 E6 56 4N 2 42W
North Berwick, U.S.A. 79 C14 43 18N 70 44W
North C., Canada 71 C7 47 5N 64 0W
North C., N.Z. 59 F4 34 23S 173 4 E
North Canadian →, U.S.A. 81 H7 35 16N 95 31W
North Canton, U.S.A. 78 F3 40 53N 81 24W
North Cape = Nordkapp, Norway 8 A21 71 10N 25 50 E
North Cape = Nordkapp, Svalbard 4 A9 80 31N 20 0 E
North Caribou L., Canada 70 B1 52 50N 90 40W
**North Carolina** □, U.S.A. 77 H6 35 30N 80 0W
North Cascades National Park, U.S.A. 82 B3 48 45N 121 10W
North Channel, Canada 70 C3 46 0N 83 0W
North Channel, U.K. 12 F3 55 13N 5 52W
North Charleston, U.S.A. 77 J6 32 53N 79 58W
North Chicago, U.S.A. 76 D2 42 19N 87 51W
North Creek, U.S.A. 79 C11 43 41N 73 59W
**North Dakota** □, U.S.A. 80 B5 47 30N 100 15W
North Downs, U.K. 11 F8 51 19N 0 21 E
North East, U.S.A. 78 D5 42 13N 79 50W
North East Frontier Agency = Arunachal Pradesh □, India 41 F19 28 0N 95 0 E
North East Lincolnshire □, U.K. 10 D7 53 34N 0 2W
North Eastern □, Kenya 54 B5 1 30N 40 0 E
North Esk →, U.K. 12 E6 56 46N 2 24W
North European Plain, Europe 6 E10 55 0N 25 0 E
North Foreland, U.K. 11 F9 51 22N 1 28 E
North Fork, U.S.A. 84 H7 37 14N 119 21W
North Fork American →, U.S.A. 84 G5 38 57N 120 59W
North Fork Feather →, U.S.A. 84 F5 38 33N 121 30W
North Fork Grand →, U.S.A. 80 C3 45 47N 102 16W
North Fork Red →, U.S.A. 81 H5 34 24N 99 14W
North Frisian Is. = Nordfriesische Inseln, Germany 16 A5 54 40N 8 20 E
North Gower, Canada 79 A9 45 8N 75 43W
North Hd., Australia 61 F1 30 14S 114 59 E
North Henik L., Canada 73 A9 61 45N 97 40W
North Highlands, U.S.A. 84 G5 38 40N 121 23W
North Horr, Kenya 54 B4 3 20N 37 8 E
North I., Kenya 54 B4 4 5N 36 5 E
**North I.**, N.Z. 59 H5 38 0S 175 0 E
North Kingsville, U.S.A. 78 E4 41 54N 80 42W
North Knife →, Canada 73 B10 58 53N 94 45W
North Koel →, India 43 G10 24 45N 83 50 E
**North Korea** ■, Asia 35 E14 40 0N 127 0 E
North Lakhimpur, India 41 F19 27 14N 94 7 E
North Lanarkshire □, U.K. 12 F5 55 52N 3 56W
North Las Vegas, U.S.A. 85 J11 36 12N 115 7W
North Lincolnshire □, U.K. 10 D7 53 36N 0 30W
North Little Rock, U.S.A. 81 H8 34 45N 92 16W
North Loup →, U.S.A. 80 E5 41 17N 98 24W
North Magnetic Pole, Canada 4 B2 77 58N 102 8W
North Minch, U.K. 12 C3 58 5N 5 55W
North Moose L., Canada 73 C8 54 11N 100 6W
North Myrtle Beach, U.S.A. 77 J6 33 48N 78 42W

# O

Oglio →, Italy 20 B4 45 2N 10 39 E
Ogmore, Australia 62 C4 22 37S 149 35 E
Ogoki, Canada 70 B2 51 38N 85 58W
Ogoki →, Canada 70 B2 51 38N 85 57W
Ogoki L., Canada 70 B2 50 50N 87 10W
Ogoki Res., Canada 70 B2 50 45N 88 15W
Ogooué →, Gabon 52 E1 1 0S 9 0 E
Ogowe = Ogooué →, Gabon 52 E1 1 0S 9 0 E
Ogre, Latvia 9 H21 56 49N 24 36 E
Ogurchinskiy, Ostrov, Turkmenistan 45 B7 38 55N 53 2 E
Ohai, N.Z. 59 L2 45 55S 168 0 E
Ohakune, N.Z. 59 H5 39 24S 175 24 E
Ohata, Japan 30 D10 41 24N 141 10 E
Ohau, L., N.Z. 59 L2 44 15S 169 53 E
**Ohio** □, U.S.A. 78 F2 40 15N 82 45W
**Ohio** →, U.S.A. 76 G1 36 59N 89 8W
Ohře →, Czech Rep. 16 C8 50 30N 14 10 E
Ohrid, Macedonia 21 D9 41 8N 20 52 E
Ohridsko Jezero, Macedonia 21 D9 41 8N 20 52 E
Ohrigstad, S. Africa 57 C5 24 39S 30 36 E
Oiapoque, Brazil 93 3 50N 51 50W
Oikou, China 35 E9 38 35N 117 42 E
Oil City, U.S.A. 78 E5 41 26N 79 42W
Oil Springs, Canada 78 D2 42 47N 82 7W
Oildale, U.S.A. 85 K7 35 25N 119 1W
Oise →, France 18 B5 49 0N 2 4 E
Ōita, Japan 31 H5 33 14N 131 36 E
Ōita □, Japan 31 H5 33 15N 131 30 E
Oiticica, Brazil 93 E10 5 3S 41 5W
Ojacaliente, Mexico 86 C4 22 34N 102 15W
Ojai, U.S.A. 85 L7 34 27N 119 15W
Ojinaga, Mexico 86 B4 29 34N 104 25W
Ojiya, Japan 31 F9 37 18N 138 48 E
Ojos del Salado, Cerro, Argentina 94 B2 27 0S 68 40W
Oka →, Russia 24 C7 56 20N 43 59 E
Okaba, Indonesia 37 F9 8 6S 139 42 E
Okahandja, Namibia 56 C2 22 0S 16 59 E
Okahukura, N.Z. 59 H5 38 48S 175 14 E
Okanagan L., Canada 72 D5 50 0N 119 30W
Okanogan, U.S.A. 82 B4 48 22N 119 35W
Okanogan →, U.S.A. 82 B4 48 6N 119 44W
Okaputa, Namibia 56 C2 20 5S 17 0 E
Okara, Pakistan 42 D5 30 50N 73 31 E
Okarito, N.Z. 59 K3 43 15S 170 9 E
Okaukuejo, Namibia 56 B2 19 10S 16 0 E
Okavango Swamps, Botswana 56 B3 18 45S 22 45 E
Okaya, Japan 31 F9 36 5N 138 10 E
Okayama, Japan 31 G6 34 40N 133 54 E
Okayama □, Japan 31 G6 35 0N 133 50 E
Okazaki, Japan 31 G8 34 57N 137 10 E
Okeechobee, U.S.A. 77 M5 27 15N 80 50W
Okeechobee, L., U.S.A. 77 M5 27 0N 80 50W
Okefenokee Swamp, U.S.A. 77 K4 30 40N 82 20W
Okehampton, U.K. 11 G4 50 44N 4 0W
Okha, India 42 H3 22 27N 69 4 E
Okha, Russia 27 D15 53 40N 143 0 E
Okhotsk, Russia 27 D15 59 20N 143 10 E
**Okhotsk, Sea of**, Asia 27 D15 55 0N 145 0 E
Okhotskiy Perevoz, Russia 27 C14 61 52N 135 35 E
Okhtyrka, Ukraine 25 D5 50 25N 35 0 E
Oki-Shotō, Japan 31 F6 36 5N 133 15 E
Okiep, S. Africa 56 D2 29 39S 17 53 E
**Okinawa** □, Japan 31 L4 26 40N 128 0 E
Okinawa-Guntō, Japan 31 L4 26 40N 128 0 E
Okinawa-Jima, Japan 31 L4 26 32N 128 0 E
Okino-erabu-Shima, Japan 31 L4 27 21N 128 33 E
**Oklahoma** □, U.S.A. 81 H6 35 20N 97 30W
**Oklahoma City**, U.S.A. 81 H6 35 30N 97 30W
Okmulgee, U.S.A. 81 H7 35 37N 95 58W
Oknitsa = Ocniţa, Moldova 17 D14 48 25N 27 30 E
Okolo, Uganda 54 B3 2 37N 31 8 E
Okolona, U.S.A. 81 J10 34 0N 88 45W
Okotoks, Canada 72 C6 50 43N 113 58W
Oksibil, Indonesia 37 E10 4 59S 140 35 E
Oksovskiy, Russia 24 B6 62 33N 39 57 E
Oktabrsk = Oktyabrsk, Kazakstan 25 E10 49 28N 57 25 E
Oktyabrsk, Kazakstan 25 E10 49 28N 57 25 E
Oktyabrskiy = Aktsyabrski, Belarus 17 B15 52 38N 28 53 E
Oktyabrskiy, Russia 24 D9 54 28N 53 28 E
Oktyabrskoy Revolyutsii, Ostrov, Russia 27 B10 79 30N 97 0 E
Okuru, N.Z. 59 K2 43 55S 168 55 E
Okushiri-Tō, Japan 30 C9 42 15N 139 30 E
Okwa →, Botswana 56 C3 22 30S 23 0 E
Ola, U.S.A. 81 H8 35 2N 93 13W
Ólafsfjörður, Iceland 8 C4 66 4N 18 39W
Ólafsvík, Iceland 8 D2 64 53N 23 43W
Olancha, U.S.A. 85 J8 36 17N 118 1W
Olancha Pk., U.S.A. 85 J8 36 15N 118 7W
Olanchito, Honduras 88 C2 15 30N 86 30W
Öland, Sweden 9 H17 56 45N 16 38 E
Olary, Australia 63 E3 32 18S 140 19 E
Olascoaga, Argentina 94 D3 35 15S 60 39W
Olathe, U.S.A. 80 F7 38 53N 94 49W
Olavarría, Argentina 94 D3 36 55S 60 20W
Oława, Poland 17 C9 50 57N 17 20 E
Ólbia, Italy 20 D3 40 55N 9 31 E
Olcott, U.S.A. 78 C6 43 20N 78 42W
Old Bahama Chan. = Bahama, Canal Viejo de, W. Indies 88 B4 22 10N 77 30W
Old Baldy Pk. = San Antonio, Mt., U.S.A. 85 L9 34 17N 117 38W
Old Castile = Castilla y Leon □, Spain 19 B3 42 0N 5 0W
Old Crow, Canada 68 B6 67 30N 139 55W
Old Dale, U.S.A. 85 L11 34 8N 115 47W
Old Forge, N.Y., U.S.A. 79 C10 43 43N 74 58W
Old Forge, Pa., U.S.A. 79 E9 41 22N 75 45W
Old Perlican, Canada 71 C9 48 5N 53 1W
Old Shinyanga, Tanzania 54 C3 3 33S 33 27 E
Old Speck Mt., U.S.A. 79 B14 44 34N 70 57W
Old Town, U.S.A. 77 C11 44 56N 68 39W
Old Washington, U.S.A. 78 F3 40 2N 81 27W
Old Wives L., Canada 73 C7 50 5N 106 0W
Oldbury, U.K. 11 F5 51 38N 2 33W
Oldcastle, Ireland 13 C4 53 46N 7 10W
Oldeani, Tanzania 54 C4 3 22S 35 35 E
Oldenburg, Germany 16 B5 53 9N 8 13 E
Oldenzaal, Neths. 15 B6 52 19N 6 53 E
Oldham, U.K. 10 D5 53 33N 2 7W
Oldman →, Canada 72 D6 49 57N 111 42W
Oldmeldrum, U.K. 12 D6 57 20N 2 19W
Olds, Canada 72 C6 51 50N 114 10W
Oldziyt, Mongolia 34 B5 44 40N 109 1 E
Olean, U.S.A. 78 D6 42 5N 78 26W
Olekma →, Russia 27 C13 60 22N 120 42 E
Olekminsk, Russia 27 C13 60 25N 120 30 E
Oleksandriya, Ukraine 17 C14 50 37N 26 19 E
Olema, U.S.A. 84 G4 38 3N 122 47W
Olenegorsk, Russia 24 A5 68 9N 33 18 E
Olenek, Russia 27 C12 68 28N 112 18 E
Olenek →, Russia 27 B13 73 0N 120 10 E
Oléron, Î. d', France 18 D3 45 55N 1 15W
Oleśnica, Poland 17 C9 51 13N 17 22 E
Olevsk, Ukraine 17 C14 51 12N 27 39 E
Olga, Russia 27 E14 43 50N 135 14 E
Olga, L., Canada 70 C4 49 47N 77 15W
Olga, Mt., Australia 61 E5 25 20S 130 50 E
Olhão, Portugal 19 D2 37 3N 7 48W
Olifants →, Africa 57 C5 23 57S 31 58 E
Olifantshoek, S. Africa 56 D3 27 57S 22 42 E
Ólimbos, Óros, Greece 21 D10 40 6N 22 23 E
Olímpia, Brazil 95 A6 20 44S 48 54W
Olinda, Brazil 93 E12 8 1S 34 51W
Oliva, Argentina 94 C3 32 0S 63 38W
Olivehurst, U.S.A. 84 F5 39 6N 121 34W
Olivenza, Spain 19 C2 38 41N 7 9W
Oliver, Canada 72 D5 49 13N 119 37W
Oliver L., Canada 73 B8 56 56N 103 22W
Ollagüe, Chile 94 A2 21 15S 68 10W
Olney, Ill., U.S.A. 76 F1 38 44N 88 5W
Olney, Tex., U.S.A. 81 J5 33 22N 98 45W
Olomane →, Canada 71 B7 50 14N 60 37W
Olomouc, Czech Rep. 17 D9 49 38N 17 12 E
Olonets, Russia 24 B5 61 0N 32 54 E
Olongapo, Phil. 37 B6 14 50N 120 18 E
Olot, Spain 19 A7 42 11N 2 30 E
Olovyannaya, Russia 27 D12 50 58N 115 35 E
Oloy →, Russia 27 C16 66 29N 159 29 E
Olsztyn, Poland 17 B11 53 48N 20 29 E
Olt →, Romania 17 G13 43 43N 24 51 E
Olteniţa, Romania 17 F14 44 7N 26 42 E
Olton, U.S.A. 81 H3 34 11N 102 8W
Olymbos, Cyprus 23 D12 35 21N 33 45 E
**Olympia**, Greece 21 F9 37 39N 21 39 E
**Olympia**, U.S.A. 84 D4 47 3N 122 53W
Olympic Dam, Australia 63 E2 30 30S 136 55 E
Olympic Mts., U.S.A. 84 C3 47 55N 123 45W
Olympic Nat. Park, U.S.A. 84 C3 47 48N 123 30W
Olympus, Cyprus 23 E11 34 56N 32 52 E
**Olympus, Mt.** = Ólimbos, Óros, Greece 21 D10 40 6N 22 23 E
Olympus, Mt. = Uludağ, Turkey 21 D13 40 4N 29 13 E
Olympus, Mt., U.S.A. 84 C3 47 48N 123 43W
Olyphant, U.S.A. 79 E9 41 27N 75 36W
Om →, Russia 26 D8 54 59N 73 22 E
Om Koi, Thailand 38 D2 17 48N 98 22 E
Ōma, Japan 30 D10 41 45N 141 5 E
Ōmachi, Japan 31 F8 36 30N 137 50 E
Omae-Zaki, Japan 31 G9 34 36N 138 14 E
Ōmagari, Japan 30 E10 39 27N 140 29 E
Omagh, U.K. 13 B4 54 36N 7 19W
Omagh □, U.K. 13 B4 54 35N 7 15W
**Omaha**, U.S.A. 80 E7 41 17N 95 58W
Omak, U.S.A. 82 B4 48 25N 119 31W
Omalos, Greece 23 D5 35 19N 23 55 E
**Oman** ■, Asia 46 C6 23 0N 58 0 E
Oman, G. of, Asia 45 E8 24 30N 58 30 E
Omaruru, Namibia 56 C2 21 26S 16 0 E
Omaruru →, Namibia 56 C1 22 7S 14 15 E
Omate, Peru 92 G4 16 45S 71 0W
Ombai, Selat, Indonesia 37 F6 8 30S 124 50 E
Omboué, Gabon 52 E1 1 35S 9 15 E
Ombrone →, Italy 20 C4 42 42N 11 5 E
Omdurmân, Sudan 51 E12 15 40N 32 28 E
Omemee, Canada 78 B6 44 18N 78 33W
Omeo, Australia 63 F4 37 6S 147 36 E
Omeonga, Dem. Rep. of the Congo 54 C1 3 40S 24 22 E
Ometepe, I. de, Nic. 88 D2 11 32N 85 35W
Ometepec, Mexico 87 D5 16 39N 98 23W
Ominato, Japan 30 D10 41 17N 141 10 E
Omineca →, Canada 72 B4 56 3N 124 16W
Omitara, Namibia 56 C2 22 16S 18 2 E
Ōmiya, Japan 31 G9 35 54N 139 38 E
Ommen, Neths. 15 B6 52 31N 6 26 E
Ömnögovĭ □, Mongolia 34 C3 43 15N 104 0 E
Omo →, Ethiopia 46 F2 6 25N 36 10 E
Omodhos, Cyprus 23 E11 34 51N 32 48 E
Omolon →, Russia 27 C16 68 42N 158 36 E
Omono-Gawa →, Japan 30 E10 39 46N 140 3 E
**Omsk**, Russia 26 D8 55 0N 73 12 E
Omsukchan, Russia 27 C16 62 32N 155 48 E
Ōmu, Japan 30 B11 44 34N 142 58 E
Omul, Vf., Romania 17 F13 45 27N 25 29 E
Ōmura, Japan 31 H4 32 56N 129 57 E
Omuramba Omatako →, Namibia 53 H4 17 45S 20 25 E
Ōmuta, Japan 31 H5 33 5N 130 26 E
Onaga, U.S.A. 80 F6 39 29N 96 10W
Onalaska, U.S.A. 80 D9 43 53N 91 14W
Onancock, U.S.A. 76 G8 37 43N 75 45W
Onang, Indonesia 37 E5 3 2S 118 49 E
Onaping L., Canada 70 C3 47 3N 81 30W
Onavas, Mexico 86 B3 28 28N 109 30W
Onawa, U.S.A. 80 D6 42 2N 96 6W
Oncócua, Angola 56 B1 16 30S 13 25 E
Onda, Spain 19 C5 39 55N 0 17W
Ondaejin, N. Korea 35 D15 41 34N 129 40 E
Ondangua, Namibia 56 B2 17 57S 16 4 E
Ondjiva, Angola 56 B2 16 48S 15 50 E
Öndörshil, Mongolia 34 B5 45 13N 108 5 E
Öndverðarnes, Iceland 8 D1 64 52N 24 0W
One Tree, Australia 63 E3 34 11S 144 43 E
Onega, Russia 24 B6 64 0N 38 10 E
Onega →, Russia 24 B6 63 58N 38 2 E
Onega, G. of = Onezhskaya Guba, Russia 24 B6 64 24N 36 38 E
**Onega, L.** = Onezhskoye Ozero, Russia 24 B6 61 44N 35 22 E
Onehunga, N.Z. 59 G5 36 55S 174 48 E
Oneida, U.S.A. 79 C9 43 6N 75 39W
Oneida L., U.S.A. 79 C9 43 12N 75 54W
O'Neill, U.S.A. 80 D5 42 27N 98 39W
Onekotan, Ostrov, Russia 27 E16 49 25N 154 45 E
Onema, Dem. Rep. of the Congo 54 C1 4 35S 24 30 E
Oneonta, U.S.A. 79 D9 42 27N 75 4W
Oneşti, Romania 17 E14 46 15N 26 45 E
Onezhskaya Guba, Russia 24 B6 64 24N 36 38 E
Onezhskoye Ozero, Russia 24 B6 61 44N 35 22 E
Ongarue, N.Z. 59 H5 38 42S 175 19 E
Ongerup, Australia 61 F2 33 58S 118 28 E
Ongjin, N. Korea 35 F13 37 56N 125 21 E
Ongkharak, Thailand 38 E3 14 8N 101 1 E
Ongniud Qi, China 35 C10 43 0N 118 38 E
Ongoka, Dem. Rep. of the Congo 54 C2 1 20S 26 0 E
Ongole, India 40 M12 15 33N 80 2 E
Ongon = Havirga, Mongolia 34 B7 45 41N 113 5 E
Onida, U.S.A. 80 C4 44 42N 100 4W
Onilahy →, Madag. 57 C7 23 34S 43 45 E
Onitsha, Nigeria 50 G7 6 6N 6 42 E
Onoda, Japan 31 G5 34 2N 131 25 E
Onpyŏng-ni, S. Korea 35 H14 33 25N 126 55 E
Onslow, Australia 60 D2 21 40S 115 12 E
Onslow B., U.S.A. 77 H7 34 20N 77 15W
Ontake-San, Japan 31 G8 35 53N 137 29 E
Ontario, Calif., U.S.A. 85 L9 34 4N 117 39W
Ontario, Oreg., U.S.A. 82 D5 44 2N 116 58W
**Ontario** □, Canada 70 B2 48 0N 83 0W
**Ontario, L.**, N. Amer. 75 B11 43 20N 78 0W
Ontonagon, U.S.A. 80 B10 46 52N 89 19W
Onyx, U.S.A. 85 K8 35 41N 118 14W
Oodnadatta, Australia 63 D2 27 33S 135 30 E
Ooldea, Australia 61 F5 30 27S 131 50 E
Oombulgurri, Australia 60 C4 15 15S 127 45 E
Oorindi, Australia 62 C3 20 40S 141 1 E
Oost-Vlaanderen □, Belgium 15 C3 51 5N 3 50 E
Oostende, Belgium 15 C2 51 15N 2 54 E
Oosterhout, Neths. 15 C4 51 39N 4 47 E
Oosterschelde →, Neths. 15 C4 51 33N 4 0 E
Oosterwolde, Neths. 15 B6 53 0N 6 17 E
Ootacamund = Udagamandalam, India 40 P10 11 30N 76 44 E
Ootsa L., Canada 72 C3 53 50N 126 2W
Opala, Dem. Rep. of the Congo 54 C1 0 40S 24 20 E
Opanake, Sri Lanka 40 R12 6 35N 80 40 E
Opasatika, Canada 70 C3 49 30N 82 50W
Opasquia Prov. Park, Canada 70 B1 53 33N 93 5W
Opava, Czech Rep. 17 D9 49 57N 17 58 E
Opelika, U.S.A. 77 J3 32 39N 85 23W
Opelousas, U.S.A. 81 K8 30 32N 92 5W
Opémisca, L., Canada 70 C5 49 56N 74 52W
Opheim, U.S.A. 82 B10 48 51N 106 24W
Ophthalmia Ra., Australia 60 D2 23 15S 119 30 E
Opinaca →, Canada 70 B4 52 15N 78 2W
Opinaca, Rés., Canada 70 B4 52 39N 76 20W
Opinnagau →, Canada 70 B3 54 12N 82 25W
Opiscoteo, L., Canada 71 B6 53 10N 68 10W
Opole, Poland 17 C9 50 42N 17 58 E
**Oporto** = Porto, Portugal 19 B1 41 8N 8 40W
Opotiki, N.Z. 59 H6 38 1S 177 19 E
Opp, U.S.A. 77 K2 31 17N 86 16W
Oppdal, Norway 9 E13 62 35N 9 41 E
Opportunity, U.S.A. 82 C5 47 39N 117 15W
Opua, N.Z. 59 F5 35 19S 174 9 E
Opunake, N.Z. 59 H4 39 26S 173 52 E
Ora, Cyprus 23 E12 34 51N 33 12 E
Oracle, U.S.A. 83 K8 32 37N 110 46W
Oradea, Romania 17 E11 47 2N 21 58 E
Öræfajökull, Iceland 8 D5 64 2N 16 39W
Orai, India 43 G8 25 58N 79 30 E
Oral = Zhayyq →, Kazakstan 25 E9 47 0N 51 48 E
Oral, Kazakstan 25 D9 51 20N 51 20 E
**Oran**, Algeria 50 A5 35 45N 0 39W
Orange, Australia 63 E4 33 15S 149 7 E
Orange, France 18 D6 44 8N 4 47 E
Orange, Calif., U.S.A. 85 M9 33 47N 117 51W
Orange, Mass., U.S.A. 79 D12 42 35N 72 19W
Orange, Tex., U.S.A. 81 K8 30 6N 93 44W
Orange, Va., U.S.A. 76 F6 38 15N 78 7W
**Orange** →, S. Africa 56 D2 28 41S 16 28 E
Orange, C., Brazil 93 C8 4 20N 51 30W
Orange Cove, U.S.A. 84 J7 36 38N 119 19W
**Orange Free State** = Free State □, S. Africa 56 D4 28 30S 27 0 E
Orange Grove, U.S.A. 81 M6 27 58N 97 56W
Orange Walk, Belize 87 D7 18 6N 88 33W
Orangeburg, U.S.A. 77 J5 33 30N 80 52W
Orangeville, Canada 78 C4 43 55N 80 5W
Oranienburg, Germany 16 B7 52 45N 13 14 E
Oranje = Orange →, S. Africa 56 D2 28 41S 16 28 E
Oranje Vrystaat = Free State □, S. Africa 56 D4 28 30S 27 0 E
Oranjemund, Namibia 56 D2 28 38S 16 29 E
Oranjerivier, S. Africa 56 D3 29 40S 24 12 E
Orapa, Botswana 53 J5 21 15S 25 30 E
Oras, Phil. 37 B7 12 9N 125 28 E
Oraşul Stalin = Braşov, Romania 17 F13 45 38N 25 35 E
Orbetello, Italy 20 C4 42 27N 11 13 E
Orbisonia, U.S.A. 78 F7 40 15N 77 54W
Orbost, Australia 63 F4 37 40S 148 29 E
Orcas I., U.S.A. 84 B4 48 42N 122 56W
Orchard City, U.S.A. 83 G10 38 50N 107 58W
Orchila, I., Venezuela 89 D6 11 48N 66 10W
Orcutt, U.S.A. 85 L6 34 52N 120 27W
Ord, U.S.A. 80 E5 41 36N 98 56W
Ord →, Australia 60 C4 15 33S 128 15 E
Ord, Mt., Australia 60 C4 17 20S 125 34 E
Orderville, U.S.A. 83 H7 37 17N 112 38W
Ordos = Mu Us Shamo, China 34 E5 39 0N 109 0 E
Ordu, Turkey 25 F6 40 55N 37 53 E
Ordway, U.S.A. 80 F3 38 13N 103 46W
Ordzhonikidze = Vladikavkaz, Russia 25 F7 43 0N 44 35 E
Ore, Dem. Rep. of the Congo 54 B2 3 17N 29 30 E
Ore Mts. = Erzgebirge, Germany 16 C7 50 27N 12 55 E
Örebro, Sweden 9 G16 59 20N 15 18 E
Oregon, U.S.A. 80 D10 42 1N 89 20W
**Oregon** □, U.S.A. 82 E3 44 0N 121 0W
Oregon City, U.S.A. 84 E4 45 21N 122 36W
Orekhovo-Zuyevo, Russia 24 C6 55 50N 38 55 E
Orel, Russia 24 D6 52 57N 36 3 E
Orem, U.S.A. 74 B4 40 19N 111 42W
Ören, Turkey 21 F12 37 3N 27 57 E
Orenburg, Russia 24 D10 51 45N 55 6 E
Orense = Ourense, Spain 19 A2 42 19N 7 55W
Orepuki, N.Z. 59 M1 46 19S 167 46 E
Orestiás, Greece 21 D12 41 30N 26 33 E
Orestos Pereyra, Mexico 86 B3 26 31N 105 40W
Orford Ness, U.K. 11 E9 52 5N 1 35 E
Organos, Pta. de los, Canary Is. 22 F2 28 12N 17 17W
Orgaz, Spain 19 C4 39 39N 3 53W
Orgeyev = Orhei, Moldova 17 E15 47 24N 28 50 E
Orhaneli, Turkey 21 E13 39 54N 28 59 E
Orhangazi, Turkey 21 D13 40 29N 29 18 E
Orhei, Moldova 17 E15 47 24N 28 50 E
Orhon Gol →, Mongolia 32 A5 50 21N 106 0 E
Oriental, Cordillera, Colombia 92 B4 6 0N 73 0W
Orientale □, Dem. Rep. of the Congo 54 B2 2 20N 26 0 E
Oriente, Argentina 94 D3 38 44S 60 37W
Orihuela, Spain 19 C5 38 7N 0 55W
Orillia, Canada 78 B5 44 40N 79 24W
**Orinoco** →, Venezuela 92 B6 9 15N 61 30W
Orion, Canada 73 D6 49 27N 110 49W
Oriskany, U.S.A. 79 C9 43 10N 75 20W
**Orissa** □, India 41 K14 20 0N 84 0 E
Orissaare, Estonia 9 G20 58 34N 23 5 E
Oristano, Italy 20 E3 39 54N 8 36 E
Oristano, G. di, Italy 20 E3 39 50N 8 29 E
Orizaba, Mexico 87 D5 18 51N 97 6W
Orkanger, Norway 8 E13 63 18N 9 52 E
Orkla →, Norway 8 E13 63 18N 9 51 E
Orkney, S. Africa 56 D4 26 58S 26 40 E
Orkney □, U.K. 12 B5 59 2N 3 13W
**Orkney Is.**, U.K. 12 B6 59 0N 3 0W
Orland, U.S.A. 84 F4 39 45N 122 12W
**Orlando**, U.S.A. 77 L5 28 33N 81 23W
Orléanais, France 18 C5 48 0N 2 0 E
**Orléans**, France 18 C4 47 54N 1 52 E
Orleans, U.S.A. 79 B12 44 49N 72 12W
Orléans, I. d', Canada 71 C5 46 54N 70 58W
Ormara, Pakistan 40 G4 25 16N 64 33 E
Ormoc, Phil. 37 B6 11 0N 124 37 E
Ormond, N.Z. 59 H6 38 33S 177 56 E
Ormond Beach, U.S.A. 77 L5 29 17N 81 3W
Ormskirk, U.K. 10 D5 53 35N 2 54W
Ormstown, Canada 79 A11 45 8N 74 0W
Örnsköldsvik, Sweden 8 E18 63 17N 18 40 E
Oro, N. Korea 35 D14 40 1N 127 27 E
Oro →, Mexico 86 B3 25 35N 105 2W
Oro Grande, U.S.A. 85 L9 34 36N 117 20W
Oro Valley, U.S.A. 83 K8 32 26N 110 58W
Orocué, Colombia 92 C4 4 48N 71 20W
Orofino, U.S.A. 82 C5 46 29N 116 15W
Orol Dengizi = Aral Sea, Asia 26 E7 44 30N 60 0 E
Oromocto, Canada 71 C6 45 54N 66 29W
Orono, Canada 78 C6 43 59N 78 37W
Orono, U.S.A. 77 C11 44 53N 68 40W
Oronsay, U.K. 12 E2 56 1N 6 15W
Oroqen Zizhiqi, China 33 A7 50 34N 123 43 E
Oroquieta, Phil. 37 C6 8 32N 123 44 E
Orosháza, Hungary 17 E11 46 32N 20 42 E
Orotukan, Russia 27 C16 62 16N 151 42 E
Oroville, Calif., U.S.A. 84 F5 39 31N 121 33W
Oroville, Wash., U.S.A. 82 B4 48 56N 119 26W
Oroville, L., U.S.A. 84 F5 39 33N 121 29W
Orroroo, Australia 63 E2 32 43S 138 38 E
Orrville, U.S.A. 78 F3 40 50N 81 46W
Orsha, Belarus 24 D5 54 30N 30 25 E
Orsk, Russia 26 D6 51 12N 58 34 E
Orşova, Romania 17 F12 44 41N 22 25 E
Ortaca, Turkey 21 F13 36 49N 28 45 E
Ortegal, C., Spain 19 A2 43 43N 7 52W
Orthez, France 18 E3 43 29N 0 48W
Ortigueira, Spain 19 A2 43 40N 7 50W
Orting, U.S.A. 84 C4 47 6N 122 12W
Ortles, Italy 18 C9 46 31N 10 33 E
Ortón →, Bolivia 92 F5 10 50S 67 0W
Ortonville, U.S.A. 80 C6 45 19N 96 27W
Orūmīyeh, Iran 44 B5 37 40N 45 0 E
Orūmīyeh, Daryācheh-ye, Iran 44 B5 37 50N 45 30 E
Oruro, Bolivia 92 G5 18 0S 67 9W
Orust, Sweden 9 G14 58 10N 11 40 E
Oruzgān □, Afghan. 40 C5 33 30N 66 0 E
Orvieto, Italy 20 C5 42 43N 12 7 E
Orwell, N.Y., U.S.A. 79 C9 43 35N 75 50W
Orwell, Ohio, U.S.A. 78 E4 41 32N 80 52W
Orwell →, U.K. 11 F9 51 59N 1 18 E
Orwigsburg, U.S.A. 79 F8 40 38N 76 6W
Oryakhovo, Bulgaria 21 C10 43 40N 23 57 E
Osa, Russia 24 C10 57 17N 55 26 E
Osa, Pen. de, Costa Rica 88 E3 8 0N 84 0W
Osage, U.S.A. 80 D8 43 17N 92 49W
Osage →, U.S.A. 80 F9 38 35N 91 57W
Osage City, U.S.A. 80 F7 38 38N 95 50W
**Ōsaka**, Japan 31 G7 34 40N 135 30 E
Osan, S. Korea 35 F14 37 11N 127 4 E
Osawatomie, U.S.A. 80 F7 38 31N 94 57W
Osborne, U.S.A. 80 F5 39 26N 98 42W
Osceola, Ark., U.S.A. 81 H10 35 42N 89 58W
Osceola, Iowa, U.S.A. 80 E8 41 2N 93 46W
Oscoda, U.S.A. 78 B1 44 26N 83 20W
Ösel = Saaremaa, Estonia 9 G20 58 30N 22 30 E
Osgoode, Canada 79 A9 45 8N 75 36W
Osh, Kyrgyzstan 26 E8 40 37N 72 49 E
Oshakati, Namibia 53 H3 17 45S 15 40 E
Oshawa, Canada 78 C6 43 50N 78 50W
Oshkosh, Nebr., U.S.A. 80 E3 41 24N 102 21W
Oshkosh, Wis., U.S.A. 80 C10 44 1N 88 33W
Oshmyany = Ashmyany, Belarus 9 J21 54 26N 25 52 E
Oshnovīyeh, Iran 44 B5 37 2N 45 6 E
Oshogbo, Nigeria 50 G6 7 48N 4 37 E
Oshtorīnān, Iran 45 C6 34 1N 48 38 E
Oshwe, Dem. Rep. of the Congo 52 E3 3 25S 19 28 E
Osijek, Croatia 21 B8 45 34N 18 41 E
Osipenko = Berdyansk, Ukraine 25 E6 46 45N 36 50 E
Osipovichi = Asipovichy, Belarus 17 B15 53 19N 28 33 E
Osiyan, India 42 F5 26 43N 72 55 E

# P

Panjang, Hon, *Vietnam* .... **39 H4** 9 20N 103 28 E
Panjgur, *Pakistan* ........ **40 F4** 27 0N 64 5 E
Panjim = Panaji, *India* .... **40 M8** 15 25N 73 50 E
Panjin, *China* ............ **35 D12** 41 3N 122 2 E
Panjinad Barrage, *Pakistan* **40 E7** 29 22N 71 15 E
Panjnad →, *Pakistan* .... **42 E4** 28 57N 70 30 E
Panjwai, *Afghan.* ......... **42 D1** 31 26N 65 27 E
Panmunjŏm, *N. Korea* .... **35 F14** 37 59N 126 38 E
Panna, *India* ............ **43 G9** 24 40N 80 15 E
Panna Hills, *India* ........ **43 G9** 24 40N 81 15 E
Pannawonica, *Australia* ... **60 D2** 21 39S 116 19 E
Pano Akil, *Pakistan* ....... **42 F3** 27 51N 69 7 E
Pano Lefkara, *Cyprus* ..... **23 E12** 34 53N 33 20 E
Pano Panayia, *Cyprus* ..... **23 E11** 34 55N 32 38 E
Panorama, *Brazil* ......... **95 A5** 21 21S 51 51W
Pánormon, *Greece* ....... **23 D6** 35 25N 24 41 E
Pansemal, *India* .......... **42 J6** 21 39N 74 42 E
Panshan = Panjin, *China* .. **35 D12** 41 3N 122 2 E
Panshi, *China* ............ **35 C14** 42 58N 126 5 E
Pantanal, *Brazil* ......... **92 H7** 17 30S 57 40W
Pantar, *Indonesia* ........ **37 F6** 8 28S 124 10 E
Pante Macassar, *Indonesia* **37 F6** 9 30S 123 58 E
Pantelleria, *Italy* ......... **20 F4** 36 50N 11 57 E
Pánuco, *Mexico* .......... **87 C5** 22 0N 98 15W
Paola, *Malta* ............. **23 D2** 35 52N 14 30 E
Paola, *U.S.A.* ............ **80 F7** 38 35N 94 53W
Paonia, *U.S.A.* ........... **83 G10** 38 52N 107 36W
Paoting = Baoding, *China* . **34 E8** 38 50N 115 28 E
Paot'ou = Baotou, *China* .. **34 D6** 40 32N 110 2 E
Paoua, *C.A.R.* ............ **52 C3** 7 9N 16 20 E
Pápa, *Hungary* ........... **17 E9** 47 22N 17 30 E
Papa Stour, *U.K.* ......... **12 A7** 60 20N 1 42W
Papa Westray, *U.K.* ....... **12 B6** 59 20N 2 55W
Papagayo →, *Mexico* .... **87 D5** 16 36N 99 43W
Papagayo, G. de, *Costa Rica* **88 D2** 10 30N 85 50W
Papakura, *N.Z.* ........... **59 G5** 37 4S 174 59 E
Papantla, *Mexico* ......... **87 C5** 20 30N 97 30W
Papar, *Malaysia* .......... **36 C5** 5 45N 116 0 E
**Papeete**, *Tahiti* ......... **65 J13** 17 32S 149 34W
Paphos, *Cyprus* .......... **23 E11** 34 46N 32 25 E
Papigochic →, *Mexico* ... **86 B3** 29 9N 109 40W
Paposo, *Chile* ............ **94 B1** 25 0S 70 30W
Papoutsa, *Cyprus* ........ **23 E12** 34 54N 33 4 E
**Papua New Guinea** ■,
*Oceania* ............... **64 H6** 8 0S 145 0 E
Papudo, *Chile* ........... **94 C1** 32 29S 71 27W
Papun, *Burma* ........... **41 K20** 18 2N 97 30 E
Papunya, *Australia* ....... **60 D5** 23 15S 131 54 E
Pará = Belém, *Brazil* ...... **93 D9** 1 20S 48 30W
Pará □, *Brazil* ............ **93 D8** 3 20S 52 0W
Paraburdoo, *Australia* ..... **60 D2** 23 14S 117 32 E
Paracatu, *Brazil* .......... **93 G9** 17 10S 46 50W
Paracel Is., *S. China Sea* .. **36 A4** 15 50N 112 0 E
Parachilna, *Australia* ..... **63 E2** 31 10S 138 21 E
Parachinar, *Pakistan* ...... **42 C4** 33 55N 70 5 E
Paradhísi, *Greece* ........ **23 C10** 36 18N 28 7 E
Paradip, *India* ........... **41 J15** 20 15N 86 35 E
Paradise, *Calif., U.S.A.* .... **84 F5** 39 46N 121 37W
Paradise, *Nev., U.S.A.* .... **85 J11** 36 9N 115 10W
Paradise →, *Canada* ..... **71 B8** 53 27N 57 19W
Paradise Hill, *Canada* ..... **73 C7** 53 32N 109 28W
Paradise River, *Canada* ... **71 B8** 53 27N 57 17W
Paradise Valley, *U.S.A.* .... **82 F5** 41 30N 117 32W
Parado, *Indonesia* ........ **37 F5** 8 42S 118 30 E
Paragould, *U.S.A.* ........ **81 G9** 36 3N 90 29W
Paragua →, *Venezuela* ... **92 B6** 6 55N 62 55W
Paraguaçu →, *Brazil* ..... **93 F11** 12 45S 38 54W
Paraguaçu Paulista, *Brazil* . **95 A5** 22 22S 50 35W
Paraguaná, Pen. de,
*Venezuela* ............. **92 A5** 12 0N 70 0W
Paraguarí, *Paraguay* ...... **94 B4** 25 36S 57 0W
Paraguarí □, *Paraguay* .... **94 B4** 26 0S 57 10W
**Paraguay** ■, *S. Amer.* .... **94 A4** 23 0S 57 0W
Paraguay →, *Paraguay* .. **94 B4** 27 18S 58 38W
Paraíba = João Pessoa,
*Brazil* ................. **93 E12** 7 10S 34 52W
Paraíba □, *Brazil* ........ **93 E11** 7 0S 36 0W
Paraíba do Sul →, *Brazil* . **95 A7** 21 37S 41 3W
Parainen, *Finland* ........ **9 F20** 60 18N 22 18 E
Paraiso, *Mexico* .......... **87 D6** 18 24N 93 14W
Parak, *Iran* .............. **45 E7** 27 38N 52 25 E
Parakou, *Benin* .......... **50 G6** 9 25N 2 40 E
Paralimni, *Cyprus* ........ **23 D12** 35 2N 33 58 E
**Paramaribo**, *Surinam* .... **93 B7** 5 50N 55 10W
Paramushir, Ostrov, *Russia* **27 D16** 50 24N 156 0 E
Paran →, *Israel* ......... **47 E4** 30 20N 35 10 E
Paraná, *Argentina* ........ **94 C3** 31 45S 60 30W
Paranã, *Brazil* ........... **93 F9** 12 30S 47 48W
Paraná □, *Brazil* ......... **95 A5** 24 30S 51 0W
**Paraná** →, *Argentina* ... **94 C4** 33 43S 59 15W
Paranaguá, *Brazil* ........ **95 B6** 25 30S 48 30W
Paranaíba, *Brazil* ......... **93 G8** 19 40S 51 11W
Paranaíba →, *Brazil* ..... **93 H8** 20 6S 51 4W
Paranapanema →, *Brazil* . **95 A5** 22 40S 53 9W
Paranapiacaba, Serra do,
*Brazil* ................. **95 A6** 24 31S 48 35W
Paranavaí, *Brazil* ......... **95 A5** 23 4S 52 56W
Parang, *Jolo, Phil.* ........ **37 C6** 5 55N 120 54 E
Parang, *Mindanao, Phil.* .... **37 C6** 7 23N 124 16 E
Parângul Mare, Vf., *Romania* **17 F12** 45 20N 23 37 E
Parbati →, *India* ........ **42 F6** 26 54N 77 53 E
Parbati →, *India* ........ **42 G7** 25 50N 76 30 E
Parbhani, *India* .......... **40 K10** 19 8N 76 52 E
Parchim, *Germany* ....... **16 B6** 53 26N 11 52 E
Pardes Hanna-Karkur, *Israel* **47 C3** 32 28N 34 57 E
Pardo →, *Bahia, Brazil* ... **93 G11** 15 40S 39 0W
Pardo →, *Mato Grosso,*
*Brazil* ................. **95 A5** 21 46S 52 9W
Pardubice, *Czech Rep.* .... **16 C8** 50 3N 15 45 E
Pare, *Indonesia* .......... **37 G15** 7 43S 112 12 E
Pare Mts., *Tanzania* ...... **54 C4** 4 0S 37 45 E
Parecis, Serra dos, *Brazil* .. **92 F7** 13 0S 60 0W
Paren, *Russia* ........... **27 C17** 62 30N 163 15 E
Parent, *Canada* .......... **70 C5** 47 55N 74 35W
Parent, L., *Canada* ....... **70 C4** 48 31N 77 1W
Parepare, *Indonesia* ...... **37 E5** 4 0S 119 40 E
Párga, *Greece* ........... **21 E9** 39 15N 20 29 E
Pargo, Pta. do, *Madeira* ... **22 D2** 32 49N 17 17W
Pariaguán, *Venezuela* ..... **92 B6** 8 51N 64 34W
Paricutín, Cerro, *Mexico* ... **86 D4** 19 28N 102 15W
Parigi, *Indonesia* ......... **37 E6** 0 50S 120 5 E
Parika, *Guyana* .......... **92 B7** 6 50N 58 20W
Parima, Serra, *Brazil* ..... **92 C6** 2 30N 64 0W
Parinari, *Peru* ........... **92 D4** 4 35S 74 25W
Pariñas, Pta., *S. Amer.* .... **90 D2** 4 30S 82 0W
Parintins, *Brazil* ......... **93 D7** 2 40S 56 50W
Pariparit Kyun, *Burma* .... **41 M18** 14 55N 93 45 E
Paris, *Canada* ........... **78 C4** 43 12N 80 25W
**Paris**, *France* ........... **18 B5** 48 50N 2 20 E
Paris, *Idaho, U.S.A.* ....... **82 E8** 42 14N 111 24W
Paris, *Ky., U.S.A.* ......... **76 F3** 38 13N 84 15W
Paris, *Tenn., U.S.A.* ....... **77 G1** 36 18N 88 19W
Paris, *Tex., U.S.A.* ........ **81 J7** 33 40N 95 33W
Parish, *U.S.A.* ........... **79 C8** 43 25N 76 8W
Parishville, *U.S.A.* ........ **79 B10** 44 38N 74 49W
Park, *U.S.A.* ............. **84 B4** 48 45N 122 18W
Park City, *U.S.A.* ......... **81 G6** 37 48N 97 20W
Park Falls, *U.S.A.* ......... **80 C9** 45 56N 90 27W
Park Head, *Canada* ....... **78 B3** 44 36N 81 9W
Park Hills, *U.S.A.* ......... **81 G9** 37 53N 90 28W
Park Range, *U.S.A.* ....... **82 G10** 40 0N 106 30W
Park Rapids, *U.S.A.* ....... **80 B7** 46 55N 95 4W
Park River, *U.S.A.* ........ **80 A6** 48 24N 97 45W
Park Rynie, *S. Africa* ..... **57 E5** 30 25S 30 45 E
Parkā Bandar, *Iran* ....... **45 E8** 25 55N 59 35 E
Parkano, *Finland* ........ **9 E20** 62 1N 23 0 E
Parker, *Ariz., U.S.A.* ...... **85 L12** 34 9N 114 17W
Parker, *Pa., U.S.A.* ....... **78 E5** 41 5N 79 41W
Parker Dam, *U.S.A.* ....... **85 L12** 34 18N 114 8W
Parkersburg, *U.S.A.* ...... **76 F5** 39 16N 81 34W
Parkes, *Australia* ........ **63 E4** 33 9S 148 11 E
Parkfield, *U.S.A.* ......... **84 K6** 35 54N 120 26W
Parkhill, *Canada* ........ **78 C3** 43 15N 81 38W
Parkland, *U.S.A.* ......... **84 C4** 47 9N 122 26W
Parkston, *U.S.A.* ......... **80 D6** 43 24N 97 59W
Parksville, *Canada* ....... **72 D4** 49 20N 124 21W
Parla, *Spain* ............. **19 B4** 40 14N 3 46W
**Parma**, *Italy* ............ **18 D9** 44 48N 10 20 E
Parma, *Idaho, U.S.A.* ..... **82 E5** 43 47N 116 57W
Parma, *Ohio, U.S.A.* ...... **78 E3** 41 23N 81 43W
Parnaguá, *Brazil* ......... **93 F10** 10 10S 44 38W
Parnaíba, *Brazil* ......... **93 D10** 2 54S 41 47W
Parnaíba →, *Brazil* ..... **93 D10** 3 0S 41 50W
**Parnassós**, *Greece* ...... **21 E10** 38 35N 22 30 E
Pärnu, *Estonia* .......... **9 G21** 58 28N 24 33 E
Paroo →, *Australia* ..... **63 E3** 31 28S 143 32 E
Páros, *Greece* ........... **21 F11** 37 5N 25 12 E
Parowan, *U.S.A.* ......... **83 H7** 37 51N 112 50W
Parral, *Chile* ............ **94 D1** 36 10S 71 52W
Parras, *Mexico* .......... **86 B4** 25 30N 102 20W
Parrett →, *U.K.* ........ **11 F4** 51 12N 3 1W
Parris I., *U.S.A.* ......... **77 J5** 32 20N 80 41W
Parrsboro, *Canada* ....... **71 C7** 45 30N 64 25W
Parry I., *Canada* ......... **78 A4** 45 18N 80 10W
Parry Is., *Canada* ........ **4 B2** 77 0N 110 0W
Parry Sound, *Canada* ..... **78 A5** 45 20N 80 0W
Parsnip →, *Canada* ..... **72 B4** 55 10N 123 2W
Parsons, *U.S.A.* ......... **81 G7** 37 20N 95 16W
Parsons Ra., *Australia* .... **62 A2** 13 30S 135 15 E
Partinico, *Italy* .......... **20 E5** 38 3N 13 7 E
Partridge I., *Canada* ...... **70 A2** 55 59N 87 37W
Paru →, *Brazil* ......... **93 D8** 1 33S 52 38W
Parvān □, *Afghan.* ....... **40 B6** 35 0N 69 0 E
Parvatipuram, *India* ...... **41 K13** 18 50N 83 25 E
Parvatsar, *India* ......... **42 F6** 26 52N 74 49 E
Parys, *S. Africa* .......... **56 D4** 26 52S 27 29 E
Pas, Pta. des, *Spain* ...... **22 C7** 38 46N 1 26 E
Pasadena, *Canada* ....... **71 C8** 49 1N 57 36W
Pasadena, *Calif., U.S.A.* ... **85 L8** 34 9N 118 9W
Pasadena, *Tex., U.S.A.* .... **81 L7** 29 43N 95 13W
Pasaje →, *Argentina* .... **94 B3** 25 39S 63 56W
Pascagoula, *U.S.A.* ....... **81 K10** 30 21N 88 33W
Pascagoula →, *U.S.A.* ... **81 K10** 30 23N 88 37W
Paşcani, *Romania* ........ **17 E14** 47 14N 26 45 E
Pasco, *U.S.A.* ........... **82 C4** 46 14N 119 6W
Pasco, Cerro de, *Peru* ..... **92 F3** 10 45S 76 10W
Pasco I., *Australia* ....... **60 D2** 20 57S 115 20 E
Pascoag, *U.S.A.* ......... **79 E13** 41 57N 71 42W
Pascua, I. de, *Pac. Oc.* .... **65 K17** 27 0S 109 0W
Pasfield L., *Canada* ...... **73 B7** 58 24N 105 20W
Pashiwari, *Pakistan* ...... **43 B6** 34 40N 75 10 E
Pashmakli = Smolyan,
*Bulgaria* ............... **21 D11** 41 36N 24 38 E
Pasir Mas, *Malaysia* ...... **39 J4** 6 2N 102 8 E
Pasir Putih, *Malaysia* ..... **39 K4** 5 50N 102 24 E
Pasirian, *Indonesia* ...... **37 H15** 8 13S 113 8 E
Pasirkuning, *Indonesia* .... **36 E2** 0 30S 104 33 E
Paskūh, *Iran* ............ **45 E9** 27 34N 61 39 E
Pasley, C., *Australia* ..... **61 F3** 33 52S 123 35 E
Pašman, *Croatia* ......... **16 G8** 43 58N 15 20 E
Pasni, *Pakistan* ......... **40 G3** 25 15N 63 27 E
Paso Cantinela, *Mexico* ... **85 N11** 32 33N 115 47W
Paso de Indios, *Argentina* . **96 E3** 43 55S 69 0W
Paso de los Libres,
*Argentina* .............. **94 B4** 29 44S 57 10W
Paso de los Toros, *Uruguay* **94 C4** 32 45S 56 30W
Paso Robles, *U.S.A.* ...... **83 J3** 35 38N 120 41W
Paspébiac, *Canada* ....... **71 C6** 48 3N 65 17W
Pasrur, *Pakistan* ......... **42 C6** 32 16N 74 43 E
Passage West, *Ireland* .... **13 E3** 51 52N 8 21W
Passaic, *U.S.A.* .......... **79 F10** 40 51N 74 7W
Passau, *Germany* ........ **16 D7** 48 34N 13 28 E
Passero, C., *Italy* ........ **20 F6** 36 41N 15 10 E
Passo Fundo, *Brazil* ...... **95 B5** 28 10S 52 20W
Passos, *Brazil* ........... **93 H9** 20 45S 46 37W
Pastavy, *Belarus* ......... **9 J22** 55 4N 26 50 E
Pastaza →, *Peru* ....... **92 D3** 4 50S 76 52W
Pasto, *Colombia* ......... **92 C3** 1 13N 77 17W
Pasuruan, *Indonesia* ..... **37 G15** 7 40S 112 44 E
**Patagonia**, *Argentina* .... **96 F3** 45 0S 69 0W
Patagonia, *U.S.A.* ........ **83 L8** 31 33N 110 45W
Patambar, *Iran* .......... **45 D9** 29 45N 60 17 E
Patan, *India* ............ **40 H8** 23 54N 72 14 E
Patan, *Maharashtra, India* . **42 H5** 23 54N 72 14 E
Patan, *Nepal* ............ **41 F14** 27 40N 85 20 E
Patani, *Indonesia* ........ **37 D7** 0 20N 128 50 E
Pataudi, *India* ........... **42 E7** 28 18N 76 48 E
Patchewollock, *Australia* .. **63 F3** 35 22S 142 12 E
Patchogue, *U.S.A.* ....... **79 F11** 40 46N 73 1W
Patea, *N.Z.* ............. **59 H5** 39 45S 174 30 E
Patensie, *S. Africa* ....... **56 E3** 33 46S 24 49 E
Paternò, *Italy* ........... **20 F6** 37 34N 14 54 E
Pateros, *U.S.A.* ......... **82 B4** 48 3N 119 54W
Paterson, *U.S.A.* ........ **79 F10** 40 55N 74 11W
Paterson Ra., *Australia* ... **60 D3** 21 45S 122 10 E
Pathankot, *India* ......... **42 C6** 32 18N 75 45 E
Pathfinder Reservoir, *U.S.A.* **82 E10** 42 28N 106 51W
Pathiu, *Thailand* ......... **39 G2** 10 42N 99 19 E
Pathum Thani, *Thailand* ... **38 E3** 14 1N 100 32 E
Pati, *Indonesia* .......... **37 G14** 6 45S 111 1 E
Patía →, *Colombia* ...... **92 C3** 2 13N 78 40W
Patiala, *India* ........... **42 D7** 30 23N 76 26 E
Patiala, *India* ........... **43 F8** 27 43N 79 1 E
Patkai Bum, *India* ....... **41 F19** 27 0N 95 30 E
Pátmos, *Greece* ......... **21 F12** 37 21N 26 36 E
Patna, *India* ............ **43 G11** 25 35N 85 12 E
Pato Branco, *Brazil* ...... **95 B5** 26 13S 52 40W
Patonga, *Uganda* ........ **54 B3** 2 45N 33 15 E
Patos, *Brazil* ............ **93 E11** 6 55S 37 16W
Patos, L. dos, *Brazil* ...... **95 C5** 31 20S 51 0W
Patos, Río de los →,
*Argentina* .............. **94 C2** 31 18S 69 25W
Patos de Minas, *Brazil* .... **93 G9** 18 35S 46 32W
Patquía, *Argentina* ....... **94 C2** 30 2S 66 55W
Pátrai, *Greece* .......... **21 E9** 38 14N 21 47 E
Pátraikós Kólpos, *Greece* .. **21 E9** 38 17N 21 30 E
Patras = Pátrai, *Greece* ... **21 E9** 38 14N 21 47 E
Patrocínio, *Brazil* ........ **93 G9** 18 57S 47 0W
Patta, *Kenya* ............ **54 C5** 2 10S 41 0 E
Pattani, *Thailand* ........ **39 J3** 6 48N 101 15 E
Pattaya, *Thailand* ........ **36 B2** 12 52N 100 55 E
Patten, *U.S.A.* .......... **77 C11** 46 0N 68 38W
Patterson, *Calif., U.S.A.* ... **84 H5** 37 28N 121 8W
Patterson, *La., U.S.A.* ..... **81 L9** 29 42N 91 18W
Patterson, Mt., *U.S.A.* ..... **84 G7** 38 29N 119 20W
Patti, *Punjab, India* ....... **42 D6** 31 17N 74 54 E
Patti, *Ut. P., India* ....... **43 G10** 25 55N 82 12 E
Pattoki, *Pakistan* ........ **42 D5** 31 5N 73 52 E
Patton, *U.S.A.* .......... **78 F6** 40 38N 78 39W
Patuakhali, *Bangla.* ...... **41 H17** 22 20N 90 25 E
Patuanak, *Canada* ....... **73 B7** 55 55N 107 43W
Patuca →, *Honduras* .... **88 C3** 15 50N 84 18W
Patuca, Punta, *Honduras* .. **88 C3** 15 49N 84 14W
Pátzcuaro, *Mexico* ....... **86 D4** 19 30N 101 40W
Pau, *France* ............ **18 E3** 43 19N 0 25W
Pauk, *Burma* ............ **41 J19** 21 27N 94 30 E
Paul I., *Canada* .......... **71 A7** 56 30N 61 20W
Paul Smiths, *U.S.A.* ...... **79 B10** 44 26N 74 15W
Paulatuk, *Canada* ....... **68 B7** 69 25N 124 0W
Paulis = Isiro,
*Dem. Rep. of the Congo* . **54 B2** 2 53N 27 40 E
Paulistana, *Brazil* ........ **93 E10** 8 9S 41 9W
Paulo Afonso, *Brazil* ..... **93 E11** 9 21S 38 15W
Paulpietersburg, *S. Africa* . **57 D5** 27 23S 30 50 E
Pauls Valley, *U.S.A.* ...... **81 H6** 34 44N 97 13W
Pauma Valley, *U.S.A.* ..... **85 M10** 33 16N 116 58W
Pauri, *India* ............. **43 D8** 30 9N 78 47 E
Pāveh, *Iran* ............. **44 C5** 35 3N 46 22 E
Pavia, *Italy* ............. **18 D8** 45 7N 9 8 E
Pavilion, *U.S.A.* ......... **78 D6** 42 52N 78 1W
Pāvilosta, *Latvia* ......... **9 H19** 56 53N 21 14 E
Pavlodar, *Kazakstan* ..... **26 D8** 52 33N 77 0 E
Pavlograd = Pavlohrad,
*Ukraine* ................ **25 E6** 48 30N 35 52 E
Pavlohrad, *Ukraine* ...... **25 E6** 48 30N 35 52 E
Pavlovo, *Russia* ......... **24 C7** 55 58N 43 5 E
Pavlovsk, *Russia* ........ **25 D7** 50 26N 40 5 E
Pavlovskaya, *Russia* ..... **25 E6** 46 17N 39 47 E
Pawayan, *India* .......... **43 E9** 28 4N 80 6 E
Pawhuska, *U.S.A.* ........ **81 G6** 36 40N 96 20W
Pawling, *U.S.A.* .......... **79 E11** 41 34N 73 36W
Pawnee, *U.S.A.* .......... **81 G6** 36 20N 96 48W
Pawnee City, *U.S.A.* ...... **80 E6** 40 7N 96 9W
Pawtucket, *U.S.A.* ....... **79 E13** 41 53N 71 23W
Paximádhia, *Greece* ...... **23 E6** 35 0N 24 35 E
Paxoí, *Greece* ........... **21 E9** 39 14N 20 12 E
Paxton, *Ill., U.S.A.* ....... **76 E1** 40 27N 88 6W
Paxton, *Nebr., U.S.A.* ..... **80 E4** 41 7N 101 21W
Payakumbuh, *Indonesia* ... **36 E2** 0 20S 100 35 E
Payette, *U.S.A.* ......... **82 D5** 44 5N 116 56W
Payne Bay = Kangirsuk,
*Canada* ................ **69 C13** 60 0N 70 0W
Payne L., *Canada* ........ **69 C12** 59 30N 74 30W
Paynes Find, *Australia* .... **61 E2** 29 15S 117 42 E
Paynesville, *U.S.A.* ....... **80 C7** 45 23N 94 43W
Paysandú, *Uruguay* ...... **94 C4** 32 19S 58 8W
Payson, *Ariz., U.S.A.* ..... **83 J8** 34 14N 111 20W
Payson, *Utah, U.S.A.* ..... **74 B4** 40 3N 111 44W
Paz →, *Guatemala* ...... **88 D1** 13 44N 90 10W
Paz, B. la, *Mexico* ........ **86 C2** 24 15N 110 25W
Pāzanān, *Iran* ........... **45 D6** 30 35N 49 59 E
Pazardzhik, *Bulgaria* ..... **21 C11** 42 12N 24 20 E
Pe Ell, *U.S.A.* ........... **84 D3** 46 34N 123 18W
Peabody, *U.S.A.* ......... **79 D14** 42 31N 70 56W
Peace →, *Canada* ....... **72 B6** 59 0N 111 25W
Peace Point, *Canada* ..... **72 B6** 59 7N 112 27W
Peace River, *Canada* ..... **72 B5** 56 15N 117 18W
Peach Springs, *U.S.A.* .... **83 J7** 35 32N 113 25W
Peachland, *Canada* ...... **72 D5** 49 47N 119 45W
Peachtree City, *U.S.A.* .... **77 J3** 33 25N 84 35W
Peak, The = Kinder Scout,
*U.K.* ................... **10 D6** 53 24N 1 52W
**Peak District**, *U.K.* ...... **10 D6** 53 10N 1 50W
Peak Hill, *N.S.W., Australia* **63 E4** 32 47S 148 11 E
Peak Hill, *W. Austral.,*
*Australia* ............... **61 E2** 25 35S 118 43 E
Peak Ra., *Australia* ...... **62 C4** 22 50S 148 20 E
Peake Cr. →, *Australia* .. **63 D2** 28 2S 136 7 E
Peale, Mt., *U.S.A.* ....... **83 G9** 38 26N 109 14W
Pearblossom, *U.S.A.* ..... **85 L9** 34 30N 117 55W
Pearl →, *U.S.A.* ........ **81 K10** 30 11N 89 32W
Pearl City, *U.S.A.* ....... **74 H16** 21 24N 157 59W
Pearl Harbor, *U.S.A.* ..... **74 H16** 21 21N 157 57W
Pearl River, *U.S.A.* ...... **79 E10** 41 4N 74 2W
Pearsall, *U.S.A.* ......... **81 L5** 28 54N 99 6W
Peary Land, *Greenland* ... **4 A6** 82 40N 33 0W
Pease →, *U.S.A.* ....... **81 H5** 34 12N 99 2W
Peawanuck, *Canada* ...... **69 C11** 55 15N 85 12W
Pebane, *Mozam.* ......... **55 F4** 17 10S 38 8 E
Pebas, *Peru* ............. **92 D4** 3 10S 71 46W
Pebble Beach, *U.S.A.* ..... **84 J5** 36 34N 121 57W
Peć, *Yugoslavia* ......... **21 C9** 42 40N 20 17 E
Pechenga, *Russia* ........ **24 A5** 69 29N 31 4 E
Pechenizhyn, *Ukraine* .... **17 D13** 48 30N 24 48 E
Pechiguera, Pta., *Canary Is.* **22 F6** 28 51N 13 53W
Pechora, *Russia* ......... **24 A10** 65 10N 57 11 E
Pechora →, *Russia* ...... **24 A9** 68 13N 54 15 E
Pechorskaya Guba, *Russia* . **24 A9** 68 40N 54 0 E
Pečory, *Russia* .......... **9 H22** 57 48N 27 40 E
Pecos, *U.S.A.* ........... **81 K3** 31 26N 103 30W
Pecos →, *U.S.A.* ....... **81 L3** 29 42N 101 22W
Pécs, *Hungary* .......... **17 E10** 46 5N 18 15 E
Pedder, L., *Australia* ..... **62 G4** 42 55S 146 10 E
Peddie, *S. Africa* ........ **57 E4** 33 14S 27 7 E
Pédernales, *Dom. Rep.* ... **89 C5** 18 2N 71 44W
Pedieos →, *Cyprus* ..... **23 D12** 35 10N 33 54 E
Pedirka, *Australia* ....... **63 D2** 26 40S 135 14 E
Pedra Azul, *Brazil* ....... **93 G10** 16 2S 41 17W
Pedreiras, *Brazil* ........ **93 D10** 4 32S 44 40W
Pedro Afonso, *Brazil* ..... **93 E9** 9 0S 48 10W
Pedro Cays, *Jamaica* ..... **88 C4** 17 5N 77 48W
Pedro de Valdivia, *Chile* ... **94 A2** 22 55S 69 38W
Pedro Juan Caballero,
*Paraguay* .............. **95 A4** 22 30S 55 40W
Pee Dee →, *U.S.A.* ..... **77 J6** 33 22N 79 16W
Peebinga, *Australia* ...... **63 E3** 34 52S 140 57 E
Peebles, *U.K.* ............ **12 F5** 55 40N 3 11W
Peekskill, *U.S.A.* ......... **79 E11** 41 17N 73 55W
Peel, *U.K.* ............... **10 C3** 54 13N 4 40W
Peel →, *Australia* ...... **63 E5** 30 50S 150 29 E
Peel →, *Canada* ........ **68 B6** 67 0N 135 0W
Peel Sound, *Canada* ...... **68 A10** 73 0N 96 0W
Peera Peera Poolanna L.,
*Australia* ............... **63 D2** 26 30S 138 0 E
Peerless Lake, *Canada* .... **72 B6** 56 37N 114 40W
Peers, *Canada* ........... **72 C5** 53 40N 116 0W
Pegasus Bay, *N.Z.* ........ **59 K4** 43 20S 173 10 E
Pegu, *Burma* ............ **41 L20** 17 20N 96 29 E
Pegu Yoma, *Burma* ....... **41 K20** 19 0N 96 0 E
Pehuajó, *Argentina* ....... **94 D3** 35 45S 62 0W
Pei Xian = Pizhou, *China* .. **34 G9** 34 44N 116 55 E
Peine, *Chile* ............. **94 A2** 23 45S 68 8W
Peine, *Germany* ......... **16 B6** 52 19N 10 14 E
Peip'ing = Beijing, *China* .. **34 E9** 39 55N 116 20 E
Peipus, L. = Chudskoye,
Ozero, *Russia* ........... **9 G22** 58 13N 27 30 E
Peixe, *Brazil* ............ **93 F9** 12 0S 48 40W
Peixe →, *Brazil* ......... **93 H8** 21 31S 51 58W
Pekalongan, *Indonesia* .... **37 G13** 6 53S 109 40 E
Pekan, *Malaysia* ......... **39 L4** 3 30N 103 25 E
Pekanbaru, *Indonesia* .... **36 D2** 0 30N 101 15 E
Pekin, *U.S.A.* ........... **80 E10** 40 35N 89 40W
**Peking** = Beijing, *China* .. **34 E9** 39 55N 116 20 E
Pelabuhan Kelang, *Malaysia* **39 L3** 3 0N 101 23 E
Pelabuhan Ratu, Teluk,
*Indonesia* .............. **37 G12** 7 5S 106 30 E
Pelabuhanratu, *Indonesia* . **37 G12** 7 0S 106 32 E
Pelagie, Is., *Italy* ......... **20 G5** 35 39N 12 33 E
Pelaihari, *Indonesia* ...... **36 E4** 3 55S 114 45 E
Peleaga, Vf., *Romania* .... **17 F12** 45 22N 22 55 E
Pelée, Mt., *Martinique* .... **89 D7** 14 48N 61 10W
Pelee, Pt., *Canada* ....... **70 D3** 41 54N 82 31W
Pelee I., *Canada* ......... **78 E2** 41 47N 82 40W
Pelekech, *Kenya* ......... **54 B4** 3 52N 35 8 E
Peleng, *Indonesia* ....... **37 E6** 1 20S 123 30 E
Pelican, *U.S.A.* ......... **72 B1** 57 58N 136 14W
Pelican L., *Canada* ...... **73 C8** 52 28N 100 20W
Pelican Narrows, *Canada* .. **73 B8** 55 10N 102 56W
Pelješac, *Croatia* ........ **20 C7** 42 55N 17 25 E
Pelkosenniemi, *Finland* .... **8 C22** 67 6N 27 28 E
Pella, *S. Africa* .......... **56 D2** 29 1S 19 6 E
Pella, *U.S.A.* ............ **80 E8** 41 25N 92 55W
Pello, *Finland* ........... **8 C21** 66 47N 23 59 E
Pelly →, *Canada* ....... **68 B6** 62 47N 137 19W
Pelly Bay, *Canada* ....... **69 B11** 68 38N 89 50W
Peloponnese =
Pelopónnisos □, *Greece* . **21 F10** 37 10N 22 0 E
**Pelopónnisos** □, *Greece* . **21 F10** 37 10N 22 0 E
Pelorus Sd., *N.Z.* ........ **59 J4** 40 59S 173 59 E
Pelotas, *Brazil* .......... **95 C5** 31 42S 52 23W
Pelotas →, *Brazil* ....... **95 B5** 27 28S 51 55W
Pelvoux, Massif du, *France* **18 D7** 44 52N 6 20 E
Pemalang, *Indonesia* ..... **37 G13** 6 53S 109 23 E
Pemanggil, Pulau, *Malaysia* **39 L5** 2 37N 104 21 E
Pematangsiantar, *Indonesia* **36 D1** 2 57N 99 5 E
Pemba, *Mozam.* .......... **55 E5** 12 58S 40 30 E
Pemba, *Zambia* .......... **55 F2** 16 30S 27 28 E
Pemba Channel, *Tanzania* . **54 D4** 5 0S 39 37 E
Pemba I., *Tanzania* ...... **54 D4** 5 0S 39 45 E
Pemberton, *Australia* ..... **61 F2** 34 30S 116 0 E
Pemberton, *Canada* ...... **72 C4** 50 25N 122 50W
Pembina, *U.S.A.* ......... **80 A6** 48 58N 97 15W
Pembroke, *Canada* ....... **70 C4** 45 50N 77 7W
Pembroke, *U.K.* .......... **11 F3** 51 41N 4 55W
Pembrokeshire □, *U.K.* .... **11 F3** 51 52N 4 56W
Pen-y-Ghent, *U.K.* ....... **10 C5** 54 10N 2 14W
**Penang** = Pinang, *Malaysia* **39 K3** 5 25N 100 15 E
Penápolis, *Brazil* ........ **95 A6** 21 30S 50 0W
Peñarroya-Pueblonuevo,
*Spain* .................. **19 C3** 38 19N 5 16W
Penarth, *U.K.* ........... **11 F4** 51 26N 3 11W
Peñas, C. de, *Spain* ...... **19 A3** 43 42N 5 52W
Penas, G. de, *Chile* ...... **96 F2** 47 0S 75 0W
Peñas del Chache,
*Canary Is.* .............. **22 E6** 29 6N 13 33W
Pench'i = Benxi, *China* .... **35 D12** 41 20N 123 48 E
Pend Oreille →, *U.S.A.* ... **82 B5** 49 4N 117 37W
Pend Oreille, L., *U.S.A.* ... **82 C5** 48 10N 116 21W
Pendembu, *S. Leone* ..... **50 G3** 9 7N 11 14W
Pender B., *Australia* ..... **60 C3** 16 45S 122 42 E
Pendleton, *U.S.A.* ........ **82 D4** 45 40N 118 47W
Pendra, *India* ............ **43 H9** 22 46N 81 57 E
Penedo, *Brazil* ........... **93 F11** 10 15S 36 36W
Penetanguishene, *Canada* . **78 B5** 44 50N 79 55W
Penfield, *U.S.A.* ......... **78 E6** 41 13N 78 35W
Pengalengan, *Indonesia* ... **37 G12** 7 9S 107 30 E
Penge, *Kasai-Or.,*
*Dem. Rep. of the Congo* . **54 D1** 5 30S 24 33 E
Penge, *Sud-Kivu,*
*Dem. Rep. of the Congo* . **54 C2** 4 27S 28 25 E
Penglai, *China* .......... **35 F11** 37 48N 120 42 E
Penguin, *Australia* ....... **62 G4** 41 8S 146 6 E
Penhalonga, *Zimbabwe* .... **55 F3** 18 52S 32 40 E
Peniche, *Portugal* ........ **19 C1** 39 19N 9 22W
Penicuik, *U.K.* .......... **12 F5** 55 50N 3 13W
Penida, *Indonesia* ....... **36 F5** 8 45S 115 30 E
Peninsular Malaysia □,
*Malaysia* ............... **39 L4** 4 0N 102 0 E
Penitente, Serra do, *Brazil* . **93 E9** 8 45S 46 20W
Penkridge, *U.K.* ......... **10 E5** 52 44N 2 6W
Penmarch, Pte. de, *France* . **18 C1** 47 48N 4 22W
Penn Hills, *U.S.A.* ........ **78 F5** 40 28N 79 52W
Penn Yan, *U.S.A.* ........ **78 D7** 42 40N 77 3W
Pennant, *Canada* ........ **73 C7** 50 32N 108 14W
Penner →, *India* ........ **40 M12** 14 35N 80 10 E
**Pennines**, *U.K.* ......... **10 C5** 54 45N 2 27W
Pennington, *U.S.A.* ....... **84 F5** 39 15N 121 47W
Pennsburg, *U.S.A.* ....... **79 F9** 40 23N 75 29W
**Pennsylvania** □, *U.S.A.* ... **76 E7** 40 45N 77 30W
Penny, *Canada* .......... **72 C4** 53 51N 121 20W
Penobscot →, *U.S.A.* ... **77 C11** 44 30N 68 48W
Penobscot B., *U.S.A.* ..... **77 C11** 44 35N 68 50W
Penola, *Australia* ........ **63 F3** 37 25S 140 48 E
Penong, *Australia* ....... **61 F5** 31 56S 133 1 E

Piura, *Peru* **92 E2** 5 15S 80 38W
Pixley, *U.S.A.* **84 K7** 35 58N 119 18W
Pizhou, *China* **34 G9** 34 44N 116 55 E
Placentia, *Canada* **71 C9** 47 20N 54 0W
Placentia B., *Canada* **71 C9** 47 0N 54 40W
Placerville, *U.S.A.* **84 G6** 38 44N 120 48W
Placetas, *Cuba* **88 B4** 22 15N 79 44W
Plainfield, *N.J., U.S.A.* **79 F10** 40 37N 74 25W
Plainfield, *Ohio, U.S.A.* **78 F3** 40 13N 81 43W
Plainfield, *Vt., U.S.A.* **79 B12** 44 17N 72 26W
Plains, *Mont., U.S.A.* **82 C6** 47 28N 114 53W
Plains, *Tex., U.S.A.* **81 J3** 33 11N 102 50W
Plainview, *Nebr., U.S.A.* **80 D6** 42 21N 97 47W
Plainview, *Tex., U.S.A.* **81 H4** 34 11N 101 43W
Plainwell, *U.S.A.* **76 D3** 42 27N 85 38W
Plaistow, *U.S.A.* **79 D13** 42 50N 71 6W
Pláka, Ákra, *Greece* **23 D8** 35 11N 26 19 E
Plana Cays, *Bahamas* **89 B5** 22 38N 73 30W
Planada, *U.S.A.* **84 H6** 37 16N 120 19W
Plano, *U.S.A.* **81 J6** 33 1N 96 42W
Plant City, *U.S.A.* **77 M4** 28 1N 82 7W
Plaquemine, *U.S.A.* **81 K9** 30 17N 91 14W
Plasencia, *Spain* **19 B2** 40 3N 6 8W
Plaster City, *U.S.A.* **85 N11** 32 47N 115 51W
Plaster Rock, *Canada* **71 C6** 46 53N 67 22W
Plastun, *Russia* **30 B8** 44 45N 136 19 E
**Plata, Río de la**, *S. Amer.* **94 C4** 34 45S 57 30W
Plátani →, *Italy* **20 F5** 37 23N 13 16 E
Plátanos, *Greece* **23 D5** 35 28N 23 33 E
Platte, *U.S.A.* **80 D5** 43 23N 98 51W
Platte →, *Mo., U.S.A.* **75 C8** 39 16N 94 50W
Platte →, *Nebr., U.S.A.* **80 E7** 41 4N 95 53W
Platteville, *U.S.A.* **80 D9** 42 44N 90 29W
Plattsburgh, *U.S.A.* **79 B11** 44 42N 73 28W
Plattsmouth, *U.S.A.* **80 E7** 41 1N 95 53W
Plauen, *Germany* **16 C7** 50 30N 12 8 E
Plavinas, *Latvia* **9 H21** 56 35N 25 46 E
Playa Blanca, *Canary Is.* **22 F6** 28 55N 13 37W
Playa Blanca Sur, *Canary Is.* **22 F6** 28 51N 13 50W
Playa de las Americas, *Canary Is.* **22 F3** 28 5N 16 43W
Playa de Mogán, *Canary Is.* **22 G4** 27 48N 15 47W
Playa del Inglés, *Canary Is.* **22 G4** 27 45N 15 33W
Playa Esmerelda, *Canary Is.* **22 F5** 28 8N 14 16W
Playgreen L., *Canada* **73 C9** 54 0N 98 15W
Pleasant Bay, *Canada* **71 C7** 46 51N 60 48W
Pleasant Hill, *U.S.A.* **84 H4** 37 57N 122 4W
Pleasant Mount, *U.S.A.* **79 E9** 41 44N 75 26W
Pleasanton, *Calif., U.S.A.* **84 H5** 37 39N 121 52W
Pleasanton, *Tex., U.S.A.* **81 L5** 28 58N 98 29W
Pleasantville, *N.J., U.S.A.* **76 F8** 39 24N 74 32W
Pleasantville, *Pa., U.S.A.* **78 E5** 41 35N 79 34W
Plei Ku, *Vietnam* **38 F7** 13 57N 108 0 E
Plenty →, *Australia* **62 C2** 23 25S 136 31 E
Plenty, B. of, *N.Z.* **59 G6** 37 45S 177 0 E
Plentywood, *U.S.A.* **80 A2** 48 47N 104 34W
Plesetsk, *Russia* **24 B7** 62 43N 40 20 E
Plessisville, *Canada* **71 C5** 46 14N 71 47W
Plétipi, L., *Canada* **71 B5** 51 44N 70 6W
Pleven, *Bulgaria* **21 C11** 43 26N 24 37 E
Plevlja, *Montenegro, Yug.* **21 C8** 43 21N 19 21 E
Plevna, *Canada* **78 B8** 44 58N 76 59W
Płock, *Poland* **17 B10** 52 32N 19 40 E
Plöckenstein, *Germany* **16 D7** 48 46N 13 51 E
Ploieşti, *Romania* **17 F14** 44 57N 26 5 E
Plonge, Lac la, *Canada* **73 B7** 55 8N 107 20W
Plovdiv, *Bulgaria* **21 C11** 42 8N 24 44 E
Plum, *U.S.A.* **78 F5** 40 29N 79 47W
Plum I., *U.S.A.* **79 E12** 41 11N 72 12W
Plumas, *U.S.A.* **84 F7** 39 45N 120 4W
Plummer, *U.S.A.* **82 C5** 47 20N 116 53W
Plumtree, *Zimbabwe* **55 G2** 20 27S 27 55 E
Plungė, *Lithuania* **9 J19** 55 53N 21 59 E
**Plymouth**, *U.K.* **11 G3** 50 22N 4 10W
Plymouth, *Calif., U.S.A.* **84 G6** 38 29N 120 51W
Plymouth, *Ind., U.S.A.* **76 E2** 41 21N 86 19W
Plymouth, *Mass., U.S.A.* **79 E14** 41 57N 70 40W
Plymouth, *N.C., U.S.A.* **77 H7** 35 52N 76 43W
Plymouth, *N.H., U.S.A.* **79 C13** 43 46N 71 41W
Plymouth, *Pa., U.S.A.* **79 E9** 41 14N 75 57W
Plymouth, *Wis., U.S.A.* **76 D2** 43 45N 87 59W
Plynlimon = Pumlumon Fawr, *U.K.* **11 E4** 52 28N 3 46W
**Plzeň**, *Czech Rep.* **16 D7** 49 45N 13 22 E
**Po** →, *Italy* **20 B5** 44 57N 12 4 E
Po Hai = Bo Hai, *China* **35 E10** 39 0N 119 0 E
Pobeda, *Russia* **27 C15** 65 12N 146 12 E
Pobedy, Pik, *Kyrgyzstan* **26 E8** 42 0N 79 58 E
Pocahontas, *Ark., U.S.A.* **81 G9** 36 16N 90 58W
Pocahontas, *Iowa, U.S.A.* **80 D7** 42 44N 94 40W
Pocatello, *U.S.A.* **82 E7** 42 52N 112 27W
Pochutla, *Mexico* **87 D5** 15 50N 96 31W
Pocito Casas, *Mexico* **86 B2** 28 32N 111 6W
Pocomoke City, *U.S.A.* **76 F8** 38 5N 75 34W
Poços de Caldas, *Brazil* **95 A6** 21 50S 46 33W
Podgorica, *Montenegro, Yug.* **21 C8** 42 30N 19 19 E
Podilska Vysochyna, *Ukraine* **17 D14** 49 0N 28 0 E
Podolsk, *Russia* **24 C6** 55 25N 37 30 E
Podporozhye, *Russia* **24 B5** 60 55N 34 2 E
Pofadder, *S. Africa* **56 D2** 29 10S 19 22 E
Pogranitšnyi, *Russia* **30 B5** 44 25N 131 24 E
Poh, *Indonesia* **37 E6** 0 46S 122 51 E
P'ohang, *S. Korea* **35 F15** 36 1N 129 23 E
Pohjanmaa, *Finland* **8 E20** 62 58N 22 50 E
Pohnpei, *Micronesia* **64 G7** 6 55N 158 10 E
Pohri, *India* **42 G6** 25 32N 77 22 E
Poinsett, C., *Antarctica* **5 C8** 65 42S 113 18 E
Point Arena, *U.S.A.* **84 G3** 38 55N 123 41W
Point Baker, *U.S.A.* **72 B2** 56 21N 133 37W
Point Edward, *Canada* **70 D3** 43 0N 82 30W
Point Hope, *U.S.A.* **68 B3** 68 21N 166 47W
Point L., *Canada* **68 B8** 65 15N 113 4W
Point Pedro, *Sri Lanka* **40 Q12** 9 50N 80 15 E
Point Pleasant, *N.J., U.S.A.* **79 F10** 40 5N 74 4W
Point Pleasant, *W. Va., U.S.A.* **76 F4** 38 51N 82 8W
Pointe-à-Pitre, *Guadeloupe* **89 C7** 16 10N 61 30W
Pointe-Claire, *Canada* **79 A11** 45 26N 73 50W
Pointe-Gatineau, *Canada* **79 A9** 45 28N 75 42W
Pointe-Noire, *Congo* **52 E2** 4 48S 11 53 E
Poisonbush Ra., *Australia* **60 D3** 22 30S 121 30 E
Poissonnier Pt., *Australia* **60 C2** 19 57S 119 10 E
**Poitiers**, *France* **18 C4** 46 35N 0 20 E
Poitou, *France* **18 C3** 46 40N 0 10W
Pojoaque, *U.S.A.* **83 J11** 35 54N 106 1W
Pokaran, *India* **40 F7** 27 0N 71 50 E
Pokataroo, *Australia* **63 D4** 29 30S 148 36 E
Pokhara, *Nepal* **43 E10** 28 14N 83 58 E
Poko, *Dem. Rep. of the Congo* **54 B2** 3 7N 26 52 E
Pokrovsk = Engels, *Russia* **25 D8** 51 28N 46 6 E
Pokrovsk, *Russia* **27 C13** 61 29N 129 0 E
Pola = Pula, *Croatia* **16 F7** 44 54N 13 57 E
Polacca, *U.S.A.* **83 J8** 35 50N 110 23W
Polan, *Iran* **45 E9** 25 30N 61 10 E
**Poland** ■, *Europe* **17 C10** 52 0N 20 0 E
Polar Bear Prov. Park, *Canada* **70 A2** 55 0N 83 45W
Polatsk, *Belarus* **24 C4** 55 30N 28 50 E
Polcura, *Chile* **94 D1** 37 17S 71 43W
Polessk, *Russia* **9 J19** 54 50N 21 8 E
Polesye = Pripet Marshes, *Europe* **17 B15** 52 10N 28 10 E
Polevskoy, *Russia* **24 C11** 56 26N 60 11 E
Pŏlgyo-ri, *S. Korea* **35 G14** 34 51N 127 21 E
Police, *Poland* **16 B8** 53 33N 14 33 E
Polillo Is., *Phil.* **37 B6** 14 56N 122 0 E
Polis, *Cyprus* **23 D11** 35 2N 32 26 E
Políyiros, *Greece* **21 D10** 40 23N 23 25 E
Polk, *U.S.A.* **78 E5** 41 22N 79 56W
Pollachi, *India* **40 P10** 10 35N 77 0 E
Pollença, *Spain* **22 B10** 39 54N 3 1 E
Pollença, B. de, *Spain* **22 B10** 39 53N 3 8 E
Polnovat, *Russia* **26 C7** 63 50N 65 54 E
Polonne, *Ukraine* **17 C14** 50 6N 27 30 E
Polonnoye = Polonne, *Ukraine* **17 C14** 50 6N 27 30 E
Polson, *U.S.A.* **82 C6** 47 41N 114 9W
Poltava, *Ukraine* **25 E5** 49 35N 34 35 E
Põltsamaa, *Estonia* **9 G21** 58 41N 25 58 E
Polunochnoye, *Russia* **26 C7** 60 52N 60 25 E
Põlva, *Estonia* **9 G22** 58 3N 27 3 E
Polyarny, *Russia* **24 A5** 69 8N 33 20 E
**Polynesia**, *Pac. Oc.* **65 J11** 10 0S 162 0W
Polynésie française = French Polynesia ■, *Pac. Oc.* **65 K13** 20 0S 145 0W
Pomaro, *Mexico* **86 D4** 18 20N 103 18W
Pombal, *Portugal* **19 C1** 39 55N 8 40W
Pómbia, *Greece* **23 E6** 35 0N 24 51 E
Pomeroy, *Ohio, U.S.A.* **76 F4** 39 2N 82 2W
Pomeroy, *Wash., U.S.A.* **82 C5** 46 28N 117 36W
Pomézia, *Italy* **20 D5** 41 40N 12 30 E
Pomona, *Australia* **63 D5** 26 22S 152 52 E
Pomona, *U.S.A.* **85 L9** 34 4N 117 45W
Pomorskie, Pojezierze, *Poland* **17 B9** 53 40N 16 37 E
Pomos, *Cyprus* **23 D11** 35 9N 32 33 E
Pomos, C., *Cyprus* **23 D11** 35 10N 32 33 E
Pompano Beach, *U.S.A.* **77 M5** 26 14N 80 8W
Pompeys Pillar, *U.S.A.* **82 D10** 45 59N 107 57W
Pompton Lakes, *U.S.A.* **79 F10** 41 0N 74 17W
Ponape = Pohnpei, *Micronesia* **64 G7** 6 55N 158 10 E
Ponask L., *Canada* **70 B1** 54 0N 92 41W
Ponca, *U.S.A.* **80 D6** 42 34N 96 43W
Ponca City, *U.S.A.* **81 G6** 36 42N 97 5W
Ponce, *Puerto Rico* **89 C6** 18 1N 66 37W
Ponchatoula, *U.S.A.* **81 K9** 30 26N 90 26W
Poncheville, L., *Canada* **70 B4** 50 10N 76 55W
Pond, *U.S.A.* **85 K7** 35 43N 119 20W
Pond Inlet, *Canada* **69 A12** 72 40N 77 0W
Pondicherry, *India* **40 P11** 11 59N 79 50 E
Ponds, I. of, *Canada* **71 B8** 53 27N 55 52W
Ponferrada, *Spain* **19 A2** 42 32N 6 35W
Ponnani, *India* **40 P9** 10 45N 75 59 E
Ponnyadaung, *Burma* **41 J19** 22 0N 94 10 E
Ponoka, *Canada* **72 C6** 52 42N 113 40W
Ponorogo, *Indonesia* **37 G14** 7 52S 111 27 E
Ponoy, *Russia* **24 A7** 67 0N 41 13 E
Ponoy →, *Russia* **24 A7** 66 59N 41 17 E
Ponta do Sol, *Madeira* **22 D2** 32 42N 17 7W
Ponta Grossa, *Brazil* **95 B5** 25 7S 50 10W
Ponta Pora, *Brazil* **95 A4** 22 20S 55 35W
Pontarlier, *France* **18 C7** 46 54N 6 20 E
Pontchartrain L., *U.S.A.* **81 K10** 30 5N 90 5W
Ponte do Pungué, *Mozam.* **55 F3** 19 30S 34 33 E
Ponte Nova, *Brazil* **95 A7** 20 25S 42 54W
Ponteix, *Canada* **73 D7** 49 46N 107 29W
Pontevedra, *Spain* **19 A1** 42 26N 8 40W
Pontiac, *Ill., U.S.A.* **80 E10** 40 53N 88 38W
Pontiac, *Mich., U.S.A.* **76 D4** 42 38N 83 18W
Pontian Kecil, *Malaysia* **39 M4** 1 29N 103 23 E
Pontianak, *Indonesia* **36 E3** 0 3S 109 15 E
Pontine Is. = Ponziane, Ísole, *Italy* **20 D5** 40 55N 12 57 E
Pontine Mts. = Kuzey Anadolu Dağlari, *Turkey* **25 F6** 41 30N 35 0 E
Pontivy, *France* **18 B2** 48 5N 2 58W
Pontoise, *France* **18 B5** 49 3N 2 5 E
Ponton →, *Canada* **72 B5** 58 27N 116 11W
Pontypool, *Canada* **78 B6** 44 6N 78 38W
Pontypool, *U.K.* **11 F4** 51 42N 3 2W
Ponziane, Ísole, *Italy* **20 D5** 40 55N 12 57 E
Poochera, *Australia* **63 E1** 32 43S 134 51 E
Poole, *U.K.* **11 G6** 50 43N 1 59W
Poole □, *U.K.* **11 G6** 50 43N 1 59W
Poona = Pune, *India* **40 K8** 18 29N 73 57 E
Pooncarie, *Australia* **63 E3** 33 22S 142 31 E
Poopelloe L., *Australia* **63 E3** 31 40S 144 0 E
Poopó, L. de, *Bolivia* **92 G5** 18 30S 67 35W
Popayán, *Colombia* **92 C3** 2 27N 76 36W
Poperinge, *Belgium* **15 D2** 50 51N 2 42 E
Popilta L., *Australia* **63 E3** 33 10S 141 42 E
Popio L., *Australia* **63 E3** 33 10S 141 52 E
Poplar, *U.S.A.* **80 A2** 48 7N 105 12W
Poplar →, *Canada* **73 C9** 53 0N 97 19W
Poplar Bluff, *U.S.A.* **81 G9** 36 46N 90 24W
Poplarville, *U.S.A.* **81 K10** 30 51N 89 32W
**Popocatépetl, Volcán**, *Mexico* **87 D5** 19 2N 98 38W
Popokabaka, *Dem. Rep. of the Congo* **52 F3** 5 41S 16 40 E
Poprad, *Slovak Rep.* **17 D11** 49 3N 20 18 E
Porali →, *Pakistan* **42 G2** 25 58N 66 26 E
Porbandar, *India* **40 J6** 21 44N 69 43 E
Porcher I., *Canada* **72 C2** 53 50N 130 30W
Porcupine →, *Canada* **73 B8** 59 11N 104 46W
Porcupine →, *U.S.A.* **68 B5** 66 34N 145 19W
Pordenone, *Italy* **20 B5** 45 57N 12 39 E
Pori, *Finland* **9 F19** 61 29N 21 48 E
Porlamar, *Venezuela* **92 A6** 10 57N 63 51W
Poronaysk, *Russia* **27 E15** 49 13N 143 0 E
Poroshiri-Dake, *Japan* **30 C11** 42 41N 142 52 E
Poroto Mts., *Tanzania* **55 D3** 9 0S 33 30 E
Porpoise B., *Antarctica* **5 C9** 66 0S 127 0 E
Porreres, *Spain* **22 B10** 39 31N 3 2 E
Porsangen, *Norway* **8 A21** 70 40N 25 40 E
Porsgrunn, *Norway* **9 G13** 59 10N 9 40 E
Port Alberni, *Canada* **72 D4** 49 14N 124 50W
Port Alfred, *S. Africa* **56 E4** 33 36S 26 55 E
Port Alice, *Canada* **72 C3** 50 20N 127 25W
Port Allegany, *U.S.A.* **78 E6** 41 48N 78 17W
Port Allen, *U.S.A.* **81 K9** 30 27N 91 12W
Port Alma, *Australia* **62 C5** 23 38S 150 53 E
Port Angeles, *U.S.A.* **84 B3** 48 7N 123 27W
Port Antonio, *Jamaica* **88 C4** 18 10N 76 30W
Port Aransas, *U.S.A.* **81 M6** 27 50N 97 4W
Port Arthur = Lüshun, *China* **35 E11** 38 45N 121 15 E
Port Arthur, *Australia* **62 G4** 43 7S 147 50 E
Port Arthur, *U.S.A.* **81 L8** 29 54N 93 56W
Port au Choix, *Canada* **71 B8** 50 43N 57 22W
Port au Port B., *Canada* **71 C8** 48 40N 58 50W
**Port-au-Prince**, *Haiti* **89 C5** 18 40N 72 20W
Port Augusta, *Australia* **63 E2** 32 30S 137 50 E
Port Austin, *U.S.A.* **78 B2** 44 3N 83 1W
Port Bell, *Uganda* **54 B3** 0 18N 32 35 E
Port Bergé Vaovao, *Madag.* **57 B8** 15 33S 47 40 E
Port Blandford, *Canada* **71 C9** 48 20N 54 10W
Port Bradshaw, *Australia* **62 A2** 12 30S 137 20 E
Port Broughton, *Australia* **63 E2** 33 37S 137 56 E
Port Burwell, *Canada* **78 D4** 42 40N 80 48W
Port Campbell, *Australia* **63 F3** 38 37S 143 1 E
Port Canning, *India* **43 H13** 22 23N 88 40 E
Port-Cartier, *Canada* **71 B6** 50 2N 66 50W
Port Chalmers, *N.Z.* **59 L3** 45 49S 170 30 E
Port Charlotte, *U.S.A.* **77 M4** 26 59N 82 6W
Port Chester, *U.S.A.* **79 F11** 41 0N 73 40W
Port Clements, *Canada* **72 C2** 53 40N 132 10W
Port Clinton, *U.S.A.* **76 E4** 41 31N 82 56W
Port Colborne, *Canada* **78 D5** 42 50N 79 10W
Port Coquitlam, *Canada* **72 D4** 49 15N 122 45W
Port Credit, *Canada* **78 C5** 43 33N 79 35W
Port Curtis, *Australia* **62 C5** 23 57S 151 20 E
Port d'Alcúdia, *Spain* **22 B10** 39 50N 3 7 E
Port Dalhousie, *Canada* **78 C5** 43 13N 79 16W
Port Darwin, *Australia* **60 B5** 12 24S 130 45 E
Port Darwin, *Falk. Is.* **96 G5** 51 50S 59 0W
Port Davey, *Australia* **62 G4** 43 16S 145 55 E
Port-de-Paix, *Haiti* **89 C5** 19 50N 72 50W
Port de Pollença, *Spain* **22 B10** 39 54N 3 4 E
Port de Sóller, *Spain* **22 B9** 39 48N 2 42 E
Port Dickson, *Malaysia* **39 L3** 2 30N 101 49 E
Port Douglas, *Australia* **62 B4** 16 30S 145 30 E
Port Dover, *Canada* **78 D4** 42 47N 80 12W
Port Edward, *Canada* **72 C2** 54 12N 130 10W
Port Elgin, *Canada* **78 B3** 44 25N 81 25W
Port Elizabeth, *S. Africa* **56 E4** 33 58S 25 40 E
Port Ellen, *U.K.* **12 F2** 55 38N 6 11W
Port Erin, *U.K.* **10 C3** 54 5N 4 45W
Port Essington, *Australia* **60 B5** 11 15S 132 10 E
Port Etienne = Nouâdhibou, *Mauritania* **50 D2** 20 54N 17 0W
Port Ewen, *U.S.A.* **79 E11** 41 54N 73 59W
Port Fairy, *Australia* **63 F3** 38 22S 142 12 E
Port Gamble, *U.S.A.* **84 C4** 47 51N 122 35W
Port-Gentil, *Gabon* **52 E1** 0 40S 8 50 E
Port Germein, *Australia* **63 E2** 33 1S 138 1 E
Port Gibson, *U.S.A.* **81 K9** 31 58N 90 59W
Port Glasgow, *U.K.* **12 F4** 55 56N 4 41W
Port Harcourt, *Nigeria* **50 H7** 4 40N 7 10 E
Port Hardy, *Canada* **72 C3** 50 41N 127 30W
Port Harrison = Inukjuak, *Canada* **69 C12** 58 25N 78 15W
Port Hawkesbury, *Canada* **71 C7** 45 36N 61 22W
Port Hedland, *Australia* **60 D2** 20 25S 118 35 E
Port Henry, *U.S.A.* **79 B11** 44 3N 73 28W
Port Hood, *Canada* **71 C7** 46 0N 61 32W
Port Hope, *Canada* **78 C6** 43 56N 78 20W
Port Hope, *U.S.A.* **78 C2** 43 57N 82 43W
Port Hope Simpson, *Canada* **71 B8** 52 33N 56 18W
Port Hueneme, *U.S.A.* **85 L7** 34 7N 119 12W
Port Huron, *U.S.A.* **78 D2** 42 58N 82 26W
Port Jefferson, *U.S.A.* **79 F11** 40 57N 73 3W
Port Jervis, *U.S.A.* **79 E10** 41 22N 74 41W
Port Kelang = Pelabuhan Kelang, *Malaysia* **39 L3** 3 0N 101 23 E
Port Kenny, *Australia* **63 E1** 33 10S 134 41 E
Port Lairge = Waterford, *Ireland* **13 D4** 52 15N 7 8W
Port Laoise, *Ireland* **13 C4** 53 2N 7 18W
Port Lavaca, *U.S.A.* **81 L6** 28 37N 96 38W
Port Leyden, *U.S.A.* **79 C9** 43 35N 75 21W
Port Lincoln, *Australia* **63 E2** 34 42S 135 52 E
Port Loko, *S. Leone* **50 G3** 8 48N 12 46W
**Port Louis**, *Mauritius* **49 H9** 20 10S 57 30 E
Port Lyautey = Kenitra, *Morocco* **50 B4** 34 15N 6 40W
Port MacDonnell, *Australia* **63 F3** 38 5S 140 48 E
Port McNeill, *Canada* **72 C3** 50 35N 127 6W
Port Macquarie, *Australia* **63 E5** 31 25S 152 25 E
Port Maria, *Jamaica* **88 C4** 18 25N 76 55W
Port Matilda, *U.S.A.* **78 F6** 40 48N 78 3W
Port Mellon, *Canada* **72 D4** 49 32N 123 31W
Port-Menier, *Canada* **71 C7** 49 51N 64 15W
Port Moody, *Canada* **84 A4** 49 17N 122 51W
Port Morant, *Jamaica* **88 C4** 17 54N 76 19W
**Port Moresby**, *Papua N. G.* **64 H6** 9 24S 147 8 E
Port Musgrave, *Australia* **62 A3** 11 55S 141 50 E
Port Neches, *U.S.A.* **81 L8** 30 0N 93 59W
Port Nolloth, *S. Africa* **56 D2** 29 17S 16 52 E
Port Nouveau-Québec = Kangiqsualujjuaq, *Canada* **69 C13** 58 30N 65 59W
**Port of Spain**, *Trin. & Tob.* **89 D7** 10 40N 61 31W
Port Orange, *U.S.A.* **77 L5** 29 9N 80 59W
Port Orchard, *U.S.A.* **84 C4** 47 32N 122 38W
Port Orford, *U.S.A.* **82 E1** 42 45N 124 30W
Port Pegasus, *N.Z.* **59 M1** 47 12S 167 41 E
Port Perry, *Canada* **78 B6** 44 6N 78 56W
Port Phillip B., *Australia* **63 F3** 38 10S 144 50 E
Port Pirie, *Australia* **63 E2** 33 10S 138 1 E
Port Radium = Echo Bay, *Canada* **68 B8** 66 5N 117 55W
Port Renfrew, *Canada* **72 D4** 48 30N 124 20W
Port Roper, *Australia* **62 A2** 14 45S 135 25 E
Port Rowan, *Canada* **78 D4** 42 40N 80 30W
Port Safaga = Bûr Safâga, *Egypt* **44 E2** 26 43N 33 57 E
**Port Said** = Bûr Sa'îd, *Egypt* **51 B12** 31 16N 32 18 E
Port St. Joe, *U.S.A.* **77 L3** 29 49N 85 18W
Port St. Johns, *S. Africa* **57 E4** 31 38S 29 33 E
Port St. Lucie, *U.S.A.* **77 M5** 27 20N 80 20W
Port Sanilac, *U.S.A.* **78 C2** 43 26N 82 33W
Port Severn, *Canada* **78 B5** 44 48N 79 43W
Port Shepstone, *S. Africa* **57 E5** 30 44S 30 28 E
Port Simpson, *Canada* **72 C2** 54 30N 130 20W
Port Stanley = Stanley, *Falk. Is.* **96 G5** 51 40S 59 51W
Port Stanley, *Canada* **78 D3** 42 40N 81 10W
Port Sudan = Bûr Sûdân, *Sudan* **51 E13** 19 32N 37 9 E
Port Sulphur, *U.S.A.* **81 L10** 29 29N 89 42W
Port Talbot, *U.K.* **11 F4** 51 35N 3 47W
Port Townsend, *U.S.A.* **84 B4** 48 7N 122 45W
Port-Vendres, *France* **18 E5** 42 32N 3 8 E
Port Vila, *Vanuatu* **64 J8** 17 45S 168 18 E
Port Vladimir, *Russia* **24 A5** 69 25N 33 6 E
Port Wakefield, *Australia* **63 E2** 34 12S 138 10 E
Port Washington, *U.S.A.* **76 D2** 43 23N 87 53W
Port Weld = Kuala Sepetang, *Malaysia* **39 K3** 4 49N 100 28 E
Porta Orientalis, *Romania* **17 F12** 45 6N 22 18 E
Portadown, *U.K.* **13 B5** 54 25N 6 27W
Portaferry, *U.K.* **13 B6** 54 23N 5 33W
Portage, *Pa., U.S.A.* **78 F6** 40 23N 78 41W
Portage, *Wis., U.S.A.* **80 D10** 43 33N 89 28W
Portage La Prairie, *Canada* **73 D9** 49 58N 98 18W
Portageville, *U.S.A.* **81 G10** 36 26N 89 42W
Portalegre, *Portugal* **19 C2** 39 19N 7 25W
Portales, *U.S.A.* **81 H3** 34 11N 103 20W
Portarlington, *Ireland* **13 C4** 53 9N 7 14W
Portbou, *Spain* **19 A7** 42 25N 3 9 E
Porter L., *N.W.T., Canada* **73 A7** 61 41N 108 5W
Porter L., *Sask., Canada* **73 B7** 56 20N 107 20W
Porterville, *S. Africa* **56 E2** 33 0S 19 0 E
Porterville, *U.S.A.* **84 J8** 36 4N 119 1W
Porthcawl, *U.K.* **11 F4** 51 29N 3 42W
Porthill, *U.S.A.* **82 B5** 48 59N 116 30W
Porthmadog, *U.K.* **10 E3** 52 55N 4 8W
Portile de Fier, *Europe* **17 F12** 44 44N 22 30 E
Portimão, *Portugal* **19 D1** 37 8N 8 32W
Portishead, *U.K.* **11 F5** 51 29N 2 46W
Portknockie, *U.K.* **12 D6** 57 42N 2 51W
Portland, *N.S.W., Australia* **63 E5** 33 20S 150 0 E
Portland, *Vic., Australia* **63 F3** 38 20S 141 35 E
Portland, *Canada* **79 B8** 44 42N 76 12W
Portland, *Conn., U.S.A.* **79 E12** 41 34N 72 38W
**Portland**, *Maine, U.S.A.* **69 D12** 43 39N 70 16W
Portland, *Mich., U.S.A.* **76 D3** 42 52N 84 54W
**Portland**, *Oreg., U.S.A.* **84 E4** 45 32N 122 37W
Portland, *Pa., U.S.A.* **79 F9** 40 55N 75 6W
Portland, *Tex., U.S.A.* **81 M6** 27 53N 97 20W
Portland, I. of, *U.K.* **11 G5** 50 33N 2 26W
Portland B., *Australia* **63 F3** 38 15S 141 45 E
Portland Bill, *U.K.* **11 G5** 50 31N 2 28W
Portland Canal, *U.S.A.* **72 B2** 55 56N 130 0W
Portmadoc = Porthmadog, *U.K.* **10 E3** 52 55N 4 8W
Porto, *Portugal* **19 B1** 41 8N 8 40W
Pôrto Alegre, *Brazil* **95 C5** 30 5S 51 10W
Porto Amboim = Gunza, *Angola* **52 G2** 10 50S 13 50 E
Porto Cristo, *Spain* **22 B10** 39 33N 3 20 E
Pôrto de Móz, *Brazil* **93 D8** 1 41S 52 13W
Porto Empédocle, *Italy* **20 F5** 37 17N 13 32 E
Pôrto Esperança, *Brazil* **92 G7** 19 37S 57 29W
Pôrto Franco, *Brazil* **93 E9** 6 20S 47 24W
Porto Mendes, *Brazil* **95 A5** 24 30S 54 15W
Porto Moniz, *Madeira* **22 D2** 32 52N 17 11W
Pôrto Murtinho, *Brazil* **92 H7** 21 45S 57 55W
Pôrto Nacional, *Brazil* **93 F9** 10 40S 48 30W
**Porto-Novo**, *Benin* **50 G6** 6 23N 2 42 E
Porto Petro, *Spain* **22 B10** 39 22N 3 13 E
Porto Santo, *Madeira* **50 B2** 33 45N 16 25W
Pôrto São José, *Brazil* **95 A5** 22 43S 53 10W
Pôrto Seguro, *Brazil* **93 G11** 16 26S 39 5W
Porto Tórres, *Italy* **20 D3** 40 50N 8 24 E
Pôrto União, *Brazil* **95 B5** 26 10S 51 10W
Pôrto Válter, *Brazil* **92 E4** 8 15S 72 40W
Porto-Vecchio, *France* **18 F8** 41 35N 9 16 E
Pôrto Velho, *Brazil* **92 E6** 8 46S 63 54W
Portobelo, *Panama* **88 E4** 9 35N 79 42W
Portoferráio, *Italy* **20 C4** 42 48N 10 20 E
Portola, *U.S.A.* **84 F6** 39 49N 120 28W
Portoscuso, *Italy* **20 E3** 39 12N 8 24 E
Portoviejo, *Ecuador* **92 D2** 1 7S 80 28W
Portpatrick, *U.K.* **12 G3** 54 51N 5 7W
Portree, *U.K.* **12 D2** 57 25N 6 12W
Portrush, *U.K.* **13 A5** 55 12N 6 40W
Portsmouth, *Domin.* **89 C7** 15 34N 61 27W
**Portsmouth**, *U.K.* **11 G6** 50 48N 1 6W
Portsmouth, *N.H., U.S.A.* **77 D10** 43 5N 70 45W
Portsmouth, *Ohio, U.S.A.* **76 F4** 38 44N 82 57W
Portsmouth, *R.I., U.S.A.* **79 E13** 41 36N 71 15W
**Portsmouth**, *Va., U.S.A.* **76 G7** 36 50N 76 18W
Portsmouth □, *U.K.* **11 G6** 50 48N 1 6W
Portsoy, *U.K.* **12 D6** 57 41N 2 41W
Portstewart, *U.K.* **13 A5** 55 11N 6 43W
Porttipahtan tekojärvi, *Finland* **8 B22** 68 5N 26 40 E
**Portugal** ■, *Europe* **19 C1** 40 0N 8 0W
Portumna, *Ireland* **13 C3** 53 6N 8 14W
Portville, *U.S.A.* **78 D6** 42 3N 78 20W
Porvenir, *Chile* **96 G2** 53 10S 70 16W
Porvoo, *Finland* **9 F21** 60 24N 25 40 E
Posadas, *Argentina* **95 B4** 27 30S 55 50W
Poshan = Boshan, *China* **35 F9** 36 28N 117 49 E
Posht-e-Badam, *Iran* **45 C7** 33 2N 55 23 E
Poso, *Indonesia* **37 E6** 1 20S 120 55 E
Posong, *S. Korea* **35 G14** 34 46N 127 5 E
Posse, *Brazil* **93 F9** 14 4S 46 18W
Possession I., *Antarctica* **5 D11** 72 4S 172 0 E
Possum Kingdom L., *U.S.A.* **81 J5** 32 52N 98 26W
Post, *U.S.A.* **81 J4** 33 12N 101 23W
Post Falls, *U.S.A.* **82 C5** 47 43N 116 57W
Postavy = Pastavy, *Belarus* **9 J22** 55 4N 26 50 E
Poste-de-la-Baleine = Kuujjuarapik, *Canada* **70 A4** 55 20N 77 35W
Postmasburg, *S. Africa* **56 D3** 28 18S 23 5 E
Postojna, *Slovenia* **16 F8** 45 46N 14 12 E
Poston, *U.S.A.* **85 M12** 34 0N 114 24W
Postville, *Canada* **71 B8** 54 54N 59 47W
Potchefstroom, *S. Africa* **56 D4** 26 41S 27 7 E

Poteau, U.S.A. 81 H7 35 3N 94 37W
Poteet, U.S.A. 81 L5 29 2N 98 35W
Potenza, Italy 20 D6 40 38N 15 48 E
Poteriteri, L., N.Z. 59 M1 46 5S 167 10 E
Potgietersrus, S. Africa 57 C4 24 10S 28 55 E
Poti, Georgia 25 F7 42 10N 41 38 E
Potiskum, Nigeria 51 F8 11 39N 11 2 E
**Potomac** →, U.S.A. 76 G7 38 0N 76 23W
Potosí, Bolivia 92 G5 19 38S 65 50W
Potosi Mt., U.S.A. 85 K11 35 57N 115 29W
Pototan, Phil. 37 B6 10 54N 122 38 E
Potrerillos, Chile 94 B2 26 30S 69 30W
**Potsdam**, Germany 16 B7 52 25N 13 4 E
Potsdam, U.S.A. 79 B10 44 40N 74 59W
Pottersville, U.S.A. 79 C11 43 43N 73 50W
Pottstown, U.S.A. 79 F9 40 15N 75 39W
Pottsville, U.S.A. 79 F8 40 41N 76 12W
Pottuvil, Sri Lanka 40 R12 6 55N 81 50 E
Pouce Coupé, Canada 72 B4 55 40N 120 10W
Poughkeepsie, U.S.A. 79 E11 41 42N 73 56W
Poulaphouca Res., Ireland 13 C5 53 8N 6 30W
Poulsbo, U.S.A. 84 C4 47 44N 122 39W
Poultney, U.S.A. 79 C11 43 31N 73 14W
Poulton-le-Fylde, U.K. 10 D5 53 51N 2 58W
Pouso Alegre, Brazil 95 A6 22 14S 45 57W
Pouthisat, Cambodia 38 F4 12 34N 103 50 E
Považská Bystrica, Slovak Rep. 17 D10 49 8N 18 27 E
Povenets, Russia 24 B5 62 50N 34 50 E
Poverty B., N.Z. 59 H7 38 43S 178 2 E
Póvoa de Varzim, Portugal 19 B1 41 25N 8 46W
Povungnituk = Puvirnituq, Canada 69 B12 60 2N 77 10W
Powassan, Canada 70 C4 46 5N 79 25W
Poway, U.S.A. 85 N9 32 58N 117 2W
Powder →, U.S.A. 80 B2 46 45N 105 26W
Powder River, U.S.A. 82 E10 43 2N 106 59W
Powell, U.S.A. 82 D9 44 45N 108 46W
Powell, L., U.S.A. 83 H8 36 57N 111 29W
Powell River, Canada 72 D4 49 50N 124 35W
Powers, U.S.A. 76 C2 45 41N 87 32W
**Powys** □, U.K. 11 E4 52 20N 3 20W
Poyang Hu, China 33 D6 29 5N 116 20 E
Poyarkovo, Russia 27 E13 49 36N 128 41 E
Poza Rica, Mexico 87 C5 20 33N 97 27W
Požarevac, Serbia, Yug. 21 B9 44 35N 21 18 E
**Poznań**, Poland 17 B9 52 25N 16 55 E
Pozo, U.S.A. 85 K6 35 20N 120 24W
Pozo Almonte, Chile 92 H5 20 10S 69 50W
Pozo Colorado, Paraguay 94 A4 23 30S 58 45W
Pozoblanco, Spain 19 C3 38 23N 4 51W
Pozzuoli, Italy 20 D6 40 49N 14 7 E
Prachin Buri, Thailand 38 F3 14 0N 101 25 E
Prachuap Khiri Khan, Thailand 39 G2 11 49N 99 48 E
Prado, Brazil 93 G11 17 20S 39 13W
**Prague** = Praha, Czech Rep. 16 C8 50 5N 14 22 E
Praha, Czech Rep. 16 C8 50 5N 14 22 E
Praia, C. Verde Is. 49 E1 14 55N 23 30W
Prainha, Amazonas, Brazil 92 E6 7 10S 60 30W
Prainha, Pará, Brazil 93 D8 1 45S 53 30W
Prairie, Australia 62 C3 20 50S 144 35 E
Prairie City, U.S.A. 82 D4 44 28N 118 43W
Prairie Dog Town Fork →, U.S.A. 81 H5 34 30N 99 23W
Prairie du Chien, U.S.A. 80 D9 43 3N 91 9W
Prairies, L. of the, Canada 73 C8 51 16N 101 32W
Pran Buri, Thailand 38 F2 12 23N 99 55 E
Prapat, Indonesia 36 D1 2 41N 98 58 E
Prasonísi, Ákra, Greece 23 D9 35 42N 27 46 E
Prata, Brazil 93 G9 19 25S 48 54W
Pratabpur, India 43 H10 23 28N 83 15 E
Pratapgarh, Raj., India 42 G6 24 2N 74 40 E
Pratapgarh, Ut. P., India 43 G9 25 56N 81 59 E
Prato, Italy 20 C4 43 53N 11 6 E
Pratt, U.S.A. 81 G5 37 39N 98 44W
Prattville, U.S.A. 77 J2 32 28N 86 29W
Pravia, Spain 19 A2 43 30N 6 12W
Praya, Indonesia 36 F5 8 39S 116 17 E
Precordillera, Argentina 94 C2 30 0S 69 1W
Preeceville, Canada 73 C8 51 57N 102 40W
Preiļi, Latvia 9 H22 56 18N 26 43 E
Premont, U.S.A. 81 M5 27 22N 98 7W
Prentice, U.S.A. 80 C9 45 33N 90 17W
Preobrazheniye, Russia 30 C6 42 54N 133 54 E
Preparis North Channel, Ind. Oc. 41 M18 15 12N 93 40 E
Preparis South Channel, Ind. Oc. 41 M18 14 36N 93 40 E
Přerov, Czech Rep. 17 D9 49 28N 17 27 E
Prescott, Canada 79 B9 44 45N 75 30W
Prescott, Ariz., U.S.A. 83 J7 34 33N 112 28W
Prescott, Ark., U.S.A. 81 J8 33 48N 93 23W
Prescott Valley, U.S.A. 83 J7 34 40N 112 18W
Preservation Inlet, N.Z. 59 M1 46 8S 166 35 E
Presho, U.S.A. 80 D4 43 54N 100 3W
Presidencia de la Plaza, Argentina 94 B4 27 0S 59 50W
Presidencia Roque Saenz Peña, Argentina 94 B3 26 45S 60 30W
Presidente Epitácio, Brazil 93 H8 21 56S 52 6W
Presidente Hayes □, Paraguay 94 A4 24 0S 59 0W
Presidente Prudente, Brazil 95 A5 22 5S 51 25W
Presidio, Mexico 86 B4 29 29N 104 23W
Presidio, U.S.A. 81 L2 29 34N 104 22W
Prešov, Slovak Rep. 17 D11 49 0N 21 15 E
Prespa, L. = Prespansko Jezero, Macedonia 21 D9 40 55N 21 0 E
Prespansko Jezero, Macedonia 21 D9 40 55N 21 0 E
Presque I., U.S.A. 78 D4 42 9N 80 6W
Presque Isle, U.S.A. 77 B12 46 41N 68 1W
Prestatyn, U.K. 10 D4 53 20N 3 24W
Presteigne, U.K. 11 E5 52 17N 3 0W
Preston, Canada 78 C4 43 23N 80 21W
Preston, U.K. 10 D5 53 46N 2 42W
Preston, Idaho, U.S.A. 82 E8 42 6N 111 53W
Preston, Minn., U.S.A. 80 D8 43 40N 92 5W
Preston, C., Australia 60 D2 20 51S 116 12 E
Prestonburg, U.S.A. 76 G4 37 39N 82 46W
Prestwick, U.K. 12 F4 55 29N 4 37W
**Pretoria**, S. Africa 57 D4 25 44S 28 12 E
Préveza, Greece 21 E9 38 57N 20 47 E
Prey Veng, Cambodia 39 G5 11 35N 105 29 E
Pribilof Is., U.S.A. 68 C2 57 0N 170 0W
Příbram, Czech Rep. 16 D8 49 41N 14 2 E
Price, U.S.A. 82 G8 39 36N 110 49W
Price I., Canada 72 C3 52 23N 128 41W
Prichard, U.S.A. 77 K1 30 44N 88 5W
Priekule, Latvia 9 H19 56 26N 21 35 E
Prienai, Lithuania 9 J20 54 38N 23 57 E
Prieska, S. Africa 56 D3 29 40S 22 42 E
Priest L., U.S.A. 82 B5 48 35N 116 52W
Priest River, U.S.A. 82 B5 48 10N 116 54W
Priest Valley, U.S.A. 84 J6 36 10N 120 39W
Prievidza, Slovak Rep. 17 D10 48 46N 18 36 E
Prikaspiyskaya Nizmennost = Caspian Depression, Eurasia 25 E8 47 0N 48 0 E
Prilep, Macedonia 21 D9 41 21N 21 32 E
Priluki = Pryluky, Ukraine 25 D5 50 30N 32 24 E
Prime Seal I., Australia 62 G4 40 3S 147 43 E
Primrose L., Canada 73 C7 54 55N 109 45W
Prince Albert, Canada 73 C7 53 15N 105 50W
Prince Albert, S. Africa 56 E3 33 12S 22 2 E
Prince Albert Mts., Antarctica 5 D11 76 0S 161 30 E
Prince Albert Nat. Park, Canada 73 C7 54 0N 106 25W
Prince Albert Pen., Canada 68 A8 72 30N 116 0W
Prince Albert Sd., Canada 68 A8 70 25N 115 0W
Prince Alfred, C., Canada 4 B1 74 20N 124 40W
Prince Charles I., Canada 69 B12 67 47N 76 12W
Prince Charles Mts., Antarctica 5 D6 72 0S 67 0 E
**Prince Edward I.** □, Canada 71 C7 46 20N 63 20W
Prince Edward Is., Ind. Oc. 3 G11 46 35S 38 0 E
Prince Edward Pt., Canada 78 C8 43 56N 76 52W
Prince George, Canada 72 C4 53 55N 122 50W
Prince of Wales, C., U.S.A. 66 C3 65 36N 168 5W
Prince of Wales I., Australia 62 A3 10 40S 142 10 E
Prince of Wales I., Canada 68 A10 73 0N 99 0W
Prince of Wales I., U.S.A. 68 C6 55 47N 132 50W
Prince Patrick I., Canada 4 B2 77 0N 120 0W
Prince Regent Inlet, Canada 4 B3 73 0N 90 0W
Prince Rupert, Canada 72 C2 54 20N 130 20W
Princess Charlotte B., Australia 62 A3 14 25S 144 0 E
Princess May Ranges, Australia 60 C4 15 30S 125 30 E
Princess Royal I., Canada 72 C3 53 0N 128 40W
Princeton, Canada 72 D4 49 27N 120 30W
Princeton, Calif., U.S.A. 84 F4 39 24N 122 1W
Princeton, Ill., U.S.A. 80 E10 41 23N 89 28W
Princeton, Ind., U.S.A. 76 F2 38 21N 87 34W
Princeton, Ky., U.S.A. 76 G2 37 7N 87 53W
Princeton, Mo., U.S.A. 80 E8 40 24N 93 35W
**Princeton**, N.J., U.S.A. 79 F10 40 21N 74 39W
Princeton, W. Va., U.S.A. 76 G5 37 22N 81 6W
Príncipe, I. de, Atl. Oc. 48 F4 1 37N 7 27 E
Principe da Beira, Brazil 92 F6 12 20S 64 30W
Prineville, U.S.A. 82 D3 44 18N 120 51W
Prins Harald Kyst, Antarctica 5 D4 70 0S 35 1 E
Prinsesse Astrid Kyst, Antarctica 5 D3 70 45S 12 30 E
Prinsesse Ragnhild Kyst, Antarctica 5 D4 70 15S 27 30 E
Prinzapolca, Nic. 88 D3 13 20N 83 35W
Priozersk, Russia 24 B5 61 2N 30 7 E
Pripet = Prypyat →, Europe 17 C16 51 20N 30 15 E
Pripet Marshes, Europe 17 B15 52 10N 28 10 E
Pripyat Marshes = Pripet Marshes, Europe 17 B15 52 10N 28 10 E
Pripyats = Prypyat →, Europe 17 C16 51 20N 30 15 E
Priština, Yugoslavia 21 C9 42 40N 21 13 E
Privas, France 18 D6 44 45N 4 37 E
Privolzhskaya Vozvyshennost, Russia 25 D8 51 0N 46 0 E
Prizren, Yugoslavia 21 C9 42 13N 20 45 E
Probolinggo, Indonesia 37 G15 7 46S 113 13 E
Proctor, U.S.A. 79 C11 43 40N 73 2W
Proddatur, India 40 M11 14 45N 78 30 E
Prodhromos, Cyprus 23 E11 34 57N 32 50 E
Profítis Ilías, Greece 23 C9 36 17N 27 56 E
Profondeville, Belgium 15 D4 50 23N 4 52 E
Progreso, Mexico 87 C7 21 20N 89 40W
Progreso, Yucatán, Mexico 86 B4 21 17N 89 40W
Prokopyevsk, Russia 26 D9 54 0N 86 45 E
Prokuplje, Serbia, Yug. 21 C9 43 16N 21 36 E
Prome = Pyè, Burma 41 K19 18 49N 95 13 E
Prophet →, Canada 72 B4 58 48N 122 40W
Prophet River, Canada 72 B4 58 6N 122 43W
Propriá, Brazil 93 F11 10 13S 36 51W
Proserpine, Australia 62 C4 20 21S 148 36 E
Prosna →, Poland 17 B9 52 6N 17 44 E
Prospect, U.S.A. 79 C9 43 18N 75 9W
Prosser, U.S.A. 82 C4 46 12N 119 46W
Prostějov, Czech Rep. 17 D9 49 30N 17 9 E
Proston, Australia 63 D5 26 8S 151 32 E
**Provence**, France 18 E6 43 40N 5 46 E
Providence, Ky., U.S.A. 76 G2 37 24N 87 46W
**Providence**, R.I., U.S.A. 79 E13 41 49N 71 24W
Providence Bay, Canada 70 C3 45 41N 82 15W
Providence Mts., U.S.A. 85 K11 35 10N 115 15W
Providencia, I. de, Colombia 88 D3 13 25N 81 26W
Provideniya, Russia 27 C19 64 23N 173 18W
Provins, France 18 B5 48 33N 3 15 E
Provo, U.S.A. 82 F8 40 14N 111 39W
Provost, Canada 73 C6 52 25N 110 20W
Prudhoe Bay, U.S.A. 68 A5 70 18N 148 22W
Prudhoe I., Australia 62 C4 21 19S 149 41 E
Prud'homme, Canada 73 C7 52 20N 105 54W
Pruszków, Poland 17 B11 52 9N 20 49 E
Prut →, Romania 17 F15 45 28N 28 10 E
Pruzhany, Belarus 17 B13 52 33N 24 28 E
Prydz B., Antarctica 5 C6 69 0S 74 0 E
Pryluky, Ukraine 25 D5 50 30N 32 24 E
Pryor, U.S.A. 81 G7 36 19N 95 19W
Prypyat →, Europe 17 C16 51 20N 30 15 E
Przemyśl, Poland 17 D12 49 50N 22 45 E
Przhevalsk, Kyrgyzstan 26 E8 42 30N 78 20 E
Psará, Greece 21 E11 38 37N 25 38 E
Psíra, Greece 23 D7 35 12N 25 52 E
Pskov, Russia 24 C4 57 50N 28 25 E
Pskovskoye, Ozero, Russia 9 H22 58 0N 27 58 E
Ptich = Ptsich →, Belarus 17 B15 52 9N 28 52 E
Ptolemaís, Greece 21 D9 40 30N 21 43 E
Ptsich →, Belarus 17 B15 52 9N 28 52 E
Pu Xian, China 34 F6 36 24N 111 6 E
Pua, Thailand 38 C3 19 11N 100 55 E
Puán, Argentina 94 D3 37 30S 62 45W
Puan, S. Korea 35 G14 35 44N 126 44 E
Pucallpa, Peru 92 E4 8 25S 74 30W
Pudasjärvi, Finland 8 D22 65 23N 26 53 E
Pudozh, Russia 24 B6 61 48N 36 32 E
Pudukkottai, India 40 P11 10 28N 78 47 E
Puebla, Mexico 87 D5 19 3N 98 12W
Puebla □, Mexico 87 D5 18 30N 98 0W
Pueblo, U.S.A. 80 F2 38 16N 104 37W
Pueblo Hundido, Chile 94 B1 26 20S 70 5W
Puelches, Argentina 94 D2 38 5S 65 51W
Puelén, Argentina 94 D2 37 32S 67 38W
Puente Alto, Chile 94 C1 33 32S 70 35W
Puente-Genil, Spain 19 D3 37 22N 4 47W
Puerco →, U.S.A. 83 J10 34 22N 107 50W
Puerto, Canary Is. 22 F2 28 5N 17 20W
Puerto Aisén, Chile 96 F2 45 27S 73 0W
Puerto Ángel, Mexico 87 D5 15 40N 96 29W
Puerto Arista, Mexico 87 D6 15 56N 93 48W
Puerto Armuelles, Panama 88 E3 8 20N 82 51W
Puerto Ayacucho, Venezuela 92 B5 5 40N 67 35W
Puerto Barrios, Guatemala 88 C2 15 40N 88 32W
Puerto Bermejo, Argentina 94 B4 26 55S 58 34W
Puerto Bermúdez, Peru 92 F4 10 20S 74 58W
Puerto Bolívar, Ecuador 92 D3 3 19S 79 55W
Puerto Cabello, Venezuela 92 A5 10 28N 68 1W
Puerto Cabezas, Nic. 88 D3 14 0N 83 30W
Puerto Cabo Gracias á Dios, Nic. 88 D3 15 0N 83 10W
Puerto Carreño, Colombia 92 B5 6 12N 67 22W
Puerto Castilla, Honduras 88 C2 16 0N 86 0W
Puerto Chicama, Peru 92 E3 7 45S 79 20W
Puerto Coig, Argentina 96 G3 50 54S 69 15W
Puerto Cortés, Costa Rica 88 E3 8 55N 84 0W
Puerto Cortés, Honduras 88 C2 15 51N 88 0W
Puerto Cumarebo, Venezuela 92 A5 11 29N 69 30W
Puerto de Alcudia = Port d'Alcúdia, Spain 22 B10 39 50N 3 7 E
Puerto de Andraitx, Spain 22 B9 39 32N 2 23 E
Puerto de Cabrera, Spain 22 B9 39 8N 2 56 E
Puerto de Gran Tarajal, Canary Is. 22 F5 28 13N 14 1W
Puerto de la Cruz, Canary Is. 22 F3 28 24N 16 32W
Puerto de Pozo Negro, Canary Is. 22 F6 28 19N 13 55W
Puerto de Sóller = Port de Sóller, Spain 22 B9 39 48N 2 42 E
Puerto del Carmen, Canary Is. 22 F6 28 55N 13 38W
Puerto del Rosario, Canary Is. 22 F6 28 30N 13 52W
Puerto Deseado, Argentina 96 F3 47 55S 66 0W
Puerto Escondido, Mexico 87 D5 15 50N 97 3W
Puerto Heath, Bolivia 92 F5 12 34S 68 39W
Puerto Inírida, Colombia 92 C5 3 53N 67 52W
Puerto Juárez, Mexico 87 C7 21 11N 86 49W
Puerto La Cruz, Venezuela 92 A6 10 13N 64 38W
Puerto Leguízamo, Colombia 92 D4 0 12S 74 46W
Puerto Limón, Colombia 92 C4 3 23N 73 30W
Puerto Lobos, Argentina 96 E3 42 0S 65 3W
Puerto Madryn, Argentina 96 E3 42 48S 65 4W
Puerto Maldonado, Peru 92 F5 12 30S 69 10W
Puerto Manotí, Cuba 88 B4 21 22N 76 50W
Puerto Montt, Chile 96 E2 41 28S 73 0W
Puerto Morazán, Nic. 88 D2 12 51N 87 11W
Puerto Morelos, Mexico 87 C7 20 49N 86 52W
Puerto Natales, Chile 96 G2 51 45S 72 15W
Puerto Padre, Cuba 88 B4 21 13N 76 35W
Puerto Páez, Venezuela 92 B5 6 13N 67 28W
Puerto Peñasco, Mexico 86 A2 31 20N 113 33W
Puerto Pinasco, Paraguay 94 A4 22 36S 57 50W
Puerto Plata, Dom. Rep. 89 C5 19 48N 70 45W
Puerto Pollensa = Port de Pollença, Spain 22 B10 39 54N 3 4 E
Puerto Princesa, Phil. 37 C5 9 46N 118 45 E
Puerto Quepos, Costa Rica 88 E3 9 29N 84 6W
Puerto Rico, Canary Is. 22 G4 27 47N 15 42W
**Puerto Rico** ■, W. Indies 89 C6 18 15N 66 45W
Puerto Rico Trench, Atl. Oc. 89 C6 19 50N 66 0W
Puerto San Julián, Argentina 96 F3 49 18S 67 43W
Puerto Sastre, Paraguay 94 A4 22 2S 57 55W
Puerto Suárez, Bolivia 92 G7 18 58S 57 52W
Puerto Vallarta, Mexico 86 C3 20 36N 105 15W
Puerto Wilches, Colombia 92 B4 7 21N 73 54W
Puertollano, Spain 19 C3 38 43N 4 7W
Pueyrredón, L., Argentina 96 F2 47 20S 72 0W
Puffin I., Ireland 13 E1 51 50N 10 24W
Pugachev, Russia 24 D8 52 0N 48 49 E
Pugal, India 42 E5 28 30N 72 48 E
Puge, Tanzania 54 C3 4 45S 33 11 E
Puget Sound, U.S.A. 82 C2 47 50N 122 30W
Pugŏdong, N. Korea 35 C16 42 5N 130 0 E
Pugu, Tanzania 54 D4 6 55S 39 4 E
Pūgūnzī, Iran 45 E8 25 49N 59 10 E
Puig Major, Spain 22 B9 39 48N 2 47 E
Puigcerdà, Spain 19 A6 42 24N 1 50 E
Puigpunyent, Spain 22 B9 39 38N 2 32 E
Pujon-chŏsuji, N. Korea 35 D14 40 35N 127 35 E
Pukaki L., N.Z. 59 L3 44 4S 170 1 E
Pukapuka, Cook Is. 65 J11 10 53S 165 49W
Pukaskwa Nat. Park, Canada 70 C2 48 20N 86 0W
Pukatawagan, Canada 73 B8 55 45N 101 20W
Pukchin, N. Korea 35 D13 40 12N 125 45 E
Pukch'ŏng, N. Korea 35 D15 40 14N 128 10 E
Pukekohe, N.Z. 59 G5 37 12S 174 55 E
Pukhrayan, India 43 F8 26 14N 79 51 E
Pula, Croatia 16 F7 44 54N 13 57 E
Pulacayo, Bolivia 92 H5 20 25S 66 41W
Pulandian, China 35 E11 39 25N 121 58 E
Pularumpi, Australia 60 B5 11 24S 130 26 E
Pulaski, N.Y., U.S.A. 79 C8 43 34N 76 8W
Pulaski, Tenn., U.S.A. 77 H2 35 12N 87 2W
Pulaski, Va., U.S.A. 76 G5 37 3N 80 47W
Pulau →, Indonesia 37 F9 5 50S 138 15 E
Puławy, Poland 17 C11 51 23N 21 59 E
Pulga, U.S.A. 84 F5 39 48N 121 29W
Pulicat L., India 40 N12 13 40N 80 15 E
Pullman, U.S.A. 82 C5 46 44N 117 10W
Pulo-Anna, Pac. Oc. 37 D8 4 30N 132 5 E
Pulog, Phil. 37 A6 16 40N 120 50 E
Pułtusk, Poland 17 B11 52 43N 21 6 E
Pumlumon Fawr, U.K. 11 E4 52 28N 3 46W
Puná, I., Ecuador 92 D2 2 55S 80 5W
Punakha, Bhutan 41 F16 27 42N 89 52 E
Punasar, India 42 F5 27 6N 73 6 E
Punata, Bolivia 92 G5 17 32S 65 50W
Punch, India 43 C6 33 48N 74 4 E
Punch →, Pakistan 42 C5 33 12N 73 40 E
Pune, India 40 K8 18 29N 73 57 E
P'ungsan, N. Korea 35 D15 40 50N 128 9 E
Pungue, Ponte de, Mozam. 55 F3 19 0S 34 0 E
**Punjab** □, India 42 D7 31 0N 76 0 E
**Punjab** □, Pakistan 42 E6 32 0N 74 30 E
Puno, Peru 92 G4 15 55S 70 3W
Punpun →, India 43 G11 25 31N 85 18 E
Punta Alta, Argentina 96 D4 38 53S 62 4W
Punta Arenas, Chile 96 G2 53 10S 71 0W
Punta de Díaz, Chile 94 B1 28 0S 70 45W
Punta Gorda, Belize 87 D7 16 10N 88 45W
Punta Gorda, U.S.A. 77 M5 26 56N 82 3W
Punta Prieta, Mexico 86 B2 28 58N 114 17W
Punta Prima, Spain 22 B11 39 48N 4 16 E
Puntarenas, Costa Rica 88 E3 10 0N 84 50W
Punto Fijo, Venezuela 92 A4 11 50N 70 13W
Punxsatawney, U.S.A. 78 F6 40 57N 78 59W
Puquio, Peru 92 F4 14 45S 74 10W
Pur →, Russia 26 C8 67 31N 77 55 E
Purace, Vol., Colombia 92 C3 2 21N 76 23W
Puralia = Puruliya, India 43 H12 23 17N 86 24 E
Puranpur, India 43 E9 28 31N 80 9 E
Purbeck, Isle of, U.K. 11 G6 50 39N 1 59W
Purcell, U.S.A. 81 H6 35 1N 97 22W
Purcell Mts., Canada 72 D5 49 55N 116 15W
Puri, India 41 K14 19 50N 85 58 E
Purmerend, Neths. 15 B4 52 32N 4 58 E
Purnia, India 43 G12 25 45N 87 31 E
Pursat = Pouthisat, Cambodia 38 F4 12 34N 103 50 E
Purukcahu, Indonesia 36 E4 0 35S 114 35 E
Puruliya, India 43 H12 23 17N 86 24 E
Purus →, Brazil 92 D6 3 42S 61 28W
Purvis, U.S.A. 81 K10 31 9N 89 25W
Purwa, India 43 F9 26 28N 80 47 E
Purwakarta, Indonesia 37 G12 6 35S 107 29 E
Purwodadi, Indonesia 37 G14 7 7S 110 55 E
Purwokerto, Indonesia 37 G13 7 25S 109 14 E
Puryŏng, N. Korea 35 C15 42 5N 129 43 E
Pusa, India 43 G11 25 59N 85 41 E
**Pusan**, S. Korea 35 G15 35 5N 129 0 E
Pushkino, Russia 25 D8 51 16N 47 0 E
Putahow L., Canada 73 B8 59 54N 100 40W
Putao, Burma 41 F20 27 28N 97 30 E
Putaruru, N.Z. 59 H5 38 2S 175 50 E
Puthein Myit →, Burma 41 M19 15 56N 94 18 E
Putignano, Italy 20 D7 40 51N 17 7 E
Puting, Tanjung, Indonesia 36 E4 3 31S 111 46 E
Putnam, U.S.A. 79 E13 41 55N 71 55W
Putorana, Gory, Russia 27 C10 69 0N 95 0 E
Puttalam, Sri Lanka 40 Q11 8 1N 79 55 E
Puttgarden, Germany 16 A6 54 30N 11 10 E
Putumayo →, S. Amer. 92 D5 3 7S 67 58W
Putussibau, Indonesia 36 D4 0 50N 112 56 E
Puvirnituq, Canada 69 B12 60 2N 77 10W
Puy-de-Dôme, France 18 D5 45 46N 2 57 E
Puyallup, U.S.A. 84 C4 47 12N 122 18W
Puyang, China 34 G8 35 40N 115 1 E
Pūzeh Rīg, Iran 45 E8 27 20N 58 40 E
Pwani □, Tanzania 54 D4 7 0S 39 0 E
Pweto, Dem. Rep. of the Congo 55 D2 8 25S 28 51 E
Pwllheli, U.K. 10 E3 52 53N 4 25W
Pya-ozero, Russia 24 A5 66 5N 30 58 E
Pyapon, Burma 41 L19 16 20N 95 40 E
Pyasina →, Russia 27 B9 73 30N 87 0 E
Pyatigorsk, Russia 25 F7 44 2N 43 6 E
Pyè, Burma 41 K19 18 49N 95 13 E
Pyetrikaw, Belarus 17 B15 52 11N 28 29 E
Pyhäjoki, Finland 8 D21 64 28N 24 14 E
Pyinmana, Burma 41 K20 19 45N 96 12 E
Pyla, C., Cyprus 23 E12 34 56N 33 51 E
Pymatuning Reservoir, U.S.A. 78 E4 41 30N 80 28W
Pyŏktong, N. Korea 35 D13 40 50N 125 50 E
Pyŏnggang, N. Korea 35 E14 38 24N 127 17 E
P'yŏngt'aek, S. Korea 35 F14 37 1N 127 4 E
**P'yŏngyang**, N. Korea 35 E13 39 0N 125 30 E
Pyote, U.S.A. 81 K3 31 32N 103 8W
Pyramid L., U.S.A. 82 G4 40 1N 119 35W
Pyramid Pk., U.S.A. 85 J10 36 25N 116 37W
**Pyrénées**, Europe 18 E4 42 45N 0 18 E
Pyu, Burma 41 K20 18 30N 96 28 E


# Q


Qaanaaq = Thule, Greenland 4 B4 77 40N 69 0W
Qachasnek, S. Africa 57 E4 30 6S 28 42 E
Qa'el Jafr, Jordan 47 E5 30 20N 36 25 E
Qa'emābād, Iran 45 D9 31 44N 60 2 E
Qā'emshahr, Iran 45 B7 36 30N 52 53 E
Qagan Nur, China 34 C8 43 30N 114 55 E
Qahar Youyi Zhongqi, China 34 D7 41 12N 112 40 E
Qahremānshahr = Bākhtarān, Iran 44 C5 34 23N 47 0 E
Qaidam Pendi, China 32 C4 37 0N 95 0 E
Qajarīyeh, Iran 45 D6 31 1N 48 22 E
Qala, Ras il, Malta 23 C1 36 1N 14 20 E
Qala-i-Jadid = Spīn Búldak, Afghan. 42 D2 31 1N 66 25 E
Qala Viala, Pakistan 42 D2 30 49N 67 17 E
Qala Yangi, Afghan. 42 B2 34 20N 66 30 E
Qal'at al Akhḑar, Si. Arabia 44 E3 28 0N 37 10 E
Qal'at Dīzah, Iraq 44 B5 36 11N 45 7 E
Qal'at Şāliḩ, Iraq 44 D5 31 31N 47 16 E
Qal'at Sukkar, Iraq 44 D5 31 51N 46 5 E
Qal'eh Shaharak, Afghan. 40 B4 34 10N 64 20 E
Qamdo, China 32 C4 31 15N 97 6 E
Qamruddin Karez, Pakistan 42 D3 31 45N 68 20 E
Qandahār, Afghan. 40 D4 31 32N 65 30 E
Qandahār □, Afghan. 40 D4 31 0N 65 0 E
Qapān, Iran 45 B7 37 40N 55 47 E
Qapshaghay, Kazakstan 26 E8 43 51N 77 14 E
Qaqortoq = Julianehåb, Greenland 4 C5 60 43N 46 0W

Qara Qash →, *India* **43 B8** 35 0N 78 30 E
Qarabutaq, *Kazakstan* **26 E7** 49 59N 60 14 E
Qaraghandy, *Kazakstan* **26 E8** 49 50N 73 10 E
Qārah, *Si. Arabia* **44 D4** 29 55N 40 3 E
Qarataū, *Kazakstan* **26 E8** 43 10N 70 28 E
Qareh →, *Iran* **44 B5** 39 25N 47 22 E
Qareh Tekān, *Iran* **45 B6** 36 38N 49 29 E
Qarqan He →, *China* **32 C3** 39 30N 88 30 E
Qarqaraly, *Kazakstan* **26 E8** 49 26N 75 30 E
Qarshi, *Uzbekistan* **26 F7** 38 53N 65 48 E
Qartabā, *Lebanon* **47 A4** 34 4N 35 50 E
Qaryat al Gharab, *Iraq* **44 D5** 31 27N 44 48 E
Qaryat al 'Ulyā, *Si. Arabia* **44 E5** 27 33N 47 42 E
Qasr 'Amra, *Jordan* **44 D3** 31 48N 36 35 E
Qaşr-e Qand, *Iran* **45 E9** 26 15N 60 45 E
Qasr Farâfra, *Egypt* **51 C11** 27 0N 28 1 E
Qatanā, *Syria* **47 B5** 33 26N 36 4 E
**Qatar** ■, *Asia* **45 E6** 25 30N 51 15 E
Qatlīsh, *Iran* **45 B8** 37 50N 57 19 E
Qattâra, Munkhafed el, *Egypt* **51 C11** 29 30N 27 30 E
Qattâra Depression = Qattâra, Munkhafed el, *Egypt* **51 C11** 29 30N 27 30 E
Qawām al Ḩamzah, *Iraq* **44 D5** 31 43N 44 58 E
Qāyen, *Iran* **45 C8** 33 40N 59 10 E
Qazaqstan = Kazakstan ■, *Asia* **26 E8** 50 0N 70 0 E
Qazimämmäd, *Azerbaijan* **45 A6** 40 3N 49 0 E
Qazvin, *Iran* **45 B6** 36 15N 50 0 E
Qena, *Egypt* **51 C12** 26 10N 32 43 E
Qeqertarsuaq = Disko, *Greenland* **4 C5** 69 45N 53 30W
Qeqertarsuaq = Godhavn, *Greenland* **4 C5** 69 15N 53 38W
Qeshlāq, *Iran* **44 C5** 34 55N 46 28 E
Qeshm, *Iran* **45 E8** 26 55N 56 10 E
Qeys, *Iran* **45 E7** 26 32N 53 58 E
Qezel Owzen →, *Iran* **45 B6** 36 45N 49 22 E
Qezi'ot, *Israel* **47 E3** 30 52N 34 26 E
Qi Xian, *China* **34 G8** 34 40N 114 48 E
Qian Gorlos, *China* **35 B13** 45 5N 124 42 E
Qian Xian, *China* **34 G5** 34 31N 108 15 E
Qianyang, *China* **34 G4** 34 40N 107 8 E
Qibā', *Si. Arabia* **44 E5** 27 24N 44 20 E
Qikiqtarjuaq, *Canada* **69 B13** 67 33N 63 0W
Qila Safed, *Pakistan* **40 E2** 29 0N 61 30 E
Qila Saifullāh, *Pakistan* **42 D3** 30 45N 68 17 E
Qilian Shan, *China* **32 C4** 38 30N 96 0 E
Qin He →, *China* **34 G7** 35 1N 113 22 E
Qin Ling = Qinling Shandi, *China* **34 H5** 33 50N 108 10 E
Qin'an, *China* **34 G3** 34 48N 105 40 E
Qing Xian, *China* **34 E9** 38 35N 116 45 E
Qingcheng, *China* **35 F9** 37 15N 117 40 E
Qingdao, *China* **35 F11** 36 5N 120 20 E
Qingfeng, *China* **34 G8** 35 52N 115 8 E
**Qinghai** □, *China* **32 C4** 36 0N 98 0 E
Qinghai Hu, *China* **32 C5** 36 40N 100 10 E
Qinghecheng, *China* **35 D13** 41 28N 124 15 E
Qinghemen, *China* **35 D11** 41 48N 121 25 E
Qingjian, *China* **34 F6** 37 8N 110 8 E
Qingjiang = Huaiyin, *China* **35 H10** 33 30N 119 2 E
Qingshui, *China* **34 G4** 34 48N 106 8 E
Qingshuihe, *China* **34 E6** 39 55N 111 35 E
Qingtongxia Shuiku, *China* **34 F3** 37 50N 105 58 E
Qingxu, *China* **34 F7** 37 34N 112 22 E
Qingyang, *China* **34 F4** 36 2N 107 55 E
Qingyuan, *China* **35 C13** 42 10N 124 55 E
Qingyun, *China* **35 F9** 37 45N 117 20 E
Qinhuangdao, *China* **35 E10** 39 56N 119 30 E
Qinling Shandi, *China* **34 H5** 33 50N 108 10 E
Qinshui, *China* **34 G7** 35 40N 112 8 E
Qinyang = Jiyuan, *China* **34 G7** 35 7N 112 57 E
Qinyuan, *China* **34 F7** 36 29N 112 20 E
Qinzhou, *China* **32 D5** 21 58N 108 38 E
Qionghai, *China* **38 C8** 19 15N 110 26 E
Qiongzhou Haixia, *China* **38 B8** 20 10N 110 15 E
Qiqihar, *China* **27 E13** 47 26N 124 0 E
Qiraîya, W. →, *Egypt* **47 E3** 30 27N 34 0 E
Qiryat Ata, *Israel* **47 C4** 32 47N 35 6 E
Qiryat Gat, *Israel* **47 D3** 31 32N 34 46 E
Qiryat Mal'akhi, *Israel* **47 D3** 31 44N 34 44 E
Qiryat Shemona, *Israel* **47 B4** 33 13N 35 35 E
Qiryat Yam, *Israel* **47 C4** 32 51N 35 4 E
Qishan, *China* **34 G4** 34 25N 107 38 E
Qitai, *China* **32 B3** 44 2N 89 35 E
Qixia, *China* **35 F11** 37 17N 120 52 E
Qızılağac Körfäzi, *Azerbaijan* **45 B6** 39 9N 49 0 E
Qojūr, *Iran* **44 B5** 36 12N 47 55 E
**Qom**, *Iran* **45 C6** 34 40N 51 0 E
Qomolangma Feng = Everest, Mt., *Nepal* **43 E12** 28 5N 86 58 E
Qomsheh, *Iran* **45 D6** 32 0N 51 55 E
Qostanay, *Kazakstan* **26 D7** 53 10N 63 35 E
Quabbin Reservoir, *U.S.A.* **79 D12** 42 20N 72 20W
Quairading, *Australia* **61 F2** 32 0S 117 21 E
Quakertown, *U.S.A.* **79 F9** 40 26N 75 21W
Qualicum Beach, *Canada* **72 D4** 49 22N 124 26W
Quambatook, *Australia* **63 F3** 35 49S 143 34 E
Quambone, *Australia* **63 E4** 30 57S 147 53 E
Quamby, *Australia* **62 C3** 20 22S 140 17 E
Quan Long = Ca Mau, *Vietnam* **39 H5** 9 7N 105 8 E
Quanah, *U.S.A.* **81 H5** 34 18N 99 44W
Quang Ngai, *Vietnam* **38 E7** 15 13N 108 58 E
Quang Tri, *Vietnam* **38 D6** 16 45N 107 13 E
Quantock Hills, *U.K.* **11 F4** 51 8N 3 10W
Quanzhou, *China* **33 D6** 24 55N 118 34 E
Qu'Appelle, *Canada* **73 C8** 50 33N 103 53W
Quaqtaq, *Canada* **69 B13** 60 55N 69 40W
Quaraí, *Brazil* **94 C4** 30 15S 56 20W
Quartu Sant'Elena, *Italy* **20 E3** 39 15N 9 10 E
Quartzsite, *U.S.A.* **85 M12** 33 40N 114 13W
Quatsino Sd., *Canada* **72 C3** 50 25N 127 58W
Quba, *Azerbaijan* **25 F8** 41 21N 48 32 E
Qūchān, *Iran* **45 B8** 37 10N 58 27 E
Queanbeyan, *Australia* **63 F4** 35 17S 149 14 E
**Québec**, *Canada* **71 C5** 46 52N 71 13W
**Québec** □, *Canada* **71 C6** 48 0N 74 0W
Queen Alexandra Ra., *Antarctica* **5 E11** 85 0S 170 0 E
Queen Charlotte City, *Canada* **72 C2** 53 15N 132 2W
Queen Charlotte Is., *Canada* **72 C2** 53 20N 132 10W
Queen Charlotte Sd., *Canada* **72 C3** 51 0N 128 0W
Queen Charlotte Strait, *Canada* **72 C3** 50 45N 127 10W
Queen Elizabeth Is., *Canada* **66 B10** 76 0N 95 0W
Queen Elizabeth Nat. Park, *Uganda* **54 C3** 0 0 30 0 E
Queen Mary Land, *Antarctica* **5 D7** 70 0S 95 0 E
Queen Maud G., *Canada* **68 B9** 68 15N 102 30W
Queen Maud Land, *Antarctica* **5 D3** 72 30S 12 0 E
Queen Maud Mts., *Antarctica* **5 E13** 86 0S 160 0W
Queens Chan., *Australia* **60 C4** 15 0S 129 30 E
Queenscliff, *Australia* **63 F3** 38 16S 144 39 E
**Queensland** □, *Australia* **62 C3** 22 0S 142 0 E
Queenstown, *Australia* **62 G4** 42 4S 145 35 E
Queenstown, *N.Z.* **59 L2** 45 1S 168 40 E
Queenstown, *S. Africa* **56 E4** 31 52S 26 52 E
Queets, *U.S.A.* **84 C2** 47 32N 124 20W
Queguay Grande →, *Uruguay* **94 C4** 32 9S 58 9W
Queimadas, *Brazil* **93 F11** 11 0S 39 38W
Quelimane, *Mozam.* **55 F4** 17 53S 36 58 E
Quellón, *Chile* **96 E2** 43 7S 73 37W
Quelpart = Cheju do, *S. Korea* **35 H14** 33 29N 126 34 E
Quemado, *N. Mex., U.S.A.* **83 J9** 34 20N 108 30W
Quemado, *Tex., U.S.A.* **81 L4** 28 58N 100 35W
Quemú-Quemú, *Argentina* **94 D3** 36 3S 63 36W
Quequén, *Argentina* **94 D4** 38 30S 58 30W
Querétaro, *Mexico* **86 C4** 20 36N 100 23W
Querétaro □, *Mexico* **86 C5** 20 30N 100 0W
Queshan, *China* **34 H8** 32 55N 114 2 E
Quesnel, *Canada* **72 C4** 53 0N 122 30W
Quesnel →, *Canada* **72 C4** 52 58N 122 29W
Quesnel L., *Canada* **72 C4** 52 30N 121 20W
Questa, *U.S.A.* **83 H11** 36 42N 105 36W
Quetico Prov. Park, *Canada* **70 C1** 48 30N 91 45W
Quetta, *Pakistan* **42 D2** 30 15N 66 55 E
Quezaltenango, *Guatemala* **88 D1** 14 50N 91 30W
**Quezon City**, *Phil.* **37 B6** 14 38N 121 0 E
Qufār, *Si. Arabia* **44 E4** 27 26N 41 37 E
Qui Nhon, *Vietnam* **38 F7** 13 40N 109 13 E
Quibaxe, *Angola* **52 F2** 8 24S 14 27 E
Quibdo, *Colombia* **92 B3** 5 42N 76 40W
Quiberon, *France* **18 C2** 47 29N 3 9W
Quiet L., *Canada* **72 A2** 61 5N 133 5W
Quiindy, *Paraguay* **94 B4** 25 58S 57 14W
Quila, *Mexico* **86 C3** 24 23N 107 13W
Quilán, C., *Chile* **96 E2** 43 15S 74 30W
Quilcene, *U.S.A.* **84 C4** 47 49N 122 53W
Quilimarí, *Chile* **94 C1** 32 5S 71 30W
Quilino, *Argentina* **94 C3** 30 14S 64 29W
Quill Lakes, *Canada* **73 C8** 51 55N 104 13W
Quillabamba, *Peru* **92 F4** 12 50S 72 50W
Quillagua, *Chile* **94 A2** 21 40S 69 40W
Quillaicillo, *Chile* **94 C1** 31 17S 71 40W
Quillota, *Chile* **94 C1** 32 54S 71 16W
Quilmes, *Argentina* **94 C4** 34 43S 58 15W
Quilon, *India* **40 Q10** 8 50N 76 38 E
Quilpie, *Australia* **63 D3** 26 35S 144 11 E
Quilpué, *Chile* **94 C1** 33 5S 71 33W
Quilua, *Mozam.* **55 F4** 16 17S 39 54 E
Quimilí, *Argentina* **94 B3** 27 40S 62 30W
Quimper, *France* **18 B1** 48 0N 4 9W
Quimperlé, *France* **18 C2** 47 53N 3 33W
Quinault →, *U.S.A.* **84 C2** 47 21N 124 18W
Quincy, *Calif., U.S.A.* **84 F6** 39 56N 120 57W
Quincy, *Fla., U.S.A.* **77 K3** 30 35N 84 34W
Quincy, *Ill., U.S.A.* **80 F9** 39 56N 91 23W
Quincy, *Mass., U.S.A.* **79 D14** 42 15N 71 0W
Quincy, *Wash., U.S.A.* **82 C4** 47 22N 119 56W
Quines, *Argentina* **94 C2** 32 13S 65 48W
Quinga, *Mozam.* **55 F5** 15 49S 40 15 E
Quinns Rocks, *Australia* **61 F2** 31 40S 115 42 E
Quintana Roo □, *Mexico* **87 D7** 19 0N 88 0W
Quintanar de la Orden, *Spain* **19 C4** 39 36N 3 5W
Quintero, *Chile* **94 C1** 32 45S 71 30W
Quirihue, *Chile* **94 D1** 36 15S 72 35W
Quirindi, *Australia* **63 E5** 31 28S 150 40 E
Quirinópolis, *Brazil* **93 G8** 18 32S 50 30W
Quissanga, *Mozam.* **55 E5** 12 24S 40 28 E
Quitilipi, *Argentina* **94 B3** 26 50S 60 13W
Quitman, *U.S.A.* **77 K4** 30 47N 83 34W
**Quito**, *Ecuador* **92 D3** 0 15S 78 35W
Quixadá, *Brazil* **93 D11** 4 55S 39 0W
Quixaxe, *Mozam.* **55 F5** 15 17S 40 4 E
Qul'ân, Jazâ'ir, *Egypt* **44 E2** 24 22N 35 31 E
Qumbu, *S. Africa* **57 E4** 31 10S 28 48 E
Quneitra, *Syria* **47 B4** 33 7N 35 48 E
Qūnghirot, *Uzbekistan* **26 E6** 43 6N 58 54 E
Quoin I., *Australia* **60 B4** 14 54S 129 32 E
Quoin Pt., *S. Africa* **56 E2** 34 46S 19 37 E
Quorn, *Australia* **63 E2** 32 25S 138 5 E
Qŭqon, *Uzbekistan* **26 E8** 40 30N 70 57 E
Qurnat as Sawdā', *Lebanon* **47 A5** 34 18N 36 6 E
Quşaybā', *Si. Arabia* **44 E4** 26 53N 43 35 E
Qusaybah, *Iraq* **44 C4** 34 24N 40 59 E
Quseir, *Egypt* **44 E2** 26 7N 34 16 E
Qūshchī, *Iran* **44 B5** 37 59N 45 3 E
Quthing, *Lesotho* **57 E4** 30 25S 27 36 E
Qūţīābād, *Iran* **45 C6** 35 47N 48 30 E
Quwo, *China* **34 G6** 35 38N 111 25 E
Quyang, *China* **34 E8** 38 35N 114 40 E
Quynh Nhai, *Vietnam* **38 B4** 21 49N 103 33 E
Quyon, *Canada* **79 A8** 45 31N 76 14W
Quzhou, *China* **33 D6** 28 57N 118 54 E
Quzi, *China* **34 F4** 36 20N 107 20 E
Qyzylorda, *Kazakstan* **26 E7** 44 48N 65 28 E


## R


Ra, Ko, *Thailand* **39 H2** 9 13N 98 16 E
Raahe, *Finland* **8 D21** 64 40N 24 28 E
Raalte, *Neths.* **15 B6** 52 23N 6 16 E
Raasay, *U.K.* **12 D2** 57 25N 6 4W
Raasay, Sd. of, *U.K.* **12 D2** 57 30N 6 8W
Raba, *Indonesia* **37 F5** 8 36S 118 55 E
Rába →, *Hungary* **17 E9** 47 38N 17 38 E
Rabai, *Kenya* **54 C4** 3 50S 39 31 E
Rabat, *Malta* **23 D1** 35 53N 14 25 E
**Rabat**, *Morocco* **50 B4** 34 2N 6 48W
Rabaul, *Papua N. G.* **64 H7** 4 24S 152 18 E
Rābigh, *Si. Arabia* **46 C2** 22 50N 39 5 E
Râbniţa, *Moldova* **17 E15** 47 45N 29 0 E
Rābor, *Iran* **45 D8** 29 17N 56 55 E
Race, C., *Canada* **71 C9** 46 40N 53 5W
Rach Gia, *Vietnam* **39 G5** 10 5N 105 5 E
Rachid, *Mauritania* **50 E3** 18 48N 11 41W
Racibórz, *Poland* **17 C10** 50 7N 18 18 E
Racine, *U.S.A.* **76 D2** 42 41N 87 51W
Rackerby, *U.S.A.* **84 F5** 39 26N 121 22W
Radama, Nosy, *Madag.* **57 A8** 14 0S 47 47 E
Radama, Saikanosy, *Madag.* **57 A8** 14 16S 47 53 E
Rădăuţi, *Romania* **17 E13** 47 50N 25 59 E
Radcliff, *U.S.A.* **76 G3** 37 51N 85 57W
Radekhiv, *Ukraine* **17 C13** 50 25N 24 32 E
Radekhov = Radekhiv, *Ukraine* **17 C13** 50 25N 24 32 E
Radford, *U.S.A.* **76 G5** 37 8N 80 34W
Radhanpur, *India* **42 H4** 23 50N 71 38 E
Radhwa, Jabal, *Si. Arabia* **44 E3** 24 34N 38 18 E
Radisson, *Canada* **70 B4** 53 47N 77 37W
Radisson, *Sask., Canada* **73 C7** 52 30N 107 20W
Radium Hot Springs, *Canada* **72 C5** 50 35N 116 2W
Radnor Forest, *U.K.* **11 E4** 52 17N 3 10W
Radom, *Poland* **17 C11** 51 23N 21 12 E
Radomsko, *Poland* **17 C10** 51 5N 19 28 E
Radomyshl, *Ukraine* **17 C15** 50 30N 29 12 E
Radstock, C., *Australia* **63 E1** 33 12S 134 20 E
Radviliškis, *Lithuania* **9 J20** 55 49N 23 33 E
Radville, *Canada* **73 D8** 49 30N 104 15W
Rae, *Canada* **72 A5** 62 50N 116 3W
Rae Bareli, *India* **43 F9** 26 18N 81 20 E
Rae Isthmus, *Canada* **69 B11** 66 40N 87 30W
Raeren, *Belgium* **15 D6** 50 41N 6 7 E
Raeside, L., *Australia* **61 E3** 29 20S 122 0 E
Raetihi, *N.Z.* **59 H5** 39 25S 175 17 E
Rafaela, *Argentina* **94 C3** 31 10S 61 30W
Rafah, *Gaza Strip* **47 D3** 31 18N 34 14 E
Rafai, *C.A.R.* **54 B1** 4 59N 23 58 E
Rafḩā, *Si. Arabia* **44 D4** 29 35N 43 35 E
Rafsanjān, *Iran* **45 D8** 30 30N 56 5 E
Raft Pt., *Australia* **60 C3** 16 4S 124 26 E
Raga, *Sudan* **51 G11** 8 28N 25 41 E
Ragachow, *Belarus* **17 B16** 53 8N 30 5 E
Ragama, *Sri Lanka* **40 R11** 7 0N 79 50 E
Ragged, Mt., *Australia* **61 F3** 33 27S 123 25 E
Raghunathpalli, *India* **43 H11** 22 14N 84 48 E
Raghunathpur, *India* **43 H12** 23 33N 86 40 E
Raglan, *N.Z.* **59 G5** 37 55S 174 55 E
Ragusa, *Italy* **20 F6** 36 55N 14 44 E
Raha, *Indonesia* **37 E6** 4 55S 123 0 E
Rahaeng = Tak, *Thailand* **38 D2** 16 52N 99 8 E
Rahatgarh, *India* **43 H8** 23 47N 78 22 E
Raḩīmah, *Si. Arabia* **45 E6** 26 42N 50 4 E
Rahimyar Khan, *Pakistan* **42 E4** 28 30N 70 25 E
Rāhjerd, *Iran* **45 C6** 34 22N 50 22 E
Rahon, *India* **42 D7** 31 3N 76 7 E
Raichur, *India* **40 L10** 16 10N 77 20 E
Raiganj, *India* **43 G13** 25 37N 88 10 E
Raigarh, *India* **41 J13** 21 56N 83 25 E
Raijua, *Indonesia* **37 F6** 10 37S 121 36 E
Raikot, *India* **42 D6** 30 41N 75 42 E
Railton, *Australia* **62 G4** 41 25S 146 28 E
Rainbow Lake, *Canada* **72 B5** 58 30N 119 23W
Rainier, *U.S.A.* **84 D4** 46 53N 122 41W
**Rainier, Mt.**, *U.S.A.* **84 D5** 46 52N 121 46W
Rainy L., *Canada* **73 D10** 48 42N 93 10W
Rainy River, *Canada* **73 D10** 48 43N 94 29W
Raippaluoto, *Finland* **8 E19** 63 13N 21 14 E
Raipur, *India* **41 J12** 21 17N 81 45 E
Raisen, *India* **42 H8** 23 20N 77 48 E
Raisio, *Finland* **9 F20** 60 28N 22 11 E
Raj Nandgaon, *India* **41 J12** 21 5N 81 5 E
Raj Nilgiri, *India* **43 J12** 21 28N 86 46 E
Raja, Ujung, *Indonesia* **36 D1** 3 40N 96 25 E
Raja Ampat, Kepulauan, *Indonesia* **37 E8** 0 30S 130 0 E
Rajahmundry, *India* **41 L12** 17 1N 81 48 E
Rajang →, *Malaysia* **36 D4** 2 30N 112 0 E
Rajanpur, *Pakistan* **42 E4** 29 6N 70 19 E
Rajapalaiyam, *India* **40 Q10** 9 25N 77 35 E
**Rajasthan** □, *India* **42 F5** 26 45N 73 30 E
Rajasthan Canal, *India* **42 F5** 28 0N 72 0 E
Rajauri, *India* **43 C6** 33 25N 74 21 E
Rajgarh, *Mad. P., India* **42 G7** 24 2N 76 45 E
Rajgarh, *Raj., India* **42 F7** 27 14N 76 38 E
Rajgarh, *Raj., India* **42 E6** 28 40N 75 25 E
Rajgir, *India* **43 G11** 25 2N 85 25 E
Rajkot, *India* **42 H4** 22 15N 70 56 E
Rajmahal Hills, *India* **43 G12** 24 30N 87 30 E
Rajpipla, *India* **40 J8** 21 50N 73 30 E
Rajpur, *India* **42 H6** 22 18N 74 21 E
Rajpura, *India* **42 D7** 30 25N 76 32 E
Rajshahi, *Bangla.* **41 G16** 24 22N 88 39 E
Rajshahi □, *Bangla.* **43 G13** 25 0N 89 0 E
Rajula, *India* **42 J4** 21 3N 71 26 E
Rakaia, *N.Z.* **59 K4** 43 45S 172 1 E
Rakaia →, *N.Z.* **59 K4** 43 36S 172 15 E
Rakan, Ra's, *Qatar* **45 E6** 26 10N 51 20 E
Rakaposhi, *Pakistan* **43 A6** 36 10N 74 25 E
Rakata, Pulau, *Indonesia* **36 F3** 6 10S 105 20 E
Rakhiv, *Ukraine* **17 D13** 48 3N 24 12 E
Rakhni, *Pakistan* **42 D3** 30 4N 69 56 E
Rakhni →, *Pakistan* **42 E3** 29 31N 69 36 E
Rakitnoye, *Russia* **30 B7** 45 36N 134 17 E
Rakops, *Botswana* **56 C3** 21 1S 24 28 E
Rakvere, *Estonia* **9 G22** 59 20N 26 25 E
**Raleigh**, *U.S.A.* **77 H6** 35 47N 78 39W
Raleigh B., *U.S.A.* **75 D11** 34 50N 76 15W
Ralls, *U.S.A.* **81 J4** 33 41N 101 24W
Ralston, *U.S.A.* **78 E8** 41 30N 76 57W
Ram →, *Canada* **72 A4** 62 1N 123 41W
Rām Allāh, *West Bank* **47 D4** 31 55N 35 10 E
Ram Hd., *Australia* **63 F4** 37 47S 149 30 E
Rama, *Nic.* **88 D3** 12 9N 84 15W
Ramakona, *India* **43 J8** 21 43N 78 50 E
Raman, *Thailand* **39 J3** 6 29N 101 18 E
Ramanathapuram, *India* **40 Q11** 9 25N 78 55 E
Ramanetaka, B. de, *Madag.* **57 A8** 14 13S 47 52 E
Ramanujganj, *India* **43 H10** 23 48N 83 42 E
Ramat Gan, *Israel* **47 C3** 32 4N 34 48 E
Ramatlhabama, *S. Africa* **56 D4** 25 37S 25 33 E
Ramban, *India* **43 C6** 33 14N 75 12 E
Rambipuji, *Indonesia* **37 H15** 8 12S 113 37 E
Ramechhap, *Nepal* **43 F12** 27 25N 86 10 E
Ramganga →, *India* **43 F8** 27 5N 79 58 E
Ramgarh, *Bihar, India* **43 H11** 23 40N 85 35 E
Ramgarh, *Raj., India* **42 F6** 27 16N 75 14 E
Ramgarh, *Raj., India* **42 F4** 27 30N 70 36 E
Rāmhormoz, *Iran* **45 D6** 31 15N 49 35 E
Ramīān, *Iran* **45 B7** 37 3N 55 16 E
Ramingining, *Australia* **62 A2** 12 19S 135 3 E
Ramla, *Israel* **47 D3** 31 55N 34 52 E
Ramnad = Ramanathapuram, *India* **40 Q11** 9 25N 78 55 E
Ramnagar, *India* **43 E8** 29 24N 79 7 E
Ramnagar, *Jammu & Kashmir, India* **43 C6** 32 47N 75 18 E
Râmnicu Sărat, *Romania* **17 F14** 45 26N 27 3 E
Râmnicu Vâlcea, *Romania* **17 F13** 45 9N 24 21 E
Ramona, *U.S.A.* **85 M10** 33 2N 116 52W
Ramore, *Canada* **70 C3** 48 30N 80 25W
Ramotswa, *Botswana* **56 C4** 24 50S 25 52 E
Rampur, *H.P., India* **42 D7** 31 26N 77 43 E
Rampur, *Mad. P., India* **42 H5** 23 25N 73 53 E
Rampur, *Ut. P., India* **43 E8** 28 50N 79 5 E
Rampur Hat, *India* **43 G12** 24 10N 87 50 E
Rampura, *India* **42 G6** 24 30N 75 27 E
Ramrama Tola, *India* **43 J8** 21 52N 79 55 E
Ramree I. = Ramree Kyun, *Burma* **41 K19** 19 0N 94 0 E
Ramree Kyun, *Burma* **41 K19** 19 0N 94 0 E
Rāmsar, *Iran* **45 B6** 36 53N 50 41 E
Ramsey, *U.K.* **10 C3** 54 20N 4 22W
Ramsey, *U.S.A.* **79 E10** 41 4N 74 9W
Ramsey L., *Canada* **70 C3** 47 13N 82 15W
Ramsgate, *U.K.* **11 F9** 51 20N 1 25 E
Ramtek, *India* **40 J11** 21 20N 79 15 E
Rana Pratap Sagar Dam, *India* **42 G6** 24 58N 75 38 E
Ranaghat, *India* **43 H13** 23 15N 88 35 E
Ranahu, *Pakistan* **42 G3** 25 55N 69 45 E
Ranau, *Malaysia* **36 C5** 6 2N 116 40 E
Rancagua, *Chile* **94 C1** 34 10S 70 50W
Rancheria →, *Canada* **72 A3** 60 13N 129 7W
Ranchester, *U.S.A.* **82 D10** 44 54N 107 10W
Ranchi, *India* **43 H11** 23 19N 85 27 E
Rancho Cucamonga, *U.S.A.* **85 L9** 34 10N 117 30W
Randalstown, *U.K.* **13 B5** 54 45N 6 19W
Randers, *Denmark* **9 H14** 56 29N 10 1 E
Randfontein, *S. Africa* **57 D4** 26 8S 27 45 E
Randle, *U.S.A.* **84 D5** 46 32N 121 57W
Randolph, *Mass., U.S.A.* **79 D13** 42 10N 71 2W
Randolph, *N.Y., U.S.A.* **78 D6** 42 10N 78 59W
Randolph, *Utah, U.S.A.* **82 F8** 41 40N 111 11W
Randolph, *Vt., U.S.A.* **79 C12** 43 55N 72 40W
Randsburg, *U.S.A.* **85 K9** 35 22N 117 39W
Råne älv →, *Sweden* **8 D20** 65 50N 22 20 E
Rangae, *Thailand* **39 J3** 6 19N 101 44 E
Rangaunu B., *N.Z.* **59 F4** 34 51S 173 15 E
Rangeley, *U.S.A.* **79 B14** 44 58N 70 39W
Rangeley L., *U.S.A.* **79 B14** 44 55N 70 43W
Rangely, *U.S.A.* **82 F9** 40 5N 108 48W
Ranger, *U.S.A.* **81 J5** 32 28N 98 41W
Rangia, *India* **41 F17** 26 28N 91 38 E
Rangiora, *N.Z.* **59 K4** 43 19S 172 36 E
Rangitaiki →, *N.Z.* **59 G6** 37 54S 176 49 E
Rangitata →, *N.Z.* **59 K3** 43 45S 171 15 E
Rangkasbitung, *Indonesia* **37 G12** 6 21S 106 15 E
Rangon →, *Burma* **41 L20** 16 28N 96 40 E
**Rangoon**, *Burma* **41 L20** 16 45N 96 20 E
Rangpur, *Bangla.* **41 G16** 25 42N 89 22 E
Rangsit, *Thailand* **38 F3** 13 59N 100 37 E
Ranibennur, *India* **40 M9** 14 35N 75 30 E
Raniganj, *Ut. P., India* **43 F9** 27 3N 82 13 E
Raniganj, *W. Bengal, India* **41 H15** 23 40N 87 5 E
Ranikhet, *India* **43 E8** 29 39N 79 25 E
Raniwara, *India* **40 G8** 24 50N 72 10 E
Rāniyah, *Iraq* **44 B5** 36 15N 44 53 E
Ranka, *India* **43 H10** 23 59N 83 47 E
Ranken →, *Australia* **62 C2** 20 31S 137 36 E
Rankin, *U.S.A.* **81 K4** 31 13N 101 56W
Rankin Inlet, *Canada* **68 B10** 62 30N 93 0W
Rankins Springs, *Australia* **63 E4** 33 49S 146 14 E
Rannoch, L., *U.K.* **12 E4** 56 41N 4 20W
Rannoch Moor, *U.K.* **12 E4** 56 38N 4 48W
Ranobe, Helodranon' i, *Madag.* **57 C7** 23 3S 43 33 E
Ranohira, *Madag.* **57 C8** 22 29S 45 24 E
Ranomafana, *Toamasina, Madag.* **57 B8** 18 57S 48 50 E
Ranomafana, *Toliara, Madag.* **57 C8** 24 34S 47 0 E
Ranong, *Thailand* **39 H2** 9 56N 98 40 E
Rānsa, *Iran* **45 C6** 33 39N 48 18 E
Ransiki, *Indonesia* **37 E8** 1 30S 134 10 E
Rantauprapat, *Indonesia* **36 D1** 2 15N 99 50 E
Rantemario, *Indonesia* **37 E5** 3 15S 119 57 E
Rantoul, *U.S.A.* **76 E1** 40 19N 88 9W
Raoyang, *China* **34 E8** 38 15N 115 45 E
Rapa, *Pac. Oc.* **65 K13** 27 35S 144 20W
Rapallo, *Italy* **18 D8** 44 21N 9 14 E
Rapar, *India* **42 H4** 23 34N 70 38 E
Rāpch, *Iran* **45 E8** 25 40N 59 15 E
Raper, C., *Canada* **69 B13** 69 44N 67 6W
Rapid City, *U.S.A.* **80 D3** 44 5N 103 14W
Rapid River, *U.S.A.* **76 C2** 45 55N 86 58W
Rapla, *Estonia* **9 G21** 59 1N 24 52 E
Rapti →, *India* **43 F10** 26 18N 83 41 E
Raquette →, *U.S.A.* **79 B10** 45 0N 74 42W
Raquette Lake, *U.S.A.* **79 C10** 43 49N 74 40W
Rarotonga, *Cook Is.* **65 K12** 21 30S 160 0W
Ra's al 'Ayn, *Syria* **44 B4** 36 45N 40 12 E
Ra's al Khaymah, *U.A.E.* **45 E8** 25 50N 55 59 E
Ra's an Naqb, *Jordan* **47 F4** 30 0N 35 29 E
Ras Dashen, *Ethiopia* **46 E2** 13 8N 38 26 E
Râs Timirist, *Mauritania* **50 E2** 19 21N 16 30W
Rasca, Pta. de la, *Canary Is.* **22 G3** 27 59N 16 41W
Raseiniai, *Lithuania* **9 J20** 55 25N 23 5 E
Rashmi, *India* **42 G6** 25 4N 74 22 E
Rasht, *Iran* **45 B6** 37 20N 49 40 E
Rasi Salai, *Thailand* **38 E5** 15 20N 104 9 E
Rason L., *Australia* **61 E3** 28 45S 124 25 E
Rasra, *India* **43 G10** 25 50N 83 50 E
Rasul, *Pakistan* **42 C5** 32 42N 73 34 E
Rat Buri, *Thailand* **38 F2** 13 30N 99 54 E
Rat Islands, *U.S.A.* **68 C1** 52 0N 178 0 E
Rat L., *Canada* **73 B9** 56 10N 99 40W
Ratangarh, *India* **42 E6** 28 5N 74 35 E
Raţāwī, *Iraq* **44 D5** 30 38N 47 13 E
Ratcatchers L., *Australia* **63 E3** 32 38S 143 10 E

# S

Salisbury Plain, *U.K.* ...... **11 F6** 51 14N 1 55W
Şalkhad, *Syria* .......... **47 C5** 32 29N 36 43 E
Salla, *Finland* .......... **8 C23** 66 50N 28 49 E
Salliq, *Canada* .......... **69 B11** 64 8N 83 10W
Sallisaw, *U.S.A.* .......... **81 H7** 35 28N 94 47W
Salluit, *Canada* .......... **69 B12** 62 14N 75 38W
Salmās, *Iran* ............ **44 B5** 38 11N 44 47 E
Salmo, *Canada* .......... **72 D5** 49 10N 117 20W
Salmon, *U.S.A.* .......... **82 D7** 45 11N 113 54W
Salmon —►, *Canada* ..... **72 C4** 54 3N 122 40W
Salmon —►, *U.S.A.* ...... **82 D5** 45 51N 116 47W
Salmon Arm, *Canada* ..... **72 C5** 50 40N 119 15W
Salmon Gums, *Australia* .. **61 F3** 32 59S 121 38 E
Salmon River Mts., *U.S.A.* . **82 D6** 45 0N 114 30W
Salo, *Finland* ........... **9 F20** 60 22N 23 10 E
Salome, *U.S.A.* .......... **85 M13** 33 47N 113 37W
Salon, *India* ............ **43 F9** 26 2N 81 27 E
Salon-de-Provence, *France* **18 E6** 43 39N 5 6 E
Salonica = Thessaloníki,
*Greece* .............. **21 D10** 40 38N 22 58 E
Salonta, *Romania* ........ **17 E11** 46 49N 21 42 E
Salpausselkä, *Finland* ..... **9 F22** 61 0N 27 0 E
Salsacate, *Argentina* ...... **94 C2** 31 20S 65 5W
Salsk, *Russia* ........... **25 E7** 46 28N 41 30 E
Salso —►, *Italy* .......... **20 F5** 37 6N 13 57 E
Salt —►, *Canada* ........ **72 B6** 60 0N 112 25W
Salt —►, *U.S.A.* ......... **83 K7** 33 23N 112 19W
Salt Fork Arkansas —►,
*U.S.A.* ................ **75 C7** 36 36N 97 3W
**Salt Lake City**, *U.S.A.* ... **82 F8** 40 45N 111 53W
Salt Range, *Pakistan* ...... **42 C5** 32 30N 72 25 E
Salta, *Argentina* ......... **94 A2** 24 57S 65 25W
Salta □, *Argentina* ....... **94 A2** 24 48S 65 30W
Saltash, *U.K.* ........... **11 G3** 50 24N 4 14W
Saltburn by the Sea, *U.K.* . **10 C7** 54 35N 0 58W
Saltcoats, *U.K.* .......... **12 F4** 55 38N 4 47W
Saltee Is., *Ireland* ........ **13 D5** 52 7N 6 37W
Saltfjellet, *Norway* ....... **8 C16** 66 40N 15 15 E
Saltfjorden, *Norway* ...... **8 C16** 67 15N 14 10 E
Saltillo, *Mexico* .......... **86 B4** 25 25N 101 0W
Salto, *Argentina* ......... **94 C3** 34 20S 60 15W
Salto, *Uruguay* .......... **94 C4** 31 27S 57 50W
Salto —►, *Italy* .......... **20 C5** 42 26N 12 25 E
Salto del Guaíra, *Paraguay* **95 A5** 24 3S 54 17W
Salton City, *U.S.A.* ....... **85 M11** 33 29N 115 51W
Salton Sea, *U.S.A.* ....... **85 M11** 33 15N 115 45W
Saltsburg, *U.S.A.* ........ **78 F5** 40 29N 79 27W
Saluda —►, *U.S.A.* ....... **77 J5** 34 1N 81 4W
Salûm, *Egypt* ........... **51 B11** 31 31N 25 7 E
Salur, *India* ............. **41 K13** 18 27N 83 18 E
**Salvador**, *Brazil* ......... **93 F11** 13 0S 38 30W
Salvador, *Canada* ........ **73 C7** 52 10N 109 32W
Salvador, L., *U.S.A.* ...... **81 L9** 29 43N 90 15W
**Salween** —►, *Burma* ..... **41 L20** 16 31N 97 37 E
Salyan, *Azerbaijan* ....... **25 G8** 39 33N 48 59 E
Salzach —►, *Austria* ...... **16 D7** 48 12N 12 56 E
**Salzburg**, *Austria* ........ **16 E7** 47 48N 13 2 E
Salzgitter, *Germany* ...... **16 B6** 52 9N 10 19 E
Salzwedel, *Germany* ...... **16 B6** 52 52N 11 10 E
Sam, *India* ............. **42 F4** 26 50N 70 31 E
Sam Ngao, *Thailand* ...... **38 D2** 17 18N 99 0 E
Sam Rayburn Reservoir,
*U.S.A.* ................ **81 K7** 31 4N 94 5W
Sam Son, *Vietnam* ....... **38 C5** 19 44N 105 54 E
Sam Teu, *Laos* .......... **38 C5** 19 59N 104 38 E
Sama de Langreo =
Langreo, *Spain* ........ **19 A3** 43 18N 5 40W
Samagaltay, *Russia* ...... **27 D10** 50 36N 95 3 E
Samales Group, *Phil.* ..... **37 C6** 6 0N 122 0 E
Samana, *India* ........... **42 D7** 30 10N 76 13 E
Samaná □, *Dom. Rep.* .... **89 C6** 19 15N 69 27W
Samana Cay, *Bahamas* ... **89 B5** 23 3N 73 45W
Samanga, *Tanzania* ...... **55 D4** 8 20S 39 13 E
Samangwa,
*Dem. Rep. of the Congo* . **54 C1** 4 23S 24 10 E
Samani, *Japan* .......... **30 C11** 42 7N 142 56 E
Samar, *Phil.* ............. **37 B7** 12 0N 125 0 E
Samara, *Russia* .......... **24 D9** 53 8N 50 6 E
Samaria = Shōmrōn,
*West Bank* ............ **47 C4** 32 15N 35 13 E
Samariá, *Greece* ......... **23 D5** 35 17N 23 58 E
Samarinda, *Indonesia* ..... **36 E5** 0 30S 117 9 E
**Samarkand** = Samarqand,
*Uzbekistan* ............ **26 F7** 39 40N 66 55 E
Samarqand, *Uzbekistan* ... **26 F7** 39 40N 66 55 E
Sāmarrā, *Iraq* ........... **44 C4** 34 12N 43 52 E
Samastipur, *India* ........ **43 G11** 25 50N 85 50 E
Samba,
*Dem. Rep. of the Congo* . **54 C2** 4 38S 26 22 E
Samba, *India* ........... **43 C6** 32 32N 75 10 E
Sambalpur, *India* ........ **41 J14** 21 28N 84 4 E
Sambar, Tanjung, *Indonesia* **36 E4** 2 59S 110 19 E
Sambas, *Indonesia* ....... **36 D3** 1 20N 109 20 E
Sambava, *Madag.* ........ **57 A9** 14 16S 50 10 E
Sambawizi, *Zimbabwe* .... **55 F2** 18 24S 26 13 E
Sambhal, *India* .......... **43 E8** 28 35N 78 37 E
Sambhar, *India* .......... **42 F6** 26 52N 75 6 E
Sambhar L., *India* ........ **42 F6** 26 55N 75 12 E
Sambiase, *Italy* .......... **20 E7** 38 58N 16 17 E
Sambir, *Ukraine* ......... **17 D12** 49 30N 23 10 E
Sambor, *Cambodia* ....... **38 F6** 12 46N 106 0 E
Samborombón, B.,
*Argentina* ............. **94 D4** 36 5S 57 20W
Samch'ŏk, *S. Korea* ...... **35 F15** 37 30N 129 10 E
Samch'onp'o, *S. Korea* .... **35 G15** 35 0N 128 6 E
Same, *Tanzania* ......... **54 C4** 4 2S 37 38 E
Samfya, *Zambia* ......... **55 E2** 11 22S 29 31 E
Samhah, *Si. Arabia* ....... **44 E3** 25 10N 37 15 E
Samo Alto, *Chile* ........ **94 C1** 30 22S 71 0W
Samokov, *Bulgaria* ....... **21 C10** 42 18N 23 35 E
Sámos, *Greece* .......... **21 F12** 37 45N 26 50 E
Samothráki = Mathráki,
*Greece* .............. **23 A3** 39 48N 19 31 E
Samothráki, *Greece* ...... **21 D11** 40 28N 25 28 E
Sampacho, *Argentina* ..... **94 C3** 33 20S 64 50W
Sampang, *Indonesia* ...... **37 G15** 7 11S 113 13 E
Sampit, *Indonesia* ........ **36 E4** 2 34S 113 0 E
Sampit, Teluk, *Indonesia* .. **36 E4** 3 5S 113 3 E
Samrong, *Cambodia* ...... **38 E4** 14 15N 103 30 E
Samrong, *Thailand* ....... **38 E3** 15 10N 100 40 E
Samsø, *Denmark* ......... **9 J14** 55 50N 10 35 E
Samsun, *Turkey* ......... **25 F6** 41 15N 36 22 E
Samui, Ko, *Thailand* ...... **39 H3** 9 30N 100 0 E
Samusole,
*Dem. Rep. of the Congo* . **55 E1** 10 2S 24 0 E
Samut Prakan, *Thailand* ... **38 F3** 13 32N 100 40 E
Samut Songkhram —►,
*Thailand* ............. **36 B1** 13 24N 100 1 E
Samwari, *Pakistan* ....... **42 E2** 28 30N 66 46 E
San, *Mali* .............. **50 F5** 13 15N 4 57W
San —►, *Cambodia* ...... **38 F5** 13 32N 105 57 E
San —►, *Poland* ......... **17 C11** 50 45N 21 51 E
San Agustin, C., *Phil.* ..... **37 C7** 6 20N 126 13 E
San Agustín de Valle Fértil,
*Argentina* ............. **94 C2** 30 35S 67 30W
San Ambrosio, *Pac. Oc.* ... **90 F3** 26 28S 79 53W
San Andreas, *U.S.A.* ...... **84 G6** 38 12N 120 41W
San Andrés, I. de, *Caribbean* **88 D3** 12 42N 81 46W
San Andres Mts., *U.S.A.* .. **83 K10** 33 0N 106 30W
San Andrés Tuxtla, *Mexico* **87 D5** 18 30N 95 20W
San Angelo, *U.S.A.* ....... **81 K4** 31 28N 100 26W
San Anselmo, *U.S.A.* ..... **84 H4** 37 59N 122 34W
San Antonio, *Belize* ...... **87 D7** 16 15N 89 2W
San Antonio, *Chile* ....... **94 C1** 33 40S 71 40W
San Antonio, *N. Mex.*,
*U.S.A.* ................ **83 K10** 33 55N 106 52W
**San Antonio**, *Tex., U.S.A.* **81 L5** 29 25N 98 30W
San Antonio —►, *U.S.A.* .. **81 L6** 28 30N 96 54W
San Antonio, C., *Argentina* **94 D4** 36 15S 56 40W
San Antonio, C., *Cuba* .... **88 B3** 21 50N 84 57W
San Antonio, Mt., *U.S.A.* .. **85 L9** 34 17N 117 38W
San Antonio de los Baños,
*Cuba* ................ **88 B3** 22 54N 82 31W
San Antonio de los Cobres,
*Argentina* ............. **94 A2** 24 10S 66 17W
San Antonio Oeste,
*Argentina* ............. **96 E4** 40 40S 65 0W
San Ardo, *U.S.A.* ......... **84 J6** 36 1N 120 54W
San Augustín, *Canary Is.* .. **22 G4** 27 47N 15 32W
San Augustine, *U.S.A.* .... **81 K7** 31 30N 94 7W
San Bartolomé, *Canary Is.* . **22 F6** 28 59N 13 37W
San Bartolomé de Tirajana,
*Canary Is.* ............. **22 G4** 27 54N 15 34W
San Benedetto del Tronto,
*Italy* ................. **20 C5** 42 57N 13 53 E
San Benedicto, I., *Mexico* . **86 D2** 19 18N 110 49W
San Benito, *U.S.A.* ....... **81 M6** 26 8N 97 38W
San Benito —►, *U.S.A.* ... **84 J5** 36 53N 121 34W
San Benito Mt., *U.S.A.* .... **84 J6** 36 22N 120 37W
San Bernardino, *U.S.A.* ... **85 L9** 34 7N 117 19W
San Bernardino Mts., *U.S.A.* **85 L10** 34 10N 116 45W
San Bernardino Str., *Phil.* . **37 B7** 13 0N 125 0 E
San Bernardo, *Chile* ...... **94 C1** 33 40S 70 50W
San Bernardo, I. de,
*Colombia* ............. **92 B3** 9 45N 75 50W
San Blas, *Mexico* ........ **86 B3** 26 4N 108 46W
San Blas, Arch. de, *Panama* **88 E4** 9 50N 78 31W
San Blas, C., *U.S.A.* ...... **77 L3** 29 40N 85 21W
San Borja, *Bolivia* ........ **92 F5** 14 50S 66 52W
San Buenaventura, *Mexico* **86 B4** 27 5N 101 32W
San Carlos = Sant Carles,
*Spain* ................ **22 B8** 39 3N 1 34 E
San Carlos, *Argentina* .... **94 C2** 33 50S 69 0W
San Carlos, *Chile* ........ **94 D1** 36 10S 72 0W
San Carlos, *Mexico* ...... **86 B4** 29 0N 100 54W
San Carlos, *Mexico* ...... **86 C2** 24 47N 112 6W
San Carlos, *Nic.* ......... **88 D3** 11 12N 84 50W
San Carlos, *Phil.* ......... **37 B6** 10 29N 123 25 E
San Carlos, *Uruguay* ..... **95 C5** 34 46S 54 58W
San Carlos, *U.S.A.* ....... **83 K8** 33 21N 110 27W
San Carlos, *Venezuela* .... **92 B5** 9 40N 68 36W
San Carlos de Bariloche,
*Argentina* ............. **96 E2** 41 10S 71 25W
San Carlos de Bolívar,
*Argentina* ............. **96 D4** 36 15S 61 6W
San Carlos del Zulia,
*Venezuela* ............ **92 B4** 9 1N 71 55W
San Carlos L., *U.S.A.* ..... **83 K8** 33 11N 110 32W
San Clemente, *Chile* ...... **94 D1** 35 30S 71 29W
San Clemente, *U.S.A.* ..... **85 M9** 33 26N 117 37W
San Clemente I., *U.S.A.* ... **85 N8** 32 53N 118 29W
San Cristóbal = Es Migjorn
Gran, *Spain* ........... **22 B11** 39 57N 4 3 E
San Cristóbal, *Argentina* .. **94 C3** 30 20S 61 10W
San Cristóbal, *Dom. Rep.* .. **89 C5** 18 25N 70 6W
San Cristóbal, *Venezuela* .. **92 B4** 7 46N 72 14W
San Cristóbal de la Casas,
*Mexico* ............... **87 D6** 16 50N 92 33W
**San Diego**, *Calif., U.S.A.* .. **85 N9** 32 43N 117 9W
San Diego, *Tex., U.S.A.* ... **81 M5** 27 46N 98 14W
San Diego, C., *Argentina* .. **96 G3** 54 40S 65 10W
San Diego de la Unión,
*Mexico* ............... **86 C4** 21 28N 100 52W
San Dimitri, Ras, *Malta* ... **23 C1** 36 4N 14 11 E
San Estanislao, *Paraguay* .. **94 A4** 24 39S 56 26W
San Felipe, *Chile* ........ **94 C1** 32 43S 70 42W
San Felipe, *Mexico* ....... **86 A2** 31 0N 114 52W
San Felipe, *Venezuela* .... **92 A5** 10 20N 68 44W
San Felipe —►, *U.S.A.* ... **85 M11** 33 12N 115 49W
San Felix, *Chile* ......... **94 B1** 28 56S 70 28W
San Félix, *Pac. Oc.* ....... **90 F2** 26 23S 80 0W
San Fernando = Sant
Ferran, *Spain* .......... **22 C7** 38 42N 1 28 E
San Fernando, *Chile* ...... **94 C1** 34 30S 71 0W
San Fernando, *Mexico* .... **86 B1** 29 55N 115 10W
San Fernando, *Tamaulipas*,
*Mexico* ............... **87 C5** 24 51N 98 10W
San Fernando, *La Union*,
*Phil.* ................. **37 A6** 16 40N 120 23 E
San Fernando, *Pampanga*,
*Phil.* ................. **37 A6** 15 5N 120 37 E
San Fernando, *Spain* ..... **19 D2** 36 28N 6 17W
San Fernando, *Trin. & Tob.* **89 D7** 10 20N 61 30W
San Fernando, *U.S.A.* ..... **85 L8** 34 17N 118 26W
San Fernando de Apure,
*Venezuela* ............ **92 B5** 7 54N 67 15W
San Fernando de Atabapo,
*Venezuela* ............ **92 C5** 4 3N 67 42W
San Francisco, *Argentina* .. **94 C3** 31 30S 62 5W
**San Francisco**, *U.S.A.* ... **84 H4** 37 47N 122 25W
San Francisco —►, *U.S.A.* . **83 K9** 32 59N 109 22W
San Francisco, Paso de,
*S. Amer.* .............. **94 B2** 27 0S 68 0W
San Francisco de Macorís,
*Dom. Rep.* ............ **89 C5** 19 19N 70 15W
San Francisco del Monte de
Oro, *Argentina* ......... **94 C2** 32 36S 66 8W
San Francisco del Oro,
*Mexico* ............... **86 B3** 26 52N 105 50W
San Francisco Javier = Sant
Francesc de Formentera,
*Spain* ................ **22 C7** 38 42N 1 26 E
San Francisco Solano, Pta.,
*Colombia* ............. **90 C3** 6 18N 77 29W
San Gabriel, *Chile* ........ **94 C1** 33 47S 70 15W
San Gabriel Mts., *U.S.A.* .. **85 L9** 34 20N 118 0W
San Gorgonio Mt., *U.S.A.* . **85 L10** 34 7N 116 51W
San Gottardo, P. del, *Switz.* **18 C8** 46 33N 8 33 E
San Gregorio, *Uruguay* ... **95 C4** 32 37S 55 40W
San Gregorio, *U.S.A.* ..... **84 H4** 37 20N 122 23W
San Ignacio, *Belize* ....... **87 D7** 17 10N 89 0W
San Ignacio, *Bolivia* ...... **92 G6** 16 20S 60 55W
San Ignacio, *Mexico* ...... **86 B2** 27 27N 113 0W
San Ignacio, *Paraguay* .... **88 C2** 26 52S 57 3W
San Ignacio, L., *Mexico* ... **86 B2** 26 50N 113 11W
San Ildefonso, C., *Phil.* .... **37 A6** 16 0N 122 1 E
San Isidro, *Argentina* ..... **94 C4** 34 29S 58 31W
San Jacinto, *U.S.A.* ....... **85 M10** 33 47N 116 57W
San Jaime = Sant Jaume,
*Spain* ................ **22 B11** 39 54N 4 4 E
San Javier, *Misiones*,
*Argentina* ............. **95 B4** 27 55S 55 5W
San Javier, *Santa Fe*,
*Argentina* ............. **94 C4** 30 40S 59 55W
San Javier, *Bolivia* ....... **92 G6** 16 18S 62 30W
San Javier, *Chile* ........ **94 D1** 35 40S 71 45W
San Jeronimo Taviche,
*Mexico* ............... **87 D5** 16 38N 96 32W
San Joaquin, *U.S.A.* ...... **84 J6** 36 36N 120 11W
San Joaquin —►, *U.S.A.* .. **84 G5** 38 4N 121 51W
San Joaquin Valley, *U.S.A.* **84 J6** 37 20N 121 0W
San Jon, *U.S.A.* .......... **81 H3** 35 6N 103 20W
San Jordi = Sant Jordi,
*Spain* ................ **22 B9** 39 33N 2 46 E
San Jorge, *Argentina* ..... **94 C3** 31 54S 61 50W
San Jorge, *Spain* ......... **22 C7** 38 54N 1 24 E
San Jorge, B. de, *Mexico* .. **86 A2** 31 20N 113 20W
San Jorge, G., *Argentina* .. **96 F3** 46 0S 66 0W
San Jorge, G. of, *Argentina* **90 H4** 46 0S 66 0W
San José = San Josep,
*Spain* ................ **22 C7** 38 55N 1 18 E
**San José**, *Costa Rica* ..... **88 E3** 9 55N 84 2W
San José, *Guatemala* ..... **88 D1** 14 0N 90 50W
San José, *Mexico* ........ **86 C2** 25 0N 110 50W
San Jose, *Luzon, Phil.* .... **37 A6** 15 45N 120 55 E
San Jose, *Mind. Or., Phil.* . **37 B6** 12 27N 121 4 E
**San Jose**, *U.S.A.* ........ **84 H5** 37 20N 121 53W
San Jose —►, *U.S.A.* .... **83 J10** 34 25N 106 45W
San Jose Buenavista, *Phil.* . **37 B6** 10 45N 121 56 E
San José de Chiquitos,
*Bolivia* ............... **92 G6** 17 53S 60 50W
San José de Feliciano,
*Argentina* ............. **94 C4** 30 26S 58 46W
San José de Jáchal,
*Argentina* ............. **94 C2** 30 15S 68 46W
San José de Mayo, *Uruguay* **94 C4** 34 27S 56 40W
San José del Cabo, *Mexico* **86 C3** 23 0N 109 40W
San José del Guaviare,
*Colombia* ............. **92 C4** 2 35N 72 38W
San Josep, *Spain* ........ **22 C7** 38 55N 1 18 E
San Juan, *Argentina* ..... **94 C2** 31 30S 68 30W
San Juan, *Mexico* ........ **86 C4** 21 20N 102 50W
**San Juan**, *Puerto Rico* .... **89 C6** 18 28N 66 7W
San Juan □, *Argentina* .... **94 C2** 31 9S 69 0W
San Juan □, *Dom. Rep.* ... **89 C5** 18 45N 71 25W
San Juan —►, *Argentina* .. **94 C2** 32 20S 67 25W
San Juan —►, *Nic.* ....... **88 D3** 10 56N 83 42W
San Juan —►, *U.S.A.* ..... **83 H8** 37 16N 110 26W
San Juan Bautista = Sant
Joan Baptista, *Spain* .... **22 B8** 39 5N 1 31 E
San Juan Bautista, *Paraguay* **94 B4** 26 37S 57 6W
San Juan Bautista, *U.S.A.* . **84 J5** 36 51N 121 32W
San Juan Bautista Valle
Nacional, *Mexico* ....... **87 D5** 17 47N 96 19W
San Juan Capistrano, *U.S.A.* **85 M9** 33 30N 117 40W
San Juan Cr. —►, *U.S.A.* .. **84 J5** 35 40N 120 22W
San Juan de Guadalupe,
*Mexico* ............... **86 C4** 24 38N 102 44W
San Juan de la Costa,
*Mexico* ............... **86 C2** 24 23N 110 45W
San Juan de los Morros,
*Venezuela* ............ **92 B5** 9 55N 67 21W
San Juan del Norte, *Nic.* .. **88 D3** 10 58N 83 40W
San Juan del Norte, B. de,
*Nic.* .................. **88 D3** 11 0N 83 40W
San Juan del Río, *Mexico* .. **87 C5** 20 25N 100 0W
San Juan del Sur, *Nic.* .... **88 D2** 11 20N 85 51W
San Juan I., *U.S.A.* ....... **84 B3** 48 32N 123 5W
San Juan Mts., *U.S.A.* .... **83 H10** 37 30N 107 0W
San Justo, *Argentina* ..... **94 C3** 30 47S 60 30W
San Kamphaeng, *Thailand* . **38 C2** 18 45N 99 8 E
San Lázaro, C., *Mexico* ... **86 C2** 24 50N 112 18W
San Lázaro, Sa., *Mexico* ... **86 C3** 23 25N 110 0W
San Leandro, *U.S.A.* ...... **84 H4** 37 44N 122 9W
San Lorenzo = Sant Llorenç
des Cardassar, *Spain* ... **22 B10** 39 37N 3 17 E
San Lorenzo, *Argentina* ... **94 C3** 32 45S 60 45W
San Lorenzo, *Ecuador* .... **92 C3** 1 15N 78 50W
San Lorenzo, *Paraguay* ... **94 B4** 25 20S 57 32W
San Lorenzo —►, *Mexico* . **86 C3** 24 15N 107 24W
San Lorenzo, I., *Mexico* ... **86 B2** 28 35N 112 50W
San Lorenzo, Mte.,
*Argentina* ............. **96 F2** 47 40S 72 20W
San Lucas, *Bolivia* ....... **92 H5** 20 5S 65 7W
San Lucas, *Baja Calif. S.*,
*Mexico* ............... **86 C3** 22 53N 109 54W
San Lucas, *Baja Calif. S.*,
*Mexico* ............... **86 B2** 27 10N 112 14W
San Lucas, *U.S.A.* ........ **84 J5** 36 8N 121 1W
San Lucas, C., *Mexico* .... **86 C3** 22 50N 110 0W
San Luis, *Argentina* ...... **94 C2** 33 20S 66 20W
San Luis, *Cuba* .......... **88 B3** 22 17N 83 46W
San Luis, *Guatemala* ..... **88 C2** 16 14N 89 27W
San Luis, *Ariz., U.S.A.* .... **83 K6** 32 29N 114 47W
San Luis, *Colo., U.S.A.* .... **83 H11** 37 12N 105 25W
San Luis □, *Argentina* .... **94 C2** 34 0S 66 0W
San Luis, I., *Mexico* ...... **86 B2** 29 58N 114 26W
San Luis, Sierra de,
*Argentina* ............. **94 C2** 32 30S 66 10W
San Luis de la Paz, *Mexico* **86 C4** 21 19N 100 32W
San Luis Obispo, *U.S.A.* ... **85 K6** 35 17N 120 40W
San Luis Potosí, *Mexico* ... **86 C4** 22 9N 100 59W
San Luis Potosí □, *Mexico* . **86 C4** 22 10N 101 0W
San Luis Reservoir, *U.S.A.* . **84 H5** 37 4N 121 5W
San Luis Río Colorado,
*Mexico* ............... **86 A2** 32 29N 114 58W
San Manuel, *U.S.A.* ...... **83 K8** 32 36N 110 38W
San Marcos, *Guatemala* ... **88 D1** 14 59N 91 52W
San Marcos, *Mexico* ...... **86 B2** 27 13N 112 6W
San Marcos, *Calif., U.S.A.* . **85 M9** 33 9N 117 10W
San Marcos, *Tex., U.S.A.* .. **81 L6** 29 53N 97 56W
San Marino, *San Marino* .. **16 G7** 43 55N 12 30 E
**San Marino** ■, *Europe* ... **20 C5** 43 56N 12 25 E
San Martín, *Argentina* .... **94 C2** 33 5S 68 28W
San Martín —►, *Bolivia* ... **92 F6** 13 8S 63 43W
San Martín, L., *Argentina* .. **96 F2** 48 50S 72 50W
San Martín de los Andes,
*Argentina* ............. **96 E2** 40 10S 71 20W
San Mateo = Sant Mateu,
*Spain* ................ **22 B7** 39 3N 1 23 E
San Mateo, *U.S.A.* ....... **84 H4** 37 34N 122 19W
San Matías, *Bolivia* ...... **92 G7** 16 25S 58 20W
San Matías, G., *Argentina* . **96 E4** 41 30S 64 0W
San Miguel = Sant Miquel,
*Spain* ................ **22 B7** 39 3N 1 26 E
San Miguel, *El Salv.* ...... **88 D2** 13 30N 88 12W
San Miguel, *Panama* ..... **88 E4** 8 27N 78 55W
San Miguel, *U.S.A.* ....... **84 K6** 35 45N 120 42W
San Miguel —►, *Bolivia* ... **92 F6** 13 52S 63 56W
San Miguel de Tucumán,
*Argentina* ............. **94 B2** 26 50S 65 20W
San Miguel del Monte,
*Argentina* ............. **94 D4** 35 23S 58 50W
San Miguel I., *U.S.A.* ..... **85 L6** 34 2N 120 23W
San Nicolás, *Canary Is.* ... **22 G4** 27 58N 15 47W
San Nicolás de los Arroyas,
*Argentina* ............. **94 C3** 33 25S 60 10W
San Nicolas I., *U.S.A.* .... **85 M7** 33 15N 119 30W
San Onofre, *U.S.A.* ....... **85 M9** 33 22N 117 34W
San Pablo, *Bolivia* ....... **94 A2** 21 43S 66 38W
San Pablo, *U.S.A.* ........ **84 H4** 37 58N 122 21W
San Pedro, *Argentina* .... **94 C4** 33 40S 59 40W
San Pedro, *Buenos Aires*,
*Argentina* ............. **95 B5** 26 30S 54 10W
San Pedro, *Chile* ......... **94 C1** 33 54S 71 28W
San Pedro, *Ivory C.* ....... **50 H4** 4 50N 6 33W
San Pedro, *Mexico* ....... **86 C2** 23 55N 110 17W
San Pedro □, *Paraguay* ... **94 A4** 24 0S 57 0W
San Pedro —►, *Chihuahua*,
*Mexico* ............... **86 B3** 28 20N 106 10W
San Pedro —►, *Nayarit*,
*Mexico* ............... **86 C3** 21 45N 105 30W
San Pedro —►, *U.S.A.* ... **83 K8** 32 59N 110 47W
San Pedro, Pta., *Chile* .... **94 B1** 25 30S 70 38W
San Pedro Channel, *U.S.A.* **85 M8** 33 30N 118 25W
San Pedro de Atacama,
*Chile* ................ **94 A2** 22 55S 68 15W
San Pedro de Jujuy,
*Argentina* ............. **94 A3** 24 12S 64 55W
San Pedro de las Colonias,
*Mexico* ............... **86 B4** 25 50N 102 59W
San Pedro de Macorís,
*Dom. Rep.* ............ **89 C6** 18 30N 69 18W
San Pedro del Norte, *Nic.* . **88 D3** 13 4N 84 33W
San Pedro del Paraná,
*Paraguay* ............. **94 B4** 26 43S 56 13W
San Pedro Mártir, Sierra,
*Mexico* ............... **86 A1** 31 0N 115 30W
San Pedro Mixtepec, *Mexico* **87 D5** 16 2N 97 7W
San Pedro Ocampo =
Melchor Ocampo, *Mexico* **86 C4** 24 52N 101 40W
San Pedro Sula, *Honduras* . **88 C2** 15 30N 88 0W
San Pietro, *Italy* ......... **20 E3** 39 8N 8 17 E
San Quintín, *Mexico* ...... **86 A1** 30 29N 115 57W
San Rafael, *Argentina* .... **94 C2** 34 40S 68 21W
San Rafael, *Calif., U.S.A.* .. **84 H4** 37 58N 122 32W
San Rafael, *N. Mex., U.S.A.* **83 J10** 35 7N 107 53W
San Rafael Mt., *U.S.A.* .... **85 L7** 34 41N 119 52W
San Rafael Mts., *U.S.A.* ... **85 L7** 34 40N 119 50W
San Ramón de la Nueva
Orán, *Argentina* ........ **94 A3** 23 10S 64 20W
San Remo, *Italy* ......... **18 E7** 43 49N 7 46 E
San Roque, *Argentina* .... **94 B4** 28 25S 58 45W
San Roque, *Spain* ........ **19 D3** 36 17N 5 21W
San Rosendo, *Chile* ...... **94 D1** 37 16S 72 43W
San Saba, *U.S.A.* ......... **81 K5** 31 12N 98 43W
**San Salvador**, *El Salv.* ... **88 D2** 13 40N 89 10W
San Salvador, *Spain* ...... **22 B10** 39 27N 3 11 E
San Salvador de Jujuy,
*Argentina* ............. **94 A3** 24 10S 64 48W
San Salvador I., *Bahamas* . **89 B5** 24 0N 74 40W
San Sebastián = Donostia-
San Sebastián, *Spain* ... **19 A5** 43 17N 1 58W
San Sebastián, *Argentina* . **96 G3** 53 10S 68 30W
San Sebastian de la
Gomera, *Canary Is.* ..... **22 F2** 28 5N 17 7W
San Serra = Son Serra,
*Spain* ................ **22 B10** 39 43N 3 13 E
San Severo, *Italy* ........ **20 D6** 41 41N 15 23 E
San Simeon, *U.S.A.* ...... **84 K5** 35 39N 121 11W
San Simon, *U.S.A.* ....... **83 K9** 32 16N 109 14W
San Telmo = Sant Telm,
*Spain* ................ **22 B9** 39 35N 2 21 E
San Telmo, *Mexico* ...... **86 A1** 30 58N 116 6W
San Tiburcio, *Mexico* ..... **86 C4** 24 8N 101 32W
San Valentin, Mte., *Chile* .. **96 F2** 46 30S 73 30W
San Vicente de la Barquera,
*Spain* ................ **19 A3** 43 23N 4 29W
San Vito, *Costa Rica* ...... **88 E3** 8 50N 82 58W
**Sana'**, *Yemen* ........... **46 D3** 15 27N 44 12 E
Sana —►, *Bos.-H.* ........ **16 F9** 45 3N 16 23 E
Sanaga —►, *Cameroon* ... **52 D1** 3 35N 9 38 E
Sanaloa, Presa, *Mexico* ... **86 C3** 24 50N 107 20W
Sanana, *Indonesia* ....... **37 E7** 2 4S 125 58 E
Sanand, *India* ........... **42 H5** 22 59N 72 25 E
Sanandaj, *Iran* .......... **44 C5** 35 18N 47 1 E
Sanandita, *Bolivia* ....... **94 A3** 21 40S 63 45W
Sanawad, *India* ......... **42 H7** 22 11N 76 5 E
Sancellas = Sencelles,
*Spain* ................ **22 B9** 39 39N 2 54 E
Sanchahe, *China* ........ **35 B14** 44 50N 126 2 E
Sánchez, *Dom. Rep.* ...... **89 C6** 19 15N 69 36W
Sanchor, *India* .......... **42 G4** 24 45N 71 55 E
Sancti Spíritus, *Cuba* ..... **88 B4** 21 52N 79 33W
Sancy, Puy de, *France* .... **18 D5** 45 32N 2 50 E
Sand —►, *S. Africa* ...... **57 C5** 22 25S 30 5 E
Sand Hills, *U.S.A.* ........ **80 D4** 42 10N 101 30W
Sand Springs, *U.S.A.* ..... **81 G6** 36 9N 96 7W
Sanda, *Japan* ........... **31 G7** 34 53N 135 14 E
Sandakan, *Malaysia* ...... **36 C5** 5 53N 118 4 E
Sandan = Sambor,
*Cambodia* ............. **38 F6** 12 46N 106 0 E
Sandanski, *Bulgaria* ..... **21 D10** 41 35N 23 16 E
Sanday, *U.K.* ............ **12 B6** 59 16N 2 31W

Sauðarkrókur, Iceland 8 D4 65 45N 19 40W
**Saudi Arabia** ■, Asia 46 B3 26 0N 44 0 E
Sauerland, Germany 16 C4 51 12N 7 59 E
Saugeen →, Canada 78 B3 44 30N 81 22W
Saugerties, U.S.A. 79 D11 42 5N 73 57W
Saugus, U.S.A. 85 L8 34 25N 118 32W
Sauk Centre, U.S.A. 80 C7 45 44N 94 57W
Sauk Rapids, U.S.A. 80 C7 45 35N 94 10W
Sault Ste. Marie, Canada 70 C3 46 30N 84 20W
Sault Ste. Marie, U.S.A. 69 D11 46 30N 84 21W
Saumlaki, Indonesia 37 F8 7 55S 131 20 E
Saumur, France 18 C3 47 15N 0 5W
Saunders C., N.Z. 59 L3 45 53S 170 45 E
Saunders I., Antarctica 5 B1 57 48S 26 28W
Saunders Point, Australia 61 E4 27 52S 125 38 E
Saurimo, Angola 52 F4 9 40S 20 12 E
Sausalito, U.S.A. 84 H4 37 51N 122 29W
Savá, Honduras 88 C2 15 32N 86 15W
Sava →, Serbia, Yug. 21 B9 44 50N 20 26 E
Savage, U.S.A. 80 B2 47 27N 104 21W
Savage I. = Niue, Cook Is. 65 J11 19 2S 169 54W
Savage River, Australia 62 G4 41 31S 145 14 E
Savai'i, W. Samoa 59 A12 13 28S 172 24W
Savalou, Benin 50 G6 7 57N 1 58 E
Savane, Mozam. 55 F4 19 37S 35 8 E
Savanna, U.S.A. 80 D9 42 5N 90 8W
Savanna-la-Mar, Jamaica 88 C4 18 10N 78 10W
**Savannah**, Ga., U.S.A. 77 J5 32 5N 81 6W
Savannah, Mo., U.S.A. 80 F7 39 56N 94 50W
Savannah, Tenn., U.S.A. 77 H1 35 14N 88 15W
Savannah →, U.S.A. 77 J5 32 2N 80 53W
Savannakhet, Laos 38 D5 16 30N 104 49 E
Savant L., Canada 70 B1 50 16N 90 44W
Savant Lake, Canada 70 B1 50 14N 90 40W
Savanur, India 40 M9 14 59N 75 21 E
Save →, Mozam. 57 C5 21 16S 34 0 E
Sāveh, Iran 45 C6 35 2N 50 20 E
Savelugu, Ghana 50 G5 9 38N 0 54W
Savo, Finland 8 E22 62 45N 27 30 E
Savoie □, France 18 D7 45 26N 6 25 E
Savona, Italy 18 D8 44 17N 8 30 E
Savona, U.S.A. 78 D7 42 17N 77 13W
Savonlinna, Finland 24 B4 61 52N 28 53 E
**Savoy** = Savoie □, France 18 D7 45 26N 6 25 E
Savur, Turkey 44 B4 37 34N 40 53 E
Sawahlunto, Indonesia 36 E2 0 40S 100 52 E
Sawai, Indonesia 37 E7 3 0S 129 5 E
Sawai Madhopur, India 42 G7 26 0N 76 25 E
Sawang Daen Din, Thailand 38 D4 17 28N 103 28 E
Sawankhalok, Thailand 38 D2 17 19N 99 50 E
Sawara, Japan 31 G10 35 55N 140 30 E
Sawatch Range, U.S.A. 83 G10 38 30N 106 30W
Sawel Mt., U.K. 13 B4 54 50N 7 2W
Sawi, Thailand 39 G2 10 14N 99 5 E
Sawmills, Zimbabwe 55 F2 19 30S 28 2 E
Sawtooth Range, U.S.A. 82 E6 44 3N 114 58W
Sawu, Indonesia 37 F6 10 35S 121 50 E
Sawu Sea, Indonesia 37 F6 9 30S 121 50 E
Saxby →, Australia 62 B3 18 25S 140 53 E
Saxmundham, U.K. 11 E9 52 13N 1 30 E
**Saxony** = Sachsen □, Germany 16 C7 50 55N 13 10 E
Saxony, Lower = Niedersachsen □, Germany 16 B5 52 50N 9 0 E
Saxton, U.S.A. 78 F6 40 13N 78 15W
Sayabec, Canada 71 C6 48 35N 67 41W
Sayaboury, Laos 38 C3 19 15N 101 45 E
Sayán, Peru 92 F3 11 8S 77 12W
Sayan, Vostochnyy, Russia 27 D10 54 0N 96 0 E
Sayan, Zapadnyy, Russia 27 D10 52 30N 94 0 E
Saydā, Lebanon 47 B4 33 35N 35 25 E
Sayhandulaan = Oldziyt, Mongolia 34 B5 44 40N 109 1 E
Sayḥūt, Yemen 46 D5 15 12N 51 10 E
Saynshand, Mongolia 34 B6 44 55N 110 11 E
Sayre, Okla., U.S.A. 81 H5 35 18N 99 38W
Sayre, Pa., U.S.A. 79 E8 41 59N 76 32W
Sayreville, U.S.A. 79 F10 40 28N 74 22W
Sayula, Mexico 86 D4 19 50N 103 40W
Sayward, Canada 72 C3 50 21N 125 55W
Sazanit, Albania 21 D8 40 30N 19 20 E
Sázava →, Czech Rep. 16 D8 49 53N 14 24 E
Sazin, Pakistan 43 B5 35 35N 73 30 E
**Scafell Pike**, U.K. 10 C4 54 27N 3 14W
Scalloway, U.K. 12 A7 60 9N 1 17W
Scalpay, U.K. 12 D3 57 18N 6 0W
Scandia, Canada 72 C6 50 20N 112 0W
Scandicci, Italy 20 C4 43 45N 11 11 E
**Scandinavia**, Europe 6 C8 64 0N 12 0 E
Scapa Flow, U.K. 12 C5 58 53N 3 3W
Scappoose, U.S.A. 84 E4 45 45N 122 53W
Scarba, U.K. 12 E3 56 11N 5 43W
Scarborough, Trin. & Tob. 89 D7 11 11N 60 42W
Scarborough, U.K. 10 C7 54 17N 0 24W
Scariff I., Ireland 13 E1 51 44N 10 15W
Scarp, U.K. 12 C1 58 1N 7 8W
Scebeli, Wabi →, Somali Rep. 46 G3 2 0N 44 0 E
Schaffhausen, Switz. 18 C8 47 42N 8 39 E
Schagen, Neths. 15 B4 52 49N 4 48 E
Schaghticoke, U.S.A. 79 D11 42 54N 73 35W
Schefferville, Canada 71 B6 54 48N 66 50W
Schelde →, Belgium 15 C4 51 15N 4 16 E
Schell Creek Ra., U.S.A. 82 G6 39 15N 114 30W
Schellsburg, U.S.A. 78 F6 40 3N 78 39W
Schenectady, U.S.A. 79 D11 42 49N 73 57W
Schenevus, U.S.A. 79 D10 42 33N 74 50W
Schiedam, Neths. 15 C4 51 55N 4 25 E
Schiermonnikoog, Neths. 15 A6 53 30N 6 15 E
Schio, Italy 20 B4 45 43N 11 21 E
Schleswig, Germany 16 A5 54 31N 9 34 E
Schleswig-Holstein □, Germany 16 A5 54 30N 9 30 E
Schoharie, U.S.A. 79 D10 42 40N 74 19W
Schoharie →, U.S.A. 79 D10 42 57N 74 18W
Scholls, U.S.A. 84 E4 45 24N 122 56W
Schouten I., Australia 62 G4 42 20S 148 20 E
Schouten Is. = Supiori, Indonesia 37 E9 1 0S 136 0 E
Schouwen, Neths. 15 C3 51 43N 3 45 E
Schreiber, Canada 70 C2 48 45N 87 20W
Schroon Lake, U.S.A. 79 C11 43 50N 73 46W
Schuler, Canada 73 C6 50 20N 110 6W
Schumacher, Canada 70 C3 48 30N 81 16W
Schurz, U.S.A. 82 G4 38 57N 118 49W
Schuyler, U.S.A. 80 E6 41 27N 97 4W
Schuylerville, U.S.A. 79 C11 43 6N 73 35W
Schuylkill →, U.S.A. 79 G9 39 53N 75 12W
Schuylkill Haven, U.S.A. 79 F8 40 37N 76 11W
Schwäbische Alb, Germany 16 D5 48 20N 9 30 E
Schwaner, Pegunungan, Indonesia 36 E4 1 0S 112 30 E
Schwarzwald, Germany 16 D5 48 30N 8 20 E
Schwedt, Germany 16 B8 53 3N 14 16 E
Schweinfurt, Germany 16 C6 50 3N 10 14 E
Schweizer-Reneke, S. Africa 56 D4 27 11S 25 18 E
Schwenningen = Villingen-Schwenningen, Germany 16 D5 48 3N 8 26 E
Schwerin, Germany 16 B6 53 36N 11 22 E
Schwyz, Switz. 18 C8 47 2N 8 39 E
Sciacca, Italy 20 F5 37 31N 13 3 E
Scilla, Italy 20 E6 38 15N 15 43 E
**Scilly, Isles of**, U.K. 11 H1 49 56N 6 22W
Scioto →, U.S.A. 76 F4 38 44N 83 1W
Scituate, U.S.A. 79 D14 42 12N 70 44W
Scobey, U.S.A. 80 A2 48 47N 105 25W
Scone, Australia 63 E5 32 5S 150 52 E
Scoresbysund, Greenland 4 B6 70 20N 23 0W
Scotia, Calif., U.S.A. 82 F1 40 29N 124 6W
Scotia, N.Y., U.S.A. 79 D11 42 50N 73 58W
Scotia Sea, Antarctica 5 B18 56 5S 56 0W
Scotland, Canada 78 C4 43 1N 80 22W
**Scotland** □, U.K. 12 E5 57 0N 4 0W
Scott, C., Australia 60 B4 13 30S 129 49 E
Scott City, U.S.A. 80 F4 38 29N 100 54W
Scott Glacier, Antarctica 5 C8 66 15S 100 5 E
Scott I., Antarctica 5 C11 67 0S 179 0 E
Scott Is., Canada 72 C3 50 48N 128 40W
Scott L., Canada 73 B7 59 55N 106 18W
Scott Reef, Australia 60 B3 14 0S 121 50 E
Scottburgh, S. Africa 57 E5 30 15S 30 47 E
Scottdale, U.S.A. 78 F5 40 6N 79 35W
Scottish Borders □, U.K. 12 F6 55 35N 2 50W
Scottsbluff, U.S.A. 80 E3 41 52N 103 40W
Scottsboro, U.S.A. 77 H3 34 40N 86 2W
Scottsburg, U.S.A. 76 F3 38 41N 85 47W
Scottsdale, Australia 62 G4 41 9S 147 31 E
Scottsdale, U.S.A. 83 K7 33 29N 111 56W
Scottsville, Ky., U.S.A. 77 G2 36 45N 86 11W
Scottsville, N.Y., U.S.A. 78 C7 43 2N 77 47W
Scottville, U.S.A. 76 D2 43 58N 86 17W
Scranton, U.S.A. 79 E9 41 25N 75 40W
Scugog, L., Canada 78 B6 44 10N 78 55W
Scunthorpe, U.K. 10 D7 53 36N 0 39W
Seabrook, L., Australia 61 F2 30 55S 119 40 E
Seaford, U.K. 11 G8 50 47N 0 7 E
Seaford, U.S.A. 76 F8 38 39N 75 37W
Seaforth, Australia 62 C4 20 55S 148 57 E
Seaforth, Canada 78 C3 43 35N 81 25W
Seaforth, L., U.K. 12 D2 57 52N 6 36W
Seagraves, U.S.A. 81 J3 32 57N 102 34W
Seaham, U.K. 10 C6 54 50N 1 20W
Seal →, Canada 73 B10 59 4N 94 48W
Seal L., Canada 71 B7 54 20N 61 30W
Sealy, U.S.A. 81 L6 29 47N 96 9W
Searchlight, U.S.A. 85 K12 35 28N 114 55W
Searcy, U.S.A. 81 H9 35 15N 91 44W
Searles L., U.S.A. 85 K9 35 44N 117 21W
Seascale, U.K. 10 C4 54 24N 3 29W
Seaside, Calif., U.S.A. 84 J5 36 37N 121 50W
Seaside, Oreg., U.S.A. 84 E3 46 0N 123 56W
Seaspray, Australia 63 F4 38 25S 147 15 E
**Seattle**, U.S.A. 84 C4 47 36N 122 20W
Seaview Ra., Australia 62 B4 18 40S 145 45 E
Sebago L., U.S.A. 79 C14 43 52N 70 34W
Sebago Lake, U.S.A. 79 C14 43 51N 70 34W
Sebastián Vizcaíno, B., Mexico 86 B2 28 0N 114 30W
Sebastopol = Sevastopol, Ukraine 25 F5 44 35N 33 30 E
Sebastopol, U.S.A. 84 G4 38 24N 122 49W
Sebewaing, U.S.A. 76 D4 43 44N 83 27W
Sebha = Sabhah, Libya 51 C8 27 9N 14 29 E
Şebinkarahisar, Turkey 25 F6 40 22N 38 28 E
Sebring, Fla., U.S.A. 77 M5 27 30N 81 27W
Sebring, Ohio, U.S.A. 78 F3 40 55N 81 2W
Sebringville, Canada 78 C3 43 24N 81 4W
Sebta = Ceuta, N. Afr. 19 E3 35 52N 5 18W
Sebuku, Indonesia 36 E5 3 30S 116 25 E
Sebuku, Teluk, Malaysia 36 D5 4 0N 118 10 E
Sechelt, Canada 72 D4 49 25N 123 42W
Sechura, Desierto de, Peru 92 E2 6 0S 80 30W
Secretary I., N.Z. 59 L1 45 15S 166 56 E
Secunderabad, India 40 L11 17 28N 78 30 E
Security-Widefield, U.S.A. 80 F2 38 45N 104 45W
Sedalia, U.S.A. 80 F8 38 42N 93 14W
Sedan, France 18 B6 49 43N 4 57 E
Sedan, U.S.A. 81 G6 37 8N 96 11W
Seddon, N.Z. 59 J5 41 40S 174 7 E
Seddonville, N.Z. 59 J4 41 33S 172 1 E
Sedé Boqér, Israel 47 E3 30 52N 34 47 E
Sedeh, Fārs, Iran 45 D7 30 45N 52 11 E
Sedeh, Khorāsān, Iran 45 C8 33 20N 59 14 E
Sederot, Israel 47 D3 31 32N 34 37 E
Sédhiou, Senegal 50 F2 12 44N 15 30W
Sedley, Canada 73 C8 50 10N 104 0W
Sedona, U.S.A. 83 J8 34 52N 111 46W
Sedova, Pik, Russia 26 B6 73 29N 54 58 E
Sedro Woolley, U.S.A. 84 B4 48 30N 122 14W
Seeheim, Namibia 56 D2 26 50S 17 45 E
Seekoei →, S. Africa 56 E4 30 18S 25 1 E
Seeley's Bay, Canada 79 B8 44 29N 76 14W
Seferihisar, Turkey 21 E12 38 10N 26 50 E
Seg-ozero, Russia 24 B5 63 20N 33 46 E
Segamat, Malaysia 39 L4 2 30N 102 50 E
Segesta, Italy 20 F5 37 56N 12 50 E
Seget, Indonesia 37 E8 1 24S 130 58 E
Segezha, Russia 24 B5 63 44N 34 19 E
Ségou, Mali 50 F4 13 30N 6 16W
Segovia = Coco →, Cent. Amer. 88 D3 15 0N 83 8W
Segovia, Spain 19 B3 40 57N 4 10W
Segre →, Spain 19 B6 41 40N 0 43 E
Séguéla, Ivory C. 50 G4 7 55N 6 40W
Seguin, U.S.A. 81 L6 29 34N 97 58W
Segundo →, Argentina 94 C3 30 53S 62 44W
Segura →, Spain 19 C5 38 3N 0 44W
Seh Konj, Kūh-e, Iran 45 D8 30 6N 57 30 E
Seh Qal'eh, Iran 45 C8 33 40N 58 24 E
Sehitwa, Botswana 56 C3 20 30S 22 30 E
Sehore, India 42 H7 23 10N 77 5 E
Sehwan, Pakistan 42 F2 26 28N 67 53 E
Seil, U.K. 12 E3 56 18N 5 38W
Seiland, Norway 8 A20 70 25N 23 15 E
Seiling, U.S.A. 81 G5 36 9N 98 56W
Seinäjoki, Finland 9 E20 62 40N 22 51 E
**Seine** →, France 18 B4 49 26N 0 26 E
Sekayu, Indonesia 36 E2 2 51S 103 51 E
Seke, Tanzania 54 C3 3 20S 33 31 E
Sekenke, Tanzania 54 C3 4 18S 34 11 E
Sekondi-Takoradi, Ghana 50 H5 4 58N 1 45W
Sekuma, Botswana 56 C3 24 36S 23 50 E
Selah, U.S.A. 82 C3 46 39N 120 32W
Selama, Malaysia 39 K3 5 12N 100 42 E
Selaru, Indonesia 37 F8 8 9S 131 0 E
Selby, U.K. 10 D6 53 47N 1 5W
Selby, U.S.A. 80 C4 45 31N 100 2W
Selçuk, Turkey 21 F12 37 56N 27 22 E
Selden, U.S.A. 80 F4 39 33N 100 34W
Sele →, Italy 20 D6 40 29N 14 56 E
Selebi-Pikwe, Botswana 57 C4 21 58S 27 48 E
Selemdzha →, Russia 27 D13 51 42N 128 53 E
Selenga = Selenge Mörön →, Asia 32 A5 52 16N 106 16 E
Selenge Mörön →, Asia 32 A5 52 16N 106 16 E
Seletan, Tanjung, Indonesia 36 E4 4 10S 114 40 E
Sélibabi, Mauritania 50 E3 15 10N 12 15W
Seligman, U.S.A. 83 J7 35 20N 112 53W
Selîma, El Wâhât el, Sudan 51 D11 21 22N 29 19 E
Selinda Spillway, Botswana 56 B3 18 35S 23 10 E
Selinsgrove, U.S.A. 78 F8 40 48N 76 52W
Selkirk, Canada 73 C9 50 10N 96 55W
Selkirk, U.K. 12 F6 55 33N 2 50W
Selkirk I., Canada 73 C9 53 20N 99 6W
Selkirk Mts., Canada 68 C8 51 15N 117 40W
Selliá, Greece 23 D6 35 12N 24 23 E
Sells, U.S.A. 83 L8 31 55N 111 53W
Selma, Ala., U.S.A. 77 J2 32 25N 87 1W
Selma, Calif., U.S.A. 84 J7 36 34N 119 37W
Selma, N.C., U.S.A. 77 H6 35 32N 78 17W
Selmer, U.S.A. 77 H1 35 10N 88 36W
Selowandoma Falls, Zimbabwe 55 G3 21 15S 31 50 E
Selpele, Indonesia 37 E8 0 1S 130 5 E
Selsey Bill, U.K. 11 G7 50 43N 0 47W
Seltso, Russia 24 D5 53 22N 34 4 E
Selu, Indonesia 37 F8 7 32S 130 55 E
Selva, Argentina 94 B3 29 50S 62 0W
Selvas, Brazil 92 E5 6 30S 67 0W
Selwyn L., Canada 73 B8 60 0N 104 30W
Selwyn Mts., Canada 68 B6 63 0N 130 0W
Selwyn Ra., Australia 62 C3 21 10S 140 0 E
Semani →, Albania 21 D8 40 47N 19 30 E
Semarang, Indonesia 37 G14 7 0S 110 26 E
Sembabule, Uganda 54 C3 0 4S 31 25 E
Semeru, Indonesia 37 H15 8 4S 112 55 E
Semey, Kazakstan 26 D9 50 30N 80 10 E
Seminoe Reservoir, U.S.A. 82 F10 42 9N 106 55W
Seminole, Okla., U.S.A. 81 H6 35 14N 96 41W
Seminole, Tex., U.S.A. 81 J3 32 43N 102 39W
Seminole Draw →, U.S.A. 81 J3 32 27N 102 20W
Semipalatinsk = Semey, Kazakstan 26 D9 50 30N 80 10 E
Semirara Is., Phil. 37 B6 12 0N 121 20 E
Semitau, Indonesia 36 D4 0 29N 111 57 E
Semiyarka, Kazakstan 26 D8 50 55N 78 23 E
Semiyarskoye = Semiyarka, Kazakstan 26 D8 50 55N 78 23 E
Semmering P., Austria 16 E8 47 41N 15 45 E
Semnān, Iran 45 C7 35 40N 53 23 E
Semnān □, Iran 45 C7 36 0N 54 0 E
Semporna, Malaysia 37 D5 4 30N 118 33 E
Semuda, Indonesia 36 E4 2 51S 112 58 E
Sen →, Cambodia 36 B3 13 45N 105 12 E
Senā, Iran 45 D6 28 27N 51 36 E
Sena, Mozam. 55 F4 17 25S 35 0 E
Sena Madureira, Brazil 92 E5 9 5S 68 45W
Senador Pompeu, Brazil 93 E11 5 40S 39 20W
Senanga, Zambia 56 B3 16 2S 23 14 E
Senatobia, U.S.A. 81 H10 34 37N 89 58W
Sencelles, Spain 22 B9 39 39N 2 54 E
Sendai, Kagoshima, Japan 31 J5 31 50N 130 20 E
Sendai, Miyagi, Japan 30 E10 38 15N 140 53 E
Sendai-Wan, Japan 30 E10 38 15N 141 0 E
Sendhwa, India 42 J6 21 41N 75 6 E
Seneca, U.S.A. 77 H4 34 41N 82 57W
Seneca Falls, U.S.A. 79 D8 42 55N 76 48W
Seneca L., U.S.A. 78 D8 42 40N 76 54W
Senecaville L., U.S.A. 78 G3 39 55N 81 25W
**Senegal** ■, W. Afr. 50 F3 14 30N 14 30W
Senegal →, W. Afr. 50 E2 15 48N 16 32W
Senegambia, Africa 48 E2 12 45N 12 0W
Senekal, S. Africa 57 D4 28 20S 27 36 E
Senga Hill, Zambia 55 D3 9 19S 31 11 E
Senge Khambab = Indus →, Pakistan 42 G2 24 20N 67 47 E
Sengua →, Zimbabwe 55 F2 17 7S 28 5 E
Senhor-do-Bonfim, Brazil 93 F10 10 30S 40 10W
Senigállia, Italy 20 C5 43 43N 13 13 E
Senj, Croatia 16 F8 45 0N 14 58 E
Senja, Norway 8 B17 69 25N 17 30 E
Senkaku-Shotō, Japan 31 L1 25 45N 124 0 E
Senlis, France 18 B5 49 13N 2 35 E
Senmonorom, Cambodia 38 F6 12 27N 107 12 E
Senneterre, Canada 70 C4 48 25N 77 15W
Seno, Laos 38 D5 16 35N 104 50 E
Sens, France 18 B5 48 11N 3 15 E
Senta, Serbia, Yug. 21 B9 45 55N 20 3 E
Sentani, Indonesia 37 E10 2 36S 140 37 E
Sentery, Dem. Rep. of the Congo 54 D2 5 17S 25 42 E
Sentinel, U.S.A. 83 K7 32 52N 113 13W
Seo de Urgel = La Seu d'Urgell, Spain 19 A6 42 22N 1 23 E
Seohara, India 43 E8 29 15N 78 33 E
Seonath →, India 43 J10 21 44N 82 28 E
Seondha, India 43 F8 26 9N 78 48 E
Seoni, India 43 H8 22 5N 79 30 E
Seoni Malwa, India 42 H8 22 27N 77 28 E
**Seoul** = Sŏul, S. Korea 35 F14 37 31N 126 58 E
Sepīdān, Iran 45 D7 30 20N 52 5 E
Sepo-ri, N. Korea 35 E14 38 57N 127 25 E
Sepone, Laos 38 D6 16 45N 106 13 E
Sept-Îles, Canada 71 B6 50 13N 66 22W
Sequim, U.S.A. 84 B3 48 5N 123 6W
**Sequoia National Park**, U.S.A. 84 J8 36 30N 118 30W
Seraing, Belgium 15 D5 50 35N 5 32 E
Seraja, Indonesia 39 L7 2 41N 108 35 E
Serakhis →, Cyprus 23 D11 35 13N 32 55 E
Seram, Indonesia 37 E7 3 10S 129 0 E
Seram Sea, Indonesia 37 E7 2 30S 128 30 E
Serang, Indonesia 37 G12 6 8S 106 10 E
Serasan, Indonesia 39 L7 2 29N 109 4 E
**Serbia** □, Yugoslavia 21 C9 43 30N 21 0 E
Serdobsk, Russia 24 D7 52 28N 44 10 E
Seremban, Malaysia 39 L3 2 43N 101 53 E
Serengeti Plain, Tanzania 54 C4 2 40S 35 0 E
Serenje, Zambia 55 E3 13 14S 30 15 E
Sereth = Siret →, Romania 17 F14 45 24N 28 1 E
Sergino, Russia 26 C7 62 25N 65 12 E
Sergipe □, Brazil 93 F11 10 30S 37 30W
Sergiyev Posad, Russia 24 C6 56 20N 38 10 E
Seria, Brunei 36 D4 4 37N 114 23 E
Serian, Malaysia 36 D4 1 10N 110 31 E
Seribu, Kepulauan, Indonesia 36 F3 5 36S 106 33 E
Sérifos, Greece 21 F11 37 9N 24 30 E
Sérigny →, Canada 71 A6 56 47N 66 0W
Seringapatam Reef, Australia 60 B3 13 38S 122 5 E
Sermata, Indonesia 37 F7 8 15S 128 50 E
Serov, Russia 24 C11 59 29N 60 35 E
Serowe, Botswana 56 C4 22 25S 26 43 E
Serpentine Lakes, Australia 61 E4 28 30S 129 10 E
Serpukhov, Russia 24 D6 54 55N 37 28 E
Serra do Navio, Brazil 93 C8 0 59N 52 3W
Sérrai, Greece 21 D10 41 5N 23 31 E
Serrezuela, Argentina 94 C2 30 40S 65 20W
Serrinha, Brazil 93 F11 11 39S 39 0W
Sertanópolis, Brazil 95 A5 23 4S 51 2W
Serua, Indonesia 37 F8 6 18S 130 1 E
Serui, Indonesia 37 E9 1 53S 136 10 E
Serule, Botswana 56 C4 21 57S 27 20 E
Sese Is., Uganda 54 C3 0 20S 32 20 E
Sesepe, Indonesia 37 E7 1 30S 127 59 E
Sesfontein, Namibia 56 B1 19 7S 13 39 E
Sesheke, Zambia 56 B3 17 29S 24 13 E
S'Espalmador, Spain 22 C7 38 47N 1 26 E
S'Espardell, Spain 22 C7 38 48N 1 29 E
S'Estanyol, Spain 22 B9 39 22N 2 54 E
Setana, Japan 30 C9 42 26N 139 51 E
Sète, France 18 E5 43 25N 3 42 E
Sete Lagôas, Brazil 93 G10 19 27S 44 16W
Sétif, Algeria 50 A7 36 9N 5 26 E
Seto, Japan 31 G8 35 14N 137 6 E
Setonaikai, Japan 31 G6 34 20N 133 30 E
Settat, Morocco 50 B4 33 0N 7 40W
Setting L., Canada 73 C9 55 0N 98 38W
Settle, U.K. 10 C5 54 5N 2 16W
Settlement Pt., Bahamas 77 M6 26 40N 79 0W
Setúbal, Portugal 19 C1 38 30N 8 58W
Setúbal, B. de, Portugal 19 C1 38 40N 8 56W
Seul, Lac, Canada 68 C10 50 20N 92 30W
Sevan, Ozero = Sevana Lich, Armenia 25 F8 40 30N 45 20 E
Sevana Lich, Armenia 25 F8 40 30N 45 20 E
**Sevastopol**, Ukraine 25 F5 44 35N 33 30 E
Seven Sisters, Canada 72 C3 54 56N 128 10W
Severn →, Canada 70 A2 56 2N 87 36W
**Severn** →, U.K. 11 F5 51 35N 2 40W
Severn L., Canada 70 B1 53 54N 90 48W
Severnaya Zemlya, Russia 27 B11 79 0N 100 0 E
Severnyye Uvaly, Russia 24 C8 60 0N 50 0 E
Severo-Kurilsk, Russia 27 D16 50 40N 156 8 E
Severo-Yeniseyskiy, Russia 27 C10 60 22N 93 1 E
Severodvinsk, Russia 24 B6 64 27N 39 58 E
Severomorsk, Russia 24 A5 69 5N 33 27 E
Severouralsk, Russia 24 B10 60 9N 59 57 E
Sevier, U.S.A. 83 G7 38 39N 112 11W
Sevier →, U.S.A. 83 G7 39 4N 113 6W
Sevier Desert, U.S.A. 82 G7 39 40N 112 45W
Sevier L., U.S.A. 82 G7 38 54N 113 9W
Sevilla, Spain 19 D2 37 23N 5 58W
**Seville** = Sevilla, Spain 19 D2 37 23N 5 58W
Sevlievo, Bulgaria 21 C11 43 2N 25 6 E
Sewani, India 42 E6 28 58N 75 39 E
Seward, Alaska, U.S.A. 68 B5 60 7N 149 27W
Seward, Nebr., U.S.A. 80 E6 40 55N 97 6W
Seward, Pa., U.S.A. 78 F5 40 25N 79 1W
Seward Peninsula, U.S.A. 68 B3 65 30N 166 0W
Sewell, Chile 94 C1 34 10S 70 23W
Sewer, Indonesia 37 F8 5 53S 134 40 E
Sewickley, U.S.A. 78 F4 40 32N 80 12W
Sexsmith, Canada 72 B5 55 21N 118 47W
Seychelles ■, Ind. Oc. 29 K9 5 0S 56 0 E
Seyðisfjörður, Iceland 8 D6 65 16N 13 57W
Seydişehir, Turkey 25 G5 37 25N 31 51 E
Seydvān, Iran 44 B5 38 34N 45 2 E
Seyhan →, Turkey 44 B2 36 43N 34 53 E
Seym →, Ukraine 25 D5 51 27N 32 34 E
Seymour, Australia 63 F4 37 0S 145 10 E
Seymour, S. Africa 57 E4 32 33S 26 46 E
Seymour, Conn., U.S.A. 79 E11 41 24N 73 4W
Seymour, Ind., U.S.A. 76 F3 38 58N 85 53W
Seymour, Tex., U.S.A. 81 J5 33 35N 99 16W
Sfântu Gheorghe, Romania 17 F13 45 52N 25 48 E
Sfax, Tunisia 51 B8 34 49N 10 48 E
Shaanxi □, China 34 G5 35 0N 109 0 E
Shaba = Katanga □, Dem. Rep. of the Congo 54 D2 8 0S 25 0 E
Shabogamo L., Canada 71 B6 53 15N 66 30W
Shabunda, Dem. Rep. of the Congo 54 C2 2 40S 27 16 E
Shache, China 32 C2 38 20N 77 10 E
Shackleton Ice Shelf, Antarctica 5 C8 66 0S 100 0 E
Shackleton Inlet, Antarctica 5 E11 83 0S 160 0 E
Shādegān, Iran 45 D6 30 40N 48 38 E
Shadi, India 43 C7 33 24N 77 14 E
Shadrinsk, Russia 26 D7 56 5N 63 32 E
Shadyside, U.S.A. 78 G4 39 58N 80 45W
Shafter, U.S.A. 85 K7 35 30N 119 16W
Shaftesbury, U.K. 11 F5 51 0N 2 11W
Shagram, Pakistan 43 A5 36 24N 72 20 E
Shah Alizai, Pakistan 42 E2 29 25N 66 33 E
Shah Bunder, Pakistan 42 G2 24 13N 67 56 E
Shahabad, Punjab, India 42 D7 30 10N 76 55 E
Shahabad, Raj., India 42 G7 25 15N 77 11 E
Shahabad, Ut. P., India 43 F8 27 36N 79 56 E
Shahadpur, Pakistan 42 G3 25 55N 68 35 E
Shahba, Syria 47 C5 32 52N 36 38 E

Shahdād, Iran 45 D8 30 30N 57 40 E
Shahdād, Namakzār-e, Iran 45 D8 30 20N 58 20 E
Shahdadkot, Pakistan 42 F2 27 50N 67 55 E
Shahdol, India 43 H9 23 19N 81 26 E
Shahe, China 34 F8 37 0N 114 32 E
Shahganj, India 43 F10 26 3N 82 44 E
Shahgarh, India 40 F6 27 15N 69 50 E
Shahjahanpur, India 43 F8 27 54N 79 57 E
Shahpur, India 42 H7 22 12N 77 58 E
Shahpur, Baluchistan, Pakistan 42 E3 28 46N 68 27 E
Shahpur, Punjab, Pakistan 42 C5 32 17N 72 26 E
Shahpur Chakar, Pakistan 42 F3 26 9N 68 39 E
Shahpura, Mad. P., India 43 H9 23 10N 80 45 E
Shahpura, Raj., India 42 G6 25 38N 74 56 E
Shahr-e Bābak, Iran 45 D7 30 7N 55 9 E
Shahr-e Kord, Iran 45 C6 32 15N 50 55 E
Shāhrakht, Iran 45 C9 33 38N 60 16 E
Shahrig, Pakistan 42 D2 30 15N 67 40 E
Shahukou, China 34 D7 40 20N 112 18 E
Shaikhabad, Afghan. 42 B3 34 2N 68 45 E
Shajapur, India 42 H7 23 27N 76 21 E
Shakargarh, Pakistan 42 C6 32 17N 75 10 E
Shakawe, Botswana 56 B3 18 28S 21 49 E
Shaker Heights, U.S.A. 78 E3 41 29N 81 32W
Shakhty, Russia 25 E7 47 40N 40 16 E
Shakhunya, Russia 24 C8 57 40N 46 46 E
Shaki, Nigeria 50 G6 8 41N 3 21 E
Shallow Lake, Canada 78 B3 44 36N 81 5W
Shalqar, Kazakstan 26 E6 47 48N 59 39 E
Shaluli Shan, China 32 C4 30 40N 99 55 E
Shām, Iran 45 E8 26 39N 57 21 E
Shām, Bādiyat ash, Asia 44 C3 32 0N 40 0 E
Shamâl Kordofân □, Sudan 48 E6 15 0N 30 0 E
Shamattawa, Canada 70 A1 55 51N 92 5W
Shamattawa →, Canada 70 A2 55 1N 85 23W
Shamīl, Iran 45 E8 27 30N 56 55 E
Shāmkūh, Iran 45 C8 35 47N 57 50 E
Shamli, India 42 E7 29 32N 77 18 E
Shammar, Jabal, Si. Arabia 44 E4 27 40N 41 0 E
Shamo = Gobi, Asia 34 C6 44 0N 110 0 E
Shamo, L., Ethiopia 46 F2 5 45N 37 30 E
Shamokin, U.S.A. 79 F8 40 47N 76 34W
Shamrock, U.S.A. 81 H4 35 13N 100 15W
Shamva, Zimbabwe 55 F3 17 20S 31 32 E
Shan □, Burma 41 J21 21 30N 98 30 E
Shan Xian, China 34 G9 34 50N 116 5 E
Shanchengzhen, China 35 C13 42 20N 125 20 E
Shāndak, Iran 45 D9 28 28N 60 27 E
Shandon, U.S.A. 84 K6 35 39N 120 23W
Shandong □, China 35 G10 36 0N 118 0 E
Shandong Bandao, China 35 F11 37 0N 121 0 E
Shang Xian = Shangzhou, China 34 H5 33 50N 109 58 E
Shanga, Nigeria 50 F6 11 12N 4 33 E
Shangalowe, Dem. Rep. of the Congo 55 E2 10 50S 26 30 E
Shangani →, Zimbabwe 55 F2 18 41S 27 10 E
Shangbancheng, China 35 D10 40 50N 118 1 E
Shangdu, China 34 D7 41 30N 113 30 E
**Shanghai**, China 33 C7 31 15N 121 26 E
Shanghe, China 35 F9 37 20N 117 10 E
Shangnan, China 34 H6 33 32N 110 50 E
Shangqiu, China 34 G8 34 26N 115 36 E
Shangrao, China 33 D6 28 25N 117 59 E
Shangshui, China 34 H8 33 42N 114 35 E
Shangzhi, China 35 B14 45 22N 127 56 E
Shangzhou, China 34 H5 33 50N 109 58 E
Shanhetun, China 35 B14 44 33N 127 15 E
Shannon, N.Z. 59 J5 40 33S 175 25 E
**Shannon** →, Ireland 13 D2 52 35N 9 30W
Shannon, Mouth of the, Ireland 13 D2 52 30N 9 55W
Shannon Airport, Ireland 13 D3 52 42N 8 57W
Shansi = Shanxi □, China 34 F7 37 0N 112 0 E
Shantar, Ostrov Bolshoy, Russia 27 D14 55 9N 137 40 E
Shantipur, India 43 H13 23 17N 88 25 E
Shantou, China 33 D6 23 18N 116 40 E
Shantung = Shandong □, China 35 G10 36 0N 118 0 E
Shanxi □, China 34 F7 37 0N 112 0 E
Shanyang, China 34 H5 33 31N 109 55 E
Shanyin, China 34 E7 39 25N 112 56 E
Shaoguan, China 33 D6 24 48N 113 35 E
Shaoxing, China 33 D7 30 0N 120 35 E
Shaoyang, China 33 D6 27 14N 111 25 E
Shap, U.K. 10 C5 54 32N 2 40W
Shapinsay, U.K. 12 B6 59 3N 2 51W
Shaqra', Si. Arabia 44 E5 25 15N 45 16 E
Shaqrā', Yemen 46 E4 13 22N 45 44 E
Sharafkhāneh, Iran 44 B5 38 11N 45 29 E
Sharbot Lake, Canada 79 B8 44 46N 76 41W
Shari, Japan 30 C12 43 55N 144 40 E
**Sharjah** = Ash Shāriqah, U.A.E. 45 E7 25 23N 55 26 E
Shark B., Australia 61 E1 25 30S 113 32 E
Sharon, Mass., U.S.A. 79 D13 42 7N 71 11W
Sharon, Pa., U.S.A. 78 E4 41 14N 80 31W
Sharon Springs, Kans., U.S.A. 80 F4 38 54N 101 45W
Sharon Springs, N.Y., U.S.A. 79 D10 42 48N 74 37W
Sharp Pt., Australia 62 A3 10 58S 142 43 E
Sharpe L., Canada 70 B1 54 24N 93 40W
Sharpsville, U.S.A. 78 E4 41 15N 80 29W
Sharya, Russia 24 C8 58 22N 45 20 E
Shashemene, Ethiopia 46 F2 7 13N 38 33 E
Shashi, Botswana 57 C4 21 15S 27 27 E
Shashi, China 33 C6 30 25N 112 14 E
Shashi →, Africa 55 G2 21 14S 29 20 E
Shasta, Mt., U.S.A. 82 F2 41 25N 122 12W
Shasta L., U.S.A. 82 F2 40 43N 122 25W
**Shatt al'Arab** →, Iraq 45 D6 29 57N 48 34 E
Shaunavon, Canada 73 D7 49 35N 108 25W
Shaver L., U.S.A. 84 H7 37 9N 119 18W
Shaw →, Australia 60 D2 20 21S 119 17 E
Shaw I., Australia 62 C4 20 30S 149 2 E
Shawanaga, Canada 78 A4 45 31N 80 17W
Shawangunk Mts., U.S.A. 79 E10 41 35N 74 30W
Shawano, U.S.A. 76 C1 44 47N 88 36W
Shawinigan, Canada 70 C5 46 35N 72 50W
Shawnee, U.S.A. 81 H6 35 20N 96 55W
Shay Gap, Australia 60 D3 20 30S 120 10 E
Shaybārā, Si. Arabia 44 E3 25 26N 36 47 E
Shaykh, J. ash, Lebanon 47 B4 33 25N 35 50 E
Shaykh Miskīn, Syria 47 C5 32 49N 36 9 E
Shaykh Sa'īd, Iraq 44 C5 32 34N 46 17 E
Shcherbakov = Rybinsk, Russia 24 C6 58 5N 38 50 E
Shchuchinsk, Kazakstan 26 D8 52 56N 70 12 E
She Xian, China 34 F7 36 30N 113 40 E
Shebele = Scebeli, Wabi →, Somali Rep. 46 G3 2 0N 44 0 E
Sheboygan, U.S.A. 76 D2 43 46N 87 45W
Shediac, Canada 71 C7 46 14N 64 32W
Sheelin, L., Ireland 13 C4 53 48N 7 20W
Sheep Haven, Ireland 13 A4 55 11N 7 52W
Sheerness, U.K. 11 F8 51 26N 0 47 E
Sheet Harbour, Canada 71 D7 44 56N 62 31W
**Sheffield**, U.K. 10 D6 53 23N 1 28W
Sheffield, Ala., U.S.A. 77 H2 34 46N 87 41W
Sheffield, Mass., U.S.A. 79 D11 42 5N 73 21W
Sheffield, Pa., U.S.A. 78 E5 41 42N 79 3W
Sheikhpura, India 43 G11 25 9N 85 53 E
Shekhupura, Pakistan 42 D5 31 42N 73 58 E
Shelburne, N.S., Canada 71 D6 43 47N 65 20W
Shelburne, Ont., Canada 78 B4 44 4N 80 15W
Shelburne, Vt., U.S.A. 79 B11 44 22N 73 13W
Shelburne, Vt., U.S.A. 79 B11 44 23N 73 14W
Shelburne B., Australia 62 A3 11 50S 142 50 E
Shelburne Falls, U.S.A. 79 D12 42 36N 72 45W
Shelby, Mich., U.S.A. 76 D2 43 37N 86 22W
Shelby, Miss., U.S.A. 81 J9 33 57N 90 46W
Shelby, Mont., U.S.A. 82 B8 48 30N 111 51W
Shelby, N.C., U.S.A. 77 H5 35 17N 81 32W
Shelby, Ohio, U.S.A. 78 F2 40 53N 82 40W
Shelbyville, Ill., U.S.A. 80 F10 39 24N 88 48W
Shelbyville, Ind., U.S.A. 76 F3 39 31N 85 47W
Shelbyville, Ky., U.S.A. 76 F3 38 13N 85 14W
Shelbyville, Tenn., U.S.A. 77 H2 35 29N 86 28W
Sheldon, U.S.A. 80 D7 43 11N 95 51W
Sheldrake, Canada 71 B7 50 20N 64 51W
Shelikhova, Zaliv, Russia 27 D16 59 30N 157 0 E
Shell Lakes, Australia 61 E4 29 20S 127 30 E
Shellbrook, Canada 73 C7 53 13N 106 24W
Shellharbour, Australia 63 E5 34 31S 150 51 E
Shelter I, U.S.A. 79 E12 41 5N 72 21W
Shelton, Conn., U.S.A. 79 E11 41 19N 73 5W
Shelton, Wash., U.S.A. 84 C3 47 13N 123 6W
Shen Xian, China 34 F8 36 15N 115 40 E
Shenandoah, Iowa, U.S.A. 80 E7 40 46N 95 22W
Shenandoah, Pa., U.S.A. 79 F8 40 49N 76 12W
Shenandoah, Va., U.S.A. 76 F6 38 29N 78 37W
Shenandoah →, U.S.A. 76 F7 39 19N 77 44W
Shenandoah National Park, U.S.A. 76 F6 38 35N 78 22W
Shenchi, China 34 E7 39 8N 112 10 E
Shendam, Nigeria 50 G7 8 49N 9 30 E
Shendî, Sudan 51 E12 16 46N 33 22 E
Shengfang, China 34 E9 39 3N 116 42 E
Shenjingzi, China 35 B13 44 40N 124 30 E
Shenmu, China 34 E6 38 50N 110 29 E
Shenqiu, China 34 H8 33 25N 115 5 E
Shenqiucheng, China 34 H8 33 24N 115 2 E
Shensi = Shaanxi □, China 34 G5 35 0N 109 0 E
**Shenyang**, China 35 D12 41 48N 123 27 E
Sheo, India 42 F4 26 11N 71 15 E
Sheopur Kalan, India 40 G10 25 40N 76 40 E
Shepetivka, Ukraine 17 C14 50 10N 27 10 E
Shepetovka = Shepetivka, Ukraine 17 C14 50 10N 27 10 E
Shepparton, Australia 63 F4 36 23S 145 26 E
Sheppey, I. of, U.K. 11 F8 51 25N 0 48 E
Shepton Mallet, U.K. 11 F5 51 11N 2 33W
Sheqi, China 34 H7 33 12N 112 57 E
Sher Qila, Pakistan 43 A6 36 7N 74 2 E
Sherborne, U.K. 11 G5 50 57N 2 31W
Sherbro I., S. Leone 50 G3 7 30N 12 40W
Sherbrooke, Canada 71 C7 45 8N 61 59W
Sherbrooke, Qué., Canada 79 A13 45 28N 71 57W
Sherburne, U.S.A. 79 D9 42 41N 75 30W
Shergarh, India 42 F5 26 20N 72 18 E
Sherghati, India 43 G11 24 34N 84 47 E
Sheridan, Ark., U.S.A. 81 H8 34 19N 92 24W
Sheridan, Wyo., U.S.A. 82 D10 44 48N 106 58W
Sheringham, U.K. 10 E9 52 56N 1 13 E
Sherkin I., Ireland 13 E2 51 28N 9 26W
Sherkot, India 43 E8 29 22N 78 35 E
Sherman, U.S.A. 81 J6 33 40N 96 35W
Sherpur, India 43 G10 25 34N 83 47 E
Sherridon, Canada 73 B8 55 8N 101 5W
**Sherwood Forest**, U.K. 10 D6 53 6N 1 7W
Sherwood Park, Canada 72 C6 53 31N 113 19W
Sheslay →, Canada 72 B2 58 48N 132 5W
Shethanei L., Canada 73 B9 58 48N 97 50W
Shetland □, U.K. 12 A7 60 30N 1 30W
**Shetland Is.**, U.K. 12 A7 60 30N 1 30W
Shetrunji →, India 42 J5 21 19N 72 7 E
Sheyenne →, U.S.A. 80 B6 47 2N 96 50W
Shibām, Yemen 46 D4 16 0N 48 36 E
Shibata, Japan 30 F9 37 57N 139 20 E
Shibecha, Japan 30 C12 43 17N 144 36 E
Shibetsu, Japan 30 B11 44 10N 142 23 E
Shibogama L., Canada 70 B2 53 35N 88 15W
Shibushi, Japan 31 J5 31 25N 131 8 E
Shickshinny, U.S.A. 79 E8 41 9N 76 9W
Shickshock Mts. = Chic-Chocs, Mts., Canada 71 C6 48 55N 66 0W
Shidao, China 35 F12 36 50N 122 25 E
Shido, Japan 31 G7 34 19N 134 10 E
Shiel, L., U.K. 12 E3 56 48N 5 34W
Shield, C., Australia 62 A2 13 20S 136 20 E
Shiga □, Japan 31 G8 35 20N 136 0 E
Shiguaigou, China 34 D6 40 52N 110 15 E
Shihchiachuangi = Shijiazhuang, China 34 E8 38 2N 114 28 E
Shijiazhuang, China 34 E8 38 2N 114 28 E
Shikarpur, India 42 E8 28 17N 78 7 E
Shikarpur, Pakistan 42 F3 27 57N 68 39 E
Shikohabad, India 43 F8 27 6N 78 36 E
**Shikoku** □, Japan 31 H6 33 30N 133 30 E
Shikoku-Sanchi, Japan 31 H6 33 30N 133 30 E
Shiliguri, India 41 F16 26 45N 88 25 E
Shilka, Russia 27 D12 52 0N 115 55 E
Shilka →, Russia 27 D13 53 20N 121 26 E
Shillelagh, Ireland 13 D5 52 45N 6 32W
Shillington, U.S.A. 79 F9 40 18N 75 58W
Shillong, India 41 G17 25 35N 91 53 E
Shilo, West Bank 47 C4 32 4N 35 18 E
Shilou, China 34 F6 37 0N 110 48 E
Shimabara, Japan 31 H5 32 48N 130 20 E
Shimada, Japan 31 G9 34 49N 138 10 E
Shimane □, Japan 31 G6 35 0N 132 30 E
Shimanovsk, Russia 27 D13 52 15N 127 30 E
Shimizu, Japan 31 G9 35 0N 138 30 E
Shimodate, Japan 31 F9 36 20N 139 55 E
Shimoga, India 40 N9 13 57N 75 32 E
Shimoni, Kenya 54 C4 4 38S 39 20 E
Shimonoseki, Japan 31 H5 33 58N 130 55 E
Shimpuru Rapids, Angola 56 B2 17 45S 19 55 E
Shin, L., U.K. 12 C4 58 5N 4 30W
Shinano-Gawa →, Japan 31 F9 36 50N 138 30 E
Shināş, Oman 45 E8 24 46N 56 28 E
Shīndand, Afghan. 40 C3 33 12N 62 8 E
Shinglehouse, U.S.A. 78 E6 41 58N 78 12W
Shingū, Japan 31 H7 33 40N 135 55 E
Shinjō, Japan 30 E10 38 46N 140 18 E
Shinshār, Syria 47 A5 34 36N 36 43 E
Shinyanga, Tanzania 54 C3 3 45S 33 27 E
Shinyanga □, Tanzania 54 C3 3 50S 34 0 E
Shio-no-Misaki, Japan 31 H7 33 25N 135 45 E
Shiogama, Japan 30 E10 38 19N 141 1 E
Shiojiri, Japan 31 F8 36 6N 137 58 E
Shipchenski Prokhod, Bulgaria 21 C11 42 45N 25 15 E
Shiping, China 32 D5 23 45N 102 23 E
Shipki La, India 40 D11 31 45N 78 40 E
Shippegan, Canada 71 C7 47 45N 64 45W
Shippensburg, U.S.A. 78 F7 40 3N 77 31W
Shippenville, U.S.A. 78 E5 41 15N 79 28W
Shiprock, U.S.A. 83 H9 36 47N 108 41W
Shiqma, N. →, Israel 47 D3 31 37N 34 30 E
Shiquan, China 34 H5 33 5N 108 15 E
Shiquan He = Indus →, Pakistan 42 G2 24 20N 67 47 E
Shīr Kūh, Iran 45 D7 31 39N 54 3 E
Shiragami-Misaki, Japan 30 D10 41 24N 140 12 E
Shirakawa, Fukushima, Japan 31 F10 37 7N 140 13 E
Shirakawa, Gifu, Japan 31 F8 36 17N 136 56 E
Shirane-San, Gumma, Japan 31 F9 36 48N 139 22 E
Shirane-San, Yamanashi, Japan 31 G9 35 42N 138 9 E
Shiraoi, Japan 30 C10 42 33N 141 21 E
**Shīrāz**, Iran 45 D7 29 42N 52 30 E
Shire →, Africa 55 F4 17 42S 35 19 E
Shiretoko-Misaki, Japan 30 B12 44 21N 145 20 E
Shirinab →, Pakistan 42 D2 30 15N 66 28 E
Shiriya-Zaki, Japan 30 D10 41 25N 141 30 E
Shiroishi, Japan 30 F10 38 0N 140 37 E
Shīrvān, Iran 45 B8 37 30N 57 50 E
Shirwa, L. = Chilwa, L., Malawi 55 F4 15 15S 35 40 E
Shivpuri, India 42 G7 25 26N 77 42 E
Shixian, China 35 C15 43 5N 129 50 E
Shizuishan, China 34 E4 39 15N 106 50 E
Shizuoka, Japan 31 G9 34 57N 138 24 E
Shizuoka □, Japan 31 G9 35 15N 138 40 E
Shklov = Shklow, Belarus 17 A16 54 16N 30 15 E
Shklow, Belarus 17 A16 54 16N 30 15 E
Shkoder = Shkodra, Albania 21 C8 42 4N 19 32 E
Shkodra, Albania 21 C8 42 4N 19 32 E
Shkumbini →, Albania 21 D8 41 2N 19 31 E
Shmidta, Ostrov, Russia 27 A10 81 0N 91 0 E
Shō-Gawa →, Japan 31 F8 36 47N 137 4 E
Shoal L., Canada 73 D9 49 33N 95 1W
Shoal Lake, Canada 73 C8 50 30N 100 35W
Shōdo-Shima, Japan 31 G7 34 30N 134 15 E
Sholapur = Solapur, India 40 L9 17 43N 75 56 E
Shologontsy, Russia 27 C12 66 13N 114 0 E
Shōmrōn, West Bank 47 C4 32 15N 35 13 E
Shoreham by Sea, U.K. 11 G7 50 50N 0 16W
Shori →, Pakistan 42 E3 28 29N 69 44 E
Shorkot Road, Pakistan 42 D5 30 47N 72 15 E
Shoshone, Calif., U.S.A. 85 K10 35 58N 116 16W
Shoshone, Idaho, U.S.A. 82 E6 42 56N 114 25W
Shoshone →, U.S.A. 82 D8 44 22N 110 43W
Shoshone Mts., U.S.A. 82 G5 39 20N 117 25W
Shoshong, Botswana 56 C4 22 56S 26 31 E
Shoshoni, U.S.A. 82 E9 43 14N 108 7W
Shouguang, China 35 F10 37 52N 118 45 E
Shouyang, China 34 F7 37 54N 113 8 E
Show Low, U.S.A. 83 J9 34 15N 110 2W
Shreveport, U.S.A. 81 J8 32 31N 93 45W
Shrewsbury, U.K. 11 E5 52 43N 2 45W
Shri Mohangarh, India 42 F4 27 17N 71 18 E
Shrirampur, India 43 H13 22 44N 88 21 E
**Shropshire** □, U.K. 11 E5 52 36N 2 45W
Shu, Kazakstan 26 E8 43 36N 73 42 E
Shu →, Kazakstan 28 E10 45 0N 67 44 E
Shuangcheng, China 35 B14 45 20N 126 15 E
Shuanggou, China 35 G9 34 2N 117 30 E
Shuangliao, China 35 C12 43 29N 123 30 E
Shuangshanzi, China 35 D10 40 20N 119 8 E
Shuangyang, China 35 C13 43 28N 125 40 E
Shuangyashan, China 33 B8 46 28N 131 5 E
Shuguri Falls, Tanzania 55 D4 8 33S 37 22 E
Shuiye, China 34 F8 36 7N 114 8 E
Shujalpur, India 42 H7 23 18N 76 46 E
Shukpa Kunzang, India 43 B8 34 22N 78 22 E
Shulan, China 35 B14 44 28N 127 0 E
Shule, China 32 C2 39 25N 76 3 E
Shumagin Is., U.S.A. 68 C4 55 7N 160 30W
Shumen, Bulgaria 21 C12 43 18N 26 55 E
Shumikha, Russia 26 D7 55 10N 63 15 E
Shuo Xian = Shuozhou, China 34 E7 39 20N 112 33 E
Shuozhou, China 34 E7 39 20N 112 33 E
Shūr →, Fārs, Iran 45 D7 28 30N 55 0 E
Shūr →, Kermān, Iran 45 D8 30 52N 57 37 E
Shūr →, Yazd, Iran 45 D7 31 45N 55 15 E
Shūr Āb, Iran 45 C6 34 23N 51 11 E
Shūr Gaz, Iran 45 D8 29 10N 59 20 E
Shūrāb, Iran 45 C8 33 43N 56 29 E
Shūrjestān, Iran 45 D7 31 24N 52 25 E
Shurugwi, Zimbabwe 55 F3 19 40S 30 0 E
Shūsf, Iran 45 D9 31 50N 60 5 E
Shūshtar, Iran 45 D6 32 0N 48 50 E
Shuswap L., Canada 72 C5 50 55N 119 3W
Shuyang, China 35 G10 34 10N 118 42 E
Shūzū, Iran 45 D7 29 52N 54 30 E
Shwebo, Burma 41 H19 22 30N 95 45 E
Shwegu, Burma 41 G20 24 15N 96 26 E
Shweli →, Burma 41 H20 23 45N 96 45 E
Shymkent, Kazakstan 26 E7 42 18N 69 36 E
Shyok, India 43 B8 34 13N 78 12 E
Shyok →, Pakistan 43 B6 35 13N 75 53 E
Si Chon, Thailand 39 H2 9 0N 99 54 E
Si Kiang = Xi Jiang →, China 33 D6 22 5N 113 20 E
Si-ngan = Xi'an, China 34 G5 34 15N 109 0 E
Si Prachan, Thailand 38 E3 14 37N 100 9 E
Si Racha, Thailand 38 F3 13 10N 100 48 E
Si Xian, China 35 H9 33 30N 117 50 E
Siahaf →, Pakistan 42 E3 29 3N 68 57 E
Siahan Range, Pakistan 40 F4 27 30N 64 40 E
Siaksriindrapura, Indonesia 36 D2 0 51N 102 0 E
Sialkot, Pakistan 42 C6 32 32N 74 30 E
**Siam** = Thailand ■, Asia 38 E4 16 0N 102 0 E
**Sian** = Xi'an, China 34 G5 34 15N 109 0 E
Siantan, Indonesia 36 D3 3 10N 106 15 E
Sīāreh, Iran 45 D9 28 5N 60 14 E
Siargao, Phil. 37 C7 9 52N 126 3 E
Siari, Pakistan 43 B7 34 55N 76 40 E
Siasi, Phil. 37 C6 5 34N 120 50 E
Siau, Indonesia 37 D7 2 50N 125 25 E
Šiauliai, Lithuania 9 J20 55 56N 23 15 E
Sibâi, Gebel el, Egypt 44 E2 25 45N 34 10 E
Sibay, Russia 24 D10 52 42N 58 39 E
Sibayi, L., S. Africa 57 D5 27 20S 32 45 E
Šibenik, Croatia 20 C6 43 48N 15 54 E
**Siberia**, Russia 4 D13 60 0N 100 0 E
Siberut, Indonesia 36 E1 1 30S 99 0 E
Sibi, Pakistan 42 E2 29 30N 67 54 E
Sibil = Oksibil, Indonesia 37 E10 4 59S 140 35 E
Sibiti, Congo 52 E2 3 38S 13 19 E
Sibiu, Romania 17 F13 45 45N 24 9 E
Sibley, U.S.A. 80 D7 43 24N 95 45W
Sibolga, Indonesia 36 D1 1 42N 98 45 E
Sibsagar, India 41 F19 27 0N 94 36 E
Sibu, Malaysia 36 D4 2 18N 111 49 E
Sibuco, Phil. 37 C6 7 20N 122 10 E
Sibuguey B., Phil. 37 C6 7 50N 122 45 E
Sibut, C.A.R. 52 C3 5 46N 19 10 E
Sibutu, Phil. 37 D5 4 45N 119 30 E
Sibutu Passage, E. Indies 37 D6 4 50N 120 0 E
Sibuyan, Phil. 37 B6 12 25N 122 40 E
Sibuyan Sea, Phil. 37 B6 12 30N 122 20 E
Sicamous, Canada 72 C5 50 49N 119 0W
Siccus →, Australia 63 E2 31 26S 139 30 E
**Sichuan** □, China 32 C5 31 0N 104 0 E
Sicilia, Italy 20 F6 37 30N 14 30 E
**Sicily** = Sicilia, Italy 20 F6 37 30N 14 30 E
Sicuani, Peru 92 F4 14 21S 71 10W
Sidári, Greece 23 A3 39 47N 19 41 E
Siddhapur, India 42 H5 23 56N 72 25 E
Siddipet, India 40 K11 18 5N 78 51 E
Sidhauli, India 43 F9 27 17N 80 50 E
Sidheros, Ákra, Greece 23 D8 35 19N 26 19 E
Sidhi, India 43 G9 24 25N 81 53 E
Sidi-bel-Abbès, Algeria 50 A5 35 13N 0 39W
Sidlaw Hills, U.K. 12 E5 56 32N 3 2W
Sidley, Mt., Antarctica 5 D14 77 2S 126 2W
Sidmouth, U.K. 11 G4 50 40N 3 15W
Sidmouth, C., Australia 62 A3 13 25S 143 36 E
Sidney, Canada 72 D4 48 39N 123 24W
Sidney, Mont., U.S.A. 80 B2 47 43N 104 9W
Sidney, N.Y., U.S.A. 79 D9 42 19N 75 24W
Sidney, Nebr., U.S.A. 80 E3 41 8N 102 59W
Sidney, Ohio, U.S.A. 76 E3 40 17N 84 9W
Sidney Lanier L., U.S.A. 77 H4 34 10N 84 4W
Sidoarjo, Indonesia 37 G15 7 27S 112 43 E
Sidon = Saydā, Lebanon 47 B4 33 35N 35 25 E
Sidra, G. of = Surt, Khalīj, Libya 51 B9 31 40N 18 30 E
Siedlce, Poland 17 B12 52 10N 22 20 E
Sieg →, Germany 16 C4 50 46N 7 6 E
Siegen, Germany 16 C5 50 51N 8 0 E
Siem Pang, Cambodia 38 E6 14 7N 106 23 E
Siem Reap = Siemreab, Cambodia 38 F4 13 20N 103 52 E
Siemreab, Cambodia 38 F4 13 20N 103 52 E
**Siena**, Italy 20 C4 43 19N 11 21 E
Sieradz, Poland 17 C10 51 37N 18 41 E
Sierra Blanca, U.S.A. 83 L11 31 11N 105 22W
Sierra Blanca Peak, U.S.A. 83 K11 33 23N 105 49W
Sierra City, U.S.A. 84 F6 39 34N 120 38W
Sierra Colorada, Argentina 96 E3 40 35S 67 50W
Sierra Gorda, Chile 94 A2 22 50S 69 15W
**Sierra Leone** ■, W. Afr. 50 G3 9 0N 12 0W
**Sierra Madre**, Mexico 87 D6 16 0N 93 0W
Sierra Mojada, Mexico 86 B4 27 19N 103 42W
Sierra Nevada, U.S.A. 84 H8 37 30N 119 0W
Sierra Vista, U.S.A. 83 L8 31 33N 110 18W
Sierraville, U.S.A. 84 F6 39 36N 120 22W
Sífnos, Greece 21 F11 37 0N 24 45 E
Sifton, Canada 73 C8 51 21N 100 8W
Sifton Pass, Canada 72 B3 57 52N 126 15W
Sighetu-Marmaţiei, Romania 17 E12 47 57N 23 52 E
Sighişoara, Romania 17 E13 46 12N 24 50 E
Sigli, Indonesia 36 C1 5 25N 96 0 E
Siglufjörður, Iceland 8 C4 66 12N 18 55W
Signal, U.S.A. 85 L13 34 30N 113 38W
Signal Pk., U.S.A. 85 M12 33 20N 114 2W
Sigsig, Ecuador 92 D3 3 0S 78 50W
Sigüenza, Spain 19 B4 41 3N 2 40W
Siguiri, Guinea 50 F4 11 31N 9 10W
Sigulda, Latvia 9 H21 57 10N 24 55 E
Sihanoukville = Kampong Saom, Cambodia 39 G4 10 38N 103 30 E
Sihora, India 43 H9 23 29N 80 6 E
Siikajoki →, Finland 8 D21 64 50N 24 43 E
Siilinjärvi, Finland 8 E22 63 4N 27 39 E
Sijarira Ra., Zimbabwe 55 F2 17 36S 27 45 E
Sika, India 42 H3 22 26N 69 47 E
Sikao, Thailand 39 J2 7 34N 99 21 E
Sikar, India 42 F6 27 33N 75 10 E
Sikasso, Mali 50 F4 11 18N 5 35W
Sikeston, U.S.A. 81 G10 36 53N 89 35W
Sikhote Alin, Khrebet, Russia 27 E14 45 0N 136 0 E
Sikhote Alin Ra. = Sikhote Alin, Khrebet, Russia 27 E14 45 0N 136 0 E
Síkinos, Greece 21 F11 36 40N 25 8 E
Sikkani Chief →, Canada 72 B4 57 47N 122 15W
**Sikkim** □, India 41 F16 27 50N 88 30 E
Sikotu-Ko, Japan 30 C10 42 45N 141 25 E
Sil →, Spain 19 A2 42 27N 7 43W
Silacayoapan, Mexico 87 D5 17 30N 98 9W
Silawad, India 42 J6 21 54N 74 54 E
Silchar, India 41 G18 24 49N 92 48 E
Siler City, U.S.A. 77 H6 35 44N 79 28W
**Silesia** = Śląsk, Poland 16 C9 51 0N 16 30 E

Silgarhi Doti, *Nepal* 43 E9 29 15N 81 0 E
Silghat, *India* 41 F18 26 35N 93 0 E
Silifke, *Turkey* 25 G5 36 22N 33 58 E
Siliguri = Shiliguri, *India* 41 F16 26 45N 88 25 E
Siling Co, *China* 32 C3 31 50N 89 20 E
Silistra, *Bulgaria* 21 B12 44 6N 27 19 E
Silivri, *Turkey* 21 D13 41 4N 28 14 E
Siljan, *Sweden* 9 F16 60 55N 14 45 E
Silkeborg, *Denmark* 9 H13 56 10N 9 32 E
Silkwood, *Australia* 62 B4 17 45S 146 2 E
Sillajhuay, Cordillera, *Chile* 92 G5 19 46S 68 40W
Sillamäe, *Estonia* 9 G22 59 24N 27 45 E
Silloth, *U.K.* 10 C4 54 52N 3 23W
Siloam Springs, *U.S.A.* 81 G7 36 11N 94 32W
Silsbee, *U.S.A.* 81 K7 30 21N 94 11W
Šilutė, *Lithuania* 9 J19 55 21N 21 33 E
Silva Porto = Kuito, *Angola* 53 G3 12 22S 16 55 E
Silvani, *India* 43 H8 23 18N 78 25 E
Silver City, *U.S.A.* 83 K9 32 46N 108 17W
Silver Cr. →, *U.S.A.* 82 E4 43 16N 119 13W
Silver Creek, *U.S.A.* 78 D5 42 33N 79 10W
Silver L., *U.S.A.* 84 G6 38 39N 120 6W
Silver Lake, *Calif., U.S.A.* 85 K10 35 21N 116 7W
Silver Lake, *Oreg., U.S.A.* 82 E3 43 8N 121 3W
Silver Streams, *S. Africa* 56 D3 28 20S 23 33 E
Silverton, *Colo., U.S.A.* 83 H10 37 49N 107 40W
Silverton, *Tex., U.S.A.* 81 H4 34 28N 101 19W
Silvies →, *U.S.A.* 82 E4 43 34N 119 2W
Simaltala, *India* 43 G12 24 43N 86 33 E
Simanggang = Bandar Sri Aman, *Malaysia* 36 D4 1 15N 111 32 E
Simard, L., *Canada* 70 C4 47 40N 78 40W
Simav, *Turkey* 21 E13 39 4N 28 58 E
Simba, *Tanzania* 54 C4 2 10S 37 36 E
Simbirsk, *Russia* 24 D8 54 20N 48 25 E
Simbo, *Tanzania* 54 C2 4 51S 29 41 E
Simcoe, *Canada* 78 D4 42 50N 80 20W
Simcoe, L., *Canada* 78 B5 44 25N 79 20W
Simdega, *India* 43 H11 22 37N 84 31 E
Simeria, *Romania* 17 F12 45 51N 23 1 E
Simeulue, *Indonesia* 36 D1 2 45N 95 45 E
Simferopol, *Ukraine* 25 F5 44 55N 34 3 E
Sími, *Greece* 21 F12 36 35N 27 50 E
Simi Valley, *U.S.A.* 85 L8 34 16N 118 47W
Simikot, *Nepal* 43 E9 30 0N 81 50 E
Simla, *India* 42 D7 31 2N 77 9 E
Simmie, *Canada* 73 D7 49 56N 108 6W
Simmler, *U.S.A.* 85 K7 35 21N 119 59W
Simojoki →, *Finland* 8 D21 65 35N 25 1 E
Simojovel, *Mexico* 87 D6 17 12N 92 38W
Simonette →, *Canada* 72 B5 55 9N 118 15W
Simonstown, *S. Africa* 56 E2 34 14S 18 26 E
Simplonpass, *Switz.* 18 C8 46 15N 8 3 E
Simpson Desert, *Australia* 62 D2 25 0S 137 0 E
Simpson Pen., *Canada* 69 B11 68 34N 88 45W
Simpungdong, *N. Korea* 35 D15 40 56N 129 29 E
Simrishamn, *Sweden* 9 J16 55 33N 14 22 E
Simsbury, *U.S.A.* 79 E12 41 53N 72 48W
Simushir, Ostrov, *Russia* 27 E16 46 50N 152 30 E
Sin Cowe I., *S. China Sea* 36 C4 9 53N 114 19 E
Sinabang, *Indonesia* 36 D1 2 30N 96 24 E
Sinadogo, *Somali Rep.* 46 F4 5 50N 47 0 E
Sinai = Es Sînâ', *Egypt* 47 F3 29 0N 34 0 E
Sinai, Mt. = Mûsa, Gebel, *Egypt* 44 D2 28 33N 33 59 E
**Sinai Peninsula**, *Egypt* 47 F3 29 30N 34 0 E
Sinaloa □, *Mexico* 86 C3 25 0N 107 30W
Sinaloa de Leyva, *Mexico* 86 B3 25 50N 108 20W
Sinarádhes, *Greece* 23 A3 39 34N 19 51 E
Sincelejo, *Colombia* 92 B3 9 18N 75 24W
Sinch'ang, *N. Korea* 35 D15 40 7N 128 28 E
Sinchang-ni, *N. Korea* 35 E14 39 24N 126 8 E
Sinclair, *U.S.A.* 82 F10 41 47N 107 7W
Sinclair Mills, *Canada* 72 C4 54 5N 121 40W
Sinclair's B., *U.K.* 12 C5 58 31N 3 5W
Sinclairville, *U.S.A.* 78 D5 42 16N 79 16W
Sincorá, Serra do, *Brazil* 93 F10 13 30S 41 0W
**Sind**, *Pakistan* 42 G3 26 0N 68 30 E
Sind □, *Pakistan* 42 G3 26 0N 69 0 E
Sind →, *India* 43 F8 26 26N 79 13 E
Sind →, *Jammu & Kashmir, India* 43 B6 34 18N 74 45 E
Sind Sagar Doab, *Pakistan* 42 D4 32 0N 71 30 E
Sindangan, *Phil.* 37 C6 8 10N 123 5 E
Sindangbarang, *Indonesia* 37 G12 7 27S 107 1 E
Sinde, *Zambia* 55 F2 17 28S 25 51 E
Sindri, *India* 43 H12 23 45N 86 42 E
Sines, *Portugal* 19 D1 37 56N 8 51W
Sines, C. de, *Portugal* 19 D1 37 58N 8 53W
Sineu, *Spain* 22 B10 39 38N 3 1 E
Sing Buri, *Thailand* 38 E3 14 53N 100 25 E
Singa, *Sudan* 51 F12 13 10N 33 57 E
**Singapore** ■, *Asia* 39 M4 1 17N 103 51 E
Singapore, Straits of, *Asia* 39 M5 1 15N 104 0 E
Singaraja, *Indonesia* 36 F5 8 6S 115 10 E
Singida, *Tanzania* 54 C3 4 49S 34 48 E
Singida □, *Tanzania* 54 D3 6 0S 34 30 E
Singitikós Kólpos, *Greece* 21 D11 40 6N 24 0 E
Singkaling Hkamti, *Burma* 41 G19 26 0N 95 39 E
Singkang, *Indonesia* 37 E6 4 8S 120 1 E
Singkawang, *Indonesia* 36 D3 1 0N 108 57 E
Singkep, *Indonesia* 36 E2 0 30S 104 25 E
Singleton, *Australia* 63 E5 32 33S 151 0 E
Singleton, Mt., *N. Terr., Australia* 60 D5 22 0S 130 46 E
Singleton, Mt., *W. Austral., Australia* 61 E2 29 27S 117 15 E
Singoli, *India* 42 G6 25 0N 75 22 E
Singora = Songkhla, *Thailand* 39 J3 7 13N 100 37 E
Singosan, *N. Korea* 35 E14 38 52N 127 25 E
Sinhung, *N. Korea* 35 D14 40 11N 127 34 E
Sînî □, *Egypt* 47 F3 30 0N 34 0 E
Sinjai, *Indonesia* 37 F6 5 7S 120 20 E
Sinjār, *Iraq* 44 B4 36 19N 41 52 E
Sinkat, *Sudan* 51 E13 18 55N 36 49 E
Sinkiang Uighur = Xinjiang Uygur Zizhiqu □, *China* 32 C3 42 0N 86 0 E
Sinmak, *N. Korea* 35 E14 38 25N 126 14 E
Sinnamary, *Fr. Guiana* 93 B8 5 25N 53 0W
Sinni →, *Italy* 20 D7 40 8N 16 41 E
Sinop, *Turkey* 25 F6 42 1N 35 11 E
Sinor, *India* 42 J5 21 55N 73 20 E
Sinp'o, *N. Korea* 35 E15 40 0N 128 13 E
Sinsk, *Russia* 27 C13 61 8N 126 48 E
Sintang, *Indonesia* 36 D4 0 5N 111 35 E
Sinton, *U.S.A.* 81 L6 28 2N 97 31W
Sintra, *Portugal* 19 C1 38 47N 9 25W
Sinŭiju, *N. Korea* 35 D13 40 5N 124 24 E
Siocon, *Phil.* 37 C6 7 40N 122 10 E
Siófok, *Hungary* 17 E10 46 54N 18 3 E
Sioma, *Zambia* 56 B3 16 25S 23 28 E
Sion, *Switz.* 18 C7 46 14N 7 20 E
Sion Mills, *U.K.* 13 B4 54 48N 7 29W
Sioux City, *U.S.A.* 80 D6 42 30N 96 24W
Sioux Falls, *U.S.A.* 80 D6 43 33N 96 44W
Sioux Lookout, *Canada* 70 B1 50 10N 91 50W
Sioux Narrows, *Canada* 73 D10 49 25N 94 10W
Siping, *China* 35 C13 43 8N 124 21 E
Sipiwesk L., *Canada* 73 B9 55 5N 97 35W
Sipra →, *India* 42 H6 23 55N 75 28 E
Sipura, *Indonesia* 36 E1 2 18S 99 40 E
Siquia →, *Nic.* 88 D3 12 10N 84 20W
Siquijor, *Phil.* 37 C6 9 12N 123 35 E
Siquirres, *Costa Rica* 88 D3 10 6N 83 30W
Şīr Banī Yās, *U.A.E.* 45 E7 24 19N 52 37 E
Sir Edward Pellew Group, *Australia* 62 B2 15 40S 137 10 E
Sir Graham Moore Is., *Australia* 60 B4 13 53S 126 34 E
Sir James MacBrien, Mt., *Canada* 68 B7 62 8N 127 40W
Sira →, *Norway* 9 G12 58 23N 6 34 E
**Siracusa**, *Italy* 20 F6 37 4N 15 17 E
Sirajganj, *Bangla.* 43 G13 24 25N 89 47 E
Sirathu, *India* 43 G9 25 39N 81 19 E
Sīrdān, *Iran* 45 B6 36 39N 49 12 E
Sirdaryo = Syrdarya →, *Kazakstan* 26 E7 46 3N 61 0 E
Siren, *U.S.A.* 80 C8 45 47N 92 24W
Sirer, *Spain* 22 C7 38 56N 1 22 E
Siret →, *Romania* 17 F14 45 24N 28 1 E
Sirghāyā, *Syria* 47 B5 33 51N 36 8 E
Sirmaur, *India* 43 G9 24 51N 81 23 E
Sirohi, *India* 42 G5 24 52N 72 53 E
Sironj, *India* 42 G7 24 5N 77 39 E
Síros, *Greece* 21 F11 37 28N 24 57 E
Sirretta Pk., *U.S.A.* 85 K8 35 56N 118 19W
Sīrrī, *Iran* 45 E7 25 55N 54 32 E
Sirsa, *India* 42 E6 29 33N 75 4 E
Sirsa →, *India* 43 F8 26 51N 79 4 E
Sisak, *Croatia* 16 F9 45 30N 16 21 E
Sisaket, *Thailand* 38 E5 15 8N 104 23 E
Sishen, *S. Africa* 56 D3 27 47S 22 59 E
Sishui, *Henan, China* 34 G7 34 48N 113 15 E
Sishui, *Shandong, China* 35 G9 35 42N 117 18 E
Sisipuk L., *Canada* 73 B8 55 45N 101 50W
Sisophon, *Cambodia* 38 F4 13 38N 102 59 E
Sisseton, *U.S.A.* 80 C6 45 40N 97 3W
Sīstān, *Asia* 45 D9 30 50N 61 0 E
Sīstān, Daryācheh-ye, *Iran* 40 D2 31 0N 61 0 E
Sīstān va Balūchestān □, *Iran* 45 E9 27 0N 62 0 E
Sisters, *U.S.A.* 82 D3 44 18N 121 33W
Siswa Bazar, *India* 43 F10 27 9N 83 46 E
Sitamarhi, *India* 43 F11 26 37N 85 30 E
Sitapur, *India* 43 F9 27 38N 80 45 E
Siteki, *Swaziland* 57 D5 26 32S 31 58 E
Sitges, *Spain* 19 B6 41 17N 1 47 E
Sitía, *Greece* 23 D8 35 13N 26 6 E
Sitka, *U.S.A.* 72 B1 57 3N 135 20W
Sitoti, *Botswana* 56 C3 23 15S 23 40 E
Sittang Myit →, *Burma* 41 L20 17 20N 96 45 E
Sittard, *Neths.* 15 C5 51 0N 5 52 E
Sittingbourne, *U.K.* 11 F8 51 21N 0 45 E
Sittwe, *Burma* 41 J18 20 18N 92 45 E
Situbondo, *Indonesia* 37 G16 7 42S 114 0 E
Siuna, *Nic.* 88 D3 13 37N 84 45W
Siuri, *India* 43 H12 23 50N 87 34 E
Sīvand, *Iran* 45 D7 30 5N 52 55 E
Sivas, *Turkey* 25 G6 39 43N 36 58 E
Siverek, *Turkey* 44 B3 37 50N 39 19 E
Sivomaskinskiy, *Russia* 24 A11 66 40N 62 35 E
Sivrihisar, *Turkey* 25 G5 39 30N 31 35 E
Sîwa, *Egypt* 51 C11 29 11N 25 31 E
Sîwa Oasis, *Egypt* 48 D6 29 10N 25 30 E
Siwalik Range, *Nepal* 43 F10 28 0N 83 0 E
Siwan, *India* 43 F11 26 13N 84 21 E
Siwana, *India* 42 G5 25 38N 72 25 E
Sixmilebridge, *Ireland* 13 D3 52 44N 8 46W
Sixth Cataract, *Sudan* 51 E12 16 20N 32 42 E
Siziwang Qi, *China* 34 D6 41 25N 111 40 E
Sjælland, *Denmark* 9 J14 55 30N 11 30 E
Sjumen = Shumen, *Bulgaria* 21 C12 43 18N 26 55 E
Skadarsko Jezero, *Montenegro, Yug.* 21 C8 42 10N 19 20 E
Skaftafell, *Iceland* 8 D5 64 1N 17 0W
Skagafjörður, *Iceland* 8 D4 65 54N 19 35W
Skagastølstindane, *Norway* 9 F12 61 28N 7 52 E
Skagaströnd, *Iceland* 8 D3 65 50N 20 19W
Skagen, *Denmark* 9 H14 57 43N 10 35 E
Skagerrak, *Denmark* 9 H13 57 30N 9 0 E
Skagit →, *U.S.A.* 84 B4 48 23N 122 22W
Skagway, *U.S.A.* 68 C6 59 28N 135 19W
Skala-Podilska, *Ukraine* 17 D14 48 50N 26 15 E
Skala Podolskaya = Skala-Podilska, *Ukraine* 17 D14 48 50N 26 15 E
Skalat, *Ukraine* 17 D13 49 23N 25 55 E
Skåne, *Sweden* 9 J15 55 59N 13 30 E
Skaneateles, *U.S.A.* 79 D8 42 57N 76 26W
Skaneateles L., *U.S.A.* 79 D8 42 51N 76 22W
Skara, *Sweden* 9 G15 58 25N 13 30 E
Skardu, *Pakistan* 43 B6 35 20N 75 44 E
Skarżysko-Kamienna, *Poland* 17 C11 51 7N 20 52 E
Skeena →, *Canada* 72 C2 54 9N 130 5W
Skeena Mts., *Canada* 72 B3 56 40N 128 30W
Skegness, *U.K.* 10 D8 53 9N 0 20 E
Skeldon, *Guyana* 92 B7 5 55N 57 20W
Skellefte älv →, *Sweden* 8 D19 64 45N 21 10 E
Skellefteå, *Sweden* 8 D19 64 45N 20 50 E
Skelleftehamn, *Sweden* 8 D19 64 40N 21 9 E
Skerries, The, *U.K.* 10 D3 53 25N 4 36W
Ski, *Norway* 9 G14 59 43N 10 52 E
Skíathos, *Greece* 21 E10 39 12N 23 30 E
Skibbereen, *Ireland* 13 E2 51 33N 9 16W
Skiddaw, *U.K.* 10 C4 54 39N 3 9W
Skidegate, *Canada* 72 C2 53 15N 132 1W
Skien, *Norway* 9 G13 59 12N 9 35 E
Skierniewice, *Poland* 17 C11 51 58N 20 10 E
Skikda, *Algeria* 50 A7 36 50N 6 58 E
Skilloura, *Cyprus* 23 D12 35 14N 33 10 E
Skipton, *U.K.* 10 D5 53 58N 2 3W
Skirmish Pt., *Australia* 62 A1 11 59S 134 17 E
Skíros, *Greece* 21 E11 38 55N 24 34 E
Skive, *Denmark* 9 H13 56 33N 9 2 E
Skjálfandafljót →, *Iceland* 8 D5 65 59N 17 25W
Skjálfandi, *Iceland* 8 C5 66 5N 17 30W
Skoghall, *Sweden* 9 G15 59 20N 13 30 E
Skole, *Ukraine* 17 D12 49 3N 23 30 E
Skópelos, *Greece* 21 E10 39 9N 23 47 E
Skopí, *Greece* 23 D8 35 11N 26 2 E
**Skopje**, *Macedonia* 21 C9 42 1N 21 26 E
Skövde, *Sweden* 9 G15 58 24N 13 50 E
Skovorodino, *Russia* 27 D13 54 0N 124 0 E
Skowhegan, *U.S.A.* 77 C11 44 46N 69 43W
Skull, *Ireland* 13 E2 51 32N 9 34W
Skunk →, *U.S.A.* 80 E9 40 42N 91 7W
Skuodas, *Lithuania* 9 H19 56 16N 21 33 E
Skvyra, *Ukraine* 17 D15 49 44N 29 40 E
**Skye**, *U.K.* 12 D2 57 15N 6 10W
Skykomish, *U.S.A.* 82 C3 47 42N 121 22W
Skyros = Skíros, *Greece* 21 E11 38 55N 24 34 E
Slættaratindur, *Færoe Is.* 8 E9 62 18N 7 1W
Slagelse, *Denmark* 9 J14 55 23N 11 19 E
Slamet, *Indonesia* 37 G13 7 16S 109 8 E
Slaney →, *Ireland* 13 D5 52 26N 6 33W
Śląsk, *Poland* 16 C9 51 0N 16 30 E
Slate Is., *Canada* 70 C2 48 40N 87 0W
Slatina, *Romania* 17 F13 44 28N 24 22 E
Slatington, *U.S.A.* 79 F9 40 45N 75 37W
Slaton, *U.S.A.* 81 J4 33 26N 101 39W
Slave →, *Canada* 72 A6 61 18N 113 39W
Slave Coast, *W. Afr.* 50 G6 6 0N 2 30 E
Slave Lake, *Canada* 72 B6 55 17N 114 43W
Slave Pt., *Canada* 72 A5 61 11N 115 56W
Slavgorod, *Russia* 26 D8 53 1N 78 37 E
Slavonski Brod, *Croatia* 21 B8 45 11N 18 1 E
Slavuta, *Ukraine* 17 C14 50 15N 27 2 E
Slavyanka, *Russia* 30 C5 42 53N 131 21 E
Slavyansk = Slovyansk, *Ukraine* 25 E6 48 55N 37 36 E
Slawharad, *Belarus* 17 B16 53 27N 31 0 E
Sleaford, *U.K.* 10 D7 53 0N 0 24W
Sleaford B., *Australia* 63 E2 34 55S 135 45 E
Sleat, Sd. of, *U.K.* 12 D3 57 5N 5 47W
Sleeper Is., *Canada* 69 C11 58 30N 81 0W
Sleepy Eye, *U.S.A.* 80 C7 44 18N 94 43W
Slemon L., *Canada* 72 A5 63 13N 116 4W
Slide Mt., *U.S.A.* 79 E10 42 0N 74 25W
Slidell, *U.S.A.* 81 K10 30 17N 89 47W
Sliema, *Malta* 23 D2 35 54N 14 30 E
Slieve Aughty, *Ireland* 13 C3 53 4N 8 30W
Slieve Bloom, *Ireland* 13 C4 53 4N 7 40W
Slieve Donard, *U.K.* 13 B6 54 11N 5 55W
Slieve Gamph, *Ireland* 13 B3 54 6N 9 0W
Slieve Gullion, *U.K.* 13 B5 54 7N 6 26W
Slieve Mish, *Ireland* 13 D2 52 12N 9 50W
Slievenamon, *Ireland* 13 D4 52 25N 7 34W
Sligeach = Sligo, *Ireland* 13 B3 54 16N 8 28W
Sligo, *Ireland* 13 B3 54 16N 8 28W
Sligo, *U.S.A.* 78 E5 41 6N 79 29W
Sligo □, *Ireland* 13 B3 54 8N 8 42W
Sligo B., *Ireland* 13 B3 54 18N 8 40W
Slippery Rock, *U.S.A.* 78 E4 41 3N 80 3W
Slite, *Sweden* 9 H18 57 42N 18 48 E
Sliven, *Bulgaria* 21 C12 42 42N 26 19 E
Sloan, *U.S.A.* 85 K11 35 57N 115 13W
Sloansville, *U.S.A.* 79 D10 42 45N 74 22W
Slobodskoy, *Russia* 24 C9 58 40N 50 6 E
Slobozia, *Romania* 17 F14 44 34N 27 23 E
Slocan, *Canada* 72 D5 49 48N 117 28W
Slonim, *Belarus* 17 B13 53 4N 25 19 E
Slough, *U.K.* 11 F7 51 30N 0 36W
Slough □, *U.K.* 11 F7 51 30N 0 36W
Sloughhouse, *U.S.A.* 84 G5 38 26N 121 12W
**Slovak Rep.** ■, *Europe* 17 D10 48 30N 20 0 E
Slovakia = Slovak Rep. ■, *Europe* 17 D10 48 30N 20 0 E
Slovakian Ore Mts. = Slovenské Rudohorie, *Slovak Rep.* 17 D10 48 45N 20 0 E
**Slovenia** ■, *Europe* 16 F8 45 58N 14 30 E
Slovenija = Slovenia ■, *Europe* 16 F8 45 58N 14 30 E
Slovenské Rudohorie, *Slovak Rep.* 17 D10 48 45N 20 0 E
Slovyansk, *Ukraine* 25 E6 48 55N 37 36 E
Sluch →, *Ukraine* 17 C14 51 37N 26 38 E
Sluis, *Neths.* 15 C3 51 18N 3 23 E
Słupsk, *Poland* 17 A9 54 30N 17 3 E
Slurry, *S. Africa* 56 D4 25 49S 25 42 E
Slutsk, *Belarus* 17 B14 53 2N 27 31 E
Slyne Hd., *Ireland* 13 C1 53 25N 10 10W
Slyudyanka, *Russia* 27 D11 51 40N 103 40 E
Småland, *Sweden* 9 H16 57 15N 15 25 E
Smalltree L., *Canada* 73 A8 61 0N 105 0W
Smallwood Res., *Canada* 71 B7 54 0N 64 0W
Smara, *Morocco* 50 B4 32 9N 8 16W
Smarhon, *Belarus* 17 A14 54 20N 26 24 E
Smartt Syndicate Dam, *S. Africa* 56 E3 30 45S 23 10 E
Smartville, *U.S.A.* 84 F5 39 13N 121 18W
Smeaton, *Canada* 73 C8 53 30N 104 49W
Smederevo, *Serbia, Yug.* 21 B9 44 40N 20 57 E
Smerwick Harbour, *Ireland* 13 D1 52 12N 10 23W
Smethport, *U.S.A.* 78 E6 41 49N 78 27W
Smidovich, *Russia* 27 E14 48 36N 133 49 E
Smith, *Canada* 72 B6 55 10N 114 0W
Smith Center, *U.S.A.* 80 F5 39 47N 98 47W
Smith Sund, *Greenland* 4 B4 78 30N 74 0W
Smithburne →, *Australia* 62 B3 17 3S 140 57 E
Smithers, *Canada* 72 C3 54 45N 127 10W
Smithfield, *S. Africa* 57 E4 30 9S 26 30 E
Smithfield, *N.C., U.S.A.* 77 H6 35 31N 78 21W
Smithfield, *Utah, U.S.A.* 82 F8 41 50N 111 50W
Smiths Falls, *Canada* 79 B9 44 55N 76 0W
Smithton, *Australia* 62 G4 40 53S 145 6 E
Smithville, *Canada* 78 C5 43 6N 79 33W
Smithville, *U.S.A.* 81 K6 30 1N 97 10W
Smoky →, *Canada* 72 B5 56 10N 117 21W
Smoky Bay, *Australia* 63 E1 32 22S 134 13 E
Smoky Hill →, *U.S.A.* 80 F6 39 4N 96 48W
Smoky Hills, *U.S.A.* 80 F5 39 15N 99 30W
Smoky Lake, *Canada* 72 C6 54 10N 112 30W
Smøla, *Norway* 8 E13 63 23N 8 3 E
**Smolensk**, *Russia* 24 D5 54 45N 32 5 E
Smolikas, Óros, *Greece* 21 D9 40 9N 20 58 E
Smolyan, *Bulgaria* 21 D11 41 36N 24 38 E
Smooth Rock Falls, *Canada* 70 C3 49 17N 81 37W
Smoothstone L., *Canada* 73 C7 54 40N 106 50W
Smorgon = Smarhon, *Belarus* 17 A14 54 20N 26 24 E
**Smyrna** = İzmir, *Turkey* 21 E12 38 25N 27 8 E
Smyrna, *U.S.A.* 76 F8 39 18N 75 36W
Snæfell, *Iceland* 8 D6 64 48N 15 34W
Snaefell, *U.K.* 10 C3 54 16N 4 27W
Snæfellsjökull, *Iceland* 8 D2 64 49N 23 46W
Snake →, *U.S.A.* 82 C4 46 12N 119 2W
Snake I., *Australia* 63 F4 38 47S 146 33 E
Snake Range, *U.S.A.* 82 G6 39 0N 114 20W
Snake River Plain, *U.S.A.* 82 E7 42 50N 114 0W
Snåsavatnet, *Norway* 8 D14 64 12N 12 0 E
Sneek, *Neths.* 15 A5 53 2N 5 40 E
Sneeuberge, *S. Africa* 56 E3 31 46S 24 20 E
Snelling, *U.S.A.* 84 H6 37 31N 120 26W
Sněžka, *Europe* 16 C8 50 41N 15 50 E
Snizort, L., *U.K.* 12 D2 57 33N 6 28W
Snøhetta, *Norway* 9 E13 62 19N 9 16 E
Snohomish, *U.S.A.* 84 C4 47 55N 122 6W
Snoul, *Cambodia* 39 F6 12 4N 106 26 E
Snow Hill, *U.S.A.* 76 F8 38 11N 75 24W
Snow Lake, *Canada* 73 C8 54 52N 100 3W
Snow Mt., *Calif., U.S.A.* 84 F4 39 23N 122 45W
Snow Mt., *Maine, U.S.A.* 79 A14 45 18N 70 48W
Snow Shoe, *U.S.A.* 78 E7 41 2N 77 57W
Snowbird L., *Canada* 73 A8 60 45N 103 0W
**Snowdon**, *U.K.* 10 D3 53 4N 4 5W
Snowdrift →, *Canada* 73 A6 62 24N 110 44W
Snowflake, *U.S.A.* 83 J8 34 30N 110 5W
Snowshoe Pk., *U.S.A.* 82 B6 48 13N 115 41W
Snowtown, *Australia* 63 E2 33 46S 138 14 E
Snowville, *U.S.A.* 82 F7 41 58N 112 43W
Snowy →, *Australia* 63 F4 37 46S 148 30 E
Snowy Mt., *U.S.A.* 79 C10 43 42N 74 23W
Snowy Mts., *Australia* 63 F4 36 30S 148 20 E
Snug Corner, *Bahamas* 89 B5 22 33N 73 52W
Snyatyn, *Ukraine* 17 D13 48 27N 25 38 E
Snyder, *Okla., U.S.A.* 81 H5 34 40N 98 57W
Snyder, *Tex., U.S.A.* 81 J4 32 44N 100 55W
Soahanina, *Madag.* 57 B7 18 42S 44 13 E
Soalala, *Madag.* 57 B8 16 6S 45 20 E
Soan →, *Pakistan* 42 C4 33 1N 71 44 E
Soanierana-Ivongo, *Madag.* 57 B8 16 55S 49 35 E
Sobat, Nahr →, *Sudan* 51 G12 9 22N 31 33 E
Sobhapur, *India* 42 H8 22 47N 78 17 E
Sobradinho, Reprêsa de, *Brazil* 93 E10 9 30S 42 0 E
Sobral, *Brazil* 93 D10 3 50S 40 20W
Soc Trang, *Vietnam* 39 H5 9 37N 105 50 E
Socastee, *U.S.A.* 77 J6 33 41N 79 1W
Soch'e = Shache, *China* 32 C2 38 20N 77 10 E
Sochi, *Russia* 25 F6 43 35N 39 40 E
Société, Is. de la, *Pac. Oc.* 65 J12 17 0S 151 0W
**Society Is.** = Société, Is. de la, *Pac. Oc.* 65 J12 17 0S 151 0W
Socompa, Portezuelo de, *Chile* 94 A2 24 27S 68 18W
Socorro, *N. Mex., U.S.A.* 83 J10 34 4N 106 54W
Socorro, *Tex., U.S.A.* 83 L10 31 39N 106 18W
Socorro, I., *Mexico* 86 D2 18 45N 110 58W
**Socotra**, *Ind. Oc.* 46 E5 12 30N 54 0 E
Soda L., *U.S.A.* 83 J5 35 10N 116 4W
Soda Plains, *India* 43 B8 35 30N 79 0 E
Soda Springs, *U.S.A.* 82 E8 42 39N 111 36W
Sodankylä, *Finland* 8 C22 67 29N 26 40 E
Soddy-Daisy, *U.S.A.* 77 H3 35 17N 85 10W
Söderhamn, *Sweden* 9 F17 61 18N 17 10 E
Söderköping, *Sweden* 9 G17 58 31N 16 20 E
Södermanland, *Sweden* 9 G17 58 56N 16 55 E
Södertälje, *Sweden* 9 G17 59 12N 17 39 E
Sodiri, *Sudan* 51 F11 14 27N 29 0 E
Sodus, *U.S.A.* 78 C7 43 14N 77 4W
Soekmekaar, *S. Africa* 57 C4 23 30S 29 55 E
Soest, *Neths.* 15 B5 52 9N 5 19 E
**Sofia** = Sofiya, *Bulgaria* 21 C10 42 45N 23 20 E
Sofia →, *Madag.* 57 B8 15 27S 47 23 E
Sofiya, *Bulgaria* 21 C10 42 45N 23 20 E
Sōfu-Gan, *Japan* 31 K10 29 49N 140 21 E
Sogamoso, *Colombia* 92 B4 5 43N 72 56W
Sogār, *Iran* 45 E8 25 53N 58 6 E
Sognadalsfjøra, *Norway* 9 F12 61 14N 7 5 E
Søgne, *Norway* 9 G12 58 5N 7 48 E
Sognefjorden, *Norway* 9 F11 61 10N 5 50 E
Sŏgwipo, *S. Korea* 35 H14 33 13N 126 34 E
Soh, *Iran* 45 C6 33 26N 51 27 E
Sohâg, *Egypt* 51 C12 26 33N 31 43 E
Sohagpur, *India* 42 H8 22 42N 78 12 E
Sŏhori, *N. Korea* 35 D15 40 7N 128 23 E
Soignies, *Belgium* 15 D4 50 35N 4 5 E
Soissons, *France* 18 B5 49 25N 3 19 E
Sōja, *Japan* 31 G6 34 40N 133 45 E
Sojat, *India* 42 G5 25 55N 73 45 E
Sokal, *Ukraine* 17 C13 50 31N 24 15 E
Söke, *Turkey* 21 F12 37 48N 27 28 E
Sokelo, *Dem. Rep. of the Congo* 55 D1 9 55S 24 36 E
Sokhumi, *Georgia* 25 F7 43 0N 41 0 E
Sokodé, *Togo* 50 G6 9 0N 1 11 E
Sokol, *Russia* 24 C7 59 30N 40 5 E
Sokółka, *Poland* 17 B12 53 25N 23 30 E
Sokołów Podlaski, *Poland* 17 B12 52 25N 22 15 E
Sokoto, *Nigeria* 50 F7 13 2N 5 16 E
Sol Iletsk, *Russia* 24 D10 51 10N 55 0 E
Solai, *Kenya* 54 B4 0 2N 36 12 E
Solan, *India* 42 D7 30 55N 77 7 E
Solano, *Phil.* 37 A6 16 31N 121 15 E
Solapur, *India* 40 L9 17 43N 75 56 E
Soldotna, *U.S.A.* 68 B4 60 29N 151 3W
Soléa □, *Cyprus* 23 D12 35 5N 33 4 E
Soledad, *Colombia* 92 A4 10 55N 74 46W
Soledad, *U.S.A.* 84 J5 36 26N 121 20W
Soledad, *Venezuela* 92 B6 8 10N 63 34W
Solent, The, *U.K.* 11 G6 50 45N 1 25W
Solfonn, *Norway* 9 F12 60 2N 6 57 E
Solhan, *Turkey* 44 B4 38 57N 41 3 E
Soligalich, *Russia* 24 C7 59 5N 42 10 E
Soligorsk = Salihorsk, *Belarus* 17 B14 52 51N 27 27 E
Solihull, *U.K.* 11 E6 52 26N 1 47W
Solikamsk, *Russia* 24 C10 59 38N 56 50 E
Solila, *Madag.* 57 C8 21 25S 46 37 E
Solimões = Amazonas →, *S. Amer.* 93 D9 0 5S 50 0W
Solingen, *Germany* 16 C4 51 10N 7 5 E

Staveley, N.Z. 59 K3 43 40S 171 32 E
Stavelot, Belgium 15 D5 50 23N 5 55 E
Stavern, Norway 9 G14 59 0N 10 1 E
Stavoren, Neths. 15 B5 52 53N 5 22 E
Stavropol, Russia 25 E7 45 5N 42 0 E
Stavros, Cyprus 23 D11 35 1N 32 38 E
Stavrós, Greece 23 D6 35 12N 24 45 E
Stavros, Ákra, Greece 23 D6 35 26N 24 58 E
Stawell, Australia 63 F3 37 5S 142 47 E
Stawell →, Australia 62 C3 20 20S 142 55 E
Stayner, Canada 78 B4 44 25N 80 5W
Stayton, U.S.A. 82 D2 44 48N 122 48W
Steamboat Springs, U.S.A. 82 F10 40 29N 106 50W
Steele, U.S.A. 80 B5 46 51N 99 55W
Steelton, U.S.A. 78 F8 40 14N 76 50W
Steen River, Canada 72 B5 59 40N 117 12W
Steenkool = Bintuni, Indonesia 37 E8 2 7S 133 32 E
Steens Mt., U.S.A. 82 E4 42 35N 118 40W
Steenwijk, Neths. 15 B6 52 47N 6 7 E
Steep Pt., Australia 61 E1 26 8S 113 8 E
Steep Rock, Canada 73 C9 51 30N 98 48W
Stefanie L. = Chew Bahir, Ethiopia 46 G2 4 40N 36 50 E
Stefansson Bay, Antarctica 5 C5 67 20S 59 8 E
Steiermark □, Austria 16 E8 47 26N 15 0 E
Steilacoom, U.S.A. 84 C4 47 10N 122 36W
Steinbach, Canada 73 D9 49 32N 96 40W
Steinkjer, Norway 8 D14 64 1N 11 31 E
Steinkopf, S. Africa 56 D2 29 18S 17 43 E
Stellarton, Canada 71 C7 45 32N 62 30W
Stellenbosch, S. Africa 56 E2 33 58S 18 50 E
Stendal, Germany 16 B6 52 36N 11 53 E
Steornabhaigh = Stornoway, U.K. 12 C2 58 13N 6 23W
Stepanakert = Xankändi, Azerbaijan 25 G8 39 52N 46 49 E
Stephens Creek, Australia 63 E3 31 50S 141 30 E
Stephens I., Canada 72 C2 54 10N 130 45W
Stephens L., Canada 73 B9 56 32N 95 0W
Stephenville, Canada 71 C8 48 31N 58 35W
Stephenville, U.S.A. 81 J5 32 13N 98 12W
Stepnoi = Elista, Russia 25 E7 46 16N 44 14 E
Steppe, Asia 28 D9 50 0N 50 0 E
Sterkstroom, S. Africa 56 E4 31 32S 26 32 E
Sterling, Colo., U.S.A. 80 E3 40 37N 103 13W
Sterling, Ill., U.S.A. 80 E10 41 48N 89 42W
Sterling, Kans., U.S.A. 80 F5 38 13N 98 12W
Sterling City, U.S.A. 81 K4 31 51N 101 0W
Sterling Heights, U.S.A. 76 D4 42 35N 83 0W
Sterling Run, U.S.A. 78 E6 41 25N 78 12W
Sterlitamak, Russia 24 D10 53 40N 56 0 E
Stérnes, Greece 23 D6 35 30N 24 9 E
Stettin = Szczecin, Poland 16 B8 53 27N 14 27 E
Stettiner Haff, Germany 16 B8 53 47N 14 15 E
Stettler, Canada 72 C6 52 19N 112 40W
Steubenville, U.S.A. 78 F4 40 22N 80 37W
Stevenage, U.K. 11 F7 51 55N 0 13W
Stevens Point, U.S.A. 80 C10 44 31N 89 34W
Stevenson, U.S.A. 84 E5 45 42N 121 53W
Stevenson L., Canada 73 C9 53 55N 96 0W
Stevensville, U.S.A. 82 C6 46 30N 114 5W
Stewart, B.C., Canada 72 B3 55 56N 129 57W
Stewart, N.W.T., Canada 68 B6 63 19N 139 26W
Stewart, U.S.A. 84 F7 39 5N 119 46W
Stewart, C., Australia 62 A1 11 57S 134 56 E
Stewart, I., Chile 96 G2 54 50S 71 15W
Stewart I., N.Z. 59 M1 46 58S 167 54 E
Stewarts Point, U.S.A. 84 G3 38 39N 123 24W
Stewartville, U.S.A. 80 D8 43 51N 92 29W
Stewiacke, Canada 71 C7 45 9N 63 22W
Steynsburg, S. Africa 56 E4 31 15S 25 49 E
Steyr, Austria 16 D8 48 3N 14 25 E
Steytlerville, S. Africa 56 E3 33 17S 24 19 E
Stigler, U.S.A. 81 H7 35 15N 95 8W
Stikine →, Canada 72 B2 56 40N 132 30W
Stilfontein, S. Africa 56 D4 26 51S 26 50 E
Stillwater, N.Z. 59 K3 42 27S 171 20 E
Stillwater, Minn., U.S.A. 80 C8 45 3N 92 49W
Stillwater, N.Y., U.S.A. 79 D11 42 55N 73 41W
Stillwater, Okla., U.S.A. 81 G6 36 7N 97 4W
Stillwater Range, U.S.A. 82 G4 39 50N 118 5W
Stillwater Reservoir, U.S.A. 79 C9 43 54N 75 3W
Stilwell, U.S.A. 81 H7 35 49N 94 38W
Štip, Macedonia 21 D10 41 42N 22 10 E
Stirling, Canada 78 B7 44 18N 77 33W
Stirling, U.K. 12 E5 56 8N 3 57W
Stirling □, U.K. 12 E4 56 12N 4 18W
Stirling Ra., Australia 61 F2 34 23S 118 0 E
Stittsville, Canada 79 A9 45 15N 75 55W
Stjernøya, Norway 8 A20 70 20N 22 40 E
Stjørdalshalsen, Norway 8 E14 63 29N 10 51 E
Stockerau, Austria 16 D9 48 24N 16 12 E
**Stockholm**, Sweden 9 G18 59 20N 18 3 E
Stockport, U.K. 10 D5 53 25N 2 9W
Stocksbridge, U.K. 10 D6 53 29N 1 35W
Stockton, Calif., U.S.A. 84 H5 37 58N 121 17W
Stockton, Kans., U.S.A. 80 F5 39 26N 99 16W
Stockton, Mo., U.S.A. 81 G8 37 42N 93 48W
**Stockton-on-Tees**, U.K. 10 C6 54 35N 1 19W
Stockton-on-Tees □, U.K. 10 C6 54 35N 1 19W
Stockton Plateau, U.S.A. 81 K3 30 30N 102 30W
Stoeng Treng, Cambodia 38 F5 13 31N 105 58 E
Stoer, Pt. of, U.K. 12 C3 58 16N 5 23W
**Stoke-on-Trent**, U.K. 10 D5 53 1N 2 11W
Stoke-on-Trent □, U.K. 10 D5 53 1N 2 11W
Stokes Pt., Australia 62 G3 40 10S 143 56 E
Stokes Ra., Australia 60 C5 15 50S 130 50 E
Stokksnes, Iceland 8 D6 64 14N 14 58W
Stokmarknes, Norway 8 B16 68 34N 14 54 E
Stolac, Bos.-H. 21 C7 43 5N 17 59 E
Stolbovoy, Ostrov, Russia 27 D17 74 44N 135 14 E
Stolbtsy = Stowbtsy, Belarus 17 B14 53 30N 26 43 E
Stolin, Belarus 17 C14 51 53N 26 50 E
Stomíon, Greece 23 D5 35 21N 23 32 E
Stone, U.K. 10 E5 52 55N 2 9W
Stoneboro, U.S.A. 78 E4 41 20N 80 7W
Stonehaven, U.K. 12 E6 56 59N 2 12W
Stonehenge, Australia 62 C3 24 22S 143 17 E
Stonehenge, U.K. 11 F6 51 9N 1 45W
Stonewall, Canada 73 C9 50 10N 97 19W
Stony L., Man., Canada 73 B9 58 51N 98 40W
Stony L., Ont., Canada 78 B6 44 30N 78 5W
Stony Point, U.S.A. 79 E11 41 14N 73 59W
Stony Pt., U.S.A. 79 C8 43 50N 76 18W
Stony Rapids, Canada 73 B7 59 16N 105 50W
Stony Tunguska = Tunguska, Podkamennaya →, Russia 27 C10 61 50N 90 13 E
Stonyford, U.S.A. 84 F4 39 23N 122 33W
Stora Lulevatten, Sweden 8 C18 67 10N 19 30 E
Storavan, Sweden 8 D18 65 45N 18 10 E
Stord, Norway 9 G11 59 52N 5 23 E
Store Bælt, Denmark 9 J14 55 20N 11 0 E
Storm B., Australia 62 G4 43 10S 147 30 E
Storm Lake, U.S.A. 80 D7 42 39N 95 13W
Stormberge, S. Africa 56 E4 31 16S 26 17 E
Stormsrivier, S. Africa 56 E3 33 59S 23 52 E
Stornoway, U.K. 12 C2 58 13N 6 23W
Storozhinets = Storozhynets, Ukraine 17 D13 48 14N 25 45 E
Storozhynets, Ukraine 17 D13 48 14N 25 45 E
Storrs, U.S.A. 79 E12 41 49N 72 15W
Storsjön, Sweden 8 E16 63 9N 14 30 E
Storuman, Sweden 8 D17 65 5N 17 10 E
Storuman, sjö, Sweden 8 D17 65 13N 16 50 E
Stouffville, Canada 78 C5 43 58N 79 15W
Stoughton, Canada 73 D8 49 40N 103 0W
Stour →, Dorset, U.K. 11 G6 50 43N 1 47W
Stour →, Kent, U.K. 11 F9 51 18N 1 22 E
Stour →, Suffolk, U.K. 11 F9 51 57N 1 4 E
Stourbridge, U.K. 11 E5 52 28N 2 8W
Stout L., Canada 73 C10 52 0N 94 40W
Stove Pipe Wells Village, U.S.A. 85 J9 36 35N 117 11W
Stow, U.S.A. 78 E3 41 10N 81 27W
Stowbtsy, Belarus 17 B14 53 30N 26 43 E
Stowmarket, U.K. 11 E9 52 12N 1 0 E
Strabane, U.K. 13 B4 54 50N 7 27W
Strahan, Australia 62 G4 42 9S 145 20 E
Stralsund, Germany 16 A7 54 18N 13 4 E
Strand, S. Africa 56 E2 34 9S 18 48 E
Stranda, Møre og Romsdal, Norway 9 E12 62 19N 6 58 E
Stranda, Nord-Trøndelag, Norway 8 E14 63 33N 10 14 E
Strangford L., U.K. 13 B6 54 30N 5 37W
Stranraer, U.K. 12 G3 54 54N 5 1W
Strasbourg, Canada 73 C8 51 4N 104 55W
**Strasbourg**, France 18 B7 48 35N 7 42 E
Stratford, Canada 78 C4 43 23N 81 0W
Stratford, N.Z. 59 H5 39 20S 174 19 E
Stratford, Calif., U.S.A. 84 J7 36 11N 119 49W
Stratford, Conn., U.S.A. 79 E11 41 12N 73 8W
Stratford, Tex., U.S.A. 81 G3 36 20N 102 4W
**Stratford-upon-Avon**, U.K. 11 E6 52 12N 1 42W
Strath Spey, U.K. 12 D5 57 9N 3 49W
Strathalbyn, Australia 63 F2 35 13S 138 53 E
Strathaven, U.K. 12 F4 55 40N 4 5W
Strathcona Prov. Park, Canada 72 D3 49 38N 125 40W
Strathmore, Canada 72 C6 51 5N 113 18W
Strathmore, U.K. 12 E5 56 37N 3 7W
Strathmore, U.S.A. 84 J7 36 9N 119 4W
Strathnaver, Canada 72 C4 53 20N 122 33W
Strathpeffer, U.K. 12 D4 57 35N 4 32W
Strathroy, Canada 78 D3 42 58N 81 38W
Strathy Pt., U.K. 12 C4 58 36N 4 1W
Strattanville, U.S.A. 78 E5 41 12N 79 19W
Stratton, U.S.A. 79 A14 45 8N 70 26W
Stratton Mt., U.S.A. 79 C12 43 4N 72 55W
Straubing, Germany 16 D7 48 52N 12 34 E
Straumnes, Iceland 8 C2 66 26N 23 8W
Strawberry →, U.S.A. 82 F8 40 10N 110 24W
Streaky B., Australia 63 E1 32 48S 134 13 E
Streaky Bay, Australia 63 E1 32 51S 134 18 E
Streator, U.S.A. 80 E10 41 8N 88 50W
Streetsboro, U.S.A. 78 E3 41 14N 81 21W
Streetsville, Canada 78 C5 43 35N 79 42W
Strelka, Russia 27 D10 58 5N 93 3 E
Streng →, Cambodia 38 F4 13 12N 103 37 E
Streymoy, Færoe Is. 8 E9 62 8N 7 5W
Strezhevoy, Russia 26 C8 60 42N 77 34 E
Strimón →, Greece 21 D10 40 46N 23 51 E
Strimonikós Kólpos, Greece 21 D11 40 33N 24 0 E
Stroma, U.K. 12 C5 58 41N 3 7W
Strómboli, Italy 20 E6 38 47N 15 13 E
Stromeferry, U.K. 12 D3 57 21N 5 33W
Stromness, U.K. 12 C5 58 58N 3 17W
Stromsburg, U.S.A. 80 E6 41 7N 97 36W
Strömstad, Sweden 9 G14 58 56N 11 10 E
Strömsund, Sweden 8 E16 63 51N 15 33 E
Strongsville, U.S.A. 78 E3 41 19N 81 50W
Stronsay, U.K. 12 B6 59 7N 2 35W
Stroud, U.K. 11 F5 51 45N 2 13W
Stroud Road, Australia 63 E5 32 18S 151 57 E
Stroudsburg, U.S.A. 79 F9 40 59N 75 12W
Stroumbi, Cyprus 23 E11 34 53N 32 29 E
Struer, Denmark 9 H13 56 30N 8 35 E
Strumica, Macedonia 21 D10 41 28N 22 41 E
Struthers, Canada 70 C2 48 41N 85 51W
Struthers, U.S.A. 78 E4 41 4N 80 39W
Stryker, U.S.A. 82 B6 48 41N 114 46W
Stryy, Ukraine 17 D12 49 16N 23 48 E
Strzelecki Cr. →, Australia 63 D2 29 37S 139 59 E
Stuart, Fla., U.S.A. 77 M5 27 12N 80 15W
Stuart, Nebr., U.S.A. 80 D5 42 36N 99 8W
Stuart →, Canada 72 C4 54 0N 123 35W
Stuart Bluff Ra., Australia 60 D5 22 50S 131 52 E
Stuart L., Canada 72 C4 54 30N 124 30W
Stuart Ra., Australia 63 D1 29 10S 134 56 E
Stull, L., Canada 70 B1 54 24N 92 34W
Stung Treng = Stoeng Treng, Cambodia 38 F5 13 31N 105 58 E
Stupart →, Canada 70 A1 56 0N 93 25W
Sturgeon B., Canada 73 C9 52 0N 97 50W
Sturgeon Bay, U.S.A. 76 C2 44 50N 87 23W
Sturgeon Falls, Canada 70 C4 46 25N 79 57W
Sturgeon L., Alta., Canada 72 B5 55 6N 117 32W
Sturgeon L., Ont., Canada 70 C1 50 0N 90 45W
Sturgeon L., Ont., Canada 78 B6 44 28N 78 43W
Sturgis, Canada 73 C8 51 56N 102 36W
Sturgis, Mich., U.S.A. 76 E3 41 48N 85 25W
Sturgis, S. Dak., U.S.A. 80 C3 44 25N 103 31W
Sturt Cr. →, Australia 60 C4 19 8S 127 50 E
Stutterheim, S. Africa 56 E4 32 33S 27 28 E
**Stuttgart**, Germany 16 D5 48 48N 9 11 E
Stuttgart, U.S.A. 81 H9 34 30N 91 33W
Stuyvesant, U.S.A. 79 D11 42 23N 73 45W
Stykkishólmur, Iceland 8 D2 65 2N 22 40W
Styria = Steiermark □, Austria 16 E8 47 26N 15 0 E
Su Xian = Suzhou, China 34 H9 33 41N 116 59 E
Suakin, Sudan 51 E13 19 8N 37 20 E
Suan, N. Korea 35 E14 38 42N 126 22 E
Suaqui, Mexico 86 B3 29 12N 109 41W
Suar, India 43 E8 29 2N 79 3 E
Subang, Indonesia 37 G12 6 34S 107 45 E
Subansiri →, India 41 F18 26 48N 93 50 E
Subarnarekha →, India 43 H12 22 34N 87 24 E
Subayhah, Si. Arabia 44 D3 30 2N 38 50 E
Subi, Indonesia 39 L7 2 58N 108 50 E
Subotica, Serbia, Yug. 21 A8 46 6N 19 39 E
Suceava, Romania 17 E14 47 38N 26 16 E
Suchan, Russia 30 C6 43 8N 133 9 E
Suchitoto, El Salv. 88 D2 13 56N 89 0W
Suchou = Suzhou, China 33 C7 31 19N 120 38 E
Süchow = Xuzhou, China 35 G9 34 18N 117 10 E
Suck →, Ireland 13 C3 53 17N 8 3W
**Sucre**, Bolivia 92 G5 19 0S 65 15W
Sucuriú →, Brazil 93 H8 20 47S 51 38W
Sud, Pte. du, Canada 71 C7 49 3N 62 14W
Sud-Kivu □, Dem. Rep. of the Congo 54 C2 3 30S 28 0 E
Sud-Ouest, Pte. du, Canada 71 C7 49 23N 63 36W
Sudan, U.S.A. 81 H3 34 4N 102 32W
**Sudan** ■, Africa 51 E11 15 0N 30 0 E
Sudbury, Canada 70 C3 46 30N 81 0W
Sudbury, U.K. 11 E8 52 2N 0 45 E
Sûdd, Sudan 51 G12 8 20N 30 0 E
Sudeten Mts. = Sudety, Europe 17 C9 50 20N 16 45 E
Sudety, Europe 17 C9 50 20N 16 45 E
Suðuroy, Færoe Is. 8 F9 61 32N 6 50W
Sudi, Tanzania 55 E4 10 11S 39 57 E
Sudirman, Pegunungan, Indonesia 37 E9 4 30S 137 0 E
Sueca, Spain 19 C5 39 12N 0 21W
Suemez I., U.S.A. 72 B2 55 15N 133 20W
Suez = El Suweis, Egypt 51 C12 29 58N 32 31 E
Suez, G. of = Suweis, Khalîg el, Egypt 51 C12 28 40N 33 0 E
**Suez Canal** = Suweis, Qanâ es, Egypt 51 B12 31 0N 32 20 E
Suffield, Canada 72 C6 50 12N 111 10W
Suffolk, U.S.A. 76 G7 36 44N 76 35W
**Suffolk** □, U.K. 11 E9 52 16N 1 0 E
Sugargrove, U.S.A. 78 E5 41 59N 79 21W
Sugarive →, India 43 F12 26 16N 86 24 E
Sugluk = Salluit, Canada 69 B12 62 14N 75 38W
Şuḩār, Oman 45 E8 24 20N 56 40 E
Sühbaatar □, Mongolia 34 B8 45 30N 114 0 E
Suhl, Germany 16 C6 50 36N 10 42 E
Sui, Pakistan 42 E3 28 37N 69 19 E
Sui Xian, China 34 G8 34 25N 115 2 E
Suide, China 34 F6 37 30N 110 12 E
Suifenhe, China 35 B16 44 25N 131 10 E
Suihua, China 33 B7 46 32N 126 55 E
Suining, China 35 H9 33 56N 117 58 E
Suiping, China 34 H7 33 10N 113 59 E
Suir →, Ireland 13 D4 52 16N 7 9W
Suisun City, U.S.A. 84 G4 38 15N 122 2W
Suiyang, China 35 B16 44 30N 130 56 E
Suizhong, China 35 D11 40 21N 120 20 E
Sujangarh, India 42 F6 27 42N 74 31 E
Sukabumi, Indonesia 37 G12 6 56S 106 50 E
Sukadana, Indonesia 36 E4 1 10S 110 0 E
Sukagawa, Japan 31 F10 37 17N 140 23 E
Sukaraja, Indonesia 36 E4 2 28S 110 25 E
Sukarnapura = Jayapura, Indonesia 37 E10 2 28S 140 38 E
Sukch'ŏn, N. Korea 35 E13 39 22N 125 35 E
Sukhona →, Russia 24 C6 61 15N 46 39 E
Sukhothai, Thailand 38 D2 17 1N 99 49 E
Sukhumi = Sokhumi, Georgia 25 F7 43 0N 41 0 E
Sukkur, Pakistan 42 F3 27 42N 68 54 E
Sukkur Barrage, Pakistan 42 F3 27 40N 68 50 E
Sukri →, India 42 G4 25 4N 71 43 E
Sukumo, Japan 31 H6 32 56N 132 44 E
Sukunka →, Canada 72 B4 55 45N 121 15W
Sula, Kepulauan, Indonesia 37 E7 1 45S 125 0 E
Sulaco →, Honduras 88 C2 15 2N 87 44W
Sulaiman Range, Pakistan 42 D3 30 30N 69 50 E
Sūlār, Iran 45 D6 31 53N 51 54 E
**Sulawesi** □, Indonesia 37 E6 2 0S 120 0 E
Sulawesi Sea = Celebes Sea, Indonesia 37 D6 3 0N 123 0 E
Sulawesi Selatan □, Indonesia 37 E6 2 30S 120 0 E
Sulawesi Utara □, Indonesia 37 D6 1 0N 122 30 E
Sulima, S. Leone 50 G3 6 58N 11 32W
Sulina, Romania 17 F15 45 10N 29 40 E
Sulitjelma, Norway 8 C17 67 9N 16 3 E
Sullana, Peru 92 D2 4 52S 80 39W
Sullivan, Ill., U.S.A. 80 F10 39 36N 88 37W
Sullivan, Ind., U.S.A. 76 F2 39 6N 87 24W
Sullivan, Mo., U.S.A. 80 F9 38 13N 91 10W
Sullivan Bay, Canada 72 C3 50 55N 126 50W
Sullivan I. = Lambi Kyun, Burma 39 G2 10 50N 98 20 E
Sulphur, La., U.S.A. 81 K8 30 14N 93 23W
Sulphur, Okla., U.S.A. 81 H6 34 31N 96 58W
Sulphur Pt., Canada 72 A6 60 56N 114 48W
Sulphur Springs, U.S.A. 81 J7 33 8N 95 36W
Sultan, Canada 70 C3 47 36N 82 47W
Sultan, U.S.A. 84 C5 47 52N 121 49W
Sultanpur, India 43 F10 26 18N 82 4 E
Sultanpur, Mad. P., India 42 H8 23 9N 77 56 E
Sultanpur, Punjab, India 42 D6 31 13N 75 11 E
Sulu Arch., Phil. 37 C6 6 0N 121 0 E
Sulu Sea, E. Indies 37 C6 8 0N 120 0 E
Suluq, Libya 51 B10 31 44N 20 14 E
Sulzberger Ice Shelf, Antarctica 5 D10 78 0S 150 0 E
Sumalata, Indonesia 37 D6 1 0N 122 31 E
Sumampa, Argentina 94 B3 29 25S 63 29W
Sumatera □, Indonesia 36 D2 0 40N 100 20 E
Sumatera Barat □, Indonesia 36 E2 1 0S 101 0 E
Sumatera Utara □, Indonesia 36 D1 2 30N 98 0 E
**Sumatra** = Sumatera □, Indonesia 36 D2 0 40N 100 20 E
Sumba, Indonesia 37 F5 9 45S 119 35 E
Sumba, Selat, Indonesia 37 F5 9 0S 118 40 E
Sumbawa, Indonesia 36 F5 8 26S 117 30 E
Sumbawa Besar, Indonesia 36 F5 8 30S 117 26 E
Sumbawanga □, Tanzania 52 F6 8 0S 31 30 E
Sumbe, Angola 52 G2 11 10S 13 48 E
Sumburgh Hd., U.K. 12 B7 59 52N 1 17W
Sumdeo, India 43 D8 31 26N 78 44 E
Sumdo, India 43 B8 35 6N 78 41 E
Sumedang, Indonesia 37 G12 6 52S 107 55 E
Šumen = Shumen, Bulgaria 21 C12 43 18N 26 55 E
Sumenep, Indonesia 37 G15 7 1S 113 52 E
Sumgait = Sumqayıt, Azerbaijan 25 F8 40 34N 49 38 E
Summer L., U.S.A. 82 E3 42 50N 120 45W
Summerland, Canada 72 D5 49 32N 119 41W
Summerside, Canada 71 C7 46 24N 63 47W
Summersville, U.S.A. 76 F5 38 17N 80 51W
Summerville, Ga., U.S.A. 77 H3 34 29N 85 21W
Summerville, S.C., U.S.A. 77 J5 33 1N 80 11W
Summit Lake, Canada 72 C4 54 20N 122 40W
Summit Peak, U.S.A. 83 H10 37 21N 106 42W
Sumner, Iowa, U.S.A. 80 D8 42 51N 92 6W
Sumner, Wash., U.S.A. 84 C4 47 12N 122 14W
Sumoto, Japan 31 G7 34 21N 134 54 E
Šumperk, Czech Rep. 17 D9 49 59N 16 59 E
Sumqayıt, Azerbaijan 25 F8 40 34N 49 38 E
Sumter, U.S.A. 77 J5 33 55N 80 21W
Sumy, Ukraine 25 D5 50 57N 34 50 E
Sun City, Ariz., U.S.A. 83 K7 33 36N 112 17W
Sun City, Calif., U.S.A. 85 M9 33 42N 117 11W
Sun City Center, U.S.A. 77 M4 27 43N 82 18W
Sun Lakes, U.S.A. 83 K8 33 10N 111 52W
Sun Valley, U.S.A. 82 E6 43 42N 114 21W
Sunagawa, Japan 30 C10 43 29N 141 55 E
Sunan, N. Korea 35 E13 39 15N 125 40 E
Sunart, L., U.K. 12 E3 56 42N 5 43W
Sunburst, U.S.A. 82 B8 48 53N 111 55W
Sunbury, Australia 63 F3 37 35S 144 44 E
Sunbury, U.S.A. 79 F8 40 52N 76 48W
Sunchales, Argentina 94 C3 30 58S 61 35W
Suncho Corral, Argentina 94 B3 27 55S 63 27W
Sunch'ŏn, S. Korea 35 G14 34 52N 127 31 E
Suncook, U.S.A. 79 C13 43 8N 71 27W
Sunda, Selat, Indonesia 36 F3 6 20S 105 30 E
Sunda Is., Indonesia 28 K14 5 0S 105 0 E
Sunda Str. = Sunda, Selat, Indonesia 36 F3 6 20S 105 30 E
Sundance, Canada 73 B10 56 32N 94 4W
Sundance, U.S.A. 80 C2 44 24N 104 23W
Sundar Nagar, India 42 D7 31 32N 76 53 E
Sundarbans, The, Asia 41 J16 22 0N 89 0 E
Sundargarh, India 41 H14 22 4N 84 5 E
Sundays = Sondags →, S. Africa 56 E4 33 44S 25 51 E
Sunderland, Canada 78 B5 44 16N 79 4W
**Sunderland**, U.K. 10 C6 54 55N 1 23W
Sundre, Canada 72 C6 51 49N 114 38W
Sundsvall, Sweden 9 E17 62 23N 17 17 E
Sung Hei, Vietnam 39 G6 10 20N 106 2 E
Sungai Kolok, Thailand 39 J3 6 2N 101 58 E
Sungai Lembing, Malaysia 39 L4 3 55N 103 3 E
Sungai Petani, Malaysia 39 K3 5 37N 100 30 E
Sungaigerong, Indonesia 36 E2 2 59S 104 52 E
Sungailiat, Indonesia 36 E3 1 51S 106 8 E
Sungaipenuh, Indonesia 36 E2 2 1S 101 20 E
Sungari = Songhua Jiang →, China 33 B8 47 45N 132 30 E
Sunghua Chiang = Songhua Jiang →, China 33 B8 47 45N 132 30 E
Sunland Park, U.S.A. 83 L10 31 50N 106 40W
Sunndalsøra, Norway 9 E13 62 40N 8 33 E
Sunnyside, U.S.A. 82 C3 46 20N 120 0W
Sunnyvale, U.S.A. 84 H4 37 23N 122 2W
Suntar, Russia 27 C12 62 15N 117 30 E
Suomenselkä, Finland 8 E21 62 52N 24 0 E
Suomussalmi, Finland 8 D23 64 54N 29 10 E
Suoyarvi, Russia 24 B5 62 3N 32 20 E
Supai, U.S.A. 83 H7 36 15N 112 41W
Supaul, India 43 F12 26 10N 86 40 E
Superior, Ariz., U.S.A. 83 K8 33 18N 111 6W
Superior, Mont., U.S.A. 82 C6 47 12N 114 53W
Superior, Nebr., U.S.A. 80 E5 40 1N 98 4W
Superior, Wis., U.S.A. 80 B8 46 44N 92 6W
**Superior, L.**, N. Amer. 70 C2 47 0N 87 0W
Suphan Buri, Thailand 38 E3 14 14N 100 10 E
Suphan Dağı, Turkey 44 B4 38 54N 42 48 E
Supiori, Indonesia 37 E9 1 0S 136 0 E
Supung Shuiku, China 35 D13 40 35N 124 50 E
Sūq Suwayq, Si. Arabia 44 E3 24 23N 38 27 E
Suqian, China 35 H10 33 54N 118 8 E
Sūr, Lebanon 47 B4 33 19N 35 16 E
Sūr, Oman 46 C6 22 34N 59 32 E
Sur, Pt., U.S.A. 84 J5 36 18N 121 54W
Sura →, Russia 24 C8 56 6N 46 0 E
Surab, Pakistan 42 E2 28 25N 66 15 E
**Surabaja** = Surabaya, Indonesia 37 G15 7 17S 112 45 E
Surabaya, Indonesia 37 G15 7 17S 112 45 E
Surakarta, Indonesia 37 G14 7 35S 110 48 E
Surat, Australia 63 D4 27 10S 149 6 E
Surat, India 40 J8 21 12N 72 55 E
Surat Thani, Thailand 39 H2 9 6N 99 20 E
Suratgarh, India 42 E5 29 18N 73 55 E
Surendranagar, India 42 H4 22 45N 71 40 E
Surf, U.S.A. 85 L6 34 41N 120 36W
Surgut, Russia 26 C8 61 14N 73 20 E
Suriapet, India 40 L11 17 10N 79 40 E
Surigao, Phil. 37 C7 9 47N 125 29 E
Surin, Thailand 38 E4 14 50N 103 34 E
Surin Nua, Ko, Thailand 39 H1 9 30N 97 55 E
**Surinam** ■, S. Amer. 93 C7 4 0N 56 0W
Suriname = Surinam ■, S. Amer. 93 C7 4 0N 56 0W
Suriname →, Surinam 93 B7 5 50N 55 15W
Sūrmaq, Iran 45 D7 31 3N 52 48 E
**Surrey** □, U.K. 11 F7 51 15N 0 31W
Sursand, India 43 F11 26 39N 85 43 E
Sursar →, India 43 F12 26 14N 87 3 E
Surt, Libya 51 B9 31 11N 16 39 E
Surt, Khalīj, Libya 51 B9 31 40N 18 30 E
Surtanahu, Pakistan 42 F4 26 22N 70 0 E
Surtsey, Iceland 8 E3 63 20N 20 30W
Suruga-Wan, Japan 31 G9 34 45N 138 30 E
Susaki, Japan 31 H6 33 22N 133 17 E
Sūsangerd, Iran 45 D6 31 35N 48 6 E
Susanville, U.S.A. 82 F3 40 25N 120 39W
Susner, India 42 H7 23 57N 76 5 E

Susquehanna, *U.S.A.* 79 E9 41 57N 75 36W
Susquehanna →, *U.S.A.* 79 G8 39 33N 76 5W
Susques, *Argentina* 94 A2 23 35S 66 25W
Sussex, *Canada* 71 C6 45 45N 65 37W
Sussex, *U.S.A.* 79 E10 41 13N 74 37W
Sussex, E. □, *U.K.* 11 G8 51 0N 0 20 E
Sussex, W. □, *U.K.* 11 G7 51 0N 0 30W
Sustut →, *Canada* 72 B3 56 20N 127 30W
Susuman, *Russia* 27 C15 62 47N 148 10 E
Susunu, *Indonesia* 37 E8 3 20S 133 25 E
Susurluk, *Turkey* 21 E13 39 54N 28 8 E
Sutherland, *S. Africa* 56 E3 32 24S 20 40 E
Sutherland, *U.S.A.* 80 E4 41 10N 101 8W
Sutherland Falls, *N.Z.* 59 L1 44 48S 167 46 E
Sutherlin, *U.S.A.* 82 E2 43 23N 123 19W
Suthri, *India* 42 H3 23 3N 68 55 E
Sutlej →, *Pakistan* 42 E4 29 23N 71 3 E
Sutter, *U.S.A.* 84 F5 39 10N 121 45W
Sutter Creek, *U.S.A.* 84 G6 38 24N 120 48W
Sutton, *Canada* 79 A12 45 6N 72 37W
Sutton, *Nebr., U.S.A.* 80 E6 40 36N 97 52W
Sutton, *W. Va., U.S.A.* 76 F5 38 40N 80 43W
Sutton →, *Canada* 70 A3 55 15N 83 45W
Sutton Coldfield, *U.K.* 11 E6 52 35N 1 49W
Sutton in Ashfield, *U.K.* 10 D6 53 8N 1 16W
Sutton L., *Canada* 70 B3 54 15N 84 42W
Suttor →, *Australia* 62 C4 21 36S 147 2 E
Suttsu, *Japan* 30 C10 42 48N 140 14 E
**Suva**, *Fiji* 59 D8 18 6S 178 30 E
Suva Planina, *Serbia, Yug.* 21 C10 43 10N 22 5 E
Suvorov Is. = Suwarrow Is., *Cook Is.* 65 J11 15 0S 163 0W
Suwałki, *Poland* 17 A12 54 8N 22 59 E
Suwannaphum, *Thailand* 38 E4 15 33N 103 47 E
Suwannee →, *U.S.A.* 77 L4 29 17N 83 10W
Suwanose-Jima, *Japan* 31 K4 29 38N 129 43 E
Suwarrow Is., *Cook Is.* 65 J11 15 0S 163 0W
Suwayq aş Şuqban, *Iraq* 44 D5 31 32N 46 7 E
Suweis, Khalîg el, *Egypt* 51 C12 28 40N 33 0 E
Suweis, Qanâ es, *Egypt* 51 B12 31 0N 32 20 E
Suwŏn, *S. Korea* 35 F14 37 17N 127 1 E
Suzdal, *Russia* 24 C7 56 29N 40 26 E
Suzhou, *Anhui, China* 34 H9 33 41N 116 59 E
**Suzhou**, *Jiangsu, China* 33 C7 31 19N 120 38 E
Suzu, *Japan* 31 F8 37 25N 137 17 E
Suzu-Misaki, *Japan* 31 F8 37 31N 137 21 E
Suzuka, *Japan* 31 G8 34 55N 136 36 E
**Svalbard**, *Arctic* 4 B8 78 0N 17 0 E
Svappavaara, *Sweden* 8 C19 67 40N 21 3 E
Svartisen, *Norway* 8 C15 66 40N 13 50 E
Svay Chek, *Cambodia* 38 F4 13 48N 102 58 E
Svay Rieng, *Cambodia* 39 G5 11 9N 105 45 E
Svealand □, *Sweden* 9 G16 60 20N 15 0 E
Sveg, *Sweden* 9 E16 62 2N 14 21 E
Svendborg, *Denmark* 9 J14 55 4N 10 35 E
Sverdlovsk = Yekaterinburg, *Russia* 26 D7 56 50N 60 30 E
Sverdrup Is., *Canada* 4 B3 79 0N 97 0W
Svetlaya, *Russia* 30 A9 46 33N 138 18 E
Svetlogorsk = Svyetlahorsk, *Belarus* 17 B15 52 38N 29 46 E
Svir →, *Russia* 24 B5 60 30N 32 48 E
Svishtov, *Bulgaria* 21 C11 43 36N 25 23 E
Svislach, *Belarus* 17 B13 53 3N 24 2 E
Svobodnyy, *Russia* 27 D13 51 20N 128 0 E
Svolvær, *Norway* 8 B16 68 15N 14 34 E
Svyetlahorsk, *Belarus* 17 B15 52 38N 29 46 E
Swabian Alps = Schwäbische Alb, *Germany* 16 D5 48 20N 9 30 E
Swainsboro, *U.S.A.* 77 J4 32 36N 82 20W
Swakopmund, *Namibia* 56 C1 22 37S 14 30 E
Swale →, *U.K.* 10 C6 54 5N 1 20W
Swan →, *Australia* 61 F2 32 3S 115 45 E
Swan →, *Canada* 73 C8 52 30N 100 45W
Swan Hill, *Australia* 63 F3 35 20S 143 33 E
Swan Hills, *Canada* 72 C5 54 43N 115 24W
Swan Is., *W. Indies* 88 C3 17 22N 83 57W
Swan L., *Canada* 73 C8 52 30N 100 40W
Swan Peak, *U.S.A.* 82 C7 47 43N 113 38W
Swan Ra., *U.S.A.* 82 C7 48 0N 113 45W
Swan Reach, *Australia* 63 E2 34 35S 139 37 E
Swan River, *Canada* 73 C8 52 10N 101 16W
Swanage, *U.K.* 11 G6 50 36N 1 58W
Swansea, *Australia* 62 G4 42 8S 148 4 E
Swansea, *Canada* 78 C5 43 38N 79 28W
**Swansea**, *U.K.* 11 F4 51 37N 3 57W
Swansea □, *U.K.* 11 F3 51 38N 4 3W
Swar →, *Pakistan* 43 B5 34 40N 72 5 E
Swartberge, *S. Africa* 56 E3 33 20S 22 0 E
Swartmodder, *S. Africa* 56 D3 28 1S 20 32 E
Swartruggens, *S. Africa* 56 D4 25 39S 26 42 E
Swastika, *Canada* 70 C3 48 7N 80 6W
Swatow = Shantou, *China* 33 D6 23 18N 116 40 E
**Swaziland** ■, *Africa* 57 D5 26 30S 31 30 E
**Sweden** ■, *Europe* 9 G16 57 0N 15 0 E
Sweet Home, *U.S.A.* 82 D2 44 24N 122 44W
Sweetgrass, *U.S.A.* 82 B8 48 59N 111 58W
Sweetwater, *Nev., U.S.A.* 84 G7 38 27N 119 9W
Sweetwater, *Tenn., U.S.A.* 77 H3 35 36N 84 28W
Sweetwater, *Tex., U.S.A.* 81 J4 32 28N 100 25W
Sweetwater →, *U.S.A.* 82 E10 42 31N 107 2W
Swellendam, *S. Africa* 56 E3 34 1S 20 26 E
Świdnica, *Poland* 17 C9 50 50N 16 30 E
Świdnik, *Poland* 17 C12 51 13N 22 39 E
Świebodzin, *Poland* 16 B8 52 15N 15 31 E
Świecie, *Poland* 17 B10 53 25N 18 30 E
Swift Current, *Canada* 73 C7 50 20N 107 45W
Swiftcurrent →, *Canada* 73 C7 50 38N 107 44W
Swilly, L., *Ireland* 13 A4 55 12N 7 33W
Swindon, *U.K.* 11 F6 51 34N 1 46W
Swindon □, *U.K.* 11 F6 51 34N 1 46W
Swinemünde = Świnoujście, *Poland* 16 B8 53 54N 14 16 E
Swinford, *Ireland* 13 C3 53 57N 8 58W
Świnoujście, *Poland* 16 B8 53 54N 14 16 E
**Switzerland** ■, *Europe* 18 C8 46 30N 8 0 E
Swords, *Ireland* 13 C5 53 28N 6 13W
Swoyerville, *U.S.A.* 79 E9 41 18N 75 53W
Sydenham →, *Canada* 78 D2 42 33N 82 25W
**Sydney**, *Australia* 63 E5 33 53S 151 10 E
Sydney, *Canada* 71 C7 46 7N 60 7W
Sydney L., *Canada* 73 C10 50 41N 94 25W
Sydney Mines, *Canada* 71 C7 46 18N 60 15W
Sydprøven, *Greenland* 4 C5 60 30N 45 35W
Sydra, G. of = Surt, Khalīj, *Libya* 51 B9 31 40N 18 30 E
Sykesville, *U.S.A.* 78 E6 41 3N 78 50W
Syktyvkar, *Russia* 24 B9 61 45N 50 40 E
Sylacauga, *U.S.A.* 77 J2 33 10N 86 15W
Sylarna, *Sweden* 8 E15 63 2N 12 13 E
Sylhet, *Bangla.* 41 G17 24 54N 91 52 E
Sylt, *Germany* 16 A5 54 54N 8 22 E
Sylvan Beach, *U.S.A.* 79 C9 43 12N 75 44W
Sylvan Lake, *Canada* 72 C6 52 20N 114 3W
Sylvania, *U.S.A.* 77 J5 32 45N 81 38W
Sylvester, *U.S.A.* 77 K4 31 32N 83 50W
Sym, *Russia* 26 C9 60 20N 88 18 E
Symón, *Mexico* 86 C4 24 42N 102 35W
Synnott Ra., *Australia* 60 C4 16 30S 125 20 E
Syracuse, *Kans., U.S.A.* 81 G4 37 59N 101 45W
Syracuse, *N.Y., U.S.A.* 79 C8 43 3N 76 9W
Syracuse, *Nebr., U.S.A.* 80 E6 40 39N 96 11W
Syrdarya →, *Kazakstan* 26 E7 46 3N 61 0 E
**Syria** ■, *Asia* 44 C3 35 0N 38 0 E
Syrian Desert = Shām, Bādiyat ash, *Asia* 44 C3 32 0N 40 0 E
Syzran, *Russia* 24 D8 53 12N 48 30 E
**Szczecin**, *Poland* 16 B8 53 27N 14 27 E
Szczecinek, *Poland* 17 B9 53 43N 16 41 E
Szczeciński, Zalew = Stettiner Haff, *Germany* 16 B8 53 47N 14 15 E
Szczytno, *Poland* 17 B11 53 33N 21 0 E
**Szechwan** = Sichuan □, *China* 32 C5 31 0N 104 0 E
Szeged, *Hungary* 17 E11 46 16N 20 10 E
Székesfehérvár, *Hungary* 17 E10 47 15N 18 25 E
Szekszárd, *Hungary* 17 E10 46 22N 18 42 E
Szentes, *Hungary* 17 E11 46 39N 20 21 E
Szolnok, *Hungary* 17 E11 47 10N 20 15 E
Szombathely, *Hungary* 17 E9 47 14N 16 38 E


# T


Ta Khli Khok, *Thailand* 38 E3 15 18N 100 20 E
Ta Lai, *Vietnam* 39 G6 11 24N 107 23 E
Tabacal, *Argentina* 94 A3 23 15S 64 15W
Tabaco, *Phil.* 37 B6 13 22N 123 44 E
Ţābah, *Si. Arabia* 44 E4 26 55N 42 38 E
Ţabas, *Khorāsān, Iran* 45 C9 32 48N 60 12 E
Ţabas, *Khorāsān, Iran* 45 C8 33 35N 56 55 E
Tabasará, Serranía de, *Panama* 88 E3 8 35N 81 40W
Tabasco □, *Mexico* 87 D6 17 45N 93 30W
Tabāsin, *Iran* 45 D8 31 12N 57 54 E
Tabatinga, Serra da, *Brazil* 93 F10 10 30S 44 0W
Taber, *Canada* 72 D6 49 47N 112 8W
Taberg, *U.S.A.* 79 C9 43 18N 75 37W
Tablas, *Phil.* 37 B6 12 25N 122 2 E
Table B. = Tafelbaai, *S. Africa* 56 E2 33 35S 18 25 E
Table B., *Canada* 71 B8 53 40N 56 25W
Table Mt., *S. Africa* 56 E2 34 0S 18 22 E
Table Rock L., *U.S.A.* 81 G8 36 36N 93 19W
Tabletop, Mt., *Australia* 62 C4 23 24S 147 11 E
Tábor, *Czech Rep.* 16 D8 49 25N 14 39 E
Tabora, *Tanzania* 54 D3 5 2S 32 50 E
Tabora □, *Tanzania* 54 D3 5 0S 33 0 E
Tabou, *Ivory C.* 50 H4 4 30N 7 20W
**Tabrīz**, *Iran* 44 B5 38 7N 46 20 E
Tabuaeran, *Pac. Oc.* 65 G12 3 51N 159 22W
Tabūk, *Si. Arabia* 44 D3 28 23N 36 36 E
Tacámbaro de Codallos, *Mexico* 86 D4 19 14N 101 28W
Tacheng, *China* 32 B3 46 40N 82 58 E
Tach'ing Shan = Daqing Shan, *China* 34 D6 40 40N 111 0 E
Tacloban, *Phil.* 37 B6 11 15N 124 58 E
Tacna, *Peru* 92 G4 18 0S 70 20W
Tacoma, *U.S.A.* 84 C4 47 14N 122 26W
Tacuarembó, *Uruguay* 95 C4 31 45S 56 0W
Tademaït, Plateau du, *Algeria* 50 C6 28 30N 2 30 E
Tadjoura, *Djibouti* 46 E3 11 50N 42 55 E
Tadmor, *N.Z.* 59 J4 41 27S 172 45 E
Tadoule, L., *Canada* 73 B9 58 36N 98 20W
Tadoussac, *Canada* 71 C6 48 11N 69 42W
Tadzhikistan = Tajikistan ■, *Asia* 26 F8 38 30N 70 0 E
Taechŏn-ni, *S. Korea* 35 F14 36 21N 126 36 E
**Taegu**, *S. Korea* 35 G15 35 50N 128 37 E
Taegwan, *N. Korea* 35 D13 40 13N 125 12 E
Taejŏn, *S. Korea* 35 F14 36 20N 127 28 E
Tafalla, *Spain* 19 A5 42 30N 1 41W
Tafelbaai, *S. Africa* 56 E2 33 35S 18 25 E
Tafermaar, *Indonesia* 37 F8 6 47S 134 10 E
Tafí Viejo, *Argentina* 94 B2 26 43S 65 17W
Tafīhān, *Iran* 45 D7 29 25N 52 39 E
Tafresh, *Iran* 45 C6 34 45N 49 57 E
Taft, *Iran* 45 D7 31 45N 54 14 E
Taft, *Phil.* 37 B7 11 57N 125 30 E
Taft, *U.S.A.* 85 K7 35 8N 119 28W
Taftān, Kūh-e, *Iran* 45 D9 28 40N 61 0 E
Taga Dzong, *Bhutan* 41 F16 27 5N 89 55 E
Taganrog, *Russia* 25 E6 47 12N 38 50 E
Tagbilaran, *Phil.* 37 C6 9 39N 123 51 E
Tagish, *Canada* 72 A2 60 19N 134 16W
Tagish L., *Canada* 72 A2 60 10N 134 20W
Tagliamento →, *Italy* 20 B5 45 38N 13 6 E
Tagomago, *Spain* 22 B8 39 2N 1 39 E
Taguatinga, *Brazil* 93 F10 12 16S 42 26W
Tagum, *Phil.* 37 C7 7 33N 125 53 E
**Tagus** = Tejo →, *Europe* 19 C1 38 40N 9 24W
Tahakopa, *N.Z.* 59 M2 46 30S 169 23 E
Tahan, Gunong, *Malaysia* 39 K4 4 34N 102 17 E
Tahat, *Algeria* 50 D7 23 18N 5 33 E
Tāherī, *Iran* 45 E7 27 43N 52 20 E
**Tahiti**, *Pac. Oc.* 65 J13 17 37S 149 27W
Tahlequah, *U.S.A.* 81 H7 35 55N 94 58W
Tahoe, L., *U.S.A.* 84 G6 39 6N 120 2W
Tahoe City, *U.S.A.* 84 F6 39 10N 120 9W
Tahoka, *U.S.A.* 81 J4 33 10N 101 48W
Taholah, *U.S.A.* 84 C2 47 21N 124 17W
Tahoua, *Niger* 50 F7 14 57N 5 16 E
Tahrūd, *Iran* 45 D8 29 26N 57 49 E
Tahsis, *Canada* 72 D3 49 55N 126 40W
Tahta, *Egypt* 51 C12 26 44N 31 32 E
Tahulandang, *Indonesia* 37 D7 2 27N 125 23 E
Tahuna, *Indonesia* 37 D7 3 38N 125 30 E
Tai Shan, *China* 35 F9 36 25N 117 20 E
Tai'an, *China* 35 F9 36 12N 117 8 E
Taibei = T'aipei, *Taiwan* 33 D7 25 2N 121 30 E
Taibique, *Canary Is.* 22 G2 27 42N 17 58W
Taibus Qi, *China* 34 D8 41 54N 115 22 E
T'aichung, *Taiwan* 33 D7 24 9N 120 37 E
Taieri →, *N.Z.* 59 M3 46 3S 170 12 E
Taigu, *China* 34 F7 37 28N 112 30 E
Taihang Shan, *China* 34 G7 36 0N 113 30 E
Taihape, *N.Z.* 59 H5 39 41S 175 48 E
Taihe, *China* 34 H8 33 20N 115 42 E
Taikang, *China* 34 G8 34 5N 114 50 E
Tailem Bend, *Australia* 63 F2 35 12S 139 29 E
Taimyr Peninsula = Taymyr, Poluostrov, *Russia* 27 B11 75 0N 100 0 E
Tain, *U.K.* 12 D4 57 49N 4 4W
T'ainan, *Taiwan* 33 D7 23 0N 120 10 E
Taínaron, Ákra, *Greece* 21 F10 36 22N 22 27 E
**T'aipei**, *Taiwan* 33 D7 25 2N 121 30 E
Taiping, *Malaysia* 39 K3 4 51N 100 44 E
Taipingzhen, *China* 34 H6 33 35N 111 42 E
Tairbeart = Tarbert, *U.K.* 12 D2 57 54N 6 49W
Taita Hills, *Kenya* 54 C4 3 25S 38 15 E
Taitao, Pen. de, *Chile* 96 F2 46 30S 75 0W
T'aitung, *Taiwan* 33 D7 22 43N 121 4 E
Taivalkoski, *Finland* 8 D23 65 33N 28 12 E
**Taiwan** ■, *Asia* 33 D7 23 30N 121 0 E
Taïyetos Óros, *Greece* 21 F10 37 0N 22 23 E
Taiyiba, *Israel* 47 C4 32 36N 35 27 E
**Taiyuan**, *China* 34 F7 37 52N 112 33 E
Taizhong = T'aichung, *Taiwan* 33 D7 24 9N 120 37 E
Ta'izz, *Yemen* 46 E3 13 35N 44 2 E
Tājābād, *Iran* 45 D7 30 2N 54 24 E
**Tajikistan** ■, *Asia* 26 F8 38 30N 70 0 E
Tajima, *Japan* 31 F9 37 12N 139 46 E
Tajo = Tejo →, *Europe* 19 C1 38 40N 9 24W
Tajrīsh, *Iran* 45 C6 35 48N 51 25 E
Tak, *Thailand* 38 D2 16 52N 99 8 E
Takāb, *Iran* 44 B5 36 24N 47 7 E
Takachiho, *Japan* 31 H5 32 42N 131 18 E
Takada, *Japan* 31 F9 37 7N 138 15 E
Takahagi, *Japan* 31 F10 36 43N 140 45 E
Takaka, *N.Z.* 59 J4 40 51S 172 50 E
Takamatsu, *Japan* 31 G7 34 20N 134 5 E
Takaoka, *Japan* 31 F8 36 47N 137 0 E
Takapuna, *N.Z.* 59 G5 36 47S 174 47 E
Takasaki, *Japan* 31 F9 36 20N 139 0 E
Takatsuki, *Japan* 31 G7 34 51N 135 37 E
Takaungu, *Kenya* 54 C4 3 38S 39 52 E
Takayama, *Japan* 31 F8 36 18N 137 11 E
Take-Shima, *Japan* 31 J5 30 49N 130 26 E
Takefu, *Japan* 31 G8 35 50N 136 10 E
Takengon, *Indonesia* 36 D1 4 45N 96 50 E
Takeo, *Japan* 31 H5 33 12N 130 1 E
Tākestān, *Iran* 45 C6 36 0N 49 40 E
Taketa, *Japan* 31 H5 32 58N 131 24 E
Takev, *Cambodia* 39 G5 10 59N 104 47 E
Takh, *India* 43 C7 33 6N 77 32 E
Takht-Sulaiman, *Pakistan* 42 D3 31 40N 69 58 E
Takikawa, *Japan* 30 C10 43 33N 141 54 E
Takla L., *Canada* 72 B3 55 15N 125 45W
Takla Landing, *Canada* 72 B3 55 30N 125 50W
Takla Makan = Taklamakan Shamo, *China* 32 C3 38 0N 83 0 E
Taklamakan Shamo, *China* 32 C3 38 0N 83 0 E
Taku →, *Canada* 72 B2 58 30N 133 50W
Tal Halāl, *Iran* 45 D7 28 54N 55 1 E
Tala, *Uruguay* 95 C4 34 21S 55 46W
Talagang, *Pakistan* 42 C5 32 55N 72 25 E
Talagante, *Chile* 94 C1 33 40S 70 50W
Talamanca, Cordillera de, *Cent. Amer.* 88 E3 9 20N 83 20W
Talara, *Peru* 92 D2 4 38S 81 18W
Talas, *Kyrgyzstan* 26 E8 42 30N 72 13 E
Talâta, *Egypt* 47 E1 30 36N 32 20 E
Talaud, Kepulauan, *Indonesia* 37 D7 4 30N 127 10 E
Talaud Is. = Talaud, Kepulauan, *Indonesia* 37 D7 4 30N 127 10 E
Talavera de la Reina, *Spain* 19 C3 39 55N 4 46W
Talayan, *Phil.* 37 C6 6 52N 124 24 E
Talbandh, *India* 43 H12 22 3N 86 20 E
Talbot, C., *Australia* 60 B4 13 48S 126 43 E
Talbragar →, *Australia* 63 E4 32 12S 148 37 E
Talca, *Chile* 94 D1 35 28S 71 40W
Talcahuano, *Chile* 94 D1 36 40S 73 10W
Talcher, *India* 41 J14 21 0N 85 18 E
Taldy Kurgan = Taldyqorghan, *Kazakstan* 26 E8 45 10N 78 45 E
Taldyqorghan, *Kazakstan* 26 E8 45 10N 78 45 E
Tālesh, *Iran* 45 B6 37 58N 48 58 E
Ţalesh, Kūhhā-ye, *Iran* 45 B6 37 42N 48 55 E
Tali Post, *Sudan* 51 G12 5 55N 30 44 E
Taliabu, *Indonesia* 37 E6 1 50S 125 0 E
Talibon, *Phil.* 37 B6 10 9N 124 20 E
Talibong, Ko, *Thailand* 39 J2 7 15N 99 23 E
Talihina, *U.S.A.* 81 H7 34 45N 95 3W
Taliwang, *Indonesia* 36 F5 8 50S 116 55 E
Tall 'Afar, *Iraq* 44 B4 36 22N 42 27 E
Tall Kalakh, *Syria* 47 A5 34 41N 36 15 E
Talladega, *U.S.A.* 77 J2 33 26N 86 6W
**Tallahassee**, *U.S.A.* 77 K3 30 27N 84 17W
Tallangatta, *Australia* 63 F4 36 15S 147 19 E
Tallering Pk., *Australia* 61 E2 28 6S 115 37 E
Talli, *Pakistan* 42 E3 29 32N 68 8 E
**Tallinn**, *Estonia* 9 G21 59 22N 24 48 E
Tallmadge, *U.S.A.* 78 E3 41 6N 81 27W
Tallulah, *U.S.A.* 81 J9 32 25N 91 11W
Taloyoak, *Canada* 68 B10 69 32N 93 32W
Talpa de Allende, *Mexico* 86 C4 20 23N 104 51W
Talsi, *Latvia* 9 H20 57 10N 22 30 E
Taltal, *Chile* 94 B1 25 23S 70 33W
Taltson →, *Canada* 72 A6 61 24N 112 46W
Talwood, *Australia* 63 D4 28 29S 149 29 E
Talyawalka →, *Australia* 63 E3 32 28S 142 22 E
Tam Chau, *Vietnam* 39 G5 10 48N 105 12 E
Tam Ky, *Vietnam* 38 E7 15 34N 108 29 E
Tam Quan, *Vietnam* 38 E7 14 35N 109 3 E
Tama, *U.S.A.* 80 E8 41 58N 92 35W
Tamale, *Ghana* 50 G5 9 22N 0 50W
Tamano, *Japan* 31 G6 34 29N 133 59 E
Tamanrasset, *Algeria* 50 D7 22 50N 5 30 E
Tamaqua, *U.S.A.* 79 F9 40 48N 75 58W
Tamar →, *U.K.* 11 G3 50 27N 4 15W
Tamarinda, *Spain* 22 B10 39 55N 3 49 E
Tamashima, *Japan* 31 G6 34 32N 133 40 E
Tamaulipas □, *Mexico* 87 C5 24 0N 99 0W
Tamaulipas, Sierra de, *Mexico* 87 C5 23 30N 98 20W
Tamazula, *Mexico* 86 C3 24 55N 106 58W
Tamazunchale, *Mexico* 87 C5 21 16N 98 47W
Tambacounda, *Senegal* 50 F3 13 45N 13 40W
Tambelan, Kepulauan, *Indonesia* 36 D3 1 0N 107 30 E
Tambellup, *Australia* 61 F2 34 4S 117 37 E
Tambo, *Australia* 62 C4 24 54S 146 14 E
Tambo de Mora, *Peru* 92 F3 13 30S 76 8W
Tambohorano, *Madag.* 57 B7 17 30S 43 58 E
Tambora, *Indonesia* 36 F5 8 12S 118 5 E
Tambov, *Russia* 24 D7 52 45N 41 28 E
Tambuku, *Indonesia* 37 G15 7 8S 113 40 E
Tâmega →, *Portugal* 19 B1 41 5N 8 21W
Tamenglong, *India* 41 G18 25 0N 93 35 E
Tamiahua, L. de, *Mexico* 87 C5 21 30N 97 30W
Tamil Nadu □, *India* 40 P10 11 0N 77 0 E
Tamluk, *India* 43 H12 22 18N 87 58 E
Tammerfors = Tampere, *Finland* 9 F20 61 30N 23 50 E
Tammisaari, *Finland* 9 F20 60 0N 23 26 E
Tamo Abu, Pegunungan, *Malaysia* 36 D5 3 10N 115 5 E
Tampa, *U.S.A.* 77 M4 27 57N 82 27W
Tampa B., *U.S.A.* 77 M4 27 50N 82 30W
Tampere, *Finland* 9 F20 61 30N 23 50 E
Tampico, *Mexico* 87 C5 22 20N 97 50W
Tampin, *Malaysia* 39 L4 2 28N 102 13 E
Tamu, *Burma* 41 G19 24 13N 94 12 E
Tamworth, *Australia* 63 E5 31 7S 150 58 E
Tamworth, *Canada* 78 B8 44 29N 77 0W
Tamworth, *U.K.* 11 E6 52 39N 1 41W
Tamyang, *S. Korea* 35 G14 35 19N 126 59 E
Tan An, *Vietnam* 39 G6 10 32N 106 25 E
Tan-Tan, *Morocco* 50 C3 28 29N 11 1W
Tana →, *Kenya* 54 C5 2 32S 40 31 E
Tana →, *Norway* 8 A23 70 30N 28 14 E
Tana, L., *Ethiopia* 46 E2 13 5N 37 30 E
Tana River, *Kenya* 54 C4 2 0S 39 30 E
Tanabe, *Japan* 31 H7 33 44N 135 22 E
Tanafjorden, *Norway* 8 A23 70 45N 28 25 E
Tanaga, Pta., *Canary Is.* 22 G1 27 42N 18 10W
Tanahbala, *Indonesia* 36 E1 0 30S 98 30 E
Tanahgrogot, *Indonesia* 36 E5 1 55S 116 15 E
Tanahjampea, *Indonesia* 37 F6 7 10S 120 35 E
Tanahmasa, *Indonesia* 36 E1 0 12S 98 39 E
Tanahmerah, *Indonesia* 37 F10 6 5S 140 16 E
Tanakpur, *India* 43 E9 29 5N 80 7 E
Tanakura, *Japan* 31 F10 37 10N 140 20 E
Tanami, *Australia* 60 C4 19 59S 129 43 E
Tanami Desert, *Australia* 60 C5 18 50S 132 0 E
Tanana →, *U.S.A.* 68 B4 65 10N 151 58W
Tananarive = Antananarivo, *Madag.* 57 B8 18 55S 47 31 E
Tánaro →, *Italy* 18 D8 44 55N 8 40 E
Tancheng, *China* 35 G10 34 25N 118 20 E
Tanch'ŏn, *N. Korea* 35 D15 40 27N 128 54 E
Tanda, *Ut. P., India* 43 F10 26 33N 82 35 E
Tanda, *Ut. P., India* 43 E8 28 57N 78 56 E
Tandag, *Phil.* 37 C7 9 4N 126 9 E
Tandaia, *Tanzania* 55 D3 9 25S 34 15 E
Tandaué, *Angola* 56 B2 16 58S 18 5 E
Tandil, *Argentina* 94 D4 37 15S 59 6W
Tandil, Sa. del, *Argentina* 94 D4 37 30S 59 0W
Tandlianwala, *Pakistan* 42 D5 31 3N 73 9 E
Tando Adam, *Pakistan* 42 G3 25 45N 68 40 E
Tando Allahyar, *Pakistan* 42 G3 25 28N 68 43 E
Tando Bago, *Pakistan* 42 G3 24 47N 68 58 E
Tando Mohommed Khan, *Pakistan* 42 G3 25 8N 68 32 E
Tandou L., *Australia* 63 E3 32 40S 142 5 E
Tandragee, *U.K.* 13 B5 54 21N 6 24W
Tane-ga-Shima, *Japan* 31 J5 30 30N 131 0 E
Taneatua, *N.Z.* 59 H6 38 4S 177 1 E
Tanen Tong Dan, *Burma* 38 D2 16 30N 98 30 E
Tanezrouft, *Algeria* 50 D6 23 9N 0 11 E
Tang, Koh, *Cambodia* 39 G4 10 16N 103 7 E
Tang, Ra's-e, *Iran* 45 E8 25 21N 59 52 E
Tang Krasang, *Cambodia* 38 F5 12 34N 105 3 E
Tanga, *Tanzania* 54 D4 5 5S 39 2 E
Tanga □, *Tanzania* 54 D4 5 20S 38 0 E
**Tanganyika, L.**, *Africa* 54 D3 6 40S 30 0 E
Tanger = Tangier, *Morocco* 50 A4 35 50N 5 49W
Tangerang, *Indonesia* 37 G12 6 11S 106 37 E
Tanggu, *China* 35 E9 39 2N 117 40 E
Tanggula Shan, *China* 32 C4 32 40N 92 10 E
Tanghe, *China* 34 H7 32 47N 112 50 E
**Tangier**, *Morocco* 50 A4 35 50N 5 49W
Tangorin, *Australia* 62 C3 21 47S 144 12 E
Tangshan, *China* 35 E10 39 38N 118 10 E
Tangtou, *China* 35 G10 35 28N 118 30 E
Tanimbar, Kepulauan, *Indonesia* 37 F8 7 30S 131 30 E
Tanimbar Is. = Tanimbar, Kepulauan, *Indonesia* 37 F8 7 30S 131 30 E
Taninthari = Tenasserim □, *Burma* 38 F2 14 0N 98 30 E
Tanjay, *Phil.* 37 C6 9 30N 123 5 E
Tanjong Malim, *Malaysia* 39 L3 3 42N 101 31 E
Tanjore = Thanjavur, *India* 40 P11 10 48N 79 12 E
Tanjung, *Indonesia* 36 E5 2 10S 115 25 E
Tanjungbalai, *Indonesia* 36 D1 2 55N 99 44 E
Tanjungbatu, *Indonesia* 36 D5 2 23N 118 3 E
Tanjungkarang Telukbetung, *Indonesia* 36 F3 5 20S 105 10 E
Tanjungpandan, *Indonesia* 36 E3 2 43S 107 38 E
Tanjungpinang, *Indonesia* 36 D2 1 5N 104 30 E
Tanjungredeb, *Indonesia* 36 D5 2 9N 117 29 E
Tanjungselor, *Indonesia* 36 D5 2 55N 117 25 E
Tank, *Pakistan* 42 C4 32 14N 70 25 E
Tankhala, *India* 42 J5 21 58N 73 47 E
Tannersville, *U.S.A.* 79 E9 41 3N 75 18W
Tannu-Ola, *Russia* 27 D10 51 0N 94 0 E
Tannum Sands, *Australia* 62 C5 23 57S 151 22 E
Tanout, *Niger* 50 F7 14 50N 8 55 E
Tanta, *Egypt* 51 B12 30 45N 30 57 E
Tantoyuca, *Mexico* 87 C5 21 21N 98 10W
Tantung = Dandong, *China* 35 D13 40 10N 124 20 E
Tanunda, *Australia* 63 E2 34 30S 139 0 E
**Tanzania** ■, *Africa* 54 D3 6 0S 34 0 E
Tanzilla →, *Canada* 72 B2 58 8N 130 43W
Tao, Ko, *Thailand* 39 G2 10 5N 99 52 E
Tao'an = Taonan, *China* 35 B12 45 22N 122 40 E
Tao'er He →, *China* 35 B13 45 45N 124 5 E

Taolanaro, *Madag.* 57 D8 25 2S 47 0 E
Taole, *China* 34 E4 38 48N 106 40 E
Taonan, *China* 35 B12 45 22N 122 40 E
Taos, *U.S.A.* 83 H11 36 24N 105 35W
Taoudenni, *Mali* 50 D5 22 40N 3 55W
Tapa, *Estonia* 9 G21 59 15N 25 50 E
Tapa Shan = Daba Shan, *China* 33 C5 32 0N 109 0 E
Tapachula, *Mexico* 87 E6 14 54N 92 17W
Tapah, *Malaysia* 39 K3 4 12N 101 15 E
Tapajós →, *Brazil* 93 D8 2 24S 54 41W
Tapaktuan, *Indonesia* 36 D1 3 15N 97 10 E
Tapanahoni →, *Surinam* 93 C8 4 20N 54 25W
Tapanui, *N.Z.* 59 L2 45 56S 169 18 E
Tapauá →, *Brazil* 92 E6 5 40S 64 21W
Tapes, *Brazil* 95 C5 30 40S 51 23W
Tapeta, *Liberia* 50 G4 6 29N 8 52W
Taphan Hin, *Thailand* 38 D3 16 13N 100 26 E
Tapirapecó, Serra, *Venezuela* 92 C6 1 10N 65 0W
Tapuaenuku, Mt., *N.Z.* 59 K4 42 0S 173 39 E
Tapul Group, *Phil.* 37 C6 5 35N 120 50 E
Tapurucuará, *Brazil* 92 D5 0 24S 65 2W
Ţaqţaq, *Iraq* 44 C5 35 53N 44 35 E
Taquara, *Brazil* 95 B5 29 36S 50 46W
Taquari →, *Brazil* 92 G7 19 15S 57 17W
Tara, *Australia* 63 D5 27 17S 150 31 E
Tara, *Canada* 78 B3 44 28N 81 9W
Tara, *Russia* 26 D8 56 55N 74 24 E
Tara, *Zambia* 55 F2 16 58S 26 45 E
Tara →, *Montenegro, Yug.* 21 C8 43 21N 18 51 E
Tarabagatay, Khrebet, *Kazakstan* 26 E9 48 0N 83 0 E
Tarābulus, *Lebanon* 47 A4 34 31N 35 50 E
Tarābulus, *Libya* 51 B8 32 49N 13 7 E
Taradehi, *India* 43 H8 23 18N 79 21 E
Tarajalejo, *Canary Is.* 22 F5 28 12N 14 7W
Tarakan, *Indonesia* 36 D5 3 20N 117 35 E
Tarakit, Mt., *Kenya* 54 B4 2 2N 35 10 E
Tarama-Jima, *Japan* 31 M2 24 39N 124 42 E
Taran, Mys, *Russia* 9 J18 54 56N 19 59 E
Taranagar, *India* 42 E6 28 43N 74 50 E
Taranaki □, *N.Z.* 59 H5 39 25S 174 30 E
Tarancón, *Spain* 19 B4 40 1N 3 0W
Taranga Hill, *India* 40 H8 24 0N 72 40 E
Taransay, *U.K.* 12 D1 57 54N 7 0W
Táranto, *Italy* 20 D7 40 28N 17 14 E
Táranto, G. di, *Italy* 20 D7 40 8N 17 20 E
Tarapacá, *Colombia* 92 D5 2 56S 69 46W
Tarapacá □, *Chile* 94 A2 20 45S 69 30W
Tarapoto, *Peru* 92 E3 6 30S 76 20W
Tararua Ra., *N.Z.* 59 J5 40 45S 175 25 E
Tarashcha, *Ukraine* 17 D16 49 30N 30 31 E
Tarauacá, *Brazil* 92 E4 8 6S 70 48W
Tarauacá →, *Brazil* 92 E5 6 42S 69 48W
**Tarawa**, *Kiribati* 64 G9 1 30N 173 0 E
Tarawera, *N.Z.* 59 H6 39 2S 176 36 E
Tarawera L., *N.Z.* 59 H6 38 13S 176 27 E
Tarazona, *Spain* 19 B5 41 55N 1 43W
Tarbat Ness, *U.K.* 12 D5 57 52N 3 47W
Tarbela Dam, *Pakistan* 42 B5 34 8N 72 52 E
Tarbert, *Arg. & Bute, U.K.* 12 F3 55 52N 5 25W
Tarbert, *W. Isles, U.K.* 12 D2 57 54N 6 49W
Tarbes, *France* 18 E4 43 15N 0 3 E
Tarboro, *U.S.A.* 77 H7 35 54N 77 32W
Tarcoola, *Australia* 63 E1 30 44S 134 36 E
Tarcoon, *Australia* 63 E4 30 15S 146 43 E
Taree, *Australia* 63 E5 31 50S 152 30 E
Tarfaya, *Morocco* 50 C3 27 55N 12 55W
Târgovişte, *Romania* 17 F13 44 55N 25 27 E
Târgu-Jiu, *Romania* 17 F12 45 5N 23 19 E
Târgu Mureş, *Romania* 17 E13 46 31N 24 38 E
Ţarif, *U.A.E.* 45 E7 24 3N 53 46 E
Tarifa, *Spain* 19 D3 36 1N 5 36W
Tarija, *Bolivia* 94 A3 21 30S 64 40W
Tarija □, *Bolivia* 94 A3 21 30S 63 30W
Tariku →, *Indonesia* 37 E9 2 55S 138 26 E
**Tarim Basin** = Tarim Pendi, *China* 32 B3 40 0N 84 0 E
Tarim He →, *China* 32 C3 39 30N 88 30 E
Tarim Pendi, *China* 32 B3 40 0N 84 0 E
Taritatu →, *Indonesia* 37 E9 2 54S 138 27 E
Tarka →, *S. Africa* 56 E4 32 10S 26 0 E
Tarkastad, *S. Africa* 56 E4 32 0S 26 16 E
Tarkhankut, Mys, *Ukraine* 25 E5 45 25N 32 30 E
Tarko Sale, *Russia* 26 C8 64 55N 77 50 E
Tarkwa, *Ghana* 50 G5 5 20N 2 0W
Tarlac, *Phil.* 37 A6 15 29N 120 35 E
Tarma, *Peru* 92 F3 11 25S 75 45W
Tarn →, *France* 18 E4 44 5N 1 6 E
Târnăveni, *Romania* 17 E13 46 19N 24 13 E
Tarnobrzeg, *Poland* 17 C11 50 35N 21 41 E
Tarnów, *Poland* 17 C11 50 3N 21 0 E
Tarnowskie Góry, *Poland* 17 C10 50 27N 18 54 E
Ţārom, *Iran* 45 D7 28 11N 55 46 E
Taroom, *Australia* 63 D4 25 36S 149 48 E
Taroudannt, *Morocco* 50 B4 30 30N 8 52W
Tarpon Springs, *U.S.A.* 77 L4 28 9N 82 45W
Tarragona, *Spain* 19 B6 41 5N 1 17 E
Tarraleah, *Australia* 62 G4 42 17S 146 26 E
Tarrasa = Terrassa, *Spain* 19 B7 41 34N 2 1 E
Tarrytown, *U.S.A.* 79 E11 41 4N 73 52W
Tarshiha = Me'ona, *Israel* 47 B4 33 1N 35 15 E
Tarso Emissi, *Chad* 51 D9 21 27N 18 36 E
Tarsus, *Turkey* 25 G5 36 58N 34 55 E
Tartagal, *Argentina* 94 A3 22 30S 63 50W
Tartu, *Estonia* 9 G22 58 20N 26 44 E
Ţarţūs, *Syria* 44 C2 34 55N 35 55 E
Tarumizu, *Japan* 31 J5 31 29N 130 42 E
Tarutao, Ko, *Thailand* 39 J2 6 33N 99 40 E
Tarutung, *Indonesia* 36 D1 2 0N 98 54 E
Taseko →, *Canada* 72 C4 52 8N 123 45W
Tash-Kömür, *Kyrgyzstan* 26 E8 41 40N 72 10 E
Tash-Kumyr = Tash-Kömür, *Kyrgyzstan* 26 E8 41 40N 72 10 E
Tashauz = Dashhowuz, *Turkmenistan* 26 E6 41 49N 59 58 E
Tashi Chho Dzong = Thimphu, *Bhutan* 41 F16 27 31N 89 45 E
Ţashk, Daryācheh-ye, *Iran* 45 D7 29 45N 53 35 E
**Tashkent** = Toshkent, *Uzbekistan* 26 E7 41 20N 69 10 E
Tashtagol, *Russia* 26 D9 52 47N 87 53 E
Tasikmalaya, *Indonesia* 37 G13 7 18S 108 12 E
Tåsjön, *Sweden* 8 D16 64 15N 15 40 E
Taskan, *Russia* 27 C16 62 59N 150 20 E
Tasman B., *N.Z.* 59 J4 40 59S 173 25 E
Tasman Mts., *N.Z.* 59 J4 41 3S 172 25 E
Tasman Pen., *Australia* 62 G4 43 10S 148 0 E
Tasman Sea, *Pac. Oc.* 64 L8 36 0S 160 0 E
**Tasmania** □, *Australia* 62 G4 42 0S 146 30 E
Tassili n'Ajjer, *Algeria* 50 C7 25 47N 8 1 E
Tatabánya, *Hungary* 17 E10 47 32N 18 25 E
Tatahouine, *Tunisia* 51 B8 32 56N 10 27 E
**Tatar Republic** = Tatarstan □, *Russia* 24 C9 55 30N 51 30 E
Tatarbunary, *Ukraine* 17 F15 45 50N 29 39 E
Tatarsk, *Russia* 26 D8 55 14N 76 0 E
Tatarstan □, *Russia* 24 C9 55 30N 51 30 E
Tateyama, *Japan* 31 G9 35 0N 139 50 E
Tathlina L., *Canada* 72 A5 60 33N 117 39W
Tathra, *Australia* 63 F4 36 44S 149 59 E
Tati →, *India* 40 J8 21 8N 72 41 E
Tatinnai L., *Canada* 73 A9 60 55N 97 40W
Tatla L., *Canada* 72 C4 52 0N 124 20W
Tatnam, C., *Canada* 73 B10 57 16N 91 0W
Tatra = Tatry, *Slovak Rep.* 17 D11 49 20N 20 0 E
Tatry, *Slovak Rep.* 17 D11 49 20N 20 0 E
Tatshenshini →, *Canada* 72 B1 59 28N 137 45W
Tatsuno, *Japan* 31 G7 34 52N 134 33 E
Tatta, *Pakistan* 42 G2 24 42N 67 55 E
Tatuí, *Brazil* 95 A6 23 25S 47 53W
Tatum, *U.S.A.* 81 J3 33 16N 103 19W
Tat'ung = Datong, *China* 34 D7 40 6N 113 18 E
Tatvan, *Turkey* 25 G7 38 31N 42 15 E
Taubaté, *Brazil* 95 A6 23 0S 45 36W
Tauern, *Austria* 16 E7 47 15N 12 40 E
Taumarunui, *N.Z.* 59 H5 38 53S 175 15 E
Taumaturgo, *Brazil* 92 E4 8 54S 72 51W
Taung, *S. Africa* 56 D3 27 33S 24 47 E
Taungdwingyi, *Burma* 41 J19 20 1N 95 40 E
Taunggyi, *Burma* 41 J20 20 50N 97 0 E
Taungup, *Burma* 41 K19 18 51N 94 14 E
Taungup Pass, *Burma* 41 K19 18 40N 94 45 E
Taungup Taunggya, *Burma* 41 K18 18 20N 93 40 E
Taunsa, *Pakistan* 42 D4 30 42N 70 39 E
Taunsa Barrage, *Pakistan* 42 D4 30 42N 70 50 E
Taunton, *U.K.* 11 F4 51 1N 3 5W
Taunton, *U.S.A.* 79 E13 41 54N 71 6W
Taunus, *Germany* 16 C5 50 13N 8 34 E
Taupo, *N.Z.* 59 H6 38 41S 176 7 E
Taupo, L., *N.Z.* 59 H5 38 46S 175 55 E
Tauragė, *Lithuania* 9 J20 55 14N 22 16 E
Tauranga, *N.Z.* 59 G6 37 42S 176 11 E
Tauranga Harb., *N.Z.* 59 G6 37 30S 176 5 E
Taureau, Rés., *Canada* 70 C5 46 46N 73 50W
Taurianova, *Italy* 20 E7 38 21N 16 1 E
Taurus Mts. = Toros Dağları, *Turkey* 25 G5 37 0N 32 30 E
Tavda, *Russia* 26 D7 58 7N 65 8 E
Tavda →, *Russia* 26 D7 57 47N 67 18 E
Taveta, *Tanzania* 54 C4 3 23S 37 37 E
Taveuni, *Fiji* 59 C9 16 51S 179 58W
Tavira, *Portugal* 19 D2 37 8N 7 40W
Tavistock, *Canada* 78 C4 43 19N 80 50W
Tavistock, *U.K.* 11 G3 50 33N 4 9W
Tavoy = Dawei, *Burma* 38 E2 14 2N 98 12 E
Taw →, *U.K.* 11 F3 51 4N 4 4W
Tawa →, *India* 42 H8 22 48N 77 48 E
Tawas City, *U.S.A.* 76 C4 44 16N 83 31W
Tawau, *Malaysia* 36 D5 4 20N 117 55 E
Tawitawi, *Phil.* 37 C6 5 10N 120 0 E
Taxco de Alarcón, *Mexico* 87 D5 18 33N 99 36W
Taxila, *Pakistan* 42 C5 33 42N 72 52 E
**Tay** →, *U.K.* 12 E5 56 37N 3 38W
Tay, Firth of, *U.K.* 12 E5 56 25N 3 8W
Tay, L., *Australia* 61 F3 32 55S 120 48 E
Tay, L., *U.K.* 12 E4 56 32N 4 8W
Tay Ninh, *Vietnam* 39 G6 11 20N 106 5 E
Tayabamba, *Peru* 92 E3 8 15S 77 16W
Taylakova, *Russia* 26 D8 59 13N 74 0 E
Taylakovy = Taylakova, *Russia* 26 D8 59 13N 74 0 E
Taylor, *Canada* 72 B4 56 13N 120 40W
Taylor, *Nebr., U.S.A.* 80 E5 41 46N 99 23W
Taylor, *Pa., U.S.A.* 79 E9 41 23N 75 43W
Taylor, *Tex., U.S.A.* 81 K6 30 34N 97 25W
Taylor, Mt., *U.S.A.* 83 J10 35 14N 107 37W
Taylorville, *U.S.A.* 80 F10 39 33N 89 18W
Taymā, *Si. Arabia* 44 E3 27 35N 38 45 E
Taymyr, Oz., *Russia* 27 B11 74 20N 102 0 E
Taymyr, Poluostrov, *Russia* 27 B11 75 0N 100 0 E
Tayport, *U.K.* 12 E6 56 27N 2 52W
Tayshet, *Russia* 27 D10 55 58N 98 1 E
Taytay, *Phil.* 37 B5 10 45N 119 30 E
Taz →, *Russia* 26 C8 67 32N 78 40 E
Taza, *Morocco* 50 B5 34 16N 4 6W
Tāzah Khurmātū, *Iraq* 44 C5 35 18N 44 20 E
Tazawa-Ko, *Japan* 30 E10 39 43N 140 40 E
Tazin, *Canada* 73 B7 59 48N 109 55W
Tazin L., *Canada* 73 B7 59 44N 108 42W
Tazovskiy, *Russia* 26 C8 67 30N 78 44 E
**Tbilisi**, *Georgia* 25 F7 41 43N 44 50 E
Tchad = Chad ■, *Africa* 51 F8 15 0N 17 15 E
Tchad, L., *Chad* 51 F8 13 30N 14 30 E
Tch'eng-tou = Chengdu, *China* 32 C5 30 38N 104 2 E
Tchentlo L., *Canada* 72 B4 55 15N 125 0W
Tchibanga, *Gabon* 52 E2 2 45S 11 0 E
Tch'ong-k'ing = Chongqing, *China* 32 D5 29 35N 106 25 E
Tczew, *Poland* 17 A10 54 8N 18 50 E
Te Anau, L., *N.Z.* 59 L1 45 15S 167 45 E
Te Aroha, *N.Z.* 59 G5 37 32S 175 44 E
Te Awamutu, *N.Z.* 59 H5 38 1S 175 20 E
Te Kuiti, *N.Z.* 59 H5 38 20S 175 11 E
Te Puke, *N.Z.* 59 G6 37 46S 176 22 E
Te Waewae B., *N.Z.* 59 M1 46 13S 167 33 E
Teague, *U.S.A.* 81 K6 31 38N 96 17W
Teapa, *Mexico* 87 D6 18 35N 92 56W
Tebakang, *Malaysia* 36 D4 1 6N 110 30 E
Tébessa, *Algeria* 50 A7 35 22N 8 8 E
Tebicuary →, *Paraguay* 94 B4 26 36S 58 16W
Tebingtinggi, *Indonesia* 36 D1 3 20N 99 9 E
Tebintingii, *Indonesia* 36 E2 1 0N 102 45 E
Tecate, *Mexico* 85 N10 32 34N 116 38W
Tecka, *Argentina* 96 E2 43 29S 70 48W
Tecomán, *Mexico* 86 D4 18 55N 103 53W
Tecopa, *U.S.A.* 85 K10 35 51N 116 13W
Tecoripa, *Mexico* 86 B3 28 37N 109 57W
Tecuala, *Mexico* 86 C3 22 23N 105 27W
Tecuci, *Romania* 17 F14 45 51N 27 27 E
Tecumseh, *Canada* 78 D2 42 19N 82 54W
Tecumseh, *Mich., U.S.A.* 76 D4 42 0N 83 57W
Tecumseh, *Okla., U.S.A.* 81 H6 35 15N 96 56W
Tedzhen = Tejen, *Turkmenistan* 26 F7 37 23N 60 31 E
Tees →, *U.K.* 10 C6 54 37N 1 10W
Tees B., *U.K.* 10 C6 54 40N 1 9W
Teeswater, *Canada* 78 C3 43 59N 81 17W
Tefé, *Brazil* 92 D6 3 25S 64 50W
Tegal, *Indonesia* 37 G13 6 52S 109 8 E
Tegid, L. = Bala, L., *U.K.* 10 E4 52 53N 3 37W
**Tegucigalpa**, *Honduras* 88 D2 14 5N 87 14W
Tehachapi, *U.S.A.* 85 K8 35 8N 118 27W
Tehachapi Mts., *U.S.A.* 85 L8 35 0N 118 30W
Tehoru, *Indonesia* 37 E7 3 19S 129 37 E
**Tehrān**, *Iran* 45 C6 35 44N 51 30 E
Tehri, *India* 43 D8 30 23N 78 29 E
Tehuacán, *Mexico* 87 D5 18 30N 97 30W
Tehuantepec, *Mexico* 87 D5 16 21N 95 13W
Tehuantepec, G. de, *Mexico* 87 D5 15 50N 95 12W
Tehuantepec, Istmo de, *Mexico* 87 D6 17 0N 94 30W
Teide, *Canary Is.* 22 F3 28 15N 16 38W
Teifi →, *U.K.* 11 E3 52 5N 4 41W
Teign →, *U.K.* 11 G4 50 32N 3 32W
Teignmouth, *U.K.* 11 G4 50 33N 3 31W
Tejam, *India* 43 E9 29 57N 80 11 E
Tejen, *Turkmenistan* 26 F7 37 23N 60 31 E
Tejen →, *Turkmenistan* 45 B9 37 24N 60 38 E
Tejo →, *Europe* 19 C1 38 40N 9 24W
Tejon Pass, *U.S.A.* 85 L8 34 49N 118 53W
Tekamah, *U.S.A.* 80 E6 41 47N 96 13W
Tekapo, L., *N.Z.* 59 K3 43 53S 170 33 E
Tekax, *Mexico* 87 C7 20 11N 89 18W
Tekeli, *Kazakstan* 26 E8 44 50N 79 0 E
Tekirdağ, *Turkey* 21 D12 40 58N 27 30 E
Tekkali, *India* 41 K14 18 37N 84 15 E
Tekoa, *U.S.A.* 82 C5 47 14N 117 4W
**Tel Aviv-Yafo**, *Israel* 47 C3 32 4N 34 48 E
Tel Lakhish, *Israel* 47 D3 31 34N 34 51 E
Tel Megiddo, *Israel* 47 C4 32 35N 35 11 E
Tela, *Honduras* 88 C2 15 40N 87 28W
Telanaipura = Jambi, *Indonesia* 36 E2 1 38S 103 30 E
Telavi, *Georgia* 25 F8 42 0N 45 30 E
Telde, *Canary Is.* 22 G4 27 59N 15 25W
Telegraph Creek, *Canada* 72 B2 58 0N 131 10W
Telekhany = Tsyelyakhany, *Belarus* 17 B13 52 30N 25 46 E
Telemark, *Norway* 9 G12 59 15N 7 40 E
Telén, *Argentina* 94 D2 36 15S 65 31W
Teleng, *Iran* 45 E9 25 47N 61 3 E
Teles Pires →, *Brazil* 92 E7 7 21S 58 3W
Telescope Pk., *U.S.A.* 85 J9 36 10N 117 5W
Telfer Mine, *Australia* 60 C3 21 40S 122 12 E
Telford, *U.K.* 11 E5 52 40N 2 27W
Telford and Wrekin □, *U.K.* 10 E5 52 45N 2 27W
Telkwa, *Canada* 72 C3 54 41N 127 5W
Tell City, *U.S.A.* 76 G2 37 57N 86 46W
Tellicherry, *India* 40 P9 11 45N 75 30 E
Telluride, *U.S.A.* 83 H10 37 56N 107 49W
Teloloapán, *Mexico* 87 D5 18 21N 99 51W
Telpos Iz, *Russia* 24 B10 63 16N 59 13 E
Telsen, *Argentina* 96 E3 42 30S 66 50W
Telšiai, *Lithuania* 9 H20 55 59N 22 14 E
Teluk Anson = Teluk Intan, *Malaysia* 39 K3 4 3N 101 0 E
Teluk Betung = Tanjungkarang Telukbetung, *Indonesia* 36 F3 5 20S 105 10 E
Teluk Intan, *Malaysia* 39 K3 4 3N 101 0 E
Telukbutun, *Indonesia* 39 K7 4 13N 108 12 E
Telukdalem, *Indonesia* 36 D1 0 33N 97 50 E
Tema, *Ghana* 50 G5 5 41N 0 0 E
Temax, *Mexico* 87 C7 21 10N 88 50W
Temba, *S. Africa* 57 D4 25 20S 28 17 E
Tembagapura, *Indonesia* 37 E9 4 20S 137 0 E
Tembe, *Dem. Rep. of the Congo* 54 C2 0 16S 28 14 E
Temblor Range, *U.S.A.* 85 K7 35 20N 119 50W
Teme →, *U.K.* 11 E5 52 11N 2 13W
Temecula, *U.S.A.* 85 M9 33 30N 117 9W
Temerloh, *Malaysia* 36 D2 3 27N 102 25 E
Teminabuan, *Indonesia* 37 E8 1 26S 132 1 E
Temir, *Kazakstan* 25 E10 49 1N 57 14 E
Temirtau, *Kazakstan* 26 D8 50 5N 72 56 E
Temirtau, *Russia* 26 D9 53 10N 87 30 E
Temiscamie →, *Canada* 71 B5 50 59N 73 5W
Témiscaming, *Canada* 70 C4 46 44N 79 5W
Témiscamingue, L., *Canada* 70 C4 47 10N 79 25W
Temosachic, *Mexico* 86 B3 28 58N 107 50W
Tempe, *U.S.A.* 83 K8 33 25N 111 56W
Tempiute, *U.S.A.* 84 H11 37 39N 115 38W
Temple, *U.S.A.* 81 K6 31 6N 97 21W
Temple B., *Australia* 62 A3 12 15S 143 3 E
Templemore, *Ireland* 13 D4 52 47N 7 51W
Templeton, *U.S.A.* 84 K6 35 33N 120 42W
Templeton →, *Australia* 62 C2 21 0S 138 40 E
Tempoal, *Mexico* 87 C5 21 31N 98 23W
Temuco, *Chile* 96 D2 38 45S 72 40W
Temuka, *N.Z.* 59 L3 44 14S 171 17 E
Tenabo, *Mexico* 87 C6 20 2N 90 12W
Tenaha, *U.S.A.* 81 K7 31 57N 94 15W
Tenakee Springs, *U.S.A.* 72 B1 57 47N 135 13W
Tenali, *India* 40 L12 16 15N 80 35 E
Tenancingo, *Mexico* 87 D5 19 0N 99 33W
Tenango, *Mexico* 87 D5 19 7N 99 33W
Tenasserim, *Burma* 39 F2 12 6N 99 3 E
Tenasserim □, *Burma* 38 F2 14 0N 98 30 E
Tenby, *U.K.* 11 F3 51 40N 4 42W
Tenda, Colle di, *France* 18 D7 44 7N 7 36 E
Tendaho, *Ethiopia* 46 E3 11 48N 40 54 E
Tendukhera, *India* 43 H8 23 24N 79 33 E
Ténéré, *Niger* 50 E7 19 0N 10 30 E
**Tenerife**, *Canary Is.* 22 F3 28 15N 16 35W
Tenerife, Pico, *Canary Is.* 22 G1 27 43N 18 1W
Teng Xian, *China* 35 G9 35 5N 117 10 E
Tengah □, *Indonesia* 37 E6 2 0S 122 0 E
Tengah, Kepulauan, *Indonesia* 36 F5 7 5S 118 15 E
Tengchong, *China* 32 D4 25 0N 98 28 E
Tengchowfu = Penglai, *China* 35 F11 37 48N 120 42 E
Tenggara □, *Indonesia* 37 E6 3 0S 122 0 E
Tenggarong, *Indonesia* 36 E5 0 24S 116 58 E
Tenggol, Pulau, *Malaysia* 39 K4 4 48N 103 41 E
Tengiz, Ozero, *Kazakstan* 26 D7 50 30N 69 0 E
Tenino, *U.S.A.* 84 D4 46 51N 122 51W
Tenkasi, *India* 40 Q10 8 55N 77 20 E
Tenke, *Katanga, Dem. Rep. of the Congo* 55 E2 11 22S 26 40 E
Tenke, *Katanga, Dem. Rep. of the Congo* 55 E2 10 32S 26 7 E
Tennant Creek, *Australia* 62 B1 19 30S 134 15 E
**Tennessee** □, *U.S.A.* 77 H2 36 0N 86 30W
**Tennessee** →, *U.S.A.* 76 G1 37 4N 88 34W
Teno, Pta. de, *Canary Is.* 22 F3 28 21N 16 55W
Tenom, *Malaysia* 36 C5 5 4N 115 57 E
Tenosique, *Mexico* 87 D6 17 30N 91 24W
Tenryū-Gawa →, *Japan* 31 G8 35 39N 137 48 E
Tenterden, *U.K.* 11 F8 51 4N 0 42 E
Tenterfield, *Australia* 63 D5 29 0S 152 0 E
Teófilo Otoni, *Brazil* 93 G10 17 50S 41 30W
Tepa, *Indonesia* 37 F7 7 52S 129 31 E
Tepalcatepec →, *Mexico* 86 D4 18 35N 101 59W
Tepehuanes, *Mexico* 86 B3 25 21N 105 44W
Tepetongo, *Mexico* 86 C4 22 28N 103 9W
Tepic, *Mexico* 86 C4 21 30N 104 54W
Teplice, *Czech Rep.* 16 C7 50 40N 13 48 E
Tepoca, C., *Mexico* 86 A2 30 20N 112 25W
Tequila, *Mexico* 86 C4 20 54N 103 47W
Ter →, *Spain* 19 A7 42 2N 3 12 E
Ter Apel, *Neths.* 15 B7 52 53N 7 5 E
Teraina, *Kiribati* 65 G11 4 43N 160 25W
Téramo, *Italy* 20 C5 42 39N 13 42 E
Terang, *Australia* 63 F3 38 15S 142 55 E
Tercero →, *Argentina* 94 C3 32 58S 61 47W
Terebovlya, *Ukraine* 17 D13 49 18N 25 44 E
Terek →, *Russia* 25 F8 44 0N 47 30 E
Teresina, *Brazil* 93 E10 5 9S 42 45W
Terewah, L., *Australia* 63 D4 29 52S 147 35 E
Teridgerie Cr. →, *Australia* 63 E4 30 25S 148 50 E
Termez = Termiz, *Uzbekistan* 26 F7 37 15N 67 15 E
Términi Imerese, *Italy* 20 F5 37 59N 13 42 E
Términos, L. de, *Mexico* 87 D6 18 35N 91 30W
Termiz, *Uzbekistan* 26 F7 37 15N 67 15 E
Térmoli, *Italy* 20 C6 42 0N 15 0 E
Ternate, *Indonesia* 37 D7 0 45N 127 25 E
Terneuzen, *Neths.* 15 C3 51 20N 3 50 E
Terney, *Russia* 27 E14 45 3N 136 37 E
Terni, *Italy* 20 C5 42 34N 12 37 E
Ternopil, *Ukraine* 17 D13 49 30N 25 40 E
Ternopol = Ternopil, *Ukraine* 17 D13 49 30N 25 40 E
Terowie, *Australia* 63 E2 33 8S 138 55 E
Terra Bella, *U.S.A.* 85 K7 35 58N 119 3W
Terra Nova Nat. Park, *Canada* 71 C9 48 33N 53 55W
Terrace, *Canada* 72 C3 54 30N 128 35W
Terrace Bay, *Canada* 70 C2 48 47N 87 5W
Terracina, *Italy* 20 D5 41 17N 13 15 E
Terralba, *Italy* 20 E3 39 43N 8 39 E
Terranova = Ólbia, *Italy* 20 D3 40 55N 9 31 E
Terrassa, *Spain* 19 B7 41 34N 2 1 E
Terre Haute, *U.S.A.* 76 F2 39 28N 87 25W
Terrebonne B., *U.S.A.* 81 L9 29 5N 90 35W
Terrell, *U.S.A.* 81 J6 32 44N 96 17W
Terrenceville, *Canada* 71 C9 47 40N 54 44W
Terry, *U.S.A.* 80 B2 46 47N 105 19W
Terryville, *U.S.A.* 79 E11 41 41N 73 3W
Terschelling, *Neths.* 15 A5 53 25N 5 20 E
Teruel, *Spain* 19 B5 40 22N 1 8W
Tervola, *Finland* 8 C21 66 6N 24 49 E
Teryaweyna L., *Australia* 63 E3 32 18S 143 22 E
Teshio, *Japan* 30 B10 44 53N 141 44 E
Teshio-Gawa →, *Japan* 30 B10 44 53N 141 45 E
Tesiyn Gol →, *Mongolia* 32 A4 50 40N 93 20 E
Teslin, *Canada* 72 A2 60 10N 132 43W
Teslin →, *Canada* 72 A2 61 34N 134 35W
Teslin L., *Canada* 72 A2 60 15N 132 57W
Tessalit, *Mali* 50 D6 20 12N 1 0 E
Test →, *U.K.* 11 G6 50 56N 1 29W
Testigos, Is. Las, *Venezuela* 89 D7 11 23N 63 7W
Tetachuck L., *Canada* 72 C3 53 18N 125 55W
Tetas, Pta., *Chile* 94 A1 23 31S 70 38W
Tete, *Mozam.* 55 F3 16 13S 33 33 E
Tete □, *Mozam.* 55 F3 15 15S 32 40 E
Teterev →, *Ukraine* 17 C16 51 1N 30 5 E
Teteven, *Bulgaria* 21 C11 42 58N 24 17 E
Tethul →, *Canada* 72 A6 60 35N 112 12W
Tetiyev, *Ukraine* 17 D15 49 22N 29 38 E
Teton →, *U.S.A.* 82 C8 47 56N 110 31W
Tétouan, *Morocco* 50 A4 35 35N 5 21W
Tetovo, *Macedonia* 21 C9 42 1N 20 59 E
Teuco →, *Argentina* 94 B3 25 35S 60 11W
Teulon, *Canada* 73 C9 50 23N 97 16W
Teun, *Indonesia* 37 F7 6 59S 129 8 E
Teutoburger Wald, *Germany* 16 B5 52 5N 8 22 E
Tevere →, *Italy* 20 D5 41 44N 12 14 E
Teverya, *Israel* 47 C4 32 47N 35 32 E
Teviot →, *U.K.* 12 F6 55 29N 2 38W
Tewantin, *Australia* 63 D5 26 27S 153 3 E
Tewkesbury, *U.K.* 11 F5 51 59N 2 9W
Texada I., *Canada* 72 D4 49 40N 124 25W
Texarkana, *Ark., U.S.A.* 81 J8 33 26N 94 2W
Texarkana, *Tex., U.S.A.* 81 J7 33 26N 94 3W
Texas, *Australia* 63 D5 28 49S 151 9 E
**Texas** □, *U.S.A.* 81 K5 31 40N 98 30W
Texas City, *U.S.A.* 81 L7 29 24N 94 54W
Texel, *Neths.* 15 A4 53 5N 4 50 E
Texline, *U.S.A.* 81 G3 36 23N 103 2W
Texoma, L., *U.S.A.* 81 J6 33 50N 96 34W
Tezin, *Afghan.* 42 B3 34 24N 69 30 E
Teziutlán, *Mexico* 87 D5 19 50N 97 22W
Tezpur, *India* 41 F18 26 40N 92 45 E
Tezzeron L., *Canada* 72 C4 54 43N 124 30W
Tha-anne →, *Canada* 73 A10 60 31N 94 37W
Tha Deua, *Laos* 38 D4 17 57N 102 53 E
Tha Deua, *Laos* 38 C3 19 26N 101 50 E
Tha Pla, *Thailand* 38 D3 17 48N 100 32 E
Tha Rua, *Thailand* 38 E3 14 34N 100 44 E
Tha Sala, *Thailand* 39 H2 8 40N 99 56 E
Tha Song Yang, *Thailand* 38 D1 17 34N 97 55 E
Thaba Putsoa, *Lesotho* 57 D4 29 45S 28 0 E
Thabana Ntlenyana, *Lesotho* 57 D4 29 30S 29 16 E
Thabazimbi, *S. Africa* 57 C4 24 40S 27 21 E
Thādiq, *Si. Arabia* 44 E5 25 18N 45 52 E
Thai Muang, *Thailand* 39 H2 8 24N 98 16 E
**Thailand** ■, *Asia* 38 E4 16 0N 102 0 E
Thailand, G. of, *Asia* 39 G3 11 30N 101 0 E
Thakhek, *Laos* 38 D5 17 25N 104 45 E

Thal, Pakistan 42 C4 33 28N 70 33 E
Thal Desert, Pakistan 42 D4 31 10N 71 30 E
Thala La, Burma 41 E20 28 25N 97 23 E
Thalabarivat, Cambodia 38 F5 13 33N 105 57 E
Thallon, Australia 63 D4 28 39S 148 49 E
Thames, N.Z. 59 G5 37 7S 175 34 E
Thames →, Canada 78 D2 42 20N 82 25W
**Thames** →, U.K. 11 F8 51 29N 0 34 E
Thames →, U.S.A. 79 E12 41 18N 72 5W
Thames Estuary, U.K. 11 F8 51 29N 0 52 E
Thamesford, Canada 78 C4 43 4N 81 0W
Thamesville, Canada 78 D3 42 33N 81 59W
Than, India 42 H4 22 34N 71 11 E
Than Uyen, Vietnam 38 B4 22 0N 103 54 E
Thana Gazi, India 42 F7 27 25N 76 19 E
Thandla, India 42 H6 23 0N 74 34 E
Thane, India 40 K8 19 12N 72 59 E
Thanesar, India 42 D7 30 1N 76 52 E
Thanet, I. of, U.K. 11 F9 51 21N 1 20 E
Thangool, Australia 62 C5 24 38S 150 42 E
Thanh Hoa, Vietnam 38 C5 19 48N 105 46 E
Thanh Hung, Vietnam 39 H5 9 55N 105 43 E
Thanh Pho Ho Chi Minh = Phanh Bho Ho Chi Minh, Vietnam 39 G6 10 58N 106 40 E
Thanh Thuy, Vietnam 38 A5 22 55N 104 51 E
Thanjavur, India 40 P11 10 48N 79 12 E
Thano Bula Khan, Pakistan 42 G2 25 22N 67 50 E
Thaolinta L., Canada 73 A9 61 30N 96 25W
Thap Sakae, Thailand 39 G2 11 30N 99 37 E
Thap Than, Thailand 38 E2 15 27N 99 54 E
**Thar Desert**, India 42 F5 28 0N 72 0 E
Tharad, India 42 G4 24 30N 71 44 E
Thargomindah, Australia 63 D3 27 58S 143 46 E
Tharrawaddy, Burma 41 L19 17 38N 95 48 E
Tharthār, Mileh, Iraq 44 C4 34 0N 43 15 E
Tharthār, W. ath →, Iraq 44 C4 33 59N 43 12 E
Thásos, Greece 21 D11 40 40N 24 40 E
Thatcher, Ariz., U.S.A. 83 K9 32 51N 109 46W
Thatcher, Colo., U.S.A. 81 G2 37 33N 104 7W
Thaton, Burma 41 L20 16 55N 97 22 E
Thaungdut, Burma 41 G19 24 30N 94 40 E
Thayer, U.S.A. 81 G9 36 31N 91 33W
Thayetmyo, Burma 41 K19 19 20N 95 10 E
Thazi, Burma 41 J20 21 0N 96 5 E
The Alberga →, Australia 63 D2 27 6S 135 33 E
The Bight, Bahamas 89 B4 24 19N 75 24W
The Coorong, Australia 63 F2 35 50S 139 20 E
The Dalles, U.S.A. 82 D3 45 36N 121 10W
The English Company's Is., Australia 62 A2 11 50S 136 32 E
The Frome →, Australia 63 D2 29 8S 137 54 E
The Great Divide = Great Dividing Ra., Australia 62 C4 23 0S 146 0 E
The Hague = 's-Gravenhage, Neths. 15 B4 52 7N 4 17 E
The Hamilton →, Australia 63 D2 26 40S 135 19 E
The Macumba →, Australia 63 D2 27 52S 137 12 E
The Neales →, Australia 63 D2 28 8S 136 47 E
The Officer →, Australia 61 E5 27 46S 132 30 E
The Pas, Canada 73 C8 53 45N 101 15W
The Range, Zimbabwe 55 F3 19 2S 31 2 E
The Rock, Australia 63 F4 35 15S 147 2 E
The Salt L., Australia 63 E3 30 6S 142 8 E
The Sandheads, India 43 J13 21 10N 88 20 E
The Stevenson →, Australia 63 D2 27 6S 135 33 E
The Warburton →, Australia 63 D2 28 4S 137 28 E
The Woodlands, U.S.A. 81 K7 30 9N 95 27W
**Thebes** = Thívai, Greece 21 E10 38 19N 23 19 E
Thebes, Egypt 51 C12 25 40N 32 35 E
Thedford, Canada 78 C3 43 9N 81 51W
Thedford, U.S.A. 80 E4 41 59N 100 35W
Theebine, Australia 63 D5 25 57S 152 34 E
Thekulthili L., Canada 73 A7 61 3N 110 0W
Thelon →, Canada 73 A8 62 35N 104 3W
Theodore, Australia 62 C5 24 55S 150 3 E
Theodore, Canada 73 C8 51 26N 102 55W
Theodore, U.S.A. 77 K1 30 33N 88 10W
Theodore Roosevelt National Memorial Park, U.S.A. 80 B3 47 0N 103 25W
Theodore Roosevelt Res., U.S.A. 83 K8 33 46N 111 0W
Thepha, Thailand 39 J3 6 52N 100 58 E
Theresa, U.S.A. 79 B9 44 13N 75 48W
Thermaïkós Kólpos, Greece 21 D10 40 15N 22 45 E
Thermopolis, U.S.A. 82 E9 43 39N 108 13W
Thermopylae P., Greece 21 E10 38 48N 22 35 E
Thessalon, Canada 70 C3 46 20N 83 30W
**Thessaloníki**, Greece 21 D10 40 38N 22 58 E
Thessaloniki, Gulf of = Thermaïkós Kólpos, Greece 21 D10 40 15N 22 45 E
Thetford, U.K. 11 E8 52 25N 0 45 E
Thetford Mines, Canada 71 C5 46 8N 71 18W
Theun →, Laos 38 C5 18 19N 104 0 E
Theunissen, S. Africa 56 D4 28 26S 26 43 E
Thevenard, Australia 63 E1 32 9S 133 38 E
Thibodaux, U.S.A. 81 L9 29 48N 90 49W
Thicket Portage, Canada 73 B9 55 19N 97 42W
Thief River Falls, U.S.A. 80 A6 48 7N 96 10W
Thiel Mts., Antarctica 5 E16 85 15S 91 0W
Thiers, France 18 D5 45 52N 3 33 E
Thiès, Senegal 50 F2 14 50N 16 51W
Thika, Kenya 54 C4 1 1S 37 5 E
Thikombia, Fiji 59 B9 15 44S 179 55W
Thimphu, Bhutan 41 F16 27 31N 89 45 E
þingvallavatn, Iceland 8 D3 64 11N 21 9W
Thionville, France 18 B7 49 20N 6 10 E
Thíra, Greece 21 F11 36 23N 25 27 E
Third Cataract, Sudan 51 E12 19 49N 30 19 E
Thirsk, U.K. 10 C6 54 14N 1 19W
Thisted, Denmark 9 H13 56 58N 8 40 E
Thistle I., Australia 63 F2 35 0S 136 8 E
Thívai, Greece 21 E10 38 19N 23 19 E
þjórsá →, Iceland 8 E3 63 47N 20 48W
Thlewiaza →, Man., Canada 73 B8 59 43N 100 5W
Thlewiaza →, N.W.T., Canada 73 A10 60 29N 94 40W
Thmar Puok, Cambodia 38 F4 13 57N 103 4 E
Tho Vinh, Vietnam 38 C5 19 16N 105 42 E
Thoa →, Canada 73 A7 60 31N 109 47W
Thoen, Thailand 38 D2 17 43N 99 12 E
Thoeng, Thailand 38 C3 19 41N 100 12 E
Thohoyandou, S. Africa 53 J6 22 58S 30 29 E
Tholdi, Pakistan 43 B7 35 5N 76 6 E
Thomas, U.S.A. 81 H5 35 45N 98 45W
Thomas, L., Australia 63 D2 26 4S 137 58 E
Thomaston, U.S.A. 77 J3 32 53N 84 20W
Thomasville, Ala., U.S.A. 77 K2 31 55N 87 44W
Thomasville, Ga., U.S.A. 77 K4 30 50N 83 59W
Thomasville, N.C., U.S.A. 77 H5 35 53N 80 5W
Thompson, Canada 73 B9 55 45N 97 52W
Thompson, U.S.A. 79 E9 41 52N 75 31W
Thompson →, Canada 72 C4 50 15N 121 24W
Thompson →, U.S.A. 80 F8 39 46N 93 37W
Thompson Falls, U.S.A. 82 C6 47 36N 115 21W
Thompson Pk., U.S.A. 82 F2 41 0N 123 0W
Thompson Springs, U.S.A. 83 G9 38 58N 109 43W
Thompsontown, U.S.A. 78 F7 40 33N 77 14W
Thomson, U.S.A. 77 J4 33 28N 82 30W
Thomson →, Australia 62 C3 25 11S 142 53 E
Thomson's Falls = Nyahururu, Kenya 54 B4 0 2N 36 27 E
þórisvatn, Iceland 8 D4 64 20N 18 55W
Thornaby on Tees, U.K. 10 C6 54 33N 1 18W
Thornbury, Canada 78 B4 44 34N 80 26W
Thorne, U.K. 10 D7 53 37N 0 57W
Thornhill, Canada 72 C3 54 31N 128 32W
Thorold, Canada 78 C5 43 7N 79 12W
þórshöfn, Iceland 8 C6 66 12N 15 20W
Thouin, C., Australia 60 D2 20 20S 118 10 E
Thousand Oaks, U.S.A. 85 L8 34 10N 118 50W
Thrace, Turkey 21 D12 41 0N 27 0 E
Three Forks, U.S.A. 82 D8 45 54N 111 33W
Three Hills, Canada 72 C6 51 43N 113 15W
Three Hummock I., Australia 62 G3 40 25S 144 55 E
Three Points, C., Ghana 50 H5 4 42N 2 6W
Three Rivers, Calif., U.S.A. 84 J8 36 26N 118 54W
Three Rivers, Tex., U.S.A. 81 L5 28 28N 98 11W
Three Sisters, U.S.A. 82 D3 44 4N 121 51W
Three Springs, Australia 61 E2 29 32S 115 45 E
Throssell, L., Australia 61 E3 27 33S 124 10 E
Throssell Ra., Australia 60 D3 22 3S 121 43 E
Thuan Hoa, Vietnam 39 H5 8 58N 105 30 E
Thubun Lakes, Canada 73 A6 61 30N 112 0W
Thuin, Belgium 15 D4 50 20N 4 17 E
Thule, Greenland 4 B4 77 40N 69 0W
Thun, Switz. 18 C7 46 45N 7 38 E
Thunder B., U.S.A. 78 B1 45 0N 83 20W
Thunder Bay, Canada 70 C2 48 20N 89 15W
Thung Song, Thailand 39 H2 8 10N 99 40 E
Thunkar, Bhutan 41 F17 27 55N 91 0 E
Thuong Tra, Vietnam 38 D6 16 2N 107 42 E
Thüringer Wald, Germany 16 C6 50 35N 11 0 E
Thurles, Ireland 13 D4 52 41N 7 49W
Thurrock □, U.K. 11 F8 51 31N 0 23 E
Thursday I., Australia 62 A3 10 30S 142 3 E
Thurso, Canada 70 C4 45 36N 75 15W
Thurso, U.K. 12 C5 58 36N 3 32W
Thurso →, U.K. 12 C5 58 36N 3 32W
Thurston I., Antarctica 5 D16 72 0S 100 0W
Thutade L., Canada 72 B3 57 0N 126 55W
Thyolo, Malawi 55 F4 16 7S 35 5 E
Thysville = Mbanza Ngungu, Dem. Rep. of the Congo 52 F2 5 12S 14 53 E
Ti Tree, Australia 62 C1 22 5S 133 22 E
**Tian Shan**, Asia 32 B3 42 0N 76 0 E
**Tianjin**, China 35 E9 39 8N 117 10 E
Tianshui, China 34 G3 34 32N 105 40 E
Tianzhen, China 34 D8 40 24N 114 5 E
Tianzhuangtai, China 35 D12 40 43N 122 5 E
Tiaret, Algeria 50 A6 35 20N 1 21 E
Tibagi, Brazil 95 A5 24 30S 50 24W
Tibagi →, Brazil 95 A5 22 47S 51 1W
Tiber = Tevere →, Italy 20 D5 41 44N 12 14 E
Tiberias = Teverya, Israel 47 C4 32 47N 35 32 E
Tiberias, L. = Yam Kinneret, Israel 47 C4 32 45N 35 35 E
Tibesti, Chad 51 D9 21 0N 17 30 E
**Tibet** = Xizang Zizhiqu □, China 32 C3 32 0N 88 0 E
Tibet, Plateau of, Asia 28 F12 32 0N 86 0 E
Tibnī, Syria 44 C3 35 36N 39 50 E
Tibooburra, Australia 63 D3 29 26S 142 1 E
Tiburón, I., Mexico 86 B2 29 0N 112 30W
Ticino →, Italy 18 D8 45 9N 9 14 E
Ticonderoga, U.S.A. 79 C11 43 51N 73 26W
Ticul, Mexico 87 C7 20 20N 89 31W
Tidaholm, Sweden 9 G15 58 12N 13 58 E
Tiddim, Burma 41 H18 23 28N 93 45 E
Tidioute, U.S.A. 78 E5 41 41N 79 24W
Tidjikja, Mauritania 50 E3 18 29N 11 35W
Tidore, Indonesia 37 D7 0 40N 127 25 E
Tiel, Neths. 15 C5 51 53N 5 26 E
Tieling, China 35 C12 42 20N 123 55 E
Tielt, Belgium 15 C3 51 0N 3 20 E
Tien Shan = Tian Shan, Asia 32 B3 42 0N 76 0 E
Tien-tsin = Tianjin, China 35 E9 39 8N 117 10 E
Tien Yen, Vietnam 38 B6 21 20N 107 24 E
T'ienching = Tianjin, China 35 E9 39 8N 117 10 E
Tienen, Belgium 15 D4 50 48N 4 57 E
Tientsin = Tianjin, China 35 E9 39 8N 117 10 E
Tieri, Australia 62 C4 23 2S 148 21 E
Tierra Amarilla, Chile 94 B1 27 28S 70 18W
Tierra Amarilla, U.S.A. 83 H10 36 42N 106 33W
Tierra Colorada, Mexico 87 D5 17 10N 99 35W
Tierra de Campos, Spain 19 A3 42 10N 4 50W
**Tierra del Fuego, I. Gr. de**, Argentina 96 G3 54 0S 69 0W
Tiétar →, Spain 19 C3 39 50N 6 1W
Tieté →, Brazil 95 A5 20 40S 51 35W
Tiffin, U.S.A. 76 E4 41 7N 83 11W
Tiflis = Tbilisi, Georgia 25 F7 41 43N 44 50 E
Tifton, U.S.A. 77 K4 31 27N 83 31W
Tifu, Indonesia 37 E7 3 39S 126 24 E
Tighina, Moldova 17 E15 46 50N 29 30 E
Tigil, Russia 27 D16 57 49N 158 40 E
Tignish, Canada 71 C7 46 58N 64 2W
Tigre →, Peru 92 D4 4 30S 74 10W
Tigre →, Venezuela 92 B6 9 20N 62 30W
**Tigris** = Dijlah, Nahr →, Asia 44 D5 31 0N 47 25 E
Tigyaing, Burma 41 H20 23 45N 96 10 E
Tījara, India 42 F7 27 56N 76 31 E
Tijuana, Mexico 85 N9 32 30N 117 10W
Tikal, Guatemala 88 C2 17 13N 89 24W
Tikamgarh, India 43 G8 24 44N 78 50 E
Tikhoretsk, Russia 25 E7 45 56N 40 5 E
Tikhvin, Russia 24 C5 59 35N 33 30 E
Tikrīt, Iraq 44 C4 34 35N 43 37 E
Tiksi, Russia 27 B13 71 40N 128 45 E
Tilamuta, Indonesia 37 D6 0 32N 122 23 E
Tilburg, Neths. 15 C5 51 31N 5 6 E
Tilbury, Canada 78 D2 42 17N 82 23W
Tilbury, U.K. 11 F8 51 27N 0 22 E
Tilcara, Argentina 94 A2 23 36S 65 23W
Tilden, U.S.A. 80 D6 42 3N 97 50W
Tilhar, India 43 F8 28 0N 79 45 E
Tilichiki, Russia 27 C17 60 27N 166 5 E
Tílissos, Greece 23 D7 35 20N 25 1 E
Till →, U.K. 10 B5 55 41N 2 13W
Tillamook, U.S.A. 82 D2 45 27N 123 51W
Tillsonburg, Canada 78 D4 42 53N 80 44W
Tillyeria □, Cyprus 23 D11 35 6N 32 40 E
Tílos, Greece 21 F12 36 27N 27 27 E
Tilpa, Australia 63 E3 30 57S 144 24 E
Tilsit = Sovetsk, Russia 9 J19 55 6N 21 50 E
Tilt →, U.K. 12 E5 56 46N 3 51W
Tilton, U.S.A. 79 C13 43 27N 71 36W
Tiltonsville, U.S.A. 78 F4 40 10N 80 41W
Timagami, L., Canada 70 C3 47 0N 80 10W
Timanskiy Kryazh, Russia 24 A9 65 58N 50 5 E
Timaru, N.Z. 59 L3 44 23S 171 14 E
Timau, Kenya 54 B4 0 4N 37 15 E
Timbákion, Greece 23 D6 35 4N 24 45 E
Timber Creek, Australia 60 C5 15 40S 130 29 E
Timber Lake, U.S.A. 80 C4 45 26N 101 5W
Timber Mt., U.S.A. 84 H10 37 6N 116 28W
**Timbuktu** = Tombouctou, Mali 50 E5 16 50N 3 0W
Timi, Cyprus 23 E11 34 44N 32 31 E
Timimoun, Algeria 50 C6 29 14N 0 16 E
**Timişoara**, Romania 17 F11 45 43N 21 15 E
Timmins, Canada 70 C3 48 28N 81 25W
Timok →, Serbia, Yug. 21 B10 44 10N 22 40 E
**Timor**, Indonesia 37 F7 9 0S 125 0 E
Timor Sea, Ind. Oc. 60 B4 12 0S 127 0 E
Timor Timur □, Indonesia 37 F7 9 0S 125 0 E
Tin Can Bay, Australia 63 D5 25 56S 153 0 E
Tin Mt., U.S.A. 84 J9 36 50N 117 10W
Tinaca Pt., Phil. 37 C7 5 30N 125 25 E
Tinajo, Canary Is. 22 E6 29 4N 13 42W
Tindal, Australia 60 B5 14 31S 132 22 E
Tindouf, Algeria 50 C4 27 42N 8 10W
Tinggi, Pulau, Malaysia 39 L5 2 18N 104 7 E
Tingo Maria, Peru 92 E3 9 10S 75 54W
Tingrela, Ivory C. 50 F4 10 27N 6 25W
Tinh Bien, Vietnam 39 G5 10 36N 104 57 E
Tinnevelly = Tirunelveli, India 40 Q10 8 45N 77 45 E
Tinogasta, Argentina 94 B2 28 5S 67 32W
Tínos, Greece 21 F11 37 33N 25 8 E
Tinpahar, India 43 G12 24 59N 87 44 E
Tintina, Argentina 94 B3 27 2S 62 45W
Tintinara, Australia 63 F3 35 48S 140 2 E
Tioga, N. Dak., U.S.A. 80 A3 48 23N 102 56W
Tioga, Pa., U.S.A. 78 E7 41 55N 77 8W
Tioman, Pulau, Malaysia 39 L5 2 50N 104 10 E
Tionesta, U.S.A. 78 E5 41 30N 79 28W
Tipongpani, India 41 F19 27 20N 95 55 E
Tipperary, Ireland 13 D3 52 28N 8 10W
**Tipperary** □, Ireland 13 D4 52 37N 7 55W
Tipton, Calif., U.S.A. 84 J7 36 4N 119 19W
Tipton, Iowa, U.S.A. 80 E9 41 46N 91 8W
Tipton Mt., U.S.A. 85 K12 35 32N 114 12W
Tiptonville, U.S.A. 81 G10 36 23N 89 29W
Tīrān, Iran 45 C6 32 45N 51 8 E
**Tirana**, Albania 21 D8 41 18N 19 49 E
Tiranë = Tirana, Albania 21 D8 41 18N 19 49 E
Tiraspol, Moldova 17 E15 46 55N 29 35 E
Tire, Turkey 21 E12 38 5N 27 45 E
Tirebolu, Turkey 25 F6 40 58N 38 45 E
Tiree, U.K. 12 E2 56 31N 6 55W
Tiree, Passage of, U.K. 12 E2 56 30N 6 30W
Tîrgovişte = Târgovişte, Romania 17 F13 44 55N 25 27 E
Tîrgu-Jiu = Târgu-Jiu, Romania 17 F12 45 5N 23 19 E
Tîrgu Mureş = Târgu Mureş, Romania 17 E13 46 31N 24 38 E
Tirich Mir, Pakistan 40 A7 36 15N 71 55 E
Tírnavos, Greece 21 E10 39 45N 22 18 E
Tirodi, India 40 J11 21 40N 79 44 E
**Tirol** □, Austria 16 E6 47 3N 10 43 E
Tirso →, Italy 20 E3 39 53N 8 32 E
Tiruchchirappalli, India 40 P11 10 45N 78 45 E
Tirunelveli, India 40 Q10 8 45N 77 45 E
Tirupati, India 40 N11 13 39N 79 25 E
Tiruppur, India 40 P10 11 5N 77 22 E
Tiruvannamalai, India 40 N11 12 15N 79 5 E
Tisa, India 42 C7 32 50N 76 9 E
Tisa →, Serbia, Yug. 21 B9 45 15N 20 17 E
Tisdale, Canada 73 C8 52 50N 104 0W
Tishomingo, U.S.A. 81 H6 34 14N 96 41W
Tisza = Tisa →, Serbia, Yug. 21 B9 45 15N 20 17 E
Tit-Ary, Russia 27 B13 71 55N 127 2 E
Tithwal, Pakistan 43 B5 34 21N 73 50 E
**Titicaca, L.**, S. Amer. 92 G5 15 30S 69 30W
Titograd = Podgorica, Montenegro, Yug. 21 C8 42 30N 19 19 E
Titule, Dem. Rep. of the Congo 54 B2 3 15N 25 31 E
Titusville, Fla., U.S.A. 77 L5 28 37N 80 49W
Titusville, Pa., U.S.A. 78 E5 41 38N 79 41W
Tivaouane, Senegal 50 F2 14 56N 16 45W
Tiverton, U.K. 11 G4 50 54N 3 29W
Tívoli, Italy 20 D5 41 58N 12 45 E
Tizi-Ouzou, Algeria 50 A6 36 42N 4 3 E
Tizimín, Mexico 87 C7 21 0N 88 1W
Tjeggelvas, Sweden 8 C17 66 37N 17 45 E
Tjirebon = Cirebon, Indonesia 37 G13 6 45S 108 32 E
Tjörn, Sweden 9 G14 58 0N 11 35 E
Tlacotalpan, Mexico 87 D5 18 37N 95 40W
Tlahualilo, Mexico 86 B4 26 20N 103 30W
Tlaquepaque, Mexico 86 C4 20 39N 103 19W
Tlaxcala, Mexico 87 D5 19 20N 98 14W
Tlaxcala □, Mexico 87 D5 19 30N 98 20W
Tlaxiaco, Mexico 87 D5 17 18N 97 40W
Tlemcen, Algeria 50 B5 34 52N 1 21W
To Bong, Vietnam 38 F7 12 45N 109 16 E
Toad →, Canada 72 B4 59 25N 124 57W
Toad River, Canada 72 B3 58 51N 125 14W
Toamasina, Madag. 57 B8 18 10S 49 25 E
Toamasina □, Madag. 57 B8 18 0S 49 0 E
Toay, Argentina 94 D3 36 43S 64 38W
Toba, Japan 31 G8 34 30N 136 51 E
Toba, Danau, Indonesia 36 D1 2 30N 97 30 E
Toba Kakar, Pakistan 42 D3 31 30N 69 0 E
Toba Tek Singh, Pakistan 42 D5 30 55N 72 25 E
**Tobago**, W. Indies 89 D7 11 10N 60 30W
Tobelo, Indonesia 37 D7 1 45N 127 56 E
Tobermory, Canada 78 A3 45 12N 81 40W
Tobermory, U.K. 12 E2 56 38N 6 5W
Tobi, Pac. Oc. 37 D8 2 40N 131 10 E
Tobin, U.S.A. 84 F5 39 55N 121 19W
Tobin, L., Australia 60 D4 21 45S 125 49 E
Tobin L., Canada 73 C8 53 35N 103 30W
Toboali, Indonesia 36 E3 3 0S 106 25 E
Tobol →, Russia 26 D7 58 10N 68 12 E
Toboli, Indonesia 37 E6 0 38S 120 5 E
Tobolsk, Russia 26 D7 58 15N 68 10 E
Tobruk = Tubruq, Libya 51 B10 32 7N 23 55 E
Tobyhanna, U.S.A. 79 E9 41 11N 75 25W
Tobyl = Tobol →, Russia 26 D7 58 10N 68 12 E
Tocantinópolis, Brazil 93 E9 6 20S 47 25W
Tocantins □, Brazil 93 F9 10 0S 48 0W
Tocantins →, Brazil 93 D9 1 45S 49 10W
Toccoa, U.S.A. 77 H4 34 35N 83 19W
Tochi →, Pakistan 42 C4 32 49N 70 41 E
Tochigi, Japan 31 F9 36 25N 139 45 E
Tochigi □, Japan 31 F9 36 45N 139 45 E
Toconao, Chile 94 A2 23 11S 68 1W
Tocopilla, Chile 94 A1 22 5S 70 10W
Tocumwal, Australia 63 F4 35 51S 145 31 E
Tocuyo →, Venezuela 92 A5 11 3N 68 23W
Todd →, Australia 62 C2 24 52S 135 48 E
Todeli, Indonesia 37 E6 1 38S 124 34 E
Todenyang, Kenya 54 B4 4 35N 35 56 E
Todgarh, India 42 G5 25 42N 73 58 E
Todos os Santos, B. de, Brazil 93 F11 12 48S 38 38W
Todos Santos, Mexico 86 C2 23 27N 110 13W
Toe Hd., U.K. 12 D1 57 50N 7 8W
Tofield, Canada 72 C6 53 25N 112 40W
Tofino, Canada 72 D3 49 11N 125 55W
Tofua, Tonga 59 D11 19 45S 175 5W
Tōgane, Japan 31 G10 35 33N 140 22 E
Togian, Kepulauan, Indonesia 37 E6 0 20S 121 50 E
Togliatti, Russia 24 D8 53 32N 49 24 E
**Togo** ■, W. Afr. 50 G6 8 30N 1 35 E
Togtoh, China 34 D6 40 15N 111 10 E
Tōhoku □, Japan 30 E10 39 50N 141 45 E
Töhöm, Mongolia 34 B5 44 27N 108 2 E
Toinya, Sudan 51 G11 6 17N 29 46 E
Toiyabe Range, U.S.A. 82 G5 39 30N 117 0W
Tojikiston = Tajikistan ■, Asia 26 F8 38 30N 70 0 E
Tojo, Indonesia 37 E6 1 20S 121 15 E
Tōjō, Japan 31 G6 34 53N 133 16 E
Tok, U.S.A. 68 B5 63 20N 142 59W
Tok-do, Japan 31 F5 37 15N 131 52 E
Tokachi-Dake, Japan 30 C11 43 17N 142 5 E
Tokachi-Gawa →, Japan 30 C11 42 44N 143 42 E
Tokala, Indonesia 37 E6 1 30S 121 40 E
Tōkamachi, Japan 31 F9 37 8N 138 43 E
Tokanui, N.Z. 59 M2 46 34S 168 56 E
Tokara-Rettō, Japan 31 K4 29 37N 129 43 E
Tokarahi, N.Z. 59 L3 44 56S 170 39 E
Tokashiki-Shima, Japan 31 L3 26 11N 127 21 E
Tokat □, Turkey 25 F6 40 15N 36 30 E
Tŏkch'ŏn, N. Korea 35 E14 39 45N 126 18 E
Tokeland, U.S.A. 84 D3 46 42N 123 59W
Tokelau Is., Pac. Oc. 64 H10 9 0S 171 45W
Tokmak, Kyrgyzstan 26 E8 42 49N 75 15 E
Toko Ra., Australia 62 C2 23 5S 138 20 E
Tokoro-Gawa →, Japan 30 B12 44 7N 144 5 E
Tokuno-Shima, Japan 31 L4 27 56N 128 55 E
Tokushima, Japan 31 G7 34 4N 134 34 E
Tokushima □, Japan 31 H7 33 55N 134 0 E
Tokuyama, Japan 31 G5 34 3N 131 50 E
**Tōkyō**, Japan 31 G9 35 45N 139 45 E
Tolaga Bay, N.Z. 59 H7 38 21S 178 20 E
Tolbukhin = Dobrich, Bulgaria 21 C12 43 37N 27 49 E
Toledo, Brazil 95 A5 24 44S 53 45W
**Toledo**, Spain 19 C3 39 50N 4 2W
Toledo, Ohio, U.S.A. 76 E4 41 39N 83 33W
Toledo, Oreg., U.S.A. 82 D2 44 37N 123 56W
Toledo, Wash., U.S.A. 82 C2 46 26N 122 51W
Toledo, Montes de, Spain 19 C3 39 33N 4 20W
Toledo Bend Reservoir, U.S.A. 81 K8 31 11N 93 34W
Tolga, Australia 62 B4 17 15S 145 29 E
Toliara, Madag. 57 C7 23 21S 43 40 E
Toliara □, Madag. 57 C8 21 0S 45 0 E
Tolima, Colombia 92 C3 4 40N 75 19W
Tolitoli, Indonesia 37 D6 1 5N 120 50 E
Tollhouse, U.S.A. 84 H7 37 1N 119 24W
Tolo, Teluk, Indonesia 37 E6 2 20S 122 10 E
Toluca, Mexico 87 D5 19 20N 99 40W
Tom Burke, S. Africa 57 C4 23 5S 28 0 E
Tom Price, Australia 60 D2 22 40S 117 48 E
Tomah, U.S.A. 80 D9 43 59N 90 30W
Tomahawk, U.S.A. 80 C10 45 28N 89 44W
Tomakomai, Japan 30 C10 42 38N 141 36 E
Tomales, U.S.A. 84 G4 38 15N 122 53W
Tomales B., U.S.A. 84 G3 38 15N 123 58W
Tomar, Portugal 19 C1 39 36N 8 25W
Tomaszów Mazowiecki, Poland 17 C10 51 30N 20 2 E
Tomatlán, Mexico 86 D3 19 56N 105 15W
Tombador, Serra do, Brazil 92 F7 12 0S 58 0W
Tombigbee →, U.S.A. 77 K2 31 8N 87 57W
Tombouctou, Mali 50 E5 16 50N 3 0W
Tombstone, U.S.A. 83 L8 31 43N 110 4W
Tombua, Angola 56 B1 15 55S 11 55 E
Tomé, Chile 94 D1 36 36S 72 57W
Tomelloso, Spain 19 C4 39 10N 3 2W
Tomini, Indonesia 37 D6 0 30N 120 30 E
Tomini, Teluk, Indonesia 37 E6 0 10S 122 0 E
Tomintoul, U.K. 12 D5 57 15N 3 23W
Tomkinson Ranges, Australia 61 E4 26 11S 129 5 E
Tommot, Russia 27 D13 59 4N 126 20 E

Tomnop Ta Suos, Cambodia 39 G5 11 20N 104 15 E
Tomo →, Colombia 92 B5 5 20N 67 48W
Toms Place, U.S.A. 84 H8 37 34N 118 41W
Toms River, U.S.A. 79 G10 39 58N 74 12W
Tomsk, Russia 26 D9 56 30N 85 5 E
Tonalá, Mexico 87 D6 16 8N 93 41W
Tonantins, Brazil 92 D5 2 45S 67 45W
Tonasket, U.S.A. 82 B4 48 42N 119 26W
Tonawanda, U.S.A. 78 D6 43 1N 78 53W
Tonbridge, U.K. 11 F8 51 11N 0 17 E
Tondano, Indonesia 37 D6 1 35N 124 54 E
Tone →, Australia 61 F2 34 25S 116 25 E
Tone-Gawa →, Japan 31 F9 35 44N 140 51 E
Tonekābon, Iran 45 B6 36 45N 51 12 E
Tong Xian, China 34 E9 39 55N 116 35 E
**Tonga** ■, Pac. Oc. 59 D11 19 50S 174 30W
Tonga Trench, Pac. Oc. 64 J10 18 0S 173 0W
Tongaat, S. Africa 57 D5 29 33S 31 9 E
Tongareva, Cook Is. 65 H12 9 0S 158 0W
Tongatapu, Tonga 59 E12 21 10S 174 0W
Tongchŏn-ni, N. Korea 35 E14 39 50N 127 25 E
Tongchuan, China 34 G5 35 6N 109 3 E
Tongeren, Belgium 15 D5 50 47N 5 28 E
Tongguan, China 34 G6 34 40N 110 25 E
Tonghua, China 35 D13 41 42N 125 58 E
Tongjosŏn Man, N. Korea 35 E15 39 30N 128 0 E
Tongking, G. of, Asia 32 E5 20 0N 108 0 E
Tongliao, China 35 C12 43 38N 122 18 E
Tongling, China 33 C6 30 55N 117 48 E
Tongnae, S. Korea 35 G15 35 12N 129 5 E
Tongobory, Madag. 57 C7 23 32S 44 20 E
Tongoy, Chile 94 C1 30 16S 71 31W
Tongres = Tongeren, Belgium 15 D5 50 47N 5 28 E
Tongsa Dzong, Bhutan 41 F17 27 31N 90 31 E
Tongue, U.K. 12 C4 58 29N 4 25W
Tongue →, U.S.A. 80 B2 46 25N 105 52W
Tongwei, China 34 G3 35 0N 105 5 E
Tongxin, China 34 F3 36 59N 105 58 E
Tongyang, N. Korea 35 E14 39 9N 126 53 E
Tongyu, China 35 B12 44 45N 123 4 E
Tonj, Sudan 51 G11 7 20N 28 44 E
Tonk, India 42 F6 26 6N 75 54 E
Tonkawa, U.S.A. 81 G6 36 41N 97 18W
Tonkin = Bac Phan, Vietnam 38 B5 22 0N 105 0 E
Tonle Sap, Cambodia 38 F5 13 0N 104 0 E
Tono, Japan 30 E10 39 19N 141 32 E
Tonopah, U.S.A. 83 G5 38 4N 117 14W
Tonosí, Panama 88 E3 7 20N 80 20W
Tons →, Haryana, India 42 D7 30 30N 77 39 E
Tons →, Ut. P., India 43 F10 26 1N 83 33 E
Tønsberg, Norway 9 G14 59 19N 10 25 E
Toobanna, Australia 62 B4 18 42S 146 9 E
Toodyay, Australia 61 F2 31 34S 116 28 E
Tooele, U.S.A. 82 F7 40 32N 112 18W
Toompine, Australia 63 D3 27 15S 144 19 E
Toora, Australia 63 F4 38 39S 146 23 E
Toora-Khem, Russia 27 D10 52 28N 96 17 E
Toowoomba, Australia 63 D5 27 32S 151 56 E
Top-ozero, Russia 24 A5 65 35N 32 0 E
Top Springs, Australia 60 C5 16 37S 131 51 E
Topaz, U.S.A. 84 G7 38 41N 119 30W
**Topeka**, U.S.A. 80 F7 39 3N 95 40W
Topley, Canada 72 C3 54 49N 126 18W
Topocalma, Pta., Chile 94 C1 34 10S 72 2W
Topock, U.S.A. 85 L12 34 46N 114 29W
Topoľčany, Slovak Rep. 17 D10 48 35N 18 12 E
Topolobampo, Mexico 86 B3 25 40N 109 4W
Toppenish, U.S.A. 82 C3 46 23N 120 19W
Toraka Vestale, Madag. 57 B7 16 20S 43 58 E
Torata, Peru 92 G4 17 23S 70 1W
Torbalı, Turkey 21 E12 38 10N 27 21 E
Torbat-e Heydārīyeh, Iran 45 C8 35 15N 59 12 E
Torbat-e Jām, Iran 45 C9 35 16N 60 35 E
Torbay, Canada 71 C9 47 40N 52 42W
Torbay □, U.K. 11 G4 50 26N 3 31W
Tordesillas, Spain 19 B3 41 30N 5 0W
Torfaen □, U.K. 11 F4 51 43N 3 3W
Torgau, Germany 16 C7 51 34N 13 0 E
Torhout, Belgium 15 C3 51 5N 3 7 E
Tori-Shima, Japan 31 J10 30 29N 140 19 E
Torin, Mexico 86 B2 27 33N 110 15W
Torino, Italy 18 D7 45 3N 7 40 E
Torit, Sudan 51 H12 4 27N 32 31 E
Torkamān, Iran 44 B5 37 35N 47 23 E
Tormes →, Spain 19 B2 41 18N 6 29W
Tornado Mt., Canada 72 D6 49 55N 114 40W
Torne älv →, Sweden 8 D21 65 50N 24 12 E
Torneå = Tornio, Finland 8 D21 65 50N 24 12 E
Torneträsk, Sweden 8 B18 68 24N 19 15 E
Tornio, Finland 8 D21 65 50N 24 12 E
Tornionjoki →, Finland 8 D21 65 50N 24 12 E
Tornquist, Argentina 94 D3 38 8S 62 15W
Toro, Spain 22 B11 39 59N 4 8 E
Toro, Cerro del, Chile 94 B2 29 10S 69 50W
Toro Pk., U.S.A. 85 M10 33 34N 116 24W
Toroníios Kólpos, Greece 21 D10 40 5N 23 30 E
**Toronto**, Canada 78 C5 43 39N 79 20W
Toronto, U.S.A. 78 F4 40 28N 80 36W
Toropets, Russia 24 C5 56 30N 31 40 E
Tororo, Uganda 54 B3 0 45N 34 12 E
Toros Dağları, Turkey 25 G5 37 0N 32 30 E
Torpa, India 43 H11 22 57N 85 6 E
Torquay, Australia 63 F3 38 20S 144 19 E
Torquay, U.K. 11 G4 50 27N 3 32W
Torrance, U.S.A. 85 M8 33 50N 118 19W
Torre de Moncorvo, Portugal 19 B2 41 12N 7 8W
Torre del Greco, Italy 20 D6 40 47N 14 22 E
Torrejón de Ardoz, Spain 19 B4 40 27N 3 29W
Torrelavega, Spain 19 A3 43 20N 4 5W
Torremolinos, Spain 19 D3 36 38N 4 30W
Torrens, L., Australia 63 E2 31 0S 137 50 E
Torrens Cr. →, Australia 62 C4 22 23S 145 9 E
Torrens Creek, Australia 62 C4 20 48S 145 3 E
Torrent, Spain 19 C5 39 27N 0 28W
Torreón, Mexico 86 B4 25 33N 103 26W
Torres, Brazil 95 B5 29 21S 49 44W
Torres, Mexico 86 B2 28 46N 110 47W
Torres Strait, Australia 64 H6 9 50S 142 20 E
Torres Vedras, Portugal 19 C1 39 5N 9 15W
Torrevieja, Spain 19 D5 37 59N 0 42W
Torrey, U.S.A. 83 G8 38 18N 111 25W
Torridge →, U.K. 11 G3 51 0N 4 13W
Torridon, L., U.K. 12 D3 57 35N 5 50W
Torrington, Conn., U.S.A. 79 E11 41 48N 73 7W
Torrington, Wyo., U.S.A. 80 D2 42 4N 104 11W
Tórshavn, Færoe Is. 8 E9 62 5N 6 56W
Tortola, Virgin Is. 89 C7 18 19N 64 45W
Tortosa, Spain 19 B6 40 49N 0 31 E
Tortosa, C., Spain 19 B6 40 41N 0 52 E
Tortue, I. de la, Haiti 89 B5 20 5N 72 57W
Torūd, Iran 45 C7 35 25N 55 5 E
Toruń, Poland 17 B10 53 2N 18 39 E
Tory I., Ireland 13 A3 55 16N 8 14W
Tosa, Japan 31 H6 33 24N 133 23 E
Tosa-Shimizu, Japan 31 H6 32 52N 132 58 E
Tosa-Wan, Japan 31 H6 33 15N 133 30 E
Toscana □, Italy 20 C4 43 25N 11 0 E
Toshkent, Uzbekistan 26 E7 41 20N 69 10 E
Tostado, Argentina 94 B3 29 15S 61 50W
Tostón, Pta. de, Canary Is. 22 F5 28 42N 14 2W
Tosu, Japan 31 H5 33 22N 130 31 E
Toteng, Botswana 56 C3 20 22S 22 58 E
Totma, Russia 24 C7 60 0N 42 40 E
Totnes, U.K. 11 G4 50 26N 3 42W
Totness, Surinam 93 B7 5 53N 56 19W
Totonicapán, Guatemala 88 D1 14 58N 91 12W
Totten Glacier, Antarctica 5 C8 66 45S 116 10 E
Tottenham, Australia 63 E4 32 14S 147 21 E
Tottenham, Canada 78 B5 44 1N 79 49W
Tottori, Japan 31 G7 35 30N 134 15 E
Tottori □, Japan 31 G7 35 30N 134 12 E
Toubkal, Djebel, Morocco 50 B4 31 0N 8 0W
Tougan, Burkina Faso 50 F5 13 11N 2 58W
Touggourt, Algeria 50 B7 33 6N 6 4 E
Toul, France 18 B6 48 40N 5 53 E
**Toulon**, France 18 E6 43 10N 5 55 E
**Toulouse**, France 18 E4 43 37N 1 27 E
Toummo, Niger 51 D8 22 45N 14 8 E
Toungoo, Burma 41 K20 19 0N 96 30 E
Touraine, France 18 C4 47 20N 0 30 E
Tourane = Da Nang, Vietnam 38 D7 16 4N 108 13 E
Tourcoing, France 18 A5 50 42N 3 10 E
Touriñán, C., Spain 19 A1 43 3N 9 18W
Tournai, Belgium 15 D3 50 35N 3 25 E
Tournon-sur-Rhône, France 18 D6 45 4N 4 50 E
**Tours**, France 18 C4 47 22N 0 40 E
Tousidé, Pic, Chad 51 D9 21 1N 16 29 E
Toussora, Mt., C.A.R. 52 C4 9 7N 23 14 E
Touwsrivier, S. Africa 56 E3 33 20S 20 2 E
Towada, Japan 30 D10 40 37N 141 13 E
Towada-Ko, Japan 30 D10 40 28N 140 55 E
Towanda, U.S.A. 79 E8 41 46N 76 27W
Towang, India 41 F17 27 37N 91 50 E
Tower, U.S.A. 80 B8 47 48N 92 17W
Towerhill Cr. →, Australia 62 C3 22 28S 144 35 E
Towner, U.S.A. 80 A4 48 21N 100 25W
Townsend, U.S.A. 82 C8 46 19N 111 31W
Townshend I., Australia 62 C5 22 10S 150 31 E
Townsville, Australia 62 B4 19 15S 146 45 E
Towson, U.S.A. 76 F7 39 24N 76 36W
Towuti, Danau, Indonesia 37 E6 2 45S 121 32 E
Toya-Ko, Japan 30 C10 42 35N 140 51 E
Toyama, Japan 31 F8 36 40N 137 15 E
Toyama □, Japan 31 F8 36 45N 137 30 E
Toyama-Wan, Japan 31 F8 37 0N 137 30 E
Toyohashi, Japan 31 G8 34 45N 137 25 E
Toyokawa, Japan 31 G8 34 48N 137 27 E
Toyonaka, Japan 31 G7 34 50N 135 28 E
Toyooka, Japan 31 G7 35 35N 134 48 E
Toyota, Japan 31 G8 35 3N 137 7 E
Tozeur, Tunisia 50 B7 33 56N 8 8 E
Trá Li = Tralee, Ireland 13 D2 52 16N 9 42W
Tra On, Vietnam 39 H5 9 58N 105 55 E
Trabzon, Turkey 25 F6 41 0N 39 45 E
Tracadie, Canada 71 C7 47 30N 64 55W
Tracy, Calif., U.S.A. 84 H5 37 44N 121 26W
Tracy, Minn., U.S.A. 80 C7 44 14N 95 37W
Trafalgar, C., Spain 19 D2 36 10N 6 2W
Trail, Canada 72 D5 49 5N 117 40W
Trainor L., Canada 72 A4 60 24N 120 17W
Trákhonas, Cyprus 23 D12 35 12N 33 21 E
Tralee, Ireland 13 D2 52 16N 9 42W
Tralee B., Ireland 13 D2 52 17N 9 55W
Tramore, Ireland 13 D4 52 10N 7 10W
Tramore B., Ireland 13 D4 52 9N 7 10W
Tran Ninh, Cao Nguyen, Laos 38 C4 19 30N 103 10 E
Tranås, Sweden 9 G16 58 3N 14 59 E
Trancas, Argentina 94 B2 26 11S 65 20W
Trang, Thailand 39 J2 7 33N 99 38 E
Trangahy, Madag. 57 B7 19 7S 44 31 E
Trangan, Indonesia 37 F8 6 40S 134 20 E
Trangie, Australia 63 E4 32 4S 148 0 E
Trani, Italy 20 D7 41 17N 16 25 E
Tranoroa, Madag. 57 C8 24 42S 45 4 E
Tranqueras, Uruguay 95 C4 31 13S 55 45W
Transantarctic Mts., Antarctica 5 E12 85 0S 170 0W
Transilvania, Romania 17 E12 46 30N 24 0 E
Transilvanian Alps = Carpaţii Meridionali, Romania 17 F13 45 30N 25 0 E
**Transvaal** □, S. Africa 53 K5 25 0S 29 0 E
**Transylvania** = Transilvania, Romania 17 E12 46 30N 24 0 E
Trápani, Italy 20 E5 38 1N 12 29 E
Trapper Pk., U.S.A. 82 D6 45 54N 114 18W
Traralgon, Australia 63 F4 38 12S 146 34 E
Trasimeno, L., Italy 20 C5 43 8N 12 6 E
Trat, Thailand 39 F4 12 14N 102 33 E
Tratani →, Pakistan 42 E3 29 19N 68 20 E
Traun, Austria 16 D8 48 14N 14 15 E
Travellers L., Australia 63 E3 33 20S 142 0 E
Travemünde, Germany 16 B6 53 57N 10 52 E
Travers, Mt., N.Z. 59 K4 42 1S 172 45 E
Traverse City, U.S.A. 76 C3 44 46N 85 38W
Travis, L., U.S.A. 81 K5 30 24N 97 55W
Travnik, Bos.-H. 21 B7 44 17N 17 39 E
Trébbia →, Italy 18 D8 45 4N 9 41 E
Třebíč, Czech Rep. 16 D8 49 14N 15 55 E
Trebinje, Bos.-H. 21 C8 42 44N 18 22 E
Trebonne, Australia 62 B4 18 37S 146 5 E
Tregaron, U.K. 11 E4 52 14N 3 56W
Tregrosse Is., Australia 62 B5 17 41S 150 43 E
Treherne, Canada 73 D9 49 38N 98 42W
Treinta y Tres, Uruguay 95 C5 33 16S 54 17W
Trelew, Argentina 96 E3 43 10S 65 20W
Trelleborg, Sweden 9 J15 55 20N 13 10 E
Tremadog Bay, U.K. 10 E3 52 51N 4 18W
Tremonton, U.S.A. 82 F7 41 43N 112 10W
Tremp, Spain 19 A6 42 10N 0 52 E
Trenche →, Canada 70 C5 47 46N 72 53W
Trenčín, Slovak Rep. 17 D10 48 52N 18 4 E
Trenggalek, Indonesia 37 H14 8 3S 111 43 E
Trenque Lauquen, Argentina 94 D3 36 5S 62 45W
Trent →, Canada 78 B7 44 6N 77 34W
**Trent** →, U.K. 10 D7 53 41N 0 42W
Trento, Italy 20 A4 46 4N 11 8 E
Trenton, Canada 78 B7 44 10N 77 34W
Trenton, Mo., U.S.A. 80 E8 40 5N 93 37W
**Trenton**, N.J., U.S.A. 79 F10 40 14N 74 46W
Trenton, Nebr., U.S.A. 80 E4 40 11N 101 1W
Trepassey, Canada 71 C9 46 43N 53 25W
Tres Arroyos, Argentina 94 D3 38 26S 60 20W
Três Corações, Brazil 95 A6 21 44S 45 15W
Três Lagoas, Brazil 93 H8 20 50S 51 43W
Tres Lomas, Argentina 94 D3 36 27S 62 51W
Tres Marías, Islas, Mexico 86 C3 21 25N 106 28W
Tres Montes, C., Chile 96 F1 46 50S 75 30W
Tres Pinos, U.S.A. 84 J5 36 48N 121 19W
Três Pontas, Brazil 95 A6 21 23S 45 29W
Tres Puentes, Chile 94 B1 27 50S 70 15W
Tres Puntas, C., Argentina 96 F3 47 0S 66 0W
Três Rios, Brazil 95 A7 22 6S 43 15W
Tres Valles, Mexico 87 D5 18 15N 96 8W
Tresco, U.K. 11 H1 49 57N 6 20W
Treviso, Italy 20 B5 45 40N 12 15 E
Triabunna, Australia 62 G4 42 30S 147 55 E
Triánda, Greece 23 C10 36 25N 28 10 E
Tribulation, C., Australia 62 B4 16 5S 145 29 E
Tribune, U.S.A. 80 F4 38 28N 101 45W
Trichinopoly = Tiruchchirappalli, India 40 P11 10 45N 78 45 E
Trichur, India 40 P10 10 30N 76 18 E
Trida, Australia 63 E4 33 1S 145 1 E
Trier, Germany 16 D4 49 45N 6 38 E
**Trieste**, Italy 20 B5 45 40N 13 46 E
Triglav, Slovenia 16 E7 46 21N 13 50 E
Trikkala, Greece 21 E9 39 34N 21 47 E
Trikomo, Cyprus 23 D12 35 17N 33 52 E
Trikora, Puncak, Indonesia 37 E9 4 15S 138 45 E
Trim, Ireland 13 C5 53 33N 6 48W
Trincomalee, Sri Lanka 40 Q12 8 38N 81 15 E
Trindade, Brazil 93 G9 16 40S 49 30W
Trindade, I., Atl. Oc. 2 F8 20 20S 29 50W
Trinidad, Bolivia 92 F6 14 46S 64 50W
Trinidad, Cuba 88 B4 21 48N 80 0W
Trinidad, Uruguay 94 C4 33 30S 56 50W
Trinidad, U.S.A. 81 G2 37 10N 104 31W
Trinidad, W. Indies 89 D7 10 30N 61 15W
Trinidad →, Mexico 87 D5 17 49N 95 9W
**Trinidad & Tobago** ■, W. Indies 89 D7 10 30N 61 20W
Trinity, Canada 71 C9 48 59N 53 55W
Trinity, U.S.A. 81 K7 30 57N 95 22W
Trinity →, Calif., U.S.A. 82 F2 41 11N 123 42W
Trinity →, Tex., U.S.A. 81 L7 29 45N 94 43W
Trinity B., Canada 71 C9 48 20N 53 10W
Trinity Is., U.S.A. 68 C4 56 33N 154 25W
Trinity Range, U.S.A. 82 F4 40 15N 118 45W
Trinkitat, Sudan 51 E13 18 45N 37 51 E
Trinway, U.S.A. 78 F2 40 9N 82 1W
**Tripoli** = Tarābulus, Lebanon 47 A4 34 31N 35 50 E
**Tripoli** = Tarābulus, Libya 51 B8 32 49N 13 7 E
Trípolis, Greece 21 F10 37 31N 22 25 E
Tripolitania, Libya 48 C5 31 0N 12 0 E
Tripolitania, N. Afr. 51 B8 31 0N 13 0 E
Tripura □, India 41 H18 24 0N 92 0 E
Tripylos, Cyprus 23 E11 34 59N 32 41 E
**Tristan da Cunha**, Atl. Oc. 49 K2 37 6S 12 20W
Trisul, India 43 D8 30 19N 79 47 E
**Trivandrum**, India 40 Q10 8 41N 77 0 E
Trnava, Slovak Rep. 17 D9 48 23N 17 35 E
Trochu, Canada 72 C6 51 50N 113 13W
Trodely I., Canada 70 B4 52 15N 79 26W
Troglav, Croatia 20 C7 43 56N 16 36 E
Troilus, L., Canada 70 B5 50 50N 74 35W
Trois-Pistoles, Canada 71 C6 48 5N 69 10W
Trois-Rivières, Canada 70 C5 46 25N 72 34W
Troitsk, Russia 26 D7 54 10N 61 35 E
Troitsko Pechorsk, Russia 24 B10 62 40N 56 10 E
Trölladyngja, Iceland 8 D5 64 54N 17 16W
Trollhättan, Sweden 9 G15 58 17N 12 20 E
Trollheimen, Norway 8 E13 62 46N 9 1 E
Trombetas →, Brazil 93 D7 1 55S 55 35W
Tromsø, Norway 8 B18 69 40N 18 56 E
Trona, U.S.A. 85 K9 35 46N 117 23W
Tronador, Mte., Argentina 96 E2 41 10S 71 50W
Trøndelag, Norway 8 D14 64 17N 11 50 E
**Trondheim**, Norway 8 E14 63 36N 10 25 E
Trondheimsfjorden, Norway 8 E14 63 35N 10 30 E
Troodos, Cyprus 23 E11 34 55N 32 52 E
Troon, U.K. 12 F4 55 33N 4 39W
Tropic, U.S.A. 83 H7 37 37N 112 5W
Trostan, U.K. 13 A5 55 3N 6 10W
Trout →, Canada 72 A5 61 19N 119 51W
Trout L., N.W.T., Canada 72 A4 60 40N 121 14W
Trout L., Ont., Canada 73 C10 51 20N 93 15W
Trout Lake, Canada 72 B6 56 30N 114 32W
Trout Lake, U.S.A. 84 E5 46 0N 121 32W
Trout River, Canada 71 C8 49 29N 58 8W
Trout Run, U.S.A. 78 E7 41 23N 77 3W
Trouville-sur-Mer, France 18 B4 49 21N 0 5 E
Trowbridge, U.K. 11 F5 51 18N 2 12W
Troy, Turkey 21 E12 39 57N 26 12 E
Troy, Ala., U.S.A. 77 K3 31 48N 85 58W
Troy, Kans., U.S.A. 80 F7 39 47N 95 5W
Troy, Mo., U.S.A. 80 F9 38 59N 90 59W
Troy, Mont., U.S.A. 82 B6 48 28N 115 53W
Troy, N.Y., U.S.A. 79 D11 42 44N 73 41W
Troy, Ohio, U.S.A. 76 E3 40 2N 84 12W
Troy, Pa., U.S.A. 79 E8 41 47N 76 47W
Troyes, France 18 B6 48 19N 4 3 E
Truchas Peak, U.S.A. 81 H2 35 58N 105 39W
Trucial States = United Arab Emirates ■, Asia 45 F7 23 50N 54 0 E
Truckee, U.S.A. 84 F6 39 20N 120 11W
Trudovoye, Russia 30 C6 43 17N 132 5 E
Trujillo, Honduras 88 C2 16 0N 86 0W
Trujillo, Peru 92 E3 8 6S 79 0W
Trujillo, Spain 19 C3 39 28N 5 55W
Trujillo, U.S.A. 81 H2 35 32N 104 42W
Trujillo, Venezuela 92 B4 9 22N 70 38W
Truk, Micronesia 64 G7 7 25N 151 46 E
Trumann, U.S.A. 81 H9 35 41N 90 31W
Trumansburg, U.S.A. 79 D8 42 33N 76 40W
Trumbull, Mt., U.S.A. 83 H7 36 25N 113 8W
Trundle, Australia 63 E4 32 53S 147 35 E
Trung-Phan = Annam, Vietnam 38 E7 16 0N 108 0 E
Truro, Canada 71 C7 45 21N 63 14W
Truro, U.K. 11 G2 50 16N 5 4W
Truskavets, Ukraine 17 D12 49 17N 23 30 E
Trutch, Canada 72 B4 57 44N 122 57W
Truth or Consequences, U.S.A. 83 K10 33 8N 107 15W
Trutnov, Czech Rep. 16 C8 50 37N 15 54 E
Truxton, U.S.A. 79 D8 42 45N 76 2W
Tryonville, U.S.A. 78 E5 41 42N 79 48W
Tsaratanana, Madag. 57 B8 16 47S 47 39 E
Tsaratanana, Mt. de, Madag. 57 A8 14 0S 49 0 E
Tsarevo = Michurin, Bulgaria 21 C12 42 9N 27 51 E
Tsau, Botswana 56 C3 20 8S 22 22 E
Tselinograd = Astana, Kazakstan 26 D8 51 10N 71 30 E
Tsetserleg, Mongolia 32 B5 47 36N 101 32 E
Tshabong, Botswana 56 D3 26 2S 22 29 E
Tshane, Botswana 56 C3 24 5S 21 54 E
Tshela, Dem. Rep. of the Congo 52 E2 4 57S 13 4 E
Tshesebe, Botswana 57 C4 21 51S 27 32 E
Tshibeke, Dem. Rep. of the Congo 54 C2 2 40S 28 35 E
Tshibinda, Dem. Rep. of the Congo 54 C2 2 23S 28 43 E
Tshikapa, Dem. Rep. of the Congo 52 F4 6 28S 20 48 E
Tshilenge, Dem. Rep. of the Congo 54 D1 6 17S 23 48 E
Tshinsenda, Dem. Rep. of the Congo 55 E2 12 20S 28 0 E
Tshofa, Dem. Rep. of the Congo 54 D2 5 13S 25 16 E
Tshwane, Botswana 56 C3 22 24S 22 1 E
Tsigara, Botswana 56 C4 20 22S 25 54 E
Tsihombe, Madag. 57 D8 25 10S 45 41 E
Tsiigehtchic, Canada 68 B6 67 15N 134 0W
Tsimlyansk Res. = Tsimlyanskoye Vdkhr., Russia 25 E7 48 0N 43 0 E
Tsimlyanskoye Vdkhr., Russia 25 E7 48 0N 43 0 E
Tsinan = Jinan, China 34 F9 36 38N 117 1 E
Tsineng, S. Africa 56 D3 27 5S 23 5 E
Tsinghai = Qinghai □, China 32 C4 36 0N 98 0 E
Tsingtao = Qingdao, China 35 F11 36 5N 120 20 E
Tsinjomitondraka, Madag. 57 B8 15 40S 47 8 E
Tsiroanomandidy, Madag. 57 B8 18 46S 46 2 E
Tsivory, Madag. 57 C8 24 4S 46 5 E
Tskhinvali, Georgia 25 F7 42 14N 44 1 E
Tsna →, Russia 24 D7 54 55N 41 58 E
Tso Moriri, L., India 43 C8 32 50N 78 20 E
Tsodilo Hill, Botswana 56 B3 18 49S 21 43 E
Tsogttsetsiy = Baruunsuu, Mongolia 34 C3 43 43N 105 35 E
Tsolo, S. Africa 57 E4 31 18S 28 37 E
Tsomo, S. Africa 57 E4 32 0S 27 42 E
Tsu, Japan 31 G8 34 45N 136 25 E
Tsu L., Canada 72 A6 60 40N 111 52W
Tsuchiura, Japan 31 F10 36 5N 140 15 E
Tsugaru-Kaikyō, Japan 30 D10 41 35N 141 0 E
Tsumeb, Namibia 56 B2 19 9S 17 44 E
Tsumis, Namibia 56 C2 23 39S 17 29 E
Tsuruga, Japan 31 G8 35 45N 136 2 E
Tsurugi-San, Japan 31 H7 33 51N 134 6 E
Tsuruoka, Japan 30 E9 38 44N 139 50 E
Tsushima, Gifu, Japan 31 G8 35 10N 136 43 E
Tsushima, Nagasaki, Japan 31 G4 34 20N 129 20 E
Tsuyama, Japan 31 G7 35 3N 134 0 E
Tsyelyakhany, Belarus 17 B13 52 30N 25 46 E
Tual, Indonesia 37 F8 5 38S 132 44 E
Tuam, Ireland 13 C3 53 31N 8 51W
Tuamotu Arch. = Tuamotu Is., Pac. Oc. 65 J13 17 0S 144 0W
Tuamotu Is., Pac. Oc. 65 J13 17 0S 144 0W
Tuamotu Ridge, Pac. Oc. 65 K14 20 0S 138 0W
Tuao, Phil. 37 A6 17 55N 121 22 E
Tuapse, Russia 25 F6 44 5N 39 10 E
Tuatapere, N.Z. 59 M1 46 8S 167 41 E
Tuba City, U.S.A. 83 H8 36 8N 111 14W
Tuban, Indonesia 37 G15 6 54S 112 3 E
Tubarão, Brazil 95 B6 28 30S 49 0W
Tūbās, West Bank 47 C4 32 20N 35 22 E
Tübingen, Germany 16 D5 48 31N 9 4 E
Tubruq, Libya 51 B10 32 7N 23 55 E
Tubuai Is., Pac. Oc. 65 K13 25 0S 150 0W
Tuc Trung, Vietnam 39 G6 11 1N 107 12 E
Tucacas, Venezuela 92 A5 10 48N 68 19W
Tuchodi →, Canada 72 B4 58 17N 123 42W
Tuckanarra, Australia 61 E2 27 7S 118 5 E
**Tucson**, U.S.A. 83 K8 32 13N 110 58W
Tucumán □, Argentina 94 B2 26 48S 66 2W
Tucumcari, U.S.A. 81 H3 35 10N 103 44W
Tucupita, Venezuela 92 B6 9 2N 62 3W
Tucuruí, Brazil 93 D9 3 42S 49 44W
Tucuruí, Reprêsa de, Brazil 93 D9 4 0S 49 30W
Tudela, Spain 19 A5 42 4N 1 39W
Tudmur, Syria 44 C3 34 36N 38 15 E
Tudor, L., Canada 71 A6 55 50N 65 25W
Tugela →, S. Africa 57 D5 29 14S 31 30 E
Tuguegarao, Phil. 37 A6 17 35N 121 42 E
Tugur, Russia 27 D14 53 44N 136 45 E
Tui, Spain 19 A1 42 3N 8 39W
Tuineje, Canary Is. 22 F5 28 19N 14 3W
Tukangbesi, Kepulauan, Indonesia 37 F6 6 0S 124 0 E
Tukarak I., Canada 70 A4 56 15N 78 45W
Tukayyid, Iraq 44 D5 29 47N 45 36 E
Tuktoyaktuk, Canada 68 B6 69 27N 133 2W
Tukums, Latvia 9 H20 56 58N 23 10 E
Tukuyu, Tanzania 55 D3 9 17S 33 35 E
Tula, Hidalgo, Mexico 87 C5 20 5N 99 20W
Tula, Tamaulipas, Mexico 87 C5 23 0N 99 40W
Tula, Russia 24 D6 54 13N 37 38 E
Tulancingo, Mexico 87 C5 20 5N 99 22W
Tulare, U.S.A. 84 J7 36 13N 119 21W
Tulare Lake Bed, U.S.A. 84 K7 36 0N 119 48W
Tularosa, U.S.A. 83 K10 33 5N 106 1W

Tulbagh, S. Africa 56 E2 33 16S 19 6 E
Tulcán, Ecuador 92 C3 0 48N 77 43W
Tulcea, Romania 17 F15 45 13N 28 46 E
Tulchyn, Ukraine 17 D15 48 41N 28 49 E
Tūleh, Iran 45 C7 34 35N 52 33 E
Tulemalu L., Canada 73 A9 62 58N 99 25W
Tuli, Zimbabwe 55 G2 21 58S 29 13 E
Tulia, U.S.A. 81 H4 34 32N 101 46W
Tulita, Canada 68 B7 64 57N 125 30W
Ţūlkarm, West Bank 47 C4 32 19N 35 2 E
Tulla, Ireland 13 D3 52 53N 8 46W
Tullahoma, U.S.A. 77 H2 35 22N 86 13W
Tullamore, Australia 63 E4 32 39S 147 36 E
Tullamore, Ireland 13 C4 53 16N 7 31W
Tulle, France 18 D4 45 16N 1 46 E
Tullow, Ireland 13 D5 52 49N 6 45W
Tully, Australia 62 B4 17 56S 145 55 E
Tully, U.S.A. 79 D8 42 48N 76 7W
Tulsa, U.S.A. 81 G7 36 10N 95 55W
Tulsequah, Canada 72 B2 58 39N 133 35W
Tulua, Colombia 92 C3 4 6N 76 11W
Tulun, Russia 27 D11 54 32N 100 35 E
Tulungagung, Indonesia 37 H14 8 5S 111 54 E
Tuma →, Nic. 88 D3 13 6N 84 35W
Tumaco, Colombia 92 C3 1 50N 78 45W
Tumatumari, Guyana 92 B7 5 20N 58 55W
Tumba, Sweden 9 G17 59 12N 17 48 E
Tumba, L., Dem. Rep. of the Congo 52 E3 0 50S 18 0 E
Tumbarumba, Australia 63 F4 35 44S 148 0 E
Tumbaya, Argentina 94 A2 23 50S 65 26W
Tumbes, Peru 92 D2 3 37S 80 27W
Tumbwe, Dem. Rep. of the Congo 55 E2 11 25S 27 15 E
Tumby Bay, Australia 63 E2 34 21S 136 8 E
Tumd Youqi, China 34 D6 40 30N 110 30 E
Tumen, China 35 C15 43 0N 129 50 E
Tumen Jiang →, China 35 C16 42 20N 130 35 E
Tumeremo, Venezuela 92 B6 7 18N 61 30W
Tumkur, India 40 N10 13 18N 77 6 E
Tump, Pakistan 40 F3 26 7N 62 16 E
Tumpat, Malaysia 39 J4 6 11N 102 10 E
Tumu, Ghana 50 F5 10 56N 1 56W
Tumucumaque, Serra, Brazil 93 C8 2 0N 55 0W
Tumut, Australia 63 F4 35 16S 148 13 E
Tumwater, U.S.A. 84 C4 47 1N 122 54W
Tuna, India 42 H4 22 59N 70 5 E
Tunas de Zaza, Cuba 88 B4 21 39N 79 34W
Tunbridge Wells = Royal Tunbridge Wells, U.K. 11 F8 51 7N 0 16 E
Tuncurry-Forster, Australia 63 E5 32 17S 152 29 E
Tundla, India 42 F8 27 12N 78 17 E
Tunduru, Tanzania 55 E4 11 8S 37 25 E
Tundzha →, Bulgaria 21 C11 41 40N 26 35 E
Tunga Pass, India 41 E19 29 0N 94 14 E
Tungabhadra →, India 40 M11 15 57N 78 15 E
Tungla, Nic. 88 D3 13 24N 84 21W
Tungsten, Canada 72 A3 61 57N 128 16W
Tunguska, Nizhnyaya →, Russia 27 C9 65 48N 88 4 E
Tunguska, Podkamennaya →, Russia 27 C10 61 50N 90 13 E
Tunica, U.S.A. 81 H9 34 41N 90 23W
Tunis, Tunisia 51 A8 36 50N 10 11 E
Tunisia ■, Africa 51 A7 33 30N 9 10 E
Tunja, Colombia 92 B4 5 33N 73 25W
Tunkhannock, U.S.A. 79 E9 41 32N 75 57W
Tunliu, China 34 F7 36 13N 112 52 E
Tunnsjøen, Norway 8 D15 64 45N 13 25 E
Tunungayualok I., Canada 71 A7 56 0N 61 0W
Tunuyán, Argentina 94 C2 33 35S 69 0W
Tunuyán →, Argentina 94 C2 33 33S 67 30W
Tuolumne, U.S.A. 84 H6 37 58N 120 15W
Tuolumne →, U.S.A. 84 H5 37 36N 121 13W
Tūp Āghāj, Iran 44 B5 36 3N 47 50 E
Tupã, Brazil 95 A5 21 57S 50 28W
Tupelo, U.S.A. 77 H1 34 16N 88 43W
Tupinambaranas, Brazil 92 D7 3 0S 58 0W
Tupiza, Bolivia 94 A2 21 30S 65 40W
Tupman, U.S.A. 85 K7 35 18N 119 21W
Tupper, Canada 72 B4 55 32N 120 1W
Tupper Lake, U.S.A. 79 B10 44 14N 74 28W
Tupungato, Cerro, S. Amer. 94 C2 33 15S 69 50W
Tuquan, China 35 B11 45 18N 121 38 E
Túquerres, Colombia 92 C3 1 5N 77 37W
Tura, Russia 27 C11 64 20N 100 17 E
Turabah, Si. Arabia 46 C3 28 20N 43 15 E
Tūrān, Iran 45 C8 35 39N 56 42 E
Turan, Russia 27 D10 51 55N 95 0 E
Ţurayf, Si. Arabia 44 D3 31 41N 38 39 E
Turda, Romania 17 E12 46 34N 23 47 E
Turek, Poland 17 B10 52 3N 18 30 E
Turen, Venezuela 92 B5 9 17N 69 6W
Turfan = Turpan, China 32 B3 43 58N 89 10 E
Turfan Depression = Turpan Hami, China 28 E12 42 40N 89 25 E
Turgeon →, Canada 70 C4 50 0N 78 56W
Tŭrgovishte, Bulgaria 21 C12 43 17N 26 38 E
Turgutlu, Turkey 21 E12 38 30N 27 43 E
Turia →, Spain 19 C5 39 27N 0 19W
Turiaçu, Brazil 93 D9 1 40S 45 19W
Turiaçu →, Brazil 93 D9 1 36S 45 19W
Turin = Torino, Italy 18 D7 45 3N 7 40 E
Turkana, L., Africa 54 B4 3 30N 36 5 E
Turkestan = Türkistan, Kazakstan 26 E7 43 17N 68 16 E
Turkey ■, Eurasia 25 G6 39 0N 36 0 E
Turkey Creek, Australia 60 C4 17 2S 128 12 E
Türkistan, Kazakstan 26 E7 43 17N 68 16 E
Türkmenbashi, Turkmenistan 25 G9 40 5N 53 5 E
Turkmenistan ■, Asia 26 F6 39 0N 59 0 E
Turks & Caicos Is. ■, W. Indies 89 B5 21 20N 71 20W
Turks Island Passage, W. Indies 89 B5 21 30N 71 30W
Turku, Finland 9 F20 60 30N 22 19 E
Turkwel →, Kenya 54 B4 3 6N 36 6 E
Turlock, U.S.A. 84 H6 37 30N 120 51W
Turnagain →, Canada 72 B3 59 12N 127 35W
Turnagain, C., N.Z. 59 J6 40 28S 176 38 E
Turneffe Is., Belize 87 D7 17 20N 87 50W
Turner, U.S.A. 82 B9 48 51N 108 24W
Turner Pt., Australia 62 A1 11 47S 133 32 E
Turner Valley, Canada 72 C6 50 40N 114 17W
Turners Falls, U.S.A. 79 D12 42 36N 72 33W
Turnhout, Belgium 15 C4 51 19N 4 57 E
Turnor L., Canada 73 B7 56 35N 108 35W
Tŭrnovo = Veliko Tŭrnovo, Bulgaria 21 C11 43 5N 25 41 E
Turnu Măgurele, Romania 17 G13 43 46N 24 56 E
Turnu Roşu, P., Romania 17 F13 45 33N 24 17 E
Turpan, China 32 B3 43 58N 89 10 E
Turpan Hami, China 28 E12 42 40N 89 25 E
Turriff, U.K. 12 D6 57 32N 2 27W
Tursāq, Iraq 44 C5 33 27N 45 47 E
Turtle Head I., Australia 62 A3 10 56S 142 37 E
Turtle L., Canada 73 C7 53 36N 108 38W
Turtle Lake, U.S.A. 80 B4 47 31N 100 53W
Turtleford, Canada 73 C7 53 23N 108 57W
Turukhansk, Russia 27 C9 65 21N 88 5 E
Tuscaloosa, U.S.A. 77 J2 33 12N 87 34W
Tuscany = Toscana □, Italy 20 C4 43 25N 11 0 E
Tuscarawas →, U.S.A. 78 F3 40 24N 81 25W
Tuscarora Mt., U.S.A. 78 F7 40 55N 77 55W
Tuscola, Ill., U.S.A. 76 F1 39 48N 88 17W
Tuscola, Tex., U.S.A. 81 J5 32 12N 99 48W
Tuscumbia, U.S.A. 77 H2 34 44N 87 42W
Tuskegee, U.S.A. 77 J3 32 25N 85 42W
Tustin, U.S.A. 85 M9 33 44N 117 49W
Tuticorin, India 40 Q11 8 50N 78 12 E
Tutóia, Brazil 93 D10 2 45S 42 20W
Tutong, Brunei 36 D4 4 47N 114 40 E
Tutrakan, Bulgaria 21 B12 44 2N 26 40 E
Tuttle Creek L., U.S.A. 80 F6 39 22N 96 40W
Tuttlingen, Germany 16 E5 47 58N 8 48 E
Tutuala, Indonesia 37 F7 8 25S 127 15 E
Tutuila, Amer. Samoa 59 B13 14 19S 170 50W
Tutume, Botswana 53 J5 20 30S 27 5 E
Tututepec, Mexico 87 D5 16 9N 97 38W
Tuva □, Russia 27 D10 51 30N 95 0 E
Tuvalu ■, Pac. Oc. 64 H9 8 0S 178 0 E
Tuxpan, Mexico 87 C5 20 58N 97 23W
Tuxtla Gutiérrez, Mexico 87 D6 16 50N 93 10W
Tuy = Tui, Spain 19 A1 42 3N 8 39W
Tuy Ān, Vietnam 38 F7 13 17N 109 16 E
Tuy Duc, Vietnam 39 F6 12 15N 107 27 E
Tuy Hoa, Vietnam 38 F7 13 5N 109 10 E
Tuy Phong, Vietnam 39 G7 11 14N 108 43 E
Tuya L., Canada 72 B2 59 7N 130 35W
Tuyen Hoa, Vietnam 38 D6 17 50N 106 10 E
Tūysarkān, Iran 45 C6 34 33N 48 27 E
Tuz Gölü, Turkey 25 G5 38 42N 33 18 E
Ţūz Khurmātū, Iraq 44 C5 34 56N 44 38 E
Tuzla, Bos.-H. 21 B8 44 34N 18 41 E
Tver, Russia 24 C6 56 55N 35 55 E
Twain, U.S.A. 84 E5 40 1N 121 3W
Twain Harte, U.S.A. 84 G6 38 2N 120 14W
Tweed, Canada 78 B7 44 29N 77 19W
Tweed →, U.K. 12 F6 55 45N 2 0W
Tweed Heads, Australia 63 D5 28 10S 153 31 E
Tweedsmuir Prov. Park, Canada 72 C3 53 0N 126 20W
Twentynine Palms, U.S.A. 85 L10 34 8N 116 3W
Twillingate, Canada 71 C9 49 42N 54 45W
Twin Bridges, U.S.A. 82 D7 45 33N 112 20W
Twin Falls, Canada 71 B7 53 30N 64 32W
Twin Falls, U.S.A. 82 E6 42 34N 114 28W
Twin Valley, U.S.A. 80 B6 47 16N 96 16W
Twinsburg, U.S.A. 78 E3 41 18N 81 26W
Twitchell Reservoir, U.S.A. 85 L6 34 59N 120 19W
Two Harbors, U.S.A. 80 B9 47 2N 91 40W
Two Hills, Canada 72 C6 53 43N 111 52W
Two Rivers, U.S.A. 76 C2 44 9N 87 34W
Two Rocks, Australia 61 F2 31 30S 115 35 E
Twofold B., Australia 63 F4 37 8S 149 59 E
Tyachiv, Ukraine 17 D12 48 1N 23 35 E
Tychy, Poland 17 C10 50 9N 18 59 E
Tyler, U.S.A. 75 D7 32 18N 95 17W
Tyler, Minn., U.S.A. 80 C6 44 18N 96 8W
Tyler, Tex., U.S.A. 81 J7 32 21N 95 18W
Tynda, Russia 27 D13 55 10N 124 43 E
Tyndall, U.S.A. 80 D6 43 0N 97 50W
Tyne →, U.K. 10 C6 54 59N 1 32W
Tyne & Wear □, U.K. 10 B6 55 6N 1 17W
Tynemouth, U.K. 10 B6 55 1N 1 26W
Tyre = Sūr, Lebanon 47 B4 33 19N 35 16 E
Tyrifjorden, Norway 9 F14 60 2N 10 8 E
Tyrol = Tirol □, Austria 16 E6 47 3N 10 43 E
Tyrone, U.S.A. 78 F6 40 40N 78 14W
Tyrone □, U.K. 13 B4 54 38N 7 11W
Tyrrell →, Australia 63 F3 35 26S 142 51 E
Tyrrell, L., Australia 63 F3 35 20S 142 50 E
Tyrrell L., Canada 73 A7 63 7N 105 27W
Tyrrhenian Sea, Medit. S. 20 E5 40 0N 12 30 E
Tysfjorden, Norway 8 B17 68 7N 16 25 E
Tyulgan, Russia 24 D10 52 22N 56 12 E
Tyumen, Russia 26 D7 57 11N 65 29 E
Tywi →, U.K. 11 F3 51 48N 4 21W
Tywyn, U.K. 11 E3 52 35N 4 5W
Tzaneen, S. Africa 57 C5 23 47S 30 9 E
Tzermiádhes, Greece 23 D7 35 12N 25 29 E
Tzukong = Zigong, China 32 D5 29 15N 104 48 E

# U

U Taphao, Thailand 38 F3 12 35N 101 0 E
U.S.A. = United States of America ■, N. Amer. 74 C7 37 0N 96 0W
Uatumã →, Brazil 92 D7 2 26S 57 37W
Uaupés, Brazil 92 D5 0 8S 67 5W
Uaupés →, Brazil 92 C5 0 2N 67 16W
Uaxactún, Guatemala 88 C2 17 25N 89 29W
Ubá, Brazil 95 A7 21 8S 43 0W
Ubaitaba, Brazil 93 F11 14 18S 39 20W
Ubangi = Oubangi →, Dem. Rep. of the Congo 52 E3 0 30S 17 50 E
Ubauro, Pakistan 42 E3 28 15N 69 45 E
Ubayyid, W. al →, Iraq 44 C4 32 34N 43 48 E
Ube, Japan 31 H5 33 56N 131 15 E
Úbeda, Spain 19 C4 38 3N 3 23W
Uberaba, Brazil 93 G9 19 50S 47 55W
Uberlândia, Brazil 93 G9 19 0S 48 20W
Ubolratna Res., Thailand 38 D4 16 45N 102 30 E
Ubombo, S. Africa 57 D5 27 31S 32 4 E
Ubon Ratchathani, Thailand 38 E5 15 15N 104 50 E
Ubondo, Dem. Rep. of the Congo 54 C2 0 55S 25 42 E
Ubort →, Belarus 17 B15 52 6N 28 30 E
Ubundu, Dem. Rep. of the Congo 54 C2 0 22S 25 30 E
Ucayali →, Peru 92 D4 4 30S 73 30W
Uchiura-Wan, Japan 30 C10 42 25N 140 40 E
Uchquduq, Uzbekistan 26 E7 41 50N 62 50 E
Uchur →, Russia 27 D14 58 48N 130 35 E
Ucluelet, Canada 72 D3 48 57N 125 32W
Uda →, Russia 27 D14 54 42N 135 14 E
Udagamandalam, India 40 P10 11 30N 76 44 E
Udainagar, India 42 H7 22 33N 76 13 E
Udaipur, India 42 G5 24 36N 73 44 E
Udaipur Garhi, Nepal 43 F12 27 0N 86 35 E
Udala, India 43 J12 21 35N 86 34 E
Uddevalla, Sweden 9 G14 58 21N 11 55 E
Uddjaur, Sweden 8 D17 65 56N 17 49 E
Uden, Neths. 15 C5 51 40N 5 37 E
Udgir, India 40 K10 18 25N 77 5 E
Udhampur, India 43 C6 33 0N 75 5 E
Údine, Italy 20 A5 46 3N 13 14 E
Udmurtia □, Russia 24 C9 57 30N 52 30 E
Udon Thani, Thailand 38 D4 17 29N 102 46 E
Udupi, India 40 N9 13 25N 74 42 E
Udzungwa Range, Tanzania 55 D4 9 30S 35 10 E
Ueda, Japan 31 F9 36 24N 138 16 E
Uedineniya, Os., Russia 4 B12 78 0N 85 0 E
Uele →, Dem. Rep. of the Congo 52 D4 3 45N 24 45 E
Uelen, Russia 27 C19 66 10N 170 0W
Uelzen, Germany 16 B6 52 57N 10 32 E
Ufa, Russia 24 D10 54 45N 55 55 E
Ufa →, Russia 24 D10 54 40N 56 0 E
Ugab →, Namibia 56 C1 20 55S 13 30 E
Ugalla →, Tanzania 54 D3 5 8S 30 42 E
Uganda ■, Africa 54 B3 2 0N 32 0 E
Ugie, S. Africa 57 E4 31 10S 28 13 E
Uglegorsk, Russia 27 E15 49 5N 142 2 E
Ugljan, Croatia 16 F8 44 12N 15 10 E
Uhrichsville, U.S.A. 78 F3 40 24N 81 21W
Uibhist a Deas = South Uist, U.K. 12 D1 57 20N 7 15W
Uibhist a Tuath = North Uist, U.K. 12 D1 57 40N 7 15W
Uig, U.K. 12 D2 57 35N 6 21W
Uíge, Angola 52 F2 7 30S 14 40 E
Uijŏngbu, S. Korea 35 F14 37 48N 127 0 E
Ŭiju, N. Korea 35 D13 40 15N 124 35 E
Uinta Mts., U.S.A. 82 F8 40 45N 110 30W
Uitenhage, S. Africa 56 E4 33 40S 25 28 E
Uithuizen, Neths. 15 A6 53 24N 6 41 E
Ujh →, India 42 C6 32 10N 75 18 E
Ujhani, India 43 F8 28 0N 79 6 E
Uji-guntō, Japan 31 J4 31 15N 129 25 E
Ujjain, India 42 H6 23 9N 75 43 E
Ujung Pandang, Indonesia 37 F5 5 10S 119 20 E
Uka, Russia 27 D17 57 50N 162 0 E
Ukara I., Tanzania 54 C3 1 50S 33 0 E
Uke-Shima, Japan 31 K4 28 2N 129 14 E
Ukerewe I., Tanzania 54 C3 2 0S 33 0 E
Ukhrul, India 41 G19 25 10N 94 25 E
Ukhta, Russia 24 B9 63 34N 53 41 E
Ukiah, U.S.A. 84 F3 39 9N 123 13W
Ukki Fort, India 43 C7 33 28N 76 54 E
Ukmergė, Lithuania 9 J21 55 15N 24 45 E
Ukraine ■, Europe 25 E5 49 0N 32 0 E
Uku, Angola 53 G2 11 24S 14 22 E
Ukwi, Botswana 56 C3 23 29S 20 30 E
Ulaan-Uul, Mongolia 34 B6 44 13N 111 10 E
Ulaanbaatar, Mongolia 27 E11 47 55N 106 53 E
Ulaangom, Mongolia 32 A4 50 5N 92 10 E
Ulaanjirem, Mongolia 34 B3 45 5N 105 30 E
Ulamba, Dem. Rep. of the Congo 55 D1 9 3S 23 38 E
Ulan Bator = Ulaanbaatar, Mongolia 27 E11 47 55N 106 53 E
Ulan Ude, Russia 27 D11 51 45N 107 40 E
Ulaya, Morogoro, Tanzania 54 D4 7 3S 36 55 E
Ulaya, Tabora, Tanzania 54 C3 4 25S 33 30 E
Ulcinj, Montenegro, Yug. 21 D8 41 58N 19 10 E
Ulco, S. Africa 56 D3 28 21S 24 15 E
Ulefoss, Norway 9 G13 59 17N 9 16 E
Ulhasnagar, India 40 K8 19 15N 73 10 E
Uliastay, Mongolia 32 B4 47 56N 97 28 E
Ulithi Atoll, Pac. Oc. 37 B9 10 0N 139 30 E
Uladulla, Australia 63 F5 35 21S 150 29 E
Ullapool, U.K. 12 D3 57 54N 5 9W
Ullswater, U.K. 10 C5 54 34N 2 52W
Ullŭng-do, S. Korea 31 F5 37 30N 130 30 E
Ulm, Germany 16 D5 48 23N 9 58 E
Ulmarra, Australia 63 D5 29 37S 153 4 E
Ulonguè, Mozam. 55 E3 14 37S 34 19 E
Ulricehamn, Sweden 9 H15 57 46N 13 26 E
Ulsan, S. Korea 35 G15 35 20N 129 15 E
Ulsta, U.K. 12 A7 60 30N 1 9W
Ulster □, U.K. 13 B5 54 35N 6 30W
Ulubat Gölü, Turkey 21 D13 40 9N 28 35 E
Uludağ, Turkey 21 D13 40 4N 29 13 E
Uluguru Mts., Tanzania 54 D4 7 15S 37 40 E
Ulungur He →, China 32 B3 47 1N 87 24 E
Uluru = Ayers Rock, Australia 61 E5 25 23S 131 5 E
Uluru Nat. Park, Australia 61 E5 25 15S 131 20 E
Ulutau, Kazakstan 26 E7 48 39N 67 1 E
Ulva, U.K. 12 E2 56 29N 6 13W
Ulverston, U.K. 10 C4 54 13N 3 5W
Ulverstone, Australia 62 G4 41 11S 146 11 E
Ulya, Russia 27 D15 59 10N 142 0 E
Ulyanovsk = Simbirsk, Russia 24 D8 54 20N 48 25 E
Ulyasutay = Uliastay, Mongolia 32 B4 47 56N 97 28 E
Ulysses, U.S.A. 81 G4 37 35N 101 22W
Umala, Bolivia 92 G5 17 25S 68 5W
Uman, Ukraine 17 D16 48 40N 30 12 E
Umaria, India 41 H12 23 35N 80 50 E
Umarkot, Pakistan 40 G6 25 15N 69 40 E
Umarpada, India 42 J5 21 27N 73 30 E
Umatilla, U.S.A. 82 D4 45 55N 119 21W
Umba, Russia 24 A5 66 42N 34 11 E
Umbagog L., U.S.A. 79 B13 44 46N 71 3W
Umbakumba, Australia 62 A2 13 47S 136 50 E
Umbrella Mts., N.Z. 59 L2 45 35S 169 5 E
Ume älv →, Sweden 8 E19 63 45N 20 20 E
Umeå, Sweden 8 E19 63 45N 20 20 E
Umera, Indonesia 37 E7 0 12S 129 37 E
Umfuli →, Zimbabwe 55 F2 17 30S 29 23 E
Umgusa, Zimbabwe 55 F2 19 29S 27 52 E
Umkomaas, S. Africa 57 E5 30 13S 30 48 E
Umlazi, S. Africa 53 L6 29 59S 30 54 E
Umm ad Daraj, J., Jordan 47 C4 32 18N 35 48 E
Umm al Qaywayn, U.A.E. 45 E7 25 30N 55 35 E
Umm al Qittayn, Jordan 47 C5 32 18N 36 40 E
Umm Bāb, Qatar 45 E6 25 12N 50 48 E
Umm el Fahm, Israel 47 C4 32 31N 35 9 E
Umm Keddada, Sudan 51 F11 13 36N 26 42 E
Umm Lajj, Si. Arabia 44 E3 25 0N 37 23 E
Umm Ruwaba, Sudan 51 F12 12 50N 31 20 E
Umnak I., U.S.A. 68 C3 53 15N 168 20W
Umniati →, Zimbabwe 55 F2 16 49S 28 45 E
Umpqua →, U.S.A. 82 E1 43 40N 124 12W
Umreth, India 42 H5 22 41N 73 4 E
Umtata, S. Africa 57 E4 31 36S 28 49 E
Umuarama, Brazil 95 A5 23 45S 53 20W
Umvukwe Ra., Zimbabwe 55 F3 16 45S 30 45 E
Umzimvubu = Port St. Johns, S. Africa 57 E4 31 38S 29 33 E
Umzingwane →, Zimbabwe 55 G2 22 12S 29 56 E
Umzinto, S. Africa 57 E5 30 15S 30 45 E
Una, India 42 J4 20 46N 71 8 E
Una →, Bos.-H. 16 F9 45 0N 16 20 E
Unadilla, U.S.A. 79 D9 42 20N 75 19W
Unalakleet, U.S.A. 68 B3 63 52N 160 47W
Unalaska, U.S.A. 68 C3 53 53N 166 32W
Unalaska I., U.S.A. 68 C3 53 35N 166 50W
'Unayzah, Si. Arabia 44 E4 26 6N 43 58 E
'Unāzah, J., Asia 44 C3 32 12N 39 18 E
Uncía, Bolivia 92 G5 18 25S 66 40W
Uncompahgre Peak, U.S.A. 83 G10 38 4N 107 28W
Uncompahgre Plateau, U.S.A. 83 G9 38 20N 108 15W
Underbool, Australia 63 F3 35 10S 141 51 E
Ungarie, Australia 63 E4 33 38S 146 56 E
Ungarra, Australia 63 E2 34 12S 136 2 E
Ungava, Pén. d', Canada 69 C12 60 0N 74 0W
Ungava B., Canada 69 C13 59 30N 67 30W
Ungeny = Ungheni, Moldova 17 E14 47 11N 27 51 E
Unggi, N. Korea 35 C16 42 16N 130 28 E
Ungheni, Moldova 17 E14 47 11N 27 51 E
União da Vitória, Brazil 95 B5 26 13S 51 5W
Unimak I., U.S.A. 68 C3 54 45N 164 0W
Union, Miss., U.S.A. 81 J10 32 34N 89 7W
Union, Mo., U.S.A. 80 F9 38 27N 91 0W
Union, S.C., U.S.A. 77 H5 34 43N 81 37W
Union City, Calif., U.S.A. 84 H4 37 36N 122 1W
Union City, N.J., U.S.A. 79 F10 40 45N 74 2W
Union City, Pa., U.S.A. 78 E5 41 54N 79 51W
Union City, Tenn., U.S.A. 81 G10 36 26N 89 3W
Union Gap, U.S.A. 82 C3 46 33N 120 28W
Union Springs, U.S.A. 77 J3 32 9N 85 43W
Uniondale, S. Africa 56 E3 33 39S 23 7 E
Uniontown, U.S.A. 76 F6 39 54N 79 44W
Unionville, U.S.A. 80 E8 40 29N 93 1W
United Arab Emirates ■, Asia 45 F7 23 50N 54 0 E
United Kingdom ■, Europe 7 E5 53 0N 2 0W
United States of America ■, N. Amer. 74 C7 37 0N 96 0W
Unity, Canada 73 C7 52 30N 109 5W
University Park, U.S.A. 83 K10 32 17N 106 45W
Unjha, India 42 H5 23 46N 72 24 E
Unnao, India 43 F9 26 35N 80 30 E
Unst, U.K. 12 A8 60 44N 0 53W
Unuk →, Canada 72 B2 56 5N 131 3W
Uozu, Japan 31 F8 36 48N 137 24 E
Upata, Venezuela 92 B6 8 1N 62 24W
Upemba, L., Dem. Rep. of the Congo 55 D2 8 30S 26 20 E
Upernavik, Greenland 4 B5 72 49N 56 20W
Upington, S. Africa 56 D3 28 25S 21 15 E
Upleta, India 42 J4 21 46N 70 16 E
Upolu, W. Samoa 59 A13 13 58S 172 0W
Upper Alkali L., U.S.A. 82 F3 41 47N 120 8W
Upper Arrow L., Canada 72 C5 50 30N 117 50W
Upper Foster L., Canada 73 B7 56 47N 105 20W
Upper Hutt, N.Z. 59 J5 41 8S 175 5 E
Upper Klamath L., U.S.A. 82 E3 42 25N 121 55W
Upper Lake, U.S.A. 84 F4 39 10N 122 54W
Upper Musquodoboit, Canada 71 C7 45 10N 62 58W
Upper Red L., U.S.A. 80 A7 48 8N 94 45W
Upper Sandusky, U.S.A. 76 E4 40 50N 83 17W
Upper Volta = Burkina Faso ■, Africa 50 F5 12 0N 1 0W
Uppland, Sweden 9 F17 59 59N 17 48 E
Uppsala, Sweden 9 G17 59 53N 17 38 E
Upshi, India 43 C7 33 48N 77 52 E
Upstart, C., Australia 62 B4 19 41S 147 45 E
Upton, U.S.A. 80 C2 44 6N 104 38W
Ur, Iraq 44 D5 30 55N 46 25 E
Urad Qianqi, China 34 D5 40 40N 108 30 E
Urakawa, Japan 30 C11 42 9N 142 47 E
Ural = Zhayyq →, Kazakstan 25 E9 47 0N 51 48 E
Ural, Australia 63 E4 33 21S 146 12 E
Ural Mts. = Uralskie Gory, Eurasia 24 C10 60 0N 59 0 E
Uralla, Australia 63 E5 30 37S 151 29 E
Uralsk = Oral, Kazakstan 25 D9 51 20N 51 20 E
Uralskie Gory, Eurasia 24 C10 60 0N 59 0 E
Urambo, Tanzania 54 D3 5 4S 32 0 E
Urana, Australia 63 F4 35 15S 146 21 E
Urandangi, Australia 62 C2 21 32S 138 14 E
Uranium City, Canada 73 B7 59 34N 108 37W
Uraricoera →, Brazil 92 C6 3 2N 60 30W
Urawa, Japan 31 G9 35 50N 139 40 E
Uray, Russia 26 C7 60 5N 65 15 E
'Uray'irah, Si. Arabia 45 E6 25 57N 48 53 E
Urbana, Ill., U.S.A. 76 E1 40 7N 88 12W
Urbana, Ohio, U.S.A. 76 E4 40 7N 83 45W
Urbino, Italy 20 C5 43 43N 12 38 E
Urbión, Picos de, Spain 19 A4 42 1N 2 52W
Urcos, Peru 92 F4 13 40S 71 38W
Urdinarrain, Argentina 94 C4 32 37S 58 52W
Urdzhar, Kazakstan 26 E9 47 5N 81 38 E
Ure →, U.K. 10 C6 54 5N 1 20W
Ures, Mexico 86 B2 29 30N 110 30W
Urfa = Sanliurfa, Turkey 25 G6 37 12N 38 50 E
Urganch, Uzbekistan 26 E7 41 40N 60 41 E
Urgench = Urganch, Uzbekistan 26 E7 41 40N 60 41 E

Ürgüp, *Turkey* **44 B2** 38 38N 34 56 E
Uri, *India* **43 B6** 34 8N 74 2 E
Uribia, *Colombia* **92 A4** 11 43N 72 16W
Uriondo, *Bolivia* **94 A3** 21 41S 64 41W
Urique, *Mexico* **86 B3** 27 13N 107 55W
Urique →, *Mexico* **86 B3** 26 29N 107 58W
Urk, *Neths.* **15 B5** 52 39N 5 36 E
Urla, *Turkey* **21 E12** 38 20N 26 47 E
Urmia = Orūmīyeh, *Iran* **44 B5** 37 40N 45 0 E
Urmia, L. = Orūmīyeh, Daryācheh-ye, *Iran* **44 B5** 37 50N 45 30 E
Uroševac, *Yugoslavia* **21 C9** 42 23N 21 10 E
Uruaçu, *Brazil* **93 F9** 14 30S 49 10W
Uruapan, *Mexico* **86 D4** 19 30N 102 0W
Urubamba →, *Peru* **92 F4** 10 43S 73 48W
Uruçara, *Brazil* **92 D7** 2 20S 57 50W
Uruçuí, *Brazil* **93 E10** 7 20S 44 28W
Uruguai →, *Brazil* **95 B5** 26 0S 53 30W
Uruguaiana, *Brazil* **94 B4** 29 50S 57 0W
**Uruguay** ■, *S. Amer.* **94 C4** 32 30S 56 30W
**Uruguay** →, *S. Amer.* **94 C4** 34 12S 58 18W
Urumchi = Ürümqi, *China* **26 E9** 43 45N 87 45 E
Ürümqi, *China* **26 E9** 43 45N 87 45 E
Urup, Ostrov, *Russia* **27 E16** 46 0N 151 0 E
Usa →, *Russia* **24 A10** 66 16N 59 49 E
Uşak, *Turkey* **25 G4** 38 43N 29 28 E
Usakos, *Namibia* **56 C2** 21 54S 15 31 E
Usedom, *Germany* **16 B8** 53 55N 14 2 E
Useless Loop, *Australia* **61 E1** 26 8S 113 23 E
Ush-Tobe, *Kazakstan* **26 E8** 45 16N 78 0 E
Ushakova, Ostrov, *Russia* **4 A12** 82 0N 80 0 E
Ushant = Ouessant, Î. d', *France* **18 B1** 48 28N 5 6W
Ushashi, *Tanzania* **54 C3** 1 59S 33 57 E
Ushibuka, *Japan* **31 H5** 32 11N 130 1 E
Ushuaia, *Argentina* **96 G3** 54 50S 68 23W
Ushumun, *Russia* **27 D13** 52 47N 126 32 E
Usk, *Canada* **72 C3** 54 38N 128 26W
Usk →, *U.K.* **11 F5** 51 33N 2 58W
Uska, *India* **43 F10** 27 12N 83 7 E
Usman, *Russia* **24 D6** 52 5N 39 48 E
Usoke, *Tanzania* **54 D3** 5 8S 32 24 E
Usolye Sibirskoye, *Russia* **27 D11** 52 48N 103 40 E
Uspallata, P. de, *Argentina* **94 C2** 32 37S 69 22W
Uspenskiy, *Kazakstan* **26 E8** 48 41N 72 43 E
Ussuri →, *Asia* **30 A7** 48 27N 135 0 E
Ussuriysk, *Russia* **27 E14** 43 48N 131 59 E
Ussurka, *Russia* **30 B6** 45 12N 133 31 E
Ust-Aldan = Batamay, *Russia* **27 C13** 63 30N 129 15 E
Ust Amginskoye = Khandyga, *Russia* **27 C14** 62 42N 135 35 E
Ust-Bolsheretsk, *Russia* **27 D16** 52 50N 156 15 E
Ust Chaun, *Russia* **27 C18** 68 47N 170 30 E
Ust Ilimpeya = Yukta, *Russia* **27 C11** 63 26N 105 42 E
Ust-Ilimsk, *Russia* **27 D11** 58 3N 102 39 E
Ust Ishim, *Russia* **26 D8** 57 45N 71 10 E
Ust-Kamchatsk, *Russia* **27 D17** 56 10N 162 28 E
Ust-Kamenogorsk = Öskemen, *Kazakstan* **26 E9** 50 0N 82 36 E
Ust Khayryuzovo, *Russia* **27 D16** 57 15N 156 45 E
Ust-Kut, *Russia* **27 D11** 56 50N 105 42 E
Ust Kuyga, *Russia* **27 B14** 70 1N 135 43 E
Ust Maya, *Russia* **27 C14** 60 30N 134 28 E
Ust-Mil, *Russia* **27 D14** 59 40N 133 11 E
Ust-Nera, *Russia* **27 C15** 64 35N 143 15 E
Ust-Nyukzha, *Russia* **27 D13** 56 34N 121 37 E
Ust Olenek, *Russia* **27 B12** 73 0N 120 5 E
Ust-Omchug, *Russia* **27 C15** 61 9N 149 38 E
Ust Port, *Russia* **26 C9** 69 40N 84 26 E
Ust Tsilma, *Russia* **24 A9** 65 28N 52 11 E
Ust Urt = Ustyurt Plateau, *Asia* **26 E6** 44 0N 55 0 E
Ust Usa, *Russia* **24 A10** 66 2N 56 57 E
Ust Vorkuta, *Russia* **24 A11** 67 24N 64 0 E
Ústí nad Labem, *Czech Rep.* **16 C8** 50 41N 14 3 E
Ústica, *Italy* **20 E5** 38 42N 13 11 E
Ustinov = Izhevsk, *Russia* **24 C9** 56 51N 53 14 E
Ustyurt Plateau, *Asia* **26 E6** 44 0N 55 0 E
Usu, *China* **32 B3** 44 27N 84 40 E
Usuki, *Japan* **31 H5** 33 8N 131 49 E
Usulután, *El Salv.* **88 D2** 13 25N 88 28W
Usumacinta →, *Mexico* **87 D6** 17 0N 91 0W
Usumbura = Bujumbura, *Burundi* **54 C2** 3 16S 29 18 E
Usure, *Tanzania* **54 C3** 4 40S 34 22 E
Uta, *Indonesia* **37 E9** 4 33S 136 0 E
**Utah** □, *U.S.A.* **82 G8** 39 20N 111 30W
Utah L., *U.S.A.* **82 F8** 40 10N 111 58W
Utarni, *India* **42 F4** 26 5N 71 58 E
Utatlan, *Guatemala* **88 C1** 15 2N 91 11W
Ute Creek →, *U.S.A.* **81 H3** 35 21N 103 50W
Utena, *Lithuania* **9 J21** 55 27N 25 40 E
Utete, *Tanzania* **54 D4** 8 0S 38 45 E
Uthai Thani, *Thailand* **38 E3** 15 22N 100 3 E
Uthal, *Pakistan* **42 G2** 25 44N 66 40 E
Utiariti, *Brazil* **92 F7** 13 0S 58 10W
Utica, *N.Y., U.S.A.* **79 C9** 43 6N 75 14W
Utica, *Ohio, U.S.A.* **78 F2** 40 14N 82 27W
Utikuma L., *Canada* **72 B5** 55 50N 115 30W
Utopia, *Australia* **62 C1** 22 14S 134 33 E
Utraula, *India* **43 F10** 27 19N 82 25 E
**Utrecht**, *Neths.* **15 B5** 52 5N 5 8 E
Utrecht, *S. Africa* **57 D5** 27 38S 30 20 E
Utrecht □, *Neths.* **15 B5** 52 6N 5 7 E
Utrera, *Spain* **19 D3** 37 12N 5 48W
Utsjoki, *Finland* **8 B22** 69 51N 26 59 E
Utsunomiya, *Japan* **31 F9** 36 30N 139 50 E
**Uttar Pradesh** □, *India* **43 F9** 27 0N 80 0 E
Uttaradit, *Thailand* **38 D3** 17 36N 100 5 E
Uttoxeter, *U.K.* **10 E6** 52 54N 1 52W
Uummannarsuaq = Farvel, Kap, *Greenland* **4 D5** 59 48N 43 55W
Uusikaarlepyy, *Finland* **8 E20** 63 32N 22 31 E
Uusikaupunki, *Finland* **9 F19** 60 47N 21 25 E
Uva, *Russia* **24 C9** 56 59N 52 13 E
Uvalde, *U.S.A.* **81 L5** 29 13N 99 47W
Uvat, *Russia* **26 D7** 59 5N 68 50 E
Uvinza, *Tanzania* **54 D3** 5 5S 30 24 E
Uvira, *Dem. Rep. of the Congo* **54 C2** 3 22S 29 3 E
Uvs Nuur, *Mongolia* **32 A4** 50 20N 92 30 E
'Uwairidh, Harrat al, *Si. Arabia* **44 E3** 26 50N 38 0 E
Uwajima, *Japan* **31 H6** 33 10N 132 35 E
Uweinat, Jebel, *Sudan* **51 D10** 21 54N 24 58 E
Uxbridge, *Canada* **78 B5** 44 6N 79 7W
Uxin Qi, *China* **34 E5** 38 50N 109 5 E
Uxmal, *Mexico* **87 C7** 20 22N 89 46W
Üydzin, *Mongolia* **34 B4** 44 9N 107 0 E
Uyo, *Nigeria* **50 G7** 5 1N 7 53 E
Uyûn Mûsa, *Egypt* **47 F1** 29 53N 32 40 E
Uyuni, *Bolivia* **92 H5** 20 28S 66 47W
**Uzbekistan** ■, *Asia* **26 E7** 41 30N 65 0 E
Uzen, *Kazakstan* **25 F9** 43 29N 52 54 E
Uzen, Mal →, *Kazakstan* **25 E8** 49 4N 49 44 E
Uzerche, *France* **18 D4** 45 25N 1 34 E
Uzh →, *Ukraine* **17 C16** 51 15N 30 12 E
Uzhgorod = Uzhhorod, *Ukraine* **17 D12** 48 36N 22 18 E
Uzhhorod, *Ukraine* **17 D12** 48 36N 22 18 E
Užice, *Serbia, Yug.* **21 C8** 43 55N 19 50 E
Uzunköprü, *Turkey* **21 D12** 41 16N 26 43 E


# V


Vaal →, *S. Africa* **56 D3** 29 4S 23 38 E
Vaal Dam, *S. Africa* **57 D4** 27 0S 28 14 E
Vaalwater, *S. Africa* **57 C4** 24 15S 28 8 E
Vaasa, *Finland* **8 E19** 63 6N 21 38 E
Vác, *Hungary* **17 E10** 47 49N 19 10 E
Vacaria, *Brazil* **95 B5** 28 31S 50 52W
Vacaville, *U.S.A.* **84 G5** 38 21N 121 59W
Vach = Vakh →, *Russia* **26 C8** 60 45N 76 45 E
Vache, Î. à, *Haiti* **89 C5** 18 2N 73 35W
Vadnagar, *India* **42 H5** 23 47N 72 40 E
Vadodara, *India* **42 H5** 22 20N 73 10 E
Vadsø, *Norway* **8 A23** 70 3N 29 50 E
Vaduz, *Liech.* **18 C8** 47 8N 9 31 E
Værøy, *Norway* **8 C15** 67 40N 12 40 E
Vágar, *Færoe Is.* **8 E9** 62 5N 7 15W
Vågsfjorden, *Norway* **8 B17** 68 50N 16 50 E
Váh →, *Slovak Rep.* **17 D9** 47 43N 18 7 E
Vahsel B., *Antarctica* **5 D1** 75 0S 35 0W
Váï, *Greece* **23 D8** 35 15N 26 18 E
Vaigach, *Russia* **26 B6** 70 10N 59 0 E
Vail, *U.S.A.* **74 C5** 39 40N 106 20W
Vaisali →, *India* **43 F8** 26 28N 78 53 E
Vakh →, *Russia* **26 C8** 60 45N 76 45 E
Val-d'Or, *Canada* **70 C4** 48 7N 77 47W
Val Marie, *Canada* **73 D7** 49 15N 107 45W
Valahia, *Romania* **17 F13** 44 35N 25 0 E
Valandovo, *Macedonia* **21 D10** 41 19N 22 34 E
Valcheta, *Argentina* **96 E3** 40 40S 66 8W
Valdayskaya Vozvyshennost, *Russia* **24 C5** 57 0N 33 30 E
Valdepeñas, *Spain* **19 C4** 38 43N 3 25W
Valdés, Pen., *Argentina* **96 E4** 42 30S 63 45W
Valdez, *U.S.A.* **68 B5** 61 7N 146 16W
Valdivia, *Chile* **96 D2** 39 50S 73 14W
Valdosta, *U.S.A.* **77 K4** 30 50N 83 17W
Valdres, *Norway* **9 F13** 61 5N 9 5 E
Vale, *U.S.A.* **82 E5** 43 59N 117 15W
Vale of Glamorgan □, *U.K.* **11 F4** 51 28N 3 25W
Valemount, *Canada* **72 C5** 52 50N 119 15W
Valença, *Brazil* **93 F11** 13 20S 39 5W
Valença do Piauí, *Brazil* **93 E10** 6 20S 41 45W
Valence, *France* **18 D6** 44 57N 4 54 E
**Valencia**, *Spain* **19 C5** 39 27N 0 23W
Valencia, *U.S.A.* **83 J10** 34 48N 106 43W
**Valencia**, *Venezuela* **92 A5** 10 11N 68 0W
Valencia □, *Spain* **19 C5** 39 20N 0 40W
Valencia, G. de, *Spain* **19 C6** 39 30N 0 20 E
Valencia de Alcántara, *Spain* **19 C2** 39 25N 7 14W
Valencia I., *Ireland* **13 E1** 51 54N 10 22W
Valenciennes, *France* **18 A5** 50 20N 3 34 E
Valentim, Sa. do, *Brazil* **93 E10** 6 0S 43 30W
Valentin, *Russia* **30 C7** 43 8N 134 17 E
Valentine, *Nebr., U.S.A.* **74 B6** 42 52N 100 33W
Valentine, *Tex., U.S.A.* **81 K2** 30 35N 104 30W
Valera, *Venezuela* **92 B4** 9 19N 70 37W
Valga, *Estonia* **9 H22** 57 47N 26 2 E
Valier, *U.S.A.* **82 B7** 48 18N 112 16W
Valjevo, *Serbia, Yug.* **21 B8** 44 18N 19 53 E
Valka, *Latvia* **9 H21** 57 42N 25 57 E
Valkeakoski, *Finland* **9 F20** 61 16N 24 2 E
Valkenswaard, *Neths.* **15 C5** 51 21N 5 29 E
Vall de Uxó = La Vall d'Uixó, *Spain* **19 C5** 39 49N 0 15W
Valladolid, *Mexico* **87 C7** 20 40N 88 11W
**Valladolid**, *Spain* **19 B3** 41 38N 4 43W
Valldemossa, *Spain* **22 B9** 39 43N 2 37 E
Valle de la Pascua, *Venezuela* **92 B5** 9 13N 66 0W
Valle de las Palmas, *Mexico* **85 N10** 32 20N 116 43W
Valle de Santiago, *Mexico* **86 C4** 20 25N 101 15W
Valle de Suchil, *Mexico* **86 C4** 23 38N 103 55W
Valle de Zaragoza, *Mexico* **86 B3** 27 28N 105 49W
Valle Fértil, Sierra del, *Argentina* **94 C2** 30 20S 68 0W
Valle Hermoso, *Mexico* **87 B5** 25 35N 97 40W
Valledupar, *Colombia* **92 A4** 10 29N 73 15W
Vallehermoso, *Canary Is.* **22 F2** 28 10N 17 15W
Vallejo, *U.S.A.* **84 G4** 38 7N 122 14W
Vallenar, *Chile* **94 B1** 28 30S 70 50W
**Valletta**, *Malta* **23 D2** 35 54N 14 31 E
Valley Center, *U.S.A.* **85 M9** 33 13N 117 2W
Valley City, *U.S.A.* **80 B6** 46 55N 98 0W
Valley Falls, *Oreg., U.S.A.* **82 E3** 42 29N 120 17W
Valley Falls, *R.I., U.S.A.* **79 E13** 41 54N 71 24W
Valley Springs, *U.S.A.* **84 G6** 38 12N 120 50W
Valley View, *U.S.A.* **79 F8** 40 39N 76 33W
Valley Wells, *U.S.A.* **85 K11** 35 27N 115 46W
Valleyview, *Canada* **72 B5** 55 5N 117 17W
Vallimanca, Arroyo, *Argentina* **94 D4** 35 40S 59 10W
Valls, *Spain* **19 B6** 41 18N 1 15 E
Valmiera, *Latvia* **9 H21** 57 37N 25 29 E
Valognes, *France* **18 B3** 49 30N 1 28W
Valona = Vlóra, *Albania* **21 D8** 40 32N 19 28 E
Valozhyn, *Belarus* **17 A14** 54 3N 26 30 E
**Valparaíso**, *Chile* **94 C1** 33 2S 71 40W
Valparaíso, *Mexico* **86 C4** 22 50N 103 32W
Valparaiso, *U.S.A.* **76 E2** 41 28N 87 4W
Valparaíso □, *Chile* **94 C1** 33 2S 71 40W
Vals →, *S. Africa* **56 D4** 27 23S 26 30 E
Vals, Tanjung, *Indonesia* **37 F9** 8 26S 137 25 E
Valsad, *India* **40 J8** 20 40N 72 58 E
Valverde, *Canary Is.* **22 G2** 27 48N 17 55W
Valverde del Camino, *Spain* **19 D2** 37 35N 6 47W
Vammala, *Finland* **9 F20** 61 20N 22 54 E
Vámos, *Greece* **23 D6** 35 24N 24 13 E
Van, *Turkey* **25 G7** 38 30N 43 20 E
Van, L. = Van Gölü, *Turkey* **25 G7** 38 30N 43 0 E
Van Alstyne, *U.S.A.* **81 J6** 33 25N 96 35W
Van Blommestein Meer, *Surinam* **93 C7** 4 45N 55 5W
Van Buren, *Canada* **71 C6** 47 10N 67 55W
Van Buren, *Ark., U.S.A.* **81 H7** 35 26N 94 21W
Van Buren, *Maine, U.S.A.* **77 B11** 47 10N 67 58W
Van Buren, *Mo., U.S.A.* **81 G9** 37 0N 91 1W
Van Canh, *Vietnam* **38 F7** 13 37N 109 0 E
Van Diemen, C., *N. Terr., Australia* **60 B5** 11 9S 130 24 E
Van Diemen, C., *Queens., Australia* **62 B2** 16 30S 139 46 E
Van Diemen G., *Australia* **60 B5** 11 45S 132 0 E
Van Gölü, *Turkey* **25 G7** 38 30N 43 0 E
Van Horn, *U.S.A.* **81 K2** 31 3N 104 50W
Van Ninh, *Vietnam* **38 F7** 12 42N 109 14 E
Van Rees, Pegunungan, *Indonesia* **37 E9** 2 35S 138 15 E
Van Wert, *U.S.A.* **76 E3** 40 52N 84 35W
Vanadzor, *Armenia* **25 F7** 40 48N 44 30 E
Vanavara, *Russia* **27 C11** 60 22N 102 16 E
**Vancouver**, *Canada* **72 D4** 49 15N 123 10W
Vancouver, *U.S.A.* **84 E4** 45 38N 122 40W
Vancouver, C., *Australia* **61 G2** 35 2S 118 11 E
**Vancouver I.**, *Canada* **72 D3** 49 50N 126 0W
Vandalia, *Ill., U.S.A.* **80 F10** 38 58N 89 6W
Vandalia, *Mo., U.S.A.* **80 F9** 39 19N 91 29W
Vandenburg, *U.S.A.* **85 L6** 34 35N 120 33W
Vanderbijlpark, *S. Africa* **57 D4** 26 42S 27 54 E
Vandergrift, *U.S.A.* **78 F5** 40 36N 79 34W
Vanderhoof, *Canada* **72 C4** 54 0N 124 0W
Vanderkloof Dam, *S. Africa* **56 E3** 30 4S 24 40 E
Vanderlin I., *Australia* **62 B2** 15 44S 137 2 E
Vänern, *Sweden* **9 G15** 58 47N 13 30 E
Vänersborg, *Sweden* **9 G15** 58 26N 12 19 E
Vang Vieng, *Laos* **38 C4** 18 58N 102 32 E
Vanga, *Kenya* **54 C4** 4 35S 39 12 E
Vangaindrano, *Madag.* **57 C8** 23 21S 47 36 E
Vanguard, *Canada* **73 D7** 49 55N 107 20W
Vanino, *Russia* **27 E15** 48 50N 140 5 E
Vanna, *Norway* **8 A18** 70 6N 19 50 E
Vännäs, *Sweden* **8 E18** 63 58N 19 48 E
Vannes, *France* **18 C2** 47 40N 2 47W
Vanrhynsdorp, *S. Africa* **56 E2** 31 36S 18 44 E
Vansbro, *Sweden* **9 F16** 60 32N 14 15 E
Vansittart B., *Australia* **60 B4** 14 3S 126 17 E
Vantaa, *Finland* **9 F21** 60 18N 24 58 E
Vanua Levu, *Fiji* **59 C8** 16 33S 179 15 E
Vanua Mbalavu, *Fiji* **59 C9** 17 40S 178 57W
**Vanuatu** ■, *Pac. Oc.* **64 J8** 15 0S 168 0 E
Vanwyksvlei, *S. Africa* **56 E3** 30 18S 21 49 E
Vanzylsrus, *S. Africa* **56 D3** 26 52S 22 4 E
Vapnyarka, *Ukraine* **17 D15** 48 32N 28 45 E
**Varanasi**, *India* **43 G10** 25 22N 83 0 E
Varanger-halvøya, *Norway* **8 A23** 70 25N 29 30 E
Varangerfjorden, *Norway* **8 A23** 70 3N 29 25 E
Varaždin, *Croatia* **16 E9** 46 20N 16 20 E
Varberg, *Sweden* **9 H15** 57 6N 12 20 E
Vardar = Axiós →, *Greece* **21 D10** 40 57N 22 35 E
Varde, *Denmark* **9 J13** 55 38N 8 29 E
Vardø, *Norway* **8 A24** 70 23N 31 5 E
Varella, Mui, *Vietnam* **38 F7** 12 54N 109 26 E
Varėna, *Lithuania* **9 J21** 54 12N 24 30 E
Varese, *Italy* **18 D8** 45 48N 8 50 E
Varginha, *Brazil* **95 A6** 21 33S 45 25W
Varillas, *Chile* **94 A1** 24 0S 70 10W
Varkaus, *Finland* **9 E22** 62 19N 27 50 E
Varna, *Bulgaria* **21 C12** 43 13N 27 56 E
Värnamo, *Sweden* **9 H16** 57 10N 14 3 E
Vars, *Canada* **79 A9** 45 21N 75 21W
Varysburg, *U.S.A.* **78 D6** 42 46N 78 19W
Varzaneh, *Iran* **45 C7** 32 25N 52 40 E
Vasa Barris →, *Brazil* **93 F11** 11 10S 37 10W
Vascongadas = País Vasco □, *Spain* **19 A4** 42 50N 2 45W
Vasht = Khāsh, *Iran* **40 E2** 28 15N 61 15 E
Vasilevichi, *Belarus* **17 B15** 52 15N 29 50 E
Vasilkov = Vasylkiv, *Ukraine* **17 C16** 50 7N 30 15 E
Vaslui, *Romania* **17 E14** 46 38N 27 42 E
Vassar, *Canada* **73 D9** 49 10N 95 55W
Vassar, *U.S.A.* **76 D4** 43 22N 83 35W
**Västerås**, *Sweden* **9 G17** 59 37N 16 38 E
Västerbotten, *Sweden* **8 D18** 64 36N 20 4 E
Västerdalälven →, *Sweden* **9 F16** 60 30N 14 7 E
Västervik, *Sweden* **9 H17** 57 43N 16 33 E
Västmanland, *Sweden* **9 G16** 59 45N 16 20 E
Vasto, *Italy* **20 C6** 42 8N 14 40 E
Vasylkiv, *Ukraine* **17 C16** 50 7N 30 15 E
Vatersay, *U.K.* **12 E1** 56 55N 7 32W
**Vatican City** ■, *Europe* **20 D5** 41 54N 12 27 E
Vatili, *Cyprus* **23 D12** 35 6N 33 40 E
Vatnajökull, *Iceland* **8 D5** 64 30N 16 48W
Vatoa, *Fiji* **59 D9** 19 50S 178 13W
Vatólakkos, *Greece* **23 D5** 35 27N 23 53 E
Vatoloha, *Madag.* **57 B8** 17 52S 47 48 E
Vatomandry, *Madag.* **57 B8** 19 20S 48 59 E
Vatra-Dornei, *Romania* **17 E13** 47 22N 25 22 E
Vatrak →, *India* **42 H5** 23 9N 73 2 E
Vättern, *Sweden* **9 G16** 58 25N 14 30 E
Vaughn, *Mont., U.S.A.* **82 C8** 47 33N 111 33W
Vaughn, *N. Mex., U.S.A.* **83 J11** 34 36N 105 13W
Vaujours L., *Canada* **70 A5** 55 27N 74 15W
Vaupés = Uaupés →, *Brazil* **92 C5** 0 2N 67 16W
Vaupes □, *Colombia* **92 C4** 1 0N 71 0W
Vauxhall, *Canada* **72 C6** 50 5N 112 9W
Vav, *India* **42 G4** 24 22N 71 31 E
Vava'u, *Tonga* **59 D12** 18 36S 174 0W
Vawkavysk, *Belarus* **17 B13** 53 9N 24 30 E
Växjö, *Sweden* **9 H16** 56 52N 14 50 E
Vaygach, Ostrov, *Russia* **26 C7** 70 0N 60 0 E
Váyia, Ákra, *Greece* **23 C10** 36 15N 28 11 E
Vechte →, *Neths.* **15 B6** 52 34N 6 6 E
Vedea →, *Romania* **17 G13** 43 42N 25 41 E
Vedia, *Argentina* **94 C3** 34 30S 61 31W
Veendam, *Neths.* **15 A6** 53 5N 6 52 E
Veenendaal, *Neths.* **15 B5** 52 2N 5 34 E
Vefsna →, *Norway* **8 D15** 65 48N 13 10 E
Vega, *Norway* **8 D14** 65 40N 11 55 E
Vega, *U.S.A.* **81 H3** 35 15N 102 26W
Vegreville, *Canada* **72 C6** 53 30N 112 5W
Vejer de la Frontera, *Spain* **19 D3** 36 15N 5 59W
Vejle, *Denmark* **9 J13** 55 43N 9 30 E
Velas, C., *Costa Rica* **88 D2** 10 21N 85 52W
Velasco, Sierra de, *Argentina* **94 B2** 29 20S 67 10W
Velddrif, *S. Africa* **56 E2** 32 42S 18 11 E
Velebit Planina, *Croatia* **16 F8** 44 50N 15 20 E
Veles, *Macedonia* **21 D9** 41 46N 21 47 E
Vélez-Málaga, *Spain* **19 D3** 36 48N 4 5W
Vélez Rubio, *Spain* **19 D4** 37 41N 2 5W
Velhas →, *Brazil* **93 G10** 17 13S 44 49W
Velika Kapela, *Croatia* **16 F8** 45 10N 15 5 E
Velikaya →, *Russia* **24 C4** 57 48N 28 10 E
Velikaya Kema, *Russia* **30 B8** 45 30N 137 12 E
Veliki Ustyug, *Russia* **24 B8** 60 47N 46 20 E
Velikiye Luki, *Russia* **24 C5** 56 25N 30 32 E
Veliko Tŭrnovo, *Bulgaria* **21 C11** 43 5N 25 41 E
Velikonda Range, *India* **40 M11** 14 45N 79 10 E
Velletri, *Italy* **20 D5** 41 41N 12 47 E
Vellore, *India* **40 N11** 12 57N 79 10 E
Velsk, *Russia* **24 B7** 61 10N 42 5 E
Velva, *U.S.A.* **80 A4** 48 4N 100 56W
Venado Tuerto, *Argentina* **94 C3** 33 50S 62 0W
Vendée □, *France* **18 C3** 46 50N 1 35W
Vendôme, *France* **18 C4** 47 47N 1 3 E
Venézia, *Italy* **20 B5** 45 27N 12 21 E
Venézia, G. di, *Italy* **20 B5** 45 15N 13 0 E
**Venezuela** ■, *S. Amer.* **92 B5** 8 0N 66 0W
Venezuela, G. de, *Venezuela* **92 A4** 11 30N 71 0W
Vengurla, *India* **40 M8** 15 53N 73 45 E
**Venice** = Venézia, *Italy* **20 B5** 45 27N 12 21 E
Venice, *U.S.A.* **77 M4** 27 6N 82 27W
Venkatapuram, *India* **41 K12** 18 20N 80 30 E
Venlo, *Neths.* **15 C6** 51 22N 6 11 E
Vennesla, *Norway* **9 G12** 58 15N 7 59 E
Venray, *Neths.* **15 C6** 51 31N 6 0 E
Ventana, Punta de la, *Mexico* **86 C3** 24 4N 109 48W
Ventana, Sa. de la, *Argentina* **94 D3** 38 0S 62 30W
Ventersburg, *S. Africa* **56 D4** 28 7S 27 9 E
Venterstad, *S. Africa* **56 E4** 30 47S 25 48 E
Ventnor, *U.K.* **11 G6** 50 36N 1 12W
Ventotène, *Italy* **20 D5** 40 47N 13 25 E
Ventoux, Mt., *France* **18 D6** 44 10N 5 17 E
Ventspils, *Latvia* **9 H19** 57 25N 21 32 E
Ventuarí →, *Venezuela* **92 C5** 3 58N 67 2W
Ventucopa, *U.S.A.* **85 L7** 34 50N 119 29W
Ventura, *U.S.A.* **85 L7** 34 17N 119 18W
Venus B., *Australia* **63 F4** 38 40S 145 42 E
Vera, *Argentina* **94 B3** 29 30S 60 20W
Vera, *Spain* **19 D5** 37 15N 1 51W
Veracruz, *Mexico* **87 D5** 19 10N 96 10W
Veracruz □, *Mexico* **87 D5** 19 0N 96 15W
Veraval, *India* **42 J4** 20 53N 70 27 E
Verbánia, *Italy* **18 D8** 45 56N 8 33 E
Vercelli, *Italy* **18 D8** 45 19N 8 25 E
Verdalsøra, *Norway* **8 E14** 63 48N 11 30 E
Verde →, *Argentina* **96 E3** 41 56S 65 5W
Verde →, *Goiás, Brazil* **93 G8** 18 1S 50 14W
Verde →, *Mato Grosso do Sul, Brazil* **93 H8** 21 25S 52 20W
Verde →, *Chihuahua, Mexico* **86 B3** 26 29N 107 58W
Verde →, *Oaxaca, Mexico* **87 D5** 15 59N 97 50W
Verde →, *Veracruz, Mexico* **86 C4** 21 10N 102 50W
Verde →, *Paraguay* **94 A4** 23 9S 57 37W
Verde →, *U.S.A.* **74 D4** 33 33N 111 40W
Verde, Cay, *Bahamas* **88 B4** 23 0N 75 5W
Verden, *Germany* **16 B5** 52 55N 9 14 E
Verdi, *U.S.A.* **84 F7** 39 31N 119 59W
Verdun, *France* **18 B6** 49 9N 5 24 E
Vereeniging, *S. Africa* **57 D4** 26 38S 27 57 E
Verga, C., *Guinea* **50 F3** 10 30N 14 10W
Vergara, *Uruguay* **95 C5** 32 56S 53 57W
Vergemont Cr. →, *Australia* **62 C3** 24 16S 143 16 E
Vergennes, *U.S.A.* **79 B11** 44 10N 73 15W
Verín, *Spain* **19 B2** 41 57N 7 27W
Verkhnevilyuysk, *Russia* **27 C13** 63 27N 120 18 E
Verkhniy Baskunchak, *Russia* **25 E8** 48 14N 46 44 E
Verkhoyansk, *Russia* **27 C14** 67 35N 133 25 E
Verkhoyansk Ra. = Verkhoyanskiy Khrebet, *Russia* **27 C13** 66 0N 129 0 E
Verkhoyanskiy Khrebet, *Russia* **27 C13** 66 0N 129 0 E
Vermilion, *Canada* **73 C6** 53 20N 110 50W
Vermilion, *U.S.A.* **78 E2** 41 25N 82 22W
Vermilion →, *Alta., Canada* **73 C6** 53 22N 110 51W
Vermilion →, *Qué., Canada* **70 C5** 47 38N 72 56W
Vermilion, B., *U.S.A.* **81 L9** 29 45N 91 55W
Vermilion Bay, *Canada* **73 D10** 49 51N 93 34W
Vermilion L., *U.S.A.* **80 B8** 47 53N 92 26W
Vermillion, *U.S.A.* **80 D6** 42 47N 96 56W
**Vermont** □, *U.S.A.* **79 C12** 44 0N 73 0W
Vernal, *U.S.A.* **82 F9** 40 27N 109 32W
Vernalis, *U.S.A.* **84 H5** 37 36N 121 17W
Verner, *Canada* **70 C3** 46 25N 80 8W
Verneukpan, *S. Africa* **56 E3** 30 0S 21 0 E
Vernon, *Canada* **72 C5** 50 20N 119 15W
Vernon, *U.S.A.* **81 H5** 34 9N 99 17W
Vernonia, *U.S.A.* **84 E3** 45 52N 123 11W
Vero Beach, *U.S.A.* **77 M5** 27 38N 80 24W
Véroia, *Greece* **21 D10** 40 34N 22 12 E
Verona, *Canada* **79 B8** 44 29N 76 42W
**Verona**, *Italy* **20 B4** 45 27N 10 59 E
Verona, *U.S.A.* **80 D10** 42 59N 89 32W
**Versailles**, *France* **18 B5** 48 48N 2 8 E
Vert, C., *Senegal* **50 F2** 14 45N 17 30W
Verulam, *S. Africa* **57 D5** 29 38S 31 2 E
Verviers, *Belgium* **15 D5** 50 37N 5 52 E
Veselovskoye Vdkhr., *Russia* **25 E7** 46 58N 41 25 E
Vesoul, *France* **18 C7** 47 40N 6 11 E
Vesterålen, *Norway* **8 B16** 68 45N 15 0 E
Vestfjorden, *Norway* **8 C15** 67 55N 14 0 E
Vestmannaeyjar, *Iceland* **8 E3** 63 27N 20 15W
Vestspitsbergen, *Svalbard* **4 B8** 78 40N 17 0 E
Vestvågøy, *Norway* **8 B15** 68 18N 13 50 E
Vesuvio, *Italy* **20 D6** 40 49N 14 26 E
**Vesuvius, Mt.** = Vesuvio, *Italy* **20 D6** 40 49N 14 26 E
Veszprém, *Hungary* **17 E9** 47 8N 17 57 E

Wakkanai, Japan 30 B10 45 28N 141 35 E
Wakkerstroom, S. Africa 57 D5 27 24S 30 10 E
Wakool, Australia 63 F3 35 28S 144 23 E
Wakool →, Australia 63 F3 35 5S 143 33 E
Wakre, Indonesia 37 E8 0 19S 131 5 E
Wakuach, L., Canada 71 A6 55 34N 67 32W
Walamba, Zambia 55 E2 13 30S 28 42 E
Wałbrzych, Poland 16 C9 50 45N 16 18 E
Walbury Hill, U.K. 11 F6 51 21N 1 28W
Walcha, Australia 63 E5 30 55S 151 31 E
Walcheren, Neths. 15 C3 51 30N 3 35 E
Walcott, U.S.A. 82 F10 41 46N 106 51W
Wałcz, Poland 16 B9 53 17N 16 27 E
Waldburg Ra., Australia 61 D2 24 40S 117 35 E
Walden, Colo., U.S.A. 82 F10 40 44N 106 17W
Walden, N.Y., U.S.A. 79 E10 41 34N 74 11W
Waldport, U.S.A. 82 D1 44 26N 124 4W
Waldron, U.S.A. 81 H7 34 54N 94 5W
Walebing, Australia 61 F2 30 41S 116 13 E
**Wales** □, U.K. 11 E3 52 19N 4 43W
Walgett, Australia 63 E4 30 0S 148 5 E
Walgreen Coast, Antarctica 5 D15 75 15S 105 0W
Walker, U.S.A. 80 B7 47 6N 94 35W
Walker, L., Canada 71 B6 50 20N 67 11W
Walker L., Canada 73 C9 54 42N 95 57W
Walker L., U.S.A. 82 G4 38 42N 118 43W
Walkerston, Australia 62 C4 21 11S 149 8 E
Walkerton, Canada 78 B3 44 10N 81 10W
Wall, U.S.A. 80 D3 44 0N 102 8W
Walla Walla, U.S.A. 82 C4 46 4N 118 20W
Wallace, Idaho, U.S.A. 82 C6 47 28N 115 56W
Wallace, N.C., U.S.A. 77 H7 34 44N 77 59W
Wallaceburg, Canada 78 D2 42 34N 82 23W
**Wallachia** = Valahia, Romania 17 F13 44 35N 25 0 E
Wallal, Australia 63 D4 26 32S 146 7 E
Wallam Cr. →, Australia 63 D4 28 40S 147 20 E
Wallambin, L., Australia 61 F2 30 57S 117 35 E
Wallan, Australia 63 F3 37 26S 144 59 E
Wallangarra, Australia 63 D5 28 56S 151 58 E
Wallaroo, Australia 63 E2 33 56S 137 39 E
Wallenpaupack, L., U.S.A. 79 E9 41 25N 75 15W
Wallingford, U.S.A. 79 E12 41 27N 72 50W
**Wallis & Futuna, Is.**, Pac. Oc. 64 J10 13 18S 176 10W
Wallowa, U.S.A. 82 D5 45 34N 117 32W
Wallowa Mts., U.S.A. 82 D5 45 20N 117 30W
Walls, U.K. 12 A7 60 14N 1 33W
Wallula, U.S.A. 82 C4 46 5N 118 54W
Wallumbilla, Australia 63 D4 26 33S 149 9 E
Walmsley, L., Canada 73 A7 63 25N 108 36W
Walney, I. of, U.K. 10 C4 54 6N 3 15W
Walnut Creek, U.S.A. 84 H4 37 54N 122 4W
Walnut Ridge, U.S.A. 81 G9 36 4N 90 57W
Walpole, Australia 61 F2 34 58S 116 44 E
Walpole, U.S.A. 79 D13 42 9N 71 15W
Walsall, U.K. 11 E6 52 35N 1 58W
Walsenburg, U.S.A. 81 G2 37 38N 104 47W
Walsh, U.S.A. 81 G3 37 23N 102 17W
Walsh →, Australia 62 B3 16 31S 143 42 E
Walterboro, U.S.A. 77 J5 32 55N 80 40W
Walters, U.S.A. 81 H5 34 22N 98 19W
Waltham, U.S.A. 79 D13 42 23N 71 14W
Waltman, U.S.A. 82 E10 43 4N 107 12W
Walton, U.S.A. 79 D9 42 10N 75 8W
Walton-on-the-Naze, U.K. 11 F9 51 51N 1 17 E
Walvis Bay, Namibia 56 C1 23 0S 14 28 E
Walvisbaai = Walvis Bay, Namibia 56 C1 23 0S 14 28 E
Wamba, Dem. Rep. of the Congo 54 B2 2 10N 27 57 E
Wamba, Kenya 54 B4 0 58N 37 19 E
Wamego, U.S.A. 80 F6 39 12N 96 18W
Wamena, Indonesia 37 E9 4 4S 138 57 E
Wamsutter, U.S.A. 82 F9 41 40N 107 58W
Wamulan, Indonesia 37 E7 3 27S 126 7 E
Wan Xian, China 34 E8 38 47N 115 7 E
Wana, Pakistan 42 C3 32 20N 69 32 E
Wanaaring, Australia 63 D3 29 38S 144 9 E
Wanaka, N.Z. 59 L2 44 42S 169 9 E
Wanaka L., N.Z. 59 L2 44 33S 169 7 E
Wanapitei L., Canada 70 C3 46 45N 80 40W
Wandel Sea = McKinley Sea, Arctic 4 A7 82 0N 0 0 E
Wanderer, Zimbabwe 55 F3 19 36S 30 1 E
Wandhari, Pakistan 42 F2 27 42N 66 48 E
Wandoan, Australia 63 D4 26 5S 149 55 E
Wanfu, China 35 D12 40 8N 122 38 E
Wang →, Thailand 38 D2 17 8N 99 2 E
Wang Noi, Thailand 38 E3 14 13N 100 44 E
Wang Saphung, Thailand 38 D3 17 18N 101 46 E
Wang Thong, Thailand 38 D3 16 50N 100 26 E
Wanga, Dem. Rep. of the Congo 54 B2 2 58N 29 12 E
Wangal, Indonesia 37 F8 6 8S 134 9 E
Wanganella, Australia 63 F3 35 6S 144 49 E
Wanganui, N.Z. 59 H5 39 56S 175 3 E
Wangaratta, Australia 63 F4 36 21S 146 19 E
Wangary, Australia 63 E2 34 35S 135 29 E
Wangdu, China 34 E8 38 40N 115 7 E
Wangerooge, Germany 16 B4 53 47N 7 54 E
Wangi, Kenya 54 C5 1 58S 40 58 E
Wangiwangi, Indonesia 37 F6 5 22S 123 37 E
Wangqing, China 35 C15 43 12N 129 42 E
Wankaner, India 42 H4 22 35N 71 0 E
Wanless, Canada 73 C8 54 11N 101 21W
Wanning, Taiwan 38 C8 23 15N 121 17 E
Wanon Niwat, Thailand 38 D4 17 38N 103 46 E
Wanquan, China 34 D8 40 50N 114 40 E
Wanrong, China 34 G6 35 25N 110 50 E
Wantage, U.K. 11 F6 51 35N 1 25W
Wanxian, China 33 C5 30 42N 108 20 E
Wapakoneta, U.S.A. 76 E3 40 34N 84 12W
Wapato, U.S.A. 82 C3 46 27N 120 25W
Wapawekka L., Canada 73 C8 54 55N 104 40W
Wapikopa L., Canada 70 B2 52 56N 87 53W
Wapiti →, Canada 72 B5 55 5N 118 18W
Wappingers Falls, U.S.A. 79 E11 41 36N 73 55W
Wapsipinicon →, U.S.A. 80 E9 41 44N 90 19W
Warangal, India 40 L11 17 58N 79 35 E
Waraseoni, India 43 J9 21 45N 80 2 E
Waratah, Australia 62 G4 41 30S 145 30 E
Waratah B., Australia 63 F4 38 54S 146 5 E
Warburton, Vic., Australia 63 F4 37 47S 145 42 E
Warburton, W. Austral., Australia 61 E4 26 8S 126 35 E
Warburton Ra., Australia 61 E4 25 55S 126 28 E
Ward, N.Z. 59 J5 41 49S 174 11 E
Ward →, Australia 63 D4 26 28S 146 6 E
Ward Mt., U.S.A. 84 H8 37 12N 118 54W
Warden, S. Africa 57 D4 27 50S 29 0 E
Wardha, India 40 J11 20 45N 78 39 E
Wardha →, India 40 K11 19 57N 79 11 E
Ware, Canada 72 B3 57 26N 125 41W
Ware, U.S.A. 79 D12 42 16N 72 14W
Waregem, Belgium 15 D3 50 53N 3 27 E
Wareham, U.S.A. 79 E14 41 46N 70 43W
Waremme, Belgium 15 D5 50 43N 5 15 E
Warialda, Australia 63 D5 29 29S 150 33 E
Wariap, Indonesia 37 E8 1 30S 134 5 E
Warin Chamrap, Thailand 38 E5 15 12N 104 53 E
Warkopi, Indonesia 37 E8 1 12S 134 9 E
Warm Springs, U.S.A. 83 G5 38 10N 116 20W
Warman, Canada 73 C7 52 19N 106 30W
Warmbad, Namibia 56 D2 28 25S 18 42 E
Warmbad, S. Africa 57 C4 24 51S 28 19 E
Warminster, U.K. 11 F5 51 12N 2 10W
Warminster, U.S.A. 79 F9 40 12N 75 6W
Warner Mts., U.S.A. 82 F3 41 40N 120 15W
Warner Robins, U.S.A. 77 J4 32 37N 83 36W
Waroona, Australia 61 F2 32 50S 115 58 E
Warracknabeal, Australia 63 F3 36 9S 142 26 E
Warragul, Australia 63 F4 38 10S 145 58 E
Warrego →, Australia 63 E4 30 24S 145 21 E
Warrego Ra., Australia 62 C4 24 58S 146 0 E
Warren, Australia 63 E4 31 42S 147 51 E
Warren, Ark., U.S.A. 81 J8 33 37N 92 4W
Warren, Mich., U.S.A. 76 D4 42 30N 83 0W
Warren, Minn., U.S.A. 80 A6 48 12N 96 46W
Warren, Ohio, U.S.A. 78 E4 41 14N 80 49W
Warren, Pa., U.S.A. 78 E5 41 51N 79 9W
Warrenpoint, U.K. 13 B5 54 6N 6 15W
Warrensburg, Mo., U.S.A. 80 F8 38 46N 93 44W
Warrensburg, N.Y., U.S.A. 79 C11 43 29N 73 46W
Warrenton, S. Africa 56 D3 28 9S 24 47 E
Warrenton, U.S.A. 84 D3 46 10N 123 56W
Warri, Nigeria 50 G7 5 30N 5 41 E
Warrina, Australia 63 D2 28 12S 135 50 E
Warrington, U.K. 10 D5 53 24N 2 35W
Warrington, U.S.A. 77 K2 30 23N 87 17W
Warrington □, U.K. 10 D5 53 24N 2 35W
Warrnambool, Australia 63 F3 38 25S 142 30 E
Warroad, U.S.A. 80 A7 48 54N 95 19W
Warruwi, Australia 62 A1 11 36S 133 20 E
Warsa, Indonesia 37 E9 0 47S 135 55 E
Warsak Dam, Pakistan 42 B4 34 11N 71 19 E
**Warsaw** = Warszawa, Poland 17 B11 52 13N 21 0 E
Warsaw, Ind., U.S.A. 76 E3 41 14N 85 51W
Warsaw, N.Y., U.S.A. 78 D6 42 45N 78 8W
Warsaw, Ohio, U.S.A. 78 F3 40 20N 82 0W
Warszawa, Poland 17 B11 52 13N 21 0 E
Warta →, Poland 16 B8 52 35N 14 39 E
Warthe = Warta →, Poland 16 B8 52 35N 14 39 E
Waru, Indonesia 37 E8 3 30S 130 36 E
Warwick, Australia 63 D5 28 10S 152 1 E
Warwick, U.K. 11 E6 52 18N 1 35W
Warwick, N.Y., U.S.A. 79 E10 41 16N 74 22W
Warwick, R.I., U.S.A. 79 E13 41 42N 71 28W
**Warwickshire** □, U.K. 11 E6 52 14N 1 38W
Wasaga Beach, Canada 78 B4 44 31N 80 1W
Wasagaming, Canada 73 C9 50 39N 99 58W
Wasatch Ra., U.S.A. 82 F8 40 30N 111 15W
Wasbank, S. Africa 57 D5 28 15S 30 9 E
Wasco, Calif., U.S.A. 85 K7 35 36N 119 20W
Wasco, Oreg., U.S.A. 82 D3 45 36N 120 42W
Waseca, U.S.A. 80 C8 44 5N 93 30W
Wasekamio L., Canada 73 B7 56 45N 108 45W
Wash, The, U.K. 10 E8 52 58N 0 20 E
Washago, Canada 78 B5 44 45N 79 20W
Washburn, N. Dak., U.S.A. 80 B4 47 17N 101 2W
Washburn, Wis., U.S.A. 80 B9 46 40N 90 54W
Washim, India 40 J10 20 3N 77 0 E
Washington, U.K. 10 C6 54 55N 1 30W
**Washington**, D.C., U.S.A. 76 F7 38 54N 77 2W
Washington, Ga., U.S.A. 77 J4 33 44N 82 44W
Washington, Ind., U.S.A. 76 F2 38 40N 87 10W
Washington, Iowa, U.S.A. 80 E9 41 18N 91 42W
Washington, Mo., U.S.A. 80 F9 38 33N 91 1W
Washington, N.C., U.S.A. 77 H7 35 33N 77 3W
Washington, N.J., U.S.A. 79 F10 40 46N 74 59W
Washington, Pa., U.S.A. 78 F4 40 10N 80 15W
Washington, Utah, U.S.A. 83 H7 37 8N 113 31W
**Washington** □, U.S.A. 82 C3 47 30N 120 30W
Washington, Mt., U.S.A. 79 B13 44 16N 71 18W
Washington Court House, U.S.A. 76 F4 39 32N 83 26W
Washington I., U.S.A. 76 C2 45 23N 86 54W
Washougal, U.S.A. 84 E4 45 35N 122 21W
Wasian, Indonesia 37 E8 1 47S 133 19 E
Wasilla, U.S.A. 68 B5 61 35N 149 26W
Wasior, Indonesia 37 E8 2 43S 134 30 E
Waskaganish, Canada 70 B4 51 30N 78 40W
Waskaiowaka, L., Canada 73 B9 56 33N 96 23W
Waskesiu Lake, Canada 73 C7 53 55N 106 5W
Wasserkuppe, Germany 16 C5 50 29N 9 55 E
Waswanipi, Canada 70 C4 49 40N 76 29W
Waswanipi, L., Canada 70 C4 49 35N 76 40W
Watampone, Indonesia 37 E6 4 29S 120 25 E
Water Park Pt., Australia 62 C5 22 56S 150 47 E
Water Valley, U.S.A. 81 H10 34 10N 89 38W
Waterberge, S. Africa 57 C4 24 10S 28 0 E
Waterbury, Conn., U.S.A. 79 E11 41 33N 73 3W
Waterbury, Vt., U.S.A. 79 B12 44 20N 72 46W
Waterbury L., Canada 73 B8 58 10N 104 22W
Waterdown, Canada 78 C5 43 20N 79 53W
Waterford, Canada 78 D4 42 56N 80 17W
**Waterford**, Ireland 13 D4 52 15N 7 8W
Waterford, Calif., U.S.A. 84 H6 37 38N 120 46W
Waterford, Pa., U.S.A. 78 E5 41 57N 79 59W
Waterford □, Ireland 13 D4 52 10N 7 40W
Waterford Harbour, Ireland 13 D5 52 8N 6 58W
Waterhen L., Canada 73 C9 52 10N 99 40W
Waterloo, Belgium 15 D4 50 43N 4 25 E
Waterloo, Ont., Canada 78 C4 43 30N 80 32W
Waterloo, Qué., Canada 79 A12 45 22N 72 32W
Waterloo, Ill., U.S.A. 80 F9 38 20N 90 9W
Waterloo, Iowa, U.S.A. 80 D8 42 30N 92 21W
Waterloo, N.Y., U.S.A. 78 D8 42 54N 76 52W
Watersmeet, U.S.A. 80 B10 46 16N 89 11W
Waterton Nat. Park, U.S.A. 82 B7 48 45N 115 0W
Watertown, Conn., U.S.A. 79 E11 41 36N 73 7W
Watertown, N.Y., U.S.A. 79 C9 43 59N 75 55W
Watertown, S. Dak., U.S.A. 80 C6 44 54N 97 7W
Watertown, Wis., U.S.A. 80 D10 43 12N 88 43W
Waterval-Boven, S. Africa 57 D5 25 40S 30 18 E
Waterville, Canada 79 A13 45 16N 71 54W
Waterville, Maine, U.S.A. 77 C11 44 33N 69 38W
Waterville, N.Y., U.S.A. 79 D9 42 56N 75 23W
Waterville, Pa., U.S.A. 78 E7 41 19N 77 21W
Waterville, Wash., U.S.A. 82 C3 47 39N 120 4W
Watervliet, U.S.A. 79 D11 42 44N 73 42W
Wates, Indonesia 37 G14 7 51S 110 10 E
Watford, Canada 78 D3 42 57N 81 53W
Watford, U.K. 11 F7 51 40N 0 24W
Watford City, U.S.A. 80 B3 47 48N 103 17W
Wathaman →, Canada 73 B8 57 16N 102 59W
Wathaman L., Canada 73 B8 56 58N 103 44W
Watheroo, Australia 61 F2 30 15S 116 0 E
Wating, China 34 G4 35 40N 106 38 E
Watkins Glen, U.S.A. 78 D8 42 23N 76 52W
Watling I. = San Salvador I., Bahamas 89 B5 24 0N 74 40W
Watonga, U.S.A. 81 H5 35 51N 98 25W
Watrous, Canada 73 C7 51 40N 105 25W
Watrous, U.S.A. 81 H2 35 48N 104 59W
Watsa, Dem. Rep. of the Congo 54 B2 3 4N 29 30 E
Watseka, U.S.A. 76 E2 40 47N 87 44W
Watson, Australia 61 F5 30 29S 131 31 E
Watson, Canada 73 C8 52 10N 104 30W
Watson Lake, Canada 72 A3 60 6N 128 49W
Watsontown, U.S.A. 78 E8 41 5N 76 52W
Watsonville, U.S.A. 84 J5 36 55N 121 45W
Wattiwarriganna Cr. →, Australia 63 D2 28 57S 136 10 E
Watuata = Batuata, Indonesia 37 F6 6 12S 122 42 E
Watubela, Kepulauan, Indonesia 37 E8 4 28S 131 35 E
Watubela Is. = Watubela, Kepulauan, Indonesia 37 E8 4 28S 131 35 E
Wau, Sudan 49 F6 7 45N 28 1 E
Waubamik, Canada 78 A4 45 27N 80 1W
Waubay, U.S.A. 80 C6 45 20N 97 18W
Wauchope, N.S.W., Australia 63 E5 31 28S 152 45 E
Wauchope, N. Terr., Australia 62 C1 20 36S 134 15 E
Waukarlycarly, L., Australia 60 D3 21 18S 121 56 E
Waukegan, U.S.A. 75 B9 42 22N 87 50W
Waukesha, U.S.A. 76 D1 43 1N 88 14W
Waukon, U.S.A. 80 D9 43 16N 91 29W
Waupaca, U.S.A. 80 C10 44 21N 89 5W
Waupun, U.S.A. 80 D10 43 38N 88 44W
Waurika, U.S.A. 81 H6 34 10N 98 0W
Wausau, U.S.A. 80 C10 44 58N 89 38W
Wautoma, U.S.A. 80 C10 44 4N 89 18W
Wauwatosa, U.S.A. 76 D2 43 3N 88 0W
Waveney →, U.K. 11 E9 52 35N 1 39 E
Waverley, N.Z. 59 H5 39 46S 174 37 E
Waverly, Iowa, U.S.A. 80 D8 42 44N 92 29W
Waverly, N.Y., U.S.A. 79 E8 42 1N 76 32W
Wavre, Belgium 15 D4 50 43N 4 38 E
Wâw, Sudan 51 G11 7 45N 28 1 E
Wāw al Kabīr, Libya 51 C9 25 20N 16 43 E
Wawa, Canada 70 C3 47 59N 84 47W
Wawanesa, Canada 73 D9 49 36N 99 40W
Wawona, U.S.A. 84 H7 37 32N 119 39W
Waxahachie, U.S.A. 81 J6 32 24N 96 51W
Way, L., Australia 61 E3 26 45S 120 16 E
Waycross, U.S.A. 77 K4 31 13N 82 21W
Wayland, U.S.A. 78 D7 42 34N 77 35W
Wayne, Nebr., U.S.A. 80 D6 42 14N 97 1W
Wayne, W. Va., U.S.A. 76 F4 38 13N 82 27W
Waynesboro, Ga., U.S.A. 77 J4 33 6N 82 1W
Waynesboro, Miss., U.S.A. 77 K1 31 40N 88 39W
Waynesboro, Pa., U.S.A. 76 F7 39 45N 77 35W
Waynesboro, Va., U.S.A. 76 F6 38 4N 78 53W
Waynesburg, U.S.A. 76 F5 39 54N 80 11W
Waynesville, U.S.A. 77 H4 35 28N 82 58W
Waynoka, U.S.A. 81 G5 36 35N 98 53W
Wazirabad, Pakistan 42 C6 32 30N 74 8 E
We, Indonesia 36 C1 5 51N 95 18 E
Weald, The, U.K. 11 F8 51 4N 0 20 E
Wear →, U.K. 10 C6 54 55N 1 23W
Weatherford, Okla., U.S.A. 81 H5 35 32N 98 43W
Weatherford, Tex., U.S.A. 81 J6 32 46N 97 48W
Weaverville, U.S.A. 82 F2 40 44N 122 56W
Webb City, U.S.A. 81 G7 37 9N 94 28W
Webequie, Canada 70 B2 52 59N 87 21W
Webster, Mass., U.S.A. 79 D13 42 3N 71 53W
Webster, N.Y., U.S.A. 78 C7 43 13N 77 26W
Webster, S. Dak., U.S.A. 80 C6 45 20N 97 31W
Webster City, U.S.A. 80 D8 42 28N 93 49W
Webster Springs, U.S.A. 76 F5 38 29N 80 25W
Weda, Indonesia 37 D7 0 21N 127 50 E
Weda, Teluk, Indonesia 37 D7 0 30N 127 50 E
Weddell I., Falk. Is. 96 G4 51 50S 61 0W
Weddell Sea, Antarctica 5 D1 72 30S 40 0W
Wedderburn, Australia 63 F3 36 26S 143 33 E
Wedgeport, Canada 71 D6 43 44N 65 59W
Wedza, Zimbabwe 55 F3 18 40S 31 33 E
Wee Waa, Australia 63 E4 30 11S 149 26 E
Weed, U.S.A. 82 F2 41 25N 122 23W
Weed Heights, U.S.A. 84 G7 38 59N 119 13W
Weedsport, U.S.A. 79 C8 43 3N 76 35W
Weedville, U.S.A. 78 E6 41 17N 78 30W
Weenen, S. Africa 57 D5 28 48S 30 7 E
Weert, Neths. 15 C5 51 15N 5 43 E
Wei He →, Hebei, China 34 F8 36 10N 115 45 E
Wei He →, Shaanxi, China 34 G6 34 38N 110 15 E
Weichang, China 35 D9 41 58N 117 49 E
Weichuan, China 34 G7 34 20N 113 59 E
Weiden, Germany 16 D7 49 41N 12 10 E
Weifang, China 35 F10 36 44N 119 7 E
Weihai, China 35 F12 37 30N 122 6 E
**Weimar**, Germany 16 C6 50 58N 11 19 E
Weinan, China 34 G5 34 31N 109 29 E
Weipa, Australia 62 A3 12 40S 141 50 E
Weir →, Australia 63 D4 28 20S 149 50 E
Weir →, Canada 73 B10 56 54N 93 21W
Weir River, Canada 73 B10 56 49N 94 6W
Weirton, U.S.A. 78 F4 40 24N 80 35W
Weiser, U.S.A. 82 D5 44 10N 117 0W
Weishan, China 35 G9 34 47N 117 5 E
Weiyuan, China 34 G3 35 7N 104 10 E
Wejherowo, Poland 17 A10 54 35N 18 12 E
Wekusko L., Canada 73 C9 54 40N 99 50W
Welch, U.S.A. 76 G5 37 26N 81 35W
Welkom, S. Africa 56 D4 28 0S 26 46 E
Welland, Canada 78 D5 43 0N 79 15W
Welland →, U.K. 11 E7 52 51N 0 5W
Wellesley Is., Australia 62 B2 16 42S 139 30 E
Wellingborough, U.K. 11 E7 52 19N 0 41W
Wellington, Australia 63 E4 32 35S 148 59 E
Wellington, Canada 78 C7 43 57N 77 20W
**Wellington**, N.Z. 59 J5 41 19S 174 46 E
Wellington, S. Africa 56 E2 33 38S 19 1 E
Wellington, Somst., U.K. 11 G4 50 58N 3 13W
Wellington, Telford & Wrekin, U.K. 11 E5 52 42N 2 30W
Wellington, Colo., U.S.A. 80 E2 40 42N 105 0W
Wellington, Kans., U.S.A. 81 G6 37 16N 97 24W
Wellington, Nev., U.S.A. 84 G7 38 45N 119 23W
Wellington, Ohio, U.S.A. 78 E2 41 10N 82 13W
Wellington, Tex., U.S.A. 81 H4 34 51N 100 13W
Wellington, I., Chile 96 F2 49 30S 75 0W
Wellington, L., Australia 63 F4 38 6S 147 20 E
Wells, U.K. 11 F5 51 13N 2 39W
Wells, Maine, U.S.A. 79 C14 43 20N 70 35W
Wells, N.Y., U.S.A. 79 C10 43 24N 74 17W
Wells, Nev., U.S.A. 82 F6 41 7N 114 58W
Wells, L., Australia 61 E3 26 44S 123 15 E
Wells, Mt., Australia 60 C4 17 25S 127 8 E
Wells Gray Prov. Park, Canada 72 C4 52 30N 120 15W
Wells-next-the-Sea, U.K. 10 E8 52 57N 0 51 E
Wells River, U.S.A. 79 B12 44 9N 72 4W
Wellsboro, U.S.A. 78 E7 41 45N 77 18W
Wellsburg, U.S.A. 78 F4 40 16N 80 37W
Wellsville, N.Y., U.S.A. 78 D7 42 7N 77 57W
Wellsville, Ohio, U.S.A. 78 F4 40 36N 80 39W
Wellsville, Utah, U.S.A. 82 F8 41 38N 111 56W
Wellton, U.S.A. 83 K6 32 40N 114 8W
Wels, Austria 16 D8 48 9N 14 1 E
Welshpool, U.K. 11 E4 52 39N 3 8W
Welwyn Garden City, U.K. 11 F7 51 48N 0 12W
Wem, U.K. 10 E5 52 52N 2 44W
Wembere →, Tanzania 54 C3 4 10S 34 15 E
Wemindji, Canada 70 B4 53 0N 78 49W
Wen Xian, China 34 G7 34 55N 113 5 E
Wenatchee, U.S.A. 82 C3 47 25N 120 19W
Wenchang, China 38 C8 19 38N 110 42 E
Wenchi, Ghana 50 G5 7 46N 2 8W
Wenchow = Wenzhou, China 33 D7 28 0N 120 38 E
Wenden, U.S.A. 85 M13 33 49N 113 33W
Wendeng, China 35 F12 37 15N 122 5 E
Wendesi, Indonesia 37 E8 2 30S 134 17 E
Wendover, U.S.A. 82 F6 40 44N 114 2W
Wenlock →, Australia 62 A3 12 2S 141 55 E
Wenshan, China 32 D5 23 20N 104 18 E
Wenshang, China 34 G9 35 45N 116 30 E
Wenshui, China 34 F7 37 26N 112 1 E
Wensleydale, U.K. 10 C6 54 17N 2 0W
Wensu, China 32 B3 41 15N 80 10 E
Wensum →, U.K. 10 E8 52 40N 1 15 E
Wentworth, Australia 63 E3 34 2S 141 54 E
Wentzel L., Canada 72 B6 59 2N 114 28W
Wenut, Indonesia 37 E8 3 11S 133 19 E
Wenxi, China 34 G6 35 20N 111 10 E
Wenxian, China 34 H3 32 43N 104 36 E
Wenzhou, China 33 D7 28 0N 120 38 E
Weott, U.S.A. 82 F2 40 20N 123 55W
Wepener, S. Africa 56 D4 29 42S 27 3 E
Werda, Botswana 56 D3 25 24S 23 15 E
Weri, Indonesia 37 E8 3 10S 132 38 E
Werra →, Germany 16 C5 51 24N 9 39 E
Werrimull, Australia 63 E3 34 25S 141 38 E
Werris Creek, Australia 63 E5 31 18S 150 38 E
Weser →, Germany 16 B5 53 36N 8 28 E
Wesiri, Indonesia 37 F7 7 30S 126 30 E
Weslemkoon L., Canada 78 A7 45 2N 77 25W
Wesleyville, Canada 71 C9 49 8N 53 36W
Wesleyville, U.S.A. 78 D4 42 9N 80 0W
Wessel, C., Australia 62 A2 10 59S 136 46 E
Wessel Is., Australia 62 A2 11 10S 136 45 E
Wessington Springs, U.S.A. 80 C5 44 5N 98 34W
West, U.S.A. 81 K6 31 48N 97 6W
West →, U.S.A. 79 D12 42 52N 72 33W
West Baines →, Australia 60 C4 15 38S 129 59 E
**West Bank** □, Asia 47 C4 32 6N 35 13 E
West Bend, U.S.A. 76 D1 43 25N 88 11W
**West Bengal** □, India 43 H13 23 0N 88 0 E
West Berkshire □, U.K. 11 F6 51 25N 1 17W
West Beskids = Západné Beskydy, Europe 17 D10 49 30N 19 0 E
West Branch, U.S.A. 76 C3 44 17N 84 14W
West Branch Susquehanna →, U.S.A. 79 F8 40 53N 76 48W
West Bromwich, U.K. 11 E6 52 32N 1 59W
West Burra, U.K. 12 A7 60 5N 1 21W
West Canada Cr. →, U.S.A. 79 C10 43 1N 74 58W
West Cape Howe, Australia 61 G2 35 8S 117 36 E
West Chazy, U.S.A. 79 B11 44 49N 73 28W
West Chester, U.S.A. 79 G9 39 58N 75 36W
West Columbia, U.S.A. 81 L7 29 9N 95 39W
West Covina, U.S.A. 85 L9 34 4N 117 54W
West Des Moines, U.S.A. 80 E8 41 35N 93 43W
West Dunbartonshire □, U.K. 12 F4 55 59N 4 30W
West End, Bahamas 88 A4 26 41N 78 58W
West Falkland, Falk. Is. 96 G5 51 40S 60 0W
West Fargo, U.S.A. 80 B6 46 52N 96 54W
West Farmington, U.S.A. 78 E4 41 23N 80 58W
West Fjord = Vestfjorden, Norway 8 C15 67 55N 14 0 E
West Fork Trinity →, U.S.A. 81 J6 32 48N 96 54W
West Frankfort, U.S.A. 80 G10 37 54N 88 55W
West Hartford, U.S.A. 79 E12 41 45N 72 44W
West Haven, U.S.A. 79 E12 41 17N 72 57W
West Hazleton, U.S.A. 79 F9 40 58N 76 0W
West Helena, U.S.A. 81 H9 34 33N 90 38W
West Hurley, U.S.A. 79 E10 41 59N 74 7W
West Ice Shelf, Antarctica 5 C7 67 0S 85 0 E
**West Indies**, Cent. Amer. 89 D7 15 0N 65 0W
West Jordan, U.S.A. 82 F8 40 36N 111 56W
West Lorne, Canada 78 D3 42 36N 81 36W
West Lothian □, U.K. 12 F5 55 54N 3 36W
West Lunga →, Zambia 55 E1 13 6S 24 39 E
West Memphis, U.S.A. 81 H9 35 9N 90 11W

**West Midlands** □, U.K. 11 E6 52 26N 2 0W
West Mifflin, U.S.A. 78 F5 40 22N 79 52W
West Milton, U.S.A. 78 E8 41 1N 76 50W
West Monroe, U.S.A. 81 J8 32 31N 92 9W
West Newton, U.S.A. 78 F5 40 14N 79 46W
West Nicholson, Zimbabwe 55 G2 21 2S 29 20 E
West Palm Beach, U.S.A. 77 M5 26 43N 80 3W
West Plains, U.S.A. 81 G9 36 44N 91 51W
West Point, N.Y., U.S.A. 79 E11 41 24N 73 58W
West Point, Nebr., U.S.A. 80 E6 41 51N 96 43W
West Point, Va., U.S.A. 76 G7 37 32N 76 48W
West Pt. = Ouest, Pte. de l', Canada 71 C7 49 52N 64 40W
West Pt., Australia 63 F2 35 1S 135 56 E
West Road →, Canada 72 C4 53 18N 122 53W
West Rutland, U.S.A. 75 B12 43 38N 73 5W
West Schelde = Westerschelde →, Neths. 15 C3 51 25N 3 25 E
West Seneca, U.S.A. 78 D6 42 51N 78 48W
West Siberian Plain, Russia 28 C11 62 0N 75 0 E
**West Sussex** □, U.K. 11 G7 50 55N 0 30W
West-Terschelling, Neths. 15 A5 53 22N 5 13 E
West Valley City, U.S.A. 82 F8 40 42N 111 57W
**West Virginia** □, U.S.A. 76 F5 38 45N 80 30W
West-Vlaanderen □, Belgium 15 D2 51 0N 3 0 E
West Walker →, U.S.A. 84 G7 38 54N 119 9W
West Wyalong, Australia 63 E4 33 56S 147 10 E
West Yellowstone, U.S.A. 82 D8 44 40N 111 6W
**West Yorkshire** □, U.K. 10 D6 53 45N 1 40W
Westall Pt., Australia 63 E1 32 55S 134 4 E
Westbrook, U.S.A. 77 D10 43 41N 70 22W
Westbury, Australia 62 G4 41 30S 146 51 E
Westby, U.S.A. 80 A2 48 52N 104 3W
Westend, U.S.A. 85 K9 35 42N 117 24W
Westerland, Germany 9 J13 54 54N 8 17 E
Westerly, U.S.A. 79 E13 41 22N 71 50W
Western □, Kenya 54 B3 0 30N 34 30 E
Western □, Uganda 54 B3 1 45N 31 30 E
Western □, Zambia 55 F1 15 15S 24 30 E
**Western Australia** □, Australia 61 E2 25 0S 118 0 E
**Western Cape** □, S. Africa 56 E3 34 0S 20 0 E
Western Dvina = Daugava →, Latvia 9 H21 57 4N 24 3 E
Western Ghats, India 40 N9 14 0N 75 0 E
**Western Isles** □, U.K. 12 D1 57 30N 7 10W
**Western Sahara** ■, Africa 50 D3 25 0N 13 0W
**Western Samoa** ■, Pac. Oc. 59 B13 14 0S 172 0W
Westernport, U.S.A. 76 F6 39 29N 79 3W
Westerschelde →, Neths. 15 C3 51 25N 3 25 E
Westerwald, Germany 16 C4 50 38N 7 56 E
Westfield, Mass., U.S.A. 79 D12 42 7N 72 45W
Westfield, N.Y., U.S.A. 78 D5 42 20N 79 35W
Westfield, Pa., U.S.A. 78 E7 41 55N 77 32W
Westhill, U.K. 12 D6 57 9N 2 19W
Westhope, U.S.A. 80 A4 48 55N 101 1W
Westland Bight, N.Z. 59 K3 42 55S 170 5 E
Westlock, Canada 72 C6 54 9N 113 55W
Westmar, Australia 63 D4 27 55S 149 44 E
**Westmeath** □, Ireland 13 C4 53 33N 7 34W
Westminster, U.S.A. 76 F7 39 34N 76 59W
Westmont, U.S.A. 78 F6 40 19N 78 58W
Westmorland, U.S.A. 85 M11 33 2N 115 37W
Weston, Oreg., U.S.A. 82 D4 45 49N 118 26W
Weston, W. Va., U.S.A. 76 F5 39 2N 80 28W
Weston I., Canada 70 B4 52 33N 79 36W
Weston-super-Mare, U.K. 11 F5 51 21N 2 58W
Westover, U.S.A. 78 F6 40 45N 78 40W
Westport, Canada 79 B8 44 40N 76 25W
Westport, Ireland 13 C2 53 48N 9 31W
Westport, N.Z. 59 J3 41 46S 171 37 E
Westport, N.Y., U.S.A. 79 B11 44 11N 73 26W
Westport, Oreg., U.S.A. 84 D3 46 8N 123 23W
Westport, Wash., U.S.A. 84 D2 46 53N 124 6W
Westray, Canada 73 C8 53 36N 101 24W
Westray, U.K. 12 B5 59 18N 3 0W
Westree, Canada 70 C3 47 26N 81 34W
Westville, U.S.A. 84 F6 39 8N 120 42W
Westwood, U.S.A. 82 F3 40 18N 121 0W
Wetar, Indonesia 37 F7 7 30S 126 30 E
Wetaskiwin, Canada 72 C6 52 55N 113 24W
Wete, Tanzania 52 F7 5 4S 39 43 E
Wetherby, U.K. 10 D6 53 56N 1 23W
Wethersfield, U.S.A. 79 E12 41 42N 72 40W
Wetteren, Belgium 15 D3 51 0N 3 53 E
Wetzlar, Germany 16 C5 50 32N 8 31 E
Wewoka, U.S.A. 81 H6 35 9N 96 30W
Wexford, Ireland 13 D5 52 20N 6 28W
**Wexford** □, Ireland 13 D5 52 20N 6 25W
Wexford Harbour, Ireland 13 D5 52 20N 6 25W
Weyburn, Canada 73 D8 49 40N 103 50W
Weymouth, Canada 71 D6 44 30N 66 1W
Weymouth, U.K. 11 G5 50 37N 2 28W
Weymouth, U.S.A. 79 D14 42 13N 70 58W
Weymouth, C., Australia 62 A3 12 37S 143 27 E
Wha Ti, Canada 68 B8 63 8N 117 16W
Whakatane, N.Z. 59 G6 37 57S 177 1 E
Whale →, Canada 71 A6 58 15N 67 40W
Whale Cove, Canada 73 A10 62 11N 92 36W
Whales, B. of, Antarctica 5 D12 78 0S 165 0W
Whalsay, U.K. 12 A8 60 22N 0 59W
Whangamomona, N.Z. 59 H5 39 8S 174 44 E
Whangarei, N.Z. 59 F5 35 43S 174 21 E
Whangarei Harb., N.Z. 59 F5 35 45S 174 28 E
Wharfe →, U.K. 10 D6 53 51N 1 9W
Wharfedale, U.K. 10 C5 54 6N 2 1W
Wharton, N.J., U.S.A. 79 F10 40 54N 74 35W
Wharton, Pa., U.S.A. 78 E6 41 31N 78 1W
Wharton, Tex., U.S.A. 81 L6 29 19N 96 6W
Wheatland, Calif., U.S.A. 84 F5 39 1N 121 25W
Wheatland, Wyo., U.S.A. 80 D2 42 3N 104 58W
Wheatley, Ont., Canada 78 D2 42 6N 82 27W
Wheatley, Ont., Canada 78 D2 42 6N 82 27W
Wheaton, Md., U.S.A. 76 F7 39 3N 77 3W
Wheaton, Minn., U.S.A. 80 C6 45 48N 96 30W
Wheelbarrow Pk., U.S.A. 84 H10 37 26N 116 5W
Wheeler, Oreg., U.S.A. 82 D2 45 41N 123 53W
Wheeler, Tex., U.S.A. 81 H4 35 27N 100 16W
Wheeler →, Canada 71 A6 57 2N 67 13W
Wheeler L., U.S.A. 77 H2 34 48N 87 23W
Wheeler Pk., N. Mex., U.S.A. 83 H11 36 34N 105 25W
Wheeler Pk., Nev., U.S.A. 83 G6 38 57N 114 15W
Wheeler Ridge, U.S.A. 85 L8 35 0N 118 57W
Wheeling, U.S.A. 78 F4 40 4N 80 43W
Whernside, U.K. 10 C5 54 14N 2 24W
Whiskey Jack L., Canada 73 B8 58 23N 101 55W
Whistleduck Cr. →, Australia 62 C2 20 15S 135 18 E
Whistler, Canada 72 C4 50 7N 122 58W
Whitby, Canada 78 C6 43 52N 78 56W
**Whitby**, U.K. 10 C7 54 29N 0 37W
White →, Ark., U.S.A. 81 J9 33 57N 91 5W
White →, Ind., U.S.A. 76 F2 38 25N 87 45W
White →, S. Dak., U.S.A. 80 D5 43 42N 99 27W
White →, Tex., U.S.A. 81 J4 33 14N 100 56W
White →, Utah, U.S.A. 82 F9 40 4N 109 41W
White →, Vt., U.S.A. 79 C12 43 37N 72 20W
White →, Wash., U.S.A. 84 C4 47 12N 122 15W
White, L., Australia 60 D4 21 9S 128 56 E
White B., Canada 71 C8 50 0N 56 35W
White Bird, U.S.A. 82 D5 45 46N 116 18W
White Butte, U.S.A. 80 B3 46 23N 103 18W
White City, U.S.A. 82 E2 42 26N 122 51W
White Cliffs, Australia 63 E3 30 50S 143 10 E
White Hall, U.S.A. 80 F9 39 26N 90 24W
White Haven, U.S.A. 79 E9 41 4N 75 47W
White Horse, Vale of, U.K. 11 F6 51 37N 1 30W
White I., N.Z. 59 G6 37 30S 177 13 E
White L., Canada 79 A8 45 18N 76 31W
White L., U.S.A. 81 L8 29 44N 92 30W
White Mountain Peak, U.S.A. 83 G4 37 38N 118 15W
White Mts., Calif., U.S.A. 84 H8 37 30N 118 15W
White Mts., N.H., U.S.A. 75 B12 44 15N 71 15W
White Mts., N.H., U.S.A. 76 C10 44 10N 71 20W
White Nile = Nîl el Abyad →, Sudan 51 E12 15 38N 32 31 E
White Otter L., Canada 70 C1 49 5N 91 55W
White Pass, U.S.A. 84 D5 46 38N 121 24W
White Plains, U.S.A. 79 E11 41 2N 73 46W
White River, Canada 70 C2 48 35N 85 20W
White River, S. Africa 57 D5 25 20S 31 0 E
White River, U.S.A. 80 D4 43 34N 100 45W
White Rock, Canada 84 A4 49 2N 122 48W
White Russia = Belarus ■, Europe 17 B14 53 30N 27 0 E
White Sea = Beloye More, Russia 24 A6 66 30N 38 0 E
White Sulphur Springs, Mont., U.S.A. 82 C8 46 33N 110 54W
White Sulphur Springs, W. Va., U.S.A. 76 G5 37 48N 80 18W
White Swan, U.S.A. 84 D6 46 23N 120 44W
Whitecliffs, N.Z. 59 K3 43 26S 171 55 E
Whitecourt, Canada 72 C5 54 10N 115 45W
Whiteface Mt., U.S.A. 79 B11 44 22N 73 54W
Whitefield, U.S.A. 79 B13 44 23N 71 37W
Whitefish, U.S.A. 82 B6 48 25N 114 20W
Whitefish L., Canada 73 A7 62 41N 106 48W
Whitefish Point, U.S.A. 76 B3 46 45N 84 59W
Whitegull, L., Canada 71 A7 55 27N 64 17W
Whitehall, Mich., U.S.A. 76 D2 43 24N 86 21W
Whitehall, Mont., U.S.A. 82 D7 45 52N 112 6W
Whitehall, N.Y., U.S.A. 79 C11 43 33N 73 24W
Whitehall, Wis., U.S.A. 80 C9 44 22N 91 19W
Whitehaven, U.K. 10 C4 54 33N 3 35W
Whitehorse, Canada 72 A1 60 43N 135 3W
Whitemark, Australia 62 G4 40 7S 148 3 E
Whiteriver, U.S.A. 83 K9 33 50N 109 58W
Whitesand →, Canada 72 A5 60 9N 115 45W
Whitesboro, N.Y., U.S.A. 79 C9 43 7N 75 18W
Whitesboro, Tex., U.S.A. 81 J6 33 39N 96 54W
Whiteshell Prov. Park, Canada 73 D9 50 0N 95 40W
Whitesville, U.S.A. 78 D7 42 2N 77 46W
Whiteville, U.S.A. 77 H6 34 20N 78 42W
Whitewater, U.S.A. 76 D1 42 50N 88 44W
Whitewater Baldy, U.S.A. 83 K9 33 20N 108 39W
Whitewater L., Canada 70 B2 50 50N 89 10W
Whitewood, Australia 62 C3 21 28S 143 30 E
Whitewood, Canada 73 C8 50 20N 102 20W
Whithorn, U.K. 12 G4 54 44N 4 26W
Whitianga, N.Z. 59 G5 36 47S 175 41 E
Whitman, U.S.A. 79 D14 42 5N 70 56W
Whitney, Canada 78 A6 45 31N 78 14W
**Whitney, Mt.**, U.S.A. 84 J8 36 35N 118 18W
Whitney Point, U.S.A. 79 D9 42 20N 75 58W
Whitstable, U.K. 11 F9 51 21N 1 3 E
Whitsunday I., Australia 62 C4 20 15S 149 4 E
Whittier, U.S.A. 85 M8 33 58N 118 3W
Whittlesea, Australia 63 F4 37 27S 145 9 E
Wholdaia L., Canada 73 A8 60 43N 104 20W
Whyalla, Australia 63 E2 33 2S 137 30 E
Wiarton, Canada 78 B3 44 40N 81 10W
Wiay, U.K. 12 D1 57 24N 7 13W
Wibaux, U.S.A. 80 B2 46 59N 104 11W
Wichian Buri, Thailand 38 E3 15 39N 101 7 E
**Wichita**, U.S.A. 81 G6 37 42N 97 20W
Wichita Falls, U.S.A. 81 J5 33 54N 98 30W
Wick, U.K. 12 C5 58 26N 3 5W
Wicked Pt., Canada 78 C7 43 52N 77 15W
Wickenburg, U.S.A. 83 K7 33 58N 112 44W
Wickepin, Australia 61 F2 32 50S 117 30 E
Wickham, Australia 60 D2 20 42S 117 11 E
Wickham, C., Australia 62 F3 39 35S 143 57 E
Wickliffe, U.S.A. 78 E3 41 36N 81 28W
Wicklow, Ireland 13 D5 52 59N 6 3W
**Wicklow** □, Ireland 13 D5 52 57N 6 25W
Wicklow Hd., Ireland 13 D6 52 58N 6 0W
Wicklow Mts., Ireland 13 C5 52 58N 6 26W
Widgeegoara Cr. →, Australia 63 D4 28 51S 146 34 E
Widgiemooltha, Australia 61 F3 31 30S 121 34 E
Widnes, U.K. 10 D5 53 23N 2 45W
Wieluń, Poland 17 C10 51 15N 18 34 E
Wien, Austria 16 D9 48 12N 16 22 E
Wiener Neustadt, Austria 16 E9 47 49N 16 16 E
**Wiesbaden**, Germany 16 C5 50 4N 8 14 E
Wigan, U.K. 10 D5 53 33N 2 38W
Wiggins, Colo., U.S.A. 80 E2 40 14N 104 4W
Wiggins, Miss., U.S.A. 81 K10 30 51N 89 8W
**Wight, I. of** □, U.K. 11 G6 50 40N 1 20W
Wigston, U.K. 11 E6 52 35N 1 6W
Wigton, U.K. 10 C4 54 50N 3 10W
Wigtown, U.K. 12 G4 54 53N 4 27W
Wigtown B., U.K. 12 G4 54 46N 4 15W
Wilber, U.S.A. 80 E6 40 29N 96 58W
Wilberforce, Canada 78 A6 45 2N 78 13W
Wilberforce, C., Australia 62 A2 11 54S 136 35 E
Wilburton, U.S.A. 81 H7 34 55N 95 19W
Wilcannia, Australia 63 E3 31 30S 143 26 E
Wilcox, U.S.A. 78 E6 41 35N 78 41W
Wildrose, U.S.A. 85 J9 36 14N 117 11W
Wildspitze, Austria 16 E6 46 53N 10 53 E
Wilge →, S. Africa 57 D4 27 3S 28 20 E
Wilhelm II Coast, Antarctica 5 C7 68 0S 90 0 E
Wilhelmshaven, Germany 16 B5 53 31N 8 7 E
Wilhelmstal, Namibia 56 C2 21 58S 16 21 E
Wilkes-Barre, U.S.A. 79 E9 41 15N 75 53W
Wilkie, Canada 73 C7 52 27N 108 42W
Wilkinsburg, U.S.A. 78 F5 40 26N 79 53W
Wilkinson Lakes, Australia 61 E5 29 40S 132 39 E
Willandra Creek →, Australia 63 E4 33 22S 145 52 E
Willapa B., U.S.A. 82 C2 46 40N 124 0W
Willapa Hills, U.S.A. 84 D3 46 35N 123 25W
Willard, N.Y., U.S.A. 78 D8 42 40N 76 50W
Willard, Ohio, U.S.A. 78 E2 41 3N 82 44W
Willcox, U.S.A. 83 K9 32 15N 109 50W
**Willemstad**, Neth. Ant. 89 D6 12 5N 69 0W
Willet, U.S.A. 79 D9 42 28N 75 55W
William →, Canada 73 B7 59 8N 109 19W
William 'Bill' Dannely Res., U.S.A. 77 J2 32 10N 87 10W
William Creek, Australia 63 D2 28 58S 136 22 E
Williams, Australia 61 F2 33 2S 116 52 E
Williams, Ariz., U.S.A. 83 J7 35 15N 112 11W
Williams, Calif., U.S.A. 84 F4 39 9N 122 9W
Williams Harbour, Canada 71 B8 52 33N 55 47W
Williams Lake, Canada 72 C4 52 10N 122 10W
Williamsburg, Ky., U.S.A. 77 G3 36 44N 84 10W
Williamsburg, Pa., U.S.A. 78 F6 40 28N 78 12W
Williamsburg, Va., U.S.A. 76 G7 37 17N 76 44W
Williamson, N.Y., U.S.A. 78 C7 43 14N 77 11W
Williamson, W. Va., U.S.A. 76 G4 37 41N 82 17W
Williamsport, U.S.A. 78 E7 41 15N 77 0W
Williamston, U.S.A. 77 H7 35 51N 77 4W
Williamstown, Australia 63 F3 37 51S 144 52 E
Williamstown, Ky., U.S.A. 76 F3 38 38N 84 34W
Williamstown, Mass., U.S.A. 79 D11 42 41N 73 12W
Williamstown, N.Y., U.S.A. 79 C9 43 26N 75 53W
Willimantic, U.S.A. 79 E12 41 43N 72 13W
Willingboro, U.S.A. 76 E8 40 3N 74 54W
Willis Group, Australia 62 B5 16 18S 150 0 E
Williston, S. Africa 56 E3 31 20S 20 53 E
Williston, Fla., U.S.A. 77 L4 29 23N 82 27W
Williston, N. Dak., U.S.A. 80 A3 48 9N 103 37W
Williston L., Canada 72 B4 56 0N 124 0W
Willits, U.S.A. 82 G2 39 25N 123 21W
Willmar, U.S.A. 80 C7 45 7N 95 3W
Willoughby, U.S.A. 78 E3 41 39N 81 24W
Willow Bunch, Canada 73 D7 49 20N 105 35W
Willow L., Canada 72 A5 62 10N 119 8W
Willow Wall, The, China 35 C12 42 10N 122 0 E
Willowick, U.S.A. 78 E3 41 38N 81 28W
Willowlake →, Canada 72 A4 62 42N 123 8W
Willowmore, S. Africa 56 E3 33 15S 23 30 E
Willows, U.S.A. 84 F4 39 31N 122 12W
Willowvale = Gatyana, S. Africa 57 E4 32 16S 28 31 E
Wills, L., Australia 60 D4 21 25S 128 51 E
Wills Cr. →, Australia 62 C3 22 43S 140 2 E
Willsboro, U.S.A. 79 B11 44 21N 73 24W
Willunga, Australia 63 F2 35 15S 138 30 E
Wilmette, U.S.A. 76 D2 42 5N 87 42W
Wilmington, Australia 63 E2 32 39S 138 7 E
**Wilmington**, Del., U.S.A. 76 F8 39 45N 75 33W
Wilmington, N.C., U.S.A. 77 H7 34 14N 77 55W
Wilmington, Ohio, U.S.A. 76 F4 39 27N 83 50W
Wilmington, Vt., U.S.A. 79 D12 42 52N 72 52W
Wilmslow, U.K. 10 D5 53 19N 2 13W
Wilpena →, Australia 63 E2 31 25S 139 29 E
Wilsall, U.S.A. 82 D8 45 59N 110 38W
Wilson, N.C., U.S.A. 77 H7 35 44N 77 55W
Wilson, N.Y., U.S.A. 78 C6 43 19N 78 50W
Wilson, Pa., U.S.A. 79 F9 40 41N 75 15W
Wilson →, Australia 60 C4 16 48S 128 16 E
Wilson Bluff, Australia 61 F4 31 41S 129 0 E
Wilson Inlet, Australia 61 G2 35 0S 117 22 E
Wilsons Promontory, Australia 63 F4 38 55S 146 25 E
Wilton, U.S.A. 80 B4 47 10N 100 47W
Wilton →, Australia 62 A1 14 45S 134 33 E
**Wiltshire** □, U.K. 11 F6 51 18N 1 53W
Wiltz, Lux. 15 E5 49 57N 5 55 E
Wiluna, Australia 61 E3 26 36S 120 14 E
Wimborne Minster, U.K. 11 G6 50 48N 1 59W
Wimmera →, Australia 63 F3 36 8S 141 56 E
Winam G., Kenya 54 C3 0 20S 34 15 E
Winburg, S. Africa 56 D4 28 30S 27 2 E
Winchendon, U.S.A. 79 D12 42 41N 72 3W
**Winchester**, U.K. 11 F6 51 4N 1 18W
Winchester, Conn., U.S.A. 79 E11 41 53N 73 9W
Winchester, Idaho, U.S.A. 82 C5 46 14N 116 38W
Winchester, Ind., U.S.A. 76 E3 40 10N 84 59W
Winchester, Ky., U.S.A. 76 G3 38 0N 84 11W
Winchester, N.H., U.S.A. 79 D12 42 46N 72 23W
Winchester, Nev., U.S.A. 85 J11 36 6N 115 10W
Winchester, Tenn., U.S.A. 77 H2 35 11N 86 7W
Winchester, Va., U.S.A. 76 F6 39 11N 78 10W
Wind →, U.S.A. 82 E9 43 12N 108 12W
Wind River Range, U.S.A. 82 E9 43 0N 109 30W
Windau = Ventspils, Latvia 9 H19 57 25N 21 32 E
Windber, U.S.A. 78 F6 40 14N 78 50W
Winder, U.S.A. 77 J4 34 0N 83 45W
**Windermere**, Cumb., U.K. 10 C5 54 23N 2 55W
Windermere, Cumb., U.K. 10 C5 54 22N 2 56W
**Windhoek**, Namibia 56 C2 22 35S 17 4 E
Windom, U.S.A. 80 D7 43 52N 95 7W
Windorah, Australia 62 D3 25 24S 142 36 E
Window Rock, U.S.A. 83 J9 35 41N 109 3W
Windrush →, U.K. 11 F6 51 43N 1 24W
Windsor, Australia 63 E5 33 37S 150 50 E
Windsor, N.S., Canada 71 D7 44 59N 64 5W
Windsor, Ont., Canada 78 D2 42 18N 83 0W
Windsor, U.K. 11 F7 51 29N 0 36W
Windsor, Colo., U.S.A. 80 E2 40 29N 104 54W
Windsor, Conn., U.S.A. 79 E12 41 50N 72 39W
Windsor, Mo., U.S.A. 80 F8 38 32N 93 31W
Windsor, N.Y., U.S.A. 79 D9 42 5N 75 37W
Windsor, Vt., U.S.A. 79 C12 43 29N 72 24W
Windsor & Maidenhead □, U.K. 11 F7 51 29N 0 40W
Windsorton, S. Africa 56 D3 28 16S 24 44 E
**Windward Is.**, W. Indies 89 D7 13 0N 61 0W
Windward Passage = Vientos, Paso de los, Caribbean 89 C5 20 0N 74 0W
Winefred L., Canada 73 B6 55 30N 110 30W
Winfield, U.S.A. 81 G6 37 15N 96 59W
Wingate Mts., Australia 60 B5 14 25S 130 40 E
Wingham, Australia 63 E5 31 48S 152 22 E
Wingham, Canada 78 C3 43 55N 81 20W
Winisk, Canada 70 A2 55 20N 85 15W
Winisk →, Canada 70 A2 55 17N 85 5W
Winisk L., Canada 70 B2 52 55N 87 22W
Wink, U.S.A. 81 K3 31 45N 103 9W
Winkler, Canada 73 D9 49 10N 97 56W
Winlock, U.S.A. 84 D4 46 30N 122 56W
Winnebago, L., U.S.A. 76 D1 44 0N 88 26W
Winnecke Cr. →, Australia 60 C5 18 35S 131 34 E
Winnemucca, U.S.A. 82 F5 40 58N 117 44W
Winnemucca L., U.S.A. 82 F4 40 7N 119 21W
Winnett, U.S.A. 82 C9 47 0N 108 21W
Winnfield, U.S.A. 81 K8 31 56N 92 38W
Winnibigoshish, L., U.S.A. 80 B7 47 27N 94 13W
**Winnipeg**, Canada 73 D9 49 54N 97 9W
Winnipeg →, Canada 73 C9 50 38N 96 19W
**Winnipeg, L.**, Canada 73 C9 52 0N 97 0W
Winnipeg Beach, Canada 73 C9 50 30N 96 58W
Winnipegosis, Canada 73 C9 51 39N 99 55W
Winnipegosis L., Canada 73 C9 52 30N 100 0W
Winnipesaukee, L., U.S.A. 79 C13 43 38N 71 21W
Winnisquam L., U.S.A. 79 C13 43 33N 71 31W
Winnsboro, La., U.S.A. 81 J9 32 10N 91 43W
Winnsboro, S.C., U.S.A. 77 H5 34 23N 81 5W
Winnsboro, Tex., U.S.A. 81 J7 32 58N 95 17W
Winokapau, L., Canada 71 B7 53 15N 62 50W
Winona, Minn., U.S.A. 80 C9 44 3N 91 39W
Winona, Miss., U.S.A. 81 J10 33 29N 89 44W
Winooski, U.S.A. 79 B11 44 29N 73 11W
Winooski →, U.S.A. 79 B11 44 32N 73 17W
Winschoten, Neths. 15 A7 53 9N 7 3 E
Winsford, U.K. 10 D5 53 12N 2 31W
Winslow, Ariz., U.S.A. 83 J8 35 2N 110 42W
Winslow, Wash., U.S.A. 84 C4 47 38N 122 31W
Winsted, U.S.A. 79 E11 41 55N 73 4W
Winston-Salem, U.S.A. 77 G5 36 6N 80 15W
Winter Garden, U.S.A. 77 L5 28 34N 81 35W
Winter Haven, U.S.A. 77 M5 28 1N 81 44W
Winter Park, U.S.A. 77 L5 28 36N 81 20W
Winterhaven, U.S.A. 85 N12 32 47N 114 39W
Winters, U.S.A. 84 G5 38 32N 121 58W
Wintersville, U.S.A. 78 F4 40 23N 80 42W
Winterswijk, Neths. 15 C6 51 58N 6 43 E
Winterthur, Switz. 18 C8 47 30N 8 44 E
Winthrop, U.S.A. 82 B3 48 28N 120 10W
Winton, Australia 62 C3 22 24S 143 3 E
Winton, N.Z. 59 M2 46 8S 168 20 E
Wirrulla, Australia 63 E1 32 24S 134 31 E
Wisbech, U.K. 11 E8 52 41N 0 9 E
**Wisconsin** □, U.S.A. 80 C10 44 45N 89 30W
Wisconsin →, U.S.A. 80 D9 43 0N 91 15W
Wisconsin Rapids, U.S.A. 80 C10 44 23N 89 49W
Wisdom, U.S.A. 82 D7 45 37N 113 27W
Wishaw, U.K. 12 F5 55 46N 3 54W
Wishek, U.S.A. 80 B5 46 16N 99 33W
Wisła →, Poland 17 A10 54 22N 18 55 E
Wismar, Germany 16 B6 53 54N 11 29 E
Wisner, U.S.A. 80 E6 41 59N 96 55W
Witbank, S. Africa 57 D4 25 51S 29 14 E
Witdraai, S. Africa 56 D3 26 58S 20 48 E
Witham, U.K. 11 F8 51 48N 0 40 E
Witham →, U.K. 10 E7 52 59N 0 2W
Withernsea, U.K. 10 D8 53 44N 0 1 E
Witney, U.K. 11 F6 51 48N 1 28W
Witnossob →, Namibia 56 D3 26 55S 20 37 E
**Wittenberge**, Germany 16 B6 53 0N 11 45 E
Wittenoom, Australia 60 D2 22 15S 118 20 E
Wkra →, Poland 17 B11 52 27N 20 44 E
Wlingi, Indonesia 37 H15 8 5S 112 25 E
Włocławek, Poland 17 B10 52 40N 19 3 E
Włodawa, Poland 17 C12 51 33N 23 31 E
Woburn, U.S.A. 79 D13 42 29N 71 9W
Wodian, China 34 H7 32 50N 112 35 E
Wokam, Indonesia 37 F8 5 45S 134 28 E
Woking, U.K. 11 F7 51 19N 0 34W
Wokingham □, U.K. 11 F7 51 25N 0 51W
Wolf →, Canada 72 A2 60 17N 132 33W
Wolf Creek, U.S.A. 82 C7 47 0N 112 4W
Wolf L., Canada 72 A2 60 24N 131 40W
Wolf Point, U.S.A. 80 A2 48 5N 105 39W
Wolfe I., Canada 79 B8 44 7N 76 20W
Wolfeboro, U.S.A. 79 C13 43 35N 71 13W
Wolfsberg, Austria 16 E8 46 50N 14 52 E
Wolfsburg, Germany 16 B6 52 25N 10 48 E
Wolin, Poland 16 B8 53 50N 14 37 E
Wollaston, Is., Chile 96 H3 55 40S 67 30W
Wollaston L., Canada 73 B8 58 7N 103 10W
Wollaston Lake, Canada 73 B8 58 3N 103 33W
Wollaston Pen., Canada 68 B8 69 30N 115 0W
Wollongong, Australia 63 E5 34 25S 150 54 E
Wolmaransstad, S. Africa 56 D4 27 12S 25 59 E
Wolseley, S. Africa 56 E2 33 26S 19 7 E
Wolsey, U.S.A. 80 C5 44 24N 98 28W
Wolstenholme, C., Canada 66 C12 62 35N 77 30W
Wolvega, Neths. 15 B6 52 52N 6 0 E
Wolverhampton, U.K. 11 E5 52 35N 2 7W
Wondai, Australia 63 D5 26 20S 151 49 E
Wongalarroo L., Australia 63 E3 31 32S 144 0 E
Wongan Hills, Australia 61 F2 30 51S 116 37 E
Wŏnju, S. Korea 35 F14 37 22N 127 58 E
Wonosari, Indonesia 37 G14 7 58S 110 36 E
Wonosobo, Indonesia 37 G13 7 22S 109 54 E
Wonowon, Canada 72 B4 56 44N 121 48W
Wŏnsan, N. Korea 35 E14 39 11N 127 27 E
Wonthaggi, Australia 63 F4 38 37S 145 37 E
Wood Buffalo Nat. Park, Canada 72 B6 59 0N 113 41W
Wood Is., Australia 60 C3 16 24S 123 19 E
Wood L., Canada 73 B8 55 17N 103 17W
Woodah I., Australia 62 A2 13 27S 136 10 E
Woodbourne, U.S.A. 79 E10 41 46N 74 36W
Woodbridge, Canada 78 C5 43 47N 79 36W
Woodbridge, U.K. 11 E9 52 6N 1 20 E
Woodburn, U.S.A. 82 D2 45 9N 122 51W
Woodenbong, Australia 63 D5 28 24S 152 39 E
Woodend, Australia 63 F3 37 20S 144 33 E
Woodford, Australia 63 D5 26 58S 152 47 E
Woodfords, U.S.A. 84 G7 38 47N 119 50W
Woodlake, U.S.A. 84 J7 36 25N 119 6W
Woodland, Calif., U.S.A. 84 G5 38 41N 121 46W
Woodland, Maine, U.S.A. 77 C12 45 9N 67 25W
Woodland, Pa., U.S.A. 78 F6 40 59N 78 21W

Woodland, *Wash., U.S.A.* .. **84 E4** 45 54N 122 45W
Woodland Caribou Prov. Park, *Canada* .......... **73 C10** 51 0N 94 45W
Woodridge, *Canada* ...... **73 D9** 49 20N 96 9W
Woodroffe, Mt., *Australia* .. **61 E5** 26 20S 131 45 E
Woods, L., *Australia* ...... **62 B1** 17 50S 133 30 E
Woods, L. of the, *Canada* .. **73 D10** 49 15N 94 45W
Woodside, *Australia* ...... **63 F4** 38 31S 146 52 E
Woodstock, *Australia* ..... **62 B4** 19 35S 146 50 E
Woodstock, *N.B., Canada* .. **71 C6** 46 11N 67 37W
Woodstock, *Ont., Canada* .. **78 C4** 43 10N 80 45W
Woodstock, *U.K.* .......... **11 F6** 51 51N 1 20W
Woodstock, *Ill., U.S.A.* .... **80 D10** 42 19N 88 27W
Woodstock, *Vt., U.S.A.* .... **79 C12** 43 37N 72 31W
Woodsville, *U.S.A.* ....... **79 B13** 44 9N 72 2W
Woodville, *N.Z.* .......... **59 J5** 40 20S 175 53 E
Woodville, *Miss., U.S.A.* ... **81 K9** 31 6N 91 18W
Woodville, *Tex., U.S.A.* .... **81 K7** 30 47N 94 25W
Woodward, *U.S.A.* ....... **81 G5** 36 26N 99 24W
Woody, *U.S.A.* ........... **85 K8** 35 42N 118 50W
Woody →, *Canada* ....... **73 C8** 52 31N 100 51W
Woolamai, C., *Australia* .... **63 F4** 38 30S 145 23 E
Wooler, *U.K.* ............ **10 B5** 55 33N 2 1W
Woolgoolga, *Australia* .... **63 E5** 30 6S 153 11 E
Woomera, *Australia* ...... **63 E2** 31 5S 136 50 E
Woonsocket, *R.I., U.S.A.* .. **79 E13** 42 0N 71 31W
Woonsocket, *S. Dak., U.S.A.* **80 C5** 44 3N 98 17W
Wooramel →, *Australia* .. **61 E1** 25 47S 114 10 E
Wooramel Roadhouse, *Australia* ............. **61 E1** 25 45S 114 17 E
Wooster, *U.S.A.* .......... **78 F3** 40 48N 81 56W
Worcester, *S. Africa* ...... **56 E2** 33 39S 19 27 E
**Worcester**, *U.K.* ......... **11 E5** 52 11N 2 12W
Worcester, *Mass., U.S.A.* .. **79 D13** 42 16N 71 48W
Worcester, *N.Y., U.S.A.* ... **79 D10** 42 36N 74 45W
Worcestershire □, *U.K.* .... **11 E5** 52 13N 2 10W
Workington, *U.K.* ......... **10 C4** 54 39N 3 33W
Worksop, *U.K.* ........... **10 D6** 53 18N 1 7W
Workum, *Neths.* ......... **15 B5** 52 59N 5 26 E
Worland, *U.S.A.* ......... **82 D10** 44 1N 107 57W
**Worms**, *Germany* ........ **16 D5** 49 37N 8 21 E
Worsley, *Canada* ......... **72 B5** 56 31N 119 8W
Wortham, *U.S.A.* ......... **81 K6** 31 47N 96 28W
Worthing, *U.K.* .......... **11 G7** 50 49N 0 21W
Worthington, *Minn., U.S.A.* **80 D7** 43 37N 95 36W
Worthington, *Pa., U.S.A.* .. **78 F5** 40 50N 79 38W
Wosi, *Indonesia* .......... **37 E7** 0 15S 128 0 E
Wou-han = Wuhan, *China* . **33 C6** 30 31N 114 18 E
Wousi = Wuxi, *China* ..... **33 C7** 31 33N 120 18 E
Wowoni, *Indonesia* ....... **37 E6** 4 5S 123 5 E
Wrangel I. = Vrangelya, Ostrov, *Russia* ......... **27 B19** 71 0N 180 0 E
Wrangell, *U.S.A.* ......... **72 B2** 56 28N 132 23W
Wrangell Mts., *U.S.A.* ..... **68 B5** 61 30N 142 0W
Wrath, C., *U.K.* .......... **12 C3** 58 38N 5 1W
Wray, *U.S.A.* ............ **80 E3** 40 5N 102 13W
Wrekin, The, *U.K.* ........ **11 E5** 52 41N 2 32W
Wrens, *U.S.A.* ........... **77 J4** 33 12N 82 23W
Wrexham, *U.K.* .......... **10 D4** 53 3N 3 0W
Wrexham □, *U.K.* ........ **10 D5** 53 1N 2 58W
Wright, *U.S.A.* ........... **80 D2** 43 47N 105 30W
Wright Pt., *Canada* ....... **78 C3** 43 48N 81 44W
Wrightson Mt., *U.S.A.* .... **83 L8** 31 42N 110 51W
Wrightwood, *U.S.A.* ...... **85 L9** 34 21N 117 38W
Wrigley, *Canada* ......... **68 B7** 63 16N 123 37W
**Wrocław**, *Poland* ........ **17 C9** 51 5N 17 5 E
Września, *Poland* ........ **17 B9** 52 21N 17 36 E
Wu Jiang →, *China* ...... **32 D5** 29 40N 107 20 E
Wu'an, *China* ........... **34 F8** 36 40N 114 15 E
Wubin, *Australia* ......... **61 F2** 30 6S 116 37 E
Wubu, *China* ............ **34 F6** 37 28N 110 42 E
Wuchang, *China* ......... **35 B14** 44 55N 127 5 E
Wucheng, *China* ......... **34 F9** 37 12N 116 20 E
Wuchuan, *China* ......... **34 D6** 41 5N 111 28 E
Wudi, *China* ............ **35 F9** 37 40N 117 35 E
Wuding He →, *China* ..... **34 F6** 37 2N 110 23 E
Wudinna, *Australia* ....... **63 E2** 33 0S 135 22 E
Wudu, *China* ............ **34 H3** 33 22N 104 54 E
**Wuhan**, *China* .......... **33 C6** 30 31N 114 18 E
Wuhe, *China* ............ **35 H9** 33 10N 117 50 E
Wuhsi = Wuxi, *China* ..... **33 C7** 31 33N 120 18 E
Wuhu, *China* ............ **33 C6** 31 22N 118 21 E
Wukari, *Nigeria* .......... **50 G7** 7 51N 9 42 E
Wulajie, *China* .......... **35 B14** 44 6N 126 33 E
Wulanbulang, *China* ...... **34 D6** 41 5N 110 55 E
Wular L., *India* .......... **43 B6** 34 20N 74 30 E
Wulian, *China* ........... **35 G10** 35 40N 119 12 E
Wuliaru, *Indonesia* ....... **37 F8** 7 27S 131 0 E
Wuluk'omushih Ling, *China* **32 C3** 36 25N 87 25 E
Wulumuchi = Ürümqi, *China* .............. **26 E9** 43 45N 87 45 E
Wundowie, *Australia* ..... **61 F2** 31 47S 116 23 E
Wunnummin L., *Canada* ... **70 B2** 52 55N 89 10W
Wuntho, *Burma* .......... **41 H19** 23 55N 95 45 E
Wuppertal, *Germany* ...... **16 C4** 51 16N 7 12 E
Wuppertal, *S. Africa* ..... **56 E2** 32 13S 19 12 E
Wuqing, *China* .......... **35 E9** 39 23N 117 4 E
Wurtsboro, *U.S.A.* ....... **79 E10** 41 35N 74 29W
**Würzburg**, *Germany* ..... **16 D5** 49 46N 9 55 E
Wushan, *China* .......... **34 G3** 34 43N 104 53 E
Wusuli Jiang = Ussuri →, *Asia* ................. **30 A7** 48 27N 135 0 E
Wutai, *China* ............ **34 E7** 38 40N 113 12 E
Wuting = Huimin, *China* .. **35 F9** 37 27N 117 28 E
Wutonghaolai, *China* ..... **35 C11** 42 50N 120 5 E
Wutongqiao, *China* ....... **32 D5** 29 22N 103 50 E
Wuwei, *China* ........... **32 C5** 37 57N 102 34 E
Wuxi, *China* ............ **33 C7** 31 33N 120 18 E
Wuxiang, *China* ......... **34 F7** 36 49N 112 50 E
Wuyang, *China* .......... **34 H7** 33 25N 113 35 E
Wuyi, *China* ............ **34 F8** 37 46N 115 56 E
Wuyi Shan, *China* ........ **33 D6** 27 0N 117 0 E
Wuyuan, *China* .......... **34 D5** 41 2N 108 20 E
Wuzhai, *China* .......... **34 E6** 38 54N 111 48 E
Wuzhi Shan, *China* ....... **38 C7** 18 45N 109 45 E
Wuzhong, *China* ......... **34 E4** 38 2N 106 12 E
Wuzhou, *China* .......... **33 D6** 23 30N 111 18 E
Wyaaba Cr. →, *Australia* . **62 B3** 16 27S 141 35 E
Wyalkatchem, *Australia* ... **61 F2** 31 8S 117 22 E
Wyalusing, *U.S.A.* ........ **79 E8** 41 40N 76 16W
Wyandotte, *U.S.A.* ....... **76 D4** 42 12N 83 9W
Wyandra, *Australia* ...... **63 D4** 27 12S 145 56 E
Wyangala Res., *Australia* . **63 E4** 33 54S 149 0 E
Wyara, L., *Australia* ...... **63 D3** 28 42S 144 14 E
Wycheproof, *Australia* .... **63 F3** 36 5S 143 17 E
Wye →, *U.K.* ........... **11 F5** 51 38N 2 40W
Wyemandoo, *Australia* .... **61 E2** 28 28S 118 29 E
Wymondham, *U.K.* ....... **11 E9** 52 35N 1 7 E
Wymore, *U.S.A.* ......... **80 E6** 40 7N 96 40W
Wyndham, *Australia* ...... **60 C4** 15 33S 128 3 E
Wyndham, *N.Z.* .......... **59 M2** 46 20S 168 51 E
Wynne, *U.S.A.* ........... **81 H9** 35 14N 90 47W
Wynyard, *Australia* ....... **62 G4** 41 5S 145 44 E
Wynyard, *Canada* ........ **73 C8** 51 45N 104 10W
Wyola L., *Australia* ....... **61 E5** 29 8S 130 17 E
Wyoming, *Canada* ........ **78 D2** 42 57N 82 7W
**Wyoming** □, *U.S.A.* ...... **82 E10** 43 0N 107 30W
Wyomissing, *U.S.A.* ...... **79 F9** 40 20N 75 59W
Wyong, *Australia* ........ **63 E5** 33 14S 151 24 E
Wytheville, *U.S.A.* ....... **76 G5** 36 57N 81 5W


# X


Xaçmaz, *Azerbaijan* ...... **25 F8** 41 31N 48 42 E
Xai-Xai, *Mozam.* ........ **57 D5** 25 6S 33 31 E
Xainza, *China* ........... **32 C3** 30 58N 88 35 E
Xangongo, *Angola* ....... **56 B2** 16 45S 15 5 E
Xankändi, *Azerbaijan* ..... **25 G8** 39 52N 46 49 E
Xánthi, *Greece* .......... **21 D11** 41 10N 24 58 E
Xanxerê, *Brazil* .......... **95 B5** 26 53S 52 23W
Xapuri, *Brazil* ........... **92 F5** 10 35S 68 35W
Xar Moron He →, *China* . **35 C11** 43 25N 120 35 E
Xátiva, *Spain* ........... **19 C5** 38 59N 0 32W
Xau, L., *Botswana* ....... **56 C3** 21 15S 24 44 E
Xavantina, *Brazil* ........ **95 A5** 21 15S 52 48W
Xenia, *U.S.A.* ........... **76 F4** 39 41N 83 56W
Xeropotamos →, *Cyprus* . **23 E11** 34 42N 32 33 E
Xhora, *S. Africa* ......... **57 E4** 31 55S 28 38 E
Xhumo, *Botswana* ....... **56 C3** 21 7S 24 35 E
Xi Jiang →, *China* ....... **33 D6** 22 5N 113 20 E
Xi Xian, *China* .......... **34 F6** 36 41N 110 58 E
Xia Xian, *China* ......... **34 G6** 35 8N 111 12 E
Xiachengzi, *China* ....... **35 B16** 44 40N 130 18 E
Xiaguan, *China* ......... **32 D5** 25 32N 100 16 E
Xiajin, *China* ........... **34 F9** 36 56N 116 0 E
**Xiamen**, *China* ......... **33 D6** 24 25N 118 4 E
**Xi'an**, *China* ........... **34 G5** 34 15N 109 0 E
Xian Xian, *China* ........ **34 E9** 38 12N 116 6 E
Xiang Jiang →, *China* .... **33 D6** 28 55N 112 50 E
Xiangcheng, *Henan, China* **34 H8** 33 29N 114 52 E
Xiangcheng, *Henan, China* **34 H7** 33 50N 113 27 E
Xiangfan, *China* ......... **33 C6** 32 2N 112 8 E
Xianggang = Hong Kong □, *China* ............. **33 D6** 22 11N 114 14 E
Xianghuang Qi, *China* .... **34 C7** 42 2N 113 50 E
Xiangning, *China* ........ **34 G6** 35 58N 110 50 E
Xiangquan, *China* ....... **34 F7** 36 30N 113 1 E
Xiangquan He = Sutlej →, *Pakistan* ............. **42 E4** 29 23N 71 3 E
Xiangshui, *China* ........ **35 G10** 34 12N 119 33 E
Xiangtan, *China* ......... **33 D6** 27 51N 112 54 E
Xianyang, *China* ........ **34 G5** 34 20N 108 40 E
Xiao Hinggan Ling, *China* . **33 B7** 49 0N 127 0 E
Xiao Xian, *China* ........ **34 G9** 34 15N 116 55 E
Xiaoyi, *China* ........... **34 F6** 37 8N 111 48 E
Xiawa, *China* ........... **35 C11** 42 35N 120 38 E
Xiayi, *China* ............ **34 G9** 34 15N 116 10 E
Xichang, *China* ......... **32 D5** 27 51N 102 19 E
Xichuan, *China* ......... **34 H6** 33 0N 111 30 E
Xieng Khouang, *Laos* .... **38 C4** 19 17N 103 25 E
Xifei He →, *China* ...... **34 H9** 32 45N 116 40 E
Xifeng, *Gansu, China* .... **34 G4** 35 40N 107 40 E
Xifeng, *Liaoning, China* ... **35 C13** 42 42N 124 45 E
Xifengzhen = Xifeng, *China* **34 G4** 35 40N 107 40 E
Xigazê, *China* ........... **32 D3** 29 5N 88 45 E
Xihe, *China* ............ **34 G3** 34 2N 105 20 E
Xihua, *China* ........... **34 H8** 33 45N 114 30 E
Xiliao He →, *China* ...... **35 C12** 43 32N 123 35 E
Xin Xian = Xinzhou, *China* **34 E7** 38 22N 112 46 E
Xinavane, *Mozam.* ....... **57 D5** 25 2S 32 47 E
Xinbin, *China* ........... **35 D13** 41 40N 125 2 E
Xing Xian, *China* ........ **34 E6** 38 27N 111 7 E
Xing'an, *China* ......... **33 D6** 25 38N 110 40 E
Xingcheng, *China* ....... **35 D11** 40 40N 120 45 E
Xinghe, *China* .......... **34 D7** 40 55N 113 55 E
Xinghua, *China* ......... **35 H10** 32 58N 119 48 E
Xinglong, *China* ........ **35 D9** 40 25N 117 30 E
Xingping, *China* ........ **34 G5** 34 20N 108 28 E
Xingtai, *China* .......... **34 F8** 37 3N 114 32 E
**Xingu** →, *Brazil* ....... **93 D8** 1 30S 51 53W
Xingyang, *China* ........ **34 G7** 34 45N 112 52 E
Xinhe, *China* ........... **34 F8** 37 30N 115 15 E
Xining, *China* .......... **32 C5** 36 34N 101 40 E
**Xinjiang**, *China* ........ **34 G6** 35 34N 111 11 E
Xinjiang Uygur Zizhiqu □, *China* ............... **32 C3** 42 0N 86 0 E
Xinjin = Pulandian, *China* . **35 E11** 39 25N 121 58 E
Xinkai He →, *China* ..... **35 C12** 43 32N 123 35 E
Xinle, *China* ............ **34 E8** 38 25N 114 40 E
Xinlitun, *China* ......... **35 D12** 42 0N 122 8 E
Xinmin, *China* ......... **35 D12** 41 59N 122 50 E
Xintai, *China* ........... **35 G9** 35 55N 117 45 E
Xinxiang, *China* ........ **34 G7** 35 18N 113 50 E
Xinzhan, *China* ......... **35 C14** 43 50N 127 18 E
Xinzheng, *China* ........ **34 G7** 34 20N 113 45 E
Xinzhou, *China* ......... **34 E7** 38 22N 112 46 E
Xiong Xian, *China* ....... **34 E9** 38 59N 116 8 E
Xiongyuecheng, *China* ... **35 D12** 40 12N 122 5 E
Xiping, *Henan, China* .... **34 H8** 33 22N 114 5 E
Xiping, *Henan, China* .... **34 H6** 33 25N 111 8 E
Xique-Xique, *Brazil* ...... **93 F10** 10 50S 42 40W
Xisha Qundao = Paracel Is., *S. China Sea* ......... **36 A4** 15 50N 112 0 E
Xiuyan, *China* .......... **35 D12** 40 18N 123 11 E
Xixabangma Feng, *China* . **41 E14** 28 20N 85 40 E
Xixia, *China* ............ **34 H6** 33 25N 111 29 E
Xixiang, *China* .......... **34 H4** 33 0N 107 44 E
Xiyang, *China* .......... **34 F7** 37 38N 113 38 E
Xizang Zizhiqu □, *China* .. **32 C3** 32 0N 88 0 E
Xlendi, *Malta* .......... **23 C1** 36 1N 14 12 E
Xuan Loc, *Vietnam* ...... **39 G6** 10 56N 107 14 E
Xuanhua, *China* ......... **34 D8** 40 40N 115 2 E
Xuchang, *China* ......... **34 G7** 34 2N 113 48 E
Xun Xian, *China* ......... **34 G8** 35 42N 114 33 E
Xunyang, *China* ......... **34 H5** 32 48N 109 22 E
Xunyi, *China* ........... **34 G5** 35 8N 108 20 E
Xúquer →, *Spain* ....... **19 C5** 39 5N 0 10W
Xushui, *China* .......... **34 E8** 39 2N 115 40 E
Xuyen Moc, *Vietnam* ..... **39 G6** 10 34N 107 25 E
Xuzhou, *China* .......... **35 G9** 34 18N 117 10 E
Xylophagou, *Cyprus* ..... **23 E12** 34 54N 33 51 E


# Y


Ya Xian, *China* ........... **38 C7** 18 14N 109 29 E
Yaamba, *Australia* ....... **62 C5** 23 8S 150 22 E
Yaapeet, *Australia* ....... **63 F3** 35 45S 142 3 E
Yablonovy Ra. = Yablonovyy Khrebet, *Russia* ................ **27 D12** 53 0N 114 0 E
Yablonovyy Khrebet, *Russia* **27 D12** 53 0N 114 0 E
Yabrai Shan, *China* ...... **34 E2** 39 40N 103 0 E
Yabrūd, *Syria* ........... **47 B5** 33 58N 36 39 E
Yacheng, *China* ......... **33 E5** 18 22N 109 6 E
Yacuiba, *Bolivia* ......... **94 A3** 22 0S 63 43W
Yacuma →, *Bolivia* ...... **92 F5** 13 38S 65 23W
Yadgir, *India* ........... **40 L10** 16 45N 77 5 E
Yadkin →, *U.S.A.* ....... **77 H5** 35 29N 80 9W
Yaeyama-Rettō, *Japan* .... **31 M1** 24 30N 123 40 E
Yagodnoye, *Russia* ....... **27 C15** 62 33N 149 40 E
Yahila, *Dem. Rep. of the Congo* . **54 B1** 0 13N 24 28 E
Yahk, *Canada* ........... **72 D5** 49 6N 116 10W
Yahuma, *Dem. Rep. of the Congo* . **52 D4** 1 0N 23 10 E
Yaita, *Japan* ............ **31 F9** 36 48N 139 56 E
Yaiza, *Canary Is.* ........ **22 F6** 28 57N 13 46W
Yakima, *U.S.A.* .......... **82 C3** 46 36N 120 31W
Yakima →, *U.S.A.* ....... **82 C3** 47 0N 120 30W
Yakobi I., *U.S.A.* ......... **72 B1** 58 0N 136 30W
Yakovlevka, *Russia* ....... **30 B6** 44 26N 133 28 E
Yaku-Shima, *Japan* ...... **31 J5** 30 20N 130 30 E
Yakumo, *Japan* .......... **30 C10** 42 15N 140 16 E
Yakutat, *U.S.A.* .......... **68 C6** 59 33N 139 44W
**Yakutia** = Sakha □, *Russia* **27 C14** 66 0N 130 0 E
Yakutsk, *Russia* ......... **27 C13** 62 5N 129 50 E
Yala, *Thailand* .......... **39 J3** 6 33N 101 18 E
Yale, *U.S.A.* ............ **78 C2** 43 8N 82 48W
Yalgoo, *Australia* ........ **61 E2** 28 16S 116 39 E
Yalinga, *C.A.R.* .......... **52 C4** 6 33N 23 10 E
Yalkubul, Punta, *Mexico* ... **87 C7** 21 32N 88 37W
Yalleroi, *Australia* ........ **62 C4** 24 3S 145 42 E
Yalobusha →, *U.S.A.* .... **81 J9** 33 33N 90 10W
Yalong Jiang →, *China* ... **32 D5** 26 40N 101 55 E
Yalova, *Turkey* .......... **21 D13** 40 41N 29 15 E
Yalta, *Ukraine* .......... **25 F5** 44 30N 34 10 E
Yalu Jiang →, *China* ..... **35 E13** 40 0N 124 22 E
Yam Ha Melah = Dead Sea, *Asia* .................. **47 D4** 31 30N 35 30 E
Yam Kinneret, *Israel* ..... **47 C4** 32 45N 35 35 E
Yamada, *Japan* .......... **31 H5** 33 33N 130 49 E
Yamagata, *Japan* ........ **30 E10** 38 15N 140 15 E
Yamagata □, *Japan* ...... **30 E10** 38 30N 140 0 E
Yamaguchi, *Japan* ....... **31 G5** 34 10N 131 32 E
Yamaguchi □, *Japan* ..... **31 G5** 34 20N 131 40 E
Yamal, Poluostrov, *Russia* . **26 B8** 71 0N 70 0 E
Yamal Pen. = Yamal, Poluostrov, *Russia* ...... **26 B8** 71 0N 70 0 E
Yamanashi □, *Japan* ..... **31 G9** 35 40N 138 40 E
Yamantau, Gora, *Russia* ... **24 D10** 54 15N 58 6 E
Yamba, *Australia* ........ **63 D5** 29 26S 153 23 E
Yambarran Ra., *Australia* .. **60 C5** 15 10S 130 25 E
Yâmbiô, *Sudan* .......... **51 H11** 4 35N 28 16 E
Yambol, *Bulgaria* ........ **21 C12** 42 30N 26 30 E
Yamdena, *Indonesia* ..... **37 F8** 7 45S 131 20 E
Yame, *Japan* ............ **31 H5** 33 13N 130 35 E
Yamethin, *Burma* ........ **41 J20** 20 29N 96 18 E
Yamma-Yamma, L., *Australia* ............... **63 D3** 26 16S 141 20 E
Yamoussoukro, *Ivory C.* ... **50 G4** 6 49N 5 17W
Yampa →, *U.S.A.* ........ **82 F9** 40 32N 108 59W
Yampi Sd., *Australia* ...... **60 C3** 16 8S 123 38 E
Yampil, *Moldova* ......... **17 D15** 48 15N 28 15 E
Yampol = Yampil, *Moldova* **17 D15** 48 15N 28 15 E
**Yamuna** →, *India* ....... **43 G9** 25 30N 81 53 E
Yamunanagar, *India* ..... **42 D7** 30 7N 77 17 E
Yamzho Yumco, *China* .... **32 D4** 28 48N 90 35 E
Yana →, *Russia* ......... **27 B14** 71 30N 136 0 E
Yanagawa, *Japan* ........ **31 H5** 33 10N 130 24 E
Yanai, *Japan* ............ **31 H6** 33 58N 132 7 E
Yan'an, *China* ........... **34 F5** 36 35N 109 26 E
Yanaul, *Russia* .......... **24 C10** 56 25N 55 0 E
Yanbu 'al Baḥr, *Si. Arabia* . **46 C2** 24 0N 38 5 E
Yanchang, *China* ........ **34 F6** 36 43N 110 1 E
Yancheng, *Henan, China* .. **34 H8** 33 35N 114 0 E
Yancheng, *Jiangsu, China* . **35 H11** 33 23N 120 8 E
Yanchep Beach, *Australia* . **61 F2** 31 33S 115 37 E
Yanchi, *China* ........... **34 F4** 37 48N 107 20 E
Yanchuan, *China* ........ **34 F6** 36 51N 110 10 E
Yanco, *Australia* ......... **63 E4** 34 38S 146 27 E
Yanco Cr. →, *Australia* ... **63 F4** 35 14S 145 35 E
Yandoon, *Burma* ........ **41 L19** 17 0N 95 40 E
Yang Xian, *China* ........ **34 H4** 33 15N 107 30 E
Yangambi, *Dem. Rep. of the Congo* . **54 B1** 0 47N 24 20 E
Yangcheng, *China* ....... **34 G7** 35 28N 112 22 E
Yangch'ü = Taiyuan, *China* **34 F7** 37 52N 112 33 E
Yanggao, *China* ......... **34 D7** 40 21N 113 55 E
Yanggu, *China* .......... **34 F8** 36 8N 115 43 E
Yangliuqing, *China* ...... **35 E9** 39 2N 117 5 E
Yangon = Rangoon, *Burma* **41 L20** 16 45N 96 20 E
Yangpingguan, *China* .... **34 H4** 32 58N 106 5 E
Yangquan, *China* ........ **34 F7** 37 58N 113 31 E
**Yangtse** = Chang Jiang →, *China* ....... **33 C7** 31 48N 121 10 E
Yangtze Kiang = Chang Jiang →, *China* ....... **33 C7** 31 48N 121 10 E
Yangyang, *S. Korea* ...... **35 E15** 38 4N 128 38 E
Yangyuan, *China* ........ **34 D8** 40 1N 114 10 E
Yangzhou, *China* ........ **33 C6** 32 21N 119 26 E
Yanji, *China* ............ **35 C15** 42 59N 129 30 E
Yankton, *U.S.A.* ......... **80 D6** 42 53N 97 23W
Yanonge, *Dem. Rep. of the Congo* . **54 B1** 0 35N 24 38 E
Yanqi, *China* ............ **32 B3** 42 5N 86 35 E
Yanqing, *China* ......... **34 D8** 40 30N 115 58 E
Yanshan, *China* ......... **35 E9** 38 4N 117 22 E
Yanshou, *China* ......... **35 B15** 45 28N 128 22 E
Yantabulla, *Australia* ..... **63 D4** 29 21S 145 0 E
Yantai, *China* ........... **35 F11** 37 34N 121 22 E
Yanzhou, *China* ......... **34 G9** 35 35N 116 49 E
Yao Xian, *China* ......... **34 G5** 34 55N 108 59 E
Yao Yai, Ko, *Thailand* .... **39 J2** 8 0N 98 35 E
**Yaoundé**, *Cameroon* ..... **52 D2** 3 50N 11 35 E
Yaowan, *China* .......... **35 G10** 34 15N 118 3 E
Yap I., *Pac. Oc.* .......... **64 G5** 9 30N 138 10 E
Yapen, *Indonesia* ........ **37 E9** 1 50S 136 0 E
Yapen, Selat, *Indonesia* ... **37 E9** 1 20S 136 10 E
Yapero, *Indonesia* ........ **37 E9** 4 59S 137 11 E
Yappar →, *Australia* ..... **62 B3** 18 22S 141 16 E
Yaqui →, *Mexico* ........ **86 B2** 27 37N 110 39W
Yar-Sale, *Russia* ......... **26 C8** 66 50N 70 50 E
Yaraka, *Australia* ........ **62 C3** 24 53S 144 3 E
Yaransk, *Russia* ......... **24 C8** 57 22N 47 49 E
Yare →, *U.K.* ........... **11 E9** 52 35N 1 38 E
Yaremcha, *Ukraine* ...... **17 D13** 48 27N 24 33 E
Yarensk, *Russia* ......... **24 B8** 62 11N 49 15 E
Yarí →, *Colombia* ....... **92 D4** 0 20S 72 20W
Yarkand = Shache, *China* . **32 C2** 38 20N 77 10 E
Yarker, *Canada* .......... **79 B8** 44 23N 76 46W
Yarkhun →, *Pakistan* .... **43 A5** 36 17N 72 30 E
Yarmouth, *Canada* ....... **71 D6** 43 50N 66 7W
Yarmūk →, *Syria* ........ **47 C4** 32 42N 35 40 E
**Yaroslavl**, *Russia* ....... **24 C6** 57 35N 39 55 E
Yarqa, W. →, *Egypt* ...... **47 F2** 30 0N 33 49 E
Yarra Yarra Lakes, *Australia* **61 E2** 29 40S 115 45 E
Yarram, *Australia* ........ **63 F4** 38 29S 146 39 E
Yarraman, *Australia* ...... **63 D5** 26 50S 152 0 E
Yarras, *Australia* ........ **63 E5** 31 25S 152 20 E
Yartsevo, *Russia* ........ **27 C10** 60 20N 90 0 E
Yarumal, *Colombia* ...... **92 B3** 6 58N 75 24W
Yasawa Group, *Fiji* ....... **59 C7** 17 0S 177 23 E
Yaselda, *Belarus* ......... **17 B14** 52 7N 26 28 E
Yasin, *Pakistan* ......... **43 A5** 36 24N 73 23 E
Yasinski, L., *Canada* ..... **70 B4** 53 16N 77 35W
Yasinya, *Ukraine* ........ **17 D13** 48 16N 24 21 E
Yasothon, *Thailand* ...... **38 E5** 15 50N 104 10 E
Yass, *Australia* .......... **63 E4** 34 49S 148 54 E
Yatağan, *Turkey* ......... **21 F13** 37 20N 28 10 E
Yates Center, *U.S.A.* ..... **81 G7** 37 53N 95 44W
Yathkyed L., *Canada* ..... **73 A9** 62 40N 98 0W
Yatsushiro, *Japan* ........ **31 H5** 32 30N 130 40 E
Yatta Plateau, *Kenya* ..... **54 C4** 2 0S 38 0 E
Yavari →, *Peru* ......... **92 D4** 4 21S 70 2W
Yávaros, *Mexico* ........ **86 B3** 26 42N 109 31W
Yavatmal, *India* ......... **40 J11** 20 20N 78 15 E
Yavne, *Israel* ........... **47 D3** 31 52N 34 45 E
Yavoriv, *Ukraine* ........ **17 D12** 49 55N 23 20 E
Yavorov = Yavoriv, *Ukraine* **17 D12** 49 55N 23 20 E
Yawatahama, *Japan* ...... **31 H6** 33 27N 132 24 E
Yazd, *Iran* ............. **45 D7** 31 55N 54 27 E
Yazd □, *Iran* ........... **45 D7** 32 0N 55 0 E
Yazd-e Khvāst, *Iran* ..... **45 D7** 31 31N 52 7 E
Yazman, *Pakistan* ....... **42 E4** 29 8N 71 45 E
Yazoo →, *U.S.A.* ........ **81 J9** 32 22N 90 54W
Yazoo City, *U.S.A.* ....... **81 J9** 32 51N 90 25W
Yding Skovhøj, *Denmark* .. **9 J13** 55 59N 9 46 E
Ye Xian = Laizhou, *China* . **35 F10** 37 8N 119 57 E
Ye Xian, *China* .......... **34 H7** 33 35N 113 25 E
Yebyu, *Burma* .......... **38 E2** 14 15N 98 13 E
Yechŏn, *S. Korea* ........ **35 F15** 36 39N 128 27 E
Yecla, *Spain* ............ **19 C5** 38 35N 1 5W
Yécora, *Mexico* ......... **86 B3** 28 20N 108 58W
Yedintsy = Edineţ, *Moldova* **17 D14** 48 9N 27 18 E
Yegros, *Paraguay* ....... **94 B4** 26 20S 56 25W
Yehuda, Midbar, *Israel* .... **47 D4** 31 35N 35 15 E
Yei, *Sudan* ............. **51 H12** 4 9N 30 40 E
Yekaterinburg, *Russia* ..... **26 D7** 56 50N 60 30 E
Yekaterinodar = Krasnodar, *Russia* ............... **25 E6** 45 5N 39 0 E
Yelarbon, *Australia* ...... **63 D5** 28 33S 150 38 E
Yelets, *Russia* ........... **24 D6** 52 40N 38 30 E
Yelizavetgrad = Kirovohrad, *Ukraine* .............. **25 E5** 48 35N 32 20 E
Yell, *U.K.* .............. **12 A7** 60 35N 1 5W
Yell Sd., *U.K.* ........... **12 A7** 60 33N 1 15W
Yellow Sea, *China* ....... **35 G12** 35 0N 123 0 E
Yellowhead Pass, *Canada* . **72 C5** 52 53N 118 25W
Yellowknife, *Canada* ..... **72 A6** 62 27N 114 29W
Yellowknife →, *Canada* .. **72 A6** 62 31N 114 19W
Yellowstone →, *U.S.A.* .. **80 B3** 47 59N 103 59W
Yellowstone L., *U.S.A.* ... **82 D8** 44 27N 110 22W
Yellowstone National Park, *U.S.A.* ............... **82 D9** 44 40N 110 30W
Yelsk, *Belarus* .......... **17 C15** 51 50N 29 10 E
**Yemen** ■, *Asia* ......... **46 E3** 15 0N 44 0 E
Yenangyaung, *Burma* .... **41 J19** 20 30N 95 0 E
Yenbo = Yanbu 'al Baḥr, *Si. Arabia* ............. **46 C2** 24 0N 38 5 E
Yenda, *Australia* ........ **63 E4** 34 13S 146 14 E
Yenice, *Turkey* .......... **21 E12** 39 55N 27 17 E
**Yenisey** →, *Russia* ..... **26 B9** 71 50N 82 40 E
Yeniseysk, *Russia* ....... **27 D10** 58 27N 92 13 E
Yeniseyskiy Zaliv, *Russia* .. **26 B9** 72 20N 81 0 E
Yennádhi, *Greece* ....... **23 C9** 36 2N 27 56 E
Yenyuka, *Russia* ........ **27 D13** 57 57N 121 15 E
Yeo →, *U.K.* ........... **11 G5** 51 2N 2 49W
Yeo, L., *Australia* ........ **61 E3** 28 0S 124 30 E
Yeo I., *Canada* .......... **78 A3** 45 24N 81 48W
Yeola, *India* ............ **40 J9** 20 2N 74 30 E
Yeoryioúpolis, *Greece* .... **23 D6** 35 20N 24 15 E
Yeovil, *U.K.* ............ **11 G5** 50 57N 2 38W
Yeppoon, *Australia* ...... **62 C5** 23 5S 150 47 E
Yerbent, *Turkmenistan* .... **26 F6** 39 30N 58 50 E
Yerbogachen, *Russia* .... **27 C11** 61 16N 108 0 E
**Yerevan**, *Armenia* ....... **25 F7** 40 10N 44 31 E
Yerington, *U.S.A.* ........ **82 G4** 38 59N 119 10W
Yermak, *Kazakstan* ...... **26 D8** 52 2N 76 55 E
Yermo, *U.S.A.* .......... **85 L10** 34 54N 116 50W
Yerólakkos, *Cyprus* ...... **23 D12** 35 11N 33 15 E
Yeropol, *Russia* ......... **27 C17** 65 15N 168 40 E
Yeropótamos →, *Greece* . **23 D6** 35 3N 24 50 E
Yeroskipos, *Cyprus* ...... **23 E11** 34 46N 32 28 E
Yershov, *Russia* ......... **25 D8** 51 23N 48 27 E
Yerushalayim = Jerusalem, *Israel* ................. **47 D4** 31 47N 35 10 E
Yes Tor, *U.K.* ........... **11 G4** 50 41N 4 0W
Yesan, *S. Korea* ......... **35 F14** 36 41N 126 51 E
Yeso, *U.S.A.* ............ **81 H2** 34 26N 104 37W
Yessey, *Russia* .......... **27 C11** 68 29N 102 10 E
Yetman, *Australia* ....... **63 D5** 28 56S 150 48 E
Yeu, Î. d', *France* ........ **18 C2** 46 42N 2 20W
Yevpatoriya, *Ukraine* ..... **25 E5** 45 15N 33 20 E
Yeysk, *Russia* ........... **25 E6** 46 40N 38 12 E
Yezd = Yazd, *Iran* ....... **45 D7** 31 55N 54 27 E
Yhati, *Paraguay* ......... **94 B4** 25 45S 56 35W
Yhú, *Paraguay* .......... **95 B4** 25 0S 56 0W
Yi →, *Uruguay* ......... **94 C4** 33 7S 57 8W
Yi 'Allaq, G., *Egypt* ...... **47 E2** 30 22N 33 32 E
Yi He →, *China* ......... **35 G10** 34 10N 118 8 E
Yi Xian, *Hebei, China* ..... **34 E8** 39 20N 115 30 E

Yi Xian, *Liaoning, China* ... **35 D11** 41 30N 121 22 E
Yialiás →, *Cyprus* ....... **23 D12** 35 9N 33 44 E
Yialousa, *Cyprus* ......... **23 D13** 35 32N 34 10 E
Yianisádhes, *Greece* ...... **23 D8** 35 20N 26 10 E
Yiannitsa, *Greece* ........ **21 D10** 40 46N 22 24 E
Yibin, *China* ............ **32 D5** 28 45N 104 32 E
Yichang, *China* .......... **33 C6** 30 40N 111 20 E
Yicheng, *China* .......... **34 G6** 35 42N 111 40 E
Yichuan, *China* .......... **34 F6** 36 2N 110 10 E
Yichun, *China* ........... **33 B7** 47 44N 128 52 E
Yidu, *China* ............. **35 F10** 36 43N 118 28 E
Yijun, *China* ............ **34 G5** 35 28N 109 8 E
Yıldız Dağları, *Turkey* ..... **21 D12** 41 48N 27 36 E
Yilehuli Shan, *China* ...... **33 A7** 51 20N 124 20 E
Yimianpo, *China* ......... **35 B15** 45 7N 128 2 E
Yinchuan, *China* ......... **34 E4** 38 30N 106 15 E
Yindarlgooda, L., *Australia* **61 F3** 30 40S 121 52 E
Ying He →, *China* ....... **34 H9** 32 30N 116 30 E
Ying Xian, *China* ......... **34 E7** 39 32N 113 10 E
Yingkou, *China* .......... **35 D12** 40 37N 122 18 E
Yining, *China* ........... **26 E9** 43 58N 81 10 E
Yinmabin, *Burma* ........ **41 H19** 22 10N 94 55 E
Yiofiros →, *Greece* ...... **23 D7** 35 20N 25 6 E
Yirga Alem, *Ethiopia* ...... **46 F2** 6 48N 38 22 E
Yirrkala, *Australia* ....... **62 A2** 12 14S 136 56 E
Yishan, *China* ........... **32 D5** 24 28N 108 38 E
Yishui, *China* ........... **35 G10** 35 47N 118 30 E
Yíthion, *Greece* .......... **21 F10** 36 46N 22 34 E
Yitiaoshan, *China* ........ **34 F3** 37 5N 104 2 E
Yitong, *China* ........... **35 C13** 43 13N 125 20 E
Yiyang, *Henan, China* ..... **34 G7** 34 27N 112 10 E
Yiyang, *Hunan, China* ..... **33 D6** 28 35N 112 18 E
Yli-Kitka, *Finland* ........ **8 C23** 66 8N 28 30 E
Ylitornio, *Finland* ........ **8 C20** 66 19N 23 39 E
Ylivieska, *Finland* ........ **8 D21** 64 4N 24 28 E
Yoakum, *U.S.A.* .......... **81 L6** 29 17N 97 9W
Yog Pt., *Phil.* ............ **37 B6** 14 6N 124 12 E
**Yogyakarta**, *Indonesia* ... **37 G14** 7 49S 110 22 E
Yoho Nat. Park, *Canada* ... **72 C5** 51 25N 116 30W
Yojoa, L. de, *Honduras* .... **88 D2** 14 53N 88 0W
Yŏju, *S. Korea* ........... **35 F14** 37 20N 127 35 E
Yokadouma, *Cameroon* ... **52 D2** 3 26N 14 55 E
Yokkaichi, *Japan* ......... **31 G8** 34 55N 136 38 E
Yoko, *Cameroon* ......... **52 C2** 5 32N 12 20 E
**Yokohama**, *Japan* ....... **31 G9** 35 27N 139 28 E
Yokosuka, *Japan* ......... **31 G9** 35 20N 139 40 E
Yokote, *Japan* ........... **30 E10** 39 20N 140 30 E
Yola, *Nigeria* ............ **51 G8** 9 10N 12 29 E
Yolaina, Cordillera de, *Nic.* **88 D3** 11 30N 84 0W
Yoloten, *Turkmenistan* .... **45 B9** 37 18N 62 21 E
Yom →, *Thailand* ........ **36 A2** 15 35N 100 1 E
Yonago, *Japan* ........... **31 G6** 35 25N 133 19 E
Yonaguni-Jima, *Japan* .... **31 M1** 24 27N 123 0 E
Yŏnan, *N. Korea* .......... **35 F14** 37 55N 126 11 E
Yonezawa, *Japan* ......... **30 F10** 37 57N 140 4 E
Yong Peng, *Malaysia* ..... **39 M4** 2 0N 103 3 E
Yong Sata, *Thailand* ...... **39 J2** 7 8N 99 41 E
Yongamp'o, *N. Korea* ..... **35 E13** 39 56N 124 23 E
Yongcheng, *China* ........ **34 H9** 33 55N 116 20 E
Yŏngch'ŏn, *S. Korea* ...... **35 G15** 35 58N 128 56 E
Yongdeng, *China* ......... **34 F2** 36 38N 103 25 E
Yŏngdŏk, *S. Korea* ....... **35 F15** 36 24N 129 22 E
Yŏngdŭngpo, *S. Korea* .... **35 F14** 37 31N 126 54 E
Yonghe, *China* ........... **34 F6** 36 46N 110 38 E
Yŏnghŭng, *N. Korea* ...... **35 E14** 39 31N 127 18 E
Yongji, *China* ........... **34 G6** 34 52N 110 28 E
Yŏngju, *S. Korea* ........ **35 F15** 36 50N 128 40 E
Yongnian, *China* ......... **34 F8** 36 47N 114 29 E
Yongning, *China* ......... **34 E4** 38 15N 106 14 E
Yongqing, *China* ......... **34 E9** 39 25N 116 28 E
Yŏngwŏl, *S. Korea* ....... **35 F15** 37 11N 128 28 E
Yonibana, *S. Leone* ...... **50 G3** 8 30N 12 19W
**Yonkers**, *U.S.A.* ......... **79 F11** 40 56N 73 54W
Yonne →, *France* ....... **18 B5** 48 23N 2 58 E
York, *Australia* .......... **61 F2** 31 52S 116 47 E
**York**, *U.K.* .............. **10 D6** 53 58N 1 6W
York, *Nebr., U.S.A.* ...... **80 E6** 40 52N 97 36W
York, *Pa., U.S.A.* ........ **76 F7** 39 58N 76 44W
York, C., *Australia* ....... **62 A3** 10 42S 142 31 E
York, City of □, *U.K.* ..... **10 D6** 53 58N 1 6W
York, Kap, *Greenland* ..... **4 B4** 75 55N 66 25W
York, Vale of, *U.K.* ....... **10 C6** 54 15N 1 25W
York Haven, *U.S.A.* ...... **78 F8** 40 7N 76 46W
York Sd., *Australia* ...... **60 C4** 15 0S 125 5 E
Yorke Pen., *Australia* .... **63 E2** 34 50S 137 40 E
Yorketown, *Australia* .... **63 F2** 35 0S 137 33 E
Yorkshire Wolds, *U.K.* .... **10 C7** 54 8N 0 31W
Yorkton, *Canada* ......... **73 C8** 51 11N 102 28W
Yorkville, *U.S.A.* ........ **84 G3** 38 52N 123 13W
Yoro, *Honduras* .......... **88 C2** 15 9N 87 7W
Yoron-Jima, *Japan* ....... **31 L4** 27 2N 128 26 E
Yos Sudarso, Pulau =
*Dolak, Pulau, Indonesia* . **37 F9** 8 0S 138 30 E
**Yosemite National Park**,
*U.S.A.* ................. **84 H7** 37 45N 119 40W
Yosemite Village, *U.S.A.* .. **84 H7** 37 45N 119 35W
Yoshkar Ola, *Russia* ...... **24 C8** 56 38N 47 55 E
Yŏsu, *S. Korea* ........... **35 G14** 34 47N 127 45 E
Yotvata, *Israel* .......... **47 F4** 29 55N 35 2 E
Youbou, *Canada* ......... **84 B2** 48 53N 124 13W
Youghal, *Ireland* ......... **13 E4** 51 56N 7 52W
Youghal B., *Ireland* ...... **13 E4** 51 55N 7 49W
Young, *Australia* ......... **63 E4** 34 19S 148 18 E
Young, *Canada* .......... **73 C7** 51 47N 105 45W
Young, *Uruguay* ......... **94 C4** 32 44S 57 36W
Younghusband, L., *Australia* **63 E2** 30 50S 136 5 E
Younghusband Pen.,
*Australia* .............. **63 F2** 36 0S 139 25 E
Youngstown, *Canada* ..... **73 C6** 51 35N 111 10W
Youngstown, *N.Y., U.S.A.* . **78 C5** 43 15N 79 3W
Youngstown, *Ohio, U.S.A.* . **78 E4** 41 6N 80 39W
Youngsville, *U.S.A.* ...... **78 E5** 41 51N 79 19W
Youngwood, *U.S.A.* ...... **78 F5** 40 14N 79 34W
Youyu, *China* ........... **34 D7** 40 10N 112 20 E
Yozgat, *Turkey* .......... **25 G5** 39 51N 34 47 E
Ypané →, *Paraguay* ..... **94 A4** 23 29S 57 19W
Ypres = Ieper, *Belgium* .... **15 D2** 50 51N 2 53 E
Yreka, *U.S.A.* ........... **82 F2** 41 44N 122 38W
Ystad, *Sweden* .......... **9 J15** 55 26N 13 50 E
Ysyk-Köl, *Kyrgyzstan* .... **28 E11** 42 26N 76 12 E
Ysyk-Köl, Ozero, *Kyrgyzstan* **26 E8** 42 25N 77 15 E
Ythan →, *U.K.* .......... **12 D7** 57 19N 1 59W
Ytyk Kyuyel, *Russia* ...... **27 C14** 62 30N 133 45 E
Yu Jiang →, *China* ...... **33 D6** 23 22N 110 3 E
Yu Xian = Yuzhou, *China* . **34 G7** 34 10N 113 28 E
Yu Xian, *Hebei, China* .... **34 E8** 39 50N 114 35 E
Yu Xian, *Shanxi, China* ... **34 E7** 38 5N 113 20 E
Yuan Jiang →, *China* .... **33 D6** 28 55N 111 50 E
Yuanqu, *China* .......... **34 G6** 35 18N 111 40 E
Yuanyang, *China* ........ **34 G7** 35 3N 113 58 E
Yuba →, *U.S.A.* ........ **84 F5** 39 8N 121 36W
Yuba City, *U.S.A.* ....... **84 F5** 39 8N 121 37W
Yūbari, *Japan* ........... **30 C10** 43 4N 141 59 E
Yūbetsu, *Japan* .......... **30 B11** 44 13N 143 50 E
**Yucatán** □, *Mexico* ...... **87 C7** 21 30N 86 30W
Yucatán, Canal de,
*Caribbean* ............. **88 B2** 22 0N 86 30W
Yucatán, Península de,
*Mexico* ................ **66 H11** 19 30N 89 0W
Yucatán Basin, *Cent. Amer.* **66 H11** 19 0N 86 0W
Yucatan Str. = Yucatán,
Canal de, *Caribbean* .... **88 B2** 22 0N 86 30W
Yucca, *U.S.A.* ........... **85 L12** 34 52N 114 9W
Yucca Valley, *U.S.A.* ..... **85 L10** 34 8N 116 27W
Yucheng, *China* ......... **34 F9** 36 55N 116 32 E
Yuci, *China* ............. **34 F7** 37 42N 112 46 E
Yuendumu, *Australia* .... **60 D5** 22 16S 131 49 E
**Yugoslavia** ■, *Europe* ... **21 B9** 43 20N 20 0 E
**Yukon** →, *U.S.A.* ....... **68 B3** 62 32N 163 54W
**Yukon Territory** □,
*Canada* ............... **68 B6** 63 0N 135 0W
Yukta, *Russia* ........... **27 C11** 63 26N 105 42 E
Yukuhashi, *Japan* ........ **31 H5** 33 44N 130 59 E
Yulara, *Australia* ........ **61 E5** 25 10S 130 55 E
Yule →, *Australia* ....... **60 D2** 20 41S 118 17 E
Yuleba, *Australia* ........ **63 D4** 26 37S 149 24 E
Yulin, *Shaanxi, China* .... **34 E5** 38 20N 109 30 E
Yulin, *Shensi, China* ..... **38 C7** 38 15N 109 30 E
Yuma, *Ariz., U.S.A.* ...... **85 N12** 32 43N 114 37W
Yuma, *Colo., U.S.A.* ...... **80 E3** 40 8N 102 43W
Yuma, B. de, *Dom. Rep.* ... **89 C6** 18 20N 68 35W
Yumbe, *Uganda* ......... **54 B3** 3 28N 31 15 E
Yumbi,
*Dem. Rep. of the Congo* . **54 C2** 1 12S 26 15 E
Yumen, *China* ........... **32 C4** 39 50N 97 30 E
Yun Ho →, *China* ....... **35 E9** 39 10N 117 10 E
Yuna, *Australia* ......... **61 E2** 28 20S 115 0 E
Yuncheng, *Henan, China* .. **34 G8** 35 36N 115 57 E
Yuncheng, *Shanxi, China* .. **34 G6** 35 2N 111 0 E
Yungas, *Bolivia* ......... **92 G5** 17 0S 66 0W
Yungay, *Chile* ........... **94 D1** 37 10S 72 5W
**Yunnan** □, *China* ....... **32 D5** 25 0N 102 0 E
Yunta, *Australia* ......... **63 E2** 32 34S 139 36 E
Yunxi, *China* ............ **34 H6** 33 0N 110 22 E
Yupyongdong, *N. Korea* ... **35 D15** 41 49N 128 53 E
Yurga, *Russia* ........... **26 D9** 55 42N 84 51 E
Yurimaguas, *Peru* ........ **92 E3** 5 55S 76 7W
Yuryung Kaya, *Russia* .... **27 B12** 72 48N 113 23 E
Yuscarán, *Honduras* ..... **88 D2** 13 58N 86 45W
Yushe, *China* ........... **34 F7** 37 4N 112 58 E
Yushu, *Jilin, China* ...... **35 B14** 44 43N 126 38 E
Yushu, *Qinghai, China* ... **32 C4** 33 5N 96 55 E
Yutai, *China* ............ **34 G9** 35 0N 116 45 E
Yutian, *China* ........... **35 E9** 39 53N 117 45 E
Yuxan Qarabağ = Nagorno-
*Karabakh, Azerbaijan* ... **25 F8** 39 55N 46 45 E
Yuxi, *China* ............. **32 D5** 24 30N 102 35 E
Yuzawa, *Japan* .......... **30 E10** 39 10N 140 30 E
Yuzhno-Sakhalinsk, *Russia* **27 E15** 46 58N 142 45 E
Yuzhou, *China* .......... **34 G7** 34 10N 113 28 E
Yvetot, *France* .......... **18 B4** 49 37N 0 44 E


# Z


Zaanstad, *Neths.* ......... **15 B4** 52 27N 4 50 E
Zāb al Kabīr →, *Iraq* .... **44 C4** 36 1N 43 24 E
Zāb aş Şagīr →, *Iraq* .... **44 C4** 35 17N 43 29 E
Zabaykalsk, *Russia* ...... **27 E12** 49 40N 117 25 E
Zābol, *Iran* .............. **45 D9** 31 0N 61 32 E
Zābolī, *Iran* ............. **45 E9** 27 10N 61 35 E
Zabrze, *Poland* .......... **17 C10** 50 18N 18 50 E
Zacapa, *Guatemala* ...... **88 D2** 14 59N 89 31W
Zacapu, *Mexico* ......... **86 D4** 19 50N 101 43W
Zacatecas, *Mexico* ....... **86 C4** 22 49N 102 34W
Zacatecas □, *Mexico* .... **86 C4** 23 30N 103 0W
Zacatecoluca, *El Salv.* .... **88 D2** 13 29N 88 51W
Zachary, *U.S.A.* ......... **81 K9** 30 39N 91 9W
Zacoalco, *Mexico* ........ **86 C4** 20 14N 103 33W
Zacualtipán, *Mexico* ..... **87 C5** 20 39N 98 36W
Zadar, *Croatia* ........... **16 F8** 44 8N 15 14 E
Zadetkyi Kyun, *Burma* .... **39 H2** 10 0N 98 25 E
Zafarqand, *Iran* ......... **45 C7** 33 11N 52 29 E
Zafra, *Spain* ............ **19 C2** 38 26N 6 30W
Żagań, *Poland* .......... **16 C8** 51 39N 15 22 E
Zagaoua, *Chad* ......... **51 E10** 15 30N 22 24 E
Zagazig, *Egypt* .......... **51 B12** 30 40N 31 30 E
Zāgheh, *Iran* ........... **45 C6** 33 30N 48 42 E
Zagorsk = Sergiyev Posad,
*Russia* ................ **24 C6** 56 20N 38 10 E
**Zagreb**, *Croatia* ........ **16 F9** 45 50N 15 58 E
Zāgros, Kūhhā-ye, *Iran* ... **45 C6** 33 45N 48 5 E
Zagros Mts. = Zāgros,
*Kūhhā-ye, Iran* ......... **45 C6** 33 45N 48 5 E
Zāhedān, *Fārs, Iran* ...... **45 D7** 28 46N 53 52 E
Zāhedān,
*Sīstān va Balūchestān,*
*Iran* ................... **45 D9** 29 30N 60 50 E
Zahlah, *Lebanon* ........ **47 B4** 33 52N 35 50 E
**Zaïre** = Congo →, *Africa* **52 F2** 6 4S 12 24 E
Zaječar, *Serbia, Yug.* ..... **21 C10** 43 53N 22 18 E
Zakamensk, *Russia* ...... **27 D11** 50 23N 103 17 E
Zakhodnaya Dzvina =
*Daugava →, Latvia* .... **9 H21** 57 4N 24 3 E
Zākhū, *Iraq* ............. **44 B4** 37 10N 42 50 E
Zákinthos, *Greece* ....... **21 F9** 37 47N 20 57 E
Zakopane, *Poland* ....... **17 D10** 49 18N 19 57 E
Zákros, *Greece* .......... **23 D8** 35 6N 26 10 E
Zalaegerszeg, *Hungary* ... **17 E9** 46 53N 16 47 E
Zalău, *Romania* ......... **17 E12** 47 12N 23 3 E
Zaleshchiki = Zalishchyky,
*Ukraine* ................ **17 D13** 48 45N 25 45 E
Zalew Wiślany, *Poland* ... **17 A10** 54 20N 19 50 E
Zalingei, *Sudan* .......... **51 F10** 12 51N 23 29 E
Zalishchyky, *Ukraine* ..... **17 D13** 48 45N 25 45 E
Zama L., *Canada* ........ **72 B5** 58 45N 119 5W
Zambeke,
*Dem. Rep. of the Congo* . **54 B2** 2 8N 25 17 E
Zambeze →, *Africa* ...... **55 F4** 18 35S 36 20 E
**Zambezi** = Zambeze →,
*Africa* ................ **55 F4** 18 35S 36 20 E
Zambezi, *Zambia* ........ **53 G4** 13 30S 23 15 E
Zambezia □, *Mozam.* .... **55 F4** 16 15S 37 30 E
**Zambia** ■, *Africa* ....... **55 F2** 15 0S 28 0 E
Zamboanga, *Phil.* ........ **37 C6** 6 59N 122 3 E
Zamora, *Mexico* ......... **86 D4** 20 0N 102 21W
Zamora, *Spain* .......... **19 B3** 41 30N 5 45W
Zamość, *Poland* ......... **17 C12** 50 43N 23 15 E
Zandvoort, *Neths.* ........ **15 B4** 52 22N 4 32 E
Zanesville, *U.S.A.* ........ **78 G2** 39 56N 82 1W
Zangābād, *Iran* .......... **44 B5** 38 26N 46 44 E
Zangue →, *Mozam.* ...... **55 F4** 17 50S 35 21 E
Zanjān, *Iran* ............ **45 B6** 36 40N 48 35 E
Zanjān □, *Iran* .......... **45 B6** 37 20N 49 30 E
Zanjān →, *Iran* ......... **45 B6** 37 8N 47 47 E
Zante = Zákinthos, *Greece* **21 F9** 37 47N 20 57 E
Zanthus, *Australia* ....... **61 F3** 31 2S 123 34 E
**Zanzibar**, *Tanzania* ...... **54 D4** 6 12S 39 12 E
Zaouiet El-Kala = Bordj
*Omar Driss, Algeria* .... **50 C7** 28 10N 6 40 E
Zaouiet Reggane, *Algeria* .. **50 C6** 26 32N 0 3 E
Zaozhuang, *China* ....... **35 G9** 34 50N 117 35 E
Zap Suyu = Zāb al
*Kabīr →, Iraq* ......... **44 C4** 36 1N 43 24 E
Zapadnaya Dvina =
*Daugava →, Latvia* .... **9 H21** 57 4N 24 3 E
Západné Beskydy, *Europe* . **17 D10** 49 30N 19 0 E
Zapala, *Argentina* ....... **96 D2** 39 0S 70 5W
Zapaleri, Cerro, *Bolivia* ... **94 A2** 22 49S 67 11W
Zapata, *U.S.A.* .......... **81 M5** 26 55N 99 16W
Zapolyarnyy, *Russia* ..... **24 A5** 69 26N 30 51 E
**Zaporizhzhya**, *Ukraine* ... **25 E6** 47 50N 35 10 E
Zaporozhye = Zaporizhzhya,
*Ukraine* ............... **25 E6** 47 50N 35 10 E
Zara, *Turkey* ........... **44 B3** 39 58N 37 43 E
Zaragoza, *Coahuila, Mexico* **86 B4** 28 30N 101 0W
Zaragoza, *Nuevo León,*
*Mexico* ................ **87 C5** 24 0N 99 46W
**Zaragoza**, *Spain* ......... **19 B5** 41 39N 0 53W
Zarand, *Kermān, Iran* .... **45 D8** 30 46N 56 34 E
Zarand, *Markazī, Iran* .... **45 C6** 35 18N 50 25 E
Zaranj, *Afghan.* .......... **40 D2** 30 55N 61 55 E
Zarasai, *Lithuania* ....... **9 J22** 55 40N 26 20 E
Zarate, *Argentina* ....... **94 C4** 34 7S 59 0W
Zard, Kūh-e, *Iran* ....... **45 C6** 32 22N 50 4 E
Zāreh, *Iran* ............. **45 C6** 35 7N 49 9 E
Zaria, *Nigeria* ........... **50 F7** 11 0N 7 40 E
Zarneh, *Iran* ............ **44 C5** 33 55N 46 10 E
Zarós, *Greece* ........... **23 D6** 35 8N 24 54 E
Zarqā', Nahr az →, *Jordan* **47 C4** 32 10N 35 37 E
Zarrīn, *Iran* ............ **45 C7** 32 46N 54 37 E
Zaruma, *Ecuador* ........ **92 D3** 3 40S 79 38W
Żary, *Poland* ............ **16 C8** 51 37N 15 10 E
Zarzis, *Tunisia* .......... **51 B8** 33 31N 11 2 E
Zaskar →, *India* ........ **43 B7** 34 13N 77 20 E
Zaskar Mts., *India* ....... **43 C7** 33 15N 77 30 E
Zastron, *S. Africa* ....... **56 E4** 30 18S 27 7 E
Zavāreh, *Iran* ........... **45 C7** 33 29N 52 28 E
Zavitinsk, *Russia* ........ **27 D13** 50 10N 129 20 E
Zavodovski, I., *Antarctica* .. **5 B1** 56 0S 27 45W
Zawiercie, *Poland* ........ **17 C10** 50 30N 19 24 E
Zāwiyat al Bayḑā = Al
*Bayḑā, Libya* ........... **51 B10** 32 50N 21 44 E
Zāyā, *Iraq* .............. **44 C5** 33 33N 44 13 E
Zāyandeh →, *Iran* ...... **45 C7** 32 35N 52 0 E
Zaysan, *Kazakstan* ....... **26 E9** 47 28N 84 52 E
Zaysan, Oz., *Kazakstan* ... **26 E9** 48 0N 83 0 E
Zayü, *China* ............ **32 D4** 28 48N 97 27 E
Zbarazh, *Ukraine* ........ **17 D13** 49 43N 25 44 E
Zdolbuniv, *Ukraine* ...... **17 C14** 50 30N 26 15 E
Zduńska Wola, *Poland* ... **17 C10** 51 37N 18 59 E
Zeballos, *Canada* ........ **72 D3** 49 59N 126 50W
Zebediela, *S. Africa* ..... **57 C4** 24 20S 29 17 E
Zeebrugge, *Belgium* ..... **15 C3** 51 19N 3 12 E
Zeehan, *Australia* ....... **62 G4** 41 52S 145 25 E
Zeeland □, *Neths.* ....... **15 C3** 51 30N 3 50 E
Zeerust, *S. Africa* ....... **56 D4** 25 31S 26 4 E
Zefat, *Israel* ............ **47 C4** 32 58N 35 29 E
Zeil, Mt., *Australia* ...... **60 D5** 23 30S 132 23 E
Zeila, *Somali Rep.* ....... **46 E3** 11 21N 43 30 E
Zeist, *Neths.* ............ **15 B5** 52 5N 5 15 E
Zeitz, *Germany* ......... **16 C7** 51 2N 12 7 E
Zelenograd, *Russia* ...... **24 C6** 56 1N 37 12 E
Zelenogradsk, *Russia* .... **9 J19** 54 53N 20 29 E
Zelienople, *U.S.A.* ....... **78 F4** 40 48N 80 8W
Zémio, *C.A.R.* ........... **54 A2** 5 2N 25 5 E
Zemun, *Serbia, Yug.* ..... **21 B9** 44 51N 20 25 E
Zenica, *Bos.-H.* .......... **21 B7** 44 10N 17 57 E
Žepče, *Bos.-H.* .......... **21 B8** 44 28N 18 2 E
Zevenaar, *Neths.* ........ **15 C6** 51 56N 6 5 E
Zeya, *Russia* ............ **27 D13** 53 48N 127 14 E
Zeya →, *Russia* ........ **27 D13** 51 42N 128 53 E
Zêzere →, *Portugal* ..... **19 C1** 39 28N 8 20W
Zghartā, *Lebanon* ....... **47 A4** 34 21N 35 53 E
Zgorzelec, *Poland* ....... **16 C8** 51 10N 15 0 E
Zhabinka, *Belarus* ....... **17 B13** 52 13N 24 2 E
Zhailma, *Kazakstan* ...... **26 D7** 51 37N 61 33 E
Zhambyl, *Kazakstan* ..... **26 E8** 42 54N 71 22 E
Zhangaqazaly, *Kazakstan* .. **26 E7** 45 48N 62 6 E
Zhangbei, *China* ......... **34 D8** 41 10N 114 45 E
Zhangguangcai Ling, *China* **35 B15** 45 0N 129 0 E
Zhangjiakou, *China* ...... **34 D8** 40 48N 114 55 E
Zhangwu, *China* ......... **35 C12** 42 43N 123 52 E
Zhangye, *China* ......... **32 C5** 38 50N 100 23 E
Zhangzhou, *China* ....... **33 D6** 24 30N 117 35 E
Zhanhua, *China* ......... **35 F10** 37 40N 118 8 E
Zhanjiang, *China* ........ **33 D6** 21 15N 110 20 E
Zhannetty, Ostrov, *Russia* . **27 B16** 76 43N 158 0 E
Zhanyi, *China* ........... **32 D5** 25 38N 103 48 E
Zhanyu, *China* ........... **35 B12** 44 30N 122 30 E
Zhao Xian, *China* ........ **34 F8** 37 43N 114 45 E
Zhaocheng, *China* ....... **34 F6** 36 22N 111 38 E
Zhaotong, *China* ........ **32 D5** 27 20N 103 44 E
Zhaoyuan, *Heilongjiang,*
*China* ................. **35 B13** 45 27N 125 0 E
Zhaoyuan, *Shandong, China* **35 F11** 37 20N 120 23 E
Zhashkiv, *Ukraine* ....... **17 D16** 49 15N 30 5 E
Zhashui, *China* ......... **34 H5** 33 40N 109 8 E
Zhayyq →, *Kazakstan* .... **25 E9** 47 0N 51 48 E
Zhdanov = Mariupol,
*Ukraine* ............... **25 E6** 47 5N 37 31 E
Zhecheng, *China* ........ **34 G8** 34 7N 115 20 E
**Zhejiang** □, *China* ...... **33 D7** 29 0N 120 0 E
Zheleznodorozhnyy, *Russia* **24 B9** 62 35N 50 55 E
Zheleznogorsk-Ilimskiy,
*Russia* ................ **27 D11** 56 34N 104 8 E
Zhen'an, *China* ......... **34 H5** 33 27N 109 9 E
Zhengding, *China* ....... **34 E8** 38 8N 114 32 E
Zhengzhou, *China* ...... **34 G7** 34 45N 113 34 E
Zhenlai, *China* .......... **35 B12** 45 50N 123 5 E
Zhenping, *China* ........ **34 H7** 33 10N 112 16 E
Zhenyuan, *China* ........ **34 G4** 35 35N 107 30 E
Zhetiqara, *Kazakstan* .... **26 D7** 52 11N 61 12 E
Zhezqazghan, *Kazakstan* .. **26 E7** 47 44N 67 40 E
Zhidan, *China* .......... **34 F5** 36 48N 108 48 E
Zhigansk, *Russia* ........ **27 C13** 66 48N 123 27 E
Zhilinda, *Russia* ........ **27 C12** 70 0N 114 20 E
Zhitomir = Zhytomyr,
*Ukraine* ............... **17 C15** 50 20N 28 40 E
Zhlobin, *Belarus* ........ **17 B16** 52 55N 30 0 E
Zhmerinka = Zhmerynka,
*Ukraine* ............... **17 D15** 49 2N 28 2 E
Zhmerynka, *Ukraine* ..... **17 D15** 49 2N 28 2 E
Zhob, *Pakistan* ......... **42 D3** 31 20N 69 31 E
Zhob →, *Pakistan* ...... **42 C3** 32 4N 69 50 E
Zhodino = Zhodzina,
*Belarus* ............... **17 A15** 54 5N 28 17 E
Zhodzina, *Belarus* ....... **17 A15** 54 5N 28 17 E
Zhokhova, Ostrov, *Russia* . **27 B16** 76 4N 152 40 E
Zhongdian, *China* ....... **32 D4** 27 48N 99 42 E
Zhongning, *China* ....... **34 F3** 37 29N 105 40 E
Zhongtiao Shan, *China* .... **34 G6** 35 0N 111 10 E
Zhongwei, *China* ........ **34 F3** 37 30N 105 12 E
Zhongyang, *China* ....... **34 F6** 37 20N 111 11 E
Zhoucun, *China* ........ **35 F9** 36 47N 117 48 E
Zhouzhi, *China* ......... **34 G5** 34 10N 108 12 E
Zhuanghe, *China* ....... **35 E12** 39 40N 123 0 E
Zhucheng, *China* ....... **35 G10** 36 0N 119 27 E
Zhugqu, *China* ......... **34 H3** 33 40N 104 30 E
Zhumadian, *China* ...... **34 H8** 32 59N 114 2 E
Zhuo Xian = Zhuozhou,
*China* ................. **34 E8** 39 28N 115 58 E
Zhuolu, *China* .......... **34 D8** 40 20N 115 12 E
Zhuozhou, *China* ....... **34 E8** 39 28N 115 58 E
Zhuozi, *China* .......... **34 D7** 41 0N 112 25 E
Zhytomyr, *Ukraine* ...... **17 C15** 50 20N 28 40 E
Zīārān, *Iran* ............ **45 B6** 36 7N 50 32 E
Ziarat, *Pakistan* ......... **42 D2** 30 25N 67 49 E
Zibo, *China* ............ **35 F10** 36 47N 118 3 E
Zichang, *China* ......... **34 F5** 37 18N 109 40 E
Zielona Góra, *Poland* .... **16 C8** 51 57N 15 31 E
Zierikzee, *Neths.* ........ **15 C3** 51 40N 3 55 E
Zigey, *Chad* ............ **51 F9** 14 43N 15 50 E
Zigong, *China* .......... **32 D5** 29 15N 104 48 E
Ziguinchor, *Senegal* ..... **50 F2** 12 35N 16 20W
Zihuatanejo, *Mexico* ..... **86 D4** 17 38N 101 33W
Žilina, *Slovak Rep.* ...... **17 D10** 49 12N 18 42 E
Zillah, *Libya* ............ **51 C9** 28 30N 17 33 E
Zima, *Russia* ........... **27 D11** 54 0N 102 5 E
Zimapán, *Mexico* ........ **87 C5** 20 54N 99 20W
Zimba, *Zambia* ......... **55 F2** 17 20S 26 11 E
**Zimbabwe**, *Zimbabwe* .... **55 G3** 20 16S 30 54 E
Zimbabwe ■, *Africa* ..... **55 F3** 19 0S 30 0 E
Zimnicea, *Romania* ...... **17 G13** 43 40N 25 22 E
Zinder, *Niger* ........... **50 F7** 13 48N 9 0 E
Zinga, *Tanzania* ......... **55 D4** 9 16S 38 49 E
Zion National Park, *U.S.A.* . **83 H7** 37 15N 113 5W
Ziros, *Greece* ........... **23 D8** 35 5N 26 8 E
Zitácuaro, *Mexico* ....... **86 D4** 19 28N 100 21W
Zitundo, *Mozam.* ........ **57 D5** 26 48S 32 47 E
Ziway, L., *Ethiopia* ...... **46 F2** 8 0N 38 50 E
Ziyang, *China* .......... **34 H5** 32 32N 108 31 E
Zlatograd, *Bulgaria* ..... **21 D11** 41 22N 25 7 E
Zlatoust, *Russia* ........ **24 C10** 55 10N 59 40 E
Zlín, *Czech Rep.* ........ **17 D9** 49 14N 17 40 E
Zmeinogorsk, *Kazakstan* .. **26 D9** 51 10N 82 13 E
Znojmo, *Czech Rep.* ..... **16 D9** 48 50N 16 2 E
Zobeyrī, *Iran* ........... **44 C5** 34 10N 46 40 E
Zobia,
*Dem. Rep. of the Congo* . **54 B2** 3 0N 25 59 E
Zoetermeer, *Neths.* ...... **15 B4** 52 3N 4 30 E
Zolochev = Zolochiv,
*Ukraine* ............... **17 D13** 49 45N 24 51 E
Zolochiv, *Ukraine* ....... **17 D13** 49 45N 24 51 E
Zomba, *Malawi* ......... **55 F4** 15 22S 35 19 E
Zongo,
*Dem. Rep. of the Congo* . **52 D3** 4 20N 18 35 E
Zonguldak, *Turkey* ...... **25 F5** 41 28N 31 50 E
Zonqor Pt., *Malta* ....... **23 D2** 35 51N 14 34 E
Zorritos, *Peru* ........... **92 D2** 3 43S 80 40W
Zou Xiang, *China* ....... **34 G9** 35 30N 116 58 E
Zouar, *Chad* ............ **51 D9** 20 30N 16 32 E
Zouérate = Zouîrât,
*Mauritania* ............ **50 D3** 22 44N 12 21W
Zouîrât, *Mauritania* ..... **50 D3** 22 44N 12 21W
Zoutkamp, *Neths.* ....... **15 A6** 53 20N 6 18 E
Zrenjanin, *Serbia, Yug.* ... **21 B9** 45 22N 20 23 E
Zufār, *Oman* ............ **46 D5** 17 40N 54 0 E
Zug, *Switz.* ............. **18 C8** 47 10N 8 31 E
Zugspitze, *Germany* ..... **16 E6** 47 25N 10 59 E
Zuid-Holland □, *Neths.* ... **15 C4** 52 0N 4 35 E
Zuidbeveland, *Neths.* .... **15 C3** 51 30N 3 50 E
Zuidhorn, *Neths.* ........ **15 A6** 53 15N 6 23 E
Zula, *Eritrea* ............ **46 D2** 15 17N 39 40 E
Zumbo, *Mozam.* ......... **55 F3** 15 35S 30 26 E
Zumpango, *Mexico* ...... **87 D5** 19 48N 99 6W
Zunhua, *China* .......... **35 D9** 40 18N 117 58 E
Zuni, *U.S.A.* ............ **83 J9** 35 4N 108 51W
Zunyi, *China* ........... **32 D5** 27 42N 106 53 E
Zuoquan, *China* ........ **34 F7** 37 5N 113 22 E
Zurbātīyah, *Iraq* ........ **44 C5** 33 9N 46 3 E
**Zürich**, *Switz.* .......... **18 C8** 47 22N 8 32 E
Zutphen, *Neths.* ........ **15 B6** 52 9N 6 12 E
Zuwārah, *Libya* ......... **51 B8** 32 58N 12 1 E
Zūzan, *Iran* ............ **45 C8** 34 22N 59 53 E
Zverinogolovskoye, *Russia* **26 D7** 54 26N 64 50 E
Zvishavane, *Zimbabwe* ... **55 G3** 20 17S 30 2 E
Zvolen, *Slovak Rep.* ..... **17 D10** 48 33N 19 10 E
Zwelitsha, *S. Africa* ..... **53 L5** 32 55S 27 22 E
Zwettl, *Austria* ......... **16 D8** 48 35N 15 9 E
Zwickau, *Germany* ...... **16 C7** 50 44N 12 30 E
Zwolle, *Neths.* .......... **15 B6** 52 31N 6 6 E
Zwolle, *U.S.A.* .......... **81 K8** 31 38N 93 39W
Żyrardów, *Poland* ....... **17 B11** 52 3N 20 28 E
Zyryan, *Kazakstan* ...... **26 E9** 49 43N 84 20 E
Zyryanka, *Russia* ....... **27 C16** 65 45N 150 51 E
Zyryanovsk = Zyryan,
*Kazakstan* ............. **26 E9** 49 43N 84 20 E
Żywiec, *Poland* ......... **17 D10** 49 42N 19 10 E
Zyyi, *Cyprus* ............ **23 E12** 34 43N 33 20 E

ENCYCLOPEDIA

ENCYCLOPEDIA

ENCYCLOPEDIA

ENCYCLOPEDIA

ENCYCLOPEDIA

ENCYCLOPEDIA

ENCYCLOPEDIA

ENCYCLOPEDIA

ENCYCLOPEDIA

# A

*A/a, first letter of the Roman alphabet. It evolved from the ancient Egyptian hieroglyph representing the head of an ox through the Hebrew word* **aleph,** *meaning* **ox,** *to the Greek* **alpha.**

**Aachen** (Aix-la-Chapelle) City in SW North Rhine-Westphalia, W Germany. Aachen is noted for its hot sulfur baths, used by the Romans and the hottest in N Europe. It was the site of medieval imperial diets and the coronations of the monarchs of the Holy Roman Empire from 1349 to 1531. Industries: machinery, iron and steel, textiles. Pop. (1993) 246,100.

**Aalto, Alvar** (1898–1976) Finnish architect and furniture designer, famous for his imaginative handling of floor levels and use of natural materials and irregular forms. Aalto's work includes the municipal library at Viipuri (1927–35), the Baker House at the Massachusetts Institute of Technology (1947–49), the Säynätsalo town hall complex (1950–52), and Finlandia House, Helsinki (1967–71). *See also* INTERNATIONAL STYLE

**aardvark** Nocturnal, bristly haired mammal of central and S Africa. It lives on termites and ants, which it scoops up with its sticky 12in (30cm) tongue. Length: up to 5ft (1.5m); weight: up to 154lb (70kg). It is the only representative of the order *Tubulidentata*.

**Aaron** Brother of MOSES chosen by God to be the first Jewish high priest. According to the biblical book of Exodus, he helped to obtain the release of the Israelites from slavery in Egypt. He lapsed into idolatry, and made a golden calf for the people to worship, but was later restored to divine favor.

**Aaron, Hank (Henry Louis)** (1934– ) US baseball player. Aaron was one of the first African-Americans to play in the major leagues when he joined (1954) the Milwaukee (later Atlanta) Braves. In 1974 he surpassed Babe RUTH's major-league career home run record of 714. In 1976 Aaron retired from playing, having hit a record 755 home runs. He was elected to the Baseball Hall of Fame in 1982.

**abacus** Archaic mathematical tool used since ancient times in the Middle and Far East for addition and subtraction. One form of abacus consists of beads strung on wires and arranged in columns.

**abalone** Seashore gastropod MOLLUSK with a single flattened spiral shell perforated by a row of respiratory holes; it is found on Mediterranean, Atlantic, and N Pacific shores and off the coasts of South Africa and Australia. Length: to 12in (30cm). Family Haliotidae; species include *Haliotis rufescens*.

**Abbado, Claudio** (1933– ) Italian conductor. Abbado was musical director at LA SCALA, Milan (1972–86), London Symphony Orchestra (1983–88), Vienna State Opera (1986– ), and Berlin Philharmonic (1989– ). He is noted for his interpretations of 20th-century music.

**Abbas I (the Great)** (1571–1629) Shah of Persia (1588–1629). The outstanding ruler of the SAFAVID dynasty, Abbas restored Persia as a great power, waging war successfully against the invading Uzbeks and Ottoman Turks and recapturing Hormuz from the Portuguese. Tolerant in religion, he encouraged Dutch and English merchants and admitted Christian missionaries. Abbas made ISFAHAN his capital.

**Abbasid** Muslim CALIPH dynasty (750–1258). They traced their descent from al-Abbas, the uncle of MUHAMMAD, and came to power by defeating the Umayyads. The Abbasids moved the caliphate from Damascus to Baghdad in 862, where it achieved great splendor. From the 10th century Abbasid caliphs ceased to exercise political power, becoming religious figureheads. After the family's downfall in 1258, following the fall of Baghdad to the Mongols, one member was invited by the Mameluke sultan to Cairo where the dynasty was recognized until the 16th century.

**abbey** Complex of buildings that constitute a religious community, the center of which is the abbey church.

**Abbey Theatre** Theater erected on Abbey St., Dublin (1904), by Annie E.F. Horniman to house the Irish National Theatre Society. In 1925 the Abbey became the National Theatre of Ireland. Works by W.B. YEATS, Lady Gregory, J.M. SYNGE, and Sean O'CASEY have been introduced here and the theater is renowned for its support of new writers.

**Abd al-Kadir** (1808–83) Algerian leader, and emir of Mascara. Abd al-Kadir displaced (1832–39) the French and Turks from N Algeria before launching a holy war against the French. In 1843 he was forced into Morocco where he enlisted the support of the sultan. Abd al-Kadir and his Moroccan forces were beaten at Isly (1844). He was imprisoned in France (1847–52).

**abdomen** In VERTEBRATES, that portion of the body between the chest and the pelvis containing the abdominal cavity and the abdominal viscera, including most of the digestive organs. In arthropods it is the posterior part of the body, containing the reproductive organs and part of the digestive system.

**Abdul-Jabbar, Kareem** *See* Jabbar, Kareem Abdul

**Abdullah** (1882–1951) King of Jordan (1946–51), son of Hussein. In 1921, after aiding Britain in World War I, Abdullah became emir of Trans-Jordan. He lost control of Hejaz to Ibn Saud. In World War II he resisted the Axis. Abdullah fought Israel, annexed land, and signed an armistice (1949). He was assassinated in Jerusalem, and Talal ascended the throne.

**Abel** In the Bible (Genesis), primal farmer killed by his brother CAIN, the primal hunter.

**Abel, John Jacob** (1857–1938) US biochemist, best known for the first identification (1898) of a hormone, adrenaline (epinephrine). He made his key discovery after many years of studying the chemical composition of body tissues. Later, Abel isolated amino acids from blood by the process of DIALYSIS, and discovered insulin in crystalline form.

**Abélard, Pierre** (1079–1142) French philosopher noted for his application of logic in approaching theological questions. In his famous work *Sic et Non*, he attempted to reconcile differences between the Fathers of the Church by using the Aristotelian method of DIALECTIC. His views were condemned by the Council of Sens (1140). Abélard is known for his tragic love for his young pupil Héloise. The affair scandalized his contemporaries. He was castrated and became a monk, while Héloise was forced to enter a convent. These events inspired his work *Historia Calamitatum Mearum*.

**Aberdeen** City and seaport in NE Scotland, called the "Granite City" for its grey granite architecture. Aberdeen gained in importance since the development of the North Sea oil fields in the late 1970s. Pop. (1991) 204,885.

**aberration** In physics, defect in lens and mirror images arising when the incident light is not at or near the center of the lens or mirror. **Spherical** aberration occurs when rays falling on the periphery of a lens or mirror are not brought to the same focus as light at the center; the image is blurred. **Chromatic** aberration occurs when the wavelengths of the dispersed light are not brought to the same focus; the image is falsely colored.

**aberration of light** Apparent slight change of position of a star due to the effect of the Earth's orbital motion on the direction of the light's arrival. A telescope must be inclined by an angle of up to about 20° to compensate for it. Aberration of light was discovered in 1728 and used to prove the Earth orbits the Sun.

**Abidjan** Former capital of the Ivory Coast (and the largest city in W Africa) situated on the Ebrié Lagoon, inland from the Gulf of Guinea. The country's chief port and commercial center, Abidjan was founded by French colonists at the end of the 19th century. Although it lost capital status to YAMOUSSOUKRO in 1983, it remains Ivory Coast's cultural and economic center. Industries: textiles, sawmilling. Pop. (1988) 1,929,079.

**Abington School District v. Schempp** (1963) US Supreme Court case that ruled unconstitutional a law requiring bible readings in public schools, citing First Amendment restriction on laws "respecting an establishment of religion."

◄ **aardvark** Found throughout much of Africa, the termite-eating aardvark (*Orycteropus afer*) is a shy, nocturnal animal. Its presence may be detected by the large burrows it digs, using the hooflike claws on its front feet.

A

**Abkhazia** Autonomous republic on the Black Sea coast of Georgia. The capital is Sukhumi. The area was conquered by Romans, Byzantines, Arabs, and the Turks before becoming a Russian protectorate in 1910. It was made a Soviet republic in 1921 and an autonomous republic within Georgia in 1930. After the establishment of an independent Georgia, the Abkhazian parliament declared independence in 1992 and Abkhazian forces seized the capital in 1993. In 1994 a May ceasefire was followed in November by a new constitution. Its independent status was confirmed by a new Georgian constitution in 1995. Tobacco, tea, grapes, and citrus fruits are the main crops. Area: 3,320sq mi (8,600sq km). Pop. (1990) 537,500.

**abolitionist** Person who sought to end SLAVERY. In the US and the UK the abolitionist movement was particularly active in the early 19th century. In the US the American Anti-Slavery Society was formed in 1833, while in the UK, William WILBERFORCE headed the movement that led to the abolition of Britain's role in the slave trade in 1807.

**aborigines** Strictly, the indigenous inhabitants of a country. The term is usually applied to NATIVE AUSTRALIANS.

**abortion** Loss of a fetus before it is sufficiently advanced to survive outside the womb; commonly called a miscarriage. A medical abortion is the termination of pregnancy by drugs or surgery. The rights of the fetus and the mother's right to choose provoke much political and ethical debate.

**Abraham** In the Old Testament, progenitor of the Hebrews and founder of Judaism. God tested his loyalty by demanding he sacrifice his son, ISAAC. He is esteemed by Muslims who regard him as the ancestor, through another son ISHMAEL, of the Arabs.

**Abrams v. United States** (1919) Supreme Court decision that upheld the espionage convictions of anti-World War I pamphleteers and broadened the "clear and present danger" doctrine first outlined in *Schenck v. United States*.

**abrasion** In geology, mechanical wearing down of rock surface by wind, water, glacial movements, tides, or currents. Common agents of abrasion are the bed load of streams, rock debris at the base of glaciers, and sand transported by wind or waves. *See also* EROSION

**abrasive** Hard and rough substance used to grind and polish surfaces. Some abrasives are used as fine powders, others in larger fragments with sharp cutting edges. Most natural abrasives are minerals.

**Absalom** In the Old Testament, third and favorite son of King DAVID. A youth of uncontrollable arrogance, he murdered his brother Amnon, led a rebellion against David, and was routed. Trapped in flight when his hair became entangled in the branches of an oak, he was killed by David's general Joab.

**abscess** Collection of pus anywhere in the body, contained in a cavity of inflamed tissue. It is caused by bacterial infection.

**absolute zero** Temperature at which all parts of a system are at the lowest energy permitted by the laws of QUANTUM MECHANICS; zero on the kelvin temperature scale, which is −459.67°F (−273.16°C). At this temperature the system's ENTROPY is also zero, although the total energy of the system may not be zero.

**absolution** Formal rite carried out by a Christian priest in which repentant sinners are forgiven the sins they have confessed. *See also* CONFESSION; PENANCE

**absorption** Taking up chemically or physically of molecules of one substance into another. The absorbed matter permeates all of the absorber. This includes a gas taken in by a liquid and a liquid or gas absorbed by a solid. The process is often utilized commercially, such as the purification of natural gas by the absorption of hydrogen sulfide in aqueous ethanolamine. *See also* ADSORPTION

**abstract art** Art in which recognizable objects are reduced to schematic marks. Although abstraction was evident in impressionist, neo- and post-impressionist work of the late 19th century, the movement did not become established until the early 20th century. Its most radical form is called **nonobjective** or noniconic art. In this, the artist creates marks, signs, or three-dimensional constructions which have no connection with images or objects in the visible world. There are two main types of nonobjective art: **expressionist**, which is fundamentally emotional, spontaneous, and personal; and **geometrical**, which works from the premise that geometry is the only discipline precise and universal enough to express our intellectual and emotional longings. Art historians often credit Wassily KANDINSKY with being the first to explore expressionist abstraction in 1910. It was Kandinsky's influence that inspired the BLAUE REITER group and his work which helped to pave the way toward abstract expressionism, ACTION PAINTING, and Tachism. Geometrical abstraction found its most adept, early exponents in Russia in *c*.1913. The pioneers included Kasimir MALEVICH who invented SUPREMATISM and El LISSITZKY, a leading proponent of CONSTRUCTIVISM. The French *Section d'Or* worked in parallel to the Russians. Other individuals who provided landmarks in geometrical abstraction include Piet MONDRIAN, Naum GABO, and Ben NICHOLSON; influential movements include De STIJL and Concrete Art.

**abstract expressionism** Mainly US art movement in which the creative process itself is examined and explored. It is neither wholly abstract nor wholly expressionist. The term originally applied to paintings created (1945–55) by about 15 artists from the New York School. Although very different in temperament and style, these individuals shared a fascination with SURREALISM and "psychic automatism" as well as other progressive European styles. Toward the early 1950s, two distinct groups emerged with Willem DE KOONING and Jackson POLLOCK heading the most aggressive trend (also loosely known as ACTION PAINTING) which involved dripping or throwing paint on the canvas. Barnett NEWMAN, Ad Reinhardt, and Mark ROTHKO were more contemplative.

**Absurd, Theater of the** Dramatic and literary critical term developed from the philosophy of Albert CAMUS to describe discordant human experience in an inhuman world. It was first applied in 1961 to describe contemporary drama which depicted the irrationality of life in an unconventional dramatic style. Exponents include Samuel BECKETT, Eugène IONESCO, Jean GENET, and Edward ALBEE. Such drama attempts to abandon logical, linguistic processes. The connection between language

► **abstract expressionism** *Black and White* (1948) by Jackson Pollock. Pollock is generally seen as the father of abstract expressionism, a modern art style that was dominant in the USA in the late 1940s and 1950s.

and meaning is fractured (often by the use of repetition) and dramatic characters appear dislocated from their surroundings. Beckett's play *Waiting for Godot* is a classic of the genre.

**Abu Bakr** (573–634) First Muslim CALIPH. One of the earliest converts to Islam, Abu Bakr was chief adviser to the Prophet MUHAMMAD. After Muhammad's death he was elected leader of the Muslim community. During his short reign (632–34), he defeated the tribes that had revolted against Muslim rule in Medina after the death of Muhammad and restored them to Islam. By invading the Byzantine Christian provinces of Syria and Palestine and the Iranian province of Iraq, he launched the series of Holy Wars through which the first major expansion of the Islamic world was accomplished.

**Abu Dhabi** (Abu Zaby) Largest and wealthiest of the seven UNITED ARAB EMIRATES, lying on the s coast of the Persian Gulf. Also the name of its capital city (1984 pop. 242,975), federal capital of the UAE. It has been ruled since the 18th century by the Al-bu-Falah clan of the Bani Yas tribe. There are longstanding frontier disputes with Saudi Arabia and Oman. Since the discovery of oil in the late 1950s, Abu Dhabi's economy has been based almost entirely on crude oil production. Area: 26,000sq mi (67,340sq km). Pop. (1985) 670,125.

**Abuja** Nigeria's administrative capital since December 1991. The new city was designed by the Japanese architect Kenzo Tange, and work began in 1976. Government offices began moving in the 1980s to relieve pressure on the infrastructure of LAGOS. Pop. (1992 est.) 305,900.

**Abu Simbel** Ancient Egyptian village on the w bank of the River Nile, near the border with Sudan, and location of two rock-cut sandstone temples built by RAMSES II (*c*.1292–1225 BC). In a huge operation (1963–66), the temples and statuary were moved farther inland. This was to prevent their disappearance under the waters of Lake Nasser, created by the construction of the new ASWAN High Dam.

**abyssal** Term to describe oceanic features occurring at great depths, usually more than *c*.3,000m (10,000ft) below sea level. Abyssal **plains** cover *c*.30% of the Atlantic and nearly 75% of the Pacific ocean floors. They are covered by deposits of biogenic oozes formed by the remains of microscopic plankton, and nonbiogenic sediments (red clays). The gradient is less than 1:1,000, except for the occasional low, oval-shaped abyssal **hills**. The plains are characterized by stable temperatures from 30°F to 41°F (−1°C to 5°C) and the relative absence of water currents. The abyssal **zone** is the deepest area of the ocean. It receives no sunlight, so there are no seasons and no plants, but there are many forms of life, such as glass sponges, crinoids (sea lilies), and brachiopods (lamp shells).

**acacia** (mimosa) Evergreen shrubs and trees widely distributed in tropical and subtropical regions, especially Australia. They have compound leaves made up of many small leaflets, and yellow or white flowers. Height: 4–59ft (1.2–18m). Family Leguminosae; genus *Acacia*.

**Académie Française** Official French literary society, now part of the Institut de France. Originating as a private discussion group whose members were persuaded by Cardinal RICHELIEU to become an official body in 1635, the society is the guardian of the French language and of literary conventions. Past members have included many of the giants of French literature, such as RACINE, VOLTAIRE, and HUGO.

**Academy** School of philosophy founded (*c*.387 BC) by PLATO. Plato met his pupils in a garden outside Athens, said to have belonged to a Greek hero called Academus. Academies were founded in Europe, notably in the Renaissance era. By the 18th century they had become known generally as universities, but the name continues to be applied to scholarly institutions.

**Academy Award** *See* OSCAR

**Acadia** (Acadie) Historic region in North America. It was settled by the French in the early 17th century and includes present-day Nova Scotia, New Brunswick, Prince Edward Island, and parts of Quebec and Maine.

**acanthus** PERENNIAL plant with thistlelike leaves, found in Africa, the Mediterranean region, India, and Malaysia. It has lobed, often spiny leaves and white or colored flower spikes. The pattern of the leaves in a stylized form is a common classical architectural motif.

◀ **accordion** Invented in the 1820s, the accordion is a reed organ working along the same principle as the mouth organ – that is a separate reed is provided for each note. Air is forced through the reeds by bellows that form the center of the instrument. The right hand plays the melody on the keyboard, while the left hand operates the buttons for accompanying chords.

**Acapulco** (Acapulco de Juárez) City-port on the sw coast of Mexico. Founded in 1550, Acapulco was for 250 years an important port on the galleon route linking Spain and the Philippines. Now the country's most famous Pacific resort, it is noted for beautiful scenery, deep-sea fishing, and luxury hotels. Exports: cotton, fruit, hides, and tobacco. Pop. (1990) 593,212.

**acceleration** Amount by which the VELOCITY of an object increases in a certain time. It can be found by applying the equation acceleration = (change in velocity)/(time taken for change). It is measured in feet or meters per second per second ($ft/s^2$ or $m/s^2$).

**accelerator, particle** Machine for increasing the energy of charged particles by increasing their speed. Accelerators are used mostly in PARTICLE PHYSICS' experiments, in which high-energy particles are forced to collide with other particles. The way the fragments of particles behave following the collision provides information on the forces found within atoms. In a linear accelerator, particles travel in a straight line. The world's longest is 2mi (3.2km) long. In a cyclotron, particles are accelerated in a spiral path between pairs of D-shaped magnets with an alternating electric field between them. A synchrotron synchronizes the accelerating electric current to the time it takes to make one revolution. The CERN synchrotron accelerator in Geneva, Switzerland has a circumference of 16.7mi (27km).

**accessory** In law, a person associated with a criminal act. An accessory before the fact consults, encourages, and advises the criminal. An accessory after the fact is one who, with knowledge of a crime, receives or assists the criminal in some way.

**accommodation** Process by which the EYE focuses on objects at various distances. In the human eye, focusing is achieved when the muscles of the ciliary body contract or relax to change the curvature of the lens and bring light rays into focus on the light-sensitive RETINA at the back of the eye.

**accomplice** In law, person associated with another or others in the commission of a crime. Unlike an ACCESSORY, an accomplice generally takes an active part in the crime.

**accordion** Musical instrument of the reed organ type. It has an organlike tone produced by air from the bellows vibrating reeds. It was invented in *c*.1822 and is widely used in folk music.

**accounting** Profession that assesses and produces financial information for and about a company or individual for the benefit of the company's management, the investing public, and official tax, regulatory, and financial authorities. *See also* BOOKKEEPING

**Accra** Capital and largest city of Ghana, on the Gulf of Guinea. Occupied by the Ga people since the 15th century, Accra became the capital of Britain's Gold Coast colony in 1875. Today, it is a major port and economic center and the headquarters of the Defense Commission of the Organization of African Unity. Industries: engineering, timber, textiles, chemicals. The main export is cacao. Pop. (1988 est.) 949,113.

**acetaldehyde** *See* ETHANAL

**acetaminophen** Ingredient used as a substitute for or in combination with ASPIRIN in many over-the-counter drugs. It has fever-reducing and pain-killing properties.

**acetate** (ethanoate) Salt or ester of acetic (ethanoic) acid. It is used in synthetic acetate fibers, in lacquers, and in acetate film.

**acetic acid** *See* ETHANOIC ACID

**acetone** (propanone) Colorless flammable liquid ($CH_3COCH_3$) made by oxidizing isopropyl alcohol. It is a raw material for the manufacture of many organic chemicals and is a widely used solvent. Properties: sp.gr. 0.79; m.p. −94.8°C (−138.6°F); b.p. 56.2°C (133.2°F).

**Achaemenids** Ruling dynasty of the first PERSIAN EMPIRE, which stretched from the Nile River as far E as modern Afghanistan. The dynasty was founded by CYRUS THE GREAT (r.559–529 BC) and named for his ancestor, Achaemenes. Its last ruler, DARIUS III (r.336–330 BC), was defeated by ALEXANDER THE GREAT.

**Achebe, (Albert) Chinua (Chinualumogu)** (1930– ) Nigerian novelist. Achebe's work deals primarily with the search for identity in modern Africa and explores the effects of cultural change. His highly acclaimed first novel, *Things Fall Apart* (1958), depicts life in an African village before and after the arrival of missionaries. He received the Nobel Prize for literature in 1989. Other works include *No Longer at Ease* (1960), *Arrow of God* (1964) and *Anthills of the Savannah* (1987). The volume of poems *Beware Soul Brothers* (1971) deals with Achebe's experience of the Nigerian civil war.

**Acheson, Dean** (1893–1971) US statesman, secretary of state (1949–53) under Harry S TRUMAN. Acheson's desire to restrict the growth of communism was fundamental to the establishment of the North Atlantic Treaty Organization (NATO), the ANZUS Pact, and the Marshall Plan. He was criticized for his lack of support for the new state of Taiwan and his advocacy of US military involvement in South Korea.

**Achilles** In the Greek epic tradition, a formidable warrior, the most fearless Greek fighter of the Trojan War, and the hero of Homer's *Iliad*. Legend held him invulnerable from weapons because he had been dipped by his mother, Thetis, in the Styx River at birth, except for the heel by which he was held. Achilles sought glory fighting at TROY, but an arrow shot by PARIS struck his heel and killed him.

**Achilles tendon** Strong band of elastic connective tissue at the back of the ankle. One of the largest tendons in the body, it connects the calf muscles to the heel bone. The spring provided by this tendon is very important in walking, running, and jumping.

**acid** Chemical compound containing hydrogen that can be replaced by a metal or other positive ION to form a SALT. Acids dissociate in water to yield aqueous hydrogen ions ($H^+$), thus acting as proton donors. The solutions are corrosive, have a sour taste, and have a PH below 7. *See also* BASE

**acid rain** Rain that is highly acidic because of sulfur oxides, nitrogen oxides, and other air pollutants dissolved in it. Acid rain may have a pH value as low as 2.8. Acid rain can severely damage both plant and animal life. Certain lakes, for example, have lost all fish and plant life because of acid rain.

**acne** Inflammatory disorder of the sebaceous (oil-producing) glands of the SKIN resulting in skin eruptions such as blackheads and infected pimples; it is seen mostly on the face, neck, back, and chest. Acne is extremely common in both sexes at PUBERTY, but is usually more pronounced in boys. It does not usually persist beyond early adulthood.

**Aconcagua** Mountain in the Andes range on the border between Argentina and Chile. The highest peak outside Asia at 6,960m (22,834ft), the snow-capped extinct volcano was first climbed in 1897. The River Aconcagua rises at its NW foot and enters the Pacific N of Valparaiso.

► **acropolis** The fortified high point of many Greek cities, the most famous acropolis is that of Athens. It is dominated by the Parthenon, one of the world's most impressive structures. Built as an expression of Athens' supremacy, it housed a vast ivory and gold statue of Athena, the Greek goddess of war, wisdom and the arts.

**aconite** Flowering plant of the genus *Aconitum*. Its roots provide the ALKALOID aconitine, used in medicine; in ancient times it was used as a poison. Species of *Aconitum* include monkshood and wolfsbane. Family Ranunculaceae.

**acorn** Fruit of an OAK tree

**acoustics** Study of sound, especially the behavior of sound waves. Experts apply acoustics in the design of concert and lecture halls, microphones, loudspeakers, and musical instruments. Audiologists use acoustics to assess degrees of abnormality in their patients' hearing. *See also* ANECHOIC CHAMBER

**Acquired Immune Deficiency Syndrome (AIDS)** Fatal disease caused by a RETROVIRUS, called Human Immunodeficiency Virus (HIV), that renders the body's IMMUNE SYSTEM incapable of resisting infection. The first diagnosis was in New York in 1979. In 1983–84 scientists at the Pasteur Institute in France and the National Cancer Institute in the US isolated HIV as the cause of the disease. The virus can remain dormant in infected cells for up to 10 years. Initial AIDS-related complex (ARC) symptoms include severe weight loss and fatigue. It may develop into the AIDS syndrome, characterized by secondary infections, neurological damage, and cancers. AIDS is transmitted only by a direct exchange of body fluids, most commonly through sexual intercourse, the sharing of contaminated needles by intravenous drug users, and the uterus of infected mothers to their babies. Before effective screening was introduced, many hemophiliacs were infected through transfusions of contaminated blood. In the US and Europe, more than 90% of victims have been homosexual or bisexual men. However, 90% of reported cases are in the developing world and many victims are heterosexual. Combinations of drugs have met with some success in controlling symptoms. By 1996 more than 6.4 million people had died from AIDS.

**acre** Unit of area measurement in English-speaking countries, equal to 4,840sq yd (0.405ha).

**acropolis** Hilltop fortress of an ancient Greek city. The earliest known examples were fortified castles built for the Mycenaean kings, and it was only later that they became the symbolic homes of the gods. The most famous acropolis is in Athens; it includes the PARTHENON.

**acrostic** Piece of prose or poetry in which the initial letters of each word or line spell a word or phrase. For example: Aesthetic Conceit, Relying On Studying The Initial Characters.

**acrylic** Type of plastic, one of a group of synthetic, short-chain, unsaturated, carboxylic acid derivatives. Variations include hard and transparent, soft and resilient, or liquid forms. They are used for molded structural parts, adhesives, and paints.

**actinide series** Group of radioactive elements with similar chemical properties. Their atomic numbers range from 89 to 103. Each element is analogous to the corresponding LANTHANIDE SERIES (rare-earth) group. The most important of the group is uranium. Those having atomic numbers greater than 92 are called TRANSURANIC ELEMENTS.

**actinium** Radioactive metallic element (symbol Ac), the first of the ACTINIDE SERIES, discovered in 1899 by the French chemist André Debierne. It is found associated with uranium ores. $^{227}Ac$, a decay product of $^{235}U$, emits beta particles (electrons) during disintegration. Properties: at.no. 89; at.wt. 227 (of most stable isotope); sp.gr. 10.07 (calc.); m.p. 1,900°F (1,100°C); b.p. 5,800°F (3,200°C); most stable isotope $^{227}Ac$ (half-life 21.8 yr).

**action painting** Act and result of applying paint spontaneously. A dynamic style, it gained momentum in 1952 when painters such as Willem DE KOONING and Jackson POLLOCK moved away from ABSTRACT EXPRESSIONISM to make pictures with spontaneous gestures such as dripping and pouring paint onto their canvases. Its purpose is to stimulate vision and to show a record of passing emotions. Other practitioners include Alan Davie, Mathieu Emilio, Robert MOTHERWELL, and Jean-Paul Riopelle.

**action potential** Change that occurs in the electrical potential between the outside and the inside of a nerve fiber or muscle fiber when stimulated by the transmission of a nerve impulse. At rest the fiber is electrically negative inside and positive outside. When the nerve or muscle is stimulated, the charges are momentarily reversed.

**Actium, Battle of** (31 BC) Naval battle in which the fleet of Octavian (later Emperor AUGUSTUS) defeated the fleets of MARK ANTONY and CLEOPATRA. Mark Antony's army surrendered a week later.

**active transport** Energy-requiring process by which molecules or ions are transported across the membranes of living cells against a concentration gradient. It is particularly important in the uptake of food across the gut lining, in the reabsorption of water and salts from the urine in the kidney before excretion, and in the uptake of minerals by the plant root. Active transport enables cells to maintain an internal chemical environment which is of a different composition from that of their surroundings.

**act of Congress** Statute adopted by the US CONGRESS. It overrides conflicting legislation from any other source, although the SUPREME COURT may rule that an act of Congress is unconstitutional.

**act of Parliament** Statute created in Britain when a bill, having passed through a variety of stages in both the House of Commons and House of Lords, receives the royal assent. An act remains in force until it is repealed by Parliament.

**Act of Union** *See* UNION, ACTS OF

**Actors' Studio** Theater workshop founded by Elia KAZAN, Cheryl Crawford, and Robert Lewis in New York in 1947. It became noted for the "method" approach to acting, particularly under Lee STRASBERG. In the early 1960s, it also began to produce plays on Broadway. An enduring and influential workshop, its many eminent members include Marlon BRANDO, Dustin HOFFMAN, and Robert DE NIRO.

**Acts of the Apostles** Book of the New Testament describing the spread of the Gospel of Christ immediately after his death and resurrection. It mainly focuses on St. PETER and St. PAUL. The book was probably written *c*.65 AD by the author of St. Luke's gospel.

**acupuncture** System of medical treatment in which long needles are inserted into the body to assist healing, relieve pain, or for anesthetic purposes. Of ancient Chinese origin, it has so far defied scientific explanation.

**Adam** In the Old Testament (Genesis 2), first man and progenitor of all mankind, created from dust by God in his own image. He and his wife EVE were cast out of the Garden of EDEN to become mortal after they ate forbidden fruit from the Tree of the Knowledge of Good and Evil.

**Adam, Robert** (1728–92) Scottish architect, best known of four brothers who were all architects. Adam was the greatest British architect of the late-18th century and his refined neo-Classical style was widely influential. He was equally brilliant as an interior decorator and furniture designer. The vast Adelphi complex, London, begun in 1768, was his most ambitious project; his interior designs include Kenwood House, London (1767) and Syon House, Middlesex (1762–69).

**Adams, Ansel** (1902–84) US photographer. Concentrating on the scenic grandeur of the West, Adams produced magnificent prints that are widely exhibited and reproduced. A co-founder of the *f*/64 group, he was instrumental in forming museum and university photographic departments and was a celebrated teacher. He wrote the *Basic Photo-Books* series of technical manuals (1968).

**Adams, Brooks** (1848–1927) US historian. His *Law of Civilization and Decay* (1895) held that civilizations rise and fall with the growth and decline of commerce. In *America's Economic Supremacy* (1900), he predicted the decline of Western Europe and proposed that within 50 years only the US and Russia would be great powers.

**Adams, Gerry** (1948– ) Northern Irish politician, president of SINN FÉIN (1983– ). Adams was interned (1972–78) by the British for his involvement in the IRISH REPUBLICAN ARMY (IRA). He was vice president (1978–83) of Sinn Féin. Adams is seen as a pivotal figure between the "ballot box" and "bullet" factions of the Republican movement. Adams served (1983–92, 1997– ) as a member of parliament for Belfast West, but refused to take his seat at Westminster. His negotiations with John HUME led to an IRA ceasefire (1994). He headed the Sinn Féin delegation in the 1997 peace talks, and became the first Republican leader to meet a British prime minister since 1921.

**ADAPTATION**

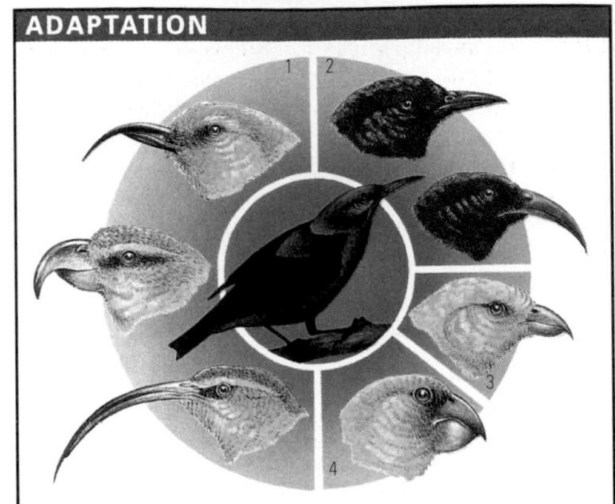


The various honeycreepers of Hawaii in the Pacific evolved from one species of bird now long extinct (center). Over millions of years the honeycreepers evolved different methods of feeding. This ensured the island's various habitat niches could be exploited, resulting in less competition among the birds and therefore allowing more to survive. The main adaptation was the dramatic change in the shape of the beaks. A few species evolved beaks best suited to feed on nectar (1), others feed purely on insects (2), while some feed on fruit (3) or seeds (4).

**Adams, Henry Brooks** (1838–1918) US historian and writer. A direct descendant of John ADAMS and John Quincy ADAMS, his best-known work is an autobiography, *The Education of Henry Adams* (1907), which is also an ironic analysis of a technological society.

**Adams, John** (1735–1826) Second US president (1797–1801). Influenced by his radical cousin Samuel ADAMS, he helped draft the DECLARATION OF INDEPENDENCE (1776) and the Treaty of Paris (1783) which ended the AMERICAN REVOLUTION. He was George WASHINGTON's vice president (1789–97). His presidency was marked by conflict between Alexander HAMILTON's FEDERALIST PARTY and Thomas JEFFERSON's DEMOCRATIC-REPUBLICAN PARTY. Adams' moderate stance enabled a negotiated settlement of the XYZ AFFAIR (1797–98). He reluctantly endorsed the ALIEN AND SEDITION ACTS (1798).

**Adams, John** (1947– ) US composer. He became interested in electronics, jazz, and the music of experimental US composers such as John Cage and Morton Feldman. Most of his output is written in an intentionally accessible minimalist style. In 1989 Adams won a Grammy Award for Best Contemporary Composition for his opera *Nixon in China* (1987).

**Adams, John Quincy** (1767–1848) Sixth US president (1825–29), son of the second president John ADAMS. Adams served in his father's administration, before acting (1803–08) as FEDERALIST PARTY member in the US Senate. Adams was secretary of state (1817–24) for James MONROE. He was largely responsible for formulating the MONROE DOCTRINE and negotiating the ADAMS-ONÍS TREATY (1819). Adams became president without an electoral majority, his appointment confirmed by the House of Representatives. Adams' lack of a mandate and non-partisan approach contributed to his electoral defeat by Andrew JACKSON. Adams served in the House of Representatives (1830–48).

**Adams, Samuel** (1722–1803) American revolutionary leader. As a member and clerk of the Massachusetts legislature (1765–74), he was the chief spokesman for revolution. He helped form several radical organizations, led the STAMP ACT protest in 1765, helped plan the BOSTON TEA PARTY of 1773, and was a signatory of the DECLARATION OF INDEPENDENCE (1776). He was a delegate to the CONTINENTAL CONGRESS until 1781.

**Adams-Onís Treaty** (1819) Agreement between the US and Spain. Negotiated by secretary of state John Quincy ADAMS and Spanish minister Luis de Onís, Spain gave up its land E of the Mississippi River and its claims to the Oregon Territory; the US assumed debts of $5 million and gave up claims to Texas.

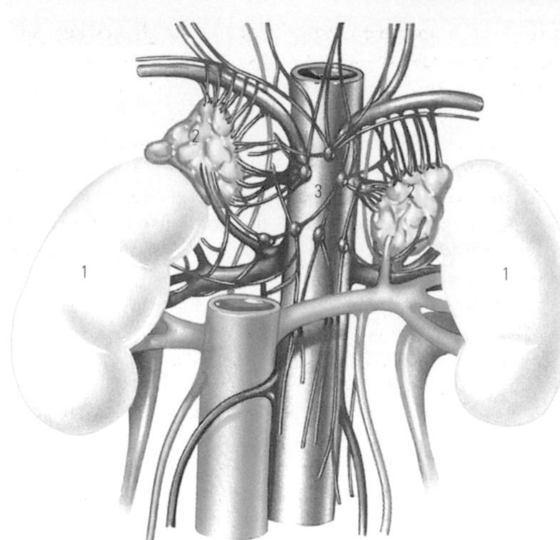


► **adrenal gland** Located just above the kidneys (1), the two adrenal glands (2) are well supplied with blood entering from the aorta (3). Each gland consists of an outer layer (the cortex) and a central medulla. The cortex produces steroid hormones and hormones involved in maintaining water balance, and small quantities of sex hormones. The medulla produces epinephrine and norepinephrine, both of which prepare the body for an emergency situation.

**adaptation** Adjustment by a living organism to its surroundings. Animals and plants adapt to changes in their environment through variations in structure, reproduction, or organization within communities. Some such changes are temporary (ACCLIMATIZATION), while others may involve changes in the genetic material (DNA) and be inherited by offspring (EVOLUTION). The word is also used to describe a particular characteristic, as body size, shape, color, physiology, or behavior, that fits an organism to survive in its environment.

**adaptive radiation** In biology, the EVOLUTION of different forms of living organisms from a common ancestral stock, as different populations adapt to different environmental conditions or modes of life. Eventually the populations may become so different that they constitute separate species. Examples are the many different kinds of finches in the GALÁPAGOS ISLANDS, which diversified to specialize in different kinds of food, feeding methods, and HABITATS. *See also* ADAPTATION

**Addams, Jane** (1860–1935) US reformer. Addams shared the 1931 Nobel Peace Prize with Nicholas Murray Butler. In 1889 she founded Hull House, Chicago – an early settlement house. She pioneered labor, housing, health, and legal reforms, and campaigned for female suffrage, pacifism, and the rights of immigrants.

**adder** Any of several snakes in various parts of the world, some poisonous and others harmless. The European viper (*Vipera berus*) is called an adder in Britain. The puff adder (*Bitis arietans*) is a large African viper, and the death adder (*Acanthophis antarticus*) is a dangerous Australian elapid.

**addiction** Inability to control the use of a particular substance, resulting in physiological or psychological dependence. It is most frequently associated with DRUG ADDICTION. In a medical context, addiction requires a physical dependence. When the dose of a drug is reduced or withdrawn from the user, the addict experiences withdrawal syndromes. Psychological dependence on activities such as gambling or exercise are difficult to distinguish from a disorder or MANIA.

**Addis Ababa** Capital and largest city in Ethiopia, located on a plateau at *c.*8,000ft (2,400m) in the highlands of Shewa province. It was made capital of Ethiopia in 1889. It is the headquarters of the ORGANIZATION OF AFRICAN UNITY (OAU). It is the main center for the country's coffee trade. Industries: tanning, textiles, wood products. Pop. (1990 est.) 1,700,000.

**Addison, Joseph** (1672–1719) English essayist, poet and politician. Addison's poetic celebration of Marlborough's victory at the Battle of Blenheim, *The Campaign* (1704), led to a government appointment. He is chiefly remembered as a brilliant essayist. His stylish articles were a major reason for the success of the newly-established *Tatler* and *Spectator* periodicals. He was England's secretary of state (1717–18).

**addition reaction** Chemical reaction in which two substances combine to form a third substance, with no other substance being produced. Addition reactions are most commonly used in ORGANIC CHEMISTRY, particularly by adding a simple molecule across a carbon-carbon double bond in an UNSATURATED COMPOUND. *See also* SUBSTITUTION

**Adelaide** Capital of the state of SOUTH AUSTRALIA, situated at the mouth of the Torrens River on the Gulf of St. Vincent. Founded in 1836, Adelaide is noted for its churches and fine cathedrals. There are two universities. The port provides facilities for an extensive hinterland and exports wool, fruit, wine, and wheat. Industries: oil refining, machinery, motor vehicle assembly, electronics, chemicals, textiles. Pop. (1994) 1,076,400.

**Aden** Commercial capital and largest city of Yemen, historic capital of the Aden Protectorate (1937–67) and the former (southern) People's Democratic Republic of Yemen (1967–90). A seaport city on the Gulf of Aden, 100mi (160km) E of the Red Sea, Aden was an important Roman trading port. With the opening of the SUEZ CANAL in 1869, its importance increased. It was made a British crown colony in 1937; the surrounding territory became the Aden Protectorate. In 1970 Aden became the sole capital of the new People's Democratic Republic of Yemen. When the (northern) Yemen Arab Republic and the (southern) People's Democratic Republic of Yemen combined to form a united Republic of Yemen in 1990, SANA'A became the official capital. Industries: cigarette manufacture, oil, and salt refining. Pop. (1995) 562,000.

**Adenauer, Konrad** (1876–1967) German statesman, first chancellor of the Federal Republic of Germany (1949–63). He was twice imprisoned by the Nazis. He helped to create the Christian Democratic Union (CDU), West Germany's dominant post-war party, and was its leader (1946–66). Adenauer led West Germany into NATO (1955) and campaigned for the establishment of the EUROPEAN ECONOMIC COMMUNITY.

**adenoids** Masses of LYMPH tissue in the upper part of the PHARYNX (throat) behind the NOSE; part of a child's defenses against disease, they normally disappear by the age of ten.

**adenosine diphosphate (ADP)** Chemical involved in energy-generating reactions (*see* RESPIRATION) during METABOLISM.

**adenosine triphosphate (ATP)** Chemical found in all plant and animal cells. It is fundamental in the biochemical reactions required to support life. *See also* RESPIRATION

**adhesion** In chemistry, attraction of molecules of one substance to those of another. GUM, GLUE, and paste use the property of adhesion to join substances together. *See also* COHESION

**adhesion** In medicine, fibrous band of connective tissue developing at a site of inflammation or damage; it may bind together adjacent tissues, such as loops of intestine, occasionally causing obstruction.

**adipose tissue** (fatty tissue) Connective tissue made up of body cells which store large globules of fat.

**Adirondack Mountains** Circular mountain group located in NE New York State, reaching from Mohawk Valley in the S to the St. Lawrence River in the N. There are many gorges, waterfalls, and lakes. Much of the area makes up the Adirondack Forest Preserve. Noted for its resorts (including Lake Placid), its highest point is Mount Marcy, 5,344 ft (1,629m).

**adjutant stork** Large scavenging bird found in Africa, India, and SE Asia, named for its military gait. It has white, black, and gray plumage and throat pouches; it feeds on carrion. Length: up to 60in (152cm). Species *Leptoptilos crumeniferus*.

**Adler, Alfred** (1870–1937) Austrian psychiatrist. After working with Sigmund FREUD (1902–11), Adler broke away to found his own school of "individual psychology." He believed that striving for social success and power was fundamental in human motivation. According to his theory, individuals develop problems and maladjustments when they cannot surmount feelings of inferiority acquired in childhood.

**Adler, Felix** (1851–1933) US ethical philosopher, b. Germany. Like KANT he stressed the importance of the individual and believed that ETHICS need not be founded on religious or philosophical beliefs nor assume the existence of a supreme being. In 1876 he founded the Society for Ethical Culture, the forerunner of the international Ethical Movement. Among its aims were the economic, social, and intellectual development of disadvantaged people. Adler also supported social reforms, such as improved housing and the abolition of child labor. His books include *Creed and Deed* (1877), *The Moral Instruction of Children* (1892), and *An Ethical Philosophy of Life* (1918).

A

**administrative law** Laws that regulate the powers, procedures, and acts of administrative agencies of the executive branch of government.

**Admiral's Cup** International yachting competition, established in 1957 and held biennially at Cowes, Isle of Wight, England. Teams of three yachts from each participating country compete in four events.

**Adonis** In Phoenician and Greek myth, a youth of remarkable beauty, loved by PERSEPHONE and APHRODITE. Adonis was gored to death by a boar and during his afterlife Zeus decided that Adonis should spend part of the year with Persephone, queen of the underworld, and part with Aphrodite.

**adrenal gland** One of a pair of small endocrine glands situated on top of the KIDNEYS. They produce many STEROIDS that regulate the blood's salt and water balance and are concerned with the METABOLISM of carbohydrates, proteins, and fats, and the HORMONES EPINEPHRINE and norepinephrine. *See also* ENDOCRINE SYSTEM

**Adrian IV** (*c*.1100–59) Pope (1154–59), b. Nicholas Breakspear, the only English pope. In 1155 he crowned emperor FREDERICK I, Barbarossa.

**Adriatic Sea** Shallow arm of the Mediterranean Sea, separated from the Ionian Sea by the Strait of Otranto, between Albania and the "heel" of Italy. Lobsters and sardines are the chief catches of local fisheries. Length: *c*.500mi (800km); Max. depth: 4,035ft (1,230m).

**adsorption** Attraction of a gas or liquid to the surface of a solid or liquid. It involves attraction of molecules at the surface, unlike ABSORPTION, which implies incorporation. The amounts adsorbed and the rate of adsorption depend on the structure exposed, the chemical identities and concentrations of the substances involved, and the temperature.

**Advent** (Lat. coming) Liturgical season preceding Christmas. It begins on the Sunday nearest 30 November (St Andrew's Day). In many countries, observances during Advent include the lighting of candles. Advent refers both to Christ's birth and his coming in glory as judge at the end of history.

**Adventists** Christians belonging to any of a group of churches whose distinctive belief concerns the imminent Second Coming of Christ. William Miller (1782–1849) formed the first organized Adventist movement in the US in 1831. Christ's failure to return on dates forecast by Miller led to splits in the movement. The largest group to emerge was the SEVENTH-DAY ADVENTISTS.

**Aegean civilization** (*c*.3000–1100 BC) Bronze Age cultures, chiefly MINOAN and MYCENAEAN, of Greece and the Aegean islands. The artistically brilliant Minoan civilization flourished in Crete, reaching its height between *c*.1700 and 1100 BC, when it was probably overrun by Mycenaens from mainland Greece. In the 13th century BC Mycenaean sea power imposed a roughly uniform civilization over the whole region. From *c*.1200 BC, for reasons still uncertain, Mycenaean civilization began to disintegrate and ultimately disappeared.

**Aegean Sea** Part of the Mediterranean Sea between Greece and Turkey, bounded by Crete to the S and connected to the Black Sea and the Sea of Marmara by the Dardanelles to the NE. Oil and natural gas have been discovered in the area, but the principal income is derived from tourism, fishing, and crops such as citrus fruits, olives, and grapes.

**Aeneas** In Greek mythology, the son of Anchises and Aphrodite. Active in the defense of TROY, he led the Trojans to Italy. The Romans acknowledged Aeneas and his Trojan company as their ancestors.

**Aeneid** Poem written by the Roman poet VIRGIL between 30–19 BC. Written in 12 books, the *Aeneid* recounts the legendary founding of the town of Lavinium by the Trojan AENEAS.

**Aeolians** Ancient Greek people. In *c*.1100 BC, they settled on Lesbos and other islands. They were famous for their music and poetry.

**aerobic** Connected with or dependent on the presence of free oxygen or air. An aerobic organism can only survive in the presence of oxygen and depends on it for breaking down GLUCOSE and other foods to release energy. This process is called aerobic respiration. **Aerobics** are physical exercises whose purpose is to improve physical fitness through walking, jogging, running, and similar activities. *See also* ANAEROBIC

**aerodynamics** Science of gases in motion and the forces acting on objects, such as aircraft, in motion through the air. An aircraft designer must consider four main factors and their interrelationships: **weight** of the aircraft and the load it will carry; **lift** to overcome the pull of gravity; **drag**, or the forces that retard motion; and **thrust**, the driving force. Engineers use the WIND TUNNEL and computer systems to predict aerodynamic performance.

**aeronautics** Study of flight and the control of AIRCRAFT involving AERODYNAMICS, aircraft structures, and methods of propulsion. Aeronautics started with the study of the BALLOON, which mainly concerned BUOYANCY. It later included the heavier-than-air flight of gliders, planes, helicopters, and rockets. The increased speeds of modern aircraft to supersonic (speeds in excess of that of sound, *c*.750mph or 1,200km/h) and the accompanying shock waves this produces has brought changes in wing and fuselage designs to improve streamlining. With hypersonic speeds (in excess of five times the speed of sound or Mach 5), the forces involved again change fundamentally, requiring further design adjustments.

**aerosol** Suspension of liquid or solid particles in a gas. Fog – millions of tiny water droplets suspended in air – is a liquid-based example; airborne dust or smoke is a solid-based equivalent. Manufactured aerosols are used in products such as deodorants, cosmetics, paints, and household sprays. CHLOROFLUOROCARBONS (CFCs) are being phased out as aerosol propellants because they damage the OZONE LAYER.

**Aeschylus** (525–456 BC) Earliest of the great Greek playwrights. Aeschylus is said to have been responsible for the development of TRAGEDY as a dramatic form through his addition of a second actor, and for his reduction of the role of the chorus. He was also the first to introduce scenery. His best-known work is the trilogy *Oresteia*, which comprises *Agamemnon*, *The Choephori*, and *The Eumenides*.

**Aesir** Primary group of Nordic gods who lived in Asgard. Woden (Odin), Thor (Donar), and Tyr (Tiw), with a few others, were the object of a cult that extended throughout the lands inhabited by Germanic peoples. Secondary to the Aesir was a group of gods known as the Vanir.

**Aesop** (620–560 BC) Semi-legendary Greek fabulist. The reputed creator of numerous short tales about animals, all illustrating human virtues and failings (they are almost certainly written by several people). According to one tradition, he was a former slave.

**AERODYNAMICS**

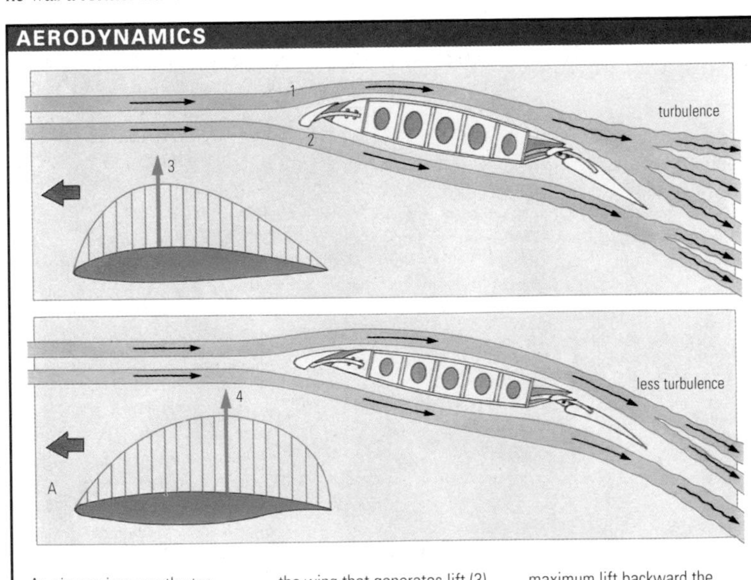


As air passing over the top edge of an airfoil (1) has to travel further than the air flowing beneath it (2), an area of low pressure forms above the wing that generates lift (3). In modern high-lift airfoils (A) the center of pressure is further toward the rear of the wing (4). By moving the point of maximum lift backward the airfoil has a more even distribution of lift allowing a plane to fly more slowly without stalling.

A

**aesthetic movement** Late 19th-century English cult of beauty. It grew out of aestheticism, a philosophy which spread across Europe in reaction to industrialization and UTILITARIANISM. The principal figures of the movement were Aubrey BEARDSLEY, Walter Pater, J.M. WHISTLER and Oscar WILDE.

**aesthetics** (Gk. *aisthēsis*, perception) Specialized branch of philosophy concerned with the arts. PLATO's classical formulation of art as a mirror of nature was developed by ARISTOTLE in his *Poetics*. As a distinct discipline, aesthetics dates from Alexander Baumgarten's *Reflections on Poetry* (1735). Common problems in aesthetics include a definition of beauty and the ascribing of artistic value. For Plato and Aristotle beauty is objective, it resides in the object. David HUME argued that the value of art was dependent on subjective perception. Immanuel KANT in his *Critique of Judgement* (1790) mediated between the two, arguing that artistic value may be subjective, but it has universal validity in the form of pleasure. Later philosophers, such as George SANTANYANA and Benedetto Croce, have focused on art as a socially symbolic act.

**affidavit** Formal written statement tstifying on oath that a specified fact or account is true. Countersigned (usually with an official seal) by a witness of juridical authority, affidavits may be used as evidence in court and tribunal proceedings, or to guarantee the identity of a person claiming legal rights.

**Africa** Second-largest continent (after Asia), straddling the equator and lying largely within the tropics. **Land** Africa forms a plateau between the Atlantic and Indian oceans. Its highest features include the ATLAS and Ahaggar mountains in the NW, the Ethiopian Highlands in the E, the Drakensberg Mountains in the S, and KILIMANJARO. Lake Assal in the Afar Depression of Djibouti is the lowest point at −502ft (−153m). The huge sunken strip in the E is the African section of the Great RIFT VALLEY. The SAHARA stretches across the N and the KALAHARI and NAMIB are smaller deserts in the S and SW. MADAGASCAR lies off the SE coast. **Structure and geology** Africa is composed largely of ancient metamorphic rocks overlain with tertiary Mesozoic and Paleozoic sediments. The mountains of the NW are folded sedimentary material, roughly contemporaneous with the Alps. The Great Rift Valley, formed by the progressive movement of the Arabian Peninsula away from Africa, is mainly igneous in the N and mainly older pre-Cambrian in the S. **Lakes and rivers** The Rift Valley contains the lakes ALBERT, MALAWI, and TANGANYIKA. Lake VICTORIA to the E is Africa's largest; Lake CHAD lies in the S Sahara. Rivers include the

## AFGHANISTAN

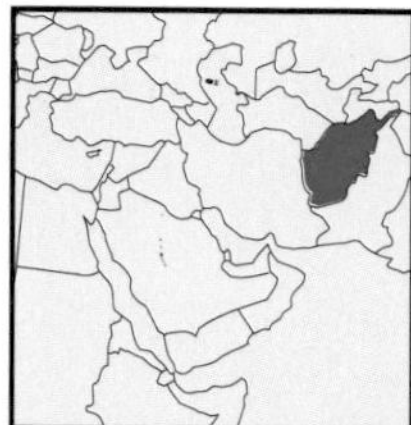

Introduced in December 1992, this flag uses the colors of the Mujaheddin (holy warriors) who fought against Afghanistan's Socialist government and then the Soviet occupation from the 1970s. The flag bears the new national arms of the country.

**AREA:** 251,773sq mi (652,090sq km)
**POPULATION:** 19,062,000
**CAPITAL (POPULATION):** Kabul (700,000)
**GOVERNMENT:** Islamic republic
**ETHNIC GROUPS:** Pathan (Pashtun) 52%, Tajik 20%, Uzbek 9%, Hazara 9%, Chahar 3%, Turkmen 2%, Baluchi 1%
**LANGUAGES:** Pashto, Dari (Persian) – both official
**RELIGIONS:** Islam (Sunni Muslim 74%, Shiite Muslim 25%)
**CURRENCY:** Afghani = 100 puls

The Republic of Afghanistan is a landlocked country in S Asia bordered by Turkmenistan, Uzbekistan, Tajikistan, China, Pakistan, and Iran. The central highlands reach a height of more than 24,930ft (7,600m) in the E and make up nearly 75% of Afghanistan. The main range is the HINDU KUSH, which is cut by deep, fertile valleys. North of the central highlands are broad plateaus and hilly areas. To the S are lowlands, consisting largely of stony desert or semidesert.

### CLIMATE

The height of the land and the country's remote position have a great effect on the climate. In winter northerly winds bring cold weather to the mountains, but summers are hot and dry. To the S rainfall decreases and temperatures are higher all year.

### VEGETATION

Grasslands cover much of the N, while the vegetation in the dry S is sparse. Trees are rare in both regions, but forests of coniferous trees such as pine and fir grow on the higher mountain slopes, with cedars lower down. Alder, ash, juniper, oak, and walnut trees grow in the mountain valleys.

### HISTORY

In ancient times, Afghanistan was in turn invaded by Aryans, Persians, Greeks, Macedonians, and warrior armies from central Asia. Arab armies introduced Islam in the late 7th century, and founded several short-lived Muslim dynasties.

The modern history of Afghanistan began in 1747, when the various tribes in the area united for the first time. In the 19th century, Russia and Britain struggled for control of the area. Russia was seeking an outlet to the Indian Ocean, while Britain was looking for a means to protect its Indian territories against Russia. British troops invaded Afghanistan in 1839–42 and again in 1878. In 1921 Afghanistan became fully independent.

### POLITICS

After World War II the country remained neutral during the Cold War, siding neither with the US nor the Soviet Union. In 1973 the army leaders overthrew the monarchy and made the country a republic. In 1978 the government was taken over by a Socialist group, which turned to the Soviet Union for aid. Many people rebelled against the pro-Communist government, and, in late 1979, Soviet troops invaded the country. During the 1980s, the Soviet troops fought unsuccessfully to put down the rebel Muslim forces, who were called the MUJAHEDDIN. In 1988–89 Soviet troops withdrew, but the civil war raged on and the number of refugees continued to mount. In 1992 Mujaheddin forces captured Kabul and set up a moderate Islamic government. Fundamentalists continued to agitate. In 1996 the TALIBAN (Persian, "students"), based in the S city of KANDAHAR, captured Kabul and formed an interim government. An anti-Taliban coalition (United Islamic Front for the Salvation of Afghanistan) failed to prevent further gains, and by 1998 the Taliban controlled 90% of the country.

### ECONOMY

Afghanistan is one of the world's poorest countries, depending heavily on agriculture, which employs about 60% of the work force. Many people are seminomadic, moving around with their herds of sheep and other animals, while wheat is the chief crop of the settled farmers in the valleys.

The country has many mineral deposits, but most are undeveloped. Natural gas is produced, together with some coal, copper, gold, precious stones, and salt, but Afghanistan has few manufacturing industries. The main exports are karakul skins, which are used to make hats and jackets, cotton, dried and fresh fruit, and nuts.

Nile, Niger, Congo, and Zambezi. **Climate and vegetation** Much of the continent is hot and (outside the desert areas) humid. The belt along the equator receives more than 100in (250cm) of precipitation a year and is covered by tropical rain forest. The forest gives way both in the N and S to areas of acacia and brush and then through savanna grassland to desert. The N strip of the continent and the area around the Cape have a Mediterranean climate. **Peoples** Africa is home to over 13% of the world's population divided into more than 700 culturally distinct tribes and groups. N of the Sahara Arabs and Berbers predominate, while to the S some of the many black tribes include the Akan, Fulani, Galla, Hausa, Hottentots, Ibo, Masai, Mossi, San, Yoruba, and Zulu. Indians and Europeans also form significant minorities. Africa is relatively thinly populated and c.75% of the population is rural. **Economy** Agriculture is restricted in central Africa by the large expanse of tropical rain forest, though cash crops such as cocoa, rubber, and peanuts are grown on plantations. Along the N coast, crops such as citrus fruits, olives, and cereals are grown. The Sahara is largely unproductive, supporting only a nomadic herding community. E and S Africa are the richest agricultural areas, containing large mixed farms and cattle ranching. Apart from South Africa, the continent is industrially underdeveloped. Mining is important. Zambia contains the largest deposits of copper ore in the world, bauxite is extracted in W Africa, and oil is produced in Libya, Algeria, and Nigeria. South Africa is extremely rich in minerals, with gold, diamonds, and coal being the most important. **Recent History** Before the 1880s Europeans were, except in South Africa, largely confined to the coastal regions. By the end of the 19th century the whole continent, except for Liberia and Ethiopia, was under foreign domination either by European powers or (in the N) by the Ottoman Empire. Beginning in the 1950s, the former colonies secured their independence within the space of 40 years, but the process of rapid decolonization brought unrest and instability to many parts of the continent. A major factor in this unrest was, and continues to be, the artificial boundaries created by colonialism. Area: c.11,700,000sq mi (30,000,000sq km)

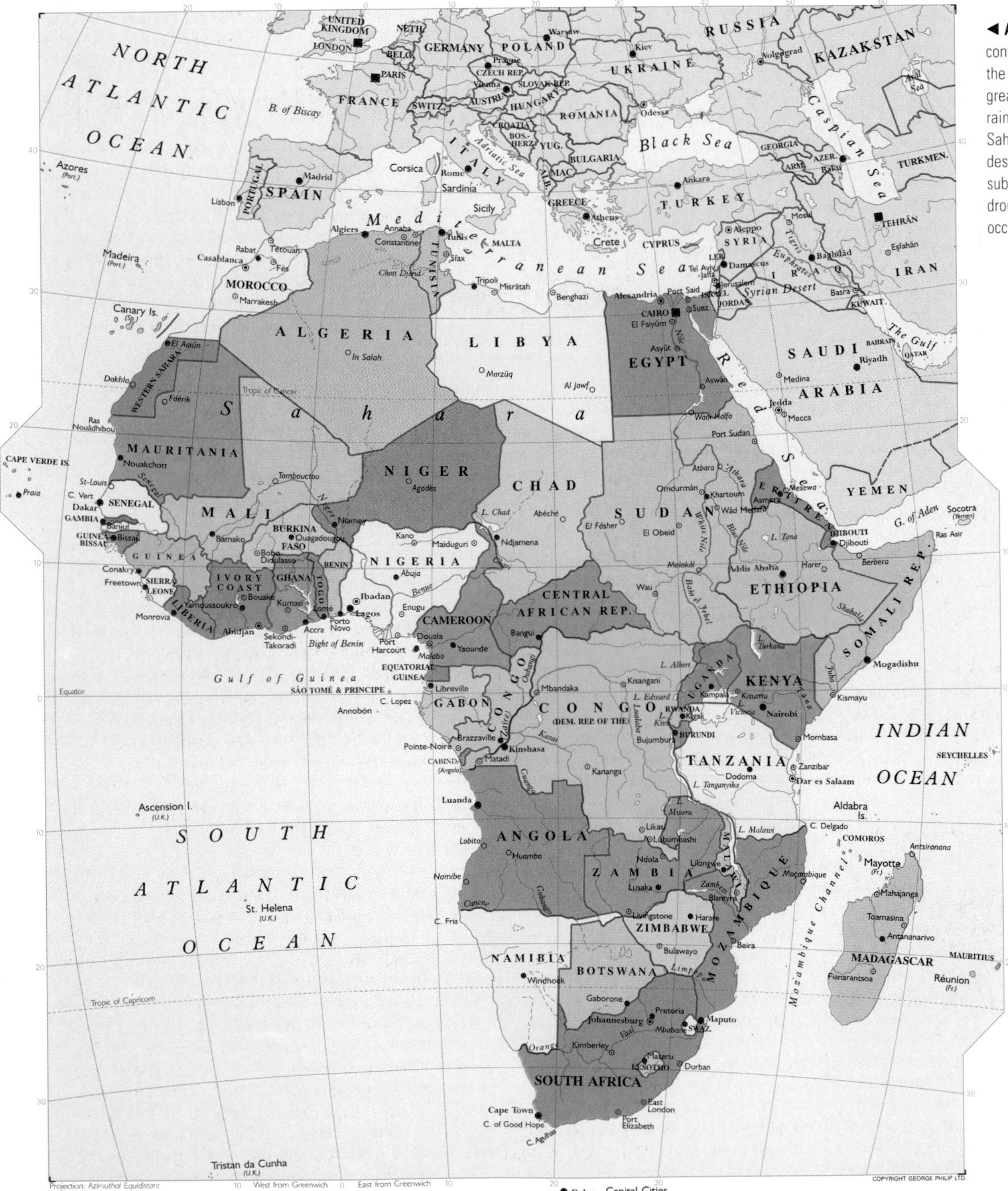


◀ **Africa** Earth's second largest continent, Africa stretches across the equator. Its vegetation varies greatly from the equatorial rainforests to the the vast Sahara, Kalahari, and Namib deserts. The harsh climate of sub-Saharan Africa makes droughts an all too regular occurrence.

*Highest mountain* Kilimanjaro (Tanzania) 19,340ft (5,895m) *Longest river* Nile 4,140mi (6,670km) *Population* (1990 est.) 647,518,000 *Largest cities* CAIRO (6,663,000); KINSHASA (3,804,000); ALEXANDRIA (3,170,000); CAPE TOWN (2,350,000) *See also* articles on individual countries

**African art** Naturalistic rock paintings and engravings, from before 4000 BC are found in the Sahara Desert. They are similar to European PALAEOLITHIC ART. Later African tribal art is inseparable from the ritual life of the community. Examples include: body painting and dance; music and musical instruments (especially the drum); ceremonial masks and small sculptures used in ANCESTOR WORSHIP; weapons and everyday utensils (such as bowls and stools). Wood is the most commonly used material. Artists were usually professionals and received great respect and cultural status. Except for EGYPTIAN ART, the most fertile artistic region is sub-Saharan Africa. The Nok terracotta heads from Nigeria are the earliest examples of African sculpture yet discovered (*c*.500 BC). The naturalistic bronze heads produced by the YORUBA at Ife, SW Nigeria, reveal an early (12th–15th century) mastery of the CIRE PERDUE process. This skill passed to the ASHANTI of Ghana, who produced highly exaggerated figurative sculpture. The Dogon of Mali are renowned for their wooden sculpture, especially stylized wooden masks featuring recessed rectangles. The stonework of GREAT ZIMBABWE reveals a highly advanced grasp of architectural design. Traditional African art influenced early modern European art, especially PICASSO's development of CUBISM and MODIGLIANI's figurative paintings. *See also* ISLAMIC ART AND ARCHITECTURE

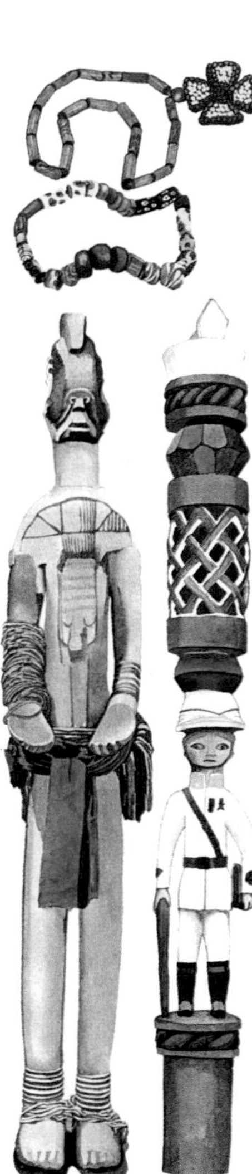

▲ **African art** Sculpture and the decorative arts are among the most varied and finest throughout Africa. The illustration shows beads, a large carved ancestral figure from Nigeria, and a colonial carving.

**African mythology** North Africans are predominantly Islamic, but the many peoples in sub-Saharan Africa have a rich collection of traditional beliefs. Almost all recognize a supreme being who created the universe. There are also innumerable other gods, whose cults flourish in W Africa. Many Africans believe in the power of the spirit world. Belief in reincarnation is also widespread and ANCESTOR WORSHIP is an important social ritual. The dead are feared because they possess greater powers than the living. Many Africans believe that people are reborn in living animals or in inanimate objects. MAGIC plays an important part in people's everyday lives. Medicine men make amulets, necklaces, and other kinds of charms which are believed to ward off evil. Other objects are used to protect crops and houses or to bring rain. Belief in magic has proved more enduring than the traditional mythologies, which have declined with the advance of CHRISTIANITY and ISLAM.

**African National Congress (ANC)** South African political party. It was formed in 1912 with the aim of securing racial equality and full political rights for nonwhites. By the 1950s it had become the principal opposition to the APARTHEID regime. A military wing, *Umkhonte We Sizwe* (Spear of the Nation), was set up in the aftermath of the SHARPEVILLE Massacre. It engaged in economic and industrial sabotage. In 1961 the ANC was banned and many of its leaders were arrested or forced into exile. In 1964 the leaders of the ANC, Nelson MANDELA and Walter SISULU, began long sentences as political prisoners. In 1990 the ANC was legalized, Mandela was released from Robben Island, and many of the legislative pillars of apartheid were dismantled. In 1994, in South Africa's first multiracial elections, the ANC gained more than 60% of the popular vote. Nelson Mandela became the first post-apartheid president of South Africa. In 1997 he was succeeded as ANC leader by Thabo MBEKI.

**Afrikaans** One of 11 official languages of the Republic of South Africa. It is derived from the language spoken by the Dutch settlers of the 17th century but quickly evolved its own forms to become a distinct language. Afrikaans is regarded as a cultural focal point by South Africans of Dutch origin. It is the everyday means of communication for some three million speakers of European, African, and mixed descent.

**Afrika Korps** German armored force in World War II that operated in the N African desert. Under its commander General Erwin ROMMEL it had spectacular but transient success against the British in 1941–42.

**Afrikaner** (*Boer*, farmer) Descendant of the predominantly Dutch settlers in SOUTH AFRICA. Afrikaners first settled around the Cape region in the 17th century. To avoid British control, the Afrikaners spread N and E from the Cape in the GREAT TREK and founded the independent South African Republic (TRANSVAAL) and Orange Free State. Defeat in the SOUTH AFRICAN WAR (1899–1902) led to the republics merging in the Union of South Africa (1910). *See also* CAPE PROVINCE

**Afro-Asiatic languages** (Hamito-Semitic) Family of languages common to both Asia and Africa. They are spoken by *c*.130 million people in N Africa, the Sahara, parts of E, W and central Africa, and W Asia. On the African continent, it includes such languages as Berber and the now extinct Coptic and ancient Egyptian. It also includes the SEMITIC LANGUAGES, notably Arabic and Hebrew, that originated in Syria, Mesopotamia, Arabia and Palestine. With a few exceptions, the family uses a script that is read from right to left.

**Agadir** Atlantic seaport, SW Morocco. In 1960 Agadir suffered a disastrous earthquake, but it was rebuilt as a tourist center and is now a popular European tourist destination. Fishing is the other main economic activity. Pop. (1990) 439,000.

**Aga Khan** Since 1818, title of the leader of the ISHMAILI sect of SHIITE Muslims. Aga Khan III (1877–1957) was the best known. He headed the All-India Muslim League in support of British rule in 1906. He moved to Europe and was known for his enormous wealth and love of horse racing. His son, Karim, became Aga Khan IV in 1957.

**Agamemnon** In Greek mythology, king of Mycenae, and brother of Menelaus. According to Homer's *Iliad*, he led the Greeks at the siege of TROY. When Troy fell, Agamemnon returned home but was murdered by his wife CLYTEMNESTRA and her lover Aegisthus.

**agar** Complex substance extracted from seaweed; its powder forms a "solid" gel in solution. It is used as a thickening agent in foods; as an adhesive; as a medium for growing bacteria, MOLD, YEAST, and other microorganisms; as a medium for TISSUE CULTURE; and as a gel for ELECTROPHORESIS.

**agaric** Order of FUNGI that includes edible mushrooms, ink caps, and the poisonous AMANITA. Their spores are born on the surface of gills or pores on the undersurface of the cap.

**Agassi, Andre** (1970– ) US tennis player. Agassi turned professional at 16, and within two years was ranked third in the world. He won the men's singles titles at Wimbledon (1992), the US Open (1994), and the Australian Open (1995).

**Agassiz, Alexander** (1835–1910) US marine zoologist, b. Switzerland. Agassiz was influential in the development of modern systematic zoology, and made important studies of the SEAFLOOR. In 1874 he succeeded his father, Louis, as curator of the Harvard Museum of Natural History.

**agate** Microcrystalline form of quartz with parallel bands of color. It is regarded as a semiprecious stone and is used for making jewelry. Hardness *c*.6.5; sp.gr. *c*.2.6.

**agave** Succulent, flowering plant found in tropical, subtropical, and temperate regions. Agaves have narrow, lance-shaped leaves clustered at the base of the plant, and many have large flower clusters. The flower of the well-known century plant (*Agave americana*) of SW North America grows up to 25ft (7.6m) in one season. Other species are SISAL (*A. sisalana*) and mescal (*Lophophora williamsii*), whose fermented sap forms the basis of the liqueur tequila. Family Agavaceae.

**Agee, James** (1909–55) US writer. A novelist, poet, influential film critic, and screenwriter for films such as *The African Queen* (1951, co-scripted with John HUSTON) and *The Night of the Hunter* (1955). Agee is perhaps best known for his study of rural poverty, *Let Us Now Praise Famous Men* (1941). His novel *A Death in the Family* (1957) won a Pulitzer Prize.

**Agency for International Development (AID)** US government agency (now under the control of the International Development Cooperation Agency) that carries out assistance programs designed to help peoples of less developed countries develop human and economic resources and increase production capacities.

**agglutination** Clumping of BACTERIA or red blood cells by ANTIBODIES that react with ANTIGENS on the cell surface.

**Agincourt** Village in Pas de Calais, NE France. It was the site of the English King HENRY V's victory over the French in 1415 during the HUNDRED YEARS WAR. Despite being outnumbered,

England won due to poor French tactics and the superiority of the English longbow over the French crossbow.

**Agnew, Spiro Theodore** (1918–96) US statesman, vice president (1969–73) to Richard NIXON. Agnew became (1967) governor of his native Maryland. He was a staunch advocate of US involvement in the VIETNAM WAR. During his second term as vice president, he was forced to resign after the discovery of political bribery and corruption in Maryland. Agnew did not contest further charges of tax evasion and was given a three-year probationary sentence and fined $10,000.

**agnosticism** Philosophical viewpoint according to which it is impossible either to demonstrate or refute the existence of a supreme being or ultimate cause on the basis of available evidence. It was particularly associated with RATIONALISM of Thomas HUXLEY, and is used as a reasoned basis for the rejection of both Christianity and ATHEISM.

**agora** Civic center or market-place of ancient Greek towns and cities. Situated in the center of the town or near the harbor, the agora was a special place for male citizens to conduct their religious, commercial, judicial, and social activities. It was usually surrounded by public buildings, temples, and colonnades of shops, and was ornamented with statues and fountains.

**Agra** City in Uttar Pradesh, and site of the TAJ MAHAL, N central India. It was founded (1566) by AKBAR I. Agra's importance declined after 1658 when the Mogul capital moved to DELHI. It was annexed to the British empire in 1803 and later became the capital of North-West Province (1835–62). Agra's fine Mogul architecture make it a major tourist destination. It is an important rail junction and commercial and administrative center. Industries: glass, shoes, textiles. Pop. (1991) 892,200.

**Agricultural Revolution** Series of changes in farming practice in the 18th and early 19th centuries. The main changes comprised crop rotation, new machinery, increased capital investment, scientific breeding, land reclamation, and enclosure of common lands. Originating in Britain, these advances led to greatly increased agricultural productivity in Europe.

**agriculture** Practice of cultivating crops and raising livestock. Modern archaeological dating techniques suggest that the production of CEREALS and the domestication of animals were widespread throughout E Mediterranean countries by *c*.7000 BC. The Egyptians and Mesopotamians (*c*.3000 BC) were the earliest peoples to organize agriculture on a large scale, using irrigation techniques and manure as fertilizer. Farming formed the foundations of later societies in China, India, Europe, Mexico, and Peru. By Roman times (200 BC–AD 400), crop farming and the domestication of animals were commonplace in W Europe. In 17th- and 18th-century Europe, selective breeding improved milk and meat yields. The use of the four-field system of crop rotation meant that fields could be used continuously for production with no deterioration in yield or quality of the crops. The greatest changes in agriculture came with the INDUSTRIAL REVOLUTION. Many items of farm machinery were introduced in the 19th century. In Western Europe and North America, mechanization has advanced greatly and a large proportion of agricultural production is now carried out by FACTORY FARMING methods. In much of the underdeveloped world, agriculture (especially RICE production) is still labor intensive. Three-quarters of the world's workforce is engaged in farming.

**Agriculture, US Department of** US cabinet-level department within the executive branch. Established in 1862, it is directed by the secretary of agriculture. It accumulates and makes available agricultural information. It engages in research, education, conservation, marketing, agricultural adjustment, surplus disposal, and rural development. Among its important agencies are the Food and Nutrition Service, Soil Conservation Service, Forest Service, and Federal Crop Insurance Corporation.

**Agrippa, Marcus Vipsanius** (b. 63 BC) Roman general, adviser to Octavian (later AUGUSTUS). He helped Octavian to power by winning naval battles against Sextus Pompeius (36 BC) and MARK ANTONY at the Battle of ACTIUM in 31 BC.

**agronomy** Science of soil management and improvement in the interests of agriculture. It includes the studies of particular plants and soils and their interrelationships. Agronomy involves disease-resistant plants, selective breeding, and the development of chemical fertilizers.

**Ahern, Bertie** (1951– ) Irish statesman, taoiseach (1997– ). Ahern was first elected to the Dáil Éireann in 1977. He served as vice president (1983–94) of FIANNA FÁIL, before becoming leader. He succeeded John BRUTON as taoiseach.

**ahimsa** Non-violence or non-injury to both people and animals. It is a central concept of JAINISM and BUDDHISM, and is also important in HINDUISM. This belief inspired the passive resistance of Mahatma GANDHI.

**Ahmadabad** (Ahmedabad) City on the Sabarmati River, in W India. Founded in 1411 by Ahmad Shah, the Muslim ruler of Gujurat, it is the cultural, commercial, and transportation center of the state, with many magnificent mosques, temples, and tombs. It is the headquarters of the INDIAN NATIONAL CONGRESS movement. Industries: cotton. Pop. (1991) 2,954,526.

**Ahmad Shah Durrani** (1722–73) Emir of Afghanistan (1747–73) and founder of the Durrani dynasty. He united the Afghan tribes and is sometimes known as the founder of modern Afghanistan.

**Ahura Mazdah** (Ormazd or Ormuzd) In the Zoroastrian religion of ancient Persia, the supreme deity and the god of light and wisdom. Ahura Mazdah created the universe and the twin spirits of good and evil. He later became identified with the good spirit, who was in constant conflict with AHRIMAN.

**aid, development** Funds, goods, equipment, and expertise donated or loaned by the world's richer countries to poorer countries and used to promote development. The largest amount of development aid is paid out by the WORLD BANK, specifically through its International Development Association (IDA). All industrialized member states of the UNITED NATIONS (UN) allocate a specific proportion of their own GROSS NATIONAL PRODUCT (GNP) to foreign aid.

**Aidan, Saint** (d.651) Irish monk from Iona who brought Christianity to NE England. He became the first Bishop of Lindisfarne, where he established a monastery and sent out missionaries all over N England. His feast day is August 31, the date on which he died.

**AIDS** Acronym for ACQUIRED IMMUNE DEFICIENCY SYNDROME.

**Aiken, Conrad Potter** (1889–1973) US poet, novelist, and critic. Aiken's *Selected Poems* (1929) won him a Pulitzer Prize. His interest in psychoanalysis and musical form are evident in *Collected Poems* (1953). His also wrote five novels and an autobiography, *Ushant* (1952).

**aileron** Hinged control surface on the outer trailing edge of each wing of an AIRCRAFT. By moving down or up in opposite directions, ailerons cause the airplane to roll, or bank.

**Ailey, Alvin** (1931–89) US modern dancer and choreographer. Ailey studied dance with Martha GRAHAM. In 1958 he formed the American Dance Theater and acted as its artistic director (1958–89). The company introduced many leading African-American and Asian dancers to worldwide audiences. His works, such as *Roots of the Blues* (1961), incorporate elements of jazz, African and MODERN DANCE.

**Ainu** Aboriginal people of Hokkaido (N Japan), Sakhalin, and the Kuril islands. Traditionally hunters, fishermen, and trappers, they practice ANIMISM and are famed for their bear cult.

**air** Gases above the Earth's surface. *See* ATMOSPHERE

**aircraft** Any vehicle capable of traveling in the Earth's atmosphere. By far the most common aircraft is the airplane. An airplane is a heavier-than-air flying machine that depends upon fixed wings for LIFT in the air, as it moves under the THRUST of its engines. This thrust may be provided by an airscrew (propeller) turned by a piston or turbine engine, or by the exhaust gases of a JET engine or rocket motor. Gliders differ from planes only in their dependence upon air currents to keep them airborne. The main body of a plane is the fuselage, to which are attached the wings and tail assembly. Engines may be incorporated into or slung below the wings, but are sometimes mounted on the fuselage toward the tail or, as in some fighter aircraft, built into the fuselage near the wings. The landing gear or undercarriage, with its heavy wheels and stout shock absorbers, is usually completely retractable into the wings or fuselage. Wing design varies with the type of plane, high-speed

A

**AIR-CUSHION VEHICLE (ACV)**

ACVs, or hovercraft, float on a bed of air allowing them to operate on both land and water. A turbine (1) powers a propeller (2) for forward motion. Two main fans (3) pull air in and force it into the skirt (4) beneath the vehicle providing lift. Two smaller fans (5) blow air through directable nozzles on top of the craft providing maneuverability. The skirt, divided into cells (6), forms a seal around the air cushion and acts as a giant shock absorber.

fighters having slim, often swept-back or adjustable wings that create minimal air resistance (drag) at high speeds. At the other extreme, heavy air freighters need broader wings in order to achieve the necessary lift at takeoff. A plane is steered by the pilot moving flaps and ailerons on the wings and rudder and elevators on the tail assembly. This deflects the pressure of air on the airfoil surfaces, causing the plane to rise or descend, to bank (tilt) or swing and turn in the air. RADAR systems aid navigation, an AUTOMATIC PILOT keeps the aircraft on a fixed course, and pressurized cabins allow passenger planes to fly at heights exceeding 33,000ft (10,000m). *See also* AERODYNAMICS; AIRFOIL; AIRSHIP; BALLOON; GLIDING; HELICOPTER

**aircraft carrier** Military vessel with a wide open deck which serves as a runway for the launching and landing of aircraft. A modern nuclear-powered carrier may have a flight deck about 1,000ft (300m) long, a displacement of about 75,000 metric tons, a 4,000-man crew and carry 90 aircraft of various types.

**air-cushion vehicle (ACV)** Vehicle that is lifted from the ground by air as it is forced out from under the craft. The best-known example is a HOVERCRAFT.

**airfoil** Any shape or surface, such as a wing, tail, or propeller blade on an aircraft, that has as its major function the deflection of airflow to produce a pressure differential or LIFT. A typical airfoil has a leading and trailing edge, and an upper and lower camber. *See also* AERODYNAMICS

**air force** Military air power, first used in World War I. In 1918 the British government formed the Royal AIR FORCE (RAF), the world's first separate air force. The United States AIR FORCE (USAF) was created in 1947.

**Air Force, Royal (RAF)** Youngest of the British armed services, formed in 1918 by the amalgamation of the Royal Naval Air Service and the Royal Flying Corps. It was controlled by the Air Ministry from 1919–64, when it was merged into the Ministry of Defense. Total personnel (1996): 68,000.

**Air Force, United States (USAF)** One of the three major military services established under the Department of Defense in the National Security Act of 1947. It began as the Aeronautical Division of the Army in 1907, became the Aviation Section of the Signal Corps in 1914, the Air Service in 1918, the Army Air Corps in 1926, and the Army Air Forces in 1941. It is the world's largest air force. Total personnel (1994): 426,000

**airplane** *See* AIRCRAFT

**air pollution** *See* POLLUTION

**airship** (dirigible) Powered lighter-than-air craft able to control its direction of motion. A gas that is less dense than air, nowadays helium, provides lift. A rigid airship, or **Zeppelin**, maintains its form with a framework of girders covered by fabric or aluminum alloy. Non-rigid airships, or **blimps**, have no internal structure. They rely on the pressure of the contained gas to maintain the shape.

**air traffic control** System of guidance to allow the safe and orderly movement of aircraft. Air traffic controllers organize ground and local control for airport vehicles and emergency services. Other operators in radar rooms control aircraft arrivals and departures and monitor the "stacking" and timing of aircraft traffic. A system of route control allows operators to hand over a flight to the next control station on the route.

**Aix-en-Provence** City in SE France, 17mi (27km) N of Marseilles. Founded in 123 BC by the Romans, it is a cultural center with a university (1409), an 11th–13th-century cathedral and several art galleries. Industries: wine-making equipment, electrical apparatus, olives, almonds. Pop. (1990) 123,842.

**Aix-la-Chapelle, Treaty of** (1748) Diplomatic agreement, principally between France and Britain, that ended the War of the AUSTRIAN SUCCESSION (1740–48). The treaty provided for the restitution of conquests made during the war, contributed to the rise of Prussian power, and confirmed British control of the slave trade to Spanish America. An earlier treaty signed at Aix-la-Chapelle ended the War of Devolution (1668).

**Ajax** In Greek mythology, name given to two heroes who fought for Greece against TROY. The Greater Ajax is depicted in Homer's *Iliad* as a warrior who led the troops of Salamis against Troy. The Lesser Ajax was shipwrecked by ATHENA for raping CASSANDRA.

**Akbar I (the Great)** (1542–1605) Emperor of India (1556–1605). Generally regarded as the greatest ruler of the MOGUL EMPIRE, he assumed personal control in 1560 and set out to establish Mogul control of the whole of India, extending his authority as far S as Ahmadnagar. Akbar built a new capital at Fatehpur Sikri and endeavored to unify his empire by conciliation with Hindus. He also tolerated Christian missionaries.

**Akhmatova, Anna** (1889–1966) Russian poet. Her simple, intense lyrics and personal themes are best represented in the volumes *The Rosary* (1914) and *The Willow Tree* (1940). Her longest work, *Poem Without a Hero* (trans. 1971), is her masterpiece. Although officially ostracized for "bourgeois decadence," she remained popular in the Soviet Union.

**Akhnaten** (d.1362 BC) (Akhnaten) Ancient Egyptian king of the 18th dynasty (r. *c*.1379–1362 BC). He succeeded his father, AMENHOTEP III, as Amenhotep IV. In an attempt to overthrow the influence of the priests of the temple of AMON at LUXOR, he renounced the old gods and introduced an almost monotheistic worship of the sun god, Aten. He adopted the name Akhnaten and established a new capital at Akhetaten (modern Tell el-Amarna). After his death TUTANKHAMEN reinstated Amon as national god, and the capital reverted to Luxor.

**Akiba Ben Joseph** (50–135) Jewish rabbi and martyr in Palestine. He developed a new method of interpreting the Halakah, Hebrew oral laws, and supported a revolt (132) against the Roman emperor, Hadrian. He was imprisoned by the Romans and tortured to death.

**Akihito** (1933– ) Emperor of Japan (1989– ). In 1959 Akihito married a commoner, Michiko Shoda, the first such marriage in the history of the imperial dynasty. Akihito succeeded his father, HIROHITO.

**Akron** City on the Cuyahoga River, NE Ohio. The Ohio and Erie Canal (1827) promoted the city's growth. Once "the rubber capital of the world," the first tire factory opened there in 1871. Products include plastics and chemicals. Pop. (1992) 223,621.

**Alabama** Southeastern state, in the chief cotton-growing

**ALABAMA**
**Statehood :**
14 December 1819
**Nickname :**
The Heart of Dixie
**State bird :**
Yellowhammer
**State flower :**
Camellia
**State tree :**
Southern pine
**State motto :**
We dare defend our rights

region; the state capital is Montgomery. Birmingham is the largest city and a leading iron and steel center. Settled by the French in 1702, the region was acquired by Britain in 1763. Most of it was ceded to the US in 1783, and Alabama was admitted as the 22nd state of the Union in 1819. It seceded in 1861 as one of the original six states of the Confederacy, and was readmitted to the Union in 1868. In the 1960s it was a center of the Civil Rights movement. The N of the state lies in the Appalachian highlands, which have coal, iron ore, and other mineral deposits, and the rest consists of the Gulf coastal plain, crossed by a wide strip of rich soil valuable for agriculture. The Mobile River and its tributaries form the chief river system. The principal crops are peanuts, soybeans, and corn, with cotton decreasingly important. Industries: chemicals, textiles, electronics, metal and paper products. Area: 51,705sq mi (133,915sq km ). Pop. (1992) 4,137,511.

**Alabama claims** (1872) Award of $155 million compensation to the US against the UK for damage inflicted by Confederate ships built in England during the American Civil War (1861–65). An international tribunal ruled that the British government violated its neutrality by allowing the ships to be built on its territory.

**alabaster** Fine-grained, massive variety of gypsum (calcium sulfate), snow-white and translucent in its natural form. It can be dyed or made opaque by heating and is used for making statues and other ornaments.

**Alain-Fournier, Henri** (1886–1914) French writer. His reputation was secured by his only completed novel, *Le Grand Meaulnes* (1913), a lyrical and semi-autobiographical account of the experiences of a schoolboy. He was killed in action at the Battle of the Marne.

**Alamo** Mission in San Antonio, Texas, scene of a battle between Mexico and the Republic of Texas (1836). About 180 Texans, led by William Travis, Davy Crockett, and James Bowie, were overwhelmed by superior Mexican forces numbering in the thousands following a siege of 11 days.

**Alaric** (370–410) King and founder of a group of Goths called the Visigoths (395–410). His forces ravaged Thrace, Macedonia, and Greece and occupied Epirus (395–96). He invaded Italy and besieged (408) and sacked (410) Rome when the emperor Honorius would not grant him a position at court. He planned an invasion of Sicily and Africa, but his fleet was destroyed in a storm.

**Alaska** State in NW North America, separated from the rest of continental US by the province of British Columbia, Canada, and from Russia by the Bering Strait. The capital is Juneau. The largest city is Anchorage on the S coast. The US purchased the area from Russia in 1867 for $7.2 million. Fishing drew settlers and, after the gold rush of the 1890s, the population doubled in ten years. It became the 49th state of the Union in 1959. About 25% lies inside the Arctic Circle. The main Alaska Range includes Mount McKinley (Denali), the highest peak in North America. The chief river is the Yukon. The Alaskan economy is based on fish, natural gas, timber, quartz and, primarily, oil. Tourism to the national parks is also becoming important. Because of its strategic position and oil reserves, Alaska has been developed as a military area and is linked to the rest of the US by the 1,523mi (2,450km) Alaska Highway. Although by far the largest US state, it has the second smallest population (after Vermont). Of the total state population, 85,698 were registered as Native Americans in the 1990 census (the majority of them Inuit-Aleut Eskimos). Area: 591,004sq mi (1,530,700sq km). Pop. (1992) 587,766.

**Alaskan Boundary Dispute** (1902–03) Dispute between the US and Britain, representing Canada, over possession of the inlets between Alaska and Canada after the Klondike gold strike. It was settled by a six-man panel in favor of the US.

**Alban, Saint** First British martyr, from the Roman town of Verulamium (now St. Albans). He was killed for hiding a Christian priest from the Romans. In 797 King Offa founded an abbey on the site of Alban's execution. His feast day is June 22.

**Albania** Balkan republic; the capital is Tirana. **Land and climate** About 70% of Albania is mountainous, rising to Mount Korab at 2,764m (9,068ft) on the Macedonian border. Most Albanians live in the farming regions of the W coastal lowlands. Albania is subject to severe earthquakes. The coastal regions have a typical Mediterranean climate, with fairly dry, sunny summers and cool, moist winters. The highlands have heavy winter snowfalls. Maquis covers much of the lowlands. **History** In ancient times, Albania was part of Illyria, and in 167 BC, became part of the Roman empire. Between 1469 and 1912 Albania formed part of the Ottoman empire. Italy invaded Albania in 1939, and German forces occupied Albania in 1943. In 1944 Albanian communists, led by Enver Hoxha, took power. In the early 1960s, Albania broke with the Soviet Union after Soviet criticism of the Chinese Communist Party to which it was allied until the late 1970s. In the early 1990s the Albanian government abandoned communism and allowed the formation of opposition parties. **Recent events** In 1996 the Democratic Party, headed by Sali Berisha, won a sweeping victory. In 1997 the collapse of nationwide pyramid finance schemes sparked a large-scale rebellion in S Albania and a state of emergency was proclaimed. Berisha formed a government of national reconciliation and agreed to new elections. The Socialist Party of Albania was victorious and Rexhep Mejdani became president. **Economy** Albania is Europe's poorest country, and 56% of the workforce are engaged in agriculture. Under communism, the land was divided into large state and collective farms, but private ownership has been encouraged

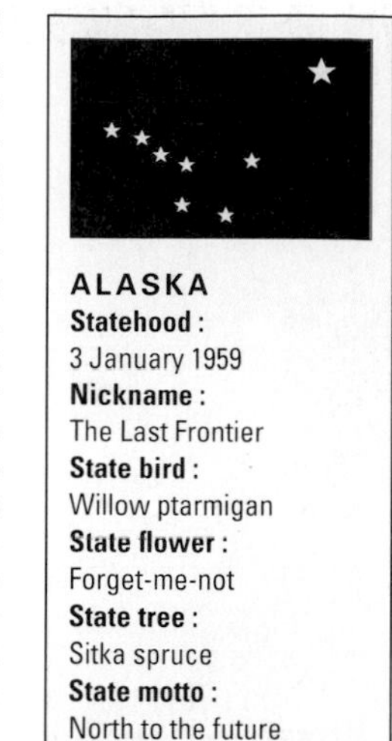

**ALASKA**
**Statehood:** 3 January 1959
**Nickname:** The Last Frontier
**State bird:** Willow ptarmigan
**State flower:** Forget-me-not
**State tree:** Sitka spruce
**State motto:** North to the future

**ALBANIA**

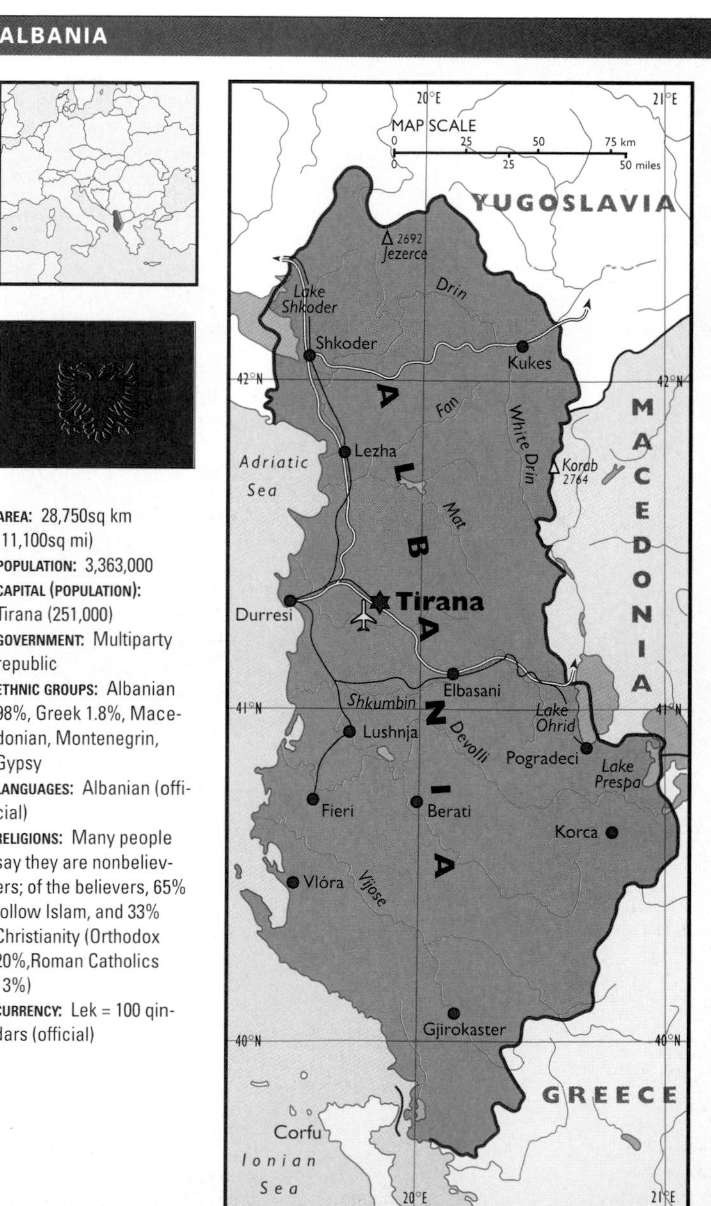


**AREA:** 28,750sq km (11,100sq mi)
**POPULATION:** 3,363,000
**CAPITAL (POPULATION):** Tirana (251,000)
**GOVERNMENT:** Multiparty republic
**ETHNIC GROUPS:** Albanian 98%, Greek 1.8%, Macedonian, Montenegrin, Gypsy
**LANGUAGES:** Albanian (official)
**RELIGIONS:** Many people say they are nonbelievers; of the believers, 65% follow Islam, and 33% Christianity (Orthodox 20%,Roman Catholics 13%)
**CURRENCY:** Lek = 100 qindars (official)

A

## ALBINO

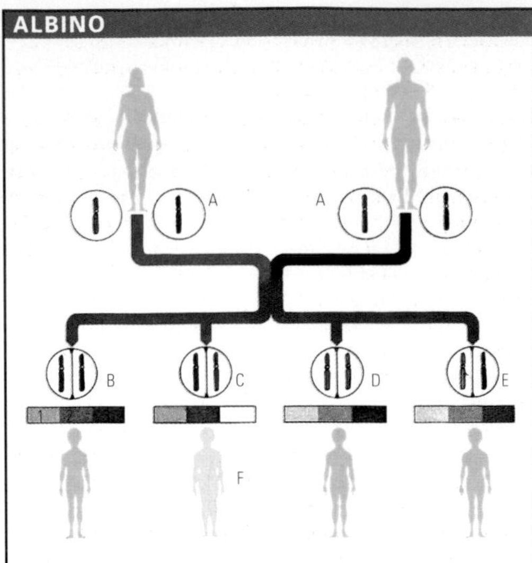


A male and female both carrying a recessive gene (green) for albinism (A) will have three normally pigmented children (B, D, and E) to every one albino (C). The corresponding normal gene (orange or purple) in both produces normal skin color. This is due to an amino acid, phenylalanine (1), which has been converted to tyrosine (2) and then to the pigment melanin (3). However, a recessive gene in double quantity only allows the conversion of phenylalanine to tyrosine (F) resulting in an albino with a lack of pigment in the skin, hair, and eyes.

since 1991. Crops include fruits, maize, olives, potatoes, sugar beet, vegetables, and wheat. Livestock farming is also important. Albania has some mineral reserves. Chromite, copper, and nickel are exported. Other resources include oil, brown coal, and hydroelectricity. Albania's heavy industry has caused severe pollution in some areas.

**Albany** Capital of New York State, on the Hudson River. Settled by the Dutch in 1614 and British from 1664, it replaced New York City as state capital in 1797. It grew from the 1820s with the building of the Erie Canal, linking it to the Great Lakes, and it is still an important river port. Industries: paper, brewing, machine tools, metal products, textiles. Pop. (1992) 99,708.

**Albany Congress** (1754) North American colonial conference to discuss Native American relations. Representatives from seven northern and middle colonies met Iroquois leaders and negotiated an alliance against the French. At this meeting Benjamin FRANKLIN proposed a plan for union of the colonies, which was rejected by the colonial governments.

**Albany Regency** (1820–48) Organization of Democratic Party leaders in New York state. It successfully controlled conventions and appointments until the defeat of Martin VAN BUREN's presidential bid (1848).

**albatross** Large, migratory oceanic bird of the Southern Hemisphere famed for its effortless gliding flight. There are 13 species. The wandering albatross has a long, hooked bill, short tail, webbed toes, and the greatest wingspan of any living bird – 11.5ft (3.5m) or more. Length: 2.3–4.4ft (0.7–1.4m). Family Diomedeidae.

**albedo** Fraction of light or other radiation that is reflected from a surface. An ideal reflector has an albedo of 1; those of real reflectors are less; that of the Earth, viewed from satellites, is 0.35.

**Albee, Edward Franklin** (1928– ) US playwright. Albee's debut play *The Zoo Story* (1959) is a classic text of the Theater of the ABSURD. His best-known play *Who's Afraid of Virginia Woolf?* (1962) is an portrait of a destructive marriage. *A Delicate Balance* (1966) and *Seascape* (1975) won Pulitzer prizes.

**Albéniz, Isaac** (1860–1909) Spanish Romantic composer and pianist. Most of his compositions are for piano. He often used Spanish folk elements in his compositions, notably in the piano suite *Iberia* (1906–09).

**Albert, Lake** Lake in the Rift Valley of E central Africa on the border between Zaire and Uganda. It is fed by the Semliki River and the Victoria Nile and drained by the Albert Nile (Bahr el Jebel). Ugandans call it Lake Nyanza and the Zairians named it Lake Mobuto Sese Seko. Some 100mi (160km) long, it has an average width of 22mi (35km) and its maximum depth is 168ft (51m). Area: 2,065sq mi (5,350sq km).

**Alberta** Province of W Canada bounded on the W mainly by the Rocky Mountains and in the S by the US; the capital is EDMONTON. Other major cities include CALGARY. Most of Alberta is prairie land. The principal rivers are the Athabasca, Peace, North and South Saskatchewan. Lesser Slave Lake is the largest of the many lakes. The area was part of a large territory granted (1670) by Charles II to the HUDSON'S BAY COMPANY, and in 1870 the government of Canada bought the region from the company. In 1882 Northwest Territories was divided into four districts and Alberta was created (named after Queen Victoria's fourth daughter). Alberta was admitted to the confederation as a province in 1905. The fertile plains support wheat farming and livestock. Major resources are coal, minerals, and wood from the forests in the N. Oil and natural gas fields in central Alberta have been a major stimulus to the post-1945 economy. Industries: petroleum products, metals, chemicals, food, wood products. Area: 661,188sq km (255,285sq mi). Pop. (1991) 2,545,553.

**Alberti, Leon Battista** (1404–72) Italian architect, humanist, and writer. The first major art theorist of the RENAISSANCE, Alberti's treatise *On Painting* (1435) was highly influential. His buildings include the Rucellai Palace, Florence; Tempio Malatestiano, Rimini; and the Church of San Andrea, Mantua.

**Albigenses** (Cathars) Members of a heretical religious sect that existed in southern France from the 11th to the early 14th centuries and took its name from the French city of Albi. Pope Innocent III ordered a crusade against them in 1200, which caused much damage in Languedoc and Provence.

**albino** Person or animal with a rare hereditary absence of pigment from the skin, hair, and eyes. The hair is white and the skin and eyes are pink because the blood vessels are visible. The eyes are abnormally sensitive to light and vision is often poor.

**Albinoni, Tomaso** (1671–1750) Italian violinist and composer. He worked mainly in Venice, where he was a friend of VIVALDI. He was one of the first composers of CONCERTOS for a solo instrument; he also wrote nearly 50 operas.

**Albright, Madeleine Korbel** (1937– ) US stateswoman, secretary of state (1997– ), b. Czechoslovakia. Following Bill CLINTON's re-election (1996), Albright became the first woman to hold the office of secretary of state. She was a hawkish advocate of US involvement in the GULF WAR and Bosnia. Middle Eastern politics consumed much of her time.

**albumin** (albumen) Type of water-soluble PROTEIN occurring in animal tissues and fluids. The principal forms are egg albumin (egg white), milk albumin, and blood albumin. In a healthy human, it constitutes about 5% of the body's total weight. It is composed of a colorless, transparent fluid called plasma in which are suspended microscopic ERYTHROCYTES (red blood cells), LEUKOCYTES (white blood cells), and PLATELETS.

**Albuquerque, Afonso d'** (1453–1515) Portuguese military commander, founder of the Portuguese empire of the East Indies. After serving as a soldier in North Africa, Albuquerque became governor-general of the Portuguese settlements in W India. He established control over the spice trade by capturing Goa (1510), Malacca (1511), Calicut (1512), and the Malabar Coast.

**Albuquerque** City in W central New Mexico, on the Upper Rio Grande River, the state's largest city. Traditionally a center for transportation and the livestock trade, it now has a high-tech profile in electronics and solar and nuclear research (home to the federal Atomic Energy Commission). A popular health resort, its population increased by nearly 20% between 1980 and 1992. Pop. (1992) 398,492.

**Alcatraz** (Sp. *álcatraces*, pelican) Island in San Francisco Bay, famous as an escape-proof prison surrounded by shark-infested waters. Discovered by the Spanish in 1769, the island served as a fort and then US federal prison (1933–63). In 1972 it became part of the Golden Gate National Recreational Area.

**alchemy** Primitive form of chemistry practiced in Western Europe from early Christian times until the 17th century, popularly supposed to involve a search for the philosopher's stone – capable of transmuting base metals into gold – and the elixir of life. It actually involved a combination of practical chemistry, astrology, philosophy, and mysticism. Similar movements existed in China and India.

**Alcock, Sir John William** (1892–1919) Pioneer British airman who, together with Arthur Whitten-Brown, was the first to fly nonstop across the Atlantic Ocean. Their transatlantic flight began in St. John's, Newfoundland on June 14, 1919, and landed 16.5 hours later near Clifden, Ireland.

**alcohol** Organic compound having a hydroxyl (-OH) group bound to a carbon atom. ETHANOL, the alcohol found in alcoholic drinks, has the formula $C_2H_5OH$. Alcohols are used to make dyes and perfumes and as SOLVENTS in lacquers and varnishes.

**Alcott, (Amos) Bronson** (1799–1888) US philosopher, teacher and reformer, father of Louisa May ALCOTT. A leading figure in TRANSCENDENTALISM, Alcott helped found the utopian community of Fruitlands, Massachusetts.

**Alcott, Louisa May** (1832–88) US writer, daughter of Bronson ALCOTT. Her first book, *Flower Fables* (1854), helped ease the family's financial troubles. *Hospital Sketches* (1863) is an account of Alcott's experiences as a nurse in the Civil War. *Little Women* (1868) is one of the most successful children's books ever written. It was originally published in two parts: *Good Wives* appeared in 1869. They form the first of a semi-autobiographical quartet of novels about the New England upbringing of the four March sisters, which includes *An Old-Fashioned Girl* (1870), *Little Men* (1871), and *Jo's Boys* (1886).

**Aldrin, "Buzz" (Edwin)** (1930– ) US astronaut. Aldrin piloted the Gemini XII orbital-rendezvous space flight (November 1966) and the lunar module for the first Moon landing (July 20, 1969). He followed Neil ARMSTRONG to become the second man on the Moon.

**aleatoric** Word used to describe 20th-century music in which the sequence of notes is determined partly by chance, either at the time of composition or at the discretion of the performers.

**Aleichem, Sholem** (1859–1916) Yiddish novelist, dramatist, and short story writer, b. Sholem Yakov Rabinowitz. He portrayed the oppression of Russian Jews with humor and compassion. Aleichem's numerous works include *Tevye the Dairyman* (*c*.1949), which was later adapted as the musical *Fiddler on the Roof* (1964).

**Alembert, Jean le Rond d'** (1717–83) French mathematician and philosopher. D'Alembert was a leading figure in the ENLIGHTENMENT. He was DIDEROT's co-editor on the first edition of the *Encyclopédie* (1751) and contributed the "Preliminary Discourse." His systematic *Treatise on Dynamics* (1743) provided a solution (D'Alembert's principle) that enables Newton's third law of motion to be applied to moving objects.

**Aleppo** (Halab) City in NW Syria; Syria's second largest city. Like the capital DAMASCUS, it claims to be the oldest continually inhabited city in the world. It has been part of Syria since 1924. Industries: cotton products, silk weaving, dried nuts and fruit. Pop. (1993) 1,494,000.

**Aleut** Branch of the Eskimo people who occupy the ALEUTIAN ISLANDS and Alaska Peninsula. They are divided into two major language groups, the Unalaska and Atka. About 4,000 Aleuts live in scattered villages throughout SW Alaska.

**Aleutian Islands** Volcanic island chain separating the Bering Sea from the Pacific Ocean. They were purchased with Alaska by the US in 1867. The islands have several US military bases and wildlife reserves. Industries: fishing and furs. Area: 6,821sq mi (17,666sq km). Pop. (1990) 11,942.

**Alexander III** (*c*.1105–81) Pope (1159–81). His election to the papacy was opposed by the Holy Roman emperor FREDERICK I, who had an antipope, Victor IV, elected. The ensuing schism ended 17 years later with the victory of the LOMBARD LEAGUE over Frederick at the Battle of Legnano.

**Alexander I** (1777–1825) Russian czar (1801–25). After repulsing Napoleon's attempt to conquer Russia (1812), he led his troops across Europe and into Paris (1814). Under the influence of various mystical groups, he helped form the Holy Alliance with other European powers. He was named constitutional monarch of Poland in 1815 and also annexed Finland, Georgia and Bessarabia to Russia.

**Alexander II** (1818–81) Russian czar (1855–81). He was known as the "Czar Liberator" for his emancipation of the serfs in 1861. He warred with Turkey (1877–78) and gained much influence in the Balkans. He sold Alaska (1867), but expanded the eastern part of the empire. He brutally put down a revolt in Poland (1863). In 1881 he was assassinated by revolutionaries.

**Alexander III** (1845–94) Russian czar (1881–94). He introduced reactionary measures limiting local government; censorship of the press was enforced and arbitrary arrest and exile became common. Ethnic minorities were persecuted. Toward the end of his career, he formed an alliance with France.

**Alexander I** (1888–1934) King of the Serbs, Croats, and Slovenes (1921–29) and of Yugoslavia (1929–34). In his efforts to forge a united country from the rival national groups and ethnically divided political parties, he created an autocratic police state. He was assassinated by a Croatian terrorist.

**Alexander, Grover Cleveland** (1887–1950) US baseball player. A right-handed pitcher, Alexander set a major league record (1916) for 16 shutouts in 33 victories. He played for the Philadelphia Phillies, the Chicago Cubs, and the St. Louis Cardinals.

**Alexander Nevski, Saint** (1220–63) Russian ruler, Grand Duke of Novgorod and Grand Duke of Vladimir. He pragmatically submitted to Mongol rule following their invasion of Russia, and the Great Khan appointed him Grand Duke of Kiev. He defeated the Swedes on the River Neva in 1240 (hence the name "Nevski") and the Teutonic Knights on Lake Peipus in 1242. He was canonized by the Russian Orthodox Church in 1547.

**Alexander the Great** (356–323 BC) King of Macedonia (336–323 BC), considered the greatest conqueror of classical times. Son of PHILIP II of Macedonia, he became king at the age of 20. Destroying rivals, he rapidly consolidated Macedonian power in Greece. In 334 BC he began his destruction of the vast Achaemenid Persian empire, conquering W Asia Minor and storming Tyre in 332 BC. He subdued Egypt and occupied Babylon, conquering central Asia in 328 BC. In 327 BC he invaded India but was prevented from advancing beyond the Punjab by the threat of mutiny. He died in Babylon, planning new conquests in Arabia. Although his empire did not outlive

ALEXANDER THE GREAT

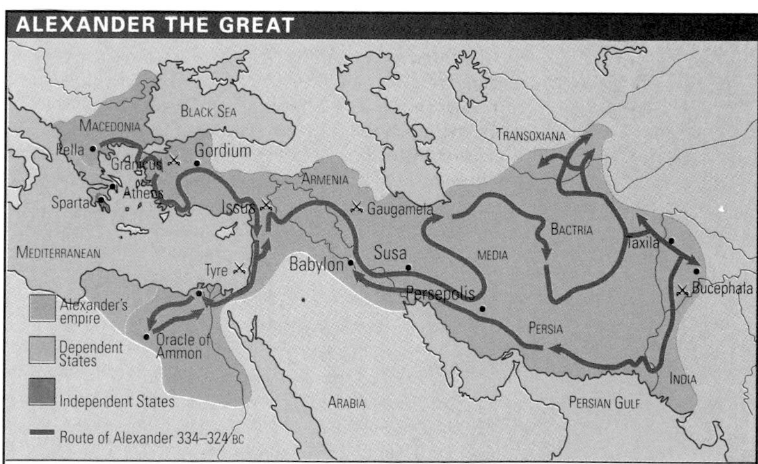


In the spring of 334 BC Alexander's army of 32,000 infantry, 5,000 cavalry, and 160 ships crossed the Hellespont and defeated the Persians at the battle of Granicus. The following year, he won another victory against the Persians at Issus. He then marched on and besieged Tyre, before advancing into Egypt where he founded the city of Alexandria. In 331 BC he left Egypt and again defeated the Persians at Guagamela before capturing Babylon and the Persian capitals of Susa and Persepolis. In pursuit of Darius, king of Persia, he went E into Asia, overcoming the Iranians. At the foot of the Himalayas, his army refused to go further and he turned S, following the Indus River to the Indian Ocean, before marching W through the desert of Gedrosia. Alexander returned to Babylon where he died at the age of 32.

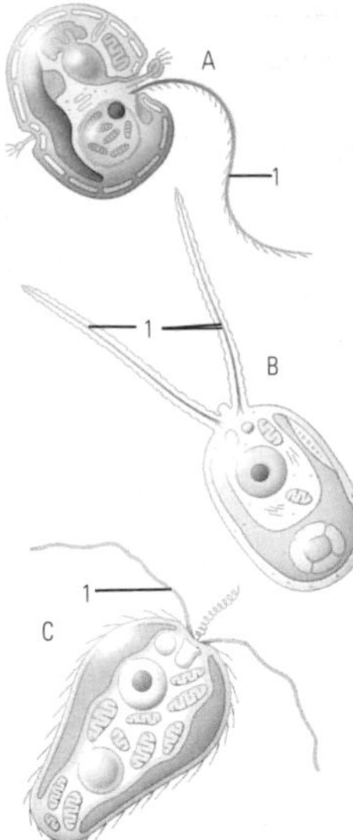


▲**algae** Many unicellular (single-celled) algae are said to be motile, that is they move in response to changes in their environment, in particular to light. This is achieved with tail-like flagella (1) which propel them through the water. The illustration shows three different types of algae. (A) *Gonyaulax tamarensis*, (B) *Chlamydomonas* and (C) *Prymnesium parvum* all have two flagella, but some have one flagella and others have four.

him, for he left no heir, he was chiefly responsible for the spread of Greek civilization in the Mediterranean and W Asia.

**Alexandria** Chief port and second largest city of Egypt, situated on the W extremity of the Nile delta. Founded by ALEXANDER THE GREAT in 332 BC, it became a great center of Greek (and Jewish) culture. An offshore island housed the 3rd-century BC Pharos lighthouse, one of the SEVEN WONDERS OF THE WORLD, and the city contained a great library (founded by Ptolemy I and said to contain 700,000 volumes). Today, Alexandria is a deep-water port handling over 75% of the country's trade. The city is the Middle East headquarters for the WORLD HEALTH ORGANIZATION (WHO). Industries: oil refining, cotton textiles, plastics, paper. Pop. (1990 est.) 3,170,000.

**Alexandrian school** Group of Greek poets including Apollonius Rhodius and THEOCRITUS who worked in Alexandria between the 3rd and 1st centuries BC.

**Alexius I (Alexius Comnenus)** (1048–1118) Byzantine emperor (1081–1118), founder of the Comnenian dynasty. He held off the Normans, who threatened Constantinople and turned the Western armies of the First CRUSADE to his own advantage by using them to reconquer parts of Anatolia.

**alfalfa** (lucerne) Leguminous perennial plant with spiral pods and purple, cloverlike flowers. Like other legumes, it has the ability to enrich the soil with nitrogen and is often grown by farmers and then plowed under. It is a valuable fodder plant. Height: 1.5–4ft (0.5–1.2m). Species *Medicago sativa*. Family Leguminosae. *See also* NITROGEN FIXATION

**Alfonso** Name of a number of rulers of Spanish kingdoms. **Alfonso V** (994–1028) became king of León and Asturias after his supporters took the city of León in 999. He was killed in battle against the MOORS. **Alfonso VIII** (1155–1214) was king of Castile (1158–1214). He took personal control of his kingdom in 1166 and at first opposed both Moors and fellow Christian kings. In 1212 he forged a coalition with the Christian rulers and won a major victory over the ALMOHADS at Las Navas de Tolosa. **Alfonso X** (1221–84), king of Castile and León (1252–84), was the son and successor of Ferdinand III. He continued his father's wars against the Moors but his ambition was to become Holy Roman emperor. A distinguished scholar, he codified the law and wrote histories of Spain and the world. **Alfonso V** (1396–1458) was king of Aragon (1416–58). He pursued military activity to protect his Eastern trade and to curb Turkish power. **Alfonso XIII** (1886–1941) was born after the death of his father, Alfonso XII, and his mother acted as regent until 1902. Although popular, he could not satisfy the conflicting demands of nationalist groups, socialists, republicans, and others. In 1923 he supported the establishment of a military dictatorship under General Miguel PRIMO DE RIVERA. The dictatorship fell in 1930 and a republic was proclaimed.

**Alfred the Great** (849–99) King of WESSEX (871–99). A warrior and scholar, Alfred saved Wessex from the Danes and laid the foundations of a united English kingdom. After the Danish invasion of 878, he escaped to Athelney in Somerset, returning to defeat the Danes at Edington and recover the kingdom. In a pact with the Danish leader, Guthrum (who accepted Christian baptism), England was roughly divided in two; the DANELAW occupied the NE. Although he controlled only Wessex and part of Mercia, Alfred's leadership was widely recognized throughout England after his capture of London (886).

**algae** Large group of essentially aquatic photosynthetic organisms found in salt and fresh water throughout the world. Algae are a primary source of food for mollusks, fish, and other aquatic animals. Algae are directly important to humans as food (especially in Japan) and as FERTILIZERS. They range in size from unicellular microscopic organisms such as those that form green pond scum to huge brown SEAWEEDS more than 150ft (45m) long. Algae belong to the kingdom Protista. *See also* GREEN ALGAE; RED ALGAE; PHOTOSYNTHESIS

**Algarve** Southernmost province of Portugal, and the most popular of the country's tourist areas. The capital is Faro. Irrigated orchards produce almonds, oranges, figs, and olives, and the main fish catches are tuna and sardines. Area: 1,925sq mi (4,986sq km). Pop. (1994 est.) 344,300.

**algebra** Form of arithmetic in which symbols replace numbers. Thus $3 + 5 = 8$ is a statement in arithmetic; $x + y = 8$ is one in algebra, involving the VARIABLES $x$ and $y$. Boolean algebra (an example of a higher algebra) can be applied to sets and to logical propositions. Algebraic operations are the arithmetical operations addition, subtraction, multiplication, and division. Operations that involve infinite series and functions such as log $x$ are not algebraic because they depend on the use of limits. *See also* MATHEMATICS

**Alger, Horatio** (1832–99) US author and minister who wrote more than 135 books for young boys on the theme of self-help. The Horatio Alger hero became one who, through hard work, rose from rags to riches. His works include *Fame and Fortune*, *Struggling Upward*, and *Strive and Succeed*.

**Algeria** Republic in nw Africa. See country feature

**Algiers** Capital and largest city of Algeria, on the Bay of Algiers, N Africa's chief port on the Mediterranean. Founded by the Phoenicians, it has been colonized by Romans, Berber Arabs, Turks (Barbarossa), and Muslim Barbary pirates. In 1830 the French invaded and made Algiers the capital of the French colony of Algeria. In World War II it was the headquarters of the Allies and seat of the French provisional government. During the 1950s and 1960s it was a focus for the violent struggle for independence. The 11th-century Sidi Abderrahman Mosque is a major destination for Muslim pilgrims. Industries: oil refining, phosphates, wine, metallurgy, cement, tobacco. Pop. (1995) 2,168,000.

**Algol** (Beta Persei) Prototype of a class of eclipsing binaries known as Algol-type variables. The variability in its appearance was first noted in 1669. Algol lies about 100 light years away. *See also* BINARY STAR

**Algonquian** (Algonkin) Group of Canadian Native American tribes that gave their name to the Algonquian languages of North America. The Algonquian people occupied the Ottawa River area *c.*AD 1600. Driven from their home by the IROQUOIS in the 17th century, they were eventually absorbed into other related tribes in Canada.

**algorithm** Step-by-step set of instructions needed to obtain some result from given starting data. The term is also used in computer science for the method of a computer in following an established series of steps in the solution of a problem.

**Algren, Nelson** (1909–81) US novelist. Algren's debut novel was *Somebody in Boots* (1935). His novel about drug addiction, *The Man with the Golden Arm* (1949), won the National Book Award. His work is often set in the slums of Chicago. Other novels include *A Walk on the Wild Side* (1956) and *The Devil's Stocking* (1983).

**Alhambra** Spanish citadel of the sultans of Granada, a world heritage site and a major tourist attraction. Standing on a plateau overlooking Granada, s Spain, it is one of the most beautiful and well-preserved examples of medieval ISLAMIC ART AND ARCHITECTURE. Most of the complex dates from the period of the Nasrid dynasty (1238–1358).

►**Alhambra** Built in the 13th–14th centuries, the Alhambra complex in Granada, s Spain, is considered a masterpiece of Moorish architecture. The Court of the Lions (shown) is surrounded by delicate columns and features a marble fountain supported by a circle of stone-carved lions. It is believed to represent the Muslim idea of paradise.

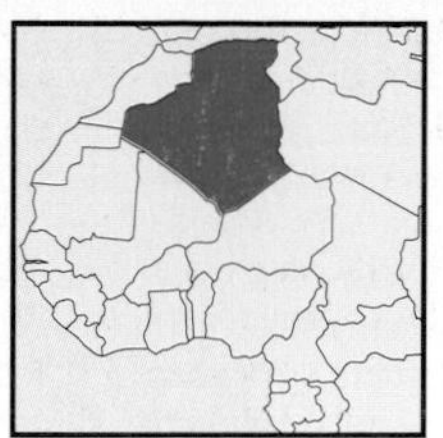

The star and crescent and the color green on Algeria's flag are traditional symbols of the Islamic religion. The liberation movement which fought for independence from French rule from 1954 used this design, which was adopted as the national flag when Algeria became independent in 1962.

**AREA:** 919,590sq mi (2,381,700sq km)
**POPULATION:** 26,346,000
**CAPITAL (POPULATION):** Algiers (2,168,000)
**GOVERNMENT:** Socialist republic
**ETHNIC GROUPS:** Arab, Berber, French
**LANGUAGES:** Arabic (official), Berber, French
**RELIGIONS:** Sunni Muslim 98%, Christianity (Roman Catholic)
**CURRENCY:** Algerian dinar = 100 centimes

The Democratic and Popular Republic of Algeria is the second largest country in Africa. Most of the people live in the N, on the fertile coastal plains and hill country bordering the Mediterranean Sea, and in Algeria's two largest cities, ALGIERS and ORAN. South of this region are high plateaus and ranges of the ATLAS Mountains, but over 80% of Algeria lies in the empty wastes of the SAHARA, which is the the world's largest desert. The majority of people who live in the Sahara are found at oases, where springs and wells supply water. A few Tuareg nomads roam the desert in search of pasture for their animals.

### CLIMATE

Algiers has a Mediterranean climate: summers are warm and dry, and winters are mild and moist. The highlands in the N tend to have colder winters and warmer summers. The Sahara is very hot by day but becomes cool at night, and the annual rainfall is everywhere less than 8in (200mm). Salah, in the far S, has an average rainfall of less than 0.7in (17mm). In the summer the hot, dusty wind called the sirocco blows from the Sahara.

### VEGETATION

The N has areas of scrub and farmland, with forests of Aleppo pine and cork oak on mountain slopes. The Sahara contains regions of sand dunes, known to geographers as erg, but most of the desert is gravel-strewn plains and areas of bare rock. Few plants or animals are able to survive here, though grasses grow in the highlands and date palms and crops flourish around every oasis.

### HISTORY AND POLITICS

In early times, N Algeria came under the rule of many invaders, including the Phoenicians and the Carthaginians. By the 4th century it had become an integral part of the Roman empire but was later overrun by the Vandals. Arabs invaded the area in the 7th century and converted the local Berber people, who had reached the area about 3,000 years before, to Islam. Arabic became the chief language, although Berber dialects are still sometimes spoken in the highlands and by about 17% of the population overall.

France ruled Algeria from 1830 but finally relinquished power after a bitter civil war between the government and the National Liberation Front (FLN), which began in 1954 and resulted in the death of around 250,000 people. Most of the French *colons*, who numbered about one million, had opposed Algerian independence and left Algeria in 1961, when the peace talks began. In 1962 an agreement was signed providing for an end to the fighting and the establishment of Algeria as an independent one-party state.

The government, led by Ahmed BEN BELLA, an advocate of socialist policies, was overthrown in 1965 by a military group. The country was then ruled by a Revolutionary Council led by the authoritarian Houari Boumédienne, who sought to diversify the economy by founding new industries with revenue from oil and gas sales. After Boumédienne's death in 1978, Chadli Benjedid became president. and in 1989 his government introduced constitutional changes which permitted the formation of opposition parties.

In January 1992, with the opposition Islamic Salvation Front (FIS) on course for electoral victory, President Benjedid decided to cancel the second round of voting and declared a national state of emergency. He was forced to resign, and a military government took charge. The FIS was banned and many of their leaders were arrested and imprisoned. Benjedid's successor, President Muhammad Boudiaf, was assassinated in June 1992 as part of a terrorist campaign launched by anti-Western Muslim fundamentalists.

In 1995 elections General Liamine Zeroual won a second term as president. Between 1992 and 1997 it is estimated that the civil war has claimed 100,000 civilian lives. Algeria continues to suffer from political violence.

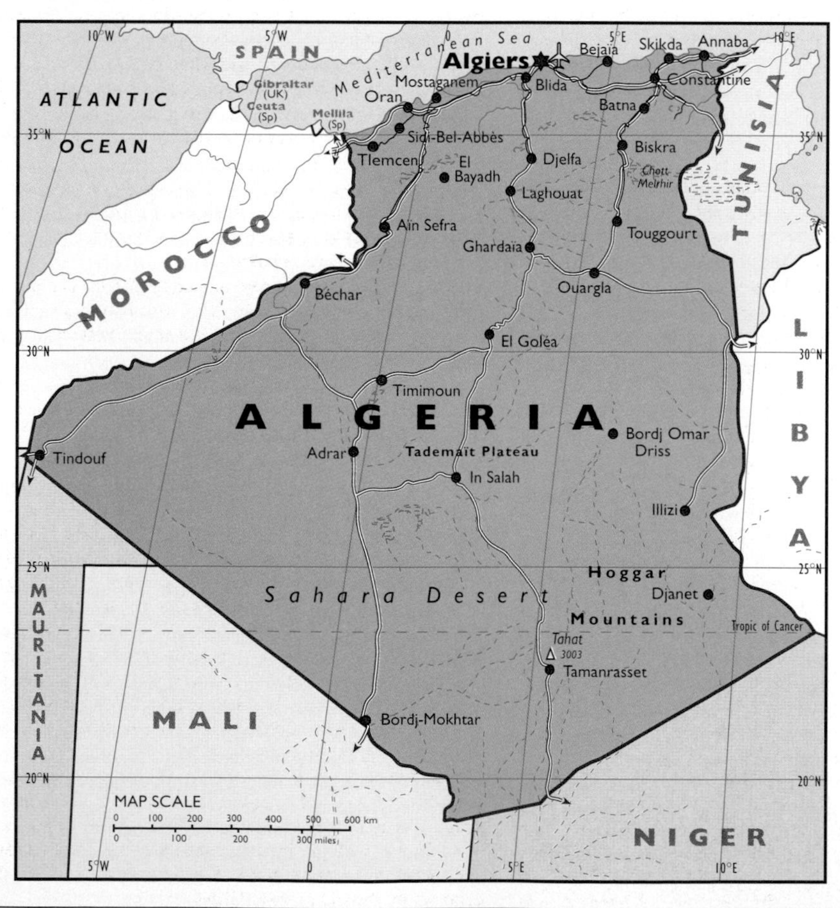


### ECONOMY

Algeria is a developing country (1995 GDP per capita, US$5,300). Its chief resources are oil and natural gas, which were first discovered under the Sahara in 1956. Its natural gas reserves are the fifth-largest in the world; oil the 14th-largest. Gas and oil account for more than 90% of Algeria's exports. Manufactures include cement, iron and steel, textiles and vehicles (Algeria is one of the few African states to have its own car plant).

While most larger industries are owned by the government, much of light industry is under private control. Farming employs *c.*14% of the workforce. Barley, citrus fruits, dates, grapes, olives, potatoes and wheat are the major crops. In 1995 unemployment stood at over 25% of the workforce, and many Algerians work abroad, especially in France.

A

▲ **Ali** Considered one of the greatest heavyweight boxers of all time, Muhammad Ali was loved as much for his showmanship as for his extraordinary boxing talent.

**Ali** (*c*.600–61) Fourth Muslim caliph (656–61), cousin and son-in-law of the Prophet Muhammad. Ali was married to Fatima. He is regarded by the Shiites as the first Imam and rightful heir of Muhammad. Ali succeeded Othman as caliph, despite opposition from Aishah and Muawiya. He was assassinated and his first son, Hasan, abdicated in favor of Muawiya, who founded the Umayyad dynasty. His second son, Husayn, led the insurrection against the Umayyads, but was defeated and killed at the Battle of Karbala (680).

**Ali, Muhammad** (1942– ) US boxer, b. Cassius Marcellus Clay. As Cassius Clay, he defeated Sonny Liston to gain the world heavyweight championship (1964). Clay converted to Islam and joined the Black Muslims. Ali successfully defended the title nine times. In 1967 he refused to fight in the Vietnam War. The World Boxing Association (WBA) took away his title. In 1971 the US Supreme Court upheld Ali's appeal against the ban, but he was defeated by reigning champion Joe Frazier. He regained the title from George Foreman in the 1974 "rumble in the jungle" fight. In 1978 Ali was defeated by Leon Spinks, but won the rematch, becoming the first heavyweight to win the title three times.

**Alice Springs** Town on the Todd River, Northern Territory, central Australia. Founded in 1860, Alice Springs is a crucial railhead, livestock shipping center, and supply source for a vast area that includes Ayers Rock. It is the state's largest town after Darwin. Pop. (1994) 24,852.

**Alien and Sedition Acts** (1798) Four US acts designed to curb criticism of the government at a time when war with France seemed imminent. Many of the severest critics were refugees from Europe who were regarded as disloyal. The acts imposed stringent rules on residency before naturalization, and gave the president unprecedented powers to deport undesirable foreigners or imprison them in time of war.

**alienation** Term used in psychology to mean a feeling of estrangement and separation from other people. In existential psychology this meaning is extended to include the perception that one is alienated or estranged from one's "real self" because of being forced to conform to society's expectations. In the US "alienist" refers to a psychiatrist who deals with the legal aspects of insanity.

**alimentary canal** Digestive tract of an animal that begins with the mouth, continues through the esophagus to the stomach and intestines, and ends at the anus. It is about 30ft (9m) long in humans. *See also* digestive system

**aliphatic compound** Any organic chemical compound whose carbon atoms are linked in straight chains, not closed rings. They include the alkanes (paraffins), alkenes (olefins), and alkynes (acetylenes).

**alkali** Soluble base that reacts with an acid to form a salt and water. A solution of an alkali has a pH greater than 7. Alkali solutions are used as cleaning materials. Strong alkalis include the hydroxides of the alkali metals and ammonium hydroxide. The carbonates of these metals are weak alkalis.

**alkali metals** Univalent metals forming Group I of the periodic table: lithium, sodium, potassium, rubidium, cesium, and francium. They are soft silvery white metals that tarnish rapidly in air and react violently with water to form hydroxides.

**alkaline-earth metals** Bivalent metals forming Group II of the periodic table: beryllium, magnesium, calcium, strontium, barium, and radium. They are all light, soft, and highly reactive. All, except beryllium and magnesium, react with cold water to form hydroxides (though magnesium reacts with hot water). Radium is important for its radioactivity.

**alkaloid** Member of a class of complex nitrogen-containing organic compounds found in certain plants. They are sometimes bitter and highly poisonous substances, used as drugs. Examples include codeine, morphine, nicotine, and quinine.

**alkane** ($C_nH_{2n+2}$) Hydrocarbon compound. Alkanes have a single carbon-carbon bond and form an homologous series whose first members are methane, ethane, propane and butane. Because alkanes are saturated compounds they are relatively unreactive. Alkanes are used as fuels. *See also* paraffin

**alkene** (olefin, $C_nH_{2n}$) Unsaturated hydrocarbon compound. Alkenes have a carbon-carbon double bond and form an homologous series whose first members are ethene and propene. They are reactive, particularly in addition reactions. Alkenes are made by the dehydration of alcohols.

**alkyne** (acetylene, $C_nH_{2n-2}$) Unsaturated hydrocarbon compound. Alkynes have a carbon-carbon triple bond and form an homologous series whose first members are ethyne and propyne.

**Allah** One and only God of Islam. His name is probably derived from Arabic *al-Ilāh*, meaning "the God." Allah is the omnipresent and merciful rewarder, the creator and judge. Unreserved surrender to Allah, as preached in the Koran, is the heart of the Islamic faith.

**Allahabad** City at the confluence of the Ganges and Yamuna rivers, Uttar Pradesh state, N central India. Allahabad is a pilgrimage center for Hindus because of the belief that the goddess Saraswati joined the two rivers at this point. The Kumbh Mela fair, a religious celebration, takes place here every 12 years. It is also an agricultural trade center. Pop. (1991) 806,000.

**allegory** Literary work in either prose or verse in which more than one level of meaning is expressed simultaneously. The fables of Aesop and La Fontaine are examples of simple allegory. *Pilgrim's Progress* (1684) by John Bunyan is a sophisticated religious allegory.

**Allegri, Gregorio** (1582–1652) Italian composer. Allegri composed many works for the papal choir. His most famous work is the beautiful *Miserere*, which is still widely performed today. He also composed five masses and several other books of church music.

**allele** One of two or more alternative forms of a particular gene. Different alleles may give rise to different forms of the characteristic for which the gene codes. Different flower color in peas is due to the presence of different alleles of a single gene. *See* Gregor Mendel

**Allen, Ethan** (1738–89) US frontiersman and soldier. He moved to the New Hampshire grants (now Vermont) in 1768 and became commander (*c*.1770) of the Green Mountain Boys, a volunteer militia. In the American Revolution, Allen and his troops (with sympathizers from Connecticut and Massachusetts) captured Fort Ticonderoga (May 10, 1775), and Crown Point (May 11, 1775). During the invasion of Canada, Allen was captured (September 25, 1775) and imprisoned in England until 1778, when he returned to Vermont.

**Allen, Woody** (1935– ) US film director, writer, and actor, b. Allen Stewart Konigsberg. Allen made his film debut as an actor and screenwriter in *What's New Pussycat?* (1965). In the 1970s he established his trademark style of urbane, angst-ridden, New York-based comedies. Allen won Academy awards for Best Picture, Best Screenplay, and Best Director for *Annie Hall* (1977). He gained an Oscar nomination for his first serious drama, the Bergman-like *Interiors* (1978). His next film, *Manhattan* (1979), marked a return to the semi-autobiographical format. *Hannah and Her Sisters* (1986) won Allen an Oscar for Best Screenplay. Other films include *Zelig* (1983), *The Purple Rose of Cairo* (1985), *Crimes and Misdemeanors* (1989), and *Mighty Aphrodite* (1996). His separation (1992) from Mia Farrow, his long-standing partner and co-star, was acrimonious and litigious.

**Allende Gossens, Salvador** (1908–73) Chilean statesman, president (1970–73). Allende was one of the founders of the Chilean Socialist Party (1933), and served as minister of health (1939–42) and head of the senate (1965–69). His narrow election victory led to the introduction of democratic socialist reforms, which antagonized the Chilean establishment. The nationalization of the US-owned copper industry resulted in a US trade embargo. The CIA began a covert campaign of destabilization, aided by a deteriorating economy. Allende was overthrown and died in a military coup led by General Pinochet.

**allergy** Disorder in which the body mounts a hypersensitive reaction to one or more substances (allergens) not normally considered harmful. Typical allergic reactions are sneezing (hay fever), "wheezing" and difficulty in breathing (asthma), and skin eruptions and itching (eczema). A tendency to allergic reactions is often hereditary.

**Allies** Term used in World War I and World War II for the forces that fought the Central Powers and Axis Powers respectively. In World War I they numbered 23 and included Belgium, Britain and its Commonwealth, France, Italy, Japan,

Russia, and the US. In World War II the 49 Allies included Belgium, Britain and the Commonwealth, France, the Netherlands, the Soviet Union, and the US.

**alligator** Broad-snouted crocodilian reptile found only in the US and China. The American alligator, *Alligator mississippiensis*, is found in the SE US; it grows up to 19ft (5.8m) long. The almost extinct smaller Chinese alligator, *A. sinensis*, is restricted to the Yangtze-Kiang river basin. Length: up to 5ft (1.5m). Family Alligatoridea.

**allium** *See* ONION

**allotropy** Property of some chemical elements that enables them to exist in two or more distinct physical forms. Each form (called an allotrope) can have different chemical properties but can be changed into another allotrope – given suitable conditions. Examples of allotropes are molecular oxygen and ozone; white and yellow phosphorus; and graphite and diamond (carbon).

**alloy** Combination of two or more metals. An alloy's properties are different from those of its constituent elements. Alloys are generally harder and stronger, and have lower melting points. Some mixtures composed of a metal and a non-metal, such as STEEL, are also referred to as alloys.

**All Saints' Day** In the Christian liturgical calendar, the day on which all the saints are commemorated. The feast is observed on November 1 in the West and on the first Sunday after Pentecost in the East. The eve of the day is celebrated in some western countries as Halloween.

**All Souls' Day** Day of remembrance and prayer for all the departed souls. Observed by Roman Catholics and High Church Anglicans on November 2, or on November 3 if the former falls on a Sunday.

**allspice** (pimento) Aromatic tree native to the West Indies and Central America. The fruits are used as a spice, in perfume, and in medicine. Height: up to 40ft (12m). Family Myrtaceae; species *Pimenta officinalis*

**Allston, Washington** (1779–1843) US romantic painter. A pupil of Benjamin WEST at London's Royal Academy, Allston was the pioneer of romantic LANDSCAPE PAINTING in the US and a precursor of the HUDSON RIVER SCHOOL. His work in England includes a portrait of Coleridge (1814). In 1818 he returned to the US. Allston's most famous work is the lyrical *Moonlit Landscape* (1819). He spent 20 years working on the disappointing *Belshazzar's Feast*. It remained unfinished.

**alluvial fan** Generally fan-shaped area of ALLUVIUM (waterborne sediment) deposited by a river when the stream reaches a plain on lower ground and the water velocity is abruptly reduced. Organic matter is also transported, making the soil highly fertile. Valuable minerals are often found in alluvial fans.

**alluvium** General term that describes the sediments sand, silt and mud deposited by flowing water along the banks, delta, or floodplain of a river or stream. Fine-textured sediments that contain organic matter form soil.

**Almaty** (formerly Alma-Ata) Largest city and, until 2000, capital of Kazakstan, near the SE border with Kyrgyzstan. In 1991 it hosted the meeting of 11 former Soviet republics that led to the Alma-Ata Declaration, which created the COMMONWEALTH OF INDEPENDENT STATES (CIS). In 1995 the government decided to move the capital to AQMOLA. Industries: foodstuffs, tobacco, timber, printing, film-making, leather, machinery. Pop. (1991) 1,515,300.

**Almodóvar, Pedro** (1951– ) Spanish film director and screenwriter. Almodóvar's debut film was *Dos Putas* (1974). A master of kitsch, black comedies, he achieved international success with *Women on the Verge of a Nervous Breakdown* (1988), and *Tie Me Up! Tie Me Down!* (1990).

**Almohad** BERBER Muslim dynasty (1145–1269) in North Africa and Spain, the followers of a reform movement within ISLAM. It was founded by Muhammad ibn Tumart, who set out from the Atlas Mountains to purify Islam and oust the ALMORAVIDS from Morocco and eventually Spain. In 1212 Alfonso VIII of Castile routed the Almohads, and in 1269 their capital, MARRAKESH, fell to the Marinids.

**almond** Small tree native to the E Mediterranean region and SW Asia; also the seed of its nutlike fruit. Family Rosaceae; species *Prunus dulcis*.

**ALLOTROPY**

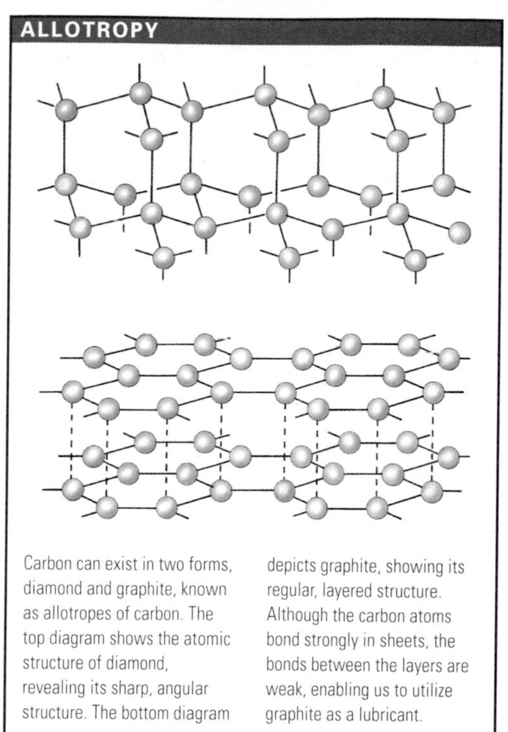

Carbon can exist in two forms, diamond and graphite, known as allotropes of carbon. The top diagram shows the atomic structure of diamond, revealing its sharp, angular structure. The bottom diagram depicts graphite, showing its regular, layered structure. Although the carbon atoms bond strongly in sheets, the bonds between the layers are weak, enabling us to utilize graphite as a lubricant.

**Almoravid** BERBER Muslim dynasty (1054–1145) in Morocco and Spain. They rose to power under Abdullah ibn Yasin who converted Saharan tribes in a religious revival. ABU BAKR founded MARRAKESH as their capital in 1070; his brother Yusuf ibn Tashufin defeated Alfonso VI of Castile in 1086. Almoravid rule was ended by the rise of the ALMOHADS.

**aloe** Genus of plants native to S Africa, with spiny-edged, fleshy leaves. They grow in dense rosettes and have drooping red, orange, or yellow flower clusters. Family Liliaceae.

**alpaca** *See* LLAMA

**alphabet** System of letters representing the sounds of speech. The word alphabet is derived from the first two letters of the Greek alphabet, *alpha* and *beta*. The most important alphabets in use today are Roman, CYRILLIC, GREEK, ARABIC, HEBREW, and Devanagari. The Latin alphabet, which grew out of the Greek by way of the Etruscans, was perfected around AD 100 and is the foundation on which Western alphabets are based. In some alphabets, such as the Devanagari of India, each character represents a syllable. BRAILLE and MORSE code are alphabets invented to meet special needs.

**Alpha Centauri** Brightest star in the constellation Centaurus, and the third-brightest star in the sky. It is a visual BINARY.

**alpha particles** (alpha rays) Stable, positively charged particles emitted spontaneously from the nuclei of certain radioactive isotopes undergoing alpha decay. They consist of two protons and two neutrons and are identical to the nuclei of HELIUM atoms. Their penetrating power is low compared with that of beta particles (electrons) but they cause intense ionization along their track. This ionization is used to detect them. *See also* RADIOACTIVITY; Ernest RUTHERFORD

**Alps** Mountain system in S central Europe, extending *c.*750mi (1,200km) in a broad arc from near the Gulf of Genoa on the Mediterranean Sea through France, Italy, Switzerland, Liechtenstein, Austria, Germany, and Slovenia. The system was formed by the collision of the European and African tectonic plates. The highest peak is MONT BLANC at 15,771ft (4,807m).

**Alsace** Region in E France, comprising the departments of Bas-Rhin and Haut-Rhin. STRASBOURG is the leading city, Mulhouse and Colmar are the main industrial centers. Separated from Germany by the RHINE River, the Alsace-Lorraine region has often caused friction between France and Germany. The culture and architecture reflect both national influences. There are rich deposits of iron ore and potash. Most of the region is fertile and productive, with German-style, riesling wines the

▼ **almond** Bitter and sweet almonds are related to the stone fruits such as the peach, and are cultivated in temperate climates. Sweet almonds are edible, but the kernel of the bitter variety is inedible and used only for the extraction of its oil.

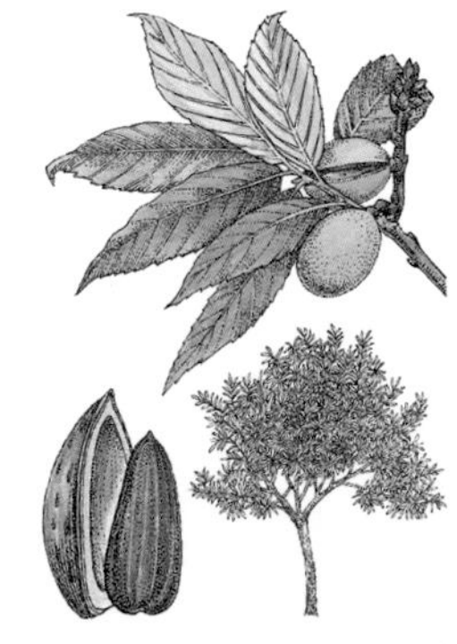

A

major agricultural product. Industries: steel, textiles, chemicals. Area: 3,197sq mi (8,280sq km). Pop. (1990) 1,624,400.

**Altai** (Altajsk) Complex mountain system in central Asia stretching from Kazakstan into N China and W Mongolia, and from S Siberia to the Gobi Desert. A densely forested area, it is the source of the Irtysand Ob rivers. The average height is 6,500–10,000ft (2,000–3,000m), and the highest peak is Mount Belukha at 14,783ft (4,506m).

**Altaic languages** Family of languages spoken by *c*.80 million people in Turkey, Iran, parts of the former Soviet Union, Mongolia, and parts of China. It consists of three branches: the Turkic, the Mongolian, and the Tungusic languages.

**Altair** Star Alpha Aquilae, whose luminosity is ten times that of the Sun. Characteristics: apparent mag. 0.77; spectral type A7; distance 16 light-years.

**Altamira** World heritage site of Paleolithic cave paintings and engravings (*c*.14,000–9,500 BC) near Santander, N Spain. The roof of the lateral chamber is covered with paintings of animals, including boars, deer, horses, and particularly bison, boldly executed in vivid black, red and violet. There are also eight engraved anthropomorphic figures.

**Altdorfer, Albrecht** (*c*.1480–1538) German painter and engraver, one of the most original German painters of his day. Altdorfer concentrated mainly on religious and historic themes but was also one of the first European artists to take a real interest in landscape. His patrons included the Emperor Maximilian, who commissioned him along with DÜRER and others to illuminate his prayer book (*c*.1515), and Duke William of Bavaria for whom Altdorfer painted a series of Classical and Christian histories including *The Battle of Alexander at Issus* (1529).

**alternating current (AC)** *See* ELECTRIC CURRENT

**alternation of generations** Two-generation cycle by which plants and some algae reproduce. The asexual diploid SPOROPHYTE form produces haploid SPORES that, in turn, grow into the sexual (GAMETOPHYTE) form. The gametophyte produces the egg cell that is fertilized by a male gamete to produce a diploid zygote that grows into another sporophyte.

**alternative energy** *See* RENEWABLE ENERGY

**alternator** Electrical generator that produces an alternating ELECTRIC CURRENT.

**altimeter** Instrument for measuring altitude. The simplest type is a form of aneroid BAROMETER. As height increases, air pressure decreases, so the barometer scale can be calibrated to show altitude. Some aircraft have a radar altimeter, which measures the time taken to bounce a radar signal off the ground.

**Altiplano** High plain in the South American Andes of Peru and W Bolivia, at an elevation of about 12,000ft (3,650m).

**altitude** In astronomy, the angular distance of a celestial body above the observer's horizon. It is measured in degrees from 0 (on the horizon) to 90 (at the zenith) along the GREAT CIRCLE passing through the body and the zenith. If the object is below the horizon, the altitude is negative.

**altitude sickness** Metabolic problems occurring at high altitudes, notably deficiency of oxygen in the blood and tissues. Symptoms include dizziness, palpitations, headache, nosebleed, and nausea.

**Altman, Robert** (1925– ) US independent film director. Altman gained his first Academy Award nomination for *MASH* (1970). A second Oscar nomination followed for *Nashville* (1975). Following a series of theater adaptations, he returned to exposing the reality behind the myth in *The Player* (1992). *Short Cuts* (1993) was a successful adaptation of Raymond Carver's short stories.

**alto** In singing, the highest male voice, also called COUNTERTENOR; or the lowest female voice, also called CONTRALTO. It is also used to describe that member of a family of instruments with a range that corresponds to the alto voice; for example, an alto FLUTE is a fourth lower than a standard one.

**alumina** (aluminum oxide, $Al_2O_3$) Mineral used as an abrasive, electrical insulator, and furnace lining. Other forms of alumina include corundum, two impure varieties of which are the gemstones SAPPHIRE and RUBY.

**aluminum** (symbol Al) Metallic silvery white element of Group III of the periodic table. It is the most common metal in the Earth's crust; the chief ore is BAUXITE, from which the metal is extracted by electrolysis. Alloyed with other metals, it is extensively used in machined and molded articles, particularly where lightness is important, as in aircraft. It is protected from oxidation (corrosion) by a thin, natural layer of oxide. Properties: at.no. 13; at.wt. 26.98; sp.gr. 2.69; m.p. 1,220.38°F (660.2°C); b.p. 3272°F (1800°C); most common isotope $^{27}$Al. *See also* ANODIZING

**Alvarez, Luis Walter** (1911–88) US physicist who won the 1968 Nobel Prize for physics for developing the liquid-hydrogen bubble chamber. Alvarez used it to identify many "resonances" (very short-lived particles). He also helped construct the first proton linear accelerator. Alvarez worked on the MANHATTAN PROJECT to develop the atom bomb and invented the radar guidance system for aircraft landings.

**alveolus** One of a cluster of microscopic air sacs that open out from the alveolar ducts at the far end of each bronchiole in the LUNGS. The alveolus is the site for the exchange of gases between the air and the bloodstream, and is covered in a network of CAPILLARY blood vessels. *See also* GAS EXCHANGE; RESPIRATORY SYSTEM

**Alzheimer's disease** Degenerative condition characterized by memory loss and progressive mental impairment; it is the most common cause of DEMENTIA. Sometimes seen in the middle years, Alzheimer's becomes increasingly common with advancing age. Many factors have been implicated, but the precise cause is unknown.

**AM** Abbreviation of AMPLITUDE MODULATION

**Amado, Jorge** (1912– ) Brazilian novelist. Amado's early novels, such as *Sweat* (1934) and *The Violent Land* (1942), are powerful realist novels on poverty in Brazil. His later works, such as *Dona Flor and Her Two Husbands* (1966), are more lyrical, using folklore and humor to examine contemporary Brazilian society.

**Amal** (Arabic *Afwaj al-Muqawama al-Lubnaniyya*, "masses of the Lebanese resistance"; the acronym means hope) Lebanese SHIITE political movement. Amal was established in 1974 by Musa Sadr to press for greater Shiite political representation in Lebanon. It split into extremist and moderate groups in 1982. Backed variously by Syria and the Palestinian Liberation Organization (PLO), its members have perpetrated a number of terrorist acts, such as the kidnappings in Lebanon during the 1980s. In 1991 the National Assembly decreed the dissolution of all militias and the moderated their stance.

**amalgam** Solid or liquid alloy of mercury with other metals. Dentists once filled teeth with amalgams usually containing copper and zinc. Most metals dissolve in mercury, although iron and platinum are exceptions.

**amanita** Large, widely distributed genus of fungi. Amanitas usually have distinct stalks and the prominent remains of a veil in a fleshy ring under the cap and at the bulbous base. They include some of the most poisonous fungi known, such as the DEATH CAP and destroying angel. *See also* FLY AGARIC

**amaryllis** Genus consisting of a single species of bulbous plant, *Amaryllis belladona*, the belladonna lily, which has several trumpet-shaped pink or white flowers. Amaryllis is also the common name for *Hippeastrum*, a bulbous houseplant.

**Amaterasu** Sun goddess of the SHINTO pantheon (hierarchy of gods), considered to be the ancestor of the Japanese imperial clan.

**Amati** Family of Italian violinmakers in Cremona in the 16th and 17th centuries. They included Andrea (*c*.1520–78), the founder of the Cremona school of violinmaking. The Amati family are credited with establishing the design of the violin as it is today.

**Amazon** World's second-longest river, draining the vast Amazon RAIN FOREST basin of N South America. It carries by far the greatest volume of water of any river in the world: the average rate of discharge is *c*.3,355,000ft$^3$ (95,000m$^3$) every second, nearly three times as much as its nearest rival, the Zaire. The flow is so great that its silt discolors the water up to 125mi (200km) into the Atlantic. At around 2.7 million sq mi (7 million sq km), the Amazon river basin comprises nearly 40% of the continent of South America. Length: *c*.3,990mi (6,430km).

**Amazon** In Greek mythology, a race of female warriors who lived in a totally matriarchal society. As allies of the

Trojans, they took part in the defense of TROY, where their queen Penthesilea was slain by ACHILLES after she had killed many Greek warriors.

**ambassador** Diplomatic representative of the highest rank, appointed to represent a goverment abroad.

**amber** Hard, yellow or brown, translucent fossil resin, mainly from pine trees. Amber is most often found in alluvial soils, in lignite beds, or around seashores, especially the Baltic Sea. The resin sometimes occurs with embedded fossil insects or plants. Amber can be polished to a high degree and is used to make necklaces and other items of jewelry.

**ambergris** Musky, waxy, solid formed in the intestine of a SPERM WHALE. It is used in perfumes as a fixative for the scent.

**Ambrose, Saint** (339–97) Roman cleric who as Bishop of Milan from 374 resisted demands to surrender Milan's churches to the Arians and refused to compromise his orthodox position. He was the author of works on theology and ethics that greatly influenced the thought of the Western church. His feast day is December 7. *See also* ARIANISM

**ameba** Microscopic, almost transparent, single-celled protozoan animal that has a constantly changing, irregular shape. Found in ponds, damp soil, and animal intestines, it consists of a thin outer cell membrane, a large nucleus, food and contractile vacuoles, and fat globules. It reproduces by binary fission. Length: up to 0.1in (3mm). Class Sarcodina; species include the common *Ameba proteus* and *Entameba histolytica*, which causes amebic DYSENTERY. *See illustration on page 23*

**Amenhotep III** (*c*.1417–*c*.1379 BC) King of ancient Egypt. Amenhotep succeeded his father, Thutmose IV. The 18th dynasty was at its height during his reign. His wife, Queen Tiy, played an important role in state affairs. He was succeeded by his son, who took the name AKHNATEN.

**Amenhotep IV** *See* AKHNATEN

**America** Western Hemisphere, consisting of the continents of NORTH AMERICA and SOUTH AMERICA, joined by the isthmus of CENTRAL AMERICA. It extends from N of the Arctic Circle to 56° S, separating the Atlantic Ocean from the Pacific. NATIVE AMERICANS settled the entire continent by 8000 BC. Norsemen were probably the first Europeans to explore America in the 8th century, but Christopher COLUMBUS is popularly credited with the first European discovery in 1492. The name "America" was first applied to the lands in 1507 and derives from Amerigo Vespucci, a Florentine navigator who was falsely believed to be the first European to set foot on the mainland.

**American Academy and Institute of Arts and Letters** Association formed in 1977 by the merger of the National Institute of Arts and Letters and the American Academy of Arts and Letters. The association's membership is limited to 250 individuals of literary, musical, or artistic achievement. Awards are given annually for distinguished and creative work in painting, sculpture, the novel, poetry, and drama.

**American art** During the colonial era, American art reflected the taste of European settlers. In Spanish territories, the main demand was for religious art; while in Dutch and English areas, there was a greater emphasis on portraiture. In the 18th century, America produced its first artists of international standing, John Singleton COPLEY and Benjamin WEST. Both spent much of their career in England, where they became leading exponents of history painting (historical, biblical and mythological scenes). After independence, there was a gradual movement away from European traditions. This was most evident in the field of landscape painting, where artists from the HUDSON RIVER SCHOOL and the Rocky Mountain School recorded the beauty of the wilderness. Thomas EAKINS and Winslow HOMER also celebrated the American way of life, although in a more realistic vein. Realism was the cornerstone of the ASHCAN SCHOOL. In the 20th century, the key event was the ARMORY SHOW of 1913, which encouraged the spread of modern art. Alfred STIEGLITZ was a seminal figure in the development of modern art in the US. Georgia O'KEEFFE and Edward HOPPER were arguably its two greatest stylists. With the development of abstract expressionism in the 1940s, US artists became the standard-bearers of the avant-garde, a role they have never relinquished. *See also* LUMINISM; NATIVE NORTH AMERICAN ART

**American Bar Association (ABA)** Organization whose members are attorneys admitted to the bar of any state. Founded in 1878, the association attempts to ensure parity of law across the country, improve the efficiency of the legal system, and maintain high standards. By the mid-1990s the association boasted more than 400,000 members.

**American Colonization Society** Group founded in 1817 by Robert Finley to return free African Americans to Africa for settlement. More than 11,000 African Americans were transported to Sierra Leone and, after 1821, MONROVIA. Leading members of the society included James Monroe, James Madison, and John Marshall.

**American Federation of Labor and Congress of Industrial Organizations (AFL-CIO)** Labor organization, the largest union in North America. It is a federation of individual trade unions from the US, Canada, Mexico, Panama, and some US dependencies. Established in 1955, it merged the American Federation of Labor (AFL) and Congress of Industrial Organizations (CIO). Although each union within the federation is fully autonomous, the ultimate governing body of the AFL-CIO is an executive council made up of president, vice presidents, and secretary-treasurer. In recent years, the reduction of union membership (*c*.15% of US workers in 1995) has seen the AFL-CIO concentrate on organizing public sector workers.

**American Fur Company** First US business monopoly, owned by John Jacob ASTOR. John JAY's Treaty of 1794 permitted US fur trading in the Pacific Northwest. Fort Astoria was set up in Oregon in 1805. During the WAR OF 1812 the US was unable to defend Astoria, and Astor was forced to sell. As the fur trade declined in the 1840s, Fort Astoria reverted to US control.

**American Indians** Alternative name for NATIVE AMERICANS

**American Labor Party** US political party formed in 1936, primarily to support President Franklin D. ROOSEVELT's NEW DEAL. Based in New York state, the Party was an influential power-broker in New York City. In 1944 the Party split over its relationship with the Soviet Union, the anti-communists forming the Liberal Party. In the 1948 presidential elections, the Party gained more than 500,000 votes for Henry A. WALLACE. It was officially dissolved in 1956.

**American Legion** Association of US military veterans. Founded (1919) in Paris, its US headquarters are in Indianapolis, Indiana. Qualifications for membership are honorable service or honorable discharge. It sponsors many social causes, notably education and sports for young people and care of sick and disabled veterans.

**American literature** English explorers and early colonists produced literary accounts of North America. The first English

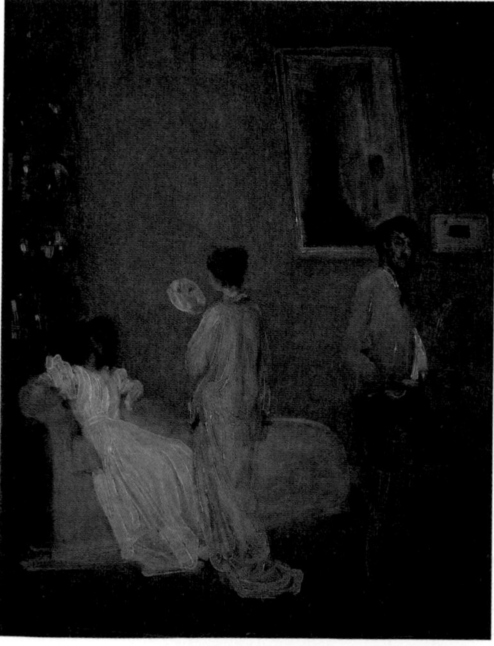

◄ **American art** *The Actor's Studio* by James Abbot McNeil Whistler (1834–1903). Although active in Europe for much of his working life, Whistler was an influential US artist, whose style is thought by some to have been a precursor of abstract art. He asserted that art did not have to provide a message and should exist for its own sake.

language work published in New England was the *Bay Psalm Book* (1640). Early colonial literature was often an expression of Puritan piety. Many of the leading figures in the AMERICAN REVOLUTION, such as Thomas PAINE and Benjamin FRANKLIN, produced important literary works. Early 19th-century writers, such as Washington IRVING and James Fenimore COOPER, were influenced by European romanticism. The preeminent US romantic poet was Henry Wadsworth LONGFELLOW. TRANSCENDENTALISM was the first truly distinctive national literary movement. Leading writers included the essayists Henry David THOREAU, Ralph Waldo EMERSON, Oliver Wendell HOLMES, and Louisa May ALCOTT. Walt WHITMAN's free-verse epic *Leaves of Grass* (1855–92) is perhaps the most fully realized poetic expression of transcendentalism. The 1840s and 1850s produced many American fiction classics, such as Herman MELVILLE's *Moby Dick* (1851) and Nathaniel HAWTHORNE's *The Scarlet Letter* (1850). Harriet Beecher Stowe's antislavery story *Uncle Tom's Cabin* (1852) was the best-selling novel of the century. Literature of the immediate post-Civil War period is characterized by parochialism. The two great exceptions to the trend were Henry JAMES and Mark TWAIN. While James emigrated to Europe and embraced psychological realism in novels such as *Portrait of a Lady* (1881), Twain used national dialects in humorous classics such as *Huckleberry Finn* (1885). Realism fed into NATURALISM, producing writers who either focused on the development of cities (Theodore DRIESER and Edith WHARTON), or those who concentrated on a hostile wilderness (Jack LONDON). Stephen CRANE's *Red Badge of Courage* (1895) was groundbreaking in its naturalistic treatment of the Civil War. In the early 20th century many US writers went into exile. In Paris, Gertrude STEIN held court over the "Lost Generation," a large group of emigrés that included Ernest HEMINGWAY and Henry MILLER. T.S. ELIOT and Ezra POUND led the search for experimental poetic forms. Eliot's bleak and fragmentary poem *The Wasteland* (1922) is often viewed as the archetype of high MODERNISM. Wallace STEVENS and William Carlos WILLIAMS developed the new poetry. The HARLEM RENAISSANCE witnessed the emergence of African-American writers, such as Langston HUGHES. The style and decadence of the "jazz age" in 1920s New York was captured by F. Scott FITZGERALD in *The Great Gatsby* (1925). The 1920s also witnessed the debut of the first great American dramatist, Eugene O'NEILL. Writers such as John STEINBECK, Carson MCCULLERS, and Eudora WELTY emerged in the 1930s. Post-World War II literature and drama can be characterized by a sense of despair when confronted by the violence of the 20th century. In the 1950s major dramatists such as Arthur MILLER, Edward ALBEE, and Sam SHEPARD developed the American theater. African-American writers, such as Richard Wright, Ralph ELLISON, and James BALDWIN, dealt with racial inequality and violence in contemporary US society. Maya ANGELOU and Toni MORRISON focused on the 20th-century US history of African-American women. During the 1960s novelists such as Saul BELLOW, Philip ROTH, and Joseph HELLER examined the Jewish urban intellectual approach to American society, often adopting a deeply ironic tone. Humor was also a major outlet for writers such as John UPDIKE, Kurt VONNEGUT, and Thomas PYNCHON. Norman MAILER used a more muscular, Hemingway-like approach. The BEAT MOVEMENT (including Jack KEROUAC and Allen GINSBERG) urged the rejection of the established order. A major trend in American poetry was the "confessional" style of personal revelation by poets such as Robert LOWELL and Sylvia PLATH. POSTMODERNISM has informed the work of authors such as Kathy Acker and Bret Easton Ellis.

**American Medical Association (AMA)** Federation of 54 state and territorial medical associations, founded in 1847. The AMA develops programs to provide scientific information for the profession and health-education materials for the public. By the mid-1990s there were *c.*300,000 members.

**American Revolution** (1775–83) (Revolutionary War) Successful revolt by the THIRTEEN COLONIES in North America against British rule. A number of issues provoked the conflict including restrictions on trade and manufacturing imposed by the NAVIGATION ACTS, restrictions on land settlement in the West, and attempts to raise revenue in America by such means as the STAMP ACT (1765) and the Tea Act (1773) that led to the BOSTON TEA PARTY. "No taxation without representation" became the colonial radicals' rallying cry. The intellectual battle for independence was led by Thomas PAINE, Thomas JEFFERSON, and Benjamin FRANKLIN. A CONTINENTAL CONGRESS was summoned in 1774, and the first shots were fired at LEXINGTON AND CONCORD, Massachusetts, in April 1775. In May the second Continental Congress met at Philadelphia, established an army under George WASHINGTON, and assumed the role of a revolutionary government. On 4 July 1776 the DECLARATION OF INDEPENDENCE made the break with Britain decisive. Initially the colonials suffered a series of military defeats, and Washington retreated from New York to Pennsylvania. Crossing the Delaware River, he surprised and captured the British at TRENTON (December 26, 1776). On January 3, 1777, he defeated the British at PRINCETON, further strengthening American morale. The British attempted a three-pronged attack, focusing on New York State. The strategy failed with the first decisive colonial victory at SARATOGA (October 17, 1777), and brought France into the war against Britain. During the winter of 1777, Washington's forces reorganized in Pennsylvania. In 1778 the British forces focused on the South, taking SAVANNAH in December 1778. Following the defeat at King's Mountain in 1780, the British, under General Charles Cornwallis, were forced to withdraw N to YORKTOWN, Virginia. In 1781, surrounded by American forces and the French navy, Cornwallis surrendered. Fighting ceased and the war was formally ended by the Peace of Paris (1783), which recognized US independence.

**American Samoa** US-administered group of five volcanic islands and two coral atolls of the SAMOA island chain in the S Pacific, *c.*650mi (1,050km) NE of Fiji. The principal islands are Tutuila, the Manua group (Ta'u, Ofu and Olosega), and Aun'u. Rose Island (uninhabited) and Swain's Island are coral atolls. In 1899 a treaty between the US, Germany, and the UK granted the US rights to the islands E of 171° longitude, and Germany the rights to the W sector. American Samoa remained under the jurisdiction of the US Navy until 1951, when the US naval base at the capital Pago Pago closed down. Administration was transferred to the Department of the Interior. In 1978 the first gubernatorial elections took place. The population is largely Polynesian, who are considered US nationals. The US government and the tuna fish canning industry are the main sources of employment. Pop. (1990) 46,773.

**America's Cup** International competition for racing yachts. A trophy was established in 1857 by the New York Yacht Club. Several countries compete in a series of elimination races, before challenging the previous winner. The US has won the best-of-seven series on almost every occasion and traditionally hosted the contest off Newport, Rhode Island.

**americium** (symbol Am) Radioactive metallic element of the ACTINIDE SERIES, first made in 1944 by neutron bombardment of plutonium. It is used in home smoke detectors, and $^{241}$Am is a source of gamma rays. Properties: at.no. 95; at.wt. 243.13; sp.gr. 13.67; m.p. 1,821°F (995°C); b.p. unknown; most stable isotope $^{243}$Am (half-life 7,650 yr).

**amethyst** Transparent, violet variety of crystallized QUARTZ, containing more iron oxide than other varieties. It is found mainly in Brazil, Uruguay, Canada, and North Carolina. Amethyst is a semiprecious gem.

**Amharic** Official language of Ethiopia since *c.* 1300. It is a Semitic language belonging to the SE Semitic subgroup of Afro-Asiatic languages and has many words in common with the ancient form of Ethiopic, the language of religious ritual in the Christian Church in Ethiopia.

**Amin, Idi** (1925– ) President of Uganda (1971–79). He gained power by a military coup in 1971, overthrowing Milton OBOTE. He established a dictatorship marked by atrocities, and expelled *c.*80,000 Asian Ugandans in 1972. When Tanzanian forces joined rebel Ugandans in a march on KAMPALA, Amin fled to Libya.

**amine** Any of a group of organic compounds derived from AMMONIA by replacing hydrogen atoms with alkyl groups. Methylamine ($CH_3NH_2$) has one hydrogen replaced. Replacement of two hydrogens gives a secondary amine and of three hydrogens, a tertiary amine. Amines are produced in the putrefaction of organic matter and are weakly basic. *See also* ALKALOID

**amino acid** Organic acid containing at least one carboxyl group (COOH) and at least one amino group ($NH_2$). Amino acids are of great biological importance because they combine to form PROTEIN. Amino acids form PEPTIDES by the reaction of adjacent amino and carboxyl groups. Proteins are polypeptide chains consisting of hundreds of amino acids. About 20 amino acids occur in proteins; not all organisms are able to synthesize all of them. **Essential** amino acids are those that an organism has to obtain from its environment. There are ten such essential amino acids for humans: arginine, histidine, isoleucine, leucine, lysine, methionine, phenylalanine, threonine, tryptophan, and valine.

**Amis, Kingsley** (1922–95) British novelist, father of Martin AMIS. Amis' debut novel *Lucky Jim* (1954) is a classic of post-1945 British fiction. A satire on academia, it established Amis as one of the ANGRY YOUNG MEN. Other novels include *That Uncertain Feeling* (1955), *Take a Girl Like You* (1960), *Girl, 20* (1971) and *Stanley and the Women* (1984). His tragicomedy *The Old Devils* (1986) won the Booker Prize.

**Amis, Martin** (1949– ) British novelist and journalist, son of Kingsley AMIS. Amis' debut novel, *The Rachel Papers* (1974), won the Somerset Maugham Award. His humor is more bawdy and dark than his father's. *Money* (1984) is a stylish critique of the dehumanizing tendencies of late capitalism. *Einstein's Monsters* (1987) is a collection of five short stories on nuclear war. *Time's Arrow* (1991) is a complex work on the Holocaust. Other novels include *Success* (1978) and *Night Train* (1997).

**Amish** Highly conservative, Protestant sect of North America, whose members form an offshoot of the ANABAPTIST MENNONITE Church. The strict Old Order Amish Mennonite Church, to which most sect members belong, was founded in Switzerland in 1693 by Jakob Ammann (*c*.1645–*c*.1730). The Amish began migrating to North America in 1720 and eventually died out in Europe. In the US and Canada they established small closed agricultural communities. After 1850 tensions between traditionalist "old order" Amish and more liberal "new order" communities split the sect. Today, a few groups of traditionalist Amish still work the land, practice noncooperation with the state, wear plain, homemade clothes, and shun modern conveniences such as telephones and cars.

**Amman** Capital and largest city of Jordan, 50mi (80km) ENE of Jerusalem. Known as Rabbath-Ammon, it was the chief city of the Ammonites in biblical times. A new city was built on seven hills from 1875, and it became the capital of Trans-Jordan in 1921. From 1948 it grew rapidly, partly as a result of the influx of Palestinian refugees. Industries: cement, textiles, tobacco, leather. Pop. (1994 est.) 1,300,042.

**ammeter** Instrument for measuring ELECTRIC CURRENT in AMPERES. An ammeter is connected in series in a circuit. In the moving-coil type for DIRECT CURRENT (DC), the current to be measured passes through a coil suspended in a magnetic field and deflects a needle attached to the coil. In the moving-iron type for both direct and ALTERNATING CURRENT (AC), current through a fixed coil magnetizes two pieces of soft iron that repel each other and deflect the needle. Digital ammeters are now also commonly used.

**ammonia** Colorless, nonflammable, pungent gas ($NH_3$) manufactured by the HABER PROCESS. It is used to make nitrogenous fertilizers. Ammonia solutions are used in cleaning and bleaching. The gas is extremely soluble in water, forming an alkaline solution of ammonium hydroxide ($NH_4OH$), which gives rise to ammonium salts containing the ion $NH_4^+$. Properties: sp.gr. 0.59; m.p. −107.9°F (−77.7°C); b.p. −28.1°F (−33.4°C).

**ammonite** Any of an extinct group of shelled cephalopod MOLLUSKS. Most ammonites had a spiral shell, and they are believed to be related to the nautiloids, whose only surviving form is the pearly NAUTILUS. They are common as FOSSILS in marine rocks.

**amnesia** Loss of or impairment of memory. It can be caused by disease or physical injury, especially to the brain, or by psychological disturbance. Selective amnesia, in which only certain unpleasant memories are eliminated, is generally due to emotional disorder.

**AMMONITE**

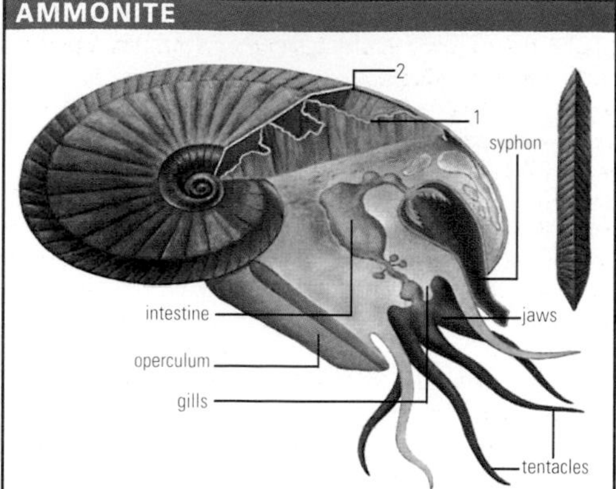


Ammonites had a soft anatomy similar to that of the modern nautilus, which lives in the open end of its shell. As the animal grew it secreted more shell and moved forward into the new part, walling off the old section with a septum (1). The walled-off chambers were used for buoyancy, being supplied with air from a tissue filament or siphuncle (2) connecting them all. The septa met the shell wall in suture lines that had identifiable patterns for each species and became more complex as the group advanced.

**Amnesty International** Human rights organization, founded (1961) by Peter Berenson. It campaigns on behalf of prisoners of conscience. Based in the UK and funded entirely by private donations, it champions the rights of individuals detained for political or religious reasons. By the mid-1990s, Amnesty had more than one million members and offices in more than 40 countries. It was awarded the Nobel Peace Prize in 1977.

**amnion** Membrane or sac that encloses the EMBRYO of a reptile, bird, or mammal. The embryo floats in the amniotic fluid within the sac. *See also* WOMB

**Amon** (Amun) Ancient Egyptian deity of reproduction or the animating force. The "invisible one," Amon is commonly represented as a human being wearing ram's horns and a twin-feathered crown. He gradually assimilated other Egyptian gods, becoming Amon-Re (the supreme creator). His cult temple was at Weset (LUXOR).

**Amos** (active *c*.750 BC) Old Testament prophet. He was named as the author of the Book of Amos, the third of the 12 books of the Minor Prophets.

**Ampère, André Marie** (1775–1836) French physicist and mathematician. Ampère founded electrodynamics (now called ELECTROMAGNETISM) and performed numerous experiments to investigate the magnetic effects of electric currents. He devised techniques for detecting and measuring currents, and constructed an early type of galvanometer. Ampère's law – proposed by him – is a mathematical description of the magnetic force between two electric currents. His name is also commemorated in the fundamental unit of current, the AMPERE (A). *See also* ELECTRIC CURRENT

**ampere** SI unit of ELECTRIC CURRENT (symbol A). It is defined as the current in a pair of straight, parallel conductors of infinite length and 1m (39in) apart in a vacuum that produces a force of $2 \times 10^{-7}$ newton per meter in their length. This force may be measured on a current balance instrument, the standard against which current meters, such as an AMMETER, are calibrated.

**amphetamine** DRUG that stimulates the CENTRAL NERVOUS SYSTEM. The use of amphetamines (known as "pep pills" or "speed") can lead to drug abuse and dependence. They can induce a temporary sense of well-being, often followed by fatigue and depression. *See also* ADDICTION

**amphibian** Class of egg-laying VERTEBRATES, whose larval stages (tadpoles) are usually spent in water but whose adult life is normally spent on land. Amphibians have smooth, moist skin and are cold-blooded. Larvae breathe through gills; adults usually have lungs. All adults are carnivorous but larvae are

▼ **ameba** In order to move, an ameba pushes out projections called *pseudopods* (lit. fake foot) from its body. Cytoplasm – the fluid content of the cell – flows into the pseudopod, constantly enlarging it until all the cytoplasm has entered and the ameba as a whole has moved. Pseudopods are also used in feeding: they move out to engulf a food particle (1) which then becomes enclosed in a membrane-bound food vacuole (2). Digestive enzymes enter the vacuole, which gradually shrinks as the food is broken down (3). Undigested material is discharged by the vacuole and left behind as the ameba moves on (4).

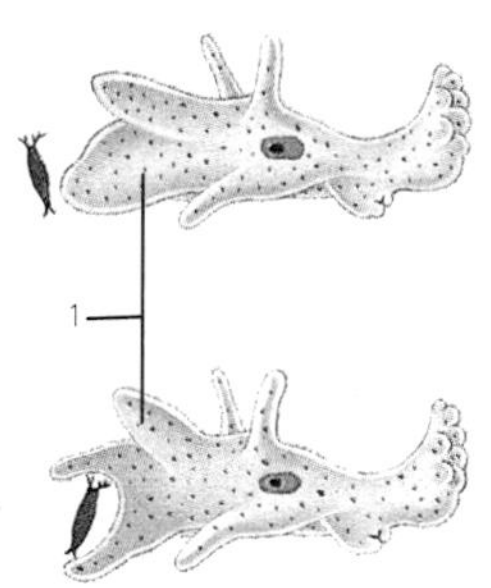


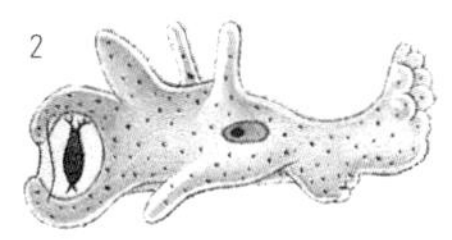


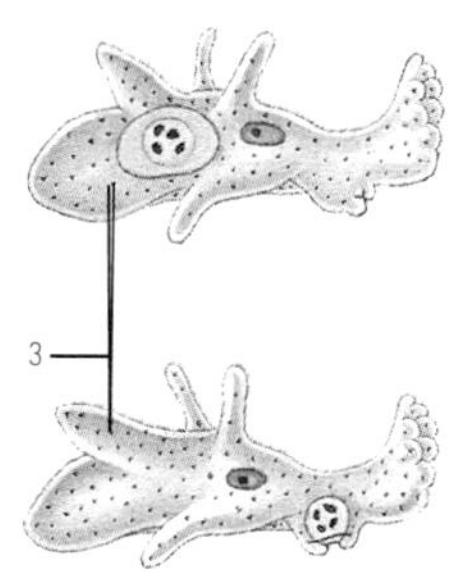


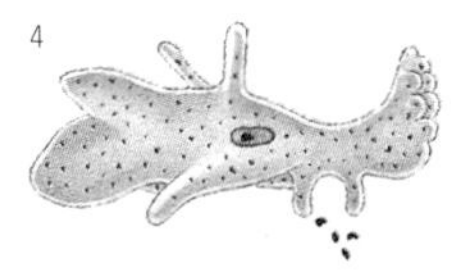

A

▲ **Amritsar** The Golden Temple of Amritsar in the NW Indian state of Punjab is a holy Sikh shrine. In 1984, armed Sikh extremists demanding greater autonomy in the Punjab, took refuge in the Temple and fierce gun battles with security forces followed. Some 400 people were killed, and the assault on the Sikh extremists led to the assassination of the prime minister, Indira Gandhi.

frequently herbivorous. There are three living orders: Urodela (NEWTS and SALAMANDERS); Anura (FROGS and TOADS); and Apoda (CAECILIANS).

**amphibole** Any of a large group of complex rock-forming minerals characterized by a double-chain silicate structure ($Si_4O_{11}$). They all contain water as $OH^-$ ions and usually calcium, magnesium, and iron. Found in IGNEOUS and METAMORPHIC rocks, they form wedge-shaped fragments on cleavage. Crystals are orthorhombic or monoclinic.

**amphitheater** In ancient Rome and the Roman empire, a large circular or oval building with the performance space surrounded by tiered seating. It was used as a theater for gladiatorial contests, wild-animal shows, and similar events. Many ruined amphitheaters remain; the best-known is the COLOSSEUM in Rome. The term is now used generically to refer to any open, banked arena.

**amplifier** Device for changing the magnitude (size) of a signal, such as voltage or current, but not the way it varies. Amplifiers are used in radio and television transmitters and receivers, and in audio equipment. *See also* THERMIONICS

**amplitude** *See* WAVE AMPLITUDE

**amplitude modulation (AM)** Form of RADIO transmission. Broadcasts on the short-, medium-, and long-wave bands are transmitted by amplitude modulation. The sound signals to be transmitted are superimposed on a constant-amplitude radio signal called the carrier. The resulting modulated radio signal varies in amplitude according to the strength of the sound signal. *See also* FREQUENCY MODULATION (FM)

**Amritsar** City in Punjab state, NW India, founded in 1577. Religious center of SIKHISM, and site of its holiest shrine, the Golden Temple. It was the scene of the Amritsar Massacre in 1919, when hundreds of Indian nationalists were killed by British troops. The city is noted for handicrafts. Industries: textiles, silk weaving, food processing. Pop. (1991) 709,000.

**Amsterdam** Capital and largest city in the Netherlands, on the River Amstel and linked to the North Sea by the North Sea Canal. The city was chartered in *c.*1300 and joined the Hanseatic League in 1369. The Dutch East India Company (1602) brought great prosperity to the city. It became a notable center of learning and book printing in the 17th century. Its commerce and importance declined when captured by the French in 1795 and blockaded by the British during the Napoleonic Wars. A major European port and one of its leading financial and cultural centers, it has an important stock exchange and diamond-cutting industry. Industries: iron and steel, oil refining, rolling stock, chemicals, glass, shipbuilding. Pop. (1994) 724,096.

**Amundsen, Roald** (1872–1928) Norwegian explorer and the first man to reach the SOUTH POLE. In 1903–06 Amundsen became the first man to sail through the NORTHWEST PASSAGE and determined the exact position of the magnetic NORTH POLE. He was beaten by Robert PEARY in the race to the North Pole and turned to ANTARCTICA. Amundsen reached the South Pole on 14 December 1911 (35 days before SCOTT). In 1926 Amundsen and Umberto Nobile made the first flight across the North Pole.

**amylase** Digestive enzyme secreted by the SALIVARY GLANDS (salivary amylase) and the PANCREAS (pancreatic amylase). It aids digestion by breaking down starch into MALTOSE (a disaccharide) and then GLUCOSE (a monosaccharide).

**amyotrophic lateral sclerosis (ALS)** (Lou Gehrig's disease) Disease of middle life primarily affecting men, with no known cause, brought to public attention by its affliction of baseball player Lou Gehrig (1903–41). It is a neurological disease that affects the lower brainstem and the spinal cord. Symptoms are gradual weakness and atrophy of the muscles of the hands, then arms and legs, with some spasticity. There is no known cure, and death ultimately results.

**Anabaptists** Radical Protestant sects in the REFORMATION who shared the belief that infant baptism is not authorized by Scripture, and that it was necessary to be baptized as an adult. The first such baptisms were conducted by the Swiss Brethren sect in Zurich (1525). The sect was the first to completely separate church from state, when they rejected Ulrich ZWINGLI's Reformed Church. Aided by social upheavals (such as the PEASANTS WAR) and the theological arguments of Martin LUTHER and Thomas Münzer, Anabaptism spread rapidly to Germany and the Netherlands. It stressed the community of believers. The communal theocracy established by John of Leiden at Münster was brutally suppressed (1535).

**anabolic steroid** Any of a group of hormones that stimulate the growth of tissue. Synthetic versions are used in medicine to treat OSTEOPOROSIS and some types of ANEMIA; they may also be prescribed to aid weight gain in severely ill or elderly patients. These drugs are associated with a number of side-effects, including acne, fluid retention, liver damage, and masculinization in women. Some athletes have been known to abuse anabolic steroids in order to increase muscle bulk.

**anabolism** *See* METABOLISM

**anaconda** Large constricting SNAKE of South America, the heaviest snake in the world. It feeds mainly on birds and small mammals. Females give birth to up to 75 live young. Species *Eunectes murinus*. Length: up to 30ft (9m).

**anaerobic** Connected with the absence of oxygen or air, or not dependent on oxygen or air for survival. An anaerobic organism, or anaerobe, is a microorganism that can survive by releasing energy from GLUCOSE and other foods in the absence of oxygen. The process by which it does so is called anaerobic respiration. Most anaerobes can survive in oxygen but do not need it for RESPIRATION. *See also* AEROBIC

**Anaheim** City in Orange County, part of the greater LOS ANGELES conurbation, S California, US. Anaheim was founded (1857) by German immigrants, and developed rapidly as a manufacturing center. It is home to the Disneyland amusement park (founded 1955), and the National Football League's Los Angeles Rams. Industries: electronics, aerospace, tourism. Pop. (1992) 274,162.

**analgesic** DRUG that relieves or prevents pain without causing loss of consciousness. It does not cure the cause of the pain, but helps to deaden the sensation. Some analgesics are also NARCOTICS, and many have anti-inflammatory properties. Common analgesics include aspirin, codeine, and morphine. *See also* ANESTHESIA

**analog computer** Machine that processes continuously variable information. Information is usually first converted into proportional electrical quantities. These are manipulated by amplifiers and other circuits that perform various mathematical operations. In other words, the computer works out problems by dealing with quantities (voltages) that are analogous (similar) to the quantities in the problem. Analogue computers are time-consuming to set up and operate. Most work once done on analogue computers is now carried out on digital computers, which are simpler and quicker to use.

**analog signal** In telecommunications and electronics, transmission of information by means of variation in a continuous waveform. An analog signal varies (usually in AMPLITUDE or FREQUENCY) in direct proportion to the information content of the signal.

**anarchism** (Gk. "no government") Political theory that regards the abolition of the state as a prerequisite for equality and social justice. In place of government, anarchy is a social form based upon voluntary cooperation between individuals. The STOICS leader, ZENO OF CITIUM, is regarded as the father of anarchism. Millenarian movements of the Reformation, such as the Anabaptists, espoused a form of anarchism. As a modern political philosophy, anarchism dates from the mid-19th century, and writers such as P.J. PROUDHON. Often in conflict with emerging communism, MIKHAIL BAKUNIN's brand of violent, revolutionary anarchism led to his expulsion from the First International (1872). Anarchism has been a popular political force only in conjunction with SYNDICALISM. Its support of civil disobedience and sometimes political biolence has led to its marginalization. following the assassination (1901) of President MCKINLEY, the US has barred anarchists from its shores. The Sacco and Vanzetti Case (1920) led to further hysteria over the threat of anarchism.

**Anatolia** *See* ASIA MINOR

**anatomy** Branch of biological science that studies the structure of an organism. The study of anatomy can be divided in several ways. On the basis of size, there is **gross** anatomy, which is studying structures with the naked eye; **microscopic** anatomy, studying finer detail with a light microscope; **submicroscopic** anatomy, studying even finer structural detail with an electron microscope; and **molecular** anatomy, studying with sophisticated instruments the molecular make-up of an organism. Microscopic and submicroscopic anatomy involve two closely related sciences: HISTOLOGY and CYTOLOGY. Anatomy can also be classified according to the type of organism studied: plant, invertebrate, vertebrate, or human anatomy. *See also* PHYSIOLOGY

**Anaximander** (611–547 BC) Greek philosopher, student of THALES. Anaximander's lasting reputation is based on his notion of *apeiron* (Gr. infinite), a non-perceivable substance which he regarded as the primary source material of the natural world. His ideas are considered the precursor of a modern conception of the indestructibility of matter. Anaximander also anticipated the theory of evolution and is said to have made the first map of the Earth, which he conceived of as a self-supporting immobile cylindrical object at the center of the universe.

**ancestor worship** Any of various religious beliefs and practices found in societies where kinship is strong. The spirits of dead ancestors or tribal members, believed capable of good or harm, are propitiated by prayers and sacrifices.

**Anchorage** City in S central Alaska. The state's largest city, Anchorage was founded as a railroad town in 1914 and became the supply center for the gold- and coal-mining regions to the N. Industries: tourism, oil and natural gas. Pop. (1992) 245,866.

**anchovy** Commercially valuable food fish found worldwide in large shoals in temperate and tropical seas. There are more than 100 species. Length: 4–10in (10–25cm). Family Engraulidae.

**ancien régime** Term used to describe the political, legal, and social system in France before the FRENCH REVOLUTION of 1789. It was characterized by a rigid social order, a fiscal system weighted in favor of the rich, and an absolutist monarchy.

**Andalusia** (Andalucía) Largest, most populous, and southernmost region of Spain, crossed by the Guadalquivir River, and comprising eight provinces. The capital is SEVILLE; other major cities include MÁLAGA, GRANADA, and CÓRDOBA. In the N are the Sierra Morena mountains, which are rich in minerals. In the S are the Sierra Nevada, rising to Mulhacén (Spain's highest point), at 11,411ft (3,378m). Farms in the low-lying SW raise horses and cattle (including fighting bulls) and grow most of the country's cereals; other important crops are citrus fruits, olives, sugar, and grapes. Sherry is made from grapes grown in the neighborhood of Jerez de la Frontera, near Cádiz. Area: 33,707sq mi (87,268sq km). Pop. (1991) 6,940,522.

**Andaman and Nicobar Islands** Territory of India comprising two chains of islands in the Bay of Bengal. The capital is Port Blair (on South Andaman). The main exports are timber, coffee, coconuts, and copra. The population of the islands (one of India's seven union territories) almost doubled in the decade to 1991. Total area: 3,200sq mi (8,300sq km). Pop. (1991) 280,661.

◀ **anchovy** A member of the herring family, the tiny anchovy is fished mainly in the Mediterranean. Once caught the anchovy is used either as a concentrated sauce, or a salted and dried filet, or is canned in oil.

**Andean Indians** *See* NATIVE AMERICANS

**Andersen, Hans Christian** (1805–1875) Danish writer of some of the world's best-loved fairy tales. He gained a reputation as a poet and novelist before his talent found its true expression. His humorous, delicate but frequently also melancholy stories, were first published in 1835. They include *The Ugly Duckling*, *The Little Mermaid*, *The Little Match Girl*, and *The Emperor's New Clothes*.

**Anderson, Carl David** (1905–91) US physicist who shared the 1936 Nobel Prize for physics with Victor HESS. In 1932 Anderson discovered the first known particle of antimatter, the POSITRON or anti-electron. He later helped discover the muon, an elementary particle.

**Anderson, Elizabeth Garrett** (1836–1917) British physician and pioneer of women's rights. She had to overcome intense prejudice against women doctors to become one of the first English women to practice. Later she became England's first woman mayor.

**Anderson, Marian** (1902–93) US contralto. She secured her reputation as a singer by touring America and Europe in recitals (1925–35). She made her debut with the METROPOLITAN OPERA COMPANY in 1955 as Ulrica in Verdi's *Un Ballo in Maschera*; this was the first appearance of a black singer in a leading role at the Metropolitan Opera.

**Anderson, Sherwood** (1876–1941) US short-story writer and novelist. Anderson's best known work is *Winesburg, Ohio* (1919), a series of interrelated stories of life in a small Midwestern town. His novel, *Poor White* (1920), expanded on the theme of conflict between industrial technology and the individual. Other short-story collections include *The Triumph of the Egg* (1921) and *Death in the Woods* (1933). His flat, spare style was a formative influence on Ernest HEMINGWAY and William FAULKNER.

**Andersonville Prison** Historic prison in Andersonville, SW Georgia. It was used during the CIVIL WAR by the Confederacy to confine Union prisoners. Harsh conditions led to the deaths of nearly 14,000 Union soldiers. Area: 495 acres (200ha).

**Andes** Chain of mountains in South America, extending along the whole length of the W coast. The longest mountain range in the world, it stretches for 5,500mi (8,900km). At their widest it is *c.*500mi (800km) across. There are more than 50 peaks over 21,980ft (6,700m) high. It contains many active volcanoes, including COTOPAXI in Ecuador. Earthquakes are common, and cities such as LIMA, CALLAO, and VALPARAÍSO have been severely damaged. The highest peak is ACONCAGUA, rising 22,834ft (6,960m) in Argentina. Lake TITICACA (the highest lake in the world) lies in the Andes at 12,500ft (3,810m) above sea-level on the Peru-Bolivia border.

**Andhra Pradesh** State in SE India on the Bay of Bengal; the capital is HYDERABAD. It was created in 1953 from part of MADRAS, and in 1956 incorporated the princely state of Hyderabad. Though mountainous to the NE, most of the region is flat coastal plain. Products include rice and peanuts; coal, chrome, and manganese are mined. The principal language is Teluga. Area: 106,878sq mi (276,814sq km). Pop. (1991) 66,508,008.

**Andorra** Small independent state situated high in the E Pyrenees between France and Spain. Andorra consists mainly of six valleys that drain to the Valira River. These deep glaciated valleys lie at altitudes of 3,300–9,500ft (1,000–2,900m). In the N a lofty watershed forms the frontier with France, and to the S the land falls away to the Segre Valley in Spain. It is a rare surviving example of a medieval principality. In 1993, a new democratic constitution was adopted. The main sources of income include agriculture; the sale of water and hydroelectricity to Catalonia; tourism, particularly skiing; and the sale of duty-free goods. Area: 175sq mi (453sq km). Pop. (1993) 61,599.

**Andrea del Sarto** (1486–1531) (Andrea d'Agnolo di Francesco) Florentine artist. A contemporary of MICHELANGELO and RAPHAEL, he was one of the outstanding painters and

▲ **anemone** The white wood anemone *A. nemorosa* is found in Europe and Asia growing in wooded areas. Like all anemones, what appear to be petals are actually sepals.

draftsmen of the High RENAISSANCE. He was an excellent portraitist, a master of composition, and he produced many frescos and altarpieces. His frescos include the cycles in the cloister of SS. Annunziata (1514–24) and the terra verde grisailles in the Chiostro dello Scalzo (1511–26), Florence.

**Andrew, Saint** In the New Testament, brother of Simon Peter and one of the original 12 disciples of Jesus. According to tradition he was crucified on an x-shaped cross. He is patron saint of Scotland and Russia; his feast day is November 30.

**Androcles** In Roman legend, a slave who ran away from his master. Androcles removed a thorn from the paw of a suffering lion. When he later faced the same lion in the Roman Arena, the lion refused to harm him.

**androgen** General name for male sex HORMONES, such as TESTOSTERONE.

**Andromeda** In Greek mythology, daughter of Cepheus and Cassiopea, king and queen of Ethiopia. When her country was under threat from a sea dragon, Andromeda was chained to a rock by the sea as a sacrifice. She was saved by PERSEUS.

**Andromeda** Large constellation of the Northern Hemisphere, adjoining the Square of Pegasus. The main stars lie in a line leading away from Pegasus. The most famous object in the constellation is the ANDROMEDA GALAXY

**Andromeda Galaxy** Spiral GALAXY in the constellation ANDROMEDA, 2.2 million light-years away, the most distant object visible to the naked eye. The Andromeda Galaxy has a mass of more than 300,000 million Suns. Its diameter is *c.*150,000 light-years, somewhat larger than our own Galaxy.

**Andropov, Yuri Vladimirovich** (1914–84) Soviet statesman, president of the Soviet Union (1983–84), general secretary of the Communist Party (1982–84). Andropov first gained attention for his role in the suppression of the Hungarian uprising (1956). As head of the KGB (1967–82), Andropov took a hard line against political dissidence, supporting Soviet intervention in Czechoslovakia (1968) and Poland (1981). He joined the Politburo in 1973. Andropov succeeded Leonid BREZHNEV as leader. His term in office was the shortest in Soviet history. Perhaps his most significant decision was the promotion of Mikhail GORBACHEV. He was succeeded by Konstantin Chernenko.

**anechoic chamber** (dead room) Room designed to be echo-free so that it can be used in ACOUSTIC laboratories to measure sound reflection and transmission, and to test audio equipment. The walls, floor, and ceiling must be insulated and all surfaces covered with an absorbent material such as rubber, often over inward-pointing pyramid shapes to reduce reflection. The room is usually asymmetrical to reduce stationary waves.

**anemia** Condition in which there is a shortage of HEMOGLOBIN, the oxygen-carrying pigment contained in ERYTHROCYTES (red blood cells). Symptoms include weakness, pallor, breathlessness, faintness, palpitations, and lowered resistance to infection. It may be due to a decrease in the production of hemoglobin or red blood cells or excessive destruction of red blood cells or blood loss. Worldwide, iron deficiency is the most common cause of anemia.

**anemometer** Instrument using pressure tubes or rotating cups, vanes, or propellers to measure the speed or force of the wind.

**anemone** (windflower) Perennial plant found worldwide. Anemones have sepals resembling petals, and numerous stamens and pistils covering a central knob; two or three deeply toothed leaves appear in a whorl midway up the stem. Many are wild flowers, such as the wood anemone

► **Angel Falls** Measuring 3,212ft (980m), the Angel Falls of Venezuela, S America, is the highest uninterrupted waterfall in the world.

▲ **Angelou, Maya** Best known for her writing, Angelou was originally a dancer and a singer. She was also a prominent figure in the Civil Rights movement.

(*Anemone nemorosa*). There are 120 species. Family Ranunculaceae. *See also* BUTTERCUP; SEA ANEMONE

**anesthesia** State of insensibility or loss of sensation produced by disease or by various anesthetic drugs used during surgical procedures. During general, or total, anesthesia the entire body becomes insensible and the individual sleeps; in local anesthesia only a specific part of the body is rendered insensible and the patient remains conscious. A **general** anesthetic may be either an injected drug, such as the barbiturate thiopentone, used to induce unconsciousness, or an inhalation agent such as halothane, which is used to maintain anesthesia for surgery. **Local** anesthetics, such as lignocaine, numb the relevant part of the body by blocking the transmission of impulses through the sensory nerves which supply it.

**angel** (Gk. messenger) Spiritual being superior to man but inferior to God. In the Bible, angels appear on Earth as messengers and servants of God. Angels also form an integral part of Judaism and Islam.

**Angel Falls** World's highest uninterrupted waterfall, in La Gran Sabrana, E Venezuela. Part of the Caroni River, it was discovered in 1935 and named after Jimmy Angel, a US aviator who died in a crash near the Falls. Total drop: 3,212ft (980m).

**angelfish** Tropical fish found in the Atlantic and Indo-Pacific oceans, popular as an aquarium fish because of its graceful, trailing fins and beautiful markings. Length: 0.75–4in (2–10cm). Family Cichlidae.

**Angelico, Fra** (1400–55) (Guido di Pietro) Florentine painter and Dominican friar. Angelico and his assistants painted a cycle of some 50 devotional frescos in the friary of San Marco, Florence (*c.*1438–45). These pictures show great technical skill and are the key to Angelico's reputation as an artist of extraordinary sweetness and serenity. International Gothic influenced his early work but he found great inspiration in representations of architectural perspective by MASACCIO. His style showed a marked change toward narrative detail in frescos carried out for Pope Nicholas V's Vatican chapel (1447–50).

**Angelou, Maya** (1928– ) US writer and editor. She is best known for five volumes of autobiography, starting with *I Know Why the Caged Bird Sings* (1970), which evokes her childhood in 1930s Arkansas. The fourth volume, *The Heart of a Woman*, deals with her involvement in the 1960s CIVIL RIGHTS movement as the Northern Coordinator for Martin Luther KING. She read her poem "On the Pulse of Morning" at the inauguration of President CLINTON in 1993.

**Angevins** English royal dynasty named after King HENRY II, son of the Count of Anjou (and grandson of Henry I), who ascended the throne in 1154. The Angevins, who later became the PLANTAGENET royal line, retained the crown until 1485.

**angina** Pain in the chest due to insufficient blood supply to the heart, usually associated with diseased coronary arteries. Generally induced by exertion or stress, it is treated with drugs, such as glyceryl trinitrate, or surgery.

**angiosperm** Plants with true flowers, as distinct from GYMNOSPERM and other nonflowering plants. They include most trees, bushes, and nonwoody herbs. There are two main groups: MONOCOTYLEDONS, such as grasses and daffodils (which have one seed leaf); and DICOTYLEDONS, such as peas and oak (which have two seed leaves).

**Angkor** Ancient KHMER capital and temple complex, NW Cambodia. The site contains the ruins of several stone temples erected by Khmer rulers, many of which lie within the walled enclosure of Angkor Thom, the capital built 1181–95 by Jayavarman VII (*c.* 1120–1215). **Angkor Wat**, the greatest structure in terms of its size and the quality of its carving, lies outside the main complex. Thai invaders destroyed the Angkor complex in 1431, and it remained neglected until French travelers rediscovered it in 1858. After restoration, Angkor Wat suffered again when the followers of POL POT ravaged Cambodia in the civil war (1970–75).

**angle** Measure of the inclination of two straight lines or planes to each other. One revolution is divided into 360 degrees or $2\pi$ radians. One degree may be subdivided into 60 minutes, and one minute into 60 seconds.

**Angles** Germanic tribe from a district of Schleswig-Holstein now called Angeln. In the 5th century they invaded England with neighboring tribes, JUTES, SAXONS, and others. They settled mainly in Northumbria and East Anglia. The name England (Angle-land) derives from them.

**Anglican Communion** Fellowship of 37 independent national or provincial worldwide churches, many of which are in Commonwealth nations. It originated from missionary work by the CHURCH OF ENGLAND. An exception is the EPISCOPAL CHURCH in the US, founded by the Scottish Episcopal Church. There is no single governing authority, but all recognize the leadership of the Archbishop of CANTERBURY. Worship is liturgical, based on the Book of COMMON PRAYER. In 1997 there were *c.*70 million Anglicans organized into about 30,000 parishes.

**angling** *See* FISHING

**Anglo-Irish Agreement** (Hillsborough Agreement) Treaty on the status of Northern IRELAND, signed (1985) by Margaret THATCHER and Garret FITZGERALD. Aiming to clarify the status of Northern Ireland, it gave the Republic of Ireland the right of consultation; it asserted that any future changes would have to be ratified by a majority of the people of Northern Ireland; and it set up the Anglo-Irish Intergovernmental Conference (AIIC) to promote cooperation. The agreement was denounced by the Northern Irish Unionists.

**Anglo-Saxon art and architecture** Style of art and architecture in Britain following the ANGLO-SAXON invasions from

## ANGOLA

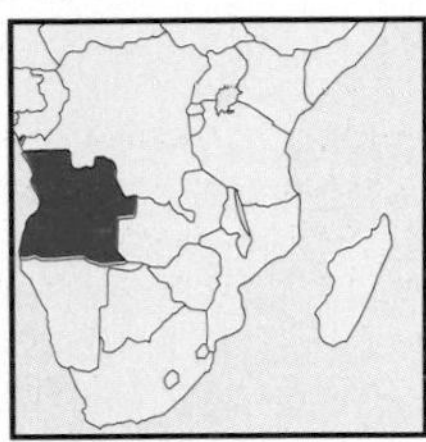

The flag is based on the flag of the MPLA (the Popular Movement for the Liberation of Angola) during the independence struggle. The emblem includes a star symbolizing Socialism, one half of a gearwheel to represent industry, and a machete to illustrate agriculture.

**AREA:** 481,351sq mi (1,246,700sq km)
**POPULATION:** 10,609,000
**CAPITAL (POPULATION):** Luanda (1,544,000)
**GOVERNMENT:** Multiparty republic
**ETHNIC GROUPS:** Ovimbundu 37%, Mbundu 22%, Kongo 13%, Luimbe-Nganguela 5%, Nyaneka-Humbe 5%, Chokwe, Luvale, Luchazi
**LANGUAGES:** Portuguese (official)
**RELIGIONS:** Christianity (Roman Catholic 69%, Protestant 20%), traditional beliefs 10%
**CURRENCY:** Kwanza = 100 lwe

The Republic of Angola is a large country, more than twice the size of France, on the SW coast of Africa. Most of the country is part of the huge plateau which makes up the interior of S Africa, with a narrow coastal plain in the W.

Angola has many rivers. In the NE, several flow N to the Zaire (CONGO) River. In the S some rivers, including the Cubango (also known as the Okavango) and the Cuanda, flow SE into the interior of Africa.

### CLIMATE

Angola has a tropical climate with temperatures of over 68°F (20°C) throughout the year, though the highest areas are cooler. The coastal regions are dry, increasingly so S of LUANDA, but the rainfall increases to the N and E. The rainy season is between November and April.

### VEGETATION

Grasslands cover much of Angola. The coastal plain has little vegetation and the S coast is a desert merging into the NAMIB DESERT. Some rainforest grows in N Angola towards Zaire.

### HISTORY

Bantu-speaking people from the N settled in Angola around 2,000 years ago. In the later part of the 15th century Portuguese navigators, seeking a route to Asia round Africa, explored the coast and, in the early 1600s, the Portuguese set up supply bases.

Angola became important as a source of slaves for Brazil, Portugal's huge colony in South America. After the decline of the slave trade, Portuguese settlers began to develop the land, and the Portuguese population increased greatly in the 20th century.

In the 1950s, local nationalists began to demand independence and, in 1956, the MPLA (Popular Movement for the Liberation of Angola) was founded, drawing support from the Mbundu tribe and mestizos (people of African and European descent). The MPLA led a revolt in Luanda in 1961, but it was put down by Portuguese troops. Other opposition movements developed among different ethnic groups. In the N, the Kongo set up the FNLA (Front for the Liberation of Angola), and in 1966 southern peoples, including many of the Ovimbundu, formed the National Union for the Total Independence of Angola (UNITA).

### POLITICS

Portugal granted independence in 1975, but a power struggle developed among rival nationalists. The MPLA formed the government but UNITA troops, opposed to the MPLA's austere Marxist policies, and supported by South Africa, began a civil war. After 16 crippling years a peace treaty was signed in 1991 and multiparty elections were held in 1992. After a victory for the MPLA, which had renounced socialism, civil strife resumed when UNITA refused to abide by the result. A new peace accord was signed in 1994, but the political climate remained unstable. In April 1997 the new government was inaugurated. DOS SANTOS remained president, but UNITA leader, Jonas SAVIMBI, rejected the vice presidency. UNITA retained military control of *c.*50% of Angola. In September 1997 the UN imposed sanctions on UNITA for failing to comply with the 1994 Lusaka Protocol.

### ECONOMY

Angola is a poor, developing country (1995 GDP per capita US$1,310) where *c.*70% of the people subsist by farming. The main food crops are cassava and corn; coffee is exported. Angola has huge economic potential. It has oil reserves near Luanda and in the Cabinda exclave (separated from Angola by a strip of land belonging to the Democratic Republic of Congo) and oil is the leading export. The country is a major diamond producer and has reserves of copper, manganese, and phosphates. It also has a manufacturing sector, much of it based on hydroelectric power.

the 5th to the 11th centuries. The most famous archeological find is the pagan shipburial at SUTTON HOO. Anglo-Saxon art is predominantly Christian, consisting of stone crosses, ivory carvings, and illuminated manuscripts (the most important being the LINDISFARNE GOSPELS). Anglo-Saxon churches are characterized by square apses, aisles or side chambers (*porticus*), pilaster strips, and distinctive timber work.

**Anglo-Saxon Chronicle** Monastic chronicles written in England between the 9th century and 1155. The four surviving versions of the Chronicle are the chief documentary source for ANGLO-SAXON English history.

**Anglo-Saxons** People of Germanic origin comprising ANGLES, SAXONS, and other tribes who began to invade England from the mid-5th century, when Roman power was in decline. By 600 they were well established in most of England. They were converted to Christianity in the 7th century. Early tribal groups were led by warrior lords whose thegns (noblemen) provided military service in exchange for rewards and protection. The tribal groups eventually developed into larger kingdoms, such as Northumbria and WESSEX. The term Anglo-Saxon was first used in the late 8th century to distinguish the Saxon settlers in England from the "Old Saxons" of N Germany, and became synonymous with "English." The Anglo-Saxon period of English history ended with the NORMAN CONQUEST (1066).

**Angola** Republic in SW Africa. *See* country feature page 27

**Angora** *See* ANKARA

**Angry Young Men** Loose literary and dramatic term, applied to an anti-establishment group of British writers in the 1950s. Taken from Leslie Allen Paul's autobiography *Angry Young Man* (1951), it was popularized through John OSBORNE's play *Look Back in Anger* (1956). The group included Kingsley AMIS, Arnold WESKER, and Alan SILLITOE.

**angstrom** (angstrom unit) Obsolete unit of length, equal to $10^{-10}$ m or 0.1nm (nanometer). It is used to express the wavelength of light and ultraviolet radiation, interatomic and intermolecular distances. Symbol: Å.

**Anguilla** Island in the West Indies, most northerly of the Leeward Islands. Settled in the 17th century by English colonists, it eventually became part of the St. Kitts-Nevis-Anguilla group. Declared independent in 1967, it re-adopted British colonial status in 1980, and is now a self-governing dependency. The economy of the flat, coral island is based on fishing and tourism. Area: 35sq mi (91sq km). Pop. (1992) 8,960.

**anhydride** Chemical compound derived from another compound by removing water. Thus, sulphur trioxide ($SO_3$) is the anhydride of sulphuric acid ($H_2 SO_4$)

**aniline** (phenylamine, $C_6H_5NH_2$) Highly poisonous, colorless oily liquid made by the reduction of nitrobenzene. It is an important starting material for making organic compounds such as drugs, explosives, and dyes. Properties: sp.gr. 1.02; m.p. 20.8°F (−6.2°C); b.p. 363.4°F (184.1°C). *See also* AMINE

**animal** Living organism of the animal kingdom, usually distinguishable from members of the PLANT kingdom by its power of locomotion (at least during some stage of its existence); a well-defined body shape; limited growth; its feeding exclusively on organic matter; the production of two different kinds of sex cells; and the formation of an embryo or larva during the developmental stage. Higher animals, such as the VERTEBRATES, are easily distinguishable from plants, but the distinction becomes blurred with the lower forms. Some one-celled organisms could easily be assigned to either category. Scientists have classified about a million different kinds of animals in more than twenty phyla. The simplest (least highly evolved) animals include the PROTOZOA, SPONGES, JELLYFISH, and WORMS. Other invertebrate phyla include ARTHROPODS (arachnids, crustaceans, and insects), MOLLUSKS (shellfish, octopus and, squid) and ECHINODERMS (sea urchins and starfish). Vertebrates belong to the CHORDATA phylum, which includes fish, amphibians, reptiles, birds, and mammals.

**animal classification** Systematic grouping of animals into categories based on shared characteristics. The first major classification was drawn up by Aristotle. The method in current use was devised by Carl LINNAEUS. *See* TAXONOMY

**animal rights** Freedom from subjection to pain and distress, especially applied to those animals used in scientific experimentation for human purposes. Experiments using animals decreased considerably during the 1980s, but continue particularly in determining the effects of new medicinal preparations, and of the long-term use of consumer products such as alcoholic drinks, cigarettes, and cosmetics. Animal rights campaigners wish to extend animal rights to include all farm animals kept, transported, or slaughtered in conditions perceived to be inhumane. *See also* VIVISECTION

**animation** Illusion of motion created by projecting successive images of still drawings or objects. Drawn cartoons are the most common form. Each of a series of drawings is photographed singly. The illusion of motion is created when the photographs are displayed in rapid succession. Computer animation programs have advanced to a point where the drawings themselves are no longer a necessity.

**animism** Belief that within every animal, plant, or inanimate object dwells an individual spirit capable of governing its existence and influencing human affairs. Natural objects and phenomena are regarded as possessing life, consciousness, and a spirit. In animism the spirits of dead animals live on, and (if the animals have been killed improperly) can inflict harm. These beliefs are widespread among tribal peoples.

**anion** Negative ION attracted to the ANODE during electrolysis.

**Anjou** Region and former province in W France straddling the lower Loire valley. It was ruled by HENRY II of England after his marriage to Eleanor of Aquitaine, and Louis XI annexed it to the French crown in 1480. Known for its wine, it ceased to be a province in 1790.

**Ankara** Capital of Turkey, at the confluence of the Cubuk and Ankara rivers. In ancient times it was known as Ancyra, and was an important commercial center as early as the 8th century BC. It was a Roman provincial capital and flourished particularly under AUGUSTUS. TAMERLANE took the city in 1402. In the late 19th century it declined in importance until Kemal ATATÜRK set up a provisional government here in 1920. It replaced Istanbul as the capital in 1923. It is noted for its angora wool and mohair products. Pop. (1990) 2,541,899.

**Annam** Former kingdom on the E coast of INDOCHINA, now in Vietnam; the capital was Hué. The ancient empire fell to China in 214 BC. It regained self-government but was again ruled by China from 939–1428. The French obtained missionary and trade agreements in 1787, and a protectorate was established (1883–84). During World War II it was occupied by the Japanese; in 1949 it was incorporated into the Republic of VIETNAM.

**Annan, Kofi** (1938– ) Ghanaian diplomat, seventh secretary-general of the UN (1997– ). Annan became the first black African secretary-general. In 1993 Annan was elected under secretary-general for peacekeeping, handling the removal of UN troops from Bosnia. His diplomacy helped secure a peaceful resolution (1998) to the weapons inspection crisis in Iraq.

**Annapolis** Seaport capital of Maryland, on the S bank of the Severn River on Chesapeake Bay. It was founded in 1649 by Puritans from Virginia, and in 1694 was laid out as the state capital. The site of the signing of the peace treaty ending the American Revolution, it has many buildings dating from colonial times. It is also the seat of the US Naval Academy (founded 1845). Industries: boatyards, seafood packing. Pop. (1992) 34,070.

**Annapurna** Mountain massif in the HIMALAYAS, in N central Nepal, notoriously dangerous to climbers. It has two of the world's highest peaks: Annapurna I in the W rises to 26,504ft (8,078m); Annapurna II in the E rises to 26,041ft (7,937m).

**Anne** (1665–1714) Queen of Great Britain and Ireland (1702–14), second daughter of JAMES II. Anne succeeded WILLIAM III as the last STUART sovereign and, after the Act of UNION (1707), the first monarch of the United Kingdom of England and Scotland. Brought up a Protestant, she married Prince George of Denmark (1683). Despite 18 pregnancies, no child survived her. The War of the SPANISH SUCCESSION (1701–14) dominated her reign, and is often called Queen Anne's War. Anne was the last English monarch to exercise the royal veto over legislation (1707), but the rise of parliamentary government was inexorable. The JACOBITE cause was crushed when

Anne was succeeded by GEORGE I. The most lasting aspect of her reign was the strength of contemporary arts and culture.

**annealing** Slow heating and cooling of a metal, alloy, or glass to relieve internal stresses and make up dislocations or vacancies introduced during mechanical shaping, such as rolling or extruding (ejection). Annealing increases the material's workability and durability. *See also* TEMPERING

**Anne Boleyn** *See* BOLEYN, ANNE

**annelid** Animal phylum of segmented WORMS. All have encircling grooves usually corresponding to internal partitions of the body. A digestive tube, nerves, and blood vessels run through the entire body, but each segment has its own set of internal organs. Annelids form an important part of the diets of many animals. The three main classes are: Polychaeta, marine worms; Oligochaeta, freshwater or terrestrial worms; and Hirudinea, LEECHES.

**Anne of Austria** (1601–66) Daughter of Philip III of Spain, wife of LOUIS XIII of France and mother of LOUIS XIV. Her husband died in 1643, and she ruled France as regent in close alliance with Cardinal MAZARIN until her death.

**Anne of Cleves** (1515–57) Fourth wife of HENRY VIII of England. Her marriage (1540) was a political alliance joining Henry with the German Protestants, and was never consummated, being declared null after only six months. Anne received a pension, and remained in England until her death.

**annual** Plant that completes its life cycle in one growing season, such as the sweet pea, sunflower, or wheat. Annual plants overwinter as seeds. *See also* BIENNIAL; PERENNIAL

**annual ring** (growth ring) Concentric circles visible in cross-sections of woody stems or trunks. Each year the CAMBIUM layer produces a layer of XYLEM, the vessels of which are large and thin-walled in the spring and smaller and thick-walled in the summer, creating the contrast between the rings. Used to determine the age of trees, the thickness of these rings also reveals environmental conditions during a tree's lifetime.

**Annunciation** Announcement made to the Virgin Mary by the Angel GABRIEL that she was to be the mother of Christ (Luke 1). In many Christian churches the Feast of the Annunciation is kept on March 25, a date often called "Lady Day." The Annunciation was a common subject for painters during medieval and Renaissance times.

**anode** Positive electrode of an electrolytic cell that attracts ANIONS during electrolysis. *See also* ELECTROLYSIS

**anodizing** Electrolytic process to coat ALUMINUM or MAGNESIUM with a thin layer of oxide to help prevent corrosion. The process makes the metal the ANODE in an acid solution. The protective coating, steamed to seal the pores, is insoluble and a good insulator. It can be dyed bright colors.

**anorexia nervosa** Abnormal loss of the desire to eat. The condition is seen mainly in young women. It can result in severe emaciation and in rare cases can be life-threatening.

**Anouilh, Jean** (1910–87) French playwright and screenwriter. A major dramatist of the mid-20th century, Anouilh was influenced by neoclassicism and often reinterpreted Greek myth as a means of exploring oppression. *Antigone* (1944) is perhaps his most celebrated play. The underlying theme of many of his plays is the contrast between innocence and bitter experience. Other works include *Becket* (1959).

**anoxia** Deficiency of oxygen in the tissues. It can occur at high altitudes or as a result of underlying disease (such as lung or heart malfunction) or toxic agents. Symptoms include troubled breathing, rapid pulse and cyanosis (bluish discoloration of the skin).

**Anschluss** Unification of Austria and Germany in 1938. Prohibited by treaty at the end of World War I, to limit the strength of Germany, Anschluss was nevertheless favored by many Germans and Austrians. Unification took place through a show of force under HITLER. It was dissolved by the Allies in 1945.

**Anselm of Canterbury, Saint** (1033–1109) English theologian, b. Italy. Anselm was an early scholastic philosopher and became Archbishop of Canterbury in 1093. His belief in the rational character of Christian belief led him to propose an ontological argument for the existence of God. His feast day is April 21. *See also* ONTOLOGY

**ant** Social insect belonging to a family that also includes the BEE and WASP. A typical ant colony consists of one or more queens (fertile females), workers (sterile females), and winged males. Some species also have a caste of soldier ants which guard the colony. Ants range in length from 0.08–1.0in (2–25mm) and are found worldwide except Antarctica. They typically feed on plants, nectar, and other insects. Most ants are wingless except at times of dispersal. Family Formicidae.

**Antakya** (formerly Antioch, now also Hatay) City in s Turkey on the Orontes River and capital of Hatay province. Founded in *c.*300 BC by SELEUCUS I, it earned the title "queen of the east." It was taken by POMPEY (64 BC). The modern city occupies only a small part of the ancient Roman site. Products: olives, tobacco, cotton, cereals. Pop. (1990) 118,433.

**Antananarivo** (Tananarive) Capital and largest city of Madagascar. Founded *c.*1625, Antananarivo became the residence for

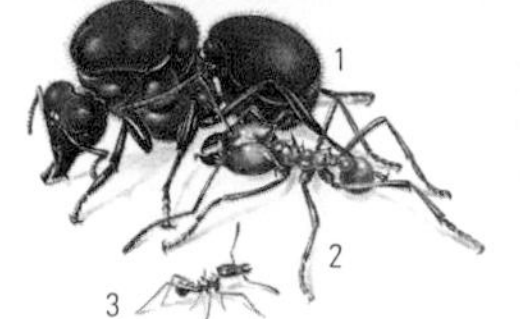

▲ **ant** Most ant societies are made up of different types of ant known as castes. Shown here are the queen (1), soldier (2) and small worker (3) of the leaf-cutter species *Atta caphalotes.*

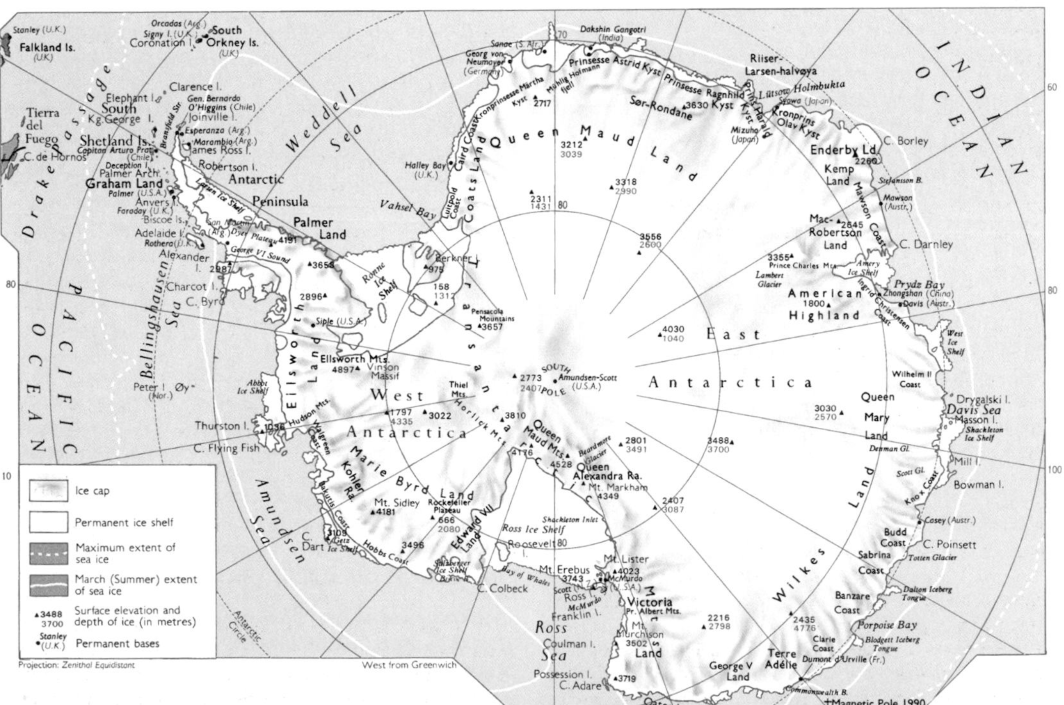

◀ **Antarctica** Containing more than 90% of the world's ice, Antarctica is cold throughout the year. In the early 20th century, exploration of the area turned into a race to reach the South Pole. It was won by Roald Amundsen.

Imerina rulers in 1794 and the capital of Madagascar. The city was captured by the French in 1895 and became part of a French protectorate. A trade center for a rice-producing region, it has textile, tobacco, and leather industries. Pop. (1990) 802,000.

**Antarctica** Fifth-largest continent (larger than Europe or Australasia), covering almost 10% of the world's total land area. Surrounding the SOUTH POLE, it is bordered by the Antarctic Ocean and the S sections of the Atlantic, Pacific, and Indian oceans. Almost entirely within the ANTARCTIC CIRCLE, it is of great strategic and scientific interest. No people live here permanently, although scientists frequently stay for short periods to conduct research and exploration. Seven nations lay claim to sectors of it. Covered by an ice sheet with an average thickness of *c*.5,900ft (1,800m), it contains *c*.90% of the world's ice and more than 70% of its fresh water. **Land** Resembling an open fan, with the Antarctic Peninsula as a handle, the continent is a snowy desert covering c.5.5 million sq mi (14.2 million sq km). The land is a high plateau, having an average elevation of 6,000ft (1,800m) and rising to 16,863ft (5,140m) in the Vinson Massif. Mountain ranges occur near the coasts. The interior, or South Polar Plateau, lies beneath *c*.6,500ft (2,000m) of snow, accumulated over tens of thousands of years. Mineral deposits exist in the mountains, but their recovery has not become practicable. Coal may be plentiful, but the value of known deposits of copper, nickel, gold, and iron will not repay the expenses of extracting and exporting them. **Seas and glaciers** Antarctic rivers are frozen, inching toward the sea, and instead of lakes there are large bodies of ice along the coasts. The great Beardmore Glacier creeps down from the South Polar Plateau, and eventually becomes part of the Ross Ice Shelf. The southernmost part of the Atlantic is the portion of the Antarctic Ocean known as the Weddell Sea. **Climate and vegetation** Antarctica remains cold all year, with only a few coastal areas being free from snow or ice in summer (December to February). On most of the continent the temperature remains below freezing, and in August it has been recorded at nearly −130°F (−90°C). Precipitation generally amounts to 7–15in (17.5–38cm) of snow a year, but melting is less than that, allowing a buildup over the centuries. Nevertheless, mosses manage to survive on rocks along the outer rim of the continent. Certain algae grow on the snow, and others appear in pools of fresh water when melting occurs. **History** Antarctic islands were sighted first in the 18th century, and in 1820 Nathaniel Palmer reached the Antarctic Peninsula. Between 1838 and 1840 the US explorer Charles Wilkes discovered enough of the coast to prove that a continent existed, and the English explorer James Clark Ross made coastal maps. Toward the end of the 19th century, exploration reached inland developing into a race for the South Pole. Roald AMUNDSEN reached the Pole on December 14, 1911, a month before Robert Falcon SCOTT. The airplane brought a new era of exploration, and Richard E. BYRD became the best known of the airborne polar explorers. The Antarctic Treaty (1959), which pledged international scientific cooperation, was renewed and extended in 1991, banning commercial exploitation of the continent.

**Antarctic Circle** Southernmost of the Earth's parallels, 66.5° S of the equator. At this latitude the sun neither sets on the day of summer SOLSTICE (December 22) nor rises on the day of winter solstice (June 21). *See also* ARCTIC CIRCLE

**Antares** (Alpha Scorpii) Supergiant, or very large and bright star. Its luminosity and distance are not well determined.

**anteater** Toothless, mainly nocturnal, insect-eating mammal that lives in swamps and savannahs of tropical America. It has a long, sticky tongue and powerful claws. Length: up to 60in (152cm). Family Myrmecophagidae. *See also* EDENTATE

▶ **anteater** The giant anteater (*Myrmecophaga tridactyla*) is found in South America, particularly in the swampy regions of the Chaco in Argentina. It uses its powerful claws to rip open termite mounds before scooping up the termites with its long sticky tongue.

**antelope** Hollow-horned, speedy RUMINANT found throughout the Old World except in Madagascar, Malaya, and Australasia; most antelopes are found in Africa. They range in size from that of a rabbit to that of an ox. In some species both sexes bear horns of varied shapes and sizes; in others, only the males are horned. Family Bovidae.

**antenna** In communications, a conductor component of radio and television systems for the broadcast and transmission of signals. An antenna's design usually depends on the wavelength of the signal.

**anthem** Choral composition in Anglican and other English-language church services analogous to the Roman Catholic MOTET in Latin. Developed in the 16th century as a verse anthem with soloists, the anthem was later performed with orchestral accompaniment and by a choir without soloists. Composers of anthems include Henry PURCELL and Ralph VAUGHAN WILLIAMS.

**anther** In botany, the fertile part of a male sex organ in a flower. The anther produces and distributes pollen, and together with its connecting filament forms a STAMEN.

**Anthony, Saint** (*c*.250–*c*.355) Egyptian saint and first Christian monk. He withdrew into complete solitude at the age of 20 to practice ascetic devotion. By the time of St. Anthony's death, Christian MONASTICISM was well established. His feast day is January 17.

**Anthony, Susan Brownell** (1820–1906) US reformer and woman suffragist. Anthony organized the first woman's TEMPERANCE association and, with Elizabeth Cady STANTON, cofounded the National Woman Suffrage Association (1869). It later became (1890) the National American Woman Suffrage Association, and she acted as president (1892–1900). *See also* SUFFRAGETTE MOVEMENT

**anthracite** Form of COAL consisting of more than 90% CARBON, relatively hard, black and with a metallic luster. It burns with the hot pale-blue flame of complete combustion. It is the final form in the series of fuels: PEAT, lignite, bituminous COAL, and black coal.

**anthrax** Contagious disease, chiefly of livestock, caused by the microbe *Bacillus anthracis*. Human beings can catch anthrax from contact with infected animals or their hides.

**anthropoidea** Suborder of primates including monkeys, apes, and human beings. Anthropoids have flatter, more humanlike faces, larger brains and are larger in size than prosimian PRIMATES.

**anthropology** Scientific study of human development and how different societies are interrelated. It is concerned with the chronological and geographical range of human societies. Modern anthropology stems from the first half of the 19th century. Public interest in cultural EVOLUTION followed the publication of *On the Origin of Species* by Charles DARWIN (1859). **Physical** anthropologists are concerned with the history of human evolution in its biological sense. **Social** anthropologists study living societies in order to learn about cultural and social evolution. **Applied** anthropology is the specific study of a particular community and its collective and individual relationships. *See also* ETHNOGRAPHY; ETHNOLOGY

**antibiotic** Substance that is capable of stopping the growth of (or destroying) BACTERIA and other microorganisms. Many antibiotics are themselves produced by microorganisms. Antibiotics are GERMICIDES that are safe enough to be eaten or injected into the body. The introduction of antibiotics post-1945 has revolutionized medical science, making possible the virtual elimination of once widespread and often fatal diseases, including TYPHOID FEVER, PLAGUE, and CHOLERA. Some antibiotics are selective, that is, effective against specific microorganisms; those effective against a large number of microorganisms are known as broad-spectrum antibiotics. Some important antibiotics are PENICILLIN, the first widely used antibiotic, streptomycin, and the tetracyclines. Some bacteria have developed ANTIBIOTIC RESISTANCE. *See also* ANTISEPTIC

**antibiotic resistance** Resistance to antibiotic drugs acquired by many bacteria and other PATHOGENS. Because they survive while nonresistant strains are killed, they pass their resistance to their progeny and resistance increases in the population. Some bacteria have the ability to pass the genes for antibiotic resistance to other organisms of different species on plasmids (small lengths of DNA). Spread of resistance is accelerated by routine prescription of antibiotics to humans and unregulated application to farm animals for the purpose of disease prevention rather than cure. An inadequate dose or failure to complete a course of antibiotics increases the chances of resistant microorganisms surviving to breed. This may lead to the return of epidemics of untreatable infectious disease.

**antibody** PROTEIN synthesized in the BLOOD in response to the entry of "foreign" substances or organisms into the body. Each episode of bacterial or viral infection prompts the production of a specific antibody to fight the disease in question. After the infection has cleared, the antibody remains in the blood to fight off any future invasion.

**Antichrist** Term loosely referring to the supreme enemy of Christ. It is used in the letters of St. JOHN to refer to a force that will appear at the end of time. Martin LUTHER and other leaders of the REFORMATION applied it to the PAPACY.

**anticline** Arch-shaped fold in rock strata. Unless the formation has been overturned, the oldest rocks are found in the center with younger rocks symmetrically on each side of it.

**anticoagulant** Substance that prevents or counteracts coagulation, or clotting. Anticoagulants are used to treat diseases caused by blood clots, such as THROMBOSIS. Heparin is a common blood anticoagulant.

**Anti-Corn Law League** Organization formed (1839) in Manchester, England, to agitate for the removal of import duties on grain. It was led by the Radical members of Parliament, Richard COBDEN and John BRIGHT. By holding mass meetings, distributing pamphlets, and contesting elections it helped bring about the repeal of the CORN LAWS in 1846.

**anticyclone** Area of high atmospheric pressure around which air circulates. The circulation is clockwise in the Northern Hemisphere and counterclockwise in the Southern Hemisphere. Anticyclones are often associated with settled weather conditions. In middle latitudes, they bring periods of hot, dry weather in summer and cold, often foggy, weather in winter.

**antidepressant** *See* DRUG

**Antietam, Battle of** (September 17, 1862) Fought around Sharpsburg, Maryland, during the CIVIL WAR. General George MCCLELLAN's Army of the Potomac made a series of assaults on the Confederates of General Robert E. LEE. Casualties were very heavy. McClellan's forces, *c.*12,000, were slightly greater, but Lee was forced to retreat to Virginia.

**Anti-Federalist Party** Organized in 1792 to oppose the proposed Constitution, mainly on the grounds that it gave the central government power. Anti-Federalist leaders included Richard Henry Lee and Patrick Henry of Virginia and George Clinton of New York. Their support came mostly from agricultural sections.

**antifreeze** Substance dissolved in a liquid to lower its freezing point. Ethylene glycol ($HOC_2H_4OH$) is commonly used in car radiators.

**antigen** Any substance or organism that induces the production of an ANTIBODY, part of the body's defense mechanism against disease. The antibody reacts specifically with the antigen.

**Antigonus I** (382–301 BC) General of ALEXANDER THE GREAT. Antigonus became governor of Phrygia in 333 BC and, in the struggles over the regency, he defeated challengers to gain control of Mesopotamia, Syria, and Asia Minor. At Salamis in 306 BC he defeated his former ally, Ptolemy I, but was himself killed at Ipsus.

**Antigua and Barbuda** Caribbean islands in the LEEWARD ISLANDS group, part of the Lesser ANTILLES. The capital is St. John's (on Antigua). **Antigua** is atypical of the Leeward Islands in that it has no rivers or forests; **Barbuda**, by contrast, is a well-wooded low coral atoll. Only 1,400 people live on the game reserve island of Barbuda, where lobster fishing is the main occupation, and none on the rocky island of Redondo. Antigua and Barbuda were linked by Britain after 1860, gained internal self-government in 1967 and independence in 1981. Both islands rely heavily on tourism, though some attempts at diversification (notably Sea Island cotton) have been successful. Other industries: livestock rearing, market gardening, fishing. Area: 170sq mi (440sq km). Pop. (1994) 65,000.

**antihistamine** Any one of certain drugs that counteracts or otherwise prevents the effects of histamine, a natural substance released by the body in response to injury, or more often as part of an allergic reaction. Histamine can produce symptoms such as sneezing, running nose, and burning eyes. *See also* HAY FEVER

**Antilles** Collective name for the two major island groups in the West Indies archipelago, between the Atlantic Ocean and the Caribbean Sea, stretching in an arc from Puerto Rico to the N coast of Venezuela. The Greater Antilles (the larger group) includes CUBA, HISPANIOLA, JAMAICA, PUERTO RICO, and the CAYMAN ISLANDS. The Lesser Antilles comprises the British VIRGIN ISLANDS, the US VIRGIN ISLANDS, the LEEWARD ISLANDS, and WINDWARD ISLANDS, plus small islands off South America.

**antimatter** Matter made up of antiparticles, identical to ordinary particles in every way except the charge, SPIN, and magnetic moment are reversed. When an antiparticle, such as a positron (anti-electron), antiproton, or antineutron meets its respective particle, both are annihilated. Since a PHOTON is its own antiparticle, the possibility exists that there are stars or galaxies composed entirely of antimatter. *See also* SUBATOMIC PARTICLES

**antimony** (symbol Sb) Toxic semimetallic element of Group V of the periodic table. Stibnite (a sulfide) is its commonest ore. It is used in some alloys, particularly in hardening lead for batteries and type metal, and in semiconductors. The element has two allotropes: a silvery white metallic and an amorphous gray form. Properties: at.no. 51; at.wt. 121.75; sp.gr. 6.68; m.p. 1,166.9°F (630.5°C); b.p. 3,182°F (1,750°C); most common isotope $^{121}$Sb (57.25%).

**Antioch** *See* ANTAKYA

**Antiochus III** (242–187 BC) King of Syria (223–187 BC), son of SELEUCUS II. After his defeat at Rafa (217 BC) by Ptolemy IV, he invaded Egypt (212–202 BC), seizing land from Ptolemy V with the help of Philip V of Macedon. He recaptured Palestine, Asia Minor, and the Thracian Cheronese. The Romans overwhelmed him at Thermopylae (191 BC) and at Magnesia (190 BC). The rebuilt Seleucid empire shrank when he gave up all possessions W of the Taurus. Seleucus IV succeeded him.

**antiphon** Alternate short verses or phrases (usually of a psalm or canticle) sung by two spatially separated halves of a choir (designated *decani* and *cantoris*). More generally, antiphon refers to a short piece of PLAINSONG, during the recitation of divine office. The text of the antiphon usually serves to reinforce a psalm's meaning or Christian significance.

**antipope** Name given to rivals of legitimately elected popes, generally "appointed" by unauthorized religious factions. The first was HIPPOLYTUS (AD 217–35), a Trinitarian heretic and rival of Calixtus I. The most famous were the AVIGNON popes, who rivaled those of ROME during the Great Schism (1378–1417).

**antiseptic** Chemicals that destroy or stop the growth of many microorganisms. Antiseptics are weak germicides that can be used on the skin. The English surgeon Joseph Lister pioneered the use of antiseptics in 1867. One commonly used is ALCOHOL. *See also* ANTIBIOTIC

**antitoxin** ANTIBODY produced by the body in response to a TOXIN. It is specific in action and neutralizes the toxin. Antitoxin sera are used to treat and prevent bacterial diseases such as TETANUS and DIPHTHERIA.

**antler** Bony outgrowth on the skulls of male DEER (and female reindeer). In temperate-zone species, antlers begin to grow in early summer. They are soft, well supplied with blood, and covered with thin, velvety skin. Later, the blood recedes and the dried skin is rubbed off. Antlers then serve as sexual ornaments and weapons until they are shed the following spring.

**ant lion** Larva of the neuropteran family Myrmeleontidea, found in most parts of the world. Carnivorous, with large, sickle-shaped jaws, it digs a pit in dry sand where it lies waiting for ants and other insects to fall in. *See also* LACEWING

**Antofagasta** Seaport and rail center on the coast of N Chile and the capital of Antofagasta province. Built in 1870 to provide port facilities for the nitrate and copper deposits in the ATACAMA DESERT, it has both ore refining and concentrating plants. The Chuquicamata open-cast copper mine, 135mi (220km) to the NE, is the world's largest. Pop. (1992) 226,749.

**Antonello da Messina** (1430–79) Sicilian artist. A pioneer of oil painting in Italy, Antonello spent much of his working life in Milan, Naples, Venice, and Rome. He probably learned the oil technique in Naples, a center for Dutch artists. His work married Netherlandic taste for detail with Italian clarity. Apart from religious paintings such as *Salvator Mundi* (1465) and *Ecce Homo* (1470), he produced some remarkable male portraits. His knowledge of oil glazes had a great influence on Venetian painters, notably Giovanni BELLINI.

**Antony, Mark** (82–30 BC) (Marcus Antonius) Roman general and statesman. Antony fought with distinction in Julius CAESAR's campaign (54–50 BC) in Gaul. In 49 BC he became tribune. Civil war broke out between POMPEY and Caesar, and after the decisive Battle of Pharsala, Antony was made consul. After Caesar's assassination (44 BC), he inspired the mob to drive the conspirators, BRUTUS and CASSIUS, from Rome. Octavian (later AUGUSTUS) emerged as Antony's main rival. Octavian and Brutus joined forces and Antony retreated to Transalpine Gaul. He sued for peace. Antony, Octavian and Lepidus formed the Second Triumverate, which divided up the ROMAN EMPIRE: Antony received Asia. He and CLEOPATRA, queen of Egypt, became lovers. In 40 BC Antony married Octavian's sister Octavia, but Antony continued to live with Cleopatra in Alexandria and became isolated from Rome. In 32 BC the senate deprived Antony of his posts. He was defeated at the Battle of ACTIUM (31 BC). Antony and Cleopatra committed suicide.

**Antrim** County in Northern Ireland, bounded N by the Atlantic Ocean and NE and E by the North Channel. The capital is BELFAST; other notable centers are Ballymena, Antrim (on the N shore of Lough Neagh), and Larne. Mainly a low basalt plateau, it is noted for the GIANT'S CAUSEWAY. It is chiefly an agricultural region. Industries: linen and shipbuilding, concentrated in Belfast. Area: 1,175sq mi (3,043sq km). Pop. (1991) 665,013.

**Antwerp** (Flemish *Antwerpen* Fr. *Anvers*) Port city on the Scheldt River, capital of Antwerp province and Belgium's second-largest city. Antwerp rose to prominence in the 15th century and became a center for English mercantile interests. It was the site of Europe's first stock exchange (1460). Although heavily bombed during World War II, it retains many attractive old, narrow streets and fine buildings. Industries: oil refining, food processing, tobacco, diamond cutting. Pop. (1993 est.) 462,880.

**Anubis** In Egyptian mythology, a jackal-headed god. Son of Nephthys and OSIRIS, he conducted the souls of the dead to the underworld and presided over mummification and funerals. Anubis accompanied Osiris on his world conquest and buried him after his murder.

**ANZAC** (acronym for Australian and New Zealand Army Corps) Volunteer force of 30,000 men that spearheaded the disastrous GALLIPOLI CAMPAIGN in World War I. Troops landed at GALLIPOLI on April 25, 1915. Anzac Day (April 25) is a public holiday in Australia and New Zealand. About 8,500 Anzac troops were killed during World War I.

**ANZUS Pact** (Australia-New Zealand-United States Treaty Organization) Military alliance organized by the US in 1951. ANZUS was set up in response to waning British power, the Korean War, and alarm at increasing Soviet influence in the Pacific. The treaty stated that an attack on any one of the three countries would be considered as an attack on them all. It was replaced in 1954 by the SOUTHEAST ASIA TREATY ORGANIZATION (SEATO).

**aorta** Principal ARTERY in the body. Carrying freshly oxygenated blood, the aorta leaves the left ventricle of the heart and descends the length of the trunk, finally dividing to form the two main arteries that serve the legs. *See also* CIRCULATORY SYSTEM; HEART

**Apache** Athabascan-speaking tribe of Native North Americans that live in Arizona, New Mexico, and Colorado. Divided culturally into Eastern Apache (including Mescalero and Kiowa) and Western Apache (including Coyotero and Tonto), they migrated from the NW with the NAVAJO in about AD 1000 but separated to form a distinct tribal group. They retained their earlier nomadic raiding customs, which brought them into military conflict with Mexico and the US during the 19th century. The total population is now *c*.11,000.

**Apache Wars** Series of battles in Arizona, New Mexico, Texas, and Oklahoma between Apaches and white settlers. One Apache chief, COCHISE, made peace in 1872, but GERONIMO fought on until 1886. Atrocities occurred on both sides.

**apartheid** Policy of racial segregation practiced by the South African government from 1948 to 1990. Racial inequality and restricted rights for nonwhites was institutionalized when the AFRIKANER-dominated National Party came to power in 1948. Officially a framework for "separate development" of races, in practice apartheid confirmed white-minority rule. It was based on segregation in all aspects of life including residence, land ownership, and education. Nonwhites, around 80% of the population, were also given separate political structures, quasi-autonomous homelands or bantustans. The system was underpinned by extensive repression, and measures such as pass laws, which severely restricted the movements of nonwhites. Increasingly isolated internationally and beset by economic difficulties and domestic unrest, the government pledged to dismantle the system in 1990. The transition to nonracial democracy was completed with the elections in April 1994. *See also* AFRICAN NATIONAL CONGRESS (ANC)

**ape** Term usually applied to the anthropoid apes (PRIMATES) that are the closest relatives of humans. There are three great apes – CHIMPANZEE, GORILLA, and ORANGUTAN – and one lesser, the GIBBON. An ape differs from a MONKEY in being larger, having no visible tail, and in possessing a more complex brain. Two monkeys are also called "apes" – the BARBARY APE of N Africa and Gibraltar, and the black ape of Celebes.

**Apennines** (Appennino) Mountain range extending the length of Italy, a continuation of the Pennine Alps. The Apennines form the "backbone" of Italy, stretching *c*.840mi (1,350km) from the Genoese Riviera to the tip of the country's "toe." Unselective deforestation over the years has caused deep erosion and landslides. Sheep and goats are grazed on its slopes. The highest point is Mount Corno, at 9,560ft (2,914m).

**aperture** In photography, a hole that allows light to pass through the lens onto the film. Modern cameras usually have a diaphragm aperture which works like the iris of a human eye. The photographer can widen or narrow the diaphragm according to a series of points on the lens dial called "f-numbers" or "f-stops." The individual f-numbers represent the focal length of the lens divided by the diameter of the aperture. As the aperture narrows, it gives a longer depth of field.

**aphasia** Group of disorders of language arising from disease of or damage to the brain. In aphasia, a person has problems formulating or comprehending speech and difficulty in reading and writing. *See also* BRAIN DISORDERS

**aphid** (plant louse) Winged or wingless, soft-bodied insect found worldwide. It transmits viral diseases of plants when sucking plant juices. Females reproduce with or without mating, producing one to several generations annually. Common species are also known as blackfly and greenfly. Length: to 0.2in (5mm). Family Aphididae.

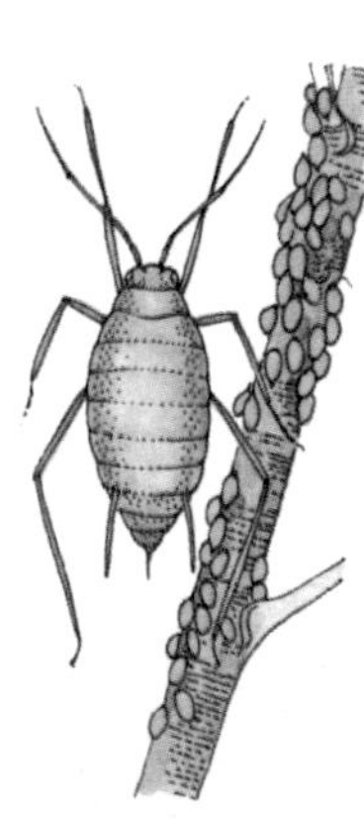

▲ **aphid** The greenfly (*Aphis* sp) occurs in enormous numbers, and the 2,000 or species probably inflict more damage on crops worldwide than any other insect pest. Their remarkable power of reproduction is due to the fact that the females are parthenogenetic, that is they can produce young without fertilization by a male.

**Aphrodite** Greek goddess of love, beauty, and fruitfulness, identified by the Romans as VENUS. She was the daughter of ZEUS and Dione. Her husband was HEPHAESTUS (in Roman mythology, VULCAN). Among her lovers were ARES, ADONIS, and Anchises, the father of AENEAS. Statues of her include the Venus de Milo (Paris) and Aphrodite of Cnidus (Rome).

**Apocrypha** Certain books included in the Bible as an appendix to the OLD TESTAMENT in the SEPTUAGINT and in St. Jerome's Vulgate translation but not forming part of the Hebrew canon. Nine books are accepted as canonical by the Roman Catholic Church. They are: Tobit, Judith, Wisdom, Ecclesiasticus, Baruch (including the Letter to Jeremiah), 1 and 2 Maccabees, and parts of Esther and Daniel. Other books are found in Eastern Orthodox Bibles and in the appendix to the Roman Catholic Old Testament.

**Apollinaire, Guillaume** (1880–1918) (Wilhelm Apollinaris de Kostrowitzky) French experimental poet, essayist, and playwright. One of the most extraordinary artists of early 20th-century Paris, Apollinaire's *Peintres Cubistes* (1913) was the first attempt to define CUBISM. He also experimented with typography in his poetry collection *Calligrams* (1918). His masterpiece was the wholly unpunctuated *Alcools* (1913), in which he relived the wild romances of his youth.

**Apollo** In Greek mythology, god of the Sun, archery, and prophecy; patron of musicians, poets, and physicians; founder of cities and giver of laws. He was the son of ZEUS and Leto, twin to ARTEMIS. In the Trojan War he sided with Troy, sending a plague against the Greeks.

**Apollonius of Perga** (*c*.262–190 BC) Greek mathematician and astronomer. He built on the foundations laid by EUCLID. In *Conics*, he showed that an ELLIPSE, a PARABOLA, and a HYPERBOLA can be obtained by taking plane sections at different angles through a cone. In astronomy, he described the motion of the planets in terms of epicycles which remained the basis of the system used until the time of COPERNICUS.

**Apollo program** US SPACE EXPLORATION project to land men on the Moon. Initiated in May 1961 by President Kennedy, it achieved its objective on July 20, 1969, when Neil ARMSTRONG set foot on the Moon. The program terminated with the successful Apollo-Soyuz linkup in space during July 1975. It placed more than 30 astronauts in space and 12 on the Moon.

**Apostle** Missionary sent out and empowered by divine authority to preach the gospel and heal the sick. Jesus commissioned his 12 DISCIPLES to carry out the purpose of God for man's salvation (Mark 3, Matthew 10, Luke 6). The first qualification for being an apostle was to have "seen the Lord." The 12 disciples thus became the first and original Apostles. The term is also applied in the New Testament to St. PAUL. In modern usage it is sometimes given to the leader of the first Christian mission to a country. For example, St PATRICK is described as the "Apostle of Ireland."

**Apostles' Creed** Statement of Christian faith. The last section affirms the tradition of the "holy Catholic Church; the communion of saints; the forgiveness of sins; the resurrection of the body; and the life everlasting." The text evolved gradually, and its present form was fixed by the early 7th century. It is used widely in private and public worship in all the major churches in the West. *See also* NICENE CREED

**Appalachians** Mountain system stretching 1,600mi (2,570km) from E Canada to Alabama. Comprising a series of parallel ridges divided by wide valleys, the mountains restricted early European settlers to the E coast. It includes the White Mountains, Green Mountains, Catskills, Alleghenies, and the Blue Ridge and Cumberland mountains; the highest point is Mount Mitchell in North Carolina at 6,684ft (2,037m). Rich in timber and coal, the ranges are home to many NATIONAL PARKS.

**appeasement** Policy in which one government grants unilateral concessions to another to forestall a political, economic, or military threat. The 1938 MUNICH AGREEMENT is considered a classic example of appeasement.

**Appel, Karel** (1921– ) Dutch painter, sculptor, and muralist. In the 1940s, Appel was one of several painters who reacted against the strict formalism of De STIJL, and invented a wildly expressionist language of his own, similar to abstract expressionism. His most powerful work, often portraying fantastic, aggressive and tragic figures, anticipated *Art Informel*.

**appendicitis** Inflammation of the APPENDIX caused by obstruction and infection. Symptoms include severe pain in the central abdomen, nausea, and vomiting. Acute appendicitis is generally treated by surgery. A ruptured appendix can cause peritonitis and even death.

**appendix** In some mammals, finger-shaped organ, *c*.4in (10cm) long, located near the junction of the small and large intestines, usually in the lower right part of the abdomen. It has no known function in humans but can become inflamed or infected (APPENDICITIS).

**apple** Common name for the most widely cultivated fruit tree of temperate climates. Developed from a tree native to Europe and SW Asia, apple trees are propagated by budding or grafting. From the flowers, which require cross-pollination to produce a desirable fruit, the fleshy fruit grows in a variety of sizes, shapes, and acidities; it is generally roundish, 2–4in (5–10cm) in diameter, and a shade of yellow, green, or red. A mature tree may yield up to 30 bushels (1cu m) of fruit in a single growing season. Europe produces 50–60% of the world's annual crop, and the US 16–20%. Family Rosaceae; genus *Malus*.

**Appomattox** Town in Virginia, 18mi (29km) E of Lynchburg; the seat of Appomattox county. It is near Appomattox Court House National Historical Park. Nearby is the site of General LEE's surrender of his Confederate troops to Union forces under General GRANT (April 9, 1865), ending the CIVIL WAR.

**apricot** Tree, cultivated throughout temperate regions, that originated in China. The large, spreading tree with dark green leaves and white blossoms bears yellow or yellowish-orange edible fruit, with a large stone. Family Rosaceae; species *Prunus armeniaca*.

**apsis** (pl. apsides) Either of two points in an object's orbit. The closest point to the primary body is known as the **periapsis**, and the farthest the **apapsis**. The apsides of the Earth's orbit are its perihelion and aphelion; in the Moon's orbit they are its perigee and apogee.

**aptitude test** Test used to measure potential for educational achievement. Some (such as "intelligence tests") purport to measure general capacity. Others are designed to measure potential for a specific aptitude, such as playing a musical instrument.

**Aqaba** (Al 'Aqabah) Only seaport of Jordan, at the head of the Gulf of AQABA on the NE end of the Red Sea. It was an important part of medieval Palestine. In 1917 it was captured from the Turks by T.E. LAWRENCE, and finally ceded to Jordan in 1925. It is crucial to Jordan's phosphate exports, and is expanding as a port and diving resort. Pop. (1992 est) 58,000.

**Aqaba, Gulf of** NE arm of the Red Sea between the Sinai Peninsula and Saudi Arabia. AQABA and ELAT lie at the N end of the Gulf. The gulf has played an important role in ARAB-ISRAELI WARS. It was blockaded by the Arabs (1949–56), and again in 1967, when Israel held strategic points along the Strait of Tiran to guarantee open passage for ships. The Gulf has excellent coral beds and rich marine life.

**Aqmola** (Akmola, lit. "white grave") Capital-designate of Kazakstan. Aqmola lies on Ishim River in the steppes of N central Kazakstan. Under Soviet rule, Aqmola functioned as capital of the Virgin Lands. From 1961 to 1993 it was known as Tselinograd. Pop. (1990) 281,400.

**aqualung** *See* SCUBA DIVING

**aquamarine** *See* BERYL

**Aquarius** (Water Bearer) Eleventh constellation of the zodiac, represented by a figure pouring water from a jar.

**aquatint** Method of engraving on metal plates. The process was invented in the mid-18th century to imitate the effect of brush drawing or watercolor. It involves sprinkling a plate with fine grains of acid-resistant resin, fusing the resin to the metal (modern enamel sprays allow you to avoid this step) and letting acid bite around and through some of the grains. Printmakers can achieve extremely varied effects depending on the thickness of the resin and the immersion time. Aquatint enables line engraving or to draw on top of the resin with an acid-resistant varnish. GOYA and PICASSO were masters of the process.

**aqueduct** Artificial channel for conducting water from its source to its distribution point. While the ancient Romans were not the first to build these conduits, their aqueducts are the most famous because of their graceful architectural structures. One of their most extensive water systems, which served Rome itself, consisted of 11 aqueducts and took 500 years to complete. California has the world's largest conduit system: it carries water over a distance of more than 500mi (800km).

**aquifer** Rock, often sandstone or limestone, which is capable of both storing and transmitting water owing to its porosity and permeability. Much of the world's human population depends on aquifers for its water supply. They may be directly exploited by sinking wells.

**Aquinas, Saint Thomas** (1225–74) Italian theologian and philosopher, Doctor of the Church. St Thomas is the greatest figure of SCHOLASTICISM. His *Summa Theologiae* (Theological Digest, 1267–73) was declared (1879) by Pope Leo XIII to be the basis of official Catholic philosophy. Aquinas argued that faith and reason are two complementary realms; both are gifts of God, but reason is autonomous. His four hymns for the feast of Corpus Christi are among the greatest devotional pieces. Thomas was canonized in 1323. Thomist METAPHYSICS, a moderate form of REALISM, was the dominant world view until the mid-17th century. Other writings include *Commentary in the Sentences* (1254–56) and *Summa Contra Gentiles* (Against the Errors of the Infidels, 1259–64). His feast day is March 7.

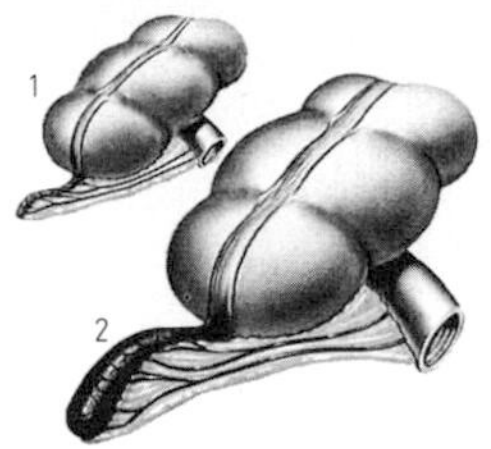


▲ **appendicitis** In appendicitis, the tissues lining the appendix become infected and inflamed, which causes the organ to swell (1) and its vascularization to increase (2). Prompt surgical removal is usually carried out to prevent the appendix bursting and causing peritonitis by the spread of its infection.

▼ **apple** Grown predominantly in temperate regions, apples have been cultivated since prehistoric times. They are commerically important.

A

**Aquino, (Maria) Cory (Corazon)** (1933– ) Philippine stateswoman, president (1986–92), b. Maria Corazon. In 1954 she married Benigno Aquino (1932–83), an outspoken opponent of the MARCOS regime. While he was in prison (1973–81), Cory campaigned tirelessly for his release. Benigno was assassinated by Marcos' agents. Cory claimed to have defeated Marcos in the 1986 presidential election and accused the government of vote-rigging. A bloodless "people's revolution" forced Marcos into exile. Aquino's administration was beset by economic obstacles and she survived a coup attempt only with US help (1989). Aquino declined to run for re-election in 1992, but supported the campaign of her successor Fidel Ramos.

**Aquitaine** Historic region in SW France, named after a Celtic tribe, the Aquitani. Named Aquitania by the Romans, it became (56 BC) an integral part of their empire and included all the land between the Pyrenees and the River Garonne. Aquitaine later formed part of the Carolingian empire. Independent for a time during the early Middle Ages, it became part of France and then, following the marriage of Eleanor of Aquitaine to HENRY II in the 12th century, part of England. In the early 13th century all but the southern part (Gascony) was returned to France, the rest being restored in 1453 at the end of the HUNDRED YEARS WAR. The modern region, comprising the départements of Dordogne, Gironde, Landes, Lot-et-Garonne, and Pyrénées-Atlantiques, is an important wine-producing region centered on BORDEAUX. Area: 15,950sq mi (41,308sq km). Pop. (1990) 2,795,800.

**Arab** Peoples of many nationalities, found predominantly in the Middle East and North Africa, who share a common heritage in the religion of Islam and their language (ARABIC). The patriarchal family is the basic social unit in a strongly traditional culture that has been little affected by external influences. Wealth from oil has brought rapid modernization in some Arab countries, but a great deal of economic inequality exists.

**Arabia** Peninsular region of SW Asia bordered by the Persian Gulf (E), the Arabian Sea (S), the Syrian Desert (N), and the Red Sea (W). The original homeland of the ARABS, it is the world's largest peninsula, consisting largely of a plateau of crystalline rock. It is mostly desert, including the vast, barren Rub al-Khali ("Empty Quarter") in the S and the An Nafud in the N. The area was unified by the Muslims in the 7th century, and dominated by Ottoman Turks after 1517. Hussein ibn Ali led a successful revolt against the Turks and founded an independent state in the Hejaz region in 1916, but was subsequently defeated by the Saud family, who founded SAUDI ARABIA in 1925. After World War II independent Arab states emerged, many of them exploiting the peninsula's vast reserves of oil. Area: *c.*1,000,000sq mi (2,600,000sq km).

▶ **Arafat** Following a 30-year struggle with Israel, Palestine Liberation Organization (PLO) leader Yasir Arafat returned to Jericho on 1 July, 1994 as head of the Palestinian National Authority. He was elected president in 1996. His leadership was criticized by some Palestinians for relinquishing too much to Israel, and by Israeli prime minister Benjamin Netanyahu for harboring Palestinian extremists. Arafat's ill heath prompted speculation concerning a crisis of succession.

**Arabic** Language originating in the Arabian Peninsula and now spoken in a variety of dialects throughout North Africa and the Middle East. It is a Semitic language, belonging to a major subfamily of Afro-Asiatic languages. Classical Arabic is the language of the KORAN. It began to spread during the Islamic expansion of the 7th and 8th centuries. It is estimated that more than 100 million people are native speakers. Arabic uses a script written from right to left. The script has been borrowed for rendering other languages such as Urdu.

**Arab-Israeli Wars** (1948–49, 1956, 1967, 1973–74) Conflicts between Israel and the Arab states. After Israeli independence (May 14, 1948), troops from Egypt, Iraq, Lebanon, Syria, and Transjordan (modern Jordan) invaded the country. Initial Arab gains were halted and armistices arranged at Rhodes (January–July 1949). UN security forces upheld the truce until October 1956, when Israeli forces under Moshe DAYAN attacked the SINAI PENINSULA with support from France and Britain, alarmed at Egypt's nationalization of the SUEZ CANAL. International opinion forced a ceasefire in November. In 1967 guerrilla raids led to Israeli mobilization, and in the ensuing SIX DAY WAR, Israel captured Sinai, the GOLAN HEIGHTS on the Syrian border, and the Old City of JERUSALEM. In the October War of 1973 (after intermittent hostilities) Egypt and Syria invaded on the Jewish holiday of YOM KIPPUR (October 6), and Israel pushed back their advance after severe losses. Fighting lasted 18 days. Subsequent disengagement agreements were supervised by the UN. In 1979 Israel signed a peace treaty with Egypt, but relations with other Arab states remained hostile. Israeli forces invaded Lebanon in 1982 in an effort to destroy bases of the PALESTINE LIBERATION ORGANIZATION (PLO). They were withdrawn (1984) after widespread international criticism. After 1988 the PLO renounced terrorism and gained concessions, including limited autonomy in parts of the occupied territories. Israeli relations with some Arab neighbors generally improved after the GULF WAR.

**Arab League** Organization formed in 1945 to give a collective political voice to the Arab nations. Its members include Syria, Lebanon, Iraq, Jordan, Sudan, Algeria, Kuwait, Saudi Arabia, Libya, Morocco, Tunisia, Yemen, Qatar, and the United Arab Emirates. It has often been divided, notably by the Egyptian peace treaty with Israel (1979) and over the GULF WAR (1991) and has been politically less effective than its founders hoped.

**arachnid** Arthropod of the class Arachnida, which includes the SPIDER, TICK, MITE, SCORPION, and HARVESTMAN. Arachnids have four pairs of jointed legs, two distinct body segments (cephalothorax and abdomen), and chelicerate jaws (consisting of clawed pincers). They lack antennae and wings.

**Arafat, Yasir** (1929– ) Palestinian statesman, first president of Palestine (1996– ), leader of the PALESTINE LIBERATION ORGANIZATION (PLO). From a base in Lebanon, Arafat led the anti-ISRAEL guerrilla organization, Fatah. He sought the abolition of Israel and the creation of a secular Palestinian state. The INTIFADA in Israel's occupied territories (GAZA and the WEST BANK) prompted secret talks between Israel and the PLO. In 1993 Arafat and Yitzhak Rabin signed an agreement in which Arafat renounced terrorism and recognized the state of Israel. In return, Rabin recognized the PLO as the legitimate representative of Palestinians and agreed to a withdrawal of Israeli troops from parts of the occupied territories. In 1994 the Palestinian National Authority, headed by Arafat, assumed limited self-rule in the territories relinquished by the Israeli army. In 1996 elections Arafat became president.

**Aragón** Region in NE Spain. In 1479 the Kingdom of Aragón became part of Spain, but retained its own government, currency, and military forces until the early 18th century. It is now an autonomous region, comprising the provinces of Huesca, Teruel, and Zaragoza. It produces grapes, wheat, and sugarbeet. Industries: textiles, chemicals, iron ore, marble, limestone. Area: 18,500sq mi (47,670sq km). Pop. (1991) 1,188,817.

**Aral Sea** (Aralskoye More) Inland sea in central Asia, SW Kazakstan, and NW Uzbekistan. Once the world's fourth largest inland body of water, it has no outlet, contains many small islands, and is fed by the rivers Syrdarya in the NE and Amudarya (Oxus) in the S. It is generally shallow and only slightly saline. The diversion of the rivers for irrigation by the Soviet government led to a disastrous drop in the water level and the area of the lake shrunk by more than a third between 1960 and 1995. Many fishing communities were left literally stranded. Area: 26,518sq mi (68,681sq km).

**Aramaic** Ancient Semitic language used as a means of everyday communication in Palestine and other parts of the Middle East at the time of Christ. Originally the language of nomadic groups who established small states in MESOPOTAMIA during the late 2nd millennium BC, it became the common spoken and written language of the Middle East under the Persian Empire until replaced by ARABIC. Parts of the Old Testament were originally written in Aramaic. Minor dialects persist today in small Christian communities of the Near and Middle East.

**Arapaho** ALGONQUIAN-speaking tribe of Native North Americans. Their original home was in the Red River Valley; they moved across the Missouri River and split into two groups. After the Treaty of Medicine Lodge (1847), one group joined the Southern Cheyennes in Oklahoma, while the northern band went onto Wind River Reservation with the SHOSHONE. Today, they number *c*.3,000.

**Ararat, Mount** (Ağri Daği) Two extinct volcanic peaks in the E extremity of Turkey. The highest peaks in Turkey, they are just N of where Noah's Ark is said to have come to rest (Genesis 8). There are two peaks: Great Ararat, 16,945ft (5,165m), (last eruption 1840), and Little Ararat, 12,877ft (3,925m).

**Araucanian** Independent language family of South American Indians who live in Chile and Argentina. A loose confederation of Araucanian-speaking subtribes (including the Picunche, Mapuche, and Huilliche) offered strong resistance to the Spanish invasion under Diego de Almagro in 1536. They drove the Spaniards back to the Bio-Bio River in 1598, and retained possession of interior portions of Chile to the present time. Their descendants prefer the name *Mapuche* (land people). The population has declined from *c*.1 million in the 16th century to *c*.300,000 today.

**Arawak** Largest and most widely spread Native South American language family, once spoken from the Caribbean to the GRAN CHACO. Some 40 Arawak tribes remain in Brazil today.

**arbitration** Resolution of a dispute by an unbiased referee (arbiter) chosen by the parties in conflict. While arbitration may be utilized by individuals in conflict, the procedure is most commonly applied in commercial and industrial disputes and overseen by independent bodies such as the American Arbitration Association in the US. International cases are often brought before the United Nations International Court of Justice, based at The Hague, Netherlands.

**arbor vitae** Common name for five species of trees or shrubs of the genus *Thuja*, resinous, evergreen conifers of the cypress family native to North America and E Asia. They have thin outer bark, fibrous inner bark, and flattened branches. Family Cupressaceae.

**arc** Portion of a curve. For a circle, the length ($s$) of an arc is found either by $2\pi \times \theta/360$ or the product of the radius ($r$) and the angle ($\theta$), measured in RADIANS, that it subtends at the center: that is, $s = r\theta$.

**Arc de Triomphe** TRIUMPHAL ARCH in the Place Charles de Gaulle, Paris, France. The Arc de Triomphe de l'Etoile is a generalized copy of the triumphal arches erected in ancient Rome to commemorate the victories of individual emperors. Napoleon I commissioned J.F. Chalgrin to design this version, completed in 1836. It is one of the city's most celebrated landmarks.

**arch** Upward-pointing or curving arrangement of masonry blocks or other load-bearing materials; also used in architectural decoration. The ancient Romans invented traditional masonry arches but later cultures extended their repertoire to include many different and sometimes quite elaborate shapes. The basic structure of a masonry arch consists of wedge-shaped blocks (*voussoirs*) placed on top of each other and a central keystone which holds them together at the top. Modern materials, such as steel and reinforced concrete, are strong and flexible enough to stand on their own and they can also stretch across much wider areas. *See also* VAULT

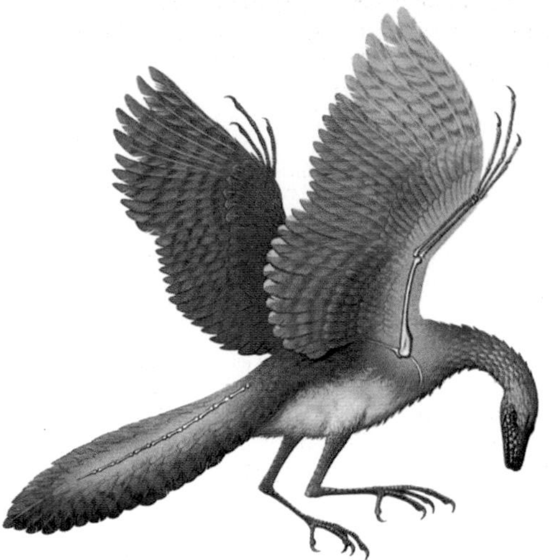

◀ **archaeopteryx** The earliest known recognizable bird, archaeopteryx dates from the upper Jurassic period. The presence of wings and feathers define it as a bird, but the skeleton is quite reptilian. The wings, instead of being the specialized flying limbs of modern birds, were really elongated forelimbs, complete with claws. The tail resembles a lizard's and the skull had teeth. The small breastbone shows it was a poor flyer.

**Archaebacteria** Subkingdom of the kingdom PROKARYOTAE, which on the basis of both RNA and DNA composition and biochemistry differ significantly from other BACTERIA. They are thought to resemble ancient bacteria that first arose in extreme environments such as sulfur-rich deep-sea vents. Archaebacteria have unique proteinlike cell walls and cell membrane chemistry, and distinctive RIBOSOMES. They include methane-producing bacteria, which use simple organic compounds such as methanol and acetate as food, combining them with carbon dioxide and hydrogen gas from the air, and releasing methane as a by-product. The bacteria of hot springs and saline areas have a variety of ways of obtaining food and energy, including the use of minerals instead of organic compounds. They include both AEROBIC and ANAEROBIC bacteria. Some taxonomists consider Archaebacteria to be so different from other living organisms that they constitute a higher grouping called a domain.

**archaeopteryx** First known bird. About the size of a crow and fully feathered, its fossilized skeleton is more like that of a reptile than a modern bird, and its beak had pronounced jaws with teeth. It was probably capable only of weak flight.

**Archangel** (Archangel'sk) City and major port on the North Dvina delta, NW Russia. Archangel was opened (*c*.1600) to European trade, and was Russia's major port until the founding (1703) of St Petersburg. The monastery of Archangel Michael was built here (1685–99). In the winter, icebreakers keep the large harbor clear, but the port remains ice-free for about six months, essential for commerce in N European Russia. Industries: paper, fishing, shipbuilding. Pop. (1994) 407,000.

**archbishop** Chief or highest-ranking bishop who is head of an ecclesiastical province or archdiocese. The main function of an archbishop is to supervise and guide the work of subordinate BISHOPS.

**Archean** Subdivision of pre-Cambrian geological time. It ended *c*.2.5 billion years ago.

**archeology** Scientific study of former human life and activities through material remains such as artifacts and buildings. An archeologist excavates and retrieves remains from the ground or seabed, recording and interpreting the circumstances in which objects were found, such as their level in the soil and association with other objects. This information can then be used to build a picture of the culture that produced the objects.

**archerfish** Fish found in brackish waters of SE Asia and Australia. It is yellowish-green to brown with dark markings, and catches insect prey by spitting water "bullets." Length: up to 8in (20cm). Family Toxotidae.

**archery** Target sport that makes use of a bow and arrow or a crossbow and bolt. Commonly, archers use a longbow to shoot arrows at a target that consists of concentric scoring rings of five colors. The three other divisions of archery are field, flight, and crossbow. Archery's world governing body is the *Fédération Internationale de Tir à l'Arc (FITA)*, based in Milan, Italy. The sport returned to the Olympic Games in 1972.

**Archimedes** (287–212 BC) Greek mathematician and engineer. He developed a method for expressing large numbers and made outstanding discoveries about the determination of areas and volumes, which led to a new accurate method of measuring π (pi). In his work *On Floating Bodies* he stated ARCHIMEDES' PRINCIPLE. He also invented the ARCHIMEDES' SCREW.

**Archimedes' principle** Observation by ARCHIMEDES that a body immersed in a FLUID is pushed up by a force equal to the weight of the displaced fluid. He supposedly formulated this principle after stepping into a bath and watching it overflow.

**Archimedes' screw** Machine used for raising water, thought to have been invented by Archimedes in the 3rd century BC. The most common form of the machine is a cylindrical pipe enclosing a helix, inclined at a 45° angle to the horizontal with its lower end in the water. When the machine rotates, water rises through the pipe.

**Archipenko, Alexander** (1887–1964) Russian-US modernist sculptor, one of the most radical innovators of his day. Largely self-taught, Archipenko helped to introduce the idea of making space an integral element of sculpture, as in the cubist *Walking Woman* (1912). He also developed a form of sculpture using light. Archipenko took part in the ARMORY SHOW (1913) and opened a sculpture school in New York in the late 1930s. His work influenced GABO and Henry MOORE.

**architecture** Art and science of designing permanent buildings for human use. Architecture can express aesthetic ideas from the most restrained UTILITARIANISM to extravagantly ornate decoration. The difference between "architecture" and "building" is a subject that has exercised theorists since the discipline was invented. In reality, architecture is usually a compromise between aesthetic creation and the demands of practicality. There are many different areas of architecture and apart from the stylistic and historical periods (*See* individual articles), it comes under such broad categories as civic, commercial, religious, recreational, and domestic. In the 20th century, traditional barriers between separate artistic disciplines have gradually dissolved, so that it is possible to see architecture as a type of sculpture. Key figures in the development of Western architectural theory include VITRUVIUS, who believed that architecture was merely a form of applied mathematics, and ALBERTI whose pioneering treatise *De re Aedificatoria* (1485) introduced the idea that architecture was an art form in its own right. After the 18th century, European architects tended to regard "building" as a cheap substitute for their profession and something carried ou by engineers. Architects began to swing back in the other direction with the arrival of the ARTS AND CRAFTS MOVEMENT, and the introduc-

## ARGENTINA

The sky blue and white stripes were the symbols of independence around the city of Buenos Aires, where an independent government was set up in 1810.
It became the national flag in 1816, and the gold May Sun was added two years later.

**AREA:** 1,068,296sq mi (2,766,890sq km)
**POPULATION:** 33,101,000
**CAPITAL (POPULATION):** Buenos Aires (11,662,050)
**GOVERNMENT:** Federal republic
**ETHNIC GROUPS:** European 85%, Mestizo, Native American
**LANGUAGES:** Spanish (official)
**RELIGIONS:** Christianity (Roman Catholic 92%)
**CURRENCY:** Peso = 100 centavos

The Argentine Republic is the second largest country in South America and the eighth largest in the world. The high ANDES Mountains in the W contain Aconcagua, the highest peak outside Asia. In S Argentina the Andes overlook PATAGONIA, a plateau region. In east-central Argentina lies a fertile plain called the Pampas, while the NE also contains lowland plains. The GRAN CHACO lies W of the PARANÁ River, while Mesopotamia is another fertile plain between the Paraná and the URUGUAY rivers.

### CLIMATE

Argentina's climates range from subtropical in the N to temperate in the S, with extremly harsh conditions in the high Andes. The rainfall is abundant in the NE, but less to the W and S. Though dry, Patagonia is crossed by rivers rising in the Andes.

### VEGETATION

The Gran Chaco is a forested region, known for quebracho trees, which yield tannin used in the leather industry. Mesopotamia and the Pampas are grassy regions, and large areas are farmed. Patagonia is too dry for crops; the main activity on the grassy tablelands is sheep raising.

### HISTORY AND POLITICS

Spanish explorers first reached the coast in 1516, and Spanish settlers quickly followed. At first they came in search of silver and gold, but they soon began to establish huge farms and ranches. Spanish rule continued until BUENOS AIRES declared itself independent in 1810; the provinces followed in 1816. In 1853 the country adopted a federal constitution, giving the provinces the power to control most of their own internal affairs.

Argentina's economy developed steadily in the late 19th and early 20th centuries. Since the 1930s, however, political instability has marred progress, with frequent power coups, high unemployment, and rampant inflation. From 1976, during the so-called "dirty war," torture, political murders, and wrongful imprisonment were commonplace. In 1982, partly to divert attention from the poor state of the economy, Argentina invaded the FALKLAND ISLANDS (Islas Malvinas), precipitating the FALKLANDS WAR. Britain quickly recaptured the islands and in 1983 the junta was forced to hold elections. Civilian government was restored. In 1989 the Perónist Carlos MENEM was elected president. He was re-elected in 1995.

### ECONOMY

According to the World Bank, Argentina is an "upper-middle-income" developing country (1995 GDP per capita, US$8,310). It has large areas of fertile farmland, and its main products are beef, corn and wheat. Wool is also important. Other major crops include citrus fruits, cotton, grapes, sorghum, soybeans, sugarcane, and tea.

Almost 90% of the people live in cities and towns, where many factories process farm products. Many other industries have been set up, including the manufacture of automobiles, electrical equipment, and textiles. The main exports remain agricultural: meat, wheat, maize, vegetable oils, hides and skins, and wool.

tion of efficient, mass-produced materials. The 20th-century modernists, such as Walter GROPIUS, believed that the form of a building should follow its function. The relationship between the two extremes is continually changing.

**Arctic** Vast region of icy seas and cold lands around the NORTH POLE, often defined as extending from the Pole to the ARCTIC CIRCLE. In areas N of latitude 66° 30'N, the sun neither sets during the height of summer nor rises during the depths of winter. The more southerly areas are frequently referred to as the subarctic. At the center of the Arctic is the ARCTIC OCEAN, with its many seas and inlets. In the region around the North Pole, the waters of the Arctic are permanently covered with sheet ice or a floating mass of ice debris called the ice pack, but some parts of the ocean are frozen only in winter. When the ice starts to melt in the spring it disintegrates into floes and drifting pack ice. Icebergs have their origins in freshwater glaciers flowing into the ocean from the surrounding lands. **Lands and climate** Bordering the Arctic Ocean are the most northerly lands of Asia, Europe, and North America. By far the greater part of the huge frozen island of GREENLAND lies N of the Arctic Circle. Arctic lands generally have a summer free from ice and snow. Most of the Arctic tundra is flat and marshy in summer but the subsoil is PERMAFROST. For most of the year Arctic temperatures are below freezing point. In spring the sun appears, and some Arctic lands have sunshine every day from March or April to September. **People** Despite the severity of the climate and the restricted food resources, many peoples live in the Arctic. The most scattered are the *c.*60,000 ESKIMOS spread across polar North America, Greenland, and NE Siberia. Several culturally separate groups of people live in N Siberia. In the European part of Russia there are the numerous Zyryans, and in LAPLAND the LAPPS. Most of these peoples follow ancient, traditional patterns of life, but the discovery of great mineral wealth, especially in Alaska and Russia, has brought huge change to their homelands. **History** The region was first explored by Norsemen as early as the 9th century. The search for the NORTHWEST PASSAGE gave impetus to further explorations in the 16th and 17th centuries, though a route was not found until the early 1900s. The North Pole was first reached in 1909 by the American Robert Peary, and the first crossing of the Arctic Ocean under the polar ice-cap was completed in 1959.

**Arctic Circle** Northernmost of the Earth's parallels, 66.5° N of the equator. At this latitude the sun neither sets on the day of summer SOLSTICE (June 21) nor rises on the day of winter solstice (December 22). *See also* ANTARCTIC CIRCLE

**Arctic fox** (white fox or polar fox) Fox found on tundra or mountains of the Arctic. Its fur changes color in winter either from gray-brown to white or gray to gray-blue. Length: 50–60cm (20–24in).

**Arctic Ocean** Ocean N of the Arctic Circle, between North America and Eurasia. Almost totally landlocked and the Earth's smallest ocean, it is bordered by Greenland, Canada, Alaska, Russia, and Norway. Connected to the Pacific Ocean by the Bering Strait, and to the Atlantic Ocean by the Davis Strait and Greenland Sea, it includes the Barents, Beaufort, Chukchi, Greenland, and Norwegian seas. There is animal life (plankton) in all Arctic water and polar bears, seals, and gulls up to about 88° N. Area: 5.4 million sq mi (14 million sq km).

**Arctic tern** Sea bird whose migrations are the longest of any bird, from summer breeding areas in the far N to wintering areas in Antarctica, a round trip of *c.*22,000mi (35,500km). It has gray, black, and white feathers and a reddish bill and feet. It nests in colonies and lays one to four eggs in a sandy scrape nest. Length: 15in (38cm). Species *Sterna paradisaea.*

**Ardennes** (Forest of Ardennes) Sparsely populated wooded plateau in SE Belgium, N Luxembourg, and the Ardennes département of N France. The capital is Charleville-Mézières. It was the scene of heavy fighting in both world wars, notably in the Battle of the BULGE. In the well-preserved forest regions wild game is abundant, and cleared areas support farming.

**area** Two-dimensional measurement of a plane figure or body given in square units, such as $in^2$ or $cm^2$. The area of a rectangle of sides $a$ and $b$ is $ab$; the areas of triangles and other polygons can be determined using TRIGONOMETRY. Areas of curved figures and surfaces can be determined by integral CALCULUS.

**Arequipa** Second-largest city of Peru and capital of Arequipa department. It was established in 1540 by Francisco PIZARRO on the site of an INCA settlement. Located at the foot of the extinct volcano El Misti (19,100ft/5,822m), it is known as the "White City" because many of its buildings are made of white volcanic stone. Industries: wool processing, textiles, leather. Pop. (1993) 619,156.

**Ares** In Greek mythology, the god of war, identified with the Roman god MARS. He was the son of Zeus and HERA and lover of APHRODITE. In the Trojan War he sided with the Trojans.

**argon** (symbol Ar) Monatomic (single-atom), colorless and odorless gaseous element that is the most abundant NOBLE GAS (inert gas). Argon was discovered (1894) in air by the chemists Lord Rayleigh and Sir William Ramsay. It makes up 0.93% of the atmosphere by volume. Obtained commercially by the fractionation of liquid air, it is used in electric light bulbs, fluorescent tubes, argon lasers, arc welding, and semiconductor production. The element has no known true compounds. Properties: at.no. 18; at.wt. 39.948; sp.gr. 0.0017837g $cm^{-3}$; m.p. −308.9°F (−189.4°C); b.p. −302.6°F (−185.9°C).

**argonaut** (paper nautilus) Ocean-dwelling cephalopod MOLLUSK found in many parts of the world. Related to the OCTOPUS, it has eight arms with suckers. Two of the female's arms are modified to secrete a coiled, paper-thin, ridged shell that is an egg-case. Length: to 40cm (16in). Family Argonautidae.

**Argonauts** In Greek legend, 50 heroes, including HERACLES, ORPHEUS, and CASTOR AND POLLUX, who sailed the ship *Argo* to Colchis, a kingdom at the E end of the Black Sea, in search of the GOLDEN FLEECE. Their leader was JASON, husband of MEDEA.

**Argus** Name of three figures in Greek legend. One was a giant with 100 eyes, half of which remained open at all times. Another was the shipbuilder who built the ship Argo for JASON and became a member of the crew. Argus was also the name of the dog who recognized ODYSSEUS on his return to Ithaca.

**aria** Solo song with instrumental accompaniment, or a lyrical instrumental piece. An important element of operas, cantatas, and oratorios, the aria form originated in the 17th century.

**Ariadne** In Greek mythology, Cretan princess (daughter of MINOS) who fell in love with THESEUS but was abandoned by him after saving him from the Minotaur. She was consoled by the god DIONYSUS, whom she later married.

**Arianism** Theological school based on the teachings of Arius (*c.*AD 250–336), considered heretical by orthodox Christianity. Arius taught that Christ was a created being, and that the Son, though divine, was neither equal nor co-eternal with the Father. Arianism was condemned by the first Council of NICAEA (325).

**Aries** (Ram) First constellation of the zodiac. In mythology, it represents the lamb with the golden fleece.

**Ariosto, Ludovico** (1474–1533) Italian Renaissance poet. In 1503 Ariosto became a servant of Cardinal d'Este and from 1517 until his death served the duke of Ferrara. Ariosto's masterpiece, *Orlando Furioso* (published 1532), was intended to glorify the Este family. *Orlando Furioso* follows several love stories from the era of Charlemagne, when Christian knights and Saracens fought for control of Christendom.

**Aristarchus of Samos** (310–230 BC) Greek mathematician and astronomer. Aristarchus tried to calculate the distances of the Sun and Moon from Earth, as well as their sizes. Although his method was sound the results were inaccurate. He was the first to propose that the Sun is the center of the Universe (heliocentric theory); the idea was not taken up because it did not seem to make the calculation of planetary positions any easier.

**Aristophanes** (448–380 BC) Greek comic playwright. Of his more than 40 plays, only 11 survive, the only extant comedies from the period. All follow the same basic plan: caricatures of contemporary Athenians become involved in absurd situations. Graceful, choral lyrics frame caustic personal attacks. A conservative, Aristophanes parodied EURIPIDES' innovations in drama, and satirized the philosophical radicalism of SOCRATES and Athens' expansionist policies. The importance of the chorus in the early works is reflected in the titles, such as *The Wasps* (422 BC) *The Birds* (414 BC) and *The Frogs* (405 BC). Other notable plays include *The Clouds* (423 BC) and *Lysistrata* (411 BC).

A

## ARMENIA

**AREA:** 11,506sq mi (29,800sq km)
**POPULATION:** 3,667,000
**CAPITAL (POPULATION):** Yerevan (1,254,000)
**GOVERNMENT:** Multiparty republic
**ETHNIC GROUPS:** Armenian 93%, Azerbaijani 3%, Russian, Kurd
**LANGUAGES:** Armenian (official)
**RELIGIONS:** Christianity (mainly Armenian Apostolic)
**CURRENCY:** Dram = 100 couma

**Aristotle** (384–322 BC) Greek philosopher, founder of the science of LOGIC and one of the greatest figures in Western philosophy, b. Macedonia. Aristotle studied (367–347 BC) under PLATO at the ACADEMY in Athens. After Plato's death he tutored the young ALEXANDER THE GREAT, before founding the Lyceum (335 BC). In direct opposition to Plato's IDEALISM, Aristotle's METAPHYSICS is based on the principle that all knowledge proceeds directly from observation of the particular. Aristotle argued that a particular object can only be explained through an understanding of causality. He outlined four causes: the **material** cause (an object's substance); **formal** cause (design); **efficient** cause (maker); and the **final** cause (function). For Aristotle this final cause was the primary one. Form was inherent in matter. His ethical philosophy stressed the exercise of rationality in political and intellectual life. Aristotle's writings cover nearly every branch of human knowledge, from statecraft to astronomy. His principal works are the *Organon* (six treatises on logic and SYLLOGISM); *Politics* (the conduct of the state); *Poetics* (analysis of poetry and TRAGEDY); and *Rhetoric*.

**arithmetic** Calculations and reckoning using numbers and such operations as addition, subtraction, multiplication, and division. The study of arithmetic traditionally involved learning procedures for operations such as long division and extraction of square roots. The procedures of arithmetic were put on a formal axiomatic basis by Giuseppe Peano in the late 19th century. Using certain postulates, including that there is a unique natural number, 1, it is possible to give formal definition of the set of natural numbers and the arithmetical operations. Thus, addition is interpretable in terms of combining sets: in $2 + 7 = 9$, 9 is the cardinal number of a set produced by combining sets of 2 and 7. Multiplication can be thought of as repeated additions: subtraction and division are the inverse operations of addition and multiplication.

**arithmetic progression** Sequence of numbers in which each term is produced by adding a constant term (the common difference $d$) to the preceding one. It has the form $a, a + d, a + 2d$, and so on. An example is the sequence 1, 3, 5, .... The sum of such a progression, $a + (a + d) + (a + 2d) + ...$ is an arithmetic series. For $n$ terms, it has a value $\frac{1}{2}n\,[2a + 0.5(n - 1)d]$.

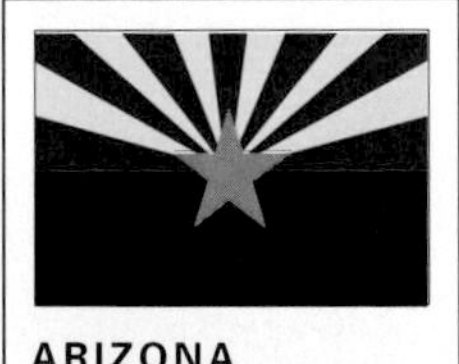

**ARIZONA**
**Statehood:**
14 February 1912
**Nickname:**
The Grand Canyon State
**State bird:**
Cactus wren
**State flower:**
Saguaro (giant cactus)
**State tree:**
Paloverde
**State motto:**
God enriches

**Arizona** Southwestern state, bordering on Mexico. The capital is PHOENIX; other cities include Tucson and Mesa. After the end of the MEXICAN WAR (1848), Mexico ceded most of the present state to the US, and it became the 48th state of the Union in 1912. The Colorado Plateau occupies the N part of the state, and is cut by many steep canyons, notably the GRAND CANYON, through which the COLORADO RIVER flows. Arizona's mineral resources, grazing, and farmland have long been mainstays of the economy. Mining and agriculture are still important, but since the 1950s manufacturing has been the most profitable sector. The state has many scenic attractions (including the Petrified Forest, Fort Apache, and the reconstructed London Bridge at Lake Havasu). Tourism is now a major source of income. It also has the largest Native American population of any US state (203,527 in 1990), with Indian reservations comprising 28% of the land area. Between 1950 and 1970 Arizona's population more than doubled; in the 1970s its annual growth rate was more than 35%, and it grew a further 41.1% between 1980 and 1992. Area: 113,909sq mi (295,025sq km). Pop. (1992) 3,832,368.

**ark** According to Genesis 6, the floating house Noah was ordered to build and live in with his family and one pair of each living creature during the flood. As the flood waters receded, it came to rest on a mountain top, believed to be Mount ARARAT.

**Arkansas** South-central state, bounded on the E by the Mississippi River. The capital (and only large city) is LITTLE ROCK. It was acquired by the LOUISIANA PURCHASE (1803) and was admitted to the Union as the 25th state in 1836. Arkansas was one of the 11 Confederate states during the American Civil War. In the E and S the land is low, providing excellent farmland for cotton, rice, and soybeans. The principal waterway is the ARKANSAS River, which (like all the state's rivers) drains into the Mississippi. The NW of the state, including part of the Ozarks, is higher land. Forests are extensive and economically important. Bauxite processing, timber and chemicals are the main industries. Noted for its resistance to black equality in the 1960s, Arkansas is home to President Bill CLINTON. Area: 53,104sq mi (137,539sq km). Pop. (1992) 2,394,253.

**Arkansas** River with its source high up in the Rockies of central Colorado, and flowing 1,450mi (2,335km) to the Mississippi River in SE Arkansas. Fourth-longest river in the US, it flows E through Kansas and SE across the NE corner of Oklahoma, and SE to Arkansas.

**Ark of the Covenant** In Jewish tradition, a gold-covered chest of acacia that contained the stone tablets on which the TEN COMMANDMENTS were inscribed. It rested in the Holy of Holies within the tabernacle. Only the high priest could look upon the Ark, and no one could touch it. In Palestine, the Israelites set up a resting place for the Ark in Shiloh. In the 10th century BC, the Ark was moved to the temple built by SOLOMON in Jerusalem. After the destruction of the temple in 586 BC, there is no further record of the Ark's location. In today's synagogues, the Ark of the Covenant is a closet or recess in which the sacred scrolls of the congregation are kept.

**Arkwright, Sir Richard** (1732–92) English inventor and industrialist. Arkwright introduced powered machinery to the textile industry with his water-driven frame for spinning; he started work on the machine in 1764 and patented his invention in 1769.

**Arlington** County in N Virginia, across the Potomac River from Washington, D.C. Since 1943 it has been the location of the PENTAGON as well as Arlington National Cemetery (1864). The 500 acre (200ha) cemetery, built on the former estate of Robert E. LEE, contains the Tomb of the Unknown Soldier, a memorial amphitheater, and the graves of many servicemen and prominent Americans. Originally a part of the District of Columbia, it was made a county of Virginia in 1847. Pop. (1990) 170,936.

**Armada, Spanish** (1588) Fleet launched by the Catholic PHILIP II of Spain against England to overthrow the Protestant ELIZABETH I. English support for the rebels in the Spanish Netherlands and pirate attacks on Spanish possessions convinced Philip that England must be conquered. The 130 ships of the Armada were supposed to collect troops from the Netherlands but, hampered by English attacks and poor planning, this proved impossible. After an indecisive engagement with the English off Gravelines, the Spanish ships ran out of ammunition. They withdrew around N Scotland. Though a blow to Spanish prestige, the defeat had little effect on the balance of naval power.

**armadillo** Nocturnal burrowing mammal found from Texas to Argentina, noted for the armor of bony plates that protect its back and sides. When attacked, some species roll into a defensive ball. It eats insects, carrion, and plants. Length: 5–60in (30–150cm). Family Dasypodidae.

**Armageddon** Place referred to in Revelation 16, where the final battle between the demonic kings of the Earth and the forces of God will be fought at the end of the world. The name is derived from the Hebrew *har megiddo* ("hill of MEGIDDO").

**Armagh** City and county in SE Northern Ireland, near the border with the Republic of Ireland. The town became an ecclesiastical center in the 5th century and is now the seat of Roman Catholic and Protestant archbishops. It was settled by Protestants in the 16th century. The county is low-lying in the N and hilly in the S. Much of the land is used for farming and the town is a market center for agricultural produce. Lurgan and Portadown are centers for textiles and light industries. Area: 261sq mi (676sq km). Pop. (county, 1991) 67,128; (town, 1991) 14, 625.

**Armagnacs** Faction supporting the Duke of Orléans in the early 15th-century civil war in France. Led by Bernard VII, Count of Armagnac, they opposed the BURGUNDIANS led by John, Duke of Burgundy, who was allied with the English in this phase of the HUNDRED YEARS WAR.

**Armenia** Republic in the S Caucasus; the capital is YEREVAN. **Land and climate** Armenia is a rugged mountainous republic. The highest peak is Mount Aragats, 13,420ft (4,090m). Armenia has severe winters and cool summers, but the total yearly rainfall is generally low, between 8–30in (200–800mm). The lowest land is in the NE and NW, where Yerevan is situated. Armenia has many fast-flowing rivers, which have cut deep gorges in the plateau. The major river is the Araks. The largest lake is Lake Sevan, containing 90% of all Armenia's standing water. Vegetation ranges from tundra to grassy steppe. Oak forests are found in the SE, beech in the NE. **History and politics** Armenia was an advanced ancient kingdom, considered to be one of the original sites of iron and bronze smelting. A nation was established in the 6th century BC, and Alexander the Great expelled the Persians in 330 BC. In 69 BC Armenia was incorporated into the Roman empire. In AD 303 Armenia became the first country to adopt Christianity as its state religion. From 886–1046 Armenia was an independent kingdom. From the 11th–15th centuries the Mongols were the greatest power in the region. By the 16th century Armenia was controlled by the Ottoman empire. Despite religious discrimination, the Armenians generally prospered under Turkish rule. In 1828 Russia acquired Persian Armenia, and (with promises of religious toleration) many Armenians moved into the Russian-controlled area. In Turkish Armenia, nationalist movements were encouraged by British promises of protection. The Turkish response was uncompromising and it is estimated that 200,000 Armenians were killed in 1896 alone. In the Russian sector, a process of Russification was enforced. During World War I, Armenia was the battleground for the Turkish and Russian armies. Armenians were accused of aiding the Russians, and Turkish atrocities intensified. Over 600,000 Armenians were killed by Turkish troops, and 1.75 million were deported to Syria and Palestine. In 1918 Russian Armenia became the Armenian Autonomous Republic, the W part remained part of Turkey, and the NW part of Iran. In 1922 Armenia, Azerbaijan, and Georgia were federated to form the Transcaucasian Soviet Socialist Republic (one of the four original republics in the Soviet Union). In 1936 Armenia became a separate republic. Earthquakes in 1984 and 1988 destroyed many cities and killed more than 80,000 people. In 1988 war broke out between Armenia and Azerbaijan over NAGORNO-KARABAKH (an Armenian enclave in Azerbaijan). In 1990 the Armenian parliament voted to break from the Soviet Union, and in 1991 joined the newly-established COMMONWEALTH OF INDEPENDENT STATES (CIS). In 1992 Armenia invaded Azerbaijan and occupied Nagorno-Karabakh. In 1994, an uneasy ceasefire left Armenia in control of about 20% of Azerbaijan. **Economy** Armenia is a lower-middle-income nation. The economy, badly hit by war with Azerbaijan, is in a state of transition. Under communist rule, most economic activity was controlled by the state. Since 1991 the government has encouraged free enterprise, selling farmland and state-owned businesses. Armenia is highly industrialized, production is dominated by mining and chemicals. Copper is the chief metal; gold, lead, and zinc are also mined. Agriculture (centered around the River Araks) is the second-largest sector, with cotton, tobacco, fruit, and rice the main products. Despite significant increases in production, Armenia is still dependent on food imports.

**Arminius, Jacobus** (1560–1609) Dutch theologian whose system of beliefs, especially concerning salvation, became widespread and was later known as Arminianism. Arminius rejected the notion of PREDESTINATION developed by John CALVIN, in favor of a more liberal concept of conditional election and universal redemption. He believed that God will elect to everlasting life those who are prepared to respond in faith to the offer of divine salvation. Arminianism finally achieved official recognition in the Netherlands in 1795. It was a major influence on METHODISM.

**Armistice Day** *See* VETERANS' DAY

**Armory Show** Landmark exhibition of contemporary American and European art held in New York in 1913. The European section caused the greatest excitement. It looked back to IMPRESSIONISM, tracing the history of modernism through NEO-IMPRESSIONISM and POSTIMPRESSIONISM, but came right up to date with examples of CUBISM, ORPHISM, and DADA. Marcel Duchamps's painting *Nude Descending a Staircase* caused the most controversy. The exhibition traveled successfully to Chicago and Boston, attracting an estimated half a million visitors. It put avant-garde European art on the American map and revolutionized the country's attitudes, provoking an interest in contemporary art.

**arms control** Activity undertaken by powerful nations to prevent mutual destruction in warfare, especially with nuclear weapons. The nations attempt to maintain a balance of power by regulating each other's stockpile of weapons. *See also* DISARMAMENT; STRATEGIC ARMS LIMITATION TALKS (SALT)

**arms race** Rivalry between states or blocs of states to achieve supremacy in military strength. The first modern instance was the race between Germany and Britain to build up their navies before World War I. The term refers principally to the race in nuclear weapons between the Soviet Union and the US after World War II, during the COLD WAR. Examples of arms races at regional level are that of Israel and the Arab states in the Middle East, which started in the 1950s, and of Iran and Iraq in the 1980s.

**Armstrong, (Daniel) Louis** (1900–71) US jazz trumpeter, singer and bandleader, nicknamed "Satchmo" (satchel mouth). Armstrong was one of the most distinctive sounds in 20th-century music. His career spanned over half a century. Armstrong learned to play in New Orleans, and in 1922 joined the King Oliver band. The Hot Fives and Hot Sevens recordings (1925–29) are some of the most influential in the history of jazz. In the 1930s he became a successful bandleader. He also appeared in films such as *Pennies from Heaven* (1936), *New Orleans* (1947), and *High Society* (1956).

**Armstrong, Neil Alden** (1930– ) US astronaut. Armstrong was chosen as a NASA astronaut in 1962 and was the command pilot for the Gemini 8 orbital flight in 1966. On July 20, 1969, he became the first man to walk on the Moon, remarking that it was "one small step for man, one giant leap for mankind."

◄ **Armstrong** Following his highly successful career as an astronaut, during which time he became the first man to walk on the Moon, Neil Armstrong remained a highly influential figure in the world of aerospace and aeronautics.

**ARKANSAS**
**Statehood:** 15 June 1836
**Nickname:** The Land of Opportunity
**State bird:** Mockingbird
**State flower:** Apple Blossom
**State tree:** Pine tree
**State motto:** The people rule

A

▲ **arrowroot** The West Indian island of St. Vincent is the main source of arrowroot (*Maranta arundinacea*). It has rhizomes that produce a starchy powder used for thickening sauces.

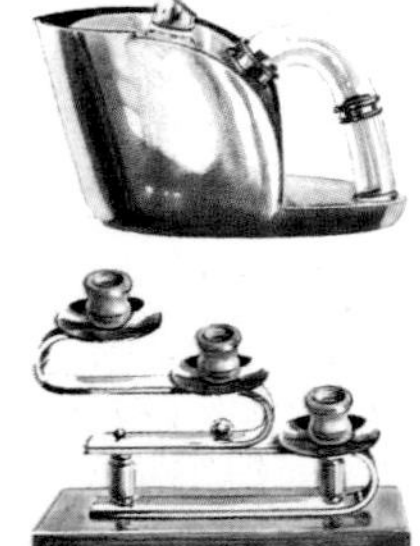

▲ **art deco** Examples of art deco-style goods, fashionable during the 1920s and 1930s.

**army** Organized group of soldiers trained to fight on land, usually rigidly hierarchical in structure. The first evidence of an army comes from Sumer in the third millennium BC. The Hittites were first to use cavalry and the Assyrians added archers and developed siege machines. In the Middle Ages armies used improved armor and weapons. The short-term feudal levy by which these armies were raised proved inflexible, and this led to the use of mercenaries. Heavy cavalry was replaced by a combination of infantry and archery. The end of the Hundred Years War saw the inception of royal standing armies and an end to the chaos caused by mercenary armies. Muskets and bayonets replaced the combinations of longbow, pike, and infantry, and ARTILLERY was much improved. In the French Revolutionary Wars a citizen army was raised by CONSCRIPTION and contained various specialist groups. Other European armies followed suit and the age of the mass national army began. The invention of the MACHINE GUN brought about the deadlock of the trench warfare of World War I, which was broken by the TANK, and World War II saw highly mechanized and mobile armies whose logistics of supply and support demanded an integration of the land, sea, and air forces. Since World War II nuclear weapons have been deployed both tactically and strategically, and again the nature of weaponry has determined an army's structure.

**Army, British** Ground service of the UK armed forces. In 1995 Regular Army personnel numbered *c.*116,000, including *c.*6,000 women and *c.*10,000 personnel overseas. Since 1945 it has formed part of NORTH ATLANTIC TREATY ORGANIZATION (NATO) forces and maintained overseas garrisons in such areas as Falklands, Cyprus, and Gibraltar. The monarch is the official head of the British Army. Control of all British armed forces is exercised by the Ministry of Defence, headed by the secretary of state for defense. In addition to the Regular Army there is a reserve force of *c.*230,000, over 80,000 of which is in the Territorial Army (TA) and the remainder in the Regular Army Reserve.

**Army, US** Ground service of the US armed forces. In 1995 active army personnel numbered *c.*525,000, 32% stationed overseas. Army personnel are under the general supervision of the secretary of the army and his adviser, the army chief of staff, who is the army's highest ranking officer and a member of the Joint Chiefs of Staff. The president is commander in chief of the armed forces. The Department of the Army is charged with the organization, training, and equipping of these forces, but not their military deployment. The army also provides assistance in disaster relief, conducts weapons research, carries on training at civilian colleges, and administers the US Military Academy at West Point. The army has active divisions and helps to maintain National Guard and reserve divisions; major overseas commands are the Seventh Army in Europe and the Eighth Army in Korea. The Continental Army existed from 1775, but the first regular standing army was authorized by Congress in 1785. The War Department was established in 1789. The Department of War became the Department of the Army in 1947, and in 1949 it became a part of the Department of DEFENSE. The US Army has taken part in all major wars between the War of 1812 and the Vietnam War. A draft was occasionally employed and was used in peacetime after World War II. In 1973, Congress established an all-volunteer Army. In 1980, Congress resumed draft registration for 18-year-old men, and women were, for the first time, among the graduates at West Point.

**Arnhem** City in E central Netherlands. An important trading center since medieval times, Arnhem was almost destroyed by an abortive Allied airborne attack in 1944. Industries: metallurgy, textiles, electrical equipment, chemicals. Pop. (1994 est.) 133,670.

**Arnold, Benedict** (1741–1801) American colonial soldier. During the American Revolution Arnold commanded Philadelphia (1778), after being wounded at the Battle of SARATOGA. In 1780 he became commander of West Point, a fort he planned to betray to the British for money. After the plot was discovered, Arnold fled to the British. His name has become proverbial in modern US usage for treachery

**Arnold, Malcolm** (1921– ) English composer. Arnold started his career as principal trumpet with the London Philharmonic Orchestra but won immediate acclaim for his compositions. His style is easily accessible and his output includes symphonies, concertos, overtures (*Beckus the Dandipratt*, 1943), ballets (*Homage to the Queen*, 1953), and movie scores (*The Bridge on the River Kwai*, 1957).

**Arnold, Matthew** (1822–88) English poet and critic. His writings include literary criticism, such as *Essays in Criticism* (series 1, 1865; series 2, 1888), and social commentary, such as *Culture and Anarchy* (1869), as well as such classic Victorian poems as "Dover Beach" and "The Scholar Gypsy." His theories about the social and moral benefits of culture are largely responsible for the establishment of English literature as a "core" subject in schools and universities.

**Arnulf** (850–99) King of the East FRANKS (887–99); last CAROLINGIAN Holy Roman emperor (896–99). Arnulf defeated his uncle CHARLES III (THE FAT) and was proclaimed king. He successfully resisted the Norse invasion (891). At the request of the pope, Arnulf invaded Italy (894), captured Rome (895), and was crowned emperor (896).

**Aroostook War** (1838–39) Dispute over the Maine-New Brunswick boundary. The Aroostook Valley was claimed by both Canada and the US, and a conflict arose over Canadian lumber operations in the area. In 1839 a contingent of 50 Maine militia men also moved into the valley. War loomed, but US general Winfield Scott negotiated a truce, and the dispute was submitted to a commission. It was settled by the Webster-Ashburton Treaty (1842).

**Arp, Jean (Hans)** (1887–1966) Alsatian sculptor, painter and poet. Arp founded the Zurich DADA movement with the Romanian artists Tristan Tzara, Marcel Janco, and others during World War I. He worked briefly with the BLAUE REITER group, and in the 1920s joined the SURREALISM movement. Arp's sculpture spans the divide between Dada humor and the purity of noniconic ABSTRACT ART. *Navel Shirt and Head* (1926) and *Human Concretion* (1935) are typical.

**arrhythmia** Irregularity in the rhythm of the heartbeat. Various abnormalities include atrial tachycardia (fast heartbeat), atrial flutter, and atrial fibrillation, in which there is erratic and ineffective atrial contraction. In the course of normal activity, however, the heart rate of a healthy person will have some variety.

**arrowroot** Tropical and subtropical perennial plant found in wet habitats of North and South America, and some islands of the West Indies. Its leaves are lance-shaped and the flowers are usually white. The dried and ground roots are used in cooking. Family Marantaceae; species *Maranta undinaceae*.

**arsenic** (symbol As) Semimetallic element of Group V of the periodic table, probably obtained (1250) by Albertus Magnus. Compounds containing arsenic are used as a poison, and to harden lead and make semiconductors. Three allotropes are known: white arsenic, black arsenic, and a yellow nonmetallic form. Properties: at.no. 33; at.wt. 74.9216; sp.gr. 5.7; sublimes 613°C (1,135°F); most common isotope $^{75}$As.

**art** See PAINTING, SCULPTURE, DRAWING, ARCHITECTURE

**Artaud, Antonin** (1896–1948) Influential French drama theorist and director. In 1927 Artaud cofounded the Théâtre Alfred Jarry, which produced surreal, symbolist plays. His most significant contribution to 20th-century drama was the concept of the theater of CRUELTY. Influenced by the psychoanalytical theories of Carl JUNG, Artaud proposed a physical theater based on unconscious myth and symbol, rather than narrative and psychological realism. His most important work was the volume of essays *The Theater and its Double* (1938).

**art deco** Fashionable style of design and interior decoration in the 1920s and 1930s. It took its name from the *Exposition Internationale des Arts Décoratifs et Industriels Modernes* held in Paris (1925). The art deco style is characterized by sleek forms, simplified lines, and geometric patterns.

**Artemis** In Greek mythology, the goddess of hunting and light, identified as DIANA by the Romans. She was the daughter of ZEUS and Leto, and twin sister of APOLLO. Associated with the Moon, she was a virgin who assisted in childbirth and protected infants and animals.

**arteriosclerosis** Blanket term for degenerative diseases of the arteries, in particular ATHEROSCLEROSIS (hardening of the arteries). It is caused by deposits of fatty materials and scar tissue on the ARTERY walls, which narrow the channel and restrict blood flow, causing an increased risk of heart disease, stroke or gangrene. Evidence suggests that predisposition to the disease is hereditary. Risk factors include cigarette smoking, inactivity, obesity, and a diet rich in animal fats and refined sugar. Treatment is by drugs and, in some cases, surgery.

**artery** One of the BLOOD VESSELS that carry BLOOD away from the HEART. The **pulmonary** artery carries deoxygenated blood from the heart to the lungs, but all other arteries carry oxygenated blood to the body's tissues. An artery's walls are thick, elastic, and muscular and pulsate as they carry the blood. A severed artery causes major HEMORRHAGE.

**artesian well** Well from which water is forced out naturally under pressure. Artesian wells are bored where water in a layer of porous rock is sandwiched between two layers of impervious rock. The water-filled layer is called an AQUIFER. Water flows up to the surface because distant parts of the aquifer are higher than the wellhead.

**arthritis** Inflammation of the joints, with pain and restricted mobility. The most common forms are osteoarthritis and rheumatoid arthritis. **Osteoarthritis**, common among the elderly, occurs with erosion of joint cartilage and degenerative changes in the underlying bone. It is treated with analgesics and anti-inflammatories and, in some cases (especially a diseased hip), by joint replacement surgery. **Rheumatoid arthritis**, more common in women, is generally more disabling. It is an autoimmune disease which may disappear of its own accord but is usually slowly progressive. Treatment includes analgesics to relieve pain. The most severe cases may need to be treated with CORTISONE injections, drugs to suppress immune activity or joint replacement surgery. *See also* RHEUMATISM

**arthropod** Member of the largest animal phylum, Arthropoda. Living forms include CRUSTACEA, ARACHNID, CENTIPEDE, MILLIPEDE, and INSECT. The species (numbering well over one million) are thought to have evolved from ANNELIDS. All have a hard outer skin of CHITIN that is attached to the muscular system on the inside. The body is divided into segments, modified among different groups, with each segment originally carrying a pair of jointed legs. In some animals some of the legs have evolved into jaws, sucking organs or weapons. Arthropods have well-developed digestive, circulatory and nervous systems.

**Arthur** Legendary British king who was said to rule the Knights of the Round Table. Two medieval chroniclers, Gildas and Nennius, tell of Arthur's fighting against the invading West Saxons and his final defeat of them at Mount Badon (possibly Badbury Hill, Dorset) in the early 6th century. However, some consider these sources unreliable and a modern view is that Arthur was a professional soldier in service to the British kings after the Roman occupation. Geoffrey of Monmouth's 12th century *Historia Regum Brittaniae*, based on Nennius and Welsh folklore, gave the legend – with the Round Table, Camelot, Lancelot, Guinevere, and the Holy Grail – the form in which it was transmitted through the Middle Ages.

**Arthur, Chester Alan** (1830–86) 21st US president (1881–85). In 1880 Arthur was nominated by the Republican Party as vice president in the (justified) hope that he could deliver New York. He became president after the assassination of James GARFIELD and tried to reform the spoils system, in which incoming presidents replaced government staff with their own appointees. A Civil Service Commission with a merit system was created, but Arthur's modest reforms were often frustrated by Congress. Gentlemanly but uninspiring, and suffering from incurable illness, he was not renominated (1884). He was succeeded by Grover CLEVELAND.

**Arthurian romance** In literature, the numerous medieval stories based on the largely apocryphal life of King ARTHUR of Britain and his knights. The 9th century *Historia Brittonum* by Nennius contains the first references to Arthur as a Christian warrior. Geoffrey of Monmouth's *Historia Regum Brittaniae* (*c*.1135) embellishes the tale with details of Excalibur (his sword), Merlin the prophet, the CHIVALRY of Arthur's knights, Mordred's treachery and Arthur's voyage to Avalon. Wace's *Roman de Brut* (1155) translated the tale into French. CHRÉTIEN DE TROYES added the story of the quest for the Holy Grail, which in turn inspired von Eschenbach's *Parzival* (1200–12). Sir Thomas Malory's *Morte d'Arthur* (1485) synthesized all the previous Arthurian material into a coherent cycle. More recent interpretations of the legend include Tennyson's *Idylls of the King* (1859–88).

**ARTHRITIS**

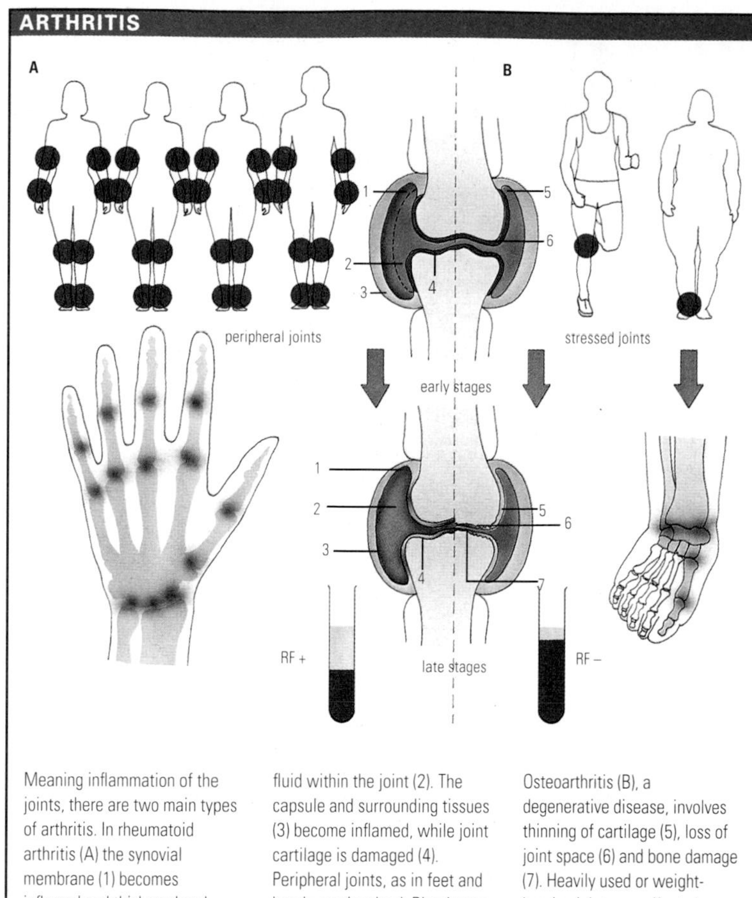


Meaning inflammation of the joints, there are two main types of arthritis. In rheumatoid arthritis (A) the synovial membrane (1) becomes inflamed and thickened and produces increased synovial fluid within the joint (2). The capsule and surrounding tissues (3) become inflamed, while joint cartilage is damaged (4). Peripheral joints, as in feet and hands, are involved. Blood tests show rheumatoid factor. Osteoarthritis (B), a degenerative disease, involves thinning of cartilage (5), loss of joint space (6) and bone damage (7). Heavily used or weight-bearing joints are affected. Blood tests are normal.

**artichoke** (globe artichoke) Tall, thistlelike perennial plant with large, edible, immature flower heads, native to the Mediterranean region. It has spiny leaves and blue flowers. Height: 3–5ft (0.9–1.5m). Family Asteraceae/Compositae; species *Cynara scolymus*. A different plant, the Jerusalem artichoke, is grown for its edible tubers. Family Asteraceae/Compositae; species *Helianthus tuberosus*.

**Articles of Confederation** (1781) First Federal constitution of the US, drafted by the Continental Congress in 1777. Distrust of central authority and state rivalries produced a weak central government, with Congress dependent on the states and unable to enforce its own legislation. The weakness of the Articles was analyzed by Alexander Hamilton and James MADISON in *The Federalist*, and the CONSTITUTIONAL CONVENTION met in 1787 to draft a new constitution.

**artificial insemination** Method of inducing PREGNANCY without sexual intercourse by injecting SPERM into the female genital tract. Used extensively in livestock farming, artificial insemination allows proven sires to breed with many females at low cost.

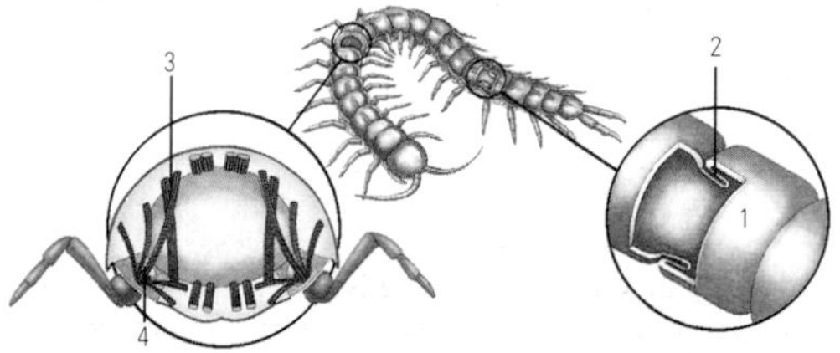


◀ **arthropod** The most numerous invertebrates (animals without a backbone) are the arthropods (joint-legged animals), such as the centipede. They owe their success to the exoskeleton that covers their bodies and allows the development of jointed limbs. Body segments are encased in a rigid protein cuticle (1) and body flexibility is permitted by an overlapping membrane (2). The strength of the exoskeleton ensures that muscles (3) can be anchored to the inside of the cuticle. Groups of muscles (4) are used to move the legs.

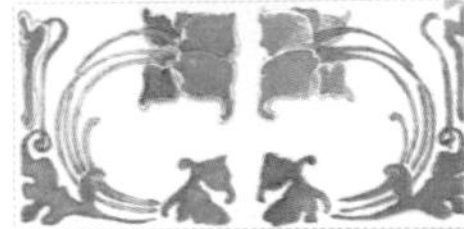

▲ **art nouveau** Examples of art nouveau style, popular during the early 1890s through the 1910s.

▼ **ash** The white ash (*Fraxinus americana*) of E North America grows to 135ft (41m). The leaves of the ash are distinctive in being split into many small leaflets giving the impression of very fine foliage.

**artificial intelligence (AI)** Science concerned with developing computers and computer programs that model human intelligence. The most common form of AI involves a computer being programmed to answer questions on a specialized subject. Such "expert systems" are said to display the human ability to perform expert analytical tasks. A closely related science, sometimes known as "artificial life," is concerned with more low-level intelligence. For example, a ROBOT may be programmed to find its way around a maze, displaying the basic ability to interact physically with its surroundings.

**artificial selection** Breeding of plants, animals, or other organisms in which the parents are individually selected in order to perpetuate certain desired traits and eliminate others from the captive population. By this means, most of our domestic crops, livestock, and pets have arisen. Artificial selection can be accelerated by techniques such as plant TISSUE CULTURE and the ARTIFICIAL INSEMINATION of livestock. *See also* GENETIC ENGINEERING; CLONE

**artillery** Projectile-firing weapons with a carriage or mount. An artillery piece is generally one of four types: gun, howitzer, mortar, or missile launcher. Modern artillery is classified according to caliber; ranging from under 105mm for light artillery to more than 155mm for heavy. Advances in the 19th century such as smokeless powder, elongated shells, rifling and rapid-fire breach loading, made artillery indispensable in battle. *See also* CANNON

**art nouveau** Ornamental style which flourished in most of central and W Europe and the US from *c.*1890 to World War I. The idea originated in England with the ARTS AND CRAFTS MOVEMENT. Focusing mainly on the decorative arts, its most characteristic forms come from sinuous distortions of plant forms and asymmetrical lines. Outstanding art nouveau graphic artists included BEARDSLEY, TIFFANY, and Mucha. Charles Rennie MACKINTOSH, Antonio GAUDI, and Victor Horta were among its most gifted architects.

**Arts and Crafts Movement** Late 19th- and early 20th-century British movement led by artists who wanted to revitalize the decorative arts by returning to the ideals of medieval craftsmanship. Inspired by William MORRIS, the movement contributed to European ART NOUVEAU, but was eventually transformed by the acceptance of modern industrial methods.

**Aruba** Dutch island in the Caribbean, off the coast of NW Venezuela; the capital is Oranjestad. It is an autonomous part of the Netherlands. Industries: oil refining, phosphates, tourism. Area: 193sq km (75sq mi). Pop. (1991) 68,897.

**Arunachal Pradesh** State of the eastern Himalayas in the far NE of India. The capital is Itanagar. Once a district of ASSAM, it was invaded by the Chinese (1962), but returned to India in 1963. It became a union territory in 1972 and the 24th state of India in 1986. Most of the state is mountainous forest and jungle. Its main products are coffee, rubber, fruit, spices, and rice. It is India's least densely populated state. Area: 31,438sq mi (81,426sq km). Pop. (1991) 864,558.

**Aryan** Language of an ancient people in the region between the Caspian Sea and Hindu Kush mountains. About 1500 BC one branch entered India, introducing the SANSKRIT language; another branch migrated to Europe. In their 1930s racist propaganda, the Nazis traced German descent from Aryans.

**asbestos** Group of fibrous, naturally occurring, silicate minerals used in insulating, fireproofing, brake lining, and in astronaut suits. Several types exist, the most common being white asbestos. Many countries have banned the use of asbestos, as it can cause lung cancer and asbestosis, a lung disease.

**Ascension** Island in the S Atlantic Ocean; a UK dependency administered from the colony of ST. HELENA. Discovered by the Portuguese (1501), it was occupied by Britain in the early 19th century. It now serves as an Anglo-American intercontinental telecommunications center, and was an important base for British forces and supplies during the FALKLANDS WAR. Area: 34sq mi (88sq km). Pop. (1993) 1,117.

**Ascension Day** Christian feast day that commemorates Christ's ascension into heaven, 40 days after his resurrection. It falls on a Thursday, the 40th day after EASTER. It used to be called Holy Thursday.

**ascorbic acid** *See* VITAMIN

**asexual reproduction** Type of reproduction in organisms that does not involve the union of male and female reproductive cells. It occurs in several forms: FISSION, BUDDING and VEGETATIVE REPRODUCTION. *See also* CLONE; SEXUAL REPRODUCTION

**Asgard** In ancient TEUTONIC MYTHOLOGY, the domain of the gods, who resided there in a variety of splendid palaces. The most famous of these was VALHALLA, to which heroes slain in battle were carried in triumph.

**ash** Group of mainly deciduous trees of the genus *Fraxinus* growing in temperate regions, usually having leaves made up of many small leaflets and winged fruits. The wood is elastic, strong, and shock-resistant, and is widely used for furniture. Species include manna ash, *F. ornus*, the flowering ash of S Europe and Asia Minor; the European ash, *F. excelsior*, which grows to 148ft (45m) tall; and *F. floribunda*, a native of the Himalayas. Family Oleaceae. The mountain ash of Europe and Asia (*Sorbus aucuparia*) comes from a different family.

**Ashanti** Administrative region and ethnic group of central Ghana, W Africa. The capital is KUMASI. The Ashanti people (a matrilineal society) established a powerful empire based on the slave trade with the British and Dutch. In the 18th century their influence extended into Togo and the Ivory Coast. Conflicts with the British throughout the 19th century were finally resolved in 1902, when the Ashanti territories (a British protectorate since 1896) were declared a crown colony. The society is traditionally agricultural. The region is the main area of Ghana's vital cocoa production. The Ashanti are renowned for their crafts, including high-quality goldwork and weaving. Today, Ashanti is the most populous of Ghana's ten regions. Area: 9,414sq mi (24,390sq km). Pop. (1984) 2,090,100.

**Ashcan school** Nickname given to a group of late 19th- and early 20th-century US artists, including George BELLOWS, Robert HENRI, and Edward HOPPER, who rejected academic and traditional artistic subjects for the seamier aspects of city life (especially in New York). The inspiration for the group's interest in everyday life came from four core members, William Glackens, John Sloan, George Luks, and Everett Shinn, all of whom worked as artist-reporters in Philadelphia before joining Henri's circle.

**Ashdown, Paddy (Jeremy John Durham)** (1941– ) British politician, first leader of the Social and LIBERAL DEMOCRATS (1988– ), b. India. Ashdown entered parliament in 1983 and quickly became a leading spokesman for the LIBERAL PARTY. He succeeded David STEEL, who stood down as Liberal leader when the merger with the SOCIAL DEMOCRATIC PARTY (SDP) was formalized.

**Ashe, Arthur Robert** (1943–93) US tennis player. Ashe won the US (1968), Australian (1970), and Wimbledon (1975) championships. Heart surgery (1979) ended his tournament career, but in 1980 he became the nonplaying captain of the US Davis Cup team. He died of AIDS contracted from a blood transfusion.

**Ashgabat** (formerly Ashkhabad) Capital of the central Asian republic of Turkmenistan, located 25mi (40km) from the Iranian border. Founded in 1881 as a Russian fortress between the Kara-Kum Desert and the Kopet Dagh Mountains, it was largely rebuilt after an earthquake in 1948. Its present name was adopted after the republic attained independence from the former Soviet Union in 1992. Industries: textiles, carpets, silk, metalware, glass, light machinery. Pop. (1990) 411,000.

**Ashikaga** City in central Japan, 50mi (80km) N of Tokyo. An ancient silk-weaving center, it was the home of the Ashikaga shōgunate (1338–1573). Sites include a sacred 12th century temple and an important library of Chinese classics. Pop. (1990) 167,687

**Ashkenazim** Jews who originally settled in NW Europe, as distinguished from the SEPHARDIM, who settled in Spain and Portugal.

**Ashkenazy, Vladimir** (1937– ) Icelandic pianist and conductor, b. Russia. Ashkenazy's interpretations of Russian piano music (especially Rachmaninov) earned international praise, and he shared first prize in the Tchaikovsky Piano Competition (1962). He was principal conductor of the Philharmonia Orchestra (1981–86) and the Royal Philharmonic Orchestra (1987– ).

**Ashoka** (*c*.271–238 BC) Indian emperor (r.264–238 BC). The greatest emperor of the MAURYA EMPIRE, he at first fought to expand his empire. Ashoka was disgusted by the bloodshed of war and, renouncing conquest by force, embraced BUDDHISM. He became one of its most fervent supporters and spread its ideas through missionaries to neighboring countries and through edicts engraved on pillars. His empire encompassed most of India and large areas of Afghanistan.

**Ashton, Sir Frederick** (1904–88) British choreographer and ballet director. In 1935 Ashton joined the Sadler's Wells Ballet (now the Royal Ballet) in London and was its chief choreographer until 1963, then its director (1963–70). His gifted work for dancers such as Margot FONTEYN and Ninette de VALOIS earned him a reputation as Britain's greatest choreographer. His major pieces include *Cinderella* (1948), *Ondine* (1958) and *Marguèrite and Armand* (1963).

**Ashurbanipal** (d. *c*.627 BC) (Assurbanipal) Last great king of ASSYRIA (668–*c*.627 BC). The Assyrian empire was at its height in his reign, reaching into Upper Egypt, before a rapid decline. Excavations at NINEVEH after 1850 revealed an advanced civilization.

**Ash Wednesday** First day of LENT

**Asia** World's largest continent. Entirely in the Eastern Hemisphere, it extends from N of the Arctic Circle in Russia to S of the Equator in Indonesia. **Land** On the W, Asia's boundary with Europe follows a line through the Ural Mountains, W of the CASPIAN SEA and along the Caucasus. Geographically, Europe and Asia are one enormous continent (Eurasia) but historically they have always been regarded as separate continents. Asia has six regions, each defined largely by mountain ranges. Northern Asia includes the massive inhospitable region of SIBERIA. A large part lies within the Arctic Circle, forming a vast cold, treeless plain (tundra). Southern Siberia includes great coniferous forests (taiga) and the Russian steppes. Its S boundary runs through the TIEN SHAN and Yablonovy Mountains and Lake BAIKAL, the world's deepest lake. The high plateau area of Central Asia extends S to the Himalayas and includes the W Chinese provinces of TIBET and SINKIANG as well as MONGOLIA. This is a region of low rainfall and very low winter temperatures. Much of the area is desert, the largest being the GOBI and TAKLA MAKAN. The Tibetan Plateau is mostly barren. Eastern Asia lies between the plateaus of Central Asia and the Pacific. It is a region of highlands and plains, watered by broad rivers. Off the E coast there are many islands, the most important being the Japanese islands of HOKKAIDŌ, HONSHŪ, and KYUSHŪ, and the Chinese island of TAIWAN. Southeast Asia includes the INDOCHINA peninsula, part of which forms the MALAY PENINSULA, BURMA, and a large number of islands, among which the PHILIPPINES and INDONESIA are the most important. The N of this region is mountainous and the S mainly low-lying. Southern Asia consists of the Indian subcontinent and the island of SRI LANKA. In the N it is bounded by the HINDU KUSH, Pamir, KARAKORAM, and the Himalayan Mountains. In the HIMALAYAS is Mount EVEREST, the world's highest mountain. To the S of the mountains lie wide plains, crossed by rivers flowing from the Himalayas. Farther S is the DECCAN Plateau that rises on its E and W edges, culminating in the E and W GHATS. Southwest Asia includes most of the region known as the MIDDLE EAST. It is made up largely of two peninsulas; Anatolia (Asia Minor) and the vast Arabian Peninsula. It is also a region of large inland seas: the Aral, Caspian, Dead and Black

▼ **Asia** The largest continent, Asia is geographically part of an even larger continent, Eurasia. It is home to more than half of the world's population. The people are unevenly distributed; some areas in the centre of the continent are practically uninhabited, whereas parts of India and China are among the world's most densely populated regions.

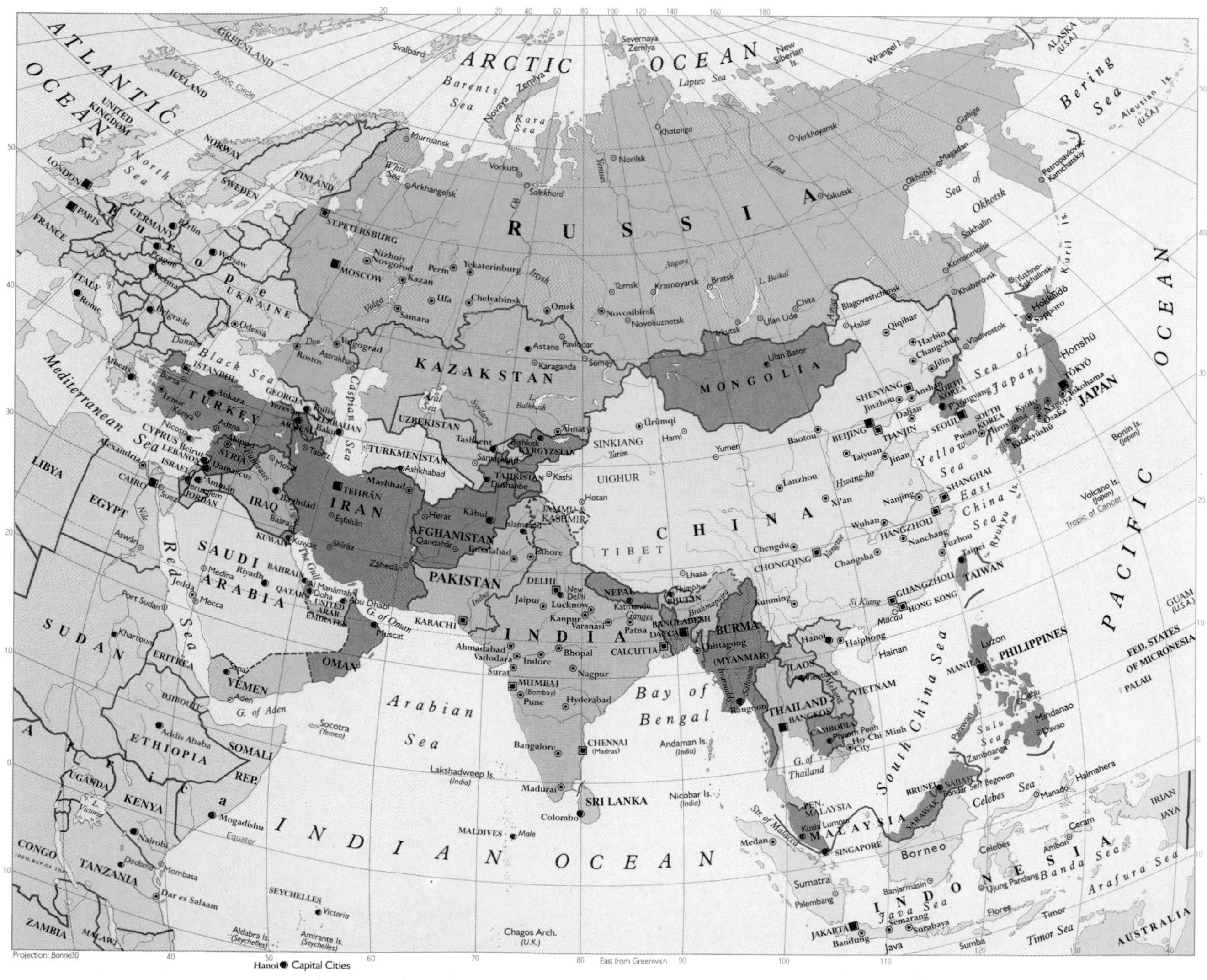

seas. **Structure and geology** The most striking feature of the continent is the massive range of Himalayan fold mountains that were formed when the Indo-Australian and Eurasian tectonic plates collided in the Mesozoic era. Most of China and S central Asia is composed of folded Paleozoic and Mesozoic sediments, and large expanses of central Siberia consist of flat-lying sediments of the same age, some completely exposed. The Indian subcontinent is largely pre-Cambrian except for the Deccan Plateau, which is a complex series of lava flows. **Lakes and rivers** Most of the major Asian lakes are found in the center of the continent, and include the Caspian Sea (the largest landlocked body of water in the world), the ARAL SEA, and lake BALKHASH. The YANGTZE River in China, is Asia's longest. The HUANG HE (Yellow) River is China's other major river. Like these rivers, the three principal waterways of SE Asia (IRRAWADDY, SALWEEN, Mekong) rise on the Tibetan Plateau but flow S instead of E. The INDUS, BRAHMAPUTRA, and GANGES are the largest rivers of the Indian subcontinent, and the OB, YENISEI, and LENA are the continent's major N-flowing rivers, emptying into the Arctic Ocean. **Climate and vegetation** Except for the climate found on W temperate seaboards, all the world's major climatic divisions (with local variations) are represented in the continent. The monsoon climates of India and W Southeast Asia are peculiar to these regions. Large expanses are covered by desert and semi-arid grassland, with belts of coniferous forest to the N and tropical forest to the S. **People** Asians constitute half the world's population. The main language groups are Indo-Aryan, Sino-Tibetan, Ural-Altaic, Malayan, and Semitic. Mandarin Chinese has more speakers than any other single language. HINDUISM is the religion with the most adherents, although it is confined to India and SE Asia. ISLAM, CONFUCIANISM, BUDDHISM, SHINTO, CHRISTIANITY, TAOISM, and JUDAISM are also important, with the Islamic influence stretching from Turkey to Indonesia. **Economy** Agriculture is important, although less than 10% of the continent is cultivated. Asia produces more than 90% of the world's rice, rubber, cotton, and tobacco. Rice is the major crop in the E and S, wheat and barley are grown in the W and N. China, Japan, and Russia are the most highly industrialized countries in terms of traditional heavy materials. Since the 1960s there has been dramatic commercial growth in several countries of SE and E Asia based on a combination of household and high-tech products. Following Japan's example, South Korea, Taiwan, Hong Kong, Singapore, Malaysia, and Thailand form the "tiger" economies. Oil is the most important export of many Middle East countries. **Recent history** Since World War II, the history of Asia has been dominated by three main themes: the legacy of COLONIALISM, the growth of COMMUNISM, and the rise of Islamic FUNDAMENTALISM. The Indian subcontinent gained its independence from Britain in 1947, when India and Pakistan became separate nations. Indonesia achieved formal independence from the Netherlands in 1949. During the 1950s, Indochina and Malaysia won independence from France and Britain respectively after military confrontations. The spread of communism began with the victory of MAO ZEDONG in China in 1949. North Korea failed, in its war with South Korea (1950–53), to establish a united communist state, and communism was also repulsed with Western help in Indonesia. Communism did finally gain control of Vietnam and Cambodia, following the VIETNAM WAR. The breakup of the Soviet Union led to the creation of eight "new" countries in central Asia, few of which were politically stable or economically strong. In the Middle East, Israel remained on uneasy terms with its Arab neighbors, and Iraq was involved in prolonged war with fundamentalist Iran (1980–88) and later with an international coalition, headed by the US, following Iraq's invasion of Kuwait. Total area: 17,139,445sq mi (44,391,206sq km) *Highest mountain* Mount Everest (Nepal) 29,029ft (8,848m) *Longest river* Yangtze (China) 3,716mi (5,980km) *Population* 3,193,000,000 *Largest cities* Shanghai (8,760,000); Tokyo (7,927,000); Beijing (6,560,000) *See also* articles on individual countries

**Asia Minor** (Anatolia) Great peninsula of W Asia making up most of modern Turkey. The Bosporus, the Sea of Marmara, and the Dardanelles divide both Turkey and Europe from Asia. Apart from a very narrow coastal plain, the area is a high, arid plateau. In the SE the Taurus Range rises to more than 12,000ft (3,750m). The area has been inhabited since the Bronze Age, with civilizations such as Troy. The HITTITES established a kingdom here in *c*.1800 BC. From the 8th century BC the Greeks established colonies in the area; the Persians invaded in the 6th century BC and the PERSIAN WARS followed. ALEXANDER THE GREAT's empire included this region, although it split into several states after his death. The Romans unified the area in the 2nd century AD. By the 6th century it had become part of the Byzantine empire. In the 13th–15th centuries it was conquered by the Ottoman Turks and remained part of the Ottoman Empire until the establishment of the Republic of Turkey in 1923.

**Asimov, Isaac** (1920–92) US author and scientist, b. Russia. Although he published several serious scientific works, Asimov is best known for his science fiction novels and short stories. His prolific output contains some of the finest works in the genre, including *I, Robot* (1950) and *The Foundation Trilogy* (1951–53).

**Asmara** (Asmera) Capital of Eritrea, NE Africa. Occupied by Italy in 1889, it was their colonial capital and the main base for the invasion of Ethiopia (1935–36). Asmara was captured by the British in 1941 and, in the 1950s, the US built Africa's biggest military communications center here. The city was absorbed by Ethiopia in 1952, and was the main garrison in the fight against Eritrean rebels seeking independence. In 1993 Asmara became the capital of independent ERITREA. Though ravaged by drought, famine, and war, it began a strong recovery based on numerous light industries, including ceramics, footwear, and textiles. Pop. (1991) 367,300.

**asp** Popular name for two species of VIPER, the asp viper of S Europe (*Vipera aspis*), and the Egyptian asp, a horned, side-winding viper of N Africa (*Cerastes cerastes*). Both are weakly venomous and eat small animals. Family: Viperidae.

**Aspen** Town on Rolling Fork River, W central Colorado, US. Aspen was founded (1878) as silver-mining camp, but the collapse in the silver price led to depopulation. Today Aspen is a major ski resort. Pop. (1995) 7,250.

**aspen** One of three species of trees of the genus *Populus*, with toothed, rounded leaves. Closely related to poplars, they are native to temperate Eurasia, North Africa, and North America. They grow up to 100ft (30m). Family Salicaceae.

**asphalt** *See* BITUMEN

**aspirin** (acetylsalicylic acid) DRUG widely used to reduce fever, and as an ANALGESIC to relieve minor pain. Recent evidence indicates aspirin can inhibit the formation of blood clots and in low doses can reduce the danger of heart attack and stroke. Aspirin can irritate the stomach and in overdose is toxic and can cause death.

**Asquith, Herbert Henry, 1st Earl of Oxford and Asquith** (1852–1928) British statesman, last Liberal prime minister (1908–16). Asquith entered parliament in 1886 and served as GLADSTONE's home secretary (1892–95). He was chancellor of the exchequer under Sir Henry Campbell-Bannerman, and succeeded him as prime minister. His administration was notable for its social welfare legislation, such as the introduction of old age pensions (1908) and unemployment insurance (1911). He also passed the Parliament Act (1911), which ended the Lords' power of veto over Commons legislation. His attempts to establish Home Rule for Ireland were rejected by Conservatives and Unionists. Asquith took Britain into WORLD WAR I but was an ineffective wartime leader. In 1915 he formed a coalition government with the Conservative Party. He was replaced as prime minister in a cabinet coup led by Lloyd George. Asquith stayed on as LIBERAL PARTY leader until 1926.

**ass** Wild, speedy, long-eared member of the HORSE family found in African and Asian desert and mountain areas. Smaller than the horse, it has a short mane and tail, small hoofs, and dorsal stripes. The three African races (species *Equus asinus*) are the Nubian, North African, and the rare Somali. Height: 3–5ft (90–150cm) at shoulder. Asian races are the kiang and the onager. Family Equidae.

**Assad, Hafez al-** (1928– ) Syrian statesman, president (1970– ). Assad served as minister of defense (1965–70), before seizing power in a military coup. He was elected president in 1971. Assad took a hardline stance against Israel, and Syrian troops participated in the 1973 Arab-Israeli War. He was accused of harboring terrorists. In 1976 Syrian troops were deployed in the Lebanese civil war. In 1987 the Syrian army moved into Beirut to restore order. In the mid-1990s, Assad's stance toward Israel softened and he played an vital role in the Israeli-Palestinian peace negotiations. Syria supported the coalition forces arrayed against Iraq in the Gulf War.

**Assam** State in NE India, almost separated from the rest of the country by Bangladesh. The capital is Dispur and the largest city is Guwahati. It became a state in 1950, but its people have resented, and forcibly resisted, immigration from West Bengal and Bangladesh. The Bodo minority continue to push for a separate state N of the Brahmaputra River. The state's main products are tea, jute, timber, and oil. Area: 30,277sq mi (78,438sq km). Pop. (1991) 22,414,322.

**assassin** (Arabic, users of hashish) Name given to a Muslim sect of Ismailis, founded *c.*1090 by Hasan ibn al-Sabbah. They fought against orthodox Muslims and Christian Crusaders, and committed many political murders, until their defeat in the 13th century.

**assay** Test to determine the amount of a metal present in a sample of material such as ores and alloys. The term is normally reserved for finding the proportion of gold, silver, or platinum present.

**Assemblies of God** Largest Pentecostal religious sect in the US. Founded in 1914 by preachers of the Church of God in Hot Springs, Arkansas, in 1916 it was incorporated and titled General Council of Assemblies of God. There are *c.*600,000 current members.

**assembly language** Computer language for writing computer programs in a form that is closely related to the form that computers can understand directly. Assembly language is a low-level language. Each instruction to be carried out by the computer is represented by a simple code. Programs written using these codes are translated by an "assembler" into a form the computer can understand.

**asset** Anything owned by a person or a company that has a money value. **Current** assets can be easily liquidated to produce their cash value. **Fixed** assets include buildings, machinery, and land. Goodwill and patents are described as **intangible** assets, because they have potential, rather than actual, money value. Asset stripping is the practice of taking over a business and selling off its assets.

**assimilation** Process by which an organism uses substances taken in from its surroundings to make new living protoplasm or to provide energy for metabolic processes. It includes the incorporation of the products of food digestion into living tissues in animals, and the synthesis of new organic material by a plant during photosynthesis.

**Assiniboine** Nomadic Native North American tribe. Their language is Siouan, and they are related to the Dakotas, although they migrated W from Minnesota to Saskatchewan and the Lake Winnepeg area. Their culture is that of the Plains Indians. They were peaceful trading partners of the English Hudson's Bay Company, and their trade helped to destroy the French monopoly among tribes of the region. Today, they number *c.*5,000; 4,000 on reservations in Montana and 1,000 in Canada.

**Association of Southeast Asian Nations (ASEAN)** Regional alliance formed in 1967 to promote economic cooperation. Its membership comprises Indonesia, Malaysia, Philippines, Singapore, Thailand, and Brunei. Based in Jakarta, Indonesia, it took over the nonmilitary aspects of the Southeast Asia Treaty Organization (SEATO) in 1975.

**associative law** Rule of combination in mathematics, in which the result of two or more operations on terms does not depend on the way in which they are grouped. Thus, normal addition and multiplication of numbers follows the associative law, since $a + (b + c) = (a + b) + c$, and $a \times (b \times c) = (a \times b) \times c$.

**Assumption** In the Roman Catholic Church, principal feast of the Blessed Virgin Mary. It is celebrated on August 15, and marks the occasion when she was taken up into heaven at the end of her life on Earth.

▲ **Assyria** The alabaster relief, originally painted, shows King Ashurbanipal's lion hunt. This is part of a series of narrative wall reliefs, *c.*650 found in the Northern Palace, Nineveh, and represents the highest achievement of Assyrian art.

**Assyria** Ancient empire of the Middle East. It took its name from the city of Ashur (Assur) on the River Tigris near modern Mosul, Iraq. The Assyrian empire was established in the 3rd millennium BC and reached its zenith between the 9th and 7th centuries BC, when it extended from the Nile to the Persian Gulf and N into Anatolia. Thereafter it was absorbed by the Persian empire. Under Ashurbanipal, art and learning reached their peak. The luxuriance of Ashurbanipal's court at Nineveh was legendary and, combined with the cost of maintaining his armies, weakened the empire. The capture of Nineveh in 612 BC marked the terminal decline of Assyria.

**Assyro-Babylonian mythology** Early mythology of the Middle East (Mesopotamia) that described a cosmic order of heaven, Earth, and an underworld. Some 4,000 deities and demons directed the physical and spiritual activities of the world.

**Astaire, Fred** (1899–1987) US dancer, actor, and choreographer. Astaire's sparkling, improvised solo dances redefined the musical with their energy and zany sophistication. In 1933 cinema's greatest partnership was formed, when he starred opposite Ginger Rogers in *Flying Down to Rio*. Fred and Ginger made ten films together. Their first major MGM musical was *The Gay Divorcee* (1934). Classics include *Top Hat* (1935) and *Swing Time* (1936). *The Barkleys of Broadway* (1949) was their last film together. Other dance partners included: Audrey Hepburn, Rita Hayworth, and Judy Garland.

**Astarte** (Ashtar or Ashtoreth) Phoenician goddess of fertility and love, the equivalent of Ishtar of the Assyro-Babylonians and Aphrodite of the Greeks. She is represented by a crescent, perhaps symbolic of the Moon or the horns of a cow.

**astatine** (symbol At) Semimetallic radioactive element that is one of the halogens (group VII of the periodic table). It is rare in nature, and is found in radioactive decay. $^{211}$At will collect in the thyroid gland and is used in medicine as a radioactive tracer. Properties: at.no. 85; at.wt. 211; m.p. 575.6°F (302°C); b.p. 710.6°F (377°C); most stable isotope $^{210}$At (half-life 8.3hr).

**aster** Genus of mostly perennial, leafy, stemmed plants native to the Americas and Eurasia. Asters are popular garden plants and most bear daisylike flowers. Family Asteraceae/Compositae.

**asteroid** Small body in an independent orbit around the Sun. The majority move between the orbits of Mars and Jupiter, in the main asteroid belt. The largest asteroid (and the first to be discovered) was Ceres, with a diameter of 567mi (913km). There are thought to be a million asteroids with a diameter greater than 0.6mi (1km); below this, they decrease in size to dust particles. Some very small objects find their way to Earth as meteorites. So far nearly 6,000 asteroids have been catalogued and have had their orbits calculated. This figure is increasing by several hundred a year. At least 10,000 more have been observed, but not often enough for an orbit to be calculated. Asteroids almost certainly originate from the time of the formation of the solar system.

**asthma** Disorder of the respiratory system in which the bronchi (air passages) of the lungs go into spasm, making breathing difficult. It can be triggered by infection, air pollution, allergy, certain drugs, exertion, or emotional stress. Allergic asthma may be treated by injections aimed at lessening sensitivity to specific allergens. Otherwise treatment is with bronchodilators to relax the bronchial muscles and ease breathing.

A

## ASTRONAUT

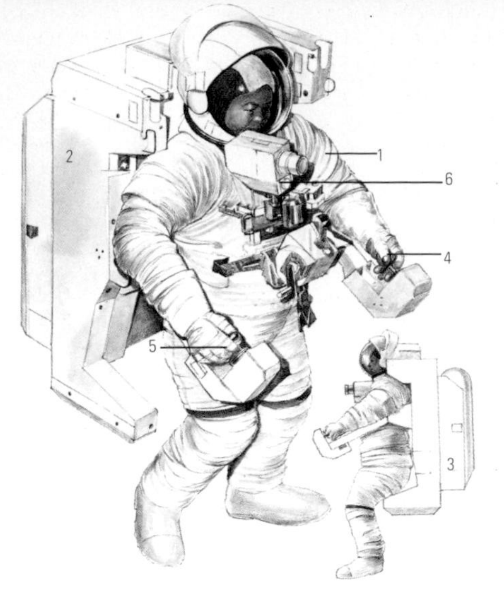

Astronauts on NASA's shuttle use spacesuits (1) that allow the crew members to work in space for up to seven hours. The suit is multilayered with eight materials combined. The outside is treated nylon to stop damage from tiny meteorites. Four layers of aluminum material then provide a heat shield from solar radiation backed by a fire- and tear-resistant layer. The astronaut is protected from the vacuum of space by a pressure suit of nylon coated with polyeurathane and is kept comfortable in extremes of heat and cold by water pumped through a network of tubes in a nylon chiffon undergarment. The MMU (manned manoeuvering unit) (2) allows an astronaut to move away from the shuttle. Power comes from 24 thrusters arranged at the corners of the MMU. By releasing pressurized nitrogen from two tanks (3) through nozzles, the astronaut can propel himself/herself through the vacuum. The hand controllers regulate rotation (4) and speed (5). A video camera (6) sends pictures to the shuttle and records the work carried out.

**astigmatism** Defect of vision in which the curvature of the lens differs from one perpendicular plane to another. It can be compensated for by use of corrective lenses.

**Aston, Francis William** (1877–1945) British physicist awarded the 1922 Nobel Prize for chemistry for his work on ISOTOPES. Astor developed the MASS SPECTROGRAPH, which he used to identify 212 naturally occurring isotopes.

**Astor, John Jacob** (1763–1848) US financier, b. Germany. Astor founded the AMERICAN FUR COMPANY in 1808. After 1812 he acquired a virtual monopoly of the US fur trade. In the 1830s he concentrated on land investment and became the wealthiest man in the US. His great-great-grandson William Waldorf Astor (Viscount Astor) (1879–1952) was married to Vicountess Nancy ASTOR.

**Astor, Nancy Witcher (Langhorne), Viscountess** (1879–1964) British politician, b. US, the first woman elected to the House of Commons (1919–45). A Conservative, she advocated temperance, educational reform, and women's and children's welfare. In the 1930s she and her husband William Waldorf Astor (Viscount Astor) were at the center of a group of influential proponents of appeasement toward Nazi Germany.

**Astrakhan** (Astrachan) City in S Russia, a port on the Caspian Sea. It was developed by the Mongols in the 13th century. In the Russian civil war (1917–20) the city remained in "White" Russian hands, becoming a base for the Caspian Sea conquest of 1920. Industries: fishing, shipbuilding, engineering, oil-refining. Pop. (1992) 512,000.

**astrobiology** *See* EXOBIOLOGY

**astrolabe** Early astronomical instrument for showing the appearance of the celestial sphere at a given moment and for determining the altitude of celestial bodies. The basic form consisted of two concentric disks, one with a star map and one with a scale of angles around its rim, joined and pivoted at their centers (rather like a modern planisphere), with a sighting device attached. Astrolabes were used from the time of the ancient Greeks until the 17th century for navigation, measuring time, and terrestrial measurement of height and angles.

**astrology** Study of the influence supposedly exerted by stars and planets on the natures and lives of human beings. Western astrology draws specifically on the movements of the Sun, Moon, and major planets of the Solar System in relation to the stars that make up the 12 constellations known as the ZODIAC. Astrology originated in ancient Babylon and Persia about 3,900 years ago, and rapidly spread through Europe, the Middle East, and Asia. In Europe the growing influence of Christianity saw the demise of astrologers. Popular HOROSCOPES still appear in some daily newspapers.

**astronaut** (Rus. *cosmonaut*) Person who navigates or rides in a space vehicle. The first man to orbit the Earth was the Russian Yuri GAGARIN in 1961. The first man to walk on the Moon was the American Neil ARMSTRONG in 1969. The first woman in space was the Russian Valentina Tereshkova in 1963.

**astronomical unit (AU)** Mean distance between the Earth and the Sun, used as a fundamental unit of distance, particularly for distances in the Solar System. It is equal to 92,956,000mi (149,598,000km).

**astronomy** Branch of science concerned with the universe and its components in terms of the relative motions of celestial bodies, their positions on the celestial sphere, physical and chemical structure, evolution, and the phenomena occurring on them. It includes celestial mechanics, ASTROPHYSICS, COSMOLOGY, and astrometry. **History** Astronomy was first practically used to develop a CALENDAR, the units of which were determined by observing the heavens. The Chinese had a calendar in the 14th century BC. The Greeks developed astronomy significantly between 600 BC and AD 200. THALES introduced geometrical ideas and PYTHAGORAS saw the universe as a series of concentric spheres. ARISTOTLE believed the Earth to be stationary but he explained lunar eclipses correctly. ARISTARCHUS put forward a heliocentric theory. HIPPARCHUS used trigonometry to determine astronomical distances. The system devised by PTOLEMY was a geometrical representation of the SOLAR SYSTEM that predicted the motions of the planets with great accuracy. From then on astronomy remained dormant until the scientific revolution of the 16th and 17th centuries, when COPERNICUS stated his theory that the Earth rotates on its axis and, with all the other planets, revolves round the Sun. KEPLER and his laws of planetary motion refined the theory of heliocentric motion, and his contemporary, GALILEO, made use of the TELESCOPE and discovered the moons of JUPITER. Isaac NEWTON combined the sciences of astronomy and physics. His laws of motion and universal theory of GRAVITATION provided a physical basis for Kepler's laws and the work of many astronomers from then on, such as the prediction of HALLEY'S COMET and the discovery of the planets URANUS, NEPTUNE, and PLUTO. By the early 19th century the science of celestial mechanics (the study of the motions of bodies in space as they move under the influence of their mutual gravitation) had become highly advanced and new mathematical techniques permitted the solution of the remaining problems of classical gravitation theory as applied to the Solar System. In the second half of the 19th century astronomy was revolutionized by the introduction of techniques based on photography and SPECTROSCOPY. These encouraged investigation into the physical composition of stars, rather than their position. By this time larger telescopes were being constructed, which extended the limits of the universe known to man. Harlow SHAPLEY determined the shape and size of our galaxy and E.P. HUBBLE's study of distant galaxies led to his theory of an expanding universe. BIG BANG and STEADY STATE THEORY of the origins of the universe were formulated. In recent years space exploration and observation in different parts of the electromagnetic spectrum have contributed to the discovery and postulation of such phenomena as the QUASAR, PULSAR, and BLACK HOLE. There are various branches of modern astronomy: **Optical** astronomy is the oldest branch and studies sources of light in space. Light rays can penetrate the atmosphere but, because of disturbances, many observations are now made from above the atmosphere. **Gamma-ray**, INFRARED, **ultraviolet,** and **x-ray** astronomy are branches that study the emission of radiation (at all wavelengths) from astronomical objects. Higher wavelengths can be studied from the ground while lower wavelengths require the use of satellites and balloons. Other branches within astronomy include RADAR ASTRONOMY and RADIO ASTRONOMY.

**astrophysics** Branch of ASTRONOMY that studies the physical and chemical nature and evolution of celestial bodies. Many branches of physics, including nuclear physics, plasma physics, RELATIVITY, and SPECTROSCOPY, are used to predict properties of stars, planets, and other celestial bodies. Astrophysicists also interpret information obtained from studies of the electromagnetic spectrum, including light, x-rays, and radio waves.

**Asturias, Miguel Angel** (1899–1974) Guatemalan novelist, poet, and diplomat. Asturias is best known for his debut novel, *The President* (1946), about the fall and trial of a hated Latin American dictator. A major theme of his novels is the impact of colonialism and industrialization on traditional modes of existence in Latin America. Asturias won the 1967 Nobel Prize for literature.

**Asturias** Region in NW Spain, bordering the Bay of Biscay and traversed by the Cantabrian Mountains. The capital is Oviedo. The region was named by the Iberians in the 2nd century BC and is famous for its cider and coal mines, the richest in Spain. Industries: coal, manganese, mining, steel and nonferrous metal production, fishing, fruit. Pop. (1991) 1,093,937.

**Asunción** Capital, chief port and largest city of Paraguay, located on the E bank of the Paraguay River near its junction with the Pilcomayo River. Founded by the Spanish *c.*1536 as a trading post, it was the scene of the Communeros rebellion against Spanish rule in 1721 and was later occupied by Brazil (1868–76). It is an administrative, industrial, and cultural center. Industries: vegetable oil, textiles. Pop. (1992) 637,737.

**Aswan** City SE Egypt, on the E bank of the Nile River just above Lake Nasser. Aswan was of strategic importance to the Egyptians and Greeks because it controlled all shipping and communications above the first cataract of the NILE. The modern city is a commercial and winter resort center and has benefited greatly from the construction of the Aswan High Dam. The dam, built with Soviet aid between 1960 and 1970, has a generating capacity of 10 billion kilowatt-hours and supersedes the first Aswan Dam completed in 1902 to establish flood control on the Nile. Many Nubians displaced by the dam's construction have moved to the city. The rock terrain surrounding the lake abounds in Egyptian and Greek temples and, although some sites were submerged, the temples of ABU SIMBEL were saved. Industries: copper, steel, textiles. Pop. (1992) 220,000.

**Atacama Desert** Desert of N Chile, stretching *c.*620m (1,000km) S from the Peru border. Despite its proximity to the Pacific Ocean it is considered to be the most arid desert in the world; some areas had no recorded rainfall in 400 years. Except where it is artificially irrigated, it is devoid of vegetation. Until the advent of synthetic fertilizers, the desert was mined for sodium nitrate. Large deposits of copper and other minerals remain; nitrates and iodine are extracted from the salt basins.

**Atahualpa** (1502–33) (Atabalipa) Last Inca ruler of Peru. The son of Huayna Capac, upon his father's death he inherited Quito, while his half-brother Huáscar controlled the rest of the Inca kingdom. In 1532 Atahualpa defeated Huáscar, but his period of complete dominance was to be short-lived. In November 1532 Francisco PIZARRO captured Atahualpa and he was later executed.

**Atalanta** In Greek mythology, a swift-footed huntress who was suckled by a she-bear. She offered to marry any man who could outrun her, but to kill those who failed. Aphrodite gave three of the golden apples of the Hesperides to a challenger, Hippomenes. During the race he dropped them one by one, distracting and delaying Atalanta. They married, but to punish them for consummating their union within the precincts of a temple, Zeus turned them into lions.

**Atatürk, (Mustafa) Kemal** (1881–1938) Turkish general and statesman, first president (1923–38) of the Turkish republic. As a young soldier he joined the YOUNG TURKS and was chief of staff to ENVER PASHA in the successful revolution (1908). He fought against the Italians in Tripoli (1911) and defended Gallipoli in the BALKAN WARS. During World War I he led resistance to the Allies' GALLIPOLI CAMPAIGN. The defeat of the OTTOMAN EMPIRE and the capitulation of the sultan persuaded Mustafa Kemal to organize the Turkish Nationalist Party (1919) and set up a rival government in ANKARA. The Treaty of SÈVRES (1920) forced him on the offensive. His expulsion of the Greeks from ASIA MINOR (1921–22) led the sultan to flee Istanbul. The Treaty of Lausanne (1923) saw the creation of a independent republic. His dictatorship undertook sweeping reforms, which transformed Turkey into a secular, industrial nation. In 1934 he adopted the title Atatürk (Turkish, father of the Turks). He was succeeded by Ismet INÖNÜ.

**atavism** Reversion by an organism to a characteristic of its ancestors after an interval of at least one generation in which the trait was absent. The term is no longer in scientific use since the reappearance of ancestral traits is now understood to be the expression of RECESSIVE genes.

**ataxia** In medicine, a condition where muscles are uncoordinated. It results in clumsiness, irregular and uncontrolled movements, and difficulties with speech. It may be caused by physical injury to the brain or nervous system, by a STROKE, or by disease.

**Aten** Ancient Egyptian god. Originally referring to the disk of the Sun, Aten entered into the Egyptian pantheon as the sun god. AKHNATEN elevated his status and virtually established the first monotheistic religion. After Akhnaten's death, the worship of AMON was restored.

**Athabasca** Lake in W central Canada, on the border between NE Alberta and NW Saskatchewan. Covering about 3,120sq mi (8,080sq km) and the fourth largest lake in Canada, it is fed by the Athabasca River from the S and drained by the Slave River to the N. Fort Chipewyan (1788) is preserved at the W end of the lake. There are gold and uranium deposits nearby.

**Athabascan** (Athapascan or Slave Indians) Tribe and language group of Native North Americans, inhabiting NW Canada. They were forced N to the Great Slave Lake and Fort Nelson by the Cree. The term Slave Indian derives from the domination and forced labor exacted by the Cree. The Athabascan tribe has always been closely linked to the Chipewyan people and some authorities regard them as one group. The Athabascan language is a subgroup of the Na-Dene linguistic phylum; there are over 30 languages. Athabascan languages cover the largest geographical area of all Native North American language groups, including Alaska, Yukon, N and W Canada, Oregon, California, New Mexico, and W Arizona. By the mid-1980s the number of Athabascan speakers was believed to exceed 160,000, including the APACHE and NAVAJO.

**Athanasian Creed** Christian profession of faith, probably written in the 6th century, that explains the teachings of the Church on the Trinity and the incarnation. The Roman Catholic and some Protestant churches accept its authority.

**Athanasius, Saint** (d.373) Early Christian leader. As patriarch of Alexandria he confuted ARIANISM, and in various writings defended the teaching that the Son and the Holy Spirit were of equal divinity with God the Father and so shared a threefold being. He is no longer considered the author of the ATHANASIAN CREED, but he did write the *Life of St Anthony*. His feast day is May 2.

**atheism** Philosophical denial of the existence of God or any supernatural or spiritual being. The first Christians were called atheists because they denied Roman religions but the term is now used to indicate the denial of Christian theism. During the 18th-century ENLIGHTENMENT, David HUME, Immanuel KANT, and the Encyclopedists laid the foundations for atheism. In the 19th century Karl MARX, Friedrich NIETZSCHE, and Sigmund FREUD all accommodated some form of atheism into their respective philosophical creeds. In the 20th century, many individuals and groups advocate atheism. *See also* AGNOSTICISM

**Athena** In Greek mythology, the goddess of wisdom, and patroness of the arts and industry, identified with MINERVA. Athena emerged from the head of Zeus fully grown and armed; thereafter, she was her father's most reliable supporter, and the sponsor of heroes such as Heracles, Perseus, and Odysseus. In the Trojan War she sided with the Greeks. She helped Argus build the ship *Argo* for JASON and the ARGONAUTS. She received special worship at Athens, where her main temples were the PARTHENON and the Erechtheum.

**Athens** (Athínai) Capital and largest city of Greece. The ancient city was built around the Acropolis, a fortified citadel, and was the greatest artistic and cultural center in ancient Greece, gaining importance after the PERSIAN WARS (500–449 BC). The city prospered under Cimon and PERICLES during the 5th century BC and provided a climate in which the great classical works of philosophy and drama were created. The most noted artistic treasures are the PARTHENON (438 BC); the Erechtheum (406 BC); and the Theater of Dionysus (*c*.500 BC, the oldest of the Greek theaters). Modern Athens and its port of PIRAEUS form a major Mediterranean transportation and economic center. Overcrowding and severe air pollution are damaging the ancient sites. Industries: shipbuilding, tourism, paper, steel machinery, textiles, pottery, brewing, chemicals, glass. Pop. (1991) 3,072,922.

**atherosclerosis** Most common form of arterial disease. An early stage of ARTERIOSCLEROSIS, it is a thickening of artery walls.

**Athos** Holy mountain, 6,667ft (2,032m) high, at the E end of the Acte Peninsula, NE Greece, . It is located inside the autonomous Mount Athos community of 20 Byzantine monasteries of the Eastern Orthodox Church established in 962. No women or "beardless boys," or even female animals, are allowed to set foot on the peninsula, and foreign visitors are restricted to ten a day. It forms a special department of Greece in the Macedonia Central region. Area: 336sq km (130sq mi). Pop. (1991) 1,536 (all male).

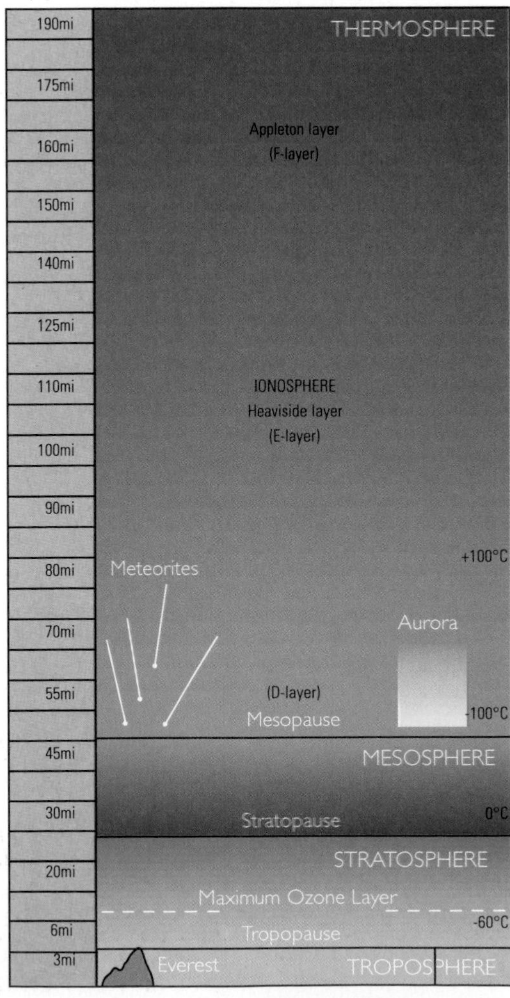


► **atmosphere** The Earth's atmosphere is formed of various layers. It is believed that the atmosphere has changed three times during the Earth's history. The present atmosphere consists mainly of nitrogen and oxygen.

**athlete's foot** Contagious, fungus-caused infection usually appearing first between the last two toes. Itching, macerated skin, and blisters are usual symptoms.

**Atlanta** Capital of Georgia, in the NW center of the state. The land was ceded to Georgia in 1821 by the CREEK and was settled in 1833. The city was founded in 1837 at the E end of the Western and Atlantic Railroad. Originally called Terminus, it became Marthasville in 1845 and Atlanta in 1847. It served as a Confederate supply depot and communications center during the CIVIL WAR. On September 2, 1864, it fell to General Sherman, whose army razed the city. Atlanta was rapidly rebuilt and soon recovered its importance as a transportation and cotton manufacturing center. It became the permanent state capital in 1887. During the late 20th century, Atlanta has become a major US city. Industries: textiles, chemicals, iron and steel, electronics. Pop. (1992) 394,848.

**Atlantic, Battle of the** (1939–43) Campaign for control of the Atlantic sea routes waged by air and naval forces during World War II. The Germans hoped to starve Britain into submission by U-boat attacks on merchant shipping, and later to prevent US reinforcements reaching the Mediterranean and Europe. More than 14 million metric tons of shipping were destroyed.

**Atlantic Charter** Joint declaration of peace aims issued in August 1941 by US President Franklin D. ROOSEVELT and British Prime Minister Winston CHURCHILL. It affirmed the right of all nations to choose their own form of government, promised to restore sovereignty to all nations that had lost it, and advocated the disarmament of aggressor nations.

**Atlantic City** Resort city in SE New Jersey, built on a 10mi (16km) sandbar in the Atlantic Ocean and settled as a fishing village in 1790. Famous for its 4mi (6km) boardwalk (1896) and its annual Miss America pageant (started in 1921), it became a center for political and business conventions. In 1976 gambling was legalized and, after the first casinos were opened in 1978, Atlantic City has become a popular tourist center and stage for sporting events (notably boxing). Pop. (1990) 37,986.

**Atlantic Intracoastal Waterway** System of inland waterways (bays, rivers, sounds, and canals) along the Atlantic coast from Cape Cod, Massachusetts, to Florida Bay. Main points are Trenton, New Jersey; Norfolk, Virginia; Beaufort, North Carolina; Jacksonville, Florida; and Miami, Florida.

**Atlantic Ocean** World's second largest ocean stretching from the Arctic Circle in the N to the Antarctic Ocean in the S. Its name derives from the ATLAS Mountains, which, for the ancient Greeks, marked the western boundary between the known and the unknown world. Its most striking feature is the MID-ATLANTIC RIDGE which runs N–S for its entire length. At the crest the ridge is cleft by a deep rift valley which is frequently offset by E–W transform faults. The age of the crust steadily increases with distance from the central rift, and so there is little doubt that the rift has evolved by seafloor spreading and is associated with the movement of the Americas away from Europe and Africa at a rate of 0.8–1.6in (2–4cm) a year. The average depth of the Atlantic is 12,100ft (3,700m). The greatest known depth is the Milwaukee Deep in the Puerto Rico Trench, which has a depth of 28,370ft (8,650m). The N clockwise gyre is dominated by the fast-flowing GULF STREAM, traveling at speeds of up to 80mi (130km) a day, and forming the W boundary current of the gyre. The S counterclockwise gyre is atypical in having a weak western boundary current, the Brazil Current. Apart from oil (found mainly in the Gulf of Guinea), sand and gravel are the most important minerals from the Atlantic. The largest single offshore mining operation in the world is located at Ocean Cay on the Grand Bahamas bank, where calcium carbonate is extracted in the form of aragonite. The North Atlantic contains the most valuable fishing grounds in the world, namely the cod fisheries around Iceland, S Greenland, and the Grand Banks of Newfoundland. The relatively unexploited fisheries of the South Atlantic are probably less stable than those of the N. Area: 32 million sq mi (82 million sq km).

**Atlantis** Mythical island in the Atlantic Ocean from which, according to PLATO, a great empire tried to subdue the Mediterranean countries. It has been identified by some with the Greek island of Thera, destroyed by an earthquake *c.*1450 BC.

**Atlas** Mountain system in NW Africa, comprising several folded and roughly parallel chains extending 1,500mi (2,415km) from the coast of SW Morocco to the coast of N Tunisia. North Africa's highest peak, Djebel Toubkal, 13,671ft (4,170m), is found in the Grand Atlas range in W Morocco.

**Atlas** In Greek mythology, one of the TITANS, brother of PROMETHEUS. Having fought against Zeus, he was condemned to hold up the heavens.

**atman** Human soul or self in Hindu religion. *See* BRAHMAN

**atmosphere** Envelope of gases surrounding the Earth that shields the planet from the harsh environment of space. The gases it contains are vital to life. About 95% by weight of the Earth's atmosphere lies below 15mi (25km); the mixture of gases in the lower atmosphere is commonly called air. The atmosphere's composition by weight is: nitrogen 78.09%, oxygen 20.9%, argon 0.93%, 0.03% carbon dioxide, plus 0.05% of hydrogen, the inert gases and varying amounts of water vapor. The atmosphere can be conceived as concentric shells; the innermost is the **troposphere**, in which dust and water vapor create the clouds and weather. The **stratosphere** extends from 8–36mi (10–55km) and is cooler and clearer and contains ozone. Above, to a height of 43mi (70km), is the **mesosphere** in which chemical reactions occur, powered by sunlight. The temperature climbs steadily in the **thermosphere**, which gives way to the **exosphere** at *c.*250mi (400km), where helium and hydrogen may be lost into space. The **ionosphere** ranges from about 30mi (50km) out into the VAN ALLEN RADIATION BELTS.

**atmospheric pressure** Pressure exerted by the atmosphere because of its gravitational attraction to the Earth (or other body), measured by barometers and usually expressed in units of mercury. Standard atmospheric pressure at sea level is 29.92in (760mm) of mercury. The column of air above each in$^2$ of Earth's surface weighs *c.*14.7lb (6.7kg); the column above each cm$^2$ weighs *c.*2.2 lb (1kg).

**atoll** Ring-shaped REEF of CORAL enclosing a shallow LAGOON. An atoll begins as a reef surrounding a slowly subsiding island, usually volcanic. As the island sinks the coral continues to grow upward until eventually the island is below sea level and only a ring of coral is left at the surface.

**atom** Smallest particle of matter that can take part in a chemical reaction. Every element has its own characteristic atoms. The atom, once thought indivisible, consists of a central, positively charged NUCLEUS orbited by negatively charged ELECTRONS. The nucleus (identified in 1911 by Ernest RUTHERFORD) is composed of tightly packed protons and neutrons. It occupies a small fraction of the atomic space but accounts for almost all of the mass of the atom. In 1913 Niels BOHR suggested that electrons moved in fixed orbits. The study of QUANTUM MECHANICS has since modified the concept of orbits: the Heisenberg UNCERTAINTY PRINCIPLE says it is impossible to know the exact position and MOMENTUM of a subatomic particle. The number of electrons in an atom and their configuration determine its chemical properties. Adding or removing one or more electrons produces an ION.

**atomic bomb** *See* NUCLEAR WEAPON

**atomic clock** Most accurate of terrestrial clocks. It is an electric clock regulated by such natural periodic phenomena as emitted radiation or atomic vibration; the atoms of CESIUM are most commonly used. Clocks that run on radiation from hydrogen atoms lose one second in 1.7 million years.

**atomic energy** *See* NUCLEAR ENERGY

**atomic mass number** (nucleon number) Number of nucleons (protons and neutrons) in the nucleus of an atom. It is represented by the symbol *A*. In nuclear notation, such as $^7_3$Li, the mass number is the upper number and the ATOMIC NUMBER (the number of protons) is the lower one. ISOTOPES of an element have different mass numbers but identical atomic numbers.

**atomic mass unit (amu)** Unit of mass used to compare relative atomic masses, defined since 1961 as 1/12th the mass of the most abundant isotope of carbon, carbon$^{-12}$ (6 electrons, 6 protons and 6 neutrons). One amu is equal to $1.66033 \times 10^{-27}$ kg.

**atomic number** (proton number) Number of protons in the nucleus of an atom of an element, which is equal to the number

## ATOM

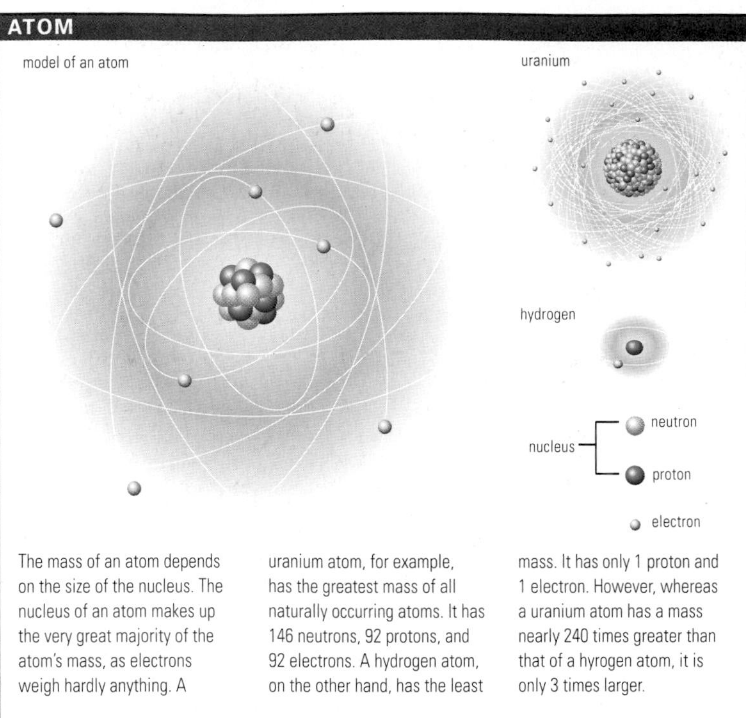


The mass of an atom depends on the size of the nucleus. The nucleus of an atom makes up the very great majority of the atom's mass, as electrons weigh hardly anything. A uranium atom, for example, has the greatest mass of all naturally occurring atoms. It has 146 neutrons, 92 protons, and 92 electrons. A hydrogen atom, on the other hand, has the least mass. It has only 1 proton and 1 electron. However, whereas a uranium atom has a mass nearly 240 times greater than that of a hyrogen atom, it is only 3 times larger.

of electrons moving around that nucleus. It is abbreviated to at. no. and represented by the symbol *Z*. The atomic number determines the chemical properties of an element and its position in the PERIODIC TABLE. ISOTOPES of an element all have the same atomic number but a different ATOMIC MASS NUMBER.

**atomic weight** *See* RELATIVE ATOMIC MASS (R.A.M.)

**atomism** (Gk. *atmos*, "uncuttable") Philosophical theory originated in Greece by Leucippus and elaborated by DEMOCRITUS during the 5th and 4th centuries BC. It held that everything is made of immutable and indivisible particles called atoms. It was an attempt to reconcile the single immutable substance theory of being espoused by Parmenides and other Eleatic philosophers with HERACLITUS' view that all things are subject to change.

**atonality** Style of music composed using the 12 tones of the chromatic scale without reference to traditional KEYS and HARMONY. Examples include *Pierrot Lunaire* (1912) by Arnold SCHOENBERG. *See also* SERIALISM

**atonement** In religion, the process by which a sinner seeks forgiveness from and reconciliation with God, through an act of expiation such as prayer, fasting or good works.

**atrophy** In medicine, shrinking or wastage of tissues or organs. It may be associated with disease, malnutrition, or, in the case of muscle atrophy, with disuse.

**atropine** Poisonous ALKALOID drug ($C_{17}H_{23}NO_3N$) obtained from certain plants such as *Atropa belladonna* (DEADLY NIGHTSHADE). Atropine is used medicinally to regularize the heartbeat during anesthesia, to dilate the pupil of the eye, and to treat motion sickness.

**attar of roses** Essential oil obtained from rose petals, and used as a perfume and perfumery agent. Also called otto, attar is any fragrant oil derived from plants, though attar of roses (produced by crushing and distilling petals from the damask rose cultivated in the Balkans) is by far the best known.

**Attenborough, Sir David Frederick** English naturalist and broadcaster; brother of Sir Richard ATTENBOROUGH. Attenborough was controller of BBC2 television (1965–68). Since 1954, he has travelled on zoological and ethnographical filming expeditions, which have formed the basis of such landmark natural history series as *Life on Earth* (1979), *The Living Planet* (1984), *The Trials of Life* (1990), and *The Private Life of Plants* (1995). He was knighted in 1985.

**Attenborough, Sir Richard** (1923– ) British film actor and director. Attenborough's career has spanned more than 50 years beginning with *In Which We Serve* (1942). He delivered a menacing performance in *Brighton Rock* (1947). Attenborough's directorial debut was the World War I satire *Oh! What a Lovely War* (1971). His acting and directorial style appear to suit biographical films: *Gandhi* (1982) won Best Film and Best Director Oscars. *Shadowlands* (1993), his biopic of C.S. Lewis, brought further critical praise.

**Attila** (406–453) King of the HUNS (*c*.439–53), co-ruler with his elder brother until 445. Attila defeated the Eastern Roman emperor THEODOSIUS II, extorting land and tribute, and invaded Gaul in 451. Although his army suffered heavy losses, he invaded Italy in 452, but disease forced his withdrawal. Attila has a reputation as a fierce warrior, but was fair to his subjects and encouraged learning. On his death the empire fell apart.

**Attlee, Clement Richard, 1st Earl** (1883–1967) British statesman, prime minister (1945–51). He became leader of the LABOUR PARTY in 1935. During World War II, he served in Winston CHURCHILL's wartime cabinet. Attlee won a landslide victory in the 1945 general election. His administration was notable for the introduction of important social reforms, such as the NATIONAL HEALTH SERVICE (NHS) and the nationalization of the power industries, the railways, and the BANK OF ENGLAND. He also granted independence to India (1947) and Burma (1948). Attlee was re-elected in 1950, but was defeated by Winston Churchill in the 1951 general election. He continued to serve as leader of the opposition until he retired and accepted an earldom in 1955.

**attorney general** Principal law officer. In the US, the attorney general is the highest law officer of the government and head of the Department of Justice and advises the president and heads of the executive department. In the UK, the attorney general is the chief law officer of the crown and head of the English bar and also legal advisor to the House of Commons and the government.

**Atwood, Margaret Eleanor** (1939– ) Canadian novelist, poet, and critic. Best known outside Canada for her novels, Atwood has also published numerous volumes of poetry. Her debut novel, *The Edible Woman* (1969), received immediate acclaim for its stylish and articulate treatment of complex gender relationships. Other novels include *Surfacing* (1972), the award-winning *The Handmaid's Tale* (1985), *The Robber Bride* (1993), and *Alias Grace* (1996).

**Auber, Daniel-François-Esprit** (1782–1871) French composer. Auber studied under Cherubini and is regarded as the founder of French grand opera. He often collaborated with the librettist Scribe. His 40 operas include *La Muette de Portici* (1828), *Fra Diavolo* (1830), and *La Sirène* (1844).

**Auckland** Largest city and chief port of New Zealand, lying on an isthmus on NW North Island. The port, built on land purchased from the Maoris in 1840, handles around 60% of New Zealand's trade. The first immigrants arrived from Scotland in 1842, and in 1854 the first New Zealand parliament opened here. It remained the capital until 1865. Industries: vehicle assembly, boatbuilding, footwear, food canning, chemicals. Auckland has the largest Polynesian population (*c*.65,000) of any city in the world. Pop. (1994) 929,300.

**Auden, W.H. (Wystan Hugh)** (1907–73) Anglo-American poet, b. England, one of the major poets of the 20th century. Auden's first volume of poetry, *Poems* (1930), established him as the leading voice in a group of left-wing writers, which included Stephen SPENDER, Louis MACNEICE, Cecil DAY-LEWIS, and Christopher ISHERWOOD. Auden and Isherwood collaborated on a series of plays, such as *The Ascent of F6* (1936). Auden joined the Republican cause in the Spanish Civil War and wrote *Spain* (1937). In 1939 he emigrated to New York and became a US citizen in 1946. His volume *The Age of Anxiety* (1947) won a Pulitzer Prize. From 1956 to 1961 he was professor of poetry at Oxford University. Auden's poetry adopts many tones, often utilizing colloquial and everyday language. His later poetry is more serious and epistolary, reflecting his conversion to Anglicanism.

**auditory canal** Tube leading from the outer EAR to the eardrum. It is *c*.1in (2.5cm) long.

**Audubon, John James** (1785–1851) US ornithologist and artist. His remarkable series of some 400 watercolors of birds, often in action, were published in *Birds of America* (1827–38).

**Augsburg** Historical city on the River Lech, in Bavaria. Founded by the Romans (*c*.15 BC) and named for the Emperor Augustus, it became a free imperial city in 1276 and was a prosperous banking and commercial center in the 15th and 16th centuries. The AUGSBURG CONFESSION was presented and the Peace of Augsburg (1555) signed here. The cathedral (started 994) claims the oldest stained-glass windows in Europe (11th century). Industries: textiles, engineering, motor vehicles. Pop. (1993) 265,000.

**Augsburg, League of** (1686) Alliance of the enemies of the French King LOUIS XIV. Composed of Spain, Sweden, the Holy Roman Empire and lesser states, its formation under the Emperor Leopold I was a reaction to French encroachment on the land bordering the Holy Roman Empire. Following the French attack on the PALATINATE in 1688, a new coalition against the French, the Grand Alliance, was formed (1689).

**Augsburg, Peace of** (1555) Agreement reached by the Diet of the Holy Roman Empire in Augsburg ending the conflict between Roman Catholics and Lutherans in Germany. It established the right of each prince to decide on the nature of religious practice in his lands. Dissenters were allowed to sell their lands and move. Free cities and imperial cities were open to both Catholics and Lutherans. The exclusion of other Protestant sects proved to be a source of future conflict.

**Augsburg Confession** (1530) Summation of the Lutheran faith, presented to Emperor Charles V at the Diet of Augsburg. Its 28 articles were formulated from earlier Lutheran statements principally by Philip MELANCHTHON. It was denounced by the Roman Catholic Church, but became a model for later Protestant creeds.

**augur** In ancient Rome, an interpreter of signs from the gods. Augurs belonged to a priestly college whose job was to "take the auspices" – to perform certain rituals and to study omens, such as the flight of birds. Roman state officials consulted the augurs on the timing of important meetings, battles, or other actions.

**Augusta** State capital of Maine, on the Kennebec River, 45mi (72km) from the Atlantic Ocean. Founded by settlers from Plymouth as a trading post in 1628, it was incorporated in 1797. A dam built across the Kennebec River in 1837 led to Augusta's industry changing from shipping to manufacturing textiles, paper, and steel. The city also benefits from tourism. Pop. (1990) 21,325.

**Augustine, Saint** (354–430) Christian theologian and philosopher. Augustine's *Confessions* provide an intimate psychological self-portrait of a spirit in search of ultimate purpose. This he believed he found in his conversion to Christianity in 386. As Bishop of Hippo (396–430), North Africa, he defended Christian orthodoxy against Manicheism, Donatism, and Pelagianism. *The City of God* (426) is a model of Christian apologetic literature. Of the Four Fathers of the Latin Church, AMBROSE, JEROME, and GREGORY I, Augustine is considered the greatest. His feast day is August 28.

**Augustine of Canterbury, Saint** (d.604) First Archbishop of CANTERBURY. He was sent from Rome in 596 by Pope GREGORY I, at the head of a 40-strong mission. Arriving in Kent in 597, Augustine converted King ETHELBERT and introduced Roman ecclesiastical practices into England. This brought him into conflict with the Celtic monks of Britain and Ireland whose traditions had developed in isolation from the continent. The Synod of Whitby (663) settled disputes in favor of Roman custom. St. Augustine's feast day is May 28 (May 26 in England and Wales).

**Augustinian** Name of two distinct and long-established Christian orders. The order of Augustinian Canons was founded in the 11th century. Based on the recommendations of St. AUGUSTINE OF HIPPO, its discipline was milder than those of full monastic orders. The mendicant order of Augustinian Hermits or Friars was founded in the 13th century and modeled on the DOMINICANS.

**Augustus** (63 BC–AD 14) (Gaius Julius Caesar Octavianus) First Roman emperor (27 BC–AD 14), also called **Octavian**. Nephew and adopted heir of Julius CAESAR, he formed the Second Triumvirate with Mark ANTONY and Lepidus after

Caesar's assassination. They defeated BRUTUS and CASSIUS at Philippi in 42 BC and divided the empire between them. Rivalry between Antony and Octavian was resolved by the defeat of Antony at Actium in 31 BC. While preserving the form of the republic, Octavian held supreme power. He introduced peace and prosperity after years of civil war. He built up the power and prestige of Rome, encouraging patriotic literature and rebuilding much of the city in marble. He extended the frontiers and fostered colonization, took general censuses, and attempted to make taxation more equitable. He tried to arrange the succession to avoid future conflicts, though had to acknowledge an unloved stepson, TIBERIUS, as his successor.

**Augustus II** (1670–1733) King of Poland (1697–1704, 1709–33) and, as Frederick Augustus I, elector of Saxony (1694–1733). Augustus was elected by the Polish nobles in order to secure an alliance with Saxony, but the result was to draw Poland into the Great NORTHERN WAR on the side of Russia. He was forced to give up the crown to Stanislas I Leszcyński in 1704. Civil war (1704–09) and invasion by Charles XII of Sweden weakened the Polish state. Augustus was restored to the throne after Peter the Great defeated Sweden at the Battle of Poltava in 1709, but at the cost of growing Russian dominance in Polish affairs.

**auk** Squat-bodied sea bird of colder Northern Hemisphere coastlines. The flightless great auk (*Pinguinus impennis*), or the Atlantic penguin, became extinct in the 1840s; height: 30in (76cm). The razorbill auk (*Alca torda*) is the largest of living species. Family Alcidae.

**Aung San** (1914–47) Burmese politician who opposed British rule, father of AUNG SAN SUU KYI. Initially collaborating with the Japanese (1942), he later helped expel the invaders. He was assassinated shortly after his appointment as deputy chairman of the executive council.

**Aung San Suu Kyi, Daw** (1945– ) Burmese civil rights activist, daughter of AUNG SAN. She was placed under house arrest in 1989 for leadership of the National League for Democracy, a coalition opposed to Myanmar's oppressive military junta. In 1991 she was awarded the Nobel Peace Prize and the European Parliament's Sakharov Prize (for human rights).

**Aurangzeb** (1619–1707) Emperor of India (1659–1707). The last of the great Mogul emperors, Aurangzeb seized the throne from his enfeebled father, SHAH JEHAN. He reigned over an even greater area and spent most of his reign defending it. Aurangzeb was a devout Muslim, whose intolerance of Hindus provoked long wars with the MARATHA. The empire was already breaking up before his death.

**Aurelian** (*c.*215–75) Roman emperor. Having risen through the army ranks, Aurelian succeeded CLAUDIUS in 270. His victories against the Goths, reconquest of Palmyra, and recovery of Gaul and Britain earned him the title "Restorer of the World." He built the Aurelian Wall to protect Rome and was assassinated in an obscure military plot.

**Aurelius, Marcus** *See* MARCUS AURELIUS (ANTONINUS)

**Auric, Georges** (1899–1983) French composer. Auric was artistic director of the Paris Opéra (1962–67). His many compositions include ballets, songs, and film scores, such as those for *Caesar and Cleopatra* (1946) and *Moulin Rouge* (1952). He was a member of Les SIX.

**Auriga** Large northern constellation, containing the first-magnitude star Capella. Mythologically, it represents Erichthonius, a king of Athens, who invented the four-horse chariot.

**aurochs** (urus) Extinct European wild ox, the long-horned ancestor of modern domesticated cattle. Once found throughout the forests of Europe and central and SE Asia, it became extinct in 1627. A dark, shaggy animal, it stood up to 7ft (2m) tall at the shoulder. Family Bovidae; species *Bos primigenius*. *See also* BISON

**Aurora** In Roman mythology, the goddess of dawn, equivalent to the Greek goddess EOS.

**aurora** Sporadic, radiant display of colored light in the night sky, caused by charged particles from the Sun interacting with air molecules in the Earth's magnetic field. Auroras occur in polar regions and are known as **aurora borealis** in the N, and **aurora australis** in the S.

**Auschwitz** (Oświçim) Town in Poland. It was the site of a German concentration camp during World War II. A group of three main camps, with 39 smaller camps nearby, Auschwitz was Hitler's most "efficient" extermination center. Between June 1940 and January 1945 more than 4 million people were executed here, mostly Jews. The buildings have been preserved as the National Museum of Martyrology. Together with the world's largest burial ground at Brzezinka (Birkenau), one of the other two main camps, Auschwitz is now a place of pilgrimage. Pop. (1989) 45,400.

**Austen, Jane** (1775–1817) English novelist. Austen completed six novels of great art, insight, and wit, casting an ironic but ultimately sympathetic light on the society of upper-middle-class England. In order of composition they are: *Northanger Abbey* (1818), a parody on the contemporary Gothic novel; *Sense and Sensibility* (1811); *Pride and Prejudice* (1813); *Mansfield Park* (1814); *Emma* (1816); and *Persuasion* (1818). Not particularly successful in their time, they have since established their place among the most popular and well-crafted works in English literature. Her work has recently undergone an enthusiastic revival in the public imagination, following several film adaptations, most notably *Sense and Sensibility* (1995).

**Austerlitz, Battle of** (December 2, 1805) Conflict in Bohemia between the French under NAPOLEON and the Russians led by Mikhail Kutuzov. One of Napoleon's greatest victories, it was also called the Battle of the Three Emperors.

**Austin, Stephen** (1793–1836) US pioneer. On his father's death in 1821, Austin acquired a grant in the Spanish territory that was to become Texas. He settled the first English-speaking

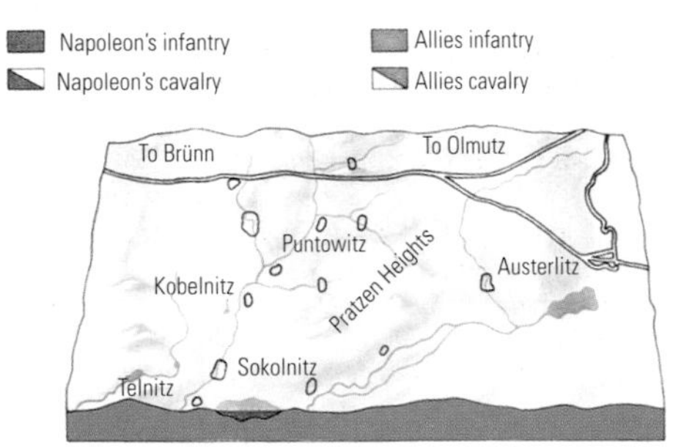


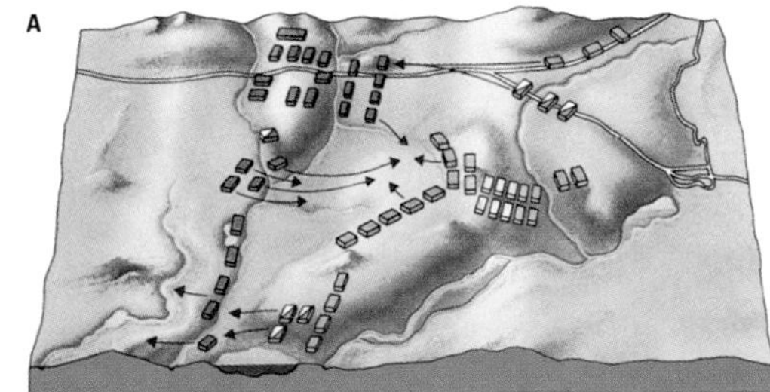


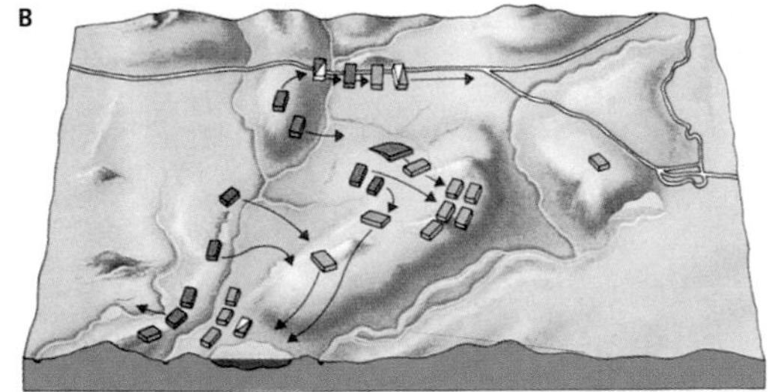


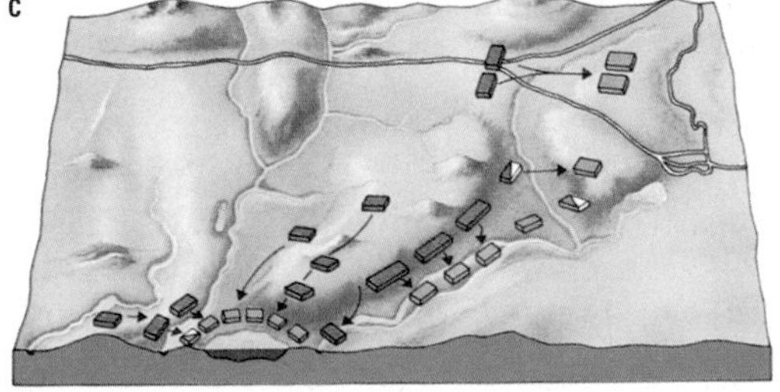


◀ **Austerlitz, Battle of**
Napoleon's defeat of the Allied forces at the Battle of Austerlitz was one of his greatest triumphs. By evacuating Austerlitz and the Pratzen Heights, Napoleon feigned weakness. The Allied forces camped on the heights (A). Their plan was to overwhelm the (deliberately) weak French right flank, before heading north to envelop the French as they headed for Brünn. Beneath the cover of mist, elements of the French forces maneuvered beneath the Pratzen Heights. The Allies attacked the French right flank. While the Allies were engaged in battle to the south, French forces marched up and occupied the Pratzen Heights (B). Additional support was provided by other French forces that had initially engaged the Allies to the north. Together the French forces dispersed the Allies, driving them on to the frozen lakes near Telnitz, where many drowned as Napoleon ordered his artillery to open fire, breaking the ice (C).

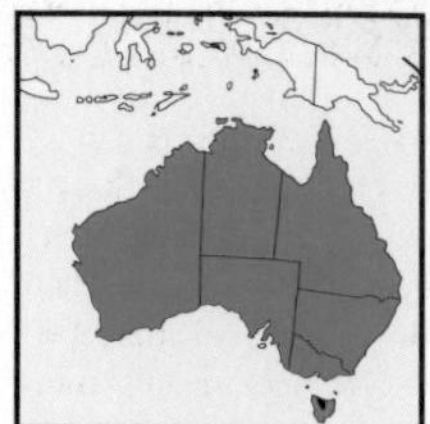

The national flag, top right, was adopted in 1901. It includes the British Union Flag, revealing Australia's historic links with Britain. In 1995, the Australian government put the flag used by Native Australians, bottom right, on the same footing as the national one.

**AREA:** 2,967,893sq mi (7,686,850sq km)
**POPULATION:** 17,529,000
**CAPITAL (POPULATION):** Canberra (324,600)
**GOVERNMENT:** Federal constitutional monarchy
**ETHNIC GROUPS:** White 95%, Aboriginal 1.5%, Asian 1.3%
**LANGUAGES:** English (official)
**RELIGIONS:** Christianity (Roman Catholic 26%, Anglican 24%, others 20%), Islam, Buddhism, Judaism
**CURRENCY:** Australian dollar = 100 cents

The Commonwealth of Australia, the world's sixth largest country, is a continental landmass. The main highland zone is the GREAT DIVIDING RANGE in the E, which contains the country's highest peak, Mount KOSCIUSKO, in NEW SOUTH WALES. The range extends from the Cape York peninsula to VICTORIA; the mountains of Tasmania are a southerly extension. These mountains separate the E coastal plains from the Central Lowlands. The SE lowlands are drained by the MURRAY and the Darling, Australia's two longest rivers. Lake EYRE, in the desert to the W, is the continent's largest lake, though it is a dry salt flat for most of the time. The huge Western Plateau, which makes up two thirds of Australia, is flat with a few low mountain ranges.

### CLIMATE

Only 10% of Australia has an average annual rainfall of more than 39in (1,000mm). These areas include some of the tropical N, where DARWIN is situated, the NE coast and the SE. The coasts are usually warm and many parts of the S and W, including PERTH, enjoy a Mediterranean climate of dry summers and moist winters. The interior is dry and water is quickly evaporated, making many of the rivers only seasonal.

### VEGETATION

Much of the Western Plateau is desert, although areas of grass and low shrubs are found on the desert margins. The Central Lowlands are grasslands used to raise farm animals, taking their water from artesian wells that tap underground rock strata. The N has areas of savanna and rain forest. In dry areas, shrubs called acacias are common, while in wetter areas eucalyptus (gum) trees are found. Australia has many

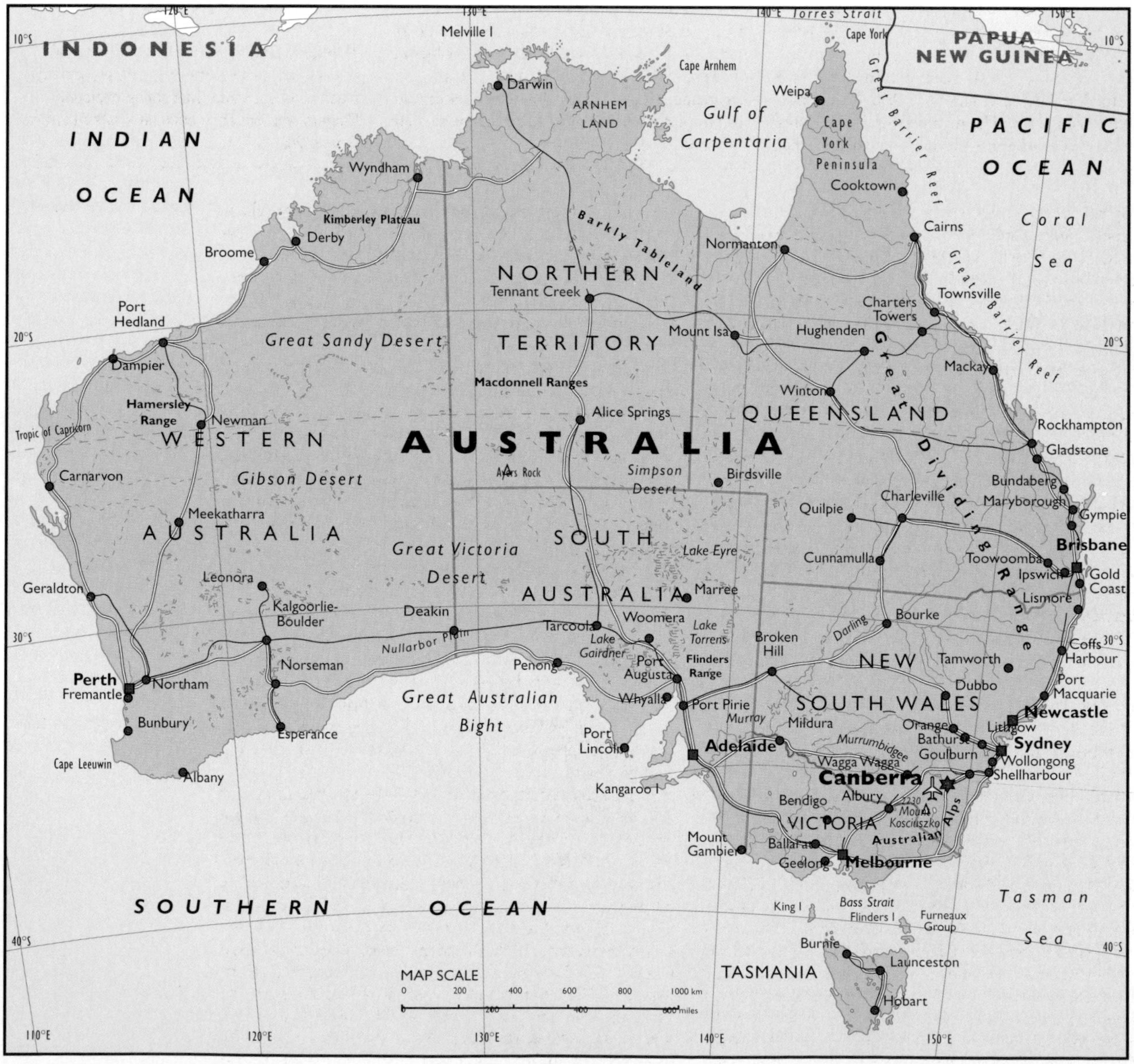

INDONESIA
PAPUA NEW GUINEA
INDIAN OCEAN
PACIFIC OCEAN
Coral Sea
Tasman Sea
SOUTHERN OCEAN
Torres Strait
Gulf of Carpentaria
Great Barrier Reef
Great Australian Bight
Bass Strait
AUSTRALIA
WESTERN AUSTRALIA
NORTHERN TERRITORY
QUEENSLAND
SOUTH AUSTRALIA
NEW SOUTH WALES
VICTORIA
TASMANIA
Great Sandy Desert
Gibson Desert
Great Victoria Desert
Simpson Desert
Great Dividing Range
Australian Alps
Kimberley Plateau
Hamersley Range
Macdonnell Ranges
Barkly Tableland
Flinders Range
Nullarbor Plain
ARNHEM LAND
Cape York Peninsula
Melville I
Cape Arnhem
Darwin
Wyndham
Derby
Broome
Port Hedland
Dampier
Newman
Carnarvon
Meekatharra
Geraldton
Leonora
Kalgoorlie-Boulder
Norseman
Perth
Fremantle
Northam
Bunbury
Esperance
Albany
Cape Leeuwin
Tropic of Capricorn
Tennant Creek
Alice Springs
Ayers Rock
Deakin
Tarcoola
Lake Gairdner
Woomera
Lake Torrens
Lake Eyre
Marree
Penong
Port Augusta
Whyalla
Port Pirie
Port Lincoln
Adelaide
Kangaroo I
Mount Gambier
Birdsville
Weipa
Cape York
Cooktown
Cairns
Normanton
Townsville
Charters Towers
Mount Isa
Hughenden
Mackay
Winton
Rockhampton
Gladstone
Bundaberg
Maryborough
Gympie
Brisbane
Gold Coast
Toowoomba
Ipswich
Lismore
Charleville
Quilpie
Cunnamulla
Bourke
Darling
Broken Hill
Tamworth
Coffs Harbour
Port Macquarie
Dubbo
Newcastle
Orange
Bathurst
Lithgow
Sydney
Goulburn
Wollongong
Shellharbour
Mildura
Murray
Murrumbidgee
Wagga Wagga
Canberra
Albury
2230 Mount Kosciusko
Bendigo
Ballarat
Geelong
Melbourne
King I
Flinders I
Furneaux Group
Burnie
Launceston
Hobart
MAP SCALE
0 200 400 600 800 1000 km
200 400 600 miles
10°S 20°S 30°S 40°S
110°E 120°E 130°E 140°E 150°E

## AUSTRALIA

flowering plants, and when heavy rains occur in dry areas these burst into life transforming the dry landscape into a carpet of colors.

### History

Native Australians (Aborigines) entered the continent from Southeast Asia more than 50,000 years ago. They settled throughout the country and remained isolated from the rest of the world until the first European explorers, the Dutch, arrived in the 17th century. The Dutch did not settle, but in 1770 Britain's Captain Cook explored the E coast and in 1788 the first British settlement was established (for convicts) on the site of what is now Sydney. The first free settlers arrived three years later.

In the 19th century, the continent was divided into colonies, which later became states. In 1901 the states united to create the Commonwealth of Australia. The federal capital was established at Canberra, in the Australian Capital Territory, in 1927.

### Politics

Australia has strong ties with the British Isles, but since World War II people from other parts of Europe and, most recently, from Asia have settled in Australia. Ties with Britain were also weakened by the UK membership in the European Union. Many Australians now believe that they should become more involved economically and politically with their neighbors in eastern Asia and the Americas rather than with Europe. In the early 1990s, Australia's prime minister, Paul Keating, suggested that Australia should become a republic (rather than a constitutional monarchy with the British sovereign as its head of state) by the year 2001. Opinion polls suggest that the majority of Australians share this view. In 2000 Sydney will host the Olympic Games and the following year will be the centenary of Australia's nationhood.

An important political issue concerns the position of Native Australians. In 1993 the government passed the Native Title Act which restored to Native Australians land rights over their traditional hunting and sacred areas.

### Economy

Australia is a prosperous country (1995 GDP per capita, US$18,940). Its economy was originally based on agriculture, although crops can be grown on only 6% of the land; dry pasture covers another 58%. The country remains a major producer and exporter of farm products, particularly cattle, wheat, and wool, followed by dairy products, various kinds of fruits and sugarcane. Grapes grown for wine-making are also important and quality Australian wines are now sold all around the world.

The country is also rich in natural resources and is a major producer of minerals, including bauxite, coal, copper, diamonds, gold, iron ore, manganese, nickel, silver, tin, tungsten, and zinc. Australia also produces some oil and natural gas. These three commodities – metals, minerals, and farm products – account for the bulk of Australia's exports.The majority of Australia's imports are manufactured products. They include machinery and other capital goods required by factories. The country has a highly developed manufacturing sector; the major products include consumer goods, notably foodstuffs and household articles. Tourism is a vital industry (1992 receipts, US$4,000 million).

**Matthew Flinders,** a British explorer, sailed around Australia in 1801–02, accurately mapping much of its coastline. This stamp depicting Flinders was issued to commemorate Australia Day in 1980.

colony here and was followed by many other colonists. Mexico opposed this colonization, and Austin went to Mexico City to argue his case, but was arrested. On his return in 1835 he became a leader in the fight for Texan independence.

**Austin** Capital of Texas, on the Colorado River. Originally called Waterloo, it was first settled in 1835 and renamed after Stephen AUSTIN (the "father of Texas") in 1839. The market center for a farming and ranching area, Austin hosts national conventions. Industries: high-tech electronics, furniture, machinery, building materials, food processing. Pop. (1992) 492,329.

**Australasia** Region that includes Australia, New Zealand, and Papua New Guinea. The term Australasia is not exact. It is sometimes used to include various Asian countries (principally Indonesia and Malaysia) or extended to include Pacific island groups and the Australian and New Zealand territories in Antarctica – all the lands coming within the same sphere of influence.

**Australia** Earth's smallest continent, between the Pacific and Indian Oceans. Combined with the island of TASMANIA, it forms the independent Commonwealth nation of Australia. *See* country feature

**Australia Day** Annual national holiday in Australia, on the Monday following January 26. It commemorates the arrival of the First Fleet (carrying the first colonists) at Port Jackson, Sydney on January 26, 1788.

**Australian art** Term applied to art produced by Native Australians and also that introduced by European settlers, which has developed its own distinctive style. The art of Native Australians dates back to prehistoric times. They painted on a variety of surfaces, including rock, bark, and shells. The most remarkable examples are the so-called x-ray paintings in Arnhem Land, in which hunters depicted the internal anatomy of the beasts they killed, and the *wondjina* figures, which were found near water holes in the NW. European influence on the continent dates from 1788, when the first penal colony was established. The Australian landscape attracted a significant number of foreign painters, such as John Glover (1767–1849) and Conrad Martens (1801–78); however, Australian artists still felt the need to train in Europe. The late 19th-century Heidelberg School, based in Heidelberg, Victoria, represented the first truly national movement in Australian art. It was led by Tom Roberts, and their impressionist-inspired landscapes influenced Australian art for many decades. In the 20th century, the Melbourne journal *Angry Penguins* (1940–46) proved a seminal influence, fostering the talents of many avant-garde painters. Among these were the two most celebrated names in Australian art, Sir Sidney NOLAN and Arthur Boyd.

**Australian Capital Territory (ACT)** (Commonwealth Territory) District within NEW SOUTH WALES but administratively independent of it. It contains the Australian capital, CANBERRA. The area was first settled in 1824 and was set aside as the capital territory in 1908. In 1915 an additional 28sq mi (72sq km) were added, making a total of 939sq mi (2,432sq km). Pop. (1993 est.) 299,400.

**Australopithecus** *See* HUMAN EVOLUTION

**Austria** Republic in central Europe. *See* country feature

**Austrian Succession, War of the** (1740–48) Overall name for several related wars. They included the war for the Austrian succession itself, in which France supported Spain's claim to part of the Hapsburg domains; the first and second Silesian wars, in which Frederick II of Prussia took Silesia from Austria; and the war between France and Britain over colonial possessions, known in North America as King George's War.

**Austro-Hungarian empire** (1867–1918) Organization of the old Austrian Empire into the kingdom of Hungary and the empire of Austria, also known as the "Dual Empire." The emperor of Austria and the king of Hungary were the same person but each nation had its own parliament and controlled its internal affairs. This arrangement ignored other nationalist minorities and pleased neither the Hungarians, who wanted greater autonomy, nor the Austrians, many of whom wanted a realignment with other German states. After World War I Hungary and Czechoslovakia declared their independence, the Emperor Charles abdicated and Austria became a republic.

**Austronesian languages** (Malayo-Polynesian) Family that includes Malay, Indonesian, Tagalog, Malagasy, and numerous other languages spoken in Indonesia, the Philippines, and the islands of the Pacific Ocean. There are four branches: Indonesian, Melanesian (which includes Fijian), Micronesian (which includes Chamorro, spoken on Guam), and the Polynesian languages, which include Maori, Tongan, Tahitian, and Samoan. There are *c*.175 million speakers.

**Austro-Prussian War** (1866) Conflict between Prussia and Austria, also known as the Seven Weeks War. Otto von BISMARCK engineered the war to further Prussia's supremacy in Germany and reduce Austrian influence. Defeat at Sadowa forced Austria out of the German Confederation (a federation of 39 German principalities set up by the Congress of Vienna to replace the HOLY ROMAN EMPIRE).

**auteur** In film theory, the notion that the director is the prime creator, or "author" of a film. Developed by François TRUFFAUT in 1954, the theory focuses on directorial style and use of recurring motifs to develop a canon of auteurs. Its popularity has waned because it minimizes the collaborative nature of filmmaking.

**authoritarianism** System of government that concentrates power in the hands of one person or small group of people not responsible to the population as a whole. Freedom of the press and of political organization are suppressed. Many authoritarian regimes arise from military takeovers.

**autism** Disorder, usually first appearing in early childhood, characterized by a withdrawal from social behavior, communication difficulties, and ritualistic behavior. The causes of autism may originate in genetics, brain damage, or psychology.

**autobiography** Narrative account of a person's life, written by the subject. The first important example of the genre was the 4th-century *Confessions* of Saint AUGUSTINE. The modern, introspective autobiography, dealing frankly with all aspects of life, is usually dated from the remarkable *Confessions* of ROUSSEAU (written 1765–72; pub. 1782). *See also* BIOGRAPHY

**autochrome** Method developed by the LUMIÈRE brothers for color photography, first marketed in 1907. The screen plate consisted of glass on one side coated with round particles of starch grains dyed red, blue, and green and mixed at random and compressed. Carbon black was laid between the dots and the whole plate covered with a varnish. An emulsion was applied to the reverse side. In widespread use for over 30 years, this method was an improvement over the earlier three-color screen method.

**autocracy** System of government in which a single person or small group of people wields absolute power. It is imposed and generally aimed at furthering the interests of an individual or group. Now rarely used, the term is applied

## AUSTRIA

According to legend, the simple colors on Austria's flag date back to a battle in 1191, during the Third Crusade, when an Austrian duke's tunic was stained with blood except under his swordbelt, where it remained white. The flag was officially adopted in 1918.

**AREA:** 32,347sq mi (83,850sq km)
**POPULATION:** 7,884,000
**CAPITAL (POPULATION):** Vienna (1,589,052)
**GOVERNMENT:** Federal republic
**ETHNIC GROUPS:** Austrian 93%, Slav 2%, Turkish, German
**LANGUAGES:** German (official)
**RELIGIONS:** Christianity (Roman Catholic 78%, Protestant 6%), Islam
**CURRENCY:** Schilling = 100 Groschen

The Republic of Austria is a landlocked country in the heart of Europe. About 75% of the land is mountainous, with much magnificent scenery. Northern Austria contains the valley of the DANUBE River, which rises in Germany and flows to the Black Sea, and the Vienna Basin, Austria's main farming region. Southern Austria contains ranges of the E ALPS, which rise to their highest point with Gross Glockner at 3,979m (12,457ft).

### CLIMATE AND VEGETATION

The climate of Austria is influenced by westerly and easterly winds. Moist westerlies bring rain, snow, and also moderate temperatures, but the dry easterlies bring cold weather in winter and hot weather in summer. Thus, E Austria has a more continental climate than the W parts of the country.

Woods and meadows cover much of the land, and Austria has a higher proportion of forest than any other European country. The trees include beech, larch, oak, and spruce.

### HISTORY AND POLITICS

Austria was once part of the HOLY ROMAN EMPIRE, and, under rulers from the HAPSBURG family, it became the most important state in the empire. When the empire ended in 1806, the Hapsburg ruler became emperor of Austria. In 1867, Austria and Hungary set up a powerful dual monarchy, the AUSTRO-HUNGARIAN EMPIRE, which finally collapsed in 1918 at the end of World War I. In 1938 Germany annexed Austria, and Austria fought alongside Germany in World War II. In 1945 the Allies partitioned Austria but the occupation was ended in 1955 when Austria became a neutral federal republic. In 1994, the people voted overwhelmingly in favor of joining the European Union, and Austria became a member on January 1, 1995.

### ECONOMY

Austria is a prosperous country, with plenty of hydroelectric power, some oil and gas, and good reserves of lignite (brown coal). These sources of energy do not meet the needs, and fossil fuels are imported.

The country's leading economic activity is manufacturing metals and metal products, including iron and steel, vehicles, and machines. VIENNA is the main industrial center. Craft industries are important, producing fine glassware, jewelry, and porcelain.

Crops are grown on 18% of the land, and another 24% is pasture. Dairy and livestock farming are leading activities; barley, potatoes, rye, sugarbeets, and wheat are the major crops. Tourism is a major industry, with nearly 20 million visitors to the country in 1995. Visitors are drawn to the cities of Vienna and SALZBURG (especially during the music festival) and for winter sports, as at INNSBRUCK.

A

## AUTOMOBILE

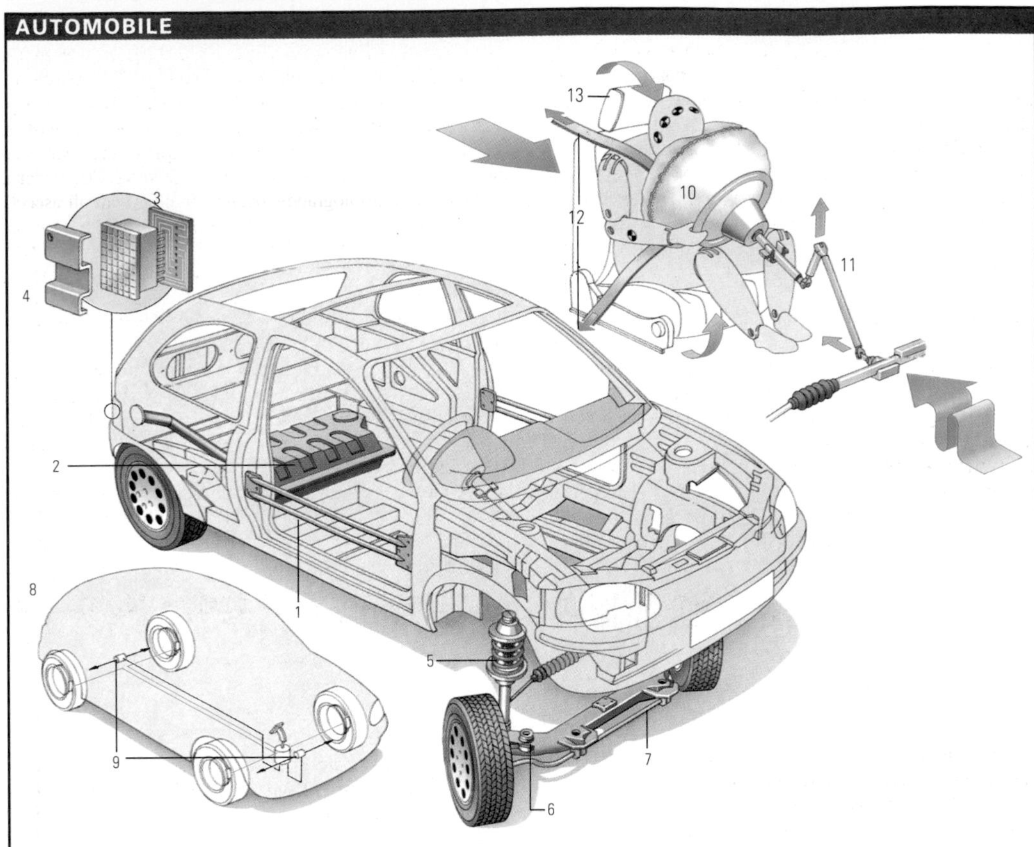


A modern car is designed with crumple zones at the front and rear to absorb the energy of a crash and protect the part of the car in which people sit. Side-impact protection bars (1) give strength to the side of the vehicle and spread energy to either side of the passenger cell. Fuel tanks (2) are situated in front of the rear axle to protect the tank if the car is hit from behind. Some manufacturers have replaced the traditional rear brake lights with LEDs (3) which light more quickly. The cover is stepped (4) to prevent the light being obscured by dirt. The suspension, a MacPherson strut system, allows vertical movement through the spring (5) while the wishbone (6) and antiroll bar (7) keep the wheels in position and stop excessive roll respectively. Antilock braking systems (ABS) (8) prevent the wheels locking under heavy braking or in poor weather. Sensors (9) detect when a wheel is about to lock and release the brake pads for a fraction of a second. An explosive charge inflates the air bag (10), which prevents the driver or passenger from hitting the steering wheel or dashboard. The steering column (11) is designed to collapse so the driver is not impaled. Seat belt tensioners use the impact to pull the belt tight (12), holding the passenger in place. The headrest (13) helps stop whiplash injuries when heads snap back in the aftermath of the impact.

to those regimes which came before the development of modern technology and state institutions which made TOTALITARIANISM possible.

**autoimmune disease** Any one of a group of disorders caused by the body's production of antibodies which attack the body's own tissues. One example of such an autoimmune disease is systemic LUPUS ERYTHEMATOSUS.

**Autolycus** In Greek mythology, son of Hermes and the mortal Chione. He received from his father the gift of making whatever he touched invisible. In this way he was able to commit numerous thefts until one day he was caught by SISYPHUS, whose oxen he had stolen.

**automatic pilot** (autopilot) Electronic and mechanical control system that ensures an aircraft follows a preprogramed flight plan. It monitors the course and speed of the aircraft and corrects any deviations from the flight plan. Systems range from simple wing-levelers in light aircraft to computer-operated units consisting of: a GYROSCOPE; an electric SERVOMECHANISM unit; and an accelerometer, which measures the aircraft's acceleration.

**automation** Use of self-governing machines to carry out manufacturing, distribution, and other processes automatically. By using FEEDBACK, sensors check a system's operations and send signals to a computer that automatically regulates the process. *See also* MASS PRODUCTION; ROBOT

**automobile** Road vehicle that first appeared in the 19th century. The first cars were propelled by steam, but were not a success. The age of the automobile really dates from the introduction of the gasoline-driven carriages of Gottlieb DAIMLER and Karl BENZ (1885–86). The INTERNAL COMBUSTION ENGINE for these cars had been developed earlier by several engineers (most notably Nikolaus Otto in 1876). The main components of an automobile remain unchanged. A body (**chassis**) to which are attached all other parts including: an **engine** or power plant; a **transmission** system for transferring the drive to the wheels, and steering, braking, and suspension for guiding, stopping, and supporting the car. Early cars were assembled by a few experts, but modern mass-production began in the early 1900s by Henry FORD and R. E. Olds in the US. In most modern motor factories, component parts are put together on assembly lines. Each worker has a specific task (such as fitting doors or crankshafts). Bodies and engines are made on separate assembly lines which converge when the engine is installed. Overhead rail conveyors move heavy components along the assembly lines, lowering them into position. The assembled car is tested before sale. Recent technology has seen the introduction of robots (properly, robotic arms secured to the workshop floor) on the assembly line. They are usually used for welding and painting. Increasing concern over the environmental impact of the car (such as congestion, pollution, and energy consumption) has encouraged governments to examine alternative forms of mass transportation, oil companies to produce cleaner fuels, and car manufacturers to look at alternative power plants (such as electric- or gas-powered motors).

**autonomic nervous system** Part of the body's nervous system that regulates the body's involuntary functions. It helps to regulate the body's internal environment by controlling the rate of heartbeat, PERISTALSIS and sweating. *See also* HOMEOSTASIS; INVOLUNTARY MUSCLE

**Auvergne** Region and former province of S France, comprising the departments of Allier, Puy-de-Dôme, Cantal, and Haute-Loire. The capital is Clermont-Ferrand. Running N–S are the Auvergne Mountains, a scenic chain of extinct volcanoes, with the highest peak at Puy de Sancy, 6,188ft (1,886m). Area: 10,047sq mi (26,013sq km). Pop. (1990) 1,321,200.

**auxin** Plant hormone produced mainly in the growing tips of plant stems. Auxins accelerate plant growth by stimulating cell division and enlargement and by interacting with other hormones. Actions include the elongation of cells (by increasing the elasticity of cell walls, allowing the cells to take up more water) in geotropism and PHOTOTROPISM, fruit drop, and leaf fall. *See also* GIBBERELLIN

**AUTOMATIC PILOT**

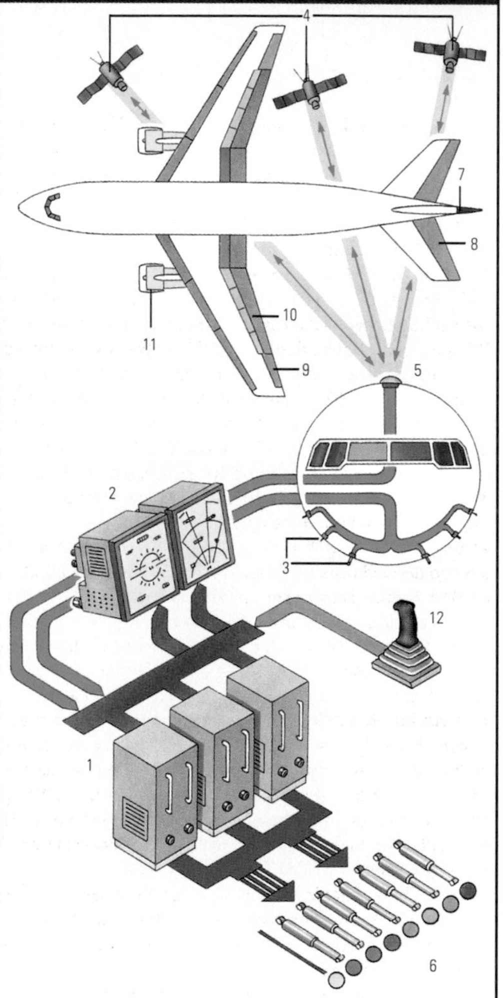

The diagram shows how a typical automatic pilot system works. A preprogramed flight plan is loaded into the aircraft's computers (1). After takeoff the automatic pilot is engaged. Two visual display units (2) show the aircraft's position, its intended route and its attitude. The change in movement of small vanes (3) on the outside of the aircraft alert the computers to any change in the aircraft's orientation. The aircraft uses the Global Positioning System (4) to determine its position. The receiver is located on top of the aircraft (5). The computers track the aircraft's route and automatically make any adjustments via servos (6) which control the rudder (7), elevators (8), ailerons (9), flaps (10), and throttle settings on the engines (11). The pilots can override the automatic system at any time and revert to manual controls (12).

**Avalokitesvara** In Buddhism, one of the most distinguished of the BODHISATTVAS. He is noted for his compassion and mercy, and has remained on Earth in order to bring help to the suffering and knowledge to those who have not yet been converted. DALAI LAMAS are considered reincarnations of Avalokitesvara.

**Avalon** Mythical island where King ARTHUR is supposed to have died, following his battle against Mordred. Avalon was ruled by Morgan Le Fey, and many identify it with Glastonbury, SW England.

**avatar** In HINDUISM, an incarnation of a god (especially VISHNU) in human or animal form that appears on Earth to combat evil and restore virtue. In Hindu tradition there have been nine incarnations of VISHNU and a tenth is yet to come: these include BUDDHA, KRISHNA and RAMA.

**Avedon, Richard** (1923– ) US photographer, famed for his portraits of celebrities. After serving in the photography section of the US Merchant Marines, Avedon worked as staff photographer for *Harper's Bazaar* and *Vogue* in 1965. At one stage he was the world's highest-paid fashion photographer.

**average** In statistics, the one score that most typifies an entire set of scores. It is the arithmetic MEAN of the scores. Other calculations that are also used to express what is typical in a set of scores are the MODE (the one score that occurs most often) and the MEDIAN (the middle score in a range which thus divides the set of scores into upper and lower halves).

**Averröes** (Abu-al-Walid Ibn-Rushd) (1126–98) Leading Islamic philosopher in Spain. Averröes became physician to the Caliph of Marrakesh in 1182, but was banished in to Seville, Spain, in 1795 for advocating reason over religion. His major work, *Incoherence of the Incoherence*, defends Neoplatonism and ARISTOTLE. He exercised a powerful influence on Christian thought that persisted into the Renaissance. *See also* Saint Thomas AQUINAS; SCHOLASTICISM

**Avesta** (Zend-Avesta) Sacred book of ZOROASTRIANISM. Most of the original was apparently lost when ALEXANDER THE GREAT burned Persepolis, the capital of ancient Persia, in 331 BC. The Gathas, forming the oldest part, originated with Zoroaster. The other remaining parts are the Yashts, Yasna and Vendidad, and prayers. The writings were systematized under the Sassanid kings of Persia between the 3rd and 7th centuries AD.

**Avicenna** (979–1037) (Abu Ali al-Husayn ibn abd Allah ibn Sina) Persian physician and philosopher whose work influenced the science of medicine for many centuries. Avicenna was the greatest philosopher and scientist of the golden age of Islamic learning. His *Canon Medicinae* became a standard work. He also made enduring contributions in the field of Aristotelian philosophy.

**Avignon** City at the confluence of the Rhône and Durance rivers, Vaucluse department, Provence, SE France. A thriving city under Roman rule, Avignon was the seat of the popes during their exile from Rome in the 14th century. There is a Papal Palace begun in 1316 and a Romanesque cathedral. The papacy held Avignon until 1791, when it was annexed to France by the Revolutionary authorities. Industries: tourism, soap, wine, grain, leather. Pop. (1990) 83,939.

**Avignon popes** During the BABYLONIAN CAPTIVITY (1309–77), popes who resided in Avignon instead of Rome. The papal court was established in Avignon by the French pope Clement V. In 1348 the city was bought by CLEMENT VI. The GREAT SCHISM occurred shortly after the court returned to Rome.

**avocado** Evergreen, broad-leafed tree native to the tropical New World. The name is extended to its green to dark purple, pear-shaped fruit. Avocados have a high oil content and a nutty flavor. Weight: 7oz (200g) but exceptionally up to 4.4lb (2kg). Family Lauraceae; species *Persea americana.*

**Avogadro, Amedeo, Conte di Quaregna** (1776–1856) Italian physicist and chemist. His hypothesis, **Avogadro's law** (1811), states that equal volumes of gases at the same pressure and temperature contain an equal number of molecules. This led later physicists to determine that the number of molecules in one gram molecule (the relative molecular mass expressed in grams) is constant for all gases. This number, called **Avogadro's number**, equals $6.02257 \times 10^{23}$. It is both the ratio of the universal gas constant to Boltzmann's constant and of Faraday's constant to the charge of the electron.

**Avon** Former county in SW England, created in 1974 from areas of Gloucestershire and Somerset. It was replaced in 1996 by the unitary authorities of BATH and North-East Somerset, BRISTOL, North-West SOMERSET, and South GLOUCESTERSHIRE.

**Avon** Name of four British rivers. The **Bristol** (Lower) Avon rises in the Cotswold Hills in Gloucestershire and flows S and then W through Bristol, entering the Severn estuary at Avonmouth. Length: 75mi (121km). The **Warwickshire** (Upper) Avon rises in Northamptonshire, and flows SW through Stratford-on-Avon to join the River Severn at Tewkesbury. Length: 96mi (155km). The **Wiltshire** (East) Avon rises near Devizes and flows S into the English Channel. Length: 48mi (77km). The **Scottish** Avon flows E into the Firth of Forth. Length: 18mi (29km).

**axiom** Assumption used as a basis for deductive reasoning. The axiomatic method is fundamental to the philosophy of modern mathematics: it was used by the Greeks and formalized early in the 20th century by David HILBERT. In an axiomatic system, certain undefined entities (**terms**) are taken and described by a set of axioms. Other, often unsuspected, relationships (**theorems**) are then deduced by logical reasoning. For example, the points, lines, and angles of Euclidean geometry are connected by postulates; theorems, such as Pythagoras' theorem, can be deduced.

**axis** Imaginary straight line about which a body rotates. In mechanics an axis runs longitudinally through the center of an axle or rotating shaft. In geography and astronomy, it is a line through the center of a planet or star, about which the planet or star rotates. The Earth's axis between the North and South geographic poles is 7,900mi (12,700km) long and is inclined at an angle of 66.5° to the plane in which the Earth orbits the Sun. A mathematical axis is a fixed line, such as the $x$, $y$, or $z$ axis, chosen for reference.

**Axis Powers** Term applied to Germany and Italy after they signed the Rome-Berlin Axis in October 1936. It included Japan after it joined them in the Tripartite Pact (September 1940). Other states that joined the Axis were Hungary and Romania (1940) and Bulgaria (1941).

**axolotl** Larval form of certain species of SALAMANDER native to W US and Mexico. Axolotls are aquatic amphibians that normally mature and reproduce without developing into adult salamanders. Length: *c.*10in (25cm). Family Ambystomidae.

**ayatollah** (Arabic, reflection of God) Honorific title bestowed upon a Muslim leader who has attained significant distinction and, often, political influence. *See also* Ayatollah Ruhollah KHOMEINI

**aye-aye** (aare) Primitive, squirrellike LEMUR of Madagascar. Nocturnal and tree-dwelling, it has dark shaggy fur and an elongated third finger with which it scrapes insects and pulp from bamboo canes. Length: 16in (40cm) excluding tail. Species *Daubentonia madagascariensis*.

**Ayer, Sir A.J. (Alfred Jules)** (1910–89) British philosopher. Building on the ideas of the Vienna Circle of positivists and of George BERKELEY, David HUME, Bertrand RUSSELL, and Ludwig WITTGENSTEIN, Ayer introduced LOGICAL POSITIVISM into US and British philosophy. His works include *Language, Truth and Logic* (1936), and *Philosophy and Language* (1960).

**Ayers Rock** (Uluru) Outcrop of rock, 280mi (448km) SW of Alice Springs, Northern Territory, Australia. Named for the prominent South Australian politician Sir Henry Ayers (1821–97), it remained undiscovered by Europeans until 1872. It stands 1,142ft (348m) high, and is the largest single rock in the world – the distance around its base is about 6mi (10km). The rock, caves of which are decorated with ancient paintings, is of great religious significance to Native Australians. It is known to them as Uluru.

**Aymara** Major tribe of Native South Americans who live in the highlands of Bolivia and Peru. By 1500 they had been brought into the INCA empire, which was subsequently conquered by the Spanish. Today, the Aymara number *c.*1,360,000. Their struggle to survive in a harsh, semidesert region accounts for their lack of an artistic heritage. The Aymara language is spoken by about a million people in Bolivia and 3 million people in Peru.

▲ **Ayers Rock** The site of many ancient cave paintings, Ayers Rock is known as *Uluru* to Native Australians. Lying in Northern Territory, Australia, it is the largest outcrop of free-standing rock in the world.

**Ayub Khan, Muhammad** (1907–74) Pakistani general and statesman, president (1958–69). After the partition of British India, Ayub Khan assumed control of the army in East Pakistan (now Bangladesh). In 1951 he became commander in chief of the army and served as defense minister (1954–56). In 1958 Ayub Khan led the military coup that overthrew Iskander Mirza. He was confirmed as president in a 1960 referendum. His administration was notable for its economic modernization and reforms to the political system. The failure of his regime to deal with poverty and social inequality forced him to resign.

**Ayurveda** System of medicine practiced by the ancient Hindus and derived from the VEDAS. It is still practiced in India.

**azalea** Name given to certain shrubs and small trees of the genus *Rhododendron*, from temperate regions of Asia and North America. Mostly deciduous, they have leathery leaves and funnel-shaped red, pink, magenta, orange, yellow, or white flowers, sometimes variegated. Family Ericaceae.

**Azerbaijan** Republic in SW Asia. See country feature page 58

**azimuth** Angle between the vertical plane through a celestial body and the N–S direction. Astronomers measure the angle eastward from the N point of the observer's horizon. Navigators and surveyors measure it westward from the S point. Altitude and azimuth form an astronomical coordinate system for defining position.

**Aznar, Jose Maria** (1953– ) Spanish statesman, prime minister (1996– ). Aznar became president of the Popular Party in 1990. His centrist policies helped him to form a minority government.

**Azores** Portuguese island group in the N Atlantic Ocean, 800mi (1,290km) W of Portugal. The capital and chief port is Ponta Delgada (on Sãn Miguel). Although they were known to early explorers such as the Phoenicians and the Norsemen, they were first settled by the Portuguese in the 15th century. In both world wars they were used as military bases. Volcanic in origin, they consist of nine main islands, divided into three groups. A variety of fruits, vegetables, and fish are exported. The islands' economy, dependent on small-scale farming and fishing, has improved with the development of tourism. Since 1976 the islands have formed an autonomous region of Portugal. Pico Alto at 7,713ft (2,351m) is Portugal's highest mountain. Area: 868sq mi (2,247sq km). Pop. (1994 est.) 239,900.

**Azov, Sea of** (Azovskoye More) N arm of the Black Sea. A shallow sea with only slight salinity, it has fishing ports on its E and S coasts. The marshes and lagoons at the W (Crimean peninsula) end were so noxious that the sea was known as *Sivash* (putrid lake). Area: 14,520sq mi (37,607sq km).

▼ **avocado** The fruit of the avocado tree (*Persea americana*) contains a single large seed surrounded by pale green flesh. When the skin of an avocado is soft it is ripe to eat.

A

**Aztec** Native American civilization that rose to a position of dominance in the central valley of Mexico in *c.*AD 1450. A warlike group, the Aztec (or Tenochca) settled near Lake Texcoco in about 1325, where they founded their capital Tenochtitlan (now Mexico City). They established an empire that included most of modern Mexico and extended S as far as Guatemala. The state was theocratic, with a number of deities whose worship included human sacrifice. The Aztec built temples, pyramids, and palaces and adorned them with stone images and symbolic carvings. At the time of the Spanish conquest, Aztec society was based on the exploitation of labor. As a result Hernán CORTÉS used disaffected tribesmen to help him defeat the Aztec in 1521. *See also* CENTRAL AND SOUTH AMERICAN MYTHOLOGY

## AZERBAIJAN

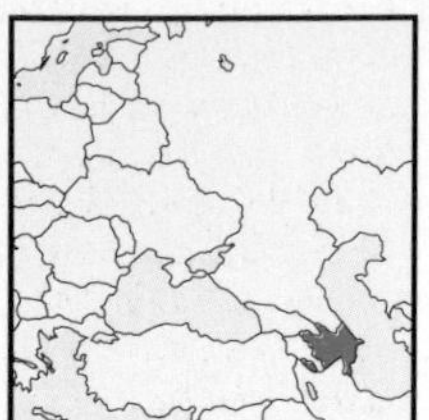

Azerbaijan's flag was adopted in 1991. The blue stands for the sky, the red for freedom, and the green for the land and for Islam. The crescent and the star also symbolize Islam. The points of the star represent the eight groups of people in Azerbaijan.

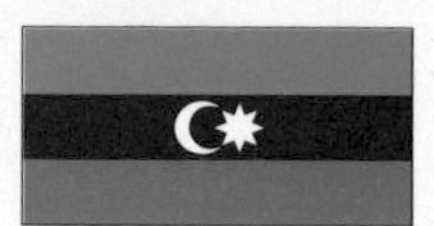

**AREA:** 86,600sq km (33,436sq mi)
**POPULATION:** 7,398,000
**CAPITAL (POPULATION):** Baku (1,100,000)
**GOVERNMENT:** Federal multiparty republic
**ETHNIC GROUPS:** Azerbaijani 83%, Russian 6%, Armenian 6%, Lezgin, Avar, Ukrainian, Tatar
**LANGUAGES:** Azerbaijani (official)
**RELIGIONS:** Islam (Shiite Muslim)
**CURRENCY:** Manat = 100 gopik

The Azerbaijani Republic is a country in the SW of Asia, bordering the Caspian Sea to the E. The CAUCASUS Mountains are in the N and another highland region, including the Little Caucasus Mountains and part of the rugged Armenian Plateau, is in the SW. Between these regions lies a broad plain drained by the Kura River. Its eastern part S of BAKU lies below sea level. The country also includes the NAKHICHEVAN Autonomous Republic on the Iran frontier, which is totally cut off from the rest of Azerbaijan by Armenian territory.

### CLIMATE AND VEGETATION

Azerbaijan has hot summers and cool winters. The rainfall is low on the plains, ranging from about 5–15in (130–380mm) a year, but is much higher in the highlands and on the subtropical SE coast. Forests of beech, oak, and pine trees grow on the mountain slopes, while the dry lowlands comprise grassy steppe or semidesert.

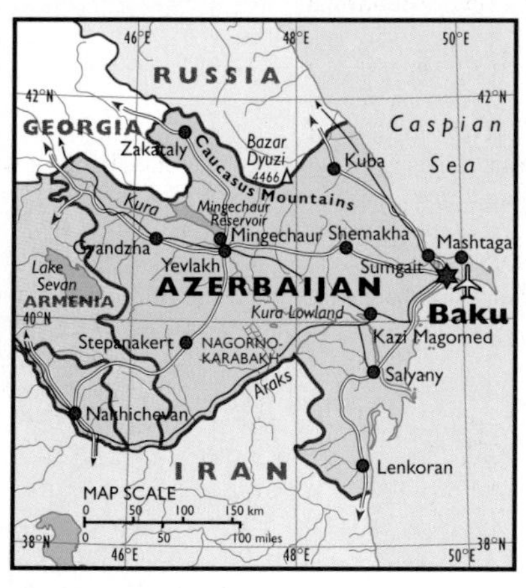


### HISTORY

In ancient times the area now called Azerbaijan was invaded many times. Arab armies introduced Islam in 642, but most modern Azerbaijanis are descendants of Persians and Turkic peoples who had migrated to the area from the E by the 9th century. The area later came under the MONGOLS between the 13th and 15th centuries and was then ruled by the Persian SAFAVID dynasty.

By the early 19th century Azerbaijan was under Russian rule. After the Russian Revolution of 1917, attempts were made to form a Transcaucasian Federation made up of Armenia, Azerbaijan and Georgia. When these attempts failed, Azerbaijanis set up an independent state, but Russian forces again occupied the area in 1920.

In 1922, the Russians did set up a Soviet Republic of TRANSCAUCASIA, but in 1936 the three areas became separate Socialist Republics within the SOVIET UNION.

### POLITICS

In the late 1980s, the government of the Soviet Union began to introduce social and political reforms, giving the people greater freedom. In 1991, the Soviet Union was voted out of existence and, like its neighbors, Azerbaijan became an independent nation.

After independence, economic progress was slow, partly because of civil unrest in NAGORNO-KARABAKH, a large enclave well within Azerbaijan where the majority of the people are Christian Armenians.

In 1992, Armenia occupied the area between its eastern border and Nagorno-Karabakh, while ethnic Armenians took over Nagorno-Karabakh itself. This conflict led to thousands of deaths and large migrations of both Armenians and Azerbaijanis. A ceasefire was agreed in 1994, with about 20% of Azerbaijan territory under Armenian control. There is little sign of a long-term solution to this problem, however, and sporadic fighting continued into 1998.

### ECONOMY

With its economy in disarray since the breakup of the Soviet Union, Azerbaijan now ranks among the world's "lower-middle-income" countries (1995 GDP per capita, US$1,460). Its chief resource is its oil – Azerbaijan is one of the world's oldest centers of production – with the main oil fields in the Baku region, both on the shore of the Caspian Sea and in the sea itself. In 1994, Azerbaijan invited Western companies to develop and exploit the offshore oil deposits.

Manufacturing, including oil refining and the production of chemicals, machinery, and textiles, is the most valuable activity. Large areas of land are irrigated and crops include cotton, tea, fruit, grains, tobacco, and vegetables. Fishing is still important, although the Caspian Sea has become increasingly polluted. Under the Communists, most economic activity was subject to state control, but (as with most former Soviet republics) private enterprise is now being encouraged.

B

*B/b, second letter of the alphabet. It is probably derived from an Egyptian hieroglyph for a house (c.3000 BC), which entered the Semitic alphabet 1,500 years later as the letter* **beth.** *From there it was taken to Greece to become* **beta,** *which was a similar shape to the modern B.*

**Baade, Walter** (1893–1960) US astronomer, b. Germany. From Mount Wilson Observatory, in the 1943 wartime blackout, he was able to observe individual stars in the ANDROMEDA GALAXY and distinguish the younger, bluer Population I stars from the older, redder Population II stars. He went on to show that the Universe was older and larger than previously thought.

**Baal** Chief god of the Semitic pantheon, akin to the Greek ZEUS. In the ancient Middle East he was linked with fertility as lord of the Earth, the rain and the dew. The Canaanites looked upon him as the foe of Mot, god of death and barrenness.

**Baalbek** Town in E Lebanon. An early Phoenician settlement, it was occupied by the Greeks in 323 BC and renamed Heliopolis. It was colonized by the Romans in the 1st century BC. It is noted for its Greek and Roman remains, especially the Temple of Jupiter.

**Ba'ath Party** Arab political party, founded in 1943. Its major objectives are socialism and Arab unity. It is strongest in Iraq and Syria, and militaristic elements of the Ba'ath Party seized power in those countries in 1968 and 1970 respectively. *See also* SADDAM HUSSEIN

**Babbage, Charles** (1791–1871) British mathematician. Babbage compiled the first actuarial tables and planned a mechanical calculating machine, the forerunner of the modern COMPUTER. He failed to complete the construction of the machine because the financial support recommended by the Royal Society was refused by the British government.

**Babbitt, Milton** (1916– ) US composer, musicologist, and teacher. Babbitt's mathematical background influenced his musical style. He systematized the analysis of TWELVE-TONE MUSIC. His compositions include vocal, piano, and chamber music. Works include *Ensembles for Synthesizer* (1962–64).

**Babel, Isaac Emmanuelovich** (1894–1941) Russian short-story writer. His works, many of which are informed by his military service and experience of persecution, include *Tales of Odessa* (1924) and *Red Cavalry* (1926). He died a victim of Stalinist purges in a Siberian concentration camp.

**Babel, Tower of** Tower begun on the plain of Shinar, in Babylonia, by the descendants of NOAH as a means of reaching heaven (Genesis 11). God prevented its completion by confusing the speech of the people and scattering them throughout the world. The Genesis story was probably inspired by a ZIGGURAT in Babylon, seven stories high and with a shrine to the god Marduk on its top.

**Babi faith** (Babism) Muslim religious sect founded in 1844 in Persia (Iran) by Sayyid Ali Muhammad, the self-proclaimed prophet Bab (Arabic gate). Babists believed in the imminent coming of the Promised One. In 1848 they declared secession from ISLAM, but their rebellion against the new shah was crushed and their founder was executed in 1850.

**Babi Yar** Ravine near Kiev, Ukraine, in which *c*.34,000 Jews were massacred by Nazi German soldiers in 1941. The massacre is commemorated in an eponymous poem (1961) by Yevgeny YEVTUSHENKO and a novel by Anatoly KUZNETSOV.

**baboon** Large African MONKEY with a doglike face, which walks on all fours. Its buttocks have callus-like pads surrounded by brilliantly colored skin. Baboons are ground dwellers and active by day, traveling in families and larger troops led by old males, usually in open, rocky country. Their diet consists of plants, insects, and small animals. The males have large canine teeth up to 2in (5cm) long. Weight: 30-90lb (14–41kg). Genus *Chaeropithecus* (or *Papio*).

**Babur** (1483–1530) First Mogul emperor of India (1526–30) b. Zahir ud-Din Muhammad; Babur (Turk. tiger) became ruler of FERGANA in 1495 and engaged in a long conflict for control of SAMARKAND, but ultimately lost both territories. Raising an army, he captured Kabul and carved out a new kingdom for himself in Afghanistan. From here he invaded India, gaining Delhi (1526) and Agra (his future capital, 1527) and conquering N India as far as Bengal.

**Babylon** Ancient city on the Euphrates River in MESOPOTAMIA, capital of the empire BABYLONIA. It was rebuilt after being destroyed by ASSYRIA *c*.689 BC, and its new buildings included the HANGING GARDENS, one of the SEVEN WONDERS OF THE WORLD. This was the period, under NEBUCHADNEZZAR, of the BABYLONIAN CAPTIVITY of the Jews. After 275 BC Babylon declined , as Seleucia gained ascendancy.

**Babylonia** Ancient region and empire of MESOPOTAMIA, based on the city of BABYLON. The Babylonian empire was first established in the early 18th century BC by HAMMURABI the Great, but declined under the impact of HITTITES and Kassites in *c*.1595 BC. The empire eventually fell to ASSYRIA in the 8th century BC. Babylon's greatness was restored and in *c*.625 BC its independence was won by Nabopolassar, who captured the Assyrian capital of NINEVEH. This New Babylonian (Chaldaean) empire defeated Egypt and took the Jews to captivity in Babylon in 586 BC. In 538 BC it fell to the Persians.

**Babylonian Captivity** Deportation of the Jews to BABYLON between the capture of Jerusalem in 586 BC by NEBUCHADNEZZAR and the reformation of a Palestinian Jewish state (*c*.538 BC) by CYRUS THE GREAT. Many Jewish religious institutions, such as SYNAGOGUES, were founded in the period of exile, and parts of the Hebrew Bible also date from this time. The term was later applied to the exile of the popes at AVIGNON (1309–77). *See also* DIASPORA; GREAT SCHISM

**Bacall, Lauren** (1924– ) US film actress. Following Bacall's screen debut opposite Humphrey BOGART in *To Have and Have Not* (1944) the two married in 1945. They starred together in a further three films, including the classics *The Big Sleep* (1946) and *Key Largo* (1948).

**Bacchus** In Roman mythology, the god of wine and fertility, identified with the Greek god DIONYSUS.

**Bach, C.P.E. (Carl Philipp Emanuel)** (1714–88) German composer, second surviving son of J.S. BACH. The most prolific and famous of Bach's sons, he wrote over 150 keyboard sonatas, 20 symphonies, *c*.50 harpsichord concertos, numerous chamber works, much sacred music, and *c*.300 songs. He was widely esteemed as a keyboard player and became a leading theorist with his *Essay on the True Art of Keyboard Playing* (1753–62).

**Bach, J.C. (Johann Christian)** (1735–82) German composer, youngest son of J.S. BACH. He was organist at Milan cathedral, composed operas that were staged in Turin and Naples, but soon moved to London where his operas were better received. In 1763 he was made music-master to Queen Charlotte. Besides 11 operas, he wrote many instrumental and vocal works.

**Bach, Johann Sebastian** (1685–1750) Prolific German BAROQUE composer. He held a series of court positions as organist and music director and had 20 children, four of whom were also composers. Bach brought contrapuntal forms to their highest expression and is unrivaled in his ability to interweave melodies within the exacting rules of baroque harmony and counterpoint. While at the court in Weimar (1708–17), he wrote many of his great organ works (preludes, fugues, toccatas), such as the Fugue in C minor. At Köthen (1717–23), he wrote Book I of the *The Well-Tem-*

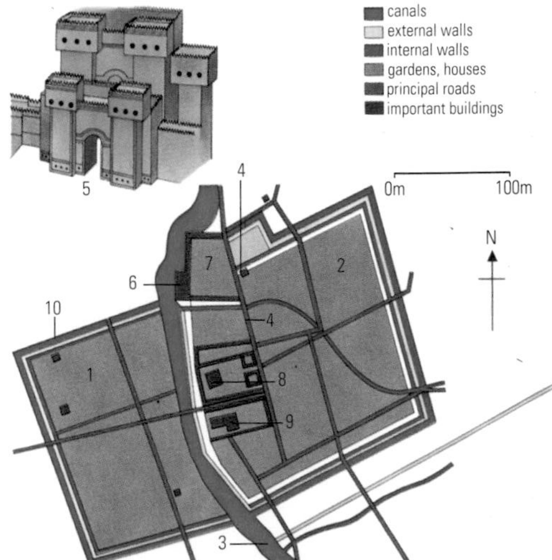


◄ **Babylon** Early Babylon was often rebuilt. The excavated, sophisticated layout we see today was created mainly by Nebuchadnezzar II (*c*.604-561 BC). Old city (1) and new (2) are separated by the Euphrates River (3), and contained within two fortification walls, reinforced by a moat (10) and accessible through fortified gateways connected to the major streets. A SE outer wall gave additional protection. The ritual Processional Way (4) enters the new city through the Ishtar Gate (5), passing a fortress (6) and the main citadel complex (7) of administration and garrison buildings, palaces, and vaulted Hanging Gardens. Skirting Etemenanki enclosure with its ziggurat (8) – possibly that of Babel – it turns W past the temple of Marduk (9) and crosses the five-pier bridge to the old city. Navigable canals irrigated the dry soil and helped prevent flooding of the Euphrates.

**BACTERIA**

Bacteria occur in three basic shapes: spherical forms called cocci (A), rodlike bacilli (B), and spiral spirilla (C). Cocci can occur in clumps known as staphylococci (1), groups of two called diplococci (2), or chains called streptococci (3). Unlike cocci, which do not move, bacilli are freely mobile; some are termed peritrichous and use many flagellae (4) to swim about, while other monotrichous forms use a single flagellum (5). Bacilli can also form spores (6) to survive unfavorable conditions. Spirilla may be either corkscrew-shaped spirochetes like Leptospira (7), or less coiled and flagellated, such as Spirillum (8) (magnification x 5,000).

*pered Clavier* and the six *Brandenburg Concertos*. As musical director of St. Thomas, Leipzig (1723–50), Bach wrote his celebrated church music, including *St. Matthew Passion* (1729) and Mass in B Minor. Other works included the *Goldberg Variations* (1742).

**bacillus** Genus of rodlike BACTERIA present in the air and soil. One example of a species that is pathogenic in man is *Bacillus anthracis*, which causes ANTHRAX.

**background radiation** Radiation that is normally present in an environment. Such radiation must be taken into account when measuring radiation from a particular source. On Earth, background radiation is caused by the decay of naturally occurring radioactive substances in surface rocks. In space, the so-called "microwave background" is attributed to the BIG BANG.

**Bacon, Francis** (1561–1626) British philosopher, statesman, and early advocate of the scientific method. Bacon was also an important essayist. He held important government offices but was forced to resign in 1621. None of this interrupted his efforts to break the hold of Aristotelian LOGIC and establish an inductive EMPIRICISM. Bacon entertained the idea of cataloguing all useful knowledge in his *Advancement of Learning* (1605) and *Novum Organum* (1620).

**Bacon, Francis** (1909–92) British painter, one of the most controversial artists of his generation. Bacon changed the face of English painting in 1945 when he exhibited his triptych, *Three Studies for Figures at the Base of a Crucifixion*. The shock of the distorted representations of grieving people in his work stems from his violent handling of paint as much as from the subjects themselves. The religious focus of his work continued in a savage series of portraits of Roman Catholic popes.

**Bacon's Rebellion** (1676) Revolt in colonial Virginia, led by Nathaniel Bacon (1647–76). High taxes and the low value of tobacco angered colonists and Governor William Berkeley's failure to defend the frontier from attack by Native Americans precipitated the rebellion. After leading the defence of the frontier, Bacon was elected to the house of burgesses but was arrested by Berkeley. Upon his release, he led a march on Jamestown and Berkeley fled. Berkeley's attempt to recapture the capital ended in failure and the razing of the city. However, Bacon died of a fever and the rebellion collapsed. Berkeley exacted bloody revenge.

**bacteria** Simple unicellular microscopic organisms. They lack a clearly defined nucleus and most are without CHLOROPHYLL. Many are motile, swimming around by using whiplike flagella. Most multiply by FISSION. Under adverse conditions many can remain dormant inside highly resistant SPORES with thick protective coverings. Bacteria may be AEROBIC or ANAEROBIC. Although pathogenic bacteria are a major cause of human disease, many bacteria are harmless or even beneficial to humans by providing an important link in FOOD CHAINS, as in decomposing plant and animal tissue, and in converting free nitrogen and sulfur into AMINO ACIDS and other compounds that plants and animals can use. Some contain a form of CHLOROPHYLL and carry out PHOTOSYNTHESIS. Bacteria belong to the kingdom PROKARYOTAE. *See also* ARCHAEBACTERIA; EUBACTERIA

**bacteriology** Scientific study of BACTERIA. They were first observed in the 17th century by Anton van LEEUWENHOEK, but it was not until the mid-19th century researches of Louis PASTEUR and Robert KOCH that bacteriology was established as a scientific discipline.

**bacteriophage** VIRUS that lives on and infects BACTERIA. It has a protein head containing a core of DNA and a protein tail. Discovered in 1915, it is important in the study of GENETICS.

**Baden-Powell, Robert Stephenson Smyth, Baron of Gilwell** (1857–1941) British soldier and founder of the BOY SCOUT movement. He held Mafeking against the Boers (1899–1900). His sister **Agnes** (1858–1945) founded the Girl Guides (1910). His wife, Lady Olave (1889–1977), also did much to promote these movements worldwide.

**Baden-Württemberg** Federal state in SW Germany, formed in 1952 by the merger of Baden, Württemberg-Baden, and Württemberg-Hohenzollern; the capital is STUTTGART. A forested and fertile region drained by the Rhine and Danube rivers, agriculture and livestock rearing are important, but industry is the main economic activity. Chief manufactures include electrical freight, machinery, and vehicle-assembly at Stuttgart, MANNHEIM, and Karlsruhe. There are famous universities at HEIDELBERG and Freiburg im Breisgau. Visitors are drawn to the spa at Baden-Baden and the natural beauty of the Neckar Valley and the Black Forest. Area: 13,803sq mi (35,750sq km). Pop. (1993) 10,234,000.

**badger** Burrowing, nocturnal mammal that lives in Eurasia, North America, and Africa. It has a stocky body with short legs and tail. Eurasian badgers (*Meles meles*) have gray bodies with black-and-white striped heads. American badgers (*Taxidea taxus*) are smaller and have gray-brown to red fur with a white head stripe. Length: 16-28in (41–71cm); weight: 22-44lb (10–20kg). Family Mustelidae.

**badlands** Eroded, barren plateau in an arid or semi-arid area characterized by steep gullies and ravines. Because of the lack of adequate vegetation (due to climate or human intervention), the rainwater runs off very quickly and erodes soft and exposed rock. The best-known examples are the badlands of SW South Dakota and NW Nebraska, US.

**Badlands National Park** Park in SW South Dakota, US. Established as a National Park in 1929, the arid region is characterized by steep ravines, sparse vegetation and layers of sandstone rock. Area: 170sq mi (440sq km)

**badminton** Court game for two or four players, popular in England from the 1870s. The rules were drawn up in Pune, India and codified with the formation of the Badminton Asso-

► **badger** Eurasian badgers (*Meles meles*) of S China live in large family groups in large burrows known as sets. Sets have a complex network of tunnels and chambers, each serving a particular function.

ciation (1893). The object is to use light rackets to volley a shuttlecock over a net until missed or hit out of bounds by an opponent. Only the player serving can score a point; games are played to 15 points.

**Baekeland, Leo Hendrik** (1863–1944) US chemist, b. Belgium. Baekeland invented a type of photographic paper, Velox, capable of being developed under artificial light. He also invented the first thermosetting plastic, BAKELITE, a substance that led to the development of the plastics industry.

**Baffin, William** (1584–1622) English navigator and explorer. Baffin took part in several expeditions (1612–16) in search of the NORTHWEST PASSAGE. He discovered the Canadian Arctic seaways, the island now named after him, and Lancaster Sound. An outstanding navigator, he published a method of determining longitude by the stars, using nautical tables.

**Baffin Island** Largest and most easterly island of the Canadian Arctic Archipelago, separated from QUEBEC province by the Hudson Strait. It is the fifth-largest island in the world, with largely mountainous terrain and an almost entirely Inuit population. Area: 195,928sq mi (507,451sq km).

**Bagehot, Walter** (1826–77) British economist and writer. Editor of *The Economist* (1860–77), he is chiefly remembered for his influential treatise *The English Constitution* (1867).

**Baghdad** Capital of Iraq, on the Tigris River. Established in 762 as capital of the ABBASID caliphate, it became a center of Islamic civilization and focus of caravan routes between Asia and Europe. In 1921, Baghdad became the capital of newly independent Iraq. In 1991 it was badly damaged during the Persian Gulf War. Notable sights include the 13th-century Abbasid Palace. Industries: building materials, textiles, tanning, bookbinding. Pop. (1987 est.) 3,850,000.

**bagpipes** Musical instrument with reed pipes connected to a windbag held under the arm and filled by mouth or bellows. The chanter pipe has finger holes for melody, while drone pipes produce monotone accompaniment.

**Baha'i** Religion founded in the 1860s by BAHAULLAH as an outgrowth of the BABI FAITH. Its headquarters are in HAIFA, Israel. It seeks world peace through the unification of all religions and stresses a simple life dedicated to serving others. It recognizes Bahaullah as the latest prophet of God.

**Bahamas** Small independent state in the West Indies, in the W Atlantic, SE of Florida. It consists of *c*.700 islands, 2,000 cays, and numerous coral reefs. The largest island is Grand Bahama; the capital is NASSAU (on New Providence). The islands consist mainly of limestone and coral, and the rocky terrain provides little chance for agricultural development. Most of the islands are low, flat, and riverless with mangrove swamps. The climate is subtropical, with temperatures averaging between 70–90°F (21–32°C). The population is 90% African or African-European; the majority live on New Providence. Anglicanism is the predominant religion, and English the official language. San Salvador island is traditionally believed to have been the first stop of Christopher Columbus in his quest for the New World (1492). Charles II granted the islands to six lord proprietors of Carolina in 1670, but development was continually hindered by pirates. Britain assumed direct control by 1729, expelling militants and restoring civil order. Held briefly by Spain (1782) during the American Revolution, the islands were given back to England by the Treaty of Versailles (1783) in exchange for E Florida. In 1834 slavery was abolished. In 1963 a new constitution was drawn up providing for a parliamentary form of government. In 1973 the Bahamas became an independent nation. The main industry is tourism; commercial fishing, salt, rum, and handicrafts are also important. Area: 5,350sq mi (13,860sq km). Pop. (1992 est.) 264,000.

**Bahaullah** (1817–92) Name adopted by Mirza Husayn Ali Nuri, Persian religious leader and founder of the BAHA'I faith. He embraced the BABI FAITH in 1850 but broke away in 1867, proclaiming himself Bahaullah ("The Glory of Allah"), the Promised One foretold by Bab. His work, the *Katabi ikan* (*The Book of Certitude*) is the Baha'i holy book.

**Bahia** Coastal state in E Brazil; the capital is SALVADOR. Portuguese explorers reached the area in 1501. Declared a province in 1823, it achieved statehood in 1889. Products: cacao, tobacco, hardwoods, natural gas, lead, titanium, asbestos, hydroelectricity. Area: 216,612sq mi (561,026sq km). Pop. (1991) 11,801,810.

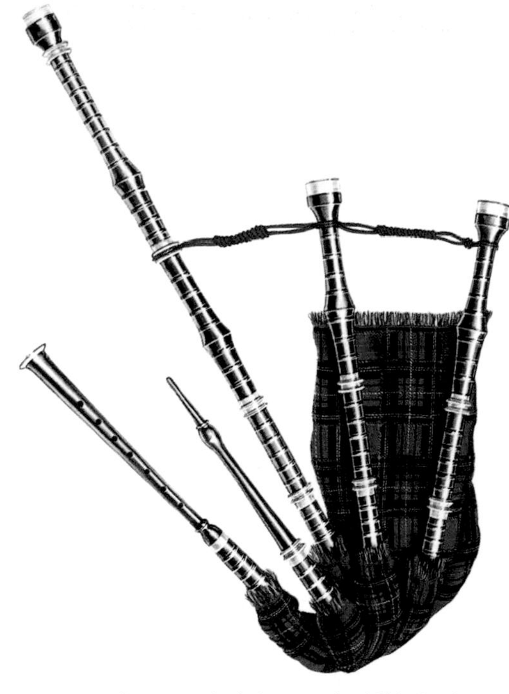

◀ **bagpipes** Although closely associated with Scotland and to some degree Ireland, the bagpipes actually originated in Greece and Asia.

**Bahrain** Emirate archipelago in the Persian (Arabian) Gulf, SW Asia; the capital is MANAMA. It comprises 34 small islands and the largest island of Bahrain. Oil was discovered in 1932 and the sheikhdom led the regional development of oil production. It is a hot, desert kingdom linked by a causeway to the Saudi Arabian mainland. From 1861 to 1971 the country was a British protectorate. Since the late 18th century Bahrain has been governed by the Khalifa family. The 1970s drop in oil production led to economic diversification. Bahrain's aluminum-smelting plant is the Gulf's largest non-oil industrial complex. While other economic sectors have grown, oil still accounts for 80% of Bahrain's exports and 20% of its GDP. Bahrain is a predominantly Muslim nation. Tensions exist between the SUNNI and majority SHIITE population. During the IRAN-IRAQ WAR (1980–88) Bahrain supported Iraq. Area: 262sq mi (678sq km). Pop. (1995 est.) 558,000.

**Baikal, Lake** (Baykal) World's deepest lake in S Siberia, Russia; the largest freshwater feature in Asia. Fed by numerous small rivers, its outlet is the ANGARA River. It has rich fish stocks and includes the only freshwater seal species. Its ecology has been threatened by industrial pollutants from lakeside factories, and government schemes have been introduced to protect the environment. The city of Irkutsk lies on its N shore. Area: 12,160sq mi (31,494sq km). Max. depth: 5,714ft (1,743m).

**Baird, John Logie** (1888–1946) Scottish electrical engineer, inventor of TELEVISION. In 1926 Baird demonstrated the first working television to members of the Royal Institution, London. In 1928 he transmitted to a ship at sea, and in 1929 was granted experimental broadcasting facilities by the British Broadcasting Corporation (BBC). His 240-line, part-mechanical television system was used for the world's first public television service by the BBC in 1936. In 1937 it was superseded by MARCONI's fully electronic scanning.

**Baja California** (Lower California) Peninsula of NW Mexico, extending SSE for 760mi (1,220km) between the Gulf of California and the Pacific Ocean. The peninsula consists of two states, Baja California Norte (capital Mexicali) and Baja California Sur (capital La Paz). The chief product of the region is long-staple cotton and the main industry is tourism. Area: 55,517sq mi (143,790sq km). Pop. (1990) 1,978,619.

B

**Bakelite** Trade name (coined by Leo BAEKELAND) for a thermosetting PLASTIC used for insulating purposes and in making paint. It was the first plastic (1909) made by the process of condensation, in which many molecules of two chemicals (in this case PHENOL and METHANAL) are joined together to form large polymer molecules.

**Baker, James Addison** (1930– ) US Republican Party politician. After serving under Ronald REAGAN as White House chief of staff (1981–85) and secretary of the treasury (1985–88), Baker managed the successful 1988 presidential election campaign of George BUSH. As Bush's secretary of state (1989–92), much of his focus was on the Middle East, particularly Iraq's invasion of Kuwait (1990) and the subsequent GULF WAR (1991). In 1992 Baker became Bush's chief of staff and supervised his unsuccessful bid for re-election.

**Baker, Josephine** (1906–75) US dancer and singer. After a sensational 1925 Paris debut in *La Revue Nègre*, she became internationally famous for her jazz singing and dancing. She took French citizenship in 1937 and became a member of the French Legion of Honor for her work in the resistance.

**Baker v. Carr** (1962) Landmark US Supreme Court decision holding that apportionment of state legislatures and redistricting to assure proper representation were proper issues that should be decided in federal courts. The court overruled *Colegrove v. Green* (1946).

**Bakke Case** (Regents of the University of California v. Bakke) US Supreme Court case (1978) involving Allan Bakke, who was refused admission (1972) to the University of California at Davis medical school, despite his excellent academic record. He sued the university on a charge that he had been passed over in favor of less qualified minority students. The Court ruled that Bakke had been a victim of reverse discrimination and must be admitted to the university.

**Baku** Capital of Azerbaijan, a port on the W coast of the Caspian Sea. A trade and craft center in the Middle Ages, Baku prospered under the Shirvan shahs in the 15th century. Commercial oil production began in the 1870s. At the beginning of the 20th century Baku lay at the center of the world's largest oil field. The port handles a vast quantity of oil and petroleum products. Industries: oil processing and equipment, shipbuilding, electrical machinery, chemicals. Pop. (1993) 1,100,000.

**Bakunin, Mikhail Alexandrovich** (1814–76) Russian political philosopher. Bakunin became a believer in violent revolution while in Paris in 1848, and was active in the first Communist International until expelled by Karl MARX in 1872. His approach, known as revolutionary ANARCHY, repudiates all forms of governmental authority as fundamentally at variance with human freedom and dignity. In *God and the State* (1882) Bakunin argued that only natural law is consistent with liberty.

**Balaclava** (Balaklava) Town in the Crimea, site of an inconclusive battle (1854) during the CRIMEAN WAR. The British, French, and Turks held off a Russian attack on the supply port of Balaclava. The battle is famous for a disastrous charge by Lord Cardigan's Light Brigade to capture Russian guns, as recorded in a poem by Alfred TENNYSON.

**Balakirev, Mili Alexeyevich** (1837–1910) Russian composer. Balakirev was one of the RUSSIAN FIVE dedicated to promoting Russian nationalism in 19th-century music. To this end he incorporated Russian folk idioms into his compositional style. Balakirev's best-known compositions are two symphonies, *Islamey* (1869), and incidental music to *King Lear* (1858–61). He founded the St. Petersburg Free School of Music in 1862.

**balalaika** Triangular musical instrument popular in Russia. Strings (usually three) are fingered on a fretted neck and may be picked, or plucked with the fingers. It sounds similar to the MANDOLIN.

**balance of payments** Overall surplus or deficit that occurs as a result of the exchange of all freight and services between one nation and the rest of the world. A country with a balance of payments deficit must finance it by borrowing from other countries or the INTERNATIONAL MONETARY FUND (IMF), or by using foreign currency reserves. Such deficits, if frequent, can pose a serious problem, because they cause a reduction in the reserves. This in turn leads to economic pressure for DEVALUATION in order to correct the imbalance.

**balance of trade** Surplus or deficit incurred by a country in its trading. It is the difference between the sum of its imports and the sum of its exports. *See also* BALANCE OF PAYMENTS

**Balanchine, George** (1904–83) US choreographer and ballet dancer. One of the greatest artists in 20th-century ballet, Balanchine defected (1924) from Russia to work as principal dancer and choreographer for DIAGHILEV and the BALLETS RUSSES. He moved to the US in 1933, established the School of American Ballet, and was director (1934–37) of the Metropolitan Opera ballet. He became the first artistic director and choreographer of the New York City Ballet (1948). Credited with creating US neoclassical ballet, he also undertook film choreography. Ballet pieces include *The Nutcracker* (1954) and *Don Quixote* (1965).

**Balaton** Largest lake in central Europe, SW of Budapest, central Hungary. Rich in fish, many holiday resorts and vineyards line its shores. Area: 232sq mi (600sq km).

**Balboa, Vasco Núñez de** (1475–1519) Spanish conquistador, the first European to see the Pacific Ocean. Balboa went to Hispaniola in 1500 and to Darién (Panama) ten years later. In September 1513, accompanied by a group of locals, he crossed the isthmus and saw the Pacific, which he called the South Sea. He was later executed on a false charge.

**bald cypress** (swamp cypress) Deciduous tree growing in shallow water in the SE US. They have woody growth on the roots that grow above water, and lose their feathery, light green needles in fall. Height: to 15ft (4.6m). Family Taxodiaceae; species *Taxodium distichum*.

**bald eagle** Large bird of prey that lives in North America, where it feeds on fish and small mammals. It is brown with a white head and tail and a yellow bill. Its tail feathers were used in the headdresses of some Native Americans, and it is the national emblem of the US. Although now protected by law, it is still an endangered species. Species *Haliaeetus leucocephalus*

**Baldwin, James** (1924–87) US novelist and essayist. Baldwin's first novel, *Go Tell It on the Mountain* (1953), was semi-autobiographical and has become an American classic. His prose is inflected with blues and gospel rhythms. His most celebrated novel is *Another Country* (1962). Essay collections include *Notes of a Native Son* (1955) and *The Fire Next Time* (1963). Baldwin was prominent in the US CIVIL RIGHTS movement.

**Baldwin, Stanley, 1st Earl of Bewdley** (1867–1947) British statesman, prime minister (1923–24, 1924–29, 1935–37). Baldwin was chancellor of the exchequer (1922–23) before succeeding Bonar LAW as Conservative prime minister. Baldwin responded to the General Strike (1926) by passing the Trades Disputes Acts (1927), which made any subsequent general strikes illegal. Baldwin opposed EDWARD VIII's marriage to Wallis Simpson and secured his abdication (1936). His APPEASEMENT of European fascism is often cited as a cause of Britain's lack of preparedness at the start of World War II.

**Balearic Islands** Group of Spanish islands in the W Mediterranean, off the E coast of Spain; the capital is PALMA. The islands were successively occupied by all the great Mediterranean civilizations of antiquity. In the 11th century a Moorish kingdom used them as a base for piracy. The chief islands are MAJORCA, Minorca, and IBIZA. Industries: tourism, silverworking, olive oil, wine, fruit. Area: 1,936sq mi (5,014sq km). Pop. (1991) 709,138.

**Balfour, Arthur James Balfour, 1st Earl of** (1848–1930) British statesman, prime minister (1902–05), b. Scotland. Balfour succeeded his uncle, the Marquess of SALISBURY, as prime minister. His government introduced educational reforms (1902), but the CONSERVATIVE PARTY fractured over the tariff reform proposed by Joseph CHAMBERLAIN. Balfour resigned and the Conservatives lost the ensuing general election. He returned to the cabinet in the coalition governments of Herbert ASQUITH and David LLOYD GEORGE. As foreign secretary, he issued the BALFOUR DECLARATION (1917).

**Balfour Declaration** (1917) Letter written by British foreign minister Arthur BALFOUR to the British Zionist Federation pledging cooperation for the settlement of Jews in PALESTINE. Jews were admitted to the area when it became a British mandate under the League of Nations after World War I. *See also* ZIONISM

**Bali** Island province of Indonesia, off the E tip of Java, between the Bali Sea and the Indian Ocean. The main town is Denpasar. Under Javanese control from the 10th century, Bali was a Dutch possession from 1908 to 1949, apart from Japanese occupation during World War II. It is the center of Majaphit Hinduism. Its scenic beauty and native culture make it a popular tourist resort. Industries: rice, sweet potatoes, cassava, copra, meat processing. Area: 2,147sq mi (5,561sq km). Pop. (1990) 2,777,811.

**Balkan Mountains** Major mountain range of the Balkan Peninsula extending from E Serbia through central Bulgaria to the Black Sea; a continuation of the CARPATHIAN MOUNTAINS. It is rich in minerals and forms a climatic barrier for the inland regions. The highest peak is Botev, 7,793ft (2,375m).

**Balkan states** Group of countries in the Balkan Peninsula, in SE Europe, consisting of ALBANIA, BOSNIA-HERZEGOVINA, BULGARIA, CROATIA, GREECE, MACEDONIA, ROMANIA, SERBIA, and European TURKEY. From the 3rd century AD the region was ruled by Byzantium. It was later invaded by Slav peoples, and then for 500 years formed part of the Ottoman Empire. The individual countries regained independence in the 19th century.

**Balkan Wars** (1912–13) Two wars involving the BALKAN STATES and the OTTOMAN EMPIRE. In the first, the Balkan League (Serbia, Bulgaria, Greece, and Montenegro) conquered most of the European territory of the OTTOMAN EMPIRE. The second war (mainly between Serbia and Bulgaria) arose out of dissatisfaction with the distribution of these lands. Serbia's victory added to regional tension before World War I.

**Balkhash** (Balchaš) Lake in SE Kazakstan extending from the Kazak Hills (NE) to the desert steppes (SW). It has no outlet. The chief inlet is the freshwater Ili River, therefore the W half of the lake is freshwater. Area: 7,115sq mi (18,428sq km). Max. depth: 85ft (26m).

**Balla, Giacomo** (1871–1958) Italian artist. Influenced by the poet MARINETTI, founder of FUTURISM, Balla adopted the movement's philosophical outlook and urged artists to use art as a means to change Italy's culture through the acceptance of science and technology. His works include *The Street Light – Study of Light* (1909) and *Dynamism of Dog on a Leash* (1912).

**ballad** (Lat. *ballare*, to dance) Form of popular poetry which is regularly sung, narrative in style with simple meter, rhyme, and often a refrain. The first surviving examples date from medieval times, and typically consist of four-line stanzas. The ballad was a vital means of perpetuating community myth, the traditions of storytelling, and the celebration of rites. Notable later examples include *Lyrical Ballads* (1798), written by WORDSWORTH in collaboration with COLERIDGE. The late-18th century revival of the ballad was central to the rise of ROMANTICISM. It was espoused by SWINBURNE, LONGFELLOW, Sir Walter SCOTT, and Rudyard KIPLING.

**ballade** Non-narrative poem of three (typically eight-line) rhymed stanzas and a final (typically four-line) rhymed stanza (envoy) in which the poet's conclusion or moral is drawn. A widely used form, especially in France where its greatest exponent was François Villon, it flourished in the Middle Ages and was often sung.

**Balladur, Edouard** (1929– ) French statesman, Gaullist prime minister (1993–95). Balladur was elected to parliament in 1986 and became (1988) minister of economy and finance. In 1995 his lackluster campaign for the presidency was tainted by charges of corruption, and he lost to Jacques CHIRAC.

**Ballard, J.G. (James Graham)** (1930– ) British novelist and short-story writer. Ballard is best known for his highly stylized science fiction. Novels such as *The Wind from Nowhere* (1962), *The Drought* (1965), *The Crystal World*, and *Crash* (1973), explore psychological reactions to catastrophic situations. The popular novel *Empire of the Sun* (1984) dealt with his childhood experiences of a World War II Japanese prisoner of war camp. Its sequel was *The Kindness of Women* (1991).

**Ballesteros, Severiano** (1957– ) Spanish golfer. Ballesteros was the 20th-century's youngest winner of the British Open (1979). A brilliant stroke-maker, He won the British Open twice more (1984, 1988) and the US Masters in 1980 and 1983. Ballesteros was an inspiring member of the European Ryder Cup teams from 1985 and captained them to victory in 1997.

**ballet** Theatrical dance form set to music. The first formal ballet, *Ballet comique de la Reine*, was performed at the court of Catherine de' Medici (1581). Louis XIV founded the Royal Academy of Dance in 1661. *The Triumph of Love* (1681) was the first ballet to use trained female dancers. The first public performance of a ballet was in 1708. Choreographic notation was developed, and Pierre Beauchamp (1631–1719) established the five classical positions. Jean-Georges NOVERRE (1727–1810), the most influential choreographer of the 18th century, argued for a greater naturalism. The 1832 performance of *Les Sylphides* set the choreographic model for 19th-century romantic ballets, stressing the role of the prima ballerina. Dancing on the toes (*sur les pointes*) was introduced. At the end of the 19th century Russian ballet emphasized technique and virtuosity. Subsequently, Sergei DIAGHILEV and his BALLETS RUSSES revolutionized ballet with dynamic choreography and dancing. Today, the preeminence of Russian ballet is maintained by the KIROV and BOLSHOI companies. In 1930 Dame Marie RAMBERT founded the first English ballet school, and in 1931 Dame Ninette de VALOIS established the Sadler's Wells Ballet (now the Royal Ballet). Rudolf NUREYEV's influential work for the Royal Ballet enlarged the role and dramatic range of the male dancer. In 1934 the first major US ballet school was instituted under the direction of George BALANCHINE. In 1948 the New York City Ballet was established. It is now one of the world's principal ballet companies. American ballet introduced a more abstract style and eclectic approach, fusing elements of classical ballet, jazz, popular, and MODERN DANCE. *See also* MASQUE

**Ballets Russes** Dance company founded (1909) in Paris by Sergei DIAGHILEV, with Michel FOKINE as chief choreographer. It revitalized and reshaped ballet by bringing together great dancers (PAVLOVA and NIJINSKY) and choreographers (MASSINE, NIJINSKY, and BALANCHINE). Leading composers, such as STRAVINSKY, DEBUSSY, and Richard STRAUSS composed music for the company, and top artists such as PICASSO, CHAGALL, and MATISSE designed sets and costumes. It disbanded soon after Diaghilev's death in 1929.

◀ **balloon** Man's first balloon flight took place on 21 November 1783, when a balloon designed by the Montgolfier brothers, and carrying Jean-François Pilâtre de Rozier and the Marquis of d'Arlandes, flew about 5mi (8km) across Paris. The flight is believed to have lasted 23min, during which time the balloon is thought to have reached a height of 3,000ft (900m). Made of paper-lined linen and coated with alum to reduce the fire risk, the balloon was 50ft (15m) high, and weighed 785kg (1,730lb). The air inside was heated by a large mass of burning straw resting on a wire grid in the centre of the gallery.

► **bamboo** Woody members of the grass family, bamboos can vary in height from a few inches to many feet. While most bamboo grows in dense clumps in tropical regions, some bamboo such as *Arundinaria alpina* (shown here) grows on mountainsides and can withstand cold conditions. Although hollow, bamboo is surprisingly strong for its weight, and is used in some parts of the world for building houses and making furniture.

**balloon** Unsteerable, lighter-than-air craft, usually made of nylon. Balloons are used for recreation, scientific, and military purposes. A gas that is lighter than air lifts the balloon from the ground. The first balloons to fly were of the open-necked hot-air type. This type of balloon uses propane gas to inflate the balloon. Controlled descent is achieved through regulated deflation. Unmanned military, meteorological, or other scientific balloons are usually filled with hydrogen. Manned balloons are generally filled with safer helium gas, or hot air.
**ballooning** Traveling in a basket suspended beneath a balloon inflated with a gas lighter than air. Now largely a leisure activity, ballooning was the first means of human "flight". Generally credited with the achievement are the French brothers Jacques and Joseph MONTGOLFIER, who devised a hot-air balloon in which Jean François Pilâtre de Rozier and the Marquis d'Arlandes made the first ascent (21 November, 1783). Although hydrogen ballooning is considered by many to be the purest form of the sport, because it is completely silent, it has been largely superseded by the cheaper hot air method. In this, burning propane gas is used to heat the air through an opening in the bottom of the balloon, which is usually made of nylon fabric. An Anglo-Swiss .team completed the first non-stop circumnavigation of the world in a balloon in March 1999.
**ballot** Object used to cast a vote, or process of voting in an election. The word derives from the Italian *ballotta* (little ball) and since 5th-century BC Athens, balls have been used to cast votes. Today, the ballot is often a sheet (or sheets) of paper, although voting machines are frequently used to register votes.
**balm** Resin from a BALSAM plant and the name of various aromatic plants, particularly those of the genera *Melissa* and *Melittis*, both family Lamiaceae/Labiatae. Also, an old name for any soothing ointment.
**Balmoral** Private residence of the British monarch, in the Scottish Highlands, 53mi (85km) W of Aberdeen. Built in the reign of Queen Victoria, it was left to her by Prince Albert on his death in 1861.
**balsa** Lightweight wood obtained from a South American tree, used for modeling, and for building rafts. Family Bombacaceae; species *Ochroma lagopus*.
**balsam** Aromatic RESIN obtained from plants; or healing preparations, especially those with benzoic and cinnamic acid added to the resin; or balsam-yielding trees, such as the balsam fir and balsam poplar. The name is also given to numerous species of the family Balsaminaceae that are plants of moist areas, with pendent flowers. *See also* IMPATIENS
**balsam fir** Evergreen tree native to NE North America. It has flat needles and 2.5in (6.3cm) cones. It is often grown for pulpwood and Christmas trees. Height: to 70ft (21.3m). Family Pinaceae; species *Abies balsamea.*
**Baltic Sea** Part of the Atlantic extending past Denmark, along the N coasts of Germany and Poland, and the E coasts of the BALTIC STATES, separating Sweden from Russia and Finland. The sea extends N–S with an arm reaching out to the E. The N part is the Gulf of Bothnia, the E part of the Gulf of Finland. The Baltic is the largest body of brackish water in the world. Its low salinity accounts for the ease with which the Gulf of Bothnia freezes in the winter. The tidal range is low and currents are weak. Area: 160,000sq mi (414,400sq km).
**Baltic states** Countries of ESTONIA, LATVIA, and LITHUANIA, on the E coast of the Baltic Sea. The region was settled by various tribes in the 7th century AD, but until the 20th century remained mostly under Danish, Russian, or Polish rule. Following the Russian Revolution in 1918, each state became independent, but came under the control of the Soviet Union in 1940. They regained their independence following the breakup of the Soviet Union in 1991.
**Baltimore** City and port in N Maryland, at the mouth of the Patapsco River, on Chesapeake Bay. Founded by the Irish baronial family of Baltimore as a tobacco port in 1729. During the 19th century it became an important shipbuilding center. It is a notable center of commerce and education, with three universities, and a major port. Industries: steelworks, oil refineries, shipbuilding, aerospace equipment. Pop. (1990) 736,014.
**Baltimore oriole** American songbird named because its colors are the same as the coat of arms of the Baltimore family, founders of Maryland. The male has black head, neck, back, and wings and orange breast, rump, and outer tail feathers. Females (olive upper and yellow lower body), build long, slender weed-and-bark nests in high trees. Length: to 8in (20cm). Species *Icterus galbula.*
**Baluchistan** Region and province in central and SW Pakistan, bordered by Iran (W), Afghanistan (N), and the Arabian Sea (S). Quetta is the capital. The boundaries with Iran and Afghanistan were settled in 1885–96. The region became part of Pakistan in 1947. The terrain is mostly hilly desert, and is inhabited by nomadic tribes such as the Baluchi. Much of the population is employed in sheep raising. Some cotton is grown, and fishing is the chief occupation on the coast. Natural gas is extracted and exported, along with salt and fish. Area: 134,102sq mi (347,190sq km). Pop. (1985 est.) 4,908,000.
**Balzac, Honoré de** (1799–1850) French novelist. One of the greatest novelists of the 19th century, Balzac's first success was *Les Chouans* (1829). More than 90 novels and short stories followed during a lifetime of extraordinary creative effort. He organized these works into a grand fictional scheme, intended as a detailed, realistic study of contemporary French society, which he called *La Comédie Humaine*. Among his best-known novels are *Le Pére Goriot* (1834–35) and *La Cousine Bette* (1846).
**Bamako** Capital of Mali, on the Niger River, 90mi (145km) NE of the border with Guinea, W Africa. Once a center of Muslim learning (11th–15th centuries), it was occupied by the French in 1883 and became capital of the French Sudan (1908). Industries: shipping, peanuts, meat, metal products. Pop. (1990 est.) 646,000.
**bamboo** Tall, tree-like GRASS native to tropical and subtropical regions. The hollow, woody stems grow in branching clusters from a thick rhizome and the leaves are stalked blades. It is used in house construction and for household implements. Some bamboo shoots are eaten. The pulp and fiber may form a basis for paper production. Height: to 131ft (40m). There are 1,000 species. Family Poaceae/Gramineae; genus *Bambusa*.
**banana** Long, curved, yellow or reddish fruit of the tree of the same name. It has soft, creamy flesh. A spike of yellow, clustered flowers grows from the center of the crown of the tree and bends downward and develops into bunches of 50–150 fruits in "hands" of 10–20. More than 100 varieties are cultivated. Height: 10-30ft (3–9m). Family Musaceae; genus *Musa*.
**Bancroft, George** (1800–91) US diplomat and historian. Bancroft was appointed secretary of the navy in 1845 and established the US Naval Academy at Annapolis, Maryland. He served as ambassador to Britain (1846–49) and to Germany (1867–74). Bancroft's *History of the United States* (10 vols., 1834–74) is a classic account.
**band** Instrumental ensemble, usually consisting of wind and percussion instruments. A **big** band performs swing music and has about 16 musicians in four sections: trumpets, trombones, saxophones, and a rhythm section. A **brass** band contains only

brass and percussion instruments. A **dance** band has a rhythm section to provide the strict beat and melody instruments such as saxophone and violin to play the tunes. A **jazz** band varies according to the style of JAZZ: a traditional jazz band usually has a clarinet, trumpet, trombone, and a rhythm section. A **military** (marching) **band** contains brass and woodwind instruments with percussion. A ROCK band has a core of electric guitar, bass guitar, and drums.

**Banda, Hastings Kamuzu** (1902–97) Malawian statesman, the country's first president (1966–94). Banda guided Nyasaland to independence as MALAWI (1964) establishing an autocratic regime. He was named president-for-life in 1971. Banda was the only African leader to maintain friendly relations with the South African apartheid regime. He was forced to allow multiparty elections in 1994, which he lost.

**Bandaranaike, Sirimavo Ratwatte Dias** (1916– ) Sri Lankan stateswoman, prime minister (1960–65, 1970–77, 1994– ). Following the assassination (1959) of her husband, Solomon BANDARANAIKE, she assumed control of the Sri Lanka Freedom Party and became the world's first woman prime minister. Her daughter, Kumaratunga, became president in 1994, and Sirimavo returned as prime minister.

**Bandaranaike, Solomon West Ridgeway Dias** (1899–1959) Ceylonese statesman, prime minister (1956–59). He made Sinhalese the official language and founded the Sri Lanka Freedom Party to unite nationalists and socialists. He was assassinated and his wife, Sirimavo BANDARANAIKE, succeeded him.

**Bandar Seri Begawan** (formerly Brunei Town) Capital of BRUNEI, Borneo, SE Asia. The town port was superseded in 1972 by a new deepwater harbor at Maura. The capital includes the Sultan Omar Ali Saifuddin Masjid, SE Asia's largest mosque. Pop. (1991) 45,867.

**bandicoot** Australian MARSUPIAL about the size of a rabbit and with similarly long ears, hopping gait, and burrowing habits. It eats insects rather than vegetation, and its long pointed snout is probably an adaptation for its insectivorous diet. Genus *Perameles.*

**Bandung** Capital of West Java province, Indonesia. Founded in 1810, it was the administrative center of the Dutch East Indies, and is now the third largest city in Indonesia. A center for Sundanese culture; educational institutions include the Bandung Institute of Technology and two universities. Industries: canning, chemicals, quinine, textiles. Pop. (1990) 2,026,893.

**Bandung Conference** (1955) International meeting in BANDUNG, Indonesia. Representatives of 29 non-aligned countries of Asia and Africa, including China, met to express their united opposition to COLONIALISM and to gain recognition for the Third World.

**Bangalore** (Bangalur) Capital of Karnataka state, S central India. Established in 1537 by the Mysore dynasty, the city was retained by Britain as a military headquarters until 1947. It is the sixth largest city in India, and an important industrial and communications center. Main products include aircraft and machine tools. Pop. (1991) 3,302,296.

**Bangkok** Capital and chief port of Thailand, on the E bank of the Menam River (Chao Phraya). Bangkok became the capital in 1782 when King Rama I built a royal palace here. It quickly became Thailand's largest city. The Grand Palace (including the sacred Emerald Buddha) and more than 400 Buddhist temples (*wats*) are notable examples of Thai culture and help make the capital a popular tourist destination. It has a large Chinese minority. During World War II it was occupied by the Japanese. Today, Bangkok is a busy market center, much of the commerce taking place on the numerous canals. Industries: building materials, rice processing, textiles, jewelry. Pop. (1993) 5,572,712

**Bangladesh** Republic in S Asia. *See* country feature page 66

**Bangui** Capital of the Central African Republic, on the Ubangi River, near the Zaire border. Founded in 1889 by the French, it is the nation's chief port for international trade. Industries: textiles, food processing, beer, soap. Pop. (1988) 451,690.

**banjo** Musical instrument with four to nine strings, a body of stretched parchment on a metal hoop, and a long, fretted neck. It is played with a plectrum or the fingers. Probably of African origin, it was taken to the US by slaves. It is most often used in Dixieland jazz and folk music.

**Banjul** (Bathurst) Capital of Gambia, W Africa, on St. Mary's Island, where the Gambia River enters the Atlantic Ocean. Founded as a trading post by the British in 1816, it is the country's chief port and commercial center. The main industry is peanut processing, although tourism is rapidly expanding. Pop. (1983) 44,188.

**banking** Commercial process providing a wide range of financial services such as holding and transferring money, providing loans, and giving stability to the financial sector of the economy. **Commercial** banks in the US and **clearing** banks in the UK deal with the general public, as well as with small and medium-sized businesses and corporations; MERCHANT BANKS or investment banks provide services to business and industry, such as investment loans or share flotations. In many countries there are other providers of banking services, such as insurance companies and credit card issuers, as well as SAVINGS AND LOAN ASSOCIATIONS. A country's CENTRAL BANK, sometimes under government control, can be used as an economic regulator.

**Bank of England** Britain's central banking institution, founded in 1694 by a group of London merchants. Nationalized in 1946, it regulates foreign exchange, issues bank notes, advises the government on monetary matters, such as the setting of interest rates, and acts as the government's financial agent. It is situated in Threadneedle Street, City of London. The governor of the Bank of England is appointed by the national government.

**Bank of the United States** Two US national banks. The first was established in 1791. Although it was soundly operated, autonomous state banking interests defeated its rechartering in 1811. Following the War of 1812, a second national bank was chartered by Congress in 1816. There was much opposition to its power to establish local branches. President Andrew JACKSON supported the bank's opponents, and vetoed its rechartering. The bank became obsolete in 1836.

**bankruptcy** Legally determined status of a person or company, usually when debts greatly exceed income and assets. A person or company may ask to be declared bankrupt by the court, or else the creditors may do so. A court-appointed receiver takes charge of the bankrupt's property with the aim of meeting, as far as possible, the bankrupt's financial obligations to his or her creditors.

**Banks, Sir Joseph** (1743–1820) English botanist. Banks was the senior scientist of the group who sailed to Tahiti with Captain James COOK aboard *HMS Endeavour* in 1768. At Botany Bay, Australia (1770), he collected examples of plants hitherto unknown in Europe, including the shrub BANKSIA named in his honor. Upon his return, Banks helped set up the Royal Botanic Gardens at Kew, W London. In 1778 he became president of the Royal Society.

**banksia** Any of about 70 species of flowering shrubs and small trees found in Australia and New Guinea that belong to the genus *Banksia*. Their evergreen leaves are long and leathery, and they bear tube-shaped heads of yellowish or reddish flowers. The genus was discovered by Sir Joseph BANKS. Family Proteaceae.

**Bannister, Sir Roger Gilbert** (1929– ) British track athlete. On May 6, 1954, Bannister became the first man to run a mile in less than four minutes (3min 59.4sec). He was knighted in 1975.

**Bannock** Shoshonean-speaking tribe that broke off from the Northern Paiute and settled in SE Idaho. They are primarily noted for their role in the Bannock War (1878). The bulk of the tribe – some 500 individuals – share Fort Hall, Idaho, with the Shoshone tribe.

**Bannockburn** Town and moor in central Scotland, scene of a Scottish victory over the English in 1314. The English army of EDWARD II, advancing on Stirling, was intercepted by Scottish troops under ROBERT I (THE BRUCE). Fighting began at dawn and before noon the English survivors were in flight. Although conflict continued for many years, the victory secured Scottish independence from the English.

▲ **banjo** Originating in the 18th century, the banjo is popularly supposed to have been brought by slaves from Africa to the US. By the middle of the 19th century it had become the traditional instrument of African Americans. It has four or more strings, which are plucked, and a resonating body consisting of parchment stretched over a metal hoop.

**Banting, Sir Frederick Grant** (1891–1941) Canadian physician. Banting shared, with J.J.R. Macleod, the 1923 Nobel Prize for physiology or medicine for his work in extracting the hormone INSULIN from the PANCREAS. This made possible the effective treatment of DIABETES.

**Bantu** Group of African languages generally considered as forming part of the Benue-Congo branch of the Niger-Congo family. Among the most widely-spoken of the several hundred tongues used from the Congo Basin to South Africa are Swahili, Xhosa, and Zulu. There are more than 70 million speakers of Bantu languages.

**banyan** Evergreen tree of E India. The branches send down antenna shoots that take root, forming new trunks. Such trunks from a single tree may form a circle up to 330ft (100m) across. Height: to 100ft (30m). Family Moraceae; species *Ficus benghalensis*.

**baobab** Tropical tree native to Africa. It has a stout trunk containing water storage tissue, and short, stubby branches with sparse foliage. Fiber from its bark is used for rope. Its gourdlike fruit has edible pulp. Height: to 60ft (18m); trunk diameter: to 40ft (12m). Family Bombacaceae; species *Adansonia digitata*.

**baptism** Pouring of water on a person's forehead or the immersion of the body in water, used as a rite of initiation into the Christian church. Baptism is one of the SACRAMENTS of the Christian church. Total immersion is practiced by the BAPTISTS. In churches which practice infant baptism, the rite is often referred to as christening and is the occasion when a child is given its names.

**Baptist** Member of various Protestant and Evangelical sects who practice BAPTISM of believers and regard immersion as the only legitimate form sanctioned by the New Testament. Like the ANABAPTISTS, to whom they have an affinity but no formal links, they generally reject the practice of infant baptism, insisting that initiates must have freedom of thought and expression and must already be believers. Baptists originated among English dissenters of the 17th century, but have spread worldwide. Baptists cherish the principle of religious liberty. There is no official creed, no hierarchy, and individual churches are autonomous. In the mid-1990s, the number of Baptists worldwide was estimated at more than 31 million.

**bar** Unit of pressure, the pressure created by a column of mercury 29.53in high. It is equal to $10^5$ pascals. Standard atmospheric pressure (at sea level) is 1.01325 bars, or 1,013.25 millibars.

## BANGLADESH

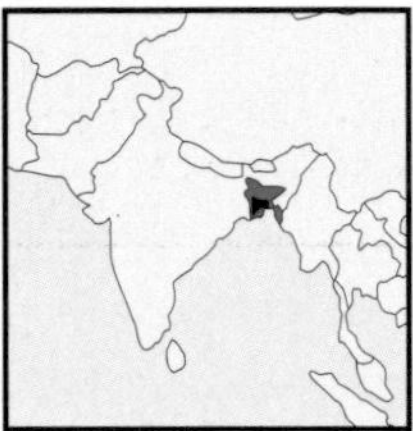

Bangladesh adopted this flag in 1971, following the country's break from Pakistan. The green is said to represent the fertility of the land. The red disk is the sun of independence, and commemorates the blood shed during the struggle for freedom.

**AREA:** 55,598sq mi (144,000sq km)
**POPULATION:** 119,288,000
**CAPITAL (POPULATION):** Dhaka (Dacca, 3,397,187)
**GOVERNMENT:** Multiparty republic
**ETHNIC GROUPS:** Bengali 98%, tribal groups
**LANGUAGES:** Bengali (official)
**RELIGIONS:** Islam (Sunni Muslim) 87%, Hinduism 12%, Buddhism, Christianity
**CURRENCY:** Taka = 100 paisa

The People's Republic of Bangladesh is the world's most densely populated country: the 1990 figure was 2,080 people per sq mi (803 per sq km). Apart from hilly regions in the far NE and SE, most of the land is flat and covered by fertile alluvium spread over the land by the GANGES, BRAHMAPUTRA, and Meghna rivers. These rivers overflow when they are swollen by the annual monsoon rains. Floods also occur along the coast, which is about 357mi (575km) long, when cyclones (hurricanes) drive seawater inland. These periodic storms cause great human suffering: the official death toll from the 1991 delta cyclone was 132,000, although it was almost certainly higher, and more than an estimated 5 million people were made homeless. DHAKA is situated on the Ganges delta.

### CLIMATE

Bangladesh has a tropical monsoon climate. In winter, dry winds blow from the N, but in spring the land heats up and moist winds blow from the S, bringing heavy rain. The coldest month is January and the hottest is April, although it remains hot throughout the monsoon season from June to August.

### VEGETATION

Although most of Bangladesh is low and cultivated, forests cover about 16% of the landmass. These include bamboo forests in the NE and mangrove swamps in the Sundarbans region in the SW, which is a sanctuary for the Bengal tiger. On the misty, jungle border with Burma there are large areas of mahogany forests and rubber plantations.

### HISTORY AND POLITICS

Islam, the chief religion today, was introduced into Bengal in the 13th century. In 1576, Bengal became part of the MOGUL EMPIRE, which also included most of Afghanistan, Pakistan, and India. European influence increased in the 16th century and, in 1858, Bengal became part of British India.

In 1947, British India was partitioned between the mainly Hindu India and Muslim PAKISTAN. Pakistan consisted of two parts, West and East Pakistan, separated by about 1,000mi (1,600km) of Indian territory. Differences developed between the West and East "wings" and in 1971 the East Pakistanis, claiming both ethnic and economic discrimination, rebelled against Islamabad. After a bitter nine-month civil war, they declared East Pakistan to be a separate nation called Bangladesh.

Bangladesh became a one-party state in 1975, but military leaders seized control and dissolved parliament. In the years that followed, several military coups occurred. In 1991, Bangladesh held its first free elections since independence. The Bangladesh National Party (BNP) gained a parliamentary majority. In 1996 elections the Awami League, led by Sheikh Hasina, returned to power. In 1998 Begum Zia, the former prime minister, was charged with corruption.

### ECONOMY

Bangladesh is one of the world's poorest countries (1995 GDP per capita, US$1,380) and its economy depends mainly on agriculture, which employs more than half of the people. Rice is the chief crop, but jute, sugar-cane, tobacco, and wheat are also grown. Jute processing is still the biggest manufacturing industry and export. Some 60% of internal trade is by boat, although this is becoming more difficult as the delta silts up. The direct cause is the deforestation of hillsides in Nepal.

**Bar, the** *See* AMERICAN BAR ASSOCIATION

**Barabbas** In the New Testament, convicted criminal or terrorist who was in prison at the time of Jesus Christ's trial before PONTIUS PILATE. In accordance with a PASSOVER custom, Pilate offered to release a prisoner. The Jerusalem mob, given the choice, nominated Barabbas and called for Christ to be crucified (Matthew 27, Mark 15, Luke 23, John 18).

**Barbados** Island state in the Windward Islands, West Islands; the capital is BRIDGEPORT. Barbados' warm climate has encouraged the growth of its two largest industries, sugar cane and tourism. Barbados was settled by the British in 1627, and dominated by British plantation owners (using African slave labor until the abolition of slavery) for the next three hundred years. It was not until 1966 that it gained its independence. Area: 166sq mi (430sq km). Pop. (1993) 263,900.

**Barbarossa** (1466–1546) (Redbeard) Name given by Christians to two Muslim privateers in the Mediterranean, **Aruj** (d.1518) and Khizr, or **Khayr ad-Din** (d.1546). Aruj was killed in battle against the Spanish, but Khayr seized Algiers from Spain (1533), took Tunis (1534), raided Christian coasts and shipping, and gained control of the Barbary States. He acknowledged the Ottoman sultan as his overlord, and from 1533 to 1544 he was the commander of the fleet of SULEIMAN the Magnificent. His forces were finally defeated by Spain and Italy in the famous naval battle of Lepanto.

**Barbary ape** Tailless, yellowish-brown ape-like MONKEY native to Algeria and Morocco, and introduced into Gibraltar. It is the size of a small dog. The Gibraltar Barbary apes are the only wild monkeys in Europe. Species *Macaca sylvana*. *See also* MACAQUE; PRIMATE

**barbastelle** BAT found in Europe and Asia. Up to 2.5in (6cm) long with grayish fur, it catches insects and roosts in buildings or caves. Genus *Barbastella*.

**barbel** (barb) CARP-like freshwater fish of W Asia and S central Europe. A game and food fish, it has an elongated body, flattened underside and two pairs of fleshy mouth whiskers (barbels). It is a strong swimmer well adapted to fast-flowing rivers. Length: 20–35in (50–90cm); weight: 35lb (16kg). Family Cyprinidae; species *Barbus barbus*.

**Barber, Samuel** (1910–81) US composer. Barber composed chamber music, notably *Dover Beach* (1931) for voice and string quartet, two symphonies, a piano concerto (1962), and three operas, including *Vanessa* (1958). His style, initially quite romantic, became more dissonant. Barber won two Pulitzer Prizes.

**barberry** *See* BERBERIS

**barbet** Brightly colored, poor-flying tropical bird, known for its monotonous call. It is stout-bodied with a large head, heavy bill, beard-like bristles, and short legs. The female lays 2–5 white eggs. Length: 3.5–12in (9–30cm). Family Capitonidae. Genus *Megalaima*.

**Barbie, Klaus** (1913–91) Nazi chief of the German Gestapo in France during World War II. Barbie was known as the "Butcher of Lyon" for his persecution and murder of French Resistance fighters and Jews. He sent thousands of people to AUSCHWITZ. After the war, he worked for US counterintelligence before escaping to Bolivia in 1951. Barbie was captured in 1987, brought back to Lyon, and sentenced to life imprisonment.

**Barbirolli, Sir John** (1899–1970) English conductor. Barbirolli succeeded TOSCANINI as conductor (1937–42) of the New York Philharmonic. He returned to England to lead (1943–68) the Hallé Orchestra, Manchester.

**barbiturate** DRUG used as sedative or to induce sleep. Highly addictive and dangerous in high doses, or in combination with other drugs, most barbiturates are no longer prescribed. Short-acting barbiturates are used in surgery to induce general anesthesia; long-acting formulations are prescribed for epilepsy.

**Barbizon School** French school of landscape painting in the 19th century. Led by Théodore ROUSSEAU in the late 1840s, the group worked in the forest of Fontainebleau near Barbizon, N France. Artists included Charles Daubigny, Diaz de la Peña, Jules Dupré, and Constant Troyon. They embraced a longing for the freedom of nature, escaping the restraints of Parisian art. In working directly from nature they were forerunners of IMPRESSIONISM.

### BAR CODE

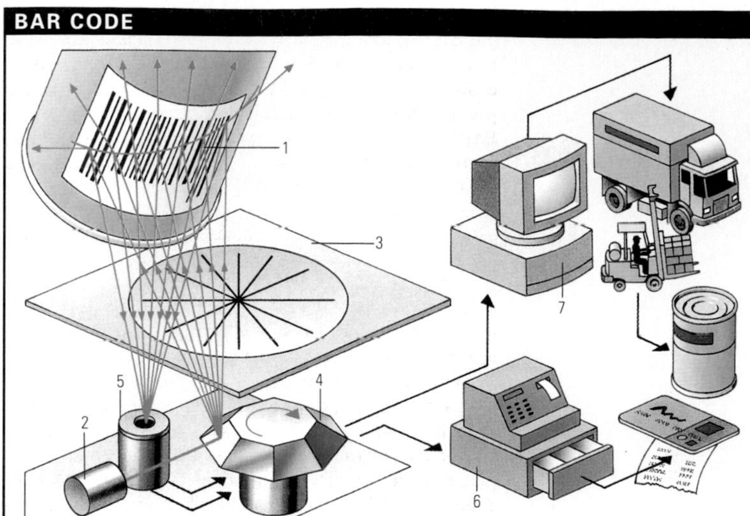


Bar codes represent information concerning a product and its manufacturer in a series of thick and thin black and white lines (1). A laser (2) is reflected through a glass screen (3) onto the bar code by a rotating multi-faceted mirror (4). The laser light is scattered by the white lines and absorbed by the black lines. A sensor (5) detects the reflected laser light and compares the relative width of the lines. Because the relative widths are compared, the bar code does not have to be on a flat surface. The sensor passes the bar code information to the till (6) for billing the customer, and a central store computer (7) can automatically order supplies of fast-selling freight.

**Barbuda** Coral island in the West Indies, a dependency of ANTIGUA, with which, along with Redonda, it forms an independent state of the Lesser Antilles. The chief industry is cotton. Area: 101sq mi (161sq km) Pop. (1994) 1,450.

**Barcelona** City and Mediterranean port in NE Spain, capital of CATALONIA and Spain's second-largest city. Reputedly founded by the Carthaginian Barca family, it was ruled by Romans, Visigoths, and Moors, and by the late Middle Ages had become a major trading center. It is the focus of radical political and Catalan separatist movements. The autonomous Catalan government based here (1932–39) was swept away by the Spanish CIVIL WAR. Modern Barcelona is the cosmopolitan, cultural capital of Spain. In 1992 the Summer Olympics were held here. Historic buildings include the gothic Cathedral of Santa Eulalia (13th–15th century), the Church of the Sagrada Familia designed by Antonio GAUDÍ (begun 1882), and a Monument to Christopher Columbus. There are two universities, a Museum of Modern Art, and the Picasso Museum. Industries: vehicles, textiles, machinery, petrochemicals, electrical goods. Pop. (1991) 1,625,542.

**bar code** (Universal Product Code) Coded information consisting of thick and thin lines, and designed for computer recognition. A laser beam scans the bar code and a light-sensitive detector picks up the reflected signal, which consists of a pattern of pulses. Bar codes are used on many products for sale in stores and supermarkets. The store's computer translates the bar code into information, including the product's name, weight or size.

**Bardeen, John** (1908–91) US physicist known for his research into SEMICONDUCTORS. Bardeen worked for the Bell Telephone Laboratories (1945–51) and was professor of physics (1951–75) at the University of Illinois. He was the first person to win the Nobel Prize twice in the same field, physics: in 1956 he shared it with William SHOCKLEY and Walter BRATTAIN, for their joint invention of the TRANSISTOR, and in 1972 with Leon Cooper and John Schrieffer, for their theory of SUPERCONDUCTIVITY.

**Bardot, Brigitte** (1934– ) French film actress and 1950s sex symbol. Bardot became famous for her roles in *And God Created Woman* (1956) and *Heaven Fell that Night* (1957), directed by her then husband, Roger Vadim. Despite Bardot's long retirement from film-making, she has maintained a high public profile, largely due to her animal rights campaigns.

**Barebone's Parliament** (Parliament of the Saints, July–December 1653) Last Parliament of the English COMMONWEALTH. Successor to the RUMP PARLIAMENT, it was named after a prominent member, Praise-God Barebone, and representatives were handpicked by Oliver CROMWELL and the Puritan army chiefs. Religious disputes ruined its effectiveness. It voted its own dissolution and handed over power to Cromwell as Lord Protector.

**Barenboim, Daniel** (1942– ) Israeli pianist and conductor, b. Argentina. An eclectic musician, Barenboim has performed with many of the world's leading orchestras, such as the New York and Berlin philharmonics, the London Symphony Orchestra, and the Orchestre de Paris. He was married to the cellist Jacqueline DU PRÉ.

**Barents, Willem** (d.1597) Dutch navigator and explorer. Barents made three expeditions in search of the NORTHEAST PASSAGE (1594–97). On his third voyage he discovered SVALBARD and, crossing the sea now named after him, reached Novaya Zemlya. The ship was trapped by ice and the Dutch sailors built a shelter; most survived until the following year, when they escaped, but Barents died before they reached safety.

**Barents Sea** Part of the ARCTIC OCEAN lying between Svalbard and NOVAYA ZEMLYA, it was named after Willem BARENTS. The seabed consists of an uneven surface distribution of Quaternary sediments. Deeper, older sediments bear evidence of long periods above sea level. The fishing grounds are particularly rich in cod and herring. Area: 529,096sq mi (1,370,360sq km).

**barite** Translucent, white or yellow mineral, barium sulfate ($BaSO_4$), found in sedimentary rocks and in ore veins in limestone. It occurs as a gangue mineral with ores of lead, copper, and zinc, and as a replacement for limestone. It is used as a weighting agent in oil rig drilling, and in the chemical industry for papermaking, rubber manufacture, high-quality paints, and in x-rays. Hardness: 3–3.5; s.g. 4.5.

**barium** (symbol Ba) Silver-white element of the ALKALINE-EARTH METALS, discovered in 1808 by Sir Humphry DAVY. It is a soft metal whose chief sources are heavy spar (barium sulfate) and witherite (barium carbonate). Barium compounds are used as rodent poison, pigments for paints, and as drying agents. Barium sulfate ($BaSO_4$) is swallowed to allow x-ray examination of the stomach and intestines because barium atoms are opaque to x-rays; this is a "barium meal." Properties: at.no. 56; at.wt. 137.34; sp.gr. 3.51; m.p. 1,337°F (725°C); b.p. 2,984°F (1,640°C); most common isotope $^{138}Ba$ (71.66%).

**bark** Outer protective covering of a woody plant stem. It is made up of several layers. The CORK layer, waxy and waterproof, is the thickest and hardens into the tough, fissured outer covering. Lenticels (pores) in the bark allow GAS EXCHANGE between the stem and the atmosphere. *See also* CAMBIUM

**Barker, Pat** (1943– ) English novelist. Barker's novels focus on the plight of women, usually in the N of England. Her debut novel was *Union Street* (1982). *Regeneration* (1991) and *The Eye in the Door* (1993) were the first volumes of a World War I trilogy. The final part, *The Ghost Road*, won the 1995 Booker Prize.

**Barlach, Ernst** (1870–1938) German sculptor, graphic artist, writer, and dramatist. Barlach was a major pioneer of the German EXPRESSIONISM movement. His distinctive style was influenced by medieval German wood carving and art nouveau. Barlach's sculptures, such as the bronze angel in Güstrow Cathedral, Germany, have a raw, emotional quality and vigor.

**barley** Cereal GRASS native to Asia and Ethiopia, cultivated perhaps since 5000 BC. Three cultivated species are: *Hordeum distichum*, commonly grown in Europe; *H. vulgare*, favored in the US; and *H. irregulare*, grown in Ethiopia. Barley is eaten by humnas and many other animals, and is used to make malt beverages, Family Poaceae/Gramineae.

**bar mitzvah** Jewish ceremony in which a young male is initiated into the religious community. Girls may participate in a simlar ceremony, called bas mitzvah. At the ceremony, which traditionally takes place when he is aged 13 years and 1 day, he reads a portion of the TORAH in a synagogue. The rite is followed by a social celebration.

**barn** (symbol *b*) Scientific unit of area used in nuclear physics to measure the cross sections in interactions of particles. A barn equals $10^{-24}$ $cm^2$ per nucleus. This area is a measure of the probability that fission will occur when a neutron moves toward a heavy nucleus.

**Barnabas, Saint** Early Christian apostle, originally named Joseph, who was a companion of St. PAUL. Barnabas traveled with Paul on two proselytizing missions to Cyprus and the European mainland. His feast day is June 11.

**barnacle** Crustacean that lives mostly on rocks and floating timber. Some barnacles live on whales, turtles, and fish without being parasitic, although there are also parasitic species. The larvae swim freely until ready to become adults, when they settle permanently on their heads; their bodies become covered with calcareous plates. Two main types are those with stalks (**goose** barnacles) and those without (**acorn** barnacles). Subclass Cirripedia.

**Barnard, Christiaan** (1922– ) South African surgeon. Barnard was the first to perform a human heart transplant (December 3, 1967). In 1974 he was the first to implant a second heart into a patient and to link the circulations of the hearts so that they worked together as one.

**Barnardo, Thomas John** (1845–1905) British philanthropist who founded the Dr. Barnardo homes for destitute children. In 1867 Barnardo founded the East End Mission for orphan children, the first of his famous homes. These spread rapidly through the UK and still flourish today.

**barn owl** Generally nocturnal bird of prey that lives mainly in the Eastern Hemisphere. The widely distributed common barn OWL (*Tyto alba*) has a heart-shaped face and long legs. It sometimes lives in buildings, and acute hearing enables it to locate rodents and other prey in almost total darkness. Family Tytonidae.

**Barnum, Phineas Taylor** (1810–91) US showman. Barnum established the American Museum in New York City (1842), where he presented the "dwarf" Tom Thumb, the Fijian mermaid, and other "freaks." In 1847 he introduced the Swedish soprano Jenny Lind to US audiences. In 1871 he opened his circus, billed as "The Greatest Show on Earth." He merged with rival James Bailey in 1881, to form Barnum and Bailey's Circus.

**barometer** Instrument for measuring atmospheric pressure. Barometers are of two basic types. A **mercury** barometer has a vertical column of mercury that changes length with changes in atmospheric pressure. An **aneroid** barometer has a chamber containing a partial vacuum, and the chamber changes shape with changes in pressure. Barometers are used in WEATHER FORECASTING to predict local weather changes: a rising barometer (increasing pressure) indicates dry weather; a falling barometer indicates wet weather. A barometer can also be used in an ALTIMETER to measure altitude by indicating changes in atmospheric pressure. *See also* BAR

**baroque** Term (perhaps derived from the Portuguese *barroca*, a misshapen pearl) applied to the style of art and architecture prevalent in Europe in the 17th and early 18th centuries. Baroque was at its height in the Rome (*c*.1630–80) of BERNINI, BORROMINI,'and Pietro de Cortona and in S Germany (*c*.1700–50) with Balthazar Neumann and Fischer von Erlach. High baroque at its best was a blend of light, color, and movement calculated to overwhelm the spectator by a direct emotional appeal. Paintings contained visual illusions; sculpture exploited the effect of light on surface and contour. Buildings were heavily decorated with stucco ornament and freestanding sculpture. Baroque became increasingly florid before merging with the lighter style of ROCOCO. The term is often used to describe the period as well as the style. In music, the period is notable for several stylistic developments. Musical textures became increasingly contrapuntal (polyphonic), culminating in the masterpieces of J.S. BACH and HANDEL. Many purely instrumental forms, such as the fugue, sonata, concerto, suite, toccata, passacaglia, and chaconne, emerged and became popular and involved increasing virtuosity.

**barracuda** Marine fish found in tropical Atlantic and Pacific waters. Known to attack people, it has a large mouth with many large, razor-sharp teeth. It is long, slender and olive green. Length: usually 4–6ft (1.2–1.8m); weight: 3–50lb (1.4–22.7kg). The great barracuda of the Florida coast grows to 8ft (2.5m). Family Sphyraenidae; there are 20 species.

**Barranquilla** City and major port on the River Magdalena, N Colombia. It became a river port in the mid-19th century, and the river was deepened to take seagoing ships in 1935. Located in an agricultural region, industries include textiles, food processing, chemicals, shipbuilding and glass. Pop. (1992) 1,018,763.

**Barrie, Sir James Matthew** (1860–1937) Scottish dramatist and novelist. Barrie is chiefly remembered as the writer of *Peter Pan* (1904), an ever-popular play about a boy who refuses to grow up. Although criticized for his sentimentality, his best works are clever, romantic fantasies. Other plays include *The Admirable Crichton* (1902) and *What Every Woman Knows* (1908).

**barrier reef** Long, narrow CORAL REEF some distance from and roughly parallel to the shore, and separated from it by a lagoon. Australia's GREAT BARRIER REEF is the most famous.

**barrister** Name given to lawyers entitled to practice as advocates in the higher courts. In Britain the right to "call to the bar" is vested in the four INNS OF COURT.

**barrow** In archeology, a prehistoric burial mound. In North America, barrows were built by Native Americans known as MOUND BUILDERS. In Europe, barrows are usually either long or round. **Long** barrows were built in the NEOLITHIC period, and consist of a vault built of stones, roofed with stone slabs and covered with soil; many were used for multiple burials. **Round** barrows primarily date to the early BRONZE AGE, but some in England were built as late as Roman and Saxon times. Usually containing a single body, they vary in diameter from 4.5 to 160ft (1.5–50m).

**Barry, Sir Charles** (1795–1860) British architect. Barry redesigned the HOUSES OF PARLIAMENT at Westminster, London, in a Gothic style after the original building burned down. Barry's preference for Italian Renaissance architecture shows in the classical ground plan for the parliament building.

**Barrymore** US family of actors. **Maurice** (1847–1905) made his stage debut in London in 1872. In 1875 he immigrated to the US, where he married the actress Georgiana Drew. They had three children. **Lionel** (1878–1954), a fine character actor, made many films, including *Dinner at Eight* (1933), and *A Free Soul* (1931) for which he won an Oscar for Best Actor. **Ethel** (1879–1959) was best known for her stage performances in plays such as *A Doll's House* (1905) and *The Corn is Green* (1942). She won an Oscar for her part in the film *None But the Lonely Heart* (1944). **John** (1882–1942) was a matinee idol. His many films include *Beau Brummel* (1924), *Don Juan* (1926), and *Grand Hotel* (1932). **Drew** Barrymore (1975– ) became a child star for *E.T., The Extra-Terrestrial* (1982).

**Barth, John Simmons** (1930– ) US writer, founder of postmodern literary pastiche. Among Barth's best known works are the novels *The Sot-Weed Factor* (1960) and *Giles Goat-Boy* (1966). In 1973 he won the US National Book Award for his three novellas, collectively entitled *Chimera* (1972). Later works include *Sabbatical* (1982), *The Tidewater Tales* (1987), and *The Last Voyage of Somebody the Sailor* (1991).

**Barth, Karl** (1886–1968) Swiss theologian. Barth was a leading thinker of 20th-century PROTESTANTISM. He tried to lead theology back to the principles of the REFORMATION, and emphasized the revelation of God through Jesus Christ. Barth's school has been called dialectical theology or theology of the word. In 1935 he was suspended from his position at the University of Bonn for his anti-Nazi stance, and he returned to Switzerland.

**Barthes, Roland** (1915–80) French academic, writer, and cultural critic. A leading proponent of STRUCTURALISM and SEMIOTICS, his notion of the literary text as a "system of signs" was informed by the linguistics of Ferdinand de SAUSSURE. Perhaps his best-known contribution to literary theory was the notion of the "death of the author," in which the meaning of a text is generated by the reader. His diverse works include *Mythologies* (1957), *S/Z* (1970), and *Camera Lucida* (1980).

**Bartholdi, Frédéric Auguste** (1834–1904) French sculptor. His most famous piece is *Liberty Enlightening the World* (Statue of Liberty) in New York harbor, which was dedicated in 1886.

**Bartók, Béla** (1881–1945) Hungarian composer and pianist. With Zoltán KODÁLY, Bartók amassed a definitive collection of Hungarian folk music. His orchestral works include *Music for Strings, Percussion, and Celesta* (1936), two violin concertos (1908 and 1938), and the Concerto for Orchestra (1943). He wrote one opera, *Bluebeard's Castle* (1911). His compositional style combines folk-music idioms with dissonance and great rhythmic energy.

**Bartolommeo, Fra** (1457–1517) (Bartolommeo della Porta) Florentine painter, draftsman, and Dominican friar. In parallel with RAPHAEL, he contributed to the development of a new type of Madonna with Saints, specific to the High RENAISSANCE, in which the Madonna acts as a central point for the whole composition. Bartolommeo's characteristic style is one of restraint combined with monumentality, exemplified by *The Mystical Marriage of St. Catherine* (1511).

**Barton, Clara (Clarissa Harlowe)** (1821–1912) US humanitarian, founder (1882) of the American National RED CROSS. Barton cared for wounded soldiers during the CIVIL WAR, and was active in the International Red Cross during the FRANCO-PRUSSIAN WAR. She was responsible for the "American amendment" at the 1884 Geneva Convention which enabled the Red Cross to be active in peacetime emergencies.

**baryon** Any ELEMENTARY PARTICLE affected by the strong interaction of nuclear force. The baryon consists of three QUARKS. Baryons are subclasses of HADRONS. The only stable baryons are the proton and (provided it is inside a nucleus) the neutron. Heavier baryons are called hyperons. *See also* LEPTON; MESON

**Baryshnikov, Mikhail** (1948– ) US ballet dancer, b. Russia. A leading member (1969–74) of the Kirov Ballet, Baryshnikov's defection to the West received much publicity. He was with the American Ballet Theatre as principal dancer (1974–78) and artistic director (1980–89). He starred in several films and set up the White Oak Dance Project.

**basal metabolic rate (BMR)** Minimum amount of energy required by the body to sustain basic life processes, including breathing, circulation, and tissue repair. It is calculated by measuring oxygen consumption. Metabolic rate increases well above basal metabolic rate (BMR) during vigorous physical activity or fever or under the influence of some DRUGS (including CAFFEINE). It falls below BMR during sleep, general ANESTHESIA, or starvation. BMR is higher in children.

**basalt** Hard, fine-grained, basic IGNEOUS ROCK, which may be intrusive or extrusive. Its color can be dark green, brown, dark gray, or black. It can have a glassy appearance. There are many types of basalt with different proportions of elements. It may be compact or vesicular (porous). If the vesicles are subsequently filled with secondary minerals, such as quartz or calcite, it is called **amygdaloidal** basalt. Basalts are the main rocks of ocean floors, and form the world's major lava flows, such as the Deccan Trap, India

**base** In chemistry, a compound that accepts protons. A base will neutralize an ACID to form a SALT and water. Most are oxides or hydroxides of metals; others, such as ammonia, are compounds that yield hydroxide IONS in water. Soluble bases are called ALKALIS. Strong bases are fully dissociated into ions; weak bases are partially dissociated in solution. *See also* NEUTRALIZATION

**base** In mathematics, the number of units in a number system that is equivalent to one unit in the next higher counting place. Thus 10 is the base of the decimal system: only the ten digits 0–9 can be used in the units, tens, hundreds, and so on. Each

▲ **Baryshnikov** Fomerly one of the world's leading ballet dancers, Baryshnikov was known for the brilliance of his technique and the strength of his character interpretations. As well as performing in all the standard ballets, Baryshnikov has starred in several films, including *The Turning Point* (1977), *White Nights* (1985), and *The Cabinet of Dr. Ramirez* (1991).

▲ **bat** The large mouse-eared bat (*Myotis myotis*) is the biggest of all European bats. It has a wingspan of up to 15in (38cm) and migrates up to 125mi (200km) from its summer habitat in S Europe to the Middle East where it spends the winter months. Although it prefers open farmland and woodland, the large mouse-eared bat is sometimes known to live in cellars or the attics of houses. A nocturnal animal, it lives on insects, particularly moths.

number system has a number of symbols equal to its base. In the BINARY SYSTEM (base 2) there are two symbols, 0 and 1.

**baseball** National summer sport of the US and Canada, also popular in Japan, Korea, Taiwan, Latin America, Australia, and parts of Europe. Baseball evolved during the 19th century from various ball games, particularly the English "rounders." The field comprises an inner diamond 90ft (27m) on each side, and an outfield. The diamond has a central pitcher's mound and bases at three corners. The batter stands at the fourth, home plate. Each team has nine players. A run is scored when a batter reaches first base and eventually home plate. To get back to home base with a single hit is a **home run**. A game has nine innings (during which each team bats once). A team's innings ends when a third batter or runner is put out, such as by missing three consecutive valid pitches ("**strikes**"); by making fouls; by a field catch; or if a runner does not reach the next base before the ball is thrown there. Games tied after nine innings are played until there is a winner. Every fall the top teams of the two North American major leagues (American and National) compete in a World Series.

**Basel** (Bâle or Basle) City and river port on the Rhine River; capital of Basel-Stadt canton, NW Switzerland. It joined the Swiss Confederation in 1501. It is an economic, financial, and historically important cultural center. There is a cathedral (where Erasmus is buried), a 15th-century university and a 16th-century town hall. It is the center of the Swiss chemical and pharmaceutical industries. Pop. (1992) 173,800.

**Basel, Council of** Ecumenical council convoked at Basel in 1431. It instituted church reforms and conciliated the Hussites in Bohemia. Conflict with Pope Eugene IV led the pope to denounce the council in 1437. In 1439 the council declared Eugene deposed and chose an anti-pope, Amadeus of Savoy, as Pope Felix V. Felix resigned in 1449 and the council was dissolved.

**BASIC** (**B**eginners' **A**ll-purpose **S**ymbolic **I**nstruction **C**ode) Computer programming language that is relatively easy to learn and uses many ordinary words. It is used by both amateur and professional programmers.

**Basie, Count (William)** (1904–84) US jazz band leader, pianist, and composer. Basie formed his own band in Kansas City in 1935, centered around a rhythm section of himself, Freddie Green, Walter Page, and Jo Jones. The Count Basie Orchestra recordings for Decca (1937–39) are among the most powerful works of the swing era. Basie formed a new orchestra in 1952, which made the explosive *The Atomic Mr. Basie* (1957).

**Basil I** (*c*.813–86) Byzantine emperor (r.867–86) and founder of the Macedonian dynasty. Emperor Michael III assisted Basil in his rise to power. After Michael designated him co-emperor, Basil had his former patron murdered. His most effective policies concerned the conversion of the Bulgars to Orthodox Christianity; military campaigns against the Paulician religious sect in Asia Minor; and a revision of Roman legal codes.

**Basil II** (*c*.958–1025) Byzantine emperor (976–1025), surnamed Bulgaroctonus ("Bulgar-slayer"). One of Byzantium's ablest rulers, Basil reigned during the heyday of the empire. He is best known for his military victory over the Bulgarian czar Samuel in 1014, which brought the entire Balkan peninsula under Byzantine control.

**basil** Common name for a tropical plant of the MINT family, whose dried leaves are used for flavoring. It has white or purple flowers. Family Lamiaceae/Labiatae; species *Ocimum basilicum*.

**basilica** Roman colonnaded hall used for public business; also an early Christian church based on this design. The main characteristics of a basilica church, established by the 4th century AD, were a rectangular plan with a longitudinal axis, a wooden roof, and an E end which was either rectangular or contained a semicircular apse. The body of the church usually had a central nave and two flanking aisles, lower and narrower than the nave.

**basilisk** Semiaquatic LIZARD found in trees near streams of tropical America. It has a compressed greenish body, whip-like tail, a crest along its back, and an inflatable pouch on its head. It can run over water for short distances on its hind legs, and eats plants and insects. Length: up to 2ft (61cm). Family Iguanidae; genus *Basiliscus*. The basilisk is also a legendary serpent with the body of a cockerel.

**Basil the Great, Saint** (329–79) Doctor of the Church and one of the four Fathers of the Greek Church. He founded a monastic community and in 370 was ordained bishop of Caesarea, Cappadocia. Basil established the dominance of the NICENE CREED and was a fierce opponent of ARIANISM. He is thought to have composed the *Liturgy of St. Basil*, which is still used in the Eastern Orthodox Church. His feast day is January 2 in the West; January 1 in the East.

**Baskerville, John** (1706–75) British typographer and pioneer of the English tradition of fine printing. Baskerville set up his own printing house in 1757 and became (1758) printer to Cambridge University. He produced a folio edition of the Bible (1763) and editions of John Milton's* poetry. Baskerville's clear typefaces remain in common use.

**basketball** Game that originated in the US, and is now played worldwide. Devised in 1891 by Dr. James Naismith, it has been an Olympic sport since 1936. It is played by two teams of five (plus substitutes), usually indoors. The court is up to 91ft (27.8m) long and 49ft (15m) wide. At each end is a backboard on which a bottomless netting basket hangs from a hoop 10ft (3m) above the floor. The object is to put the ball down through the opposing team's basket, scoring points. In normal play, 2 points are scored when the ball is thrown from within a zone close to the basket, and 3 points from farther away; a free throw (for a foul) counts 1 point. Players may move with the ball when dribbling it one-handed. With growing commercialization and the worldwide transmission of National Basketball Association (NBA) games, basketball is one of the most popular spectator sports.

**Basle** *See* BASEL

**Basov, Nikolai Gennadiyevich** (1922– ) Soviet physicist who developed the MASER that amplifies microwaves, and the LASER that amplifies light. For these contributions, Basov and his coworker Alexander PROKHOROV shared the 1964 Nobel Prize for physics with Charles TOWNES.

**Basque Country** Region of the W Pyrenees in both Spain and France, consisting of the provinces of Alava, Guipúzcoa, part of Navarra, and Vizcaya in Spain and Basse-Navarre, Labord, and Soule in France. The main towns are BILBAO and San Sebastian. The region is populated by the BASQUES. It lost its autonomy in the late 18th and early 19th centuries. Separatist movements were formed in response.

**Basques** Indigenous people of the western Pyrenees in N Spain and SW France, numbering *c*.3.9 million. Their language is not related to any other European tongue. Throughout history they have tenaciously maintained their cultural identity. The kingdom of NAVARRE, which existed for 350 years, was the home to most of the Basques. After its dissolution in 1512, most of the Spanish Basques enjoyed a degree of political autonomy. This autonomy was removed in 1873, and Basque unrest followed. Basque separatists known as ETA continue to agitate for an independent state.

**Basra** (Al-Basrah) City and chief port on the Shatt al-Arab channel, S Iraq; capital of Basra province. An ancient center of Arabic learning, it was captured by the Turks in 1668. In the early 20th century, large oil fields were discovered nearby. It suffered serious damage during the Iran-Iraq and Gulf wars. Industries: oil refining, flour milling, wool. Pop. (1992 est.) 746,000.

**bass** Any of several bony fish, both freshwater and marine, and not all closely related. Together they make up a valuable commercial and sport fish. They include the white, black, striped, rock, and calico basses. The two main bass families are Serranidae and Centrarchidae.

**bass** Term denoting low or deep pitch. It is used of the lowest-pitched part of a composition, or the lowest-pitched member of a family of instruments. It applies to the deepest male singing voice. The bass line in a composition is the bottom note of a chord or the lowest line in polyphony.

B

**basset** Short-legged hunting hound, originally bred in France to flush out game. After the BLOODHOUND, it has the most highly developed sense of smell among dogs. Bassets have long bodies and long floppy ears. The short coat is generally tan and white. Standard size: 12–15in (30–38cm) at the shoulder; weight: 25–50lb (11.3–22.7kg).

**Basseterre** Capital and chief port of the federated state of ST. KITTS-NEVIS, on the SW coast of St. Kitts, in the Leeward Islands group, E Caribbean. Founded in 1627, it is an important commercial center. Industries: sugar refining. Pop. (1990) 14,283.

**Basse-Terre** Capital of GUADELOUPE in the French West Indies. Founded by the French in 1643, it is an important trade center. Pop. (1988) 13,796.

**bassoon** Bass WOODWIND instrument with a range of three octaves, corresponding to that of the CELLO. It has a double-reed mouthpiece and a conical bore, the tube bending back on itself to reduce the instrument's length. Bassoons are used in symphonic and chamber music. The double bassoon or contrabassoon is the lowest-pitched woodwind instrument, sounding an octave below the bassoon.

**Bastille** Fortress and prison in Paris, built in the late 14th century and destroyed during the FRENCH REVOLUTION. Political prisoners were incarcerated here, and it became a symbol of royal oppression. On July 14, 1789, now a national holiday in France, a revolutionary mob stormed it and released its seven prisoners. The Bastille was pulled down soon afterward.

**bat** Only MAMMAL that has true flight (although a few others can glide). Bats are nocturnal and found in all tropical and temperate regions. Most are brown, gray, or black. A bat's wing is formed by a sheet of skin. Bats are able to navigate in complete darkness by means of a kind of SONAR. Many bats live largely on insects, some are carnivorous, some drink blood, some live on nectar and pollen, and one group – flying foxes – subsist on fruit. Most are small, although they range in wingspan from 10–58in (25cm–147cm). The 178 genera of bats make up the order Chiroptera.

**Bates, H.E. (Herbert Ernest)** (1905–74) British novelist, playwright, and short-story writer. Bates' novels include *Fair Stood the Wind for France* (1944), *The Jacaranda Tree* (1949), and a popular series featuring the Larkin family, including *The Darling Buds of May* (1958) and *A Little of What You Fancy* (1970).

**Bath** Spa city on the River Avon, in SW England. The center of the new unitary authority of Bath and North-East Somerset, Bath has been designated a world heritage site. Its hot springs were discovered in the 1st century AD by the Romans, who named the city *Aquae Solis* (waters of the sun). The bathing complex and temple are the finest Roman remains in Britain. The city flourished as a center for the cloth and wool industries. In the 18th century (under the direction of Beau Nash) the city became a fashionable resort. John Wood transformed the city into a showcase for Georgian architecture. The Royal Crescent, Queen Square, and the Circus are among his notable achievements. The city hosts an annual arts festival. The University of Bath was established in 1966. Industries: tourism, printing, bookbinding. Pop. (1991) 79,900.

**batholith** Huge mass of igneous rock at the Earth's surface that has an exposed surface of more than 40sq mi (100sq km). It may have originated as an intrusive igneous structure that was gradually eroded and which became surface material. Most batholiths consist of granite rock types, and are associated with the mountain-building phases of PLATE TECTONICS.

**batik** Method of decorating textiles, practiced for centuries in Indonesia and introduced into Europe by Dutch traders. Molten wax is applied to the parts of a fabric that are to remain undyed, before the fabric is dipped into cool vegetable dye. The fabric is then dipped in hot water to remove the wax from the undyed areas. The process may be repeated, using different colored dyes.

**Batista y Zaldívar, Fulgencio** (1901–73) Cuban political leader. A sergeant in the army, he led a successful coup in 1933 and in 1940 was elected president. He retired in 1944 and moved to Florida, but in 1952 a military coup returned him to power. In 1959 he was overthrown by Fidel CASTRO.

**Baton Rouge** Capital city of Louisiana, on the Mississippi River. Founded in 1719 by French colonists, it was ceded to Britain by France in 1763, and to the US with the Louisiana Purchase (1803). It became the state capital in 1849. The city contains both Louisiana State University and Southern University and is the site of a large petrochemical complex. Pop. (1990) 219,531.

**Battambang** (Batdambung) Second-largest town in Cambodia, and capital of Battambang province, W Cambodia. It was ceded to Thailand in 1809, became part of French INDOCHINA in 1907, and was returned to Cambodia in 1946. It is a market center in a major rice-producing area. Pop. (1981 est.) 551,860.

**Batten, Jean Gardner** (1909–82) New Zealand aviator who in 1935 became the first woman to make a solo flight from Australia to Britain. Batten also flew solo across the S Atlantic Ocean to South America.

**battery** Collection of voltaic cells that convert chemical energy into direct current (DC) electricity. The term is also commonly used for a single cell, particularly a dry cell as used in portable electronic equipment. Most primary cell batteries are not rechargeable; some types of primary cell – such as nickel-cadmium (Nicad) batteries – and all accumulators (storage batteries) can be recharged.

**battleship** Most powerful type of naval warship in use during the late 19th and early 20th centuries. The largest battleships, the *Musachi* and the *Yamato*, displaced over 72,000 tons and were built by the Japanese. Both were sunk during World War II. Modern battleships carry a variety of missile systems. *See also* AIRCRAFT CARRIER; CRUISER

**baud** Unit for measuring the speed of at which a digital communications device carries information. One baud is equal to one BIT per second. Although the term baud rate is still widely used, the speed of modern equipment is often expressed in kilobits per second.

**Baudelaire, Charles Pierre** (1821–67) French poet and critic. Baudelaire's collection of poems, *Les Fleurs du Mal* (1857), represents one of the highest achievements of 19th-century French poetry. The poems were condemned by the censor and six were subsequently suppressed. Baudelaire was influenced by Edgar Allan POE.

**BATTERY**

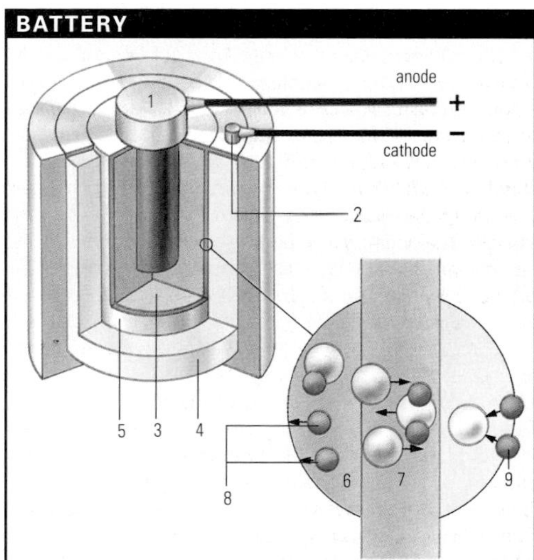


Sodium sulfur batteries are the newest type of battery and are much lighter than nickel cadmium types. They have a carbon anode (1) and a metal cathode (2). The reactants are arranged in rings around the central anode. An inner core of sodium (3) is separated from an outer ring of sulfur (4) by a layer of aluminum (5). The sodium (6) reacts with the aluminum layer (7) giving up electrons (8) which stream to the anode. The cathode gives electrons to the sulfur atoms (9) which bond with the sodium ions to form sodium sulfide. The process creates a voltage.

B

▲ **Bayeux tapestry** The tapestry (strictly an embroidery) depicts the history of the Norman Conquest of England. It begins with Harold's visit to France, and ends with his defeat by the forces of William the Conqueror. This section of the tapestry depicts Breton cavalry forces floundering in marshy ground having failed to break the English line of foot soldiers located on the top of a small hill. The English soldiers are always shown with large mustaches.

**Bauhaus** German school for architecture and the applied arts that played an important role in developing links between design and industry. Founded by Walter GROPIUS in 1919, it aimed to combine great craftsmanship with an ideal of an all-embracing modern art. Although the Bauhaus specialized in architecture and design, several progressive painters, including KANDINSKY and KLEE, taught there. The studios focused on designing products for manufacturing industry, especially furniture, textiles, and electric light fittings. In 1928 Hannes Meyer succeeded Gropius as director. MIES VAN DER ROHE took Meyer's place in 1930 but in 1933, after it moved to Berlin, the Nazis closed the school. Many students and staff emigrated. The school's teaching had an enormous influence on Western design. MOHOLY-NAGY, a Hungarian designer who taught at the Bauhaus in the 1920s, founded the New Bauhaus in Chicago in 1937. This later became the Institute of Design.

**bauxite** Rock from which most aluminum is extracted. Bauxite is a mixture of minerals, such as diaspore, gibbsite, boehmite, and iron. It is formed by weathering and leaching of rocks containing aluminum silicates.

**Bavaria** (Bayern) Largest state in Germany; the capital is MUNICH. Part of the Roman empire until the 6th century, it was taken by CHARLEMAGNE in 788, forming part of the Holy Roman Empire until the 10th century. Incorporated into Germany in 1871, it became a state within the German Federal Republic in 1946. Industries: glass, porcelain, brewing. Area: 27,256sq mi (70,553sq km). Pop. (1993) 11,863,313.

**Bayeux tapestry** (*c.*1080) Strip of linen embroidered in wool, measuring 231ft×19in (70m×48cm), and depicting (in more than 70 scenes) the life of HAROLD I of England and the NORMAN CONQUEST. An unfounded tradition attributes its design to Matilda, wife of WILLIAM I (THE CONQUEROR), but it was probably commissioned by William's half-brother Odo, Bishop of Bayeux. It is now in a museum in Bayeux, N France.

**Bay of Pigs** (April 17, 1961) Unsuccessful effort by Cuban exiles (aided by the US) to overthrow Fidel CASTRO by invading Cuba near the Bay of Pigs. About 1,500 Cubans trained, equipped, and transported by the US government were involved. The invasion was badly planned and the Cuban army defeated the exiles within three days. President John F. KENNEDY initially denied US involvement and was later subject to much criticism for its failure. *See also* CUBAN MISSILE CRISIS

**Bayreuth** City in Bavaria, S Germany, where an annual festival is held, staging exclusively the work of composer Richard WAGNER. The festivals are held in the *Festspielhaus*, built to Wagner's specifications. The first festival was held in 1876.

**BCG** (Bacille Calmette Guérin) Vaccine against tuberculosis. It was named for its discoverers, the French bacteriologists Albert Calmette and Camille Guérin.

**beach** Sloping zone of the shore, covered by sediment, sand, or pebbles, that extends from the low-water line to the limit of the highest storm waves. The sediment is derived from coastal erosion or river alluvium.

**Beach Boys** US pop group. Formed in 1961 around the three Wilson brothers. Their surf music, built around close vocal harmonies, generated a series of hit records including "Surfin' USA" (1963), "I Get Around" (1964), "Help Me Rhonda" (1965), and "Good Vibrations" (1966).

**Beadle, George Wells** (1903–89) US geneticist. During his study of MUTATIONS in bread mold (*Neurospora crassa*), he and Edward Tatum found that GENES are responsible for the synthesis of ENZYMES that control each step of all biochemical reactions occurring in an organism. For this discovery they shared, with J. Lederberg, the 1958 Nobel Prize for physiology or medicine.

**beagle** Hunting dog, used to chase and follow small game. Of ancient origin, the modern breed was developed in England in the mid-1800s. It has a long, slightly domed head with a square-cut muzzle, long, hanging ears, and widely set, large eyes. Average size: (two varieties) not exceeding 15in (38cm) at the shoulder; weight: 18-31lb (8–14kg).

**Beagle, HMS** British survey ship that carried Charles DARWIN as ship's naturalist. The *Beagle* left England in December 1831 and for five years explored parts of South America and the Pacific islands. Darwin's observations formed the basis for his theory of EVOLUTION by NATURAL SELECTION.

**bean** Plant grown for its edible seeds and seed pods. The broad bean (*Vicia faba*) is native to N Africa. The string bean (*Phaseolus vulgaris*) is native to tropical South America, and is common in the US; several varieties are cultivated. Its long pods or kidney-shaped seeds are eaten as vegetables. The runner (*Phaseolus coccineus*) has scarlet, rather than white or lilac flowers, and shorter, broader seeds. *See also* SOYBEAN

**bear** Large, omnivorous mammal with a stocky body, thick coarse fur, and a short tail. Bears are native to the Americas and Eurasia. The sun bear is the smallest species, the Kodiak brown bear the largest. Bears have poor sight and only fair hearing, but an excellent sense of smell. They kill prey with a blow from their powerful forepaws. In cold regions most bears become dormant or hibernate in winter. Length: 4–10ft (1.3–3m); weight: 100–1,600lb (45–725kg). Order Carnivora; family Ursidae; there are approximately nine species.

**Beardsley, Aubrey** (1872–98) British illustrator. Beardsley's highly wrought, stylized black-and-white drawings epitomize the English ART NOUVEAU style. Associated with the Decadent writers of the 1890s and the AESTHETIC MOVEMENT, he illustrated the first four volumes of the *Yellow Book* (1894–95) and Oscar Wilde's play *Salome*. Beardsley's mainstream work, such as *Isolde* (1895), enabled him to produce more outrageous, erotic "Japonesque" illustrations.

**Bear Flag Revolt** (1846) Uprising by US settlers in California. During the MEXICAN WAR a group of US emigrants in Mexico's territory of California proclaimed the Republic of California at Sonoma in June, and raised the "bear flag." The republic lasted until US troops arrived in July.

**bear market** In terms of the stock market, a declining market. A bear is an investor who sells shares or stocks that he does not own in anticipation of a fall in prices, at which time he will buy them back. This sort of speculative deal is called "selling short." An investor who actually owns the shares he sells is called a "protected bear." Bears are generally regarded as pessimists. The opposite of a bear is a bull. *See also* BULL MARKET

**beatitudes** Blessings spoken by Jesus at the opening of his SERMON ON THE MOUNT upon those worthy of admission to the Kingdom of God. (Luke 6, Matthew 5).

**Beatles, The** British rock group. Perhaps the most influential band in the history of 20th-century popular music. Formed in Liverpool in 1960, The Beatles initially consisted of John LENNON (1940–80), Paul MCCARTNEY (1942– ), George Harrison (1943– ), and Pete Best (1941– ). In 1962, Best was replaced by Ringo Starr (Richard Starkey, 1940– ). The Beatles' early style was US-derivative rhythm and blues blended with Lennon and McCartney's songwriting talent and attractive harmonies. From 1964 to 1970, they dominated pop music with 18 albums, including *Revolver* (1966) and *Sgt. Pepper's Lonely Hearts Club Band* (1967). After 1966 they never publicly performed live. The group disbanded in 1970 to pursue individual careers.

**beat movement** Term derived from John Clellon Holmes' novel *Go* (1952) and applied to a group of US writers in the 1950s, who rejected middle-class values and commercialism. They also experimented with different states of perception through drugs and meditation, and included the poets Allen

GINSBERG and Lawrence FERLINGHETTI and novelists Jack KEROUAC and William BURROUGHS.

**Beaton, Sir Cecil Walter Hardy** (1904–80) British photographer, costume and stage designer, and writer. Beaton began his career as a fashion photographer in the 1920s, and took up stage design in the 1930s. His film and stage designs include *Gigi* (film, 1951), *My Fair Lady* (stage, 1956; film, 1964), and *Coco* (1969).

**Beaufort, Henry** (1374–1447) English statesman and prelate, illegitimate son of John of Gaunt. As chancellor to Henry IV and Henry V, Beaufort considerably influenced English domestic and foreign policy. Guardian of Henry VI (1422), he controlled England in the 1430s.

**Beaufort wind scale** Range of numbers from 0 to 17 representing the force of winds, together with descriptions of the corresponding land or sea effects. The Beaufort number 0 means calm wind less than 0.6214mph (1km/h), with smoke rising vertically. Beaufort 3 means light breeze, 8–12mph (12–19km/h), with leaves in constant motion. Beaufort 11 is a storm, 64–72mph (103–116km/h) and Beaufort 12–17 is a hurricane, 73–136+mph (117.5–219+km/h), with devastation. The scale is named for its inventor, Admiral Sir Francis Beaufort (1774–1857).

**Beauharnais, Eugène de** (1781–1824) French general, son of NAPOLEON I's wife JOSÉPHINE. Beauharnais was a lieutenant in the Napoleonic battles of Marengo and Lützen. He was rewarded (1895) with the title of viceroy of Italy. After Napoleon's downfall, he lived in Bavaria as the duke of Leuchtenberg.

**Beaumarchais, Pierre Augustin Caron de** (1732–99) French dramatist. His principal plays were the related court satires *The Barber of Seville* (1775) and *The Marriage of Figaro*, which were transformed into operas by ROSSINI and MOZART respectively. Beaumarchais was also employed as a secret agent by the French to supply arms to the Americans during the American Revolution.

**Beaumont, Sir Francis** (1584–1616) English dramatist closely associated with the dramatist John FLETCHER. Between 1607–13 they produced at least ten outstanding plays, including *Philaster, The Maid's Tragedy*, and *A King and No King*. Beaumont is usually credited with sole authorship of two plays, *The Woman Hater* (1607) and *The Knight of the Burning Pestle* (*c*.1607).

**Beauregard, Pierre Gustave Toutant de** (1818–93) Confederate general in the Civil War. Beauregard served in the Mexican War and was superintendent of West Point until just before the Civil War broke out (1861). On April 13, 1861 he forced the Union surrender of Fort Sumter in the first action of the war.

**Beauvais** Town in France, 42mi (68km) NW of Paris. Founded by the Romans, the famed Beauvais tapestry factory was established in the 17th century by Jean Baptiste COLBERT. In 1940 the factory was destroyed and the industry moved to Paris. Landmarks include the unfinished Gothic cathedral of St. Pierre (begun 1227), which has the world's highest choir vault at 154ft (47m). Industries: ceramics, textiles, machinery. Pop. (1990) 56,280.

**Beauvoir, Simone de** (1908–86) French novelist, essayist, and critic. De Beauvoir's novels *She Came to Stay* (1943) and *The Mandarins* (1954) are portraits of the existentialist intellectual circle of which she and her lifelong companion, Jean-Paul SARTRE, were members. Her best-known work remains the feminist treatise *The Second Sex* (1949). Other significant works include *The Prime of Life* (1960) and *Old Age* (1970).

**beaver** Large RODENT with fine brown to black fur, webbed hind feet, and a broad scaly tail; it lives in streams and lakes of Europe, North America, and Asia. Beavers build "lodges" of trees and branches above water level and dam streams and rivers with stones, sticks, and mud. In many places they are hunted for fur. Length: to 4ft (1.2m); weight: up to 70lb (32kg). Family Castoridae; species *Castor fiber*.

**Beaverbrook, William Maxwell Aitken, 1st Baron** (1879–1964) British newspaper proprietor and politician, b. Canada. Beaverbrook entered Parliament in 1910 and was made a peer in 1917. He was a member of Winston CHURCHILL's war cabinet (1940–45). Beaverbrook bought a majority interest in the *Daily Express* (1916) and later founded the *Sunday Express* and the *Evening Standard*.

**Bebel, Ferdinand August** (1840–1913) German politician. One of the founders (1869) of the Social Democratic Party of Germany (SPD), Bebel was its leader for more than 40 years.

**bebop** (bop) Form of jazz with subtle harmonies and shifting rhythms. It arose in the late 1940s as a development from the simpler SWING style. Complex and dynamic, involving the extensive use of improvisation, the movement was pioneered by musicians such as Charlie PARKER and Dizzy GILLESPIE.

**Becker, Boris** (1967– ) German tennis player. Becker rose from obscurity to win the 1985 Wimbledon singles title. His booming serve and athleticism gained him two more Wimbledon titles (1986, 1989). He won the US Open (1989) and the Australian Open (1991, 1996). Becker retired in 1997.

**Becket, Saint Thomas à** (1118–70) English church leader. He was appointed chancellor of England (1155) and became a friend of HENRY II. In 1162 Henry made him archbishop of Canterbury, hoping for his support in asserting royal control, but Becket devoted his loyalty to the church. His defense of clerical privileges against the crown led to fierce conflict. Becket spent six years in exile. Reconciliation was short-lived, as Becket turned on those, including the king, who had violated his rights during his exile. Four of Henry's knights, assuming wrongly they would gain the king's gratitude, killed Becket in Canterbury Cathedral. Henry did penance, and Becket was acclaimed a martyr. He was canonized in 1173.

**Beckett, Samuel** (1906–89) Irish playwright and novelist. One of the most influential European writers of the 20th century, Beckett wrote in both French and English. He emigrated to Paris in the 1920s, and became an assistant to James JOYCE. Beckett's reputation is largely due to his three full-length plays, *Waiting for Godot* (1952), *Endgame* (1957), and *Happy Days* (1961), which explore notions of suffering, paralysis, and survival. His work is often linked to the Theater of the ABSURD with its repetitive, inventive language, and obsession with futility and meaninglessness. His short plays include *Krapp's Last Tape* (1958), *Not I* (1973), and *Footfalls* (1975). His novels include the French trilogy *Molloy* (1951), *Malone Dies* (1951), and *The Unnameable* (1953). Beckett was awarded the 1969 Nobel Prize for literature.

**Beckmann, Max** (1884–1950) German expressionist painter. Beckmann was disturbed by his experiences as a medical orderly in World War I and changed his painting style to reflect his awareness of human brutality. His EXPRESSIONISM often took the form of allegory. In 1933, after being dismissed from teaching by the Nazis, he started work on *Departure*, the first of nine TRIPTYCHS that express the sense of dislocation he felt in the modern world. As a result of Nazi harassment, Beckmann moved to Amsterdam and then to the US.

▼ **Beatles** Early in their career, the clean-cut image of the Beatles, and the extraordinary songwriting talents of Paul McCartney and John Lennon, ensured that they were a huge success all over the world. Although the group split up in 1970, they remain one of the most influential popular music groups of all time.

B

▲ **beech** Beech trees are found in the Northern and Southern Hemispheres. The northern beech (A) (European *Fagus sylvatica*; US *Fagus grandifolia*) thrives on chalky soil. Male flowers grow in clusters, separate from the female. The Antarctic beech (C) (*Nothofagus antarctica*) grows to 100ft (30m) and is found in the Andes, SE Australia, and New Zealand. It differs from its northern cousin in being an evergreen species. Although the eastern beech (B) belongs to the same genus as the Antarctic, like the northern it grows up to 120ft (36m) high.

**BEE**

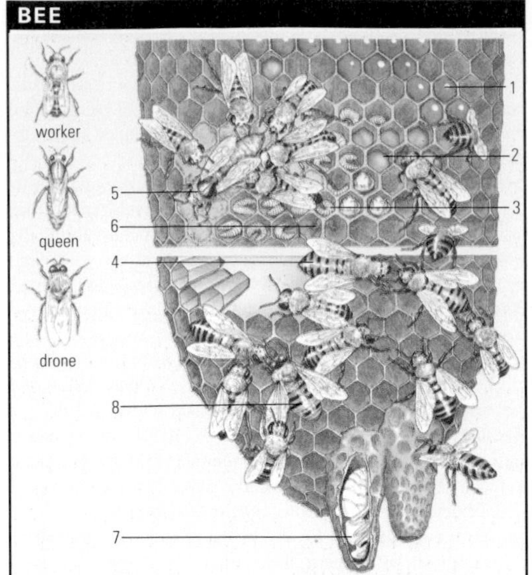


The nest of the honeybee consists of a number of wax combs suspended in a shelter, such as a hollowed-out tree. The cells of the outer edges of the comb (1) contain nectar mixed with saliva, which the workers fan with their wings to evaporate excess water before the cell is capped with wax; this mixture eventually turns into honey. Other cells are used to contain reserves of pollen (2). Developing larvae (3) in open cells are kept clean by worker bees to prevent fungal infestations. They are fed by young workers with regurgitated food, and with honey and pollen from the storage cells. When a newly formed worker emerges from its cell it is fed regurgitated pollen and nectar from another worker (4). Its vacated cell is thoroughly cleaned and re-used. The queen (5), surrounded by a retinue of workers, here rests on a group of capped cells, each of which contains a worker pupa. Eggs (6) are laid by the queen in the center of the comb. When new queens are needed, the workers construct extra large cells of the edge of the comb (7) in order to hold them.

**Becquerel, Antoine Henri** (1852–1908) French physicist. Becquerel was professor of physics at the Paris Museum of Natural History, and later at the Ecole Polytechnique. In 1896 he discovered RADIOACTIVITY in uranium salts, for which he shared the 1903 Nobel Prize for physics with Pierre and Marie CURIE. The Becquerel standard unit for measuring radioactivity, which has replaced the CURIE, was named for him. *See also* BETA PARTICLE

**bed** In geology, a layer of sedimentary rock. Usually deposited in a broadly horizontal sheet, it underlies the surface material (regolith) except where regolith has been removed by EROSION.

**bedbug** Broad, flat, wingless insect found worldwide. It feeds by sucking blood from mammals, including human beings. Bedbugs usually gorge themselves at night and remain hidden during the day. Length: to 0.25in (6mm). Family Cimicidae; species *Cimex lectularius*.

**Bede, Saint** (673–735) (Venerable Bede) English monk and scholar. Bede spent his life in the Northumbrian monasteries of Wearmouth and Jarrow. His most important work is the *Ecclesiastical History of the English Nation*, which remains a primary source for English history from 54 BC–AD 697. His works were profoundly influential in early medieval Europe.

**Bedfordshire** County in central S England; the county town is Bedford, other major towns include Luton and Dunstable. There are traces of early Bronze Age settlements. The land is mostly flat with low chalk hills, the Chilterns, in the S. The region (drained by the River Ouse) is fertile, and agriculture is the chief economic activity. Industries: motor-vehicle manufacture, electrical equipment. Area: 477sq mi (1,235sq km). Pop. (1991) 524,105.

**Bedouin** Nomadic, desert-dwelling ARAB peoples of the Middle East, followers of ISLAM. Traditionally they live in tents, moving with their herds of camels, goats, sheep, and sometimes cattle across vast areas. Their society is patrilineal and they are renowned for their hospitality, honesty, and fierce independence. In the 20th century many Bedouin have been forced to abandon the nomadic way of life and work in agriculture or in towns.

**bee** Insect distinguished from other members of the order Hymenoptera, such as ants and wasps, by the presence of specially adapted hairs, with which they collect POLLEN; all bees feed their young NECTAR and pollen. Although the honeybee and BUMBLEBEE are social insects living in well-organized colonies, many other bees are solitary. Found worldwide, except in polar regions, they are important pollinators of flowers. Entomologists recognize *c*.12,000 species, but only the honeybee provides the HONEY that we eat. It builds combs of six-sided cells with wax from glands on its abdomen. A honeybee colony may have up to 60,000 individuals, consisting mainly of infertile female workers, with a few male drones and one egg-laying queen.

**beech** Deciduous tree native to the Northern Hemisphere. Beeches have wide-spreading branches, smooth gray bark, and alternate, coarse-toothed leaves. Male flowers hang from thin stems; pairs of female flowers hang on hairy stems and develop into triangular, edible nuts enclosed by burs. The American beech (*Fagus grandifolia*) and the European beech (*F. sylvatica*) are important timber trees used for furniture and tool handles. Height: to 117ft (36m). Family Fagaceae; there are 10 species. All belong to the genus *Nothofagus*.

**Beecham, Sir Thomas** (1869–1961) English conductor, one of the greatest of his era. Beecham founded the New Symphony Orchestra (1906), the London Philharmonic (1932), and the Royal Philharmonic (1947). In 1933 he became artistic director of Covent Garden Opera, where he gave the first English performances of the operas of Richard Strauss.

**Beecher, Henry Ward** (1813–87) US Congregational minister, outstanding preacher, and influential advocate of social reform, brother of Harriet Beecher Stowe. In 1847 Beecher became pastor of the Plymouth Congregational Church, Brooklyn, New York. Famed for his opposition to slavery, he supported women's voting rights and the scientific theory of evolution. He wrote several books of sermons, a life of Jesus Christ, and a novel.

**bee-eater** Tropical bird of the Eastern Hemisphere that catches flying bees and wasps. It has a long, curved beak, bright, colorful plumage, and a long tail. It nests in large colonies and builds a tunnel to its egg chamber. Length: 6–15in (15–38cm). Family Meropidae.

**Beelzebub** Name used for Satan or the Devil. The word was originally *Beelzebul* ("Lord of demons") but was corrupted deliberately in Syrian texts and the (Latin) Vulgate to *Beelzebub* ("Lord of flies") as a gesture of contempt. Originally an aspect of Baal, it was used in its present sense in the New Testament (Matthew 10, Mark 3, and Luke 11).

**beer** Alcoholic beverage produced by the soaking, boiling, and fermentation of a cereal extract (often malted barley) flavored with a bitter substance (hops). Other ingredients are water, sugar, and yeast. The alcohol content of most beer ranges from *c*.2.5% to 12%, with the majority between 3% and 6%. Among the major types of beer are: ales, which classically have fewer hops added; stouts and porters, which are darker, with a persistent head and a hint of sweetness; lagers and pilsners, which are light, usually fizzy, and matured over a longer period of time at low temperature; bitter, which features additional hops; mild, which has few hops and is low in alcohol; and brown ale, which is similar to stout.

**Beersheba** (Be'er Sheva) Chief city of the Negev region, S Israel. Beersheba was the most S point of biblical PALESTINE. It flourished under Byzantine rule, but declined until restored by the Ottoman Turks *c*.1900. Industries: chemicals, textiles. Pop. (1992 est.) 128,400.

**beet** Vegetable native to Europe and parts of Asia, and cultivated in most cool regions. Its leaves are green or red and edible, although it is generally grown for its thick red or golden root. Some varieties are eaten as a vegetable, others are a source of sugar and some are used as fodder. Family Chenopodiaceae; species *Beta vulgaris See also* SUGAR BEET

**Beethoven, Ludwig van** (1770–1827) German composer, a profound influence on the development of musical styles. He provides a link between the formal CLASSICAL style of HAYDN and MOZART and the ROMANTICISM of WAGNER, BRAHMS, and BRUCKNER. Born in Bonn, Beethoven visited Vienna in 1787 and was taught briefly by Mozart; he made Vienna his home from 1792 and took lessons from Haydn. Beethoven's early works, such as the piano sonatas *Pathétique* (1789) and *Moonlight* (1801), betray the influences of his teachers. The year 1801 marks the onset of Beethoven's deafness and a shift in style. His third SYMPHONY (Eroica, 1803) was a decisive break from the classical tradition. This middle period also includes his fifth piano concerto (Emperor, 1809) and his only opera, *Fidelio* (1805). Beethoven's final period coincides with his complete loss of hearing (1817) and is marked by works of even greater length and complexity. These include his ninth symphony (1817–23).

**beetle** Insect characterized by horny front wings that serve as protective covers for the membranous hind wings. These protective sheaths are often brightly colored. Beetles are usually stout-bodied, and their mouthparts are adapted for biting and chewing. They are poor fliers, but (like all insects) are protected from injury and drying up by an EXOSKELETON. Beetles are the most numerous of the insects. More than 250,000 species are known, and new ones are still being discovered. They include SCARAB BEETLES, LADYBUGS, and WEEVILS. Most feed on plants, some prey on small animals, including other insects, whereas others are scavengers. Beetles undergo complete METAMORPHOSIS. Length: 0.02–6.3in (0.5mm– 6cm). Order Coleoptera.

**Begin, Menachem** (1913–92) Israeli statesman, prime minister (1977–83). A Polish-born Zionist, Begin was sentenced to eight years slave-labor but was released in 1941 to fight in the new Polish army. As commander of the paramilitary Irgun Zeva'i Leumi, he led resistance to British rule until Israeli independence in 1948. In 1973 Begin became leader of the Likud coalition. In 1977 Likud formed a coalition government with Begin as prime minister. Though a fervent nationalist, he sought reconciliation with Egypt and signed a peace treaty with Anwar SADAT in 1979. In recognition of their efforts they shared the 1978 Nobel Peace Prize. His popularity waned after Israel's 1982 invasion of Lebanon and he was succeeded by Yitzhak Shamir.

**begonia** Member of the genus *Begonia*, which includes plants, shrubs or trees native to tropical America and SE Asia. Begonias make popular houseplants, with their white, pink, or red flowers. There are three types: **rex**, with ornamental leaves of green, red, and silver; **rhizomatous**, with fleshy, creeping stems and glossy leaves; and **basket**, with trailing stems and brightly colored leaves. Family Begoniaceae.

**Behan, Brendan** (1923–64) Irish writer, notorious for his riotous lifestyle. Behan became a member of the IRA at the age of 14 and served several years in reform school, as described in his autobiography *Borstal Boy* (1958). His first play, *The Quare Fellow*, was produced in 1954, and his second was *The Hostage* (1959).

**behavioral ecology** Study of the complex relationship between environment and animal behavior. This involves drawing on natural history to study the adaptive features of an organism within its habitat. Human behavior is similarly studied. *See also* ADAPTATION; ECOLOGY; ETHOLOGY

**behaviorism** School of psychology that seeks to explain all animal and human behavior primarily in terms of observable and measurable responses to stimuli. Its method of research often involves laboratory experiments. PAVLOV's work on conditioned reflexes was a source for the early behaviorists such as J.B. WATSON. Later behaviorists, such as B.F. SKINNER, explain learning and development by "operant conditioning." *See also* DEVELOPMENTAL PSYCHOLOGY

**behavior therapy** (behavior modification) Treatment of psychological disorders by using principles and methods of BEHAVIORISM. It assumes that all behavior, desirable and otherwise, is learned through CONDITIONING and reinforcement. The therapy is designed to change people's behavior by rewarding desirable conduct and punishing or ignoring undesirable behavior.

**Behn, Aphra** (1640–89) English playwright, poet, and novelist. The first English professional female writer. A protofeminist, Behn attracted much contemporary scandal. She produced 15 risqué comic plays, the most well-known being *The Rover* (1677). She also wrote poetry, but is principally remembered for the first English philosophical novel, *Oroonoko* (1688).

**Behring, Emil Adolph von** (1854–1917) German bacteriologist and pioneer immunologist. Behring was awarded (1901) the first Nobel Prize for physiology or medicine for his work on serum therapy, developing immunization against DIPHTHERIA (1890) and TETANUS (1892) by injections of antitoxins. His discoveries led to the treatment of many childhood diseases.

**Beijing** (Peking) Capital of the People's Republic of CHINA, on a vast plain between the Pei and Hun Rivers, NE China. A settlement since *c.*1000 BC, Beijing served as China's capital from 1421 to 1911. After the establishment of the Chinese Republic (1911–12), Beijing remained the political center of the country. The seat of government was transferred to NANKING in 1928. Beijing ("northern capital") became known as Pei-p'ing ("northern peace"). Occupied by the Japanese in 1937, it was restored to China in 1945 and came under Communist control in 1949. Its name was restored as capital of the People's Republic. The city comprises two walled sections: the Inner (Tatar) City, which houses the Forbidden City (imperial palace complex), and the Outer (Chinese) city. Since 1949 heavy industry has been introduced, and textiles, iron, and steel are produced. Pop. (1993 est.) 6,560,000. *See also* TIANANMEN SQUARE

**Beirut** (Bayrūt) Capital and chief port of Lebanon, on the Mediterranean coast at the foot of the Lebanon Mountains. Beirut was taken by the Arabs in AD 635. In 1110 it was captured by the Christian crusaders, and remained part of the Latin Kingdom of Jerusalem until 1291. In 1516, under DRUZE control, Beirut became part of the Ottoman empire. During the 19th century it was the center of the revolt against the Ottoman empire led by MUHAMMAD ALI. In 1830 Beirut was captured by Egyptians, but in 1840 British and French forces restored Ottoman control. In 1920 it became capital of Lebanon under French mandate. During the 1950s and 1960s Beirut was a popular tourist destination. In 1976 the civil war began and

◄ **Beethoven, Ludwig van** Considered one of the finest composers, Beethoven's work is often divided into three periods. Until 1800 he generally followed the conventions of Haydn and Mozart; from about 1800–14 he wrote passionate works, now among his most popular, including the Third and Fifth symphonies, the Violin Concerto, and *Appassionata* piano sonata; and from 1814 date his most sublime compositions, among them the last five string quartets, the Ninth Symphony, and the *Missa Solemnis*.

Beirut rapidly fractured along religious lines. In 1982 West Beirut was devastated by an Israeli invasion in the war against the Palestine Liberation Organization (PLO). Following a series of atrocities, the Israelis began a phased withdrawal in 1985 and Syrian troops entered (1987) as part of an Arab peacekeeping force. By 1991 all militias had withdrawn from the city and restoration work began. Pop. (1993 est.) 1,500,000.

**Béjart, Maurice Jean** (1927– ) French ballet dancer and choreographer. One of the most innovative modern choreographers, Béjart experimented with avant-garde modern dance techniques and acrobatics. He founded and became director of the Ballet of the 20th Century in Brussels in 1960.

**Bekaa Valley** (Al Biqa) Highest part of the Rift Valley, between the Lebanon and Anti-Lebanon mountains, central Lebanon. The town of BAALBEK is located in the N of the valley. To the N of Baalbek, nomadic pastoralism is dominant. To the S lies the granary of Lebanon. The Litani River winds through this fertile region to the Mediterranean Sea. The valley has been a battleground for centuries, contested by the Persians, Seleucids, and Ptolemies. Today, it is a center of HIZBOLLAH activity. Length: 75mi (121km). Width: 5–9mi (8–14.5km).

**Belarus** (Belorussia) Republic in NE Europe. *See* country feature

**Belau** (formerly Palau) Self-governing island group in the Caroline Islands of the W Pacific, consisting of about 200 islands, eight of which are inhabited. The capital is Koror. A Spanish possession from 1710 to 1898, Belau was then held by Germany until 1914, when Japan occupied it. At the end of World War II control passed to the US. Self-government was instituted in 1981, and full independence followed in 1994. Most of the inhabitants are Micronesian, engaged in subsistence agriculture. Industries: fishing, copra processing. Area: 189sq mi (460sq km). Pop. (1986) 13,870.

**Belfast** Capital of Northern Ireland, at the mouth of the River Legan on Belfast Lough. The city was founded in 1177, but did not develop until after the Industrial Revolution. Belfast is now the center for the manufacture of Irish linen. Since the 19th century, religious and political differences between Protestants and Catholics have been a source of tension. In the late 1960s these differences erupted into violence and civil unrest. Belfast's harbor includes the Harland and Wolff yard, which has produced many of the largest liners in the world. Other industries: aircraft, machinery, tobacco. Pop. (1991) 283,746.

## BELARUS

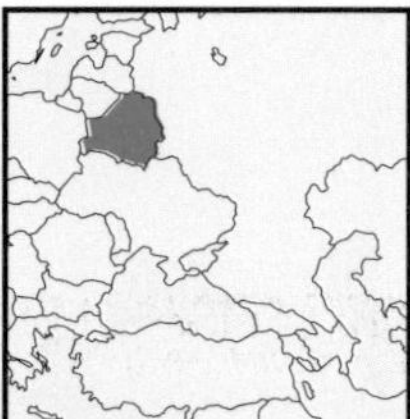

In September 1991, Belarus adopted a red and white flag to replace the flag used in the Soviet era. In June 1995, following a referendum in which Belarussians voted to improve relations with Russia, this was replaced with a design similar to the flag of 1958 but without the hammer and sickle.

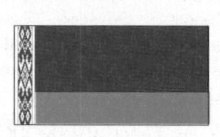

**AREA:** 80,154sq mi (207,600sq km)
**POPULATION:** 10,297,000
**CAPITAL (POPULATION):** Minsk (1,633,600)
**GOVERNMENT:** Multiparty republic
**ETHNIC GROUPS:** Belarussian 80%, Russian, Polish, Ukrainian, Jewish
**LANGUAGES:** Belarussian, Russian (both official)
**RELIGIONS:** Christianity (mainly Belarussian Orthodox, with Roman Catholics in the W and Evangelicals in the SW)
**CURRENCY:** Belarussian ruble = 100 kopecks

The Republic of Belarus, or Belorussia as it is also called, is a landlocked country in eastern Europe which was formerly part of the SOVIET UNION. The land is low-lying and mostly flat and, in the S, much of the land is marshy. This area contains Europe's largest marsh and peat bog, the Pripet Marshes. A hilly region, extending from NE to SW through the center of the country, includes the highest point in Belarus, a hill near the capital of MINSK, which reaches a height of 1,135ft (346m).

### CLIMATE

Belarus is affected both by the moderating influence of the Baltic Sea and by continental conditions to the E. Winters are cold and summers warm and the average annual rainfall is about 22–28in (550–700mm).

### VEGETATION

Forests cover about a third of Belarus. The colder N has such trees as alder, birch, and pine, while ash, oak, and hornbeam grow in the warmer S. Farmland and pasture have replaced most of the original forest.

### HISTORY AND POLITICS

Slavic people settled in the region 1,500 years ago. In the 9th century the area became part of the first East Slavic state, Kievan Rus. In the 13th century MONGOL armies overran the area and, later, Belarus became part of LITHUANIA. In 1569 Lithuania, including Belarus, became part of Poland. In the 18th century, Russia took over most of eastern Poland, including Belarus.

In 1918 Belarus became an independent republic, however Russia invaded the country and, in 1919, a Communist state was established. In 1922, Belarus became a founder republic of the Soviet Union. In 1991, after the breakup of the Soviet Union, Belarus again became an independent republic, though it retained ties with Russia through the organization called the CIS (COMMONWEALTH OF INDEPENDENT STATES), whose administrative center is located in Minsk.

During World War II, Belarus was once more a battlefield for major European powers and a quarter of its population perished. The Nazis murdered most of the Jewish population. In 1991, after the breakup of the Soviet Union, Belarus declared its independence and was a founder member of the COMMONWEALTH OF INDEPENDENT STATES (CIS). The administrative center of the CIS is located in Minsk. In 1997, despite opposition from nationalists, Belarus signed a Union Treaty with Russia, committing it to integration with Russia.

### ECONOMY

Belarus is an upper-middle-income economy (1995 GDP per capita, US$4,220). It has faced problems in the transition to a free-market economy. In 1995 an agreement with Russia enabled Belarus to receive subsidized fuel supplies. Agriculture, especially meat and dairy farming, is important.

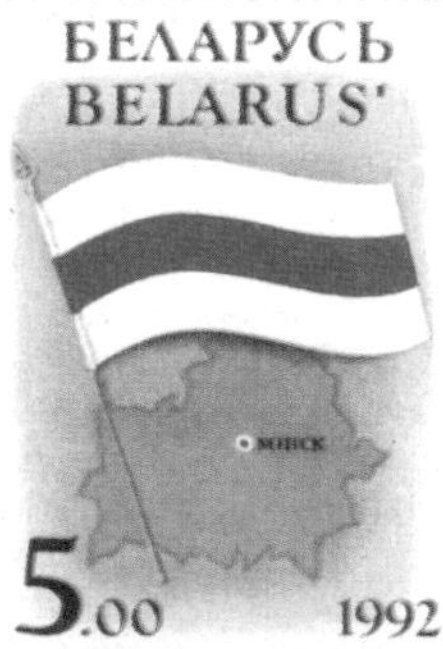


**The former national flag,** adopted in 1991 but replaced in 1995, flying above an outline of Belarus, was the subject of this 5-ruble stamp issued in 1992. The site of the capital city, Minsk, whose name is written in the Cyrillic alphabet, is marked on the center of the map.

**Belgium** Kingdom in NW Europe. *See* country feature page 78

**Belgrade** (Beograd) Capital of Serbia and of Yugoslavia, situated at the confluence of the Sava and Danube rivers. In the 12th century it became the capital of Serbia but was later ruled by the Ottoman Turks. It was incorporated into the area which came to be known as Yugoslavia in 1929 and suffered much damage under German occupation in World War II. In 1996 Belgrade witnessed huge demonstrations against the government. The many museums and art galleries include the National Museum (1844). Industries: chemicals, metals, machine tools, textiles. Pop. (1991) 1,168,454.

**Belize** (formerly British Honduras) Republic in Central America, on the Caribbean Sea. **Land and climate** Swamp vegetation and rain forest cover large areas. N Belize is mostly low-lying and swampy. Behind the swampy coastal plain in the S, the land rises to 3,681ft (1,122m) at Victoria Peak in the Maya Mountains. The Belize River flows across the center of the country. Belize has a humid tropical climate, with high temperatures throughout the year, and an average annual rainfall ranging from 51in (1,300mm) in the N to over 150in (3,800mm) in the S. In the N, ironwood, mahogany, and sapote (date plum) are common trees, while cedar, oak, and pine predominate in the S. The coastal plains are covered by savanna, while mangrove swamps line the coast. **Economy** Belize is a lower-middle-income developing country. The economy is based on agriculture; sugar cane is the chief commercial crop. Other crops include bananas, beans, citrus fruits, corn, and rice. Forestry, fishing and tourism are important activities. **History and Politics** Between *c*.300 BC and AD 1000, Belize was part of the MAYA empire, which had declined long before Spanish explorers reached the coast in the early 16th century. Shipwrecked British sailors founded the first European settlement in 1638, and over the next 150 years Britain gradually took control of Belize and established sugar plantations using slave labor. In 1862 Belize became the colony of British Honduras. In 1973 it became known as Belize and achieved independence in 1981. Guatemala has claimed Belize and British troops remained in Belize to prevent a possible invasion. In 1992 Guatemala recognized its independence and in 1993 Britain began to withdraw its troops.

**Bell, Alexander Graham** (1847–1922) US inventor of the TELEPHONE, b. Scotland. He first worked with his father, inventor of a system for educating the deaf. The family moved to Canada in 1870, and Bell taught speech at Boston University (1873–77). His work on the transmission of sound by electricity led to the first demonstration of the telephone in 1876 and the founding of the Bell Telephone Co. in 1877.

**Bell, John** US statesman. Bell served (1827–41) in the House of Representatives and was secretary of war (1841). Bell was a senator (1847–59) for Tennessee. Although he supported slavery, Bell supported the Union. In 1860, as the presidential candidate for the Constitutional Union Party, he won the southern states of Tennessee, Kentucky, and Virginia.

**belladonna** *See* ATROPINE; NIGHTSHADE

**belles-lettres** (Fr. fine letters) Type of literature valued more for its elegant style than for the information it contains. It was once used to describe all literature.

**bellflower** Plant native to northern temperate regions and tropical mountains, with bell-shaped flowers, alternate leaves and milky sap. Bellflowers are now widely cultivated. There are 250–300 species. Family CAMPANULACEAE; genus *Campanula*.

**Bellini, Giovanni** (*c*.1430–1516) Italian painter, from an artistic family. Giovanni's father, **Jacopo** (*c*.1400–*c*.1470), was a pupil of GENTILE DA FABRIANO. His major surviving works are two sketchbooks, the source of many works by his son-in-law Andrea MANTEGNA and his two sons Giovanni and Gentile. **Gentile** (*c*.1429–1507) was famous for his narrative works (such as *The Miracle of the True Cross*) which became the prototype of the genre in Venice. **Giovanni** was the greatest painter of the family and single-handedly transformed Venice into a great center of the RENAISSANCE. In his early works, the treatment of nature was precise and realistic but it gradually became poetic and monumental. He is chiefly remembered as a religious painter. His pictures emphasize light and color as a means of expression. Many of the leading painters of Venice trained in his studio, including TITIAN.

**Bellini, Vincenzo** (1801–35) Italian composer of operas. Bellini's most notable works are *Norma* and *La Sonnambula* (both 1831) and *I Puritani* (1835). His flowing melodies require great vocal skill. These *bel canto* operas were popular during the 19th century.

**Belloc, (Joseph) Hilaire (Pierre-René)** (1870–1953) British writer, b. France. Belloc became a British citizen in 1902 and was a Liberal member of Parliament (1906–10). His work includes satirical novels (some illustrated by his long-term collaborator, G.K. CHESTERTON), biographies, historical works, and travel writing. Belloc is best-known for his light verse, especially the children's classic, *Cautionary Tales* (1907).

**Bellow, Saul** (1915– ) US writer, b. Canada. Bellow's work demonstrates intense moral preoccupation with the plight of the individual. His debut novel was *The Dangling Man* (1944). Later novels include *The Adventures of Augie March* (1953), *Herzog* (1964), *Humboldt's Gift* (1975), and *The Dean's December* (1982). Awarded the 1976 Nobel Prize for literature, Bellow has also written plays and short stories.

**Bellows, George Wesley** (1882–1925) US painter and printmaker. Bellows was taught by Robert HENRI and worked with the ASHCAN SCHOOL. He is best known for his paintings of boxing matches and street scenes such as the impressionistic *Stag at Sharkey's* (1907).

**bell-ringing** (campanology) Art of ringing church bells or handbells. In Britain, the most widely practiced form is **change-ringing** in which bells are rung by rope in strict sequences. In the US and Europe, the most common forms are the **carillon** and the **chime**, in which the bells remain stationary as they are struck by hammers.

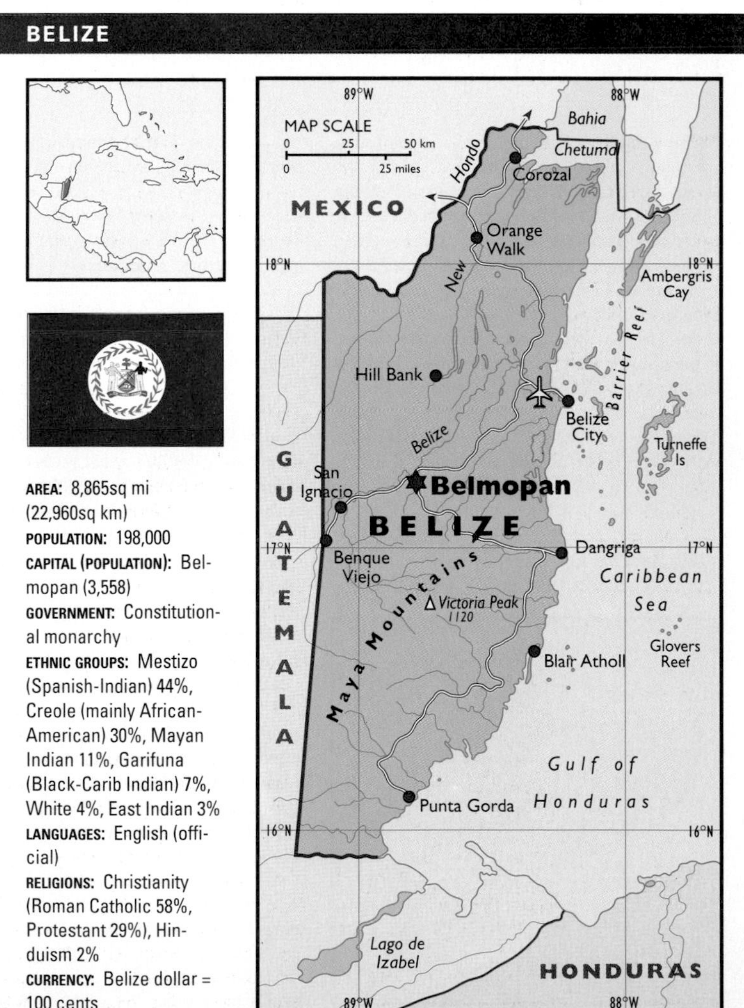

**Bell's palsy** Paralysis of a facial nerve causing weakness of the muscles on one side of the face. The condition, which may be due to viral infection, usually disappears, or may be treated with drugs or, rarely, surgery.

**Belmopan** Capital of Belize, on the Belize River, 50mi (80km) upstream from Belize City. It replaced Belize City as capital in 1970, the latter having been largely destroyed by a hurricane in 1961. Pop. (1991) 3,558.

**Belsen** Village in Lower Saxony, Germany, site of a CONCENTRATION CAMP established by the Nazi government during World War II. An estimated 30,000 people were murdered or died here of starvation and disease, before the camp was liberated in April 1945.

**Belshazzar** In the Old Testament, the son of Nebuchadnezzar and last king of BABYLON. The Book of DANIEL relates how Belshazzar organized a great feast during which a disembodied hand wrote upon the wall, "*Mene, mene tekel upharsin.*" Daniel translated it as "Thou art weighed in the balance and found wanting," and said it signified Babylon's downfall. Modern archeological investigations have identified Belshazzar with Bel-shar-usur (d.539 BC), the son of Nabonidus, king of Babylon (556–539 BC).

**beluga** (white whale) Small, toothed Arctic WHALE that is milky white when mature. It preys on fish, squid, and crustaceans and is valued by Eskimos for its meat, hide, and blubber. Length: *c.*13ft (4m). Species: *Delphinapterus leucas*. Beluga is also a type of STURGEON.

**Benares** *See* VARANASI

**bends** (decompression sickness) Syndrome, mostly seen in divers, featuring pain in the joints, dizziness, nausea, and paralysis. It is caused by the release of nitrogen into the tissues and blood. This occurs if there is a too rapid return to normal atmospheric pressure after a period of breathing high-pressure air (when the body absorbs more nitrogen). Treatment involves gradual decompression in a hyperbaric chamber.

**Benedict (of Nursia), Saint** (480–547) Roman founder of Western monasticism and of the BENEDICTINE order. St. Benedict was of noble birth. Shocked by the city's lawlessness, he retired to a cave above Subiaco, where he acquired a reputation for austerity and sanctity. A community grew up around him and he established 12 monasteries. His feast day is July 11.

**Benedict XV** (1854–22) Pope (1914–22), b. Giacomo della Chiesa. During World War I, Benedict strove for peace among nations, stressing pacifist idealism. He tried to unite

## BELGIUM

Belgium's national flag was adopted in 1830, when the country won its independence from the Netherlands. The colors come from the arms of the province of Brabant, in central Belgium, which rebelled against Austrian rule in 1787.

**AREA:** 11,780sq mi (30,510sq km)
**POPULATION:** 9,998,000
**CAPITAL (POPULATION):** Brussels (Brussel, Bruxelles, 949,070)
**GOVERNMENT:** Federal constitutional monarchy
**ETHNIC GROUPS:** Belgian 91% (Fleming 55%, Walloon 34%), Italian, French, Dutch, Turkish, Moroccan
**LANGUAGES:** Dutch, French, German (all official)
**RELIGIONS:** Christianity (Roman Catholic 72%)
**CURRENCY:** Belgian franc = 100 centimes

The Kingdom of Belgium is a densely populated country in W Europe. Behind the North Sea coastline, which extends for about 39mi (63km), lie coastal plains, including some polders – low-lying areas which have been drained and are protected from the sea by dikes (sea walls). Central Belgium consists of low plateaus and the only hilly region is the ARDENNES, in the SE. The chief rivers, which occupy fertile valleys, are the Schelde in the W and the Sambre and Meuse flowing between the central plateau and the Ardennes. The capital is BRUSSELS, other major cities include BRUGES, ANTWERP, GHENT, and LIÈGE.

### CLIMATE

Belgium has a cool temperate climate. Moist winds from the Atlantic bring fairly heavy rain, and the Ardennes has heavy winter snowfalls.

Brussels enjoys mild winters and warm summers, but the hills are cooler.

### VEGETATION

Farmland and pasture cover about 50% of Belgium. The forests, especially in the Ardennes, contain trees such as beech, birch, elm, and oak, but in the N, the birch forests and heathland have largely been replaced by plantations of evergreen trees.

### HISTORY

In the Middle Ages, Belgium was split into small states, but the country was united by the dukes of BURGUNDY in the 14th and 15th centuries. It later came, at various times, under Austrian, Spanish, and French rule.

In 1815 Belgium and the Netherlands united as the LOW COUNTRIES, but Belgium became independent in 1830. In 1885 Belgium became a colonial power when the Congo Free State (now Zaire) became a Belgian possession.

Belgium's economy was weakened by German invasions in both world wars, but the country recovered quickly post-1945 – initially through collaboration with the Netherlands and Luxembourg, which formed a customs union called Benelux, and later through its membership of the EUROPEAN COMMUNITY.

### POLITICS

A central political issue in Belgium has been the tensions between Dutch-speaking Flemings and French-speaking WALLOONS. In the 1970s, the government divided the country into three economic regions: FLANDERS, Wallonia, and bilingual BRUSSELS. In 1993, Belgium adopted a federal system of government, and each of the regions now has its own parliament, which is responsible for local matters. Elections under this new system were held in 1995. During 1996 and 1997 Belgium was shocked by a large-scale child-abuse scandal.

### ECONOMY

Belgium is a major trading nation (1995 GDP per capita, US$21,660) with a highly developed transport system and economy. It does have coal reserves, though most of its mines have been closed over the last 30 years because they are uneconomic. While Belgium has to import many raw materials and fuels, its leading activity is manufacturing, the main products including steel, chemicals, and processed foods. The other main industries are oil-refining, textiles, diamond cutting, and glassware.

Agriculture employs only 3% of the people, but Belgian farmers produce most of the basic foods needed by the population. Barley and wheat are the chief crops, followed by flax, hops, potatoes, and sugar beets, but the most valuable activities are dairy farming and livestock rearing.

Belgium's economic profile is essentially European, and it regards itself as at the heart of Europe. Brussels has provided the headquarters of the European Union since its inception and is also the site of the headquarters of the North Atlantic Treaty Organization (NATO).

all Roman Catholics, made changes in the Curia, and published a new Code of Canon Law.

**Benedictines** Monks and nuns of the monastic Order of St. Benedict, who follow the Rule laid down by St. BENEDICT (OF NURSIA) in the 6th century. The order played a leading role in bringing Christianity and civilization to western Europe in the 7th century, and in preserving Christianity in the medieval period. During the REFORMATION most Benedictine monasteries and nunneries in Europe, including 300 in England, were suppressed. The order revived in France and Germany during the 17th century. Benedictine monks and nuns returned to England in the late 19th century, and the Order spread to North and South America.

**Beneš, Eduard** (1884–1948) Czech statesman, president (1935–38). Beněs promoted Czech independence while abroad during World War I and became the first foreign minister of Czechoslovakia (1918–35). He resigned from the presidency in protest against the MUNICH AGREEMENT. Reelected in 1946, he resigned again 1948 after the communist takeover.

**Bengal** Former province of India. Now a region of the Indian subcontinent that includes WEST BENGAL state in India, and East Bengal, which became part of BANGLADESH. Much of Bengal lies in the deltas of the Ganges and Brahmaputra rivers. Bengal was the richest region in the 16th-century Mogul empire of AKBAR I (THE GREAT). Conquered by the British in 1757, it became the center of British India, with CALCUTTA as the capital. It was made an autonomous region in 1937. Area: 77,442sq mi (200,575sq km).

**Bengal, Bay of** NE Gulf of the Indian Ocean, bounded by India and Sri Lanka (W), India and Bangladesh (N), Burma (E), and the Indian Ocean (S). Many rivers empty into the Bay, including the GANGES and BRAHMAPUTRA. The chief ports are MADRAS and CALCUTTA.

**Bengali** Major language of the Indian subcontinent. It is spoken by virtually all of the 85 million inhabitants of Bangladesh and by 45 million in the Indian province of West Bengal. Bengali belongs to the Indic branch of the Indo-European family of languages.

**Benghazi** (Banghazi) City on the NE shore of the Gulf of Sidra, Libya. Founded by the Greeks in the 6th century BC, the Italians captured it in 1911. Libya's second largest city, Benghazi contains several government offices, and is a commercial and industrial center for Cyrenaica province. Industries: salt processing, shipping, oil refining. Pop. (1988 est.) 446,250.

**Ben-Gurion, David** (1886–1973) Israeli statesman, one of the founders of the state of Israel, prime minister (1948–53, 1955–63). Born in Poland, Ben-Gurion became leader of the Zionist labor movement in Palestine, and founded (1930) the Mapai (Labor) Party. After World War II, he led the campaign for an independent Jewish state and became Israel's first prime minister.

**Benin** Republic in W Africa. *See* country feature page 81

**Benin City** Capital of Edo state, S Nigeria. A port on the River Benin, the city is the center of Nigeria's rubber industry. From the 13th to 17th centuries, Benin served as the capital of a powerful African kingdom. In the 15th century it acted as a market for the trade in slaves and ivory with the Portuguese. In 1898 Britain captured Benin and destroyed many of its famous bronze portrait busts. The city remains a center for traditional arts and crafts. Pop. (1992 est.) 207,200.

**Benn, Tony (Anthony Neil Wedgwood)** (1925– ) British politician. Benn was elected to Parliament in 1950, and in 1963 disclaimed an inherited peerage in order to remain a member of the House of Commons. He held several ministerial posts in the Labour governments of the 1960s and 1970s, and was a leading opposition spokesman for the left wing of the LABOUR PARTY.

**Bennett, (Enoch) Arnold** (1867–1931) British author. Bennett is best known for his novels of the "Five Towns," which portray provincial life in the industrial Midlands, England. They include *Anna of the Five Towns* (1902), *The Old Wives' Tale* (1908), and the trilogy, *Clayhanger* (1910), *Hilda Lessways* (1911), and *These Twain* (1916). He was also a playwright, short-story writer, and journalist.

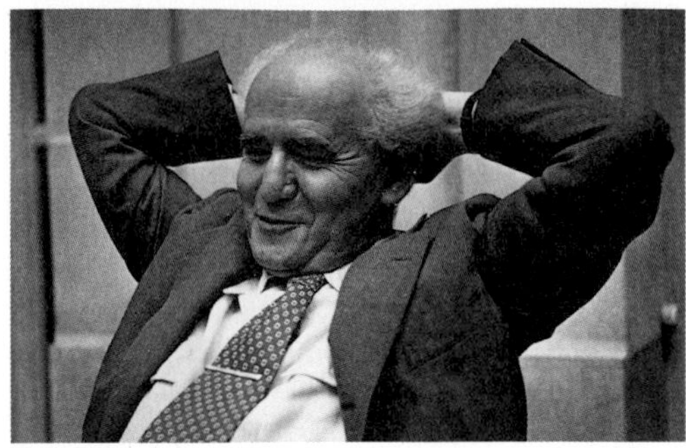

◀ **Ben-Gurion, David** Known as the "Father of the Nation", Ben-Gurion was Israel's first prime minister. He played a key role in establishing a Jewish state in Palestine as set out in the Balfour Declaration.

**Ben Nevis** Highest peak in the British Isles, in the Highlands region of W central Scotland. Ben Nevis is in the central Grampian Mountain range (overlooking Glen Nevis), near Fort William. It rises to 4,406ft (1,343m).

**Bentham, Jeremy** (1748–1832) British philosopher, jurist, and social reformer. Bentham developed the theory of UTILITARIANISM, based on the premise that "the greatest happiness of the greatest number" should be the object of individual and government action. His theories influenced much of England's early reform legislation.

**benthos** Flora and fauna of the seafloor. They include sedentary forms such as sponges, creeping creatures such as crabs and snails, burrowing animals such as worms, and countless bacteria.

**Bentley, John Francis** (1839–1902) British church architect. Bentley's most famous design is the Byzantine-style Roman Catholic cathedral in Westminster, London.

**Benton, Thomas Hart** (1889–1975) US painter. A realist, Benton concentrated on painting rural and small-town US life. His work includes several murals, notably in the New School for Social Research, New York City (1930–31) and the Whitney Museum of American Art. Jackson POLLOCK was his most famous pupil.

**Benz, Karl** (1844–1929) German pioneer of the INTERNAL COMBUSTION ENGINE. After some success with an earlier TWO-STROKE ENGINE, he built a FOUR-STROKE ENGINE in 1885. Benz achieved great success when he installed the new engine in a four-wheel vehicle in 1893. Benz was the first to make and sell light, self-propelled vehicles built to a standardized pattern.

**benzene** ($C_6H_6$) Colorless, volatile, sweet smelling, flammable liquid HYDROCARBON, a product of petroleum refining. A benzene molecule is a hexagonal ring of six unsaturated carbon atoms (benzene ring). It is a raw material for manufacturing many organic chemicals and plastics, drugs, and dyes. Properties: sp.gr. 0.88; m.p. 41.9°F (5.5°C); b.p. 176.2°F (80.1°C). Benzene is carcinogenic and should be handled with caution.

**benzodiazepine** Any of a group of mood-altering DRUGS, such as librium and valium, that are used primarily to treat severe anxiety or insomnia. They intervene in the transmission of nerve signals and were originally developed as muscle relaxants. Today, they are the most widely prescribed tranquilizers.

**benzoin** Fragrant, resinous polymer, once obtained from the balsam resin found in the trees of the genus *Styrax* in tropical SE Asia, now made synthetically. It is used in perfumes and decongestant cough medicines.

**Ben-zvi, Itzhak** (1884–1963) Israeli statesman, president (1952–63). After fleeing his native Russia, Ben-zvi settled in PALESTINE in 1907. Exiled (1915–18), he worked with David BEN-GURION and other Zionist leaders to create the institutions basic to the formation of the state of Israel, including Histadrut, the leading labor organization, and the Mapai (Labor) Party.

**Beowulf** Oldest English epic poem, dating from around the 8th century, and the most important example of Anglo-Saxon verse. It tells how the young prince, Beowulf, slays the monster Grendel and his vengeful mother. Some 50 years later, Beowulf (now king of the Geats) fights and slays a fire-breathing dragon but dies from his wounds. The text, which exists in a single 10th-century manuscript, was transcribed by more than one hand and the many explicitly Christian interpretations were probably added by monks.

B

**berberis** (barberry) Genus of *c*.450 species of shrubs native to temperate regions. The bark and wood are yellow, the stems are usually spiny, and the golden flowers give way to sour blue berries. The stamens are sensitive to touch. It is a host for the plant disease RUST, especially those that attack cereal crops. Family Berberidaceae.

**Berbers** Caucasian Muslim people of N Africa and the Sahara. Some are herdsmen and subsistence farmers; others, like the TUAREG, roam the desert with their great animal herds. Their stable culture dates back to before 2400 BC. Berber languages are spoken by more than 10 million people.

**Berg, Alban** (1885–1935) Austrian composer. A student of Arnold SCHOENBERG, Berg composed his later works in a complex, highly individualized style based on Schoenberg's TWELVE-TONE MUSIC technique. His *Wozzeck* (1925) is regarded as one of the masterpieces of 20th-century opera.

**Bergen** Port on the N Atlantic Ocean; capital of Hordaland county, SW Norway. Founded in the 11th century, Bergen was Norway's chief city and the residence of medieval kings. It is now an industrial and cultural center with a university (1948), a national theater (1850), and a 13th-century Viking hall. Industries: shipbuilding, textiles, fish processing. Pop. (1990) 212,944.

**Bergman, Ingmar** (1918– ) Swedish film director. With a versatile company of artists and a strong personal vision, Bergman created dark allegories, satires on sex, and complex studies of human relationships. Major films include *The Seventh Seal* (1956), *Wild Strawberries* (1957), *The Virgin Spring* (1960), *Scenes from a Marriage* (1974), and *The Magic Flute* (1975). *Fanny and Alexander* (1983) was considered his finest achievement.

**Bergman, Ingrid** (1915–82) Swedish actress. Bergman's first major film was *Intermezzo* (1936). In 1939 she moved to Hollywood, starring in films such as *Casablanca* (1943). She won an Academy Award for Best Actress in *Gaslight* (1944). Other classics followed, such as *Spellbound* (1945) and *Notorious* (1946). Bergman gained another Best Actress Oscar for *Anastasia* (1956). Towards the end of her career, she won a third Oscar as Best Supporting Actress in *Murder on the Orient Express* (1974). She was married (1950–58) to the film director Roberto ROSSELLINI.

**Bergson, Henri** (1859–1941) French philosopher of evolution. Bergson saw existence as a struggle between human life force (*élan vital*) and the material world. He received the Nobel Prize for literature in 1927. Bergson's works include *Time and Free Will* (1889) and *Creative Evolution* (1907).

**Beria, Lavrenti Pavlovich** (1899–1953) Soviet politician, chief (1938–53) of the secret police (NKVD). Beria headed the Cheka, predecessor of the NKVD, in Transcaucasia in the 1920s. He helped STALIN to conduct the purges of the Communist Party. When Stalin died, Beria was arrested and executed for treason.

**beriberi** Disease caused by a deficiency of vitamin $B_1$ (thiamine), and other vitamins in the diet. Symptoms include weakness, edema and degeneration of nerves. The disease is rare in the developed world.

▲ **Bergman** One of Hollywood's most enduring stars, Ingrid Bergman will perhaps be best remembered for the film *Casablanca*, in which she starred opposite Humphrey Bogart.

**Bering, Vitus Jonassen** (1680–1741) Danish naval officer and explorer in Russian service who gave his name to the Bering Strait and Bering Sea. In 1728 he sailed N from Kamchatka, NE Siberia, to the Bering Strait to discover whether Asia and North America were joined. Bering turned back before he was certain, but set out again in 1741, reaching Alaska. Returning, he was shipwrecked and died on what is now Bering Island.

**Bering Sea** Northernmost reach of the Pacific Ocean, bounded by Siberia (NW), Alaska (NE), and separated from the Pacific by the ALEUTIAN ISLANDS; it is connected to the Arctic Ocean by the BERING STRAIT. It is icebound in the winter. Vitus BERING's explorations in the early 18th century drew attention to the seal-fur resource. Widespread disagreement over the protection of seals resulted in the BERING SEA CONTROVERSY (1886). Seal hunting regulations were imposed in 1893. Area: *c*.885,000sq mi (2,292,000sq km).

**Bering Sea Controversy** Dispute between various nations (mainly the US, Britain, and Canada) concerning control of the E Bering Sea and its lucrative seal-fur trade. In 1881 US citizens demanded control of the entire region, seized British ships, and weakened Canadian commercial interests. In 1893 an international board ruled in favor of the British. An agreement (1911) between Britain, Japan, Russia, and the US limited hunting and made concessions to Canadian interests.

**Bering Strait** Strait at the N end of the BERING SEA separating W Alaska from E Siberia and connecting the Bering Sea to the ARCTIC OCEAN. It was named for Vitus BERING, who sailed through it in 1728. Min. width: 53mi (85km).

**Berio, Luciano** (1925– ) Italian composer. Berio was in the forefront of postwar avant-garde composers, and used electronic and chance effects in many of his works, which include *Nones* (1953), *Différences* (1958–60), *Visage* (1961), and *Opera* (1970).

**Berkeley, Busby** (1895–1976) US film choreographer and director. Berkeley was first employed in Hollywood by Samuel Goldwyn. In 1933 he joined Warner Brothers. Berkeley's lavish, spectacular dance sequences and innovative camera techniques, notably in films such as *42nd Street* (1933) and the *Gold Diggers* series, overwhelmed audiences.

**Berkeley, George** (1685–1753) Irish philosopher and clergyman. Drawing on the EMPIRICISM of John LOCKE, he argued that there is no existence independent of subjective perception (*esse est percipi*). For Berkeley, the apparently ordered physical world is the work of God. This standpoint is often called subjective IDEALISM.

**Berkeley, Sir Lennox Randal Francis** (1903–89) English composer. His early works, such as *Serenade for Strings* and *Symphony* (1939–40), reveal the influence of Igor STRAVINSKY. His major choral work is the *Stabat Mater* (1946); he also wrote four operas, four symphonies, sacred and chamber music.

**Berkeley** City on the E shore of San Francisco bay, N California, US. Originally part of a land grant made by Spain to the Peralta family in 1820, it was annexed to the US in 1853 and named Oceanview. The name was changed to Berkeley in 1866 and incorporated as a city in 1878. It is one of the campuses of the University of California (1868), and also the site of the Lawrence Radiation Laboratory and the Lawrence Hall of Science. Industries: food processing, chemicals. Pop. (1990) 102,724.

**berkelium** (symbol Bk) Radioactive metallic element, of the ACTINIDE SERIES. It does not occur in nature and was first made in 1949 by alpha-particle bombardment of americium-241 at the University of California at Berkeley (after which it is named). Nine isotopes are known. Properties: at.no. 97; sp.gr. (calculated) 14; m.p. 1,807°F (986°C); most stable isotope $^{247}$Bk (half-life $1.4 \times 10^3$ yr).

**Berkshire** County in S central England within the Thames River basin; the county town is Reading. The Berkshire Downs run across the county. It is an agricultural area; dairy cattle and poultry are important, and barley is the main crop. Industries: nuclear research. Area: 485sq mi (1,255sq km). Pop. (1991) 734,246.

**Berlin, Irving** (1888–1989) US songwriter and composer. A prolific artist, Berlin wrote nearly 1,000 songs. His most popular tunes include "Alexander's Ragtime Band," "God Bless America," and "There's No Business Like Show Business." Berlin's successful Broadway musicals include *Annie Get Your Gun* (1946) and *Call Me Madam* (1950). He composed the scores for the films *Easter Parade* (1948) and *White Christmas* (1954).

**Berlin** Capital of Germany, lying on the Spree River, NE Germany. Berlin was founded in the 13th century. It became the residence of the Hohenzollerns and the capital of Brandenburg, and later of Prussia. It became the capital of the newly formed state of Germany in 1871. In the early 20th century Berlin was the second-largest city in Europe. Virtually destroyed at the end of WORLD WAR II, the city was divided into four sectors; British, French, US, and Soviet. On the formation of East Germany, the Soviet sector became East Berlin and the rest West Berlin. The BERLIN WALL was erected in 1961 by the East Germans, and separated the two parts of the city until 1989. On the reunification of Germany in 1990, East and West Berlin were amalgamated. Sights include the Brandenburg Gate and the Victory Column in Tiergarten Park. Parts of the Berlin Wall remain as a monument. Berlin has two universities, important museums and art galleries, a famous opera house, and is home to the Berlin Philharmonic Orchestra. Industries: chemicals, electronics. Pop. (1993) 3,466,000.

**Berlin, Congress of** (1878) Meeting of European powers to revise the Treaty of San Stefano (1878) that had increased Russian power in SE Europe. The purpose of the Congress, under the presidency of BISMARCK, was to modify its terms. The main territorial adjustment was to reduce the Russian-sponsored Greater Bulgaria.

**Berlin Airlift** (1948–49) Operation to supply BERLIN with food and other necessities after the Soviet Union closed all road and rail links between the city and West Germany. For 15 months US and British aircraft flew more than 270,000 flights, delivering food and supplies.

**Berlin Wall** Heavily fortified and defended wall 30mi (49km) long, that divided East and West BERLIN. It was built in 1961 by the East Germans to stop refugees fleeing to West Germany. Some individuals succeeded in crossing it, others were killed in the attempt. It was dismantled after the collapse of the Communist regime in 1989.

**Berlioz, (Louis) Hector** (1803–69) Preeminent French Romantic composer. Berlioz is noted for innovative, progressive orchestral writing. His best-known works include the *Symphonie Fantastique* (1830), *Harold in Italy* (1834) for viola and orchestra, the operas *Benvenuto Cellini* (1838) and *The Trojans* (1855–58), and the *Requiem* (1837).

**Bermuda** (formerly Somers Island) British colony of *c*.300 islands in the W Atlantic Ocean, 580mi (940km) E of North Carolina; the capital is Hamilton. Discovered *c*.1503, the islands were claimed for Britain by Sir George Somers in the early 17th century. They became a crown colony in 1684, eventually achieving self-government in 1968. Tourism is important. Agricultural products include vegetables, bananas, and citrus fruits. Area: 21sq mi (53sq km). Pop. (1994 est.) 60,500.

**Bern** (Berne) Capital of Switzerland, on the Aare River in the Bern region. Founded in 1191 as a military post, it became part of the Swiss Confederation in 1353. Bern was occupied by French troops during the French Revolutionary Wars (1798). It has a notable Gothic cathedral and a 15th-century town hall. Industries: precision instruments, chemicals, textiles, chocolate manufacture, tourism. Pop. (1992) 135,600.

## BENIN

The colors on this flag, used by Africa's oldest independent nation, Ethiopia, symbolize African unity. Benin adopted this flag after independence in 1960. A flag with a red star replaced it between 1975 and 1990, after which Benin dropped its Communist policies.

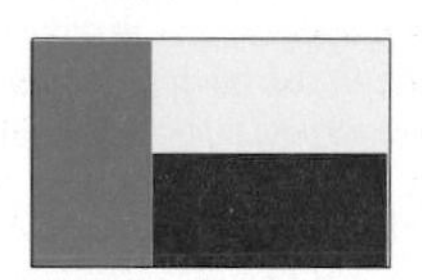

**AREA:** 43,483sq mi (112,620sq km )
**POPULATION:** 4,889,000
**CAPITAL (POPULATION):** Porto-Novo (208,258)
**GOVERNMENT:** Multiparty republic
**ETHNIC GROUPS:** Fon, Adja, Bariba, Yoruba, Fulani, Somba
**LANGUAGES:** French (official)
**RELIGIONS:** Traditional beliefs 60%, Christianity 23%, Islam 15%
**CURRENCY:** CFA franc = 100 centimes

The Republic of Benin is one of Africa's smallest countries, extending about 390mi (620km) from N to S. Its Atlantic coastline, which is only 62mi (100km) long, is lined by lagoons. The country has no natural harbors and the one at COTONO, Benin's main port and biggest city, is artificial. PORTO-NOVO, the capital, is farther E.

Behind the lagoons is a flat plain partly covered by rain forests, while about 50mi (80km) inland there is a large marshy depression. In central Benin the land rises to low plateaus, with the highest land in the NW. Northern Benin is covered by savanna (grassland with scattered trees), the habitat of such animals as water buffaloes, elephants, and lions. The N has two national parks, the Penjari and the "W", which Benin shares with Burkina Faso and Niger.

### CLIMATE

Benin has a hot, wet climate, with an average annual temperature on the coast of about 77°F (25°C) and an average rainfall around 52in (1,330mm). The inland plains are wetter than the coast, but the rainfall decreases to the N, which is hot throughout the year, with a rainy summer season and a very dry winter.

### HISTORY

The ancient kingdom of Dahomey had its capital at Abomey, in modern S Benin. In the 17th century the kings of Dahomey became involved in the lucrative slave trade, and by 1700 over 200,000 slaves were being annually transported from the "slave coast". The Portuguese shipped many Dahomeans to Brazil. Despite the abolition of slavery, the trade persisted well into the 19th century. In 1892 the French established a protectorate in Dahomey, and in 1904 the colony became part of the federation of French West Africa. The French developed the country's infrastructure and institutions. In 1958 Dahomey achieved self-governing status within the French Community. In 1960 it achieved independence. The new nation was beset with economic and social difficulties and in 1963 the military seized power. In 1972 a power-sharing arrangement between N and S Benin collapsed and the army, led by General Kerekou, again intervened. In 1975 Dahomey became the People's Republic of Benin.

### POLITICS

Adopting Marxism-Leninism as the state ideology, alliances were sought with European communism. In 1989 communism was abandoned and 1991 multi-party elections led to the formation of a provisional government. In 1996 elections Kerekou returned to power.

### ECONOMY

Benin is a developing country (1995 GDP per capita, US$1,760), and about 70% of the people earn their living by farming. Many farmers live at subsistence level, however, growing little more than they need to feed their families. Major food crops include beans, cassava, corn, millet, rice, sorghum, and yams, while the chief cash crops grown for export are cotton, palm oil, and palm kernels. Forestry is an important activity. Benin also produces oil and limestone.

B

**Bernard of Clairvaux, Saint** (1090–1153) French mystic and religious leader. Bernard was abbot of the Cistercian monastery of Clairvaux from 1115 until his death. Under his direction nearly 100 new monasteries were founded. He was canonized in 1174. His feast day is August 20.

**Bernhardt, Sarah** (1845–1923) French actress and the greatest tragedienne of the late 19th century. Bernhardt rose to prominence in the Comédie Française (1872–80). Her superb portrayals in *Phédre* (1874) and *Hernani* (1877) earned her the title "Divine Sarah." In 1899 she founded and managed the Théâtre Sarah Bernhardt in Paris, where she played the lead in *Hamlet* (1899). Bernhardt also appeared in silent films.

**Bernini, Gianlorenzo** (1598–1680) Italian architect and sculptor. The outstanding personality of the Italian BAROQUE, Bernini's work combines astonishing, flamboyant energy with great clarity of detail. He was also a skillful painter. As the favorite of several popes, Bernini was given unparalleled design opportunities. His large-scale commissions in and around St. Peter's include the *baldacchino* (canopy) above the high altar (1633), Cathedra Petri (1657–66), and (from 1656 onward) the great elliptical piazza and enclosing colonnades in front of St. Peter's. Bernini, more than any other architect, gave Rome its Baroque character.

**Bernoulli, Daniel** (1700–82) Swiss mathematician and physicist. Bernoulli demonstrated that pressure in a FLUID decreases as the velocity of fluid flow increases. This fact, which explains the LIFT of an aircraft wing, has become known as Bernoulli's principle. Bernoulli also formulated BERNOULLI'S LAW and made the first statement of the KINETIC THEORY of gases.

**Bernoulli's law** For a steadily flowing fluid, the sum of the pressure, kinetic energy, and potential energy per unit volume is constant at any point in the fluid. Using this relationship, formulated by Daniel BERNOULLI, it is possible to measure the velocity of a liquid.

**Bernstein, Leonard** (1918–90) US conductor, composer, and pianist. Bernstein was musical director (1958–69) of the New York Philharmonic, winning world fame through his diverse recordings. His works include three symphonies, such as *The Age of Anxiety* (1949) and *Kaddish* (1963), the *Chichester Psalms* (1965), the *Mass* (1971) for John F. Kennedy, ballets, and music for the shows *Candide* (1956) and *West Side Story* (1957).

**Berryman, John** (1914–72) US poet and critic. His works include the critical biography *Stephen Crane* (1950). Berryman's major work, *The Dream Songs* (1969), combines *77 Dream Songs* (1964), winner of the 1965 Pulitzer Prize, and *His Toy, His Dream, His Rest* (1968), winner of the 1969 National Book Award.

**Bertolucci, Bernardo** (1940– ) Italian film director. Bertolucci's most influential film was probably *The Conformist* (1969). His two greatest commercial successes were *Last Tango in Paris* (1972) and *The Last Emperor* (1987), a Chinese dynastic saga that gained Bertolucci Academy Awards for Best Director and Best Film.

**beryl** Mineral, beryllium silicate. Its crystals are usually hexagonal prisms of the hexagonal system. Gemstone varieties are aquamarine (pale blue-green); emerald (deep green); and morganite (pink). Cut stones have little brilliance, but are valued for their intense color. Hardness 8; sp.gr. 2.6–2.8.

**beryllium** (symbol Be) Strong, light, silver-gray, metallic alkaline-earth element, first isolated in 1828. It is used in alloys that combine lightness with rigidity. Properties: at.no. 4; at.wt. 9.012; sp.gr. 1.85; m.p. 2,345°F (1,285°C); b.p. 5,378°F (2,970°C ); most common isotope $^{9}$Be (100%).

**Berzelius, Jöns Jakob, Baron** (1779–1848) Swedish chemist, one of the founders of modern chemistry. Berzelius' accomplishments include the discovery of cerium, selenium, and thorium; the isolation of the elements silicon, zirconium, and titanium; the determination of relative atomic masses; and the devising of a modern system of chemical symbols. He prepared the first of relative atomic masses. *See also* PERIODIC TABLE

**Bessel, Friedrich Wilhelm** (1784–1846) German astronomer and mathematician. Bessel devised a system for analyzing and reducing astronomical observations, made the first accepted measurements of the distance of a star (61 Cygni), and accurately predicted that SIRIUS and PROCYON are binary stars.

**Bessemer process** First method for the mass production of steel. The process was patented in 1856 by the British engineer and inventor Sir Henry Bessemer (1813–98). In a Bessemer converter, cast iron is converted into steel by blowing air through the molten iron to remove impurities. Precise amounts of carbon and metals are then added to give the desired properties to the steel.

**Best, Charles Herbert** (1899–1978) Canadian physiologist. Best and F.G. BANTING discovered INSULIN in 1921. He was head (1929–65) of the department of physiology at the University of Toronto, and chief of the Banting-Best department of medical research there.

**beta-blocker** Any of a class of DRUGS that block impulses to beta nerve receptors in various tissues throughout the body, including the heart, airways, and peripheral arteries. These drugs are mainly prescribed to regulate the heartbeat, reduce blood pressure, relieve ANGINA, and improve survival following a heart attack. They are not suitable for patients with asthma.

**beta particle** Energetic electron emitted spontaneously by certain radioactive ISOTOPES. Beta decay results from the breakdown of a neutron to a proton, electron, and antineutrino. *See also* RADIOACTIVITY

**Betelgeuse** (Alpha Orionis) Red supergiant star, the second-brightest in the constellation of Orion. It is a pulsating variable whose diameter fluctuates between 300 to 400 times that of the Sun. Characteristics: apparent mag. 0.85 (mean); absolute mag. −5.5 (mean); spectral type M2; distance 500 light-years.

**Bethe, Hans Albrecht** (1906– ) US nuclear physicist, b. Germany. Bethe left Germany when Hitler came to power and became professor of theoretical physics (1935–75) at Cornell University. He worked on stellar energy processes and helped develop the atomic bomb. Bethe was awarded the 1967 Nobel Prize for physics for his work on the origin of solar and stellar energy.

**Bethlehem** (Bayt Lahm) Town on the W bank of the Jordan River, 5mi (8km) SSW of Jerusalem, administered by the Palestinian National Authority since 1994. The traditional birthplace of JESUS CHRIST, it was the early home of King David and the site of the biblical Massacre of the Innocents. The Church of the Nativity, built by Constantine in AD 330, is the oldest Christian church still in use. Under the rule of the Ottoman empire (1571–1916), it was part of the British Palestine mandate until 1948 when it became part of Jordan. After the SIX DAY WAR (1967) it was occupied by Israel. Tourism is the main industry. Pop. (1993 est.) 20,300.

**Bethune, Mary McLeod** (1875-1955) US educator. Bethune founded (1904) the Daytona Normal and Industrial Institute for Negro Girls. In 1923 it merged with Cookham Institute to form Bethune-Cookman College. Bethune acted as president (1904–42, 1946–47). She founded (1935) the National Council of Negro Women.

**Betjeman, Sir John** (1906–84) English poet. Betjeman's poetry is traditional in form, accessible in sentiment, and often apparently parochial in its concern with English social and domestic life. His *Collected Poems* (1958; rev. 1962) was a bestseller. Poet Laureate from 1972, Betjeman was also a broadcaster.

**Bevan, Aneurin** (1897–1960) British politician. A former active labor unionist, Bevan entered Parliament in 1929. A stirring orator, he assumed leadership of the left wing of the LABOUR PARTY. As minister of health (1945–51), Bevan founded the NATIONAL HEALTH SERVICE (1946).

**Beveridge, William Henry, Baron** (1879–1963) British academic and social reformer. A director (1909–16) of the labor exchanges, Beveridge later became director (1919–37) of the London School of Economics and master (1937–45) of University College, Oxford. He wrote the "Beveridge Report," the basis of the British WELFARE STATE.

**Bevin, Ernest** (1881–1951) British labor unionist and politician. As general secretary (1922–40) of the Transport and General Workers' Union (TGWU), Bevin helped to plan the GENERAL STRIKE (1926). As foreign minister (1945–51) in Clement ATTLEE's government, he helped to establish the NORTH ATLANTIC TREATY ORGANIZATION (NATO).

**Bhagavad Gita** (Hindi, "Song of the Lord") Popular episode in the sixth book of the Hindu epic, the MAHABHARATA. Written in Sanskrit verse probably in the 1st or 2nd century AD, it presents KRISHNA as an incarnation of the god VISHNU who, if worshiped, will save people.

**Bharatiya Janata Party (BJP)** Indian political party. In 1975–77, most non-Communist left-of-center and right-wing parties formed the coalition Janata Party in opposition to Indira Gandhi's ruling CONGRESS PARTY. The alliance collapsed in 1979, and the BJP emerged as one of the principal remnants. Broadly right-wing, the BJP is in favor of the creation of a Hindu state, Hindustan.

**Bhopal** State capital of MADHYA PRADESH, central India. Founded in 1728, it is noted for its terraced lakes, mosques, and prehistoric paintings. In 1984 poisonous gas from the Union Carbide insecticide plant killed 2,500 people, the world's worst industrial disaster. Industries: food processing, electrical engineering, flour milling, cotton textiles. Pop. (1991) 1,063,000.

**Bhutan** Mountainous kingdom in the E Himalayas, bordered N by Tibet (China), E and S by India, and W by SIKKIM. The capital is Thimbu. **Land and climate** The Great Himalayas in the N rise majestically to Kula Shan at 24,741ft (7,543m). The River BRAHMAPUTRA and its tributaries flow through thickly forested valleys. Torrential rain is common; annual rainfall on the S plains averages more than 200in (500mm). Bhutan is the world's most rural country; more than 90% of the workforce are engaged in agriculture, mostly at subsistence level. Only 10% of the land is arable or grassland; forests account for 56%. **History and politics** In the 17th century, the leader of the *Drukpa Kagyu* (Thunder Dragon) sect of TIBETAN BUDDHISM unified the country. Villages developed around the *dzong* (castle-monastery), and many Bhutanese continue to live in these monastic communities. In 1720 the Chinese invaded Tibet and Bhutan, but met fierce resistance. War with Britain (1865) resulted in the British annexation of S Bhutan. In 1907 Britain supported the establishment of an hereditary monarchy and Sir Ugyen Wangchuk became king. Bhutanese foreign policy was directed by Britain. After India gained independence (1949) it assumed Britain's former role. King Jigme Dorji Wangchuk (r.1952–72) reformed Bhutanese society, abolishing slavery (1958), and establishing a national assembly. In 1971 Bhutan was admitted into the United Nations (UN). Jigme Singye Wangchuk succeeded his father as king (r.1972– ). In 1990 prodemocracy demonstrations were suppressed and political parties remain banned. The Nepalese, Hindu minority complain of discrimination. **Economy** Bhutan is one of the world's poorest nations (1992 GDP per capita US$750). It produces mainly rice and corn as staple crops, and fruit and cardamon as cash crops. Other products include cement, talcum, and wood. Tourism, a vital source of foreign currency, is restricted. Area: 18,000sq mi (47,000sq km). Pop. (1995 est.) 1,600,000.

**Bhutto, Benazir** (1953– ) Pakistani stateswoman, prime minister (1988–90, 1993–96), daughter of Zulfikar Ali BHUTTO. She was long considered the leader of the Pakistani People's Party, but was subject to house arrest and forced into exile. Bhutto's return (1986) was marked by jubilation and violence. In 1988 Bhutto proclaimed a "people's revolution" and became the first woman prime minister of Pakistan. Amid charges of corruption, she was removed from office. Bhutto was re-elected in 1993. Further charges of corruption led to her dismissal in 1996.

**Bhutto, Zulfikar Ali** (1928–79) Pakistani statesman, prime minister (1973–77), father of Benazir BHUTTO. He founded (1967) the Pakistan People's Party. In 1970 elections, Bhutto gained a majority in West Pakistan but the Awami League controlled East Pakistan. Bhutto's refusal to grant autonomy to East Pakistan led to civil war (1971). Defeat led to the formation of BANGLADESH and Bhutto became president. He was overthrown in a military coup, led by General Zia. Bhutto was convicted of conspiracy to murder and executed.

**Biafra** Former state in W Africa, formed from the E region of Nigeria. It was established in 1967 when the IBO attempted to secede from Nigeria. A bitter civil war ensued, ending in 1970 when Biafra surrendered and was reincorporated into Nigeria.

**Bible** Sacred scriptures of Judaism and Christianity. Partly a history of the tribes of Israel, it is regarded as a source of divine revelation and of prescriptions and prohibitions for moral living. The Bible consists of two main sections. The OLD TESTAMENT, excluding the APOCRYPHA, is accepted as sacred by both Jews and Christians. The Roman Catholic and Eastern Orthodox Churches accept parts of the Apocrypha as sacred and include them in the Old Testament. Jews and Protestants for the most part reject them. The NEW TESTAMENT is accepted as sacred only by Christians.

**Bichat, Marie François Xavier** (1771–1802) French anatomist, pathologist, and physiologist. His study of TISSUE laid the foundations of modern HISTOLOGY.

**bicycle** Two-wheeled vehicle propelled by the rider. The earliest design dates from *c.*1790. Karl von Drais of Germany developed an improved version around 1816. An Englishman, J. Starley, demonstrated the first successful chain drive in 1871. *See also* CYCLING

**biennial** Plant with a life cycle of two years, producing flowers and seed during the second year, such as an onion. This distinguishes it from an ANNUAL and a PERENNIAL.

**Bierce, Ambrose Gwinett** (1842–1914) US satirical writer and journalist. Bierce published several collections of short stories, and was a onetime associate of Mark TWAIN. He is best-known for his collection of epigrammatic definitions, *The Devil's Dictionary* (1906).

**BICYCLE**

New designs of mountain bikes have reduced weight without sacrificing strength and have added suspension to both front (1) and rear wheels (2) to allow greater speed over rough terrain. The front suspension has twin pistons in the forks with elastomer cores (3) that allow travel and absorb vibration. Oil and air can also be used in the pistons. The rear suspension has a single, oil-filled piston (4) damped by a spring (5). Rear suspension units come in different forms (6). New frame materials include carbon fiber, titanium, and aluminum. A V-shaped frame (7) allows bike designers to use the more exotic substances which are difficult to use in a traditional tubular frame. Some bikes have softer compounds of rubber for the back wheels to give greater grip on steep slopes.

B

**Big Bang** Theory advanced to explain the origin of the Universe. It states that a giant explosion 10 to 20 billion years ago began the expansion of the Universe, which still continues. Everything in the Universe once constituted an exceedingly hot and compressed gas with a temperature exceeding 10 billion degrees. As it cooled, nuclear reactions took place that led to material emerging from the fireball consisting of *c*.75% hydrogen and *c*.25% helium by mass – the composition of the Universe as we observe it today. Slightly denser regions of gas whose expansion rate lagged behind the mean value collapsed to form galaxies when the Universe was perhaps 10% of its present age. The cosmic microwave background radiation detected in 1965 is considered to be the residual radiation of the Big Bang.

**Big Ben** Bell in the clock tower of Britain's Houses of Parliament, London. Its name comes from Sir Benjamin Hall, commissioner of works when the bell was installed (1859). The name can refer to the whole tower.

**Bihar** State in NE India; the capital is Patna. Bihar was a center of Indian civilization from the 6th century BC to the 7th century AD. It became a province in the Mogul empire. A rich agricultural region, drained by the Ganges River, it produces more than 40% of India's mineral output. Industries: mica, coal, copper. Area: 57,160sq mi (173,877sq km). Pop. (1994 est.) 93,080,000.

**Bikini Atoll** Group of 36 islands in the W central Pacific and part of the US-administered MARSHALL ISLANDS. The US used the area to conduct atomic weapons tests (1946–56). The islands (although considered safe in 1969) were re-evacuated in 1978. Area: 2sq mi (5sq km).

**Bilbao** Seaport on the estuary of the Nervión River, near the Bay of Biscay, Spain; capital of the BASQUE COUNTRY province of Vizcaya. Founded *c*.1300, it grew prosperous through the export of wool and later by trade with Spain's American colonies. It is the home of the University of Bilbao (1968). Lying at the center of an industrial region, it is now Spain's major port and a flourishing commercial center. Industries: iron and steel, fishing, shipbuilding. Pop. (1991) 368,710.

**bilberry** (blueberry or whortleberry) Deciduous evergreen shrub native to N Europe and E North America, which produces a small, dark purple fruit. Family Ericaceae; genus *Vaccinium*.

**bile** Bitter yellow, brown, or green alkaline fluid, secreted by the LIVER and stored in the GALLBLADDER. Important in digestion, it enters the duodenum via the bile duct. The bile salts it contains emulsify fats (allowing easier digestion) and neutralize stomach acids.

**Bill of Rights** (1689) British statute enshrining the constitutional principles won during the GLORIOUS REVOLUTION. It confirmed the abdication of James II and bestowed the throne on William III and Mary II. It excluded Roman Catholics from the succession and outlawed certain of James' abuses of the royal prerogative, such as his manipulation of the legal system and use of a standing army. It hastened the trend toward the supremacy of parliament over the crown.

**Bill of Rights** Name given to the first ten amendments to the US Constitution, ratified 1791. Several states had agreed to ratify the CONSTITUTION (1787) only after George Washington promised to add such a list of liberties. The main rights confirmed are: freedom of worship, of speech, of the press, and of assembly; the right to bear arms; freedom from unreasonable search and seizure; the right to a speedy trial by jury; and protection from self-incrimination. Powers not granted specifically to the federal government were reserved for the states.

**"Billy the Kid" (William H. Bonney)** (1859–81) US frontier outlaw. Traditionally 21 murders are ascribed to him but there is no evidence for this figure. In 1878 he killed a sheriff and led a gang of cattle rustlers. He was sentenced in 1880. He escaped from jail but was caught and killed by Sheriff Pat Garrett.

**binary star** Two stars in orbit around a common center of mass. **Visual** binaries can be seen as separate stars. In an **eclipsing** binary, one star periodically passes in front of the other, so that the total light output appears to fluctuate. Most eclipsing binaries are also spectroscopic binaries. A **spectroscopic** binary is a system too close for their separation to be measured visually.

**binary system** In mathematics, number system having a BASE of 2 (the decimal system has a base of 10). It is most appropriate to computers since it is simple and corresponds to the open (0), and closed (1) states of switch, or logic gate, on which computers are based.

**Binchois, Gilles de** (*c*.1400–60) Franco-Flemish composer and organist. After Dufay, the most influential composer of the early to mid-15th century. De Binchois was organist at Mons (1419–23), and served at the Burgundian court (1430–53), after which he was made provost of St. Vincent, Soignies. He is best known for his secular songs, of which 60 survive.

**bindweed** Climbing plant with white or pink trumpet-shaped flowers. Species include *Calystegia sepium*, or hedge bindweed, and *Convolvulus arvensis*, field bindweed. Family Convolvulaceae.

**Binet, Alfred** (1857–1911) French psychologist. Binet established the first French psychology laboratory (1889) and the first French psychology journal (1895). His best-known achievement was devising the first practical intelligence tests (1905–11). *See also* APTITUDE TEST

**Bingham, George Caleb** (1811–79) US painter. Largely self-taught, Bingham is best known for his genre paintings of Missouri, such as *Shooting for the Beef* (1850) and *Fur Traders Descending the Missouri* (1845). The latter is his most famous work.

**Bingham, Hiram** (1875–1956) US archeologist. Bingham's discovery (1911), and excavation, of the INCA city of MACHU PICCHU in the Peruvian Andes helped historians unravel the story of Peru before the Spanish conquest.

**binoculars** Optical instrument, used with both eyes simultaneously, that produces a magnified image of a distant object or scene. It consists of a pair of identical telescopes, one for each eye, both containing an objective lens, an eyepiece lens, and an optical system.

**binomial nomenclature** System of categorizing organisms by giving them a two-part Latin name. The first part of the name is the GENUS and the second the SPECIES. *Homo sapiens* is the binomial name for humans. The system was developed by the botanist Carolus LINNAEUS. *See also* TAXONOMY

**binomial theorem** Mathematical rule for expanding (as a series) an algebraic expression of the form $(x + y)^n$, where $x$ and $y$ are numerical quantities and $n$ is a positive integer. For $n = 2$, its expansion is given by $(x + y)^2 = x^2 + 2xy + y^2$.

**biochemistry** Science of the CHEMISTRY of life. It uses the methods and concepts of organic and physical chemistry to investigate living matter and systems. Biochemists study both the structure and properties of all the constituents of living matter, such as FATS, PROTEINS, ENZYMES, HORMONES, VITAMINS, DNA, CELLS, MEMBRANES, and ORGANS – together with METABOLISM.

**biodegradable** Property of a substance that enables it to be decomposed by microorganisms. The end result of decay is stable, simple compounds (such as water and carbon dioxide). This property has been designed into materials such as plastics to aid refuse disposal.

**bioengineering** Application of engineering techniques to medical and biological problems such as devices to aid or replace defective or inadequate body organs, as in the production of artificial limbs and hearing aids.

**biofeedback** In alternative medicine, the use of monitoring systems to provide information about body processes to enable them to be controlled voluntarily. By observing data on events which are normally involuntary, such as breathing and the heartbeat, many people learn to gain control over them to some extent in order to improve well-being. The technique has proved helpful in a number of conditions, including headaches and hypertension.

**biogenesis** Biological principle maintaining that living organisms derive from parent(s) generally similar to themselves. This long-held principle was originally established in opposition to the idea of SPONTANEOUS GENERATION of life. *See also* GENETICS

**biogenetic law** (recapitulation theory) Principle that the stages that an organism goes through during embryonic development reflect the stages of that organism's evolutionary development.

**biography** Literary form that describes the events of a person's life. The first known biographies were *Lives* by PLUTARCH in the 1st century AD. In English literature, the first biographies appeared in the 17th century, notably *Lives* (1640–70) by Izaak Walton and *Lives of Eminent Men* (1813) by John AUBREY. The first modern biography was the monumental *Life of Samuel Johnson* (1791) by BOSWELL, which is rich in detail and first-hand recollections. *See also* AUTOBIOGRAPHY

**biological clock** Internal system in organisms that relates behavior to natural rhythms. Functions, such as growth, feeding, or reproduction, coincide with certain external events, including day and night, tides, and seasons. These "clocks" seem to be set by environmental conditions, but if organisms are isolated from these conditions, they still function according to the usual rhythm. If conditions change gradually, the organisms adjust their behavior gradually.

**biological warfare** Use of disease microbes and their toxins in warfare. The extensive use of mustard gas during World War I prompted the prohibition of biological warfare by the GENEVA CONVENTION (1925). However, many nations have maintained costly research programs. The microbes include plant pathogens for the destruction of food crops. None has yet been used, although US forces employed a variety of biological warfare, such as the use of the defoliant Agent Orange, during the Vietnam War.

**biology** Science of life and living organisms. Its branches include BOTANY, ZOOLOGY, ECOLOGY, PHYSIOLOGY, CYTOLOGY, GENETICS, TAXONOMY, EMBRYOLOGY, and MICROBIOLOGY. These sciences deal with the origin, history, structure, development, and function of living organisms, their relationships to each other and their environment.

**bioluminescence** Production of light, with very little heat, by some living organisms. Its biological function is varied: in some species, such as fireflies, it is a recognition signal in mating; in others, such as squid, it is a method of warding off predators, and in anglerfish it is used to attract prey. The light-emitting substance (luciferin) in most species is an organic molecule that emits light when it is oxidized by molecular oxygen in the presence of an enzyme (luciferase).

**biomass** Total mass (excluding water content) of the plants and/or animals in a particular place. The term is often used to refer to the totality of living things on Earth; or those occupying a part of the Earth, such as the oceans. It may also refer to plant material that can be exploited.

**biome** Extensive community of animals and plants whose makeup is determined by soil type and climate. There is generally distinctive, dominant vegetation, and characteristic climate and animal life in each biome. Ecologists divide the Earth (including the seas, lakes, and rivers) into ten biomes.

**biophysics** Study of biological phenomena in terms of the laws and techniques of physics. Techniques include x-ray diffraction and SPECTROSCOPY. Subjects studied include the structure and function of molecules, the conduction of electricity by nerves, the visual mechanism, the transport of molecules across cell membranes, and energy transformations in living organisms.

**biopsy** Removal of a small piece of tissue from a patient for examination for evidence of disease. An example is the cervical biopsy ("Pap smear") to screen for changes that can lead to cervical cancer.

**biosphere** Portion of the Earth from its crust to the surrounding atmosphere, encompassing and including all living organisms. It is self-sufficient except for energy and extends a few miles above and below sea level.

**biosynthesis** Process in living cells by which complex chemical substances, such as PROTEIN, are made from simpler substances. A GENE "orders" a molecule of RNA to be made, which carries the genetic instructions from the DNA. On the RIBOSOMES of the cell, the protein is built up from molecules of AMINO ACIDS, in the order determined by the genetic instructions carried by the RNA.

## BIOTECHNOLOGY

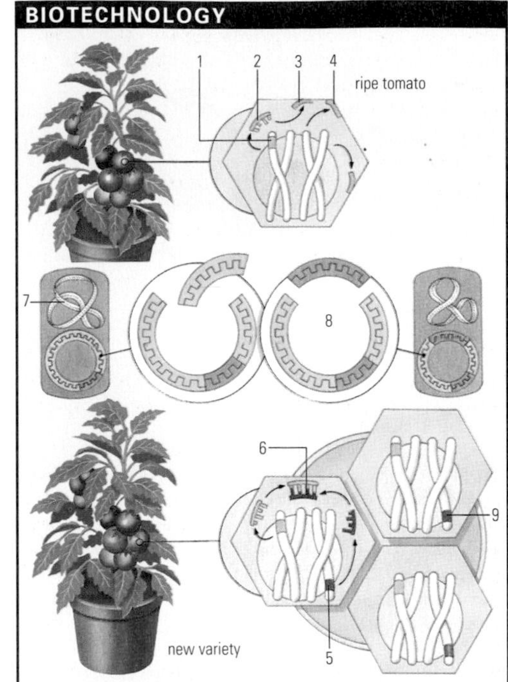


In a ripe tomato, rotting is caused by an enzyme formed by the copying of a gene in the plant DNA (1) in a messenger molecule mRNA (2). The mRNA is changed into the enzyme (3) which damages the cell wall (4). In a genetically altered tomato, a mirror duplicate of the gene that starts the process is present (5). The result is that two mirror-image mRNA molecules are released (6) and they bind together, preventing the creation of the rotting enzyme. The result is longer-lasting tomatoes. Introducing the necessary DNA through the rigid cell wall is accomplished by using a bacteria (7) which naturally copies its own DNA onto that of a plant. It is easy to introduce the mirror DNA (8) into the bacteria and once the bacteria has infected the cell the DNA is transferred (9). All cells then replicated have the new DNA in their chromosomes and can be grown to create the new variety of plant.

**biotechnology** Use of biological processes for medical, industrial, or manufacturing purpose. Humans have long used yeast for brewing and bacteria for products such as cheese and yoghurt. Biotechnology now enjoys a wider application. By growing microorganisms in the laboratory, new drugs and chemicals are produced. GENETIC ENGINEERING techniques of cloning, splicing, and mixing genes facilitate, for example, the growing of crops outside their normal environment, and vaccines that fight specific diseases. Hormones are also produced, such as INSULIN for treating diabetes.

**biotite** Common mineral of the MICA group. It is a silicate of aluminum, iron, potassium and magnesium. Its color ranges from greenish-brown to black. Its lustrous, monoclinic crystals are opaque to translucent, and cleave to form flexible sheets. It is found in IGNEOUS ROCK (such as granite), METAMORPHIC ROCK (such as schist and gneiss) and SEDIMENTARY ROCK (such as flakes).

**birch** Any of *c*.40 species of trees and shrubs native to cooler areas of the Northern Hemisphere. The double-toothed leaves are oval or triangular with blunt bases and arranged alternately along branches. The smooth resinous bark peels off in papery sheets. Species include the gray, silver, sweet, and yellow birches. Height: up to 98ft (30m). Family Betulaceae; genus *Betula*.

**bird** Any one of *c*.8,600 species of feathered vertebrates that occupy most natural habitats. Birds are warm-blooded and have forelimbs modified as wings, hindlimbs for walking, and jaws elongated into a toothless beak. They lay eggs (usu-

▲ **birch** From the Betulaceae family, birches are found throughout the Northern Hemisphere. The paper birch (*Betula papyrifera*) is found in many regions of North America and grows to a height of 130ft (39m). Native Americans used the tree to make birch-bark canoes.

► **bird of paradise** The magnificent bird of paradise (*Diphyllodes magnificus*) is found in the tropical forest regions of New Guinea. Like other species of bird of paradise, the male performs elaborate courtship displays, involving ruffling the feathers on his breast and neck. Before he displays, he clears an area on the ground, using the branches of young saplings as perches on which he also performs.

ally in nests), incubate the eggs, and care for young. As a group they feed on seeds, nectar, fruit, and carrion, and hunt live prey ranging from insects to small mammals. Sight is the dominant sense, smell the poorest. Size ranges from the bee hummingbird, 2.5in (6.4cm), to the wandering albatross, whose wingspread reaches 11.5ft (3.5m). The 8ft (2.4m) tall ostrich is the largest of living birds, but several extinct flightless birds were even bigger. Of the 27 orders of birds, the perching birds (Passeriformes) include more species than all others combined. There are several groups of large flightless land birds, including the ostrich, rhea, emu, cassowary, kiwi, and penguin. Birds are descended from Theocodonts (reptiles), and the first fossil bird, ARCHAEOPTERYX, dates from the late Jurassic period. Class Aves. *See* individual species

**bird of paradise** Brightly colored, ornately plumed, perching bird of Australia, New Guinea forests, and nearby regions. Most species have stocky bodies, rounded wings, short legs, and a squarish tail. The males' plumes are black, orange, red, yellow, blue, or green and are raised during courtship and rituals. Length: 5–40in (12.5–100cm). Family Paradisaeidae.

**bird of prey** Bird that usually has a sharp, hooked beak and curved talons with which it captures its prey. Two orders of birds fit this description: the hawks, falcons, eagles, vultures, and secretary bird (order Falconiformes); and the owls (order Strigiformes).

**Birdseye, Clarence** (1886–1956) US industrialist and inventor, who developed a technique for deep-freezing foods. Birdseye experimented on freezing food in 1917 and sold frozen fish in 1924. He was a founder of the General Foods Corporation.

**Birmingham** Britain's second-largest city, in the West Midlands, England. A small town in the Middle Ages, during the Industrial Revolution it became one of Britain's chief manufacturing cities. James WATT designed and built his steam-engine here. Later it became known for the manufacture of cheap goods ("Brummagem ware"). The Birmingham Repertory Theatre (opened 1913) has a high reputation. The city also has a well-known symphony orchestra, three universities, and a museum and art gallery. An important center for rail, road, and water transportation, the town's intersecting highways are known as "Spaghetti Junction." Industries: car manufacture, engineering, machine tools, metallurgy. Pop. (1990) 961,041.

**Birmingham** Largest city in Alabama. It was founded in 1871 as a railroad junction at the center of a mineral-rich region. It has two universities and two colleges. Industries: iron and steel, metalworking, construction materials, transportation equipment. Pop. (1990) 265,968.

**Birmingham Six** Six Irishmen convicted by an English court in 1974 of carrying out terrorist bombings in two public houses (pubs) in Birmingham, England. Their life sentences were reversed in 1991. The Court of Appeal ruled that methods used by the police in producing some written statements were inappropriate. Five of the men were duly released; the sixth had died in prison. Their case became notorious as a modern miscarriage of British justice. *See also* GUILDFORD FOUR

**birth, Cesarean** Delivery of a baby by a surgical incision made through the abdomen and UTERUS of the mother. It is carried out for various medical reasons; the mother usually recovers quickly, without complications. The procedure is named for Julius Caesar, who is reputed to have been born in this manner.

**birth control** Alternative term for CONTRACEPTION

**Birtwistle, Harrison** (1934– ) English composer. Birtwistle has written a wide variety of works consolidating his position as a leading modern composer. His instrumental pieces include *The World is Discovered* (1960) and *The Triumph of Time* (1972). Birtwistle has written four operas: the one-act chamber opera *Punch and Judy* (1967), *The Mask of Orpheus* (performed 1986), *Gawain* (1991), and *The Second Mrs. Kong* (1995).

**Biscay, Bay of** Inlet of the Atlantic Ocean, W of France and N of Spain. It is noted for its strong currents, sudden storms, and sardine fishing grounds. The chief ports are BILBAO, San Sebastián, and Santander in Spain, and LA ROCHELLE, Bayonne, and Saint-Nazaire in France.

**Bishkek** (formerly Frunze) Capital of Kyrgyzstan, central Asia, on the Chu River. Founded (1862) as Pishpek, it was the birthplace of a Soviet general, Mikhail Frunze, after whom it was renamed in 1926 when it became administrative center of the Kirghiz Soviet Republic. Its name changed to Bishkek in 1991, when Kyrgyzstan declared its independence. The city has a university. Industries: textiles, food processing, agricultural machinery. Pop. (1991 est.) 641,400.

**bishop** In Christian Churches, the highest order in the ministry. Bishops are distinguished from priests chiefly by their powers to confer holy orders and to administer CONFIRMATION.

**Bismarck, Otto von** (1815–98) German statesman responsible for 19th-century German unification. Bismarck first made an impression as a diehard reactionary during the REVOLUTIONS OF 1848. Keen to strengthen the Prussian army, WILLIAM I appointed (1862) him chancellor of Prussia. Bismarck dissolved parliament and raised taxes to pay for military improvements. The status of SCHLESWIG-HOLSTEIN enabled him to engineer the AUSTRO-PRUSSIAN WAR (1866) and expel Austria from the German Confederation. Bismarck then provoked the FRANCO-PRUSSIAN WAR (1870–71), in order to bring the S German states into the Prussian-led North German Confederation. Victory saw Bismarck become (1871) the first chancellor of the empire. Through skillful diplomacy and alliance-building he consolidated Germany's position in the heart of Europe. In 1882 he formed the TRIPLE ALLIANCE with Austro-Hungary and Italy. Bismarck's domestic policies were similarly based on the principle of "divide-and-rule." He passed an antisocialist law (1878) to stem the rise of German SOCIALISM, but was forced to adopt (1883–87) a paternalist program of social welfare. The rapid process of industrialization encouraged COLONIALISM, and the building of a German

► **bison** The American bison (*Bison bison*) was almost hunted to extinction by European settlers who wanted to free the land for farming and deprive some of the Native Americans of their herds. Strict conservation programs subsequently have ensured the survival of large numbers of this animal in protected areas.

overseas empire. The accession (1888) of WILLIAM II saw the demise of Bismarck's political influence, and in 1890 the "Iron Chancellor" was forced to resign.

**Bismarck** State capital of North Dakota, overlooking the Missouri River. It originated in the 1830s, becoming a distribution center for grain and cattle, and was later an important stop on the Northern Pacific Railroad. Industries: livestock raising, dairying. Pop. (1990) 49,256.

**bismuth** (symbol Bi) Metallic silvery-white element of group V of the periodic table, first identified as a separate element in 1753. The chief ores are bismite ($Bi_2O_3$) and bismuthnite ($Bi_2S_3$). A poor heat conductor, it is put into low-melting alloys used in automatic sprinkler systems. Bismuth is also used in insoluble compounds to treat gastric ulcers and skin injuries. It expands when it solidifies, a property exploited in several bismuth alloys for castings. Properties: at.no. 83; at.wt. 208.98; sp.gr. 9.75; m.p. 520.3°F (271.3°C); b.p. 2,840°F (1,560°C); most common isotope $^{209}Bi$ (100%).

**bison** Two species of wild oxen formerly ranging over the grasslands and open woodlands of most of North America and Europe. Once numbered in millions, the American bison (often incorrectly called BUFFALO) is now almost extinct in the wild. The wisent (European bison) was reduced to two herds by the 18th century. Both species now survive in protected areas. The American species is not as massive or as shaggy as the European. Length: to 138in (3.5m); height: to 118in (3m); weight: to 2,976lb (1,350kg). Family Bovidae; species American *Bison bison*; wisent *Bison bonasus*.

**Bissau** Capital of Guinea-Bissau, near the mouth of the Geba River, W Africa. Established in 1687 by the Portuguese as a slave-trading center, it became a free port in 1869. It replaced Bonama as capital in 1941. Oil processing is the principal industry. Pop. (1985 est.) 126,900.

**bit** In computing, abbreviation for BINARY system digit, a 1 or 0 used in binary arithmetic. A bit is the smallest element of storage. Groups of bits form a BYTE of binary code representing letters and other characters. Binary code is used in computing because it is easy to represent each 1 or 0 using electrical components that can be switched between two states (such as on and off). The code is also easy to store on disk.

**bittern** Solitary heronlike wading bird with a characteristic booming call found in marshes worldwide. A heavy-bodied bird, it is brownish with streaks and spots which help to hide it in swamplands. The female lays 3–6 brownish eggs. Length: 10in–3ft (25–90cm). Family Ardeidae, species *Botaurus stellaris*.

**bittersweet** *See* NIGHTSHADE

**bitumen** (asphalt) Material used for roadmaking and for proofing timber against rot. It consists of a mixture of hydrocarbons and other organic chemical compounds. Some bitumen occurs naturally in pitch lakes, notably in Trinidad. The material is also made by distilling tar from coal or wood.

**bivalent** In biology, describing a pair of homologous chromosomes formed during MEIOSIS. In chemistry, the term is used to describe an atom or group that has a VALENCE of two.

**bivalve** Animal that has a shell with two halves or parts hinged together. The term most usually applies to a class of MOLLUSKS – Pelecypoda or Lamellibranchiata – with left and right shells, such as clams, cockles, mussels, and oysters. It also refers to animals of the phylum BRACHIOPODA (lamp shells) with dorsal and ventral shells. Length: 0.17in–4ft (2mm–1.2m).

**Biwa** Lake in W central Honshū, Japan, and namesake of the Japanese musical instrument whose shape it resembles. It is the largest lake in Japan and yields freshwater fish. Length: 40mi (64km); width 2–12mi (3–19km); depth 315ft (96m).

**Bizet, Georges** (1838–75) French romantic composer. Bizet's opera *Carmen* (1875), although a failure at its first performance, has become one of the most popular operas of all time. Bizet also composed other operas, notably *Les pêcheurs de perles* (1863) and orchestral works, including the Symphony in C (1855).

**Black, Joseph** (1728–99) British chemist and physicist. Rediscovering "fixed air" (carbon dioxide), Black found that this gas is produced by respiration (burning of charcoal and FERMENTATION), that it behaves as an ACID, and that it is found in the atmosphere. He also discovered hydrogen carbonates (bicarbonates) and investigated LATENT HEAT and specific heat.

**black bear** BEAR found in North America and Asia. The American black bear lives in forests from Canada to central Mexico. It eats a variety of plant and animal foods, including carrion. It is timid and avoids humans. Length: 5–6ft (1.5–1.8m); weight: 265–330lb (120–150kg). Species *Euarctos americanus*. The Asiatic black bear lives in bush or forest areas of E and S Asia. Smaller than the American black bear, it has a white crescent marking on the chest. Aggressive, it sometimes kills livestock and humans. Species *Selenarctos thibetanos*.

**blackberry** (bramble) Fruit-bearing bush, native to northern temperate regions. The prickly stems may be erect or trailing, the leaves oval and toothed, and the blossoms white, pink, or red. The edible berries are black or dark red. Family Rosaceae; genus *Rubus*.

**blackbird** Songbird of the THRUSH family, common in gardens and woodland throughout most of Europe, the Near East, Australia, and New Zealand. The male has jet-black plumage and a bright orange bill. The female is brown, with a brown bill. Length: to 10in (25cm). Species *Turdus merula*. In America, the blackbird is a bird of the Icteridae family. The typical red-winged blackbird (*Agelaius phoeniceus*) has a straight bill, long pointed wings, and rounded tail. Length: 8–10in (20–25cm).

**black body** In physics, an ideal body that absorbs all incident radiation and reflects none. Such a body would look "perfectly" black. Wien's law, Stefan's law, and PLANCK's law of black body radiation grew out of the study of black bodies, as did Planck's discoveries in quantum mechanics.

**blackbuck** (Indian antelope) Medium-sized ANTELOPE of the open plains of India. Females and young are fawn-colored and males are dark. The underparts are white, and there are patches of white on the muzzle. Only males carry long, spiral horns. Length: to 47in (1.2m); height: to 32in (81cm) at the shoulder. Family Bovidae; species *Antilope cervicapra*.

**Black Codes** (1865–66) Laws passed in former Confederate states restricting the civil and political rights of newly freed blacks. The Black Codes were outlawed by the 14th amendment to the Constitution (1868).

**Black Death** (1348–50) Pandemic of PLAGUE, both bubonic and pneumonic, that killed about one-third of the popula-

▼ **Black Death** Orginating in China (*c.*1333), the Black Death spread W across Asia and Europe via trade and pilgrimage routes, reaching the Crimea in 1347. Rats were the disease's original hosts, but when they died their infected fleas would transfer to humans. Contemporary descriptions suggest that the infection was bubonic plague, a disease characterized by swollen lymphatic glands, or buboes, and an extremely high mortality rate. Recurring for short spells throughout much of the late 1300s, by 1400, it is estimated that the European population declined by 50%.

Area infected by plague

Regions spared partly or wholly from the plague

Route of plague's spread

Approximate extent of plague in Europe at 6-monthly intervals from December 31, 1347 to June 30, 1350

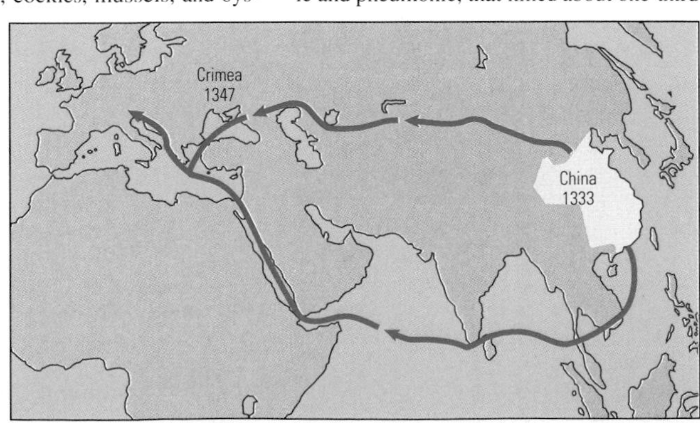


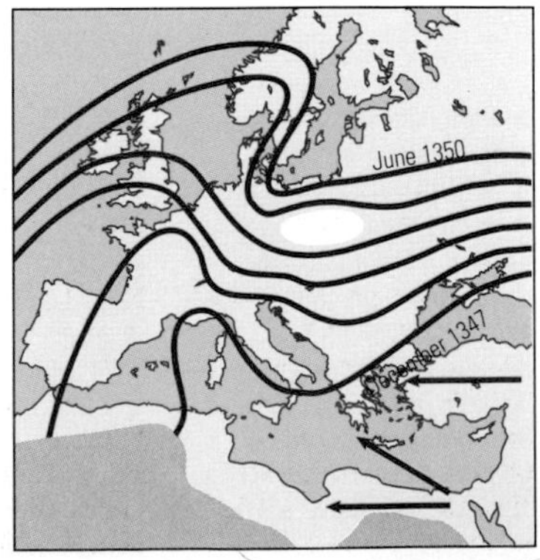

▲ **black widow** The European black widow spider (*Latrodectus tredecimguttatus*) has characteristic red marks on its rounded abdomen that warn other animals that it is poisonous. On rare occasions, the female will eat the male once he has fertilized the eggs.

tion of Europe. It was first carried to Mediterranean ports from the Crimea and spread throughout Europe, carried by fleas infesting rats. Plague recurred intermittently and less severely until the 18th century.

**blackfly** *See* APHID

**Blackfoot** Nomadic, warlike Native North American tribes. They are made up of three Algonquian-speaking tribes: the Siksika, or Blackfeet proper; the Kainah; and the Pikuni (Piegan). Living on the N Great Plains E of the Rockies, they depended largely on the bison (buffalo), which was hunted on horseback. Something of their richly ceremonial culture survives among the *c*.8,000 Blackfeet living today on reservations in Alberta and Montana.

**Black Forest** (Schwarzwald) Mountainous region between the Rhine and Neckar rivers, Baden-Württemburg, SW Germany. It is heavily forested in the higher areas, particularly around the sources of the Danube and the Neckar rivers. The highest peak is Feldberg, 4,898ft (1,493m). Industries: tourism, timber, mechanical toys, clocks. Area: *c*.2,300sq mi (6,000sq km).

**Black Friday** (September 24, 1869) Day of financial panic in the US. The financiers Jay GOULD and James Fisk attempted to corner the gold market and drove the price of gold up. The price fell after the US government sold part of its gold reserve, and many speculators were ruined.

**Black Hawk War** (1832) Conflict between the Sac and Fox and the US army. The Sac chief, Black Hawk (1767–1838), denounced treaties (1804, 1832) that sought to remove the Native Americans from land W of the Mississippi. The shooting of his peace emissary stung Black Hawk into attack. Initial victories against larger white armies were overturned at the Battle of Bad Axe (1832). Black Hawk's surrender was ignored and most of the tribe were massacred.

**black hole** Postulated end product of the total gravitational collapse of a massive star into itself following exhaustion of its nuclear fuel; the matter inside is crushed to unimaginably high density. It is an empty region of distorted space-time that acts as a center of gravitational attraction; matter is drawn toward it and once inside nothing can escape. Its boundary (the event horizon) is a demarcation line, rather than a material surface. Since no light or other radiation can escape from black holes, they are extremely difficult to detect. Not all black holes result from stellar collapse. During the Big Bang, some regions of space might have become so compressed that they formed so-called primordial black holes. *See also* Stephen HAWKING

**Black Hole of Calcutta** Prison in Calcutta, India, where 64 or more British soldiers were placed by the Nawab Siraj-ad-Dawlah of Bengal in June 1756. The cell was 18×15ft (5.5×4.5m) and most of the soldiers died of suffocation.

**Blackmore, R.D. (Richard Doddridge)** (1825–1900) English novelist and poet. He is chiefly known for his historical romance *Lorna Doone* (1869).

**Black Mountain Poets** Designation for writers affiliated to Black Mountain College in North Carolina in the 1950s. There the writers came under the influence of Charles Olson. Poets from this school include Robert Creeley, Robert Duncan, and Denise Levertov.

**Blackmun, Harry Andrew** (1908– ) US associate justice of the Supreme Court of the US (1970–94). He wrote the majority opinion in the 1973 landmark case *Roe v. Wade*, which in effect legalized abortion. Blackmun retired in 1994.

► **Blair** Britain's youngest prime minister since the Earl of Liverpool (1812), Tony Blair's modernization of the Labour Party helped to achieve a landslide victory in 1997. His government introduced important constitutional reforms, such as devolution for Scotland and Wales. More controversial policies included the "Welfare to Work" package of reforms to social security.

**Black Muslims** African-American nationalist movement in the US. It aims to establish a separatist black Muslim state. Founded (1930) in Detroit by Wallace D. Farad, the movement was led (1934–76) by Elijah MUHAMMAD. The Black Muslims grew rapidly from 1945 to 1960, helped by the rhetorical power of the preacher MALCOLM X. Factions developed within the movement and, in 1963, Malcolm's membership was suspended. In 1976 the movement split into the American Muslim Mission and the Nation of Islam. The former (led by Elijah's son, Wallace D. Muhammad) preach a more integrationist message. The Nation of Islam, led by Louis FARRAKHAN, claims to uphold the true doctrines of Elijah Muhammad, and preaches a more racially exclusive message. During the 1980s and 1990s, the Nation of Islam has gained greater popularity in the US. Mass demonstrations, such as the "Million Man March" in Washington, D.C., have generated great media attention. Total membership is *c*.10,000.

**Black Panthers** Revolutionary party of African-Americans in the 1960s and 1970s. It was founded by Huey Newton and Bobby Seale in 1966. The Black Panthers called for the establishment of an autonomous black state and armed resistance to white repression. Armed clashes with police occurred and several leaders, including Newton, fled abroad to escape prosecution. Leadership conflicts and the decline of black militancy reduced the influence of the Panthers in the 1970s.

**black power** Doctrine of radical black movements in the US in the 1960s and later. Principal organizations involved were the Student Nonviolent Coordinating Committee (SNCC), the BLACK MUSLIMS, the Organization of Afro-American Unity and the BLACK PANTHERS. Black Power groups rejected the policy of nonviolent civil disobedience associated with Martin Luther KING and advocated autonomy and self-determination for black communities.

**Black Sea** (Kara Sea) Inland sea between Europe and Asia, connected to the Aegean Sea by the Bosporus, the Sea of Marmara, and the Dardanelles. It receives many rivers (including the Danube) and is a major outlet for Russian shipping. Subject to violent storms in winter, it remains free of ice except in the remote NW. The Black Sea yields large quantities of fish (especially sturgeon). Area: 159,662sq mi (413,365sq km).

**black snake** Wide-ranging North American rat snake. A good climber, it is shiny black, sometimes with small, light spots between its scales; it has a paler belly. Length: to 8.2ft (2.5m). Family Colubridae; species *Elaphe obsoleta*.

**blackthorn** Tree or shrub of the rose family that bears white flowers early in the year and has small plumlike fruits (sloes) and long black thorns that give it its name. Family Rosaceae; species *Prunus spinosa*.

**black widow** Common name for a small SPIDER found in many warm regions of the world. It is black and has red hourglass-shaped marks on the underside. Its bite is poisonous, though rarely fatal to humans. Length: 1in (25mm); the male is smaller. Family Therididae; genus *Latrodectus*.

**bladder** Large, elastic-walled organ in the lower abdomen in which URINE is stored. Urine passes from each KIDNEY by way of two narrow tubes (ureters) to the bladder, where it is stored until it can be voided. When pressure in the bladder becomes too great, nervous impulses signal the need for emptying. Urine leaves the bladder through a tube called the URETHRA.

**bladderwort** Matlike, aquatic INSECTIVOROUS PLANT found in bogs and ponds. It has feathery threadlike leaves with small bladders in which insects and other small creatures are trapped and drowned. Upright stems bear purple or dark pink flowers. Family Lentibulariaceae; genus *Utricularia*.

**Blaine, James Gillespie** (1830–93) US statesman, secretary of state (1881, 1889–92). An influential Maine Republican, he served as US senator (1876–81). He ran for president in 1884 but lost the election to the Democratic candidate, Grover CLEVELAND, partly because of the defection of reform Republicans (MUGWUMPS).

**Blair, Tony (Anthony Charles Lynton)** (1953– ) British statesman, prime minister (1997– ). Blair entered Parliament in 1983 and joined the shadow cabinet in 1988. He was elected leader of the LABOUR PARTY after the death of John SMITH (1994), and rapidly established himself as a moderniser. His reform of the party's structure and constitution ("new Labour") helped him achieve a landslide victory in the 1997 general election. Britain's youngest prime minister of the 20th century, Blair succeeded John MAJOR. Adopting a more presidential approach, his reforms included giving the Bank of England independence in the setting of interest rates and devolution for Scotland and Wales.

**Blake, Robert** (1599–1657) English admiral. A staunch parliamentarian, Blake defended (1643–45) Bristol, Lyme, and Taunton against royalist attack in the English Civil War. In 1649 he took command of the parliamentary fleet, and destroyed the royalist navy. In the first (1652–54) of the DUTCH WARS, Blake gained some notable victories against a strong Dutch navy. In 1657 he sank the Spanish fleet at Tenerife (1657), but died on the voyage home.

**Blake, William** (1757–1827) British poet, philosopher, and artist, one of the most extraordinary personalities of ROMANTICISM. A visionary, he believed that spiritual reality lies hidden behind the visible world of the senses and he attempted to create a visual symbolism to represent his spiritual visions. Blake worked as a commercial engraver in the 1780s, but from *c.*1787 he began printing his own illustrated poems in color. The first example was *Songs of Innocence* (1789). Toward the end of his life, he joined a circle of younger artists who appreciated his remarkable powers, including Samuel PALMER and Edward Calvert. It was not until the late 19th century that Blake's work achieved general recognition. Among his productions were *Songs of Experience* (1794), prophetic books portraying his private mythologies such as *The Book of Urizen* (1794) and *The Four Zoas* (1797), and illustrations to *The Book of Job* and to the *Divine Comedy* by DANTE.

**Blanc, Mont** *See* MONT BLANC

**blank verse** Unrhymed verse, especially iambic pentameter or unrhymed heroic couplets, widely used in English dramatic and epic poetry. Henry HOWARD introduced blank verse into England in the 16th century. A highly adaptable form, Christopher MARLOWE and William SHAKESPEARE transformed it into the characteristic medium of Elizabethan and JACOBEAN drama. John MILTON employed it in *Paradise Lost* (1667), and William WORDSWORTH used it notably in *The Prelude* (1850). It continues to be popular in contemporary poetry.

**Blanqui, Louis Auguste** (1805–81) French socialist leader. A legendary revolutionary campaigner who spent much of his life in prison. Blanqui participated in the revolutions of 1830 and 1848, and in the overthrow of NAPOLEON III in 1870. He became a symbol for European socialists and was president of the PARIS COMMUNE.

**Blasco Ibáñez, Vicente** (1867–1928) Spanish novelist. Blasco Ibáñez's best works, such as *The Cabin* (1898) and *Reeds and Mud* (1902), deal with rural life in Valencia and express his Republican beliefs. *Blood and Sand* (1908) and *The Four Horsemen of the Apocalypse* (1916) established his international reputation.

**blasphemy** Speech or action manifesting contempt for God or religion. Severe penalties were prescribed for it in the Old Testament and also by medieval CANON LAW. Jesus Christ was crucified for blasphemy against Judaism. The statutes of many secular countries still include laws against blasphemy. Britain, for example, retains its law, originally designed to ensure social conformity to ANGLICANISM.

**blast furnace** Cylindrical smelting furnace. It is used in the extraction of metals, mainly iron and copper, from their ores. The ore is mixed with coke and a FLUX (limestone in the case of iron ore). A blast of hot compressed air is piped in at the bottom of the furnace to force up temperatures to where the reduction of the oxide ore to impure metal occurs. The molten metal sinks to the bottom and is tapped off. Waste "slag" floats to the top of the metal and is piped off. *See also* OXIDATION-REDUCTION

**blastula** Stage in the development of the EMBRYO in animals. The blastula consists of a hollow cavity (blastocoel) surrounded by one or more spherical layers of cells. Commonly called the hollow ball of cells stage, it occurs at or near the end of cleavage.

**Blaue Reiter, der** Loosely organized group of German expressionist painters. Formed in 1911, it took its name from a picture by Wassily KANDINSKY, one of the group's leading members. Other members included Paul KLEE, August MACKE, Alexei von Jawlensky, and Franz Marc. Influenced by CUBISM, the group was the most important manifestation of German modern art before World War I. *See also* EXPRESSIONISM

**Blenheim, Battle of** (1704) Decisive battle for the English in the War of the SPANISH SUCCESSION. The Duke of MARLBOROUGH and Prince EUGÈNE OF SAVOY defeated the French at Blenheim in Bavaria. Marlborough was granted a royal manor near Oxford where he built Blenheim Palace, birthplace of his descendant Winston Churchill.

**Blériot, Louis** (1872–1936) French aircraft designer and aviator. In 1909 Blériot became the first man to fly an aircraft across the English Channel. The flight from Calais to Dover took 37 minutes. As a designer, he was responsible for a system by which the pilot could operate AILERONS by remote control.

**blesbok** Small South African antelope that has a large white mark on its face. Both sexes have horns that grow up to 20in (50cm) long. They are raised successfully as livestock. Family Bovidae, species *Damaliscus dorcas*.

**Bleuler, Paul Eugen** (1857–1939) Swiss psychiatrist, pioneer in the diagnosis and treatment of PSYCHOSIS. Bleuler coined the term SCHIZOPHRENIA and, unlike his predecessors, attributed the symptoms to psychological rather than physiological origins.

**Bligh, William** (1754–1817) British naval officer. Bligh was captain of the *Bounty* in 1789, when his mutinous crew cast him adrift. With a few loyal companions, he sailed nearly 4,000mi (6,500km) to Timor. While governor of New South Wales (1805–08) he was arrested by mutineers led by his deputy and sent back to England. He was exonerated.

**blight** Yellowing, browning, and withering of plant tissues caused by various diseases; alternatively, the diseases themselves. Blights may be caused by microorganisms, such as bacteria and fungi, or by environmental factors such as drought. Common blights induced by microorganisms include fire, bean, late, and potato blight. They typically affect leaves the most.

**blindness** Severe impairment (or complete absence of) vision. It may be due to heredity, accident, disease, or old age. Worldwide, the commonest cause of blindness is TRACHOMA. In developed countries, it is most often due to severe DIABETES, GLAUCOMA, CATARACT, or degenerative changes associated with aging.

**Bliss, Sir Arthur** (1891–1975) English composer. Bliss was a pupil of Charles Villiers Stanford, Ralph Vaughan Williams, and Gustav Holst. His works include the *Color Symphony* (1932), a piano concerto (1938), two operas, and a number of choral works. From 1953 he was Master of the Queen's Music.

**Blitz** Name used by the British to describe the night bombings of British cities by the German Luftwaffe (air force) in 1940–41. It is an abbreviation of *Blitzkrieg* (lightning war), the name used by the German army to describe hard-hitting, surprise attacks on enemy forces.

**Blixen, Karen** *See* DINESEN, ISAK

◀ **Blitz** The aerial bombardment of London and other major cities in Britain, such as Coventry (shown here) by the German air force in World War II. It was at its height during the Battle of Britain (July–December 1940). The Blitz aimed not only to destroy key industrial centers, but also to undermine the spirit of British civilians and overseas forces. Some 23,000 civilians died during the Blitz.

## BLOOD

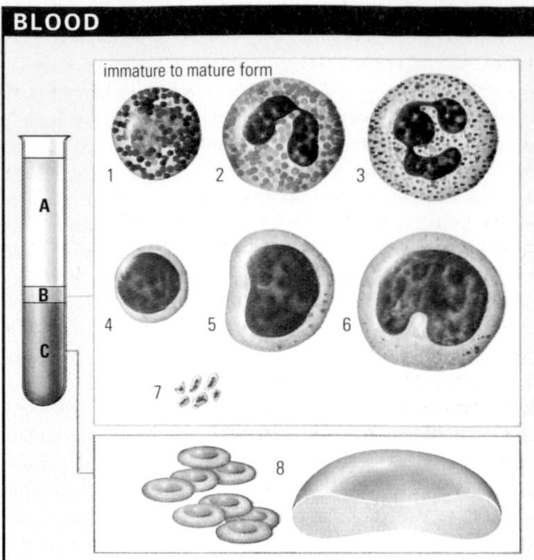


Spun in a high-speed centrifuge, blood separates out into plasma (A), layers of white cells and platelets (B), and red cells (C). Fluid plasma, almost 90% water, contains salts and proteins. Three main types of white cells shown in magnification are polymorphonuclearcytes (1–3), responsible for the destruction of invading bacteria and removal of dead or damaged tissue; small and large lymphocytes (4 and 5), which are involved in the body's immunity; and monocytes (6), which form a further line of the body's defense. Platelets (7) are vital clotting agents. Red cells (8) are the most numerous, and are concerned with the transport of oxygen around the body.

**Bloch, Felix** (1905–83) US nuclear physicist, b. Switzerland. Bloch shared the 1952 Nobel Prize for physics with the US physicist Edward Mills Purcell for their separate development of the technique of nuclear MAGNETIC RESONANCE (NMR), used to study the interactions between atomic nuclei. He was the first director (1954–55) of *Conseil Européen pour la Recherche Nucléaire* (CERN), the European center in Geneva for research into high-energy PARTICLE PHYSICS.

**Bloemfontein** City and judicial capital of South Africa; capital of FREE STATE. Dutch farmers settled here in the early 19th century. It contains the oldest Dutch Reformed church in South Africa. The modern city is an important educational center. Industries: furniture, glassware. Pop. (1991) 300,150.

**blood** Fluid circulating in the body that transports oxygen and nutrients to all the cells and removes wastes such as carbon dioxide. In a healthy human, it constitutes *c.*5% of the body's total weight; by volume, it comprises *c.*5.8qts (5.5l). It is composed of plasma in which are suspended microscopic ERYTHROCYTES, LEUKOCYTES, and PLATELETS.

**blood clotting** Protective mechanism that prevents excessive blood loss after injury. A mesh of tight fibers (of insoluble FIBRIN) coagulates at the site of injury through a complex series of chemical reactions. This mesh traps blood cells to form a clot which dries to form a scab. This prevents further loss of blood, and also prevents bacteria getting into the wound. Normal clotting takes place within five minutes. The clotting mechanism is impaired in some diseases such as HEMOPHILIA.

**blood group** Type into which blood is classified according to which ANTIGENS are present on the surface of its red cells. There are four major types: A, B, AB, and O. Each group in the ABO system may also contain the rhesus factor (Rh), in which case it is Rh-positive; otherwise it is Rh-negative. Such typing is essential before BLOOD TRANSFUSION. *See also* Karl LANDSTEINER

**bloodhound** Hunting DOG with long tapered head, loose hanging jowls and ears, and a characteristically wrinkled skin. The body is strong and the legs muscular, and the dog weighs up to 110lb (50kg). The smooth coat may be black, tan, or red and tan. Height: (at shoulder) up to 27in (69cm).

**blood poisoning** (septicemia) Presence in the blood of bacteria or their toxins in sufficient quantity to cause illness. Symptoms include chills and fever, sweating, and collapse. It is most often seen in people who are already vulnerable, such as the old, the critically ill, or those whose immune systems have been suppressed.

**blood pressure** Force exerted by circulating BLOOD on the walls of blood vessels due to the pumping action of the HEART. This is measured by a SPHYGMOMANOMETER. It is greatest when the heart contracts and lowest when it relaxes. High blood pressure is associated with an increased risk of heart attack and stroke; abnormally low blood pressure is mostly seen in people in shock or following excessive loss of fluid or blood.

**blood transfusion** Transfer of blood or a component of blood from one body to another to make up for a deficiency. This is possible only if the BLOOD GROUPS of the donor and recipient are compatible. It is often done to counteract life-threatening SHOCK following excessive blood loss. Donated blood is scrutinized for readily transmissible diseases such as HEPATITIS B and ACQUIRED IMMUNE DEFICIENCY SYNDROME (AIDS).

**blood vessel** Closed channel that carries blood throughout the body. An ARTERY carries oxygenated blood away from the heart; these give way to smaller arterioles and finally to tiny capillaries deep in the tissues, where oxygen and nutrients are exchanged for cellular wastes. The deoxygenated blood is returned to the heart by way of the VEINS.

**Bloody Assizes** (1685) Trials held in the W of England following MONMOUTH's Rebellion against James II. Judge Jeffreys conducted the trials. He sentenced about 200 people to be hanged, 800 to transportation, and hundreds more to flogging, imprisonment, or fines. *See also* MONMOUTH, JAMES SCOTT, DUKE OF

**bloom** Dense population of microscopic algae or CYANOBACTERIA on the surface of lakes or seas, often coloring the

## BLOOD VESSELS

Arteries (A) and veins (B) conduct blood around the body. They have a common structure consisting of four layers: a protective fibrous coat (1); a middle layer of smooth muscle and elastic tissue (2), which is thickest in the largest arteries; a thin layer of connective tissue (3); and a smooth layer of cells – endothelium (4). Arteries have thicker walls and a smaller diameter. In veins, inner coat layers are often indistinguishable. A comparison of the two vessels is shown in half sections of arteries and veins found in the body. Arteries divide into smaller ones, and finally into arterioles (5), where the blood flow can be controlled by autonomic nerves supplying the layer of smooth muscle.

B

water. They may appear suddenly through migration of the population to the water surface. This occurs when the cells float or swim to the surface under calm conditions. They may arise also in response to large increases in nutrients. This happens when sewage, or other mineral-rich water, enters a lake or sea. Some blooms produce toxins harmful to marine life.

**Bloomer, Amelia Jenks** (1818–94) US women's rights campaigner. Bloomer published (1849–54) *Lily*, the first US magazine for women. She subsequently continued as editor and wrote articles on education, marriage laws, and female suffrage. She popularized the full trousers for women that became known as "bloomers."

**Bloomsbury Group** Intellectuals who met in Bloomsbury, London, from about 1907. They included the art critics Roger Fry and Clive Bell; novelists E.M. FORSTER and Virginia WOOLF; her husband Leonard, a publisher; economist John Maynard KEYNES; and biographer Lytton STRACHEY.

**bluebell** Spring-flowering blue flower, native to Europe. It grows from a bulb, especially in woodlands, and bears a drooping head of bell-shaped flowers. Height: 8–20in (20–50cm). Family Liliaceae; species *Hyacinthoides non-scripta*.

**blueberry** *See* BILBERRY

**bluebird** North American songbird with blue plumage, a member of the thrush subfamily. There are three species. Typically, a bluebird lays its eggs (usually 4–6) in a grass-and-weed-lined nest in a hole in a tree or fence post. Length: 7in (17.8cm). Genus *Sialia*.

**bluebottle** Black or metallic blue-green FLY, slightly larger but similar in habits to the housefly. The larvae (maggots) usually feed on carrion and refuse containing meat. Like the greenbottle, it is often also called a blowfly. Family Calliphoridae. Genus *Calliphora*. Length: 0.23–0.43in (6–11mm).

**bluefish** Marine fish found in most tropical and temperate seas. Fished widely for food and sport, it has an elongated blue/green body, and a large mouth with sharp teeth. Length: 4ft (1.2m). Family Pomatomidae; species *Pomatomus saltatrix*.

**bluegrass** Type of grass that grows in temperate and Arctic regions and is used extensively for food by grazing animals. Family Poaceae/Gramineae; genus *Poa*.

**blue-green algae** *See* CYANOBACTERIA

**blueprint** Photographic image on paper with white lines against a blue background, often used for engineering drawings. The paper is coated with a solution of ammonium ferric citrate and potassium ferricyanide and exposed to intense light under the sheet of drawings to be copied. The blueprint is "developed" in water.

**Blue Rider** *See* BLAUE REITER, DER

**Blue Ridge Mountains** East and SE range of the APPALACHIAN Mountains, extending from S Pennsylvania into Georgia. A narrow ridge, 10mi (16km) wide in the N, widens to 70mi (113km) in North Carolina. Heavily forested, with few lakes, it includes Great Smoky Mountains National Park, North Carolina, and the Shenandoah National Park, Virginia. The Appalachian Trail takes hikers across the top of range. Industries: timbering, apple growing, tourism. The highest peak is Mount Mitchell, North Carolina, at 6,684ft (2,039m).

**blues** Form of African-American music, originating in the late 19th-century, primarily in the South. It evolved from gospel and work songs. The first published blues piece was *The Memphis Blues* by W.C. HANDY (1912). "Jelly Roll" MORTON incorporated a jazzier style in *Jelly Roll Blues*. Great blues vocalists such as Bessie SMITH ("Empress of the Blues"), Robert JOHNSON, Huddie LEDBETTER, and "Ma" Rainey, popularized the form. The 1930s northerly migration of African-Americans saw the emergence of a more assertive, urban blues tradition based around Chicago. After World War II, the electric guitar became the dominant voice, with artists such as Muddy Waters and John Lee Hooker. In the 1950s, new forms such as RHYTHM AND BLUES and ROCK and roll drew on the blues. During the 1960s rock and pop bands, such as the Rolling Stones and Grateful Dead, were also directly influenced by the tradition.

**blue shift** In astronomy, an effect in which the lines in the SPECTRUM of a celestial object are displaced toward the blue end of the spectrum. It results from the DOPPLER EFFECT because the object and the observer are moving toward each other. The closing speed can be calculated from the extent of the shift. *See also* RED SHIFT

**blue whale** Largest animal to have lived on Earth, related to the rorquals. It has been overhunted and is in danger of extinction. Species *Balaenoptera musculus*.

**Blum, Léon** (1872–1950) French statesman, prime minister (1936–37). He served in the chamber of deputies (1919–40) as a leader of the Socialist Party. Blum formed the Popular Front, which became a coalition government. His administration rapidly embarked on a program of nationalization. Opposed by Conservatives, Blum was forced to resign and became deputy prime minister. He opposed the MUNICH AGREEMENT (1938). Interned by the VICHY GOVERNMENT (1940–45), he briefly (1946–47) led a provisional government.

**Blunt, Anthony** (1907–83) English art historian. Blunt was director (1947–74) of the Courtauld Institute of Art, London, and surveyor of the king's (later queen's) pictures (1945–72). In 1979 his reputation was tarnished when it was disclosed that he was a Soviet spy during World War II.

**boa** Large, constricting SNAKE. The boa constrictor (*Constrictor constrictor*) of the American tropics can grow to 12ft (3.7m) in length. The iridescent rainbow boa, the emerald tree boa, and the rosy boa are smaller species. Most boas are tree-dwellers, but the rubber boa of the W US is a burrowing species. Family Boidae.

**Boadicea** (Boudicca) (d. AD 62) Queen of the ICENI in East Britain. She was the wife of King Prasutagus who, on his death, left his daughters and the Roman emperor as coheirs. The Romans seized his domain and Boadicea led a revolt against them. After initial successes, during which her army is thought to have killed as many as 70,000 Roman soldiers, she was defeated and poisoned herself. *See also* ROMAN BRITAIN

**boar** Male domestic PIG (particularly one that has not been castrated) or, more specifically, the wild pig of Europe, Africa, and Asia. It is hunted, either for food or sport. The European wild boar is species *Sus scrofa*.

**boat** Vehicle for passenger and freight transportation by water. Today, it usually refers to craft that can be removed from the water; a larger vessel is called a SHIP. The first boats, made in prehistoric times, included rafts, hollowed-out logs, and vessels made from plaited reeds. Among the first maritime peoples were the Phoenicians. They built fleets of galleys, propelled by sails and oars. The later Viking long-boats, also square-sailed, were slimmer and speedier. Lateen (triangular) sails were probably introduced to the West by the empire-building Arabs. Modern boats include SAILING vessels, used mainly for pleasure, motorboats, and launches.

**boat people** Refugees that flee their country by sea to avoid political persecution, or to find greater economic opportunities. The term is closely associated with South Vietnamese refugees, of whom, since 1975, some 150,000 have sailed to Hong Kong and to Southeast Asian countries. Other boat people include Cubans and Haitians attempting to reach the US, usually Florida.

**Boat Race** In England, annual rowing contest between Oxford and Cambridge University eights, first held in 1829. It is rowed on a 4.25mi (6.8km) course on the River Thames in London, from Putney to Mortlake. Staged on the present course since 1845, the race takes place in March or April.

**bobcat** (wild cat or red lynx) Vicious, short-tailed cat found throughout swamp, forest, and grassland regions of the US, S Canada, and Central America. Its reddish-brown coat has black spots with white underparts. The bobcat feeds on

▲ **bluebell** A spring flowering bulb, the bluebell (*Endymion non-scriptus*) is a monocotyledon. The bulb is a storage organ for the plant and provides a means of vegetative reproduction.

◀ **boa** The boa constrictor (*Constrictor constrictor*) is found in many areas of South America. It feeds on birds and small mammals such as rats and agoutis, which it kills by restricting their ability to breath. A large snake, it grows to about 12ft (3.5m) in length.

▲ **Bolsheviks** Following the 1917 October Revolution, the Bolsheviks, led by Lenin, gained power. A significant element of support was provided by soldiers and sailors, seen here at a rally in the Catherine Hall of the Tauride Palace, Petrograd (now St Petersburg).

rodents and gives birth to 2–4 young following a gestation period of 50–60 days. Length: body 25–30in (64–76cm). Family Felidae; species *Lynx rufus*

**bobsleigh** One of the fastest and most dangerous of winter sports. Two- or four-men teams ride in an open steel-bodied vehicle with sledlike runners on an icy downhill course that is steeply banked with twisting inclines. Bobsledding was developed in the late 19th century at St. Moritz, Switzerland, and was first included in the Winter Olympic Games in 1924. The only bobsled course in the US is in Lake Placid, New York.

**Boccaccio, Giovanni** (1313–75) Italian poet, prose writer, and scholar, considered to be one of the founders of the Italian RENAISSANCE. His early work, the *Filocolo* (*c*.1336) is considered by many to be the first European novel. Boccaccio is best known for his masterpiece the *Decameron* (1348–58), a series of prose stories of contemporary mores, which exercised a tremendous influence on the development of Renaissance literature. His poetry includes *Il Filostrato* (*c*.1338) and *Il Ninfale Fiesolano* (*c*.1344–45).

**Boccherini, Luigi** (1743–1805) Italian composer and cellist. He was the main exponent of Latin instrumental music during the Viennese classical period. Boccherini was a prolific composer of chamber music, writing over 120 string quintets and nearly 100 string quartets. His orchestral work includes over 20 symphonies.

**Bode's law** In astronomy, empirical numerical relationship for the mean distances of the planets from the Sun, named after the German astronomer Johann Bode (1747–1826). If 4 is added to the sequence 0, 3, 6, 12, 24, 48, 96 and 192, the result corresponds reasonably with the mean planetary distances, Earth's distance being equal to 10. This aided the discovery of Uranus (1781), but does not work for Neptune.

**Bodhidharma** (active 6th century AD) Indian Buddhist monk who traveled to China and there founded ZEN (or Ch'an) Buddhism.

**bodhisattva** (bodhista) In THERAVADA Buddhism, an individual who is about to reach NIRVANA. In MAHAYANA Buddhism, the term is used to denote an individual on the verge of enlightenment who delays his salvation in order to help mankind.

**Bodin, Jean** (1530–96) French lawyer and political philosopher. In *Six Books of the Republic* (1576) Bodin treated ANARCHY as the supreme political evil and order as the supreme human need.

**Boer** (Afrikaans, farmer) Alternative name for an AFRIKANER

**Boer Wars** *See* SOUTH AFRICAN WARS

**Boethius** (*c*.480–524) (Anicius Manlius Severinus) Roman statesman and philosopher under the Emperor Theodoric. He attempted to eliminate governmental corruption, but was imprisoned on a charge of conspiracy. In prison at Pavia, where he was subsequently tortured and executed, Boethius wrote *On the Consolation of Philosophy* (523). Next to the Bible, this was medieval Europe's most influential book.

**bog** Spongy, wet soil of decayed vegetable matter; often called a peat bog. It develops in a depression with little or no drainage, where the water is cold and acidic and almost devoid of oxygen and nitrogen. A bog rarely has standing water like a MARSH, but plants such as cranberry and the SUNDEW readily grow there.

**Bogart, Humphrey DeForest** (1899–1957) Legendary US film actor, often cast as a cynical, wisecracking anti-hero. His association with FILM NOIR and John HUSTON began with roles in *High Sierra* and *The Maltese Falcon* (both 1941). Bogart starred in *Casablanca* (1942). In 1945 he married Lauren BACALL; their sexual magnetism was evident in the *film noir* classic *The Big Sleep* (1946). In 1948 Bogart starred in two Huston classics, *The Treasure of the Sierra Madre* and *Key Largo*. He won a Best Actor Oscar for *The African Queen* (1951).

**Bogotá** Capital of Colombia, on a fertile plateau in central Columbia. Bogotá was founded (1538) by the Spanish on the site of a CHIBCHA Indian settlement. In 1819 it was made the capital of Greater Colombia, part of which later became Colombia. Today, it is a center for culture, education, and finance. It has some fine examples of Spanish colonial architecture. Industries: tobacco, sugar, flour, textiles. Pop. (1992) 4,921,264.

**Bohemia** Historic region which (with MORAVIA) now comprises the CZECH REPUBLIC. Bohemia was first unified in the 10th century as part of the Holy Roman Empire, coming under Hapsburg control in 1526. It was the center of occasional revolts against Austrian rule, including that of the Hussites and the episode (1618) that sparked the Thirty Years' War. It became part of CZECHOSLOVAKIA in 1918 and the Czech Republic in 1992.

**Bohr, Aage Niels** (1922– ) Danish physicist, son of Niels BOHR. Bohr shared the 1975 Nobel Prize for physics with Benjamin Mottelson and James Rainwater for devising a "collective model" of the atomic nucleus that assumes the collective vibration of all nucleons.

**Bohr, Niels Henrik David** (1885–1962) Danish physicist, major contributor to QUANTUM THEORY and the first person to apply it successfully to atomic structure. Bohr worked with J.J. THOMSON and Ernest RUTHERFORD in Britain before teaching theoretical physics at the University of Copenhagen. He escaped from German-occupied Denmark during World War II, and worked briefly on developing the atom bomb in the US. He later returned to Copenhagen and worked for international cooperation. In the 1920s Bohr helped to develop the "standard model" of quantum theory, known as the Copenhagen Interpretation. He was awarded the 1922 Nobel Prize for physics for his work on atomic structure, and in 1957 received the first Atoms for Peace Award.

**boil** (furuncle) Small, pus-filled swelling on the skin, often occurring around a hair follicle or SEBACEOUS GLAND. Most boils are caused by infection by a bacterium called a STAPHYLOCOCCUS.

**boiling point** Temperature at which a substance changes phase (state) from a liquid to a vapor or gas. The boiling point increases as the external pressure increases and falls as pressure decreases. It is usually measured at standard pressure of one atmosphere (760mm of mercury). The boiling point of pure water at standard pressure is 212°F (100°C).

**Boise** Capital and largest city of Idaho, in the valley of the Boise River. Founded in 1863 as a supply post for gold miners, Boise is now a trade center for the agricultural region of SW Idaho and E Oregon. Crops: sugar beets, potatoes, alfalfa, onions. Industries: steel, sheet metal, furniture. Pop. (1990) 125,738.

**Bokassa, Jean Bédel** (1921–96) Emperor of the Central African Empire (1977–79). Bokassa came to power in 1966 in a military coup. After serving as president (1966–77) of the Central African Republic, he crowned himself emperor. His regime was brutal. A 1979 coup (with French military aid) removed Bokassa, who went into French exile.

**boletus** Genus of terrestrial fungi, whose spore-bearing parts are tubes instead of the usual gills. There are many species, all of which have a fleshy cap on a central stem and many of which are edible. Some poisonous kinds have red tube mouths. The edible cep is *Boletus edulis*.

**Boleyn, Anne** (1507–36) Second wife of HENRY VIII of England, mother of ELIZABETH I. Henry and Anne were married in 1533, when his first marriage, to Catherine of Aragon, had been annulled. Henry was desperate for an heir, and following the birth of a stillborn boy (1536), Anne was accused of adultery and executed for treason. It is thought that her Protestant sympathies pushed the king toward the break with Rome that unleashed the English REFORMATION.

**Bolingbroke** *See* HENRY IV (of England)

**Bolingbroke, Henry St. John, Viscount** (1678–1751) English political leader. A prominent Tory minister under ANNE, he fled to France in 1714 and joined the JACOBITES. Bolingbroke was allowed to return to England in 1723, and continued to oppose the Whig regime under Robert WALPOLE.

**Bolívar, Simón** (1783–1830) Latin American revolutionary leader, known as "the Liberator." Bolívar achieved no real success until 1819, when his victory at Boyacá led to the liberation of New Granada (later Colombia) in 1821. The liberation of Venezuela (1821), Ecuador (1822), Peru (1824), and Upper Peru (1825) followed, the latter renaming itself Bolivia in his honor. Despite the removal of Spanish hegemony from the continent, his hopes of uniting South America into one confederation were dashed by rivalry between the new states.

**Bolivia** Republic in W central South America. *See* country feature

**Böll, Heinrich Theodor** (1917–85) German novelist and short-story writer. Böll's narratives often contain strident criticisms of German society and Catholic morality, such as the popular novel *The Clown* (1963). Strongly affected by his experiences as a German soldier in World War II, novels such as *Billiards at Half past Nine* (1961) attempt to come to terms with the Holocaust. Other novels include *Group Portrait with Lady* (1971) and *The Lost Honor of Katharina Blum* (1974). He was awarded the 1972 Nobel Prize for literature.

**Bologna** City in N central Italy, at the foot of Apennines; capital of Bologna and Emilia-Romagna province. Originally an Etruscan town, Felsina, it was colonized by Rome in the 2nd century BC. It has an 11th-century university and the incomplete Church of San Petronio (1390). Industries: mechanical and electrical engineering, publishing. Pop. (1992) 401,308.

**Bolsheviks** (Rus. majority) Marxist revolutionaries led by LENIN who seized power in the RUSSIAN REVOLUTION of

## BOLIVIA

This flag, which has been Bolivia's national and merchant flag since 1888, dates back to 1825 when the country became independent. The red stands for Bolivia's animals and the courage of the army, the yellow for its mineral resources, and the green for its agricultural wealth.

**AREA:** 424,162sq mi (1,098,580sq km)
**POPULATION:** 7,832,000
**CAPITAL (POPULATION):** La Paz (1,126,000), Sucre (103,952)
**GOVERNMENT:** Multiparty republic
**ETHNIC GROUPS:** Mestizo 31%, Quechua 25%, Aymará 17%, White 15%
**LANGUAGES:** Spanish, Aymará, Quechua (all official)
**RELIGIONS:** Christianity (Roman Catholic 94%)
**CURRENCY:** Boliviano = 100 centavos

The Republic of Bolivia is a landlocked country which straddles the ANDES Mountains in central South America. The Andes range, which rises to a height of 21,464ft (6,542m) at Nevado Sajama in the W, contains part of Lake TITICACA in the N, with Lake Poopó to the S.

### CLIMATE AND VEGETATION

The climate of LA PAZ in the Andean region is greatly affected by its altitude, and it has frosts in winter. The highest of the Andean peaks are always covered by snow, while the E plains have a humid climate. The main rainy season in Bolivia is between December and February.

The windswept altiplano, a high plateau between the E and W Andes, is a treeless grassland zone, merging higher up into the puna, a region of scrub. Tropical rain forests cover much of the E, together with areas of open grassland and swamps. In the SE is the semiarid Chaco, a vast lowland plain drained by headwaters of the Madeira River, a tributary of the mighty AMAZON.

### HISTORY

Native Americans have lived in Bolivia for some 10,000 years and the main groups today are the AYMARÁ and QUECHUA people. When Spanish soldiers arrived in the 16th century, Bolivia was part of the INCA empire. Following the defeat of the Incas, Spain ruled from 1532 to 1825, when Antonio José de SUCRE, one of Simón BOLÍVAR's generals, defeated the Spaniards and became the country's first president.

### POLITICS

Since independence, Bolivia has lost much territory to its neighbors. In 1932, Bolivia fought Paraguay unsuccessfully for control of the GRAN CHACO region, most of which passed to Paraguay in 1938.

From 1964 to 1982, Bolivia was ruled by a succession of repressive military regimes, most prominently that of Colonel Hugo Banzer Suárez (1971–78). In 1982 civilian rule was restored. In 1997 Banzer became president, promising to maintain, with US support, the war against the growing of coca.

### ECONOMY

Despite its many natural resources, including tin, silver, and natural gas, Bolivia remains South America's poorest republic (1995 GDP per capita, US$2,540) and the chief activity is agriculture, which employs 47% of the workforce. Potatoes, wheat, and grain are important crops on the altiplano, while bananas, cocoa, coffee, and corn are grown at lower, warmer levels. Manufacturing is on a small scale, and the chief exports are mineral ores, especially tin. Some experts believe that the main export may be coca, which is used to make cocaine and is highly profitable. Coca is exported illegally, mostly through Peru and Colombia, although the government is trying to stamp out the industry.

**Bolivia's coat of arms,** shown on this 1972 stamp, contains a central graphic including a mountain where silver is mined, a breadfruit tree, and an alpaca, which is raised for its fine wool. At the top is the magnificent Andean condor, the world's heaviest bird of prey.

B

1917. They narrowly defeated the MENSHEVIKS at the Second Congress of the All-Russian Soviet Democratic Workers' Party in London (1903). The split centered on the means of achieving revolution. The Bolsheviks believed it could be obtained only by professional revolutionaries leading the PROLETARIAT. The Bolsheviks were able to defeat KERENSKY'S provisional government with the support of the SOVIETS in Moscow and Petrograd. *See also* MARXISM

**Bolshoi Ballet** One of the world's leading ballet companies. It adopted its present name in 1825 but was founded as the Petrovsky Theater in 1776. Based at the Bolshoi Theater, its choreographers have included Yuri Grigorovich and Alexander Gorsky, and its leading dancers Galina ULANOVA and Mikhail Lavrovsky.

**Bolshoi Opera** Leading Russian opera company, founded in 1780 in Moscow. It performs mostly Russian works and a few foreign operas translated into Russian.

**Boltzmann, Ludwig** (1844–1906) Austrian physicist, acclaimed for his major contribution to statistical mechanics and to the kinetic theory of gases. His research extended the theories of James MAXWELL. Boltzmann's general law asserts that a system will approach a state of thermodynamic equilibrium. He introduced the "Boltzmann equation" (1877) relating the kinetic energy of a gas atom or molecule to temperature. Symbol K in the formula, the gas constant per molecule, is called the "Boltzmann constant." In 1884 he derived a law, often termed the "Stefan-Boltzmann law," for BLACK BODY radiation discovered by his Viennese teacher, Josef Stefan (1835–93). After being attacked for his belief in the atomic theory of MATTER, Boltzmann committed suicide.

**bomb** Projectile filled with an explosive charge exploded by a fuse or by impact, and used as a weapon to cause destruction and death. The many specialized types include NUCLEAR WEAPONS, high-explosive bombs, smoke bombs to provide a smokescreen, gas bombs to spread poison gas, and fire (or incendiary) bombs, the purpose of which is to set alight buildings.

**Bombay** See MUMBAI

**Bonaparte, Joseph** (1768–1844) King of Spain, b. Corsica. He was the eldest brother of NAPOLEON I. He served as diplomat for the First Republic of France. Napoleon made him king of Naples (1806), and he was king of Spain from 1808–13. After Napoleon's defeat at Waterloo, he resided in the US (1815–32).

**Bonaparte, Louis** (1778–1846) King of Holland (1806–10), brother of NAPOLEON I and father of NAPOLEON III. He accompanied his brother in the Italian and Egyptian campaigns, became a general (1804) and governor of Paris (1805). Forced by Napoleon to take the Dutch throne, he worked to restore its economy and welfare. Napoleon felt he was too lenient and the conflict led Louis to abdicate.

**Bonaparte, Napoleon** *See* NAPOLEON I

**Bonar Law, Andrew** *See* LAW, ANDREW BONAR

**bond** Promissory note guaranteeing the repayment of a specific amount of money on a particular date at a particular fixed rate of interest. Bonds may be issued by corporations, states, cities or the federal government. The quality of the bond, and the interest rate paid on it, is determined by the period of the outstanding loan and the risk involved. Thus the US federal government normally pays a lower rate of interest than cities because US bonds are relatively risk-free. Bonds pay out fixed amounts of interest on a regular basis and appeal to investors seeking a regular income.

**Bond, Edward** (1935– ) English playwright. His early works, such as *Saved* (1965), were controversial in their use of violent imagery to express the cruelty of modern society. *Early Morning* (1968) was the last play to be banned in the UK. Other major plays include *Lear* (1971) and *War Plays* (1985). He has written several film scripts, including *Blow Up* (1966).

**Bond, William Cranch** (1789–1859) US astronomer who discovered Hyperion, Saturn's eighth satellite, and the Crêpe Ring, the faint innermost ring around the planet. Both discoveries were made with his son, George. Bond founded (1839) and was the first director of the Harvard College Observatory. He also produced a Daguerreotype of the Moon in 1850.

**▼ bone** A magnified cross-section of bone shows that it is composed of rodlike units (1) which have a central channel (2) containing blood vessels (3). These are surrounded by concentric layers, or lamellae, of collagen fibers, each arranged in a different direction from those in adjacent layers. Calcium salt crystals and bone cells (4) are embedded between the fibers.

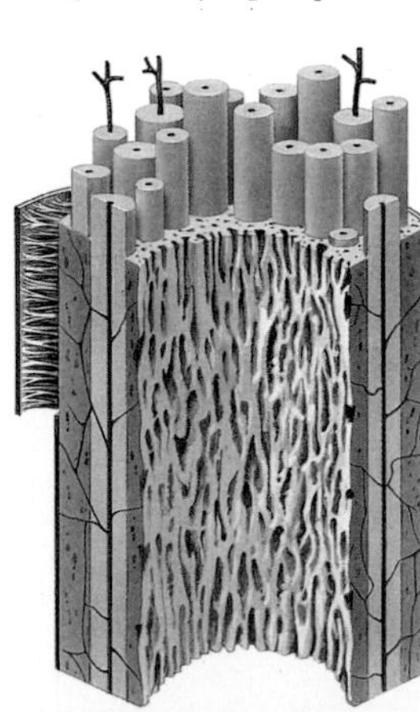


**Bondfield, Margaret Grace** (1873–1953) British Labour politician and labor unionist. In 1923 she became chairman of the TRADES UNION CONGRESS (TUC). As minister of labor (1923–31), she was the first woman member of a British cabinet.

**bone** CONNECTIVE TISSUE that forms the skeleton of the body, protects its internal organs, serves as a lever during locomotion and when lifting objects, and stores calcium and phosphorus. Bone is composed of a strong, compact layer of COLLAGEN and calcium phosphate and a lighter, porous inner spongy layer containing MARROW, in which ERYTHROCYTES and some LEUKOCYTES are produced.

**bone china** Hard-paste PORCELAIN, consisting of kaolin, china stone, and bone ash. Josiah SPODE perfected the manufacture of bone china in the 19th century.

**Bonhoeffer, Dietrich** (1906–45) German theologian. A Lutheran pastor, he opposed the rise of National Socialism. Arrested by the Nazis in 1943, Bonhoeffer was executed for treason after being linked with a failed conspiracy to assassinate Hitler in 1944. Among his works are *Letters from Prison* (1953) and *Christology* (1966). Bonhoeffer espoused a kind of "secular" Christianity.

**Boniface, Saint** (675–754) English missionary. He left England in 716 to convert the pagan Germans. For his success he was rewarded with the Archbishopric of Mainz in 751. Boniface was martyred by pagans in Friesland. He is buried in Fulda, Bavaria, and is venerated as the Apostle of Germany. His feast day is June 5.

**Boniface VIII** (1235–1303) Pope (1294–1303), b. Benedetto Gaetani. To bring order to Rome and prevent schism, he imprisoned his predecessor, Celestine V. He offered the first plenary indulgence (1300) for all who made a pilgrimage to Rome.

**bonito** Speedy streamlined tunalike fish found in all warm and temperate waters, usually in schools. Bonitos are blue, black, and silver, and highly valued as food and game fish. The ocean bonito (*Katsuwonus pelamis*) is also called skipjack tuna or bluefin. Family Scombridae.

**Bonn** City and capital of former West Germany, on the Rhine River, 16mi (26km) SSE of Cologne. Founded in the 1st century AD as a Roman military establishment, it later became the seat of the electors of Cologne, and was awarded to Prussia by the Congress of Vienna (1815). Bonn was capital of West Germany from 1949 until German reunification in 1990. There is some fine architecture, including a Romanesque cathedral and the Poppelsdorf Palace. Beethoven was born here. Industries: engineering, laboratory equipment. Pop. (1990) 297,400.

**Bonnard, Pierre** (1867–1947) French painter and graphic artist. Together with his lifelong friend, Jean-Edouard Vuillard, he adapted the traditions of IMPRESSIONISM to create a repertoire of sensuous domestic interiors. Known as *intimiste*, his paintings are drenched in gorgeous colors. Examples include *The Terrasse Family*, *Luncheon* (1922), and *Martha in a Red Blouse* (1928).

**Bonnie and Clyde** American couple, Bonnie Parker (1910–34) and Clyde Barrow (1909–34), who robbed banks and shops during the era of the Depression. Their story was filmed in 1967 by Arthur Penn, and the film quickly developed a cult following.

**Bonnie Prince Charlie** *See* STUART, CHARLES EDWARD

**bonsai** Japanese art of dwarfing woody plants and shrubs by pruning and restraining root growth; they are primarily outdoor plants and occur naturally in cliff areas. Bonsai can be 2–24in (5–60cm) tall, depending on the plant used.

**Bonus Army** (1932) Unemployed veterans who marched on Washington, D.C., and demanded cash payment of bonus certificates. The 17,000 veterans camped out during June and July until President HOOVER sent troops led by Douglas MacArthur to disperse them. In 1936 the veterans were given cashable bonds.

**booby** *See* GANNET

**boogie-woogie** Type of JAZZ popular in the 1930s. It has a rapid, driving beat, uses BLUES themes, and is generally played on the piano. The melody is played over a consistently repeated bass motif played by the left hand.

B

**book** Primarily a bound volume of printed pages, it may also be a division within a book (as in the Bible) or a statement of accounts. The earliest books were Egyptian writings on papyrus, of which the BOOK OF THE DEAD is often considered the first. Roman books were mostly in the form of rolls, although the Roman period also saw the emergence of the codex, the forerunner of the paged book. In the Middle Ages, vellum, a fine parchment made from animal skins, became the standard material for books, but by the 15th century they were often written on paper. Modern printed books date from the invention of movable metal type in 1454 by GUTENBERG, and the first printed book was a German Latin Bible of 1455. *See also* PRINTING

**Booker Prize** British literary prize. The Booker is the most prestigious award for new English-language novels by UK, Commonwealth, or Irish writers. Recipients of the prize, first presented in 1969, have included Iris MURDOCH and V.S. NAIPAUL. In 1993 Salman RUSHDIE's *Midnight's Children* (1981) won the "Booker of Bookers."

**bookkeeping** Regular and systematic recording in ledgers of the amounts of money involved in business transactions. These records provide the basis for ACCOUNTING.

**booklouse** Transparent to white, usually wingless insect found worldwide. Booklice feed on molds in hot, humid, dusty places such as shelves, books, and behind loose wallpaper. Length: to 0.2in (5mm). Order Psocoptera; genus *Liposcelis*.

**Book of Changes** (I-Ching) Ancient Chinese book of wisdom. Although the oldest parts of the text are thought to predate CONFUCIUS, he is credited with the commentaries that form a part of the collection.

**Book of Common Prayer** *See* COMMON PRAYER, BOOK OF

**book of hours** Book containing the prescribed order of prayers, rites for the canonical hours, and readings from the Bible. Such books, developed in the 1300s, were often lavishly decorated by miniaturists and served as status symbols. The most famous extant book of hours is the Très Riches Heures du Duc de Berry, illustrated in part by the Limbourg brothers.

**Book of Kells** Illuminated manuscript of the four GOSPELS in Latin. Probably begun in the late 8th century at the Irish monastery of Iona, which later migrated to Kells, County Meath, Ireland, its intricate illumination and superb penmanship have earned it the title of "the most beautiful book in the world." After its collation in 1621 by James Usher, it was presented to Trinity College, Dublin, where it has remained.

**Book of the Dead** Collection of Old Egyptian texts probably dating from the 16th century BC. The papyrus texts, which incorporate mortuary texts from as early as 2350 BC, were placed in the tombs of the dead in order to help them combat the dangers of the afterlife.

**Boole, George** (1815–64) English mathematician. Largely self-taught, Boole was appointed (1849) professor of mathematics of Cork University. He is remembered for his invention of Boolean algebra, commonly used in COMPUTERS.

**boomslang** Venomous snake of the savannas of Africa. It is green or brown with a slender body and a small head. Commonly found in trees or bushes, it lies in wait for lizards and small birds, often with the front portion of its body extended motionless in midair. Length: to 4.9ft (1.5m). Species *Dispholidus typus*.

**Boone, Daniel** (1734–1820) US frontier pioneer. In 1775 he blazed the famous Wilderness Road from Virginia to Kentucky and founded the settlement of Boonesborough. During the American Revolution Boone was captured by the Shawnee, but escaped and reached Boonesborough in time to prevent it from falling to the British and their Native American allies.

**Booth, Charles** (1840–1916) English social reformer who pioneered the method of social survey in his *Life and Labour of the People in London* (1891–1903). He was instrumental in gaining the passage of the Old Age Pensions Act in 1908.

**Booth, John Wilkes** (1838–65) US actor and assassin of Abraham LINCOLN. He was a Confederate sympathizer. On April 14, 1865, during a performance at Ford's Theater in Washington, D.C., Booth shot Lincoln, who died the next day. He escaped but was either shot, or killed himself, two weeks later.

**Booth, William** (1829–1912) English religious leader, founder and first general of the SALVATION ARMY. A Methodist, Booth started his own revivalist movement, which undertook evangelistic and social work among the poor. It became known as the Salvation Army in 1878 and spread to many countries. On his death he was succeeded by his son, William Bramwell Booth.

**bootlegging** Illegal supply and sale of goods that are subject to government prohibition or taxation. Bootleg also refers to unlicensed copies or cheap imitations of goods that are packaged to deceive the buyer. The name is said to derive from the practice of American frontiersmen who carried bottles of illicit liquor in the tops of their boots, for sale to Native Americans. Bootlegging blossomed during the PROHIBITION era (1920–33) in the US.

**borage** Hairy, annual plant native to S Europe. It has rough, oblong leaves and drooping clusters of pale blue flowers and is cultivated as a food and flavoring. Height: up to 2ft (60cm). Family Boraginaceae; species *Borago officinalis*.

**Borah, William Edgar** (1865–1940) US senator from Idaho (1907–40). He led opposition to US entry into the League of Nations and was chairman (1924–33) of the Senate committee on foreign affairs. Borah promoted the Kellogg-Briand Pact (1927) and opposed US intervention in Latin America. He was a leading prohibitionist and strongly opposed much of the NEW DEAL legislation.

**borax** (hydrated sodium borate, $Na_2B_4O_7.10H_2O$) Most common borate mineral. It is found in large deposits in dried-up alkaline lakes as crusts or masses of crystals. Borax may be colorless or white, transparent, or opaque. It is used to make heat-resistant glass, pottery glaze, fertilizers, and pharmaceuticals.

**Bordeaux** City and port on the Garonne River; capital of Gironde department, SW France. There is an 11th-century Gothic cathedral, a university (1441), and many fine 18th-century buildings, from a period when the slave trade brought prosperity. Bordeaux is a good deepwater inland port and serves an area famous for its fine wines and brandies. Industries: shipbuilding, oil refining, pharmaceuticals. Pop. (1990) 210,336.

**Borders** Region of SE Scotland; its S boundary forms the border between Scotland and England. The administrative center is Newtown St. Boswells, other towns include Hawick and Jedburgh. The Tweed and Teviot rivers flow E through the region and meet near Kelso. The Cheviot Hills form most of its S border and the Southern Uplands its E border. Livestock farming and forestry are the major economic activities. It was the scene of many battles between the English and Scots. Area: 1,820sq mi (4,714sq km). Pop. (1991) 103,881.

**boreal forest** Wooded zone of northern latitudes with a cold dry climate and a poor sandy soil. It consists primarily of conifers and stretches like a broad ribbon across the Northern Hemisphere. Its northern edge is bordered by frozen tundra.

**Borg, Björn** (1956– ) Swedish tennis player. Borg won five consecutive men's singles titles at Wimbledon (1976–80). He also won six French Open titles (1974–75, 1978–81) and helped Sweden win the 1975 Davis Cup. He retired in 1983.

**Borges, Jorge Luis** (1899–1986) Argentinian short-story writer, poet, and critic. Borges is best known for his short-story collections *Dreamtigers* (1960), *The Book of Imaginary Beings* (1967), and *Dr. Brodie's Report* (1970). Dream-like and poetic, they often use intellectual puzzles, and they established Borges as one of the most significant literary talents of the 20th century.

**Borghese** Italian princely family, originally of Siena, later Rome. Camillo Borghese (1552–1621) became pope as PAUL V in 1605. Another Camillo (1775–1832) married Marie Pauline Bonaparte, the sister of NAPOLEON I, and was made governor of Piedmont.

B

▲ **Borobudur** One of the world's greatest Buddhist shrines, Borobudur was built in about the middle of the 9th century to a unique plan involving colossal resources; 2 million cu ft (570,000cu m) of stone were moved from a riverbed, dressed, positioned, and carved with countless spouts, urns, and other embellishments. The walls are covered with reliefs relating to Buddhist doctrine and altogether there are 504 shrines with seated Buddhas.

**Borgia, Cesare** (1475–1507) Italian general and political figure, brother of Lucrezia BORGIA. He was made a cardinal (1493) by his father, Pope Alexander VI, but forsook the church to embark on a military campaign (1498–1503) to establish his dominion in central Italy. Borgia's ruthless campaigns lend credence to the theory that he was the model for Machiavelli's *The Prince*. Imprisoned by Pope Julius II, Borgia escaped to Spain, where he was killed in battle.

**Borgia, Lucrezia** (1480–1519) Daughter of Pope Alexander VI and sister of Cesare BORGIA. Her marriage to Giovanni Sforza (1493) was annulled by Alexander in 1497 when it failed to produce anticipated political advantages. Lucrezia's marriage to Alfonso, nephew of Alfonso II of Naples, ended with Alfonso's murder (1500) by Cesare's henchman. After the collapse of Borgia aspirations in 1503, she forsook the political intrigue for which she was notorious and lived quietly, a patron of art, at Ferrara with her third husband.

**Borglum, John Gutzon** (1867–1941) US sculptor. He fashioned a head of Abraham LINCOLN, which now stands in the Capitol rotunda in Washington, D.C. His last and most exacting project was to carve the heads of WASHINGTON, JEFFERSON, LINCOLN, and Theodore ROOSEVELT in a rock face at Mount Rushmore, South Dakota. The final details were completed by his son.

**boric acid** (boracic acid, $H_3BO_3$) Soft, white crystalline solid, that occurs naturally in certain volcanic hot springs. It is used as a metallurgical flux, preservative, antiseptic, and an insecticide for ants and cockroaches.

**Born, Max** (1882–1970) German-British physicist. He was professor of physics at Göttingen University from 1921 but left Germany in 1933, teaching at the universities of Cambridge (1933–36) and Edinburgh (1936–53). Born returned to Germany in 1954. For his work in QUANTUM MECHANICS, he shared the 1954 Nobel Prize for physics with Walther BOTHE.

**Borneo** Island in the Malay Archipelago, 400mi (650km) E of Singapore, SE Asia. Mostly undeveloped, Borneo is the world's third largest island, and is divided into four political regions: SARAWAK (W) and SABAH (N) are states of Malaysia; BRUNEI (NW) is a former British protectorate; KALIMANTAN (E, central, and S) covers 70% of the island and forms part of Indonesia. Industries: timber, fishing. Area: 287,000sq mi (743,330sq km).

**Borden, Lizzie** (1860–1927) US woman who, in 1892, was accused of murdering her father and stepmother with an ax, but was acquitted in a sensational trial. Many books, and a humorous poem, were written about the case, and she and her trial have become part of legend.

**Borden, Sir Robert Laird** (1854–1937) Canadian statesman, prime minister (1911–20). Borden was elected to Parliament in 1896, and in 1901 became leader of the Conservative Party. He succeeded Sir Wilfrid Laurier as prime minister. From 1917 to 1920 Borden headed a coalition government. He steered Canada through World War I and helped to shape the future constitutional status of the Dominion.

**Bornu** Province and former kingdom in NE Nigeria, SW of Lake Chad. From the 14th to the 19th centuries it was the center of a powerful Muslim empire, which exported slaves and fabrics to N Africa.

**Borobudur** Ruins of a Buddhist monument in Central Java, built under the Sailendra dynasty *c*.800. It comprises a stupa (relic mound), mandalas (ritual diagrams), and the temple mountain, all forms of Indian GUPTA DYNASTY religious art.

**Borodin, Alexander Porfirevich** (1833–87) Russian composer and chemist, one of the RUSSIAN FIVE group of composers. Borodin's works include the tone poem *In the Steppes of Central Asia* (1880) and the *Polovtsian Dances* from his opera *Prince Igor* (completed after his death by GLAZUNOV and RIMSKY-KORSAKOV).

**boron** (symbol B) Nonmetallic element of group III of the periodic table, first isolated in 1808 by Sir Humphry DAVY. It occurs in several minerals, notably kernite (its chief ore) and BORAX. It has two allotropes: **amorphous** boron is an impure brown powder; **metallic** boron is a black to silver-gray, hard crystalline material. The element is used in semiconductor devices and the stable isotope $^{10}$B is a good neutron absorber, used in nuclear reactors and particle counters. Properties: at.no. 5; at.wt. 10.81; sp.gr. 2.34 (cryst.), 2.37 (amorph.); m.p. 3,774°F (2,079°C); sublimes 4,622°F (2,550°C); most common isotope $^{11}$B (80.22%).

**Borromini, Francesco** (1599–1667) Italian Baroque architect. He was the most inventive figure of the three masters (with BERNINI and Pietro da Cortona) of Roman Baroque. Borromini's hallmark was a dynamic, hexagonal design, such as the spectacular Sant'Ivo della Sapienza (begun 1642). His masterpieces include San Carlo alle Quattro Fontane (1638–41) and Sant'Agnese in Piazza Navona (1653–55).

**borough** Originally, in medieval England, a town which had a charter granting privileges and autonomy; now it refers to an urban area, granted a charter of incorporation and administered internally. Large metropolitan areas, such as New York City and London, may be divided into separate boroughs. *See also* LOCAL GOVERNMENT

**borstal** British system of rehabilitation for juvenile offenders between the ages of 16 and 21. The idea originated in 1895 with the Gladstone Committee, and the first institution was established at Borstal Prison, Kent, in 1902. Borstals are residential, providing education, vocational training, regular work, and group counseling.

**borzoi** (Russian wolfhound) Sharp-sighted, speedy hunting DOG, with a long narrow head. The body is deep and streamlined, with long legs and curved tail. The coat is long and silky and is usually white with darker markings. Height: (at shoulder) up to 31in (79cm).

**Bosch, Hieronymus** (*c*.1450–1516) Flemish painter, b. Jerome van Aken, in 's Hertogenbosch. His paintings of grotesque and fantastic visions based on religious themes led to accusations of heresy and greatly influenced 20th-century SURREALISM. Most of his paintings explore the distressing

▶ **Bosch** A detail of the "Hell" section of *The Garden of Earthly Delights*. The triptych by Hieronymous Bosch shows the surreal nature of his work. Among his patrons was the devout Catholic Philip II of Spain, and it is thought that Bosch's work was to serve as a warning against sin.

consequences of human sin and innocent figures besieged by horrifying physical torements. About 40 examples of his work survive, including *The Temptation of St. Anthony*, *The Garden of Earthly Delights* (often considered his masterpiece), and *Adoration of the Magi*.

**Bose, Satyendranath** (1894–1974) Indian physicist and mathematician. Bose significantly extended a theory of QUANTUM MECHANICS by Albert EINSTEIN, concerning the gaslike properties of ELECTROMAGNETIC RADIATION. He developed an important statistical model for the behavior of a collection of subatomic particles.

**Bosnia-Herzegovina** Balkan republic in SE Europe. *See* country feature

**boson** ELEMENTARY PARTICLE that transmits FUNDAMENTAL FORCES, such as PHOTONS and gluons (the particles that hold QUARKS together). Bosons have an integer SPIN and are not covered by the EXCLUSION PRINCIPLE. This means that the number of bosons occupying the same quantum state is not restricted. They are named for the physicist Satyendranath BOSE. *See also* FERMION

**Bosporus** (Karadeniz Bogazi) Narrow strait joining the Sea of Marmara with the Black Sea, and separating European and Turkey. It is an important strategic and commercial waterway, controlled by the Turks since 1452. Length: 19mi (30km).

**Boston** State capital and seaport of Massachusetts, at the mouth of the Charles River, on Massachusetts Bay. Founded in 1630, it became a Puritan stronghold and the scene of several incidents leading to the outbreak of the American Revolution. A religious and cultural center, Boston is the home of many important educational establishments, including Boston University and Harvard Medical School. HARVARD UNIVERSITY and the Massachusetts Institute of Technology (MIT) are in nearby Cambridge. Industries: publishing, banking and insurance, shipbuilding. Pop. (1990) 574,283.

**Boston Massacre** (1770) Riot by American colonists angered over the quartering of troops in private homes. Starting with some snowballing, it was put down by British soldiers and resulted in the death of five civilians, including Crispus Attucks. The riot was exploited for anti-British propaganda by Samuel ADAMS and the Boston radicals. The soldiers were tried for murder, defended by John Adams, and acquitted.

**Boston Tea Party** (1773) Protest by a group of Massachusetts colonists, disguised as Mohawks and led by Samuel ADAMS, against the Tea Act and, more generally, against "tax-

## BOSNIA-HERZEGOVINA

Bosnia-Herzegovina adopted a new flag in 1998 because the previous flag was thought by Croats and Serbs to be synonymous with the wartime Muslim regime. The blue background and white stars represent the country's links with the EU, and the triangle stands for the three ethnic groups within the country.

**AREA:** 19,745 sq mi (51,129sq km)
**POPULATION:** 4,366,000
**CAPITAL (POPULATION):** Sarajevo (526,000)
**GOVERNMENT:** Transitional
**ETHNIC GROUPS:** Muslim 49%, Serb 31%, Croat 17%
**LANGUAGES:** Serbo-Croatian
**RELIGIONS:** Islam 40%, Christianity (Serbian Orthodox 31%, Roman Catholic 15%, Protestant 4%)
**CURRENCY:** Dinar = 100 paras

The Republic of Bosnia-Herzegovina, which is often called Bosnia for short, is one of the five republics that emerged from the former Federal People's Republic of YUGOSLAVIA. Much of the country is mountainous or hilly, with an arid limestone plateau in the SW. The Sava River, which forms most of the N border with Croatia, is a tributary of the Danube. The coastline is limited to a short stretch of 13mi (20km) on the Adriatic Sea coast.

### CLIMATE AND VEGETATION

A Mediterranean climate, with dry, sunny summers and mild, moist winters, prevails near the coast. Inland the weather becomes more severe, with hot, dry summers and bitterly cold winters, the most severe weather being in the N. Forests of beech, oak, and pine grow in the N, while the S has bare limestone landscapes interspersed with farmland and pasture.

### HISTORY

SLAVS settled in the area that is now Bosnia-Herzegovina around 1,400 years ago. In the late 15th century, the area was conquered by the OTTOMAN Turks, who introduced Islam.

In 1878 the AUSTRO-HUNGARIAN EMPIRE gained temporary control over Bosnia-Herzegovina, and it formally took over the area in 1908. In 1914, World War I began when Austro-Hungary's Archduke FRANZ FERDINAND was assassinated in SARAJEVO. At the end of the war, in 1918, Bosnia-Herzegovina became part of the Kingdom of the Serbs, Croats, and Slovenes, which was renamed Yugoslavia in 1929.

Germany occupied the area during World War II, but from 1945 Communist governments ruled Yugoslavia as a federation consisting of six republics, one of which was Bosnia-Herzegovina. During the 1980s, the Socialist policies proved unsuccessful and differences arose between the region's three rival ethnic groups.

### POLITICS

In 1990, free elections were held in Bosnia-Herzegovina, and non-Communists won a majority, with a Muslim, Alija IZETBEGOVIĆ, becoming president. In 1991, Croatia and Slovenia, other parts of the former Yugoslav federation, declared themselves independent, and in 1992 Bosnia-Herzegovina held a referendum on independence. Most Bosnian Serbs boycotted it, but the Muslims and Bosnian Croats voted in favor.

Many Bosnian Serbs, opposed to independence, started a war against the non-Serbs, and soon occupied more than two-thirds of the land. The Bosnian Serbs were accused of "ethnic cleansing" – the killing or expulsion of other ethnic groups from Serb-occupied areas. The war was later extended when Croat forces seized other parts of the country.

The United Nations, while attempting a peacekeeping operation, tried to find a way of ending the war by dividing Bosnia-Herzegovina into self-governing provinces, under a unified, multi-ethnic central government. Finally, in 1995, the Dayton peace accord affirmed that Bosnia-Herzegovina was a single state, but partitioned it into a Muslim-Croat federation, given 51% of the area, and a Serbian republic, occupying the remaining 49%. The agreement deployed 60,000 NATO troops as part of a Peace Implementation Force (IFOR). KARADŽIĆ and the Bosnian Serb army leader Ratko MLADIĆ were forced to resign. In 1996 elections Izetbegović was re-elected as head of a tripartite presidency, including a Serb and a Croat representative. In 1998 the Serbian nationalist Nikola Poplasen was elected president of Republika Srpska. NATO troops remained as a "dissuasion" force (DFOR).

### ECONOMY

Excluding Macedonia, Bosnia was the least developed of the former republics of Yugoslavia. Its economy has been shattered by the war.

B

## BOTFLY

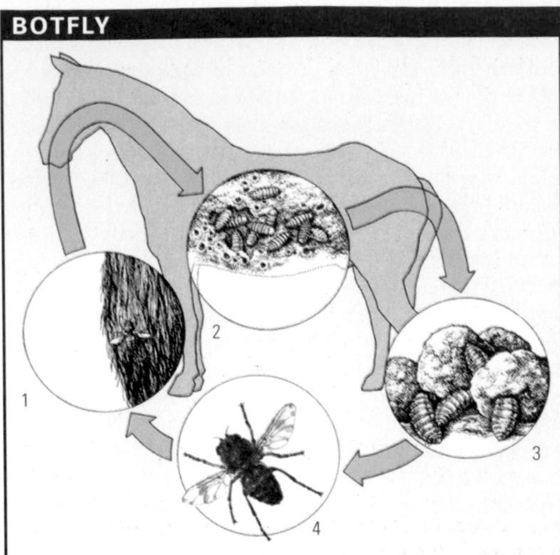


The families of botflies, Cuterebridae, Oestridae, and Gaterophilidae, are parasitic on humans, sheep, and horses respectively. The life cycle of the common horse botfly (*Gasterophilus intestinalis*) begins (1) as eggs are glued by the adult to the hairs, usually on the front legs of the horse. The stimulus of the moisture and friction provided by the horse's tongue when cleaning itself near the eggs causes the larvae to emerge and attach themselves to the animal's tongue and lips. The larvae pass to the stomach (2) where they attach themselves to the walls. The fully developed larvae release their hold on the walls and pass out with excrement (3). The larvae pupate in the ground and emerge as adults (4).

ation without representation." The Tea Act, passed by the British Parliament in 1773, withdrew duty on tea exported to the colonies. It enabled the EAST INDIA COMPANY to sell tea directly to the colonies without first going to Britain and resulted in colonial merchants being undersold. The protesters boarded three British ships and threw their cargo of tea into Boston harbor. The British retaliated by closing the harbor.

**Boswell, James** (1740–95) Scottish biographer and author. As a young man, he traveled widely in Europe, meeting VOLTAIRE and Jean-Jacques ROUSSEAU. An inveterate hero-worshiper, Boswell found his vocation as the friend and biographer of Samuel JOHNSON. His monumental *Life of Samuel Johnson* (1791) is regarded as one of the greatest biographies in English. Boswell's other works include *An Account of Corsica* (1768) and *The Journal of a Tour to the Hebrides* (1785), an account of his travels with Johnson. His often disconcertingly frank journals paint a colorful picture of contemporary life.

**Bosworth Field** English battleground, 12mi (19km) W of Leicester, England, where RICHARD III was defeated by Henry Tudor (1485). Henry, who claimed to represent the Lancastrian royal house, invaded England from France. Richard was killed, and Henry claimed the throne as HENRY VII.

**botanical garden** Large garden preserve for display, research, and teaching purposes. The first botanical gardens were established during the Middle Ages. In the 16th century, gardens existed in Pisa, Bologna, Padua, and Leiden. Aromatic and medicinal herbs still exist in the Botanical Garden of Padua. The first US botanical garden was established by John Bartram in Philadelphia in 1728. Famous botanical gardens include the Royal Botanical Gardens in Kew, near London (1759); Botanical Gardens of Berlin-Dahlem (1646); and Botanical Gardens in Schönbrunn, Vienna (1753).

**botany** Study of PLANTS and ALGAE, including their classification, structure, physiology, reproduction, and evolution. The disciplie used to be studied in two parts: lower (non-flowering) plants, which included the algae, mosses, and ferns; and higher (see-bearing) plants, including most flowers, trees, and shrubs. Botany also studies the importance of plants to humans.

**Botany Bay** Large, shallow inlet immediately S of Port Jackson, Sydney Harbor, New South Wales, Australia. It was visited in 1700 by Captain James COOK, who named it because of its flora. It is fed by the Georges and Woronora rivers, and is *c.*1mi (1.6km) wide at its mouth.

**botfly** Any of several families of stout, hairy, black-and-white to gray fly. Its larvae are parasites of livestock, small animals, and even humans. The botfly that attacks deer is possibly the swiftest insect, flying at 50mph (80km/h). Order Diptera; family Oestridae.

**Botha, Louis** (1862–1919) South African statesman and military leader. During the SOUTH AFRICAN WAR (1899–1902) he was an outstanding commander. A moderate, Botha advocated reconciliation with the British and in 1910 became first prime minister of the Union of SOUTH AFRICA.

**Botha, P.W. (Pieter Willem)** (1916– ) South African statesman. The longest-serving member of the APARTHEID regime, Botha entered parliament in 1948. As defense minister (1966–78), he increased South Africa's armed forces and was responsible for the military involvement in Angola. Botha became prime minister (1978) and undertook limited reform of apartheid. In 1980 he established the Southwest Africa Territorial Force, as part of a destabilization policy of South Africa's neighbors. Botha became (1980) South Africa's first president and was re-elected in 1987. In 1989 he suffered a stroke and, amid increasing National party factionalism, resigned and was replaced by F.W. DE KLERK.

**Bothe, Walther Wilhelm Georg Franz** (1891–1957) German physicist. During World War II he worked on Germany's nuclear energy project and built Germany's first cyclotron. Bothe shared the 1954 Nobel Prize for physics with Max BORN for his development of the coincidence method, which can detect two particles emitted simultaneously from the same nucleus during radioactive decay.

**Botswana** Landlocked republic in the heart of S Africa; the capital is GABORONE. **Land and climate** Most of the land is flat or gently rolling, with an average height of *c.*3,300ft (1,000m) with more hilly country in the E. The KALAHARI covers much of Botswana. Most of the S has no permanent streams, but large depressions form inland drainage basins in the N, such as the swamps of the Okavango River delta.

## BOTSWANA

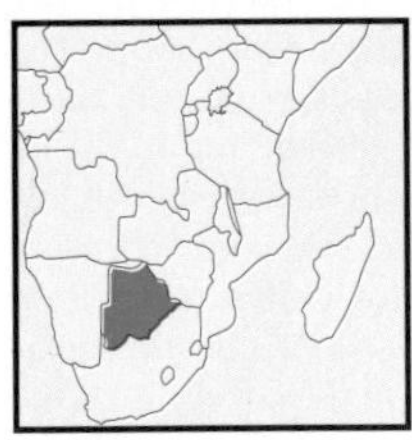

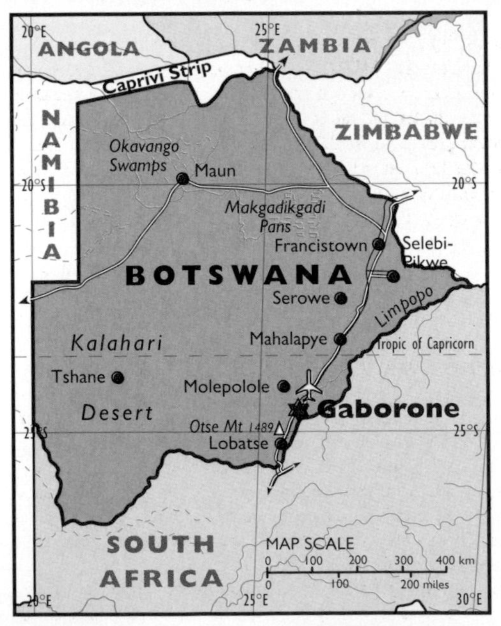


**AREA:** 224,606sq mi (581,730sq km)
**POPULATION:** 1,373,000
**CAPITAL (POPULATION):** Gaborone (138,471)
**GOVERNMENT:** Multiparty republic
**ETHNIC GROUPS:** Tswana 75%, Shona 12%, San (Bushmen) 3%
**LANGUAGES:** English (official), Setswana (national language)
**RELIGIONS:** Traditional beliefs 49%, Christianity 50%
**CURRENCY:** Pula = 100 thebe

Gaborone lies in the wetter and more populous E. Temperatures are high in the summer months (October–April), but winter months are much cooler. The average annual rainfall varies from more than 16in (400mm) in E Botswana to less than 18in (200mm) in the SW. **History** The earliest inhabitants of the region were the nomadic SAN. The Tswana now form the majority population. They settled in E Botswana more than 1,000 years ago. Their arrival led the San to move into the Kalahari. Today, the San form a tiny minority of the population, and many live in permanent settlements. Britain ruled the area as the Bechuanaland Protectorate between 1885–1966, when the country became the republic of Botswana. Botswana remains a stable multiparty democracy. **Economy** At the time of independence, Botswana was one of Africa's poorest countries. Many people migrated to work in the mines of South Africa. Today, Botswana is one of the continent's wealthiest nation, its economy boosted by the discovery of diamonds. It is the world's third-largest diamond producer. Diamonds account for 70% of its exports. Coal, copper and nickel are also valuable resources. Agriculture employs over 40% of the workforce.

**Botticelli, Sandro** (1444–1510) (Alessandro di Mariano Filipepi) Florentine RENAISSANCE painter. Loved by the PRE-RAPHAELITE BROTHERHOOD and an important influence on ART NOUVEAU, Botticelli was part of a late 15th-century movement which admired the ornamental, linear qualities of GOTHIC ART. He is best known for his mythological allegories, *Primavera* (*c*.1478), *The Birth of Venus*, and *Pallas and the Centaur*. Botticelli was one of the few privileged to decorate the Sistine Chapel in Rome (1481) and was the most popular painter in Florence. He made a series of delicate pen drawings for a copy of Dante's *Divine Comedy*.

**botulism** Rare but potentially lethal form of food poisoning caused by a toxin produced by the bacterium *Clostridium botulinum*. The toxin attacks the nervous system, causing paralysis and cessation of breathing. The most likely source of botulism is imperfectly canned meat. Botulinum toxin is used medicinally as a treatment for some neuromuscular disorders.

**Boucher, François** (1703–70) French painter, decorator, and engraver. Boucher's style was the epitome of ROCOCO frivolity and was distinctly risqué in tone. He was immensely successful and widely imitated. He produced over 11,000 historical, mythological, genre, and landscape paintings. Boucher was first painter to Louis XV.

**Boucicault, Dion (Dionysius Lardner)** (*c*.1822–90) Anglo-Irish playwright and actor-manager. Boucicault was responsible for the growth of the touring company. A prolific dramatist, he wrote and adapted nearly 300 plays. The most successful were his comedies and romantic melodramas, such as *London Assurance* (1841) and *The Octoroon* (1859). He was one of the greatest figures of Victorian theater.

**Bougainville, Louis Antoine de** (1729–1811) French navigator. A veteran of the French and Indian Wars in Canada, in 1763 Bougainville joined the navy and commanded the first French naval force to circumnavigate the globe (1766–69). Important botanical and astronomical studies were made during the voyage and he claimed many of the Pacific islands for France, rediscovering the Solomon Islands. He fought in the American Revolution, but was disgraced by a French defeat (1782) in the Caribbean.

**Bougainville** Volcanic island in the SW Pacific Ocean, E of New Guinea; a territory of Papua New Guinea. It was discovered in 1768 by Louis de BOUGAINVILLE. The island was under German control from 1884, and then under Australian administration after 1914 and again in 1945. It has been the scene of guerrilla warfare since the late 1980s. Kieta is the chief port. Industries: copper mining, copra, cocoa, timber. Area: 3,880sq mi (10,049sq km). Pop. (1990 est.) 128,000.

**bougainvillea** Tropical, flowering woody vine native to S America, often grown as a garden plant in warm climates. Its flowers have showy purple or red bracts. It was named for Louis de BOUGAINVILLE. Family Nyctaginaceae; genus *Bougainvillea*.

**Boulanger, Nadia** (1887–1979) French music teacher. She was one of the foremost teachers of composition in the 20th century; her pupils included Aaron Copland and Jean Françaix. In the 1930s Boulanger became the first woman to conduct the Boston Symphony Orchestra and the New York Philharmonic. Her sister, Lili Boulanger (1893–1918), was a composer.

**Boulez, Pierre** (1925– ) French conductor and composer. Boulez aimed to extend serialism into all aspects of a composition, including rhythm and dynamics. His works for voice and orchestra have received much attention, especially *Le Marteau sans maître* (1954) and *Pli selon pli* (1960). Boulez was conductor of the BBC Symphony Orchestra (1971–74) and the New York Philharmonic (1971–78). As director (1975– ) of the French Institute for Acoustic and Musical Research (IRCAM), he explored the use of computers in musical composition.

**Boulle (Buhl), André Charles** (1642–1732) French cabinetmaker maintained in the Louvre Palace by Louis XIV to design for the court. Boulle created a distinctive marquetry of tortoiseshell and gilded brass, to which he gave his name. There are examples of his work at Versailles and in the Louvre.

**Boult, Sir Adrian** (1889–1983) English conductor, widely known for his interpretation of early 20th-century English composers. Boult was musical director and principal conductor (1930–50) of the BBC Symphony Orchestra and principal conductor of the London Philharmonic Orchestra (1950–57).

**Bourbons** European dynastic family, descendants of the CAPETIANS. The ducal title was created in 1327 and continued until 1527. A cadet branch, the Bourbon-Vendôme line, won the kingdom of Navarre. The Bourbons ruled France from 1589 (when Henry of Navarre became HENRY IV) until the FRENCH REVOLUTION (1789). Two members of the family, LOUIS XVIII and CHARLES X, reigned (1814–30) after the restoration of the monarchy. The Bourbons became the ruling family of Spain in 1700 when PHILIP V, grandson of LOUIS XIV of France, assumed the throne. His descendants mostly continued to rule Spain until 1931, when the Second Republic was declared. JUAN CARLOS I, a Bourbon, was restored to the Spanish throne in 1975.

**bourgeoisie** (middle class) Term originally applied to artisans and craftsmen who lived in medieval French towns. Up to the late 18th century it was a propertied but relatively unprivileged class, often of urban merchants and tradesmen, who helped speed the decline of the FEUDAL SYSTEM. The 19th century advent of capitalism led to the expansion of the bourgeoise, and its division into the high (industrialists and financiers) and petty (tradesmen, clerical workers) bourgeoisie.

**Bourguiba, Habib** (1903– ) Tunisian statesman, first president of Tunisia (1957–87). In 1954 he began negotiations that culminated in Tunisian independence (1956). He became prime minister and, after the abolition of the monarchy, was elected president. In 1975 Bourguiba was proclaimed president-for-life. He maintained a pro-French, autocratic rule until, old and ill, he was overthrown in a coup led by Ben Ali.

**Bourke-White, Margaret** (1906–71) US photo-journalist. Bourke-White produced dramatic photo-essays for *Time*, *Life*, and *Fortune* magazines on a variety of subjects, including the rural South of the 1930s, World War II, concentration camp victims, the Korean War, South Africa, India, and world political leaders.

**Boutros-Ghali, Boutros** (1922– ) Egyptian statesman, sixth secretary-general of the UN (1992–96). As Egypt's foreign affairs minister (1977–91), he was involved in much of the Middle East peace negotiations. Boutros-Ghali briefly served as Egypt's prime minister (1991–92), before becoming the first African secretary general of the UN. Early in his term he faced civil-war crises in the Balkans, Somalia, and Rwanda. A fiercely independent secretary general, Boutros-Ghali managed to alienate US opinion.

**bovine spongiform encephalopathy (BSE)** In cattle, degeneration of the brains caused by infectious particles or PRIONS; it may be transmitted by feeding on infected meat. It is also known as "mad cow disease." *See also* CREUTZFELD-JAKOB DISEASE (CJD)

▲ **bowerbird** The tooth-billed bowerbird (*Scenopoeetes dentirostris*) is found in the highland forests of NE Australia. It grows up to 9in (23cm).

B

**bowerbird** Forest bird of New Guinea and Australia. The male builds a simple but brightly ornamented bower to attract the female. After mating, the female lays 1–3 eggs. Adults, mainly terrestrial, have short wings and legs, and variously colored plumage. Length: 10–15in (25-38cm). Family Ptilonorhynchidae.

**Bowie, David** (1947– ) British pop singer, b. David Jones. Fusing a bizarre theatricality to progressive pop, he graduated to international stardom with his record *Ziggy Stardust* (1972). Other records include *Hunky Dory* (1972) and *Heroes* (1977).

**Bowie, Jim (James)** (1796–1836) US frontiersman. He moved to Texas from Louisiana in 1828 and married the daughter of the Mexican vice-governor. By 1832 he had joined the US colonists who opposed the Mexican government. Bowie was appointed a colonel in the Texas army (1835) and killed at the ALAMO (1836).

**bowling** Indoor sport in which a ball is bowled at pins. It originated in Germany and was brought to the US by Dutch immigrants in the 17th century. Known as ninepins, it soon became a popular gambling game and, when it was banned, a tenth pin was added to circumvent the law. Ten-pin bowling is now an extremely popular sport. Two players or teams bowl at pins set on a triangular base. Points are scored according to the number of pins knocked over. *See also* SKITTLES

**bowls** Game popular in Britain and Commonwealth countries, in which a series of bowls (woods) are delivered underarm to stop as close as possible to a small white target ball (jack). A point is scored for each bowl closer to the jack than the best opposition bowl.

**box** Evergreen tree or shrub found in tropical and temperate regions in Europe, North American, and w Asia. The shrub is popular for TOPIARY, and boxwood is used for musical instruments. The 100 species include English or common *Buxus sempervirens* and larger *Buxus balearica* that grows to 80ft (24m). Family *Buxaceae*.

**boxer** Smooth-haired, working DOG bred originally in Germany. It has a broad head with a deep, short, square muzzle, and its deep-chested body is set on strong, medium-length legs. The tail is commonly docked, and its coat is generally red or brown, with black and white markings. Height: to 24in (61cm) at the shoulder.

**BRACHIOPODA**

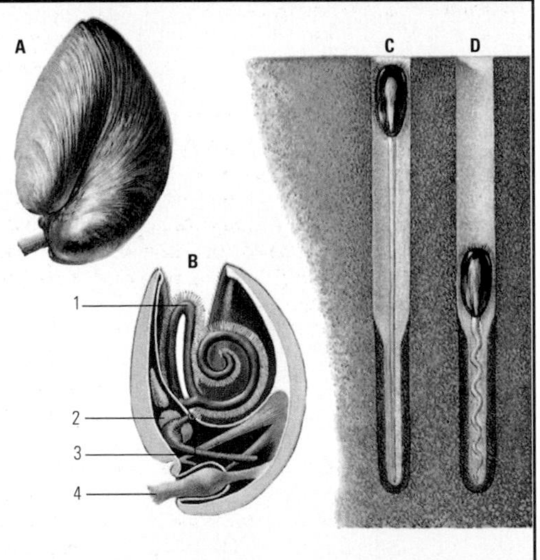

A
B
C
D
1
2
3
4

The marine animal known as a brachiopod, or lampshell, lives in holes in mudflats. It comprises (A) a hinged shell and a stalk with which it grips the rocks. The cross section (B) shows; lophophore (1) which bears ciliated tentacles for feeding; digestive gland (2); mouth (3) and stalks (4). When feeding *Lingula* (C), which resembles fossil forms of 500 million years ago, rests at the surface of its burrow using feathery cilia to filter water for food particles. When disturbed, its stalk contracts, drawing the animal into the burrow (D), out of sight and reach of its potential predator.

**Boxer Rebellion** (1900) European name for a Chinese revolt aimed at ousting foreigners from China. Forces led by the Society of Righteous and Harmonious Fists (hence the "Boxers") attacked Europeans and Chinese Christians, and besieged Beijing's foreign-legations enclave for two months. An international expeditionary force relieved the legations in August and suppressed the rising. China agreed to pay an indemnity.

**boxing** Sport of fistfighting between two people wearing padded gloves within a roped-off ring. Boxers are classified in eight divisions according to weight: minimum weight (under 105lb/48kg), fly, bantam, feather, light, welter, middle, and heavyweight (over 195lb/88kg). Professional bouts are scheduled for 4 to 15 rounds of three minutes' duration. A fight is controlled by a referee in the ring and ends when there is a knockout (a boxer is unable to get to his feet by the count of ten) or a technical knockout (one fighter is seriously injured). If both boxers finish the scheduled number of rounds, the winner is determined by a ringside referee or three judges. Boxing emerged from bareknuckle fighting when the Marquis of QUEENSBURY's rules introduced timed rounds and padded gloves in 1866. The international sport is now controlled by three major rival organizations: the World Boxing Association (WBA), the World Boxing Council (WBC), and the International Boxing Federation (IBF).

**box turtle** Turtle native to the US and Mexico with a hinge across the undershell, enabling front and back portions to close completely against the upper shell. All species have domed shells. They are terrestrial and eat animal and vegetable matter. Length: 5–6 in (127–153mm). Family Emydidae; genus *Terrapene*.

**boycott** Refusal to deal with a person, organization, or country, either in terms of trade or other activities such as sport. The term originated in 1880 when Irish tenant farmers refused to work for, supply, or speak with Captain Charles Boycott, an agent of their landlord. *See also* EMBARGO

**Boyd, William** (1952– ) British novelist and short-story writer, whose sometimes grimly comic works are often set in Africa, where he grew up. These include his first novel, *A Good Man in Africa* (1981), and *Brazzaville Beach* (1990). The location for *Stars and Bars* (1984) and *The Blue Afternoon* (1995) shifts to the US, and his most ambitious novel, *The New Confessions* (1987), ranges across the whole history of the 20th century.

**Boyle, Robert** (1627–91) British chemist, b. Ireland. He is often regarded as the father of modern chemistry. At his laboratories in Oxford and London, Boyle conducted research into air, vacuum, metals, combustion and sound. Boyle's *Sceptical Chymist* (1661) proposed an early atomic theory of MATTER. He made an efficient vacuum pump, which he used to establish (1662) BOYLE'S LAW. Boyle formulated the first chemical definitions of an element and a reaction.

**Boyle's law** Volume of a gas at constant temperature is inversely proportional to the pressure. This means as pressure increases, the volume of a gas at constant temperature decreases. First stated by Robert BOYLE in 1662, it is a special case of the ideal gas law (involving a hypothetical gas that perfectly obeys the gas laws).

**Boyne, Battle of the** (1690) Engagement near Drogheda, Ireland, which confirmed the Protestant succession to the English throne. The forces of the Protestant William III of England defeated those of the Catholic James II.

**Boy Scouts** Worldwide social organization for boys that stresses outdoor knowledge and good citizenship. It was founded (1908) in Britain by Lord BADEN-POWELL with the motto, "Be prepared." A companion organization for girls (Girl Scouts, US; Girl Guides, UK) was founded in 1910. By the 1990s the scouting movement had *c.*14 million members (including the Cub Scouts and Brownies) in more than 100 countries.

**Brabant** Province of central Belgium; the capital is BRUSSELS. Mainly Flemish-speaking, it is a densely populated and fertile agricultural region. Industries: chemicals, metallurgy, food processing. Area: 1,302sq mi (3,372sq km). Pop. (1970 est.) 2,178,000.

**brachiopoda** (lampshells) Phylum of *c*.260 species of small, bottom-dwelling, marine invertebrates. They are similar in outward appearance to BIVALVE MOLLUSKS, having a shell composed of two valves. They live attached to rocks by a pedicle (stalk), or buried in mud or sand. There are 75 genera including *Lingula*, the oldest known animal genus. Most modern brachiopods are less than 2in (5cm) across. More than 30,000 fossil species have been found and described.

**bracken** Persistent, weedy FERN found worldwide. It has an underground stem that can travel 6ft (1.8m) and sends up fronds that may reach 15ft (4.6m) in some climates. The *typica* variety is widespread in Britain. Family Dennstaedtiaceae; species *Pteridium aquilinum*.

**bracket fungus** (shelf fungus) Any of a large family (Polyporaceae) of common arboreal fungi that have spore-bearing tubes under the cap. Bracket fungi are usually hard and leathery or woodlike and have no stems. They often cover old logs and their parasitic activity may kill living trees. Some are edible when young.

**bract** Modified leaf found on a flower stalk or the flower base. Bracts are usually small and scalelike. In some species they are large and brightly colored, such as DOGWOOD and POINSETTIA.

**Bradbury, Ray Douglas** (1920– ) US novelist and short-story writer. Best known for his imaginative science fiction, Bradbury's most celebrated work includes *The Martian Chronicles* (1950), *Fahrenheit 451* (1953), and *Something Wicked This Way Comes* (1962). He has also written plays, poetry, children's stories, screenplays, and volumes of essays, such as *Journey to Far Metaphor* (1994).

**Bradford, William** (1590–1657) American colonial governor and signatory of the Mayflower Compact. He immigrated to America as one of the PILGRIMS on the *Mayflower* (1620). Bradford was elected governor of Plymouth Colony in 1621 and reelected for 30 years. He helped draw up a body of laws for the colony in 1636, and wrote a *History of Plymouth Plantation, 1620–46*.

**Bradford** City in the Aire Valley, West Yorkshire, N England. Since the 14th century it has been a center for woolen and worsted manufacturing, but industry has diversified. The city is home to one of England's largest communities from the Indian subcontinent. It has a university (established 1966). Industries: textiles, electrical engineering, microelectronics. Pop. (1991) 457,344.

**Bradley, Bill (William)** (1943– ) US basketball player and politician. Bradley played (1967–77) in the National Basketball Association (NBA) as a forward for the New York Knicks. He was elected to the Basketball Hall of Fame in 1983. Bradley served (1979–97) as a Democrat senator from New Jersey.

**Bradley, Omar Nelson** (1893–1981) US general. In World War II he commanded the 2nd Corps in N Africa and the invasion of Sicily (1943), and led the 1st Army in the Normandy invasion (1944). Bradley served (1948–49) as chief of staff of the US army and first chairman of the joint chiefs of staff (1949–53).

**Brady, Mathew B.** (1823–96) Pioneer US photographer. After studying the daguerreotype process with Samuel F.B. Morse, he became the leading US portraitist of his day. Brady organized a staff of photographers to make a record of the Civil War.

**bradycardia** Slowing of the heart rate to less than 50 beats per minute. It is often found in fit people, especially athletes, but is also seen as a symptom of various disorders, including some kinds of heart trouble.

**Braganza** Ruling dynasty of Portugal (1640–1910). The dynasty was founded by the Duke of Braganza, who ruled (1640–56) as John IV. During the NAPOLEONIC WARS, the royal family fled to Brazil, then a Portuguese colony. A branch of the house ruled as emperors of Brazil (1822–89).

**Bragg, Sir (William) Lawrence** (1890–1971) English physicist, b. Australia. He was director (1938–53) of the Cavendish Laboratory at Cambridge. With his father, Sir William Henry Bragg, he determined the mathematics involved in x-ray DIFFRACTION, showed how to compute x-ray wavelengths and studied CRYSTAL structure by x-ray diffraction. For these advances, they were jointly awarded the 1915 Nobel Prize for physics.

**Brahe, Tycho** (1546–1601) Danish astronomer. He became the most skilled observer of the pre-telescope era, expert in making accurate naked-eye measurements of the stars and planets. He built an observatory on the island of Hven (1576) and calculated the orbit of the comet seen in 1577. This, together with his study of the supernova, showed that ARISTOTLE was wrong in picturing an unchanging heaven. Brahe could not, however, accept the world system put forward by COPERNICUS. In his own planetary theory (the Tychonian system), the planets move around the Sun, and the Sun itself, like the Moon, moves round the stationary Earth. In 1597 he settled in Prague, where Johann KEPLER became his assistant.

**Brahma** Creator god in HINDUISM, later identified as one of the three gods in the Trimurti. Brahma is usually thought equal to the gods VISHNU and SHIVA, but later myths tell of him being born from Vishnu's navel. There is only one major temple to Brahma, located at Pushkar, Rajasthan, NW India.

**Brahman** (Atman) In HINDUISM, the supreme soul of the universe. The omnipresent Brahman sustains the Earth. According to the UPANISHADS, the individual soul is identified with Brahman. Brahman is not God, but rather is *neti neti* (not this, not that) or indescribable.

**Brahman cattle** (zebu) Many domestic varieties of a species of OX native to India. Tan, gray, or black with a hump over the shoulders, brahmans have drooping ears and a large dewlap. Family Bovidae; species *Bos indicus*.

**Brahmanism** Term denoting an early phase of HINDUISM. It was characterized by acceptance of the VEDAS as divine revelation. The Brahmanas, the major text of Brahmanism, are the ritualistic books comprising the greater portion of Vedic literature. They were complemented by the UPANISHADS. In the course of time deities of post-Vedic origin began to be worshiped and the influence of Brahmanist priests declined.

**Brahmaputra** River in S Asia. Rising in SW Tibet, it flows E into China, then S into India and WSW across India into Bangladesh (where it becomes the YAMUNA River). Before emptying into the Bay of BENGAL, it forms (with the GANGES and Meghna rivers) a vast delta. Length: *c*.1,800mi (2,900km).

**Brahmin** (Brahman) Priestly CASTE that was the highest-ranking of the four *varnas* (social classes) in India during the late Vedic period, the era of BRAHMANISM. The term also denotes a member of that caste. Brahmin were believed to be ritually purer than other castes, and they alone could perform certain spiritual and ritual duties. The recitation of the VEDAS was their preserve, and for hundreds of years they were the only caste to receive an education and so controlled Indian scholarship. With the later development of HINDUISM as a popular religion, their priestly influence declined, but their secular influence grew, and their social supremacy and privileged status have changed little over the centuries.

**Brahms, Johannes** (1833–97) German composer. Encouraged by his friends Robert and Clara Schumann, Brahms began to earn his living as a composer at the age of 30. He used classical forms rather than the less-strict programmatic style that was becoming popular, and was a master of contrapuntal HARMONY. Brahms composed in all major musical genres except opera. Among his major works are the *German Requiem* (1868), the *Variations on the St. Antony Chorale* (1863), the Violin Concerto in D (1878), four symphonies (1876–1885), two piano concertos (1858, 1881), and *Hungarian Dances* (1873).

**Braille** System of reading and writing for the blind. It was invented by Louis Braille (1809–52), who lost his sight at the age of three. Braille was a scholar, and later a teacher, at the National Institute of Blind Youth, Paris. He developed a system of embossed dots to enable blind people to read by touch. This was first published in 1829, and a more complete form appeared in 1837.

**brain** Mass of nerve tissue which regulates all physical and mental activity; it is continuous with the spinal cord. Weighing *c*.3.3lb (1.5kg) in the adult (*c*.2% of body weight), the

B

human brain has three parts: the **hindbrain**, where basic physiological processes such as breathing and the heartbeat are coordinated; the **midbrain** links the hindbrain and the **forebrain**, which is the seat of all higher functions and attributes (personality, intellect, memory, emotion), as well as being involved in sensation and initiating voluntary movement. *See also* CENTRAL NERVOUS SYSTEM; CEREBRUM

**brain damage** Result of any harm done to brain tissue causing the death of nerve cells. It may arise from a number of causes, such as oxygen deprivation, brain or other disease, or head injury. The nature and extent of damage varies. Sudden failure of the oxygen supply to the brain may result in widespread (global) damage, whereas a blow to the head may affect only one part of the brain (local damage). Common effects of brain damage include weakness of one or more limbs, impaired balance, memory loss, and personality change; epilepsy may develop.

**brain disorder** Disturbance of physical or mental function due to abnormality or disease of the brain. Brain disorders should be distinguished from psychological (psychogenic) mental disturbances in which the functioning of the brain itself is not impaired. Brain disorders are associated with impairment of memory, orientation, comprehension, and judgment, and also by shallowness of emotional expression. Secondary personality changes may occur, depending upon such factors as the strength and type of personality and the amount of psychological and social stress present. **Acute** disorders are temporary, and are generally due to disruption of brain function rather than destruction of brain tissue. They may be caused by such things as infection, drug intoxication, and brain trauma. **Chronic** brain disorders are irreversible, and include such things as CONGENITAL DISORDER, hereditary disease, senility, and BRAIN DAMAGE.

**BRAIN**

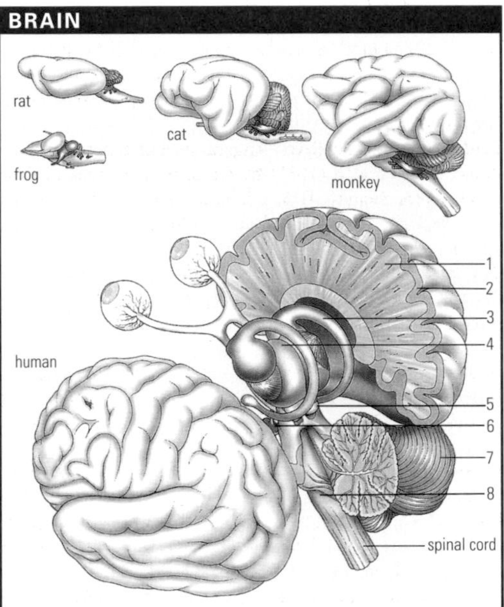


The vertebrate brain has three major structural and functional regions – the forebrain, the midbrain, and the hindbrain. In primitive animals, such as amphibians, the forebrain is concerned with smell, the midbrain with vision and the hindbrain with balance and hearing. In higher animals, such as rats, cats, monkeys and humans, parts of the brain have adapted to meet the needs of the organism. Most notably, part of the forebrain, the cerebrum (1), developed into a complex, deeply fissured structure. It comprises large regions concerned with association, reasoning, and judgment. Its outer layer, the cortex (2), contains areas that coordinate movement and sensory information. The limbic system (3) controls emotional responses, such as fear. The thalamus (4) coordinates sensory and motor signals, and relays them to the cerebrum: the hypothalamus (5) along with the pituitary glands control the body's hormonal system. Visual, tactile, and auditory inputs are coordinated by the tectum (6), part of the midbrain. In the hindbrain, the cerebellum (7) controls the muscle activity needed for refined limb movements and maintaining posture. The medulla (8) contains reflex centers that are involved in respiration, heartbeat regulation, and gastric function.

**brain stem** Stalk-like portion of the BRAIN in vertebrates that includes everything except the CEREBELLUM and the CEREBRAL HEMISPHERES. It provides a channel for all signals passing between the spinal cord and the higher parts of the brain. It also controls automatic functions such as breathing and heartbeat.

**Brain Trust** (1933–35) Name given to the advisers of US President Franklin ROOSEVELT. It first described his closest advisers in the presidential campaign of 1932. Later, the term was applied more widely to members of his administration who advised on the policies of the NEW DEAL.

**brake** Device for slowing the speed of a vehicle or machine. Braking can be accomplished by a mechanical, hydraulic (liquid), or pneumatic (air) system that presses a non-rotating part into contact with a rotating part, so that friction stops the motion. Some vehicles use electromagnetic effects to oppose the motion and cause braking. A "power" brake utilizes a vacuum system.

**Bramante, Donato** (1444–1514) Italian architect and painter. Bramante was the greatest exponent of High RENAISSANCE architecture. In 1506, he started rebuilding St. Peter's in Rome. His influence was enormous and many Milanese painters took up his interest in perspective and *trompe l'oeil.*

**Branagh, Kenneth** (1960– ) Northern Irish actor and director. He worked with the Royal Shakespeare Company (RSC) before leaving to form the Renaissance Theatre Company. He moved into directing with the film *Henry V* (1989), receiving Academy Award nominations for Best Actor and Best Director. Branagh's success in popularizing Shakespeare continued with *Much Ado About Nothing* (1993), *Othello* (1996), and *Hamlet* (1997).

**Branch Davidians** Late 20th-century religious cult. A breakaway branch of the SEVENTH-DAY ADVENTISTS, the cult had its headquarters near WACO, Texas, and was led by David Koresh, who claimed to be the reincarnated Jesus Christ. On February 28, 1993, following the shooting of federal officers, the cult was besieged by FBI agents. On April 19, 1993, a fire suddenly broke out and the corpses of more than 80 cult members, including Koresh, were found.

**Brancusi, Constantin** (1876–1957) French sculptor. Brancusi's primitive style is revealed in a series of wooden sculptures, including *Chimera* (1918). In 1919 his *Bird in Space* was not permitted into the US as a work of art, but was taxed on its value as raw metal. This decision was reversed in a suit filed by Brancusi, and the sculpture is now housed in the Museum of Modern Art, New York City. Other works include *The Kiss* (1908), *Prometheus* (1911), and *Flying Turtle* (1943).

**Brandeis, Louis Dembitz** (1856–1941) US jurist and lawyer, associate justice (1916–39) of the US Supreme Court. Brandeis became known as the "people's attorney." An advisor to President Wilson, he was instrumental in creating the Federal Reserve Act (1913) and Clayton Anti-Trust Act (1914). The first Jew to sit on the US Supreme Court, Brandeis was noted for his dissents favoring civil liberties and social welfare legislation. **Brandenburg** State in NE Germany; the capital is POTSDAM. The region formed the nucleus for the kingdom of Prussia. The March of Brandenburg was founded in 1134 by Albert I (the Bear). It came under the rule of the Hohenzollerns in 1411, and in 1417 Frederick I became the first elector of Brandenburg. Frederick II became the first king of Prussia in 1701. Pop. (1993 est.) 2,543,000

**Brando, Marlon** (1924– ) US actor. In 1951 a reprise of his Broadway role in the film *A Streetcar Named Desire* earned him the first of four consecutive Academy Award nominations. Brando finally won his first Best Actor Oscar in *On the*

B

*Waterfront* (1954). He was awarded a second Best Actor Oscar for *The Godfather* (1971), but refused the award in protest against the persecution of Native Americans. He received another Oscar nomination for his role in *Last Tango in Paris* (1972). Other supporting credits include *Apocalypse Now* (1979), and an Oscar-nominated performance in *A Dry White Season* (1989).

**Brandt, Bill** (1904–83) British photographer. He assisted Man RAY in Paris (1929–30), before returning to London where he developed a reputation as a social commentator, as shown in his collection of photographs *The English at Home* (1936). During the war he documented life during the Blitz. Brandt is perhaps better known for his nudes.

**Brandt, Willy** (1913–92) German statesman, chancellor of West Germany (1969–74), b. Karl Herbert Frahm. An active Social Democrat, he fled to Norway and then Sweden during the Nazi era. Brandt returned to Germany after World War II and was elected mayor of West Berlin in 1957. In national politics he was foreign minister (1966–68). As chancellor, he initiated a program of cooperation with the Communist bloc states, for which he was awarded the Nobel Peace Prize in 1971. Brandt resigned after a close aide was exposed as an East German spy.

**brandy** Alcoholic spirit made by distilling the fermented juice of a fruit, especially grapes in the form of wine. Armagnac and cognac are famous French wine brandies, with an alcohol content of 42%–44%. Marc is a French brandy distilled from grape mush or pomace. Applejack and calvados are brandies distilled from fermented apple juice. Other well known fruit brandies are kirsch (cherries), slivovitz (plums) and peach, apricot, cherry, and blackberry brandies.

**Brant, Joseph** (1742–1807) Mohawk chief. Brant served in the FRENCH AND INDIAN WARS (1754–63) and in PONTIAC'S REBELLION (1763–66). He attended an Anglican school and became an interpreter for missionaries. In return for securing an alliance between the Iroquois and the British he gained a commission in the British army in 1775. He fought with outstanding courage for the British during the American Revolution.

**Braque, Georges** (1882–1963) French painter who created CUBISM with PICASSO. *Head of a Woman* (1909), *Violin and Palette* (1909–10), and *The Portuguese* (1911) show his transition through the early, analytical phases of cubism. Braque was badly wounded in World War I, and afterward evolved a gentler style of painting which earned him enormous prestige. He concentrated on still-life subjects.

**Brasília** Capital of Brazil, in W central Brazil. Although the city was originally planned in 1891, building did not start until 1956. The city was laid out in the shape of an aircraft, and Oscar NIEMEYER designed the modernist public buildings. It was inaugurated as the capital in 1960. Pop. (1991) 1,596,274.

**Braşov** City at the foot of the Transylvanian Alps, E central Romania. Founded in the 13th century by Teutonic knights, many of Braşov's inhabitants are of German descent. It was held by Hungary until 1918, when it was ceded to Romania. During the 1950s the city was known as Orasul Stalin. Today, Braşov is Romania's second-largest city and a major industrial center and winter sports resort. Pop. (1992) 323,835.

**brass** Alloy of mainly copper (55%–95%) and zinc (5%–45%). Brass is yellowish or reddish, malleable and ductile, and can be hammered, machined, or cast. Its properties can be altered by varying the amounts of copper and zinc, or by adding other metals, such as tin, lead, and nickel. Brass is widely used for pipe and electrical fittings, ornamental metalwork, and musical instruments.

**brass** Family of musical wind instruments made of metal and played by means of a cupped or funnel-shaped mouthpiece. Simple brass instruments, such as the BUGLE, produce a limited range of harmonics corresponding to the length of the tube. In most other brass instruments, the length of the air column can be altered by valves or slides to produce the full range of notes. The chief brass instruments of a symphony orchestra are the TRUMPET, FRENCH HORN, TROMBONE, and TUBA.

◄ **Brando** Although considered one of America's greatest screen actors, Marlon Brando's personal life has been interspersed with tragedy, culminating in the imprisonment of his son Christian for the murder of the boyfriend of his half-sister, Cheyenne.

**Brassäi** (1899–1984) French photographer and painter, b. Hungary as Guyla Halasz. Arriving in Paris in 1923, he worked as a journalist and painter, associating with Picasso and Dali. Brassäi turned to photography in 1930, concentrating on pictures of Paris nightlife and portraits.

**brassica** Genus of plants with edible roots or leaves. It includes cabbages, cauliflowers, Brussels sprouts (all subspecies of *Brassica oleracea*), turnip (*B.rapa*), and rutabaga (*B. napobrassica*). Some, such as broccoli, have edible flowerheads. Family Brassicaceae/Cruciferae.

**Bratislava** Capital of Slovakia, on the Danube River, W Slovakia. It became part of Hungary after the 13th century, and was the Hungarian capital from 1526 to 1784. Incorporated into Czechoslovakia in 1918, it become the capital of Slovakia in 1992. Industries: oil refining, textiles. Pop. (1990) 440,421.

**Bratsk** City on the River Angara, central Siberia, Russia. Bratsk was founded (1631) by Cossacks and ruins of their watchtowers remain. Today, it is the site of an enormous hydroelectric plant. Industries: metallurgy, cellulose, construction. Pop. (1992) 259,000.

**Brattain, Walter Houser** (1902–87) US physicist. He shared the 1956 Nobel Prize for physics with John BARDEEN and William SHOCKLEY for their development of the TRANSISTOR and research into semiconductivity.

**Braun, Eva** (1912–45) Mistress of Adolf HITLER. She met Hitler in the early 1930s and they lived together for the rest of their lives. They married in Berlin the day before committing suicide.

**Braun, Wernher von** (1912–77) US rocket engineer, b. Germany. He perfected the V-2 rocket missiles in the early 1940s. In 1945 he went to the US, becoming a citizen in 1955. In 1958 von Braun was largely responsible for launching the first US satellite, *Explorer 1*. He later worked on the development of the *Saturn* rocket (for the Apollo program) and was deputy associate administrator (1970–72) of the NATIONAL AERONAUTICS AND SPACE ADMINISTRATION (NASA).

**Brazil** Republic in E South America. *See* country feature page 104

**Brazil nut** Seed of an evergreen tree, which has leathery leaves and grows to 135ft (41m) tall. Its flowers produce a thick-walled fruit 4–12in (10–30.5cm) in diameter which contain 25–40 large seeds. Family Lecythidaceae; species *Bertholletia excelsa*.

**brazing** Process in which metallic parts are joined by the fusion of alloys that have lower melting points than the parts themselves. The bonding alloy is either preplaced or fed into the joint as the parts are heated. Brazed joints are used extensively in the aerospace industry.

**Brazzaville** Capital and largest city of the Congo, W Africa, on the Congo River. Founded in 1880, it was capital (1910–58) of French Equatorial Africa. It has a university (1972) and a cathedral. It is a major port, connected by rail to the main Atlantic seaport of Pointe-Noire. Industries: foundries, chemicals, shipyards. Pop. (1992) 937,579.

**bread** Staple food made by mixing flour (containing a little yeast, salt, and sugar) with water to make a dough, allowing the yeast to ferment carbohydrates in the mixture (thus providing carbon-dioxide gas which leavens the bread), and finally baking in an oven. Bicarbonate of soda ($NaHCO_3$)

▲ **brazil** Brazil-nut trees (genus *Bertholletia*) are found along the banks of the Amazon and Orinoco rivers in Brazil. They grow in clumps and are a valuable source of natural oils.

The green symbolizes Brazil's rain forests, the yellow diamond its mineral wealth. The blue sphere bears the motto "Order and Progress". The 27 stars, arranged in the pattern of the night sky over Rio de Janeiro, represent the states and the federal district.

**AREA:** 3,286,472sq mi (8,511,970sq km)
**POPULATION:** 156,275,000
**CAPITAL (POPULATION):** Brasília (1,596,274)
**GOVERNMENT:** Federal republic
**ETHNIC GROUPS:** White 53%, Mulatto 22%, Mestizo 12%, African American 11%, Japanese 1%, Native American 0.1%
**LANGUAGES:** Portuguese (official)
**RELIGIONS:** Christianity (Roman Catholic 88%, Protestant 6%)
**CURRENCY:** Cruzeiro real

The Federative Republic of Brazil is the world's fifth largest country, accounting for 48% of South America. Brazil contains three main regions. The AMAZON basin, which is drained by a river system that carries a fifth of the world's running water, covers more than half of the country. The Amazon is the world's second longest river, though it has a far greater volume than any other river.

Brazil's second region is the NE, which consists of a coastal plain and the sertão, the inland plateaus and hill country. The main river in this region is the São Francisco. The third region is made up of the plateaus in the SE. This region, which covers about a quarter of the entire country, is the most developed and densely populated part of Brazil, and includes the cities of SÃO PAULO, RIO DE JANEIRO, SALVADOR, BELO HORIZONTE, and the capital, Brasília. Its main river is the PARANÁ, which flows S through Argentina.

### CLIMATE

Brazil lies almost entirely within the tropics and the average monthly temperatures are high, over 68°F (20°C), with little seasonal variation. The hottest regions are the arid NE lowlands and the Amazon basin. Most areas have moderate rainfall with a dry season in the months May to September.

### VEGETATION

The Amazon basin contains the world's largest rain forests, the *selvas*. The forests contain a huge variety of plant and animal species, but many species are threatened by loggers, ranchers, mining companies, government hydroelectric projects, and even landless migrants, all of them wanting to exploit the region. Forest destruction is also ruining the lives of the last surviving groups of Native Amazonians.

Forests grow on the NE coasts, but the dry interior has large areas of thorny scrub. The

## BRAZIL

SE contains fertile farmland and large ranches. A large, swampy area is located along Brazil's borders with Bolivia and Paraguay, S of the Mato Grosso.

### HISTORY

The Portuguese explorer Pedro Alvarez CABRAL claimed Brazil for Portugal in 1500. With Spain occupied in W South America, the Portuguese began to develop their colony, which was more than 90 times as big as Portugal. To do this, they enslaved many Native Americans and introduced about 4 million African slaves to work on their plantations and in the mines.

Brazil declared itself an independent empire in 1822. The first emperor, PEDRO I, was the son of King Joãs VI of Portugal. He was forced to resign in 1831 and the throne passed to his son, PEDRO II. During his long reign slavery was gradually abolished, finally coming to an end in 1888. Brazil adopted a federal system of government in 1881. In 1889 it became a republic and began a program of economic development.

### POLITICS

From the 1930s, Brazil faced many political problems, including social unrest, corruption, and frequent spells of dictatorial government by military leaders. A new constitution, which came into force in 1988, took powers from the president and transferred many of them to Congress (the parliament, consisting of an elected Senate and Chamber of Deputies). This constitution paved the way for a return to a shaky democracy in 1990. In 1995 Fernando Henrique Cardoso was elected president. In 1998 Cardosa was re-elected on a platform of austerity measures.

### ECONOMY

Brazil is a rapidly industrializing country( 1995 GDP percapita is $5,400). Its total volume of production is one of the largest in the world, but most of its people, including poor farmers and residents of the favelas (city slums), do not share in the country's fast economic growth. High rates of inflation and unemployment have caused widespread poverty and serious social and political problems.

By the early 1990s industry had become the most valuable activity, employing 25% of the people. Brazil is among the world's top producers of bauxite, chrome, diamonds, gold, iron ore, manganese, and tin. It is also a major manufacturing country, the products including aircraft, cars, chemicals, raw sugar, iron and steel, paper, and textiles.

Brazil is one of the world's leading farming countries, and agriculture employs 28% of the country's population. It is the world's largest coffee producer and a major exporter. Other leading products include bananas, citrus fruits, cocoa, corn, rice, soybeans, and sugarcane. Brazil is the top producer of eggs, meat, and milk in South America.

Forestry is a major industry, though many people fear that the exploitation of the rain forests, with 1.5% to 4% of the trees being destroyed every year, is a disaster for the entire world. Brazil may gain financially in the short term, but it may find the markets for the products have disappeared.

**Education** has long been regarded as an essential part of any development strategy in the developing world, because progress is impossible without a skilled workforce. Brazil has a good record in education, with around 80% of adults able to read and write. The stamp, issued in 1974, commemorates the bicentenary of a college.

may be used instead of yeast. Unleavened bread, favored in many Asian countries, is flat in shape and heavy.

**breadfruit** Starchy fruit of a tree of the MULBERRY family (Moraceae) native to SE Asia. The pulp is eaten fresh or cooked, or ground up and baked to make bread. Genus *Atocarpus*.

**Breakspear, Nicholas** *See* ADRIAN IV

**Bream, Julian Alexander** (1933– ) English guitarist and lutenist. He studied (1945–48) at the Royal College of Music. An outstanding classical guitarist, Bream has had pieces composed for him by, among others, Benjamin BRITTEN and William WALTON.

**bream** Freshwater fish of E and N Europe. Its stocky body is green-brown and silver, and anglers prize it for its tasty flesh. Length: 12–20in (30–50cm); weight: 9–13lb (4– 6kg). Family Cyprinidae; species *Abramis brama*.

**breast** (mammary gland) Organ of a female mammal that secretes milk to nourish newborn young. In males the glands are rudimentary and nonfunctional. The human female breast, which develops during puberty, is made up of about 15–20 irregularly shaped lobes separated by connective and fat tissues. Lactiferous ducts lead from each lobe to the nipple.

**breathing** Process by which air is taken into and expelled from the LUNGS for the purpose of GAS EXCHANGE. During inhalation, the intercostal muscles raise the ribs, increasing the volume of the THORAX and drawing air into the lungs. During exhalation, the ribs are lowered, and air is forced out.

**breccia** Rock formed by the cementation of sharp-angled fragments in a finer matrix of the same or different material. It is formed either inside the Earth by movements of the crust, from scree slopes, or from volcanic material. *See also* CONGLOMERATE

**Brecht, Bertolt** (1898–1956) German playwright, poet, and drama theorist. One of the most influential dramatists of the 20th century, his early plays, such as *Baal* (1918), won praise for their radicalism. In the 1920s, Brecht developed his distinctive, politicized theory of EPIC THEATER. It encouraged audiences to see theater as staged illusion via a range of "alienation" techniques. His major works were written in collaboration with composers: Kurt WEILL, *The Threepenny Opera* (1928); Hanns Eisler, *The Mother* (1931); and Paul Dessau, *The Caucasian Chalk Circle* (1948). With the rise of Hitler in 1933, Brecht's Marxist

## BREAST

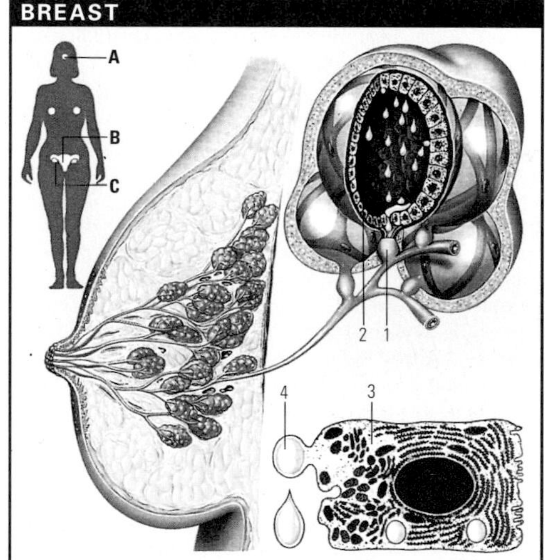


The mammary glands are composed of a mass of epithelial ducts (1) (shown enlarged) surrounded by a fibrous tissue. In females these ducts enlarge and spread, differentiating into milk-producing tissue. This process occurs under complex hormonal control from the anterior and posterior pituitary glands (A), the placenta during pregnancy (B), and from the ovaries (C). Full development of the glands involves extensive growth of mammary ducts from which specialized lobules proliferate (shown magnified x2). Each lobule, lined by milk-producing cells (shown magnified x3), opens into the ducts leading to the gland nipple. Three to four days after childbirth, milk containing fat droplets (4) and protein is available to the child.

views forced him into exile. While in the US, he wrote *Mother Courage and Her Children* (1941) and *The Good Woman of Setzuan* (1943). In 1949 Brecht returned to East Germany to direct the Berliner Ensemble.

**Breckinridge, John Cabell** (1821–75) American statesman, vice president (1857–61). He was a major in the MEXICAN WAR and a congressman (1851), before being elected vice president under James BUCHANAN. Defeated as a pro-slavery presidential candidate in 1860 by Abraham LINCOLN, Breckinridge became a Confederate general and secretary of war in Jefferson DAVIS' cabinet (1865).

**Breda** City in Noord-Brabant province, s Netherlands. It is noted for the 1566 Compromise of Breda (a Dutch alliance against Spanish rule) and Charles II's Declaration of Breda (1660) before the Restoration. Industries: engineering, textiles. Pop. (1994) 129,125.

**Breda, Treaty of** (1667) Peace agreement that ended the Second DUTCH WARS with England. England gave up its claim to the Dutch East Indies but gained control of New York and New Jersey.

**breeding** Process of producing offspring, specifically the science of changing or promoting certain genetic characteristics in animals and plants. Breeding may involve CROSSBREEDING or INBREEDING to produce the desired characteristics. Scientific breeding has resulted in disease-resistant strains of crops, and in animals that give improved food yields. *See also* GENE; GENETIC ENGINEERING

**Bremen** City on the Weser River; capital of Bremen state, N Germany. The city suffered severe damage during World War II, but many of its original buildings (including the Gothic city hall) survived. Industries: shipbuilding, electrical equipment, textiles. Pop. (1990) 553,200.

**Brendel, Alfred** (1931– ) Austrian pianist. One of the world's most critically acclaimed and widely traveled concert artists, Brendel is especially noted for his interpretations of Beethoven and Schubert.

**Brest** (formerly Brest-Litovsk) City and port at the confluence of the Bug and Muchavec rivers, near the Polish border, w Belarus. It was the site of the signing of the Treaty of BREST-LITOVSK. Industries: food processing, sawmilling, textiles. Pop. (1991) 277,000.

**Brest** City and port on the Atlantic coast of Brittany, w France. An important naval base, the town was severely damaged in World War II, when used as a German submarine base. Industries: shipbuilding and repair, chemical manufacture. Pop. (1990) 147,956.

**Brest-Litovsk, Treaty of** (March 1918) Peace treaty between Russia and the CENTRAL POWERS, confirming Russian withdrawal from World War I. The Ukraine and Georgia became independent and Russian territory was surrendered to Germany and Austria-Hungary.

**Breton, André** (1896–1966) French poet and theorist. A founder and poet of the SURREALISM movement, Breton wrote *Manifeste du surréalisme* (1924) and *Le Surréalisme et la Peinture* (1928).

**Breton** Celtic language spoken in Brittany, on the NW coast of France. It is a descendant of British, an old Celtic language, and is closely related to Welsh. Its approximately half a million users usually also speak French, which is rapidly replacing it.

**Bretton Woods Conference** (officially the United Nations Monetary and Financial Conference) It met at Bretton Woods, New Hampshire, in July 1944. It was summoned on the initiative of President Franklin ROOSEVELT to establish a system of international monetary cooperation and prevent severe financial crises such as that of 1929, which had precipitated the GREAT DEPRESSION. Representatives of 44 countries agreed to establish the INTERNATIONAL MONETARY FUND (IMF) and the International Bank for Reconstruction and Development, or WORLD BANK, to provide credit to states requiring financial investment in major economic projects.

**Breuer, Marcel** (1902–81) US architect and designer, b. Hungary. One of the great innovators of modern furniture design, Breuer studied and taught (1920–28) at the BAUHAUS, where he created his famous tubular steel chair. In 1937, he settled in the US and subsequently worked with Walter GROPIUS as a partner in architectural projects. He designed the Whitney Museum of American Art in New York (1966).

**brewing** Preparation of BEER and stout by using YEAST as a catalyst in the alcoholic fermentation of liquors containing malt and hops. In beer brewing, a malt liquor (wort) is made from crushed germinated barley grains. Hops are added to the boiling wort both to impart a bitter flavor, and also to help to clarify the beer and keep it free from spoilage by microbes. The clear, filtered wort is cooled and inoculated with brewer's yeast.

**Brezhnev, Leonid Ilyich** (1906–82) Soviet statesman, effective ruler from the mid-1960s until his death. Brezhnev rose through the Communist Party of the Soviet Union (CPSU) to become a member of the presidium (later politburo) (1957). In 1964 he helped plan the downfall of Nikita KHRUSHCHEV and became party general secretary, at first sharing power with Aleksei KOSYGIN. In 1977 Brezhnev became president of the Soviet Union. He pursued a hard line against reforms at home and in Eastern Europe, but also sought to reduce tensions with the West. After the Soviet invasion of CZECHOSLOVAKIA (1968), he promulgated the "Brezhnev Doctrine" confirming Soviet domination of satellite states, as seen in the 1979 invasion of Afghanistan.

**Briand, Aristide** (1862–1932) French statesman. A moderate, he was premier of 11 governments between 1909 and 1929. Briand advocated international cooperation and was one of the instigators of the LOCARNO PACT (1925), for which he shared the Nobel Peace Prize with Gustav STRESEMANN in 1926. He was also one of the authors of the KELLOGG-BRIAND PACT of 1928.

**Brice, Fanny** (1891–1951) US comedienne. While in VAUDEVILLE, Brice was discovered by Florenz Ziegfeld and joined his "Follies." In 1937 she created the character of "Baby Snooks" for radio. Brice's life and career formed the basis for the musical comedy, *Funny Girl* (1964).

**brick** Hardened block of clay used for building and paving. Usually rectangular, bricks are made in standard sizes by machines that either mold or cut off extruded sections of stiff clay. The first, sun-dried, bricks were used in the Tigris-Euphrates basin *c.*5,000 years ago.

**bridge** Structure providing a continuous passage over a body of water, roadway, or valley. Bridges are prehistoric in origin, the first probably being merely logs. Modern bridges take a great variety of forms including beams, arches, cantilevers, suspension bridges, and cable-stayed bridges. They can also be movable or floating pontoons. They can be made from a variety of materials, including brick or stone (for arches), steel, or concrete.

**bridge** Card game for four players. **Contract** bridge is the most international of card games, with Olympiads and world championships. It evolved from **auction** bridge, invented by the British in India. Opposite players are partners, and after the cards are dealt, each pair bids for the contract; a bid is a claim of how many "tricks" (rounds of play) will be won. The winner of the bidding must then attempt to win the number of tricks bid.

**Bridgeport** City on Long Island Sound, sw Connecticut. Settled in 1639 as a fishing community, it is now a port of entry and the chief industrial city in Connecticut. Industries: electrical appliances, transport equipment, helicopters, machine tools. Pop. (1990) 141,686.

**Bridger, Jim (James)** (1804–81) Frontiersman and scout. Bridger was the first white explorer to find the Great Salt Lake (1824), South Pass through the Rockies, and the area now Yellowstone Park. In 1843 he built Fort Bridger in sw Wyoming to supply settlers traveling West on the Oregon Trail.

**Bridgetown** Capital and port of Barbados, in the West Indies. Founded in 1628, it is the seat of Parliament. Industries: rum distilling, sugar processing, tourism. Pop. (1990 est.) 6,720.

**Bright, John** (1811–89) British parliamentary reformer. A Quaker, he and his fellow radical, Richard COBDEN, were leaders of the ANTI-CORN LAW LEAGUE (founded 1839). First elected to Parliament in 1843, Bright subsequently represented Manchester, the home of FREE TRADE. He lost his seat in 1857 after opposing the Crimean War but was reelected for Birmingham.

**Brighton** Resort town on the English Channel, East Sussex, S England. Originally a fishing village, it was popularized as a resort by the Prince Regent (George IV), who had the Royal Pavilion rebuilt here in oriental style by John Nash. It is the seat of the University of Sussex (1961) and the University of Brighton (1992). Industries: food processing, furniture, tourism. Pop. (1991) 143,582.

**brill** Flatfish similar to and related to the TURBOT. It is fished for food, but unlike the turbot lacks tentacles. Species *Scophthalmus rhombus*.

**Brindley, James** (1716–72) British engineer and pioneer canal-builder who constructed the first major canal in England, from Worsley, Lancashire to Manchester. Brindley was responsible for *c.*350mi (565km) of canals that hastened the INDUSTRIAL REVOLUTION.

**Brisbane** City and seaport on the Brisbane River; capital of Queensland, E Australia. First settled in 1824 as a penal colony, it became state capital in 1859. It is the location of Parliament House (1869) and the University of Queensland (1909) and is a major shipping and railroad center. Industries: oil refining, shipbuilding, car assembly. Pop. (1993 est.) 1,421,600.

**bristle tail** *See* SILVERFISH

**Bristol** City and unitary authority at the confluence of the Avon and Frome rivers, SW England. An important seaport and trade center since achieving city status in 1155, it was a major center for the wool and cloth industry. From the 15th to 18th century, it was England's second city and the base for many New World explorations. The 19th century witnessed a gradual decline in the city's economy. Bristol suffered intensive bombing during World War II. Clifton Suspension Bridge (designed by BRUNEL) was completed in 1864. Other sites include a 12th-century cathedral and the 14th-century church of St. Mary Redcliffe. Bristol has two universities: the University of Bristol (1909) and the University of the West of England (1992). Industries: aircraft engineering, chemicals. Pop. (1991) 376,146.

**Britain** (Great Britain) Island kingdom in NW Europe, officially the UNITED KINGDOM of Great Britain and NORTHERN IRELAND. It is made up of ENGLAND, SCOTLAND, WALES, the CHANNEL ISLANDS, and the Isle of MAN.

**Britain, ancient** British history from PREHISTORY to ROMAN BRITAIN. During the NEOLITHIC age, hunter-gatherers gradually turned to sedentary farming. Old STONE AGE remains have been found at Cheddar Gorge, Somerset, S England. There are numerous examples of New Stone Age burial mounds. During the BRONZE AGE (*c.*2300 BC), the Beaker folk, built an advanced civilization, producing the stone circles at STONEHENGE and Avebury, S England. The IRON AGE was dominated by the CELTS. Julius Caesar invaded Britain in 54 BC, and the Roman conquest began in earnest from 43 BC.

**Britain, Battle of** (1940) Series of air battles fought over Britain. Early in World War II (as a prelude to invasion) the Germans hoped to destroy Britain's industrial and military infrastructure and civilian morale by a sustained series of bombing raids. Failure to eliminate the fighters of the Royal Air Force (RAF) in August–September resulted in the abandonment of the plans for invasion, though bombing raids continued.

**British Antarctic Territory** British colony in Antarctica comprising the mainland and islands within a triangular area bounded by latitude 60°S and longitudes 20° and 80°W. It includes the South Shetland Islands, South Orkney Islands, and Graham Land. Formerly part of the FALKLAND ISLANDS, the territory became a British Crown colony in 1962, although today Argentina and Chile claim parts of it. There are no permanent settlements, but scientists occupy establishments of the British Antarctic Survey. Area: 666,000sq mi (1,725,000sq km).

**British Columbia** Province of W Canada, on the Pacific coast, bounded N by Alaska, S by Washington state. The Rocky Mountains run N to S through the province. The capital is Victoria, other major cities include VANCOUVER. The region was first sighted by Sir Francis DRAKE in 1578. Captain COOK landed here in 1778, and George Vancouver took possession of the island that bears his name for Britain in 1794. In 1846 the border with the US was finally settled. Completion of the Canadian Pacific Railway in 1885 spurred the development of the province. The many rivers (principal of which is the Fraser) provide abundant hydroelectric power. Three-fourths of the land is forested, making timber an important industry. Mineral deposits include copper, silver, gold, lead, zinc, and asbestos. Dairying and fruit-growing are the chief farming activities. Industries: fishing, paper, tourism, chemicals. Area: 366,255sq mi (948,600sq km). Pop. (1991) 3,282,061.

**British empire** Overseas territories ruled by Britain from the 16th to the 20th century. Historians distinguish two empires. The first, based mainly on commercial ventures (such as sugar and tobacco plantations), missionary activities, and slave trading, resulted in the creation of British colonies in the Caribbean and North America in the 17th century. This "First Empire" was curtailed by the loss of 13 US colonies, at the end of the AMERICAN REVOLUTION (1775–81). The "Second Empire" was created in the 19th century, with Queen Victoria its empress. British colonial expansion was predominantly in the Far East, Australia (initially with the penal colonies), Africa, and India. By 1914 the empire comprised about 25% of the Earth's land surface and population. Virtually all the constituent members gained independence in the period after World War II. Most subsequently became members of the COMMONWEALTH.

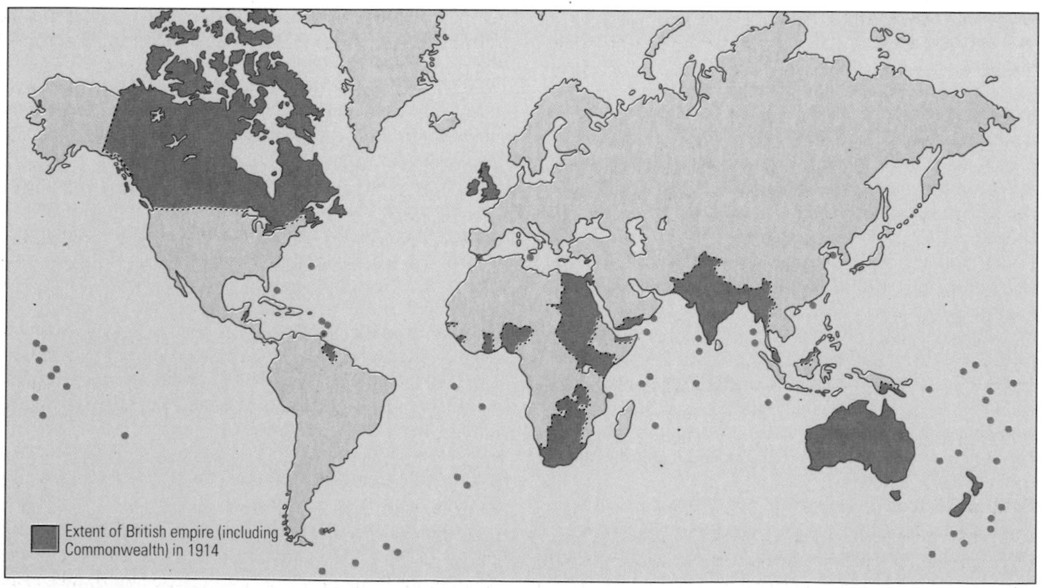


◄ **British empire** Despite the loss of the US (1783) and the strong anti-imperialist pressure of the free trade faction, the British empire continued to expand throughout the 19th century. By 1914 (shown here) the empire included all of India, Canada, Australia, most of the Cape to Nile "corridor," which ran up E Africa, and myriad small islands of strategic importance.

B

► **bromeliad** Many bromeliads, such as *Aechmea fasciata*, are epiphytes (air plants), plants that use other plants for support but are not parasitic. Its broad leaves catch water as its drips through the canopy of the tropical forest.

**British Empire, Order of the (OBE)** British military and civil order or knighthood bestowed as a reward for public service to the Commonwealth of Nations. Created in 1917, it has five different classes for men and women: Knights (or Dames) Grand Cross, Knights (or Dames) Commander, Commanders, Officers, and Members.

**British Honduras** *See* BELIZE

**British Indian Ocean Territory** British colony in the Indian Ocean comprising the islands of the Chagos Archipelago, 1,200mi (1,900km) NE of Mauritius. In 1814 France ceded the territory to Britain and it was administered by Mauritius. In 1965 Britain bought it from Mauritius in order to build a joint US/UK naval base on Diego Garcia island. In 1976 the islands of Aldabra, Farquhar, and Desroches reverted to SEYCHELLES administration. Industries: coconuts, fishing. Area: 31sq mi (80sq km).

**British Isles** Group of islands off the NW coast of Europe, made up of the UNITED KINGDOM of Great Britain and Northern IRELAND, and the Republic of IRELAND. It also includes the Isle of MAN in the Irish Sea (a self-governing island but part of the United Kingdom); and the CHANNEL ISLANDS in the English Channel (also self-governing, but a British crown dependency).

**British Legion** Organization of ex-service men and women for helping disabled and unemployed war veterans, their widows, and families. Each year during the week preceding Remembrance Day (the Sunday nearest to November 11) millions of artificial red poppies are sold to commemorate the dead of two World Wars and raise funds for the Legion.

**British Museum** One of the world's greatest public collections of art, ethnography, and archeology (established 1753). Its first displays came from a private collection purchased from the naturalist, Sir Hans Sloane. Later additions included the ROSETTA STONE and the ELGIN MARBLES. The present building by Sir Robert SMIRKE was completed in 1847. The museum's separate departments include the Museum of Mankind and the Department of Prints and Drawings which houses works by Rembrandt, Rubens, and Michelangelo.

**British North America Act** (1867) Act of the British Parliament that created the Dominion of CANADA. It provided a constitution similar to that of Britain. British powers were surrendered in the Canada Act of 1982, when the original act was renamed the Constitution Act.

**Brittany** (Bretagne) Former duchy and province in NW France, forming the peninsula between the Bay of Biscay and the English Channel. Under Roman rule from 56 BC to the 5th century AD, it was later inhabited by CELTS who gave it its name, language (BRETON), and distinctive culture. England and France disputed its possession, but the duchy retained its independence until it was formally incorporated within France in 1532. In more recent times, the French government has improved the region's infrastructure, and there has been a revival of interest in Breton culture and heritage. Pop. (1990) 2,795,600.

**Britten, (Edward) Benjamin** (1913–76) English composer. Britten is best known for his operas, among the greatest of the 20th century. He also wrote numerous songs, many especially for Peter PEARS. Britten's operas include *Peter Grimes* (1945), *Billy Budd* (1951), *The Turn of the Screw* (1954), *A Midsummer Night's Dream* (1960), and *Death in Venice* (1973). In 1948 he established the music festival held annually at his hometown of Aldeburgh, E England. He was made a peer in 1976.

**brittle star** (serpent star) Marine ECHINODERM with a small central disk body and up to twenty (though typically five) long, sinuous arms; these break off easily and are replaced by regeneration. Class Ophiuroidea; genera include the phosphorescent *Amphiopholis* and *Ophiactis*.

**Brittonic** (Brythonic) Group of languages belonging to the Celtic branch of the Italo-Celtic subfamily of Indo-European languages. Its two existing members are WELSH and BRETON. A third Brittonic language, CORNISH, died out in the 18th century, although there are speakers in Cornwall who have revived it in the 20th century. The separate languages emerged from the Celtic language spoken in Britain in the 6th century after the Germanic invasions. *See also* CELTIC LANGUAGES

**Brno** (Brünn) Capital city of central Jihomoravský (MORAVIA) region, SE Czech Republic. Founded in the 10th century, it has a 15th-century cathedral. The Bren Gun was designed here. Industries: armaments, engineering, textiles, chemicals. Pop. (1990 est.) 391,000.

**broadbill** Tropical Eurasian and African bird, named for its broad bill. It weaves a root-and-grass nest suspended over water and lays 2–4 eggs. Length: 5–11in (12–28cm). Family: Eurylaimidae.

**broadcasting** Transmission of sound or images by radio waves or through electrical or fiber-optic cables to a widely dispersed audience through RADIO or TELEVISION receivers. The first US commercial radio company, KDKA, began broadcasting in Pittsburgh in 1920. By 1992 there were over 6,000 FM stations operating in the US. In the UK, the British Broadcasting Corporation (BBC) began radio transmission in 1927. Television is a huge market in the US. By the early 1990s, there were more than 1,100 commercial television stations and 215 million TV sets. In 1962 Telstar delivered the first transatlantic, satellite television broadcast. By 1990, 60% of all US households had CABLE TELEVISION. Further developments include the introduction of digital television.

**Broads, Norfolk** Region of shallow lakes and waterways in E England, connected by the Waveney, Yare, and Bure rivers, between Norwich and the coast. It is a wildlife sanctuary and a popular sailing area, with 200mi (320km) of waterways.

**Broadway** Major thoroughfare of New York City that began as the principal N-S axis of the old town. It runs from the S tip of Manhattan to the northern city limit in the Bronx. Famous sites along the route include the Woolworth Building, the Lincoln Center for the Performing Arts, and Columbia University. In the vicinity of Times Square, its theaters and cinemas have made it known worldwide as the "show center" of the US.

**broccoli** (It. sprouts) Variety of CABBAGE cultivated for its edible immature flowers. It is the same variety (*Brassica oleracea botrytis*) as the CAULIFLOWER. **Winter** broccoli has large white heads. **Sprouting** broccoli (calabrese) has tiny green or purple flower buds which gather in compact heads. Family Brassicaceae/Cruciferae.

**Brod, Max** (1884–1968) Czech novelist, critic, and philosopher. Although chiefly remembered for bringing to public attention the work of Franz KAFKA, of whom he also wrote a biography, Brod was also a novelist. He was a Zionist and settled in Palestine in 1939, where he later became director of the Habina Theater.

**Brodsky, Joseph** (1940–96) US poet, b. Russia. Brodsky won the 1987 Nobel Prize for literature and was US poet laureate (1991–92). Before his exile in 1972, he was sent to a Soviet labor camp. His works include *Less than One,* which won the 1986 US National Book Critics award, and *History of the Twentieth Century*.

**Broglie, Prince Louis Victor de** (1892–1987) French physicist who theorized that all ELEMENTARY PARTICLES have an associated wave. He devised the formula that predicts this wavelength, and its existence was proven in 1927. Broglie developed this form of QUANTUM MECHAN-

ICS, called WAVE MECHANICS, for which he was awarded the 1929 Nobel Prize for physics.

**bromeliad** Any of 1,700 species of the PINEAPPLE family (Bromeliaceae). Most are native to the tropics and subtropics and, besides the pineapple, include many of the larger EPIPHYTES of trees of the rain forests.

**bromide** Salt of hydrobromic acid or certain organic compounds containing bromine. The bromides of ammonium, sodium, potassium, and certain other metals were once extensively used medically as sedatives. Silver bromide is light-sensitive and is used in photography.

**bromine** (symbol Br) Volatile, liquid element of the HALOGEN group in group VII of the periodic table, first isolated (1826) by the French chemist A.J. Balard. Bromine is the only liquid form of a nonmetallic element. It is extracted by treating seawater or natural brines with chlorine. A reddish-brown fuming liquid having an unpleasant odor, it is used to manufacture photographic film and additives for gasoline. Chemically it resembles CHLORINE but is less reactive. Properties: at.no. 35; at.wt. 79.904; sp.gr. 3.12; m.p. 19.04°F (−7.2°C); b.p. 137.8°F (58.8°C); the most common isotope is $^{79}$Br (50.54%).

**bronchitis** Inflammation of the bronchial tubes most often caused by a viral infection such as the common cold or influenza but exacerbated by environmental pollutants. Symptoms include coughing and the production of large quantities of mucus. It can be acute or chronic, especially in those who smoke.

**bronchus** (pl. bronchi) One of two branches into which the TRACHEA or windpipe divides, with one branch leading to each of the LUNGS. The bronchus divides into smaller and smaller branches, called bronchioles, which extend throughout the lung, opening into the air sacs or ALVEOLI.

**Brontë, Anne** (1820–49) English novelist and poet. The youngest of the Brontë sisters, she became a governess, an experience reflected in *Agnes Grey* (1847). All of her work was published under the male pseudonym Acton Bell and her best-known novel is *The Tenant of Wildfell Hall* (1848).

**Brontë, Charlotte** (1816–55) English novelist and poet. Brontë suffered from poor health, and her mother, four sisters, and dissolute brother Branwell died early. She died in childbirth within a year of her marriage. Her four novels, *The Professor* (1846), *Jane Eyre* (1847), *Shirley* (1849), and *Villette* (1853) are works of remarkable passion and imagination. Her writings initially appeared under the male pseudonym Currer Bell.

**Brontë, Emily** (1818–48) English novelist and poet. Like her sisters she wrote under a male pseudonym, Ellis Bell. Her love for her native Yorkshire moors and insight into human passion are manifested in her poetry and her only novel, *Wuthering Heights* (1847).

**brontosaurus** Former name of apatosaurus, a DINOSAUR of the Jurassic and early Cretaceous periods. It had a long neck and tail, and a small head with the eyes and nostrils on the top so that it could remain completely immersed in water. Length: 70ft (21m); weight: to 30 tons.

**Bronx, The** Residential borough of NEW YORK CITY, bordered by the Hudson River (W), Harlem River (SW), East River (S), Long Island Sound (E), and connected to MANHATTAN and QUEENS by a network of bridges. The Bronx was founded (1641) by Jonas Bronck for the Dutch West India Company. It was incorporated as part of New York City in 1898. The Bronx has 80mi (129km) of waterfront. It is the site of the Bronx Zoo and Yankee Stadium. Pop. (1990) 1,191,303.

**bronze** Traditionally an ALLOY of COPPER and no more than 33% tin. It is hard and resistant to corrosion, but easy to work. It has long been used in sculpture and bell-casting. Other metals are often added for specific properties and uses, such as aluminum in aircraft parts and tubing, silicon in marine hardware and chemical equipment, and phosphorus in springs and electrical parts.

**Bronze Age** Period between the NEOLITHIC period and the discovery of iron-working techniques (the IRON AGE). In Mesopotamia, BRONZE tools were used from *c*.3200 BC and the Bronze Age lasted until *c*.1100 BC. In Britain, bronze was used after 2000 BC.

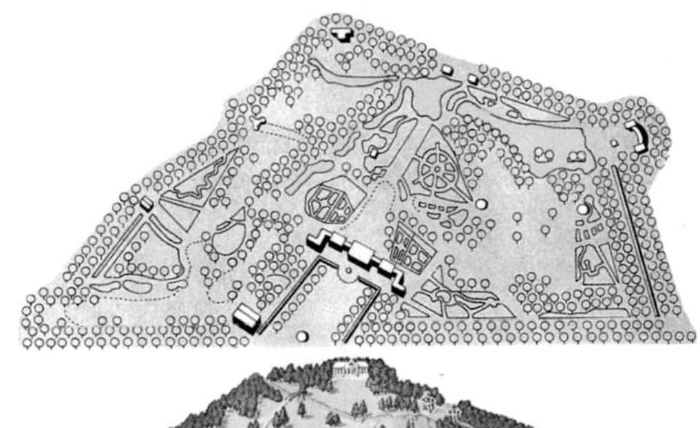

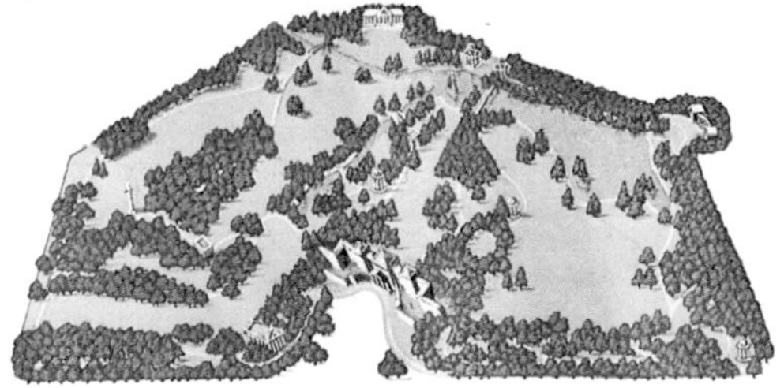

◀ **Brown** The 18th century gardens of Stowe, Buckinghamshire, S England, were worked on successively by Bridgeman, Kent, and "Capability" Brown. Bridgeman's layout moved some way from the formal geometric patterns of the French and Italian gardens, but was still characterized by a rigidity of outline. Kent's work (above) softened these outlines considerably, introducing the concept of naturalism, harmonizing house and temples with the landscape. It can be seen, however, that a certain formality persisted. The transformation of the gardens into their superbly landscaped state (below) is attributed to "Capability" Brown. The stilted outlines have gone, the whole setting has a deceptively natural breadth and ease as well as a generous fullness.

**Brook, Peter Stephen Paul** (1925– ) English director of theater, opera, and film. He joined the ROYAL SHAKESPEARE COMPANY (RSC) as co-director in 1962. His most notable productions were *King Lear* (1962, filmed 1969), *Marat/Sade* (1964), and *Midsummer Night's Dream* (1970). In 1970 Brook established the International Center for Theater Research in Paris, and directed the epic cycle *The Mahabharata* (1985, filmed 1989). Brook also directed the film *Lord of the Flies* (1963).

**Brooke, Rupert Chawner** (1887–1915) English poet. Brooke wrote some of the most anthologized poems in the English language, including "The Soldier" and "The Old Vicarage, Grantchester," but the romantic image created by his early death during World War I has tended to distort his status. His collections include *Poems* (1911) and *1914 and Other Poems* (1915).

**Brooklyn** Borough of NEW YORK CITY, coextensive with Kings County in SW Long Island; it is connected to Manhattan and Staten Island by bridges, subway trains, and ferries. First settled in 1645, it became a borough in 1898. It is the home of Coney Island. Area: 71sq mi (184sq km). Pop. (1990) 2,291,664.

**Brooks, Louise** (1906–85) US film actress. Brooks achieved most of her success in Germany under the direction of G.W. Pabst in his *Diary of a Lost Girl* (1929), and as Lulu in *Pandora's Box* (1929). She never recaptured this early brilliance, and retired in 1938.

**broom** Any of various deciduous shrubs of the PEA family (Fabaceae/Leguminosae). They have yellow, purple, or white flowers, usually in clusters. Many belong to the genus *Genista*, which gave its name to the Plantagenate kings of England (Lat. *Planta genista*), who used the broom as their emblem.

**Brown, "Capability" (Lancelot)** (1715–83) English landscape gardener who revolutionized garden and parkland layout in the 1700s. Brown designed or remodeled nearly 150 estates, including gardens at Blenheim and Kew. He worked to achieve casual effects, in contrast to the formal gardens of the 16th and 17th centuries. He earned his nickname from a habit of saying that a place had "capabilities of improvement."

**Brown, Ford Madox** (1821–93) English painter, closely associated with (although not a member of) the PRE-RAPHAELITE BROTHERHOOD, grandfather of Ford Madox FORD. The Pre-Raphaelite influence can be seen in *The Last of England* (1855) and *Work* (1852–63).

**Brown, George** (1818–80) Canadian statesman and journalist, b. Scotland. Brown immigrated to the US in 1837, but later moved to Canada. There he founded the Toronto *Globe* newspaper. Brown was elected to the Canadian assembly in 1851. He opposed proposals for increased participation of French Canadians. Brown supported land and education reforms and played a pivotal role in the establishment of the Confederation of Canada.

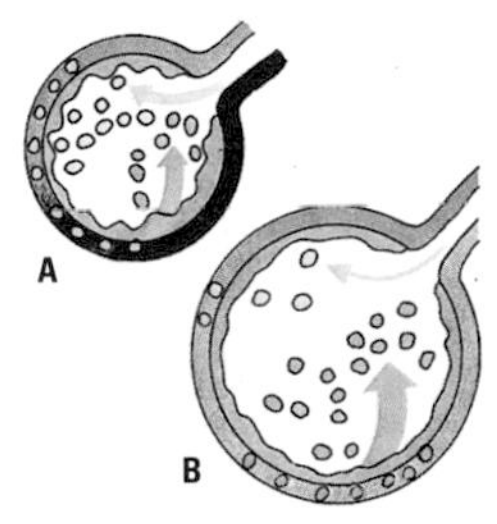


▲ **bronchitis** A common disease of industrialized areas with a cool damp climate, bronchitis involves inflammation of air passages and air sacs of the lungs. Mild attacks lasting only a few days are usually due to a cold, spreading to the chest. Chronic bronchitis is caused by heavily polluted air irritating the lining of the lungs. The lung air sacs become inflamed and lose their elasticity and air passages become constricted [normal (A) diseased (B)]. Less oxygen (yellow dots) enters the bloodstream and carbon dioxide (green dots) accumulates. Rapid shallow breathing arises to compensate.

**Brown, James** (1933– ) US singer and songwriter. An energetic performer, renowned for his dance routines, Brown is hailed as the "Godfather of Soul" and a pioneer of FUNK. His album *Live at the Apollo* (1962) is one of the best-selling pop albums of all time. Brown's hit singles include "Please, Please, Please" (1956), "Papa's Got a Brand New Bag" (1965), and "Say it Loud, I'm Black and I'm Proud" (1968).

**Brown, John** (1800–59) US antislavery crusader. He led the Pottawatomie Massacre (1856) in Kansas in which five alleged slaveowners were killed. Hoping to start a slave revolt, he led 21 men who captured the US arsenal at Harper's Ferry, Virginia, in 1859. They were driven out the next day by troops under Robert E. LEE. Brown was captured, charged with treason, and hanged. The trial aggravated North-South tensions.

**brown bear** *See* BEAR

**Brownian movement** Random, zigzag movement of particles suspended in a fluid (liquid or gas). It is caused by the unequal bombardment of the larger particles, from different sides, by the smaller molecules of the fluid. The movement is named for the Scottish botanist Robert Brown (1773–1858), who in 1827 observed the movement of plant spores floating in water.

**Browning, Elizabeth Barrett** (1806–61) English poet. In 1846 she secretly married Robert BROWNING and, from 1847, the couple lived in Florence, Italy. *The Seraphim and Other Poems* (1838) and *Poems* (1844) established her popularity, later confirmed by a collection of 1850, which included *Sonnets from the Portuguese,* and *Aurora Leigh* (1857). She was regarded as the preeminent English woman poet of her generation.

**Browning, Robert** (1812–89) English poet. "My Last Duchess" and "Soliloquy of the Spanish Cloister," both published in *Bells and Pomegranates* (1846), display his characteristic use of dramatic monologue. In 1846 he and Elizabeth Barrett (BROWNING) secretly married and moved to Florence, Italy, in 1847. Browning published the volumes *Christmas Eve and Easter Day* (1850) and *Men and Women* (1855) before returning to London after Elizabeth's death in 1861. His popularity increased with *Dramatis Personae* (1864) and *The Ring and the Book* (1868–69), often considered to be his masterpiece. One of the foremost poets of the 19th century, Browning is also at times one of the most obscure.

**Brownshirts** (officially *Sturmabteilung*, or *SA*) German Nazi stormtroopers founded in 1920. By 1933 the Brownshirts, led by Ernst Röhm, numbered *c.*500,000. After the Nazis seized power, the Brownshirts' ideology and challenge to the autonomy of the German army was perceived as a threat by Adolf HITLER. The SA leaders were shot on the "Night of the Long Knives" (June 29, 1934) and the SS emerged as their successors.

**brucellosis** (undulant fever) Infectious disease that can be passed from farm stock to man, usually in unpasteurized milk. It has virtually disappeared from the developed world.

**Brücke, Die** (1905–13) (The Bridge) First group of German expressionist painters. Founded in Dresden by E.L. KIRCHNER, the group chose their name because they wanted their work to form a bridge with the art of the future. Members of the group included Emil NOLDE, Karl Schmidt-Rottluff, Max Pechstein, and Erich Heckel. Their work was characterized by jagged edges, harshly distorted figures, and a simplification of color and form. *See also* EXPRESSIONISM

**Bruckner, Anton** (1824–96) Austrian composer. He wrote a great deal of church music – cantatas, masses, and a *Te Deum* (1881–84) – and nine symphonies. Bruckner's compositions are noted for their massive scale: the symphonies are lengthy, monumental creations greatly influenced by ROMANTICISM. His work is characterized by the use of complex musical form.

**Bruegel, Pieter the Elder** (1525–69) Netherlandish landscape painter and draftsman. The greatest 16th-century Dutch artist, Bruegel traveled extensively in France and Italy. His return journey through the Alps influenced him profoundly and he produced a series of sensitive drawings of the region. In 1563, he moved to Brussels and for the rest of his life concentrated on painting. The characteristic rural scenes crowded with tiny peasant figures of his early years gave way during his last six years to paintings with larger figures which illustrated proverbs. His son, Pieter the Younger (1564–1637), sometimes copied his father's work. Another son, Jan (1568–1625), specialized in highly detailed flower paintings.

**Bruges** (Brugge) Capital of West Flanders province, NW Belgium. Built on a network of canals, it was a great trading center in the 15th century. Its importance declined after 1500, but trade revived when the Zeebrugge ship canal was opened in 1907. It has many medieval buildings. Industries: engineering, brewing, lace, textiles, tourism. Pop. (1993 est.) 116,724.

**Brummell, "Beau" (George Bryan)** (1778–1840) Leader of fashion in gentlemen's dress in Regency England between 1798 and 1812. His evident sense of perfection in dress, accompanied by a sharp wit and a friendship with the Prince Regent (later George IV), gave him enormous social success. The demise of royal patronage and his huge gambling debts forced Brummell into exile (1816) in France, where he lived the rest of his life in poverty.

**Brunei** Sultanate in N BORNEO, SE Asia; the capital is BANDAR SERI BEGAWAN. **Land and climate** Bounded in the NW by the South China Sea, Brunei consists of humid plains with forested mountains running along its S border with Malaysia. Brunei has a moist, tropical climate. **History and politics** During the 16th century Brunei ruled over the whole of Borneo and parts of the Philippines, but gradually lost its influence. It became a British protectorate in 1888. Brunei achieved independence from Britain in 1983. **Economy** Oil and gas are the main source of income, accounting for 70% of GDP. Area: 2,225sq mi (5,765sq km). Pop. (1993) 276,300.

**Brunel, Isambard Kingdom** (1806–59) British marine and railroad engineer, who revolutionized British engineering. In 1829 he designed the Clifton Suspension Bridge (completed 1864). He is also noted for his ships: *Great Western* (designed 1837), the first trans-Atlantic wooden steamship, *Great Britain* (1843), the first iron-hulled, screw-driven steamship, and *Great Eastern* (1858), the largest steamship of its era.

**Brunel, Sir Marc Isambard** (1769–1849) Architect and engineer. A refugee from the FRENCH REVOLUTION, Brunel went to the US in 1793 and was chief engineer of New York. He went to England in 1799, where he was responsible for the construction of the first tunnel (1825–43) under the Thames River, London.

**Brunelleschi, Filippo** (1377–1446) Florentine architect, first of the great RENAISSANCE architects and a pioneer of PERSPECTIVE. Brunelleschi influenced many later architects, including MICHELANGELO. In 1420 he began to design the dome of Florence Cathedral, the largest since the HAGIA SOPHIA. Other works include the Ospedale degl'Innocenti (1419–26) and the Basilica of San Lorenzo (begun 1421), both in Florence.

**Bruno, Frank (Franklin Roy)** (1961– ) English boxer. In 1985 he challenged Tim Witherspoon for the WBA crown. Bruno retired after losing to Mike TYSON in 1989, but staged a comeback only to lose another world title challenge to Lennox Lewis in 1993. In 1995 he beat Oliver McCall on points to win the WBC title, but again lost to Tyson and retired for a second time.

**Bruno, Giordano** (1548–1600) Italian philosopher. A fierce opponent of dogmatism and a supporter of the relativity of perception, his pantheistic belief in a deity manifest in the cosmos led to his censure for unorthodoxy and his death at the stake.

**Brussels** (Bruxelles) Capital of Belgium and of Brabant province, central Belgium. During the Middle Ages it achieved prosperity through the wool trade and became capital of the Spanish Netherlands. In 1830 it became capital of newly independent Belgium. It has many fine buildings including a 13th-century cathedral, the town hall, art nouveau period buildings, and academies of fine arts. The main commercial, financial, cultural, and administrative center of Belgium, it is also the headquarters of the EUROPEAN COMMUNITY (EC) and of the NORTH ATLANTIC TREATY ORGANIZATION (NATO). Industries: textiles, chemicals. Pop. (1993 est.) 949,070.

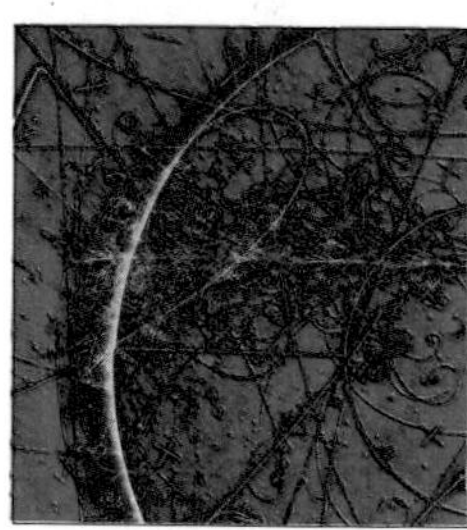

▲ **bubble chamber** Colored image showing a collection of tracks left by subatomic particles in a bubble chamber. A charged particle leaves behind a trail of tiny bubbles as the liquid hydrogen boils in its wake. The tracks are curved due to an intense applied magnetic field. The tightly wound spiral tracks are due to electrons and positrons.

**Brussels, Treaty of** (1948) Agreement signed by Britain, France, and the Low Countries for cooperation in defense, politics, economics, and cultural affairs for 50 years. The defense agreement was merged into the NORTH ATLANTIC TREATY ORGANIZATION (NATO) in 1950. In 1954 Italy and West Germany joined and the name was changed to the Western European Union. It was a forerunner of the EUROPEAN COMMUNITY (EC).

**brutalism** Architectural movement of the 1950s and early 1960s. It took its inspiration from LE CORBUSIER's pilgrimage chapel at Ronchamp and his High Court building at CHANDIGARH, India. A number of young architects, such as James STIRLING, tried to extend Le Corbusier's experiments into aggressive and chunky designs of their own. It should not be confused with the 1950s' British movement of **new brutalism**, in which Alison and Peter Smithson adopted the uncompromising simplicity of MIES VAN DER RÖHE.

**Bruton, John Gerard** (1947– ) Irish statesman, taoiseach (prime minister, 1995–97). He was elected to the Dáil in 1969. A member of FINE GAEL, Bruton rose steadily through the ministerial ranks, earning a reputation as a right-winger. He became leader of Fine Gael in 1990, and succeeded Albert REYNOLDS as prime minister.

**Brutus** (85–42 BC) (Marcus Junius Brutus) Roman republican leader, one of the principal assassins of Julius CAESAR. He sided first with POMPEY against Caesar, but Caesar made him governor of Cisalpine Gaul in 46 BC and city praetor in 44 BC. After taking part in Caesar's assassination, he raised an army in Greece but, was defeated at Philippi by MARK ANTONY and Octavian (later AUGUSTUS). Brutus committed suicide.

**Bryan, William Jennings** (1860–1925) US statesman and lawyer, secretary of state (1913–15). A Democratic congressman (1891–95) and a leading advocate of the free coinage of silver, Bryan's "Cross of Gold" speech at the 1896 Democratic convention earned him the presidential nomination. He lost the ensuing election to William MCKINLEY. Nominated again in 1900, he was again defeated by McKinley. Bryan was defeated a third time (1908) by William Howard TAFT. In return for helping Woodrow WILSON win the 1912 election, he became secretary of state. An opponent of the teaching of evolution, he acted as prosecuting attorney in the SCOPES TRIAL (1925), opposing Clarence DARROW. Bryan won the case but died five days later.

**Bryant, William Cullen** (1794–1878) US poet and editor. His debut volume, *Poems* (1821), contains some of his most famous verse, including "Thanatopsis" and "To a Waterfowl." In 1826 Bryant began working for the New York *Evening Post*, soon rising to editor (1829) and part owner.

**Brynner, Yul** (1915–85) US film actor, b. Russia. Brynner first came to prominence in the Broadway musical *The King and I*. His reprise of the role for film earned him an Academy Award for Best Actor (1956). Regularly cast as a maverick gunslinger, other films include *The Magnificent Seven* (1960) and *Westworld* (1973).

**bryony** Either of two unrelated plants, both of which are climbers in hedgerows in Europe and elsewhere. **White** bryony, *Bryonia alba*, is a member of the GOURD family (Cucurbitaceae), with large hand-shaped leaves. **Black** bryony, *Tamus communis*, is a member of the YAM family (Dioscoreaceae) and has heart-shaped leaves.

**bryophyte** Group of small, green, rootless non-VASCULAR PLANTS (phylum Bryophyta), including MOSS and LIVERWORT. Bryophytes grow on damp surfaces exposed to light, including rocks and tree bark, almost everywhere from the Arctic to the Antarctic. There are about 24,000 species. *See also* ALTERNATION OF GENERATIONS

**BSE** See BOVINE SPONGIFORM ENCEPHALOPATHY

**bubble chamber** Device for detecting and identifying SUBATOMIC PARTICLES. It consists of a sealed chamber filled with a liquefied gas, usually liquid hydrogen, kept just below its boiling point by high pressure in the chamber. When the pressure is released, the boiling point is lowered and a charged particle passing through the superheated liquid leaves a trail of tiny gas bubbles. If a magnetic field is applied to the chamber, the tracks are curved according to the charge, mass, and velocity of the particles, which can thus be identified. Donald GLASER received the 1960 Nobel Prize for physics for inventing the bubble chamber, and it was developed by Luis ALVAREZ.

**Buber, Martin** (1878–1965) Austrian Jewish philosopher, theologian, and activist. He was a native of Vienna. An ardent early advocate of ZIONISM, he edited *Der Jude* (1916–24), the leading journal of German-speaking Jewish intellectuals. Bubi defiantly opposed the Nazis in Germany until forced to move to Palestine in 1938. His most important published work is *I and Thou* (1922), on the directness of the relationship between man and God within the traditions of HASIDISM.

**bubonic plague** *See* PLAGUE

**Buchan, John, 1st Baron Tweedsmuir** (1875–1940) British writer and statesman, b. Scotland. Buchan is best-known for his adventure novels, such as *The Thirty-Nine Steps* (1915). He also wrote a four-volume history of World War I (1915–19) and biographies. He was governor-general of Canada (1935–40).

**Buchanan, James** (1791–1868) 15th US president (1857–1861). Buchanan entered Congress in 1821 and was Senator (1834–45). President POLK appointed him secretary of state (1845–49). Under President PIERCE, Buchanan served as minister to Great Britain (1853–56). His administration was unpopular, and his attempt to compromise between pro- and anti-SLAVERY factions floundered. His efforts to purchase Cuba and acceptance of a pro-slavery constitution in Kansas contributed to his electoral defeat by Abraham LINCOLN. The Southern states seceded and, shortly after Buchanan left office, the American CIVIL WAR began.

**Bucharest** (Bucuresti) Capital and largest city of Romania, on the Dimbovita River, S Romania. Founded in the 14th century on an important trade route, it became capital in 1862 and was occupied by Germany in both World Wars. It is an industrial, commercial, and cultural center. The seat of the patriarch of the Romanian Orthodox Church, it has churches, museums, and galleries. There are two universities. Industries: oil refining, chemicals. Pop. (1992) 2,350,984.

**Buchenwald** Site of a Nazi concentration camp, near Weimar in Germany. Established in 1937, it became notorious especially for the medical experiments conducted on its inmates, of whom *c*.50,000 died. The camp was liberated by US forces in 1945.

**Büchner, Georg** (1813–37) German dramatist. Büchner died young of typhoid fever, leaving only two completed plays: *Danton's Death* (1835) and *Leonce and Lena* (1850). He is best known, however, for the fragmentary tragedy *Woyzeck* (1837), which formed the basis for Alban Berg's opera *Wozzeck* (1925).

**Buck, Pearl S. (Sydenstricker)** (1892–1973) US novelist. Buck was brought up in China, which she used as the setting for many of her novels, including *The Good Earth* (1931), which won the 1932 Pulitzer Prize. Her other works include *Sons* (1932), *The Mother* (1934), and *Dragon Seed* (1942). Buck also wrote plays, screenplays, verse, and children's fiction, and was awarded the 1938 Nobel Prize for literature.

**Buckingham, George Villiers, 2nd Duke of** (1628–87) English courtier and political figure. He was educated with Charles I's sons and supported the Royalists in the CIVIL WAR (1642–48). A dashing, rakish courtier in Restoration England, he was a member of the group of ministers known as the CABAL, but later joined the opposition to CHARLES II. He wrote several comedies, notably *The Rehearsal* (1671).

**Buckingham Palace** London residence of British sovereigns since 1837. Formerly owned by the dukes of Buckingham, it was purchased by George III in 1761 and remodeled into a 600-room palace by John NASH in 1825. Sir Aston Webb redesigned the E front in 1913. The changing of the guard takes place here daily.

**Buckinghamshire** County in SE central England; the county town is Aylesbury. In the Vale of Aylesbury to the N, cereal crops and beans are grown; livestock and poultry are raised in the S. Industries: furniture, printing. Area: 725sq mi (1,877sq km). Pop. (1991) 632,487.

**Buckminsterfullerene** (buckyball) Allotrope of CARBON that consists of many carbon atoms bonded together in the

▶ **Buddhism** Founded in NE India in the 6th century BC, Buddhism has over 300 million followers in Japan, Sri Lanka, Nepal, Thailand, and other regions of the Far East. Its disdain of material wealth is finding increasing support in parts of the West.

shape of a hollow sphere. The simplest Buckminsterfullerene has 60 carbon atoms arranged as 12 regular pentagons and 20 hexagons (like the panels on a modern football). It can be made by exposing graphite to a laser beam or electric arc in an inert atmosphere. It is a yellow crystalline solid that dissolves in benzene. It gets its name from the US architect Richard Buckminster FULLER, who invented the GEODESIC DOME structure that the molecules resemble. *See also* ALLOTROPY

**bud** In plants, a small swelling or projection consisting of a short stem with overlapping, immature leaves covered by scales. Leaf buds develop into leafy twigs, and flower buds develop into blossoms. A bud at the tip of a twig is a terminal bud and contains the growing point; lateral buds develop in leaf axils along a twig.

**Budapest** Capital of Hungary, on the Danube River. It was created in 1873 by uniting the towns of Buda (capital of Hungary since the 14th century) and Pest on the opposite bank. It became one of the two capitals of the AUSTRO-HUNGARIAN EMPIRE. In 1918 it was declared capital of an independent Hungary. Budapest was the scene of a popular uprising against the Soviet Union in 1956. The old town contains a remarkable collection of buildings including: Buda Castle, the 13th-century Matthias Church, the Parliament Building, the National Museum, and Roman remains. Industries: iron and steel, chemicals. Pop. (1993 est.) 2,009,000.

**Buddha** (Enlightened One) Title adopted by Gautama Siddhartha (*c*.563–*c*.483 BC), the founder of BUDDHISM. Born at Lumbini, Nepal, Siddhartha was son of the ruler of the Sakya tribe, and his early years were spent in luxury. At the age of 29, he realized that human life is little more than suffering. He gave up his wealth and comfort, deserted his wife and small son, and took to the road as a wandering ascetic. He sought truth in a six-year regime of austerity and self-mortification. After abandoning asceticism as futile, he sought his own middle way toward enlightenment. The moment of truth came (*c*.528 BC) as he sat beneath a banyan tree in the village of Buddha Gaya, Bihar, India. After this, he taught others about his way to truth. The title "buddha" applies to those who have achieved perfect enlightenment. Buddhists believe that there have been several buddhas before Siddhartha, and there will be many to come. The term also serves to describe a variety of Buddha images.

**Buddhism** Religion and philosophy founded (*c*.528 BC) in India by Gautama Siddhartha, the BUDDHA. Buddhism is based on Four Noble Truths: existence is suffering; the cause of suffering is desire; the end of suffering comes with the achievement of NIRVANA; Nirvana is attained through the Eightfold Path: right views, right resolve, right speech, right action, right livelihood, right effort, right mindfulness, and right concentration. There are no gods. **Karma**, one of Buddhism's most important concepts, says good actions are rewarded and evil ones are punished, either in this life or throughout a long series of lives resulting from **samsara**, the cycle of death and rebirth by REINCARNATION. The achievement of Nirvana breaks the cycle. Buddhism is a worldwide religion. Its main divisions are: THERAVADA, or *Hinayana*, in SE Asia; MAHAYANA in N Asia; Lamaism or TIBETAN BUDDHISM in Tibet; and ZEN in Japan. By 1995 the total number of Buddhists was estimated at *c*.300 million.

**budding** Method of asexual reproduction that produces a new organism from an outgrowth of the parent. Hydras, for example, often bud in spring and summer. A small bulge appears on the parent and grows until it breaks away as a new individual.

**Budge, (John) Don (Donald)** (1915– ) US tennis player. In 1937 Budge won the Wimbledon and US Open singles titles. In 1938 he became the first man to complete the sport's grand slam of the four major singles titles (Wimbledon, US, Australia, France). Budge also won both the mixed and men's doubles titles at Wimbledon and the US Open (1937–38).

**budgerigar** (parakeet) Small, bright-colored seed-eating PARROT native to Australia, and a popular pet. It can be taught to mimic speech. The sexes look alike but the coloration of the cere (a waxy membrane at the base of the beak) may vary seasonally. Size: 7.5in (19cm) long. Species *Melopsittacus undulatus*.

**budget** Plan for the financial expenditure of an individual, a corporation, or a government, matching it against expected income. National budgets determine the level of direct and indirect taxation against projected expenditure and economic growth. The complexity of modern trade and finance has sometimes forced governments to make two or more budgets in a single year.

**Buena Vista, Battle of** (1847) Engagement in the MEXICAN WAR. US troops, led by Zachary TAYLOR, had disobeyed orders from the US government and advanced to Buena Vista. The Mexican army, led by General SANTA ANNA, attacked. After two days of indecisive fighting, Santa Anna withdrew, giving the US control of N Mexico.

**Buenos Aires** Capital of Argentina, on the estuary of the Río de la Plata, 150mi (240km) from the Atlantic Ocean. Originally founded by Spain in 1536, it was rebuilt in 1580 after being destroyed by the indigenous population. It became a separate federal district and capital of the country in 1880. Buenos Aires later developed as a commercial center for beef, grain, and dairy products. It is the seat of the National University (1821). Industries: meat processing, flour milling, textiles, metal works. Pop. (1992 est.) 11,662,050.

**Buffalo** Industrial city and port on the E shore of Lake Erie, NW New York State. It was first settled in 1803. Its rapid industrial growth was encouraged by its position at the W terminus of the Erie Canal (opened 1825). President MCKINLEY was assassinated at the Pan-American Exposition held here in 1901. It is home to the Albright-Knox art gallery and has two universities. Industries: flour milling, motor vehicles, chemicals. Pop. (1990) 328,123.

**buffalo** Any of several horned mammals and a misnomer for the North American BISON. The massive ox-like Indian, or water, buffalo (*Bubalus bubalis*) is often domesticated for milk and hides. Height: 5ft (1.5m). Family Bovidae.

**"Buffalo Bill" (William Frederick Cody)** (1846–1917) US frontiersman, scout, and showman. A Pony Express rider at 14, he then served as Union scout during the Civil War. Cody gained his nickname by supplying buffalo meat to railroad construction workers. He became famous through Ned Buntline's dime novels about his exploits. In 1883 "Buffalo Bill" organized a "Wild West" exhibition, co-starring Annie Oakley and Chief Sitting Bull.

**buffer solution** Solution to which a moderate quantity of a strong acid or a strong base can be added without making a significant change to its pH value (acidity or alkalinity).

**bug** Any member of the insect order Hemiptera, although in the US any insect is commonly called a bug. True bugs are flattened insects that undergo gradual or incomplete metamorphosis, have two pairs of wings, and use piercing and sucking mouthparts. Most feed on plant juices, such as the greenfly, although a number attack animals and are carriers of disease.

**bugle** Brass wind instrument resembling a small TRUMPET without valves, capable of playing notes of only one harmonic series. Because its penetrating tones carry great distances, it was often used for military signaling.

**Buhl, André Charles** *See* André Charles BOULLE

**Bujumbura** (formerly Usumbura) Capital and chief port of Burundi, E central Africa, at NE end of Lake TANGANYIKA. Founded in 1899 as part of German East Africa, it was the capital of the Belgian trust territory of Ruanda-Urundi after World War I and remained capital of Burundi when the coun-

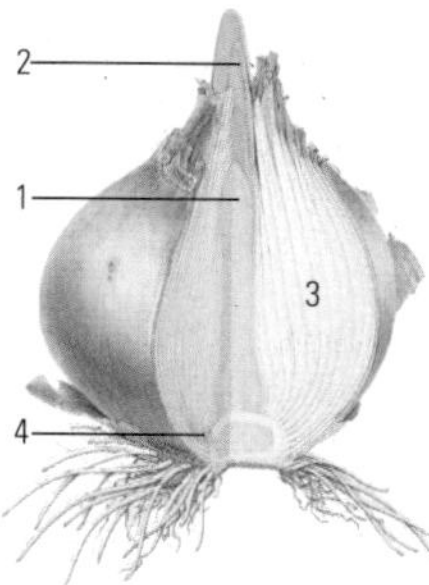


▲ **bulb** As well as serving as underground storage organs, bulbs may also provide flowering plants with a means of vegetative reproduction. In spring, the flower bud (1) and young foliage leaves (2) will develop into a flowering plant using the food and water stored in the bulb's fleshy scale leaves (3). When the flower has died, the leaves live on, and continue to make food which is transported downwards to the leaf bases. These swell and develop into new bulbs. Axillary buds (4) may develop into daughter bulbs which break off to form new independent plants.

try achieved independence in 1962. It is an administrative and commercial center. Industries: textiles, cotton. Pop. (1994 est.) 300,000.

**Bukhara** (Buchara) Ancient city in W Uzbekistan, capital of the Bukhara region. Founded *c.*1st century AD, it was ruled by Arabs (7th–9th century), by Turks and Mongols (12th–15th century), and annexed to Russia in 1868; it was included in Uzbekistan (1924). It is an important Asian trade and cultural center. Monuments include the 10th-century mausoleum of Ismail Samani. Industries: silk processing, rugs. Pop. (1990) 246,200.

**Bukharin, Nikolai Ivanovich** (1888–1938) Russian communist political theorist. After the Russian Revolution (1917), he became a leading member of the COMMUNIST INTERNATIONAL (Comintern) and editor of *Pravda*. In 1924 Bukharin joined the politburo. He opposed agricultural collectivization and was executed for treason by STALIN.

**Bulawayo** City in SW Zimbabwe, SE Africa; capital of Matabeleland North province. It was founded by the British in 1893 and was the site of the Matabele revolt in 1896. It is the second largest city in the country. Industries: textiles, motor vehicles. Pop. (1992) 620,936.

**bulb** In botany, a food storage organ consisting of a short stem and swollen scale leaves. Food is stored in the scales, which are either layered in a series of rings, as in the onion, or loosely attached to the stem, as in some lilies. Small buds between the scale leaves give rise to new shoots each year. New bulbs are produced in the axils of the outer scale leaves. *See also* ASEXUAL REPRODUCTION

**bulbul** Any of numerous species of songbird of Africa and S Asia, where they are kept as cage birds. They are short-necked dull-colored birds, ranging in size from 6–12in (15–30cm). They feed on berries and other fruits and build a grass nest for 3–5 eggs. Family Pycnonotidae; there are *c.*120 species.

**Bulfinch, Charles** (1763–1844) US architect. He is particularly noted for his public buildings, including the State House, Boston, and University Hall at Harvard, Cambridge, Massachusetts. In 1818–30 he completed the building of the Capitol in Washington, D.C.

**Bulganin, Nikolai** (1895–1975) Soviet statesman and military leader, prime minister (1955–58). He served in the army during World War II. Defense minister in 1947–49 and 1953–55, he became prime minister after the fall of MALENKOV. Bulganin was dismissed after disagreements with KHRUSHCHEV.

▲ **bulldog** The history of the bulldog goes back many centuries. The French bulldog (shown here) is considerably smaller than the pure bulldog, and is most popular in France, Britain and the US.

## BULGARIA

This flag, first adopted in 1878, uses the colors associated with the Slav people. The national emblem incorporating a lion – a symbol of Bulgaria since the 14th century – was first added to the flag in 1947. It is now added only for official government occasions.

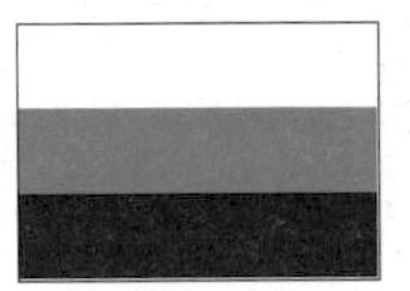

**AREA:** 42,822sq mi (110,910sq km)
**POPULATION:** 8,963,000
**CAPITAL (POPULATION):** Sofia (1,141,142)
**GOVERNMENT:** Multiparty republic
**ETHNIC GROUPS:** Bulgarian 86%, Turkish 10%, Gypsy 3%, Macedonian, Armenian, Romanian, Greek
**LANGUAGES:** Bulgarian (official)
**RELIGIONS:** Christianity (Eastern Orthodox 87%), Islam 13%
**CURRENCY:** Lev = 100 stotinki

The Republic of Bulgaria is located in the Balkan peninsula, facing the Black Sea in the E. Northern Bulgaria consists of a plateau falling to the valley of the River Danube, which forms most of Bulgaria's N frontier with Romania. The heart of Bulgaria is mountainous and the main ranges include the BALKAN MOUNTAINS (Stara Planina) in the center and the Rhodope Mountains in the S. Between these ranges is the Maritsa River valley, which forms an E–W route between the coast and the interior.

### CLIMATE

Bulgaria has hot summers and cold winters, though they are seldom severe, while the rainfall is moderate. The E has drier and warmer summers than the W, and the Black Sea coast is a popular resort area. In winter, cold winds sometimes blow from the NE, bringing bitterly cold spells to the Danubian lowlands.

### VEGETATION

More than half of Bulgaria is under crops or pasture while forests, including beech and spruce, cover about 35% of the country. Trees swathe the mountain slopes, with grassy meadows and Alpine plants above the tree line. In the warmer S, the plants are similar to those found in the lands around the Mediterranean Sea. In the Balkan Mountains are the valuable rosefields of Kazanluk, from which attar of roses is exported worldwide to the cosmetics and perfumes industries.

### HISTORY

Most of the people of Bulgaria are descendants of SLAVS and nomadic BULGAR tribes who arrived from the E in the 6th and 7th centuries. A powerful Bulgar kingdom was set up in 681, but the country became part of the BYZANTINE EMPIRE in the 11th century.

OTTOMAN Turks ruled Bulgaria from 1396 and ethnic Turks still comprise a sizable minority of the population. In 1879 Bulgaria became a monarchy and, in 1908, it achieved full independence. Bulgaria was an ally of Germany in both World War I and World War II. In 1944, Soviet troops invaded Bulgaria and, after the war, the monarchy was abolished and the country became a subservient Communist ally of the Soviet Union.

### POLITICS

In the late 1980s, reforms in the Soviet Union led Bulgaria's government to introduce a multiparty system in 1990. The Bulgarian Communist Party was renamed the Bulgarian Socialist Party (BSP). In 1990 the first non-communist president for 40 years, Zhelyu Zhelev, was elected. A new constitution (1991) saw the adoption of free-market reforms. The BSP won the 1994 general election, but virtual economic collapse and anti-government demonstrations prompted the government to resign (1996). Fresh elections (1997) were won by a center-right coalition.

### ECONOMY

Bulgaria is a lower-middle-income developing country (1995 GDP per capita, US$4,480), faced with a difficult transition to a market economy. Since 1989 Bulgaria's major trading partner has been the European Union (EU). Inflation (1994, 96%), unemployment (1993, 16%) and public debt are major economic and social obstacles. Manufacturing is the leading economic activity, but faces problems arising from outdated technology. The main products are chemicals, metals, machinery and textiles. Mineral reserves include molybdenum. Wheat and corn are the principal crops, and fruit, oilseeds, tobacco, and vegetables are also economically important. The warm south-facing valleys of the Maritsa plains are ideal for vines, plums, cotton and tobacco. Livestock farming, especially the rearing of dairy and beef cattle, sheep, and pigs, is also important across most of the country.

Tourism is increasing rapidly, with more than 2 million tourists visiting Bulgaria in 1995. Another important source of foreign currency is the production of red wine, originally a state-aided industry.

B

**Bulgaria** Balkan republic in SE Europe. *See* country feature

**Bulgars** Ancient Turkic people originating in the region N and E of the Black Sea. In about AD 650 they split into two groups. The western group moved to Bulgaria, where they became assimilated into the Slavic population and adopted Christianity. The other group moved to the VOLGA region and set up a Bulgar state, eventually converting to Islam. The Volga Bulgars were conquered by the Kievan Rus in the 10th century.

**Bulge, Battle of the** Final German offensive of WORLD WAR II. The Germans drove a wedge through the Allied lines in the Ardennes forest on the French–Belgian frontier in December 1944. Allied forces converged to extinguish the "bulge" in their lines in January 1945, and the advance into Germany was renewed.

**bulimia nervosa** EATING DISORDER that takes the form of compulsive eating, then purging by induced vomiting or the use of a LAXATIVE or DIURETIC. Confined predominantly to girls and women, the disorder most often results from an underlying psychological problem.

**bulldog** English bullbaiting breed of DOG with a distinctive large head, short upturned muzzle, and a projecting lower jaw. The body is large, with muscular shoulders, a broad chest, and short stout legs; the tail is short. The smooth coat may be white, tan, or brindle. Height: (at shoulder) up to 15in (38cm).

**bullfighting** National sport of Spain and also popular in Latin America and S France. Classically there are six bulls and three matadors, who are assigned two bulls each. Each matador has five assistants – two *picadors* (mounted on armored horses) and three *peones* or *banderilleros*. A bullfight starts when the picadors stab the bull to weaken it. The *peones* then plant *banderillas* (barbed sticks) on the withers of the bull. The matador makes several passes with his red cape (*muleta*) before attempting to kill the bull by thrusting a sword between its shoulder blades. In Spain, bullfighting is regarded as an art, to many others worldwide it is a cruel spectacle.

**bullfinch** Northern European and Asian finch, with a stout, rounded beak. Males have a crimson and gray body and a black head; females have duller colors. It grows to 5.5in (14cm) long; species *Pyrrhula pyrrhula*.

**bullfrog** FROG found in streams and ponds in the US; it is green or brown and breeds in the spring. The largest North American frog, it can jump long distances; it gets its name from its loud bass voice. Family Ranidae, genus *Rana*. Length: up to 8in (20cm).

## BURKINA FASO

This flag was adopted in 1984, when Upper Volta was renamed Burkina Faso. The red, green, and yellow colors symbolize the desire for African unity. This is because they are used on the flag of Ethiopia, Africa's oldest independent country.

**AREA:** 105,869 sq mi (274,200sq km)
**POPULATION:** 9,490,000
**CAPITAL (POPULATION):** Ouagadougou (442,223)
**GOVERNMENT:** Multiparty republic
**ETHNIC GROUPS:** Mossi 48%, Mande 9%, Fulani 8%, Bobo 7%
**LANGUAGES:** French (official)
**RELIGIONS:** Traditional beliefs 45%, Islam 43%, Christianity 12%
**CURRENCY:** CFA franc = 100 centimes

The Democratic People's Republic of Burkina Faso is a landlocked country in West Africa. Although it is a little larger than the United Kingdom, it has only one-sixth of that country's population.

Burkina Faso consists of a plateau, between about 650–2,300ft (200–700m) above sea level. It is cut by several rivers, most of which flow S into Ghana or E into the Niger River. During droughts, some of the rivers stop flowing and their valleys become marshes.

### CLIMATE

OUAGADOUGOU lies in the center of the country and its climate is representative of the nation as a whole. It is hot throughout the year, with most rain occurring between May and September, when it is often humid and uncomfortable. The rainfall is erratic and droughts are common.

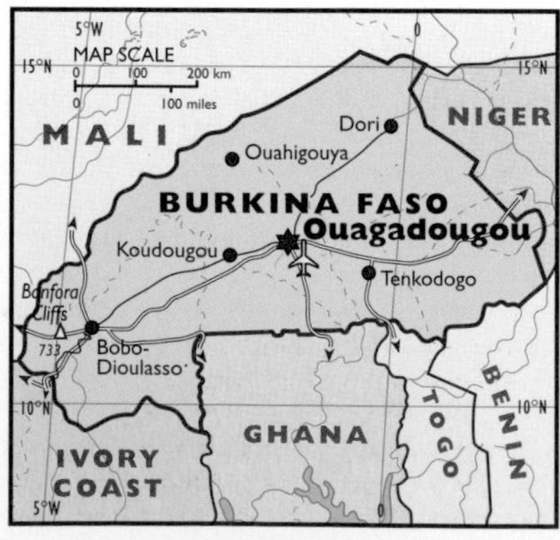


### VEGETATION

The N part of the country is covered by savanna, consisting of grassland with stunted trees and shrubs. It is part of a region called the SAHEL, where the land merges northward into the Sahara. Overgrazing of the land, deforestation, and the consequent soil erosion are common problems in the Sahel, causing desertification in many areas of the country.

Large areas of woodland border the rivers and parts of the SE are swampy. The SE contains the "W" National Park, which Burkina Faso shares with both Benin and Niger, and the Arly Park. A third wildlife area is the Po Park, S of Ouagadougou.

### HISTORY

The people of Burkina Faso are divided into two main groups. The Voltaic group includes the MOSSI, who form the largest single group, and the Bobo. The other main group is the Mande family. Some FULANI herders and HAUSA traders, who are related to the people of N Nigeria, also live here.

In early times, the ethnic groups in Burkina Faso were divided into kingdoms and chiefdoms. The leading kingdom, the Mossi for example, which was ruled by an absolute monarch called the Moro Naba, has existed since the 13th century.

The French conquered the Mossi capital of Ouagadougou in 1897 and they made the area a protectorate. In 1919 the area became a French colony called Upper Volta, and it remained under French rule until 1960, when it became a fully independent republic.

### POLITICS

After independence, Upper Volta became a one-party state, but it suffered from instability. Military groups seized control several times and political killings were common.

In 1984 the country's name was changed by Thomas Sankara to Burkina Faso. In 1991 Captain Blaise Compaoré was elected president, after 20 opposition parties joined forces to boycot what they regarded as an unfair poll. He was re-elected in 1997 .

### ECONOMY

Burkina Faso is one of the world's 20 poorest countries (1995 GDP per capita, $US780) and has become dependent on foreign aid. Nearly 90% of the people earn their living by subsistance farming or raising livestock: grazing land covers about 37% of the land and farmland 10%.

Most of Burkina Faso is dry with thin, relatively unproductive soils. The country's main food crops are beans, corn, millet, and sorghum. Cotton, peanuts, and shea nuts, whose seeds produce a fat used to make cooking oil and soap, are grown for sale abroad. Livestock are an important export.

The country has few resources and manufacturing is on a small scale. There are some deposits of manganese, zinc, lead, and nickel in the N of the country, but there is not yet a good enough transport route to exploit them adequately. Many young men seek jobs abroad, especially in Ghana and Ivory Coast, and the money they send home to their families is important to the country's economy.

**bullhead** Freshwater catfish, originally found throughout the E US. Now farmed as food, it has been introduced in Europe and Hawaii. It has four pairs of fleshy mouth whiskers and a square tail. Length: to 24in (61cm); weight: to 8lb (3.6kg). Family Ictaluridae; species include yellow *Ictalurus natalis* and brown *Ictalurus nebulosus*.

**bull market** In terms of the stock market, a rising market as opposed to a falling, BEAR MARKET. As an investor, a bull purchases shares or stocks in anticipation of a rise in prices, when he will sell them and make a profit. The activities of bulls tend to force prices upward.

**Bull Run, First Battle of** (July 21, 1861) CIVIL WAR engagement, fought near Manassas, Virginia. Under-trained Union troops commanded by General Irvin McDowell, at first successful, were eventually routed by Confederate troops under General P.G.T. BEAUREGARD, reinforced by General Thomas J. JACKSON, who earned his nickname "Stonewall" at the battle.

**Bull Run, Second Battle of** (August 28, 1862) CIVIL WAR battle. On the old battleground of 1861, 48,000 Confederates under General Robert E. LEE beat 75,000 Union soldiers under General John Pope. Union losses were 16,000 to the Confederates' 9,000. Pope was dismissed as commander of the Union army, and General George MCCLELLAN, the former commander, reassumed control.

**bull terrier** Strongly built sporting DOG, originating from England and once used for bearbaiting; it has a large oval head with small erect ears. The broad-chested body is set on strong legs and the tail is short. The "colored" variety can be any color, but the "white" is pure white, often with darker head markings. Height (at shoulder): up to 22in (56cm).

**Bülow, Bernhard von, Prince** (1849–1929) Chancellor of the German empire (1900–09). His aggressive foreign policy left Germany isolated against the TRIPLE ENTENTE and heightened the tensions in Europe that preceded the outbreak of World War I. In 1908 Bülow lost the favor of Emperor William II and was forced to resign.

**bumblebee** (humble bee) Robust, hairy black BEE with broad yellow or orange stripes. The genus *Bombus* live in organized groups in ground or tree nests, where the fertile queen lays her first eggs after the winter hibernation. These become worker bees. Later, the queen lays eggs to produce drones (males) and new queens which develop before the colony dies. The cycle is then repeated. The genus *Psithyrus*, or cuckoo bee, lays its eggs in the nests of *Bombus*, which rear them. Length: up to 1in (2.5cm). Order Hymenoptera; family Apidae.

**Bunche, Ralph Johnson** (1904–71) US diplomat. Bunche joined the staff of the UN in 1947 and helped negotiate a ceasefire (1949) in the Arab-Israeli conflict, for which he won the 1950 Nobel Peace Prize. He directed UN peacekeeping forces in Suez (1956), the Congo (1960), and Cyprus (1964) and was UN under-secretary-general (1967–71).

**Bunin, Ivan Alekseyevich** (1870–1953) Russian writer. Bunin was opposed to the 1917 Revolution and emigrated to France. His works lament the passing of the old Russian order. They include the novel *The Village* (1910), and the short story *The Gentleman from San Francisco* (1916). Bunin was the first Russian to be awarded the Nobel Prize for literature (1933).

**Bunker Hill, Battle of** (June 1775) Battle in the AMERICAN REVOLUTION fought on Boston's Charlestown peninsula. The first large-scale battle of the war, it was actually fought S of Bunker Hill on Breed's Hill. Although the Americans were driven from their position, they inflicted heavy losses on the British.

**Bunsen, Robert Wilhelm** (1811–99) German chemist, professor (1852–99) at Heidelberg University. Bunsen did important work with organo-arsenic compounds, and discovered an arsenic poisoning antidote. He later evolved a method of gas analysis. With his assistant, Gustav KIRCHHOFF, Bunsen used SPECTROSCOPY to discover two new elements (caesium and rubidium). He invented various kinds of laboratory equipment, such as the Bunsen cell, a carbon-zinc electric cell that was used in arc lamps. Bunsen also improved a gas burner that was later named after him.

**Bunsen burner** Gas burner widely used in science laboratories. It is named after the German chemist Robert W. BUNSEN. The burner is a 5-in (13-cm) upright tube, usually of brass, attached to a gas source. It has a variable air inlet at its base to control the intensity of its flame.

**Bunshaft, Gordon** (1909–90) US architect, chief designer of the Skidmore, Owings and Merril Group. Influenced by MIES VAN DER ROHE, Bunshaft is best known for Lever House, New York (1952).

**bunting** FINCH found throughout most of the world. Males of the genus *Passerina* are brightly colored, whereas the females are smaller and duller. Members of the genus *Emberiza* are larger and dull colored, although the snow bunting is almost white. Family Fringillidae.

**Buñuel, Luis** (1900–83) Spanish film director. Buñuel's films were harsh and ferociously critical of the church and social hypocrisy. Among his major works are *Un Chien Andalou* (1928), *Viridiana* (1961), *Belle de Jour* (1966), and *The Phantom of Liberty* (1974).

**Bunyan, John** (1628–88) English preacher and author. During the English CIVIL WAR (1642–52) he fought as a Parliamentarian. Bunyan became a Puritan preacher in 1655, and was twice imprisoned for his nonconformist religious activities. His writings include the Christian ALLEGORY *The Pilgrim's Progress* (1684).

**buoyancy** Upward pressure exerted on an object by the fluid in which it is immersed. The object is subjected to pressure from all sides. The result of all these pressures is a force acting upward that is equal to the weight of the fluid displaced. *See also* ARCHIMEDES' PRINCIPLE

**burbot** Bottom-dwelling, freshwater COD found in colder waters of Asia, N America and Europe. It is a slender, brown fish that spawns in winter. Length: to 38in (110cm); weight: to 36lb (16kg). Order Gadiformes; family Gadidae; species *Lota lota*.

**burdock** Oil-yielding weed found throughout Europe, North Africa, and North America. It has large basal leaves and thistlelike purple flower heads covered by stiff, hooked bracts. Common burdock, *Arctium pubens*, is biennial and grows to 3ft (0.9m). Family Asteraceae/Compositae.

**Burger, Warren Earl** (1907–95) US jurist, 15th Chief Justice (1969–86) of the US Supreme Court. Burger first served as a judge (1956–69) of the US Court of Appeals in Washington D.C. A conservative chief justice, he prevented or overturned liberal legislation. In *Gregg* v. *Georgia* (1976) capital punishment for murder was declared constitutional.

**Burgess, Anthony** (1917–93) English novelist. Burgess' early works are set in Malaya, where he lived and served (1954–60) as part of the Colonial Service. His best-known work is *A Clockwork Orange* (1962), a nightmare vision of a modern dystopia in which he deploys a macabre, invented language. Later novel include *Earthly Powers* (1980), and *The Kingdom of the Wicked* (1985).

**Burgess Shale** Layer of siltstone in a quarry in Yoho National Park, E British Columbia, Canada. Discovered in 1909 by US scientist Charles Walcott, it contains a large number of animal fossils from the CAMBRIAN period. They include animals that have completely vanished, and apparently do not belong to any of the 32 or so phyla (major groups) of animals we know today.

**Burghley, William Cecil, 1st Baron** (1520–98) English statesman and chief minister of ELIZABETH I of England. He was secretary of state (1550–53) under EDWARD VI but failed to win MARY I's favor on her accession to the throne. On Mary's death, Elizabeth I made him secretary of state (1558–72) and then lord high treasurer (1572–98). In 1587 Burghley was responsible for ordering the execution of MARY, QUEEN OF SCOTS.

**Burgos** Capital city of Burgos province, N Spain. Founded in the 9th century, it was the capital of the former kingdom of Castile. During the Spanish Civil War it was General Franco's headquarters. Sites includes the burial place of El Cid. It is an important trade and tourist center. Pop. (1991) 160,381.

**Burgundy** Historical region and former duchy of E central France that now includes the departments of Yonne, Côte-d'Or, Saône et Loire, Ain, and Nièvre. Dijon is the historical

▲ **bullfinch** The stout-beaked bullfinch (*Pyrrhula pyrrhula*) is well adapted to its woodland habitats where it feeds on the buds and flowers found on trees.

▲ **bunting** The black-headed bunting (*Emberiza melanocephala*) is found in SE Europe and SW Asia. A type of finch this species grows to about 6in (16cm) long.

▲ **bull terrier** A sporting dog bred for dogfighting and bearbaiting, the bull terrier was a cross between a bulldog and a type of terrier. No longer bred for their aggression, today's bull terriers are intelligent, loyal dogs, and make good family pets.

capital. Burgundy's golden age began in 1364 when John II of France made his son, Philip the Bold, duke of Burgundy. The succeeding dukes created a state that extended across the Rhine and included the Low Countries. The last duke, Charles the Bold (r.1467–77) failed to have himself crowned king by the Holy Roman emperor, and Burgundy was divided up after his death, France annexing the largest part. The region is a rich agricultural region renowned for its wine. Pop. (1990) 1,609,400.

**Burke, Edmund** (1729–97) British statesman and writer, b. Ireland. He played a major part in the reduction of royal influence in the House of Commons and sought better treatment for Catholics and American colonists. Burke deplored the excesses of the FRENCH REVOLUTION in his most famous work, *Reflections on the Revolution in France* (1790).

**Burke, Robert O'Hara** (1820–61) Irish explorer. In 1860 he led the first expedition to cross Australia from S to N. At the Barcoo River, Burke left most of the party and continued with three companions. They reached N Australia in 1861. Only one of the group (King) survived the return journey.

**Burkina Faso** Landlocked republic in W Africa. *See* country feature, page 114

**burlesque** (It. ridicule) Form of literary or dramatic entertainment that achieves its effect by caricature, ridicule, and distortion, often of celebrated literary genres or works. A later form, in the US, became synonymous with strip shows.

**Burlington, Richard Boyle, 3rd Earl of** (1694–1753) English architect. He was an important exponent of PALLADIANISM in England. Burlington promoted the style through his own buildings, such as his villa at Chiswick, London.

**Burlington** City on Lake Champlain, NW Vermont. Settled in 1773, it was the scene of a British naval attack in the WAR OF 1812. The largest city in the state, Burlington is the site of the University of Vermont and two colleges. Industries: electronics, textiles. Pop. (1990) 39,127.

**Burma** Republic in SE Asia. *See* country feature

## BURMA

The colors on Burma's flag were adopted in 1948 when the country became independent from Britain. The Socialist symbol, added in 1974, includes a ring of 14 stars for the country's states. The gearwheel represents industry and the rice plant agriculture.

**AREA:** 261,228 sq mi (676,577 sq km)
**POPULATION:** 43,668,000
**CAPITAL (POPULATION):** Rangoon (Yangon, 2,458,712)
**GOVERNMENT:** Military regime
**ETHNIC GROUPS:** Burman 69%, Shan 9%, Karen 6%, Rakhine 5%, Mon 2%, Kachin 1%
**LANGUAGES:** Burmese (official)
**RELIGIONS:** Buddhism 89%, Christianity 5%, Islam 4%
**CURRENCY:** Kyat = 100 pyas

The Union of Burma has been officially called the Union of Myanmar since 1989, but most people still know it as Burma. Mountains border the country in the E and W, but the highest mountains are in the N, including Hkakabo Razi at 19,294ft (5,881m). Between these ranges is central Burma, which contains the fertile valleys of the IRRAWADDY and Sittang rivers and MANDALAY, Burma's second largest city (after RANGOON). The Irrawaddy delta on the Bay of BENGAL is one of the world's leading rice-growing areas. Burma also includes the long Tenasserim coast in the SE. The capital, RANGOON, lies on the coast and the next largest city, MANDALAY, is in the interior

### CLIMATE AND VEGETATION

Burma has a tropical monsoon climate, with three seasons. The rainy season runs from late May to mid-October. A cool, dry season follows, between late-October and mid-February. The hot season lasts from late February to mid-May and temperatures remain high during the humid rainy season. Rainfall varies across the country, with the coastal areas being much wetter than the interior plains.

About 50% of the country is covered by forest. Tropical trees, such as teak, grow on low-lying areas, with mangrove swamps on the coast. Forests of oak and pine grow on mountain slopes.

### HISTORY AND POLITICS

Many groups settled in Burma in ancient times. Some, the hill peoples, live in remote mountain areas where they have retained their own cultures. The ancestors of the main group today, the Burmese, arrived in the 9th century.

At the end of the 13th century, Burma was conquered by Kublai Khan. It was reunified by Alaungapaya in 1758. A series of wars between Britain and the Konbaung dynasty (1826–85) resulted in British subjugation of the country into a province of British India. In 1937, the British granted Burma limited self-government. Japan conquered the country in 1942, but was driven out in 1945 by Allied forces and internal resistance forces led by AUNG SAN. Burma achieved independence in 1948.

Revolts by both communists and Karen tribesmen led to instability in the 1950s. In 1962 NE WIN established a military dictatorship and, in 1974, a one-party state. Attempts to control minority liberation movements and the warlords who run the opium trade have led to increasingly repressive rule. Elections in 1990 were won by the National League for Democracy (NLD), led by AUNG SAN SUU KYI, but SLORC annulled the result and placed Aung San Suu Kyi under house arrest. In 1997 SLORC was renamed the State Peace and Development Council (SPDC). In 1998 NLD calls for the reconvening of Parliament led to mass detention of political opponents by the SPDC.

### ECONOMY

Burma's internal political problems have made it one of the world's poorest countries. Agriculture is the main activity, employing 64% of the people. The chief crop is rice, and others include corn, sugarcane, pulses, oilseeds, rubber, and tobacco. Forestry is important. Teak and rice together make up about two-thirds of the total value of exports. Burma has many mineral resources, most of which are undeveloped. It is famous for its precious stones. Manufacturing is on a small scale and most products, such as processed foods and textiles, are sold locally.

**Burmese** Official language of Burma, spoken by 75% of the population, or 25 million people. It belongs to the Tibeto-Burman branch of the Sino-Tibetan family of languages.

**burn** Injury caused by exposure to flames, scalding liquids, caustic chemicals, acids, electric current, or ionizing radiation. Its severity depends on the extent of SKIN loss and the depth of tissue damage. A **superficial** burn, involving only the EPIDERMIS, causes redness, swelling, and pain; it heals within a few days. A **partial-thickness** burn (epidermis and DERMIS) causes intense pain, with mottling and blistering of the skin; it takes a couple of weeks to heal. In a **full-thickness** burn, involving both the skin and the underlying flesh, there is charring, and the damaged flesh looks dry and leathery; there is no pain because the nerve endings have been destroyed. Such a burn, serious in itself, is associated with life-threatening complications, including dehydration and infection. Treatment includes fluid replacement and antibiotics; skin grafting may be necessary.

**Burne-Jones, Sir Edward Coley** (1833–98) English painter and designer. He was associated with the PRE-RAPHAELITE BROTHERHOOD's romanticism and escapism. Burne-Jones often depicted scenes from Arthurian and similar legends, and was considered an outstanding designer of stained glass.

**Burnett, Frances Hodgson** (1849–1924) US author, b. England. Burnett is chiefly remembered as the author of the children's classics *Little Lord Fauntleroy* (1886), *The Little Princess* (1905), and *The Secret Garden* (1911).

**Burney, Fanny** (1752–1840) English novelist, dramatist, and diarist. The daughter of the musicologist Dr. Charles Burney, she came to fame with her first novel, *Evelina* (1778), a semi-satirical, semi-sentimental look at polite society through the eyes of a young innocent. This was followed by similar works such as *Cecilia* (1782), *Camilla* (1796), and *The Wanderer* (1814).

**Burnham, Daniel Hudson** (1846–1912) US architect and city planner. With his partner John W. Root, he was a pioneer in the development of early steel-frame and modern commercial architecture. They designed buildings such as the Reliance Building (1890) and the 20-story Masonic Temple Building (1891), both in Chicago.

**Burns, George** (1896–1996) US comedian. With his wife Gracie Allen, he starred in vaudeville, on radio and on TV's *Burns and Allen Show* (1950–58). Burns received an Academy Award for Best Supporting Actor in *The Sunshine Boys* (1975). Other films include *Oh, God!* (1977) and *Oh, God! Book II* (1980).

**Burns, Robert** (1759–96) Scottish poet. The success of *Poems, Chiefly in the Scottish Dialect* (1786), which includes "The Holy Fair" and "To a Mouse", enabled him to move to Edinburgh. Although popular, he could not support himself on the revenue from his poetry, and so became an excise officer. Scotland's unofficial national poet, his works include "Tam o'Shanter" (1790) and the song "Auld Lang Syne." An annual Burns night is held on his birthday, January 25.

**Burnside, Ambrose Everett** (1824–81) US Civil War general. He participated in the First Battle of BULL RUN (1861). Burnside led the Army of the Potomac in the Union defeat at Fredericksburg (1862). He was relieved of command of the 9th Corps following Petersburg (1864). After the war, he was governor of Rhode Island and a senator (1875–81).

**Burr, Aaron** (1756–1836) US statesman, vice president (1801–05). Burr was senator for New York (1791–97). His contribution to the formation of a Republican legislature in New York (1800), ensured the election of a Republican president. Burr was supposed to become vice president, but confusion in the ELECTORAL COLLEGE resulted in a tie for president between Burr and Thomas JEFFERSON. Jefferson was elected with the support of Alexander HAMILTON. This mix-up led to the adoption of the 12th amendment to the US Constitution. Burr was an able vice president and was nominated for governor of New York. Hamilton led public attacks on Burr's suitability, which resulted in a duel (1804). Burr killed Hamilton and effectively ended his own political career. Embittered, he embarked on an apparent conspiracy to establish an independent republic in sw US. He was tried for treason but was acquitted (1807).

**Burra, Edward John** (1905–76) British painter. Fascinated with Harlem, New York, and the Marseilles docks, some of his most famous paintings are the Harlem scenes (1933–34). In the mid-1930s Burra turned to fantastic imagery, akin to SURREALISM. His later paintings, such as *Soldiers* and *War in the Sun*, were provoked by the tragedies of the Spanish Civil War and World War II.

**Burroughs, Edgar Rice** (1875–1950) US author of adventure novels. A prolific writer, he is best known as the creator of Tarzan the apeman, who featured in a series of books, beginning with *Tarzan of the Apes* (1912).

**Burroughs, William S. (Seward)** (1914–97) US novelist, regarded as one of the founders of the BEAT MOVEMENT. Burrough's best-known work, *Naked Lunch* (1959), deals in part with his heroin addiction. Other works, experimental in style, include *The Ticket That Exploded* (1962) and *The Western Lands* (1987).

**Bursa** (Brusa) City in NW Turkey; capital of Bursa province. Bursa is Turkey's sixth-largest city. Founded in the 3rd century BC, it was the first capital (1327–1413) of the Ottoman Empire. In 1402 the city was sacked by Tamerlane. The city has several fine mosques and is famous for its silk manufacture. Pop. (1990) 775,388.

**bursitis** Inflammation of the fluid-filled sac (bursa) surrounding a joint. It is characterized by pain, swelling, and restricted movement. Treatment generally includes rest, heat, and gentle exercise. "Housemaid's knee," "tennis elbow," and bunions are common forms of bursitis.

**Burton, Sir Richard Francis** (1821–90) British explorer and scholar. In 1853 he traveled in disguise to Medina and Mecca, one of the first Europeans to visit the holy cities. On his second trip to E Africa, with John SPEKE in 1857, Burton discovered Lake Tanganyika. The author of many books, he was best known for his translation of the *Arabian Nights* (1885–88).

**Burton, Richard** (1925–84) Welsh stage and film actor, remembered for his deep, passionate, and fiery voice. By the 1950s he had a reputation as a leading Shakespearean actor. Burton appeared in such movies as *The Robe* (1953), *Look Back in Anger* (1959), and *Becket* (1964). He made a number of films with Elizabeth Taylor, notably *Who's Afraid of Virginia Woolf?* (1966). The couple had a tempestuous relationship and married each other twice.

**Burundi** Republic in E central Africa. *See* country feature page 118

**Bush, George Herbert Walker** (1924– ) 41st US president (1989–93). Bush served as a fighter pilot during World War II. In 1966 he entered Congress as a representative for Texas. Under President Richard NIXON, he held several political offices, including ambassador to the United Nations (1971–73). Under President Gerald FORD, Bush was head (1976–77) of the Central Intelligence Agency (CIA). In 1980, after failing to secure the presidential nomination, he became vice president (1981–88) to Ronald REAGAN. In the 1988 presidential election Bush easily defeated the challenge of Michael Dukakis. Iraq's invasion (1990) of Kuwait provided the first test of Bush's "new world order" and a threat to America's oil supplies. The Allied forces, led by General SCHWARZKOPF, won the GULF WAR (1991), but failed to remove Saddam HUSSEIN. At home, Bush was faced with a stagnant economy, high unemployment and a massive budget deficit. He was forced (1990) to break his election pledge and raise taxes. This factor, combined with a split in the conservative vote, led to a comfortable victory for his Democratic successor Bill CLINTON.

**bushbaby** (galago) Primitive, squirrel-like PRIMATE of African forests and bushlands. It is usually gray or brown with a white stripe between its large eyes. It is a gregarious nocturnal tree-dweller which can be domesticated as a pet. Length: (excluding tail) to 15in (38cm). Family Lorisidae; genus *Galago*.

**Bushehr** (Bushire) City in sw Iran, near the head of the Persian (Arabian) Gulf and 115mi (185km) sw of Shiraz. Founded in 1736, it was the chief Iranian port until the rise of Abadan. Industries: carpet-making, cotton. Pop. (1991 est.) 133,000.

**bushido** (way of the samurai) Moral discipline important in Japan between 1603 and 1868. Requiring loyalty, courage, honor, politeness, and benevolence, bushido paralleled European CHIVALRY. Although not a religion, bushido involved family worship and SHINTO rites.

**bushmaster** Largest pit VIPER, found in central America and N South America. It has long fangs and large venom glands, and is pinkish and brown with a diamond pattern. Length: up to 12ft (3.7m). Family Viperidae; subfamily Crotalidae.

**bustard** Large bird found in arid areas of the Eastern Hemisphere. Its plumage is gray, black, brown, and white and its neck and legs are long; in appearance it is quite ostrichlike. A swift runner and a strong, though reluctant flier, it feeds on small animals and lays up to five eggs. Family Otidae. Height: 4.3ft (1.3m).

**butane** ($C_4H_{10}$) Colorless flammable gas, the fourth member of the ALKANE series of HYDROCARBONS. It has two ISOMERS: n-butane is obtained from natural gas; isobutane is a by-product of PETROLEUM refining. Butane can be liquefied under pressure at normal temperatures and is used in the manufacture of fuel gas and synthetic rubber. Properties: b.p. (n-butane) 31.5°F (−0.3°C) and (isobutane) 13.46°F (−10.3°C).

**Buthelezi, Mangusuthu Gatsha** (1928– ) ZULU chief and politician. Buthelezi was installed as chief of the Buthelezi tribe in 1953 and became chief minister of KwaZulu, a black homeland within APARTHEID South Africa in 1970. In 1975 he founded the Inkatha "freedom" party. Buthelezi acted as minister for home affairs (1994– ) in the MANDELA government.

**Butler, Nicholas Murray** (1862–1947) US educationalist. Butler was president of Columbia University (1902–45) and helped to establish the Carnegie Endowment for International Peace (becoming its president, 1925–1945). He shared the 1931 Nobel Peace Prize with Jane ADDAMS.

**Butler, Samuel** (1835–1902) English satirical writer. Butler's famous novel *Erewhon* (1872) is a classic utopian criticism of contemporary social and economic injustice. He produced a sequel to his early masterpiece, *Erewhon Revisited* (1901), and the autobiographical *The Way of All Flesh* (1903), a biting attack on Victorian life.

**butter** Edible fat made from milk. A churning process changes the milk from a water-in-oil emulsion to an oil-in-water emulsion. The fat (oil) globules of the milk collide and coalesce, losing their protective shield of protein and turning into butter, thus separating out from the more

## BURUNDI

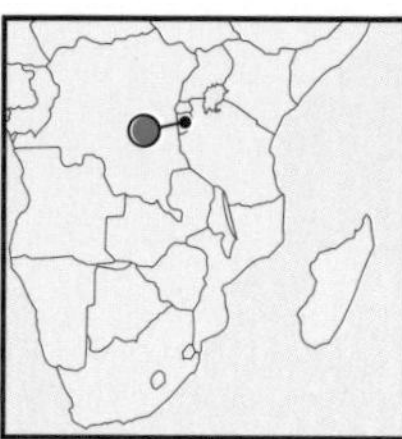

This flag was adopted in 1966 when Burundi became a republic. It contains three red stars rimmed in green, symbolizing the nation's motto of "Unity, Work, Progress". The green represents hope for the future, the red the struggle for independence, and the white the desire for peace.

**AREA:** 10,745 sq mi (27,830 sq km)
**POPULATION:** 5,786,000
**CAPITAL (POPULATION):** Bujumbura (300,000)
**GOVERNMENT:** Republic
**ETHNIC GROUPS:** Hutu 85%, Tutsi 14%, Twa (pygmy) 1%
**LANGUAGES;** French and Kirundi (both official)
**RELIGIONS:** Christianity 85% (Roman Catholic 78%), traditional beliefs 13%
**CURRENCY:** Burundi franc = 100 centimes

The Republic of Burundi is the fifth smallest country on the mainland of Africa and the second most densely populated, after its northern neighbor Rwanda. Part of the Great RIFT VALLEY, which runs throughout E Africa into SW Asia, lies in W Burundi.

East of the Rift Valley are high mountains, reaching 8,760ft (2,760m), composed partly of volcanic rocks. In central and E Burundi, the land descends in a series of steplike grassy plateaus.

### Climate and Vegetation

BUJUMBURA lies on the shore of Lake TANGANYIKA and it has a warm climate. A dry season occurs from July to September, but the other months are fairly rainy. The mountains and plateaus are cooler and wetter, but the rainfall decreases to the E.

Grasslands cover much of Burundi. The land used to be mainly forest, but farmers have cleared most of the trees. In some areas, new forests are being planted to protect the soil against the rain and wind, because soil erosion is a serious problem throughout the region.

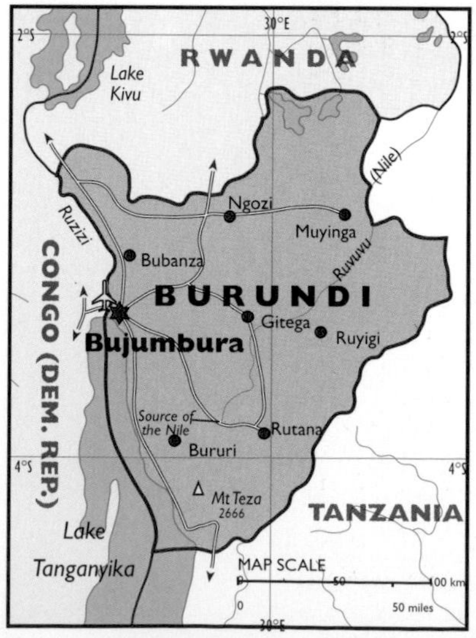


### History and Politics

The Twa, a pygmy people, were the first known inhabitants of Burundi. About 1,000 years ago the Hutu, a people who speak a Bantu language, gradually began to settle in the area, pushing the Twa into more remote areas.

From the 15th century the Tutsi, a tall,cattle-owning people from the NE, gradually took over the country. The Hutu, although greatly outnumbering the Tutsi, were forced into serfdom, serving the Tutsi overlords.

Germany conquered the area that is now Burundi and Rwanda in the 1890s. The area, called Ruanda-Urundi, was then taken by Belgium during World War 1. In 1961 the people of Urundi voted to become a monarchy, while the people of Ruanda voted to become a republic. In 1962, the two territories became fully independent as Burundi and Rwanda.

After 1962 the rivalries between the Hutu and Tutsi led to periodic outbreaks of fighting. The Tutsi monarchy was overthrown in 1966 and Burundi became a republic. Instability continued, with four coups between 1976 and 1996, and periodic massacres as Tutsis and Hutus fought for power.

### Economy

Burundi is one of the world's ten poorest countries (1995 GDP per capita, $US630). About 92% of the people are farmers, but they mostly grow little more than what they need to feed their families. The main food crops are beans, cassava, corn, and sweet potatoes. Cattle, goats are sheep are raised, while fish, caught in Lake Tanganyika, is an important supplement to the local diets. Burundi has to import food.

The main cash crops are coffee, which accounts for 80–90% of the exports; tea and cotton. Mining is unimportant and manufacturing is on a small scale, with most factories modest and based in Bujumbura.

**This 50-centime stamp,** issued in 1964, shows impalas, among the most graceful of Africa's antelopes. In 1964, Burundi was a monarchy, as shown by the wording on the stamp – the French word Royaume means Kingdom. Two years later, Burundi's mwami (king) was overthrown and the country became a republic.

watery whey. Commercial butter contains about 80% fat, 1–3% added salt, 1% milk solids, and 16% water.

**buttercup** Herbaceous flowering plant found worldwide; the many species vary considerably but usually have yellow or white flowers and deeply cut leaves. Family Ranunculaceae; genus *Ranunculus*.

**butterfly** Day-flying INSECT of the order Lepidoptera. The adult has two pairs of scale-covered wings that are often brightly colored. The female lays eggs on a selected food source and the (CATERPILLAR) larvae emerge within days or hours. The larvae have chewing mouthparts and often do great damage to crops until they reach the "resting phase" of the life cycle, the pupa (chrysalis). Within the pupa, the adult (imago) is formed with wings, wing muscles, antennae, a slender body, and sucking mouthparts. *See also* METAMORPHOSIS

**butterwort** Large group of carnivorous bog plants that trap and digest insects in a sticky secretion on their leaves. They bear single white, purple, or yellow flowers on a leafless stalk. The sides of the leaves roll over to enclose the insect while it is digested. Family Lentibulariaceae; species *Pinguicula*. *See also* INSECTIVOROUS PLANT

**buttress** Mass of masonry built against a wall to add support. Used since ancient times, buttresses became increasingly complex and decorative in medieval architecture. Gothic architecture often featured dramatically daring flying buttresses.

**Buxtehude, Diderik (Dietrich)** (1637–1707) Danish organist and composer of organ and church music. He was organist at Lübeck and became well-known for his evening concerts, *Abendmusik*, for which he composed many works. J.S. BACH was greatly influenced by him.

**buzzard** Slow-flying bird with broad, rounded wings, fan-shaped tail, and sharp hooked beak. The name is used in reference to many BIRD OF PREY types as in North America for hawks and vultures. Family Accipitridae; genus *Buteo*.

**Byatt, A.S. (Antonia Susan)** (1936– ) English novelist and critic, sister of the Margaret DRABBLE. Byatt was best known as a literary scholar until she published her third novel, *The Virgin in the Garden* (1978). *Possession*, a mystery story and romance set in the 19th and 20th centuries, became an unlikely bestseller and won the Booker Prize (1990). Her recent work includes the novellas *Angels and Insects* (1993) and *The Djinn in the Nightingale's Eye* (1994). She was awarded the CBE in 1990.

**Byblos** Ancient city of the Phoenicians, in Lebanon, 17mi (27km) N of BEIRUT. Byblos was a center of Phoenician trade with Egypt from the 2nd millennium BC, and was particularly famous as a source of PAPYRUS. The Greek word for "book" derived from its name. The city was abandoned after its capture by the Crusaders in 1103.

**Byrd, Richard Evelyn** (1888–1957) US polar explorer. A naval officer and aviator, Byrd led five major expeditions to the Antarctic (1928–57), surveying more than 845,000sq mi (2,200,000sq km) of the continent. Among other feats, he claimed to be the first man to fly over both the North Pole (1926) and the South Pole (1929).

**Byrd, William** (1543–1623) English composer. Byrd was appointed by Elizabeth I to be joint organist of the Chapel Royal with Thomas Tallis, whom he succeeded in 1585. With Tallis, he was granted England's first monopoly to print music. Byrd was especially celebrated for his madrigals and church music.

**Byron, George Gordon Noel Byron, 6th Baron** (1788–1824) British poet. After a childhood scarred by the handicap of a clubfoot and maltreatment by his mother, Byron went to Trinity College, Cambridge (1805). It was with the publication of the first two cantos of *Childe Harold's Pilgrimage* (1812) that he became famous. Byron's romantic image and reputation for dissolute living and numerous sexual affairs vied with his poetic reputation. By 1816 he was a social outcast and went into permanent exile. Abroad, Byron wrote Cantos III and IV of *Childe Harold* (1816, 1818), and *Don Juan* (1819–24), an epic satire often regarded as his masterpiece. In 1823 he traveled to Greece to fight for Greek independence against the Turks and died of fever at Missolonghi.

**BUTTERFLY**

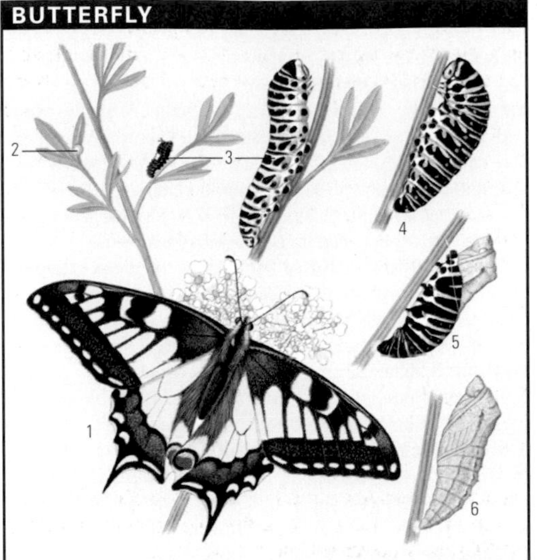


The life cycle of the European swallowtail (*Papilio machoan*) is typical of most butterflies. The female adult (1) lays her eggs (2) on the underside of leaves in batches of 100 or more. The eggs hatch into the first stage larva or caterpillar (3). The caterpillar molts several times before it is fully grown (4). After the final molt the caterpillar's skin hardens (4 and 5) to form the case of the pupa or chrysalis (6). Within the case the tissues of the caterpillar reorganize before the adult butterfly emerges (1).

**byte** Binary number used to represent letters, numbers, and other characters in a computer system. Each byte consists of the same number of BITS. Byte is a contraction of the words "by eight", and originally meant an eight-bit byte, such as 01101010 (representing j on most systems). Many computers now use 16-, 32-, or 64-bit bytes.

**Byzantine art and architecture** Art produced in the Roman empire E of the Balkans. Its greatest achievements fall within three periods. The **first Golden Age** coincided with the reign of Justinian (527–65) and saw the construction of the HAGIA SOPHIA. The **second** Golden Age refers to the artistic revival, which occurred during the time of the Macedonian emperors (867–1057). Finally, the last years of the empire, under the rule of the Palaeologs (1261–1453), are often referred to as the **Byzantine Renaissance**. Most Byzantine art was religious in subject matter and combined Christian imagery with an oriental expressive style. The MOSAIC and ICON were the most common forms. Byzantine church architecture is typically central rather than longitudinal, and the central dome is supported by means of pendentives. Construction is of brick arranged in decorative patterns and mortar. Interiors are faced with marble slabs, colored glass mosaics, gold leaf, and fresco decoration.

**Byzantine empire** Christian, Greek-speaking, Eastern ROMAN EMPIRE, which outlasted the Roman empire in the West by nearly 1,000 years. Constantinople (Byzantium or ISTANBUL) was established by the Roman emperor CONSTANTINE I in AD 330. The area of the Byzantine empire varied greatly and its history from *c.*600 was marked by continual military crisis and heroic recovery. At its height, under JUSTINIAN I, in the 6th century, it controlled, besides Asia Minor and the Balkans, much of the Near East and the Mediterranean coastal regions of Europe and North Africa. From 1204 to 1261 it was controlled by usurping Crusaders from W Europe and, although Constantinople was recovered, Byzantine territory shrank under pressure from the West and from the Ottoman Turks, who finally captured Constantinople in 1453, extinguishing the Byzantine empire.

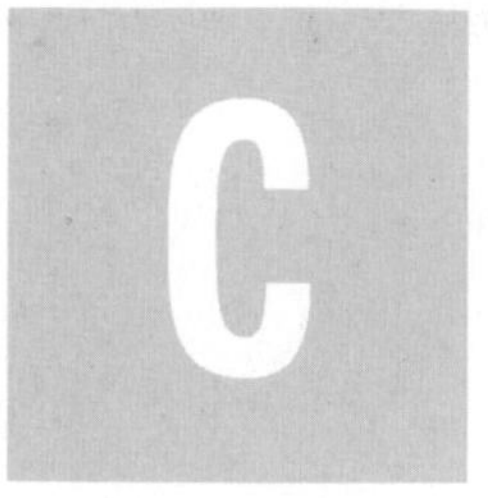

*C/c, third letter of the Roman alphabet, comes from the same root as the letter G/g. It is derived from the Semitic* **gimel**, *meaning throwing stick. It was possibly adapted from the Egyptian* **hieroglyph** *for a boomerang.*

1

2

3

4

5

▲ **cabbage** Cabbage (1), broccoli (2), cauliflower (3), and Brussels sprouts (4) all belong to the same *Brassica* genus although they differ greatly in appearance. Like curly kale (5), they are all hardy and some varieties can stand quite cold winters.

**Caballé, Montserrat** (1933– ) Spanish soprano. Caballé made her debut as Mimì in Puccini's *La Bohème* (1957) and performed at the METROPOLITAN OPERA (1965). She specializes in Verdi and Donizetti.

**cabbage** Low, stout vegetable of the genus *Brassica*. Members include Brussels sprouts, cauliflowers, broccoli, kohlrabi, and turnips. They are all biennials that produce "heads" one year and flowers the next. The common cabbage (*B. oleracea capitata*) has an edible head and large, fleshy leaves. They grow in temperate regions. Family Brassicaceae/Cruciferae.

**cabbage white butterfly** BUTTERFLY, the green caterpillar of which is a common pest on cabbage plants. The female adult is almost completely white except for black spots on its wings; the male has no forewing spots. Species *Pieris brassicae*.

**cabbala** (kabbala) Form of Jewish MYSTICISM. It holds that every word, letter, number, even accent of the Bible contains mysteries to be interpreted, often in the form of codes for YAHWEH. The earliest extant cabbalist work is the 3rd-century *Sefir Yezirah* (Book of Creation). Cabbalism spread throughout Europe in the 13th century, and is still practiced by some Hasidic Jews. *See also* HASIDISM; JUDAISM

**Cabeza de Vaca, Álvar Núñez** (1490–1557) Spanish explorer. In 1528 he was shipwrecked off the Texas coast. Cabeza and three fellow survivors became the first Europeans to explore the American Southwest, eventually settling in Mexico (1536). His published account (1542) and exaggerations encouraged dreams of treasure in the region. His *Comentarios* (1555) recount hardships endured in South America, where he served as governor (1542–45) of the province of Río de la Plata before being disgraced and impoverished through political intrigue.

**Cabinda** Province of Angola, SW Africa, N of Congo River, bounded W by the Atlantic Ocean and separated from the rest of Angola by Zaire; the seaport and chief town is Cabinda. The Simulambuco Treaty (1885) politically unified Cabinda with Angola. Cabinda refuses to recognize the treaty and claims independence from Angola. There are important offshore oil fields. Industries: oil refining, palm, timber, cacao. Area: 2,808sq mi (7,270sq km). Pop. (1992 est.) 152,100.

**cabinet** Body of people collectively advising the chief executive in a presidential system or responsible to the legislature for government in a parliamentary system. Most cabinet members have individual responsibility for the management of a department of state. In the US, cabinet members are heads of major executive departments, although the president may appoint other officials.

**cable** Wire for mechanical support, for conducting electricity, or carrying signals. In civil and mechanical engineering, a cable is made of twisted strands of steel wire. They range in size from small bowden cables to massive supporting cables on the decks of suspension bridges. In electrical engineering, a cable is a conductor consisting of one or more insulated wires. They range greatly in size, from cables used for domestic wiring to the large, armored underwater cables. These are used for telephone, radio, television, and data signals. In a **coaxial** cable one conductor is cylindrical and surrounds the other. FIBER OPTIC cables carry signals in the form of coded pulses of light.

**cable television** Generally refers to community antenna television (CATV). CATV does not broadcast, but picks up signals at a central antenna and delivers them to individual subscribers via coaxial CABLES. Originally designed for areas with poor reception and no local station, cable television, run by private franchise, now serves to increase the variety of local viewing by transmitting channels brought by microwave relay. In 1980 **Cable News Network (CNN)** was founded by US entrepreneur Ted Turner (1938– ). It provides a global 24-hour news service.

**Cabot, John** (*c*.1450–*c*.1498) Italian navigator who made the first recorded European journey to the coast of North America since the Vikings. Supported by the English king Henry VII, Cabot sailed in search of a western route to India, and reached Newfoundland (1497). He followed the coast to Cape Breton Island before returning to England. He did not return from a second voyage, but his discovery served as the basis for English claims in North America.

**Cabral, Pedro Alvares** (1467–1520) Portuguese navigator who was the first European to discover Brazil. Supported by the Portuguese king Manuel I, Cabral led an expedition (1500) to the East Indies. To avoid the Gulf of Guinea, he sailed westward and reached Brazil, which he claimed for Portugal.

**Cabrini, Saint Frances Xavier** (1850–1917) US foundress of orphanages, hospitals, schools, and convents, b. Italy. Cabrini was the first US citizen to be canonized (1946). She became a nun in 1877, founded (1880) the Institute of Missionary Sisters of the Sacred Heart, and moved to the US (1889). Her feast day is December 22.

**cacao** *See* COCOA

**cactus** Any of more than 2,000 species of succulent plants, found particularly in hot desert regions of the Western Hemisphere. A cactus has long roots, adapted to absorb moisture from desert terrains. Stems are usually spiny, cylindrical, and branched. Cactus flowers are usually borne singly in a wide range of colors. Height: 1in (2.5cm) to more than 50ft (15m). *See also* XEROPHYTE

**caddis fly** Any of several moth-like insects of the order Trichoptera. Adults have long, many-jointed antennae, hold their wings tent-like over the body, and usually grow to *c*.1in (2.5cm) long.

**cadence** In music, ending of a melodic phrase and/or its accompanying CHORD progression. In Western classical theory, the main kinds of chordal cadence are: **perfect** (dominant to tonic chords); **imperfect** (tonic or other chord to dominant); **plagal** (subdominant to tonic); and **interrupted** (dominant to chord other than tonic, often submediant).

**Cadillac, Antoine de la Mothe** (1658–1730), French colonial administrator. He arrived in Canada in 1683. Cadillac became commander (1694–97) of the fur-trading post at Mackinac. He founded Detroit (1701), and served as governor of Louisiana (1713–16).

**Cádiz** Port on the Gulf of Cádiz, SW Spain; capital of Cádiz province (founded 1100 BC). It became an important port for shipping routes to the Americas, and in 1587 a Spanish fleet was burned by Sir Francis Drake. Sights include a 13th-century cathedral. Industries: shipbuilding, sherry, olives, salt, fishing. Pop. (1991) 153,550.

**cadmium** (symbol Cd) Silvery-white, metallic element in group II of the periodic table, first isolated (1817) by the German chemist Friedrich Stromeyer. Cadmium is found in greenockite (a sulfide) but is mainly obtained as a by-product in the extraction of zinc and lead. Malleable and ductile, its main uses are as a protective electroplated coating, an absorber of neutrons in nuclear reactors and in nickel-cadmium batteries. Chemically it resembles zinc. Properties: at.no. 48; sp.gr. 112.4; r.d. 8.65; m.p. 320.9°C (609.6°F); b.p. 765°C (1,409°F); most common isotope $^{114}$Cd (28.86%).

**caecilian** Underground, burrowing amphibian found in Central and South America, S Asia, and Africa. Its worm-like body varies from *c*.7–53in (18–135cm) in length and its color from black to pink. There are sensory tentacles between the eyes, which are tiny and often useless.

**Caedmon** Earliest known English poet, dating from around the 7th century. According to BEDE, he was an illiterate herdsman of Whitby Abbey, Yorkshire, who was commanded in a vision to turn the scriptures into poetry. His only surviving work is the fragmentary *Hymn on the Creation*.

**Caernarvon** Town in Britain, on the Menai Strait, NW Wales. It has a 13th-century castle built by Edward I, whose son, Edward II, was crowned the first Prince of Wales (1301). The Princes of Wales are now invested here. Industry: tourism. Pop. (1992 est.) 9,600.

**Caesar** Name of a powerful family of ancient Rome. The most illustrious representative was Julius CAESAR. The name became the title for the Roman emperor in 27 BC on the accession of Octavius (later AUGUSTUS). *Czar* and *kaiser* are derived from it.

**Caesar, (Gaius) Julius** (?100–44 BC) Roman general and statesman. After the death of SULLA, Caesar became military tribune. As *pontifex maximus*, he directed reforms in 63 BC that resulted in the Julian CALENDAR. Caesar formed the First Triumvirate in 60 BC with POMPEY and CRASSUS, instituted agrarian reforms, and created a PATRICIAN-PLEBEIAN alliance. He conquered Gaul for Rome (58–49 BC) and invaded Britain (54 BC). Refusing Senate demands to disband his army, he provoked civil war with Pompey. Caesar defeated Pompey at Pharsalus (48 BC) and pursued him to Egypt, where he made CLEOPATRA queen. After further victories, he returned to Rome in 45 BC and was received with unprecedented honors, culminating in the title of dictator for life. Caesar introduced popular reforms, but his growing power aroused resentment. He was assassinated in the Senate on March 15 by a conspiracy led by CASSIUS and BRUTUS. His grandnephew, Octavian (later AUGUSTUS), together with Mark ANTONY, avenged his murder.

**Caesarean section** *See* BIRTH, CAESAREAN

**caffeine** ($C_8H_{10}N_4O_2$) White, bitter substance that occurs in COFFEE, TEA, and other substances, such as COCOA and ilex plants. It acts as a mild, harmless stimulant and DIURETIC, although an excessive dose can cause insomnia and delirium.

**Cage, John** (1912–92) US avant-garde composer. He believed that all sounds, including noise and silence, are valid compositional materials. Cage invented the "prepared piano," modified by fixing objects to the strings. *Imaginary Landscape* (1951) is written for 12 randomly tuned radios, *Reunion* (1968) consists of electronic sounds created by chess moves on an electric board, *4'33"* (1952) has no sound, except for the environment in which it is performed.

**Cagney, James** (1899–1986) US actor. He is best remembered as the ruthless gangster in such films as *Public Enemy* (1930) and *Angels With Dirty Faces* (1936). Cagney won a Best Actor Academy Award for his performance as US showman George M. Cohan in *Yankee Doodle Dandy* (1942). He made a comeback in *Ragtime* (1981).

**Caiaphas** Jewish high priest who presided over the SANHEDRIN that tried Jesus Christ (Matthew 2, Luke 3, John 18). Caiaphas was one of the priests at the Temple in Jerusalem.

**Cain** First-born son of ADAM and EVE, brother of ABEL. His story is recounted in Genesis 4. God accepted Abel's offering in preference to Cain's and Cain murdered Abel in anger. Marked by God to preserve him from being murdered, Cain was driven out from the Garden of EDEN and lived in exile in the land of Nod.

**Cairo** (Al-Qahirah) Capital of Egypt and port on the Nile River. The largest city in Africa, Cairo was founded (AD 969) by the Fatimid dynasty and subsequently fortified by SALADIN. Medieval Cairo became capital of the MAMELUKE empire, but declined under Turkish rule. Nearby are the SPHINX and the PYRAMIDS of GIZA. Museums include the Museum of Egyptian Antiquities and Museum of Islamic Art. Old Cairo is a world heritage site containing more than 400 mosques and other fine examples of ISLAMIC ART AND ARCHITECTURE. Its five universities include the world's oldest, housed in the mosque of Al Azhar (972) and the center of SHI'A Koranic study. Industries: tourism, textiles, leather. Pop. (1992 est.) 6,663,000. *See also* EGYPTIAN ARCHITECTURE

**Cajun** French-speaking settlers in Louisiana. They were driven from Nova Scotia (then Acadia) by the British in the 18th century. Cajun music and cookery are popular.

**calabash gourd** (bottle gourd) Tropical vine with oval leaves and white flowers. It grows to 30–40ft (9–12m). Its smooth, hard fruit is bottle-shaped and grows to 6ft (180cm) long. Family Cucurbitaceae; species *Lagenaria vulgaris*.

**Calabria** Region in S Italy, including the provinces of Catanzaro, Cosenza, and Reggio di Calabria; the capital is Reggio di Calabria. The local economy is almost exclusively agricultural. Area: 5,822sq mi (15,080sq km). Pop. (1992) 2,074,763.

**Calais** City and seaport on the Strait of Dover, N France. A major commercial center and port since the Middle Ages, it suffered much damage during World War II. Industries: lace making, chemicals, paper. Pop. (1990) 75,309.

**calamine** Pinkish, odorless powder of zinc oxide and some ferric oxide, dissolved in mineral oils and used in skin ointments to alleviate such disorders as chicken pox, poison ivy, and skin rashes.

**Calamity Jane** (*c.*1852–1903) US frontier heroine, b. Martha Jane Canary. She worked in mining and railroad camps in the West and with the US cavalry as a guide and scout. A fine horsewoman and expert shot, she appeared in various Wild West shows in the 1890s.

**calcite** (calcium carbonate, $CaCO_3$). Mineral, a major constituent of calcareous sedimentary rock, especially LIMESTONE. The crystals are in the hexagonal system and vary in form from tabular (rare) to prismatic or needle-like. Calcite is usually glassy white but may be red, pink, or yellow. It reacts with dilute hydrochloric acid. Hardness 3; s.g. 2.7.

**calcium** (symbol Ca) Common, silvery-white metallic element of the ALKALINE-EARTH METALS; first isolated (1808) by Sir Humphry DAVY. It occurs in many rocks and minerals, notably LIMESTONE and GYPSUM, and in bones. Calcium helps regulate the heartbeat and is essential for strong bones and teeth. The metal, which is soft and malleable, has few commercial applications but its compounds are widely used. It is a reactive element, combining readily with oxygen, nitrogen, and other nonmetals. Properties: at.no. 20; at.wt. 40.08; sp.gr. 1.55; m.p. 1,542°F (839°C); b.p. 2,703°F (1,484°C); most common isotope $^{40}Ca$ (96.95%).

**calcium carbide** (calcium acetylide, $CaC_2$) Chemical made commercially by heating coke and calcium oxide (CaO) in an ELECTRIC FURNACE. It reacts with water to yield ETHYNE. Calcium carbide is also used to manufacture ETHANOIC ACID and ETHANAL.

**calcium carbonate** ($CaCO_3$) White compound, insoluble in water, that occurs naturally as MARBLE, CHALK, LIMESTONE, and CALCITE. Calcium carbonate also forms the shells of mollusks. Crystals are in the hexagonal system and vary in form. Calcium carbonate is used in the manufacture of cement, iron, steel, and lime, and as a constituent of antacids. Properties: sp.gr. 2.7 (calcite).

**calcium oxide** (quicklime, CaO) White solid made by heating CALCIUM CARBONATE ($CaCO^3$) at high temperatures. It is used industrially to treat acidic soil and make porcelain, glass, caustic soda, mortar, and cement, and in the recovery of AMMONIA. Calcium oxide reacts with water to form calcium hydroxide ($Ca(OH)^2$), which dissolves in water to give lime water.

**calcium sulfate** ($CaSO_4$) Chemical compound that occurs naturally as the mineral anhydrite. The hydrated form ($CaSO^4.2H^2O$) is the mineral GYPSUM, which loses water when heated to form plaster of Paris (calcium sulfate, $(CaSO^4)^2.H^2O$).

**calculus** Branch of mathematics dealing with continuously changing quantities. DIFFERENTIAL CALCULUS is used to find slopes of curves and INTEGRAL CALCULUS is used to find the areas enclosed by curves. The fundamental theorem is: $\int_a^b f(x)dx = g(b)-g(a)$, where $g$ is any FUNCTION whose DERIVATIVE is the function $f$. For more than 200 years it was believed that this theorem was discovered (independently) by Gottfried LEIBNIZ and Isaac NEWTON. In 1934 a note written by Newton was discovered that acknowledged the work of Pierre de FERMAT.

**Calcutta** City on the Hooghly River, E India; capital of West Bengal state. Founded *c.*1690 by the EAST INDIA COMPANY, it was the capital of India under British rule (1772–1912). It has a

▼ **Caesar** Successful campaigns were waged by Julius Caesar between 58 and 51 BC against the Helvetii, Belgae, Veneti, and the Aquitani. He conquered the whole of Gaul and made it a new province, Transalpine Gaul. He twice landed in Britain. The second expedition was on quite a large scale, landing near Walmer or Deal in 54 BC and penetrating northward beyond St Albans.

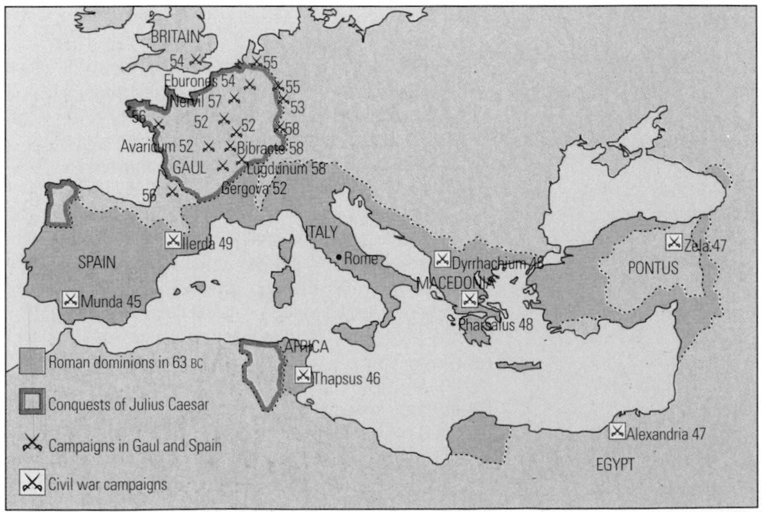

university (1857) and several important temples. The major port and industrial center of E India, Calcutta has one of the world's largest jute-milling industries. Other industries: electrical equipment, chemicals, paper, cotton. Pop. (1991) 4,309,819.

**Calder, Alexander** (1898–1976) US sculptor. Calder created the mobile, a type of colorful, kinetic sculpture with parts that move either by motors or air currents. He also developed nonmoving sculptures called "stabiles."

**caldera** Large, shallow crater formed when a volcano collapses and the MAGMA migrates under the Earth's crust. The caldera of an extinct volcano, if fed by floodwater, rain or springs, can become a crater lake.

**calendar** Way of reckoning time for regulating religious, commercial, and civil life, and for dating events in the past and future. Ancient Egyptians had a system based on the movement of the star SIRIUS and on the seasons. Calendars are based on natural and astronomical regularities: tides and seasons, movements of the Sun and Earth, and phases of the Moon. The basic units are day, month, and year. The main difficulty in compiling a calendar is that the month is not an exact number of days and the year not an exact number of months. For convenience, extra days (intercalations) are added at intervals to compensate. In the modern **Gregorian** or New Style calendar an extra day (February 29) is added every four years ( leap year). The Gregorian calendar was based on the **Julian** or Old Style solar calendar. This was introduced by Julius Caesar in the 1st century BC and was developed from an earlier Moon-based calendar.

**Calgary** City at the confluence of the Bow and Elbow rivers, S Alberta, Canada. It was founded in 1875 as a post of the Royal Canadian Mounted Police. It is an industrial and commercial center, and has a university (1945). Industries: flour milling, timber, brick, cement, oil refining. Pop. (1991) 710,677.

**Calhoun, John Caldwell** (1782–1850) US vice president (1825–32). After serving in the House of Representatives (1811–17), he was secretary of war (1817–25). Calhoun was vice president under John Quincy ADAMS and Andrew JACKSON, resigning over the NULLIFICATION issue. He was elected to the Senate and was secretary of state (1844–45). A staunch advocate of SLAVERY and STATES' RIGHTS, Calhoun strongly influenced the South in the course that led to the CIVIL WAR.

**calibration** Testing of scientific instruments for the purpose of affixing measuring scales. For example, thermometers are calibrated in degrees Fahrenheit or Celsius, or in kelvins, and pressure gauges are calibrated in N/m$^2$ or lb/sq ft.

**California** State on the Pacific coast; the largest state by population and the third largest in area. The capital is SACRAMENTO. Other major cities include LOS ANGELES, SAN FRANCISCO, SAN DIEGO, and OAKLAND. The Spanish explored the coast in 1542, but the first European settlement was in 1769, when Spaniards founded a Franciscan mission at San Diego. The area became part of Mexico. Settlers came from the US and, during the MEXICAN WAR, US forces occupied California (1846); it was ceded to the US at the war's end. After gold was discovered in 1848, the GOLD RUSH swelled the population from 15,000 to 250,000 in four years. In 1850 California joined the Union. In the 20th century, the discovery of oil and development of service industries attracted further settlers. In the W, Coast Ranges run N to S, paralleled by the Sierra Nevada Mountains in the E; between them lies the fertile Central Valley, drained by the Sacramento and San Joaquin rivers. In the SE, is a broad desert area. With a perennial growing season and vast irrigation projects, California is the leading producer of many crops, including a wide variety of fruit and vegetables. Forests cover *c*.40% of the land and support an important timber industry. Mineral deposits include oil, natural gas, and a variety of ores valuable in manufacturing (the largest economic sector). Industries: tourism, aircraft, aerospace equipment, electronic components, missiles, wine. Area: 155,973sq mi (403,971sq km). Pop. (1990) 29,760,021.

**CALIFORNIA**
**Statehood:** September 9, 1850
**Nickname:** The Golden State
**State bird:** California valley quail
**State flower:** Golden poppy
**State tree:** California redwood
**State motto:** *Eureka!*

**California, University of** State university in California (founded 1868). The university system has nine campuses throughout the state. Undergraduate study is at eight campuses: Berkeley, Davis, Irvine, Los Angeles, Riverside, San Diego, Santa Barbara, and Santa Cruz.

**California redwood** (*Sequoia sempervirens*) CONIFER that grows to more than 330ft (100m), and is one of the tallest trees. Its close relative from California is the less common big tree or wellingtonia (*Sequoiadendron giganteum*), the heaviest tree in the Western world. SEQUOIAS can live for more than 4,000 years. Family Taxodiaceae.

**californium** (symbol Cf) Radioactive, metallic element of the ACTINIDE SERIES, first synthesised (1950) at the University of California, Berkeley, by alpha-particle bombardment of the curium isotope $^{242}$Cm. Californium presents biological dangers because one microgram releases 170 million neutrons a minute. Properties: at.no. 98; most stable isotope $^{251}$Cf (half-life 800yr). *See also* TRANSURANIC ELEMENTS

**Caligula** (AD 12–41) (Gaius Caesar) Roman emperor (37–41). Son of Germanicus Caesar, he became emperor after the death of TIBERIUS. Caligoula was highly autocratic, made his horse a consul to mock the Senate, and was said to be insane. He was murdered by the Praetorian Guard and succeeded by his uncle, CLAUDIUS I.

**caliph** Leader of the Muslim community. After the death of MUHAMMAD, ABU BAKR was chosen to be his caliph (successor). The role was originally elective but later became hereditary. The title remained with the Ottoman sultans (1517–1924), after which it was abolished. *See also* OMAR; OTHMAN; ALI

**Callaghan, (Leonard) James, Baron** (1912– ) British statesman, prime minister (1976–79). He entered Parliament in 1945 and succeeded (1976) Harold WILSON as LABOUR PARTY leader. Callaghan is the only prime minister in British history to have held all three major offices of state: chancellor of the exchequer (1964–67), home secretary (1967–70), and foreign secretary (1974–76). His administration was marked by strife with the labor unions that culminated in the "winter of discontent." Callaghan was defeated by Margaret THATCHER in the 1979 general election. He was made a life peer in 1987.

**Callas, Maria** (1923–77) Greek soprano. She made her debut in 1941, but attracted international recognition for her performance as Gioconda in Verona (1947). Callas was best-known for her *bel canto* roles, singing Norma at her London (1952), and New York (1956) debuts. She combined dramatic ability with a rich, versatile voice. Callas retired in 1965.

**calligraphy** Art of fine writing. Calligraphy is freehand, with components in proportion to each other. In Europe there was a marked difference between **uncial** hands used for literary works, which are rounded, easily inscribed letters, and **cursive** hands, used for documents and letters, which are more regularized. Fragments on papyrus from the 3rd century BC show a variety of cursive hands. During the 8th century the **minuscule** superseded the uncial for ordinary, commercial purposes. The 20th century has seen a revial of calligraphy.

**Callisto** Second-largest and outermost of Jupiter's GALILEAN SATELLITES, with a diameter of 3,000mi (4,800km). It is the most heavily cratered object known. As well as the dark dense craters, there are large, multiringed impact features, the largest of which is Valhalla, with a diameter of 2,500mi (4,000km).

**callus** In botany, a protective mass of undifferentiated plant cells formed at the site of a wound in a woody plant. Callus tissue is also formed at the base of cuttings as they start to take root. Callus tissue is important as the starting point for TISSUE CULTURE of plants.

**calotype** Photographic process developed and patented in 1841 by Fox Talbot. The positive-negative process produced a print made from a paper negative that was brushed with silver iodide and other chemicals and exposed in the camera.

**calorie** Unit of heat. A calorie is the amount of heat required to raise 1 gram of water one degree CELSIUS between 58.1 and 59.9°F (14.5 –15.5°C). The SI system of units uses the JOULE (1 calorie = 4.184 joules) instead of the calorie. A dietition's "calorie" is the kilocalorie, 1,000 times larger than a calorie.

**Calvert, George, 1st Baron Baltimore** (1580–1632) English colonizer. Calvert was secretary of state (1619–25) under James I, but resigned after converting to Roman Catholicism. In 1629 he sought a charter for a colony in what became Maryland. Baltimore died before the charter was issued and the grant passed to his son, Cecil, 2nd Lord Baltimore, whose brother Leonard became the first governor.

**Calvin, John** (1509–64) French theologian of the Reformation. He prepared for a career in the Roman Catholic Church but turned to the study of classics. In *c.*1533 Calvin became a Protestant and began work on his *Institutes of the Christian Religion*. In this work he presented the basics of what came to be known as Calvinism. To avoid persecution, he went to live in Geneva, Switzerland (1536), where he advanced the Reformation.

**Calvin, Melvin** (1911–97) US chemist. Calvin used radioactive carbon-14 as a trace to label carbon dioxide and track the process by which plants turned it into glucose by photosynthesis. The series of reactions that take place during photosynthesis is known as the Calvin cycle. In 1961 he received the Nobel Prize for chemistry.

**Calvinism** Set of doctrines and attitudes derived from the Protestant theologian John Calvin. The Reformed and Presbyterian churches were established in his tradition. Rejecting papal authority and relying on the Bible, Calvinism stresses the sovereignty of God and predestination. It usually subordinates state to church, and cultivates austere morality, family piety, business enterprise, education, and science. These doctrines, particularly predestination, and the rejection of consubstantiation in its eucharistic teaching, caused a split in Protestantism between Lutheranism and Presbyterianism. Calvinist leaders include John Knox and Jonathan Edwards.

**Calypso** In Greek mythology, the daughter of Atlas and Tethys. Calypso lived on the mythical island of Ogygia. When Odysseus landed on the island during a storm, she imprisoned him for seven years. Finally Hermes was sent by Zeus to have Odysseus released.

**cambium** In botany, layer of cells parallel to the surface of stems and roots of plants that divides to produce new cells to allow for growth in diameter of the stem and roots. There are two main types of cambium. **Vascular** cambium produces new phloem on the outside and xylem on the inside. **Cork** cambium forms a cylinder just below the epidermis, and produces cork cells to replace the epidermis, which ruptures as the stem and root expand, forming the bark and corky outer layer of the older root. *See also* Meristem

**Cambodia** Kingdom in SE Asia. *See* country feature

**Cambrian** Earliest period of the Paleozoic era, lasting from *c.*590 million to 505 million years ago. Cambrian rocks are the earliest to preserve the hard parts of animals as fossils. The commonest animal forms were trilobites, brachiopods, sponges, and snails. Plant life consisted mainly of seaweeds.

## CAMBODIA

Red is the traditional color of Cambodia. Blue symbolizes the water resources that are so important to the people, 75% of whom depend on farming for a living. The silhouette is the historic temple at Angkor Wat.

**AREA:** 69,900sq mi (181,040sq km)
**POPULATION:** 9,054,000
**CAPITAL (POPULATION):** Phnom Penh (920,000)
**GOVERNMENT:** Constitutional monarchy
**ETHNIC GROUPS:** Khmer 94%, Chinese 3%, Cham 2%, Thai, Lao, Kola, Vietnamese
**LANGUAGES:** Khmer (official)
**RELIGIONS:** Buddhism 88%, Islam 2%
**CURRENCY:** Riel = 100 sen

The Southeast Asian kingdom of Cambodia is bordered by low mountains except in the SE. Most of the country consists of plains drained by the Mekong River, which enters Cambodia from Thailand in the N and exits through Vietnam in the SE. In the NW is Tonle Sap (Great Lake), which in the dry season drains into the Mekong. In the monsoon, the Mekong rises and water flows from the river into Tonle Sap.

### Climate

Cambodia has a tropical monsoon climate, with constant high humidity and temperatures. The dry season (when winds blow from the N or NE) runs from November to April. During the May–October rainy season moist winds blow from the S or SE, bringing heavy coastal rain; inland areas have less rain.

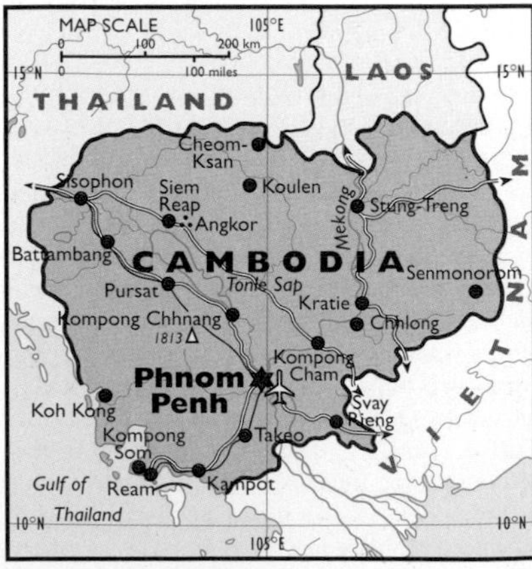


### Vegetation

Forests cover *c.*75% of Cambodia. There are dense rainforests in the N mountains, while mangrove forests line the coast.

### History and Politics

In the 6th century the Khmer established an empire roughly corresponding to modern-day Cambodia and Laos. In 889 the empire was reunited, with its capital at Angkor. The Angkor period (889–1434) was the golden age of Khmer civilization, culminating in the 12th-century construction of Angkor Wat. In 1863 Cambodia became a French protectorate, and was subsumed into the Union of Indochina in 1887. During World War II, it was occupied by Japan. In 1953 Cambodia achieved full independence from France. Prince Norodom Sihanouk became king. In 1955 he abdicated to become prime minister. The Vietnam War (1954–75) dominated Cambodian politics. Initially, Cambodia received US aid, but in 1963 Sihanouk denounced US interference. The build-up of North Vietnamese troops persuaded Sihanouk to seek US help and, in 1969, the US conducted secret bombing raids on communist bases in Cambodia. In March 1970 Sihanouk was overthrown by Lon Nol, and US and South Vietnamese troops entered Cambodia to destroy North Vietnamese camps. Many civilians were killed, and public support rallied behind the Cambodian communists (Khmer Rouge). In October 1970 the Khmer Republic was declared, but the communists already controlled most of rural Cambodia. Civil war broke out. Despite US military aid, the government continued to lose ground. In 1973 the US Congress halted air attacks. In 1975 the Khmer Rouge (led by Pol Pot) seized Phnom Penh. Cambodia was renamed **Kampuchea**. A brutal form of peasant politics ensued in which *c.*2 million people were murdered. In 1979 Vietnamese and Cambodian troops overthrew Pol Pot, but fighting continued. In 1989 Vietnamese troops withdrew. In 1993 elections were held (without the Khmer Rouge) and a coalition government was formed. Sihanouk was restored as king. In 1994 the Khmer Rouge was banned. In 1997 Hun Sen ousted his co-premier, Prince Norodom Ranaridh. In 1998 elections Hun Sen claimed victory, amid widespread accusations of fraud.

### Economy

Cambodia is a poor economy, wrecked by war (1992 GDP per capita, $1,250). Until the 1970s, it was agriculturally self-sufficient, but by 1986 it could meet only 80% of its needs. Major products include rice, rubber, and corn.

**The numbers** of wild animals in Southeast Asia have been greatly reduced as land is cleared. The stamp, issued in 1964, shows a kouprey, a rare wild ox.

**Cambridge** City on the Cam River, county town of Cambridgeshire, E England. It has one of the world's leading universities. Industries: precision engineering, electronics, printing, publishing. Pop. (1991) 91,933.

**Cambridge, University of** Founded in 1209 (with claims for an earlier origin), it is one of the oldest scholarly establishments in England. It has a collegiate system, the oldest college being Peterhouse (1284). A center of Renaissance learning and theological debate in the Reformation, it now offers almost every discipline. In the 20th century it excelled in scientific research. Its many buildings include Kings College Chapel.

**Cambridgeshire** County in E central England; the county town is CAMBRIDGE. The area is marshy with chalk hills to the S and is drained by the Ouse and Nene rivers. Ely and Peterborough both have cathedrals. Agriculture is the most important economic activity; crops include wheat, barley, and oats. Area: 1,312sq mi (3,400sq km). Pop. (1990) 645,125.

**camel** Large, hump-backed, UNGULATE mammal of the family Camelidae. There are two species – the two-humped **Bactrian** of central Asia and the single-humped Arabian **dromedary**. Its broad, padded feet and ability to travel several days without water make the camel a perfect desert animal. Camels can carry up to 600lb (270kg) and cover *c.*30mi (50km) a day. Genus *Camelus*.

**camellia** Genus of evergreen trees or shrubs of the family Theaceae, native to E Asia. It has oval, dark green leaves and waxy, rose-like flowers which may be pink, red, white, or variegated. *Camellia japonica* is the most common species.

**Camelot** In English mythology, the seat chosen by King ARTHUR for his court. Its site is not known, although many believe it was Cadbury Castle, Somerset, SW England.

**cameo** Relief carving, usually on striated gemstones, semi-precious stones, or shell. The decoration, often a portrait head, is generally cut on the light-colored vein, the dark vein being left as a background. Cameos originated from carved stone seals used by Ancient Egyptians, Greeks, and Etruscans.

**camera** Apparatus for taking photographs, consisting essentially of a light-proof box containing photographic film. When a shutter is opened, usually briefly, light from the scene is focused by a lens system onto the film. The amount of light falling on the film is controlled by the shutter speed and by the diameter of the lens APERTURE. Many cameras also have a rangefinder, enabling a focused image to be produced for a given object distance, and a built-in exposure meter to deter-

## CAMEROON

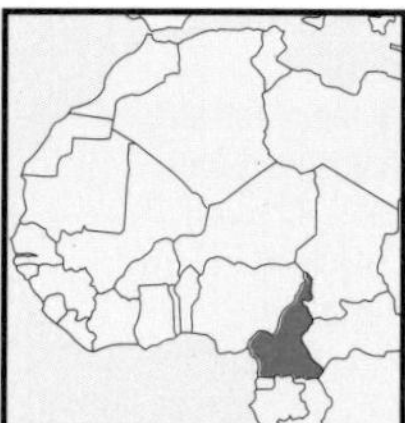

Cameroon uses the colors that appear on the flag of Ethiopia, Africa's oldest independent nation. These colors symbolize African unity. The flag is based on the tricolor adopted in 1957. The design (with a yellow liberty star) dates from 1975.

**AREA:** 183,567sq mi (475,440sq km)
**POPULATION:** 12,198,000
**CAPITAL (POPULATION):** Yaoundé (750,000)
**GOVERNMENT:** Multiparty republic
**ETHNIC GROUPS:** Fang 20%, Bamileke and Bamum 19%, Douala, Luanda and Basa 15%, Fulani 10%
**LANGUAGES:** French and English (both official)
**RELIGIONS:** Christianity (Roman Catholic 35%, Protestant 18%), traditional beliefs 25%, Islam 22%
**CURRENCY:** CFA franc = 100 centimes

The West African republic of Cameroon gets its name from the early Portuguese explorers, who fished for *camarões* (prawns) along its coast. Behind narrow coastal plains on the Gulf of Guinea, the land rises in a series of plateaus. In the N, the land slopes down towards the Lake CHAD basin. The mountainous SW region rises to the active volcano, Mount Cameroon at 13,354ft (4,070m).

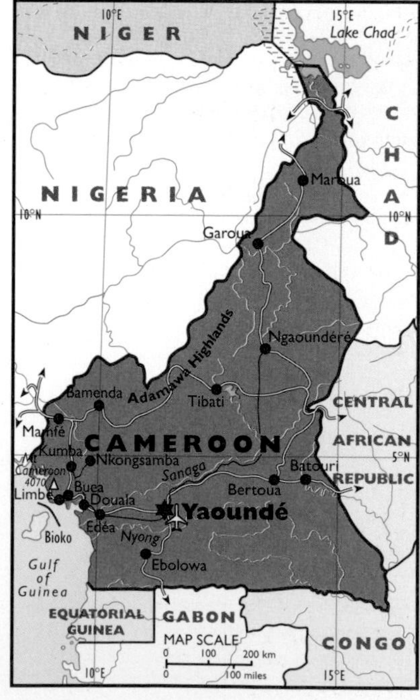


### CLIMATE

Cameroon has one of the wettest climates on Earth. The rain is heaviest in the hot and humid SW between July and September. The inland plateaus are cooler. The average annual rainfall decreases as you move N, and the far N has a hot, dry climate.

### VEGETATION

Rainforests flourish in southern Cameroon. Inland, the forests give way to savanna. Here national parks (such as Waza, N of Maroua) contain protected animals, such as antelopes, elephants, giraffes, and lions. The far N is semi-desert.

### HISTORY AND POLITICS

Cameroon is a diverse nation, with more than 160 ethnic groups. Bantu-speakers predominate in coastal areas, such as DOUALA. Islam is the dominant force in the N, major tribal groupings include the FULANI. In 1472, Portuguese explorers (seeking a sea route to Asia) reached the Cameroon coast. From the 17th century, S Cameroon was a center of the slave trade. In the early nineteenth century SLAVERY was abolished and replaced by the ivory trade, led by Britain.

In 1884 Cameroon became a German protectorate. The Germans developed the port of DOUALA. In 1916 the country was captured by Allied troops. After World War I Cameroon was divided in two and ruled by Britain and France. In 1960, following civil unrest, French Cameroon became an independent republic. In 1961 N British Cameroon voted to join the Cameroon Republic (forming the Federal Republic of Cameroon, while S British Cameroon joined Nigeria. In 1966 a one-party state was created, and in 1972 the federation became a unitary state.

From 1960 to 1982 Ahmadou Ahidjo served as Cameroon's president. His successor, Paul Biya, purged the party of Ahidjo's supporters. In 1984 a failed coup led to many executions, and Biya made Cameroon a republic. In 1992 Biya was reelected, amid charges of electoral maplpractice. His autocratic rule was regularly accused of torture and the creation of a police state. In 1995, partly to satisfy its English-speaking community, Cameroon became the 52nd member of the COMMONWEALTH OF NATIONS.

### ECONOMY

Cameroon is one of West Africa's most successful economies (1995 GDP per capita, $2,110). Its wealth, however, is extremely unevenly distributed. Northern Cameroon is impoverished and heavily dependent on cattle-raising. Agriculture employs 79% of the population. It is self-sufficient in foodstuffs. Major crops include cassava, maize, millet, and yams. It is the world's seventh largest producer of cocoa. Other commercial plantations grow coffee, bananas, peanuts, and tobacco. Oil accounts for nearly 50% of Cameroon's exports. Other mineral resources include gold and bauxite.

mine the correct combination of shutter speed and aperture for the prevailing light conditions. *See also* PHOTOGRAPHY

**Cameroon** Republic in W Africa. *See* country feature

**Camões, Luís vaz de** (1524–80) Portuguese poet and soldier. In 1572 he published *The Lusiads*, which was adopted as Portugal's national epic and established Camões as the country's greatest national poet.

**Campaign for Nuclear Disarmament (CND)** Movement in Britain, founded (1958) by Bertrand RUSSELL and Canon John Collins. Advocating unilateral nuclear DISARMAMENT, during the 1960s it organized an annual march. The end of the COLD WAR and disarmament treaties between the US and the former Soviet Union, lessened CND's political prominence.

**Campania** Region of SW Italy on the Tyrrhenian Sea, including the provinces of Avellino, Benevento, Caserta, Napoli, and Salerno; the capital is NAPLES. It is a mountainous area with fertile plains yielding wheat, potatoes, fruit, tobacco, flowers, and wine. Area: 5,249sq mi (13,595sq km). Pop. (1992) 5,668,895.

**Campanulaceae** Bellflower family of herbaceous flowering plants. There are *c.*300 species, including HAREBELL, Canterbury bell, Coventry bell, peach bellflower, and clustered bellflower. They are cultivated for their delicate blossoms, often a pale or purplish blue.

**Campbell, Donald Malcolm** (1921–67) English speed record holder, son of Sir Malcolm CAMPBELL. He set seven new world records on water. In 1964 Campbell broke the world water and speed records in Australia. On Lake Dumbleyung he achieved 276.28mph (444.7km/h), while on the salt flats of Lake Eyre he reached 403mph (648.72km/h). Campbell died trying to set a new record. In 1984 his daughter, Gina, set a new women's water speed record.

**Campbell, Sir Malcolm** (1885–1948) English world speed record holder. In 1935 Campbell became the first man to reach a land speed of 300mph (483km/h), accomplished in *Bluebird* at Utah's Bonneville Salt Flats. He also set a water record of 141mph (227km/h).

**Camp David Agreement** (September 1978) Significant step towards Arab-Israeli reconciliation. The agreement resulted from a meeting between Anwar SADAT of Egypt and Menachem BEGIN of Israel, mediated by US President Jimmy CARTER at his official country home. Condemned by other Arab leaders, the agreement formed the basis for a 1979 treaty between Egypt and Israel. Sadat and Begin shared the 1978 Nobel Peace Prize.

**camphor** ($C_{10}H_{16}O$) Organic chemical compound. It has a strong odor, which also occurs in the wood and leaves of the camphor tree, *Cinammonum camphora*, native to Taiwan. Camphor is used in medicine for liniments, in the manufacture of celluloid, lacquers, explosives, and mothballs.

**Campion, Saint Edmund** (1540–81) English Jesuit priest and martyr. He was ordained deacon in the Church of England (1569), but became a Roman Catholic (1571) and later a Jesuit missionary. In 1581 Campion published the pamphlet *Decem Rationes*, defending Roman Catholicism. He was charged with treason and executed. His feast day is December 1.

**Campion, Thomas** (1567–1620) English physician, poet, and composer. Campion's four *Books of Ayres* (1601–17) for the lute, including "There is a Garden in Her Face," rival the songs of John DOWLAND. *Pomata* (1595) is a collection of Latin epigrams and elergies. *Observations in the Art of English Poesie* (1602) argues for classical forms rather than rhyme.

**Camus, Albert** (1913–60) French novelist, playwright, and essayist. An active figure in the French Resistance, Camus achieved recognition with his first novel, *The Stranger* (1942), a work permeated with the sense of individual alienation. His later works include the novels *The Plague* (1947) and *The Fall* (1956), and the essay *The Rebel* (1951). Camus has been associated with EXISTENTIALISM and the Theater of the ABSURD. He was awarded the 1957 Nobel Prize for literature.

**Canaan** Historical region occupying the land between the Mediterranean and the Dead Sea. The Canaanites were a Semitic people, identified with the Phoenicians from *c.*1200 BC. Canaan was the Promised Land of the Israelites, who settled here on their return from Egypt.

◄ **Canaletto** The *Punta della Dogana* (1730) by Giovanni Caneletto is one of his famous series of views of Venice. The incredible attention to detail is characteristic of his work.

**Canada** Federation in N North America. *See* country feature pages 126–127

**Canada goose** North American wild goose found in wide-ranging habitats, which feeds on grasses or vegetation in streams and ponds. It has white cheek pouches and a long black neck. Nesting on stream banks or tundra, it lays white eggs (4–10). Length: 23–40in (58–100cm); weight: 3–14lb (1.3–6kg). Species *Branta canadensis*.

**Canadian art and architecture** Following Canada's colonization by the French in the 17th century, the Catholic Church provided the main source of patronage. Most art from the colonial period was documentary in nature, such as Paul Kane's portraits of Native Americans. The Royal Canadian Academy of Art, Montreal, and the National Gallery of Canada, Ottawa, were founded in 1880. Landscape painting was the predominant art form in the late 19th and early 20th centuries. Artists, such as J.W. Morrice, used the palette and approach of IMPRESSIONISM to depict the grandeur of the Canadian scenery. In the 1920s the Group of Seven (Frank Carmichael, Lawren Harris, A.Y. Jackson, Franz H. Johnston, Arthur Lismer, J.E.H. MacDonald, and F.H. Varley) rebelled against the prevailing naturalism and produced more expressionist works. Since 1945 Montreal has emerged as a vital artistic center in Canadian national culture, producing a diverse range of modern and post-modern art from surrealism to op art. Canadian civic architecture has often applied prevailing European and American trends. The Parliament building in Ottawa (*c.*1859) by Thomas Fuller is a notable example of GOTHIC REVIVAL. Devotional and domestic architecture is more distinctive.

**Canadian literature** Literary work can be divided into two distinct (yet interrelated) traditions, reflecting Canada's dual French and English linguistic and cultural history. In the 1860s a Quebec group emerged, characterized by nationalist romanticism. In the early 20th century Quebec was again the focus for a parochial pastoralism. In Montreal a more innovative poetic SYMBOLISM developed. The first North American novel, *The History of Emily Montague* (1769), was an account of Quebec by Frances Moore Brooke. The Confederation of 1867 produced the first national literary movement, the Confederation school of poets. At the turn of the 19th century prose tended to pastoral romanticism, such as L.M. Montgomery's classic *Anne of Green Gables* (1908). Literature of the 1920s was more critical of Canadian society; post-1945 literature reflected and nurtured a burgeoning national consciousness. Major poets of the period include Earle Birney, Dorothy Livesay, and Jay Macpherson. Recent novelists include Margaret ATWOOD, Robertson DAVIES, and Mordecai RICHLER.

**canal** Artificial waterway for irrigation, drainage, navigation, or in conjunction with hydroelectric dams. Canals were built 4,000 years ago in ancient Mesopotamia. Today, the longest canal able to accommodate large ships connects the Baltic and White seas in N Europe. It is 141mi (227km) long. The heyday of canal building in the US was in the early 19th century, spurred by the success of the Erie Canal.

**Canaletto** (1697–1768) (Giovanni Antonio Canal) Italian painter of the VENETIAN SCHOOL, famous for his perspectival views of Venice. Canaletto's early work is more dramatic and free-flowing than his smoother, accurate mature style. In 1746 he traveled to England, where he painted views of London and country houses. Canaletto used a camera obscura to make his

Canada's flag, with its simple 11-pointed maple leaf emblem, was adopted in 1964 after many attempts to find an acceptable design. The old flag, used from 1892, was the British Red Ensign. But this flag became unpopular with Canada's French community.

**AREA:** 3,851,788sq mi (9,976,140sq km)
**POPULATION:** 27,562,000
**CAPITAL (POPULATION):** Ottawa (313,987)
**GOVERNMENT:** Federal multiparty constitutional monarchy
**ETHNIC GROUPS:** British 34%, French 26%, German 4%, Italian 3%, Ukrainian 2%, Native American (Amerindian/Inuit) 1.5%, Chinese, Dutch
**LANGUAGES:** English and French (both official)
**RELIGIONS:** Christianity (Roman Catholic 47%, Protestant 41%, Eastern Orthodox 2%), Judaism, Islam, Hinduism, Sikhism
**CURRENCY:** Canadian dollar = 100 cents

Canada, the world's second largest country (after Russia), is thinly populated. Much of the land is too cold or mountainous for human settlement; and most Canadians live within 200mi (320km) of the S border.

Western Canada has the most rugged terrain, including the Pacific ranges and the mighty ROCKY MOUNTAINS. Mount LOGAN is Canada's highest peak, 19,850ft (6,050m). E of the Rockies are the interior plains of Canada's Prairie Provinces (S ALBERTA, MANITOBA, and SASKATCHEWAN). This vast farming area is the northward extension of the prairie regions of the United States.

In the N are the bleak Arctic islands. The Canadian Shield, in E central Canada, is a vast region of ancient rocks, which covers almost half the country, enclosing the HUDSON BAY lowlands. South of the Canadian Shield lie Canada's most populous regions, the lowlands N of Lakes ERIE and ONTARIO and the ST LAWRENCE river valley. The northernmost part of the APPALACHIAN MOUNTAINS are in the far SE.

### CLIMATE

Canada has a cold climate, with winter temperatures below freezing point throughout most of the country. In the N, along the Arctic Circle, mean temperatures are below freezing for seven months every year. But VANCOUVER on the W coast has a mild climate, and average temperatures remain above freezing in the winter months.

Western Canada has plenty of rainfall but the prairies are dry with 10–20in (250–500mm) of rain annually. SE Canada has a moist climate, and QUEBEC has an annual average of *c.*41in (1,040mm) of rain.

### VEGETATION

Forests of cedar, hemlock, and other trees grow on the western mountains, with firs and spruces at higher levels. The interior plains were once grassy prairies, but today they are used mainly for farming and ranching. The far N contains cold, treeless tundra regions. but the SE lowlands contain forests of deciduous trees, such as beech, oak, and walnut. The Appalachian region has beautiful mixed coniferous and deciduous forests.

### HISTORY

Canada's first people, ancestors of present-day Native Americans, arrived in North America from Asia *c.*40,000 years ago. Later arrivals were the INUIT, also from Asia. John CABOT was the first European to reach the Canadian coast in 1497. A race began between France and Britain for the riches in this new land, with France gaining an initial advantage when Jacques CARTIER discovered the St Lawrence River in 1534 and claimed Canada for France.

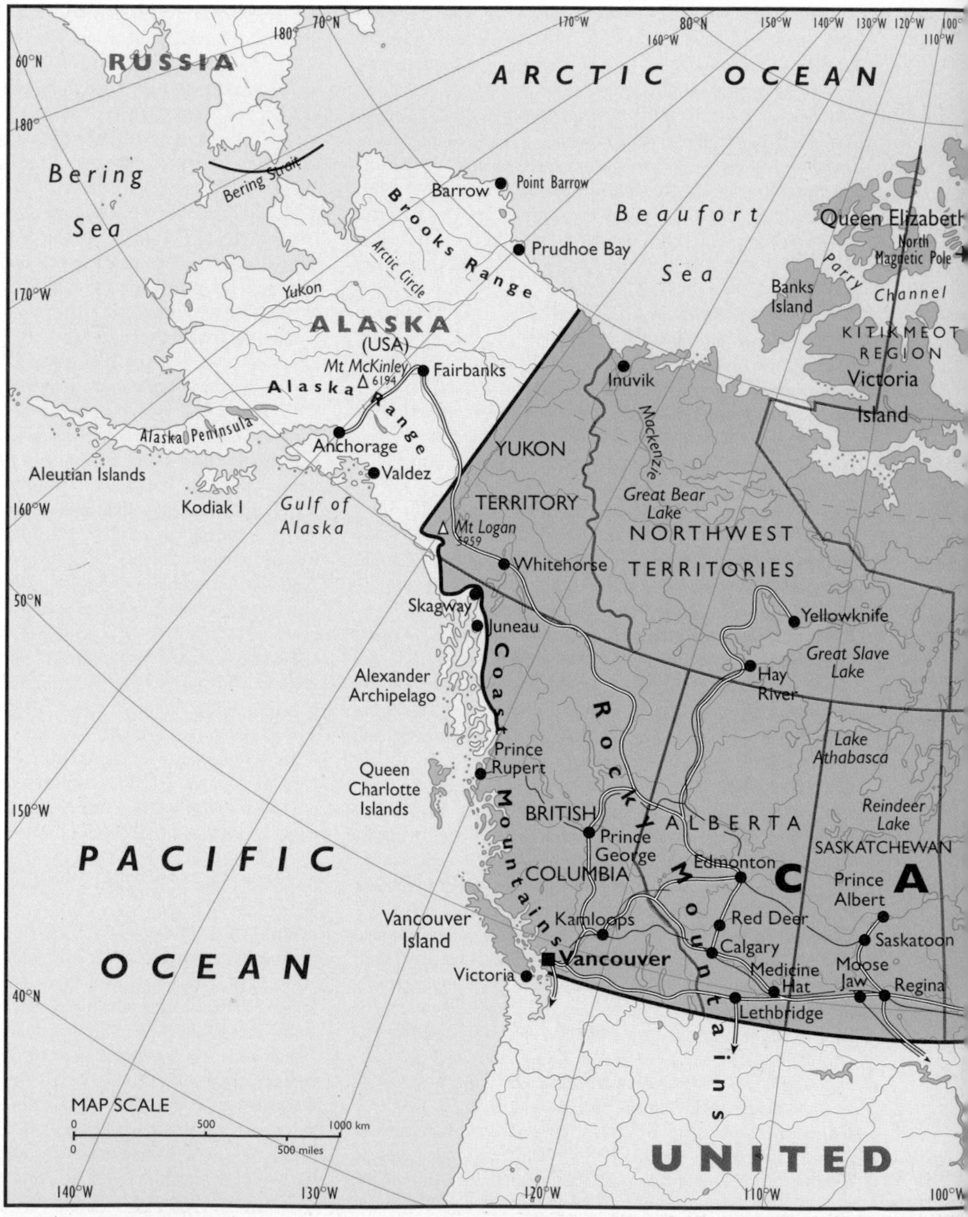

The French established the first European settlement in 1605 and founded Quebec in 1608. The empire was extended by explorers such as LA SALLE. French settlement in the W was generally much slower than English development on the Atlantic coast. The FRENCH AND INDIAN WARS (1689–1763) were a protracted battle for colonial domination of Canada. In 1713 the province of NOVA SCOTIA was ceded in the Treaty of Utrecht. In 1759 Quebec was captured by Britain, and France surrendered all of its Canadian lands in the Treaty of Paris (1763). In 1774 the French-Canadian population of Quebec gained territory to the Ohio River, the CONTINENTAL CONGRESS responded by invading Canada. During the American Revolution, Canada remained loyal to the English crown, and American attempts to capture it failed. In 1784 the province of New Brunswick was created out of Nova Scotia. The Constitutional Act (1791) divided Canada along linguistic and religious lines: Upper Canada (now Ontario) was English and Protestant; Lower Canada (now Quebec) was French and Catholic.

Explorers such as Alexander MacKenzie, George Vancouver, and James Cook enabled Britain to form the crown colony of British Columbia in 1858. Border disputes with the USA (*see* Aroostook War; War of 1812) continued into the 19th century.

Large-scale immigration from Ireland and Scotland increased tension and conflict between the English-speaking majority and the French-speaking minority. In an attempt to reduce conflict, the British passed the British North America Act (1867). This constitutional act established the federation or Dominion of Canada, consisting of Quebec, Ontario, Nova Scotia, and New Brunswick. In 1869 it acquired the lands of the Hudson's Bay Company and other provinces were added: Manitoba (1870), British Columbia (1871), Prince Edward Island (1873), Alberta and Saskatchewan (1905), and Newfoundland (1949). The Dominion's first prime minister (1867–73, 1878–91) Sir John Macdonald established the Canadian Pacific Railway, which proved disastrous to his career but provided the means for 3 million Europeans to emigrate to Canada between 1894–1914. Canadians fought as part of Allied forces in both World Wars, and in 1949 Canada was a founding member of NATO. Under the leadership of W.L. Mackenzie King, national unity was strengthened and industry developed. In 1963 Lester Pearson became prime minister and, as a sign of Canada's growing national confidence, adopted a new national flag. In 1967 Montreal hosted the influential Expo' 67. Pierre Trudeau's first administration (1968–79) was faced with violent separatist demands for Quebec's independence and martial law was imposed in 1970. In 1976 Montreal hosted the summer Olympic Games. In Trudeau's second administration, Quebec voted to remain part of the federation (1980) and Trudeau passed the Canada Act to amend the constitution (1981). This made Canada a fully sovereign state and contained a Charter of Rights and Freedoms. It was approved by all the provinces except Quebec, which claimed power of constitutional veto.

## Politics

In 1985 Brian Mulroney and provincial leaders signed the Meech Lake Accord, which provided for Quebec to be brought into the constitutional settlement as a "distinct society." Manitoba and Newfoundland failed to endorse the Accord, and Canada was plunged into constitutional crisis. In 1993 Jean Chrétien was elected prime minister. In 1995 a referendum on sovereignty for Quebec was narrowly defeated by 50.6% to 49.4%, and the issue seems unlikely to disappear. In 1997 Chrétien was reelected. Canada's new constitution has also enabled Native Americans to press land claims. In 1999 part of Northwest Territories became the Inuit territory of Nunavut.

Regional differences exist particularly between people in the E and W. Experts argue that reconciling the divisions between the E Montreal-Toronto axis and the W Vancouver-Winnipeg axis is essential for Canada's future.

## Economy

Canada is a highly developed and prosperous country (1995 GDP per capita, US$21,130). Although farmland covers only 8% of the country, farms are highly mechanized and productive, and Canada is one of the world's leading producers of barley, meat, milk, and wheat. Fishing is important in both Atlantic and Pacific waters. Forestry is a major industry and the availability of cheap hydroelectric power has encouraged the development of huge wood pulp and paper industries.

Canada is rich in mineral resources and is a major exporter of minerals, such as oil and natural gas. Canada also produces copper, gold, iron ore, uranium, and zinc. Manufacturing is highly developed, especially in the cities where 77% of the population live. Canada produces cars, chemicals, electronic freight, machinery, telecommunications equipment, and timber.

Canada has long been influenced, both culturally and economically, by the USA, and the two countries have the largest bilateral trade flow in the world. Since January 1, 1994, Canada, Mexico, and the US have been linked through the North American Free Trade Agreement (NAFTA), which created the world's largest trading area.

Issued in 1993, this stamp celebrates the bicentenary of Canada's largest metropolitan area, Toronto. The site was selected by John Graves Simcoe in 1793 and named York. But the settlement was renamed Toronto in 1834. Toronto is a Huron word for "meeting place."

## CANARY ISLANDS

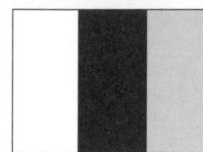

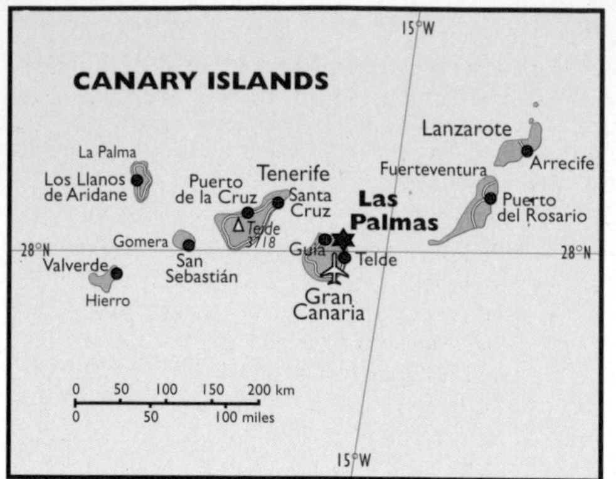


**AREA:** 2,808 sq mi (7,273 sq km)
**POPULATION:** 1,493,784
**CAPITAL (POPULATION):** Santa Cruz (189,317) / Las Palmas (372,000)
**GOVERNMENT:** Spanish autonomous region
**ETHNIC GROUPS:** Spanish
**LANGUAGES:** Spanish
**RELIGIONS:** Christianity (mainly Roman Catholic)
**CURRENCY:** Spanish currency

paintings more precise, sometimes making the finished work seem stiff and mannered. He managed to infuse his best work with energy, light, and color. Canaletto had an enormous influence on European art.

**canary** Popular cage-bird that lives wild in the Azores, Canary, and Madeira islands. These yellowish FINCHES feed on fruit, seeds, and insects, and lay spotted greenish-blue eggs. The pure yellow varieties have been domesticated since the 16th century. Family Fringillidae; species *Serinus canarius*.

**Canary Islands** Group of islands in the N Atlantic Ocean, *c*.70mi (113km) off the NW coast of Africa; they constitute two provinces of Spain, LAS PALMAS and SANTA CRUZ DE TENERIFE. Under Spanish rule since the 16th century, the islands are mountainous and the climate warm, with little rainfall. Industries: agriculture, fishing, tourism. Area: 2,808sq mi (7,273sq km). Pop. (1991) 1,493,784.

## CANCER

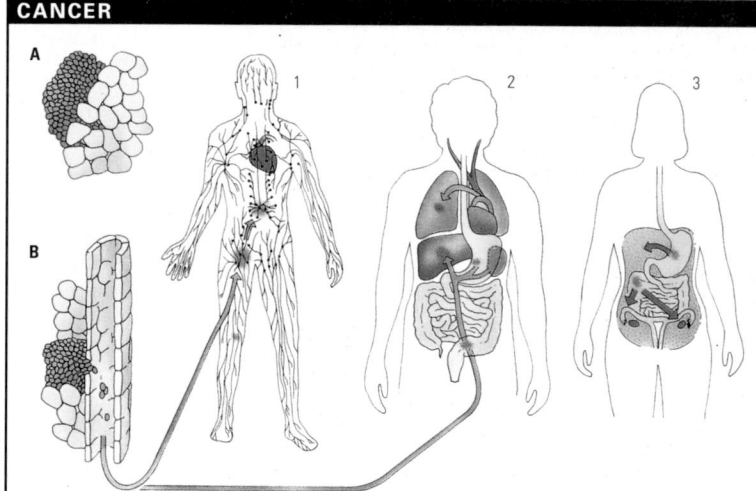

Cancer can spread in two ways. First, by direct growth into adjacent tissues, called "direct extension" (A), when cancer cells penetrate into bone, soft connective tissue, and the walls of veins and lymphatic vessels. Alternatively, a cancer cell separates from its tumor and is transported to another part of the body. This spread of cancer is called "metastasis" (B). In metastasis after the tumor has grown to some size, cancer cells or small groups of cells enter a blood or lymph vessel through the vessel wall (1). They travel through the vessel until they are stopped by a barrier, such as a lymph node, where additional tumors may develop, before releasing more cells which may develop on other lymph nodes. Such cancers, usually carcinomas, may also invade the blood stream and establish more distant secondary growths. Another type of cancer, sarcomas, tends to spread via venous blood vessels, frequently establishing tumors in the lungs, gastrointestinal tract, or the genito-urinary tract (2). In abdominal cancers, metastases may also arise as a result of travel across body cavities, such as the peritoneal, oral, or pleural cavities (3).

**Canberra** Capital of Australia on the Molonglo River, Australian Capital Territory, SE Australia. Settled in the early 1820s, it was chosen in 1908 as the new site for Australia's capital (succeeding MELBOURNE). The transfer of all governmental agencies was not completed until after World War II. Canberra has the Australian National University (1946), Royal Australian Mint (1965), Royal Military College, and Stromlo Observatory. The new Parliament House was opened in 1988. Other sites include the National Library, National Museum, and National Gallery. Pop. (1993 est.) 324,600.

**Cancer** Northern constellation between Gemini and Leo. It contains two open clusters: M44, Praesepe or the Beehive Cluster (NGC 2632), and M67 (NGC 2692). The brightest star is Beta Cancri.

**cancer** Group of diseases featuring the uncontrolled proliferation of cells (tumor formation). Malignant (cancerous) cells spread (metastasize) from their original site to other parts of the body. Known causative agents (**carcinogens**) include smoking, certain industrial chemicals, asbestos dust, and radioactivity. Viruses are implicated in some cancers. Some people have a genetic tendency towards particular types of cancer. Treatments include surgery, chemotherapy with cell-destroying drugs, and radiotherapy (or sometimes a combination of all three). Early diagnosis can lead to successful treatment.

**Cancer, Tropic of** Line of latitude, *c*.23.5° N of the Equator, which marks the N boundary of the tropics. It indicates the farthest N position at which the Sun appears directly overhead at noon. The Sun is vertical over the Tropic of Cancer on about June 21, the summer SOLSTICE in the Northern Hemisphere.

**candela** (symbol cd) SI unit of luminous intensity. It is defined as 1/60 of the luminous intensity of a BLACK BODY at atmospheric pressure and the temperature of solidification of platinum, 3,222°F (1,772°C).

**Canetti, Elias** (1905–94) British writer, b. Bulgaria. His experience of violent anti-semitism in 1930s Europe inspired his masterpiece, *Crowds and Power* (1960). Canetti's fear of the destructive power of mass psychology also informed his only novel, *Auto da Fé* (1935). He was awarded the 1981 Nobel Prize for literature.

**Canis Major** (Great Dog) Southern constellation situated S of Monoceros. It contains the bright open cluster M41 (NGC 2287). The brightest star is Alpha Canis Majoris or Sirius (Dog Star), the brightest star in the sky

**cannabis** (marijuana) Common name for the Indian hemp plant, *Cannabis sativa* (family Cannabidaceae), and for the dried plant or extracted resin (often known as hashish) when used as a psychotropic drug. The drug produces a NARCOTIC effect sometimes allied with a feeling of well-being. It is carcinogenic and can induce mild psychosis. Possession or sale of cannabis is illegal in many countries.

**Cannes** Resort on the French Riviera, SE France. During the 19th century Cannes became fashionable with visiting British aristocracy. An international film festival is held here in spring. Industries: tourism, flowers, textiles. Pop. (1990) 68,676.

**Canning, Charles John, Earl** (1812–62) British imperial administrator, son of George CANNING. He was governor general of India (1856–58). Canning repressed the INDIAN MUTINY and followed a policy of conciliation that earned him the nickname "Clemency Canning." With the transfer of the government of India to the British Crown, he became the first viceroy of India (1858–62).

**Canning, George** (1770–1827) British statesman, prime minister (1827). He was Tory foreign minister (1807–10, 1822–24), favoring vigorous measures against NAPOLEON I. He became prime minister, in coalition with the Whigs, but died four months later.

**cannon** ARTILLERY piece consisting of a metal tube, used to aim and fire missiles propelled by the explosion of gunpowder in the closed end. Cannon, first used in the 14th century, were originally made of bronze or iron.

**canoe** Light, shallow-draft boat propelled by one or more paddles. Primitive types are dug out of logs or made of skin or bark stretched over wooden frames. Modern types are made of wood, metal, or fiberglass. Canoeing became an Olympic sport in 1936.

**canon** In music, form of COUNTERPOINT using strict imitation. All the voices or parts have the same melody, but each voice starts at a different time.

**canon** Term used in Christian religion with several meanings. The basic meaning is a rule or standard, such as the official list of saints or the list of books accepted as genuine parts of the BIBLE. This is the meaning embraced by the term CANON LAW. Initially a canon was also a priest in a cathedral or collegiate church, whose life was regulated by the precepts of canon law. They were distinct from secular canons, who lived outside the cathedral and performed a largely administrative role.

**canonization** Official action by which a member of a Christian church is created a cult figure or SAINT and added to the CANON. In the Orthodox Church, a person's sainthood may be proclaimed by a bishop after examining the candidate's case. In the Anglican Church, a commission determines this. In the Roman Catholic Church, officials analyze the evidence of a candidate's reputation for sanctity or virtue and seek out evidence for any miracles done. The results are submitted to the Congregation for the Causes of Saints and, after their findings are ratified by the pope, the candidate is beatified. Further proof is required before full canonization.

**canon law** In the Roman Catholic, Anglican, and Orthodox churches, a body of ecclesiastical laws relating to faith, morals, and discipline. It is based on custom and regulations laid down by church councils, popes, or bishops.

**Canopus** (Alpha Carinae) Second-brightest star in the sky. Its luminosity and distance are not accurately known, but one estimate classifies it as a bright giant, 800 times as luminous as the Sun, and 74 light years away.

**Canova, Antonio** (1757–1822) Italian sculptor. His work expresses the elegance and allusions to antique art which characterize NEOCLASSICISM, but retains a high degree of individuality. Two important pieces of the 1780s, *Theseus and the Minotaur* and Pope Clement XIV's tomb, catapulted Canova into the limelight. He worked for many distinguished European patrons, notably the papal court.

**cantata** Musical work consisting of vocal solos and choruses, often alternating with passages of recitative, and accompanied by an orchestra. It was a popular form in the 17th and 18th centuries, when Alessandro Scarlatti and J.S. Bach wrote numerous cantatas, both secular and religious.

**Canterbury** City on the Great Stour River in Kent, SE England. It is the seat of the archbishop and primate of the Anglican Church. The present cathedral (built in the 11th–15th centuries) replaced the original Abbey of St. Augustine. Thomas à BECKET was murdered in the cathedral in 1170; after his canonization, Canterbury became a major pilgrimage center. It contains the University of Kent (1965). Industries: tourism. Pop. (1991) 123,947.

**Canterbury, archbishop of** Primate of All England and spiritual leader of the worldwide ANGLICAN COMMUNION. The archbishopric was established in 597, when Pope GREGORY I sent a mission to England to convert the Anglo-Saxons. St. AUGUSTINE, leader of the mission, became the first archbishop of Canterbury. During the REFORMATION, Archbishop Thomas CRANMER accepted the decision of the English Crown to end papal jurisdiction in England (1534). The archbishop of Canterbury traditionally crowns British monarchs and officiates at other religious ceremonies of national importance. He presides over the Lambeth Conference of worldwide Anglicanism, but exercises no jurisdiction outside his own ecclesiastical province.

**cantilever bridge** BRIDGE in which each half of the main span is rigidly supported at one end only. The other ends are joined in the middle of the bridge.

**Canton** *See* GUANGZHOU

**canton** Unit of government and administration that make up the Swiss Confederation (Switzerland). Each canton sends two members to the Council of State, which (with the National Council) forms the country's federal parliament.

**Cantonese** One of the major languages of China. Within the Chinese People's Republic it is spoken by *c.*50 million people, mainly in the extreme southern provinces of GUANGDONG and GUANGXI. It is also the language spoken by most Chinese in Southeast Asia and the US.

**Cantor, Georg** (1845–1918) German mathematician, b. Russia. He was professor of mathematics (1869–1913) at the University of Halle, Germany. His work on INFINITY challenged the existing deductive process of mathematics. Cantor developed the SET THEORY and provided a new definition of IRRATIONAL NUMBERS.

**Canute** (*c.*994–1035) King of Denmark (1014–28), England (1017–35), and Norway (1028–29). He accompanied his father, Sweyn, on the Danish invasion of England (1013). After his father's death (1014), Canute was accepted as joint king of Denmark with his brother and later became sole king. He invaded England again (1015) and divided it (1016) with the English king Edmund Ironside. Canute became king after Edmund's death. His rule was a just and peaceful one. Canute restored the church and codified English law. His reign in Scandinavia was more turbulent. Canute conquered Norway (1028), made one son king of Denmark (1028) and another king of Norway (1029).

**canyon** Deep, narrow depression in the Earth's crust. Land canyons are the result of erosion by rivers flowing through arid terrain. Marine canyons may be formed when a river bed and the surrounding terrain is submerged, or by turbulence produced by deep water currents. *See also* GRAND CANYON

**capacitance** (symbol *C*) Property of an electrical circuit or component that describes its ability to store charge in its CAPACITOR. Capacitance is measured in farads: 1 farad is a capacitance needing a charge of 1 coulomb to raise its potential by 1 volt. Most capacitances are small enough to be measured in microfarads (one millionth of a farad).

**capacitor** (condenser) Electrical circuit component that stores charge. It has at least two metal plates and is used principally in alternating current (AC) circuits. The various types include parallel-plate condensers and electrolytic capacitors. *See also* ELECTRIC CURRENT

**Cape Canaveral** Low, sandy promontory in E Florida, extending E into the Atlantic Ocean. It is the site of the John F. Kennedy Space Center which, since 1950, has been NASA's main US launch site for space flights and long-range missiles.

**Cape Cod** Hook-shaped, sandy peninsula in SE Massachusetts. The Pilgrim Fathers landed here in 1620. It extends into the Atlantic Ocean, forming Cape Cod Bay. It was originally a center for fishing, whaling, and salt extraction; tourism is now the major industry.

**Capella** (Alpha Aurigae) Star in the constellation of Auriga, magnitude 0.08 (sixth-brightest in the sky). A spectroscopic binary (comprised of two yellow giants) it is 41 light-years from Earth.

**Cape Horn** Southernmost point of South America in S Chile. It was sighted by Francis Drake in 1578, and first rounded in 1616 by Cornelis van Schouten.

**Cape of Good Hope** Peninsula, 30mi (48km) S of Cape Town, South Africa. The first European to sail around it was Bartholomeu Diaz in 1488. The Cape sea route between India and Europe was established by Vasco da Gama in 1497–99.

**Cape Province** Formerly the largest province in South Africa. In 1994 it was divided into the separate provinces of EASTERN CAPE, WESTERN CAPE, and NORTHERN CAPE. The first colony was established (1652) by the Dutch EAST INDIA COMPANY and slaves were imported to work the land. The BOER settlers' expansion led to territorial wars with indigenous tribes, such as the XHOSA (1779). In 1806 Britain established control and renamed the region, Cape of Good Hope Colony. The new British settlers clashed with the Boers, precipitating the GREAT TREK (1835). Diamonds were discovered near KIMBERLEY in 1867. The British attempt to incorporate TRANSVAAL and Orange FREE STATE into a single state with NATAL and Cape Colony, resulted in the SOUTH AFRICAN WARS (1899–1902). In 1910 the colony became a province of the Union of South Africa. During the 1960s, the apartheid government created the separate tribal areas (bantustans) of Transkei and Ciskei. In 1994 these were integrated into the new Eastern Cape Province.

▲ **Capone** Born in Naples, S Italy, Al Capone grew up in Brooklyn, New York. During prohibition he established himself as the head of a notorious Chicago gang.

**Capetians** French royal family forming the third dynasty providing France with 15 kings. It began (987) with Hugh Capet, who succeeded Louis V, the last of the CAROLINGIANS. Capetians dominated the feudal forces, extending the king's rule across the whole of France. The last Capetian king, Charles IV, was succeeded (1328) by Philip VI of the House of Valois.

**Cape Town** City and seaport at the foot of Table Mountain, South Africa. It is South Africa's legislative capital and the capital of WESTERN CAPE province. Founded in 1652 by the Dutch EAST INDIA COMPANY, it came under British rule in 1795. Places of interest include the Union Parliament, a 17th-century castle, the National Historic Museum, and the University of Cape Town (founded 1829). It is an important industrial and commercial center. Industries: clothing, engineering equipment, motor vehicles, wine. Pop. (1991) 2,350,157.

**Cape Verde** Republic in the E Atlantic Ocean. It is made up of 15 volcanic islands divided into two groups (Windward and Leeward). The capital is Praia on São Tiago. The economy is based on coffee, tobacco, and sugar cane, and the mining of salt and coal. An overseas province of Portugal, the islands became independent in 1975. Area: 1,557sq mi (4,033sq km). Pop. (1993 est.) 350,000.

**capillarity** Movement of a liquid in a narrow opening caused by the surface tension between the liquid and the surrounding material. This is most often seen in a vertical, narrow glass capillary tube, but capillarity also occurs in various directions – as when a sponge or blotting paper soaks up water.

**capillary** Smallest of BLOOD VESSELS, connecting arteries and veins. Capillary walls consist of only a single layer of cells, so that water containing dissolved oxygen and other nutrients (as well as carbon dioxide and other wastes) can pass easily between the blood and surrounding tissues.

**capital** In architecture, the block of masonry at the top of a column, often elaborately carved. The design of the capital is characteristic of the ORDERS OF ARCHITECTURE.

**capital** In ECONOMICS, different forms of wealth. **Fixed** capital includes buildings, tools, and equipment; **working** capital (variable or circulating capital) includes raw materials, stock, and cash. In accounting, capital is the obligation a business enterprise has to its owners. Capital includes not only the owner's contribution but also the profits retained within the business for future use.

**capitalism** Economic system in which property and the means of PRODUCTION are privately owned. Capitalism is based on profit motive, individual enterprise, efficiency through competition, and a notion of freedom of choice. It was first articulated by Adam SMITH in his treatise *The Wealth of Nations* (1776). Its development dates from the INDUSTRIAL REVOLUTION and the rise of the BOURGEOISIE. In practice, capitalist governments participate in economic regulation although to a lesser extent than a government within COMMUNISM or SOCIALISM. The collapse of Soviet communism removed capitalism's traditional opponent and created economic uncertainty. *See also* DIVISION OF LABOUR; FREE TRADE; FRIEDMAN, MILTON; GALBRAITH, J.K.; KEYNES, JOHN MAYNARD; LAISSEZ-FAIRE; MARXISM; MERCANTILISM; MONETARISM

**capital punishment** Punishing a criminal offense by death. Usual methods of execution include hanging, electrocution, lethal injection, lethal gas, or firing squad. The death penalty has been abolished in many Western countries. In the US, capital punishment was effectively in abeyance during the 1970s after several rulings by the Supreme Court, but today 38 states have the death penalty. The use of capital punishment is the subject of much debate: supporters claim that such punishment can be deserved and has a deterrent effect, while opponents state that it is inhuman, does not deter, and that miscarriages of justice cannot be rectified.

**Capitol** Building in WASHINGTON, D.C., in which the US CONGRESS convenes. The original architect was William Thornton and the cornerstone was laid by George Washington in 1793. It was burned to the ground by the British in 1814. Benjamin LATROBE and Charles BULFINCH worked on the restoration, which was completed in 1830. The dome reaches a height of 288ft (88m).

**Capone, Al (Alphonse)** (1899–1947) US gangster of the PROHIBITION era, b. Italy. He inherited a vast crime empire from Johnny Torio. Capone was suspected of many brutal crimes but, ironically, was only ever convicted and imprisoned for income tax evasion (1931).

**Capote, Truman** (1924–84) US writer. His works, typified by keen social observation and characters on the fringes of society, include the novella *Breakfast at Tiffany's* (1958), the novel *The Grass Harp* (1951), and volumes of shorter pieces such as *Music for Chameleons* (1980). Capote claimed that *In Cold Blood* (1966) was the first nonfiction (faction) novel.

**Capra, Frank** (1897–1991) US film director, b. Italy. During the 1930s Depression, Capra made a string of successful screwball comedies. His central theme was the unlikely triumph of idealism and the common man over materialism and bureaucracy. Capra won three Academy Awards as best director for *It Happened One Night* (1934), *Mr. Deeds Goes to Town* (1936), and *You Can't Take It With You* (1938). Capra's best film *It's a Wonderful Life* (1947) was a commercial failure.

**Capricorn, Tropic of** Line of latitude, *c*.23.54° S of the Equator which marks the southern boundary of the tropics. It indicates the farthest southern position at which the Sun appears directly overhead at noon. The Sun is vertical over the Tropic of Capricorn on about December 22, which is the summer SOLSTICE in the Southern Hemisphere.

**Capricornus** (Sea Goat) Southern constellation situated on the ecliptic between Sagittarius and Aquarius; the tenth sign of the zodiac, identified with the Greek god PAN. Usually referred to as Capricorn only for astrological purposes, this constellation contains the faint globular cluster M30 (NGC 7099).

**capsicum** *See* PEPPER

**capuchin** Small, diurnal monkey found in South and Central America. It is generally brown or black and is a tree-dweller. Omnivorous, but preferring fruit, it may grow to 22in (55cm) with a furry, prehensile tail of similar length. Family Cebidae.

**Capuchins** (officially Friars Minor of St. Francis Capuchin, O.F.M.Cap.) Roman Catholic religious order, founded in 1525 as an offshoot of the FRANCISCANS. Capuchins are so-called because of the pointed cowl (*capuche*) which forms part of their habit. They re-emphasized Franciscan ideals of poverty and austerity, and played an important role in the COUNTER-REFORMATION through their missionary activities.

**capybara** Largest living RODENT, native to Central and South America; it is semi-aquatic with webbed feet, a large, nearly hairless, body, short legs, and a tiny tail. Length: 4ft (1.2m). Species *Hydrochoerus hydrochoeris*.

**car** *See* AUTOMOBILE

**Caracalla** (188–217) (Marcus Aurelius Antoninus) Roman emperor (211–17). Caracalla murdered his brother, Geta (212). Excessive expenditure on war caused economic crisis. During his reign Roman citizenship was extended to all free men in the empire. Caracalla was assassinated by his successor, Macrinus.

**Caracas** Capital of Venezuela, on the Guaire River. The city was under Spanish rule until 1821. It was the birthplace of Simón BOLÍVAR. Caracas grew after 1930, with the exploitation of oil. It has the Central University of Venezuela (1725) and a cathedral (1614). Industries: motor vehicles, oil, brewing. Pop. (1990) 1,824,892.

**Caravaggio, Michelangelo Merisi da** (1571–1610) Italian painter, the most influential and original painter of the 17th century. His work brought a new, formidable sense of reality at a time when a feeble MANNERISM prevailed. The majestic *Supper at Emmaus* (*c*.1598–1600) with its beautifully modeled images of Christ and his disciples shows him gaining confidence. His mature phase (1599–1606) began with two large-scale religious paintings of St. Matthew. The use of dramatic shadows (CHIAROSCURO) and a living model, show Caravaggio's revolutionary approach to religious themes. *The Crucifixion of St. Peter* and *The Conversion of St. Paul* (both 1600–01) are masterpieces of psychological realism.

**caraway** Biennial herb native to Eurasia and cultivated for its small, brown seed-like fruits that are used for flavoring foods. It has feathery leaves and white flowers. Family Apiaceae/Umbelliferae; species *Carum carvi*.

**carbide** Inorganic compound of carbon with metals or other more electropositive elements. Many transition metals form

▲ **capybara** Found in central and South America, the capybara (*Hydrochoerus hydrochaeris*) is the largest rodent in the world. It grows to over 3ft (1m).

carbides, in which carbon atoms occupy spaces between adjacent atoms in the metal lattice. Some electropositive metals form ionic carbon compounds; the best known is CALCIUM CARBIDE. Carbides are commonly used as abrasives.

**carbohydrate** Organic compound of carbon, hydrogen, and oxygen that is a constituent of many foodstuffs. The simplest carbohydrates are SUGARS. GLUCOSE and FRUCTOSE are monosaccharides, naturally occurring sugars; they have the same formula ($C_6H_{12}O_6$) but different structures. One molecule of each combines with the loss of water to make SUCROSE ($C_{12}H_{22}O_{11}$), a disaccharide. Starch and cellulose are polysaccharides, carbohydrates consisting of hundreds of glucose molecules linked together. *See also* SACCHARIDE

**carbon** (symbol C) Common nonmetallic element of group IV of the periodic table. Carbon forms a vast number of compounds, which (with hydrogen–hydocarbons and other nonmetals) forms the basis of organic CHEMISTRY. Until recently, it was believed there were two crystalline ALLOTROPES: GRAPHITE and DIAMOND. In 1996 a third type, BUCKMINSTERFULLERENES (named for Richard Buckminster FULLER), which are shaped like geodesic domes, was discovered. Various amorphous (noncrystalline) forms of carbon also exist, such as coal, coke, and charcoal. A recently made synthetic form of carbon is CARBON FIBER. The isotope $^{14}C$ is used for CARBON DATING of archaeological specimens. Properties: at.no. 6; at.wt. 12.011; sp.gr. 1.9–2.3 (graphite), 3.15–3.53 (diamond); m.p. *c.*6,422°F (3,550°C); sublimes at 6,093°F (3,367°C); b.p. *c.*7,592°F (4,200°C); most common isotope $^{12}C$ (98.89%).

**carbonate** Salt of carbonic acid, formed when carbon dioxide ($CO_2$) dissolves in water. Carbonic acid is an extremely weak acid and both it and many of its salts are unstable, decomposing readily to release $CO_2$. Nevertheless, large parts of the Earth's crust are made up of carbonates, such as CALCIUM CARBONATE and DOLOMITE.

**carbon cycle** Circulation of carbon in the biosphere. It is a complex chain of events. The most important elements are the taking up of carbon dioxide ($CO_2$) by green plants during PHOTOSYNTHESIS, and the return of $CO_2$ to the atmosphere by the respiration and eventual decomposition of animals which eat the plants. The burning of fossil fuels has also, over the years, released $CO_2$ back into the atmosphere.

**carbon dating** (radiocarbon dating) Method of determining the age of organic materials by measuring the amount of RADIOACTIVE DECAY of an ISOTOPE of carbon, carbon-14 ($^{14}C$). This radio-isotope decays to form nitrogen, half-life of 5,730 years. When an organism dies, it ceases to take carbon dioxide into its body, so that the amount of $^{14}C$ it contains is fixed relative to its total weight. Over the centuries, this quantity steadily diminishes.

**carbon dioxide** ($CO_2$) Colorless, odorless gas that occurs in the atmosphere (0.03%) and as a product of the combustion of fossil fuels and respiration in plants and animals. In its solid form (dry ice) it is used in refrigeration; as a gas it is used in carbonated beverages and fire extinguishers. Research indicates that its increase in the atmosphere leads to the GREENHOUSE EFFECT and GLOBAL WARMING. Properties: m.p. −69.9°F (−56.6°C); sublimes −109.3°F (−78.5°C).

**carbon fiber** Form of carbon made by heating textile fibers to high temperatures. The result is fibers (typically 0.001cm in diameter) which are, weight-for-weight, some of the strongest of all fibers. They are too short to be woven into a super-strong yarn. Instead they are incorporated into plastics, ceramics, and glass.

**Carboniferous** Fifth geologic division of the PALEOZOIC era, lasting from 360 to 286 million years ago. It is often called the "Age of Coal" because of its extensive swampy forests that turned into most of today's COAL deposits. Amphibians flourished, marine life abounded in warm inland seas, and the first reptiles appeared.

**carbon monoxide** (CO) Colorless, odorless poisonous gas formed during the incomplete combustion of fossil fuels, occurring for example in coal gas and the exhaust fumes of automobiles. Carbon monoxide poisons by combining with the HEMOGLOBIN in red blood cells and thus preventing them from carrying oxygen around the body. It is used as a reducing agent in metallurgy. Properties: density 0.968 (air = 1); m.p. −337°F (−205°C); b.p. −312.7°F (−191.5°C).

**carcinogen** External substance or agent that causes CANCER, including chemicals, such as the tar present in cigarette smoke, large doses of radiation, and some viruses, such as polyoma.

**carcinoma** Form of CANCER arising from the epithelial cells present in skin and the membranes lining the internal organs. It is a malignant growth which tends to give rise to metastases (secondary cancers).

**cardamom** Pungent spice from seeds of a plant of the GINGER family (Zingiberaceae). Species *Elettaria cardamomum.*

**Cárdenas, Lázaro** (1895–1970) Mexican statesman, president of Mexico (1934–40). In the final phase of the MEXICAN REVOLUTION, Cárdenas accelerated the distribution of communal lands, expropriated oil properties (1938), and encouraged labor unionism.

**cardiac muscle** *See* MUSCLE

**Cardiff** (Caerdydd) Capital of Wales and port on the Severn River estuary at the mouth of the rivers Taff, Rhymney, and Ely, United Kingdom. The construction of docks (1839) led to the rapid growth of the city, and, until the early 20th century, it was a major coal exporting center. It is the seat of the University College of South Wales and Monmouthshire (1893), and has an 11th-century castle. Industries: steel manufacturing, engineering, chemicals, food processing. Pop. (1991) 279,055.

**cardinal** Priest of the highest rank in the hierarchy of the Roman Catholic Church after the pope. Some cardinals are heads of departments of the CURIA ROMANA, whereas others are PRIMATES of national churches. They are nominated by the pope, whom they advise. On the death of a pope they meet in secret CONCLAVE to elect his successor.

**cardinal** (redbird) North American songbird with a clear, whistle-like song. The male has bright red plumage and crest and a thick orange-red bill. They feed on seeds, fruits, and insects. A cup-shaped nest holds the four pale blue, heavily spotted eggs incubated by the female. Length: to 9in (23cm). Family Fringillidae; species *Richmondena cardinalis.*

**cardiology** Branch of medicine that deals with the diagno-

**CARBON CYCLE**

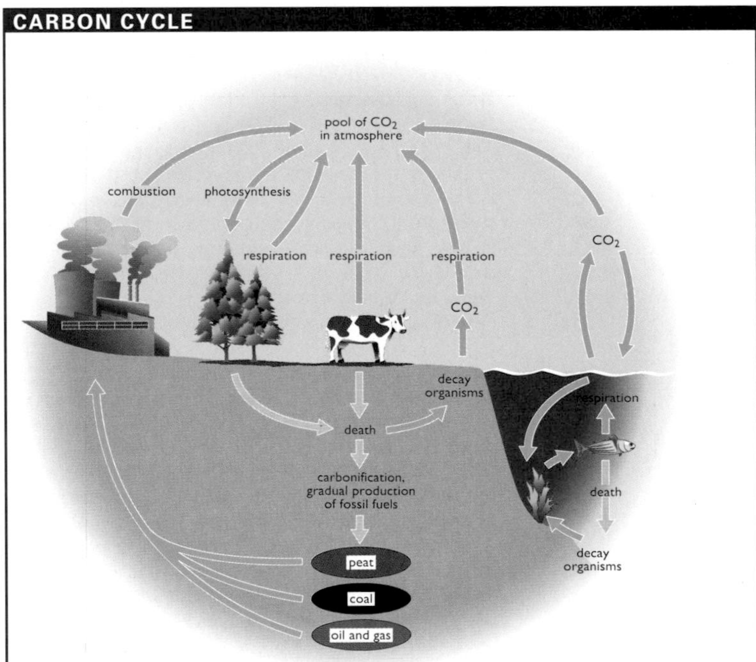


Elemental carbon is in constant flux. Gaseous carbon dioxide ($CO_2$) is first incorporated into simple sugars by photosynthesis in green plants. These may be broken down (respired) to provide energy, a process that releases $CO_2$ back into the atmosphere. Alternatively, animals that eat the plants also metabolize the sugars and release $CO_2$ in the process. Geological processes also affect the Earth's carbon balance, with carbon being removed from the cycle when it is accumulated within fossil fuels such as coal, oil, and gas. Conversely, large amounts of carbon dioxide are released into the atmosphere when such fuels are burned.

C

▲ **carnation** Native to the Mediterranean region, carnations are a species of pink (*Dianthus caryophyllaceus*). A great number of hybrids have been developed to be grown in gardens and yards in many temperate regions.

sis and treatment of the diseases and disorders of the HEART and vascular system.

**Cardozo, Benjamin Nathan** (1870–1938) US jurist. He was elected to the New York Supreme Court (1913). Appointed by Herbert HOOVER to the US Supreme Court, Cardozo served as an associate justice (1932–38). He strove to simplify the law and his decisions on NEW DEAL legislation were extremely influential.

**Carew, Thomas** (1595–1639) English poet. His poetry was largely influenced by that of his friend Ben JONSON and of John DONNE, to whom he wrote an elegy. His work includes *A Rapture* and the masque *Coelum Britannicum*.

**Carey, George Leonard** (1935– ) English Anglican churchman, archbishop of Canterbury and primate of all England (1991– ). Carey was bishop of Bath and Wells (1988–91). He belongs to the evangelical wing of the CHURCH OF ENGLAND. Carey favors the ordination of women priests and supports environmental conservation. *See also* EVANGELICALISM

**Carib** Major language group and Native American tribe. They entered the Caribbean region from NE South America. About 500 Caribs still live on the island of Dominica; 5,000 migrated to Central America, notably around Honduras, where their descendants still live.

**Caribbean Community and Common Market (CARICOM)** Caribbean economic union. CARICOM was formed (1973) by the Treaty of Chaguaramas to coordinate economic and foreign policy in the WEST INDIES. Most members rely on the export of sugar and tropical fruits and are heavily dependent on imports. The headquarters is in Georgetown, Guyana.

**Caribbean Sea** Extension of the N Atlantic Ocean linked to the Gulf of Mexico by the Yucatán Channel and to the Pacific Ocean by the Panama Canal. The first European to discover the Caribbean was Columbus in 1492, who named it after the CARIB. It soon lay on the route of many Spanish expeditions and became notorious for piracy. With the opening of the Panama Canal (1914) its strategic importance increased. Area: *c.*1,020,000sq mi (2,640,000sq km).

**caribou** *See* REINDEER

**caricature** (It. *caricare*, load or surcharge) Painting or drawing in which a person is presented in a comic, often ridiculous, light by the distortion of their features. Caricature may be used to interpret the character of a person, event, or age. The genre first appeared in the late 16th century. HOGARTH attempted to distinguish between depicting character and comic likeness, but the two traditions merged. In the 20th century many popular graphic artists have combined caricature with social and political satire, as in political CARTOONS.

**caries** Decay of teeth or BONE substance. Caries are caused by acids produced when bacteria present in the mouth break down sugars in food. Regular brushing, a reduced sugar intake, and fluoride prevent decay.

**Carina** Part of the dismembered constellation Argo Navis, the ship Argo. It is the brightest and richest part of Argo, representing the ship's keel, and contains CANOPUS.

**Carlists** Reactionary Spanish political faction in the 19th century. They favored the royal claims of Don CARLOS and his successors, and figured in several rebellions. The remnants of the Carlists eventually merged with the fascist FALANGE in 1937.

**Carlos** (1788–1855) Spanish prince and pretender to the throne. His elder brother, Ferdinand VII, changed Spanish law so that his daughter ISABELLA II succeeded him (1833). Carlos was proclaimed king by the CARLISTS, and civil war ensued. Isabella won (1840), and Carlos went into exile. In 1845 he resigned his claim in favor of his son, Don Carlos II.

**Carlson, Chester** (1906–68) US physicist, inventor of XEROGRAPHY (1938). He patented it in 1940 and in 1947 signed an agreement with the Haloid Company (now Xerox). Carlson's royalties made him a multimillionaire.

**Carlyle, Thomas** (1795–1881) Scottish philosopher, critic, and historian. His most successful work, *Sartor Resartus* (1836), combined philosophy and autobiography. His histories include *The French Revolution* (1837). Influenced by romanticism and Goethe in particular, Carlyle was a powerful advocate of the significance of great leaders in history.

**Carmelites** (officially Order of Our Lady of Mount Carmel) Order founded by St. Berthold in Palestine *c.*1154. An order of Carmelite sisters was founded in 1452. The Carmelites devote themselves to contemplation and missionary work.

**carnation** Slender-stemmed, herbaceous plant native to Europe. It has narrow leaves, swollen stem joints, and produces several dense blooms with serrated petals which range from white to yellow, pink, and red. Family Caryophyllaceae; species *Dianthus caryophyllus*.

**Carnegie, Andrew** (1835–1919) US industrialist and philanthropist, b. Scotland. He foresaw the demand for iron and steel, and founded the Keystone Bridge Company. From 1873 Carnegie concentrated on steel, pioneering mass production techniques. By 1901 the Carnegie Steel Company was producing 25% of US steel. He endowed 2,800 libraries and donated more than $350 million to charitable foundations.

**carnival** Strictly speaking, a Christian celebration (with parades, masques, and pageants) that takes place on Shrove Tuesday (*see* MARDI GRAS). Examples include the street carnivals in Rio de Janeiro, New Orleans, Venice, and Rome. Such celebrations have their origins in pagan spring festivals, and during the Roman empire reached a peak of debauchery and civil disorder. Unable to suppress these pagan revels, the Catholic Church attempted to adopt them as church ritual. The medieval Feast of Fools parodied Church practice by staging elaborate mock Masses. Eventually the Church managed to relate the festival to the advent of LENT, though carnival retains many of its pre-Christian features such as sexual license and social leveling.

**carnivore** Any member of the order of flesh-eating mammals. Mustelids (weasels, martens, minks, and the wolverine) make up the largest family. CATS are the most specialized killers among the carnivores; dogs, bears, and raccoons are much less exclusively meat eaters; and civets, mongooses, and their relatives also have a mixed diet. Related to the civets, but in a separate family, are the hyenas, large dog-like scavengers. More distantly related to living land carnivores are the seals, sea lions, and walruses; they evolved from ancient land carnivores who gave rise to early weasel- or civet-like forms. Other extinct carnivores include the sabertooth cats, which died out during the Pliocene epoch, 2 million years ago.

**carnivorous plant** *See* INSECTIVOROUS PLANT

**Carnot, Lazare Nicolas Marguerite** (1753–1823) French general. Carnot was the outstanding commander of the FRENCH REVOLUTIONARY WARS, his strategy being largely responsible for French victories. Ousted in 1797, he was recalled by Napoleon (1800), who made him minister of war.

**Carnot, Marie François Sadi** (1837–94) French statesman, president of the Third Republic (1887–94). After quashing the antirepublican movement, Carnot defended the regime during the Panama Canal scandal (1892). He was stabbed to death by an Italian anarchist.

**Carnot, (Nicolas Léonard) Sadi** (1796–1832) French engineer and physicist whose work laid the foundation for the science of THERMODYNAMICS. His major work, *Réflexions sur la puissance motrice du feu* (1824), provided the first theoretical background for the STEAM ENGINE and introduced the concept of the second law of thermodynamics (involving ENTROPY), which was formulated later by Rudolf CLAUSIUS. Carnot's work was recognized in 1848 by William KELVIN.

**Carnot cycle** In THERMODYNAMICS, a cycle of events that demonstrates the impossibility of total efficiency in heat engines. Named for Sadi CARNOT, it shows how an engine can never convert all the heat energy supplied to it into mechanical energy. Some heat energy always remains unused in a "cold sink." In an internal combustion engine, this can be thought of as the engine itself.

**Caro, Sir Anthony** (1924– ) English sculptor. He worked as an assistant to Henry MOORE, before making his own sculptures. Caro's distinctive "structures" are made from prefabricated metal, welded and bolted together. He often places his work on the floor to create a greater intimacy.

**carob** Plant of the E Mediterranean. It belongs to the pea family (Fabaceae/Leguminosae) and bears leguminous fruits that are a foodstuff. Its seeds are used as a substitute for coffee beans. Species *Ceratonia siliqua*.

**Carol I** (1839–1914) Prince of Romania (1866–81); first king (1881–1914). He aided Russia in the first Russo-Turkish War (1877–78). Romanian independence and Carol's sovereignty were recognized by the Congress of Berlin (1878). By 1913 Romania had become the strongest Balkan power. He preserved the neutrality of Romania at the start of World War I.

**Carol II** (1893–1953) King of Romania (1930–40), grandnephew of CAROL I. In 1925 he renounced the throne. Carol returned in 1930 and supplanted his son, Michael, as king. He supported the growing fascist movement and hoped to become dictator. German pressure forced him to abdicate in favor of Michael, leaving power in the hands of the fascist leader, Ion Antonescu.

**carol** Traditional song usually of religious joy and associated with Christmas. Earliest examples date to the 14th century.

**Caroline Islands** Archipelago of *c.*600 volcanic islands, coral islets, and reefs in the W Pacific Ocean, N of the Equator; part of the US Trust Territory of the Pacific Islands. Politically, the islands exist as two entities. In 1979 all the islands, except the BELAU group, became the Federated States of MICRONESIA. Area: 450sq mi (1,130sq km).

**Carolingian renaissance** Cultural revival in France and Italy under the encouragement of CHARLEMAGNE. The illiterate monarch gathered notable educators and artists from all over the world to his court at Aachen. He promoted Catholicism, art, and learning by founding abbeys and encouraging church building. As the first Roman emperor in the West for more than 300 years, Charlemagne imposed a new culture in Europe, combining Christian, Roman, and Frankish elements. The outstanding building of the period is the Palatine Chapel, Aachen (805).

**Carolingians** Second Frankish dynasty of early medieval Europe. Founded in the 7th century by Pepin of Landen, it rose to power under the weak kingship of the MEROVINGIANS. In 732 CHARLES MARTEL defeated the Muslims at Poitiers; in 751 his son, PEPIN III (THE SHORT), deposed the last Merovingian and became king of the Franks. The dynasty peaked under Pepin's son, CHARLEMAGNE (after whom the dynasty is called), who united the Frankish dominions and much of W and central Europe, and was crowned Holy Roman emperor by the pope in 800. His empire was later broken up by civil wars. Carolingian rule finally ended in 987.

**carp** Freshwater fish native to temperate waters of Asia. Introduced to the US and Europe, it is an important food fish. It is brown or golden and has four fleshy mouth whiskers called barbels. Length: to 3.2ft (1m). Family Cyprinidae; species *Cyprinus carpio*.

**Carpaccio, Vittore** (1460–1525) Venetian painter. His narrative paintings relate incidents against a background of an idealized Venice. His cycle of scenes, *The Legend of St. Ursula* (1490–98) and *SS. George and Jerome* (1502–07), have an exceptional vitality. Carpaccio's range of subjects varied from religious paintings to the enchanting *Two Venetian Ladies*.

**Carpathian Mountains** Mountain range in central and E Europe, extending NE from the central Czech Republic to the Polish-Czech border and into Romania and the Ukraine. The N Carpathians (Beskids and Tatra) run E along the border and SE through W Ukraine; the S Carpathians (Transylvanian Alps) extend SW to the Danube River. The highest peak is Gerlachovka, at 8,711ft (2,655m). Length: 950mi (1,530km).

**carpel** Female reproductive part of a flowering plant. A carpel consists of a STIGMA, a STYLE, and an OVARY. A group of carpels make up the **gynoecium**, the complete female reproductive structure within a flower.

**carpetbaggers** Term used after the CIVIL WAR to refer to Northern whites who entered the South as opportunists. They were despised by many white Southerners for seeking political office for economic gain with the aid of the votes of former slaves. They were alleged to have arrived with nothing more than a traveling carpetbag.

**Carranza, Venustiano** (1859–1920) Mexican statesman, president (1914). Carranza supported Francisco Madero's revolution against Porfirio DÍAZ. When Madero was overthrown by Victoriano HUERTA, Carranza joined Álvaro OBREGÓN, "Pancho" VILLA and Emiliano ZAPATA to defeat Huerta. Villa and Zapata's refusal to recognize Carranza's authority prolonged the civil war. Carranza supported John PERSHING's expedition against Villa. His attempts to prevent the accession of Obregón led to a revolt. Carranza fled and was murdered. *See also* MEXICAN REVOLUTION

**Carreras, José Maria** (1946– ) Spanish tenor. He made his debut in Barcelona (1970), going on to sing in opera houses worldwide. At the height of his career, Carreras developed leukemia. After treatment, he successfully returned to the stage in 1988, becoming a household name as one of the Three Tenors, with Placido DOMINGO and Luciano PAVAROTTI.

**Carroll, Lewis** (1832–98) English mathematician, photographer, and writer, b. Charles Lutwidge Dodgson. An Oxford don, much of whose output consisted of mathematical textbooks, Carroll is remembered for *Alice's Adventures in Wonderland* (1865) and its sequel, *Through the Looking Glass* (1872), along with his nonsense poem *The Hunting of the Snark* (1876).

**carrot** Herbaceous, generally biennial, root vegetable, cultivated widely as a food crop. The edible, orange taproot is the plant's store of food for the following year. The plant is topped by delicate fern-like leaves and white or pink flower clusters. Family UMBELLIFERAE; Species *Daucus carota*.

**Carson, Edward Henry** (1854–1935) Northern Irish political leader. A famous barrister, he was the leader of resistance to Irish Home Rule. Organizing the paramilitary Ulster Volunteers (1912), Carson persuaded the British government to exclude the Protestant provinces from the Home Rule Agreement of 1914.

**Carson, Kit (Christopher)** (1809–68) US guide and soldier. He achieved fame for his work as a guide on FRÉMONT's expeditions (1842–46). In 1854 Carson became an Indian agent in New Mexico and in 1861 became a colonel in the US army, fighting against Confederate forces. In 1868 he became superintendent of Indian affairs for the Colorado Territory.

**Carson, Rachel Louise** (1907–64) US writer and marine biologist. Carson is best known for her popular books on marine ecology. *The Sea Around Us* (1951) won a National Book Award. *Silent Spring* (1962) directed public attention to the dangers of agricultural pesticides and was a pioneering work in the development of the environmental movement.

**Carson City** State capital of Nevada, 30mi (50km) S of Reno. The city grew rapidly after silver was discovered in the Comstock Lode in 1859. It was named for Kit CARSON. Gambling is the main industry. Pop. (1990) 40,443.

**Cartagena** City and port in NW Colombia, on the Bay of Cartagena in the Caribbean Sea; capital of the department of Bolívar. It is the principal oil port of Colombia. There is a university (founded 1824). Industries: oil refining, sugar, tobacco, textiles, tourism. Pop. (1992) 688,306.

**Cartagena** Major seaport in SE Spain, on the Mediterranean Sea. Founded in *c.*255 BC by the Carthaginians, the settlement later fell to the Romans. Moors captured it in the 8th century, but it was retaken by Spaniards in the 13th century. In 1585, it was destroyed by Francis Drake. It is the site of the medieval Castillo de la Concepción and a modern naval base. Industries: shipbuilding, lead, zinc, iron. Pop. (1991) 166,736.

**Carte, Richard D'Oyly** (1844–1901) English impresario and producer of the operas of GILBERT and SULLIVAN. He founded the Savoy Theatre, London (1881).

**cartel** Formal agreement among the producers of a product to fix the price and divide the market among themselves. It

◀ **carp** Bony fish belonging to the order Cypriniformes, carps have large bodies usually covered evenly with scales, but these may be missing in cultivated types such as the mirror carp.

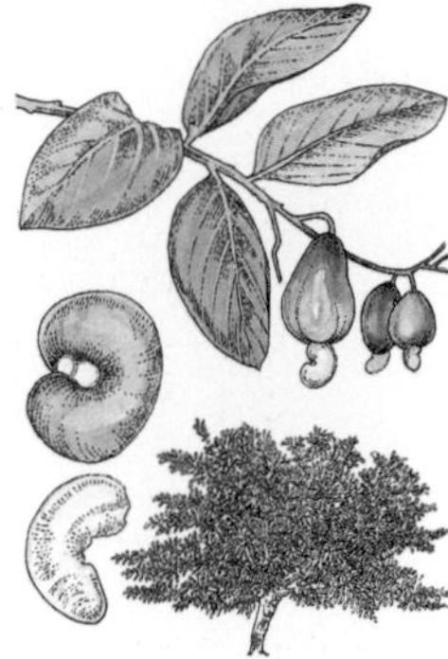

▲ **cashew** Grown in tropical regions, the cashew bears bean-shaped nuts that form beneath an apple-like fruit, and which have an inner and an outer shell which are removed before roasting.

▲ **cassava** Grown widely throughout the tropics, cassava (*Manihot utilissama*) is one of the world's most important tubers. A processed form of meal is produced from its roots and used as a cereal substitute.

usually results in higher prices for consumers and extra profits for the producers. Cartels are illegal in many countries.

**Carter, Angela** (1940–92) English novelist and short-story writer. She is closely associated with MAGIC REALISM. Carter's writing draws on legend and myth, and mixes past and present, a technique used in *Nights at the Circus* (1984). Other writings include the novels *The Magic Toyshop* (1967) and *The Passion of New Eve* (1977) and the short-story collection *The Bloody Chamber* (1979).

**Carter, Elliott Cook, Jr.** (1908– ) US composer. Carter is widely regarded as the leading modern American composer. His works are notable for elaborate COUNTERPOINT and complex structures. Compositions include a piano (1946) and a cello (1948) sonata, *Variations* (1953–55) and *Concerto* (1970) for orchestra, and four string quartets (1951, 1959, 1971, 1986). Carter received the 1960 Pulitzer Prize for his second string quartet.

**Carter, Jimmy (James Earl), Jr.** (1924– ) 39th US president (1977–81). Carter was a Democrat senator (1962–66) and governor (1971–74) for the state of Georgia. In 1976 he defeated the incumbent President Gerald FORD. Carter had a number of foreign policy successes, such as the negotiation of the CAMP DAVID AGREEMENT (1979). These were overshadowed, however, by the disastrous attempt to free US hostages in Iran (April 1980). Following the Soviet invasion of Afghanistan, Carter backed a US boycott of the 1980 Moscow Olympics. An oil price rise contributed to spiralling inflation, which was dampened only by a large increase in interest rates. In the 1980 presidential election Carter was easily defeated by Ronald REAGAN. Since then he has sought to promote human rights and acted as a international peace broker.

**Cartesian coordinates** System in which the position of a point is specified by its distances from intersecting lines (axes). In the simplest type – rectangular coordinates in two dimensions – two axes are used at right angles: $y$ and $x$. The position of a point is then given by a pair of numbers $(x, y)$. The abscissa, $x$, is the point's distance from the $y$ axis, measured in the direction of the $x$ axis, and the ordinate, $y$, is the distance from the $x$ axis. Three axes represent three dimensions.

**Carthage** Ancient port on the Bay of Tunis, N Africa. It was founded in the 9th century BC by Phoenician colonists. Carthage became a great commercial city and imperial power controlling an empire in North Africa, S Spain, and islands of the W Mediterranean. The rise of Rome in the 3rd century resulted in the PUNIC WARS, and ended with the destruction of Carthage (146 BC) in the Third Punic War. It was resettled as a Roman colony, and in the 5th century AD became the capital of the VANDALS.

**Carthusian** Monastic order founded by St. Bruno in 1084. It is based at the Grande Chartreuse monastery near Grenoble, France. It is a mainly contemplative order, in which monks and nuns solemnly vow to live in silence and solitude.

**Cartier, Jacques** (1491–1557) French navigator and explorer who discovered (1535) the St. Lawrence River. Cartier was sent (1534) to North America by Francis I. During this first voyage he discovered the Magdalen Islands and explored the Gulf of St. Lawrence. In 1535–36 he sailed up the St. Lawrence River to the site of modern Quebec and continued on foot to Hochelaga (present-day Montreal). His third voyage was part of an unsuccessful colonization scheme. Cartier's discoveries laid the basis for French settlements in Canada.

**cartilage** Flexible supporting tissue made up of the tough protein COLLAGEN. In the vertebrate EMBRYO, the greater part of the SKELETON is cartilage that is replaced by BONE during development. In humans, cartilage is also present in the larynx, nose, and external ear.

**cartoon** Originally a preparatory drawing. Italian Renaissance painters made thorough cartoons, such as RAPHAEL, for the Sistine Chapel. Its modern usage as a humorous drawing or satirical picture is derived from a 19th-century competition for fresco designs for Parliament parodied in *Punch* magazine. *See also* CARICATURE

**Cartwright, Edmund** (1743–1823) English inventor of the power loom. It was patented in 1785, but not used commercially until the early 19th century. He also invented an alcohol engine (1797).

**Caruso, Enrico** (1873–1921) Italian tenor, one of the most widely acclaimed opera singers of all time. He made his debut in Naples (1894). Caruso was a regular performer (1903–20) at the Metropolitan Opera and his recordings won him worldwide recognition. The beauty of his voice is best heard in grand opera, especially Verdi.

**Carver, George Washington** (1864–1943) US agricultural chemist. Carver is best known for his scientific research on the peanut, from which he derived more than 300 products. Born into an African-American slave family, his chief motive was to benefit the impoverished farmers of the South.

**Carver, Raymond** (1938–88) US short-story writer and poet. Carver's fiction depicts, with uncompromising realism, the lives of US citizens. His short stories are collected in *Will You Please Be Quiet, Please?* (1976), *What We Talk About When We Talk About Love* (1981) and *Cathedral* (1983). He also wrote five books of poetry.

**Cary, (Arthur) Joyce (Lunel)** (1888–1957) British novelist. His experiences in colonial service in Nigeria (1914–20) are reflected in novels, such as *Mister Johnson* (1939). Cary's best-known novel is *The Horse's Mouth* (1944).

**Casablanca** (Dar el-Beida) City in W Morocco, on Africa's Atlantic coast. The site was resettled in 1515 by the Portuguese after their destruction of the old town. An earthquake damaged the city (1755). Today, Casablanca is a thriving commercial center, exporting phosphates and importing petroleum products. Industries: tourism, textiles, fishing. Pop. (1992 est.) 2,700,000.

**Casals, Pablo (Pau)** (1876–1973) Spanish (Catalan) cellist and composer. He formed (1919) his own orchestra in Barcelona and organized the annual Casals Festival in Puerto Rico from 1957. Casal's immaculate tone and intellectual rigor are best heard on Bach's cello suites.

**Casanova de Seingalt, Giovanni Giacomo** (1725–98) Italian libertine and adventurer. From 1750 he traveled through Europe leading a dissolute existence. Casanova amassed a fortune and mixed with high society. His exploits are recounted in his *Memoirs*, not published in unexpurgated form until 1960. His name is synonymous with the amorous adventurer.

**Cascade Range** Mountain range in W North America, extending from NE California across Oregon and Washington into Canada. The Cascade Tunnel, at 8mi (13km) the longest rail tunnel in the US, passes through them. Crater Lake National Park is in the Cascades. The highest peak is Mount RAINIER, 14,410ft (4,395m). The range also includes Mount ST. HELENS, 8,363ft (2,549m).

**casein** Principal protein in milk, containing about 15 amino acids. Obtained by the addition of either acid or the enzyme rennet, casein is used to make plastics, cosmetics, adhesives, paints, cheeses, and animal feed.

**Casement, Sir Roger David** (1864–1916) Irish humanitarian and revolutionary. While a British consul (1895–1912) he exposed the exploitation of rubber-gatherers in the Belgian Congo. During World War I Casement sought aid for an Irish nationalist uprising, and was executed for treason after the British secret service tried to destroy his reputation by publishing the Casement diaries.

**cash crop** Agricultural crop cultivated for its commercial value, as opposed to a staple crop (grown for subsistence). The term is often encountered in development economics. Cash crops, such as coffee, sugar, or cotton, were introduced into Africa, Asia, and the Americas as part of the colonialist project and intensively farmed via plantation systems.

**cashew** Evergreen shrub or tree grown in the tropics, important for its nuts. The wood is used for boxes and boats and produces a gum similar to gum arabic. Height: to 39ft (12m). Family Anacardiaceae; species *Anacardium occidentale*.

**cashmere** Woolly hair of a goat native to Kashmir, India. The warm but lightweight wool is woven for clothing.

**Caspian Sea** Shallow salt lake, the world's largest inland body of water. The Caspian Sea is enclosed on three sides by Russia, Kazakstan, Turkmenistan, and Azerbaijan. The S shore forms the N border of Iran. It has been an important trade route for centuries. It is fed mainly by the Volga River; there is no outlet. The chief ports are BAKU and ASTRAKHAN. It still has important fisheries and a seal trade. Area: *c.*143,000sq mi (371,000sq km).

## CASTING

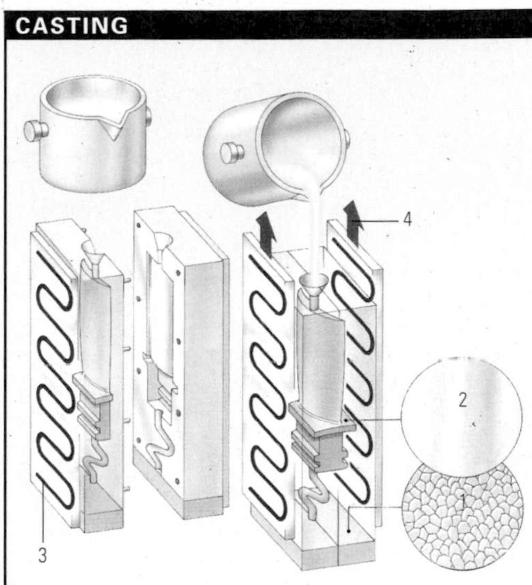


Metal alloys used to make turbine blades must withstand the huge temperatures and forces inside jet engines. The random crystalline structure formed when the alloy cools normally (as seen in the overflow ,1) can be a source of weakness. The strongest structure is achieved by making a blade from a single crystal (2). This can be done by using heating elements (3). After the molten alloy is poured, the elements move up the sides of the mold (4) ensuring the alloy cools from the bottom and forms a single crystal.

**Cassandra** In Greek mythology, the daughter of PRIAM, skilled in the art of prophecy, but condemned by Apollo never to be taken seriously. Her warning that the Greeks would capture Troy went unheeded. She was raped by the Greek Ajax the lesser, and then carried off as a concubine by AGAMEMNON; they were both murdered by Agamemnon's wife CLYTEMNESTRA and her lover Aegisthus.

**Cassatt, Mary** (1845–1926) US painter and printmaker. She was influenced by DEGAS and IMPRESSIONISM. Cassatt's finest paintings include *The Bath* (1892). She also made many DRYPOINT and AQUATINT studies of domestic life.

**cassava** (manioc) Tapioca plant native to Brazil. It is a tall woody shrub with small clustered flowers. A valuable cereal substitute is made from the tuberous roots. Height: up to 9ft (2.7m). Family Euphorbiaceae; species *Manihot esculenta*.

**Cassini, Giovanni Domenico** (1625–1712) French astronomer, who ran the Paris Observatory. Cassini was the first to accurately measure the dimensions of the SOLAR SYSTEM, and discovered the division in the rings of SATURN that now bear his name, and also four satellites. He also measured Jupiter's rotation period.

**Cassiopeia** Distinctive northern constellation, representing in mythology the mother of Andromeda. The five leading stars make up a "W" or "M" pattern.

**Cassius, Caius Longinus** (d.42 BC) Roman general who led the plot to assassinate Julius CAESAR. Cassius sided with POMPEY against Caesar, but was pardoned after Caesar defeated Pompey at the battle of Pharsalus (48 BC). After the assassination of Caesar in 44 BC he left for Sicily. Believing he had lost the battle against MARK ANTONY and Octavian (AUGUSTUS) at Philippi, Cassius committed suicide.

**cassowary** Flightless bird of rainforests in Australia and Malaysia. It has coarse black plumage, a horny crest on its brightly colored head, large feet, and sharp claws. The male incubates the eggs in a nest on the forest floor. Height: to 65in (1.6m). Family Casuariidae; species *Casuarius casuarius*.

**caste** Formal system of social stratification based on factors such as race, gender, or religion, and sanctioned by tradition. An individual is born into a position and cannot change it. It is most prevalent in Hindu society. The four main divisions (*varnas*) are BRAHMINS (priests and professionals), Kshatriyas (nobles and warriors), Vaishyas (farmers and merchants) and Sudras (servants). A fifth group, the "Untouchables" (*harijan* or *dalit*), lie outside the caste system. They perform the most polluting tasks, such as handling animal wastes.

**Castiglione, Baldassare** (1478–1529) Italian diplomat and writer. Castiglione served in the court of the duke of Milan and for the duke of Urbino. While serving as a papal envoy, he wrote *Libro del Cortegiano* (1528), a classic treatise on the role of the Renaissance courtier.

**Castile** Region and former kingdom in central Spain, traditionally comprising Old Castile (N) and New Castile (S). Old Castile was part of the kingdom of LEÓN until 1230. Castilians captured New Castile from the Moors. Queen ISABELLA I established the union with ARAGÓN in 1479, and in the 16th century Castile was the most influential power in Spain and the core of the Spanish monarchy.

**Castile-La Mancha** Region in central Spain; includes the provinces of Albacete, Ciudad Real, Cuenca, Guadalajara, and Toledo; the capital is TOLEDO. It was captured from the Moors in 1212. Its major products: are olive oil and grapes. Area: 30,590sq mi (79,226sq km). Pop. (1991) 1,658,446.

**Castile-León** Region in N Spain; includes the provinces of Ávila, Burgos, León, Palencia, Salamanca, Segovia, Soria, Valladolid, and Zamora; the capital is Valladolid. Formerly part of the kingdom of LEÓN, Castile and Aragón were united in 1479. Extreme climate and poor soil allow limited grain growing and sheep raising. Area: 36,350sq mi (94,147sq km). Pop. (1991) 2,545,926.

**casting** Forming objects by pouring molten metal into molds and allowing it to cool and solidify. Specialized processes, such as plastic molding, composite molding, CIRE PERDUE casting, and die casting give greater dimensional accuracy, smoother surfaces, and finer detail.

**castle** Fortified house or fortress, usually the medieval residences of European kings or nobles. Castles evolved from a need for strategic fortresses that could accommodate large households and offer shelter. Built of wood or stone, castles were located often on a hill and surrounded by a water-filled moat. Walls were thick and high enough to withstand attack, with parapets to enable defenders to maneuver between the turrets. WINDSOR CASTLE is a modified but recognizably medieval castle.

**Castlereagh, Robert Stewart, 2nd Viscount** (1769–1822) British statesman, b. Ireland. As chief secretary of Ireland (1799–1801), Castlereagh helped secure the passage of the Act of UNION with Britain (1800). He resigned over George III's opposition to CATHOLIC EMANCIPATION. As secretary of war (1805–06, 1807–09), Castlereagh reorganized and expanded the army. He resigned after a duel with George CANNING. As foreign secretary (1812–22), Castlereagh formed the QUADRUPLE ALLIANCE that defeated NAPOLEON I and dominated the peace terms at the Congress of VIENNA.

**Castor and Pollux** (Dioscuri) In Greek mythology, the twin sons of LEDA. They were invoked by sailors seeking favorable winds. Zeus, father of Pollux, transformed them into the Gemini constellation after Castor died and Pollux refused to be parted from him.

**castration** Removal of the sexual glands (testes or ovaries) from an animal or human. In human beings, removal of the testes has been used as punishment, to sexually incapacitate slaves to produce EUNUCHS, to artificially create soprano voices (CASTRATO), and to stop the spread of cancer.

**castrato** Male voice in the soprano or mezzo-soprano register, produced in adult males by CASTRATION during boyhood. Castratos were much used in operas in the 17th and 18th centuries and in music for the Roman Catholic Church. The most famous castrato was Farinelli. *See also* COUNTERTENOR

**Castro, Fidel** (1926– ) Cuban revolutionary leader and politician, premier (1959– ). In 1953 he was sentenced to 15 years' imprisonment after an unsuccessful coup against the BATISTA regime. Two years later, he was granted an amnesty and exiled to Mexico. In January 1959 his guerrilla forces overthrew the regime. Castro quickly instituted radical reforms, such as collectivizing agriculture and dispossessing foreign companies. In 1961, the US organized the abortive BAY OF PIGS invasion. Castro responded by allying more

▲ **cassowary** The several species of large ground-dwelling birds – ostrich, rhea, emu, and cassowary (*Casuarius casuarius*) – all resemble each other quite closely but are thought to have arisen independently and as such are examples of a phenomenon called convergent evolution.

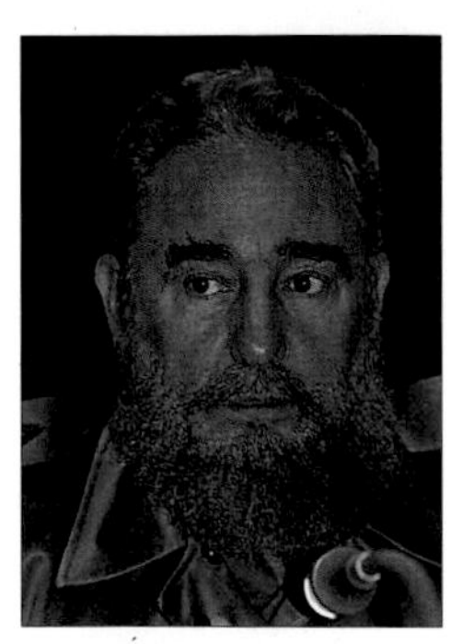

▲ **Castro** Cuba's political leader since 1959, Fidel Castro has in the past enjoyed huge support from the Cuban people. However, US trade embargoes and lack of economic support from the former Soviet Union have brought about public demand for economic and political reforms.

C

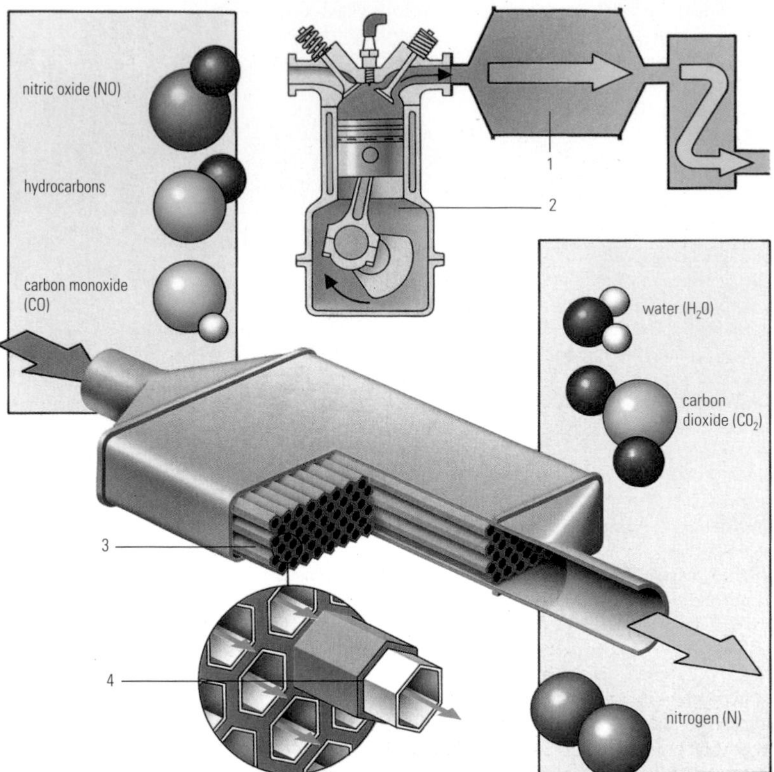


▲ **catalytic converter** A catalytic converter is placed in the exhaust system (1) to reduce the pollution produced by combustion engines (2). It comprises a ceramic honeycomb structure (3), which maximizes the surface area of the converter, covered in catalysts – normally platinum and rhodium (4). As exhaust gases, primarily carbon monoxide, nitric oxide, and hydrocarbons from the cylinder pass through the converter they react with the catalysts. The platinum and rhodium accelerate oxidation and reduction in the hot gases. The pollutants are oxidized into water, carbon dioxide, and nitrogen.

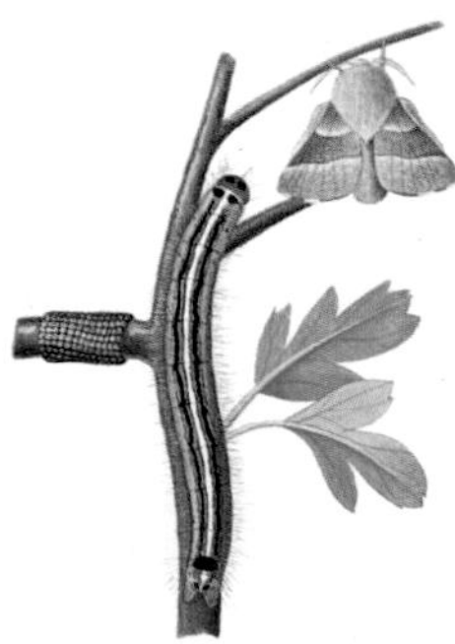

▲ **caterpillar** The lackey moth (*Malacosoma neustria*) is found throughout Europe. Its colorfully striped caterpillars live communually on hawthorn and similar bushes, which they may strip of their leaves. Eggs are laid in a collar around a twig.

closely with the Soviet Union and developing nations. In 1962 the CUBAN MISSILE CRISIS saw the US and Soviet Union on the brink of nuclear war. Castro's attempt to export revolution to the rest of Latin America was largely thwarted by the capture of his ally "Che" GUEVARA (1967). In 1980 he lifted the ban on emigration and 125,000 people left for Florida. The Cuban economy was heavily dependent on Soviet economic aid. The collapse of Soviet communism and the continuing US trade embargo dramatically worsened the Cuban economy, forcing Castro to introduce economic reforms.

**cat** Carnivorous, often solitary and nocturnal mammal of the family Felidae, ranging in size from the rare Siberian tiger to the domestic cat. It has specialized teeth and claws for hunting, a keen sense of smell, acute hearing, sensitive vision, and balances well with its long tail (only the Manx cat is tailless). Cats all have fully retractile claws, except for the CHEETAH. One of the first animals to be domesticated, cats have appeared frequently in myth and religion. Order Carnivora.

**catabolism** *See* METABOLISM

**Catalan** Romance language spoken mainly in NE Spain, but also in the Balearic Islands, Andorra, and southern France. There are *c*.6 million speakers.

**Catalonia** (Cataluña) Region in NE Spain, extending from the French border to the Mediterranean Sea; the capital is BARCELONA. Catalonia includes the provinces of Barcelona, Gerona, Lérida, and Tarragona. United with Aragón in 1137, it retained its own laws and language. During the Spanish Civil War it was a Loyalist stronghold, and recently has been a focus of separatist movements. The COSTA BRAVA is an important tourist area. Products: grain, fruit, olive oil, wool, wine. Area: 12,329sq mi (31,932sq km). Pop. (1990) 6,059,454.

**catalyst** Substance that speeds up the rate of a chemical reaction without itself being consumed. Many industrial processes rely on catalysts such as the HABER PROCESS for manufacturing AMMONIA. Metals or their compounds catalyze by adsorbing gases to their surface, forming intermediates that then readily react to form the desired product while regenerating the original catalytic surface. The METABOLISM of all living organisms depends on biological catalysts called ENZYMES.

**catalytic converter** Antipollution device used in INTERNAL COMBUSTION ENGINES. It consists of a bed of catalytic agents through which flow the gaseous exhaust of fuel combustion. Converters located in mufflers reduce harmful unburned hydrocarbons and carbon monoxide. These converters are adversely affected by tetraethyl lead found in some gasolines.

**Catania** Port near Mount ETNA, E Sicily, Italy, capital of Catania province. Catania was founded by the Greeks in 729 BC. It was devastated by a volcanic eruption in 1669 and an earthquake in 1693. It has Greek and Roman ruins, a Norman cathedral (1091), and a university (1444). Pop. (1992) 329,898.

**cataract** Opacity in the lens of an EYE, causing blurring of vision. Most cases are due to degenerative changes in old age but it can also be congenital, the result of damage to the lens, or some metabolic disorder such as diabetes. Treatment is by removal of the cataract and implanting an artificial lens.

**catastrophe theory** Mathematical technique published in 1972 by the French mathematician René Thom. It is useful for describing situations in which gradually changing motivations or inputs cause a sudden discontinuous leap in a system's behavior or output. *See also* CHAOS THEORY

**catechism** Manual of instruction in Christian church teachings for the young or any candidate preparing for membership of a church. In some sects, it provides a medium of instruction for baptized members. A catechism often takes the form of question and answer.

**caterpillar** Worm-like larva of a BUTTERFLY or MOTH; it has a segmented body, short antennae, simple eyes, three pairs of true legs, and chewing mouthparts. Nearly all feed voraciously on plants and are serious crop pests.

**catfish** Any member of a large family of scaleless fish found in tropical and subtropical waters; it has fleshy barbels on the upper jaw, sometimes with venomous spines. Most species live in freshwater and can be farmed. Length: up to 10ft (3.3m). Order Siluriformes.

**cathedral** (Gk. *kathedra*, throne or seat) Main church of a bishop's province, containing his throne. In the ROMANESQUE period, cathedrals started to become very large and many Gothic cathedrals are gigantic structures. The prototype of the true Gothic cathedral is the Abbey Church of St.-Denis near Paris. Suger, the abbot, added a chapel and pointed groin VAULT. Bigger windows and slender arches gave it a sense of lightness very different from the static solidity of the Romanesque. Among the great cathedrals of western Europe are Notre-Dame, Paris (begun 1163), and CHARTRES (begun 1194) in France, COLOGNE cathedral in Germany, and MILAN cathedral (begun 1386) in Italy. Some of the finest English examples, such as Canterbury and York, combine Romanesque and Gothic features. St. Mark's, VENICE, is a magnificent Byzantine example. Central and Eastern European cathedrals often amalgamate Byzantine and western features, while many Spanish cathedrals combine Romanesque, French, German, and Moorish features. In Latin America, cathedrals are often of Portuguese or Spanish RENAISSANCE and BAROQUE origin. The Episcopal Cathedral of St. John the Divine in New York is the world's largest Gothic cathedral. *See also* BYZANTINE ART AND ARCHITECTURE; GOTHIC ART AND ARCHITECTURE

**Cather, Willa** (1876–1947) US novelist and short-story writer. She grew up among immigrant Nebraskan farmers who became the subject of her work. Cather's fiction explores the pioneer spirit: love of the land, loyalty to family, and the struggle with nature. Her novels include *O Pioneers* (1913), *A Lost Lady* (1923), and *Death Comes for the Archbishop* (1927).

**Catherine II (the Great)** (1729–96) Empress of Russia (1762–96), b. Germany. ELIZABETH chose her (1745) as the wife of the future czar Peter III. Peter succeeded to the throne in 1761. With the help of her lover, Grigori Orlov, Catherine overthrew her husband and shortly afterward he was murdered. Catherine began her reign as an "enlightened despot," with ambitious plans for reform, but after the peasants' revolt (1773–74), led by Pugachev, she became increasingly conservative. In 1785 Catherine extended the powers of the nobility at the expense of the serfs. Catherine's foreign policy, guided by POTEMKIN, vastly extended Russian territory (chiefly at the expense of the Ottoman Empire). In 1764 she secured the accession of her former lover to the Polish throne as Stanislaus II. Russia emerged from the first Russo-Turkish War (1768–74) as the dominant power in the Middle East. Crimea was annexed in 1783 and Alaska was colonized. Her dialog with leading Enlightenment figures did much to promote her contemporary image in Europe.

**Catherine de' Medici** (1519–89) Queen of France, wife of Henry II, and daughter of Lorenzo de' MEDICI. She exerted considerable political influence after her husband's and first son's deaths in 1559. In 1560 Catherine became regent for her second son, CHARLES IX, and remained principal adviser until his death (1574). Her initial tolerance of the HUGUENOTS turned to enmity at the beginning of the French Wars of RELIGION. Catherine's concern for preserving the power of the monarchy led to a dependence on the Catholic House of GUISE, whose growing power she failed to control. Fearing the decline of her own importance at court, she planned the SAINT BARTHOLOMEW'S DAY MASSACRE (1572). When her third son, HENRY III, acceded to the throne in 1574, her effectiveness in policy-making had been compromised.

**Catherine of Aragon** (1485–1536) Daughter of FERDINAND and ISABELLA, she was the first queen of England's HENRY VIII (1509). Catherine's only surviving child was a daughter (MARY I). The need to produce a male heir, combined with Henry's desire for Anne BOLEYN, induced him to seek an annulment (1527). The pope's procrastination led to the break with Rome and to the English REFORMATION. The annulment was granted by Thomas CRANMER in 1533.

**cathode** In chemistry, the negative electrode of an electrolytic cell or electron tube. It attracts positive ions (cations) during ELECTROLYSIS.

**cathode rays** Radiation emitted by the cathode of a thermionic electron valve containing a gas at low pressure. The rays were identified in 1897 by J.J. THOMSON as streams of charged, elementary particles having extremely low mass, later called ELECTRONS. Most electrons are emitted because of collisions between the cathode and positive ions formed in the valve.

**cathode-ray tube** Evacuated electron tube used for TELEVISION picture tubes, oscilloscopes, and display screens in radar sets and computers. An electron gun shoots a beam of electrons, focused by a grid. The electrons strike a fluorescent screen and produce a spot of light. In a television tube, an electrostatic or magnetic field deflects the beam so that it scans a number of lines on the screen, controlled by the incoming picture signals.

**Catholic Church** Term used in Christianity with one of several connotations: (1) It is the Universal church, as distinct from local churches. (2) It means the church holding "orthodox" doctrines. (3) It is the undivided church before the schism of East and West in 1054. Following this, the Western church called itself "Catholic," the Eastern church "Orthodox." (4) Since the REFORMATION, the term has usually been used to denote the ROMAN CATHOLIC CHURCH, although the ANGLICAN COMMUNION and the OLD CATHOLICS use it to cover themselves as well.

**Catholic Emancipation, Act of** (1829) Measure by which the statutes (dating back to the REFORMATION) barring Roman Catholics in Britain from holding civil office or sitting in Parliament were repealed. Emancipation was achieved through a series of acts. In 1778 restrictions against land purchase and inheritance were lifted. In 1791 further restrictions were removed, and by 1793 Catholics were allowed in the services, universities, and the judiciary. The final concession allowing them to sit in Parliament was wrung from the Duke of WELLINGTON's government by Daniel O'CONNELL.

**cation** Positive ION attracted to the CATHODE during electrolysis.

**Catlin, George** (1796–1872) US painter, who concentrated on pictures of Native American life. His paintings represent 45 tribal groups and include many portraits. His books include *Notes on the Manners, Customs, and Conditions of the North American Indians* (1841).

**Cato the Elder** (234–149 BC) (Marcus Porcius) Roman leader. As censor, from 184 BC, Cato worked to restore the old ideals of Rome – courage, honesty, and simple living. His constant urging in the Senate that CARTHAGE should be destroyed precipitated the Third PUNIC WAR.

**Cato the Younger** (95–46 BC) (Marcus Porcius Cato Uticensis) Roman politician, great-grandson of CATO THE ELDER. He opposed Julius CAESAR and forced the creation of the First Triumvirate. Cato favored POMPEY in the civil war (49 BC) and, when Caesar emerged victorious, committed suicide.

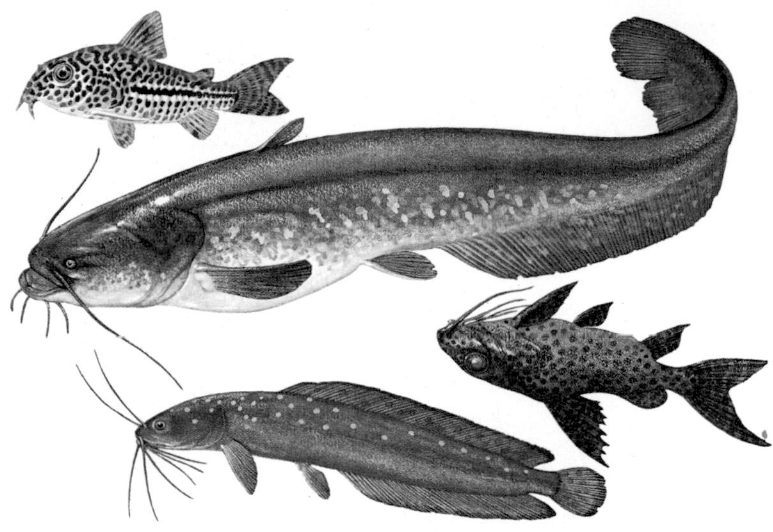

▲ **catfish** The name "catfish" is applied to a very large family of freshwater fish of the order Siluriformes. They tend to be sluggish in their movements and have barbels (whiskers) growing from their mouths.

**CAT scan** *See* COMPUTERIZED AXIAL TOMOGRAPHY

**Catskill Mountains** Plateau of the Appalachian system on the W bank of the Hudson River, SE New York. The highest peak is Slide Mountain, 4,204ft (1,282m). Site of the Rip Van Winkle legend, its natural beauty attracted the painters of the Hudson River School. Today, it is a popular resort.

**cattle** Large, ruminant mammals of the family Bovidae, including all the varieties of modern domestic cattle (*Bos taurus*), the brahman (*Bos indicus*), and hybrids of these two. The family also includes the YAK, the wild GAUR, the wild banteng, and the kouprey. The male is born as a bull calf and becomes a bull if left intact; if castrated, it becomes a steer, bullock, or ox if used as a draft animal. The female is a heifer calf, growing to become a heifer and, after calving, a cow. Horns are permanent, hollow, and unbranched. Domestic cattle are raised for meat, milk, and other dairy products. Leather, glue, gelatin, and fertilizers are made from the carcasses.

## CATHODE-RAY TUBE

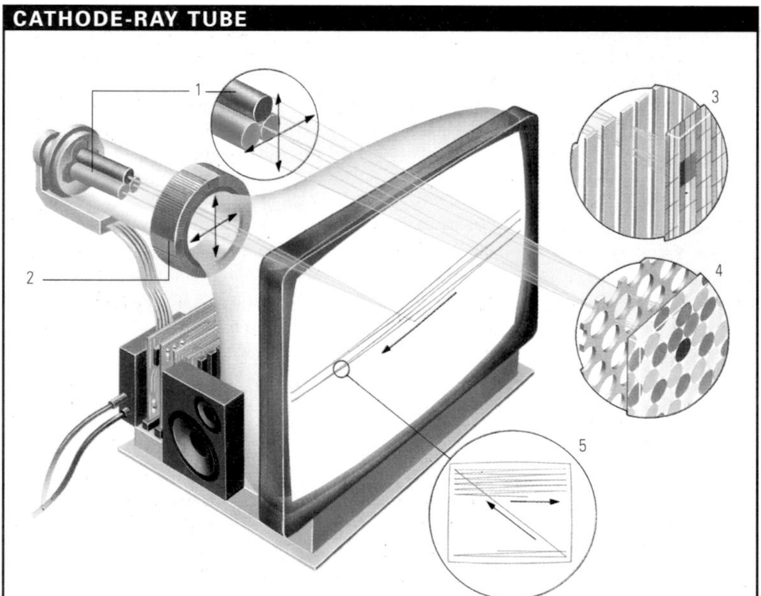


Television receivers are a type of cathode-ray tube. Three electron guns (1) receive color signals from a color decoder that splits the color signal into red, green, and blue. The guns fire three beams of electrons through vertical and horizontal deflection coils (2) onto the screen of a "shadow mask tube" (3). This is made up of about a million dots (4), a third of which glow red when bombarded, a third blue, and the remaining third, green. The dots compose the color picture received by the television. The beam of electrons scans hundreds of lines on the screen (525 in the US, 625 in Europe) making up the moving pictures. The beam scans from left to right, starting top left and finishing at the bottom right (5).

C

**Catullus, Gaius Valerius** (84–54 BC) Roman poet. He is best known for short love lyrics, the most famous of which refer to Lesbia, depicting the woman, Clodia, with whom Catullus was in love. His longer works are the poems *Attis* and *The Marriage of Peleus and Thetis*.

**Caucasus** (Bol'šoj Kavkaz) Mountain region in SE Europe, Russia, Georgia, Armenia, and Azerbaijan, extending SE from the mouth of the Kuban River on the Black Sea to the Apscheron Peninsula on the Caspian Sea. The system includes two major regions: N Caucasia (steppes) and TRANSCAUCASIA. It forms a natural barrier between Asia and Europe. There are deposits of oil, iron, and manganese. The highest peak is Mount ELBRUS, at 18,493ft (5,637m). Length: 750mi (1,210km).

**cauliflower** Form of CABBAGE with a short thick stem, large lobed leaves, and edible white or purplish flower clusters that form tightly compressed heads. Family Brassicaceae; species *Brassica oleracea botrytis*.

**caustic soda** (sodium hydroxide, NaOH) Strong ALKALI that is prepared industrially by the ELECTROLYSIS of salt (sodium chloride, NaCl). It is a white solid that burns the skin, with a slippery feel because it absorbs moisture from the air. It also absorbs atmospheric carbon dioxide, so forming a crust of sodium carbonate ($Na_2CO_3$). Caustic soda is used in many industries, such as soap-making and to manufacture ALUMINUM.

**Cavalier** (Fr. *chevalier*) Name adopted by the Royalists during the English CIVIL WAR in opposition to the ROUNDHEADS (Parliamentarians). The court party retained the name after the RESTORATION until superseded by the name TORY.

**cavalry** Mounted troops. Cavalry were first employed by the ancient Egyptians; the first use of cavalry in Europe dates from the invasions of the Huns, Magyars, and Mongols. The last prominent use of cavalry occurred in the American CIVIL WAR.

**cave** Natural underground cavity. There are several kinds, including; coastal caves, formed by wave erosion; ice caves, formed in glaciers; and lava caves. The largest are formed in carbonate rocks such as limestone.

**Cavendish, Henry** (1731–1810) English chemist and physicist. He discovered hydrogen and the compositions of water and air, and estimated the Earth's mass and density by a method now known as the "Cavendish experiment." Cavendish also discovered nitric acid ($HNO_3$), the gravitational constant, and measured the specific gravity of carbon dioxide ($CO_2$) and hydrogen. The Cavendish Laboratory at Cambridge University, England, is named for him.

**cave painting** Drawing made on the wall of a cave by humans of the upper PALAEOLITHIC period. The most famous cave paintings are those at LASCAUX in SW France and ALTAMIRA in N Spain, all of which were made between 10,000 and 30,000 years ago. Because most cave paintings depict animals that were hunted for food, such as bison, archaeologists believe they were designed to bring good fortune in hunting.

**caviar** Roe (eggs) of a STURGEON and three less common fish (also occasionally a salmon) which, salted and seasoned, is a gastronomic delicacy, especially in Russia. The roe is extracted from the fish before it can spawn.

► **Ceauşescu** The former president of Romania, Nicolae Ceauşescu, attempted massive social and political reforms while in power (1965–89), many of which were hugely unpopular. With the demise of communism in Eastern Europe, he was deposed, and executed along with his wife, Elena.

**Cavour, Camillo Benso, conte di** (1810–61) Piedmontese politician, instrumental in uniting Italy under Savoy rule. From 1852 he was prime minister under Victor EMMANUEL II. He engineered Italian liberation from Austria with French aid, expelled the French with the help of Giuseppe GARIBALDI, and finally neutralized Garibaldi's influence. This led to the formation of the kingdom of Italy (1861). *See also* RISORGIMENTO

**Caxton, William** (1422–91) First English printer. Following a period in Germany (1470–72), where he learned printing, Caxton set up his own press in 1476 at Westminster. He published more than 100 items, many of them his own translations. Among his publications were editions of CHAUCER, GOWER, and MALORY.

**Cayley, Sir George** (1773–1857) British inventor who founded the science of AERODYNAMICS. Cayley built the first GLIDER to carry a man successfully, developed the basic form of the early airplane, and invented a caterpillar tractor.

**Cayman Islands** British dependency in the West Indies, comprising Grand Cayman, Little Cayman, and Cayman Brac, *c.*200mi (325km) NW of Jamaica, in the Caribbean Sea. The capital is Georgetown. The islands were discovered by Columbus in 1503, and ceded to Britain in the 17th century. Industries: tourism, international finance, turtle and shark fishing, timber, coconuts. Area: 100sq mi (259sq km). Pop. (1989) 25,355.

**Cayuga** Major branch of the Five Nations of the IROQUOIS CONFEDERACY, originally living around Lake Cayuga, New York, and the Grand River in Ontario, Canada. The Cayuga fought alongside the British during the American Revolution and afterwards became widely scattered into Ohio, Wisconsin, and Oklahoma, where they joined the Seneca. Today, there are *c.*550 in Oklahoma and 400 Cayuga in New York.

**CD-ROM** (**c**ompact **d**isk **r**ead-**o**nly **m**emory) Optical storage device for COMPUTER data and programs. It resembles a COMPACT DISC (CD) used in hi-fi systems. A CD-ROM can store much more data than a comparably priced portable MAGNETIC DISK. Computer games, encyclopedias and other software are now available in this form. To use a CD-ROM, the disk is placed in a specialized player connected, or built in, to a computer.

**Ceauşescu, Nicolae** (1918–89) Romanian statesman, the country's effective ruler from 1965 to 1989. He became general secretary of the Romanian Communist Party in 1965 and head of state in 1967. Ceauşescu promoted Romanian nationalism, pursued an independent foreign policy, but instituted repressive domestic policies. He was deposed and executed in the December 1989 revolution.

**Cecil, Robert, 1st earl of Salisbury** (1563–1612) English statesman, son of Lord BURGHLEY. He became secretary of state to ELIZABETH I on his father's retirement in 1596. Cecil was responsible for negotiating the accession of JAMES I (1603).

**cecum** Dilated pouch at the junction of the small and large intestines, terminating in the APPENDIX. It has no known function in humans. In rabbits and horses, the cecum contains microorganisms which help to break down the cellulose cell walls of the plants they eat.

**cedar** Evergreen tree native to the Mediterranean and Asia, but found in warm temperate regions worldwide; it has clustered needle-like leaves, long cones, and fragrant, durable wood. It is a popular ornamental tree. Height: 100–180ft (30–55m). Family Pinaceae; genus *Cedrus*.

**Celebes** Former name of SULAWESI, Indonesia

**celery** Biennial plant, native to the Mediterranean and widely cultivated for its long stalks used as a vegetable. Its fruits are used as food flavoring and in medicine. Family Apiaceae/Umbelliferae; species *Apium graveolens*.

**celesta** (céleste) Percussion instrument with a range of four octaves. It consists of steel bars that are struck, producing a tinkling tone. Invented by Auguste Mustel in Paris (1886), it features on the "Dance of the Sugar Plum Fairy" in Tchaikovsky's *Nutcracker* ballet (1892).

**celestial mechanics** Branch of ASTRONOMY concerned with the relative motions of stars and planets that are associated in systems (such as the Solar System or a binary star system) by gravitational fields. Introduced by Isaac NEWTON in the 17th century, celestial mechanics, rather than general RELATIVITY, is usually sufficient to calculate the factors determining the motion of stars and planets, around a center of gravitational attraction.

**celestial sphere** Imaginary sphere of infinite radius used to define the positions of celestial bodies as seen from Earth, the center of the sphere. The sphere rotates, once in 24 hours, about a line that is an extension of the Earth's axis. The position of a celestial body is the point at which a radial line through it meets the surface of the sphere. The position is defined in terms of coordinates, such as declination and right ascension or altitude and azimuth, which refer to great circles on the sphere, such as the celestial EQUATOR or the ecliptic.

**celibacy** Commitment to a lifelong abstention from sexual relations. The status of celibacy as a religious obligation is found in Christianity and Buddhism. From the 4th century, it gradually became compulsory for Roman Catholic priests, monks, and nuns.

**cell** Basic biological unit of which all plant and animal tissues are composed. The cell is the smallest unit of life that can exist independently, with its own self-regulating chemical system. Most cells consist of a MEMBRANE surrounding jelly-like CYTOPLASM with a central NUCLEUS. The nucleus is the main structure in which DNA is stored in CHROMOSOMES. Animal cells vary widely in shape. A red blood cell, for instance, is a biconcave disk, while a nerve cell has a long fiber. The cells of plants and algae are enclosed in a cell wall, which gives them a more rigid shape. Bacterial cells also have a cell wall, but do not have nuclei or chromosomes; instead, they have a loop of DNA floating in the cytoplasm. More advanced cells (those that have nuclei), often have other membrane-bounded structures inside the cell, such as MITOCHONDRIA and CHLOROPLASTS. *See also* EUKARYOTE; PROKARYOTE

**cell** In physics, device from which electricity is obtained due to a chemical reaction. A cell consists of two electrodes (a positive ANODE and a negative CATHODE) immersed in a solution (ELECTROLYTE). A chemical reaction takes place between the electrolyte and one of the electrodes. In a **primary** cell, current is produced from an irreversible chemical reaction, and the chemicals must be renewed at intervals. In a **secondary** cell (BATTERY), the chemical reaction is reversible, and the cell can be charged by passing a current through it.

**cell division** Process by which living CELLS reproduce and enable an organism to grow. In EUKARYOTE cells, a single cell splits in two, first by division of the NUCLEUS (occurring by MITOSIS or MEIOSIS), then by fission of the CYTOPLASM. For growth and asexual reproduction, where the daughter cells are required to be genetically identical to their parents, **mitosis** is used. **Meiosis** results in daughter cells having half the number of chromosomes (HAPLOID). This type of division results in the production of GAMETES (sex cells) that allow genetic information from two parents to be combined at FERTILIZATION. *See also* ALTERNATION OF GENERATIONS; DIPLOID

**cello** (violoncello) Musical instrument, member of the violin family. It has a soft, mellow tone, one octave below the viola; its strings are tuned to C-G-D-A. It is played with a bow and supported by the knees of a seated player. It was developed in the 16th-century by the AMATI family. Among the most important players of the 20th century are Pablo CASALS and Jacqueline DU PRÉ.

**cellophane** Flexible, transparent film made of regenerated CELLULOSE and used mostly as a wrapping material. It is made by dissolving wood pulp or other plant material in an ALKALI, to which carbon disulfide is added to form viscose. This is forced through a narrow slit into a dilute acid where it precipitates as a film of cellulose.

**cellular phone** *See* MOBILE PHONE

**celluloid** Hard plastic invented (1869) in the US by John Hyatt, by mixing cellulose nitrate with pigments and fillers in a solution of camphor and alcohol. When heated it can be molded into a variety of shapes. It was the first major plastic, and used for early motion pictures. It is highly flammable.

**cellulose** $[(C^6H^{10}O^5)_n]$ POLYSACCHARIDE, CARBOHYDRATE that is the structural constituent of the cell walls of plants and algae. Consisting of parallel unbranched chains of GLUCOSE units cross-linked together it forms the basic material of the paper and textile industries.

**Celsius** Temperature scale, devised (1742) by the Swedish astronomer Anders Celsius. The difference between the temperatures of the freezing and boiling points of water is divided into 100 degrees. The freezing point is 0°C and the boiling point is 100°C. The name Celsius officially replaced centigrade in 1948. Degrees Celsius are converted to degrees FAHRENHEIT by multiplying by 1.8 and adding 32. *See also* THERMOMETER

**Celt** Someone who speaks one of the CELTIC LANGUAGES, or is descended from a Celtic language area. After 2000 BC early Celts spread from E France and W Germany over much of W Europe, including Britain. They developed a village-based, hierarchical society headed by nobles and DRUIDS. Conquered by the Romans, the Celts were pushed into Ireland, Wales, Cornwall, and Brittany by Germanic peoples. Their culture remained vigorous, and Celtic churches were important in the early spread of Christianity in N Europe.

**Celtic art** Artworks produced by Celtic peoples in Europe during the prehistoric La Tène period. Its chief characteristic was swirling, abstract design, which found its fullest expression in metalwork and jewelery. The term is sometimes also applied to the La Tène-influenced, early Christian art of western Europe, such as THE BOOK OF KELLS.

**Celtic languages** Group of languages spoken in parts of Britain, Ireland, and France, forming a division within the Italo-Celtic subfamily of Indo-European languages. There are two branches of Celtic languages: Brittonic, which includes WELSH, BRETON, and Cornish; and Goidelic, including Irish and Scots GAELIC and MANX. The Brittonic or Celtic languages were dominant in the British Isles until the 5th century AD.

**Celtic mythology** Legends of local deities of the Celtic tribes scattered throughout Europe and the British Isles. Each tribe had an omnipotent god, similar to Dagda. The gods' world was seen as a reflection of the world of men, while female divinities were more closely identified with nature.

**Cenozoic** Most recent era of geological time, beginning *c*.65 million years ago and extending up to the present. It is subdivided into the TERTIARY and Quaternary periods. It is the period during which present geographical features and plants and animals developed.

**censor** Public official of ancient Rome, from 443 to 22 BC. Two censors were elected for 18-month terms. Besides taking the census, they supervised public works, finance, and morals, and filled senatorial vacancies.

**censorship** Official ban or restriction of any expression deemed to threaten the political, social, or moral order. It is usually imposed by the state or church. Rigorous censorship is a feature of authoritarian or totalitarian regimes. In democracies it is used principally in matters relating to national security. The medieval INQUISITION was a form of censorship. The Reformation and Counter-Reformation used censorship as a means of religious persecution. Until 1948 the Roman Catholic Church published the Index – a list of banned books. Litera-

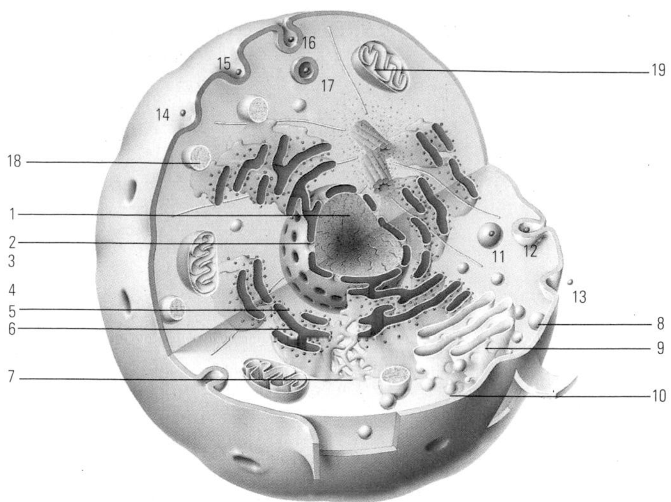


▲ **cell** Animal cells are made up of many different components called organelles. The most prominent is the nucleus (1), which contains all the information of the cell in the form of chromosomes. It is surrounded by the nuclear membrane (2) which contains many pores (3) which allow the nucleus to communicate with the rest of the cell. The center of the nucleus, the nucleolus (4) generates ribosomes (5), which provide the cell with protein. They are found on the rough endoplasmic reticulum (6), a system of flattened sacs and tubes connected to the nuclear membrane. It brings the messenger RNA molecules, which control the creation of protein, to the ribosomes. The smooth endoplasmic reticulum (7) produces small spheres called vesicles (8) which provide the Golgi apparatus (9) with protein. The Golgi apparatus modifies, sorts and packs large molecules into other vesicles which bud off (10). They are sent to other organelles, or secreted from the cell. The fusion of such vesicles with the cell membrane allows particles to be transported out of the cell (exocytosis) (11–13) or brought in (endocytosis) (14–17). Lysosomes (18) break down the molecules entering the cell into enzymes. The mitochondria (19) power the cell, using oxygen and food to generate energy in the form of ATP. ATP is then used in many metabolic processes essential for the cell to function.

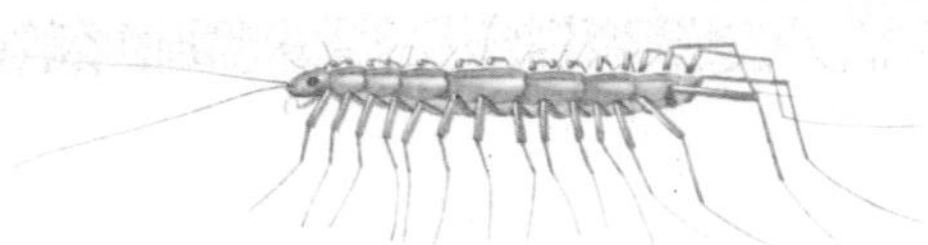

► **centipede** Despite its name the centipede rarely has 100 legs. They are placed in the class Chilopoda. The house centipede (*Scutigera coleoptrata*) is found in damp indoor places and measures up to 5cm (2in) long.

ture has often subject to censorship, mostly on political or moral grounds. Strict censorship in the Soviet Union was imposed on literary works that contradicted state ideology. In the US and Britain, literary works have been banned on the grounds of obscenity. Although the BILL OF RIGHTS in the US Constitution guarantees freedom of the press, until the 1930s many classic works of art and literature deemed as obscene were prevented from being imported. From 1934 to 1966 the US motion picture industry applied a restrictive, self-regulatory code of morals (the Hays Code). More recently, there have been calls for the censorship of PORNOGRAPHY and racist material. Advanced communications technology (such as the Internet) has made policing more problematic.

**centaur** In Greek mythology, a creature half-human, half-horse. One of a warlike and lustful race who roamed Mount Pelion in Thessaly, their debauched behavior was exacerbated by wine. *See also* CHIRON

**Centaurus** (Centaur) Brilliant southern constellation representing a centaur. The brightest star is ALPHA CENTAURI.

**center of gravity** Point at which the weight of a body is considered to be concentrated and around which its weight is evenly balanced. An object in free flight spins around its center of gravity (that is moving in a straight line). In a uniform gravitational field, the center of gravity is the same as the CENTER OF MASS.

**center of mass** Point at which the whole mass of an object or group of objects is considered to be concentrated. Isaac NEWTON first proved his inverse-square law of gravitation by assuming the respective masses of the Earth and Moon were located at their centers.

**centigrade** *See* CELSIUS

**centipede** (lit. hundred-legged) Common name for many arthropods of the class Chilopoda. Found in warm and temperate regions, they have flattened, segmented bodies. Most centipedes have *c.*70 legs (one pair per segment). Many tropical species are 6–12in (15–30cm) long; temperate ones are *c.*1in (2.5cm). Fast-moving predators, they eat small insects and other invertebrates.

**Central** Administrative region of central Scotland; the capital is STIRLING. Major towns include Falkirk, Alloa, Grangemouth, and Dunblane. In the N lie the foothills of the Highlands, including the Trossachs. The S is drained chiefly by the Forth River and is the region's industrial base. The Firth of Forth cuts into the E of the region. Historic sites include BANNOCKBURN battleground and Stirling Castle. Industries: brewing, distilling. Area: 913sq mi (2,635sq km) Pop: 267,492.

**Central African Republic** Landlocked nation in central Africa; the capital is BANGUI. **Land and climate** It lies on a plateau, mostly between 1,970 and 2,620ft (600–800m) above sea level, forming a watershed between the headwaters of two river systems. In the S, the rivers flow into the navigable Ubangi River (a tributary of the CONGO River). The Ubangi and the Bomu form much of the republic's S border. In the N, most rivers are headwaters of the Chari River, which flows into Lake CHAD to the N. Bangui has a warm climate with a high average annual rainfall of 62in (1,574mm). The N is drier, with rainfall of *c.*31in (800mm).Wooded savanna covers much of the country, with open grasslands in the N and rainforests in the SW. The republic has many forest and savanna animals. About 6% of the land is protected in national parks and reserves. **History** Between the 16th–19th centuries, the population was greatly reduced by slavery, and the country is still thinly populated. Most inhabitants migrated into the area during the past 200 years to escape the slave trade. France first occupied the area in 1887, and in 1894 established the colony of Ubangi-Shari at Bangui. In 1906 the colony was united with CHAD, and in 1910 was subsumed into French Equatorial Africa. Forced-labor rebellions occurred in 1928, 1935, and 1946. During World War II Ubangi-Shari supported the Free French. In 1958 the colony voted to become a self-governing republic within the French community, and became the Central African Republic. In 1960 it declared independence, but the next six years saw a deterioration in the economy, and increasing government corruption and inefficiency under President David Dacko. In 1966 Colonel Jean Bedel BOKASSA assumed power in a bloodless coup. In 1976 Bokassa transformed the republic into an empire, and proclaimed himself Emperor Bokassa I. His rule became increasingly brutal, and in 1979 he was deposed in a French-backed coup led by Dacko. In 1981, faced with continuing unrest, Dacko was replaced by André Kolingba. In 1991 the country adopted a new, multiparty constitution. In 1993 Ange-Felix Patasse was elected president. In 1996 an army rebellion was suppressed with the help of French troops. In 1998 a UN peacekeeping force was sent to oversee fresh elections. **Economy** Central African Republic is a low-income developing country (1995 GDP per capita, $1,070), *c.*10% of the land is cultivated, and more than 80% of the work force are engaged in subsistence agriculture. The main food crops are bananas, corn, manioc, millet, and yams. Coffee, cotton, timber, and tobacco are the main cash crops. Diamonds (the only major mineral resource) are the most valuable single export. Manufacturing is on a small scale, and products include beer and cotton. Development has been impeded by its remote position, poor transport system, untrained work force, and heavy dependence on foreign aid (especially from France).

**Central America** Geographical term for the narrow strip of land that connects NORTH AMERICA to SOUTH AMERICA and divides the Caribbean Sea from the Pacific Ocean; it consists of GUATEMALA, EL SALVADOR, HONDURAS, NICARAGUA, COSTA RICA, BELIZE, and PANAMA. Highly developed by the Mayas, the region (excluding Panama) was conquered and ruled by the Spanish from the 16th century until 1821. In 1823 the Central American Federation was formed, but broke up in 1838. The terrain is mostly mountainous; the climate tropical. It enjoys an economic, ethnic, and geological unity. Spanish is the main language. Area: 276,400sq mi (715,876sq km).

**Central and South American mythology** Traditional beliefs of the native peoples of Central and South America and Mexico. The AZTECS had a rich and complex mythology, much of it taken from the earlier cultures of the TOLTECS and MAYAS. The **Aztecs** believed that there had been four eras (suns) before the one in which they were living, and that each sun had ended in universal destruction. They expected that their own era, the fifth, would end with an earthquake. The Aztec pantheon was headed by HUITZILOPOCHTLI. Other important deities included QUETZALCOATL, Tezcatlipoca (god of the night sky), and Tlaloc (rain-god). The underworld was

## CENTRAL AFRICAN REPUBLIC

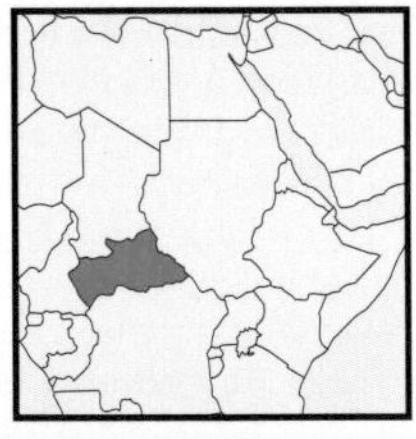

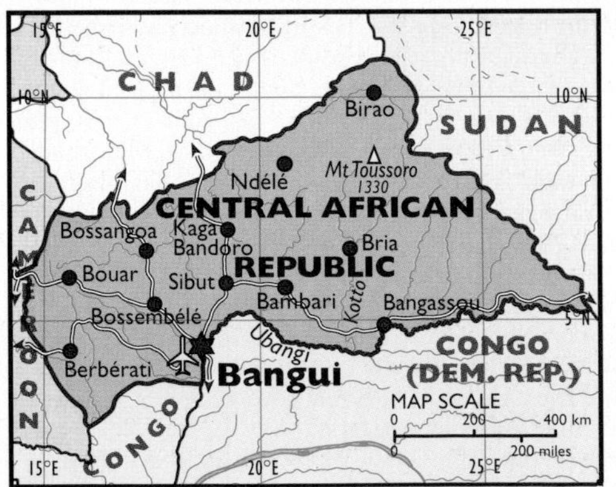


**AREA:** 240,533sq mi (622,980sq km)
**POPULATION:** 3,173,000
**CAPITAL (POPULATION):** Bangui (451,690)
**GOVERNMENT:** Multiparty republic

**ETHNIC GROUPS:** Banda 29%, Baya 25%, Ngbandi 11%, Azande 10% Sara 7%, Mbaka 4%, Mbum 4%
**LANGUAGES:** French (official), Sango (most common)

**RELIGIONS:** Traditional beliefs 57%, Christianity 35%, Islam 8%
**CURRENCY:** CFA franc = 100 centimes

ruled by Mictlantecuhtli, the god of death. Human sacrifice was a central feature of Aztec culture. They believed that the Sun would cease to rise unless constantly supplied with human blood. The **Mayas** of the Yucatán peninsula in Central America had a god of creation, Hunab Ku, remote from human affairs. His son, Itzamna, was the inventor of drawing and writing, and also offered help to the sick. In Guatemala there were creator divinities and also the ancient god Huracán who gave the Mayas fire. In South America the vast INCA empire of Peru worshiped Inti, the sun god and ancestor of the ruling dynasty. ANCESTOR WORSHIP played a central role in **Inca** religious observances. The dead were venerated and the mummies of previous emperors accorded special honors. In tribal groups the shaman still enjoys considerable authority.

**Central Asian Republics** Economic alliance among the republics of KAZAKSTAN, KYRGYZSTAN, and UZBEKISTAN. The alliance was formed in 1994 after the break-up of the Soviet Union.

**central bank** Institution that regulates and sets policy for a nation's banking system. The US central bank is the FEDERAL RESERVE SYSTEM, and in the UK it is the BANK OF ENGLAND.

**Central Intelligence Agency (CIA)** US government agency established to coordinate the intelligence activities of government departments and agencies responsible for US national security. Founded in 1947, it played a major role during the COLD WAR, supporting anticommunist movements. At times the CIA has come under attack for overstepping its mandate and interfering in the internal affairs of foreign countries. It was severely criticized for its role in the WATERGATE AFFAIR. It advises and is directed by the NATIONAL SECURITY COUNCIL (NSC), and should report any action it proposes to take to Congress and gain presidential authorization.

**central nervous system (CNS)** Term embracing the brain and spinal cord, as distinct from the PERIPHERAL NERVOUS SYSTEM. The CNS coordinates all nervous activity. *See also* NERVOUS SYSTEM

**Central Powers** Alliance of Germany and Austria-Hungary (with Bulgaria and Turkey) during World War I. The name distinguished them from their opponents in the W (Britain, France, Belgium, US) and E (Russia and others).

**central processing unit (CPU)** Part of a digital COMPUTER circuit that controls all operations. In most computers, the CPU consists of one complex INTEGRATED CIRCUIT (IC), a chip called a MICROPROCESSOR. A CPU contains temporary storage circuits that hold data and instructions; an arithmetic and logic unit (ALU) that performs calculations; and a control unit that organizes operations.

**centrifugal force** *See* CENTRIPETAL FORCE

**centrifuge** Rotating device used for separating substances. In laboratories, centrifuges separate particles from suspensions, and red blood cells from plasma. In the food industry, centrifuges separate cream from milk and sugar from syrup. In each case, the denser substance is forced to the outside of a rotating container

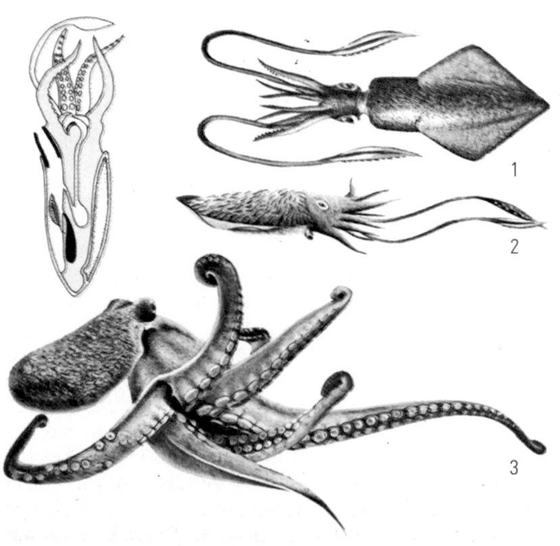


◄ **Cephalopoda** The squid (1), cuttlefish (2), and octopus (3) are all swimming mollusks of the Cephalopoda group. They have advanced, powerful eyes, tentacles lined with sucker pads which are used to catch fish and small crustaceans. The horny jawed mouth is powerful enough to break up their prey before it is digested in the gut.

**CENTRIFUGE**

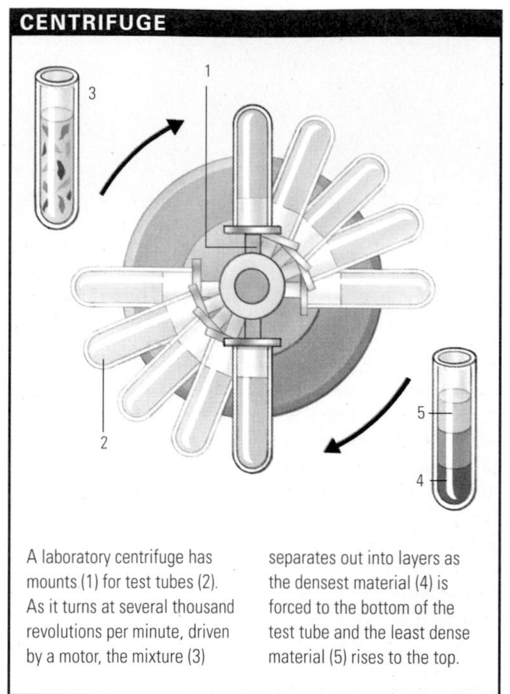


A laboratory centrifuge has mounts (1) for test tubes (2). As it turns at several thousand revolutions per minute, driven by a motor, the mixture (3) separates out into layers as the densest material (4) is forced to the bottom of the test tube and the least dense material (5) rises to the top.

**centripetal force** In circular or curved motion, the force acting on an object that keeps it moving in a circular path. For example, if an object attached to a rope is swung in a circular motion above a person's head, the centripetal force acting on the object is the tension in the rope. Similarly, the centripetal force acting on the Earth as it orbits the Sun is gravity. In accordance with NEWTON's laws, the reaction to this, the (theoretical) centrifugal force, is equal in magnitude and opposite in direction.

**centurion** Military officer of ancient Rome. He commanded 100 men, forming one sixth of a cohort, with ten cohorts making a legion. Centurions were usually soldiers who had risen through the ranks.

**Cephalopoda** Advanced class of predatory marine mollusks, including SQUID, NAUTILUS, OCTOPUS, and CUTTLEFISH. Each has eight or more arms surrounding the mouth, which has a parrot-like beak. The nervous system is well developed, permitting great speed and alertness; the large eyes have an image-forming ability equal to that of vertebrates. Most squirt an inky fluid to alarm attackers. Cephalopods move by squirting water from their mantle edge. Their heavily yolked eggs develop into larval young. Members of this class vary dramatically in size from 1.5in (4cm) to the giant squid, which may reach 65ft (20m). There are more than 600 species.

**cephalosporin** Class of ANTIBIOTIC drugs derived from fungi of the genus *Cephalosporium*. Similar to PENICILLIN, they are effective against a wide spectrum of BACTERIA, including some resistant to penicillin.

**cepheid variable** One of an important class of VARIABLE STARS that pulsate in a regular manner, accompanied by changes in luminosity. Cepheids can expand and contract up to 30% in each cycle. The average luminosity is 10,000 times that of the Sun. Cepheids became important in cosmology (1912) when US astronomer Henrietta Leavitt discovered a relationship between the period of light variation and the absolute magnitude of a cepheid. This law enables the distances of stars to be ascertained.

**ceramic** In art and technology, article made from inorganic compounds formed in a plastic condition and hardened by heating in a furnace. **Earthenware** is a porous ceramic made from kaolin, ball clay, and crushed flint. **Porcelain** is made from kaolin and feldspar, and heated to a higher temperature. It is nonporous and translucent. Special ceramics are made from pure aluminium oxide, silicon carbide, titranates, and other compounds. Ceramic ware is ornamented by inlays, relief modeling, or by incised, stamped, or impressed designs. A creamy mixture of clay and water (slip) can be used to coat the

► **Cézanne** The mountains at L'Estaque were one of Cézanne's favorite landscape subjects. The interlocking flat planes of color, representing land, water, and buildings, greatly influenced abstract artists.

ware. After drying, ceramic ware is baked in a kiln until it has hardened. **Glaze**, a silicate preparation applied to the clay surface and fused to it during firing, is used to make the pottery nonporous and to give it a smooth, colorful, decorative surface. Chinese porcelain dates from the T'ang dynasty, and Chinese stoneware goes back to *c.*3000 BC. In ancient Egypt they developed a faience with a glaze. Mesopotamia and Persia used large architectural tiles with colorful glazes. In the 6th and 5th centuries BC the Greeks developed red, black, and white glazed pottery with figures and scenes, while the Romans used relief decoration. In Spain, lusterware, the first sophisticated ceramic of the modern era, was produced by 9th-century Moors. Later refinements include Italian majolica, Dutch delft, German Meissen, and English Wedgewood. *See also* POTTERY

**cereal** Any grain of the grass family (Gramineae) grown as a food crop. Wheat, corn, rye, oats, and barley are grown in temperate regions. Rice, millet, and sorghum require more tropical climates. Cereal cultivation was the basis of early civilizations, and with the development of high-yielding strains, remains the world's most important food source.

**cerebellum** Part of the brain located at the base of the CEREBRUM. It is involved in maintaining muscle tone, balance, and finely coordinated movement.

**cerebral cortex** Deeply fissured outer layer of the CEREBRUM. The cortex (gray matter) is the most sophisticated part of the brain, responsible for sensation, initiating voluntary movement, emotions, and intellect.

**cerebral hemispheres** Lateral halves of the CEREBRUM, the largest parts of the BRAIN and the sites of higher thought. Because of the crossing of nerve fibers from one hemisphere

## CHAD

Chad's flag was adopted in 1959 as the country prepared for independence in 1960. The blue represents the sky, the streams in southern Chad, and hope. The yellow symbolizes the sun and the Sahara in the north. The red represents national sacrifice.

**AREA:** 495,752sq mi (1,284,000sq km)
**POPULATION:** 5,961,000
**CAPITAL (POPULATION):** Ndjamena (529,555)
**GOVERNMENT:** Transitional
**ETHNIC GROUPS:** Bagirmi, Kreish, and Sara 31%, Sudanic Arab 26%, Teda 7%, Mbum 6%
**LANGUAGES:** French and Arabic (both official)
**RELIGIONS:** Islam 40%, Christianity 33%, traditional beliefs 27%
**CURRENCY:** CFA franc = 100 centimes

The land-locked republic of Chad is Africa's fifth largest country. It is more than twice as big as France (the former colonial power).

Southern Chad is crossed by rivers that flow into Lake CHAD, on the W border with Nigeria. Beyond a large depression (NE of Lake Chad) are the Tibesti Mountains which rise steeply from the sands of the SAHARA Desert. The mountains contain Chad's highest peak, Emi Koussi, at 11,204ft (3,415m).

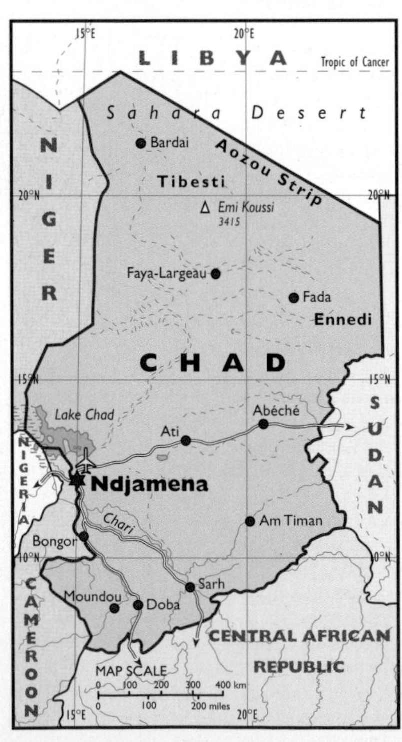


### Climate

Central Chad has a hot tropical climate, with a marked dry season between November and April. The S is wetter, with an average yearly rainfall of about 39in (1,000mm). The hot N desert has an average annual rainfall of less than 5in (130mm).

### Vegetation

The far S contains forests, while central Chad is a region of SAVANNA, merging into the dry grasslands of the SAHEL. Plants are rare in the N desert. Droughts are common in N central Chad. Long droughts, over-grazing, and felling for firewood have exposed the Sahel's soil to the elements, and wind erosion is turning the land into desert. This S creeping process of the Sahara is called DESERTIFICATION.

### History and Politics

Chad straddles two, often conflicting worlds: the N, populated by nomadic or seminomadic Muslim peoples, such as Arabs and Tuaregs; and the dominant S, where a sedentary population practice Christianity or traditional religions, such as animism.

Lake Chad was an important watering point for the trans-Saharan caravans. N African nomads founded the Kanem empire here in *c.*AD 700. In the 13th century the Islamic state of Bornu was established. In the late 19th century the region fell to Sudan.

The first major European explorations were by the French in 1890. In 1900 the French defeated the Sudanese, and in 1908 Chad became the largest province of French Equatorial Africa. In 1920 it became a separate colony.

In 1958 Chad was granted autonomous status within the French Community, and in 1960 achieved full independence. Divisions between N and S rapidly surfaced. In 1965 President François Tombalbaye declared a one-party state and the N Muslims, led by the Chad National Liberation Front (Frolinat), rebelled. By 1973 the revolt had been quashed with the aid of French troops. Libya (supporters of Frolinat) occupied N Chad. In 1981 two leaders of Frolinat came to power, Hissène Habré and Goukouni Oueddi. Splits soon emerged, and Libya's bombing of Chad in 1983 led to the deployment of 3,000 French troops. Libyan troops retreated retaining only the uranium-rich Aozou Strip. A ceasefire took effect in 1987. In 1990 Habré was removed in a coup led by Idriss Déby. In 1996 a new democratic constitution was adopted and multiparty elections confirmed Déby as president.

### Economy

Hit by drought and civil war, Chad is one of the world's poorest countries (1995, GDP per capita, $700). Subsistence agriculture employs 83% of the population. Peanuts, millet, rice, and sorghum are major crops in the wetter S. The most valuable crop is cotton, accounting for *c.*50% of Chad's exports.

to the other, the right side controls most of the movements and sensation on the left side of the body, and vice-versa.

**cerebral hemorrhage** Form of stroke in which there is bleeding from a blood vessel in the BRAIN into the surrounding tissue. It is usually caused by ARTERIOSCLEROSIS and high blood pressure. Symptoms vary from temporary numbness and weakness on one side of the body to deep coma. A major hemorrhage may be fatal.

**cerebral palsy** Disorder mainly of movement and coordination caused by BRAIN damage during or soon after birth. It may feature muscular spasm and weakness, lack of coordination, and impaired movement or paralysis and deformities of the limbs. Intelligence is not necessarily affected. The condition may result from a number of causes, such as faulty development, oxygen deprivation, birth injury, or infection.

**cerebrospinal fluid** Clear fluid that cushions the brain and spinal cord, giving some protection against shock. It is found between the two innermost meninges (membranes), in the four ventricles of the BRAIN and in the central canal of the spinal cord. A small quantity of the fluid can be withdrawn by lumbar puncture to aid diagnosis of some brain diseases.

**cerebrum** Largest and most highly developed part of the BRAIN, consisting of the CEREBRAL HEMISPHERES separated by a central fissure. It is covered by the CEREBRAL CORTEX. It coordinates all higher functions and voluntary activity.

**Cerenkov, Pavel Alekseevich** (1904–90) Russian physicist. Working at the Institute of Physics of the Soviet Academy of Science, he discovered (1934) that light (CERENKOV RADIATION) is emitted by charged particles traveling at very high speeds. Cerenkov was awarded the 1958 Nobel Prize for physics with his coworkers, I.M. Frank and I.Y. Tamm.

**Cerenkov radiation** Light emitted when energetic particles travel through a transparent medium, such as water, faster than the velocity of light in that medium. This action is called the Cerenkov effect. A cone of light is emitted, trailing the path of the particle. It is named for Pavel CERENKOV. The radiation is used in a Cerenkov counter, a detector of energetic particles.

**Ceres** Largest ASTEROID and the first to be discovered (January 1, 1801, by Guiseppe Piazzi). Ceres' diameter measures 567mi (913km). It orbits in the main asteroid belt, at an average distance from the Sun of 257 million mi (414 million km), the distance of the "missing" planet predicted by BODE'S LAW.

**cerium** (symbol Ce) Soft, ductile, iron-gray metallic element, the most abundant of the LANTHANIDE SERIES group, first isolated in 1803. The chief ore is monazite. It is used in alloys, catalysts, nuclear fuels, glass, and as the core of carbon electrodes in arc lamps. Properties: at.no. 58; at.wt. 140.12; sp.gr. 6.77; m.p. 1,468°F (798°C); b.p. 5,895°F (3,257°C). The most common isotope is $^{140}$Ce (88.48%).

**Cervantes, Miguel de** (1547–1616) Spanish novelist, poet, and dramatist. Cervantes published two volumes of his masterpiece *Don Quixote de la Mancha* (1605; 1615). Don Quixote is a great archetype of Western fiction, the picaresque hero who misapplies the logic of high Romance to the mundane situations of modern life. It established Cervantes as a towering figure in Spanish letters. Other works include two surviving plays and a collection of short stories, *Novelas Ejemplares* (1613).

**cervical smear** *See* PAP TEST

**cervix** Neck of the WOMB (uterus), projecting downwards into the VAGINA. It dilates (expands) widely to allow the passage of the baby during childbirth.

**cesium** (symbol Cs) Rare silvery-white metallic element in group I of the periodic table; the most alkaline and electropositive element. Discovered in 1860 by Robert BUNSEN and Gustav KIRCHHOFF, cesium is ductile and used commercially in photoelectric cells. The isotope $^{137}$Cs is used in cancer treatments. The decay rate of its most common isotope $^{133}$Cs is the standard for measuring time. Properties: at.no. 55; at.wt. 132.9055; sp.gr. 1.87; m.p. 83.1°F (28.4°C); b.p. 1,252.4°F (678°C). *See also* ALKALI METALS; ATOMIC CLOCK

**Cetshwayo** (d.1884) King of the Zulus (1873–79). Nephew of SHAKA, he sought British aid against the BOERS, but British demands for him to disarm led to the ZULU WAR (1879). Eventually defeated, he was deposed, restored briefly in 1883 but died in exile.

**Ceylon** *See* SRI LANKA

**Cézanne, Paul** (1839–1906) French painter. He exhibited at the first impressionist show in 1874. *House of the Hanged Man* (1873–74) is characteristic of this period. Cézanne later moved away from IMPRESSIONISM in favor of a more analytical approach using color to model and express form. Figure paintings, such as *The Card Players* (1890–92), *Madame Cézanne* (*c*.1885), and *The Bathers* (1895–1905), and landscapes, such as *Mont Sainte Victoire* (1904–06), were painted on this principle. Cézanne ranks as one of the great influences on modern art, especially CUBISM. *See also* POSTIMPRESSIONISM

**Chaco War** (1932–35) *See* GRAN CHACO

**Chad** Republic in N central Africa. *See* country feature

**Chadwick, Sir James** (1891–1974) English physicist who discovered and named the NEUTRON. He worked on radioactivity with Ernest RUTHERFORD at the Cavendish Laboratory, Cambridge, UK. In 1920 Rutherford had predicted a particle without electric charge in the NUCLEUS of an ATOM, and in 1932 Chadwick proved the neutron's existence and calculated its mass. For this, he received the 1935 Nobel Prize for physics. During World War II, Chadwick moved to the US to head British research for the MANHATTAN PROJECT to develop the atomic bomb.

**chafer** Any of a large number of beetles, particularly of the SCARAB BEETLE family (Scarabaeidae), that feed on the leaves of plants.

**chaffinch** Small songbird common throughout Europe. It generally perches on low trees, bushes, and fences, feeding on plants and insects. The blue and buff colors and pink breast belong to the male only. In winter, flocks consisting solely of males can be seen. Family Fringillidae; species *Fringilla coelebs.*

**Chagall, Marc** (1887–1985) Russian-French painter. His paintings, with their dream-like imagery, considerably influenced SURREALISM. *I and the Village* (1911) is characteristic of his early style. Chagall worked using ceramics, mosaics, and tapestry, and in theater design. He designed stained-glass windows for Hadassah-Hebrew Medical Center, Jerusalem (1962), murals for the Metropolitan Opera House, New York (1966), and mosaics and tapestries for the Knesset in Jerusalem (1969).

**Chain, Sir Ernst Boris** (1906–79) British biochemist, b. Germany. Chain shared the 1945 Nobel Prize for physiology or medicine with Howard FLOREY and Alexander FLEMING for the isolation and development of PENICILLIN as an antibiotic.

**chain reaction** Self-sustaining nuclear reaction in which one reaction is the cause of a second, the second of a third, and so on. The initial conditions are critical, in that the quantity of fissionable material must exceed the CRITICAL MASS. The explosion of a NUCLEAR WEAPON is an uncontrolled chain reaction.

**Chalcedon, Council of** (451) Meeting of all the bishops of the Christian church in the city of Chalcedon, Asia Minor. Convoked by the Emperor Marcian, it reaffirmed the doctrine of two natures (divine and human) in Christ and condemned NESTORIANISM.

**chalcedony** Microscrystalline form of QUARTZ. When cut and polished, it is used by gem engravers. It is waxy, lustrous, and there are white, gray, blue, and brown varieties. Often colored by artificial methods, some varieties contain impurities giving a distinctive appearance, such as AGATE (colored bands), ONYX (striped), and bloodstone (dark green with red flecks).

**chalcopyrite** (copper pyrites, copper iron sulfide $CuFeS_2$) Most important copper ore. Opaque and brass-colored, it is found in sulfide veins, igneous and contact metamorphic rocks. The crystals are tetragonal but often occur in masses. Hardness 3.5–4; s.g. 4.2.

**Chaliapin, Fyodor Ivanovich** (1873–1938) Russian operatic bass. After singing with the Bolshoi, Chaliapin embarked on international tours, performing at La Scala, Milan (1901), the Metropolitan Opera, New York (1907–08), and with Diaghilev in Paris. He left Russia in 1921 and joined the Metropolitan. Chaliapin was noted for the title role in Mussorgsky's *Boris Godunov*.

**chalk** Mineral, mainly calcium carbonate ($CaCO_3$), formed from the shells of minute marine organisms. It varies in properties and appearance; pure forms, such as calcite, contain up

▲ **Chagall** The Russian-born artist Marc Chagall influenced many later "surrealist" painters. His paintings draw heavily from folklore and have a fairy tale or dreamlike appeal.

▲ **Chamberlain** Having been instrumental in the formation of the National Government (1931), British prime minister Neville Chamberlain's firm belief in appeasement resulted in Britain's slow preparation for war. A succession of victories for the Axis powers in the early stages of World War II forced Chamberlain to resign.

to 99% calcium carbonate. It is used in making putty, plaster, and cement. Blackboard chalk is now made from calcium sulfate ($CaSO_4$) or chemically produced calcium carbonate.

**Challenger disaster** *See* SPACE SHUTTLE

**Challenger expedition** (1872–76) British expedition in oceanographic research. The *Challenger* ship comprised a staff of six naturalists headed by Charles Wyville Thompson. She sailed *c*.69,000 nautical mi (128,000km) making studies of the life, water, and seabed in the three main oceans.

**Chamberlain, Joseph** (1836–1914) British political leader, father of Neville CHAMBERLAIN. He entered Parliament as a Liberal in 1876. In 1880 Chamberlain became president of the board of trade. In 1886 he resigned over GLADSTONE's Home Rule Bill and was leader of the Liberal Unionists from 1889. In 1895 Chamberlain returned to government as colonial secretary, where his aggressive, imperialist stance helped provoke the SOUTH AFRICAN WAR (1899).

**Chamberlain, (Arthur) Neville** (1869–1940) British statesman, prime minister (1937–40). Son of Joseph CHAMBERLAIN, he entered Parliament in 1918. During the 1920s, Chamberlain served as chancellor of the exchequer (1923–24, 1931–37) and minister of health (1924–29). He succeeded Stanley BALDWIN as prime minister and leader of the Conservative Party. Chamberlain approached HITLER with a policy of APPEASEMENT and signed the MUNICH AGREEMENT (1938). After Hitler's invasion of Poland, Chamberlain declared war in September 1939. After the loss of Norway, he was replaced by Winston CHURCHILL in May 1940.

**Chamberlain, Wilt (Wilton Norman)** (1936– ) US basketball player. Perhaps the greatest offensive player in basketball history, he had a career total of 31,419 points. Chamberlain played in the NBA for Philadelphia (1960–62, 1965–68), San Francisco (1963–65), and Los Angeles (1969–73). He was elected to the Basketball Hall of Fame in 1978.

**chamber music** Music intended for performance in intimate surroundings. It is usually written for two to eight instruments (or voices). The string quartet (two violins, viola, and cello) is the most common arrangement. The term dates from the 17th century, and was applied to music played privately in the homes of wealthy patrons. The form has been revived in the late 20th century.

**chameleon** Arboreal LIZARD, found chiefly in Madagascar, Africa, and Asia, notable for its ability to change color. The compressed body has a curled, prehensile tail and bulging eyes that move independently. Length: 7–24in (17–60cm). Family Chamaeleontidae; genus *Chamaeleo*; there are 80 species.

**chamois** Nimble, goat-like RUMINANT that lives in mountain ranges of Europe and W Asia. It has coarse, reddish-brown fur with a black tail and horns. Its skin is made into chamois leather. Length: up to 50in (1.3m); weight: 55–110lb (25–50kg). Family Bovidae; species *Rupicapra rupicapra*.

**chamomile** (camomile) Low-growing, yellow- or white-flowered herb. Several species are cultivated as ground cover. Flowers of the European chamomile (*Chamaemelum nobile*) are used to make herbal tea. Family Asteraceae; genus *Chamaemelum*.

**Chamorro, Violeta Barrios de** (1939– ) Nicaraguan stateswoman, president (1990–96). Chamorro entered politics in 1978 when her husband, Pedro Joáin Chamorro, was assassinated. In 1989, supported by the US, she became leader of the right-wing coalition, the National Opposition Union (UNO). Chamorro became president after defeating the SANDINISTA government in 1990. Her presidency was marked by skirmishes between CONTRA rebels and the Sandinistas, and many of her policies were blocked by reactionary elements in the UNO and by members of the Sandinista Liberation Front.

**Champagne** District in NE France, made up of the Aube, Marne, Haute-Marne, and Ardennes departments. The major city is REIMS. It was a center for European trade in the 11th–13th centuries. During World War II there was heavy fighting along the Marne River. It is an arid region, renowned for its champagne, a sparkling white wine that can only be produced in the district. Area: 9,886sq mi (25,606sq km). Pop. (1990) 1,347,800.

**Champaigne, Philippe de** (1602–74) French painter, b. Flanders. He was the greatest French portraitist of the 17th century and a remarkable religious painter. In 1628 Champaigne became artist to Queen Marie de' Medici and Cardinal Richelieu. His beliefs in JANSENISM produced religious paintings characterized by a serene realism. Champaigne's best-known works include portraits and frescos at Vincennes and in the Tuileries.

**Champlain, Samuel de** (1567–1635) French explorer, founder of New France (Canada). In 1603, following the discoveries of Jacques CARTIER, Champlain traveled up the St. Lawrence River as far as Lachine. He returned to New France in 1604 and established a fur-trading colony at Port Royal (now Annapolis Royal, Nova Scotia). Champlain explored the Atlantic coast from Cape Breton to Cape Cod, making the first detailed maps of the area, and in 1608 he founded Quebec. With the help of the HURON, he continued to explore the region for the next six years, discovering the lake that bears his name in 1609. In 1615 he traveled up the Ottawa River as far as Lake Huron. The last 20 years of his life were spent as a colonial administrator and patron of further explorations.

**Champlain, Lake** Lake that lies on the border of New York State and Vermont and extends into Quebec, Canada. It serves as a link in the Hudson-St. Lawrence waterway. Explored by Samuel de CHAMPLAIN (1609), it was the scene of many battles in the French and Indian wars, the American Revolution, and the defeat of the British in the War of 1812. Today, the lake is a popular resort area. Area: 435sq mi (1,101sq km).

**Champollion, Jean François** (1790–1832) French scholar, one of the founders of Egyptology. In 1822 he revealed his decipherment of Egyptian HIEROGLYPHICS through study of the ROSETTA STONE. He was later curator at the Louvre in Paris, and first professor of Egyptology at the Collège de France.

**chancellor of the exchequer** British minister responsible for national finances. The office evolved from the 13th-century clerk of the court of exchequer, assistant to the chancellor. Since the 1850s, it has become probably the second most high-profile cabinet office (after the prime minister).

**Chancellorsville, Battle of** (May 2–4, 1863) CIVIL WAR battle. Union forces under General Joseph HOOKER, advancing on Richmond, were opposed by General Robert E. LEE in N Virginia. Outflanked by General "Stonewall" JACKSON, the Union forces were decisively defeated, although Jackson, accidentally shot by his own men, died a week later.

**Chancery** In England, court developed in the 15th century for the lord chancellor to deal with petitions from aggrieved persons for redress when no remedy was available in the COMMON LAW courts.

**Chandigarh** City in NW India, at the foot of the Siwalik Hills. The joint capital of Punjab and Haryana states, it is a planned city, designed by LE CORBUSIER and built in the 1950s. Pop. (1991) 511,000.

**Chandler, Raymond Thornton** (1888–1959) US novelist. His DETECTIVE FICTION features the tough private eye Philip Marlowe, in novels such as *The Big Sleep* (1939), *Farewell, My Lovely* (1940), and *The Long Goodbye* (1953). Many have been made into successful films. Chandler's crackling dialog and seedy plots are distinctive and much copied.

**Chandragupta** Founder of the MAURYA EMPIRE in India (ruled *c*.321–297 BC) and grandfather of ASHOKA. He seized the throne of Magadha and defeated SELEUCUS, gaining dominion over most of N India and part of Afghanistan. His reign was characterized by religious tolerance. He established a vast bureaucracy at Patna. He abdicated and, it is thought, become a Jain monk.

**Chandrasekhar, Subrahmanyan** (1910–95) US astrophysicist, b. India. He formulated theories about the creation, life, and death of stars, and calculated the maximum mass (Chandrasekhar limit) of a WHITE DWARF STAR before it becomes a neutron star. Chandrasekhar shared the 1983 Nobel Prize for physics with William Fowler.

**Chanel, "Coco" (Gabrielle)** (1883–1971) French fashion designer. Chanel revolutionized women's fashion, borrowing elements from men's clothing. She is associated with the Chanel suit, jersey dresses, bell-bottom trousers, trench coats, and Chanel No.5 perfume.

## CHANNEL TUNNEL

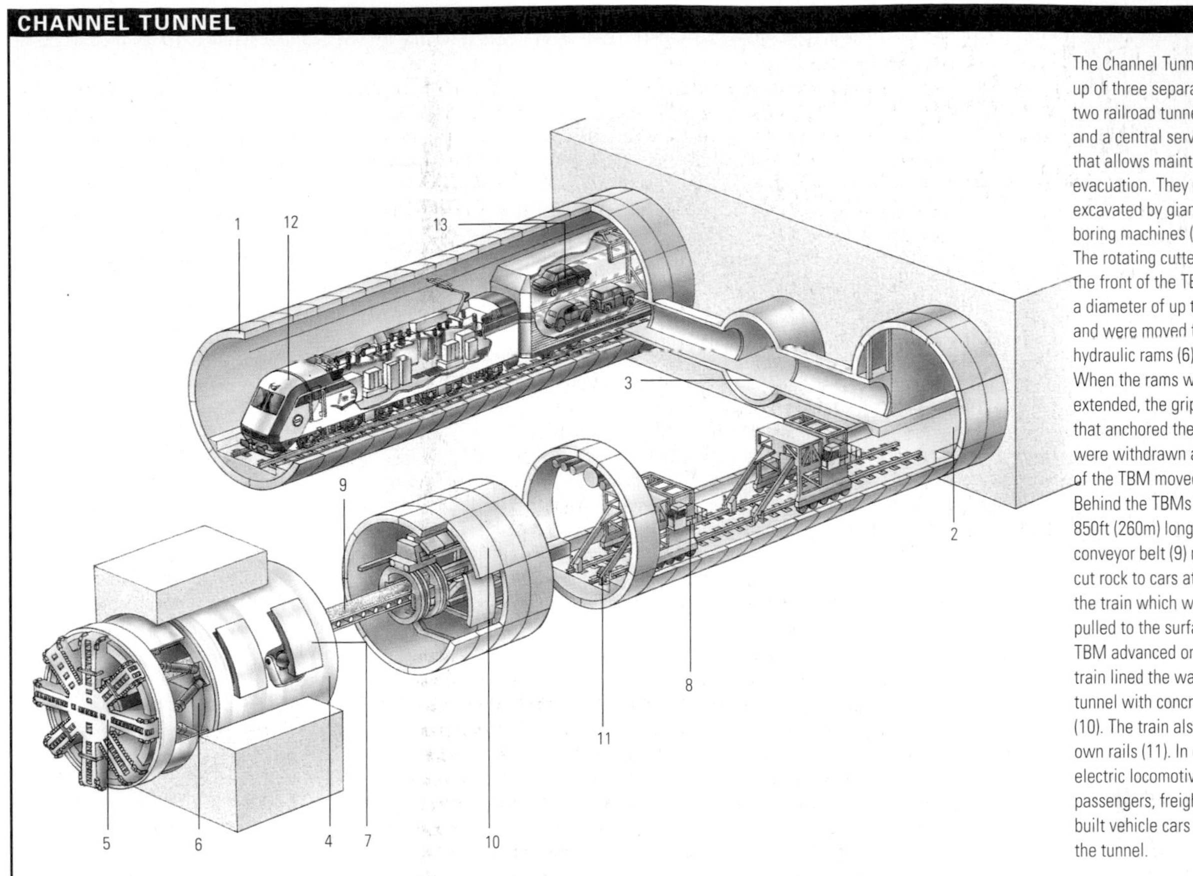


The Channel Tunnel is made up of three separate tunnels – two railroad tunnels (1 and 2) and a central service tunnel (3) that allows maintenance and evacuation. They were excavated by giant tunnel boring machines (TBMs) (4). The rotating cutter heads at the front of the TBMs (5) had a diameter of up to 30ft (9m) and were moved forward by hydraulic rams (6) as they cut. When the rams were fully extended, the gripper pads (7) that anchored the machines were withdrawn and the body of the TBM moved forward. Behind the TBMs was a train 850ft (260m) long (8). A conveyor belt (9) removed the cut rock to cars at the rear of the train which were then pulled to the surface. As the TBM advanced one part of the train lined the walls of the tunnel with concrete segments (10). The train also laid its own rails (11). In operation electric locomotives (12) pull passengers, freight, or specially built vehicle cars (13) through the tunnel.

**Changchun** (Ch'ang-ch'un) Capital of Jilin province, NE China. As Hsinking, it was the capital (1932–45) of the former state of Manchukuo. Industries: chemicals, textiles, motor vehicles. Pop. (1993 est.) 2,400,000.

**Chang Jiang** *See* YANGTZE

**Channel Islands** Group of islands at the SW end of the English Channel, *c.*10mi (16km) off the W coast of France. The main islands are Jersey, Guernsey, Alderney, and Sark; the chief towns are St. Helier on Jersey and St. Peter Port on Guernsey. A dependency of the British crown since the Norman Conquest, they were under German occupation during World War II. Guernsey and Jersey each have its own parliament. The islands have a warm climate and fertile soil. Industries: tourism, agriculture. Area: 75sq mi (194sq km). Pop. (1991) 142,949.

**Channel Tunnel** (Chunnel) Railroad tunnel under the English Channel, 30.6mi (49km) long. The first Channel tunnel was proposed in 1802 by a French engineer. A start was made in 1882 but soon abandoned for defense reasons. Another false start was made in the 1970s. In 1985 Eurotunnel, a joint French-English private company, was granted a 55-year concession to finance and operate the tunnel. The French and English sections were linked in 1990, and the tunnel became operational in 1994. It consists of two railroad tunnels and one service tunnel and links Folkestone, S England, with Calais, N France.

**chansons de geste** (Fr. songs of deeds) Epic poems, written in Old French between the 11th and 14th centuries, generally dealing with the campaigns of CHARLEMAGNE. These anonymous narratives, of which some 80 survive, describe semi-imaginary events.

**Chanson de Roland, La** French epic, written in Old French by an unnamed author of the late 11th century. It recounts the defeat of CHARLEMAGNE's rearguard at Roncesvalles Pass in the Pyrenees on August 15, 778. A typical CHANSON DE GESTE, the poem alters historical fact.

**chant** Unaccompanied liturgical singing, especially of PSALMS. Anglican chant developed from the earlier Gregorian tones, which were melody formulas defining pitch relationships only. Later, harmonies were added to the melodies and note values designated to English texts of the psalms.

**chaos theory** Theory that attempts to describe and explain the highly complex behavior of apparently chaotic or unpredictable systems which show an underlying order. The behavior of some physical systems is impossible to describe using the standard laws of physics, the mathematics needed to describe these systems being too difficult for even the largest supercomputers. Such systems are sometimes known as "nonlinear" or "chaotic" systems, and they include complex machines, electrical circuits, and natural phenomena such as the weather. Nonchaotic systems can become chaotic, such as when smoothly flowing water hits a rock. Chaos theory provides mathematical methods needed to describe chaotic systems, and even allows some general prediction of a system's behavior. Because it is impossible to know the precise starting conditions of a system, accurate prediction is also impossible.

**chapel** Place of worship such as a small church or a separate area with its own altar within a church or cathedral. Side chapels are small rooms set into the wall of a cathedral apse, which often house the relics of saints. Many state and civic buildings, monasteries, and convents have chapels. A chapel may be a place of worship subordinate to a larger parish church, or a building used for services by nonconformists.

**Chaplin, Charlie (Sir Charles Spencer)** (1889–1977) English film actor and director, often considered the greatest silent film comedian. In his short films, such as *The Immigrant* (1917) and *A Dog's Life* (1918), he developed his famous character; a jaunty, wistful figure of pathos in baggy trousers and bowler hat, with a cane and a mustache. Chaplin's major films include *The Kid* (1920), *The Gold Rush* (1924), *City Lights* (1931), *Modern Times* (1936), *The Great Dictator* (1940), and *Limelight* (1952). He was attacked for his left-wing politics and in 1952 left the US to live in Switzerland.

▲ **Chaplin** Although he made several films with sound, Charlie Chaplin will always be remembered as one of the great stars of the silent movie era. His comedies were sophisticated enough to evoke sympathy and romance, unlike many of his contemporaries who relied solely on slapstick. Chaplin married the daughter of Eugene O'Neill.

**Chapman, George** (1560–1634) English poet, dramatist, and translator. He completed Christopher Marlowe's unfinished poem *Hero and Leander* (1598), and worked with Ben JONSON and John Marston. His own works include the plays *The Blind Beggar of Alexandria* (1598) and *Bussy D'Ambois* (1604), and translations of Homer's *Iliad* (1611) and *Odyssey* (1614–15).

**charcoal** Porous form of CARBON, made traditionally by heating wood in the absence of air, and used in western Europe until late medieval times for smelting iron ore. Today, charcoal is chiefly used for its absorptive properties, to decolorize food liquids such as syrups, and to separate chemicals. Artists use charcoal sticks for sketching.

**Charcot, Jean Martin** (1825–93) French physician and founder of neurology. He made classical studies of HYPNOSIS and HYSTERIA, and taught Sigmund FREUD. Charcot's work centered on discovering how behavioral symptoms of patients relate to neurological disorders.

**charge-coupled device (CCD)** Type of SILICON CHIP designed to capture images. The CCD is divided into a number of microscopic areas (pixels), arranged in rows. When a photon hits a pixel, it knocks off an ELECTRON from a silicon atom, which becomes charged. An opposite charge in a layer on the base of the CCD confines this charged silicon atom, and a charge builds up in each pixel relative to the number of photons hitting it. The contents of each pixel are read off 50 times a second, a row at a time, forming an electrical signal used to create television pictures. Charge-couled devices are found in video cameras, fax machines, and digital cameras.

**Charge of the Light Brigade** (October 25, 1854) British cavalry charge in the CRIMEAN WAR, one of the most notorious mistakes in British military history. It stemmed from Lord Lucan's misreading of an ambiguous order by the British commander, Lord Raglan. As a result, Lord Cardigan led the unsupported Light Brigade straight at a battery of Russian guns. More than 600 men took part, nearly half of whom were casualties. The incident is commemorated in a famous poem by Alfred TENNYSON.

**charismatic movement** Movement within the Christian church. It emphasizes the presence of the Holy Spirit in the life of an individual and in the work of the church. It is particularly associated with PENTECOSTAL CHURCHES.

▼ **Charles V** The map illustrates how Charles V gained his vast European empire by succeeding his father Philip as duke of Burgundy in 1506, and his grandfather Ferdinand as king of Aragon and Castile in 1516, and by being elected Holy Roman emperor in 1519.

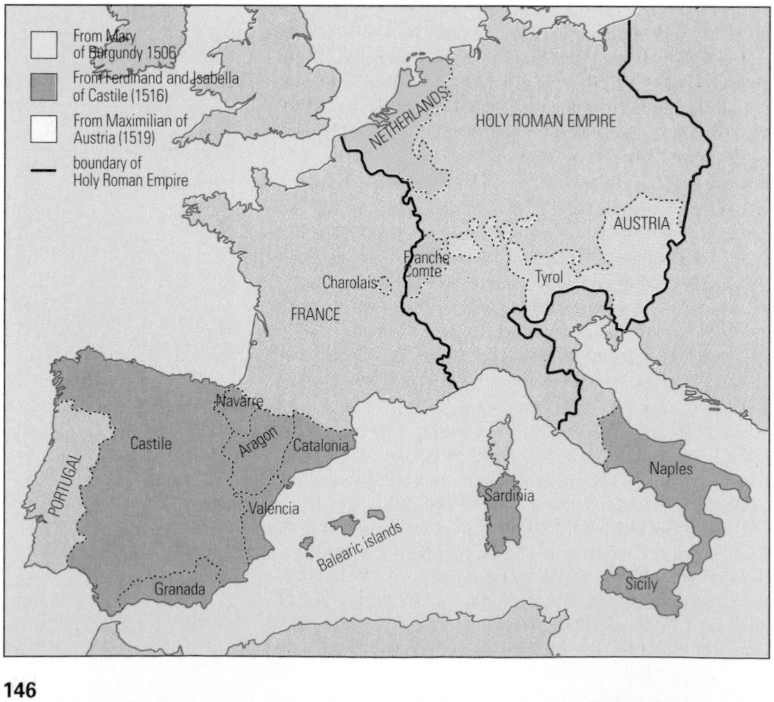

**Charlemagne** (742–814) (lit. Charles the Great) King of the Franks (768–814) and Holy Roman emperor (800–14). The eldest son of PEPIN III (THE SHORT), Charlemagne inherited half the Frankish kingdom (768), annexed the remainder on his brother Carloman's death (771), and built a large empire. He invaded Italy twice and took the Lombard throne (773). Charlemagne undertook a long and brutal conquest of Saxony (772–804), annexed Bavaria (788), and defeated the Avars of the middle Danube (791–96, 804). He undertook campaigns against the Moors in Spain. In 800 Charlemagne was consecrated as emperor by Pope Leo II, thus reviving the concept of the Roman empire, and confirming the separation of the West from the Eastern, BYZANTINE EMPIRE. He encouraged the intellectual awakening of the CAROLINGIAN RENAISSANCE, set up a strong central authority, and maintained provincial control through court officials. Charlemagne's central aim was Christian reform, both of church and laity.

**Charles II (the Bald)** (823–77) King of the West Franks (843–77) and Holy Roman emperor (875–77). Younger son of Emperor Louis I, he was involved in the ambitious disputes of his elder brothers. The Treaty of VERDUN (843) made him king of the West Franks, in effect the first king of France. After the death of Louis II, Charles was recognized as Holy Roman emperor.

**Charles III (the Fat)** (839–88) Holy Roman emperor (881–87) and king of France (884–87) as Charles II. Through the death or incapacity of relatives, he inherited the kingdoms of the East and West Franks. Charles almost reunited the territories of Charlemagne in the 880s, but was deposed by his nephew, Arnulf.

**Charles IV** (1316–78) Holy Roman emperor (1355–78) and king of Bohemia (1347–78). Supported by Pope Clement VI, Charles was a rival of the Wittelsbach Emperor Louis IV, and when Louis died, was elected king of the Germans (emperor-elect). A skillful diplomat, he blocked or appeased his Wittelsbach and Hapsburg rivals and improved relations with the papacy. In 1356 Charles introduced a stable system of imperial government. He ruled from PRAGUE, his birthplace, where he founded Charles University (1348) and built the Charles Bridge. Czech culture reached a peak under his patronage. Charles was succeeded by his son, Wenceslas.

**Charles V** (1500–58) Holy Roman emperor (1519–56) and king of Spain, as Charles I (1516–56). He ruled the Spanish kingdoms, s Italy, the Netherlands, and the Austrian Hapsburg lands by inheritance and, when elected emperor in succession to his grandfather, MAXIMILIAN I, headed the largest European empire since CHARLEMAGNE. In addition, the Spanish conquistadores made him master of a New World empire. Charles' efforts to unify his possessions were unsuccessful, largely due to the hostility of FRANCIS I of France, the Ottoman Turks in central Europe, and the conflicts arising from the advance of LUTHERANISM in Germany. The struggle with France was centered in Italy: Spanish control was largely confirmed by 1535, but French hostility was never overcome. The Turks were held in check but not defeated, and Charles' attempt to capture Algiers failed (1541). In Germany, Charles, who saw himself as the defender of the Catholic Church, nevertheless recognized the need for reform, but other commitments prevented him following a consistent policy, and LUTHERANISM expanded. Charles increasingly delegated power in Germany to his brother and successor, FERDINAND I, and in 1554–56 surrendered his other titles to his son, PHILIP II of Spain.

**Charles VI** (1685–1740) Holy Roman emperor (1711–40) and king of Hungary as Charles III. His claim to the Spanish throne against the grandson of Louis XIV, Philip V, caused the War of the SPANISH SUCCESSION. After his election as emperor (1711), Charles gave up his Spanish claim. He spent much of his reign trying to secure the succession of his daughter, MARIA THERESA, to his Austrian possessions.

**Charles I** (1887–1922) Austrian emperor (1916–18) and king (as Charles IV) of Hungary (1916–18). When Hungary and Czechoslovakia declared their independence and Austria became a republic in 1918, Charles, the last Hapsburg emperor, was forced into exile in Switzerland.

**Charles I** (1600–49) King of England, Scotland, and Ireland (1625–49). Son of JAMES I, he was criticized by Parliament for his reliance on the Duke of BUCKINGHAM and for his marriage to the Catholic Henrietta Maria. Although he accepted the PETITION OF RIGHT, Charles' insistence on the "divine right of kings" provoked further conflict with Parliament and led him to rule without it for 11 years (1629–40). With the support of the archbishop of Canterbury, William LAUD, Charles enforced harsh penalties on nonconformists. When attempts to impose Anglican liturgy on Scotland led to the Bishops' War, Charles was obliged to recall Parliament to raise revenue. The LONG PARLIA-

MENT insisted on imposing conditions, and impeached Charles' advisor, the earl of STRAFFORD. In 1641 it presented the GRAND REMONSTRANCE. Relations steadily worsened, and Charles' attempt to arrest five leading opponents (including John PYM) in the Commons precipitated the English CIVIL WARS. After the defeat of the Royalists, attempts by Oliver CROMWELL and other parliamentary and army leaders to reach a compromise with the king failed, and he was tried and executed. *See also* PRIDE'S PURGE; VANE, SIR HENRY

**Charles II** (1630–85) King of England, Scotland, and Ireland (1660–85). After the execution of his father, CHARLES I, he fled to France, but in 1650 was invited to Scotland by the COVENANTERS and crowned king in 1651. Charles' attempted invasion of England was repulsed by Oliver CROMWELL, and he was forced back into exile. In 1660 Charles issued the Declaration of Breda, in which he promised religious toleration and an amnesty for his enemies. Parliament agreed to the Declaration and Charles was crowned king in May 1660, ushering in the RESTORATION. He attempted to preserve royal power, accepting secret subsidies from LOUIS XIV in exchange for promoting Roman Catholicism. Charles' support of Louis led to a war with the Netherlands (1672–74). He clashed with Parliament over both the war and his support of the Catholics. Conflict was further fuelled by strong anti-Catholic feeling, manifest in the "Popish Plot" rumor spread by Titus OATES and the Exclusion Crisis (1679–81), when attempts were made to exclude Charles' brother, the Catholic Duke of York (later JAMES II), from the succession. Unable to resolve his differences with Parliament, Charles dissolved it and ruled with financial support from Louis XIV. Known as the Merry Monarch, Charles had many mistresses (including Nell Gwyn), but left no legitimate heir.

**Charles V (the Wise)** (1337–80) King of France (1364–80). He regained most of the territory lost to the English in the HUNDRED YEARS WAR. Charles strengthened royal authority by introducing a regular taxation system, standing army, and powerful navy. He established a royal library, encouraged literature and art, and built the BASTILLE. He was succeeded by his son, CHARLES VI.

**Charles VI (the Mad)** (1368–1422) King of France (1380–1422). Until 1388 he was controlled by his uncle, Philip the Bold of Burgundy. After ruling for four years, Charles suffered recurrent bouts of insanity. Philip and Louis d'Orléans, the king's brother, fought for control of the kingdom. Louis was murdered in 1407, and Philip allied himself with HENRY V of England. English victories at Agincourt (1415) and elsewhere forced Charles to sign the Treaty of Troyes (1420), acknowledging Henry as his successor.

**Charles VII** (1403–61) King of France (1422–61). The son of CHARLES VI, he was excluded from the throne by the Treaty of Troyes (1420). When his father died, Charles controlled lands S of the Loire River, while the N remained in English hands. With the support of JOAN OF ARC, he checked the English at Orléans and was crowned king at Reims (1429). The Treaty of Arras (1435) ended the hostility of Burgundy, and by 1453 the English had been driven out of most of France.

**Charles VIII** (1470–98) King of France (1483–98). He succeeded his father Louis XI and until 1491 was controlled by his sister Anne de Beaujeu and her husband. In 1494 Charles invaded Italy, beginning the long Italian Wars. In 1495 he entered Naples. A league of Italian states, the papacy, and Spain forced him to retreat. One positive result was the introduction of Italian Renaissance culture into France. He was succeeded by his cousin, LOUIS XII.

**Charles IX** (1550–74) King of France (1560–74). He succeeded his brother FRANCIS II aged ten, and his mother CATHERINE DE' MEDICI acted as regent. Her authority waned when, in 1571, the young king fell under the influence of Gaspard de Coligny, leader of the HUGUENOTS. Coligny and thousands of his followers were slain in the SAINT BARTHOLOMEW'S DAY MASSACRE (1572), ordered by Charles at the instigation of his mother. He was succeeded by his brother, HENRY III.

**Charles X** (1757–1836) King of France (1824–30), brother of LOUIS XVI and LOUIS XVIII. He fled France at the outbreak of the FRENCH REVOLUTION (1789). He remained in England until the BOURBON restoration (1814). Charles opposed the moderate policies of LOUIS XVIII. After the assassination of his son in 1820, his reactionary forces triumphed. In 1825 he signed a law indemnifying émigrés for land confiscated during the Revolution. In 1830 Charles issued the July Ordinance, which restricted suffrage and press freedom, and dissolved the newly elected chamber of deputies. The people rebelled and Charles was forced to abdicate.

**Charles III** (1716–88) King of Spain (1759–88) and of Naples and Sicily (1735–59), son of PHILIP V and Elizabeth Farnese. Charles conquered Naples and Sicily in 1734, and inherited the Spanish crown in 1759 from his half-brother Ferdinand VI. He handed Naples and Sicily to his son Ferdinand. Charles was a highly competent ruler. He encouraged commercial and agrarian reform, and brought the Spanish Catholic Church under state control, expelling the Jesuits in 1767. Allied with France in the SEVEN YEARS WAR, he received LOUISIANA in 1763. He was succeeded by his son, CHARLES IV.

**Charles IV** (1748–1819) King of Spain (1788–1808), son and successor of CHARLES III. Unable to cope with the upheavals of NAPOLEON I, Charles virtually turned over government to his wife Maria Luisa and her lover Manuel de Godoy. Spain was occupied by French troops in the PENINSULAR WAR. He was forced to abdicate in favor of his son Ferdinand VII, who in turn was forced from the throne by Napoleon.

**Charles IX** (1550–1611) King of Sweden (1604–11), youngest son of Gustav I. He opposed his brother, John III's, Catholicism. At John's death he became regent (1599–1604) and established Lutheranism. John's son SIGISMUND III, king of Poland, claimed the throne but was deposed by Charles. Sigismund launched an abortive invasion (1598). In 1600 Charles invaded Livonia, starting the 60-year conflict with Poland. At the end of his reign, he embarked on the disastrous Kalmar War (1611–13) with Denmark.

**Charles X** (1622–60) King of Sweden (1654–60). Charles ascended the throne when his cousin, Queen Christina, abdicated. His efforts to dominate the Baltic resulted in a reign of continuous military activity. Charles invaded Poland unsuccessfully and twice invaded Denmark. He established the natural frontiers in Scandinavia, recovering the S provinces of Sweden from Denmark. He was succeeded by his son, CHARLES XI.

**Charles XI** (1655–97) King of Sweden (1660–97), son and successor of CHARLES X. A council of regency ruled until he reached his majority (1672). As part of his restriction on the powers of the nobility, Charles restored lands to the crown. He led Sweden into the third of the DUTCH WARS. Charles lost (1675) Swedish Pomerania to FREDERICK WILLIAM of Brandenburg. The Peace of Lund (1679) signaled greater unity within Scandinavia, cemented by Charles' marriage to Princess Ulrika of Denmark. His son succeeded him as CHARLES XII.

**Charles XII** (1682–1718) King of Sweden (1697–1718), son and successor of CHARLES XI. He was one of the greatest military leaders in European history. Charles defeated Denmark, Poland, Saxony, and Russia in a series of brilliant campaigns. Leading the battle, he destroyed the army of PETER I (THE GREAT) at Narva (1700). In 1708 he renewed his assault on Russia, but his army, depleted by the severe winter, was decisively defeated at Poltava (1709). He fled to the Ottomans and persuaded the sultan to attack Russia (1711). The sultan turned against him and, in disguise, Charles escaped back to Sweden and devoted his energy to the domestic economy. He was killed while fighting in Norway and was succeeded by his sister, Ulrika Eleanora.

**Charles XIV** (1763–1844) (Jean Baptiste Bernadotte) King of Sweden and Norway (1818–44), b. France. He fought in the French Revolution and in the Battle of AUSTERLITZ. In effective control of Sweden from 1810, he joined the Allies against Napoleon at the Battle of Leipzig (1814) and forced Denmark to cede Norway to Sweden in the Treaty of Kiel (1814). Charles' subsequent reign brought peace and prosperity to Sweden and he founded the present Swedish dynasty.

**Charles (Prince of Wales)** (1948– ) Eldest son of ELIZABETH II and heir to the British throne. In 1969 he was invested as the Prince of Wales at Caernarvon. Charles married Lady DIANA Spencer in 1981. A fairy-tale marriage rapidly

► **cheetah** Also known as the hunting leopard, the cheetah (*Acinonyx jubatus*) is well adapted to catching its prey of antelope, hares, and some species of birds, such as guinea fowl and young ostriches. It is the fastest land mammal and hunts by sight not scent. The cheetah is distinguished by its pattern of solid black spots, a striped tail, and a dark line running from the inner eye to the mouth. It is tameable.

and publicly disintegrated. Their eldest son, Prince William (1982– ), is second in line to the throne. Charles is well-known for his work with charities, such as the Prince's Trust, and his advocacy of COMMUNITY ARCHITECTURE.

**Charles Edward Stuart** *See* STUART, CHARLES EDWARD

**Charles, Ray** (1930– ) US singer and pianist. Blind since the age of six, Charles' fusion of gospel harmonies, jazz instrumentation, and blues lyrics have proved successful since his first hit, "I Got A Woman," (1955). Other standards include "Georgia on My Mind" (1960).

**Charles' law** Volume of a gas at constant pressure is directly proportional to its absolute temperature. As temperature increases, the volume of a gas also increases at a constant pressure. The relationship was discovered by a French scientist Jacques Charles in 1787. The law is a special case of the ideal gas law. It is sometimes called Gay-Lussac's law, because Joseph GAY-LUSSAC established it more accurately in 1802.

**Charleston** Capital of West Virginia, W central West Virginia, at the confluence of the Elk and Kanawha rivers; seat of Kanawha county. Founded in 1788, the city grew around Fort Lee, home of Daniel BOONE, and was incorporated in 1794. Industries: chemicals, glass, metal, timber, oil, coal. Pop. (1990) 57,287.

**Charlotte** Largest city in North Carolina. Charlotte was named (*c.*1750) after the wife of King George III of England. The Mecklenburg Declaration of Independence was signed here (1775). Its citizens were vocal opponents of British rule, and the city was occupied briefly (1780) by the British army. The discovery of gold (1799) swelled the city population. President James K. POLK was born in Charlotte and the last Confederate cabinet meeting was held here (1865). Charlotte has become the transportation, commercial and industrial center of the Piedmont region. Industries: textiles, chemicals, machinery. Pop. (1990) 395,934.

**Charon** In Greek mythology, boatman of the Lower World who ferried the souls of the dead across the STYX to HADES.

**Charpentier, Gustave** (1860–1956) French composer, taught by MASSENET. His best-known compositions are the operas *Louise* (1900) and *Julien* (1913), and the orchestral *Impressions d'Italie* (1892).

**Chartism** (1838–48) British working-class movement for political reform. The Chartists organized mass petitions (1839, 1842, 1848). The movement faded away after a major demonstration in 1848.

**Chartres** Town on the Eure River, NW France; capital of Eure-et-Loire department. The stained glass and sculptures in the 12th–13th century gothic Cathedral of Notre Dame, make it one of Europe's finest cathedrals. It is a world heritage site. Industries: brewing, leather, agricultural equipment. Pop. (1990) 41,850.

**Charybdis** In Greek mythology, a female monster of the Straits of Messina. Daughter of Poseidon and Gaea, Zeus hurled her into the sea for stealing Heracles' cattle. A whirlpool formed where she lay.

**Chase, Salmon Portland** (1808–73) Chief justice of the US Supreme Court (1864–73). Known as the defender of fugitive slaves, he was appointed chief justice by President LINCOLN. Chase presided over the Senate impeachment proceedings against President Andrew JOHNSON (1868). His dissenting opinion in the Slaughterhouse Cases (1873) became a standard court judgment on the restrictive clause of the 14th Amendment.

**Chase, Samuel** (1741–1811) US jurist. A signer of the Declaration of Independence and member of the Maryland assembly (1764–84), he was appointed an associate justice of the US Supreme Court in 1796. A Federalist, impeached in 1804 for his conduct at the trials of two Jeffersonians, Chase won acquittal on the ground that holding opposing political views is not misconduct.

**Chateaubriand, François René, vicomte de** (1768–1848) French writer and diplomat, whose works contributed to French ROMANTICISM. *The Genius of Christianity* (1802) was a reaction to ENLIGHTENMENT attacks on Catholicism and established his literary reputation. *Atala* (1801) and *René* (1805) are tragic love stories set in the American

wilderness. After 1803 Chateaubriand held important diplomatic posts for both Napoleon and the Bourbons and was minister of foreign affairs (1823–24).

**Chattanooga** City on the Tennessee River, SE Tennessee. Founded as a trading post in the early 19th century, it was an important strategic center in the Civil War. Since 1935 it has been the headquarters of the Tennessee Valley Authority (TVA). Industries: iron and steel, synthetic fibers, tourism. Pop. (1992) 152,888.

**Chaucer, Geoffrey** (1346–1400) English medieval poet. His writings are remarkable for their range, narrative sense, power of characterization, and humor. They include *The Book of the Duchess* (1369), *The Parliament of Fowls,* and *Troilus and Criseyde* (both *c.*1385). Chaucer's most famous and popular work is *The Canterbury Tales* (*c.*1387–1400), an extraordinarily varied collection of narrative poems, each told by one of a group of pilgrims while traveling to the shrine of Thomas á Becket. Ranging from the courtly "Knight's Tale" to the bawdy "Miller's Tale", they provide a panoramic view of 14th-century English society and are a landmark in medieval fiction. Chaucer's writings exercised a powerful influence on the future direction of ENGLISH LITERATURE.

**Chávez, Cesar Estrada** (1927–93) US labor leader. Born of Mexican-American parents, he migrated to California as a field worker. In 1962 Chávez founded the National Farm Workers Association (NFWA), which in 1966 merged with the Agricultural Workers Organizing Committee of the AFL-CIO, to become the United Farm Workers Organizing Committee. In 1968–70 he led a successful national boycott of California grapes, and later a lettuce boycott.

**Chechenia** (formerly Checheno-Ingush Republic) Republic of the Russian Federation, in the N Caucasus; the capital is GROZNYY. The region's chief rivers are the Terek and Sunzha, whose valleys are the main source of agricultural products. Chechens, who are Sunni Muslims, constitute 50% of the population and 40% live in urban areas. Groznyy oilfield is a major source of Russian oil. The Chechens fiercely resisted czarist Russia's conquest of the Caucasus, even after absorption in 1859. In the 1920s separate autonomous regions were created by the Soviet Union for the Chechen and Ingush peoples. In 1934 the two were united to form a single region which, in 1936, became the Checheno-Ingush Autonomous Republic. The republic was dissolved in 1943–44 because of alleged collaboration with the German occupying forces in World War II. The region was reconstituted in 1957. In 1991 the Checheno-Ingush Republic split in two. General Dudayev was elected president of Chechenia. In 1994, following a period of bloody internal strife, Russia invaded but met fierce resistance. In 1995 Russian troops completed the capture of Groznyy at the cost of *c*.25,000 civilian lives. This lead to a protracted guerrilla war. Industries: oil refining, chemicals. Area: 7,452sq mi (19,301sq km). Pop. (1992) 1,308,000.

**cheese** Food made by curdling MILK and then processing the curd. The commonest source is cows' milk. Blue cheeses are pierced in order to channel air to a reactive fungus previously introduced. The simplest product is cottage cheese, formed when skimmed milk coagulates.

**cheetah** Spotted, large CAT found in hot, arid areas of Africa, the Middle East, and India. A long-legged animal with blunt, nonretractable claws, it has a tawny brown coat with round black spots. Capable of running at more than 60mph (95km/h), it hunts gazelles and antelopes by sight. Length: body: 55–60in (140–150cm); tail: 30–32in (75–80cm); weight: 132lb (60kg). Family Felidae; subfamily Acinonchinae; species *Acinonyx jubatus*.

**Cheever, John** (1912–82) US short-story writer and novelist. His works satirize the morals of American suburban life. Cheever's novel *The Wapshot Chronicle* (1957) won a National Book award and its sequel, *The Wapshot Scandal* (1964), was also well-received. His short-story collection *The Stories of John Cheever* (1978) won a Pulitzer Prize.

**Cheka** First secret police force in the Soviet Union. Formed shortly after the Russian Revolution (1917). A ferocious reign of terror alienated many Bolshevik organizations and it was disbanded in 1922, replaced first by the GPU and then by the KGB.

**Chekhov, Anton Pavlovich** (1860–1904) Russian dramatist, who worked closely with Konstantin STANISLAVSKY at the MOSCOW ART THEATRE. His major plays, *The Seagull* (1896), *Uncle Vanya* (1897), *The Three Sisters* (1901) and *The Cherry Orchard* (1904), reveal a deep awareness of human nature and a fine blend of comedy and tragedy. They are detailed portraits of provincial life. Characters often reveal as much by what they leave unsaid as the subtleties of the dialog itself.

**chemical bond** Mechanism that holds together atoms to form molecules. There are several types which arise either from the attraction of unlike charges or from the formation of stable configurations through electron-sharing. The number of bonds an atom can form depends upon its valency. The main types are IONIC, COVALENT, metallic, and hydrogen bonds.

**chemical engineering** Application of engineering principles to the making of chemical products on an industrial scale. Unit processes of chemical engineering include OXIDATION-REDUCTION, hydrogenation, nitration and sulfonation, ELECTROLYSIS, polymerization, ion exchange, and FERMENTATION.

**chemical equation** Set of symbols used to represent a CHEMICAL REACTION. Equations show how atoms are rearranged by a reaction, with reactants on the left-hand side and products on the right-hand side. For example, the formation of magnesium oxide when magnesium burns in oxygen is represented by $2Mg + O_2 \rightarrow 2MgO$. The number of atoms of an element on the left-hand side of an equation must equal the number on the right.

**chemical equilibrium** Balance in a REVERSIBLE REACTION, when two opposing reactions proceed at constant equal rates with no net change in the system. The initial rate of the reactions falls off as the concentrations of reactants decrease and the build-up of products causes the rate of the reverse reaction to increase.

**chemical reaction** Change or process in which chemical substances convert into other substances. This involves the breaking and formation of CHEMICAL BONDS. Reaction mechanisms include ENDOTHERMIC, EXOTHERMIC, ADDITION, CONDENSATION, combination (formation of a COMPOUND), DECOMPOSITION, and OXIDATION-REDUCTION reaction.

**chemical warfare** Use of chemical weapons such as poison and nerve gases, defoliants, and HERBICIDES. Poison gas and mustard gas were used in World War I. Chemical weapons were not used in World War II, but the Germans developed a nerve gas. A defoliant, Agent Orange, was employed by the US in the Vietnam War. Although the use of chemical and biological weapons is prohibited by the Geneva Convention (1925), their production, possession, and exchange are not. In 1990 the US and Soviet Union agreed to reduce their stockpiles of chemical weapons by 80%. In the 1980s Iraq used chemical weapons in both the Iran-Iraq War and against the Kurds in N Iraq. *See also* BIOLOGICAL WARFARE

**chemistry** Branch of science concerned with the properties, structure and composition of substances and their reactions with one another. Today, chemistry forms a vast body of knowledge with a number of subdivisions: the major division is between organic and inorganic. **Inorganic** chemistry studies the preparation, properties, and reactions of all chemical elements and their COMPOUNDS, except most of CARBON. The historic separation from organic chemistry is a false one, since many "inorganic" compounds are found in living organisms, such as common salt (NaCl) in human blood. In education and industry, however, the distinction is frequently still made. **Organic** chemistry studies the reactions of carbon compounds. Organic compounds are *c*.100 times more numerous than nonorganic ones. Organic chemistry also studies an immense variety of molecules, including those of industrial compounds such as plastics, rubbers, dyes, drugs, and solvents. **Analytical** chemistry deals with the composition of substances. PHYSICAL CHEMISTRY deals with the physical properties of substances, such as their boiling and melting points. Its subdivisions include ELECTROCHEMISTRY, thermochemistry and chemical KINETICS.

**Chemnitz** (formerly Karl-Marx-Stadt) City on the Chemnitz River, Saxony, SE Germany. Chartered in 1143, Chemnitz's linen trade was devastated by the Thirty Years War. Recovery followed the opening of cotton mills in the late 17th century. From 1953 until German reunification (1990), it was called Karl-Marx-Stadt. Chemnitz is one of the most heavily polluted cities in Europe. Industries: machine tools, chemicals, textiles, electronics. Pop. (1991) 287,510.

**chemoreceptor** Tiny region on the outer membrane of some biological cells that is sensitive to chemical stimuli. The chemoreceptor transforms a stimulus from an external molecule into a sensation, such as smell or taste.

**chemotherapy** Treatment of a disease (usually cancer) by a combination of chemical substances, or DRUGS, that kill or impair disease-producing cells or organisms in the body.

**CHEMICAL REACTION**

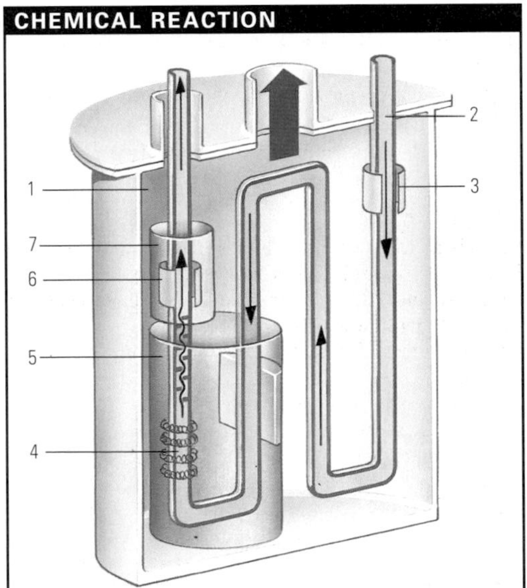


Calorimeters measure the amount of heat absorbed or let out during a chemical reaction. In a high-pressure flow calorimeter the apparatus is contained in a vacuum (1) for insulation. A constant flow of liquid or gas enters the calorimeter (2). A platinum resistance thermometer (3) measures the temperature of the substance on entry. A heater (4) puts a known amount of energy into the liquid or gas inside a radiation shield (5) which further lessens any dispersion of energy. The change in temperature is measured by a second thermometer (6) again shielded (7).

▶ **cherry** Grown for its fruit in many parts of the world, the cherry forms a type of fruit known as a drupe. It takes the form of a single seed surrounded by fleshy fruit. Cherries date from Roman times. The black variety shown here is known as Early Rivers.

Specific drug treatment was first introduced in the early 1900s by Paul EHRLICH.

**Chennai** (formerly Madras) City in SE India, on the Bay of Bengal; capital of Tamil Nadu state. India's second-largest port and fourth-largest city, Chennai was founded in 1639 as a British trading post. As Fort St. George, it became the seat of the EAST INDIA COMPANY and rapidly developed as a commercial centre. It was occupied by the French in 1746, but returned to Britain in 1748. The harbor was constructed in the second half of the 19th century. Industries: textiles, Tamil films, railroad stock, transport equipment. Pop. (1991) 3,841,396.

**Chernobyl** (Ukrainian, Chornobyl) City on the Pripyat River, N central Ukraine. It is 12mi (20km) from the Chernobyl power plant. On April 26, 1986 an explosion in one of the plant's reactors released 8 tons of radioactive material into the atmosphere. Within the first few hours 31 people died. Fallout spread across E and N Europe, contaminating much agricultural produce. Containment efforts began with the evacuation of more than 100,000 people from the vicinity of the plant. The reactor was encased in cement and boron. About 25,000 local inhabitants have died prematurely. Two of the three remaining reactors were reworking by the end of 1986. In 1991 Ukraine pledged to shut down the plant, but energy needs dictated its continued output. In 1994 the West pledged economic aid to ensure the plant's closure.

**Chernomyrdin, Viktor** (1938– ) Russian statesman, prime minister (1992–98). A member (1986–90) of the Central Committee of the Communist Party of the Soviet Union (CPSU), he became prime minister despite the objections of Boris YELTSIN. He broadly supported economic reform, but was critical of the pace of privatization. Yeltsin's illness meant that Chernomyrdin acted as caretaker-president throughout much of 1996–97.

**Cherokee** Largest tribe of Native Americans in the US, member of the Iroquoian language family. The Cherokee migrated S into the Appalachian region of Tennessee, Georgia, and the Carolinas. They sided with the British during the American Revolution. When gold was discovered on their land in Georgia in the 1830s, they were forced to move W. This tragic "Trail of Tears" (1838) reduced the population by 25%. One of the Five Civilized Tribes, *c.*47,000 Cherokee descendants now live in Oklahoma and *c.*3,000 in North Carolina.

**cherry** Widely grown fruit tree of temperate regions, probably native to W Asia and E Europe. Various types are grown for their fruit – round yellow, red or almost black with a round stone. The wood is used in furniture. Height: to 100ft (30m). Family Rosaceae; genus *Prunus*; there are *c.*50 species.

**Chesapeake Bay** Inlet of the Atlantic Ocean between Virginia (S) and Maryland (N) at the mouth of the Susquehanna River. Linked to the Delaware River by the Chesapeake and Delaware Canal, it has the world's longest bridge-tunnel system, the Chesapeake Bay Bridge-Tunnel, 18mi- (29km-) long. The first permanent English settlement in North America was on Chesapeake Bay, at Jamestown, Virginia, (1607). In 1608 John Smith explored and charted the bay. Length: *c.*200mi (320km). Width: 3–30mi (5–50km).

**Cheshire** County in NW England, bounded W by Wales and N by Greater Manchester and Merseyside. The county town is Chester. Cheshire is drained by the Mersey, Weaver, and Dee rivers. It is an important industrial and dairy farming region, noted for its cheese. Industries: salt, chemicals, textiles, motor vehicles. Area: 900sq mi (2,331sq km). Pop. (1991) 956,616.

**chess** Board game of strategic attack and defense, played on a 64-square checkered board. Two players start with 16 pieces each, white or black, set out along the outer two ranks (rows) of the board. With a black square in the left corner, white's pieces are set out: rook (castle), knight, bishop, queen, king, bishop, knight, rook. Black's pieces align directly opposite. Pawns stand on the second rank. White takes first move, and players move alternately on either rank (horizontal), file (vertical), or diagonal, until the king is captured (checkmate). Chess originated in ancient India. Extant references date the game back to the 6th century AD. Modern chess is a high-profile, international game. Since 1948 all male world champion grandmasters (except Bobby FISHER from the US) have come from Russia or the former Soviet Union.

**Chester** City and county district on the Dee River, NW England, Cheshire. A Roman garrison town, Chester was a major port until the Dee became silted and Liverpool's port facilities were expanded. Notable sights include the city wall, a Roman amphitheater, and a medieval cathedral. Industries: tourism, engineering. Area: 173sq mi (448sq km). Pop. (1991) 115,971.

**Chesterton, G.K. (Gilbert Keith)** (1874–1936) British essayist, novelist, biographer, and poet. Best-known for his *Father Brown* stories, which began in 1911, Chesterton also wrote literary criticism and essays on social and political themes. His novels include *The Napoleon of Notting Hill* (1904), and *The Man who was Thursday* (1908).

**chestnut** Deciduous tree native to temperate areas of the Northern Hemisphere. It has lance-shaped leaves and furrowed bark. Male flowers hang in long catkins, females are solitary or clustered at the base of catkins. The prickly husked fruits open to reveal two or three edible nuts. Family Fagaceae; genus *Castanea*; there are four species. *See also* HORSE CHESTNUT

**Cheyenne** Native North American tribe. Tribal competition forced them to migrate W from Minnesota along the Cheyenne River. The tribe split (*c.*1830), with the Northern Cheyenne remaining near the Platte River, and the Southern Cheyenne settling near the Arkansas River. The Colorado Gold Rush (1858) brought rapid white migration and the Cheyenne were restricted to a reservation. War broke out following a US army massacre of Cheyenne (1864). Colonel George CUSTER crushed the Southern Cheyenne, but the Northern Cheyenne helped in his eventual defeat at LITTLE BIGHORN. The Cheyenne surrendered in 1877, and were forced to move to Oklahoma, then to Montana where *c.*2,000 Cheyenne remain.

**Cheyenne** State capital of Wyoming and county seat of Laramie County. Founded in 1867 as a center for transporting freight and livestock by railroad, it became famous for its connections with figures such as BUFFALO BILL, Calamity Jane, and Wild Bill Hickok. Industries: packing plants, oil refineries. Pop. (1990) 50,008.

**Chiang Ching-kuo** (1909–88) Taiwanese statesman, president (1978–88). The eldest son of CHIANG KAI-SHEK, Chiang rose through the ranks of the KUOMINTANG. He was minister of defense (1965–72) and premier (1972–78), before becoming president. He began the process of democratization in Taiwan

**Chiang Kai-shek** (1887–1975) (Jiang Jieshi) Chinese nationalist leader. After taking part in resistance against the QING dynasty, he joined the KUOMINTANG, succeeding SUN YAT-SEN as leader (1925). From 1927 he purged the party of communists, and headed a nationalist government in Nanking. During World War II, with US support, Chiang led the fight against Japan. Civil war resumed in 1945. In 1948 Chiang was elected president of China, but in 1949 the communists led by MAO ZEDONG drove his government into exile in TAIWAN. Here, Chiang established a dictatorship and maintained that the Kuomintang were the legitimate Chinese government. He remained president of Taiwan until his death.

**Chiangmai** City in NW Thailand. Founded in the 13th century, it is the commercial, cultural, and religious center of N Thailand. It has air, rail, and road links with BANGKOK and is an export point for local produce. Industries: handicrafts, silk. Pop. (1991 est.) 161,541.

**chiaroscuro** Term for the opposition of light and dark in painting and drawing. CARAVAGGIO and REMBRANDT were masters of the dramatic use of chiaroscuro.

**Chiba** City and port in Japan, on Tokyo Bay, central Honshu; capital of Chiba prefecture. It has an 8th-century Buddhist temple. Industries: textiles, paper. Pop. (1993 est.) 834,000.

▲ **chestnut** Sweet chestnuts have had a variety of uses for many hundreds of years. They may be roasted, boiled or ground into flour or fed to livestock. The best quality chestnuts grow in S Europe.

Chile's flag was adopted in 1817. It was designed by an American serving in the Chilean army, who was inspired by the US Stars and Stripes. The white represents the snow-capped Andes, the blue the sky, and the red the blood of the nation's patriots.

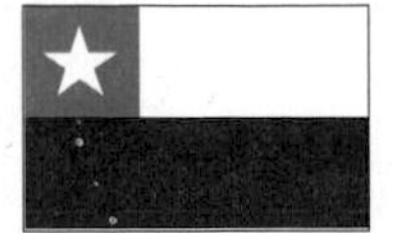

**AREA:** 292,258sq mi (756,950sq km)
**POPULATION:** 13,599,000
**CAPITAL (POPULATION):** Santiago (4,385,381)
**GOVERNMENT:** Multiparty republic
**ETHNIC GROUPS:** Mestizo 92%, Native American 7%
**LANGUAGES:** Spanish (official)
**RELIGIONS:** Christianity (Roman Catholic 81%, Protestant 6%)
**CURRENCY:** Peso = 100 centavos



The Republic of Chile stretches *c.*2,650mi (4,260km) from N to S, while the maximum E-W distance is only *c.*267mi (430km). The high Andes mountains form the country's E borders with Argentina and Bolivia. They include Ojos del Salado, at 22,516ft (6,863m), the second-highest peak in South America. To the W are basins and valleys, with coastal uplands overlooking the shore. EASTER ISLAND lies 2,200mi (3,500km) off Chile's W coast.

Western Chile contains three main land regions. In the N is the sparsely populated ATACAMA DESERT. The Central Valley, which contains the capital, SANTIAGO, the main port of VALPARAISO, and the city of Concepción, is by far the most densely populated region. In the S, the land has been heavily glaciated: coastal uplands have been worn into islands, while the inland valleys are arms of the sea.

In the far S, the Strait of MAGELLAN separates the Chilean mainland from TIERRA DEL FUEGO, a bleak group of islands divided between Chile and Argentina. Punta Arenas is the world's southernmost city.

## CLIMATE

Chile's great N-S extent, ranging from the tropics in the N to 55° 50's at Cape HORN, gives it a variety of climates. Santiago has a Mediterranean climate, with hot, dry summers from November to March and mild, moist winters from April to October. Northern Chile has a desert climate, with an average annual rainfall in places of only 0.004in (0.1mm). Southern Chile has a cool, temperate climate with frequent storms.

## VEGETATION

The few plants that live in the Atacama Desert, stretching *c.*1,000mi (1,600km) S from the Peruvian border, include varieties of cactus, and shrub. Central Chile has mixed forests of beech and laurel, while the wet S is a region of thick forests, glaciers, scenic lakes, and windswept, rocky slopes. Industrial growth has led to widespread deforestation.

## HISTORY AND POLITICS

ARAUCANICIANS reached the S tip of South America more than 8,000 years ago. In 1520 Ferdinand MAGELLAN became the first European to sight Chile. In 1541 Pedro de Valdivia founded Santiago. Chile became a Spanish colony. The Native Americans acted as bonded labour on colonial ranches. In 1817 an army, led by José de SAN MARTÍN, surprised the Spanish by crossing the Andes. In 1818 Bernardo O'HIGGINS proclaimed Chile's independence. His dictatorship was followed by democratic reforms. In the War of the Pacific (1879–84), Chile gained mineral-rich areas from Peru and Bolivia. In the late 19th century, Chile's economy rapidly industrialized, but a succession of autocratic regimes and its dependence on nitrate exports hampered growth. In 1964 Eduardo FREI Montalvo of the Christian Democratic Party was elected. Frei embarked on a process of reform, such as assuming a majority share in the US-owned copper mines. In 1970 Salvador ALLENDE was elected president. He introduced many socialist policies, such as land reform and the nationalization of industries. In 1973 soaring inflation and public disturbances led to a military coup, with covert US backing. Allende and many of his supporters were executed. General Augusto PINOCHET assumed control and instigated a series of sweeping market reforms and pro-Western foreign-policy initiatives. In 1977 Pinochet banned all political parties. His regime was characterized by repression and human-rights violations. Many political opponents simply "disappeared". In 1981 a new constitution was introduced. In 1989 Patricio Aylwyn was elected president in Chile's first democratic elections. Despite public protests Pinochet was made a senator-for-life, ensuring his immunity from prosecution in Chile. In 1993 Eduardo Frei Ruiz-Tagle was elected president. The process of social liberalization was accelerated. In 1998 Pinochet was arrested in England after Spain had applied for his extradition on charges of "crimes of genocide and terrorism". The UK law lords ruled that Pinochet did not enjoy sovereign immunity under international law for crimes committed since 1989. His arrest provoked unrest in Chile.

## ECONOMY

Chile is a lower-middle-incomedeveloping country (1995 GDP per capita, $9,520). Mining is important. Chile is the world's largest producer of copper ore; accounting for 22% of total world production in 1993. The industry is based in N Chile, especially around Chaquicamata. Minerals dominate Chile's exports, but the most valuable activity is manufacturing and the main products include iron and steel, wood products, transport equipment, cement, and textiles.

Agriculture employs 18% of the work force; the chief crop is wheat. Chile's major economic problem is its lack of an adequate domestic food supply. Climate and landscape combine to make Chile dependent on imports for more than 50% of its food consumption. Yet Chile's wine industry is expanding rapidly, and its fishing industry is the world's fifth largest.

Chile's economy has become one of the strongest in Latin America. In 1995 it began negotiations to become the first South American member of the North American Free Trade Agreement (NAFTA), alongside Canada, Mexico, and the US.

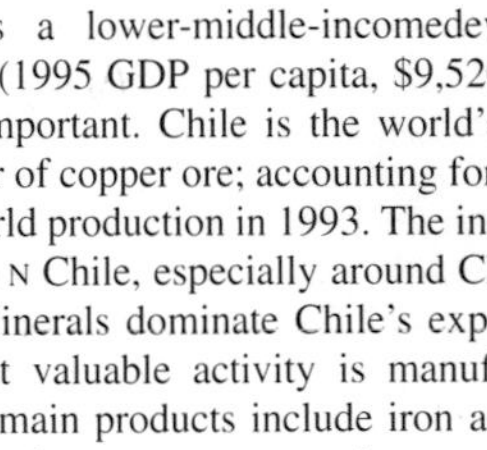

**Chile's shape** and its inhospitable terrain have hampered the development of an effective transportation system. Air transport is important in linking Chilean cities.

China's flag was adopted in 1949, when the country became the Communist People's Republic. Red is the traditional color of both China and communism. The large star represents the Communist Party program. The smaller stars symbolize the four main social classes.

**AREA:** 3,705,386 sq mi (9,596,960 sq km)
**POPULATION:** 1,187,997,000
**CAPITAL (POPULATION):** Beijing (6,560,000)
**GOVERNMENT:** Single-party Communist republic
**ETHNIC GROUPS:** Han (Chinese) 92%, 55 minority groups
**LANGUAGES:** Mandarin Chinese (official)
**RELIGIONS:** The government encourages atheism; though Confucianism, Buddhism, Taoism, and Islam are practiced
**CURRENCY:** Renminbi (yuan) = 10 jiao = 100 fen

The People's Republic of China is the world's third largest country (after Russia and Canada). Most people live on the E coastal plains, in the highlands or the fertile river valleys of the HUANG HE and YANGTZE, Asia's longest river, at 3,960mi- (6,380km-) long.

Western China includes the bleak Tibetan plateau, bounded by the HIMALAYAS (the world's highest mountain range). EVEREST, the world's highest peak, lies on the Nepal-TIBET border. Other ranges include the TIAN SHAN and Kunlun Shan. China also has deserts, such as the GOBI on the Mongolian border.

### CLIMATE

BEIJING in NE China has cold winters and warm summers, with moderate rainfall. SHANGHAI, in the E central region, has milder winters and more rain. The SE region has a wet, subtropical climate. In the W, the climate is severe.

### VEGETATION

Large areas in the W are covered by sparse grasses or desert. The most luxuriant forests are in the SE, such as the bamboo forest habitat of the rare giant panda.

### HISTORY AND POLITICS

The first documented dynasty was the SHANG (*c*.1523–*c*.1030 BC), when bronze casting was perfected. The ZHOU dynasty (*c*.1030–221 BC) was the age of Chinese classical literature, in particular CONFUCIOUS and LAO TZU. China was unified by QIN SHIHUANGDI, whose tomb near XIAN contains the famous Terracotta Army. The QIN dynasty (*c*.221–206 BC) also built the majority of the GREAT WALL. The HAN dynasty (*c*.202 BC–AD 220) developed the empire, a bureaucracy based on CONFUCIANISM, and introduced BUDDHISM. China then split into three kingdoms (Wei, Shu, and Wu) and the influence of Buddhism and TAOISM grew. The T'ANG dynasty (618–907) was a golden era of artistic achievement, especially in poetry and fine art. In the 1210s GENGHIS KHAN conquered most of China and established the MONGOL empire. KUBLAI KHAN founded the YÜAN dynasty (1271–1368), a period of dialog with Europe. The MING dynasty (1368–1644) reestablished Chinese rule and is famed for its fine porcelain. The Manchu QING dynasty (1644–1912) began by vastly extending the empire, but the 19th century was marked by foreign interventions, such as the OPIUM WAR (1839–42), when Britain occupied HONG KONG. Popular disaffection culminated in the BOXER REBELLION (1900). The last emperor (Henry PU YI) was overthrown in a revolution led by SUN YAT-SEN and a republic established.

## CHINA

China rapidly fragmented between a Beijing government supported by warlords, and Sun Yat-sen's nationalist KUOMINTANG government in GUANGZHOU. The COMMUNIST PARTY OF CHINA initially allied with the nationalists. In 1926 CHIANG KAI-SHEK's nationalists emerged victorious and turned on their communist allies. In 1930 a rival communist government was established, but was uprooted by Kuomintang troops and began the LONG MARCH (1934). Japan, taking advantage of the turmoil, established the puppet state of MANCHUKUO (1932) under Henry Pu Yi. Chiang was forced into an alliance with the communists. Japan launched a full-scale invasion in 1937 and conquered much of N and E China. From 1941 Chinese forces, with Allied support, began to regain territory. After World War 2, civil war resumed: nationalists supported by the USA and communists by Russia. The communists, with greater popular support, triumphed and the Kuomintang fled to TAIWAN. MAO ZEDONG established the People's Republic of China on 1 October 1949. In 1950 China seized Tibet.

Domestically, Mao began to collectivize agriculture and nationalize industry. In 1958 the GREAT LEAP FORWARD was a five-year plan to revolutionize industrial production. The CULTURAL REVOLUTION (1966–76) mobilized Chinese youth against bourgeois and bureaucratic culture. By 1971 China had become a world power with a seat on the UN security council and its own nuclear capability. Following Mao's death (1976), a power struggle developed within the party leadership between the GANG OF FOUR and moderates led by DENG XIAOPING; the latter emerged victorious. Deng began a process of modernization, forging closer links with the West. In 1979 special economic zones were created to encourage inward investment. Despite China's economic reforms, political, cultural, and intellectual pluralism were often suppressed by the party. In 1989 a pro-democracy demonstration was crushed in TIANANMEN SQUARE. In 1997 JIANG ZEMIN succeeded Deng as paramount leader. China enjoys most-favored nation status with the US. In 1998 China regained HONG KONG. In 1999 Portugal returned MACAO. China has one of the world's largest economies (1995 GDP per capita, $US2,920), agriculture employs *c*.70% of the work force. It has vast mineral resources and a huge steel industry.

**Chibcha** (Muisca) Late prehistoric culture in South America. Bogotá and Tunja were the main centers. Chibcha culture flourished between 1000 and 1541, and rivaled the INCA in political sophistication. The population, *c*.750,000, developed city-states. Chibcha pottery, weaving, and goldsmithing were inferior to Inca work. They were conquered by the Spanish (1536–41). Today, Chibcha refers to a Native American language family, whose speakers inhabit S Panama and N Colombia.

**Chicago** City on the SW shore of Lake Michigan, NE Illinois. In the late 18th century it was a trading post and became Fort Dearborn military post (1803). With the construction of the Erie Canal and railroads, and the opening up of the prairies, Chicago attracted settlers and industry. Large areas of the city were destroyed by fire in 1871. It became a noted cultural center in the late 19th century, including the establishment of the Chicago Symphony Orchestra (1891) and several literary magazines. Chicago is the major industrial, commercial, cultural, and shipping center of the Midwest. It has many colleges and universities, the largest railroad terminal in the world, and the world's busiest airport, O'Hare. Chicago is renowned for its architecture. The world's first SKYSCRAPER was built here in 1885 and, until 1996, the Sears Tower was the world's tallest building, at 1,454ft (443m). Industries: steel, chemicals, machinery, food processing, metal working. Pop. (1990) 2,783,726.

**Chichén Itzá** Chief city and shrine of MAYA and TOLTEC peoples between the 9th and 13th centuries AD, in YUCATÁN, Mexico. The earlier Maya city was abandoned *c*.900. The new Toltec city was built *c*.1mi (1.5km) away. Remains include temple-pyramids, a court for ball games, and a sacrificial well. In *c*.1200 Chichén Itzá lost its pre-eminence to nearby Mayapan.

**chickadee** Any of several North American titmice whose calls resemble a whistled "chick-a-dee." Chickadees are small and plump, with short, rounded wings, stubby bills, dark caps and bibs, and light cheeks. The black-capped chickadee (*Parus atricapillus*) of E North America is an active bird that feeds on seeds and insects. It grows to *c*.5in (13cm). Family Paridae; genus *Parus*.

**Chickasaw** Muskogean-speaking Native Americans, who originated in Mississippi and Tennessee and who cultivated corn. One of the Five Civilized Tribes, in the 1830s the Chickasaw were resettled in Indian Territory (now Oklahoma). Pop. (1995) *c*.9,000.

**chicken** *See* POULTRY

**chickenpox** (varicella) Infectious disease of childhood caused by a virus of the HERPES group. After an incubation period of two to three weeks, a fever develops and red spots (which later develop into blisters) appear. Recovery is usually within a week, although the possibility of contagion remains until the last scab has been shed.

**chickpea** (dwarf pea, garbanzo, chich, or gram) Bushy annual plant cultivated from antiquity in S Europe and Asia for its pea-like seeds. It is grown widely in the Western Hemisphere. Family Fabaceae/Leguminosae; species *Cicer arietinum*.

**chicory** Perennial weedy plant whose leaves are cooked and eaten, or served raw in salads. The fleshy roots are dried and ground for mixing with (or a substitute for) COFFEE. Chicory has bright blue, daisy-like flowers. Height: 5ft (1.5m). Family Asteraceae/Compositae; species *Chichorium intybus*.

**chigger** (harvest mite or red bug) Tiny, red larva of some kinds of MITES. Adults lay eggs on plants and hatched larvae find an animal host. On humans their bites cause a severe rash and itching. Length: 0.004–0.6in (0.1–16mm). Order Acarina; family Trombiculidae.

**Chihuahua** Largest state in Mexico, on the N Mexican plateau. The climate and terrain vary from cool mountains (W) to arid desert (E). The state capital, Chihuahua, has a Spanish colonial cathedral. Industries: mining, forestry, tourism, cotton. Area: 95,400sq mi (247,086sq km). Pop. (state, 1990) 2,441,873; (city, 1990) 530,783.

**child abuse** Emotional and/or physical (often sexual) maltreatment of a child. Neglect is considered a form of abuse. Physical abuse may be apparent in bruising and lacerations, burns, or scars. Sexual abuse is often concealed by the abused out of fear or guilt. Mental effects may result in remoteness or crudely violent outbursts.

**childbirth** *See* LABOR

**child psychology** *See* DEVELOPMENTAL PSYCHOLOGY

**Children's Crusade** Name given to two 13th-century CRUSADES by children. French children were offered free transport from Marseilles to the Holy Land, but were sold as slaves in North Africa. A group of German children bound for the Holy Land traveled to Italy, where the crusade floundered, many dying of starvation and disease.

**Chile** Republic in SW South America. *See* country feature, page 151

**chili** (chilli) Hot red PEPPER. It is an annual with oval leaves and white or greenish-white flowers that produce red or green seedpods. When dried, the pods are ground to powder. Cayenne pepper comes from the same plant. Height: 6–8ft (2–2.5m). Family Solanaceae; species *Capsicum annuum*.

**chimaera** (ratfish or ghost shark) One of *c*.28 species of cartilaginous, deep-sea fish with a long poisonous dorsal spine and a slender tail. Some species have an elongated snout. An oil, derived from its liver, is used as a lubricant in precision equipment. Length: 23–80in (60cm–2m). Families Chimaeridae, Collorhinchidae, and Rhinochimaeridae. The term is also used in biology for an animal formed from several different embryos.

**Chimera** In Greek mythology, a female monster with a lion's head, goat's body, and dragon's tail. She was the sister of Cerberus, HYDRA, and the SPHINX and was slain by Bellerophon.

**chimpanzee** Intelligent great APE of tropical Africa. Chimpanzees are mostly black and powerfully built. A smaller chimpanzee of the Congo is sometimes classified as a separate species. Chimpanzees often nest in trees, but spend the day on the ground searching for fruit and nuts. The closest relative to man, they are communicative and highly social. Height: *c*.4.5ft

▲ **chickpea** A staple crop in certain regions of India, the chickpea (*Cicer arietinum*) is grown for its seed, which is then boiled.

**▶ Chirac** Becoming president of France in 1995, Jacques Chirac's austerity measures to ensure that the French economy met the stringent convergence criteria for European monetary union in 1999, caused some civil unrest and strikes.

(1.3m); weight: *c.*150lb (68kg). Family Pongidae. Species *Pan troglodytes* (Congo *P. paniscus*). *See also* PRIMATE

**Ch'in** Alternative transliteration for the QIN dynasty

**China** Republic in E Asia. *See* country feature, page 152

**China Sea** Western part of the Pacific Ocean, divided by Taiwan into the SOUTH CHINA SEA and the EAST CHINA SEA.

**chinchilla** Genus of small, furry RODENTS native to South America. Chinchillas were hunted almost to extinction. They are now bred for their soft fur, the most expensive of all animal furs. Length: 9–15in (23–38cm); weight; 1–2lb (450–900g). Family Chinchilidae.

**Chinese** Group of languages spoken by *c.*95% of the population of China and by millions more in Taiwan, Hong Kong, Southeast Asia, and other countries. There are six major languages, which are not mutually intelligible; the most numerous is MANDARIN, spoken by *c.*66% of the Chinese population. All Chinese languages are written in a single common nonalphabetic script, whose characters number in the thousands and in some cases date back several thousand years. This single writing-system leads to the classification of all Chinese languages as dialects of one language. Chinese has twice as many users as any other language in the world. *See also* CANTONESE

**Chinese architecture** Style that as early as the neolithic period, used columns to support roofs, faced houses south, and used bright colors. The characteristic Chinese roof with wide overhang and upturned eaves was probably developed in the ZHOU period (*c.*1030–221 BC). A walled complex with a central axis for temples and palaces was established in the HAN dynasty (*c.*202 BC–AD 220), and building residential units around a central courtyard with elaborately planned garden became standard. The pagoda derives from Buddhist influences, notably the Indian stupa, and dates from the 6th century.

**Chinese art** Longest pedigree of any school in world art, its earliest artifacts (painted pottery) date back to the late Neolithic period. By the time of the SHANG dynasty (*c.*1523–1030 BC), native craftsmen were proficient at casting bronze and making jade carvings, many of which have survived as grave freight. The most elaborate of these belonged to the first emperor of the QIN dynasty, QIN SHIHUANGDI (d.210 BC). It contains a fabulous Terracotta Army of *c.*7,500 life-sized figures and horses. Painting and sculpture were established during the HAN dynasty, though little survives. The T'ANG dynasty (618–907) marked China's artistic zenith. Sculpture reached a peak of refinement, and there were early attempts at landscape painting. The SUNG dynasty saw the first true porcelain. Important technical advances, such as colored enamels, took place during the MING period (1368–1644). Chinese porcelain became highly valuable in European markets in the QING period. The advent of communism created a rift in this long tradition, as artists adopted Soviet-inspired SOCIALIST REALISM.

**Chinese literature** Earliest literary texts date from the ZHOU dynasty (*c.*1030–221 BC). This period produced the canonical writings of CONFUCIANISM: the Five Classics, including the first poetry anthology *Shih ching* (Classic of Odes); and the Four Books, containing doctrinal writings. Traditionally attributed to CONFUCIUS, the *Shih ching* is probably earlier still. In this era, LAO TZU is credited with founding TAOISM. During the HAN dynasty (202 BC–AD 220), elaborate *fu* prose poems which praised the dynasty flourished. The T'ANG dynasty (618–907) marked the golden age of Chinese literature; LI PO, TU FU, and Wang Wei were the outstanding poets of the period. In the SUNG dynasty (960–1279), the novel (often historical) and drama came into being. From the late-17th to early 19th century, much emphasis was placed on formal technique. Ts'ao Chan produced the most memorable work of the period, the novel *Dream of the Red Chamber*. The lyric poem has been the dominant form in Chinese literature. It is normally philosophical, with a quietness of tone and an emphasis on simple, routine experiences. In the first half of the 20th century, Chinese literature became modernized, with the new Chinese republic striving to formulate a new, politicized literary language. During the CULTURAL REVOLUTION, strict censorship was imposed. Recent years have seen a slight liberalization.

**Chinese mythology** During the SHANG dynasty, divination by means of animal bones was used to consult the spirits of royal ancestors. These ancestors were divine and provided a means of communication with the spirit world. A supreme god, Shang Ti, ruled in heaven as Chinese sovereigns did on earth. During the ZHOU dynasty, Shang Ti was replaced by T'ien ("Heaven") as the supreme being. The emperor, the "Son of Heaven," was responsible for maintaining harmony on earth and assumed the role of both priest and monarch. Chinese creation myths are essentially the reduction of chaos to order. Later, there existed a formal Chinese pantheon ruled by a father-god, the August Personage of Jade. His heavenly court was an almost exact replica of the imperial court at BEIJING. The Sun and the Moon were the objects of an official cult, and the Festival of the Moon was a major annual celebration.

**Chinese theater** In its purest form, the traditions of Chinese theater date back to the SUNG dynasty (960–1279). Traditional theater is highly stylized and the symbolism of the various dramatic parts, the actors' costumes, make-up, and gestures are considered of far greater importance than the dialog. Although much recent Chinese theater has become Westernized, the old dramatic tradition remains enormously popular.

**Ch'ing** Alternative transliteration for the QING dynasty

**chinook** Warm, dry foehn wind experienced on the E side of the Rocky Mountains in Canada and the US, and in the European Alps.

**Chinook** Native American tribe living along the Pacific coast from the Columbia River to The Dalles, Oregon. Although fewer than 1,000, the Chinook traveled widely and the Chinook language was used by others, native and European, during the settlement of the West.

**chip** *See* SILICON CHIP

**chipmunk** Small, ground-dwelling SQUIRREL native to North America and Asia. It carries nuts, berries, and seeds in cheek pouches, to store underground. Active tree-climbers in summer, they hibernate in winter. Most chipmunks are brown with one or more black-bordered, light stripes. Length: 5–6in (13–15cm) excluding the tail. Family Sciuridae; genera *Eutamias* and *Tamias*.

**Chippendale, Thomas** (1718–79) British furniture designer. One of the great English craftsmen, much of his fame rested upon his *The Gentleman and Cabinet Maker's Directory* (1754–62), a trade catalog illustrating the designs of his factory. Many of Chippendale's finest pieces were marquetry and inlaid items of NEOCLASSICISM.

**Chirac, Jacques René** (1932– ) French statesman, president (1995– ). He entered the National Assembly in 1967. In 1974 Chirac was appointed prime minister by President GISCARD D'ESTAING. In 1976 he resigned and formed a new Gaullist party, the Rally for the Republic (RPR). In 1977 Chriac became mayor of Paris. He was again prime minister (1986–88), this time under President MITTERRAND. In 1995 Chirac succeeded Mitterrand as president. Confronted by the lead-up to European monetary union, he called a surprise prime ministerial election (1997). Victory for the socialists, led by Lionel JOSPIN, was a personal setback for Chirac.

**Chirico, Giorgio de** (1888–1978) Italian painter, b. Greece. Chirico was the quasi-surrealist "metaphysical painting" movement. He painted still lifes and empty, dreamlike landscapes in exaggerated perspective. In the 1930s he repudiated all modern art in favor of the style of the Old Masters. *See also* SURREALISM

**Chiron** In Greek mythology, wisest and most famous

CENTAUR. He taught many of the lesser gods and heroes, including ACHILLES, and was accidently killed by Hercules with a poisoned arrow.

**chiropractic** Nonorthodox medical practice based on the theory that the nervous system integrates all of the body's functions, including defense against disease. Chiropractors aim to remove nerve interference by manipulations of the affected musculoskeletal parts.

**Chisholm v. Georgia** (1793) First important Supreme Court decision in which the court upheld the right of a citizen of one state to sue the government of another. Strong opposition to this ruling led to the 11th Amendment (1796), which overturned the decision.

**Chisinau** (Kishinev) Capital of Moldova, on the Byk River. Founded in the early 15th century, it came under Turkish and then Russian rule. Romania held the city from 1918 to 1940 when it was annexed by the Soviet Union. In 1991 it became capital of independent Moldova. It has a 19th-century cathedral and a university (1945). Industries: plastics, rubber. Pop. (1994) 700,000.

**chitin** Hard, tough substance that occurs widely in nature, particularly in the hard shells (exoskeletons) of arthropods, such as crabs, insects, and spiders. The walls of hyphae (microscopic tubes of fungi) are composed of slightly different chitin. Chemically, chitin is a polysaccharide, derived from glucose.

**chiton** (coat-of-mail shell) MOLLUSK that lives on rocks along marine shores. Bilaterally symmetrical, its upper surface has eight overlapping shells. Underneath is a large fleshy foot and a degenerate head with mouth, gills, and mantle. Length: to 13in (33cm). Class Amphineura; order Polyplacophora; family Chitonidae.

**Chittagong** Seaport on the Karnaphuli River, near the Bay of Bengal, SE Bangladesh. Under Mogul rule in the 17th century, it was ceded to the British East India Company in 1760. It is Bangladesh's chief port. Industries: jute, tea, oil, engineering. Pop. (1991) 1,363,998.

**chive** Perennial herb whose long, hollow leaves have an onion-like flavor used for seasoning. The flowers grow in rose-purple clusters. Family Liliaceae; species *Allium schoenoprasum*.

**chlamydia** Small, virus-like BACTERIA that live as PARASITES in animals and cause disease. One strain, *C. trachomatis*, is responsible for TRACHOMA and is also a major cause of pelvic inflammatory disease (PID) in women. *C. psittaci* causes PSITTACOSIS. Chlamydial infection is the most common SEXUALLY TRANSMITTED DISEASE (STD) in many developed countries.

**chlamydomonas** Genus of microscopic, single-celled GREEN ALGAE that can be so common in ponds as to turn the water bright green. The cell of *Chlamydomonas* is only *c.*20 micrometers (20 millionths of a meter) across and has two flagella, which the cell beats to swim. *See also* FLAGELLATE

**chloride** Salt of HYDROCHLORIC ACID or some organic compounds containing CHLORINE, especially those with the negative ion $Cl^-$. The best-known example is common salt, sodium chloride (NaCl). Most chlorides are soluble in water, except mercurous and silver chlorides.

**chlorine** (symbol Cl) Common nonmetallic element that is one of the HALOGENS, first discovered in 1774 by the Swedish chemist Karl Scheele. It occurs in common salt (NaCl). It is a greenish-yellow poisonous gas extracted by the electrolysis of brine (salt water) and is widely used to disinfect drinking water and swimming pools, to bleach wood pulp, and in the manufacture of plastics, chloroform, and pesticide. Chemically, it is a reactive element, and combines with most metals. Properties: at.no. 17; at.wt. 35.453; m.p. 149.8°F (101°C); b.p. 30.28°F (34.6°C). The most common isotope is $^{35}Cl$ (75.53%).

**chlorofluorocarbon (CFC)** Chemical compound in which hydrogen atoms of a hydrocarbon, such as an alkane, are replaced by atoms of fluorine, chlorine, carbon, and sometimes bromine. CFCs are inert, stable at high temperatures and are odorless, colorless, nontoxic, noncorrosive and nonflammable. Under the trade name of Freons, CFCs were widely used in aerosols, fire-extinguishers, refrigerators, and in the manufacture of foam plastics. When CFCs are used they slowly drift into the stratosphere and are broken down by the Sun's ultraviolet radiation into chlorine atoms that destroy the OZONE LAYER. It often takes more than 100 years for CFCs to disappear from the atmosphere. In 1990 many governments agreed to reduce and eventually phase out the use of CFCs and other chemicals harming the ozonosphere.

**chloroform** ($CHCl_3$, trichloromethane) Colorless, volatile, sweet-smelling liquid, prepared by the chlorination of methane. Formerly a major anesthetic, it is used in the manufacture of fluorocarbons, in cough medicines, for insect bites, and as a solvent. Properties: sp.gr. 1.48; m.p. 82.3°F (63.5°C); b.p. 142.2°F (61.2°C).

**chlorophyll** Group of green pigments in the CHLOROPLASTS of plants and ALGAE that absorb light for PHOTOSYNTHESIS. There are five types: chlorophyll *a* is present in all photosynthetic organisms except bacteria; chlorophyll *b*, in plants and GREEN ALGAE; and chlorophylls *c*, *d*, and *e*, in some algae. It is similar in structure to HEMOGLOBIN, with a magnesium atom replacing an iron atom.

**chloroplast** Microscopic green structure within a plant cell in which PHOTOSYNTHESIS takes place. The chloroplast is enclosed in an "envelope" and contains internal membranes to increase the surface area for reactions. Molecules of the light-absorbing pigment CHLOROPHYLL are embedded in these internal membranes.

**chocolate** Like COCOA, chocolate was originally a drink (introduced to Europe in the 1500s) produced from the seeds of the tropical tree *Theobroma cacao*. The seeds are beans contained in an elliptical pod, and do not have the flavor or color of chocolate until they have been fermented and roasted. The beans are then ground up to make chocolate powder. The first chocolate bar was produced in the late 1700s.

**Choctaw** One of the largest tribes of Muskogean-speaking Native North Americans, located in SE Mississippi and part of Alabama. An agricultural people closely related to the CHICKASAW, they were generally at peace with the settlers and remained neutral during the Revolution. As large slave-owners, they supported the South during the Civil War. A majority of the Choctaw moved to Oklahoma in 1830, where some 40,000 of their descendants still reside.

**choir** Group of singers who perform together as a musical unit. The earliest choirs were ecclesiastical and sang PLAINSONG in church services. From the 10th century onwards, polyphonic composition gradually replaced unharmonized PLAINSONG in liturgical use. The beginnings of OPERA marked the development of the secular choir or CHORUS. Most modern choirs are mixed.

**Choiseul, Etienne François, duc de** (1719–85) French statesman, chief minister (1758–1770) of LOUIS XV. As ambassador to Vienna (1757–58), he negotiated the marriage of Marie Antoinette and the future Louis XVI. As minister of foreign affairs he negotiated the Family Compact (1761), allying the BOURBON rulers of France and Spain, and the Treaty of Paris (1763), in which France was forced to surrender French Canada and India to Britain. Choiseul approved the suppression of the Jesuits (1764).

**Chola** Dynasty of S India. From 985 to 1024, they established an empire that included Sri Lanka, Bengal, parts of Sumatra, and Malaya. A great era of Hindu culture finally ended in 1279.

**cholera** Infectious disease caused by the bacterium *Vibrio cholerae*, transmitted in contaminated water. Cholera, prevalent in many tropical regions, produces almost continuous, watery diarrhea often accompanied by vomiting and muscle cramps, and leads to severe dehydration. Untreated it can be fatal, but proper treatment, including fluid replacement and antibiotics, result in a high recovery rate. There is a vaccine.

**cholecystitis** Inflammation of the GALL BLADDER, often associated with GALLSTONES. Most gallstones produce no pain, but inflammation may set in, causing severe pain, nausea, and vomiting, and possibly JAUNDICE. It is most common in relatively young, overweight women with a high-fat diet. Treatment is with antibiotics and pain-killers, although severe attacks may require removal of the gall bladder (cholecystectomy).

**cholesterol** White, fatty STEROID, occurring in large concentrations in the brain, spinal cord, and liver. It is synthesized in

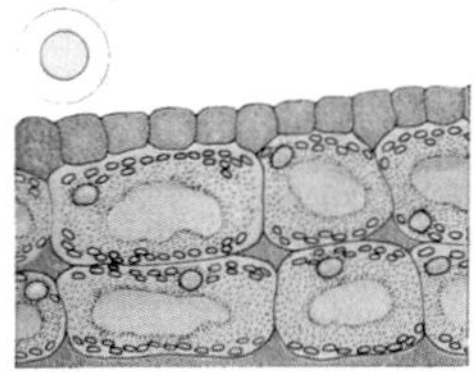

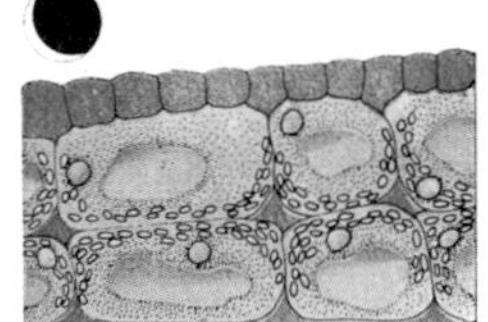

▲ **chloroplast** Chloroplasts, found mostly in the cells of plant leaves, absorb sunlight and use it to manufacture special types of sugar. They are able to move about in order to receive the maximum amount of light possible. A section through a leaf reveals that during the day (top) chloroplasts have moved to the outer and inner walls in the direct line of light. During the night (bottom) they move to the inner and side walls only.

▶ **Chopin** As well as a successful composer, Frédéric Chopin, was a virtuoso pianist. He left his native Poland due to political repression, and moved to Paris in 1831; much of his music reflects traditional Polish folk songs.

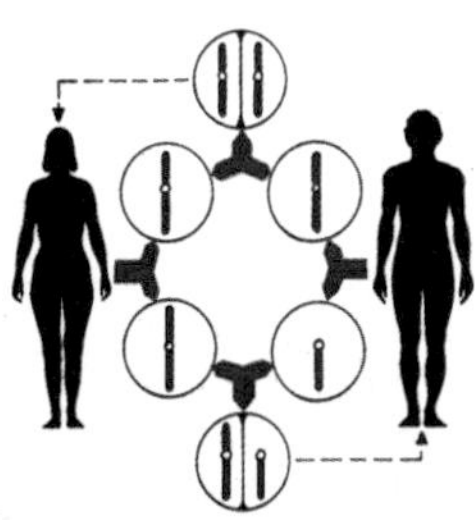

▲ **chromosome** The 46 chromosomes in somatic (non-reproductive) cells contain a single sex-determining pair, which consists of an X and Y chromosome in males, or an XX pair in females. Ova contain only the X chromosome, while spermotozoa contain X or Y chromosomes in equal proportions. At fertilization therefore there is a 50% chance of an XX or XY pair being formed.

▲ **chrysanthemum** Native to E Asia, the chrysanthemum, along with the cherry blossom, is the national flower of Japan. Today there are some 200 species cultivated around the world.

the liver, intestines, and skin and is an intermediate in the synthesis of vitamin D and many hormones. GALLSTONES are composed mainly of cholesterol. Meat-rich diets may produce high cholesterol in blood vessels, and can lead to ARTERIOSCLEROSIS.

**Chomsky, (Avram) Noam** (1928– ) US academic and writer. In *Syntactic Structures* (1957), he developed the concept of a transformational generative grammar, embodying his theories about the relationship between language and the human mind and an underlying universal structure of language. Opposed to BEHAVIORISM, Chomsky argued that the human capacity for language is partially innate. He has been a consistent critic of US imperialist tendencies and was an outspoken opponent of the Vietnam War.

**Chongjin** City on the Sea of Japan, NE North Korea. From 1910 to 1945 it was controlled by the Japanese, who developed the Musan iron mines. Chongjin was severely damaged during the Korean War. Industries: iron, steel, shipbuilding. Pop. (1984 est.) 754,128.

**Chongqing** *See* CHUNGKING

**Chopin, Frédéric François** (1810–49) Composer for the piano, b. Poland. He gave his first public piano recital in Warsaw at the age of eight. Political repression forced Chopin to move (1831) to Paris, where he rapidly endeared himself in the *salons*. His restrained and delicate style contrasted strongly with contemporary trends. In 1836 Liszt introduced Chopin to the novelist George SAND. In 1838 the couple moved to Majorca, and he composed 24 préludes. Chopin composed almost exclusively for the piano and established it as a solo instrument. His improvisational method produced radical new ideas of HARMONY. Chopin's major works include two piano concertos and three piano sonatas. He died of tuberculosis.

**choral music** Music written for several voices. Choral compositions were originally religious, CANTATA and ORATORIO being the most usual forms. The foremost composer of cantatas was J.C. BACH, and of oratorios HANDEL. Choral music varies from the small-scale madrigals of the 16th century to the large-scale works of the 19th and 20th centuries, such as Verdi's *Requiem* (1874), and Elgar's *Dream of Gerontius* (1900).

**chord** In music, the simultaneous occurrence of three or more musical tones of different pitch. Chords are categorized as anomalous, characteristic, common, inverted, or transient. *See also* HARMONY

**chordata** Name of a large phylum of VERTEBRATES and some marine invertebrates, which, at some stage in their lives, have rod-like, cartilaginous supporting structures (notochords). Invertebrate chordates are divided into three subphyla: TUNICATES (seasquirts), Cephalochordata (amphioxus), and Hemichordata (acorn worms).

**chorus** In Greek tragedy, the *choros* danced and chanted commentary. Today, the term refers to a group of voices. Major works with chorus parts include CANTATAS, OPERAS, and ORATORIOS. *See also* CHOIR

**Chou** Alternative transliteration for the ZHOU dynasty

**Chouteau, (Jean) Pierre** (1758–1849) US fur trader and political figure. With his half-brother, **René Auguste** Chouteau (1749–1829), he controlled the important trade with the Osage Native Americans. In 1796 Chouteau established the first permanent white settlement in Oklahoma. In 1804 he became US agent for the Osage and founded (1809) the St. Louis Missouri Fur Company. His sons, **Auguste Pierre** (1786–1838) and **Pierre** (1789–1865), developed the firm so that by the 1850s it controlled most of the FUR TRADE from the Mississippi to the Rockies.

**Chrétien, Jean (Joseph-Jacques)** (1934– ) 20th Canadian prime minister (1993– ). He entered Parliament in 1963. Chrétien served under Pierre TRUDEAU before succeeding him as leader of the Liberal Party (1990). In 1993 his populist election campaign secured a landslide victory. His administration was faced with rising unemployment and demands for an independent Quebec. He was reeleted in 1997.

**Chrétien de Troyes** (active 1160–85) Romance writer of N France, noted for his tales of King ARTHUR. He influenced Geoffrey CHAUCER and Thomas MALORY.

**Christ** (Gk. *christos*, anointed one) Epithet for the MESSIAH in Old Testament prophecies. Later applied to JESUS, in recognition that he was the expected Messiah.

**Christchurch** City on South Island, New Zealand; main town of Canterbury. It was founded as a Church of England settlement (1850). The University of Canterbury (1873) is here. Industries: fertilizers, rubber, woolen freight, electrical freight, furniture. Pop. (1993) 312,600.

**christening** *See* BAPTISM

**Christian IV** (1577–1648) King of Denmark and Norway (1588–1648), son of Frederick II. Despite a costly war with Sweden (1611–13) and his disastrous participation (1625–29) in the THIRTY YEARS WAR, Christian's reign brought culture and economic prosperity. He founded OSLO, Norway.

**Christian X** (1870–1947) King of Denmark (1912–47) and Iceland (1919–44), succeeding Frederick VIII. During his reign universal suffrage was established (1915) and social welfare policies were consolidated. Christian defied the Germans during occupation (1940–45).

**Christian** Follower of JESUS CHRIST. The major Christian Churches regard belief in the divinity of Christ and the Holy TRINITY as the minimum requirement for a Christian.

**Christian Democrats** Political group combining Christian conservative principles with progressive social responsibility. Christian Democrats have achieved power in many European countries, notably Germany and Italy. Its political principles include: individual responsibility allied with collective action; social equality within a welfare state; and progress through evolutionary change.

**Christianity** Religion based on faith in JESUS CHRIST as the Son of God. The orthodox Christian faith, summarized in the APOSTLES' and NICENE CREEDS, affirms belief in the TRINITY and Christ's incarnation, atoning death on the cross, resurrection, and ascension. The moral teachings of Jesus are contained in the NEW TESTAMENT. The history of Christianity has been turbulent and often sectarian. The first major SCHISM took place in 1054, when the eastern and western churches separated. The next occurred in the 16th-century REFORMATION, with the split of PROTESTANTISM and the ROMAN CATHOLIC CHURCH. In recent times, the ECUMENICAL MOVEMENT, which aims at the reunion of all Christians, has gained strength. Today, the number of Christians worldwide is estimated at more than one billion.

**Christian Science** (officially Church of Christ Scientist) Religious sect founded in 1879 by Mary Baker EDDY, and based on her book *Science and Health With Key to the Scriptures* (1875). Its followers believe that physical illness and moral problems can only be cured by spiritual and mental activity. They refuse medical treatment. "Divine Mind" is used as a synonym for God. Each human being is regarded as a complete and flawless manifestation of the Divine Mind.

**Christie, Dame Agatha Mary Clarissa** (1891–1976) English author. A prolific and popular writer of DETECTIVE FICTION, *The Mysterious Affair at Styles* (1920) introduced her most famous character, the Belgian detective Hercule

Poirot. *The Murder of Roger Ackroyd* (1926), and *Murder at the Vicarage* (1930) featured the aged sleuth Miss Marple. Other novels include *Murder on the Orient Express* (1934), and *And Then There Were None* (1939). *Curtain* (1975) killed Poirot off. Christie's plays include *The Mousetrap* (1952), the longest-running play in London.

**Christie, Linford** (1960– ) British athlete, b. Jamaica. In the 1992 Olympics, he captained the British men's team and won the 100m gold medal. Christie won another gold in the 1993 World Championship. He won a hat-trick of gold medals in the European Championships (1986, 1990, 1994).

**Christina** (1626–89) Queen of Sweden (1632–54). An intellectual of great energy, she brought foreign scholars, such as DESCARTES, to her court. Ruling a Lutheran country, Christina abdicated to become a Roman Catholic. She tried unsuccessfully to obtain the Polish crown (1667).

**Christmas** Feast in celebration of the birth of JESUS CHRIST, common in Christendom since the 4th century. Although the exact date of Christ's birth is unknown, the feast takes place on December 25. Christmas is also a secular holiday, marked by the exchange of presents.

**Christmas Island** *See* KIRITIMATI

**Christmas Island** Island in the E Indian Ocean, 200mi (320km) S of JAVA. Once under British domination, it was annexed to Australia in 1958. It has important lime phosphate deposits. Area: 52sq mi (135sq km). Pop. (1994 est.) 2,500.

**Christophe, Henri** (1767–1820) Haitian revolutionary leader, president (1806–11), and king (1811–20). Born a free man on the island of Grenada, he participated in the armed struggle against the French in Haiti. Christophe ordered the construction of the citadel of La Ferrière, a fort overlooking CAP-HAITIEN, the building of which cost many Haitian lives.

**Christopher, Saint** Patron saint of ferrymen and travelers. His feast day, July 25, is not officially recognized.

**Christopher, Warren** (1925– ) US statesman, secretary of state (1993–97). He served under President Bill CLINTON. Christopher launched an economic assistance program for Russia, and reopened the Middle East peace negotiations. He was succeeded by Madeline ALBRIGHT.

**chromatic** Musical term used in melodic and harmonic analysis for notes not in the SCALE of the KEY of a passage. Such notes are marked with accidentals; the chords in which they occur are termed chromatic. A chromatic scale is one containing all 12 notes of an octave rather than the seven notes of a DIATONIC scale. *See also* HARMONY; MELODY

**chromatid** Either of the two duplicate strands into which each CHROMOSOME in a biological CELL nucleus divides in the first phase of MITOSIS or MEIOSIS (cell division). The pairs of identical chromatids are separated by a long fibrous structure made of proteins, called a mitotic spindle. The separated chromatids become identical daughter chromosomes of the same kind as those of the parent cell on opposite sides of the nucleus.

**chromatography** Technique of chemical analysis by which substances are separated from one another, identified and measured. All involve a **mobile** phase consisting of a liquid or gaseous mixture of the substances to be separated, and a **stationary** phase consisting of a material that differentially absorbs the substances in the mixture. The two major types are gas chromatography and paper chromatography. *See also* ELECTROPHORESIS

**chromite** ($FeOCr_2O_3$) Black mineral, ferrous chromic oxide, separated from magma in the formation of igneous rock. It is weakly magnetic and opaque. Hardness 5.5; s.g. 4.6.

**chromium** (symbol Cr) Dull gray metal, one of the TRANSITION ELEMENTS, first isolated in 1797. Its chief ore is CHROMITE. Chromium is extensively used as an electroplated coating. Chromium compounds are used in tanning and dyeing. Properties: at.no. 24; at.wt. 51.996; sp.gr. 7.19; m.p. 3,434°F (1,890°C); b.p. 4,842°F (2,672°C); most common isotope $^{52}Cr$ (83.76%).

**chromosome** Structure carrying the genetic information of an organism, found only in the cell nucleus of EUKARYOTES. Thread-like and composed of DNA, chromosomes carry a specific set of GENES. Each species usually has a characteristic number of chromosomes; these occur in pairs, members of which carry identical genes, so that most cells have a DIPLOID number of chromosomes. GAMETES carry a HAPLOID number. *See also* HEREDITY

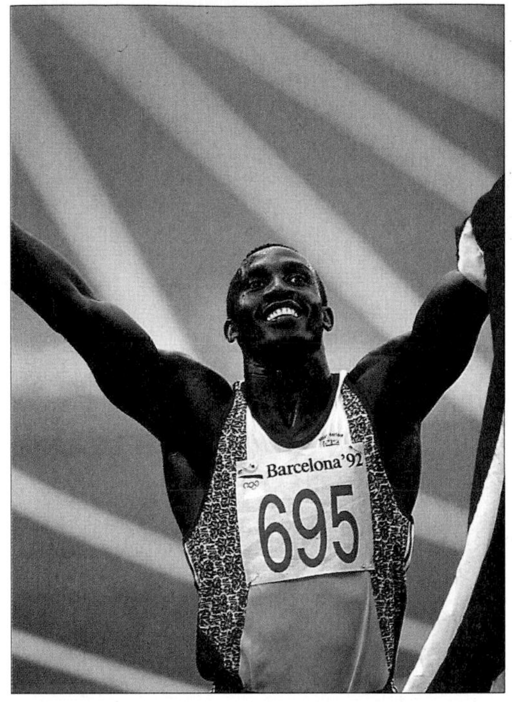


◀ **Christie** Former Olympic and world 100m champion, Linford Christie, despite ruling out competing in the 1996 Olympic games did eventually take part. Although he made the finals of the 100m event, he made three false starts and was automatically disqualified.

**chromosphere** Layer of the SUN's atmosphere between the PHOTOSPHERE and the CORONA. The chromosphere is *c*.6,000mi (10,000km) thick and is normally invisible because of the glare of the photosphere. It is briefly visible near the beginning and end of a total solar eclipse as a spiky red rim around the Moon's disk, and at other times can be studied by SPECTROSCOPY. At its base the temperature of the chromosphere is *c*.4,000K, rising to 100,000K at the top. Powerful magnetic fields are believed to cause this rise in temperature.

**Chronicles** Two historical books of the OLD TESTAMENT. They trace the history of Israel and Judah from the Creation to the return of the Jews from exile in Babylon (538 BC). *See* BABYLONIAN CAPTIVITY

**chrysalis** Intermediate or pupal stage in the life cycle of all insects that undergo complete METAMORPHOSIS. The chrysalis is usually covered with a hard case, but some pupae, such as the silk moth, spin a silk cocoon. Within the chrysalis, the final stages of the development take place. *See also* LEPIDOPTERA

**chrysanthemum** Large genus of annual and perennial

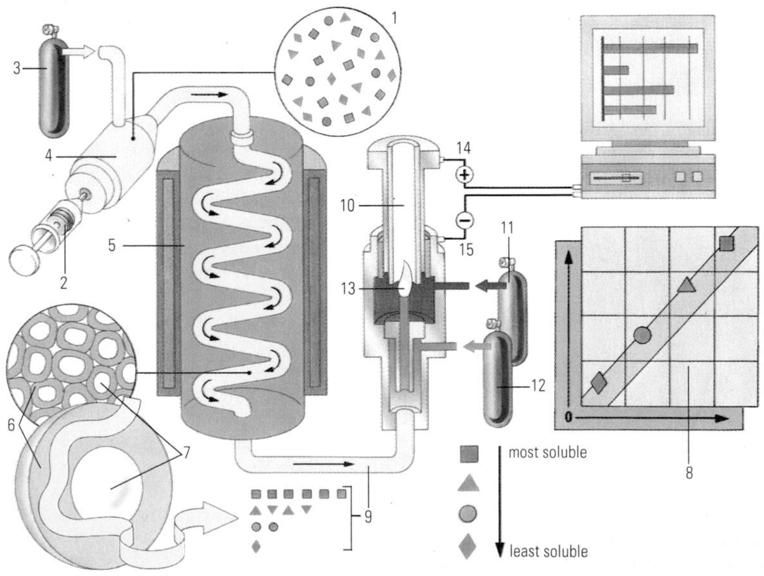


▼ **chromatography** Gas-liquid chromatographs can separate the components of tiny amounts of an unknown mixture. A sample of the mixture (1) is injected (2) into a stream of helium (3), or another inert gas. Heating ensures the vaporized gas mixes fully with the helium. After impurities are removed (4) the gas mixture passes into a tube (5) packed with coated granules of silicon (6). A liquid with a very high boiling point (7) covers the 0.15in (4mm) granules. The components of the vaporized mixture have different solubilities (8) and so pass through the liquid around the silicon, and the whole tube, at different speeds. The whole tube is kept at a high temperature to prevent the vaporized gas condensing. As the now-separated parts of the mixture exit the tube (9) they enter a detector (10). Hydrogen (11) and oxygen (12) are added and the gas stream is then burnt (13). During burning each compound produces ions which pass a charge between an anode (14) and a cathode (15). This charge is measured and can be compared to known results to determine the makeup of the initial mixture.

► **Churchill** During World War II, British prime minister Winston Churchill encouraged a "bulldog" spirit of resistance to the German forces that had amassed in Europe preparing to invade in Britain. His charismatic radio broadcasts and public speeches provided a focus for British patriotism in times of great hardship.

plants that are native to temperate Eurasia and now widely cultivated. Centuries of selective breeding have modified the original plain daisy-like flowers, and most species have large white, yellow, bronze, pink or red flower-heads. Family Asteraceae/COMPOSITAE.

**chub** Freshwater CARP found in flowing waters. It has a large head, wide mouth, and is gray-brown. Length 4–25in (10–60cm). Family Cyprinidae. Chub is also the name of a marine fish of warm seas – oval-shaped with a small mouth and bright colors. Family Kyphosidae.

**Chungking** (Chongqing, Ch'ung-ch'ing) City on the YANGTZE River, s China. From the 14th century AD it was part of a unified China. It became a treaty port in 1891 and was the wartime capital of China (1937–45). It is a transportation and shipping center. Industries: chemicals, steel, iron, silk, cotton. Pop. (1993 est.) 3,780,000.

**church** Community of believers. Although adopted by non-Christian movements, such as SCIENTOLOGY, it is usually refers to CHRISTIANITY. The characteristics of the Christian Church as the whole body of Christ's followers are described in the NICENE CREED. The church is also the name of the building used for worship by Christians. See also CHAPEL; CATHEDRAL

**Churches of God** US Pentecostal religious sect. It grew out of the Later Rain revival that began (1886) in the Great Smokey Mountains led by R.G. Spurling and W.F. Bryant. They preached that a second rain of gifts of the Holy Spirit similar to the first Pentecostal would occur. Members practice speaking in tongues. There have been many splits in the church since its founding. Today, the various sects of the Churches of God have *c*.500,000 members. *See* PENTECOSTAL CHURCHES

**Churchill, Lord Randolph Henry Spencer** (1849–95) British statesman, secretary of state for India (1885–86), chancellor of the exchequer (1886). A gifted speaker and loyal member of the Tory Party, he nevertheless attempted widespread Party reform. Churchill's first budget as chancellor proposed deep cuts in military expenditure and was defeated. He was forced to resign. In 1874 he married Jennie Jerome, a US citizen. Their son, Winston CHURCHILL, achieved the success denied his father.

**Churchill, Sir Winston Leonard Spencer** (1874–1965) British statesman, son of Lord Randolph CHURCHILL. He was a reporter in the SOUTH AFRICAN WARS. Elected to Parliament in 1900 as a Conservative, Churchill joined the Liberals in 1904. As first lord of the admiralty under Herbert ASQUITH, he expanded Britain's navy in preparation for World War I. In LLOYD GEORGE's cabinet, Churchill served as secretary of state for war (1918–21). As colonial secretary (1921–22), he oversaw the creation of the Irish Free State. Churchill returned to power as chancellor of the exchequer (1924–29) in Stanley BALDWIN's Conservative government. On the outbreak of WORLD WAR II, he was reappointed first lord of the admiralty. In 1940 Churchill replaced Neville CHAMBERLAIN as prime minister. He proved an inspiring wartime leader, resolute in his opposition to fascism. Cultivating close relations with President ROOSEVELT, he was the principal architect of the grand alliance of Britain, the US, and the Soviet Union. In 1945 he was succeeded by Clement ATTLEE. In 1950 Churchill was re-elected and reversed some of Labour's nationalizations. He remained an MP until 1964. His writings include a history of World War II and the *History of the English-Speaking Peoples* (1956–58). In 1953 he was awarded the Nobel Prize for literature.

**Church of England** Christian Church in England, established by law in the 16th century. During the reign of King HENRY VIII, a process of separation from the Roman Catholic Church began. The initial impetus for this was the pope's refusal to grant Henry a divorce from CATHERINE OF ARAGON. By the Act of Supremacy (1534), the English monarch became head of the church. As the REFORMATION extended to England, the Church of England finally emerged independent of papal jurisdiction and adopted the Elizabethan Settlement. This agreement, while espousing PROTESTANTISM, aimed at preserving religious unity by shaping a national church acceptable to all persons of moderate theological views. This middle course found expression in the doctrinal *Thirty-nine Articles* (1571). The liturgy of the Church of England is contained in the Book of COMMON PRAYER (1662), but since the 1960s alternative forms of worship have come into use. The sovereign bears the title Supreme Governor of the Church of England, and formally nominates the bishops. The church is episcopally governed, but priests and laity share in all major decisions by virtue of their representation in the General Synod. Territorially, the church is divided into two provinces, Canterbury and York. The archbishop of Canterbury is Primate of All England. The overseas expansion of the Church of England during the period of the growth of the British empire resulted in the gradual development of the worldwide ANGLICAN COMMUNION. The Church of England is the only part of the Anglican Communion still established by law as an official state church. In 1992 the General Synod voted in favor of the ordination of women as priests. The first women priests were ordained in 1994.

**Church of Ireland** Anglican Church in Ireland. It claims to be heir to the ancient Church of the island of Ireland. At the time of the REFORMATION, it ended papal jurisdiction and introduced doctrinal and disciplinary reforms similar to the CHURCH OF ENGLAND. It is territorially divided into two provinces, Armagh and Dublin. The archbishop of Armagh is Primate of All Ireland. It was the legally established Church until 1869.

**Church of Scotland** National non-episcopal form of CHRISTIANITY in Scotland, adopting PRESBYTERIANISM by constitutional act in 1689. The church arose as a separate entity during the REFORMATION. Under the leadership of John KNOX, it abolished papal authority and accepted many of the teachings of John CALVIN. The doctrinal position of the Church is based on the Scottish Confession (1560) and the Westminster Confession of 1643. The highest authority resides in the General Assembly, presided over by an annually elected moderator. The Disruption of 1843 led to about one-third of its ministers and members leaving to form the FREE CHURCH OF SCOTLAND. The Church has *c*.850,000 members.

**CIA** Abbreviation of CENTRAL INTELLIGENCE AGENCY

**cicada** GRASSHOPPER-like insect found in most parts of the world. Males make a loud sound by the vibration of a pair of plates in their abdomen. Females lay eggs in tree branches. The dog-day cicada appears annually in summer. The larvae of the 17-year LOCUST spends up to 17 years in the ground feeding on roots and lives only a week as a winged adult. Length: up to 2in (5cm).

**Cicero, Marcus Tullius** (106–43 BC) Roman politician, philosopher, and orator. A leader of the Senate, he exposed CATILINE's conspiracy (63 BC). Cicero criticized MARK ANTONY, and when Octavian (later AUGUSTUS) came to power Antony persuaded him to have Cicero executed. His fame rests largely on his political philosophy and oratory. Among Cicero's greatest speeches were *Orations Against Catiline* and the *Phillipics*. His rhetorical and philosophical works include *De Amicitia*.

**Cid, El** (1043–99) (Rodrigo Díaz de Vivar) Spanish national hero. He was a knight in the service of the king of Castile, who spent his whole life fighting, often against the Moors. His greatest achievement was the conquest of Valencia (1094), which he ruled until his death. His exploits have been romanticized in Spanish legend.

**cigarette** Roll of shredded TOBACCO wrapped in thin paper for inhalation by smoking. Because of tar, NICOTINE (the addictive substance), and other chemicals in the smoke, cigarettes are highly carcinogenic. However, cigarettes continue to represent a huge industry and source of taxation for governments despite increasing controls, including clear warnings on packets, bans on smoking in public places, and restrictions on advertising.

**cilia** Small, hair-like filaments on cell walls whose wafting motion is used for propulsion or moving matter along a surface. Cilia are present in great quantities on some lining cells of the body, such as those along the respiratory tract. Cilia are also found on single-celled PROTOZOA, known as CILIATES.

**ciliate** Member of the phylum Ciliophora, characterized by hair-like CILIA used for locomotion and food collecting. Ciliates are the largest (*c*.8,000 species) and the most complex of the PROTOZOA. They are found in aquatic and terrestrial habitats and many are carnivorous. Ciliates have two nuclei and a variety of organelles, such as a cystome (mouth). Subclasses include Holotrichs (*Paramecium*), Spirotrichs (*Stentor*), and Peritrichs (*Vorticella*).

**Cimabue, Giovanni** (*c*.1240–*c*.1302) Florentine painter, an important transitional link between the rigid Byzantine style of painting and the greater realism of the 14th-century School of Florence. His best-known work is *Madonna and Child Enthroned*.

**Cimarosa, Domenico** (1749–1801) Italian composer. He wrote more than 60 operas, the best-known of which is the opera buffa *The Secret Marriage* (1792). Cimarosa also wrote seven cantatas and six oratorios.

**cinchona** Genus of evergreen trees native to the Andes and grown in South America, Indonesia, and Zaire. The dried bark of the trees is a source of QUININE and other medicinal products. Family Rubiaceae.

**Cincinnati** City on the Ohio River, SW Ohio. Originally named Losantiville, it grew around Fort Washington (established 1789). The completion (1832) of the Miami and Erie Canal made the city a shipping center for farm produce, and the railroad arrived in 1880. Cincinnati has a university (1819). Industries: machine tools, soap products, brewing, meat packing. Pop. (1990) 364,040.

**cine camera** Apparatus that takes a number of consecutive still photographs or frames, on film. The illusion of motion is created when the developed film is projected on to a screen. Big-screen cine cameras use 70mm cine film, most professional cameras 35mm, and some smaller cameras 16 or 8mm. *See also* CINEMA; CINEMATOGRAPHY; PHOTOGRAPHY; VIDEO RECORDING

**cinema** Motion pictures as an industry and artistic pursuit. For much of its history cinema has been commercially dominated by HOLLYWOOD. Public showings of silent moving pictures, with live musical accompaniment, began in the 1890s, but speech was not heard in a full-length film until *The Jazz Singer* (1927). By then cinema was big business with mass appeal. D.W. GRIFFITH's *The Birth of a Nation* (1915) used innovative close-ups and editing techniques. In Russia, EISENSTEIN used MONTAGE to enhance his political message. In Germany, the influence of EXPRESSIONISM on the work of Fritz LANG further revealed the creative possibilities of the medium. Technicolor was introduced in 1933, but black-and-white was the dominant medium until the 1950s. The growth of television in the US during the 1950s profoundly altered film economics; the decline of Hollywood led to the rise of the independent producer and director. Experiments in framing, such as CINEMASCOPE and CINERAMA, attempted to draw audiences back to the cinema. FILM NOIR in the US and NEOREALISM in Europe explored in different ways the social and psychological effects of World War II. In the 1960s NOUVELLE VAGUE used faster film stocks and more mobile cameras to develop the notions of the AUTEUR and CINEMA VERITÉ. In the 1970s and 1980s the box-office success of Steven SPIELBERG and the development of VIDEO revolutionized the motion picture industry. In the 1990s the development of computer-generated images has brought a new dimension to film. *See also* ANIMATION, CINEMA; CINE CAMERA; CINEMATOGRAPHY; DOCUMENTARY; PHOTOGRAPHY

**cinematography** Technique of taking and projecting cine film, the basis of the CINEMA industry. Based on the inventions pioneered during the 1880s and 1890s by Thomas EDISON in the US and the LUMIÈRE brothers in France, cinematography was applied professionally soon after the turn of the century.

**cinéma vérité** Style of film-making, popular during the 1960s, but first practiced by Dziga Vertov in the 1920s. It attempted to record truthful action, employing a documentary-like style, often using 16mm cameras. The style was also used in dramas, particularly by François TRUFFAUT and Jean-Luc GODARD.

**cinnamon** Light-brown SPICE made from the dried inner bark of the cinnamon tree. Its delicate aroma and sweet flavor make it a common ingredient in food. It was also used for religious rites and witchcraft. The tree is a bushy evergreen native to India and Burma and cultivated in the West Indies and South America. Family Lauraceae; species *Cinnamomum zeylanicum*.

**cipher** *See* CRYPTOGRAPHY

**circadian rhythm** Internal "clock" mechanism found in most organisms that normally corresponds roughly with the 24-hour day. It relates most obviously to the cycle of waking and sleeping, but is also involved in other cyclic variations, such as body temperature.

**Circe** In Greek mythology, seductive but baleful enchantress whose spells could change men into animals. Mistress of the island of Aeaea, she kept ODYSSEUS with her for a year, changing his men into pigs.

**circle** Plane geometric figure that is the locus of points equidistant from a fixed point (the center). This distance is the radius ($r$). The area of a circle is $\pi r^2$ and its perimeter (circumference) is $2\pi r$.

**circuit** System of electric conductors, appliances, or electronic components connected so they form a continuously conducting path. Modern circuits are often printed in copper on a plastic card (printed circuit). *See also* CAPACITOR; INTEGRATED CIRCUIT (IC); SILICON CHIP; TRANSISTOR

**circulation, atmospheric** Flow of the ATMOSPHERE around the Earth. The poleward circulation due to CONVECTION, gives rise to large-scale eddies such as the CYCLONE and ANTICYCLONE, low-pressure troughs, and high-pressure ridges. The eddies are also caused by the Earth's rotation maintaining easterly winds towards the Equator and westerly winds towards the poles.

**circulatory system** Means by which oxygen and nutrients are carried to the body's tissues, and carbon dioxide and other waste products are removed. It consists of BLOOD VESSELS that carry the BLOOD, propelled by the pumping action of the HEART. In humans and other mammals, blood travels to the lungs, where it picks up OXYGEN and loses CARBON DIOXIDE. It then flows to the heart, from where it is pumped out into the AORTA, which branches into smaller arteries, arterioles, and CAPILLARIES. Oxygen and other nutrients diffuse out of the blood, and carbon dioxide and other tissue wastes pass into the capillaries, which join to form veins leading back to the heart. Blood then returns to the lungs and the entire cycle is repeated. In fish and many other animals, there is a single circulatory system, with blood passing through the GILLS and on to the rest of the body without an extra boost from the heart. Insects and many other invertebrates have an open circulatory system,

▲ **cinchona** The medicinal significance of the 40 or so species of the genus *Cinchona* lies in its bark which yields quinine and cinchona. Until relatively recently, quinine was the major drug used in the treatment and prevention of malaria, while cinchona eased coughs. However with ever increasingly sophisticated ways of synthesizing natural products, cheaper synthetic drugs are now available.

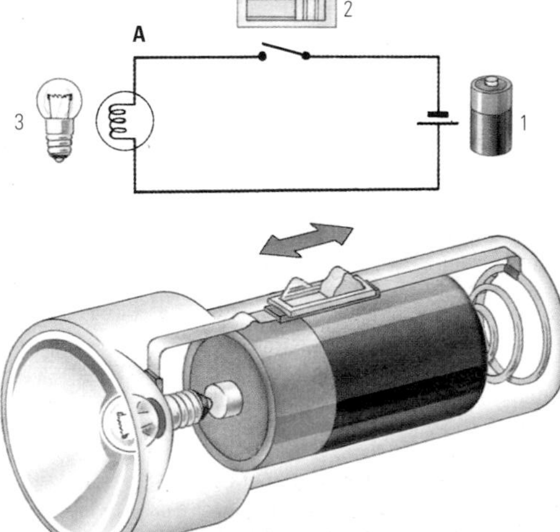


◄ **circuit** This simple electric circuit (A) represents a flashlight. The power source is a battery (1) The switch (2) breaks the circuit when it is in the off position. When closed, in the on position, power flows to the resistor (3), the bulb, which emits light.

► **citrus** Most fruits belonging to the genus *Citrus* originated in China and SE Asia. The fruits are commercially important throughout the world, and some hybrids have been created to increase the number of varieties available. The orange (1) is probably the most economically important and popular citrus fruit. It is sweet and contains a great amount of vitamin C. The grapefruit (2) is less sweet, but also popular and has been crossed with the tangerine to produce the sweet, juicy fruit known as the ugli (3). The lemon (4) is one of the few citrus fruits with a sour taste. Rather than eaten as a whole fruit, the lemon is used most frequently to flavor other foods and drinks.

where the blood flows freely within the body cavity, but passes through a series of open blood vessels and heart(s).

**circumcision** Operation of removing part or the whole of the foreskin of the penis or of removing the clitoris. Male circumcision is ritual in some groups, notably Jews and Muslims, and is believed to have sanitary benefits. Female circumcision (genital mutilation) is intended to reduce sexual pleasure and has no medical benefit.

**circumference** Distance around the boundary of a plane geometric figure, nearly always applied to a circle, for which it has the value $2\pi r$, where $r$ is the radius.

**circumnavigation** Voyage around the world. It was first accomplished in 1519–22 by the *Victoria*, from the expedition commanded by Ferdinand MAGELLAN. Magellan died during the voyage.

**cire perdue** (Fr. lost wax) Method of casting metal objects (usually bronzes) used since classical antiquity. First the object is covered in wax then covered in a heat-proof mold. When heated the wax melts away and the metal is poured into the space it occupied.

**cirrhosis** Degenerative disease with excessive growth of fibrous tissue in an organ, most often the LIVER, causing inflammation and scarring. Cirrhosis of the liver may be caused by viral hepatitis, prolonged obstruction of the common bile duct, chronic abuse of alcohol or other drugs, blood disorder, heart failure, or malnutrition.

**Cistercian** Religious order of monks founded by St. Robert of Molesme (1098), based on ideals of strict Benedictinism. A community dedicated to contemplation, the Cistercians were noted agricultural pioneers. *See also* BENEDICTINES; TRAPPISTS

**citric acid** ($C_6H_8O_7$) Colorless, crystalline solid with a sour taste. It is found in a free form in citrus fruits such as lemons and oranges, and is used for flavoring, in effervescent salts, and as a mordant (color-fixer) in dyeing. Properties: sp.gr. 1.54; m.p. 307.4°F (153°C).

**citron** Evergreen shrub or small tree of the rue family, native to Asia. It has short spines and oval leaves. It bares large, oblong, lemon-yellow fruit. Height: up to 11.5ft (3.5m). Family Rutaceae; species *Citrus medica*.

**citrus** Group of trees and shrubs of the genus *Citrus* in the rue family, native to subtropical regions. They include GRAPEFRUIT, kumquat, LEMON, LIME, ORANGE, MANDARIN, tangerine, and ugli. The stems are usually thorny, the leaves bright green, shiny, and pointed. The flowers are usually white, waxy, and fragrant. The fruit (hesperidium) is usually ovoid with a thick, aromatic rind. The inside of the fruit is pulpy and juicy and is divided into segments that contain the seeds. Most citrus fruits contain significant amounts of vitamin C. Family Rutaceae.

**Ciudad Juárez** City on the Rio Bravo del Norte (Río Grande), Chihuahua state, N Mexico. Lying between the US–Mexico borders, it is connected by bridges to El Paso, Texas. It has processing industries for the surrounding cotton-growing region. Pop. (1990) 798,499.

**civet** (civet cat) Small, nocturnal, carnivorous mammal, related to the GENET and MONGOOSE, found in Africa, Asia, and S Europe. It has a narrow body set on long legs, and its coat is gray-yellow with black markings. There are *c.*20 species. Length: (overall) 21–59in (53–150cm). Family Viverridae.

**civil engineering** Field of engineering dealing with large structures and systems. Civil engineers provide facilities for living, industry, and transportation, such as roads, bridges, airports, dams, harbors, and tunnels.

**Civilian Conservation Corps (CCC)** US organization established in 1933 to provide employment for young men aged 18 to 25 during the Depression. As part of the NEW DEAL, more than two million men in 1,500 camps were engaged in conservation work.

**civil law** Legal system derived from ROMAN LAW. It is different from COMMON LAW, the system generally adhered to in England and other English-speaking countries. Civil law is based on a system of codes, the most famous of which is the CODE NAPOLÉON (1804), and decisions are precisely worked out from general basic principles *a priori*. Thus, a civil law judge follows the evidence and is bound by the conditions of the written law and not by previous judicial interpretation. Civil law influences common law in jurisprudence and in admiralty, testamentary, and domestic relations; it is also the basis for the system of EQUITY. It is prevalent in Louisiana, Quebec (Canada), Latin America, and continental Europe.

**civil liberties** Basic rights that every citizen possesses in a democracy. In some countries, the courts ensure freedom from government control or restraint, except as the public good may require. *See also* CIVIL RIGHTS

**civil rights** Rights conferred legally upon the individual by the state. There is no universal conception of civil rights. The modern use of the phrase is most common in the US, where it refers to relations between individuals as well as between individuals and the state. It is especially associated with the movement to achieve equal rights for African-Americans. The modern civil rights movement may be said to have begun with the foundation (1910) of the NATIONAL ASSOCIATION FOR THE ADVANCEMENT OF COLORED PEOPLE (NAACP). It gathered pace after the 1954 Supreme Court decision against segregation in schools, and the foundation of organizations such as the CONGRESS OF RACIAL EQUALITY (CORE), the Southern Christian Leadership Conference led by Martin Luther KING, Jr., and the Student Nonviolent Coordinating Committee (SNCC). Subsequently, a series of CIVIL RIGHTS ACTS protected individuals from discrimination.

**Civil Rights Acts** (1866, 1870, 1875, 1957, 1960, 1964, 1968) US legislation. The **Civil Rights Act** (1866) gave African Americans citizenship and extended civil rights to all persons born in the US (except Native Americans). The **1870 Act** was passed to reenact the previous measure, which was considered to be of dubious constitutionality. The 1870 Act was declared unconstitutional by the US Supreme Court in 1883. The **1875 Act** was passed to outlaw discrimination in public places because of race or previous servitude. The Act was declared unconstitutional by the Supreme Court (1883–85), which stated that the 14th Amendment protected individual rights against infringement by states, not by other individuals. The **1957 Act** established the Civil Rights Commission to investigate violations of the 15th Amendment. The **1960 Act** enabled court-appointed federal officials to protect African-American voting rights. An act of violence to obstruct a court order became a federal offense. The **1964 Act** established as law equal rights for all citizens in voting, education, public accommodations, and in federally assisted programs. The **1968 Act** guaranteed equal treatment in housing and real estate to all citizens.

**Civil Rights Commission** Federal commission that investigates complaints alleging that citizens are being deprived of their right to vote because of their race, color, religion, sex, or national origin, or, in the case of federal elections, by fraudulent practices. It submits reports of its activities, findings, and recommendations to the president and Congress.

**civil service** Administrative establishment for carrying on the work of government. In the US, the civil service evolved from the ineffective "SPOILS SYSTEM" (1828) established during Andrew JACKSON's presidency, whereby posts were given as rewards for political support. This system remained in place until the Pendleton Act (1883) created the Civil Service Commission. The commission implemented a merit system, and following the Hatch Acts (1939, 1940), federal employees were no longer allowed to take an active role in party politics. In Britain the civil service was developed between 1780 and 1870, as the burden of Parliamentary business became too heavy for ministers to deal with policy-making and administration.

**Civil War** (1861–65) War fought between the northern states (the Union) and the forces of the 11 southern states which seceded from the Union to form the CONFEDERATE STATES OF AMERICA (the Confederacy). Its immediate cause was the determination of the southern states to withdraw from a Union that the northern states regarded as indivisible. The more general cause was the question of slavery, a well-established institution in the South but one that the northern ABOLITIONISTS opposed. By the 1850s slavery, abolition, and STATES' RIGHTS had created insurmountable differences between North and South. The abolitionists formed the new REPUBLICAN PARTY and those campaigning for the rights of southern states remained in the DEMOCRATIC PARTY. The 1860 election of a Republican, Abraham LINCOLN, virtually assured southern withdrawal from the Union. The North had superior numbers, greater economic power, and command of the seas. The Confederates had passionate conviction, were fighting for their homeland, and, at least early in the war, had superior generals, such as Robert E. LEE and "Stonewall" JACKSON. The war began on April 12, 1861 when Confederate forces attacked FORT SUMTER, South Carolina. The Union's first objective was to take the Confederate capital at Richmond, Virginia, in the First Battle of BULL RUN (July 1861). This campaign was unsuccessful, and the Confederates continued to be victorious, with Lee winning the PENINSULAR CAMPAIGN (April–June 1862) and Jackson victorious in the Shenandoah Valley (March–June 1862). The Confederates were also successful in the SEVEN DAYS' BATTLES (June–July 1862) and the Second Battle of BULL RUN (August 1862). However, Lee's army was checked by the strengthening Union troops (led by General George MCCLELLAN) in the Battle of ANTIETAM (September 1862). The Union was defeated at the Battle of FREDERICKSBURG (December 1862) under Ambrose BURNSIDE and at CHANCELLORSVILLE (May 1863) under Joseph HOOKER. The Union victory in the Battle of GETTYSBURG (June–July 1863) was a turning point. The Union Navy had blocked southern ports, thereby denying the Confederacy essential trade with Europe. The Union strategy was to divide the South by taking control of the Mississippi, Tennessee, and Cumberland rivers. The first big Union victory was at Fort Donelson on the Tennessee River (February 1862) under the command of Ulysses S. GRANT. Grant won a victory in the siege of VICKSBURG (November 1862–July 1863) which, with the fall of Memphis (June 1862), gave Union troops control of the Mississippi. In 1864 Grant became supreme commander. He confronted Lee's army in the WILDERNESS CAMPAIGN (May–June 1864) and began the long siege of Petersburg, Virginia – the defense of which was vital to the survival of RICHMOND. Meanwhile, the Union's General William T. SHERMAN cut a devastating swathe across Georgia in 1864, burning ATLANTA on the way. The Union victory at the Battle of Five Forks (1865) blocked the retreat route for Confederate troops in Richmond. Petersburg fell two days later, and Richmond was indefensible. The war ended with Lee's surrender to Grant at APPOMATTOX Court House in April 1865. The Civil War claimed *c.*620,000 lives, more than the combined American dead from all other wars between 1775 and 1975. The Union lost c.360,000 soldiers, and the Confederacy c.260,000. The South was economically ruined by the war, and RECONSTRUCTION policies poisoned relations between North and South for a century.

**Civil Wars, English** (1642–45, 1648, 1651) Conflicts in Britain between Crown and Parliament. Following years of dispute between the king and state over the power of the crown, war began when King CHARLES I raised his standard at Nottingham. Royalist forces were at first successful at Edgehill (1642) but there were no decisive engagements, and Parliament's position was stronger, as it controlled the SE, London, and the navy, and formed an alliance with Scotland. Parliament's victory at Marston Moor (1644) was a turning point, and in 1645 FAIRFAX and Oliver CROMWELL won a decisive victory at Naseby with their NEW MODEL ARMY. Charles surrendered in 1646. While negotiating with Parliament, he secretly secured an agreement with the Scots that led to what is usually called the second civil war (1648). A few local Royalist risings came to nothing, and the Scots, invading England, were swiftly defeated. The execution of Charles I (1649) provoked further conflict in 1650, in which Scots and Irish Royalists supported the future CHARLES II. Cromwell suppressed the Irish and the Scots, the final battle being fought at Worcester (1651).

**Civil War, Spanish** (1936–39) Conflict developing from a military rising against the republican government in Spain. The revolt began in Spanish Morocco, led by General FRANCO. It was supported by conservatives and reactionaries of many kinds, collectively known as the Nationalists and including the fascist FALANGE. The leftist, POPULAR FRONT government was supported by republicans, socialists, and a variety of ill-coordinated leftist groups, collectively known as Loyalists or Republicans. The Nationalists swiftly gained control of most of rural W Spain. The war represented the first major clash between the forces of the extreme right and the extreme left in Europe. Franco received extensive military support, especially aircraft, from the fascist dictators MUSSOLINI AND HITLER. The Soviet Union provided more limited aid for the Republicans. Liberal and socialist sympathizers from countries such as Britain and France fought as volunteers for the Republicans, but their governments remained neutral. The Nationalists extended their control in 1937, while the Republicans were weakened by internal quarrels. In 1938 the Nationalists reached the Mediterranean, splitting the Republicans' forces. The fall of Madrid to the Nationalists, after a long siege, in March 1939 ended the war. More than one million Spaniards had been killed.

**Cixi** (1835–1908) (Tz'u Hsi or Zi Xi) Empress Dowager of China. As mistress of the Emperor Xian Feng and mother of his only son, she became co-regent in 1861 and remained in power until her death by arranging for the succession of her infant nephew in 1875 and displacing him in a palace coup in 1898. Ruthless and reactionary, she abandoned the modernization programme of the "Hundred Days of Reform" and supported the BOXER REBELLION (1900).

**clam** Bivalve mollusk found mainly in marine waters. It is usually partly buried in sand or mud. With a large foot for burrowing, its soft, flat body lies between two muscles for opening and closing the shells. A fleshy part called the mantle, lies next to the shells. Clams feed on PLANKTON. Class Pelecypoda.

**Clapham Sect** (*c.*1790–*c.*1830) Group of British evangelical reformers. Many of them, including William WILBERFORCE, lived in Clapham, S London, and several were members of Parliament. Originally known as the "Saints," they were especially influential in the abolition of SLAVERY and in prison reform.

**Clare, John** (1793–1864) English poet. The son of an agricultural laborer, his verse contained vivid descriptions of the countryside from the viewpoint of a class that seldom found a poetic voice. His works include *Poems Descriptive of Rural Life and Scenery* (1820), *The Village Minstrel* (1821), and *The Rural Muse* (1835). Briefly lionized as a "peasant" poet, he was declared insane in 1837.

**Clare** County between Galway Bay and the Shannon River estuary, Munster province, W Republic of Ireland; the county

▼ **Civil War** Loyalties to South or North crossed state lines and divided families during the Civil War. Three of Abraham Lincoln's brothers-in-law died fighting for the Confederates. The "border states," the slave states of Kentucky, Maryland, and Missouri, were most divided. Their allegiance to the "Stars and Stripes" proved to be stronger than their purely regional interests.

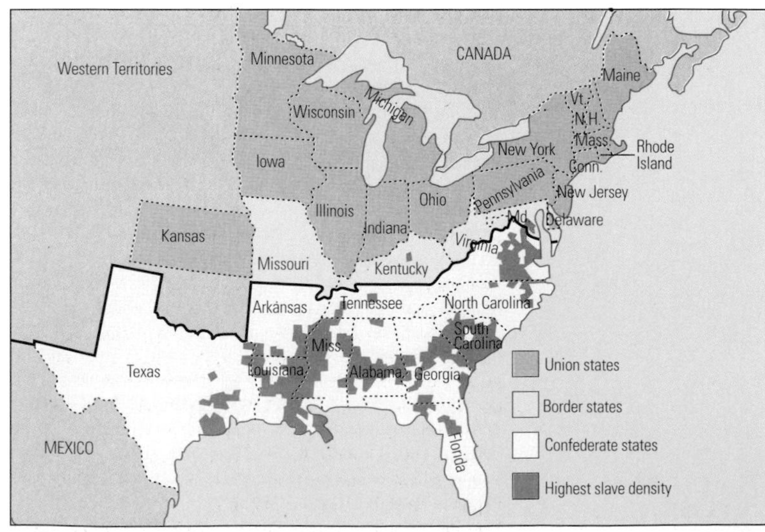

town is Ennis. The area is hilly and infertile. The chief crops are oats and potatoes. Sheep, cattle, pigs, and poultry are raised. Area: 1,231sq mi (3,188sq km). Pop. (1991) 90,918.

**Clarendon, Edward Hyde, 1st earl of** (1609–74) British statesman and historian. A leading adviser to Charles I, he joined Charles II in exile, and negotiated the Restoration (1660). As chief minister to Charles II, he initiated (but disapproved of) four statutes collectively known as the Clarendon Code. The statutes restricted gatherings of Puritans and Nonconformists, and the movement of their ministers. In addition, all ministers were forced to use the Anglican Book of Common Prayer. Following disagreements with Charles II he was impeached and forced into exile in 1667, where he completed his *History of the Rebellion*. *See also* Nonconformism

**Clarendon, Constitutions of** (1164) Sixteen articles issued by Henry II of England to limit the powers of the church. The most controversial article required clergy who had been convicted in church courts to be punished by royal courts. They played a significant role in the dispute between Henry and Thomas à Becket.

**clarinet** Single-reed woodwind instrument. It is commonly pitched in B♭ and has a range of over 3 octaves. Other members of the family include the alto clarinet in E♭, the bass in B♭, and the high sopranino in E♭.

**Clark, George Rogers** (1752–1818) US revolutionary general. In 1778 Clark led an expedition from Kentucky against the British in Illinois country, capturing Kaskaskia, Cahokia, and Vincennes. His conquests were responsible for gaining the Midwestern territories for the US.

**Clarke, Arthur C. (Charles)** (1917– ) British science-fiction writer. He is noted for the realism of his works, such as *Childhood's End* (1953), and *Voices from the Sky* (1965). Stanley Kubrick's film *2001: A Space Odyssey* (1969) was based on his short story *The Sentinel* (1951). Clarke has written two sequels, *2010: Odyssey Two* (1982), and *2061: Odyssey Three* (1987).

**class** In social science, a section of society sharing similar socio-economic status. A person's class is usually determined by the income and wealth of their parents. A class society is a system based on the unequal distribution of wealth. In Marxism, class is defined in relation to the means of production (land, capital). The bourgeoisie own the means of production and the proletariat provide the labour. In the *Communist Manifesto* (1848), Karl Marx and Friedrich Engels asserted that "the history of all society to date is the history of class struggle."

**classical** Term used in many different and apparently conflicting ways. Literally, it refers to the period between the Archaic and the Hellenistic phases of ancient Greek culture. It is used more generally, however, to mean the opposite of romantic or to refer to the artistic styles whose origins can be traced in ancient Greece or Rome. As the antithesis of romanticism, it is an art which follows recognized aesthetic formulas rather than a style which focuses on individual expression. The Renaissance architect, Alberti, took his inspiration from ancient Greek and Roman buildings and classicism often suggests descent from antique sources. A classical style of Greek and Roman architecture dominated Europe from 1500 to 1900.

**classical economics** Term applied to the work of British economists from the late-18th to the mid-19th century. Classical economists range from Adam Smith to John Stuart Mill. They maintained that if left to their own devices, without the interference of government, markets would find a natural equilibrium. *See also* capitalism; laissez-faire; Malthus, Thomas

**classical music** Music composed between *c.*1750 and *c.*1820, whose style is characterized by emotional restraint, the dominance of homophonic melodies (melodies with accompaniment), and clear structures and forms underlying the music. The classical period saw the development of forms such as concerto, sonata, symphony, and string quartet, and the piano replace the harpsichord. The greatest composers of this period were Haydn, Mozart, Beethoven, and Schubert.

**classical revival** Art and architecture in the style of the Ancient Greeks and Romans. The style reflects simplicity, harmony, and balance. The Italian Renaissance and the neoclassical style of the early 19th century are examples of classical revivals. *See also* classicism; neoclassicism

**classicism** Art history term used for an aesthetic attitude and an artistic tradition. The artistic tradition refers to the classical antiquity of Greece and Rome, its art, literature, and criticism, and the subsequent periods that looked back to it for their prototypes, such as the Carolingian Renaissance, Renaissance, and neoclassicism. Its aesthetic use suggests the classical characteristics of clarity, order, balance, unity, symmetry, and dignity.

**classification** *See* taxonomy

**Claude Lorrain** (*c.*1604–82) (Claude Gellée) French landscape painter, the most influential ideal landscapist. After settling in Rome (1627), he developed a style that combined poetic idealism and his own observations. His mature style evolved between 1640 and 1660, when he explored the natural play of light on different textures. Turner was among those to absorb his ideas, and he inspired the style known as picturesque.

**Claudius I** (10 BC–AD 54) (Tiberius Claudius Nero Germanicus) Roman emperor (AD 41–54), nephew of Tiberius. Claudius was the first emperor chosen by the army. He had military successes in Germany, conquered Britain in AD 43, and built both the harbor of Ostia and the Claudian aqueduct. Agrippina the Younger (his fourth wife) supposedly poisoned him and made her son, Nero, emperor.

**Clausius, Rudolf Julius Emanuel** (1822–88) German physicist, regarded as the founder of thermodynamics. Clausius was the first to formulate the second law of thermodynamics that heat cannot pass from a colder to a hotter object. He also introduced the term entropy.

**clavichord** Earliest stringed instrument with mechanical action controlled by a keyboard. Possibly originating in the 13th century, it was used extensively from the 16th–18th centuries. The clavichord has a delicate, tone; it was superseded by the harpsichord.

**clavicle** (collarbone) Thin, slightly curved bone attached by ligaments to the top of the sternum (breast-bone). The clavicle and shoulder-blade make up the shoulder girdle, linking the arms to the axis of the body.

**Clay, Cassius Marcellus** Former name of Muhammad Ali

**Clay, Henry** (1777–1852) US statesman. He served in both the House of Representatives (1811–14, 1815–21, 1823–25), several times as speaker, and in the Senate (1831–42, 1849–52). Clay was one of the "war hawks" who favored the War of 1812. He ran for president (1824), and when the election went to the House of Representatives, he supported John Quincy Adams. When Adams named Clay secretary of state (1825–29), charges of political corruption were made. One of the founders of the Whig Party, he ran against Andrew Jackson in 1832. He ran for president again (1844) but was defeated by James Polk. Clay's last years in the Senate were spent trying to work out a compromise between the slave-owning states of the South and the free northern states. The Compromise of 1850 was one result of those efforts.

**cleavage** In embryology, progressive series of cell divisions that transform a fertilized egg into the earliest embryonic stage (blastula). The egg is divided into blastomeres (smaller cells), each containing a diploid number of chromosomes.

**cleft palate** Congenital deformity in which there is an opening in the roof of the mouth, causing direct communication between the nasal and mouth cavities. It is often associated with harelip and makes normal speech difficult. Usual treatment includes surgery, special dental care, and speech therapy if necessary.

**clematis** Genus of perennial, mostly climbing shrubs found worldwide. Many have attractive deep blue, violet, white, pink, or red flowers or flower clusters. The leaves are usually compound. Family Ranunculaceae.

**Clemenceau, Georges** (1841–1929) French statesman, premier (1906–09, 1917–20). A moderate republican, he served in the Chamber of Deputies (1876–1893), favored compromise in the revolt of the Paris Commune (1871) and strongly supported Dreyfus. Clemenceau returned to the Senate in 1902. Concerned with the growing power of Germany, his first term as premier saw the strengthening of relations with Britain. He was succeeded by Aristide Briand. After World War I Clemenceau returned to power and led the French delegation at the Versailles peace conference. *See also* Dreyfus Affair

**Clement I, Saint** (active late 1st century AD) (Clement of Rome) Pope (*c*.88–*c*.97). His epistle to the church at Corinth (*c*.96) stated the need for unity within the church. Clement was probably martyred. His feast day is 23 November.

**Clement VII** (1478–1534) Pope (1523–34), b. Giulio de Medici. He sided with FRANCIS I in the League of Cognac, thus opposing the Holy Roman emperor CHARLES V. The imperial troops attacked Rome, and a compromise was won. Clement was unable to deal with the rise of Protestantism and his indecisiveness over the divorce of Catherine of Aragon and HENRY VIII is thought to have hastened the REFORMATION in England.

**Cleopatra** (69–30 BC) Queen of Egypt (51–30 BC). In 47 BC she overthrew her husband, brother, and coruler Ptolemy XIII with the aid of Julius CAESAR, who became her lover. Cleopatra went to Rome with Caesar, but after his assassination in 44 BC she returned to Alexandria, once again as queen. MARK ANTONY, who had become her lover following Caesar's death, followed her to Egypt, and they married (37 BC). The marriage infuriated Octavian (later AUGUSTUS), the brother of Mark Antony's former wife. Rome declared war on Egypt in 31 BC and defeated Antony and Cleopatra's forces at the Battle of ACTIUM. Mark Antony committed suicide. Cleopatra surrendered to Octavian but then killed herself.

**Cleopatra's needles** Popular name for two Egyptian obelisks of red granite that were acquired separately in the 1870s. Erected by King Thutmose III in Egypt in the 15th century BC, they are nearly 70ft (21m) tall and weigh *c*.180 tons. One stands in New York's Central Park, the other on the Thames Embankment, London, UK.

**clergy** Collective organization of ordained or consecrated priests and ministers, especially of the Christian church. In the Roman Catholic, Orthodox, and Anglican churches, the clergy comprise the orders of bishop, priest, and deacon, and may also include members of religious orders. In these churches, bishops exercise authority over priests and deacons. In nonepiscopal Protestant churches, the clergy consist of pastors and ministers. Functions of the clergy include administration of the sacrament, preaching, and the exercise of spiritual guidance. *See also* ORDINATION OF WOMEN

**Cleveland, (Stephen) Grover** (1837–1908) 22nd and 24th US president (1885–89, 1893–97). He rose to prominence as a reforming Democratic mayor of Buffalo (1881–82) and governor of New York (1883–84). With the help of Republican MUGWUMPS, Cleveland defeated James G. BLAINE to become the first Democratic president since the Civil War. His attempt to reduce the tariff contributed to Benjamin HARRISON's electoral victory in 1888. In his second term, Cleveland was faced with a monetary crisis (1893), and secured repeal of the Sherman Silver Purchase Act. He sent troops to crush the Pullman Strike (1894) called by Eugene V. DEBS. His attempt to maintain the gold standard angered radical Democrats. Cleveland was not renominated in 1896.

**Cleveland** City and port at the mouth of the Cuyahoga River, on Lake Erie, NE Ohio. Founded in 1796 by Moses Cleaveland, it grew rapidly with the opening of the Ohio and Erie Canal and the arrival of the railroad in 1851. John D. Rockefeller founded Standard Oil Company here in 1870. Cleveland has a symphony orchestra, three universities, and an art institute. It is a major Great Lakes shipping port, and an iron and steel center. NASA maintains a research center here. Industries: chemicals, oil refining, engineering, electronics. Pop. (1990) 505,616.

**click language** Any of several southern African languages belonging chiefly to the Khoisan group and characterized by the use of suction speech sounds called clicks. Clicks are also found in some Bantu languages.

**client-server** Type of relationship between computers in a COMPUTER NETWORK. A client computer makes requests of a designated server computer. The server performs the requested functions and delivers the results.

**Cliff, Clarice** (1899–1972) English ART DECO pottery designer. Cliff created geometrically shaped ceramics, decorated with bold, brightly colored abstract designs. Extremely popular in the 1930's, her innovative work was sold under the title "Bizarre."

**climate** Weather conditions of a place or region prevailing over a long time. The major factors influencing climate are temperature, air movement, incoming and outgoing radiation, and moisture movements.

**climate change** *See* GLOBAL WARMING

**climate modeling** Use of a computer to simulate the Earth's climate. Physical data, such as temperature, pressure and wind direction, are manipulated mathematically by a powerful computer to give a model of the Earth's whole climatic system. Researchers can vary various parameters to see what changes occur. In this way they can study the effects of the greenhouse effect and possible global warming. *See also* CHAOS THEORY

**climatology** Scientific study of the Earth's climates. Physical climatology investigates relationships between temperature, pressure, winds, precipitation, and other weather phenomena. Regional climatology considers latitude and other geographical factors, such as the influence of large land masses.

▼ **climate** The map shows the world's various major climatic regions.

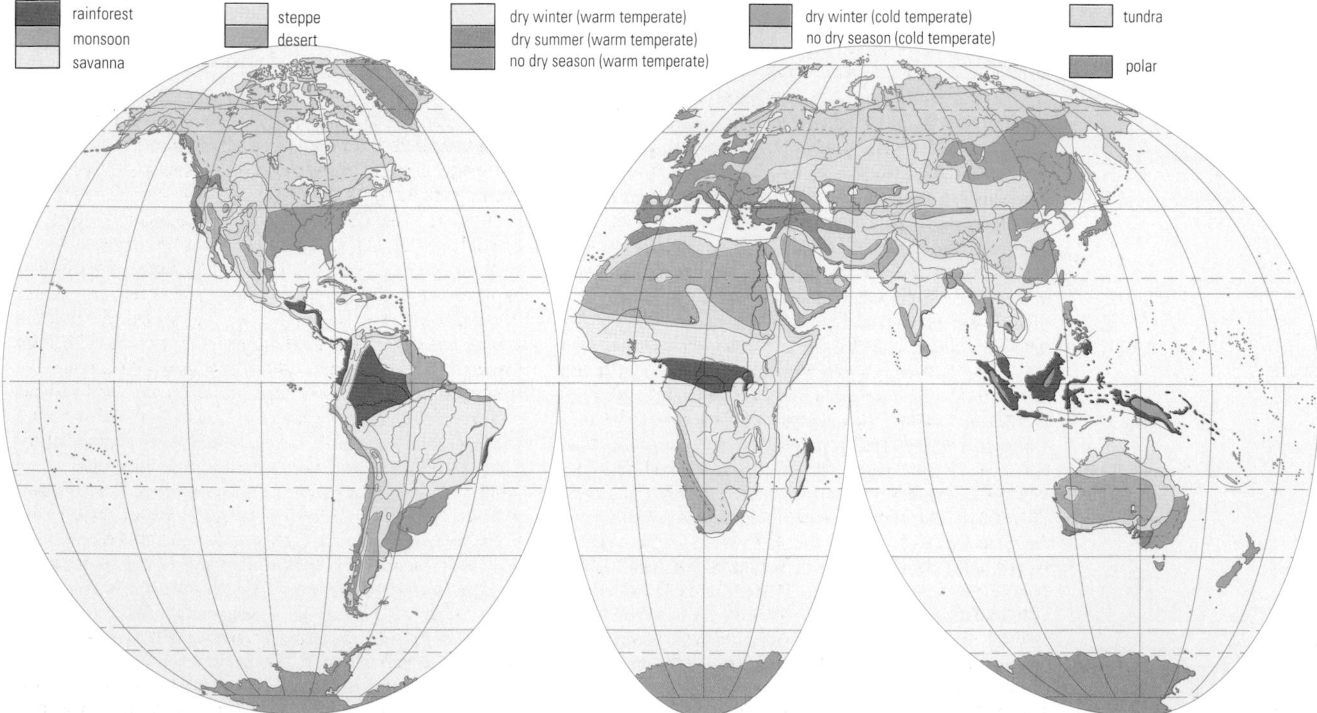

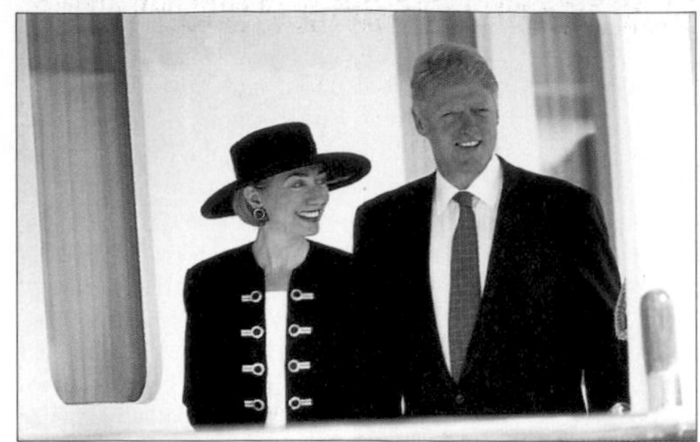

▶ **Clinton** Bill Clinton's second presidential term was dominated by the scandal of his relationship with a White House intern, Monica Lewinsky. Special prosecutor Kenneth Starr released a graphic account of the affair, claiming that Clinton had committed perjury and conspired in the obstruction of justice. Clinton's public popularity remained undimmed by the intensive scrutiny of his private life and he survived the impeachment proceedings.

**clinical psychology** Field of psychology concerned with diagnosis and treatment of behavioral disorders. Clinical psychologists are engaged in treatment including behavior therapy and other forms of psychotherapy. Clinical psychologists may work with psychiatrists, but do not usually have medical training themselves.

**Clinton, Bill (William Jefferson)** (1946– ) 42nd US president (1993– ). He became the youngest-ever US governor when he was elected to represent Arkansas (1978–80, 1983–92). Economic recession and Clinton's reformist agenda led to an easy electoral victory (1992) over the incumbent president, George BUSH. As president, he made health-care an immediate priority, appointing his wife, Hillary CLINTON, to head a commission on reform. Bill Clinton was a chief advocate of the NORTH AMERICAN FREE TRADE AGREEMENT (NAFTA), which won congressional approval in 1993. His first term was dogged by the Whitewater investigation and the blocking of reforms and appointments by a Republican-dominated Congress. Despite allegations of financial and personal impropriety, a buoyant domestic economy and Bob DOLE's lackluster campaign enabled Clinton to become the first Democratic president since Franklin D. ROOSEVELT to serve successive terms in office. The priorities for his second term were education and welfare reforms, and the expansion of NATO. Economic growth enabled Clinton to announce a balanced budget for 1998. His second term was dogged by sexual scandal. Following the investigations of special prosecutor Kenneth Starr, Clinton was forced to admit that he had an improper relationship with Monica Lewinsky, a White House intern. In 1998, he became only the second US president (after Andrew JOHNSON) to be impeached. Clinton refused to resign and showed his ability to make tough political decisions by launching Operation Desert Fox (December 1998), a concerted bombing campaign against Iraq for failing to comply with UN resolutions. In 1999 he survived the impeachment vote and supported NATO's actions against Serbia.

**Clinton, De Witt** (1769–1828) US politician. He was a successful mayor of New York City (1803–15) and in 1812 he ran for president but lost to James MADISON. Clinton was governor of New York (1817–21, 1825–28), and was responsible for the construction of the Erie Canal (1817–25).

**Clinton, George** (1739–1812) US statesman, vice president (1805–12). He led the anti-British faction in the New York assembly and was a delegate to the Second Continental Congress. Clinton served as a brigadier general in the Revolution before becoming the first elected governor of New York (1777–95, 1800–04). Clinton became vice president in Thomas JEFFERSON's second term. He stood for president in 1808, but had to accept the vice presidency under James MADISON.

**Clinton, Hillary Rodham** (1947– ) US attorney and first lady, wife of Bill CLINTON. In 1993 she drafted a plan to provide health insurance for all Americans. Hillary Clinton was removed as head of the commission on health-care reform and her proposals were not implemented. She has been involved with women's rights around the world. Along with her husband she was implicated in the Whitewater land and banking scandal. Hillary's popularity soared as she firmly supported her husband through a series of allegations of extra-marital liaisons. She was strongly tipped to run for high public office.

**clitoris** *See* VULVA

**Clive, Robert (Baron Clive of Plassey)** (1725–74) British soldier and administrator. In 1751 Clive captured Arcot, which prevented the French gaining control of s India. In 1757 he recaptured Calcutta from the nawab of Bengal. As first governor of Bengal (1757–60), Clive established British supremacy in India but his administration was tarnished by corruption. Clive returned to Bengal to serve a second term as governor (1765–67). He reformed the civil service and extended the British EAST INDIA COMPANY's control to Bihar. Clive faced charges of embezzling state funds, but was finally acquitted in 1773. He committed suicide.

**cloaca** Cavity into which intestinal, urinary, and genital tracts open in fish, reptiles, birds, and some primitive mammals.

**clock** Instrument for measuring time. The earliest timekeeping instruments were designed to measure the movements of the Sun, Moon, and stars. Examples include neolithic stone columns, ancient Egyptian sundials, and water clocks. Candle clocks and sandglasses were later types of non-mechanical clocks. The central feature of all mechanical clocks is an **escapement** mechanism, which enables a clock to tick off time at discrete intervals. This movement is transmitted through a series of gears to the hands which are pushed forward a small distance with every escapement movement. Motive power for mechanical clocks has been provided variously by falling weights, pendulums, and coiled springs. In some modern wristwatches the coiled spring is rewound continually by natural wrist movements. Other modern clocks include those using an electrically oscillated quartz crystal. The latter are accurate, but even more accurate are ATOMIC CLOCKS, which rely upon the natural oscillations of atoms and which measure time to an accuracy of thousandths of a second per year.

**cloisonné** Enameling technique in which the design is constructed of wires soldered to a plate, and the cells (cloisons) formed are filled with colored ENAMEL paste and fired. It was developed in Mycenaean Greece.

**clone** Set of organisms obtained from a single original parent through some form of ASEXUAL REPRODUCTION or by ARTIFICIAL SELECTION. Clones are genetically identical and may arise naturally from PARTHENOGENESIS in animals. Cloning is often used in plant propagation (including TISSUE CULTURE) to produce new plants from parents with desirable qualities such as high yield. In 1997 scientists in Scotland announced that they had cloned a female sheep. *See also* GENETIC ENGINEERING

**cloud** Masses of water particles or ice crystals suspended in the lower atmosphere. Clouds are formed when water from the

**CLOCK**

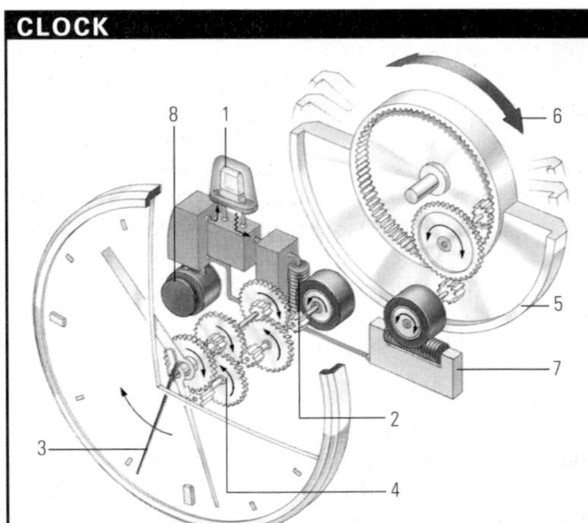


Many modern clocks and watches use a quartz crystal (1) to tell the time accurately. When electricity is passed through a quartz crystal, it oscillates exactly 32,768 times each second. The oscillations are counted and on every 32,768th, a pulse of electricity is sent to a motor (2) that moves the hands (3) via gears (4). The need for a battery for power can be removed if a swinging weight (5) is used to generate a current. As the watch moves, the weight rotates (6) turning a generator (7). The current produced by the generator is stored in a capacitor (8) and is smoothed before reaching the quartz crystal.

Earth's surface becomes vapor through EVAPORATION. As the water vapor rises, it cools and condenses around microscopic salt and dust particles, forming droplets. Where the atmosphere is below the freezing temperature of water the droplets turn to ice. There are ten different classifications of clouds: **cirrus** are high (above 20,000ft/6,000m), white, and thread-like. **Cirrocumulus** are also high, but are often thin sheets. **Cirrostratus** are white, almost transparent, sheets. **Altocumulus** are grayish-white, globular clouds found between 8,000ft (2,400m) and 20,000ft (6,000m). **Altostratus** are gray and streaky, and often cover the whole sky. They produce drizzle. **Nimbostratus** are thick and dark, and usually shed rain or snow. **Stratocumulus** are masses of white, gray or dark cloud. **Stratus** are low-lying and gray. **Cumulus** are white and fluffy-looking. **Cumulonimbus** are towering, dark clouds that generally produce thunderstorms. Their bases almost touch the ground and extend upward to 75,000ft (23,000m). By day, clouds reflect the rays of the Sun back into the atmosphere, keeping the ground cool. At night, clouds trap and reradiate heat rising from the Earth, keeping surface temperatures warm. *See also* FOG; HYDROLOGICAL CYCLE

**cloud chamber** Instrument used to detect and identify charged particles, invented in the 1880s by C.T.R. WILSON to study atomic radiation. The principle is the same as the later BUBBLE CHAMBER, except liquefied gas is replaced by air supersaturated with water or alcohol vapor, and the tracks left are droplets which form around the ionizing particle. The tracks are deflected by a magnetic field and photographed for analysis.

**clove** Tall, aromatic, evergreen tree native to the Molucca Islands. The small purple flowers appear in clusters; the dried flower buds are widely used in cookery. Oil of cloves is distilled from the stems. Height: to 40ft (12m). Family Myrtaceae; species *Syzygium aromaticum*.

**clover** Low-growing annual, biennial, and perennial plants, native to temperate regions of Europe, but now found throughout warmer regions of the Northern Hemisphere. The leaves have three leaflets, rarely four (considered good luck), and the dense flower clusters are white, red, purple, pink, or yellow. Some species are grown as food for cattle. Most species are good nitrogen-fixers, due to the bacteria in their ROOT NODULES, which help to enrich soil. Family Fabaceae/Leguminosae; genus *Trifolium*. *See also* NITROGEN CYCLE; NITROGEN FIXATION

**Clovis I** (465–511) Frankish king. He overthrew the Romanized kingdom of Soissons and conquered the Alemanni near Cologne. He and his army later converted to Christianity in fulfillment of a promise made before the battle. In 507 he defeated the Visigoths under Alaric II near POITIERS. He established MEROVINGIAN power throughout most of GAUL.

**club moss** Any of *c*.200 species of small evergreen spore-bearing plants which, unlike true MOSSES, have specialized tissues for transporting water, food, and minerals. They are related to FERNS and HORSETAILS. The small leaves are arranged in tight whorls around the antenna stems. Millions of years ago their ancestors formed the large trees of CARBONIFEROUS coal forests. Phylum LYCOPODOPHYTA, Family Lycopodiaceae.

**Cluny, Order of** Religious order founded (910) by William the Pious, Duke of Aquitaine, at the Monastery of Cluny, France. It was known for its high standards, reflected in strict observance of the BENEDICTINE rule and emphasis on dignified worship, a personal spiritual life, and sound economics. Its influence spread throughout S France and Italy, reaching its climax in the 12th century. The monastery survived until 1790.

**cluster, stellar** *See* GLOBULAR CLUSTER; OPEN CLUSTER

**clutch, electromagnetic** Device that uses magnetic attraction to connect two rotating shafts. Forms include disk clutches with energized coils and magnetic clutch plates. Eddy current clutches induce rotational movement in the shaft to be engaged and rotated. Hysteresis clutches also transmit rotation without slip. Other electromagnetic clutches employ magnetic metal particles.

**Clwyd** County in N Wales, bordered by the Irish Sea, Cheshire, Shropshire, Powys, and Gwynedd. The county town is Mold. The Vale of Clwyd is a rich agricultural region. Industries: iron and steel, tourism. Area: 937sq mi (2,426sq km). Pop. (1991) 408,090.

**COAL**

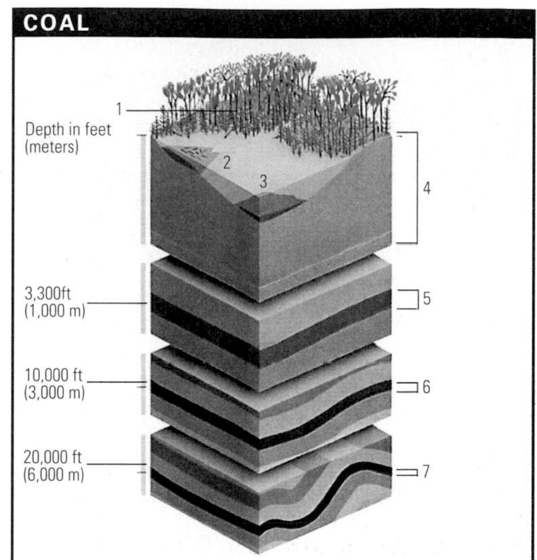


The process of making coal begins with plant debris (1). Dead vegetation lies in a swampy environment and forms peat (4), the first stage of coal formation. Underwater bacteria remove some oxygen, nitrogen and hydrogen from the organic material. Debris carried elsewhere and deposited by water forms a product called cannel coal (2). Algal material collected underwater forms boghead coal (3). If the dead organic material is buried by sediment, the weight on top of the peat and the higher temperature will turn the peat into lignite (5). With more heat and pressure at increasing depths lignite becomes bituminous coal (6) and then anthracite (7).

**Clyde** River in SW Scotland. It rises in the Southern Uplands, flows N, then NW, passing over the Falls of Clyde and widening into the Firth of Clyde at Dumbarton. Clydebank, below GLASGOW, was Scotland's main shipbuilding region. Length: 106mi (170km).

**Clytemnestra** In Greek legend, the unfaithful wife of AGAMEMNON, King of Mycenae, and mother of his son ORESTES. On Agamemnon's return from TROY he was murdered by Clytemnestra and her lover Aegisthus.

**CND** Abbreviation of CAMPAIGN FOR NUCLEAR DISARMAMENT

**cnidarian** (coelenterate) Any one of the 9,000 species of marine invertebrates of the phylum Cnidaria. The phylum includes JELLYFISH, SEA ANEMONE, and CORAL. Characterized by a digestive cavity that forms the main body, they may have been the first animal group to reach the tissue level of organization. Cnidarians are radially symmetrical, jelly-like and have a nerve net and one body opening. Reproduction is sexual and asexual; REGENERATION also occurs.

**coal** Blackish, solid fuel formed from the remains of fossil plants. In the carboniferous and tertiary periods, swamp vegetation subsided to form PEAT bogs. Sedimentary deposits buried the bogs, and the resultant increase in pressure and heat produced lignite (brown coal), then bituminous coal, and ANTHRACITE if temperature increased sufficiently. This is termed the coal rank series; each rank represents an increase in carbon content. Lignite is a poorer fuel than anthracite.

**coal tar** Byproduct from the manufacture of coke. Coal tar comes from bituminous coal used in the distillation process. It is a volatile substance, important for its organic chemical constituents (coal-tar crudes), which are extracted by further distillation. These are the basic ingredients for the synthesis of many products, such as explosives, drugs, dyes, and perfumes.

**coati** (coatimundi) Three species of raccoon-like rodents of SW US and South America. Most have long, slender reddish-brown to black bodies with tapering snouts and long, ringed tails. Length: 26in (67cm); weight: 25lb (11.3kg). Family Procyonidae; genus *Nasua*.

**coaxial cable** Communications CABLE consisting of a central conductor with surrounding insulator and tubular shield.

▲ **coca** Native to regions of South America, the leaves of the coca tree (*Erythroxylon coca*) have been used for centuries as medicine and to relieve hunger. The leaves are harvested and used in the illegal manufacture of cocaine.

▲ **cockle** Bivalves, such as the cockle (*Cardium* sp.), have calcareous shells, the two halves of which are hinged, and can be closed by muscular action.

▲ **coconut palm** Its ability to survive in sandy, salty soil makes the coconut palm (*Cocus nucifera*) a common sight close to beaches. The nut is found within an outer skin and thick fibrous layer or husk. A hard shell covers the edible white "meat."

**cobalt** (symbol Co) Grey TRANSITION ELEMENT first discovered in 1737. Cobalt is found in cobaltite and smaltite, but mostly obtained as a by-product during the processing of other ores. It is a constituent of vitamin $B_{12}$. Cobalt is used in high-temperature steel, artists' colors (cobalt blue), jet engine manufacture, cutting tools, and magnets. $^{60}$Co (half-life 5.26yr) is an artificial isotope used as a source of gamma rays in radiotherapy and tracer studies. Properties: at.no. 27; at.wt. 58.9332; sp.gr. 8.9; m.p. 2,723°F (1,495°C); b.p. 5,198°F (2,870°C); most common isotope $^{59}$Co (100%).

**Cobb, Ty (Tyrus) Raymond** (1886–1961) US baseball player. Cobb is major league baseball's all-time leading hitter with a .367 lifetime batting average. He played for the Detroit Tigers (1905–26) and the Philadelphia Athletics (1927–28), winning 12 batting championships. His career total of 4,191 hits remained a record until 1985. The "Georgia Peach"was also an expert base runner, stealing 892 bases. Cobb was the first member of the Baseball Hall of Fame (1936).

**Cobbett, William** (1763–1835) English journalist and political reformer. He fought for the British in the American Revolution, and (as Peter Porcupine) his criticism of the fledgling democracy in the United States forced his return to England. In 1802 Cobbett founded his weekly *Political Register*. Cobbett was was forced into exile (1817–19) in the US. On his return, Cobbett toured England in the campaign for parliamentary reform. His resultant masterpiece, *Rural Rides* (1830), describes the living conditions of rural workers.

**Cobden, Richard** (1804–65) British Radical politician. With John BRIGHT he led the campaign for the repeal of the CORN LAWS and was the chief spokesman in Parliament (1841–57, 1859–65) for the "Manchester School" of FREE TRADE.

**COBOL (Common Business-Oriented Language)** Widely used COMPUTER LANGUAGE developed in 1959 for processing business data.

**cobra** Any of several highly poisonous snakes in the family Elapidae, including the MAMBA, CORAL SNAKE, kraits, and true cobras. It can expand its neck ribs to form a hood. Found primarily in Africa and Asia, cobras feed on rats, toads, and small birds. It is the only snake to make a nest for its young. The king cobra (*Ophiophagus hannah*) reaches 18ft (5.5m) in length, and is the largest venomous snake in the world. The Indian cobra (*Naja naja*) has spectacle-like markings on its hood. Some African species can spit venom into a victim's eyes from more than 7ft (2m), causing temporary or permanent blindness.

**coca** Shrub native to Colombia and Peru which contains the ALKALOID drug COCAINE. Native Americans chew the leaves. The plant has yellow-white flowers growing in clusters, and red berries. Height: *c*.8ft (2.4m). Family Erythroxylaceae; species *Erythroxylon coca*.

**cocaine** White, crystalline ALKALOID extracted from the leaves of the COCA plant. Once used as a local anesthetic, it is now primarily an illegal narcotic, with stimulant and hallucinatory effects. It is psychologically habit-forming, but increasing doses are not needed, as the body does not develop tolerance. Habitual use results in physical and nervous deterioration, and withdrawal results in severe depression. *See also* CRACK

**coccolith** Any microscopic, single-celled flagellate of the Coccolithophorida, a class of ALGAE of the phylum Chrysophyta. The cell is covered with round, chalky platelets only one or two thousandths of a millimeter in diameter. Many limestone and chalk cliffs are made up entirely of the remains of platelets.

**coccus** Small spherical or spheroid bacterium. Average diameter, 0.5–1.25 micrometers. Some, such as *Streptococcus* and *Staphylococcus*, are causes of infection.

**cochineal** Crimson dye produced from the pulverized dried bodies of certain female scale insects, found in Central America. The dye is still used in cosmetics and foodstuffs, although now often replaced by aniline dyes.

**Cochise** (1815–1874) Chief of the Chiricahua APACHE. In 1861 the US army falsely imprisoned him, killing five of his relatives. Cochise escaped to lead his tribe in an 11-year war against the army in Arizona. He concluded a treaty that created a reservation. Cochise lived peacefully here until his death, after which the treaty was broken and his people forcibly moved.

**cochlea** Fluid-filled structure in the inner EAR which is essential to hearing. It has a shape like a coiled shell, and is lined with hair cells which move in response to incoming sound waves, stimulating nerve cells to transmit impulses to the BRAIN.

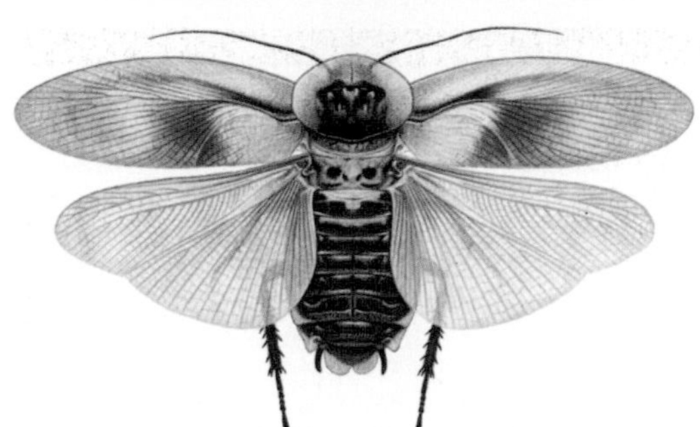

▲ **cockroach** The *Blaberus giganticus* species of cockroach is found in Central America. Its wingspan measures 3in (8cm).

**cockatoo** Large PARROT with a long, erectile crest. Cockatoos live mainly in Australia and SW Asia. Most are predominantly white, tinged with pink or yellow. They feed on fruit and seeds. Females lay 1–4 white eggs. Length: 15in (38cm). Family Psittacidae.

**Cockcroft, Sir John Douglas** (1897–1967) English physicist who, with Ernest WALTON, was the first person to split the ATOM. He and Walton constructed a particle ACCELERATOR, and created the first artificial nuclear reaction by bombarding lithium atoms with protons (1932). They shared the 1951 Nobel Prize for physics.

**Cockerell, Sir Christopher Sydney** (1910– ) English engineer who invented the HOVERCRAFT. In 1955 Cockerell filed the first patent for an AIR-CUSHION VEHICLE (ACV).

**cockle** Bivalve mollusk in marine waters. Its varicolored, heart-shaped shell has 20–24 strong, radiating ribs. There are *c*.200 recognized species, many edible. Average length: 1.5–3in (4–8cm). Class Bivalvia; family Cardiidae; species include *Cardium aculeatum*.

**cockroach** (roach) Member of a group of insects with long antennae and a flat, soft body found worldwide, but mostly in the tropics. Its head is hidden under a shield (pronotum) and it may be winged or wingless. Eggs are laid in special egg cases. Some species are household pests. Length: 0.5–2in (13–50mm). Family Blattidae.

**cocoa** Drink obtained from the seeds of the tropical American evergreen tree *Theobroma cacao*. The seeds are crushed and some fatty substances are removed to produce cocoa powder. Cocoa is the basic ingredient of CHOCOLATE. The Ivory Coast is one of the world's largest producers. Family Sterculiaceae.

**coconut palm** (copra plant) Tall palm tree native to the shores of the Indo-Pacific region and the Pacific coast of South America; commercially the most important of all palms. Growing to 100ft (30.5m) tall, it has a leaning trunk and a crown of feather-shaped leaves. Copra, the dried kernel of the coconut fruit, is a valuable source of oil used in the manufacture of margarine and soap. The fibrous husk is used for matting. Family Arecacae/Palmae; species *Cocos nucifera*.

**cocoon** Case or wrapping produced by larval forms of animals (such as some MOTHS, BUTTERFLIES, and WASPS) for the resting or pupal stage in their life cycle. Most cocoons are made of SILK, and those of the domestic silkworm provide most of the world's commercial silk. *See also* CHRYSALIS; PUPA

**Cocos Islands** (Keeling Islands) Archipelago in the Indian

▲ **cod** The characteristic configuration of the fins – three dorsal fins, two anal fins – reveal this to be a species of cod (*Gadus morhua*). A carnivorous fish, cod can grow to 5ft (1.5m).

## COIN

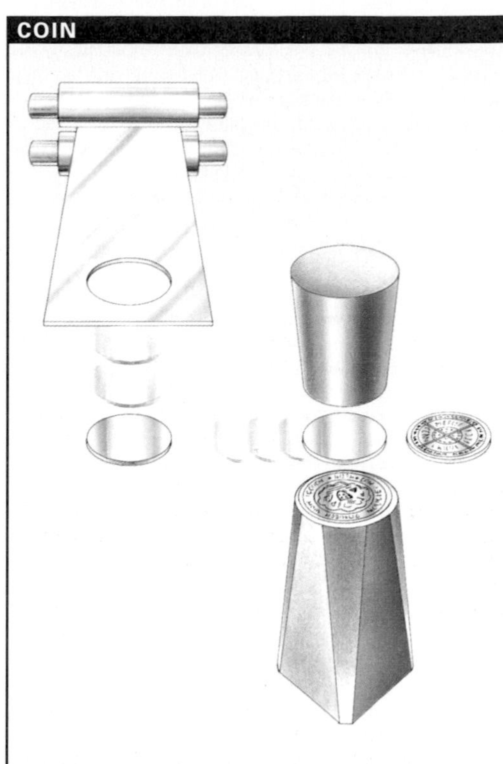

Coins and medals, though they serve different purposes, are made in the same way. The principles of their manufacture have not changed, although the processes are now mechanized. The metal used to be hand-beaten into fillets of coin thickness and the blanks cut out with shears; now coin-thick sheets are rolled out by machines and the blanks stamped. An operator with two dies and a hammer was superseded by the screw press in the 18th century, capable of producing about 20–25 coins a minute. Since it was automated 200–250 coins per minute can be produced.

Ocean, an external territory of Australia, 750mi (1,200km) sw of Java. The 28 small coral islands were discovered (1609) by William Keeling. They came under British control in 1857, but since 1955 have been administered by Australia. The main product is copra. Area: 5sq mi (13sq km). Pop. (1992) 586.

**Cocteau, Jean** (1889–1963) French writer and filmmaker, an experimental leader of the French avant-garde. He was associated with many leading artistic figures of the 1920s, such as Apollinaire, Picasso, Diaghilev, and Stravinsky. His works of surrealist fantasy include the novel *Les enfants terribles* (1929; filmed, 1950); the play *Orphée* (1926; filmed 1950); and the films *Le sand d'un poète* (1930) and *La belle et la bête* (1946).

**cod** Bottom-dwelling, marine fish found in cold to temperate waters of the Northern Hemisphere. It is gray, green, brown, or red with darker speckled markings. Cod is one of the chief food fishes. Length: up to 6ft (1.8m). Family Gadidae.

**code** *See* CRYPTOGRAPHY

**codeine** White, crystalline ALKALOID extracted from OPIUM by the methylation of MORPHINE, and with the properties of weak morphine. It is used in medicine as an analgesic to treat mild to moderate pain, as a cough suppressant, and to treat diarrhea.

**Code Napoléon** French CIVIL LAW, introduced (1804) by Napoleon I. Based on ROMAN LAW, the Code was intended to end the disunity of French law and was applied to all French territories. It banned social inequality, permitted freedom of person and contract, and upheld the right to own private property. It was revised in 1904.

**Cody, Samuel Franklin** (1862–1913) US pioneer aviator. In 1896 he went to England, where he subsequently took out British citizenship. Cody helped to plan and build the first British airship. In 1908 he built his own airplane. Cody was killed in a flying accident.

**Cody, William Frederick** *See* "BUFFALO BILL"

**coefficient** Term multiplying a specified unknown quantity in an algebraic expression. In the expression $1 + 5x + 2x^2$: 5 and 2 are the coefficients of $x$ and $x^2$ respectively. In physics, it is a ratio that yields a pure number or a quantity with dimensions.

**coelacanth** Bony fish of the genus *Latimeria*. Thought to have become extinct 60 million years ago, it was found in deep waters off the African coast in 1938. It is gray-brown with lobed fins that have fleshy bases. The scales and bony plates are unlike those of modern fish. Length: 5ft (1.5m). Order Crossopterygii; species *Latimeria chalumnae*.

**coelenterate** *See* CNIDARIAN

**coeliac disease** Disorder in which the small intestine fails to absorb food properly. It is caused by intolerance to gluten, a protein in wheat and rye products. Symptoms include depression, diarrhea and malnutrition.

**Coetzee, J.M. (John Michael)** (1940– ) South African novelist and critic. His novels deal with life under forms of imperialism, including the South African apartheid system in *In the Heart of the Country* (1977) and *Age of Iron* (1990). Coetzee won the Booker Prize for *Life and Times of Michael K* (1983).

**coffee** Plant and the popular CAFFEINE beverage produced from its seeds (coffee beans). The plants of the genus *Coffea* are evergreen with white fragrant flowers. Native to Ethiopia, they are now cultivated in the tropics, especially Brazil (the world's biggest producer), Colombia, and the Ivory Coast. Family Rubiaceae.

**cognitive psychology** Broad area of psychology concerned with perceiving, thinking, and knowing. It investigates such matters as the way in which people perceive by sight or hearing; how they organize information; and the use they make of language. *See also* BEHAVIORISM

**cognitive therapy** Form of PSYCHOTHERAPY that aims to treat psychological problems through changing patients' attitudes and beliefs. It is used in the treatment of various behavioral problems, phobias, and sometimes for children with learning problems.

**Cohen, William** (1940– ) US statesman, secretary of defense (1997– ). He was appointed by President CLINTON following his reelection in 1996. A former Republican senator from Maine, Cohen was nominated partly as an attempt to ensure closer support for foreign policy initiatives from a Republican-dominated Senate.

**cohesion** Mutual attraction between the component atoms, ions, or molecules of a substance. Weak cohesive forces permit the fluidity of liquids; those of solids are much stronger. Liquids form droplets because of surface tension caused by cohesion.

**coin** Stamped metal disks of standard sizes used as tokens of money in commercial transactions. The earliest coins are of Lydian origin, from the 7th century BC. Early coinage also appeared in China and India. Ancient coins usually contained a specific quantity of precious metal, often gold or silver, and were stamped with the symbol of the issuing authority. With the introduction of banknotes in the late 17th century, and the gradual decline of the quantity of precious metal in each coin, they became used for smaller money transactions.

**Colbert, Claudette** (1905–96) (Claudette Chauchoin) US actress, b. France. Her screwball performance in *It Happened One Night* (1934) earned her an Academy Award for best actress. Other credits include *Private Worlds* (1934), and *Since You Went Away* (1936).

**Colbert, Jean Baptiste** (1619–83) French statesman, the principal exponent of MERCANTILISM. He came to prominence as an adviser to Cardinal MAZARIN. From 1661, when LOUIS

▲ **cocoa** The cacao tree (*Theobroma cacao*) sprouts pendulous pods 6–14in (15–35cm) long from its branches and trunk. Each pod contains 30–40 beans from which cocoa and chocolate are made.

▼ **coffee** The Arabian coffee plant (*Coffea arabica*) is the most common kind of coffee plant. It is a small evergreen tree which can grow to a height of 25ft (7.5m), but is pruned to 10ft (3m) on plantations. Its leaves are some 3–6in (7.5–15cm) long. The white blossoms are followed by tiny green berries, each holding two tough-skinned, greenish beans. The berries ripen to a deep red after six or seven months and are then ready for picking.

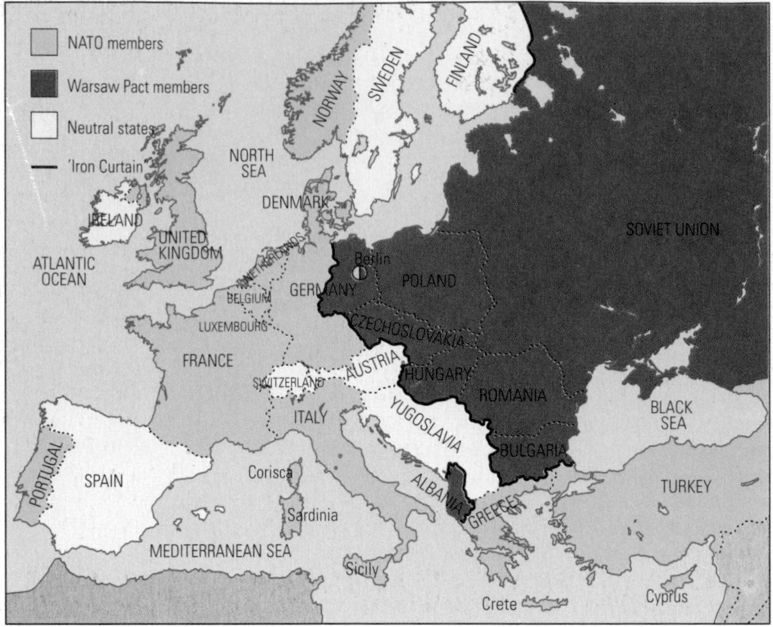


▲ **Cold War** The map shows the division of Europe in 1955 between the members of NATO and the Soviet-dominated Warsaw Pact.

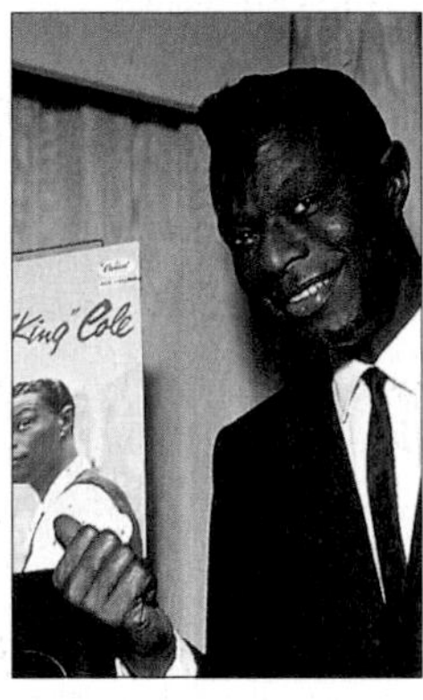

▲ **Cole** Popular US singer and jazz pianist, Nat King Cole had a string of successful songs during the 1950s and 1960s.

▲ **collie** Bred in Scotland during the 17th and 18th centuries, the collie is still used on farms for rounding up livestock, most commonly sheep. Collies are highly intelligent dogs and one of the most popular US breeds.

XIV began his personal rule, Colbert controlled most aspects of government: reforming taxation and manufacturing, reducing tariffs, establishing commercial companies such as the French EAST INDIA COMPANY, and strengthening the navy.

**Colchester** City on the Colne River, Essex, SE England. The first Roman colony in Britain was settled here in AD 43 and attacked by Boadicea in AD 61. It has a Roman wall and a fine Norman castle. It is a market center for the surrounding area. Pop. (1991) 142,515.

**colchicum** Genus of *c.*30 species of flowering plants, including *C. fallale*. Species grow throughout Eurasia, and have pink, white, or purple crocus-like flowers. The CORM contains colchicine, an ALKALOID used to treat rheumatism and gout. Colchicine's ability to inhibit MITOSIS make it a valuable IMMUNOSUPPRESSIVE DRUG and aid to cancer research. Family Liliaceae.

**cold, common** Minor disease of the upper respiratory tract caused by viral infection. Symptoms include inflammation of the nose, headache, sore throat, and a cough. A cold usually disappears within a few days. Fever-reducing and pain-relieving drugs, as well as decongestants, may relieve symptoms; rest is recommended for heavy colds. Antibiotics may be prescribed where a bacterial infection is also present.

**cold-blooded** *See* POIKILOTHERMAL

**Cold War** Political, ideological, and economic confrontation between the US and the Soviet Union and their allies from the end of World War II until the late 1980s. Despite incidents such as the BERLIN AIRLIFT (1948–49) and the CUBAN MISSILE CRISIS (1962), open warfare never occurred between the NORTH ATLANTIC TREATY ORGANIZATION (NATO) and the WARSAW PACT. Indirect confrontation occurred in the KOREAN WAR and the VIETNAM WAR. Detente ushered in an era of ARMS-CONTROL negotiations, including the STRATEGIC ARMS LIMITATION TALKS (SALT). In 1991 the Cold War officially ended with the collapse of Soviet COMMUNISM and the dissolution of the Warsaw Pact. *See also* DISARMAMENT

**Cole, Nat King (Nathaniel Adams)** (1917–65) US singer and pianist, father of Natalie Cole. He was a jazz pianist in the King Cole Trio from 1939, but achieved popularity as a singer with his velvety soft and rich voice. Cole's many hit songs include "Unforgettable," "When I Fall in Love," "Mona Lisa," and "Nature Boy."

**Cole, Thomas** (1801–48) US landscape painter, b. England. A founder of the HUDSON RIVER SCHOOL, his romantic landscapes depict the grandeur of the Hudson River Valley and Catskill Mountains.

**Coleridge, Samuel Taylor** (1772–1834) English poet, critic and philosopher. In 1798 Coleridge and William WORDSWORTH published *Lyrical Ballads*, a fundamental work of English ROMANTICISM that opened with Coleridge's ballad "The Rime of the Ancient Mariner". *Christabel and Other Poems* (1816) included the ballad "Christabel" and the fragment "Kubla Khan". Battling with opium-addiction, Coleridge produced little poetry in his later life, concentrating instead on his lectures. *Biographia Literaria* (1817) is both a meditation on German philosophy and a work of literary criticism.

**Colette** (1873–1954) French novelist. Her early works, including the first four *Claudine* novels (1900–03), were published under her first husband's pseudonym, Willy. Among her best-known works are *Chéri* (1920), *The Last of Chéri* (1926), and *Gigi* (1944).

**colic** Severe pain in the abdomen, usually subsiding and then recurring. Intestinal colic may be associated with obstruction of the intestine or constipation.

**colitis** Inflammation of the lining of the colon, or large intestine, that produces bowel changes, usually diarrhea, and cramp-like pains. In severe chronic ulcerative colitis, the colon lining ulcerates and bleeds.

**collage** Composition of various materials (such as cardboard, string, and fabric), pasted on to a canvas or other background. Cubist artists, such as PICASSO, BRAQUE, and GRIS developed it into a serious art form.

**collagen** Protein substance that is the main constituent of bones, tendons, cartilage, connective tissue, and skin. It is made up of inelastic fibers.

**collective unconscious** According to JUNG's psychological theory, the inherited aspect of the UNCONSCIOUS that is common to all members of the human race. The collective unconscious has evolved over many centuries and contains images (archetypes), which are found in dreams and numerous religious and mystical symbols.

**collectivism** Political and economic theory, opposed to individualism. It emphasizes the need to replace competition with cooperation. SOCIALISM and COMMUNISM are both expressions of the collectivist idea.

**collectivization** Agricultural policy enforced in the SOVIET UNION under STALIN in 1929, and adopted by China after the communist takeover in 1949. With the object of modernizing agriculture and making it more efficient, small peasant holdings were combined and agriculture brought under state control.

**collie** Smooth-coated or long-haired working dog. It has a lean, wedge-shaped head with small triangular ears. The long body is set on strong straight legs and the tail is long and curved. The coat, usually black-and-white or tan, may be rough or smooth. Height: to 26in (66cm) at the shoulder.

**Collins, Michael** (1890–1922) Irish revolutionary. Collins was imprisoned for a year for his role in the EASTER RISING (1916). A leading member of Sinn Féin, he helped establish (1918) the Dáil Eireann (Irish assembly). Collins was the leader of the IRISH REPUBLICAN ARMY (IRA) campaign against British troops. He and Arthur GRIFFITH negotiated the treaty (1921) that created the Irish Free State and the partition of Ireland. Collins was assassinated by extremist republicans.

**Collins, (William) Wilkie** (1824–89) British novelist. Collins made important contributions to the development of DETECTIVE FICTION, especially in his two enduringly popular novels, *The Woman in White* (1860) and *The Moonstone* (1868). He also collaborated with Charles DICKENS.

**colloid** Substance composed of fine particles which can be readily dispersed throughout a second substance. A **sol** is a solid dispersed in a liquid, an **aerosol** is a solid or liquid in a gas, an **emulsion** is a liquid in a liquid, and a **foam** is a gas in either a liquid or solid.

**Cologne** (Köln) City on the Rhine River, Nordrhein Westfalen, W Germany. The Romans built a fortress at Cologne in AD 50. It was made an archbishopric by Charlemagne in 785 and enjoyed great influence during the Middle Ages. It was heavily bombed during World War II. Notable buildings include a cathedral (started 1248, completed 1880) and the Gürzenich (a Renaissance patrician's house). Its university was founded in 1388. Cologne is a commercial, industrial, and transportation center. Industries: oil refining, petrochemicals, chemicals, engineering, textiles. Pop. (1990) 958,600.

**Colombia** Republic in NW South America. *See* country feature

**Colombo** Capital and chief seaport of Sri Lanka, on the SW coast. Settled in the 6th century BC, it was taken by Portugal in the 16th century and later by the Dutch. In 1796, it was captured by the British and gained its independence in 1948. Colombo has one of the world's largest artificial harbors. Apart from shipping, the city has light industries. Pop. (1992 est.) 684,000.

**Colombo Plan** International organization with headquarters in COLOMBO, Sri Lanka, which seeks to promote the economic and social development in S and SE Asia. Initiated by the Commonwealth of Nations (1951), it now includes 26 states including the US, Canada, Japan, and the UK.

**colon** Part of the large INTESTINE that extends from the small intestine to the RECTUM. The colon absorbs water from digested food and allows bacterial action for the formation of feces. *See also* DIGESTIVE SYSTEM

**colonialism** Control by one country over a dependent area or people. Although associated with modern political history, the practice is ancient. In European colonial history, economic, political, and strategic factors were involved in the world empires of countries such as Britain and France, subjugating mainly African and Asian states and often creating artificial boundaries. After World War II, colonialist exploitation was widely recognized, and colonial powers conceded, willingly or not, independence to their colonies. *See also* IMPERIALISM

**color** Sensation experienced when light of sufficient brightness and of a particular wavelength strikes the retina of the eye. Normal daylight (white light) is made up of a spectrum of colors, each a different wavelength. These colors can be placed in seven bands – red, orange, yellow, green, blue, indigo, and violet – of decreasing wavelength. A pure spectral color is called a **hue**. If the color is not pure but contains some white, it is "desaturated" (**tint**). A color may also have luminosity (brightness) which determines its shade. Any color is perceived as a mixture of three primary colors: red, green, and blue.

**Colorado** State in W central USA; the capital is DENVER. Other major cities include Colorado Springs and Pueblo. It is the highest state in the nation, with an average elevation of 6,800ft (2,073m). In the W half are the ranges of the ROCKY MOUNTAINS, and in the E the GREAT PLAINS. Major rivers are the Colorado, Rio Grande, Arkansas, and South Platte. The US acquired the E of the state from France in the LOUISIANA PURCHASE (1803). The remainder was ceded by Mexico after the MEXICAN WAR (1848). The discovery of gold and silver encouraged immigration, and Colorado was made a territory

**COLORADO**
**Statehood:**
1 August 1876
**Nickname:**
The Centennial State
**State bird:**
Lark bunting
**State flower:**
Rocky Mountain columbine
**State tree:**
Blue spruce
**State motto:**
Nothing without providence

## COLOMBIA

The yellow on Colombia's flag depicts the land, separated from the tyranny of Spain by the blue of the Atlantic Ocean. The red symbolizes the blood of the people who fought for Colombia's independence. The flag has been used since 1806.

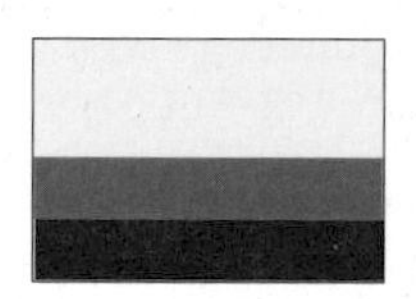

**AREA:** 439,733sq mi (138,910sq km)
**POPULATION:** 33,424,000
**CAPITAL (POPULATION):** Bogotá (4,921,000)
**GOVERNMENT:** Multiparty republic
**ETHNIC GROUPS:** Mestizo 58%, White 20%, Mulatto 14%, Black 4%, mixed Black and Indian 3%, Native American 1%
**LANGUAGES:** Spanish (official)
**RELIGIONS:** Christianity (Roman Catholic 93%)
**CURRENCY:** Peso = 100 centavos

The Republic of Colombia is the only South American country to have coastlines on both the Pacific Ocean and the Caribbean Sea. Colombia contains the 3 northernmost ranges of the ANDES Mountains. The fertile valleys between the ranges contain *c*.75% of Colombia's population. E of the Andes lie plains drained by headwaters of the AMAZON and ORINOCO rivers: this area covers *c*.66% of the country but less than 2% of the population live here. W of the mountains lie the Caribbean lowlands in the N and the Pacific lowlands in the W.

### CLIMATE AND VEGETATION

The lowlands have a tropical climate, but altitude greatly affects the climate of the Andean highlands. BOGOTÁ, on a plateau in the E Andes at *c*.9,200ft (2,800m), has mild annual temperatures. Rainfall is heavy, especially on the Pacific coast, though the Caribbean lowlands and the Andean Magdalena valley have dry seasons. Plant life in the Andes varies with altitude, from tundra at the highest levels to grassy meadows and forests on lower slopes. The W lowlands have some dense forests,with coastal mangrove swamps. The original forests of the Caribbean lowlands have been largely cleared. The NE plains are covered by tropical grassland (*llanos*) while rainforest grows in the SE.

### HISTORY AND POLITICS

The advanced, pre-Colombian CHIBCHA civilization lived undisturbed in the E cordillera for many thousands of years. In 1525 the Spanish established the first European settlement at Santa Marta. By 1538 the conquistador Gonzalo Jiménez de Quesada had conquered the Chibcha and established Bogotá. Colombia became part of the New Kingdom of Granada, whose territory also included Ecuador, Panama and Venezuela. In 1819 Simón BOLÍVAR liberated the land and established Greater Colombia. In 1830 Ecuador and Venzuela became independent nations. The first civil war (1899–1902) killed nearly 100,000 people. In 1903, aided by the US, Panama achieved independence. The second civil war *La Violencia* (1949–1957) was even more bloody. Political corruption, violence, and repression were endemic. In 1957 Liberal and Conservative parties formed the National Front Coalition that remained in power until 1974. Throughout the 1970s Colombia's illegal trade in cocaine grew steadily, creating wealthy drug barons. In the 1980s armed cartels (such as the Cali) became a destabilizing force, and political and media assassinations were frequent. In 1991 a new constitution protected human rights. In 1994 the Liberal leader Ernesto Samper was elected president. In 1998 elections Samper was defeated by the Social Conservative Party (PSC) leader, Andrés Pastrana Arango. In an effort to end the guerrilla war that has lasted for 30 years, Pastrana negotiated with the Revolutionary Armed Forces of Colombia (FARC) and the National Liberation Army (ELN).

### ECONOMY

Colombia is a lower-middle-income developing country (1995 GDP per capita, $US1,105). Agriculture is important with coffee the leading export. Other crops include bananas, cocoa, and corn. Colombia also exports coal, oil, emeralds, and gold. Manufacturing is based mainly in Bogotá, CALI, and MEDELLÍN. In 1997, the collapse of the world coffee and banana markets led to a massive budget deficit and added to the high unemployment rate. In 1998, as part of austerity measures, the peso was devalued by 20%. It triggered the longest general strike in Colombia's history (20 days).

in 1861. It achieved statehood in 1876. The most important agricultural activity is the raising of sheep and cattle. Sugar beets, corn, and hay are grown. Industries: tourism, transport, electrical equipment. Area: 103,729sq mi (268,658sq km). Pop. (1990) 3,294,394.

**Colorado** Major river in SW US, which rises in the Rocky Mountains of N Colorado and flows SW into the Gulf of California, passing through the GRAND CANYON. There are many national parks and hydroelectric power projects on the river. Length: 1,450mi (2,333km).

**color blindness** General term for various disorders of color vision. The most common involves red-green vision, a hereditary defect almost exclusively affecting males, in which the person cannot tell red from green. Total color blindness, an inherited disorder in which the person sees only black, white, and gray, is rare.

**Colosseum** Amphitheater in Rome built (AD 72–81) by Emperor Vespasian. It measures 620 × 513ft (189 × 156m) by 150ft (45.7m) high, and seated *c.*50,000 people. Citizens of Rome came here to watch gladiatorial contests and, according to tradition, the martyrdom of Christians.

**Colossians, Epistle to the** Book of the New Testament taking the form of a letter written by either St. PAUL or a disciple to the Church at Colossae, a city in SW Phrygia (now central Turkey). The letter, written from prison in Rome (*c.*AD 61), is a warning to the Colossians not to adopt ideas from other faiths.

**Colossus of Rhodes** One of the SEVEN WONDERS OF THE WORLD, a bronze statue of the Sun god overlooking the harbor at Rhodes. It stood more than 100ft (30.5m) high. It was built, at least in part, by Chares of Lindos between *c.*292 BC and *c.*280 BC and destroyed by an earthquake *c.*224 BC.

**colostomy** Operation to bring the COLON out through the wall of the abdomen in order to bypass the lower section of the bowel. An artificial opening is created so that fecal matter is passed into a bag, worn outside the body. *See also* DIGESTION

**Colt, Samuel** (1814–62) US inventor. In 1835 Colt patented the revolver, a single-barreled pistol with an automatic revolving set of chambers, brought into successive alignment. He also invented a submarine battery and, a submarine telegraph cable. His Colt's Patent Firearms Manufacturing Company at Hartford, Connecticut, was the first assembly-line in manufacturing.

**Coltrane, John William** (1926–67) US jazz saxophonist. Coltrane first attracted attention as a member (1955–61) of the Miles DAVIS quintet, on albums such as *Kind as Blue* (1959). In 1957 he worked with Theolonious MONK and became a bandleader. *Giant Steps* (1959) was a landmark recording in the development of modern jazz. In 1961 he formed a quartet. After making the masterpiece *A Love Supreme* (1964), the quartet disbanded. Other albums include *Africa/Brass Vols. 1&2* (1961) *Impressions* (1963), *Ascension* (1965) and *Interstellar Space* (1967).

**Colum, Padraic** (1881–1972) Irish writer. A key figure in the Irish literary renaissance, Colum helped found the Abbey Theatre and wrote a memoir of James JOYCE. From 1914 he lived mainly in the US. His verse is collected in *Collected Poems* (1953).

**Columba, Saint** (521–97) Irish Christian missionary in Ireland and Scotland. He founded several monasteries in Ireland before leaving in 563 to found an important monastery on the island of Iona. His feast day is June 9.

**Columbia** Capital of South Carolina, in the center of the state at the junction of the Broad and Saluda rivers. Founded as state capital in 1786, it was nearly destroyed in the Civil War. It is home to the University of South Carolina (1801), Columbia College (1854), Allen University (1870), and the Woodrow Wilson Museum. Industries: textiles, printing. Pop. (1990) 98,052.

**Columbia** River in SW Canada and NW US. It flows from Columbia Lake in British Columbia, Canada, through Washington and Oregon, and enters the Pacific Ocean N of Portland. It has one of the largest drainage basins on the continent, *c.*258,000sq mi (668,220sq km). Length: 1,214mi (1,953km).

**Columbia, District of** *See* WASHINGTON, D.C.

**columbine** Any of *c.*100 species of perennial herbaceous plant native to cool climates of the Northern Hemisphere. They have five-petaled, spurred flowers and notched leaflets. Height: to 3ft (90cm). Family Ranunculaceae; genus *Aquilegia*.

**columbium** *See* NIOBIUM

**Columbus, Christopher** (1451–1506) Italian explorer credited with the discovery of America. Columbus believed he could establish a route to China and the East Indies by sailing across the Atlantic since, along with many learned contemporaries, he believed the circumference of the Earth to be much smaller than it is. He secured Spanish patronage from Ferdinand and Isabella. In 1492 Columbus set out with three ships (*Niña*, *Pinta*, and *Santa Maria*) and made landfall in the Bahamas, the first European to reach the Americas since the Vikings. Believing he had reached the East, he called the inhabitants "Indians." On a second, larger expedition (1493), a permanent colony was established in Hispaniola. Columbus made two more voyages (1498 and 1502), exploring the Caribbean region. He never surrendered his belief that he had reached Asia. His discoveries laid the basis for the Spanish empire in the Americas.

▲ **Columbus** Although Columbus was not the first European to sail to the New World (the Vikings had arrived in *c.*1000 AD), his voyages mark the start of intensive European exploration of the Americas. On his final voyage (1502), he sailed past Hispaniola and S along the coast of Honduras. Attempting to return to Hispaniola, he was shipwrecked on Jamaica and forced to return to Spain, abandoning his travels.

**Columbus** Capital of Ohio, on the Scioto River. Founded in 1812, it grew rapidly with the arrival of the railroad in 1850. It is a major transport, industrial, and trading center. Columbus has numerous universities and colleges. The Battelle Memorial Institute (1929) conducts scientific, technological, and economic research. Industries: machinery, aircraft. Pop. (1990) 632,910.

**column** In architecture, a vertical post, supporting part of a building. A column may be free-standing, with a CAPITAL, base, and shaft, or it may be partly attached to a wall. Triumphal columns such as the Roman Trajan's Column, had narrative reliefs depicting military victories. *See also* ORDERS OF ARCHITECTURE

**coma** Unconsciousness caused by a head injury, brain disease, drugs, or lack of blood supply to the BRAIN.

**Comanche** Shoshonean-speaking Native American nation. They separated from the parent SHOSHONE in the distant past and migrated from E Wyoming into Kansas. Numbering *c.*15,000, they introduced the horse to the Northern Plains tribes. Conflict with US forces resulted in their near extinction by 1874. Today, *c.*4,500 Comanche live on reservations in SW Oklahoma.

**Combination Acts** British acts of Parliament of 1799 and 1800 making combinations (or labor unions) of workers illegal. The government feared they were potentially subversive. Labor unions nevertheless multiplied after 1815, and in 1824 the acts were repealed. A later Combination Act (1825) restricted the right to strike and, as the TOLPUDDLE MARTYRS (1834) demonstrated, union organizers could still be prosecuted.

**combustion** Burning, usually in oxygen. The combustion of fuels is used to produce heat and light. An example is a fire. Industrial techniques harness the energy produced using combustion chambers and furnaces.

**COMECON** *See* COUNCIL FOR MUTUAL ECONOMIC ASSISTANCE

**Comédie-Française** French national theater, founded (1680) by Louis XIV. There are two kinds of members: *pensionnaires*, chosen by audition, and *sociétaires*, to which position the *pensionnaire* can be elevated only upon the death, retirement, or resignation of a *sociétaire*.

**comedy** One of the two main types of DRAMA. It differs from TRAGEDY in its lightness of style and theme and its tendency to resolve happily. It originated in early Greek fertility rites and, in modern usage, refers not only to a humorous play or film, but also to the growing tradition of stand-up routines. As theater has developed, the once clear division between the two dramatic forms has been blurred. *See also* ARISTOPHANES; GREEK DRAMA

**comet** Small, icy solar system body in an independent orbit around the Sun. F.L. Whipple's (1906– ) "dirty snowball" theory of comets is largely accepted. The solid nucleus of a comet is small, that of HALLEY'S COMET measures just 16 × 8km (10 × 5mi), and comprises rock and dust particles embedded in ice. As the comet approaches the Sun and gets warmer, evaporation begins, and jets of gas and dust form the luminous, spherical coma. Later, radiation pressure from the Sun and the SOLAR WIND may send dust and gas streaming away as a tail, as much as 150 million kilometres in length. They are three main types of comet: **short-period** comets often have their aphelia at approximately the distance of Jupiter's orbit. **Long-period** comets (such as Halley's) have aphelia near or beyond Neptune's orbit. Comets with **very long periods** have such great orbital eccentricities that their paths are almost parabolic. It is now thought that comets originated with the rest of the solar system. *See also* METEOR

**comfrey** Any plant of the genus *Symphytum* of the BORAGE family (Boraginaceae), native to Eurasia. Comfreys have small yellow or purple flowers and hairy leaves. Boiled concoctions of *S. officinale* were once used to treat wounds.

**comic** Magazine consisting of stories told by means of strip cartoons with "balloons" containing the characters' speech. Comics evolved from the comic strip in the 1930s and cover many subjects. A tradition of adult, politicized, subversive, and often erotic comics, along with explicit graphic novels, has established itself during the latter part of the 20th century.

**comic opera** Musico-dramatic work with some spoken dialog and a light or amusing plot. The term is used indiscriminately and includes musical comedy and OPERETTA. In operatic works, it approximates most closely to early 18th-century Italian OPERA BUFFA, but bears little relation to the French OPÉRA COMIQUE.

**Cominform** (acronym for **Com**munist **Inform**ation Bureau) Agency established in 1947 to coordinate and provide information to the Communist Party of the Soviet Union and other European communist parties. It replaced the COMMUNIST INTERNATIONAL, abolished in 1943. Cominform was dissolved in 1956.

**Comintern** Acronym for COMMUNIST INTERNATIONAL

**commedia dell' arte** Style of Italian comedy, popular from the mid-16th to late-18th century, which spread throughout Europe. Professional players performed on street stages or at court functions. Plays were comic, often coarse, and crudely improvised on briefly outlined scenarios. Commedia produced several (now standard) masked characters: Harlequin (clown), Capitano (braggart soldier), Pantalone (deceived father or cuckolded husband), Colombina (maid), and Inamorato (lover).

**commensalism** Situation in nature in which two species live in close association but only one benefits. One of the species (the commensal) may gain from increased food supply, or by procuring shelter, support, or means of locomotion, but the other (the host) neither gains nor loses. *See also* MUTUALISM; SYMBIOSIS

**Commerce, US Department of** Executive department that promotes economic development and technological advancement through activities that encourage and assist states, regions, communities, and industries. Its agencies include the Bureau of the Census, Office of Business Economics, Patent Office, and National Bureau of Standards. It was founded in 1903 as the Department of Commerce and Labor, and became a separate department in 1913.

**commodity market** Market in which freight or services are bought and sold. Commodities are raw materials such as tea, rubber, tin, or copper. The actual commodities are seldom present, and what is traded is their ownership. The largest commodity exchange in the world is in Chicago, Illinois.

**Commodus, Lucius Aelius Aurelius** (161–192) Roman emperor (180–192), son and successor of MARCUS AURELIUS. Commodus' profligate, perhaps insane, rule was mainly spent organizing gladiatorial contests. He was assassinated by a wrestler.

**Common Agricultural Policy (CAP)** System of support for agriculture within the EUROPEAN UNION (EU). The CAP was incorporated in the Treaty of ROME (1957). It was designed to increase food production within the EU, and to ensure a reasonable income for farmers. The EU sets target prices for commodities. If prices fall below target, the EU buys up surplus product, creating the so-called "beef mountains" and "wine lakes." In 1988, to prevent overproduction, the EU introduced a policy of paying farmers to set aside part of their land as fallow. By 1994 the CAP accounted for 51% of the total EU budget, having soared to 75% in the 1970s. It is one of the most contentious issues in the EU and demands for reform are frequent.

**Common Cause** US nationwide, nonpartisan citizens' lobby working for legislative action and for political reform, founded (1970) by John W. Gardner. Within a year of its formation, the organization had 215,000 dues-paying member.

**common law** Legal system developed in England and adopted in most English-speaking countries. Distinguished from CIVIL LAW, its chief characteristics are judicial precedents, trial by jury, and the doctrine of the supremacy of law. Based originally on the king's court, "common to the whole realm," rather than local or manorial courts, it dates back to the constitutions of CLARENDON (1164). It is the customary and traditional element in the law accumulating from court decisions. A proliferation of statutes have come to supersede common law. *See also* ROMAN LAW

**Common Prayer, Book of** Official liturgy of the ANGLICAN COMMUNION. It was prepared originally as a reformed version of the old Roman Catholic liturgy for England's Henry VIII by Thomas CRANMER in 1549. In 1552 it was revised under the Protestant government of Edward VI. The final version (1559), a combination of the two, was produced by Elizabeth I's archbishop of Canterbury, Matthew Parker. The Prayer Book was further revised in 1662 after the RESTORATION of Charles II.

**Commons, House of** Lower chamber of UK PARLIAMENT

**Commonwealth** (1649–60) Official name of the republic established in England after the execution of King CHARLES I. The PROTECTORATE was set up in 1653 and Oliver CROMWELL became lord protector. The Commonwealth ended with the RESTORATION of CHARLES II. *See also* RUMP PARLIAMENT

**Commonwealth Games** Sports competition originating as the British Empire Games (1930). Competitors are members of the COMMONWEALTH OF NATIONS. Based on the OLYMPIC GAMES, they are held every four years.

**Commonwealth of Independent States (CIS)** Alliance of 12 of the former republics of the SOVIET UNION. The CIS was formed in 1991 with ARMENIA, AZERBAIJAN, BELARUS, GEORGIA, KAZAKSTAN, KYRGYZSTAN, MOLDOVA, RUSSIA, TAJIKISTAN, TURKMENISTAN, UKRAINE, and UZBEKISTAN. The BALTIC STATES (ESTONIA, LATVIA, and LITHUANIA) did not join. All members, except Ukraine, signed a treaty of economic union in 1993, creating a free trade zone. Russia is the dominant power, with an overall responsibility for defense and peacekeeping.

**Commonwealth of Nations** Voluntary association of 53 states, consisting of English-speaking countries formerly part of the BRITISH EMPIRE. Headed by the British sovereign, it exists largely as a forum for discussion of issues of common concern. A Commonwealth secretariat is located in London.

**commune** Usually a community of people who choose to live together for a shared purpose. In the 19th century many communes tried to apply utopian socialist ideals. In the 1960s communes were formed intending to be cooperative, self-supporting and free of the values of mainstream society. In China farming communes exist, similar to the state farms of the former Soviet Union.

**communications** Processes for sharing information and ideas. Facial expressions, hand signals, writing, and speech are examples. The 15th-century invention of the PRINTING press revolutionized communications. The 20th century has witnessed a further revolution, primarily in terms of increased access. TELECOMMUNICATIONS inventions, such as the TELEPHONE, RADIO, TELEVISION, and COMPUTER NETWORK, have facilitated rapid, global, mass communication. The INTERNET is the latest in a long line of technological innovations.

**Communications Satellite (COMSAT)** A private company that provides worldwide SATELLITE communications systems. COMSAT, established by the US Congress, began with the launch of the Early Bird satellite in 1965. Other nations now participate in projects.

**communism** Political outlook based on the principle of communal ownership of property. The theory is derived from the interpretation placed by Karl MARX and Friedrich ENGELS on the course of human history. As outlined in the *Communist Manifesto* (1848), *Capital* (vol. 1, 1867), and other writings, Marx asserted that social and political relations depend ultimately upon relations of economic production. All value (and so wealth) is produced by labor, yet in a capitalist system,

C

## COMPACT DISK

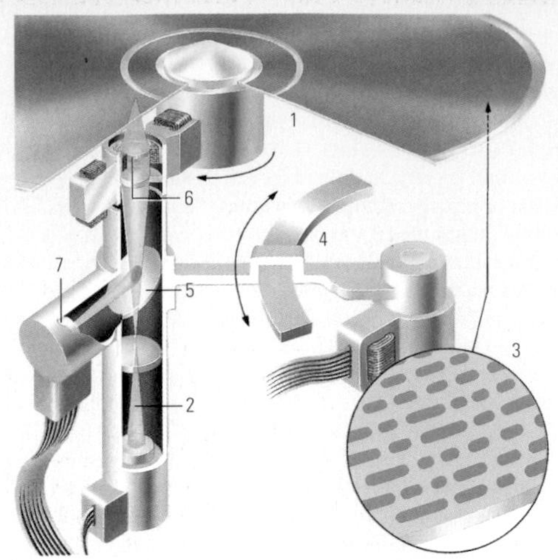


A compact disc player reads digital information from a compact disc (1) using a focused laser (2). Music or other information is written on the underside of the disc in a spiral track of pits (3) representing a digital code of zeros and ones. The disc spins and the laser, mounted on a swing arm (4), moves as the disc plays. The laser passes through a semi-silvered mirror (5) and is focused on the disc (6). When the laser hits a flat area it is reflected back via the mirror to a sensor (7) and the information sent to a chip. When the laser hits a pit it is scattered.

workers' salaries do not represent the full value of their labor. Thus, the working class (PROLETARIAT) and the class that is in control of capital and production (BOURGEOISIE) have conflicting interests. CAPITALISM, it is asserted, is merely one stage in the progress of human institutions. As the forces of production (technology and capital stock) increase, the relations of production must change in order to accommodate them. Marx postulated that the bourgeoisie (by the nature of its operations) brought into being the urban proletariat. Conflicting interests within capitalism would inevitably lead to the overthrow of the bourgeoisie by the proletariat and so the collapse of the system itself. This would be replaced, first by SOCIALISM and eventually by a communist society in which production and distribution would be democratically controlled, summarized in the slogan "From each according to their ability, to each according to their need." A socialist experiment was attempted by LENIN in Russia following the revolution (1917). STALIN turned communism into an ideology to justify the use of dictatorial state power to drive rapid economic development. This process was used as a model for other communist countries, such as China and Cuba.

**Communist International** (Comintern, Third International) Communist organization founded by LENIN in 1919. He feared that the reformist Second International might re-emerge and wished to secure control of the world socialist movement. The Comintern was made up mainly of Russians, and failed to organize a successful revolution in Europe in the 1920s and 1930s. The Soviet Union abolished the Comintern in 1943.

**Communist Party, Chinese** Political organization established in July 1921 by Li Ta-chao and Ch'en Tu-hsiu. The party was strengthened by its alliance (1924) with CHIANG KAI-SHEK's nationalist KUOMINTANG, but virtually shattered when the communists were expelled from Chiang's group in 1927. MAO ZEDONG was the guiding force in revitalizing the party in the early 1930s. Under his leadership, solidified during the LONG MARCH (1934–35), the party revised the Soviet proletariat-based model to fit the peasant-oriented economy of China and, after another four years of civil war from 1945, the People's Republic was proclaimed in TIANANMEN SQUARE (October 1949). The party had achieved complete political and military power. Its structure and hierarchy was nearly destroyed during the CULTURAL REVOLUTION, but reestablished after Mao's death (1976) by DENG XIAOPING. Following pro-democracy demonstrations (May 1989) the party swung away from political reform. Yet, its flexible approach to economic reform enabled it to survive the collapse of Soviet COMMUNISM. Jiang ZEMIN became president in 1993. The National People's Congress is the supreme legislative body, and nominally elects the highest officers of state. Today, the party has more than 40 million members.

**Communist Party of America** Radical party organized in 1919 to represent the interest of workers, farmers, and the lower middle class. The party was strongest in 1932 when it polled more than 100,000 votes in the presidential election. In 1940, following the passage of the Voorhis Act, the party severed its connection with the COMMUNIST INTERNATIONAL and began to lose strength. Subsequently, the Smith Act (1940), the McCarran Act (1950), and the Communist Control Act (1954) drastically reduced its rights and possible influence.

**Communist Party of the Soviet Union (CPSU)** Former ruling party of the SOVIET UNION. It wielded all effective political power in the country and, via the COMMUNIST INTERNATIONAL, had considerable influence over Communist parties in other countries. At its height the CPSU had *c.*15 million members, organized into *c.*400,000 local units (cells) throughout the Soviet Union. Party organization paralleled the hierarchy of local government administration, thus enabling party control of every level of government. There were party cells in almost all areas of Soviet life, such as the school system, armed forces, factories, collective farms, and the media. After the break up of the Soviet Union in 1991, the party was dissolved following a number of decrees by Boris YELTSIN. There remains a strong, traditional conservative power base of ex-party members who are politically active in Russia. *See also* COMMUNISM; LENIN; individual party leaders

**community architecture** Programs, mainly for housing, that involve a study of the prevailing social conditions and consultation with the people who are going to use them. In Britain, the idea developed during the 1970s as a reaction to mass housing developments. Its leading supporter is Prince CHARLES.

**commutative law** Rule of combination in mathematics; it requires that an operation on two terms is independent of the order of the terms. Addition and multiplication of numbers is commutative, since $a + b = b + a$ and $ab = ba$. Vector cross-multiplication does not obey the commutative law.

**Comoros** (Comores) Independent republic off the E coast of Africa between Mozambique and Madagascar in the Indian Ocean, made up of a group of volcanic islands. The three major islands are Grande Comore (home of the capital, Moroni), Anjouan, and Mohéli. The islands are mountainous, the climate tropical, and the soil fertile. Farming is the chief occupation. Coconuts, copra, vanilla, cocoa, and sisal are the main crops. France owned the islands between 1841 and 1909. They gained independence in 1975 and there have been several attempted revolutions. Area: 719sq mi (1,862sq km). Pop. (1994) 535,600.

**compact disk (CD)** Disk used for high-quality digital sound reproduction. The disk has a shiny metal layer and a transparent, protective plastic coating. The sound signal consists of millions of minute pits, pressed into one side of the metal. On replay, a narrow laser beam is reflected from the rotating disk's surface. A sensor detects changes in the beam, and forms an electrical signal of pulses. This is processed and decoded to form a sound signal that can be amplified for reproduction on loudspeakers. *See also* CD-ROM

**company** Group of people who agree to work together as a firm or business. The legal responsibility of running a company rests with its board of directors which, if the business has raised finance by selling shares in the company, has to account to its shareholders. In a **private** company, the directors sell shares to whomever they please. The shares of a **public** company can be bought and sold by anyone through a STOCK EXCHANGE. *See also* CORPORATION

**compass** Direction-finding instrument also used to show direction of a magnetic field. It is a horizontal magnetic needle on a vertical pivot whose north-seeking end can turn to point towards magnetic N. Adjustments can be made to give true N. The compass has been used in Europe since the 12th century when the "needle" was a piece of lodestone. NAVIGATION today often uses the motor-driven GYROCOMPASS.

**compass plant** Large, coarse, perennial plant native to North America. It has a tall flower stalk with a number of large, solitary, yellow flowers and long, deeply cut leaves that are said to face north and south. Height: 11ft (3.5m). Family Asteraceae/Compositae; species *Silphium laciniatum*.

**compiler** Computer PROGRAM that translates the symbols of a programing language into instructions readable directly by a COMPUTER. Most programs are written in high-level languages, such as "C," Pascal or BASIC, which are made up of words and symbols easily comprehended by humans. *See also* COMPUTER

**complex number** Number of the form $a + bi$, where $i = \sqrt{-1}$, and $a$ and $b$ are REAL NUMBERS. To obtain a solution to the equation $x^2 + 1 = 0$, we need to introduce a new number i, such that $i^2 = -1$. The solutions to similar equations then give rise to a set of numbers of the general form $a + bi$. These are known as the complex numbers. Since $b$ can be equal to zero, the set of complex numbers includes the real numbers.

**Compositae** Family of *c.*20,000 species of plants in which the "flower" is actually a composite flower-head consisting of a cluster of many, usually tiny, individual flowers (florets). In a typical composite, such as the DAISY, the flower-head has a central yellow disk, consisting of a cluster of tiny bisexual florets lacking visible petals. The outer ring of female ray florets has large white petals. In composites such as the DANDELION and CHICORY, the flower-head consists entirely of ray florets. Others, such as THISTLES, consist entirely of disk florets. Composites make up by far the largest family of plants. The Compositae are often known as the Asteraceae.

**COMPUTER**

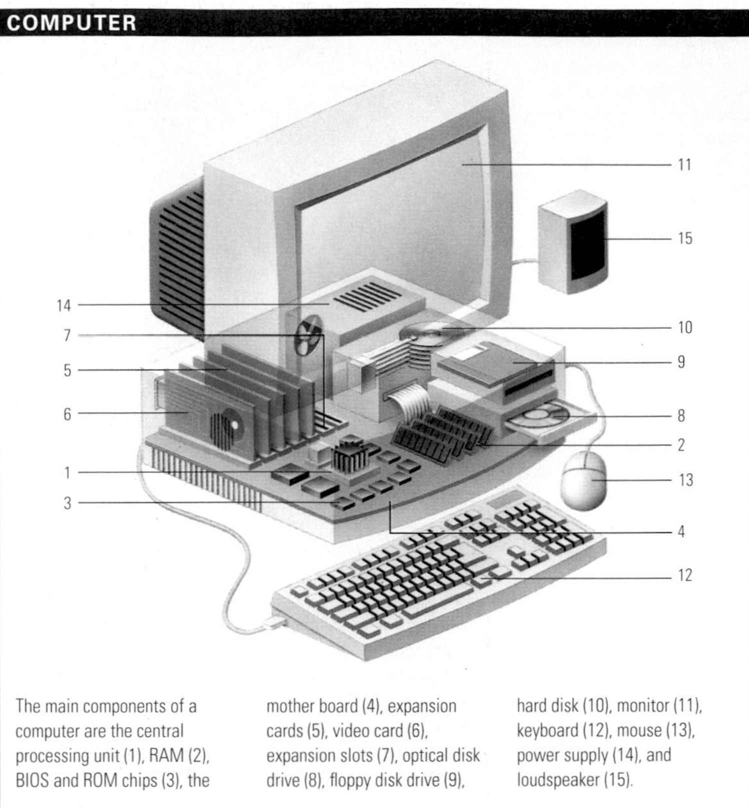


The main components of a computer are the central processing unit (1), RAM (2), BIOS and ROM chips (3), the mother board (4), expansion cards (5), video card (6), expansion slots (7), optical disk drive (8), floppy disk drive (9), hard disk (10), monitor (11), keyboard (12), mouse (13), power supply (14), and loudspeaker (15).

**COMPUTER**

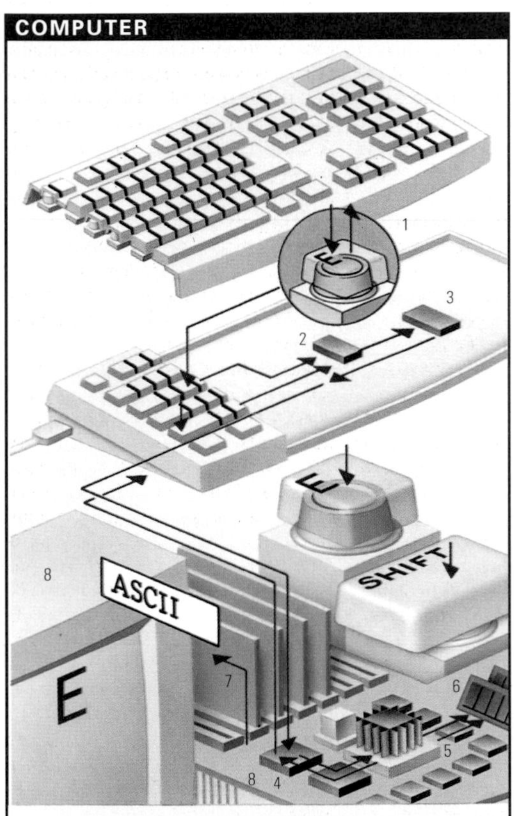


Pressing a key (1) or pair of keys changes the current flowing through the key's circuit. A microprocessor (2) scans the circuits and detects when they change. A scan code is transmitted by the microprocessor to the memory buffer in the keyboard (3). The scan code then travels through the cable connecting the keyboard to its controller chip (4), in the body of the computer. The controller chip informs the CPU (5) which finds the keyboard program in ROM (6) and cancels the scan code in the keyboard's memory buffer. The ROM converts the scan code into the PC's language, ASCII (7), and then instructs the monitor (8) to display the character, an uppercase E.

**compound** Substance formed by chemical combination of two or more elements that cannot be separated by physical means. Compounds are produced by the rearrangement of VALENCE electrons (outer ELECTRONS of an atom) seeking to attain more stable configurations. They usually have properties quite different from those of their constituent elements. IONIC COMPOUNDS have ionic bonds – they are collections of oppositely charged ions. The ions are packed together in a regular arrangement called a CRYSTAL lattice. Ionic compounds, such as sodium chloride, are solids at room temperature and have high melting and boiling points. COVALENT bonding occurs where nonmetal atoms share electrons. Such compounds can be classified as simple molecular structures (such as carbon dioxide) – with low melting and boiling points; or giant molecular structures (such as graphite and diamond). Their properties depend on the arrangement of the atoms in the macromolecule. *See also* MOLECULE

**Compromise of 1850** Set of balanced resolutions by Senator Henry CLAY to prevent civil war. The US Congress agreed to admit California as a free state, organize New Mexico and Utah as territories without mention of slavery, provide for a tougher fugitive slave law, and abolish the slave trade in Washington, D.C.

**Compton, Arthur Holly** (1892–1962) US physicist. He discovered that wavelengths of X-RAYS increase when the rays collide with ELECTRONS (the Compton effect). This helped prove that X-rays could act as particles. Compton shared the 1927 Nobel Prize for physics with C.T.R. WILSON. Head of the early phase of the MANHATTAN PROJECT to develop the atom bomb, he helped create the first sustained nuclear CHAIN REACTION.

**computer** Device that processes data (information) by following a set of instructions called a PROGRAM. All digital computers work by manipulating data represented as numbers. The origins of the computer can be traced back to the ABACUS and mechanized adding machines. Charles BABBAGE first conceived of a machine that could be given instructions to perform many different calculating tasks. By the mid-1940s mechanical machines were replaced by electronic versions. Some used

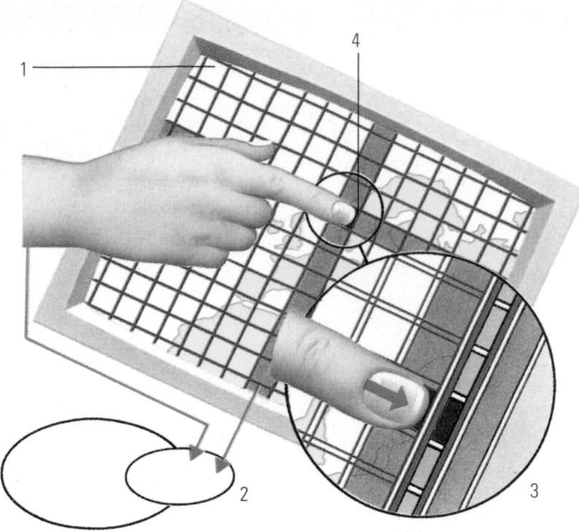


► **computer graphics** Touch-screens detect physical contact with the screen (1). Most screens have two plastic layers with a thin transparent coating of a conducting material (2). The pressure of a finger brings the two sheets slightly closer together (3). The screen reads the position of the touch horizontally and vertically (4) to ascertain its position. In consumer touch-screens, such as automated teller machines, a small selection of options is presented to the user with each section of the screen relating to one of them.

groups of electromagnetic switches, called relays, to register binary numbers. At any instant, each switch could be either on or off, corresponding to the digits 1 or 0 in the BINARY SYSTEM. Stages in the long term development of electronic digital computers are termed **computer generations**. A first generation computer was developed by engineers at the University of Pennsylvania in 1946. The 27-ton machine called ENIAC (Electronic Numerical Indicator and Computer) used electronic VALVES instead of relays. Programming ENIAC to do a particular task was a lengthy process that consisted of changing wired connections. John VON NEUMANN helped to develop techniques for storing programs in code to avoid this problem. In 1951 UNIVAC 1 became the first computer offered for general sale. This second-generation computer used TRANSISTORS and became smaller and more practical. In the 1960s, a third generation of computers appeared with the invention of INTEGRATED CIRCUITS, leading to a further reduction in size. Fourth-generation computers, developed in the 1980s, are even smaller, utilizing powerful MICROPROCESSORS. Microprocessors contain a complete CENTRAL PROCESSING UNIT (CPU) which controls operations. The latest microprocessors contain more than a million transistors and other components, all in a package little bigger than a postage stamp. Fifth-generation computers using **very large-scale integration (VLSI)** chips will utilize the developments of ARTIFICIAL INTELLIGENCE (AI) and commonly may be controlled by spoken commands. Read-Only Memory (ROM) and Random Access Memory (RAM) SILICON CHIPS act as permanent and temporary electronic memories for storing data. A typical desktop computer system consists of: a CENTRAL PROCESSING UNIT (CPU) together with memory chips and storage devices (usually MAGNETIC DISKS); a monitor containing a CATHODE-RAY TUBE; a keyboard and a mouse; and a printer. Computer programs are usually stored on disks and transferred to the machine's RAM when required. The keyboard and mouse are called **input devices**, since they allow the user to feed information into the computer. The **keyboard** enables the user to enter letters, numbers and other symbols. The **mouse** is a small device moved by hand, which enables the user to control the computer by positioning a pointer on the monitor screen, to select functions. A magnetic disk drive, such as a HARD DISK can supply programs and data to the computer, and store its output. Many computers have CD-ROM drives. Many other **peripherals** are used, such as a scanner which converts images into an electronic signal so that they can be stored and displayed by the computer. The modern computer market is dominated by PCs – the generic term used to refer to machines based on the original IBM personal computer produced in the early 1980s. All these machines use an operating system (such as DOS or Windows) produced by the giant SOFTWARE corporation, Microsoft. Other popular operating systems include Apple Macintosh (MacOS) and UNIX.

**computer-aided design (CAD)** Use of COMPUTER GRAPHICS to assist the design of, for example, fabrics, electronic circuits, buildings, and vehicles. With CAD, designers can make alterations and analyze their effect.

► **computer graphics** A graphics pad is a method for inputting information to a computer. It allows the operator to "draw" on the computer with a pen or stylus (1) via the pad (2). Just below the surface of the pad are current-carrying filaments (shown blue and green). The pen has a magnet in the tip (3). As the pen moves across the pad the magnet interferes with the magnetic fields (4) created by the filaments sending the location of the pen to the computer. The location of the interference is read hundreds of times a second by a chip providing a constant stream of coordinates.

**computer graphics** Illustrations produced on a COMPUTER. Simple diagrams and shapes may be produced by typing on the keyboard. Complex images require a mouse, painting or drawing SOFTWARE, and often special graphics HARDWARE.

**computerized axial tomography (CAT)** Method of taking X-RAYS that provides images of "slices" through the body. Inside a CAT scanner is an X-ray source, which produces a narrow beam of radiation. This passes through a patient's body and is detected by an electronic sensor. The X-ray source and detector are rotated around the patient's body so that views are taken from all angles. A computer analyzes the output to build up a picture of the slice of the body.

**computer language** System of words and rules used to PROGRAM a COMPUTER. Most computers work using a binary-coded language (using 1s and 0s) called **machine code**. A language consisting of words and symbols that relate more directly to normal language can be used to instruct a computer. A COMPILER, assembler, or other such program then translates this into machine code. Several kinds of programming language have been designed for different purposes. **Fortran** is for scientific and mathematical use, COBOL (Common Business-Oriented Language) for business programs, **Algol** for mathematical applications, and BASIC and **Pascal** were originally for use by learners. Today, the majority of applications for personal computers are written in a language called "**C**".

**computer network** Number of computers linked together for communications purposes. A typical **local area network (LAN)** links computers within the same building, enabling staff to exchange data and share printers. A **wide area network (WAN)** covers longer distances and may link LANs. The interconnections are made through public TELEPHONE services via electronic units called MODEMS, or through the INTEGRATED SERVICES DIGITAL NETWORK (ISDN), a dedicated high-speed line that carries digital signals. *See also* INTERNET

**computer program** *See* PROGRAM

**computer virus** Sequence of computer PROGRAM code that is able to copy itself from one COMPUTER to another and is usually designed to disrupt the normal operation of a computer. Some viruses find their way into computers all over the world. A virus may remain undetected for months and then suddenly go into action. The worst can cause loss or alteration of data held on the computer

**COMSAT** *See* COMMUNICATIONS SATELLITE

**Comte, Auguste** (1798–1857) French philosopher, founder of POSITIVISM. He proposed the law of the three stages (theological, metaphysical, and positive) that represent the development of the human race. In the first two stages the human mind finds religious or abstract causes to explain phenomena, while in the third, explanation of a phenomenon is found in a scientific law. Comte influenced John Stuart MILL and was the founder of SOCIOLOGY. His works include *System of Positive Polity* (1830–42).

**Conakry** Capital city of Guinea, W Africa, on Tombo Island,

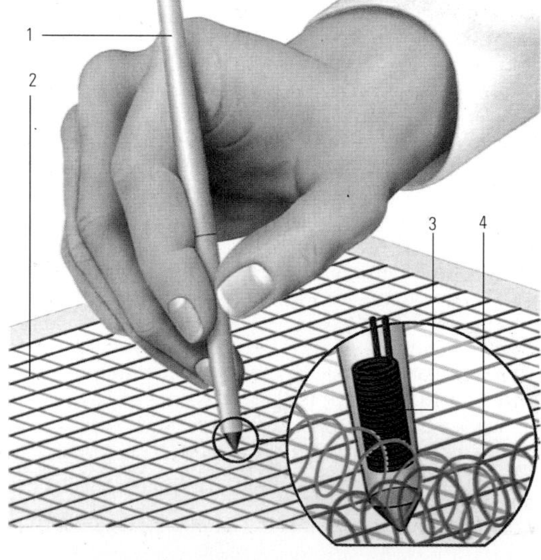

in the Atlantic Ocean. Founded in 1884, it is a major port and the administrative and commercial center of Guinea. It has an airport. It exports alumina and bananas. Pop. (1983) 705,300.

**concentration camp** Detention center for military or political prisoners. The first were set up by the British for Afrikaner civilians during the SOUTH AFRICAN WARS (1899-1902). The most notorious were those established by the Nazi regime in Germany in the 1930s for people considered racially or socially undesirable and political opponents. Some of these camps provided slave labor while others were the sites of mass execution. In Poland, more than 6 million people, mostly Jews, were murdered in the gas chambers. GULAGS were widely employed during Stalin's purges, and reeducation camps were used in the Chinese CULTURAL REVOLUTION and by the KHMER ROUGE. *See also* AUSCHWITZ; BELSEN; BUCHENWALD; DACHAU

**conceptualism** Philosophical theory in which the universal is found in the particular, a position between NOMINALISM and REALISM. It asserts that the mind is the individual that universalizes by experiencing particulars.

**concerto** Musical work for instrumental soloists accompanied by orchestra. Alessandro Stradella (1644–1682) is credited with originating the **concerto grosso**, in which a small section of soloists on various instruments, the *concertino*, is contrasted with the full orchestra, the *ripieno*. J.S. BACH's Brandenburg Concertos are fine examples of this form. VIVALDI composed most of his concertos for one soloist and orchestra and used the three-movement form (fast-slow-fast) which was to become standard in CLASSICAL MUSIC, such as the brilliant concertos of MOZART and BEETHOVEN. In the 19th century, concertos involved increasing virtuosity, as in the works of LISZT and RACHMANINOV.

**conclave** Originally a place of private or secret assembly, then the assembly itself. More particularly, the assembly of CARDINALS that elects a new pope.

**Concord** Capital of New Hampshire, on the Merrimack River. Founded as a trading post (1660), it was settled in 1727. It was the scene of New Hampshire's ratification of the Constitution as the deciding state on June 21, 1788, and designated state capital in 1808. Quarries N of the city produce the famous white granite used for the Library of Congress, Washington, D.C. Industries: electrical equipment. Pop. (1992) 36,364.

**Concord** Town on the Concord River, E Massachusetts, US. Settled in 1635, it was the site of one of the early battles in the American Revolution (April 19, 1775). British forces were sent from Boston to destroy ammunition and supplies stockpiled in the city, but were met by MINUTEMEN. Concord was a center of the 19th century TRANSCENDENTALISM movement. Pop. (1990) 17,076. *See also* LEXINGTON AND CONCORD, BATTLES OF

**concrete** Hard, strong building material made by mixing CEMENT, sand, gravel, and water. It is an important building material. It can be reinforced by embedded steel rods. Prestressed concrete contains piano wires instead of steel. Its modern use dates from the early 19th century, although the Romans made extensive use of concrete.

**concussion** Temporary loss of consciousness due to a blow to the head. It may last from a few seconds to a few hours. There may be no structural damage to the brain, but a scan will detect signs of bruising. It is often associated with confusion and AMNESIA. Treatment consists of rest and close observation.

**Condé** (1530–1830) Junior branch of the French royal house of BOURBON. Notable members of the line included **Louis I**, Prince de Condé (1530–69), a HUGUENOT leader. The third prince was **Henry II** (1588–1646), a Catholic, who was arrested for blackmail and sedition (1616), but was reconciled to the crown under LOUIS XIII. **Louis II**, the Great Condé (1621–86), was a famous general. Victorious against Spain at Rocroi (1643), he was later involved in the civil conflict known as the FRONDES. **Louis Joseph** de Bourbon-Condé (1736–1818) led the émigré nobility during the FRENCH REVOLUTION.

**condensation** Formation of a liquid from a gas or vapor, caused by cooling or an increase in pressure. It changes water vapor in the air into water droplets, forming mist, cloud, rain, or drops on cold surfaces.

**condenser** *See* CAPACITOR

**conditioning** In experimental psychology, learning in

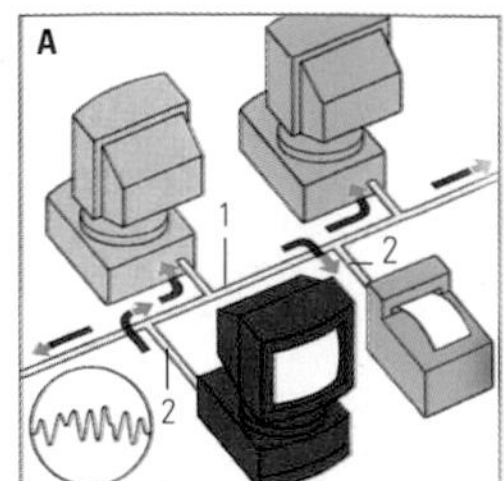

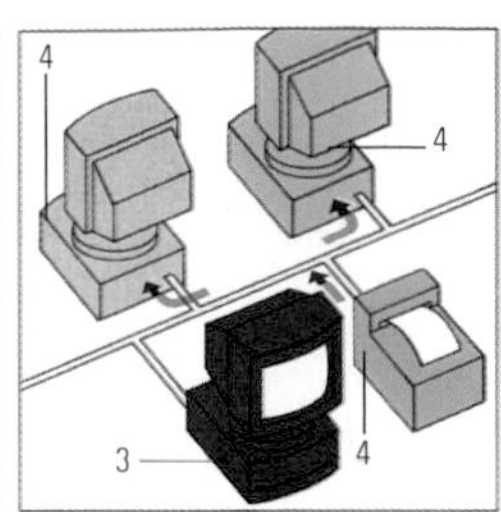

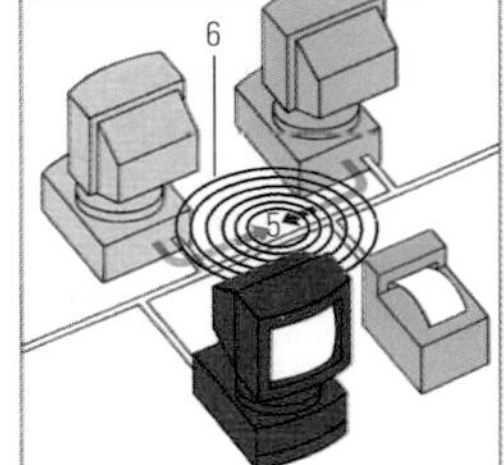

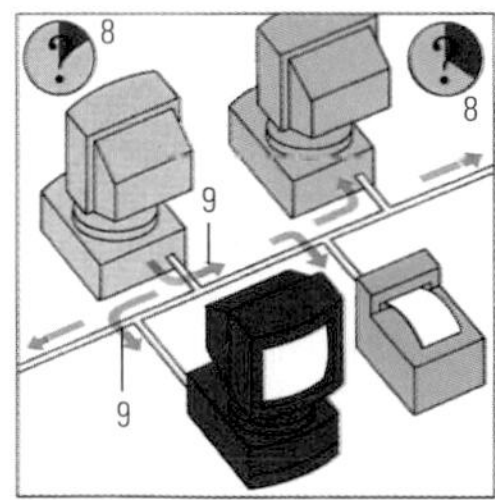


▲ **computer network** The most common local area network (LAN) provides a communication link for all office computers and printers (A). From a single cable (1), spurs (2) lead to individual machines. A machine sends (3) an address code at the start of each message. Receiving machines (4) return a message, consisting of an address code and confirmation. When two machines send messages simultaneously they collide (5). The electronic shock wave (6), produced when the messages hit, are picked up by all the machines on the LAN. The machines suspend message-sending for a random length of time (8) before repeating the message (9).

which human or animal subjects learn to respond in a certain way to a stimulus. Classical conditioning stems from the work of Ivan PAVLOV, while operant conditioning was first described by B.F. SKINNER.

**condom** *See* CONTRACEPTION

**condor** Common name for two species of the American VULTURE: the black Andean condor (*Vultur gryphus*) and the rare gray-brown California condor (*Gymnogyps californianus*). They are two of the largest flying birds and feed on partly rotted carrion. Length: up to 50in (127cm). Wing-span: up to 10ft (3.5m).

**conductance** Ability of a material to conduct ELECTRICITY. In a direct current (DC) circuit, it is the reciprocal of electrical resistance. In an alternating current (AC) circuit, it is the resistance divided by the square of impedance (the opposition of a circuit to the passage of a current). SI units of conductance are siemens (symbol S). *See also* ELECTRIC CURRENT

**conduction** **Thermal** conduction is the transfer of heat from a hot region of a body to a cold region. If one end of a metal rod is placed in a flame, the heat energy received causes increased vibratory motion of the molecules in that end. These molecules bump into others farther along the rod, and the increased motion is passed along until finally the end not in the flame becomes hot. **Electrical** conduction is the progress of charged particles through a substance resulting in an electric charge. In metals it is the flow of free ELECTRONS. In gases it is the flow of IONS. *See also* SEMICONDUCTOR; SUPERCONDUCTIVITY

**conductivity** Measure of the ease with which a material allows electricity or heat to pass through it. For a solid substance, the electrical conductivity is the CONDUCTANCE. *See also* ELECTRIC CURRENT

**conductor** In music, a person who coordinates the performance of a band, orchestra, or choir, and directs and inspires the interpretation of the music. Before the 19th century a harpsichordist or first violinist "directed" orchestral playing.

**conductor** In physics, substance or object that allows easy passage of free electrons. Conductors have a low electrical RESISTANCE. Metals, the best conductors, have free electrons that become an ELECTRIC CURRENT when made to move. The resistance of a metallic conductor increases with temperature.

**cone** Solid geometric figure swept out by a line (generator) that joins a point moving in a closed curve in a plane, to a fixed point (vertex) outside the plane. In a right circular cone, the vertex lies above the center of a circle (base), and the cone's generators join the vertex to points on the circle. Such a cone has a volume $\frac{1}{3}\pi r^2 h$ and a curved surface area $\pi rs$, where $h$ is the vertical height, $s$ the slant height, and $r$ the radius of the base.

**Confederate States of America** (1861–65) (Confederacy) Southern states which seceded from the Union following the election of Abraham LINCOLN. South Carolina left in December 1860, and was followed closely by Alabama, Florida, Georgia, Louisiana, Mississippi, and Texas. In March 1861, Jefferson DAVIS was elected president and a new constitution protected STATE'S RIGHTS and retained SLAVERY.

▲ **condor** The Andean condor (*Vultur gryphus*) is a type of vulture. With a wing span of up to 10ft (3m), the Andean condor feeds mainly on carrion, but will attack young lambs or deer.

A capital was established at MONTGOMERY, Alabama. On April 12 the CIVIL WAR began, and Arkansas, North Carolina, Tennessee, and Virginia joined the Confederacy. The capital was moved to RICHMOND, Virginia. The Confederacy received little external support, and internal problems contributed to its defeat and dissolution in April 1865.

**Confederation, Articles of** *See* ARTICLES OF CONFEDERATION

**confession** Acknowledgment of SINS. In the Jewish and Christian traditions, it may be made by a congregation in the course of worship, or by individual penitents.

**confirmation** Sacrament of the Christian Church by which the relationship between God and an individual, established by BAPTISM, is confirmed or strengthened in faith. Candidates for confirmation take the baptismal vows previously made on their behalf by godparents.

**Confucianism** Philosophy that dominated China until the early 20th century and still has many followers, mainly in Asia. It is based on the *Analects*, sayings attributed to CONFUCIUS. Strictly an ethical system to ensure a smooth-running society, it gradually acquired quasi-religious characteristics. Confucianism views man as potentially the most perfect form of *li*, the ultimate embodiment of good. It stresses the responsibility of sovereign to subject, of family members to one other, and of friend to friend. Politically, it helped to preserve the existing order, upholding the status of the MANDARINS. When the monarchy was overthrown (1911–12), Confucian institutions were ended, but after the Communist Revolution (1949); many Confucian elements were incorporated into Maoism.

**Confucius** (*c.*551–479 BC) (K'ung-fu-tzu) Founder of CONFUCIANISM. Born in Lu, he was an excellent scholar and became an influential teacher of the sons of wealthy families. He is said to have been prime minister of Lu. In his later years he sought a return to the political morality of the early ZHOU dynasty. *See also* CHINESE LITERATURE

**congenital disorder** Abnormal condition present from birth caused by faulty development, infection, or the mother's exposure to drugs or other toxic substances during pregnancy. SPINA BIFIDA is such a condition.

**CONGO**

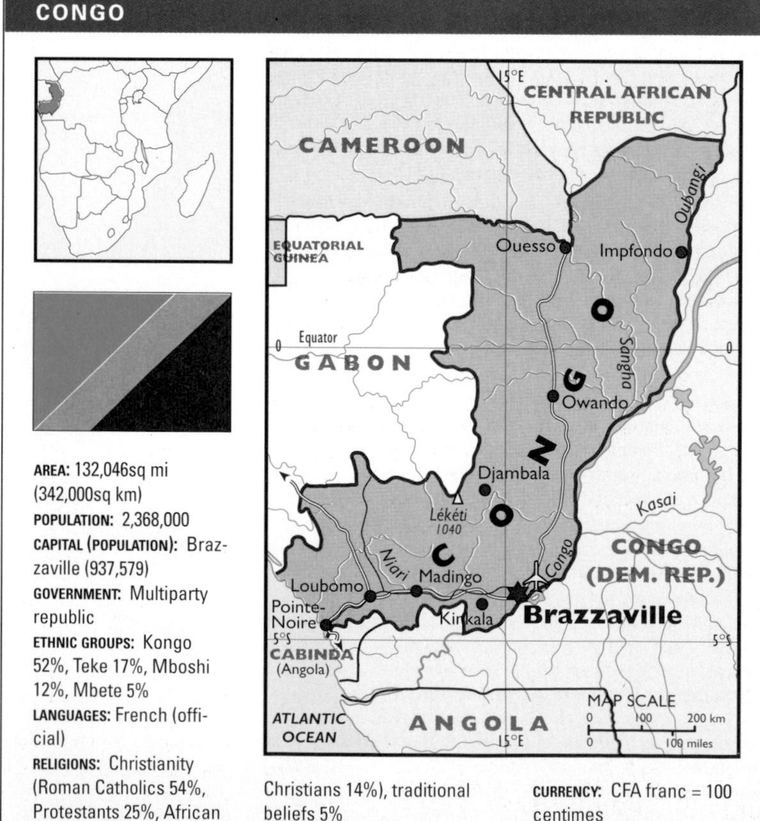


**AREA:** 132,046sq mi (342,000sq km)
**POPULATION:** 2,368,000
**CAPITAL (POPULATION):** Brazzaville (937,579)
**GOVERNMENT:** Multiparty republic
**ETHNIC GROUPS:** Kongo 52%, Teke 17%, Mboshi 12%, Mbete 5%
**LANGUAGES:** French (official)
**RELIGIONS:** Christianity (Roman Catholics 54%, Protestants 25%, African Christians 14%), traditional beliefs 5%
**CURRENCY:** CFA franc = 100 centimes

**conglomerate** In geology, a sedimentary rock made up of rounded pebbles embedded in a fine matrix of sand or silt, commonly formed along beaches or on river beds.

**Congo** Equatorial republic in W central Africa; the capital is BRAZZAVILLE. The main port is Pointe Noire on the Gulf of Guinea. **Land and climate** Congo generally has a hot, wet equatorial climate. Its narrow, treeless coastal plain is dry and cool. Inland, the Niari River has carved a fertile valley through the forested highlands. Central Congo consists of luxuriant savanna with valley forests. Tree species include the valuable okoumé and mahogany. The N contains large swamps in the tributary valleys of the Zaire and Ubangi rivers. **History** Between the 15th and 18th centuries, part of Congo probably belonged to the huge Kongo kingdom. The Congo coast became a center of the European slave trade. European exploration of the interior took place in the late 19th century, and the area came under French protection in 1880. It was later governed as part of a larger region called French Equatorial Africa and remained under French control until 1960. In 1964 Congo adopted Marxism-Leninism as the state ideology. In 1968 the military, led by Marien Ngouabi, seized power. Ngouabi created the Congolese Workers Party (PCT). In 1977 Ngouabi was assassinated, but the PCT retained power under Colonel Sassou-Nguesso. In 1990 the PCT renounced Marxism and Sassou-Nguesso was deposed. In 1992 democratic elections were won by the Pan-African Union for Social Democracy (UPADS), led by Pascal Lissouba. In 1997 Lissouba was deposed and Sassou-Nguesso was reinstalled as president. **Economy** Congo is a lower-middle-income developing country (1995 GDP per capita, US$2,050). More than 60% of the work force is engaged in subsistence agriculture. Major food crops include bananas, cassava, corn, and rice, while cash crops are coffee and cocoa. Congo's main exports are oil (70% of the total) and lumber.

**Congo, Democratic Republic of** *See* ZAIRE

**Congo** (Zaire River) River in central and W Africa; the second-longest in the continent. It rises in S Zaire and flows in a massive curve to the Atlantic Ocean for 2,900mi (4,670km). Its rate of flow and size of drainage basin make it Africa's largest untapped source of hydroelectric power. The chief ocean port is Matadi. The main headstream is the Lualaba, and the Kasai and Ubangi are among its many large tributaries.

**Congregationalism** Christian church denomination in which local churches are autonomous; members have been called Brownists, Separatists, and Independents. It is based on the belief that Christ is the head of the church and all members are priests. Modern Congregationalism began in England in *c.*1580. In the US, the Congregational Christian Churches united with others as the United Church of Christ (1957). In the UK, the Congregational Church in England and Wales merged with others as the United Reformed Church (1972).

**Congress** Legislative branch of the federal government established by the US CONSTITUTION (1789). Congress comprises the SENATE (the upper house) and the HOUSE OF REPRESENTATIVES (the lower house). The main powers of Congress include the right to assess and collect taxes, introduce legislation, regulate commerce, propose constitutional amendments, mint money, raise and maintain armed forces, establish lower courts, and declare war. Legislation must be passed by both houses and the president to become law. If the president uses his power of veto, Congress can still pass the bill with a two-thirds majority in each house. The first meeting of Congress took place in 1789 in New York City. The Senate can approve treaties and presidential appointments and tries the president if he is impeached. The House of Representatives initiates all tax bills and has the power to impeach the president. The Constitution requires that Congress meet at least once every year, and the president may call special sessions. The preparation and consideration of legislation is largely accomplished by the 17 standing committees in the Senate and the 21 in the House of Representatives. There are additional commissions and committees.

**Congress of Industrial Organizations (CIO)** *See* AMERICAN FEDERATION OF LABOR AND CONGRESS OF INDUSTRIAL ORGANIZATIONS (AFL-CIO)

**Congress of Racial Equality (CORE)** US civil rights organization, founded (1942) in Chicago by James Farmer. CORE first attracted national attention for its sponsorship of the FREEDOM RIDES (1961) to end segregation on public transport. Using the tactics of nonviolence, espoused by Martin Luther KING, Jr., it organized sit-ins, pickets, and boycotts to combat racial discrimination. CORE cosponsored the March on Washington (1963).

**Congress Party** (officially Indian National Congress) Oldest political party in India, whose fortunes were often intertwined with the Nehru dynasty. It was founded in 1885, but was not prominent until after World War I, when Mahatma GANDHI transformed it into a mass independence movement. Jawaharlal NEHRU became president of the Congress in 1929 and at independence (1947) became prime minister. Nehru's daughter, Indira GANDHI, became prime minister in 1966, but the party later split, and Indira's Congress (I) suffered a landslide defeat at the elections of 1977. The party regained power in 1979, and in 1984 (after Indira's assassination) her son, Rajiv GANDHI, became leader. Following a further split, Congress was defeated in 1989, and Rajiv was assassinated in 1991. After defeats in 1996 and 1998 elections, Sonia Gandhi (Rajiv's wife) became leader.

**congress system** Attempt during the early 19th century to conduct diplomacy through regular conferences between the European allies that had defeated Napoleonic France. It originated in the Treaty of PARIS (1815). The four powers (Austria, Britain, Prussia, and Russia) met in 1818, 1820, and 1821. Britain withdrew (1822) after opposing proposals to intervene against revolutionary forces in South America and elsewhere. Differences between the three remaining powers at St. Petersburg in 1825 caused the abandonment of the system.

**CONIFER**

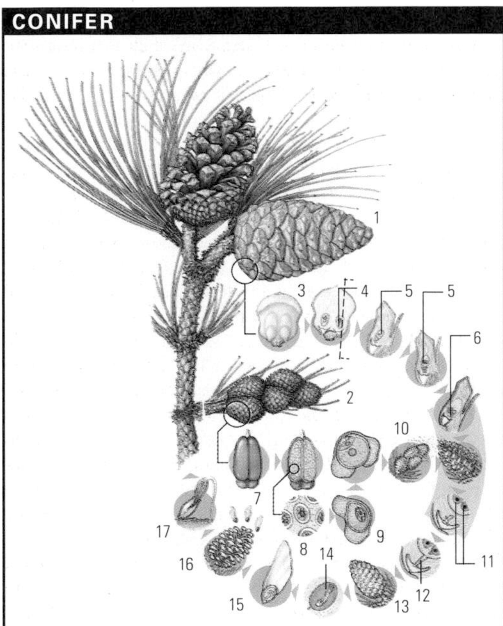

The reproductive cycle of the ponderosa pine is typical of many conifers. In summer the mature tree bears both female cones (1) and male cones (2). A scale from the female cone (3) contains two ovules (4). Within each ovule, a spore cell (5) divides to develop into a female gametophyte (6). A scale from the male cone (7) contains many spores (8). Each of these develops into a male gametophyte within a winged pollen grain (9). This process lasts one year. Pollination occurs early the next summer, when female cones open so that airborne pollen grains enter an ovule. Inside the ovule, the female gametophyte develops two ova (11). Fertilization occurs during the spring of the following year, after the male gametophyte has matured and grown a pollen tube, and the cone closes (13). Within the female gametophyte, the fertilized ova (zygote) develops into an embryo (14); and around it, a tough, winged seed case is formed (15). In the fall of the second year, the female cone opens (16), and seeds are dispersed by wind, ready to germinate (17).

**Congreve, William** (1670–1729) English dramatist. His elegant satire represents the peak of RESTORATION DRAMA. His comedies include *Love for Love* (1695), and *The Way of the World* (1700). Congreve also wrote a tragedy, *The Mourning Bride* (1697).

**conic** (conic section) Curve found by the intersection of a plane with a CONE. Circles, ellipses, parabolas, or hyperbolas are conic sections. Alternatively, a conic is the locus of a point that moves so that the ratio of its distances from a fixed point (the focus) and a fixed line (the directrix) is constant. This ratio is called the eccentricity ($e$): $e = 1$ gives a parabola, $e > 1$ a hyperbola, $e < 1$ an ellipse, and $e = 0$ a circle.

**conifer** Cone-bearing trees, generally evergreen, such as pines, firs, and redwoods. Some are the Earth's largest plants, reaching heights of up to 325ft (99m). They are a major natural resource of the Northern Hemisphere. *See also* GYMNOSPERM

**conjunctivitis** Inflammation of the conjunctiva, the fine membrane that lines the eyelid and covers the front of the eye. It can be caused by infection, usually bacterial, by exposure to irritants, or by allergy, and produces watery, burning, and itching eyelids.

**Connecticut** Northeastern state; its state capital and largest city is HARTFORD. One of the original 13 colonies, Connecticut was first settled by the English in the 1630s. Puritans flocked to the area, and in 1662 the colony received a charter from Charles II. Connecticut was one of the first states to ratify the Constitution and joined the union in 1788. The Connecticut River valley separates the W and E highlands. The economy is based on manufacturing. Industries: transportation equipment, machinery. Hartford is one of the world's leading insurance centers. Dairy produce, eggs, and tobacco are the main farm products. Fishing is also important. Area: 4,845sq mi (12,549sq km). Pop. (1990) 3,287,116.

**CONNECTICUT**
**Statehood:** 9 January 1788
**Nickname:** Constitution State
**State bird:** Robin
**State flower:** Mountain laurel
**State tree:** White oak
**State motto:** He who transplanted still sustains

**Connecticut Compromise** (1787) Compromise at the Philadelphia Constitutional Convention between large states, which favored representation based on population (**Virginia Plan**), and small states, which wanted equal representation regardless of size (**New Jersey Plan**). Proposed by Oliver Ellsworth of Connecticut, the plan was incorporated into the CONSTITUTION and included representation by population (House of Representatives) and equal representation for the states (Senate).

**connective tissue** Supporting and packing tissue that helps to maintain the body's shape and hold it together. Bones, ligaments, cartilage, and skin are types.

**Connery, Sean** (1930– ) Scottish film actor. Connery starred in *Dr. No* (1962), the first adaptation of Ian FLEMING's James Bond spy stories. He made a further six Bond films. Connery became a versatile character actor in films such as *The Name of the Rose* (1986). He won an Academy Award as best supporting actor for *The Untouchables* (1987). Other films include *Marnie* (1964) and *Russia House* (1990).

**Connolly, James** (1870–1916) Irish nationalist leader. He went to the US in 1903 and helped establish the INDUSTRIAL WORKERS OF THE WORLD (IWW). Returning to Ireland, he was a leader in the EASTER RISING of 1916 and was executed by the British authorities.

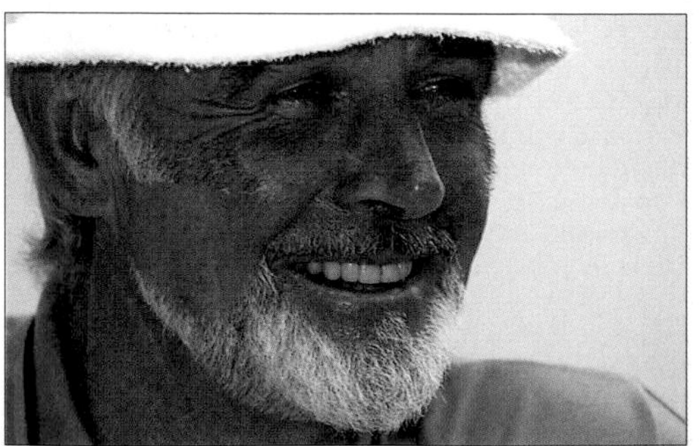

◄ **Connery** Sean Connery appeared in seven Bond films: *Dr. No* (1962), *From Russia with Love* (1963), *Goldfinger* (1964), *Thunderball* (1965), *You Only Live Twice* (1967), *Diamonds are Forever* (1971), and *Never Say Never Again* (1983). His performance in *The Untouchables* (1987) led to a succession of roles in Hollywood actioon films, such as *Indiana Jones and the Last Crusade* (1989).

**Connors, Jimmy (James Scott)** (1952– ) US tennis player. He won more Grand Prix singles titles (109) than any player. In 1974 Connors won the US, Australian, and Wimbledon singles titles. He won the US Open four more times (1976, 1978, 1982–83) and Wimbledon in 1982. Connors also won doubles titles with Ilie Nastase.

**conquistador** (Sp. conqueror) Leader of the Spanish conquest of the New World in the 16th century. Conquistadores were often ex-soldiers unemployed since the Christian reconquest of Spain. The most famous were Hernán CORTÉS and Francisco PIZARRO.

**Conrad IV** (1228–54) German king (1237–54), king of Sicily and Jerusalem (1250–54), son of FREDERICK II. The conflict between Frederick and Pope INNOCENT IV saw the election (1246) of an antiking and Germany lurched into civil war. Conrad inherited Sicily and Jerusalem upon Frederick's death, but was never crowned emperor. The pope excommunicated him (1254).

**Conrad, Joseph** (1857–1924) British novelist and short-story writer, b. Poland. His eventful years as a ship's officer in Asian, African and Latin American waters permeated the exotic settings of many of his novels. Conrad was a central figure in the development of literary MODERNISM. His major works include *Lord Jim* (1900), *Heart of Darkness* (1902), *Nostromo* (1904), *The Secret Agent* (1907), *Under Western Eyes* (1911), and *Chance* (1914).

**conscription** (military draft) Compulsory enlistment in the armed forces. In the US conscription was used during the Civil War, but dropped until 1940 when it was reintroduced, finally being abolished in 1973. In Britain conscription was used in both World Wars and continued in peacetime as National Service until 1962.

**conservation** Preservation of nature and its resources. Conservation requires planning and organization to make the best use of resources or to preserve the natural landscape and wildlife. It is also used to describe the preservation, and sometimes renovation, of ancient and historic man-made structures. *See also* ECOLOGY

**conservation, laws of** Physical laws stating that some property of a closed system is unaltered by change in the system. The most important are the laws of conservation of MATTER and ENERGY. Mass and energy are interconvertible according to the equation $E = mc^2$; what is conserved is the total mass and its equivalent in energy.

**conservatism** Political philosophy seeking to preserve the historic continuity of a society's laws, customs, social structure and institutions. Its modern expression derives from the response, first in Germany, to the liberal doctrines of the Enlightenment and the French Revolution. Originally conservatives supported MERCANTILISM in preference to LAISSEZ-FAIRE economics, but in the 20th century they adopted the principles of the free-market and MONETARISM. *See also* BURKE, EDMUND; CHRISTIAN DEMOCRATS; CONSERVATIVE PARTY; LIBERALISM; SOCIALISM

**Conservative Party** (officially Conservative and Unionist Party) Oldest political party in Britain. Its origins lie in the transformation of the early 19th-century TORY PARTY into the Conservative Party under Sir Robert PEEL in the 1830s; it was mainly a party of landed interests. After the Reform Act of 1867 the urban and commercial element in the party increased. It held power for 31 of the 71 years between 1834 and 1905 and for most of the 1920s and 1930s, either alone or in coalition. In the post-war period it held office in 1951–64 and 1970–74. In 1979 the party swung to the right under the leadership (1975–90) of Margaret THATCHER. With the support of traditional LABOUR PARTY voters, it was able (under Thatcher and John MAJOR) to win four consecutive elections. In 1997 William Hague became the youngest leader of the party since William PITT (1783).

**Constable, John** (1776–1837) English painter, a leading Western landscapist. He attended the Royal Academy (1795–1802) and studied the paintings of CLAUDE LORRAIN. Constable studied every effect of clouds and light on water. His first success came when *The Haywain* (1821) and *View on the Stour* (1817) were shown at the 1824 Paris Salon, although recognition in England only came after his death.

**Constance, Council of** (1414–18) Ecumenical council that ended the GREAT SCHISM. It was convoked by the antipope John XXIII. MARTIN V was elected pope in 1417. The Council also attempted to combat heresy, notably that of Jan HUS.

**Constant (de Rebecque), (Henri) Benjamin** (1761–1830) French political writer, b. Switzerland. A member of Napoleon's tribunate (1799–1802), he went into exile in 1803. After the BOURBON restoration he led the liberal opposition (1819–22, 1824–30). His chief work was the psychological novel *Adolphe* (1816).

**constant** In mathematics, a quantity or factor that does not change. It may be universal, such as the ratio of the circumference of a circle to its diameter, or it may be particular, such as a symbol that has a fixed value in an algebraic equation.

**Constanţa** City on the Black Sea, E Romania. Founded in the 7th century BC as a Greek colony, it was taken by the Romans in 72 BC and named in the 4th century AD by Emperor Constantine. It is Romania's chief port and a major trade center. It has Roman and Byzantine ruins, several mosques, and a naval and air base. Industries: shipbuilding, oil refining. Pop. (1992) 350,476.

**Constantine I (the Great)** (285–337) Roman emperor (306–37) and founder of the Christian empire. A series of feuds for control of Italy ended when Constantine adopted Christianity and defeated Maxentius (312). Constantine and Licinius signed the Edict of Milan (313), which extended tolerance to Christians throughout the empire. In 324 Constantine defeated Licinius and became sole ruler. He presided over the first council of the Christian church at NICAEA (325), which condemned ARIANISM. Constantine rebuilt (330) Byzantium as his capital and renamed it Constantinople (modern-day ISTANBUL). Constantine centralized imperial power, but divided the empire before his death.

**Constantinople** Former name of ISTANBUL

**constellation** Grouping of stars, forming an imaginary figure traced on the sky. The groupings have no physical basis as each star is a different distance from Earth. There are 88 constellations that have been assigned boundaries on the CELESTIAL SPHERE by the International Astronomical Union in 1930.

**constitution** Code of laws or collection of customary practices delineating the powers and organization of the various organs of government within a nation, and some of the rights and obligations of its citizens. *See also* CONSTITUTIONAL LAW

**Constitutional Convention** (1787) Meeting of delegates, in Philadelphia, from 12 of the 13 US states (Rhode Island abstained), which resulted in the creation of the US CONSTITUTION. The Convention was called to revise the ARTICLES OF CONFEDERATION (1781) and to redress the lack of power wielded by the existing government structure. There was demand for a more stable and centralized federal government that had tighter monetary control. The major disagreement centered on how each state should determine its share of this centralized power. A bicameral system was agreed, whereby the House of Representatives was elected according to population, and the Senate was chosen by the states.

**constitutional law** Procedures and doctrines defining the operation of the constitution of a state. In states with a written constitution, courts often have specific powers relating to the constitution and likely points of conflict. In the US, where there is a federal system of government, the SUPREME COURT often resolves conflict between the individual states and the central government. In countries without a written constitution, such as Britain, constitutional law is more imprecise and problems are addressed within the political process.

**Constitution of the United States** Fundamental laws and basis of US government. Adopted (September 1787) by the CONSTITUTIONAL CONVENTION in Philadelphia, it was ratified in 1788 and came into effect in 1789. It replaced the ARTICLES OF CONFEDERATION (1781), which had proved inadequate, giving too much power to each state. It was designed to create a system of "checks and balances" to prevent one branch of government gaining dominance over others. Opponents who feared that the federal government would be too powerful and the rights of the individual unprotected succeeded in having ten amendments, collectively known as the BILL OF RIGHTS, added. Seventeen other amendments have been ratified, the most recent in 1992.

The Constitution was designed not as a code of laws, but as a statement of principles to which laws should adhere, thus allowing considerable flexibility in judicial interpretation.

**constructivism** Russian abstract art movement founded *c.*1913 by the sculptor Vladimir TATLIN. Other members were the brothers Naum GABO and Antoine PEVSNER. Influenced by CUBISM and FUTURISM, their sculptures attempted to relate to contemporary technology. From 1921 the Soviet regime condemned the movement and Gabo and Pevsner left Russia. Through them, and other exiles, constructivism spread and informed modern European architecture and sculpture.

**consul** One of the two chief magistrates of ancient Rome. The office was said to have been established in 510 BC. Consuls were elected each year to administer civil and military matters. After 367 BC, one consul was a PATRICIAN, the other a PLEBEIAN, each having the power to veto the other's decisions.

**consumerism** Belief that consumers should influence the policies and practices regulating the standards and methods of manufacturers, advertisers, and sellers. Interest in consumerism first arose in the 1960s, with Ralph NADER raising the issue in the public consciousness.

**consumption** In economics, expenditure on goods and services, excluding expenditure on capital goods such as machinery. Consumption can be divided into public and private sectors. **Public** consumption consists of government spending on services, such as health and education. Private consumption is household expenditure on nondurables, such as cars and clothing. It is the largest component of national income. The primary importance of private consumption was first stated by Jeremy BENTHAM. Adam SMITH made it the sole reason for production. John Maynard KEYNES proposed the theory of **consumptive function**, which describes the relationship between consumer income and consumption. Governments seek to control consumption by TAXATION and INTEREST rates.

**consumption** *See* TUBERCULOSIS

**contact lens** Lens worn on the CORNEA to aid defective vision. They were invented (1887) by Adolf Frick and were initially made of glass. Modern contact lenses, developed (1948) by Kevin Tuohy, are made of plastic. Hard (corneal) lenses cover the pupil and part of the cornea. They are usually gas-permeable (allowing oxygen to reach the cornea). Soft (hydrophilic) lenses cover the whole cornea and are hydrated in saline solution.

**contempt** In law, disorderly conduct in a court or legislative body, or action performed elsewhere that tends to obstruct the work of a court or legislative body, or bring it into disrepute.

**continent** Large land masses on the Earth's surface. The continents are EUROPE and ASIA (or Eurasia), AFRICA, NORTH AMERICA, SOUTH AMERICA, AUSTRALIA, and ANTARCTICA. They cover *c.*30% of the Earth above sea level and extend below sea level forming continental shelves. All continents have four components, which make up the continental crust. **Shields** are areas of relatively level land within several hundred feet height above sea level consisting of crystalline rocks. **Stable platforms** are areas that have a thin covering of sedimentary rock. **Sedimentary basins** are broad deep depressions filled with sedimentary rocks formed in shallow seas. **Folded mountain** belts are younger sedimentary rocks in long, linear zones of intensely folded and faulted rocks that have been metamorphosed and intruded by igneous and volcanic activity. The continental crust is composed of rocks, moving position over the surface of the Earth very slowly by CONTINENTAL DRIFT. Its thickness is mainly between 20 and 25mi (30–40km) except under large mountain chains where thickness can be 45mi (70km). *See also* PLATE TECTONICS

**continental divide** Line of separation running the length of a continent that determines to which side of the continent rivers flow. Such divides exist in the US, Canada, s America, and Australia.

**Continental Congress** (1774–89) Federal legislature of the American colonies during the AMERICAN REVOLUTION and the period of Confederation. Its first meeting at Philadelphia in September 1774, resulted in unified opposition to British rule and agreed on a boycott of trade with Britain. The Congress reconvened in May 1775 and appointed George WASHINGTON to command the American army. In July 1776 the Second Congress adopted the DECLARATION OF INDEPENDENCE and drafted the ARTICLES OF CONFEDERATION. The adoption of the CONSTITUTION (1787) made it redundant, although it continued to meet until 1789.

**continental drift** Theory that the continents change position very slowly, moving over the Earth's surface at a rate of a only a few centimeters per year, adding up to thousands of kilometers over geological time. Early supporters of continental drift claimed that the jigsaw shapes of the present day continents could be pieced together to form an ancient land mass which, at sometime in the past, split and drifted apart. Continental drift became accepted with the development of PLATE TECTONICS in the 1960s. In recent years continental movement has been measured by global positioning satellites using laser beams.

**continental margin** Region of the ocean floor that lies between the shoreline and the abyssal ocean floor. It includes the continental shelf, the continental slope, and the continental rise.

**Contra** Right-wing Nicaraguan revolutionary group active between 1979 and 1990. In support of the former dictator General Anastasio SOMOZA, ousted in 1979, the Contra aimed to overthrow the elected, left-wing SANDINISTA government. The Contra received financial and military assistance from the US Government from mid-1986. Elections were subsequently held in Nicaragua in 1990, at which the US-funded Union of National Opposition (UNO), effectively the political wing of the Contra, was victorious. The Contra were officially disbanded. *See also* IRAN-CONTRA AFFAIR

**contraception** (birth control) Use of devices or techniques to prevent pregnancy. The PILL is a hormone preparation that prevents the release of an egg (OVUM) and thickens the cervical mucus. The intrauterine device (IUD) is a small spring made from plastic or metal inserted into the womb. It stops the fertilized egg embedding itself in the uterine lining. Barrier methods include the male and female condom and the diaphragm. The male condom is a latex sheath which covers the penis and collects the ejaculated semen; the female condom lines the inside of the vagina, preventing any sperm entering the womb. The use of condoms is widely advocated because they help protect against some SEXUALLY TRANSMITTED DISEASES, including ACQUIRED IMMUNE DEFICIENCY SYNDROME (AIDS). Devices such as diaphragms or caps cover the cervix thus preventing sperm entering the womb. Less effective is the "rhythm method" which involves the avoidance of sex on days when conception is most likely (when the woman is ovulating). It is not a reliable method. Emergency contraception, known as the "morning-after pill," can be taken up to 72 hours after unprotected sexual intercourse; it prevents the fertilized ovum embedding itself in the womb. It is not suitable to be used regularly. *See also* SEXUAL REPRODUCTION

**contract** In law, an agreement between parties that can be legally enforced. A contract creates rights and obligations which can be enforced by law.

**contralto** Lowest range (below SOPRANO and MEZZO-SOPRANO) of the female singing voice. A male voice in this range is called a COUNTERTENOR. *See also* ALTO

▼ **continental drift** About 200 million years ago, the original Pangaea land mass began to split into two continental groups, which further separated over time to produce the present-day configuration.

trench
rift
new ocean floor
zones of slippage

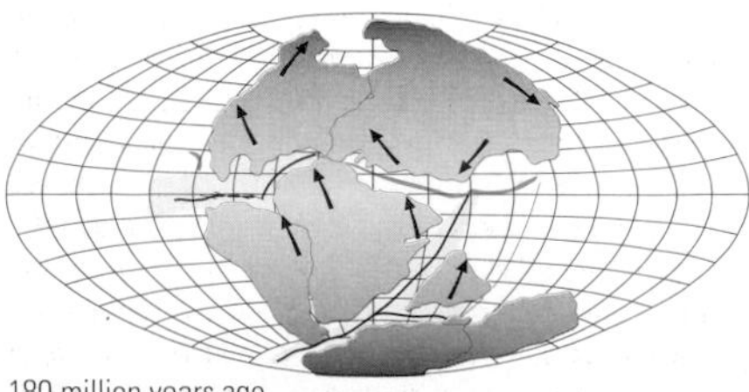

180 million years ago

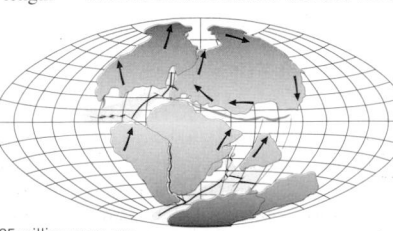

135 million years ago

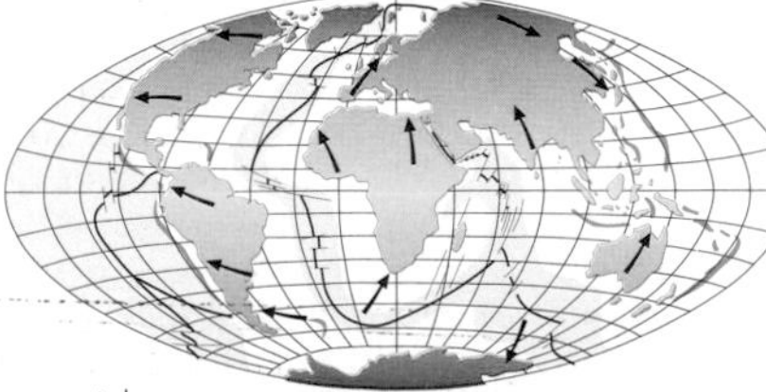

present day

▶ **Cook** The map shows the three voyages of the British explorer Captain James Cook between 1768 and 1779. By sailing south into Antarctic waters and accurately charting the coastline of Australia and New Zealand, he won a new continent for the British crown. On Cook's third voyage, he set out to discover a western entrance to possible Northwest Passage. After surveying the Bering Strait, he was killed by Hawaiian islanders.

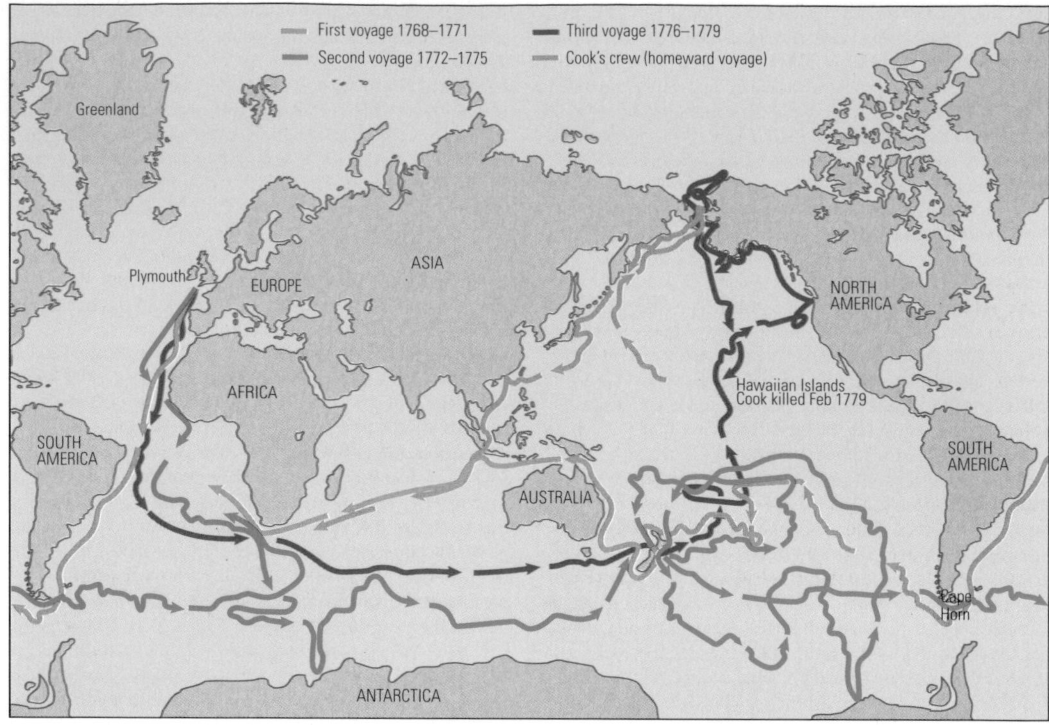


**convection** Transfer of heat by flow of currents within fluids (gases or liquids). Warm fluids have a natural tendency to rise (because they are less dense), whereas cooler fluids tend to fall. This movement subsides when all areas of the fluid are at the same temperature. Convection in the form of winds is the main method of heat transfer from one part of the Earth to another. Liquid convection is used in a car's cooling system.

**convection current** In geology, heat generated from radioactivity deep within the Earth's MANTLE causing rock to flow towards the CRUST. At the top of the mantle the rising rock is deflected laterally below the crust before sinking. This mantle convection is thought to be the process driving PLATE TECTONICS.

**convolvulus** *See* BINDWEED

**convulsion** Intense, involuntary contraction of the muscles, sometimes accompanied by loss of consciousness. A seizure may indicate EPILEPSY although there are other causes, including intoxication, brain abscess or HYPOGLYCEMIA.

**Conway Cabal** (1771) In US history, a failed plot (supposedly led by Thomas Conway) to remove George WASHINGTON as Revolutionary War commander and replace him with Horatio Gates. Investigations later revealed that the plot was not instigated by Conway.

**Cook, James** (1728–79) British naval officer and explorer. He charted the approaches to Quebec during the Seven Years War. In 1768–71 Cook led an expedition to Tahiti to observe an eclipse of the Sun and to investigate the strategic and economic potential of the South Pacific. He conducted a survey of the unknown coasts of New Zealand and charted the E coast of Australia, naming it New South Wales and claiming it for Britain. On a second expedition to the S Pacific (1772–75), Cook charted much of the Southern Hemisphere and circumnavigated Antarctica. On his last voyage (1776–79) he discovered the Sandwich (Hawaiian) Islands, where he was killed in a dispute with the inhabitants. Cook is generally regarded as the greatest European explorer of the Pacific in the 18th century.

**Cook, Mount** Mountain in W central South Island, New Zealand. The highest peak in New Zealand, it lies in Mount Cook National Park and has the Tasman Glacier on its SE slope. Height: 12,349ft (3,764m).

**Cook Islands** Group of 15 islands in the S Pacific Ocean, NE of New Zealand, consisting of the Northern (Manihiki) Cook Islands and the Southern (Lower) Cook Islands; a self-governing territory in free association with New Zealand. Discovered by James Cook in 1773, the islands became a British protectorate in 1888 and were annexed to New Zealand in 1901. They achieved self-governing status in 1965. Products: copra, citrus fruits. Area: 113sq mi (293sq km). Pop. (1986) 17,463.

**Coolidge, (John) Calvin** (1872–1933) 30th US President (1923–29). Stern action in the Boston police strike of 1919 earned him the Republican nomination as vice president in 1920. He became president on the death of Warren HARDING in 1923 and was reelected in 1924. A conservative with no dramatic political program, his administration was characterized by a laissez-faire approach to business and commerce, summed up by his phrase, "the business of America is business." Many argue that this attitude was partly responsible for the unsustainable bullishness of the US stock market.

**Cooper, Gary** (1901–61) US film actor. His laconic style soon became an archetype for the cowboy hero in Westerns such as *The Virginian* (1929). In the 1930s Cooper's acting diversified in films such as *Mr. Deeds Goes to Town* (1936). He won two Academy Awards for best actor: *Sergeant York* (1941), and *High Noon* (1952).

**Cooper, James Fenimore** (1789–1851) US novelist. One of the earliest American novelists and among the first to gain international recognition. His most successful works were the romantic "Leatherstocking Tales" about the frontier, of which

▶ **Coolidge** His frankness and sincerity made Calvin Coolidge a popular president with the people. His term in office was distinguished by his "laissez-faire" approach to business. He strongly advocated a policy of government non-interference.

the best known are *The Pioneers* (1823), *The Last of the Mohicans* (1826), and *The Deerslayer* (1841).

**cooperative movement** Variety of worldwide organizations, founded to provide mutual assistance in economic enterprises for the benefit of their members. The first such movement was founded in England in 1844 by the Rochdale Pioneers, who established a cooperative retail society to eliminate the middleman and share profits among its members. The cooperative movement has been extended to include cooperative agriculture, cooperative manufacturing and cooperative banking and finance. *See also* COOPERATIVE WHOLESALE SOCIETY; OWEN, ROBERT

**Cooperative Wholesale Society** Organization formed (1863) in N England to provide for consumer cooperation. It was a development of the early cooperative plans of Robert OWEN and the Rochdale Pioneers, which encouraged consumers to form their own retail societies and share the profits.

**coordinate geometry** (algebraic geometry) Branch of mathematics combining the methods of pure GEOMETRY with those of ALGEBRA. Any geometrical point can be given an algebraical value by relating it to coordinates, marked off from a frame of reference. Thus, if a point is marked on a square grid so that it is $x_1$ squares along the x axis and $y_1$ squares along the y axis, it has the coordinates ($x_1$, $y_1$). Polar coordinates can also be used. It was first introduced in the 17th century by René DESCARTES. *See also* CARTESIAN COORDINATE

**coot** Aquatic bird of freshwater marshes. Related to the RAILS, it takes flight awkwardly but is a strong swimmer and diver and feeds in or near water. All coots have white bills and foreheads. The female lays 8–12 buff-colored, brown-spotted eggs on a floating reed nest. Family Rallidae; genus *Fulica*.

**Copenhagen** (København) Capital and chief port of Denmark on E Sjaelland and N Amager Island, in the Øresund. A trading and fishing center by the early 12th century, it became the capital in 1443. It has a 17th-century stock exchange, the Amalienborg palace (home of the royal family), and the Christianborgs Palace. Other sights include the Tivoli amusement park and the Little Mermaid sculpture. The commercial and cultural center of Denmark, it has shipbuilding, chemical, and brewing industries. Pop. (1994) 620,970.

**Copernicus, Nicolas** (1473–1543) (Mikolaj Kopernik) Polish astronomer. Through his study of planetary motions, Copernicus developed a heliocentric (Sun-centred) theory of the universe in opposition to the accepted geocentric (Earth-centred) theory conceived by PTOLEMY nearly 1,500 years before. In the **Copernican system** (as it is now called) the planets' motions in the sky were explained by their orbit of the Sun. The motion of the sky was simply a result of the Earth turning on its axis. An account of his work, *De revolutionibus orbium coelestium*, was published in 1543. *See also* ARISTOTLE; GALILEO; KEPLER

**Copland, Aaron** (1900–90) US composer, especially known for combining folk and jazz elements with 20th-century symphonic techniques. His highly popular ballet music includes *Billy the Kid* (1938), *Rodeo* (1942), and *Appalachian Spring* (1944), which won a Pulitzer Prize. Copland wrote symphonies, chamber music, and patriotic pieces such as *A Lincoln Portrait* (1942). He was also a conductor and an admired teacher.

**Copley, John Singleton** (1738–1815) US painter. A gifted draftsman and colorist, he produced some ground-breaking historical paintings which introduced the notion of portraying subjects just because they were exciting. Copley's paintings include *Colonel Epes Sargent* (*c*.1760), and *The Death of Major Peirson* (1783).

**copper** (symbol Cu) Orange-pink TRANSITION ELEMENT. Reddish copper occurs native (free or uncombined) and in several ores including cuprite (an oxide) and chalcopyrite (a sulphide). Ores are often treated with acids and the copper recovered by ELECTROLYSIS. It is malleable, a good thermal and electrical conductor, second only to silver, and is extensively used in boilers, pipes, electrical equipment and alloys, such as brass and bronze. Copper tarnishes in air, oxidizes at high temperatures and is attacked only by oxidizing acids. It forms two series of salts, termed copper(I) (cuprous) and copper(II) (cupric). Properties: at.no. 29; at.wt. 63.546; r.d. 8.96; m.p. 1.083°C (1,981°F); b.p. 2,567°C (4,653°F); most common isotope $^{63}$Cu (69.09%).

**copperhead** Any of various species of snakes, so-called because of their head color. The N American copperhead is a pit viper, rarely more than 3ft (1m) long. The Australian copperhead is a venomous snake of the cobra family, often reaching 5ft (1.5m) in length. The Indian copperhead is a rat snake.

**Coppola, Francis Ford** (1939– ) US film director, producer and screenwriter. In 1969 he established Zoetrope, an independent production company. Coppola won an Academy Award for best picture for *The Godfather* (1972). Its sequel, *Godfather II* (1974), won him Oscars for best picture and best director. Coppola followed this success with *Apocalypse Now* (1975). Other credits include *Peggy Sue Got Married* (1986), *Godfather III* (1990) and *Dracula* (1992).

▲ **Coppola** His *Godfather* trilogy of films on the history of the fictional Corleone mafia family earned Coppola a place in cinema history. *Apocalypse Now* (1975) was both a creative updating of the Joseph Conrad novel *Heart of Darkness* (1902) and an expression of the horrors of the Vietnam War.

**copra** Dried kernel (meat) of the COCONUT and the principal commercial product of that nut. The husk is usually removed and the exposed kernel dried by the sun and later by artificial heat. The oil is pressed out and the residue sold as animal feed.

**Coptic Church** Largest Christian church in Egypt. Its members form 5–10% of Egypt's population. The Coptic Church is led by the patriarch of Alexandria. Of ancient origin, the Copts trace the history of the church to St. MARK. As a result of its Monophysite creed (denying the humanity of Christ), the Coptic Church was declared heretical by the Council of Chalcedon (451) and became isolated from other Christian churches. In 642 Arab conquest brought mass conversion to Islam.

**copyright** Legal authority protecting an individual's or company's works of art, literature, music, and computer programs from reproduction or publication without the consent of the owner of the copyright. Since the Universal Copyright Convention (1952), works must carry the copyright symbol (©) followed by the owner's name and the first year of publication.

**coral** Small, coelenterate marine animal of class Anthozoa, often found in colonies. The limestone skeletons secreted by each animal polyp accumulate to form a CORAL REEF. Reef-building corals are found only in waters with temperatures in excess of 68°F (20°C).

**coral reef** Rock formation found in shallow tropical seas. Such reefs are formed from the calcium carbonate secreted by living CORAL organisms as protection against predators and wave action. The way in which the coral, and therefore the reef, grows is strongly influenced by the currents and temperature of the sea-water.

**Coral Sea** Arm of the SW Pacific Ocean between the Great Barrier Reef off the E coast of Australia, Vanuatu (E), and New Guinea (NW). It was the scene of a US naval victory over the Japanese in 1942.

**coral snake** Poisonous burrowing snake of the Americas and SE Asia. It is shy and docile, but has fatal venom. Most species are brightly colored, ringed with red, yellow, and black. It feeds on lizards, frogs, and other snakes. Family Elapidae.

**cor anglais** *See* ENGLISH HORN

**Corbett, "Gentleman Jim" (James John)** (1866–1933) US boxer. In 1892 Corbett won the world heavyweight crown after defeating John L. SULLIVAN in the first championship boxing match fought with gloves. He lost the title to Bob Fitzsimmons in 1897.

**Corbusier, Le** *See* LE CORBUSIER

**Corday, Charlotte** (1768–93) French patriot. A noblewoman, she was one of the GIRONDINS who disagreed with the radical policies espoused by the Jacobin Jean Paul MARAT. On July 13, 1793 Corday stabbed Marat to death in his bath and was guillotined on July 17.

**Córdoba** (Cordova) City on the Guadalquivir River, S Spain; capital of Córdoba province. A flourishing center of learning under Abd ar-Rahman III (first caliph of Córdoba), it was captured by Ferdinand III of Castile in 1236, who imposed Christian culture on the city. There are many historic sites. Industries: tourism, coal mining, engineering. Pop. (1991) 300,229.

**core** Central area of the Earth from a depth of *c*.1,750mi (2,850km). It accounts for 16% of the Earth's volume and 31% of its mass. Measurement of seismic waves indicate that the outer part is liquid, because shear (S) waves will not travel through it, whereas the inner core from *c*.3,000mi (5,000km) to

▲ **cormorant** The common cormorant (*Phalacrocorax carbo*) is the largest of the cormorant species. It grows to a height of up to 3ft (1m). This particular species is found in or near coastal regions of N Europe, Iceland, W Greenland, Africa, Asia, Australia, and New Zealand.

the center of the Earth is interpreted as solid because seismic velocities are lower. The core is thought to be composed of iron-nickel alloy (90% iron, 10% nickel). Temperature estimates for the core vary from 7,200 to 12,600°F (4,000–7,000°C). Convection in the iron liquid outer core is thought to be responsible for producing the Earth's magnetic field.

**Corelli, Arcangelo** (1653–1713) Italian BAROQUE composer. He achieved early distinction as a violinist. Corelli helped to develop the CONCERTO grosso, composed many sonatas, and did much to consolidate the principles behind modern violin playing.

**Corfu** (Kérkyra) Island in NW Greece, second largest of the Ionian island group; the major town is Corfu. The island was allied with Athens in 433 BC against Corinth. The Romans held Corfu from 229 BC, and it was part of the Byzantine empire until the 11th century. It was occupied by the Venetians (1386–1797), and then fell under British protection (1809–64), before passing to Greece. Products: olives, fruit. Industries: tourism, fishing. Area: 229sq mi (593sq km). Pop. (1991) 107,592.

**Cori, Carl Ferdinand** (1896–1984) US biochemist, b. Czechoslovakia. Cori shared the 1947 Nobel Prize for physiology or medicine with his wife, Gerty Theresa (1896–1957), and B.A. HOUSSAY for their discovery of how the chemical energy of GLYCOGEN, a carbohydrate, is broken down to be used by the body.

**coriander** (cilantro) Strong-smelling herb of the CARROT family native to the Mediterranean and Near East. The leaves, the seeds, and oil from the seeds are used as an aromatic flavoring in foods, medicines, and liqueurs. Family Apiaceae/Umbelliferae; species *Coriandrum sativum*.

**Corinth** (Kórinthos) Capital of Corinth department, NE Peloponnesos, at the SW tip of the Isthmus of Corinth, Greece. One of the largest and most powerful cities of Ancient Greece, it was a rival of Athens and friend of Sparta, with which it was allied in the Peloponnesian War (431–404 BC). Destroyed by the Romans in 146 BC, it was rebuilt by Julius Caesar in 44 BC. Ruled by the Venetians (1687–1715), then by the Turks, it became part of Greece in 1822. The modern city is 3mi (5km) NE of ancient Corinth, which was destroyed by an earthquake in 1858. The ruins include a temple of Apollo and amphitheater. It is a major transportation center. Industries: chemicals, winemaking. Pop. (1991 est.) 29,000.

**Corinthian order** *See* ORDERS OF ARCHITECTURE

**Corinthians, Epistles to the** Two books of the New Testament that are two letters of St. PAUL addressed to the Christian Church in Corinth, Greece. The letters cover a number of issues but center on the teething troubles of the newly founded Christian community at Corinth.

**Coriolis effect** (Coriolis force) Apparent force on particles or objects due to the rotation of the Earth under them. The motion of particles or objects is deflected towards the right in the Northern Hemisphere and towards the left in the Southern Hemisphere, but their speed is unaffected. The direction of water swirling round in a drain or whirlpool demonstrates this force.

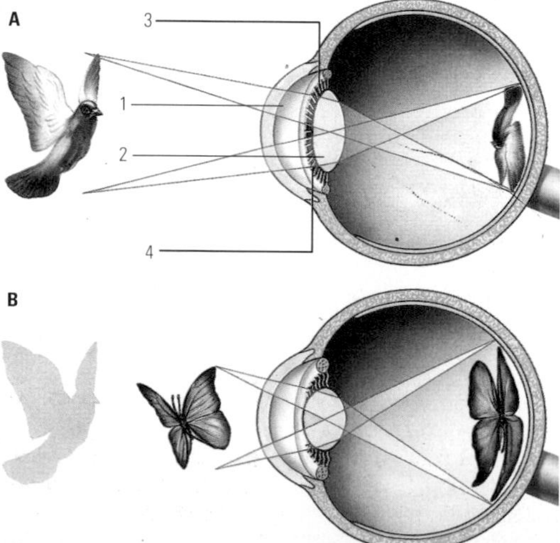


► **cornea** Focusing of light rays from distant objects (A) is mainly done by the cornea (1) with a little help from the lens (2). Ciliary muscles (3) encircling the lens relax and stretch ligaments (4), which pull the lens flat. Rays from a near object (B) are bent by a thick lens produced when the ligaments slacken as the ciliary muscles contract. This process, which is called accommodation, is essential for sharp focusing.

**Cork** County and county town in S Republic of Ireland, in Munster province. The largest Irish county, it has a rugged terrain with fertile valleys. The chief occupations are farming and fishing. In the 9th century the Danes took Cork, but were driven out in 1172 by Dermot McCarthy who swore allegiance to the English throne. In 1649 Oliver Cromwell occupied Cork. In 1920 many public buildings were destroyed in nationalist uprisings. Sites include Catholic and Protestant cathedrals, the University College of Cork (1845), and a large harbor. The largest export is farm produce, but it is also famous for tweed and linen. Area: 2,881sq mi (7,462sq km). Pop. (1991) 410,369.

**cork** Outer dead, waterproof layer of the BARK of woody plants. The bark of the cork oak, native to Mediterranean countries, is the chief source of commercial cork. Family Fagaceae; species *Quercus ruber*

**corm** Fleshy underground stem that produces a plant such as the CROCUS. In most plants, new corms form on top of old ones, which last for one season. *See also* ASEXUAL REPRODUCTION

**cormorant** Bird found in coastal and inland waters throughout the world. It has a hooked bill, a black body, and webbed feet. It dives well and in some areas of SE Asia it is trained to catch and retrieve fish. There are 30 species. Length: to 3.3ft (1m). Family Phalacrocoracidae; genus *Phalacrocorax*.

**corn** CEREAL plant of the grass family. Originally from Central America, it is the key cereal in subtropical zones. Edible seeds grow in rows upon a cob, protected by a leafy sheath. Height: to 16ft (5m). Species *Zea mays*.

**corncrake** Bird of the RAIL family common in grain fields of N Europe. It has a brown body and a short bill, and its specific name describes its call. Family Rallidae; species *Crex crex*.

**cornea** Transparent membrane at the front of the EYE. It is curved and acts as a fixed LENS, so that light is to some extent focused before it reaches the lens.

**Corneille, Pierre** (1606–84) French dramatist. Corneille and RACINE are regarded as the masters of classical French tragedy. His comedy *Mélite* (1629) attracted the attention of Cardinal Richelieu. Corneille's masterpiece is the epic tragedy *Le Cid* (1637). Other tragedies include *Horace* (1640), *Cinna* (1641), and *Polyeucte* (1643). His tragedies assert the human will against fate in classically precise ALEXANDRINE lines.

**cornet** BRASS musical instrument similar to a TRUMPET. It was one of the first brass instruments to have valves and, therefore, capable of playing a full range of notes. Hector Berlioz was one of the many 19th-century composers to take advantage of this ability. Its range is about the same as a trumpet's, but its tone is mellower. It is used in brass and military bands.

**cornflower** (bachelor's button) Annual of the composite family common in many parts of Europe. Family Asteraceae/Compositae; species *Centaurea cyanus*.

**Corn Laws** Series of acts regulating the import and export of grain in Britain. The Act of 1815 prevented the import of wheat until the domestic price exceeded a certain figure. This kept the price of bread high. Opposition led to repeal by the ANTI-CORN LAW LEAGUE (1846).

**Cornwall** County in SW England, on a peninsula bounded by the Atlantic Ocean, the English Channel, and Devon; the county town is Bodmin. Major towns include Truro, St. Austell, and Penzance. A rocky coast with hills and moors inland, it is drained by the Camel, Fowey, Tamar, and Fal rivers. It is a popular tourist region. Area: (including Scilly Isles) 1,356sq mi (3,512sq km). Pop. (1991) 468,425.

**Cornwallis, Charles, 1st marquess** (1738–1805) British general and statesman. In 1778 he became second in command of British forces in the AMERICAN REVOLUTION. In 1780 Cornwallis took command of the Carolina Campaign. His surrender at the Siege of YORKTOWN (1781) signalled the end of the war. As governor-general of India (1786–93, 1805), he reformed the civil service and defeated Tipu Sahib of Mysore.

**corona** Outermost layer of the SUN's atmosphere, extending for many millions of kilometers into space. The corona emits strongly in the x-ray region, and has been studied by X-ray satellites. The corona has a temperature of 1–2 million K.

**Coronado, Francisco Vásquez de** (1510–54) Spanish explorer. He went to Mexico in 1535, and in 1540 headed an expedition to locate the seven cities of Cibola, reportedly the repositories of untold wealth. Coronado explored the W coast of Mexico, found the Colorado River and the Grand Canyon, followed the route of the Rio Grande, and then headed N through the Texas Panhandle, Oklahoma, and E Kansas.

**coronary heart disease** ARTERIOSCLEROSIS of the coronary ARTERIES. It is the most common cause of death in the western world. Atheriosclerosis can lead to the formation of a blood clot in one or other of the coronary arteries supplying the HEART (**coronary thrombosis**). The patient experiences sudden pain in the chest (ANGINA) and the result may be a HEART ATTACK (**myocardial infarction**), when the flow of blood to the heart is suddenly stopped. Smokers are much more likely to die suddenly from atheriosclerosis. Evidence suggests that a high intake of POLYUNSATURATES can protect against coronary heart disease. *See also* ANGIOPLASTY

**Corot, Jean-Baptiste Camille** (1796–1875) French painter, a leading 19th-century landscapist. After 1827 Corot gained success at the Paris Salon with traditionally romantic paintings in a soft-edged style, unlike the precisely observed scenes of his earlier work. He was a major influence on CÉZANNE and POSTIMPRESSIONISM.

**corporation** Business organization that is legally a separate entity, which gives it limited liability, as compared to a proprietorship or partnership. The owners or shareholders are not individually responsible for the legal dealings of the corporation, except in the extent of their holdings. The corporation form is most usual in large organizations, especially in the US. In Britain the term COMPANY is often used.

**Correggio** (*c.*1490–1534) (Antonio Allegri) Italian painter from Correggio who worked mainly in Parma. His oil paintings and frescos produced daring foreshortening effects. One of the first painters to experiment with the dramatic effects of artificial light, Corregio is the major link between the early illusionism of MANTEGNA and the great Baroque ceiling painters.

**correlation** In STATISTICS, a number that summarizes the direction and degree of relationship between two or more dimensions or variables. Correlations range between 0 (no relationship) and 1.00 (a perfect relationship), and may be positive (as one variable increases, so does the other) or negative (as one variable increases, the other decreases).

**corrosion** Gradual tarnishing of surface or major structural decomposition by chemical action on solids, especially metals and alloys. It commonly appears as a greenish deposit on copper and brass, RUST on iron, or a gray deposit on aluminum, zinc, and magnesium. Some metals, such as aluminum, corrode readily to form an oxide.

**Corsica** (Corse) Mountainous island in the Mediterranean Sea, *c.*100mi (160km) SE of the French coast. It is a region of France comprising two departments. The capital is Ajaccio. It was a Roman colony, before passing into the hands of a series of Italian rulers. In 1768 France purchased all rights to the island. Napoleon was born here in 1769. Products: grapes, olives, mutton. Area: 3,352sq mi (8,681sq km). Pop. (1990) 250,400.

**Cortés, Hernán** (1485–1547) Spanish CONQUISTADOR and conqueror of Mexico. In 1518 Cortés sailed from Cuba to Central America with 550 men. He marched inland toward the Aztec capital, Tenochtitlan (Mexico City), gaining allies among the subject peoples of the Aztec king, Montezuma II. While Cortés was absent conflict broke out. He recaptured the city after a three-month siege in 1521, gaining the Aztec empire for Spain.

**cortex** In animal and plant anatomy, outer layer of a gland or tissue. Examples are the cortex of the ADRENAL GLANDS; the cerebral cortex or outer layer of the brain; the cortical layers of tissue in plant roots and stems lying between the bark or EPIDERMIS and the hard wood or conducting tissues.

**cortisone** HORMONE produced by the cortex of the ADRENAL GLANDS and essential for carbohydrate, protein, and fat metabolism, kidney function, and disease resistance. Synthetic cortisone is used to treat adrenal insufficiency, rheumatoid arthritis and other inflammatory diseases, and rheumatic fever.

**corundum** (aluminium oxide, $Al_2O_3$) Translucent to transparent mineral in many hues. It is found in igneous, pegmatitic, and metamorphic rocks, occurring as pyramidal or prismatic crystals in the rhombohedral class and as granular masses. It is the hardest natural substance after DIAMOND. Gemstone varieties are sapphire and ruby. It is an industrial abrasive. Hardness 9; s.g. 4.

**Cosby, Bill** (1937– ) US comedian, actor, and writer. He was one of the first leading African Americans in a television series (*I Spy*, 1965–68). Cosby's situation comedy, *The Cosby Show* (1984–92), was one of the most successful shows in the history of television.

**cosecant** In TRIGONOMETRY, ratio of the length of the hypotenuse to the length of the side opposite an acute angle in a right-angled triangle. The cosecant of angle $A$ is usually abbreviated cosec $A$ and is equal to the reciprocal of its SINE.

**cosine** In TRIGONOMETRY, ratio of the length of the side adjacent to an acute angle to the length of the hypotenuse in a right-angled triangle. The cosine of angle $A$ is abbreviated cos $A$.

**cosmic radiation** (cosmic rays) Charged particles from space that constantly bombard the Earth at velocities approaching the speed of light. The extraterrestrial nature of cosmic RADIATION was discovered (*c.*1912) by Victor HESS and has contributed greatly to the development of PARTICLE PHYSICS. **Primary** cosmic radiation consists mainly of PROTONS (hydrogen nuclei) and some ALPHA PARTICLES (helium nuclei). These are the most energetic particles known; as high as $10^{20}$ electron volts (eV), or nearly a billion times more energetic than the highest energy yet produced in a particle ACCELERATOR. There are two main types of primary radiation, galactic and solar. It is believed that **galactic** rays originate chiefly from SUPERNOVAE. The energy for **solar** rays appears to be obtained from **solar flares**. Some primary nuclei penetrate Earth's magnetic field and enter the upper atmosphere, where they collide with other nuclei to produce **secondary** cosmic radiation of nucleons (protons and NEUTRONS), MESONS, LEPTONS (such as ELECTRONS), and high-energy GAMMA RADIATION. Cosmic radiation contributes to BACKGROUND RADIATION.

**cosmology** Branch of scientific study that brings together ASTRONOMY, MATHEMATICS, and PHYSICS in an effort to understand the makeup and evolution of the Universe. Once considered the province of theologians and philosophers, it is now an all-embracing science. The discovery by the US astronomer Edwin HUBBLE in the 1920s that galaxies are receding from each other promoted the BIG BANG theory. Associated with this is the OSCILLATING UNIVERSE THEORY. The other main theory of cosmology is the STEADY-STATE THEORY.

**Cosmos** (Gk. order) Universe considered as an ordered whole. PLATO and ARISTOTLE conceived of the Universe as

## COSTA RICA

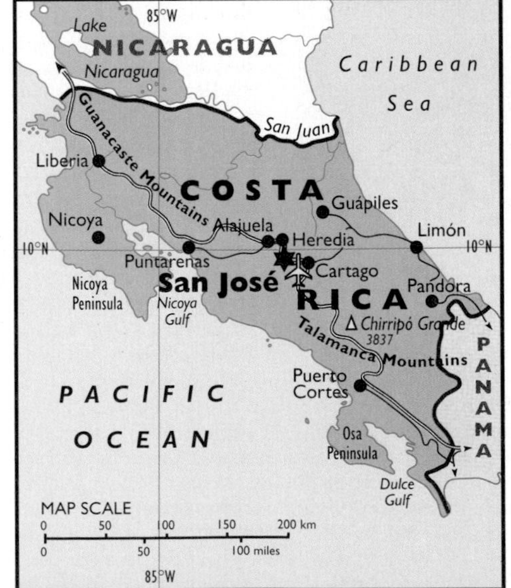


**AREA:** 19,730sq mi (51,100sq km)
**POPULATION:** 3,099,000
**CAPITAL (POPULATION):** San José (303,000)
**GOVERNMENT:** Multiparty republic
**ETHNIC GROUPS:** White 85%, Mestizo 8%, Black and Mulatto 3%, East Asian (mostly Chinese) 3%
**LANGUAGES:** Spanish (official)
**RELIGIONS:** Christianity (Roman Catholic 81%)
**CURRENCY:** Colón = 100 céntimos

► **Costner** After a string of acting and directing successes, Kevin Costner suffered a huge setback with the spectacular flop *Waterworld* (1995), the most expensive film made to date.

ordered by an intelligent principle. The conviction of an ordered nature became the basis of modern natural science.

**Cossacks** Bands of Russian adventurers who undertook the conquest of Siberia in the 17th century. Of ethnically mixed origins, they were escaped serfs, renegades, and vagabonds who formed independent, semi-military groups on the fringe of society. After the Russian Revolution (1917), the Cossacks opposed the BOLSHEVIKS and strongly resisted collectivization.

**Costa Rica** Republic in Central America; the capital is SAN JOSÉ. **Land and climate** Central Costa Rica consists of mountain ranges and plateaus with many volcanoes. In the SE, the densely populated Meseta Central and Valle del General have rich volcanic soils. The highlands descend to the Caribbean lowlands and the Pacific coast region. San José stands at *c.*3,840ft (1,170m) above sea-level, and has a pleasant climate with an average annual temperature of 68°F (20°C), compared with more than 81°F (27°C) on the coast. The NE trade winds bring heavy rains to the Caribbean coast. Evergreen forests (including mahogany and tropical cedar) cover *c.*50% of Costa Rica. **History** Christopher Columbus reached the Caribbean coast in 1502, and rumors of treasure soon attracted many Spanish settlers. Spain ruled the country until 1821; in 1822 Spain's Central American colonies broke away to join Mexico. In 1823 the Central American states broke from Mexico and set up the Central American Federation. This large union gradually disintegrated and Costa Rica achieved full independence in 1838. From the late 19th century, Costa Rica experienced a number of revolutions. In 1948 a revolt led to the abolition of the armed forces. Since then, Costa Rica has been a stable democracy. **Economy** Costa Rica is a lower-middle-income developing nation with one of the most prosperous economies in Central America (1995 GDP per capita, US$5,850). Agriculture employs 24% of the work force. Major crops include coffee, bananas, and sugar. Other crops include beans, citrus fruits, and cocoa. Cattle ranching is important. Costa Rica has rich timber resources, but lacks minerals. Tourism is a fast-growing industry. *See map, page 183*

**Costner, Kevin** (1955– ) US film actor and director. His breakthrough film was *The Untouchables* (1987). Other leading roles followed, such as *Bull Durham* (1988). Costner won Academy Awards for best director and best actor in his directorial debut *Dances With Wolves* (1990). Other acting credits include *JFK* (1991) and *The Bodyguard* (1992).

**cotangent** Ratio of the length of the side adjacent to an acute angle, to the length of the side opposite the angle in a right-angled triangle. The cotangent of angle $A$ is usually abbreviated cot $A$ and is equal to the reciprocal of its TANGENT.

**cot death** *See* SUDDDEN INFANT DEATH SYNDROME (SIDS)

**Côte d'Ivoire** *See* IVORY COAST

**Cotman, John Sell** (1782–1842) British landscape painter and etcher, cofounder (with John CROME) of the Norwich School. One of Britain's most important 19th-century watercolorists, Cotman's paintings include *Greta Bridge* (*c.*1805).

**cotoneaster** Genus of *c.*50 species of deciduous shrubs of the ROSE family (Rosaceae), mostly native to China. They have small white flowers and small, red or black, round berry-like fruit, and are often cultivated as ornamental plants.

**Cotonou** City in S Benin, W Africa, *c.*15mi (24km) SW of Porto-Novo. The former capital and largest city in Benin, it is an important port and distribution center for the offshore oil industry. Industries: textiles, brewing. Pop. (1982) 487,020.

▲ **cotton** The cotton plant (*Gossypium* sp.) is a shrub-like annual native to the world's subtropical regions. After rapid flowering, small green seedpods (bolls) develop. The cotton seeds within the bolls sprout a mass of fine fiber hairs. When mature the bolls rupture and soft cloud of cotton erupts. The crop is either harvested by hand or machine and then taken to be ginned (separating the seed from the fibers), cleaned, carded, and spun into yarn.

**Cotopaxi** Active volcano in N central Ecuador, 40mi (65km) S of Quito, in the Andes Mountains. It is the highest continually active volcano in the world and its frequent eruptions have caused severe damage. Height: 19,344ft (5,896m).

**Cotswolds** Range of limestone hills in W England lying mainly in Gloucestershire, and extending 50mi (80km) NE from Bath. The local stone is widely used as a building material. The region is also known for its breed of sheep.

**cotton** Annual shrub native to subtropical regions. Most cotton is grown for the fibers that envelop the seeds and are made into fabric. Family Malvaceae; genus *Gossypium*.

**cotton gin** Machine for separating cotton lint from seeds, a task previously done by hand. The gin, patented (1794) by Eli WHITNEY contributed to the prosperity of US cotton plantations and to the industrialization of the textile industry.

**cottonmouth** *See* WATER MOCCASIN

**cotyledon** First leaf or pair of leaves produced by the embryo of a flowering plant. Its function is to store and digest food for the embryo plant, and, if it emerges above ground, to photosynthesize for seedling growth. *See also* DICOTYLEDON; MONOCOTYLEDON

**cougar** *See* PUMA

**Coulomb, Charles Augustin de** (1736–1806) French physicist. He invented the torsion balance which led to the discovery of **Coulomb's law**: the force between two point electric charges is proportional to the product of the charges, and inversely proportional to the square of the distance between them. The SI unit of electric charge is the coulomb.

**Council for Mutual Economic Assistance (COMECON)** International organization (1949–91) aimed at the coordination of economic policy among communist states, especially in Eastern Europe. Led by the Soviet Union, its original members were Bulgaria, Czechoslovakia, East Germany, Hungary, Poland, and Romania; later joined by Cuba, Mongolia, and Vietnam. Cooperation took the form of bilateral trade agreements.

**Council of Europe** European organization founded (1949) with the aim of strengthening pluralist democracy and human rights, and promoting European cultural identity. Originally a Western European organization, it admitted former communist countries in the 1990s. It has adopted around 150 conventions, the most important of which is the EUROPEAN CONVENTION ON HUMAN RIGHTS. The organization is based in Strasbourg, France.

**counterfeiting** Illegal manufacture of coins or printed "money." Although counterfeiting is a form of forgery, it is considered a more serious offense as it is perpetrated against the government.

**counterpoint** In music, technique in composition involving independent melodic lines sung or played simultaneously to produce HARMONY. Counterpoint (contrapuntal) writing reached its height in the 16th century in the work of William Byrd, Orlando di Lasso, and Giovanni Palestrina, the organ compositions of J.S. Bach in the 18th century, and in the late works of Beethoven.

**Counter Reformation** Revival of the Roman Catholic Church in Europe during the 16th and early 17th centuries. It began as a reaction to the Protestant REFORMATION and was intended to strengthen the Church against PROTESTANTISM and the prevailing HUMANISM of the RENAISSANCE. The reforms were essentially conservative, trying to remove many of the abuses that had crept into the late medieval church, and win new prestige for the papacy. Girolamo SAVARONAROLA highlighted the secularisation, corruption, and growing materialism within the church hierarchy, but his prescription for change was too radical. The fifth LATERAN COUNCIL introduced minor changes and CLEMENT VII founded new monastic orders to act as evangelical bulwarks against LUTHERANISM, but the major impetus for reform emerged from the pontificate of PAUL III and the founding of the Society of Jesus (JESUITS). The Council of TRENT (1545–63) was the engine of the Counter Reformation. It eradicated simony (such as the sale of indulgences), standardized Roman Catholic theology, and undertook institutional reforms. Paul IV brought discipline and morality back to the papal court. Pius IV oversaw the last session of the Council.

The second phase (1563–90) of the Counter Reformation was administered by PIUS V, GREGORY XIII, and SIXTUS V. *See also* CAMPION, ST. EDMUND; ST. VINCENT DE PAUL

**countertenor** Male voice of the same register as the female CONTRALTO. It is most common in Britain, where some traditional church choirs prefer male altos.

**country and western** Popular music originally associated with rural areas of s US. The music typically features sentimental lyrics and instrumental music played with stringed instruments such as the guitar, banjo, or fiddle. Its origins lie in the folk music of British immigrants. NASHVILLE, Tennessee, is the music's spiritual home.

**county** One of the main administrative divisions of local government in the US, the UK, and some Commonwealth countries. Counties are usually responsible for policing, local judicial administration, maintaining public roads, and other public facilities, such as a fire service. *See also* LOCAL GOVERNMENT

**coup d'état** Swift stroke of policy, either against the ruling power of a state or by the state against an element within it. Of the former, the most usual is a military takeover of civilian government. An example of the latter is Hitler's murder of the *Sturm Abteilung* (SA) leaders in Germany (1934).

**Couperin, François** (1668–1733) French composer. He was organist and harpsichordist at the court of Louis XIV. "Le Grand," as he was known, is now principally remembered for his many harpsichord pieces.

**Courbet, Gustave** (1819–77) French painter, the leading exponent of REALISM. Largely self-taught, Courbet rejected traditional subject matter and instead painted peasant groups and scenes from life in Paris. His nudes shocked contemporary society. His controversial political activity forced him into exile in Switzerland in 1873. Courbet's rejection of both romantic and classical ideals prepared the way for IMPRESSIONISM.

**Court, Margaret** (1942– ) Australian tennis player. Her singles titles include the US Open (1962, 1965, 1968–70, 1973), Wimbledon (1963, 1965, 1970), the Australian Open (1960–66, 1969–71, 1973), and the French Open (1962, 1964, 1969–70, 1973). Court won more Grand Slam titles (64) than any other player in the history of women's tennis.

**Courtauld, Samuel** (1793–1881) British industrialist. He founded the firm of Courtaulds in 1816. At first it specialized in the production of silks, and from 1904 produced viscose rayon, nylon, and other artificial fibers. In 1931 he bequeathed his London house (Home House) and his collection of 19th-century French painting to the University of London, to form a department for the research and study of art (the Courtauld Institute).

**court martial** Court of the armed services for trial of service persons accused of breaking military law. Offenses range from murder to desertion. Courts martial do not utilize the JURY system. Members of the court martial are serving officers, in certain cases advised by a judge advocate.

**courts of law** Judicial assemblies to try legal cases and to impose punishment or remedy a damage. The history of the court system lies in the English assumption of COMMON LAW as its legal basis (which Britain introduced to its former colonies, including the US and Canada) as opposed to ROMAN LAW in many other countries around the world. In the US and the UK, courts are hierarchically organized, and try suits of two different types, CIVIL or CRIMINAL. In the US there are two court systems. **Federal** courts administer cases involving the nation, federal laws, interstate disputes, and non-US nationals. Federal courts include the SUPREME COURT, courts of appeal, district courts, and special courts that cover issues such as tax or patents. **State** courts are divided into superior and inferior courts. **Superior** courts include the state supreme court and county and municipal courts. **Inferior** courts include magistrates' courts, and tribunals such as traffic courts, juvenile courts, and small claims courts. In the UK, civil law cases are heard by county courts and the HIGH COURT OF JUSTICE, while those of criminal law are heard by CROWN COURTS or MAGISTRATES' court. The Court of Appeal is divided into civil and criminal divisions and hears appeals from crown courts, county courts, and the High Court. Appeals from the High Court are heard by the HOUSE OF LORDS, the Supreme Court of Appeal.

**Cousteau, Jacques Yves** (1910–97) French oceanographer. Cousteau and Emile Gagnan invented the AQUALUNG. He also invented a process of underwater television and conducted a series of undersea living experiments (1962–65). Many of the expeditions made by his research ship *Calypso* were filmed for television.

**covalent bond** Chemical bond in which two atoms share a pair of electrons, one from each atom. Covalent bonds with one shared pair of electrons are called single bonds; double and triple bonds also exist. The molecules tend to have low melting and boiling points and to be soluble in nonpolar solvents. Covalent bonding is most common in organic compounds.

**Covenanters** Scottish Presbyterians pledged by the National Covenant (1638) to uphold their religion. They opposed CHARLES I's efforts to impose an Anglican episcopal system and supported Parliament in the English CIVIL WAR, in exchange for a promise to introduce PRESBYTERIANISM in England and Ireland. The Scots changed sides when this promise was broken, but were defeated by Oliver CROMWELL. Covenanter revolts against Charles II were suppressed, but Presbyterianism was restored in Scotland in 1688.

**Coventry** City and county district in West Midlands, central England. An important weaving center in the Middle Ages, it later became known for its clothing manufacture. Coventry was badly damaged by bombing during World War II and the 14th-century cathedral was destroyed. A new cathedral (designed by Sir Basil Spence) was completed in 1962. It is the home of the University of Warwick (1965) and Coventry University (1992). Industries: motor vehicles, telecommunications, engineering. Pop. (1991) 294,387.

**Coverdale, Miles** (1488–1569) English cleric who issued the first printed English Bible (1535) and the "Great Bible" (1539). Influenced by the REFORMATION, he helped William TYNDALE on his Bible translation.

**cow** Of CATTLE, a mature female that has borne at least one calf. It is also applied to other female mammals, such as elephants and seals.

**Coward, Sir Noel Pierce** (1899–1973) English playwright, composer, and performer. He was known for his urbane comedies such as *Hay Fever* (1925), *Bitter Sweet* (1929), *Private Lives* (1930), and *Blithe Spirit* (1941). Coward's plays frequently lampooned drab high-society etiquette. Other works include the films *In Which We Serve* (1942) and *Brief Encounter* (1945). He also composed hundreds of songs, including "Mad Dogs and Englishmen."

**cowboy** (cowhand) Ranch hand. Traditionally living and working in the West, cowboys increased after the Civil War. They have been romanticized in books and films as a symbol of the rugged independence, color, and vigor of the old "Wild West." *See also* GAUCHO

**Cowell, Henry Dixon** (1887–1965) US composer, influenced by non-Western music. Cowell created "tone clusters" (dissonances produced by striking piano keys with the fist or forearm), used in such pieces as *Advertisement* (1914). Other piano pieces are played directly on the strings by plucking or striking, for example *Aeolian Harp* (1923).

**Cowper, William** (1731–1800) English poet and hymn writer. Despite bouts of near insanity, Cowper's poetry is lucid and direct, often drawing engagingly on the countryside or the details of domestic life, as in the long blank-verse poem *The Task* (1785) and the comic ballard *John Gilpin* (1782).

**cowrie** (cowry) Gastropod MOLLUSK identified by an ovoid, highly polished shell with a long toothed opening and varied markings. It is found on tropical coral shores. Length: 0.33–6in (8.3–152mm). Family Cypraeidae; more than 160 species, including the map cowry *Cypraea mappa*.

**cowslip** Most commonly either the marsh MARIGOLD (*Caltha palustris*) or the English PRIMROSE native to Europe (*Primula veris*), both yellow-flowered herbs. The term is also sometimes used for the shooting star and the Virginia cowslip.

**coyote** Wild DOG originally native to w North America. Coyotes have moved into many E areas of the US formerly inhabited by wolves. Usually grayish-brown, they have pointed muzzles, big ears, and bushy tails. Length: 35in (90cm); weight: *c.*26lb (12kg). Species *Canis latrans*.

▶ **coypu** Native to swamps, lakes and streams of central and South America, the coypu (*Myocastor coypus*) is now found in the wild of wetter regions of the US and Europe, a number having escaped from fur farms.

**coypu** Large, aquatic RODENT, native to South America. It now also lives in North America and parts of Europe. Coypus have brown outer fur and soft gray underfur, commercially known as nutria. Overall length: 3.5ft (1m); weight: 20lb (8kg). Species *Myocastor coypus*.

**crab** Flattened, triangular, or oval ten-legged crustacean covered with a hard shell. Primarily marine, some crabs are found in freshwater and a few are terrestrial. Their short abdomen, often called a tail, is bent under. Most have a pair of large foreclaws, a pair of movable eyestalks, and a segmented mouth. Crabs usually move sideways. Size: pea-sized to 12ft (3m). Order Decapoda.

**Crabbe, George** (1754–1832) English poet. Crabbe's poetry is imbued with the atmosphere of his native Suffolk and is unflinchingly antisentimental, as in *The Village* (1783) and *The Borough* (1810), the basis for Benjamin Britten's opera *Peter Grimes* (1945).

▲ **crane fly** The hindwings of crane flies have evolved into small balancing organs known as halterers. In flight they vibrate with the wings, detecting and helping to correct any deviation from the stable flight path.

**crab nebula** NEBULA located *c*.6,500 light years away in Taurus. It is the remnant of a supernova noted by Chinese astronomers in July 1054, when it shone as brightly as Venus, visible even in daylight. The nebula was discovered in 1731 by the English astronomer John Bevis and independently by Charles Messier in 1758.

**crack** Street DRUG that is a COCAINE derivative. It is supplied in the form of hard, crystalline lumps, which are heated to produce smoke inhaled for its stimulant effects. It imposes considerable strain on the heart and blood vessels, and may result in heart failure or a stroke. Psychotic episodes may also occur.

**cracking** Stage in oil-refining during which the products of the first distillation are treated to break up large HYDROCARBONS into smaller molecules by the controlled use of heat, catalysts, and often pressure. The cracking of PETROLEUM yields heavy oils, gasoline, and gases such as ETHANE, ETHYLENE and PROPENE, which are used in the manufacture of plastics, textiles, detergents, and agricultural chemicals.

**Craig, Edward Gordon** (1872–1966) English stage designer, son of Ellen TERRY. In *On the Art of the Theatre* (1905), Craig proposed that actors become "supermarionettes" controlled by the director-designer-creator. He advocated non-representational scenery and atmospheric lighting. Among his numerous productions were *Dido and Aeneas* (1900) and *Hamlet* (1912).

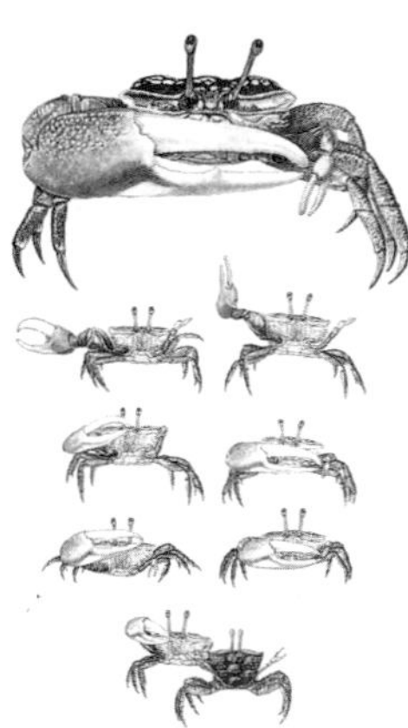

▲ **crab** Fiddler crabs (*Uca* sp.), like most crustaceans, recognize potential mates by sight. During courtship, the male waves his one enormous claw in a complex series of signals, while at the same time raising and lowering his body.

**Craig, James** (1871–1940) Northern Irish statesman and soldier, first prime minister of Northern Ireland (1921–40). With Sir Edward CARSON, Craig helped organize Unionist resistance and was instrumental in keeping Ulster part of the United Kingdom. As prime minister, he abolished (1929) proportional representation and through boundary changes ensured a Protestant majority.

**crake** *See* RAIL

**Cranach, Lucas, the Elder** (1472–1553) German painter and engraver, court artist to the electors of Saxony. A friend and follower of Martin Luther, Cranach designed many propaganda woodcuts for the Protestant cause. He also produced some of the first full-length portraits.

**cranberry** Plant of the HEATH family, distributed widely in N temperate regions. It is a creeping or trailing shrub and bears red berries with an acid taste used to make sauce and juice. Family Ericaceae; Genus *Vaccinium*.

**Crane, (Harold) Hart** (1899–1932) US poet. He is acclaimed as one of the most brilliant and creative 20th-century US poets. Crane's major work, *The Bridge* (1930), is a series of related poems in which New York City's Brooklyn Bridge serves as a mystical symbol of the creative power of civilization.

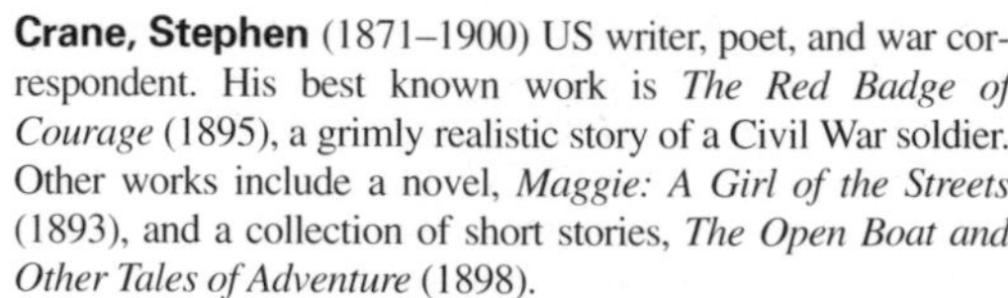

**Crane, Stephen** (1871–1900) US writer, poet, and war correspondent. His best known work is *The Red Badge of Courage* (1895), a grimly realistic story of a Civil War soldier. Other works include a novel, *Maggie: A Girl of the Streets* (1893), and a collection of short stories, *The Open Boat and Other Tales of Adventure* (1898).

**crane** Any of several species of tall, wading birds found in most parts of the world except S America. It has brownish, grayish, or white plumage with a bright ornamental head and feeds on almost anything. After courtship dances, the female lays two eggs in a bulky nest. Height: to 60in (150cm). Family Gruidae.

**crane fly** Nonbiting true fly of the order Diptera. It has a slender body, long fragile legs, and one pair of wings. The larvae, leatherjackets, live in the soil where they feed on plant roots and stems, frequently becoming serious agricultural pests. Family Tipulidae; species *Tipula simplex*. Length: to 1.2in (3cm).

**cranesbill** Common name for certain species of wild GERANIUM. Some species are cultivated for ornamental ground cover.

**cranium** Dome-shaped part of the SKULL that protects the brain. It is composed of eight bones that are fused together.

**Cranmer, Thomas** (1489–1556) English prelate and religious reformer. He was appointed archbishop of Canterbury by HENRY VIII in 1533. Cranmer secured the annulment of Henry's marriage to Catherine of Aragon despite opposition from the pope, Cranmer, a friend of Thomas CROMWELL, promoted the introduction of PROTESTANTISM into England and compiled the first Book of COMMON PRAYER in 1549. Following the accession of the Roman Catholic MARY I in 1553, Cranmer's reforms were halted. He was burned at the stake.

**Crassus, Marcus Licinius** (115–53 BC) Roman political and military leader. He amassed a vast personal fortune, and raised and led the troops who defeated the slave rebellion of Spartacus in 71. With POMPEY and Julius CAESAR Crassus formed the First Triumvirate in 60 BC and was governor of Syria in 54 BC.

**crater** Roughly circular depression found in the surface of some planets, notably the Moon, usually with steep sides. It is formed either by meteoric impact, when shock waves blast out a hole in the ground, or at the vent of a volcano, when lava is expelled explosively.

**crater lake** Accumulation of water, usually by precipitation of rain or snow but sometimes groundwater, in a volcanic crater (caldera). Should an eruption occur, the resulting mud flow (lahar) is often more destructive than a lava flow, owing to its greater speed. Crater Lake in Crater Lake Park, Oregon, was formed by precipitation and the waters are maintained solely by rain and snow.

**Crawford, Joan** (1904–77) US film actor, b. Lucille Fay le Sueur. Determined and versatile, she remained a star for nearly half a century. Crawford started in musicals before graduating to dramatic roles in films, such as *Grand Hotel* (1932) and *The Women* (1939). She won an Academy Award for best actress in *Mildred Pierce* (1945). Other films include *Possessed* (1947) and *What Ever Happened to Baby Jane?* (1962).

**Crawford, Thomas** (1814–57) US sculptor who studied in Rome and brought a neo-classical style to his art. Crawford's most famous works are his equestrian statue of George Washington and his enormous *Freedom* statue (1862) on top of the US Capitol.

**crayfish** Edible, freshwater, ten-legged crustacean in rivers and streams of temperate regions. Smaller than lobsters, crayfish burrow into the banks of streams and feed on animal and vegetable matter. Some cave-dwelling species are blind. Length: normally 3–4in (8–10cm). Families Astacidae (Northern Hemisphere), Parastacidae (Southern Hemisphere), Austroastacidae (Australia).

**Crazy Horse** (1842–77) Chief of the Oglala SIOUX. He was a leader of Sioux resistance to the advance of white settlers in the Black Hills and assisted SITTING BULL in the destruction of Colonel George CUSTER at the BATTLE OF LITTLE BIGHORN in 1876. Persuaded to surrender, he was killed a few months later, allegedly while trying to escape.

**creationism** Belief that all things owe their origin to God's acts of creation. Some conservative Christians believe in the literal truth of the biblical account of the creation given in the Book of Genesis, which states that God created Heaven and Earth in six days. Such people oppose Charles DARWIN's theory of EVOLUTION. Roman Catholics use the term creationism to denote the doctrine that God creates a soul for every single human being at conception. *See also* ORIGINAL SIN

**creation myth** In most mythologies and religions, an account of the origin of the world, as well as of the human race and all the other creatures on Earth. There is a remarkable similarity in the creation stories as recounted in the holy books of major religions, and in the myths and legends of ethnic groups.

**Crécy, Battle of** (1346) First major battle of the HUNDRED YEARS WAR. The English led by EDWARD III and his son, the Black Prince, defeated the French led by PHILIP VI. The English longbow, as well as superior tactics, accounted for their victory.

**Cree** People belonging to the ALGONQUIAN language family of Native Americans in Canada, who ranged from James Bay to the Saskatchewan River. Like the closely related Chippewa, the Cree served as guides and hunters for French and British fur traders. Many of the Plains Cree intermarried with the French. Today, the Cree number *c.*130,000.

**creed** (Lat. *credo*, I believe) In Christian churches, personal yet formal statement of commitment to doctrinal belief. *See also* APOSTLES' CREED; ATHANASIAN CREED; NICENE CREED.

**Creek** Confederation of NATIVE AMERICANS, part of the Muskogean-language group. One of the largest groups of SE US, they ranged from Georgia to Alabama. They formed a settled, agricultural society, with land owned communally. Individual settlements had a degree of autonomy. After the Creek Wars (1813–14), they were removed to Oklahoma, where *c.*60,000 remain.

**cremation** Ritual disposal of a corpse by burning. It was a common custom in parts of the ancient civilized world, and is still the only funeral practice among Hindus and Buddhists. Early Christians rejected cremation because of their belief in the physical resurrection of the body. Its legitimacy is now recognized by all Christian churches.

**Creole** Person born in the S US, West Indies, or Latin America but of foreign or mixed descent. Generally a Creole's ancestors were either African slaves or French, Spanish or English settlers. In the US it can also refer to someone of mixed European and African ancestry. Creole language is a PIDGIN, adopted as the native language of a community (English, French, Portuguese).

▲ **crane** The crowned crane (*Balearica pavonina*) is a tall, elegant bird of desert and grassland regions of Africa, S from the Nile Valley. It grows to a height of 3ft (95cm).

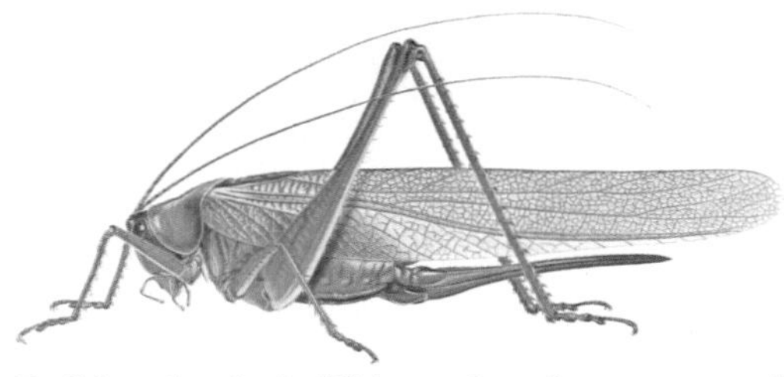

◀ **cricket** The great green bush cricket (*Tettigonia viridissima*) of S Europe, N Africa, and Asia is bright green in color to blend in well with its surroundings. Large examples of this insect can reach 3in (7cm) long.

**crescent** Symbol of the MOON in its first quarter. The symbol has been associated with ISLAM since the capture of Constantinople by the Ottoman Turks in 1453. It is on the Turkish and other Islamic nation flags.

**cress** Any of several small, pungent-leaved plants of the mustard family (Brassicaceae/Cruciferae), generally used in salads and as garnishes. The best known is WATERCRESS. Species *Nasturtium officinale*.

**Cretaceous** Last period of the MESOZOIC era, lasting from 144 to 65 million years ago. DINOSAURS became extinct at the end of this period. The first true placental and MARSUPIAL mammals appeared and modern flowering plants were common.

**Crete** (Kreti, Kríti) Largest island of Greece, in the E Mediterranean Sea, SSE of the Greek mainland; the capital is IRÁKLION. Minoan civilization flourished on Crete from 2000 BC, and the palace of KNOSSOS was built *c.*1700 BC. Crete was conquered by Rome in 68–67 BC and later came under Byzantine (395), Arab (826), and Venetian (1210) rule. In 1669 Crete fell to Turkey. Foreign intervention forced Turkey to evacuate Crete (1898) and it was eventually united with Greece (1908). It was occupied by German forces in World War II. Crete has a mountainous terrain upon which sheep and goats are raised. The mild climate supports the cultivation of cereals, grapes, olives, and oranges. Products: wool, hides, cheese, olive oil, wine. Tourism is important. Area: 3,218sq mi (8,336sq km). Pop. (1991) 540,054.

**Creutzfeldt-Jakob disease (CJD)** Rare, degenerative brain disease that results in dementia and death. It is believed to be caused by an infective agent, possibly a slow virus. Some scientists believe that CJD can be acquired by eating meat products from cattle infected with BOVINE SPONGIFORM ENCEPHALOPATHY (BSE).

**Crick, Francis Harry Compton** (1916– ) English biophysicist. In the 1950s, with James WATSON and Maurice Wilkins, he established the double-helix molecular structure of deoxyribonucleic acid (DNA). The three were jointly awarded the Nobel Prize for physiology or medicine in 1962.

**cricket** Brown to black insect with long antennae and hind legs adapted for jumping, found worldwide. Males produce a chirping sound by rubbing their wings together. Length: 0.8–2in (3–50mm). Family Gryllidae.

**cricket** Bat and ball game popular in Britain and other Commonwealth nations originating *c.*1700. Two teams of 11 players compete on an oval or round field. The game revolves around two wickets, 66ft, 22yd (20.1m) apart. A wicket comprises three wooden stumps 28in (71.1cm) high, connected at the top with two small crosspieces (bails). Leading nations compete against each other in a series of test matches. A test match is held over five days with two innings per side. In an innings all the players of one team bat once, while the other team fields, providing the bowlers and a wicket-keeper. A batsman stands within a marked area (crease) on the pitch (the strip between the wickets), 4ft (1.2m) from the wicket. A bowler is allowed to bowl six consecutive overarm deliveries (an over) at the wicket defended by a batsman, this is followed by another over from the opposite end of the pitch by a different bowler. A run is usually scored by a batsman making contact with the ball and running between the wickets before the ball can be returned to either wicket. If the ball reaches the boundary of the field it scores four runs, or six if it does not bounce. A batsman can be given out in a number of ways: by being bowled (when the ball delivered by a bowler hits the wicket); by being caught (the ball struck by the bat or glove is caught before bouncing by a fielder); by being run out or "stumped" (a player dislodges the bails with the ball when a batsman is outside the crease), by being "leg before wicket," (the ball hits a batsman's padded leg and would, in the opinion of the umpire, have hit the wicket); or by hitting his own wicket. Since 1975 cricketing nations have competed every four years in the World Cup, a competition of one-day matches. The sport's administrative and historical headquarters is at Lord's Cricket Ground, London.

**Crimea** (Krym) Peninsula in S Ukraine that extends into the Black Sea, W of the Azov Sea and joined to the mainland by the Perekop Isthmus. Simferopol is the capital. The Crimea was inhabited from the 10th to 8th centuries BC by the Cimmerians. During the 5th century it was colonized by the Greeks and then by Romans, Ostrogoths, Huns, Mongols, Byzantines, and Turks, before being annexed to Russia in 1783. In 1921 it became an autonomous republic of Russia, and in 1954 was transferred to the Ukraine as the Krymskaya oblast. In 1991 it was made an autonomous republic of an independent Ukraine. The region has many mineral resources and much intensive agriculture. Area: *c*.10,400sq mi (27,000sq km). Pop. (1991 est.) 2,549,800.

**Crimean War** (1853–56) Fought by Britain, France, and the Ottoman Turks against Russia. In 1853 Russia occupied Turkish territory and France and Britain, determined to preserve the Ottoman empire, invaded the Crimea (1854) to attack SEVASTOPOL. The war was marked on both sides by incompetent leadership and organization. The CHARGE OF THE LIGHT BRIGADE is the best-known example. Sevastopol was eventually captured (1855). At the Treaty of Paris (1856) Russia surrendered its claims on the Ottoman empire.

**criminal law** Body of law that defines crimes, lays down rules of procedure for dealing with them, and establishes penalties for those convicted. Broadly, a crime is distinguished from a TORT by being deemed injurious to the state. In many countries the criminal law has been codified. Criminal law remains what it was originally, a part of COMMON LAW, although since the 18th century it has been greatly added to by statute law.

**Cripps, Sir (Richard) Stafford** (1889–1952) British statesman. He belonged to the left wing of the LABOUR PARTY and was ambassador to Russia (1940–42), later serving in Winston CHURCHILL's war cabinet. As chancellor of the exchequer (1947–50) in the reforming government of

## CROATIA

Croatia adopted a red, white, and blue flag in 1848. Under communist rule, a red star appeared at the center. In 1990 the red star was replaced by the present coat of arms, which symbolizes the various parts of the country.

**AREA:** 21,824sq mi (56,538sq km)
**POPULATION:** 4,764,000
**CAPITAL (POPULATION):** Zagreb (726,770)
**GOVERNMENT:** Multiparty republic
**ETHNIC GROUPS:** Croat 78%, Serb 12%, Bosnian, Hungarian, Slovene
**LANGUAGES:** Croatian
**RELIGIONS:** Christianity (Roman Catholic 77%, Eastern Orthodox 11%), Islam 1%
**CURRENCY:** Kuna

The Republic of Croatia was one of the six republics that made up the former republic of YUGOSLAVIA. It achieved independence in 1991. The region of DALMATIA borders the Adriatic Sea and includes limestone coastal ranges, which reach 6,276ft (1,913m) at Mount Troglav. Other highlands lie in the NE, but Croatia chiefly consists of the fertile Pannonian plains, drained by Croatia's two main rivers, the Drava and the Sava.

### Climate

The coastal area has a Mediterranean climate, with hot, dry summers and mild, moist winters. Inland, the climate becomes more continental. Winters are often bitterly cold, while summer temperatures often soar to 100°F (38°C).

### Vegetation

Farmland, including pasture, covers 70% of Croatia, with forest and woodland occupying only 15%. Sparse Mediterranean scrub predominates in Dalmatia.

### History and Politics

Slav people settled in the area *c*.1,400 years ago. In 803 Croatia became part of the Holy Roman Empire and the Croats soon adopted Christianity. Croatia was an independent kingdom in the 10th and 11th centuries. In 1102 an 800-year union of the Hungarian and Croatian crowns was formed.

In 1526 part of Croatia came under the Turkish Ottoman empire, while the rest of Croatia came under the Austrian HABSBURGS. In 1699 all of Croatia came under Habsburg rule. In 1867 the Habsburg empire became the dual monarchy of Austria-Hungary.

Following the defeat of Austria-Hungary in World War I, Croatia became part of the new Kingdom of the Serbs, Croats, and Slovenes, renamed Yugoslavia (1929). Germany occupied Yugoslavia during World War II, and Croatia was proclaimed independent, though it was really a pro-Nazi puppet state (*Ustashe*).

After the war, communists took power, and Josip Broz (TITO) became the country's leader. Despite ethnic differences, Tito held Yugoslavia together until his death (1980). During the 1980s, economic and ethnic problems (including a deterioration in relations between Croatia and SERBIA) threatened the country's stability. In 1990 the Croatian Democratic Union (HDZ), led by Franjo TUDJMAN, won Croatia's first democratic elections. A 1991 referendum voted overwhelmingly in favor of Croatia becoming an independent republic. The Yugoslav National Army was deployed and Serb-dominated areas took up arms in support of the federation. Serbia supplied arms to Croatian Serbs, and war broke out between Serbia and Croatia. In 1992 United Nations peacekeeping troops were deployed to maintain an uneasy ceasefire. Croatia had lost more than 30% of its territory. Tudjman was re-elected president. In 1992 war broke out in BOSNIA-HERZEGOVINA, and Bosnian Croats occupied parts of Croatia. In 1993 Croatian Serbs in Eastern Slavonia voted to establish the separate republic of Krajina. In 1994 the Bosnian, Bosnian Croat, and Croatian governments formed a federation. In 1995 Croatian government forces seized Krajina and 150,000 Serbs fled. Following the Dayton Peace Accord (1995), Croatia and the rump Yugoslav state formally established diplomatic relations (August 1996). In 1998 an agreement between the Croatian government and Croatian Serbs led to the reintegration of Eastern Slavonia into Croatia.

### Economy

The wars of the early 1990s disrupted Croatia's relatively prosperous economy. Before the crisis, Dalmatia had been a major European tourist destination. Croatia has a wide range of manufacturing industries, such as steel, chemicals, oil refining and wood products. Agriculture remains the principal employer. Crops include corn, soyabeans, sugar beet, and wheat.

Clement ATTLEE, Cripps played a significant role in the reconstruction of the post-war economy.

**critical angle** Angle at which a significant transition occurs. In optics, it is the angle of incidence with a medium at which total internal REFLECTION occurs. In telecommunications, it is the angle at which radio waves are reflected by the IONOSPHERE.

**critical mass** Minimum mass of fissionable material required in a FISSION bomb or nuclear reactor to sustain a CHAIN REACTION. The fissionable material of a fission bomb is divided into portions less than the critical mass; when brought together at the moment of detonation they exceed the critical mass.

**Crittenden, John Jordan** (1787–1863) US statesman and lawyer. He was a senator from Kentucky (1817–19, 1835–41, 1842–48, 1855–61). Crittenden served as attorney general under William Henry HARRISON (1841) and Millard FILLMORE (1850–53). "Crittenden's Propositions" of 1860 sought to reach a compromise on slavery with the southern states and prevent civil war, but it was defeated.

**Crivelli, Carlo** (1430–93) Italian painter. A distinctive artist, he combined a linear approach with an intensely decorative style of drawing. Crivelli's masterpiece is *The Annunciation* (1486).

**Croatia** Balkan republic in SE Europe. *See* country feature

**Croce, Benedetto** (1866–1952) Italian idealist philosopher and politician. He was a senator (1910–20) and minister of education (1920–21). When Mussolini came to power, Croce retired from politics in protest against fascism. He re-entered politics following the fall of Mussolini in 1943. As leader of the Liberal Party, he played a prominent role in resurrecting Italy's democratic institutions. Among his writings is the idealistic *Philosophy of the Spirit* (1902–17)

**Crockett, Davy (David)** (1786–1836) US politician and frontiersman. He served in the Tennessee legislature (1821–26) and the US Congress (1827–31, 1833–35). A Whig, Crockett opposed the policies of Andrew JACKSON and the Democrats. He died at the ALAMO.

**crocodile** Carnivorous, lizard-like REPTILE found in warm parts of every continent except Europe. Most crocodiles have a longer snout than ALLIGATORS. All lay hard-shelled eggs in nests. Length: up to 23ft (7m). There are about 12 species including two dwarf species in Africa. The Asian saltwater crocodile (*Crocodylus porosus*) sometimes attacks humans. Family Crocodylidae.

**crocus** Hardy perennial flowering plant. It is low growing with a single tubular flower and grass-like leaves rising from an underground corm. Family Iridaceae; genus *Crocus*.

**Croesus** (d. *c*.546 BC) King of Lydia in Asia Minor (r. *c*.560–546 BC). Renowned for his wealth, he was overthrown and captured by CYRUS THE GREAT. According to HERODOTUS, Croesus threw himself upon a funeral pyre.

**Crohn's disease** Chronic inflammatory condition that may affect any part of the human gastrointestinal tract. The cause is unknown, but possibly represents an exaggerated response to an allergen or infective agent. The ileum and colon are most commonly affected.

**Cro-Magnon** Tall, Upper Paleolithic race of humans, possibly the earliest form of modern *Homo sapiens*. Cro-Magnon people settled in Europe *c*.35,000 years ago. They made a variety of sophisticated flint tools, as well as bone, shell, and ivory jewelery and artifacts. Cro-Magnon artists produced the cave paintings of France and N Spain. Cro-Magnon remains were first found (1868) in Les Eyzies-de-Tayac, Dordogne, France.

**Crompton, Richmal** (1890–1969) British writer. Crompton created one of the most popular characters in British children's fiction, William, a scruffy, prankish schoolboy. The stories were first collected as *Just William* (1922), and more than 30 William novels followed.

**Crompton, Samuel** (1753–1827) British inventor of a spinning machine. His "spinning mule" of 1779 proved a boon to the textile industry, reducing thread-breakage and producing very fine yarn.

**Cromwell, Oliver** (1599–1658) Lord protector of England (1653–58). An ardent Puritan, Cromwell entered Parliament in 1628 and was an active critic of CHARLES I in the LONG PARLIAMENT (1640). In the first English CIVIL WAR, his Ironsides helped defeat the Cavaliers at MARSTON MOOR (1644). In 1645 he helped to form the NEW MODEL ARMY. After a decisive victory at NASEBY (1645), Cromwell emerged as the leading voice of the army faction. He favored compromise with CHARLES I, but Charles' duplicity convinced him of the need to execute the king. In the second civil war he defeated the Scottish Royalists at Preston (1648). His influence was strengthened in PRIDE'S PURGE (1648) of parliament. The RUMP PARLIAMENT pressed for Charles' execution and established the COMMONWEALTH republic (1649). Cromwell ruthlessly suppressed opposition in Ireland and defeated CHARLES II in the third civil war (1651). The failure of BAREBONE'S PARLIAMENT (1653) led to the "Instrument of Government" that established the PROTECTORATE. Cromwell became a virtual military dictator as "lord protector." The Humble Petition and Advice (1657) offered Cromwell the throne, but he refused. Cromwell's expansionist foreign policy was both anti-Stuart and pro-Protestant. The DUTCH WARS (1652–54) and the war (1655–58) with Spain were financially exorbitant. He was succeeded by his son, Richard CROMWELL.

**CROCODILE**

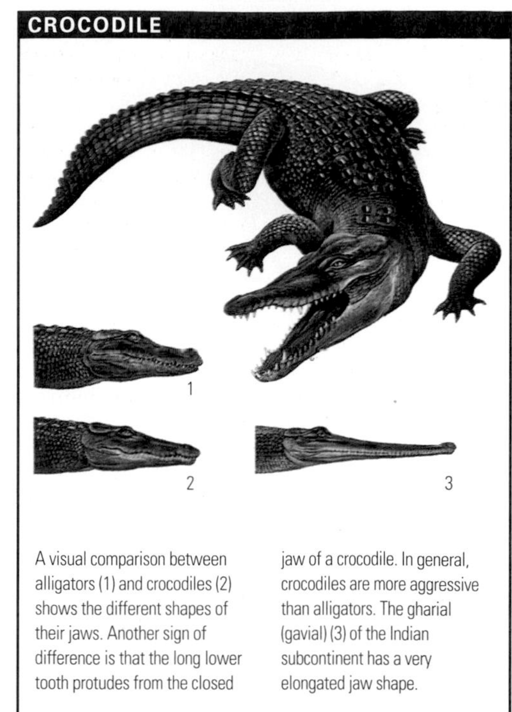


A visual comparison between alligators (1) and crocodiles (2) shows the different shapes of their jaws. Another sign of difference is that the long lower tooth protudes from the closed jaw of a crocodile. In general, crocodiles are more aggressive than alligators. The gharial (gavial) (3) of the Indian subcontinent has a very elongated jaw shape.

**Cromwell, Richard** (1626–1712) Lord protector of England (1658–59), son of Oliver CROMWELL. Richard lacked his father's qualities of leadership. He was ousted from power after eight months and spent 20 years in exile before returning to England in 1680.

**Cromwell, Thomas, earl of Essex** (1485–1540) English statesman. Cromwell was secretary to Cardinal WOLSEY and succeeded him as HENRY VIII's chief minister in 1531. He was responsible for the acts of the REFORMATION parliament that established the CHURCH OF ENGLAND with the king as supreme head. Cromwell's ruthless management of the DISSOLUTION OF THE MONASTERIES (1536–40) was demonstrated by the Pilgrimage of Grace (1536). He fell from power after the failure of Henry's marriage to ANNE OF CLEVES, and was executed.

**Cronin, A.J. (Archibald Joseph)** (1896–1981) Scottish novelist. He was a medical inspector of mines and physician until the success of his first work, *Hatter's Castle* (1931). Many of his novels, such as *The Stars Look Down* (1935), *The Citadel* (1937), *The Keys of the Kingdom* (1942), and *The Green Years* (1944), have been made into films.

**Cronkite, Walter Leland, Jr.** (1916– ) US journalist and broadcaster. Cronkite served as a war correspondent (1942–45) and reporter on the Nuremberg trials. He was anchorman (1962–81) of "The CBS Evening News with Walter Cronkite."

**Crookes, Sir William** (1832–1919) English chemist and physicist. He invented the radiometer (which measures ELEC-

▲ **crocus** Native to Europe and Asia, the crocus is grown in temperate climates, usually appearing in spring months.

▶ **crow** The American crow (*Corvus brachyrhynchas*) is found throughout North America. A large crow, its wingspan can reach up to 3ft (90cm). It feeds on some eggs and nesting chicks as well as insects and small rodents.

TROMAGNETIC RADIATION) and the Crookes tube, which led to the discovery of the electron by J.J. THOMSON. He was the first to suggest that CATHODE RAYS consist of negatively charged particles. He also discovered THALLIUM. *See also* X-RAY

**croquet** Lawn game in which wooden balls are hit with wooden mallets through a series of six wire hoops towards a peg. The first to complete 12 hoops (each hoop in both directions) and reach the peg wins. Croquet developed in France in the 17th century.

**Crosby, "Bing" (Harry Lillis)** (1904–77) US popular singer and actor. He became one of the most successful "crooners" in the US. Crosby worked with Bob HOPE on the acclaimed *Road* series and won a Academy Award for best actor in *Going My Way* (1944). His recording of the Irving BERLIN song "White Christmas" (1942) is one of the best-selling records of all time.

**cross** Ancient symbol with different significance to many cultures. In Christianity, it is associated with Christ's sacrificial death by crucifixion for the redemption of mankind. An image of a cross is usually placed on, above, or near the altar in churches and is often carried in religious processions. Other crosses are still used as religious or secular symbols. They include the crosses of St. George, St. Andrew, the Victoria Cross, the Red Cross, and the Maltese cross. As a religious symbol the cross existed in ancient Egypt, Babylonia, and Assyria.

**crossbill** Parrot-like, forest FINCH found in the N of the Northern Hemisphere. It has a heavy, curved, scissor-like bill in which the upper and lower mandibles cross, which it uses to pry seeds from cones of evergreens. Length: 6in (15cm). Family Fringillidae; genus *Loxia.*

**crossbow** *See* ARCHERY

**croup** Respiratory disorder of small children caused by inflammation of the LARYNX and airways. It is mostly triggered by viral infection. Symptoms are a harsh cough, difficult breathing, restlessness, and fever.

**Crow** Large tribe of Siouan-speaking Native Americans that separated in the early 18th century from the HIDATSA. They migrated into the Rocky Mountains region from the upper Missouri River. Today, they occupy a large reservation in Montana, where they were settled in 1868. They are noted for their fine costumes, artistic culture, and complex social system.

**crow** Large, black bird found in many temperate woodlands and farm areas worldwide. Living in large flocks, crows prey on small animals and eat plants and carrion. They can be crop pests. They are intelligent birds and can sometimes be taught to repeat phrases. The female lays three to six greenish eggs. Family Corvidae. *See also* JAY; MAGPIE; RAVEN; ROOK

**Cruelty, Theater of** French dramatic movement of the late 1920s. It developed under the influence of Antonin ARTAUD, who advocated a physical theater expressing stark emotions. Violence was used as a theatrical device to disturb audience perception. Performance was considered more important than a specific text.

**Cruikshank, George** (1792–1878) English illustrator and cartoonist, well known for his political and theatrical illustrations. Cruikshank illustrated more than 800 books, of which the best known are Dickens' *Sketches by Boz* and *Oliver Twist*.

**Cruise, Tom** (1962– ) US film actor. His career began in teenage oriented films. His roles in *Top Gun* (1986) and *Rain-man* (1988) gained him a wider audience. Cruise earned Academy Award nominations for his performance as a disabled Vietnam veteran in *Born on the Fourth of July* (1989), and in *Jerry Maguire* (1996). Other films include *Eyes Wide Shut* (1999).

**cruise missile** Self-propelled MISSILE that travels, generally at low altitudes, following the contours of the terrain. This allows it to avoid conventional radar defenses. The siting of American cruise missiles on European soil during the 1980s led to large-scale public demonstrations. In the GULF WAR (1991), the US navy used Tomahawk cruise missiles on ground targets in Iraq. In 1999 cruise missiles were also deployed against Serbia.

**cruiser** Warship smaller, lighter and faster than a BATTLESHIP, ranging in size from 8,300 to 23,000 tons. After World War I, arms limitation treaties restricted its guns to 8in (200mm). Since World War II, cruisers have replaced battleships as the major warships of a modern navy.

**Crusades** Series of military expeditions (11th–14th centuries) from Christian Europe to recover the Holy Land (Palestine) from the Muslims. In the 7th century JERUSALEM was captured by the caliph OMAR. In 1071 control of Jerusalem passed to the SELJUK Turks. The Seljuk capture (1085) of Antioch (ANTAKYA) from the BYZANTINE EMPIRE presaged Turkish domination of ASIA MINOR, and Emperor ALEXIUS I appealed to the West for assistance. In 1095 Pope URBAN II convoked the Council of Clermont. The **First Crusade** (1095–99) was the most successful. In 1097 the crusaders captured Antioch and Nicaea. In July 1099 they celebrated the recapture of Jerusalem by slaughtering the entire Muslim and Jewish population. The victorious factions established four crusader states in the Levant, including the Latin kingdom of Jerusalem. The **Second Crusade** (1147–49), led by Emperor CONRAD III and the French king LOUIS VII, was an unmitigated failure. The **Third Crusade** (1189–92) was called by Pope Gregory VIII in response to SALADIN's capture (1187) of Jerusalem. In 1190 Emperor FREDERICK I (BARBAROSSA) drowned and leadership of the Crusade passed to RICHARD I of England and PHILIP II of France. In 1191 they captured Acre, but disagreements forced a truce with Saladin. The **Fourth Crusade** (1202–04) was diverted to Constantinople by the Venetians. After the disastrous CHILDREN'S CRUSADE (1212), Pope INNOCENT III made Egypt the target of the **Fifth Crusade** (1218–21). Emperor FREDERICK II embarked on the diplomatic **Sixth Crusade** (1228–29), which saw him crowned king of Jerusalem. In 1244 Jerusalem was retaken for Islam. LOUIS IX of France responded by launching the **Seventh Crusade** (1248–54) against Egypt. In 1268 Jaffa and Antioch were recaptured for Islam. Louis IX launched the **Eighth Crusade** (1270) but died in Tunis. The **Ninth Crusade** (1271–72) was led by Prince Edward (later EDWARD I of England). In 1291 Acre, the last Christian foothold in the Levant, fell to Islam. *See also* KNIGHTS HOSPITALLERS; KNIGHTS TEMPLAR; TEUTONIC KNIGHTS

**crust** In geology, the thin outermost solid layer of the Earth. The crust represents less than 1% of the Earth's volume and varies in thickness from *c*.3mi (5km) beneath the oceans to *c*.45mi (70km) beneath mountain chains such as the Himalayas. Oceanic crust is generally thinner averaging 4.5mi (7km) thick and is basaltic in composition, whereas continental crust is mainly between 20 and 25mi (30–40km) thick and of granitic composition. The lower boundary of the crust is defined by a marked increase in seismic velocity, known as the Mohorovičić discontinuity. *See also* MOHO

**crustacea** Class of *c*.30,000 species of ARTHROPODS. The class includes the decapods (crabs, lobsters, shrimp, and crayfish), isopods (pill millipedes and woodlice), and many varied forms Most crustaceans are aquatic (marine or freshwater) and breathe through gills or the body surface. They are typically covered by a hard exoskeleton. They range in size from the ocean plankton, as little as 0.04in (1mm) in diameter, to the Japanese spider crab up to 12ft (3m) across.

**cryogenics** Branch of physics that studies materials and effects at temperatures approaching ABSOLUTE ZERO. Some materials exhibit highly unusual properties such as SUPERCONDUCTIVITY or SUPERFLUIDITY at such temperatures. Cryogenics has been used to freeze human bodies in the uncertain hope that future technology may be able to revive the subjects.

**cryolite** (kryolite, sodium-aluminum fluoride ($Na_3AlF_6$) Brittle, icy-looking, red, brown, or black halide mineral, found in pegmatite dikes and used in aluminum processing. It occurs as crystals in the monoclinic system, occasionally the cubic system, sometimes as granular masses. The crystals are frequently twinned. Greenland has the only large deposit. Cryolite is also a source of aluminum salts and fluorides.

**cryptography** Form of written message in which the original text (plaintext) is replaced by a series of other signs according to a prearranged system, in order to keep the message confidential. Unlike a **code**, in which each letter of the plaintext is replaced by another sign, a **cipher** cannot be "cracked" without a key. Typically, a key is a complex pattern of letters or symbols forming the basis upon which the plaintext is enciphered. The receiver reverses this process to decipher the message. Ciphers were used by the ancient Greeks and were employed widely during the medieval and Renaissance periods. Mechanical devices for producing complex ciphers were developed between the two World Wars. The best-known cipher machine was the German Enigma device. Today, fast computers are used by intelligence services for constructing and breaking constantly changing complex ciphers.

**crystal** Solid with a regular geometrical form and with characteristic angles between its faces, having limited chemical composition. The structure of a crystal, such as common salt, is based upon a regular 3–D arrangement of atoms, ions, or molecules (a crystal or ionic **lattice**). Crystals are produced when a substance passes from a gaseous or liquid phase to a solid state, or comes out of solution by evaporation or precipitation. Slow cooling produces large crystals, whereas fast cooling produces small crystals.

**crystallography** Study of the formation and structure of crystalline substances. It includes the study of crystal formation, chemical bonding in crystals, and the physical properties of solids. In particular, crystallography is concerned with the internal structure of crystals. *See also* X-RAY CRYSTALLOGRAPHY

**Crystal Palace** First building of its size, 408 × 1,850ft (124 × 564m), to be made of glass and iron. England's Sir Joseph PAXTON designed it for the Great Exhibition held in Hyde Park, London (1851). It was the first building prefabricated in sections and assembled on site. After the exhibition it was dismantled and reerected on Sydenham Hill, SE London, where it stood until accidentally destroyed by fire in 1936.

**Cuba** Caribbean island republic, at the entrance to the Gulf of Mexico. *See* country feature

**Cuban Missile Crisis** (October 1962) US and Soviet Union confrontation over the installation of Soviet nuclear rockets in Cuba, perhaps the closest the world has yet come to

## CUBA

Cuba's flag, the "Lone Star" banner, was designed in 1849, but not adopted as the national flag until 1901, after Spain had withdrawn from the country. The red triangle represents the Cuban people's bloody struggle for independence.

**AREA:** 42,803sq mi (110,860sq km)
**POPULATION:** 10,822,000
**CAPITAL (POPULATION):** Havana (2,096,054)
**GOVERNMENT:** Socialist republic
**ETHNIC GROUPS:** White 66%, Mulatto 22%, Black 12%
**LANGUAGES:** Spanish (official)
**RELIGIONS:** Christianity (Roman Catholic 40%, Protestant 3%)
**CURRENCY:** Cuban peso = 100 centavos

The Republic of Cuba, largest and most westerly of the WEST INDIES archipelago, consists of one large island, Cuba, together with the *Isla de la Juventud* (Isle of Youth) and many small islets. Cuba is strategically situated at the mouth of the Gulf of MEXICO.

The highest mountain range, the Sierra Maestra in the SE, reaches 6,562ft (2,000m) at Pico Turquino. The rest of the land consists of gently rolling hills or coastal plains.

### CLIMATE

Cuba has a semitropical climate. The dry season runs from November to April, while May to October is the rainy season. Fierce hurricanes may occur between August and October.

### VEGETATION

Farmland covers about 50% of Cuba and 66% of this is given over to sugarcane. Pine forests still grow, especially in the SE. Mangrove swamps line some coastal areas.

### HISTORY AND POLTICS

When Christopher Columbus discovered Cuba in 1492, it was inhabited by Native Americans. The first Spanish colony was established in 1511. The indigenous population was quickly killed, replaced by African slave labor. Cuba formed a base for Spanish exploration of the American mainland and became a prime target for pirates. Discontent at Spanish rule erupted into war in 1868. Slavery was abolished in 1886. In 1895 a second war of independence was led by José MARTÍ. In 1898 the sinking of the US battleship *Maine* precipitated the SPANISH-AMERICAN WAR. From 1898–1902 Cuba was under US military occupation before becoming an independent republic. The US occupied Cuba again in 1906–09 and in 1912 to protect US-owned plantations.

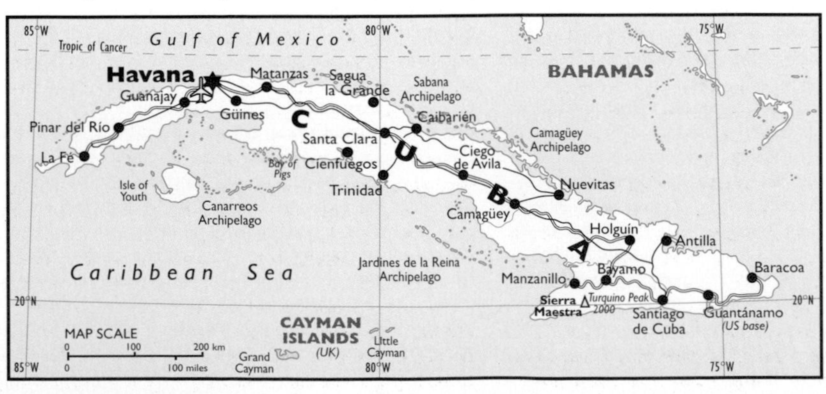


During World War I, Cuba's economy flourished as the price of sugar rose dramatically. From 1933 to 1959 Fulgencio BATISTA ruled Cuba, maintaining good relations with the US. In 1952 he imposed martial law. After an abortive coup attempt in 1953, Fidel CASTRO, supported by Che GUEVARA, launched a revolution in 1956. In 1959 Castro became premier. Castro's brand of revolutionary socialism included the nationalization of many US-owned industries. In 1961 the US broke off diplomatic ties and imposed a trade embargo. Castro turned to the Soviet Union. Cuban exiles, supported by the US government, launched the disastrous BAY OF PIGS invasion. In 1962 the potential siting of Soviet missiles on Cuba fueled the CUBAN MISSILE CRISIS. Castro's early attempts to export revolution to the rest of Latin America ended in diplomatic alienation. Cuba turned to acting as a leader of developing nations and providing support for revolutionary movements. Between 1965 and 1973, more than 250,000 Cubans became exiles. In 1980 emigration was legalized and many disaffected Cubans chose to leave.

### ECONOMY

Despite major advances in health care and education, Cuba's economy has been devastated by the dissolution of the Soviet Union (its primary market and source of aid), the US embargo, and over-dependence on the sugar industry (1992 GDP per capita, $US3,412). Nickel ore is the second largest export. Other exports include cigars, fish, and rum.

▲ **cuckoo** The common European cuckoo (*Cuculus canorus*) is famous for its parasitic behavior. The female lays its egg in the smaller host's nest. The cuckoo nestling ejects its nest fellows and receives all the attention of its foster parents.

nuclear war. President John KENNEDY warned Premier Nikita KHRUSHCHEV that any missile launched from Cuba would be met by a full-scale nuclear strike on the Soviet Union. On October 24, Cuba-bound Soviet ships bearing missiles turned back, and Khrushchev ordered the bases to be dismantled.

**cube** In mathematics, the result of multiplying a given number by itself twice. Thus the cube of $a$ is $a \times a \times a$, written $a^3$. A cube is also described as the third power of a number. The cube root is the number that must be multiplied by itself twice over to give a specified number. A cube is a regular six-sided solid figure (all its edges are equal in length and all its faces are squares).

**cubism** Revolutionary, 20th-century art movement. It originated in *c.*1907 when PICASSO and BRAQUE began working together to develop a new pictorial language able to represent ideas as well as objective reality. They built up three-dimensional images on the canvas using fragmented solids and volumes. In 1908 Braque held an exhibition of his new paintings that provoked the critic Louis Vauxcelles to describe them as bizarre arrangements of "cubes." The initial experimental, "analytical," phase (1907–12), of which Picasso and Braque were the main exponents, was inspired mainly by African sculpture and the later works of CÉZANNE. The "synthetic" phase (1912–14) introduced much more color and decoration and the techniques of COLLAGE and papiers collés were very popular. Cubist painters included LÉGER, Robert DELAUNAY and Sonia DELAUNAY-TERK, and Frantisek KUPKA. The most important cubist sculptors (apart from Picasso) were ARCHIPENKO, LIPCHITZ, and Ossip Zadkine. Cubism revolutionized artistic expression, and lent itself easily to adaptation and development. It is probably the most important single influence on 20th-century progressive art.

**Cuchulainn** Irish legendary hero. He was king of Ulster during the 1st century BC and hero of the legend *The Cattle Raid of Cooley*, in which he defended his kingdom against the rest of Ireland. The Cuillin Hills in Skye, NW Scotland, are named after him.

**cuckoo** Widely distributed forest bird. Related species are the ani, ROAD RUNNER, and coucal. True Old World cuckoos are generally brownish, although a few species are brightly colored and notable for parasitic behavior. Their chief food is insects. Length: 6–30in (15–75cm). Family Cuculidae; genus *Cuculus*.

**cuckoopint** (wake robin or lords-and-ladies) Tuberous plant native to Europe. It has arrow-shaped leaves and sends up stout spathes which unfurl to reveal a spadix that gives off a fetid carrion scent, attractive to insects. Red poisonous berries form as the spathe dies off. Family Araceae; species *Arum maculatum*.

**cucumber** Trailing annual vine covered in coarse hairs; it has yellowish flowers and the immature fruit is eaten raw or pickled. Family Cucurbitaceae; species *Cucumis sativus*.

**Culloden, Battle of** (1746) Decisive battle of the JACOBITE rising of 1745. The Jacobites, predominantly Highlanders, led by Charles Edward STUART, were defeated near Inverness by government forces under the Duke of Cumberland, son of George II. Culloden ended STUART attempts to regain the throne by force.

**cult** System of religious beliefs, rites, and observances connected with a divinity or group of divinities, or the sect devoted to such a system. Within a religion such as HINDUISM, many gods have their own cults, notably SHIVA. Animals are the focus of some cults, such as the INUIT whale cult. A deified human being may also be the object of worship, as in the emperor cults of ancient Rome. In the 20th century a cult often denotes a quasi-religious organization that controls its followers by means of psychological manipulation. Leaders of cults are usually forceful, charismatic personalities.

**Cultural Revolution** (1966–76) The "Great Proletarian Cultural Revolution" was initiated by MAO ZEDONG and his wife, JIANG QING, to purge the Chinese COMMUNIST PARTY of his opponents and to instill correct revolutionary attitudes. Senior party officials were removed from their posts, and intellectuals and others suspected of revisionism were victimized and humiliated. A new youth corps, the RED GUARDS, violently attacked reactionistic ideas. By 1968 China was near civil war. The Red Guards were disbanded and the army restored order.

**culture** In ANTHROPOLOGY, all knowledge that is acquired by human beings by virtue of their membership of a society. A culture incorporates all the shared knowledge, expectations, and beliefs of a group. Culture in general distinguishes human beings from animals since only humans can pass on accumulated knowledge.

**Cumbria** County in NW England, bounded by the Solway Firth (N), and the Irish Sea (W); the county town is CARLISLE. The region includes the LAKE DISTRICT and the Cumbrian Mountains. Area: 2,629sq mi (6,808sq km). Pop. (1991) 483,163.

**cumin** Annual herb native to the Middle East and widely cultivated for its seed-like fruit used as a food flavoring. It has a branching stem and small pink or white flowers. Height: to 6in (15cm). Family Apiaceae/Umbelliferae; species *Cuminum cyminum*.

**cummings, e.e. (Edward Estlin)** (1894–1962) US poet. His first work was a novel, *The Enormous Room* (1922). Cummings' reputation rests on his poetry, which usually exhibits sentimental emotion and/or cynical realism. It is characterized by unconventional spelling, punctuation, and typography. His verse was collected in *Complete Poems 1913–1962* (1972).

**cuneiform** System of writing developed in Mesopotamia *c.*3000 BC. The system consists of wedge-shaped strokes, derived from the practice of writing on soft clay with a triangular stylus as a "pen." Cuneiform developed from pictograms that came to serve as an "alphabet" of more than 500 characters. Most stood for words but some stood for syllables or speech-sounds.

**Cunningham, Merce** (1919– ) US dancer and choreographer. He was a soloist (1940–55) with the Martha GRAHAM Company. In 1952 Cunningham formed his own MODERN DANCE company. He is best-known for his work with avant-garde artists and composers, such as Andy Warhol and John Cage. Cunningham incorporated improvisational techniques into dance through his method of "chance composition", in which dances are performed according to the roll of a die. His productions include *How to Pass, Kick, Fall, and Run* (1965).

**Cuomo, Mario Matthew** (1932– ) US politician. He was governor of New York (1982–92), the first Italian-American to hold the office. Extremely popular, he was urged to run for the presidency in 1984, 1988, and 1992.

**Cupid** In Roman mythology, god of love, equivalent to the Greek god EROS.

**cuprite** (cuprous oxide, $Cu_2O$) Reddish-brown, brittle, translucent oxide mineral. Formed by the oxidation of other ores, such as copper sulfide, it is an important source of copper.

**Curaçao** Largest island of the NETHERLANDS ANTILLES in the West Indies, in the S Caribbean Sea; the capital is Willemstad. Most inhabitants are descended from African slaves imported during the 17th and 18th centuries; the indigenous Arawak are now extinct. Curaçao derives most income from tourism and oil-refining. Products: peanuts, tropical fruits, Curaçao liqueur. Area: 171sq mi (444sq km). Pop. (1993 est.) 146,828.

**curare** Poisonous, resinous extract obtained from various tropical South American plants of the genera *Chondodendron* and *Strychnos*. Most of its active elements are ALKALOIDS. Causing muscle paralysis, it is used on the poisoned arrows of Native South Americans when hunting. It is also used as a muscle relaxant in abdominal surgery and setting fractures.

**curate** (Lat. *cura*, charge) Clergyman who assists the incumbent priest of a parish in the performance of his duties. The term was originally used to denote a priest who had the charge of a parish.

**Curia Romana** Official administrative body of the Roman Catholic Church. It is based in the VATICAN and consists of a court of officials through which the pope governs the Church. It includes three groups – congregations, tribunals, and curial offices – and is concerned with all aspects of the life of the Church and its members.

**Curie, Marie** (1867–1934) Polish scientist, who specialized in work on RADIATION. Marie and her husband Pierre Curie (who specialized in the electrical and magnetic properties of crystals) worked together on a series of radiation experiments. In 1898 they discovered RADIUM and POLONIUM. In 1903 they shared the Nobel Prize for physics with A.H. BECQUEREL. In

▲ **cucumber** Large, watery fruits are a common feature of the cucumber (*Cucumis sativus*) and its relatives. The plants are generally large and covered in coarse hairs and many have tendrils that help them climb.

1911 Marie became the first person to be awarded a second Nobel Prize (this time for chemistry), for her work on radium and its compounds. She died of leukemia caused by laboratory radiation. Their daughter, Irène **Joliot-Curie** and her husband, Frédéric Joliot-Curie, were awarded the 1935 Nobel Prize for chemistry for producing artificial radioactive substances.

**curie** (symbol Ci) Unit formerly used to measure the activity of a radioactive substance. Named for Marie CURIE, it is defined as that quantity of a radioactive isotope that decays at the rate of $3.7 \times 10^{10}$ disintegrations per second. The curie has been replaced by an SI unit, the becquerel (symbol Bq).

**curium** (symbol Cm) Synthetic, radioactive metallic element of the ACTINIDE SERIES. It was first made in 1944 by the US nuclear chemist Glenn Seaborg and his colleagues by the alpha particle bombardment of plutonium-239 in a cyclotron. Silvery in color, curium is chemically reactive, intensely radioactive, and is toxic if absorbed by the body. It provides power for orbiting satellites. Properties: at.no. 96; sp.gr. (calculated) 13.51; m.p. 2,444°F (1,340°C); 14 isotopes, most stable $^{247}Cm$ (half-life $1.6 \times 10^7$ yr).

**curlew** Long-legged, wading bird with a down-curved bill and mottled brown plumage. Often migrating long distances, it feeds on small animals, insects, and seeds, and nests on the ground, laying two to four eggs. Length: to 19–25in (48–62cm). Species *Numenius arquata*.

**curling** Game resembling lawn bowling on ice that is a major winter sport of Scotland, and popular in Canada, N US, and Nordic countries. The game is played by two teams of four players on an ice surface 138ft (42m) long by 14ft (4.3m) wide. Each player has two smooth circular stones with a handle. At each end of the ice is a circular target with a central area known as the tee. One player sends his stone towards the tee, teammates use brooms to sweep the surface in front of it to give it a smoother surface over which to glide. Each player delivers two stones. One point is scored for each stone lying nearer the tee than an opponent's stone.

**currant** Any of several mainly deciduous shrubs and their fruits, rich in vitamin C. Black, red, and white currants are included in the genus *Ribes*: they are popular plants, cultivated widely. The fruits are used in pies, preserves, and syrups. Family Grossulariaceae.

**current** *See* OCEANIC CURRENT

**curvature of the spine** Exaggerated shaping of the SPINE. There are three major types. **Scoliosis**, or lateral curvature, can be due to bad posture or to abnormality. **Lordosis**, an accentuation of the inward curve of the neck region or more commonly of the lower back region, results in a sway-back appearance. **Kyphosis**, an accentuation of the outward curve behind the chest, can in severe form result in a hunchback appearance.

**Curzon, George Nathaniel, 1st marquess of Kedleston** (1859–1925) British statesman. He entered Parliament as a Conservative in 1886 and became viceroy of India (1899–1905). Curzon reformed administration and education and established (1901) the North-West Frontier Province. He resigned after a dispute with Lord KITCHENER. During World War I he served in the coalition cabinets of Herbert ASQUITH and LLOYD GEORGE. As foreign secretary (1919–24) in Bonar LAW's government, he helped negotiate the Treaty of Lausanne.

**Cushing, Harvey** (1869–1939) US surgeon. His pioneering techniques for surgery on the brain and spinal cord helped advance neurosurgery. He first described the syndrome produced by over-secretion of adrenal hormones that is now known as Cushing's syndrome. It is characterized by weight-gain in the face and trunk, high blood pressure, excessive growth of facial and body hair, and diabetes-like effects.

**Custer, George Armstrong** (1839–76) US military leader. A flamboyant, headstrong character, Custer was the youngest Union general in the Civil War. Following the war he was posted to the frontier, but was court-martialed for disobeying orders in 1867 and suspended. In 1868 he returned to service and led campaigns against the Cheyenne. His decision to divide his regiment and attack a superior force of Sioux at the Battle of LITTLE BIGHORN (1876) resulted in the death of Custer and his entire regiment.

**cuticle** Exposed outer layer of an animal. In humans it is the EPIDERMIS, especially the dead skin at the edge of fingers. In botany, it is the waxy layer on the outer surface of epidermal cells of leaves and stems of vascular plants. It helps to prevent excessive water loss.

**cuttlefish** Cephalopod MOLLUSK related to the SQUID and OCTOPUS. Like squid, cuttlefish swim rapidly by the propulsion of a jet of water forced out through a siphon. They have ten sucker-covered arms on the head, two much longer than the rest. Their flattened bodies contain the familiar chalky cuttlebone. Capable of rapid color changes, they can also eject blue-black "ink" as a means of protection. Family Sepiidae; species *Sepia officinalis*.

**Cuvier, Georges, baron de** (1769–1832) French geologist and zoologist, a founder of comparative anatomy and paleontology. His scheme of classification stressed the form of organs and their correlation within the body. He applied this system to fossils, and came to accept the theory of catastrophic changes.

**Cuzco** City in S central Peru; capital of Cuzco department. An ancient capital of the Inca empire from *c*.1200, it fell to the Spaniards in 1533. Cuzco was destroyed by earthquakes in 1650 and then rebuilt. It is a center of archeological research. Pop. (1993) 255,568.

**cyanide** Salt or ester of hydrocyanic acid (prussic acid, HCN). The most important cyanides are sodium cyanide (NaCN) and potassium cyanide (KCN), both of which are deadly poisonous. Cyanides have many industrial uses – in electroplating, for the heat treatment of metals, in the extraction of silver and gold, in photography, and in insecticides and pigments.

**cyanobacteria** (blue-green algae) One of the major BACTERIA phyla, distinguished by the presence of the green pigment CHLOROPHYLL and the blue pigment phycocyanin. They perform PHOTOSYNTHESIS with the production of oxygen. Many cyanobacteria perform NITROGEN FIXATION. They occur in soil, mud, and deserts; they are most abundant in lakes, rivers, and oceans. Some produce toxic BLOOMS.

**cybernetics** Study of communication and control systems in animals, organizations, and machines. It makes analogies between the BRAIN and nervous system, and COMPUTERS and other electronic systems, such as the analysis of FEEDBACK and data processing.

**cyberspace** Popular term for the perceived "virtual" space within computer memory or networks. The term is a product of science fiction, where it usually refers to direct INTERFACE between brain and computer. It is often used to refer to the INTERNET and the worldwide web.

**cycad** Phylum (Cycadophyta) of primitive palm-like shrubs and trees that grow in tropical and subtropical regions. Although they are GYMNOSPERMS, they have feathery palm- or fern-like leaves (poisonous in most species) at the top of stout (usually unbranched) stems. In addition to their main roots, they also have special roots containing CYANOBACTERIA that carry out NITROGEN FIXATION. These plants first flourished *c*.225 million years ago. Most of the 100 or so surviving species are less than 20ft (6.1m) tall.

**Cyclades** (Kikládhes) Large group of Greek islands in the S Aegean Sea, off the SE coast of Greece; the capital is Hermoupolis (on Síros). The name is derived from the Greek *kyklos* (ring), since in antiquity it was held that the islands encircled the sacred island of Delos. They were annexed to Greece in 1829 from the Ottoman Empire. Mineral deposits include bauxite, lead, and sulfur. Products: wheat, grapes, fish, olive oil, tobacco, marble. Area: 993sq mi (2,572sq km). Pop. (1991) 100,100.

**cyclamen** Genus of 20 species of low-growing perennial herbs, native to central Europe and the Mediterranean region. They have swollen, tuberous corms, and heart- or kidney-shaped leaves. The drooping blooms are white, pink, lilac, or crimson. Family Primulaceae.

**cycle** In physics, series of changes through which any system passes which brings it back to its original state. For example, alternating current starts from zero voltage, rises to a maximum, declines through zero to a minimum, and rises again to zero. In the INTERNAL COMBUSTION ENGINE, a two-stroke engine completes one cycle each downward plunge and return.

▲ **Custer** One of the most successful officers of the US Civil War, George Custer was eventually defeated and killed by Sioux at the Battle of the Little Bighorn.

▲ **cyclamen** Often cultivated for its pink or white flowers, the cyclamen (genus *Cyclamen*) has characteristic petals that are twisted at the base and bent back.

▲ **cypress** The Lawson cypress (*Chamaecyparis lawsonia*) can grow to a height of 200ft (60m) and live for up to 600 years. Also known as the Oregon cedar, this tree is native to Oregon and California, where it is grown for its timber and natural beauty.

**cycling** Sport for individuals and teams competing on BICYCLES. Now a regular event at the Olympic Games, cycle racing first became popular following the invention of the pneumatic tire (1888). There is a diversity of formats and events, road racing being the best-known form. The most famous cycle race is the TOUR DE FRANCE (inaugurated 1903).

**cyclone** System of winds, or a storm, that rotates inwards, around a center of low atmospheric pressure (depression). The winds flow counterclockwise in the Northern Hemisphere and clockwise in the Southern Hemisphere. Cyclones in middle latitudes are associated with cloudiness and high humidity, and the development of a FRONT. A strong tropical cyclone can give rise to a HURRICANE. *See also* TORNADO

**Cyclopes** In Greek mythology, three demons, each having one eye in the center of its forehead, who forged the thunderbolts of ZEUS. They were depicted by Homer as giant herdsmen living on an island. ODYSSEUS escaped from Cyclops Polyphemus by blinding him.

**Cygnus** One of the most distinctive constellations, often nicknamed the Northern Cross.

**cylinder** Solid figure or surface formed by rotating a rectangle using one side as an axis. If the vertical height is $h$ and the radius of the base $r$, then the volume is $\pi r^2 h$ and the curved surface area $2\pi rh$.

**Cymbeline** (Cunobelinus) (d. *c.*AD 42) Ancient British king. An ally of the Romans, he was king of the Catuvellauni tribe. After conquering the Trinovantes, he became the strongest ruler of S Britain.

**Cynewulf** English poet of the early 8th century, presumed to be the author of *Elene*, *The Fates of the Apostles*, *The Ascension*, and *Juliana*. The poems suggest that he was a priest in Mercia or Northumbria.

**Cynics** School of philosophy founded (*c.*440 bc) by Antisthenes, a pupil of SOCRATES. Cynics considered virtue to be the only good. Its teachings were developed by DIOGENES. *See also* STOICS

**cypress** Tall, evergreen tree native to North America and Eurasia. It has scale-like leaves, roundish cones, and a distinctive symmetrical shape. The wood is durable and fragrant and is of value commercially. Height: 20–80ft (6–24m). Family Cupressaceae; genus *Cupressus*. There are *c.*20 species.

**Cyprus** Island republic in the NE Mediterranean Sea; the capital is NICOSIA. **Land and climate** Cyprus has scenic mountain ranges, the Kyrenia and the Troodos, the latter rising to 6,401ft (1,951m) at Mount Olympus. The island contains fertile lowlands, used extensively for agriculture. It has a Mediterranean climate, with hot, dry summers and mild winters. Pine forests grow on the mountain slopes. **History and Politics** Greeks settled on Cyprus *c.*3,200 years ago. From AD 330 the island was part of the Byzantine empire. In the 1570s it became part of the Ottoman empire. Turkish rule continued until 1878 when Cyprus was leased to Britain. Britain proclaimed it a colony in 1925. In the 1950s Greek Cypriots, who made up 80% of the population, began a campaign for *enosis* (union) with Greece. Their leader was the Greek Orthodox Archbishop Makarios. A guerrilla force (EOKA) attacked the British, who exiled Makarios. Cyprus became an independent country in 1960 and Makarios was its first president. The constitution provided for power-sharing between the Greek and Turkish Cypriots. It proved unworkable, however, and fighting broke out between the two communities. In 1964 the UN sent in a peacekeeping force. In 1974 Greek-led Cypriot forces overthrew Makarios. This led Turkey to invade N Cyprus, occupying *c.*40% of the island. Many Greek Cypriots fled from the Turkish-occupied area, which in 1979 was proclaimed to be a self-governing region. In 1983 the Turkish Cypriots declared the N to be an independent state called the Turkish Republic of Northern Cyprus; the only country to recognize it is Turkey. The UN regards Cyprus as a single nation under the Greek Cypriot government in the S. It is estimated that over 30,000 Turkish troops are deployed in N Cyprus. Despite UN-brokered peace negotiations (1997), there are frequent border clashes between the two communities. In 1998 Cyprus applied for memebership of the European Union (EU). **Economy** Cyprus got its name from the Greek word *Kypros*, meaning copper, but little copper remains; the chief minerals today are asbestos and chromium. Industry employs 37% of the work force, and manufactures include cement, footwear, tiles, and wine. Farming employs 14% and crops include barley, citrus fruits, grapes, olives, potatoes and wheat. The most valuable activity in Cyprus is tourism. The economy of the Turkish Cypriot North lags behind that of the Greek Cypriot South (1992 GDP per capita, $US19,050).

**CYPRUS**

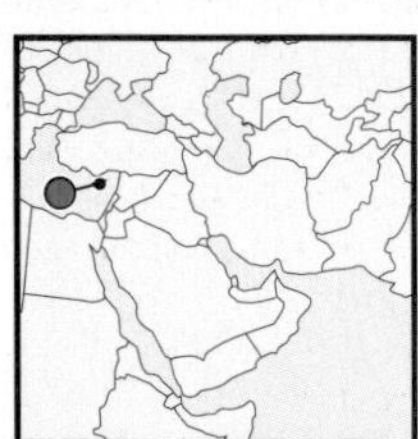

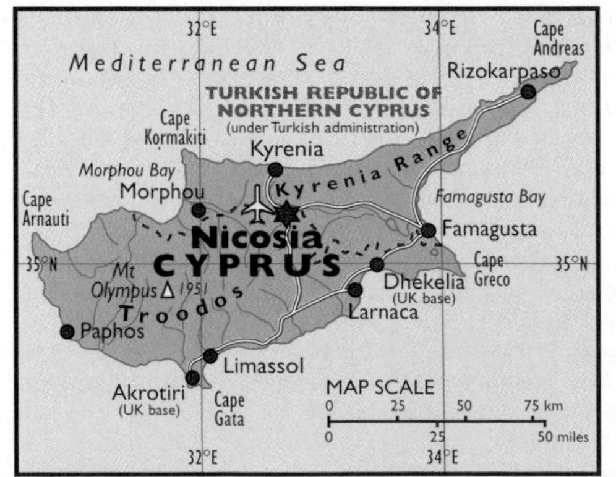


**AREA:** 3,571 sq mi (9,250 sq km)
**POPULATION:** 725,000
**CAPITAL (POPULATION):** Nicosia (177,451)
**GOVERNMENT:** Multiparty republic
**ETHNIC GROUPS:** Greek Cypriot 81%, Turkish Cypriot 19%
**LANGUAGES:** Greek and Turkish (both official)
**RELIGIONS:** Christianity (Greek Orthodox), Islam
**CURRENCY:** Cyprus pound = 100 cents

**Cyrano de Bergerac, Savinien** (1619–55) French writer. His novels and plays combine free thinking, humor, and burlesque romance. As an author, he is best known for two posthumously published prose fantasies, *Journey to the Moon* (1656) and *The Comical Tale of the States and Empires of the Sun* (1662). He is perhaps equally famous as the eponymous hero of the popular but historically inaccurate play by Edmond ROSTAND.

**Cyril, Saint** Greek Christian missionary. With his brother, Methodius, he is one of the two so-called "Apostles to the Slavs" who were sent to convert the Khazars and Moravians to Christianity. Cyril is said to have invented the CYRILLIC alphabet. His feast day is February 14 in the West and May 11 in the East.

**Cyrillic** ALPHABET based on Greek letter forms that is now used for writing several Slavic languages, most notably Russian and Serbian.

**Cyrus the Great** (600–529 BC) King of Persia, founder of the ACHAEMENID Persian empire. He overthrew the Medes, then rulers of Persia, in 549 BC, defeated King CROESUS of Lydia (*c.*546 BC), and captured BABYLON (539 BC) and the Greek cities in Asia Minor. His empire stretched from the Mediterranean to India. He delivered the Jews from their BABYLONIAN CAPTIVITY.

**cystic fibrosis** Hereditary glandular disease in which the body produces abnormally thick mucus that obstructs the breathing passages, causing chronic lung disease. There is a deficiency of pancreatic enzymes, an abnormally high salt concentration in the sweat, and a failure to gain weight. The disease is treated with antibiotics, pancreatic enzymes, and a high-protein diet.

**cystitis** Inflammation of the urinary bladder, usually caused by bacterial infection. It is more common in women. Symptoms include frequent and painful urination, low back pain, and slight fever.

**cytokinin** (kinetin or kinin) Any of a group of plant hormones that stimulate cell division. Cytokinins work in conjunction with AUXINS to promote swelling and division in the plant cells producing lateral buds. They are used commercially to produce seedless grapes, to stimulate germination of barley in brewing, and to prolong the life of green, leaf vegetables.

**cytology** Study of living CELLS and their structure, behavior, and function. Cytology began with Robert HOOKE's microscopic studies of cork in 1665, and the microscope is still the main tool. In the 19th century, a theory was developed which suggested that cells are the basic units of organisms. Recently cytochemistry has focused on the study of the chemistry of cell components.

**cytoplasm** Jelly-like matter inside a CELL and surrounding the NUCLEUS. Cytoplasm contains various bodies known as organelles, with specific metabolic functions. The proteins needed for cell growth and repair are produced in the cytoplasm.

**Czartoryski, Adam Jerzy** (1770–1861) Polish politician. A hostage at the Russian court, he befriended the future czar ALEXANDER I who appointed him foreign minister (1803–06). Czartoryski was responsible for the adoption (1815) of the Polish constitution. He opposed NICHOLAS I's ambitions and, following an insurrection, headed (1830–31) a Polish provisional government. After its failure he was forced into exile in Paris.

**Czech** Language spoken in the Czech Republic (Bohemia and Moravia) by *c.*10 million people. A Slavic language, it is closely related to SLOVAK.

**Czechoslovakia** Former federal state in central Europe. Formed after World War I from parts of the old AUSTRO-HUNGARIAN EMPIRE, Czechoslovakia was formally recognized as a new republic by the Treaty of St. Germain (1918). A democratic constitution was established in 1920, and the nation was first led by Tomás MASARYK and then by Eduard BENEŠ. Nationalist tensions caused unrest: the SLOVAKS had long wanted autonomy and the large German population in the N wanted to join with Germany. Hitler's rise to power and annexation of Austria led to the Munich Agreement (1938), which ceded land to Germany. Poland and Hungary also acquired territory and Beněs resigned. Hitler occupied the country in 1939 and Beněs formed a government-in-exile in London. In 1945 the country was liberated by Soviet and US troops and Beněs was restored as president. A 1946 election gave the communists a majority in the coalition. By 1948 they had assumed complete control, and Beněs resigned. Czechoslovakia became a Soviet-style state. Unrest during the 1950s led to some liberalization, but it was not until the PRAGUE SPRING (1968) and the reforms of Alexander DUBČEK that any great democratization occurred. Soviet troops crushed the revolution. When democratic reforms were introduced in the Soviet Union in the late 1980s, CZECHS also demanded reforms. In 1989 antigovernment demonstrations and the democratization of Eastern Europe finally led to the resignation of Communist Party leaders. Noncommunists came to power and the "Velvet Revolution" was complete when Vaclav HAVEL became president. Free elections were held in 1990, but differences between the Czechs and Slovaks led to the partitioning of the country on January 1, 1993. The break was peaceful and the two new nations, the CZECH REPUBLIC and the SLOVAK REPUBLIC, have retained many ties. *See also* BOHEMIA; MORAVIA

**Czech Republic** Republic in central Europe. *See* country feature

## CZECH REPUBLIC

After independence on 1 January 1993, the Czech Republic adopted the flag of the former Czechoslovakia. It features the red and white of Bohemia, together with the blue of Moravia and Slovakia. Red, white and blue are the colors of pan-Slavic liberation.

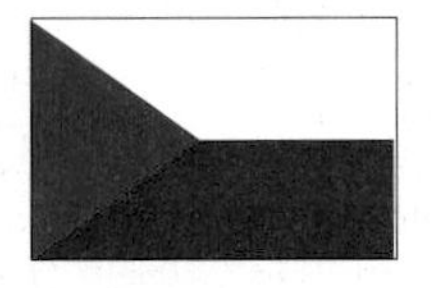

**AREA:** 30,449sq mi (78,864sq km

**POPULATION:** 10,310,000

**CAPITAL (POPULATION):** Prague (1,216,005)

**GOVERNMENT:** Multiparty republic

**ETHNIC GROUPS:** Czech 81%, Moravian 13%, Slovak 3%, Polish, German, Silesian, Gypsy, Hungarian, Ukrainian

**LANGUAGES:** Czech (official)

**RELIGIONS:** Christianity (Roman Catholic 39%, Protestant 4%)

**CURRENCY:** Czech koruna = 100 halura

The Czech Republic lies in central E Europe and contains two regions: the plateau of BOHEMIA in the W and the lowland of MORAVIA in the E. PRAGUE and PLZEN are Bohemia's largest cities; BRNO is the major Moravian city. Mountains form most of the N border. Rivers are vital to this landlocked republic. Some rivers, such as the ELBE, Oder and Vltava flow N into Germany, while others in the S flow into the DANUBE basin.

### CLIMATE

The climate is continental. Moderate Atlantic air streams give Prague warm summers, while easterly winds from Russia bring bitterly cold winters. The average annual rainfall is moderate, with 20–30in (500–750mm) common in lowland areas.

### VEGETATION

Many of the republic's forests have been cut down to create farmland, but oak and spruce remain. Acid rain is damaging trees in the N.

### HISTORY AND POLITICS

The CZECH people began to settle in the area *c.*1,500 years ago. Bohemia became important in the 10th century as a kingdom within the Holy Roman Empire. In 1526 the Austrian Habsburgs assumed control, but a Czech rebellion in 1618 led to the THIRTY YEARS' WAR. German culture dominated the area until the late 18th century. Although Austria continued to rule Bohemia and Moravia, Czech nationalism continued to grow throughout the 19th century.

After World War I CZECHOSLOVAKIA was created. Germany occupied the country in World War II. In 1946 the Communists emerged as the strongest party, but Eduard BENEŠ became president. By 1948 Communist leaders had assumed absolute control. Democratic reforms culminated in the PRAGUE SPRING of 1968. Warsaw Pact troops invaded to crush the liberals. In 1989 mass demonstrations resulted in the "Velvet Revolution" and the formation of a noncommunist administration. Free elections were held in 1991 resulting in the reelection of Vaclav HÁVEL. In 1992 the government agreed to the secession of the SLOVAK REPUBLIC, and on January 1, 1993, the Czech Republic was created. The break was peaceful and the two new nations retain many ties.

### ECONOMY

Under communist rule, Czechoslovakia became one of the most industrialized parts of Eastern Europe (1995 GDP per capita, US$9,770). The country has deposits of coal, uranium, iron ore, magnesite, tin, and zinc. Manufacturing employs 40% of the workforce. Industries include chemicals, beer, iron and steel, and machinery. Light industries include glassware and textiles. The Czech Republic is mainly self-sufficient in food. Private ownership of land is gradually being restored. Agriculture employs 12% of the workforce. Livestock raising is important. Crops include grains, fruit, and hops for brewing.

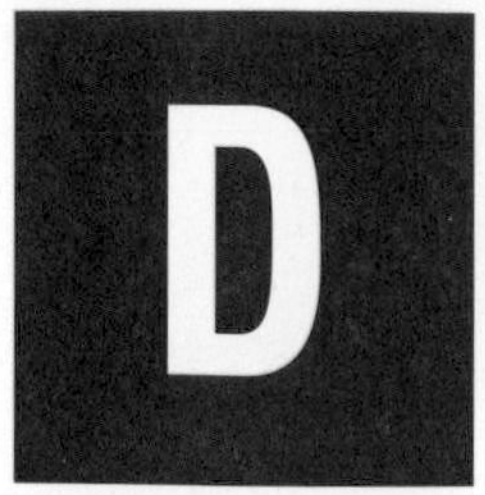

D

*D/d, fourth letter of the Roman alphabet. It is derived from the Semitic* **daleth**, *meaning door, and the Greek delta. It took its current form* c.*AD 114. In Roman numerals, D stands for 500.*

▲ **daffodil** Originally native to Europe and N Africa, the daffodil (*Narcissus* genus) is grown worldwide for its attractive, yellow, trumpet-shaped flower. In many regions it heralds the beginning of spring.

▲ **dahlia** Numbering over 7,000 varieties, the dahlia (*Dahlia* genus) is named for the Swiss botanist Anders Dahl. Most varieties have been developed from the original South American species *D. pinnata*.

**dace** Any of several small freshwater fish of the CARP family, Cyprinidae. The common European dace (*Leuciscus leuciscus*) is silvery and may grow 12in (30cm) long. The Moapa dace (*Moapa coriacea*) is an endangered species.

**Dachau** Town in Bavaria, SW Germany, site of the first Nazi CONCENTRATION CAMP established in March 1933. Up to 70,000 people died or were murdered here before liberation in 1945. The site is preserved as a memorial.

**Dacia** Ancient region of Europe (now in Romania). It was colonized (101–106) by TRAJAN. Dacia was later overrun by Goths, Huns, and Avars. The language was retained and is the basis of modern Romanian.

**Dada** (Dadaism) Movement in literature and the visual arts, started in Zürich (1915). Members included Jean ARP, Tristan Tzara, and Marcel Janco. The group promulgated complete NIHILISM, espoused satire, and ridiculed civilization. Dadaists participated in deliberately irreverent art events, designed to shock a complacent public. In the early 1920s, conflicts of interest led to the demise of Dadaism. *See also* SURREALISM

**Daedalus** In Greek mythology, an architect and sculptor. He constructed the LABYRINTH for King MINOS of Crete. Denied permission to leave the island, he made wings of wax and feathers to escape with his son ICARUS.

**daffodil** Bulbous flowering plant, family Amaryllidaceae. The single flowers are yellow or yellow and white, with a bell-like central cup and oval petals. Height: to 18in (45cm). Genus *Narcissus*.

**Dagestan** Republic in the Russian Federation, bounded on the E by the CASPIAN SEA, SE European Russia. The capital is Makhachkala. Islam was introduced in the 7th century, and the majority of the present population is Muslim. Annexed by Russia in the early 19th century, Dagestan's autonomy was granted in 1921. In 1991 it claimed full republic status. The region is dominated by the CAUCASUS mountains. Lowlands to the N support wheat, corn, and grapes. The rivers Samur and Sulak provide hydroelectric power. Difficulty of access has left mineral resources untapped. Industries: engineering, oil, chemicals. Area: 19,416sq mi (50,300sq km). Pop. (1994) 1,953,000.

**Daguerre, Louis Jacques Mandé** (1789–1851) French painter and inventor. In 1829 Daguerre and Niepce invented the daguerreotype, an early photographic process in which a unique image is produced on a copper plate without an intervening negative. Their process was announced in 1839.

**Dahl, Roald** (1913–90) English writer, chiefly of short stories. He is best-known for his witty, imaginative children's fiction. Dahl's books, such as *James and the Giant Peach* (1961) and *Charlie and the Chocolate Factory* (1964), are popular with all ages. He is also noted for his adult stories, such as *Someone Like You* (1953) and *Kiss, Kiss* (1959).

**dahlia** Genus of perennial plants with tuberous roots and large flowers. The common garden dahlia (*Dahlia pinnata*) has been developed into more than 2,000 varieties. Height: to 5ft (1.5m). Family Asteraceae/Compositae.

**Dáil Éireann** Lower house of the two-chamber Parliament of the Republic of Ireland (the upper house is the *Seanad Éireann*). It has 166 members elected for five-year terms by a system of proportional representation.

**Daimler, Gottlieb** (1834–1900) German engineer and automobile manufacturer. In 1883, with Wilhelm Maybach, Daimler developed an INTERNAL COMBUSTION ENGINE. He used this to power his first car (1886). In 1890 he founded the Daimler Motor Company, which made Mercedes cars and became Daimler-BENZ (1926).

**daisy** Any of several members of the family Asteraceae/Compositae, especially the common English garden daisy, *Bellis perennis*. It has long stalks with solitary flower heads, each of which has a large, yellow, central disk and small, radiating white petal-like florets.

**Dakar** Capital and largest city on the Atlantic coast, Senegal, W Africa. Founded in 1857 as a French fort, it later became capital of French West Africa. There is a Roman Catholic cathedral and a Presidential Palace. Dakar has excellent educational and medical facilities, including the Pasteur Institute. Industries: textiles, oil refining, brewing. Pop. (1992 est.) 1,729,823.

**Dakota** *See* NORTH DAKOTA and SOUTH DAKOTA

**Dakota** *See* SIOUX

**Daladier, Édouard** (1884–1970) French statesman, prime minister (1933, 1934, 1938–40). As prime minister and minister of defence, he signed the MUNICH AGREEMENT (1938). In 1940 he was arrested by the new VICHY GOVERNMENT and deported (1942) to Germany. He was released at the end of World War II and became a member of the National Assembly (1946–58).

**Dalai Lama** (Grand Lama) Supreme head of the Yellow Hat Buddhist monastery at LHASA, TIBET. The title was bestowed upon the third Grand Lama by the Mongol ruler Altan Khan (d.1583). In 1950–51, **Tenzin Gyatso** (1935– ), 14th Dalai Lama, temporarily fled Tibet after it was annexed by the People's Republic of China. Following a brutally suppressed Tibetan uprising (1959), he went into exile in India. In TIBETAN BUDDHISM the Dalai Lama is revered as the BODHISATTVA *Avalokitesvara*. When a Dalai Lama dies, his soul is believed to pass into the body of an infant, born 49 days later.

**Dali, Salvador** (1904–89) Spanish artist. His style, a blend of meticulous realism and hallucinatory transformations of form and space, made him an influential exponent of SURREALISM. His dreamlike paintings exploit the human fear of distortion, as in *The Persistence of Memory* (1931).

**Dallapiccola, Luigi** (1904–75) Italian composer. He was the first Italian composer to use ATONALITY, adopting the TWELVE-TONE system of SCHOENBERG in the 1930s as in the opera *Volo di notte* (1940). Persecuted by Mussolini during World War II, he wrote pieces concerned with freedom, notably *Canti di Prigonia* (1941).

**Dallas** City in NE Texas. First settled in the 1840s, Dallas expanded with the 20th-century development of its oil fields. President John F. Kennedy was assassinated here on November 22, 1963. A commercial and transportation center of the Southwest, it has many educational and cultural institutions. Industries: oil refining, electronic equipment. Pop. (1990) 1,006,877.

**Dalmatia** Region of Croatia on the E coast of the ADRIATIC SEA; the provincial capital is SPLIT. From the 10th century it was divided N and S between Croatia and Serbia. By 1420, most of Dalmatia was controlled by Venice. The Treaty of Campo Formio (1797) ceded the region to Austria. After World War I it became part of Yugoslavia. The coastline stretches along the Adriatic from Rijeka to the border with Montenegro and from the 1960s has been a popular tourist destination. Most of the inland area is mountainous. In 1991 Dalmatia was the scene of

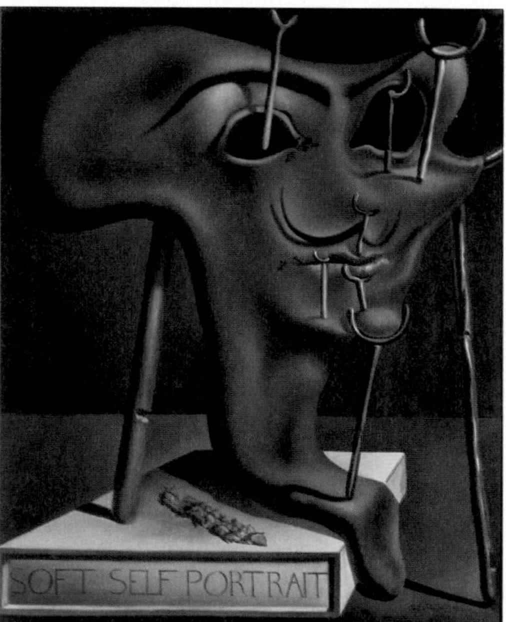


▲ **Dali** *Soft Self Portrait* (1941) by Salvador Dali. The Spanish painter Dali was influenced by the work of Sigmund Freud, and his surrealist images convey powerful dream and hallucinatory elements.

heavy fighting between Croats and Serbs. Other major cities include Zadar (the historic capital) and DUBROVNIK.

**dalmatian** Dog characterized by its white coat with black or brown spots. It has a long, flat head with long muzzle and high-set ears. Its powerful body is set on strong legs and the tail is long and tapered. Height: to 23in (58cm) at the shoulder.

**Dalton, John** (1766–1844) English chemist, physicist, and meteorologist. He researched TRADE WINDS, the cause of rain, and the AURORA borealis. Dalton described COLOR BLINDNESS based on personal experience. His study of gases led to Dalton's law of partial pressures: the total pressure of a gas mixture is equal to the sum of the partial pressures of the individual gases, provided no chemical reaction occurs. Dalton's atomic theory states that each element is made up of indestructible, small particles. He also constructed a table of relative atomic masses.

**dam** Barrier built to confine water (or check its flow) for irrigation, flood control, or electricity generation. The first dams were probably constructed by the Egyptians 4,500 years ago. **Gravity** dams are anchored by their own weight. **Single-arch** dams are convex to the water they retain, supported at each end by river banks. **Multiple-arch** and buttress dams are supported by buttresses rooted in the bedrock. The cheapest commercial source of electricity comes from hydroelectric projects made possible by dams, such as the ASWAN High Dam, Egypt.

**Damascus** Capital of Syria, on the Barada River, SW Syria. Perhaps the oldest continuously occupied city in the world, today it is Syria's administrative and financial center. In 2000 BC Damascus formed part of the Egyptian empire. In 332 BC ALEXANDER THE GREAT captured the city from Persia and it was subsumed into the SELEUCID empire. Under Roman rule Damascus became a prosperous commercial city and an early center of Christianity. THEODOSIUS I built (AD 379) a Christian church that, under UMAYYAD rule (661–750) was converted into the Great Mosque. The city withstood the CRUSADES and was part of the Ottoman empire for 400 years (1516–1918). In 1918 it was captured by the British and came under French administration. It became capital of independent Syria in 1941. Industries: damask fabric, metalware. Pop. (1993 est.) 1,497,000.

**Damocles** In Greek history, a courtier of Dionysius I of Syracuse (Sicily). Dionysius suspended a sword by a fragile thread above Damocles' head to make him realize that wealth and power were insecure.

**damselfly** Delicate insect resembling the DRAGONFLY. Almost all have a slender, elongated, blue abdomen and one pair of membranous wings that are held vertically over the body when at rest. Length: to 2in (5cm). Order Odonata.

**damson** Small tree and its edible fruit. The name is often applied to varieties of PLUM (*Prunus domestica*). The fleshy DRUPE is generally borne in clusters, has a tart flavor, and is made into jam. Family Rosaceae. The damson-plum of tropical America is a separate species, *Chrysophyllum oliviforme*, Family Sapotaceae.

**Dana, Richard Henry** (1815–82) US writer and lawyer. He sailed (1834) as an ordinary seaman around Cape Horn to California. Dana's concern for the injustices suffered by sailors prompted his book *Two Years Before the Mast* (1840), a classic in American literature of the sea.

**Danby, Thomas Osborne, Earl of** (1632–1712) (subsequently Marquis of Carmarthen, Duke of Leeds) Leading minister of CHARLES II. He was impeached and imprisoned (1679–84) for trying to secure a secret subsidy from France. Danby organized a group, later known as Tories, who supported the succession of the future James II, but later changed sides and served William III (1690–95) until again impeached for bribery.

**dance** Ancient art of ordered, stylized body movements, normally performed to music or voices. Primitive dance was probably part of courtship and religious ritual. In China, Japan, and India, graceful MIME is the distinctive feature, whereas the dances of Africa have rapid, athletic movements. In 18th-century Europe, Bach and Handel, among others, composed music for formal courtly dances, such as the gavotte and minuet. Ballroom dances, such as the waltz, foxtrot, tango, and quickstep, became popular in the 19th and early 20th centuries. From the 1940s to the 1960s many new dances, from the jitterbug to the twist, were introduced. *See also* BALLET; FOLK DANCE; MODERN DANCE

**dandelion** Widespread perennial weed, with leaves growing from the base and yellow composite flowers. It reproduces by means of parachute seeds. The leaves are used in salads, the flowers in winemaking. Family Asteraceae (COMPOSITAE); species *Taraxacum officinale*.

**Danelaw** Large region of NE England occupied by Danes in the late 9th century. Its independence was confirmed by Alfred and Guthrum's Pact (886). Alfred's son, Edward the Elder, and grandson, Athelstan, restored it to English control in the early 10th century.

**Daniel** Legendary Jewish hero and visionary of the 6th century BC, who was at the court of the Babylonian kings NEBUCHADNEZZAR and BELSHAZZAR. The OLD TESTAMENT Book of Daniel, probably written *c*.165 BC, relates events in Daniel's life during the BABYLONIAN CAPTIVITY. The last six of its 12 chapters consist of visions and prophesies.

**D'Annunzio, Gabriele** (1863–1938) Italian writer and soldier. His erotic novel *The Flame of Life* (1900) describes his affair with Eleanora DUSE. D'Annunzio's masterpiece is the impressionistic collection of lyrics, *Halcyon* (1903). His rhetoric was instrumental in persuading Italy to join the Allies in World War I. D'Annunzio fought with spectacular bravery. He established personal rule (1919–21) of Fiume (Rijeka). D'Annunzio supported the rise of Mussolini's fascist movement.

**Dante Alighieri** (1265–1321) Italian poet. He helped defeat the GHIBELLINES at the battle of Campaldino (1289). *La Vita Nuova* (*The New Life*, *c*.1292) celebrates Dante's idealized love for Beatrice Portinari (1266–90), who remained the inspiration for much of his life's work. Dante's support for the moderate White GUELPHS against the papal faction of Black Guelphs led to his exile (1302). He never returned to Florence, but wrote under the patronage of various nobles until his death in Ravenna. His masterpiece, *The Divine Comedy*, a three-book epic in *terza rima*, represents one of the pinnacles of Western literature. It depicts the poet's spiritual journey through Hell, Purgatory, and Paradise. Other works include *The Banquet* (*c*.1304–07) and *On Monarchy* (*c*.1313). *See also* ALLEGORY

**Danton, Georges Jacques** (1759–94) French statesman, a leader of the FRENCH REVOLUTION. He was instrumental in the arrest of LOUIS XVI (August 10, 1792). Danton, DESMOULINS, ROBESPIERRE, and MARAT formed a revolutionary tribunal. Danton dominated the first Committee of Public Safety (April–July 1793), but was ousted by Robespierre and the JACOBINS. He called for an end to the REIGN OF TERROR and leniency towards the GIRONDINS. Danton was arrested for conspiracy, tried, and guillotined.

**Danube** (Donau) River in central and SE Europe. Europe's second-longest river, it rises in SW Germany, flows NE then SE across Austria to form the border between Slovakia and Hungary. It then flows S into Serbia, forming part of Romania's borders with Serbia and Bulgaria. It continues N across SE Romania to the Black Sea. Length: *c*.1,770mi (2,859km).

**Danzig** *See* GDAŃSK

**Daphne** Nymph in GREEK MYTHOLOGY. APOLLO, struck by a gold-tipped arrow of EROS, fell in love with Daphne. She had been shot with one of Eros' leaden points, and so scorned all men. To protect her from Apollo, the gods transformed her into a laurel tree.

**Dardanelles** (Çanakkale Bogazi) Narrow strait between the Sea of Marmara and the Aegean Sea, separating Çanakkale in Asian Turkey from GALLIPOLI in European Turkey. With the BOSPORUS Strait, the Dardanelles forms a waterway whose strategic and commercial importance has been recognized since ancient times (known then as the Hellespont). In the Byzantine and Ottoman empires and both World Wars it was of strategic importance in the defense of Constantinople (ISTANBUL). The strait was the scene of the GALLIPOLI CAMPAIGN in World War 1. Length: 38mi (61km). Width: 0.75–4mi (1.2–6km).

**Dar es Salaam** Former capital of Tanzania, on the Indian Ocean, E Tanzania. Founded in the 1860s by the sultan of Zanzibar, it was capital of German East Africa (1891–1916) and of Tanganyika (1916–74). It is Tanzania's

▲ **dalmatian** Perhaps best known from the film *101 Dalmatians*, dalmatians are thought to have been developed as carriage dogs in the Croatian region of Dalmatia.

▲ **dandelion** Found throughout the Northern Hemisphere, the leaves of the common dandelion (*Taraxacum officinale*) have teeth-shaped edges. It is from this shape that the dandelion derives its name (Fr. *dents de lion*, teeth of the lion.)

D

commercial center, largest city, and port. Industries: textiles, chemicals. Pop. (1988 est.) 1,360,850.

**Darío, Rubén** (1867–1916) (Félix Rubén García Sarmiento) Nicaraguan poet, father of the *modernismo* movement. Darío influenced both Latin American and Spanish writers. Darío's finest book of verse, *Songs of Life and Hope* (1905), is noted for its eloquence and universality of vision.

**Darius I** (*c*.558–486 BC) King of Persia (521–486 BC) of the ACHAEMENID dynasty. Troubled by revolts, particularly in BABYLON, Darius restored order by dividing the empire into provinces, allowing some local autonomy, and tolerating religious diversity. He was defeated at Marathon in 490 BC.

**Darjeeling** City at the foot of the Himalayas, West Bengal, NE India. A former British hill station, it is noted for its teas. Pop. (1981) 57,603.

**Dark Ages** Period of European history from the fall of the Roman empire in the 5th century to the 9th or 10th century. The term appears to imply cultural and economic backwardness, but in fact indicates ignorance of the period due to lack of historical evidence.

**Darmstadt** City in Hesse state, W central Germany. The old town dates from the Middle Ages. The city was severely damaged during World War II. It is a cultural center, with a music school. Industries: chemicals, aerospace engineering, steel. Pop. (1990) 140,900.

**Darrow, Clarence Seward** (1857–1938) US lawyer. He unsuccessfully defended (1894) Eugene V. DEBS (1894) following the PULLMAN STRIKE. A staunch opponent of capital punishment, none of the 100 people charged with murder that Darrow defended were ever sentenced to death. In 1906 he secured the acquittal of William HAYWOOD. In the famous SCOPES TRIAL (1925), Darrow unsuccessfully defended the right to teach evolution in school, but his cross-examination of William Jennings BRYAN discredited the Fundamentalist stance.

**Dartmouth College case** (1819) US Supreme Court case. In 1816 the New Hampshire legislature unilaterally amended the charter of 1769 to make Dartmouth College a state university. The Court held that a corporate charter was a contract with which state laws could not interfere. This ruling greatly aided the early growth of US capitalism and big business.

**darts** Indoor target game developed in 15th-century England. Three weighted, metal-pointed darts are thrown at a board 8ft (2.4m) away. The standard board is divided into 20 even wedges, with a triple scoring band in the middle and a double scoring band on the outside, fanning out from two small circles in the center (the bull's-eye, worth 50 points, and around it the "25"). Starting with a certain number of points (usually 501), the object is to reach zero, finishing with a "double."

**Darwin, Charles Robert** (1809–82) English naturalist, who developed the organic theory of EVOLUTION. In 1831, he joined a five-year, round-the-world expedition on HMS BEAGLE. Observations made of the flora and fauna of South America (especially the Galápagos Islands) formed the basis of his work on animal variation. The development of a similar theory by A.R. WALLACE led Darwin to present his ideas to the Linnean Society in 1858. In 1859 he published *The Origin of Species*. Thomas HUXLEY championed Darwin's ideas and engaged in a heated debate with theologians, since Darwin's notion of a common ancestral origin contradicted a literal interpretation of the Book of GENESIS. Drawing on the work of Thomas MALTHUS, Darwin argued that organisms reproduce more than is necessary to replenish their population, creating competition for survival. Opposed to the ideas of LAMARCK, Darwin argued that each organism was a unique combination of genetic variations. The variations that prove helpful in the struggle to survive are passed down to the offspring of the survivors. He termed this process NATURAL SELECTION. NEO-DARWINISM supplemented his ideas with modern research into HEREDITY, especially MUTATION.

▲ ▶ **date palm** Today, grown as an ornament as well as for its fruit, the date palm (*Phoenix dactylifera*) has been cultivated for over 4,000 years. The tallest examples reach a height of 100ft (30m).

**Darwin** Port on the Beagle Gulf, N Australia, capital of Northern Territory. Founded in the late 1860s as Palmerston, it became Port Darwin in 1911. Allied headquarters in N Australia during World War II, it was bombed by the Japanese (1942). In 1974 most of the city was destroyed by a cyclone. Darwin's harbor is the major shipping point. Pop. (1993 est.) 77,900.

**Darwinism** *See* EVOLUTION

**dasyurus** Genus of mainly nocturnal, carnivorous MARSUPIALS found in Australia, New Guinea, and Tasmania. They have large canine teeth, separate digits, and long tails. Family Dasyuridae.

**data** Information, such as lists of words, quantities, or measurements, or codes representing a picture. A computer PROGRAM works by processing data, which may be entered using a keyboard or other input device, stored as a data file on a MAGNETIC DISK. Data may come from a variety of sources, including the INTERNET.

**database** Collection of DATA produced and retrieved by a COMPUTER. The data is usually stored on MAGNETIC DISK or tape. A database PROGRAM enables the computer to generate files of data and later search for and retrieve specific items or groups of items.

**data processing** Systematic sequence of operations performed on DATA, especially by a COMPUTER, in order to calculate or revise information stored on MAGNETIC DISK or tape. The main processing operations performed by a computer are arithmetical addition, subtraction, multiplication, and division, and logical operations that involve decision-making based on comparison of data.

**data protection** Measures taken to guard DATA against unauthorized access. Many governments have passed legislation ensuring that such DATABASES are registered and that the information they contain is protected.

**date palm** Tree native to the Near East. It has large flower clusters that produce the popular edible fruit. Height: up to 100ft (30m). Family Arecacae/Palmae.

**dating, radioactive** (radiometric dating) Any of several methods using the laws of RADIOACTIVE DECAY to assess the ages of archaeological remains, fossils, rocks, and of the Earth itself. The specimens must contain a long-lived radioisotope of known HALF-LIFE, which, with a measurement of the ratio of radioisotope to a stable ISOTOPE (usually the decay product), gives the age.

**Daumier, Honoré** (1808–79) French painter, sculptor, and caricaturist. Daumier produced more than 4,000 lithographs lampooning French middle-class society.

**David, Saint** (d. *c*.600) Patron saint of Wales. He founded a monastery at what is now St. Davids. Little is known of his life, but legends abound. His feast day is March 1.

**David** (1000–962 BC) (d. *c*.962 BC) King of Israel. His career is related in the OLD TESTAMENT. David became a hero by defeating GOLIATH in a duel and was made king of Judah on SAUL'S death. He united Judah and Israel and made Jerusalem his capital. God is said to have promised that his dynasty would be eternal. *See* MESSIAH

**David, Gerard** (1460–1523) Flemish painter. Influenced by van EYCK and van der WEYDEN, David has a distinctive, austere grace. He was commissioned by the town of BRUGES to paint several works: *The Judgment of Cambyses* and *The Flaying of Sisamnes* warned officials of the retribution for injustice.

**David, Jacques Louis** (1748–1825) French painter, a leader of NEOCLASSICISM. David's work was tied up with his JACOBIN views and support of Napoleon I. His most famous work is *Oath of the Horatii* (1784). Others include *Death of Socrates* (1787), and *Death of Marat* (1793).

**Davies, Sir Peter Maxwell** (1934– ) British composer. Prolific and varied in his compositions, he has written four operas, including *Taverner* (1972) and *Resurrection* (1988). Much of his work reflects the landscape and culture of his adopted home, the remote Orkney Islands, N Scotland.

**Davies, Robertson** (1913–95) Canadian writer. Davies is best known for *The Deptford Trilogy* (1970–75), which exhibits his characteristic mixture of myth, satire, and psychological symbolism. Other works include *The Salterton Trilogy* (1951–58), and a number of plays, including *A Jig for the Gypsy* (1954).

**Da Vinci, Leonardo** *See* LEONARDO DA VINCI

**Davis, Alexander Jackson** (1803–92) US architect. With Ithiel Town he designed many public buildings in the Greek revival style, notably the US Customs House, New York City (1832), and the state capitols of North Carolina, Indiana, Illinois, and Ohio.

**Davis, Angela** (1944– ) US political activist. Beginning in the 1960s, Davis was an advocate for both African-Americans' and women's CIVIL RIGHTS. In 1970 a judge was murdered with guns registered in Davis's name. Charged with conspiracy, murder, and kidnapping, Davis was acquitted after a sensational trial.

**Davis, Benjamin Oliver, Jr** (1912– ) US air force general, son of Benjamin Oliver Davis, the first African-American general in the US army. Davis was the first African-American graduate of West Point (1936). In World War II he earned the Distinguished Flying Cross. In 1959 Davis became the first African-American major general in the air force. He was chief of staff in South Korea (1965). After retiring from the air force (1970), he was (1971–75) assistant transportation secretary.

**Davis, Bette** (1908–89) US film actress. She is remembered for her intense character portrayals in films such as *Of Human Bondage* (1934). Davis won two Best Actress Academy Awards – *Dangerous* (1935), and *Jezebel* (1938). Other films include *All About Eve* (1950), and *What Ever Happened to Baby Jane* (1962).

**Davis, Jefferson** (1808–89) American statesman, president of the CONFEDERATE STATES during the CIVIL WAR (1861–65). Davis was elected to Congress in 1845 but resigned to fight in the MEXICAN WAR. A strong advocate for the extension of SLAVERY, he acted as senator for Mississippi (1849–51). In 1853 Franklin PIERCE made him secretary of war. In 1857 he rejoined the Senate and acted as leader of the Southern bloc. He resigned when Mississippi seceded from the Union (1861) and was soon elected leader of the Confederacy. Following Lee's surrender, Davis was captured and imprisoned (1865–67).

**Davis, Miles Dewey** (1926–91) US jazz trumpeter and composer. During the 1940s Davis played bebop with Charlie PARKER. *The Birth of the Cool* (1949), marked a change of style with greater texture and restraint. In 1955 Davis formed a quintet (including the saxophonist John COLTRANE) that made such landmark recordings as *Relaxin'* (1956). *Kind of Blue* (1959) is widely regarded as the first exercise in "modal" jazz. In the late 1960s Davis pioneered a fusion of jazz and rock music. He retired from playing (1975–80), but returned with a series of pop-jazz records such as *You're Under Arrest* (1985).

**Davis, Stuart** (1894–1964) US painter, leading US exponent of CUBISM. The greatest impact on his style was the ARMORY SHOW (1913). After a visit to Paris (1928–29), he turned toward cubism's synthetic phase, introducing natural forms arranged in flat areas of pattern in bright, contrasting colors. His later abstract style used lettering that resembled advertising slogans, such as *Owh! in San Pao* (1951).

**Davitt, Michael** (1846–1906) Irish nationalist. Imprisoned in 1870 as a member of the FENIAN MOVEMENT. He and Charles Stewart PARNELL established the Irish Land League (1879) to organize Irish tenant farmers against exploitative landlords.

**Davy, Sir Humphry** (1778–1829) English chemist, who discovered that electrolytic cells produce electricity by chemical means. This led to his isolation of the elements sodium, potassium, barium, strontium, calcium, and magnesium. His investigation into the conditions under which firedamp (methane and other gases) and air explode, led to his invention of a miner's safety lamp.

**Dawes, Charles Gates** (1865–1951) US statesman, vice president (1925–29). He served (1897–1902) as comptroller of the currency under President William MCKINLEY. Dawes was awarded the 1925 Nobel Peace Prize for his work that produced the DAWES PLAN (1924) for stabilizing the German economy.

**Day, Doris** (1924– ) US singer and actress. Her recordings, such as "Secret Love" (1954), sold millions during the 1940s and 1950s. Day's wholesome, energetic performances in films such as *Calamity Jane* (1953), and *Send Me No Flowers* (1964) won her an even greater audience. She received an Academy Award nomination for *Pillow Talk* (1959).

**Dayan, Moshe** (1915–81) Israeli army officer and statesman. He led a Palestinian Jewish force against the Vichy French in World War II. Dayan led the invasion of the Sinai Peninsula in 1956 and, as minister of defense, became a hero of the SIX DAY WAR (1967). He also served as foreign minister (1977–79).

**Day-Lewis, Cecil** (1904–72) British poet and critic, b. Ireland. Day-Lewis was associated with the leftist AUDEN circle. His concern for social justice is evident in *Transitional Poem* (1929), and *Collected Poems* (1954). He was Poet Laureate from 1968. He also wrote detective fiction under the pseudonym Nicholas Blake.

**Day-Lewis, Daniel Michael** (1957– ) Irish actor, b. London, son of Cecil DAY-LEWIS. He first achieved recognition in *My Beautiful Laundrette* (1986). Day-Lewis won an Academy Award as Best Actor for *My Left Foot* (1989). Other films include *The Age of Innocence* (1993), and *In the Name of the Father* (1993).

**Dayton** City at the confluence of the Great Miami and Stillwater rivers, SW Ohio. Settled in 1796, it is a commercial center for the surrounding agricultural region. In 1995 the Dayton Peace Accord ended the Bosnian civil war. Pop. (1990) 182,044.

**D-day** (June 6, 1944) Codename for the Allied invasion of Normandy during WORLD WAR II. Commanded by General EISENHOWER, Allied forces landed on the French coast between Cherbourg and Le Havre. It was the largest amphibious operation in history, involving *c.*5,000 ships. Despite fierce resistance, bridgeheads were established by June 9. It was the first step in the liberation of Europe.

**DDT** (dichlorodiphenyltrichloroethane) Organic compound used as an insecticide. It acts as a contact poison, disorganizing the nervous system. Though effective against most insect pests, it proved to have long-lasting toxic effects and is now banned in many countries.

**deacon** (Gk. *diakonas*, helper) Ordained minister who serves as a priest's assistant in Christian churches. The institution of the diaconate can be traced to the New Testament, which describes the ordination of seven deacons (Acts 6).

**deadly nightshade** (belladonna) Poisonous perennial plant native to Europe and W Asia. It has large leaves, purple flowers, and black berries. ALKALOIDS, such as ATROPINE, are obtained from its roots and leaves. Eating the fruit can be fatal. Family Solanaceae; species *Atropa belladonna*.

**Dead Sea** (Al-Bahr-al-Mayyit) Salt lake in the Jordan valley, on the Jordan-Israel border. It is fed by the JORDAN River. The surface, 1,302ft (396m) below sea level, is the lowest point on Earth. It is situated in a hot, dry region. One of the world's saltiest waters, it supports no life, and much salt is commercially extracted.

**Dead Sea Scrolls** Ancient manuscripts discovered from 1947 in caves at Qumran near the DEAD SEA. Written in Hebrew or Aramaic, they date from between the 1st century BC and the 1st century AD. They include versions of much of the OLD TESTAMENT. Some are a thousand years older than any other biblical manuscript.

**deafness** Partial or total hearing loss. **Conductive** deafness is usually due to infection or inherited abnormalities of the middle ear. **Perceptive** deafness may be hereditary or due to injury or disease of the COCHLEA, auditory nerve, or hearing

▲ **Davis** Trumpeter Miles Davis was among the first jazz musicians to experiment with other contemporary forms of music, such as funk and rap. Beginning in the 1940s be-bop era, his musical career spanned half a century.

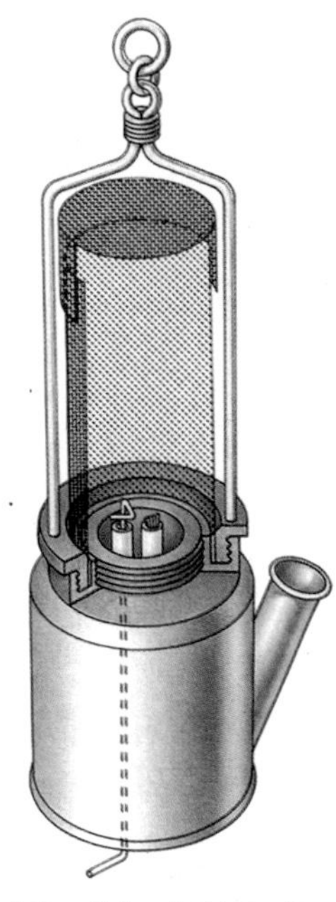

▲ **Davy** Perhaps best known for the invention of a miner's safety lamp (Davy lamp), English chemist Sir Humphry Davy was a significant chemist who inspired Michael Faraday.

▶ **Death Valley** The desert region of SE California, known as Death Valley, is among the hottest places on Earth. It acquired its name from gold and silver prospectors, many of whom lost their lives trying to cross it.

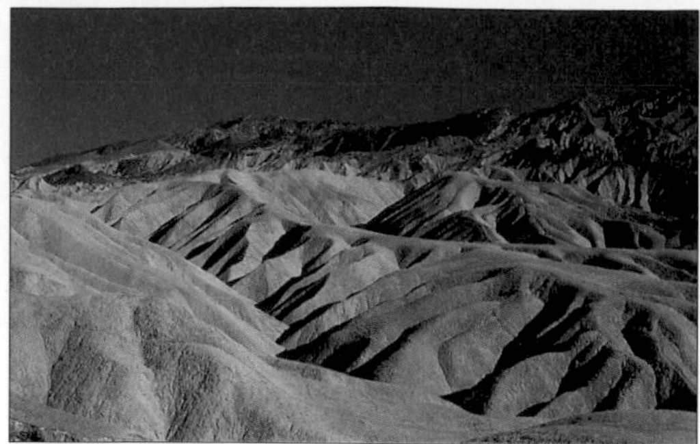

centers in the brain. Treatment ranges from removal of wax to delicate microsurgery. Hearing aids, sign language, and lip-reading are techniques which help the deaf to communicate.

**Dean, "Dizzy" (Jay Hanna)** (1911–74) US baseball player. He played (1930–37) for the St. Louis Cardinals and helped them win the 1934 World Series. Dean injured his arm in 1937 and was traded to the Chicago Cubs. He retired in 1941 and became a sports commentator. Dean was elected to the Baseball Hall of Fame in 1953.

**Dean, James** (1931–55) US film actor. Dean played the restless son in the film of John Steinbeck's *East of Eden* (1954) and appeared as a misunderstood teenager in *Rebel Without a Cause* (1955). He was killed in a car crash, a year before the release of his third and final film *Giant*. Dean has become a cult hero.

**death** Cessation of life. In medicine, death has traditionally been pronounced on cessation of the heartbeat. However, modern resuscitation and life-support techniques have led to the revival of patients whose hearts have stopped. In a tiny minority of cases, while breathing and heartbeat can be maintained artificially, the potential for life is extinct. In this context, death may be pronounced when it is clear that the brain no longer controls vital functions. The issue is highly controversial.

**death cap** (deadly amanita) Highly poisonous FUNGUS that grows in woodlands. It has a yellowish-green cap and a white stem with a drooping ring and sheathed base. If eaten, the poison causes great pain and, in most cases, death. Species *Amanita phalloides*.

**death penalty** *See* CAPITAL PUNISHMENT

**Death Valley** Desert basin in E California. It has the lowest point in the Western Hemisphere, 282ft (86m) below sea level. Temperatures can reach 134°F (57°C), the highest in the US. Gold and silver were mined in the 1850s and borax in the late 19th century. Length: 140mi (225km).

**deathwatch beetle** Small beetle that tunnels through wood. It makes a faint ticking sound once said to presage death. It is the mating signal of the female as it taps against the wood. Length: to 0.3in (0.9cm). Family Anobiidae; species *Xestobium rufovillosum*.

**de Broglie, Louis** *See* BROGLIE, LOUIS VICTOR DE

**Debs, Eugene Victor** (1855–1926) US labor organizer. He was a founder and first president (1893–97) of the American Railroad Union (ARU). When federal troops broke up the PULLMAN STRIKE (1894) Debs was imprisoned. In 1898 he formed the Social Democratic Party (renamed the Socialist Party, 1901) and was its presidential candidate (1900, 1904, 1908, 1912). Debs was also a founder (1905) of the INDUSTRIAL WORKERS OF THE WORLD (IWW). He condemned US participation in World War I and was convicted (1918) under the Espionage Act. Debs ran for president (1920) while still in prison and polled nearly one million votes.

**debt, national** Public debt of a government. National debt accumulates if governments spend more than they generate through taxation; it consists largely of borrowings from individuals and other governments.

**Debussy, Claude Achille** (1862–1918) French composer, exponent of IMPRESSIONISM. He wrote highly individual music that was delicate and suggestive. Debussy explored new techniques of harmony and orchestral color. Some critics cite his *Prélude à l'après-midi d'un faune* (1894) as the beginning of 20th-century music. Other orchestral works are *Nocturnes* (1899), *La Mer* (1905) and *Images* (1912). His piano works, such as *Suite Bergamasque* (1890) and *Etudes* (1915), are among the most important in the repertoire. His one completed opera was *Pelléas and Mélisande* (1902).

**Debye, Peter Joseph Wilhelm** (1884–1966) US chemist, b. Netherlands. He was best known for his work on molecular structure and ionization. Debye pioneered X-RAY CRYSTALLOGRAPHY and was awarded the 1936 Nobel Prize for chemistry.

**decathlon** Sports event comprising ten different track and field activities: 100m, long jump, shot put, high jump, 400m, 110m hurdles, discus, pole vault, javelin, and 1,500m. It has been an Olympic event since 1912.

**Decatur, Stephen** (1779–1820) US naval officer. In the TRIPOLITAN WAR (1801–05), Decatur's daring destruction of the captured US frigate *Philadelphia* earned him a captaincy. His capture of the British frigate *Macedonian* in the WAR OF 1812 saw him rise to commodore. Decatur was killed in a duel with James Barron. He is noted for his toast "Our country! In her intercourse with foreign nations may she always be right; but our country, right or wrong!"

**Deccan** Plateau in central India, S of the Narmada River. In attempting to conquer it in the 17th century, Aurangzeb fatally weakened the MOGUL dynasty. In the late 18th century, the British defeated the French here. On its E and W edges, the Deccan rises to the GHATS. The plateau is covered with rich volcanic soils. Cotton, cereal, coffee, and tea are grown.

**decibel** (symbol dB) Logarithmic unit, one tenth of a bel, used for comparing two power levels and for expressing the loudness of a sound. The faintest audible sound ($2 \times 10^{-5}$ pascal) is given an arbitrary value of 0dB. Ordinary conversations occur at 50 to 60 dB.

**deciduous** Annual or seasonal loss of all leaves from a tree or shrub; it is the opposite of EVERGREEN.

**decimal system** Commonly used system of writing numbers, using a base ten and the Arabic numerals 0 to 9. It is a positional number system, each position to the left representing an extra power of ten. Thus 6,741 is $(6 \times 10^3) + (7 \times 10^2) + (4 \times 10^1) + (1 \times 10^0)$. Note that $10^0 = 1$. Decimal fractions are represented by negative powers of ten placed to the right of a decimal point.

**Declaration of Independence** (July 4, 1776) Statement of principles, in which the THIRTEEN COLONIES of North America justified the AMERICAN REVOLUTION and separation from Britain. Its blend of idealism and practical statements have ensured its place as one of the world's most important political documents. The Declaration was drafted by a committee that included Thomas JEFFERSON, and was based on the theory of NATURAL RIGHTS, propounded by John LOCKE to justify the GLORIOUS REVOLUTION in England. It was approved by the CONTINENTAL CONGRESS on July 4. The Declaration states the necessity of government having the consent of the governed, of government's responsibility to its people, and contains the famous paragraph: "We hold these truths to be self-evident, that all men are created equal, that they are endowed by their Creator with certain unalienable Rights, that among these are Life, Liberty, and the Pursuit of Happiness."

**Declaration of Rights** *See* BILL OF RIGHTS

**Declaration of the Rights of Man and Citizen** (1789) Statement of principles of the FRENCH REVOLUTION, adopted by the National Assembly, accepted by Louis XVI and included in the 1791 constitution. Influenced by the American DECLARATION OF INDEPENDENCE and the ideas of Jean Jacques ROUSSEAU, it established the sovereignty of the people and a balance of rights and responsibilities embodied in "liberty, equality, and fraternity."

**decomposition** Natural degradation of organic matter into simpler substances, such as carbon dioxide and water. Organisms of decay are usually BACTERIA and FUNGI. Decomposition recycles nutrients by releasing them back into the ECOSYSTEM.

**decompression sickness** *See* BENDS

**deconstruction** In architecture, a term used to describe work dating from the early 1980s that explores ways of reconciling traditional oppositions in building design, such as structure–decoration or abstraction–figuration. Deconstruction is also a literary and philosophical term of critical analysis, pioneered by the philosopher Jacques DERRIDA. Patterns of opposition, which form a given text, are broken down and considered.

**Decorated style** Style of English Gothic architecture which flourished *c.*1250–1350. The most exuberant phase of English Gothic, it featured the double-curving ogee arch and intricate, curvilinear window tracery. The windows of Exeter Cathedral are excellent examples of Decorated stone carving. *See also* GOTHIC ART AND ARCHITECTURE

**deep scattering layer (DSL)** Sound-reflecting layers in the oceans that are distinct enough at times to create a "false bottom." Various layers that can be detected during the day by sonar equipment disappear at night. Shoals of small deep-dwelling fish, crustaceans, and squid that feed at the water surface at night seem to be the cause. DSLs are found usually at depths of 600 to 1,200ft (400–800m).

**deer** Long-legged, hoofed RUMINANT. There are 53 species in 17 genera distributed worldwide. In most species, the male (buck, hart, or stag) bears ANTLERS. Only in REINDEER does the female (hind or doe) bear antlers. Deer often gather in herds. They are generally brown, with spotted young (fawns). They eat bark, shoots, twigs, and grass. Humans exploit them for their meat (venison), hides, and antlers (for hunting trophies). The deer family Cervidae has existed since the Oligocene epoch. The Chinese water deer is the smallest, measuring only 22in (55cm) tall at the shoulder; the ELK at 6.5ft (2m), is the largest.

**Defense, US Department of** Federal executive department, based in the PENTAGON. It consists of the secretary of defense, JOINT CHIEFS OF STAFF (JCS), service departments, and operational military commands. The secretary of defense, with the president, is responsible for all operational military activities, providing civilian control for the ARMY, NAVY, and AIR FORCE. Established as the war department in 1789, in 1947 the National Security Act brought the three branches of the military forces together as the National Military Establishment, which in 1949 became the Department of Defense.

**defense mechanism** Unconscious or involuntary reaction adopted by people to protect themselves from threatening and anxiety-producing mental or physical events. The term was first used by Sigmund FREUD and includes repression and mannerisms.

**deflation** Falling prices, accompanied by falls in output and employment. The opposite of INFLATION, it normally occurs during a RECESSION or DEPRESSION and can be measured by the price index. Excess production capacity leads to an excess of supply that usually causes deflation.

**Defoe, Daniel** (1660–1731) English journalist and novelist. Defoe championed William III in his first notable poem, *The True-born Englishman* (1701). A politically controversial journalist, he was twice imprisoned, once for *The Shortest Way with the Dissenters* (1702). Defoe's enduringly popular novels include *Robinson Crusoe* (1719), *Moll Flanders* (1722), *Colonel Jack* (1722), and *Roxana* (1724). He is among the most prolific writers in the English language.

**De Forest, Lee** (1873–1961) US inventor of the audion triode valve (1907). It could amplify signals, and had numerous applications. Valves became essential in radio, television, radar, and computer systems; they were replaced by the TRANSISTOR (1947).

**deforestation** Clearing away forests and their ECOSYSTEMS, usually on a large scale, by humans. There is an immediate danger that the vital topsoil will be eroded by wind (such as the DUST BOWL) or, in hilly areas, by rain. Proposals to clear whole regions of the Amazonian rain forests, which play a key role in maintaining the oxygen balance of the Earth, could cause an environmental catastrophe.

**Degas, (Hilaire Germain) Edgar** (1834–1917) French painter and sculptor. He studied (1854–59) Renaissance art in Italy, and exhibited in the Salon (1865–70). After meeting Édouard MANET, Degas took part in exhibitions of IMPRESSIONISM. While sharing an interest in depicting scenes of everyday life, he differed from his colleagues in the stress he placed on composition, draftsmanship, and the use of the studio. His favorite themes, ballet and horse racing, reveal his preoccupation with the depiction of movement. Inspired by photography and Japanese prints, Degas' paintings, such as *Foyer of the Dance* (1874), are characterized by informal poses and unusual viewpoints. For the last 20 years of his life he was almost blind and produced much freer work in glowing pastels or sculpting in wax.

**De Gasperi, Alcide** (1881–1954) Italian statesman, prime minister (1945–53). He was born in Trentino, then under Austrian rule. De Gasperi struggled successfully for its reunification with Italy. A staunch anti-fascist, he was imprisoned twice in the 1920s. During World War II he founded the Italian Christian Democratic Party. De Gasperi is regarded as the chief architect of Italy's post-war recovery.

**De Gaulle, Charles André Joseph Marie** (1890–1970) French general and statesman, first president (1959–69) of the fifth republic. In 1940 he became undersecretary of war, but fled to London after the German invasion. De Gaulle organized French resistance (Free French) forces, and in June 1944 was proclaimed president of the provisional French government. Following liberation he resigned, disenchanted with the political settlement. In 1958 De Gaulle emerged from retirement to deal with the war in Algeria. In 1962 he was forced to cede Algerian independence. France gained an independent nuclear capability, but alienated the UK and US by its temporary withdrawal from NATO and by blocking British entry into the EEC. De Gaulle was reelected (1965), but resigned after defeat in a 1969 referendum.

**degree** In mathematics, unit of angular measure equal to 1/360 of a complete revolution. One degree is written 1°, and can be divided into 60 parts called minutes (e.g. 20'), which may in turn be divided into 60 parts called seconds (e.g. 25"). In physics and engineering, a degree is one unit on any of various scales, such as the CELSIUS temperature scale.

**dehydration** Removal or loss of water from a substance or tissue. Water molecules can be removed by heat, catalysts, or a dehydrating agent such as concentrated sulfuric acid. Dehydration is used to preserve food. In medicine, excessive water loss is often a symptom or result of disease or injury.

**deism** System of natural religion, first developed in England in the late 17th century. It affirmed belief in one God, but held that He detached himself from the universe after its creation and made no revelation. Reason was man's only guide. Deist writings include John Toland's *Christianity not Mysterious* (1696) and Matthew Tindal's *Christianity as Old as the Creation* (1730). Deism was a great influence on the ENLIGHTENMENT. VOLTAIRE, ROUSSEAU, and DIDEROT were its chief exponents.

**deity** God or goddess, or the condition, rank, or quality of divinity. Deity is applied broadly to any divine being who is the object of worship, regardless of religious creed. In the 18th century, the deists used the term to signify a supreme being.

**de Klerk, F.W. (Frederik Willem)** (1936– ) South African statesman, president (1989–94). He entered Parliament in

▼ **Degas** The French painter Degas was an unusual impressionist, because of the emphasis he placed on drawing and composition of indoor scenes. Perhaps his most popular theme was movement, in particular dance, such as *Dancers on a Bench* (1898).

1972 and joined the cabinet in 1978. In 1989 De Klerk led a "palace coup" against P.W. BOTHA, and became president and National Party leader. Following a narrow electoral victory, he began the process of dismantling APARTHEID. In 1990 the ban on the AFRICAN NATIONAL CONGRESS (ANC) was lifted, and Nelson MANDELA was released. In 1991 the main apartheid laws were repealed and victory in a 1992 whites-only referendum marked an end to white minority rule. In 1993 de Klerk shared the Nobel Peace Prize with Nelson Mandela. Following the 1994 elections, de Klerk became deputy president in Mandela's government of national unity. In 1996 he resigned and led the Nationalists out of the coalition. In 1997 he retired as leader of the National Party.

**de Kooning, Willem** (1904–97) US painter, b. Netherlands. In the 1930s he explored several different styles, and in 1948 became one of the leaders of abstract expressionism. Unlike POLLOCK, he kept a figurative element in his work and shocked the public with violently distorted images such as the *Women* series (1953). His emphasis on technique is known as ACTION PAINTING.

**Delacroix, (Ferdinand Victor) Eugène** (1798–1863) French painter, the greatest French artist of ROMANTICISM. He was heralded as the leader of the romantic movement following the exhibition of his first major painting *The Barque of Dante* (1822). Opposed to the prevailing NEOCLASSICISM, he was inspired by history, politics, mythology, and literature (especially Shakespeare and Byron). *Massacre at Chios* (1824), and *Greece Expiring on the Ruins of Missolonghi* (1827) were inspired by the Greek War of Independence. A visit to Morocco (1832) inspired sketches that developed into paintings such as *Women of Algiers* (1834). In the 1830s Delacroix's work underwent a major change as he began to exploit divisionism. From 1833 he worked on decorations for civic buildings, such as the Louvre. His portraits of contemporaries include *Paganini* (1832), and *Chopin and George Sand* (1838).

**De la Mare, Walter** (1873–1956) British poet, short-story writer, and anthologist. His technically accomplished collections of poems include *Songs of Childhood* (1902), *Winged Chariot* (1951), and the anthology *Come Hither* (1923). His prose includes the novel *Memoirs of a Midget* (1921).

**Delaunay, Robert** (1885–1941) French painter, cofounder (with his wife Sonia DELAUNAY-TERK) of ORPHISM. Delaunay was an influence on the BLAUE REITER group. Many of his works are abstract cityscapes. The Eiffel Tower series is his most famous.

**Delaunay-Terk, Sonia** (1885–1979) French painter, b. Russia. Cofounder (with her husband Robert DELAUNAY) of ORPHISM. Among her most notable works are the lyrical *Simultaneous Contrasts* (1912), and delightful abstract illustrations for the *Prose du Trans-Sibérien.*

**Delaware** Confederation of Algonquian-speaking NATIVE AMERICANS. The main members were the Unami, Munsee, and Unalachtigo, who occupied land from Long Island to Pennsylvania and Delaware. Pressured by settlers and the IROQUOIS CONFEDERACY, they migrated to the Ohio region in the 18th century. They lost these lands by a treaty of 1795 and became scattered.

**Delaware** State in E US, on the Atlantic coast, occupying a peninsula between Chesapeake and Delaware bays. The capital is DOVER, the largest city is WILMINGTON. Discovered by Henry Hudson in 1609, it was named for the British governor of Virginia, Baron De la Warr. Delaware was settled by Swedes in 1638. The Dutch, under Peter Stuyvesant, conquered the territory by 1655. It was under English control from 1664 to 1776. One of the original THIRTEEN COLONIES, it was the first to ratify the Articles of Confederation (1789). Despite being a slave state, it remained in the Union during the CIVIL WAR. It is the second smallest state (after Rhode Island) and most of its land is coastal plain. The Delaware River, an important shipping route, forms part of the E boundary. Industries: chemicals, rubber, plastics. Agriculture: cereal crops, soya, dairy produce. Area: 2,057sq mi (5,328sq km). Pop. (1990) 666,168.

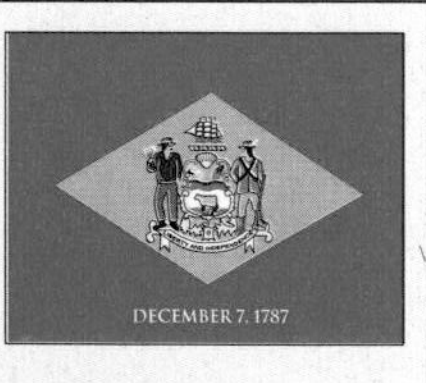


**DELAWARE**
**Statehood:**
December 7, 1787
**Nickname:**
The First State
**State bird:**
Blue hen chicken
**State flower:**
Peach blossom
**State tree:**
American holly
**State motto:**
Liberty and independence

**Delaware** River in NE US. The Delaware rises in two branches in the Catskill Mountains, SE New York. The branches meet at Hancock, New York, and it then flows SE and S along the New York-Pennsylvania and Pennsylvania-New Jersey borders. The Delaware becomes navigable at Trenton, New Jersey, and travels through a highly industrialized area before emptying into Delaware Bay. The Delaware is second only to the Mississippi River in annual freight tonnage carried. Length: 280mi (450km).

**Delft** City in South Holland province, SW Netherlands. Founded in the 11th century, it was an important commercial center until the 17th century. Industries: Delftware pottery, ceramics, china. Pop. (1994) 91,941.

**Delhi** Union territory and city on the Yamuna River, N central India. Strategically placed midway between the Ganges and Indus valleys, the city has been of strategic importance for more than 2,000 years. The union territory consists of NEW DELHI, the capital of India since 1912, and **Old Delhi** whose walls were built (1638) by SHAH JAHAN. With the construction of the Red Fort imperial palace, Delhi became capital of the MOGUL empire. Shah Jahan also built the Jami Masjid. Other sites include Rajghat (a shrine where Gandhi was cremated). Industries: cotton textiles, handicrafts. Pop. (1991) 7,206,704. *See also* DELHI SULTANATE

**Delibes, (Clément Philibert) Léo** (1836–91) French composer. He was famous for his ballet music, especially *Coppélia* (1870), and also wrote several operas (such as *Lakmé*, 1883), and sacred and secular choral works.

**Delilah** Philistine woman in the Old Testament (Judges 16). The mistress of SAMSON, she betrayed him to the Philistines by cutting his hair, the source of his strength, while he slept.

**Delius, Frederick** (1862–1934) English composer. He combined ROMANTICISM with IMPRESSIONISM, most notably in orchestral pieces, such as *Brigg Fair* (1907) and *On Hearing the First Cuckoo in Spring* (1912). His love of nature is evident in the operas *A Village Romeo and Juliet* (1901) and *Fennimore and Gerda* (1910).

**De Long, George Washington** (1844–81) US naval officer and Arctic explorer. He set sail in 1879, but his ship was caught in polar ice and drifted until 1881 when it was crushed. De Long was one of 14 survivors to reach Siberia, only to die of cold and starvation.

**Delphi** Ancient city state in Greece, near Mount Parnassus. The presence of the ORACLE of APOLLO made it a sacred city. The Pythian Games were held at Delphi every four years. The Temple of Apollo was sacked in Roman times, and the oracle closed with the spread of Christianity (AD 390).

**delphinium** (larkspur) Any of *c*.250 species of herbaceous plants native to temperate areas, with spirally arranged leaves and loose clusters of flowers. Petals form a tubular spur. Garden delphiniums are varieties of *Delphinium elatum*. Family Ranunculaceae.

**delta** Fan-shaped body of ALLUVIUM deposited at the mouth of a river. It is formed when a river deposits sediment as its speed decreases while it enters the sea. Most deltas are fertile areas, but subject to frequent flooding.

**delusion** False or irrational belief based upon a misinterpretation of reality. Mild delusions are quite common, but fixed delusions can be a symptom of PARANOIA.

**dementia** Deterioration of personality and intellect that can result from disease of or damage to the BRAIN. It is characterized by memory loss, impaired mental processes, personality change, confusion, lack of inhibition, and poor personal hygiene. Dementia is more common in the elderly. *See also* ALZHEIMER'S DISEASE

**Demeter** In GREEK MYTHOLOGY, the goddess of nature, sister of ZEUS and mother of PERSEPHONE.

**De Mille, Agnes George** (1906–93) US dancer and choreographer. Her choreography for the Broadway musical *Oklahoma* (1943) rendered dance integral to the plot and turned it into a serious art form. Other musicals include *Carousel* (1945), *Brigadoon* (1947), *Gentlemen Prefer Blondes* (1949), *Paint Your Wagon* (1951), and *Come Summer* (1969). De Mille also created ballets, such as *Rodeo* (1942) and *Fall River Legend* (1948).

**De Mille, Cecil B. (Blount)** (1881–1959) US film producer and director. His debut film, *The Squaw Man* (1913), established Hollywood as the world's film production capi-

▲ **Dempsey** The first boxer to generate a $1 million gate, Dempsey will always be remembered for his "Battle of the Long Count" fight with Gene Tunney (1927). After flooring Tunney, Dempsey failed to return to a neutral corner and delayed the start of the referee's count. Tunney won the fight.

tal. Many of his films deal with biblical themes, such as *The Ten Commandments* (1923, 1956), and *King of Kings* (1927). Other films include *Union Pacific* (1939), and *The Greatest Show on Earth* (1952).

**Demirel, Süleyman** (1924– ) Turkish statesman, prime minister (1965–71, 1975–77, 1979–80, 1991–93) and president (1993– ). In 1964 he became leader of the Justice Party. Demirel was ousted by military coups in 1971 and 1980. He led the Truth Path Party (1987–93).

**democracy** (Gk. *demos kratia*, people authority) Rule of the people, as opposed to rule by one (autocracy) or a few (oligarchy). Ancient Greece is regarded as the birthplace of democracy, in particular ATHENS (5th century BC). Small Greek city-states enabled direct political participation, but only among its citizens (a small political elite). As societies grew, more refined systems were needed. In a FEUDAL SYSTEM, the king selected tenants-in-chief to provide counsel. In late 13th-century England, a PARLIAMENT evolved, but remained answerable to the monarchy. The Roundheads' victory in the English CIVIL WAR was a victory for parliamentary sovereignty. A fundamental shift in emphasis was the transition from natural law to NATURAL RIGHTS, as expounded by John LOCKE: in addition to responsibility (to crown or church), people possessed inalienable rights. ROUSSEAU developed these notions into the SOCIAL CONTRACT, which influenced the FRENCH and AMERICAN REVOLUTIONS: government was limited by law from impinging on individual freedoms. During the 19th century, the FRANCHISE was extended. In the 20th century, democratic representation has been a matter of debate and sometimes bloody dispute. Common to modern liberal democracy is the principle of free multiparty elections with universal adult suffrage.

**Democratic Party** US political party, descendant of the ANTI-FEDERALIST PARTY and DEMOCRATIC-REPUBLICAN PARTY. From the election of Thomas JEFFERSON (1801) until James BUCHANAN in 1857, the party was the dominant force in US politics. The party was split by the Civil War (1861–65), with support mainly restricted to the South and West. It regained power in 1932 with Franklin D. ROOSEVELT's "New Deal" policies. Democratic presidents were in office from 1961 to 1969 (John F. KENNEDY, Lyndon B. JOHNSON), a period marked by progressive economic and social policy, such as the passing of CIVIL RIGHTS legislation. In the 1970s and 1980s, only Jimmy CARTER (1977–81) held the presidency. The REPUBLICAN PARTY dominated until Bill CLINTON recaptured the center ground (1992).

**Democratic-Republican Party** Early US political party, and precursor to the modern DEMOCRATIC PARTY. It was formed in the late 1790s in opposition to the FEDERALIST PARTY, and led by Thomas JEFFERSON and James MADISON. It opposed strong central government and advocated a liberal agrarian democracy, while also appealing to poor townsfolk. It became the Democratic Party in the era of Andrew JACKSON.

**Democritus** (460–370 BC) Greek philosopher and scientist. Democritus contributed to the theory of ATOMISM, propounded by his teacher Leucippus, by suggesting that all matter consisted of tiny, indivisible particles.

**demography** Term introduced (1855) by Achille Guillard for the scientific study of human populations, their changes, movements, size, distribution, and structure.

**Demosthenes** (383–322 BC) Athenian orator and statesman. Demosthenes devoted his life to speaking and fighting on behalf of the Greek states in their resistance to PHILIP II of Macedon.

**Dempsey, Jack** (1895–1983) US heavyweight boxer. Nicknamed the "Manassa Mauler," Dempsey was the first boxer to generate a $1 million gate. He became world heavyweight champion after knocking out Jess Willard (1919). Dempsey lost the title to Gene Tunncy (1926) on points. In the "Battle of the Long Count" rematch (1927), Dempsey floored Tunney but failed to return to a neutral corner thereby delaying the referee's count. Tunney went on to win.

**dendrochronology** Means of estimating time by the growth rings in trees. Chronology based on the bristlecone pine extends back more than 7,000 years.

**Deneb** (Alpha Cygni) White supergiant star in the constellation of Cygnus. It is 60,000 times more luminous than the Sun and located *c.*1,500 light-years away.

**dengue** Infectious virus disease transmitted by the *Aedes aegypti* MOSQUITO. Occurring in the tropics and some temperate areas, it produces fever, headache, and fatigue, followed by severe joint pains, aching muscles, swollen glands, and a reddish rash. Recovery usually follows, but relapses are common.

**Deng Xiaoping** (1904–97) Chinese statesman. He took part in the LONG MARCH, served in the Red Army, and became a member of the central committee of the Chinese COMMUNIST PARTY in 1945. After the establishment of the People's Republic (1949) Deng held several important posts, becoming general secretary of the party in 1956. During the CULTURAL REVOLUTION, he was denounced for capitalist tendencies and dismissed. Deng returned to government in 1973, was purged by the GANG OF FOUR in 1976, but reinstated in 1977. Within three years he had become the paramount leader of party and government. Deng introduced rapid economic modernization, encouraging foreign investment, but without social and political liberalization. He officially retired in 1987, but was still in control at the time of the TIANANMEN SQUARE massacre (1989).

**De Niro, Robert** (1943– ) US film actor. An powerful presence, he first gained critical acclaim in Martin SCORSESE's *Mean Streets* (1973). De Niro won an Academy Award as Best Supporting Actor for *The Godfather, Part II* (1974). After a powerful performance in *Taxi Driver* (1976), he was nominated for an Oscar in *The Deer Hunter* (1978). De Niro won a Best Actor Academy Award for *Raging Bull* (1981). His first film as director was *A Bronx Tale* (1993).

**Denmark** Kingdom in W Europe. *See* country feature page 204

**density** Ratio of mass to volume for a given substance, usually expressed in SI UNITS as kg/m$^3$. It is an indication of the concentration of particles within a material. The density of a solid or liquid changes little over a wide range of temperatures and pressures. Specific gravity (sp.gr.), or relative density, is the ratio of the density of one substance to that of a reference substance (usually water) at the same temperature and pressure. The density of a gas depends on both pressure and temperature.

**dentistry** Profession concerned with the care and treatment of the mouth, particularly the TEETH and their supporting tissues. Dentistry includes specialties such as oral surgery, periodontics, and orthodontics.

**dentition** Type, number, and arrangement of TEETH. An adult human has 32 teeth. In each jaw are four incisors, two canines, four premolars, four molars and, in most adults, up to four wisdom teeth. Children lack the premolars and four molars. The incisors are used for cutting; the canines for gripping and tearing; the molars and premolars for crushing and grinding food.

**Denver** Capital and largest city of Colorado, at the foot of the Rocky Mountains. At an altitude of 5,280ft (1,608m), it is nick-

▲ **Deng Xiaoping** Chinese political leader for much of the 1980s, Deng saw the advantage of introducing economic reforms to China and encouraged a more open and free market. However, he was still deeply opposed to political reforms, and cracked down heavily on the pro-democracy movement.

D

▲ **De Niro** Academy Award-winning US actor Robert De Niro is well known for his method approach to acting. Many of his characters retain surprising sensitivity in a world of violence. He is closely associated with the director Martin Scorsese.

named the "Mile High City." Founded in 1860, it became state capital in 1867. Its prosperity was boosted with the discovery of gold and silver. After World War II, Denver's dramatic growth and high altitude led to serious pollution problems. During the 1970s, exploitation of oil deposits created further growth. Denver is the site of many government agencies, including a US mint. Other places of note are the Denver Art Museum, the Boettcher Botanical Gardens, and a university (1864). It has the world's largest airport, Denver International, and its proximity to the Rockies and the ski resort of Aspen make it a major tourist center. Denver has many high-technology industries, especially aerospace and electronics. Pop. (1990) 467,610.

**deoxyribonucleic acid** *See* DNA

**Depardieu, Gérard** (1948– ) French film actor. Burly and charismatic, he was France's principal actor in the 1980s. He is equally adroit at playing an historical figure such as *Danton* (1982), or a hunchback tax-collector in *Jean de Florette* (1986). *Green Card* (1990) was his first major English-speaking role. Depardieu's performance as *Cyrano de Bergerac* (1990) was definitive.

**deposition** In geology, layering or placing of any material that may become rock. It is the accumulation of sediment, ore body, or organic material by any natural process that would result in stratification of rock-forming material.

**depreciation** Decline in the value of an ASSET over the asset's economic life. It includes the decrease in value or usefulness because of wear and tear, obsolescence, or fall in market prices, but does not cover unexpected losses due to accident or natural disaster.

**depression** In economics, a period of economic hardship, more severe than a RECESSION. It is usually measured by a fall in output and a rise in unemployment. The most severe and widespread was the GREAT DEPRESSION of the 1930s.

**depression** In meteorology, a region of low atmospheric pressure with the lowest pressure at the center. It usually brings unsettled or stormy weather. *See also* CYCLONE

**depression** Disorder characterized by feelings of guilt, failure, or worthlessness. Often stress-related, depression leads to low self-esteem, self-recrimination, and obsessive thoughts. Insomnia, loss of appetite, and lethargy can be present; in severe cases there is a risk of suicide. *See also* MANIC DEPRESSION.

**De Quincey, Thomas** (1785–1859) English essayist and critic. He was an associate of WORDSWORTH and COLERIDGE, whom he memorialized in *Recollections of the Lakes and the*

## DENMARK

Denmark's flag is the *Dannbrog*, "spirit of Denmark." It may be the oldest national flag in continuous use. It represents a vision thought to have been seen by King Waldemar II before the Battle of Lyndanisse (1219) in Estonia

**AREA:** 16,629sq mi (43,070sq km)
**POPULATION:** 5,170,000
**CAPITAL (POPULATION):** Copenhagen (620,970)
**GOVERNMENT:** Parliamentary monarchy
**ETHNIC GROUPS:** Danish 97%
**LANGUAGES;** Danish (official)
**RELIGIONS:** Christianity (Lutheran 91%, Roman Catholic 1%)
**CURRENCY:** Krone = 100 ore

The Kingdom of Denmark is the smallest country in Scandinavia. It consists of a peninsula, Jutland (which is joined to Germany), and more than 400 islands, 89 of which are inhabited. The capital, COPENHAGEN, lies on Sjaelland (the largest island) facing Sweden across a narrow strait, The Sound, which leads from the Baltic Sea to the Kattegat and the North Sea. To the NW of Denmark lie the self-governing Danish dependencies of GREENLAND and the FARÖE ISLANDS. The granite island of Bornholm, off the S tip of Sweden, is also a Danish possession and is a separate administrative region.

Denmark is flat and mostly covered by rocks deposited here by huge ice sheets during the last Ice Age. The highest point is only 561ft (171m) above sea level.

### Climate

Denmark has a cool but pleasant climate due to North Atlantic Drift. In cold winter spells The Sound may freeze over. Summers are warm, and rainfall occurs throughout the year. The wettest seasons are summer and fall. Atlantic storms sometimes occur.

### Vegetation

Much of Denmark is a patchwork of green fields, lakes, and sandy beaches. Forests of oak and elm trees once covered the land, but most of the original forests have been felled. Today planted belts of beech, pine, and spruce help to break the force of strong westerly winds.

### History

In *c.*2000 BC the Danes developed an advanced Bronze Age culture. Between the 9th–11th centuries AD, VIKINGS terrorized much of W Europe and Danes were among the invaders who conquered much of England. In the 11th century King CANUTE ruled over Denmark, Norway, and England. Queen Margaret unified the crowns of Denmark, Sweden, and Norway in 1397. Sweden broke away in 1523, while Norway was lost to Sweden in 1814.

Denmark adopted LUTHERANISM as the national religion in the 1530s and Danish culture flourished in the 16th and early 17th centuries. A succession of wars with Sweden, including the THIRTY YEARS WAR, weakened Danish aristocratic rule. Serfdom was abolished in 1788.

In the late 19th century, the Danes developed their economy. They set up cooperatives and improved farming techniques. Denmark was neutral in World War I. In 1918 ICELAND was granted independence. During the 1920s Denmark passed much progressive social welfare legislation. In 1940 Germany occupied Denmark, and in 1943 martial law was declared. Many Jews escaped to Sweden. In 1945 Denmark was liberated by British forces.

### Politics

Denmark played an important part in European reconstruction. In 1949 it relinquished its neutrality and joined NATO. In 1973 Denmark became the first Scandinavian member of the European Economic Community (EEC). In 1992 Denmark rejected the MAASTRICHT TREATY by a slender majority, but reversed the decision in a second referendum (1993). In 1998 the Amsterdam Treaty, which broadly expanded the power of the European Parliament, was ratified by a further referendum.

### Economy

Danes enjoy a high standard of living (1995 GDP per capita, $US21,230). During the 1980s and 1990s, the Danish economy suffered from high unemployment. Other problems include pollution and the high cost of welfare provision. Despite being self-sufficient in oil and natural gas, Denmark has few natural resources. The economy is highly developed, with manufacturing employing 27% of the workforce. Products include furniture, electrical goods and textiles. Services, including tourism, form the largest sector, accounting for 63% of GDP. Farms cover *c.*75% of the land. Farming employs only 4% of the workforce but is highly technological and productive.

*Lake Poets* (1834–39). De Quincy is best known for his famous *Confessions of an English Opium Eater* (1822).

**Derby, Edward George Geoffrey Smith Stanley, 14th Earl of** (1799–1869) British statesman, three times prime minister (1852, 1858–59, 1866–68). He entered Parliament as a WHIG in 1827, and acted as chief secretary for Ireland (1830–33). He resigned shortly after becoming colonial secretary (1833), and joined the CONSERVATIVE PARTY. He was colonial secretary (1841–45) under Robert PEEL, but resigned over the repeal of the CORN LAWS. From 1846 to 1868, Derby led the Tory protectionists, briefly heading two administrations. In 1866 he became prime minister for the last time, and introduced the REFORM ACT (1867). Derby was succeeded by Benjamin DISRAELI.

**Derby** City and county district on the Derwent River, Derbyshire, central England. Industries: railroad and aerospace engineering, textiles, ceramics. Rolls-Royce cars are made here. Pop. (1991) 218,802.

**Derbyshire** County in N central England; the county town is DERBY, other major towns are Chesterfield and Alfreton. Low-lying in the S, it rises to the PEAK DISTRICT in the N, and is drained by the Trent River and its tributaries the Dove, Derwent, and Wye. Agriculture is important, such as dairy farming, wheat, and oats. There are coal deposits in the E. Industries: steel, textiles. Area: 1,016sq mi (2,631sq km). Pop. 887,600.

**derivative** Rate of change of the value of a mathematical FUNCTION with respect to a change in the independent VARIABLE. The derivative is an expression of the instantaneous rate of change of the function's value: in general it is itself a function of the variable. An example is obtaining the velocity and acceleration of an object that moves distance $x$ in time $t$ according to the equation $x = at^n$. The velocity increases with time. The expression dx/dt, called the first derivative of distance with respect to time, is equal to the velocity of the object; in this example it equals $nat^{(n-1)}$. The result is obtained by DIFFERENTIAL CALCULUS. In this example, the second derivative, written $d^2x/dt^2$, is equal to the acceleration.

**dermatitis** Inflammation of the skin. In acute form it produces itching and blisters. In chronic form it causes thickening, scaling, and darkening of the skin. *See also* ECZEMA

**dermatology** Branch of medicine that deals with the diagnosis and treatment of skin diseases.

**dermis** Thick inner layer of the SKIN, which lies beneath the EPIDERMIS. It consists mainly of loose CONNECTIVE TISSUE, richly supplied with BLOOD and lymph vessels, nerve endings, sensory organs, and sweat glands.

**Derrida, Jacques** (1930– ) French philosopher, b. Algeria. Drawing on the work of STRUCTURALISM, Derrida proposed a philosophy of DECONSTRUCTION. He argued that Western philosophy is based on a series of metaphysical binary oppositions, such as speech/text, which privilege one term over another, in this instance speech. Derrida revealed the limits or margins of these oppositions and sought to **defer** assimilation (*différance*) through an appeal to intertextuality, multiple meanings, and the free play of language. His work proved most influential in the field of literary theory. Writings include *Writing and Difference* (1967), and *Margins of Philosophy* (1972).

**Derry** City and administrative district on the Foyle River near Lough Foyle, NW Northern Ireland. In AD 546, St. Columba founded a monastery here. In 1600 English forces seized the city, and in 1613 James I granted Derry to the citizens of London. It was renamed **Londonderry**, a new city was laid out, and Protestant colonization began. In 1688–89 James II unsuccessfully besieged the city. In recent years the city has been plagued by sectarian violence. In 1984 its name reverted to Derry. Industries: clothing manufacture. Area: 149sq mi (347sq km). Pop. (1991) 95,371.

**dervish** Member of a Muslim fraternity. Communities arose within SUFISM and by the 12th century had established themselves in the Middle East. The chief devotion of dervishes is *dhikr* (remembering of God). Its encouragement of emotional display and hypnotic trances has earned dervishes the epithet "whirling."

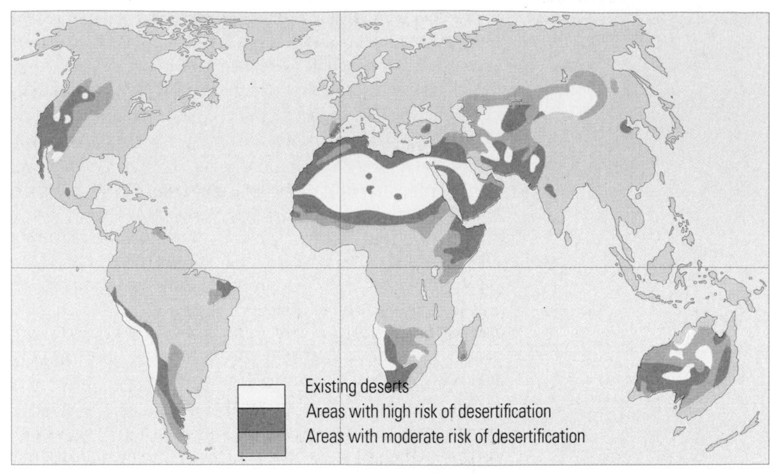


▲ **desertification** The true causes of desertification are still not entirely understood, but it is generally accepted that recent desertification is directly attributable to increased human intervention. On a large scale, the burning of fossil fuels is likely to shift climatic belts and increase areas of desert. More localized problems have occurred due to overgrazing of livestock and ill-planned irrigation projects.

**desalination** Extraction of pure water from water containing dissolved salts, usually seawater. The commonest and oldest method is DISTILLATION. Another method is to freeze the salt solution; salt is excluded from the ice crystals which can then be melted.

**Descartes, René** (1596–1650) French philosopher and mathematician. Descartes is often regarded as the father of modern philosophy. His philosophical principles are outlined in *Discourse on Method (*1637), *Meditations on the First Philosophy (*1641), and *Principles of Philosophy* (1644). His methods of deduction and intuition inform modern metaphysics. He reached one indubitable proposition: "I am thinking," and from this he concluded that he existed: *cogito ergo sum* (I think, therefore I am). Descartes also founded analytic geometry, introduced the CARTESIAN COORDINATE SYSTEM, and helped establish the science of optics.

**desert** Arid region of the Earth, at any latitude, characterized by scant, intermittent rainfall of less than 10in (25cm) per year, and little or no vegetation. Regions with 10–20in (25–50cm) are semideserts. Cold deserts, areas almost permanently covered with snow or ice, extend over one-sixth of the Earth's surface; and hot deserts over one-fifth. Most desert regions lie between 20° and 30° N and S of the Equator. The SAHARA in Africa is the world's largest desert.

**desertification** Process by which a DESERT gradually spreads into neighboring areas of semidesert. The change may result from a natural event, such as fire or climatic change, but occurs most frequently as a result of human activity.

**De Sica, Vittorio** (1901–74) Italian film director and actor. He is noted for his use of amateur actors in realistic dramas. Working with Cesare Zavattini, he made a significant contribution to Italian NEOREALISM with films such as *Shoeshine* (1946) and *Bicycle Thieves* (1948). Other films include *Umberto D* (1952), *Two Women* (1961), and *A Brief Vacation* (1975).

**Des Moines** Capital and largest city of Iowa, near the confluence of the Des Moines and Raccoon rivers. Founded in 1843, it is an industrial and transport center for the Corn Belt. Flooded in 1954, the city is protected by dams and reservoirs. Industries: mechanical and aerospace engineering. Pop. (1990) 193,187.

**Desmoulins, Camille** (1760–94) French revolutionary. His pamphlets, such as *Révolutions de France et de Brabant* (1789), were widely read, and he was responsible for inciting the mob to attack the BASTILLE on July 12, 1789, precipitating the FRENCH REVOLUTION. Initially Desmoulins attacked the Girondins, but later (with DANTON) urged moderation. He was arrested and guillotined.

**De Soto, Hernando** (1500–42) Spanish explorer. After taking part in the conquest of the Inca under Francisco PIZARRO, he was appointed governor of Cuba (1537) with permission to conquer the North American mainland. His expedition landed in Florida (1539) and advanced as far north as the Carolinas and as west as the Mississippi. The ruthless search for nonexistent treasure and extreme brutality toward the native inhabitants led to a costly battle at Maubilia (1540).

D

**Des Prés, Josquin** *See* JOSQUIN DESPREZ
**Dessalines, Jean Jacques** (1758–1806) Haitian ruler. He succeeded TOUSSAINT L'OUVERTURE as leader of the revolution in 1802. Having driven out the French, He declared independence in 1804, changing the country's name from St. Domingue to Haiti. As Emperor Jacques, he ruled despotically and was assassinated.
**destroyer** Warship, smaller than a CRUISER, usually equipped with guns, torpedoes, depth charges, and missiles. It evolved from torpedo boats in the British Royal Navy in the 1890s and played a major role in both world wars convoying Allied merchant ships. The first nuclear-powered destroyer was built by the US in 1962.
**detective fiction** Literary form in which a crime (almost always murder) is solved by a detective (usually amateur). The greatest exponents of the genre include: Edgar Allan POE, Wilkie COLLINS, Arthur Conan DOYLE, G.K. CHESTERTON, Agatha CHRISTIE, Raymond CHANDLER, and Dorothy L. SAYERS.
**detente** Term in international relations for the reduction of tension between states. It chiefly refers to the efforts of the US, the Soviet Union, and their respective allies to end the COLD WAR and to establish closer links of mutual understanding. Detente was marked by a series of ARMS-CONTROL agreements and confidence-building measures, such as the STRATEGIC ARMS LIMITATION TREATY (SALT), signed in 1974. *See also* DISARMAMENT
**detergent** Synthetic chemical cleansing substance. The most common type is alkyl sulfonate. Detergents have molecules that possess a long hydrocarbon chain attached to an ionized group. This chain attaches to grease, while the ionized group has an affinity for water (so the grease is washed away with the water).
**determinism** Philosophical thesis that every event is the result of its causes. Nothing is accidental. It usually involves the denial of FREE WILL, though Thomas HOBBES and David HUME struggled to reconcile the two ideas. CALVIN'S PREDESTINATION is a form of determinism.
**Detroit** City on the Detroit River, SE Michigan. Founded (1710) as a French trading post, the British captured it in 1760 and used it as a base during the American Revolution. Britain took it in the WAR OF 1812, but retaken by US forces in 1813. The largest city in Michigan, Detroit is a GREAT LAKES center and headquarters of General Motors, Chrysler, and Ford. Industries: motor vehicles, steel. Pop. (1990) 1,027,974.
**deuterium** ISOTOPE (D or $H^2$) of hydrogen whose nuclei contain a neutron in addition to a proton. Deuterium occurs in water as $D_2O$ (heavy water), from which it is obtained by ELECTROLYSIS. Heavy water is used as a moderator in some FISSION reactors. Mass no. 2; at.wt. 2.0144.
**Deuteronomy** Biblical book, fifth and last of the PENTATEUCH or TORAH. It contains three discourses ascribed to MOSES, which frame a code of civil and religious laws. The book was probably written long after Moses.
**De Valera, Eamon** (1882–1975) Irish statesman, prime minister (1932–48, 1951–54, 1957–59). De Valera was active in the Irish independence movement and after the Easter Rising (1916) was elected president of SINN FÉIN while imprisoned in England. He founded FIANNA FÁIL in 1924. He defeated Cosgrave in 1932. In 1959 De Valera became president of the republic. He retired in 1973.
**developing countries** *See* LESS DEVELOPED COUNTRIES (LDCs)
**developmental psychology** Study of behavior through all life stages, from fetus to old age. Psychologists study normal growth, change, and self-actualization.
**devil** Evil spirit considered in many religions to be the arch-enemy of the Supreme being. In Christianity, the Devil is the chief of the fallen angels cast out of heaven for their sins. The devil was named as SATAN, BEELZEBUB, or the Prince of Darkness. The biblical account of Christ's temptation in the desert leads to the perception of the Devil as the tempter of men's souls. In Islam, Iblis is the name of the devil figure, the supreme tempter.
**Devon** County in SW England, bounded by the English Channel (S) and the Bristol Channel (N); the county town is EXETER. During the Middle Ages, tin mining was a major industry. Devon is a hilly region that includes Dartmoor and Exmoor. Industries: tourism, fishing, dairy products, textiles. Area: 2,591sq mi (6,711sq km). Pop. (1991) 1,009,950.
**Devonian** Fourth-oldest period of the PALEOZOIC era, lasting from 408 to 360 million years ago. Many marine and freshwater remains include jawless fishes and forerunners of today's bony and cartilaginous fishes. The first known land vertebrate, the amphibian *Ichthyostega*, appeared at this time. Land animals included scorpions, mites, spiders, and the first insects. Land plants consisted of CLUB MOSS and ferns.
**De Vries, Hugo** (1848–1935) Dutch botanist. His experimental methods led to the rediscovery (1900) of MENDEL's laws of HEREDITY and the development of a theory of MUTATION. De Vries argued that GENETIC mutation was the chief engine of EVOLUTION.
**dew** Water droplets formed, usually at night, by condensation on vegetation and other surfaces near the ground.
**Dewey, George** (1837–1917) US admiral, hero of the battle of Manila (1898). He served on the USS *Mississippi* in the Civil War and was naval commander of the Asiatic squadron when the SPANISH-AMERICAN WAR broke out. Dewey sailed for the Philippines, and on May 1, 1898, entered Manila Bay. By noon the Spanish fleet had been destroyed without the loss of a single American life. He was promoted (1899) to admiral of the navy.
**Dewey, John** (1859–1952) US educator and philosopher. He was professor of philosophy (1904–30) at Columbia University. Influenced by PRAGMATISM and UTILITARIANISM, Dewey proposed a philosophy of **instrumentalism**. He regarded intelligence as an instrument to overcome practical problems. In works such as *Democracy and Education* (1916) Dewey emphasised the importance of experimentation and practical application in education. A leading figure in the development of PROGRESSIVE EDUCATION, he urged that learning should be vocational, equipping students with the skills to integrate into society.
**Dewey decimal system** Means of classifying books, devised (1873) by US librarian Melvil Dewey (1851–1931). Books are divided by subject into ten main classes, each class containing 100 numbers. The main disciplines within each subject are subdivided into groups of ten and decimal numbers are used for even more precise definitions. For example, class 600-699 is technology and applied sciences; 630-639 is agriculture; useful insects is 638; beekeeping is 638.1.
**dew point** Temperature at which a vapor begins to condense, for example when water vapor in the air condenses into cloud as the air becomes saturated with vapor.
**Dhaka** (Dacca) Capital of Bangladesh, a port on the Ganges delta, E Bangladesh. In the 17th century it was the Mogul capital of Bengal. In 1765 it came under British control. At independence (1947) it became capital of the province of East Pakistan. Severely damaged during the war of independence from Pakistan, it became capital of independent Bangladesh (1971). Sites include the Dakeshwari temple. It is in the center of the world's largest jute-producing area. Industries: engineering, textiles, printing. Pop. (1991) 3,397,187.
**dharma** Religious concept relating to what is true or right, found in the principal religions of India. In HINDUISM, it is the moral law or code governing an individual's conduct in life. In BUDDHISM, dharma is the doctrine of universal truth proclaimed by the BUDDHA. In JAINISM, dharma is moral virtue.
**diabetes** Disease characterised by lack of INSULIN needed for sugar METABOLISM. This leads to HYPERGLYCAEMIA and an excess of SUGAR in the blood. Symptoms include abnormal thirst, over-production of urine and weight loss; degenerative changes occur in blood vessels. Untreated, it progresses to diabetic coma and death. **Type 1** usually begins in childhood and is an autoimmune disease. Those affected owe their survival to insulin injections. Milder **type 2** mostly begins in middle-age; there is some insulin output. The disease is managed with dietary restrictions and oral insulin. Susceptibility to *diabetes mellitus* is inherited and more common in males.
**diagenesis** Physical and chemical processes whereby sediments are transformed into solid rock, usually at low pressure and temperature.

**Diaghilev, Sergei Pavlovich** (1872–1929) Russian ballet impresario. He was active in the Russian avant-garde before moving to Paris, where he formed (1911) the BALLETS RUSSES and acted as its director until his death. Diaghilev was responsible for revolutionizing the world of BALLET, integrating music and scene design with innovative choreography. Dancers such as NIJINSKY, PAVLOVA, and MARKOVA performed pieces choreographed by the likes of Michel FOKINE, and George BALANCHINE. STRAVINSKY, DEBUSSY, RAVEL, and Richard STRAUSS composed for the company, while artists such as Pablo PICASSO designed the sets and costumes.

**dialect** Regional variety of a language, distinguished by features of pronunciation, grammar, and vocabulary. Dialectal differences may be relatively slight (as in the dialects of American English), or so great (Italian) that mutual comprehension becomes difficult or impossible.

**dialectic** Method of argument through conversation and dialogue; based on the philosophy of SOCRATES, in particular the *Dialogues*. HEGEL went on to argue that ordinary logic is static and lifeless. In the *Science of Logic* (1812–16) he claimed to satisfy the need for a dynamic method. Logic was to be dialectical, or a process of resolution by means of conflict of categories. *See also* DIALECTICAL MATERIALISM

**dialectical materialism** Scientific theory and philosophical basis of MARXISM. It asserts that everything is material, and that change results from the struggle of opposites according to definite laws. Its main application was in the analysis of human history. Karl MARX agreed with HEGEL that history is logically dialectical, so that true social change can only occur when two opposing views are resolved through a new synthesis, rather than one establishing itself as true. According to Marx's theory of historical materialism, history was derived from economic or social realities.

**dialysis** Process for separating particles from a solution by differing rates of diffusion through a semipermeable membrane. In the artificial KIDNEY, molecules of waste products are separated out to purify the blood. Electrodialysis uses a direct electric current to accelerate the process, especially useful for isolating proteins.

**diamond** Crystalline form of carbon (C). The hardest natural substance known. It is found in kimberlite pipes and alluvial deposits. Appearance varies according to its impurities. Nongem varieties are used in industry. Industrial diamonds are used as abrasives, bearings in precision instruments such as watches, and in the cutting heads of drills for mining. Synthetic diamonds, made by subjecting GRAPHITE, with a catalyst, to high pressure and temperatures of *c*.5,400°F (3,000°C) are fit only for industry. Diamonds are weighed in carats (0.2gm) and points (1/100 carat). The largest producer is Australia. Hardness 10; sp.gr. 3.5.

**Diana** In Roman religion, the virgin huntress and patroness of domestic animals. She was identified with ARTEMIS. A fertility deity, she was invoked to aid conception and childbirth.

**Diana, Princess of Wales** (1961–97) Former wife of the heir to the British throne. The daughter of Earl Spencer, Diana married CHARLES, Prince of Wales in 1981, and they had two sons, William (1982– ) and Harry (1984– ). A popular, glamorous figure, she worked for many public health and children's charities. Their marriage fell apart acrimoniously and publicly, and they divorced in 1996. Diana continued to campaign for humanitarian causes, particularly for a worldwide ban on the use of landmines, until her tragic death in a car crash in Paris the following year.

**diaphragm** Sheet of muscle that separates the abdomen from the THORAX. During exhalation it relaxes and allows the chest to subside; on inhalation it contracts and flattens, causing the chest cavity to enlarge.

**diarrhea** Frequent elimination of loose, watery stools, accompanied by cramps and stomach pains. It arises from infection, intestinal irritants, or food allergy. Mild attacks can be treated by replacement fluids.

**diaspora** (Gr. dispersion) Jewish communities outside Palestine. Although there were communities of Jews outside Palestine from the time of the BABYLONIAN CAPTIVITY (6th century BC), the diaspora essentially dates from the destruction of Jerusalem by the Romans (AD 70). Six million European JEWS perished in the Nazi HOLOCAUST. The majority of Jews remain in the diaspora. *See also* JUDAISM; ZIONISM

**diatom** Any of a group of tiny microscopic single-celled ALGAE (phylum Bacillariophyta) characterized by a shell-like cell wall made of silica. Diatoms live in salt and fresh water, and even soil and tree bark.

**Diaz, Bartholomeu** (*c*.1450–1500) Portuguese navigator, the first European to round the CAPE OF GOOD HOPE. In 1487 Diaz sailed three ships around the Cape, opening the long-sought route to India. He took part in the expedition of CABRAL that discovered Brazil, but was drowned when his ship foundered.

**Díaz, Porfirio** (1830–1915) Mexican statesman, president (1876–80, 1884–1911). He supported Benito JUÁREZ in the war (1861–67) against Emperor MAXIMILIAN. Díaz refused to accept defeat in the 1871 and 1876 presidential elections and began a revolt that overthrew President Sebastián Lerdo. His 35-year dictatorship was brutally effective. His fraudulent reelection (1910) sparked a popular uprising led by Francisco MADERO and Díaz was forced into exile.

**Dickens, Charles John Huffam** (1812–70) English novelist. After a difficult early life, he began his writing career as a parliamentary reporter for the *Morning Chronicle*. Dickens' first success was a series of satirical pieces collected as *Sketches by Boz* (1836). *The Pickwick Papers* (1836–37) launched his literary career. All of Dickens' novels first appeared in serial form. His early work includes *Oliver Twist* (1838), *Nicholas Nickleby* (1839), *The Old Curiosity Shop* (1841), and *Barnaby Rudge* (1841). In 1842 Dickens traveled to America, recording his thoughts in *American Notes*. In 1843 he finished *Martin Chuzzlewit* and wrote *A Christmas Carol*. His mature novels included *David Copperfield* (1850), *Bleak House* (1853), *Hard Times* (1854), *Little Dorrit* (1857), and *A Tale of Two Cities* (1859). Dickens' last novels, *Great Expectations* (1861), *Our Mutual Friend* (1865), and the incomplete *The Mystery of Edwin Drood*, are bleak depictions of the destructive powers of money and ambition. His prolific output provided some of the most memorable characters in ENGLISH LITERATURE and captured the mood of Victorian London.

**Dickinson, Emily Elizabeth** (1830–86) US poet. From the age of 30 she lived in almost total seclusion in Amherst, Massachusetts. Dickinson wrote 1,775 short lyrics, only seven of which were published in her lifetime. *Poems by Emily Dickinson* appeared in 1890, and her collected works were not published until 1955. They rank among the greatest works in AMERICAN LITERATURE. Her rich verse explores the world of emotion and the beauty of simple things.

◀ **Diana, Princess of Wales** Following her divorce from Charles, Prince of Wales, Diana's future public role was uncertain. Her self-appointed role as "Queen of Hearts," has meant increasing involvement with humanitarian causes, particularly in less-developed areas of Africa and Asia. Her glamorous appearance ensured that she remained a popular figure and one of the world's most photographed women both in the UK and abroad until her death in 1997.

D

**dicotyledon** Larger of the two subgroups of flowering plants or ANGIOSPERMS, characterized by two seed leaves (COTYLEDONS) in the seed embryo. Dicotyledons have broad leaves with branching veins; flower parts in whorls of fours or fives; vascular bundles in a ring in the stem and root; and a taproot. There are *c.*250 families of dicotyledons, such as the ROSE and DAISY.
**dictatorship** Absolute rule without consent of the governed. In many modern dictatorships, all power resides in the dictator, with DEMOCRACY abolished or existing as mere formality. Personal freedom is severely limited, censorship is generally enforced, education is tightly controlled, and legal restraints on governmental authority are abolished.
**dictionary** Book that lists words and their definitions in alphabetical order. A dictionary may be general or subject oriented. In the former category, Samuel JOHNSON's *A Dictionary of the English Language* (1755) is the pioneering work in English. The first great US lexicographer was Noah WEBSTER, who published *An American Dictionary of the English Language* in 1828. The authoritative *Oxford English Dictionary (OED)* was first published in 1884.
**Diderot, Denis** (1713–84) French philosopher and writer. He was chief editor of the *Encyclopédie* (1751–72), an influential publication of the ENLIGHTENMENT. A friend of ROUSSEAU, he was imprisoned briefly (1749) for irreligious writings. He broadened the scope of the *Encyclopédie* and with d'ALEMBERT recruited contributors, such as VOLTAIRE. As a philosopher, Diderot progressed gradually from Christianity through DEISM to ATHEISM. *On the Interpretation of Nature* (1754), and *d'Alembert's Dream* (1769) reveal his scientific MATERIALISM. *Jacques the Fatalist* (1796) illustrates his DETERMINISM. He also wrote plays, and art and literary criticism.
**Dido** In Greek and Roman legend, Phoenician princess and founder of CARTHAGE. Dido's hand was sought by the king of Libya. To escape him she stabbed herself. VIRGIL made Dido a lover of AENEAS, and attributes her suicide to his decision to abandon her.
**Diem, Ngo Dinh** (1901–63) Vietnamese statesman, prime minister of South Vietnam (1954–63). A nationalist, he at first received strong US support, but corruption and setbacks in the war against communism led to growing discontent. With covert US help, army officers staged a coup in which Diem was murdered.
**Dien Bien Phu** Fortified village in N Vietnam. In a 1954 battle the French stronghold was captured by the Vietnamese Viet Minh after a siege lasting 55 days. French casualties were *c.*15,000. The resultant ceasefire ended eight years of war.
**diesel engine** (compression-ignition engine) INTERNAL COMBUSTION ENGINE, invented by Rudolf Diesel (1897). Heat for igniting the light fuel oil is produced by compressing air.
**diet** Range of food and drink consumed by an animal. The human diet falls into five main groups of necessary nutrients: PROTEIN, CARBOHYDRATE, FAT, VITAMIN, and MINERAL. An adult's daily requirement is about one gram of protein for each two pounds of body weight. Beans, fish, eggs, milk, and meat are important protein sources. Carbohydrates (stored as GLYCOGEN) and fat, are the chief sources of energy and are found in cereals, root vegetables, and sugars. Carbohydrates make up the bulk of most diets. Fats are a concentrated source of energy, and aid the absorption of fat-soluble vitamins (vitamins A, D, E, and K). Water and minerals such as iron, calcium, potassium, and sodium are also essential.
**Dietrich, Marlene** (1904–92) German film star and cabaret singer. Her glamorous, sultry image evolved in films directed by Josef von Sternberg, such as *The Blue Angel* (1930) and *Blonde Venus* (1932). Later films include *Destry Rides Again* (1939), and *Rancho Notorious* (1956).
**differential** In mathematics, small change in the value of a mathematical expression due to a change in a VARIABLE. If $f(x)$ is a function of $x$, the differential of the function, written $df$, is given by $f'(x)\,dx$, where $f'(x)$ is the DERIVATIVE of $f(x)$.
**differential** In mechanics, a set of circular gears that transmits power from an engine to the wheels. When a car is turning a corner, the differential allows the outside drive wheel to rotate faster than the inner one.
**differential calculus** (differentiation) Form of CALCULUS used to calculate the rate of change (DERIVATIVE) of one quantity with respect to another of which it is the FUNCTION.
**diffraction** Spreading of a wave, such as a LIGHT beam, on passing through a narrow opening or hitting the edge of an obstacle, such as sound being heard around corners. It is evidence for the wave nature of light. All waves are diffracted by obstacles.
**diffusion** Movement of a substance in a mixture from regions of high concentration to regions of low concentration, due to the random motion of atoms or molecules. Diffusion ceases when there is no longer a concentration gradient. Its rate increases with temperature.
**digestion** Process of the DIGESTIVE SYSTEM, in which food is broken down into smaller molecules that can be readily absorbed. Digestion occurs mainly by means of chemical agents called ENZYMES.
**digestive system** (alimentary system) Group of organs of the body concerned with the DIGESTION of foodstuffs. In

## DIGESTION

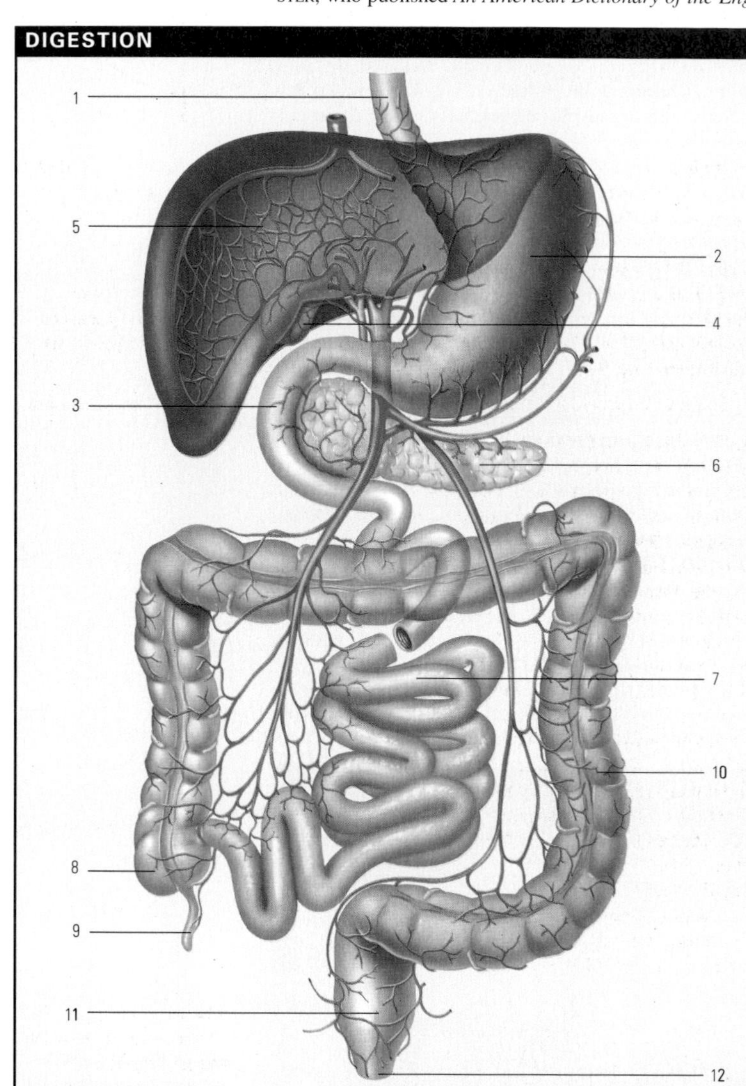


The digestion and absorption of food takes place within the digestive tract, a coiled tube some 33ft (10m) long which links mouth to anus. Food is passed down the esophagus (1) to the stomach (2), where it partially digested. Chyme is released into the duodenum (3), the first part of 23ft (7m) of small intestine. The duodenum receives bile secreted by the gall bladder (4) in the liver (5), and enzymes secreted by the pancreas (6). Most absorption occurs in the jejunum and ileum, the remaining parts of the small intestine (7). Any residue passes into the caecum (8), the pouch at the start of the large intestine. At one end of the caecum is the 4in (10cm) long vermiform appendix (9), which serves no useful purpose in humans. Water is reabsorbed in the colon (10). Feces form and collect in the rectum (11) before being expelled as waste through the anus (12).

humans, it begins with the mouth, and continues into the ESOPHAGUS, which carries food into the STOMACH. The stomach leads to the small INTESTINE, which then opens into the COLON. After food is swallowed, it is pushed through the digestive tract by PERISTALSIS. On its journey, food is transformed into small molecules that can be absorbed into the bloodstream and carried to the tissues. CARBOHYDRATE is broken down to sugars, PROTEIN to AMINO ACIDS, and FAT to FATTY ACIDS and GLYCEROL. Indigestible matter, mainly CELLULOSE, passes into the RECTUM, and is eventually eliminated from the body (as feces) through the ANUS.

**Diggers** (1649–50) English millenarian social and religious sect, an extreme group of the LEVELERS. Their egalitarian agrarian community was destroyed by local farmers. The main Digger theorist, Gerrard Winstanley, proposed communalization of property.

**digital** DATA expressed in terms of a few discrete quantities, often associated with a digital COMPUTER. Data is represented as a series of zeros and ones in a BINARY SYSTEM. Digital can also refer to displaying information in numbers, as opposed to continuously varying analog.

**digital audio tape (DAT)** Technology for recording data in DIGITAL form on magnetic TAPE. DATs are smaller and longer than analog cassettes. They are used primarily for computer backups and studio-recording.

**digitalis** Drug obtained from the leaves of the FOXGLOVE (*Digitalis purpurea*), used to treat HEART disease. It increases heart contractions and slows the heartbeat.

**digital signal** Group of electrical or other pulses in a COMPUTER or COMMUNICATIONS system. They may represent DATA, sounds, or pictures. Pulses are represented by zeros and ones in the BINARY SYSTEM.

**Dijon** City in E France; capital of Côte-d'Or department. In the 11th century the dukes of BURGUNDY made it their capital. It was annexed to France (1477). Sites include Dijon University (1722) and the Church of Notre Dame. Exports: wine, mustard. Pop. (1990) 146,703.

**dill** Aromatic annual herb native to Europe. Its small oval seeds and feathery leaves are used in cooking. Family Apiaceae/Umbelliferae; species *Anethum graveolens*.

**DiMaggio, Joe (Joseph Paul)** (1914–99) US baseball player. He played for the New York Yankees (1936–42, 1946–51) and held the record for hitting safely in 56 consecutive games. He married Marilyn MONROE (1954) and was elected to the Baseball Hall of Fame (1955).

**dimension** In mathematics, the spatial dimension is the number specifying the extent of an object in different directions. A figure with length only, is one-dimensional; a figure having area but not volume, two-dimensional; and a figure having volume, three-dimensional.

**diminishing returns, law of** (law of increasing costs) In economics, if more of a variable input, such as labor, is added to the production process, while all other factors are held constant, the addition to total output per unit input begins to decline at some point.

**Dinaric Alps** (Dinara Planina) Mountain range parallel to the E coast of the Adriatic Sea. Forming part of the E Alps, it extends from the Istrian peninsula (Croatia) to NW Albania, with peaks over 7,900ft (2,400m). Length: 400mi (640km).

**D'Indy, Vincent** (1851–1931) French composer and teacher. He cofounded the *Schola Cantorum* for the study of church music (1894). D'Indy taught composition here until his death. His pupils included SATIE. He composed several operas, orchestral, choral, chamber, and piano music.

**Dinesen, Isak** (1885–1962) (Karen Blixen) Danish writer. She described her life on a Kenyan coffee plantation in *Out of Africa* (1937). Her collections of short stories include *Shadows on the Grass* (1960).

**dingo** Yellowish-brown wild DOG found in Australia; it is probably a descendant of early domestic dogs introduced by Native Australians. It feeds mainly on rabbits and other small mammals. Height (at shoulder): *c*.24in (61cm). Family Canidae; species *Canis dingo*.

**dinosaur** (Gr. terrible lizard) Any of a large number of REPTILES that lived during the MESOZOIC era, between 225 and 65 million years ago. They appeared during the Triassic period, survived the JURASSIC, and became extinct at the end of the Cretaceous. Dinosaurs were mostly egg-laying animals, ranging in size from 30in (91cm) to the 90-ft (27-m) DIPLODOCUS. There were two orders: **Saurischia** ("lizard hips"), included the bipedal carnivores and the giant herbivores; the **Ornithiscia** ("bird hips") were smaller herbivores. There is evidence that some birds are the living descendants of ornithischians. Many theories are advanced to account for their extinction. One theory is that they died because of the devastating atmospheric effects from the impact of a large meteor. *See also* BRONTOSAURUS; PTERODACTYL; TRICERATOPS; TYRANNOSAURUS

**Diocletian** (245–313) Roman emperor (284–305). Of low birth, he was made emperor by the army. He reorganized the empire to resist the barbarians, sharing power with Maximilian, Constantius I, and Galerius. He ordered the last great persecution of the Christians (303).

**diode** Electronic component with two electrodes, used as a RECTIFIER to convert alternating current (AC) to direct current (DC). Semiconductor diodes have largely replaced electron-tubes, and allow ELECTRIC CURRENT to flow freely

**DIGITAL AUDIO TAPE**

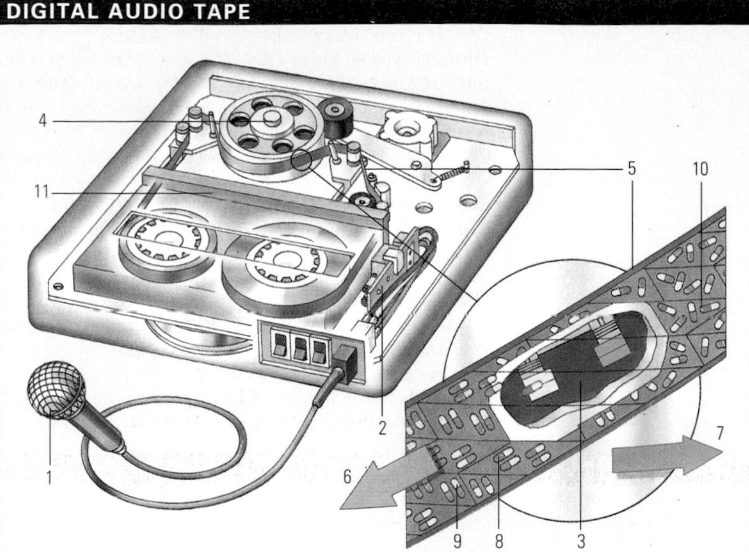


A digital audio tape (DAT) recorder records sound, an analog signal, in digital form. The analog signal enters via a microphone (1) and passes through a converter (2), which transcribes the sound wave into a series of zeros and ones. Two magnetic heads, tiny electromagnets (3) in a rotating drum (4), receive the digital signal as electrical pulses which polarize diagonal strips of magnetic tape (5) (moving right to left) (6) as it is scanned diagonally (7). The heads align the magnetic elements of the tape representing a zero or a one. Each head records one half of a stereo recording. One head records parallel to the tape (8), one perpendicular (9) to avoid interference. The units of an unrecorded tape are jumbled (10). When a tape (11) is played the head reads the polarization of the tape.

◀ **dinosaur** The first dinosaurs appeared on Earth *c*.220 million years ago. They were the dominant land animals until they died out suddenly *c*.63 million years ago. The stegosaurus (left) was a plant-eating dinosaur that lived *c*.140 million years ago. They grew to 20ft (6m) long and 8ft (2.4m) high at the hip. The bony plates along the spine and the spikes on the tail are thought to have offered protection against carnivorous dinosaurs, but may also have acted like radiators, regulating the animal's temperature.

in only one direction. A Zener diode blocks current until a critical voltage is reached.

**Dionysius the Elder** (430–367 BC) Tyrant of Syracuse (405–367 BC). His ambitions were to spread Hellenism beyond the city. He tried to form an empire in Lower Italy by seizing Rhegium (387), Caulonia, and Croton (379). He then mixed the various populations. An erstwhile playwright, he once sold Plato as a slave.

**Dionysus** Greek god of wine and fertility, identified with the Roman god BACCHUS. Son of ZEUS and Semele, he was reared by nymphs and taught men the secrets of cultivating grapes and making wine.

**Dior, Christian** (1905–57) French fashion designer. In 1947 he launched the "New Look," whose wide shoulders and long, shapely skirts signaled an end to war austerity. Dior created the A-line dress in 1956.

**dioxin** Any of various poisonous chemicals. The compound most commonly known as dioxin is 2,3,7,8-tetrachlorodibenzo-p-dioxin (TCDD), a by-product and impurity in the manufacture of various disinfectants and HERBICIDES. Dioxin causes skin disfigurement and is associated with birth defects, cancer, and miscarriages. Accidental releases of dioxin from chemical plants have caused major disasters. TCCD was a constituent of Agent Orange.

**diphtheria** Acute, infectious disease characterized by the formation of a membrane in the throat which can cause asphyxiation; there is also release of a toxin which can damage the nerves and heart. Caused by a bacterium, *Corynebacterium diphtheriae*, it is treated with antitoxin and antibiotics

**diplodocus** DINOSAUR that lived in N US during the JURASSIC period. The longest land animal that has ever lived. It had a long slender neck and tail and was a swamp-dwelling herbivore. Length: up to 90ft (27m).

**diploid** CELL that has its CHROMOSOMES in pairs. Diploids are found in almost all animal cells, except GAMETES which are HAPLOID. Cells of flowering plants and gymnosperms are also diploid. In diploids, the chromosomes of each pair carry the same GENES. *See also* ALTERNATION OF GENERATIONS

**dipole** Separation of electric charge in a molecule. In a COVALENT BOND, the electron pair is not equally shared. In hydrogen chloride (HCl), electrons are attracted toward the more electronegative chlorine atom, giving it a partial negative charge and leaving an equal positive charge on the hydrogen atom. Dipoles contribute to the chemical properties of molecules.

**dipper** Bird found near mountain streams. It feeds on small fish and aquatic invertebrates. It has a thin, straight bill, short wings, and grayish-brown plumage. Length: to 7.5in (19cm). Family Cinclidae; genus *Cinclus*.

**dip pole** Either of two imaginary points on the Earth's surface where the direction of the Earth's magnetic field is vertical (downward at the magnetic North Pole, upward at the magnetic South Pole).

**Dirac, Paul Adrien Maurice** (1902–84) English physicist who devised a version of QUANTUM MECHANICS. He extended this to combine RELATIVITY and quantum-mechanical descriptions of ELECTRON properties. He also predicted the existence of the POSITRON. Dirac shared the 1933 Nobel Prize for physics with Erwin SCHRÖDINGER for their work on QUANTUM THEORY.

**direct current (DC)** *See* ELECTRIC CURRENT

**Directory** (1795–99) Government of the First Republic of France, consisting of five directors elected by the Council of Five Hundred and the Council of Ancients. It was established as part of the Thermidorian reaction to the REIGN OF TERROR. Success in the FRENCH REVOLUTIONARY WARS inspired greater independence among the generals, and the coup of 18 Brumaire (November 9), 1799, led to the accession of NAPOLEON I. *See also* Lazare CARNOT; FRENCH REVOLUTION

**disarmament** Refers principally to attempts post-1918 (and especially post-1945) to reach international agreements to reduce armaments. The United Nations established the Atomic Energy Commission (1946), and the Commission for Conventional Armaments (1947). In 1952 these were combined into the Disarmament Commission. It produced no results and the Soviet Union withdrew in 1957. The US and the Soviet Union signed the Nuclear Test Ban Treaty (1963) and the Nuclear Non-Proliferation Treaty (1968), which provided for an international inspectorate. This was followed by a series of STRATEGIC ARMS LIMITATION TALKS (SALT). In 1986 SALT was superseded by START (strategic arms reduction talks), resulting in the Intermediate Nuclear Forces (INF) Treaty (1987) that reduced the superpowers' arsenal of short-range, intermediate missiles by *c.*2,000 (4% of the total stockpile) and provided for on-site inspection. Conventional Forces in Europe Treaty (1990) set limits on equipment and troop levels. Attempts to sign a comprehensive Test Ban Treaty have been thwarted by China, France, India, and Pakistan. Following the break-up of the Soviet Union, the four republics with nuclear weapons (Russia, Ukraine, Belarus, Kazakstan) agreed in 1991 to implement the START treaties.

**disciple** One of the followers of Jesus Christ during his life on Earth, especially one of his 12 close personal associates. These 12 men were his first APOSTLES.

**Disciples of Christ** US Protestant church, claiming to derive all its beliefs from the BIBLE. Beginning in the 19th-century religious revival movements of frontier America, there is no single founder and no creed but Christ. There are *c.*1,200,000 members.

**discontinuity** *See* MOHO

**discus** Field event, in which a wooden and metal disk is thrown. The thrower rotates in a circle (diameter 8.2ft/2.5m) several times before releasing the discus. Originally an ancient Greek sport, it was revived for the first modern Olympic Games held in Athens (1896).

**disease** Any departure from health, with impaired functioning of the body. Disease may be **acute**, severe symptoms for a short time; **chronic**, lasting a long time; or **recurrent**, returning periodically. There are many types and causes of disease: infectious, caused by harmful BACTERIA or VIRUSES; hereditary and metabolic; growth and development; IMMUNE SYSTEM diseases; neoplastic (TUMOR-producing); nutritional; deficiency; ENDOCRINE SYSTEM diseases; or diseases due to environmental agents. Treatment may be **symptomatic** (relieving symptoms) or **specific** (attempting to cure an underlying cause). Disease prevention includes eradication of harmful organisms, VACCINES, public health measures, and medical checks.

**disk** Form of computer DATA storage. Disks come in many different forms, some using magnetic methods to store data, such as the HARD DISK, while others use optical systems like the COMPACT DISC (CD) and CD-ROM.

**disk operating system (DOS)** COMPUTER operating system, developed in the early 1980s by Bill GATES and Microsoft for early International Business Machines (IBM) personal computers. DOS is the SOFTWARE that governs a computer's data storage and PROGRAM execution. It is rapidly being replaced by Windows-based operating systems (also developed by Microsoft).

**Disney, Walt (Walter Elias)** (1901–66) US film animator, producer, and executive. Disney has become synonymous with family entertainment and a menagerie of cartoon characters, such as Mickey Mouse, Donald Duck, and Pluto. Disney's first success, *Steamboat Willie* (1928), was the first cartoon to use sound and featured his own voice as Mickey Mouse. Disney's first feature was *Snow White and the Seven Dwarfs* (1937). A series of popular classics followed: *Pinocchio* (1940), *Fantasia* (1940), *Dumbo* (1941), and *Bambi* (1942). In 1950 Disney diversified into live action features with *Treasure Island* (1950). In 1955 Disneyland amusement park opened in Anaheim, California. Disney collected a total of 29 Academy Awards. The Walt Disney Company (founded 1923) is one of the world's most powerful media corporations.

**Disraeli, Benjamin, 1st Earl of Beaconsfield** (1804–81) British statesman and novelist, prime minister (1868, 1874–80). Disraeli was elected to Parliament in 1837. His brand of Toryism is expressed in the trilogy of novels *Coningsby* (1844), *Sybil* (1846), and *Tancred* (1847). Following the split in the TORY PARTY over the repeal of the CORN LAWS (1846), Disraeli became leader of the land-owning faction. His opposition to Robert PEEL was rewarded when he became chancellor of the exchequer (1852, 1858–59, 1866–68) under Lord DERBY. Disraeli succeeded Derby as prime minister, but soon was ousted by William GLADSTONE. His second term coincided with the greatest expansion of the second British EMPIRE. Disraeli led Britain into the Zulu War (1879), the second Afghan War (1878–79), and sought to diminish the strength of Russia. In 1875 Britain purchased the Suez Canal from Egypt. In 1880 Disraeli was defeated for a second time by Gladstone.

**Dissolution of the Monasteries** (1536–40) Abolition of English MONASTICISM in the reign of HENRY VIII. The operation, led by Thomas CROMWELL, was a result of the break with Rome, but also provided additional revenue, since the monasteries owned *c*.25% of the land in England, all of which passed to the crown.

**distemper** Contagious, often fatal, disease of young dogs, wild canines, and weasels. Symptoms include fever, shivering, muscular spasms, and loss of appetite. Death is caused by inflammation of the brain.

**distillation** Extraction of a liquid by boiling a solution and cooling the vapor so that it condenses and can be collected. Distillation is used to separate liquids in solution, or liquid solvents from dissolved solids, to yield drinking water from sea water, or to produce alcoholic spirit. Fractional distillation, which uses a vertical column for condensation, is used in OIL refining.

**distilling** Production of liquor by DISTILLATION, especially of ethyl ALCOHOL. In wine, yeast FERMENTATION produces a maximum alcohol content of *c*.15%. Distillation concentrates alcohol to a much higher degree to produce spirit. Most spirits are *c*.40% proof.

**distributive law** Rule of combination in mathematics, in which an operation applied to a combination of terms is equal to the combination of the operation applied to each individual term. Thus, in arithmetic $3\times(2+1) = (3\times2)+(3\times1)$ and, in algebra $a(x + y) = ax + ay$.

**District of Columbia** Federal district, coextensive with the city of WASHINGTON, D.C., the US capital. It is governed under federal law. It was created in 1790–91 from land taken from the states of Maryland and Virginia. The Virginia portion was returned in 1846. Area: 69sq mi (179sq km).

**diuretic** Drug used to increase the output of URINE. It is used to treat raised blood pressure and EDEMA.

**diverticulitis** Inflammation of diverticula, pockets of herniation on the wall of the large intestine, usually caused by infection. Symptoms include abdominal pain and either diarrhea or constipation. It usually responds to antibiotics and a bland diet.

**dividend** Net earnings of a public company that is paid to its stockholders. The dividend is a percentage of the par value of the stock or is calculated on a per share basis. It is a share of the profits.

**divination** Foretelling the future by interpreting various signs. Divination is a form of magic with worldwide distribution. OMENS are often thought to be found in the entrails of sacrificed animals, cards, and palms.

**division of labor** In economics, the specialization of the functions and roles involved in production. The term was introduced by Adam SMITH in his *Wealth of Nations* (1776). Modern MASS PRODUCTION is based on **occupational** division of labor, where each worker is allocated to a specific task.

**diving** Water sport in which acrobatic maneuvers are performed off a springboard or platform. Points are awarded for level of difficulty, technique and grace of flight, and cleanness of entry into the water. Techniques include tuck, pike, twist, and somersault.

**diving, deep-sea** Underwater activity for commercial or leisure purposes. Deep-sea diving developed with the introduction of the diving bell and diving suit. It refers to descents to depths of more than *c*.36ft (11m). Divers need to ascend slowly from such depths to avoid the BENDS. *See also* SCUBA DIVING

**divorce** Legal dissolution of marriage. The ease with which a divorce may be obtained, if at all, varies greatly. In most Western countries, adultery was for many years the only ground for divorce. Desertion, insanity, and mental cruelty were added over the years. More recently, irretrievable breakdown, which apportions blame on neither partner is cited. In many contemporary Western societies, more than one in three marriages ends in divorce.

**Dix, Dorothea Lynde** (1802–87) US pioneer in the treatment of the mentally ill. Dix exposed the inhumane treatment of the insane and inspired legislation resulting in patients being treated in state mental hospitals.

**Dix, Otto** (1891–1969) German painter and engraver. He was a pitiless satirist of inhumanity, notably in a series of 50 etchings called *The War* (1924). Dix attacked the corruption of post-World War I Germany. The Nazis banned him from teaching (1933), and he was jailed for an alleged plot to kill Hitler (1939). After World War II, he concentrated on religious themes.

**Djibouti** (Jibouti) Republic on the NE coast of Africa; the capital is DJIBOUTI. **Land and Climate** Djibouti occupies a strategic position around the Gulf of Tadjoura, where the RED SEA meets the Gulf of Aden. Behind the coastal plain lie the Mabla Mountains, rising to Moussa Ali at 6,627ft (2,020m). Djibouti contains the lowest point on the African continent, Lake Assal, at 509ft (155m) below sea-level. Djibouti has one of the world's hottest and driest climates; summer temperatures regularly exceed 100°F (42°C) and average annual rainfall is 5in (130mm). In the wooded Mabla Mountains the annual rainfall reaches *c*.20in (500mm). Nearly 90% of the land is semidesert, and shortage of pasture and water make farming difficult. **History and politics** ISLAM was introduced in the 9th century. The subsequent conversion of the Afars led to conflict with Christian Ethiopians. France set up French Somaliland (1888). Full independence as the Republic of Djibouti was achieved in 1977, and Hassan Gouled Aptidon of the Popular Rally for Progress (RPP) was elected president. He declared a one-party state in 1981. Continuing protests against the Issas-dominated regime forced the introduction of a multiparty constitution in 1992. The Front for the Restoration of Unity and Democracy (FUUD), supported primarily by Afars, boycotted 1993 elections, and Aptidon was reelected for a fourth six-year term. FUUD rebels continued an armed campaign for political representation. In 1996 government and FUUD forces signed a peace agreement, recognizing FUUD as a political party. **Economy** Djibouti is a poor country, heavily reliant on food imports. A free trade zone, it has no major resources and manufacturing is on a very small scale. The only important activity is livestock raising, and 50% of the population are pastoral nomads.

▲ **Disney** Creator of the world's most famous cartoon characters, Walt Disney first introduced Mickey Mouse in a series of short cartoons in 1928. He went on to make full-length animated features, the first of which, *Snow White and the Seven Dwarfs* (1937), became one of the most popular movies ever made. The Walt Disney Company, with theme parks in the US, Japan, and France, and merchandising, home-video, publishing, television, and recording interests, is one of the most successful entertainment companies.

## DJIBOUTI

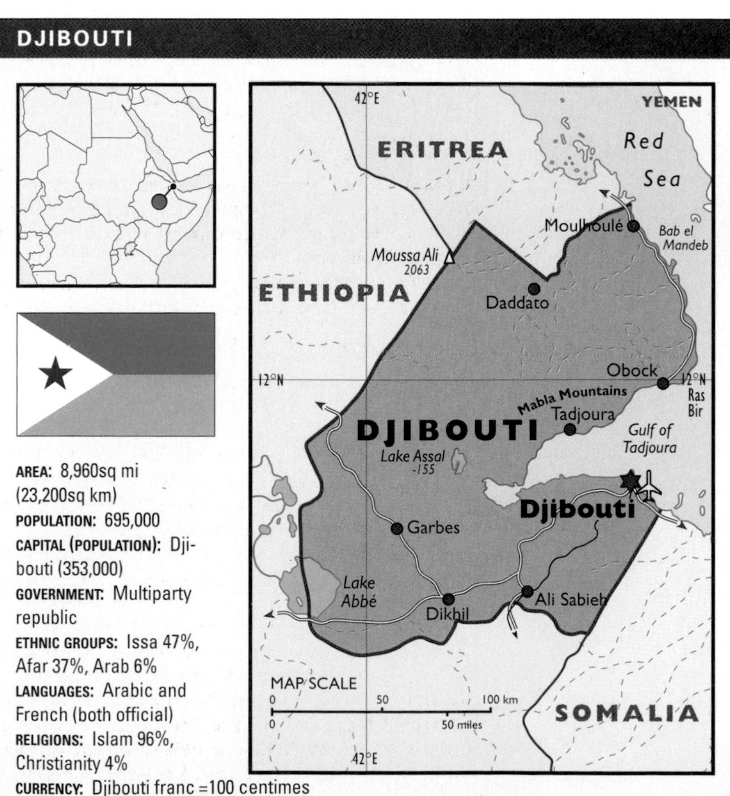


**AREA:** 8,960sq mi (23,200sq km)
**POPULATION:** 695,000
**CAPITAL (POPULATION):** Djibouti (353,000)
**GOVERNMENT:** Multiparty republic
**ETHNIC GROUPS:** Issa 47%, Afar 37%, Arab 6%
**LANGUAGES:** Arabic and French (both official)
**RELIGIONS:** Islam 96%, Christianity 4%
**CURRENCY:** Djibouti franc =100 centimes

D

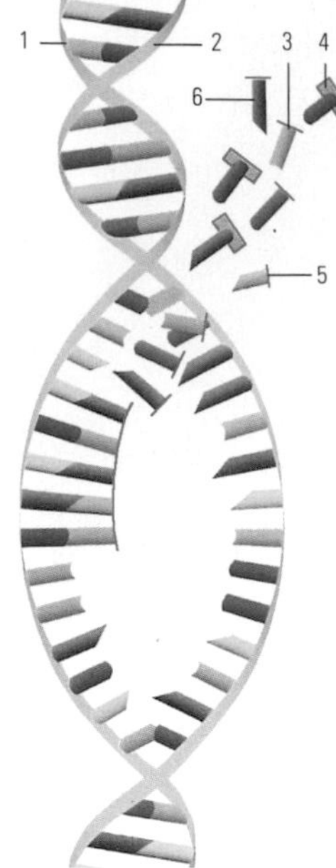


▲ **DNA** molecules form a double helix, with two spiral backbones (1,2). These are made of sugar and phosphate units. Linking the backbones, like rungs on a ladder, are the bases; adenine (3), thymine (4), guanine (5), and cytosine (6). Each backbone contributes one base to each rung, which are strictly paired; adenine with thymine, and cytosine with guanine.

**Djibouti** (Jibouti) Capital of DJIBOUTI, on the S shore of the Gulf of Tadjoura, NE Africa. Founded in 1888, it became capital in 1892, and a free port in 1949. Ethiopian emperor Menelik II built a railroad from ADDIS ABABA, and Djibouti became the chief port for Ethiopian trade. When ERITREA was federated with ETHIOPIA (1952–93), it lost this status. Pop. (1993 est.) 353,000.

**Djilas, Milovan** (1911–95) Yugoslav politician and writer. Djilas was an architect of Yugoslavia's independence from the Soviet Union. In 1954 he was dismissed suddenly from office by TITO. Djilas' support for the Hungarian revolution (1956) and criticism of the authoritarian regime in *New Class* (1957) led to a prison term (1956–61). His next work *Conversations with Stalin* (1962) brought a second prison sentence (1962–66).

**DNA** (deoxyribonucleic acid) NUCLEIC ACID that is the major constituent of the CHROMOSOMES of EUKARYOTE cells and some viruses. DNA is often referred to as the "building block" of life since it stores the GENETIC CODE that functions as the basis of HEREDITY. The molecular structure of DNA was first proposed by J.D. WATSON and F.H. CRICK in 1953. It consists of a double helix of two long strands of alternating SUGAR molecules and PHOSPHATE groups linked by nitrogenous bases. The whole molecule is shaped like a twisted rope ladder with the nitrogenous bases forming the rungs. The sugar is deoxyribose, and the four bases are adenine (A), cytosine (C), guanine (G), and thymine (T). The bases are always paired in the same way: adenine always binds with thymine, guanine with cytosine. This regularity ensures accurate self-replication. During replication the two DNA strands separate, each providing a template for the synthesis of a new strand of RNA (MESSENGER RNA). This process of transcription, mediated by ENZYMES, results in an identical copy of the original helix. In the process of replication the amount of DNA doubles as the chromosomes replicate themselves before MITOSIS; in the ovum and sperm the amount is half that of the body cells (*see* MEIOSIS). A base and its associated sugar and phosphate are known as a **nucleotide**; the whole strand is a polynucleotide chain. The genetic code is stored in terms of the sequence of nucleotides: three nucleotides code for one specific AMINO ACID and a series of them constitute a GENE. *See also* BIOTECHNOLOGY; GENETIC ENGINEERING; RECOMBINANT DNA RESEARCH

## DNA FINGERPRINTING

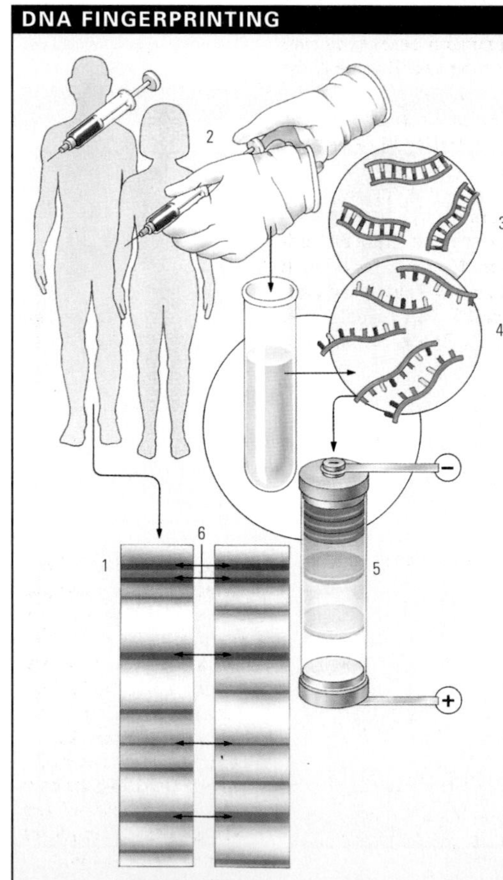


Using a technique known as DNA fingerprinting, a person can be accurately identified. The process allows a person's DNA to be represented in visual form (1). Each DNA pattern is unique (like a fingerprint) – with the exception of identical twins. In a case of disputed paternity, DNA fingerprinting allows the relationship to be settled beyond doubt. DNA is present in all cells, so a sample can be taken from blood (2), skin, or even sweat. DNA is separated out (3) and an enzyme that divides DNA is added. The enzyme attacks the minisatellite region between the genes (4). The genes are then sorted by size by an electric field (5). Gel electrophoresis exploits the fact that snippets of DNA carry a charge to force them through a gel. The size of the snippets controls how far they travel, giving a pattern unique to each individual. A child combines DNA from both parents, so will have a partially similar pattern. Paternity is confirmed by the matching marks (6).

**Dnieper** (Dnepr) River in E Europe. Rising in the Valdai Hills, W of Moscow, it flows S through Belarus and Ukraine to the Black Sea. It is the third longest river in Europe. The Dneproges dam (completed 1932) made the river entirely navigable. It has several hydroelectric power stations. Length: 1,420mi (2,286km).

**doberman** Strong guard dog, bred in late 19th-century Germany. It has a long head; its ears are often clipped to a short, erect shape. The smooth coat may be black, red, or fawn. Height: to 28in (71cm) at the shoulder.

**Dobzhansky, Theodosius** (1900–75) US geneticist, b. Russia. He was influential in the development of population GENETICS as a separate study. His writings include *Genetics and the Origin of Species* (1937), and *Genetics of the Evolutionary Process* (1970).

**dock** Any of more than 200 species of flowering plants native to N US and Europe. Curled dock (*Rumex crispus*) has scaly brown flowers. Dock leaves are a country remedy for nettle stings. Family Polygonaceae.

**Doctorow, E.L. (Edgar Lawrence)** (1931– ) US author. Doctorow's novels have a strong political edge and concern for history. *Ragtime* (1975), his best known novel, deals with late 19th-century racism in the US. Other works include *The Book of Daniel* (1971), *Billy Bathgate* (1988), and *The Waterworks* (1994).

**documentary** Factual film. The term was first applied to Robert Flaherty's *Nanook of the North* (1921), a firsthand account of life among the Inuit. Documentaries soon rivaled newspapers and became a major means of television news, current affairs, and science presentation.

**dodder** Leafless, parasitic, twining plant with a threadlike stem and clusters of small yellow flowers. It feeds using haustoria, modified roots that enter the host plant. Family Convolvulaceae; species *Cuscuta europaea*.

**Dodecanese** (Dhodhekánisos) Group of 20 islands in the SE Aegean Sea, between Turkey and Crete; a department of Greece. The capital and largest island is RHODES. The islands were under Ottoman control (1500–1912), before passing to Greece (1947). The main occupation is agriculture, such as fruit growing, livestock raising, and diving for sponges. Area: 839sq mi (2174sq km). Pop. (1991) 163,476.

**dodo** Extinct, flightless bird that lived on the Mascarene Islands in the Indian Ocean. The last dodo died in *c.*1790. The true dodo (*Raphus cucullatus*) of Mauritius was a heavy-bodied bird with a large head and large hooked bill. Weight: to 50lb (23kg).

**Dodge City** City on the Arkansas River, SW Kansas. The city was founded with the arrival of the Sante Fe Railroad in 1872 and rapidly became the world's largest cattle market. A frontier town, Dodge City became notorious for its gunfights and Wyatt EARP was called upon to keep the peace. Boot Hill, the old burial ground for cowboys, has been preserved. Today, it is the commercial center of an agricultural region. Pop. (1990) 21,129

**Dodoma** Capital of Tanzania, central Tanzania. In 1974 Dodoma replaced DAR ES SALAAM as capital. It is in an agricultural region, crops include grain, seeds, and nuts. Pop. (1988) 203,833.

**dog** Domesticated, carnivorous mammal closely related to the jackal, wolf, and fox. Typically it has a slender, muscular body; long head with slender snout; small paws, five toes on the forefeet, four on the hind; non-retractile claws; and well-developed teeth. Smell is the dog's keenest sense; its hearing is also acute. The gestation period is 49 to 70 days; one or more puppies are born. Dogs developed from the tree-dwelling *miacis*, which lived *c.*40 million years ago. The dog was domesticated *c.*10–14,000 years ago. There are *c.*400 breeds, classified in various ways, such as TERRIER, sporting, hound, working, and toy. Length: 13.4–53.2in (34–135cm); tail 4.3–21.3in (11–54cm); weight: 2–150lb (0.1kg–70kg). Family Canidae; species *Canis familiaris*. *See also* individual breeds

**Doge's Palace** Residence of the *doge* (chief magistrate of Venice, 697–1797), in ST. MARK'S Square, VENICE, Italy. Begun in the 9th century and rebuilt several times. The present version (by Giovanni and Bartolomeo Buon) is Venetian Gothic architecture.

**dogfish** SHARK found in marine waters worldwide. Generally grayish with white spots, it lacks a lower tail lobe. Eggs are laid in cases (mermaids' purses). Dogfish are divided into two groups: spiny and spineless. A food fish, they are sold as rock salmon. Length: spiny, 2–4ft (0.6–1.2m); spineless, 24ft (7.3m). Suborder Squalidae.

**dogwood** Any of several small trees and shrubs in the genus *Cornus* of the family Cornaceae. Wild flowering dogwoods are in deciduous forests. They have small flowers in four large, petal-like, white bracts.

**Doha** Capital of QATAR, on the E coast of the Qatar peninsula, in the Persian (Arabian) Gulf. Doha was a small fishing village until oil production began in 1949. It is now a modern city and trade center. Industries: oil refining, shipping, engineering. Pop. (1992 est.) 313,639.

**Doisy, Edward Adelbert** (1893–1986) US biochemist. He researched BLOOD buffers, VITAMINS, and METABOLISM. He also isolated the female sex HORMONES, estrone (1929) and estradiol (1935). Doisy shared the 1943 Nobel Prize for physiology or medicine with Henrik Dam, for their analysis of vitamin K.

**doldrums** Region of the ocean near the EQUATOR, characterized by calms, and light winds. It corresponds approximately to low pressure around the Equator.

**Dole, Bob (Robert Joseph)** (1923– ) US politician. Dole served as a Republican representative from Kansas (1960–69), before joining the Senate. He was President Gerald FORD's running mate in the unsuccessful Republican campaign (1976). Dole served as majority leader of the Senate (1984–86, 1994–96). In 1996 he finally gained the Republican presidential nomination, but ran a lackluster campaign and lost the election to Bill CLINTON.

**Dole, Sanford** (1844–1926) Hawaiian statesman. He was appointed (1893) leader of a provisional government following the overthrow of Queen Liliuokalani. Dole became (1894) the republic's first president. He secured US annexation of Hawaii (1898) and served (1900–03) as the territory's first governor .

**Dolin, Sir Anton** (1904–83) English ballet dancer and choreographer, b. Patrick Kay. He joined Diaghilev's BALLETS RUSSES in 1921, becoming principal dancer in 1924. Dolin is best-known for his partnership with Alicia MARKOVA and the couple formed the Markova-Dolin Ballet (1935) and the London Festival Ballet (1949). Dolin was knighted in 1981.

**dollar** Standard monetary unit of the US since 1792. It was derived from the Spanish *dolar*, the most widely used coin in the American colonies. Divided into a hundred cents, the value was based on the gold price until 1934. Many other countries have adopted the dollar.

**Dollfuss, Engelbert** (1892–1934) Austrian chancellor (1932–34). Determined to preserve Austrian independence, he dissolved the National Socialist (Nazi) Party, which had demanded union with Germany (1933) and assumed authoritarian powers. He was assassinated by Austrian Nazis in an unsuccessful coup.

**dolmen** Megalithic monument of a stone lintel supported by upright stones. Dolmens were used as burial chambers and covered by mounds. They are most common in Cornwall, SW England, and Brittany, NW France.

**dolomite** ($CaMg(CO_3)_2$, calcium-magnesium carbonate) Carbonate mineral found in altered limestones. It is usually colorless or white. A rhombohedral class prismatic crystal, it is often found as a gangue mineral in hydrothermal veins. It is also a sedimentary rock, probably formed by the alteration of limestone by seawater.

**Dolomites** (Dolomiti or Dolomiten) Alpine range in NE Italy. The Dolomites are composed of dolomitic limestone, eroded to form a striking landscape popular with mountaineers and tourists. The highest peak is Marmolada, 10,964ft (3,342m) high.

**dolphin** Aquatic mammal, any of the small toothed WHALES of the family Delphinidae. There are *c*.50 species, both salt and freshwater. The best-known are the dark-blue-backed common dolphin (*Delphinus delphis*), the blue-gray bottlenosed (*Tursiops truncatus*), and the KILLER WHALE. Larger than a PORPOISE, a dolphin has a distinct beak and slender body, a tail fin for propulsion and a dorsal fin for steering. A dolphin breathes through a single blowhole, and can remain underwater for 15 minutes. It is the fastest and most agile of the whales, achieving speeds up to 24mph (39km/h) and leaps of 30ft (9m). Dolphins swim in large, hierarchically-organized schools, feeding on fish and crustacea. Their intelligence and playful behavior have contributed to a wealth of maritime literature and mythology. They communicate through a complex language and map their environment by ECHOLOCATION. Dolphins have a gestation period of 12 months. Length: to 13ft (4m).

**domain** In mathematics, a set of values that can be assigned to the independent VARIABLE in a function or relation; the set of values of the dependent variable is called the range. For example, let the function be $y = x^2$, with $x$ restricted to 0, 1, 2, 3, and $-3$. Then y takes the values 0, 1, 4, 9, and 9 respectively. The domain is $\{0, 1, 2, 3, -3\}$ and the range is $\{0, 1, 4, 9\}$.

**domain** In TAXONOMY, the domain is sometimes seen as a higher category than KINGDOM. In this scheme, the two subkingdoms of PROKARYOTAE (ARCHAEBACTERIA and EUBACTERIA) constitute two domains, called Archaea and Bacteria. All other living organisms are included in a third domain, EUKARYOTES. *See also* PHYLOGENETICS; PLANT CLASSIFICATION

**dome** In architecture, a hemispherical roof. One of the earliest monumental domes is the PANTHEON, Rome. It was an important element in ISLAMIC ART AND ARCHITECTURE, especially MOSQUES. It was a significant element in Renaissance and Baroque styles.

**Domenichino** (1581–1641) Leading painter of the Italian BAROQUE. In 1602 he worked with Annibale Carracci on the FARNESE Palace. His landscapes include *The Hunt of Diana.*

**Dome of the Rock** (Qubbat al-Sakhrah) MOSQUE and shrine built (685–692) by Abd al-Malik on a Jewish temple site in JERUSALEM. The Dome covers the summit of Mount Moriah, where the prophet Muhammad is believed to have ascended to Heaven. According to the Old Testament, the Rock is also where Abraham was to have sacrificed Isaac.

**Domesday Book** (1085–86) Census of the English kingdom commissioned by WILLIAM I (THE CONQUEROR) to ascertain potential crown revenue. The most complete survey in medieval Europe, it is an important primary historical source. It lists property and resources by manors.

**Domingo, Placido** (1941– ) Spanish tenor, one of the leading opera singers of his generation. He made his debut at Monterrey, Mexico (1961). Domingo is an outstanding interpreter of the Italian romantic repertoire. In the 1990s, he achieved popularity as one of the Three Tenors. *See also* José CARRERAS; Luciano PAVAROTTI

▲ **dock** The curled dock (*Rumex crispus*) of Europe and Asia, is related to sorrel. It gets its name from the wavy margins of its leaves. Application of dock leaves is a country remedy for nettle stings.

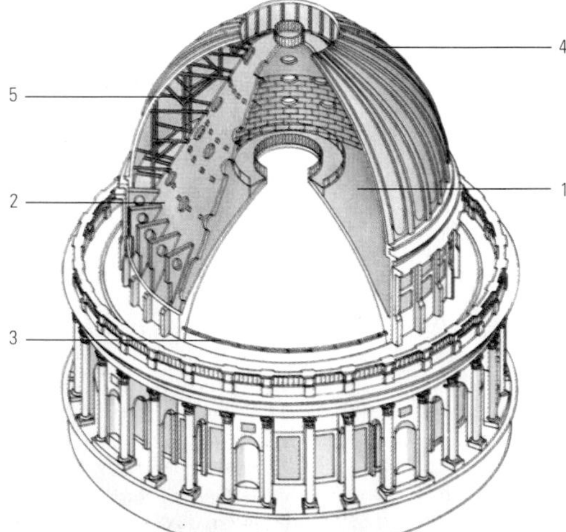


◀ **dome** The dome of St. Paul's Cathedral, London, was designed by Christopher Wren. To make it as airy and as light as possible it has a triple construction: a brick inner dome (1), its "eye" rising 213ft (65m) above the floor; an intermediate brick cone (2), reinforced with iron chains (3); and an outer dome (4), resting on the intermediate cone, and built out with wooden framing (5) and lead covering to obtain the desired silhouette.

## DOMINICAN REPUBLIC

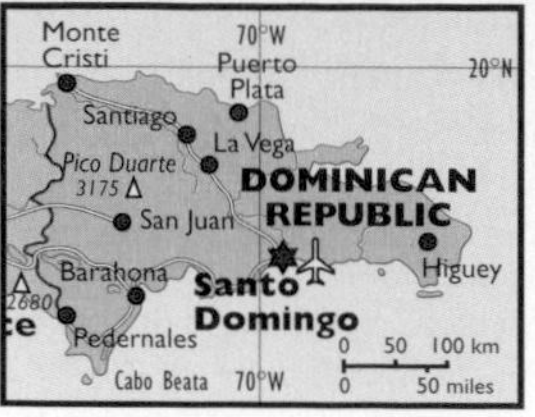




**Dominic, Saint** (1170–1221) (Domingo de Guzmán) Spanish priest, founder of the Dominicans. In 1203 Pope Innocent III sent him to preach to the Albigenses. Dominic founded a monastery at Prouille, s France. He developed an order based on scholastic and democratic principles, and rules derived from St. Augustine. His feast day is August 4.

**Dominica** Independent island nation in the E Caribbean Sea, West Indies; the capital and chief port is Roseau. The largest of the Windward Islands, it was named for *dies dominica* (Sunday), the day it was discovered by Christopher Columbus (1493). The original inhabitants were Carib, but the present population are mainly the descendants of African slaves. Dominica is mountainous and heavily forested, and the climate is tropical. Possession of Dominica was disputed between Britain and France, until it was awarded to Britain in 1783. It became a British crown colony in 1805, and was a member of the Federation of the West Indies (1958–62). It achieved complete independence as a republic within the Commonwealth of Nations in 1978. Dominica is one of the poorest Caribbean countries. Agriculture is the dominant economic sector. Exports: copra, bananas, citrus fruit. Area: 290sq mi (750sq km). Pop. (1994 est.) 74,200.

**Dominican Republic** Independent nation occupying the E two-thirds of the island of Hispaniola in the West Indies; the capital is Santo Domingo. Dominican Republic is mountainous: the Cordillera Central range includes the highest point in the Caribbean, Duarte Peak, at 10,417ft (3,175m). The most fertile agricultural region is the Cibao Valley. Hispaniola was visited by Christopher Columbus in 1492, and a Spanish settlement was established at Santo Domingo. In 1697 the W third of the island (now Haiti) was ceded to France. In 1795 the whole island came under French rule but the E part was returned to Spain in 1809. In 1821 the colony declared itself the independent Dominican Republic, but was annexed by Haiti. It won independence a second time in 1844. Its subsequent history was punctuated by dictatorships and US military interventions. The most notorious dictator was Rafael Trujillo, who ruled from 1930 to 1961. A new constitution was introduced (1966). Mineral deposits are an increasingly important export, though agriculture is still the economic mainstay. Tourism is encouraged. Chief crops: sugarcane, coffee. Area: 18,703sq mi (48,442sq km). Pop. (1994 est.) 7,770,000.

**Dominicans** (officially *Ordo Praedicatorum*, Order of Preachers, O.P.) Roman Catholic religious order, founded by St. Dominic in 1215. Dominicans are one of the four great mendicant orders of Roman Catholicism. Devoted to preaching and study, the order operates worldwide and includes a contemplative order of nuns.

**domino theory** Political doctrine that affected US foreign policy during the Cold War. It held that if one country became communist, its neighbors would inevitably follow. The doctrine was widely used in support of US military involvement in Vietnam.

**Domitian** (51–96) Roman emperor (81–96). A son of Vespasian, he succeeded his brother Titus. His rule was at first orderly but became increasingly tyrannical. After several attempts, he was assassinated. Domitian was partly responsible for building the Colosseum.

**Don** River of SW Russia. Rising SE of Tula, it flows S, then SW to the Sea of Azov. Rostov is the major port. Annual floods are controlled by the Tsimlyansk Reservoir. The Don is navigable for 850mi (1,370km) and is an important shipping route for grain, timber, and coal. It is linked to the Volga River. Length: 1,200mi (1,930km).

▲ **donkey** Smaller than a horse, the donkey has a large head and long ears in proportion to its body. Its coarse hair is tight and matted giving the coat a very rough appearance. Male donkeys are crossed with female horses to breed mules.

**Donatello** (1386–1466) Greatest European sculptor of the 15th century, joint creator of Renaissance art in Florence. His work is a turning point in European sculpture, moving from a formulaic Gothic style to a more vital means of expression. Inspired by humanism, his initial innovations included standing figures of saints in Orsanmichele, Florence. Donatello invented the technique of *stiacciato* ("like drawing in marble"). After a visit to Rome (1430–32), his work, such as the bronze *David*, adopted a more classical feel. His late work, such as *Judith and Holofernes*, and a wood carving of *Mary Magdalene* (1455), shows even greater emotional intensity. Donatello greatly influenced Michelangelo.

**Donegal** County in NW Republic of Ireland, bounded by Northern Ireland (E) and the Atlantic Ocean (N and W). The county town is Lifford. There is a rocky, indented coastline and much of the county is hilly. The chief rivers are the Finn, Foyle, and Erne. Agriculture is the main activity. Tourism and fishing are also important. Area: 1,865sq mi (4,830sq km). Pop. (1991) 128,117.

**Donets Basin** (Donbas or Donec) Industrial region in E Ukraine and S Russia; the capital is Donetsk. It is a major coal and steel producer. Development of one of the world's most concentrated industrial areas began *c.*1870. By 1989 it was producing over 200 million tons of coal a year. In the 1990s there was a slump in production due to exhausted deposits and antiquated technology. Area: *c.*10,000sq mi (25,900sq km).

**Donizetti, Gaetano** (1797–1848) Italian composer. He wrote 75 comic and serious operas. Initially influenced by Rossini, he formed his own melodic style. Operas include *L'Elisir d'Amore* (1832), *Lucia di Lammermoor* (1835), *Roberto Devereux* (1837), and *Don Pasquale* (1843).

**donkey** Domesticated ass, used by humans since well before 3000 BC. Crossed with a horse it produces a mule.

**Donleavy, J.P. (James Patrick)** (1926– ) Irish author, b. US. Donleavy's first novel, *The Ginger Man* (1955), was not published in uncensored form in Britain and the US until 1963. Other novels include *A Singular Man* (1963), *The Beastly Beatitudes of Balthazar B.* (1968)*The Onion Eaters* (1971), and *That Darcy, That Dancer, That Gentleman* (1991).

**Donne, John** (1572–1631) English poet and cleric. Donne's metaphysical poetry is among the greatest work in English literature. His early poetry, mostly written in the 1590s, consists mainly of love poems, elegies, and satires. The love poetry is intense, erotic, and rhetorical; the elegies, colloquial and racy; the satires, witty and cynical. Donne's marriage (1601) to a minor, Anne More, ruined his court career. His poetry, such as *An Anatomy of the World* (1611), and *Of the Progress of the Soul* (1612), became more philosophical. Donne's rejection of Catholicism and conversion to Anglicanism is evident in the prose-work *Pseudo-Martyr* (1610). He was ordained in 1615 and became dean (1621) of St. Paul's Cathedral, London (1621). Donne's late poetry is devotional in tone, such as the powerful *Holy Sonnets*. Donne's *Collected Poems* were published in 1633.

**Donner Party** California-bound group, led by George and Jacob Donner, who traveled overland from Illinois. In October 1846 the party reached Truckee in the High Sierras, where they were trapped by early snowstorms. They escaped starvation by eating the flesh of those who died. Of the 87 members of the party, 47 survived.

**Doolittle, Hilda** (1886–1961) (H.D.) US poet associated with Ezra Pound and Imagism. Her published verse includes the collections *Sea Garden* (1916), and *The Flowering of the Rod* (1946). She also wrote prose, such as *Palimpsest*, and *Hermione* (1981).

**dopamine** Chemical normally found in the corpus striatum region of the brain. Insufficient levels are linked with Parkinson's disease. Dopamine is a neurotransmitter. *See also* epinephrine; norepinephrine

**Doppler, Christian Johann** (1803–53) Austrian physicist and mathematician. Doppler is famous for his prediction (1842) of the Doppler effect.

**Doppler effect** Change in frequency of a wave, when there is relative motion between the wave source and the observer. The amount of change depends on the velocities of the wave, source, and observer. With a sound wave, the effect is the drop in pitch of a vehicle's siren as it passes an observer. With light, the velocity must be large for an appreciable effect, such as the RED SHIFT of a rapidly receding galaxy. *See also* NAVIGATION

**Dordogne** River in SW France. Rising in the AUVERGNE hills, it is formed by the convergence of the Dor and Dogne rivers. It flows SW then W to meet the Garonne River, and forms the Gironde estuary. It has famous vineyards along its 293mi (471km) course.

**Doré, Gustave** (1832–83) French illustrator, painter, and sculptor. He is best known for his engraved book illustrations, such as *Inferno* (1861), *Don Quixote* (1862), and the Bible (1866).

**Dorian** Greek-speaking people, who settled in N Greece *c.*1200 BC. They displaced the culturally superior MYCENAEAN CIVILIZATION because they mastered the use of iron. Their arrival marks the start of a 400-year "dark age" of ancient Greece.

**Doric order** One of the five ORDERS OF ARCHITECTURE .

**dormouse** Squirrel-like RODENT of Eurasia and Africa in temperate climates. Most dormice are active at night. They eat nuts, fruit, seeds, insects, and other tiny animals. They were once bred for human food. Length: 4–8in (10–20cm), excluding tail. Family Gliridae.

**Dorset** County on the English Channel, SW England; the county town is Dorchester. Dorset's most famous prehistoric monument is the Iron Age hill fort, Maiden Castle. It is traversed W to E by the North Dorset and South Dorset Downs. Cereal crop cultivation and livestock raising are important. Industries: tourism, marble quarrying. Area: 1,025sq mi (2,654sq km). Pop. (1991) 361,919.

**Dortmund** City and port on the Dortmund-Ems Canal, Nodrhein-Westfalen state, NW Germany. In the 13th century Dortmund flourished as a member of the HANSEATIC LEAGUE. It declined in the late 17th century but grew as an industrial center from the mid-19th century. Industries: iron and steel. Pop. (1990) 600,700.

**dory** (John Dory) Marine fish found worldwide. It is deep-bodied with a large mouth. The species *Zeus faber* of the Mediterranean Sea and Atlantic Ocean is a valuable food fish. Length: to 3.3ft (1m). Family Zeidae.

**DOS** Acronym for DISK OPERATING SYSTEM

**Dos Passos, John Roderigo** (1896–1970) US novelist. His characteristic style was first evident in *Manhattan Transfer* (1925). Dos Passos' masterpiece, the trilogy *United States*, consisting of *The 42nd Parallel* (1930), *1919* (1932), and *The Big Money* (1936), develops his ambitious idea of a "collective" portrait of early 20th-century America using multiple narrative forms, including STREAM OF CONSCIOUSNESS.

**Dos Santos, José Eduardo** (1942– ) Angolan statesman, president (1979– ). Dos Santos' succession to the presidency was marked by violence between the Cuban-backed People's Movement for the Liberation of Angola (MPLA) government, and the South African-backed National Union for the Total Independence of Angola (UNITA), led by Jonas SAVIMBI. The Lusaka Protocol (1994) paved the way for a government of national unity, headed by Dos Santos.

**Dostoevsky, Fyodor Mikhailovich** (1821–81) Russian novelist, one of the greatest 19th century authors. After completing *Poor Folk* and *The Double* (both 1846), he joined a revolutionary group, was arrested, and sentenced to death (1849). He was reprieved at the eleventh hour, and his sentence was commuted to four years' hard labor. Dostoevsky returned to St. Petersburg in 1859, where he wrote *Notes from the Underground* (1864). After *Crime and Punishment* was published (1866), he left Russia, partly to escape creditors. His last major work was his masterpiece *The Brothers Karamazov* (1879–80).

**Douai Bible** English translation (from the Latin Vulgate) of the BIBLE, authorized by the Roman Catholic Church for use after the REFORMATION. Gregory Martin, living in exile at Douai, France, was the main translator. The NEW TESTAMENT was published at Reims (1582), the OLD TESTAMENT at Douai (1609–10). It was revised by Richard Challoner (1749–50).

◀ **dormouse** Found in Europe and Asia, the dormouse (*Glis glis*) usually lives in trees. The hands and feet of the dormouse are equipped with rough pads which assist in climbing. The diet is chiefly vegetarian, but may include insects and small birds.

**Douala** Chief port of Cameroon, on the Bight of Biafra, W Africa. As Kamerunstadt, it was capital of the German Kamerun Protectorate (1885–1901), became Douala (1907), and was capital of French Cameroon (1940–46). Industries: ship repairing, textiles, palm oil. Pop. (1991 est.) 810,000.

**double bass** Largest stringed instrument. It has four strings tuned in fourths (E-A-D-G) and sounds one OCTAVE below the musical notation. It resembles a large violin but has sloping shoulders. The double bass is held vertically. A bow is generally used for classical music, but the strings are usually plucked in jazz.

**double star** Two stars that appear close together. There are two types of double star: BINARY STARS and **optical doubles** (two stars quite distant from each other, but appear close as a result of chance alignment).

**Douglas, Stephen Arnold** (1813–61) US statesman. He served in the House of Representatives (1843–47). Known as the "Little Giant," he was a senator (1847–61). Douglas helped to secure the passage of the COMPROMISE OF 1850. His doctrine of "popular sovereignty" proposed that each territory be given the right to chose whether they wanted SLAVERY or not. Douglas sponsored the KANSAS-NEBRASKA ACT (1854). In 1858 he campaigned for reelection to the Senate against Abraham LINCOLN. The contest involved a series of public meetings (the Lincoln-Douglas debates) on the issue of slavery. Douglas was returned to the Senate, but had alienated many Southern Democrats. In 1860 his nomination as presidential candidate for the Democrats split the party as the Southern delegates voted for John C. BRECKENRIDGE. Lincoln won the election and Douglas supported him when the CIVIL WAR broke out.

**Douglas, William Orville** (1898–1980) US jurist, associate justice of the US Supreme Court (1939–75). Douglas served the longest period in the Court's history. He was a strong supporter of civil rights, conservation, and civil liberties. In 1953 Douglas granted a stay of execution to Julius and Ethel Rosenberg. He also wrote the majority opinion in *Griswold v. Connecticut* (1965) that struck down anti-birth control legislation.

**Douglas-Home, Sir Alec** (1903–95) British statesman, prime minister (1963–64). He served as parliamentary private secretary (1937–39) to Neville CHAMBERLAIN. He joined the House of Lords as Lord Home of the Hirsel (1951), and had a succession of cabinet posts, including foreign secretary (1960–63). Douglas-Home renounced his peerage to succeed Harold MACMILLAN as Conservative prime minister. He was also foreign secretary under Edward HEATH (1970–74).

**Douglass, Frederick** (1817–95) African-American abolitionist and social reformer. An escaped slave, he became (1841) a lecturer for the Massachusetts Anti-Slavery Society. Douglass wrote *Narrative of the Life of Frederick Douglass* (1845) and, fearing capture, went into exile in England. In 1847 he bought his freedom and returned to the US to found the abolitionist newspaper, *North Star*. Douglass' home was a station on the UNDERGROUND RAILROAD. A lifelong supporter of equal rights, he served as minister to Haiti (1889–91).

**Douro** (Duero) River in Spain and Portugal. Rising in N central Spain, it flows W to form part of the Spanish-Portuguese border. It then turns W through N Portugal to empty into the Atlantic Ocean near OPORTO. Length: 556mi (895km).

**dove** Cooing, plump-bodied bird found almost worldwide. Doves are related to PIGEONS, and have small heads, short legs, and dense, varied plumage. They feed mostly on vegetable matter. Length: 6–33in (15–83cm). Family Columbidae.

**Dover** Seaport on the Strait of Dover, Kent, SE England. One of the cinque ports, Dover is a resort and cross-Channel ferry port. The nearest point to France on mainland Britain, it was fortified by the Romans. In World War I it was an important naval base and suffered intensive bombing during World War

D

► **dragonfly** An incomplete metamorphosis, such as occurs in dragonflies (order Odonata), may be an adaptation to take advantage of different habitats. The adult form (A) of *Anax imperator* is a fast-flying predator on other insects, while the nymph (B) is aquatic, preying on a variety of life in freshwater ponds.

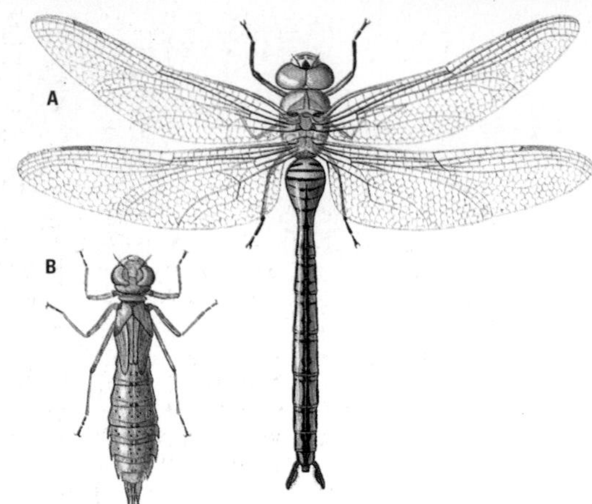


II. Its medieval castle contains the remains of a Roman lighthouse and a Saxon stronghold. Pop. (1991) 34,322.

**Dover** Capital of Delaware, on the St. Jones River. Founded in 1683, it has been state capital since 1777. Dover contains fine examples of Georgian architecture. It is a shipping and canning center for the surrounding agricultural region. Industries: gelatin food products, synthetic polymers. Pop. (1990) 27,630.

**Dowell, Sir Anthony** (1943– ) English ballet dancer, director of the Royal Ballet (1986– ). He joined the Royal Ballet in 1961 and was principal dancer (1966–86). Dowell's most famous partnership was with Antoinette Sibley. In 1978–79 he danced with the American Ballet Theater. Dowell was knighted in 1973.

**Down** District on the Irish Sea coast, SE Northern Ireland; the administrative center is Downpatrick. The Mountains of Mourne lie in the S. Anglo-Normans invaded (12th century), and from the 16th century English and Scottish settlers made their home here. Agriculture dominates the economy. Industries: agricultural machinery, textiles. Area: 250sq mi (650sq km). Pop. (1991) 58,008.

**Downing Street** Street in London, off Whitehall, named for the diplomat Sir George Downing (1623–84). It includes the official residence of the British prime minister at No. 10, chancellor of the exchequer at No. 11, chief whip at No. 12.

**Downing Street Declaration** (December 15, 1993) Joint declaration issued by the UK prime minster John MAJOR and the Irish leader Albert REYNOLDS. Continuing the momentum of the ANGLO-IRISH AGREEMENT, it set a framework for peace talks in NORTHERN IRELAND. It stated that all political parties (including SINN FÉIN) could be involved in an all-Ireland forum, if they committed themselves to permanently ending paramilitary violence. The UK and Irish governments also agreed that the status of Northern Ireland could only change with majority consent of its people, and Ireland's future would be determined only by the peoples of the island of Ireland.

**Down's syndrome** Human condition caused by the presence of an extra copy of CHROMOSOME 21. It gives rise to varying degrees of mental retardation, decreased life expectancy, and perhaps physical problems, such as heart and respiratory disorders. The syndrome was first described by British physician J.L.H. Down. There is evidence that the risk of having a Down's child increases with maternal age. Originally called "Mongolism" by Down, this term is now obsolete.

**Doyle, Sir Arthur Conan** (1859–1930) English physician and novelist. The novel *A Study in Scarlet* (1887) introduced his famous characters Sherlock Holmes and Dr. Watson. A succession of highly popular Sherlock Holmes stories followed, including *The Adventures of Sherlock Holmes* (1892), *The Memoirs of Sherlock Holmes* (1894), and *The Hound of the Baskervilles* (1902). Other works include *The Lost World* (1912).

**D'Oyly Carte, Richard** *See* CARTE, RICHARD D'OYLY

**Drabble, Margaret** (1939– ) English novelist, sister of A.S. BYATT. *The Millstone* (1965) was filmed as *A Touch of Love*. Later work includes the trilogy *The Radiant Way* (1987), *A Natural Curiosity* (1989), and *The Gates of Ivory* (1991).

**Draco** (active 7th century BC) Athenian political leader and lawmaker. He drew up the first written code of laws in Athens. Famous for their severity, the death penalty was prescribed even for minor offenses.

**Draco** (Dragon) Long, winding N constellation, representing the dragon slain by Hercules. It extends between URSA MAJOR and URSA MINOR, with the dragon's head near the star VEGA.

**draft riots** Uprisings against Union CONSCRIPTION in the CIVIL WAR. The Union Conscription Act (March 1863) provoked nationwide disturbances. The most serious riots were in New York City (July 13–16, 1863), where a mob beat many blacks to death, and razed buildings. New York troops were deployed to restore order. The riots left *c.*1,000 dead and caused $2 million worth of damage.

**drag** (air resistance) Force opposing the motion of a body through a gas or liquid. Aircraft experience drag as the friction of air over external surfaces. To combat drag, aircraft and cars have streamlined designs.

**dragonfly** Swift-flying insect of the order Odonata. It has a long, slender, often brightly colored abdomen, and two pairs of large membranous wings. Like the DAMSELFLY, it mates while flying. The carnivorous nymphs are aquatic. Wingspan: to 7in (17cm).

**Drake, Sir Francis** (1540–96) English mariner. In 1577–80 he circumnavigated the world in the *Golden Hind*, looting Spanish ships and settlements, and claiming California for England. Drake was knighted by Elizabeth I on his return. His raid on CADIZ in 1587 postponed the Spanish ARMADA, which he helped to defeat in 1588. Drake died in a raid on the Spanish colonies.

**Dravidian** Family of languages spoken in S India by *c.*10 million people. The four major Dravidian languages are Telugu, Tamil, Kannada, and Malayalam. Tamil is also spoken in Sri Lanka. Brahui is spoken in Pakistan.

**dream** Mental activity associated with rapid-eye-movement (REM) sleep. It is usually a train of thoughts, scenes, and desires expressed in visual images and symbols. On average, a person dreams for a total of 1.5–2 hours in eight hours of sleep. For centuries, dreams have been regarded as a source of prophecy or visionary insight. In PSYCHOANALYSIS, patients' dreams are often examined to reveal a latent content.

**Dred Scott Case** (1856–57) US Supreme Court trial on the issue of Federal jurisdiction over SLAVERY in the territories. In 1834 Dred Scott, a slave of John Emerson, was taken from the slave state of Missouri to the free state of Illinois and then Wisonsin territory, where slavery was prohibited by the MISSOURI COMPROMISE. After Emerson's death, Scott sued for his freedom because he had lived in a free state. The case went to Federal court. In the case of *Scott vs. Sanford*, Roger B. TANEY delivered the verdict that the Missouri Compromise was unconstitutional. Three of the justices also held that slaves were not entitled to the rights of US citizens.

► **Drake** This portrait of Sir Francis Drake by Samuel Lane reflects Drake's life as an explorer, adventurer, and mariner. An English national hero, Drake is sometimes credited with establishing the absolute authority of the captain on a ship at sea.

**Dreiser, Theodore Herman Albert** (1871–1945) US writer. His first novel, *Sister Carrie* (1900), was considered immoral by its publisher and Dreiser distributed it himself. *Jennie Gerhardt* (1911) was attacked for its uncompromising NATURALISM. Dreiser's masterpiece, *An American Tragedy* (1925), is based on a real murder case.

**Dresden** City on the Elbe River, capital of Saxony state, SE Germany. First settled by Germans in the early 13th century. It suffered almost total destruction from Allied bombing in World War II. Industries: optical and precision instruments. Pop. (1990) 483,400.

**Dreyer, Carl Theodor** (1889–1968) Danish film director. His silent masterpiece, *The Passion of Joan of Arc* (1928), used prolonged close-ups and elaborate sets. His best-known film, *Day of Wrath* (1943), is a slow-burning allegory on the Nazi occupation of Denmark.

**Dreyfus Affair** French political crisis arising from the conviction of Captain Alfred Dreyfus for treason in 1894. Dreyfus was a Jewish army officer, convicted on false evidence. In 1898 publication of *J'accuse*, an open letter by Emile ZOLA in defense of Dreyfus, provoked a bitter national controversy. Dreyfus, initially imprisoned, later received a presidential pardon.

**dromedary** Large domesticated CAMEL, a pack and riding animal. It has a long neck and legs, wide feet suited to walking on sand and snow, and a single fatty hump on its back. Height: to 7ft (2m) at the shoulder.

**drug** In medicine, a substance used to diagnose, prevent, or treat disease, or aid recovery from injury. Although many drugs are still obtained from natural sources, scientists are continually developing synthetic drugs. Such drugs include ANTIBIOTICS. Some drugs interfere in physiological processes, such as anticoagulants which render the blood less prone to clotting. Drugs also may be given to make good some deficiency, such as hormone preparations for an underactive gland.

**drug addiction** Psychological or physical dependence on a DRUG. **Physical** addiction is often manifested by symptoms of withdrawal (such as vomiting and convulsions) if the drug dose is decreased or stopped. Long-term drug use often produces tolerance, increasing doses are required to reproduce the psychological effect. Physical dependence on drugs has only been medically proven for NARCOTICS (such as HEROIN), depressants (such as BARBITURATES or ALCOHOL), and some STIMULANTS (such as NICOTINE). Other drugs, such as hallucinogens or hashish, are not thought to be physically addictive, but can produce PSYCHOSIS or PARANOIA. Two of the most common addictions are alcohol and nicotine, since these are legal and easily available. In comparison, addiction to "hard" (addictive) drugs (such as HEROIN or CRACK cocaine) is not common, yet drug-related crime makes up a significant percentage of crime statistics in many countries.

**druids** Pre-Christian Celtic religious leaders of ancient Britain, Ireland, and Gaul. Little is known of them but they appear to have been judges and teachers as well as priests. In Britain and Gaul, druidism was suppressed by the Romans, but survived in Ireland until the 5th century.

**drum** Percussion instrument, generally a hollow cylinder or vessel with a skin stretched across the openings. It is struck with hands or a variety of sticks. Drums were among the earliest musical instruments; examples have been found dating from 6000 BC. Drums first appeared in European CLASSICAL MUSIC in the 18th century. In the 20th century, the role of drums in popular music has greatly expanded. Since the 1980s, electronic drum machines have developed the sound of much contemporary dance music.

**drupe** (stone fruit) Any FRUIT with a thin skin, fleshy pulp, and hard stone or pit enclosing a single seed.

**Druse** (Druze) Middle Eastern religious sect. A breakaway group of the ISMAILIS, the Druse originated in the reign of al-Hakim (996–1021), sixth Fatimid CALIPH of Egypt. They are named for al-Darazi, the first to proclaim the cult. Stressing pure MONOTHEISM, they emphasize the possibility of direct communication with divinity as a living presence. There are *c.*500,000 Druses living in Syria, LEBANON, and Israel.

**dryads** In Greek mythology, nymphs of the woodlands and guardian spirits of trees.

◀ **Dublin** One of the world's most famous cultural centers, Dublin is the capital of the Republic of Ireland. It is closely associated with many literary figures, in particular George Bernard Shaw, Oscar Wilde and James Joyce. Each year many tourists who visit the city follow the route around Dublin taken by Leopold Bloom, the central character of Joyce's modernist masterpiece *Ulysses*.

**Dryden, John** (1631–1700) English poet and playwright. He first attracted attention for his *Heroic Stanzas* (1659) on the death of Oliver Cromwell. Dryden also celebrated the RESTORATION with *Astraea Redux* (1660). His account of the events of 1666, *Annus Mirabilis* (1667), saw him become the first official poet laureate (1668–88). For the next decade, Dryden concentrated on dramatic writing, such as *Tyrannic Love* (1669) and the comedy *Marriage à la mode* (1673). *All for Love* (1678) was his first play in blank verse. *MacFlecknoe* (1684) lampooned Thomas Shadwell, his eventual successor as poet laureate. Dryden converted to Catholicism, and *The Hind and the Panther* (1687) is a religious ALLEGORY.

**dry ice** Popular name for frozen CARBON DIOXIDE

**drypoint** Quick ENGRAVING technique, probably originating in the 15th century, using a sharply pointed tool to draw lines in a metal plate. Qualities of line are determined by the amount of pressure.

**dualism** Doctrine in philosophy and metaphysics that recognizes two basic and mutually independent principles, such as mind and matter, body and soul, or good and evil. Dualism contrasts with MONISM. Both PLATO and DESCARTES were dualists, but modern philosophers have tended toward monism.

**Dubai** One of the seven federated states of the UNITED ARAB EMIRATES (UAE), on the Persian (Arabian) Gulf, SE Arabia; the capital is Dubai. First settled in the late 18th century, it was a dependency of ABU DHABI until 1833. At the end of the 19th century, it became a British protectorate. Dubai was at war with Abu Dhabi from 1945 to 1948. In 1971 it became a founder member of the UAE. Oil was discovered in the early 1960s, and is the largest sector of Dubai's prosperous, export-driven economy. Area: *c.*3,890sq km (1,500sq mi). Pop. (1985) 419,104.

**Du Barry, Marie Jeanne Bécu, Comtesse** (1743–93) French courtesan and noblewoman. She was mistress of Jean du Barry, who engineered her acceptance as last mistress of Louis XV in 1769. A great patron of the arts, she was arrested and executed for treason by the Revolutionary Tribunal.

**Dubček, Alexander** (1921–92) Czechoslovak statesman, Communist Party secretary (1968–69). Dubček was elected party leader at the start of the PRAGUE SPRING. His liberal reforms led to a Soviet invasion in August 1968, and Dubček was forced to resign and expelled from the party. Following the collapse of Czech communism, he was publicly rehabilitated and served as speaker (1989–92) of the federal parliament.

**Dublin** (Baile Átha Cliath) Capital of the Republic of Ireland, at the mouth of the Liffey River on Dublin Bay. In 1014 Brian Boru recaptured it from the Danish. In 1170 it was taken by the English and became the seat of colonial government. Dublin suffered much bloodshed in nationalist attempts to free Ireland from English rule. From 1913 a series of strikes culminated in the EASTER RISING (1916). Dublin was the center of the late-19th-century Irish literary renaissance. George Bernard SHAW, James JOYCE, and Oscar WILDE were born here. It is now the commercial and cultural center of the Republic. Notable sites include Christ Church Cathedral (1053), St. Patrick's Cathedral (1190), Trinity College (1591), and the ABBEY THEATRE (1904). Industries: brewing, textiles, clothing. Pop. (1992) 915,516.

**Dublin** County in E Republic of Ireland, in Leinster province, on the Irish Sea; the county town is DUBLIN. Low lying in the N, the land rises to the Wicklow Mountains in the S and is drained chiefly by the Liffey River. Cattle are raised; crops include wheat, barley and potatoes. Area: 922sq km (356sq mi). Pop. (1991) 1,025,304.

**dubnium** (symbol Db) Synthetic, radioactive, metallic element, the first of the transactinide elements, atomic number 104. The longest-lived of its ten ISOTOPES has a half-life of 70 seconds (the longest yet identified). Previously named "unnilquodium," "dubnium" was adopted in 1995 as a compromise between the proposed US name of "Rutherfordium" (now assigned to element 106) and the Russian proposal of "Kurchatovium."

**Dubrovnik** Adriatic seaport, DALMATIA, Croatia. As a free city, it was an important trading post between the Ottoman empire and Europe, and a traditional place of asylum for persecuted peoples. It was devastated by an earthquake (1979), and a 1991 Serbian siege. Sites include a 14th-century mint. It is an important tourist center. Products: grapes, cheese, olives. Pop. (1981) 66,131.

**Dubuffet, Jean** (1901–85) French painter and sculptor. Among his best-known works are assemblages of materials (such as glass, sand, rope) arranged into crude shapes, called *pâtes*. He collected the work of untrained artists, coining the phrase *art brut*.

**Duccio di Buoninsegna** (*c*.1265–1319) Italian painter, first great artist of the Sienese School. He infused the rigid Byzantine style of figure painting with humanity and lyricism. Surviving works include *Rucellai Madonna* (1285) and Maestà altarpiece (1308–11).

**Duchamp, Marcel** (1887–1968) French painter and theorist, one of the most radical art theorists of the 20th century. His *Nude Descending a Staircase* outraged visitors to the 1913 ARMORY SHOW. Duchamp produced relatively few paintings, concentrating on abolishing the concept of aesthetic beauty. He was a leading member of New York DADA, inventing the "ready-made." His main work, *The Bride Stripped Bare by Her Bachelors, Even* (1915–23), is a "definitively unfinished" painting of metal COLLAGE elements on glass.

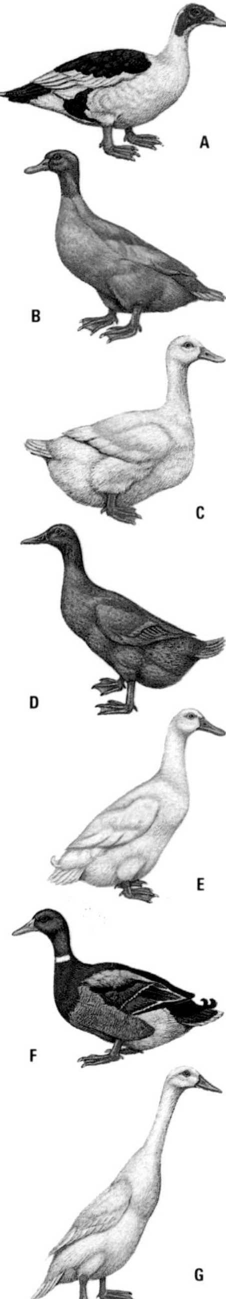


▲ **duck** Ducks were domesticated over 3,000 years ago. The picture shows Muscovy (A), buff Orpington (B), Aylesbury (C), khaki campbell (D), Pekin (E), Rouen (F), and Indian runner white (G).

**duck** Worldwide waterfowl, related to the SWAN and GOOSE. Most nest in cool areas and migrate to warm areas in winter. All have large bills, short legs, and webbed feet. Their color is varied, and dense plumage is underlaid by down and waterproof feathers. There are two groups: **dabbling** ducks, which feed from the surface, and **diving** ducks. All eat seeds, insects, crustacea, and mollusks. Most lay a large clutch of eggs. There are seven tribes: EIDERS, shelducks, dabbling ducks, perching ducks, pochards, sea ducks, and stiff-tailed ducks. There are *c*.200 species. Length: 1–2ft (30–60cm); weight: to 16lb (7.2kg). Family Anatidae.

**duck-billed platypus** *See* PLATYPUS

**duckweed** Family (Lemnaceae) of four genera including 25 species of tiny, floating, aquatic flowering plants. The disc-like leaflets have a single 6in (15cm) trailing root.

**due process of law** Formal legal procedure to ensure that no one is deprived of life, freedom, or property before proper legal authority has been obtained. It is enshrined in England's MAGNA CARTA and the 5th and 14th amendments of the US CONSTITUTION. A major element of the process is a TRIAL.

**Dufay, Guillaume** (1400–74) Burgundian composer. His MOTETS were grand, compex compositions written for specific events. Dufay also wrote masses.

**Dufy, Raoul** (1877–1953) French painter. Dufy was associated with IMPRESSIONISM and FAUVISM, and is famous for his decorative racing and boating scenes. The bright, luminous colors and linear simplicity of *Riders in the Wood* (1931) is typical of his work.

**dugong** (sea cow) Large, plant-eating aquatic mammal found in shallow coastal waters of Africa, Asia, and Australia. Gray and hairless, the dugong has no hind legs, and its forelegs are weak flippers. Length: 8–13ft (2.5–4m); weight: 600lb (270kg). Family Dugongidae.

**duiker** (duikerbok) Small sub-Saharan African ANTELOPE. The female is larger than the male and occasionally carries stunted horns; the horns of the male are short and spiky. Duikers are gray to reddish-yellow. Height: up to 26in (66cm) at the shoulder; weight: up to 37lb (17kg). Family Bovidae; species *Sylvicapra grimmia*.

**Duisburg** City at the confluence of the Rhine and Ruhr rivers, Nordrhein-Westfalen state, NW Germany. Chartered in 1129, it remained a free imperial city until the late 13th century. During World War II, it was the center of the German armaments industry, and suffered extensive bombing damage. Industries: iron, steel, textiles, chemicals. Pop. (1990) 538,300.

**Dukas, Paul** (1865–1935) French composer. His best-known work, the orchestral scherzo *The Sorcerer's Apprentice* (1897), shows his skillful orchestration and individual style.

**dulcimer** Medieval stringed instrument, originally Persian, with a flat, triangular sounding board and ten or more strings struck with handheld hammers.

**Dulles, John Foster** (1888–1959) US statesman, secretary of state (1953–59). He served (1945–49) as a US delegate to the United Nations. Dulles drew up the peace treaty with Japan (1951). As secretary of state to Dwight D. EISENHOWER, he advocated the expansion of a nuclear weapons program to counteract the perceived threat of communism.

**Dumas, Alexandre** (1802–70) (*père*) French novelist and dramatist. He achieved success with romantic historical plays, such as *La Tour de Nesle* (1832). Dumas wrote popular swashbuckling novels, such as *The Count of Monte Cristo*, *The Three Musketeers* (1844–45) and *The Black Tulip* (1850).

**Dumas, Alexandre** (1824–95) (*fils*) French dramatist and novelist, illegitimate son of Alexandre DUMAS (*père*). His first great success was *La Dame aux Camélias* (1852), the basis of Verdi's opera *La Traviata*. His didactic later plays, such as *Les idées de Madame Aubray* (1867), helped to provoke French social reform.

**Du Maurier, Dame Daphne** (1907–89) English novelist. Du Maurier's romantic novels include *Jamaica Inn* (1936), *Rebecca* (1938), *Frenchman's Creek* (1941), and *My Cousin Rachel* (1951). She also wrote plays, and short stories (including *The Birds*).

**Dumfries and Galloway** Region in SW Scotland, bounded SE by England, S by the Solway Firth; the capital is Dumfries. Major towns include Castle Douglas, Lockerbie, and Stranraer. An agricultural region, sites include the Galloway Hills and the runic Ruthwell Cross. Area: 2,470sq mi (6,396sq km). Pop. (1991) 147,805.

**dump** In computing, information copied from COMPUTER memory to an output or storage device. It may be the entire contents of a file copied to another DISK, or a printout of the screen (screen dump).

**Dunbar, Paul Laurence** (1872–1906) US author. His poetry, written in African-American dialect, is a bittersweet mixture of sadness and humor. Dunbar's *Lyrics of Lowly Life* (1896) concerns Southern black life before the Civil War. His novels include *The Love of Landry* (1900).

**Duncan, Isadora** (1877–1927) US dancer, pioneer of MODERN DANCE. She achieved fame in Europe for her emotional, expressive style. Duncan died tragically when her scarf caught in the wheel of her car and strangled her.

**Dundee** City on the N shore of the Firth of Tay, Tayside, E Scotland. A center of the REFORMATION in Scotland, Dundee is an important port and has a university (founded 1881). Industries: textiles, confectionery, engineering. Pop. (1991) 165,873.

**dune** Ridge of windblown particles, most often sand. They occur in deserts in many shapes: **barchans** (crescent-shaped) are formed by a constant wind; **seifs** are narrow ridges.

**Dunedin** (Gaelic, Edinburgh) City on SE South Island, New Zealand. Founded in 1848 by Scottish Free Church settlers, Dunedin grew after the discovery of gold in the

1860s. It has the University of Otago (1871). Industries: agricultural machinery. Pop. (1993) 111,200.

**dung beetle** Small to medium-sized SCARAB BEETLE. Some species form balls of dung as food for their larvae, and may roll the balls some distance before burying them. Family Scarabaeidae; species *Geotrupus stercorarius*.

**Dunkirk** (Dunkerque) City on the Strait of Dover, NW France. It came under French rule in 1662. In World War II, more than 300,000 Allied troops were evacuated from its beaches between May 29 and June 3, 1940, when the German army broke through to the English Channel. Now it is a leading port, and one of the principal iron and steel producers in W Europe. Industries: oil refining, shipbuilding. Pop. (1990) 70,331.

**Duns Scotus, John** (1265–1308) Scottish theologian and scholastic philosopher. He founded a school of SCHOLASTICISM called Scotism.

**Dunstan, Saint** (*c*.910–88) English monk, archbishop of Canterbury (960–88). He negotiated a peace treaty with the Danes that helped to unify England. Dunstan revived English monasticism and acted as advisor to several kings of Wessex. His feast day is May 19.

**duodenum** First section of the small INTESTINE, shaped like a horseshoe. The pyloric sphincter, a circular muscle, separates it from the STOMACH. Alkaline BILE and pancreatic juices are released into the duodenum to aid the DIGESTION of food.

**Du Pont de Nemours, Eleuthère Irénée** (1771–1834) US industrialist, b. France. Founder of a huge chemical company and family empire that continues as E.I. Du Pont de Nemours and Co. In 1799 he came to the US with his father, Pierre Samuel Du Pont de Nemours (1739–1817). They started a business producing high-quality gunpowder and prospered from the War of 1812. The Du Pont company pioneered the production of nylon and other synthetic fibers.

**Du Pré, Jacqueline** (1945–87) English cellist, wife of Daniel BARENBOIM. Du Pré's interpretation of Elgar, Beethoven, and Brahms drew special acclaim. In 1973 her career was cut short by multiple sclerosis.

**Durango** State in NW Mexico. In W Durango, the SIERRA MADRE Occidental contains mineral deposits such as silver, gold, and lead. The capital, Victoria de Durango, has been the major mining town since its foundation in 1563. To the E, the arid plains provide excellent pastures, and many crops are cultivated in the fertile Nazas River valley. Industries: timber, tanning, textiles, tourism. Area: 119,648sq km (46,196sq mi). Pop. (1990) 1,349,378.

**Duras, Marguérite** (1914–96) French novelist and playwright, b. Indochina. Her novels include *The Sea Wall* (1950), *Destroy, She Said* (1969), *The Lover* (1984), and *Summer Rain* (1990). Duras also wrote the screenplay for *Hiroshima Mon Amour* (1959).

**Durban** Seaport on the N shore of Durban Bay, South Africa. Founded in 1835, the national convention initiating the Union of South Africa was held here. It has the University of Natal (1949) and Natal University College (1960). Industries: shipbuilding, oil refining, chemicals. Pop. (1991) 1,137,378.

**Dürer, Albrecht** (1471–1528) German painter, engraver, and designer of woodcuts; the greatest artist of the northern RENAISSANCE. During his visits to Italy, Dürer was influenced by artists such as LEONARDO DA VINCI. Dürer's personal synthesis of N and S European traditions deeply affected European art. His album of woodcuts, *The Apocalypse* (1498), has remarkable paint-like tones. His paintings include *The Feast of the Rose Garlands* (1506) and *Four Apostles* (1526), which reveal his preoccupation with Lutheranism. Dürer is often credited as the founder of etching.

**Durga** In the Hindu pantheon, one of the names of the wife of SHIVA. Depicted as a 10-armed goddess, she is both destructive and beneficent but is worshiped today as a warrior against evil. Her festival, the Durga-puja, which occurs around September, is a time for family reunions.

**Durham, John George Lambton, 1st Earl of** (1792–1840) British statesman. One of the drafters of the Great REFORM ACT of 1832, he led the radical wing of the Whig Party. Governor-general of Canada (1838), he formulated the basis of British colonial policy.

◀ **Dürer** German artist, Albrecht Dürer's *Self-portrait* (1500), depicts the artist resembling Christ. The greatest artist of the northern Renaissance, he is perhaps best known for his albums of woodcuts, such as *The Apocalypse* (1498). These have a remarkably dense and subtle texture, creating paintlike tones. The Emperor Maximilian was a patron and commissioned his famous *Rhinoceros* woodcut.

**Durham** City and administrative district on the Wear River, NE England; the county town of Co. Durham. Founded by monks in the 10th century, it became a defensive outpost against the Scots and the seat of prince-bishops. Its cathedral (1093) contains the tomb of the Venerable BEDE, and an 11th-century castle is now part of the university (founded 1832). Industries: textiles, carpet-weaving, engineering. Pop. (1991) 85,800.

**Durkheim, Emile** (1858–1917) French sociologist. Influenced by the POSITIVISM of Auguste COMTE, Durkheim used the methods of natural science to study human society, and is considered (with Max WEBER) a founder of SOCIOLOGY. In *The Division of Labor in Society* (1893) and the *Elementary Forms of Religious Life* (1912), Durkheim argued that religion and labor were basic organizing principles of society. *Suicide* (1897) outlines his theory of alienation.

**Durrell, Gerald Malcolm** (1925–95) British naturalist and author, brother of Lawrence DURRELL, b. India. His humorous and stylish novels include *My Family and Other Animals* (1956), and *A Zoo in My Luggage* (1960).

**Durrell, Lawrence George** (1912–90) British novelist and poet, brother of Gerald DURRELL, b. India. His life in Greece and Egypt provided inspiration for most of his writing. His major work is the inventive tetralogy, *The Alexandria Quartet*: *Justine* (1957), *Balthazar* (1958), *Mountolive* (1958), and *Clea* (1960).

**Dürrenmatt, Friedrich** (1921–90) Swiss dramatist, novelist, and essayist. Influential in the post-1945 revival of German theater, his works are ironic and display a nihilistic, black humor. *Woyzeck* (1972) is his most frequently performed play.

**Duse, Eleanora** (1859–1924) Italian actress. She was regarded as the greatest actress of her generation. Duse is best-known for her roles in plays by her lover Gabriele D'ANNUNZIO, and Henrik Ibsen.

**Dushanbe** (Dušanbe) Capital of Tajikistan, at the foot of the Gissar Mountains, Central Asia. Founded in the 1920s, it was known as Stalinabad from 1929 to 1961. An industrial, trade, and transportation center, it has Tadzhik University and Academy of Sciences. Industries: cotton, engineering. Pop. (1991 est.) 592,000.

**Düsseldorf** Capital of North Rhine-Westphalia, at the confluence of the rivers Rhine and Düssel, NW Germany. Founded in the 13th century, it was the residence of the dukes of Berg in the 14th–16th centuries. It became part of Prussia in 1815 and was under French occupation from 1921 to 1925. It is a cultural center. Industries: chemicals, textiles. Pop. (1990) 577,400.

**dust bowl** Area of *c*.100 million acres (40 million ha) of the GREAT PLAINS, that suffered from wind erosion. Due to drought, overplanting, and mismanagement, much of the topsoil was blown away in the 1930s. Soil conservation programs have helped restore productivity.

**Dutch** Official language of the Netherlands, spoken by almost all of the country's 13 million inhabitants, and also in

▲ **Dvořák** Czech composer Antonín Dvořák drew heavily on folk music, both Czech (for the polka rhythms) and American, which he would have picked up during his stay in the US. Although he was intrigued with opera, it is generally accepted that his stage works are of less significance than his orchestral pieces.

Netherlands Antilles and Surinam. Dutch is a Germanic language, belonging to the Indo-European family.

**Dutch art** Before the 16th century, most Netherlandish art was commissioned by the church. Artists such as LUCAS VAN LEYDEN produced elaborate altarpieces. After independence from Spain, the chief patrons were the merchant class. The 17th century was a golden age, producing artists of the caliber of REMBRANDT, Jan VERMEER, Frans HALS, and Jacob van RUISDAEL. The 19th-century Hague School rekindled the Dutch landscape tradition. Vincent VAN GOGH, though Dutch-born, had closer links with 19th-century FRENCH ART. In the 20th century, the main artistic contributions have come from Piet MONDRIAN and the De STIJL group.

**Dutch East India Company** *See* EAST INDIA COMPANY

**Dutch East Indies** Until 1949 the part of Southeast Asia that is now INDONESIA. An overseas territory of the Netherlands, it comprised the Malay Archipelago, including SUMATRA, JAVA, BORNEO (except North Borneo), SULAWESI, MOLUCCAS, and the Lesser Sunda Islands (except Portuguese TIMOR). The islands were first colonized by the Dutch in the early 17th century.

**Dutch elm disease** Highly infective fungus infection that attacks the bark of elm trees and spreads inward until it kills the tree. It is spread by beetles whose grubs make a series of linked tunnels in the wood below the bark.

**Dutch Wars** Three 17th-century naval conflicts between Holland and England arising from commercial rivalry. The first war (1652–54) ended, with England holding the advantage. The second war (1665–67) followed England's seizure of New Amsterdam (New York). The Dutch inflicted heavy losses and destroyed Chatham naval base, England; England modified its trade laws. The third war (1672–74) arose from English support of a French invasion of the Netherlands. The Dutch naval victory forced England to make peace.

**Duvalier, "Baby Doc" (Jean-Claude)** (1951– ) President of Haiti (1971–86). He succeeded his father, "Papa Doc" DUVALIER, as president-for-life. Although he introduced several important reforms and disbanded the Tonton Macoutes, he retained his father's brutal methods. Civil unrest forced his exile to France in 1986.

**DYSENTERY**

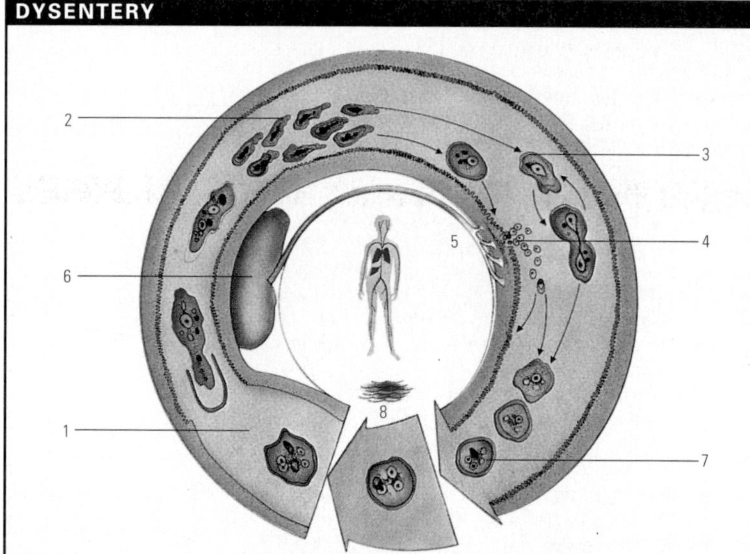


Amebic dysentery is a widespread disease caused by a microscopic organism (*Entameba histolytica*),found in contaminated water and food. *Entameba* is a natural inhabitant of the gut but under certain conditions invasion of the gut wall occurs. Ingested *Entameba* cysts undergo division and multiplication in the large intestine (1). After division, eight trophozoites (feeding protozoa) are produced (2), non-infective trophozoites remain in the intestine (3) feeding on bacteria and food particles. Infective trophozoites invade the gut wall (4), multiply and dissolve away tissues by producing protein-digesting enzymes. If organisms enter the blood stream (5) they can be carried to the lungs (6), liver, and brain, where abscesses develop. Those released from gut abscesses reinvade tissues or form cysts (7) and are passed in the feces. The disease is transmitted if flies carry cysts from feces to food or more usually if contaminated water is drunk (8).

**Duvalier, "Papa Doc" (François)** (1907–71) President of Haiti (1957–71). He declared himself president-for-life and relied on the feared Tonton Macoutes, a vigilante group, to consolidate his rule. Under Duvalier's ruthless regime, the longest in Haiti's history, the country's economy severely declined.

**Dvořák, Antonín** (1841–1904) Czech composer. He adapted Czech FOLK MUSIC to a classical style. Best known for his orchestral works, which include nine symphonies, two sets of *Slavonic Dances*, and several symphonic poems, Dvořák's Cello Concerto (1895) is one of the supreme achievements of the form. His stay in the US (1892–95) inspired his most popular work, the Symphony in E minor ("From the New World").

**dye** Substance, natural or synthetic, used to impart color to various substances. Natural dyes have mostly been replaced by synthetic dyes, many derived from coal tar. Dyes are classified according to their application: **direct** dyes, such as sulfur and vat dyes, can be applied directly to fabric because they bind to the fibers. **Indirect** dyes, such as ingrain and mordant dyes, require a secondary process to fix the dye.

**Dyfed** County in SW Wales; the administrative center is Carmarthen. The Cambrian Mountains extend to the coast. Agriculture is based on livestock rearing, and crops. Industries: fishing, timber, textiles, tourism. Area: 2,226sq mi (5,765sq km). Pop. (1990) 343,543.

**Dyke, Sir Anthony van** *See* VAN DYCK, SIR ANTHONY

**dyke** (dike) In engineering, a barrier or embankment designed to confine or regulate the flow of water. Dykes are used in reclaiming land from the sea by sedimentation (as practiced in The Netherlands), and also as controls against river flooding. In geology, a dyke is an intrusion of igneous rock whose surface is different from that of the adjoining material.

**Dylan, Bob** (1941– ) US popular singer and composer, b. Robert Allen Zimmerman. Dylan successfully combined social protest poetry and FOLK MUSIC on records such as *The Times They Are A-Changin'* (1963), and *Highway 61 Revisited* (1965). His switch to ROCK music and electric instrumentation initially alienated many fans. Classic albums from this period include *Blood on the Tracks* (1975).

**dynamics** Branch of MECHANICS that studies objects in motion. Its two main branches are: kinematics, which examines motion; and KINETICS, which also studies the causes of motion. *See also* INERTIA; MOMENTUM

**dynamite** Solid, blasting explosive. It contains NITROGLYCERINE incorporated in an absorbent base, such as charcoal or wood pulp. Dynamite is used in mining, quarrying, and engineering. It was invented by Alfred NOBEL in 1866.

**dynamo** (generator) Device that converts mechanical energy into electrical energy by the principle of ELECTROMAGNETIC INDUCTION. In a simple dynamo, a CONDUCTOR, usually an open coil of wire (armature), is placed between the poles of a permanent magnet. This armature is rotated within the magnetic field, inducing an ELECTRIC CURRENT. *See also* ALTERNATOR

**dysentery** Infectious disease characterized by DIARRHEA, bleeding, and abdominal cramps. It is spread in contaminated food and water, especially in the tropics. There are two types: **bacillary** dysentery, caused by BACTERIA of the genus *Shigella*; and **amebic** dysentery, caused by a type of PROTOZOA. Both are treated with antibacterials and fluid replacement.

**dyslexia** Impairment in reading ability. Dyslexia is usually diagnosed when difficulty in learning to read is clearly not due to inadequate intelligence, brain damage, or emotional problems. Symptoms may include difficulty with writing, especially in spelling correctly.

**dyspepsia** (indigestion) Pain or discomfort in the stomach or abdomen arising from digestive upset.

**dysprosium** (symbol Dy) Silvery-white, metallic rare-earth element of the LANTHANIDE SERIES, first identified (1886) by Lecoq de Boisbaudran. Its chief ores are monazite and bastnaesite. Its capacity to absorb neutrons makes it important in nuclear technology. Its compounds are also used in lasers. Properties: at.no. 66; at.wt. 162.5; sp.gr. 8.54; m.p. 2,568°F (1,409°C); b.p. 4,235°F (2,335°C); most common isotope $^{164}$Dy (28.18%).

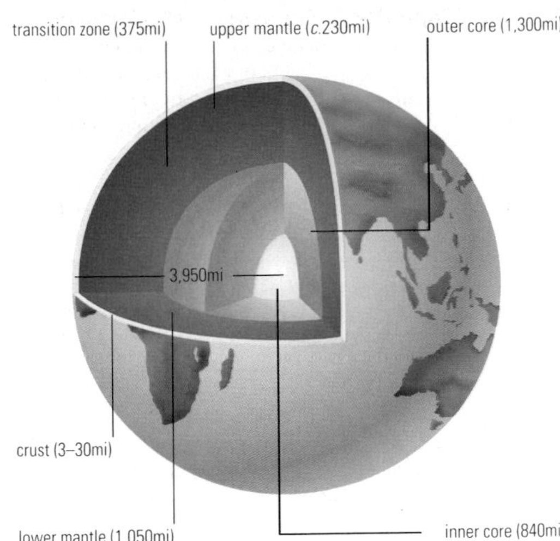


▲ **Earth** Formed c.4.6 billion years ago, the Earth first supported life some 1 billion years later. The Earth consists of concentric rings, from the uppermost crust to a solid inner core of nickel and iron.

**eagle** Strong, carnivorous diurnal BIRD OF PREY. Sea and fishing eagles, such as the bald eagle, are large birds found by sea coasts and lakes, where they feed on fish, small animals, and carrion. Serpent eagles are stocky, reptile-eating birds. Large, harpy eagles inhabit tropical forests. True (booted) eagles (*Aquila*) have long hooked bills, broad wings, powerful toes with long curved talons, and feathered legs. They nest high on sea coasts or island mountains, building massive stick nests (eyries). One or two light-brown or spotted eggs are laid. Length: 16–40in (40–100cm) Family Accipitridae. *See also* FALCON

**Eakins, Thomas** (1844–1916) US painter and photographer, regarded as one of the greatest artists of the 19th century. Eakin's painstaking search for anatomical accuracy aroused much controversy. His use of CHIAROSCURO and psychological insight attract comparison with Rembrandt. Eakin's most celebrated paintings are *Gross Clinic* (1875), *The Chess Players* (1876), *The Swimming Hole* (1883), and *Agnew Clinic* (1889). He had a profound impact on the ASHCAN SCHOOL. *See also* LUMINISM

**ear** Organ of hearing and balance. It converts sound waves to nerve impulses which are carried to the BRAIN. In most mammals it consists of the outer, middle, and inner ear. The **outer** ear carries sound to the eardrum. The **middle** ear is air-filled, and has three tiny bones (ossicles) that pass on and amplify sound vibrations to the fluid-filled inner ear. The **inner** ear contains the COCHLEA. Vibrations stimulate tiny hairs which cause impulses to be sent via the auditory nerve to the brain. The inner ear also contains semicircular canals that maintain orientation and balance.

**Earhart, Amelia** (1898–?1937) US aviator, first woman to fly solo across the Atlantic (1932). In 1937, she attempted to fly around the world, but disappeared in the Pacific Ocean.

**Early, Jubal Anderson** (1816–94) Confederate general in the CIVIL WAR. He was brigadier general of the Virginia troops at the first battle of BULL RUN (1861) and fought in the battle of CHANCELLORSVILLE, the GETTYSBURG CAMPAIGN (1863), and the WILDERNESS CAMPAIGN (1864). Early was routed by General CUSTER at Waynesboro (March 1865), and General LEE relieved him of command.

**Early English** First phase of English GOTHIC ARCHITECTURE (13th century). It followed NORMAN ARCHITECTURE. In c.1250 French-inspired English stonemasons developed a native Gothic idiom: CANTERBURY Cathedral is a very early example. Later works emphasized appearance rather than structure: builders ornamented and enhanced visible walls, or made prominent use of VAULT ribbing. *See also* DECORATED STYLE; PERPENDICULAR STYLE

**Early English** (Anglo-Saxon, or Old English) ENGLISH language from c.AD 450 to 1100. It constitutes the earliest form of English, directly descended from the Germanic languages of the early ANGLO-SAXONS. It had a vocabulary of c.50,000 words. It comprised four main dialects: Northumbrian, Mercian, Kentish, and West Saxon. The best of Early English literature, such as the epic poem BEOWULF, was written in Northumbrian. West Saxon became the chief dialect as a result of ALFRED THE GREAT's unification of England.

**Earp, Wyatt Berry Stapp** (1848–1929) US law officer. In 1879 he became deputy sheriff of Tombstone, Arizona. The Earp brothers and Doc Holliday fought the Clanton gang in the famous gunfight at the O.K. Corral in 1881.

**Earth** Third major planet from the Sun, and the largest of the four inner, or terrestrial planets. Some 70% of the surface is covered by water. This fact and the Earth's average surface temperature of 55°F (13°C), make it suitable for life. Continental land masses make up the other 30%. Our planet has one natural satellite, the MOON. Like all the terrestrial planets, there is a dense CORE rich in iron and nickel, surrounded by a MANTLE of silicate rocks. The thin, outermost layer of lighter rock is the CRUST, which can vary in depth from between 30mi (50km) – the thickest **continental** crust – to 3mi (5km) – the thinnest **oceanic** crust. The boundary between the crust and the mantle is called the MOHO. The solid, inner core rotates at a different rate from the molten, outer layers, and this, together with currents in the outer core, gives rise to the Earth's MAGNETIC FIELD. The crust and the uppermost mantle together form the **lithosphere**, which consists of tightly fitting slabs called **plates**. The plates, which float on a semi-molten layer of mantle called the **asthenosphere**, move in interactions known collectively as PLATE TECTONICS. *See also* ATMOSPHERE; GEOLOGICAL TIME

**earthquake** Tremor below the surface of the Earth which causes shaking to occur in the crust. Shaking lasts only for a few seconds, but widespread devastation can result. According to PLATE TECTONICS, earthquakes are caused by the movement of crustal plates, which produces FAULT lines. The main earthquake regions are found along plate margins, especially on the edges of the Pacific, such as the SAN ANDREAS FAULT. A large earthquake is usually followed by smaller "aftershocks." An earthquake beneath the sea is called a TSUNAMI. Earthquake prediction is a branch of SEISMOLOGY. The world's largest recorded earthquake (1976) at Tangshan, China, killed more than 250,000 people and measured 8.2 on the RICHTER SCALE.

**Earth sciences** General term used to describe all the sciences concerned with the EARTH. It includes the basic subject of GEOLOGY, with its subclassifications of GEOCHEM-

***E/e, fifth letter of the Roman alphabet. Derived from an Egyptian* hieroglyph *of a man rejoicing, it entered the Semitic alphabet as the letter* he. *It was adopted by the Greeks as the letter* epsilon *before taking its present form.***

**EARTH: DATA**

Diameter (equatorial): 7,923mi (12,756km)
Mass: 5,378 billion billion tons
Volume: 260 billion cubic mi (1,083 billion cubic km)
Density (water = 1): 5.52
Orbital period: 365.3 days
Rotation period: 23h 56m 04s

**EAR**

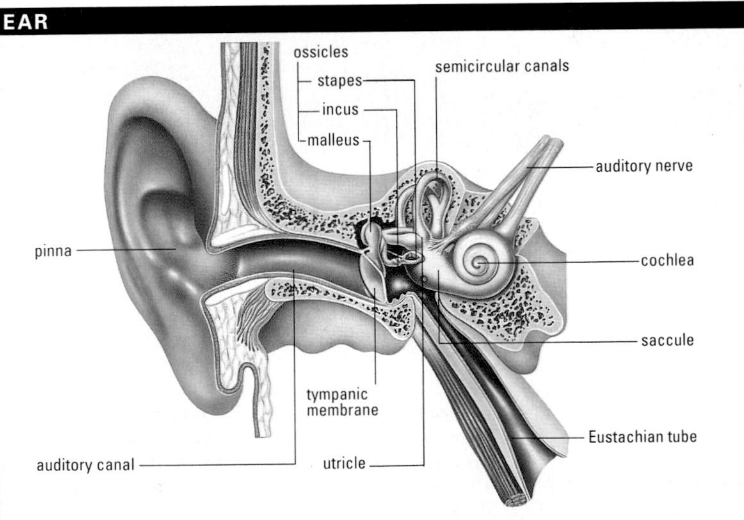


The ear is divided into three parts – the outer, middle and inner ear. The outer consists of the pinna, and the auditory canal. The pinna funnels sound waves via the canal to the ear drum, tympanic membrane, of the middle ear. The sound waves are amplified and transmitted by tiny bones, the ossicles, which cause the oval window to vibrate. This sets the fluids of the inner ear in motion. Hair cells in structures of the inner ear, the cochlea and semicircular canals, are stimulated and generate impulses interpreted by the brain as sound.

▲ **Eastwood** Charismatic leading actor and director, Clint Eastwood has enjoyed a career spanning 40 years. He is best-known for his tough, tight-lipped action roles in films such as *Dirty Harry* (1971). His love of jazz music is revealed in his direction of the film biography of Charlie Parker, *Bird* (1988). He won Best Film and Best Actor Oscars for his western *Unforgiven* (1992).

ISTRY, GEOMORPHOLOGY, GEOPHYSICS; MINERALOGY and PETROLOGY; SEISMOLOGY and VOLCANISM; OCEANOGRAPHY; METEOROLOGY; PALEONTOLOGY

**Earth Summit** (June 1992) United Nations Conference on Environment and Development, held in Rio de Janeiro, Brazil. The first serious global acknowledgment of the problems created by the impact of industrial society on the ENVIRONMENT. The Rio Declaration imposed limits on the emission of gases, responsible for the GREENHOUSE EFFECT. A second Earth Summit (June 1997) called for progress in the reduction of carbon dioxide emissions.

**earthworm** Annelid with a cylindrical, segmented body and tiny bristles. Most worms live in moist soil. Their burrowing aerates the soil, helping to make it fertile. Length: 2in–11ft (5cm–33m). There are several hundred species. Class Oligochaeta; genus *Lumbricus*.

**earwig** Slender, flattened, brownish-black insect found in crevices and under tree bark. There are some 900 species worldwide. All have a pair of forceps at the hind end. Order Dermaptera; genus *Forficula*.

**East Anglia** Region of E England, made up of the counties of NORFOLK and SUFFOLK, and parts of CAMBRIDGESHIRE and ESSEX. The protection afforded by the fenlands made it one of the most powerful Anglo-Saxon kingdoms of the late 6th century. A fertile agricultural land, farming includes grain and vegetable growing and livestock raising. Industries: farming, tourism, fishing.

**East China Sea** Northern branch of the China Sea, bordered by Korea and Japan (N), China (W), Taiwan (S), and the Ryukyu Islands (E). Area: *c*.482,300sq mi (1,249,160sq km).

**Easter** Feast in celebration of the resurrection of JESUS CHRIST on the third day after his crucifixion. It is the oldest and greatest Christian feast, celebrated on the Sunday following the first full moon between March 21 and April 25. The exchange of Easter eggs is a pre-Christian rite.

**Easter Island** (Isla de Pascua) Volcanic island in the SE Pacific; the chief town is Hanga Roa. The most isolated island in Polynesia, it was discovered by a Dutch navigator on Easter Day, 1722, and has been under Chilean administration since 1888. It is famous for the curious hieroglyphs (*rongorongo*) and statues carved in stone, standing up to 40ft (12m) high. Industries: farming, tourism. Area: 63sq mi (163sq km). Pop. (1982) 1,867.

**Eastern Cape** Province in SE South Africa; the capital is East London. Eastern Cape was created in 1994 from the E part of the former CAPE PROVINCE. It incorporates the former, apartheid-created homelands of Transkei and Ciskei. Area: 65,466sq mi (169,600sq km). Pop. (1994 est.) 6,436,790

**Eastern Orthodox Church** (Orthodox Church) Community of *c*.130 million Christians living mainly in E and SE Europe, parts of Asia, and a significant minority in the US. The Church is a federation of groups that share forms of worship and episcopal organization, but each group has its own national head. The patriarch of Istanbul is recognized as titular head. Eastern Orthodox Christians reject the jurisdiction of the Roman pope. When CONSTANTINE moved his capital to Byzantium (Istanbul) in 330, a separate non-Roman culture developed. Conflicts grew between the Eastern patriarchs and Rome. In the 1054 SCHISM, the Western and Eastern arms of Christendom excommunicated each other's followers, and the split became irreparable when Crusaders invaded Constantinople (1204). In 1963 the Eastern Orthodox Churches agreed to open a dialogue with Rome.

**Easter Rising** (April 24, 1916) Rebellion by Irish nationalists against British rule. Led by Patrick PEARSE, James CONNOLLY, and Joseph Plunkett, *c*.1,200 men seized buildings in Dublin and proclaimed Ireland a republic. The British crushed the rising within a week and executed 15 of the ringleaders. Nationalist sentiment produced an electoral victory for SINN FÉIN in 1917.

**East India Company** Name of several organizations set up by European countries in the 17th century to trade E of Africa. The British company was set up in 1600 to compete for the East Indian spice trade, but competition with the Dutch led it to concentrate on India, where it gradually won a monopoly. Under government control, the company continued to administer the British colony in India until the Indian Mutiny (1857). The Dutch Company was founded (1602), with headquarters in Jakarta from 1619. It was dissolved in 1799. The French Company was founded by Louis XIV (1664) and set up colonies on several islands in the Indian Ocean. It was defeated by the English company and abolished in 1789.

**Eastman, George** (1854–1932) US inventor, industrialist, and philanthropist, who popularized the art of PHOTOGRAPHY. Eastman invented (1879) a dry-plate process and began to mass produce photographic plates. In 1884 he designed a roll film. The first Kodak camera was produced in 1888. The Eastman Kodak Company was founded in 1892.

**East Sussex** County of SE England. The county town is Lewes, other major towns include BRIGHTON, and Eastbourne. Its S border is the English Channel. The chalky South Downs run parallel to the coast. In the N, the Weald plains are drained by the Ouse River. Most of the region was included in the kingdom of WESSEX. In 1066 William the Conqueror met the forces of Harold II in the Battle of HASTINGS. Industries: agriculture, services, tourism. Area: 693sq mi (1,795sq km) Pop. (1991) 670,600.

**East Timor** *See* TIMOR

**Eastwood, Clint** (1930– ) US film actor and director. He played the drifter in the "spaghetti WESTERNS" *A Fistful of Dollars* (1964), *For a Few Dollars More* (1965), and *The Good, the Bad, and the Ugly* (1967). *Dirty Harry* (1971) and its four sequels were also tough and uncompromising. Eastwood won Best Picture and Best Director Academy Awards for *Unforgiven* (1992).

**eating disorders** Range of disorders involving eating habits and appetites. The most common are ANOREXIA NERVOSA and bulimia nervosa.

**ebony** Hard, fine-grained dark heartwood of various Asian and African trees of the genus *Diospyros* in the ebony family (Ebenaceae). Its major commercial tree is the macassar ebony (*D. ebenum*) of S India and Malaysia.

**Ebro** River in N Spain. Rising at Fontibre in the Catabrian Mountains, it flows ESE and then SE through Logrono and ZARAGOZA, and into the Mediterranean below Tortosa. It is the longest river whose entire course is in Spain. Length: 565mi (910km).

**eccentricity** (symbol *e*) One of the elements of an ORBIT. It indicates how much an elliptical orbit departs from a circle. A circle has an eccentricity of 0, a parabola an eccentricity of 1.

**Ecclesiastes** Old Testament book of aphorisms, compiled under the pseudonym "the Preacher, the son of David." An example of WISDOM LITERATURE, the book is traditionally ascribed to SOLOMON but clearly dates from after the BABYLONIAN CAPTIVITY. Its theme is the vanity and emptiness of life, relieved only by faith in God.

**Ecclesiastical court** Tribunal system set up by European church authorities during the later Middle Ages for matters involving the church and the clergy, religious offenses, and secular matters. They had wide social jurisdiction. The best known was the INQUISITION.

**Ecclesiasticus** Book of the APOCRYPHA, an example of Jewish WISDOM LITERATURE. The work of a Jewish scribe, Jesus ben Sirach, written in *c*.180 BC. A handbook of practical and moral advice, the central theme is the relationship between wisdom and God.

**echidna** (spiny anteater) MONOTREME related to the PLATYPUS, found in Australia, Tasmania, and New Guinea. It is a primitive egg-laying mammal with a CLOACA, spines on the upper body, and an elongated snout. Length: 12–30in (30–77cm).

**echinoderm** Any member of the phylum Echinodermata, a group of spiny-skinned, marine invertebrate animals. Radially symmetrical with five axes, they have a skeleton of calcareous plates in their skin. Their body cavity includes a complex, internal fluid-pumping system and tube feet. They reproduce sexually, and produce a bilaterally symmetrical larva. Species include SEA URCHIN, SEA CUCUMBER, and STARFISH.

**Echo** In Greek mythology, a mountain nymph condemned to speak only in echoes, because her chattering distracted the goddess HERA from the infidelity of ZEUS.

**echo** Reflected portion of a wave, such as SOUND or radar, from a surface so that it returns to the source and is heard after a short interval. High notes provide a better echo than low notes. Echoes are useful in NAVIGATION.

**echolocation** In animals, system of navigation used principally by WHALES and BATS. The animal emits a series of short, high-frequency sounds, and from the returning ECHO it gauges its environment. Bats also use the system for hunting. *See also* SONAR

**Eck, Johann Maier von** (1486–1543) German Roman Catholic theologian. He held a public debate (1519) with Martin LUTHER in Leipzig. Eck forced Luther to deny the authority of the Council of CONSTANCE, and engineered his excommunication for heresy (1521). He helped produce the AUGSBURG CONFESSION (1530).

**Eckhart, Johannes** (*c.*1260–*c.*1327) (Meister Eckhart) German Dominican theologian and mystic. An evangelical preacher, his sermons stressed the path to salvation through personal spiritual development. In 1526 he was accused of heresy, but died before his condemnation by Pope John XXII.

**eclipse** Celestial body completely or partially obscuring another, as seen from Earth. Eclipses are transitory, the most familiar are solar and lunar eclipses. A **solar** eclipse occurs when the MOON passes between the EARTH and the SUN, so that the Sun's light is blocked from the part of the Earth on which the Moon's shadow (umbra) falls. It provides a unique research opportunity for scientists, such as checking Einstein's theory of RELATIVITY. A **lunar** eclipse is caused by the Earth when it moves between Sun and Moon, so that the Moon passes into the Earth's umbra, and cannot shine by reflected sunlight. This happens, at most, seven times a year.

**Eco, Umberto** (1932– ) Italian writer and academic. Eco's best-known work is the erudite philosophical thriller *The Name of the Rose* (1981). Other novels include *Foucault's Pendulum* (1989), and *The Island Before Time* (1994). He is a professor of SEMIOTICS.

**ecology** Biological study of relationships of organisms to their ENVIRONMENT and to one another. The term was coined (1866) by Ernst Haeckel. Ecologists study **populations** (groups of individual organisms), **communities** (different organisms sharing the same environment), or ECOSYSTEMS (a community and its physical environment). The maximum population that can be sustained by a particular environment's resources is called its **carrying capacity**. The role of a species within its community is termed its **ecological niche**. Within the BIOSPHERE, natural cycles (CARBON CYCLE, HYDROLOGICAL CYCLE, NITROGEN CYCLE, and oxygen cycle) are assisted when the biological diversity of species fill these various ecological niches. This diversity produces **climax communities**, and an extensive climax community is called a BIOME. **Applied ecology** is the practical management and preservation of natural resources and environments.

**econometrics** Branch of ECONOMICS that seeks to explain economic relationships by using mathematical methods and statistical tests. It is widely used in economic forecasting.

**economics** Social science studying the allocation of scarce RESOURCES in the PRODUCTION of commodities, and the distribution of these commodities for consumption in society. Adam Smith's *The Wealth of Nations* (1776) is often cited as the first economic treatise. Smith's arguments in favor of FREE TRADE form the basis of CLASSICAL ECONOMICS. Thomas MALTHUS argued that population would outstrip food supply and lead to famine. David RICARDO's theory of labor value was adopted by Karl MARX. Marx provided a detailed critique of CAPITALISM and a prescription for change. Refinements to classical economics included the theory of marginal utility, which argued that value was determined by need. John Maynard KEYNES produced more fundamental modifications. His *General Theory of Employment, Interest, and Money* (1936) was an attempt to deal with economic DEPRESSION and mass UNEMPLOYMENT. The pressures of INFLATION led to the development of MONETARISM and the reemergence of high unemployment. In recent years, economics has developed into two broad areas: **microeconomics** studies the economics of firms and individuals, and the workings of individual market mechanisms; and **macroeconomics** studies whole economic systems. *See also* DIVISION OF LABOR; FEUDAL SYSTEM; LAISSEZ-FAIRE; MERCANTILISM

**economies of scale** Theory that as a business expands and produces more, its profitability increases due to lower unit costs, higher productivity, better use of plant and machinery, and greater bargaining power. It is often used to support mergers and acquisitions, but there can be diseconomies of scale, such as greater difficulty in monitoring and control, and increased bureaucracy.

**ecosystem** Basic unit in ECOLOGY, consisting of a community of organisms in a physical ENVIRONMENT. Study of these systems is based often on energy flow. The chemicals necessary for life are recycled by the FOOD CHAIN, CARBON CYCLE, HYDROLOGICAL CYCLE, NITROGEN CYCLE, and oxygen cycle. Interference with these natural processes, such as POLLUTION, climate change, or the loss of a species, can disrupt the entire ecosystem.

**ecstasy (MDMA)** (3,4–methylnedioxymethylamphetamine) AMPHETAMINE-based drug, which raises body temperature and blood pressure by inducing the release of epinephrine and targeting the neurotransmitter, SEROTONIN. Users experience short-term feelings of euphoria, rushes of energy, and increased tactility. Withdrawal can involve bouts of depression and insomnia. Some deaths have resulted from using the drug.

**ectopic** Occurrence of a pregnancy outside the UTERUS, such as in the FALLOPIAN TUBE. The EMBRYO cannot develop normally and spontaneous ABORTION often occurs. If not, urgent surgery is necessary to save the mother from serious hemorrhage.

**Ecuador** Republic in NW South America. *See* country feature page 224

**ecumenical council** (general council) Ecclesiastical convention of worldwide church representatives. Pronouncements are considered binding on all church members. All Christians recognize the first seven councils, the last of which was held in NICAEA in 787. Since then, the Roman Catholic Church has recognized 21 convened by popes. Since the REFORMATION, the councils have been restricted to Roman Catholics. The most recent was the Second Vatican Council (1962–65).

**ecumenical movement** Movement to restore the lost unity of Christendom. In its modern sense, the movement began with the Edinburgh Missionary Conference of 1910 and led to the foundation of the WORLD COUNCIL OF CHURCHES in 1948.

**eczema** Inflammatory condition of the skin, a form of DERMATITIS characterized by dryness, itching, rashes, and blister formation. It can be caused by contact with a substance, such as a detergent, or a general ALLERGY. Treatment is usually with a corticosteroid ointment.

**Edda** One of two collections of Old Icelandic literature. The *Poetic Edda* or *Elder Edda* is a collection of 34 mythological and heroic poems written between AD 800 and 1200. It is the most valuable collection of Norse literature. The *Prose Edda* or *Younger Edda* (*c.*1220) by Snorri Sturluson is a guide to early Icelandic poetry, the first half of which deals with TEUTONIC MYTHOLOGY.

**Eddington, Sir Arthur Stanley** (1882–1944) English astronomer and physicist. Eddington pioneered the use of atomic theory to study the internal constitution of stars. Among his discoveries were the mass-luminosity relationship and the degeneration of matter by white dwarfs. Eddington helped pop-

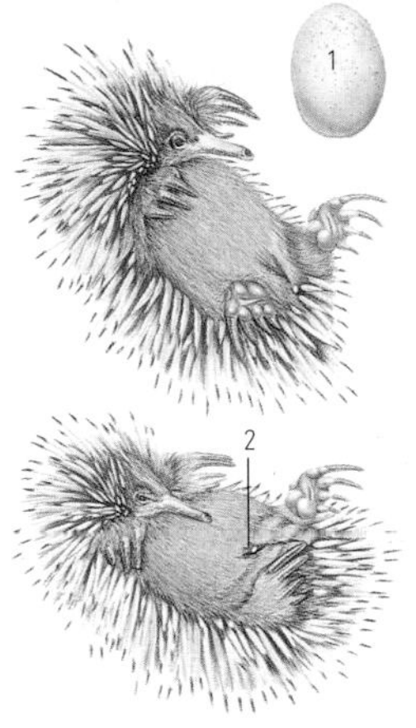


▲ **echidna** An example of a primitive mammal, the echidna (spiny anteater) is classified as a monotreme. Instead of giving birth to live young like other mammals, it lays a tiny egg. The egg (1) is soft-shelled and resembles a reptile's egg. Once the egg is laid, the echidna uses its hind limbs to roll it to a special incubation groove (2). The minute hatchling is about 0.5in (1.25cm) long.

▼ **eclipse** When the Moon passes between the Sun and the Earth it causes a partial eclipse of the Sun (1) if the Earth passes through the Moon's outer shadow (P), or a total eclipse (2) if the inner cone shadow crosses the Earth's surface. In a lunar eclipse, the Earth's shadow crosses the Moon and, again, provides either a partial or total eclipse. Eclipses of the Sun and the Moon do not occur every month because of the 5° difference between the plane of the Moon's orbit and the plane in which the Earth moves.

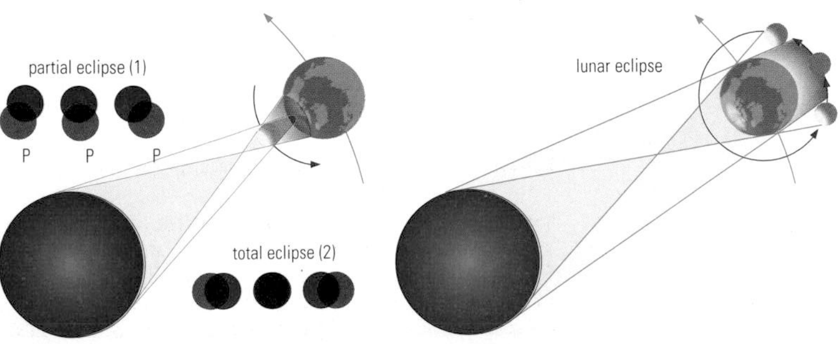

ularize Einstein's theory of RELATIVITY, and in 1919 obtained experimental proof of the general theory that gravity bends light by measuring stars close to the Sun during a solar eclipse.

**Eddy, Mary Baker** (1821–1910) US founder of CHRISTIAN SCIENCE (1879). Her doctrine of healing based on the Bible was expounded in *Science and Health With Key to the Scriptures* (1875). In 1879 Eddy organized the Chuch of Christ, Scientist, and actively directed the movement until her death.

**edelweiss** Small, perennial plant native to the Alps and other high Eurasian mountains. It has white, downy leaves and small yellow flower heads enclosed in whitish-yellow bracts. Family Asteraceae (COMPOSITAE); species *Leontopodium alpinum*.

**edema** Abnormal accumulation of fluid in the tissues; it may be generalized or confined to one part, such as the ankles. It may be due to heart failure, obstruction of veins, or increased permeability of the capillary walls.

**Eden, Sir Anthony, 1st Earl of Avon** (1897–1977) British statesman, prime minister (1955–57). He was Britain's youngest foreign secretary (1935). Eden resigned (1938) in protest at the APPEASEMENT policy of Neville CHAMBERLAIN. He served again as foreign secretary (1940–45, 1951–55), and succeeded Winston CHURCHILL as Conservative prime minister. Ill health and his mishandling of the SUEZ CANAL Crisis forced Eden to resign. He was succeeded by Harold MACMILLAN.

**Eden, Garden of** In GENESIS 2, garden created by God as the home of ADAM and EVE. Adam and Eve lived in the garden and enjoyed its fruits without toil, until they were banished for eating the forbidden fruit from the tree of knowledge. The garden of Eden is also mentioned in the KORAN and is popularly equated with paradise.

**edentate** (Lat. with all the teeth removed) Any of a small order of North and South American mammals found from Kansas to Patagonia. There are *c*.30 species of edentates, including ARMADILLO, SLOTH, and ANTEATER. Only anteaters are truly toothless.

**Ederle, Gertrude Caroline** (1906– ) US swimmer. At the 1924 Olympics she won a gold medal as a member of the US women's relay team and two individual bronze medals. In 1926 Ederle became the first woman to swim the English Channel.

**Edinburgh, Duke of** *See* PHILIP, PRINCE, DUKE OF EDINBURGH

**Edinburgh** Capital of Scotland, in Lothian region. The city grew steadily when Malcolm III made Edinburgh Castle his

## ECUADOR

Ecuador's flag was created by a patriot, Francisco de Miranda, in 1806. The armies of Simón Bolívar, who liberated much of South America, fought under this flag. At the center is Ecuador's coat-of arms, showing a condor over Mount Chimborazo, Ecuador's highest peak at 20,561ft (6,267m).

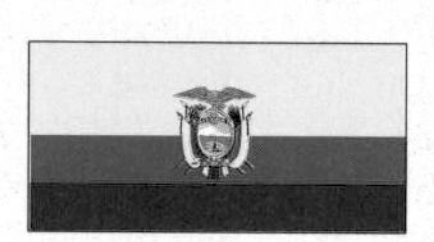

**AREA:** 109,483sq mi (283,560sq km)
**POPULATION:** 10,980,972
**CAPITAL (POPULATION):** Quito (1,100,847)
**GOVERNMENT:** Multiparty republic
**ETHNIC GROUPS:** Mestizo 40%, Native American 40%, White 15%, Black 5%
**LANGUAGES:** Spanish (official)
**RELIGIONS:** Christianity (Roman Catholic 92%)
**CURRENCY:** Sucre = 100 centavos

The Republic of Ecuador straddles the Equator on the W side of South America. Three ranges of the high ANDES Mountains form Ecuador's backbone. The snowcapped Andean peaks include Chimborazo and the world's highest active volcano, Cotopaxi, at 19,344ft (5,896m). Nearly half of Ecuador's population live in the high Andean plateaux.

West of the Andes lie the flat coastal lowlands, including Ecuador's largest city and port, GUAYAQUIL. The E lowlands (Oriente) are drained by headwaters of the River Amazon.

The GALÁPAGOS ISLANDS form a province of Ecuador, in the Pacific Ocean, *c*.650mi (1,050km) off the W coast of Ecuador.

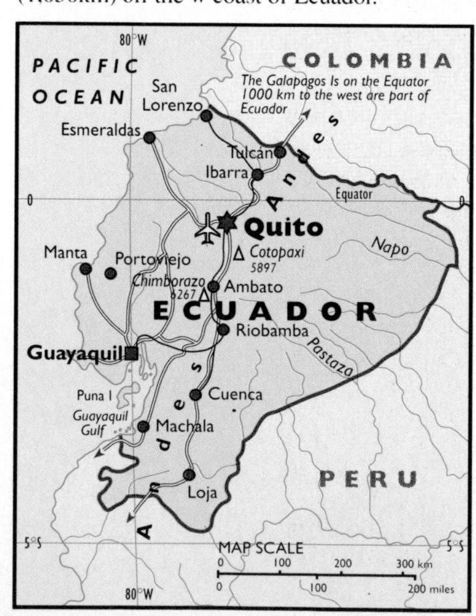


### CLIMATE

Ecuador's climate fluctuates according to height above sea level. Although the coast is cooled by the cold Peruvian current, temperatures remain from 73°F–77°F (23°–25°C) throughout the year. The capital, QUITO, just S of the Equator at 8,200ft (2,500m) above sea level, experiences temperatures of 57°F–59°F (14°C–15°C). Rainfall is low in the SW, but the low-lying Oriente region is hot and wet.

### VEGETATION

The vegetation in the Andes varies from high snowfields to grassy meadows on the lower slopes. The N coastal lowlands contain large tropical forests, with deciduous woodland in the central coastal regions. Palm trees are common, and the fiber from *Carludovica palmata* is used to make Panama hats. Balsa trees grow in the Guayas valley, N of Guayaquil. The S coast, bordering Peru, is desert. Dense rain forest covers the Oriente.

### HISTORY AND POLITICS

The INCA conquered the kingdom of Quito in the late 15th century. They introduced their language, QUECHUA, and this remains widely spoken. In 1532 Spanish forces, under Francisco PIZARRO, defeated the Incas at Cajamarca and established the Spanish viceroyalty of Quito. A revolutionary war, launched in 1809, culminated in the defeat of the Spanish at the battle of Mount Pichincha (1822). Simón Bolívar negotiated the admittance of Quito to the federation of Gran Colombia, along with Colombia and Venezuela. Ecuador seceded in 1830. The 19th century was characterized by wars with Peru, and internal instability, with Conservatives and the Roman Catholic Church attempting to preserve the status quo against the Liberals desire for socio-economic reform. For the first half of the 20th century, the army dominated politics. In the Treaty of Rio (1942), Ecuador was forced to cede over 50% of its Amazonian territory to Peru. Post-1945 politics was dominated by José María Velasco Ibarro. During the 1950s, his authoritarian regime improved Ecuador's infrastructure. In 1970, faced with student riots and economic recession, Velasco established a dictatorship. In 1972 he was deposed by an army coup. Ecuador returned to democracy in 1979. Failure to implement land reforms and lack of recognition for minorities saw continual unrest during the 1980s. Durán Ballen's presidency (1992–96) saw the start of privatization. Austerity measures provoked civil unrest. Ballen was defeated by Abdala Bucaram in 1996 elections. In 1997 Bucaram was declared mentally incompetent and removed from office. The 1998 election was won by Jamil Mahaud.

### ECONOMY

Ecuador is a lower-middle-income developing nation (1995 GDP per capita, US$4,220). Agriculture employs 33% of the workforce. Ecuador is the world's third largest producer of bananas. Cocoa and coffee are also vital crops. Fishing is important, but periodically disrupted by EL NIÑO. Forestry is a vital industry, and mining is increasingly important. The economy was transformed by the discovery (1972) of oil in the Oriente. Energy crises are a recurrent feature.

residence (11th century), and became the capital of Scotland in the early 15th century. It flourished as a cultural center in the 18th and 19th centuries around figures such as David HUME, Adam SMITH, Robert BURNS, and Sir Walter SCOTT. Sites include: Palace of Holyroodhouse (official residence of the monarch in Scotland); Chapel of St. Margaret (part of Edinburgh Castle and the city's oldest building); the Royal Mile (linking the Castle with Holyroodhouse); the 15th-century St. Giles Cathedral; the home of the Protestant reformer John KNOX; and Princes Street. The University of Edinburgh was founded in 1583. Edinburgh has held an international arts festival since 1947. Industries: brewing, tourism, chemicals, printing and publishing. Pop. (1991) 418,914.

**Edirne** (Adrianople) Fortified city at the confluence of the Meric and Tundzha rivers. Rebuilt by the Roman emperor Hadrian (*c.*AD 125) as Adrianopolis, it was the scene of a Roman defeat by the Visigoths in 378. Edirne was capital of Ottoman Turkey from 1361 to 1453. Captured by the Russians (1829, 1879) and the Bulgarians (1913), Edirne was ceded to Greece in 1920. It was returned to Turkey in 1923. It is an agricultural trading center. Industries: textiles, tanning. Pop. (1990) 102,300.

**Edison, Thomas Alva** (1847–1931) US inventor. With little formal education, he became the most prolific inventor of his generation. In 1876 Edison opened a laboratory in Menlo Park, New Jersey. Here, he invented the carbon transmitter for TELEPHONES (1876), and the phonograph or RECORD PLAYER (1877). Using a carbon filament, Edison's invention of the first commercially viable ELECTRIC LIGHT (October 21, 1879) ensured his fame. In New York City, he built (1881–82) the world's first permanent electric power plant for distributing electric light. In 1892 most of his companies were merged into the General Electric Company (GEC). In 1914 Edison developed an experimental talking motion picture. By the time of his death, he had patented more than 1,300 inventions.

**Edmonton** Capital of ALBERTA, on the North Saskatchewan River, Canada. The "Gateway to the North," Edmonton is the northernmost city in North America. Founded as a fur-trading post by the Hudson's Bay Company in 1795, it developed with the arrival of the railroad in 1891 and the Klondike goldrush (1898). It became the capital of Alberta in 1905. The discovery of oil (1947) made Edmonton a major metropolitan area. The city is home to the University of Alberta (1906). Industries: coal mining, natural gas. Pop. (1991) 616,741.

**Edo** *See* TOKYO

**education** Process, either formal or informal, of acquiring knowledge and skills, leading to the development of understanding, attitudes, and values. **Formal** education is organized instruction undertaken by society. In *c.*3000 BC the first SCHOOLS for reading and writing were founded by the Egyptians and Sumerians. Western education is based largely on the ancient Greek model. In c.387 BC Plato founded a school of philosophy, known as the ACADEMY. SOCRATES' and CICERO's works proved highly influential in the development of teaching and LEARNING techniques. In medieval Europe, education was usually undertaken by the church. The establishment of the first modern universities, especially in Paris and Oxford, contributed to the growth of SCHOLASTICISM. The humanist ideals of the Renaissance and the invention of printing saw an expansion in formal education. The ENLIGHTENMENT brought new disciplines and teaching methods. The early 19th century saw the beginnings of state education. In 1841 Friedrich FROEBEL opened the first kindergarten. Elementary education became free and compulsory throughout most of Europe by the early 20th century. Maria MONTESSORI's theories on the importance of creative learning proved highly influential. John DEWEY emphasized the importance of VOCATIONAL EDUCATION. DEVELOPMENTAL PSYCHOLOGY, in particular the work of Jean PIAGET, has informed new educational models.

**Education, US Department of** Federal government department, formed from part of the Department of Health, Education and Welfare (HEW). It was created in 1979 and consolidated 170 educational programs from various agencies. The department establishes policy, and coordinates federal assistance to EDUCATION.

**educational psychology** Branch of PSYCHOLOGY that deals with the process and context of learning. It includes measurement of intelligence and ability.

**Edward I** (1239–1307) King of England (1272–1307), son and successor of HENRY III. His suppression of the baronial revolt (1263–65), led by Simon de Montfort, made him king in all but name. Edward joined the Ninth CRUSADE (1270), and was crowned on his return (1274). He conquered Wales and incorporated it into England (1272–84). In 1296 Edward captured the Scottish coronation stone from Scone. His reforms are central to Britain's legal and constitutional history. The Statutes of WESTMINSTER codified common law. Edward's foreign ambitions led to the formation of the MODEL PARLIAMENT (1295). His son, EDWARD II, inherited high taxation and the enmity of Scotland.

**Edward II** (1284–1327) King of England (1307–27), son and successor of EDWARD I. His reliance on his friend and advisor, Piers Gaveston, alienated his barons. In 1312 they killed Gaveston. Renewing his father's campaign against the Scots, Edward was routed at BANNOCKBURN (1314). In 1325, his estranged queen, Isabella, went as envoy to France. In 1326, she formed an army with her lover, Roger Mortimer, which invaded England and forced Edward to abdicate in favor of his son, EDWARD III. Edward II was murdered.

**Edward III** (1312–77) King of England (1327–77), son and successor of EDWARD II. For the first three years of his reign, his mother, Isabella, and Roger Mortimer wielded political power. In 1330 Edward mounted a successful coup. His reign was dominated by the outbreak of the HUNDRED YEARS WAR (1337). Edward led several campaigns to France, won victory at CRÉCY (1346), and claimed to be king of France, although only conquering Calais. PARLIAMENT was divided into two houses, and permanently sited at Westminster. In his old age, his sons, EDWARD THE BLACK PRINCE and JOHN OF GAUNT, took over government. He was succeeded by his grandson, RICHARD II.

**Edward IV** (1442–83) King of England (1461–70, 1471–83). On the death (1460) of his father, Richard, Duke of York, in the Wars of the ROSES, Edward became the Yorkist candidate for the throne. He became king after the defeat of the Lancastrians at Towton. When the powerful Earl of WARWICK changed sides, Edward was forced into exile, but returned to defeat Warwick at Barnet (1471). He encouraged trade, restored order and enforced royal absolutism. Edward died leaving two young sons, "the Princes in the Tower," but the throne was usurped by his brother, RICHARD III.

**Edward V** (1470–83) King of England for 77 days in 1483. He succeeded his father, EDWARD IV (1483). His uncle, duke of Gloucester, placed Edward and his younger brother, Richard, in the Tower of London, taking the throne for himself as RICHARD III. The disappearance of "the Princes in the Tower" was attributed to Richard although some suspect HENRY VII.

**Edward VI** (1537–53) King of England (1547–53), only legitimate son of HENRY VIII. He reigned under two regents, the dukes of Somerset (1547–49) and Northumberland (1549–53). Clever, but frail, Edward died after willing the crown to Northumberland's daughter-in-law, Lady Jane GREY, to exclude his Catholic sister, MARY I.

**Edward VII** (1841–1910) King of Great Britain and Ireland (1901–10), son of Queen VICTORIA. As Prince of Wales, his views and lifestyle led to his exclusion from government by his mother. As king, he restored court pageantry and contributed to the ENTENTE CORDIALE with France. He was succeeded by his son, GEORGE V.

**Edward VIII** (1894–1972) King of Great Britain and Ireland (1936), subsequently Duke of Windsor. Edward's proposed marriage to an American divorcee, Wallis Simpson, was opposed by Stanley BALDWIN's government. Edward refused to back down, and was forced to abdicate after a 325-day reign.

**Edwards, Jonathan** (1703–58) US revivalist minister and theologian. A powerful preacher in Northampton, Massachusetts (1729–50), he gained a wide following. With his Calvinist themes of PREDESTINATION and man's dependence on God, Edwards brought about the GREAT AWAKENING.

**Edward the Black Prince** (1330–76) Son and heir of EDWARD III of England. He distinguished himself at the Battle

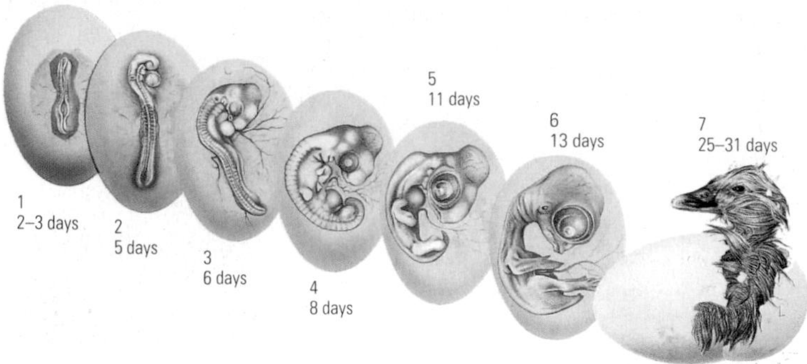


▲ **egg** A duck embryo grows from a patch of cells on the surface of the egg yolk. The yolk is its food store. First, a network of tiny blood vessels spreads over the yolk and a simple heart develops. The developing embryo (enlarged here for clarity) begins to elongate and develops a vertebral column (1). A head and bulging eye start to form, and the heart folds around into its final position (2). The gut forms, the brain begins to enlarge and the embryo starts to curl (3–4). The limbs appear as tiny buds; and the tail and mouth form (5). By 13 days (6) it is possible to identify the bird from its bill. Some species of bird hatch shortly after this stage, others, such as the mallard duck (7) continue to develop in the egg. Feathers grow, limbs become stronger and the bird hatches with its eyes open and able to see.

Rebus pectoral
Signet ring
Shell pendant
Bezel ring
Faience collar

▲ **Egyptian art and architecture** Examples of the work of ancient Egyptian jewelers survive as evidence of their craftsmanship. Gold was the major material, and silver and the alloy electrum were also used. Semi-precious stones, such as carnelians, turquoise and lapiz lazuli were also used.

of Crécy (1346) and captured the French king at Poitiers (1356). As ruler (1362–71) of Aquitaine, Edward was responsible for the massacre at Limoges (1371). He insured the accession of his son as Richard II.

**Edward the Confessor** (1002–66) King of England (1042–66), son of Ethelred II (the Unready). Before succeeding Hardecanute, Edward was resident in Normandy. His perceived favoritism towards Normans resulted in a rebellion, led by his father-in-law, Godwin. Edward's reign is noted for the rebuilding of Westminster Abbey. His name resulted from his piety and, having taken a vow of chastity, he produced no heir. Though said to have promised the throne to William I (the Conqueror), Edward acknowledged Harold I as his rightful heir.

**Edward the Elder** (d.925) King of Wessex (899–925), son and successor to Alfred the Great. Edward completed the reconquest of the s Danelaw (918), and was considered overlord by the rulers of Northumbria and Wales (920).

**Edward the Martyr** (d.978) King of England (975–78). He was murdered, perhaps by his stepmother, and succeeded by his step-brother Ethelred II (the Unready). Miracles were reported at his grave, and he was popularly regarded as a saint.

**eel** Marine and freshwater fish found worldwide in shallow temperate and tropical waters. Eels have snake-like bodies, dorsal and anal fins, and an air bladder at the throat. Length: up to 10ft (3m). Types include freshwater, moray and conger. Order Anguilliformes.

**eelworm** Tiny, thread-like nematode found worldwide in soil, fresh and saltwater. Most species are parasitic, and can cause extensive damage to crops. They have been used to control other pests. *See* Roundworm

**efficiency** Work a machine does (output) divided by the work put in (input) It is usually expressed as a percentage. In mechanical systems there are energy losses, such as those caused by friction. Output never equals input, and the efficiency is always less than 100%.

**egg** (ovum) Reproductive cell of female organisms. Its nucleus supplies half the chromosome complement of a future zygote, and almost all the cytoplasm, upon union with the male gamete (sperm). Once fertilized, an animal egg is surrounded by albumin, shell, egg case, or membrane, depending on the species. The egg provides a reserve of food for the embryo in the form of yolk.

**eggplant** (aubergine) Shrublike plant of the nightshade family, native to Africa and India. The leaves are large and the 2in (5.1cm) -wide violet flowers produce a berry fruit ranging from a small egg-shape to a large pear-shape. Height: 2-3ft (61-92cm). Species: cultivated *Solanum melongena*; wild *S. incanum*.

**ego** Self or "I" which the individual consciously experiences. According to Sigmund Freud, it is the conscious level of personality that deals with the external world, and also mediates the internal demands made by the impulses of the id and the prohibitions of the superego.

**egret** White heron of temperate and tropical marshy regions. It is known for its plumes. Egrets are long-legged, long-necked, slender-bodied wading birds with dagger-like bills. They feed on small animals and nest in colonies. Height: 20–40in (50–100cm). Family Ardeidae; genus *Egretta*.

**Egypt** Country in NE Africa. *See* country feature

**Egypt, ancient** Civilization that flourished along the Nile River in NW Africa from *c*.3400 BC–30 BC. The dynasties are numbered from 1 to 30, and the kingdoms of Upper and Lower Egypt were united *c*.3100 BC by the legendary Menes. Ancient Egyptian history is separated into a number of periods. The highlight of the **Old Kingdom** was the building of the Pyramids of Giza during the 4th dynasty. After the death of Pepy II in the 6th dynasty, central government disintegrated. This was the **First Intermediate Period**. Central authority was restored in the 11th dynasty and the capital was moved to Thebes (now Luxor). The **Middle Kingdom** (*c*.2040–1640 BC) saw Egypt develop into a great power. Amenemhet I, founder of the 12th dynasty (*c*.1991 BC), secured Egypt's borders and created a new capital. Art, architecture, and literature flourished. At the end of this Kingdom, Egypt again fell into disarray (**Second Intermediate Period**) and control was seized by the Hyksos. The **New Kingdom** began *c*.1550 BC and brought great wealth. Massive temples and tombs, such as Tutankhamun's, were built. Wars with the Hittites under Ramses II weakened Egypt and subsequent ineffectual rulers led to the decline of the New Kingdom. The 21st to 25th dynasties (**Third Intermediate Period**) culminated in Assyrian domination. The Persians ruled from 525 until 404 BC, when the last native dynasties appeared. In 332 BC, Egypt fell to the armies of Alexander the Great, who moved the capital to Alexandria. After Alexander's death, his general became ruler of Egypt, as Ptolemy I. The Ptolemies maintained a powerful empire for three centuries, and Alexandria became a centre of learning. Roman power was on the ascendancy, and when Ptolemy XII asked Pompey for aid in 58 BC, it marked the end of Egyptian independence. Cleopatra tried to assert independence through associations with Julius Caesar and Mark Antony, but she was defeated at Actium. Her son, Ptolemy XV (whose father was probably Julius Caesar), was the last Ptolemy; he was killed by Octavian (Augustus), and Egypt became a province of Rome.

**Egyptian architecture** Architecture developed since 3000 BC and characterized by post and lintel construction, massive walls covered with hieroglyphic and pictorial carving, flat roofs, and structures such as the mastaba, obelisk, pylon, and Pyramid. Perhaps the great architect of the ancient period was Imhotep.

**Egyptian art** (2686–2181 BC) Works were chiefly relief sculpture and painting, characterized by front and side views of the human figure, flat color tones, symmetry in sculpture, and static figures. Relief-decorated private tombs and temples portrayed daily life.

**Egyptian mythology** Ancient Egyptians worshipped many deities that represented every aspect of nature and human activity. Early tribal deities took the form of totemic animals that gradually acquired human characteristics. The sun-god Ra emerged out of primeval chaos to create the air, and father the sky-goddess Nut and the Earth-god Geb. Ra was the chief deity. His symbol, the pyramid, became the design for the tombs of ancient Egypt's rulers. The pharaohs administered the will of the gods and built huge temples in their honor at Luxor. Nut and Geb gave birth to Osiris. Osiris was both protector of nature and judge of the dead. He was murdered by his brother, Seth, but restored to life by his sister and wife, the mother goddess Isis. Their son, Horus, represented the triumph of good over evil. By the XIX dynasty, Ra had become united with the god Amon. Akhnaten asserted the supremacy of the god Aten. The ancient Egyptians believed in reincarnation, and the Book of the Dead outlines the precautions needed to ensure immortality *See also* Hathor; mummy; Thoth

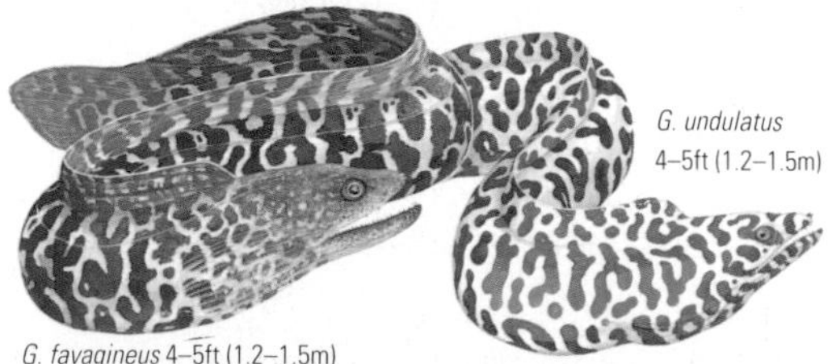


▲ **eel** Moray eels (*Gymnothorax undulatus* and *G. favagineus*) are found in all tropical seas. They can inflict severe bites if disturbed.

**Egyptology** Study of ancient EGYPT, its people and its antiquities. Important landmarks in Egyptology include the discovery of the ROSETTA STONE, the temple of AMON, and the tomb of TUTANKHAMEN at LUXOR, and the moving of the temples at ABU SIMBEL.

**Ehrlich, Paul** (1854–1915) German bacteriologist. He shared with Ilya Metchnikoff the 1908 Nobel Prize for physiology or medicine for his work on immunization. Ehrlich's search for a "magic bullet" against disease, and his discovery of salvarsan, a chemical effective against syphilis microorganisms, introduced CHEMOTHERAPY.

**eider** Large sea DUCK found in N Europe and North America. Its down is used to fill pillows and comforters. When breeding, the male grows striking black and white plumage. Family Anatidae; genus *Somateria*.

**Eiffel Tower** Landmark built for the Paris *Exposition* of 1889. Designed by Alexandre Gustave Eiffel, the iron-framed tower rises 984ft (300m). Elevators and stairs lead to observation platforms.

**Einstein, Albert** (1879–1955) US physicist, b. Germany, best known for his theories of RELATIVITY. In 1905 Einstein published four papers that revolutionized physical science. "The Electrodynamics of Moving Bodies" announced his special theory of relativity. Drawing on the work of H.A. LORENTZ, Einstein discarded the notion of absolute motion in favor of the hypothesis that the speed of light is constant for all observers in uniform (unaccelerated) motion. Measurements in one uniformly moving system can be correlated with measurements in another uniform system, if their **relative** velocity is known. It asserted that the speed of light was the maximum velocity attainable in the Universe. A corollary of this special theory – the equivalence of MASS and ENERGY ($E = mc^2$) – was put forward in a second paper. A third paper, on BROWNIAN MOVEMENT, confimed the atomic theory of MATTER. Lastly, Einstein explained the PHOTOELECTRIC EFFECT in terms of quanta or photons of light. For this insight, which forms the basis of modern QUANTUM THEORY, Einstein received the 1921 Nobel Prize for physics. In 1911 he asserted the equivalence of GRAVITATION and INERTIA. Einstein extended his special theory into a general theory of relativity (1916) that incorporated systems in non-uniform (accelerated) motion. He asserted that matter in space causes curvature in the space-time continuum, resulting in gravitational fields. This explained the peculiar motion of the planet Mercury and was confirmed (1919) by EDDINGTON's

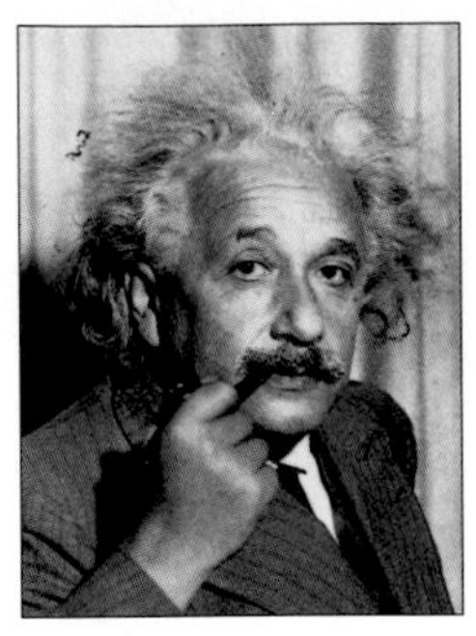

▲ **Einstein** One of the greatest physicists of all time, Albert Einstein was forced to flee Nazi Germany in 1933, moving to the US and working at Princeton University. He formulated the special theory of relativity and advanced quantum theory (1905).



## EGYPT

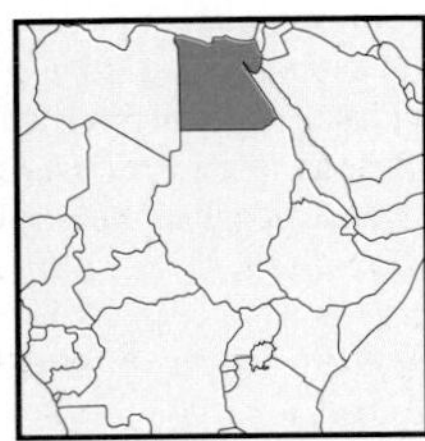

A flag consisting of three bands of red, white, and black, the colors of the Pan-Arab movement, was adopted in 1958. The design includes a gold eagle in the center: symbolizing Saladin, the warrior who led the Arabs in the 12th century.

**AREA:** 386,660 sq mi (1,001,450sq km)
**POPULATION:** 55,163,000
**CAPITAL (POPULATION):** Cairo (6,663,000)
**GOVERNMENT:** Republic
**ETHNIC GROUPS:** Egyptian 99%
**LANGUAGES:** Arabic (official), French, English
**RELIGIONS:** Islam (Sunni Muslim 94%), Christianity (mainly Coptic Christian 6%)
**CURRENCY:** Pound = 100 piastres

The Arab Republic of Egypt is Africa's second most populous country (after Nigeria), and its capital, CAIRO, is Africa's largest city. Most of Egypt is desert, and almost all the people live either in the NILE valley and its fertile delta, or along the SUEZ CANAL, a vital artificial waterway between the Mediterranean and Red seas. The region N of Cairo is often called Lower Egypt and S of Cairo, Upper Egypt. On the Sudanese border, S of the ASWAN High Dam, lies Lake Nasser.

Egypt has three other, largely uninhabited, regions: the Western and Eastern deserts (parts of the SAHARA), and the SINAI PENINSULA, which contains Egypt's highest peak, Gebel Katherina, at 8,650ft (2,637m).

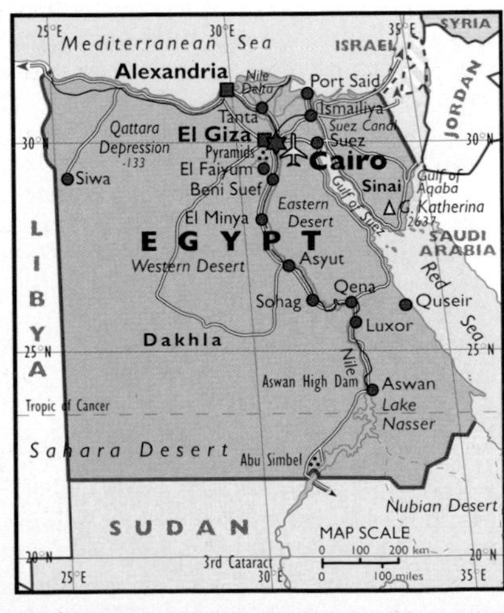


### CLIMATE

Egypt is a dry country, and sparse rainfall occurs in winter. It has mild winters and hot summers. Hot, dusty, desert winds blow into the Nile valley.

### VEGETATION

The Nile valley forms a long, green ribbon of fertile farmland. Dry landscape covers 90% of Egypt; the Western Desert alone covers *c*.75%.

### HISTORY

The Egyptian state was formed (*c*.3100 BC). The Old Kingdom marked the building of the PYRAMIDS at GIZA. The ruins of the Middle Kingdom's capital at LUXOR bear testament to Egypt's imperial power. In 332 BC it was conquered by Alexander the Great, and the capital moved to ALEXANDRIA. After CLEOPATRA, the Roman empire was dominant. *See* EGYPT, ANCIENT

In AD 642, Egypt was conquered by the UMAYYAD dynasty, then the ABBASIDS. ARABIC became the official language. Under the FATIMIDS, Cairo became a center of SHIITE culture. SALADIN's rule (1169–93) is notable for his defeat of the CRUSADES. His dynasty was overthrown (1250) by MAMELUKE soldier slaves. In 1517 Egypt was conquered by the OTTOMANS.

Egypt was occupied (1798–1801) by Napoleon I. France was expelled by MUHAMMAD ALI, who established the modern Egyptian state. The construction of the Suez Canal (1867) encouraged British imperial ambitions. Britain subdued Cairo (1882) and maintained a military presence even after Egypt became an independent monarchy under FUAD I. (1922). Fuad was succeeded by FAROUK (1936–52). The creation of ISRAEL (1948) saw the involvement of Egypt in the first of the ARAB-ISRAELI WARS. In 1953 the monarchy fell. NASSER emerged to head (1954–70) the new republic. Nasser's nationalization of the Suez Canal (1956) was briefly contested by Israel, Britain and France. In 1958 Egypt, Syria and Yemen formed the short-lived United Arab Republic. Nasser promoted Egypt as leader of the Arab world. Egypt was defeated by Israel in the SIX DAY WAR (1967). Nasser was succeeded by SADAT, who ended Egypt's dependence on Soviet aid. The Yom Kippur War (1973) marked another Egyptian defeat. Sadat signed the Camp David Agreement (1979) with Israel, and Israel withdrew from Sinai (1982). Egypt was expelled from the Arab League, and Sadat assassinated by Islamic extremists. Hosni MUBARAK (1981– ) assumed control. A state of emergency has been in force since 1981. Mubarak led Egypt back into the Arab League (1989) and improved relations with the West. In 1992 Muslim fundamentalists re-launched an armed struggle. Terrorist attacks included the massacre of 58 tourists in Luxor (1997), damaging the vital tourist industry.

### ECONOMY

Egypt is Africa's second most industrialized country (after South Africa), but it remains a poor developing country (1995 GDP per capita, US$3,820). Farming employs 34% of the workforce. Most peasants grow staple crops. The main cash crop is cotton and textiles are the second most valuable export after oil.

## ELECTRICITY SOURCES

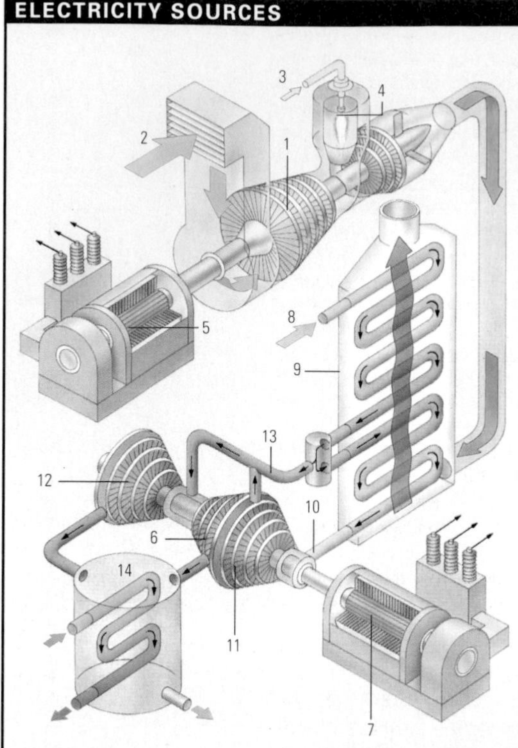


A combined cycle power station burns gas to generate electricity. It is considerably more efficient than traditional fossil fuel power plants. The first turbine (1) sucks in air (2) compressing it before mixing it with the fuel (3) and burning the mixture (4). Exhaust gases spin a second turbine, connected to the first turbine and a generator (5). The energy of the gases is harnessed to power a second multiple turbine (6) connected to another generator (7). Gases are used to superheat water (8) looping through a special vessel (9). To maximize power generation, superheated steam (10) turns a high-pressure turbine (11) before passing (at a slightly lower temperature) into a lower-pressure turbine (12) .Steam is fed into the turbine directly from the heating loops (13), and is cooled (14) before going back into the circuit.

study of starlight. Fearful of the rise of Nazism, Einstein accepted a post (1933–55) at the Institute of Advanced Study, Princeton, New Jersey. In 1940 he became a US citizen. Einstein devoted the rest of his career to a UNIFIED FIELD THEORY.

**einsteinium** Radioactive, synthetic metallic element (symbol Es) of the ACTINIDE SERIES. The isotope, $^{253}$Es, was first identified in 1952 at the University of California at Berkeley. Eleven isotopes have been identified. Properties: at.no. 99; most stable isotope $^{254}$Es (half-life 276 days). *See also* TRANSURANIC ELEMENTS

**Eisenhower, Dwight David ("Ike")** (1890–1969) 34th US president (1953–61). Supreme commander of the Allied Expeditionary Force from 1943, Eisenhower was largely responsible for the integration of Allied forces in the liberation of Europe. In 1950 he became Supreme Allied Commander (Europe) and helped establish the NORTH ATLANTIC TREATY ORGANIZATION (NATO). In 1952 he gained the Republican nomination and secured an easy victory over Adlai STEVENSON in the election. He enforced a prompt end to the KOREAN WAR and, with John Foster DULLES, established an anti-communist foreign policy. Eisenhower was resoundingly re-elected in 1956. In 1957 he ordered Federal troops into Little Rock, Arkansas, to end segregation in schools. His second term was dominated by the COLD WAR. He was succeeded by John F. KENNEDY.

**Eisenstein, Sergei** (1898–1948) Soviet film director. Although he completed just six films in 25 years, he is one of the most influential artists in the history of CINEMA. Eisenstein developed the use of creative editing for narrative and expressive effect. His films include *The Battleship Potemkin* (1925), and *October/Ten Days That Shook the World* (1928). *See also* MONTAGE

**El Alamein** Village in N Egypt. In October 1942 the British 8th Army (under General MONTGOMERY) successfully attacked Axis forces here, and eventually drove them back to Tunisia. The battle was a turning point in the North Africa campaign of World War II.

**Elam** Ancient country of MESOPOTAMIA; the capital was Susa. Elamite civilization became dominant *c.*2000 BC, with the capture of BABYLON. It flourished until the Muslim conquest in the 7th century. Susa was an important center under the ACHAEMENID kings of Persia and the palace of DARIUS I: archaeological finds include the stele of HAMMURABI, inscribed with his code of law.

▲ **elder** Native to Europe, the elder (family Caprifoliaceae) grows to a height of 40ft (12m). In early summer the tree bears clusters of white flowers. The species shown here is *Sambucus nigra*.

**eland** Largest living ANTELOPE, native to central and S Africa. Gregarious and slow-moving, elands have heavy, spiral horns. Height: up to 5.8ft (1.8m) at the shoulder; weight: up to 2,000lb (900kg). Family Bovidae.

**elasticity** Capability of a material to recover its size and shape after deformation by STRESS and strain. When an external force is applied, a material develops stress, which results in strain (a change in dimensions). *See also* HOOKE'S LAW

**Elat** (Eilat) Seaport in S Israel on the Gulf of AQABA. A holiday resort, it is also the site of an oil pipeline terminal. Its location close to the SINAI PENINSULA and its harbor make it a vital gateway for Israel's trade with Africa. Industries: fishing, tourism. Pop. (1990 est.) 26,000.

**Elba** Italian island in the Tyrrhenian Sea; largest of the Tuscan Archipelago; the chief port and town is Portoferraio. Napoleon I was exiled here (1814–15). Industries: fisheries, wine, tourism. Area: 86sq mi (223sq km). Pop. (1984 est.) 28,907.

**Elbe** River in central Europe. It rises as the Labe on the S slopes of the Riesengebirge in the Czech Republic, flows N and NW through Germany, and enters the North Sea at Cuxhaven. Length: 725mi (1 167km).

**Elbert, Mount** Mountain in the Sawatch Range of the Rocky Mountain system, central Colorado. It is the highest peak in the ROCKY MOUNTAINS, at 14,433ft (4,402m).

**Elbrus, Mount** (Gora El'Brus) Two peaks in S European Russia, in the Caucasus range, on the border with Georgia. Extinct volcanoes, the W peak, rising to 18,481ft (5,633m), is the highest in Europe.

**elder** Shrub or small tree found in temperate and subtropical areas. It has divided leaves and clusters of small white flowers. Its small, shiny black berries are used for making wine, jelly, and in medicine. There are 40 species. Family Caprifoliaceae, genus *Sambucus*.

**El Dorado** (Sp. The Golden One) Mythical city of fabulous wealth, supposedly in South America, the focus of many Spanish expeditions in the 16th century.

**election** Process of choosing candidates for office. In the modern world, elections have been inseparable from the rise of DEMOCRACY. In most countries, age and residency qualifications govern a person's eligibility to vote; candidates must also meet certain requirements. In the US, congressional elections are held every two years and presidential elections every four years. The first elections to PARLIAMENT in England were held in the 13th century. In the 19th century various reform acts widened the FRANCHISE and a secret BALLOT was introduced in 1872. Under the US CONSTITUTION, elections to the House of REPRESENTATIVES are **direct** or popular, whereas the elections of the SENATE, President and Vice President are **indirect**. Senators are selected by state legislatures, and the President and Vice President through an ELECTORAL COLLEGE of electors chosen by the public. *See also* PRIMARY; PROPORTIONAL REPRESENTATION

**electoral college** Body, elected by voters in the states, which casts the votes to elect the president and vice president. The number of electors from each state equals the number of its representatives in both houses of Congress. State committees or conventions of each political party select candidates for electors. In the ELECTION, the candidate who wins a plurality of a state's popular vote usually receives all the state's electoral vote. Thus, a candidate may be elected to the presidency without a majority of the popular vote.

**Electra** Daughter of AGAMEMNON, leader of the Greeks in the Trojan war. She helped her brother Orestes avenge their father's murder by plotting to kill their mother CLYTEMNESTRA and stepfather Aegisthus.

**Electra complex** *See* OEDIPUS COMPLEX

**electric charge** Quantity of ELECTRICITY. Electric charges (measured in coulombs) are either positive or negative. They can be stored on insulated metal spheres (VAN DE GRAAFF GENERATOR), insulated plates (CAPACITOR) or in chemical solutions (electric BATTERY).

**electric current** Movement of electric charges, usually the flow of ELECTRONS along a CONDUCTOR or the movement of ions through an ELECTROLYTE. Current (symbol $I$) flows from a positive to a negative terminal, although electrons actually flow along a wire in the opposite direction. It is measured in

AMPERES. Direct current (DC) flows continuously in one direction, whereas alternating current (AC) regularly reverses direction. The frequency of AC current is measured in HERTZ (Hz). *See also* ELECTRICITY

**electric field** (electrostatic field) Region around an ELECTRIC CHARGE in which any charged particle experiences a force. The strength of the field (E) upon unit charge at a distance $r$ from a charge $Q$ is equal to $Q/4\pi r^2 E$, where E is the permittivity (degree to which molecules polarize). *See also* ELECTROMAGNETISM

**electric furnace** FURNACE heated to a very high temperature by an ELECTRIC CURRENT. Electric furnaces are used in industry for melting metals and other materials.

**electricity** Form of energy associated with static or moving charges. Charge has two forms – positive and negative. Like charges repel, and unlike attract, as described by Charles COULOMB in Coulomb's law. ELECTRIC CHARGES are acted upon by forces when they move in a MAGNETIC FIELD; this movement generates an opposing magnetic field (FARADAY'S LAWS). Electricity and MAGNETISM are different aspects of ELECTROMAGNETISM. The flow of charges constitutes a current, which in a CONDUCTOR consists of negatively charged ELECTRONS. For an ELECTRIC CURRENT to exist in a conductor there must be an ELECTROMOTIVE FORCE (EMF) or POTENTIAL DIFFERENCE between the ends of the conductor. If the source of potential difference is a BATTERY, the current flows in one direction as a direct current (DC). If the source is the power supply, the current reverses direction twice every cycle, as alternating current (AC). The AMPERE is the unit of current, the coulomb is the unit of charge, the OHM the unit of RESISTANCE and the VOLT is the unit of ELECTROMOTIVE FORCE. OHM'S LAW and the laws of KIRCHHOFF are the basic means of calculating circuit values.

**electricity sources** Devices that convert other forms of energy into ELECTRICITY. Most of the world's electricity is produced in power stations from the chemical energy of fossil fuels. The heat from burning coal, oil, or natural gas turns water into steam. The steam drives a TURBINE, linked to an electricity GENERATOR. In a nuclear power station, heat comes from the FISSION of nuclei in a NUCLEAR REACTOR. A BATTERY and fuel cell converts chemical energy directly into electricity. SOLAR CELLS convert SOLAR ENERGY into electricity. Wind generators and water turbines produce electricity from the energy of movement in wind and water. *See also* ENERGY SOURCES; HYDROELECTRICITY; RENEWABLE ENERGY

**ELECTRIC MOTOR**

Electric motors work using the interaction of a magnet (1) and a wire with a current passing through it (2). With the current flowing, the magnetic field produced by the loop interacts with the field of the magnet. A downward force acts on the right side, an upward force on the left side. When the loop reaches the vertical the split ring (through which the current reaches the loop) (3) reverses the current and so the magnetic field. Electric motors use multiple coils (4) to ensure constant power. In an electric drill, the turning shaft (5) emerges from the magnetic coils and is then geared (6) through to a chuck (7) to the drill bit (8).

**electric motor** Machine that converts electrical energy into mechanical energy. In a simple form of electric motor, an ELECTRIC CURRENT powers a set of ELECTROMAGNETS on a rotor in the MAGNETIC FIELD of a permanent MAGNET. Magnetic forces set up between the permanent magnet and the electromagnet cause the rotor to turn. Electric motors may use alternating current (AC) or direct current (DC).

**electrocardiogram (ECG)** Recording of the electrical activity of the heart traced on a moving strip of paper by an electrocardiograph. It is used to diagnose heart disease.

**electrochemistry** Branch of chemistry concerned with the relationship between ELECTRICITY and chemical changes. It includes the properties of IONS in solution, the CONDUCTIVITY of ELECTROLYTES, and the study of the processes in electrochemical cells and in ELECTROLYSIS.

**electroconvulsive therapy (ECT)** Controversial treatment of mental disturbance by an electric current passed via ELECTRODES to one or both sides of the brain to induce convulsions. Given under anesthesia, it is mainly for severe depression which has failed to respond to other forms of treatment. It can produce unpleasant side effects, such as confusion, memory loss, and headache.

**electrocution** Death caused by the passage of an ELECTRIC CURRENT through the body. The current may come from a low- or (more often) a high-voltage source or from lightning. A major shock either causes chaotic disruption of the heartbeat (fibrillation) or stops the heart completely. Severe burns may be visible where the current has entered the body and also at its point of exit.

**electrode** Conductor, usually a wire or rod, through which an ELECTRIC CURRENT flows into or leaves a medium. In ELECTROLYSIS, two electrodes – a positive (ANODE) and a negative (CATHODE) – are immersed in an ELECTROLYTE.

**electroencephalogram (EEG)** Recording of electrical activity of the brain. Electrodes are attached to the scalp to pick up the tiny oscillating currents produced by brain activity. Electroencephalography is used mainly in the diagnosis and monitoring of EPILEPSY.

**electrolysis** Chemical reaction caused by passing a direct current (DC) through an ELECTROLYTE. This results in positive IONS migrating to the negative ELECTRODE (CATHODE) and negative ions migrating to the positive electrode (ANODE). Electrolysis is an important method of obtaining chemicals. *See* ELECTROPLATING

**electrolyte** Solution or molten salt that can conduct ELECTRICITY, as in ELECTROLYSIS. In electrolytes, current is carried by IONS, rather than by ELECTRONS.

**electromagnet** Magnet constructed from a soft iron core around which is wound a coil of wire. A MAGNETIC FIELD is set up when an ELECTRIC CURRENT is passed through the wire.

**electromagnetic force** One of the four FUNDAMENTAL FORCES in nature. Within an atom, the electromagnetic force binds the negatively charged electrons to the positively charged nucleus. *See also* GRAND UNIFIED THEORY (GUT); UNIFIED FIELD THEORY

**electromagnetic induction** Use of MAGNETISM to produce an ELECTROMOTIVE FORCE (EMF). If a bar magnet is pushed through a wire coil, an ELECTRIC CURRENT is induced in the coil when the magnet is moving. An electric current is also induced in the coil if it is rotated around the magnet, as in a DYNAMO, ELECTRIC MOTOR, or transformer. *See also* INDUCTANCE; INDUCTION

**electromagnetic radiation** Energy in the form of waves. It travels through empty space at the speed of light, *c.*186,000mi (300,000km) per second. In general, electromagnetic waves are set up by electrical and magnetic vibrations that occur universally in ATOMS. These waves, which make up the **electromagnetic spectrum**, range from low-frequency radio waves, through the visible spectrum to very high-frequency gamma rays. They can undergo REFLECTION, REFRACTION, INTERFERENCE, DIFFRACTION, and polarization.

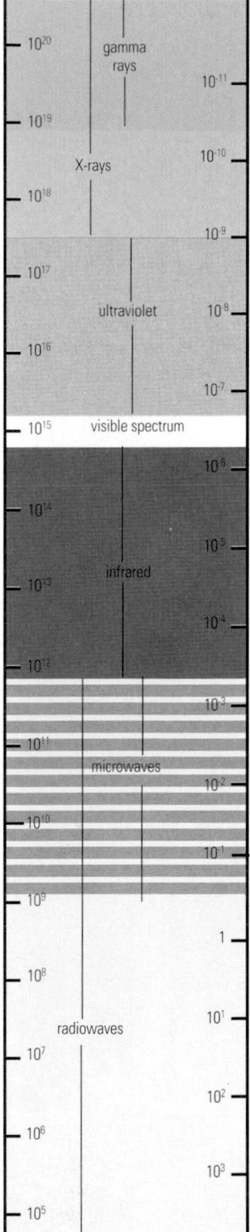


▲ **electromagnetic radiation** can be ordered by either frequency or wavelength, to make up the **electromagnetic spectrum** shown here. It ranges from low-frequency (high-wavelength) radio waves, through microwaves, infrared waves, light (the visible spectrum – red, orange, yellow, green, blue, indigo, and violet), continuing with ultraviolet waves and X-rays, to very high-frequency (short wavelength) gamma rays.

**electromagnetic series** (electrochemical series) List of METALS and the gas hydrogen, whose order indicates their relative tendency to be oxidized, or to lose electrons in chemical reactions (*see* OXIDATION-REDUCTION). The series starts with the metal that tends to lose the most electrons in reaction. Those that lose electrons more readily than hydrogen are termed **electropositive**; those that lose electrons less readily are called **electronegative**. The order of some common metals is: potassium, aluminum, zinc, iron, cobalt, nickel, tin, lead, hydrogen, copper, mercury, silver, and gold.

**electromagnetism** Branch of physics dealing with the laws and phenomena that involve the interaction or interdependence of ELECTRICITY and MAGNETISM. The region in which the effect of an electromagnetic system can be detected is known as an **electromagnetic field**. When a magnetic field changes, an electric field can always be detected. When an electric field varies, a magnetic field can always be detected.

**electromotive force (emf)** Potential difference between the terminals in a source of ELECTRIC CURRENT, measured in volts. It is equal to the energy liberated when this voltage drives the current round an electric circuit. *See also* ELECTRICITY

**electron** (symbol *e*) Stable ELEMENTARY PARTICLE with a negative charge and a rest mass of $9.1 \times 10^{-31}$ kg. First identified (1879) by J.J. THOMSON, electrons are constituents of matter, moving around the nucleus of an atom in complex orbits. In a neutral atom, the electrons' total negative charge balances the positive charge of the PROTONS in the nucleus. Removal or addition of an atomic electron produces a charged ION. When not bound to an atom, electrons are responsible for electrical conduction. Beams of electrons are used in electronic devices, such as television tubes, OSCILLOSCOPES, and ELECTRON MICROSCOPES. An electron is classified as a LEPTON. Its antiparticle is the POSITRON.

## ELECTRON MICROSCOPE

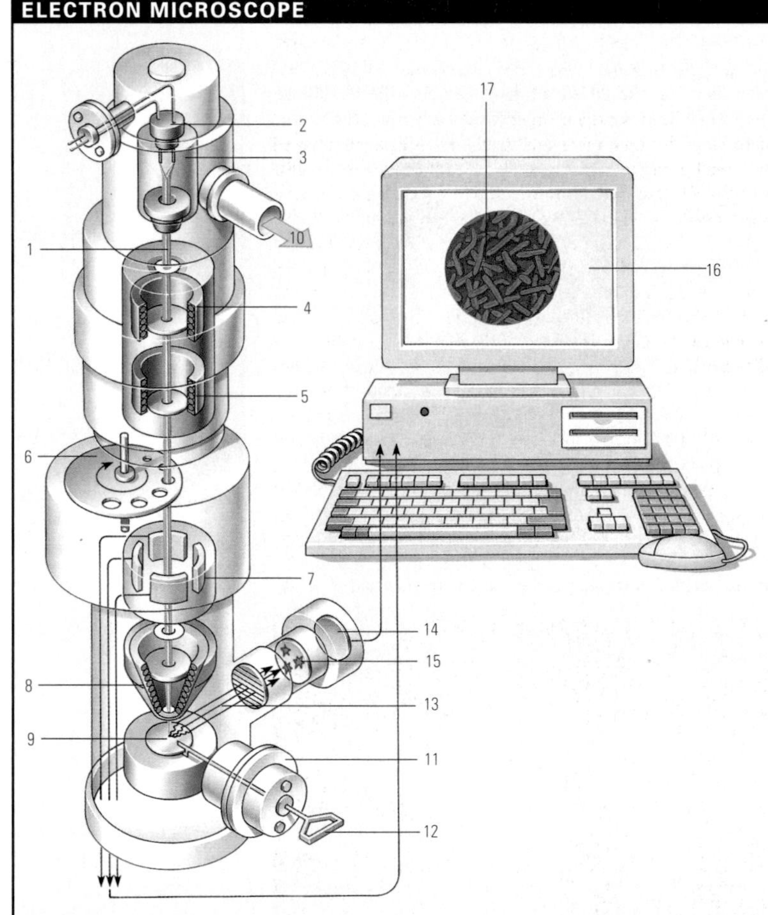


In an electron microscope, a beam of electrons (1) streams from the heated tungsten cathode (2) of an electron gun (3), and is focused by upper (4) and lower (5) electromagnetic lenses. It then passes through an aperture ring (6) and a scan coil (7) before being focused by a projector lens (8) onto the sample (9). The process takes place in a vacuum with air evacuated (10) by a pump. A computer controls the scan coil, which directs the beam across the sample. The sample is placed in an airlock (11) and manipulated into position (12). An image of the sample is created by detecting electrons dislodged (13) from the sample. These electrons correlate to the topography of the sample and are measured by a flash detector (14) when they hit a fluorescent target (15). The image is displayed on a computer monitor (16): here Lactobacillus bulgaricus magnified 1,000 times (17).

**electronic mail (e-mail)** Correspondence sent via a COMPUTER NETWORK. Messages produced using word-processing programs are transmitted over a network and stored in a computer called a **mail server** until people transfer them to their own computer.

**electronic music** Music in which electronic methods are used to generate or modulate sounds. The first pieces produced on tape recorders were composed in the 1920s. In Paris, Pierre Schaeffer and Pierre Henry manipulated recorded sounds, producing one of the first major works, *Symphonie pour un homme seul* (1950). The invention of the SYNTHESIZER inspired many composers, particularly Karlheinz STOCKHAUSEN. In the 1960s it became possible to use computers for complex electronic sounds; Yannis XENAKIS and Pierre BOULEZ are two of the many composers to have used computers.

**electronics** Study and use of CIRCUITS based on the conduction of ELECTRICITY through valves and semiconducting devices. The DIODE valve, invented by John FLEMING, and the triode valve, invented by Lee DE FOREST, provided the basic components for all the electronics of radio, television, and radar until the end of World War II. In 1948 a team led by William SHOCKLEY produced the first semiconducting TRANSISTOR. Semiconductor devices do not require the high operating voltages of valves and can be miniaturized as an INTEGRATED CIRCUIT (IC). This has led to the production of COMPUTERS and automatic control devices. *See also* MICROELECTRONICS; PRINTED CIRCUIT

**electron microscope** MICROSCOPE used for producing an image of a minute object. It "illuminates" the object with a stream of ELECTRONS, and the "lenses" consist of magnets that focus the electron beam. The image is obtained by converting the pattern (made by electrons passing through the object) into a video display, which may be photographed. These microscopes can magnify from 2,000 to a million times.

**electrophoresis** Movement of electrically charged colloidal particles through a fluid from one ELECTRODE to another when a voltage is applied across the electrodes. It is used in the analysis and separation of colloidal suspensions, especially colloidal proteins. *See also* COLLOID

**electroplating** Deposition of a coating of metal on another by making the object to be coated the CATHODE in ELECTROLYSIS. Positive ions in the ELECTROLYTE are discharged at the cathode and deposited as metal. Electroplating is used in silver-plated utensils and chromium-plated automobile parts.

**electroscope** Instrument to detect the presence of an ELECTRIC CHARGE or radiation. The commonest type is the gold-leaf electroscope, in which two gold leaves hang from a conducting rod held in an insulated container. A charge applied to the rod causes the leaves to separate, and the amount of separation indicates the amount of charge.

**electrostatics** *See* STATIC ELECTRICITY

**element** Substance that cannot be split into simpler substances by chemical means. All atoms of a given element have the same ATOMIC NUMBER (at.no.) and thus the same number of PROTONS and ELECTRONS. The atoms can have different ATOMIC MASS NUMBERS and a natural sample of an element is generally a mixture of ISOTOPES. The known elements range from hydrogen (at.no. 1) to unnilenium (at.no. 109); elements of the first 95 atomic numbers exist in nature, the higher numbers have been synthesized. *See also* PERIODIC TABLE

**element 104** *See* DUBNIUM

**element 105** *See* HAHNIUM

**element 106** *See* RUTHERFORDIUM

**elementary particle** In physics, a SUBATOMIC PARTICLE that cannot be subdivided. Such particles are the basic constituents of matter. There are three groups of elementary particles: QUARKS, LEPTONS (light particles), and gauge BOSONS (messenger particles). All elementary particles have an associated antiparticle.

**elephant** Largest land animal, the only surviving member of the mammal family Proboscidea, which included the MAMMOTH and the MASTODON. It is native to Africa (*Loxodonta africana*) and India (*Elephas maximus*). The tusks, the source of ivory, are elongated upper incisors, which it uses for digging up roots. The Indian cow (female) elephant has no tusks. The trunk is an elongated nose and upper lip, which it uses for drinking and picking up food. The African elephant is taller and heavier than its Indian counterpart. A bull (male) elephant may weigh as much as eight tons (7,000kg), and can charge at speeds up to 30mph (48km/h). It also has much larger ears, up to 40in (100cm) in diameter. Elephants are herbivores, and browse in herds led by a bull. The cow (female) gives birth to its calf after 18 to 22 months gestation. Elephants live for 60 to 70 years. Indian elephants are used as beasts of burden, but do not breed in captivity.

**elephantiasis** Condition in which there is gross swelling of the tissues due to blockage of lymph vessels. It is usually caused by parasitic worms, as in FILARIASIS.

**Eleusinian Mysteries** Religious rites in ancient Greece at Eleusis, Attica, to honor DEMETER and PERSEPHONE. The rites probably began as a fertility festival.

**Elgar, Sir Edward** (1857–1934) English composer. His most popular works include "Land of Hope and Glory," one of the five *Pomp and Circumstance* marches (1901–30), and *Variations on an Original Theme* (1899), popularly known as *Enigma Variations*.

**Elgin, James Bruce, 8th Earl of** (1811–63) British colonial official. He was governor-general of Canada (1847–54), where he oversaw the transition to responsible government. In 1861 he was appointed viceroy of India, where he died.

**Elgin Marbles** Group of sculptures from the Acropolis of Athens, including sculptures of the PARTHENON. They were collected by the 7th Earl of Elgin, sold to the British Government in 1816, and are now on display in the British Museum, London. The Greek government has campaigned for their return.

**Elijah** Old Testament prophet who appeared in Israel in the 9th century BC and attacked the Phoenician cult of Baal (1 Kings 17, 2 Kings 2). Elijah, aided by ELISHA, set out to prove that there was no God but Yahweh.

**Eliot, Charles William** (1834–1926) US educator, president of Harvard University (1869–1909). Under Eliot's administration, Harvard was transformed into a leading modern university.

**Eliot, George** (1819–80) English novelist, b. Mary Ann Evans. Her relationship with G.H. LEWES began in 1853. Her first work of fiction was the collection *Scenes of Clerical Life* (1858). Three novels of provincial life followed: *Adam Bede* (1859), *The Mill on the Floss* (1860), and *Silas Marner* (1861). The historical romance *Romola* (1862–63) was published in Cornhill Magazine. *Middlemarch* (1871–72) is regarded as her masterpiece. Eliot's last novel was *Daniel Deronda* (1874–76).

**Eliot, John** (1604–90) American missionary, b. England. He traveled to Massachusetts (1631) as the first Christian missionary in New England. He became known as the "Apostle of the Indians" for his evangelistic work.

**Eliot, T.S. (Thomas Stearns)** (1888–1965) British poet, playwright, and critic, b. US. His first volume, *Prufock and Other Observations* (1917), includes "The Love Song of J. Alfred Prufock." Eliot's poem *The Waste Land* (1922) is a keystone of literary MODERNISM. Later poems, notably *Ash Wednesday* (1930) and the *Four Quartets* (1935–43), concerned religious faith. Eliot also wrote verse plays, including *Murder in the Cathedral* (1935). His children's poems, *Old Possum's Book of Practical Cats* (1939), formed the basis for the musical *Cats*. Eliot was awarded the 1948 Nobel Prize for literature.

**Elisha** Old Testament prophet of Israel, disciple and successor of ELIJAH (2 Kings 2–13). He appeared in the 9th century BC and destroyed the Phoenician cult of Baal. Elisha is portrayed as a miracle worker, healer, and fulfiller of God's commissions to his master Elijah.

◄ **elephant** Over many thousands of years the numerous front teeth of the elephant have been reduced to two upper incisors which form two long tusks, and the nose too has extended to form the trunk. The African elephant (*Loxodonta africana*) was once found over much of that continent, but it is now relatively rare due to destruction of its habitat and hunting

**Elizabeth, Saint** In the New Testament, wife of Zacharias and mother of JOHN THE BAPTIST. She was related to Mary, mother of Jesus. Her feast day is 5 November.

**Elizabeth** (1709–62) Empress of Russia (1741–62). The daughter of PETER I (THE GREAT), she came to the throne after overthrowing her nephew, Ivan VI. She waged war against Sweden (1741–43), and annexed the southern portion of Finland (1743). A great patron of the arts, she was succeeded by her nephew, Peter III.

**Elizabeth I** (1533–1603) Queen of England (1558–1603), daughter of HENRY VIII and Anne BOLEYN. During the reigns of her half-brother and half-sister, EDWARD VI and MARY I, she avoided political disputes. Once crowned, she reestablished Protestantism. Various plots to murder Elizabeth and place the Catholic MARY, QUEEN OF SCOTS on the throne resulted in Mary's imprisonment and execution (1587), and increasing discrimation against Catholics. Elizabeth adhered to a small group of advisers, such as Lord BURGHLEY and Sir Francis WALSINGHAM. For most of her reign, England was at peace and commerce and industry prospered. ELIZABETHAN DRAMA reflected this "golden age." The expansion of the navy saw the development of the first BRITISH EMPIRE and the defeat of the Spanish ARMADA (1588). Despite pressure to marry, Elizabeth remained single. She was the last of the TUDORS, and the throne passed to the JAMES I, a STUART.

**Elizabeth II** (1926– ) Queen of Great Britain and Northern Ireland and head of the Commonwealth of Nations (1952– ). Daughter of GEORGE VI, she married Philip Mountbatten, Duke of Edinburgh, in 1947, with whom she had four children, CHARLES, Anne, Andrew, and Edward. Popular and dutiful, Elizabeth has had to contend with criticism of royal wealth and scandals associated with the marriage failures in the royal family, particularly that of Charles and DIANA, PRINCESS OF WALES.

**Elizabeth** (1900– ) (Queen Mother) British queen consort of GEORGE VI. Born Lady Bowes-Lyon, she married George in

◄ **Elizabeth I** Her rule was a "Golden Age" of increasing prosperity and a flowering of the arts. Elizabeth I of England became known as "Good Queen Bess." Throughout her reign friction with Spain grew, culminating in the Armada, and there were attempts to place the Catholic Mary, Queen of Scots on the throne.

**EMBRYO**

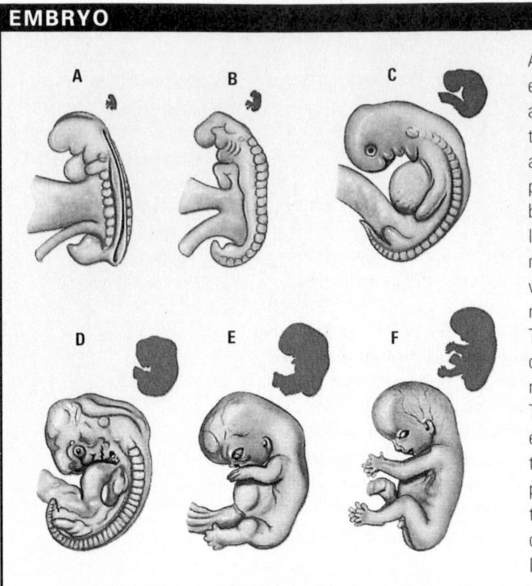


After three weeks a human embryo bears a primitive heart and head (A). By the fourth week, the heart is pumping blood around the body and into the placenta and 25 pairs of tissue blocks (somites) appear, which later give rise to bone and muscle tissue (B). After five weeks, limb buds and rudimentary eyes are visible (C). The limbs become well developed and the tail region recedes by the sixth week (D). The head grows rapidly; eyes, ears, and teeth buds appear by the seventh week (E). The tail portion vanishes and almost all the organs and tissues have developed by the eighth week (F). It is now known as a fetus.

1923. They had two children, Elizabeth (ELIZABETH II) and Margaret. In 1936 she became queen when George's brother, EDWARD VIII, abdicated. A popular figure, she continues to perform public duties in her nineties.

**Elizabethan drama** Drama staged in England during the reign of ELIZABETH I (1558–1603). Drawing on classical and medieval thought, as well as folk drama, Elizabethan drama is characterized by a spiritual vitality and creativity. Dramatists of the period include SHAKESPEARE, MARLOWE, and JONSON.

**elk** Alternative name for the WAPITI; also sometimes used to refer to the MOOSE.

**Ellesmere Island** Mountainous island in the Arctic Ocean, NW of Greenland, forming part of the Northwest Territories of Canada. It is the second largest and northernmost island of the Arctic Archipelago. Area: 75,767sq mi (196,236sq km).

**Ellice Islands** Former name of TUVALU

**Ellington, "Duke" (Edward Kennedy)** (1899–1974) US jazz composer, pianist, and bandleader. Ellington's early pieces, performed (1927–32) at the Cotton Club, Harlem, New York, include "Black and Tan Fantasy" (1927) and "Mood Indigo" (1930). The "jungle" style gave way to the elegance of standards such as "Take the A Train" (1941). *Black, Brown and Beige* (1943) was written for a concert at Carneige Hall.

**ellipse** CONIC section formed by cutting a right circular cone with a plane inclined at such an angle that the plane does not intersect the base of the cone. When the intersecting plane is parallel to the base, the conic section is a circle. Most planetary orbits are ellipses.

**Ellis, (Henry) Havelock** (1859–1939) British psychologist and author. His seven volume *Studies in the Psychology of Sex* (1897–1928) promoted the scientific study of sex and helped change public attitudes.

**Ellis Island** Island in Upper New York Bay, near MANHATTAN, SE New York. It acted as the main US immigration center from 1892 to 1943. The Ellis Island Immigration Museum opened in 1990. Area: 27 acres (11ha).

**Ellison, Ralph Waldo** (1914–94) US writer. Ellison wrote *Invisible Man* (1952), a semi-autobiographical novel about an African American's struggle for identity.

**Ellsworth, Lincoln** (1880–1951) US polar explorer. In 1926 he and Roald AMUNDSEN became the first humans to fly over the North Pole. In 1935 Ellsworth became the first person to fly over Antarctica.

**Ellsworth, Oliver** (1745–1807) Chief justice of the US Supreme Court (1796–99). He served as a delegate to the Constitutional Convention (1787), and helped draft the "Connecticut Compromise". Ellsworth was responsible for the term "United States" in the Constitution. As senator from Connecticut (1789–96), he drafted the bill that established the federal judiciary.

**elm** Hardy, tall, deciduous tree of N temperate zones. Elms have fan-shaped crowns, which make them ideal shade trees. Species include the American (*Ulmus americana*), and the Wych elm (*U. procera*). Both species are attacked by the fungus known as Dutch elm disease. Height: more than 100ft (30m). Family Ulmaceae.

**El Niño** (Sp. child Christ) Warm surface current that sometimes flows in the equatorial Pacific Ocean toward the South American coast. It occurs approximately every 7–11 years around Christmas time. Its effects include dramatic reductions in fish catches and short-term changes in worldwide climate patterns.

**El Paso** City and port of entry in W Texas, across the Rio Grande from Juárez, Mexico; seat of El Paso county. The area was visited by Spanish missionaries in the 16th century, but no settlement was made until 1827. The coming of the railroad (1881) spurred development. In 1963 the border with Mexico was settled finally. Industries: cotton clothing, oil refining. Pop. (515,342).

**El Salvador** Republic in Central America. *See* country feature

**Elysium** In Greek mythology, the Elysian fields. The abode of blessed mortals after their removal from the Earth, it is the realm to which heroes departed.

**Emancipation Proclamation** (January 1, 1863) Declaration issued by Abraham LINCOLN abolishing SLAVERY in the CONFEDERATE STATES of America. It was designed to enhance the Union's support from abroad, especially Britain, and reduce the South's fighting force. By the end of the war more than 500,000 slaves had fled to the Union side. Slavery was finally abolished by the 13th Amendment (December 1865).

**embalming** Artificial preservation of dead bodies. The custom was highly advanced in ancient Egypt as early as 4000 BC. The body was soaked in a soda solution and the cavities filled with spices, oils, and resins. Viscera were sometimes embalmed separately and placed in canopic jars. The science of anatomy revived the process, commonly by injecting formaldehyde into the vascular system and draining the blood.

**embargo** Order prohibiting exchange of goods. It usually refers to the restriction by government on the depaparture of merchant ships from its ports. Embargoes are used for economic and political purposes and may be part of a package of SANCTIONS imposed on another country.

**Embargo Act** (1807) Act passed by Thomas JEFFERSON to force England and France to remove restrictions on US trade, following attacks on US merchant shipping. It prohibited all ships from entering or leaving US ports. The act hurt the US economy and merchants resorted to smuggling. Resistance led to the Nonintercourse Act (1809) that ended the 14-month embargo.

**embolism** Blocking of a blood vessel by an obstruction called an embolus, usually a blood clot, air bubble, or particle of fat. The effects depend on where the embolus lodges; a cerebral embolism causes a STROKE. Treatment is with anticoagulants or surgery. *See also* ARTERIOSCLEROSIS

**embroidery** Decorative needlework (specifically stitching) on cloth. It has sometimes served as a means to depict historic events, such as the BAYEUX TAPESTRY. During the Renaissance, it was an important art of many courts. There was also a tradition of rural and folk embroidery, particularly in E Europe and in the quilting of the early English settlers in N America.

**embryo** Early developing stage of an animal or plant. In animals, the embryo stage starts at FERTILIZATION, and ends when the organism emerges from the egg or from its mother's UTERUS. In plants, the embryo is found in the seed and the embryo stage ends on GERMINATION. An embryo results when the nuclei of an EGG and a SPERM or male sex cell fuse to form a single cell, called a ZYGOTE. The zygote then divides into a ball of cells called an embryo. The embryo undergoes rapid changes in which the cells differentiate themselves to form features, such as limbs and organs. *See also* MEIOSIS; MITOSIS

**embryology** Biological study of the origin, development, and activities of an EMBRYO.

**emerald** Variety of BERYL, highly valued as a gemstone. The color varies from light to dark green according to the amount of chromium. The finest emeralds are found in Colombia.

**Emerson, Ralph Waldo** (1803–82) US essayist, philosopher, and poet. He was a minister in the Unitarian Church, but became disillusioned and resigned (1832). Emerson settled in New England, where he formed a circle that included Nathaniel HAWTHORNE, Henry David THOREAU, and Bronson ALCOTT. Emerson's essay *Nature* (1836) set forth the principles of TRANSCENDENTALISM. His speech at Harvard "The American Scholar" (1837) argued for an independent AMERICAN LITERATURE. In 1840 he cofounded *The Dial* magazine. Emerson's lectures formed the basis of *Essays* (1841, 1844). His poetry was collected in *Poems* (1847), and *May-Day* (1867). Other collections of lectures include *Representative Men* (1850), *The Conduct of Life* (1860), and *Society and Solitude* (1870).

**Emilia-Romagna** Region in N central Italy, bordering the Adriatic Sea; the capital is BOLOGNA. It was incorporated in the kingdom of Italy in 1860. The N part forms a vast plain. In the S lies the central part of the APENNINES. Industries: tourism, motor vehicles. Area: 8,542sq mi (22,124sq km). Pop. (1991) 3,909,512.

**Empedocles** (*c*.495–*c*.435 BC) Greek scientist and philosopher. He taught the doctrine of the four elements (earth, water, air, and fire) and, anticipating modern physics, he explained change as being alterations in the proportions of the four elements.

**emphysema** Accumulation of air in tissues, most often in the lungs (pulmonary emphysema). Pulmonary emphysema includes breathlessness, the result of damage to and enlargement of the ALVEOLUS. It is associated with chronic bronchitis and smoking.

**Empire Style** Neoclassical style in interior decoration, associated with the reign of NAPOLEON I. It made affected use of Egyptian decorative motifs.

**empiricism** Philosophical doctrine that all knowledge is derived from experience. It was developed mainly by LOCKE, BERKELEY, and HUME, in reaction to the RATIONALISM of DESCARTES, SPINOZA, and LEIBNIZ, who claimed the existence of *a priori* knowledge (innate ideas). *See also* LOGICAL POSITIVISM

**emu** Large, dark-plumed, flightless Australian bird. It is a strong runner with powerful legs. Large greenish eggs (8–10) are hatched by the male in a ground nest. Height: 5ft (1.5m); weight: to 120lb (54kg). Species *Dromaius novaehollandiae.*

## EL SALVADOR

This flag was adopted in 1912, replacing the earlier "Stars and Stripes." The blue and white stripes are featured on the flags of several Central American countries which gained their independence from Spain at the same time in 1821.

**AREA:** 8,124sq mi (21,040sq km)
**POPULATION:** 5,047,925
**CAPITAL (POPULATION):** San Salvador (422,570)
**GOVERNMENT:** Republic
**ETHNIC GROUPS:** Mestizo 89%, Native American 10%, White 1%
**LANGUAGES:** Spanish (official)
**RELIGIONS:** Christianity (Roman Catholic 94%)
**CURRENCY:** Colón = 100 centavos

The Republic of El Salvador is the smallest and most densely populated country in Central America. It has a narrow coastal plain along the Pacific Ocean. The majority of the interior is mountainous with many extinct volcanic peaks, overlooking a heavily populated central plateau. Earthquakes are common; in 1854 an earthquake destroyed the capital, SAN SALVADOR, and another in October 1986 killed 400 people and caused widespread damage.

### CLIMATE

The coast has a hot tropical climate. Inland, the climate is moderated by altitude. There is a wet season between May and October.

### VEGETATION

Grassland and some virgin forests of original oak and pine are found in the highlands. The central plateau and valleys have areas of grass and deciduous woodland, while coastal regions are covered by tropical savanna or forest.

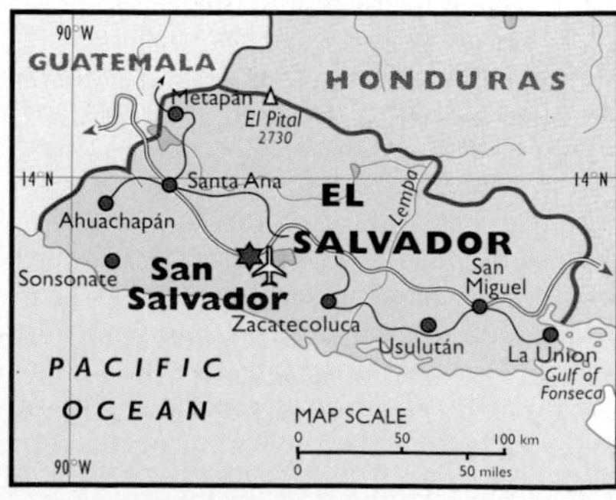


### HISTORY

From 1524–26, the Spanish explorer Pedro de Alvarado conquered Native-American tribes such as the Pipil, and the region formed part of the Spanish viceroyalty of Guatemala. Independence was achieved (1821), and in 1823 El Salvador joined the Central American Federation. The federation was dissolved in 1839. El Salvador declared its independence in 1841, but was continually subject to foreign interference (especially from Guatemala and Nicaragua). El Salvador's coffee plantations were developed.

Following a collapse in the world coffee market, Maximiliano Hernández Martínez seized power in a palace coup (1931). His brutal dictatorship was overthrown by a general strike (1944). A period of progressive government was followed by a military junta headed by Julio Adalberto Rivera (1962–67) and Fidel Sánchez Hernández (1967–72). Border tension with Honduras was exacerbated by Honduras' discriminatory immigration laws. The "Soccer War" (1969) broke out following an ill-tempered World Cup qualifying match between the two countries. Within four days, El Salvador had captured much of Honduras. A ceasefire was announced and the troops withdrew. In the 1970s, El Salvador's problems of overpopulation, unequal distribution of wealth, and social unrest were compounded by the repressive National Republican Alliance (ARENA) regime. Civil war broke out in 1979 between US-backed government forces and the Farabundo Marti National Liberation Front (FMLN). The 12-year war claimed 75,000 lives and caused mass homelessness.

### POLITICS

A ceasefire came into effect in 1992, and the FMLN became a recognized political party. In 1993 a UN Truth Commission led to the removal of senior army officers for human rights abuses, and FMLN arms were decommissioned. In 1994 Armando Calderón Sol of the ruling ARENA party was elected president.

### ECONOMY

El Salvador is a lower-middle-income developing country (1995 GDP per capita, US$2,610). Farmland and pasture account for *c*.60% of land use. El Salvador is the world's 10th largest producer of coffee. Its reliance on the crop has caused profound economic structural imbalance. The Salvadorean Coffee Company is being privatized. Sugar and cotton are grown on the coastal lowlands. Fishing is important, but manufacturing is small. The civil war has devastated the economy. From 1993–95 El Salvador has received over $100 million of credit from the IMF.

Francisco Antonio Gavidia, the El Salvadorean philosopher and humanist, was honored by a set of six stamps issued in 1965.

▲ **Engels** A founder of 19th-century communism, Friedrich Engels' success in the textile industry helped finance the work of Karl Marx, and they collaborated on the *Communist Manifesto* (1848). Engels' work on dialectical materialism contributed much to subsequent Marxist philosophy. *The Origin of the Family, Private Property and the State* (1884) is a seminal work.



**emulator** Computer configured in such a way that it acts like another type of computer. Emulators are often used in the development of new microprocessors.

**enamel** Decorative or protective glazed coating produced on metal surfaces, or a type of paint. Ceramic enamels are made from powdered glass and calx, with metal oxides to add color. Enamel paints consist of zinc oxide, lithopone, and high-grade varnish. The finish is hard, glossy, and durable.

**encephalitis** Inflammation of the brain, usually associated with a viral infection; often there is an associated MENINGITIS. Symptoms include fever, headache, lassitude, and intolerance of light; in severe cases there may be sensory and behavioral disturbances, paralysis, convulsions, and coma.

**encyclical** Letter addressed by the Pope to all members of the Roman Catholic Church. Recent encyclicals have condemned contraception (Paul VI, 1968) and ecumenism (John Paul II, 1995).

**encyclopedia** Compendium of knowledge, containing information in all fields (general) or in a particular field (specialist). Some of the first encyclopedic works were compiled by Aristotle and Pliny, but the first modern work was probably John Harris's *Lexicon Technicum* (1704), which contained sophisticated bibliographies and cross-referencing. Perhaps the most influential work was the *Encyclopédie* (1772) compiled by DIDEROT. The *Encyclopaedia Britannica* was published first in 1771.

**endangered species** Animals or plants threatened with extinction as a result of such activities as habitat destruction and overhunting. More than 1,000 animals and 20,000 plants are considered endangered.

**Enders, John Franklin** (1897–1985) US microbiologist. He shared the 1954 Nobel Prize for physiology or medicine with Frederick C. Robbins and Thomas H. Weller for the discovery that poliomyelitis viruses can be grown in cultures of various types of tissues. This work was fundamental to the development of the polio vaccine.

**endive** Leafy annual or biennial plant widely cultivated for its sharp-flavored leaves. There are two main types: curly CHICORY (escarole), with slender, wavy-edged leaves, and a variety with broad, flat leaves. Family Asteraceae/Compositae; species *Cichorium endivia*.

**endocrine system** Body system made up of all the endocrine (ductless) glands that secrete HORMONES directly into the bloodstream to control body functions. The chief endocrine glands are the PITUITARY GLAND, the THYROID GLAND, the ADRENAL GLAND, and the sex gland or GONAD (TESTIS in males and OVARY in females).

**endocytosis** In biology, process by which a CELL takes in substances. When a cell's MEMBRANE comes into contact with food, a portion of the cytoplasm surrounds the substance and a depression forms within the cell wall. There are two types of endocytosis: **pinocytosis** is the incoporation and digestion of dissolved substances, and **phagocytosis** is the engulfing and digestion of microscopic particles. In higher animals, PHAGOCYTE cells are an important part of the IMMUNE SYSTEM.

**endometriosis** Gynecological disorder in which tissue similar to the ENDOMETRIUM occurs elsewhere in the pelvic cavity. It is treated with analgesics, hormone preparations, or surgery.

**endometrium** Mucous membrane, well supplied with blood vessels, that lines the UTERUS. It is shed each month during menstruation.

**endoplasmic reticulum** Network of membranes and channels in the CYTOPLASM of EUKARYOTE cells. It helps to transport material inside the CELL.

**endorphin** NEUROTRANSMITTER that occurs naturally in the HYPOTHALAMUS and PITUITARY GLAND connected to the brain. Endorphins are PEPTIDES that reduce pain. *See also* ANALGESIC

**endoscope** Instrument used to examine the interior of the body. Generally a light source and lenses are included in a flexible tube. MINIMAL ACCCESS SURGERY uses fine instruments passed through the endoscope.

**endosperm** Tissue that surrounds the developing embryo of a seed and provides food for growth. It is triploid (each cell has three sets of chromosomes), being derived from the fusion of one of the male GAMETES from the germinated pollen grain and two of the haploid nuclei in the embryo sac.

**endosymbiosis** Mutually beneficial relationship in which one organism lives inside another. For example, bacteria were engulfed by EUKARYOTE cells and formed symbiotic relationships with them, eventually becoming so interdependent that the cells behaved as a single organism; the bacteria became MITOCHONDRIA and CHLOROPLASTS. *See also* SYMBIOSIS

**endothermic reaction** Chemical reaction in which heat is absorbed from the surroundings, causing a fall in temperature – as in the manufacture of water-gas from coal and steam.

**energy** In physics, capacity for doing WORK. It is measured in JOULES. The many forms of energy include POTENTIAL, KINETIC, electrical, NUCLEAR, thermal, LIGHT, and chemical. The law of conservation of energy states that energy cannot be created or destroyed. The concept of energy began with GALILEO and Sir Isaac NEWTON. The idea that MASS is a form of energy was established by Albert EINSTEIN, who recognized that energy (E) and mass (m) could be transformed into each other according to the relation $E = mc^2$, where c is the velocity of light.

**Energy, US Department of** Federal government department. Established in 1977, it is responsible for administering a comprehensive national energy plan, including research and development, regulatory functions, and the nuclear energy program.

**energy sources** Naturally occurring substances, processes, and phenomena from which we obtain ENERGY. Most energy is derived originally from the Sun. FOSSIL FUELS are the remains of life that was dependent on the Sun's energy. HYDROELECTRICITY derives from the solar energy that maintains the HYDROLOGICAL CYCLE, while wind is generated by uneven heating of the atmosphere and its energy harnessed by wind farms. The movements of the oceans – waves and tides – are caused by wind and the pull of the Moon and have been used to generate energy. Increasingly, SOLAR ENERGY is being used to heat some domestic water supplies directly, and for providing electricity from PHOTOELECTRIC CELLS. GEOTHERMAL ENERGY is obtained from underground hot rocks. Other major energy sources are radioactive metals, such as URANIUM and PLUTONIUM, which provide NUCLEAR ENERGY.

**Engels, Friedrich** (1820–95) German political writer. Engels and MARX formulated the theory of DIALECTICAL MATERIALISM, and cowrote the *Communist Manifesto* (1848). From 1870 until Marx's death in 1883, Engels helped financially with Marx's research and continued to help him with his writings, particularly *Das Kapital*. His materialist reorientation of the dialectics of Hegel is most evident in his *Socialism, Utopian and Scientific* (1882).

**engine** Machine that produces useful energy of motion from some other form of energy. The term is usually restricted to combustion engines, which burn fuel. These machines include the STEAM ENGINE, DIESEL ENGINE, JET ENGINE, and ROCKET engine. Such engines are distinct from ELECTRIC MOTORS. An external combustion engine burns its fuel outside the chamber in which motion is produced. An INTERNAL COMBUSTION ENGINE burns its fuel and develops motion in the same place.

**engineering** Application of scientific principles for practical purposes, such as construction and developing power sources. There are many different fields in engineering including MECHANICAL, CIVIL, CHEMICAL, electrical, and nuclear. *See also* ELECTRONICS

**England** Largest nation within the United Kingdom, bounded by the North Sea (E), the English Channel (S), Wales and the Irish Sea (W), and Scotland (N); the capital is LONDON. **Land and economy** In general, the N and W are higher and geologically older than the S and E. The chief rivers are the SEVERN, THAMES, Trent, Ouse, Humber, and Mersey. The principal lakes include Windermere and Derwentwater in the Lake District. The S of the country has low hills and downs, while much of E England is flat fenland. The N is predominantly upland and includes the Pennines, Cheviot Hills, and Cumbrian Mountains. **History** There are traces of PALEOLITHIC settlements in England. Occupied by the CELTS from *c*.400 BC, England was later conquered by the Romans, whose rule lasted until the 5th century. Germanic tribes began arriving in the 3rd century AD and gradually established independent kingdoms. Christianity was introduced into the country in the

6th century. In the 9th century Alfred the Great led a united England against the Danes. The Norman Conquest (1066) brought strong central government and inaugurated the feudal system. Ireland was conquered in the late 12th century, and Wales became a principality of England in 1284. The 13th century saw the foundations of Parliament and the development of statute law. During the Middle Ages, English kings laid claim to French territory. The Wars of the Roses curbed the power of the nobility. Under the Tudors, Wales was united politically with England and became a strong Protestant monarchy. The reign of Elizabeth I was one of colonial expansion and growing naval power. In 1603 James I merged the English and Scottish crowns. For the subsequent history of England, *see* United Kingdom. Area: 50,333sq mi (130,362sq km). Pop. (1991) 47,055,204.

**English** Language belonging to the Germanic branch of the Indo-European family. It may be said to have come into existence with the arrival of the Anglo-Saxons in England in the 5th century AD. During more than 1,500 years of development, it has been transformed from an inflected language with grammatical gender to one with very few inflections and employing a sex-correlated gender system (he, she, and it). Its vocabulary has been massively expanded by the inclusion of numerous foreign, technical, and slang words. It is the mother tongue of *c*.300 million people, and a second language for hundreds of millions more worldwide.

**English architecture** Between the 6th and the 17th centuries, there were at least five distinctive styles of English architecture, including Saxon, Norman and Gothic, and Renaissance and Baroque. England was influenced by European trends in architecture toward the end of their development. For example, Inigo Jones brought his revolutionary Renaissance ideas relatively late to the 17th-century Stuart court, and Christopher Wren introduced Baroque forms to England at the end of his career. The Georgian period (1702–1830) is subdivided into English Baroque, Palladianism, and Neoclassicism. In the 19th century, the Victorian age was marked by earnestness and solidity, while the Great Exhibition (1851) paved the way for modernism. William Morris and the Arts and Crafts Movement encouraged purity of design in the late 19th century, and continued into the early 20th century with the work of Lutyens and Voysey. In the late 20th century, notable English modernist and postmodernist architects include Richard Rogers and Norman Foster.

**English art** England's earliest artistic traditions were shaped by invading forces. The Anglo-Saxons had an enduring influence. Their most notable achievement came with the Bayeux Tapestry. A native tradition eventually emerged in the 18th century, with William Hogarth, Thomas Gainsborough, and Joshua Reynolds. In the 19th century, England's two most influential artists were J.M.W. Turner and John Constable. The work of the Pre-Raphaelite Brotherhood bridged romanticism and symbolism, while William Morris was a seminal influence on the Arts and Crafts Movement. The major 20th-century figures were Stanley Spencer and Francis Bacon. Modern English sculptors, including Henry Moore and Barbara Hepworth, have exerted a widespread influence.

**English Channel** Arm of the Atlantic Ocean between France and Britain, joining the North Sea at the Strait of Dover. A cross-channel train-ferry service was started in 1936 and the Channel Tunnel was completed in 1994. Width: 20–100mi (30–160km); length: 350mi (564km).

**English horn** (cor anglais) Reed instrument of the oboe family. Longer than the oboe, its range is a fifth lower. Its bell is pear-shaped and its double reed is inserted in a curved mouthpiece.

**English literature** Earliest surviving works are from the Old English period (475–1000). Mainly poems in the heroic mold, epics such as Beowulf belong to an oral tradition but were written down in the 7th century. King Alfred began a tradition of English prose by translating a number of Latin works into the vernacular, and initiating the *Anglo Saxon Chronicle*. Norman French replaced Old English as the language of the ruling classes after 1066, and the influence of French literature was reflected in the numerous romances centered around the stories of Charlemagne and the legends of King Arthur. The native tradition of alliterative poetry reemerged in the 14th century in the works of Langland, Malory, and Geoffrey Chaucer. William Shakespeare and Christopher Marlowe were the leading figures in Elizabethan drama. Shakespeare's late works formed a bridge with the Jacobean era. Edmund Spenser and Philip Sidney ensured the period was also a golden age for poetry. John Donne and the Metaphysical poets continued this tradition, but the poetry of Milton was unsurpassed in the 17th century. English prose flourished with the production of the Authorized Version of the Bible in 1611. After the Restoration, drama revived in the comedies of Congreve; the classical ideals of the Augustan age (*c*.1690–1740) are typified in the satiric prose of Swift, the poetry of Pope, and the criticism of Samuel Johnson. The novel emerged during the early 18th century, with works by Defoe, Richardson, Fielding, Sterne, and Smollett, and was developed in the 19th century by Jane Austen, Walter Scott, Thackeray, the Brontës, George Eliot, and Dickens. The romantic movement, heralded in Blake's poetry, gained full flight with Wordsworth and Coleridge, and was developed by Keats, Byron, and Shelley. The major Victorian poets were Tennyson, and Robert and Elizabeth Browning. The wit of Shaw and Wilde, and the bleak novels of Hardy, gave way to the cynicism of war poets such as Siegfried Sassoon. The formal experiments of modernism were realized best in the the novels of James Joyce, Virginia Woolf, and D.H. Lawrence, and the verse dramas of T.S. Eliot. W.B. Yeats looked back to the visions of Blake. The novel diversified with the writings of Aldous Huxley, Evelyn Waugh, and Graham Greene. In the 1930s, W.H. Auden produced explicitly political poems and Noel Coward lampooned the British class system. The 1950s saw the emergence of the "Angry Young Men," including John Osborne and Kingsley Amis, and the absurdist plays of Samuel Beckett. Post-war novel-

## ENGINE

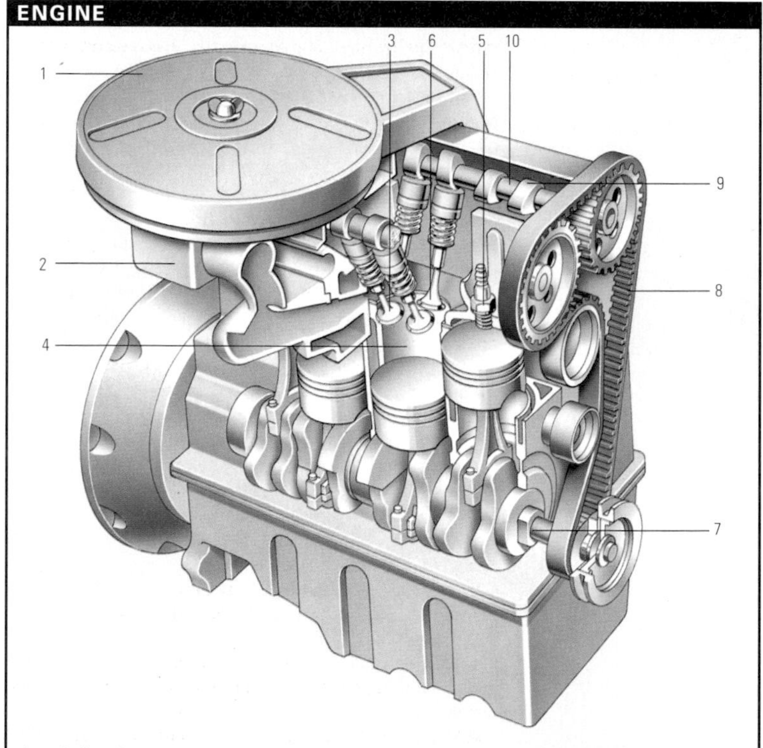


In an in-line, four-cylinder gasoline engine air is sucked through a filter (1) into the carburetor (2). The air mixes with gasoline which enters through the dual inlet valves (3) on each cylinder (4). The spark plug (5) then ignites the mixture, forcing the cylinder down rapidly. The burnt gases are expelled through the outlet valves (6). The reciprocal motion of the cylinders is converted into rotation by the crankshaft (7). The crankshaft also turns the timing belt (8), which controls the opening of the valves and the firing of the spark plug through the cams (9) located on the camshaft (10).

ists include Anthony BURGESS, William GOLDING, Iris MURDOCH, Angela CARTER, and Salman RUSHDIE; dramatists include Harold PINTER, Tom STOPPARD, Joe ORTON, and David HARE; poets include Dylan THOMAS, Philip LARKIN, Ted HUGHES, and Seamus HEANEY.

**engraving** INTAGLIO printing process; it describes various methods of making prints by cutting lines into metal or wood. Variations include ETCHING and AQUATINT. *See also* WOODCUT

**Enlightenment** (Age of Reason) Philosophical movement of 18th-century Europe and America. It was inspired by the scientific and philosophical revolutions of the late 17th century. The spirit of rational inquiry of the Scientific Revolution embodied by the work of Issac NEWTON, the RATIONALISM of DESCARTES, the religious ideas of SPINOZA and PASCAL, and the EMPIRICISM of Francis BACON and John LOCKE, filtered into the fabric of 18th-century society. The *Encyclopédie* was the central text of the Enlightenment. In France, the Philosophes (VOLTAIRE, de MONTESQUIEU, Jean-Jacques ROUSSEAU, and DIDEROT) championed a scientific approach to sociopolitical, and economic affairs. They attacked established religion (*see* DEISM) and viewed the state as the instrument for social change. Rational human behavior was at the center of the economic theories of Adam SMITH, Jeremy BENTHAM, and Baron TURGOT. The importance of the individual was underlined in the philosophies of Immanuel KANT and David HUME. The work of Thomas PAINE, Thomas JEFFERSON, and Benjamin FRANKLIN, in creating the United States of America epitomized the political spirit of the age.

**Enoch** Name of several Old Testament figures. One was the father of METHUSELAH, and writer of PSEUDEPIGRAPHA, such as the Books of Enoch. Another was the eldest son of CAIN.

**Entebbe** City on the NW shore of Lake Victoria, S central Uganda, E Africa. Founded in 1893, it was capital of the British protectorate of Uganda (1894–1962). Pop. (1991) 41,638.

**Entente Cordiale** Anglo-French alliance, formalized in April 1904. Outstanding differences, especially over colonies, were solved. The Entente was the first step leading to the TRIPLE ENTENTE.

**enthalpy** (symbol H) Amount of thermodynamic heat energy possessed by a substance. The enthalpy of a system equals the sum of its internal energy and the product of the pressure and volume.

**entomology** (Gk. *entomon*, insect) Term for the scientific study of INSECTS, coined by ARISTOTLE. The ancient Greeks were the first serious entomologists.

**entropy** Quantity that specifies the disorder of a physical system; the greater the disorder, the greater the entropy. In THERMODYNAMICS, it expresses the degree to which thermal energy is available for work – the less available it is, the greater the entropy.

**environment** Physical and biological surroundings of an organism. The environment covers both nonliving (abiotic) factors such as temperature, soil, atmosphere, and radiation, and also living (biotic) organisms such as plants, microorganisms, and animals. *See also* ECOLOGY

**Environmental Protection Agency (EPA)** US federal government agency. It was created (1970) to reduce and control POLLUTION by a variety of research, monitoring, and enforcement activities.

**enzyme** (Gk. *zymosis*, fermentation) PROTEIN that functions as a CATALYST in biochemical reactions. The FERMENTATION properties of yeast cells have long been utilized in the brewing trade. In 1926 the US biochemist James B. Sumner became the first person to isolate an enzyme, urase, in pure crystal form and proved that enzymes are protein molecules. In the next decade, PEPSIN, TRYPSIN, and CHYMOTRYPSIN were crystallized. Today, more than 1,500 catalysts have been identified. In 1969 scientists first synthesized an enzyme, ribonulease. Chemical reactions can occur several thousand or million times faster with enzymes than without them. They operate within a narrow temperature range (usually 30°C to 40°C) and have optimal pH ranges. Many enzymes have to be bound to nonprotein molecules in order to function effectively. These molecules include **trace elements** (such as metals) and **coenzymes** (such as vitamins). The lack or malfunction of enzymes can cause a variety of metabolic diseases. Enzymes are widely used in the manufacture of detergents and food.

**Eocene** Second of the five epochs of the TERTIARY period, *c*.55–38 million years ago. The fossil record shows members of modern plant genera, including beeches, walnuts, and elms, and indicates the apparent dominance of mammals, including the ancestors of camels, horses, rodents, bats, and monkeys.

**Eos** In Greek mythology, the goddess of dawn, identified with the Roman goddess Aurora. Daughter of HYPERION, and of HELIOS and SELENE, she drove through the sky in a horse-drawn chariot.

**ephemeris** (pl. Ephemerides) Table giving the predicted positions of a celestial object, such as a planet or comet, at given intervals.

**Ephesians** New Testament epistle dictated, according to tradition, by St. PAUL during his captivity in Rome (*c*.AD 60) and addressed to the Christian Church at Ephesus. The letter describes the supreme power and authority invested by God in Christ and stresses the unity of love and faith in the Christian church.

**Ephesus** (Efes) Ancient Ionian city of W Asia Minor (modern Turkey). A prosperous port under the Greeks and Romans, it was a center of the cult of Artemis (Diana). The Temple of Artemis was the largest Greek temple ever built and one of the SEVEN WONDERS OF THE WORLD. Ephesus was captured by CROESUS (*c*.550 BC), CYRUS THE GREAT (*c*.546 BC), and ALEXANDER THE GREAT (334 BC), falling under Roman control (133 BC). Today, it is one of the world's principal archaeological sites.

**epic** Long, narrative poem in grandiose style. The earliest known form of Greek literature, epics were originally used to transmit history orally. Using highly formalized language, epics tend to involve gods, men, and legendary battles. HOMER is the author of two of the most famous epics, the *Iliad* and the *Odyssey*. Later examples include the *Aeneid* by VIRGIL, *Paradise Lost* (1667) by MILTON, and *The Faerie Queene* (1589–96) by SPENSER.

**epic theater** *See* Bertolt BRECHT; Erwin PISCATOR

**epicureanism** School of Greek philosophy founded by EPICURUS. He proposed that the sensations of pleasure and pain were the ultimate measures of good and evil, and that pleasure should be actively pursued.

**Epicurus** (341–270 BC) Greek philosopher, founder of EPICUREANISM. Born on the island of Samos, he began teaching philosophy at the age of 32. He embraced a theory of physics derived from the ATOMISM of DEMOCRITUS.

**epidemic** Outbreak of an infectious disease rapidly spreading to many people. The study of epidemics is known as EPIDEMIOLOGY. An epidemic sweeping across many countries, such as the BLACK DEATH, is termed a pandemic.

**epidemiology** Study of the incidence and patterns of disease, with a view to finding means of prevention or control. Modern epidemiology is concerned with environmental and lifestyle factors in disease causation.

**epidermis** In animals, outer layer that contains no blood vessels. In many invertebrates it is only one cell thick, in vertebrates it may comprise several layers, and forms part of the SKIN. In plants, it is the outermost layer of a leaf or of an unthickened stem or root.

**epiglottis** Small flap of CARTILAGE projecting upward behind the root of the tongue. It closes off the LARYNX during swallowing to prevent food entering the airway.

**epigram** (Gk. inscription) In classical literature, a brief Greek or Latin poem expressing, in a pointed, witty manner, a single thought. The epigrams of the 1st century Latin poet Martial served as the model for epigrammatists, such as Ben JONSON and Oscar WILDE.

**epilepsy** Disorder characterized by abnormal electrical discharges in the brain that provoke seizures. Attacks are often presaged by warning symptoms, the "aura." Seizure types vary from the momentary loss of awareness seen in *petit mal* attacks ("absences") to the major convulsions of *grand mal* epilepsy. They may be triggered by a number of factors, including sleep deprivation, flashing lights, or excessive noise. Epilepsy is controlled with anti-convulsant drugs.

**epinephrine** HORMONE secreted by the ADRENAL GLANDS, important in preparing the body's response to stress. It increases the strength and rate of the heart beat and the rate of BREATHING, diverts blood from the SKIN and DIGESTIVE SYSTEM to the heart and muscles, and stimulates the release of GLUCOSE from the LIVER to increase energy supply by promoting increased RESPIRATION. Epinephrine is used in the resuscitation of patients in shock or following cardiac arrest.

**Epiphany** Christian feast celebrated on January 6. It originated in the Eastern Church as an observance of the baptism of Jesus. In the West it became associated with the manifestation of Christ to the Gentiles, and the coming of the Magi (Three Wise Men).

**epiphyte** (air plant) Plant that grows on another plant but is not a parasite. Epiphytes usually have aerial roots and produce their own food by PHOTOSYNTHESIS. They are common in tropical forests. Examples are some FERNS, orchids, Spanish moss, and many BROMELIADS.

**Episcopal Church** Anglican church of the US. CHURCH OF ENGLAND services were held in the first American colonies. With the American Revolution, the Church of England was disestablished and a national church organized in its place. Known as the Protestant Episcopal Church, its constitution and its own version of the Book of COMMON PRAYER were established in 1789. In 1989 it appointed the first woman bishop in the ANGLICAN COMMUNION. The church has more than 2.5 million members.

**epistemology** Branch of philosophy that critically examines the nature, limits, and validity of knowledge and the difference between knowledge and belief. In RATIONALISM, the existence of innate ideas are maintained along with ideas derived from experience. EMPIRICISM rejected the existence of innate ideas. Immanuel KANT attempted to combine both positions. A.N. WHITEHEAD proposed a causal theory of knowledge. PRAGMATISM focused on the practical data derived from the senses. Sir Karl POPPER rejected the certainity of scientific knowledge, since it depends on unpredicatble insight.

**epistles** Collection of 20 letters forming most of the middle section of the New Testament. More than half of them are attributed to the apostle St. PAUL.

**epithelium** Layer of cells, closely packed to form a surface for a body tube or cavity. Epithelium covers the SKIN, and various internal organs and surfaces such as the intestines, nasal passages, and mouth. Epithelial cells may also produce protective modifications such as hair and nails, or secrete substances such as ENZYMES.

**epoxy resin** Group of thermosetting polymers with outstandingly good mechanical and electrical properties, stability, heat and chemical resistance, and adhesion. Epoxy resins are used as adhesives, in casting and protective coatings.

**Epstein, Sir Jacob** (1880–1959) British sculptor, b. USA. His series of 18 nude figures (1907–08) caused a public outcry. Epstein scandalized Paris with the angel for Oscar Wilde's tomb (1912). His most revolutionary sculpture was *The Rock Drill* (1913–14), an ape that has mutated into a robot. Epstein also produced religious works, including the bronze *Visitation* (1926).

**Equal Employment Opportunities Commission (EEOC)** US government agency created in 1964 to end job discrimination based on race, color, religion, age, sex, national origin, or handicap. The commission investigates charges of discrimination and works for conciliation. If a voluntary settlement is not found, the commission may sue in federal court.

**Equal Rights Amendment (ERA)** Proposed amendment to the US Constitution, passed by Congress in 1972. The amendment states that "equality of rights under the law shall not be denied or abridged by the United States or by any State on account of sex." It provoked great controversy and by the 1982 deadline had been ratified by only 35 of the necessary 38 states.

**equation** Mathematical statement of variables, equal to some subset of all possible variables. The equation $x^2 = 8 - 2x$ is true only for certain values (solutions) of $x$ ($x = 2$ and $x = -4$). This type of equation is contrasted with an identity, such as $(x + 2)^2 = x^2 + 4x + 4$, which is true for all values of $x$. Equations are said to be linear, quadratic, cubic, quartic, etc., according to whether their degree (the highest power of the variable) is 1, 2, 3, 4, etc. *See also* SIMULTANEOUS EQUATIONS

**equator** Name given to two imaginary circles. The **terrestrial** Equator lies midway between the North Pole and South Pole and is the zero line from which latitude is measured. It divides the Earth into the Southern and Northern hemispheres. The **celestial** equator lies directly above the Earth's Equator and is used as a reference to determine the position of a star.

**Equatorial Guinea** (formerly Spanish Guinea) Republic in W central Africa, consisting of a mainland territory between Cameroon and Gabon, Mbini (Río Muni), and five islands in the Gulf of Guinea, the largest of which is Bioko (Fernando Póo). The capital is MALABO (on Bioko). **Land and climate** Bioko is a volcanic island with fertile soils. It is also mountainous, rising to 9,869ft (3,008m), and has heavy rainfall. There is a marked dry season from December to February. Mainland Mbini (90% of Equatorial Guinea's land area) consists mainly of hills and plateaus behind the coastal plains. Its main river, the Lolo, rises in Gabon. Mbini has a similar climate to Bioko. Dense rain forest covers most of Mbini. **History and Politics** Portuguese navigators reached the area in 1471. In 1778 Portugal ceded the islands and commercial mainland rights to Spain. In 1827 Spain leased bases on Bioko to Britain, and the British settled some freed slaves. Descendants of these former slaves (*Fernandinos*) remain on the island. Spain returned to the area in the mid-19th century. Bioko and Mbini were made provinces of overseas Spain (1959). They achieved independence in 1968. In 1979 the nation's first president, Francisco Macias Nguema, was deposed by a Supreme Military Council, led by Colonel Mbasogo. A 1991 referendum voted to set up a multiparty democracy, consisting of the ruling Equatorial Guinea Democratic Party (PDGE) and ten opposition parties. Elections (1993) were boycotted by the main parties and most of the electorate. The PDGE formed a government. In 1996 elections, again boycotted by opposition parties, President Mbasogo claimed 99% of the vote. **Economy** Agriculture employs 66% of the work force. The main food crops are bananas, cassava, and sweet potatoes. The most valuable crop is cocoa. Timber and coffee are also exported.

**equestrian sports** Three Olympic equestrian disciplines of dressage, show jumping, and trials (or eventing). This tests a horse's training, development, and ability to execute defined movements; showjumping tests its speed and jumping ability over obstacles set in a confined area; trials, held over 1–3 days, test its ability at dressage, over obstacles across country, and in showjumping.

**equilibrium** In physics, a stable state in which any variety of forces acting on a particle or object negate each other, resulting in no net force. An object with constant velocity is

**EQUATORIAL GUINEA**

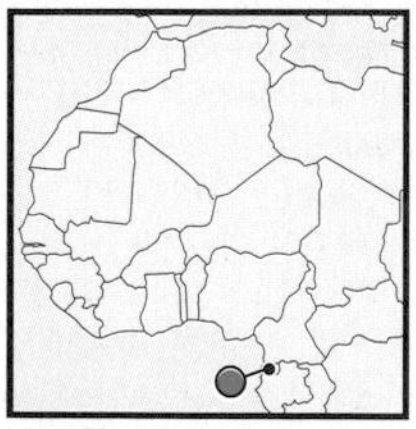

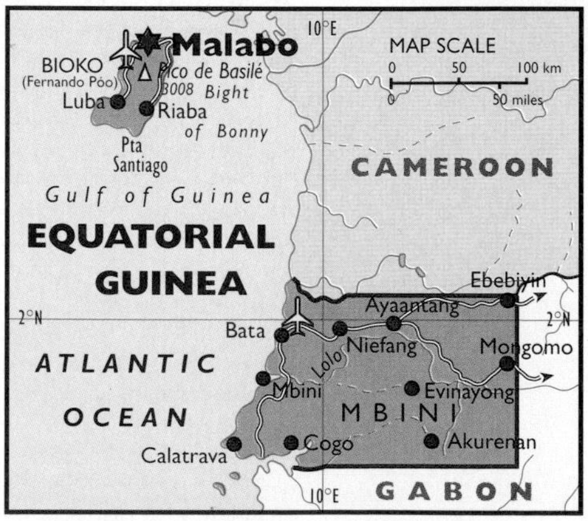

**AREA:** 10,830 sq mi (28,050sq km)
**POPULATION:** 420,000
**CAPITAL (POPULATION):** Malabo (35,000)
**GOVERNMENT:** Multiparty republic (transitional)
**ETHNIC GROUPS:** Fang 83%, Bubi 10%, Ndowe 4%
**LANGUAGES:** Spanish (official)
**RELIGIONS:** Christianity (mainly Roman Catholic) 89%, traditional beliefs 5%
**CURRENCY:** CFA franc = 100 centimes

▲ **Erasmus** The artist Hans Holbein the Younger was often commissioned by the great Dutch humanist Erasmus. Erasmus' scholarly attempts at internal reform of the Roman Catholic Church were denounced by Martin Luther. Erasmus was critical of clerical abuse, and church involvement in material matters. *The Education of a Christian Prince* (1515) is his greatest work.

E

also said to be in equilibrium. The term can also be ascribed to a body with a constant temperature; this is known as **thermic** equilibrium. *See also* GRAVITY; LEVER; THERMODYNAMICS

**equinox** Either of the two days each year when day and night are of equal duration. They occur on the two occasions, (one spring, one fall) when the Sun crosses the celestial EQUATOR.

**equity** In law, a field of jurisdiction that enables the judiciary to apply principles or morals. In medieval England it became clear that the strict application of COMMON LAW produced cases of injustice. In such cases, the chancellor reviewed petitions made to the king and made remedies where appropriate. Eventually, the chancellor became head of a court of equity known as the CHANCERY. Equity was based on ROMAN LAW and CANON LAW, but soon established its own set of precedents. In 1873 law and equity were merged in a High Court of Justice. Only a few US states retain a distinction between law and equity.

**Erasmus, Desiderius** (1466–1536) (Gerhard Gerhards) Dutch scholar and teacher, considered the greatest of the RENAISSANCE humanists. His Latin translation of the Greek New Testament revealed flaws in the VULGATE text. Among his original works, the *Manual of the Christian Knight* (1503) called for reform of the church. Erasmus had an early influence on Martin LUTHER and other Protestant reformers, but sought change from within the Catholic Church and disagreed with the course of the REFORMATION. In *On Free Will* (1524) he openly clashed with Luther. *See also* HUMANISM

**Eratosthenes** (276–194 BC) Greek scholar who first measured the Earth's circumference by geometry. Eratosthenes administered the library of ALEXANDRIA.

**erbium** (symbol Er) Metallic element of the LANTHANIDE SERIES. There are six isotopes naturally occurring, and the chief ores are monazite and bastnaesite. Nine radioactive isotopes have been identified. Soft and malleable, erbium is used in some alloys. Erbium oxide is used as a pink colorant for glass. Properties: at.no. 68; at.wt. 167.26; m.p. 2,772°F (1,522°C); b.p. 5,185°F (2,863°C); sp.gr. 9.045; most common isotope $^{166}$Er (33.41%).

**Eric the Red** (active late 10th century) Norse chieftain, discoverer of Greenland. He settled in Iceland, from which he was banished after a murder. Eric the Red set off to the west and discovered the land he named Greenland in *c.*981.

**Erie** City on Lake Erie, NW Pennsylvania. It was first settled by the French in 1753, occupied by the British in 1760, and destroyed during PONTIAC'S REBELLION. Pennsylvania's only port on the Great Lakes, Erie exports timber, coal, iron ore, petroleum, grain and fish. Industries: machinery, plastics, paper. Pop. (1990) 108,718.

**Erie, Lake** Great Lake in North America, bordered by Ontario (W), New York (E), Ohio and Pennsylvania (S), and Michigan (SW); part of the GREAT LAKES–ST. LAWRENCE SEAWAY. Site of a British defeat in the WAR OF 1812, it is the shallowest and second smallest of the lakes. Lake Erie has been polluted by the cities (Buffalo, Erie, Cleveland, and Toledo) that lie on its shores. Government regulations are aiding its recovery. Area: 9,910sq mi (25,667sq km). Max. depth: 210ft (64m).

**Erie Canal** Artificial waterway in New York, connecting Buffalo on Lake Erie to Albany on the Hudson River. The first major waterway to be built (1817–25) in the US, it aided the commercial growth of New York City by joining the Great Lakes to the Atlantic Ocean. Largely superseded by the railroads, it was revitalized and lengthened to 524mi (843km) in 1918.

**Erikson, Erik** (1902–94) US psychoanalyst, b. Germany. He extended Freudian theory into adolescence and adulthood, coining the term identity crisis. He wrote the Pulitzer Prize-winning work *Gandhi's Truth* (1969).

**Eritrea** Independent state in NE Africa, on the Red Sea; the capital is ASMARA. The chief ports are Aseb and Massawa. **Land** Much of Eritrea is a continuation of the high Ethiopian plateau, sloping down to plains to the E and W. Unreliable rainfall is a frequent cause of drought. **History** Eritrea was a dependency of Ethiopia until the 16th century, when it was annexed to the Ottoman empire. During the 19th century, control of the region was disputed between Ethiopia, Egypt, and Italy. In 1890 it became an Italian colony. From 1941 to 1952 it was under British military administration. In 1952 it was federated with Ethiopia, becoming a province in 1962. Eritrean separatists began a 30-year campaign of guerrilla warfare. 700,000 refugees fled to Somalia. In 1991 the Eritrean People's Liberation Front (EPLF) helped topple Mengistu's Ethiopian government, and won a referendum on independence. Eritrea formally gained independence in 1993. **Economy** The war-devastated economy is mainly agricultural. Industries: textiles, leather goods, salt. Area: 45,405sq mi (117,599sq km). Pop. (1994 est.) 3,530,000.

**ermine** Known as a short-tailed WEASEL in North America, or a STOAT in Eurasia.

**Ernst, Max** (1891–1976) German painter and sculptor, founder of Cologne DADA (1919), later influential in SURREALISM. Ernst developed ways of adapting COLLAGE, photomontage, and other radical pictorial techniques. His most important works include *L'Eléphant Célèbes* (1921) and *Two Children Threatened by a Nightingale* (1924). He lived in New York (1941–48).

**Eros** Elongated asteroid with an irregular-shaped orbit. In 1931 and 1975 it approached to within 15 million mi (24 million km) of Earth. Longer diameter: 17mi (27km). Mean distance from the Sun: 144 million mi (232 million km). Mean sidereal period: 1.76 yr.

**Eros** In Greek mythology, god of love, equivalent to the Roman god Cupid. Depicted as a winged boy carrying a bow and arrows, and often blindfold, he was the youngest and most mischievous of the gods. He married PSYCHE.

**erosion** In geology, alteration of landforms by the wearing away of rock and soil, and the removal of any debris (as opposed to WEATHERING). Erosion is carried out by the actions of wind, water, glaciers, and organisms. *See also* GEOMORPHOLOGY

**erratic** In geology, a rock that has been transported some distance from its source by glacial action, and is therefore of a different type to the surrounding rocks.

**Erving, Julius** (1950– ) US basketball player. He played in the American Basketball Association (ABA) before joining the Philadephia 76ers of the NBA (1976–87). One of basketball's most prolific scorers, his career total of 30,026 ranks third on the all-time scoring list. "Dr. J." was named most valuable player four times (1974–76, 1981). He retired in 1987.

**erysipelas** Contagious skin infection caused by a STREPTOCOCCUS bacterium. Symptoms include pain and heat in the affected part and coarse skin rashes that become red, shiny, and swollen.

**erythrocyte** Red BLOOD cell, usually disk-shaped and without a nucleus. It contains HEMOGLOBIN that combines with oxygen and gives blood its red color. Normal human blood contains an average of 300 million such cells per cu in of blood.

**Esaki, Leo** (1925– ) Japanese physicist, who developed the tunnel DIODE, a SEMICONDUCTOR that allows electrons to cross normally impassable electronic barriers. US physicist Ivar Giaever extended Esaki's research to the field of SUPERCONDUCTIVITY. For this work, they shared the 1973 Nobel Prize for physics with Brian JOSEPHSON.

**Esau** (Heb. hairy) Old Testament figure, son of Isaac and Rebecca. Esau sold his inheritance for a bowl of stew to his scheming brother, JACOB.

**escape velocity** Minimum velocity required to free a body from the gravitational field of a celestial body or stellar system. Escape velocities are, for the Earth 7mi/s (11.2km/sec) and Moon 1.5mi/s (2.4km/sec).

**eschatology** In systematic theology, the formalized doctrine concerning the end of the world, or the end of time. It comprises the study of teaching and theory on the coming of the kingdom of God.

**Escher, Maurits Cornelis** (1898–1972) Dutch graphic artist. He is best known for his prints based on mathematical ideas. These contain metamorphoses, illusions, and paradoxes, as in *Ascending and Descending* (1960).

**Escorial** Spanish monastery and palace near Madrid. Built 1563–84 for PHILIP II, it comprises a massive group of buildings and houses a notable art collection.

**Esfahan** *See* ISFAHAN

**Eskimo** (Algonquian, eaters of raw flesh) Aboriginal inhabitants (*c*.60,000) of Arctic and sub-Arctic regions of North America (the INUIT), Greenland, and Siberia. Sharing the common language family of Eskimo-ALEUT, Eskimos have adapted to harsh climates and are proficient hunters of sea mammals. In some areas, a nomadic existence has been replaced by village settlements and work in the oil and mining industries. The eating of raw meat preserves scarce resources and provides essential nutrients. In winter, igloos (snow huts) provide temporary shelter. In summer, tents are made from animal skins. Eskimos are skilled artisans, producing kayaks and finely crafted tools from skin, ivory, bone, copper, or stone. Their spiritual life is dominated by invisible forces of nature (*innua*). SHAMANISM plays an important part in everyday life.

**esophagus** Part of the ALIMENTARY CANAL of the digestive system, a muscular tube that connects the pharynx to the stomach. Secretions of the mucous lining of the esophagus provide lubrication to aid PERISTALSIS.

**ESP** Abbreviation of EXTRASENSORY PERCEPTION

**Esperanto** Language devised in 1887 by Ludwik Zamenhof (1859–1917), as a language of international communication. Its vocabulary is mostly derived from W European languages.

**espionage** Act of obtaining secret information, especially for one state about the political, military and industrial matters of a rival. The importance of espionage in military affairs was recognized in ancient China, Greece, and Egypt. Nathan HALE and Benedict ARNOLD are famous spies from the American Revolution. MATA HARI was the most renowned spy in World War I. The secret police (KGB) in the Soviet Union wielded considerable political power. In the US, the CENTRAL INTELLIGENCE AGENCY (CIA) was established in 1947. The COLD WAR witnessed a dramatic increase in espioniage activity. Famous spy cases of the period include Alger HISS, and the ROSENBERG CASE.

**essay** (Fr. *essai*, attempt) Usually short, non-fictional prose composition, written expressing a personal point of view. It originated with the 16th-century French writer Montaigne. Famous US essayists include Ralph Waldo EMERSON, Henry David THOREAU, Oliver Wendell HOLMES JR., and George SANTAYANA. Noted British essayists include Francis BACON, Henry FIELDING, Dr. Samuel JOHNSON, Oliver GOLDSMITH, Matthew ARNOLD, and Charles LAMB.

**Essen** City on the Ruhr River, Nordrhein-Westfalen state, NW Germany. With a major coalfield, Essen underwent a huge industrial expansion during the 19th century. The city was heavily bombed in World War II. Industries: mining, iron and steel. Pop. (1990) 627,800.

**Essenes** Jewish religious sect which existed in Palestine, from the 2nd century BC to the end of the 2nd century AD. A secrecy developed about the sect, and they shunned public life and temple worship. The DEAD SEA SCROLLS are said to contain their sacred books.

**essential oil** Oil found in flowers, fruits, or plants. It is the source of their odor and is widely used in aromatherapy, potpourri, and perfumed toiletries.

**Essex, Robert Devereux, 2nd Earl of** (1566–1601) English courtier and soldier. A favorite of ELIZABETH I, he attacked Cadiz in 1596. Following a quarrel with Elizabeth, he was made the reluctant lord lieutenant of a rebellious Ireland. Essex returned in disgrace six months later, attempted a coup d'état, and was executed for treason.

**Essex** County in SE England; the county town is Chelmsford. Colonized by the Romans at COLCHESTER, it was invaded by the Anglo-Saxons in the 5th century and later came under Danish control. Low-lying on the E coast, the land rises to the NW providing pasture for dairy and sheep farming. Wheat, barley, and sugar-beet are important crops. Industries: machinery, electrical goods. Area: 1,419sq mi (3,674sq km). Pop. (1991) 1,528,577.

**ester** Any of a class of organic compounds formed by reaction between an ALCOHOL and an ACID.

**Esther** Old Testament book narrating how the legendary Queen Esther averted the killing of her people, the Jews, by the Persians in Babylon.

**Estonia** Republic on the E coast of the Baltic Sea, Estonia is the smallest of the three Baltic states that gained independence from the Soviet Union in 1991. **Land and Climate** Estonia is mostly flat. The area is strewn with moraine. It is dotted with more than 1,500 small lakes. Lake Peipus and the Narva River make up most of Estonia's Russian border. Estonia has more than 800 islands that make up *c*.10% of total area; the largest is Saaremaa. Despite its northerly position, it has a fairly mild climate. Rainfall averages from 19 to 23in (480–580mm). Farmland and pasture account for more than 33% of land use. **History and Politics** The original settlers were related to the Finns. The TEUTONIC KNIGHTS introduced Christianity in the 13th century, and by the 16th century German noblemen owned much of the land. In 1561 Sweden took the N part of the country and Poland the S. In 1625 Sweden assumed complete control, but surrendered the region to Russia in 1721. Estonia became independent in 1918. In 1940 Soviet forces occupied Estonia, but were driven out by Germany in 1941. Soviet troops returned in 1944 and Estonia became one of the 15 socialist republics of the Soviet Union. Estonians strongly opposed Soviet rule, and many were deported to Siberia. In 1990 Estonia declared its independence, and the Soviet Union recognized this in 1991. Estonia adopted a new constitution in 1992 and multiparty elections were held. In 1995 elections a center-left government was elected. **Economy** Under Soviet rule, Estonia was the

## EROSION

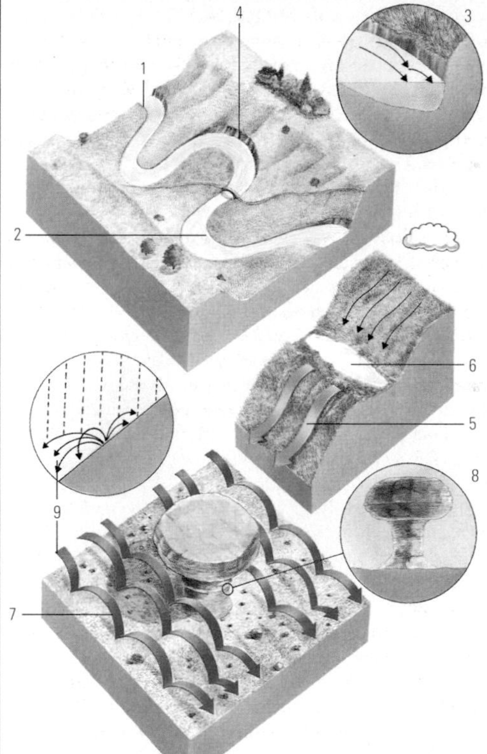


**▼ Coastal erosion** The powerful action of the waves produces recognizable features. Horse-shoe bays (below), for example, are formed when rock layers of different hardness lie parallel to the coast. The erosive power of the sea exploits areas of weakness in a hard rock deposit (1). Waves will then cut away any softer rock behind (2), eroding back until they reach another strata of harder rock (3). When bays join (4), islands of hard rock can be left across the mouth (5)

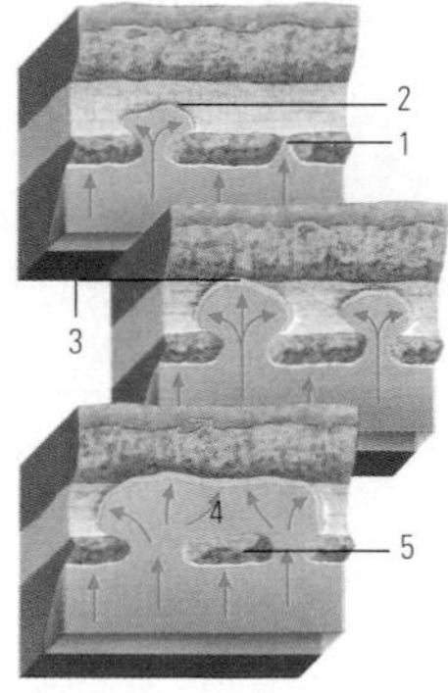


Erosion is the breakdown and transportation of rock due to the action of an outside agent. There are three main forms: river, glacial, and wind. Rivers (1) erode their channels through the flow of water and the abrasion of the load they are carrying against the banks and riverbed. Erosion is most forceful at the outside of bends (2) where the banks are undercut (3) often creating cliffs or bluffs (4) down which material moves. Flood surges dramatically increase the power of the river and correspondingly magnify the erosive force.On a smaller scale water in the form of rain will move material down a hillside (5). Particles of soil are carried by rivulets and the impact of raindrops throws soil down a slope. Vegetation reduces such erosion by binding the soil together. Where vegetation is removed, as on tracks (6), erosion is accentuated. In arid conditions wind erosion can carve distinctive features. Sand and stones blown by the wind (7) have the same effect as shot-blasting. Mushroom-shaped formations, pedestals (8), are often the result. This is due to the maximum height at which the erosive sand is carried by the wind as it bounces across the surface (9), above which the rock is untouched.

## ESTONIA

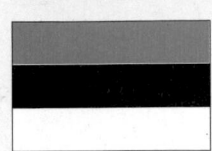

**AREA:** 17,300sq mi (44,700sq km)
**POPULATION:** 1,491,583
**CAPITAL (POPULATION):** Tallinn (490,000)
**GOVERNMENT:** Multiparty republic
**ETHNIC GROUPS:** Estonian 62%, Russian 30%, Ukrainian 3%, Belorussian 2%, Finnish 1%
**LANGUAGES:** Estonian (official)
**RELIGIONS:** Christianity (Lutheran, with Orthodox and Baptist minorities)
**CURRENCY:** Kroon = 100 senti

most prosperous of the Baltic states. Chief natural resources are oil shale and forests. Manufactures include petrochemicals, fertilizers, and textiles. Agriculture and fishing are important. Barley, potatoes, and oats are major crops. Since 1988, Estonia has begun a process of privatization.

**estrogen** Female SEX HORMONE. First produced by a girl at PUBERTY, estrogen leads to the development of the secondary sexual characteristics: breasts, body hair, and redistributed fat. It regulates the MENSTRUAL CYCLE and prepares the UTERUS for pregnancy. It is also a constituent of the contraceptive PILL.

**estuary** Coastal region where a river mouth opens into the ocean and freshwater from the land mixes with saltwater from the sea. Estuaries usually provide good harbors and breeding grounds for many kinds of marine life.

**etching** Method of INTAGLIO (incised) printing used for black-and-white designs. A metal plate, usually copper, is coated with an acid-proof ground. A design is etched with a needle so that the lines penetrate the ground. The plate is then placed in an acid that eats away the exposed line so that it will hold ink. When the plate is finished, it is rolled with ink and placed in an etching press to be printed.

**ethanal** (acetaldehyde, $CH_3CHO$) Colorless volatile flammable liquid manufactured now by catalytic oxidation of ethene, ethanol, or catalytic hydration of acetylene. It is used in the breathalyzer test and to silver mirrors. Properties: sp.gr. 0.788; m.p. −190.3°F (−123.5°C); b.p. 69.4°F (20.8°C).

**ethane** ($CH_3CH_3$) Colorless, odorless gas, the second member of the ALKANE series of HYDROCARBONS. It is a minor constituent of natural gas. *See also* SATURATED COMPOUND

**ethanoic acid** (acetic acid, $CH_3COOH$) Colorless corrosive liquid made by the oxidation of ETHANOL, by catalysis or by the action of bacteria. It is the active ingredient in VINEGAR, and has many uses in the organic chemicals industry. Properties: sp.gr. 1.049; m.p. 61.9°F (16.6°C); b.p. 244.4°F (117.9°C).

**ethanol** (ethyl alcohol, $C_2H_5OH$)) Colorless, flammable, and volatile ALCOHOL, produced by the FERMENTATION of sugars, molasses, and grains, or by the catalytic hydration of ethylene. Its many uses include alcoholic beverages, rocket fuels, cosmetics, and pharmaceuticals. Properties: sp.gr. 0.789; b.p. 173.3°F (78.5°C).

**Ethelbert** (d.616) King of Kent (560–616). He was the strongest ruler in England S of the Humber River, and was the first Christian king in Anglo-Saxon England.

**Ethelred II (the Unready)** (968–1016) (Old English, evil *rede* or counsel) King of England (978–1013; 1014–16). Following continuous Danish attacks, he paid off the raiders with money raised by the Danegeld (994). The Danes returned nevertheless in 997 and again in 1002 when they were massacred by Ethelred's forces. The Danish King Sweyn retaliated and conquered England (1013). Ethelred was made king again on Sweyn's death, but was succeeded by Sweyn's son, CANUTE II.

**ethene** (ethylene, $CH_2H_4$) Colorless gas derived from the cracking of propane and other compounds. Vast quantities are used in polyethylene production. Ethene is also used for many other chemical syntheses.

**ether** In physics, hypothetical medium that was supposed to fill all space and offer no resistance to motion. It was was disproved (1887) by MICHELSON and MORLEY.

**ether** (diethyl ether, $C_2H_5OC_2H_5$) Colorless, volatile inflammable liquid prepared by the action of sulfuric acid on ethanol followed by distillation. It is used as an industrial solvent, fuel additive, and decreasingly as an anesthetic. Diethyl ether is a typical member of the ethers with the general formula ROR', where R,R' are hydrocarbon radicals. Properties: m.p. −117.2°F (−116.2°C); b.p. 94.1°F (34.5°C).

**ethics** (moral philosophy) Study of voluntary human actions, both individual and collective, according to moral precepts. Judaism, Chistianity, Islam, Hinduism, and Buddhism all incorporate moral teachings. For ARISTOTLE, happiness was achieved through the cultivation of virtue. PLATO's ethical system was based on metaphysical IDEALISM. HEDONISM taught that the pursuit of pleasure was the highest good. STOICS advocated virtue achieved through harmony with nature. RATIONALISM postulated conscience as the basis of moral behavior. EMPIRICISM argued that conscience was acquired by experience. Immanuel KANT put moral duty above happiness. He argued that an act is only truly moral if it is motivated solely by duty. The ethics of UTILTARIANISM are based on the principle of the greatest good for the greatest number. *See also* A.J. AYER; John DEWEY

**Ethiopia** Landlocked republic in E Africa. *See* country feature

**ethnic group** In sociology, any social group that shares a complex of characteristics distinguishing it from larger society. Such groups are usually based on national origins, religion, language, culture, or race.

**ethnography** *See* ANTHROPOLOGY; ETHNOLOGY

**ethnology** Comparative study of cultures. Historical ethnology was developed in the late 19th century in an attempt to trace cultural diffusion.

**ethology** Study of animal behavior especially in the natural environment, first outlined in the 1920s by Konrad LORENZ. Ethologists study natural processes, such as courtship, mating, and self-defense.

**ethyl alcohol** *See* ETHANOL

**ethylene** *See* ETHENE

**ethyne** (acetylene, $C_2H_2$) Colorless flammable gas, manufactured by cracking of petroleum fractions. The simplest ALKYNE, it is explosive if mixed with air. When burned with oxygen, it produces extremely high temperatures up to 6,300°F (3,480°C) and is used in oxyacetylene torches. It is polymerized to manufacture plastics, synthetic fibers, resins, and neoprene (synthetic rubber). It is also used to produce ethanal and ethanoic acid. Properties: sp.gr. 0.625; m.p. −80.8°C (−113.4°F); b.p. −84°C (−119.2°F).

**Etna** Volcanic mountain on the E coast of Sicily, Italy. The first known eruption was in 475 BC, others occurring in 1169, 1669, and 1971. It is the highest active volcano in Europe and the highest mountain in Italy S of the Alps. Height: *c*.10,958ft (3,340m).

**Eton** Town on the Thames River, Berkshire, S England. It is the site of a famous private school, Eton College, founded by Henry VI in 1440. Pop. (1981) 3,559.

**Etruscan** Inhabitant of ancient Etruria (modern Tuscany and Umbria), central Italy. Etruscan civilization flourished in the first millennium BC. Their sophisticated society was influenced by Greece and organized in city states. Etruscan civilization reached its peak in the 6th century BC. Their wealth and power was based primarily on their skill at ironworking and their control of the iron trade. They are famed for their naturalistic bronze busts, and black *bucchero* pottery. The Etruscan cult of the dead led them to produce elaborate tombs. From the 5th to the 3rd century BC they were gradually overrun by neighboring peoples, particularly the Romans.

**etymology** Branch of PHILOLOGY dealing with the origin and history of words. The word *telephone*, for example, is a combination of two elements derived from Greek, *tele* (distant) and *phone* (sound or voice).

**Eubacteria** Subkingdom of the kingdom PROKARYOTAE, sometimes considered a separate DOMAIN. Eubacteria include all multicellular BACTERIA, including those that photosynthesize, deriving their carbon from the air. They do not have the unique types of cell walls, RIBOSOMES, and RNA of the other subkingdom, ARCHAEBACTERIA. *See also* PHOTOSYNTHESIS

**Euboea** (Évvoia) Island in the W Aegean Sea, SE central Greece; the capital is Khalkís. Under Athenian domination from 506 to 411 BC, it was taken by Philip II of Macedon in 338, then held successively by the Romans, Byzantines, Venetians, and Turks, before being incorporated into Greece in 1830. Industries: livestock, grapes. Area: 1,411sq mi (3,654sq km). Pop. (1991) 208,408.

**eucalyptus** (gum tree) Genus of evergreen shrubs and slender trees, native to Australia and cultivated in warm and temperate regions. They are valuable sources of hardwood and oils. Leaves are blue/white, and they bear woody fruits and flowers without petals. Height: to 400ft (122m). There are *c*.600 species. Family Myrtaceae.

**Eucharist** (Gk. thanksgiving) Central act of Christian worship, in which the priest and congregation partake in Holy Communion – one of the principal SACRAMENTS. The Eucharist is a commemorative reenactment of the LAST SUPPER. *See also* TRANSUBSTANTIATION

**Euclid** (*c*.330–*c*.260 BC) Ancient Greek mathematician, who taught at Alexandria, Egypt. He is remembered for his textbooks on geometry, such as *The Elements* (Lat. pub. 1482) and *Data*.

**Eudoxus of Cnidus** (*c*.408–*c*.355 BC) Greek mathematician and astronomer. His greatest contribution was to give a precise definition of a REAL NUMBER in the framework of a general theory of proportion. In astronomy, he proposed the first system for describing the motions of the heavenly bodies.

**Eugène of Savoy** (1663–1736) French-born prince and Austrian general. He displayed courage for Austria against the Ottoman Turks at Vienna (1683) and Zenta (1697). In the War of the SPANISH SUCCESSION (1702–13), Eugène joined the Duke of MARLBOROUGH in victories over the French at BLENHEIM (1704), Oudenarde (1708), and Malplaquet (1709).

## ETHIOPIA

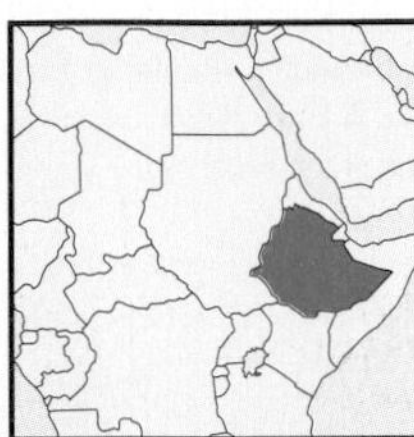

The tricolour flag of Ethiopia was first flown as three separate pennants, one above the other. The red, yellow, and green combination dates from the late 19th century. It appeared in flag form in 1897. The present sequence was adopted in 1914. The central pentangle was introduced in 1996 and represents the common will of the country's 68 ethnic groups.

**AREA:** 435,521sq mi (1,128,000sq km)
**POPULATION:** 55,500,000
**CAPITAL (POPULATION):** Addis Ababa (1,700,000)
**GOVERNMENT:** Federation of nine provinces
**ETHNIC GROUPS:** Oromo (Galla) 40%, Semitic (Amhara and Tigreans) 33%, Shangalla 5%, Somalis 5%, Others 17%
**LANGUAGES:** Amharic (de facto official)
**RELIGIONS:** Christianity 53%, Islam 36%, traditional beliefs 11%
**CURRENCY:** Birr = 100 cents

Ethiopia is a land-locked republic in NE Africa. The dominant feature is the Ethiopian Plateau, a block of volcanic mountains. Its average height is 6,000–8,000ft (1,800–2,400m), and rises to 15,157ft (4,620m), at Ras Dashen. The plateau is bisected by the Great RIFT VALLEY. The Eastern Highlands include the Somali Plateau and the desert of the Ogaden Plateau. The Western Highlands include the Blue Nile (Abbay) and its source, Lake Tana, Ethiopia's largest lake. The Danakil Desert forms Ethiopia's border with ERITREA.

### CLIMATE

The climate in Ethiopia is greatly affected by the altitude. The capital, ADDIS ABABA, at 8,000ft (2,450m), has an average annual temperature of 68°F (20°C). The rainfall is generally over 40in (1,000mm), with a rainy season from April to September. The NE and SW lowlands are extremely hot and arid with less than 20in (500mm) annual rainfall and frequent droughts.

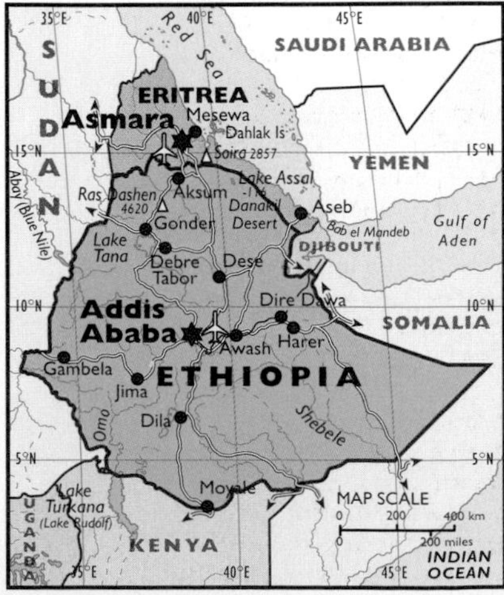


### VEGETATION

Grass, farmland, and trees cover most of the highlands. Semidesert and tropical savanna cover parts of the lowlands. Dense rain forest grows in the SW.

### HISTORY AND POLITICS

According to tradition, the Ethiopian kingdom was founded in *c*.1000 BC by Solomon's son, Menelik I. Coptic Christianity was introduced to the N kingdom of Axum in the 4th century. In the 6th century, Judaism flourished. The expansion of Islam led to the isolation of Axum. The kingdom fragmented in the 16th century. In 1855 Kasa reestablished unity, proclaimed himself *negus* (emperor) Theodore, and founded the modern state. The late 19th century was marked by European intervention, and Menelik II became emperor with Italian support. He expanded the empire, made Addis Ababa his capital (1889), and defeated an Italian invasion (1895). In 1930 Menelik II's grandnephew, Ras Tafari Makonnen, was crowned Emperor HAILE SELASSIE I. In 1935 Italian troops invaded Ethiopia (Abyssinia). In 1936 Italy combined Ethiopia with Somalia and Eritrea to form Italian East Africa. During World War II, British and South African forces recaptured Ethiopia, and Haile Selassie was restored as emperor.

In 1952, Eritrea was federated with Ethiopia. The 1960s witnessed violent demands for Eritrean secession and economic equality. Following famine in N Ethiopia, Selassie was deposed by a military coup in 1974. The Provisional Military Administrative Council (PMAC) abolished the monarchy. Military rule was repressive and civil war broke out. In 1977, Somalia seized land in the Ogaden Desert. The new PMAC leader, Mengistu Mariam, with Soviet military assistance, recaptured territory in Eritrea and the Ogaden. In 1984–85 widespread famine received global news coverage, and 10,000 FALASHAS were airlifted to Israel. In 1987 Mengistu established the People's Democratic Republic of Ethiopia. In 1991 the Tigrean-based Ethiopian People's Revolutionary Democratic Front (EPRDF) and the Eritrean People's Liberation Front (EPLF) brought down Mengistu's regime. In 1993 Eritrea achieved independence. In 1994 a federal constitution was adopted. In 1995 multiparty elections were won by the EPRDF. Negasso Gidada was elected president.

### ECONOMY

Ethiopia is the world's poorest country (1992 GDP per capita, US$330), 88% of the workforce are engaged in agriculture (mostly subsistence) and 67% of exports are food products. Coffee is the main cash crop, shipped through the port of DJIBOUTI. During the 1970s and 1980s, it was plagued by civil war and famine (partly caused by long droughts). Ethiopia remains heavily dependent on food and financial aid.

**eugenics** Study of human improvement by selective breeding, founded in the 19th century by Sir Francis GALTON. Eugenics was discredited in the early 20th century owing to its ethical implications and its racist and class-based assumptions. Advances in GENETICS have given rise to the modern field of genetic counseling, through which people known to have defective genes that could cause disorders in offspring are warned of the risks.

**Eugénie** (1826–1920) Consort of NAPOLEON III and French empress. She became the wife of Napoleon III shortly after he declared the Second Empire in 1852. Regent in her husband's absences at war (1859, 1865, 1870), her influence as a Catholic and conservative was often felt in French affairs. After Napoleon was deposed in 1870, the couple fled to England.

**Euglenophyta** Phylum of single-celled ALGAE which includes the genus *Euglena*. Members of this group have both animal and plant characteristics. They swim by means of flagella. Many species contain CHLOROPLASTS and employ PHOTOSYNTHESIS, but some are colorless and feed on BACTERIA and DIATOMS.

**eukaryote** Organism whose CELLS have a membrane-bound NUCLEUS, with DNA contained in CHROMOSOMES. Making up one of the three domains, eukaryotes include all ANIMALS, PLANTS, FUNGUS, and PROTISTA. They have a complex CYTOPLASM with an ENDOPLASMIC RETICULUM, and most of them possess MITOCHONDRIA. *See also* KINGDOM; PROKARYOTAE

**Euler, Leonhard** (1707–83) Swiss mathematician. He is best known for his geometric theorem, which states that for any polyhedron (many-sided figure), $V-E+F = 2$, where $V$ is the number of vertices, $E$ the number of edges, and $F$ the number of faces. He published on subjects as diverse as mechanics, algebra, optics, and astronomy.

**eunuch** Castrated man, originally used as keeper of a HAREM. They were employed as servants in royal and wealthy households, especially in the Byzantine and Ottoman empires. *See also* CASTRATO

**Euphrates** (Firat) River of SW Asia. Formed by the confluence of the rivers Murat and Karasu, it flows from E Turkey across Syria into central Iraq, where it joins the TIGRIS River NW of BASRA to form the SHATT AL-ARAB, and eventually flows into the PERSIAN GULF. The ancient civilizations of BABYLONIA and ASSYRIA developed along the lower Euphrates. Length: 1,740mi (2,800km).

**eurhythmics** System of musical and dance training which has influenced ballet and acting. Developed in Switzerland and Germany by Emile Jaques-Dalcroze during the early 20th century, it evolved from interpretive gymnastic exercises performed to music.

**Euripides** (480–450 BC) Greek playwright. With AESCHYLUS and SOPHOCLES, one of the three great writers of Greek TRAGEDY. Euripides' plays caused contemporary controversy, with their cynical depiction of human motivation. The significance of the CHORUS is reduced in favor of an examination of individual behavior, especially women in love. His works, such as *Medea*, *Electra*, *Hecuba*, and the antiwar satire *Trojan Women* achieved great posthumous popularity.

**Euro** Single currency unit for the EUROPEAN UNION (EU). The MAASTRICHT TREATY (1992) established a timetable for economic and monetary union (EMU). A European Currency Unit (ECU) acted as a theoretical unit until the birth of the Euro on 1

▼ **Europe** Although it is the Earth's second smallest continent, Europe features a huge diversity in climate – from the hot, dry Spanish plains to the Arctic tundra of the far N. This diversity of climate has created equally diverse populations of plants and animals

January 1999. In this first stage, 11 member states (Austria, Belgium, Finland, Fránce, Germany, Ireland, Italy, Luxembourg, Netherlands, Portugal and Spain) fixed their exchange rates against each other and against the Euro.

**Europa** Smallest of Jupiter's GALILEAN SATELLITES, with a diameter of 1,950mi (3,138km). Mainly rock, Europa's smooth water-ice crust is crisscrossed by a network of light and dark linear markings. There are very few craters.

**Europa** Beautiful Phoenician princess of Greek legend. She was abducted and ravished by ZEUS who carried her across the sea to Crete. She bore three sons, including MINOS, who became king of Crete.

**Europe** Earth's second smallest continent, comprising the western fifth of the Eurasian landmass. It is separated from Asia by the Urals (E), Caspian Sea and the Caucasus (SE), Black Sea and Dardanelles (S), and from Africa by the Mediterranean Sea. **Land** Europe is dominated by the Alpine mountain chain, the principal links of which are the PYRENEES, ALPS, CARPATHIAN MOUNTAINS, BALKAN STATES, and the CAUCASUS. Between the Scandinavian peninsula and the Alpine chain is the great European plain, which extends from the Atlantic coast in France to the Urals. Much of the plain is fertile farmland. Major islands include the British Isles, Sicily, Sardinia, Corsica, and Iceland. **Structure and geology** Much of N Europe is made up of large sedimentary plains overlying an ancient Precambrian shield, outcrops of which remain in N Scandinavia, Scotland, and the Urals. There are also worn-down Paleozoic highlands. Many upland areas N of the Alps were formed during the Carboniferous period, including Ireland, the moorlands of Devon and Cornwall and the PENNINES, England. Southern Europe is geologically younger. Alpine folding began in the Oligocene period. Europe's longest river is the VOLGA, other major rivers are (from W to E) the TAGUS, LOIRE, RHÔNE, RHINE, ELBE, and DANUBE. The CASPIAN SEA is the world's largest lake. **Climate and vegetation** Europe's climate varies from subtropical to polar. The Mediterranean climate of the S is dry and warm. Much of the land is scrub (maquis), with some hardwood forests. Further N, the climate is mild and quite humid, moderated by prevailing westerly winds and the GULF STREAM. The natural vegetation is mixed forest, but this has been extensively depleted. Mixed forest merges into boreal forests of conifers. In SE European Russia, wooded and grass steppe merge into semi-desert to the N of the Caspian Sea. In the far N, lies the tundra. **History** The Mediterranean region was the cradle of the ancient Greek and Roman civilizations. The collapse of the Western Roman empire and the barbarian invasions brought chaos to much of Europe. During the Middle Ages Christianity was the unifying force throughout the continent. The postmedieval period witnessed the SCHISM in the Catholic Church, and the emergence of the nation state. European powers began to found vast empires in other parts of the globe (*see* COLONIALISM; EXPLORATION; IMPERIALISM), and the FRENCH REVOLUTION ushered in an era of momentous political changes. During the 20th century, a period overshadowed by two World Wars and the rise of COMMUNISM, Europe began to lose some of its preeminence in world affairs. After World War II the countries of Europe became divided into two ideological blocs: Eastern Europe, dominated by the Soviet Union, and Western Europe, closely aligned with the US. The rivalry was known as the COLD WAR. The NORTH ATLANTIC TREATY ORGANIZATION (NATO) was established to act as a deterrent to the spread of COMMUNISM; the Warsaw Pact was its E European counterpart. Several economic organizations, in particular the EUROPEAN COMMUNITY (EC), worked toward closer intra-national cooperation. In 1991 the collapse of Soviet communism added to the momentum for a kind of supranational union in the form of a EUROPEAN UNION (EU). **Economy** Almost half of European land is unproductive because of climate, relief, soil, or urbanization. A quarter of land is forested; the lumber industry is particularly important in Scandinavia and the mountainous areas of E Europe. Fishing is a major industry in countries with Atlantic or North Sea coastlines. Two-thirds of cultivated land is arable. Cereals are the principal crop: wheat is the most important, replaced by oats in the N and sometimes by corn in the S. Rice is grown with the aid of irrigation. Sheep are grazed on many upland areas, but dairy farming is by far the most important form of animal husbandry. In Mediterranean areas many fruits, early vegetables, and grapevines (mainly for wine) are cultivated. Europe produces over a third of the world's coal. Other mineral deposits include bauxite, mercury, lead, zinc, and potash. Romania was the largest producer of oil in Europe until North Sea states, especially Britain, began to exploit their resources. Europe is highly industrialized and manufacturing employs a high proportion of the work force. There are many industrial areas. The largest are in W central Europe, in particular N and NE France, the RUHR, and around the North Sea ports of ANTWERP, AMSTERDAM, ROTTERDAM, and HAMBURG. There are other major industrial regions in Britain, n Italy, and central European Russia. **History** the Mediterranean region was the cradle of the ancient Greek and Roman civilizations. The collapse of the Western Roman empire and the barbarian invasions brought chaos to much of Europe, although Byzantium remained intact until the 15th century. During the Middle Ages Christianity was a unifying force throughout the continent. the postmedieval period witnessed a fundamental split in the Catholic Church, and the emergence of the nation state. European powers began to found vast empires in other parts of the globe (*See* COLONIALISM; IMPERIALISM), and the FRENCH REVOLUTION ushered in an era of momentous political changes. During the 20th century, a period overshadowed by two World Wars and the rise of COMMUNISM, Europe began to lose some of its preeminence in world affairs. After World War II the countries of Europe became divided into two idological blocs: Eastern Europe, dominated by the Soviet Union, and Western Europe, closely aligned with the US. The rivalry was known as the COLD WAR. The NORTH ATLANTIC TREATY ORGANIZATION (NATO) was established to act as a deterrent to the spread of communism; the Warsaw Pact was its E European counterpart. Several economic organizations, in particular the EUROPEAN COMMUNITY (EC), worked toward closer intra-national cooperation. In 1991 the collapse of European communism added to the momentum for a kind of supranational union in the form of a EUROPEAN UNION (EU) *Area c.*4,000,000sq mi (10,360,000sq km) *Highest mountain* Mount Elbrus (Russia) 18,481ft (5,633m) *Longest river* Volga 2,330mi (3,750km) *Population* (1990 est.) 785,700,000 *Largest cities* MOSCOW (8,881,000); LONDON (6,679,700); ST. PETERSBURG (4,952,000); BERLIN (3,419,000) *See also* individual countries

**European Atomic Energy Commission (Euratom)** Organization formed following the second of the Treaties of ROME (1958). It was founded to coordinate nonmilitary nuclear research and production, and provide capital for investment, specialists, and equipment. It is administered by the European Commission.

**European Community (EC)** Economic and political body dedicated to European development. Its history lies in the establishment (1952) of the European Coal and Steel Community (ECSC). The purpose of the ECSC was to integrate the coal and steel industries primarily of France and West Germany to create a more unified Europe. The success of the ECSC led to the formation of the European Economic Community (EEC), or Common Market, and the EUROPEAN ATOMIC ENERGY COMMUNITY (EURATOM). Established by the Treaties of ROME (1957, 1958), the aim was to create a common economic approach to agriculture, employment, trade, and social development, and to give Western Europe more influence in world affairs. Original members included France, West Germany, Italy, Belgium, The Netherlands, and Luxembourg; UK, Ireland, and Denmark joined (1973), Greece (1981), Spain and Portugal (1986); Austria, Finland, and Sweden joined (1995). The Community's institutional structure comprises the European Commission (responsible for implementing EC legislation), the Council of Ministers (which votes on Commission proposals), the Economic and Social Committee (which advises on draft EC legislation), the European Investment Bank, the EUROPEAN PARLIAMENT, and the EUROPEAN COURT OF JUSTICE. *See also* EUROPEAN UNION (EU)

**European Convention on Human Rights** Agreement to protect the rights and freedoms of the individual, signed by the members of the COUNCIL OF EUROPE in 1950. *See also* HUMAN RIGHTS

E

**European Court of Human Rights** Created in 1959, the court is presided over by one judge from member states that are signatories of the 1950 EUROPEAN CONVENTION ON HUMAN RIGHTS. It decides whether or not an individual's rights have been disregarded by a member state in cases when the two parties have already failed to reach a settlement through the European Commission of Human Rights.

**European Court of Justice** (officially Court of Justice of the European Communities) Court responsible for the interpretation and implementation of European Community laws. The court will also rule in cases where member states are alleged to have broken EC laws.

**European Free Trade Association (EFTA)** Organization seeking to promote free trade among its European members. Established in 1960, it originally comprised Austria, Denmark, Ireland, Norway, Portugal, Sweden, Switzerland, and the UK. By 1995 all but Norway and Switzerland had joined the EUROPEAN UNION (EU), while Iceland and Liechtenstein joined EFTA in 1970 and 1991 respectively.

**European Monetary System (EMS)** System set up in 1979 to bring about monetary stability among members of the EUROPEAN COMMUNITY (EC). There are three parts to the system: the European Currency Unit (ECU) or Euro; the EXCHANGE RATE MECHANISM (ERM); and the credit mechanisms. As part of the original vision, the Euro will become (1999) a pan-European currency. The ERM sets a central rate of exchange for the currency of each country, which is required to keep within a certain percentage (originally 2% or 6%) above or below the rate.

**European Monetary Union (EMU)** Union of EU member states who will share common economic policies and a common currency. Those member states who meet certain economic criteria will initially relinquish control of their own money supplies. Then, following the creation of a European Central Bank, exchange rates would become fixed and a single European currency, the Euro, created. The "first wave" of the Union occurred in early 1999, when international financial transactions began to be calculated in Euros, the "second wave," in 2002, will involve the introduction of Euros to the public and its use as an alternative to national currencies. Not all EU member states will join the EMU. Some will be unable to meet the strict economic criteria; for others, such as the UK, the choice to enter or not is a political issue.

**European Parliament** Institution of the EUROPEAN COMMUNITY. The Parliament forms part of the permanent structure of the European Community. It meets in Strasbourg, Brussels, and Luxembourg. It has 626 members, representing the 15 member states, elected for five-year terms. It has limited legislative powers.

**European Space Agency (ESA)** Organization founded by several European nations in 1962 as the European Space Research Agency (ESRO) to promote international cooperation in space research.

**European Union (EU)** Political entity established following the ratification of the MAASTRICHT TREATY in 1993. The EU aims to use the existing framework and institutions of the EUROPEAN COMMUNITY (EC) to implement greater integration of member states; particularly in areas such as foreign and security policies, and internal and judicial policies. Some member states, particularly the UK and Denmark, have resisted moves toward closer integration, particularly in the areas of a single European currency and a common social policy. Many argue that the union will create a federalist Europe. *See also* EUROPEAN MONETARY SYSTEM (EMS); EUROPEAN PARLIAMENT

**europium** (symbol Eu) Silvery-white metallic rare earth element of the LANTHANIDE SERIES. Its chief ores are monazite and bastnaesite. The metal is used in the manufacture of color television screens, lasers, and in control rods in nuclear reactors. Properties: at.no. 63; at.wt. 151.96; sp.gr. 5.25; m.p. 1,512°F (822°C); b.p. 2,907°F (1,597°C); most common isotope $^{153}$Eu (52.18%).

**Eurydice** In Greek mythology, the nymph married to ORPHEUS.

**eustachian tube** Small channel that connects the middle EAR to the back of the throat. It opens when swallowing, to allow the pressure in the middle ear to remain the same as the pressure of air outside the body.

**euthanasia** Inducing the painless death of a person (usually with a terminal illness), often by a drug. Active euthanasia is illegal in most countries.

**eutrophication** Process by which a stream or lake becomes rich in inorganic nutrients, such as compounds of nitrogen, phosphorus, iron, sulfur, and potassium, by agricultural runoff or other artificial means.

**Evangelical and Reformed Church** Protestant denomination formed (1934) by the merger of the Reformed Chuch in the United States and the Evangelical Synod of North America. The Reformed Chuch in the United States (German Reformed Church) organized its first synod in 1747. The Evangelical Synod of North America was founded in 1840. In 1957 the combined church united with the Congregational Christian Churches to form the UNITED CHURCH OF CHRIST

**Evangelicalism** (Gk. *euangelos*, good news or gospel) Term applied to several, generally Protestant, tendencies within the Christian Church. Evangelicalism denotes the school which stresses personal conversion and witness of salvation by faith in the atoning death of Jesus Christ.

**Evangelical United Brethren Church** Protestant denomination formed (1946) by the union of the Evangelical Church and the United Brethren in Christ. Both these Protestant churches had existed since the early 19th century. The Evangelical United Brethren Church merged with the Methodist Church in 1968 to form the United Methodist Church.

**evangelist** Person who preaches the gospel, announcing the good news of redemption through Jesus Christ and the hope of everlasting life. The word also applies by extension to the authors of the four gospels of the New Testament: Saints MATTHEW, MARK, LUKE, and JOHN. *See also* GREAT AWAKENING; METHODISM

**Evans, Sir Arthur John** (1851–1941) English archaeologist. He excavated the ruins of KNOSSOS in Crete and found evidence of a Bronze Age (2000–1400 BC) civilization, which he named the MINOAN CIVILIZATION.

**Evans, Walker** (1903–75) US photographer. He is famed for his portrait images of the poverty-stricken South of the 1930s, many published in *Let Us Now Praise Famous Men* (1941).

**evaporation** Process by which a liquid or solid becomes a vapor. The reverse process is CONDENSATION. Solids and liquids cool when they evaporate because they give up energy (LATENT HEAT) to the escaping molecules.

**Eve** In the Bible (GENESIS 2), the first woman, created by God from Adam's rib to be his companion and wife in the Garden of EDEN. She succumbed to temptation and disobeyed God by eating the fruit of the tree of the knowledge of good and evil and sharing it with Adam. For this act the couple became mortal and were banished from the garden. She was the mother of CAIN, ABEL, and Seth.

**evening primrose** Any of various plants of the genus *Oenothera*, many of which are native to w North America. They have yellow, pink, or white flowers that open in the evening. Height: 5.3ft (1.8m). Family Onagraceae.

**Everest, Mount** (Nepalese *Sagarmatha*; Tibetan *Chomo-Langma*, Mother Goddess of the World) Highest mountain in the world, in the central Himalayas on the borders of Tibet and Nepal. It is named for George Everest, first surveyor-general of India. Everest was conquered on May 29, 1953, by Sir Edmund HILLARY and Tenzing Norgay. Height: 29,029ft (8,848m).

**Everett, Edward** (1794–1865) US orator and statesman. He was a member of the House of Representatives (1824–34), governor of Massachusetts (1835–39), US minister to England (1841–45), and president of Harvard (1846–49). In 1852 Everett became secretary of state in Millard Fillmore's administration. During the Civil War at Gettysburg (1863) he delivered the main speech shortly before Lincoln's famous address.

**Everglades** Large tract of marshland in s Florida, extending from Lake Okeechobee to Florida Bay. The region is made up of mangrove forests, saw grass, and hummocks (island masses of vegetation). In the late 19th and early 20th century large areas of the Everglades were drained for agricultural use. Water shortages and fires damaged the fragile ecosytem and the Everglades National Park was established in 1947. The third-largest national park, 1,398,800acres (566,074ha), it supports abundant animal life, including alligators, snakes, turtles, egrets, and bald eagles. Total area: *c*.4,000sq mi (10,000sq km).

**evergreen** Plant that retains its green foliage, unlike DECIDUOUS plants. There are two groups: narrow-leaved, or CONIFERS, and broad-leaved. Conifers include fir, spruce, pine, and juniper. Among the broad-leaved evergreens are holly and rhododendron.

**Evert, Chris (Christine Marie)** (1954– ) US tennis player. She won a total of 18 Grand Slam titles. Evert won seven French Open titles (1975–75, 1979–80, 1983, 1985–86), six US Opens (1975–77, 1978, 1980, 1982), three Wimbledon titles (1974, 1976, 1981), and two Australian Opens (1982, 1984). She was the first woman to win $1 million in prize money. Evert retired in 1989.

**evidence** In law, information placed before a court of law to resolve disputed questions of fact. Most evidence is presented by witnesses. In many COMMON LAW cases, a JURY is the trier of facts. Evidence must be relevant and admissable in court. **Direct** evidence can provide proof without corroboration, while **circumstantial** evidence provides surrounding circumstances from which the principal fact may be inferred.

**evolution** Theory that a species undergoes gradual changes to survive and reproduce in a competitive, and often changing, environment, and that a new species is the result of change from the ancestral forms. Early work on evolutionary theory was initiated by Jean LAMARCK, but it was not until Charles DARWIN wrote *The Origin of Species* that the theory was considered worthy of argument. Present-day evolutionary theory is largely derived from the work of Darwin and MENDEL and maintains that in any population or gene pool, there is VARIATION, including random MUTATION, in genetic forms and characteristics. Most species produce greater quantities of offspring than their environment can support, so only those members best adapted to the environment survive. When new characteristics provide survival advantages those individuals that possess them pass on these characteristics to their offspring. *See also* ADAPTATION; ADAPTIVE RADIATION; NATURAL SELECTION; PUNCTUATED EQUILIBRIUM

**Ewing, William Maurice** (1906–74) US geophysicist. First to take seismic measurements in open seas (1935), he aided understanding of marine sediments and ocean basins. He took the first deep-sea photographs (1939).

**exchange rate** In economics, the rate at which one nation's currency can be converted to that of another. It varies according to fluctuations on the world's FOREIGN EXCHANGE markets. *See also* GOLD STANDARD

**exclusion principle** Basic law of QUANTUM MECHANICS, proposed by Wolfgang PAULI in 1925, stating that no two ELECTRONS in an atom can possess the same energy and SPIN. More precisely, the set of four QUANTUM NUMBERS characterizing certain ELEMENTARY PARTICLES called FERMIONS must be unique.

**excommunication** Formal expulsion from the communion of the faithful, from sacraments, and from rites of a religious body. Largely abandoned by Protestants, excommunication has been retained by Jewish congregations and by the Roman Catholic Church. In the days when the church held great temporal (as well as spiritual) authority, excommunication was a severe punishment for HERESY or BLASPHEMY.

**excretion** Elimination of materials from the body that have been involved in METABOLISM. Such waste materials, particularly nitrogenous wastes, would be toxic if allowed to accumulate. In mammals these wastes are excreted mainly as URINE, and to some extent also by sweating. Carbon dioxide is excreted through the lungs during breathing.

**executive** Branch of government responsible for the execution of laws and the administration of policies. The US Constitution separates the powers of government into three parts, legislative, executive, and judicial. In general, legislative power rests with Congress; judicial power rests with the courts, and supreme executive power with the President.

**executor** Person responsibile for carrying out the provisions of a WILL. Normally the executor is named in the will by the testator (person who has made the will). The executor's duties are to arrange the funeral of the deceased, to pay outstanding debts, and to distribute the property among the beneficiaries.

**Exeter** City on the Exe River; county town of Devon, sw England. Ancient buildings include the Norman cathedral (*c*.1275), the 12th-century Guildhall, and the remains of Roman walls. Exeter University was established in 1955. Industries: tourism, textiles, leather. Pop. (1991) 98,125.

**existentialism** Any of several philosophical systems concerned with the nature of existence or being. Søren KIERKEGAARD is regarded as the founder of the movement. He rejected metaphysics, arguing that an individual is forced to make their own ethical decisions. Martin HEIDEGGER developed these ideas in relation to the PHENOMENOLOGY of Edmund HUSSERL. Karl JASPERS argued that the greatest insights into existence were experienced in extreme situations. For Jean-Paul SARTRE, the central tenet of existentialism was that existence precedes essence. He declared that there was no God and that individuals were "condemned to be free." Sartre's writings influenced Simone de BEAUVOIR and Albert CAMUS.

**exobiology** Search for life on other planets. Exobiology is concerned with attempts to detect environmental conditions beyond Earth.

**Exodus** Old Testament book of the Bible, the second book of the PENTATEUCH or TORAH. The first part details the flight of the Israelites from Egypt; the second part contains a catalog of religious instructions that formed the basis of Mosaic law.

**exorcism** Ritual expulsion of evil spirits from a person, place, or thing, usually performed by a priest or shaman. Exorcism is a practice common to many religions. In the Christian Church it is performed by means of the laying-on of hands and incantation.

**exoskeleton** Protective skeleton or hard supporting structure forming the outside of the soft bodies of certain animals, notably ARTHROPODS and MOLLUSKS.

**exothermic reaction** CHEMICAL REACTION in which heat is evolved. A common example is COMBUSTION. *See also* ENDOTHERMIC REACTION

**expansion** Change in the size of an object with change in temperature. Most substances expand on heating, although there are exceptions (ice expands on cooling). The expansivity (coefficient of expansion) of a substance is its increase in length, area, or volume per unit temperature rise.

**exploration** Phoenicians, Greeks, and Carthaginians undertook vast journeys across the oceans for the purposes of trade and colonization. The conquests of Alexander the Great opened up intercourse between East and West. For almost 1,000 years after the collapse of the Roman empire in the 5th century AD the Chinese and Arabs dominated exploration. European knowledge of Asia was advanced by MARCO POLO. The European "age of discovery" was motivated by financial gain and the missionary zeal of Christianity. In 1487 Bartholomeu DIAZ rounded the Cape of Good Hope in search of a sea route to the spices of India. In 1498 Vasco da GAMA completed the first voyage from Portugal to India. In 1492 Chirstopher COLUMBUS sailed westward toward Asia, landing In America. Similarly, in 1500 Pedro CABRAL accidentally discovered Brazil on route to India. The search for a trade route to the East spurred Ferdinand MAGELLAN's circumnavigation of the globe (1519–22). The lure of gold in South America prompted the explorations of

◄ **Everest** The world's highest peak, at 29,028ft (8,848m) high. Since Everest was first climbed in 1953, mountaineering technology has greatly improved and the Himalayan summit is now reached without the need for oxygen tanks. The mountain is imbued with local religious significance.

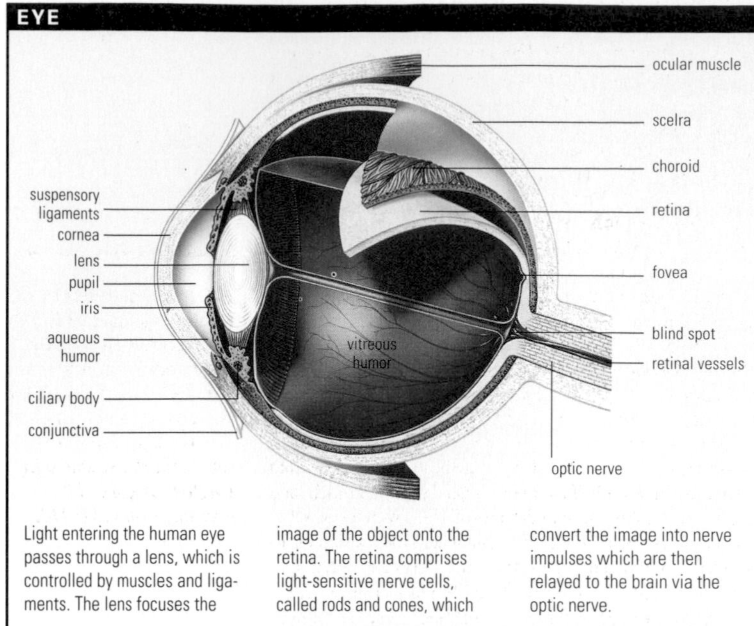


Light entering the human eye passes through a lens, which is controlled by muscles and ligaments. The lens focuses the image of the object onto the retina. The retina comprises light-sensitive nerve cells, called rods and cones, which convert the image into nerve impulses which are then relayed to the brain via the optic nerve.

Hernán CORTÉS and Francisco PIZARRO. In the 17th century the interior of North America was revealed by Samuel de CHAMPLAIN, Sieur de LA SALLE, Louis JOLIET, and Jacques MAQUETTE. The Portuguese and Spanish monopoly of the Atlantic trade routes led to the search for new routes. Francis DRAKE, James COOK, and Vitus BERING explored the Pacific and Indian oceans. In the mid-19th century the interior of Africa was mapped by H.M. STANLEY and David LIVINGSTONE. European exploration and colonization devastated indigenous peoples, either through the spread of new diseases or SLAVERY. In the late 19th century explorations began to motivated more by science than economics. In 1909 Richard E. PEARY reached the North Pole. In 1911 Roald AMUNDSEN beat Robert SCOTT to the South Pole. Richard BYRD was a pioneer of exploration by airplane. The launch of Sputnik 1 (1957) opened up the era of SPACE EXPLORATION.

**Explorer I** First of a series of US scientific satellites. It was launched in 1958, and the program continued into the 1970s. The early Explorers provided information about the VAN ALLEN RADIATION BELTS.

**explosive** Substance that reacts rapidly and violently, emitting heat, light, sound, and shock waves. Chemical explosives are mostly highly nitrated compounds or mixtures that decompose violently. Nuclear explosives are radioactive metals, the atoms of which can undergo nuclear FISSION or FUSION to release radiant energy and devastating shock waves.

**exponent** Superscript number placed to the right of a symbol indicating its power, e.g. in $a^4$ ($= a\times a\times a\times a$), 4 is the exponent.

**exponential** In general, a function of $x$ of the form $a^x$, where $a$ is a constant The exponential function $e^x$, where e is the base of natural logarithms, 2.7182818..., can be represented by a power series $1 + x + x^2/2! + x^3/3! + ...$

**expressionism** Style of art in which conventional methods of NATURALISM are replaced by distorted and exaggerated images to express intense, subjective emotion. The term is often used in relation to a radical German art movement between the 1880s and *c.*1905 that reached its apogee in the work of the BLAUE REITER. The term also applies to drama, such as the works of STRINDBERG and WEDEKIND. *See also* BRÜCKE, DIE

**extensor** *See* MUSCLE

**extinction** Dying out of a species or population. Extinction is part of the process of EVOLUTION in which certain species of plants and animals die out, often to be replaced by others.

**extrasensory perception (ESP)** Perception that takes place outside the known sensory systems. The term covers alleged parapsychological phenomena such as clairvoyance, telepathy, and precognition. ESP has been the subject of serious investigation, beginning with the establishment in 1882 in London of the Society for Psychical Research.

**extraterritoriality** State of legal immunity granted to members of the diplomatic corps, their families, and the premises they occupy. This includes exemption from arrest or prosecution and from search or seizure.

**extroversion** Personality type characterized by outgoing behavior; the opposite of INTROVERSION. The term was popularized by Carl JUNG.

**extrusion** In geology, the breaking out of IGNEOUS ROCK from below the Earth's surface. In industry, extrusion is the forcing of metals or plastics at optimum temperature through a die to make rods or tubes. *See also* VOLCANO

**Eyck, Jan van** (*c.*1390–1441) Flemish painter. His best-known work is the altarpiece for the Church of St. Bavon, Ghent, which includes the *Adoration of the Lamb* (1432) and the *Arnolfini Wedding* (1434). He perfected the manufacture and technique of oil paint. His brother **Hubert** van Eyck (*c.*1370–1426) probably assisted Jan on the St. Bavon alterpiece.

**eye** Organ of vision. It converts light energy to nerve impulses that are transmitted to the visual center of the brain. Most of the mass of a human eye lies in a bony protective socket, called the orbital cavity, which also contains muscles and other tissues to hold and move the eye. The eyeball is spherical and composed of three layers: the sclera (white of the eye), which contains the transparent CORNEA; the choroid, which connects with the IRIS, PUPIL, and LENS and contains blood vessels to provide nutrients and oxygen; and the RETINA, which contains rods and cones for converting the image into nerve impulses. The aqueous humor (a watery liquid between the cornea and iris) and the vitreous humor (a jelly-like substance behind the lens) both help to maintain the shape of the eye. *See also* SIGHT

**Eyre, Lake** Salt lake in NE South Australia. It is the lowest point on the continent, *c.*50ft (15m) below sea level, and the largest salt lake in Australia. Area: 3,600sq mi (9,324sq km). Max. depth: 4ft (1.2m).

**Eysenck, Hans Jurgen** (1916–97) British psychologist and pioneer of behavior therapy, b. Germany. Much of Eysenck's work focused on developing a biological definition of personality.

**Ezekiel** Old Testament prophet who was among the Jews deported during the BABYLONIAN CAPTIVITY. He is traditionally considered the author of the Old Testament Book of Ezekiel. He was the last of the "greater" Old Testament prophets, the successor of ISAIAH and JEREMIAH.

**Ezra** In the Old Testament, a continuation of Chronicles I and II. It records the priest Ezra's journey from Babylon to Jerusalem to spread the law of Moses.

**Fabergé, Peter Carl** (1846–1920) Russian jeweler. He took over his father's business in 1870, making decorative objects in gold and precious stones. He was famed for his many jeweled Easter eggs for European royalty, the first for Czar Alexander III in 1884. Fabergé left Russia after the revolution of 1917.

**Fabian Society** British society of non-Marxists founded in 1883, who believed that SOCIALISM could be attained through gradual political change. With George Bernard SHAW and Sidney and Beatrice WEBB as leaders, the society gained widespread recognition and helped found the Labour Representation Committee (1900) that became the British LABOUR PARTY in 1906. Today, the Fabian Society is affiliated to the Labour Party and publishes a journal and pamphlets.

**fable** Literary genre that takes the form of a short allegorical tale, intended to convey a moral. The oldest fables are the Greek tales of AESOP and the Indian stories of the *Panchatantra*. Other notable collections of fables were made by Jean de LA FONTAINE and John GAY. More recent fables include James Thurber's *Fables for Our Time* (1940). *See also* ALLEGORY

**facies** In geology, all the features of a rock that show the history of its formation. Geologists often distinguish age by facies. It is also applied to gradations of IGNEOUS ROCK.

**factor** In mathematics, any number that divides exactly into a given number. For example, the factors of 72 are 1, 2, 3, 4, 6, 8, 9, 12, 18, 24, and 36.

**Fahrenheit, Gabriel Daniel** (1686–1736) German physicist and instrument-maker. He invented the alcohol THERMOMETER (1709), the first mercury thermometer (1714), and devised the FAHRENHEIT TEMPERATURE SCALE. He also showed that the boiling points of liquids vary with changes in pressure.

**Fahrenheit temperature scale** System for measuring temperature based on the freezing point (32°F) and the boiling point (212°F) of water. The interval between them is divided into 180 equal parts. The Fahrenheit scale is still used in the US for nonscientific measurements. Fahrenheit is converted to Celsius by substracting 32 and then dividing by 1.8. *See also* THERMOMETER

**fainting** (syncope) Loss of consciousness accompanied by general weakness of the muscles. A faint may be preceded by giddiness, nausea, and sweating. Its causes include insufficient flow of blood to the brain and shock.

**Fairbanks, Douglas, Sr.** (1883–1939) US film actor. He founded United Artists films (1919) with his wife, Mary Pickford, Charlie CHAPLIN, and D.W. GRIFFITH. Fairbanks' swashbuckling acrobatics made him a screen idol in adventures such as *The Mark of Zorro* (1920) and *Robin Hood* (1922). His son, **Douglas Fairbanks, Jr.** (1909– ), appeared in films such as *Catherine the Great* (1934), and *The Prisoner of Zenda* (1937).

**Fairbanks** City on the Tanana and Chena rivers, central Alaska, 150mi (240km) S of the Arctic Circle. The second-largest city in Alaska, Fairbanks was settled after the discovery of gold (1902). The discovery of oil (1968) at Prudhoe Bay and the construction of the trans-Alaskan oil pipeline (1970–77) accelerated growth. Industries: oil, industrial chemicals, fur, gold. Pop. (1990) 30,843.

**Fair Deal** *See* TRUMAN, HARRY S.

**fakir** (Arabic, poverty) Initiate in SUFISM, who practices self-denial in order to be closer to God. *See also* DERVISH; ISLAM

**Falange** (Sp. phalanx) Spanish political party founded in 1933 by José Antonio PRIMO DE RIVERA. Modeled on other European followers of FASCISM, it was merged with other groups under the FRANCO regime and became the sole legal political party. It was heavily defeated in free elections in 1977.

**Falashas** Ethnic group of black Jews in Ethiopia, probably descended from early converts to JUDAISM. Their religion relies solely on observance of the OLD TESTAMENT. Israel acknowledged them as Jews in 1975, and, suffering discrimination at home, many migrated to Israel.

**falcon** Widely distributed, BIRD OF PREY, sometimes trained by man to hunt game (falconry). Similar to HAWKS, falcons have keen eyesight, short hooked bills, long pointed wings, streamlined bodies, strong legs with hooked claws, and gray or brownish plumage with lighter markings. The females are much larger than the males. Falcons feed on insects, smaller birds, and small ground animals. Sweeping down (stoops) at speeds of up to 175mph (280km/h), they can kill on the wing using their talons. They lay two to five brown-spotted white eggs, often in abandoned nests. The best-known species are the KESTREL, and PEREGRINE FALCON. Length: 6–25in (15–64cm). Family Falconidae.

**Faldo, Nick (Nicholas Alexander)** (1957– ) English golfer. He has won the British Open (1987, 1990, 1992), and the US Masters (1989, 1990, 1996), the only player apart from Jack NICKLAUS to win in successive years. Faldo was also a member of the victorious European Ryder Cup teams (1995, 1997).

**Falkland Islands** (Islas Malvinas) British crown colony in the S Atlantic Ocean, *c.*320mi (520km) off the E coast of Argentina; the capital is STANLEY (on East Falkland). It includes two large islands (East and West Falkland) and 200 smaller ones. First explored by Europeans in the late 16th century, the Falklands have been under Spanish, French, and British control. Argentinian denials of UK sovereignty led to the FALKLANDS WAR (1982). The main activity is sheep farming. Area: *c.*4,600sq mi (12,200sq km). Pop. (1991) 2,121.

**Falklands War** (April–June 1982) Military conflict fought between the UK and Argentina on the question of sovereignty over the FALKLAND ISLANDS. On April 2, after the breakdown of negotiations, Argentine forces invaded and occupied the Falklands, South Georgia, and South Sandwich Islands, administered by Great Britain since the 19th century. The British blockaded the islands and landed at Port San Carlos. They surrounded the Argentine troops at the capital, Port Stanley, and forced them to surrender on June 14. The war cost 254 British and 750 Argentine lives. The victory helped secure a second term for Margaret THATCHER. Although the British resumed their administration of the islands, the basic issue of sovereignty remains unresolved.

**Falla, Manuel de** (1876–1946) Spanish composer. He developed a Spanish style by using folk songs combined with rich modern harmonies. Among his works are the opera *La Vida Breve* (1905), *Nights in the Gardens of Spain* (1916) for piano and orchestra, and the music for the ballet *The Three-Cornered Hat* (1919).

**Fallopian tube** (oviduct) In mammals, either of two narrow ducts leading from the upper part of the UTERUS into the pelvic cavity and ending near each OVARY. After ovulation, the OVUM travels through the Fallopian tube where FERTILIZATION can occur. The fertilized ovum, or EMBRYO, is then implanted into the uterus.

**family planning** Alternative term for CONTRACEPTION

**famine** Extreme prolonged shortage of food, produced by both natural and man-made causes. If it persists, famine results in widespread starvation and death. Famine is often associated with drought or alterations in weather patterns which lead to crop failure and the destruction of livestock. However, warfare and complex political situations are equally likely causes.

**Faneuil Hall** Public market and meeting place in Boston, Massachusetts. It was built (1742) by Peter Faneuil

◄ **Faldo** Nick Faldo is one of Britain's most successful golfers of all time. Famous for his powers of concentration and attention to detail, he won the British Open (1987, 1990, and 1992), and the US Masters (1989, 1990, and 1996)

F

***F/f, sixth letter of the Roman alphabet. It is derived from the Semite letter* waw, *meaning* hook. *It entered the Greek alphabet as* digamma. *The Greeks used it to represent the sound w in English. It gained its present form* c.*AD 114.***

FAULT

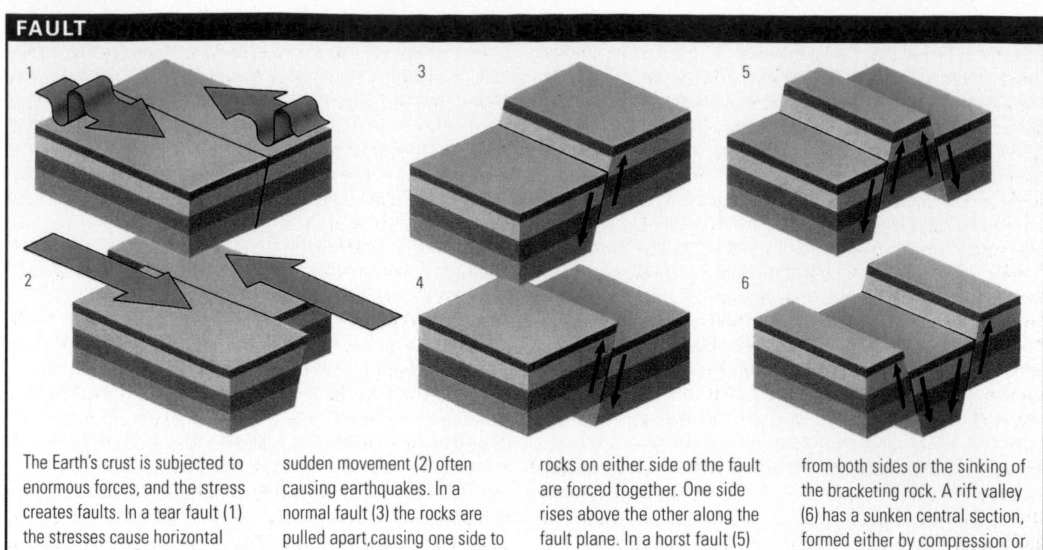


The Earth's crust is subjected to enormous forces, and the stress creates faults. In a tear fault (1) the stresses cause horizontal movement. The forces build up until they are released in a sudden movement (2) often causing earthquakes. In a normal fault (3) the rocks are pulled apart,causing one side to slip down along the plane of the fault. In a reverse fault (4) the rocks on either side of the fault are forced together. One side rises above the other along the fault plane. In a horst fault (5) the central section is left protruding due to compression from both sides or the sinking of the bracketing rock. A rift valley (6) has a sunken central section, formed either by compression or the outward movement of the two valley sides.

(1700–43). The site of Revolutionary meetings, the hall became known as the "Cradle of Liberty."

**FAO** *See* FOOD AND AGRICULTURE ORGANIZATION

**Faraday, Michael** (1791–1867) English physicist and chemist. A student of Sir Humphry DAVY, in 1825 he became director of the laboratories at the Royal Institution in London. Faraday liquefied chlorine, discovered benzene, and enunciated the laws of electrolysis (FARADAY'S LAWS). He also discovered electromagnetic induction, made the first DYNAMO, built a primitive electric motor, and studied nonconducting materials (dielectrics). The unit of capacitance (the farad) is named for him.

**Faraday's laws** Two laws of ELECTROLYSIS and three of ELECTROMAGNETIC INDUCTION, formulated by Michael FARADAY. The **electrolysis** laws state that (1) the amount of chemical change during electrolysis is proportional to the charge passed, and (2) the amount of chemical change produced in a substance by a certain amount of electricity is proportional to the electrochemical equivalent of that substance. Faraday's laws of **induction** state that (1) an electromagnetic force is induced in a conductor if the magnetic field surrounding it changes, (2) the electromagnetic force is proportional to the rate of change of the field, and (3) the direction of the induced electromagnetic force depends on the field's orientation.

**farce** (lat. *farcire*, to stuff) Comic drama typified by stereotypical characterizations, improbable plot lines, and emphasis on physical humor. One of the earliest examples is Shakespeare's *Comedy of Errors* (*c*.1593). The "bedroom farce" was developed in France by Georges FEYDEAU. Oscar Wilde's *The Importance of Being Earnest* (1895) opened up new dramatic possibilities.

**Fargo, William George** (1818–81) US businessman. He organized, with Henry Wells, a carrier service between Buffalo and the West in 1844. Wells, Fargo and Company then set up an express service between New York and San Francisco to cater for the gold rush. The company merged with two others to form the American Express Company in 1850.

**farming** *See* AGRICULTURE

**Farnese** Italian family of the Roman aristocracy. The military skill of Ranuccio Farnese (d. *c*.1460) won the gratitude of Pope Eugenius IV, and his son Alessandro became Pope PAUL III (1534). The Farnese Palace, Rome, was built for Paul III.

**Faröe Islands** (Faeroe Islands) Group of 22 volcanic islands (17 inhabited) in the N Atlantic between Iceland and the Shetland Islands. The largest are Streymoy and Esturoy. Settled in the 7th century, the group was part of Norway from the 11th century until 1380, when it was ceded to Denmark. In 1852 parliament was restored, and since 1948 it has enjoyed a degree of autonomy. Capital and chief port: Tórshavn (Streymoy), pop. (1993) 14,192; Language: Faroese; Industries: fishery, sheep-rearing. Area: 540sq mi (1,339sq km). Total pop. (1993) 45,349.

**Farouk** (1920–65) King of Egypt (1936–52). Son of King FUAD I, he alienated many Egyptians by his personal extravagance and corruption. His ambitious foreign policy ended in defeat in the first ARAB-ISRAELI WAR (1948), and he was overthrown in a military coup, led by Gamal Abdel Nasser.

**Farquhar, George** (1678–1707) Irish dramatist associated with RESTORATION THEATER. His comedies were distinguished by their humor and depth of character. Among his plays are *The Constant Couple* (1699), *The Recruiting Officer* (1706), and *The Beaux Stratagem* (1707).

**Farragut, David Glasgow** (1801–70) US admiral. He served under David Porter in the WAR OF 1812. In 1862 Farragut was given command of the Western Gulf Blockading Squadron in the CIVIL WAR and sailed up the Mississippi River to defeat the Confederate flotilla protecting the New Orleans forts. Farragut's most famous victory was at the Battle of Mobile Bay (1864), where he ignored torpedoes to capture the Confederate forts. He became (1866) the first US admiral.

**Farrakhan, Louis** (1933– ) US leader of the Nation of Islam, a black separatist organization. He was recruited into the BLACK MUSLIMS in the 1950s by MALCOLM X. Farrakhan was a charismatic advocate of its racial exclusivity and in 1976 formed the Nation of Islam, claiming greater adherence to the teachings of Elijah MUHAMMAD. He has been accused of inciting anger against other US minorities, particularly Jews. In 1995 Farrakhan organized a large political demonstration, assembling 400,000 men in a "Million Man March" on Washington.

**Farrell, James Thomas** (1904–79) US author. He is best known for his trilogy about Studs Lonigan (1932–35). Set in a poor Irish community in Chicago, it is typical of his harshly realistic treatment of modern city life. Later fiction includes 10 novels of a projected 25-volume series called *A Universe of Time*.

**far sight** (hypermetropia) Defect of vision that causes distant objects to be seen more clearly than nearby ones. The focusing distance of the eyeball is too short and, as a result, light rays entering the EYE strike the RETINA before they can be properly focused. It is corrected by convex lenses. *See also* NEAR SIGHT

**fascism** Political movement founded in Italy by Benito MUSSOLINI (1919), characterized by nationalism, totalitarianism, and anticommunism. The term also applied to the regimes of Adolf HITLER in Germany (1933) and Francisco FRANCO in Spain (1936). A reaction to the RUSSIAN REVOLU-

TION (1917) and the spread of communist influence, the movement based its appeal on the fear of financial instability among the middle-classes and on a wider social discontent. Basic to fascist ideas were: glorification of the state and total subordination to its authority; suppression of all political opposition; stern enforcement of law and order; the supremacy of the leader as the embodiment of high ideals; and an aggressive militarism aimed at achieving national greatness. It also typically encouraged racist and xenophobic attitudes and policies. Fascism was discredited by defeat in World War II, but in the 1990s far-right nationalist groups have re-emerged in many countries. *See also* NATIONAL SOCIALISM

**Fassbinder, Rainer Werner** (1946–82) German film director and leader of modern German cinema. He directed his first feature in 1969, and became known for his radical, hypnotic, low-budget productions. Fiercely political, his films include *The Marriage of Eva Braun* (1979), and *Veronika Voss* (1982).

**Fast, Howard** (1914– ) US writer. His best-known novels focus on critical moments in US history. *Citizen Tom Paine* (1943) and *April Morning* (1961) deal with the American Revolution. Fast was awarded the Stalin Peace Prize in 1953. *The Naked God* (1957) describes his disenchantment with Soviet communism.

**fat** Semisolid organic substance made and used by plants and animals to store energy. In animals, fats also serve to insulate the body and protect internal organs. Fats are soluble in organic solvents such as ether, carbon tetrachloride, chloroform, and benzene. They are triglycerides: ESTERS in which one molecule of glycerol is connected to three molecules of FATTY ACIDS (such as palmitic, lauric, and stearic acid) each having 12 to 18 carbon atoms. Research indicates that the consumption of high levels of animal fats can increase the risk of heart disease. Vegetable oils are similar to fats, but are viscous liquids rather than semisolids and have a higher proportion of molecules with double carbon–carbon bonds in the chain – that is, they are unsaturated. *See also* LIPID; SOAP

**Fates** In Greek mythology, the three goddesses of human destiny. Called the *Moirae* by the Greeks, they correspond to the Roman *Parcae* and the Germanic NORNS. Clotho spun the thread of life: Lachesis, the element of chance, measured it; and Atropos, the inevitable, cut it.

**Fatima** (606–32) Daughter of the prophet MUHAMMAD, and wife of ALI. Fatima is revered by the SHI'A sect of ISLAM.

**Fatimid** SHI'A dynasty who claimed the caliphate on the basis of their descent from FATIMA. The dynasty was founded by Said ibn Husayn at the end of the 9th century. The Fatimids quickly overthrew the SUNNI rulers in most of NW Africa. By ibn Husayn's death (934), the Fatimid empire had expanded into S Europe, and in 969 they captured Egypt and established the Mosque and University of Al-Azhar. By the end of the 11th century, Egypt was all that remained of the empire.

**fatty acids** Organic compounds, present widely in nature as constituents of FAT. They contain a single carboxyl acid group (COOH). Examples of saturated fatty acids (those which lack double bonds in their hydrocarbon chain) are acetic acid and palmitic acid, the latter being a common fat constituent; unsaturated fatty acids (having one or more double carbon–carbon bonds) include oleic acid. *See also* LIPID

**Faulkner, William Cuthbert** (1897–1962) US novelist. *Sartoris* (1929) was the first in a series of novels set in the fictional Mississippi county of Yoknapatawpha. *The Sound and the Fury* (1929), and *As I Lay Dying* (1930) utilize a STREAM OF CONSCIOUSNESS narrative. *Light in August* (1932), and *Absalom, Absalom!* (1936) examine the effects of racism in the Deep South. Faulkner was awarded the 1949 Nobel Prize for literature. He won Pulitzer Prizes for *A Fable* (1951), and his final novel *The Reivers* (1962). Faulkner also wrote screenplays.

**fault** In geology, a fracture in the Earth's crust along which movement has occurred. The result of PLATE TECTONICS, faults are classified by the type of movement. Vertical movements in the crust cause **normal** and **reverse** faults, while horizontal movements result in **tear** faults. Faults can occur in groups creating **horsts** (block mountains) or **grabens** (rift valleys).

**Fauré, Gabriel Urbain** (1845–1924) French Romantic composer renowned for his intimate, restrained compositions. They include many songs, such as *Clair de lune* (1889); chamber music, such as *Elégie* (1883); and the *Requiem* (1887). Fauré was director of the Paris Conservatoire (1905–22).

**fauvism** Expressionist art style based on vivid, non-naturalistic colors. MATISSE was the leading figure and, with SIGNAC and Derain, exhibited at the Salon d'Automne (1905). A critic described their work as something produced by wild animals (*fauves*). Other members of the group included DUFY, VLAMINCK, and BRAQUE. Although fauvism was short-lived, its influence on EXPRESSIONISM was profound.

**Fawkes, Guy** (1570–1606) English conspirator in the GUNPOWDER PLOT of 1605. He was enlisted by Roman Catholic conspirators in a plot against JAMES I and Parliament. The plot was betrayed, and Fawkes was arrested, surrounded by barrels of gunpowder, and later executed. Traditionally, an effigy called a "guy," is burned on November 5, the anniversary of the intended explosion.

**fax** (facsimile transmission) Equipment by which text, photographs, and drawings can be transmitted and received through a TELEPHONE system. The image, on paper, is scanned to translate it into a series of electrical pulses. Inside the fax machine, a modem converts the pulses into a form that can be transmitted through the telephone system. At the receiving end, the fax machine's modem converts the signals back into pulses, and prints these as dots to build up a copy of the original document. *See also* SCANNING

**FBI** *See* FEDERAL BUREAU OF INVESTIGATION

**feather** One of the skin appendages that make up the plumage of birds. Feathers are composed of the fibrous protein KERATIN, and provide insulation and enable flight. They are usually replaced at least once a year.

**February Revolution** (1848) French insurrection that overthrew the government of LOUIS PHILIPPE. The Revolution

▲ **Faulkner** US novelist and Nobel Prize winner, William Faulkner is recognized as a leading writer in the "stream-of-consciousness" literary style. Much of his work describes the effects of rural disintegration in S US.

F

**FAX**

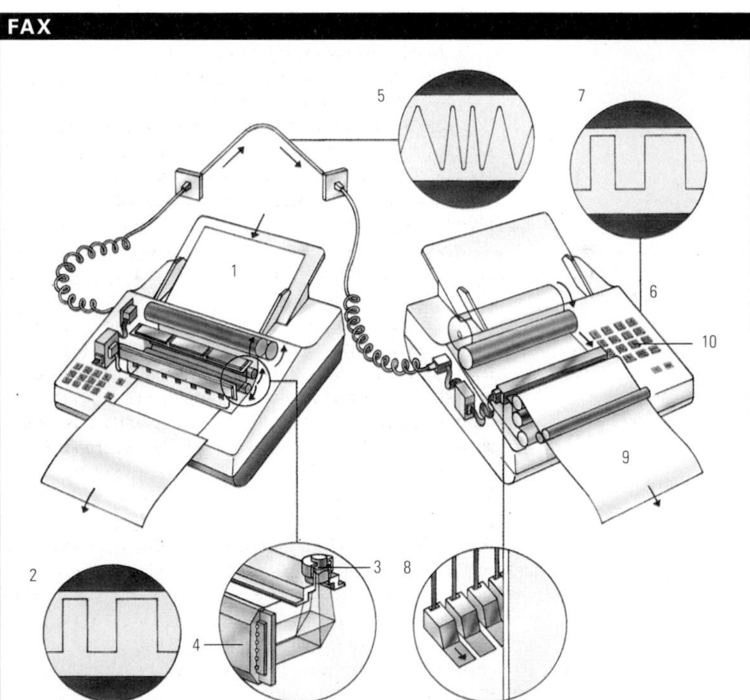


A fax machine converts text or images fed into the machine (1) into a digital code (2). The code is created by shining light on tiny strips of the document in turn (3). Sensors (4) detect the amount of light that bounces back. Where ink is present little light is reflected creating an electrical pulse of low voltage. A high voltage results when light is reflected from white paper. The digital code is converted by a modem in the fax into an analog signal (5) and transmitted to the receiving fax machine (6) via the telephone network. A modem in the second machine converts the analog code back into a digital code (7), a printer (8) interprets the digital code and produces the hard facsimile copy (9). Each machine has its own number which is dialed in via a keyboard (10) on the sending machine.

F

**FEATHER**

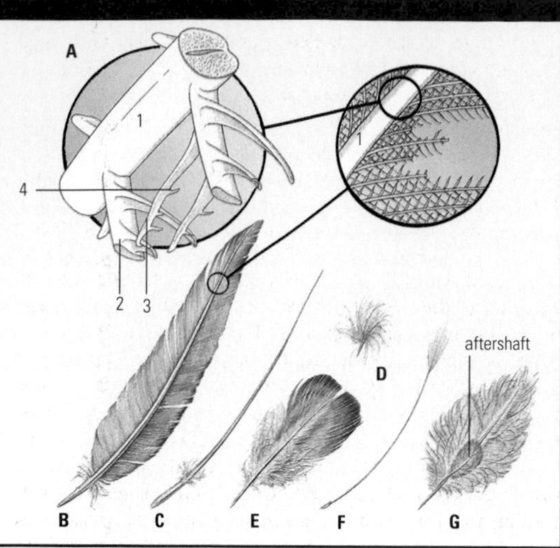


The structure of a bird's feather (A) shows how barbs (2) extend from the central midrib (1). Barbules (3) project from both sides of the barb, one side of which has tiny hooks (hamuli) (4) which catch on the next barbule. The interlocking construction adds strength to the feather. Types of feather include flight (B), bristle (C), down (D), contour feathers (E) which insulate, filoplumes (F), hair-like feathers that are either sensory or decorative, and body contour feathers (G) which have a smaller feather (aftershaft) growing from its base.

began in Paris following the economic crisis of 1847–48 and agitation for parliamentary reform. Led by bourgeois radicals and working-class revolutionaries, it created the short-lived Second Republic in France, and set off popular uprisings and unrest throughout Europe. *See also* Revolutions of 1848

**Federal Aviation Administration (FAA)** US agency of the Department of Transportation, formerly known as the Federal Aviation Agency. Its responsibilities include regulating air commerce to encourage aviation safety, promoting civil aviation and a national system of airports, and developing and operating a system of air traffic control for both civilian and military aircraft.

**Federal Bureau of Investigation (FBI)** Federal government agency that investigates violations of federal law. Its findings are reported to the Attorney General and various nationwide attorneys for decisions on prosecution. Established in 1908, its autonomy was strengthened under the directorship of J. Edgar Hoover (1924–72). The agency was criticized for its role in the Watergate scandal (1972–74). Its headquarters are in Washington, D.C., and its director is appointed by the president, subject to Senate approval.

**Federal Communications Commission (FCC)** Independent federal government agency created by the Communications Act (1934) to regulate interstate and foreign wire and broadcast communications. Its seven members are appointed by the president. The FCC licences and supervises the activities of all radio and television stations.

**Federal Deposit Insurance Corporation (FDIC)** US agency established by the Glass-Steagall Act (1933) to protect bank depositors. To protect savers from bank failures, the corporation insured individual accounts up to $5,000, raised gradually to $100,000, in all Federal Reserve banks and qualified state banks.

**federalism** Political system that allows states united under a central government to maintain a measure of independence. Examples include the US, Australia, Canada, Germany, India, and Switzerland. Central government has supreme authority, but the component states have a considerable amount of autonomy in such matters as education and health.

**Federalist Party** Early US political party that favored strong central government. Following publication of *The* Federalist, and ratification of the Constitution, George Washington formed a new government. A major split soon emerged within the cabinet, between a Federalist group led by Alexander Hamilton and an Anti-Federalist Party led by Thomas Jefferson. The Anti-Federalists later formed the Democratic Republican party then the Democratic Party. The Federalists were conservatives; favoring business and landowning interests, and pursuing a pro-British foreign policy. The election of a second Federalist president, John Adams, led to the Alien and Sedition Acts (1798). Despite the efforts of De Witt Clinton, the Federalists increasingly became the party of New England and they disintegrated after the election of 1816.

**Federal Reserve System** US central banking authority, established (1913) to maintain sound monetary and credit conditions. Twelve regional banks are supervised by a Federal Reserve Board of Governors appointed by the president. All national banks are members, as are many state and commercial banks. The Federal Reserve System regulates money flow and credit by varying its discount rate on loans to member banks and by varying the percentage of total deposits member banks must keep in reserve.

**Federal Trade Commission (FTC)** Independent US federal administrative agency, established in 1915. Its main objective is to maintain the free enterprise system and fair competition. The FTC functions in the area of interstate commerce to prevent unfair competition. The five members are appointed by the president and approved by the Senate. *See also* Sherman Antitrust Act

**feedback** In technology, process by which an electronic or mechanical control system monitors and regulates itself. Feedback works by returning part of the "output" of the system to its "input." *See also* biofeedback

**Feininger, Lyonel** (1871–1956) US painter. He left the US for Europe in 1887 and became involved with cubism in 1912. Feininger evolved a distinctive style, portraying figurative scenes in patterns of interconnecting planes colored to resemble prisms. He exhibited with the Blaue Reiter (1913) and taught at the Bauhaus (1919–33). In 1937 Feininger returned to the US and produced some of his best work, such as *Dawn* (1938).

**Feldman, Morton** (1926–87) US composer. In the 1950s he worked with John Cage. Some of his works explore chance, with decisions left for the performers to make. Works include *Rothko Chapel* (1971) and *The Viola in my Life* (1970–71).

**feldspar** (felspar) Group of common, rock-forming minerals that all contain aluminum, silicon, and oxygen, but with varying proportions of potassium, sodium, and calcium. They are essential constituents of igneous rock. Hardness 6–6.5; sp.gr. 2.5–2.8.

**Fellini, Federico** (1920–93) Italian film director. His second film, *I Vitelloni* (1953), established his characteristic blend of satire, autobiography, and humanism. *La Strada* (1954) won an Academy Award for best foreign film. Fellini won a second Oscar for *Le notti di Cabiria* (1957). *La Dolce Vita* (1960) was a controversial success. Fellini won two more Oscars for best foreign film: *8½* (1963) and *Amarcord* (1974).

**felony** Indictable criminal offense. In US federal law, felonies are distinguished from misdemeanors (less serious crimes), with a felony being any crime punishable by death or more than one year's imprisonment.

**feminism** Movement that promotes equal rights for women. One of the first feminist texts was Mary Wollstonecraft's *Vindication of the Rights of Women* (1792). In 1848 Elizabeth Cady Stanton organized the Seneca Falls Convention on women's rights. In late 19th-century Britain the suffragette movement was formed. The women's movement gained further impetus during the two World Wars, as women took on employment previously confined to men. In the latter half of the 20th century, the feminist movement has focused on attaining social and economic equality. In the US, the Equal Employment Opportunity Commission was created in 1964, and Betty Friedan organized (1966) the National Organization for Women (NOW). Feminist theorists include Simone de Beauvoir, Germaine Greer, and Gloria Steinem.

**femur** Thigh bone, extending from the hip to the knee. It is the longest and strongest bone of the human skeleton.

**fencing** Sport of swordsmanship, using blunt weapons: the foil, épée, and saber. Fencers wear protective jackets and breeches, gloves, and wire-mesh masks. In competitions, electronic sensors register hits, which score one point each. It has been an Olympic sport since 1896.

**Fenian movement** (Irish Republican Brotherhood) Irish nationalist organization set up in 1858, which sought independence from Britain by revolution. After several abortive plots, the leaders were arrested in 1867 and the focus of Fenian activity moved to the US. The movement was superseded by Sinn Féin.

**fennel** Tall, perennial herb of the PARSLEY family, native to s Europe. The seeds and extracted oil are used to add a liquorice flavor to medicines, liqueurs, and foods. It grows to 3.2ft (1m). Family Apiaceae/Umbelliferae; genus *Foeniculum vulgare*.

**Ferber, Edna** (1887–1968) US author. She won a Pulitzer Prize for her first novel, *So Big* (1924). Many of her later novels were made into films, such as *Show Boat* (1926), *Cimarron* (1930), *Giant* (1952), and *Ice Palace* (1958). Ferber also wrote several plays with George S. KAUFMAN, including *Dinner at Eight* (1932).

**Ferdinand II** (1578–1637) Holy Roman emperor (1619–37), king of Bohemia (1617–37) and Hungary (1618–37), grandson of FERDINAND I. Educated by the Jesuits, he championed the COUNTER REFORMATION. In 1619 the mainly Protestant diet of Bohemia chose FREDERICK V as their ruler, precipitating the THIRTY YEARS WAR. Ferdinand regained Bohemia (1620) and Hungary (1621). GUSTAVUS II's entry into the war turned the tide against Ferdinand. He was succeeded by his son, FERDINAND III.

**Ferdinand III** (1608–57) Holy Roman emperor (1637–57), king of Bohemia and Hungary (1625–57), son of FERDINAND II. In 1634 he succeeded WALLENSTEIN as commander of the imperial army in the THIRTY YEARS WAR. After Ferdinand's accession, the Hapsburg empire suffered a devastating series of defeats and he was forced to conclude the Peace of WESTPHALIA (1648).

**Ferdinand** (1861–1948) Prince (1887–1908) and czar (1908–18) of Bulgaria. In 1908 he declared Bulgaria independent of the Ottoman empire. Ferdinand allied Bulgaria with Serbia, Greece, and Montenegro in the first BALKAN WAR (1912–13), but Bulgaria's territorial gains were largely lost in the second war (1913) to its former allies. In a bid to regain territory, Ferdinand entered World War I on the side of the CENTRAL POWERS. Further defeats saw him abdicate in favor of his son, Boris III.

**Ferdinand V** (1452–1516) (Ferdinand the Catholic) King of Castile and León (1474–1504), of Aragon (as Ferdinand II) (1479–1516), of Sicily (1468–1516), and of Naples (as Ferdinand III) (1504–16). Ferdinand became joint king of Castile and León after marrying ISABELLA I in 1469, and inherited Aragon from his father, John II, in 1479. After he and Isabella conquered the Moorish kingdom of Granada (1492), they ruled over a united Spain. They sponsored the voyage of Christopher COLUMBUS to the New World (1492), expelled the Jews from Spain, and initiated the Spanish INQUISITION. After Isabella's death (1504), Ferdinand acted as regent in Castile for their insane daughter, Joanna, and later for her son, Charles I (Holy Roman emperor CHARLES V).

**Ferlinghetti, Lawrence** (1919– ) US poet. A leader of the BEAT MOVEMENT, he opened (1953) the City Lights bookstore in San Francisco and began publishing beat authors such as Allen GINSBERG. His colloquial poetry includes *A Coney Island of the Mind* (1958).

**Fermat, Pierre de** (1601–65) French mathematician. With Blaise PASCAL, he helped to formulate the theory of probability and, by showing that light travels along the shortest optical path (Fermat's principle), he laid the foundation for geometric optics.

**Fermat's last theorem** Theory that, for all integers $n>2$, there are no nonzero integers $x$, $y$, and $z$ that satisfy the equation $x^n+y^n=z^n$. Fermat wrote that he had found a proof, but he died without revealing it. Attempts at a valid proof, although for a long time unsuccessful, enriched the area of algebraic number theory. In 1993 Andrew Wiles of Princeton University announced a proof, but it was found to contain a gap. Further work repaired this, and the proof was widely accepted in 1995.

**fermentation** Energy-yielding metabolic process by which sugar and starch molecules are broken down to carbon dioxide and ALCOHOL in the absence of air (ANAEROBIC respiration). Catalyzed by ENZYMES, it is used for wine- and bread-making, beer-BREWING, and cheese maturation. The intoxicating effect of fermented fruits has been known since 4000 BC.

**Fermi, Enrico** (1901–54) US physicist, b. Italy. Fermi discovered NEPTUNIUM and produced the first self-sustaining CHAIN REACTION in uranium. In 1942 he built the world's first nuclear reactor. Fermi worked on the MANHATTAN PROJECT and on developing the hydrogen bomb. For his work with RADIOACTIVITY, Fermi was awarded the 1938 Nobel Prize for physics; the element FERMIUM was named for him.

**fermion** Any SUBATOMIC PARTICLE that obeys the EXCLUSION PRINCIPLE, and has a half-odd integer SPIN (such as 0.5, 1.5, or 2.5). Examples are protons, electrons, and quarks. *See also* BOSON

**fermium** (symbol Fm) Radioactive metallic TRANSURANIC ELEMENT of the ACTINIDE SERIES. First identified in 1952 as a decay product of $^{255}$U from the first large hydrogen bomb explosion. Ten isotopes have been identified. Properties: at.no. 100; most stable isotope $^{257}$Fm (half-life 80 days).

**fern** Nonflowering plant. Many ferns grow in warm, moist areas; there are *c.*10,000 species. The best-known genus *Pteridium* (BRACKEN) grows on moors and in open woodland. Ferns are characterized by two generations: the conspicuous SPOROPHYTE that possesses leafy fronds, stems, RHIZOMES, and roots, and reproduces by minute SPORES usually on the leaves; and the GAMETOPHYTE that resembles moss and produces sperm and ova. Fronds unroll from curled "fiddleheads." Phylum Filicinophyta.

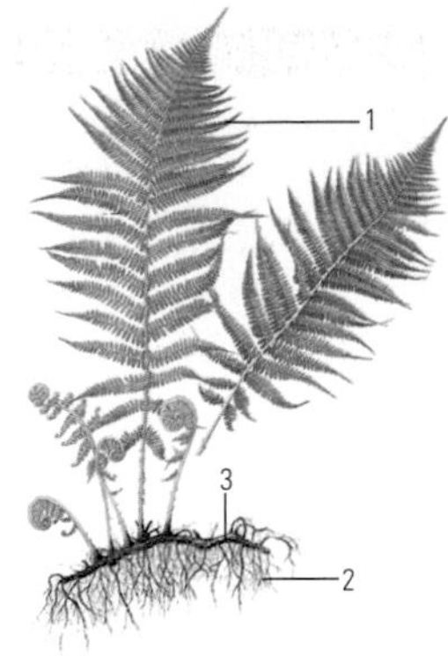


▲ **fern** A typical fern, such as the lady fern has upright leaves called fronds (1) which uncurl as they grow, and roots (2) that grow from the underground stem (3).

**Ferrari, Enzo** (1898–1988) Italian racing and sports car designer and manufacturer. He began driving in 1920 with Alfa Romeo. In 1939 Ferrari founded his own company, which produced the first Ferrari racing car in 1947. The company also manufactures production sports cars.

**Ferraro, Geraldine Anne** (1935– ) US politician. She served in the House of Representatives (1979–85). In 1984 Ferraro became the first woman to be nominated for US vice president, running on the Democratic ticket with Walter Mondale.

**ferret** European POLECAT. WEASEL-like animals, they have long necks, slender bodies, long tails, short legs, and white fur. They are agile killers, used to hunt rats and rabbits. Body length: 14in (36cm); weight: 1.5lb (700g). Family Mustelidae; species *Mustela putorius*.

**fertility drug** Drug taken to increase a woman's chances of conception and pregnancy. One of the major causes of female sterility results from insufficient secretion of pituitary hormones, and this can be treated with either human chorionic gonadotropin or clomiphene citrate, although use of the latter has resulted in multiple births. In cases where FERTILIZATION occurs, but where the uterine lining is unable to support the developing fetus, the hormone progesterone may be used.

### FERTILIZATION

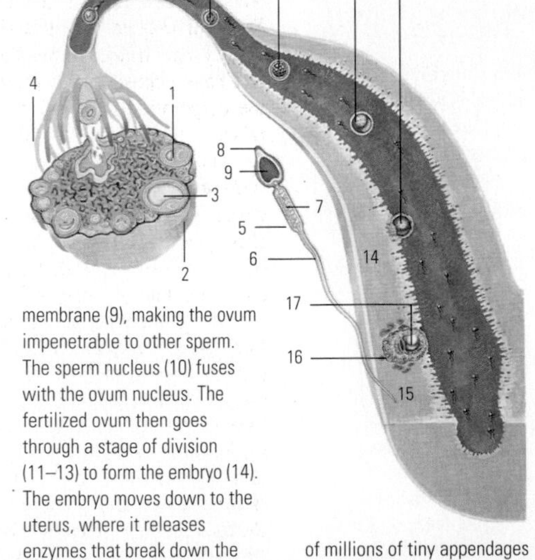


Mammalian fertilization begins with ovulation, in which an ovum (egg) (1) develops in an ovary (2) into a follicle (3). The follicle consists of the ovum, a sac of liquid and follicle cells. The pressure in the follicle increases until it bursts, releasing the ovum into the Fallopian tube (4). During ovulation, estrogen is produced by the collapsed follicle, which causes the lining of the uterus to thicken and extend its network of blood vessels, from which the ovum will be nourished. Fertilization occurs when sperm (5) are ejaculated from the penis during copulation. The sperm use their tail-like flagella (6), powered by mitochondria (7), to swim up the uterus. The first to reach the ovum penetrates the ovum membrane using enzymes secreted by the acrosomal vesicle (8). This triggers the formation of a membrane (9), making the ovum impenetrable to other sperm. The sperm nucleus (10) fuses with the ovum nucleus. The fertilized ovum then goes through a stage of division (11–13) to form the embryo (14). The embryo moves down to the uterus, where it releases enzymes that break down the lining (15), creating a hole in which the embryo sits (16). The embryo (17) develops an organ, the placenta, which is comprised of millions of tiny appendages called villi. The oxygen and food are absorbed from the mother's blood, via capillaries in the villi, into the embryo's blood.

tissue factor
plasma factor
fibrinogen
platelet
red blood cell
fibrin

A

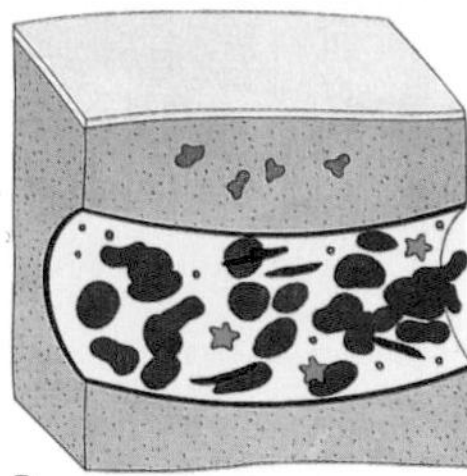

B

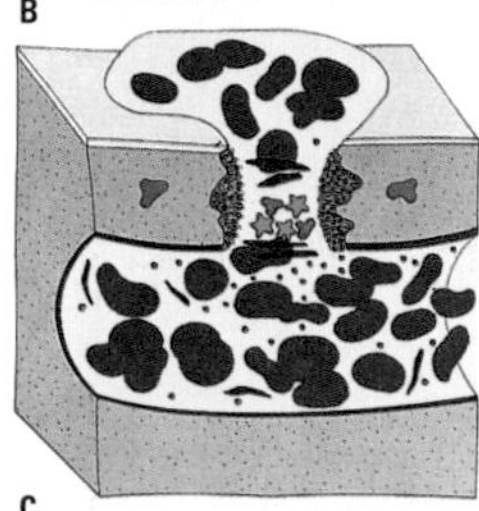

C

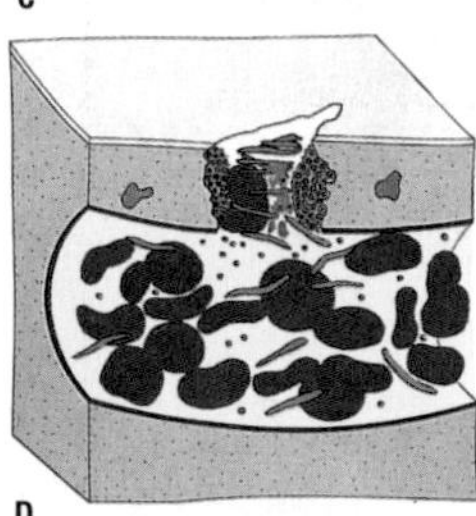

D

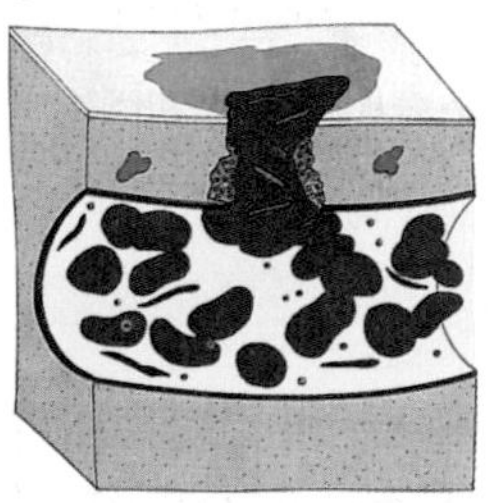

▲ **fibrin** An essential component of blood clotting, fibrin prevents excessive blood loss from a wound. Normally, circulating blood contains red cells, platelets, plasma, clotting factors, and fibrinogen. Tissue-clotting factors lie trapped within cells surrounding each blood vessel (A). When damage occurs, blood escapes from the broken vessel. Platelets congregate at the site and help plug the wound. Tissue-clotting factors are released (B). The reaction of the platelets with plasma and tissue-clotting factors converts the soluble fibrinogen into insoluble threads of fibrin. The fibrin forms a mesh across the break in the vessel (C). Platelets and blood cells become trapped in the mesh. The jellylike mass shrinks and serum oozes out, leaving a clot (D).

**fertilization** Key process in SEXUAL REPRODUCTION during which the nuclei of female and male GAMETES (sex cells) fuse to form a ZYGOTE. The zygote contains the genetic material (CHROMOSOMES) from both parents (*see* HEREDITY). In animals, the female sex cell is called the OVUM and the male cell SPERM. After fertilization, the zygote begins to divide to form an EMBRYO. Fertilization of the female OVUM by the male SPERM can be external (as in most fish, amphibians, and aquatic invetebrates) or internal (as in reptiles, birds, mammals, and insects). In PLANTS, the male gamete is found in POLLEN, and for most higher plants POLLINATION occurs before fertilization. *See also* DIPLOID; HAPLOID

**fertilizer** Organic or inorganic substance containing nutrients – mainly nitrogen, phosphorus, and potassium– that is added to soil to aid plant growth. **Organic** fertilizers include manure and compost, fish and bone meal, and guano. **Nitrogen** fertilizers are the most widely used inorganic fertilizers. Phosphorus fertilizers (**phosphates**) are made from the mineral apatite. Potassium fertilizers are extracted from deposits of potassium chloride. Nitrogen fertilizer in surface water promotes the growth of algae that degrades water quality and can cause EUTROPHICATION. Inorganic fertilizers suppress nitrogen-fixing bacteria, making agriculture increasingly dependent on artificial fertilizer.

**fetus** (foetus) Stage of EMBRYO development in a mammal after the main adult features are recognizable. In humans it dates from about eight weeks after conception.

**feudal system** Social system in most of Europe from the 9th century to the late Middle Ages, based on the tenure of land. The system originated from the need to provide a permanent group of knights to assist the king in his wars. All land was theoretically owned by the monarch and leased to his tenants-in-chief for their attendance at court and military assistance; they in turn let out fiefs to knights in return for military service and other obligations. The lowest rank, serfs, worked their lord's land in return for the right to grow their own produce. The system ended in the 16th century in England but lasted until the 18th century in parts of Europe and Russia. *See also* CAPITALISM

**fever** Elevation of the body temperature above normal, that is 98.6°F (37°C). It is mostly caused by bacterial or viral infection and can accompany virtually any infectious disease.

**Feydeau, Georges** (1862–1921) French playwright. He wrote many popular plays, with absurb plots and sparkling dialogue, in which he pioneered 19th-century French FARCE. These include *L'Hôtel du Libre Échange* (1894) and *La Dame de chez Maxim* (1899).

**Feynman, Richard Phillips** (1918–88) US physicist. He worked on the atom bomb during World War II, then with Hans BETHE on QUANTUM ELECTRODYNAMICS (QED). Feynman diagrams greatly facilitated the solution of electromagnetic interactions between ELEMENTARY PARTICLES. He was professor of physics at the California Institute of Technology from 1950 until his death. He shared the 1965 Nobel Prize for physics. With Murray GELL-MANN, Feynman developed a theory of weak interactions.

**Fez** (Fès) City in N central Morocco. Founded *c*.790, it is a former capital of Morocco and a sacred city of Islam containing many mosques. Industries: leather, pottery, traditional crafts, metalworking. Pop. (1982) 448,823.

**Fianna Fáil** ("Soldiers of Destiny") Irish political party. It was formed in 1926 by those opposed to Irish partition. The party came to power in 1932 under Eamon DE VALERA and has formed the government alone or in coalition for most years since then. It seeks the reunification of Ireland by peaceful means.

**fiber** Any of various materials consisting of thread-like strands. Natural fibers can be made into yarn, textiles, and other products, including carpets, and rope. The fibers consist of long narrow cells. **Animal** fibers are based on protein molecules and include WOOL, SILK, mohair, angora, and horsehair. **Vegetable** fibers are based mainly on CELLULOSE and include COTTON, LINEN, FLAX, JUTE, SISAL, and KAPOK. The mineral ASBESTOS is a natural, inorganic fiber. Regenerated fibers are manufactured from natural products, modified chemically. For example, RAYON is made from cellulose fiber obtained from cotton or wood. **Synthetic** fibers are made from a molten or dissolved plastic resin by forcing it through fine nozzles (spinnerets). The result is a group of filaments that are wound onto bobbins. These fibers can be used as single-strand yarn, or spun to form multistrand yarn and woven into textiles. Some synthetic fibers are made into rope, carpets, and other products. Synthetic fibers include NYLON and other polyamides, polyesters, and ACRYLICS. Other synthetic fibers, such as carbon or metals, can be used to reinforce resins to produce extremely strong materials.

**fiberglass** Spun glass used as a continuous filament in textiles and electrical insulation, and in a fibrous form to reinforce plastics or for sound or heat insulation. Molten glass is drawn through spinnerets or spun through holes in a revolving dish. Combined with layers of resin, fiberglass is a popular material for car bodies, boats, aircraft parts, and containers.

**fiber optics** Fine strands of glass or plastic, less than 0.04in (1mm) thick, able to transmit digital information in the form of pulses of light. Such transmission is possible because light entering an optical fiber is conducted, by reflection, from one end of the fiber to the other with very little loss of intensity. Fiber optic cables can carry more information than traditional copper cables and are immune to electromagnetic interference. **Single-mode fibers** have extremely small cores and accept light only along the axis of the fibers. They are used mainly in long-distance communication. **Multi-mode fibers** are larger and accept light from a variety of angles. Optical fibers have various applications, such as the ENDOSCOPE.

**Fibonacci, Leonardo** (*c*.1170–*c*.1240) Italian mathematician. He wrote *Liber abaci* (*c*.1200), the first Western work to propose the adoption of the Arabic numerical system. He produced the mathematical sequence named for him, in which each term is formed by the addition of the two terms preceding it. The sequence begins 0, 1, 1, 2, 3, 5, 8, 13, 21.... and so on. Many natural forms, such as leaf systems, are delimited by the Fibonacci series.

**fibrin** Insoluble, fibrous protein that is essential to BLOOD CLOTTING. Developed in the blood from a soluble protein, fibrinogen, fibrin is laid down at the site of a wound in the form of a mesh which then dries and hardens so that the bleeding stops.

**fibula** Long thin outer bone of the lower leg of four- and two-legged VERTEBRATES, including humans. It articulates with the other lower leg bone, the TIBIA, just below the knee.

**Field, Marshall** (1834–1906) US businessman and philanthropist. In 1856 he went to work for a Chicago store and in 1867 became a partner in a department store. In 1881 he bought out his partners and the store was renamed Marshall Field. Field's innovatory sales techniques and emphasis on customer service made him a fortune. He was a founder (1878) of the Art Institute of Chicago, and in 1893 donated $8 million for the creation of the Field Museum of Natural History.

**field hockey** Game played by two teams of 11, in which the object is to use a hooked stick to strike a small, solid ball into an opponents' goal. The field of play classically measures 300×180ft (91.47×54.9m), usually grassed. To score, a player must be within the semicircle marked out in front of the goal. Body contact is forbidden and a ball is prohibited from being hit above shoulder height. There are two 35-minute halves. The modern game dates from the mid-19th century and has been an Olympic sport since 1908. *See also* ICE HOCKEY

**Fielding, Henry** (1707–54) English novelist and playwright. In the 1730s Fielding wrote a number of satirical plays, such as *Pasquin* (1736). *Joseph Andrews* (1742) was his first NOVEL. Other works include *The Life of Mr Jonathan Wild the Great* (1743). Fielding strengthened the novel genre through his depiction of character and narrative sophistication. His masterpiece is the picaresque novel *Tom Jones* (1749). Fielding also founded Britain's first organized police force, the Bow Street Runners.

**Fields, W.C. (William Claud)** (1880–1946) US vaudeville, film, and radio comedian. He was famous for his portrayal of hard-drinking, misanthropic braggarts in such films as *My Little Chickadee* (1940) and *Never Give a Sucker an Even Break* (1941).

**Fife** Region in E central Scotland between the firths of Tay and Forth; the capital is Glenrothes. Central Fife is mostly low-lying farmland. Coalfields lie in the W and E. Along the North Sea coast there are many fishing villages. St. Andrews is the seat of Scotland's oldest university (1410), and the home of the Royal and Ancient Golf Club. Area: 504sq mi (1,305sq km). Pop. (1991) 341,199.

**fig** Tree, shrub, or climber of the MULBERRY family, growing in warm regions, especially from the E Mediterranean to India and Malaysia. The common fig (*Ficus carica*) has tiny flowers without petals that grow inside fleshy flasklike receptacles; these become the thick outer covering holding the seeds, the true, edible fruit of the fig tree. Height: to 39ft (11.8m). Family Moraceae, genus *Ficus*.

**Fiji** Independent nation in the S Pacific Ocean, consisting of more than 800 mostly volcanic islands and islets; the capital is Suva on Viti Levu island. The two largest islands, Viti Levu and Vanua Levu, rise sharply from the fertile, heavily populated coastal region to a mountainous and rugged interior. Settlement of the region dates back to the second millennium BC. Discovered by Abel TASMAN in 1643, the islands were visited by British explorers in the 18th century and became a British crown colony in 1874. Indians were subsequently imported to work on the sugar plantations and by the 1950s outnumbered the native Fijian population. In 1970 Fiji achieved independence within the Commonwealth of Nations. The election of an Indian-majority government (1987) led to a military coup by native Fijians and the proclamation of a republic. Agriculture is the most important sector of the economy; the main products are copra, sugar, and rice. Gold and silver are mined and tourism is important. Area: 7,055sq mi (18,272sq km). Pop. (1995 est.) 783,800.

**filariasis** Group of tropical diseases caused by infection with a nematode worm, *filaria*. The parasites, which are transmitted by insects, infiltrate the lymph glands, causing swelling and impaired drainage. Drug treatment reduces the symptoms. *See also* ELEPHANTIASIS

**filibuster** Method of delaying a vote of a legislative assembly by making long speeches. It has particular reference in the US Senate, which did not have any method for voting to end debate until 1917. Since then a two-thirds majority has been required to close a debate.

**Fillmore, Millard** (1800–74) 13th US president (1850–53). He served (1833–43) in the House of Representatives, and in 1834 joined the newly formed WHIGS. In 1848 Fillmore was elected vice president to Zachary TAYLOR, and succeeded as



## FINLAND

The flag of Finland was adopted in 1918 after the country had become an independent republic following a century of Russian rule. The blue represents Finland's many lakes. The white symbolizes the blanket of snow that masks the land in winter.

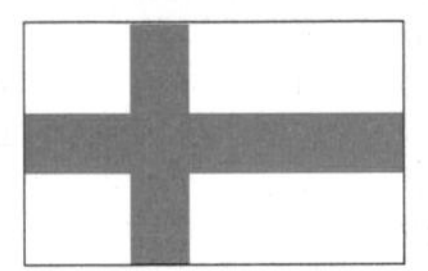

**AREA:** 130,552sq mi (338,130sq km)
**POPULATION:** 5,042,000
**CAPITAL (POPULATION):** Helsinki (508,588)
**GOVERNMENT:** Multiparty republic
**ETHNIC GROUPS:** Finnish 93%, Swedish 6%
**LANGUAGES:** Finnish and Swedish (both official)
**RELIGIONS:** Evangelical Lutheran 88%
**CURRENCY:** Markka= 100 penniä

The Republic of Finland has four geographical regions. In the S and W, on the Gulfs of Bothnia and Finland, is a low, narrow coastal strip, where most Finns live. The capital and largest city, HELSINKI, is here. Most of the interior is a beautiful wooded plateau, with over 60,000 lakes. The Saimaa area is Europe's largest inland water system. A third of Finland lies within the Arctic Circle. This "land of the midnight sun" is called *Lappi* (LAPPLAND). The ÅLAND ISLANDS lie in the entrance to the Gulf of Bothnia.

### CLIMATE

Finland has short, warm summers; Helsinki's July average is 63°F (17°C). In Lapland the temperatures are lower, and in June the sun never sets. Winters are long and cold; Helsinki's January average is 21°F (–6°C). The North Atlantic Drift keeps the Arctic coasts free of ice.

### VEGETATION

Forests (birch, pine, and spruce) cover 60% of Finland. The vegetation becomes more and more sparse to the N until it merges into Arctic tundra.

### HISTORY

In the 8th century, the LAPPS were forced N by Finnish-speaking settlers. In the 13th century Sweden conquered the country. Lutheranism was established in the 16th century. Finland was devastated by wars between Sweden and Russia. Following the NORTHERN WAR (1700–21), Russia gained much Finnish land. In the NAPOLEONIC WARS, Russia conquered Finland and it became a grand duchy (1809). Despite considerable autonomy, Finnish nationalism gained strength, fueled by important Finnish language works. Czar Nicholas II's program of russification (1899–1905) met fierce resistance.

Following the Russian Revolution, Finland declared independence. Civil war (January–May 1918) broke out between the Russian-backed Red Guard and the German-backed White Guard, led by MANNERHEIM. The conservative White Guard triumphed, and a republic was established (1919). Territorial disputes with the Soviet Union focused on KARELIA. Finland declared neutrality at the start of World War II, but Soviet troops invaded in November 1939, and in March 1940 Finland ceded part of Karelia and Lake LADOGA. In 1941 Finland allied itself with Germany, and in 1944 Soviet troops invaded and forced Finland to sign an armistice. Much of N Finland was destroyed in the ensuing war with Germany. The 1947 Paris Treaty confirmed the 1939 armistice terms. In 1955 Finland joined the UN and the Nordic Council, and was neutral during the Cold War. Urho Kaleva Kekkonen led Finland (1956–81) through reconstruction. Finland became a full member of the European Free Trade Association (EFTA) in 1986 and joined the European Union (EU) in 1995.

### ECONOMY

In 1999 Finland was one of 11 countries to participate in the "first wave" of the European single currency. Forests are Finland's most valuable resource. Forestry accounts for *c.*35% of exports. The chief manufactures are wood and paper products. Post-1945 the economy has diversified. Engineering, shipbuilding, and textile industries have grown. Farming employs only 9% of workforce. The economy is recovering from the recession caused by the collapse of the Soviet bloc.

▲ **fir** The largest Douglas firs, named for the botanical explorer David Douglas, grow to some 300ft (90m) and can live for over 400 years. In damp conditions, a Douglas fir will grow 3ft (1m) a year for the first 30 years of its life.

president when Taylor died. In an attempt to mediate between pro- and antislavery factions, he agreed to the COMPROMISE OF 1850. Fillmore's attempt to enforce the Fugitive Slave Law embittered ABOLITIONISTS and split the party. He failed to win renomination in 1852 and was succeeded by Franklin PIERCE. In the 1856 elections Fillmore stood for the KNOW-NOTHING MOVEMENT, but was defeated by Abraham LINCOLN.

**film noir** Genre of cynical, bleak films, originating in Hollywood during the 1940s and 1950s. Often bathed in gloomy shadows, the ominous mood of the films depicted an uneasy world, lacking ideals or moral absolutes. John HUSTON's *The Maltese Falcon* (1941) was the blueprint for other genre classics, such as *The Big Sleep* (1946) and *Touch of Evil* (1958).

**filter** Device for separating solid particles from a liquid or gas. The process is known as filtration. Automobiles have a number of filters that operate either by trapping solid particles in porous materials, such as paper or meshes, or by circulating the material to be filtered through a maze, such as an air filter.

**finch** Any of a family (Fringillidae) of small or medium-sized birds. Finches account for more than half of the world's known bird species, and are found on all continents, except Australasia and Antarctica. Most have a cone-shaped bill and feed on seeds. They are classified into three groups: those with small, triangular bills, such as the BUNTING, CANARY, and SPARROW, and those specifically called finches, such as the BULLFINCH, CHAFFINCH, and GOLDFINCH; those with thick, rounded bills, such as the CARDINAL, and GROSBEAK; and the crossbills. Most finches build cup-shaped nests for their three to six speckled eggs.

**Fine Gael** Irish political party. It was founded in 1933, as a successor to the party under William Cosgrave that had held power since the inception of the Irish Free State. Overshadowed by FIANNA FÁIL, Fine Gael has held office only four times, always in coalition with the Labour Party (1948–51, 1954–57, 1973–77, 1994–97).

**Finger Lakes** Series of 11 long, narrow, glacial lakes in central New York. Cayuga and Seneca are the longest, both more than *c*.37mi (60km) long. New York State's wine industry is based here. The city of Hammondsport, at the end of Keuka Lake, is the area's commercial center. Wells College and Cornell University are on Cayuga Lake. Many resorts and tourist attractions are in the Finger Lakes region.

**fingerprint** Pattern of ridges in the dermis or deeper skin on the end of the fingers and thumbs. Fingerprints are specific to an individual and remain unchanged in pattern throughout life; for this reason they are useful as a means of identification.

**Finland** Republic in N Europe. *See* country feature page 253

**Finnish** One of the two official languages of Finland and a member of the FINNO-UGRIC group of languages. It is spoken by more than 4.5 million people in Finland and by nearly a million people in Sweden, Russia, and the US. Swedish is the other official language of Finland, spoken by 300,000 inhabitants.

**Finn Mac Cumhail** (Finn MacCool) (active 2nd or 3rd century AD) Semimythical Irish leader of a group of soldiers known as the Fenians. Their exploits were recorded in many ballads and poems, including those in the 12th-century *Book of Leinster* and others said to have been written by OSSIAN.

**Finno-Ugric** Group of related languages spoken by more than 22 million people in Finland and N Norway, in Estonia, and Karelia, at the N end of the Volga river and each side of the Ural Mountains, and in Hungary. The languages are unrelated to the Indo-European family. The Finnic branch includes FINNISH, Estonian, Lappish, Mordvinian, Mari, Komi, Votyak, Cheremiss, and Zyrian; the Ugric branch comprises HUNGARIAN, Ostyak, and Mansi (Vogul). Together with the Samoyed languages, Finno-Ugric makes up the Uralic family.

**fir** Any of a number of evergreen trees of the PINE family, native to alpine regions of the Northern Hemisphere. The pyramid-shaped trees are prized for their beauty and fragrance. They have flat needles and cylindrical cones that shed their scales when mature. The North American balsam fir is the source of Canada balsam. Height: 50–300ft (15–90m). Family Pinaceae; genus *Abies*. The DOUGLAS FIR is not a true fir.

**Firdausi** (935–1020) Persian poet. He wrote the *Shah Nama* (*Book of Kings*), an epic poem about the history of Persia. The first major work in Persian literature, it was presented to Mahmud of Ghazni in 1010.

**firearm** Term used usually to describe a small arm – a weapon carried and fired by one person or a small group of people. Firearms were used in Europe in the 14th century. They were, however, ineffective in close combat until *c*.1425, when a primitive trigger to bring a lighted match into contact with the gunpowder charge was invented. These **matchlocks** were heavy and cumbersome, and needed a constantly lit match. The lighter flintlock (which used the spark produced by flint striking steel to ignite the powder) superseded the matchlock in the mid-17th century. In 1805 the explosive properties of mercury fulminate were discovered and, with the invention of the percussion cap (1815), it provided a surer, more efficient means of detonation. It permitted the development by 1865 of both the **center-fire cartridge** (which has basically been the type of ammunition used in firearms ever since) and breech-loading. Another major 19th-century advance was **rifling**, which was the cutting of spiral grooves along the inside of a barrel in order to make the bullet spin in flight. In the 1830s Samuel COLT perfected the revolver, a PISTOL which could fire several shots without the need to reload. By the 1880s magazine RIFLES were also in use and were made more effective when a bolt action was incorporated after 1889. Development of a weapon that could fire a continuous stream of bullets began with the manually operated GATLING GUN, but the first modern MACHINE GUN was the maxim gun, invented in the 1880s. Guns of this type dominated the trench warfare of World War I, and by World War II more portable automatic weapons, light machine guns such as the Bren gun and submachine gun, were in use. Newer developments include gas-operated rifles, firearms with several rotating barrels and extremely high rates of fire, and small firearms that use explosive bullets.

**fireball** (bolide) Very bright METEOR. Fireballs have been loosely defined as meteors brighter than the planets.

**firefly** Light-emitting beetle in moist places of temperate and tropical regions. Organs underneath the abdomen usually give off rhythmic flashes of light. The luminous larvae and wingless females of some species are called lightning bugs or GLOWWORMS. Length: to 1in (25mm). There are *c*.1,000 species. Family Lampyridae.

**fireweed** (willow herb) Any of several species of perennial plants, especially *Epilobium angustifolium*. It has a long, unbranched stem with narrow, willow-like leaves and purple-red flowers. Height: to 3ft (1m). Family Onagraceae; genus *Epilobium*.

**first aid** Immediate treatment of a victim of an accident, sudden illness, or other medical emergency. If the victim appears to have a broken bone or internal injuries, they should not be moved. If the victim is unconscious, their head should be turned

## FISH

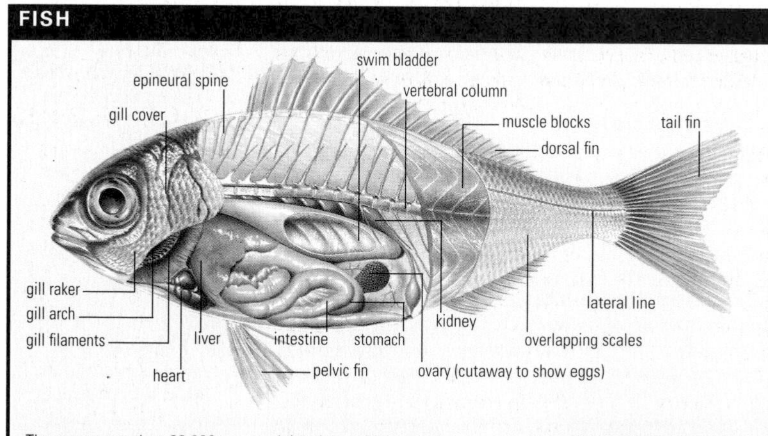


There are more than 22,000 species of bony fish. Although they vary in shape and the way they swim, they share many common features. All have a tail with equal upper and lower lobe sizes, which provides neither up nor down thrust. Such fish achieve natural buoyancy by adjusting their density using the swim bladder. The fish can expand or contract the swim bladder by secreting gas into or absorbing gas out of it, so adjusting the volume and external pressure and counteracting the tendency to sink or float to the surface.

to one side to prevent choking. Check that the victim has an open airway – if not, they may have respiratory failure (asphyxia). **Asphyxia** may be caused by the obstruction of air passages, in which case the Heimlich maneuver is recommended. For asphyxia caused by fumes or gas, such as carbon monoxide, the victim should be moved to a clear atmosphere before administering artificial respiration. The best method of **artifical respiration** is mouth-to-mouth resuscitation. Place the victim on their back, put one hand under the victim's chin and the other on the forehead. Tilt the victim's head back by lifting with the hand under the chin and pressing down on the forehead. If the victim is an adult, pinch the nostrils shut, take a deep breath, cover the mouth tightly and breathe hard. Repeat this procedure every five seconds. If the victim has swallowed a poisonous substance, identify the **poison**, and then call the emergency services. They may recommend inducing vomiting with syrup of ipecac. In an animal **bite or sting**, the wound should be cleaned with soap and water before applying antiseptic and a bandage. For poisonous SNAKEBITE, the wound should be cooled with ice to slow down the absorption of poison. A few snakebites require antivenoms. In order to stop the victim **bleeding** severly, apply direct pressure preferably with a sterile dressing. If bleeding continues, apply pressure to the artery that supplies blood to the area. To treat **shock**, place the victim on their back with their legs raised slightly, and place a blanket over the body. In the case of first- and second-degree **burns**, cold water should be applied before dressing with sterile bandages.

**Fischer, Hans** (1881–1945) German biochemist who received the 1930 Nobel Prize for chemistry for his structural studies of CHLOROPHYLL and of the red blood pigment hemin. Fischer was able to synthesize hemin, and almost completely synthesized one of the chlorophylls.

**Fischer-Dieskau, Dietrich** (1925– ) German baritone. He made his concert debut in 1947. Fischer-Dieskau is best known for his brilliant interpretations of *lieder*. His recordings of the songs and song-cycles of Schubert, Brahms, Schumann, and Wolf are definitive.

**Fish, Hamilton** (1808–93) US statesman, secretary of state (1869–77). He was US Representative (1843–45), governor of New York (1849–50), and US Senator (1951–57). After the break-up of the WHIGS, Fish joined the REPUBLICAN PARTY and served as secretary of state to Ulysses S. GRANT. He negotiated the Treaty of WASHINGTON (1871) that settled the ALABAMA CLAIMS.

**fish** Cold-blooded, aquatic vertebrate animal characterized by fins, gills for breathing, a streamlined body almost always covered by scales or bony plates onto which a layer of mucus is secreted, and a two-chambered heart. Fish are the most ancient form of vertebrate life, dating back more than 450 million years. They reproduce sexually, and fertilization may be external or internal. The eggs develop in water or inside the female, according to species. Fish have lateral line organs, which are fluid-filled pits and channels that run under the skin of the body. Sensitive fibers link these channels to the central nervous system and detect changes of pressure in the water and changes of strength and direction in currents. About 75% of all fish live in the sea. A few fish, such as SALMON and EEL, divide their lives between salt and freshwater habitats. Fish are usually divided into three classes: Agnatha, which are **jawless** fish, including the HAGFISH and LAMPREY; Chondrichthyes (**cartilaginous** fish), which includes SHARK, SKATE, RAY, and CHIMERA; and the numerous Osteichthyes (**bony** fish), including subclasses of soft-rayed fish (LUNGFISH), and the successful teleost fish, such as salmon and COD. There are *c.*22,000 species of bony fish, and they represent *c.*40% of all living vertebrates. They are divided into 34 orders and 48 families.

**Fisher, Saint John** (1469–1535) English Roman Catholic prelate. In 1529 he opposed Henry VIII's proposed divorce from Catherine of Aragon. He was tried and executed for denying that Henry was supreme head of the church under the Act of Supremacy. He was canonized in 1935. His feast day is July 9.

**fishing** and **fisheries** Harvesting fish for commercial uses. Commercial fishing boats and fleets employ several methods for catching fish, including pole and line, purse seine, gill netting, trawling, and stunning. About 70% of the commercial fish catch is taken in the Northern Hemisphere, with the greatest catches taken between the Philippines and Japan. Other fishing areas include the North Atlantic, North Pacific, and North Sea. The most significant Southern Hemisphere areas are the Pacific coast of Peru and the South African coast. Herrings, sardines, and anchovies make up the largest percentage of the total catch. Other species caught in large commercial quantities include cod, haddock, hake, redfish, sea bream, mackerel, tuna and salmon. The major fishing nations (by catch) are China, Japan, Peru, Chile, Russia, and the United States. By the late 1970s fish stocks were severely depleted. While attempts have been made to allow stocks to return to previous levels, such as the 1983 United Nations "Law of the Sea" resolution that allowed countries to enforce an exclusive 200mi (320km) limit around their coastlines, stocks are still low.

## FISSION, NUCLEAR

Most nuclear power stations use uranium-235 as fuel. When a uranium-235 nucleus is struck by a slow-moving neutron (1), it absorbs the neutron to form uranium-236. This is unstable and splits violently (2) forming two smaller nuclei, generating radiant energy (some in the form of heat), and releasing several neutrons (3). These neutrons can then start the process again (4), splitting further nuclei, which in turn release yet more neutrons (5). Such a process is known as a chain reaction and can spread at lightening speed. In a nuclear reactor, many of the neutrons are absorbed to prevent the chain reaction from running out of control and causing an excessive release of energy. Atomic bombs are designed to encourage the chain reaction to spread extremely rapidly.

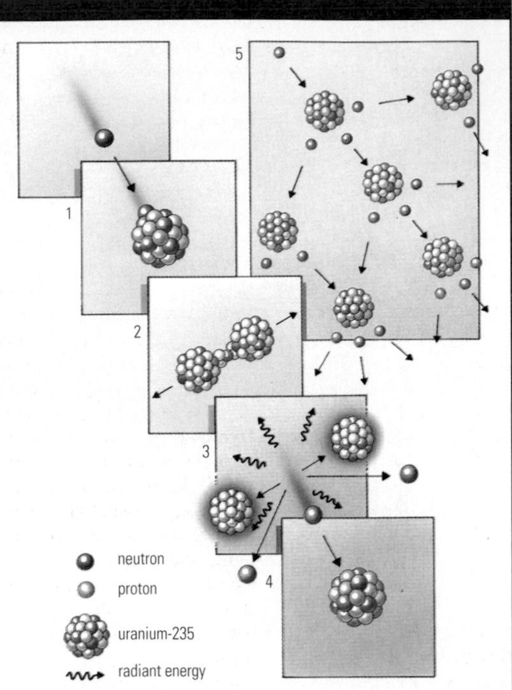


**Fisk, James** (1834–72) US financier. With Daniel Drew and Jay Gould, he gained control of Erie Railroad and manipulated the stock to acquire a fortune. Fisk and Gould's attempt to monopolize the gold market led to BLACK FRIDAY (1869). He was shot dead by a rival.

**fission** Form of ASEXUAL REPRODUCTION in unicellular organisms. The parent cell divides into two or more identical daughter cells. Binary fission produces two daughter cells (as in bacteria). Multiple fission produces 4, 8, or, in the case of some protozoa, more than 1,000 daughter cells, each developing into a new organism.

**fission, nuclear** Form of nuclear reaction in which a heavy atomic NUCLEUS splits into two, with the release of two or three NEUTRONS and large amounts of energy. It may occur spontaneously or be made to occur by bombarding certain nuclei with low-energy (slow) neutrons. The neutrons released by the initial splitting may go on to produce further fission in a nuclear CHAIN REACTION. The process is employed in atom bombs and nuclear reactors. *See also* FUSION, NUCLEAR; NUCLEAR ENERGY

**Fitzgerald, Ella** (1917–96) US jazz singer. The "First Lady of Song" was discovered by Chick Webb at Harlem's Apollo Theater (1934). Her first hit was "A-Tisket A-Tasket" (1938). Her "Songbook" series of renditions of popular "standards" by George Gershwin, Jerome Kern, and Cole Porter have become definitive.

**Fitzgerald, F. Scott (Francis Scott Key)** (1896–1940) US author. He began his first novel, *This Side of Paradise* (1920), while in the US army. Along with *The Beautiful and Damned* (1922), this established him as a chronicler of what he christened the "Jazz Age." He spent much of the 1920s in Europe,

▲ **Fitzgerald** US jazz singer Ella Fitzgerald is famous for her "scat" vocal style and classic interpretations of standards by Cole Porter, Jerome Kern, and George Gershwin.

▲ **flax** Cultivated in moist, temperate climates, only one of several species of flax (*Linum* sp.) is cultivated for its fiber and rich oil seeds. After harvesting, flax stems are retted (soaked in water) to soften the fibers which are then spun into yarn.

mingling with wealthy and sophisticated expatriates. Fitzgerald's masterpiece, *The Great Gatsby*, was published in 1925.

**fjord** (fiord) Narrow, steep-sided inlet on a sea coast. They were formed by GLACIERS moving toward the sea, and were flooded when the ice melted and sea levels rose.

**flagellant** Religious zealot who uses flagellation, or flogging, for disciplinary or devotional purposes. Now almost obsolete, the practice of flagellation has been part of many religions, including those of ancient Greece and Rome, some Native-American cultures, and Christianity. In most cases, flagellants have used self-inflicted beatings as a means of doing penance for sins or for purification.

**flagellate** Any single-celled organism that possesses, at some stage of its development, one or several whiplike structures (flagella) for locomotion and sensation. There are two major groups; the phytoflagellates resemble plants, the zooflagellates resemble animals. Most have a single nucleus. Reproduction may be asexual (FISSION) or sexual.

**Flaherty, Robert Joseph** (1884–1951) US film director. In 1922 he completed the first feature-length DOCUMENTARY film, *Nanook of the North*. Other films include *Moana* (1926), *Man of Aran* (1934), and *Louisiana Story* (1948).

**flamboyant style** Final phase of French GOTHIC ARCHITECTURE (14th–16th century). The name comes from the flame-like forms of the elaborate tracery used in cathedrals, as on the west façade of Rouen Cathedral (1370). The English DECORATED STYLE is a close equivalent.

**flamenco** Traditional song, dance, and instrumental music, thought to have developed from an amalgam of Romany, Jewish, and Arab cultures in Andalusia, S Spain. There are three types of song, of which the most demanding is the *cante hondo*. The dances epitomize pride, poise, and sensuality. Songs and dances are accompanied by handclaps, finger-snapping, and rhythmic rolls on the guitar.

**flamingo** Long-necked, long-legged wading bird of tropical and subtropical lagoons and lakes. They have webbed feet and a plumage that varies in color from pale to deep pink. Their bills have fine, hairlike filters which strain food from the muddy water. Height: to 5ft (1.5m). Family Phoenicopteridae.

**Flanders** Historic region now divided between Belgium and France. In Belgian Flanders, FLEMISH is the major language. From the 10th century, Flanders grew prosperous on the cloth industry, and the old nobility gradually lost authority to the cities, such as BRUGES, ANTWERP, and GHENT. By 1400 it was part of Burgundy, passing to the Hapsburgs in 1482, before becoming part of the Spanish Netherlands. It was frequently fought over by France, Spain, and later Austria, and was the scene of devastating trench warfare in World War I.

**flare, solar** *See* SOLAR FLARE

**flatfish** Any of more than 500 species of bottom-dwelling, mainly marine fish found worldwide. Flatfish have a laterally flattened body, with one anal and one dorsal fin. Both eyes are on the same side. The fish lie on their "blind" side, which is generally white. The upper surface is colored to blend with their surroundings, and some species are able to alter their pigmentation. Examples include HALIBUT, PLAICE, TURBOT, SOLE, dab, and flounder. Order Pleuronectiformes.

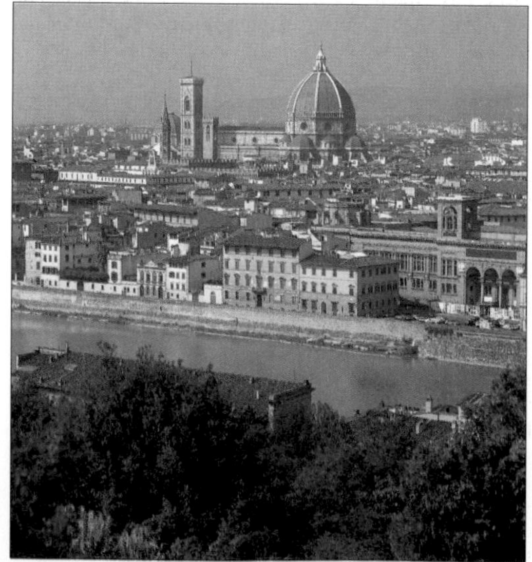

► **Florence** Located among the Tuscan foothills of N Italy, Florence is one of Italy's oldest intellectual and cultural centers.

**FLAMINGO**

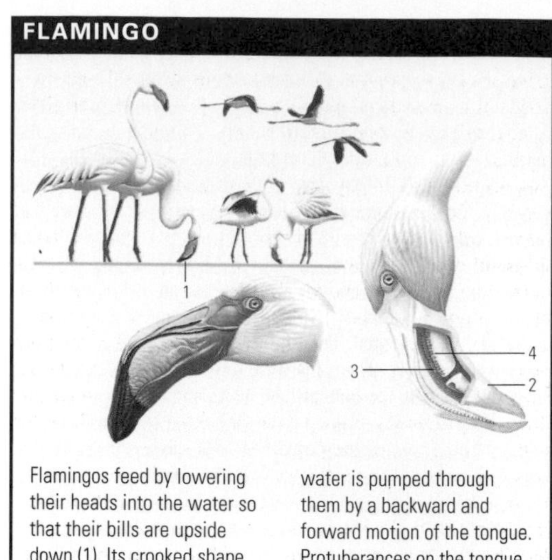


Flamingos feed by lowering their heads into the water so that their bills are upside down (1). Its crooked shape allows the front half of the bill to lie horizontally in the water (2). Tiny hook-like lamellae (3) strain food as the water is pumped through them by a backward and forward motion of the tongue. Protuberances on the tongue (4) scrape the particles of food off the lamellae for ingestion as the tongue moves back and forth.

**Flathead** *See* SALISH

**flatworm** Simple, carnivorous, ribbonlike creature which, having no circulatory system and sometimes no mouth or gut, feeds by absorption through its body wall. Almost all are hermaphrodites. The FLUKE and TAPEWORM are parasites of animals. Order Platyhelminthes.

**Flaubert, Gustave** (1821–80) French novelist of the 19th-century realist school. An extremely craftsmanlike and elegant writer, he remains one of the most highly respected of European novelists. *Madame Bovary* (1857), his masterpiece, represents the transition from ROMANTICISM to REALISM in the development of the NOVEL. Other fiction includes *The Temptation of St. Anthony* (1847) and *A Sentimental Education* (1869).

**flax** Slender, erect, flowering plant cultivated for its fibers and seeds. The fibers are spun into yarn to make LINEN. The seeds yield linseed oil. Family Linaceae; species *Linum usitatissium*.

**flea** Any of 1,000 species of wingless, leaping insects found worldwide. They are external parasites on warmblooded animals. In moving from one host to another, they can carry disease. Length: to 0.4in (1cm). Order Siphonaptera.

**fleabane** Any of *c*.250 species of plants of the genus *Erigeron* that grow in temperate climates. Most have lance-shaped leaves and daisylike flowers with yellow central discs and white, yellow, pink, or purple florets. Canada fleabane is dried and used in the treatment of diarrhea. Height: to 3.3ft (1m). Family Compositae.

**Fleming, Sir Alexander** (1881–1955) Scottish bacteriologist, discoverer of PENICILLIN. In 1922 he discovered lysozyme, a natural antibacterial substance found in saliva and tears. In 1928, while conducting research on staphylococci, Fleming noticed that a mold, identified as *Penicillium notatum*, liberated a substance that inhibited the growth of some BACTERIA. He named it penicillin; it was the first antibiotic. Howard FLOREY and Ernst CHAIN refined the drug's production, and in 1941 was produced commercially. In 1945 Fleming, Florey, and Chain shared the Nobel Prize for physiology or medicine.

**Fleming, Ian Lancaster** (1908–64) English novelist. He wrote 13 escapist spy thrillers about the agent James Bond, "007," which won great popularity for their realistic detail, and sexual and violent fantasy. They include *Casino Royale* (1952) (in which Bond makes his first appearance), *From Russia with Love* (1957), and *Goldfinger* (1959). The subsequent films based on his novels have become a movie institution.

**Fleming, Sir John Ambrose** (1849–1945) English electrical engineer, inventor of the thermionic valve. Fleming's valve was a RECTIFIER, or DIODE, consisting of two electrodes in an evacuated glass envelope. The diode permitted current to flow in one direction only. It could detect radio signals. *See also* FLEMING'S RULES

**Fleming's rules** In physics, ways of remembering the relationships between the directions of the current, field, and mechanical rotation in electric motors and generators. In the **left-hand** rule (for motors), the forefinger represents field, the second finger current, and the thumb, motion; when the digits are extended at right-angles to each other, the appropriate directions are indicated. The **right-hand** rule applies the principles to generators. The rules were devised by John FLEMING.

**Flemish** One of the two official languages of Belgium (the other being French). It is spoken mainly in the N half of the country, by *c.*50% of the population. Flemish is virtually the same language as DUTCH, but for historical and cultural reasons it is called Flemish in Belgium and Dutch in The Netherlands.

**Flemish art** (Netherlandish art) Loose art history term used to describe artists working in what roughly corresponds to modern-day Netherlands, Belgium, and Luxembourg. In the 14th and early 15th centuries, Flemish artists were masters of the International Gothic style, brilliantly characterized by the illuminated manuscripts of the LIMBOURG brothers. Naturalism became a hallmark of Flemish art, as in the portraits and altarpieces of van EYCK and van der WEYDEN and the LANDSCAPE PAINTINGS of BRUEGEL The greatest figures of the next generation were Anthony VAN DYCK, who spent much of his career in England, and Peter Paul RUBENS, the chief exponent of BAROQUE art in N Europe. After 1650, Flemish art went into decline. In the 19th century, James ENSOR was a precursor of EXPRESSIONISM. In the 20th century, MAGRITTE and Paul Delvaux both made significant contributions to the SURREALISM movement. *See also* DUTCH ART

**Fletcher, John** (1579–1625) English dramatist and poet. From *c.*1607 to 1616, he collaborated with Francis BEAUMONT on romantic tragicomedies such as *Philaster*, *The Maid's Tragedy*, and *A King and No King*. Fletcher may have worked with Shakespeare on *Henry VIII* and *The Two Noble Kinsmen*. His own work includes *The Faithful Shepherdess* (1608) and *The Chancer* (1623).

**Fletcher v. Peck** (1810) First US Supreme Court case interpreting the contract clause of the Constitution. Chief Justice John MARSHALL expanded the meaning of the term "contract" to include land grants from states.

**flight** *See* AERODYNAMICS; AERONAUTICS; AIRCRAFT; AIRFOIL

**flight recorder** (black box) Device for automatically recording data during the operation of an aircraft. Investigators analyze the data after a crash or malfunction. A small aircraft may have a simple cockpit voice recorder (CVR), which records all cockpit sounds and radio contact with air traffic control. Larger aircraft carry a separate flight data recorder (FDR). Control settings, instrument readings, and other data are recorded on magnetic wire.

**flint** ($SiO_2$) Granular variety of QUARTZ of a fine crystalline structure. It is usually brown or dark gray, although the variety known as chert is paler. It occurs in rounded nodules and is found in chalk or other sedimentary rocks containing calcium carbonate. Of great importance to early humans during the STONE AGE, when struck a glancing blow, flint is flaked, leaving sharp edges appropriate for tools and weapons; two flints struck together produce a spark which can be used to make fire.

**Flood, the** Primeval deluge, sent by God to devastate the Earth as a punishment for wickedness. As related in the Old Testament (Genesis 6–9), God sent rain upon the Earth for 40 days and nights, destroying everything he had created. Only NOAH, his family, and a pair of every living creature, contained in the Ark that he had built, were spared to start creation afresh. The Genesis account bears some resemblance to part of the epic of GILGAMESH.

**floppy disk** See MAGNETIC DISK

**Flora** In Roman mythology, personification and goddess of springtime and of budding fruits, flowers, and crops. She was honored as a fertility goddess.

**Florence** (Firenze) Capital of Tuscany and Firenze province, on the Arno River, Italy. Initially an Etruscan town, it was a Roman colony from the 1st century BC to 5th century AD. In the 12th century it became an independent commune and major trading center. The site of many factional power struggles, especially the 13th-century war between the GUELPHS and GHIBELLINES, it nevertheless became the cultural and intellectual center of Italy. Florence's period of dominance coincided with the rule of the MEDICI family. It became a city-state and one of the leading centers of the RENAISSANCE. Artists who contributed to the flourishing city included MICHELANGELO, LEONARDO DA VINCI, RAPHAEL, and DONATELLO. In 1569 Florence became the capital of the Grand Duchy of Tuscany. From 1865 to 1871 Florence was the capital of the kingdom of Italy. Its many notable churches include: the *Duomo* gothic cathedral (1296); *San Lorenzo*, Florence's first cathedral rebuilt in 1425 by BRUNELLESCHI, including the New Sacristy built by Michelangelo; and the monastery San Marco which holds FRA ANGELICO masterpieces. Major art collections include the Uffizi Museum and the Bargello Palace. Industries: tourism, craft, fashion. Pop. (1992) 397,434.

**Florence, school of** Painters and sculptors who flourished in Florence during the RENAISSANCE. Major figures include GIOTTO, Fra ANGELICO, LEONARDO, MICHELANGELO, BOTTICELLI, and RAPHAEL.

**Florey, Sir Howard Walter (Baron Florey of Adelaide)** (1898–1968) British pathologist, b. Australia. He shared, with Alexander FLEMING and Ernst CHAIN, the 1945 Nobel Prize for physiology or medicine for his part in the development of PENICILLIN. Florey isolated the antibacterial agent from the mold, thus making possible the large-scale preparation of penicillin.

**Florida** State in the extreme SE US, occupying a peninsula between the Atlantic Ocean and the Gulf of Mexico; the capital is TALLAHASSEE. Florida forms a long peninsula with thousands of lakes, many rivers, and vast areas of swampland. At the S tip there is a chain of small islands, the FLORIDA KEYS, stretching W. The biggest attractions are the EVERGLADES, Florida Keys, and Disney World. Discovered in 1513, the first permanent settlement in Florida was at St. Augustine. Originally Spanish, the land passed to the English (1763), then returned to the Spanish (1783). America purchased Florida in 1819 and, although the state seceded from the Union in 1861, it was little affected by the Civil War. It developed rapidly after 1880 when forest-clearing and drainage schemes were begun. Florida's historic ties with Cuba are particularly evident in MIAMI, Florida's second largest city after JACKSONVILLE. Industries focus on the John F. Kennedy Space Center at CAPE CANAVERAL. Chief agricultural products: citrus fruits, sugar cane, vegetables. Area: 58,560sq mi (151,670sq km). Pop. (1990) 12,938,000.

**Florida Keys** Chain of small coral and limestone islands, extending in a curve, *c.*150mi (240km) long, from Biscayne Bay, Miami, to Key West. Most of the islands are connected by the overseas Highway 1; the best-known are Key West and Key Largo. Florida Keys is a major tourist center. Other industries: fishing.

**flour** Fine or coarse powder prepared by sifting and grinding GRAIN. Most flour is made from WHEAT and is used to bake BREAD. MILLET is used in India, the former Soviet Union, and China. The main protein in wheat is GLUTEN. Bread flour contains *c.*11% protein, cake flour less than 9%. Self-rising flour contains a leavening agent, SODIUM HYDROCARBONATE. Flour is often bleached and enriched with vitamins and minerals.

**flower** Reproductive structure of all ANGIOSPERMS (flowering plants). It has four sets of organs set in whorls on a short apex (RECEPTACLE). The leaflike SEPALS protect the bud and form the calyx. The brightly colored petals form the corolla; the STAMENS are stalks (filaments) tipped by ANTHERS (pollen sacs); the CARPELS form the PISTIL with an OVARY, STYLE, and STIGMA. Flowers are bisexual if they contain stamens and carpels, and unisexual if only one of these is present. Reproduction occurs, following POLLINATION, when POLLEN is transferred from the anthers of one flower to the stigma of another flower of another plant (cross-pollination), or to the same flower or flower of the same plant (self-pollination).

**FLORIDA**
**Statehood:**
March 3, 1845
**Nickname:**
Sunshine State
**State bird:**
Mockingbird
**State flower:**
Orange blossom
**State tree:**
Sabal palm
**State motto:**
In God we trust

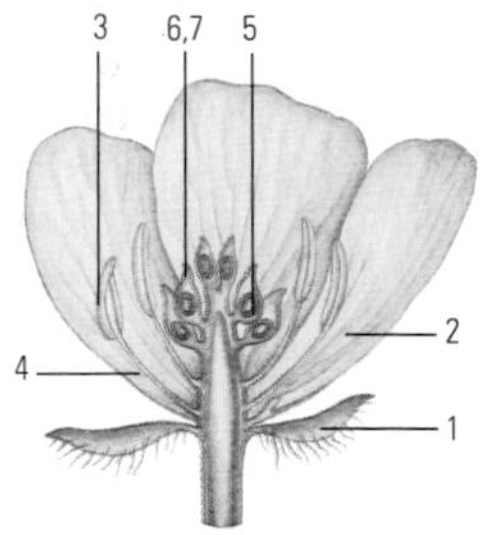


▲ **flower** A typical flower has four main parts: sepals, petals, stamens, and carpels. The sepals (1) form a protective covering (the calyx) over the developing flower bud, and lie outside the showy petals (2) which collectively are called the corolla. Each male stamen is made up of an anther (3), which contains the pollen grains, borne on a filament (4). The female carpels, which together form the pistil, are found at the center of the flower, each containing ovaries (5) which bear ovules and a style (6) which supports the stigma (7) – the structure on which pollen is deposited.

▲ **flute** Flutes, although called woodwind instruments, are metallic and covered in silver or gold plate. The illustration shows three members of the flute family: piccolo (1), flute (2), and bass flute (3).

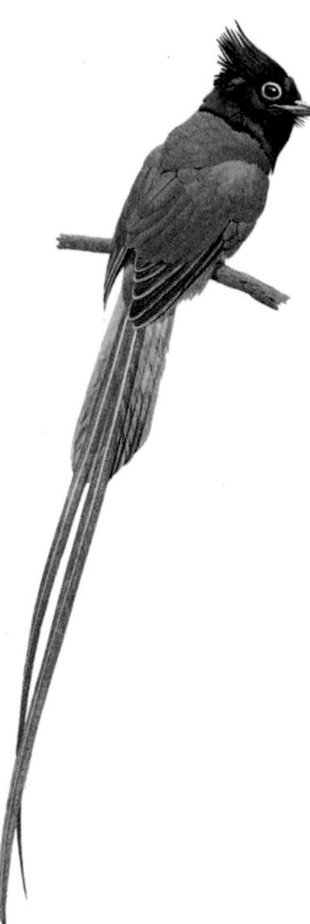

▲ **flycatcher** The paradise flycatcher (*Terpsiphone viridis*), like all flycatchers, catches its prey of small insects on the wing. It sits on its perch waiting to dart out after insects, rather than trying to catch them in continual flight.

**flu** Abbreviation of INFLUENZA

**fluid** Any substance that is able to flow. Of the three common states of matter, GAS and LIQUID are considered fluid, while a SOLID is not.

**fluidics** Use of devices operated by a fluid (gas or liquid) for controlling processes and instruments. Fluidic systems simulate electronic circuits. They were developed in the US in the 1960s for rocket and aircraft guidance.

**fluid mechanics** Study of the behavior of liquids and gases. **Fluid statics** is the study of fluids at rest and includes the study of pressure, density, and the principles of PASCAL and ARCHIMEDES. **Fluid dynamics** is the study of moving fluids and includes the study of streamline flow, BERNOULLI'S LAW, and the propagation of waves. Engineers use fluid mechanics in the design of bridges, dams, and ships. AERODYNAMICS is a branch of fluid mechanics.

**fluke** FLATWORM, an external or internal parasite of animals. Flukes have suckers for attachment to the host. Human infection can result from eating uncooked food containing encysted larvae, or from penetration of the skin by larvae in infected waters. The worms enter various body organs, such as the liver, lungs, and intestines, causing edema (swelling) and decreased function. Phylum Platyhelminthes, class Trematoda.

**fluorescence** Emission of radiation, usually light, from a substance when its atoms have acquired excess energy from a bombarding source of radiation, usually ultraviolet light or electrons. Unlike PHOSPHORESCENCE, fluorescence ceases when the source of energy is removed. Television tubes use fluorescent screens.

**fluoridation** Addition of inorganic FLUORIDES to the water supply to reduce tooth decay. The additive is usually sodium fluoride, at a concentration of about one part per million. Since its inception in the 1930s fluoridation has been adopted in many countries.

**fluoride** Any salt of hydrogen fluoride (HF); more particularly, fluoride compounds added to drinking water or toothpaste to build up resistance to tooth decay.

**fluorine** (symbol F) Gaseous toxic element of the HALOGEN group, isolated (1886) by Henri Moissan. Chief sources are fluorspar and cryolite. The pale yellow element, obtained by ELECTROLYSIS, is the most electronegative element and the most reactive nonmetallic element. It is in FLUORIDE in drinking water and is used in making FLUOROCARBONS and in extracting URANIUM. Properties: at.no. 9; at.wt. 19; m.p. −363.3°F (−219.6°C); b.p. −306.6°F (−188.1°C); single isotope $^{19}$F.

**fluorite** (fluorspar) Mineral, calcium fluoride ($CaF_2$). It has cubic system crystals with granular and fibrous masses. Brittle and glassy, it can be yellow, purple, or green. It is used as a flux in steel production, and in ceramics and chemical industries. Hardness 4; sp.gr. 3.1.

**fluorocarbon** (technically chlorofluoromethane) Organic compound that is produced by replacing the hydrogen atoms of hydrocarbons with FLUORINE atoms. Their inertness, low toxicity, and ability to withstand high temperature, make them ideal for use in plastics, such as PTFE (POLYTETRAFLUOROETHYLENE) or Teflon. Many of these chemicals also contain chlorine and are called CHLOROFLUOROCARBONS (CFCs).

**flute** WOODWIND musical instrument. Air is blown across a mouth-hole near one end of a horizontally held tube. It has a range of three octaves, with a mellow tone in the lower register and a brighter tone in the higher.

**flux** In ceramics, any substance that promotes vitrification when mixed with clay. When the ware is fired, the flux melts, filling the porous clay form. As the piece cools, it hardens, becoming glossy and nonporous. Fluxes include felspathic rock, silica, and borax. In METALLURGY, a flux is added to the charge of a smelting FURNACE to purge impurities from the ore and to lower the melting point of the slag.

**fly** Any of a large order (Diptera) of two-winged insects. They range in size from midges 0.06in (1.6mm) long to robber flies more than 3in (76mm) in length. The 60,000–100,000 species are found worldwide. All flies undergo metamorphosis. A female lays between one and 250 eggs at a time. The larva (MAGGOT) typically lives on rotting flesh or plants. Adult flies have compound eyes and sucking mouthparts. Many are pests and vectors, especially HORSEFLIES, MOSQUITOES, and TSETSE FLIES. The common housefly is species *Musca domestica*.

**flycatcher** Common name for two families (Old World Muscicapidae, New World Tyrannidae) of birds that catch insects in midflight. The Tyrannidae (tyrant flycatchers) includes the KINGBIRD.

**flying bomb** Popular name for the V1, V2 ROCKETS used by the Germans in World War II.

**flying fish** Tropical marine fish found worldwide. It is dark blue and silver, and uses its enlarged pectoral and pelvic fins to glide above the water surface for several yards. Length: to 18in (45.7cm). Family Exocoetidae; species *Cypselurus opisthopus*.

**flying fox** Popular name for a species of FRUIT BAT

**flying squirrel** Small, nocturnal SQUIRREL that lives in forests. They can glide more than 150ft (50m) by means of furry flaps of skin that stretch out flat and taut on both sides of the body when the limbs are extended. They nest high up in hollows of trees. There are 33 species of the genus *Pteromys* in Asia (one reaches SE Europe) and two species of the genus *Glaucomys* in North America. The giant flying squirrel of s Asia grows up to 4ft (120cm) long.

**FM** Abbreviation of FREQUENCY MODULATION (FM)

**focal length** Distance from the midpoint of a curved mirror or the center of a thin lens to the focal point of the system. For converging systems, it is given a positive value; for diverging systems, a negative value.

**fog** Mass of water droplets immediately above the Earth's surface that reduces visibility to less than 0.6mi (1km). A light fog is called **mist** or haze. Fog is caused by water vapor condensing as the air becomes cooler. This condensation takes place around particles of dust. **Advection** fog develops from air flowing over a surface of a different temperature, such as steam fog that results from cold air passing over warm water; **frontal** fog forms when warm rain falls through cold air near the ground; **radiation** fog occurs when the ground cools on a still, clear night, and is most common in valleys; **upslope** fog develops when air cools as it ascends a slope. *See also* DEW POINT

**Fokine, Michel** (1880–1942) Russian-American choreographer. Fokine was chief choreographer for DIAGHILEV and his BALLETS RUSSES in Paris (1909). He became a naturalized American in 1932. His best-known works include *Les Sylphides* (1909), *Firebird* (1910), and *Petrushka* (1916).

**fold** In geology, a bend in a layer of rock. An upfold is an ANTICLINE; a downfold, a SYNCLINE. A monocline (flexure) slopes in one direction only and usually passes into a FAULT. Folds occur as part of the process of PLATE TECTONICS, where rock strata buckle and bend under pressure. If the compression is fairly gentle and even, the resulting fold is "**symmetrical**." If the pressure is uneven, then **asymmetrical** folds will form. In many cases, the folds are pushed right over to form **recumbent** features. Eventually the rock strata may break under the pressure, to form an overthrust or a **nappe**.

**folic acid** Yellow crystalline derivative of glutamic acid, it forms part of the VITAMIN B complex.

**folk art** Term used to describe the art of folk cultures, especially those of rural and ethnic minority communities. It is usually practiced by people who have not had formal training and who use local craft processes. The decoration of everyday objects features strongly in folk art, often with motifs that have been handed down from generation to generation. *See also* PRIMITIVISM

**folklore** Traditions, customs, and beliefs of the people. The most prevalent form of folklore is the folk tale. In contrast to literature, which is transmitted through written texts, the folk tale has an oral basis and is transmitted primarily through memory and tradition. Often the tales take the form of myths, fables, and fairy tales. The best-known study of folklore is Sir James Frazer's anthropological study *The Golden Bough* (1890).

**folk music** Music deriving from, and expressive of, a particular national, ethnic, or regional culture; it is nearly always vocal. Its main theme tends to be the history of a people, so that folk songs are usually narrative. The musical structure is the simple repetition of a tune (with or without chorus), sometimes with a freedom of rhythm which adheres more to the natural meter of the word than to the more formal requirements of composition. Some modern writers of popular music, such as Bob DYLAN, have applied the folk idiom to their compositions.

**Folsom** Prehistoric inhabitants of North America, whose existence was proved first by the discovery (1926) of fluted stone spearheads near Folsom, New Mexico. The tools were found with the bones of extinct mammals, such as the mastodon, and appear to date from *c.*9000 BC.

**Fonda, Henry** (1905–82) US actor. Cast as the model of American decency and homespun wisdom, Fonda appeared in a series of John FORD films, such as *Young Mr. Lincoln* (1939), *The Grapes of Wrath* (1940), and *Twelve Angry Men* (1957). Fonda won his Best Actor Academy Award for his performance opposite his daughter, Jane FONDA, in *On Golden Pond* (1981). Other films include *Mister Roberts* (1955).

**Fonda, Jane** (1937– ) US film actress, daughter of Henry FONDA. Following a lauded performance in *They Shoot Horses, Don't They?* (1969), Fonda won a Best Actress Academy Award for *Klute* (1971). A second award followed for *Coming Home* (1978). She starred opposite her father in *On Golden Pond* (1981). Her personal fitness program, *Jane Fonda's Workout Book* (1981), was a worldwide bestseller.

**Fontainebleau** Town in the Forest of Fontainebleau, N France, famed for its royal palace. The 16th-century palace was commissioned by Francis I. Built on the site of a previous royal residence, it is a world heritage site and a masterpiece of French Renaissance architecture. Napoleon's imperial headquarters, it was also the location for the signing of his first abdication (1814). It is now a museum and the presidential summer residence. The town was headquarters of the military branch of NATO from 1945 to 1965. Pop. (1982) 18,750.

**Fontainebleau School** Style of painting associated with a group of artists working at the French court in the 16th century. In a bid to match the magnificence of the Italian courts, Francis I gathered an international team of artists to decorate his palace at FONTAINEBLEAU. Led by the Florentine artists Fiorentino Rosso and Francesco Primaticcio, the group evolved a unique style of MANNERISM, blending sensuality and elegance.

**Fonteyn, Dame Margot** (1919–91) English ballerina. She was a member of the Royal Ballet (1934–59) and was a guest artist with every major US and European ballet company. Fonteyn continued to dazzle audiences late in her career, especially in her appearances with Rudolf NUREYEV.

**food** Material taken into an organism to maintain life and growth. Important substances in food include: PROTEINS, FATS, CARBOHYDRATES, MINERALS, VITAMINS. *See also* FOOD CHAIN

**food additive** Substance introduced into food to enhance flavor, to act as a preservative, to effect a better external coloration or more appetizing appearance, or to restore or increase nutritional value. Other additives include thickeners, stabilizers, and anticaking agents. The use of food additives is strictly regulated by law and requires prominent labeling.

**Food and Agriculture Organization (FAO)** Specialized agency of the United Nations (UN), established in 1946. It aims to eliminate hunger and improve world nutrition. Its headquarters are in Rome.

**Food and Drug Administration (FDA)** US federal agency of the Department of Health and Human Services. Its overall purpose is to protect against impure and unsafe foods, drugs, and cosmetics, and to ensure that all products are truthfully labeled and safely packaged. The FDA was first established in 1931. Today, it has offices in more than 100 cities.

**food chain** Transfer of energy through a series of organisms. The sun provides the energy that **primary producers**, such as green plants, convert into food by PHOTOSYNTHESIS. Plants also need **abiotic** substances from the water and soil to grow. **Primary consumers** (HERBIVORES) eat the plants, and in turn serve as food for **secondary consumers** (CARNIVORES). Decomposers complete the food chain by breaking down dead organic matter into simple nutrients. *See also* DECOMPOSITION; ECOSYSTEM

**food poisoning** Acute illness caused by consumption of food which is itself poisonous or which has become contaminated with BACTERIA. Frequently implicated are SALMONELLA bacteria, found in cattle, pigs, poultry, and eggs, and listeria, sometimes found in cheese. Symptoms include abdominal pain, DIARRHEA, nausea, and vomiting. Treatment includes rest and fluids to prevent dehydration. *See also* BOTULISM; GASTROENTERITIS

**food preservation** Treatment of foodstuffs to prolong the time for which they can be kept before spoiling. Salting, pickling, and FERMENTATION preserve food chemically. Chemical preservatives, such as sodium benzoate, can also be added to foods. Cold storage at 41°F (5°C) prolongs the life of foods temporarily, while deep-freezing at −3°F (−5°C) or below greatly extends the acceptable storage period. In **freeze-drying**, frozen foods are placed in a vacuum chamber and the water in them is removed as vapor; the foods can be fully reconstituted at a later date. Since 1990, **irradiation** (the preservation of food by subjecting it to low-level radiation in order to kill microorganisms) has been increasingly used. *See also* CANNING

**foot** In poetry, unit of verse meter. Each foot is composed of a group of two or more syllables, some of which are stressed. Most commonly used feet are anapest, dactyl, iamb, and trochee.

**football** Contact sport played in the US. It is second in popularity only to baseball. It is played by two teams of 11 people on a field 100×53yd (91.5×49m). The field is marked off by latitudinal stripes every 5yd (4.6m) and is flanked on each end by an end zone, 10yd (9.1m) long. At each end of the end zone are H-shaped goal posts. An inflated leather, spheroid ball is used, with the object of moving the ball – by ground or air – across the opponent's goal line. Most football teams have defensive and offensive units that alternate on the field according to posession of the ball. The field leader is the quarterback. Before each play, the two teams face each other along the line of scrimmage. A game consists of two halves, each having two 15-minute quarters. Each half starts with a kickoff, and after the receiving team has run back the ball, it must advance 10yd in 4 attempts (downs) or turn the ball over to the opponents. The defending team must stop the ball carrier by pushing him out of bounds or tackling him. The ball is usually turned over by punting (kicking) on the last down. If a player fumbles, has a pass intercepted, or loses possession of the ball during the series of downs, the opposing team takes over the ball. Scoring can occur in four ways: a **touchdown** (crossing the opponent's goal line) scores six points ; an "**extra point**" (kicking the ball through the goal post after a touchdown) scores one point; a **conversion** (running or completing a pass into the opponent's end zone after a touchdown) scores two; a **field goal** (kicking the ball between the uprights) scores three; and a **safety** (downing the ball carrier behind his own goal line) scores two. Substitutions are freely allowed. Football has its roots in medieval England and has similarities to RUGBY and SOCCER. The US version of the game was adopted after 1874. In 1902 the first Rose Bowl was held and the popularity of collegiate football increased dramatically. The Heisman Trophy for the best college football player was founded in 1935. In 1920 the American Professional Football Association was formed, and in 1922 it was renamed the National Football League (NFL). In 1959 a separate league, the American Football League (AFL), was

▲ **flying fox** The gray-headed flying fox (*Pteropus poliocephalus*) of Australia grows to 16in (40cm) and has a wingspan of more than 3.5ft (1m). They feed in groups on various wild and cultivated fruits.

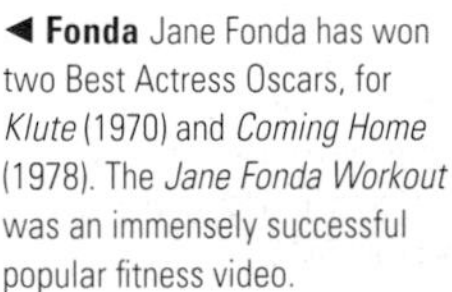

◀ **Fonda** Jane Fonda has won two Best Actress Oscars, for *Klute* (1970) and *Coming Home* (1978). The *Jane Fonda Workout* was an immensely successful popular fitness video.

formed. In January 1967 the first Super Bowl championship game was held between the winners of the AFL and the NFL. In 1970 the two leagues merged to form the present NFL, consisting of two conferences of 15 teams each.

**football, Canadian** Game similar to American FOOTBALL. The Grey Cup is the highlight of the professional season. The principal differences are that teams have 12 players, are allowed only three downs, and play on a larger field, 110×65yd (100×59.4m).

**football, Gaelic** Sport popular in Ireland and dating from the 16th century. Each side has 15 men who may kick, punch, or pass the ball, but not throw it. Players may not pick the ball up from the ground with the hands; it may be carried for four paces and then has to be bounced, kicked, or punched away. The field is 140–160yd (128–146m) long and 80–100yd (77–91m) wide with goalposts at each end. One point is scored for putting the ball over the bar and three for driving it under the bar. The game generally lasts 60 minutes with two halves.

**foraminifera** Amoeboid protozoan animals that live among plankton in the sea. They have multichambered chalky shells (tests), and vary in size from microscopic to 2in (5cm) across. Many remain as fossils and are useful in geological dating. When they die, their shells sink to the ocean floor to form large deposits, the source of chalk and limestone. Order Foraminifera.

**force** Push, pull, or turn. A force acting on an object may (1) balance an equal but opposite force or a combination of forces so that it does not move, (2) change the state of motion of the object (in magnitude or direction), or (3) change the shape or state of the object. There are four FUNDAMENTAL FORCES in nature.

**Ford, Ford Madox** (1873–1939) English novelist, poet, and critic, b. Ford Madox Hueffer. He provided influential support to such writers as Ezra POUND, while editing the *Transatlantic Review* in Paris, and Joseph CONRAD and D.H. LAWRENCE during his editorship of the *English Review*. His novels include *The Good Soldier* (1915) and the tetralogy *Parade's End* (1924–28).

**Ford, Gerald Rudolph** (1913– ) 38th US president (1974–77). Elected to the House of Representatives in 1948, he gained a reputation as an honest and hard-working Republican. He was nominated by President NIXON to replace the disgraced Spiro AGNEW as vice president (1973). When Nixon resigned, Ford became president – the only person to hold the office without winning an election. One of his first acts was to pardon Nixon. His attempts to counter economic recession with cuts in social welfare and taxes were hindered by a Democrat-dominated Congress. Renominated in 1976, he narrowly lost the election to Jimmy CARTER.

**Ford, Harrison** (1942– ) US film actor. His breakthrough film was *Star Wars* (1977). Ford's reputation as the all-action adventure hero was strengthened by *Indiana Jones* (1981) and its sequels, and the classic science-fiction film *Blade Runner* (1982). He was nominated for a Best Actor Academy Award for *Witness* (1985). Other films include *Sabrina* (1995).

**Ford, Henry** (1863–1947) US industrialist. He developed a gas-engined car in 1892 and founded Ford Motors in 1903. In 1908 Ford designed the Model T. His introduction of an assembly line (1913) revolutionized industrial production and over 15 million Model T's were sold before it was discontinued in 1928. In 1914 Ford raised the minimum wage to $5 a day and reduced the workday to eight hours. He refused, however, to allow union organization in his factories until 1941. In 1936 Ford established the philanthropic FORD FOUNDATION. In 1945, with the company losing *c.*$9 million a month, he handed control of the company to his grandson, **Henry Ford II** (1917–87). Henry Ford II transformed the business, introducing new models such as the Thunderbird and Mustang and bringing the company back into profit.

**Ford, John** (1586–1639) English playwright who, with Cyril Tourneur, pioneered post-Jacobean drama. His major plays include *The Broken Heart* (*c.*1630), *Love's Sacrifice* (*c.*1630), *'Tis Pity She's a Whore* (*c.*1633), and *Perkin Warbeck* (1634).

**Ford, John** (1895–1973) US film director. Ford won four Academy Awards for Best Director: *The Informer* (1935), *The Grapes of Wrath* (1940), *How Green Was My Valley* (1941), and *The Quiet Man* (1952). His WESTERN classics include *Stagecoach* (1939), *The Horse Soldiers* (1959), and *The Searchers* (1956).

**foreign aid** *See* AID, FOREIGN

**foreign exchange** Buying and selling national currencies. All currencies have an underlying value relative to the value of gold, registered with the INTERNATIONAL MONETARY FUND (IMF). This value may deviate and governments can control the amount of deviation by trading on foreign exchange markets. Speculators may trade in the hope of profiting from short-term fluctuations in the value, an activity known as arbitrage. International commercial companies and financial institutions also buy and sell foreign currencies.

**Foreign Legion** Professional military group of mixed national origin, created by Louis Philippe (1831) to serve in French colonies. In 1962, after fighting in the two World Wars and later French colonial struggles, the Legion moved its headquarters from Algeria to Aubagne, s France. It is renowned for its harsh discipline.

**forensic science** (medical jurisprudence) Application of medical, scientific, or technological knowledge to the investigation of crimes. Forensic medicine involves examination of living victims and suspects, as well as the pathology of the dead. The cause of death, if there is doubt, is established at an autopsy. Modern developments include testing bodily specimens (blood, semen, and so on) linked to the crime to provide a DNA "fingerprint" to be compared with the defendant's.

**Forester, C.S. (Cecil Scott)** (1899–1966) British novelist, b. Egypt. He is most famous for his 12-novel saga about Horatio Hornblower, a naval officer during the Napoleonic Wars; the series began with *The Happy Return* (1937). His other works include *The African Queen* (1935) and *The Gun* (1933).

**forestry** (silviculture) Managment of forest resources for human benefit, in particular the production of timber through reforestation. It also includes the conservation of soil, water, and wildlife. In 1907 the first national forests were created, under the administration of the NATIONAL FOREST SYSTEM. Today, more than 180 million acres (76 million ha) of forest are publicly owned and managed by the US Forest Service. In 1960 the service was directed to manage the national forests according to the principles of multiple use and sustained yield; to produce a continuous supply of timber while preserving the natural environment. In 1964 the Forest Service controversially adopted the commercial practice of clearcutting (removing all trees in a certain area of a forest). *See also* DEFORESTATION

**forgery** Imitation of a document or artifact. In most countries forgery is a serious crime punishable by imprisonment.

**forget-me-not** Any of *c.*50 species of hardy perennial and annual herbs of the genus *Myosotis* found in temperate regions. The typical five-petaled flowers are sky blue but may change color with age. Family Boraganacead (BORAGE).

**forging** Shaping of metal by hammering or by applying pressure against a shaped die. Blacksmiths forge horseshoes and other iron items by hammering the red-hot metal on an anvil. In mass-manufacturing processes, pressure from a hydraulic forging press shapes metal parts by forcing them against a hard-metal die.

**formaldehyde** *See* METHANAL

**Forman, Milos** (1932– ) Czech film director. After making several films in Czechoslovakia, including *Fireman's Ball* (1967), he moved to the US (1968). *One Flew Over the Cuckoo's Nest* (1975) is one of only three films to gain Academy Awards for Best Film, Best Director, Best Actor, and Best Actress. Forman won a further Oscar as Best Director for *Amadeus* (1984).

**formic acid** *See* METHANOIC ACID

**Formosa** *See* TAIWAN

**Forrest, Nathan Bedford** (1821–77) US Confederate general. In 1862 he headed a cavalry troop at the battles of Fort Donelson and Shiloh. In 1862 Forrest was made brigadier general and led a series of devastating raids against Union forces in Tennessee. In 1864 he captured Fort Pillow and led a brilliant victory at Brice's Cross Roads. Forrest was given control of the entire cavalry under John Bell HOOD. He was forced to surrender at Selma, Alabama, and after the war served as the first leader of the KU KLUX KLAN.

**Forster, E.M. (Edward Morgan)** (1879–1970) English novelist. He wrote six novels before giving up fiction at the age of 45: *Where Angels Fear to Tread* (1905), *The Longest Journey* (1907), *A Room with a View* (1908), *Howards End* (1910), *A Passage to India* (1924) – widely seen as his masterpiece – and the posthumously published *Maurice* (1971). Forster made a major contribution to the development of the realist novel.

**forsythia** Genus of hardy deciduous shrubs of the OLIVE family Oleaceae, named for the British botanist William Forsyth. They are commonly cultivated in temperate regions. The small yellow flowers look like golden bells. Height: to 10ft (3m).

**Fort-de-France** Capital of the French overseas department of Martinique, on Fort-de-France Bay. First settled in the 17th century, it remained undeveloped until the beginning of the 20th century, when a volcanic eruption destroyed St. Pierre. It is now a popular tourist resort. Exports: sugarcane, rum, cacao. Pop. (1990) 101,540.

**Fort Lauderdale** City on the Atlantic coast of SE Florida; seat of Broward county. It was established as a military post in 1838 by Major William Lauderdale during the wars with the Seminole. There are more than 270mi (435km) of waterways. Port Everglades is one of the world's largest passenger ports. Industries: tourism, computing. Pop. (1990) 149,377.

**Fort Sumter** Fort in South Carolina, scene of the first hostilities of the CIVIL WAR. In 1860 South Carolina seceded from the Union and demanded all Federal property to be handed to the state. President James Buchanan refused and South Carolina prepared to seize the fort held by Federal forces under Major Robert Anderson. The Confederate General BEAUREGARD called on Anderson to surrender, but he refused. On April 12 the Confederates began to bombard the fort. On April 13 it surrendered. The Confederates held Fort Sumter until 1865. It became a national monument in 1948.

**Fort Wayne** City in NE Indiana, at the confluence of the St. Joseph and St. Mary rivers. The French built a trading post here *c.*1680. It was captured by the British during the French and Indian War (1755–63) and held by Native Americans (1763) during PONTIAC'S REBELLION. Development was spurred by the opening of the Wabash and Erie canals and the railroad in the 1850s. It is also the site of the Indiana Institute of Technology (1930). Industries: heavy vehicles, copper wire, stainless steel, mining machinery. Pop. (1990) 173,072.

**Fort Worth** City in N central Texas, *c.*30mi (50km) W of Dallas. It was settled in 1843 and the US army established a post here in 1847. In the 1870s, the city was a supply center on the cattle route from Texas to Kansas. It is famous for its oil and cattle. Industries: aerospace, electronic equipment. Pop. (1990) 447,619.

**FOSSIL**

Animal fossils are not only made from their bones or shells, often their tracks can also be fossilized. Typically, a footprint (1) is left behind in soft mud, which partially hardens to form a cast. If the mud becomes flooded (2), sediment is laid over the mud especially quickly (3) helping to preserve the shape of the footprint. Over the course of time, the mud and sediment become compressed and turn to rock (4). The original mud-based rock forms a mold of the footprint (5) and the sediment-based rock forms a cast (6).

**fossil** Direct evidence of the existence of an organism more than 10,000 years old. Fossils document evolutionary change and enable geologic dating. They are original structures, such as bones, shells, or wood (often altered through mineralization or preserved as molds and casts), or imprints, such as tracks and footprints. Leaves can be preserved as a carbonized film outlining their form. Occasionally organisms are totally preserved in frozen soil (such as mammoths), peat bogs, and asphalt lakes, or trapped in hardened resin (such as insects in amber). Fossil excrement (coprolite) frequently contains undigested and recognizable hard parts.

**fossil fuels** COAL, OIL, and NATURAL GAS – FUELS that were formed millions of years ago from fossilized remains. They are a nonrenewable energy source.

**Foster, Jodie** (1962– ) US film actress and director. In 1976, aged 13, she received an Academy nomination for her role in *Taxi Driver*. Foster has won two Best Actress Oscars, one for a controversial performance as a rape victim in *The Accused* (1988) and another for *The Silence of the Lambs* (1991).

**Foster, Stephen Collins** (1826–64) US songwriter. Influenced by the Negro spiritual, his popular songs include "Camptown Races" (1850), "Old Folks at Home" (1851), "My Old Kentucky Home" (1853) and "Jeanie with the Light Brown Hair" (1854).

**Foster, William Zebulon** (1881–1961) US labor leader and politician. He was affiliated with the Socialist Party, the Industrial Workers of the World (IWW), and the American Federation of Labor (AFL). Foster led a steel strike (1919) and was the Communist Party presidential candidate (1924, 1928, and 1932).

**Foucault, Jean Bernard Léon** (1819–68) French physicist. He used a PENDULUM (Foucault's pendulum) to prove that the Earth spins on its axis. Foucault invented (1852) the GYROSCOPE and devised a method to measure the absolute velocity of light (1850), showing it to be slower in water than in air.

**Foucault, Michel** (1926–84) French philosopher and historian. He was professor of the history of systems of thought at the

◀ **Foster** One of the few child stars to enjoy a successful adult career, Jodie Foster received her first Academy Award nomination when only 13 years old.

▲ **fowl** Commercial hybrid poultry are bred for eggs and meat from pure breeding birds. The most productive egg-laying strains are derived from leghorns (1) and Rhode Island reds (2), while the Dorking (3) and Cornwall (4) are popular British meat breeds.

▲ **foxglove** Native to Old World countries, particularly those of Europe, N Africa, and Asia, foxgloves are hardy plants that bear purple and white, or less commonly, golden flowers.

*Collège de France* (1970–84). Foucault examined the social and historical contexts of ideas and institutions, such as school, prison, police force, and asylum. Foucault's main theme was how systems of knowledge (such as psychiatry) have changed humans into subjects. His works include *Madness and Civilization* (1961) and *The Order of Things* (1966).

**Fouquet, Jean** (1420–80) French court painter. His work is monumental and sculptural. Notable works include a portrait of Charles VII (*c*.1447), Books of Hours (1450–60), and the *Pietá* at Nouans.

**Fouquet, Nicolas** (1615–80) French statesman, minister of finance (1653–61). Fouquet plundered the treasury for personal gain. Jean-Baptiste COLBERT alerted King LOUIS XIV, who ordered his arrest (1661). A three-year trial led to a sentence of exile, which Louis changed to life imprisonment.

**Four Freedoms** Expression of war aims in World War II enunciated by President Franklin ROOSEVELT in his State of the Union address in January 1941. They were freedom of speech and worship, and freedom from want and fear. These aims were echoed in the ATLANTIC CHARTER of 1941.

**4-H clubs** Organizations for young people aged nine to 19. The group is part of an informal educational program designed to "learn by doing." They provide training for the development of new skills and encourage civic responsibility. The first 4-H clubs were founded in US rural communities in the early 1900s. By the 1990s, 4-H clubs had more than 5 million members.

**Fourier, (François Marie) Charles** (1772–1837) French socialist. He supported cooperativism and made detailed plans for the organization of communities (phalanxes). Fourier suggested that capital for the enterprise come from the capitalist, and he provided for payment to capital in his division of output. *See also* UTOPIANISM

**four-stroke engine** Engine in which the operation of each piston is in four stages, each stage corresponding to one movement of a piston along a cylinder. The stages are: induction (the fuel-air mixture enters the cylinder), compression, expansion (the exploding mixture forces the piston along the cylinder), and exhaust. This system, used by many INTERNAL COMBUSTION ENGINES, is called the four-stroke cycle, or Otto cycle, after its inventor, Nickolaus Otto (1832–91).

**Fourteen Points** Program presented (January 1918) by President Woodrow WILSON for a just peace settlement of World War I. In general, the program required greater liberalism in international affairs and supported national self-determination. It made useful propaganda for the Allies and was the basis on which Germany sued for peace in 1918. Some points found expression in the Treaty of VERSAILLES. The 14th Point laid the basis for the LEAGUE OF NATIONS.

**fourth estate** Name sometimes given to the press. The phrase was first used by the English author Thomas Babington MACAULAY when he wrote (1828) of the House of Commons that: "The gallery in which the reporters sit has become a fourth estate of the realm." This was an expansion of the concept of the three estates – the lords spiritual, lords temporal, and commons.

**Fourth of July** US national holiday. It celebrates the signing of the DECLARATION OF INDEPENDENCE (July 4, 1776), and has been a national holiday since then.

**fowl** Domestic birds, such as chicken or turkey, and game such as pheasant and duck. *See also* POULTRY

**Fowler, William A. (Alfred)** (1911–95) US physicist and astrophysicist, best known for his explanation of how chemical elements are built up (from heavier to lighter) within stars as they evolve. In 1983 he shared the Nobel Prize for physics with Subrahmanyan CHANDRASEKHAR.

**Fowles, John Robert** (1926– ) English novelist. His first novel, *The Collector* (1963), about an obsessive who kidnaps a young woman, was made into a successful film (1965). *The Magus* (1966) and *The French Lieutenant's Woman* (1969) were also filmed. Later novels include *Mantissa* (1983) and *A Maggot* (1985).

**Fox, Charles James** (1749–1806) British statesman and orator, the main parliamentary proponent of liberal reform in the late 18th century. Fox entered parliament in 1768 and served as lord of the Admiralty (1770–72), and lord of the Treasury (1773–74) under Lord NORTH. He was dismissed by GEORGE III for his opposition to government policy on North America. Fox became foreign secretary (1782) in Rockingham's government and formed a short-lived coalition government (1783) with Lord North. Thereafter, he led Whig opposition to the government of William PITT, urging the abolition of slavery and the extension of the franchise. On Pitt's death (1806), Fox briefly returned as foreign secretary.

**Fox, George** (1624–91) English religious leader, founder of the QUAKERS. He embarked upon his evangelical calling in 1646 in response to an "inner light." Imprisoned eight times between 1649 and 1673, he traveled to the Caribbean and America to visit Quaker colonists (1671–72).

**fox** Any of several carnivores of the DOG family. The red fox (*Vulpes vulpes*) is typical. Distinguished by its sharp features, rather large ears, and long bushy tail, it feeds on insects, fruit, carrion, small birds and mammals, and carrion. Foxes usually stalk their prey. They are solitary animals, living in dens only for the mating season. They are hunted by larger carnivores and humans. Height: 15in (38cm) at the shoulder; weight: *c*.20lb (9kg). Family Canidae.

**Foxe, John** (1516–87) English Anglican clergyman and historian, whose writings promoted Protestantism and influenced English people's perception of Roman Catholicism. He returned from exile in France in Elizabeth I's reign and wrote *Actes and Monuments of these latter and perillous Dayes*, better known as *Foxe's Book of Martyrs* (1563).

**foxglove** Hardy, Eurasian plants of the genus *Digitalis*. They have long, spiky clusters of drooping tubular flowers. The common biennial foxglove (*D. purpurea*), source of DIGITALIS, is grown for its showy purple or white flowers. Family *Scrophulariaceae*.

**foxhound** Medium-sized dog (sporting group) used in foxhunting. The coat is short and smooth, the ears droop, and the tail is carried erect. They are black, tan, and white, and are noted for their speed and stamina. The American foxhound, a separate breed, is slighter than the English variety. Height: 21–25in (53–63cm) at the shoulder.

**fractal** Geometrical figure in which an identical motif is repeated on a reducing scale; the figure is "self-similar." The term was coined by Benoit MANDELBROT and fractal geometry is closely associated with CHAOS THEORY. Fractal objects include shells, cauliflowers, mountains, and clouds. They are also produced mathematically in computer graphics.

**fraction** Quotient written in the form of one number divided by another. A fraction is $a/b$, where $a$ is the numerator and $b$ the denominator. If $a$ and $b$ are whole numbers, the quotient is a simple fraction. If $a$ is smaller than $b$, it is a **proper** fraction; if $b$ is smaller than $a$, it is an **improper** fraction. In an **algebraic** fraction the denominator, or the numerator and denominator, are algebraic expressions, e.g. $x/(x^2 + 2)$. In a **composite** fraction, both the numerator and denominator are themselves fractions.

**Fragonard, Jean-Honoré** (1732–1806) French painter. Fragonard is best known for the lighthearted spontaneity of his amorous scenes, rustic landscapes, and decorative panels.

**Frame, Janet** (1924– ) New Zealand short story writer and novelist. Her works, set in her native country, explore the situation of contemporary women. Frame's autobiographical work, *An Angel at My Table* (1984), was filmed by Jane CAMPION.

**franc** Monetary unit of France, Belgium, Switzerland, and Luxembourg, as well as of the African Financial Community (CFA) and the French Pacific Community. It is divided into 100 centimes.

**France, Anatole** (1844–1924) (Jacques Anatole François Thibault) French author. He achieved recognition with the novels *The Crime of Sylvester Bonnard* (1881) and *Thaïs* (1890). France supported Emile ZOLA during the DREYFUS AFFAIR, and his writing grew more political, as in the four-volume novel series *Contemporary History* (1897–1901) and *Penguin Island* (1908). He was awarded the 1921 Nobel Prize for literature.

**France** Republic in W Europe. *See* country feature, page 264.

**Francesca, Piero della** *See* PIERO DELLA FRANCESCA

**Franche-Comté** Historic region of E France; its capital was Dôle until 1674 and Besançon thereafter. Founded in the 12th century as the "free county" of the Burgundians, it was disputed between the Holy Roman Empire, France, Burgundy, Spain, and Switzerland throughout the Middle Ages. After LOUIS XIV's conquest of 1674, it was finally recognized as part of France in 1678. Area: 6,254sq mi (16,202sq km). Pop. (1991) 1,097,300.

**franchise** Right or privilege of an individual to vote in public political elections, granted by government. Franchise is conferred according to a set of criteria, which may include age, sex, race, and class. In contemporary democracies, the intention is that anyone over a specific age has the right to vote. In the US, the franchise is granted by each state and this is overseen by the CONSTITUTION. The 14th and 15th Amendments (1868 and 1870 respectively) forbid any state to deny voting rights to resident adult men aged over 21 on the grounds of race, color, or previous servitude. The 19th Amendment (1920) gave women the vote. In US political practice, voting rights for African Americans, especially in the South, were restricted until the 1960s through such practices as state-constitution clauses, literacy tests, and poll taxes. The 24th Amendment (1964) banned poll taxes. The Voting Rights Act outlawed literacy tests and installed poll observers to prevent voter intimidation. The 26th Amendment (1971) lowered the voting age to 18. In Britain, the modern basis of the franchise dates from the 1832 Reform Act and subsequent acts which, by 1918, ensured all men over the age of 21 and women over 30 were entitled to vote. By 1928 women aged over 21 were enfranchised, and in 1969 the voting age was lowered to 18.

**Francis I** (1708–65) Holy Roman emperor (1745–65), duke of Lorraine (1729–35) and Tuscany (1737–65). In 1736 he married the Hapsburg heiress MARIA THERESA. Her accession (1740) precipitated the War of the AUSTRIAN SUCCESSION against FREDERICK II. Francis succeeded Charles VIII as emperor, but the real ruler was his wife.

**Francis II** (1768–1835) Last Holy Roman emperor (1792–1806) and first emperor of Austria, as Francis I (1804–35), king of Bohemia and of Hungary (1792–1835). Repeatedly defeated by the armies of Napoleon Bonaparte in the FRENCH REVOLUTIONARY WARS, his territory steadily diminished, culminating in the rout at the Battle of AUSTERLITZ (1805) and the abolition of the HOLY ROMAN EMPIRE. In 1810 Prince METTERNICH secured the marriage of Francis' daughter, Marie Louise, to Napoleon. Austria was preserved by this alliance and in 1813 Francis joined the coalition that defeated Napoleon. He then formed the HOLY ALLIANCE.

**Francis I** (1494–1547) King of France (1515–47), cousin and son-in-law and successor of LOUIS XII. A leader of the Renaissance, he is best remembered for his patronage of the arts and his palace at FONTAINEBLEAU. Persecution of the WALDENSES, centralization of monarchical power, and foolish financial policies made Francis unpopular at home. A costly struggle with the Emperor CHARLES V over the imperial crown led to defeat at Pavia (1525). Francis was imprisoned and in the Treaty of Madrid (1526) forced to give up Burgundy and renounce his claims to Italy. Two more wars (1527–29, 1536–38) ended ingloriously. In 1542 Francis concluded a treaty with SULEIMAN I and attacked Italy for a fourth time. Charles, in alliance with Henry VIII, responded by invading France and Francis lost further territory. He was succeeded by his son, HENRY II.

**Franciscans** Friars belonging to an itinerant religious order founded by St. FRANCIS OF ASSISI. The first order, known as the Friars Minor, now comprises three subdivisions: the Observants; the CAPUCHIN; and the Conventual, who are allowed to own property corporately. The second order, the Poor Clares, an order of nuns founded by St. Francis and St. CLARE, came into being in 1212.

**Francis of Assisi, Saint** (1182–1226) Italian founder of the FRANCISCANS, b. Giovanni di Bernardone. The son of a wealthy merchant in Assisi, in 1205 he renounced his worldly life for one of poverty and prayer. In 1209 Francis received permission from Pope Innocent III to begin a monastic order. The Franciscans were vowed to humility, poverty, and devotion to the task of helping people. In 1212, with St. CLARE, he established an order for women, popularly called the Poor Clares. In 1224, while Francis prayed on Monte della Verna, near Florence, the stigmata wounds of the Crucifixion appeared on his body. He was canonized in 1228. His feast day is October 4.

**Francis Xavier, Saint** (1506–52) Early JESUIT missionary, often called the Apostle to the Indies. He was an associate of St. IGNATIUS OF LOYOLA, with whom he took the vow founding the Society of Jesus (JESUITS). From 1541 he traveled through India, Japan, and the East Indies, making many converts. He died while on a journey to China. His feast day is December 3.

**francium** (symbol Fr) Radioactive metallic element, discovered (1839) by Marguerite Perey. It occurs naturally in uranium ores and is a decay product of actinium. Properties: at.no. 87; most stable isotope $^{223}$Fr (half life 22 minutes).

**Franck, César Auguste** (1822–90) French Romantic composer, b. Belgium. Franck wrote major works for the organ and is best remembered for the *Symphonic Variations* for piano and orchestra (1885), the popular *Symphony in D Minor* (1888), and significant chamber works.

**Franck, James** (1882–1964) US physicist, b. Germany. With Gustav Hertz, he experimented with electron bombardment of gases, providing support for the theory of atomic structure proposed by Niels BOHR and information for the quantum theory of Max PLANCK. Franck and Hertz shared the 1925 Nobel Prize for physics. He worked on the MANHATTAN PROJECT to develop the atom bomb, and presented the "Franck petition" which opposed the use of the bomb against Japanese civilians.

**Franco, Francisco** (1892–1975) Spanish general and dictator of Spain (1939–75). He joined the 1936 military uprising that led to the Spanish CIVIL WAR and assumed leadership of the fascist FALANGE. By 1939, with the aid of Nazi Germany and Fascist Italy, Franco had won the war and become Spain's dictator. He kept Spain neutral in World War II, after which he presided over Spain's accelerating economic development, while maintaining rigid control over its politics. In 1947 Franco declared Spain a monarchy with himself as regent, and in 1969 he designated JUAN CARLOS as heir to the throne.

**Franco-Prussian War** (1870–71) Prussian victory in the AUSTRO-PRUSSIAN WAR (1866) alarmed NAPOLEON III. The Prussian chancellor, BISMARCK, used the prospect of French invasion to frighten the S German states into joining the North German Confederation dominated by Prussia. The nominal cause of the war was a dispute over the Spanish succession. Prussia was fully prepared for the French declaration of war (July 14, 1870) and General von Moltke launched a devastating offensive into Alsace. In September the emperor and 100,000 French troops were captured at Sedan. Napoleon III abdicated, and Paris was surrounded and starved into submission. An armistice was agreed in January 1871, and Alsace and Lorraine were ceded to the new German empire under WILLIAM I. Paris refused to surrender its weapons and the PARIS COMMUNE was formed.

**Frank, Anne** (1929–45) German Jew who became a symbol of suffering under the Nazis. Born in Frankfurt am Main, she fled with her family to the Netherlands in 1933. The Franks were living in Amsterdam at the time of the German invasion in 1940 and went into hiding from 1942 until they were betrayed in August 1944. Anne died in Bergen-Belsen concen-

▲ **foxhound** Foxhounds are medium-sized dogs that have been bred for their speed and stamina. They are used in foxhunting to track and chase down the fox.

F

◄ **Franco** The Spanish dictator Francisco Franco ruled Spain for 36 years. Although he allied himself with Nazi Germany and fascist Italy, he kept Spain neutral during World War II. Towards the end of his dictatorship his regime became increasingly liberal.

The colors of this flag originated during the French Revolution of 1789. The red and blue are said to represent Paris, while the white represented the monarchy. The present design was adopted in 1794. It is meant to symbolize republican principles.

**AREA:** 212,934sq mi (551,500sq km)
**POPULATION:** 57,372,000
**CAPITAL (POPULATION):** Paris (2,152,423)
**GOVERNMENT:** Multiparty republic
**ETHNIC GROUPS:** French 93%, Arab 3%, German 2%, Breton 1%, Catalan
**LANGUAGES:** French (official)
**RELIGIONS:** Christianity 90% (Roman Catholic 86%, other Christian 4%), Islam 3%
**CURRENCY:** Franc = 100 centimes

The Republic of France is Europe's second-largest country (after Ukraine). Almost half of France's 3,440mi (5,500km) of frontier is sea. The PYRENEES form its SW border with Spain. The JURA MOUNTAINS and the ALPS form its E and SE borders with Switzerland and Italy. MONT BLANC is W Europe's highest peak, 15,771ft (4,807m). The RHINE forms part of the German border. The MASSIF CENTRAL, between the RHÔNE-Saône valley and the Aquitaine basin, covers 15% of France. The ÎLE-DE-FRANCE province, W of the LOIRE River, includes the capital, PARIS. *See* individual gazetteer articles

## CLIMATE

The climate in W France is mild, moderated by the effects of the Atlantic Ocean. The E experiences greater seasonal variation. The Mediterranean Sea coast has hot, dry summers and mild, moist winters. The Alps, Jura, and Pyrenees have good snowfall and are popular for winter sports.

## VEGETATION

A patchwork of fields and meadows covers *c*.60% of the land. Forests occupy about 27%; beech and oak are common in the N, birch, pine and poplar in the center, and olive trees in the Mediterranean regions.

## HISTORY

Julius Caesar completed the Roman conquest of Gaul in 51 BC. The Roman empire began to decline in the 3rd century AD. In 486, the Franks led by CLOVIS I established the MEROVINGIAN dynasty. Following his death, the kingdom fragmented. In 687 the CAROLINGIANS reunited Gaul, and PEPIN III (THE SHORT) overthrew the Merovingians (757). His son, CHARLEMAGNE, was crowned emperor of the West (800). He expanded the empire and provided sound administration. His empire soon disintegrated, and in 843, his grandson, CHARLES II (THE BALD) became ruler of the area of present-day France. Hugh Capet is often seen as the first king of France (987), and the CAPETIANS gradually subdued the nobility. The NORMAN CONQUEST (1066) marked the start of a long history of Anglo-French rivalry. PHILIP II regained land lost through dowry to the English. In 1328 the first Valois king, PHILIP VI, acceded to the throne. The HUNDRED YEARS WAR (1337–1453) was a series of battles for the French succession. By 1422, England controlled most of France. JOAN OF ARC helped to crush the siege of Orléans (1428), and by 1453 England had been expelled from France. LOUIS XI restored royal authority and crushed the ANGEVINS. FRANCIS I's reign marked the beginning of the Renaissance in France and the struggle with the Hapsburgs. The rise of the HUGUENOTS led to the Wars of RELIGION (1562–98). The GUISE faction lost, and Henry IV became the first BOURBON king (1589). Cardinals RICHELIEU and MAZARIN led France to victory in the THIRTY YEARS WAR (1618–48). Louis XIV's court at VERSAILLES was the richest in Europe. Yet, the *ancien régime* of LOUIS XV and LOUIS XVI was bankrupted by war and incapable of reform. The FRENCH REVOLUTION (1789–99) saw the execution of the king, and ROBESPIERRE'S brutal REIGN OF TERROR. The Directory ended when NAPOLEON I proclaimed himself emperor (1799). The success of the NAPOLEONIC WARS were wiped out at WATERLOO (1815). Napoleon was forced into exile, and the Bourbons restored to the throne. The FEBRUARY REVOLUTION (1848) established a Second Republic. Napoleon I's nephew seized power as NAPOLEON III (1852). His defeat in the FRANCO-PRUSSIAN WAR (1870–71) led to the formation of the Third Republic (1870–1940). The PARIS COMMUNE (1871) was violently suppressed. The DREYFUS Affair polarized France. France was the battleground for most of WORLD WAR I. CLEMENCEAU and BRIAND led France to peace. Successive prime ministers, BLUM and DALADIER, failed to tackle Germany's increasing power. In June 1940 German troops completed the conquest of France and established the VICHY GOVERNMENT. Charles DE GAULLE became head of a government-in-exile. Paris was liberated in August 1944, and a Fourth Republic was founded (1946). Political instability and colonial war, especially in ALGERIA, slowed the postwar recovery. In 1958, Charles de Gaulle was elected president and established a Fifth Republic. Gaullist independent foreign policy alienated the US and UK. De Gaulle resigned in 1969, replaced first by POMPIDOU, then GISCARD D'ESTAING. François MITTERAND's presidency was marked by nationalization, civic rebuilding, decentralization, and advocacy of European Union. Following Mitterand's death, his conservative rival Jacques CHIRAC was elected president (1995). His welfare reforms and attempt to meet the criteria for EUROPEAN MONETARY UNION (EMU) brought strikes and unemployment and led to the election (1997) of a socialist prime minister, Lionel JOSPIN.

## ECONOMY

France is a leading industrialized nation (1995 GDP per capita, US$21,030). It is the world's fourth-largest manufacturer of cars. Industries include chemicals and steel. It is the leading producer of farm products in W Europe. Livestock and dairy farming are vital sectors. It is the world's second-largest producer of cheese and wine. Wheat is the principal crop. Tourism is a major industry (1992 receipts, US$25 million).

tration camp. The diary she kept during her years in hiding was published in 1947 and attracted worldwide readership.

**Frankenthaler, Helen** (1928– ) US painter, sculptor, and graphic artist who provides the link between ABSTRACT EXPRESSIONISM and color field painting. Her seminal work is *Mountains and Sea* (1952). She was married (1958–71) to Robert MOTHERWELL.

**Frankfort** Capital of Kentucky, on the Kentucky River, N central Kentucky. First settled in 1779, it was made the state capital in 1792. Notable buildings include "Liberty Hall" (1796), reportedly designed by Thomas Jefferson, and the Old Capitol (1827–30). Industries: tobacco, whisky distilling, textiles. Pop. (1990) 25,535.

**Frankfurt am Main** City and port, on the Main River, Hesse state, W Germany. One of the royal residences of Charlemagne, the Holy Roman emperors were elected here, and the first German National Assembly met here in 1848. Notable buildings include a Gothic cathedral, an art museum, and a university. Frankfurt is Germany's banking center and a venue for international fairs. Industries: chemicals, electrical equipment, telecommunications, publishing. Pop. (1993 est.) 660,800.

**Frankfurter, Felix** (1882–1965) US jurist and educator, associate justice of the US Supreme Court (1939–62). He helped found the American Civil Liberties Union (1920). An adviser to Franklin D. ROOSEVELT, Frankfurter was a liberal Supreme Court justice. He advocated judicial restraint and government self-regulation in civil liberties.

**Franklin, Aretha** (1942– ) US gospel and soul singer, the "Queen of Soul." Since her first hit, "I Never Loved a Man, (The Way I Love You)" (1967), she has had more million-selling singles than any other female artist. Other classics include "Respect" (1967).

**Franklin, Benjamin** (1706–90) American statesman, scientist, and inventor. A successful printer in Philadelphia, where he published *Poor Richard's Almanac* (1732–57), he gave the business up to devote his life to scientific research. His experiments in electricity, which he identified in lightning, were influential. At the ALBANY CONGRESS (1754), he proposed a union of the colonies. A leading delegate to the CONTINENTAL CONGRESS, he became an architect of the new republic. When war broke out, Franklin went to Paris and negotiated a treaty of alliance (1778). His peace proposals formed the basis of the final Treaty of Paris (1783) with Great Britain. Franklin was president of Pennsylvania's executive council (1785–88) and, as a member of the CONSTITUTIONAL CONVENTION (1787), helped form the US Constitution.

**Franklin, Sir John** (1786–1847) British Arctic explorer. He served as a naval officer in the Battle of Trafalgar (1805). His first overland exploration of N Canada (1819-22), crossed from Great Slave Lake to the Arctic coast. His second expedition (1825-27) descended the Mackenzie River. Franklin served as governor of Tasmania (1836–43). In 1845 he embarked on a fated search for the NORTHWEST PASSAGE. The first of 40 search parties was launched in 1848. These expeditions greatly advanced knowledge of the Arctic and eventually established (1859) that Franklin had died with his entire 129-man crew after they became caught in the ice in Victoria Strait.

**Franks** Germanic people who settled in the region of the Rhine River in the 3rd century. Under CLOVIS I in the late 5th century, they overthrew the remnant of Roman rule in Gaul and established the MEROVINGIAN empire. This was divided into the kingdoms of Austrasia, Neustria, and Burgundy, but was reunited by the CAROLINGIANS, notably by CHARLEMAGNE. The partition of his empire into the East and West Frankish kingdoms is the origin of Germany and France.

**Franz Ferdinand** (1863–1914) Archduke of Austria. Nephew of FRANZ JOSEPH, he became heir apparent in 1889. On an official visit to Bosnia-Herzegovina, he and his wife were assassinated by a Serb nationalist, Gavrilo Princip, in Sarajevo (June 28, 1914). The incident led directly to the outbreak of WORLD WAR I.

**Franz Josef Land** (Zemlya Franca-iosifa) Russian archipelago in the Arctic Ocean, forming part of Archangel'sk oblast. A group of *c*.85 islands, it includes Alexandra Land, George Land, and Graham Bell Island. It was discovered in 1873 by an Austrian expedition and was incorporated in the Soviet Union in 1926. Area: *c*.8,000sq mi (20,700sq km). The most northerly lands in the Eastern Hemisphere, the avearge mean temperature is 6.5°F (−14.2°C).

**Franz Joseph** (1830–1916) Emperor of Austria (1848–1916) and king of Hungary (1867–1916). He succeeded his uncle Ferdinand, who abdicated during the REVOLUTIONS OF 1848, and quickly brought the revolutions under control, defeating the Hungarians under Louis KOSSUTH in 1849. With the formation (1867) of the AUSTRO-HUNGARIAN EMPIRE, Franz Joseph was forced to grant Hungary co-equal status. He died in the midst of World War I, two years before the final collapse of the HAPSBURG empire.

**Frasch process** *See* SULFUR

**Fraser, (John) Malcolm** (1930– ) Australian statesman, prime minister (1975–83). In 1955 he entered parliament as the youngest-ever Liberal MP. Fraser served in the cabinet (1966–71) before becoming Liberal Party leader (1975) and forming a coalition government. An uncomprising politician, he was defeated in 1983 elections by Bob HAWKE and resigned from parliament.

**fraud** In law, deception or misrepresentation of facts to obtain an advantage by unfair means. It is commonly an element of crimes such as impersonation, misrepresentation, or obtaining money by false pretenses.

**Fraunhofer, Joseph von** (1787–1826) German physicist and optician, founder of astronomical spectroscopy. By studying the DIFFRACTION of light through narrow slits, he developed the earliest form of diffraction grating. He observed and began to map the dark lines in the Sun's spectrum (1814), now called **Fraunhofer lines**.

**Frazier, Joe** (1944– ) US heavyweight boxer. In 1968 he won a version of the world's heavyweight title when he beat Buster Mathis and became undisputed champion after he defeated Jimmy Ellis (1970). Frazier lost the title to George Foreman (1973). His bouts with Muhammad ALI, whom he defeated in 1971, were his most notable. After losing again to Foreman and twice to Ali, he retired in 1976.

**Frederick I (Barbarossa)** (1123–90) Holy Roman emperor (1155–90) and king of Germany (1152–90), nephew and successor to Emperor Conrad III. He hoped to end the division between the houses of HOHENSTAUFEN and GUELPH. He was crowned emperor by ADRIAN IV. In 1156 Frederick restored Bavaria to HENRY THE LION. In 1158 he captured Milan and declared himself king of the Lombards. Frederick set up an antipope to ALEXANDER III, who excomunicated him and formed the LOMBARD LEAGUE. In 1176 Frederick was defeated at Legnano by the League and was forced to recognize Alexander as pope and make peace (1183) with the Lombards. In 1180 he defeated Henry the Lion and partitioned Bavaria. Frederick was drowned on the Third Crusade. His son succeeded as HENRY VI.

**Frederick II** (1194–1250) Holy Roman emperor (1215–50) and German king (1212–20), king of Sicily (1198–1250), and king of Jerusalem (1229–50), son of Emperor HENRY VI. After his father's death, Germany was plunged into factional strife between the HOHENSTAUFENS, led by his uncle Philip of Swabia, and the GUELPHS led by OTTO IV. Otto prevailed, but his invasion of Italy prompted Pope INNOCENT III to promote Frederick. He devoted himself to Italy and Sicily, and although he promised to make his son, Henry, king of Sicily, Frederick secured his election as king of Germany (1220) instead. His claims on Lombardy and postponement of a crusade angered Pope Honorius III, who excommunicated him and revived the LOMBARD LEAGUE. He finally embarked on a crusade in 1228 and proclaimed himself *stupor mundi* (wonder of the world). In Sicily, Frederick set up a centralized royal administration, while in Germany he devolved authority to the princes. The latter policy led Henry to rebel against his father. In 1235 Frederick imprisoned Henry, gave the German throne to CONRAD IV, and issued a land peace. In 1239 he captured most of the papal states. In 1245 Pope Innocent IV deposed him.

**Frederick III** (1415–93) Holy Roman emperor (1452–93) and German king (1440–93). He attempted to win the thrones of Bohemia and Hungary after the death of his ward, Ladislas

F

V (1458). Instead, he lost Austria, Carinthia, Carniola, and Styria to Matthias Corvinus of Hungary, only recovering them on Matthias' death (1490). By marrying his son Maximilian to Mary, heiress of Burgundy, in 1477, he acquired an enormous inheritance for the HAPSBURGS.

**Frederick III** (1831–88) Emperor of Germany (1888). Son of William I, he married (1858) Victoria, eldest daughter of the British Queen VICTORIA. Liberal and popular, he died 90 days after his accession and was succeeded by his son, William II.

**Frederick II (the Great)** (1712–86) King of Prussia (1740–86). Succeeding his father, FREDERICK WILLIAM I, he made PRUSSIA a major European force. In the War of the AUSTRIAN SUCCESSION (1740–48) against MARIA THERESA, Frederick gained the province of Silesia from Austria. During the SEVEN YEARS WAR (1756–63), his brilliant generalship preserved the kingdom from a superior hostile alliance. In 1760 Austro-Russian forces occupied Berlin (1760), but Russia's subsequent withdrawal from the war enabled Frederick to emerge triumphant at the peace. He directed Prussia's remarkable recovery from the devastation of war. Gaining further territory in the first partition of Poland (1772), he renewed the contest against Austria in the War of the Bavarian Succession (1778–79). Artistic and intellectual, he was a friend and patron of Voltaire. He wrote extensively in French, built the palace of Sans Souci, and was a gifted musician.

**Frederick V** (1596–1623) (Winter King) King of Bohemia (1619–20), elector palatine (1610–20). A Calvinist prince of the Wittelsbach family, he married the daughter of James I of England (1613). In 1619 he was chosen as king by the Protestant rebels of Bohemia in preference to the Holy Roman emperor FERDINAND II, provoking the outbreak of the THIRTY YEARS WAR. Defeat at the Battle of the White Mountain (1620) resulted in the loss of both Frederick's titles.

**Fredericksburg** City on the Rappahannock River, N Virginia. Planned in 1727, the many historic landmarks make it a major tourist attraction. It is particularly associated with the American Revolution and Civil War. From 1760 the Rising Sun Tavern was a meeting place for American patriots. Many sites are connected to George WASHINGTON, including the site of the signing of a 1775 resolution of American Independence. The Civil War battle (1862) was a one-sided victory for the 72,500-strong Confederate army of Northern Virginia, led by General Robert E. LEE, over the 114,000-strong Union Army of the Potomac, led by Major General Ambrose BURNSIDE. Nearly 13,000 Union troops were killed or wounded. In comparison, the Confederate troops of Stonewall JACKSON and James Longstreet lost *c*.5,300. There is a memorial military park outside the city. Industries: tourism, clothing, shoes. Pop. (1990) 19,030.

**Frederick William I** (1688–1740) King of Prussia (1713–40), son and successor of FREDERICK I. He strengthened the army and economy and centralized the government, laying the basis for the rise of Prussia as a great power. He treated his gifted son, the future FREDERICK II (THE GREAT), with brutality, but bequeathed him a full treasury and the finest army in Europe.

**Frederick William II** (1744–97) King of Prussia (1786–97), nephew and successor of FREDERICK II (THE GREAT). He joined (1792) the alliance against France but made peace in 1795 in order to consolidate his acquisitions in the E as a result of the second (1793) and third (1795) partitions of Poland. He kept an extravagant court and left Prussia virtually bankrupt.

**Frederick William III** (1770–1840) King of Prussia (1797–1840), son and successor of FREDERICK WILLIAM II. He declared war on France (1806), suffered a disastrous defeat at Jena, and was forced to sign the Treaty of Tilsit (1807). In Prussia, some progressive reforms were made, but a constitution, though promised, was never produced, and the king later became increasingly reactionary. The reorganized Prussian army reentered the NAPOLEONIC WARS in 1813 and played a major part in his eventual defeat.

**Frederick William IV** (1795–1861) King of Prussia (1840–61), son and successor of FREDERICK WILLIAM III. He granted a constitution in response to the REVOLUTIONS OF 1848, but later amended it to eliminate popular influence. He refused the crown of Germany (1849) because it was offered by the Frankfurt Parliament, a democratic assembly. From 1858 the future Emperor WILLIAM I ruled as regent.

**Frederick William** (1620–88) (Great Elector) Elector of Brandenburg (1640–88). He inherited a collection of small, and impoverished territories ravaged by the THIRTY YEARS WAR. By the end of his reign his organizational powers had created a unified state with a centralized tax system and a formidable standing army. The powers of the provincial estates (assemblies) were reduced. The Elector encouraged commerce and industry. He acquired Eastern Pomerania at the Peace of WESTPHALIA and, by his interventions in the war between Poland and Sweden (1655–60), gained sovereignty over Prussia.

**Free Church** Any of a number of Protestant churches which are independent of the established church of a country. In England CONGREGATIONALISM, METHODISM, PRESBYTERIANISM, and the BAPTIST movements formed a National Council of Evangelical Free Churches.

**Free Church of Scotland** Grouping of Scottish Presbyterians formed as a result of the secession of nearly one-third of the membership of the established CHURCH OF SCOTLAND in the Disruption of 1843.

**Freedmen's Bureau** US government agency established in 1865 at the end of the CIVIL WAR to aid newly freed African Americans. Administered by the War Department, with General Oliver O. HOWARD as its commissioner, the agency was one of the most powerful instruments of RECONSTRUCTION. The bureau also acted as a political machine, recruiting voters for the REPUBLICAN PARTY. President Andrew JOHNSON viewed the bureau's work as an unconstitutional interference in the Southern states. It was disbanded in 1872.

**Freedom of Information Act** (1967) US law giving greater public access to government records. It permits government agencies full discretion about disclosure of information only in such areas as national defense, confidential financial information, and law enforcement. The act was weakened by agency reclassification of information under permitted exemptions.

**Freedom Rides** Civil rights trips to the South in 1961 sponsored by the CONGRESS OF RACIAL EQUALITY (CORE). They led to the desegregation of interstate terminals and subsequently to the Interstate Commerce Commission's ruling providing "nonracial" seating in buses.

**Free French** Group formed by Charles DE GAULLE on the creation of the VICHY GOVERNMENT in 1940. Its purpose was to continue French opposition to Germany. Operating outside France, the group was soon aligned with internal Resistance groups. The Free French aided the Allies throughout the war, forming a provisional government after the D-DAY invasion.

**Freeman, Morgan** (1937– ) US film actor. Freeman's measured performance in *Driving Miss Daisy* (1989) earned him an Academy nomination for Best Actor. Other credits include *Street Smart* (1987), *Unforgiven* (1992), *The Shawshank Redemption* (1995), and *Amistad* (1997).

**freemasonry** Customs and teachings of the secret fraternal order of Free and Accepted Masons, an all-male secret society with national organizations worldwide. Freemasonry is most popular in the UK and countries once in the British empire. It evolved from the medieval guilds of stonemasons and cathedral builders. The first Grand Lodge (meeting place) was founded in England (1717). The first US lodge was founded (1730) in Philadelphia. Many of the leaders of the American Revolution were masons and 13 US presidents have been lodge members. Historically associated with liberalism, freemasonry teaches morality, charity, and law-abiding behavior. In recent times, they have incurred criticism because of their strict secrecy, male exclusivity, and alleged use of influence within organizations, such as the police or local government, to benefit members. It is estimated that there are *c*.6 million Masons worldwide, with about 1 million in the US.

**free port** Area in which goods may be landed and reshipped without customs intervention. Free ports aid in quicker movement of ships and goods. When the goods are moved to the consumer, they then become subject to customs duties. Free ports include New York City, Copenhagen, and Stockholm.

**free radical** Short-lived molecule (less than 1ms) that has an unpaired ELECTRON and, therefore, rapidly binds with other molecules. Occurring as by-products of normal CELL chemistry, free radicals are highly reactive and can cause extensive damage in the body, even though cells have some protective enzymes. They are thought to play a role in ageing and a number of disease processes.

**freesia** Genus of perennial herbs of the IRIS family, native to South Africa. Species of freesia are widely cultivated for their fragrant yellow, white, or pink flowers. They are grown in greenhouses for winter blooming.

**Free Soil Party** (1848–54) US coalition political party. It was opposed, for economic reasons, to the extension of slavery into the new territories. Charles SUMNER and Salmon P. CHASE were among the members. In 1848 they chose ex-President Martin VAN BUREN as their presidential candidate. In 1854 the Free Soilers joined the Whigs and anti-slavery Democrats to form the Republican Party.

**Free State** (formerly Orange Free State) Province in E central South Africa; the capital is BLOEMFONTEIN. The region consists principally of fertile high plains, with the Drakensberg Range as part of its E border with Lesotho. The ORANGE River forms its S border with Northern Cape. Boers began to settle in large numbers after the GREAT TREK (1836). It was annexed (1848) by the British, achieved independence (1854), and after its involvement in the SOUTH AFRICAN WARS (1899–1902) was again annexed by Britain. Regaining independence in 1907, the Orange Free State joined the Union of South Africa in 1910. The economy is dominated by agriculture and gold. Pop. (1995 est.) 2,782,500.

**freethinkers** People whose opinions and ideas, especially on matters of religion, are not influenced by CANON law or dogma. The original freethinkers were part of a post-Reformation movement that sought to assert reason over religious authority. DEISM emerged as the chief expression of freethought during the 17th and 18th centuries. *See also* ATHEISM; HUMANISM

**Freetown** Capital and chief port of Sierra Leone, W Africa. Freetown was founded (1787) by the British as a settlement for freed slaves from England, Nova Scotia, and Jamaica. It was the capital of British West Africa (1808–74). In 1961 Freetown was made capital of independent Sierra Leone. Industries: platinum, gold, diamonds, oil refining, palm oil. Pop. (1985 est.) 469,776.

**free trade** Commerce conducted between nations without restrictions on imports and exports. In the 19th century, the repeal of England's CORN LAWS (1846) and the Anglo-French free trade treaty (1860) were hallmarks of free trade. Twentieth-century agreements include the EUROPEAN FREE TRADE AGREEMENT (EFTA) (1959) and the NORTH AMERICAN FREE TRADE AGREEMENT (NAFTA) (1994). Protectionists oppose free trade, advocating import duties and restrictive quotas to safeguard domestic industry from foreign competition. *See also* MERCANTILISM

**free verse** Verse with no regular meter and no apparent form, relying primarily on cadence. The rhythm is close to prose. WHITMAN and RIMBAUD were early users of free verse, which is now a common form.

**freezing** *See* FOOD PRESERVATION

**freezing point** Temperature at which a substance changes from LIQUID to SOLID. For most substances, it increases with pressure. Melting point is the change from solid to liquid and is the same as freezing point.

**Frege, Gottlob** (1848–1925) German philosopher. He was a professor of mathematics at Jena (1879–1918). With George BOOLE, Frege was one of the founders of modern symbolic LOGIC. In his *Foundations of Arithmetic* (1884), Frege attempted to derive all mathematics from logical axioms.

**Frémont, John Charles** (1813–90) US explorer and general. Following his exploration and mapping of the Oregon Trail (1842), Frémont crossed the Sierra Nevada in the winter of 1843–44. A second expedition (1845) led to the BEAR FLAG REVOLT by American settlers, and Frémont became civil governor. He resigned his commission in 1848 and made a fortune in the gold rush. Frémont served briefly (1850–51) as one of California's first two senators and was the first REPUBLICAN PARTY presidential candidate, losing to James BUCHANAN. He became governor of Arizona (1878–83).

**French** Major language, spoken in France and parts of Belgium, Switzerland, Canada, Haiti, Africa, and other areas. There are some 80–100 million French speakers worldwide. Descended from Latin, it is a Romance language of the INDO-EUROPEAN family. It is one of the six official languages of the United Nations.

**French Academy** *See* ACADÉMIE FRANÇAISE

**French and Indian Wars** (1689–1763) Collective name for four colonial wars in North America, fought between Great Britain and France with Native American nations fighting on both sides. The aim of the wars in North America was for control of the eastern part of the continent, with ports and forts that controlled trade to the Old World. **King William's War** (1689–97) was a development of the War of the GRAND ALLIANCE and ended inconclusively. **Queen Anne's War** (1702–13) corresponds to the War of the SPANISH SUCCESSION. Britain gained Newfoundland, Acadia, and Hudson Bay. **King George's War** (1744–48) grew out of the War of the Austrian Succession. It ended inconclusively. The **French and Indian War** (1754–63) was the most significant conflict, forming part of the SEVEN YEARS WAR. British efforts to capture the French forts in the west in 1754–55 were unsuccessful. After 1756 British resources improved, and forts at Louisburg and Duquesne (1758) were captured. Ticonderoga fell in 1759. In the battle for Quebec on the Plains of Abraham (1759) both the French and English generals Louis Joseph de MONTCALM and James WOLFE were killed, but Britain emerged victorious. In 1760 they captured Montreal. The Treaty of Paris (1763) established British control of Canada.

**French architecture** From the 8th to early 19th centuries, French architects were dependent on royal patronage, although the 10th-century Benedictine abbey at Cluny had an influence on church architecture. During the 11th and 12th centuries, CATHEDRALS in the ROMANESQUE style were constructed. In the 13th century, Gothic cathedrals, such as CHARTRES and NOTRE-DAME, were built. In 1494 the influence of Italian RENAISSANCE ARCHITECTURE grew and inspired kings, such as Francis I and Henry IV, to commission magnificent palaces, including FONTAINEBLEAU, the LOUVRE, and Chambord. Royal influence climaxed in the 17th century with Louis XIV's palace at VERSAILLES. After 1685, a lighter note prevailed, but in the mid-18th century, official architecture turned to NEOCLASSICISM, introducing designs based on the DORIC order. In the 19th century, patronage shifted from the court to the bourgeoisie. Baron Haussman designed the wide boulevards of Paris, and between 1850 and 1870, mansard roofs and pavilions marked a Renaissance revival. The EIFFEL TOWER (1889) heralded MODERNISM, and ART NOUVEAU faded quickly. In the 1920s and 1930s, BAUHAUS had a large influence, and the Domino frame buildings of LE CORBUSIER spearheaded the INTERNATIONAL STYLE.

**French art** Studies of French art usually begin with the 12th century. There were several important centers of manuscript illumination in Cistercian abbeys. During the Renaissance, the art of the Court was heavily influenced by Italian trends, as is evident with Jean FOUQUET and the FONTAINEBLEAU SCHOOL. It was not until the 17th century that artists of international stature emerged. Dominant figures were CLAUDE LORRAIN and Nicolas POUSSIN, both masterful exponents of classical landscape painting. The latter was particularly important, and his rigorous draftsmanship was used as a benchmark for academic standards until well into the 19th century. The twilight-years of the *ancien régime* were celebrated in the light-hearted ROCOCO fantasies of François BOUCHER and Jean-Honoré FRAGONARD. As the Revolution drew near, however, these gave way to the stern moralizing of neoclassical painters such as Jacques Louis DAVID. He remained influential into the romantic period, when the leading French artist was Eugène DELACROIX. In the second half of the 19th century, there were a succession of movements which increased artistic freedom. These began with the REALISM of COURBET and culminated in IMPRESSIONISM, POSTIMPRESSIONISM, and SYMBOLISM. This creativity continued into the 20th century, when the School of Paris fostered many new develop-

▲ **freesia** Now cultivated commercially worldwide, freesias are native to South Africa. They grow to a height of 30in (75cm).

## FRENCH GUIANA

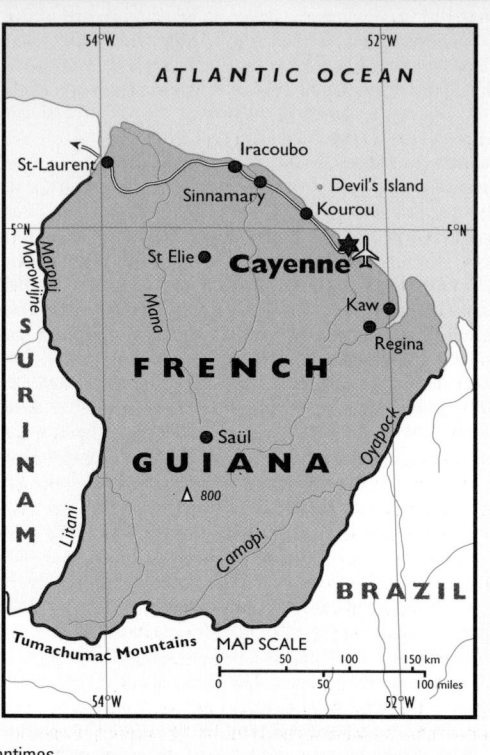

**AREA:** 37,749 sq mi (90,000 sq km)
**POPULATION:** 104,000
**CAPITAL (POPULATION):** Cayenne (41,600)
**GOVERNMENT:** Overseas department of France
**ETHNIC GROUPS:** Creole 42%, Chinese 14%, French 10%, Haitian 7%
**LANGUAGES:** French (official)
**RELIGIONS:** Catholic 80%, Protestant 4%)
**CURRENCY:** French franc = 100 centimes

ments. France remained the leading force in avant-garde art until after World War II, when its mantle passed to the US.

**French Guiana** Overseas department of France, in South America. **Land and Climate** The coastal plain includes cultivated areas, particularly near the capital, CAYENNE. Inland lies a plateau, with low mountains (Sierra Tumucumaque) in the S. The Maroni River forms the border with SURINAM, and the Oyapock River its E border with Brazil. The climate is hot and equatorial, with high annual temperatures. Rainfall is heavy, although August to October is dry. Rain forest covers *c.*90% of the land. Mangrove swamps line parts of the coast, while other areas are covered by tropical savanna. **History** Europeans first explored the coast in 1500. The French were the first settlers (1604), and Cayenne was founded in 1637 by French merchants. The area changed hands several times before becoming a French colony in the late 17th century. The colony, whose plantation economy depended on African slaves remained French except for a brief period in the early 19th century. Slavery was abolished in 1848, and Asian laborers were introduced. From the time of the French Revolution, France used the colony as a penal settlement for political and other prisoners. **Politics** In 1946 French Guiana became an overseas department of France and, in 1974, also an administrative region. **Economy** Despite rich forest and mineral resources, it is a developing country with high unemployment. It depends on France to finance services. Since 1968, Kourou has been the EUROPEAN SPACE AGENCY's rocket-launching site. Industries: fishing, forestry, gold mining, agriculture. Crops include bananas, cassava, rice, and sugar cane. Exports include shrimp, timber, and rum.

**French horn** BRASS musical instrument. It has a flared bell, long coiled conical tube, three or four valves, and a funnel-shaped mouthpiece.

**French literature** Although the earliest surviving works of French literature, written in the *langue d'oil*, date from the 10th century, major works date from the 12th century when the CHANSONS DE GESTE celebrated the military exploits of the nobility. Allegorical romances by Chrétien de TROYES and others gave way to more intimate poetry in the 15th century by writers such as Francois VILLON. The poems of the 16th century poet Pierre de Ronsard (leader of La PLÉIADE) rivaled that of Renaissance Italy, and in prose, the comic genius of RABELAIS contrasted with the pithy originality of the essayist Montaigne. The great dramatists CORNEILLE, RACINE, and MOLIÈRE, and the writings of philosophers DESCARTES and PASCAL ensured that the 17th century was a golden age of French literature. They were succeeded in the 18th century by the writers of the ENLIGHTENMENT, the rationalists ROUSSEAU, DIDEROT, and VOLTAIRE; and BEAUMARCHAIS, who wrote social farces. The Romantic movement of the early 19th century produced novels and poems by the prolific Victor HUGO, LAMARTINE, and DUMAS (*père* and *fils*). Writers such as STENDHAL, BALZAC, FLAUBERT, MAUPASSANT, and ZOLA reacted against ROMANTICISM, producing works of NATURALISM and REALISM. Poets BAUDELAIRE and RIMBAUD paved the way for SYMBOLISM and modern poetry, typified by the works of VERLAINE, and Valéry and Apollinaire in the 20th century. PROUST and GIDE dominated French fiction until 1940, backed up by MAURIAC and Duhamel, with SARTRE, de BEAUVOIR, CAMUS, MAUROIS, MALRAUX, and SAINT-EXUPÉRY producing the finest post-war work. The most original dramatists of the post-war period are Jean GENET, IONESCO, and BECKETT.

**French Polynesia** French overseas territory in the S central Pacific Ocean, consisting of more than 130 islands, divided into five scattered archipelagos: SOCIETY ISLANDS, MARQUESAS ISLANDS, Tuamotu Archipelago, Gambier Islands, and Tubuai Islands; the capital is Papeete on TAHITI (Society Islands). The larger islands are volcanic with fertile soil and dense vegetation. The more numerous coral islands are low-lying. The climate is tropical, and humidity is high. Missionaries arrived in Tahiti at the end of the 18th century, and in the 1840s France began establishing protectorates. In 1880–82, the islands were annexed by France, and became part of the colony of Oceania. In 1958 they were granted the status of an overseas territory. In the 1960s, the French government began nuclear testing on Mururoa atoll, leading to worldwide protests. In recent years there have been increasing demands for autonomy in Tahiti, the largest and most populous island. In 1995 the French government put forward proposals to grant Polynesia the status of an autonomous overseas territory. Copra and vanilla are the leading agricultural products, and cultured pearls are exported. Tourism has grown rapidly in recent years. Area: 1,260sq mi (3,265sq km). Pop. (1994 est.) 216,600.

**French Revolution** (1789–99) Series of events that removed the French monarchy, transformed government and society, and established the First Republic. Suggested causes include economic pressures, antiquated social structure, weakness of the – theoretically absolute – royal government, and the influence of the ENLIGHTENMENT. Beginning in June 1789, when the STATES GENERAL met at Versailles during a political crisis caused by attempts to tax the nobility, representatives of the bourgeoisie demanded reform and proclaimed themselves a National Assembly. Popular resistance, epitomized by the storming of the BASTILLE, forced the government to accede to demands which included the abolition of the aristocracy, reform of the clergy, and a Declaration of

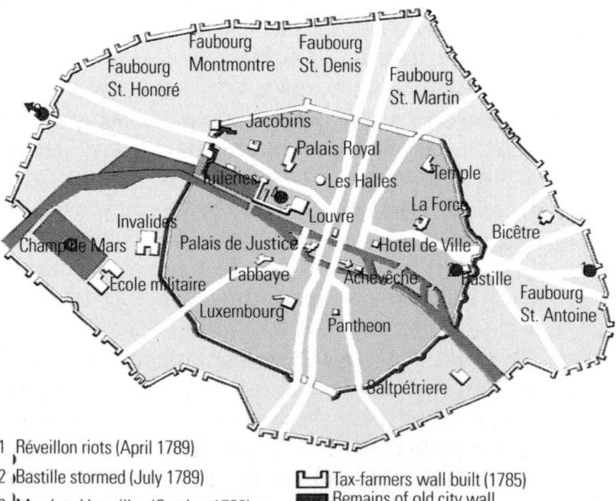


► **French Revolution** Shortly before the Revolution, Paris' city limits had been extended by the building of the "tax-farmers" wall (1785), authorized by the finance minister, Calonne, to facilitate the collection of tolls from those entering the city. The wall, 7ft (3m) high, ran concentrically with the old city boundaries and took in several of the surrounding *faubourgs*, or districts. Access was gained through 54 gates, or *barrières*, which were largely destroyed by the crowds during the Revolution. The city's population in 1789 was approximately 600,000.

the Rights of Man. The Legislative Assembly was installed (October 1791) and, faced with growing internal and external pressure, declared war on Austria (April 1792). It was soon in conflict with most other European states, whose governments viewed events in France with fear. The war hastened political change: LOUIS XVI was deposed (August 1792) and the National Convention met to proclaim a republic (September 1792). After a period of rivalry between JACOBINS and GIRONDINS (November 1792–June 1793), strong central government, marked by fanaticism and violence, was imposed during the REIGN OF TERROR, and Louis was executed. Social anarchy and runaway inflation characterized the Thermidorean Reaction (July 1794–October 1795), which followed the fall of ROBESPIERRE. Another new constitution imposed the DIRECTORY (1795–99). The Consulate (1799–1804), dominated by NAPOLEON I, put an end to the decade of revolution.

**French Revolutionary Wars** (1792–1802) Series of campaigns in which the armies of revolutionary France fought combinations of European foes. Fear and hatred of the FRENCH REVOLUTION fueled the hostility of Austria in particular. The French declared war on Austria and Prussia in April 1792. The success of the French generals Dumouriez and Kellermann at Valmy and Jemappes provoked other states, including Britain, Netherlands, and Spain, to form the First Coalition (1793). By 1794 France was once more on the offensive. After concluding peace treaties with Netherlands and Prussia (1795), France concentrated on war with Austria. Peace with Austria was concluded at Campo-Formio (1797). Napoleon Bonaparte (*see* NAPOLEON I) conducted a brilliant campaign in Italy. Britain, having established naval superiority, remained at war. Horatio NELSON defeated Napoleon's fleet at Aboukir, Egypt. A Second Coalition was formed in 1799, consisting of Russsia, Austria, Britain, Turkey, Portugal, and Naples. France defeated Naples (1799), and Russia's withdrawal weakened the alliance. In the coup of 18 Brumaire Napoleon became first consul. The events of 1800 proved decisive. Napoleon defeated the Austrians at Marengo, and Moreau crushed the Allies at Hohenlinden. Britain captured Malta and Egypt (1801), but lacked the will to fight alone and made peace at Amiens. *See* NAPOLEONIC WARS

**frequency** Rate of occurrence. In statistics, the number of times a numerical value, event, or special property occurs in a population in a given time. In physics, the number of oscillations occurring in a given time (measured in HERTZ), such as sound, light, and radio waves, or a swinging PENDULUM or vibrating springs. Frequency is the reciprocal of period.

**frequency modulation (FM)** Form of RADIO transmission. It is the variation of the FREQUENCY of a transmitted radio carrier wave by the signal being broadcast. It makes radio reception fairly free from static interference and, although restricted in range to receivers in line-of-sight of the transmitter, has become the most favored transmission method. *See also* AMPLITUDE MODULATION (AM)

**fresco** Method of painting on freshly spread plaster that is still damp. In true fresco (*buon fresco*) paint combines with moist plaster so that, when dry, the painted surface does not peel. Dry fresco (*fresco secco*) is the application of paint in a water and glue medium to a dry plaster wall. It does not last as well as true fresco. The palace at Knossos, Crete (*c*.1700 BC), was decorated with frescos. GIOTTO and MICHELANGELO created great frescos.

**Fresnel, Augustin Jean** (1788–1827) French physicist and engineer. His pioneer work in optics was instrumental in establishing the wave theory of light. He researched the conditions governing interference phenomena in POLARIZED LIGHT, studied double refraction, and devised a way of producing circularly polarized light.

**Fresno** City in S central California; seat of Fresno County. The city was settled with the arrival of the railroad in 1872 and Fresno was incorporated in 1885. In the center of the fertile San Joaquin valley, Fresno produces nearly 80% of the nation's raisins. The other major crops are grapes and cotton. The booming agribusiness saw the city's population grow by more than 60% between 1980 and 1990. Sites include Fresno City College (1910), and California State University-Fresno (1911). Industries: agriculture, wines. Pop (1990) 354,091.

**Freud, Anna** (1895–1982) British psychotherapist, youngest daughter of Sigmund FREUD, b. Austria. She applied PSYCHOANALYSIS to child development and was an early advocate of play therapy. Her books include *Normality and Pathology in Childhood* (1968).

**Freud, Lucian** (1922– ) British painter, b. Germany, grandson of Sigmund Freud. He is one of the strongest modern British figure painters. Freud's most characteristic subjects are portraits and nudes.

**Freud, Sigmund** (1856–1939) Austrian physician and founder of PSYCHOANALYSIS. With Josef Breuer he developed methods of treating mental disorders by free association and the interpretation of dreams. These methods derived from his theories of ID, EGO, and SUPEREGO, and emphasized the unconscious and subconscious as agents of human behavior. Freud developed theories of neuroses involving childhood relationships to one's parents and stressed the importance of sexuality in behavior. He believed that each personality had a tripartite structure: the **id**, the unconscious emotions, desires, and fears which may surface in dreams or madness; the **ego**, the conscious rationalizing section of the mind; and the **superego**, which may be compared to the conscience. The ego comes to mediate the selfish needs of the id and the idealistic demands of the superego. The adoption of a satisfactory superego is dependent on the resolution of the OEDIPUS COMPLEX. His works include *The Psychopathology of Everyday Life* (1904) and *The Ego and the Id* (1923).

▲ **Freud** The Austrian doctor Sigmund Freud is considered the founder of psychoanalysis. His methods of dream interpretation and employing free association were considered highly revolutionary.

**friar** Member of certain religious orders. The four main orders – the DOMINICANS, FRANCISCANS, CARMELITES, and AUGUSTINIANS – were founded in the 13th century. Friars differ from cloistered monks in that they are involved in widespread outside activity.

**friction** Resistance encountered when surfaces in contact slide or roll against each other, or when a fluid flows along a surface. Friction is directly proportional to the force pressing the surfaces together and the surface roughness. When the movement begins, it is opposed by a static friction up to a maximum "limiting friction" and then slipping occurs. Aircraft reduce air (fluid) friction by having a streamlined design.

**Friedan, Betty Naomi** (1921– ) US feminist. Her book *The Feminine Mystique* (1963) challenged the notion of woman as housewife and mother, rather than wage-earner. Friedan was founder and first president (1966–70) of the National Organization for Women (NOW).

**Friedman, Milton** (1912– ) US economist. An influential member of the Chicago School of Economics, he supported MONETARISM as the best means of controlling the economy. His works include: *A Monetary History of the United States 1867–1960* (1963), written with Anna Schwartz and a key book in monetary economics; *A Theory of the Consumption Function* (1957); and *Capitalism and Freedom* (1962). Friedman was awarded the 1976 Nobel Prize for economics.

**Friedrich, Caspar David** (1774–1840) German painter. One of the greatest romantic artists, he created eerie, symbolic landscapes, such as *Shipwreck on the Ice* (1822) and *Man and Woman Gazing at the Moon* (1824).

**Friends, The Religious Society of** *See* QUAKERS

**Frisch, Karl von** (1886–1982) Austrian zoologist. He shared the 1973 Nobel Prize for physiology or medicine with K. LORENZ and N. TINBERGEN for his pioneering work in ETHOLOGY. He deciphered the "language of bees" by studying their dance patterns in which one bee tells others in the hive the direction and distance of a food source. In his earlier work, he showed that fish and bees see colors, fish can hear, and that bees can distinguish various flower scents.

**Frisch, Max** (1911–91) Swiss novelist and dramatist. His early plays, greatly influenced by BRECHT, are experimental in form and often satirical. They include: *The Chinese Wall* (1946), *The Fire Raisers* (1953), and *Andorra* (1961). His later plays, including *Triptych* (1979), and the novels *Stiller* (1954) and *A Wilderness of Mirrors* (1964), involve man's quest for identity.

FROG

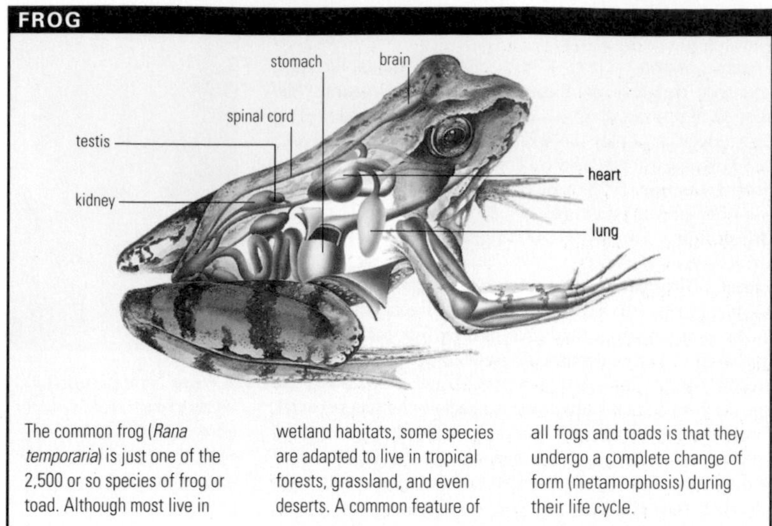


The common frog (*Rana temporaria*) is just one of the 2,500 or so species of frog or toad. Although most live in wetland habitats, some species are adapted to live in tropical forests, grassland, and even deserts. A common feature of all frogs and toads is that they undergo a complete change of form (metamorphosis) during their life cycle.

**Froebel, Friedrich Wilhelm August** (1782–1852) German educator and influential educational theorist. His main interest was in preschool-age children, and in 1841 he opened the first kindergarten. He stressed the importance of environment, self-directed activity, physical training, and play in the development of the child.

**frog** Tailless AMPHIBIAN, found worldwide. Frogs have long hind limbs, webbed feet, and external eardrums behind the eyes. Most begin life as TADPOLES after hatching from eggs, usually laid in water. Some frogs remain aquatic, some terrestrial, living in trees or underground. Most have teeth in the upper jaw and all have long sticky tongues attached at the front of the mouth to capture live food, usually insects. Length: 1–12in (2.5–30cm). Subclass Salientia (or Anura), divided into 17 families; the most typical genus is *Rana*. *See also* TOAD

**froghopper** Any of various small, hopping insects whose eggs and young are covered with a protective frothy mass called cuckoo spit. Adults are triangular and grey, greenish or brown. They feed on plants. Length: to 0.6in (1.5cm). Order Homoptera; family Cercopidae.

**Fromm, Erich** (1900–80) US psychoanalyst and writer, b. Germany. Fromm applied PSYCHOANALYSIS to the study of peoples and cultures, stressing the importance of interpersonal relationships in an impersonal, industrialized society. His books include *Escape from Freedom* (1941) and *The Art of Loving* (1956).

**Fronde** (1648–53) Series of rebellions against oppressive government in France. The **Fronde of the Parlement** (1648–49) began when ANNE OF AUSTRIA tried to reduce the salaries of court officials. It gained some concessions from the regent, LOUIS XIV. The **Fronde of the Princes** (1650–53) was a rebellion of the aristocratic followers of CONDÉ, and forced Cardinal MAZARIN into temporary exile. Condé briefly held Paris, but the rebellion soon collapsed, and promised reforms were withdrawn.

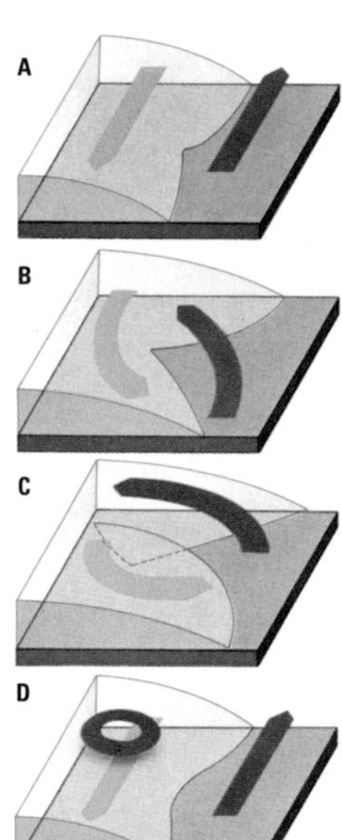


▲ **front** Fronts form in temperate latitudes where a cold air mass meets a warm air mass (A). The air masses spiral around a bulge causing cold and warm fronts to develop (B). The warm air rises above the cold front, and the cold air slides underneath the warm (C). Eventually, the cold-air areas merge, and the warm air is lifted up or occluded.

**front** In meteorology, the boundary between two air masses of different temperatures or of different densities. Cold fronts occur as a relatively cold and dense air mass moves under warmer air. With a warm front, warmer air is pushing over colder air and replacing it. An occluded front is composed of two fronts: a cold front overtakes a warm or stationary front. In a stationary front, air masses remain in the same areas and the weather is mostly unchanged.

**frontier** In US history, the westernmost region of white settlement. In the 17th century the frontier began at the foothills of the APPALACHIAN Mountains and gradually moved westward until the late 19th century, when no new land remained for pioneer homesteaders. The existence of a frontier region, where a dominant group was able to expand (usually at the expense of native inhabitants), has been an important factor in the history of other countries, such as South Africa. In the US, the frontier notions of rugged individualism and free enterprise as central to US society was promoted by Frederick Jackson Turner in *The Significance of the Frontier in American History* (1893).

**Frost, Robert Lee** (1874–1963) US poet. His work is shaped by the landscape of his native New England. Frost's first two volumes of lyric poems, *A Boy's Will* (1913) and *North of Boston* (1914), established his reputation. His best known poems include: "Stopping by Woods on a Snowy Evening," "The Road Not Taken," and "Mending Wall." Frost received the Pulitzer Prize for poetry (1924, 1931, 1937, 1943).

**frost** In meteorology, atmospheric temperatures at Earth's surface below 32°F (0°C). The visible result of a frost is usually a deposit of minute ice crystals formed on exposed surfaces from DEW and water vapor. In freezing weather the "degree of frost" indicates the number of degrees below freezing point.

**frostbite** Freezing of living body tissue in subzero temperatures. Frostbite is an effect of the body's defensive response to shut down blood vessels at the extremities in order to preserve warmth at the core of the body. It mostly occurs in the face, ears, hands, and feet. In superficial frostbite, the affected part turns white and cold; it can be treated by gentle thawing. If freezing continues, ice crystals form in the tissues; the flesh hardens, and there is no sensation. Deep frostbite, which causes tissue death, requires urgent medical treatment.

**fructose** (fruit sugar, $C_6H_{12}0_6$) Simple white monosaccharide, found in honey, sweet fruits, and flower nectar. Sweeter than SUCROSE, it is made commercially by the HYDROLYSIS of beet or cane sugar, and is used in foods as a sweetener. Its derivatives play a crucial role in providing energy for organisms.

**fruit** SEED-containing mature OVARY of an ANGIOSPERM. Fruits serve to disperse plants and are an important food source (they provide vitamins, acids, salts, calcium, iron, and phosphates). **Simple** fruits, dry or fleshy, are produced by one ripened ovary of a single pistil (unit comprising a stigma, style, and ovary) and include legumes (peas and beans) and nuts. **Aggregate** fruits develop from several simple pistils; examples are raspberry and blackberry. **Multiple** fruits develop from a flower cluster; examples are pineapples and figs. Although considered fruits in culinary terms, apples and pears are regarded botanically as "false" fruits, as the edible parts are created by the RECEPTACLE and not the carpel walls.

**fruit bat** Any of *c*.160 species of nocturnal, fruit-eating BATS found in tropical regions of the Old World. They have an independent, clawed second digit and rely on sight, rather than ECHOLOCATION for orientation. They are capable of powerful, sustained flight. The Pteropodidae, or **flying foxes**, live in SE Asia. The largest of all bats, they have a foxlike head and can cause substantial damage to fruit crops. Length: to 16in (40cm); Wingspan: to 5ft (1.5m). Genus *Pteropus*.

**fruit fly** (drosophilia) Common name for any of the flies of the families Tephritidae or Drosophilidae. The Tephritidae (**peacock flies**) contains *c*.1,200 species that lay their eggs directly in the pulp of fruit. Larvae tunnel their way through fruit, and they are a serious pest of fruit. The Drosophilidae (**pomace flies**) feed mainly on the yeasts of rotting fruit. *Drosophila melangogaster* is used extensively in GENETIC studies. Order Diptera.

**Frunze** Former name of BISHKEK

**Fry, Christopher** (1907– ) English dramatist, b. Christopher Harris. His witty blank-verse plays are often set in ancient or medieval times. They include *A Phoenix Too Frequent* (1946), *The Lady's Not for Burning* (1948), and *Venus Observed* (1950).

**Fry, Elizabeth** (1780–1845) English prison reformer and philanthropist. Horrified by conditions in Newgate Prison, London, she agitated for more humane treatment of women prisoners.

**Fuad I** (1868–1936) King of Egypt. Son of ISMAIL PASHA, he was sultan (1917–22) and first king of modern Egypt (1922–36). Fuad reigned under British influence and in conflict with the nationalist Wafd Party. His grandson reigned briefly as Fuad II (1952–53).

**Fuchs, Klaus** (1912–88) British physicist and Communist spy, b. Germany. Fuchs worked on the atom bomb in the US (1943) and returned to Britain (1946) to head the theoretical physics division of the atomic research center at Harwell.

Imprisoned (1950) for passing secrets to the Soviet Union, his British citizenship was revoked. After release (1959), he went to East Germany to work at the nuclear research center.

**fuchsia** Genus of shrubby plants found in tropical and subtropical South and Central America and parts of New Zealand. They are widely cultivated. Named for the German herbalist Leonard Fuchs (1501–66), they have oval leaves and pink, red, or purple trumpet-shaped, waxy flowers. The 100 or so species include the crimson-purple *Fuchsia procumbens* and *F. speciosa*. Family Onagraceae. *See* EVENING PRIMROSE

**fuel** Substance that is burned or otherwise modified to produce energy, usually in the form of heat. Apart from FOSSIL FUELS, firewood, and charcoal, the term also applies to radioactive materials used in nuclear power stations. *See also* ENERGY SOURCES; NATURAL GAS; OIL

**Fuentes, Carlos** (1928– ) Mexican novelist and short story writer. His first two novels, *Where the Air is Clean* (1958) and *The Death of Artemio Cruz* (1962), share a critical view of Mexican society and earned him an international reputation. Other fiction includes *The Hydra Head* (1978) and *Distant Relations* (1980). Among his recent work are the novel *The Campaign* (1991) and the essays *Geography of the Novel* (1993).

**Fugard, Athol** (1932– ) South African playwright, director, and actor. Fugard achieved international acclaim for his plays *The Blood Knot* (1961), *Sizwe Bandi is Dead* (1972), and *My Children! My Africa* (1990). His work often explores the effects of apartheid on South Africa's black population.

**fugitive slave laws** Federal acts of 1793 and 1850 that provided for the return of escaped slaves to their owners. When SLAVERY was abolished in Northern states, the UNDERGROUND RAILROAD helped Southern slaves obtain freedom. Northern states also passed laws that prevented escaped slaves from being returned to slave states. The COMPROMISE OF 1850 had a tougher fugitive slave law than the 1793 statute, with heavy penalties for aiding fugitive slaves. According to the 1850 laws, fugitive slaves were denied legal rights. The law was so harsh that it helped the abolitionists' cause and many citizens openly flouted the new regulations

**fugue** (It. flight) In music, a composition of several parts or voices where the same melodic line or theme is stated and developed in each voice. Generally the theme begins in one part and others are added in sequence. Popular in the BAROQUE period, fugue writing reached its peak with J.S. BACH.

**Fujiyama** (Mount Fuji) Highest mountain in Japan, in the Fuji-Hakone National Park. An extinct volcano, it is seen as the most sacred mountain in Japan. It is a summer and winter sports area. Height: 12,389ft (3,776m).

**Fulani** (Fulah or Fulbe) People of W Africa, numbering *c.*6 million. Their language belongs to the W Atlantic group of the NIGER-CONGO. Originally a pastoral people, they helped the spread of Islam throughout W Africa from the 16th century, establishing an empire lasting until British colonialism in the 19th century.

**Fuller, (Richard) Buckminster** (1895–1983) US architect and engineer. Believing that only technology can solve modern world problems, he invented several revolutionary designs. The most widely used is the GEODESIC DOME. His books include *Operating Manual for Spaceship Earth* (1969) and *Earth Inc.* (1973).

**Fuller, Melville Weston** (1833–1910) US lawyer, chief justice of the Supreme Court (1888–1910). He was a strict constructionist. Important cases include: *Plessy* v. *Ferguson* (1896), which upheld "separate but equal" laws of segregation; and *Lochner* v. *New York* (1905), a "due process" clause interpreted so the state could not set a 10-hour day for bakers. Fuller helped settle a boundary dispute between Venezuela and Great Britain (1899), and was a member of the Hague Tribunal (1900–10).

**fuller's earth** Claylike substance containing more than 50% SILICA. Once used for fulling (removing oil and grease from wool), it is now used to bleach petroleum and refine vegetable oils.

**Fulton, Robert** (1765–1815) US inventor and engineer. Designing torpedoes and other naval weapons, his main interest was in navigation. In 1807 he pioneered the use of steamboats for carrying passengers and freight, when his craft *Clermont* traveled between New York City and Albany.

**Funchal** Capital and chief port of MADEIRA. Founded in 1421, it was ruled by Spain from 1580 to 1640, and was briefly under British administration in the early 19th century. It is now an industrial and resort center for all the islands in the Madeira archipelago. Industries: sugar-milling, distilling, wine, handicrafts. Pop. (1981) 44,111.

**function** In mathematics, rule that assigns a unique value to each element of a given set. The given set is the **domain** of the function, and the set of values is the **range**. Two or more elements of the domain may be assigned the same value, but a function must assign only one value to each element of the domain. A function $f$ maps each element $x$ of the domain to a corresponding element (or value) $y$ in the range. Here $x$ and $y$ are variables, with $y$ dependent on $x$ through the functional relationship $f$. The dependent variable $y$ is said to be a function of the independent variable $x$. For example, the square-root is a function, its domain and range being the nonnegative real numbers. *See also* TRIGONOMETRIC FUNCTION

**functionalism** In art and architecture, an early 20th-century style based on UTILITARIANISM. Functionalism rejected ornamentation and stressed the basic structure of the work and of the materials used. Major proponents included GROPIUS, BAUHAUS, and LE CORBUSIER.

**functionalism** Sociological and anthropological theory outlined by Emile DURKHEIM. The theory attempts to understand the function of each part of society (customs, institutions, objects, roles, religion) in relation to each other and to the whole society.

**fundamental forces** Four basic forces that exist in physics. The most familiar, and the weakest, is GRAVITATION. Much stronger is the ELECTROMAGNETIC FORCE, which "binds" particles together. The two other forces operate only on the subatomic level. The WEAK NUCLEAR FORCE, associated with the decay of particles, is intermediate in strength between the gravitational and electromagnetic force, whereas the STRONG NUCLEAR FORCE, associated with the "glue" that holds nuclei together, is the strongest natural force.

**fundamentalism** Movement within some Protestant denominations, particularly in the US, which originated in the late 19th and early 20th centuries as a reaction against biblical criticism and theories of evolution. The name is derived from *The Fundamentals*, a series of 12 tracts published between 1909 and 1915 by eminent US evangelical leaders. The doctrines most emphasized are the inspiration and infallible truth of the BIBLE, the divinity of Christ, the VIRGIN BIRTH, ATONEMENT by Christ bringing expiation and salvation for all, the physical RESURRECTION, and the SECOND COMING. Fundamentalism has been loosely used to refer to any extreme orthodox element within a religion, such as Islamic fundamentalists.

**Fundamental Orders** Code of laws adopted by representatives of the settlements in Connecticut in 1639 to govern the Connecticut Colony. Sometimes called the first written constitution, it remained in force until superseded by the Connecticut Charter (1662).

**fungicide** Chemical that kills fungi. For example, creosote is used to prevent dry rot in wood.

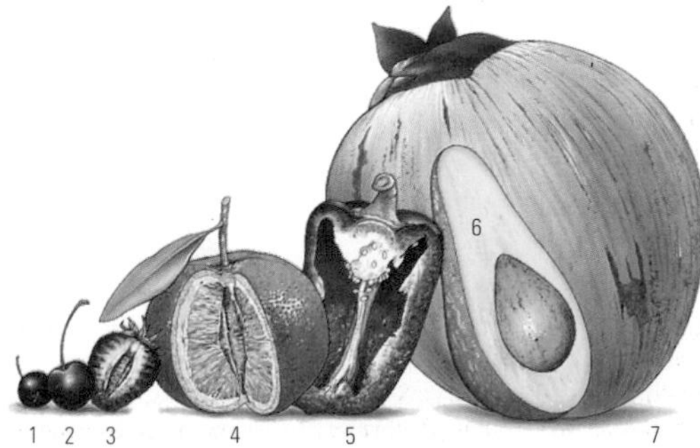


◀ **fruit** Fruits are the ripened ovary of a flowering plant which is enclosed by the fruit wall known as the pericarp. Most fruits, such as blackcurrants (1), cherries (2), strawberries (3), oranges (4), and pepper (5) contain more than one seed. The avocado (6), however, contains only one seed, about the size of a golf ball. The largest fruit, the double coconut (7), is also single-seeded.

**FUSION, NUCLEAR**

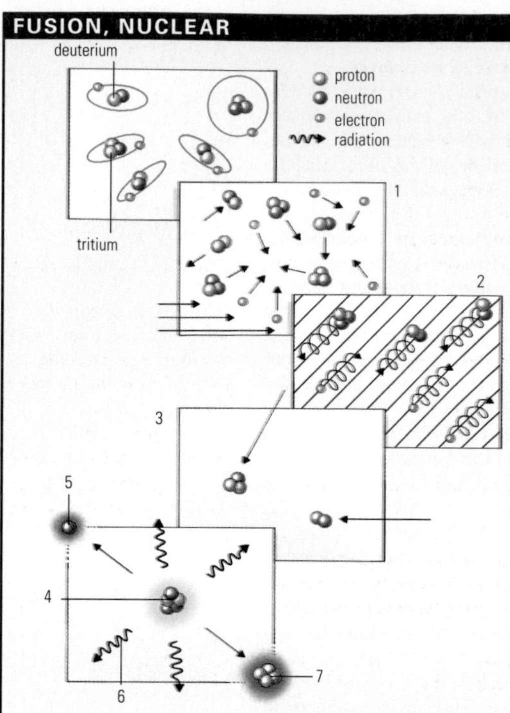


In experiments to generate power by nuclear fusion, the aim is usually to produce energy by fusing tritium and deuterium. These are isotopes of hydrogen and the process can only occur at a temperature above 100 million°C and enormous pressure. Deuterium has one proton, one neutron and one electron while tritium has one proton, two neutrons and an electron. In a fusion reactor the mixture of the two isotopes is heated by intense radio emissions, ion bombardment and electrical pulses (1). The plasma which results is suspended in a magnetic field (2). The tritium and deuterium nuclei fuse (3) creating a helium nucleus (4), a loose neutron (5), radiation (6) and energy when the products hit the edge of the plasma (7).

**fungus** Any of a wide variety of organisms of the KINGDOM Fungi, which are unable to photosynthesize and which reproduce by means of spores and never produce cells with flagella. They include MUSHROOMS, MOLDS, and YEASTS. There are *c.*100,000 species. Fungi have relatively simple structures, with no roots, stems, or leaves. Their cell walls contain the polysaccharide CHITIN. The main body of a typical multicellular fungus consists of an inconspicuous network (mycelium) of fine filaments (hyphae), which contain many nuclei and which may or may not be divided into segments by cross-walls. The hypha nuclei are HAPLOID. The mycelia may develop spore-producing, often conspicuous, fruiting bodies, mushrooms, and TOADSTOOLS. Fungal PARASITES depend on living animals or plants: SAPROPHYTES utilize the materials of dead plants and animals, and symbionts obtain food in a mutually beneficial relationship with plants. Fungi feed by secreting digestive ENZYMES onto their food, then absorbing the soluble products of digestion. Many cause diseases in crops, livestock, and humans (athlete's foot). Molds and yeasts are used in the production of BEER and CHEESE; some fungi, such as *Penicillium*, are sources of ANTIBIOTICS.

**funk** Style or energy of popular music. It was originally employed in the 1950s to summarize a form of modern JAZZ which, although influenced by BE-BOP harmonies, emphasized modern melodies. Funk was developed by such artists as James BROWN and George Clinton.

**fur** Soft, dense hair covering the skin of certain mammals. Such mammals include mink, fox, ermine, musquash, wolf, bear, squirrel, and rabbit. Most are hunted and killed for their pelts which, when manufactured into clothing, may command high prices. Some fur-bearing animals are now protected by law because overhunting has threatened extinction.

**Furies** (Erthyes and Eumenides) In Greek mythology, three hideous goddesses of vengeance whose main task was to torment those guilty of social crimes.

**furnace** Enclosed space raised to a high temperature by the combustion of fuels or by electric heating. Most furnaces are used in the extraction of metals or the making of alloys. An **arc** furnace relies on the heat generated by an electric arc (spark), often between two large carbon electrodes, which are slowly consumed. A **resistance** furnace is heated by passing an electric current through a heating element or directly through metallic material. An **induction** furnace uses ELECTROMAGNETIC INDUCTION to cause a current to flow in a metallic charge. The resulting heat is sufficient to melt the metal.

**fur trade** Vital commercial factor in the development of the North American wilderness. The fur trade began in the 1500s as a form of exchange between Native Americans and Europeans. By the late 1500s fur had become a valuable commodity in Europe, encouraging Europeans to explore further into the interior. In 1608 Samuel de CHAMPLAIN established a fur-trading post at Quebec. In 1670 the HUDSON'S BAY COMPANY was established. Control of the fur trade was a major factor in the FRENCH AND INDIAN WARS. In the 1770s the rival North West Company was formed, which merged with the Hudson's Bay Company in 1821. The LEWIS AND CLARK EXPEDITION (1804–06) led to the development of the trade in the West. John Jacob ASTOR formed the AMERICAN FUR COMPANY. Mountain men, such as Kit CARSON, explored the Rocky Mountains. In the 19th century the fur trade declined dramatically due to changes in fashion and the clearance of land for settlements.

**Furtwängler, Wilhelm** (1886–1954) German conductor. He became conductor of the Berlin Philharmonic Orchestra in 1922 (life appointment in 1952), and of the Vienna Philharmonic Orchestra in 1930. Furtwängler appeared frequently at the Bayreuth and Salzburg festivals and was a specialist in the works of Beethoven and Wagner. His ambiguous relationship with the Nazi government aroused controversy.

**furze** *See* GORSE

**fuse** In electrical engineering, a safety device to protect against overloading. Fuses are commonly strips of easily melted metal placed in series in an electrical circuit such that when overloaded, the fuse melts, breaking the circuit and preventing systemic damage.

**fusion, nuclear** Form of nuclear reaction in which nuclei of light atoms (such as hydrogen) combine to form one or more heavier nuclei with the release of large amounts of energy. The process takes place in the Sun and other stars, and has been reproduced on Earth in the HYDROGEN BOMB. In a self-sustaining fusion reaction, the combining nuclei are in the form of a PLASMA. *See also* FISSION, NUCLEAR; NUCLEAR ENERGY

**futurism** Art movement that originated in Italy (1909) with the publication of the first futurist manifesto. It aimed to glorify machines and to depict speed and motion by means of an adapted version of CUBISM. Futurists include the poet MARINETTI. Its ideas were absorbed by the DADA movement and by SURREALISM.

**Fuzhou** (Fuzhou, or Fu-chou) City and port on the Min Chiang River, capital of Fukien province, SE China. Fuzhou was founded in the T'ang dynasty (618–907). It was one of the first treaty ports to be opened to foreign trade (1842) and flourished as China's largest tea-exporting center. It declined in the early 20th century. In 1949, after the Communist takeover, Fuzhou was blockaded by the Nationalists. Industries: engineering, chemicals, textiles. Pop. (1993 est.) 1,290,000.

**fuzzy logic** System of logic able to represent statements that are true or false depending on context. For example, the statement "this is warm," applied to the inside of a freezer that is not working, is true only in the context that the freezer is not literally "freezing." Computer-controlled devices programmed on the principles of fuzzy logic are able to put into context information they receive, and respond flexibly to the environment.

**g** Symbol for the universal constant of GRAVITATION. g is also the symbol for acceleration of free fall due to Earth's gravity. One g is *c*.32ft/s² (9.8m/s²).

**Gable, Clark** (1901–60) US film actor. His magnetism made him "king" of 1930s Hollywood. Gable won an Academy Award for best actor in *It Happened One Night* (1934). His performance as Rhett Butler in *Gone With the Wind* (1939) is one of cinema's most enduring.

**Gabo, Naum** (1890–1977) US sculptor and architect, b. Russia as Naum Pevsner. A founder of CONSTRUCTIVISM, he published the *Realist Manifesto* (1920) with his brother Antoine Pevsner.

**Gabon** The Gabonese Republic lies on the Equator in W central Africa; the capital is LIBREVILLE. **Land and Climate** Behind the coastline is a narrow coastal plain. The land then rises to hills, plateaux, and mountains divided by deep valleys carved by the Ogooué River and its tributaries. Gabon has high temperatures and humidity most of the year. Dense rainforest covers *c*.75% of Gabon, with tropical savanna in the E and S. **History** Portuguese explorers reached the Gabon coast in the 1470s and the area later became a source of slaves. France established a settlement in 1839, later named Libreville. Gabon became a French colony in the 1880s. In 1960 it achieved full independence. In 1968, after the death of Gabon's first president, Leon Mba, it became a one-party state. Free elections took place in 1990. The Gabonese Democratic Party (PDG), formerly the only party, won a majority in the National Assembly. President Bongo, of the PDG, won the presidential elections in 1993, although accusations of fraud and corruption led to riots in Libreville. Under the Paris Agreement (1994), parliamentary elections were scheduled for 1996 but were not held until 1997, when the PDG was resoundingly re-elected. **Economy** Gabon's abundant natural resources, including forests, manganese, and uranium, make it one of Africa's richer nations (1992 GDP per capita, US$3,913). However, agriculture still employs *c*.75% of the workforce. Crops include bananas, cassava, maize, and sugar cane, while cocoa and coffee are grown for export. Other exports: oil, manganese, timber, uranium.

**Gaborone** Capital of Botswana, S Africa. First settled in the 1890s, it served as the administrative headquarters of the former Bechuanaland Protectorate. In 1966 it became the capital of an independent Botswana.

**Gabriel** Archangel, mentioned in the Old and New Testaments, and in the Koran. In the Old Testament, Gabriel helps DANIEL to interpret his visions. In the New Testament he foretells the birth of St. JOHN THE BAPTIST to his father, ZACHARIAS, and that of JESUS CHRIST to his mother, MARY. In the Koran, he is the angel who appears to MUHAMMAD. The Christian Church celebrates Gabriel's feast day on March 24.

**Gabrieli** Two Italian composers, uncle and nephew. Andrea Gabrieli (*c*.1533–86) was organist at St. Mark's, Venice. He wrote vocal and organ music, His nephew, Giovanni Gabrieli (*c*.1553–1612), succeeded him as organist at St. Mark's. He developed the new CONCERTO style and was a major influence on the early BAROQUE.

**Gaddafi** *See* QADDAFI, MUAMMAR AL-

**Gaddi, Taddeo** (*c*.1300–*c*.1366) Leading member in a family of Florentine artists. Taddeo's father, **Gaddo di Zanobi** (*c*.1259–*c*.1330), was a noted painter and mosaicist. Taddeo served as an apprentice to GIOTTO. His best-known work is the fresco series *Life of the Virgin* (completed in 1338). Taddeo's son, **Agnolo** (d.1396), also painted frescoes; the most famous is the *Legend of the True Cross* (*c*.1380).

**gadolinium** Silvery-white metallic element (symbol Gd) of the LANTHANIDE SERIES. Chief ores are gadolinite, monazite, and bastnaesite. Its uses include neutron absorption and the manufacture of certain alloys. Properties: at.no. 64; at.wt. 157.25; sp.gr. 7.898; m.p. 2,392°F (1,311°C); b.p. 5,851°F (3,233°C); most common isotope $^{158}$Gd (24.87%).

**Gadsden Purchase** Land purchased by the US from Mexico in 1853. It was a narrow strip, 30,000sq mi (77,000sq km) in area, now forming S Arizona and New Mexico. The deal was negotiated by James Gadsden.

**Gaelic** Language spoken in parts of Ireland and Scotland. The two branches diverged in the 15th century and are mutually unintelligible. The Irish variety is one of the official languages of the Republic of Ireland. In Scotland, Gaelic has no official status and is dying out.

**Gagarin, Yuri Alekseyevich** (1934–68) Russian cosmonaut, the first man to orbit the Earth. On April 12, 1961 he made a single orbit in 1 hour 29 minutes.

**gag rules** Series of rules that were adopted by the US Congress in 1836 to prevent the discussion of slavery. John Quincy ADAMS led the fight against the rules, and they were repealed in 1844.

**Gaia** (Gaea) In Greek mythology, mother goddess of the Earth. Wife (and in some legends, mother) of URANUS, she bore the TITANS, the CYCLOPES, and the Hecatoncheires ("those of a hundred hands").

**Gaia hypothesis** Scientific theory that interrelates the Earth's many and varied processes – chemical, physical, and biological. Popular in the 1970s, when it was proposed by James Lovelock, it conceives of Earth as a single living organism.

**Gainsborough, Thomas** (1727–88) British portrait and landscape painter. Influenced by the Dutch landscape painters, he developed a style that is remarkable for its characterization and use of color. Among his best landscapes is *The Watering Place* (1777).

**Gaitskell, Hugh Todd Naylor** (1906–63) British politician. He became a Labour member of Parliament in 1945. He was minister of fuel and power (1947–50), minister of state for economic affairs (1950), and in the same year became chancellor of the exchequer. In 1955 he was elected leader of the party.

**Galápagos Islands** (Sp. *Archipiélago de Colón*) Pacific archipelago on the Equator; a province of Ecuador, c.650mi (1,050km) W of mainland South America. The capital is Baquerizo Moreno, on San Cristóbal. Other main islands include Santa Cruz, San Salvador, and Isabela. The islands are volcanic with sparse vegetation, except for dense forests on the high lava craters, which rise to 5,633ft (1,707m) at Volcán Wolf (Isabela). Mangrove swamps and lagoons teem with wildlife. Many animal species are unique to the islands, such as the giant land tortoises. The Galápagos National Park is a world heritage site. In 1832 Ecuador annexed the archipelago

***G/g, seventh letter of the Roman alphabet. Like the letter c, it probably derived from the Egyptian hieroglyph for a boomerang. The Greeks made it the third letter of their alphabet,* gamma. *The letter g is the symbol for gravity and gram.***

G

▲ **Gable** The epitome of the rugged male, Clark Gable will perhaps be best remembered for his role as Rhett Butler in *Gone with the Wind*.

## GABON

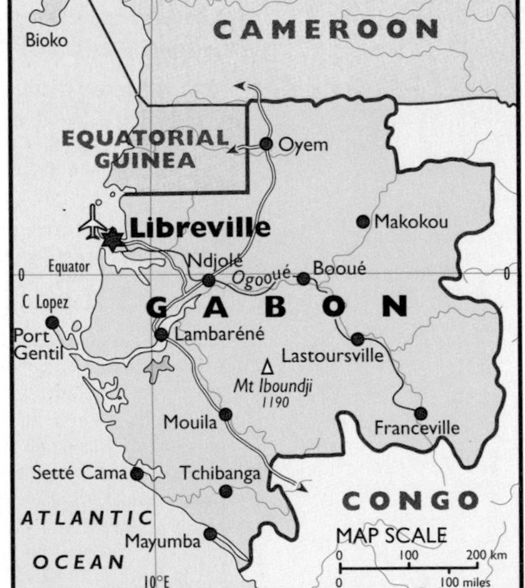

**AREA:** 103,347sq mi (267,670sq km)
**POPULATION:** 1,237,000
**CAPITAL (POPULATION):** Libreville (418,000)
**GOVERNMENT:** : Multiparty republic
**ETHNIC GROUPS:** Fang 36%, Mpongwe 15%, Mbete 14%, Punu 12%
**LANGUAGES:** French (official)
**RELIGIONS:** Christianity (Roman Catholic 65%, Protestant 19%, African churches 12%), traditional beliefs 3%, Islam 2%
**CURRENCY:** CFA franc = 100 centimes

and established a settlement. In 1835 Charles Darwin spent six weeks studying the Galápagos fauna. Area: 3,029sq mi (7,845sq km) Pop. (1990) 9,785.

**galaxy** Huge assembly of stars, dust, and gas. There are three main types, as originally classified by Edwin Hubble in 1925. **Elliptical** galaxies are round or elliptical systems, showing a gradual decrease in brightness from the center outward. **Spiral** galaxies are flattened, disk-shaped systems in which young stars, dust, and gas are concentrated in spiral arms coiling out from a central bulge, the nucleus. **Barred spiral** galaxies are distinguished by a bright central bar from which the spiral arms emerge. **Irregular** galaxies are systems with no symmetry. Current theories suggest that all galaxies were formed from immense clouds of gas soon after the Big Bang. Galaxies can exist singly or in clusters. Our Galaxy is spiral in shape and about 100,000 light-years in diameter. The Solar System is located at the edge of one of the spiral arms, about 30,000 light-years from the center. The stars of the spiral arms form the Milky Way. The whole Galaxy is rotating but the rotational rate varies with distance from the center.

**galaxy cluster** Group of associated galaxies, consisting of several separate systems moving together through space. Our Galaxy belongs to the Local Group of galaxies, which includes the Andromeda Galaxy and the Magellanic Clouds. A concentration of galaxy clusters is a galaxy supercluster.

**galena** Gray metallic mineral, lead sulfide (PbS); the major ore of lead. It is widely found in hydrothermal veins and as a replacement in limestone and dolomite rocks. Hardness 2.5–2.7; sp.gr. 7.5.

**Galicia** Region of SE Poland (Western Galicia) and W Ukraine (Eastern Galicia), on the slopes of the Carpathian Mountains (N) and bordering the Czech Republic (S). The major cities are Kraków (Poland) and Lvov (Ukraine). After passing to Austria in 1772, Galicia became the center of Hasidism. After World War I, Poland seized Western Galicia and was awarded Eastern Galicia at the 1919 Paris Peace Conference. The 1939 partition of Poland between Nazi Germany and the Soviet Union gave most of Eastern Galicia to the Ukraine, a position ratified by the 1945 Polish-Soviet Treaty. The region is mainly agricultural, though there are oil fields. Products: grain, flax, potatoes, and tobacco. Area: 30,309sq mi (78,500sq km).

**Galicia** Autonomous region in NW Spain, comprising the provinces of La Coruña, Lugo, Orense, and Pontevedra; the capital is Santiago de Compostela. It was a center of resistance to the Moorish invasions in the 8th century and passed to Castile in the 13th century. It was the focus of a literary and cultural revival in the 19th century. Galicia has a mountainous interior. Its economy is based on livestock; fishing, and mining are also important. Area: 11,361sq mi (29,434sq km). Pop. (1991) 2,731,669.

**Galilean satellites** Four chief satellites of Jupiter: Ganymede, Callisto, Io, and Europa, named for Galileo, who observed them in 1610.

**Galilee, Sea of** (Lake Tiberius or Yam Kinneret) Freshwater lake in N Israel, fed by the Jordan River. Israel's major reservoir, it is an important fishing ground and the source of water for irrigation of the Negev Desert. The surface is *c.*705ft (215m) below sea level. Area: 64sq mi (166sq km).

**Galileo** (1564–1642) (Galileo Galilei) Italian scientist. He studied falling bodies and disproved Aristotle's view that they fall at different rates according to weight. In 1610 he used one of the first astronomical telescopes to discover sunspots, Jupiter's major satellites, and the phases of Venus. In *Sidereus Muncius* (1610) he supported the Copernican view of the Universe, with Earth orbiting the Sun. This was declared a heresy, and in 1633 he was brought before the Inquisition and forced to recant.

**Galileo** Space probe to Jupiter, launched in October 1989. The probe passed the asteroids Gaspra and Ida in October 1991 and August 1993, respectively. Galileo went into orbit around Jupiter in 1995.

**gall** Abnormal swelling of plant tissue stimulated by an invasion of any of a wide variety of parasitic or symbiotic organisms, including bacteria, fungi, and insects. Most gall organisms only stunt the affected plants.

**Galla** Hamitic people who make up 40% of the population of Ethiopia, living mainly in the S. They are predominantly nomadic pastoralists, and practice Christianity, Islam, and animism.

**gall bladder** Muscular sac, found in most vertebrates, which stores bile. In humans it lies beneath the right lobe of the liver and releases bile into the duodenum by way of the bile duct.

**Gallic Wars** (58–51 BC) Campaigns in which the Romans, led by Caesar, conquered Gaul. By 57 BC Caesar had subdued SW and N Gaul. In 56 BC he conquered the Veneti, leaders of an anti-Roman confederation, and in 55–54 BC invaded Germany and Britain. He defeated a united Gallic revolt in 52 BC.

**Gallipoli** (Gelibolu) Peninsula and port in W Turkey, on the European side of the Dardanelles. Colonized by the Ancient Greeks, it has been of strategic importance in the defense of Istanbul (Constantinople). It was the first

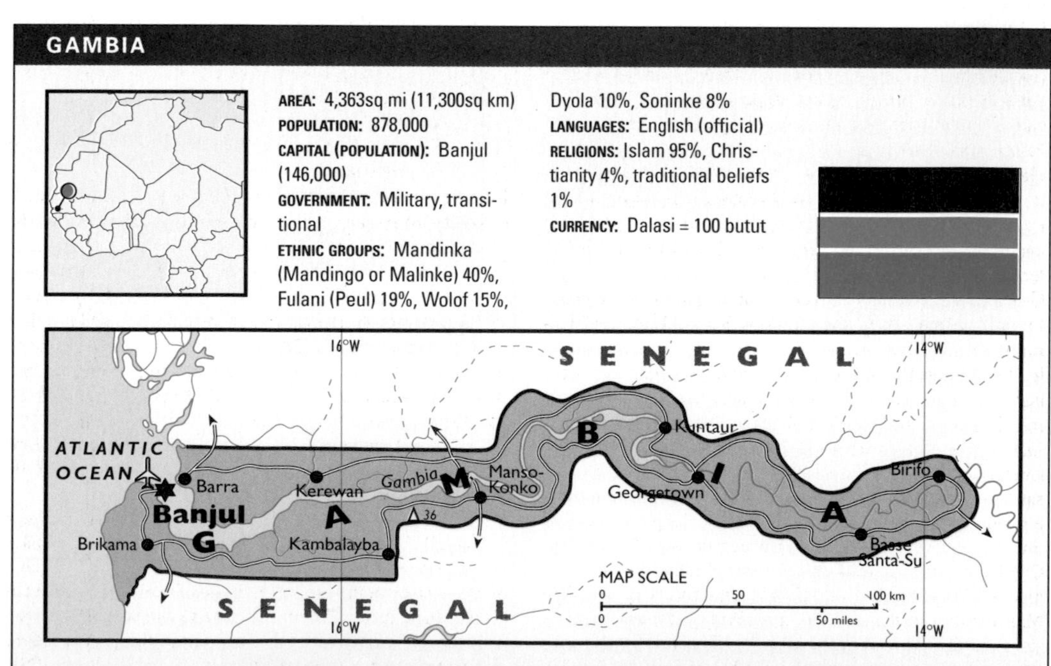

European city to be conquered by the Ottoman Turks (1354). In 1915–16 it was the scene of the GALLIPOLI CAMPAIGN. Pop. (1985) 16,715.

**Gallipoli Campaign** (1915–16) Allied operation against the Turks during WORLD WAR I. Some 45,000 British and French and 30,000 ANZAC troops were involved. After eight months of inconclusive fighting and more than 145,000 casualties, the Allies withdrew.

**gallium** (symbol Ga) Gray metallic element of Group III of the periodic table. It was discovered in 1875. Chief sources are bauxite and some zinc ores. The metal, liquid at room temperature, is used in lasers, semiconductors, and high-temperature thermometers. Properties: at.no. 31; at.wt. 69.72; sp.gr. 5.9; m.p. 85.60°F (29.78°C); b.p. 4,357°F (2,403°C); most common isotope $^{69}Ga$ (60.4%).

**gallstone** (cholelithiasis) Hard mass, usually composed of cholesterol and calcium salts, which forms in the gall bladder. Gallstones may cause severe pain (biliary colic) or become lodged in the common bile duct, causing obstructive JAUNDICE or cholecystitis. Treatment is by removal of the stones themselves or of the gall bladder.

**Gallup, George Horace** (1901–84) US pollster. His business sampling public opinion on social, political, and business matters came to wider public attention after correctly forecasting the outcome of the 1936 presidential election. Since then, Gallup pre-election polls have maintained a reputation for accuracy.

**Galsworthy, John** (1867–1933) British novelist and playwright. His novels deal with contemporary English upper-middle-class life. The most noted are *The Forsyte Saga* (1906–21), *A Modern Comedy* (1924–28), and *End of the Chapter* (1931–33). He was awarded the 1932 Nobel Prize for literature.

**Galvani, Luigi** (1737–98) Italian physician and physicist. His experiments with frogs' legs indicated a connection between muscular contraction and electricity. He believed a new type of electricity was created in the muscle and nerve.

**galvanizing** Coating of iron or steel articles with zinc in order to protect from CORROSION. The coating can be applied directly in a bath of molten zinc, electroplated from cold zinc sulfate solutions, or dusted on and baked.

**Galway** County in Connaught province, W Republic of Ireland; the county town is Galway. Bounded by the Atlantic (W), it is mountainous in the W, low-lying in the E, and drained by the SHANNON River. It is an agricultural region. Industries: tourism, agriculture, cotton-spinning, sugar-refining, handicrafts. Area: 2,293sq mi (5,939sq km). Pop. (1991) 129,511.

**Gama, Vasco da** (1469–1524) Portuguese naval commander and navigator. He led an expedition around the Cape of Good Hope (1497), which opened up the sea route to India. In 1502 he led a heavily armed expedition of 20 ships and, employing brutal tactics, secured Portuguese supremacy in the Eastern spice trade.

**Gambetta, Léon Michel** (1838–82) French politician. A parliamentary opponent of NAPOLEON III, he organized French resistance in the Franco-Prussian War (1870–71) and helped form the Third Republic. He was prime minister (1881–1882).

**Gambia** The Republic of The Gambia is the smallest country in mainland Africa; the capital is Banjul. **Land and Climate** The Gambia consists of a narrow strip of land bordering the Gambia River, and is enclosed by Senegal, except for a short Atlantic coastline. Near the sea, the land is flat. The middle part of the Gambia River is bordered by terraces (*banto faros*), which are flooded after heavy rains. The upper river flows through a deep valley that the river has cut into a sandstone plateau. Gambia has hot, humid summers. In winter, temperatures drop to *c.*61°F (16°C). Mangrove swamps line the river banks. Much land has been cleared for farming. Gambia is rich in wildlife. **History** Portuguese mariners reached Gambia's coast in 1455 when the area was part of the Mali empire. In the 16th century, Portuguese and English slave traders operated in the area. In 1664 the British established a settlement and later founded a colony, Senegambia (1765), which included parts of present-day Gambia and Senegal. In 1783 this was handed over to France. In 1816 Britain founded Bathurst (now Banjul) as a base for its anti-slavery operations. The Gambia became a British colony in 1888 and remained under British rule until it achieved full independence in 1965. **Politics** In 1970 The Gambia became a republic. In 1981 an attempted coup was defeated with the help of Senegalese troops. In 1982 The Gambia and Senegal set up a defense alliance, the Confederation of Senegambia, but this ended in 1989. In July 1994 a military group led by Yahyah Jammeh overthrew the president, Sir Dawda Jawara. In 1996 Jammeh was elected president, and in 1997 legislative elections his Patriotic Alliance for Reorientation and Construction (PARC) was victorious. **Economy** Agriculture employs more than 80% of the workforce. The main food crops are cassava, millet, and sorghum; groundnuts are the leading export. Tourism is becoming important.

**gamete** Reproductive sex cell that joins with another sex cell to form a new organism. Female gametes (ova) are usually motionless; male gametes (sperm) often have a tail (flagellum) enabling them to swim to ova. All gametes are HAPLOID.

**game theory** In mathematics, the analysis of problems involving conflict. Its application includes problems in business management, sociology, economics, and military strategy. The theory was first introduced by Émile Borel and developed by John VON NEUMANN in 1928.

**gametophyte** Generation of plants and algae that bears the female and male GAMETES. In flowering plants these are the germinated pollen grains (male) and the embryo sac (female) inside the ovule. *See also* ALTERNATION OF GENERATIONS; FERN

**gamma radiation** Form of very short wavelength ELECTROMAGNETIC RADIATION emitted from the nuclei of some radioactive atoms. High-energy gamma rays have even greater powers of penetration than X-RAYS They are used in medicine to attack cancer cells and in the food industry to kill microorganisms. *See also* RADIOACTIVITY

**Gamow, George** (1904–68) US nuclear physicist, b. Russia. He developed the BIG BANG theory, helped decipher the genetic code, developed the quantum theory of radioactivity, and proposed the liquid-drop model of atomic nuclei. With Edward TELLER, he established the Gamow-Teller theory of beta decay.

**Gandhi, Indira** (1917–84) Indian stateswoman, prime minister (1966–77, 1980–84). The daughter of Jawaharlal NEHRU, she served as president of the Indian National CONGRESS PARTY (1959–60), becoming prime minister in 1966. In 1975, amid growing social disturbance, she was found guilty of breaking electoral rules in her 1971 reelection. She refused to resign, invoked emergency powers, and imprisoned many opponents. When elections took place in 1977, the Congress Party suffered a heavy defeat, which split the party. In 1980, leading a faction of the Congress Party, she returned to power. In 1984, after authorizing the use of force against Sikh dissidents in the Golden Temple at Amritsar, she was killed by a Sikh bodyguard.

**Gandhi, "Mahatma" (Mohandas Karamchand)** (1869–1948) Indian political and spiritual leader who led the nationalist movement (1919–47). A lawyer, he practiced in South Africa (1893–1914), where he led equal-rights campaigns, before returning to his native India. Following the massacre at AMRITSAR (1919), he launched a policy of nonviolent noncooperation with the British. Resistance methods included strikes, refusal to pay taxes, and refusal to respect colonial law, such as the famous 250mi (400km) protest march against a salt tax (1930). He also strove to raise the status of lower CASTES. After frequent imprisonments, he saw India gain independence in 1947. A figure of huge international and moral stature, he was assassinated by a religious fanatic in Delhi.

**Gandhi, Rajiv** (1944–91) Indian statesman, prime minister (1984–89). The elder son of Indira GANDHI, Rajiv Gandhi was a pilot before reluctantly entering politics. He became prime minister after his mother's assassination. He worked to placate India's Sikh extremists, but his reputation was tarnished by a bribery scandal. Defeated in the 1989 election, Gandhi was assassinated campaigning for reelection in 1991.

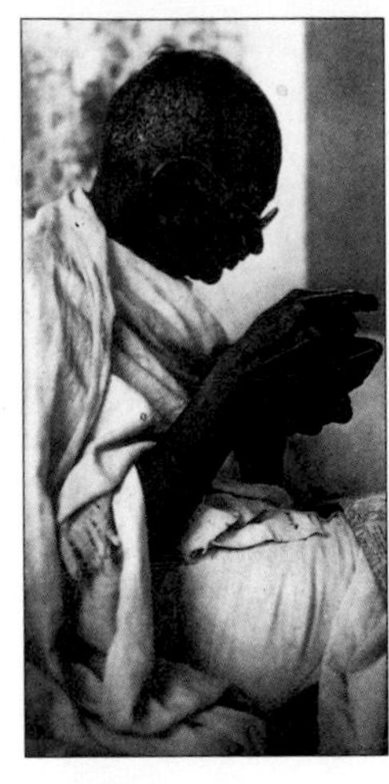

▲ **Gandhi** After years of non-violent campaigns against the British, Gandhi finally realized his dream of witnessing the creation of an independent India in May 1947. Having won this great victory for democracy, he was pained to see growing division between the Hindu and Muslim populations of India.

▲ **Ganges** The Ganges River holds great religious significance for the world's Hindu population. Certain points along the river, known as *tirath*, are holy places where bathing festivals (*mela*) occur annually. The best-known *tirath* are at Varanasi, Allahabad, and Hardwar.

**Ganges** (Ganga) River of N India. It rises in the Himalayas, then flows SE and empties into the Bay of Bengal through the Brahmaputra–Ganges delta. The plains of the Ganges are extremely fertile and support one of the world's most densely populated areas. In Hinduism, it is the earthly form of the Goddess Ganga and pilgrims purify themselves in its waters. Length: 1,560mi (2,512km).

**ganglion** Cluster of nervous tissue containing cell bodies and SYNAPSES, usually enclosed in a fibrous sheath. In a VERTEBRATE, most ganglia occur outside the CENTRAL NERVOUS SYSTEM.

**Gang of Four** Radical faction that tried to seize power in China after the death of MAO ZEDONG. In 1976 both Chairman MAO and Prime Minister ZHOU ENLAI died, leaving a power vacuum. The Gang of Four, Zhang Chunjao, Wang Hungwen, Yao Wenyuan, and their leader JIANG QING (Mao's widow), tried to launch a military coup but were arrested for treason by premier HUA GUOFENG and sentenced to life imprisonment.

**gannet** Diving seabird related to the tropical booby. Gannets are heavy-bodied with tapering bills, long pointed wings, and webbed feet. Their plumage is white with black wing tips. They nest in huge colonies on rocky islands. Length: 25–40in (63–100cm). Family Sulidae.

**Gansu** (Kansu) Province in NW central China, bordered E by Inner Mongolia; the capital is Lanzhou. The region became Chinese territory in the 3rd century BC. Wheat, cotton, rice, corn, and tobacco are grown under irrigation. Mineral deposits include iron ore, oil, and coal. Area: 141,550sq mi (366,625sq km). Pop. (1990) 22,930,000.

**Ganymede** Largest of Jupiter's GALILEAN SATELLITES, with a diameter of 3,270mi (5,262km). Its cratered terrain is covered with grooves suggesting geological activity.

**gar** Primitive freshwater bony fish found in shallow waters of North America. Its cylindrical body is covered with diamond-shaped plates. Length: to 10ft (300cm); Weight: to 300lb (135kg). Family Lepisosteidae.

**Garbo, Greta** (1905–90) Swedish film actress. Garbo's aura of mystery and enigmatic beauty made her an adored screen idol. Her first lead role was in *Torrent* (1926). Her first "talkie" was *Anna Christie* (1930). She played the lead in the classic *Camille* (1937). She retired in 1941.

**García Lorca, Federico** *See* LORCA, FEDERICO GARCÍA

**García Márquez, Gabriel** (1928– ) Colombian novelist. His popular novel *One Hundred Years of Solitude* (1967) achieves a unique combination of realism, lyricism, and mythical fantasy, making it a central text of MAGIC REALISM. Later works include *The Autumn of the Patriarch* (1975) and *Love in the Time of Cholera* (1985). He was awarded the 1982 Nobel Prize for literature.

**Garda, Lake** Largest lake in Italy, forming the border between Lombardy and Venetia. It has many tourist resorts along its shoreline. Area: 143sq mi (370sq km)

▲ **gannet** The Atlantic gannet (*Sula bassana*) is found in some coastal regions of N Europe and E North America. It grows to a length of 40in (100cm).Gannets spot their prey of surface-swimming fish from the air before dropping in a near-vertical dive to catch the fish. They snatch and swallow the prey before reemerging.

**gardenia** Genus of more than 60 species of evergreen shrubs and small trees, native to tropical and subtropical Asia and Africa. They have white or yellow fragrant, waxy flowers. Height: to 18ft (5.5m). Family Rubiaceae.

**Gardner, Erle Stanley** (1889–1970) US writer, creator of the detective lawyer Perry Mason. He wrote 80 novels featuring Perry Mason, the first of which was *The Case of the Velvet Claws* (1933).

**Garfield, James Abram** (1831–81) 20th US President (1881). He served in the Civil War until 1863, when he was elected to the House of Representatives. He became the Republican leader of the house in 1876. The 1880 Republican convention was deadlocked and, on the 36th ballot, he became the compromise presidential candidate. His four-month administration was characterized by party squabbles over federal jobs and political patronage. He was assassinated on July 2, 1881 and was succeeded by vice president Chester A. ARTHUR.

**Garibaldi, Giuseppe** (1807–82) Italian patriot and guerrilla leader who helped to bring about Italian unification. Influenced by MAZZINI, he participated in a republican rising in 1834, subsequently fleeing to South America. Returning in 1848, he defended the Roman Republic against the French. In 1860 he led his 1,000-strong band of "Red Shirts" against the Kingdom of the Two Sicilies, a dramatic episode in the RISORGIMENTO. He handed his conquests over to King VICTOR EMMANUEL II and they were incorporated into the new kingdom of Italy.

**Garland, Judy** (1922–69) US singer and film actress, b. Frances Gumm. Her performance as Dorothy in *The Wizard of Oz* (1939) made her a worldwide star. Other films include *Meet Me in St. Louis* (1944), *Easter Parade* (1948), and *A Star is Born* (1954).

**garlic** Bulbous herb native to S Europe and central Asia. It has onionlike foliage and a bulb made up of cloves, used for flavoring. It is also claimed to have medicinal properties. Family Liliaceae; species *Allium sativum*.

**Garner, John Nance** (1868–1967) US statesman, vice president (1933–41). He was a Texas legislator (1898–1902) and US Congressman (1903–33), serving as Speaker of the House (1931–33). Vice president under Franklin D. ROOSEVELT, he helped obtain passage of NEW DEAL legislation. He retired in 1941, after refusing to run as as vice president for Roosevelt's third term.

**garnet** Two series of orthosilicate minerals found in metamorphic rocks and pegmatites. Some varieties are important as gemstones. Hardness 6.5–7.5; sp.gr. 4.

**Garrick, David** (1717–79) English actor, theater manager, and dramatist. He is credited with replacing the formal declamatory style of acting with easy, natural speech.

**Garrison, William Lloyd** (1805–79) US abolitionist. In 1831 he started the *Liberator* in Boston, an influential journal in the antislavery movement. After the Civil War (1861–65), he concentrated on other reforms, including temperance and women's suffrage.

**garter snake** Nonvenomous SNAKE, native to North and Central America. They are usually olive-brown with yellow, orange, red, or blue stripes often spotted with black. They feed on frogs, insects, and earthworms. Length: to 24in (60cm). Family Colubridae; genus *Thamnophis*.

**Garvey, Marcus** (1887–1940) US black nationalist leader, b. Jamaica. In 1914 he founded the Universal Negro Improvement Association (UNIA) designed to "promote the spirit of race pride." Garvey believed that black people could not achieve equality within white-dominated Western countries, and created a "back-to-Africa" movement. He established the Black Star Line shipping company as a means of transporting black people back to Africa. By the 1920s, Garvey was the most influential black leader in the US, via his *Negro World* newspaper. In 1922 the Black Star Line and the UNIA collapsed. Garvey was convicted of fraud, jailed (1925), was pardoned (1927) by President Coolidge, and deported to Jamaica (1927). RASTAFARIANISM is influenced by his philosophy.

**gas** State of MATTER in which molecules are free to move in any direction; a gas spreads by DIFFUSION to fill a container of any size. Because of their low densities, most gases are poor conductors of heat and electricity. When cooled, gases become liquids. Some, such as carbon dioxide, can be liquefied by pressure alone. All gases follow certain laws, such as Avogadro's law, BOYLE'S LAW, CHARLES' LAW, Graham's law, and ideal gas laws. *See also* LIQUID; PLASMA; SOLID

**Gascony** Former province in SW France, bounded by the PYRENEES (S) and the Bay of BISCAY (W). Part of Roman Gaul, it was later overrun by the Visigoths and the Franks. In the 6th century it was conquered by the Vascones. It passed to Aquitaine in the 11th century. From 1154 to 1453 it was ruled by England. After the HUNDRED YEARS WAR, it was finally united to the French crown in the 16th century by HENRY IV.

**gas exchange** In biology, the uptake and output of gases, especially oxygen and carbon dioxide, by living organisms. In animals and other organisms that obtain their energy by AEROBIC respiration, gas exchange involves the uptake of oxygen and the output of carbon dioxide. In plants, algae, and bacteria that carry out PHOTOSYNTHESIS, the opposite may occur, with a carbon dioxide uptake and oxygen output. At the cellular level, gas exchange takes place by DIFFUSION across cell MEMBRANES in solution. *See also* BREATHING; CIRCULATORY SYSTEM; RESPIRATION; RESPIRATORY SYSTEM; VENTILATION

**Gaskell, Elizabeth Cleghorn** (1810–65) British writer. She explored the problems of the industrial poor in her novels *Mary Barton* (1848) and *North and South* (1855). Other works include *Cranford* (1853), and *Wives and Daughters* (1866).

**gasoline** *See* PETROLEUM

**Gasperi, Alcide de** (1881–1954) Italian statesman. He was elected to the Austro-Hungarian parliament in 1911, and in 1921 entered the Italian parliament as a founder of the Italian People's Party. A strong opponent of fascism, he was imprisoned during Mussolini's regime. During World War II, he was active in the resistance and helped to create the Christian Democratic Party. As prime minister (1945–1953), he contributed greatly to his country's postwar recovery.

**Gassendi, Pierre** (1592–1655) French physicist and astronomer. He championed atomic theory and thus sought to discredit the theories of earlier philosophers such as Aristotle. His writings summarized the state of science at his time and criticized the views of DESCARTES and other contemporaries.

**gastric juice** Fluid comprising a mixture of substances, including PEPSIN and hydrochloric acid, secreted by GLANDS of the stomach. Its principal function is to break down proteins into polypeptides during DIGESTION.

**gastroenteritis** Inflammation of the stomach and intestines causing abdominal pain, diarrhea, and vomiting. Severe cases can cause dehydration.

**gastropod** Class of MOLLUSKS, which includes the SNAIL, SLUG, WHELK, LIMPET, ABALONE, and SEA SLUG. Many possess a single spiral shell that has been produced by chemical precipitation from the mantle. Many types of gastropods live immersed in seawater, breathing through gills. Some freshwater snails, however, breathe through lungs and need to surface periodically for air. Sea slugs are entirely without shells.

**gas warfare** *See* CHEMICAL WARFARE

**Gates, Bill (William Henry)** (1955– ) US businessman. In 1975 he cofounded Microsoft Corporation, which in the 1980s became the dominant computer SOFTWARE producer. He is noted for his innovative thinking and aggressive marketing and business tactics.

**Gates, Horatio** (1727–1806) US general, b. England. He served in the British army with General Edward Braddock in the French and Indian Wars, before immigrating to Virginia in 1772 and joining the colonists' cause in the AMERICAN REVOLUTION. In 1776 he became commander of the army in the N and defeated the British at the battle at Saratoga (1777). He lost his command after his defeat at Camden, South Carolina (1780).

**gatling gun** Early MACHINE GUN invented in 1862 by US inventor Richard Gatling. Adopted by the US Army in 1866, it had several barrels mounted in a cylinder that was rotated by a crank so that each barrel fired in turn.

**GATT** Acronym for the GENERAL AGREEMENT ON TARIFFS AND TRADE

**gaucho** Colorful COWBOY of the Argentine and Uruguayan grasslands. Originally nomadic, the gauchos became farmhands and superb horse soldiers. They were an important political force in the 18th and 19th centuries.

**Gaudi, Antonio** (1852–1926) Spanish architect, He employs bizarre sculptural forms, and is often associated with ART NOUVEAU. Examples include the Palau Guell (1885–89), the Caso Battlo (1905–07), and the unfinished church of the Sagrada Familia, all in Barcelona.

**Gaudier-Brzeska, Henri** (1891–1915) French sculptor, who lived in England from 1911. A friend of Ezra POUND, he was part of the VORTICISM movement. Two of his best-known works are *The Dancer* and *Bird Swallowing Fish*. He was killed in World War I.

**Gauguin, Eugène Henri Paul** (1848–1903) French painter. He reacted against the realism of IMPRESSIONISM. His belief that form and pattern should represent mental images influenced SYMBOLISM. In 1891 he left France for Tahiti. He developed his own "synthetist" style, which was characterized by bold contours and large areas of unmodulated color. His paintings, often of South Sea islanders, convey a sense of mystery and myth. His masterpiece is *Where do we come from? What are we? Where are we going?* (1897).

**Gaul** Ancient Roman name for the region roughly equivalent to modern France, Belgium, N Italy, and Germany W of the Rhine. Most of Gaul, which was inhabited by Celts, was conquered (58–51 BC) in the GALLIC WARS. From the 3rd century, it was under attack by Germanic tribes who settled in N Gaul.

**Gaultier, Jean-Paul** (1952– ) French fashion designer. He joined Pierre Cardin at 18 before launching his own collections in 1977. His designs reveal a sense of humor, mixing textures and cuts with unconventional features and accessories for women and men.

**Gaur** Ancient, ruined city in NE India. The Hindu capital of Bengal, the town was captured by Muslims, and served as a center of Muslim government and culture (1200–late 16th century). It is the site of the Kadam Rasul Mosque (1530), the Golden Mosque, and Bara Sona Mosjid.

**gaur** (seladang) Species of wild cattle found in forested hilly country in India and Malaysia. Gaurs are dark brown in color with a white "sock" on each leg. Length: up to 12.4ft (3.8m) long. Family Bovidae; species *Bos gaurus*.

**Gauss, Karl Friedrich** (1777–1855) German mathematician and physicist. He studied electricity and magnetism. The unit of magnetic flux density is named for him.

**Gauteng** Province in N central South Africa; the capital is JOHANNESBURG. Formed in 1994 from the TRANSVAAL as PWV (PRETORIA-WITWATERSRAND-Vereeniging), the province was renamed Gauteng in 1995. It is South Africa's smallest but most populous province. Area: 7,260sq mi (18,810sq km). Pop. (1995 est.) 7,048,300.

**Gautier, Théophile** (1811–72) French poet, novelist, and critic. His poems, such as *Albertus* (1833), *España* (1845), and *Enamels and Cameos* (1852), exhibit the formalist aesthetic theory of art that influenced SYMBOLISM.

**gavial** Crocodilian native to N India. It has a long, narrow snout, an olive or brownish back, and a lighter belly. Length: to 15.4ft (5m). Family Gavialidae; species *Gavialis gangeticus*.

**Gay, John** (1685–1732) English poet and dramatist. His best-known work is the ballad-opera *The Beggar's Opera* (1728), a political satire and burlesque of Italian opera. Other works include the poem *Trivia*.

**Gaya** City on the Phalgu River, Bihar state, NE India. It is a pilgrimage center sacred to both Hindus and Buddhists. Buddha received enlightenment nearby. It is the seat of Magadha University (1962). Pop. (1991) 292,000.

**Gaye, Marvin** (1939–84) US singer-songwriter. Gaye was an influential singer throughout his recording life, from the number one gold single "I Heard It Through The Grapevine" (1968), through the best-selling album *What's Going On*, to his Grammy award-winning *Sexual Healing* (1982). His father shot him during an argument.

▲ **Gaudi** The *Sagrada Familia* (Holy Family) cathedral in Barcelona is a fine example of the Spanish architect Antonio Gaudi's extraordinary style. The cathedral, although started in 1883, remains unfinished. Gaudi's plans reveal a vast central spire, surrounded by 12 smaller spires (four are visible here). The building represents Christ surrounded by his 12 disciples. Funding for the church is still uncertain, and there is no definite completion date.

▲ **gazelle** The Thomson's gazelle (*Gazella thomsoni*) inhabits the savanna of East Africa. Its relatively small size and unremarkable coloring makes it less attractive to poachers and hunters than other African herbivores, and for this reason there exist large populations. The males' long, elegant horns are more often used for stylized, display fighting, but serious disputes do occur, often resulting in significant injury.

G

**Gay-Lussac, Joseph Louis** (1778–1850) French chemist and physicist. He discovered the law of combining gas volumes (Gay-Lussac's Law) and the law of gas expansion, often attributed to J.A.C. CHARLES.

**Gaza Strip** Strip of territory in SW Israel, bordering on the SE Mediterranean Sea. The settlement following the ARAB-ISRAELI WAR (1948–49) made it an Egyptian possession. It subsequently served as a Palestinian Arab refugee center. Occupied by Israel from 1967, it was the scene of the INTIFADA against Israel in 1988. In 1994, under a peace agreement, its administration was taken over by the Palestinian National Authority. Area: 140sq mi (363sq km). Pop. (1994) 724,500.

**gazelle** Any of several species of graceful, small to medium antelopes native to Africa and Asia, often inhabiting plains. Most are light brown with a white rump and horns. Family Bovidae; genus *Gazella*.

**Gdańsk** (Danzig) City and seaport on the Gulf of Gdańsk, N Poland; capital of Gdańsk county. Settled by Slavs in the 10th century, it was a member of the HANSEATIC LEAGUE. It was taken by Poland in the 15th century but passed to Prussia in 1793. The Treaty of VERSAILLES (1919) established Gdańsk as a free city, and annexation by Germany in 1939 precipitated World War II. In the 1980s its shipyards became a focus of opposition to Poland's communist rulers. Industries: metallurgy, chemicals, machinery, timber. Pop. (1993) 466,500.

**gear** Wheel, usually toothed, attached to a rotating shaft. The teeth of one gear engage those of another in order to transmit and modify speed of rotation and TORQUE.

**gecko** Any of about 650 species of LIZARDS, native to warm regions of the world. They owe their remarkable climbing ability to minute hooks on their feet. Length: 1–6in (3–15cm). Family Gekkonidae.

**Gehrig, (Henry) Lou (Louis)** (1903–41) US baseball player. He played for the New York Yankees (1925–39) and established a record by playing in 2,130 consecutive games. He had a lifetime batting average of .340 and hit 493 home runs. He contracted Amyotrophic Lateral Sclerosis (ALS), a degenerative muscular disease that became known as "Lou Gehrig's disease." He was elected to the Baseball Hall of Fame in 1939.

**Geiger, Hans Wilhelm** (1882–1945) German physicist who, with Ernest RUTHERFORD, devised the GEIGER COUNTER (1908). In 1909 Geiger and Ernest Marsden studied the deflection of alpha particles by thin metal foil, providing the basis of Rutherford's discovery of the atomic nucleus.

**Geiger counter** (Geiger-Müller counter) Instrument used to detect and measure the strength of radiation by counting the number of ionized particles produced.

**gel** Homogeneous mass consisting of minute particles dispersed in a liquid to form a fine network throughout the mass. A gel's appearance can be elastic or jellylike, as in GELATIN, or quite rigid and solid, as in silica gel.

**gelatin** Colorless or yellowish protein obtained from COLLAGEN in animal cartilages and bones. It is used in film emulsions, capsules for medicines, as a culture medium for bacteria, and in foodstuffs such as jellies.

**Gell-Mann, Murray** (1929– ) US theoretical physicist. He was awarded the 1969 Nobel Prize for physics for his application of group theory to ELEMENTARY PARTICLES, which led to the prediction of the QUARK as the basic constituent of the BARYON and MESON. His theory also predicted the existence of a baryon called the omega-minus particle, subsequently discovered in 1964.

► **gecko** The banded gecko (*Coleonyx variegatus*) is one of a great many species of gecko inhabiting desert regions. It is nocturnal, hiding under rocks during the day and foraging for insects at night.

**gem** Any of about 100 minerals valued for their beauty, rarity, and durability. Transparent stones, such as DIAMOND, RUBY and EMERALD are the most highly valued. PEARL, AMBER, and CORAL are gems of organic origin.

**gemeinschaft** In sociology, concept formulated by Ferdinand Toennies in 1887, denoting social systems based on spontaneous, small-group, face-to-face relationships. The family is often called Gemeinschaftlike.

**Gemini** (the Twins) Northern constellation, situated on the ecliptic between Taurus and Cancer. Its brightest stars are Castor (Alpha Geminorum) and Pollux (Beta Geminorum).

**gemma** In botany and zoology, a bud that will give rise to a new individual. The term also refers to a multicellular reproductive structure found in algae and mosses.

**gender** Any of several categories into which nouns and pronouns can be divided for grammatical purposes. In some languages, adjectives or verbs may take different forms to agree with the different genders. A three-gender system, with categories labeled masculine, feminine, and neuter, exists in such languages as German and Russian, while a two-gender system, with masculine and feminine, operates in such languages as French and Welsh.

**gene** Unit by which hereditary characteristics are passed on from one generation to another in plants and animals. A gene is a length of DNA that codes for a particular protein or peptide. Genes are usually found along the CHROMOSOMES. In most cell nuclei, genes occur in pairs, one located on each of a chromosome pair. Where different forms of a gene (ALLELES) are present in a population, some forms may be recessive to others and will not be expressed unless present on both members of a chromosome pair. *See also* GENETIC CODE; GENETIC ENGINEERING

**gene bank** Genetic material kept for possible future use. Material stored includes bacteria and molds; seeds, spores, and tubers; frozen sperm, eggs, and embryos; and even live animals and plants. The material can be used in plant and animal BREEDING, GENETIC ENGINEERING, and in medicine. Live species are used for restocking natural habitats in which species are in danger of EXTINCTION.

**General Agreement on Tariffs and Trade (GATT)** United Nations agency of international trade, subsumed into the new WORLD TRADE ORGANIZATION in 1995. Founded in 1948, GATT was designed to prevent "tariff wars" (the retaliatory escalation of tariffs) and to work toward the reduction of tariff levels. Most noncommunist states were party to GATT.

**general strike** Stoppage of work by all or most workers simultaneously. In the US, they have taken place only rarely on a local level, but in Europe, they have been a powerful means of protest.

**generator** Device for producing electrical energy. The most common is a machine that converts the mechanical energy of a turbine or internal combustion engine into electricity by employing ELECTROMAGNETIC INDUCTION. There are two types of generators: alternating current (an alternator) and direct current (a dynamo). Each has an armature (or ring) that rotates within a magnetic field creating an induced ELECTRIC CURRENT.

**gene replacement therapy (GRT)** Method of treating hereditary disorders that employs GENETIC ENGINEERING. Affected cells are removed from the patient and their faulty DNA repaired. The repaired cells are then reintroduced into the patient's body. GRT shows most promise with inherited blood disorders (such as SICKLE-CELL ANEMIA), and has been successfully carried out on animals.

**Genesis** First book of the OLD TESTAMENT and of the PENTATEUCH or TORAH. It relates the creation of the universe, from ADAM and EVE to ABRAHAM, and from Abraham to JOSEPH, and the descent into Egypt.

**Genet, Jean** (1910–86) French dramatist and novelist. In works such as the novel *Notre Dame des Fleurs* (1944) and *Journal du Voleur* (1949) he records his experiences as a homosexual in brothels and prisons. A leading exponent of the dramatic theories of the Theater of the ABSURD, he employed elements of the fantastical and the bizarre in his work.

**genet** Cat-like carnivore of the CIVET family, native to W Europe and S and E Africa. Solitary and nocturnal, genets have slender bodies, gray to brown spotted fur, and banded tails. Length: body to 22in (58cm); tail to 21in (53cm); weight: to 4.4lb (2kg). Family Viverridae; genus *Genetta*.

**genetic code** Arrangement of information stored in GENES. It is the ultimate basis of HEREDITY and forms a blueprint for the entire organism. The genetic code is based on the genes that are present, which, in molecular terms, depends on the arrangement of nucleotides in the long molecules of DNA in the cell CHROMOSOMES. Each group of three nucleotides specifies, or codes, for an amino acid, or for an action such as start or stop. By specifying which PROTEINS to make and in what quantities, the genetic code directly controls production of structural materials. It also codes for ENZYMES, which regulate all the chemical reactions in the cell, thus indirectly coding for the production of other cell materials as well.

**genetic engineering** Construction of a DNA molecule containing a desired GENE. The gene is then introduced into a bacterial, fungal, plant, or mammalian cell, so that the cell produces the desired protein. It has been used to produce substances such as human growth hormone, insulin, and enzymes for biological washing powder.

**genetic fingerprinting** Forensic technique that uses genetic material, specifically the DNA within sample body cells, to identify individuals. It is used in paternity suits to detect the true father of a child and sometimes in rape cases. The technique's first use in a court of law was in the late 1980s.

**genetics** Study of HEREDITY. Geneticists study how the characteristics of an individual organism depend on its GENES, how the characteristics are passed down to the next generation, and how changes may occur through MUTATION. A person's behavior, learning ability, and physiology may be explained partly by genetics, although the person's environment also has a considerable influence.

**Geneva** City at the S end of Lake Geneva, SW Switzerland. A Roman town, it was taken by the Franks in the 6th century and passed to the HOLY ROMAN EMPIRE in the 12th century. During the REFORMATION, it became the center of PROTESTANTISM under John CALVIN. It joined the Swiss Confederation in 1814. It was the seat of the LEAGUE OF NATIONS (1919–46), and is the headquarters of the Red Cross and the World Health Organization. Industries: banking, watchmaking and jewelry, precision instruments, tourism. Pop. (1992) 169,600.

**Geneva, Lake** (Lac de Genéve, Lac Léman) Lake in SW Switzerland and E France. Crescent-shaped, it lies between the ALPS and the JURA MOUNTAINS. Its S shore forms part of the French–Swiss border. It is drained to the W by the Rhône River. Length: 45mi (72km). Width: up to 9mi (14km). Area: 224sq mi (580sq km).

**Geneva convention** Series of agreements, beginning 1864, on the treatment of wounded soldiers and prisoners during war, and on the neutrality of the medical services.

**Genghis Khan** (1167–1227) Conqueror and founder of the MONGOL empire. He united the Mongol tribes in 1206 and demonstrated his military genius by capturing Peking (1215), annexing Iran, and invading Russia as far as Moscow. He ruled over the largest empire ever known. The empire was divided and expanded by his sons.

**Genoa** (Genova) Seaport on the Gulf of Genoa, NW Italy; capital of Liguria region. A trading power during the Middle Ages, its fortunes declined in the 15th century and it came under foreign control. It has a university (1471) and an Academy of Fine Arts (1751). Industries: oil refining, motor vehicles, textiles, chemicals, paper, shipbuilding. Pop. (1992) 667,563.

**genocide** Policy aimed at destroying a racial, religious, or ethnic group. The Nazi extermination of Jews during WORLD WAR II is an example of genocide.

**genome** Entire complement of genetic material carried within the CHROMOSOMES of a single cell. In effect, a genome carries all the genetic information about an individual; it is coded in sequence by the DNA that makes up the chromosomes. The term has also been applied to the whole range of GENES in a particular species.

**genotype** Genetic makeup of an individual. The particular set of GENES present in each cell of an organism is distinct from the PHENOTYPE, the observable characteristics of the organism.

**genre painting** Art term used to define paintings that portray scenes of everyday life. It appeared in the late 18th century to define the small paintings of household interiors popularized by 17th-century Dutch artists.

**Gentile da Fabriano** (1370–1427) Italian painter. A leader of the International Gothic style, he greatly influenced Florentine art with frescoes and the *Adoration of the Magi* (1423) for the Church of Santa Trinita, Florence.

**Gentlemen's Agreement** (1907) Agreement between the US and Japan to restrict Japanese emigration. The US agreed not to pass a law preventing immigration, and in return Japan voluntarily withheld passports from Japanese laborers coming to the US, except those with prior domiciles, a parent, spouse, or child in the US. It was later replaced by the Immigration Bill of 1924.

**genus** Group of closely related biological SPECIES with common characteristics. The genus name is usually a Latin or Greek noun. *See also* TAXONOMY

**geochemistry** Study of the chemical composition of the Earth and the changes that have resulted in it from chemical and physical processes.

**geodesic dome** Architectural structure of plastic and metal, based upon triangular or polygonal facets. They were originated (1947) by R. Buckminster FULLER.

**geodesic surveying** Method of surveying that covers areas large enough to involve consideration of the Earth's curvature. Geodesic surveying is used to establish features such as national boundaries and for mapping whole states or countries.

**Geoffrey of Monmouth** (1100–54) Welsh priest and chronicler, best known for his *History of the Kings of Britain*. Though accepted as reliable until the 17th century, Geoffrey essentially told folk tales. His book was the chief source for the legend of King ARTHUR, and it was Shakespeare's source for *King Lear* and *Cymbeline*.

**geography** Science studying the physical nature of the Earth and people's relationship to it. It includes land masses and features, seas, climate, and population.

**geological time** Time scale of the history of Earth. Until recently, only methods of relative dating were possible by studying the correlation of rock formations and fossils. The largest divisions of geological time are called eras, each of

**GENE REPLACEMENT THERAPY (GRT)**

GRT is used to treat severe combined immunodeficiency (SCID), where the gene responsible for production of the enzyme adenosine deaminase (ADA) is missing. As ADA is essential for white blood cell production, this renders the body open to infection. Two retroviruses (1) are introduced into the bone marrow. These have the ability to produce RNA from their DNA (2) using a reverse transcriptase enzyme (3). This DNA is then incorporated into the human chromosomes (4). When these chromosomes multiply, new viral RNA and viral proteins as well as ADA are produced (5). The first two produce more new viruses, while the ADA is used by the body to produce vital white blood cells. The process then repeats and spreads throughout the bone marrow.

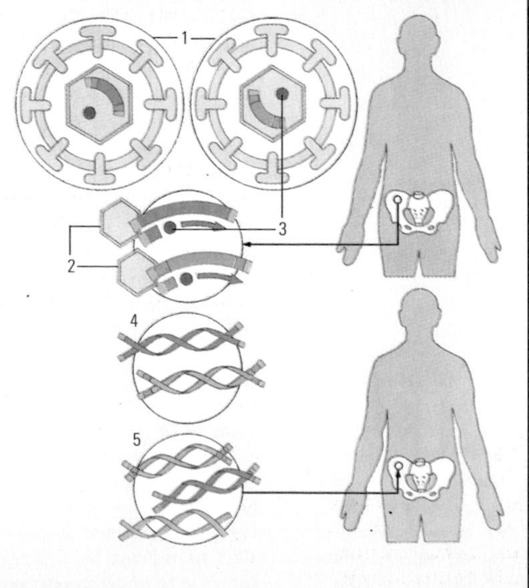

► **geological time** The 4.6 billion years since the formation of the Earth are divided into four great eras, which are further split into periods and, in the case of the most recent era, epochs. The present era is the Cenozoic ("new life"), extending backward through "middle life" and "ancient life" to the Pre-Cambrian. Although traces of ancient life have since been found, it was largely the proliferation of fossils from the beginning of the Paleozoic era onward some 570 million years ago, which first allowed precise subdivisions to be made.

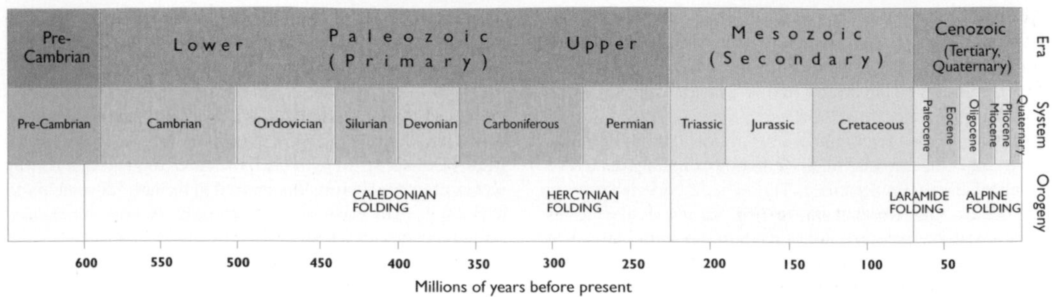


which is broken down into periods, which, in turn, are subdivided into series or epochs.

**geology** Study of the materials of the Earth, their origin, arrangement, classification, change, and history. Geology is divided into several categories, the major ones being mineralogy (arrangement of minerals), petrology (rocks and their combination of minerals), stratigraphy (succession of rocks in layers), paleontology (study of fossilized remains), geomorphology (study of landforms), structural geology (classification of rocks and the forces that produced them), and environmental geology (study of use of the environment).

**geomagnetism** Physical properties of the Earth's magnetic field. Geomagnetism is thought to be caused by the metallic composition of the Earth's core. The gradual movements of magnetic north result from currents within the MANTLE.

**geometric mean** The geometric mean of $n$ numbers is the $n$th root of their product. For example, the geometric mean of 8 and 2 is $\sqrt{(8\times2)} = 4$.

**geometry** Branch of mathematics concerned with shapes. **Euclidean** geometry deals with simple plane and solid figures. **Analytic** geometry (coordinate geometry), introduced by DESCARTES (1637), applies algebra to geometry and allows the study of more complex curves. **Projective** geometry, introduced by Jean-Victor Poncelet (1822), is concerned with projection of shapes and with properties that are independent of such changes. More abstraction occurred in the early 19th century with formulations of **non-Euclidean** geometry by Janos Bolyai and N. I. Lobachevsky, and **differential** geometry, based on the application of calculus. *See also* TOPOLOGY

**geophysics** Study of the characteristic physical properties of the Earth as a whole system. It uses CHEMISTRY, GEOLOGY, ASTRONOMY, SEISMOLOGY, METEOROLOGY, and many other disciplines. From the study of seismic waves, geophysicists have deduced the Earth's interior structure.

**George, Saint** (active 3rd–4th century) Early Christian martyr who became patron saint of England in the late Middle Ages. Many stories grew up about him, including the 12th-century tale of his killing a dragon to save a maiden. His feast day is April 23.

**George I** (1660–1727) King of Great Britain and Ireland (1714–27) and Elector of Hanover (1698–1727). A Protestant, he succeeded Queen Anne as the first Hanoverian monarch. He favored the WHIGS over the Tories, suspecting the latter of JACOBITE sympathies. As king of England, he preferred his native Hanover and spoke little English. As a result, power passed to ministers, especially Sir Robert WALPOLE, and Parliament.

**George II** (1683–1760) King of Great Britain and Ireland and Elector of Hanover (1727–1760). Son of GEORGE I, he too was more German than English. Sir Robert WALPOLE dominated politics early in the reign. George survived a JACOBITE revolt (1745) and was the last British king to lead his army in battle, at Dettingen (1746). British prosperity was growing fast, and George witnessed victories overseas in the SEVEN YEARS WAR.

**George III** (1738–1820) King of Great Britain and Ireland (1760–1820) and King of Hanover (1760–1820). Grandson of GEORGE II, he was the first thoroughly English monarch of his line. His reign saw the loss of the American colonies, wars with France, and the first stages of the Industrial Revolution. In 1765 he suffered his first attack of apparent insanity, now known to be symptoms of porphyria. They grew worse and in 1811 his son, the future GEORGE IV, was made prince regent.

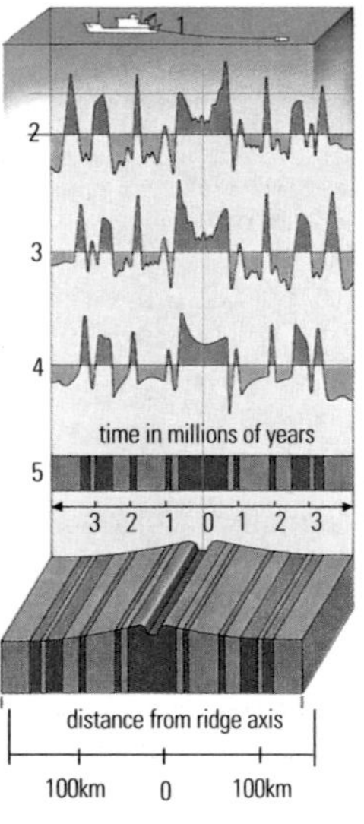


▲ **geomagnetism** A magnetic survey from a research ship (1) sailing back and forth over a mid-oceanic ridge gives readings (2, 3, 4) that indicate that the magnetism of the rocks of the seafloor points alternately N and S in a series of bands parallel to the ridge. The pattern of bands is identical at each side of the axis and corresponds to the pattern of reversals in the Earth's magnetic field for the last few million years (5). The rocks moving away from the axis carry a record of the Earth's magnetic field.

**George IV** (1762–1830) King of Great Britain and Ireland (1820–30). He served as regent for his father, GEORGE III, from 1811, ascending the throne in 1820. Self-indulgent and extravagant, he was bored by government but was a strong patron of the arts. His marriage to Caroline of Brunswick (1795) became a source of scandal and he contracted a legally invalid marriage with Mrs. Fitzherbert in 1785.

**George V** (1865–1936) King of Great Britain and Northern Ireland and Emperor of India (1910–36). The second son of EDWARD VII, he married Princess Mary of Teck in 1893. In 1917 he changed the name of the royal house from the German SAX-COBURG-GOTHA to Windsor.

**George VI** (1895–1952) King of Great Britain and Northern Ireland (1936–52) and Emperor of India (1936–47). He became king when his brother, EDWARD VIII, abdicated. In 1923 he married Lady Elizabeth Bowes-Lyon. He refused to move his family away from London during the BLITZ. In 1949 he became head of the newly formed COMMONWEALTH.

**George I** (1845–1913) King of the Hellenes (1863–1913). Made king by Great Britain, France, and Russia with approval of a Greek national assembly, he backed the constitution of 1864 giving power to an elected parliament. He gained territory for Greece through the BALKAN WARS. He was assassinated in 1913 and was succeeded by his son Constantine I.

**Georgetown** Capital and largest city of Guyana, at the mouth of the Demerara River. Founded in 1781 by the British, it was the capital of the united colonies of Essequibo and Demerara and was known as Stabroek during the brief Dutch occupation from 1784. Renamed Georgetown in 1812 by the British, it is the country's major port. Industries: shipbuilding, food processing, brewing, and rum distilling. Pop. (1985 est.) 200,000.

**Georgetown** *See* PENANG

**Georgia** State on the Atlantic Ocean, N of Florida; the capital is ATLANTA. Other major cities are Columbus, Macon, and Savannah. The Spanish were the first Europeans to arrive in the area. It was first settled by British colonists in 1732. By the end of the 18th century, cotton became the major crop. Georgia was one of the original six states of the Confederacy in the CIVIL WAR. Ravaged by the armies of General SHERMAN in 1864, Georgia was readmitted to the Union in 1870. In the S and E of the state is a broad coastal plain. The central area consists of the Piedmont plateau beyond which, in the N, are the BLUE RIDGE MOUNTAINS and the Appalachian plateau. The area is drained by the Savannah, Ogeechee, and Altamaha rivers. Cotton, once the chief crop, has declined in favor of tobacco, peanuts, livestock, and poultry. Textiles have been a major industry, but chemicals, paper, and timber, and the manufacture of ships, aircraft, and truck bodies are becoming increasingly significant. Area: 58,876sq mi (152,488sq km). Pop. (1996 est.) 7,193,700.

**Georgia** Republic in SE Europe. See country feature.

**Georgian architecture** Building styles in Britain and its colonies (1714–1830). The name derives from the Hanoverian kings who reigned during this period (George I–IV). The various Georgian styles include PALLADIANISM, ROCOCO, NEOCLASSICISM, GOTHIC REVIVAL, and REGENCY STYLE. The English town of BATH has many fine Georgian buildings.

**geostationary orbit** Location of an artificial satellite so that it remains above the same point on a planet's surface. Communications and remote-sensing satellites are often placed in geostationary orbits.

**geothermal energy** Heat contained in the Earth's crust. It is produced by RADIOACTIVITY within the Earth's core and by the movement of tectonic plates. It is released by GEYSERS and VOLCANOES, and can be used as a source for generating electricity. *See also* PLATE TECTONICS

**geranium** (Pelargonium) Genus of 400 perennial plants. They bear pink, purple, or white flowers over a long season. Family Geraniaceae.

**gerbil** Nocturnal rodent native to arid areas of Asia and Africa, and a popular pet. It has long hind legs and tail. Its fur may be fawn, gray, brown, or red. It is a subterranean herbivore and often hoards food. Family Cricetidae.

**geriatrics** Branch of medicine that deals with the problems of the elderly.

**Géricault, (Jean Louis André) Théodore** (1791–1824) French painter. A forerunner of the romantic movement, he began by painting battles. His most famous work, the *Raft of the Medusa* (1817), depicts the survivors of a shipwreck.

**germ** Popular term for any infectious agent. Germs can be bacteria, fungi, or viruses. In biology, it denotes a rudimentary stage in plant growth.

**German** Indo-European language spoken by about 120 million people in Germany, Austria, and Switzerland, and by German communities in other countries. High German (*Hochdeutsch*), of S Germany and Austria, is now the standard dialect. Low German (*Plattdeutsch*) was spoken widely in the N but is now declining.

**German architecture** Architecture of Germany including, in its early days, that of Austria. The earliest surviving buildings date from CHARLEMAGNE. They are in the ROMANESQUE style, at its best in Worms cathedral (built *c*.1180). Romanesque was superseded by GOTHIC, seen in ecclesiastical architecture and provincial buildings such as the *Rathaus* (town hall) typical of NE German towns. There is little RENAISSANCE architecture in Germany, an exception being the rebuilt facade of the *Rathaus* in Bremen. The BAROQUE period extended into the ROCOCO, examples including the elaborate Church of the *Vierzehnheiligen* (1772) by Balthasar Neuman and masterpieces by Fischer von Erlach and Matthaeus Pöppelmann. In the late 1700s NEOCLASSICISM inspired buildings in Berlin and Munich by Friedrich Schinkel, Leo von Klenze, and others. New materials such as cast iron were exploited, as in Vienna's *Dianabad* by Karl Etzel (1843). Walter GROPIUS and the BAUHAUS dominated the beginning of the 20th century. In the 1930s, MIES VAN DER ROHE exemplified the INTERNA-

**GEORGIA**
**Statehood :**
January 2, 1788
**Nickname :**
Empire state of the South
**State bird :**
Brown thrasher
**State flower :**
Cherokee rose
**State tree :**
Live oak
**State motto :**
Wisdom, justice, and moderation

G

## GEORGIA

Georgia's flag was first used between 1917 and 1921. It was readopted when Georgia became independent. The wine-red color represents the good times of the past and the future. The black symbolizes Russian rule and the white represents hope for peace.

**AREA:** 26,910sq mi (69,700sq km)
**POPULATION:** 5,456,000
**CAPITAL (POPULATION):** Tbilisi (1,279,000)
**GOVERNMENT:** Multiparty republic
**ETHNIC GROUPS:** Georgian 70%, Armenian 8%, Russian 6%, Azerbaijani 6%, Ossetes 3%, Greek 2%, Abkhazian 2%, others 3%
**LANGUAGES:** Georgian (official)
**RELIGIONS:** Christianity (Georgian Orthodox 65%, Russian Orthodox 10%, Armenian Orthodox 8%), Islam 11%
**CURRENCY:** Lary

The Transcaucasian republic of Georgia contains two autonomous republics of ABKHAZIA and Ajaria, and the province of Tskhinvali (South Ossetia). It has four geographical areas: the CAUCASUS Mountains form its N border with Russia, and include its highest peak, Mount Kazbek, at 16,541ft (5,042m); the fertile Black Sea coastal plain in the W; the E end of the Pontine Mountains form its S borders with Turkey and Armenia; and a low plateau to the E extends into Azerbaijan. Between the mountains lies the Kura valley and the capital TBILISI.

### CLIMATE

The climate varies from subtropical in the Black Sea lowlands to the permanent snow-covered, alpine Caucasus. Tbilisi has moderate rainfall, hot summers, and cold winters.

### VEGETATION

Forest and shrub cover *c*.50% of Georgia. Alpine meadows lie above the tree line. The coastal plain has apple orchards and orange groves.

### HISTORY

The land of the legendary Golden Fleece, Georgia has a strong national culture and a long literary tradition based on their own language and alphabet. Georgia was an independent kingdom from *c*.4th century BC, and the Georgians formed the two Black Sea states of Colchis and Iberia in *c*.1000 BC. The Persian SASSANIDS ruled during the 3rd and 4th centuries AD. Christianity was introduced in AD 330, and the established church is independent Eastern Orthodox. In the 11th century, independence was won from the Turkish SELJUK empire. The 12th century was Georgia's greatest period of cultural, economic, and military expansion. Thereafter it was divided and in the center of a power struggle between the rival Persian and Turkish empires. In 1555 Georgia was divided between Persia (W) and Turkey (E). In the early 19th century, Georgia was absorbed into the Russian empire.

Despite a brief period of independence after the Russian Revolution, in 1921, Georgia became a constituent republic of the SOVIET UNION. Russia combined Georgia, Armenia, and Azerbaijan into a single republic of TRANSCAUCASIA. This federation was broken up in 1936, and Georgia became a separate Soviet republic. Joseph STALIN, the Soviet Union's second leader, was born in Gori, Georgia.

Following violent demonstrations in 1989, Georgia declared its independence (May 1991). By the end of 1991, President Gamsakhurdia's authoritarian regime had led to civil war in the streets of Tbilisi. In 1992 Eduard SHEVARDNADZE was elected president. Faced by conflict from Gamsakhurdia's supporters and secessionist movements in Abkhazia and South Ossetia, Shevardnadze called in Russian troops to defeat the rebellion.

### POLITICS

In return for Russian support, Georgia joined the COMMONWEALTH OF INDEPENDENT STATES (CIS), and allowed Russia ultimate economic power. Minority demands for secession continued and in 1995 South Ossetia was renamed Tskhinvali and Abkhazia granted autonomous status. Conflict continues in the region and CIS peacekeeping forces are deployed in Abkhazia.

### ECONOMY

Georgia is a developing country (1995 GDP per capita, US$1,470), its economy devastated by civil war and the break-up of the Soviet Union. Agriculture engages 58% of the workforce. The E region is famous for its grapes, used to make wine. The coastal lowlands produce large amounts of tea and tropical fruit, and are a tourist destination. Georgia is rich in minerals, such as barite, coal, and copper. These remain relatively unexploited, though manganese is mined relatively extensively. Georgia has huge potential for generating hydroelectric power, but is desperately short of energy and dependent on Ukraine, Azerbaijan, and Russia for oil.

This flag, adopted by the Federal Republic of Germany (West Germany) in 1949, became the flag of the reunified Germany in 1990. The red, black, and gold colors date back to the Holy Roman Empire. They are associated with the struggle for a united Germany from the 1830s.

**AREA:** 137,803sq mi (356,910sq km)
**POPULATION:** 80,569,000
**CAPITAL (POPULATION):** Berlin (3,446,000)
**GOVERNMENT:** Federal multiparty republic
**ETHNIC GROUPS:** German 93%, Turkish 2%, Yugoslav 1%, Italian 1%, Greek, Polish, Spanish
**LANGUAGES:** German (official)
**RELIGIONS:** Christianity (Protestant, mainly Lutheran 45%, Roman Catholic 37%), Islam 2%
**CURRENCY:** Deutschmark = 100 Pfennige

The Federal Republic of Germany lies in the center of Europe. It is the fifth largest country (by area) in Europe (after Ukraine, France, Spain, and Sweden), but the world's 12th most populous country. Germany can be divided into three geographical regions: the N German plain, central highlands, and the S Central Alps.

The fertile N plain is drained by the rivers ELBE, Weser, and Oder. It includes the industrial centers of HAMBURG, BREMEN, HANOVER, and KIEL. In the E lies the capital, Berlin, and the former East German cities of LEIPZIG, DRESDEN, and MAGDEBURG. NW Germany (especially the RHINE, RUHR, and Saar valleys) is Germany's industrial heartland. It includes the cities of COLOGNE, ESSEN, DORTMUND, DÜSSELDORF, and DUISBURG. The central highlands include the HARZ MOUNTAINS and the cities of MUNICH, FRANKFURT AM MAIN, STUTTGART, NUREMBERG, and AUGSBURG. Southern Germany rises to the Bavarian ALPS on the border with Switzerland and Germany's highest peak, Zugspitze, at 9,721ft (2,963m). The BLACK FOREST, overlooking the Rhine valley, is a major tourist attraction. The region is drained by the DANUBE (Europe's second largest river).

## CLIMATE

Germany has a temperate climate. The NW is warmed by the North Sea. The Baltic lowlands in the NE are cooler. In the S, the climate becomes more continental.

## VEGETATION

The North German plain contains large areas of heath. The forests of central and S Germany include pine, beech, and oak.

## HISTORY

In *c.*2000 BC, German tribes began to displace the Celts. In the 5th century AD, they conquered much of the western Roman empire. In 486 CLOVIS I conquered S and W Germany and THURINGIA. His son CHARLEMAGNE expanded the territory to the Elbe and was crowned emperor (800). His empire rapidly fragmented, and the FEUDAL SYSTEM created powerful local duchies. In 918 HENRY I (THE FOWLER) began a century of SAXON rule, and his son OTTO I (THE GREAT) established the HOLY ROMAN EMPIRE (first *Reich*) (962).

In 1152 FREDERICK I founded the HOHENSTAUFEN dynasty. FREDERICK II's conflict with the papacy created civil war. In 1273 Rudolf I founded the HABSBURG dynasty. City states formed alliances, such as the HANSEATIC LEAGUE. CHARLES V's reign (1519–58) brought religious and civil unrest, such as the REFORMATION and the PEASANTS' WAR. Catholic and Protestant conflict culminated in the devastating THIRTY YEARS WAR (1618–48). The reign of FREDERICK II (THE GREAT) (1740–86) saw the emergence of the state of PRUSSIA. The NAPOLEONIC WARS (1803–15) were a humiliating defeat. The CONGRESS OF VIENNA (1815) created the German Confederation. The 19th century brought growing nationalism, fueled by German ROMANTICISM. The REVOLUTIONS OF 1848 led to the election of BISMARCK as chancellor (1862–90). Prussian victories in the AUSTRO-PRUSSIAN WAR (1866) and the FRANCO-PRUSSIAN WAR (1870–71) created the second German reich under the HOHENZOLLERN king, WILLIAM I.

Prince von BÜLOW's imperial ambitions were a cause of WORLD WAR I (1914–18). The Treaty of VERSAILLES (1919) placed a heavy price on German defeat. WILLIAM II was forced to abdicate, and the WEIMAR REPUBLIC (1919–33) was created. Mass unemployment, crippling inflation, war reparations, and world depression created the conditions for FASCISM. The leader of the National Socialist Party, Adolf HITLER, was elected (1933) to build a THIRD REICH.

NATIONAL SOCIALISM pervaded all areas of society, dissent was crushed by the GESTAPO,

## GERMANY

opposition parties and elections banned. Hitler, as *Führer,* became the father of the nation through GOEBBELS's propagandizing. CONCENTRATION CAMPS were set up, and armaments stockpiled. Hitler remilitarized the RHINELAND (1936), aided Franco in the Spanish CIVIL WAR (1936–39), and annexed Austria (1938). The MUNICH PACT (1938) marked the failure of appeasement, Germany invaded Czechoslovakia (March 1939) and Poland (September 1939), precipitating WORLD WAR II. Initial success was halted by the failure in the Battle of BRITAIN, and Hitler's disastrous Soviet offensive (June 1941). The blanket bombing of German cities devastated German industry and morale. Faced with defeat, Hitler committed suicide (April 1945). Germany surrendered (May 8, 1945), and leading Nazis faced the NUREMBERG TRIALS. Germany was divided into four military zones. COLD WAR tension increased. Following the BERLIN AIRLIFT (1949), American, British, and French zones were joined to make the Federal Republic of Germany (West Germany); the Soviet zone formed the German Democratic Republic (East Germany). Berlin was also divided: East Berlin became capital of East German, BONN *de facto* capital of West Germany.

Walter ULBRICHT became leader of **East Germany** (1950–71). Economic deprivation led to a revolt in 1953, which Soviet troops subdued. In 1955 East Germany joined the Warsaw Pact, From 1945–61, 4 million people crossed to the west. The BERLIN WALL was built to halt the exodus. Ulbricht was replaced by Erich HONECKER (1971–89). Relations with West Germany thawed, and travel was permitted between the two. Honecker's refusal to adopt reforms led to civil unrest. In November 1989, a rally of 500,000 people demanded reunification, the Wall was opened, and the regime collapsed. Christian Democrats won the first free elections (March 1990). In July 1990, East and West Germany were formally unified.

Konrad ADENAUER, was elected as the first chancellor (1949–63) of **West Germany**. He was committed to German reunification. In 1955 West Germany became a member of NATO. The economy continued to grow dramatically under KIESINGER (1963–69). Willy BRANDT's chancellorship (1969–74) was noted for his *Ostpolitik* (establishing better relations with the Soviet bloc). His successor was Helmut SCHMIDT (1974–82). Helmut KOHL's chancellorship (1982– ) was more conservative. In December 1990, Kohl was elected in the first all-German elections since 1933. In 1998 Kohl was defeated by Gerhard Schröder of the Social Democratic Party (SPD). Schröder formed a coalition government with The Greens.

### POLITICS

Reunification has meant massive investment to restructure the former East German economy, which has strained federal resources and entailed tax increases. High unemployment, unequal distribution of wealth, and the rise of neo-Nazi groups are serious political problems. Germany is a major supporter of the EUROPEAN UNION.

### ECONOMY

Germany is one of the world's greatest economic powers (1995 GDP per capita, US$20,070). Services form the largest economic sector. Machinery and transport equipment account for 50% of exports. It is the world's third-largest car producer. Other major products: ships, iron, steel, petroleum, tyres. It has the world's second-largest lignite mining industry. Other minerals: copper, potash, lead, salt, zinc, aluminum. Germany is the world's second-largest producer of hops and beer, and the fifth-largest wine-producer.

---

TIONAL STYLE, which was replaced by the readoption of neoclassicism under HITLER, with "official" Nazi architect Albert Speer. After World War II, most new buildings adopted principles of EXPRESSIONISM or MODERNISM.

**German art** It dates back to the illuminated manuscripts of the 9th and 10th centuries. By the end of the Middle Ages, a flourishing tradition in woodcarving had grown up in the s with the work of Veit Stoss and Tilman Riemenschneider. In the 16th century, Germany was at the forefront of the Northern Renaissance, led by Albrecht DÜRER and Hans HOLBEIN the Younger. This was a golden age for German painting and, although Caspar FRIEDRICH made an important contribution to ROMANTICISM, it was only in the 20th century that EXPRESSIONISM and BAUHAUS achieved comparable status.

**Germanic languages** Group of languages, a subdivision of the INDO-EUROPEAN family. One branch (West Germanic) includes English, German, Yiddish, Dutch, Flemish, and Afrikaans; another (North Germanic) includes Swedish, Danish, Icelandic, and Faroese.

**germanium** (symbol Ge) Gray-white metalloid element of Group IV of the periodic table, discovered in 1886. A by-product of zinc ores or the combustion of certain coals, it is important in semiconductor devices. Properties: at.no. 32; at.wt. 72.59; sp.gr. 5.35; m.p. 1,719°F (937°C;); b.p. 5,126°F (2,830°C); most common isotope $^{74}$Ge (36.54%).

**German literature** German-language prose, poetry, and drama. German literature has a long tradition, dating back to the 13th-century courtly poems of Hartmann von Aue, Wolfram von Eschenbach, and Gottfried von Strassburg, the *Minnesang* of Walther von der Vogelweide, and the heroic epic, the *Nibelungenlied.* During the course of the following centuries, German literature was dominated by the classical conventions of FRENCH LITERATURE. In the late 18th century a national literary movement, STURM UND DRANG, emerged. The Weimar classicists, GOETHE and SCHILLER were early proponents of the movement. CLASSICISM's major cultural expression was found in the *Bildungsroman.* Germany's foremost classicist poet was Friedrich Hölderlin. ROMANTICISM flourished during the late 18th and early 19th centuries, when writers such as SCHLEGEL, NOVALIS, BRENTANO, HOFFMANN, KLEIST, the GRIMM BROTHERS, von Arnim, Wackenroder, and Eichendorff encouraged a romanticization of German history and folklore, often through fairy tales. HEINE's work marks the beginnings of German REALISM. At the beginning of the 20th century, GEORGE and RILKE's lyrical poetry was in part a reaction against the prevailing realist tone. Among antinaturalist novelists were MANN, REMARQUE, HESSE, and Musil. German EXPRESSIONISM was a combination of formal experimentation and political content. Major figures in the movement included the novelist KAFKA and the playwright and poet BRECHT. During the Third Reich, many writers were branded as "undesirable" because of their race or politics. Many post-1945 German writers, including GRASS, FRISCH, Böll and Lenz, examine aspects of German complicity during the Nazi period.

**German measles** (rubella) Viral disease usually contracted in childhood. Symptoms include a sore throat, slight fever, and pinkish rash. Women developing rubella during the first three months of pregnancy risk damage to the fetus. Immunization is recommended for all children.

**German shepherd** (Alsatian) Working dog bred in Germany by about 1900. It has woolly underhair and is black, gray, or black and tan. Height: *c.*25in (64cm) at the shoulder; weight: 60–85lb (27–38kg).

**Germany** Federal republic in central Europe. See country feature.

**germination** Growth of the embryo in the seed of a new plant. To germinate, a seed or spore needs favorable conditions of temperature, light, moisture, and oxygen. *See also* DICOTYLEDON

**Geronimo** (1829–1908) Chief of the Chiricahua Apaches. Escaping from a reservation into which he and his tribe were force, he led a band of followers in raids against white settlers in Arizona for over ten years. After surrendering in 1886 was imprisoned in Florida, Alabama and finally confined in Fort Sill, Oklahoma. He became a farmer and national celebrity.

**Gerry, Elbridge** (1744–1814) US politician. Elected to the Massachusetts General Court (1772), he was also a delegate to the Continental Congress and to the Federal Constitutional Convention (1787). He signed the Declaration of Independence but refused to sign the Constitution until the Bill of Rights was added. He was sent to France to establish diplomatic relations and became involved in the XYZ AFFAIR. Elected vice president under James MADISON in 1813, he died in office. *See also* GERRYMANDER

**gerrymander** Practice of redrawing electoral boundaries to favor a particular party. It is named for Elbridge GERRY, gover-

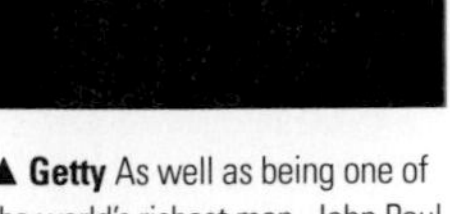

▲ **Getty** As well as being one of the world's richest men, John Paul Getty was considered an important patron of the arts.



A

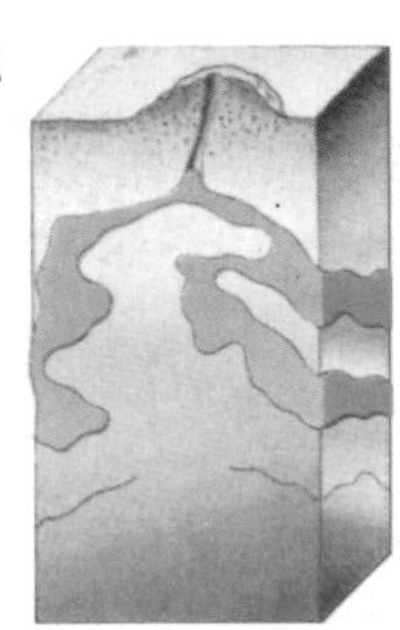

B

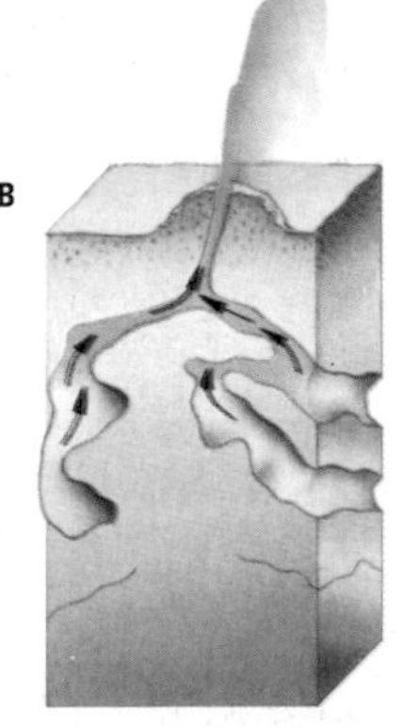

C

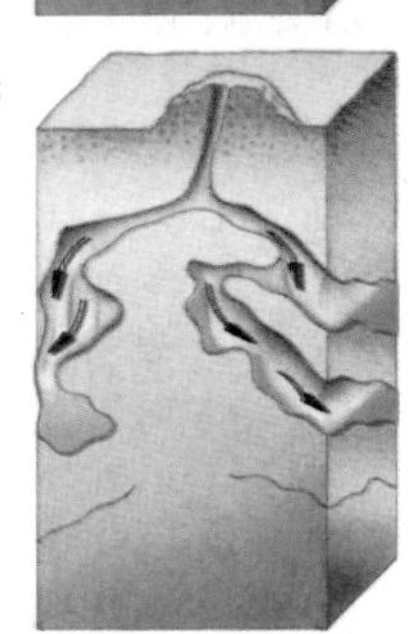

▲ **geyser** A plume of hot water and steam, a geyser is the result of the boiling of water at depth in a series of interconnecting chambers by volcanic heat (A). The expansion of steam produced drives the water and steam above it out at the surface (B), and this is followed by a period of refilling and heating, making it a periodic phenomenon (C).

nor of Massachusetts (1810–12), whose party employed the practice. One of his redefined districts was said to resemble a salamander, hence gerrymander.

**Gershwin, George** (1898–1937) US popular composer. His brother Ira Gershwin (1896–1983) mostly wrote the lyrics. He wrote scores for several musicals, such as *Lady Be Good* (1924), a jazz opera *Porgy and Bess* (1935), and some orchestral works, such as *Rhapsody in Blue* (1924).

**gestalt psychology** School of psychology holding that phenomena are perceived as relating to a whole, rather than the sum of their parts. It was developed from the end of the 19th century in Germany by Max Wertheimer, Wilhelm Wundt, Wolfgang Köhler, and Kurt Koffka.

**Gestapo** (Geheime Staatspolizei) State secret police of Nazi Germany. Founded in 1933 by Goering, it became a powerful national organization under Himmler from 1934, as an arm of the ss. With up to 50,000 members by 1945, it had unlimited powers in suppressing opposition.

**gestation** (pregnancy) Period during which a developing embryo is carried in the uterus.

**Getty, Jean Paul** (1892–1976) US businessman and art collector. He inherited his father's oil business, becoming its president in 1930. After 1959 he lived in England. He was one of the world's richest men, with a fortune estimated at more than $1,000 million.

**Gettysburg, Battle of** Decisive campaign of the Civil War, fought over three days in July 1863 near Gettysburg, Pennsylvania. The Union army of George Gordon Meade checked the invasion of Pennsylvania by the Confederate forces of Robert E. Lee. The battle was a turning point. The heavy casualties (*c.*20,000 each side) prompted Abraham Lincoln's Gettysburg Address.

**Gettysburg Address** Speech by President Abraham Lincoln on November 19, 1863 at the dedication of the national cemetery on the battlefield of Gettysburg. It ended by describing democracy as "government of the people, by the people, and for the people." One of the most famous political addresses, the text of the speech is carved onto the Lincoln Memorial in Washington, DC.

**geyser** Hot spring that erupts, throwing up jets of superheated water and steam, to a height of *c.*197ft (60m), and followed by a shaft of steam with a thunderous roar. Geysers occur in the US, Iceland, and New Zealand.

**Ghana** Republic in w Africa. See country feature.

**Ghats** Two mountain systems in India, running parallel to the coast on both sides of the Deccan Plateau. The Western Ghats extend from the Tapti River to Cape Comorin. The Eastern Ghats extend from the Mahanadi River to the Nilgiri Hills. Height: (Western) 2,950–4,920ft (900–1,500m); (Eastern) 1,970ft (600m). Length: (Western) 1,000mi (1,600km); (Eastern) 875mi (1,400km).

**Ghazali, al-** (1058–1111) Muslim scholar and mystic. He wrote on law, philosophy, theology, and mysticism. He has been called the renewer of Islam. *See also* Sufism

**Ghent** (Gent, Gand) City in NW central Belgium. A major cloth center in the 13th century, it came under Austrian control from 1714 and was captured by the French in 1792, becoming part of independent Belgium in 1830. Industries: plastics, chemicals, steel, electrical engineering, motor vehicles. Pop. (1993 est.) 228,490.

**Ghent, Treaty of** (1814) Agreement ending the War of 1812 between Britain and the US, it restored territorial allocations to the way they were before the war and appointed a commission to settle the dispute over the US–Canada boundary.

**ghetto** Section of a city inhabited almost exclusively by one ethnic group. The term originated in Europe, designating a separate area of a city for Jews. The term has come to mean a disadvantaged area.

**Ghibelline** Political faction in 13th-century Italy that supported the Hohenstaufen dynasty of the Holy Roman Empire, and opposed the pro-papal Guelphs. During the struggles between Frederick II and the popes in the mid-13th century, Ghibellines came to designate those on the imperial side. They were defeated by the Guelphs in 1268, and the family went into decline.

**Ghiberti, Lorenzo** (1378–1455) Italian sculptor, goldsmith, architect, painter, and writer; he was a major transitional figure between the late Gothic and Renaissance worlds. He made two pairs of bronze doors for the Baptistery in Florence. One pair, the "Doors of Paradise," is considered his masterpiece.

**Ghirlandaio, Domenico** (1449–94) Florentine painter, best known for his frescoes. He worked on the Sistine Chapel with Botticelli and others, his major contribution being *Christ Calling the First Apostles* (1482).

**Ghose, Aurobindo** (1872–1950) (Sri Aurobindo) Indian mystic and philosopher. For several years he was an influential nationalist leader, attracting attention for his writings on the partition issue. After his imprisonment and acquittal by the British in 1909 on charges of sedition, he renounced nationalist politics for Hindu philosophy.

**Giacometti, Alberto** (1901–66) Swiss sculptor and painter, influenced by surrealism. During the 1940s and 1950s, he produced his most characteristic works: emaciated, dreamlike figures built of plaster on a wire base. His paintings have the same agitated, visionary quality.

**gibberellin** Any of a group of plant hormones that stimulate cell division, stem elongation, and response to light and temperature. They increase crop yields.

**Gibbon, Edward** (1737–94) British historian. He conceived the idea of his great work, *The Decline and Fall of the Roman Empire* (1776–88), while among the ruins of ancient Rome. The six-volume text is still widely used.

**gibbon** Ape, native to forests in SE Asia. It has a shaggy brown, black, or silvery coat and is very agile. It has long, powerful arms. Height: 16–26in (41–66cm). Family Pongidae, genus *Hyloblates*.

**Gibbons, Grinling** (1648–1721) English wood carver, best known for his carved fruit and flowers. There are examples of his work at St. Paul's Cathedral, London, and in many palaces and country houses.

**Gibbons, Orlando** (1583–1625) English composer. He wrote church music, viol fantasies, and madrigals, such as *The Silver Swanne*. He was a master of polyphony.

**Gibbons v. Ogden (1824)** US Supreme Court decision dealing with the commerce clause of the Constitution (Article I, section 8). The case concerned the regulation of interstate commerce. The Court's broad definition of the word "commerce" is primarily responsible for the extensive power of the federal government to regulate interstate activity.

**Gibbs, James** (1682–1754) British architect. He was inspired by Sir Christopher Wren. Gibbs was an individualist, fitting into neither the Baroque style, which preceded him, nor the later Palladian. His best-known work is the church of St. Martin in the Fields, London (1722–26).

**Gibbs, Josiah Willard** (1839–1903) US mathematical physicist and chemist. His application of thermodynamics to physical processes led to statistical mechanics. He devised the phase rule and developed vector analysis.

**GI Bill** Name applied to US federal legislation to help veterans of the armed forces. The first such law, the Servicemen's Readjustment Act of 1944, provided job placement services, education grants, unemployment insurance, and guarantees for loans to buy homes, farms, or businesses. Later laws extended benefits first to Korean War veterans and then to all veterans.

**Gibraltar** British crown colony, a rocky peninsula on the s coast of Spain. The Muslim conquest of Spain began in 711, and Gibraltar remained under Moorish control until 1462. In 1704 it was captured by an Anglo-Dutch fleet and was ceded to Britain in the Peace of Utrecht (1713). In 1964 it was granted extensive self-government, and a 1967 referendum showed Gibraltarians' wish to remain British. Industries: tourism, reexportation of petroleum and petroleum products. Area: 2.5sq mi (6.5sq km). Pop. (1993 est.) 28,051.

**Gibson, Mel** (1956– ) Australian film actor and director, b. US. International recognition followed his starring roles in *Mad Max* (1979) and *Gallipoli* (1981). He showed his versatility in the Zeffirelli production of *Hamlet* (1990). Gibson won Academy Awards for Best Director and Best Picture for *Braveheart* (1995).

**Gide, André Paul Guillaume** (1869–1951) French novelist, playwright, and critic. His novels and *Journals* (1885–1950) show a constant struggle between puritan and pagan elements. Mature works, such as *Les Faux-monnayeurs* (1926), dramatize a search for spiritual truth. He was awarded the 1947 Nobel Prize for literature.

**Gideon v. Wainwright** (1963) Landmark US Supreme Court decision overruling *Betts v. Brady* (1942). The Court held that representation by an attorney is a constitutional necessity in all criminal trials. This decision led to the establishment of legal aid programs and formed the foundation for the Escobedo and Miranda decisions.

**Gielgud, Sir Arthur John** (1904– ) British stage and film actor and director. His performances in both modern and classical roles established him as one of the century's finest actors. He played almost every major Shakespearian role and appeared in *The Importance of Being Earnest* (1930/ 1939) and *The Cherry Orchard* (1961). He achieved popular success in many films, such as *Arthur* (1981), *Gandhi* (1982), and *Prospero's Books* (1991).

**gila monster** Poisonous nocturnal LIZARD that lives in deserts of SW US and N Mexico. It has a stout body, massive head, flat tail, and scales of orange, yellow, and black. It eats mammals and eggs. Length: 20in (50cm). Family Helodermatidae; species *Heloderma suspectum*.

**Gilbert, Cass** (1859–1934) US architect. He designed the US Supreme Court Building in Washington, D.C. and the Woolworth Building in New York.

**Gilbert, William** (1544–1603) English physicist and physician to Elizabeth I. He was the first to recognize terrestrial MAGNETISM and coined the terms magnetic pole, electric attraction, and electric force.

**Gilbert, Sir W.S. (William Schwenck)** (1836–1911) English librettist and playwright. He collaborated with Sir Arthur SULLIVAN on an immensely successful series of 14 comic operettas, nearly all first performed by the D'Oyly CARTE company. Their works include *HMS Pinafore* (1878), *The Pirates of Penzance* (1879), *The Mikado* (1885), and *The Gondoliers* (1889).

**Gilbert and Ellice Islands** Two groups of coral islands in the W Pacific Ocean, 2,500mi (4,000km) NE of Australia. In 1915 the islands became a British colony. Separated from the Ellice Islands in 1975, the Gilbert Islands are now part of KIRIBATI. The Ellice Islands are now called TUVALU.

G

## GHANA

Ghana's flag has red, green, and yellow bands like the flag of Ethiopia, Africa's oldest independent nation. These colors symbolize African unity. The black star is a symbol of African freedom. Ghana's flag was adopted when the country became independent in 1957.

**AREA:** 92,100sq mi (238,540sq km)
**POPULATION:** 16,944,000
**CAPITAL (POPULATION):** Accra (949,013)
**GOVERNMENT:** Republic
**ETHNIC GROUPS:** Akan 54%, Mossi 16%, Ewe 12%, Ga-Adangame 8%, Gurma 3%
**LANGUAGES:** English (official)
**RELIGIONS:** Christianity 62%, traditional beliefs 21%, Islam 16%
**CURRENCY:** Cedi = 100 pesewas

The Republic of Ghana (formerly the Gold Coast) faces the Gulf of Guinea in West Africa. The densely populated S coastal plains, including Ghana's capital, ACCRA, are lined by lagoons. In the SW plateau lies the ASHANTI region and its capital KUMASI.

Ghana's major river is the VOLTA. The Aksombo Dam was built (1964) and created one of the world's largest artificial lakes, Lake Volta. The dam is used to generate hydroelectricity.

### CLIMATE

Accra has a tropical climate, yet is cooler than many equatorial areas. Rain occurs throughout the year, especially heavily in the SW. The N is warmer than the S. The winter months (November–March) have a low average rainfall.

### VEGETATION

Tropical savanna dominates the coastal region and the far N. Rain forest covers most of the central region.

### HISTORY

Various African kingdoms existed in the region before the arrival of Portuguese explorers in 1471, who named it the Gold Coast after its precious mineral resource. The Dutch gained control (1642), and the Gold Coast was a center of the 17th-century slave trade. Following the abolition of slavery (1860s), the European powers withdrew under the advance of Ashanti. In 1874 Britain colonized the region, excluding Ashanti. In 1901 Ashanti was also subdued. The British developed cacao plantations,

After World War II, nationalist demands intensified, and in 1951 elections were held. Kwame NKRUMAH became prime minister. Ghana became the first African colony to gain full independence, in 1957. British Togoland was incorporated into the new state. The country was renamed Ghana after a powerful, medieval West African kingdom. In 1960, Ghana became a republic with Nkrumah as president. In 1964 Ghana became a one-party state. The economy slumped, burdened by debt, corruption, and the falling cacao price. Nkrumah was deposed in a military coup (1966). Ghana briefly returned to civilian rule (1969–72). The National Redemptive Council (NRC), led by Colonel Acheampong (1972–78), continued to nationalize industry. In 1979 Flight-Lieutenant Jerry Rawlings overthrew the government and executed opposition leaders. A civilian government was formed. In 1981 this was toppled by Rawlings.

### POLITICS

In 1992 a new constitution paved the way for multiparty elections. Opposition parties and voters boycotted the elections, and The National Democratic Council (NDC), led by Rawlings, secured a landslide victory. Rawlings became president in November 1992 and started a second term in 1997.

### ECONOMY

Ghana is a low-income developing country (1995 GDP per capita, US$1,990). Agriculture employs 59% of the workforce and accounts for more than 66% of exports. Ghana is the world's fifth-largest producer of cocoa beans. Other cash crops include coffee, coconuts, and palm kernels. Minerals are the second-largest export. Ghana is the world's tenth-largest producer of manganese. The Ashanti Goldfields Corporation is one of the world's largest producers. The economy has grown significantly since 1983.

**Gilgamesh** Hero of the great Assyro-Babylonian myth, the Epic of Gilgamesh. He went in search of the secret of immortality. Having overcome monsters and gods, he found the flower of life, only to have it snatched from him by a serpent.

**Gillespie, "Dizzy" (John Birks)** (1917–93) US jazz trumpeter and bandleader. One of the central figures in the history of jazz, he helped found bebop with Charlie (Bird) PARKER. After 1950 he led his own groups and made many recordings.

**gills** Organs through which most fish, some larval amphibians, and many aquatic invertebrates obtain oxygen from water. When a fish breathes it opens its mouth, draws in water, and shuts its mouth again. Water is forced through the gill slits, over the gills, and out into the surrounding water. Oxygen is absorbed into small capillary blood vessels, and at the same time, waste carbon dioxide carried by the blood diffuses into the water.

**ginger** Herbaceous PERENNIAL plant native to tropical E Asia and Indonesia and grown commercially in Jamaica and elsewhere. It has fat, tuberous roots and yellow-green flowers. The kitchen spice is made from the tubers of *Zingiber officinale*. Family Zingiberaceae.

**Gingrich, Newt (Newton Leroy)** (1943– ) US politician. He became a Republican congressman in 1979. In the 1994 Congressional election campaign, he persuaded Republicans to subscribe to his "Contract with America," a commitment to cut wasteful government spending. As Speaker of the House of Representatives (1995 –), he led the Republican-dominated Congress into conflict with President CLINTON. In 1997 financial scandals reduced his power within Congress.

**ginkgo** (maidenhair tree) Oldest living species of GYMNOSPERM, native to temperate regions of China, occurring only rarely in the wild. It dates from the late Permian period. It has fan-shaped leaves, small, foul-smelling fruits, and edible, nutlike seeds. Height: to 100ft (30m). Phylum Ginkgophyta; species *Ginkgo biloba*.

**Ginsberg, Allen** (1926–97) US poet. His work was influenced by ZEN, meditation, and the use of drugs. His most famous poems are *Howl* (1956), a condemnation of American society, which established him as the leading poet of the BEAT MOVEMENT, and *Kaddish for Naomi Ginsberg, 1894–1956* (1961), a lament for his mother.

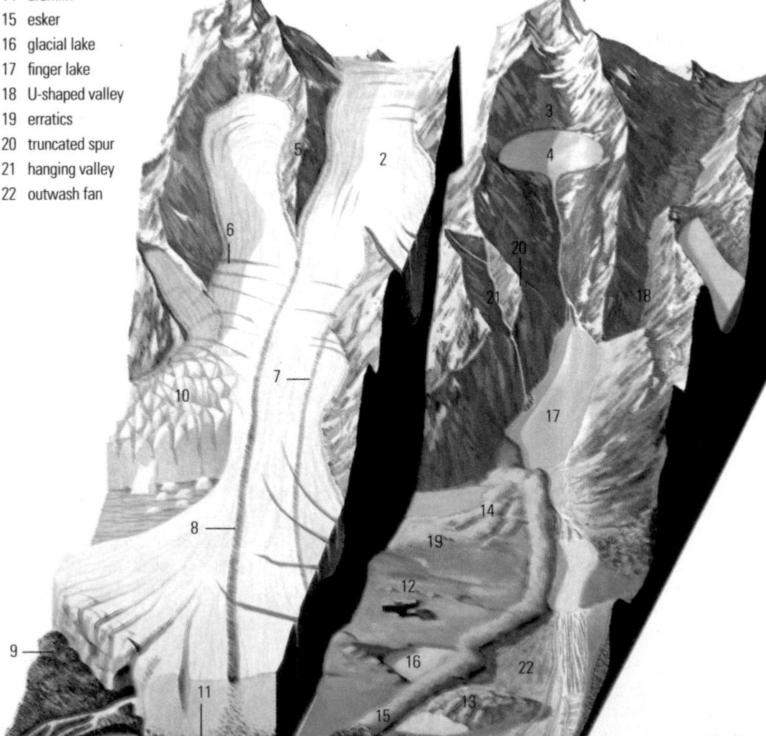


▼ **glacier** In spite of a return to warmer conditions, some regions of the world (namely those nearer the poles) are still covered by ice and are being greatly altered by its action. Glaciated regions have been subjected to erosion and deposition, the erosion mainly taking place in the highland areas, leaving features such as pyramidal peaks, corries, roches moutonnées, truncated spurs, and hanging valleys. Most deposition has occurred on lowlands, where after the retreat of the ice, moraines, drumlins, eskers, erratic boulders, and alluvial fans remain.

**Key:**
1 pyramidal peak
2 firn (granular snow)
3 corrie
4 tarn (corrie lake)
5 arête
6 marginal crevasse
7 lateral moraine
8 medial moraine
9 terminal moraine
10 sérac
11 subglacial moraine
12 glacial table
13 roche moutonnée
14 drumlin
15 esker
16 glacial lake
17 finger lake
18 U-shaped valley
19 erratics
20 truncated spur
21 hanging valley
22 outwash fan

**ginseng** Either of two perennial plants found in the US (*Panax quinquefolius* ) and E Asia (*P. ginseng*). It has yellow-green flowers and compound leaves. The dried tuberous roots are used in Chinese traditional medicine. Height: to 20in (51cm). Family Araliaceae.

**Giolitti, Giovanni** (1842–1928) Italian statesman. Five times prime minister (1892–1921), he introduced measures of social welfare and broadened the franchise. Although he instigated the Italo-Turkish War of 1911, he opposed Italy's entry into World War I. He initially backed MUSSOLINI, withdrawing support in 1924.

**Giorgione, Il** (*c.*1478–1510) Italian painter. A pupil of BELLINI, he became one of the major painters of the Venetian High RENAISSANCE. He had a mysterious romantic style as in *Tempest* (*c.*1505). Some paintings that he began were finished by others, including TITIAN.

**Giotto di Bondone** (1266–1337) (Giotto) Italian painter and architect, an important figure of the early RENAISSANCE. His best work is the *Lives of the Virgin and Christ* (*c.*1305–08) in the Arena Chapel, Padua.

**giraffe** Herbivorous mammal native to Africa. It has a very long neck, a short, tufted mane, and two to four skin-covered horns. In order to drink, giraffes bend or splay their forelegs. Their coats are pale brown with red-brown blotches. Height: to 18ft (5.5m). Family Giraffidae; species *Giraffa camelopardalis.*

**Giraudoux, Jean** (1882–1944) French novelist and dramatist. His successes include *Amphitryon '38* (1929), *La Guerre de Troie n'aura pas lieu* (1935; trans. as *Tiger at the Gates* by Christopher FRY, 1955), and *La Folle de Chaillot* (*The Madwoman of Chaillot*) (1946).

**Girl Scouts** Organization for girls. Its purpose is to inspire girls to develop personal values and to share planned activities. It was founded in Savannah, Georgia, by Juliette Gordon Low in 1912, and was modeled after the Boy Scouts and Britain's Girl Guides.

**Girondins** Political group in the French Revolution named for deputies from Gironde, SW France. From 1792 the moderate and middle-class Girondins tried to prevent the execution of Louis XVI and reduce the power of Paris. They were expelled from the National Congress by the JACOBINS in 1793, and their leaders executed.

**Giscard d'Estaing, Valéry** (1926– ) French politician. He was elected to the National Assembly (1956). In 1974, as the candidate of the right, he defeated François Mitterrand to become president, but narrowly lost to him in 1981. In 1988 he was elected leader of the Union for French Democracy (UDF).

**Gish, Lillian** (1896–1993) US stage and film actress. She was noted as a virtuous heroine in such silent films as *The Birth of a Nation* (1915), *Intolerance* (1916), and *Broken Blossoms* (1918). She was later acclaimed as a character actress in such films as *The Night of the Hunter* (1955). She also had a long and successful stage career.

**Giulio Romano** (1492–1546) Italian painter and architect. One of the founders of MANNERISM, he was the chief assistant to RAPHAEL in his youth. His later work was considered pornographic and he fled from Roma to Mantua, where in 1526 he began his famous *Palazzo del Tè*.

**Giza** (Al-Jizah) City in N Egypt. It is the site of the Great SPHINX, the PYRAMID of Khufu (Cheops), the University of Cairo (relocated in 1924), and Egypt's film industry. A suburb of Cairo, it is a resort and agricultural center. Industries: cotton textiles, footwear, cigarette-manufacturing. Pop. (1990 est.) 2,156,000.

**glacier** Large mass of ice, mainly recrystallized snow, which moves slowly downslope or outward in all directions due to the stress of its own weight. The flow terminates where the rate of melting is equal to the advance of the glacier. There are three main types: the **mountain** or **valley** glacier, originating above the snow line; the **piedmont**, which develops when valley glaciers spread out over lowland; and the **ice-sheet** and ICE-CAP.

**Glacier National Park** Park in NW Montana, along the continental divide in the Rocky Mountains (founded 1910). It is characterized by many glaciers, glacier-fed lakes, mountains, forests, and waterfalls. Area: 1,584sq mi (4,103sq km).

**gladiators** In ancient Rome, prisoners of war, slaves, or condemned convicts trained to fight one another or wild animals in public arenas. Their fate, life or death, was often decided by the spectators. Gladiatorial contests were officially abolished by Constantine I in AD 325 but persisted into the 5th century.

**gladiolus** Genus of 250 species of PERENNIAL flowering plants native to Europe and Africa but cultivated widely. A gladiolus passes the dry season as a CORM, which sprouts in spring to produce a spike of funnel-shaped flowers and tall, lance-shaped leaves. Height: to 3ft (1m). Family Iridaceae.

**Gladstone, William Ewart** (1809–98) British statesman. He entered Parliament as a Tory (1832), but joined the Whigs and then, under his leadership, the Liberals (1859). Prime minister four times (1868–74, 1880–85, 1886, 1892–94), he was a social reformer. His adoption of a policy of Home Rule for Ireland in 1886 split his party and dominated his fourth ministry.

**gland** Cell or tissue that manufactures and secretes special substances. There are two basic types. Exocrine glands make such substances as hydrochloric acid, sweat, sebaceous fluids, and ENZYMES, and secrete these usually through ducts to an external or internal body surface. Endocrine glands contain cells that secrete HORMONES directly into the bloodstream. *See also* ENDOCRINE SYSTEM

**Glaser, Donald Arthur** (1926– ) US physicist who invented the BUBBLE CHAMBER, using it to study ELEMENTARY PARTICLES. He won the 1960 Nobel Prize for physics. Since 1964, he has done research applying physics to molecular biology.

**Glasgow** Largest city and port on the Clyde River, Strathclyde Region, SW central Scotland. Founded in the 6th century, it developed with the American tobacco trade in the 18th century and the cotton trade in the 19th century. Nearby coalfields and the Clyde estuary promoted the growth of heavy industry, chiefly iron and steel, and shipbuilding (now in decline). A cultural center, Glasgow has three universities, the Glasgow School of Art, and the Kelvingrove Art Gallery and Museum. Industries: shipbuilding, heavy engineering, flour milling, brewing, textiles, tobacco, chemicals, printing. Pop (1991) 662,853.

**glasnost** (Rus. openness) Term adopted by Mikhail GORBACHEV in 1986 to express his more liberal social policy. One result was widespread popular criticism of the Soviet system and the Communist Party, leading to the breakup of the Soviet Union and the fall of Gorbachev. *See also* PERESTROIKA

**Glass, Philip** (1937– ) US composer. He studied with Vincent Persichetti at Juilliard and with Nadia BOULANGER in Paris, where he met Ravi SHANKAR and became interested in non-Western music. The hypnotic repetition of short motifs within a simple harmonic idiom characterizes him as a "Minimalist" composer. In addition to 20 operas, he has written instrumental and chamber works.

**glass** Brittle, transparent material. It behaves like a solid but is actually a liquid that is cooled to prevent particles organizing themselves into a regular pattern. It is made by melting together silica (sand), sodium carbonate (soda), and calcium carbonate (limestone). It can only be worked while hot and pliable. There are many types of glass. Soda-lime glass is used in the manufacture of bottles and drinking vessels. Flint glass refracts light well and is used in lenses and prisms. Toughened glass (laminated with plastic) is used in car windscreens.

**glass fiber** (fiberglass) Glass in the form of fine filaments. It is made by forcing molten glass through fine metal nozzles (spinnerets). The resulting continuous filaments are usually bundled together to form strands. These may then be chopped, twisted, or woven. It is used for heat insulation (as glass wool), fabrics, and with a plastic resin to make GRP (glass-reinforced plastic).

**glass snake** (glass lizard) Legless LIZARD found in North America, Eurasia, and Africa. The cylindrical body has a groove along each side and is brown or green, although some species are striped. Length: 24–48in (60–120cm). Family Anguidae; genus *Ophisaurus*.

**glaucoma** Condition in which the pressure within the eye is increased due to an excess of aqueous humor, the fluid within the chamber. It occurs when the normal drainage of fluid is interrupted, posing a threat to vision. Most frequently found in the over 40s, the disease cannot be cured but is managed with drugs and surgery.

**Glazunov, Alexander Constantinovich** (1865–1936) Russian composer, in the romantic tradition of TCHAIKOVSKY. His works include eight symphonies, chamber music, two violin concertos, and the ballets *Raymonda* (1897) and *The Seasons* (1898).

**Glendower, Owen** *See* GLYN DWR, OWAIN

**Glenn, John Herschel Jr.** (1921– ) First US astronaut to orbit the Earth (February 20, 1962). He made three orbits of the Earth in the spacecraft *Friendship 7*. Glenn became a US senator (Democrat) from Ohio, and failed to win the 1984 Democratic presidential nomination.

**gliding** Leisure activity involving flight in a glider. The unpowered glider is launched off the ground by a sling mechanism or towed by a small aircraft and then released. Once airborne, gliders descend relative to the surrounding air. If this air is a rising updraft, a glider may gain altitude, thus prolonging its flight. *See also* HANG GLIDING

**Glinka, Mikhail** (1804–57) Russian composer, the first to receive international acclaim. His two operas, *A Life for the Czar* (1836) and *Ruslan and Ludmila* (1841), inspired the RUSSIAN FIVE. Later in his life he lived in Italy and Spain, writing songs and orchestral music.

**global warming** Trend toward higher average temperatures on Earth's surface. During the last few million years, there have been several periods when surface temperatures have been significantly higher or lower than at present. During cold periods (ice ages) much of the land area has been covered by glaciers. The Earth is currently in the middle of a warm period (interglacial), which began about 10,000 years ago. Since the 1960s, some scientists have called attention to signs that the Earth is becoming unnaturally warmer as the result of an increased GREENHOUSE EFFECT caused by human activity.

**Globe Theatre** Elizabethan public theater associated with William SHAKESPEARE. Built in 1599, it had polygonal walls with a roof over the stage and galleries. Destroyed by fire in 1613 and rebuilt in 1614, it was closed down by the Puritans in 1642 and demolished in 1644. The theater was rebuilt and reopened in 1995.

**globular cluster** Near-spherical cluster of very old stars in the halo of our GALAXY and others. Globular clusters contain anything from 100,000 to several million stars, concentrated so tightly near the center that they cannot be separately distinguished by ground-based telescopes.

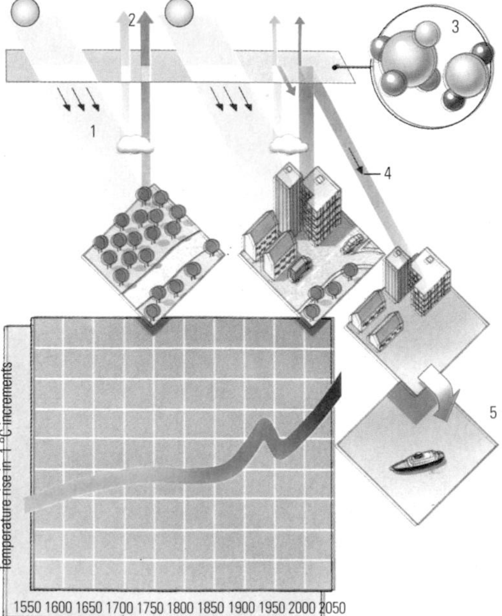


◄ **global warming** Shortwave solar radiation enters the Earth's atmosphere warming the planet (1). Cloud cover and the surface of the Earth reflect energy at a longer wavelength. Most of the energy then radiates out into space (2). When, however, the products of the burning of fossil fuels have polluted the atmosphere (3), the radiation is trapped and bounces back to the surface a second time (4), increasing the energy input into the Earth. This is known as the greenhouse effect, because the same principle warms the interior of greenhouses. The incoming shortwave rays can enter the greenhouse through the glass panels but the reflected long-wave rays are blocked by the same glass trapping the energy. On a global scale, scientists believe the greenhouse effect could raise the temperature of the Earth, resulting in the melting of the polar icecaps and subsequent sea-level rise and flooding of low-lying areas (5).

▲ **giraffe** The world's tallest mammal, the giraffe (*Giraffa camelopardalis*) reaches a height of 18ft (5.5m). The giraffe's long neck makes up about half its height and enables it to browse from the higher branches of trees of the African savanna.

▲ **goat** Bred mainly in countries where the pasture is too poor for sheep, goats are an important source of milk and meat in many desert and mountain regions worldwide. Angora goats (A) originated in Turkey, near Ankara. They have now spread to other parts of the world and are bred for their fleece, known as mohair. The quality of mohair is important and animals are carefully bred to produce long, fine-haired fleece. The Granada (B) is a black, hornless Spanish breed, kept for its milk. Although still popular in Spain, it has not spread further afield. The Toggenburg (C) is a hardy, hornless breed. It originated in Switzerland, but is now used in many countries for cross-breeding.

**glockenspiel** (Ger. *Glocken*, bells, and *spielen*, to play) Percussion instrument with a bell-like sound. Its tuned metal bars are struck with a hammer, either freehand or from a miniature keyboard.

**glomerulonephritis** Group of kidney disorders featuring damage to the glomeruli. Chronic forms may progress to kidney failure.

**Glorious Revolution** (1688–89) Abdication of JAMES II of England and his replacement with WILLIAM III (OF ORANGE) and MARY II. After James had antagonized powerful subjects by his favor toward Roman Catholics, political leaders invited William to take the throne. William landed in November and James fled to France. It was called "glorious" because it occurred virtually without violence.

**Gloucestershire** County in SW England; the county town is Gloucester. The Cotswold Hills, to the E, sustain dairy and arable farming. The fertile Severn valley is also devoted to dairying. Industries: engineering, scientific instruments, and plastics. Area: 1,020sq mi (2,642sq km). Pop. (1991) 528,370.

**glowworm** Any of a number of wingless female BEETLES or beetle larvae of the genus *Lampyris* that possess organs that emit a glow of light, and especially the European beetle *Lampyris noctiluca*. A winged male is known as a FIREFLY. Family Lampyridae.

**Gluck, Christoph Willibald von** (1714–87) German operatic composer. His early operas were composed in the Italian tradition. In *Orfeo ed Euridice* (1762) he attempted to reform opera by unifying musical and dramatic components. He turned to the French tradition in *Iphigénie en Tauride* (1779). He influenced Mozart.

**glucose** (dextrose) Colorless crystalline sugar ($C_6H_{12}O_6$) occurring in fruit and honey. It requires no digestion before absorption. A monosaccharide sugar, it is prepared commercially by the hydrolysis of starch using hydrochloric acid and is used in food and pharmaceuticals. *See also* GLYCOGEN

**glue** Adhesive traditionally made by boiling animal skin, bones, horns, and hooves. It consists of a jelly of hydrolyzed collagen (fibrous protein) and other substances. It forms a tough skin when dry. Vegetable glues are made from starch (flour and water), rubber, soybeans, and other sources. Synthetic adhesives include epoxy resins, a group of POLYMERS that have additional properties of heat and chemical resistance.

**gluten** Main protein substance in wheat flour. Not present in barley, oats, or corn, gluten contributes the elasticity to dough. It is then used to make gluten bread for diabetics, and as an additive to chocolate and coffee.

**glycerol** (glycerin) Thick, syrupy, sweet liquid (1,2,3–trihydroxypropane, $CH_2OHCH(OH)CH_2OH$) obtained from animal and vegetable fats and oils, or propylene (propene). It is used in the manufacture of various products including plastics, explosives, and foods.

**glycogen** Carbohydrate stored in the body, principally by the liver and muscles. Glycogen is a polymer of GLUCOSE. When the body needs energy, glycogen is broken down to glucose. *See also* RESPIRATION

**Glyn Dŵr, Owain** (Owen Glendower) (*c*.1359–1416) Welsh leader. He was a member of the house of Powys, and led a revolt against English rule (1400). Proclaimed Prince of Wales, he won temporary alliances with the Mortimer and Percy families in England and captured Harlech and Aberystwyth castles. He lost both castles by 1409, retreating to the hills to maintain guerrilla warfare against the English until 1412.

**GMT** Abbreviation of GREENWICH MEAN TIME

**gnat** Common name for several small flies, mainly of the family Culicidae, the female of which bites human beings. *See also* MOSQUITO.

**gneiss** METAMORPHIC ROCK with a distinctive layering or banding. The darker minerals are likely to be hornblende, augite, mica, or dark feldspar. Before metamorphism, gneiss was an IGNEOUS ROCK, possibly a granite.

**Gnosticism** Religious movement, embracing numerous sects, based on *gnosis*. This was occult knowledge that released the spiritual part of human beings from the evil bondage of the material world. Gnosticism became widespread by the 2nd century AD.

**gnu** (wildebeest) Large, oxlike African ANTELOPE. The white-tailed gnu (*Connochaetes gnou*) is almost extinct. The brindled gnu (*Connochaetes taurinus*) lives in E and S Africa, where large herds migrate annually. It has a massive, buffalo-like head and a slender body. Both sexes are horned. Length: up to 7.8ft (2.4m); height: 4ft (1.3m); weight: up to 600lb (275kg). Family Bovidae.

**Goa** State in SW India, on the Arabian Sea; the capital is Panaji. It was ruled by Hindu dynasties until it came under Muslim domination in the 15th century. Captured by the Portuguese in 1510, it became a flourishing trade center and the hub of Portugal's Asian empire. It was annexed by India in 1962 and made a Union territory of India. In 1987 Goa was created a separate state. The state's products include rice, cashews, spices, pharmaceutical products, footwear, and pesticides. Area: 1,429sq mi (3,702sq km). Pop. (1991) 1,169,793

**goat** Horned RUMINANT raised for milk, meat, leather, and hair. Closely related to sheep, they are brown or gray in color. The male is a ram or billy, the female a doe or nanny, and the young a kid. Wild species are nomadic, living in rugged mountains. The five species include the ibex (*Capra ibex*), markhor (*Capra falconeri*), and the pasang (*Capra aegagrus*). Length: to 2.8ft (0.85m); height: to 4.5ft (1.4m). Family Bovidae; genus *Capra*.

**goatsucker** Common name for various large-mouthed, nocturnal birds of the order Caprimulgiformes. Widely distributed in warm areas, they include the frogmouth, nighthawk, nightjar, potoo, and whippoorwill. Length: 6–12in (15–30cm). Family Caprimulgidae.

**Gobbi, Tito** (1915–84) Italian baritone. Following his debut in Rome in 1938 in Verdi's *La traviata*, he sang in most of the great opera houses. He was highly acclaimed for his powerful acting ability.

**Gobelins, Manufacture nationale des** State-controlled TAPESTRY factory in Paris, founded *c*.1440 by Jean Gobelin. The factory converted from a dyeworks to making tapestry (1601). Louis XIV bought the premises (1662) to create a royal tapestry and furniture works. It produced many famous tapestries.

**Gobi** (Sha-moh) Desert area in central Asia, extending over much of S Mongolia and N China. One of the world's largest deserts, it is on a plateau, 3,000–5,000ft (900–1,500m) high. The fringes are grassy and inhabited by nomadic Mongolian tribes who rear sheep and goats. The Gobi has cold winters, hot summers, and fierce winds and sandstorms. Area: *c*.500,000sq mi (1,300,000sq km).

**Gobind Singh** (1666–1708) Tenth and last Sikh guru, who laid the foundations of Sikh militarism. In 1699 he created the *Khalsa*, a military fraternity of devout Sikhs, which became the basis of the Sikh army he led against the MOGUL empire. The wearing of the turban and the common attachment of Singh ("lion") to Sikh names date from his reign.

**God** One of the supernatural, divine, and usually immortal beings worshiped by followers of a polytheistic religion such as those of ancient Greece and Rome; also a single supreme being, creator of the universe, as worshiped by the followers of monotheistic religions such as JUDAISM or ISLAM. ALLAH is God of Islam and YAHWEH is God of Judaism. CHRISTIANITY, a monotheistic religion, conceives of one God with three elements – Father, Son, and Holy Spirit. In HINDUISM, BRAHMA is considered the soul of the world, but there are lesser gods. *See also* POLYTHEISM; MONOTHEISM; AGNOSTICISM; ATHEISM; BUDDHISM; DEISM; ZEUS

**Godard, Jean-Luc** (1930– ) French film director. His imaginative flair revolutionized filmmaking. He produced the respected science-fiction film *Alphaville* (1965), and his political sketches, such as *Weekend* (1968) and *Tout va bien* (1972), transformed film as propaganda. *Breathless* (1959) and *Made in USA* (1966) also received praise.

**Goddard, Robert Hutchings** (1882–1945) US physicist and pioneer in rocket development. He developed and launched (1926) the first liquid-fueled rocket, and developed the first smokeless powder rocket and the first automatic steering for rockets.

**Gödel, Kurt** (1906–78) US logician, b. Czechoslovakia. In 1931 he published the theorem named for him. By uniquely numbering each statement in his Consistency Theorem, he proved that in any formal system that can be dealt with using NUMBER THEORY there exist true propositions that cannot be proved within the system. The implication is that the whole of human knowledge can never be systematized within one axiomatic system.

**Godiva, Lady** (d.*c*.1080) English benefactress, wife of Leofric, Earl of Mercia. According to tradition, she rode naked through the streets of Coventry in 1040 to persuade her husband to relieve the people of excessive taxation.

**Godthab** Danish name for NUUK, capital of Greenland

**Godunov, Boris** (1551–1605) Czar of Russia (1598–1605). The chief minister (and brother-in-law) of Ivan IV, he became regent to Ivan's son Fyodor after Ivan's death; he was popularly supposed to have murdered Fyodor's brother and heir, Dmitri, in 1591. On Fyodor's death in 1598, Boris was elected czar. He gained recognition for the Russian Orthodox Church as an independent patriarchate.

**Goebbels, Joseph** (1897–1945) German Nazi leader. He joined the Nazi Party in 1924 and in 1926 founded the newspaper *Der Angriff*. When the Nazis came to power in 1933, he became minister of propaganda. He took total control of the media, which he exploited to support Nazi policy. He committed suicide with his entire family in April 1945.

**Goering, Hermann Wilhelm** (1893–1946) German Nazi leader. As commander of the Luftwaffe (air force) from 1933, and overall director of economic affairs from 1936, he was second to HITLER. His reputation declined during World War II with the failure of the Luftwaffe to subdue the British or the Russians. Captured in 1945, he was sentenced to death at the NUREMBERG TRIALS but committed suicide.

**Goethe, Johann Wolfgang von** (1749–1832) German poet. He wrote simple love lyrics, profound philosophical poems, and scientific theories. Johann Gottfried von HERDER taught him to appreciate Shakespeare, and this influenced his *Götz von Berlichingen* (1773) which, like his novel *The Sorrows of Young Werther* (1774), is a seminal work of ROMANTICISM. His most famous work, the tragic drama *Faust*, is in two parts: *Part 1* (1808), *Part 2* (1832).

**Gogol, Nikolai** (1809–52) Russian novelist and dramatist. His work marks the transition from ROMANTICISM to early realism. He made his reputation with stories, such as *The Nose* (1835),, and the drama *The Government Inspector* (1836). He turned to religion and lived mostly in Rome from 1836–1848. Here he wrote the first part of his major work, *Dead Souls* (1842), and the story *The Overcoat* (1842).

**Golan Heights** (Ramat Ha Golan) Range of hills in SW Syria on the border with Israel. During the Arab-Israeli War of 1967, Israel occupied the area and later annexed it. Of great strategic importance to Israel, it has remained a source of conflict between the two countries. Area: 444sq mi (1,150sq km). Pop. (1983 est.) 19,700.

**gold** (symbol Au) Naturally occurring metallic element. It is also obtained as a byproduct in the refining of copper. Gold is used in jewelry, in connectors for electronic equipment, and as a form of money. Gold in the form of a COLLOID is sometimes used in coloring glass. The isotope Au-198 (half-life 2.7 days) is used in RADIOTHERAPY. The metal is unreactive but dissolves in aqua regia, a mixture of nitric and hydrochloric acids. Properties: at.no. 97; at.wt. 196.9665; sp.gr. 19.30; m.p. 1,945°F (1,063°C); b.p. 5,072°F (2,796°C); most common isotope $^{197}$Au (100%).

**Goldberg, Arthur Joseph** (1911– ) US public official and jurist. A labor union lawyer, he was instrumental in the AFL-CIO merger (1955). Named secretary of labor by President KENNEDY (1961–62), he was then appointed an associate justice of the US Supreme Court (1962–65), where he defended civil rights, personal liberties, and due process. In 1965 President Lyndon JOHNSON appointed him United Nations ambassador (1965–68).

**Goldberg, "Rube" (Reuben Lucius)** (1883–1970) US cartoonis. He became known for his drawings of fantastically involved machinery performing ridiculously simple operations. He was a nationally syndicated cartoonist from 1921 and created several comic characters, including "Lala Palooza" and "Boob McNutt."

**Golden Fleece** In Greek mythology, fleece of the ram that saved Helle and Phrixus from their stepmother Ino. On arrival in Colchis, Phrixus sacrificed the ram and hung the fleece in a wood guarded by a dragon. The fleece was seized by JASON and the ARGONAUTS.

**Golden Gate** Strait on the coast of California, linking the Pacific Ocean with San Francisco Bay. The first landing was made (1769) by Francisco de Ortega. It is spanned by the Golden Gate Bridge, completed in 1937.

**Golden Horde** Name given to the Mongol state established in S Russia in the early 13th century. The state derived from the conquests of GENGHIS KHAN and was extended by his successors, who took over the whole of the Russian state centered on Kiev. It was conquered by Tamerlane in the late 14th century and split up.

**goldfinch** Any of various small, seed-eating birds of the genus *Carduelis*. The males of the American goldfinches, such as *C. tristis*, have yellow body plumage in the summer. The red-faced European goldfinch (*C. carduelis*) has a brownish body with yellow and black wings. Family Fringillidae.

**goldfish** Freshwater CARP originally found in China. The most popular aquarium fish, it was domesticated in China *c*.1,000 years ago. The wild form is plain and brownish, but selective breeding has produced a variety of colors. Family Cyprinidae; species *Carassius auratus*.

**Golding, Sir William (Gerald)** (1911–93) British novelist. He achieved fame with his first novel, *Lord of the Flies* (1954). Other novels include *The Spire* (1964) and the trilogy *The Ends of the Earth* (1991), which incorporates the Booker Prize-winning *Rites of Passage* (1980). He was awarded the 1983 Nobel Prize for literature.

**gold rush** Rapid influx of population in response to reports of the discovery of gold. The largest gold rush brought about 100,000 prospectors to California (1849–50). Some of the miners, known as Forty-Niners, went on to Australia (1851–53). There were also gold rushes to South Africa (1886), to the Klondike in the Yukon, Canada (1896), and to Alaska (1898).

**Goldsmith, Oliver** (1730–74) Irish poet, novelist, essayist, and dramatist. After a colorful but penurious early life, he became known as a lively comic writer. His work includes the essay *The Citizen of the World* (1762), the poem *The Deserted Village* (1770), the novel *The Vicar of Wakefield* (1766), and the play *She Stoops to Conquer* (1773).

**gold standard** Monetary system in which the gold value of currency is set at a fixed rate and currency is convertible into gold on demand. It was adopted by Britain in 1821, by the US, France, and Germany in the 1870s, and by most of the rest of the world by the 1890s. It produced nearly fixed exchange rates and was intended to foster monetary stability. The GREAT DEPRESSION forced many countries to depreciate their exchange rates in an attempt to foster trade, and by the mid-1930s all countries had abandoned the gold standard.

**Goldwater, Barry Morris** (1909– ) US senator. As a Republican, he served in the Senate (1953–64), and was the unsuccessful candidate for president against Lyndon B. JOHNSON (1964). He was reelected to the Senate (1968, 1974, 1980). The best-known and most outspoken conservative in the Republican Party, he was a supporter of military intervention in the Vietnam War and opposed a détente with the Soviet Union. He wrote *The Conscience of a Conservative* (1960) and several other books.

**Goldwyn, Samuel** (1882–1974) US film producer, b. Poland. He was noted for his commercially successful films, including *Wuthering Heights* (1939), *The Best Years of Our Lives* (1946), *Guys and Dolls* (1955), and *Porgy and Bess* (1959). He formed Goldwyn Pictures in 1917 and later merged with Louis B. Mayer to form Metro-Goldwyn-Mayer (1924).

**golf** Game in which a small, hard ball is struck by a club. The object of the game is to hit the ball into a sequence of holes

▲ **goose** Unlike most species of birds, geese mate for life. Found in freshwater habitats all over the world, geese have been domesticated for their eggs and down. The species shown here are the Roman (A), the Egyptian (B), the Chinese (C), the graylag (D), and the embden (E).

▲ **gooseberry** The green, hairy fruit of the gooseberry (*Ribes grossularia*) is excellent for bottling, jam, and pies.

(usually 18), in the least possible number of shots. The length of each hole varies from *c*.100–550yd (90–450m). Each hole consists of a tee, from where the player hits the first shot; a fairway of mown grass bordered by trees and longer grass, known as the rough; and a green, a putting area of smooth, short grass and the site of the hole. A player may have to circumvent hazards, such as ponds or bunkers. Each hole is given a par, the number of shots it should take to complete the hole. Competition is usually over 18, 36, or 72 holes; the winner decided by the lowest total of strokes (stroke play) or the most holes won (match play). The major tournaments are the US Open, British Open, US Professional Golfer's Association (PGA), and the US Masters.

**golgi body** Collection of microscopic vesicles or packets observed near the nucleus of many living cells. It is a part of a cell's ENDOPLASMIC RETICULUM, specialized for the purpose of packaging and dispatching proteins made by the cell.

**Goliath** In the OLD TESTAMENT, the PHILISTINE giant slain by the shepherd boy DAVID (1 Samuel 17). David killed Goliath with a slingshot, hitting him between the eyes with a stone.

**Gómez, Juan Vicente** (1857–1935) Ruler of Venezuela (1908–35). Vice president under Cipriano Castro, he seized power during Castro's absence abroad and controlled the country, either as elected president (1908–15, 1922–29, 1931–35) or through puppets, until his death. His rule was autocratic and intolerant of opposition, but it provided stability during which Venezuela paid off its international debts.

**Gompers, Samuel** (1850–1924) US labor leader, b. England. As a cigarmaker in New York, he served as president of a local union (1877–81). He helped to found the Federation of Organized Trades and Labor Unions. When it was reorganized as the American Federation of Labor (1886), Gompers became its first president, serving until his death except for the year 1895. During World War I, he organized and headed the War Commission on Labor and served on the Advisory Commission to the Council of National Defense.

**Gomulka, Wladyslaw** (1905–82) Polish communist leader. He rose through party ranks to become first secretary and deputy prime minister (1945), but was dismissed during a Stalinist purge (1948). Reinstated (1956), he adopted liberal policies that made him popular at home and were accepted by Moscow. As economic problems grew, Gomulka's regime became more oppressive. Steep rises in food prices (1970) led to his resignation.

**gonad** Primary reproductive organ of male and female animals, in which develop the GAMETES or sex cells. Thus, the gonad in the male is a testis and in the female an ovary. Hermaphrodite animals possess both types.

**gonadotrophins** General term for two pituitary hormones that stimulate the development and function of the gonads (ovary and testis) and similar hormones made by the placenta. Some gonadotrophins are used to treat infertility.

**Goncourt, Huot de, Edmond Louis Antoine and Jules Alfred** French novelists and social historians, Edmond (1822–96) and Jules (1830–70). They wrote in collaboration until Jules died of syphilis. They are famous for *The Journal of the Goncourts* (1836–40). Edmond wrote the novels *La Fille Elisa* (1877) and *Les Frères Zemganno* (1879). In his will, he provided for the *prix goncourt*, France's top literary award.

**Gondwanaland** Southern supercontinent. It began to break away from the single land mass PANGAEA *c*.200 million years ago. It became South America, Africa, India, Australia, and Antarctica. The northern supercontinent, which eventually became North America and Eurasia without India, was Laurasia.

**gonorrhea** SEXUALLY TRANSMITTED DISEASE caused by the bacterium *Neisseria gonorrhoeae*, giving rise to inflammation of the genital tract. Symptoms include pain on urination and the passing of pus. The condition is treated with antibiotics. If not treated, it may spread, causing sterility and ultimately threatening other organs.

**Good Friday** Friday before EASTER Day. It is observed by all Christians as marking the day of the crucifixion of Jesus. For many, it is a day of fasting and abstinence.

**Goodman, Benny (Benjamin David)** (1909–86) US jazz clarinetist and bandleader. He formed his own band in 1934 and became famous in 1939 as the "King of Swing" with his theme songs "Let's Dance" and "Goodbye." He was the first big bandleader to use both black and white musicians in the same band. He also played with many other great jazz performers, made many best-selling recordings, appeared on television and in films, and toured worldwide.

**Good Neighbor Policy** US policy of nonintervention in the affairs of Latin America, a new approach to offset hostility bred by previous US armed intervention. President Franklin D. ROOSEVELT introduced the policy in his inaugural speech (1933) and declared his opposition to military interference. The Organization of American States, an extension of this policy, was founded (1945) to foster hemispheric solidarity.

**Goodyear, Charles** (1800–60) US inventor. he discovered the process of vulcanization, which increases the durability of rubber. Indebtedness forced him to license the process cheaply and he died in poverty.

**goose** Widely distributed waterfowl, related to the DUCK and SWAN. Geese have blunt bills, long thick necks, shortish legs, webbed feet and, in the wild, a combination of gray, brown, black, and white dense plumage underlaid by down. They live near fresh or brackish water and spend time on land, grazing on meadow grasses. Wild geese breed in colonies, mate for life, and build grass-and-twig, down-lined nests for 3–12 eggs. There are 14 species. Weight: 3–13lb (1.4–5.9kg). Family Anatidae.

**gooseberry** Hardy, deciduous, spiny shrub and its edible fruit. It is generally green and hairy, and fairly acidic. Family Grossulariaceae; species *Ribes grossularia*.

**gopher** Small, stout burrowing rodent of North and Central America. It has fur-lined external cheek pouches and long incisor teeth outside the lips. It lives underground, digging tunnels to find roots and tubers, and for shelter and food storage. Length: 5–18in (13–46cm). Family Geomyidae.

**Gorbachev, Mikhail Sergeyevich** (1931– ) Soviet statesman, president of the Soviet Union (1985–91). Secretary of the Communist Party from 1985, he embarked on a program of reform based on two principles: PERESTROIKA ("restructuring") and GLASNOST ("openness"). The benefits of radical socioeconomic change were slow to take effect, and Gorbachev became extremely unpopular as prices rose. He agreed to major arms limitation treaties with the US and acquiesced to the demolition of the communist regimes in Eastern Europe (1989–90), effectively ending the COLD WAR. Having strengthened his presidential powers in 1990, he was forced to resign in 1991 by opponents eager to grant independence to the constituent republics of the Soviet Union. He won the Nobel Peace Prize in 1990.

**Gordimer, Nadine** (1923– ) South African author. Her works, critical of apartheid, are concerned with contemporary politics and social morality. Among her collections of short stories are *Face to Face* (1949) and *Jump* (1991). Her novels include *The Lying Days* (1953), *The Conservationist* (1974), and *My Son's Story* (1990). She won the 1991 Nobel Prize for literature.

**Gordon, Charles George** (1833–85) British soldier and administrator. He fought in the CRIMEAN WAR and OPIUM WAR, and was employed by the Chinese government in the TAIPING REBELLION. He was governor-general of the Sudan (1877–80) and returned to Khartoum in 1884 to evacuate Egyptian forces threatened by the MAHDI. He was killed two days before the arrival of a relief force.

**Gore, Al (Albert Arnold)** (1948– ) US vice president (1993– ). Gore, a Democrat, became known for his commitment to environmental issues while representing Tennessee in the House of Representatives (1977–85) and Senate (1985–93). His vice presidency is characterized by a close working relationship with Bill CLINTON. He began a second term as vice president following Clinton's reelection in November 1996.

**Górecki, Henryk** (1933– ) Polish composer. Early works were influenced by Webern and serialism, but his later output is inspired more by medieval Polish chants, Renaissance polyphony, and the richness of the Wagnerian orchestra.

**Gorgon** In Greek mythology, three monsters named Stheno, Euryale, and MEDUSA. With golden wings and snakes for hair, they turned anyone who looked directly at them to stone. PERSEUS killed Medusa by using his shield as a mirror, holding it so that she saw her own reflection.

**gorilla** Powerfully built great ape native to the forests of equatorial Africa. The largest primate, it is brown or black, with long arms and short legs. It walks on all fours and is herbivorous. Height: to 70in (175cm); weight: 308–396lb (140–180kg). Family Pongidae; species *Gorilla gorilla*.

**Gorky, Arshile** (1905–48) US painter, b. Armenia. His work bridged SURREALISM and ABSTRACT EXPRESSIONISM. In 1920 he emigrated to the US, where he joined a group of European surrealists in New York in the 1940s. He became fascinated by the work of MIRÓ, who inspired some of his paintings, such as the different versions of *Garden in Sochi* (1940) and *Mojave* (1941–42).

**Gorky, Maxim** (1868–1936) Russian dramatist and writer. He championed the worker in *Sketches and Stories* (1898), in the play *The Lower Depths* (1902), and in the novel *Mother* (1907). He wrote autobiographical volumes (1913–23) and plays, including *Yegor Bulychov* (1931). He lived in intermittent exile after 1907.

**gorse** (furze) Any of several dense thorny shrubs found mainly in Europe; genus *Ulex*; family Fabaceae/Leguminosae. The common European species, *U. europaea*, bears yellow flowers and thrives in open hilly regions.

**gospel** Central content of the Christian faith, the good news (*god spell* in Old English) that human sins are forgiven. The first four books of the New Testament, ascribed to the Evangelists Matthew, Mark, Luke, and John, are known as the four Gospels.

**gospel music** African-American vocal church music. It first arose in the depression years of the 1930s from the fusion of Protestant hymn harmony with African rhythmic and melodic features. Gospel music emphasizes the "good news" aspect of revivalist Christianity. Powerfully expressive, it often uses a call-and-response form, with a choir answering a soloist/preacher.

**Gothenburg** (Göteborg) City in SW Sweden, at the confluence of the Göta and Kattegat rivers; the country's chief seaport and second largest city. Founded by Gustavus II (1619), it soon flourished as a commercial center. Its industries include shipbuilding, vehicles, food-processing, chemicals, textiles. Pop. (1993) 437,313.

**Gothic art and architecture** Architecture of medieval Europe from the 12th–16th centuries. It is characterized by the pointed arch and ribbed vault. The style is religious in inspiration and ecclesiastical in nature. Its greatest and most characteristic expression is the cathedral. The introduction of flying buttresses was a technical advance that made the large windows possible. An early prototype is the Abbey Church of St. Denis, France(1140–44). Ever higher and lighter structures followed, with increasingly intricate vaulting and tracery.

**Gothic novel** Genre of English fiction popular in the late 18th and early 19th centuries. Gothic novels often rely on eerie medieval externals, such as old castles, monasteries, and hidden trapdoors, for their symbolism. Horace WALPOLE wrote an important prototype, *The Castle of Otranto* (1764). Later examples include *The Mysteries of Udolpho* (1794) by Ann Radcliffe and *Frankenstein* (1818) by Mary Shelley.

**Gothic revival** (neo-Gothic) Architecture based on the Gothic style of the Middle Ages. Beginning in the late 18th century, it peaked in 19th-century Britain and the US, also appearing in many European countries. British exponents, notably the critic John RUSKIN and the writer and architect A.W.N. Pugin, insisted on the need for authentic, structural recreation of medieval styles. Notable examples are the Houses of Parliament in London by Pugin and Sir Charles BARRY, and Trinity Church in New York City by Richard Upjohn. *See also* GOTHIC ART AND ARCHITECTURE

**Goths** Ancient Germanic people, groups of whom settled near the Black Sea in the 2nd–3rd centuries AD. The **Visigoths** were driven westward into Roman territory by the HUNS in 376, culminating in their sacking Rome under ALARIC in 410. They settled in SW France, then, driven out by the Franks in the early 6th century, in Spain. Some groups united to create the **Ostrogoths**, who conquered Italy under THEODORIC THE GREAT (489). They held Italy until conquered by the Byzantines under Belisarius and Narses (536–553).

**Gottlieb, Adolph** (1903–74) US painter, leading exponent of abstract expressionism. His early work shows the influence of EXPRESSIONISM and SURREALISM. Best known for a series of *Pictographs* (1941–51), he portrayed Freudian or mythological concepts compartmentalized in different areas of the canvas.

**gouache** Watercolor paint made opaque by the addition of white. It lightens in color when dry and cracks if used thickly. Popular among manuscript illuminators in the Middle Ages, gouache has been used by 20th-century painters and commercial artists.

**Gould, Glenn** (1932–82) Canadian pianist and composer. He became a soloist with the Toronto Symphony Orchestra at the age of 14. He is famous for interpretations of the romantic composers and J.S. BACH. His first string quartet was premiered in 1956. In later years he concentrated on recording.

**Gould, Jay** (1836–92) US financial speculator. With his partner, James Fisk, he typified the capitalist "robber barons" who made large fortunes from corrupt dealings in stocks and shares. He and Fisk nearly cornered the gold market, forcing the Treasury to release gold stocks and leading to the panic of Black Friday (September 24, 1869).

**Gounod, Charles François** (1818–93) French composer and organist. He is best known for his operas, which include *Faust* (1859), *Mireille* (1863), and *Roméo et Juliette* (1864).

**gourd** Annual vine and its ornamental, hard-shelled fruit. These range from almost spherical, as in *Cucurbita pepo*, to irregular or bottle-shaped, as in *Lagenaria siceraria*. The rind may be smooth or warty. Family Cucurbitaceae.

▲ **Gorbachev** The former president (1985–91) of the Soviet Union, Mikhail Gorbachev was responsible for the two radical socioeconomic reforms of *glasnost* ("openness") and *perestroika* ("restructuring"). Although initially he enjoyed huge popular support, his economic reforms resulted in massive price rises and he was eventually forced to resign in 1991.

G

◄ **Gothic art and architecture** Cologne Cathedral, Germany, was begun in 1248, but the present building was completed between 1842 and 1880. The largest Gothic church in N Europe, the illustration shows the W facade. The cathedral's grandeur lies predominantly in its highly decorated, spiny twin towers, which rise to 502ft (152m).

► **Graf** German tennis star Steffi Graf is among the greatest women tennis players of all time. She has dominated the game since 1987, when she was first ranked No 1. The next ten years saw her retain the top spot every year apart from 1990 and 1991 when Monica Seles achieved the top ranking. By early 1997, Graf had won a remarkable total of 105 titles.

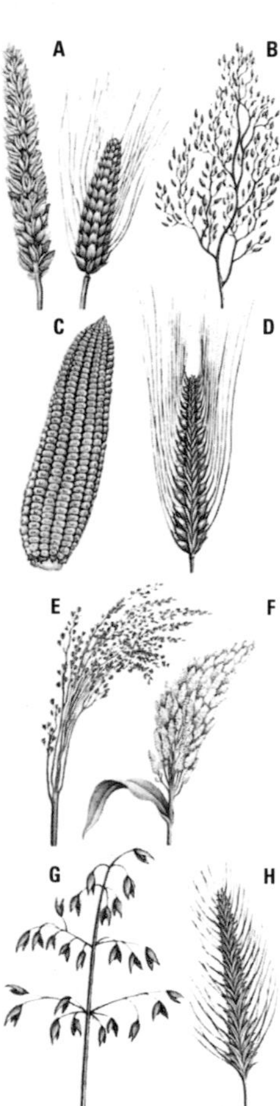


▲ **grain** The fruits of various cereal plants, the various grains together are the most important food. Wheat (A), corn (C), and barley (D) are grown in the world's temperate regions. Rice (B) needs a warm climate to grow successfully. Millet (E) is one of the oldest cultivated grains in the world and along with sorghum (F) is grown extensively in Africa. Oats (G) and rye (H) are grown extensively in Europe, and rye especially is well suited to poorer soils than those required for most cereal grains.

**gout** Form of arthritis, featuring an excess of uric acid crystals in the tissues. More common in men, it causes attacks of pain and inflammation in the joints. It is treated with anti-inflammatories.

**Gower, John** (1330–1408) English poet. Ranked in his time with Lydgate and CHAUCER, his work includes *Vox Clamantis* (1379–82), an attack on social injustice, and his most famous work, *Confessio Amantis* (1386–93), a collection of allegorical tales on the subject of Christian and courtly love.

**Goya y Lucientes, Francisco José de** (1746–1828) Spanish painter and engraver. A severe illness (1791) provoked a vein of fantastic works, one of the most vicious and sinister of which is *Los Caprichos*, a series of 82 engravings published in 1799. Goya enjoyed the royal patronage of Charles IV despite mercilessly realistic paintings such as *The family of Charles IV* (1800). His bloody scenes, *The Second of May, 1808* and *The Third of May, 1808,* portray the Spanish resistance to the French invasion. Obsessed with the dark side of the human psyche, his last works are the so-called *Black paintings*, 14 murals in somber colors in which Goya unleashed yet more horrors from his tortured imagination.

**Gozzoli, Benozzo** (1421–97) Italian painter. He is famous for his numerous frescos, such as that of the Medici family as the Magi in the chapel of the Medici Palace, Florence.

**Gracchus** (153–121 BC) (Gaius Sempronius) Roman statesman. As tribune (123–121 BC) he organized the social reforms of his brother Tiberius (d.133 BC). He sought to check the power of the Senate by uniting the plebeians and the equites and by reforming agrarian laws to benefit the poor. These reforms were short-lived; he was defeated in the election of 121 and killed during the riots that followed.

**Graces** In Greek mythology, three goddesses who represented intellectual pleasures: beauty, grace, and charm. Associated especially with poetry, Aglaia, Euphrosyne, and Thalia were often linked with the MUSES. They were also described as daughters or granddaughters of ZEUS.

**grackle** Several species of stout-billed, New World blackbirds within the genera *Quiscalus* and *Cassidix* of the family Icteridae. Sometimes called crow blackbirds, they have blackish, iridescent plumage. The common grackle, *Q. quiscula*, of the US, may reach 12in (30cm) in length. Species of Asian MINA birds of the genus *Gracula* are also called grackles.

**Graf, Steffi** (1969– ) German tennis player. Graf succeeded Martina NAVRATILOVA as the world's No 1 woman tennis player in 1987. In 1988 she completed a Grand Slam of the major tournaments. Graf's powerful serve and forehand play dominated the women's game, despite her injury problems. She has won the Australian Open (1988, 1989, 1990, 1994), the French Open (1987, 1988, 1993, 1995, 1996), Wimbledon (1988, 1989, 1991, 1992, 1993, 1995, 1996), and the US Open (1988, 1989, 1993, 1995, 1996). In 1997 her father was found guilty of tax evasion on income earned as her manager.

**graft, tissue** Organ or tissue transplanted to replace a part of the body that is damaged or diseased. The replacement tissue may be taken from elsewhere on a patient's body (an autograft) or from a donor (allograft). The use of an organ from a donor can lead to rejection, when the patient's immune system attacks the grafted tissue.

**grafting** In horticulture, method of plant propagation. A twig of one variety, called the scion, is established on the roots of a related variety, called the stock. Most fruit trees are propagated by a similar process called budding, in which the scion is a single bud.

**Graham, Billy (William Franklin)** (1918– ) US evangelist. A charismatic preacher, he led Christian revivalist crusades all over the world, including communist countries. He was consulted by several US presidents, especially Richard NIXON.

**Graham, Martha** (1894–1991) US choreographer and dancer. She was a leading figure in MODERN DANCE. In the early 1920s, she broke with traditional BALLET, employing highly individual forms based on natural movement. She established her own company in the 1930s.

**Graham, Thomas** (1805–69) British chemist best remembered for Graham's law. This states that the diffusion rate of a gas is inversely proportional to the square root of its density. This law is used in separating isotopes by the diffusion method, and has important industrial applications. He also discovered DIALYSIS.

**Grahame, Kenneth** (1859–1932) British author of children's books. He created Mole, Rat, Badger, and Mr. Toad in the classic *Wind in the Willows* (1908), which formed the basis for the A.A. MILNE play *Toad of Toad Hall* (1929).

**grain** Fruits of various CEREAL plants, or the plants themselves. The main kinds of grain are wheat, corn, and RICE. They are an important food, not only rich in carbohydrates but also containing proteins and vitamins.

**Grainger, Percy Aldridge** (1882–1961) Australian composer and pianist. He was a pupil of Ferruccio Busoni and a protégé of Edvard Grieg, who encouraged him to collect, edit and arrange English and Irish folksongs. His arrangements of *Country Gardens* and *Shepherd's Hey* were both published in 1908. He produced other songs and orchestral pieces in the same folk tradition and also wrote highly experimental music.

**grammar** Nature and structure of language, including the form, sound, and meaning of words and the construction of sentences. Traditional rules of grammar were developed in the Middle Ages and were based on Latin. They were later applied to other languages such as English, German, and Russian. In the mid-20th century, linguists such as Noam CHOMSKY developed a more scientific approach to analyzing language, which did not depend on structural similarities with Latin.

**Grampian** Region in NE Scotland, bordered by the North Sea, the Grampian Highlands, and the Cairngorms; the capital is ABERDEEN. The W of the region is mountainous, rising to 4,301ft (1,311m) at Ben Macdhui. The E is drained by the Spey, Dee, and Don rivers. Along the banks of the Spey lie many whisky distilleries. Industries: beef farming, fishing, and tourism. Area: 3,361sq mi (8,707sq km). Pop. (1991) 503,900.

**Grampians** Mountain range in N central Scotland. It is the highest mountain system in Britain, running SW – NE between Glen More and the Scottish Lowlands. Rivers rising in the Grampians include the Spey and Findhorn (flowing N), the Don and Dee (flowing E), and the Tay and Forth (flowing S). Highest peak: BEN NEVIS, 4,406ft (1,343m).

**Granada** City in Andalusia, S Spain; capital of Granada province. Founded in the 8th century as a Moorish fortress, it became the capital of the independent Muslim kingdom of Granada in 1238. The last Moorish stronghold in Spain, it surrendered to the Christian armies of Ferdinand and Isabella (1492). The central splendor of Granada is the ALHAMBRA. Industries: tourism and textiles. Pop. (1991) 254,034.

**Gran Chaco** Lowland plain of central South America, stretching across the borders of Argentina, Bolivia, and Paraguay. Arid and largely unpopulated, the region is famous for its quebracho trees, a major source of TANNIN. The discovery of oil in the Chaco Boreal, and Bolivia's subsequent need for a route to the sea, led to the Chaco War (1932–35) between Bolivia and Paraguay. More than 100,000 soldiers died before an agreement gave 75% of Gran Chaco to Paraguay, and allowed Bolivia use of the Paraguay River.

**Grand Canal** Ancient inland waterway in NE China, between Beijing and Hangzhou. The first part, between the Yangtze and Huai Ho rivers, was built in the 6th century BC. It was extended to Hangzhou in the 6th century AD and to Beijing by KUBLAI KHAN in the 13th century. Total length: c.1,000mi (1,600km).

**Grand Canyon** Deep gorge in NW Arizona, carved by the Colorado River. It is 280mi (450km) long and varies from 4mi (6km) to 11mi (18km) in width. With its magnificent multicolored rock formations revealing hundreds of millions of years of geological history, the Grand Canyon is considered one of the great natural wonders of the world.

**grand jury** In US law, a group appointed by the court to investigate a crime within its jurisdiction. It hears evidence, then decides whether a person should stand trial. It is so-called because it is usually larger than a petit, or trial, JURY.

**Grand Remonstrance** Statement of grievances by the English Parliament presented to CHARLES I in November 1641. It listed numerous objections to the royal government and demanded parliamentary approval of ministers. It was passed in the House of Commons by only 11 votes, and Charles rejected it. It hardened the division between the crown and Parliament, which culminated in the English CIVIL WAR.

**grand unified theory (GUT)** Theory that would demonstrate that three of the four FUNDAMENTAL FORCES are actually different aspects of the same fundamental force. The WEAK NUCLEAR FORCE and ELECTROMAGNETIC FORCE have been incorporated as the electroweak force, as demonstrated by particle accelerator experiments. In order to prove the GUT, the electroweak force must be unified with the STRONG NUCLEAR FORCE. If the gravitational force could be incorporated, then a UNIFIED FIELD THEORY would be produced.

**Granger Movement** US agrarian movement. The National Grange, or Order of the Patrons of Husbandry, was founded in 1867. Individual Granges, organized on a local basis, established cooperative grain elevators, mills, and stores. Together, Grangers brought pressure on state legislatures to regulate railroads and other costs. In the 1990s there were more than 5,000 local Granges in the US. They continue to be active in promoting the interests of farmers.

**granite** Coarse-grained, light-gray, durable IGNEOUS ROCK, composed chiefly of feldspar and quartz, with some mica or hornblende. It is thought to have solidified from magma (molten rock).

**Grant, Cary** (1904–86) US film star, b. Britain. A handsome and charming actor, he specialized in playing romantic leads. His many films include sophisticated comedies such as *Topper* (1937) and *Bringing Up Baby* (1938), and stylish thrillers such as *North by Northwest* (1959) and *Charade* (1963).

**Grant, Duncan** (1885–1978) British landscape painter, portraitist, and designer. He was one of the first British artists to be influenced by POSTIMPRESSIONISM. He was a member of the BLOOMSBURY GROUP.

**Grant, Ulysses S. (Simpson)** (1822–85) US Civil War general and 18th US President (1869–77). He served in the MEXICAN WAR (1846–48) and the CIVIL WAR. He masterminded the Vicksburg Campaign (1862–63). In 1864 Abraham LINCOLN gave him overall command of the Union forces. He coordinated the final campaigns and accepted the surrender of Robert E. LEE (1865). As president, he achieved foreign policy successes, but failed to prevent the growth of domestic corruption. Comfortably reelected in 1872, members of his own administration were implicated in the corruption charges and he retired at the end of his second term.

**grape** Vines that grow in temperate and subtropical climates, producing fruit that is eaten raw, dried, or used for making WINE. The classical European vine (*Vitis vinifera*) had its origins in Asia. The climate, soil, topography, and methods of cultivation all determine the quality of the crop. Family Vitaceae.

**grapefruit** Evergreen citrus-fruit tree of the family Rutaceae. Also its yellow edible fruit, which is a valuable source of vitamin C. The tree, which may reach 20ft (6m), is grown mainly in subtropical climates in the US, Israel, South Africa, and Argentina. Family Rutaceae.

**graph** Diagram representing a relationship between numbers or quantities. Many graphs use the CARTESIAN COORDINATE SYSTEM. Other forms include bar charts, in which a series of figures is represented by lines of various lengths, and pie charts, in which quantities are represented by sectors of a circle.

**graphical user interface (GUI)** Computer PROGRAM enabling a user to operate a COMPUTER using simple symbols. Early personal computers used operating systems that were text based. Commands were often obscure combinations of letters and numbers, which made using the systems difficult for the uninitiated. A GUI replaces these commands with a screen containing symbols called icons. The user manipulates these using a "mouse."

**graphite** (plumbago) Dark-gray, soft, crystalline form of CARBON. It occurs naturally in deposits of varying purity and is made synthetically by heating petroleum coke. It is used in pencils, lubricants, electrodes, brushes of electrical machines, rocket nozzles, and as a moderator that slows down neutrons in nuclear reactors. Graphite is a good conductor of heat and electricity. Hardness 1–2; sp.gr. 2.1–2.3.

**Grass, Günter Wilhelm** (1927– ) German novelist, poet, and playwright. His prose combines evocative description with historical documentation in the mannerist style. He used powerful techniques to grotesque comic effect in *The Tin Drum* (1959) and *Cat and Mouse* (1961), and he satirized the Nazi era in *Dog Years* (1963). Later works include *The Flounder* (1977) and *The Call of the Toad* (1992).

**grass** Nonwoody plants with fibrous roots that have long, narrow leaves enclosing hollow, jointed stems. The stems may be upright or bent, lie on the ground, or grow underground. The flowers are small, without PETALS and SEPALS. The leaves grow from the base, and so removal of the tips does not inhibit growth, making grass suitable for lawns and pastures. CEREAL grasses, such as rice, millet, corn, and wheat, are cultivated for their seeds. Others are grown as food for animals and for erosion control and ornament. There are *c*.8,000 species. Family Poaceae/Gramineae. *See also* MONOCOTYLEDON

**grasshopper** Plant-eating insect. It is a powerful jumper owing to enlarged hind legs. The forewings are leathery and the hind wings are membranous and fan-shaped; when the insect is at rest, the wings are folded over its back. Length: 0.3–4.3in (8–11cm). Order Orthoptera; families Acrididae and Tettingoniidae.

**Grattan, Henry** (1746–1820) Irish political leader. A compelling orator, he led the movement to free the Irish Parliament from British control, which was finally achieved in 1782. He failed to prevent the merger of the Irish and British Parliaments in the Act of UNION (1801). As a member (1805–20), Grattan fought for CATHOLIC EMANCIPATION.

**Graves, Robert von Ranke** (1895–1985) British poet, novelist, and critic. After publishing his classic World War I autobiography, *Goodbye To All That* (1929), he emigrated to Majorca, Spain. Other works include the novels *I, Claudius* (1934) and *The Crowning Privilege* (1955). His *Collected Poems* appeared in 1938 and 1975.

**gravitation** One of the four FUNDAMENTAL FORCES in nature. Gravitation is weak compared with the others, but it is apparent because of the great mass of the Earth. The gravitational force $F$ between two masses $m_1$ and $m_2$ a distance $d$ apart was found by Isaac NEWTON to be $F = Gm_1m_2/d^2$, where G is a constant of proportionality called the universal constant of gravitation. A more complete treatment of gravitation was developed by

▲ **Grant** US general and president, Ulysses S. Grant enjoyed little success in the army (1839–54) or in business until the outbreak of the Civil War. A Union hero, he was twice elected president (1868, 1872). His foreign policy successes while in office, however, were overshadowed by financial scandal and charges of corruption.

▲ **grass** Meadow grass (*Poa pratensis*) is an important hay and green pasture grass in North America and Europe, and as such it is an economically valuable member of the large and widespread grass family (Gramineae). The flower of the grass is a minute spikelet, usually arranged in open branching clusters known as panicles. The flowers are cross-fertilized by the wind and the single ovule then develops into a seed or grain. Grassland will evolve readily wherever forest or scrub cover is sparse and where there are sufficient moisture and nutrients in the soil. Vast areas of the world are natural grasslands, such as the North American prairies and the steppes of Asia.

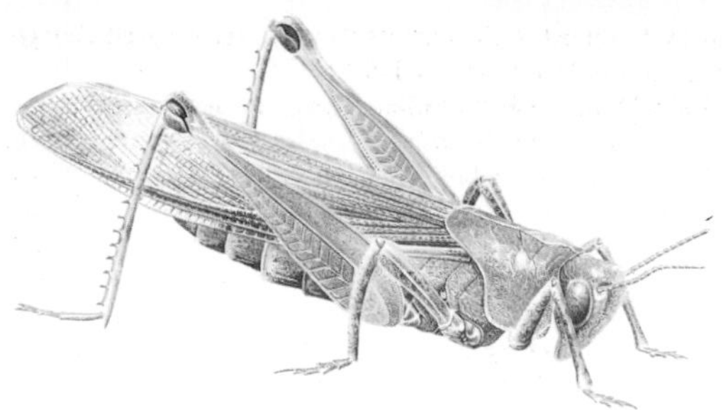

► **grasshopper** Because they have problems visually attracting mates in long grass, grasshoppers (order Orthoptera) seek partners using sound signals. By scraping a row of protruding pegs on the inside of each back leg against hardened ridges on their forewings, they make high-frequency mating calls. The calls, known as stridulation, vary from species to species depending on the number of pegs on each leg.

Albert EINSTEIN, who showed in his general theory of RELATIVITY that gravitation is a manifestation of space-time.

**Gray, Elisha** (1835–1901) US inventor. He received his first patent for a self-adjusting telegraph relay in 1867. He also patented the telegraphic repeater and the type-printing telegraph. He rivaled Alexander Graham BELL as inventor of the telephone, filing his patent just a a few hours later, but Bell's patent rights were upheld by the US Supreme Court.

**Gray, Thomas** (1716–71) English poet. His masterpiece was *Elegy Written in a Country Churchyard* (1751). Other poems include *Ode on the Death of a Favorite Cat* (1748) and *The Descent of Odin* (1768).

**gray** (symbol Gy) SI unit of absorbed radiation dose. One gray is equivalent to supplying 1 joule of energy per kilogram of irradiated material. It superseded the rad (1 gray = 100 rad).

**Graz** City at the foot of the Schlossberg mountain peak, on the Mur River, SE Austria; capital of Styria. Graz's many historic buildings include a 15th-century Gothic cathedral, the *Uhrturm* clock tower (1561), and the Renaissance Landhaus (provincial parliament). Johannes KEPLER taught at the state university (founded 1586) and Emperor Frederick II is buried here. Industries: iron and steel, paper, leather, glass, chemicals, textiles. Pop. (1991) 237,810.

**Great Awakening** Series of 18th-century religious revivals in the American colonies. They began with the preaching of Jonathan EDWARDS in New England (1734), William Tennent in New Jersey, and Samuel Davies in Virginia, and were united by George Whitefield (1739–41). Baptist revivals occurred in 1760, and METHODISM evolved in the pre-Revolutionary period. The movement inspired a great deal of Christian missionary work among the Native American tribes as well as the founding of several colleges, including Princeton and Brown.

**Great Barrier Reef** World's largest CORAL REEF, in the Coral Sea off the NE coast of Queensland, Australia. It was first explored by James COOK in 1770. It forms a natural breakwater and is up to 2,600ft (800m) wide. The reef is separated from the mainland by a shallow lagoon 7–15mi (11–24km) wide. It is a major tourist site. Length: 1,250mi (2,000km). Area: *c.*80,000sq mi (207,000sq km).

**Great Basin** Desert area in W US, comprising most of Nevada and parts of Utah, Idaho, California, Wyoming, and Oregon. It includes DEATH VALLEY, the Mojave Desert, and Carson Sink. There are mountain ranges running N – S, and the region is sparsely populated. The few streams drain into saline lakes, the biggest being GREAT SALT LAKE. Mineral deposits include gold, magnesite, mercury, and beryllium ore. Area: *c.*190,000sq mi (492,000sq km)

**Great Bear Lake** Lake in Northwest Territories, NW Canada; the largest lake in Canada and fourth largest in North America. It was first explored in 1825 by John FRANKLIN. It is drained in the W by the Great Bear River. Though the lake is one of North America's deepest, it is icebound for eight months of the year. Area: *c.*12,300sq mi (31,800sq km).

**Great Britain** Island, lying to the West of mainland Europe, and political entity containing ENGLAND, SCOTLAND, and WALES. Wales was united with England in 1536. The Act of UNION (1707) united Scotland with England, and the Act of Union (1801) established the UNITED KINGDOM of Great Britain and Ireland.

**great circle** Circle on a spherical surface, whose center is coincident with the center of the sphere. On the celestial sphere, the EQUATOR is a great circle, as are all MERIDIANS. The shortest distance between any two points on a sphere, great circles are used for mapping aircraft routes.

**Great Dane** (German mastiff) Large hunting dog, originally bred in Germany more than 400 years ago. One of the largest dog breeds, it has a long narrow head and large blunt muzzle. Its deep-chested body is set on long, strong legs. The smooth coat may be various colors. Height: up to 36in (92cm) at the shoulder.

**Great Depression** Severe economic DEPRESSION that afflicted the US throughout the 1930s. At the close of the 1920s, economic factors such as overproduction, unrealistic credit levels, stock market speculation, lack of external markets, and unequal distribution of wealth all contributed to the prolonged economic crisis. The dramatic collapse of the stock market in October 1929 saw $30 billion wiped off stock values in the first week. Bank failures became commonplace. At the depth of the Depression (1932–33), unemployment stood at 16 million, almost 33% of the total work force. The gross national product fell by almost 50%. The Hawley-Smoot Tariff Act increased US tariffs, and effectively spread the depression worldwide. Franklin D. ROOSEVELT, sensing the national emergency, instituted the NEW DEAL, which helped to mitigate the worst effects of the crisis. However, the economy only really started to pick up with increased defense spending in the 1940s.

**Great Dividing Range** (Eastern Highlands) Series of mountain ranges along the E coast of Australia. They extend S from the Atherton Tableland in Queensland to the Grampian Mountains in Victoria (S). The highest peak is Mount Kosciusko, 7,316ft (2,230m). Length: 2,300 mi (3,703km).

**Greater Antilles** Largest of three major island groups in the WEST INDIES, between the Atlantic Ocean and the Caribbean Sea. The group includes CUBA, HISPANIOLA, JAMAICA, PUERTO RICO, and the CAYMAN ISLANDS.

**Great Lakes** World's largest expanse of fresh water; five lakes in central North America, between Canada and the US. They are, from W to E, lakes SUPERIOR, MICHIGAN, HURON, ERIE, and ONTARIO. They are connected by straits, rivers, and canals, providing a continuous waterway. They are drained by the ST. LAWRENCE River, the deepening of which opened up the lakes to world shipping. The growth in industry and commerce has brought people and pollution to the lakes' shores. Major cities include CHICAGO, TORONTO, DETROIT, BUFFALO, CLEVELAND, and MILWAUKEE. Total surface area: *c.*94,700sq mi (245,300sq km).

**Great Leap Forward** Five-year economic plan begun by MAO ZEDONG in China in 1958. It aimed to double industrial production and boost agricultural output in record time. Tens of millions of workers were mobilized to smelt steel in primitive furnaces, but much of the steel proved useless. Collective farms were merged into communes, but progress was dashed by a succession of poor harvests. After four years the government was forced to admit failure.

**Great Plains** High, extensive region of grassland in central North America. The Great Plains extend from the Canadian provinces of Alberta, Saskatchewan, and Manitoba through W central US to Texas. The plateau slopes down and E from the Rocky Mountains. It is a sparsely populated region with a semiarid climate, prone to high winds. The chinook wind warms the otherwise bitter winter. Most of the land is prairie, and cattle-ranching and sheep-rearing are the main economic activities. The soil is often fertile, and wheat is the principal crop. The Great Plains were roamed by Native Americans until Europeans destroyed the herds of BISON. The railroads brought settlers in the late 19th century, but drought and soil mismanagement resulted in the 1930s DUST BOWL.

**Great Red Spot** *See* JUPITER

**Great Salt Lake** Large, shallow saltwater lake in NW Utah. It is fed by the Bear, Weber, and Jordan rivers, and its depth and area vary with climatic changes. The heavy brine supports only shrimp and algae. It is the remnant of the prehistoric Lake Bonneville, which covered much of the GREAT BASIN of North America. Bonneville Salt Flats, famous for land speed records, lies in the Great Salt Desert. Area: varies from *c.*960sq mi (2,500sq km) to *c.*2,400sq mi (6,200sq km).

**Great Schism** Division within the Roman Catholic Church resulting in the election of rival popes (1378–1417). An Italian line of popes continued in Rome, and a rival "antipope" line in AVIGNON, France. The SCHISM ended with the Council of CONSTANCE (1414–17), which established Martin V as the only pope.

**Great Slave Lake** Second largest lake in Canada, W Northwest Territories; the deepest lake in North America. It is named for the Slave tribe of Native Americans. The first European discovery was in 1771. Gold is mined on its N shore. It is drained by the Mackenzie River. Area: *c.*10,980sq mi (28,400sq km). Max. depth: 2,015ft (615m).

**Great Smoky Mountains** Part of the APPALACHIANS, on the North Carolina–Tennessee border. One of the oldest ranges on Earth, it includes the largest virgin forest of red spruce. The region is renowned for its flora and fauna. Early 20th-century exploitation of the region was restricted by the establishment of a national park. The highest point is Clingmans Dome, 6,643ft (2,026m). Area: 806sq mi (2,090sq km).

**Great Trek** (1835–40) Migration of *c.*12,000 BOERS from Cape Colony into the South African interior. Their motives were to escape British control and to acquire cheap land. The majority settled in the regions that were later called Orange FREE STATE, TRANSVAAL, and NATAL.

**Great Wall of China** Defensive frontier and world heritage site, *c.*1,500mi (2,400km) long, extending from the Huang Hai (Yellow Sea) to the central Asian desert, N China. It is an amalgamation of fortifications constructed by various dynasties. Sections of the wall were first built by the Warring States. QIN SHIHUANGDI ordered that they should be joined to form a unified boundary (214 BC). The present wall was mostly built 600 years ago by the MING dynasty. It averages 25ft (7.6m) high and up to 30ft (9m) thick. A section of the wall outside Beijing is open to tourists.

**Great Zimbabwe** Ruined city and world heritage site, SE Zimbabwe. It was the capital of a Bantu-speaking kingdom (12th–15th century). At the height of its power, the city's population probably numbered more than 15,000. The city's 30ft (9m) tower is a national symbol.

**grebe** Brown, gray and black freshwater diving bird found worldwide. It flies laboriously and has legs set so far back that it cannot walk. There are six common species in North America and five in Britain and W Europe. Length: to 19in (48cm). Family Podicepididae; genus *Podiceps.*

## GREECE

Blue and white became Greece's national colors during the war of independence (1821–29). The nine horizontal stripes on the flag, which was finally adopted in 1970, represent the nine syllables of the battle cry *Eleutheria i thanatos* ("Freedom or Death").

**AREA:** 50,961sq mi (131,990sq km)
**POPULATION:** 10,300,000
**CAPITAL (POPULATION):** Athens (3,072,922)
**GOVERNMENT:** Multiparty republic
**ETHNIC GROUPS:** Greek 96%, Macedonian 2%, Turkish 1%, Albanian, Slav
**LANGUAGES:** Greek (official)
**RELIGIONS:** Christianity (Eastern Orthodox 97%), Islam 2%
**CURRENCY:** Drachma = 100 lepta

The mountainous, maritime Hellenic Republic can be divided into four geographical regions: Northern Greece includes the historic regions of THRACE and MACEDONIA, and its second-largest city THESSALONÍKI. Central Greece, N of the Gulf of Corinth, includes the capital and largest city, ATHENS, and its highest peak, Mount OLYMPUS at 9,570ft (2,917m). Southern Greece is the PELOPONNESUS peninsula, and includes the city of CORINTH. The fourth region is the Greek islands, which constitute *c.*20% of Greece. These include CRETE (the largest) in the Mediterranean Sea, the DODECANESE group (including RHODES), EUBOEA, and LESBOS in the Aegean Sea.

### CLIMATE

Low-lying areas have mild, moist winters and hot, dry summers. The E coast has *c.*50% of the rainfall of the W. The mountains have a much more severe climate.

### VEGETATION

Much of Greece's original vegetation has been destroyed. Some areas are covered by maquis.

### HISTORY AND POLITICS

Crete was the center of MINOAN CIVILIZATION, between *c.*3000 and 1450 BC. The Minoans were followed by the MYCENAEAN CIVILIZATION, which prospered until the DORIANS settled *c.*1200 BC. Powerful city-states emerged, such as SPARTA and Athens. Solon established DEMOCRACY in Athens (5th century BC). The revolt of the IONIANS started the PERSIAN WARS (499–79 BC). *See* GREECE, ANCIENT

Athens was defeated in the PELOPONNESIAN WAR (431–04 BC), and Corinth and THEBES gained control. In 338 BC MACEDONIA, led by PHILIP II, became the dominant power. His son, ALEXANDER THE GREAT, ushered in the HELLENISTIC AGE. Greece became a Roman province in 146 BC. Greece formed part of the BYZANTINE EMPIRE from AD 330–1453. In 1456, the Ottomans conquered Greece. The Greek War of Independence (1821–27) was supported by the European powers, and an independent monarchy was established (1832). As king of the Hellenes (1863–1913), GEORGE I recovered much Greek territory. In 1913 Greece gained Crete. Greece finally entered World War I on the Allied side (1917). In 1923, 1.5 million Greeks from Asia Minor were resettled in Greece. In 1936 METAXAS became premier. His dictatorial regime remained neutral at the start of World War II. By May 1941, Germany had occupied Greece. Resistance movements recaptured most territory by 1944, and the Germans withdrew. From 1946–49 a civil war raged between communist and royalist forces. In 1951 Greece was admitted to NATO. In 1955 KARAMANLIS became prime minister, the economy improved, but tension with Turkey over CYPRUS surfaced. In 1964 a republican, George PAPANDREOU, became prime minister. In 1967 a military dictatorship seized power. The "Greek Colonels" imposed harsh controls on dissent. In 1973 the monarchy was abolished and Greece became a presidential republic. Civil unrest led to the 1974 restoration of civilian government, headed by Karamanlis. In 1981 Greece joined the EUROPEAN COMMUNITY, and Andreas PAPANDREOU became Greece's first socialist prime minister. In 1990 Karamanlis returned as president. In 1995 he was succeeded by Constantine Stephanopoulos. The 1996 general election was won by the Panhellenic Socialist Party (PASOK) led by Kostas Simitis.

### ECONOMY

Greece is one of the poorest members of the European Union (1995 GDP per capita, US$11,710). Manufacturing is important. Products: textiles, cement, chemicals. Minerals: lignite, bauxite, chromite. Farmland covers *c.*33% of Greece; grazing land covers 40%. Major crops: tobacco, fruit (olives, grapes), cotton, wheat. Shipping and tourism are major sectors.

G

**Greco, El** (1541–1614) Spanish painter, b. Crete. His early style was influenced by TITIAN. By 1577 he had settled in Toledo. His earliest work here, *The Assumption of the Virgin*, combines Spanish influences with the Italian. His characteristically elongated and distorted figures disregard normal rules of perspective. His later paintings, such as *Burial of Count Orgasz* (1586), *Agony in the Garden* (1610), and *Assumption* (1613), express his profound religious conviction.

**Greece** Republic in SE Europe. See country feature, page 295

**Greece, ancient** Period beginning with the defeat of the second Persian invasion in 479 BC and ending with the establishment of Macedonian power in 338 BC. Warring city-states flourished as centers of trade. ATHENS, the most wealthy and powerful, developed a democratic system under the guidance of PERICLES. Its main rival was the military state of SPARTA. Classical Greece was the birthplace of many ideas in art, literature, philosophy, and science – among them those of PLATO and ARISTOTLE. Hence it is traditionally regarded as the birthplace of Western civilization.

**Greek** INDO-EUROPEAN LANGUAGE spoken in Greece since *c*.2000 BC. In ancient Greece there were several dialects: Attic, spoken in Athens, is the most common in literary records. Greek was widely spoken in the Middle East during the HELLENISTIC AGE. It was the official language of the Byzantine Empire, and began to evolve into its modern form in *c*.1000 AD. After the fall of Byzantium, it developed two forms: "demotiki," the spoken language also used in most literary forms, and "katharevousa," used in official documents.

**Greek art and architecture** Greek architecture came into its own in the 6th century BC when stone replaced wood as the building material for civic and temple buildings. Distinct ORDERS OF ARCHITECTURE began to emerge. The earliest remaining Doric temple is the Temple of Hera at Olympia (late 7th century BC), and the most outstanding example is the PARTHENON. Among Ionic temples, the Erechtheum is considered the most perfect. The Corinthian mausoleum at Halicarnassus (350 BC) was one of the SEVEN WONDERS OF THE WORLD. Greek art may be divided into four chronological periods: Geometric (late 11th–late 8th century BC), Archaic (late 8th century–480 BC), Classical (480–323 BC), and Hellenistic (323–27 BC). Only a few small bronze horses survive from the Geometric period. During the Archaic period, stone sculpture appeared, vase painting proliferated, and the human figure became a common subject. Civic wealth and pride was a feature of the Classical period, and sculpture reached its peak of serene perfection. The Hellenistic period is noted for increasingly dramatic works.

**Greek drama** First form of DRAMA in Western civilization, which took three forms, TRAGEDY, COMEDY, and satyr plays. Tragedy and comedy were the two main forms. Tragedy developed from religious festivals, at which a CHORUS sang responses to a leader. AESCHYLUS introduced a second actor, and SOPHOCLES added a third. The other major tragedian was EURIPIDES. Greek tragedy usually dealt with mythical subjects, but sometimes (as in Aeschylus' *The Persians*) used recent history for its setting. A tradition of Greek comedy arose in the 5th century BC. It was often highly topical and lampooned politics and the conventions of tragedy; its best-known exponent was ARISTOPHANES. Comedy flourished in the Hellenistic Age (323–27 BC), especially in the work of MENANDER. Satyr plays were bawdy works written to accompany tragedies.

**Greek literature** One of the longest surviving traditions in world literature. The earliest Greek literature took the form of EPIC poems, as epitomized by the *Iliad* and the *Odyssey* of Homer; and the didactic poetry of Hesiod, such as *Theogony*. It also saw the development of lyric poetry, exemplified by the choric lyrics and odes of PINDAR. Throughout the Classical period (480–323 BC), there was a tradition of fine literature in poetry and prose writing. During the Hellenistic Age (323–27 BC), epic, epigrammatic, and didactic poetry flourished in the works of Apollonius of Rhodes, Aratus, and Callimachus. During the Roman period (*c*.27 BC–*c*.AD 330), important figures included PLUTARCH, MARCUS AURELIUS, and PTOLEMY. Writing in Greek died out after the Turkish invasions of the 15th century and was only revived after their overthrow in 1828. Prominent among the new generation were Dionysios Solomos and Andreas Kalvos. Modern Greek writers of international stature include KAZANTZAKIS.

**Greek mythology** Collection of stories mainly concerning the adventures of gods and heroes. In the myths, the gods are not wholly admirable figures: they have similar weaknesses to humans and are capable of great vindictiveness, revenge, and favoritism. Greek myths were often explanatory, offering answers to questions of human nature and the universe, clarifying abstract ideas, or explaining religious matters in a more rational manner.

**Greeley, Horace** (1811–72) US journalist and political leader. Greeley founded and edited the *New York Tribune* (1841). The editorials he wrote in the *Tribune* influenced national opinion. He advocated progressive social reforms, such as labor unions, and was a vigorous opponent of slavery. His advocacy of Western settlement was encapsulated in his advice, "Go West, young man, go West." A supporter of LINCOLN, he served briefly in Congress (1848–49). His bid for the presidency for the Liberal Republican Party (1872) was defeated by Ulysses S. GRANT.

**green algae** Large group of marine and freshwater ALGAE (phylum Chlorophyta). They are distinct from other algae by virtue of possessing cup-shaped CHLOROPLASTS that contain chlorophyll b, and by producing cells with flagella at some stage in their lives. Green algae range in size from microscopic single-cell types to large, complex SEAWEEDS. *See also* LICHEN

**Greenaway, Peter** (1942– ) Welsh film director and screenwriter. An innovative and painterly director, his breakthrough film was *The Draughtsman's Contract* (1983). Other films include *The Cook, the Thief, His Wife, and Her Lover* (1989), *Prospero's Books* (1991) and *The Pillow Book* (1996).

**greenback** Popular name for paper money issued by the US government during the Civil War. Greenbacks were authorized by Congress as legal tender but could not be redeemed in gold. A total of $450 million was issued. They became convertible to gold in 1878.

**Greenback Party** US political party (1875–84). Deriving its main support from Western farmers, it favored the issue of more GREENBACKS to stimulate the economy and raise farm prices. Its presidential candidate, Peter Cooper, lost the 1876 election, but the party had 14 Congressmen in 1878. It declined in the 1880s.

**Greene, (Henry) Graham** (1904–91) British novelist and dramatist. Greene converted to Catholicism in 1926; religion, guilt, and the search for redemption are consistent themes in his novels. His psychological thrillers are among the most popular and critically acclaimed works of 20th-century fiction. His first novel was *The Man Within* (1929). Important works include *Brighton Rock* (1938), *The Power and the Glory* (1940), *The Heart of the Matter* (1948), *The Quiet American* (1955), the "entertainment" *Our Man in Havana* (1958), *The Honorary Consul* (1973), and *Travels with My Aunt* (1978).

**Greene, Nathanael** (1743–86) US general. Greene was an outstanding general in the AMERICAN REVOLUTION and was WASHINGTON'S second-in-command. In 1776 he skillfully led the left wing of the American forces at Trenton, Princeton, and Brandywine. Greene assumed command of the Southern army in 1780. His reorganization and strategy ensured the success of the Carolina Campaign (1780–82), which resulted in numerous British defeats.

**greenhouse effect** Raised temperature at a planet's surface as a result of heat energy being trapped by gases in the ATMOSPHERE. As the Sun's rays pass through Earth's atmosphere, some heat is absorbed but most of the shortwave SOLAR ENERGY passes through. This energy is reemitted by the Earth as long-wave radiation, which cannot pass easily through the atmosphere. More heat is retained if there is a CLOUD layer. In recent centuries, more heat has been retained due to the increased levels of carbon dioxide ($CO_2$) from the burning of FOSSIL FUELS. Tiny particles of $CO_2$ form an extra layer, which acts like the glass in a greenhouse. Scientists argue that the greenhouse effect is contributing to GLOBAL WARMING.

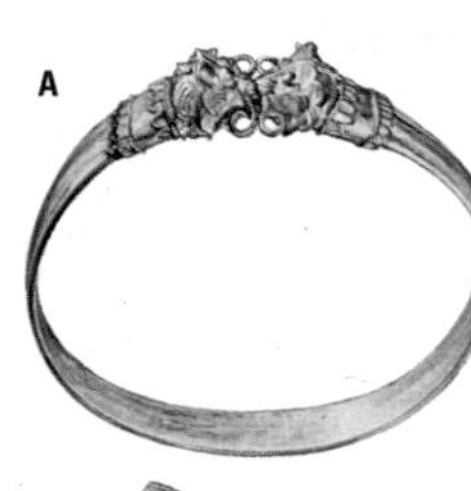

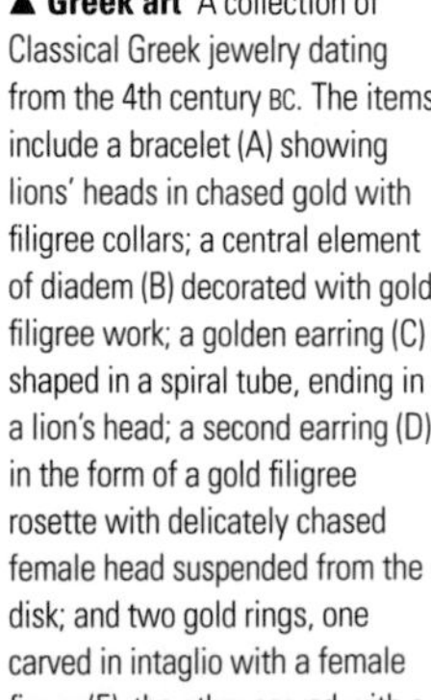


▲ **Greek art** A collection of Classical Greek jewelry dating from the 4th century BC. The items include a bracelet (A) showing lions' heads in chased gold with filigree collars; a central element of diadem (B) decorated with gold filigree work; a golden earring (C) shaped in a spiral tube, ending in a lion's head; a second earring (D) in the form of a gold filigree rosette with delicately chased female head suspended from the disk; and two gold rings, one carved in intaglio with a female figure (E), the other carved with a woman's profile (F).

**Greenland** World's largest island, in the NW Atlantic Ocean, lying mostly within the Arctic Circle. It is a self-governing province of Denmark; the capital is Nuuk (Godthåb). More than 85% of Greenland is covered by PERMAFROST, with an average depth of 5,000ft (1,500m). Settlement is confined to the SW coast, which is warmed by Atlantic currents. Most of Greenland's inhabitants are INUIT. Its European discovery is credited to ERIC THE RED, who settled in 982, founding a colony that lasted more than 500 years. Greenland became a Danish possession in 1380, and was incorporated into the kingdom in 1953. Following a referendum, Greenland achieved home rule (1979) and self-government (1981). In 1985 it withdrew from the EU. Greenland's economy is heavily dependent on subsidies from Denmark. Fish forms the basis of the economy. Lead and zinc are mined in the NW, and the S has untapped reserves of uranium. Tourism is increasing. Area: 840,000sq mi (2,175,000sq km). Pop. (1993 ) 55,117.

**Green Mountain Boys** Militia formed in 1764 to uphold the settlers' rights to the New Hampshire grants (now Vermont). Ethan Allen assumed command of the Green Mountain Boys in 1770, and they helped take Fort Ticonderoga from the British on May 10, 1775.

**green movement** Campaign to preserve the environment and to minimize pollution or destruction of the Earth's natural habitat. The green movement formed its own active pressure groups GREENPEACE and Friends of the Earth in the early 1970s. It gained political representation shortly afterward in the form of various European Green Parties. In affluent Western societies, effects of the movement have included the production of environmentally safe products and a heightened concern with the recycling of waste products such as paper and plastics.

**Green Party** Any of a number of European political parties embodying the principles of the GREEN MOVEMENT.

**Greenpeace** International pressure group. It was founded in Canada in 1971, initially to oppose US nuclear testing In Alaska. Greenpeace promotes environmental awareness and campaigns against environmental abuse. It gains wide media coverage for its active, nonviolent demonstrations against whaling, toxic-waste dumping, and nuclear testing.

**green revolution** Intensive plan of the 1960s to increase crop yields in developing countries by introducing higher-yielding strains of plant and new fertilizers. The scheme began in Mexico in the 1940s and was successfully introduced in parts of India, SE Asia, the Middle East, and Latin America.

**Greenville, Treaty of Fort** (1795) Agreement signed by Native Americans of Ohio and Indiana after their defeat by US General Anthony WAYNE in the Battle of Fallen Timbers. The Native Americans ceded most of their lands, giving the US full control of the Northwest Territory. The agreement restored peace between the US and the Native Americans and broke the British-Native American alliance.

**Greenwich** Borough in SE London, England. In Greenwich Park stands the former Royal Observatory (founded 1675). The prime meridian forms the basis of GREENWICH MEAN TIME (GMT). Greenwich has a rich maritime history. Pop. (1991) 207,650.

**Greenwich Mean Time (GMT)** Local time at GREENWICH, London, situated on the prime meridian. It has been used as the basis for calculating standard time in various parts of the world since 1884.

**Greer, Germaine** (1939– ) Australian feminist author. Her controversial book *The Female Eunuch* (1970) portrayed marriage as a legalized form of female slavery and questioned a number of gender-oriented stereotypes. Other works include *Sex and Destiny: the Politics of Human Fertility* (1984) and *The Change: Women, Aging and the Menopause* (1991).

**Gregory I, Saint** (540–604) (Gregory the Great) Pope (590–604). He devoted himself to alleviating poverty and hunger among the Romans. His reforms included changes in the Mass, and he initiated the conversion of the LOMBARDS. He sent Saint AUGUSTINE to convert the ANGLO-SAXONS. He is considered a saint and is regarded as one of the Fathers of the Church. His feast day is March 12.

**Gregory VII** (1020–85) Pope (1073–85), b. Hildebrand. He brought about various reforms to counteract abuses in the church and twice excommunicated the Holy Roman Emperor Henry IV. He increased the papacy's temporal power.

**Gregory XIII** (1502–85) Pope (1572–85), b. Ugo Buoncompagni. He supported education, training for the clergy, and missionary activity, especially the JESUITS. He promoted church reform and sought to carry out the decrees of the Council of TRENT. He is best known for his reform of the Julian CALENDAR (1582).

**Grenada** Independent island nation in the SE Caribbean Sea, the most southerly of the WINDWARD ISLANDS, *c.*100mi (160km) N of Venezuela. It consists of Grenada and the smaller islands of the Southern Grenadines dependency; the capital is St. George's. First sighted in 1498 by Christopher COLUMBUS, the islands were then inhabited by the Carib. In the mid-17th century Grenada was settled by the French. It became a permanent British possession in 1783 and a crown colony in 1877, and was a member of the West Indian Federation (1958–62). In 1974 it became an independent Commonwealth state. In 1979 the New Jewel movement seized power, and in 1983, following a military coup, US forces invaded the island. They were withdrawn in 1985 after the reestablishment of a democratic government. Elections in 1995 were won by the New National Party, led by Dr. Reith Mitchell. The country is volcanic in origin, with a ridge of mountains running N – S. It has a tropical climate with occasional hurricanes. The economy is largely agricultural, based on cocoa, bananas, sugar, spices, and citrus fruits. It is also heavily dependent on tourism. Area: 133sq mi (344sq km). Pop. (1995 est.) 96,000.

**Grenadines** Group of *c.*600 small islands in the S Windward Islands, Caribbean Sea, WEST INDIES. The S Grenadines are included in GRENADA. The N Grenadines form part of ST. VINCENT AND THE GRENADINES. Industries: cotton, limes, livestock, tourism.

**Grenville, Sir Richard** (1541–91) English naval commander and hero. He commanded the fleet that carried Sir Walter Raleigh's colonists to Roanoke, Virginia, in 1585. His adventurous career ended when he was fatally wounded and his ship, *Revenge*, captured in a 15-hour battle off the Azores (1591).

**Gretzky, Wayne** (1961– ) ("the Great Gretzky") Canadian ice hockey player. He led the Edmonton Oilers to a series of National Hockey League (NHL) titles before being traded to the Los Angeles Kings in 1988. In 1981–82 he became the first player to achieve more than 200 points (212). In 1994 he established a new NHL record for most career points (goals and assists). In 1996 he moved from the Kings to join the New York Rangers.

**Grey, Charles, 2nd Earl** (1764–1845) British Prime Minister (1830–34). During his administration the First REFORM ACT was passed (1832). Grey supported limited parliamentary reform, though as a Whig aristocrat he was no radical.

**Grey, Lady Jane** (1537–54) (Nine-Day Queen) Queen of England (1553). Great-granddaughter of Henry VII, she was married to the son of the Duke of NORTHUMBERLAND, regent for the ailing EDWARD VI. On Edward VI's death she was proclaimed queen, but the rightful heir, MARY I, was almost universally preferred. Lady Jane and her husband were executed.

**Grey, Zane** (1875–1939) US novelist. One of the best-known writers in the western genre, his most popular novel was *Riders of the Purple Sage* (1912). His cowboy stories present brawny heroes, loyal to the ethics of the frontier, who overcome callous villains. He was also a noted writer on fishing.

**Grieg, Edvard Hagerup** (1843–1907) Norwegian composer. He used Norwegian folk themes in his compositions, many of which are for piano or voice. Among his best-known works are the song *I Love Thee* (1864), the two *Peer Gynt* suites for orchestra (1876), and the Piano Concerto (1868).

**Griffith, Arthur** (1872–1922) Irish statesman, founder of SINN FÉIN. From 1899 he edited the republican newspaper *United Irishman*. Griffith regarded armed resistance as impractical and took no part in the EASTER RISING (1916). He was

▲ **Gretzky** Canadian ice-hockey star Wayne Gretzky was the first player eve to exceed 200 points (goals and assists) in a season. As well as breaking other records, he was voted Most Valuable Player in the National Hockey League from 1980–87.

elected vice president of the Dáil Éireann (1918) and led the negotiations that created the Irish Free State (1921). When DE VALERA rejected the settlement, Griffith became president.

**Griffith, D.W. (David Wark)** (1875–1948) US film director. He was the most influential figure in the development of the cinema in the US. His directorial debut was *The Adventures of Dollie* (1908). His expressive use of the camera, lighting, and dramatic editing established film as an independent art form. In 1915 he released the Civil War epic *The Birth of a Nation*, often cited as the most important document in cinematic history, but also condemned as racist. *Intolerance* (1916) was his response, examining the persistence of prejudice. In 1919 he cofounded United Artists. *Abraham Lincoln* (1930) was his first talkie and *The Struggle* (1931) his final film. In 1935 Griffith won an honorary Oscar.

**griffon** (griffon vulture) Carrion-eating bird of prey of Eurasia and N Africa, with gold or sandy-brown plumage. It is gregarious and nests in large flocks. Length: 3.3ft (1m). Family Accipitridae; species *Gyps fulvus*.

G

**Grimm brothers** German philologists and folklorists. Jakob Ludwig Karl (1785–1863) formulated **Grimm's law**, which detailed the regular shifting of consonants (such as *p* to *f*, as in the Latin word *pater* to the English *father*) in INDO-EUROPEAN LANGUAGES. It was a landmark in the study of language. He and his brother Wilhelm Karl (1786–1859) are popularly known for their enduring collection of folk tales, *Grimm's Fairy Tales* (1812–15). It was a major text of ROMANTICISM.

**Gris, Juan** (1887–1927) Spanish painter. He settled in Paris in 1906 and, with PICASSO and BRAQUE, became a leading exponent of CUBISM. Later works include collages, architectonic paintings, stage sets, and costumes for DIAGHILEV.

**Griswold v. Connecticut** (1965) Landmark US Supreme Court decision in which Justice William O. Douglas developed the "penumbra theory" of the right to privacy as protected by the First Amendment. The Court invalidated a state anti-contraceptive law.

**grizzly bear** Large BEAR, generally considered to be a variety of brown bear (*Ursus arctos*) although sometimes classified as a separate species (*Ursus horribilis*). Once widespread in W North America, the grizzly is now rare except in W Canada, Alaska, and some US national parks. Length: to 7ft (2.5m); weight: 900lb (410kg).

**Gromyko, Andrei** (1909–89) Soviet statesman, foreign minister (1957–85), president (1985–88). Soviet ambassador to the US (1943–46), Gromyko took part in the Yalta and Potsdam peace conferences (1945). He acted as the permanent Soviet delegate to the United Nations (1946–48). As foreign minister, he was influential in establishing the round of summits between the US and Soviet presidents. GORBACHEV promoted Gromyko to the presidency, but he was forced to retire in 1988.

**Groningen** City at the confluence of the Hoornse Diep and the Winschoter Diep, NE Netherlands; capital of Groningen province. A member of the HANSEATIC LEAGUE from 1284, it controlled most of Friesland. Groningen remained loyal to the Hapsburgs, but was forced to surrender to the Dutch in 1594. The surrounding fertile agricultural land makes it one of the country's biggest markets. Industries: shipbuilding, electrical equipment. Pop. (1994) 170,535.

**Gropius, Walter** (1883–1969) German-American architect, founder of the BAUHAUS (1919–28). Gropius transformed the Weimar School of Art into the Bauhaus, which was relocated to his newly designed buildings in Dessau (1926). He fled Germany (1934) and headed the Harvard school of architecture (1937–52). Gropius pioneered functional design and INTERNATIONAL STYLE in particular. The results of his cooperative, group-work design methods can be seen in the Harvard graduate center and the US embassy, Athens.

**grosbeak** Any of several birds of the FINCH family (fringillidae). They have short, thick, seed-cracking beaks. Found in woodlands of the Americas, Europe, and Asia, species include the rose-breasted grosbeak (*Pheucticus ludovicianus*) of North and South America, and the pine grosbeak (*Pinicolor enucleator*) of Canada and N Europe. Length: 7– 10in (18–25cm).

**gross domestic product (GDP)** Total amount of goods and services produced by a country annually. It does not include income from investments or overseas possessions. GDP gives an indication of the strength of national industry. *See also* GROSS NATIONAL PRODUCT (GNP)

**gross national product (GNP)** Total market value of all goods and services produced by a country annually, plus net income from abroad. GNP is a universal indicator of economic performance, and provides an assessment of different economic sectors. GNP is the sum of four types of spending: private consumption (goods and services bought by the community), government expenditure, balance of trade, and business investment. *See also* GROSS DOMESTIC PRODUCT (GDP)

**Gros Ventre** (Fr. big belly) Name given by settlers to two distinct tribes of Native North Americans: the HIDATSA and the Atsina. The Atsina were a band of Arapaho, and the Hidatsa were related to the Crow. The sign language for the names of the two tribes was similar.

**Grosz, George** (1893–1959) German illustrator and painter. A founder of the DADA movement in Berlin, he satirized capitalist and military corruption in drawings and caricatures, such as *Ecce Homo* (1923). He settled in the US in 1932. His later works showed some affinity with SURREALISM.

**groundnut** *See* PEANUT

**ground squirrel** (gopher) Terrestrial SQUIRREL native to Eurasia and North America. Ground squirrels eat plants, seeds, insects, small animals, and eggs. Most have grayish-red to brown fur; some are striped or spotted. Length: to 16in (40.5cm); weight: 0.1–2.2lb (85–1,000g). Family Sciuridae; genus *Citellus* (and others).

**ground water** Water that lies beneath the surface of the Earth. It comes chiefly from rain, although some is of volcanic or sedimentary origin. It moves through porous rocks and soil and can be collected in wells. Ground water can dissolve minerals and leave deposits, creating structures such as CAVES, STALAGMITES, and STALACTITES. *See also* WATER TABLE

**grouper** Tropical marine fish found from the coast of Florida to South America, and in the Indian and Pacific oceans. It has a large mouth, sharp teeth, a mottled body, and the ability to change color. Length: to 12ft (3.7m); weight: to 1,000lb (450kg). Family Serranidae; species: giant, *Epinephelus itajara*; Australian, *Epinephelus lanceolatus*.

**Group of Eight (G8)** (formerly Group of Seven – G7) Eight nations that meet for an annual economic summit meeting. In 1975 the heads of government of what were regarded as the world's seven wealthiest nations – the US, Japan, Germany, Britain, France, Canada, and Italy – met in the first of these meeting. The changing world economy has led other countries to seek membership. In 1997 Russia was formally admitted to the group.

**grouse** Plump game bird of N areas of the Northern Hemisphere. Grouse are fowllike, but have feathered ankles and toes, and brightly colored air sacs on the neck. Family Tetraonidae. *See also* PRAIRIE CHICKEN

**Grozny** City in the Caucasus Mountains, SW Russia; the capital of CHECHENYA. Founded in 1818, it has been an oil-producing center since 1893 and has a pipeline to the Black Sea and the Donets Basin. Grozny was severely damaged in fighting between Russian forces and Chechen rebels from 1994–96, and there were many civilian casualties. Industries: oil, petrochemicals. Pop. (1992) 388,000.

**Grünewald, Mathias** (1470–1528) German painter. He was Dürer's greatest contemporary, and one of the earliest exponents of EXPRESSIONISM. Grünewald focused on religious themes, especially crucifixions.

**Guadalajara** City in SW Mexico; capital of Jalisco state and second-largest city in Mexico. Founded in 1531, it has become a major industrial center. It has some fine Spanish colonial architecture. Noted for its mountain scenery and mild climate, it is a popular health resort. It has two universities (1792 and 1935). Industries: engineering, textiles, food processing, pottery, glassware. Pop. (1990) 1,650,205.

**Guadalcanal** Largest of the Solomon Islands, *c.*600 mi (970km) E of New Guinea, W central Pacific Ocean; the capital is Honiara. Guadalcanal was the scene of heavy fighting between Japanese and US troops in World War II. The chief products are coconuts, fish, fruit, and timber. Area: 2,047sq mi (5,302sq km). Pop. (1991 est.) 60,692.

**Guadalupe-Hidalgo, Treaty of** (1848) Peace settlement ending the Mexican War. Mexico ceded the present states of Texas, New Mexico, Arizona, California, Nevada, and Utah, plus parts of Colorado and Wyoming. The US paid $15 million in compensation.

**Guadalupe Mountains National Park** Park in w Texas. The region was established as a national park in 1966. The mountains contain portions of an extensive Permian limestone fossil reef. The park features unusual flora and fauna. Area: 127sq mi (328sq km).

**Guadeloupe** French overseas department (since 1946), consisting of the islands of Basse-Terre (w), Grande-Terre (e), and several smaller islands in the Leeward Islands, e West Indies. Discovered in 1493 by Columbus, Guadeloupe was settled by the French (1635), briefly held by Britain and Sweden, and reverted to French rule in 1816. Chief crops are sugar cane and bananas. Industries: distilling, tourism. Area: 687sq mi (1,780sq km). Pop. (1990) 378,178.

**Guam** Southernmost and largest of the Mariana Islands in the w Pacific Ocean; the capital is Agaña. An unincorporated US territory, Guam was discovered by Ferdinand Magellan (1521) and ceded to the US (1898). Guam was the first US territory to be occupied by the Japanese during World War II. Industries: oil refining, palm oil, fish products. Area: 209sq mi (541sq km). Pop (1992 est.) 140,200.

**Guangxi** (Kwangsi) Autonomous region in s China; the capital is Nanning. It was established in 1958 for the Zhuang, China's largest minority nationality. Cultivation is limited by the mountainous terrain. Minerals include manganese, zinc, tin, tungsten, and antimony. Industries: oil refining, fertilizers. Area: 85,133sq mi (220,495sq km). Pop. (1990) 21,000,000.

**Guangzhou** (Canton) Largest city in s China, on the Pearl River; capital of Guangdong province. Since 300 BC it has been an important trading port. The birthplace of Sun Yat-sen, it was the focal point of the nationalist revolution (1911). A military academy was established in 1924, under Chiang Kai-shek. It is s China's leading industrial and commercial city. Industries: textiles, rubber products, shipbuilding, sugar refining, iron, steel. Pop. (1993 est.) 3,560,000.

**Guaraní** Native South American tribe and language. The tribe's population has decreased greatly, although most Paraguayans are descended from Guaraní. Their language has survived as Paraguay's second national language.

▲ **guava** The fruit of the tropical American tree (*Psidium guajava*) is high in vitamin C. It is most commonly made into guava jelly, but it can also be stewed and canned.

G

## GUATEMALA

Guatemala's flag was adopted in 1871, but its origins go back to the days of the Central American Federation (1823–39), which was set up after the break from Spain in 1821. The Federation included Costa Rica, El Salvador, Guatemala, Honduras, and Nicaragua.

**AREA:** 42,042sq mi (108,890sq km)
**POPULATION:** 9,745,000
**CAPITAL (POPULATION):** Guatemala City (2,000,000)
**GOVERNMENT:** Republic
**ETHNIC GROUPS:** Native American 45%, Ladino (mixed Hispanic and native American) 45%, White 5%, Black 2%, others including Chinese 3%
**LANGUAGES:** Spanish (official)
**RELIGIONS:** Christianity (Roman Catholic 75%, Protestant 25%)
**CURRENCY:** Guatemalan quetzal = 100 centavos

The Central American republic of Guatemala contains a densely populated fertile mountain region. The capital, Guatemala City, is situated here. The highlands run in an e–w direction and contain many volcanoes. Guatemala is subject to frequent earthquakes and volcanic eruptions. The inactive volcano Tajmulco is the highest peak in Central America, at 13,816ft (4,211m).

South of the highlands lie the Pacific coastal lowlands. North of the highlands is the thinly populated Caribbean plain and the vast Petén tropical forest. Guatemala's largest lake, Izabal, drains into the Caribbean Sea.

### Climate

Guatemala lies in the tropics and the lowlands are hot and rainy. The central mountain region is more temperate. Guatemala City, at *c*.5,000ft (1,500m) above sea level, has a pleasant, warm climate, with a marked dry season between November and April.

### Vegetation

Hardwoods, such as mahogany, rubber, palm, and chicozapote (from which chicle, used in chewing gum, is obtained), grow in the tropical forests in the n, with mangrove swamps on the coast. Oak and willow grow in the highlands, with fir and pine at higher levels. Much of the land on the Pacific plains is farmed.

### History and Politics

Between AD 300 and 900, the Quiché branch of the Maya ruled much of Guatemala, but inexplicably abandoned their cities on the n plains. The Quiché ruins at Tikal are the tallest temple pyramids in the Americas. In 1523–24 the Spanish conquistador Pedro de Alvarado defeated the native tribes. In 1821 Guatemala became independent. From 1823–39 it formed part of the Central American Federation. Various dictatorial regimes interfered in the affairs of other Central American states, arousing much resentment and leading to the establishment of the Central American Court of Justice.

In 1941 Guatemala nationalized the German-owned coffee plantations. After World War II Guatemala embarked on further nationalization of plantations. In 1960 the mainly Quiché Guatemalan Revolutionary National Unity Movement (URNG) began a guerrilla war, which has killed over 100,000 people. During the 1960s and 1970s, Guatemala was beset by terrorism and political assassinations. In 1976 Guatemala City was devastated by an earthquake, which killed over 22,000 people.

In 1983 Guatemala reduced its claims to Belize. Civilian rule was restored in 1984, after the US withdrew backing for the Guatemalan military. In 1995 an accord was signed recognizing the rights of the indigenous population. Support for the URNG has dwindled. In 1996 Alvaro Arzú was elected president.

### Economy

Guatemala is a lower-middle-income developing nation (1995 GDP per capita, US$3,340). Agriculture employs 50% of the workforce. Coffee, sugar, bananas, and beef are leading exports. Other important crops are cardamom and cotton. Maize is the chief food crop, but Guatemala has to import food. Forestry is a major activity. Tourism and manufacturing are growing in importance. Manufactures: processed farm products, textiles, wood products, handicrafts.

**Guardi, Francesco** (1712–93) Venetian painter. His vivid, fluid views of Venice were "discovered" by the 19th-century Impressionists. His work is much freer than CANALETTO's.

**Guatemala** Republic in Central America. See country feature, page 299.

**Guatemala City** (Ciudad Guatemala) Capital of Guatemala, on a plateau in the Sierra Madre; largest city in Central America. Founded in 1776, the city was the capital of the Central American Federation from 1823–39. It was badly damaged by earthquakes in 1917–18 and in 1976. Industries: mining, furniture, textiles, handicrafts. Pop. (1989 est.) 2,000,000.

**guava** Any of 100 species of fruit-bearing trees or shrubs native to tropical America and the West Indies. The large white flowers produce a berrylike fruit, usually yellow with white, pink, or yellow flesh. Family Myrtaceae.

**Guayaquil** City on the Guayas River, near the Gulf of Guayaquil, W Ecuador; chief port and largest city of Ecuador. Founded by the Spanish in the 1530s, Guayaquil was frequently attacked by buccaneers in the 17th and 18th centuries. Industries: textiles, pharmaceuticals, leather goods, cement, iron products, oil refining, fruit. Pop. (1990) 1,508,444.

**gudgeon** Freshwater CARP found in rivers from Britain to China. It has an elongated body, variable color, and a small mouth with barbels. Length: 8in (20cm). Species *Gobio gobio*.

**guelder rose** Plant of the HONEYSUCKLE family (Caprifoliaceae). It has globular clusters of white or pink flowers. Species *Viburnum opulus*.

**Guelph** Political faction in medieval Italy, opposed to the GHIBELLINE. The two factions were linked to rival families contending for the HOLY ROMAN EMPIRE in the 12th century. In 1198 OTTO IV (a Guelph) became Holy Roman emperor. In the battle for control of Italy, the Guelphs took the side of the papacy, while the Ghibellines backed the emperor FREDERICK II. The Ghibellines were defeated by the Guelphs at Tagliacozzo in 1268, though the feud lived on.

**guenon** Any of 10–20 species of long-tailed, slender, medium-sized African MONKEYS found S of the Sahara Desert. Guenons are omnivorous tree-dwellers, living in small troops dominated by an old male. Genus *Cercopithecus*.

**Guernica** Town in Vizcaya province, N Spain. It is a center of BASQUE nationalism. The bombing of Guernica by German aircraft during the Spanish CIVIL WAR inspired Picasso's masterpiece *Guernica* (1937).

## GUINEA

Guinea's flag was adopted when the country became independent from France in 1958. It uses the colors of the flag of Ethiopia, Africa's oldest nation, which symbolize African unity. The red represents work, the yellow justice, and the green solidarity.

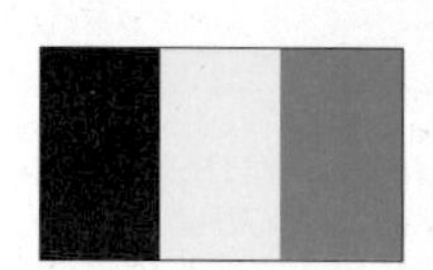

**AREA:** 94,927sq mi (245,860sq km)
**POPULATION:** 6,116,000
**CAPITAL (POPULATION):** Conakry (705,000)
**GOVERNMENT:** Multiparty republic
**ETHNIC GROUPS:** Fulani 40%, Malinke 26%, Susu 11%, Kissi 7%, Kpelle 5%
**LANGUAGES:** French (official)
**RELIGIONS:** Islam 85%, traditional beliefs 5%, Christianity 2%
**CURRENCY:** Guinean franc = 100 cauris

The Republic of Guinea, which faces the Atlantic Ocean in West Africa, can be divided into four regions: an alluvial coastal plain, which includes the capital, CONAKRY; the highland region of the Fouta Djallon, the source of one of Africa's longest rivers, the NIGER; the NE savanna; and the SE Guinea Highlands, which rise to 5,748ft (1,752m) at Mount Nimba.

### CLIMATE

Guinea has a tropical climate. Conakry has heavy rains between May and November. During the dry season, hot harmattan winds blow from the SAHARA.

### VEGETATION

Mangrove swamps grow along parts of the coast. Inland, the Fouta Djallon is largely open grassland. Northeastern Guinea is tropical savanna, with acacia and shea scattered across the grassland. Rain forests of ebony, mahogany, and teak grow in the Guinea Highlands.

### HISTORY

The NE Guinea plains formed part of the medieval empire of Ghana. The Malinke formed the Mali empire, which dominated the region in the 12th century. It was replaced by the SONGHAI empire. Portuguese explorers arrived in the mid-15th century, and the slave trade began soon afterward. From the 17th century, other European slave traders became active in Guinea. In the early 18th century, the FULANI gained control of the Fouta Djallon. Following a series of wars, France gained control and made Guinea the colony of French Guinea (1891). France exploited Guinea's bauxite deposits, and mining unions developed.

In 1958 Guinea voted to become an independent republic. France severed all aid. Its first president, Sékou Touré (1958–84), adopted a Marxist program of reform and embraced Pan-Africanism. Opposition parties were banned and dissent was brutally suppressed. In 1970 Guinea was invaded by Portuguese Guinea (GUINEA-BISSAU). Conakry acted as the headquarters for independence movements in Guinea-Bissau. A military coup followed Touré's death and established the Military Committee for National Recovery (CMRN) led by Colonel Lansana Conté (1984).

### POLITICS

Conté improved relations with the West and introduced free-enterprise policies. Civil unrest forced the introduction of a multiparty system in 1992, and Conté was elected president amid claims of electoral fraud. A military coup in February 1996 proved unsuccessful.

### ECONOMY

Guinea is a low-income developing country (1992 GDP per capita, US$592). It is the world's second-largest producer of bauxite (after Australia), which accounts for 90% of its exports. Guinea has 25% of the world's known reserves of bauxite. Other natural resources include diamonds, gold, iron ore, and uranium. Due to the mining industry, rail and road infrastructure is improving. Agriculture (mainly at subsistence level) employs 78% of the workforce. Major crops include bananas, cassava, coffee, palm kernels, pineapples, rice, and sweet potatoes. Cattle and other livestock are raised in highland areas.

**Africa's wildlife,** though seriously threatened in many areas, remain one of its chief tourist attractions. This stamp is one of a set of nine issued by Guinea in 1968.

**Guernsey** Second largest island in the CHANNEL ISLANDS; the capital is St. Peter Port. It constitutes a bailiwick with several smaller islands, including Alderney and SARK. Its mild, sunny climate is ideal for dairy farming and horticulture. Tourism is also important. Area: 30sq mi (78sq km). Pop. (1991) 58,867.

**guerrilla warfare** Small-scale ground combat operations frequently designed to harass, rather than destroy the enemy. Such tactics are especially suited to difficult terrain and rely on lightning attacks and aid from civilian sympathizers. In the 20th century, guerrilla tactics have been used by many nationalist and communist movements, such as the Viet Cong in the VIETNAM WAR.

**Guevara, "Che" (Ernesto)** (1928–67) Argentine-Cuban revolutionary leader. He became associated with Fidel CASTRO in Mexico, and returned with him to Cuba in 1956 to conduct guerrilla activities against the BATISTA regime. He disappeared from public view in 1965. Two years later he was captured and killed while trying to establish a communist guerrilla base in Bolivia. His remains were returned to Cuba in 1997.

**Guggenheim** US family of industrialists and philanthropists. **Meyer Guggenheim** (1828–1905), b. Switzerland, immigrated to Philadelphia (1847) and prospered in the lace import business. He bought silver and lead mines in Colorado. He retired, leaving control of his enterprises to his seven living sons. **Daniel Guggenheim** (1856–1930) took the leading role in expanding the family businesses. A prominent philanthropist, he established the Daniel and Florence Guggenheim Foundation. **Solomon R. Guggenheim** (1861–1949) endowed a foundation to foster nonobjective art: the Guggenheim Museum opened in New York City in 1959. **Simon Guggenheim** (1867–1941) was a US senator. In memory of his son, he established the John Simon Guggenheim Memorial Foundation, which offers fellowships to scholars and artists. **Harry Frank Guggenheim** (1890–1971) was US ambassador to Cuba (1929–33). **Peggy Guggenheim** (1898–1979) was a patron and collector of modern art.

**guided missile** Missile controlled throughout its flight by exterior or interior control systems. There are four types: surface-to-surface, surface-to-air, air-to-air, and air-to-surface. The first guided missiles were built in Germany during World War II. Postwar developments ranged from the huge intercontinental ballistic missiles (ICBMs), with ranges of 6,000mi (10,000km) and nuclear warheads, to small hand-launched antitank missiles. The multiple independently targeted reentry vehicles (MIRVs) – ICBMs with many sub-missiles – were developed in the late 1960s. The CRUISE MISSILE has wings like an airplane, making it capable of flying at low altitudes.

**guild** Association of craftsmen or merchants in medieval Europe. Merchant guilds probably developed from earlier religious associations and sometimes became more or less synonymous with municipal government. Guilds controlled economic conditions in the interest of their members, but were eclipsed by nation-states.

**Guildford Four** Three men and a woman of Irish extraction convicted in an English court of terrorist bombings in Guildford and Woolwich, s England, in 1975. The life sentences were quashed on appeal in 1989. *See also* BIRMINGHAM SIX

**guillemot** Small, usually black and white seabird of the AUK family (Alcidae). It lives on cold Northern Hemisphere coastlines and dives for food. Length: *c.*17in (43cm). Genera *Cepphus* and *Uria*.

**guillotine** Mechanized device for execution by beheading adopted during the FRENCH REVOLUTION. First used in 1792, *c.*1,400 died under it during the REIGN OF TERROR. It remained in use in France until the abolition of CAPITAL PUNISHMENT in 1981.

**Guinea** Republic in West Africa. See country feature.

**Guinea-Bissau** Small republic in West Africa; the capital and chief port is BISSAU. **Land and Climate** Guinea-Bissau is mostly low-lying, with a broad, swampy coastal plain and broad river estuaries. The land rises to low plateaus in the E. Guinea-Bissau has a tropical climate, with a dry season (December to May) and a rainy season. Mangrove forests grow along the coasts, and dense rain forest covers much of the coastal plain. Inland, forests merge into tropical savanna, with open grassland on the high ground. **History** It was first visited by Portuguese navigators in 1446. Between the 17th and early 19th centuries, Portugal used the coast as a slave trade base. In 1836 Portugal appointed a governor to administer Guinea-Bissau and the CAPE VERDE Islands, but in 1879 the two territories were separated and Guinea-Bissau became the colony of Portuguese Guinea. In 1956 African nationalists founded the African Party for the Independence of Guinea and Cape Verde (PAIGC). Portugal's determination to keep its overseas territories forced the the PAIGC to begin a guerrilla war (1963), and by 1968 it held 66% of the country. In 1972 a rebel National Assembly in the PAIGC-controlled area voted to form the independent republic of Guinea-Bissau. In 1974 it formally achieved independence (followed by Cape Verde in 1975). In 1980 an army coup led by Major João Vieira overthrew the government. The new Revolutionary Council was against unification with Cape Verde; it concentrated on national policies and socialist reforms. In 1991 the PAIGC voted to introduce a multiparty system. The PAIGC won the 1994 elections, and Vieira was reelected president. **Economy** Guinea-Bissau is a poor country (1995 GDP per capita, US$790), with agriculture employing more than 80% of the workforce. Major crops: rice, coconuts, groundnuts, the last two making up 40% of Guinea-Bissau's exports. Fishing is also important.

**guinea fowl** Pheasant-like game bird of Africa and Madagascar. The common domestic guinea hen (*Numida meleagris*) is blue, gray, or black with white spots and an ornamental crest. Length: to 20in (50cm). Family Phasianidae.

**guinea pig** Type of CAVY found in South America. The domestic *Cavia porcellus* is a popular pet. It has a large head, soft fur, short legs, and no tail. It eats grass and other green plants. *Cavia aperea* is a wild species. Family Caviidae.

**Guinevere** In Arthurian legend, King Arthur's queen who was loved by LANCELOT OF THE LAKE. In Thomas MALORY's *Morte d'Arthur* she betrayed the king and was sentenced to die. She was rescued by Lancelot and later restored to Arthur.

**Guinness, Sir Alec** (1914– ) British stage and film actor. Guinness won fame for his performances in the EALING STUDIOS comedies, such as *The Lavender Hill Mob* (1951) and *The Ladykillers* (1955). He won a Best Actor Oscar for

▲ **Guevara** The revolutionary leader "Che" Guevara was closely associated with Castro's seizure of power in Cuba, where Guevara held several government posts. A committed Marxist, he was eventually killed by Bolivian government forces while attempting to foment a peasants' revolution in that country. His actions and violent death made him an heroic figure for many revolutionaries.

**GUINEA-BISSAU**

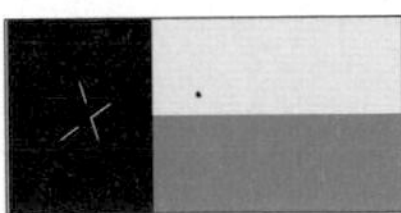

**AREA:** 13,946sq mi (36,120sq km)
**POPULATION:** 1,006,000
**CAPITAL (POPULATION):** Bissau (126,900)
**GOVERNMENT:** Multiparty republic
**ETHNIC GROUPS:** Balante 27%, Fulani (or Peul) 23%, Malinke (Mandingo or Mandinka) 12%, Mandyako 11%, Pepel 10%
**LANGUAGES:** Portuguese (official)
**RELIGIONS:** Traditional beliefs 54%, Islam 38%, Christianity 8%
**CURRENCY:** Guinea-Bissau peso = 100 centavos

*Bridge on the River Kwai* (1957). Other films include *Lawrence of Arabia* (1962), *Doctor Zhivago* (1965), *Star Wars* (1977), and *Little Dorrit* (1988).

**Guise, House of** Ducal house of Lorraine, the most powerful family in 16th-century France. Claude, duke of Lorraine (1496–1550), founded the house in 1528. His son François (1519–63) supervised the massacre of HUGUENOTS at Vassy in 1562, precipitating the French Wars of RELIGION. His brother Charles (1524–74), cardinal of Guise, played a major role at the Council of TRENT. Their sister, Marie of Scotland, married JAMES V of Scotland, and their daughter, Mary (later MARY, QUEEN OF SCOTS), married the future Francis II of France. François Guise's son, Henri (1550–88), helped to organize the SAINT BARTHOLOMEW'S DAY MASSACRE (1572) and led the Holy League, which vehemently opposed Protestantism. Guise power declined when HENRY IV took the throne.

**guitar** Plucked stringed musical instrument. The guitar is first known with the Moors, who introduced it to Spain perhaps as early as the 12th century. The early guitar had four double strings and was similar to the LUTE. The popularity of the lute in the 17th century extended to the guitar; the most famous guitarist of the time was Robert de Visée (*c.*1650–*c.*1725). The modern guitar has six (or sometimes 12) strings. The virtuoso playing of Andrés SEGOVIA inspired compositions by Manuel de FALLA and Heitor VILLA-LOBOS. In the 1940s Les Paul invented the electric guitar, now a standard instrument in blues, pop, and rock music. Acoustic (non-electric) and semiacoustic guitars are also widely used in folk and jazz.

**Guizhou** (Kweichow) Province in S China; the capital is Guiyang. Guizhou became a Chinese province in the Ming dynasty. During World War II it served as a military base for Allied forces. It was taken by Chinese communists in 1950. Industries: coal mining, iron ore, mercury. Area: 67,204sq mi (174,060sq km). Pop. (1990) 32,370,000.

**GUYANA**

**AREA:** 83,000sq mi (214,970sq km)
**POPULATION:** 808,000
**CAPITAL (POPULATION):** Georgetown (188,000)
**GOVERNMENT:** : Multiparty republic
**ETHNIC GROUPS:** Asian Indian 49%, Black 36%, Mixed 7%, Amerindian 7%, Portuguese, Chinese
**LANGUAGES:** English (official)
**RELIGIONS:** Christianity (Protestant 34%, Roman Catholic 18%), Hinduism 34%, Islam 9%
**CURRENCY:** Guyana dollar = 100 cents

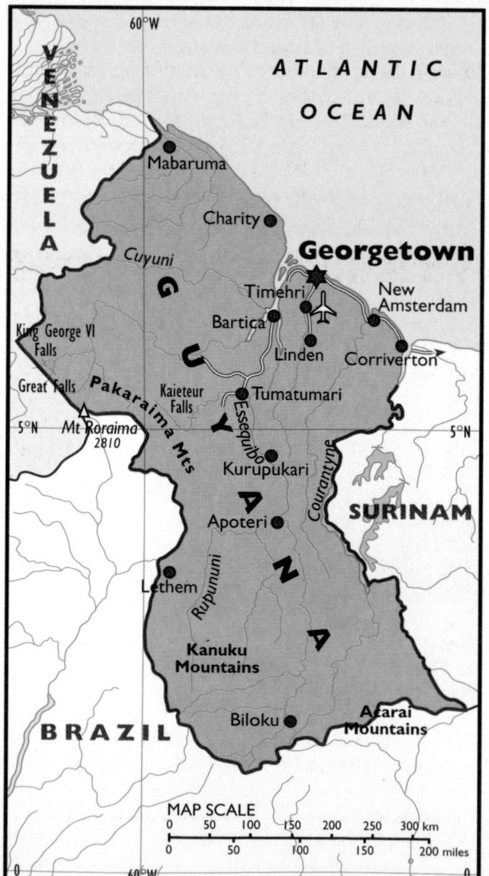

**Gujarat** State in W India, on the Arabian Sea; the capital is Gandhinagar. Absorbed into the MAURYAN EMPIRE in the 3rd century BC, it was a center of JAINISM under the Maitraka Dynasty (5th–8th centuries AD). In the early 15th century it was an autonomous Muslim sultanate. Under British rule it became a province (1857). After independence it was established as a separate state. It is highly industrialized, with substantial reserves of oil and gas. Industries: cotton textiles, salt mining, electrical engineering, petrochemicals. Area: 75,669sq mi (195,984sq km). Pop. (1994 est.) 44,235,000.

**Gulf of Mexico** *See* MEXICO, GULF OF

**Gulf Stream** Relatively fast-moving current of the N Atlantic Ocean. It flows from the straits of Florida, along the E coast of North America, then E across the Atlantic to the NW European coast. The current warms coastal climates along its course.

**Gulf War** (January 16, 1991–February 28, 1991) Military action by a US-led coalition of 32 states to expel Iraqi forces from KUWAIT. Iraqi forces invaded Kuwait (August 2, 1990) and claimed it as an Iraqi province. On August 7, 1990, Operation Desert Shield began a mass deployment of coalition forces to protect Saudi oil reserves. Economic sanctions failed to secure Iraqi withdrawal, and the UN Security Council set a deadline of January 15, 1991, for the removal of Iraqi forces. Iraqi president Saddam HUSSEIN ignored the ultimatum, and General Norman SCHWARZKOPF launched Operation Desert Storm. Within a week, extensive coalition air attacks had secured control of the skies. Iraqi ground forces were defenseless against the coalition's technologically advanced weaponry. Iraq launched Scud missile attacks on Saudi Arabia and Israel, in the hope of weakening Arab support for the coalition. On February 24, the ground war was launched. Iraqi troops burned Kuwaiti oil wells as they fled. Kuwait was liberated two days later, and a ceasefire was declared on February 28. Saddam Hussein remained in power.

**gull** (seagull) Any of various ground-nesting birds found along coastlines worldwide. They eat carrion, refuse, fish, shellfish, eggs, and young birds. The herring gull (*Larus argentatus*) is gray and white with black markings, hooked bill, pointed wings, and webbed feet. It grows to 22–26in (56–66cm). The black-headed gull (*L. ridibundus*) is smaller, with black feathers on its head in summer. Family Laridae.

**gum** Secretions of plants. Gums are chemically complex, consisting mainly of various saccharides bound to organic acids. Common examples are gum arabic, agar, and tragacanth. *See also* EUCALYPTUS; RESIN

**gun** Tubular weapon firing a projectile, usually by force of explosion. The term is now restricted to ARTILLERY pieces with a relatively high muzzle velocity and a flat trajectory. PISTOLS, RIFLES and MACHINE GUNS are usually described as guns; mortars and howitzers are not.

**gunpowder** Mixture of saltpeter (potassium nitrate), charcoal, and sulfur. It was used extensively in firearms until *c.*1900, when it was replaced by smokeless powders, such as DYNAMITE.

**Gunpowder Plot** (November 1605) Failed Roman Catholic conspiracy to blow up JAMES I of England and his Parliament. The leader was Robert Catesby, and the chief perpetrator Guy FAWKES. The plotters were arrested on November 5, a date now celebrated in Britain as Guy Fawkes Day (Bonfire Night).

**Gunther, John** (1901–70) US journalist. A foreign correspondent for the Chicago *Daily News* (1924–36), he gained intimate knowledge of Europe and wrote *Inside Europe* (1936), the first in a series of lively journalistic works surveying politics and social life abroad.

**Gupta dynasty** (*c.*320–*c.*550) Ruling house whose kingdom covered most of N India. It was founded by Chandragupta I. The Gupta dynasty embraced Buddhism, and is seen as a golden age. It reached its greatest extent at the end of the 4th century, but declined at the end of the 5th century under concerted attack from the HUNS.

**Gurdwara** (Sanskrit, Guru's doorway) Sikh temple housing a copy of the *Adi Granth*, the holy scripture of SIKHISM. There are several historically important *gurdwaras*, such as the Golden Temple of AMRITSAR, Punjab.

**Gurkha** Hindu ruling caste of Nepal since 1768. They speak a SANSKRIT language. The name also denotes a Nepalese soldier in the British or Indian army.

**gurnard** Tropical, marine, bottom-dwelling fish. It has a large spiny head and enlarged pectoral fins. Length: to 20in (50cm). Family Triglidae.

**Gustavus I (Vasa)** (1496–1560) King of Sweden (1523–60) and founder of the Vasa dynasty. He led a victorious rebellion against the invading Danes in 1520. In 1523 he was elected king. During his reign Sweden gained independence, the Protestant church was established, and the Bible was translated into Swedish.

**Gustavus II (Adolphus)** (1594–1632) King of Sweden (1611–32). His reign was distinguished by constitutional and educational reforms. He ended war with Denmark (1613) and Russia (1617). Hoping to increase Sweden's control of the Baltic, he entered the THIRTY YEARS WAR (1618–48) and died in battle.

**Gutenberg, Johann** (1400–68) German goldsmith and printer, credited with inventing PRINTING from movable metallic type. He produced the first printed Bible, known as the *Gutenberg Bible* or *Mazarin Bible* (*c*.1455).

**Guthrie, "Woody" (Woodrow Wilson)** (1912–67) US folk singer, guitarist, and songwriter. His social-protest poetry captured the spirit of the Great Depression and championed workers' rights. His most famous songs, including "This Land Is Your Land" and "So Long, It's Been Good to Know You", greatly influenced later artists. His son, Arlo Guthrie (1947– ) is also a folk singer. His best known song is "Alice's Restaurant."

**Guyana** (formerly British Guiana) Republic on the Atlantic Ocean, NE South America; the capital is GEORGETOWN. **Land and Climate** More than 80% of Guyana is forested. Its interior includes rain forests, savannas, valleys of the Essequibo River, and the Pakaraima Mountains, which rise to 9,094ft (2,772m) at Mount Roraima. The narrow, alluvial coastal plain is largely reclaimed marshland and mangrove swamp. Guyana has a hot and humid climate, but temperatures are lower in the S and W highlands. Rainfall is heavy. There are two dry seasons: February to April, and August to November. **History** The Dutch settled here in 1581, and the Treaty of Breda (1667) awarded them the area. Land reclamation for plantations began in the 18th century, under the control of the Dutch West India Company. Britain gained control in the early 19th century and set up the colony of British Guiana (1831). Slavery was abolished in 1838. After World War II, progress toward self-government was achieved with a new constitution (1952), and the election of Dr. Cheddi Jagan. British Guiana became independent in 1966, and Forbes Burnham of the socialist People's National Congress (PNC) became the first prime minister. Ethnic conflict between the majority East Indian and African minority marred much of the late 1960s. In 1970 Guyana became a republic. In 1980 Burnham became president, and a new constitution increased his power. After Burnham's death (1985), Desmond Hoyte introduced liberal reforms. Hoyte was defeated in 1992 presidential elections by Jagan. Jagan's People's Progressive Party (PPP) formed the first non-PNC government since independence. On the death of Jagan in 1997, Samuel Hinds became president. **Economy** Guyana is a poor, developing country, its economy dominated by mining and agriculture. Principal exports: sugar, rice, bauxite. Diamond and gold mining are important. Fishing and forestry industries are expanding, as is ecotourism.

**Gwent** County in SE Wales; the county town is Cwmbran. It is drained by the Usk and Wye rivers. Dairying is important in the Usk valley. Sheep are reared in upland areas. Industries: aluminum, chemicals, textiles, electronics. Area: 531sq mi (1,376sq km). Pop. (1991) 442,212.

**Gwyn, Nell** (1650–87) English actress. She first appeared in John Dryden's *The Indian Emperor* (1665). She was CHARLES II's mistress.

**Gwynedd** County in NW Wales, on the Irish Sea coast; the administrative center is CAERNARVON. Gwynedd is rugged and mountainous, and includes most of the Snowdonia National Park. Industries: slate quarrying, hydroelectric power, tourism. Area: 1,493sq mi (3,866sq km). Pop. (1990) 235,452.

**gymnastics** Multidisciplined sport requiring suppleness, strength, and poise in a variety of regulated exercises. Men and women compete separately in individual and team events. Men perform in six events: vault, parallel bars, horizontal bars, pommel horse, rings, and floor exercises. Women perform in four events: vault, balance beam, asymmetrical bars, and floor exercises. World championships were inaugurated in 1950, and women's gymnastics became an Olympic sport in 1952.

**gymnosperm** Seed plant with naked seeds borne on scales, usually cones. Most EVERGREENS are gymnosperms. However, LARCH and some other CONIFERS are DECIDUOUS. All living seed-bearing plants are divided into two main groups: gymnosperms and ANGIOSPERMS. In the Five KINGDOMS classification system, gymnosperms comprise three distinct phyla: Coniferophyta (such as PINE, SPRUCE, and CEDAR); Ginkgophyta (a single species, the GINKGO); and Gnetophyta (strange plants such as *Welwitschia*, *Ephedra*, and *Gnetum*).

**gynecology** Area of medicine concerned with the female reproductive organs. Its study and practice is often paired with OBSTETRICS.

**gypsum** (hydrated calcium sulfate, $CaSO_4.2H_2O$) Most common sulfate mineral. Huge beds of gypsum occur in sedimentary rocks, where it is associated with HALITE. It crystallizes in the monoclinic system. Varieties are ALABASTER, selenite (transparent and foliated) and satin spar (silky and fibrous). It is a source of plaster of Paris. Hardness 2; sp.gr. 2.3.

**gypsy** *See* ROMANY

**gypsy moth** Small tussock MOTH with black zigzag markings; the larger female is a lighter color. Length: 2in (5cm). Family Lepidoptera; species *Lymantria dispar*.

**gyrocompass** Navigational aid incorporating a continuously driven GYROSCOPE. The spinning axis of the gyroscope is horizontal and its direction indicates true N, irrespective of the course of the craft. *See also* COMPASS

**gyroscope** Symmetrical spinning disk that can adapt to any orientation, being mounted in gimbals (a pair of rings with one swinging freely in the other). When a gyroscope is spinning, a change in the orientation of the gimbals does not change the orientation of the spinning wheel. This means that changes in direction of an aircraft or ship can be determined without external references. *See also* AUTOMATIC PILOT

**GYROCOMPASS**

A laser gyrocompass measures rotation by comparing the wavelength of lasers (1). A current is passed from an anode (2) to two cathodes (3) creating two lasers in a gas-filled triangular chamber (4) drilled in a solid glass block (5). Part of the lasers are bled out at one end of the gyrocompass (6) and the wavelength measured. If the gyrocompass rotates to the left the path of the laser traveling to the left is reduced fractionally reducing its wavelength. The opposite occurs to the other laser. A sensor (7) compares the two lasers to measure the rotation.

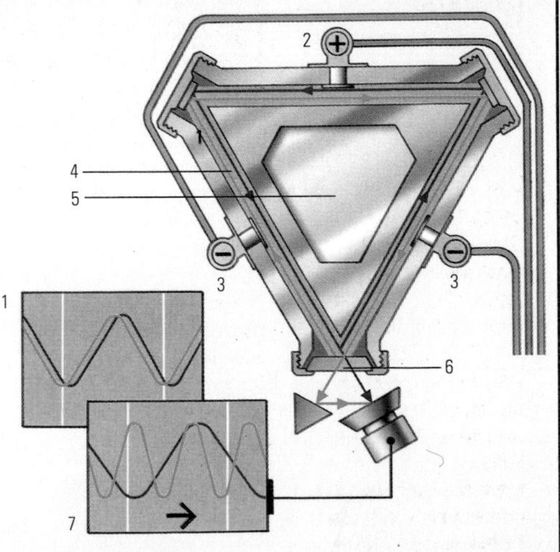


G

*H/h, eighth letter of the Roman alphabet. It is derived from an Egyptian* **hieroglyph** *for* **rope**. *The Semites modified it to form the letter* **cheth**. *It was taken into the Greek alphabet (c.600 BC) as the letter* **eta**.

**Haakon IV** (1204–63) King of Norway (1247–63). He secured the submission of Iceland and Greenland to his rule. A patron of learning and the arts, he reigned at the beginning of medieval Norway's "golden age" (1217–1319). He died in the Orkneys (Scotland) after a campaign against the Scots.

**Haarlem** City on the Spaarne River, w Netherlands; capital of North Holland province. By the 12th century Haarlem was a fortified town. A center of Dutch painting in the 16th and 17th centuries, it is famous for its tulip bulbs. Industries: electronic equipment, publishing, printing. Pop. (1994) 150,213.

**habeas corpus** (Lat. you should have the body) Writ in law for the protection of the liberty of the individual. Of the several kinds of *habeas corpus*, the most important is the *habeas corpus ad subjiciendum*, which commands a person who holds another in custody to bring the captive before the court and to state the cause of detention. The writ is part of the US Constitution (Article 1, section 9).

**Haber process** Industrial process in which nitrogen from the atmosphere is "fixed" by synthesizing ammonia. A mixture of nitrogen and hydrogen is passed over a heated catalyst at a pressure of *c.*1,000 atmospheres. The chemical reaction $N_2+3H_2 \rightarrow 2NH_3$ occurs. It was invented by German chemists Fritz Haber and Carl Bosch in 1909–10. *See also* NITROGEN FIXATION

**habitat** Place in which an organism normally lives. A habitat is defined by characteristic physical conditions and the presence of other organisms.

**Habsburg** *See* HAPSBURG

**hacker** In computing, person who obtains unauthorized access to a computer DATABASE. A hacker, who usually gains access through the public telephone system using a modem, may read or alter the information in the database.

**haddock** Marine fish found in cold and temperate waters, mainly in the Northern Hemisphere. Dark gray and silver, it has a dark blotch near the pectoral fins. Length: to about 36in (90cm); weight: to 24.5lb (11kg). Family Gadidae; species *Melanogrammus aeglefinus*.

**Hades** In Greek mythology, god of the dead; the name is also applied to the realm over which he ruled. The dead were ferried to the realm of Hades by CHARON across the river STYX. Once there, the virtuous went to ELYSIUM. The wicked were confined to Tartarus, the bottomless pit. Hades' queen was PERSEPHONE. In Roman mythology Hades was known as PLUTO.

**Hadrian, Publius Aelius** (76–138) Roman emperor (117–138). Nephew and protegé of Emperor TRAJAN, he adopted a policy of imperial retrenchment, discouraging new conquests, relinquishing territory hard to defend, and ordering the construction of HADRIAN'S WALL in Britain. One of the most cultured of the Roman emperors, he erected many fine buildings, notably the vast Hadrian's Villa at Tivoli, and also rebuilt the PANTHEON. The erection of a shrine to Jupiter on the site of the Temple in Jerusalem provoked a Jewish revolt (132–135) which was ruthlessly suppressed.

**Hadrian's Wall** Defensive fortification in N England, erected (AD 122–36) on the orders of the Roman Emperor HADRIAN. It extended 73.5mi (118.3km) and was about 7.5ft (2.3m) thick and 6–15ft (1.8–4.6m) high. Forts were built along its length. Extensive stretches survive.

**hadron** Group of SUBATOMIC PARTICLES that are influenced by the STRONG NUCLEAR FORCE. Made up of QUARKS, the group can be divided into BARYONS, such as the NEUTRON and PROTON, and MESONS. More than 150 hadrons have now been discovered and, with the exception of the proton and antiproton, they are all unstable. Unlike LEPTONS, such as electrons, they have a measurable size.

**Hafiz** (*c.*1325–*c.*1390) (Shams ud-Din Mohammad) Persian poet. His verse, in rhyming couplets, deals powerfully with sensual pleasures, most famously in the *Divan*. He was a devout Sufi and DERVISH and much of his poetry is religious in content.

**hafnium** (symbol Hf) Silvery metallic element, one of the TRANSITION ELEMENTS, discovered in 1923. Hafnium's chief source is as a byproduct in obtaining the element ZIRCONIUM. It is used as a neutron absorber in reactor control rods. Properties: at.no. 72; at.wt. 178.49; sp.gr. 13.31; m.p. 4,041°F (2,227°C); b.p. 8,316°F (4,602°C); most common isotope $^{180}$Hf (35.24%).

**Haganah** Semiunderground Zionist army formed in the 1920s to protect Jewish interests in Palestine. Allied with the extreme Irgun group in 1945, it attempted to change British policy on Jewish immigration and received financial and military aid from US Zionists. *See also* ZIONISM

**hagfish** (slime eel) Eel-like, primitive, jawless fish found in temperate to cold marine waters. It has underdeveloped eyes, and four to six fleshy whiskers around its sucking mouth. It is a scavenger and feeds on dead or dying fish. It secretes a slimy mucus from pores along its sides. Length: to 32in (80cm). Family Myxinidae.

**Haggadah** Story of the Exodus and redemption of the people of Israel by God, read during PASSOVER services. Developed over centuries, it includes excerpts from the Bible, rabbinical writings, psalms, stories, and prayers.

**Haggai** (active 6th century BC) Old Testament prophet, probably not the author of the Book of Haggai, the tenth of the 12 books of the Minor Prophets. The book records four prophesies made by Haggai in 521 BC, in which he urged the Jews to make haste in rebuilding the TEMPLE.

**Hagia Sophia** (Aya Sofia) Byzantine church in Istanbul. It was built (532–37) for Emperor JUSTINIAN I. A masterpiece of Byzantine architecture, it was the first building to use pendentives to support a central dome. A series of domes extends the lofty interior space. The church was converted into a mosque in 1453. The Hagia Sophia now acts as a museum.

**Hague, The** ('s-Gravenhage or Den Haag) City in the w Netherlands; capital of South Holland province. It is the seat of the Dutch government. Founded in the 15th century, the city has been an intellectual and political center since the 17th century. The Hague has been the seat of the International Court of Justice since 1945. Much of the city's economy depends on its diplomatic activities. Industries: textiles, pottery, furniture, chemicals. Pop. (1994) 445,279.

**Hahn, Otto** (1879–1968) German chemist. With Fritz Strassmann in 1939, he discovered nuclear fission, for which he was awarded the 1944 Nobel Prize for chemistry. With Lise Meitner, he discovered protactinium and several isomers.

**hahnium** (symbol Ha) Synthetic, radioactive, TRANSACTINIDE ELEMENT. It has atomic number 105; six isotopes have been synthesized. It was first reported by a Soviet team at the Joint Institute for Nuclear Research at Dubna. They claimed the isotopes of mass numbers 260 and 261, as a result of bombarding AMERICIUM with neon ions. In 1970 a team at the University of California claimed the isotope 260 (half-life 1.6 seconds) obtained by bombarding CALIFORNIUM with nitrogen nuclei. The element is named for Otto HAHN.

**Haifa** (Hefa) City in NW Israel, on Mount Carmel. It is the center of the BAHA'I religion. It is one of Israel's largest ports. Industries: textiles, chemicals, shipbuilding, oil-refining. Pop. (1992) 251,000.

**Haig, Alexander Meigs** (1924– ) US general and public official. He served in the army during the Korean War. During the 1960s, he held appointments as military assistant to the secretary of the army and deputy secretary of defense. After duty in Vietnam, he served as White House chief of staff for President NIXON. He was NATO commander (1974–79) and served as secretary of state (1981–82) under President REAGAN.

► **haddock** One of the mainstay species of the world's commercial fish catch, the haddock (*Melanogrammus aeglefinus*) is found in cold and temperate waters of the Northern Hemisphere. One of the main fishing areas for this member of the cod family lies off the coast of New England.

**Haig, Douglas, 1st Earl** (1861–1928) British general. Soon after the beginning of World War I, he became commander in chief of the British forces (1915). His policy of attrition produced enormous casualties but he cooperated effectively with Marshal Foch in the last stages of the war.

**haiku** Japanese poetry form consisting of 17 syllables in five-seven-five pattern. Haikus originally evoked a moment in nature. Matsuo Bashō(1644–94) is considered to be the finest exponent of the form.

**hail** Precipitation from clouds in the form of balls of ice. Hailstorms are associated with atmospheric turbulence extending to great heights together with warm, moist air nearer the ground.

**Haile Selassie I** (1892–1975) (Ras Tafari Makonnen) Emperor of Ethiopia (1930–74). When Italy invaded Ethiopia in 1935, he was forced into exile (1936). He drove out the Italians with British aid in 1941. Subsequently he became a leader among independent African nations, helping to found the ORGANIZATION OF AFRICAN UNITY (OAU) in 1963. Unrest at lack of reforms led to his being deposed by a military coup in 1974. He died while under arrest. *See also* RASTAFARIANISM

**Hainan** Island off s China, separated from the mainland by the Hainan Strait; the capital is Haikou. It has been under Chinese authority from the 2nd century BC. In 1988 it was designated a special economic zone. Products: rubber, coffee, rice, timber, tin, copper, and steel. Area: 13,124sq mi (33,991sq km). Pop. (1990) 6,420,000.

**Haiphong** Port on the Red River Delta, N Vietnam. Founded in 1874, it became the chief naval base of French Indochina. It was occupied by the Japanese during World War II, bombed by the French in 1946 during the conflict with the Viet Minh, and heavily bombed and its harbor mined by the US in the Vietnam War. Industries: cement, glass, chemicals, cotton. Pop. (1989) 456,049.

**hair** Outgrowth of mammalian skin, with insulating, protective, and sensory functions. It grows in a follicle, extending down through the EPIDERMIS to the DERMIS. New cells are added to the base of the hair; older hair cells become impregnated with KERATIN and die. Hair color depends on the presence of MELANIN in the hair cells. A small muscle attached to the base of the hair allows it to be erected in response to nerve signals sent to the follicle. Erecting the hairs traps a thicker layer of air close to the skin, which acts as INSULATION. *See also* FUR

**hairstreak** Any of a group of butterflies of the family Lycaenidae. They are gray and brown, and found in open areas on every continent, especially in the tropics. Hairstreaks have a quick, erratic flight. Genus *Strymon*.

**Haiti** Independent nation occupying the W third of the Caribbean island of Hispaniola, and including the islands of Tortuga and Gonâve; the capital is Port-au-Prince. Much of the country is mountainous, with a humid tropical climate. Discovered by Columbus in 1492, Spanish settlements were established at the E end of the island, and within 100 years most of the native Arawaks had died through disease or ill-treatment. In the 17th century, French corsairs set up plantations in the W part of the island; in 1697 the Spanish recognized the area as French territory. Known as Saint Dominque, the region prospered in the 18th century. The sugar and coffee plantations were worked by African slaves, who soon formed the majority of the population. In 1790 TOUSSAINT L'OUVERTURE led a slave revolt against the colonial rulers. In 1801, as governor general, he abolished slavery, but he was killed by the French two years later. The country was declared independent in 1804, under the name of Haiti, and Jean Jacques DESSALINES became emperor. During the 19th century, Haiti experienced much political instability. From 1915–34 it was virtually governed by the US. The election of François DUVALIER as president in 1957 inaugurated a period of corruption. Attempts to establish a democratic government in the 1980s and 1990s, after the deposition of the Duvalier family, were frustrated by the army. The democratically elected president Jean-Bertrand Aristide was removed from office by a military coup (1991), but was restored in 1994 with US backing. In 1995 René Préval was elected president. Haiti is the poorest country in the Western Hemisphere (1995 GDP per capita, US$910) and is reliant on food imports. Area: 10,714sq mi (27,750sq km). Pop. (1992 est.) 6,763,746.

**Haitink, Sir Bernard** (1929– ) Dutch conductor, principal conductor of the Amsterdam Concertgebouw Orchestra (1961–88) and the London Philharmonic (1967–79). As musical director of the ROYAL OPERA HOUSE (1987– ), he was noted for outstanding WAGNER performances.

**Hajj** (Arabic, migration) Pilgrimage to MECCA, made in the 12th month of the Muslim year. All Muslims are required to undertake the Hajj. It is the last of the Five Pillars of ISLAM, the religious duties defined by the KORAN.

**hake** Marine fish found in cold and temperate waters. It is silver and brown. Length: to 40in (1m); weight: to 30lb (14kg). Family Gadidae or Merluccidae; species Atlantic *Merluccius bilinearis*; Pacific *M. productus*.

**Halcyon** Greek mythological figure. The daughter of Aeolus, she is best known as the wife of Ceyx, king of Thessaly. When Ceyx was drowned, Halcyon ran to the seashore to find his body and drowned herself. The gods changed the couple into kingfishers.

**Hale, George Ellery** (1868–1938) US astronomer who organized a number of observatories, including the YERKES OBSERVATORY (1897), the Mount Wilson Observatory (1917), and the PALOMAR Observatory (1949). Each observatory featured in turn the largest telescope of its day. Hale also invented the spectroheliograph, and instrument that records activity in the Sun's chromosphere. .

**Hale, Nathan** (1755–76) Revolutionary War captain and hero. A Yale graduate, he was a schoolteacher before joining the Continental Army in 1775. Having volunteered to go behind British lines on Long Island to gain military secrets, he was captured on September 21, 1776, and hanged the next day. His last words are said to be, "I regret that I have but one life to lose for my country."

**Haley, Alex Palmer** (1921–92) US writer. He began his writing career while in the US Coast Guard. In 1965 he collaborated on *The Autobiography of Malcolm X*. After 12 years of research and travel he produced *Roots: The Saga of an American Family* (1976), which recounted the history of a group of black Americans from their origins in West Africa. The book earned Haley a special Pulitzer Prize in 1977.

**half-life** Time taken for one-half of the nuclei in a given amount of radioactive ISOTOPE to decay (change into another element or isotope). Only the half-life is measured because the decay is never considered to be total. Half-lives remain constant under any temperature or pressure, but there is a great variety among different isotopes. Oxygen-20 has a half-life of 14 seconds and uranium-234 of 250,000 years. A radioactive isotope disintegrates by giving off alpha or beta particles. The term "half-life" also refers to particles that spontaneously decay into new particles, such as a free neutron being transformed into an electron. *See also* DATING, RADIOACTIVE; RADIOACTIVITY

**halibut** Flatfish found worldwide in deep, cold to temperate seas. It is brownish on the eye side and white below. Family Pleuronectidae; species, Atlantic *Hippoglossus hippoglossus*, giant Pacific *H. stenolepis*.

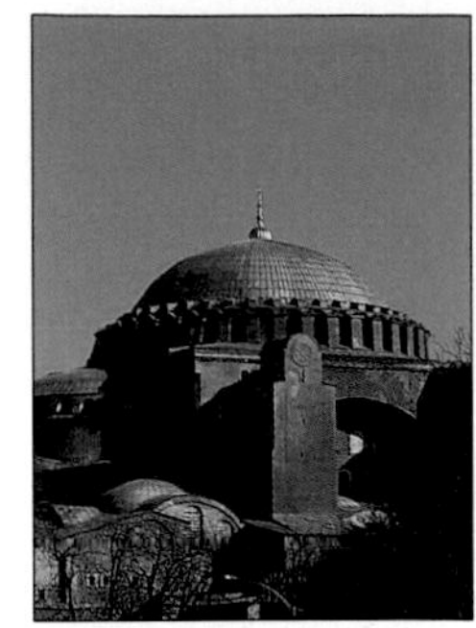

▲ **Hagia Sophia** One of the finest examples of Byzantine architecture in the world, the Hagia Sophia (Gk. holy wisdom), has been, in its lifetime, an Eastern Orthodox church, a Catholic cathedral, and a mosque. Now a museum and World Heritage site, the building is undergoing intensive restoration, which is revealing previously hidden Christian mosaics and decorations.

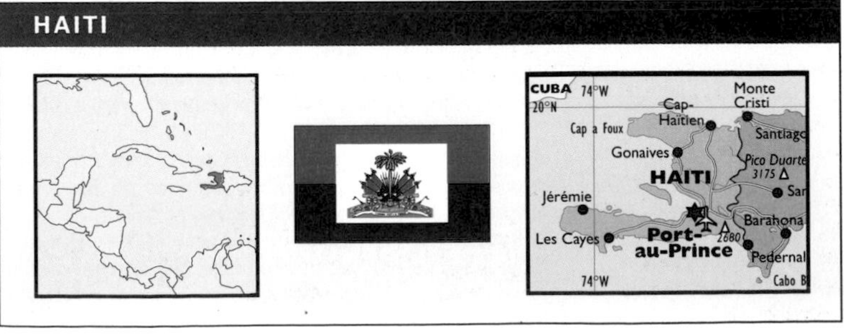

▲ **Handel** Although born in Germany, George Frideric Handel spent most of his working life in England under the patronage of George I, king of England and elector of Hanover. Among Handel's best-known works are the oratorios, including the *Messiah* (1742), and orchestral pieces, such as the *Water Music* (1717) which was written for George I. He was the first director of the Royal Academy of Music, London.



**Halicarnassus** Ancient Greek city in SW Asia Minor. Under Persian rule from the 6th century BC, it grew rich because of its advantageous trading position. In the 4th century BC it was a semi-independent state under the Persian governor, Mausolus, whose tomb was one of the SEVEN WONDERS OF THE WORLD.

**halide** Salt of one of the HALOGENS, or a compound containing a halogen and one other element; examples are sodium fluoride and potassium chloride. The alkyl halides (haloalkanes) are organic compounds, such as methyl chloride (chloromethane $CH_3Cl$).

**Halifax** City and seaport in E Canada, on the Atlantic Ocean; capital of Nova Scotia. Founded in 1749, it developed as an important naval base. In 1912 many of the victims from the *Titanic* were buried there. In 1917 it was the scene of a huge explosion on a munitions ship, which killed more than 2,000 people. Industries: commercial fishing, shipbuilding, oil refining. Pop. (1992) 114,455.

**halite** (NaCl) Sodium chloride, or common (rock) salt. It is found in evaporite sedimentary rocks, and in salt domes and dried lakes. It is colorless, white, or gray. It has a cubic system of interlocking cubic crystals, granules, and masses. It is important as table salt and as a source of CHLORINE. Hardness 2.5; sp.gr. 2.2.

**Hall, Granville Stanley** (1846–1924) US psychologist. He founded one of the first US psychology laboratories, the first US psychology journal (1887), and the American Psychological Association (1892). His books *The Contents of Children's Minds* (1883) and *Adolescence* (1904) contributed powerfully to the development of the child-study movement. In 1909 his invitation to FREUD and JUNG introduced psychoanalysis to the US.

**Haller, Albrecht von** (1708–77) Swiss biologist, physician, and poet. As a botanist, he was celebrated for his descriptions of alpine flora. During 1736 he researched the contractile properties of muscle tissue, and his resulting treatise (1757–66) laid the foundations of modern neurology.

**Halley, Edmond** (1656–1742) British astronomer and mathematician whose most famous achievement was to realize that comets could be periodic, following observations of HALLEY'S COMET. He founded modern geophysics, charting variations in Earth's magnetic field and establishing the magnetic origin of the AURORA borealis. He showed that atmospheric pressure decreases with altitude. Halley financed Isaac NEWTON to write *Principia*.

**Halley's comet** Bright periodic COMET. It takes 76 years to complete an orbit that takes it from within Venus's orbit to outside Neptune's. It was observed by Edmond HALLEY in 1682; later he deduced that it was the same comet that had been seen in 1531 and 1607, and predicted its return in 1758. There are records of every return since 240 BC. In 1986 the Giotto space probe showed the nucleus to be an irregular object measuring 9×5mi (15×8km) and consisting of ice.

**Halloween** (hallowed or holy evening) In medieval times, a holy festival observed on October 31, the eve of All Saints' Day. It was merged with the ancient Celtic festival of Samhain, when fires were lit to frighten away evil spirits and to guide the souls of the dead who were supposed to revisit their homes on this day. Halloween is observed today as a festival for masquerading and for children's "trick or treat."

**Hallstatt** Small town in W central Austria, believed to be the site of the earliest IRON AGE culture in W Europe. Iron was worked there from *c*.700 BC. The site contains a large Celtic cemetery and a deep salt mine. Fine bronze and pottery objects have also been discovered.

**hallucination** Apparent perception of something that is not present. Although they may occur in any of the five senses, auditory hallucinations and visual hallucinations are the most common. While they are usually symptomatic of psychotic disorders, hallucinations may result from fatigue or emotional upsets and can also be a side effect of certain drugs.

**hallucinogen** Drug that causes HALLUCINATIONS. Hallucinogenic drugs, such as MESCALINE, were used in primitive religious ceremonies. Today drugs such as LSD are taken illegally.

**halogen** Elements (FLUORINE, CHLORINE, BROMINE, IODINE, and ASTATINE) belonging to Group VII of the PERIODIC TABLE. They react with most other elements and with organic compounds. The halogens are highly electronegative; they react strongly because they require only one electron to achieve the "stable 8" inert gas configuration. They produce crystalline salts (HALIDES) containing negative ions of the type $F^-$ and $Cl^-$.

**halon** Any of several gases used in fire extinguishers. Chemically halons can be considered as simple HYDROCARBONS that have had some or all of their hydrogen atoms replaced by a HALOGEN. Similar to CHLOROFLUOROCARBONS (CFCs), they are much more destructive to the OZONE LAYER.

**halophyte** Any plant, usually a seed plant, that is able to live in salty conditions.

**Hals, Frans** (*c*.1580–1666) Dutch painter. He is best known for his paintings of robust figures, such as the *Laughing Cavalier* (1624), and his group portraits. His more subdued later works have a dignity and strength approaching those of his contemporary, REMBRANDT.

**Halsey, William Frederick, Jr.** (1882–1959) US admiral. He graduated from the US Naval Academy (1904). A destroyer commander in World War I, "Bull" Halsey led carrier raids against the Japanese-held Marshall and Gilbert islands early in World War II. He was fleet commander in campaigns against the Solomons and the Philippines, and the terms of Japanese surrender were signed aboard his ship, the *Missouri*.

**Hamburg** City, state, and port in N Germany, on the Elbe River. Founded in the 9th century by CHARLEMAGNE, it became one of the original members of the HANSEATIC LEAGUE. Severely bombed during World War II, it is now the country's second biggest city. It is a notable cultural center. Industries: electronic equipment, brewing, publishing, chemicals. Pop. (1990) 1,675,200.

**Hamilcar Barca** (d.228 BC) Carthaginian commander. Initially successful in the first of the PUNIC WARS, he was defeated in 241 BC. He suppressed a revolt of Carthaginian mercenaries in 238 BC and the following year conquered much of Spain. He was the father of HANNIBAL and Hasdrubal Barca.

**Hamilton, Alexander** (1755–1804) US political figure. During the American Revolution he served as George WASHINGTON's aide-de-camp and secretary. After the war he became a member of the Continental Congress, and a delegate to the Constitutional Convention. He was the principal contributor to *The Federalist Papers*, advocating the new constitution. As the first secretary of the treasury (1789–95), he established the national currency and the Bank of the United States (1791). He alienated many of his fellow Federalists by supporting Thomas JEFFERSON rather than Aaron BURR, when the 1800 election resulted in an electoral tie. In 1804 he thwarted Burr's campaign for governor of New York. Burr challenged him to a duel and killed him.

**Hamilton, James Hamilton, 1st Duke of** (1606–49) Scottish political and military leader. As CHARLES I's commissioner in Scotland (1638–39), he failed to achieve a compromise with the COVENANTERS and led an army against them in 1639. He fought for Charles in the English CIVIL WAR. In 1648 he led Scottish forces in support of the king. He was defeated by CROMWELL at Preston, and executed.

**Hamilton, Richard** (1922– ) British artist, a leader of the POP ART movement. He produced collages using images taken from commercial art. His best-known work is *Just what is it that makes today's homes so different, so appealing?* (1956).

**Hamilton** Capital and chief port of Bermuda, on Great Bermuda, at the head of Great Sound. Founded in 1790, it became the capital in 1815 and was made a free port in 1956. Tourism is the major industry. Pop. (1994) 1,100.

**Hamilton** City in Canada, in SE Ontario. Founded in 1813, it is an important communication and manufacturing center. Industries: iron, steel, vehicles, electrical equipment, textiles. Pop. (1991) 318,499.

**Hamito-Semitic languages** *See* AFRO-ASIATIC LANGUAGES

**Hamlin, Hannibal** (1809–91) US political leader. He served in the House of Representatives (1843–47), Senate (1848–57), and as Republican governor of Maine (1957). Opposed to slavery, he became vice president under President Abraham Lincoln (1861–65) during his first term. He returned to the Senate for two terms (1968–81).

**Hammarskjöld, Dag** (1905–61) Swedish diplomat and second secretary-general of the United Nations (1953–61), an office to which he brought great moral force. In 1956 he played a leading part in resolving the Suez Crisis. He sent a UN peacekeeping force to the Congo and later died there in an air crash. He was posthumously awarded the 1961 Nobel Peace Prize.

**hammer** Men's field event in which a spherical, metallic weight attached to a steel wire is thrown. The "hammer" weighs 16lb (7.26kg). The thrower stands within a circle 7ft (2.13m) in diameter, and by rotating two or three times, builds up momentum before releasing the hammer. It has been an Olympic event since 1900.

**hammerhead** Aggressive SHARK found in tropical marine waters and warmer temperate zones. It can be recognized by its head, which has extended sideways into two hammer-like lobes, with one eye and one nostril located at the tip of each. Length: to 20ft (6.1m); weight: to 2,000lb (906kg). Family Sphyrnidae.

**Hammerstein, Oscar, II** (1895–1960) US lyricist and librettist. He collaborated with Jerome KERN on *Show Boat* (1927) and with Richard RODGERS on *Oklahoma!* (1943), *Carousel* (1945), *South Pacific* (1949), *The King and I* (1951), and *The Sound of Music* (1959).

**Hammett, Dashiell** (1894–1961) US author, the originator of realistic detective fiction. Hammett drew on his own experience as a Pinkerton detective to create the investigators Sam Spade and Nick Charles. His books include *Red Harvest* (1929), *The Maltese Falcon* (1930), and *The Thin Man* (1934).

**Hammurabi** King of BABYLONIA (r. *c.*1792–*c.*1750 BC). By conquering neighbors, such as SUMERIA, he extended his rule in Mesopotamia and reorganized the empire under the Code of HAMMURABI. A good administrator, he improved productivity by building canals and granaries.

**Hammurabi, Code of** Ancient laws compiled under HAMMURABI. A copy of the code is in the Louvre, Paris. It is composed of 282 provisions with harsh penalties for offenders and includes the maxim, "An eye for an eye, a tooth for a tooth." Covering family life, property, and trade, it provides information on social and economic conditions in ancient Babylonia.

**Hampshire** County in S England, bordering the English Channel; the county town is Winchester. There are traces of Iron Age hill forts. The area was settled in Roman times. Predominantly agricultural, Hampshire contains the port of Southampton and the naval base at Portsmouth. Its coastal resorts and the New Forest woodland are tourist attractions. Industries: agriculture, oil refining, chemicals, brewing, electronics. Area: 1,460sq mi (3,782sq km). Pop. (1991) 1,541,547.

**Hampton** Seaport in SE Virginia, on the James River and Hampton Roads. First settled in 1610, it is reputedly the oldest settlement founded by the English in the US to be in continuous use. Industries: defense, tourism, seafood packing, fertilizers. Pop. (1990) 133,793.

**Hampton Court Palace** Palace situated beside the Thames River, 14mi (23km) from Westminster, London, England. Cardinal WOLSEY began construction in 1515, and he gave it to HENRY VIII in 1526, hoping to regain his favor. It is noted for the splendor of its architecture and its garden. Christopher WREN rebuilt and extended parts of the palace between 1696 and 1704.

**Hampton Roads Peace Conference** (February 1865) Abortive peace conference during the CIVIL WAR. Abraham LINCOLN and Confederate vice president Alexander H. STEPHENS met in Hampton Roads, Virginia. The talks failed, with the Confederate states declining to rejoin the Union.

**hamster** Small, mainly nocturnal, burrowing RODENT native to Eurasia and Africa. It has internal cheek pouches for carrying food. Length: up to 7in (18cm). Family Cricetidae; species *Cricetus mesocricetus*.

**Hamsun, Knut** (1859–1952) Norwegian novelist, playwright, and poet. A proponent of individualism, his work reflected his suspicion of modern Western culture. In 1920 he was awarded the Nobel Prize for literature for *The Growth of the Soil* (1917).

**Han** Imperial Chinese dynasty (202 BC–AD 220). It was founded by a rebellious peasant, Liu Pang, who established the capital at Chang'an. Under the Han, CONFUCIANISM became the state philosophy, and China achieved unprecedented power, prosperity, technological invention, and cultural growth, especially under Han Wu Ti in the 2nd century BC. A usurper, WANG MANG, interrupted the dynasty between AD 8 and 25; the dynasty is divided by that period into the Former Han and Later Han.

**Hancock, John** (1737–93) US statesman and revolutionary. He represented Massachusetts at the CONTINENTAL CONGRESS (1775–80, 1785, 1786), serving as the president (1775–77). His was the first signature, written especially large so King George III could read it easily, on the Declaration of Independence (1776). He helped to draw up the Massachusetts constitution (1780) and became that state's first governor (1780–85). He was reelected governor in 1789 and served until his death.

**Hancock, Winfield Scott** (1824–86) US general. A veteran of the MEXICAN WAR, he was a Union commander in the CIVIL WAR, fighting in the Peninsular and Antietam campaigns and at Fredericksburg, Chancellorsville, and Gettysburg (1863). In 1880, he was the unsuccessful Democratic candidate for president.

**handball** Name given to two games played mostly in Ireland and the US. One is played indoors or outdoors with a hard, small ball by two or four gloved players on courts of one, three, or four walls. A variant of this game that uses wooden rackets is called **paddleball**. The other game, sometimes called **team handball**, is played on a court where, between two goals and two goalkeepers, players catch, pass, and throw a ball with the object of hurling the ball past the opposing goalkeeper.

**Handel, George Frideric** (1685–1759) German composer. One of the greatest composers of the BAROQUE period, his many works include operas (such as *Berenice*, *Serse*, and *Semele*), oratorios (including *Samson* and *Judas Maccabaeus*), organ music, and chamber works. His most popular pieces include the *Water Music* (*c.*1717), *Music for the Royal Fireworks* (1749), and the oratorio *Messiah* (1742). He worked in Germany until 1712, when he moved to England.

**Handy, W.C. (William Christopher)** (1873–1958) US composer and musician known as the "Father of the BLUES." He led his own band in 1903 and composed several hits, including *Memphis Blues* (1911) and *St. Louis Blues* (1914).

**hang gliding** GLIDING using a lightweight craft, usually with a triangular wing, which is stabilized by the weight of the pilot's body underneath. Takeoff is made by running down a slope, assisted by a steady updraft. The pilot hangs from a harness and, by using a control bar to shift body weight, steers the glider.

**Hanging Gardens of Babylon** One of the SEVEN WONDERS OF THE WORLD. The gardens are thought to have been spectacular, rising in a series of terraces and ingeniously irrigated by water pumped up from the Euphrates. They were probably built by NEBUCHADNEZZAR. Nothing remains of them.

**hanging valley** Valley that ends high up the face of a larger valley, possibly with a stream running through it and ending in a waterfall. Most hanging valleys result from glacial deepening of the main valley.

**Hanks, Tom** (1956– ) US film actor and director. Initially typecast in comedy roles, his early films included *Splash* (1984) and *Big* (1988). His performance as a gay AIDS victim in *Philadelphia* (1993) demonstrated his dramatic versatility and won him a Best Actor Oscar. He won a second award for *Forrest Gump* (1994). Other acting roles include

▲ **Hanks** US actor and director Tom Hanks enjoyed huge success in Hollywood films of the 1980s and 1990s. He is one of only two actors (the other is Spencer Tracy) to win Best Actor Oscars in consecutive years, with *Philadelphia* (1993) and *Forrest Gump* (1994). He made his directorial debut in 1996 with *That Thing You Do!*

*Saving Private Ryan* (1998). In 1996 he made his directorial debut with *That Thing You Do!*

**Hanna, Marcus Alonzo** (1837–1904) US Republican politician. His campaign management and financial support helped William McKinley win the 1896 presidential election. His use of advertising is widely seen as the beginning of modern campaign politics.

**Hannibal** (247–183 BC) Carthaginian general in the second of the Punic Wars, son of Hamilcar Barca. One of the greatest generals of ancient times, in 218 BC he invaded N Italy after crossing the Alps with a force of elephants and 40,000 troops. He won a series of victories, but was unable to capture Rome. Recalled to Carthage to confront the invasion of Scipio Africanus, he was defeated at Zama (202 BC). After the war, as chief magistrate of Carthage, he alienated the nobility by reducing their power. They sought Roman intervention, and Hannibal fled to the Seleucid kingdom of Antiochus III. He fought under Antiochus against the Romans, was defeated, and committed suicide.

**Hanoi** Capital of Vietnam and its second largest city, on the Red River. In the 7th century the Chinese ruled Vietnam from Hanoi; it later became capital of the Vietnamese empire. Taken by the French in 1883, the city became the capital of French Indochina (1887–1945). From 1946–54 it was the scene of fighting between the French and the Viet Minh. It was heavily bombed during the Vietnam War. Industries: engineering, vehicles, textiles, rice-milling. Pop. (1989) 1,088,862.

**Hanover** (Hannover) City on the Leine River, N Germany; capital of Lower Saxony. Chartered in 1241, the city joined the Hanseatic League in 1386. George I of Britain was elector of Hanover. Hanover was badly damaged during World War II, but many old buildings were later reconstructed. Industries: machinery, steel, textiles, rubber, chemicals. Pop. (1990) 520,900.

**Hanover** (Hannover) Former kingdom and province of Germany. In 1692 Duke Ernest Augustus, one of the dukes of Brunswick-Lüneberg, was created elector of Hanover; his lands were known thereafter as Hanover. His son George succeeded to the British throne (George I) in 1714. Divided during the Napoleonic era, Hanover was reconstituted as a kingdom in 1815. Allied with Austria in the Austro-Prussian War (1866), it was annexed by Prussia after Austria's defeat. After World War II it was incorporated into the state of Lower Saxony.

**Hanover, House of** German royal family and rulers of Britain from 1714–1901. The electors of Hanover succeeded to the English throne in 1714 under the terms of the Act of Settlement (1701) and the Act of Union (1707). George I, the first elector also to be king of England, was succeeded in both England and Hanover by George II, George III, George IV, and William IV. Salic law forbade Queen Victoria's accession in Hanover; the Hanoverian title was inherited by her uncle, the Duke of Cumberland, and the crowns of Britain and Germany were separated.

**Hanseatic League** Commercial union of *c.*160 German, Dutch, and Flemish towns established in the 13th century. The League protected its merchants by controlling the trade routes from the Baltic region to the Atlantic. It began to decline in the late 15th century with the opening up of the New World and aggressive trading by the British and Dutch.

**Hanukkah** (Chanukah or Feast of Lights) Eight-day festival celebrated in Judaism. It commemorates the rededication of the Jerusalem Temple in 165 BC and the miracle of a one-day supply of oil lasting for eight days. It is celebrated with the lighting of candles on a special eight-branched holder called a menorah.

**Hanuman** In Hindu mythology, the monkey general who helped Rama to find and rescue his wife, Sita. His attributes include great strength, agility, and wisdom.

**haploid** Term describing a cell that has only one member of each chromosome pair. All human cells except gametes are diploid, having 46 chromosomes. Gametes are haploid, having 23 chromosomes. The body cells of many lower organisms, including many algae and single-celled organisms, are haploid. *See also* ALTERNATION OF GENERATIONS; MEIOSIS

**Hapsburg** (Habsburg) Austrian royal dynasty, a leading ruling house in Europe from the 13th–19th century. It became a major force when Count Rudolph was elected king of the Germans (1273). He established the core of the Hapsburg dominions in Austria. From 1438–1806 the Hapsburgs ruled the Holy Roman Empire. Under Charles V their dominions included the Low Countries, Spain and its empire, and parts of Italy. From 1556 the house was divided into Austrian and Spanish branches. The Spanish branch ended in 1700, and the male line of the Austrian branch ended in 1740. Maria Theresa reestablished the house as that of Hapsburg-Lorraine, although she lost Silesia. By 1867 the Hapsburg empire was reduced to the Austro-Hungarian empire. It finally broke up in 1918, when Charles I was deposed.

**Harare** (formerly Salisbury) Capital of Zimbabwe, in the NE part of the country. Settled by Europeans in 1890 as Fort Salisbury, it became capital of Southern Rhodesia in 1902. The city served as capital of the Federation of Rhodesia and Nyasaland (1953–63) and of Rhodesia (1965–79). It has a university (1957) and two cathedrals. Industries: gold mining, textiles, steel, tobacco, chemicals, furniture. Pop. (1992) 1,184,169.

**Harbin** (Haerbin) City on the Sungari River, NE China; capital of Heilungkiang province. It was a place of refuge for White Russians after the Revolution of 1917. Under Japanese rule from 1932–45, it was then briefly occupied by Soviet forces before falling to the Chinese Communists in 1946. Industries: oil, coal, turbines and generators, mining equipment, paper. Pop. (1993) 3,100,000.

**hard disk** Rigid magnetic disk for storing computer programs and data. The built-in hard disk drive in a typical personal computer consists of a number of hard platters coated with a magnetic material set on a common spindle. They are housed inside a sealed container, with a motor to spin the stack of platters, a head to write (record) and read (replay) each side of each platter, and associated electronic circuits. Hard-disk capacity is continually being increased: most computers are now sold with a disk of at least 500 megabytes (Mb) capacity.

**Hardie, (James) Keir** (1856–1915) British socialist politician, a founder of the Labour Party. He was chairman of the Independent Labour Party (1893–1900, 1913–14). He was the first Labour member of Parliament and for three years (1892–95) the only Labour member.

**Harding, Warren Gamaliel** (1865–1923) 29th US Presi-

**HARD DISK**

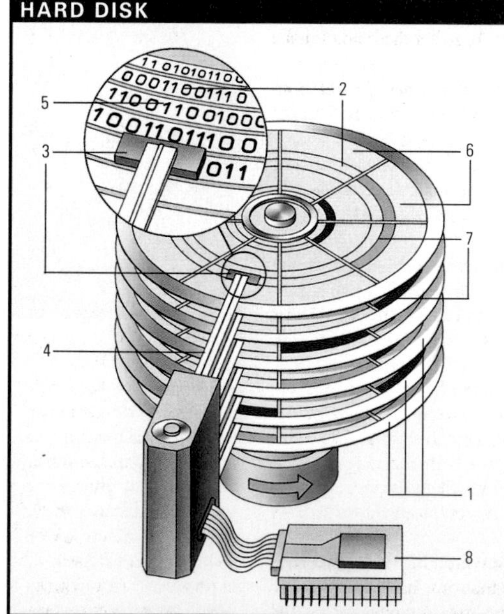


A computer hard disk is made up of multiple rotating platters (1) each one of which has circular magnetic tracks (2) that are read and written on by a magnetic head (3) held by an arm (4). The disks spin at 100 times per second. The magnetic heads, tiny electromagnets, align magnetic particles on the surface of the platters to represent a digital code of zeros and ones (5). The magnetic tracks on the platters are divided into sectors (6) and when information is written on the hard disk files are split into different sectors on the platters (7). A file allocation table tells the chip (8) controlling the hard disk where information is held on the platters.

dent (1921–23). A senator (1915–21), he was the Republican compromise candidate to run for president in 1920. His campaign for a return to "normalcy" easily defeated the Democratic challenge. While in office, he left government to his cabinet and advisers. This administration, known as the "Ohio Gang," was one of the most corrupt in US history. The TEAPOT DOME SCANDAL forced a Congressional investigation. Harding died before the worst excesses became public knowledge, and he was succeeded by the vice president, Calvin COOLIDGE.

**hardness** Resistance of a material to abrasion, cutting, or indentation. The Mohs scale is a means of expressing the comparative hardness of materials, particularly minerals, by testing them against ten standard materials. These range from (1) talc to (10) diamond (the hardest).

**hardness of water** Reluctance of water to produce a lather with soap, due to various dissolved salts, mainly those of calcium and magnesium. These salts give rise to an insoluble precipitate, which causes "scale" in boilers, pipes, and kettles. Hardness may be temporary (removed by boiling), caused by calcium bicarbonate; or permanent (not affected by boiling), caused by calcium sulfate.

**Hardouin-Mansart, Jules** (1646–1708) Royal architect to LOUIS XIV. His bold Baroque style can be seen in his major achievements, which include the Hall of Mirrors (1678–84), the Orangerie (1681–86), and the Grand Trianon (1687–88), all at Versailles.

**hardware** In computing, equipment as opposed to the programs, or SOFTWARE, with which a computer functions. The computer, keyboard, printer, and electronic circuit boards are examples of hardware.

**Hardy, Thomas** (1840–1928) English novelist and poet. His birthplace, Dorset, sw England, formed the background for most of his writing. His first major success was *Far from the Madding Crowd* (1874). The often tragic tales that followed remain among the most widely read 19th-century novels and include *The Return of the Native* (1878), *The Mayor of Casterbridge* (1886), *Tess of the d'Urbervilles* (1891), and *Jude the Obscure* (1895). The latter was attacked for its immoral tone, and thereafter Hardy devoted himself to poetry, including *Wessex Poems* (1898) and *The Dynasts* (1903–08)

**hare** Large member of the RABBIT family (Leporidae). True hares (genus *Lepus*) have ears that are longer than their heads, and are born with open eyes and a full coat of fur. Length: to 30in (76cm); weight: to 10lb (4.5kg). Hares include the JACK RABBIT and snowshoe rabbit.

**harebell** Flowering plant of the bellflower family (CAMPANULACEAE), widespread as a wildflower of pastures and also cultivated in gardens. It has drooping, bell-shaped, mid-blue flowers. Species *Campanula rotundifolia.*

**Hare Krishna** Hindu religious movement. Members of the sect celebrate the life of KRISHNA. They believe that through a combination of self-denial, meditation, chanting, and reading the Hindu scriptures they will achieve true enlightenment and escape the cycle of reincarnation.

**harelip** Congenital cleft in the upper lip caused by the failure of the two parts of the palate to unite. It is a congenital condition, often associated with CLEFT PALATE.

**harem** Women's quarters in a Muslim household. It contained a man's wives, concubines, and female servants. The most famous harems were those of the Turkish sultans in ISTANBUL, which often had several hundred women and were guarded by EUNUCHS.

**Harlem** Residential area of New York City, bounded s by 110th Street and N by 168th Street. The area is a political and cultural focus for African Americans. The Center for Research in Black Culture is located here, next to the Countee Cullen library, which has been a meeting place for black writers since the 1920s. The Apollo Theater is a noted venue for black performers.

**Harlem Renaissance** Period of creativity, particularly in literature, among African Americans in the 1920s. Centered in HARLEM, the Renaissance produced many fine writers, such as Countee Cullen, Zora Neale HURSTON, Langston HUGHES, and Claude McKay.

**harlequin** English name derived from the character Arlecchino of the COMMEDIA DELL'ARTE, who was a quick-witted, unscrupulous serving man. A harlequin today appears in comedy and pantomime as a mute jester, dressed in diamond-patterned, multicolored tights.

**HARDNESS OF WATER**

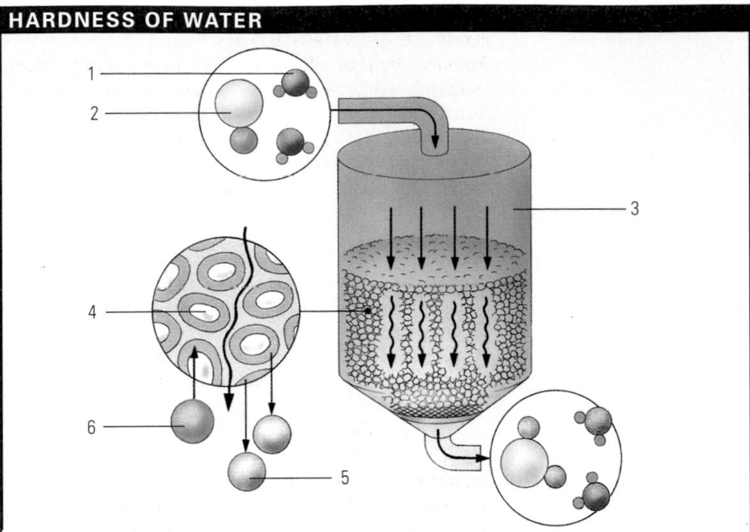


Scale in kettles and water pipes is caused by the presence in water (1) of dissolved calcium carbonate (2), usually from the chemical weathering of limestone. In hot or boiling water, calcium carbonate precipitates, forming solid limescale deposits on surfaces, such as the inside of kettles. Calcium carbonate also prevents soap from lathering. In an ion exchange tank (3), the tank is filled with grains of sodium-coated material with which the water has to come into contact (4). Sodium ions (5), which are more reactive than calcium, are exchanged for calcium ions (6). Because of the different properties of the sodium ions, the sodium salts formed remain in solution even when boiled.

**Harlow, Jean** (1911–37) US movie actress, known as the "blonde bombshell," an almost legendary figure of the Hollywood 1930s. Her first major role was in *Hell's Angels* (1930). Other films include *The Public Enemy* (1931), and *Platinum Blonde* (1931). Soon after completing *Saratoga* (1937), Harlow died of cerebral edema.

**harmonica** (mouth organ) Musical instrument consisting of a small metal case containing metal reeds. The reeds are vibrated as the player blows or inhales through slots along one edge of the case.

**harmonics** In acoustics, additional notes whose frequencies are multiples of a basic (fundamental) note. When a violin string is plucked, the sounds correspond to vibrations of the string. The loudest note corresponds to the fundamental mode of vibration. Other, weaker notes, corresponding to subsidiary vibrations, sound at the same time. Together these notes make up a harmonic series.

**harmony** In music, structure of chords and the relationships between them. The diatonic scale (from one C to the next on a piano, for example) is the basis of chord construction, and a harmonic progression from one chord to the next is defined by the KEY. The tonic, dominant, and subdominant chords are the primary chords of a key (C, G, and F chords in the key of C).

**Harold I** (d.1040) (Harold Harefoot) Danish king and ruler of England (1035–40). An illegitimate son of CANUTE II, he claimed the crown, ruling as regent (1035–37). Elected king at Oxford, he disposed of his rival, Alfred the Aethling, and displaced the heir, his half-brother Hardecanute.

**Harold II** (1022–66) Last Anglo-Saxon king of England (1066). He was elected king following the death of EDWARD THE CONFESSOR, despite having pledged to support William of Normandy's (WILLIAM I) claim to the throne. England was immediately invaded by Harold III of Norway, whom he defeated. Three days later he was defeated and killed by William at the Battle of HASTINGS.

**harp** Ancient musical instrument consisting of a frame over which strings are stretched. Variations have been found Egyptian, Greek, and Celtic civilizatons. A modern orchestral

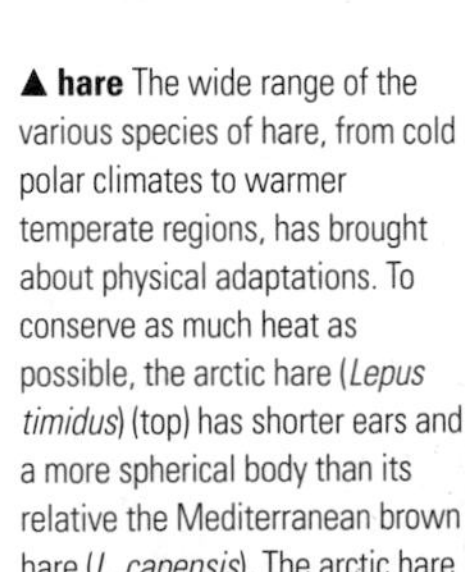

▲ **hare** The wide range of the various species of hare, from cold polar climates to warmer temperate regions, has brought about physical adaptations. To conserve as much heat as possible, the arctic hare (*Lepus timidus*) (top) has shorter ears and a more spherical body than its relative the Mediterranean brown hare (*L. capensis*). The arctic hare also has thicker fur, which turns white in winter for camouflage.

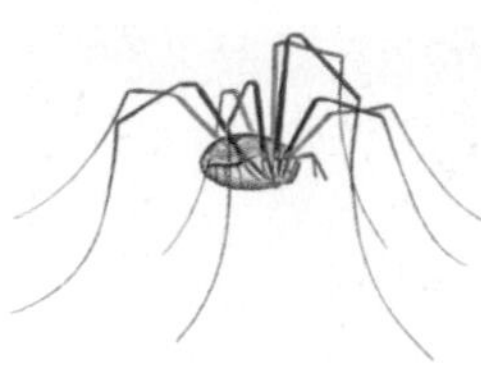

▲ **harvestman** The North African harvestman (*Phalangium africanum*) has many relatives throughout the world, including North America, where it is known as the daddy longlegs. The body measures up to 0.5in (12mm).

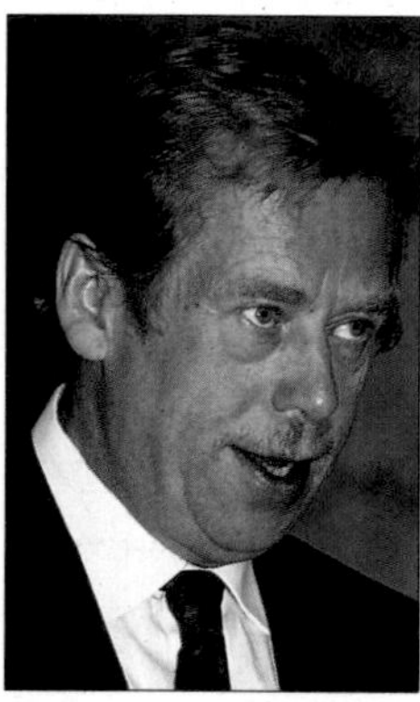

▲ **Havel** President of the Czech Republic, Vaclav Havel was imprisoned under the former communist regime, and his plays, which are centered about the lives of political dissidents, were banned. By the late 1990s, he was suffering from cancer.

▲ **hawthorn** An ideal tree for hedge-planting because of its hardiness and its display of thorns, the hawthorn (family Rosaceae) can grow to 35ft (11.5m) if left untrimmed. Its heavily scented blossoms are conspicuous in late spring and early summer in the hedgerows of Europe.

harp has a large triangular frame that carries 47 strings. Seven pedals ensure the whole chromatic range is covered by altering the pitch of the strings.

**harpsichord** Keyboard musical instrument. Its metal strings are mechanically plucked by quill plectrums. Its volume can barely be regulated, although stops may be used to bring extra strings into use. Historic instruments may have had two or, rarely, three keyboards. The harpsichord was the principal keyboard instrument from 1500 to 1750 but was later replaced by the piano.

**harrier** Bird of prey. Active by day, it frequents grasslands where it swoops on small animals. It has a small bill and long wings, legs, and tail. Length: 15–20in (38–50cm). Family Accipitridae; genus *Circus*.

**Harris, Joel Chandler** (1848–1908) US author. A journalist in the American South for much of his career, Harris is best known for the *Uncle Remus* stories, which are retellings of African-American folktales. The character of Br'er Rabbit is perhaps his most memorable.

**Harrisburg** Capital of Pennsylvania, in the SE of the state, on the Susquehanna River. Established as a trading post in *c.*1718, by 1785 a town was established, which was the scene of the Harrisburg Convention (1788). It became the state capital in 1812. Industries: textiles, machinery, electronic equipment. Pop. (1992 est.) 53,430.

**Harrison, Benjamin** (1833–1901) 23rd US President (1889–93), grandson of William Henry HARRISON. After one term in the US Senate, Harrison was selected (1888) as the Republican presidential nominee against President Grover CLEVELAND. He won with a majority of the electoral votes, although Cleveland had the most popular votes. As president, Harrison signed into law the SHERMAN ANTITRUST ACT and the McKinley Tariff Act. He was defeated by Cleveland in 1892.

**Harrison, William Henry** (1773–1841) Ninth US President (1841). He is remembered chiefly for his military career, especially his victory at Tippecanoe over Native Americans (1811) and later in the WAR OF 1812. He was elected president in 1840, with John Tyler as vice president, under the famous slogan "Tippecanoe and Tyler too." Harrison died after one month in office.

**Hart, Moss** (1904–61) US dramatist. He collaborated with George S. KAUFMAN on many comedies, including *You Can't Take It With You* (1936). His most successful musical was *Lady in the Dark* (1941) written with Kurt WEILL and Ira Gershwin. In 1956 he directed *My Fair Lady*.

**hartebeest** Large ANTELOPE native to African grasslands S of the Sahara Desert. They have sharply rising horns united at the base. Length: up to 80in (200cm); height: to 60in (150cm); weight: up to 400lb (180kg). Family Bovidae.

**Hartford** Capital of Connecticut, on the Connecticut River. More than 25 insurance companies have their headquarters here. Manufactures include precision instruments and electrical equipment. Pop. (1990) 139,739.

**Hartford Convention** (1814–15) Secret meeting of leaders from five New England states opposed to the WAR OF 1812 because it disrupted trade. Convention resolutions sought to strengthen states' rights over conscription and taxation; some delegates favored withdrawal from the Union.

**Hartley, L.P. (Lesley Poles)** (1895–1972) British novelist, short-story writer, and critic. He first won acclaim with his trilogy of novels *The Shrimp and the Anemone* (1944), *The Sixth Heaven* (1946), and *Eustace and Hilda* (1947). *The Go-Between* (1953) presents a picture of the sexual desires beneath the surface of aristocratic Edwardian society.

**Hartmann, Nicolai** (1882–1950) German realist philosopher. Although influenced by PLATO and Immanuel KANT, he proposed, in *Outlines of a Metaphysics of Knowledge* (1921), that existence is an essential prerequisite for knowledge, a reversal of Kant's idea. He finally rejected Kantian ideas in his book *New Ways of Ontology* (1942). *See also* REALISM

**Harun al-Rashid** (764–809) ABBASID caliph of Baghdad (786–809). His reign has gained romantic luster from the stories of the *Arabian Nights*. He engaged in successful war with the BYZANTINE EMPIRE, but his effort to reconcile competing interests by dividing the empire between his sons led to civil war.

**Harvard University** Oldest US college, founded in 1636 by John Harvard at Cambridge, Massachusetts. It was originally intended for the instruction of Puritan ministers. Harvard has two undergraduate divisions: Harvard College for men and Radcliffe College for women. All classes are co-educational. It has ten graduate schools.

**harvestman** (daddy longlegs) ARACHNID with legs that may be several times its body length. It feeds on insects and plant juices. Body: 0.1–0.5in (2.5–13mm). Family Phalangidae.

**Harvey, William** (1578–1657) English physician and anatomist who discovered the circulation of the blood. His findings were published in *De Motu Cordis et Sanguinis* (1628). He also studied EMBRYOLOGY.

**Haryana** State in N central India; the capital is Chandigarh. It was formed in 1966 from part of the state of Punjab. Industries: machine tools, farming implements, cement, paper, bicycles. Area: 17,074sq mi (44,222sq km). Pop. (1991) 16,403,648.

**Harz Mountains** Mountain range in central Germany, extending 60mi (96km) between the Weser and Elbe rivers. The highest peak is the Brocken, 3,747ft (1,142m).

**Hašek, Jaroslav** (1883–1923) Czech novelist and short story writer. He wrote the best-selling satirical novel *The Good Soldier Schweik* (1920–23).

**hashish** Resin obtained from the flowering tops of the hemp plant *Cannabis sativa* and used as a psychotropic drug. When smoked or eaten it generally induces heady sensations and often a feeling of detachment. Possession of the drug is illegal in the US. *See also* MARIJUANA

**Hasidism** Popular pietist movement within JUDAISM founded by Israel ben Eliezer (*c.*1699– *c.*1761), known as the Baal Shem Tov (Master of the Good Name). The movement, centered in E Europe until World War II, strongly supports Orthodox Judaism. Its main centers are now in Israel and the US.

**Hassan II** (1929– ) King of Morocco (1961– ), son of Muhammad V. He dissolved the National Assembly in 1965 and introduced a new constitution, approved by referendum (1971), which left his authority supreme.

**Hastings, Warren** (1732–1818) First British governor general of India (1774–85). He successfully defended British territory against several Indian opponents. He made many enemies and returned to England in 1785 to face a variety of charges. Though eventually acquitted, his career was ruined.

**Hastings, Battle of** (October 14, 1066) Fought near Hastings, SE England, by King HAROLD II of England against an invading army led by WILLIAM, duke of Normandy. The Norman victory and death of Harold marked the end of the Anglo-Saxon monarchy.

**hatchetfish** Marine fish found in deep temperate and tropical seas. There are light-emitting organs along the underside of its deep, muscular abdomen. Length: to 4in (10cm). Family Sternoptychidae (or Characidae).

**Hathor** Ancient Egyptian goddess of love and happiness, music and dance. She was depicted as a cow or with the horns of a cow.

**Hatshepsut** (d.1482 BC) Queen of Egypt (*c.*1494–1482 BC). Daughter of THUTMOSE I, she married Thutmose II. After his death (*c.* 1504 BC), she ruled, first as regent for her nephew, and then in her own right, the only woman to rule as pharaoh.

**Haughey, Charles** (1925– ) Irish politician. In a long and often controversial career, Haughey was prime minister three times (1979–81, March–November 1982, 1986–92). A member of the Fianna Fáil party, he entered parliament in 1957. He was dismissed from the cabinet in 1970 for alleged conspiracy in IRISH REPUBLICAN ARMY (IRA) gun-running, although he was later acquitted.

**Hauptmann, Gerhart** (1862–1946) German dramatist,

poet, and novelist. His play *Vor Sonnenaufgang* (1889) marked the birth of German naturalist drama. He was awarded the 1912 Nobel Prize for literature.

**Hausa** Mainly Muslim people, inhabiting NW Nigeria and S Niger. Hausa society is feudal and based on patrilineal descent. Its language is the official language of N Nigeria and a major trading language of W Africa. Hausa crafts include weaving, leatherwork, and silversmithing.

**Havana** (La Habana) Capital of CUBA, on the NW coast; largest city and port in the West Indies. It was founded by the Spanish explorer Diego Velázquez in 1515 and moved to its present site in 1519. Havana became Cuba's capital at the end of the 16th century. By the early 19th century its was a wealthy commercial center. The city's fortunes declined later in the century. Industries: oil refining, textiles, sugar, cigars. Pop. (1990 est.) 2,096,054.

**Havel, Vaclav** (1936– ) Czech playwright, politician, and president. Havel was imprisoned several times by the communist regime during the 1970s and 1980s, both for his satirical plays and for his work as a human-rights activist. In 1989 he became the first democratically elected president and tried to preserve a united republic. He resigned in 1992 when breakup became inevitable. In 1993 he became president of the newly formed Czech Republic and was re-elected in 1998.

**Hawaii** State in the N Pacific Ocean, 2,090mi (3,363km) WSW of San Francisco; the capital is HONOLULU. It consists of eight large and 124 small volcanic islands. Polynesians established settlements in the 9th century AD. Annexed by the US in 1898, it became the last state to be admitted to the Union in 1959. There is an important US naval base at PEARL HARBOR. The economy is based on agriculture and tourism. Exports: bananas, pineapples, sugar, nuts, and coffee. Area: 6,450sq mi (16,705sq km). Pop. (1993 est.) 1,171,592.

**hawfinch** Largest European FINCH, nesting in temperate regions. It has mostly chestnut plumage, with black and white patches. Length: 7in (18cm). Species *Coccothraustes coccothraustes*.

**hawk** Any of several species of day-active BIRDS OF PREY found in temperate and tropical climates. They have short, hooked bills for tearing meat and strong claws for killing and carrying prey. Hawks have red, brown, gray, or white plumage with streaks on the wings. Length: 11–26in (28–66 cm). Order Falconiformes; genera *Accipiter* and *Buteo*.

**Hawke, Bob (Robert)** (1929– ) Australian statesman, prime minister (1983–91). He entered Parliament in 1980, and in 1983 became leader of the Australian Labor Party. Hawke held office for an unprecedented four terms. In 1991 he was succeded by Paul Keating.

**Hawking, Stephen William** (1942– ) English theoretical physicist. Hawking supported the BIG BANG theory of the origin of the Universe and did much pioneering work on the theory of BLACK HOLES. He published a popular account of his work in *A Brief History of Time* (1988).

**Hawkins, Coleman** (1904–69) US jazz saxophonist. His definitive recording of "Body and Soul" was one of the first recordings of an extended jazz solo. From 1934–39 he lived in Europe, where he recorded with Django REINHARDT.

**Hawkins, Sir John** (1532–95) English naval commander. With the support of Elizabeth I, he led two lucrative expeditions to Africa and the West Indies (1562–63, 1564–65), but on his third expedition (1567–69) the Spanish destroyed most of his ships. He played an important role in the defeat of the Spanish ARMADA in 1588.

**hawthorn** Any of more than 200 species of thorny DECIDUOUS shrubs and trees of the genus *Crataegus*, growing in N temperate parts of the world. Their flowers are white or pink, and small berries are borne in clusters. Family Rosaceae.

**Hawthorne, Nathaniel** (1804–64) US novelist. He helped develop the American short story. His reputation was made with *The Scarlet Letter* (1850). Other works include *The House of the Seven Gables* (1851), *The Blithedale Romance* (1852), and *The Snow Image and Other Twice-Told Tales* (1851). Much of his work is set in Puritan New England and examines the conflict between emotion and repressive social strictures.

**Hay, John Milton** (1838–1905) US statesman, secretary of state under Presidents MCKINLEY and Theodore ROOSEVELT (1898–1905). His "open-door policy" was a demand for equal trading status for foreign powers in China, and he negotiated treaties ensuring US control of the Panama Canal.

**Haydn, Franz Joseph** (1732–1809) Austrian composer. He brought the SONATA form to masterful fruition in more than 100 symphonies, notably the *Military*, the *Clock*, and the *London* (all 1793–95). He also wrote many string quartets, chamber works, concertos, masses, and choral works. His most famous choral works are the oratorios *The Creation* (1798) and *The Seasons* (1801). He also wrote many string quartets, chamber works, concertos, and masses.

**Hayek, Friedrich August von** (1899–1992) British economist, b. Vienna. He wrote many books on law, economics, and philosophy, and won the 1974 Nobel Prize for economics.

**Hayes, Helen** (1900–93) US actress. In a long and distinguished stage career, she appeared in dozens of productions, notably *Dear Brutus* (1918), *Victoria Regina* (1935–39), and *The Glass Menagerie* (1948). Her film credits include *The Sin of Madelon Claudet* (1931), for which she won an Academy Award; *What Every Woman Knows* (1934); *Anastasia* (1956); and *Airport* (1969), which won her a second Academy Award.

**Hayes, Rutherford Birchard** (1822–93) 19th US President (1877–81). As governor of Ohio, he won the Republican nomination for president in 1876. Some of the electoral votes were disputed, but an electoral commission awarded all of them to Hayes, giving him victory over Samuel J. Tilden. As president, Hayes removed all federal troops from the South and tried to promote civil-service reform. He retired after one term.

**hay fever** Seasonal ALLERGY induced by grass POLLENS. Symptoms include ASTHMA, itching of the nose, ears, and eyes, and sneezing. Symptoms are controlled with an ANTIHISTAMINE.

**Haymarket Riot** (May 4, 1886) Riot in Haymarket Square, Chicago, Illinois. At a meeting organized by anarchists to protest against police brutality, a bomb was thrown and 11 people, mainly police, were killed. Although the bomb-thrower was never found, eight anarchist leaders were later convicted as accessories, and four were executed. Three others were pardoned in 1893, on the grounds that the trial was unfair; one other committed suicide while in prison. The incident turned public opinion against the labor movement.

**Hay-Pauncefote Treaty** (1901) Agreement promising equal rates through the Panama Canal to all nations and all vessels, commercial or military. It also granted the US the full right to build and manage the canal. It was negotiated by John HAY and Lord Pauncefote, British ambassador to the US.

**Haywood, William Dudley** (1869–1928) US labor leader, known as "Big Bill." He helped to organize the INDUSTRIAL WORKERS OF THE WORLD (IWW) and advocat-

▲ **Hawking** The author of the bestselling *A Brief History of Time* (1988), Professor Stephen Hawking's work has concentrated on the nature of black holes. He was the first scientist to hypothesize that the immensely powerful gravitational field around super-dense black holes can radiate matter. Since the 1960s he has suffered from a motor neuron disease, which has confined him to a wheelchair.

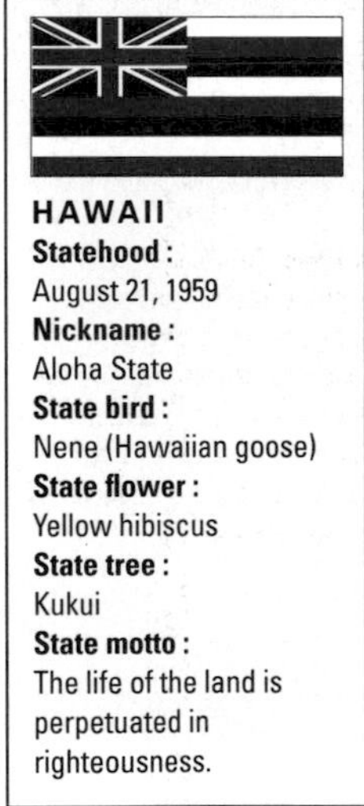

**HAWAII**
**Statehood:** August 21, 1959
**Nickname:** Aloha State
**State bird:** Nene (Hawaiian goose)
**State flower:** Yellow hibiscus
**State tree:** Kukui
**State motto:** The life of the land is perpetuated in righteousness.

◄ **Hayworth** A cousin of Ginger Rogers, the US actress and dancer Rita Hayworth came from a show business family. Known as the "Love Goddess," she was best known for her roles as the sultry temptress in films such as *Blood and Sand* (1941) and *Gilda* (1946), and as the fun-loving female lead in musicals, the most popular of which was *Cover Girl* (1944).

▲ **Heaney** Nobel Prize winning poet Seamus Heaney was deeply affected by the violence of his native Northern Ireland. Much of his poetry examines the violence and its effect on the community. He left Northern Ireland because of the troubles, and taught in Dublin, later becoming professor of rhetoric and oratory at Harvard in 1985 and professor of poetry at Oxford, UK, in 1989.

ed violence in pursuit of workers' rights. During World War I Haywood was convicted of sedition. Released on bail in 1921, he fled to the Soviet Union.

**Hayworth, Rita** (1918–87) US film actress. Her sultry, temptress image was established in *Blood and Sand* (1941). She was the dancing partner of both Gene KELLY in *Cover Girl* (1944) and Fred ASTAIRE in *You Were Never Lovelier* (1941). Orson WELLES (one of her five husbands) directed her in *The Lady From Shanghai* (1948).

**hazel** Any of about 15 bushes or small trees of the genus *Corylus*, native to N temperate regions. There are separate male and female flowers. The fruit is a hazelnut, also called cobnut or filbert. Family Betulaceae.

**Health and Human Services, US Department of** US cabinet department, formed in 1980 from parts of the Department of Health, Education, and Welfare (HEW). It consolidated the services of programs including Medicare and Medicaid, Social Security, and the Federal Drug Administration.

**Heaney, Seamus** (1939– ) Irish poet and critic, influenced by the history of sectarian violence in Northern Ireland. His volumes include *Eleven Poems* (1965), *Death of a Naturalist* (1966), *Door to the Dark* (1969), *North* (1975), and *The Spirit Level*, which won the 1996 Whitbread prize. His essays are collected in *Preoccupations* (1980) and *The Government of the Tongue* (1988). He won the 1995 Nobel Prize for literature.

**hearing** Process by which sound WAVES are experienced. SOUND waves enter the EAR and vibrate the eardrum. The vibrations are transmitted by three small bones to the COCHLEA, where receptors generate nerve impulses that pass via the auditory nerve to the brain to be interpreted.

**Hearst, William Randolph** (1863–1951) US publisher. He built a nationwide publishing empire that included newspapers, magazines, news services, radio stations, and film studios. With his rival, Joseph PULITZER, he practiced sensational journalism and promoted the Spanish-American War.

**heart** Muscular ORGAN that pumps BLOOD throughout the body. In humans, the heart is located behind the breastbone between the lower parts of the lungs. Divided longitudinally by a muscular wall, the right side contains only deoxygenated blood, the left side only oxygenated blood. Each side is divided into two chambers, an atrium and a ventricle. The average heart beat rate for an adult at rest is 70–80 beats per minute.

**heart attack** (myocardial infarction) Death of part of the heart muscle due to the blockage of a coronary artery by a blood clot (thrombosis). It is accompanied by chest pain, sweating, and vomiting. Modern drugs treat abnormal heart rhythms and dissolve clots in the coronary arteries. **Heart failure** occurs when the heart is unable to pump blood at the rate necessary to supply body tissues, and may be due to high BLOOD PRESSURE or heart disease. Symptoms include shortness of breath, edema, and fatigue. Treatment is with a DIURETIC and heart drugs. *See also* ANGINA

**heart-lung machine** Apparatus used during some surgery to take over the function of the heart and lungs. It consists of a pump to circulate blood around the body and special equipment to add oxygen to the blood and remove carbon dioxide.

**heat** Form of energy associated with the constant vibration of atoms and molecules. Currently accepted KINETIC THEORY holds that the hotness of a body depends on the extent of vibration of its atoms. Heat is distributed in three forms: CONVECTION, CONDUCTION, and RADIATION.

**heat capacity** (thermal capacity) Ratio of the heat supplied to an object to the rise in its TEMPERATURE. It is measured in joules/kelvin. *See also* SPECIFIC HEAT CAPACITY

**Heath, Sir Edward Richard George** (1916– ) British statesman, prime minister (1970–74). He entered Parliament in 1950, becoming lord privy seal (1960–63) and party leader (1965). As prime minister, he secured Britain's EC membership (1973), but poor industrial relations led to a bitter miners' strike and the "Three-Day Week" (1974) to conserve energy. After defeat in two general elections in 1974, Heath was replaced as Conservative Party leader by Margaret THATCHER (1975).

**heath** Any of various woody, evergreen shrubs of the genus *Erica*, found in North America, Europe, and Africa. They usually have bell-shaped blue or purple flowers. Family Ericaceae. The term also applies to land that supports heath.

**heather** (ling) Evergreen shrub native to Europe and Asia Minor. It has bell-shaped flowers of pink, lavender, or white. Family Ericaceae; species *Calluna vulgaris*.

**heatstroke** Condition in which the body temperature rises above 106°F (41°C). It is brought on by exposure to extreme heat. In mild cases there is lassitude and fainting; in severe cases, collapse, coma, and death may ensue.

**heaven** Abode of divine beings or a world of bliss beyond death. In the later Jewish tradition (after the 3rd or 2nd century BC), it was the dwelling place of God and the angels, and of those human beings who had died after leading a virtuous life. Christian theology adopted this conception but modified it to be the destination after death of the true followers of Jesus Christ. *See also* HADES; HELL; LIMBO; PURGATORY

**heavy metal** Metal of high density, such as platinum or lead. The term may also refer to metallic pollutants in soil that restrict plant growth.

**heavy water** *See* DEUTERIUM

**Hebrew** Language of the SEMITIC branch of the AFRO-ASIATIC family. Spoken in Palestine from ancient times, it is the language of the OLD TESTAMENT. It declined during the BABYLONIAN CAPTIVITY and was overtaken by ARAMAIC. Hebrew persisted as a literary and liturgical language among Jews. It was revived as a spoken language by the 19th century Zionist movement and became the official language of ISRAEL in 1948. *See also* YIDDISH

**Hebrews, Epistle to the** Part of the NEW TESTAMENT. It contains a letter of encouragement to a group of Jewish Christians and a review of Israel's history and Jesus' place in it. Its author is unknown.

**Hebrides** (Western Isles) Group of more than 500 islands in the Atlantic Ocean off the W coast of Scotland. They are divided into the Inner Hebrides (principal islands: Skye, Rhum, Eigg, Islay, Mull) and the Outer Hebrides (principal islands: Lewis with Harris, North and South Uist). First inhabited in the 4th millennium BC, from the 3rd century AD the islands were settled by Picts and later by Scots. In the 8th century they were invaded by Vikings and became a Norwegian dependency. In the 13th century they were ceded to Scotland by Norway. Few of the islands are inhabited, and agriculture is limited. The main occupations are fishing, farming, and the manufacture of woolens.

**Hebron** (El Khalil) City in the Israeli-occupied WEST BANK,

**HEART**

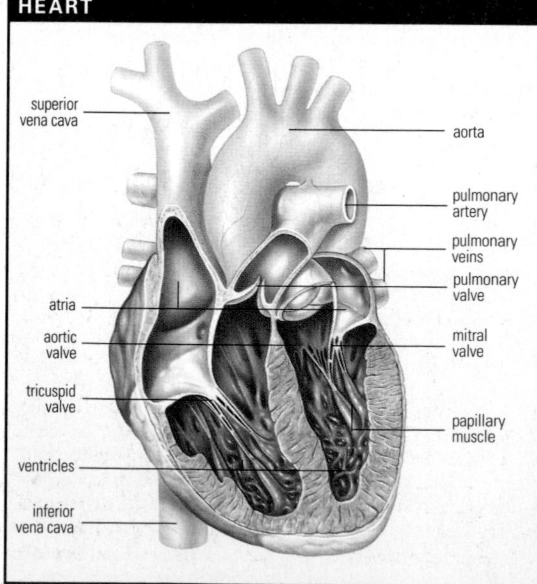


The human heart contains four chambers – two atria and two ventricles – and four sets of valves. Blood from the body passes into the right atrium, via the vena cavae. Flow of blood into the right ventricle is controlled by the tricuspid valve. Pulmonary arteries carry blood from the right ventricle to the lungs, while the pulmonary veins carry oxygenated blood back from the lungs to the left atrium. In a similar way, the mitral valve controls the flow of blood between the left atrium and the left ventricle. The aorta conducts the oxygenated blood from the left ventricle to all parts of the body.

almost entirely controlled by the Palestinian National Authority. An ancient city, it came under Arab control in the 7th century AD and was occupied by the Crusaders (12th–13th centuries) before reverting to Arab rule. It later became part of the Ottoman Empire. In 1948 it was annexed to Jordan, but was occupied by Israel during the SIX DAY WAR (1967). It has witnessed much Israeli–Arab tension, especially during the INTIFADA. The ISRAELI-PALESTINIAN ACCORD granted Palestinian self-rule to 85% of the city. After some delay, the Israeli withdrawal took place in January 1997. Hebron is sacred to both Jews and Muslims. The Tomb of the Patriarchs (the Cave of Machpelah) is the traditional burial place of Abraham, Sarah, Isaac, Rebecca, Jacob, and Leah. Industries: tanning, glass making, food processing. Pop. (1995 est.) 117,000.

**Hecate** Goddess in Greek mythology. Associated with ARTEMIS, she bestowed wealth and blessings, and presided over witchcraft, graveyards, and crossroads.

**Hector** In Greek legend, the greatest of the Trojan heroes, eldest son of PRIAM. He was slain by ACHILLES.

**hedgehog** Small, nocturnal Eurasian and African mammal of the family Erinaceidae. It has short, sharp spines and defends itself by rolling into a ball with the spines outermost. It feeds on insects and other small animals. Genus *Erinaceus*

**hedonism** Pursuit of pleasure, or any of several philosophical or ethical doctrines associated with it. Aristippus (*c.*435–*c.*356 BC) taught that pleasure was the highest good. EPICURUS advocated discrimination in the seeking of pleasure. LOCKE believed that the idea of "good" can be defined in terms of pleasure. BENTHAM and J.S. MILL adapted a psychological view of hedonism in formulating UTILITARIANISM.

**Hegel, Georg Wilhelm Friedrich** (1770–1831) German philosopher, whose method of dialectical reasoning had a strong influence on his successors, notably Karl MARX. He developed a metaphysical system that traced the self-realization of spirit by dialectical movements toward perfection. These progressions took the form of battles between a thesis (a proposition) and an antithesis (its opposite), eventually resolved in a synthesis at a higher level of truth. Hegel wrote two major books, *Phenomenology of Spirit* (1807) and *Science of Logic* (1812–16). *See also* DIALECTICAL MATERIALISM

**hegemony** Leadership or dominance of one state over others. The term originated in ancient Greece where the cities of Athens, Sparta, and Thebes held hegemony over Greece in the 5th and 4th centuries BC. The term was also employed by the Italian Marxian theorist Antonio Gramsci to refer to the phenomenon of one social class monopolizing the creation and transmission of values.

**Hegira** (Arab. *Hegira*, breaking off of relations) Flight of MUHAMMAD from MECCA to MEDINA in AD 622 to escape persecution. The Islamic calendar begins in 622.

**Heidegger, Martin** (1889–1976) German philosopher. A founder of existentialism and a major influence on modern philosophy, his most important work was *Being and Time* (1927). Influenced by hermeneutics, PHENOMENOLOGY, and Christian ONTOLOGY, his central concern was how human self-awareness is dependent on the concepts of time and death. For him, Western science and philosophy have led to nihilism and prevent people from rediscovering their true selves. His later work focused more on the role of language.

**Heidelberg** City on the Neckar River, SW Germany, in Baden-Württemberg state. Founded in the 12th century, it has the oldest university in Germany (1386) and a medieval castle. Industries: printing machinery, precision instruments, publishing, textiles. Pop. (1990) 139,900.

**Heine, Heinrich** (1797–1856) German poet and prose writer. The *Book of Songs* (1827), a collection of verse, is his best-known work. It was followed by the four-volume satirical *Pictures of Travel* (1826–31). SCHUMANN and SCHUBERT both set his lyrics to music.

**Heisenberg, Werner Karl** (1901–76) German physicist and philosopher, best known for discovering the UNCERTAINTY PRINCIPLE (1927). He won the 1932 Nobel Prize for physics for his work in QUANTUM MECHANICS.

◄ **hedgehog** The spines of the European hedgehog (*Erinaceus europus*) are actually hairs modified into hollow tubes with reinforcing ridges on the inside walls, making for a strong but light structure. The spines are raised when the animal is threatened.

**Hejaz** Region in NW Saudi Arabia, on the Red Sea coast. The center of ISLAM, it contains the Muslim holy cities of MECCA and MEDINA. It has been part of Saudi Arabia since 1932. Area: 150,000sq mi (388,500sq km).

**Helen** In Greek legend, the beautiful daughter of LEDA and ZEUS. She married Menelaus, King of Sparta, but was carried off by PARIS, Prince of TROY, thus provoking the TROJAN WAR.

**Helena** Capital of Montana, W central Montana. Settled by prospectors in 1864, by 1868 its population was 7,500 and $16 million worth of gold had been mined. In 1875 it was made the capital of Montana territory, becoming the state capital in 1889. Industries: mineral-smelting, bakery equipment, ceramics. Pop. (1990) 24,569.

**helicopter** Aircraft that gains lift from power-driven rotor(s). The helicopter is capable of vertical takeoff and landing (VTOL), hovering, and forward, backward, and lateral flight.

**Helios** In Greek mythology, god of the Sun, identified with the Roman god APOLLO. Helios appears driving a four-horse chariot through the sky.

**helium** (symbol He) Nonmetallic element, a NOBLE GAS, discovered in 1868. First obtained in 1895 from the mineral clevite, the chief source today is from natural gas. It is also found in some radioactive minerals and in the Earth's atmosphere (0.0005% by volume). It has the lowest melting and boiling points of any element. It is colorless, odorless, and nonflammable, and is used in light-air balloons, to make artificial "air" (with oxygen) for deep-sea divers, and in welding, semiconductors, and lasers. Liquid helium is used in CRYOGENICS. Properties: at.no. 2; at.wt. 4.0026; sp.gr. 0.178; m.p. −458°F (−272.2°C); b.p. −452.02°F (−268.9°C); single isotope $^{4}He$.

**HELICOPTER**

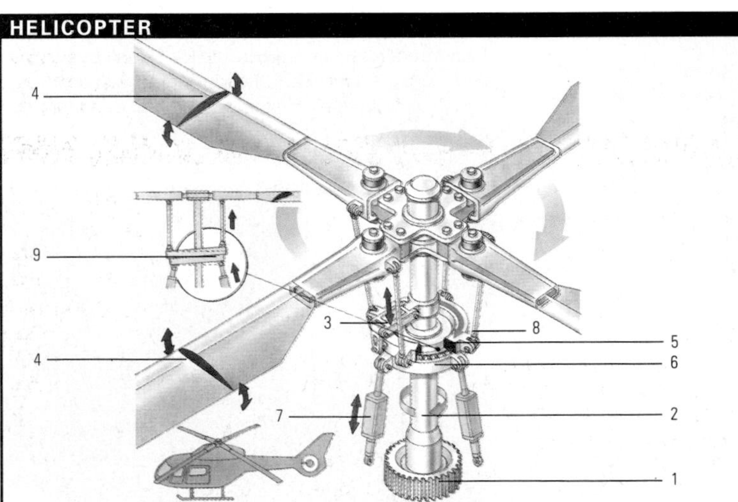


A helicopter rotor head transfers the power of the engines to the rotor blades via gears (1) and the rotor shaft (2). The swish plate controls the tilt of the rotor (3) and also the pitch of the blades (4). The upper (5) and lower (6) swish plates are controlled by hydraulic cylinders (7) attached to the lower plate. The upper plate is connected to the rotor blades by control rods (8). The pitch of the blades controls the amount of lift generated, while the attitude of the whole rotor controls how the helicopter moves horizontally. If the rear of the swish plate is raised (9) the rotor dips toward the nose of the helicopter, causing it to travel forward.

▲ **Hemingway** US novelist Ernest Hemingway was constantly seeking adventure and was a correspondent in the Spanish Civil War and World War II. Hemingway also spent time big-game hunting or deep-sea fishing. He won the Pulitzer Prize in 1953, and the following year he was awarded the Nobel Prize in literature. During his later life, he suffered increasingly from severe bouts of depression, and it is thought that this illness, combined with a fear of old age, drove him to shoot himself in 1961.

**helix** Curve generated when a point moves over the surface of a cylinder so that it traces a path inclined at a constant angle to the cylinder's axis, as in a coil spring.

**hell** Abode of evil spirits, and the place or state of eternal punishment after death for the wicked. In modern Christian theology, hell is conceived as eternal separation from God. Hell is paralleled in other religions and mythologies, for example, the Hebrew *sheol* or the Greek HADES. *See also* HEAVEN; LIMBO; PURGATORY

**hellebore** Any of about 20 species of poisonous, herbaceous plants of the genus *Helleborus,* native to Eurasia. Best known is the Christmas rose, *H. niger*, which bears white flowers from midwinter to early spring. Family Ranunculaceae.

**Hellenistic Age** (323–30 BC) Period of Classical Mediterranean history from ALEXANDER THE GREAT to the reign of AUGUSTUS. Alexander's conquests helped to spread Greek civilization over a wide area. The age was distinguished by remarkable scientific and technological advances, especially in ALEXANDRIA, and by more elaborate and naturalistic styles in the visual arts.

**Heller, Joseph** (1923– ) US author. His first novel, *Catch–22* (1961), is one of the satirical masterpieces of the 20th century. Other works include the play *We Bombed in New Haven* (1968) and the novels *Something Happened* (1974), *God Knows* (1984), and *Closing Time* (1994).

**Hellespont** *See* DARDANELLES.

**Hellman, Lillian** (1905–84) US playwright. Her first play, *The Children's Hour* (1934), set the tone for her enduring interest in Marxist theory. She became a major force in US theater and received acclaim for her memoirs, beginning with *An Unfinished Woman* (1969) and concluding with *Maybe* (1980).

**Helmholtz, Hermann Ludwig Ferdinand von** (1821–94) German anatomist, physicist, and physiologist. He made contributions in ACOUSTICS and OPTICS, expanding Thomas Young's three-color theory of vision. His experiments on the speed of nerve impulses led him to formulate a principle of conservation of energy.

**Helsinki** (Helsingfors) Capital of Finland, in the S of the country, on the Gulf of Finland. The city was ounded in 1550 by GUSTAVUS I (VASA), and it became the capital in 1812. Helsinki has two universities (1849 and 1908), a cathedral (1852), museums, and art galleries. The administrative center of Finland, Helsinki is also its largest port. Industries: shipbuilding, engineering, ceramics, textiles. Pop. (1993) 508,588.

**Helvétius, Claude Adrien** (1715–71) French philosopher and educator. His best-known work, *De L'Esprit* (1758), attacked the religious basis of morality, arousing great opposition. He claimed that everybody is intellectually equal but some have less desire to learn than others. This led him to claim, in *De l'homme* (1772), that all human problems could be solved by education.

► **Hendrix** Considered by many to be the most influential rock guitarist of all time, Jimi Hendrix enjoyed greater initial success in the UK than his native US. Although left-handed, he played a right-handed guitar turned upside down. He died aged 28, following a drug overdose.

**hematite** One of the most important iron ores, containing mainly ferric oxide, $Fe_2O_3$. Containing 70% iron by weight, it occurs in several forms and varies in color from steel-gray to black, but sometimes red.

**Hemingway, Ernest Millar** (1899–1961) US author. After serving as an ambulance driver in World War I, he became a journalist, first in Paris and later as a war correspondent in the Spanish Civil War and World War II. The novel *The Sun Also Rises* (1926) chronicled the LOST GENERATION and established his reputation. Later works include *A Farewell to Arms* (1929), *For Whom the Bell Tolls* (1940), and the novella *The Old Man and the Sea* (1952). He was also an acclaimed short-story writer. He won the 1954 Nobel Prize for literature.

**hemlock** Poisonous, herbaceous plant native to Eurasia. It has a long taproot and flat clusters of white flowers. The leaf stalks have purple spots. Family Apiaceae/Umbelliferae; species *Conium maculatum*. Hemlock is also used for conifers of the genus *Tsuga*, family Pinaceae.

**hemoglobin** Protein present in the ERYTHROCYTES of vertebrates. It carries oxygen to all cells in the body by combining with it to form oxyhemoglobin. Oxygen attaches to the haem part of the protein, which contains iron; the globin part is a globular PROTEIN.

**hemophilia** Hereditary blood clotting disorder causing prolonged external or internal bleeding, often without apparent cause. Hemophilia A is caused by inability to synthesize blood factor VIII, a substance essential to clotting. This can be managed with injections of factor VIII. The rarer hemophilia B is caused by a deficiency of blood factor IX. The gene for both types is passed on almost exclusively from mother to son.

**hemorrhage** Loss of blood from a damaged vessel. It may be external, flowing from a wound, or internal, as from internal injury or a bleeding ulcer. Blood loss from an artery is most serious, causing shock and death if untreated. Chronic bleeding can lead to ANEMIA. Internal bleeding is signaled by blood in the urine or sputum.

**hemostasis** Process by which bleeding stops. Blood vessels constrict, platelets aggregate, and plasma coagulates to form filaments of fibrin.

**hemp** Herb native to Asia and cultivated in Eurasia, North America and parts of South America. It has hollow stems with fibrous inner bark, also called hemp, which is used to make ropes and cloth. Oil from the seeds is used in soap and paint. Some strains of the plant, generally known as CANNABIS, are used to produce MARIJUANA and HASHISH. Height: to 16ft (5m). Family Cannabinaceae; species *Cannabis sativa*.

**Hendrix, Jimi (James Marshall)** (1942–70) Influential and innovative US rock musician, considered by many to be the best electric guitar player ever. He formed The Jimi Hendrix Experience in 1965 with Mitch Mitchell and Noel Redding. He was renowned for colorful, improvisational live performances. He died from a drug overdose.

**Henley Royal Regatta** Oldest rowing regatta in the world, begun (1839) in Henley-on-Thames, Oxfordshire, England. Held every July, the regatta is as famous as a social event as it is for rowing. Trophies include the Grand Challenge Cup the and Diamond Challenge Sculls.

**henna** (Egyptian privet) Small shrub native to the Middle East and N Africa. Since ancient times, people have extracted a red-brown dye from the leaves to color hair and skin. Family Lythraceae; species *Lawsonia inerma*.

**Hennepin, Louis** (1640–1701) French explorer. A Franciscan missionary, he sailed to Canada in 1675 and became chaplain to LA SALLE. He accompanied him on the 1679 expedition, writing the first description of Niagara Falls and being held prisoner by the Sioux. His exaggerated account, *Description de la Louisiane* (1683), was very popular.

**Henri, Robert** (1865–1929) US painter, a member of the ASHCAN SCHOOL. One of the most influential artists of his time, he is best known for his realistic urban scenes.

**Henrietta Maria** (1609–69) Queen consort of CHARLES I of

England. Daughter of Henry IV of France, her Catholicism and her support for Charles's absolutist tendencies incurred Parliament's hostility.

**Henry III** (1017–56) German king (1039–56) and Holy Roman emperor (1046–56). He succeeded his father, Conrad II. Imperial power reached its zenith in his reign as he subdued rebellious vassals in Saxony and Lorraine and compelled the rulers of Poland, Bohemia, and Hungary, as well as the s Italian princes, to pay him homage.

**Henry IV** (1050–1106) German king (1056–1106) and Holy Roman emperor (1084–1106). Embroiled in controversy with the popes over the lay investiture of clerics, he deposed Pope GREGORY VII and was in turn deposed by the pope (1076). Rebellion in Germany weakened Henry's position. After seeking papal absolution in 1077, he continued the struggle, setting up the antipope Clement III. In 1105 he was deposed by his son, HENRY V.

**Henry V** (1081–1125) German king (1105–25) and Holy Roman emperor (1111–25). Having deposed his father, HENRY IV, he resumed the quarrel with the papacy over investiture, while antagonizing German princes by the ruthless assertion of his power. He was defeated in Germany and compelled to compromise with the papacy. The Concordat of WORMS (1122) ended the investiture conflict.

**Henry VI** (1165–97) German king (1190–97) and Holy Roman emperor (1191–97). The son of Frederick I, he married (1186) Constance, heiress of the kingdom of Sicily, and much of his reign was devoted to securing that inheritance. After 1194, the empire was at the height of its power. Although he failed to make the empire hereditary in the HOHENSTAUFEN line, his infant son, Frederick II, was accepted as his successor.

**Henry I** (1068–1135) King of England (1100–35). He rescinded unpopular taxes and married a Scottish princess of Anglo-Saxon descent. He thus won the support that helped him to defeat his brother ROBERT II, duke of Normandy, and regain Normandy for the English crown (1106).

**Henry II** (1133–89) King of England (1154–89). Son of Geoffrey of Anjou and Matilda (daughter of HENRY I). He inherited the ANGEVIN lands and obtained Aquitaine by marrying ELEANOR in 1152. He reestablished stable royal government in England, instituting reforms in finance, local government, and justice. His efforts to extend royal justice to priests led to his famous quarrel with Thomas à BECKET. His later years were troubled by the rebellions of his sons, including two future kings, RICHARD I and JOHN.

**Henry III** (1207–72) King of England (1216–72). The influence of foreigners on his administration antagonized the nobles. He was forced to accept the Provisions of Westminster (1259), giving more power to his councilors, but renounced them in 1261, provoking the Barons' War. The leader of the barons, Simon de Montfort, was defeated at Lewes (1264) by Henry's son, the future EDWARD I, who thereafter ruled on his father's behalf.

**Henry IV** (1367–1413) King of England (1399–1413). Son of JOHN OF GAUNT, he was exiled in 1399 by RICHARD II. He returned and overthrew Richard, claiming the crown for himself. As a usurper he had to overcome revolts, notably by Owain GLYN DWR and the Percies of Northumberland.

**Henry V** (1387–1422) King of England (1413–22). Son of HENRY IV, he renewed the English claims against France of the HUNDRED YEARS WAR and won a decisive victory at AGINCOURT in 1415. Further conquests in 1417–19 resulted in the Treaty of Troyes (1420), when CHARLES VI of France recognized him as his heir.

**Henry VI** (1421–71) King of England (1422–61, 1470–71). He succeeded his father, HENRY V, as a baby and came of age in 1437. His reign was characterized by military disasters in France and by the dynastic conflict in England known as the Wars of the ROSES. Deposed by the Yorkists (1461), he was restored in 1470 but was again deposed and murdered.

**Henry VII** (1457–1509) King of England (1485–1509), founder of the TUDOR dynasty. Having come to the throne by defeating RICHARD III at Bosworth in 1485, Henry united the warring houses of LANCASTER and YORK by marrying the Yorkist heiress, Elizabeth. His financial acumen restored England's fortunes after the devastation of civil war. He took effective action against pretenders to his throne, thereby securing the future of his dynasty.

◀ **Henry VIII** Portrait by Hans Holbein. Henry's reign was most notable as the time during which England no longer acknowledged the pope as the head of the church. As the new head of the Church of England, Henry was able to grant himself a divorce from his first wife Catherine of Aragon, who was unable to provide him with an heir.

**Henry VIII** (1491–1547) King of England (1509–47). Second son of HENRY VII, he became heir on the death of his elder brother, Arthur, in 1502. His aggressive foreign policy, administered by Cardinal WOLSEY, depleted the royal treasury. Henry, supported by Thomas CROMWELL, presided over the first stages of the English REFORMATION, brought about largely because the pope refused to grant Henry a divorce from his first wife, CATHERINE OF ARAGON. With the legislation in place, Henry divorced Catherine and married Anne BOLEYN (1533), mother of the future ELIZABETH I. In 1535 Anne was executed for adultery. Thomas MORE, Henry's former chancellor, was also executed for refusing to accept Henry as head of the church. Henry then married Jane Seymour, who died shortly after the birth of the future EDWARD VI. His next marriage, to ANNE OF CLEVES, ended in divorce (1540) and with the execution of Cromwell. Shortly after, he married Catherine HOWARD (executed 1542) and finally Catherine Parr (1543) who survived him. Henry's reign will also be remembered for the DISSOLUTION OF THE MONASTERIES (1536–40), which brought temporary relief from financial problems but at the cost of social unrest.

**Henry II** (1519–59) King of France (1547–59). Son and successor of FRANCIS I, he married CATHERINE DE' MEDICI. He was dominated by his mistress, Diane de Poitiers, and by the rival families of GUISE and Montmorency. After bankrupting the royal government, the war with Spain ended with the peace of Cateau-Cambrésis (1559).

**Henry III** (1551–89) King of France (1574–89). As duke of Anjou, he fought against the HUGUENOTS in the Wars of RELIGION. By making peace with the Huguenots (1576), he antagonized extremist Roman Catholics, who formed the Catholic League led by the House of GUISE. After the League provoked a revolt in 1588, Henry had the Guise leaders killed and made an alliance with the Huguenot, Henry of Navarre (later HENRY IV). The king was assassinated by a member of the league.

**Henry IV** (1553–1610) King of France (1589–1610), first of the BOURBON dynasty. He was raised a Protestant and, escaping the St. Bartholemew's Day Massacre (1572), he became

▲ **herbivores** Mammalian herbivores may conveniently share a habitat without competing for resources. On the African plains, giraffes (1) browse in branches up to 20ft (6m) above the ground. Elephants (2) too can browse tree canopies, using their trunks to pluck off vegetation. Eland (3) attack the middle branches with their horns, twisting twigs to break them off, while gerenuk (4) stand on their hind legs to reach higher branches. The black rhino (5) uses its hook-like upper lip to feed on bark, twigs, and leaves (white rhinos have lengthened skulls and broad lips for grazing the short grasses that they favor). The wart hog (6) and dik-dik (7) eat buds and flowers, and will also dig up roots and tubers. Such sharing of a single resource also occurs among grazers. Migrating zebra (8) crop the taller, coarse grasses; wildebeest (9) feed on the leafy center layer, allowing small gazelles (10) to reach the tender new shoots.

the leader of the HUGUENOTS. On inheriting the throne, he converted to Roman Catholicism and ended the French Religious Wars by the Edict of NANTES (1598). Henry remained sympathetic to Protestantism, secretly supporting the revolt of the Protestant Netherlands against Spain.

**Henry I (the Fowler)** (*c*.876–936) King of the Germans (918–36). Duke of Saxony, he was elected to succeed Conrad I as king. He asserted his authority over the German princes and reconquered Lotharingia (Lorraine, 925). In 933 he defeated the Magyar raiders. He was succeeded by his son, OTTO I, first Holy Roman emperor.

**Henry the Lion** (1129–95) Duke of Saxony (1142–80) and of Bavaria (1156–80). A GUELPH, he recovered the lands lost by his father, Henry the Proud, to the Emperor Conrad III. As duke of Saxony he promoted German expansion beyond the Elbe River. In 1180, after refusing to support the Italian wars of the Emperor FREDERICK I (Barbarossa), he was deprived of most of his lands.

**Henry the Navigator** (1394–1460) Portuguese prince. A son of JOHN I, he sponsored Portuguese voyages to the Atlantic coast of Africa, which later led to the discovery of the route to India via the Cape of Good Hope.

**Henry, O.** (1862–1910) US short-story writer, b. William Sydney Porter. He supposedly taking his pseudonym from a contraction of Ohio Penitentiary, where he served a sentence for embezzlement. He wrote short stories about the ordinary people of New York City.

**Henry, Patrick** (1736–99) US patriot and statesman. As a member of the CONTINENTAL CONGRESS, he called the colonists to arms in March 1775 with his memorable demand, "Give me liberty or give me death." Henry served as governor of Virginia (1776–79, 1784–86). A strong believer in STATES' RIGHTS, he opposed ratification of the CONSTITUTION in 1787 but was later reconciled with the Federalists.

**Henson, Jim (James Murray)** (1936–90) US entertainer. He created The Muppets, an assemblage of characters that combine features of marionettes and puppets. The Muppets featured on *Sesame Street*, Children's Television Workshop pre-school program, from 1969.

**Hepburn, Audrey** (1929–93) US actress, b. Belgium. Her ingénue performance in *Roman Holiday* (1953) earned her an Academy Award for Best Actress. *Sabrina* (1954) and *Funny Face* (1957) won her further popular success. Other mature roles include *Breakfast at Tiffany's* (1961) and *My Fair Lady* (1964).

**Hepburn, Katharine** (1909– ) US stage and film actress. She won her first Best Actress Academy Award for *Morning Glory* (1933). Hepburn made nine films with Spencer TRACY, beginning with *Woman of the Year* (1952), and ending with an Oscar-winning performance in *Guess Who's Coming to Dinner* (1967). She won her third Best Actress Oscar for *The Lion in Winter* (1968). Her performance in *On Golden Pond* (1981) gained her a fourth award. Other films include *Bringing up Baby* (1938), *The Philadelphia Story* (1940), *The African Queen* (1951), *Suddenly Last Summer* (1959), and *Long Day's Journey into Night* (1962).

**Hephaestus** Ancient Greek god of fire and crafts. Son of ZEUS and HERA, he is equivalent to the Roman VULCAN. Blacksmith and armorer to the Olympian gods, with a forge under volcanic Mount Etna, he is depicted as crippled and uncouth. His consort was APHRODITE.

**Hepplewhite, George** (d.1786) British furniture designer and cabinetmaker. His chairs often have tapered legs with shield backs, and his furniture combines pale woods with mahogany, often in the form of inlay.

**heptathlon** Track and field discipline for women consisting of seven events contested over two days.

**Hepworth, Dame Barbara** (1903–76) English sculptor. A leading modernist sculptor, she is noted for the simplicity and elegance of her abstract works. She worked in wood, stone, and bronze.

**Hera** In Greek mythology, queen of the Olympian gods, sister and wife of ZEUS. She appears as a scold who persecuted her rivals but helped JASON and ACHILLES.

**Heracles** In Greek mythology, greatest of the Greek heroes (in Roman mythology known as Hercules). Condemned to serve King Eurystheus, he performed 12 labors: he killed the Nemean lion and the Hydra; caught the Erymanthian boar and the Cerynean hind; drove away the Stymphalian birds; cleaned the Augean stables; caught the Cretan bull and Diomedes' horses; stole the girdle of Hippolyte; killed Geryon; captured Cerberus; and stole the golden apples of Hesperides. After his death, he was allowed to ascend as a god to Olympus.

**Heraclitus** (536–470 BC) Greek philosopher, b. Ephesus, Asia Minor. Heraclitus believed that the outward, unchanging face of the universe masked a dynamic equilibrium in which all things were constantly changing, but with opposites remaining in balance. The elemental substance connecting everything was fire. He is credited with two sayings that sum up his world view: "All things change" and "You cannot step into the same river twice." Only fragments of his one book survive.

**Heraclius** (575–641) Byzantine emperor (610–41). An outstanding military leader, he came to power at a time of economic, political, and military crisis. He reestablished government and army, defeated the Persians, and took the Byzantine empire to unrivaled power. By the time of his death, however, the Arabs had conquered much of the empire.

**herb** Seed-bearing plant, usually with a soft stem that withers away after one growing season. Most herbs are ANGIOSPERMS. The term is also applied to any plant used as a flavoring, seasoning, or medicine, such as THYME, SAGE, and MINT.

**Herbert, George** (1593–1633) English poet and churchman. His verse, some of the finest METAPHYSICAL POETRY, was published posthumously as *The Temple*. It is noted for its devotional tone and technical complexity.

**herbicide** Chemical substance used to kill weeds and other unwanted plants. Selective herbicides kill the weeds growing with crops, leaving the crops unharmed; nonselective herbicides kill all the vegetation.

**herbivore** Animal that feeds solely on plants. The term is most often applied to mammals, especially ungulates (hoofed mammals). Herbivores are characterized by broad molars and blunt-edged teeth, which they use to pull, cut, and grind their food. Their digestive systems are adapted to the assimilation of cellulose.

**Herculaneum** Ancient city on the Bay of Naples, Italy, the site of modern Resina. Devastated in AD 62 by an earthquake, it was buried in AD 79 by the eruption of VESUVIUS. Archaeological excavations unearthed the Villa of the Papyri, which contained a library, well-preserved furniture, and victims who died on the seashore.

**Herder, Johann Gottfried von** (1744–1803) Prussian philosopher and historian. He believed human society to be an organic, secular totality that develops as the result of a historical process. Herder was a founder of German ROMANTICISM and an opponent of KANT. *Ideas on the Philosophy of History of Humanity* (1784–91) is regarded as his masterpiece.

**heredity** Transmission of characteristics from one generation of plants or animals to another. Characteristics, such as red hair, may be specific to individuals within a group; others, such as the possession of external ears, may be typical of a group as a whole. The combination of characteristics that makes up an organism and makes it different from others is set out in the organism's GENETIC CODE, passed on from its parents. The first studies of heredity were conducted by Gregor MENDEL.

**Hereford and Worcester** County in W central England, bounded W and SW by Wales; the county town is WORCESTER. It is drained by the Severn, Wye and Teme rivers. The Malvern Hills divide the county into two lowland plains. Agriculture is the main activity. Industries: agricultural machinery, fruit canning and processing. Area: 1,516sq mi (3,926sq km). Pop. (1991) 676,747.

**heresy** Denial of, or deviation from, orthodox religious belief. The concept is found in most organized religions with a rigid dogmatic system. The early Christian church fought against heresies such as ARIANISM and NESTORIANISM. In the Middle Ages, the Catholic Church set up the INQUISITION to fight heresy. After the REFORMATION, the Catholic Church described Protestants as heretics because of their denial of many papally defined dogmas, while Protestants applied the term to those who denied their interpretation of the major scriptural doctrines.

**hermaphrodite** Organism that has both male and female sexual organs. Most hermaphrodite animals are invertebrates, such as the EARTHWORM and SNAIL. They reproduce by the mating of two individuals, each of which receives SPERM from the other. Some hermaphrodites are self-fertilizing.

**Hermes** In Greek mythology, messenger of the gods and patron of travelers and commerce. Represented with winged hat and sandals and carrying a golden wand, he is identified with the Roman Mercury.

**hermit crab** Small, crablike CRUSTACEAN found in shallow water worldwide. It uses seasnail shells to protect its soft abdomen, changing shells as it grows. Some are terrestrial and do not use shells as adults. Family Paguridae.

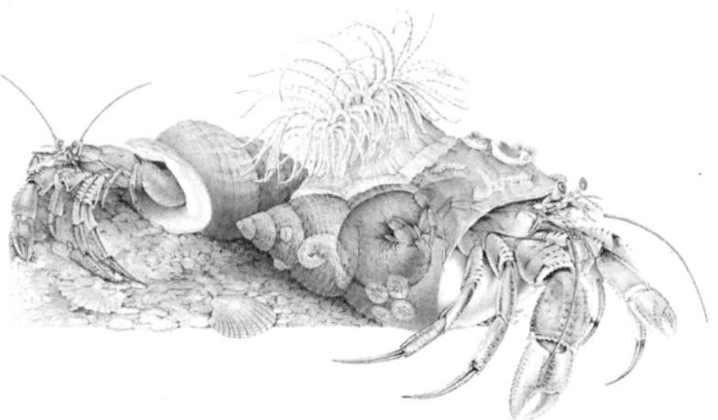

◀ **hermit crab** Unlike most other species of crab, the hermit crab (*Eupagurus* sp.) has a soft body. To protect itself, the hermit crab uses empty whelk or seasnail shells as a home. It has a modified abdomen with a twisted shape to fit the spiral snail-shell, and its last two legs and hind appendages (uropods) are specialized for gripping the shell. When the hermit crab has grown too large for its shell, it waits until it has found a suitable larger shell

**hernia** Protrusion of an organ, or part of an organ, through its enclosing wall. Common hernias include the protrusion of an intestinal loop through the umbilicus (umbilical hernia) or protrusion of part of the stomach or esophagus into the chest cavity (hiatus hernia).

**Herod Agrippa I** (10–44) King of Judaea (41–44). Grandson of HEROD THE GREAT, he attracted the favor of CALIGULA, who confirmed him as ruler of most of Palestine. He was a zealous opponent of Christianity.

**Herod Agrippa II** (27–93) King of Chalcis (50–93) and of Judaea (53–70). Son of HEROD AGRIPPA I and last of the Herodian dynasty, he tried to prevent the Jewish revolt of 66 and afterward sided with Rome.

**Herodotus** (*c*.485–*c*.425 BC) Greek historian. His *Histories* are the first great prose work in European literature. His main theme was the struggle of Greece against the Persian empire in the PERSIAN WARS, but he also provides an insight into the contemporary Mediterranean world.

**Herod the Great** (73–04 BC) King of Judaea (37–04 BC). Supported by MARK ANTONY and AUGUSTUS, he endeavored to reconcile Jews and Romans and was responsible for many public works, including the rebuilding of the Temple in Jerusalem. He later became cruel and tyrannical. According to the New Testament, Herod was king of Judaea when JESUS was born.

**heroin** Drug derived from MORPHINE. It produces effects similar to morphine, but acts more quickly and is effective in smaller doses. It is prescribed to relieve pain in terminal illness and severe injuries. Widely used illegally, it is more addictive than morphine.

**heron** Any of several species of wading bird that live near rivers. Herons have white, gray, or brown plumage, long neck and legs, and a sharp bill. They feed mainly on fish. Height: to 6ft (1.8m). Family Ardeidae.

**herpes** Infectious disease caused by one of the herpes viruses. *Herpes simplex 1* infects the skin and causes cold sores. *Herpes zoster* attacks nerve ganglia, causing SHINGLES. The same virus is responsible for CHICKENPOX.

**Herrick, Robert** (1591–1674) English poet, disciple of Ben JONSON. Ordained in 1623, he was ejected from his post (1647) for royalist sympathies. He regained the position after the RESTORATION. His poems, notably the collection *Hesperides* (1648), have great lyrical freshness.

**herring** Marine fish found worldwide. It is one of the most important food fish, and various species are canned as SARDINE or sold fresh, pickled, or smoked. Herrings have a laterally compressed body and a deeply forked tail fin. Length: 3–18in (8–46cm). Family Clupeidae; the 190 species include *Clupea harengus*.

**Herschel, Sir John Frederick William** (1792–1871) English astronomer, son of Sir William HERSCHEL He extended his father's work on double stars and nebulae. In 1834 at the Cape of Good Hope, he undertook a systematic survey of the southern sky, discovering more than 1,200 doubles and 1,700 nebulae and clusters. He combined these and his father's observations into a *General Catalog of Nebulae and Clusters*.

**Herschel, Sir William** (1738–1822) English astronomer, b. Germany. He discovered Uranus (1781) and later two SATELLITES of Uranus (1787) and two of Saturn (1789). He observed many double stars and more than 2,000 nebulae and clusters, and published catalogs of them. Herschel realized that the Milky Way is the plane of a disk-shaped uni-

◀ **heron** The purple heron (*Ardea purpurea*) is found in reed-grown waters in open country of southern Europe and Asia, and Africa. It grows to length of 2.5ft (80cm), and, like many other species of heron, feeds on fish.

verse, whose form he calculated by counting the numbers of stars visible in different directions. In 1800 he discovered and investigated infrared radiation.

**Hertfordshire** County in SE England; the county town is Hertford. The terrain is flat apart from an extension of the Chiltern Hills in the NW. The main rivers are the Lea, Stort, and Colne. Agriculture is important. Industries: engineering, electrical equipment, printing. Area 631sq mi (1,636 sq km). Pop. (1994) 1,005,400.

**Hertz, Heinrich Rudolf** (1857–94) German physicist. He discovered, broadcasted, and received the radio waves predicted by James Clerk MAXWELL. He also demonstrated that heat and light are kinds of ELECTROMAGNETIC RADIATION. The unit of frequency, the HERTZ (Hz), is named for him.

**hertz** (symbol Hz) SI unit of FREQUENCY. A periodic phenomenon with a period of one second (such as one oscillation per second) is equivalent to 1Hz.

**Hertzog, James Barry Munnik** (1866–1942) Afrikaner political leader. He was a general in the Boer forces during the SOUTH AFRICAN WARS (1899–1902). A member of the Union government under BOTHA (1910), he founded the National Party in 1914 and became prime minister in 1924. He resigned in 1939 in protest against South Africa's support for Britain in World War II.

**Hertzsprung-Russell Diagram** (HR Diagram) Plot of the absolute MAGNITUDE of stars against their spectral type; this is equivalent to plotting their LUMINOSITY against their surface temperature or color index. Brightness increases from bottom to top, and temperature increases from right to left. The diagram was devised by Henry Norris Russell in 1913, independently of Ejnar Hertzsprung, who had had the same idea some years before. The HR diagram reveals a pattern in which most stars lie on a diagonal band, the main sequence.

**Herzegovina** *See* BOSNIA-HERZEGOVINA

**Herzl, Theodor** (1860–1904) Jewish leader and founder of ZIONISM, b. Budapest. He worked as a lawyer and a journalist. He became president of the World Zionist Organization (1897), which worked throughout Europe to establish a Jewish national home in Palestine.

**Herzog, Werner** (1942– ) German film director. One of the leaders of the revival of German cinema in the 1970s, his films deal with the psychology of the individual and with mysticism. They include *Aguirre Wrath of God* (1973), *Nosferatu* (1979), and *Scream from Stone* (1991).

**Hess, Rudolf** (1894–1987) German Nazi leader. He joined the Nazi Party (1921) and took part in the abortive MUNICH PUTSCH. Hess was the nominal deputy leader under Hitler from 1933. In 1941 he flew alone to Scotland in a mysterious one-man effort to make peace with the British. He was sentenced to life imprisonment in the NUREMBERG TRIALS in 1945 and spent the rest of his life in Spandau jail, Berlin, for many years its sole inmate.

**Hess, Victor Francis** (1883–1964) US physicist, b. Austria. As a result of his investigations into the ionization of air, he suggested that radiation similar to X-rays, later named cosmic RADIATION, comes from space. He shared the 1936 Nobel Prize for physics with Carl ANDERSON.

**Hesse, Hermann** (1877–1962) German novelist. Hesse studied Indian mysticism and Jungian psychology, subjects that find expression in novels such as *Demian* (1919), *Siddhartha* (1922), and *Steppenwolf* (1927). Other novels include *Narcissus and Goldmund* (1930) and *The Glass Bead Game* (1943). He was awarded the 1946 Nobel Prize for literature.

**Hessen** Region of central Germany. It was divided by a strip of Prussian territory until 1945. Industries: chemicals, manufacturing, electrical engineering. Area 8,150sq mi (21,114sq km). Pop. (1993) 5,967,305.

**Hestia** In Greek mythology, virgin goddess of the hearth. In Rome, she was worshiped as VESTA.

**heterosexuality** Attraction of a male or female to members of the opposite sex. The word is used to distinguish such attraction from HOMOSEXUALITY.

**heterozygote** Organism possessing two contrasting forms (ALLELES) of a GENE in a CHROMOSOME pair. In cases where one of the forms is dominant and one RECESSIVE, only the dominant form will be expressed in the PHENOTYPE. *See also* HOMOZYGOTE

**Hewish, Antony** (1924– ) British radio astronomer. He shared the 1974 Nobel Prize for physics with Martin Ryle for his work on PULSARS.

**hexagon** Six-sided plane figure. Its interior angles add up to 720°. In a regular hexagon, whose sides and interior angles are all equal, each interior angle is 120°.

**Heyerdahl, Thor** (1914– ) Norwegian ethnologist. With five companions, he drifted on the balsa raft *Kon Tiki* *c*.5,000mi (8,000km) across the Pacific Ocean from Peru to Polynesia (1947) in an attempt to prove that the Polynesians came from South America and not from Southeast Asia. In 1977 he traveled from Iraq to Djibouti in a reed boat, the *Tigris*.

**Hezbollah** (Hizbollah) Iranian-backed, Islamic fundamentalist group. It was formed in the early 1980s to encourage the integration of Shiite religious militants into Middle Eastern politics. Hezbollah has been responsible for terrorist and military activities in the Middle East and elsewhere, including missile attacks on Israel from within Lebanon.

**Hiawatha** Native American leader. As chief of the Onondaga, he founded the five-nation IROQUOIS CONFEDERACY (*c*.1575) to halt intertribal wars. His semimythic reputation is partly the result of association with the fictional hero of the LONGFELLOW poem *The Song of Hiawatha* (1855).

**hibernation** Dormant (sleeplike) condition adopted by some animals to survive harsh winters. Adaptive mechanisms to avoid starvation and extreme temperatures include reduced body temperature, and slower heartbeat, breathing rate, and metabolism.

**hibiscus** Genus of plants, shrubs, and small trees native to tropical and temperate regions and cultivated worldwide. Their large white, pink, yellow, blue, or red bell-shaped flowers have darker centers. Family Malvaceae.

**Hickok, "Wild Bill" (James Butler)** (1837–76) US frontiersman. A renowned marksman, he was a scout with the Union Army during the CIVIL WAR and after the war for George CUSTER. He served as US marshal in Kansas (1869–71) and later toured with the Wild West show of "BUFFALO BILL." He was shot dead while playing poker.

**hickory** Deciduous tree of the WALNUT family native to E North America. Hickories are grown for ornament, timber, and for their nuts. Height: 80ft (25m). Family Juglandaceae; genus *Carya*. *See also* PECAN

**Hidalgo y Costilla, Miguel** (1753–1811) Mexican priest and revolutionary. Of Creole birth, he was a priest in Dolores, Guanajuato, where he plotted a revolt against Spain. With an untrained army of 80,000, he captured Guanajuato and Valladolid. Defeated by government forces at Calderón Bridge, Hidalgo fled, but was captured and executed.

**Hidatsa** Sedentary, Siouan-speaking Native American tribe of Montana. The tribe was almost entirely wiped out by a smallpox epidemic in 1837. Today *c*.1,000 Hidatsa live on Fort Berthold Reservation in North Dakota.

**hieroglyphics** Writing system used in ancient Egypt and, by extension, those of ancient Crete, Asia Minor, Central America, and Mexico. The Egyptian system of hieroglyphics (pictorial characters) arose sometime before 3100 BC. At first they were purely picture symbols. The word "sun" was represented by a circle with a dot inside. In due course, they also came to be used conceptually, with symbols such as that for "sun" also standing for "day." Eventually, many symbols were used phonetically. The "sun" symbol, for instance, stood for a syllable that contained the same combination of consonants but had a different meaning. By the 7th century, hieroglyphics were used for business and literary purposes. As ancient Egyptian was supplanted by Greek, hieroglyphics died out. Most Egyptian texts have been deciphered, thanks to the discovery of the ROSETTA STONE (1799).

**Higginson, Thomas Wentworth Storrow** (1823–1911) US social reformer. A Unitarian minister, he worked for the abolition of slavery and for women's rights. He was colonel of the first black regiment during the Civil War, an experience recorded in *Army Life in a Black Regiment* (1870). He was a close friend of many writers, notably Emily DICKINSON.

**high-definition television (HDTV)** Form of television on which the picture is made up of 1,250 or 1,125 scanning lines instead of 625 or 525. The increased number of lines makes the TV image sharper. It relies on digital transmission along OPTICAL FIBERS rather than the transmission of electronic signals by radio waves.

**high jump** Track-and-field event in which a competitor attempts to jump over a bar supported between two uprights. It has been an Olympic sport since 1896. A competitor may have a maximum of three attempts to clear each height to which the bar is raised.

**Highland Games** Series of athletic competitions featuring traditional Scottish events. The term specifically refers to the Royal Braemar Games held annually in Scotland since 1819. The program includes highland dancing, bagpipe-playing, and the tossing of the caber.

**Highlands** Scottish mountain and moorland region, lying N of a line running roughly SW to NE from Dumbarton to Stonehaven; the administrative center is Inverness. The area is split geologically into the Northwest Highlands and the Grampian Highlands (separated by Glen More). Industries: tourism, forestry, fishing. Area: 9,804sq mi (25,396sq km) Pop: (1991) 204,000

**high-level language** COMPUTER LANGUAGE that is reasonably close to spoken English. The higher the level, the further the language is removed from the BINARY SYSTEM of many other computer languages.

**Hill, Ambrose Powell** (1825–65) Confederate commander in the CIVIL WAR. He fought in the Second Battle of BULL RUN (1862) and led his troops through the GETTYSBURG and WILDERNESS campaigns. He was killed at Petersburg while trying to restore the Confederate defense.

**Hill, Graham** (1929–75) English auto racing driver. Hill's long Formula 1 career included over 176 starts and 14 winning races. In 1962 he won his first Grand Prix and the world driver's championship, winning his second in 1968. In 1972 he became the first Formula 1 world champion to win the Le Mans 24-hour race. His son **Damon** (1960– ) is also a successful Formula 1 driver, becoming world champion in 1996.

**Hill, James Jerome** (1838–1916) US railroad magnate, b. Canada. Seeing the importance of transportation to the West, Hill put together the Great Northern Railroad Company, the first private transcontinental railroad.

**Hill, Sir Rowland** (1795–1879) British administrator and postal reformer. He invented the nationwide "penny post," adopting the first adhesive, prepaid postage stamp.

**Hillary, Sir Edmund Percival** (1919– ) New Zealand explorer and mountaineer. On May 29, 1953 Hillary and the Sherpa guide Tenzing Norgay were the first climbers to reach the summit of Mount EVEREST.

**Hilliard, Nicholas** (1547–1619) English miniaturist and goldsmith. He portrayed many of the leading figures of the time in an exquisitely graceful style.

**Hillman, Sidney** (1887–1946) US labor leader. He was first president of the Amalgamated Clothing Workers (1915) and helped found the CONGRESS OF INDUSTRIAL ORGANIZATIONS (CIO) in 1935. He rallied support for President Franklin Roosevelt's NEW DEAL, established the American Labor Party, and helped form the World Federation of Trade Unions (1945).

**Himachal Pradesh** State in the W Himalayas, NW India; the capital is Simla. It suffered numerous invasions before coming under British rule in the 19th century. It is mountainous and heavily forested, with highly cultivated valleys. Timber provides the main source of income. Area: 21,495sq mi (55,673sq km). Pop. (1991) 5,170,877.

**Himalayas** System of mountains in S Asia, extending c.1,500mi (2,400km) N–S in an arc between Tibet and India-Pakistan. The mountains are divided into three ranges: the Greater Himalayas (N), which include Mount EVEREST; the Lesser Himalayas; and the Outer Himalayas (S).

**Himmler, Heinrich** (1900–45) German Nazi leader. In 1929 he became head of the SS. After the Nazis came to power in 1933, he assumed control of the German police system and of the CONCENTRATION CAMPS. He was captured by the British in 1945 and committed suicide.

**Hincks, Sir Francis** (1807–85) Canadian political leader, b. Ireland. An advocate of reform and cooperation between English and French speakers, he became joint premier with Augustin Morin (1851–54). Later, he was finance minister under John A. MACDONALD (1869–73).

**Hindemith, Paul** (1895–1963) German composer, who immigrated to the US in 1939. Among his works are symphonies, concertos, ballets, chamber music, and operas. In the 1930s he developed, with Kurt WEILL, *Gebrauchsmusik* (Ger. utility music) written for amateur performance. His best-known work is the symphony he derived from his opera *Mathis der Maler* (1934).

**Hindi** Most widespread language in India, spoken in the north-central area by 154 million people. Hindi and English are the official languages of India. It derives from SANSKRIT and belongs to the Indo-European family.

**Hinduism** Traditional religion of India, characterized by a philosophy and a way of life rather than by a dogmatic structure. It was not founded by an individual and has been developing gradually since *c*.3000 BC, absorbing external influences. There are several schools within Hinduism, but all Hindus recognize the VEDAS as sacred, believe that all living creatures have souls, follow the doctrine of TRANSMIGRATION OF SOULS, and consider *moksha* – liberation from the cycle of suffering and rebirth represented by REINCARNATION – as the chief aim in life. One of the features of Hindu society is the CASTE system, but modern Hindu scholars maintain that it is not part of the religion. In the mid-1990s, Hindus numbered *c*.800 million.

**Hindu Kush** Mountain range in central Asia, a continuation of the HIMALAYAS extending WSW for 500–600 mi (800–960km) from N Pakistan and NE Afghanistan. The highest peak is Tirich Mir, 25,260ft (7,700m).

**Hindustani** Member of the Indo-Iranian branch of INDO-EUROPEAN LANGUAGES, closely related to HINDI and URDU. More than 300 million people are thought to speak or understand Hindustani in India and Pakistan.

**hip** Joint on each side of the lower trunk, into which the head of the femur fits; the hip bones form part of the PELVIS.

◀ **Hinduism** The 800 million or so Hindus practice a complex set of rites, ceremonies, and festivals. The religion first appeared in N India *c*.5,000 years ago, and features many gods. The three chief gods (the Trimurti) are Brahma, Vishnu, and Siva, creator, preserver, and destroyer respectively. Central to Hinduism is the belief in reincarnation, which is seen as the cycle of rebirth and suffering. To escape this cycle is the chief aim for all Hindus.

▲ **hippopotamus** Hoofed mammals with an even number of toes, such as the hippopotamus (*Hippopotamus amphibius* shown here), are grouped together in the order Artiodactyla. The hippopotamus has a family of its own, the Hippopotamidae. It is a water-loving mammal that was once common all over Africa, but is now severely restricted in range.



**hip-hop** RAP music and its associated culture, originating in New York in the early 1980s. The music is characterized by a strong drumbeat, percussive "scratching" of vinyl records, and rap vocals.

**Hipparchus** (146–127 BC) Greek astronomer. He estimated the distance of the Moon from the Earth and drew the first accurate star map. He developed an organization of the Universe which, although it had the Earth at the center, provided for accurate prediction of the positions of the planets.

**Hippocrates** (460–377 BC) Greek physician, often called "the father of medicine." He emphasized clinical observation and provided guidelines for surgery. He is credited with the **Hippocratic oath**, a code of professional conduct still followed by doctors.

**Hippolytus** In Greek mythology, son of Theseus and Hippolyta. When he spurned the advances of his stepmother, Phaedra, she turned his father against him. Put to death, he came back to life when his innocence was proved.

**hippopotamus** Bulky, herbivorous mammal, native to Africa. *Hippopotamus amphibius* has a massive gray or brown body with a large head, short legs, and short tail, and spends much time in water. Males weigh up to 5 tons. Pygmy hippopotamuses, *Choeropsis liberiensis*, are much smaller and spend more time on land. They weigh about 400lbs (180kg). Family Hippopotamidae.

**Hirohito** (1901–89) Emperor of Japan (1926–89). He was the first crown prince to travel abroad (1921). Although he generally exercised little political power during his reign, he persuaded the Japanese government to surrender to the Allies in 1945. Under the new constitution of 1946, he lost all power and renounced the traditional claim of the Japanese emperors to be divine. He was succeeded by his son AKIHITO.

**Hiroshige, Ando** (1797–1858) Japanese master of the UKIYO-E (colored WOODCUT). Together with HOKUSAI and UTAMARO, he was one of the leading Japanese printmakers of his day. He is best known for his landscapes, which influenced IMPRESSIONISM.

**Hiroshima** City on the delta of the Ota River, on SW Honshū Island, Japan; the river divides the city into six islands connected by 81 bridges. Founded in 1594, it was a military headquarters in the SINO-JAPANESE and RUSSO-JAPANESE wars. In August 1945 it was the target of the first atomic bomb dropped on a populated area. The city center was obliterated and more than 70,000 people were killed. The event is commemorated in the Peace Memorial Park. Industries: brewing, shipbuilding, motor vehicles, chemicals. Pop. (1993) 1,072,000.

**Hirst, Damien** (1965– ) British sculptor. He made his name by exhibiting sculptures of animals preserved in formaldehyde. One of these pieces, *Mother and Child Divided* (1993), which consists of the severed halves of a cow and calf displayed in four tanks, helped to win him the Turner Prize in 1995.

**Hispaniola** Island in the West Indies, in the N central Caribbean Sea, between Cuba (W) and Puerto Rico (E). It was discovered in 1492 by Christopher COLUMBUS. HAITI occupies the W third of the island and the DOMINICAN REPUBLIC the remaining portion. It is a mountainous, agricultural region with a subtropical climate. Industries: coffee, cacao, tobacco, rice, sugarcane, some mining. Area: 29,521sq mi (76,480sq km).

► **Hitchcock** Known as the "master of suspense," Alfred Hitchcock is widely accepted as one of the greatest directors of all time. Audiences of his many films were treated to meticulously crafted films that were visually spectacular and contained brooding, threatening undertones. Criticized for remaining faithful to the melodramatic genre, Hitchcock never received an Academy Award for best director.

**histamine** Substance derived from the amino acid histidine, occurring naturally in many plants and in animal tissues, and released on tissue injury. It is implicated in allergic reactions that can be treated with ANTIHISTAMINES.

**histology** Biological, especially microscopic, study of TISSUES and structures in living organisms.

**historical novel** Type of novel in which the main characters, plot, and setting are based on historical persons, events, or places. Walter SCOTT's *Ivanhoe* (1819) and Charles DICKENS's *A Tale of Two Cities* (1859) are major examples.

**history** Written record of the human past; often used to mean the events themselves rather than the record of them. The Western historical tradition began with the Greek historians HERODOTUS and THUCYDIDES. China, and countries influenced by it, had a different, even older historical tradition in which the past was seen as the source of wisdom and historians strove to distinguish comprehensible patterns in it.

**Hitchcock, Sir Alfred** (1899–1980) British film director, master of the sophisticated suspense thriller. His films include *Blackmail* (1929), *The Thirty-Nine Steps* (1935), *Dial M for Murder* (1954), *Rear Window* (1954), *Psycho* (1960), *Frenzy* (1972), and *Family Plot* (1976). *Rebecca* (1940) won an Academy Award for Best Picture. His appearances as an extra, the thrilling chases, the sinister mood, and sudden shocks, greatly influenced the French New Wave.

**Hitler, Adolf** (1889–1945) German fascist dictator (1933–45), b. Austria. He served in the German army during World War I and was decorated for bravery. In 1921 he became the leader of the small National Socialist Workers' Party (Nazi Party). While imprisoned for his role in the failed MUNICH PUTSCH, he set out his extreme racist and nationalist views in *Mein Kampf*. Economic distress and dissatisfaction with the WEIMAR government led to electoral gains for the Nazis and, by forming an alliance with orthodox Nationalists, Hitler became chancellor in January 1933. He made himself dictator of a one-party state in which all opposition was ruthlessly suppressed by the SS and GESTAPO. The racial hatred he incited led to a policy of extermination of Jews and others in the HOLOCAUST. Hitler pursued an aggressive foreign policy aimed at territorial expansion in E Europe. The invasion of Poland finally goaded Britain and France into declaring war on Germany in September 1939. Hitler himself played a large part in determining strategy during WORLD WAR II. In April 1945, with Germany in ruins, he committed suicide.

**Hittites** People of Asia Minor who controlled a powerful empire in the 15th–13th centuries BC. They founded a kingdom in Anatolia (Turkey) in the 18th century BC; their capital was Hattusas (Boğazköy). They expanded E and S in the 15th century BC, and conquered N Syria before being checked by the Egyptians under RAMSES II. Under attack from ASSYRIA, the Hittite empire disintegrated *c*.1200 BC.

**hives** (urticaria or nettle rash) Transient, itchy reddish or pale raised skin patches. Hives may be caused by an ALLERGY, by irritants such as sunlight, or by stress.

**Hobart** Port and state capital of TASMANIA, SE Australia. Founded as a penal colony in the early 1800s, it became capital in 1812. It has one of the world's best natural harbors. Industries: fruit processing, textiles, zinc. Pop. (1994 est.) 52,900.

**Hobbema, Meindert** (1638–1709) Dutch painter. His serene landscapes, especially his masterpiece *The Avenue of Middelharnis* (1689), were highly influential on 18th and early 19th-century English landscape artists.

**Hobbes, Thomas** (1588–1679) English philosopher. In *De Corpore* (1655), *De Homine* (1658), and *De Cive* (1642), he maintained that matter and its motion comprise the only valid subjects for philosophy. His greatest work, *Leviathan* (1651), argued that man is not naturally social but obeys moral rules to maintain civilized society.

**Hochhuth, Rolf** (1931– ) Controversial German

dramatist. *The Representative* (1963) attacked the nonintervention of the Pope in World War II; *Soldiers* (1967) implied that Winston Churchill was inhumane for blanket-bombing Dresden.

**Ho Chi Minh** (1890–1969) (Nguyen That Thanh) Vietnamese political leader, president of North Vietnam (1954–69). He founded the Vietnamese Communist Party. Forced into exile in the 1930s, he returned to Vietnam in 1941 to lead the VIET MINH against the Japanese. In 1945 he declared Vietnamese independence and led resistance to the French colonial authorities. After the French defeat at DIEN BIEN PHU, Vietnam was divided and he became president of North Vietnam in 1954. He organized and supported the VIET CONG against South Vietnam and committed North Vietnamese forces against the US in the VIETNAM WAR.

**Ho Chi Minh City** (Saigon) City in S Vietnam, at the mouth of the Saigon River in the Mekong delta; the largest city in Vietnam. It was an ancient Khmer settlement. Saigon was seized by the French in 1859 and made capital of Cochin China, and then French Indochina (1887–1902). In 1954 it became capital of independent South Vietnam. During the VIETNAM WAR it served as the military headquarters for US and South Vietnamese forces. Taken by the North Vietnamese in 1975, it was later renamed Ho Chi Minh City. It is the commercial, and industrial center of Vietnam. Industries: shipbuilding, textiles, pharmaceuticals. Pop. (1989) 3,169,135.

**hockey** *See* FIELD HOCKEY; ICE HOCKEY

**Hockney, David** (1937– ) British painter. He made his name with witty POP ART paintings such as *Flight into Italy–Swiss Landscape* (1962). In the late 1960s and the 1970s he developed a more realistic, classical style, with pictures such as *A Bigger Splash* (1967) and his portraits in spacious interiors. His graphic work, including his series of etchings, *A Rake's Progress* (1961–63), are often regarded as being more innovative than his painting.

**Hodgkin's disease** Rare type of CANCER causing painless enlargement of the LYMPH GLANDS, lymphatic tissue, and spleen, with subsequent spread to other areas. Named for the pathologist Thomas Hodgkin (1798–1866), its treatment consists of RADIOTHERAPY, surgery, drug therapy, or a combination of these. It is curable if caught early.

**Hoffa, James Riddle** (1913–*c.*1975) US labor leader. President of the International Brotherhood of Teamsters (1957–71), he worked to consolidate the power of the union. In 1967, after the union was investigated for corrupt practices, he was imprisoned for jury tampering, mail fraud, and mishandling of union funds. His sentence was commuted by NIXON in 1971. He disappeared in 1975 and is presumed dead.

**Hoffman, Dustin** (1937– ) US film actor. Hoffman's debut performance in *The Graduate* (1967) earned him an Academy nomination for Best Actor. A dedicated character actor, he won further nominations for his roles as a derelict in *Midnight Cowboy* (1969) and as a comedian in *Lenny* (1974). He finally won a Best Actor award for *Kramer vs. Kramer* (1979). He won a second Best Actor award for *Rain Man* (1988).

**Hoffmann, E.T.A. (Ernst Theodor Amadeus)** (1776–1822) German author, musician, and music critic. He wrote many fantastic stories, several of which later formed the basis for OFFENBACH's opera *The Tales of Hoffmann* (1881). Tchaikovsky's *Nutcracker Suite* is also based on one of his stories. *The Devil's Elixir* (1815–16) and *The Educated Cat* (1820–22) are his two novels.

**Hofstadter, Robert** (1915– ) US physicist who shared the 1961 Nobel Prize for physics with Rudolf Mössbauer. He proposed that PROTONS and NEUTRONS have a positively charged core surrounded by a cloud of elementary particles (pions).

**hog** *See* PIG

**Hogan, (William) Ben (Benjamin)** (1912– ) US golfer. After winning the US PGA (1946, 1948) and the US Open (1948), Hogan was seriously injured in a car accident. He made a remarkable recovery and went on to win three further US Opens (1950, 1951, 1953), two US Masters' (1951, 1953) and the British Open (1953).

**Hogarth, William** (1697–1764) English painter and engraver. He is best known for his dark portrayals of contemporary English society, expressed in his narrative paintings (later released as engravings), *The Harlot's Progress*, *The Rake's Progress*, and *Marriage à la Mode*.

**Hogmanay** In Scotland, New Year's Eve. Traditionally more festive than Christmas, the Hogmanay celebrations date back to Celtic times.

**hognose snake** Harmless, North American snake ranging throughout the US. Variable in color, it is mostly spotted brown, gray, yellow, or orange. When alarmed, it will hiss, spread its neck, then play dead. Length: to 33in (84cm). Family Colubridae; genus *Heterodon*.

**Hohenstaufen** German dynasty that exercised great power in Germany and the HOLY ROMAN EMPIRE from 1138–1254. It is named for the castle of Staufen, built by Frederick, Count of Swabia, whose son became CONRAD III of Germany and Holy Roman emperor in 1138. From Conrad III to CONRAD IV, the family occupied the Imperial throne, except for the years 1209–15 (when Otto IV, the representative of their great rivals the GUELPHS, was emperor). The greatest of the dynasty was FREDERICK II.

**Hohenzollern** German dynasty that ruled BRANDENBURG, Prussia, and Germany. The family acquired Brandenburg in 1415, and Prussia was added in 1618. FREDERICK WILLIAM (the Great Elector) further expanded their territories, and his son, Frederick I, adopted the title "King in Prussia." FREDERICK WILLIAM I built up the famous Prussian army, and FREDERICK II used it to great effect against the Hapsburgs. Germany was finally united in 1871 under the Hohenzollern emperor, WILLIAM I. His grandson WILLIAM II abdicated at the end of World War I.

**Hokkaidō** (formerly Yezo) Most northerly and second largest of the main islands of Japan, bounded W by the Sea of Japan and E by the Pacific Ocean; the capital is Sapporo. Until the late 19th century it was the homeland of the Ainu aboriginals. It is mountainous and forested, with some active volcanoes. Linked to Honshū Island by the Seikan Tunnel, it is Japan's chief farming region and coal-producer. Crops: rice, corn, wheat, soybeans, potatoes, sugar beets. Industries: fishing, forestry, coal-mining, natural gas. Area: 32,212sq mi (83,451sq km). Pop. (1992 est.) 5,659,000.

**Hokusai, Katsushika** (1760–1849) Japanese master of UKIYO-E (colored WOODCUT), especially famous for his landscapes, who influenced late 19th-century European painters. His most famous print is *The Wave*.

**Holbein, Hans, the Younger** (1497–1543) German painter. He gained international recognition with three portraits of his friend Erasmus (1523). He settled in London (1532) and was court painter to Henry VIII. Holbein's masterpieces include *The Ambassadors* (1533) and superb portraits of *Christina of Denmark, Duchess of Milan* (1538), and *Anne of Cleves* (1540).

**Holguin** City in SE Cuba, its port on the Atlantic Ocean. Founded *c.*1720, it was the focus for rebellions against Spanish rule (1868–78, 1895–98). Located on a fertile plateau, it exports tobacco and cattle products. Industries: sugarcane, coffee, timber. Pop. (1990 est.) 228,052.

**Holiday, Billie** (1915–59) US blues and jazz singer, nicknamed Lady Day. She became famous in the 1930s with the bands of Count Basie and Artie Shaw. Holiday's melancholic renditions of "My Man, Mean to Me" (1937) and her own "God Bless the Child" (1941) are legendary in the history of jazz.

**Holland** Popular name for the NETHERLANDS, but properly referring only to a historic region, now divided into two provinces. A fief of the Holy Roman Empire in the 12th century, Holland was united with the county of Hainaut in 1299. It passed to Burgundy in 1433 and to the Hapsburgs in 1482. In the 16th century, Holland led the Netherlands in their long struggle for independence.

**Holly, Buddy** (1936–59) US singer and songwriter. Holly and his group, the Crickets, achieved success in 1957 with

▲ **Holbein** Portrait of Thomas Cromwell wearing the order of St. George, by Hans Holbein the Younger. Best known for his woodcuts and portraits, Hans Holbein the Younger painted many influential people of both German and English society, including Thomas More and Thomas Cromwell. He was also court painter to Henry VIII.

H

▶ **Hollywood** One of the most famous signs in the world, Hollywood, Los Angeles, is home to legendary film studios including MGM, Paramount, 20th Century Fox, and Colombia Pictures. Still the world's center of cinema, an increasing number of films is being made outside Hollywood as film production facilities increase.

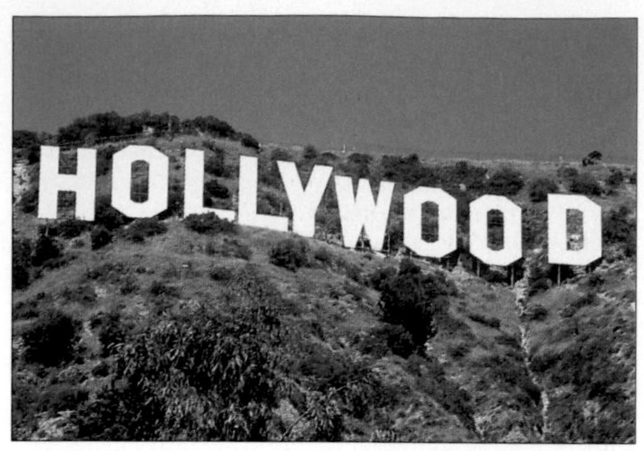


"That'll be the Day," "Oh Boy," and "Peggy Sue." Holly was a pioneer of double-tracking and the standard rock grouping of drums and bass, rhythm, and lead guitars. He was killed in an air crash.

**Hollywood** Part of LOS ANGELES, California. After 1911 it became the primary center for filmmaking in the US and by the 1930s its studios dominated world CINEMA. Tourists attractions include Hollywood Boulevard.

**Holmes, Oliver Wendell** (1809–94) US author and physician. His best literary work takes the form of humorous table talk, such as *The Autocrat of the Breakfast Table* (1857–8), *The Professor at the Breakfast Table* (1860), and *The Poet at the Breakfast Table* (1872). He was also a respected professor of medicine at Harvard University.

**Holmes, Oliver Wendell, Jr.** (1841–1935) US jurist and legal scholar. He coedited the *American Law Review* (1870–73) and *Kent's Commentaries* (1873), and wrote *The Common Law* (1881). A justice (1882–99) and then chief justice (1899–1902) of the Massachusetts Supreme Court, he became an associate justice of the US Supreme Court (1902–32). He was a champion of civil liberties.

**holmium** (symbol Ho) Metallic element of the LANTHANIDE SERIES, first identified spectroscopically in 1878. Its chief ore is monazite. The element has few commercial uses. Properties: at.no. 67; at.wt. 164.9304; sp.gr. 8.795 (25°C); m.p. 2,685°F (1,474°C); b.p. 4,883°F (2,695°C); most common isotope $^{165}$Ho (100%).

**Holocaust** Great massacre, in particular the extermination of European Jews and others by the Nazi regime in Germany (1933–45). The Nazi persecution reached its peak in the "Final Solution," a program of mass extermination adopted in 1941. Jews, as well as others considered racially inferior by the Nazis, were killed in CONCENTRATION CAMPS such as AUSCHWITZ, BELSEN, DACHAU, Majdanek, and Treblinka. Total Jewish deaths are estimated at more than 6 million.

## HONDURAS

The flag of Honduras was officially adopted in 1949. It is based on the flag of the Central American Federation, which was set up in 1823 and included Costa Rica, El Salvador, Guatemala, Honduras, and Nicaragua. Honduras left the federation in 1838.

**AREA:** 43,278 sq mi (112,090sq km)
**POPULATION:** 5,462,000
**CAPITAL (POPULATION):** Tegucigalpa (670,100)
**GOVERNMENT:** Republic
**ETHNIC GROUPS:** Mestizo 90%, Native American 7%, Garifunas (West Indian) 2%, **LANGUAGES:** Spanish (official)
**RELIGIONS:** Roman Catholic 85%, Protestant 10%)
**CURRENCY:** Honduran lempira = 100 centavos

The Republic of Honduras is the second largest country in Central America (after NICARAGUA). Honduras has two coastlines: the N Caribbean coast extends for *c*.375mi (600km), its deep offshore waters prompted the Spanish to name the country Honduras – Sp. depths); a narrow Pacific outlet to the Gulf of Fonseca is 50mi (80km) long. Along the N coast are vast banana plantations. To the E lies the MOSQUITO COAST. The Cordilleras highlands form 80% of Honduras and include the capital, TEGUCIGALPA.

### CLIMATE

Honduras has a tropical climate. The rainy season is from May to October. The N coast is sometimes hit by fierce hurricanes.

### VEGETATION

The N coastal plains contain rain forest and tropical savanna. The Mosquito Coast contains mangrove swamps and dense forests. Forests of evergreens, such as mahogany and rosewood, grow on the lower mountain slopes, while higher up are forests of oak and pine.

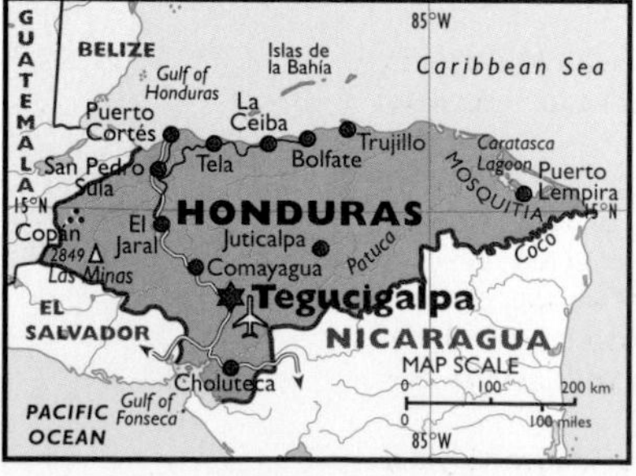


### HISTORY

From AD 400–900 the MAYA civilization flourished. The magnificent ruins at Copán in W Honduras were discovered by the Spaniards in 1576, but became covered in dense forest and were only rediscovered in 1839. Christopher Columbus sighted the coast in 1502. Pedro de Alvarado founded the first Spanish settlements (1524.) The native population gradually were subdued and gold and silver mines were established. In 1821 Honduras gained independence, forming part of the Mexican empire. From 1823–38 Honduras was a member of the Central American Federation. Throughout the rest of the 19th century, Honduras was subject to continuous political interference, especially from Guatemala. Britain controlled the Mosquito Coast. In the 1890s, US companies developed the banana plantations and exerted great political influence. Honduras became known as a "banana republic". After World War II, demands grew for greater national autonomy and workers' rights. The Liberal government was overthrown by a military coup in 1963. Honduras's expulsion of Salvadoran immigrants led to the short "Soccer War" (1969) with El Salvador, following an ill-tempered World Cup qualifying match between the two countries. In 1974 a hurricane devastated the Caribbean coast. Civilian government was restored in 1982. During the 1980s Honduras acted as a base for the US-backed CONTRA rebels from Nicaragua. Honduras was heavily dependent on US aid. Popular demonstrations against the presence of the Contras, led to the declaration of a state of emergency (1988). In 1990 the war in Nicaragua ended. In 1992 Honduras signed a treaty with El Salvador, settling the disputed border. In 1998 Hurricane Mitch killed more than 5,500 people and left 14 million homeless.

### POLITICS

The Liberal Party won the 1993 and 1997 elections. The current president is Carlos Flores.

### ECONOMY

Honduras is the least industrialized country in Central America, and the poorest developing nation in the Americas (1995 GDP per capita US$1,900). It has very few mineral resources, other than silver, lead, and zinc. Agriculture dominates the economy, forming 78% of all exports and employing 38% of the population. Bananas and coffee are the leading exports, and maize is the principal food crop. Cattle are raised in the mountain valleys and on the S Pacific plains. Fishing and forestry are also important activities. Honduras has vast timber resources. Overall development of the country is hampered by the lack of an adequate transport infrastructure.

**Holocene** (Recent epoch) Division of geological time extending from *c*.10,000 years ago to the present. It includes the emergence of humans as settled members of communities; the first known villages date from *c*.8,000 years ago.

**holography** Process of making a hologram. One or more photographs are formed on a single film or plate by interference between two parts of a split LASER beam. The photograph appears as a flat pattern until light hits the plate in the correct position; it then becomes a 3-D image.

**Holst, Gustav (Gustavus Theodore von)** (1874–1934) English composer. His early works were often influenced by Hinduism, as in the opera *Sita* (1906), and folksong, as in *Somerset Rhapsody* (1907). Among his works are several operas, including *The Perfect Fool* (1922), songs, chamber music and the popular orchestral suite *The Planets* (1914–16).

**Holy Alliance** Agreement signed by the crowned heads of Russia, Prussia, and Austria in 1815. Its purpose was to re-establish the principle of hereditary rule and to suppress democratic and nationalist movements, which had sprung up in the wake of the FRENCH REVOLUTION. The agreement, signed later by every European dynasty except the king of England and the Ottoman Sultan, came to be seen as an instrument of reaction and oppression.

**Holy Communion** *See* EUCHARIST

**Holy Grail** In medieval legend, cup supposedly used by Jesus at the LAST SUPPER and by JOSEPH OF ARIMATHEA at the crucifixion to catch the blood from Jesus' wounds. The quest for the grail, especially by the knights of Arthurian legend, became a search for mystical union with God.

**Holy Roman Empire** European empire centered on Germany (10th–19th centuries), which echoed the empire of ancient Rome. It was founded in 962 when the German king OTTO I (THE GREAT) was crowned in Rome, although some historians date it from the coronation of CHARLEMAGNE in 800. The emperor, who was elected by the German princes, claimed to be the temporal sovereign of Christendom, ruling in cooperation with the spiritual sovereign, the pope. However, the empire never encompassed all of western Christendom and relations with the papacy were often difficult. From 1438 the title was virtually hereditary in the HAPSBURG dynasty. After 1648 the empire became little more than a loose confederation, containing hundreds of virtually independent states. It was finally abolished by NAPOLEON I in 1806.

**Holy Spirit** (Holy Ghost) Third Person of the TRINITY in Christian theology. The Holy Spirit represents the spiritual agent through whom God's grace is given.

**Holy Week** Seven-day period preceding EASTER. It begins with Palm Sunday, commemorating Christ's entry into Jerusalem; Maundy Thursday marks his institution of the EUCHARIST; Good Friday marks his betrayal and crucifixion.

**homeopathy** Unorthodox medical treatment that involves administering minute doses of a drug or remedy which causes effects similar to those that are being treated. It was popularized by Christian HAHNEMANN.

**homeostasis** In biology, processes that maintain constant conditions within a cell or organism in response to either internal or external changes.

**Homer** Greek epic poet of the 8th century BC, traditionally considered to be the author of the great epics of the Trojan wars, the *Iliad* and the *Odyssey*. Nothing factual is known about Homer, but the works attributed to him represent the foundations of Greek and European literature.

**Homer, Winslow** (1836–1910) US painter and illustrator. He won international acclaim for his coverage of the Civil War in *Harper's Weekly* and particular recognition as a painter with *Prisoners from the Front* (1866). He is best known for haunting oil and watercolor paintings such as *The Country School* (1871).

**Homestead Act** (1862) US federal legislation enacted during the Civil War to encourage westward expansion. The government granted 160 acres (65 hectares) of government land to anyone who would live on it and improve it for five years. Along with the Morrill Act for education, and with subsidies for the railroads, the Homestead Act opened the west to widespread settlement.

**Homestead Massacre** (July 6, 1892) Violent labor incident. Striking workers at the Carnegie Steel Plant in Homestead, Pennsylvania, fired at 300 Pinkerton detectives hired by the company to guard the plant. During the conflict, 10 persons were killed and many injured. The state militia was sent in on July 9 and remained there for three months while strike breakers worked in the plant, weakening the power of the steelworkers union.

**homicide** In law, killing of a person by another. The various legal definitions depend on the circumstances of the killing. A distinction is made between premeditated murder, murder with some mitigating circumstances, and killing by negligence.

**homo** Genus to which humans belong. *See* HUMAN EVOLUTION.

**homoiothermic** (endothermic or warm-blooded) Describes an animal whose body temperature does not fluctuate as the temperature of its surroundings fluctuates. Mammals and birds are homoiothermic. They maintain their body temperature through metabolism. *See also* POIKILOTHERMIC

**homology** Similarity in essential structure of organisms based on a common genetic heritage. It often refers to organs that now have a different superficial appearance and function in different organisms. For example, a human arm and a seal's flipper are homologs, having evolved from a common origin. *See also* EVOLUTION

**homophony** In music, sounding in unison of voices or instruments. Also, a musical texture with a predominant melody part and an accompaniment, as opposed to monophony (music in a single part) or POLYPHONY.

**homosexuality** Emotional or sexual attraction to members of one's own sex. Male and female homosexuals are popularly known as gays and lesbians. They have long sought to gain egalitarian legislation in recognition of their rights. In the US, public policy toward homosexuality varies from state to state. In most states, private sexual acts between consenting adults are considered to be outside legislation. In 1986, however, the Supreme Court upheld the rights of those states that have prohibitive legislation on homosexuality. The threat of AIDS (ACQUIRED IMMUNE DEFICIENCY SYNDROME) has unified much of the gay community into promoting the importance of safe sex and increased funding for AIDS research.

**homozygote** Organism possessing identical forms of a GENE on a CHROMOSOME pair. It is a purebred organism and always produces the same kind of GAMETE. *See also* HETEROZYGOTE

**Honduras** Republic in Central America. See country feature.

**Honecker, Erich** (1912–94) East German communist leader (1971–89). Imprisoned by the Nazis (1935–45), he rose rapidly in the East German Communist Party after World War II and succeeded Walter ULBRICHT as party leader, pursuing policies approved by Moscow. With the reforms under Mikhail GORBACHEV and the collapse of European communism, the ailing Honecker resigned.

**Honegger, Arthur** (1892–1955) French composer. One of a group of Parisian composers known as *Les Six*, he caused a sensation with *Pacific 231* (1923), an orchestral description of a steam locomotive. His other compositions include five symphonies, two operas, and the dramatic psalm *Le Roi David* (1921).

**honey** Sweet, viscous liquid manufactured by honeybees from nectar. It consists of the sugars fructose and dextrose, traces of minerals, and about 17% water.

**honeyeater** (honey sucker) Any of a group of Australian birds that feed on nectar and fruit, pollinating the flowers they feed on. Family Meliphagidae

**honeysuckle** Woody twining or shrubby plant that grows in temperate regions worldwide. It has oval leaves and tubular flowers. In Eurasia, *Lonicera periclymenum* climbs to 20ft (6m). Family Caprifoliaceae.

**Hong Kong** (Xianggang Special Administrative Region) Former British crown colony off the coast of SE China, the capital is Victoria, on Hong Kong Island. The colony comprises Hong Kong Island, ceded to Britain by China in 1842; the mainland peninsula of Kowloon, acquired in 1860; the New Territories on the mainland, leased for 99 years in 1898; and some 230 islets in the South China Sea. The climate is subtropical, with hot, dry summers. In 1984 Britain agreed to transfer sovereignty of the colony to China in 1997. The Joint Declaration of the British and Chinese governments (1985) provided that Hong Kong would become a special administrative region, with its existing social and economic structure unchanged. It would remain a free port with its own commercial and financial policies. Under the governorship of Chris Patten (1992–97), limited democratic reforms were introduced, which China promised to reverse. The handover to China was completed on July 1, 1997 and Chief Executive Tung Chee-hwa was sworn in and a provisional legislative council appointed. Hong Kong is a vital international financial centre with a strong manufacturing base. In 1997 the financial crisis in SE Asia caused the Hang Seng index to lose half of its value. In 1998 the administration spent more than US$15.2 billion defending the Hong Kong dollar. Industries: textiles, electronic goods, cameras, toys, plastic goods, printing. Area: 1,071sq km (413sq mi). Pop. (1996) 6,311,000

**Honolulu** Capital and chief port of Hawaii, on SE Oahu Island. It became the capital of the kingdom of Hawaii in 1845 and remained the capital after the annexation of the islands by the US in 1898. Landmarks include the Iolani Palace, Waikiki Beach, and the Diamond Head Crater. Tourism is of major importance. Industries: sugar refining, pineapple-canning. Pop. (1990) 365,272. *See also* PEARL HARBOR

**Honshū** Largest of Japan's four main islands, lying between the Sea of Japan (W) and the Pacific Ocean (E). It includes Mount FUJI and Lake Biwa (BIWA-KO). Highly industrial, it has six of Japan's largest cities, including TOKYO. The majority of the population inhabit the coastal lowlands. Industries: shipbuilding, oil-refining, chemicals, textiles, rice, tea, fruit. Area: 89,105sq mi (230,782sq km). Pop. (1990) 82,569,581.

**Honthorst, Gerard** (1590–1656) Dutch painter. He was influenced by CARAVAGGIO and was particularly skillful in depicting dramatic, candle-lit interiors, notably *Samson and Delilah* (*c*.1620). He made his name, however, as a portrait painter.

**Hooch, Pieter de** (1629–84) Dutch genre painter. He is best known for his paintings of serene, domestic interiors and courtyards. His best works, such as *The Courtyard of a House in Delft* and *The Pantry*, date from the 1650s.

**Hood, John Bell** (1831–79) Confederate general in the CIVIL WAR. He fought in the Second Battle of BULL RUN and distinguished himself at Antietam, Fredericksburg, Gettysburg, and Chickamauga. Hood became commander in Georgia (1864) but was unable to stem William SHERMAN's march. He resigned in 1865.

**Hooke, Robert** (1635–1703) English physicist and inventor. Interested in astronomy, he claimed to have stated the laws of planetary motion before Isaac NEWTON. He studied the ELASTICITY of solids, which led to HOOKE'S LAW. Among his inventions were a practical telegraph system and the reflecting microscope.

**Hooke's law** Law applying to an elastic material when it is stretched. The law states that the stress (internal tension) is proportional to the strain (a change in dimensions). It was discovered in 1676 by Robert HOOKE.

**hookworm** Two species (*Necator americanus* and *Ancyclostoma duodenale*) of human PARASITE. Larvae usually enter the host through the skin of the feet and legs, and attach to the wall of the small intestine. Symptoms can include anemia and constipation. Phylum Nematoda.

**hoopoe** Striped, fawn-colored bird that inhabits open areas in warmer parts of Eurasia. It has a fanlike crest, a curved bill, and feeds on small invertebrates. Length: 12in (30cm). Family Upupidae; species *Upupa epops*.

**Hoover, Herbert Clark** (1874–1964) 31st US President (1929–33). Acclaimed for his work with victims of war, he was secretary of commerce under presidents HARDING and COOLIDGE. After winning the Republican nomination for president in 1928, he easily defeated Alfred E. Smith. During his first year in office, the economy was shattered by the Wall Street crash and the ensuing GREAT DEPRESSION. With his belief in individual enterprise and distrust of government interference, Hoover failed to provide sufficient government resources to deal with the Depression. In 1932 Hoover mobilized troops to disperse the BONUS ARMY and was resoundingly defeated by Franklin ROOSEVELT with his promised NEW DEAL.

**Hoover, J. (John) Edgar** (1895–1972) US administrator, director (1924–72) of the US FEDERAL BUREAU OF INVESTIGATION (FBI). He reorganized the Bureau, compiling a vast file of fingerprints and building a crime laboratory. During the 1930s Hoover fought organized crime. After World War II he concentrated on what he saw as the threat of communist subversion in the US.

**Hoover Dam** One of the world's largest dams, on the Colorado River between Arizona and Nevada. Opened in 1935, its waters irrigate land in S California, Arizona, and Mexico. Height: 726ft (221m). Length: 1244ft (379m).

**hop** Twining vine native to the Americas and Eurasia. It has heart-shaped leaves, and small male and female flowers on separate plants. The female flowers of *Humulus lupulus* are used to flavor BEER. Family Cannabiaceae.

**Hope, Bob** (1903– ) US comedian, b. England. He started his career in vaudeville and, in 1938, his *Bob Hope Show* began on radio. He made frequent television appearances and starred in more than 50 films, including *The Paleface* (1947) and *The Seven Little Foys* (1955).

**Hopi** Shoshonean-speaking tribe of Native Americans, famous for having retained the purest form of pre-Columbian life to have survived in the US today. About 6,000 Hopi people inhabit 11 villages in Coconino county, Arizona. In 1981, 1.8 million acres (725,000 ha) in Arizona were partitioned between the Hopi and NAVAJO.

**Hopkins, Sir Anthony** (1937– ) Welsh film and stage actor. His film career experienced several false starts before a dramatic resurgence in the 1990s. Hopkins won a Best Actor Academy Award for his hypnotic performance in *The Silence of the Lambs* (1991). He also starred in *Shadowlands* (1993) and *Nixon* (1995).

**Hopkins, Sir Frederick Gowland** (1861–1947) English biochemist. He shared with Christiaan Eijkman the 1929 Nobel Prize for physiology or medicine for his work on VITAMINS. Hopkins pointed out that some diseases, such as

## HONG KONG

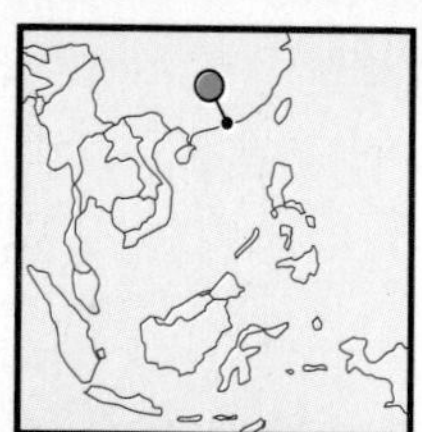

**AREA:** 413 sq mi (1,071 sq km )
**POPULATION:** 6,000,000
**CAPITAL (POPULATION):** Victoria (part of Hong Kong Island, 1,251,000)
**GOVERNMENT:** Chinese/Hong Kong provisional legislature
**ETHNIC GROUPS:** Chinese 98%, others 2% (including European)
**LANGUAGES:** English and Chinese (official)
**RELIGIONS:** Buddhism majority, Confucianism, Taoism, Christianity, Islam, Hinduism, Sikhism, Judaism
**CURRENCY:** Hong Kong dollar = 100 cents

SCURVY and RICKETS, might be caused by deficiency in the diet of a substance necessary for proper health, the so-called VITAMIN concept.

**Hopkins, Gerard Manley** (1844–89) British poet and Jesuit priest. He contributed the principle of sprung rhythm to English poetry. His writing is concerned with problems of faith. The sinking of a German ship carrying five nuns inspired *The Wreck of the Deutschland*.

**Hopper, Edward** (1882–1967) US realist painter. A pupil of Robert HENRI, he was greatly influenced by the ASHCAN SCHOOL. His paintings of scenes in New England and New York City, such as *Early Sunday Morning* (1930), convey a sense of melancholic romanticism.

**Horace** (65–08 BC) Roman poet. His first *Satires* appeared in *c*.35 BC, and were followed by *Epodes* (*c*.30 BC), *Odes* (*c*.23 BC), *Epistles* (*c*.20 BC), and *Ars Poetica* (*c*.19 BC). His simple Latin lyrics provided a vivid picture of the Augustan age.

**horizon, celestial** GREAT CIRCLE on the CELESTIAL SPHERE. It lies midway between the observer's ZENITH and NADIR.

**hormone** Chemical substance secreted by living cells. Hormones affect the metabolic activities of cells in other parts of the body. In MAMMALS, hormones are secreted by glands of the ENDOCRINE SYSTEM and are released directly into the bloodstream. They exercise chemical control of physiological functions, regulating growth, development, sexual functioning, METABOLISM, and (in part) emotional balance. They maintain a delicate equilibrium that is vital to health. The HYPOTHALAMUS is responsible for overall coordination of the secretion of hormones. Hormones include THYROXINE, EPINEPHRINE, INSULIN, ESTROGEN, PROGESTERONE, and TESTOSTERONE. In plants, hormones control many aspects of metabolism, including cell elongation and division, direction of growth, initiation of flowering, development of fruits, leaf fall, and responses to environmental factors. The most important plant hormones include AUXIN, GIBBERELLIN, and CYTOKININ. *See also* HOMEOSTASIS

**hormone replacement therapy (HRT)** Use of the female HORMONES progestogen and ESTROGEN in women who are either menopausal or who have had both ovaries removed. HRT relieves symptoms of MENOPAUSE; it also gives some protection against heart disease and OSTEOPOROSIS. The estrogen causes a thickening of the lining of the uterus, which may increase risk of cancer of the ENDOMETRIUM. The progestogen causes a regular shedding of the lining, similar to menstruation, which may lessen this risk.

**horn** BRASS musical instrument traditionally used in hunting and ceremonies. Horns appeared in the opera orchestras of 17th-century Europe and in the 19th century with Wagner and Strauss. The modern instrument (French horn) consists of a coiled tube of conical bore that widens to a flared bell; most have three valves.

**hornbill** Brownish or black-and-white bird, native to tropical Africa and SE Asia. It has a large, brightly colored bill. The female lays one to six eggs in a hole high up in a tree trunk and then sometimes erects a barricade, imprisoning herself and her eggs there for 4 to 11 weeks. The male feeds her through a slit in the wall. Length: 15–60in (38–152cm). Family Bucerotidae.

**hornblende** Black or green mineral found in IGNEOUS and METAMORPHIC ROCKS. It is the commonest form of AMPHIBOLE, and contains iron and silicates of calcium, aluminum, and magnesium. Hardness 5.5; sp.gr. 3.2.

**Horne, Marilyn** (1934– ) US mezzo-soprano. She studied with Lotte LEHMANN and made her debut in *The Bartered Bride*, Los Angeles (1954). Her international career has included a cycle of Rossini and Bellini operas with Joan SUTHERLAND.

**hornet** Large yellow-and-black WASP of the US, or the orange-and-brown wasp native to Europe. They build egg-shaped paper nests with one queen and many nectar-gathering workers. They have a powerful sting, but are less aggressive than the common wasp. Family Vespidae.

**horoscope** Map of the stars and planets at the time of a person's birth. It shows the position of the celestial bodies in relation to the 12 signs of the ZODIAC and is the basis of ASTROLOGY.

◀ **hornbill** The great hornbill (*Buceros bicornis*) is just one of the 45 species of hornbill, all of which are found in tropical Asia and Africa. The enormously developed bill seen in the great hornbill is used for display and nesting purposes rather than for feeding.

**Horowitz, Vladimir** (1904–89) US concert pianist, b. Russia. He was world-famous by the age of 20 for his virtuoso technique and great sensitivity. From 1950 he appeared only rarely on the concert platform but continued to make recordings.

**horse** Hoofed mammal. It evolved in North America but became extinct there during the late Pleistocene epoch. Early horse forms crossed the land bridge across the Bering Strait, dispersed throughout Asia, Europe, and Africa, and produced the modern horse family. The only surviving true wild horse is Przewalski's horse. The horse was first domesticated about 5,000 years ago in central Asia. Horses returned to the New World with the Spanish conquistadores in the 1500s. Horses are characterized by one large functional toe, molars with crowns joined by ridges for grazing, an elongated skull, and a simple stomach. Fast runners, they usually live in herds. Family Equideae; species *Equus caballus*.

**horse chestnut** Any of 25 species of deciduous trees that grow in temperate regions, especially the common horse chestnut, *Aesculus hippocastanum*. It has large leaves, long flower spikes, and round prickly fruits containing one or two inedible nuts. Family Hippocastanaceae. Height: to 100ft (30m).

**horsefly** Any of several species of flies in the family Tabanidae, especially *Tabanus lineola*. It is a pest to livestock and human beings. The female inflicts a painful bite and sucks blood. Length: to 1.2in (3cm).

**horsepower** (hp) Unit indicating the rate at which work is done, adopted by James WATT in the 18th century. He defined it as the weight, 550lb (250kg), a horse could raise 1ft (0.3m) in one second. The electrical equivalent of 1 hp is 746 watts.

**horse racing** Sport in which horses guided by jockeys race over a course of predetermined length. Most popular is thoroughbred racing, although harness racing (in which horses draw a light two-wheeled vehicle) is also popular in the US. Thoroughbred racing includes flat races and steeplechases, in which the course has obstacles such as hurdles, fences, and water jumps. Horse racing began in Assyria in about 1500 BC. In the US, the most popular races constitute the Triple Crown: the Kentucky Derby, Preakness, and Belmont Stakes.

**horseradish** Perennial plant native to Eastern Europe. It is cultivated for its pungent, fleshy root, which is a useful seasoning. It has lance-shaped, toothed leaves, and white flower clusters. Height: 4ft (1.2m). Family Brassicaceae/Cruciferae; species *Armoracia rusticana*.

**horsetail** Any of about 30 species of flowerless plants that are related to ferns and grow in all continents except Australasia. The hollow stems have a whorl of tiny leaves at each joint. Spores are produced in a conelike structure at the top of a stem.

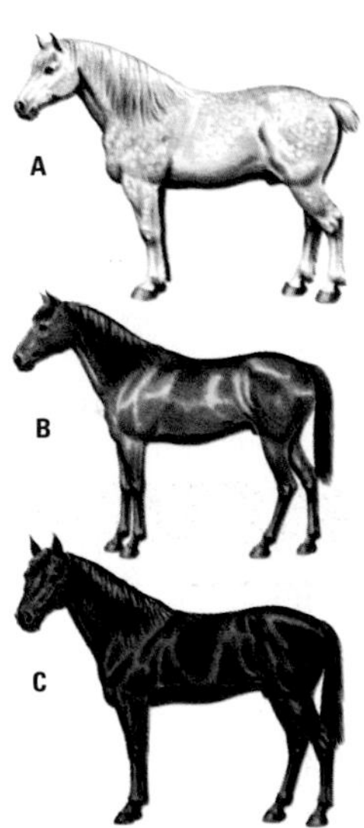


▲ **horse** Domesticated for over 5,000 years, the horse has played a significant role in the development of both agriculture and war. The species shown here are the Percheron (A) a medium-weight draft horse, bred for agricultural and industrial work. It was first bred in France, but is now found worldwide. The Holstein (B) is a saddle and harness horse, bred in Germany by crossing local strains with Spanish horses. The Hanover (C) originated in Germany and is a cross between German harness breeds and the English thoroughbred.

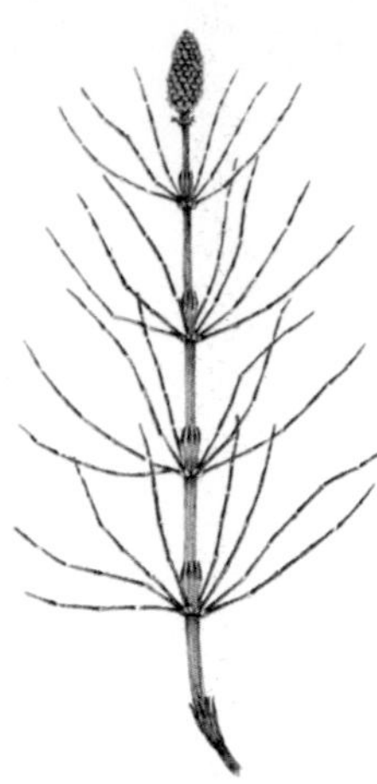

▲ **horsetail** Considered in the same group as ferns, horsetails have cylindrical "leaves", borne in whorls, and jointed stems. The spores are produced in cone-like structures at the tips of the fertile stems. They are "living fossil" relatives of giant Carboniferous trees.

▲ **Horus** One of the principal deities of ancient Egypt, Horus is depicted as a hawk or falcon, or a man's body with a falcon's head. Horus was identified with Ra and was the son of Isis and Osiris, avenging his father's death and rightfully taking the throne. For this reason, the Egyptian pharaohs were all considered Horus incarnate.

Horsetails date from the Carboniferous period. Phylum Sphenophyta, genus *Equisetum*.

**Horthy, Miklós Nagybánai** (1868–1957) Hungarian political leader and regent (1920–44). He commanded the Austro-Hungarian fleet in World War I. He took part in the counterrevolution that overthrew Béla KUN, becoming regent and effective head of state. His highly conservative regime suppressed political opposition and resisted the return of CHARLES I. Allied with the Axis Powers in 1941, he tried to arrange a separate peace with the Allies in 1944 but was arrested by the Germans.

**horticulture** Growing of vegetables, fruits, seeds, herbs, shrubs, and flowers on a commercial scale. Techniques employed include propagation by leaf, stem, and root cuttings, and by stem and bud grafting. Fruit trees, shrubs, and vines are usually propagated by grafting the fruiting stock on to a hardier rootstock. SEED is a major horticultural crop. Close scientific control of POLLINATION is essential for producing crops of specific quality.

**Horus** In Egyptian mythology, falcon-headed god, son of ISIS and OSIRIS. He came to be closely identified with all the pharaohs, who used his name as the first of their titles and were thought to rule as him on Earth.

**Hosea** (Osee) OLD TESTAMENT prophet active in the 8th century BC. The Book of Hosea is the first of the 12 books of the Minor Prophets.

**Hospitaller** *See* KNIGHTS HOSPITALLERS

**Hottentot** (Khoikhoi) KHOISAN-speaking people of S Africa, now almost extinct. Traditionally nomadic, many were displaced or exterminated by Dutch settlers. Descendants have mostly been absorbed into the South African population.

**Houdini, (Harry)** (1874–1926) US magician and escape artist, b. Erich Weiss in Hungary. He escaped from packing cases, handcuffs, and straitjackets, often while in a tank underwater. He also specialized in exposing fraudulent mediums.

**Houphouët-Boigny, Félix** (1905–93) Ivory Coast statesman, first resident (1960–93). He served in the French colonial government, becoming president on independence. He held virtually unchallenged political control. Maintaining close relations with France, the Ivory Coast became one of the more affluent West African countries. In the 1980s a recession, exacerbated by expenditure on grandiose projects, caused unrest, and he was forced to legalize opposition parties (1990).

**House, Edward Mandell** (1858–1938) US politician and diplomat. He helped Woodrow WILSON obtain the 1912 Democratic presidential nomination and became his closest adviser. House was twice sent to Europe in attempts to prevent World War I (1914) and mediate peace (1915). A member of the US peace commission, he helped draft the Treaty of VERSAILLES and the Covenant of the LEAGUE OF NATIONS.

**house music** Form of dance music popular in the US and Britain from the late 1980s. Using drum machines and sampled sound effects, often put into repetitive loops, house music increased the creative role of the disk jockey (DJ). It has produced a number of other forms of dance music.

**House of Commons** Lower house of the British PARLIAMENT. The upper house is the unelected HOUSE OF LORDS. The House of Commons dates from the 13th century. It is the major forum for discussion and voting on intended legislation and questioning of ministers. Its 659 members are elected by their constituents in a secret ballot, usually in general elections which must be held at least every five years. The prime minister is the leader of the majority party in the Commons, and most members of the Cabinet are drawn from the Commons, although some may be from the Lords. Debates and proceedings are controlled by the speaker. Select committees scrutinize legislation.

**House of Lords** Upper house of the British PARLIAMENT. In its legislative capacity, the Lords is completely subordinated to the HOUSE OF COMMONS. The Parliament Acts of 1911 and 1949 checked virtually all its power, except to delay passage of a bill for a year. Life peers, whose titles may not be inherited, and hereditary peers sit in the House.

**House of Representatives** Lower house of the US legislature, which together with the SENATE forms the CONGRESS. It has 435 members. Each state has at least one representative; the larger the population of a state the more representatives are allowed. Representatives must be at least 25 years old, US residents for no less than seven years, and resident in the state they represent. They are directly elected and serve two-year terms. The House considers bills and has exclusive authority to originate revenue bills, initiate impeachment proceedings, and elect the president if the electoral college is deadlocked.

**Houses of Parliament** (Palace of Westminster) First large-scale public building of the GOTHIC REVIVAL in Britain. After a fire destroyed the old Palace of Westminster, Charles BARRY, together with PUGIN, a passionate Gothic specialist, created a building that combined a functional plan and modern technology with Gothic detail (1868).

**Housing and Urban Development, US Department of** US federal cabinet-level department within the executive branch. It was created in 1965. The purpose of HUD is to assist in the growth and development of urban communities and metropolitan areas, so that they provide decent housing, a suitable living environment, and expanding economic opportunities.

**Housman, A.E. (Alfred Edward)** (1859–1936) British poet and classical scholar. He is best known for three volumes of poetry, *A Shropshire Lad* (1896), *Last Poems* (1922), and *More Poems* (1936), in which he treats universal themes, such as the brevity of life, in short, subtle lyrics.

**Houssay, Bernado Alberto** (1887–1971) Argentinian physiologist who greatly advanced knowledge of the ENDOCRINE SYSTEM. He shared the 1947 Nobel Prize for physiology or medicine for discovering the role played by the hormone of the anterior PITUITARY GLAND lobe in regulating the metabolism of sugar. He demonstrated the complex interlocking action between various HORMONES of the body.

**Houston, Sam (Samuel)** (1793–1863) US military and political leader. Governor of Tennessee (1827–29) before moving to Texas, he became commander in chief of the army when Texas rebelled against Mexican rule (1835). Houston was the first president of the Republic of Texas (1836–38, reelected 1841–44). When Texas was annexed by the US, he served in the Senate and as governor in 1859. Isolated by his support for the Union and for Native Americans, Houston was forced out of office when Texas voted to secede (1861).

**Houston** City and port in SE Texas, connected to the Gulf of Mexico by the Houston Ship Canal. Founded in 1836, it was capital of the Republic of Texas (1837–39, 1842–45). Its greatest growth came after the building of the canal (1912–14), as the coastal oil fields provided a rich source of income and Houston developed as a deep-water port. The largest city in the state, it is a major cultural center with five universities, a symphony orchestra, and many art galleries and museums. It is also a leading industrial, commercial, and financial center, with vast oil refineries and a massive petrochemical complex. Industries: space research (the Johnson Space Center is nearby), shipbuilding, meat-packing, electronics, chemicals, brewing, sugar and rice processing, synthetic rubber, printing, publishing. Pop. (1990) 1,630,553.

**hovercraft** (AIR-CUSHION VEHICLE) Fast, usually amphibious craft. A horizontal fan produces a cushion of air supporting the craft just above the ground or water. Vertical fans propel the craft. Most hovercraft are powered by gas turbine or diesel engines. Hovercraft travel at speeds up to about 100mph (160km/h). They are used as marine ferries and as military vehicles.

**Hovhaness, Alan** (1911– ) US composer. Influenced by Far Eastern music, he gained recognition as an original and exotic composer. His works, some of which reflect his Armenian ancestry, include *Mysterious Mountain* (1955), *Magnificat*

(1957), and *And God Created Great Whales* (1970). He has written over 60 symphonies.

**Howard, Catherine** (1520–42) Fifth queen of HENRY VIII. She was brought to Henry's attention by opponents of Thomas CROMWELL. Henry married her in July 1540, but evidence of her premarital indiscretions led to her execution.

**Howard, Henry** *See* SURREY, HENRY HOWARD, EARL OF

**Howard, John Winston** (1939– ) Australian statesman, prime minister (1996– ). Howard was elected to the House of Representatives in 1974. In 1982 he became deputy leader of the Liberal Party and was made leader in 1985. He held many shadow cabinet positions, and in 1995 was appointed leader of the Opposition. Howard led the Liberal-National coalition to victory against Paul KEATING's ruling Labor Party government.

**Howard, Oliver Otis** (1830–1909) US general. He fought in the CIVIL WAR and, commanding the Army of the Tennessee, accompanied William T. SHERMAN on his march through Georgia. After the war he headed the FREEDMEN'S BUREAU that aided former slaves and was a founder and president (1869–73) of Howard University.

**Howard, Trevor** (1916–88) British actor. He played Shakespearean roles at Stratford-upon-Avon, UK, and appeared in US stage productions. He made many films, including *Brief Encounter* (1945), *Ryan's Daughter* (1970), *Kidnapped* (1971), *The Missionary* (1982), and *Gandhi* (1982).

**Howe, Sir William** (1729–1814) British general during the AMERICAN REVOLUTION. He fought at Bunker Hill and became commander in chief of British forces in North America in 1775. He captured New York (1776) and occupied Philadelphia (September 1777). After defeat at Saratoga (1777), he resigned and returned to England (1778).

**Howells, William Dean** (1837–1920) US novelist and critic. Editor (1871–81) of the literary journal *Atlantic Monthly*, his socialist sympathies are reflected in *The Rise of Silas Lapham* (1885), *A Traveler from Altruria* (1894), and *Through the Eye of the Needle* (1907).

**Hoxha, Enver** (1908–85) Albanian statesman, prime minister (1946–54), first secretary of the Communist Party (1954–85). Hoxha was founder (1941) of the Albanian Communist Party and led the resistance to Italian occupation during World War II. In 1946 the Republic of Albania was established and Hoxha became prime minister. His dictatorial control of party, army, and state led to accusations of Stalinism. Hoxha withdrew from the Warsaw Pact in 1961. The later break with Peking led to Albania's isolation and economic impoverishment.

**Hoyle, Sir Fred (Frederick)** (1915– ) English astrophysicist and cosmologist. He developed the STEADY-STATE THEORY which, although it was subsequently displaced by the BIG BANG theory, sparked important research into NUCLEOSYNTHESIS in stars. Hoyle has often attracted controversy with unorthodox ideas.

**Hua Guofeng** (1918– ) (Hua Kuofeng) Chinese political leader, premier, chairman of the Military Commission, and chairman of the Communist Party of the People's Republic of China (1976–81). When DENG XIAOPING was ousted as prime minister in 1976, he was replaced by Hua. After the death of MAO ZEDONG, Hua also became chairman of the party and thus successor to both Mao and ZHOU ENLAI. His pragmatic approach to domestic and foreign policy led to his isolation within the party. He later resigned amid criticism, replaced by ZHAO ZIYANG as premier and HU YAOBANG as party chairman. He was ousted from the central committee (1982).

**Huang Hai** (Yellow Sea) Shallow branch of the Pacific Ocean, N of the East China Sea between the Chinese mainland and the Korean peninsula. It is connected to the Chihli and Liaodong gulfs by the Strait of Chihli. The HUANG HE, Liao, and Yalu drain into it; the yellow loess (fine-grained silt) from these rivers give the sea its popular name. Area: *c.*180,000sq mi (466,200sq km).

**Huang He** (Huang Ho, or Yellow) River in N central China; China's second longest (after the YANGTZE). It rises in the Kunlun mountains, and flows E to LANZHOU. It then takes a "great northern bend" around the Ordos Desert. Near Baotau, it turns S through Shanxi province. It then flows E through Henan province and NE through Shandong to enter the Bo Hai Gulf, an arm of the HUANG HAI. The river gets its popular name from the huge amounts of yellow silt it collects in its middle course. The silting of the riverbed makes the river prone to serious flooding, but the threat has been greatly reduced by dikes and dams. Length: *c.*3,400mi (5,500km).

**Hubbard, L. Ron (Lafayette Ronald)** (1911–86) US science fiction writer of the late 1930s and 1940s and the guiding spirit of the Church of SCIENTOLOGY. His works *Dianetics: The Modern Science of Mental Health* (1950) and *Science and Survival* (1951) formed the basis of Scientology. Hubbard was executive director of the church (1955–66).

**Hubble, Edwin Powell** (1889–1953) US astronomer. He discovered that NEBULAE were resolvable as independent star systems, and attributed the RED SHIFT of spectral lines of galaxies to their recession and hence to the expansion of the Universe, upon which modern COSMOLOGY is based. *See also* HUBBLE'S LAW

**Hubble's law** Proposed by HUBBLE (1929), it claimed a linear relation between the distance of galaxies from us and their velocity of recession, deduced from the RED SHIFT in their spectra. The **Hubble constant** (symbol $H_0$) is the rate at which the velocity of recession of galaxies increases with distance from us. The inverse of the Hubble constant is the **Hubble time**, which gives a maximum age for the Universe on the assumption that there has been no slowing of the expansion.

**Hubble Space Telescope (HST)** Optical telescope that was placed in Earth orbit by the SPACE SHUTTLE in 1990. Images transmitted back to Earth revealed that the telescope's main mirror was incorrectly shaped. A shuttle repair team corrected the fault in 1993, and it was again repaired in 1997. Hubble now produces accurate images of bodies that cannot be observed clearly by terrestrial telescopes due to atmospheric distortion.

**Hudson, Henry** (d.1611) English maritime explorer. He made several efforts to find a NORTHEAST PASSAGE. Employed by the Dutch EAST INDIA COMPANY (1609), he was blocked by ice and crossed the Atlantic to search for a NORTHWEST PASSAGE, becoming the first European to sail up the HUDSON River. In 1610 he embarked on another voyage to discover the Northwest Passage and reached HUDSON BAY. Forced by ice to winter in the Bay, his crew set him adrift to die in an open boat.

**Hudson** River in E New York state. It rises in the ADIRONDACK MOUNTAINS and flows S to New York Bay, NEW YORK CITY. First explored in 1609 by Henry HUDSON, it has become one of the world's most important waterways. The

◄ **Hubble Space Telescope**
One of the most ambitious and expensive pieces of astronomical equipment ever to be made, the Hubble Space Telescope initially was unable to relay usable images back to Earth due to an optical aberration of its main mirror. A shuttle mission in 1993 corrected this fault. A further mission in 1997 corrected problems with the telescope's power supply. Images now received on Earth have provided astronomers with the clearest views ever of distant objects.

▲ **Hughes** The son of a wealthy industrialist, Howard Hughes's passion was for film-making. Between 1926 and 1932, Hughes made six films, including *Hell's Angels* (1930) and *Scarface* (1932). He left Hollywood to pursue his other passion, for flying and designing aircrafts, building the largest-ever wooden aircraft. By this time he had returned to film-making, directing his most noted film, *The Outlaw* (1943). The last 10 years of his life he spent as a total recluse.

▼ **human evolution** Although the fossil record is not complete, we know that humans evolved from apelike creatures. Our earliest ancestor, *Australopithecus afarensis* (A), lived in NE Africa some 5 million years ago. Over the next 3–4 million years *A. africanus* (B) evolved. *Homo Habilis* (C), who used primitive stone tools, appeared c.500,000 years later. *H. erectus* (D) is believed to have spread from Africa to regions all over the world 750,000 years ago. Records indicate that from *H. erectus* evolved two species, Neanderthal man (E), who died out 40,000 years ago, and who could have been made extinct by the other species, the earliest modern man, *H. sapiens sapiens* (F).

New York State Barge Canal connects it with Lake Champlain, the Great Lakes, and the St. Lawrence River. Length: *c.*306mi (493km).

**Hudson Bay** World's largest inland sea, in E Northwest Territories, Canada, also bounded by Québec (E), Ontario (S), and Manitoba (SW). It is connected to the Atlantic by the Hudson Strait (NE) and to the Arctic Ocean by the Foxe Channel (N). Explored in 1610 by Henry HUDSON, the bay contains Southampton, Mansel, and Coats Islands. The Churchill and Nelson rivers drain into the bay, which is ice-free from July to October. Area: *c.*480,000sq mi (1,243,000sq km).

**Hudson River School** (*c.*1825–75) Group of US landscape painters influenced by European ROMANTICISM. They were so named because of their idealized scenes of the HUDSON River Valley. The group included Thomas COLE, Frederick E. Church, Henry Inman, and Asher B. DURAND.

**Hudson's Bay Company** English company chartered in 1670 to promote trade in the HUDSON BAY region of North America and to seek a NORTHWEST PASSAGE. The Company had a fur-trading monopoly and was virtually a sovereign power in the region. Throughout the 18th century, it fought with France for control of the bay. In 1763, France ceded control of CANADA to England, and the North West Company was formed. Intense rivalry forced the Hudson's Bay Company into a more active role in W exploration, and in 1771 Samuel Hearne proved the lack of a short Northwest Passage out of the Bay. The companies merged in 1821, with the new company controlling a territory from the Atlantic to the Pacific. After the Confederation of Canada (1867), challenges to its monopoly power increased, and in 1869 it was forced to cede all its territory to Canada for £300,000. As the fur trade declined in the early 20th century, the company diversified and in 1930 was divided up.

**Huerta, Victoriano** (1854–1916) Mexican general and president (1913–14). Instructed by President Francisco MADERO to suppress the revolt led by Félix Díaz, Huerta instead joined forces with the rebels. Madero was arrested and killed, and Huerta became president. Defeated by the Constitutionalists led by CARRANZA, Huerta fled to the US.

**Hughes, Charles Evans** (1862–1948) US statesman and jurist, associate justice of the Supreme Court (1910–16), secretary of state (1921–25), eleventh US chief justice (1930–41). He was the Republican presidential candidate (1916) but narrowly lost to Woodrow WILSON. He served as secretary of state under Presidents HARDING and COOLIDGE. He was a member of the Permanent Court of Arbitration (1926–30) and judge of the Permanent Court of International Justice (1928–30). Appointed chief justice by President HOOVER, he was a moderating influence. He retired in 1941.

**Hughes, Howard Robard** (1905–76) US industrialist, aviator, and film producer. He inherited an industrial corporation (1923) and became a billionaire as head of the Hughes Aircraft Company. In 1935 he set the world speed record of 352mph (567km/h) in an aircraft of his own design. He occasionally produced films, including *Hell's Angels* (1930) and *The Outlaw* (1943).

**Hughes, Ted (Edward James)** (1930–1998) British poet. One of the most distinctive voices in contemporary English verse, Hughes's work concerns raw nature. Collections include *Hawk in the Rain* (1957), *Lupercal* (1960), *Wodwo* (1967), *Crow* (1970), *Moortown* (1979), and *Wolfwatching* (1989). He was married to Sylvia PLATH (1956–62) and became poet laureate in 1984. He has also written children's books, critical essays, and plays.

**Hughes, Thomas** (1822–96) British novelist and political writer. An active member of the Christian Socialist Movement, he is best known for the novel *Tom Brown's Schooldays* (1857).

**Hugo, Victor Marie** (1802–85) French poet, dramatist, and novelist. A major force in 19th-century French literary life, he received a pension from Louis XVIII for his first collection of *Odes* (1822), and presented his manifesto of ROMANTICISM in the preface to his play *Cromwell* (1827). Later works include the plays *Hernani* (1830) and *Ruy Blas* (1838), and the novels *The Hunchback of Notre Dame* (1831) and *Les Misérables* (1862).

**Huguenots** French Protestants who arose in Roman Catholic France during the REFORMATION and suffered persecution. In 1559 a national synod of Huguenot congregations adopted an ecclesiastical structure highly influenced by CALVIN. During the Wars of RELIGION (1562–98), Huguenots continued to face persecution and thousands died. HENRY IV, a Huguenot, came to the throne in 1589 and, despite adopting the Roman Catholic faith in 1593, promulgated the Edict of NANTES (1598), which recognized Catholicism as the official religion, but gave Huguenots certain rights. It was revoked by LOUIS XIV in 1685, and thousands of Huguenots fled France. In 1789 their civil rights were restored, and the Code Napoléon (1804) guaranteed religious equality.

**Huitzilopochtli** Chief deity of the AZTEC, revered as a Sun god and god of war. He is usually shown in armor decorated with hummingbird feathers. His cult required a daily nourishment of human blood. *See also* CENTRAL AND SOUTH AMERICAN MYTHOLOGY

**Hull, Cordell** (1871–1955) US politician. He was a member of the House of Representatives (1907–21, 1923–31), author of the first federal income-tax law (1913), and served as secretary of state (1933–44) under Franklin D. ROOSEVELT. He was an important diplomatic figure in World War II, and played a key role in gaining US acceptance of the United Nations. He was awarded the 1945 Nobel Peace Prize.

**Hull** (officially Kingston upon Hull) City in NE England, on

the N bank of the Humber estuary. Britain's third largest port, it was founded in the late 13th century and grew around its fishing industry. The decline of the fishing industry has been partly offset by the construction of the Humber Bridge (1981), one of the world's longest single-span suspension bridges. Pop. (1991) 254,117

**human** Primate MAMMAL of the genus *Homo*, the only living species of which is *Homo sapiens*. When compared with near relatives, the CHIMPANZEE, GORILLA, and ORANG-UTAN, humans are distinguishable by a number of features. They walk upright, their body is only patchily hairy, their big toes are not opposable to the other toes, their backbone is more S-shaped than straight, and their forehead is higher than that of any ape. Microscopically, humans are distinguishable from great apes by the size, number, and shape of their chromosomes. Another distinction is the human capacity for language. Socially, humans are similar to lesser primates, preferring a family or other small group.

**human body** Physical structure of a HUMAN. It is composed of water, PROTEIN, and other organic compounds, and some minerals. The SKELETON consists of more than 200 bones, sheathed in voluntary MUSCLE to enable movement. A SKULL surrounds the large BRAIN. The body is fueled by nutrients absorbed from the DIGESTIVE SYSTEM and oxygen from the LUNGS, which are pumped around the body by the CIRCULATORY SYSTEM. Metabolic wastes are eliminated mainly by EXCRETION. Continuation of the species is enabled by the reproductive system. Overall control is exerted by the NERVOUS SYSTEM, working closely with the ENDOCRINE SYSTEM. The body surface is covered by a protective layer of SKIN.

**human evolution** Process by which HUMANS developed from prehuman ancestors. The FOSSIL record of human ancestors is patchy and unclear. Some scientists believe that our ancestry can be traced back to one or more species of Australopithicenes that flourished in S and E Africa *c.*4–1 million years ago. Other scientists believe that we are descended from some as yet undiscovered ancestor. The earliest fossils that can be identified as human are those of *Homo habilis* (handy people), which date from 2 million years ago. The next evolutionary stage was *Homo erectus* (upright people), who first appeared *c.*1.5 million years ago. The earliest fossils of our own species, *Homo sapiens* (wise people), date from *c.*250,000 years ago. An apparent side-branch, the NEANDERTHALS (*Homo sapiens neanderthalensis*) existed in Europe and W Asia some 130,000–40,000 years ago. Fully modern humans, *Homo sapiens sapiens*, first appeared about 50,000 years ago. All human species apart from *Homo sapiens sapiens* are now extinct.

**human immunodeficiency virus (HIV)** Organism that causes ACQUIRED IMMUNE DEFICIENCY SYNDROME (AIDS). A RETROVIRUS identified in 1983, HIV attacks the IMMUNE SYSTEM, leaving the person unable to fight infection. There are two distinct viruses: HIV-1, which has now spread worldwide; and HIV-2, which is concentrated almost entirely in W Africa. Both cause AIDS. There are three main means of transmission: from person to person by sexual contact, from mother to baby during birth, and by contact with contaminated blood or blood products (for example, during transfusions or when drug-users share needles). People can carry the virus for many years before developing symptoms.

**humanism** Philosophy based on a belief in the supreme importance of human beings and human values. The greatest flowering of humanism came during the RENAISSANCE, spreading from Italy to other parts of Europe. Early adherents included PETRARCH and ERASMUS. Modern humanism developed as an alternative to traditional Christian beliefs. This movement, which has been associated with social reform, was championed by Bertrand RUSSELL.

**human rights** Entitlements that an individual may arguably possess by virtue of being human and in accordance with what is natural. The concept of the inalienable rights of the human being has traditionally been linked to the idea of natural law, on which commentaries were written by several Greek and Roman writers. John LOCKE

◀ **hummingbird** The sword-billed hummingbird (*Ensifera ensifera*) is one of the 300 or so species of hummingbird found in the Americas. Hummingbirds live largely on nectar, and their long bills are perfectly suited to extracting the nectar from deep within the flowers.

helped to shape ideas of fundamental human rights and liberal DEMOCRACY in *Two Treatises on Government* (1690). The concept of human rights has been most notably formulated in a number of historic declarations, such as the DECLARATION OF INDEPENDENCE (1776), the CONSTITUTION (1789), and particularly its first amendments in the BILL OF RIGHTS (1791), and the French DECLARATION OF THE RIGHTS OF MAN AND CITIZEN (1789). These documents owed much to the English PETITION OF RIGHT (1628) and BILL OF RIGHTS (1689), which extended the concept of individual freedom proclaimed earlier in the MAGNA CARTA (1215). The responsibility of the international community for the protection of human rights is proclaimed in the Charter of the United Nations (1945) and the Universal Declaration of Human Rights (1948). *See also* CIVIL RIGHTS

**Humboldt, Baron Friedrich Heinrich Alexander von** (1769–1859) German scientist and explorer. On trips in Europe and Latin America, he studied volcanoes, tropical storms, and the increase in magnetic intensity from the Equator toward the poles. His five-volume *Kosmos* (1845–62) describes the physical universe.

**Hume, David** (1711–76) Scottish philosopher, historian, and man of letters. Hume's publications include *A Treatise of Human Nature* (1739–40), *History of England* (1754–63), and various philosophical "enquiries." Widely known for his humanitarianism and philosophical skepticism, Hume's philosophy was a form of empiricism that affirmed the contingency of all phenomenal events. His position was that it was impossible to go beyond the subjective experiences of impressions and ideas.

**Hume, John** (1937– ) Northern Irish politician, leader of the Social Democratic Labour Party (SDLP). A member of Parliament from 1983, his nationalist politics and commitment to peace in Northern Ireland helped secure an IRA ceasefire.

**humerus** Bone in the human upper arm. A depression on the posterior, roughened lower end of the humerus provides the point of articulation for the ULNA.

**humidity** (relative humidity) Measure of the amount of water vapor in air. It is the ratio of the actual vapor pressure to the saturation vapor pressure at which water normally condenses, and is usually expressed as a percentage. Humidity is measured by a HYGROMETER.

**hummingbird** Popular name for small, brilliantly colored birds of the family *Trochilidae*, found in S and N America. They feed in flight on insects and nectar, usually by hovering in front of flowers. Their speed can reach 60mph (100km/h) and their wings, which beat 50–75 times a second, make a humming sound. Length: 2.2–8.6in (6–22cm).

**Humperdinck, Engelbert** (1854–1921) German teacher and composer. His works include incidental music, songs, and seven operas, the first of which, *Hansel and Gretel* (1893), is his most popular work. He worked with WAGNER in the preparation of *Parsifal* (1880–81).

**Humphrey, Hubert Horatio** (1911–78) US statesman, vice president (1965–69). In 1948 he was elected to the Senate as a Democrat from Minnesota. In 1964 Lyndon B. Johnson chose him as his running mate. As vice president, Humphrey's

H

▲ **Hussein** Despite a costly war with neighboring Iran (1980–88), a crushing defeat by an Allied force following his invasion of Kuwait (1990), and international sanctions that have denied the country essential goods, Saddam Hussein has managed to retain power in Iraq. He maintains an aggressive stance toward the West and Israel, and has been accused of developing chemical-warfare agents.

▲ **Huston** US actor and director John Huston was one of the most colorful of Hollywood characters. Although he began his career acting, he was always driven to direct. He achieved this dream in 1941 with the highly acclaimed *The Maltese Falcon*. He went on to make a number of memorable films including *Key Largo* (1948), *African Queen* (1951), *The Man Who Would Be King* (1972), and *Prizzi's Honor* (1985), for which his daughter, Anjelica Huston, won an Academy Award. He increasingly performed in front of the camera in the latter part of his career, winning an Academy Award nomination for *Chinatown* (1974).

wholehearted support of the VIETNAM WAR incurred hostility. In 1968 he won the presidential nomination, but lost the election to Richard NIXON. In 1971 he returned to the Senate and was reelected in 1976.

**humus** Dark brown organic substance resulting from partial decay of plant and animal matter. It improves soil by retaining moisture, aerating, and increasing mineral nutrient content and bacterial activity.

**Hunan** Province in SE central China, S of Tungting Lake; the capital is Changsha. The region is largely forested, but agriculture is important; rice, tea, rapeseed, and tobacco are produced. The province has valuable mineral resources. Area: 81,301sq mi (210,570sq km). Pop. (1990) 60,600,000.

**hundred days** Period between the escape of NAPOLEON I from Elba and his second abdication (1815). The term has since been applied to other politically significant periods of about that duration, notably the early months of Franklin ROOSEVELT's presidency (1933).

**Hundred Years War** Conflict between France and England pursued sporadically between 1337 and 1453. EDWARD III's claim to the French crown sparked the war. Early English successes brought territorial gains in the Peace of Brétigny (1360). The French gradually regained their lost territory and a revival stimulated by JOAN OF ARC led eventually to the expulsion of the English from all of France except Calais.

**Hungarian** (Magyar) Official language of Hungary, spoken by the country's 10.3 million inhabitants and by about 3 million more in parts of Romania, Slovakia, and other countries bordering Hungary. It belongs to the Ugric branch of the FINNO-UGRIC languages.

**Hungary** Landlocked republic in central Europe. See country feature

**Huns** Nomadic people of Mongol or Turkic origin who expanded from central Asia into E Europe. Under ATTILA, they overran large parts of the Roman empire in 434–53, exacting tribute, but after his death they disintegrated.

**Hunt, (James Henry) Leigh** (1784–1859) English critic, journalist, and poet. He was instrumental in introducing the work of SHELLEY and KEATS to the public. He founded the literary periodical *The Examiner* and also contributed to *The Indicator* and *The Liberal*.

**Hunt, Richard Morris** (1827–95) US architect. Influenced by French Gothic and Italian Renaissance style, he is best known for the large town and country houses he built for the wealthy. Examples are "Biltmore" in North Carolina and "The Breakers" in Newport, Rhode Island.

**Hunt, William Holman** (1827–1910) English painter who was one of the founders of the PRE-RAPHAELITE BROTHERHOOD in 1848. His works, such as *The Light of the World* (1854) and *The Scapegoat* (1856), combine meticulous precision with heavy, didactic symbolism.

**hunting and gathering** Practice of small societies in which members subsist by hunting and by collecting plants rather than by agriculture. The groups are always small bands and have sophisticated kinship and ritualistic systems. Today hunter-gatherer societies are most numerous in lowland South America and parts of Africa.

**Huntington's disease** (Huntington's chorea) Acute degenerative disorder. It is genetically transmitted and usually occurs in early midlife. It is caused by the presence of abnormally large amounts of glutamate and aspartate. Physical symptoms include loss of motor coordination. Mental deterioration can take various forms.

**hurling** (hurley) Game that is one of the national sports of Ireland. It is played by two teams of 15 on a field 450×270ft (137×82m), at each end of which are goalposts. The object is to score points by propelling the ball between the goal uprights, either above (1 point) or below (3 points) the crossbar. Every player carries a hurley, a hooked stick, on which the ball may be balanced as the player runs, or with which it may be batted upfield toward a teammate; the ball may be kicked.

**Huron** Confederation of Iroquoian-speaking tribes of Native Americans who once occupied the St. Lawrence Valley E of Lake Huron. In wars for control of the fur trade with the IROQUOIS CONFEDERACY (1648–50), their population was reduced from 15,000 to about 500. After a period of wandering, they settled in Ohio, the Great Lakes area, and Kansas. Today, *c.*1,250 live on reservations in Ohio and Oklahoma and in Ontario.

**Huron, Lake** Second largest of the GREAT LAKES of North America, forming part of the boundary between the US and Canada. It drains Lake SUPERIOR and feeds Lake ERIE as part of the Great Lakes–St. Lawrence Seaway system and is navigable by oceangoing vessels. Area: 23,010sq mi (59,596sq km). Max. depth: 750ft (230m).

**hurricane** Wind of Force 12 or greater on the BEAUFORT WIND SCALE; intense tropical cyclone with winds ranging from 75–200mph (120–320km/h), known also as a typhoon in the Pacific. Originating over oceans around the Equator, hurricanes have a calm central hole, or eye, surrounded by inward spiraling winds and cumulonimbus clouds.

**Hus, Jan** (1369–1415) Bohemian (Czech) religious reformer. He studied and later taught at Prague, where he was ordained priest. Influenced by the beliefs of the English reformer John WYCLIFFE, he became leader of a reform movement, for which he was excommunicated in 1411. In *De Ecclesia* (1412), Hus outlined his case for reform. In 1415 he was burned at the stake as a heretic. His followers were known as HUSSITES.

**Hussein I** (1935–1999) King of Jordan (1953–1999). He sought to maintain good relations with the West while supporting the Palestinians' cause in the ARAB-ISRAELI WARS. In 1967 he led Jordan into the SIX DAY WAR, losing the WEST BANK and East JERUSALEM to Israel. In 1970 he ordered his army to suppress the activities of the PALESTINE LIBERATION ORGANIZATION (PLO) in Jordan. In 1974 he relinquished Jordan's claim to the West Bank to the PLO. In the 1990s he supported efforts to secure peace in the Middle East, signing a treaty with Israel in 1994.

**Hussein, Saddam** (1937– ) Iraqi dictator, president of Iraq (1979– ). In 1959 he was forced into exile for his part in an attempt to assassinate the Iraqi prime minister. In 1963 Saddam returned home and was imprisoned in 1964. After his release, he played a prominent role in the 1968 coup led by the BA'ATH PARTY. The civilian government was replaced by a Revolutionary Command Council (RCC). In 1979 Saddam became chairman of the RCC. His invasion of Iran marked the beginning of the IRAN-IRAQ WAR (1980–88). At home, he ruthlessly suppressed all internal opposition. His 1990 invasion of Kuwait provoked worldwide condemnation. In the GULF WAR (1991) a multinational force expelled the Iraqi forces from Kuwait. Further uprisings by KURDS and Iraqi Shiites were ruthlessly suppressed, and Saddam survived punitive economic sanctions.

**Husserl, Edmund** (1859–1938) German philosopher, founder of PHENOMENOLOGY. He studied consciousness as it related to objects and the structure of experience. His works include *Ideas: General Introduction to Pure Phenomenology* (1913) and *Cartesian Meditations* (1931).

**Hussites** Followers of the religious reformer Jan HUS in Bohemia and Moravia in the 15th century. The execution of Hus in 1415 provoked the Hussite wars against the emperor Sigismund. Peace was agreed at the Council of Basel (1431), but it was rejected by the radical wing of the Hussites, the Taborites, who were defeated at the Battle of Lipany in 1434.

**Huston, John** (1906–87) US film director, writer, and actor. His first feature as a director was *The Maltese Falcon* (1941). Huston won a Best Director Academy Award for *The Treasure of the Sierra Madre* (1946). Other classics followed, such as *Key Largo* (1948), *The Asphalt Jungle* (1950), and *The African Queen* (1951). Other credits include *The Man Who Would be King* (1975), *Prizzi's Honor* (1985), and *The Dead* (1987).

**Hutchinson, Anne Marbury** (1591–1643) Massachusetts colonist and religious leader. Her disagreement with the orthodox Puritanism of Boston led to her trial for sedition (1637) and expulsion. She moved to Pelham Bay, New York, where she was murdered by Native Americans.

**Hutton, James** (1726–97) Scottish geologist. He sought to formulate theories of the origin of the Earth and of atmospheric changes. Concluding that the Earth's history could be explained only by observing forces currently at work within it, he laid the foundations of modern geological science.

**Huxley, Aldous Leonard** (1894–1963) English novelist, grandson of Thomas HUXLEY. He published several volumes of poetry before writing novels such as *Crome Yellow* (1921), *Antic Hay* (1923), and *Point Counter Point* (1928), which satirized the hedonism of the 1920s. His best-known work, *Brave New World* (1932), presents a nightmarish vision of a future society. His later works included *Eyeless in Gaza* (1936) and *The Doors of Perception* (1954), which influenced 1960s counterculture.

**Huxley, Sir Julian Sorell** (1887–1975) English biologist, grandson of Thomas HUXLEY. His books on animal behavior and evolution include *The Individual in the Animal Kingdom* (1911) and *Evolutionary Ethics* (1943).

**Huxley, Thomas Henry** (1825–95) English biologist. Huxley was a champion of DARWIN's theory of evolution. His works include *Zoological Evidences as to Man's Place in Nature* (1863), *Manual of Comparative Anatomy of Vertebrated Animals* (1871), and *Evolution and Ethics* (1893).

**Hu Yaobang** (1915–89) Chinese statesman, general secretary of the Chinese Communist Party (1980–87). He joined the Communists in 1933 and took part in the LONG MARCH. He became associated with DENG XIAOPING during the war against Japan (1937–45), during which he served as a political commissar. In 1952 he became head of the Young Communist League but lost his post after the Cultural Revolution of 1966. He was rehabilitated in 1977 and was appointed general secretary and party chairman. Accused of sympathizing with student demonstrations for democracy, Hu was dismissed.

**Huygens, Christiaan** (1629–95) Dutch physicist and astronomer. In 1655 he discovered Saturn's largest satellite, Titan, and explained that the planet's appearance was due to a broad ring surrounding it. He introduced the convergent eyepiece for telescopes. Huygens's contributions to physics include the idea that light is a wave motion and the theory of the pendulum.

**hyacinth** Bulbous plant native to the Mediterranean region and Africa. It has long, thin leaves and spikes of bell-shaped

## HUNGARY

Hungary's flag was adopted in 1919. A state emblem was added in 1949 and removed in 1957. The colors of red, white, and green had been used in the Hungarian arms since the 15th century. The tricolor design became popular during the 1848 rebellion against Hapsburg rule.

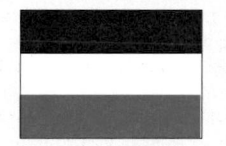

**AREA:** 35,919sq mi (93,030sq km)
**POPULATION:** 10,313,000
**CAPITAL (POPULATION):** Budapest (2,009,000)
**GOVERNMENT:** Multiparty republic
**ETHNIC GROUPS:** Magyar (Hungarian) 98%, Gypsy, German, Croat, Romanian, Slovak
**LANGUAGES:** Hungarian (official)
**RELIGIONS:** Christianity (Roman Catholic 64%, Protestant 23%, Orthodox 1%), Judaism 1%
**CURRENCY:** Forint = 100 filler

The Hungarian Republic, a landlocked country in central Europe, is mostly low-lying. The DANUBE forms much of its N border with the Slovak Republic, before turning S and bisecting Hungary. The capital, BUDAPEST, lies on the river. To the E of the Danube is the Great Hungarian Plain (*Nagyalföld*), drained by the Tisza River and including Hungary's second-largest city, DEBRECEN. In the NE, the Mátra Mountains rise to the Kékes peak, at 3,330ft (1,015m). To the E of the Danube is the Little Plain (*Kisalföld*) and the region of Transdanubia, which includes central Europe's largest lake, BALATON.

### CLIMATE

Hungary has a continental climate, with hot summers and cold winters.

### VEGETATION

Much of Hungary's original vegetation has been cleared for farmland. Large forests remain in the scenic NE highlands.

### HISTORY AND POLITICS

MAGYARS first arrived in the 9th century. In the 11th century Hungary's first king, Saint STEPHEN, made Roman Catholicism the official religion. In 1222 the Golden Bull established a parliament. In the 14th century, the ANGEVIN dynasty extended the empire. In the Battle of Mohács (1526), Hungary was defeated by the Ottomans. In 1699 LEOPOLD I expelled the Turks and established HAPSBURG control. The accession of FRANZ JOSEPH led to war with Austria (1848). Austrian defeat in the AUSTRO-PRUSSIAN WAR (1866) led to the compromise solution of the "dual monarchy" AUSTRO-HUNGARIAN EMPIRE (1867–1918). As defeat loomed in World War I, nationalist demands intensified. In 1918 independence was declared. In 1919 communists, led by Béla KUN, briefly held power. In 1920 Miklós HORTHY became regent. World War I peace terms saw the loss of all non-Magyar territory (66% of Hungarian land).

In 1941 Hungary allied with Nazi Germany, gaining much of its lost territory. Virulent anti-semitism saw the extermination of many Hungarian Jews. Hungary's withdrawal from the war led to German occupation (March 1944). The Soviet expulsion of German troops (October 1944–May 1945) devastated much of Hungary. Hungary became a republic, headed by Imre NAGY (1946). In 1948 the Communist Party gained control, forcing Nagy's resignation and declaring Hungary a People's Republic (1949). Hungary became a Stalinist state. Industry was nationalized and agriculture collectivized. Economic crisis forced the brief reinstatement of Nagy (1953–55). In 1955 Hungary joined the Warsaw Pact. In 1956 a nationwide revolution led to Nagy forming a government. János KÁDÁR formed a rival government and called for Soviet military assistance. Soviet troops brutally suppressed the uprising. Nagy was executed and 200,000 people fled. Kádár's regime adopted a more liberal social policy. Relations with the Catholic Church were restored, and a new economic policy (1968) relaxed the command economy. During the 1980s Hungary began to seek Western aid to modernize its economy. Kádár was ousted in 1988 and the Communist Party disbanded (1989). Multiparty elections were won by the conservative Democratic Forum (1990).The Hungarian Socialist Party (HSP), won the 1994 elections and set up a coalition government with the liberal Alliance of Free Democrats. Gyula Horn of the HSP became prime minister. In 1998 elections the Federation of Young Democrats-Hungarian Civic Party (Fidesz-MPP) emerged as the largest party and Viktor Orban became prime minister.

### ECONOMY

Since the early 1990s, Hungary has adopted privatization programs. The economy (1995 GDP per capita, US$6,410) has suffered from the collapse of its exports to the former Soviet Union and Yugoslavia. Transitional costs have resulted in an increase in debt, unemployment and inflation. The manufacture of machinery and transport is the most valuable sector. Hungary's resources include bauxite, coal, and natural gas. Agriculture remains important (14% of GDP). Major crops include grapes, maize, potatoes, sugar beet, and wheat. Tourism is a growing sector.

flowers, which may be white, yellow, red, blue, or purple. Family Liliaceae; genus *Hyacinthus*.

**hybrid** Offspring of two parents of different GENE composition. It often refers to the offspring of different varieties of a species or of the cross between two separate species. Most interspecies hybrids are unable to produce fertile offspring.

**hybridization** Crossbreeding of plants or animals between different species to produce offspring that differ in genetically determined traits. Changes in climate or in the environment of an organism may give rise to natural hybridization, but most hybrids are produced by human intervention to produce plants or animals that may be hardier or more economical than the original forms.

**Hyderabad** City in the Musi River valley, s India; capital of Andhra Pradesh state. Founded in 1589, it has a number of notable buildings, including the Char Minar (1591). Industries: tobacco, textiles, handicrafts, vehicle parts. Pop. (1991, core city) 3,145,939.

**Hyderabad** City on the INDUS River, Sind province, SE Pakistan. Founded in 1768, it was the capital of Sind until captured by the British in 1843. Industries: chemicals, pottery, shoes, furniture. Pop. (1981) 795,000.

**Hydra** Largest constellation in the sky. It represents the water snake killed by HERACLES in classical mythology.

**hydrangea** Genus of 80 deciduous woody shrubs, small trees, and vines, native to the w Hemisphere and Asia. They are grown for their showy clusters of flowers, which may be white, pink, or blue. Family Hydrangeaceae.

**hydraulics** Physical science and technology of the behavior of FLUIDS in both static and dynamic states. It deals with practical applications of fluid in motion and devices for its utilization and control. *See also* FLUID MECHANICS

**hydrocarbon** Organic compound containing only CARBON and HYDROGEN. There are thousands of different hydrocarbons, including open-chain compounds, such as the ALKANES (paraffins), ALKENES (olefins), and acetylenes. Petroleum, natural gas, and coal tar are sources of hydrocarbons.

**hydrocephalus** Increase in volume of cerebrospinal fluid (CSF) in the brain. A condition that exerts dangerous pressure on brain tissue, it can be due to obstruction or a failure of natural reabsorption. In babies it is congenital; in adults it may arise from injury or disease. It is treated by insertion of a shunting system to drain the CSF into the abdominal cavity.

**hydrochloric acid** Solution of hydrogen chloride (HCl) gas in water. It is obtained by the action of sulfuric acid on common salt, as a byproduct of the chlorination of hydrocarbons, or by combination of HYDROGEN and CHLORINE. Hydrochloric acid is used in industry and is produced by humans cells in the stomach lining to allow the enzyme PEPSIN to digest proteins.

**hydroelectricity** Electricity generated from the motion of water. In all installations this energy of movement, or kinetic energy, is first converted into mechanical energy in the spinning blades of a water turbine, and then into electricity by the spinning rotor of an electric GENERATOR.

**hydrofoil** Boat or ship whose hull is lifted clear of the water, when moving at speed, by submerged wings. They usually have gas-turbine or diesel engines that power propellers or water jets. Speeds range from 30 to 60 knots.

**hydrogen** (symbol H) Gaseous, nonmetallic element, first identified as a separate element in 1766 by Henry CAVENDISH. Colorless and odorless, hydrogen is the lightest and most abundant element in the universe (76% by mass), mostly found combined with oxygen in water. It is used to manufacture AMMONIA and in rocket fuels. Properties: at.no. 1; at.wt. 1.00797; sp.gr. 0.0899; m.p. −434.4°F (−259.1°C); b.p. −423.2°F (−252.9°C); most common isotope $^1$H (99.985%).

**hydrogen bomb** (H-bomb) NUCLEAR WEAPON developed by the US in the 1940s and first exploded in 1952 in the Pacific. The explosion results from nuclear FUSION when hydrogen nuclei are joined to form helium nuclei, releasing great destructive energy and radioactive fallout.

**hydrogen peroxide** ($H_2O_2$) Liquid compound of hydrogen and oxygen. It is prepared by electrolytic oxidation of sulfuric acid and by methods involving reduction of oxygen. Hydrogen peroxide is used as a bleach, a disinfectant, and an oxidizer for rocket fuel and submarine propellant. Properties: sp.gr. 1.44; m.p. 30.4°F (−0.9°C); b.p. 302°F (150°C).

**hydrogen sulfide** ($H_2S$) Colorless, poisonous gas with the smell of bad eggs. It is produced by decaying matter, found in crude oil, and prepared by the action of sulfuric acid on metal sulfides. Properties: m.p. −121.9°F (−85.5°C), b.p. −77.3°F (−60.7°C).

**hydrological cycle** (water cycle) Circulation of water around the Earth. Water is evaporated from the sea; most falls back into the oceans, but some is carried over land. There it falls as precipitation, and, by surface runoff or infiltration and seepage, it gradually finds its way back to the sea. Less than 1% of the world's water is involved in this cycle.

**hydrology** Study of the Earth's waters, their sources, circulation, uses, and chemical and physical composition. The HYDROLOGICAL CYCLE is the Earth's natural water circulation system. Hydrologists are concerned with the provision of fresh water, building dams and irrigation systems, and controlling floods and water pollution.

**hydrolysis** Chemical reaction in which molecules are split into smaller molecules by reaction with water, often assisted by a CATALYST. For example, in digestion, ENZYMES catalyze the hydrolysis of CARBOHYDRATES, PROTEINS, and FATS into smaller, soluble molecules that the body can assimilate.

**hydrophyte** (aquatic plant) Plant that grows only in water or in damp places. Examples include WATER LILIES, WATER HYACINTH, DUCKWEED, and PONDWEEDS.

**hydroponics** (soilless culture or tank farming) Growing of plants with their roots in a mineral solution or a moist inert medium (such as gravel) containing the necessary nutrients, instead of soil.

**hydrotherapy** Use of water within the body or on its surface to treat disease. It is often used in conjunction with PHYSIOTHERAPY.

**hydroxide** Inorganic chemical compound containing the hydroxyl group –OH, which acts as a BASE. The strong inorganic bases such as potassium hydroxide (KOH) dissociate (break down) in water almost completely to provide many hydroxyl ions.

**hydrozoa** Class of animals without backbones, all living in water, belonging to the phylum Coelenterata. They vary in shape and size from the large PORTUGUESE MAN-OF-WAR to the simple hydra.

**HYDROFOIL**

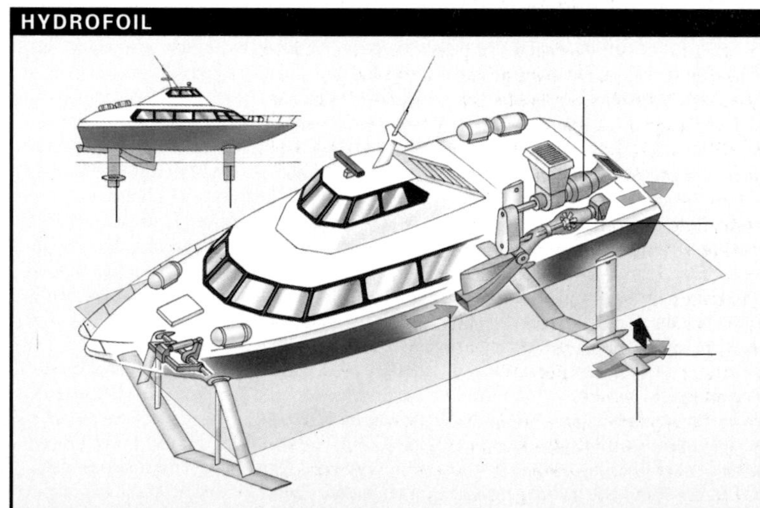

Hydrofoils use the lift of underwater wings (1) to push the body of the boat out of the water. This lessens the drag allowing the boat to travel faster. The Boeing Jetfoil (shown) scoops up water (2) and uses gas turbines (3) to drive high-pressure pumps (4) that throw the water from the rear, creating thrust. The jetfoil can reach speeds of up to 45 mph (75km/h). The hydrofoil works in water the same way an airfoil does in air. A low-pressure zone is created above the top surface of the hydrofoil, sucking and pushing the wing upward (5).

**hyena** Predatory and scavenging carnivore native to Africa and s Asia. The spotted or laughing hyena (*Crocuta crocuta*) of the sub-Sahara is the largest. The brown hyena (*Hyaena brunnea*) of s Africa is smaller. Weight: 60–176lb (27–80kg). Family Hyaenidae.

**hygrometer** Instrument to measure the HUMIDITY of the atmosphere. One type, the psychrometer, compares the wet and dry bulb temperatures of the air; other types measure absorption or condensation of moisture from the air, or chemical or electrical changes caused by that moisture.

**Hyksos** Invaders of Egypt in the 17th century BC. They probably came from Palestine and attacked Egypt at a time of weakness, perhaps possessing a military advantage in the use of chariots. They ruled Egypt from 1674 to 1567 BC as the 15th and 16th dynasties. A native revolt ended in their overthrow.

**Hymen** In Greek mythology, god of marriage. Son of APOLLO, he is represented as a youth attending APHRODITE.

**hymen** In ANATOMY, MEMBRANE that covers the entrance to the VAGINA. Intact at birth, it normally opens spontaneously before PUBERTY or at first penetration during sexual intercourse.

**hymn** Song of praise or gratitude to a god or hero. The oldest forms are found in ancient Egyptian and Greek writings and in the Old Testament psalms of rejoicing. In strict Christian church usage, hymns are religious songs sung by the choir and congregation in a church, distinct from a psalm or a canticle.

**hyperbola** Plane curve traced out by a point that moves so that its distance from a fixed point bears a constant ratio, greater than one, to its distance from a fixed straight line. The fixed point is the focus, the ratio is the eccentricity, and the fixed line is the directrix. The curve has two branches and is a CONIC section. Its standard equation in Cartesian coordinates $x$ and $y$ is $x^2/a^2 - y^2/b^2 = 1$.

**hyperbole** Rhetorical device in which an obvious exaggeration is used to create an effect without being meant literally, as in "the music is loud enough to wake the dead."

**hyperglycemia** Condition in which blood-sugar level is abnormally high. It can occur in a number of diseases, most notably DIABETES. *See also* HYPOGLYCEMIA

**Hyperion** In Greek mythology, sometimes said to be the original Sun god. He was one of the TITANS, the son of URANUS and Gaea and the father of HELIOS the Sun, SELENE the Moon, and EOS the dawn.

**hypersensitivity** Condition in which a person reacts excessively to a stimulus. Most hypersensitive reactions are synonymous with ALLERGIES, the commonest being HAY FEVER.

**hypertension** Persistent high BLOOD PRESSURE. It can damage blood vessels and may increase the risk of strokes or heart disease. *See also* HYPOTENSION

**hyperthermia** Abnormally high body temperature, usually defined as being 106°F (41°C) or more. It is usually due to overheating (as in HEATSTROKE) or FEVER.

**hyperthyroidism** Excessive production of thyroid hormone, with enlargement of the thyroid gland. Symptoms include protrusion of the eyeballs, rapid heart rate, high blood pressure, accelerated metabolism, and weight loss. *See also* HYPOTHYROIDISM

**hyperventilation** Rapid breathing that is not brought about by physical exertion. It reduces the carbon dioxide level in the blood, producing dizziness, tingling, and tightness in the chest; it may cause loss of consciousness.

**hypnosis** Artificially induced, sleeplike state during which suggestions are readily obeyed. It was first described more than two centuries ago. It is physiologically different from sleep and closer to a state of relaxed wakefulness. There is increased suggestibility, a reduction of critical faculties, and effects on memory.

**hypochondria** (hypochondriasis) Neurotic condition characterized by an exaggerated concern with ill health. Hypochondriacs imagine they have serious diseases and often consult several doctors in the hope of a "cure."

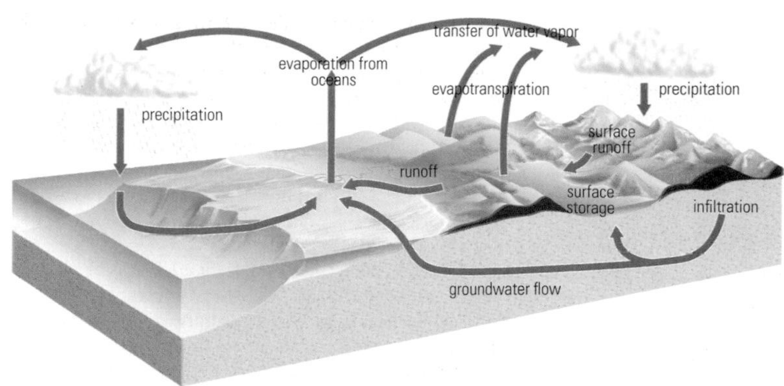


▲ **hydrological cycle** The world's water balance is regulated by the constant recycling of water between the oceans, the atmosphere, and the land. The movement of water between these three "reservoirs" is called the hydrological cycle. The oceans play a vital role in this cycle: 74% of the total precipitation falls over the oceans and 84% of the total evaporation comes from the oceans. Water vapor in the atmosphere circulates around the planet, transporting energy as well as water itself. When the vapor cools it falls as rain or other precipitation.

**hypodermic syringe** Surgical instrument for injecting fluids beneath the skin or into a muscle or blood vessel. It comprises a graduated tube containing a piston plunger, connected to a hollow needle. *See also* INJECTION

**hypoglycemia** Abnormally low blood-sugar level. It may result from fasting, excess INSULIN in the blood, or various metabolic and glandular diseases, notably DIABETES. Symptoms include dizziness, headache, sweating, and mental confusion. *See also* HYPERGLYCEMIA

**hypotension** Condition in which the blood pressure is abnormally low. It is commonly seen after heavy blood loss or excessive fluid loss due to prolonged vomiting or diarrhea. It also occurs in many kinds of serious illness. Temporary hypotension may cause sweating, dizziness, and fainting. *See also* HYPERTENSION

**hypotenuse** Side opposite the right angle in a right-angled triangle. It is the longest side of the triangle.

**hypothalamus** Region at the base of the brain containing centers that regulate body temperature, fluid balance, hunger, thirst, and sexual activity. It is also involved in emotions, sleep, and the integration of HORMONE and nervous activity.

**hypothermia** Fall in body temperature to below 95°F (35°C). Insidious in onset, it can progress to coma and death. Hypothermia is sometimes induced during surgery to lower the body's oxygen demand. It occurs naturally in animals during HIBERNATION.

**hypothyroidism** Deficient functioning of the THYROID GLAND. Congenital hypothyroidism can lead to cretinism in children. In adults the condition is called myxedema. More common in women, it causes physical and mental slowness, weight gain, sensitivity to cold, and susceptibility to infection. It can be due to a defect of the gland or a lack of iodine in the diet. It is treated with the hormone thyroxine.

**hyrax** Small, herbivorous, hoofed mammal of Africa and sw Asia. Rock hyraxes (genus *Procavia*), which live in deserts and hills, are larger than the solitary, nocturnal, tree-dwelling hyraxes (genus *Dendrohyrax*). Length: to 20in (50cm). Family Procaviidae.

**hysterectomy** Removal of the UTERUS, possibly with surrounding structures. It is performed to treat fibroids or cancer or to put an end to heavy menstrual bleeding.

**hysteresis** Phenomenon occurring in the magnetic and elastic behavior of substances in which the strain is greater when the stress is decreasing than when it is increasing because of a lag in the effect. When the stress is removed, a residual strain remains.

**hysteria** In psychology, a group of disorders characterized by emotional instability, dissociation, hallucinations, and the presence of physical symptoms of illness with no physiological cause. Hysteria is no longer used as a diagnostic term. Leading researchers in this field have included Jean Martin CHARCOT, Pierre Janet, and Sigmund FREUD.

# I

*I/i, ninth letter of the alphabet, derived from the Semitic letter* **yod**, *meaning* **hand.** *It passed through Phoenician unchanged to the Greeks, who called it* **iota.** *In the Roman alphabet it was pronounced* **ee.**

▲ **ibis** The scarlet ibis (*Eudocimus ruber*) is found in marsh regions of tropical South America. It grows to a height of some 24in (60cm). It has distinctive scarlet plumage with black wing tips.

▲ **Ibsen** Norwegian playwright Henrik Ibsen is often considered the father of modern drama. He was among the first dramatists to tackle contemporary social issues in his plays.

**Iasi** City in NE Romania, 10mi (16km) from the frontier with Moldova. It was the capital of Moldavia from 1562–1861. Notable buildings include the 15th-century Church of St. Nicholas. It remains an important commercial and administrative center. Industries: textiles, machinery, pharmaceuticals, food products. Pop. (1992) 342,994.

**Ibadan** City in SW Nigeria, *c.*90mi (145km) NNE of Lagos; capital of Oyo state. It was established in the 1830s as a Yoruba military base. Ibadan handles the regional cacao and cotton trades. Industries: plastics, cigarettes, brewing, chemicals, food processing. Pop. (1992 est.) 1,295,000.

**Ibáñez, Vicente Blasco** *See* BLASCO IBÁÑEZ, VICENTE

**Iberian Peninsula** Part of SW Europe occupied by Spain and Portugal, separated from Africa by the Strait of Gibraltar and from the rest of Europe by the Pyrenees Mountains. The early Iberian inhabitants were colonized by Phoenicians and then Carthaginians until the 2nd century BC when Rome dominated. Fourth-century Visigothic incursions were followed by the Moorish invasions from North Africa. By the 13th century, the Christian reconquest of the peninsula was virtually complete. Area: 230,264sq mi (596,384sq km).

**Iberville, Pierre Le Moyne, Sieur d'** (1661–1706) Canadian naval officer and explorer. Scion of a great Canadian family, he fought the British on land and sea in the 1690s with great success, attacking Hudson's Bay trading posts to rout them from the region. In 1698–99, he led an expedition to the Mississippi delta and established Fort Maurepas (Old Biloxi, now Ocean Springs), the first French settlement on the Gulf coast.

**ibex** Any of several species of wild Old World GOATS. The long, backward curving horns grow up to 5ft (1.5m) long on the male, and both sexes have long, yellow-brown hair. Ibexes are renowned for their agility. Height: 3ft (85cm) at shoulder. Family Bovidae.

**ibis** Tropical lagoon and marsh wading bird with long downcurved bill, long neck, and lanky legs. Closely related to the SPOONBILL, it may be black, whitish, or brightly colored. It feeds on small animals, and nests in colonies. Length: 2–3ft (60–90cm). Subfamily: Threskiornithidae.

**Ibiza** Island of Spain, 80mi (130km) off the E coast, in the W Mediterranean; part of the Balearic group. The mild climate and beautiful scenery have made Ibiza a major tourist resort. Other activities include fishing, salt mining, and of fig- and olive-growing. Area: 221sq mi (572sq km). Pop. (1981) 60,937.

**Ibn Battutah** (1304–68) Arab traveler and writer. Born in Tangier, Morocco, he began his adventures in 1325 with a pilgrimage to Mecca by way of Egypt and Syria. Travel was to occupy the next 30 years of his life, when he visited parts of Africa, Asia, and Europe. He finally returned home to Morocco in 1349.

**Ibo** (Igbo) Kwa-speaking people of E NIGERIA. Their patrilineal society originally consisted of politically and socially autonomous village units, but during the 20th century a political unity developed in reaction to British colonial rule. In 1967 the Ibo attempted to secede from Nigeria as the Republic of BIAFRA.

**Ibsen, Henrik Johan** (1828–1906) Norwegian playwright. Ibsen's first published play was *Catilina* (1850), and he came to international attention for the poetic drama *Peer Gynt* (1867). The naturalism of his presentation of social issues in tragedies such as *A Doll's House* (1879), *Ghosts* (1881), *An Enemy of the People* (1882), and *Hedda Gabler* (1890) established his reputation. His later works, such as *The Master Builder* (1892), are more symbolic.

**Icarus** In Greek mythology, the son of DAEDALUS. Daedalus made wings of feathers and wax to escape from Crete, and was successful. But Icarus flew too near the Sun, the heat of which melted his wings, and he fell into the sea and drowned.

**ice** Water frozen to 32°F (0°C) or below, when it forms complex six-sided crystals. It is less dense than water and floats. When water vapor condenses below the freezing point, ice crystals are formed. Clusters of crystals form snowflakes.

**Ice Ages** Periods in the Earth's history when ice-sheets and GLACIERS advance to cover areas previously not affected by ice. There is evidence of at least six ice ages having occurred throughout the Earth's history, the earliest dating back to 2.3 billion years ago. The best known is the most recent ice age, which began about 2 million years ago and lasted until the retreat of the ice to its present extent some 10,000 years ago. The present time may be a warmer period known as an interglacial. The last ice age produced many of the landforms seen in northern continents and affected sea level on a global scale.

**iceberg** Large drifting piece of ice, broken off from a GLACIER or polar ICECAP. In the Northern Hemisphere the main source of icebergs is the SW coast of Greenland. In the Southern Hemisphere, the glacial flow from Antarctica releases huge tabular icebergs. Icebergs can be dangerous to shipping, since only a small portion is visible above the surface of the water.

**icecap** Small ice-sheet, often in the shape of a flattened dome, which spreads over the mountains and valleys of polar islands. The floating ice fields surrounding the North Pole are sometimes incorrectly called an icecap.

**ice hockey** Fast-action sport on an oval ice rink in which two teams of six players wearing ice skates use special hockey sticks to try to propel a vulcanized rubber disk (puck) into the opponents' goal. The rink is usually 200ft (61m) long by 85ft (26m) wide and surrounded by walls about 4ft (1.2m) high. It is evenly divided into three zones – attacking, neutral, and defending – each 60ft (18.3m) long. The goals are within the playing area, 10–15ft (3–4m) from each back line. Regulation games consist of three 20-minute periods of actual timed play. Substitutions are allowed at any time, and the game is controlled by a referee and two linesmen. A penalized player may be banished to the "penalty box" for two or more minutes, and the team meanwhile remains a player short on the ice unless the opponents score. Popular in Canada, the US, Scandinavia, and central and E Europe, it has been included in the Winter Olympics since 1920, and there are also world championships.

**Iceland** Small Scandinavian republic in the North Atlantic Ocean, N Europe; the capital is REYKJAVÍK. **Land and climate** Iceland sits astride the Mid-Atlantic Ridge, which is slowly widening as the ocean is being stretched apart by CONTINENTAL DRIFT. Molten lava wells up to fill the gap in the center of Iceland. Iceland has around 200 volcanoes and eruptions are frequent. Geysers and hot springs are also common features. Icecaps and glaciers cover *c.*12% of the land; the largest is Vatnajökull in the SE. The only habitable regions are the coastal lowlands. Vegetation is sparse or nonexistent on 75% of the land. Treeless grassland or bogs cover some areas, and Iceland also has some spruce trees in sheltered areas. Deep fjords fringe the coast. **History and politics** Norwegian Vikings colonized Iceland in AD 874, and in 930 the settlers founded the world's oldest parliament (Althing). Iceland united with Norway in 1262, and when Norway united with Denmark in 1380, Iceland came under Danish rule. During the colonial period Iceland lost much of its population due to migration, disease, and natural disaster. In 1918 Iceland became a self-governing kingdom, united with Denmark. During World War II Iceland escaped German occupation, largely due to the presence of US forces. In 1944 a referendum decisively voted to sever links with Denmark, and Iceland became a fully independent republic. In 1946 it joined the North Atlantic Treaty Organization (NATO). The US maintained military bases on Iceland. In 1970 Iceland joined the European Free Trade Association. The extension of Iceland's fishing limits in 1958 and 1972 precipitated the "Cod War" with the United Kingdom. In 1977, the UK agreed not to fish within Iceland's 200 nautical mi (370km) fishing limits. The continuing US military presence remains a political issue. Vigdis Finnbogadottir has been president since 1980. In 1995 David Oddson was re-elected prime minister, leading a center right coalition. **Economy** Iceland has few resources besides its fishing grounds (1995 GDP per capita, US$20,460). Fishing and fish processing are major industries, accounting for 80% of Iceland's exports. Barely 1% of the land is used to grow crops, mainly root vegetables and fodder for livestock, and 23% is used for grazing sheep and cattle. Iceland is self-sufficient in meat and dairy products. Vegetables and fruits are grown in greenhouses. Manufacturing is important. Products: aluminum, cement, electrical equipment, and fertilizers. Geothermal power is an important energy source and heats Reykjavík. Overfishing is a major economic problem.

**ICELAND**

**AREA:** 39,768 sq mi (103,000 sq km)
**POPULATION:** 268,000
**CAPITAL (POPULATION):** Reykjavik (101,824)
**GOVERNMENT:** Multiparty republic
**ETHNIC GROUPS:** Icelandic 94%, Danish 1%
**LANGUAGES:** Icelandic (official)
**RELIGIONS:** Christianity (Evangelical Lutheran 92%, other Lutheran 3%, Roman Catholic 1%)
**CURRENCY:** Króna = 100 aurar

**Icelandic** Official language of Iceland, spoken by virtually all of the island's 268,000 inhabitants. It belongs to the Germanic family of Indo-European languages and is descended from the Old Norse that was taken to Iceland by Norwegian Vikings in the 9th and 10th centuries AD. By the time the earliest works were written in Icelandic, many dialectal characteristics had arisen to distinguish it from Norwegian. Icelandic has, however, undergone little linguistic change since the 12th century apart from pronunciation, which has altered greatly. The language has three grammatical genders, a system of noun declensions involving case forms, and complex verb conjugations similar to those of modern German.

**Icelandic literature** Early Icelandic literature emerged in the 13th century from the oral tradition of Eadic and Skaldic poetry, both of which were based on ancient Icelandic mythology. Other early writings (14th–16th centuries) include the sagas of Norse monarchs, translations of foreign romances, and religious works. From the 14th–19th centuries the rímur, a narrative verse poem, was popular. The 19th century was probably the most important period in the development of Icelandic literature, with the rise of Icelandic realism late in the period. Important 20th-century writers include Gunnar Gunnarsson (1889–1975) and Halldór LAXNESS.

**Iceni** Ancient British tribe that occupied the area now known as Norfolk and Suffolk. The territory had been ruled by Prasutagus, a client-king, but on his death (AD 60) the Romans attempted to annex it. This led to a widespread revolt led by Prasutagus's queen, BOADICEA. The Iceni sacked Colchester, London, and St. Albans before they were crushed by the Roman governor, Suetonius Paulinus.

**ice skating** Winter leisure activity and all-year-round indoor competitive sport in which participants use steel skates to glide on ice. The three disciplines of competition ice skating are solo skating, pairs skating, and (pairs) ice dancing. Solo and pairs skating comprise compulsory figure skating, a short program of compulsory elements, and free skating (to the skater's choice of music). The ice dancing competition is structured similarly but based on set styles of dancing. Speed skating has two disciplines: international-track and short-track. In international-track speed skating, competitors generally enter four races over different distances and aggregate times are calculated for individual placings. Short-track speed skaters race either as individuals or in relay teams, or in pursuit races in which two start on opposite sides of the track and race against each other and the clock for a maximum 10 laps of the track.

**I Ching** *See* BOOK OF CHANGES

**ichneumon fly** Parasitic insect that attacks other insects and spiders. Found worldwide, they are characterized by an ovipositor that is often longer than the body. They are usually 0.4in (1cm) long. Family Ichneumonidae.

**icon** Type of religious painting or sculpture, often of Christ, the Virgin and Child, or individual saints. The term is particularly used of Byzantine pictures and later Russian imitations. Icons were already being produced as early as the 5th century; they have been used as an aid to prayer from the 6th century.

**iconography** Study and interpretation of themes and symbols in the figurative arts. In the 18th century the term referred to the classification of ancient monuments by motifs and subjects, but by the 19th century it was more concerned with symbolism in Christian art. Modern iconographers also study secular art and that of religions other than Christianity.

**id** In psychoanalytic theory, the deepest level of the personality that includes primitive drives (hunger, anger, sex) demanding instant gratification. Even after the ego and the superego develop and limit these instinctual impulses, the id is a source of motivation and often of unconscious conflicts.

**Idaho** State in NW US, on the border with Canada; the capital and largest city is BOISE. Idaho remained unexplored until 1805. The discovery of gold in 1860 brought many immigrants, although the Native-American population was not subdued until 1877. The state was admitted to the Union in 1890 and by the turn of the century had begun to develop its resources. The terrain is dominated by the Rocky Mountains and is drained chiefly by the Snake River, whose waters are used to generate hydroelectricity and for irrigation. The principal crops are potatoes, hay, wheat, and sugar beets, and cattle are reared. Silver, lead, antimony, and zinc are mined, and industries include food processing and timber. Area: 83,557sq mi (216,412sq km). Pop. (1993 est.) 1,099,096.

**ideal gas law** Law relating pressure, temperature, and volume of an ideal (perfect) gas: $pV = N k T$, where $N$ is the number of molecules of the gas and k is a constant of proportionality. This law implies that at constant temperature ($T$), the product of pressure and volume ($pV$) is constant (BOYLE'S LAW); and at constant pressure, the volume is proportional to the temperature (CHARLES' LAW).

**idealism** Philosophical doctrine that assigns metaphysical priority to the mental over the material. It denies the claim within REALISM that material things exist independently of the mind. Idealism in the West dates from the teachings of PLATO. The term is also applied to artistic pursuits to denote a rendering of something "as it ought to be" rather than as it actually is.

**ideology** Collection of beliefs or ideas reflecting the interests and aspirations of a country or its political system. In the 20th century the term has been applied to various political theories, including FASCISM, MARXISM, and COMMUNISM.

**ides** Days in the Roman Republican calendar. They fell on the eighth day after the nones of each month, that is on the 15th of March, May, July, and October and on the 13th of the other months. Julius CAESAR was assassinated on the Ides of March.

**Ignatius of Antioch, Saint** (active 1st century AD) Bishop of Antioch and influential theologian of the early Christian Church. On his way to Rome, where he died for his faith, he wrote his seven *Epistles*, which are valuable sources for an assessment of the doctrine of the early Church.

**Ignatius of Loyola, Saint** (1491–1556) Spanish soldier, churchman, and founder of the JESUITS. In 1534, with FRANCIS XAVIER and other young men, he made vows of poverty, chastity, and obedience. He was ordained in 1537 and moved to Rome where, in 1540, Pope Paul III approved his request to found the Society of Jesus, or Jesuits. He spent the rest of his life in Rome supervising the growth of the order, which was to become the leading force in the COUNTER-REFORMATION.

**igneous rock** Broad class of rocks produced by the cooling and solidifying of the molten magmas deep within the Earth. Intrusive rocks, such as GRANITE, are those formed beneath the Earth's surface by the gradual cooling of molten material; extrusive rocks, such as BASALT, are formed by the rapid cooling of molten material upon the Earth's surface.

**iguana** Any of numerous species of terrestrial, arboreal (tree-dwelling), burrowing, or aquatic LIZARDS that live in tropical America and the Galápagos Islands. The common iguana

**IDAHO**
**Statehood:** July 3, 1890
**Nickname:** Gem state
**State bird:** Mountain bluebird
**State flower:** Mock orange
**State tree:** Western white pine
**State motto:** It is forever

▲ **iguana** The common iguana (*Iguana iguana*) is one of the world's largest lizards, growing up to 6.5ft (2m) or more in length. It lives near rivers in tropical America. The young feed mainly on insects, whereas adults eat leaves and fruit.

I

(*Iguana iguana*) is greenish-brown, with a serrated dewlap and a crest along its back. Length: to 6.5ft (2m). Family Iguanidae.

**Ijsselmeer** Large lake in the NW Netherlands. It was formed in 1932 by the completion of a dyke that divided the Zuider Zee into the saline Wadden Zee and the freshwater Ijsselmeer. Length of dyke: 20mi (32km).

**ileum** Major part of the small INTESTINE, about 13ft (4m) long. Its inner wall is lined with fingerlike villi, which increase the area for the absorption of nutrients.

**Iliescu, Ion** (1930– ) Romanian politician and president. He was one of the first leaders to emerge during the revolution of 1989, when Nicolae CEAUŞESCU was overthrown, and he was elected president in May 1990 and re-elected in 1992.

**Illinois** State in N central US, on the E bank of the Mississippi River; the capital is SPRINGFIELD. Illinois was explored first by the French in 1673. Ceded to the British in 1763, it was occupied by American troops during the American Revolution. Illinois became a state of the Union in 1818. The land is generally flat and is drained by many rivers flowing SW to the Mississippi. The state has fertile soil that supports crops such as hay, oats, and barley; livestock farming is also important. Mineral deposits are found in the S. CHICAGO (the largest city) is a transport center and port on Lake MICHIGAN. Area: 56,400sq mi (146,075sq km). Pop. (1993 est.) 11,697,336.

**illiteracy** Inability to read and write. The eradication of illiteracy is one aim of public and compulsory education around the world, and yet the problem remains huge. It is estimated that some one billion adults in the world (about 1 in 5 of the world's population) are unable to read.

**illumination** Colored decorations serving to beautify manuscripts of religious books. The practice of illumination began in about the 5th century. The style ranges from decoration of initial letters and borders to miniatures and full-page illustrations. Illumination reached its height during the 14th and 15th centuries with such Flemish and French artists as the LIMBOURG brothers and Jean FOUQUET.

**Illyria** Historic region on the N and E shores of the Adriatic Sea, now mainly in Albania. The tribes of Illyria were conquered by the Romans after 168 BC, and the region was later divided into the provinces of Dalmatia and Pannonia. Several late Roman emperors were of Illyrian origin.

**image, optical** Representation of an object produced by an optical instrument. A real image can be projected onto a screen and recorded in a photograph; a virtual image, such as that produced by a plane mirror, cannot. *See also* LENS

**imagism** Movement in poetry that flourished in the US and England from 1912 to 1917. The imagists believed that poetry should use the language and flexible rhythms of common speech. Amy LOWELL, the principal exponent, produced three anthologies called *Some Imagist Poets* (1915–17). Among the most distinguished contributors was Ezra POUND.

**imago** Adult, reproductive stage of an insect that has undergone full METAMORPHOSIS. Imagos are the winged insects, such as butterflies and dragonflies, that emerge from PUPAS or develop from NYMPHS.

**Imam** Leader of a Muslim community invested with spiritual or temporal authority. The word *Imam* is also a title of honor for Islamic leaders, such as the AGA KHAN.

**IMF** Abbreviation of INTERNATIONAL MONETARY FUND

**Immaculate Conception** Roman Catholic belief that the Blessed Virgin MARY was free of all ORIGINAL SIN from the moment that she was conceived. It was defined as a dogma by Pope PIUS IX in 1854.

**immigration, US** Movement of people to the US, involving more than 40 million people. Before 1890 immigrants were primarily Anglo-Saxon Protestants from the British Isles, Germany, and Scandinavia. Immigration after 1890 involved mainly Roman Catholics and Jews from E and S Europe, forced to leave because of famine, lack of social and economic opportunities, political notoriety, or religious persecution. Once a particular group of immigrants settled in an area, they urged others from their homeland to join them. The Homestead Act of 1862 encouraged potential emigrants; the steamship lines vied for their patronage; Northern Pacific Railroad agents touted land bargains; and young American industries sent out a call for workers. The rate of immigration corresponded to economic cycles in the US; increasing when prosperity was high. Attitudes of residents toward immigrants ranged from eagerness to exploit them and fear that they would denigrate the quality of life in the US, to pride in the strength the country had derived from its ethnic mix. Earlier settlers were often racially biased against those who followed. There were many who blamed immigrants for rising crime rates, labor unrest, and the deterioration of cities. Chinese immigration was restricted in 1882 and Japanese in 1908; mechanisms to control immigration included restrictions on naturalization and denial of elective office to the foreign-born. Restrictive policies won out with the passage of the Johnson Act (1924), which established a national origins quota favoring NW Europeans. The quota system, reaffirmed in the Immigration and Nationality Act (1952), was abolished in 1965. The polyglot of subcultures that immigration brought to the US offers to the mainstream a variety of life styles and values, encouraging cultural borrowing. The strong ethnicity of some immigrants has resisted the melting pot.

**immune system** System by which the body defends itself against disease. It involves many kinds of LEUKOCYTES in the blood, lymph, and bone marrow. Some of the cells make ANTIBODIES against invading microbes and other foreign substances, or neutralize TOXINS produced by PATHOGENS, while others (PHAGOCYTES) attack and digest invaders. *See also* MACROPHAGE

**immunity** Resistance to attack by disease-causing microorganisms. It can be acquired naturally, as from an infection that stimulates the body to produce protective ANTIBODIES. Alternatively, it can be conferred by IMMUNIZATION.

**immunization** Practice of conferring IMMUNITY against disease by artificial means. Passive immunity may be conferred by the injection of an antiserum containing antibodies. Active immunity involves vaccination with dead or attenuated (weakened) organisms to stimulate production of specific antibodies and so provide lasting immunity.

**immunoglobulin** PROTEIN found in the bloodstream that plays a role in the body's immune defenses. Immunoglobulins act as ANTIBODIES for specific ANTIGENS. They can be obtained from donor plasma and injected into people at risk of particular diseases.

**immunology** Study of IMMUNITY and ALLERGY. It is concerned with the preventing disease by vaccination – active immunity; or by injections of antibodies – passive immunity.

**immunosuppressive drug** Any drug that suppresses the body's immune responses to infection or "foreign" tissue. Such drugs are used to prevent rejection of transplanted organs and to treat autoimmune disease and some cancers.

**impala** (pala) Long-legged, medium-sized African antelope. Long, lyrate horns are found only on the males, but both sexes have sleek, glossy, brown fur with black markings on the rump. Length: to 5ft (1.5m); height: to 3.3ft (1m) at the shoulder. Family Bovidae; species *Aepyceros melampus.*

**impatiens** (busy lizzies) Genus of 450 species of succulent annual plants, mostly native to the tropics of Asia and Africa. They have white, red, or yellow flowers and seedpods which, when ripe, pop and scatter their seeds. Some species are known as touch-me-not. Family Balsaminaceae.

**impeachment** Prosecution of a public official by the legislature of a state. In the US it is conducted by the House of Representatives with the Senate as judge, and in Britain by the House of Commons with the House of Lords as judge.

**imperialism** Domination of one people or state by another. Imperialism can be economic, cultural, political, or religious. With the age of exploration came the setting up, from the 16th century, of trading empires by major European powers such as the British, Spanish, French, Portuguese, and Dutch. They penetrated Africa, Asia, and North America, their colonies serving as a source of raw materials and providing a market for manufactured goods. With few exceptions, imperialism imposed alien cultures on native societies. In the 20th century, most former colonies have gained independence.

**imperial system** Units of measurement developed in the UK. It is based on the foot, pound, and the second. *See also* METRIC SYSTEM.

ILLINOIS

**ILLINOIS**
**Statehood :**
December 3, 1818
**Nickname :**
Prairie state
**State bird :**
Cardinal
**State flower :**
Native violet
**State tree :**
Oak
**State motto :**
State sovereignty, national union

**impetigo** Contagious skin condition caused by streptococcal or staphylococcal infection. It causes multiple, spreading lesions with yellowish-brown crusts and primarily affects the face, hands, and feet. It is most common in children.

**impotence** In men, the inability to perform sexual intercourse. It may be temporary or permanent, brought about by illness, injury, the effects of certain drugs, fatigue, or psychological factors.

**impressionism** Major French antiacademic art movement of the late 19th century, gaining its name from a painting by MONET entitled *Impression, Sunrise* (1874). In the words of Monet, the movement's leading painter, impressionists aimed to create "a spontaneous work rather than a calculated one." In the 1860s, Monet, RENOIR, Sisley, and Frédéric Bazille formed a close-knit group exploring the possibilities of painting outdoors and the effects of light on nature. The first impressionist exhibition took place in 1874. Although not accepted at first, impressionism became widely influential from the late 1880s and spread throughout Europe. DEGAS and PISSARRO were prominent impressionists, and CÉZANNE exhibited with them twice. MANET was influenced by, and influenced, impressionism. Other impressionists include Berthe Morisot and Mary CASSATT. RODIN has been called impressionist because of his interest in the effects of light on his sculpture. In music, the term impressionism refers to a period lasting from roughly 1890 to 1930 and is usually applied to the work of Claude DEBUSSY, who influenced Maurice RAVEL, Frederick DELIUS, and Manuel DE FALLA. *See also* ROMANTICISM

**imprinting** Form of learning that occurs within a critical period in very young animals. A complex relationship develops between the newborn infant and the first animate object it encounters, which is usually a parent. The future emotional development of the infant depends upon this relationship. Imprinting in birds has been studied by Konrad LORENZ, who believed that it is an irreversible process.

**inbreeding** Mating of two closely blood-related organisms. It is the opposite of outbreeding. Over successive generations it causes much less variation in GENOTYPE and PHENOTYPE than is normal in a wild population. A form of genetic engineering, it can be used to improve breeds in domestic plants and animals. In humans, it can have harmful results, such as the persistence of HEMOPHILIA in some European royal families.

**Inca** South American people who migrated from the Peruvian highlands into the Cuzco area about AD 1250. The Incas expanded and consolidated their empire slowly and steadily until the reigns of Pachacuti (*c*.1438–71) and his son Topa (*c*.1471–93), when Inca dominance extended over most of the continent W of the Andes. Although highly organized on bureaucratic lines, the Inca empire collapsed when the Spanish invasion led by PIZARRO in 1532 coincided with a civil war.

**incandescence** Emission of light by a substance at a high temperature. An incandescent object is never at a temperature below about 750°F (400°C). An object like a fluorescent lamp can emit bright light without being incandescent.

**incarnation** Act of appearing in or assuming living or bodily form, especially the assumption of human form by a divine being, as in Hinduism or Christianity. All orthodox Christians believe that the eternal Son of God, the creator and sole deity, took on bodily form and lived on Earth as a mortal human being, JESUS of Nazareth. The doctrine of the Incarnation was confirmed amid controversy by the first general council of the Church at Nicaea in 325.

**incest** Sexual relations within a family or kinship group, the taboo on which varies between societies. In many countries incest is a crime that carries a prison sentence. It is likely that the rules of many primitive communities prohibited marriage between close relatives long before the possible adverse genetic effects of such relationships were realized.

**inch** Unit of measurement equal to 2.54cm. There are 12 inches to 1 foot.

**Inchon** City and port in NW South Korea, on the Yellow Sea. It was first opened for foreign trade in the 1880s. It was the scene of a Russo-Japanese naval battle in 1904, and US forces landed there at the beginning of the KOREAN WAR in 1950. It is one of South Korea's major commercial centers. Industries include iron and steel, textiles, and chemicals. Pop. (1990) 1,818,293.

**inclination, magnetic** Angle made by a free-floating magnet with the Earth's magnetic lines of force. At the north magnetic pole the inclination is zero; at the magnetic equator it is 90°. *See also* DECLINATION, MAGNETIC

**income tax** Federal or state annual assessment of tax on income, profits, and financial gains of any type. It is a direct tax on money earned or acquired, as distinct from a tax levied on goods or services. Tax rates are usually graduated, increasing as levels of income climb from one bracket to another. Governments can use tax rates as a means of regulating consumer demand: if tax rates rise, consumers have less disposable income and thus less money to buy goods. Income tax can also be used to redistribute wealth, using funds raised from income tax to fund social programs. In the US, federal income tax is administered by the Internal Revenue Service; similar boards administer state income tax.

**incubation** In biology, process of maintaining stable, warm conditions to ensure that eggs develop and hatch. Incubation is carried out naturally by birds and by some reptiles. It is accomplished by sitting on the eggs, by making use of volcanic or solar heat or the warmth of decaying vegetation, or by covering the eggs with an insulating layer of soil or sand.

**incubation period** In medicine, time lag between becoming infected with a disease and the appearance of the first symptoms. In many infectious diseases, the incubation period is quite short – anything from a few hours to a few days – although it may also be very variable.

**Independence Day** *See* FOURTH OF JULY

**India** Republic in S Asia and the world's second most populous country (after China). *See* country feature, pages 338–39.

**Indiana** State in N central US, S of Lake Michigan; the capital is INDIANAPOLIS. Indiana was explored first by the French in the early 18th century. It was ceded to the British in 1763 and passed to the US after the American Revolution. The Native American population was not subdued until 1811. The state remained a rural area until late 19th century industrialization. Access to Lake Michigan and to the Ohio River in the S ensures efficient distribution of the state's agricultural and manufacturing products. The area is regarded as the country's richest farming region. The development of heavy industry in the NW has made Indiana one of the leading producers of machinery. Industries: grain, soybeans, livestock, coal, limestone, steel, electrical machinery, motor vehicles, chemicals. Area: 36,291sq mi (93,993sq km). Pop. (1993 est.) 5,713,000.

**Indianapolis** State capital of INDIANA, at the center of the state, on the White River. Built on a specially selected site, it became the state capital in 1825. It is home to the Motor Speedway, where the Indianapolis 500 motor race takes place. The city is the major cereal and livestock market in a fertile agricultural area. Industries include electronic equipment, vehicle parts, pharmaceuticals, and meat packing. Pop. (1990) 741,952.

**Indian art and architecture** Earliest examples of Indian art date from the ancient civilization of the Indus Valley (*c*.2300 to 1750 BC). Art in the MAURYA EMPIRE (320–185 BC) was intensely Buddhist in motivation. The GUPTA DYNASTY (AD 320–550) was the golden age of Buddhist art. The Buddhist temple, with a porch and cella (main sanctuary), originated at this time. ISLAMIC ART AND ARCHITECTURE were introduced after the Muslim conquest (1192). Between the 16th and 18th centuries, during the MOGUL EMPIRE, an Indo-Islamic style evolved, influenced by Persian prototypes. The TAJ MAHAL stands as the most perfect example of Mogul architecture. By the late 16th century, Indian taste was emerging in bright coloring and in detailed backgrounds. Major modern painters include Rabindranath TAGORE, Jamini Roy, Amrita Sher Gil, and Francis Souza.

**Indian Mutiny** (1857–58) Indian rebellion against the British originating among Indian troops (sepoys) in the Bengal army. Delhi was captured, and atrocities were perpetrated by both sides. The revolt resulted in the British government taking over control of India from the EAST INDIA COMPANY in 1858.

**Indian National Congress** *See* CONGRESS PARTY

**INDIANA**
**Statehood:**
December 11, 1816
**Nickname:**
Hoosier state
**State bird:**
Cardinal
**State flower:**
Peony
**State tree:**
Tulip tree
**State motto:**
Crossroads of America

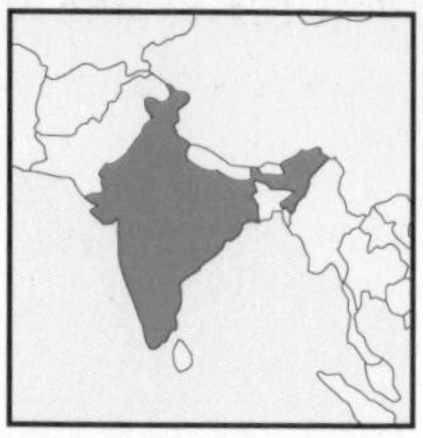

India's flag developed during the struggle for freedom against British rule. The orange symbolizes the Hindus, who form the majority of the population. The green symbolizes the Muslims, and the white peace. The blue Buddhist wheel symbol was added at independence in 1947.

**AREA:** 1,269,338sq mi (3,287,590sq km)
**POPULATION:** 879,548,000
**CAPITAL (POPULATION):** New Delhi (301,800)
**GOVERNMENT:** Multiparty federal republic
**ETHNIC GROUPS:** Indo-Aryan 72%, Dravidian (Aboriginal) 25%, Other 3%
**LANGUAGES:** Hindi and English (both official), Telugu, Bengali, Marati, Urdu, and many others
**RELIGIONS:** Hinduism 83%, Islam (Sunni) 11%, Christianity 2%, Sikhism 2%, Buddhism 1%
**CURRENCY:** Rupee = 100 paisa

The Republic of India is the world's seventh largest country, but the second most populous (after China). India can be divided into three geographical regions: N India is dominated by the HIMALAYAS. The BRAHMAPUTRA, INDUS, and GANGES rivers rise in the Himalayas and form the fertile, alluvial central plains. A densely populated area, the plains include the capital, NEW DELHI. CALCUTTA lies in the Ganges delta. In the W is the THAR DESERT and India's largest state, RAJASTHAN. Southern India consists of the large DECCAN plateau, bordered by the Western and Eastern GHATS. India's largest city is MUMBAI (Bombay). *See* individual state and city articles

### CLIMATE

India has three main seasons: a cool season, from October to February; a hot season, between March and June; and the monsoon season from mid-June to September. There are wide regional variations in temperature and rainfall.

### VEGETATION

The KARAKORAM RANGE in the far N has permanently snow-covered peaks. The E Ganges delta has mangrove swamps. Between the gulfs of Kutch and Cambay are the deciduous forest habitats of the last of India's wild lions. The Ghats are clad in heavy rain forest.

### HISTORY AND POLITICS

One of the world's oldest civilizations flourished in the lower Indus valley, *c*.2500–1700 BC. In *c*.1500 BC, Aryans conquered India, and established an early form of HINDUISM. In 327–325 BC, Alexander the Great conquered part of NW India. CHANDRAGUPTA founded the MAURYA EMPIRE. His grandson, ASHOKA, unified India and established BUDDHISM in the 3rd century BC. The CHOLA established a S trading kingdom in the 2nd century AD. In the 4th and 5th centuries AD, N India flourished under the GUPTA DYNASTY. The

## INDIA

7th century is seen as the classical period of India's history. In 1192 the DELHI Sultanate became India's first Muslim kingdom and dominated the region. In 1526 BABUR founded the MOGUL EMPIRE (1526–1857). In the 17th century, India became a center of ISLAMIC ART AND ARCHITECTURE under SHAH JAHAN (who built the TAJ MAHAL) and AURANGZEB. The MARATHA successfully resisted European imperial ambitions in the guise of the EAST INDIA COMPANY. In 1757 Robert CLIVE established the BRITISH EMPIRE (1757–1947). Growing civil unrest culminated in the INDIAN MUTINY (1857–58). Reforms failed to dampen Indian nationalism, and the CONGRESS PARTY was formed (1885). The MUSLIM LEAGUE was founded (1906) to protect Muslim minority rights. Following World War I, Mahatma GANDHI began his passive resistance campaigns. The AMRITSAR Massacre (1919) intensified Indian nationalism. In August 1947 British India was partitioned into India and the Muslim state of PAKISTAN. 500,000 people died in the ensuing mass migration. India became the world's largest democratic republic. Jawaharlal NEHRU of the Congress Party was India's first prime minister. Conflict began (1948) with Pakistan over the status of JAMMU AND KASHMIR. In 1965 Nehru's daughter, Indira GANDHI, became prime minister. In 1971 India provided military support to create an independent BANGLADESH. In 1974 India became the world's sixth nuclear power. In 1984, faced with demands for an independent Sikh state, troops stormed the Golden Temple in Amritsar. Indira Gandhi was murdered by her Sikh bodyguards (October 1984), and was succeeded by her son, Rajiv GANDHI. In 1984 India was shocked by the world's worst industrial accident at BHOPAL. Rajiv Gandhi was assassinated by TAMILS during the 1990 elections. From 1947 to 1996, India was ruled by the Congress Party (I) for all but four years. In 1996 the United Front formed a coalition government. In 1998 the withdrawal of Congress (I) support led to fresh elections and the formation of a coalition government led by the BHARATIYA JANATA PARTY (BJP). In 1999 the BJP government fell, and Congress (I), led by Sonia Gandhi, emerged once more as a power-broker.

### ECONOMY

India has rapidly industrialized; manufacturing is its largest export sector. India is rich in mineral resources; it is the world's third largest producer of bituminous coal, yet it is heavily dependent on imported fuel. Agriculture employs 62% of the work force, and food crops account for 75% of cultivated areas. India is the world's second-greatest producer of rice, and third-largest of wheat. It is the world's largest exporter of tea. In 1991, India abandoned its command economics and introduced free market reforms. Poverty and urban overcrowding remain urgent problems (1995 GDP per capita, US$1,400).

I

**Indian Ocean** Third largest ocean in the world, bounded by Asia (N), Antarctica (S), Africa (W), and Southeast Asia and Australia (E). Known in ancient times as the Erythraean Sea, the Indian Ocean was the first to be extensively navigated. Branches of the ocean include the ARABIAN SEA, the Bay of BENGAL, and the Andaman Sea. Its largest islands are MADAGASCAR and SRI LANKA. The average depth is 13,000ft (4,000m) although there is a Mid-Oceanic Ridge, extending from Asia to Antarctica; several of its peaks emerge as islands. The deepest part is the Java Trench, reaching 25,344ft (7,725m). The climate of the nearby land masses is strongly influenced by the ocean's winds and currents. There are three wind belts: the monsoons, which pick up moisture from the ocean, bringing heavy rainfall to W India and Southeast Asia; the SE TRADE WINDS; and the prevailing westerly winds, bringing tropical storms. The currents are governed by these winds, the seasonal shift of the MONSOON dictating the flow of water N of the equator. Area: *c.*28,400,000sq mi (73,600,000sq km).

**Indians, American** *See* NATIVE AMERICANS

**Indian Territory** Area set aside for Native Americans by the US government. The Indian Removal Act of 1830 gave the president authority to designate specific western lands for settlement by Native Americans removed from their native lands. In 1834 the Indian Intercourse Act set aside Kansas, Nebraska, and Oklahoma N and E of the Red River as the Indian Territory. In 1854 Kansas and Nebraska were redesignated territories open to white settlement. W Oklahoma was opened to white settlement in 1889. In 1907 the last of the Indian Territory was dissolved when Oklahoma became a state.

**Indian theater** Classical and modern dramatic traditions of the Indian subcontinent, including Sanskrit, Kutiyattam, and Kathakali. Sanskrit (Hindu) classical drama, the two great epics of which are the MAHABHARATA and the RAMAYANA, can be traced back as far as the 3rd century BC and survived into the 11th century AD, dying out probably as a result of Muslim disapproval. Sanskrit was followed by a more eclectic tradition that emphasized music, poetry, and dance in its performance. This developed in tandem with Indian folk drama. Largely as a result of Western influence, modern drama appeared during the latter half of the 20th century. There is also an enormously strong tradition of puppetry in Indian theater.

**India–Pakistan wars** Three conflicts between India and Pakistan after they became separate and independent states in 1947. The first (1947–49) arose from a dispute over KASHMIR. Inconclusive fighting continued until January 1949, when the UN arranged a truce, leaving Kashmir partitioned. It remained a source of friction and was the chief cause of the second war (1965), when fighting began over another territorial dispute. Both sides invaded the other's territory, but military stalemate resulted in a ceasefire after a few weeks. The third India–Pakistan war arose out of the civil war between East and West Pakistan in 1971. India intervened in support of East Pakistan (Bangladesh), and (West) Pakistan suffered a decisive defeat.

**indicator** In chemistry, substance used to indicate acidity or alkalinity. It does this usually by a change of color. Indicators, such as the dye LITMUS, can detect a change of PH that measures a solution's acidity (litmus turns red) or alkalinity (turns blue). Universal indicator (liquid or paper) undergoes a spectral range of color changes from pH 1 to 13.

**indigestion** *See* DYSPEPSIA

**indigo** Violet-blue dye traditionally obtained from plants of the genus *Indigofera.*, produced synthetically since the 1890s.

**indium** Silvery-white metallic element (symbol In) of Group III of the PERIODIC TABLE. Its chief source is as a by-product of zinc ores. Malleable and ductile, indium is used in semiconductors and as a mirror surface. Properties: at.no. 49; at.wt. 114.82; sp.gr. 7.31; m.p. 313.9°F (156.6°C); b.p. 3,776°F (2,080°C); most common isotope $^{115}$In (95.77%).

**Indochina** Peninsula of SE Asia, including BURMA, THAILAND, CAMBODIA, VIETNAM, West MALAYSIA, and LAOS. The name refers more specifically to the former federation of states of Vietnam, Laos, and Cambodia, associated with France within the French Union (1945–54). European penetration of the area began in the 16th century. By the 19th century France controlled Cochin China, Cambodia, ANNAM, and TONKIN, which together formed the union of Indochina in 1887; Laos was added in 1893. By the end of World War I France had announced plans for a federation within the French Union. Cambodia and Laos accepted the federation, but fighting broke out between French troops and Annamese nationalists, who wanted independence for Annam, Tonkin, and Cochin China as Vietnam. The war ended with the French defeat at DIEN BIEN PHU. French control of Indochina was officially ended by the Geneva Conference of 1954.

**Indo-European languages** Family of languages spoken throughout Europe and SW and S Asia, and used in all the areas of European colonial settlement, such as Australia and New Zealand, South Africa, Canada, the US, and Latin America. The family consists of the following subgroups: the GERMANIC LANGUAGES, the CELTIC LANGUAGES, and the Indo-Iranian languages (including Persian, Avestan, and the Indo-Aryan or Indic languages Sanskrit, Pali, and modern Hindi). Other languages and groups in the family are Armenian, Albanian, Greek, the Italic Languages (including Latin and its descendants, the ROMANCE LANGUAGES), the Baltic group (including Latvian and Lithuanian), and the Slavic group (including Old Church Slavonic, Russian, Polish, Czech, Serbian, Croatian, and others). About half the world's population speaks one or other of these Indo-European languages.

**Indonesia** Republic in SE Asia. See country feature

**Indra** In Vedic mythology, the ruler of heaven, great god of storms, thunder, and lightning, worshiped as rainmaker and bringer of fertility. In the creation myth he slew Vritra, dragon of drought, to produce the Sun and water on the Earth.

**inductance** Property of an electric circuit or component that produces an ELECTROMOTIVE FORCE (EMF) following a change in the current. The SI unit of inductance is the henry. Self-inductance (symbol $L$) occurs when the current flows through the circuit or component, and mutual inductance (symbol $M$) when current flows through two circuits or components that are linked magnetically. *See also* ELECTROMAGNETIC INDUCTION; INDUCTION

**induction** In medicine, initiation of LABOR before it starts of its own accord. It involves perforating the fetal membranes and administering the hormone oxytocin to stimulate contractions of the UTERUS.

**induction** In physics, process by which an ELECTROMOTIVE FORCE (EMF) is created in a circuit by a change in the magnetic field around the circuit. The magnitude of the current is proportional to the rate of change of magnetic flux. In a transformer, the alternating current in the primary coil creates a changing magnetic field that induces a current in the secondary coil. *See also* ELECTROMAGNETIC INDUCTION; FARADAY'S LAWS; INDUCTANCE

**indulgence** In Roman Catholic theology, remission by the Church of temporal punishment for sin. An indulgence, once granted, obviates the need for the sinner to do penance, although it does not necessarily remove guilt, and may itself be only a partial rather than a full (plenary) indulgence. Previously available from bishops, indulgences are today granted only by the pope. Abuses connected with the sale of indulgences in the later Middle Ages were among the principal causes of the REFORMATION.

**Indus** River of S Asia. It rises in the Kailas mountain range in Tibet and flows WNW through the Jammu and Kashmir region of India, then SW through Pakistan and into the Arabian Sea. Semi-navigable along its shallow lower part, the river is used chiefly for irrigation and hydroelectric power. In its lower valley there are traces of an urban civilization that flourished in the 3rd millennium BC. Length: c.1,900mi (3,060km).

**Industrial Revolution** Term applied to the profound economic changes that took place in W Europe and the US in the late 18th and 19th centuries. It was preceded by a rapid

## INDONESIA

This flag was adopted in 1945, when Indonesia proclaimed itself independent from the Netherlands. The colors, which date back to the Middle Ages, were adopted in the 1920s by political groups in their struggle against Dutch rule.

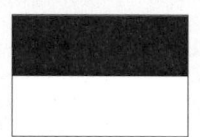

**AREA:** 735,354sq mi (1,904,570sq km)
**POPULATION:** 191,170,000
**CAPITAL (POPULATION):** Jakarta (7,885,519)
**GOVERNMENT:** Multiparty republic
**ETHNIC GROUPS:** Javanese 39%, Sundanese 16%, Indonesian (Malay) 12%, Madurese 4%, more than 300 others
**LANGUAGES:** Bahasa Indonesian (official)
**RELIGIONS:** Islam 87%, Christianity 10% (Roman Catholic 6%), Hinduism 2%, Buddhism 1%
**CURRENCY:** Indonesian rupiah = 100 sen

The Southeast Asian republic of Indonesia is the world's most populous Muslim nation and fourth most populous nation on Earth. It is also the world's largest archipelago, with 13,677 islands (fewer than 6,000 of which are inhabited). Three-quarters of its area and population is included in five main islands: the Greater Sunda Islands of SUMATRA, JAVA, SULAWESI, and KALIMANTAN; and IRIAN JAYA (W New Guinea). More than 50% of the total population live on Java, home of Indonesia's capital, JAKARTA. The Lesser Sunda Islands include BALI, TIMOR, and Lombok. Indonesia is mountainous and prone to earthquakes. It has more active volcanoes (over 100) than any other country.

### CLIMATE

Indonesia lies on the Equator and is hot and humid throughout the year. Rainfall is generally heavy; only the Sunda Islands have a dry season.

### VEGETATION

Tropical rain forests remain the major vegetation on less populated islands. Much of the larger islands has been cleared by logging.

### HISTORY AND POLITICS

In the 7th and 8th century, the Indian GUPTA DYNASTY was the dominant force, and responsible for the introduction of Buddhism and the building of BOROBUDUR, Java. By the end of the 16th century Islam had become the principal religion. In 1511 the Portuguese seized MALACCA. By 1610 the Dutch had acquired all of Portugal's holdings, except East Timor. During the 18th century, the Dutch EAST INDIA COMPANY controlled the region. In 1799 Indonesia became a Dutch colony. In 1883 KRAKATOA erupted, claiming *c.*50,000 lives. In 1927 SUKARNO formed the Indonesian Nationalist Party (PNI). During World War II, the Japanese expelled the Dutch (1942) and occupied Indonesia. In August 1945 Sukarno proclaimed its independence; the Dutch forcibly resisted. In November 1949 Indonesia became a republic, with Sukarno as its first president. During the 1950s economic hardship and secessionist demands were met with authoritarian measures. In 1962 paratroopers seized Netherlands New Guinea and, in 1969, it formally became part of Indonesia as Irian Jaya. In 1966 General SUHARTO assumed control. The Communist Party was banned and alleged members executed. In escalating violence up to 750,000 people were killed. In 1968 Suharto was elected president. In 1975 Indonesian forces seized East Timor, and declared it a province of Indonesia. Resistance to Indonesian rule has killed more than 200,000 East Timorese. In 1997 Suharto was forced to resign after economic crisis created civil disorder. He was replaced by B.J. Habibie.

### ECONOMY

Indonesia is a developing country (1995 GDP per capita, US$3,800). In 1997 the Indonesian economy collapsed. Despite the IMF agreeing a US$49.2 billion rescue package, the value of the rupiah fell by 300%. In 1998 inflation was running at 100% per annum and the economy was expected to contract by 15%. Agriculture employs 56% of the workforce. Oil is the most valuable resource. Indonesia is the world's second-largest exporter of natural gas and second-largest exporter of rubber. Coffee and rice production are important.

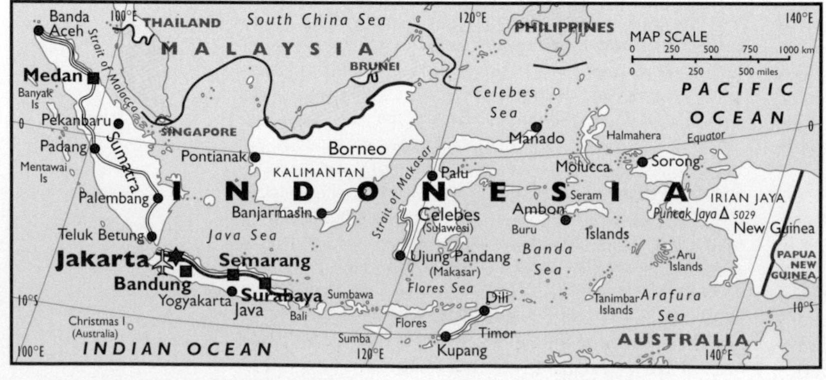

increase in population, which was both a cause and result of the AGRICULTURAL REVOLUTION. The STEAM ENGINE was the main driving force, leading to huge advances in manufacturing and transportation. The Industrial Revolution produced major social changes, in particular the creation of an industrial working class, and introduced rapid economic change that has been maintained in varying forms ever since.

**Industrial Workers of the World (IWW)** US labor union; also known as the "Wobblies." The IWW was formed in Chicago by Daniel DeLeon, Eugene V. DEBS, and William D. HAYWOOD in 1905. It was designed to combine both skilled and unskilled labor in one organization. The group advocated a socialist society and employed militant tactics. It split up after World War I.

**industry** In economic terms, all businesses that produce goods or services. The term is also used to define a group of firms producing a similar kind of product, such as the computer industry. Industries are often classified into three groups: manufacturing industries process commodities; agriculture provides food; and service industries provide largely intangible services, such as entertainment.

**inequality** Mathematical statement that one expression is less, or greater, than another. The symbols $>$, for "is greater than," and $<$, for "is less than," are used. The symbols $\geqslant$ and $\leqslant$ are also used, for "greater than or equal to" or "less than or equal to," respectively.

**inert gases** *See* NOBLE GAS

**inertia** Property possessed by all matter that is a measure of the way an object resists changes to its state of motion. Isaac NEWTON formulated the first law of motion, sometimes called the law of inertia, stating that a body will remain at rest or in a uniform motion unless acted upon by external forces.

**infantry** Foot soldiers carrying portable firearms and equipment. Modern infantry forces are equipped with rifles, machine guns, mortars, grenades, and other lightweight weapons, as well as supplies.

**infarction** Death of part of an organ caused by a sudden obstruction in an artery supplying it. In a myocardial infarction (HEART ATTACK), a section of heart muscle dies.

**infection** Invasion of the body by disease-causing organisms that become established, multiply, and give rise to symptoms.

**infertility** Inability to reproduce. In a woman it may be due to a failure to ovulate (release an egg for FERTILIZATION), obstruction of the FALLOPIAN TUBE, or disease of the ENDOMETRIUM; in a man it is due to inadequate sperm production. In plants, the term refers to inability to reproduce sexually. Infertility occurs in a HYBRID between different species, which are unable to produce viable GAMETES (eggs and male sex cells).

**infinity** Abstract quantity that represents the magnitude of an object without limit or end. In geometry, the "point at infinity" is where parallel lines can be considered as meeting. In algebra, $1/x$ approaches infinity as $x$ approaches zero. In set theory, the set of all integers is an example of an infinite set.

**inflammation** Reaction of body tissue to infection or injury, with resulting pain, heat, swelling, and redness. It occurs when damaged cells release a substance called histamine, which causes blood vessels at the damaged site to dilate. White blood cells invade the area to engulf bacteria and remove dead tissue, sometimes with the formation of pus.

**inflation** In economics, continual upward movement of prices. Although often associated with periods of prosperity, inflation may also occur during recessions. It usually occurs when there is relatively full employment. Under "cost-push" inflation, prices rise because producers' costs increase. Under "demand-pull" inflation, prices increase because of excessive consumer demand for goods.

**inflection** Variation in the form of a lexical item (word) that serves to distinguish its grammatical relationship to other words in a sentence without altering its part of speech. In a common type of inflection, affixes are added to a stem or root form in order to distinguish tense, person, number, gender, voice, or case. In English, this is usually achieved by adding different endings to the word stem singular noun "house" gives plural "houses." Another type uses internal vowel differences within the word stem – the verb "sing" gives simple past tense "sang." Even closely related languages may differ widely in inflection.

**inflorescence** FLOWER or flower cluster. Inflorescences are classified into two main types according to branching characteristics. A racemose inflorescence has a main axis and lateral flowering branches, with flowers opening from the bottom up or from the outer edge in; types include panicle, raceme, spike, and umbel. A cymose inflorescence has a composite axis, with the main stem ending in a flower and lateral branches bearing additional, later-flowering branches.

**influenza** Viral infection mainly affecting the airways, with chesty symptoms, headache, joint pains, and fever. It is treated by bed rest and painkillers. Vaccines are available to confer immunity to some strains.

**information technology (IT)** Computer and TELECOMMUNICATIONS technologies used in processing information of any kind. Word processing, the use of a DATABASE, and the sending of messages over a COMPUTER NETWORK all involve the use of information technology. Television stations use information technology to provide viewers with TELETEXT services.

**information theory** Mathematical study of the laws governing communication channels. It is primarily concerned with the measurement of information and the methods of coding, transmitting, storing, and processing this information.

**infrared astronomy** *See* ASTRONOMY

**infrared wave** ELECTROMAGNETIC RADIATION that produces a sensation of heat emitted by hot objects. Intermediate in energy between visible light and microwaves, its wavelength range is about 750 nm to 1 mm. It has applications in astronomy, medicine, and warfare.

**Inge, William** (1913–73) US playwright. His plays show the deep feelings below the surface of the lives of ordinary small-town people. *Come Back, Little Sheba* (1950), his first Broadway play, which examined the relationship between an alcoholic and his wife, was followed by *Picnic* (1953), which won a Pulitzer Prize. *Bus Stop* (1955) concerned a group of people in a diner, while *The Dark at the Top of the Stairs* (1957) examined poor family communications. Later works include *Natural Affection* (1963), and *Where's Daddy?* (1966).

**Ingres, Jean Auguste Dominique** (1780–1867) French neoclassical painter. One of the great figures of early 19th-century French art, he was an outstanding portraitist, especially of women in high society such as *Madame d'Haussonville* (1845). He also produced sensual nudes, such as *Bather of Valpinçon* (1808). Ingres was hailed as the leader of the anti-Romantic movement, with DELACROIX his rival.

**injection** In medicine, use of a syringe and needle to introduce drugs or other fluids into the body to diagnose, treat, or prevent disease. Most injections are either intravenous (into a vein), intramuscular (into a muscle), or intradermal (into the skin).

**injunction** Court order enjoining a specified party to refrain from a specified action.

**ink** Colored liquid used for writing, drawing, or printing. It may be colored by a suspended pigment or a soluble dye. Some inks dry by evaporation of a volatile solvent.

**Inkatha** South African political organization, founded in 1975 by Chief BUTHELEZI. Its initial aim was to work toward a democratic, non-racial political system. In the early 1990s, it was involved in violent conflict with the AFRICAN NATIONAL CONGRESS (ANC). In terms of representation in the National Assembly, it ranks third among political parties, and its strongest base is in KWAZULU-NATAL.

**Inness, George** (1825–94) US landscape painter. His early works showed the influence of the BARBIZON SCHOOL. His later landscapes became more delicate in color and detail, and he did some painting of the human figure.

**Innocent III** (1161–1216) Pope (1198–1216), b. Lotario di Segni. He stressed moderation; increased papal control over civil matters; and established the courts of INQUISITION. During his papacy, the term TRANSUBSTANTIATION became part of Communion dogma. He allowed the Franciscan and Dominican orders to form and backed the crusade against the ALBIGENSES.

**Innsbruck** City on the Inn River, w Austria; capital of Tirol state. Founded in the 12th century, the city grew rapidly because of its strategic position on a historic transalpine route.

Innsbruck is a commercial and industrial center and an important winter sports resort. Industries: manufacturing, metalworking, textiles, food processing. Pop. (1991) 118,112.

**Inns of Court** Four legal societies in London, England: Lincoln's Inn, Inner Temple, Middle Temple, and Gray's Inn. They date from the 13th century and have the exclusive right to admit persons to practice as barristers in English courts.

**Inönü, Ismet** (1884–1973) Turkish nationalist leader. A professional soldier, he was a close associate of ATATÜRK in the struggle to establish the Turkish republic (1923) and was prime minister for most of Atatürk's presidency (1923–37). He succeeded him as president (1938–50), but his Republican People's Party lost the election of 1950. He returned as prime minister in 1964–65.

**inorganic chemistry** *See* CHEMISTRY

**Inquisition** Court set up by the Roman Catholic Church in the Middle Ages to seek out and punish heresy. The accused were sometimes interrogated under torture. Punishments for the guilty ranged from penances to banishment and death. Kings and nobles supported the organized persecution of Jews, Protestants, and others considered enemies of church and state. The medieval Inquisition was active in Europe from the 12th to the 15th centuries. A later tribunal, the Spanish Inquisition, was instituted in 1483 at the request of the rulers of Spain and was not formally abolished until 1834. In 1542 a Roman Inquisition was set up to check the growth of Protestantism.

**In re Gault** (1967) Landmark US Supreme Court decision that extended various due process rights, including the right to counsel and to remain silent to proceedings in a juvenile court.

**insect** Any of more than a million species of small, invertebrate animals, including the BEETLE, BUG, BUTTERFLY, ANT, and BEE. There are more species of insects than all other species combined. Adult insects have three pairs of jointed legs, usually two pairs of wings, and a segmented body with a horny outer covering or exoskeleton. The head has three pairs of mouthparts, a pair of compound eyes, three pairs of simple eyes, and a pair of antennae. Most insects can detect a wide range of sounds through ultra-sensitive hairs on various parts of their bodies. Some can "sing" or make sounds by rubbing together parts of their bodies. Most insects are plant-eaters, many being serious farm and garden pests. Some prey on small animals, especially other insects, and a few are scavengers. There are two main kinds of mouthparts – chewing and sucking. Reproduction is usually sexual. Most insects go through four distinct life stages, in which complete METAMORPHOSIS is said to take place. The four stages are OVUM (egg), LARVA (caterpillar or grub), PUPA (chrysalis), and adult (IMAGO). Young grasshoppers and some other insects, called NYMPHS, resemble wingless miniatures of their parents. The nymphs develop during a series of molts (incomplete metamorphosis). SILVERFISH and a few other primitive, wingless insects do not undergo metamorphosis. Phylum Arthropoda, class Insecta. *See also* ARTHROPOD

**INSECT**

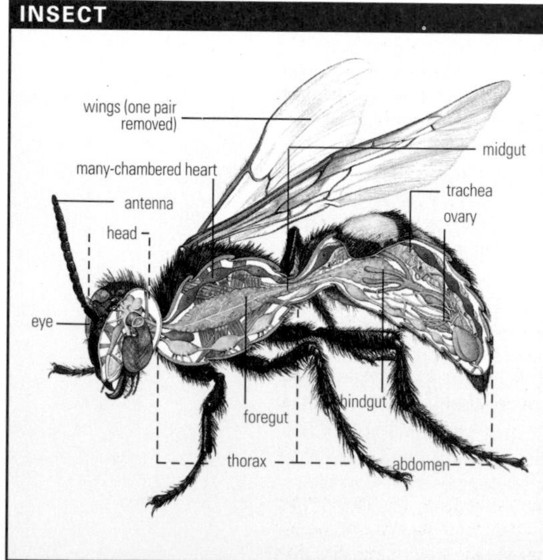


The internal anatomy of all insects, such as the honeybee, is all contained and protected within the confines of the tough, flexible exoskeleton. The typical insect body contains organs of digestion, respiration, circulation, excretion, and reproduction. There are muscles through which movement is effected and a nervous system which co-ordinates and controls insect actions on the basis of information received by the sense organs, most important of which are the large compound eyes and the feelers and antennae. All insect bodies comprise three parts: the head, thorax, and abdomen.

**insectivore** Small order of carnivorous MAMMALS (Insectivora), many of which eat insects. Almost worldwide in distribution, some species live underground, some on the ground, and some in streams and ponds. Most insectivores have narrow snouts, long skulls, and five-clawed feet. Three families are always placed in the order: Erinaceidae (moon rats, gymures, HEDGEHOGS); Talpidae (MOLES, shrew moles, desmans), and Soricidae (SHREWS). But six other families – including tree shrews, tenrecs, and solenodons – are also often included in the order.

**insectivorous plant** (carnivorous plant) Any of several plants that have poorly developed root systems and are often found in nitrogen-deficient sandy or boggy soils. They obtain the missing nutrients by trapping, "digesting," and absorbing insects. Some, such as the Venus's fly-trap (*Dionaea muscipula*), are active insect trappers. The sundews (*Drosera*) snare insects with a sticky substance and then enclose them in their leaves. Bladderworts (*Utricularia*) suck insects into their underwater bladders. Other plants have vase-shaped leaves, such as the pitcher plant (*Sarracenia flava*).

**insemination, artificial** Introduction of donor semen into a female's reproductive tract to bring about fertilization. First developed for livestock breeding, it is now routinely used to help infertile couples. *See also* IN VITRO FERTILIZATION (IVF).

**insomnia** Inability to sleep. It may be caused by anxiety, pain, or stimulants such as drugs.

**instinct** Behaviors that are innately determined, as opposed to behaviors that are learned. In the 19th century instincts were often cited to explain behavior, but the term fell into disrepute with the advent of BEHAVIORISM. The term has recently been revived in the work of such ethologists as Konrad LORENZ.

**insulation** Technique for reducing or preventing the transfer of heat, electricity, sound, or other vibrations. Wool, fiberglass, and foam plastic are good heat insulating materials because they contain air. This trapped air reduces the transfer of heat by CONDUCTION. Water is also a good heat insulator. A diver's wet suit keeps the wearer warm by trapping a layer of water around the body. Electrical insulation materials include rubber, PVC, polythene, glass, and porcelain. Sound insulating materials absorb sound and change it to heat by FRICTION.

**insulin** HORMONE secreted by the islets of Langherhans in the PANCREAS, which controls blood-glucose levels. Insulin lowers the blood-glucose level by helping the uptake of glucose into cells, and by causing the liver to convert glucose to glycogen. In the absence of insulin, glucose accumulates in the blood and urine, resulting in DIABETES.

**insurance** Procedure whereby one party (the insured) transfers the financial consequences of risk of loss to another (the insurer) for a consideration (the premium). Each insured contributes to a common fund, and the losses of the unfortunate few are reimbursed from the fund. Modern practices date back to the 16th and 17th centuries. It covers such things as life, fire, accident, and theft.

**intaglio** Incised carving on gemstones, hardstones, or glass, in which the design is sunk below the surface. In printing, the term is used to describe processes in which ink is applied to incisions and hollows in a printing plate, as in ETCHING.

**integer** Negative or positive whole number and zero, for example ... $-3, -2, -1, 0, 1, 2, 3$ ... There is a limitless (infinite) number of integers. The positive integers are the natural numbers. The existence of negative integers and zero allow any integer to be subtracted from any other integer to give an integer result.

**integral calculus** In mathematics, the branch of CALCULUS that deals with integration: the finding of a function, one or more derivatives of which are given. There are many applications of integral calculus. It is used to find the areas and volumes of curved shapes. In engineering calculations, differential equations are solved by integral calculus. Its principles are also incorporated in many measuring and control instruments.

**integrated circuit (IC)** Complete miniature electronic CIRCUIT incorporating semiconductor devices such as the TRANSISTOR and RESISTOR. Monolithic integrated circuits have all the components manufactured into or on top of a single crystal of silicon (commonly called a SILICON CHIP). Hybrid integrated circuits have separate components attached to a ceramic base. Components in both types are joined by conducting film. *See also* PRINTED CIRCUIT

**Integrated Services Digital Network (ISDN)** High-speed telephone lines designed to carry digital information. There are various grades of ISDN that can carry information more than a thousand times faster than conventional analog voice lines. ISDN lines connect directly to a computer and do not need a MODEM.

**integration** *See* INTEGRAL CALCULUS

**intelligence** General ability to learn and to deal with problems, new situations, and abstract concepts. It can be manifest in many different ways, including skills in adaptability, memory, and reasoning. Fierce debate has raged over the roles of hereditary and environmental factors in developing intelligence. Intelligence tests measure abstract reasoning and problem-solving abilities.

**intelligence quotient** *See* IQ

**intelligence service** Government organization maintained in most countries to obtain information concerning activities that might endanger the state. Intelligence services are usually secretive in their operations. In many countries there are separate organizations for internal security and foreign security. *See also* CENTRAL INTELLIGENCE AGENCY (CIA); FEDERAL BUREAU OF INVESTIGATION (FBI); KGB

**interest** In economics, price paid to the lender by the borrower for the "use" of money over a specified period of time, usually calculated as a percentage of the principal (sum lent). Simple interest is paid regularly and calculated as a percentage of the original principal. In compound interest, the interest calculated for one period (such as a year) is added to the original principal, and the interest for the next period is calculated as a percentage of this total.

**interface** Way that a computer PROGRAM or system interacts with its user. The simplest form of computer interface is the keyboard, through which the user controls the computer by typing in commands. The most common type for personal computers is the GRAPHICAL USER INTERFACE (GUI).

**interference** In optics, the interaction of two or more wave motions, such as those of light and sound, creating a disturbance pattern. Constructive interference is the reinforcement of the wave motion because the component motions are in phase. Destructive interference occurs when two waves are out of phase and cancel each other.

**interferometer** Instrument in which a wave, especially a light wave, is split into component waves that are made to travel unequal distances to recombine as INTERFERENCE patterns. The patterns have such uses as quality control of lenses and prisms, and the measurement of wavelengths.

**interferon** Protein produced by body cells when infected with a virus. Interferons can help uninfected cells to resist infection by the virus and also may impede virus replication and protein synthesis. In some circumstances they can inhibit cell growth; human interferon is now produced by GENETIC ENGINEERING for therapeutic use, to treat some CANCERS, HEPATITIS, and MULTIPLE SCLEROSIS.

**Interior, US Department of the** Federal cabinet-level department; directed by the secretary of the Interior. The department's responsibilities include the administration of *c*.500 million acres (202 million ha) of federal land and, on it, conservation of mineral and water resources, fish, and wildlife; preservation of scenic and historical areas; and promotion of mine safety. The department is also charged with the social and economic development of the US territories and administers service programs to Native Americans. It was established in 1849 as the Home Department.

**intermezzo** Light theatrical entertainment, performed to music between the acts of a drama or OPERA. The earliest intermezzi date from the late 15th century. The 18th-century intermezzi of operas were the basis for OPERA BUFFA. Today the term commonly refers to an instrumental interlude during an opera.

**internal combustion engine** Engine in which fuel is burned inside, so that the gases formed can produce motion, widely used in automobiles. An internal combustion engine may be a TWO-STROKE ENGINE or a FOUR-STROKE ENGINE. In the

**INTERFACE**

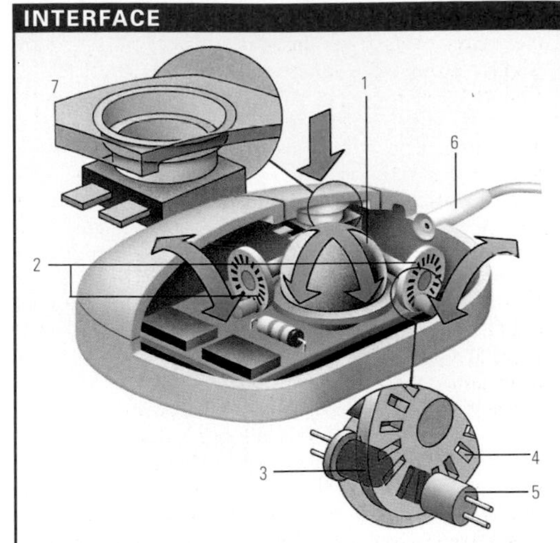


Computer operators use a variety of means to interreact with the computer. A hand-held mouse, for example, moves a cursor on a monitor screen. The central ball (1) rotates as the mouse moves. As the ball moves, spoked wheels (2) turn according to sideways and up and-down movement. An LED (3) shines through the spokes (4). The rate of rotation of both wheels is detected by sensors (5), which send information to the computer via a cable (6) moving the cursor appropriately. Buttons at the front of the mouse (7) can be used to click on areas of the monitor screen or call up menus.

most common type of engine, a mixture of gasoline vapor and air is ignited by a spark. The gases produced in the explosion usually drive a piston along a cylinder. A crankshaft changes the reciprocating (to-and-fro) movement of the pistons into rotary motion. In the WANKEL ENGINE, the gases produced in the explosions drive a triangular rotor. *See also* DIESEL ENGINE

**International Atomic Energy Agency (IAEA)** Specialized, intergovernmental agency of the United Nations. It was founded in 1956 to promote peaceful uses of nuclear energy and establish international control of nuclear weapons. The organization's headquarters are in Vienna, Austria.

**International Labor Organization (ILO)** Specialized, intergovernmental agency of the United Nations. Its aim is to facilitate improved industrial relations and conditions of work. It was formed as an agency of the LEAGUE OF NATIONS in 1919 by the Treaty of VERSAILLES, and has a membership comprising government, employer, and worker representatives. Its headquarters are in Geneva, Switzerland.

**international law** Body of rules deemed legally binding that have resulted from treaties, agreements, and customs between nations. Its sources are also decisions by agencies, conferences, or commissions of international organizations such as the United Nations, as well as decisions of international tribunals such as those of the International Court of Justice. It remains difficult to enforce.

**International Monetary Fund (IMF)** Specialized, intergovernmental agency of the United Nations, and administrative body of the international monetary system. Its main function is to provide assistance to member states troubled by BALANCE OF PAYMENTS problems and other financial difficulties. The IMF does not actually lend money to member states; rather, it exchanges the member state's currency with its own Special Drawing Rates (SDR) (a "basket" of other currencies) in the hope that this will alleviate balance of payment difficulties. These loans are usually conditional upon the recipient country agreeing to pursue prescribed policy reforms. The organization is based in Washington, D.C.

**international style** (international modern style) Name for the architectural style developed in Europe in the 1920s and 1930s that stresses function and avoids superfluous decoration in design. It characteristically features austere white walls, asymmetrical cubic shapes, and large expanses of glass. LE CORBUSIER and Walter GROPIUS were early exponents.

**Internet** Worldwide communications system consisting of hundreds of small COMPUTER NETWORKS, interconnected by telephone systems. It is a network of networks, in which messages and data are sent using short local links from place to place around the world. This enables users to send a message to the other side of the world by ELECTRONIC MAIL (E-MAIL) for the cost of a local phone call.

**interplanetary matter** Material in the space between the planets. It is made up of atomic particles (mainly protons and electrons) ejected from the Sun via the solar wind, and dust

► **Intifada** The purpose of the Intifada, an Arabic word for uprising, was to make Israeli occupied territories, particularly the West Bank and Gaza Strip, ungovernable through concerted civil unrest. Street clashes between brick-throwing Palestinian youths and armed Israeli soldiers were common.

particles (mainly from COMETS, but some possibly of cosmic origin) in the plane of the ecliptic.

**Interpol** (International Criminal Police Organization) Intergovernmental organization. Established in 1923, its main function is to provide member states with information about international criminals and to assist in their arrest. Its headquarters are in Lyon, France.

**intersection** Point, or LOCUS of points, common to two or more geometrical figures. Two non-parallel lines in the same plane meet in a point; two non-parallel planes meet in a line.

**Interstate Commerce Act** (1887) US legislation establishing the Interstate Commerce Commission (ICC), thus placing the nation's railroads under federal government supervision. Subsequently, the act has been broadened to include carrier industries (such as pipelines and trucking) that compete with railroads.

**interval** Musical term for the space between one note and another. The smallest interval on keyboard instruments is a semitone.

**intestine** Lower part of the ALIMENTARY CANAL, beyond the STOMACH. Food is moved through the intestine by the wave-like action known as PERISTALSIS. It undergoes the final stages of digestion and is absorbed into the bloodstream in the small intestine, which extends from the stomach to the large intestine. In the large intestine (cecum, colon, and rectum) water is absorbed from undigested material, which is then passed out of the body through the anus.

**Intifada** (Arabic, uprising) Campaign of violent civil disobedience by Palestinians in the Israeli-occupied territories of the WEST BANK of the JORDAN River and the GAZA STRIP. The Intifada began in 1987 and was a sustained attempt to disrupt Israel's heavy-handed policing tactics. By early 1995 the Intifada had claimed more than 1,400 Palestinian and 230 Jewish lives. It lost momentum following the ISRAELI–PALESTINIAN ACCORD.

**Intolerable Acts** (Coercive Acts) (1774) British legislation designed to punish the American colonists after the BOSTON TEA PARTY. They closed the Boston port and moved the customs house to Salem. British officials accused of capital offenses would be tried in England (Administration of Justice Act); another law (the Massachusetts Government Act) annulled the Massachusetts Charter, giving the governor power to control town meetings and making the council and judiciary appointed bodies. The colonists' opposition resulted in the calling of the First CONTINENTAL CONGRESS.

**introversion** Preoccupation with one's own responses and impressions, coupled with a preference for reflection over action and a dislike of social activity. The term was coined by C.G. JUNG as a polar opposite to EXTROVERSION. Extreme introverts can be passive and withdrawn.

**intrusion** In geology, emplacement of rock material that was either forced or flowed into spaces among other rocks. An igneous intrusion, sometimes called a pluton, consists of magma that never reached the Earth's surface but filled cracks and faults, then cooled and hardened.

**Inuit** Collective name for the Eskimo people of Alaska, Greenland, and the Northwest Territories, Arctic Quebec, and N Labrador areas of Canada. Many Inuit still live by the traditional skills of fishing, trapping, and hunting.

**invertebrate** In zoology, the term for an animal without a backbone. There are more than one million species of invertebrates, divided into 30 major groups. One of these is Arthropoda (joint-legged animals), the largest of all animal phyla in numbers of species. Most are INSECTS, but it also includes crustaceans and ARACHNIDS. MOLLUSKS make up the second largest group of invertebrates. *See also* ARTHROPODS; CRUSTACEA; PHYLUM

**investment** Employment of money with the object of providing profit or income. An element of risk accompanies investment; generally, the higher the risk the greater the potential profit. Forms of investment include personal savings placed in a bank, factory plant and machinery, insurance, and stocks.

**in vitro fertilization (IVF)** Use of artificial techniques that join an egg with sperm outside a woman's body to help infertile couples to have children of their own. The basic technique of IVF involves removing eggs from a woman's OVARIES, fertilizing them in the laboratory, and then inserting them into the woman's UTERUS. In **zygote intrafallopian transfer (ZIFT)**, a fertilized egg (ZYGOTE) is returned to the FALLOPIAN TUBE, from which it makes its own way to the uterus. In **gamete intrafallopian transfer (GIFT)**, the eggs are removed, mixed with sperm, then both eggs and sperm are inserted into a Fallopian tube to be fertilized in the natural setting.

**involuntary muscle** One of three types of MUSCLE in the body, so called because, unlike SKELETAL MUSCLE, it is not under the conscious control of the brain but is stimulated by the AUTONOMIC NERVOUS SYSTEM and by HORMONES in the bloodstream. It is of two kinds. Smooth muscle is the muscle of the alimentary canal, blood vessels, and bladder. Cardiac muscle powers the HEART.

**Io** Large innermost satellite of JUPITER. It was discovered by GALILEO in 1609–10 and is larger than the Moon. It is more than 2,200mi (3,600km) in diameter and is 262,000mi (422,000km) above the surface of the planet.

**iodine** (symbol I) Nonmetallic element that is the least reactive of the HALOGEN group (elements in Group VII of the periodic table). The black volatile solid gives a violet vapor and has an unpleasant odor that resembles CHLORINE. Iodine was discovered in 1811 by the French chemist Bernard Courtois. Existing in seawater, seaweeds, and other plants, it is also extracted from Chile saltpeter and oil-well brine. Iodine is essential for the functioning of the THYROID GLAND. It is used as a medical antiseptic and in photography. Properties: at.no. 53; at.wt. 126.9; sp.gr. 4.93; m.p. 236.3°F (113.5°C); b.p. 363.9°F (184.4°C); most stable isotope $^{127}$I (100%).

**ion** Atom or group of atoms with an electric (positive or negative) charge resulting from the loss or gain of one or more electrons. Positive ions are called cations and move toward the CATHODE in ELECTROLYSIS; negative ions are called anions and move toward the ANODE. The process of forming ions is called ionization.

**Iona** Island off the coast of W Scotland in the Inner HEBRIDES. The island has an abbey, founded in AD 563 by St. Columba. Tourism is the main source of income. Area: 5sq mi (13sq km).

**Ionesco, Eugène** (1912–94) French dramatist. A major force behind the Theater of the ABSURD, Ionesco had his first success with *The Bald Prima Donna* (1950), a satire on the futility of verbal communication.

**Ionia** Historic region on the W coast of Asia Minor (Turkey), including neighboring Aegean islands. The area was settled by people from Mycenae in Greece in the 11th and 10th centuries BC. Miletus and EPHESUS became the most important of the prosperous Ionian cities. Ionia was conquered by the Persians in the 6th century BC, then fell under Athenian domination until the Persians regained control in the 4th century BC. After the conquests of ALEXANDER THE GREAT, Ionia was ruled by Hellenistic kings and from the 2nd century BC was part of the Roman empire.

**Ionians** In ancient Greece, inhabitants of Attica, Boeotia, and IONIA. They spoke a dialect distinct from that of the DORIANS and Aeolians. There was always potential hostility between Ionians and Dorians, neither regarding the other as fully Greek, which appears in the contest between Athens and Sparta in the PELOPONNESIAN WARS. The term is also applied to the inhabitants of Ionia alone.

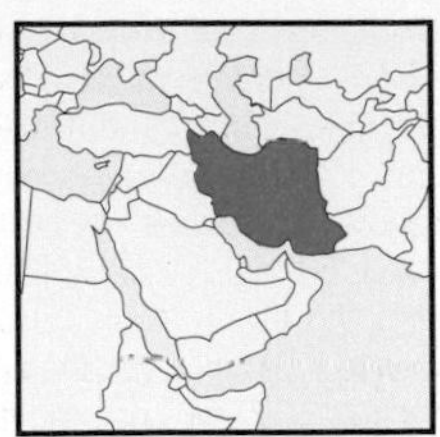

Iran's flag was adopted in 1980 by the country's Islamic government. The white strip contains the national emblem, which is the word for Allah in formal Arabic script. The words Allah Akbar (God is Great) are repeated 11 times on both the green and red stripes.

**AREA:** 636,293 sq mi (1,648,000sq km)
**POPULATION:** 59,964,000
**CAPITAL (POPULATION):** Tehran (6,475,527)
**GOVERNMENT:** Islamic republic
**ETHNIC GROUPS:** Persian 46%, Azerbaijani 17%, Kurdish 9%, Gilaki 5%, Luri, Mazandarani, Baluchi, Arab
**LANGUAGES:** Farsi (or Persian, official)
**RELIGIONS:** Islam 99%
**CURRENCY:** Rial = 100 dinars

The Islamic Republic of Iran contains a barren central plateau, which covers *c.*50% of the country. It includes the *Dasht-e-Kavir* (Great Salt Desert) and the *Dasht-e-Lut* (Great Sand Desert). The Elburz Mountains, N of the plateau, contain Iran's highest point, Damavand, at 18,368ft (5,604m) and the capital, TEHRAN. To the NE lies Iran's second city of MASHHAD. On the NW edge of the plateau lies the city of QOM. The W of the plateau is bounded by the Zagros Mountains, including the cities of ISFAHAN and SHIRAZ. In the far NW lies its largest lake, Lake Urmia, and the city of TABRIZ. The SHATT AL-ARAB forms part of its border with Iraq. Iran is susceptible to earthquakes.

## CLIMATE

Iran has hot summers and cold winters. There are wide regional variations in temperature and precipitation. Precipitation is highest in the N, often in the form of winter snow.

## VEGETATION

Forest covers *c.*10% of Iran, mainly in the Elburz and Zagros mountains. Semidesert and desert cover most of the country.

## HISTORY

Until 1935 Iran was known as PERSIA. Aryans settled in Persia *c.*2000 BC. The Persian king CYRUS THE GREAT founded the ACHAEMENID dynasty in 550 BC. The Persian empire fell to Alexander the Great in 331 BC. Persian rule was restored by the SASSANIDS in AD 224. Arabs conquered Persia in AD 641 and introduced ISLAM. For the next two centuries Persia was a center of ISLAMIC ART AND ARCHITECTURE. SELJUK Turks conquered Persia in the 11th century, but in 1220 the land was overrun by the MONGOLS. The SAFAVID dynasty (1501–1722) was founded by Shah ISMAIL, who established the SHIITE theocratic principles of modern Iran. NADIR SHAH expelled Afghan invaders. His despotic rule (1736–47) was noted for imperial ambition. The Qajar dynasty (1794–1925) witnessed the gradual decline of the Persian empire in the face of European expansion. Britain and Russia competed for influence in the area. The discovery of oil in SW Iran led to the Russian and British division of Iran (1907). In a 1919 treaty Iran effectively became a British protectorate. In 1921 Reza Khan seized power in a military coup, established the Pahlavi dynasty, and was elected shah (1925). He annulled the British treaty and began a process of modernization. In 1941 British and Soviet forces occupied Iran. Reza Pahlavi abdicated in favor of his son Muhammad Reza PAHLAVI. The 1943 Tehran Declaration guaranteed Iran's independence. In 1951 the oil industry was nationalized. The shah fled Iran, but soon returned with US backing and restored Western oil rights (1953). During the 1960s the shah undertook large-scale reforms, such as land ownership and extending the franchise to women (1963). Discontent surfaced over increasing westernization and economic inequality. The secret police crushed all dissent. Iranian clerics, led by Ayatollah KHOMEINI, openly voiced their disapproval of the secularization of society. In 1971 Britain withdrew its troops from the Persian Gulf. Iran increased its defense spending to become the largest military power in the region. Following his expulsion, Khomeini called for the abdication of the shah (1978).

In January 1979 the shah fled and Khomeini established an Islamic republic. The theocracy was profoundly conservative and anti-western. In July 1979 the oil industry was renationalized. In November 1979 militants seized the US embassy in Tehran, taking 52 American hostages. In September 1980 the Iraqi invasion marked the start of the IRAN-IRAQ WAR (1980–88). The war claimed more than 500,000 lives. In 1986 the US covertly agreed to supply Iran with arms, in return for influence over the return of hostages (*See* IRAN-CONTRA AFFAIR). In June 1989 Khomeini died and was succeeded by RAFSANJANI.

## POLITICS

Rafsanjani's regime began to ease relations with the West. Free market reforms were adopted and Iran supported international sanctions against Iraq in 1991. Allegations of support for international terrorism and development of a nuclear capability led the US to impose trade sanctions in 1995. In 1997 elections Rafsanjani was defeated by Muhammad Khatami.

## ECONOMY

Iran's prosperity is based on oil production (1995 GDP per capita, US$5,470). Oil accounts for 95% of its exports, and it is the world's 4th largest producer of crude oil. The Iran–Iraq war devastated Iran's industrial base. Oil revenue has been used to diversify the economy and develop manufacturing. Industry now employs 26% of the work force. Agriculture employs 30% of the work force. Iran is the world's largest producer of dates. Other major crops include wheat and barley. Iran is famous for its fine carpets. Tourism has great potential, but the political situation discourages many visitors.

**ionic bond** (electrovalent bond) Type of chemical bond in which ions of opposite charge are held together by electrostatic attraction.

**ionic compound** Substance formed by ionic bonding, a chemical bond of positively and negatively charged IONS. Salts, bases, and some acids are ionic compounds. As crystalline solids, such compounds have high melting points and boiling points. As solids, they are also nonconductors of electricity and are usually soluble in water but insoluble in organic solvents. In the liquid and molten states, ionic compounds are good conductors.

**Ionic order** One of the Classical ORDERS OF ARCHITECTURE.

**ionosphere** Wide region of IONS or charged particles in the ATMOSPHERE. It extends from about 37mi (60km) above the Earth's surface to the limits of the atmosphere in the VAN ALLEN RADIATION BELTS. Radio waves are deflected in the ionosphere, which makes possible long-distance radio communication.

**Iowa** State in N central US, lying between the Missouri and Mississippi rivers; the capital is DES MOINES. First explored by Europeans in 1673, the land was claimed for France in 1682. The region was sold to the US in the LOUISIANA PURCHASE of 1803. Iowa was admitted to the Union in 1846. Industrial development was encouraged after World War II. Originally prairie that was plowed to create farmland, the region is known for its fertile soil. Corn and other cereals are produced and Iowa stands second only to Texas in the raising of prime cattle. Industries include food processing and the production of farm machinery. Area: 56,290sq mi (145,790sq km). Pop. (1995 est.) 2,842,000.

**Iphigenia** In Greek legend, daughter of AGAMEMNON and CLYTEMNESTRA and sister of ELECTRA and ORESTES. She was sacrificed by her father to the goddess Artemis in exchange for favorable winds for his journey to Troy.

**IQ** (intelligence quotient) Classification of the supposed INTELLIGENCE of a person. It is computed by dividing the person's assessed "mental age" by his or her real age, then multiplying by 100. The "mental age" is determined by comparison to the average performance of people of various ages on a standard intelligence test. *See also* APTITUDE TEST

**IRA** *See* IRISH REPUBLICAN ARMY

**Iráklion** (Heraklion or Candia) Seaport and largest city on the island of Crete, S Greece; capital of Iráklion prefecture. Founded in the 9th century by the Saracens, it was conquered by the

## IRAQ

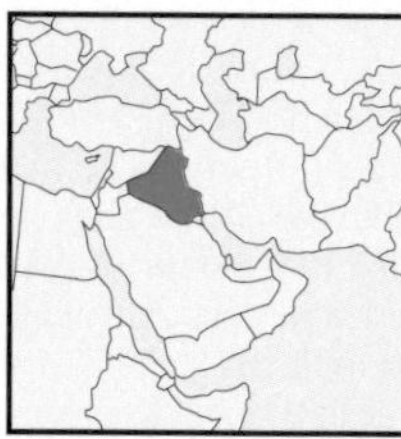

Iraq's flag was adopted in 1963, when the country was planning to federate with Egypt and Syria. It uses the four Pan-Arab colors. The three green stars symbolize the three countries. Iraq retained these stars even though the union failed to come into being.

**AREA:** 169,235sq mi (438,320sq km)
**POPULATION:** 19,290,000
**CAPITAL (POPULATION):** Baghdad (3,850,000)
**GOVERNMENT:** Republic
**ETHNIC GROUPS:** Arab 77%, Kurdish 19%, Turkmen, Persian, Assyrian
**LANGUAGES:** Arabic (official), Kurdish (official in Kurdish areas)
**RELIGIONS:** Islam 96%, Christianity 4%
**CURRENCY:** Iraqi dinar = 20 dirhams = 1,000 fils

The Republic of Iraq has only a narrow outlet, via the SHATT AL ARAB delta, to the PERSIAN GULF. Its main port of BASRA is located here. Part of the Syrian Desert forms most of W Iraq and there are mountains in the NE. Central Iraq is dominated by the valleys of the EUPHRATES and TIGRIS rivers, including the capital, BAGHDAD.

### CLIMATE

Iraq's climate varies from temperate in the N to subtropical in the S and E. The central feature is the lack of adequate rainfall, except in the NE.

### VEGETATION

Forests account for only 3% of the land. Dry grassland and low shrubs grow in the N. The desert provides good winter grazing land. The S is predominantly marshland.

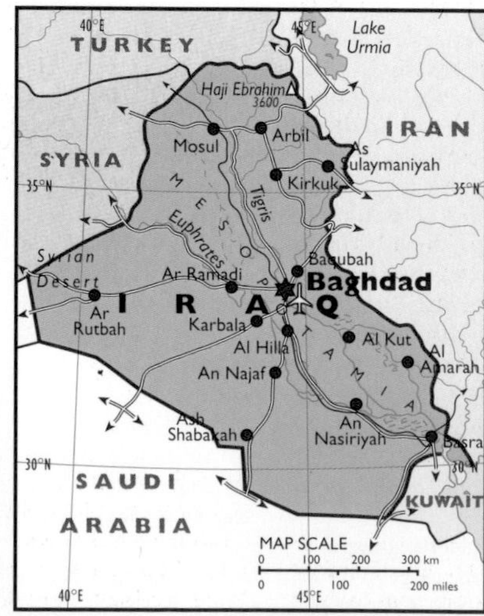


### HISTORY AND POLITICS

The ancient region of MESOPOTAMIA roughly corresponds with modern Iraq. SUMERIA was the world's first great civilization, *c.*3000 BC. In *c.*2340 BC SARGON I conquered Sumeria. In the 18th century BC, HAMMURABI established the first empire of BABYLONIA In the 8th century BC, Babylonia fell to ASSYRIA. In the 1st century BC, the Assyrian kings SARGON II, SENNACHERIB, and ASHURBANIPAL added to the splendor of NINEVEH. NEBUCHADNEZZAR extended the New Babylonian empire, and was responsible for the BABYLONIAN CAPTIVITY (from 586 BC). In 539 BC Babylon fell to CYRUS THE GREAT, who founded the Persian ACHAEMENID dynasty. Mesopotamia became part of the PERSIAN EMPIRE. ISLAM was introduced via the Arab conquest in AD 637. In the 8th century Baghdad became capital of the ABBASID caliphate (750–1258). In 1258 Mongols captured Baghdad. From 1534 Mesopotamia was part of the Ottoman empire. Britain invaded Mesopotamia in 1916. In 1920 it became a British mandated territory. Britain renamed the country Iraq, and set up an Arab monarchy. In 1932 Iraq finally became independent. Oil was first exported in 1934. As a member of the Arab League, Iraq participated in the 1948 ARAB–ISRAELI WAR. By the 1950s, oil dominated Iraq's economy and funded national development programs. In 1958 a proposal to form an Arab Union with Jordan precipitated a military coup. A republic was established and the king executed. In 1962 the KURDS of N Iraq demanded autonomy, beginning a protracted war of secession. In 1968 the BA'ATH PARTY emerged as the dominant power. Iraq also fought Israel in the YOM KIPPUR WAR (1973). In 1979 Saddam HUSSEIN became president and purged the Ba'ath Party. Iraq invaded Iran, starting the IRAN-IRAQ WAR (1980–88). The Kurdish rebellion continued and poison gas was used against villagers. In August 1990 Iraqi troops invaded Kuwait. In the ensuing GULF WAR (1991) Iraq was forced by an international coalition to withdraw from Kuwait. A revolt in the Kurdish N highlands and Shiite S marshlands was brutally suppressed. The UN formed "no fly" zones to protect the civilian population. In 1994 a Kurdish administration collapsed amid bitter infighting. In 1995 UN weapons inspectors (UNSCOM) discovered evidence of Iraq's attempts to gain a nuclear capability. Continued lack of cooperation with UNSCOM led to US and British bombing raids on Iraq in December 1998. Confrontations in the "no-fly" zones continued in 1999.

### ECONOMY

Protracted wars, sanctions, and financial mismanagement have all created economic chaos. Oil traditionally accounts for 98% of revenue and 45% of GNP. Since 1990 a UN embargo has halted oil exports. In 1996 a UN "food-for-oil" deal allowed the annual sale of $5 billion of oil. Farmland covers *c.*20% of Iraq. Major products include barley, cotton, dates, fruits, and livestock, but Iraq is dependent on food imports. Manufacturing is dominated by petroleum products.

Byzantines in 961, the Venetians in 1204, and the Ottoman Turks in 1669. It became part of Greece in 1913. The ruins of KNOSSOS are nearby. Tourism is important. Exports: wine, olive oil, almonds, raisins. Pop. (1991) 115,124.

**Iran** Islamic republic in SW Asia. *See* country feature, page 345

**Iran-Contra affair** (Irangate) US political scandal (1987–88). It involved a secret agreement to sell weapons to Iran via Israel, in order to secure the release of US hostages held in the Middle East. The profits were diverted to support the Nicaraguan CONTRAS in their attempt to overthrow the SANDINISTA government. The affair, negotiated by Colonel Oliver NORTH with the support of national security advisers to the White House, was revealed by a congressional investigative committee in 1987. North and his superiors, plus several other officials, were later convicted of various charges, including obstructing Congress. In 1992 they were controversially pardoned by President BUSH.

**Iranian languages** Group of languages forming a subdivision of the Indo-Iranian family of INDO-EUROPEAN LANGUAGES. The major Iranian languages are Persian, Pashto, Kurdish, Mazanderani, and Gilaki (of Iran), Baluchi (of Iran and Pakistan), and Tajik and Ossetic, spoken in the republic of Tajikistan and in South Ossetia (a part of Georgia) and North Ossetia (an autonomous region of the Russian Federation).

**Iran-Iraq War** (1980–88) Contest for supremacy in the Persian Gulf. The war began when Iraq, partly in response to Iranian encouragement of revolt among the Shiites of S Iraq, invaded Iran, which was disorganized after the Islamic fundamentalist revolution of 1979. Iraq's objective was the SHATT AL ARAB waterway, but stiff Iranian resistance checked its advance and forced its withdrawal (1982). The conflict bogged down in stalemate, with sporadic Iranian offensives. US-led intervention in 1987 was seen as tacit support for Iraq. A UN ceasefire resolution (1987) was accepted by Iraq and, after several Iraqi successes, by Iran also. Estimated total casualties were more than 1 million.

**Iraq** Republic in SW Asia. *See* country feature

**Ireland, John Nicholson** (1879–1962) British composer, influenced by BRAHMS, DVOŘÁK, and RAVEL. His works, firmly grounded in ROMANTICISM and often inspired by landscape, include *The Forgotten Rite* (1913), *Mai-Dun* (1921), *These Things Shall Be* (1937), and the overture *Satyricon* (1946).

**Ireland** Second largest island of the BRITISH ISLES. Ireland is W of Great Britain. The Irish Sea and St. Georges Channel run between the two islands. At present, Ireland is divided into two separate countries, the Republic of IRELAND and NORTHERN IRELAND. **Land and climate** The central area of Ireland is a lowland with a mild, wet climate. This area is covered with peat bogs (an important source of fuel) and sections of fertile limestone (the location of dairy farming). Most coastal regions are barren highlands. The interior of Ireland has many lakes and wide rivers (loughs). It boasts the longest river in the British Isles, the SHANNON. **History** From *c.*3rd century BC to the late 8th century, Ireland was divided into five kingdoms inhabited by Celtic and pre-Celtic tribes. The Danes invaded in the 8th century AD, establishing trading towns such as DUBLIN and creating new kingdoms. In 1014 Brian Boru defeated the Danes, and for the next 150 years Ireland was free from invasion but subject to clan warfare. In 1171 Henry II of England invaded Ireland and established English control. In the late 13th century, an Irish parliament was formed. English dominance was threatened by the Scottish invasion of 1315. In the late 15th century HENRY VII restored English hegemony and began the plantation of Ireland by English settlers. Edward Poynings forced the Irish Parliament to pass Poynings Law (1495), stating that future Irish legislation must be sanctioned by the English Privy Council. Under JAMES I the plantation of ULSTER was intensified. An Irish rebellion (1641–49) was eventually thwarted by Oliver Cromwell. During the GLORIOUS REVOLUTION Irish Catholics supported JAMES II, while Ulster Protestants supported WILLIAM III. After James' defeat, the English-controlled Irish Parliament passed a series of punitive laws against Catholics. In 1782 Henry GRATTAN forced trade concessions and the repeal of Poynings Law. William PITT's government passed the Act of UNION (1801), which abolished the Irish assembly and created the United Kingdom of Great Britain and Ireland. In 1829, largely due to the efforts of Daniel O'CONNELL, the Act of CATHOLIC EMANCIPATION was passed, which secured Irish representation in the British Parliament. A blight ruined the Irish potato crop and caused the Great Potato Famine (1845–49). Nationalist demands intensified. Gladstone failed to secure HOME RULE, amid mounting pressure from fearful Ulster Protestants. In 1905 Arthur GRIFFITH founded SINN FÉIN. In 1914 Home Rule was agreed, but implementation was suspended during World War I. In the EASTER RISING (April 1916) Irish Nationalists announced the creation of the Republic of Ireland. The British Army's brutal crushing of the rebellion was a propaganda victory for Sinn Féin and led to a landslide victory in Irish elections (1918). During 1918–21 the IRISH REPUBLICAN ARMY (IRA), founded by Michael COLLINS, fought a guerrilla war against British forces. In 1920 a new Home Rule bill established separate parliaments for Ulster and Catholic Ireland. Sinn Féin initially opposed the bill, but the Anglo-Irish Treaty (1921) led to the creation of an Irish Free State in January 1922 and *de facto* acceptance of partition. (For history post-1922, *see* IRELAND, NORTHERN; IRELAND, REPUBLIC OF)

**Ireland, Northern** Part of the UNITED KINGDOM, 26 districts occupying the NE of IRELAND, traditionally divided into the six counties of Antrim, Armagh, Derry, Down, Fermanagh, and Tyrone; the capital is BELFAST. Other major towns include DERRY, Coleraine, Ballymena, Lisburn, Newry, Armagh, and Enniskillen. (For land and climate, and pre-1922 history, *see* IRELAND.) **Economy** More than 80% of the land is farmed (chief crops are potatoes and barley). Heavy industry is concentrated around the port of Belfast. Industries include shipbuilding, vehicle manufacture, and textiles (especially linen). The majority population is Protestant; Catholics form a significant minority of 38%. Northern Ireland's economic prosperity is not equally shared: the Catholic community has a much higher rate of unemployment. The economy has been devastated by civil war. **History and Politics** In 1920 the six counties of Ulster became the self-governing province of Northern Ireland with a separate, Protestant-dominated parliament. The British government affirmed the inclusion of Northern Ireland within the UK under the principle of self-determination. The Irish Free State (now Republic of Ireland) constitution upheld the unity of the island of Ireland. In 1955 the IRISH REPUBLICAN ARMY (IRA) began a campaign of violence for the creation of an independent, unified Ireland. In 1962 the Republic of Ireland condemned the use of terrorism. Northern Catholics felt aggrieved at discrimination in employment, housing, and political representation. In 1967 the Civil Rights Association was established to campaign for equal rights. In 1968 civil rights marches resulted in violent clashes, especially in Derry. Catholic fear of the increasing Protestant-domination of local security forces was compounded when the Royal Ulster Constabulary (RUC) was supplemented by the sectarian Ulster Defense Regiment (UDR). The British Army was brought in to protect the Catholic populations in Belfast and Derry. The IRA and Protestant LOYALIST paramilitary organizations, such as the Ulster Defense Association (UDA), increased their campaigns of sectarian violence. In 1972 the Northern Ireland parliament (Stormont) was suspended, replaced by direct rule from Westminster. On 30 January 1972 ("Bloody Sunday"), British troops shot and killed 13 civil rights demonstrators. In 1974 the Council of Ireland, formed by the British and Irish governments to promote cooperation between Ulster and the Irish Republic, quickly collapsed under pressure from a Unionist-led general strike. The IRA campaign widened to include terrorist attacks on Great Britain and British military bases in W Europe. In 1981 hunger strikes by IRA prisoners were more successful in gaining worldwide sympathy. In 1985 the ANGLO-IRISH AGREEMENT gave the Republic of Ireland a consultative role in the government of Northern Ireland. In 1986 a Northern Ireland Assembly was reestablished, but quickly failed under the Unionists' boycott. In 1993 (following secret talks between the British government and SINN FÉIN) the DOWNING STREET DECLARATION offered all-party negotiations following a cessation of violence. A ceasefire in 1994 raised hopes of an end to a sectarian conflict that had claimed more than 2,700 lives. Disputes over arms decommissions stalled the

**IOWA**
**Statehood:**
December 28, 1846
**Nickname:**
Hawkeye state
**State bird:**
Eastern goldfinch
**State flower:**
Wild rose
**State tree:**
Oak
**State motto:**
Our liberties we prize and our rights we will maintain

▲ **iris** Grown mainly in temperate regions for displays, the many plants of the genus *iris* usually feature narrow, pointed leaves. The flowers are either purple, white, or yellow.

process and the IRA resumed its terrorist campaign in Great Britain. In July 1997 another ceasefire was agreed, and in October Sinn Féin and Unionists took part in joint peace talks for the first time since partition. On 10 April 1998 the **Good Friday Agreement** provided for an elected Northern Ireland assembly, a North-South Ministerial Council, and a British-Irish Council. The Republic of Ireland agreed to abandon its constitutional claim to Northern Ireland. In May 1998 the agreement was overwhelmingly approved in referenda in Northern Ireland and the Republic of Ireland. In June 1998 elections were held for the new Northern Ireland Assembly. David Trimble of the Ulster Unionists became First Minister. In 1999 the timing of the decommissioning of terrorist weapons continued to the main stumbling block to peace. Area: 5,452sq mi (14,121sq km). Pop. (1991) 1,573,836.

**Ireland, Republic of** Country in NW Europe. *See* country feature

**Irian Jaya** (West Irian, or Irian Barat) Province of E Indonesia, comprising the W half of New Guinea and adjacent islands; the capital is Djajapura. First explored by Europeans in the 16th century, it was formally claimed by the Netherlands in 1828 and became known as Dutch New Guinea. It achieved independence in 1962 and was incorporated into Indonesia the following year. In the central part of the province, a mountain range rising to more than 16,500ft (5,000m) runs *c.*400mi (640km) from E to W. Much of the region N of the mountain range is covered by tropical rain forest. Irian Jaya is noted for the richness of its flora and fauna. The economy is predominantly agricultural, the chief products including copra, peanuts, rice, and timber. Copper and crude oil are exported. Area: 162,900sq mi (422,170sq km). Pop. (1990) 1,648,708.

**iridium** (symbol Ir) Silver-white, metallic element discovered in 1804 by the English chemist Smithson Tennant. A platinum-type metal, iridium is hard and brittle and the most corrosion-resistant metal. It is used in making surgical tools, scientific instruments, pen tips, and electrical contacts. Properties: at.no. 77; at.wt. 192.22; sp.gr. 22.42; m.p. 4,370°F (2,410°C); b.p. 7,466°F (4,130°C); most common isotope $^{193}$Ir (62.6%).

**iris** Colored part of the EYE. It controls the amount of light that enters the PUPIL in the center of the eye by increasing or decreasing the size of the pupil. These changes are brought about by muscles in the iris contracting or relaxing.

**Iris** In Greek mythology, goddess of the rainbow and messenger of the gods. Depicted as swift-footed, golden-winged, and

## IRELAND

Ireland's flag was adopted in 1922 after the country had become independent from Britain, though nationalists had used it as early as 1848. Green represents Ireland's Roman Catholics, orange the Protestants, and the white a desire for peace between the two.

**AREA:** 27,135sq mi (70,280sq km)
**POPULATION:** 3,547,000
**CAPITAL (POPULATION):** Dublin (915,516)
**GOVERNMENT:** Multiparty republic
**ETHNIC GROUPS:** Irish 94%
**LANGUAGES:** Irish and English (both official)
**RELIGIONS:** Christianity (Roman Catholic 93%, Protestant 3%)
**CURRENCY:** Irish pound = 100 new pence

The Republic of Ireland occupies more than 80% of the island of Ireland. It is divided into 4 provinces of 26 counties (*see* individual articles). The capital is DUBLIN (Gaelic, *Baile Atha Cliath*). Other major cities include CORK and LIMERICK. (For land, climate, and pre-1922 history and politics, *see* IRELAND)

### History and Politics

In January 1922 the Irish Free State was created as a Dominion within the British empire. Arthur GRIFFITH of SINN FÉIN became taoiseach. Civil war (1922–23) ensued. The anti-settlement party, led by Eamon DE VALERA, were defeated by Irish Free State forces led by Michael COLLINS. Collins was assassinated and William Cosgrave became prime minister (1922–32). In 1926 De Valera formed a separate party, FIANNA FÁIL, and became taoiseach (1932–48, 1951–54, 1957–59). In 1933 FINE GAEL was founded. In 1937 a new constitution declared the sovereign nation of Éire to be the whole island of Ireland and abolished the oath of loyalty to the English crown. During World War II Éire remained neutral. The IRISH REPUBLICAN ARMY (IRA) pursued a pro-German line. In 1949 Ireland became a republic outside of the Commonwealth. It reiterated its claim to the six counties of Northern Ireland. In 1955 Ireland was admitted to the United Nations. In 1959 de Valera became president (1959–73). During the 1950s, the IRA was banned by both Irish governments and, as a secret organization, it conducted bombing campaigns in Northern Ireland and England. In 1973 Ireland joined the European Community (EC). During the 1980s a series of coalition governments led by Charles HAUGHEY and Dr. Garrett Fitzgerald caused political uncertainty. The ANGLO-IRISH AGREEMENT (1985) gave Ireland a consultative role in the affairs of Northern Ireland. In 1990 Mary ROBINSON became Ireland's first female president. The DOWNING STREET DECLARATION (1993), signed by John Major and Albert REYNOLDS, continued the momentum for a peaceful settlement in Northern Ireland. In 1995 elections Reynolds was defeated by John BRUTON, leader of Fine Gael. Following a 1995 referendum, divorce was legalized. In 1997 elections Bertie AHERN became taoiseach and Mary McAleese became president. In the Good Friday Agreement (1998) the Republic gave up its constitutional claim to Northern Ireland and a North-South Ministerial Council was established. In 1999 Ireland joined the EURO.

### Economy

Ireland's economy has benefited greatly from its membership of the EUROPEAN UNION (EU). COMMON AGRICULTURAL POLICY (CAP) grants have enabled the modernization of farming. Agriculture employs 14% of the work force. Food and live animals account for more than 20% of exports. There is a marked contrast in land use between the poorer W areas and the rich E lowlands of Wicklow and Westford. Major products include cereals, cattle and dairy products, sheep, sugar beets, and potatoes. Fishing is also an important economic activity. Industry has greatly expanded and accounts for 35% of GNP. Traditional sectors like brewing, distilling, and textiles have been supplemented by high-tech industries such as electronics. The service sector employs 57% of the work force and accounts for more than 50% of GDP (1995 GDP per capita, US$15,680). Tourism is the most important component; receipts from tourism totalled US$1.62 billion (1992). Unemployment is high and economic migration, though decreasing, is common.

robed in bright colors, she appears in numerous classical writings, including Euripides' *Herakles*.

**iris** Genus of *c*.300 species of monocotyledonous flowering plants widely distributed, mostly in temperate areas. They may have BULBS or RHIZOMES. Height: up to 3ft (90cm). Family Iridaceae. *See also* CROCUS; GLADIOLUS

**Irish** *See* GAELIC

**Irish literature** Earliest written works, mainly heroic sagas, date from the 7th to the 12th centuries and were composed in GAELIC. The **Fenian cycle** includes the legendary exploits of FINN MAC CUMHAIL. Leading figures in ENGLISH LITERATURE, such as Jonathan SWIFT, Laurence STERNE and Oscar WILDE, were of Irish descent. Inspired by the movement for Irish Home Rule, the late 19th and early 20th centuries saw an Irish literary renaissance. The revival, led by W.B. YEATS, drew on the traditions of Gaelic culture. The ABBEY THEATRE hosted the resurgence in Irish drama, staging plays by J.M. SYNGE, George Bernard SHAW, and Sean O'CASEY. James JOYCE and Samuel BECKETT reflected on Irish culture from self-exile. Leading contemporary Irish writers include Seamus HEANEY. *See also* BEHAN, BRENDAN; COLUM, PADRAIC; RUSSELL, GEORGE

**Irish Republican Army (IRA)** Guerrilla organization, dedicated to the forceful reunification of IRELAND. Formed in 1919 by Michael COLLINS as the militant wing of SINN FÉIN, the IRA waged war against British rule. Some members ("irregulars") rejected the Anglo-Irish Treaty of 1921, fighting a civil war until 1923. During World War 2 it was pro-German. Outlawed by both Irish governments in the 1950s, the IRA went underground. In 1970 the organization split into an "official" wing (which emphasized political activities) and a "provisional" wing (committed to armed struggle). The **Provisional IRA** perpetrated terrorist acts, including the Birmingham pub bombing (1974), the murder of Lord Mountbatten (1979), the attempted assasination of the British prime minister in Brighton (1984) and Downing Street (1991), and the Remembrance Day bombing in Enniskillen (1987). In 1994 it declared a ceasefire, but resumed its campaign in 1996. In 1997 it announced another ceasefire. The timing of the decommissioning of IRA weapons is a major issue in the peace process.

**Irish Sea** Part of the Atlantic Ocean, lying between Ireland and Britain. It is connected to the Atlantic by the North Channel (N) and by St. George's Channel (S). Scotland, Wales, and England are on its E shore and Ireland on the W shore. Area: 40,000sq mi (103,600sq km).

**Irkutsk** City on the Angara River, E Siberia, Russia; capital of Irkutsk oblast. It grew as a result of trade with China and the completion of the Trans-Siberian Railroad. Irkutsk is an important industrial and educational center. Gold from the Lena goldfields is transshipped, and there is also trade in furs. Industries: ship repairing, timber, machine tools, heavy machinery, oil refining, hydroelectricity. Pop. (1992) 639,000.

**iron** Common metallic element (symbol Fe) of the first transition series, known from the earliest times. Its chief ores are hematite ($Fe_2O_3$), magnetite ($Fe_3O_4$), and iron pyrites ($FeS_2$). It is obtained in a blast furnace by reducing the oxide with carbon monoxide from coke (carbon), using limestone to form a slag. The pure metal – a reactive soft element – is rarely used; most iron is alloyed with carbon and other elements in the various forms of STEEL. Properties: at.no. 26; at.wt. 55.847; sp.gr. 7.86; m.p. 2,795°F (1,535°C); b.p. 4,982°F (2,750°C); most common isotope $^{56}Fe$ (91.66%).

**Iron Age** Period succeeding the BRONZE AGE, dating from about 1100 BC in the Near East, later in W Europe. During this period people learned to smelt iron, although the HITTITES had probably developed the first significant iron industry in Armenia soon after 2000 BC.

**Iron Curtain** Term describing the barrier between communist East Europe and the capitalist West during the COLD WAR. The term passed into common use after it was used by Winston Churchill in a speech at Fulton, Missouri, in March 1946.

**irony** Use of words to convey, often satirically, the opposite of their literal meaning. It was first developed by Plato in his Socratic dialogues, in which Socrates often feigned ignorance to evoke admissions from other people.

**Iroquois Confederacy** League of Native North Americans occupying the Mohawk Valley and the Lakes area of New York state. They called themselves Oñgwanósioñi (Hodinonhsioni), "people of the long house," after the distinctive shape of their bark dwellings. The original tribes were the MOHAWK, SENECA, ONONDAGA, CAYUGA, and Oneida. The Tuscarora joined later. The Iroquois had a highly developed political system and were renowned warriors. Their total number has halved since 1600; in the mid-1990s they numbered *c*.10,000, living in New York, Wisconsin, Oklahoma, and Canada.

**Iroquois War** (1642–53) Territorial expansion war carried out by the IROQUOIS CONFEDERACY. The Iroquois, or Five Nations, enlarged their New York territory to the N, W, and, S by dispersing the HURONS (1649), the Tabacco, Neutral Nations (1650), the Eries (1656), Conestogas (1675), and Illinois Native Americans (1684).

**irrational number** In mathematics, any number that cannot be expressed as the ratio of two INTEGERS. An example is $\sqrt{2}$: like other irrational numbers, its expression as a decimal is infinite and nonrepeating. Irrational numbers, together with the RATIONAL NUMBERS, make up the set of REAL NUMBERS.

**Irrawaddy** (Irawadi) River in central Burma (Myanmar), formed by the union of the Mali and Nmai rivers. A vast delta extends 180mi (290km) from Henzada to the Andaman Sea. One of Asia's major rivers, it lies at the center of an important rice-producing region. Length: *c*.1,300mi (2,100km).

**irrigation** Artificial watering of land for growing crops. Irrigation enables crops to grow in regions with inadequate precipitation. The first irrigation systems date from before 3000 BC in Egypt, Asia, and the Middle East. Today, most water for irrigation is surface water (from streams, rivers, and lakes) or ground water (obtained from wells). In some regions, fresh water for irrigation is obtained by DESALINATION. Canals, ditches, pumps, and pipes are used to convey water to fields.

**Irving, Washington** (1783–1859) US essayist and short-story writer. He wrote the burlesque *History of New York* (1809) under the pseudonym Dietrich Knickerbocker. He is most famous for the stories *Rip Van Winkle* and *The Legend of Sleepy Hollow*, which were written during his 17 years in Europe. He returned to the US in 1832, where his continuing literary output included *Astoria* (1836).

**Isaac** Biblical character of the Old Testament, and one of the Patriarchs. He was the only son of ABRAHAM and Sarah. As a test of faith in God, Abraham was prepared to sacrifice Isaac as commanded, but at the last minute, Isaac was told to sacrifice a lamb instead. Isaac took as his wife Rebecca and became the father of JACOB and ESAU.

**Isabella I** (1451–1504) Queen of Castile (1474–1504), whose marriage to Ferdinand II of Aragon (FERDINAND V of Castile and León) led to the unification of Spain and its emergence as a dominant European power. Daughter of John II, she won a dispute over the succession by 1468 and married Ferdinand (1469). With his support she reformed royal administration in Castile and encouraged humanist scholarship in Spain, although she was also responsible for the Spanish INQUISITION (1487) and the expulsion of the Jews (1492). Her popularity was enhanced by the conquest of Granada (1492). She supported the voyages of COLUMBUS, which led to the establishment of the Spanish empire in the New World.

**Isabella II** (1830–1904) Queen of Spain (1833–68). The daughter of Ferdinand VII, she was challenged by her uncle, Don Carlos, resulting in the first CARLIST civil war. A liberal revolt led by army officers (1868) forced her into exile (1868), and in 1870 she abdicated in favor of her son, ALFONSO XII.

**Isaiah** (Isaias) (active *c*.8th century BC) Old Testament prophet who was active in Jerusalem from the 740s until the end of the century and gave his name to the Old Testament Book of Isaiah. Isaiah's career coincided with the westward expansion of the Assyrian empire. The Book of Isaiah was written in both verse and prose. Only part of it is attributed to Isaiah. The rest has been thought to be the work of one or even two authors from a later period. The book contrasts Judah's perilous present-day state with glimpses into the future, when God shall send a king to rule over his people.

**ISDN** Acronym for INTEGRATED SERVICES DIGITAL NETWORK

**Isfahan** (Esfahan) City in central Iran, on the Zaindeh River.

▲ **iris** Grown mainly in temperate regions for displays, the many plants of the genus *iris* usually feature narrow, pointed leaves. The flowers are either purple, white, or yellow.

► **Islamic architecture** Much of Islamic architecture, such as this mosque in Tehran, Iran, is decorated with complex and colorful geometric shapes, often inscribed with the name of the prophet Muhammad. Domes and minarets are common architectural forms.

The ancient city of Aspadana, it was occupied successively by Arabs, Seljuk Turks, and Mongols. In the late 16th century the SAFAVID dynasty made it their capital and transformed it into one of the most beautiful cities of the age. After its capture by the Afghans in 1722, the city declined. It has steel and textile industries as well as the traditional crafts of carpets and rugs, metalwork, and silverware. Pop. (1986) 986,753.

**Isherwood, Christopher William Bradshaw** (1904–86) British writer. His novels, characteristically dealing with the sensibility of the homosexual artist, include *All the Conspirators* (1928) and *Mr. Norris Changes Trains* (1935), set in pre-war Germany. The musical *Cabaret* (1966) was based on a short story from his *Goodbye to Berlin* (1939). He collaborated on three plays with W.H. AUDEN, including *The Ascent of F6* (1936). He emigrated to the US in 1939 and became interested in Hinduism.

**Ishiguro, Kazuo** (1954– ) Japanese novelist, resident in the UK since 1960. His first novels, *A Pale View of Hills* (1982) and *An Artist of the Floating World* (1986), are set in Japan. *The Remains of the Day* (1989) won the Booker Prize. *The Unconsoled* (1995) marked a departure from the elegantly crafted economy of his early style.

**Ishmael** Any of several biblical figures, most notably Abraham's son by Hagar and half brother to Isaac. He married an Egyptian and fathered 12 sons and one daughter, who married Esau, Isaac's son.

**Ishtar** Principal goddess of Assyro-Babylonian mythology. She is the daughter of both Anu, the sky god, and Sin, the moon god. Through the centuries, she came to exhibit diverse attributes, those of a compassionate mother goddess and of a lustful goddess of sex and war. Ishtar is identified with the Sumerian Inanna, Phoenician Astarte, and the biblical Ashtoreth.

**isinglass** Clear, almost pure gelatin that is prepared from the air bladders of sturgeon and other sources. It is used primarily to clarify wines and beers. The name also refers to an abundant silicate material, also called muscovite, used as an insulator.

**Isis** In Egyptian mythology, wife and sister of OSIRIS, and mother of Horus. After Osiris was murdered, Isis put together the dismembered parts of Osiris's body and magically revived him. The epitome of fidelity and maternal devotion, she was worshiped throughout the ancient world up through Roman times.

**Islam** (Arabic, submission to God) Monotheistic religion founded by MUHAMMAD in Arabia in the early 7th century. At the heart of Islam stands the KORAN, considered the divine revelation in Arabic of God to Muhammad. Members of the faith (MUSLIMS) date the beginning of Islam from AD 622, the year of the HEJIRA. Muslims submit to the will of Allah by five basic precepts (pillars). First, the *shahadah*, "there is no God but Allah, and Muhammad is his prophet." Second, *salah*, five daily ritual prayers. At the MOSQUE a Muslim performs ritual ablutions before praying to God in a attitude of submission, kneeling on a prayer mat facing MECCA with head bowed, then rising with hands cupped behind the ears to hear God's message. Third, *zakat* or alms-giving. Fourth, *sawm*, fasting during RAMADAN. Fifth, HAJJ, the pilgrimage to Mecca. The rapid growth in Islam during the 8th century can be attributed to the unification of the temporal and spiritual. The community leader (CALIPH) is both religious and social leader. The Koran was soon supplemented by the informal, scriptual elaborations of the Sunna (Muhammad's sayings and deeds), collated as the Hadith. A Muslim must also abide by the SHARIA or religious law. While Islam stresses the importance of the unity of the *summa* (nation) of Islam, several distinctive branches have developed, such as SUNNI, SHI'A, and SUFISM. Today it is estimated that there are 935 million Muslims worldwide.

**Islamabad** Capital of Pakistan, in the N of the country. Construction of a new capital to replace KARACHI began in 1960, and in 1967 Islamabad became the official capital. It lies at the heart of an agricultural region, but administrative and governmental activities predominate. Pop. (1981) 201,000.

**Islamic art and architecture** Lacking a strong, independent tradition, Islamic art began to develop as a unique synthesis of the diverse cultures of conquered countries from the 7th century. Early Islamic art and craft is perhaps best illustrated in the architecture of the MOSQUE. Two of the most impressive surviving examples of early Islamic architecture are the DOME OF THE ROCK (685–92) in Jerusalem and the UMAYYAD Mosque in Damascus (*c*.705). Common architectural forms, such as the DOME, MINARET, *sahn* (courtyard), and the often highly-decorated *mihrab* (prayer niche) and *mimbar* (prayer pulpit) developed in the 9th century. Mosques also acquired rich surface decorations of mosaic, carved stone, and paint. In Spain, Moorish architecture developed independently after the Umayyads were forced to flee there by the ABBASID dynasty. It is characterized by its use of the horseshoe arch, faience, and stone lattice screens, as seen in the ALHAMBRA. Islamic CAIRO is a world heritage site of Muslim architecture, often derived from Persian innovation. The Ibn Tulun Mosque (879) is a fine example of early brick and stucco form. The Al-Azhar mosque displays 10th century developments. The masterwork of Persian mosques, with their distinctive onion-shaped domes and slender pencil minarets, is the ISFAHAN Imperial Mosque (1585–1612). The Persians influenced the Islamic architecture of India and Turkey. Because of a religious stricture on the representation of nature, Islamic art developed stylized figures, geometrical designs, and floral-like decorations (arabesques). The KORAN was the focus for much of the development of calligraphy and illumination. Many of the cursive scripts were developed in the 10th century, and the most commonly used script, Nastaliq, was perfected in the 15th century. Muslim secular art included highly ornamented metalwork (often inlaid with red copper), which developed in the 13th century around Mosul, in N MESOPOTAMIA. The art of pottery and ceramics was extremely advanced, with excellent glazes and decoration. The Islamic *minai* (enamel) technique reached its zenith in the 16th century in Isfahan, where entire walls were decorated in faience. Perhaps the best-known art of the Islamic world is that of rugmaking.

**Isle of Man** *See* MAN, ISLE OF

**Isle of Wight** *See* WIGHT, ISLE OF

**Ismail** (1486–1524) Shah of Persia (1501–24), founder of the SAFAVID dynasty. A national and religious hero in Iran, he reestablished Persian independence and established SHI'A Islam as the state religion. He warred successfully against the UZBEKS in 1510 but was defeated by the Ottoman sultan, Selim I, at the battle of Chaldiran in 1514.

**Ismailis** (Seveners) Smaller of the two SHI'A branches of ISLAM. Ismailis believe that Muhammad, the son of ISMAIL, was the seventh and last IMAM. They are based mainly in India and Pakistan.

**Ismail Pasha** (1830–95) Viceroy and Khedive of Egypt

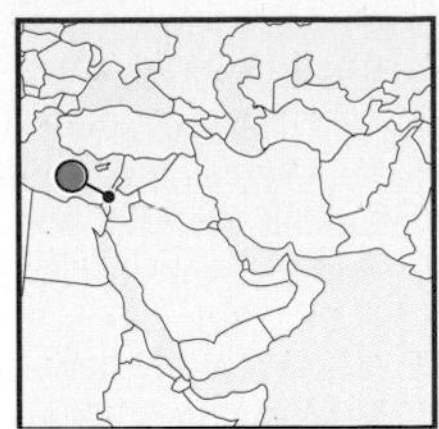

Israel's flag was adopted when the Jewish state declared itself independent in 1948. The blue and white stripes are based on the *tallit*, a Hebrew prayer shawl. The ancient, six-pointed Star of David is in the center. The flag was designed in America in 1891.

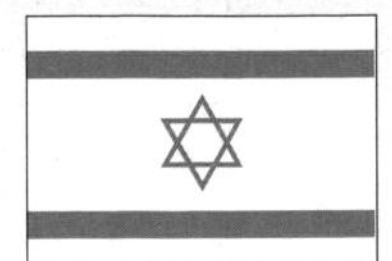

**AREA:** 10,290sq mi (26,650sq km)
**POPULATION:** 4,946,000
**CAPITAL (POPULATION):** Jerusalem (544,200)
**GOVERNMENT:** Multiparty republic
**ETHNIC GROUPS:** Jewish 82%, Arab and others 18%
**LANGUAGES:** Hebrew and Arabic (both official)
**RELIGIONS:** Judaism 82%, Islam 14%, Christianity 2%, Druse and others 2%
**CURRENCY:** New Israeli sheqel = 100 agorat

The State of Israel, a small nation in the E Mediterranean, can be divided into four geographical regions: a narrow, fertile coastal plain, site of Israel's main industrial cities, Haifa and Tel Aviv; the Judeo-Galilean highlands; the Negev Desert occupies the S half of Israel extending to Elat on the Gulf of Aqaba and includes the city of Beersheba; in the E lies part of the Great Rift Valley, including the Sea of Galilee, the Jordan River, and the Dead Sea, the world's lowest point at −1,322ft (−403m). Israeli-occupied territories are the Gaza Strip, the West Bank (including East Jerusalem), and the Golan Heights.

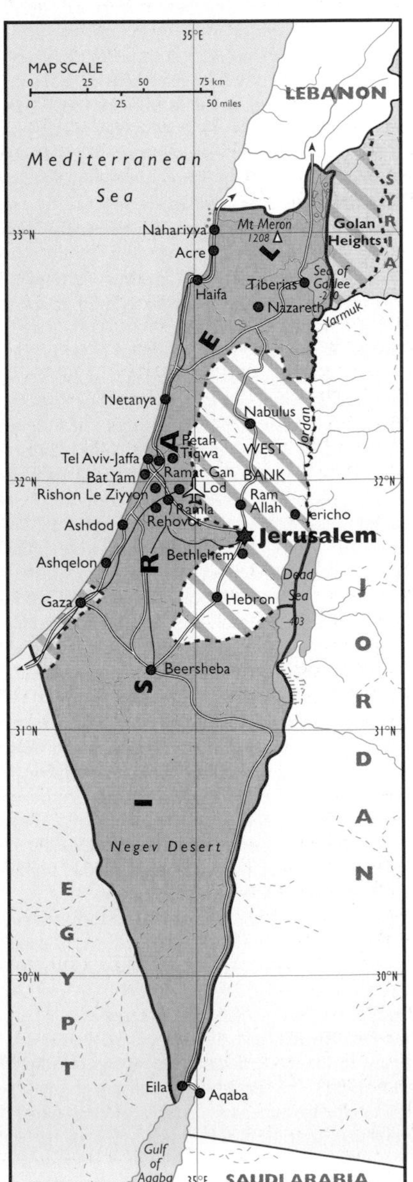


## Climate

Israel has a Mediterranean climate with hot, dry, summers and mild and rainy winters. The Dead Sea region has only 2.5in (70mm) of rainfall a year, and temperatures rise to 120°F (49°C).

## Vegetation

Despite reforestation schemes, forests account for only 6% of land use. Farmland covers *c*.20% of the land, with pasture making up another 40%. The arid Negev Desert is partly irrigated with water pumped from the Sea of Galilee.

## History and Politics

Israel is part of a historic region which makes up most of the Biblical Holy Lands. (for history pre-1947, *See* Palestine) In the late 19th century Zionism began to agitate for a Jewish homeland. In 1947 the UN agreed to partition Palestine into an Arab and a Jewish state, but the plan was rejected by the Arabs. On May 18, 1948 the State of Israel was proclaimed. Hundreds of thousands of Palestinians fled. In the first of the Arab–Israeli Wars Egypt, Iraq, Jordan, Lebanon, and Syria invaded. The Haganah successfully defended the state. An Israeli government was formed with Chaim Weizmann as president and David Ben-Gurion as prime minister. In 1949 Israel was admitted to the UN, and the capital transferred from Tel Aviv to Jerusalem. In 1950 the Law of Return provided free citizenship for all immigrant Jews. Following Egypt's nationalization of the Suez Canal, Israel captured Gaza and the Sinai peninsula. In 1957 Israel withdrew. In 1963 Ben-Gurion resigned and Levi Eshkol became prime minister (1963–69). In 1967 Nasser blockaded Elat. Israel's defense minister Moshe Dayan launched a preemptive attack against Egypt and Syria. Within six days Israel had occupied the Gaza Strip, the Sinai peninsula, the Golan Heights, the West Bank, and East Jerusalem. Eshkol died in 1969 and Golda Meir became prime minister (1969–74). On October 6, 1973 (Yom Kippur), Egypt and Syria attacked Israeli positions in Sinai and the Golan Heights. Recovering from the initial surprise, Israeli troops launched a counteroffensive and retained the 1967 gains. Yitzhak Rabin's government (1974–77) is chiefly remembered for the daring rescue of Israeli hostages at Entebbe. Rabin was succeeded by Menachem Begin (1977–83). Begin's hard-line government encouraged Jewish settlement on the West Bank and suppressed Palestinian uprisings. Following the Camp David Agreement, Egypt and Israel signed a peace treaty (1979) in which Egypt recognized the Israeli state and regained Sinai. In 1982 Begin launched a strike against nuclear installations in Iraq and a full-scale invasion of Lebanon (1982–85) to counter the Palestine Liberation Organization (PLO). In 1987 the Intifada began in Israeli-occupied territory. From 1989 to 1992 Israel's population expanded by 10%, due to the immigration of Falashas and Soviet Jews. Increasing Jewish settlement inflamed the popular uprising. During the Gulf War (1991) Israel was the target for Iraqi Scud missiles, but under US pressure did not respond. In 1992 Rabin was reelected and began "peace-for-land" negotiations with the PLO. In 1993 Rabin and Yasir Arafat signed the Israeli–Palestinian Accord. In 1994 the Palestinian National Authority (PNA) assumed limited autonomy over the West Bank town of Jericho and the Gaza Strip. On November 4, 1995 Rabin was assassinated by a Jewish extremist. His successor, Shimon Peres, continued the peace process. In 1996 elections Peres was narrowly defeated by the Likud leader Binyamin Netanyahu who, while vowing to maintain the process, favored a more hard-line policy. Jewish settlement on the West Bank intensified, despite UN disapproval. In 1997 Israeli troops withdrew from Hebron. In 1998 the US-brokered Wye Agreement broke the stalemate. Israel agreed to redeploy troops on the West Bank and the PLO promised to cancel anti-Israeli provisions in its charter. Opposition to the agreement led to new elections in 1999.

## Economy

Israel is a prosperous nation (1995 GDP per capita, US$16,490). In 1948 Israel was heavily reliant on food imports, and hit by Arab boycotts during the 1950s. Now it is self-sufficient and a major exporter of fruits (such as the Jaffa orange) and vegetables. Agriculture, which employs 4% of the work force, is highly scientific. Manufactured goods are the leading export. Major products include chemicals, electronic and military equipment, jewelry, plastics, scientific instruments, and textiles. About 66% of the work force are employed in the service sector. Tourism is a major source of foreign earnings.

**Israelis** have used modern technology and science to raise production levels. They have turned a poor country into a prosperous one. This 1968 stamp illustrates some of Israel's major food exports: the melon, avocado, and strawberry.

(1863–79). He received the title of khedive from the Ottoman sultan in 1867. Profits from cotton enabled him to build extensively in Alexandria and Cairo, but later financial difficulties forced him to sell Egypt's share in the Suez Canal Company to Britain. He resigned in favor of his son, Tewfik Pasha.

**isobar** Line on a weather map connecting points of equal pressure, either at the Earth's surface or at a constant height above it. The patterns of isobars depict the variation in atmospheric pressure, showing areas of high and low pressure on the map.

**isolationism** Avoidance by a state of foreign commitments and alliances. It is connected in particular with the foreign policy of the US. US isolationism was not applied to the Americas, considered an exclusively US area of interest under the MONROE DOCTRINE, nor did it prevent US involvement in China and elsewhere in pursuit of commercial gains. With respect to Europe, it was interrupted when the US entered World War I in 1917 and permanently abandoned in 1941, although it continues to have some advocates.

**isomers** Chemical compounds having the same molecular formula but different properties due to the different arrangement of atoms within the molecules. Structural isomers have atoms connected in different ways. Geometric isomers, also called cis-trans isomers, differ in their symmetry about a double bond. Optical isomers are mirror images of each other.

**isotope** One of two or more atoms with the same ATOMIC NUMBER but a different number of neutrons. Both mass number and mass of the nucleus are different for different isotopes. The atomic mass of an element is an average of the isotope masses. The isotopes of an element have similar chemical properties, but physical properties vary slightly. Most elements have two or more naturally occurring isotopes, some of which are radioactive (radioisotopes). Radioisotopes are used in medicine, research, and industry. Isotopes are also used in radioactive dating.

**Israel** Name given in the Old Testament to JACOB and to the nation that the Hebrews founded in Canaan. Jacob was renamed Israel after he had wrestled with the mysterious "man" who was either an angel or God Himself (Genesis 32: 28). As a geographical name, Israel at first applied to the whole territory of Canaan captured or occupied by the Hebrews after the Exodus from Egypt. This territory was united as a kingdom under DAVID in the early 10th century BC, with its capital at JERUSALEM. Following the death of David's son SOLOMON, the ten northern tribes seceded, and the name Israel thereafter applied to the kingdom they founded in N Palestine; the remaining two tribes held the southern kingdom of JUDAH.

**Israel** Republic in SW Asia. *See* country feature, page 351

**Israeli–Palestinian Accord** Agreement that aimed to end hostilities between Palestinians and Israelis, especially in the WEST BANK and GAZA STRIP. Secret talks began in the mid-1980s. On September 13, 1993, a "Declaration of Principles" was signed by Yitzhak Rabin and Yasir ARAFAT. The PLO recognized Israel's right to exist and renounced terrorism. In return, Israel recognized the PLO as the legitimate representative of Palestinians and agreed to a staged withdrawal of troops from parts of the occupied territories. On May 18, 1994, the Israeli army completed its redeployment in the Gaza Strip and withdrew from JERICHO. The Palestinian National Authority (headed by Arafat) assumed limited autonomy. In September 1995, Rabin agreed to withdraw Israeli troops from six more towns and 85% of HEBRON. In October 1995, 1,100 Palestinian prisoners were released. The assassination of Rabin and the election of Benjamin NETANYAHU halted the process, and Jewish settlement on the West Bank accelerated. During 1997 and 1998, despite the withdrawl of most Israeli troops from Hebron, and desperate attempts by the US government to encourage dialog, Israel's determination to build more Jewish settlements in E Jerusalem has stalled the process. *See also* INTIFADA

**Istanbul** City and seaport in NW Turkey, on both sides of the BOSPORUS, partly in Europe and partly in Asia, at the entrance to the Sea of Marmara. The city was founded by Greek colonists in the 7th century BC. It was known as Byzantium until AD 330 when CONSTANTINE I chose it as the capital of the Eastern Roman Empire and renamed it Constantinople. Captured by the OTTOMAN Turks in 1453, the city was largely destroyed by an earthquake in 1509 and rebuilt. When the new Turkish Republic was established after World War I, the capital was moved to ANKARA, and Constantinople was renamed Istanbul. Today it is the commercial and financial center of Turkey. Industries: shipbuilding, cement, textiles, glass, pottery, leather goods. It also derives a valuable income from tourism. Pop. (1990) 6,293,397.

**Italian** Language of Italy, where it is spoken by that country's 58 million inhabitants, and of the canton of Ticino, in Switzerland. It is one of the ROMANCE LANGUAGES descended from spoken Latin and so belongs ultimately to the Italic group of INDO-EUROPEAN LANGUAGES. There are many Italian dialects, and the official language is based on those of central Italy, particularly Tuscan. During the 20th century, broadcasting and the movies standardized the language greatly, but most Italians continue to use a regional dialect for everyday communication.

**Italian art and architecture** Painting, sculpture, and other art produced in Italy following the Roman period. By the 6th century, trade with the Byzantine Empire had brought a Byzantine influence to Italian art, which lasted through the 11th century. The chief centers of the Italo-Byzantine style were Venice, Tuscany, Rome, and the deep south. Mosaics and stylized, geometric forms became standard as decorations for GOTHIC cathedrals and churches. Icon panels were the main type of paintings during the 11th through the 13th centuries, with major schools in SIENA, Lucca, and PISA. By the time of the RENAISSANCE, the emphasis was on balance and harmony, with such masters as LEONARDO DA VINCI, GHIBERTI, DONATELLO, BOTTICELLI, and MICHELANGELO. MANNERISM developed in Florence late in the Renaissance but faded by the end of the 16th century, giving way to the BAROQUE style of the 17th century. This was typified by artists such as the painter CARAVAGGIO and the architect BERNINI. In the 18th and 19th centuries, the NEOCLASSICAL movement was inspired by Classical Roman art, the subject of PIRANESI's engravings. The 20th century saw the birth of FUTURISM, as well as the more tranquil works of MODIGLIANI and DE CHIRICO.

**Italian literature** Body of work produced in Italy from the 13th century on. Italian vernacular literature emerged in the 13th century with the work of the Sicilian poets at the court of Frederick II; they extensively employed the SONNET. Religious poetry also flourished. Major figures of the 14th century were DANTE, the poet PETRARCH, and BOCCACCIO, who influenced the works of CHAUCER. The RENAISSANCE produced outstanding poetry and philosophy, especially in the work of Torquato TASSO, Lodovico Ariosto (1474–1533), and the politician MACHIAVELLI. During the Age of Enlightenment in the 18th century, a new literary language was required to reflect modern experience. The poet Carlo Porta (1775–1821) employed regional dialects, while Giuseppe Parini (1729–99) wrote in a more conventional style. The lyrical works of Giacomo Leopardi (1798–1837) and the novels of Alessandro MANZONI helped to take Italian literature into its Romantic period. The 19th-century political movement for Italian unification and independence inspired a literary flowering. The major figure to emerge was Gabriele D'ANNUNZIO. Important 20th-century writers include Alberto MORAVIA, Cesare PAVESE, Eugenio MONTALE, Umberto ECO, and Italo Calvino (1923–85).

**italics** Style of handwriting developed by the Florentine humanist Niccolò Niccoli in the 15th century. By the 16th century it had replaced Gothic script in most European countries. The 20th century has seen its revival. It is now used in printed works for special purposes, such as to indicate emphasis or foreign words.

**Italy** Republic in S Europe. *See* country feature

**Ito, Prince Hirobumi** (1841–1909) Japanese statesman. The leading figure in the modernization of Japan after the MEIJI RESTORATION (1868), he served in several government posts and took part in the Iwakura Mission (1871–73) to study Western governments. After the RUSSO-JAPANESE WAR, he headed the Japanese administration in what was then the protectorate of Korea, and was assassinated by a Korean nationalist.

**Iturbide, Agustín de** (1783–1824) Mexican general and

The Italian flag is based on the military standard carried by the French Republican National Guard when Napoleon invaded Italy in 1796, causing great changes in Italy's map. It was finally adopted as the national flag after Italy was unified in 1861.

**AREA:** 116,320sq mi (301,270sq km)
**POPULATION:** 57,782,000
**CAPITAL (POPULATION):** Rome (2,775,250)
**GOVERNMENT:** Multiparty republic
**ETHNIC GROUPS:** Italian 94%, German, French, Greek, Albanian, Slovenian, Ladino
**LANGUAGES:** Italian 94% (official), Sardinian 3%
**RELIGIONS:** Christianity (Roman Catholic) 83%
**CURRENCY:** Lira = 100 centesimi

The Republic of Italy is bordered in the N by the ALPS, which include Italy's highest peak, Gran Paradiso, at 13,323ft (4,061m). In the NE lies Italy's largest lake, LAKE GARDA, framed by the DOLOMITES. The Alps drop down to a vast, fertile plain, drained by Italy's largest river, the PO. This is Italy's richest industrial and agricultural region. The APENNINES form Central Italy's backbone. Either side of the range are narrow coastal lowlands. On the Tyrrhenian side lies Italy's capital, ROME. SICILY is the largest Mediterranean island and includes Mount ETNA. *See* individual gazetteer articles

## CLIMATE

Italy has a Mediterranean climate, except Sicily, which is subtropical. Alpine winters are long and the frequent snow is ideal for winter sports.

## HISTORY AND POLITICS

By tradition ROMULUS AND REMUS founded ancient ROME in 753 BC. The ETRUSCANS were overthrown by the Romans, who established a republic (509 BC). In the PUNIC WARS, Rome gained a Mediterranean empire. POMPEY was defeated by Julius CAESAR, whose assassination led to the formation (27 BC) of the ROMAN EMPIRE under AUGUSTUS. DIOCLETIAN divided the empire into Eastern (BYZANTINE EMPIRE) and Western sections. The PAPACY ensured the continuation of Rome's influence. PEPIN III (THE SHORT) expelled the LOMBARDS and enabled the creation of the PAPAL STATES. In AD 800 Pepin's son, CHARLEMAGNE, was crowned emperor of the West. In 962 OTTO I conquered Italy and established the HOLY ROMAN EMPIRE. Central and N Italy were controlled by powerful city-states, while the S established a FEUDAL SYSTEM under the HOHENSTAUFEN and Angevin dynasties. The 13th-century battle between imperial and papal power divided the cities and nobles into the GUELPH and GHIBELLINE factions. The RENAISSANCE profoundly affected western civilization. ITALIAN ART AND ARCHITECTURE was a formative force across Europe. In the 16th century Spain gained Sicily, Naples, and Milan. The FRENCH REVOLUTIONARY WARS failed to bring reunification. Nationalist groups, such as the RISORGIMENTO, emerged. In 1861 MAZZINI's republicans were defeated by monarchists led by GARIBALDI, and the kingdom of Italy was unified under Victor Emmanuel II. The papacy refused to concede the loss of Rome, and VATICAN CITY was set up as a sovereign state (1929). The late 19th century was marked by industrialization and empire-building. Victor Emmanuel III's reign (1900–46) saw Italy enter World War I on the Allied side (1915). Italian discontent at the post-war settlement culminated in D'ANNUNZIO's seizure of TRIESTE and the emergence of FASCISM. In 1922 Benito MUSSOLINI assumed dictatorial powers. Aggressive foreign policy included the seizure of ETHIOPIA and Albania. In 1936 Mussolini entered an alliance with HITLER. During World War II, Italy fought on the Axis side, but after losing its North African empire, Mussolini was dismissed and Italy surrendered (1943). Germany invaded and Italy declared war. In 1944 Rome fell to the Allies. The Christian Democrat Party emerged as the dominant post-war political force, with DE GASPERI as prime minister (1945–53). In 1948 Italy became a republic and was a founding member of NATO (1949) and the European Economic Community (1958). Italy has been riven by political instability (56 governments since 1945), endemic corruption (often linked to the MAFIA), social unrest, and the wealth gap between N and S. In 1993 popular discontent with traditional parties and the political structure led to the adoption of a "first-past-the-post" system and the emergence of the Northern League and anti-corruption parties. Elections in 1996 were won by the left-wing Olive Tree alliance and Romano Prodi became prime minister (1996–98). In 1998 the Communist Refoundation (RC) withdrew its support for Prodi's government and Massimo D'Alema, leader of the Party of the Democratic Left (PDS), became prime minister. In 1999 Italy joined the EURO.

## ECONOMY

Italy's main industrial region is the NW triangle of MILAN, TURIN, and GENOA (1995 GDP per capita, US$19,870). It is the world's 8th largest auto and steel producer. Machinery and transport equipment account for 37% of exports. Italy has few mineral resources. Italy is the world's largest producer of wine. Tourism is a vital economic sector, with receipts of US$21,577 billion

politician, who helped Mexico achieve independence (1821) and was emperor (1822–23). Dissent crystallized when SANTA ANNA and Guadalupe Victoria called for the creation of a republic. Iturbide abdicated and was exiled. Early in 1824 he returned to Mexico and was promptly arrested and shot.

**Ivan III (the Great)** (1440–1505) Grand Duke of Moscow (1462–1505). He laid the foundations of the future empire of Russia. By 1480 Moscow's northern rivals, including Novgorod, were absorbed by conquest or persuasion, domestic rebellion was crushed, and the Tatar threat was ended permanently. His later years were troubled by conspiracies over succession. He began to use the title *czar* ("caesar") and employed Italian artists in the buildings of the KREMLIN.

**Ivan IV (the Terrible)** (1530–84) Grand Duke of Moscow (1533–84) and czar of Russia. Ivan was crowned czar in 1547 and married Anastasia, a ROMANOV. At first, he was an able and progressive ruler, reforming law and government. By annexing the TATAR states of Kazan and Astrakhan, he gained control of the Volga river. He established trade with W European states and began Russian expansion into Siberia. After his wife's death in 1560, he became increasingly unbalanced, killing his own son in a rage. He established a personal dominion, the *oprichnina*, inside Russia. He created a military force, the *oprichniki*, which he set against the boyars.

**Ives, Charles** (1874–1954) US composer. American folk music is often his thematic basis, as in the *Variations on America* for organ (1891) and Symphony No. 2 (1902). He also wrote symphonies and chamber music. Ives was awarded the 1947 Pulitzer Prize for music.

**IVF** Abbreviation of IN VITRO FERTILIZATION

**ivory** Hard, yellowish-white dentine of some mammals. The most highly prized variety is obtained from elephant tusks. The term also refers to the teeth of hippopotamuses, walruses, sperm whales, and several other mammals.

**Ivory Coast** (officially Côte d'Ivoire) Republic in W Africa; the capital is YAMOUSSOUKRO. **Land and climate** The SE coast features lagoons enclosed by sandbars, on one of which the former capital and chief port of ABIDJAN is situated. Rocky cliffs line the SW coast. Coastal lowlands give way to a plateau. The NW highland borders with Liberia and Guinea are an extension of the Guinea Highlands. Ivory Coast has a hot and humid tropical climate, with high temperatures throughout the year. The S has two distinct rainy seasons, May to July and October to November. Inland, rainfall decreases and the N has a dry season and only one rainy season. Rain forests of valuable trees, such as mahogany and African teak, once covered the S lowlands, but much of the land has been cleared for farming. Tropical savanna covers the plateau, and forests cover much of the Guinea Highlands. **History and Politics** European contact with the region dates back to the late 15th century, and trade in ivory and slaves soon became important. French trading posts were founded in the late 17th century, and Ivory Coast became a French colony in 1893. From 1895 Ivory Coast was governed as part of French West Africa, a massive union that also included modern-day Benin, Burkina Faso, Guinea, Mali, Mauritania, Niger, and Senegal. In 1958 Ivory Coast voted to remain within the French Community, but achieved full independence in 1960. Its first president, Félix HOUPHOUËT-BOIGNY, was the longest-serving African head of state, with an uninterrupted 33-year presidency until his death in 1993. He was a paternalistic, pro-Western leader. His dialog with South Africa's apartheid government enraged many fellow African states. In 1983 the National Assembly agreed to move the capital from Abidjan to Yamoussoukro, the president's birthplace, but economic setbacks delayed the completion of the transfer, and government offices remained in Abidjan until 1990. Civil unrest continued throughout the 1980s and led to the adoption of a new constitution (1990), which legalized opposition parties. Houphouët-Boigny was succeeded by Henri Konan Bédié. In 1995 Bédié was reelected, following an opposition boycott. **Economy** Agriculture employs *c.*66% of the work force, and agriculture makes up *c.*50% of Ivory Coast's exports. Ivory Coast is the world's largest producer of cocoa beans and fourth-largest producer of coffee (1995 GDP per capita, US$1,580). Other exports include cotton, bananas, palm oil, pineapples, and hardwoods. Food crops include cassava, rice, vegetables, and yams. Manufacturing products include fertilizers, refined oil, textiles, and lumber.

**IVORY COAST**

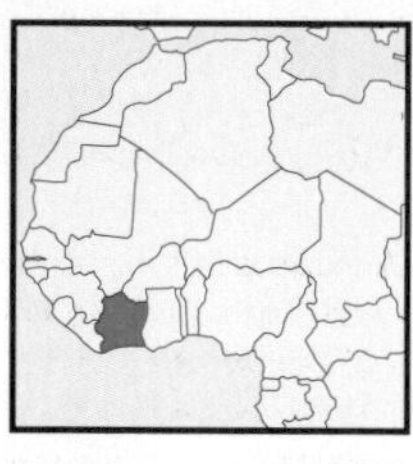

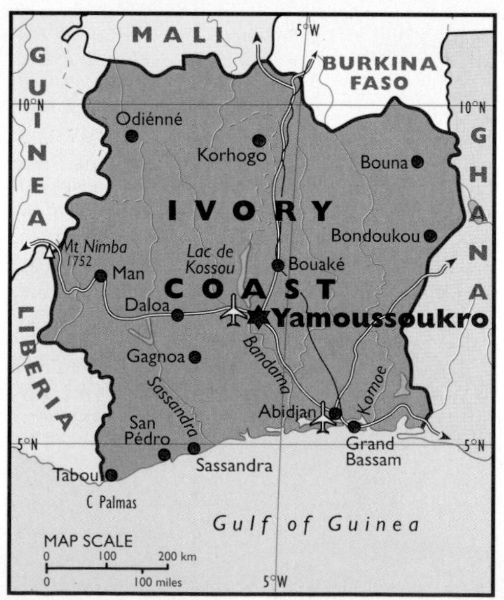


**AREA: 124,502 SQ MI (322,460 SQ KM)**
**POPULATION:** 12,910,000
**CAPITAL (POPULATION):** Yamoussoukro (106,786)
**GOVERNMENT:** Multiparty republic
**ETHNIC GROUPS:** Akan 41%, Kru 17%, Voltaic 16%, Malinke 15%, Southern Mande 10%
**LANGUAGES:** French (official)
**RELIGIONS:** Islam 38%, Christianity 28%, traditional beliefs 17%
**CURRENCY:** CFA franc = 100 centimes

**ivy** Woody, EVERGREEN vine with leathery leaves, native to Europe and Asia. Its long, climbing stems cling to upright surfaces, such as trees or walls, by aerial roots. The common English ivy (*Hedera helix*) is propagated by cuttings and grows outdoors in moist shady or sunny areas. Family Araliaceae.

**Ivy League** Group of eight long-established NE American colleges and universities. The members are HARVARD, YALE, PRINCETON, University of Pennsylvania, Brown, Columbia, Dartmouth, and Cornell. They are organized as an intercollegiate athletics league.

**Iwo Jima** (formerly Sulfur Island) Largest of the Japanese Volcano Islands in the W Pacific Ocean. During World War II, it was captured by the US at great human cost (1945). A photograph of the US flag being planted on its highest peak, Mount Suribachi, became a US symbol of the Pacific conflict and the basis for a sculpture in Arlington National Cemetery. Iwo Jima was returned to Japan in 1968. Industries: sugar refining and sulfur mining. Area: 8sq mi (21sq km).

**Izetbegović, Alija** (1925– ) Bosnian statesman, president of BOSNIA-HERZEGOVINA (1992– ). He was imprisoned (1945–48, 1983–88) by the Yugoslav government for pan-Islamic activities. In 1990 Izetbegović was elected leader of the Party of Democratic Action (PDA), promising to establish a multi-faith republic. He led Bosnia-Herzegovina's coalition government from 1990 until its declaration of independence in 1992. Izetbegović retained his position as president throughout the civil war and signed the Treaty of Paris (1995), which ended the Bosnian War. He was re-elected in 1996.

**Izmir** (formerly Smyrna) City and seaport on the Gulf of Izmir, W Turkey. It was settled by Greeks at the beginning of the 1st millennium BC. Izmir was part of the Ottoman empire from 1424–1919, when it was assigned to Greece. It passed to Turkey under the Treaty of Lausanne (1923). Industries: tourism, tobacco, silk, carpets, cotton and woolen textiles, petrochemicals, foodstuffs, cement. Pop. (1990) 2,319,188.

**jabiru** STORK of the New World, found in swamps from Mexico to Argentina. Length: 5ft (1.5m); wingspan: 7ft (2m). Family Ciconiidae, species *Jabiru mycteria*.
**jaçana** (lily trotter) Long-toed water bird of tropical lakes with a slender body, narrow bill, wrist spurs, and tapered claws. It is black or reddish-brown. It runs over floating vegetation, feeding on aquatic plants and small animals. Length: to 20in (50.8cm). Family Jacanidae.
**jacaranda** Genus of trees native to tropical America. The ornamental *Jacaranda mimosifolia* and *J. cuspidifolia* have showy blue flowers and fern-like leaves. There are 50 species. Family Bignoniaceae.
**jackal** Wild dog that resembles a COYOTE in habits, size, and general appearance. It preys on small animals and eats fruit and seeds. The species are distributed throughout Asia and Africa. Length: to 29in (74cm). Family Canidae; genus *Canis*.
**jackdaw** Gregarious, black-and-gray, European bird that frequents open country. Smaller than its relative, the CROW, it has a gray head and white-rimmed eyes. It lives in colonies. Family Corvidae; species *Corvus monedula*.
**jack rabbit** Any of several large, slender, long-eared HARES of w North America. Jack rabbits rely on their speed and agility to escape from predators. Most are gray with white underparts. Family Leporidae; genus *Lepus*.
**Jackson, Andrew** (1767–1845) Seventh US president (1829–37). He became a national hero in the WAR OF 1812 when he defeated the British at New Orleans (1815). His popular appeal narrowly failed to defeat John Quincy ADAMS in the 1824 presidential election. His supporters built the basis of the new DEMOCRATIC PARTY and in 1928 Jackson was elected with John C. CALHOUN as his vice president. He faced staunch opposition from the establishment and set up a SPOILS SYSTEM of political appointments. Calhoun resigned over the NULLIFICATION issue and Jackson faced further conflict over STATES' RIGHTS, the expansion of the FRONTIER, and the TARIFF. His second term (1832–37) was marked by his trenchant opposition to the BANK OF THE UNITED STATES. Jackson was succeeded by Martin VAN BUREN.
**Jackson, Glenda** (1936– ) British actress and politician. She won two Academy awards for Best Actress in *Women in Love* (1969), and *A Touch of Class* (1973). Other films include *Sunday Bloody Sunday* (1971), and *Hedda* (1975).
**Jackson, Jesse** (1941– ) US political leader and CIVIL RIGHTS activist. Ordained a Baptist minister in 1968, he worked with Martin Luther KING JR. in the Southern Christian Leadership Conference. In 1971 he formed Operation PUSH (People United to Save Humanity) to combat racism. An inspiring orator, Jackson campaigned for the Democratic presidential nomination in 1984 and 1988; although he did not acheive the nomination, he inspired many people to register to vote. In 1986 he became president of the National Rainbow Coalition.
**Jackson, Michael** (1958– ) US pop singer and songwriter. At the age of five, he was the youngest member of The Jackson Five. Jackson launched his solo career with the albums *Got To Be There* (1971) and *Off the Wall* (1979). His album *Thriller* (1982) sold more than 35 million copies. Later albums include *Bad* (1987) and *Dangerous* (1991). In 1993 he canceled a worldwide tour after allegations of child abuse. In 1994 Jackson married Lisa Marie Presley (1968– ), daughter of Elvis PRESLEY. The couple separated in 1996.
**Jackson, "Stonewall" (Thomas Jonathan)** (1824–63) Confederate general in the CIVIL WAR. His stand against overwhelming odds at the first battle of BULL RUN (1861) gained him the nickname "Stonewall." He fought, again greatly outnumbered, in the Shenandoah Valley (1862) and played an important part in the Confederate victories after the second battle of Bull Run. Jackson was accidentally shot and killed by his own men at Chancellorsville.
**Jackson** State capital and largest city of Mississippi, on the Pearl River, sw Mississippi. Established as a trading post in the 1790s, it was chosen as the site of the state capital in 1821. Industries: natural gas, glass, textiles. Pop. (1990) 196,637.
**Jacksonville** Seaport and largest city in Florida, in the NE part of the state, on the St. John's River. It served as a CONFEDERATE base during the Civil War, developed as a port in the 19th century, and was devastated by fire in 1901. It has shipyards and a naval air station. Industries: cigars, canning, wood products. Pop. (1994 est.) 676,718.
**Jacob** Old Testament figure, who was a grandson of ABRAHAM and, by tradition, ancestor of the nation of ISRAEL. He was the second-born son of ISAAC and Rebecca, and younger brother of ESAU. Stories about him and his family form the last part of Genesis (25:19–50:13). Jacob had 12 sons and one daughter by his two wives, Rachel and Leah, and their respective maids. The descendants of his sons became the 12 tribes of Israel.
**Jacobean** (Lat. *Jacobus*, James) Term designating the artistic styles of the reign (1603–25) of JAMES I. The major literary art form was drama, typical examples of which are the works of WEBSTER and the late plays of SHAKESPEARE. METAPHYSICAL POETRY, such as the work of John DONNE, was also a feature. In architecture the major achievement was the work of Inigo JONES. Jacobean painters were not as distinguished.
**Jacobins** French political radicals belonging to a club that played an important role during the FRENCH REVOLUTION. Begun in 1789, the club split in 1791 when the moderates left it. In 1793–94, the club was an instrument of ROBESPIERRE and became part of the government's administration. It closed soon after Robespierre's downfall in 1794.
**Jacobites** Supporters of JAMES II of England and his STUART descendants, who attempted to regain the English throne after the GLORIOUS REVOLUTION of 1688. Jacobitism was strong in the Scottish Highlands and parts of Ireland. Several Jacobite rebellions took place, most notably the rising of 1745, during which Prince Charles Edward STUART won Scotland. His Highlanders were decisively defeated at CULLODEN in 1746, and the British government embarked upon a policy of suppression of the Highland clans that ended the Jacobite threat.
**Jacob's ladder** Any of 50 species of wild and cultivated plants of temperate areas. It has clusters of delicate blue, violet, or white flowers and alternate compound leaves. Height: up to 3ft (90cm). Family Polemoniaceae.
**Jacopone da Todi** (1230–1306) Italian poet. After the death of his wife in the 1260s, he became a monk and wrote numerous fervid, personal hymns. The Latin canticle *Stabat mater dolorosa* is attributed to him.
**Jade, August Personage of** In Chinese mythology, the supreme god of heaven and, according to some traditions, the creator of human beings. He concerned himself exclusively with the affairs of the emperor, leaving his heavenly ministers to deal with lesser mortals.
**jaeger** Gull-like, predatory, fast-flying seabird that breeds in the Arctic and winters in the subtropics; also known as the skua. It has a dark, stocky body with pointed wings and long tail feathers. It feeds on small land animals and seabirds. Length: 13–20in ( 33–51cm). Genus: *Stercorarius*.
**Jaffa** City and port in w Israel, a suburb of TEL AVIV. Mentioned in the Bible, it was captured by ALEXANDER THE GREAT in 332 BC. It was taken back by the Jews during the Hasmonean revolt but was destroyed by the Roman emperor Vespasian in AD 68. It changed hands many times in the Middle Ages. In the 20th century it became a focus of Palestinian resistance to Jewish settlement. In 1948 the city was settled by Israelis and united with Tel Aviv in 1950.
**Jagiello** Medieval Polish dynasty. It began with the marriage of Grand Duke Jagiello of Lithuania to Queen Jadwiga of Poland (1386), uniting Poland and Lithuania. Members of the dynasty also reigned in Hungary and Bohemia in the 15th and 16th centuries.
**jaguar** Spotted big CAT found in wooded or grassy areas from

◄ **jaguar** The largest cat in the Americas, the jaguar (*Panthera onca*) is now extinct in most of N America. It is a solitary hunter and an excellent swimmer and tree climber. Unlike most big cats, it does not roar.

***J/j, tenth letter of the Roman-based* W *European alphabet, It evolved from the letter* i *and was the last to be incorporated into the modern alphabet; its early history is the same as that of* i*. The* j *developed from the tailed form of the* i*.***

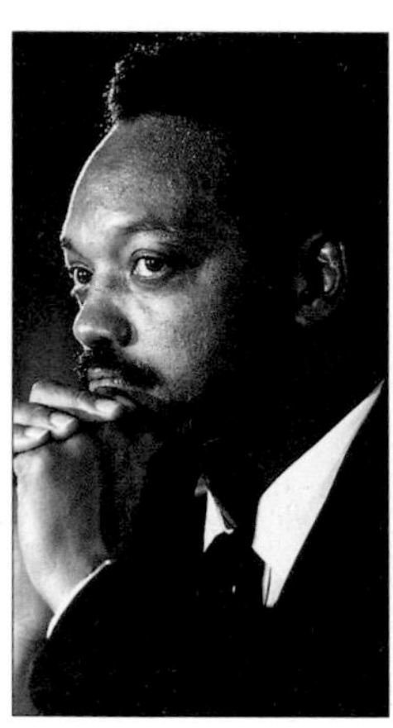

▲ **Jackson** Raised in modest circumstances, Jesse Jackson won a football scholarship to the University of Illinois. He went on to attend the Chicago Theological Seminary and became a charismatic preacher and civil rights advocate. He became president of the National Rainbow Coalition, a political organization made up of a coalition of minority groups, enivronmentalists, and peace activists.

J

SW US to Argentina. It has a chunky body and a yellowish coat with black rosettes. It eats large mammals, turtles, and fish. Length: body to 5.9ft (1.8m); tail to 35.8in (91cm); weight to 299.8lb (136kg). Family Felidae; species *Panthera onca*.

**jaguarundi** Small, ground-dwelling CAT found in Central and South America. It is black, brown, gray, or fox red. Length: to 26in (67cm), excluding the tail; weight: to 20lb (9kg). Family Felidae; species *Felis yagouaroundi*.

**Jahangir** (1569–1627) Mogul emperor of India (1605–27). He succeeded his father, AKBAR I, and continued the expansion of the empire. He granted trading privileges to the Portuguese and the British and was a patron of poetry and painting.

**Jainism** Ancient religion of India originating in the 6th century BC as a reaction against conservative BRAHMANISM. It was founded by Mahavira (599–527 BC). Jains do not accept Hindu scriptures, rituals, or priesthood, but they do accept the Hindu doctrine of TRANSMIGRATION OF SOULS. Jainism lays special stress on *ahimsa* – noninjury to all living creatures. Today, there are *c*.4 million Jains worldwide.

**Jaipur** State capital of Rajasthan. Founded in 1727, it was enclosed by a wall (still extant), and there is a system of wide, regular streets. A transport and commercial center, it is famous for its carpets, jewelry, enamels, and printed cloth. Pop. (1991) 1,458,000.

**Jakarta** Capital of Indonesia, on the NW coast of Java. It was founded (as Batavia) by the Dutch *c*.1619 as a fort and trading post, and it became the headquarters of the Dutch EAST INDIA COMPANY. It became the capital after Indonesia gained its independence in 1949. Industries: ironworking, printing, timber. Exports: rubber, tea, quinine. Pop. (1994 est.) 7,885,519.

**Jamaica** Independent island nation in the Caribbean, 145km (90mi) S of Cuba; the capital is KINGSTON. The third largest island in the Caribbean, Jamaica's coast is ringed with beautiful, palm-fringed beaches. In E Jamaica, the Blue Mountains rise to 7,402ft (2,255m). It has a tropical maritime climate. Jamaica was discovered by Christopher COLUMBUS in 1494 and remained a Spanish possession until captured by the British in 1655. Its sugar plantations brought prosperity, but the economy declined after the abolition of slavery in 1834. In 1865 British rule was threatened by a native rebellion. In 1944 the colony was granted internal self-government within the Commonwealth and in 1958 joined the Federation of the WEST INDIES. In 1962, after the collapse of the Federation, William A. Bustamente of the Jamaican Labour Party (JLP) negotiated full independence for Jamaica. In 1973 Michael Manley of the People's National Party (PNP) took Jamaica into Caricom. In 1997 Percival J. Patterson of the PNP secured a third term as prime minister. Chief crops are sugarcane, bananas, and other fruits. The economy is based on light engineering, construction, and mining. Jamaica is the world's third largest producer of bauxite (aluminium ore). Tourism is also important. Area: 4,232sq mi (10,962sq km). Pop. (1993 est.) 2,471,600. *See* West Indies map

**James I** (1566–1625) King of England (1603–25) and, as James VI, king of Scotland (1567–1625). Son of MARY, QUEEN OF SCOTS, and Lord Darnley, he acceded to the Scottish throne as an infant on his mother's abdication. In 1589 James married Anne of Denmark. He inherited the English throne on the death of ELIZABETH I. James supported the Anglican Church, at the cost of antagonizing the PURITANS, and sponsored the publication (1611) of the Authorized, or King James, Version of the BIBLE. The GUNPOWDER PLOT (1605) was foiled and James cracked down heavily on Catholics. In 1607 the first English colony in America (Jamestown) was founded. James' insistence on the "divine right" of kings brought conflict with Parliament. In 1611 he dissolved Parliament and, besides the Addled Parliament (1614) ruled without one until 1621. The death (1612) of Robert CECIL saw James' increasingly dependent on corrupt favourites such as Robert Carr and George Villiers, 1st duke of BUCKINGHAM. He was succeeded by his son, CHARLES I. *See also* JACOBEAN

**James II** (1633–1701) King of England (1685–88), second son of CHARLES I. Following the English CIVIL WARS, James spent time fighting for the French and Spanish, before becoming lord high admiral after the RESTORATION (1660). In 1669 he converted to Roman Catholicism and was forced to resign his offices. As king, he was confronted by MONMOUTH's Rebellion (1685) and his pro-Catholic policies provoked the GLORIOUS REVOLUTION. His daughter, MARY II, and her husband, WILLIAM OF ORANGE, assumed the crown and James fled to France. With French aid, he invaded Ireland but was defeated by William at the Battle of the BOYNE (1690). *See also* JACOBITES

**James I** (1394–1437) King of Scotland (1406–37). His father, Robert III, sent him to France for safety but he was intercepted by the English (1406). He was not ransomed until 1424. James then restored royal authority by ruthless methods. He carried out reforms of the financial and judicial systems and encouraged trade. His campaign against the nobility made him many enemies, and he was assassinated at Perth.

**James II** (1430–60) King of Scotland (1437–60). Succeeding his father, JAMES I, at the age of six, his minority was dominated by aristocratic factions, particularly the Douglases. In 1452 he killed the earl of Douglas and seized control. During the English Wars of the ROSES, James supported the Lancastrians against the Yorkists, who were allied with the Douglases, and was killed by an exploding cannon at Roxburgh.

**James III** (1451–88) King of Scotland (1460–88), son and successor of JAMES II. He was challenged by his brother Albany, whom Edward IV of England recognized as king in 1482. Peace was arranged, but a new rebellion resulted in James's defeat and his murder.

**James IV** (1473–1513) King of Scotland (1488–1513). He succeeded his father, JAMES III, capturing and killing those nobles responsible for his death. James defended royal authority against the nobility and the church and endeavored to promote peace with England, marrying HENRY VIII's sister, Margaret Tudor. Henry's attack on Scotland's old ally, France, drew him into war (1513), and he was killed at Flodden.

**James V** (1512–42) King of Scotland (1513–42). He made a French alliance through marriage as a safeguard against his aggressive uncle, HENRY VIII. Failure to gain the support of the nobility contributed to the defeat of his forces by the English at Solway Moss (1542). He was succeeded by his daughter, MARY, QUEEN OF SCOTS.

**James Edward Stuart** *See* STUART, JAMES EDWARD

**James, Henry** (1843–1916) US novelist, short-story writer and critic, brother of William JAMES. In 1876 he settled in England and became a British subject in 1915. James' early masterpiece, *The Portrait of a Lady* (1881), features a recurrent theme – the conflict between the values of American and European society. The novels of his middle period, such as *The Bostonians* (1886), deal with American politics. James' last novels, *The Wings of the Dove* (1902), *The Ambassadors* (1903), and *The Golden Bowl* (1904), show his mastery of the psychological novel. His shorter fiction includes *The Turn of the Screw* (1898).

**James, Jesse Woodson** (1847–82) US outlaw. With his brother Frank he fought for the Confederacy during the Civil War. In 1867 they formed an outlaw band and terrorized the frontier, robbing banks and trains in Missouri and neighboring states. He was shot dead by Robert Ford, a member of his own gang, for a large reward.

**James, William** (1842–1910) US philosopher and psychologist, elder brother of Henry JAMES. He held that the feeling of emotion is based on the sensation of a state of the body; the bodily state comes first and the emotion follows. As a philosopher, he influenced PRAGMATISM. His most famous works are *The Principles of Psychology* (1890) and *Varieties of Religious Experience* (1902).

**James, the Epistle of** Book of the New Testament consisting of a letter traditionally attributed to St. James, the brother of Jesus. Its authorship is, however, far from certain. It exhorts Christians to live righteous lives, warning that profession of Christian faith should not take the place of good works.

**Jameson, Sir Leander Starr** (1853–1917) British political leader in South Africa. He emigrated to South Africa (1878). In 1895, with Cecil RHODES, he led a failed raid on the Afrikaner republic of Transvaal and was imprisoned. After his release, he was prime minister of Cape Colony (1904–08).

**Jamestown** First successful English settlement in America. It was established in 1607 on the James River, Virginia. On the verge of collapse from disease and starvation, it was

◀ **Japanese architecture** The Shonkintei garden pavilion at the palace of Katsura in Kyoto (1641) is typical of Japanese architecture. It comprises two large rooms (1) and (2) divided by *shoji* (translucent screens), a tea room (3), lobby (4), and pantry section (5). The *tokonoma* (6) is an alcove for the display of flowers and objects of art.

saved by the leadership of Captain John SMITH (1608) and the timely arrival of new supplies and colonists (1610). From 1614 survival was assured thanks to tobacco planting.

**Jammu and Kashmir** State in NW India, bounded N by Pakistan-controlled KASHMIR, W by Pakistan, and E by China. The region is mountainous and the Himalayas stand above the heavily populated valleys of the Indus and Jhelum rivers. The capitals are Srinagar (summer) and Jammu (winter). Industries: rice, animal husbandry, silk, rice and flour milling, tourism. Area: 38,845sq mi (100,569sq km). Pop. (1994 est.) 8,435,000.

**Janáček, Leoš** (1854–1928) Moravian composer. He integrated the inflections and rhythms of the Czech language and Moravian folk music into his compositions. His pieces include orchestral works such as *Taras Bulba* (1918) and *Sinfonietta* (1926), choral works such as the *Glagolitic Mass* (1927), and operas including *Jenufa* (1904), *Kátya Kabanová* (1921), *The Cunning Little Vixen* (1924), and *The Makropoulos Affair* (1926).

**Janissaries** Elite corps of the Ottoman army, founded in the 14th century. The Janissaries were a highly effective fighting force until the 17th century, when discipline and military prestige declined. They were abolished by MAHMUD II in 1826.

**Jansen, Cornelis** (1585–1638) Dutch theologian. He studied problems raised for Catholics by Lutheran and Calvinist doctrine. In his writings, Jansen argued for a return to the views of St. AUGUSTINE OF HIPPO on grace and salvation.

**Jansenism** Theological school that grew up in the Roman Catholic Church in the 17th and 18th centuries. It was named for Cornelis JANSEN, but the movement was strongest in France. The Jansenists believed that man is incapable of carrying out the commandments of God without divine "grace," which is bestowed only on a favored few. French Jansenists incurred the hostility of the Jesuits and of the French crown, and they were condemned by the pope (1713).

**Jansky, Karl** (1905–50) US engineer. In 1931 he discovered unidentifiable radio signals from space. He concluded that they were stellar in origin and that the source lay in the direction of SAGITTARIUS. Jansky's discovery is considered to be the beginning of RADIO ASTRONOMY. The unit measuring radio emission is named for him.

**Japan** Archipelago in the N Pacific Ocean. *See* country feature

**Japanese** Official language of Japan and the native tongue of more than 120 million people in Japan and the Ryukyu and Bonin islands. Some scholars classify Japanese as a member of the Ural-Altaic family, which also includes Finnish, Hungarian, and Turkish. Japanese uses a pitch accent. There are at least four different forms of spoken Japanese, and a modern literary style. Japanese writing uses a combination of some 1,850 Chinese characters and tables of syllabic symbols called *kana*.

**Japanese art and architecture** Earliest surviving examples of **Japanese art** are Jomon pottery figurines (*c.*1000 BC). In the 6th century AD Chinese influence was strong. LACQUER work, sculpture, and ink painting developed during the Nara period (AD 674–794). The later Yamato-e tradition was based on national, rather than Chinese, aesthetic standards. It flowered during the Kamakura military rule (1185–1333). The profound influence of ZEN Buddhism on Japanese art is particularly apparent in the Muromachi period (1333–1573). Many of the best-known examples of Japanese art were produced in the Edo (TOKUGAWA) period (*c.*1600–1868). The UKIYO-E prints of UTAMARO, HOKUSAI, HIROSHIGE, and others date from this period. Modern Japanese artists have made important contributions to 20th-century art and design. **Japanese architecture** derives from 6th century Chinese Buddhist structures. Temples have curved wooden columns, overhanging roofs, and thin exterior wood and plaster walls. A gateway, drum tower, and pagoda are also built, usually on a picturesque wooded hillside. Domestic structures are traditionally built with interior wooden posts supporting the roof. The outer walls are movable panels of wood or rice paper that slide in grooves. The interior is flexibly subdivided by screens and decorated with simplicity and delicacy.

**Japanese literature** One of the oldest and richest of world literatures. The earliest extant works are the *Kojiki* (712) and the *Nihongi* (720), which are histories written in Chinese characters used phonetically. The earliest recorded Japanese poetry is in the *Manyoshu* (760), which contains poems dating from the 4th century. The **Heian Period** (794–1185) is noted for the *Kokinshu* (905), an anthology of poetry commissioned by the emperor, which provided a pattern for *tanka* (short poems). Classical prose developed during this period and accounts of court life flourished. The most significant work was Murasaki Shikibu's *Genji Monogatari* (*c.*1010), the first true novel. During the **Middle Ages** (1185–1603) NO DRAMA was refined. The "war tales" of this period are typified by *Heike Monogatari*. In the **Tokugawa Period** (1603–1868) literature, once the preserve of the aristocracy, became the field of the commoners. HAIKU became popular; Matsuo Basho (1644–94) was the greatest poet of this form. There were developments in PUPPET THEATER and KABUKI THEATER. In the **Modern Period**, foreign contacts increased and Western literature had a major influence. Poetry flourished, and major figures such as Yosano Akiko (1878–1942), Ishikawa Takuboku (1885–1912), and Hagiwara Sakutaro (1886–1942) found new means of expression. Modern writers such as Yukio MISHIMA and the Nobel prizewinners Yasunari KAWABATA and Kenzoburo Oe have won an international reputation.

**Japanese theater** Dramatic forms, including NO DRAMA, PUPPET THEATER (*bunraku*), and KABUKI THEATER. Japanese theater descended from ritual dances, and involves music, song, and dance in addition to dialog. More modern styles of drama, known as *shinpa* and *shingeki* (new theater), which were influenced by Western theater, developed out of the desire to portray modern events and ideas in a more realistic style.

**Jarry, Alfred** (1873–1907) French playwright, poet, and satirist. Jarry is best-known for his avant-garde farce *Ubu Roi* (1896). His work foreshadowed SURREALISM.

**jasmine** Any evergreen or deciduous shrub or vine of the genus *Jasminum*, common in the Mediterranean. It has fragrant yellow, pink, or white flowers. Its oil is used in perfumes. Height: to 20ft (6.5m). Family Oleaceae.

**Jason** In Greek mythology, hero and leader of the ARGONAUTS. Sent on a quest for the GOLDEN FLEECE, Jason sailed aboard the *Argo*. After surviving many perils, he found the fleece in Colchis and stole it, with the help of the sorceress MEDEA, whom he married.

**Jaspers, Karl** (1883–1969) German philosopher and psychopathologist. His major work, *Philosophy* (1932), presents an interpretation of EXISTENTIALISM. Jaspers argued that the deepest insights into human nature are revealed in "limit situations," such as death. Other works include *Truth and Symbol* (1947), and *Philosophical Faith and Revelation* (1962).

**jaundice** Yellowing of the skin and the whites of the eyes, caused by excess of BILE pigment in the blood. Mild jaundice is common in newborn babies. In adults jaundice may occur when the flow of bile to the intestine is blocked by an obstruction such as a GALLSTONE, or in diseases such as CIRRHOSIS, HEPATITIS, or ANEMIA.

**Java** Indonesian island, between the Java Sea and the Indian Ocean, SE of Sumatra; its largest city is JAKARTA. In the early centuries AD the island was ruled by Hindu kingdoms. Islam began to spread in the 16th century. By the 18th century the island was mainly under Dutch control. It was occupied by the Japanese during World War II. Java is a mountainous

▲ **Japanese art** The decorative arts in Japan were well developed by the end of the 8th cenury. Color printing was particularly advanced, along with woodcuts, and ceramic glazes. *Kakemono* are hanging scrolls executed on thin silk or paper with Chinese ink, then mounted on silk brocade and rolled on a rod.

Japan's flag was officially adopted in 1870, although Japanese emperors had used this simple design for many centuries. The flag shows a red sun on a white background. The geographical position of Japan is expressed in its name *Nippon* or *Nihon*, (source of the Sun).

**AREA:** 145,869sq mi (377,800sq km)
**POPULATION:** 124,336,000
**CAPITAL (POPULATION):** Tokyo (7,894,000)
**GOVERNMENT:** Constitutional monarchy
**ETHNIC GROUPS:** Japanese 99%, Chinese, Korean, Ainu
**LANGUAGES:** Japanese (official)
**RELIGIONS:** Shintoism 93%, Buddhism 74%, Christianity 1% (most Japanese consider themselves to be both Shinto and Buddhist)
**CURRENCY:** Yen = 100 sen

Japan is an archipelago nation in the N Pacific Ocean.

Japan's four largest islands are (in decreasing order of size): HONSHU, HOKKAIDO, KYUSHU, and SHIKOKU. These constitute 98% of the total land area and enclose the Inland Sea (Sea of Japan). Japan has thousands of other small islands, including the RYUKYU ISLANDS.

The four main islands are mostly mountainous. The highest peak is the sacred FUJIYAMA, at 12,389ft (3,776m). Japan has more than 150 volcanoes, about 60 of which are active. Many of the small islands are the tips of volcanoes. Volcanic eruptions, earthquakes, and TSUNAMI occur frequently.

Around the coast are small, densely populated fertile plains covered by alluvium deposited by the short rivers that rise in the mountains. The Kanto plain stretches from the S coast of Honshū to N Kyūshū, and is Japan's industrial heartland. The plain contains the capital and world's sixth largest city, TOKYO. If YOKOHAMA is included, this is the world's most densely populated area. Other major cities in the area include NAGOYA, KYOTO, OSAKA, KOBE, and FUKUOKA.

## CLIMATE

The climate of Japan varies greatly from cool temperate in the N to subtropical in the S. Sapporo on Hokkaido has cold, snowy winters with temperatures below -20°C (4°F). Summer temperatures sometimes exceed 86°F (30°C). Tokyo has higher rainfall and temperatures.

## VEGETATION

Forests and woodland cover *c*.66% of the land. The N forests include trees such as fir and spruce. Central Japan has mixed forests of beech, maple, and oak. Deciduous trees dominate in the S. The cherry tree is found throughout Japan.

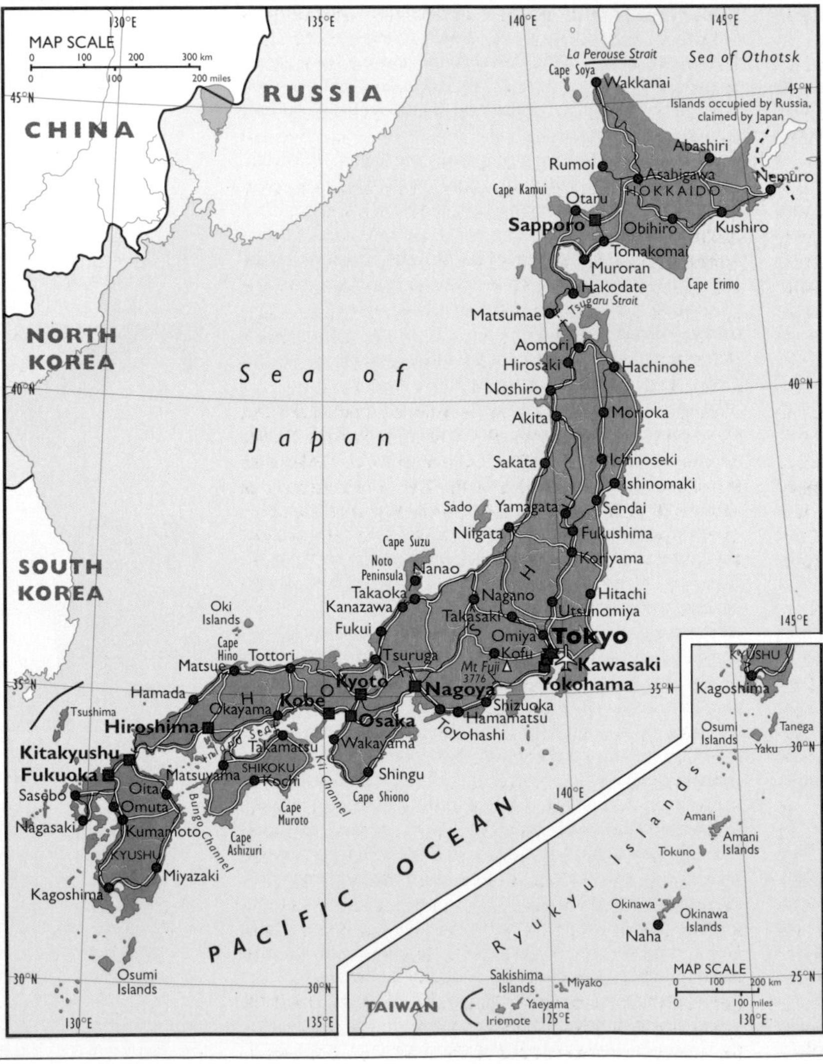

## HISTORY AND POLITICS

Most Japanese people are descendants of migrants from mainland Asia. One of the earliest groups are the AINU, *c*.15,000 of whom still live on Hokkaido. According to legend, Japan's first emperor, Jimmu, ascended the throne in 660 BC. The native religion was SHINTO. The Yamato established the Japanese state in the 5th century and made Kyōto the imperial capital. In the 6th century AD BUDDHISM was introduced to Japan, and the Chinese influence on JAPANESE ART AND ARCHITECTURE and JAPANESE LITERATURE was profound. In the 12th century civil war gave way to the power of the shōgun who ruled in the emperor's name. For the next 700 years Japan was ruled by these warrior-kings. European contact began when Portuguese sailors reached Japan in 1543. Following unsuccessful invasions of Korea and China, the TOKUGAWA shogunate (1603–1867) unified Japan and established their capital at Edo (Tokyo). Through the codes of BUSHIDO, the Tokugawa ensured total loyalty. Japan pursued an isolationalist path. In 1854 Matthew C. PERRY forced the Tokugawa shogunate to open its ports to Western trade. Western powers plotted the overthrow of the shogunate and the reestablishment of imperial power (MEIJI RESTORATION, 1868). The Emperor MEIJI's reign (1868–1912) was characterized by social and economic modernization, headed by the ZAIBATSU. Japanese nationalism created the desire for empire-building. The first of the SINO-JAPANESE WARS (1894–95) saw Japan acquire Formosa (Taiwan). Japan's decisive victory in the RUSSO–JAPANESE WAR (1904–05) marked its emergence as the dominant regional power. In 1910 Japan annexed Korea. During the 1920s Japan concentrated on building its economy. The 1923 earthquake at Kanto claimed 143,000 lives. Militarists began to dominate Japanese politics, and in 1930 Japan invaded MANCHURIA and set up the puppet state of MANCHUKUO. In 1937 Japan invaded China and precipitated the second Sino–Japanese War. At the start of WORLD WAR II Japan signed a pact with Germany and Italy. In 1941, Japan launched an attack on the US naval base at PEARL HARBOR. Japan conquered a huge swath of Pacific territory, but gradually the Allies regained ground. In 1945 the US dropped atomic bombs on the cities of HIROSHIMA and NAGASAKI and forced Japan's unconditional surrender (August 14, 1945). The US occupation of Japan under Douglas MACARTHUR (1945–52) undertook the demilitarization of industry and the adoption of a democratic constitution. Emperor HIROHITO declaimed his divinity and became a constitutional monarch. The Liberal Democratic Party (LDP) governed Japan almost continuously from 1948 to 1993. In 1951 Japan concluded a security treaty with the US that allowed US

## JAPAN

bases to be stationed on Japan in return for securing its defenses. During the 1960s and early 1970s Japan witnessed popular demonstrations against US interference. Under Eisaku Sato, the US completed the return of the Ryukyu Islands to Japan (1972). In 1989 Hirohito died and was succeeded by his son, Akihito. In the early 1990s, Japan was rocked by a series of political corruption scandals. In 1993 the LDP split: the 3 splinter parties formed a short-lived coalition government. In 1994 a new electoral system was introduced with an element of proportional representation. Tomiichi Murayama became Japan's first socialist prime minister. In 1996 he was replaced by Ryutaro Hashimoto, leader of the LDP. In 1998 the economic crisis in Southeast Asia spread to Japan. The government's slow and inadequate response forced Hashimoto to resign. He was replaced as prime minister and leader of the LDP by Keizo Obuchi.

### Economy

After the United States, Japan is the world's second largest economic power (1995 GDP per capita, US$22,110). Its success is based on the latest industrial technology, a skilled and committed labor force, vigorous export policies, and comparatively small defense expenditure. But economic success has brought problems: the rapid growth of industrial cities has led to high land prices, housing shortages, and pollution. Its aging work force also presents problems. In 1997 the economic crisis in Southeast Asia badly hit Japan's financial institutions, wiping 25% off the value of the Nikkei Dow. Unemployment rose to its highest level (4.5%) since 1945. The US government agreed a US$2 billion rescue package. Services form the largest sector of Japan's economy. Japan has seven of the world's ten largest banks. Despite having to import most of its raw materials and fuels, manufacturing is a vital sector of the Japanese economy. Machinery and transportation equipment account for over 70% of exports. Japan is the world's leading car, ship, and steel producer. It is the world's second largest iron and cement producer. Other important manufactures include electrical and electronic equipment, chemicals, and textiles. Japan has the second largest fish catch (after China). Attempts have been made to reduce whaling. Because Japan is so mountainous, only 15% of land is farmed and Japan has to import 30% of its food. Rice is the chief crop, taking up c.50% of total farmland. Japan is under increasing pressure to lift its protectionist policies of import restrictions and high tariffs.

**The kimono** is a traditional Japanese garment, worn by both women and men. It is now worn on special occasions. For everyday use, most city dwellers wear Western-style clothes.

country, with a volcanic belt in the S and an alluvial plain to the N. It is thickly forested and has many rivers. It produces rice, tea, coffee, sugarcane, textiles, tobacco, and rubber. Silver, gold, and phosphate is mined in the N. Area: 48,842sq mi (126,501sq km). Pop. (1990) 107,581,306.

**javelin** Lightweight, tapered, tubular spear thrown in a field event: the longest throw wins, provided the javelin lands point-first. The modern javelin is made of a metal alloy, is up to 8.9ft (2.7m) long, and weighs a minimum of 28.2oz (800g) for men and 21oz (600g) for women.

**Jay, John** (1745–1829) US statesman, first chief justice of the Supreme Court (1789–95). Jay was president of the Continental Congress (1778–79) and negotiated the peace treaty with Great Britain. He was secretary of foreign affairs (1784–89) and contributed to *The Federalist* (1787–88). In 1794 he concluded Jay's Treaty, which served to sharpen divisions between the Federalist Party and the Democratic-Republican Party.

**jay** Any of several species of harsh-voiced birds related to the magpie and jackdaw. It has blue wing markings. Length: 13in (34cm). Family Corvidae.

**Jay's Treaty** (1794) Agreement between the US (represented by John Jay) and Britain (represented by Lord Grenville) principally to settle points of dispute outstanding since the American Revolution. Its provisions regarding trade helped establish American commerce. The US agreed not to aid privateers hostile to Britain, and Britain withdrew from the Northwest Territory.

**jazz** Style of music that developed in the S states of the USA in the late 19th century. It evolved from Negro spirituals and African slave songs. It is traditionally characterized by a syncopated rhythm drawn from ragtime; prominence of melody, often with elements derived from the blues; and improvisation. The form was taken up by white musicians as Dixieland music. Early practitioners included Buddy Bolden, "Jelly Roll" Morton, King Oliver, and Bix Beiderbecke. Louis Armstrong's trumpet-playing developed the role of the soloist. By the end of the 1920s jazz had spread to other US cities and influenced European classical composers, such as Ravel and Stravinsky. In the late 1920s swing developed in in Kansas City and Harlem. The role of improvisation diminished in favour of big-band orchestration. Major jazz composers and bandleaders emerged, such as Duke Ellington, Count Basie, Benny Goodman, and Glenn Miller. The big bands nurtured the talents of Billie Holiday, Coleman Hawkins, and Lester Young. In the 1930s "Django" Reinhardt fused European folk music with swing. In the 1940s Charlie Parker and Dizzy Gillespie led the bebop revolution in New York City, characterized by the use of the flatted fifth, complex rhythms, and harmonic rather than melodic progression. Other leading players included Bud Powell and Theolonius Monk. In the late 1940s Miles Davis and Stan Getz pioneered "cool" jazz. In the 1950s Davis and John Coltrane introduced modes as the basis for improvisation. Charles Mingus returned to the bluesy roots of jazz. In the 1960s avant-garde or free jazz introduced atonality, polyharmonies and polyrhythms. In the 1970s Miles Davis led experiments with a fusion of jazz and other popular forms, such as funk. In the 1980s and 1990s musicians such as Wynton Marsalis reflected on the historical traditions of jazz.

**Jedda** *See* Jiddah

**Jefferson, Thomas** (1743–1826) Third US president (1801–09), vice president (1797–81). Jefferson was a leading member of the Continental Congress and the primary author of the Declaration of Independence (1776). His governorship of Virginia (1779–81) was ended by the American Revolution. Jefferson returned to Congress (1783–84), before succeeding Benjamin Franklin as minister to France (1785–89). He was persuaded by George Washington to serve as his first secretary of state (1789–93). Disagreements with Alexander Hamilton saw the formation of the Democratic Republican Party led by Jefferson. Narrowly defeated by John Adams in the 1796 presidential election, Jefferson became vice president. He led opposition to the Alien and Sedition Acts (1798). The landmarks of his first administration (1801–05) were the Louisiana Purchase (1803) and the Lewis and Clark Expedition (1804–06). His second term (1805–09) overcame the Aaron Burr conspiracy. He managed to avoid war with Britain, instead passing an Embargo Act (1807). Jefferson retired from office and was succeeded by James Madison. He was a slave owner, although in principle opposed to slavery. He founded the Univeristy of Virginia (1825).

**Jefferson City** State capital of Missouri, on the Missouri River. It was chosen as state capital in 1821. The Capitol building (1911–18) was built in the Italian Renaissance style and contains some fine murals. Industries: shoes, clothes, electrical appliances, bookbinding. Pop. (1990) 35,480.

**Jehovah** Latinized representation of the name of the God of the Israelites. The name *Jehovah* developed during the Middle Ages from the Latin framework of the sacred name Yahweh (JHVH) and the vowels from *Adonai* (a, o, and a).

**Jehovah's Witnesses** Religious sect founded in the 1870s by Charles Taze Russell (1852–1916) of Pittsburgh. The sect believes in the imminent end of the world for all except its own members. They hold to the theory of a theocratic kingdom (a kingdom ruled by God), membership in which cannot be reconciled with allegiance to any country. They deny most fundamental Christian doctrines and believe the Bible prohibits blood transfusion. The sect is active worldwide.

**jellyfish** Marine COELENTERATE found in coastal waters and characterized by tentacles with stinging cells. The adult form is the medusa. It has a bell-shaped body with a thick layer of jelly-like substance between two body cell layers, many tentacles, and four mouth lobes surrounding the gut opening. Diameter: 3–12in (7.5–30.5cm). Class Scyphozoa.

**Jenner, Edward** (1749–1823) British physician who pioneered VACCINATION. Aware that cowpox, a minor disease, seemed to protect people from smallpox, Jenner, in 1796, inoculated a healthy boy with cowpox from the sores of an infected dairymaid. The boy was later found to be immune to smallpox.

**jerboa** Nocturnal, herbivorous, burrowing RODENT of Eurasian and African deserts, with long hind legs . It has a satiny, sand-colored body and a long tail. Length: to 6in (15cm), excluding the tail. Family Dipodidae.

**Jeremiah** (active 7th century BC) Prophet who gave his name to the Old Testament Book of Jeremiah. He preached that the sinful behavior of his countrymen would be punished by God. When Babylon invaded Judah (587 BC), Jeremiah saw it as this punishment.

**Jericho** Ancient city of Palestine, on the WEST BANK of the Jordan River, N of the Dead Sea. It is one of the earliest known sites of continuous settlement, dating from *c.*9000 BC. According to the Old Testament, Joshua captured Jericho from the Canaanites (*c.*300 BC). The city was destroyed and HEROD THE GREAT built a new city to the s. In 1993 Jericho was selected as the center for Palestinian self-rule. It lies in an agricultural area, producing citrus fruit and dates.

**Jeroboam** Name of two kings of Israel (N Palestine). **Jeroboam I** (active late 10th century BC) led an unsuccessful revolt against King SOLOMON and was forced to flee to Egypt. After Solomon's death he returned to lead the secessionist kingdom of Israel in Palestine's N hills. **Jeroboam II** (reigned *c.*783–*c.*741 BC) ruled Israel during a period of relative peace. Although Israel made economic progress and saw a revival in its political power, corruption was widespread.

**Jerome, Saint** (347–420) Translator of the Bible into Latin, b. Eusebius Hieronymous. Born in what is now Slovenia, he had a literary education and spent two years as a hermit before being ordained a priest. Pope Damasus I commissioned Jerome to prepare a text of the gospels for use by Latin-speaking Christians. His work was the basis for what became the authorized Latin text of the Bible. In 384 Jerome left Rome and set up a monastic community for men and women in Bethlehem.

**Jersey** Largest of the CHANNEL ISLANDS, lying *c.*10 mi (16km) off the NW coast of Normandy in France. Fruit and dairy farming are important. The capital is St. Helier. Area: 45sq mi (117sq km). Pop. (1991) 84,082.

**Jersey City** Port city in NE New Jersey, on the Hudson River and Upper New York Bay, across from New York City; second largest city in the state. Founded in 1630, it was originally a Dutch settlement, coming under British control in 1664. In 1779 "Light-Horse Harry" Lee, under George Washington, captured it. It is the seat of Hudson county. Industries: oil refining, chemicals, locomotives, clothing. Pop. (1990) 228,517.

▼ **Jerusalem** The Dome of the Rock (*Qubbat al-Sakhrah*) is one of several major religious sites in Jerusalem. Dating to the 7th century, it is the first domed mosque, and is built on the site of a Jewish temple. In 1996 there was unrest following the opening of a tunnel that ran close to the site, which is considered sacred ground by Muslims.

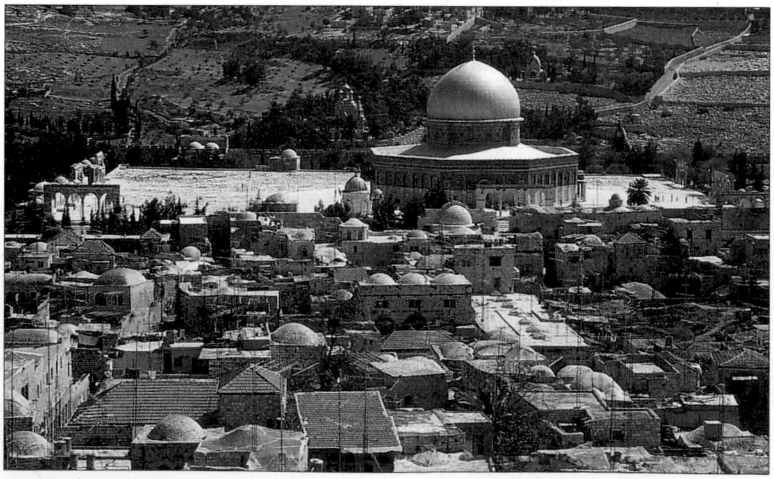

**Jerusalem** Capital of Israel, a sacred site for Christians, Jews, and Muslims. Originally a Jebusite stronghold (2000–1500 BC), the city was captured by King DAVID after 1000 BC. Destroyed by NEBUCHADNEZZAR *c.*587 BC, it was rebuilt by HEROD THE GREAT *c.*35 BC, but was again destroyed by TITUS, in AD 70. The Roman colony of Aelia Capitolina was established, and Jews were forbidden within city limits until the 5th century. Christian control was ended by the Persians in AD 614. It was conquered in 1071 by the SELJUKS, whose mistreatment of Christians precipitated the CRUSADES. It was held by the OTTOMAN Turks from 1244–1917, before becoming the capital of the British-mandated territory of Palestine. In 1948 it was divided between Jordan (the east) and Israel (the west). In 1967 the Israeli army captured the Old City of East Jerusalem. In 1980 the united city was declared the capital of Israel, although this status is not recognized by the UN. Notable monuments within the old city include the DOME OF THE ROCK, the El Aqsa Mosque, and the Western (Wailing) Wall. Jerusalem is an administrative and cultural center. Industries: banking, insurance, tourism, diamond cutting. Pop. (1992) 544,200.

**Jesuits** Members of a Roman Catholic religious order for men officially known as the Society of Jesus, founded by St. IGNATIUS OF LOYOLA in 1534. They played a significant role in the COUNTER-REFORMATION. The Jesuits were active missionaries. They antagonized many European rulers because they gave allegiance only to their general in Rome and to the pope. In 1773 Pope Clement XIV abolished the order, under pressure from the kings of France, Spain, and Portugal, but it continued to exist in Russia. The order was reestablished in 1814.

**Jesus Christ** (active 1st century AD) Hebrew preacher who founded the religion of CHRISTIANITY, hailed and worshiped by his followers as the Son of God. Knowledge of Jesus' life is based mostly on the biblical gospels of St. MATTHEW, St. MARK, and St. LUKE. The date of Jesus' birth is now given as *c.*4 BC, but may have been earlier. The birth occurred near the end of the reign of HEROD THE GREAT in Bethlehem, Judaea. MARY, believed by Christians to have been made pregnant by God, gave birth to Jesus. The birth was said to have taken place in a stable and been attended by the appearance of a bright star and other unusual events. Jesus grew up in Nazareth, and may have followed his father, JOSEPH, in becoming a carpenter. In *c.*AD 27, Jesus was baptized in the Jordan River by JOHN THE BAPTIST. Thereafter, Jesus began his own ministry, preaching to large numbers as he wandered throughout the country. He also taught a special group of 12 of his closest disciples, who were later sent out as his APOSTLES to bring his teachings to the Jews. Jesus' basic teaching, summarized in the SERMON ON THE MOUNT, was to "love God and love one's neighbor." He also taught that salvation depended on doing God's will rather than adhering to the letter and the contemporary interpretation of the Jewish Law. Such a precept angered the hierarchy of the Jewish religion. In *c.*AD 30 Jesus and his disciples went to Jerusalem. His reputation as preacher and miracle-worker went before him, and he was acclaimed as the MESSIAH. A few days later Jesus gathered his disciples to partake in the LAST SUPPER. At this meal, he instituted the EUCHARIST. Before dawn the next day, Jesus was arrested by agents of the Hebrew authorities, accompanied by JUDAS ISCARIOT, and summarily tried by the SANHEDRIN, the Supreme Council of the Jews. He was then handed to the Roman procurator, PONTIUS PILATE, on a charge of sedition. Roman soldiers crucified Jesus at Golgotha. After his death, Jesus' body was buried in a sealed rock tomb. Two days later, according to the gospel accounts, he rose from the dead and appeared to his disciples and to others. Forty days after his resurrection, he is said to have ascended into heaven.

**jet engine** Engine that derives forward motion by reaction to the rapid discharge of a jet of fluid (gas or liquid) in the opposite direction. In a jet engine, fuel burns in oxygen from the air to produce a fast-moving stream of exhaust gases. These are ejected from the back of the jet engine and produce a forward thrust in accordance with Newton's third law of motion. *See also* Newton's Laws

**Jet Propulsion Laboratory (JPL)** Space center in Pasadena, California, for the development and control of unmanned spacecraft. The California Institute of Technology runs JPL for the National Aeronautics and Space Administration (NASA). JPL scientists sent the Surveyor probes to the Moon in the 1960s. Other notable projects include the Mariner program, the Viking space mission, and the Voyager program.

**jet stream** Narrow, swiftly moving winds between slower currents at altitudes of 6–10mi (10–16km) in the upper troposphere or lower stratosphere, principally in the zone of prevailing westerlies.

**Jews** Traditionally, the descendants of Judah, fourth son of Jacob, who settled in ancient Palestine towards the end of the 2nd millennium BC; historically, followers of the religion of Judaism. In *c.*1020 BC Saul founded the Hebrew state of Israel. David united the kingdoms of Judaea and Israel. His son, Solomon, built the Temple in Jerusalem. In 587 BC the Temple was destroyed by Nebuchadnezzar and Jews were deported from Jerusalem, beginning the period of the Babylonian Captivity. In 538 BC Cyrus the Great delivered the Jews from Babylon. In AD 70 the Temple was destroyed for a second time by the Romans and the diaspora began. The descendants of Jews who emigrated to Spain and Portugal are known as the Sephardim; those who settled in NW Europe are known as the Ashkenazim. In Christian Europe Jews were victims of anti-semitism. They were forced into ghettos and given menial occupations such as usury. In 1290 Jews were driven out of England. In 1492 they were expelled from Spain. During World War II (1939–45), six million Jews were killed in the holocaust. In 1948, having struggled against British rule in modern Palestine, the modern state of Israel was proclaimed, despite opposition from Arab and other Islamic states. Today, there are *c.*17.5 million Jews worldwide, including c.7 million in the USA and c.5 million in Israel. *See also* Falashas; Semitic languages; Yiddish; Zionism

**Jezebel** (d. *c.*843 BC) Phoenician princess who became the wife of Ahab, king of Israel. She introduced into Israel the worship of the Phoenician deity Baal and came into conflict with the priests of Yahweh. She clashed most severely with the prophet Elijah, who foretold her brutal death.

**Jiang Qing** (1914–92) Chinese actress and politician, third wife of Mao Zedong. She became a high-ranking party official and the leader of the Cultural Revolution. One of the radical Gang of Four that sought power after Mao's death in 1976, she was arrested the following year, convicted of treason, and imprisoned for life.

**Jiangsu** (Kiangsu) Province in E China; the capital is Nanking. Under the rule of the Ming dynasty from 1368–1644, it became a separate province in the 18th century. Taken by Japan in 1937, the province was freed by the Chinese Nationalists in 1945 but fell to the Chinese Communists in 1949. One of China's smallest and most densely populated provinces, it is an extremely fertile region that includes the Yangtze (Changjiang) River delta. It is highly industrialized: Shanghai, the largest city, is the chief manufacturing center of China. Products: rice, cotton, wheat, barley, soybeans, peanuts, tea. Industries: silk, oil refining, textiles, food processing, cement. Area: 39,474sq mi (102,240sq km). Pop. (1990) 68,170,000.

**Jiddah** (Jedda) Administrative capital and largest port of Saudi Arabia, on the Red Sea, 46mi (74km) W of Mecca. Under Turkish rule until 1916, it was taken in 1925 by Ibn Saud. It acts as a port of entry for the Hajj. Oil wealth has also expanded the city and port. Industries: steel rolling, oil refining, cement, pottery manufacture. Pop. (1986 est.) 1,400,000.

**jihad** (jehad) Religious obligation imposed upon Muslims through the Koran to spread Islam and protect its followers by waging war on nonbelievers. There are four ways in which Muslims may fulfill their jihad duty: by the heart, by the tongue, by the hand, and by the sword.

**Jim Crow laws** Laws enacted in southern US states after Reconstruction, enforcing racial segregation in public places and on public transport. They were progressively overturned by the civil rights legislation of the 1950s and 1960s.

**JET ENGINE**

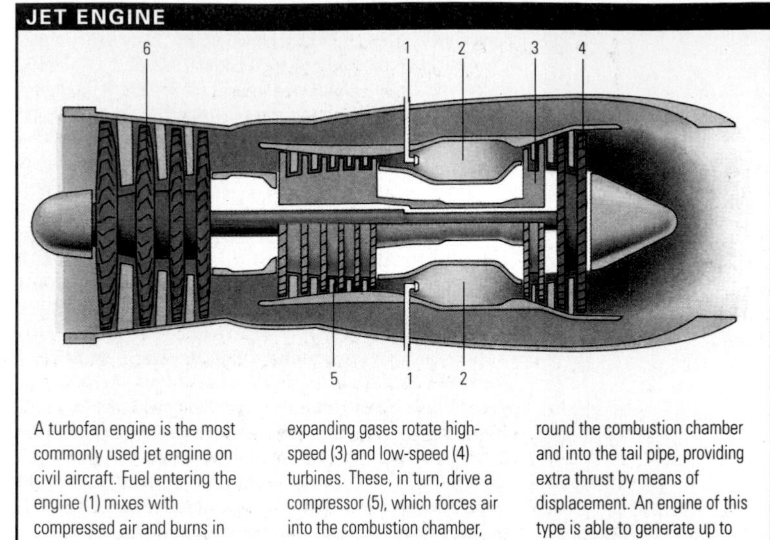


A turbofan engine is the most commonly used jet engine on civil aircraft. Fuel entering the engine (1) mixes with compressed air and burns in the combustion chamber (2). The expanding gases rotate high-speed (3) and low-speed (4) turbines. These, in turn, drive a compressor (5), which forces air into the combustion chamber, and fans (6), which push air round the combustion chamber and into the tail pipe, providing extra thrust by means of displacement. An engine of this type is able to generate up to 4,000lbs of thrust.

**Jinnah, Muhammad Ali** (1876–1948) Founder of Pakistan. A British-trained lawyer, he joined the Indian National Congress in 1906 but left it in 1920 when his demand for a separate Muslim electorate was rejected. He led the Muslim League in campaigning for political equality for Indian Muslims, while continuing to seek agreement with Hindus. By 1940 he had adopted the aim of a separate Muslim state. This was realized when India was partitioned in 1947.

**Joan of Arc** (1412–31) (Jeanne d'Arc) National heroine of France, also known as Joan of Lorraine or the Maid of Orléans. A peasant girl, she claimed to hear heavenly voices urging her to save France during the Hundred Years War. In 1429 Joan led French troops in breaking the English siege of Orléans. She drove the English from the Loire towns and persuaded the indecisive dauphin to have himself crowned at Reims as Charles VII of France. In 1430 she was captured and handed over to the English. Condemned as a heretic, she was burned at the stake.

**Job** Old Testament book describing the crises in the life of Job, a well-to-do man from a town E of Palestine. The main theme is that suffering comes to good and bad people alike.

**Jodhpur** (Marwar) Walled city on the edge of the Thar Desert, Rajasthan, NW India. Founded in 1459, it was the capital of the former princely state of Jodhpur. It is now an important road and rail junction. Industries: textiles, lacquerware, bicycles. Pop. (1991). 668,000

**Joffre, Joseph Jacques Césaire** (1852–1931) French general. He was commander in chief of the French army at the outbreak of World War I (1914). Determined to take the offensive, he was forced to retreat but recouped his forces, and his reputation, in the First Battle of the Marne. After heavy losses at Verdun and on the Somme in 1916, he resigned.

**Johannesburg** City on the Witwatersrand, capital of Gauteng province, NE South Africa. The largest city in modern South Africa, Johannesburg was founded as a gold-mining town in 1886. In 1900 it was captured by the British in the second of the South African Wars. It developed rapidly as the administrative headquarters for South Africa's gold-mining industry. Industries: pharmaceuticals, metal, machinery, textiles, engineering, diamond cutting. Pop. (1991) 1,916,063.

**John, Saint** (active 1st century AD) Apostle of Jesus Christ, one of the original 12 disciples. Known also as St. John the Apostle and St. John the Evangelist, he is widely believed to be the author of the fourth gospel and the three New Testament epistles of John. He is also identified with St. John the Divine, the author of the Book of Revelation. John was the brother of another apostle, St. James the Greater. Together with his brother and St. Peter, St. John belonged to the inner group of disciples. His feast day is December 27.

**John XXIII** (1881–1963) Pope (1958–63). b. Angelo Giuseppe Roncalli. He served in the papal diplomatic service

▲ **Jordan** Leaving North Carolina University after his junior year, Michael Jordan was selected as guard for the Chicago Bulls in 1984. He has gone on to become one of the most successful players of all time. His return to basketball saw him become the NBA's most Valuable Player (1995–96). He was a member of the US "Dream Team" in the 1992 Olympic games.

before his election as pope. Aged 77, he was regarded as a compromise choice. John convened the Second VATICAN COUNCIL to promote reform and renewal within the Church.

**John** (1167–1216) King of England (1199–1216), youngest son of HENRY II. He ruled during RICHARD I's absence on the Third Crusade. Disgraced for intriguing against Richard, John nevertheless succeeded him as king. The loss of vast territories in France (1204–05) and heavy taxation made him unpopular. In 1215 he was compelled to sign the MAGNA CARTA, and his subsequent disregard of the terms led to the first BARONS' WAR.

**John II (the Good)** (1319–64) King of France (1350–64), son of PHILIP VI. In the HUNDRED YEARS WAR he was captured by the English at Poitiers (1356) and held in England. He was released on the promise of a large ransom, but when he was unable to provide it he returned to England, where he died.

**John III (Sobieski)** (1624–96) King of Poland (1674–96). His ambition led him into conspiracy with the French against Polish interests, but his successful generalship against the Ottoman Turks gained him election as king. His greatest triumph came in 1683 when he raised the siege of Vienna and liberated Hungary by defeating the Ottoman Turks. In Poland his rule was frustrated by opposition and revolt.

**John I** (1357–1433) King of Portugal (1385–1433). After the death of his half-brother, Ferdinand I, he resisted the proposed regency of Ferdinand's daughter, and was elected king. His reign marked the beginning of Portuguese maritime expansion.

**John VI** (1767–1826) King of Portugal (1816–26). Because of the insanity of his mother, Queen Maria, he was effectively sovereign from 1792, officially regent from 1799. In 1807 he fled to Brazil to escape the invading French and did not return to claim the throne until 1822, when he accepted the constitutional government proclaimed in 1820.

**John, Gospel according to Saint** Fourth and last gospel of the New Testament, recounting the life and death of JESUS CHRIST and believed to be the work of the Apostle JOHN. It is more concerned with the spiritual meaning of events than with historical facts or even historical sequence.

**John of Gaunt** (1340–99) English nobleman, duke of Lancaster (1362–99). Fourth son of EDWARD III, he acquired the Lancastrian estates through marriage. He spent much of his life campaigning in the HUNDRED YEARS WAR. He was father of HENRY IV, first king of the Lancastrian dynasty.

**John Paul I** (1912–78) Pope (1978), b. Albino Luciani. He became the 263rd pope of the Roman Catholic Church. A modest but gregarious man, he reigned for only 34 days.

**John Paul II** (1920– ) Pope (1978– ), b. Poland as Karol Wojtyla. He studied literature before being ordained in 1946. John Paul became auxiliary bishop of Kraków (1958), archbishop (1964), and then cardinal (1967). He became the first non-Italian pope in 455 years. Theologically conservative, John Paul upheld papal infallibility and condemned artificial birth control and the ordination of women as priests.

**Johns, Jasper** (1930– ) US painter, sculptor, and printmaker. Together with Robert RAUSCHENBERG, he led the movement away from abstract expressionism toward POP ART and MINIMAL ART. His characteristic style features canvases covered with banal, everyday images, such as *Three Flags* (1958) and *Target With Four Faces* (1955).

**Johnson, Andrew** (1808–75) 17th US president (1865–69), vice president (1864–65). He was a Democrat governor (1853–57) and senator (1857–62) for Tennessee. He was the only Southerner to remain in the Senate after the outbreak of the CIVIL WAR. Johnson was elected with the incumbent Republican president Abraham LINCOLN on a National Union ticket, and became president when Lincoln was assassinated. His policy of RECONSTRUCTION saw the restoration of civil government to the South. His opposition to civil rights for blacks, conciliation of Confederate leaders and attempt to remove Edwin M. STANTON, led to his impeachment for "crimes and misdemeanours." Johnson was acquitted by one vote.

**Johnson, Jack (John Arthur)** (1878–1946) US boxer. He was the first African-American to win the world heavyweight title, defeating Tommy Burns (1908). He lost the title to Jess Willard in 1915.

**Johnson, James Weldon** (1871–1938) US writer and civil rights leader. He is best known for his poetry, especially *God's Trombones* (1927), and the novel *The Autobiography of an Ex-Colored Man* (1912). He served as a US consul and helped found the NATIONAL ASSOCIATION FOR THE ADVANCEMENT OF COLORED PEOPLE (NAACP). He also wrote music with his brother, John Rosamond Johnson (1873–1954), including the lyrics to "Lift Every Voice and Sing" (1900).

**Johnson, Lyndon Baines** (1908–73) 36th US president (1963–69), vice president (1960–63). He represented Texas as a Democrat in the House of Representatives (1937–48) and the Senate (1948–60). Johnson served as vice president to John F. KENNEDY, and became president after Kennedy's assassination (1963). He showed considerable skill in securing passage of the CIVIL RIGHTS Act (1964) and was overwhelmingly re-elected in 1964. Johnson carried out an ambitous domestic reform programme, but its success was overshadowed by the escalation of the VIETNAM WAR, which, together with severe race riots in 1965–68, dissuaded him from seeking re-election in 1968. His vice president, Hubert HUMPHREY, lost the ensuing election to Richard NIXON.

**Johnson, "Magic" (Earvin)** (1959– ) US professional basketball player. He led the Los Angeles Lakers to five National Basketball Association (NBA) championships (1980, 1982, 1985, 1987, 1988) and was voted Most Valuable Player three times (1987, 1989, 1990). In 1991 Johnson retired after announcing he was HIV-positive. He returned to win a gold medal with the US "Dream Tream" in the 1992 Olympics.

**Johnson, Philip Cortelyou** (1906– ) US architect. He studied under Marcel BREUER at Harvard University and became a proponent of the INTERNATIONAL STYLE. Johnson collaborated with MIES VAN DER ROHE on the Seagram Building, New York City, USA (1958). Other designs include the Lincoln Center, New York City (1964).

**Johnson, Samuel** (1709–84) English lexicographer, poet and critic. His reputation was established by the masterly *Dictionary of the English Language* (1755). Other works include the essay collection *The Idler* (1758–61), the philosophical romance *Rasselas* (1759), and the critical *Lives of the Poets* (1779–81). A trenchant conversationalist, Johnson co-founded (1764) "The Club" with Joshua REYNOLDS. In 1773 he toured Scotland with his biographer James BOSWELL.

**Johnson, Walter Perry** (1887–1946) US baseball player. One of the greatest pitchers of all time, he won 416 games, 110 of them shutouts, and struck out 3,508 batters in his career with the Washington Senators (1907–27). He was elected to the Baseball Hall of Fame in 1936.

**Johnston, Joseph** (1807–91) Confederate CIVIL WAR general. He commanded the Confederate troops at the First Battle of BULL RUN and in the PENINSULAR CAMPAIGN. When he was wounded at Fair Oaks, Virginia (June 1862), Robert E. LEE took command of the Confederate army.

**John the Baptist** (active 1st century AD) Prophet who heralded the appearance of JESUS CHRIST and the coming of the kingdom of God. The son of ZECHARIAH and Elizabeth, he was born in Judea six months before Jesus. Jesus was one of those who accepted his baptism, an action that marked the beginning of his ministry and was the true start of the New Testament.

**joint** In anatomy, place where one BONE meets another. In movable joints, such as those of the knee, elbow, and spine, the bones are separated and cushioned from one another by pads of CARTILAGE. In fixed joints, cartilage may be present in infancy but disappear later as the bones fuse together, as in the SKULL. In the movable joints of bony VERTEBRATES, the bones are held together by LIGAMENTS. SYNOVIAL FLUID lubricates the joint.

**Joint Chiefs of Staff (JCS)** US military body, principal advisers to the president, the National Security Council, and the Secretary of Defense. Its responsibilities include planning the strategy of the armed forces. The JCS consists of a chairman and the chiefs of staff of the Army, Air Force, and Navy, and, when necessary, the commandant of the Marine Corps.

**Jolliet, Louis** (1646–1700) French explorer, b. Quebec, Canada. In 1673 Jolliet and Jacques Marquette became the first Europeans to travel the Mississippi River, from its confluence with the Wisconsin River to the mouth of the Arkansas River.

**Joliot-Curie, Irene** *See* CURIE, MARIE

**Jolson, Al** (1886–1950) US music-hall singer and comedian, b. Russia as Asa Yoelson. He began his career working in minstrel shows. Jolson starred in *The Jazz Singer* (1927), the first major film with sound. He is remembered for his sentimental renditions of "Swanee" and "Mammy".

**Jonah** Fifth of the 12 minor prophets and central character in the Old Testament Book of Jonah. This book is an account of Jonah's adventures, showing God's mercy to non-Jews.

**Jones, Inigo** (1573–1652) English architect and painter. He introduced England to a pure CLASSICAL style based on the work of Andrea PALLADIO. His knowledge of Italian architecture gained him enormous prestige. His most noted buildings include the Queen's House, Greenwich (1616–35), and Banqueting House, Whitehall (1619–21).

**Jones, John Paul** (1747–92) American naval officer in the American Revolution, b. Scotland as John Paul. He joined the Continental navy in 1775, and proved successful at capturing supplies and enemy vessels. With his flagship *Bonhomme Richard* he engaged the British ship *Serapis* in an epic battle off the coast of England (1779). He boarded and captured the *Serapis* while his ship burned and then sank.

**Jones, Bobby Robert Tyre, Jr.** (1902–71) US golfer. Although never turning professional, he won four US Opens (1923, 1926, 1929, 1930), three British Opens (1926, 1927, 1930), and in 1930 won golf's amateur "grand slam": the US and British opens and US and British amateurs.

**Jonson, Ben** (1572–1637) English dramatist, poet, and actor. His first major play, *Every Man in His Humour* (1598), included SHAKESPEARE in its cast. Jonson's major works are the four comedies *Volpone* (1606), *Epicoene* (1609), *The Alchemist* (1610), and *Bartholomew Fair* (1614). He became the first poet laureate. His collected verse includes *Epigrams* (1616) and *The Forest* (1616), featuring "Song: To Celia".

**Joplin, Scott** (1868–1917) US composer. He wrote ragtime piano music such as "Maple Leaf Rag" (1900) and "The Entertainer" (1902), as well as the opera *Treemonisha* (1911).

**Jordan, Michael Jeffrey** (1963– ) US basketball player. He led the Chicago Bulls to six National Basketball Association titles (1991–93, 1996–98) and was named Most Valuable Player five times (1988, 1991, 1992, 1996, 1997). Jordan played in the US teams that won gold medals at the 1984 and 1992 Olympics. In 1993 he switched to baseball, but returned to the Bulls in 1995. Jordan retired in 1999.

**Jordan** Hashemite kingdom in SW Asia. *See* country feature

## JORDAN

The green, white, and black on this flag are the colors of the three tribes who led the Arab Revolt against the Turks in 1917. Red is the color of the Hussein dynasty. The star was added in 1928. Its seven points represent the first seven verses of the Holy Koran.

**AREA:** 34,444sq mi (89,210sq km)
**POPULATION:** 4,291,000
**CAPITAL (POPULATION):** Amman 1,300,042)
**GOVERNMENT:** Constitutional monarchy
**ETHNIC GROUPS:** Arab 99%, of which Palestinians make up roughly half
**LANGUAGES:** Arabic (official)
**RELIGIONS:** Islam 93%, Christianity 5%
**CURRENCY:** Jordan dinar = 1,000 fils

The Hashemite Kingdom of Jordan in SW Asia can be divided into three geographical areas. The Transjordan plateau in the E constitutes 90% of the land area and is the most populous region. It includes the capital, AMMAN. Central Jordan forms part of the Great RIFT VALLEY, and contains the JORDAN River and the DEAD SEA. West Jordan (now the WEST BANK) is part of historic PALESTINE and includes the region of SAMARIA. The area is now occupied by ISRAEL. Jordan has a coastline on the Gulf of AQABA. The ancient city of PETRA lies close to Jordan's highest peak, Jebel Ram at 5,755ft (1,754m).

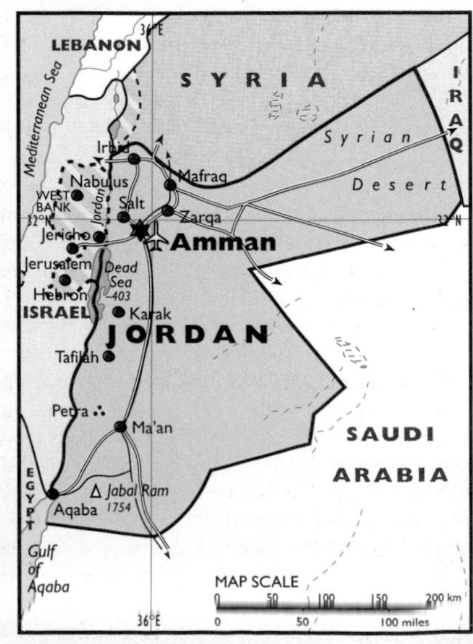


### CLIMATE

The Transjordan plateau, on which Amman stands, is a transition zone between a Mediterranean climate zone to the W and a desert climate to the E. It has much lower rainfall and a longer dry season than the Mediterranean zone.

### VEGETATION

Parts of the W plateau have scrub vegetation. Jordan has areas of dry grassland. The rest of the area is desert or semidesert.

### HISTORY AND POLITICS

The region was conquered by the SELEUCIDS in the 4th century BC. In the 1st century BC the Nabatean empire developed their capital of Petra. The Romans captured the region in the 1st century AD. In AD 636 Arab armies conquered the territory and introduced Islam. After the First CRUSADE it was incorporated into the Latin kingdom of Jerusalem (1099). In 1517 the area became part of the Ottoman Empire. After the defeat of the Ottoman Empire in World War I, the area E of the Jordan River was included in the British League of Nations mandate of Palestine. In 1921 the E region was administered separately as Transjordan. In 1928 it became a constitutional monarchy ruled by the Hashemite dynasty. In 1946 Transjordan became independent. The creation of the state of Israel (1948) led to the first of the ARAB-ISRAELI WARS (1948–49). Hundreds of thousands of Palestinians fled to Jordan. Under the peace terms Transjordan annexed the remaining Arab parts of Palestine (the West Bank and East Jerusalem). This incensed the Palestinians and King ABDULLAH was assassinated in 1951. HUSSEIN I acceded in 1953. In 1958 Jordan formed the short-lived Arab Federation with Iraq. The SIX DAY WAR (1967) ended in the Israeli occupation of East Jerusalem and the West Bank. Over 1 million Palestinian refugees now lived in E Jordan. Jordan became embroiled in a bloody civil war with Palestinian independence movements (1970). By 1971 Jordan had ejected all the guerrillas operating from its soil. In 1974 King Hussein recognized the Palestine Liberation Organization (PLO) as the legitimate representative of the Palestinian peoples. In 1988 Jordan gave up its claim to the West Bank and approved the creation of an independent Palestine. Jordan sided with Iraq in the IRAN–IRAQ WAR and the GULF WAR. In 1993 the first multiparty elections were held. In October 1994 Jordan and Israel signed a peace treaty that ended the state of war existing since 1948. The border between ELAT and Aqaba was opened and King Hussein was granted custodial rights of Islamic holy sites in Jerusalem. Elections in 1997 were boycotted by opposition parties, including the Islamic Action Front (IAF). In 1999 King Hussein died and was succeeded by his son, Abdullah

### ECONOMY

Jordan is a developing country (1995 GDP per capita, US$4,060). It is the world's seventh largest producer of phosphates and potash. Under 56% of the land is farm or pasture land. Major crops include barley, citrus fruits, grapes, olives, vegetables, and wheat. It is dependent on aid. Jordan has an oil refinery and produces natural gas. Tourism is developing rapidly and reforms are helping to expand the economy.

▲ **Joyce** Born in Dublin and educated first by Jesuits, then at University College, Dublin, James Joyce was a voracious reader and an accomplished linguist. He was plagued from a relatively early age by glaucoma and was deeply troubled by his daughter's mental illness. His seminal novel *Ulysses* (1922) was highly controversial at the time of its publication but is now regarded as a groundbreaking work of modernism.

J

**Jordan** River in the Middle East, rising in the Anti-Lebanon Mountains at the confluence of the Hasbani, Dan, and Baniyas rivers. It flows S through Israel and the Sea of Galilee and empties into the Dead Sea. Since 1967 the S part of the river has formed a section of the Israel-Jordan border. Length: 200mi (320km).

**Joseph, Saint** In the New Testament, husband of MARY and the legal father of JESUS CHRIST. He was a carpenter from Nazareth, N Palestine. His feast day is March 19 or May 1.

**Joseph I** (1678–1711) Holy Roman emperor (1705–11). His reign was dominated by revolt in Hungary, where he was king from 1687, and by the War of the SPANISH SUCCESSION. When he died, he was succeeded by his brother, CHARLES VI.

**Joseph II** (1741–90) Holy Roman emperor (1765–90). Co-ruler with his mother MARIA THERESA until 1780, he introduced sweeping liberal and humanitarian reforms while retaining autocratic powers. Some of his reforms were reversed by his successor, LEOPOLD II.

**Joseph** In the Old Testament book of Genesis, 11th of the 12 sons of JACOB. Given a richly woven, multicolored coat by his father, Joseph was sold into slavery by his jealous elder brothers. He was taken to Egypt, where he gained the pharaoh's favor by predicting the seven-year famine, thus allowing stores to be laid by from the previous seven good years. He was later reconciled with his brothers.

**Joseph, Chief** (*c*.1840–1904) Native American leader. He was chief of the Nez Percé tribe of the Wallowa Valley, succeeding his father (1873). He is best known for his brilliant tactics during his attempt (1877) to lead 800 of his people through Idaho, Washington, and Montana to Canada while fighting off the US Army. He was finally forced to surrender near the Canadian border.

**Joséphine** (1763–1814) Consort of NAPOLEON I and empress of the French (1804–09). Her first marriage, to Vicomte Alexandre de Beauharnais, ended with his death (1794) during the REIGN OF TERROR. In 1796 Joséphine married Napoleon. Her inability to bear him a son caused Napoleon to obtain annulment of their marriage in 1809.

**Joseph of Arimathea, Saint** Prosperous Jew who was a secret follower of JESUS CHRIST. He claimed Christ's body from Pontius Pilate after the crucifixion and attended to its burial. His feast day is March 17 in the West, July 31 in the East.

**Josephson, Brian David** (1940–95) Welsh physicist. In 1962 he deduced that an electric current would flow between two superconductors separated by a thin layer of insulator (the "Josephson effect"). Josephson shared the 1973 Nobel Prize for physics with Leo ESAKI and Ivar Giaever. It has helped in the understanding of SUPERCONDUCTIVITY.

**Josephus, Flavius** (AD 37–100) Jewish leader and historian, b. Joseph ben Mattityahu. As governor of Galilee, he took part in the revolt against Rome (AD 66–70) and was captured. Josephus found favour with VESPASIAN and settled in Rome (70). His writings include *The Jewish War* (75–79) and *Antiquities of the Jews* (93).

**Joshua** Heroic figure among the Israelites, who became their commander after the death of MOSES and led them into CANAAN following their exodus from Egypt. His subsequent exploits and campaigns are recorded in the Book of Joshua, the sixth book of the Old Testament.

**Jospin, Lionel** (1937– ) French statesman, prime minister (1997– ). In 1995 he succeeded François MITTERRAND as leader of the French Socialist Party (PS) but lost the ensuing presidential election to Jacques CHIRAC. In the 1997 prime ministerial elections, Jospin won a surprise victory against the incumbent, Alain Juppé.

**Joule, James Prescott** (1818–89) British physicist. Joule's law (1841) relates the current flowing through a wire to its heat loss. It laid the foundation for the law of conservation of energy. The JOULE is named for him.

**joule** SI unit of energy (symbol J). One joule is the work done by a force of one NEWTON acting over a distance of one meter. It was named for James P. JOULE and replaced the erg.

**Joyce, James** (1882–1941) Irish novelist. He renounced Catholicism and left Ireland in 1904 to live and work in Europe. Joyce's experiments with narrative form place him at the center of literary MODERNISM. His first work was the short-story collection *Dubliners* (1914). *A Portrait of the Artist as a Young Man* (1916) was a fictionalized autobiography of Stephen Daedalus. His masterpiece, the novel *Ulysses* (1922), presents a day (June 16, 1904) in the life of Leopold Bloom. *Finnegan's Wake* (1939) is an allusive mix of Irish history and myth.

**Juárez, Benito Pablo** (1806–72) Mexican statesman, president (1858–62, 1867–72). Elected governor of his native state of Oaxaca in 1847, he was exiled (1853–55) by SANTA ANNA. As president, Juárez won a victory over conservatives in the "War of Reform," and headed resistance to the French invasion (1862) until the fall of MAXIMILIAN (1867).

**Judah** Fourth son of JACOB and his first wife Leah, and forefather of the most important of the 12 tribes of ancient ISRAEL. After the exodus and Joshua's conquest of CANAAN, the tribe of Judah received the region south of JERUSALEM. This territory later became known as Judaea. The tribe of Judah eventually became the dominant one. Israel's greatest kings, DAVID and SOLOMON belonged to it, and prophets foretold that the MESSIAH would arise from among its members.

**Judaism** Monotheistic religion developed by the ancient HEBREWS in the Near East during the third millennium BC and practiced by modern JEWS. Tradition holds that Judaism was founded by ABRAHAM, who, in *c*.20th century BC, was chosen by God to receive favorable treatment in return for obedience and worship. Having entered into this covenant with God, Abraham moved to CANAAN, from where centuries later his descendants migrated to Egypt and became enslaved. God accomplished the Hebrews' escape from Egypt and renewed the covenant with their leader MOSES. Through Moses, God gave the Hebrews a set of strict laws. These laws are revealed in the TORAH, the core of Judaistic scripture. Apart from the PENTATEUCH, the other holy books are the TALMUD and several commentaries. Local worship takes place in a SYNAGOGUE, a building where the Torah is read in public and preserved in a replica of the ARK OF THE COVENANT. A RABBI undertakes the spiritual leadership and pastoral care of a community. Modern Judaism is split into four large groups: Orthodox, Reform, Conservative, and Liberal Judaism. **Orthodox** Judaism, followed by most of the world's 18 million Jews, asserts the supreme authority of the Torah and adheres most closely to traditions, such as the segregation of men and women in the synagogue. **Reform** Judaism denies the Jews' claim to be God's chosen people, and is more liberal in its interpretation of certain laws and the Torah. **Conservative** Judaism is a compromise between Orthodox and Reform Judaism, adhering to many Orthodox traditions, but seeking to apply modern scholarship in interpreting the Torah. **Liberal** Judaism, also known as Reconstructionism, is a more extreme form of Reform Judaism, seeking to adapt Judaism to the needs of society.

**Judas Iscariot** (d.*c*. AD 30) Disciple who betrayed JESUS CHRIST to the Jewish hierarchy. He was one of the 12 apostles originally chosen by Jesus. When Jesus and his disciples arrived in Jerusalem, Judas assisted the chief priests in arresting Jesus. In return for 30 pieces of silver, he led the chief priests' agents to the Garden of Gesthemane and pointed Jesus out to them by greeting him with a kiss. Later, in remorse, he committed suicide.

**Jude, Epistle of** New Testament book of the Bible. It consists of a letter exhorting all Christians to keep the faith and live righteously. The author calls himself the brother of James, probably the one mentioned in Mark 6:3.

**judge** Any officer appointed by the state to administer the law. Their chief duties are to conduct COURT cases fairly, to arrive at a conclusion (or to direct a JURY to a conclusion) and to pass sentence.

**Judges** Seventh book of the Old Testament. It covers a 200-year period in the history of ancient ISRAEL, from the death of JOSHUA to the establishment of the first Israelite kingdom (*c*.11th century BC).The judges are leaders inspired by God to fight battles on behalf of the fledgling nation against neighboring enemies. The Book of Judges contains some of the oldest material in the Bible.

**Judiciary Acts** Legislation that established the structure of the US judicial system. The first (1789) set up the Supreme

Court, with a chief justice and five associates, 13 district courts, and three circuit courts, and created the office of attorney general. Subsequent acts (1801, 1802) changed the number of Supreme Court justices and created further circuit courts.

**Judith** Heroine of an Old Testament book considered apocryphal by Protestants and Jews. She is described as a beautiful young widow who heroically rescued the Israelite city of Bethulia from siege by the Assyrians.

**judo** Form of JUJITSU and one of the most popular of the Japanese martial arts. It places emphasis on physical fitness and mental discipline. A system of belt colors displays a practitioner's standard. Maneuvers include holds, trips, and falls. Scoring is according to the finality of a throw or hold.

**Juggernaut** (Jagganath) Form of the Hindu god KRISHNA, worshipped in Puri, E India. At an annual festival, statues of the god, his brother and his sister are pulled around the town on heavy carts. The term juggernaut has come to mean any large, heavy vehicle.

**jujitsu** Method of unarmed self-defense used in hand-to-hand combat. It involves such techniques as striking, holding, throwing, choking, and joint locking. There are *c*.50 systematized variants (including JUDO, KARATE, and AIKIDO) that have been refined over a period of 2,000 years in Japan, China, and Tibet. In the early 19th century, when the SAMURAI were forbidden to carry weapons, jujitsu became a form of self-defense.

**jujube** Either of two species of small thorny trees and their fruit of the genus *Zizyphus*. *Z. jujuba*, native to China, has elliptical leaves and reddish brown, plum-sized fruits, which have a crisp, white, sweet flesh. *Z. mauritanica* of India has smaller fruit. Family Rhamnaceae.

**Julian (the Apostate)** (331–363) Roman Emperor (361–363). He achieved power on the death of Constantine II. He tried to restore paganism, without persecuting Christians.

**Julius Caesar** *See* CAESAR, (GAIUS) JULIUS

**July Revolution** Insurrection in France (1830). The immediate cause was the July Ordinances, which dissolved the chamber of deputies, reduced the electorate, and imposed rigid press censorship. CHARLES X was forced to abdicate and LOUIS PHILIPPE was proclaimed king with a more liberal constitution.

**Juneau** State capital of Alaska; a seaport on the Gastineau Channel, bordering British Columbia. It grew rapidly after the discovery of gold in 1880, was made capital of Alaska territory in 1900 and state capital in 1959. Industries: mining, timber, salmon canning, tourism. Pop. (1990) 26,751.

**Jung, Carl Gustav** (1875–1961) Swiss psychiatrist. He worked closely (1907–13) with FREUD, but disagreed that sexuality was the prime cause of NEUROSIS. Jung founded analytical psychology, based on psychic "individuation." He argued that the UNCONSCIOUS had two dimensions – the personal, and archetypes of a collective unconscious. Jung believed INTROVERSION and EXTROVERSION to be basic personality types.

**Jungfrau** Mountain peak in the Swiss Alps. First climbed in 1811, it is the site of an alpine research station. Height: 13,642ft (4,158m).

**juniper** Any evergreen shrub or tree of the genus *Juniperus*, native to temperate regions of the Northern Hemisphere. Junipers have needle-like or scale-like leaves. The aromatic timber is used for making pencils, and the berry-like cones of common juniper for flavoring gin. Family Cupressaceae.

**Junkers** Landed aristocracy of Prussia. Descendants of the knights who conquered large areas of E Germany in the Middle Ages, they came to dominate the government and army in Russia and, after 1871, the German Empire. Intensely conservative, their hostility to the WEIMAR REPUBLIC contributed to the success of the Nazis.

**Juno** Asteroid discovered by Karl Harding in 1804. It is the tenth-largest, with a diameter of 152mi (244km).

**Juno** In Roman mythology, the principal female deity and consort of Jupiter, depicted as a statuesque, matronly figure.

**Jupiter** Fifth major planet from the Sun and the largest of the giant planets. It is one of the brightest objects in the sky. Through a telescope, Jupiter's yellowish elliptical disk is seen to be crossed by brownish red bands, known as belts and zones. The most distinctive feature is the Great Red Spot (GRS), first observed by Robert HOOKE in 1664. Spots, streaks, and bands are caused by Jupiter's rapid rotation and turbulent atmosphere. Eddies give rise to the spots, which are cyclones or (like the GRS) anticyclones. Hydrogen accounts for nearly 90% of Jupiter's atmosphere and helium for most of the rest. At the center of Jupiter there is probably a massive iron–silicate core surrounded by an ice mantle. The core temperature is estimated to be 30,000K. A deep metallic hydrogen "mantle" gives Jupiter a powerful magnetic field. Its magnetosphere is huge, several times the size of the Sun, and is the source of the planet's powerful radio emissions. Jupiter has 16 known SATELLITES, the four major ones being the GALILEAN SATELLITES. Knowledge of the planet owes much to visits by space probes: Pioneers 10 and 11, Voyagers 1 and 2, Ulysses, and GALILEO.

### JUPITER: DATA

Diameter (equatorial): 88,700mi (142,800km)
Mass (Earth = 1): 317.9
Volume (Earth = 1): 1319
Density (water = 1): 1.33
Orbital period: 11.86 years
Rotation period: 9h 50m 30s
Average surface temperature: –238°F (–150°C)

**Jupiter** King of the Roman gods, identified with the Greek god ZEUS. He could take on various forms: the light-bringer (Lucetius), god of lightning and thunderbolts (Fulgur), and god of rain (Jupiter Elicius).

**Jura Mountains** Mountain range in E France and NW Switzerland. Forming part of the Alpine system, it extends from the Rhine River at Basel to the Rhône River SW of Geneva. It has several hydroelectric schemes.

**Jurassic** Central period of the MESOZOIC era, lasting from 213 to 144 million years ago. In this period there were saurischian and ornithischian DINOSAURS, such as *Allosaurus* and *Stegosaurus*. Plesiosaurs, pterosaurs, and ARCHAEOPTERYX date from this period. Primitive mammals had begun to evolve.

**jurisprudence** Philosophy and science of the law, which dates back to PLATO and ARISTOTLE. Jurisprudence seeks to discover the source and justification of the law and its scope and function in a particular society.

**jury** Group of people summoned to pass judgment under oath. The 12-member jury in criminal trials dates from the mid-12th century, but it was only in the 17th century that jury members ceased to give evidence and simply passed judgment on the basis of evidence heard in COURT.

**Justice, US Department of** Legal office of the US federal government. Directed by the ATTORNEY GENERAL, it is responsible for the enforcement of federal laws, represents the government in legal matters, and advises the president and members of the executive. It includes a number of associated agencies such as the FEDERAL BUREAU OF INVESTIGATION (FBI).

**Justinian I** (482–565) Byzantine Emperor (527–565), sometimes called the Great. His troops, commanded by Belisarius, regained much of the old Roman empire, including Italy, North Africa, and part of Spain. Longer-lasting achievements were the **Justinian Code**, a revision of the whole body of Roman law, and buildings in Constantinople. Heavy taxation to pay for wars, drained the strength of the empire.

**Justin Martyr, Saint** (AD 100–165) Greek philosopher. He became one of the first Christian apologists in the early church. Raised in a Jewish environment, he was converted to Christianity, probably while at Ephesus. He defended Christian doctrine and was put to death in Rome for his faith. His feast day is June 1.

**jute** Natural plant fiber obtained from *Corchorus capsularis* and *C. olitorius*, both native to India. The plants grow up to 15ft (4.6m) tall. The fiber is obtained from the bark by soaking (retting) and beating. Jute is used to make sacking, twine, and rope. Family Tileaceae.

**Jutes** Germanic people who invaded Britain in the 5th century along with Angles, Saxons, and others. They settled mainly in Kent and the Isle of Wight.

**Jutland, Battle of** (1916) Naval battle in the North Sea between the British and Germans in WORLD WAR I. The only full-scale engagement of the war involving the two main fleets, it ended indecisively. Although British losses were greater, the German fleet remained in harbor for the rest of the war.

**Juvarra, Filippo** (1678–1736) Italian architect, one of the finest exponents of the BAROQUE style. His greatest achievements are the Superga (1717–31), just outside Turin, and the Church of the Carmine (1732), Turin.

**Juvenal, Decimus Junius** (55–140) Roman poet. His satirical poems denounced the immorality of his time. He contrasted decadence in imperial Rome with the virtues of the republic.

▲ **jute** This tall annual plant yields a fine bast fiber that is cheap, easy to bleach and dye, and can be readily woven into coarse fabrics such as hessian scrim, and burlap for sacking and furnishing uses.

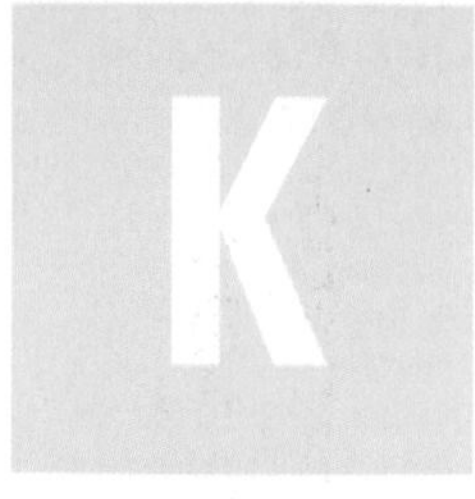

*K/k, 11th letter of the English alphabet, derived from the Semitic letter* **kaph**, *possibly from an earlier Egyptian hieroglyph for a hill-slope. In Greek it became* **kappa**, *and in that form passed into the Roman alphabet.*

**K2** Mountain in NE Pakistan, on the border with China. It is the world's second-highest peak, and the highest in the Karakoram range. It was first climbed in 1954 by Ardito Desio. Height: 28,251ft (8,611m).

**Kaaba** (Ka'abah or Ka'ba) Central shrine of ISLAM, located in the Great Mosque in MECCA. In prayer, Muslims face the meridian that passes through the Kaaba. Each pilgrim who undertakes the HAJJ circles the shrine seven times, touching the Black Stone for forgiveness.

**kabbala** Variant spelling of CABBALA

**kabuki theater** Stylized mixture of dance and music, mime, and vocal performance; a major form of moralizing entertainment in Japan since the mid-17th century. In contrast to NO DRAMA, which originated with the nobility, Kabuki was the theater of the common people. *See also* JAPANESE THEATER

**Kabul** Capital of Afghanistan, on the Kabul River, in the E part of the country. It is strategically located in a high mountain valley in the HINDU KUSH. It was taken by Genghis Khan in the 13th century. Later it became part of the MOGUL EMPIRE (1526–1738). The capital of Afghanistan since 1776, it was occupied by the British during the Afghan Wars in the 19th century. Following the Soviet invasion in 1979, Kabul was the scene of bitter fighting. Unrest continued into the mid-1990s as rival Muslim groups fought for control. Industries: textiles, leather goods, furniture, glass. Pop. (1993 est.) 700,000.

**Kádár, János** (1912–89) Hungarian statesman, premier (1956–58, 1961–65) and first secretary of the Hungarian Socialist Workers' Party (1956–88). He fought in the resistance during World War II and served as minister of the interior (1948–50). In 1956 Kádár replaced Imre NAGY as premier after crushing the Hungarian uprising. In 1968 he gave military support to the Soviet invasion of Czechoslovakia. Kádár's policy of "consumer socialism" revitalised the domestic economy.

**Kaddish** Ancient Jewish prayer used particularly at services of mourning for the dead. It is a formal statement of praise and faith in the coming of God's Kingdom.

**Kafka, Franz** (1883–1924) German novelist, b. Czechoslovakia. He suffered from intense self-doubt, publishing only essays and short stories, such as *Metamorphosis* (1916), during his lifetime. Kafka requested that his friend Max BROD destroy his works after his death. Brod overrode his wishes and published the trilogy of unfinished novels for which Kafka is best known today: *The Trial* (1925), *The Castle* (1926), and *Amerika* (1927). They are disturbing studies of the alienation of the individual in a bureaucratic and totalitarian society.

**Kahn, Louis Isadore** (1901–74) US architect, b. Estonia. He followed the example of LE CORBUSIER, GROPIUS, and MIES VAN DER ROHE, using bare concrete to create his severely beautiful designs. Kahn broke with the INTERNATIONAL STYLE drawing on NEOCLASSICISM to create a pure geometrical style that integrated form and function. His designs include the Richards Medical Center, University of Pennsylvania, Philadelphia (1958–60), and the Jonas Salk Institute of Biological Studies, La Jolla, California (1959–65).

**Kaifeng** City in Henan province, E central China. It was first settled in the 4th century BC and (as Pienching) served as capital of China during the Five Dynasty period (907–60) and the Northern Sung dynasty (960–1127). It is the site of a Jewish settlement that flourished from 1163 until the 15th century. Industries: electrical goods, agricultural machinery, chemicals, silk, flour. Pop. (1990) 690,000.

**Kaiser** German title equal to emperor. It derives from the Roman title "Caesar" and was first connected with Germany when Otto I became Holy Roman Emperor in 962. The last Kaiser was Wilhelm II (r.1888–1918), whose father had adopted the title after the Franco-Prussian War (1870–71).

**Kalahari** Desert region in S Africa, covering parts of BOTSWANA, NAMIBIA, and SOUTH AFRICA, between the ORANGE and ZAMBEZI rivers. Thorn scrub and forest grow in some parts of the desert, and it is possible to graze animals during the rainy season. The Kalahari is inhabited by the SAN, as well as by Africans and Europeans primarily engaged in rearing cattle. Area: *c.*100,000sq mi (260,000sq km).

**kale** Hardy crop plant related to the CABBAGE. It is short-stemmed and has large, bluish-green, curly-edged leaves. It may reach a height of 24in (61cm). Family Brassicaceae; (sub)species *Brassica oleracea acephala.*

**Kali** Hindu goddess of destruction, consort of SHIVA. She is also known as Chandi, DURGA, PARVATI, Sakti, Uma, and Mata. She represents the all-devouring aspect of Devi, the mother-goddess of India, who in other forms is calm and peaceful.

**Kalimantan** Region of Indonesia, forming the S part of the island of Borneo. In the 16th century, Muslim states were created. In the 17th century, the Dutch gradually established colonial rule over what became part of the Netherlands East Indies. Kalimantan came under Indonesian control in 1950. Products: rice, copra, pepper, oil, coal, industrial diamonds, timber. Area: 208,232sq mi (539,460sq km). Pop. (1990) 9,099,874.

**Kalinin, Mikhail Ivanovich** (1875–1946) Soviet statesman, head of state of the Soviet Union (1919–46). He was a founder (1912) of the newspaper *Pravda* and fought in the RUSSIAN REVOLUTION (1917). A supporter of STALIN, Kalinin served in the politburo (1925–46).

**Kaliningrad** (Königsberg) City and seaport on the Baltic coast of Russia; capital of Kaliningrad region. Founded in 1255 as Königsberg, the city was a member of the Hanseatic League. It became the residence of the dukes of Prussia in 1525. In 1946 it was incorporated into the Soviet Union. Following the break-up of the Soviet Union, Kaliningrad region is now separated from Russia proper, and shares a border with Poland and Lithuania. Industries: shipbuilding, fishing, motor vehicle parts. Pop. (1993) 411,000.

**Kalmykia** Republic of the Russian Federation on the Caspian Sea, SE European Russia; the capital is Elista. The region was made an autonomous republic in 1936. In World War II its inhabitants were deported to Soviet Central Asia for alleged collaboration with the Germans. They returned in 1957 and Kalmykia was later reestablished as an autonomous republic. After the break-up of the Soviet Union, it became a republic within the Russian Federation, acquiring its present name in 1992. Industries: fishing, animal farming. Area: *c.*29,300sq mi (75,900sq km). Pop. (1994) 320,600.

**Kamchatka Peninsula** Peninsula in E Siberia, Russia, separating the Sea of Okhotsk (W) from the Bering Sea and the Pacific Ocean (E). The region has several active volcanoes. Mineral resources include oil, coal, gold, and peat. Area: 104,260sq mi (270,034sq km).

**Kamehameha** Name of five kings of Hawaii. **Kamehameha I** (r. *c.*1758–1819) united all the Hawaiian islands. He instituted harsh laws, but abolished human sacrifice. His son, **Kamehameha II**, or Liholiho (r.1819–25), admitted the first US missionaries. **Kamehameha III**, or Kauikeaouli (r.1825–54), introduced a liberal constitution and land reform. **Kamehameha IV**, or Alexander Liholiho (r.1854–63), made social and economic reforms and resisted US influence. His brother, **Kamehameha V** (r.1863–72), abandoned the constitution and strengthened royal authority. The dynasty ended with his death.

**Kamerlingh-Onnes, Heike** (1853–1926) Dutch physicist. In 1908, using a liquid HYDROGEN cooling system, he liquefied HELIUM and found its temperature to be four degrees above ABSOLUTE ZERO. He discovered that at this temperature some metals, such as MERCURY and LEAD, become superconductors. He was awarded the 1913 Nobel Prize for physics.

**kamikaze** (Jap. divine wind) Name given to pilots or their explosive-laden aircraft used by the Japanese during World War II. Their suicidal method of attack was to dive into ships of the enemy fleet. In the Battle of Okinawa (1945) more than 1,400 pilots died in the process of destroying 26 US battleships.

**Kampala** Capital and largest city in UGANDA, on the N shore of Lake Victoria. Founded in the late 19th century on the remains of a royal palace of the kings of Buganda, it replaced Entebbe as capital when Uganda attained independence in 1962. It is the trading center for the agricultural goods and livestock produced in Uganda. Industries: textiles, food processing, tea blending, coffee, brewing. Pop. (1991) 773,463.

**Kampuchea** *See* CAMBODIA

**Kanchenjunga** (Kinchinjunga or Kanchanjanga) Third-highest mountain in the world, in the E HIMALAYAS. It was first climbed in 1955 by a British expedition led by Charles Evans. The highest of its five peaks reaches 28,169ft (8,586m).

**Kandahar** (Qandahar) City and provincial capital in S Afghanistan, *c.*300mi (483km) SW of Kabul. Because of its strategic location on important trade routes, it was occupied by many foreign conquerors before becoming the capital of the independent Afghani kingdom (1747–73). It was the scene of fighting after the Soviet invasion of Afghanistan in 1979 and became the headquarters of the TALIBAN in the 1990s. It is a commercial center. Pop. (1988 est.) 225,500.

**Kandinsky, Wassily** (1866–1944) Russian painter and theorist. His discoveries and experiments with abstraction were revolutionary. His early abstract paintings, including the many numbered *Compositions*, express great lyricism. From 1911 he was an active member of der BLAUE REITER. His writings, especially *Concerning the Spiritual in Art* (1914), show the influence of Oriental art philosophy. After World War I, his work became more controlled. *White Line* (1920) and *In the Black Circle* (1921) demonstrate the beginnings of a refinement of geometrical form that developed during his years at the BAUHAUS (1922–33).

**kangaroo** Largest MARSUPIAL mammal. Kangaroos have powerful hind legs designed for leaping and fighting. The short front legs are used for grasping. The long, muscular tail acts as a balance while hopping. They feed on roots and fungi and often live in burrows. Red kangaroos (*Macropus rufus*) graze on the Australian plains. Males (boomers) of the species may grow to more than 7ft (2m) tall and weigh up to 200lb (90kg). The gray kangaroo (*M. kanguru*) inhabits open woodland in Australia and Tasmania. The wallaroo or euro (*M. robustus*) lives in rocky hills. Kangaroos can perform single leaps of up to 26ft (8m) and travel up to 30mph (48km/h). Family Macropodidae. *See also* WALLABY

**kangaroo rat** Tiny, desert-dwelling RODENT of W North America. It has long hind legs and a long tail, and hops. It stores seeds in its cheek pouches. Length: to 16in (41cm), including the tail. Family Heteromyidae; genus *Dipodomys*.

**Kano** City in N central Nigeria; capital of Kano state. The city dates from before the 12th century and became a Muslim possession in the 16th century. It was conquered by the Fulani in the early 19th century. Today Kano is a trading center for a region producing cotton and nuts. Industries: textiles, leather goods, brewing, chemicals. Pop. (1992 est.) 699,900.

**Kanpur** (Cawnpore) City on the Ganges River, Uttar Pradesh, N India. Kanpur was ceded to the British in 1801 and became a frontier post. During the INDIAN MUTINY the entire British garrison in Kanpur was massacred. The city is now a major industrial and commercial center. Industries: chemicals, leather goods, textiles. Pop. (1991) 1,879,420.

**Kansa** Small Native American tribe that in 1854 gave its name to the state of Kansas. Linguistically it is part of the Siouan language group. The people now live in diverse clusters, mostly in Nebraska and Oklahoma.

**Kansas** State in central US; the capital is TOPEKA. Other major cities are Wichita and KANSAS CITY. First visited by Spanish explorers in the 16th century, the area passed from France to the new United States under the LOUISIANA PURCHASE of 1803. It was Native American territory until 1854, when the Territory of Kansas was created and the area opened up for settlement. It was admitted to the Union as a free state in 1861. Part of the Great Plains, the land rises from the prairies of the E to the semiarid high plains of the W. The area is drained by the Kansas and Arkansas rivers. Kansas is the leading US producer of wheat. Corn, hay, and sorghum are also grown and cattle raising is important. Manufacturing is economically significant. Industries: transport equipment, chemicals, petroleum products, machinery. Area: 82,276sq mi (213,094sq km). Pop. (1993 est.) 2,530,746.

**Kansas City** City in W Missouri, on the Missouri River, adjacent to KANSAS CITY, Kansas. Established in 1821 as a trading post, it developed in the 1860s with the introduction of the railroad and the growth in cattle trade. Industries: aerospace equipment, vehicles, chemicals, petroleum products, livestock, grain. Pop. (1990) 435,146.

**Kansas City** City in NE Kansas, at the confluence of the Kansas and Missouri rivers, adjacent to KANSAS CITY, Missouri. Part of a Native American reservation, it was acquired

◀ **Kandinsky** *Improvisation 28 (Second Version)* (1912). Throughout his life, the influential Russian painter Wassily Kandinsky explored what he saw as the deeply spiritual relationship between visual art and music. He is widely accepted as the founder of abstract art.

by Wyandotte Native Americans in 1843 and sold to the US government in 1855. The modern city was established in 1886. Industries: livestock, motor vehicles, metal products, chemicals. Pop. (1990) 149,767.

**Kansas-Nebraska Act** (May 30, 1854) US Congressional measure, sponsored by Senator Stephen A. DOUGLAS, which allowed US territories to decide for themselves such domestic matters as whether to allow slavery. The act was written to solve the growing slavery controversy, but made the problem to become worse since neither pro- nor anti-slavery forces were satisfied.

**Kant, Immanuel** (1724–1804) German metaphysical philosopher. Kant's philosophy of IDEALISM, outlined in *Critique of Pure Reason* (1781), sought to discover the nature and boundaries of human knowledge. It was much influenced by Isaac NEWTON and David HUME. Kant's system of ethics, described in the *Critique of Practical Reason* (1790), places moral duty above happiness and asserts the existence of an absolute moral law (the "categorical imperative"). His views on aesthetics are embodied in his *Critique of Judgment* (1790). Kant also produced several essays in support of religious liberalism and the ENLIGHTENMENT.

**kaolin** (china clay) Fine clay composed chiefly of KAOLINITE, a hydrous silicate of aluminum. It is used in the manufacture of coated paper, ceramics, and fine porcelains.

**kaolinite** Sheet silicate mineral of the kaolinite group, hydrous aluminum silicate ($Al_2Si_2O_5(OH)_4$). It is a product of the weathering of feldspar and has triclinic system tabular crystals. It is white with a dull luster. Hardness 2–2.5; s.g. 2.6.

**kapok** Tropical tree with compound leaves and white or pink flowers. Its seed pods burst to release silky fibers, which are commonly used for stuffing and insulation. Height: to 165ft (50m). Family Bombacaceae; species *Ceiba pentandra*.

**Karachi** City and seaport on the Arabian Sea, SE Pakistan; capital of Sind province. Settled in the early 18th century, in 1843 it passed to the British, who developed it as a major port. It was the first capital of Pakistan in 1947 and remains the country's largest city. Karachi is an important trading center for agricultural produce. Industries: steel, engineering, oil refining, motor vehicle assembly, textiles, chemicals, printing, and publishing. Pop. (1981) 5,103,000.

**Karadžić, Radovan** (1945– ) Serbian politician. In 1990 he founded the Serbian Democratic Party. In 1992 Bosnia-Herzegovina voted for independence from the Serb-dominated federation of Yugoslavia. Karadžić declared a separate Bosnian Serb state, Republika Srpska, with himself as president. With the support of Serbian president Slobodan MILOŠEVIĆ, he instituted a policy of "ethnic cleansing" of non-Serbs. In 1995 Milošević withdrew his support and Karadžić was forced to sign the Dayton peace accord with Bosnian President IZETBEGOVIĆ. In 1996 he was indicted by the United Nations (UN) for war crimes but remained at large.

**Karajan, Herbert von** (1908–89) German conductor. He conducted the Berlin State Opera (1938–45) and was director of the Vienna State Opera (1945–1964). As musical director of the Berlin Philharmonic Orchestra (1955–89) and artistic director of the Salzburg festival (1956–60), he dominated the European classical music scene.

**Kara-Kalpak** Autonomous republic in W Uzbekistan; the capital is Nukus. It was made an autonomous region of Kazakstan (1925) and an autonomous republic (1933). Three

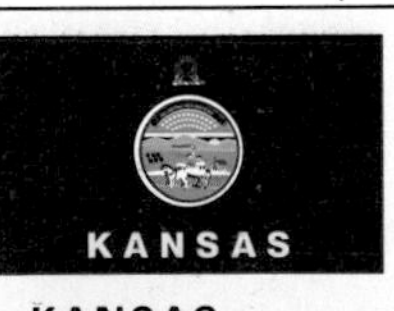


**KANSAS**
**Statehood:**
January 29, 1861
**Nickname:**
Sunflower state
**State bird:**
Western meadowlark
**State flower:**
Sunflower
**State tree:**
Cottonwood
**State motto:**
To the stars through difficulties

K

years later it became part of the Uzbek Soviet Republic and retained its autonomous status within independent Uzbekistan. Crops include alfalfa, rice, cotton, corn, and jute. Livestock raising is important, and there is some light industry. Area: 63,940sq mi (165,600sq km). Pop. (1990) 1,244,700

**Karakoram Range** Mountain range in central Asia, extending SE from E Afghanistan to Jammu and Kashmir in India. It includes some of the world's highest mountains, among them K2. Length: *c*.300mi (480km).

**Karamanlis, Koństantinos** (1907–98) Greek statesman, prime minister (1955–63, 1974–80), president (1980–85, 1990–95). He was elected to parliament in 1935. On becoming prime minister, he formed his own party, the National Radical Union (ERE). He resigned in 1963 after an election defeat. During 11 years of self-imposed exile he was an opponent of the Greek military junta, and when it fell in 1974 he returned as prime minister at the head of the new Democratic Party (ND).

**karate** Martial art popularized in Japan in the 1920s. The technique, which involves a formal method of physical and mental training, includes a variety of blows using the hand, legs, elbows, and head. In competition, scoring depends on the finality of the blow.

**Karelia** Republic of the Russian Federation in NW European RUSSIA, bounded by the White Sea to the E and FINLAND to the W; the capital is Petrozavodsk. In the Middle Ages the region was an independent Finnish state. Split in the 12th century between Sweden and NOVGOROD, it was unified under Swedish rule in the 17th century. The E was returned to Russia in 1721, while the W was part of Finland until 1940. After the 1939–40 Soviet-Finnish War the E sector absorbed 14,000sq mi (36,000sq km) of Finnish land and became a constituent republic (Karelo-Finnish SSR). During World War II the Finns occupied most of Karelia but it was returned to the Soviet Union in 1944. Declaring itself the Republic of Karelia, it became a constituent republic of the Russian Federation in 1992. Climate restricts farming to the S, where vegetables and cereal crops are grown and livestock are raised. Fishing and timber are the chief industries. The region has valuable mineral deposits. Area: 66,564sq mi (172,400sq km). Pop. (1994) 794,200.

**karma** (Sanskrit, action) Central moral doctrine in HINDUISM, BUDDHISM and JAINISM. It is a natural, impersonal law of moral cause and effect, unconnected with divine punishment for sins. In Hinduism and Jainism, karma is the sum of a person's actions which are passed on from one life to the next and

## KAZAKSTAN

Kazakstan's flag was adopted on June 4, 1992, about six months after it had become independent. The blue represents cloudless skies, while the golden sun and the soaring eagle represent love of freedom. A vertical strip of gold ornamentation is on the left.

**AREA:** 1,049,150sq mi (2,717,300sq km)
**POPULATION:** 17,038,000
**CAPITAL (POPULATION):** Aqmola (281,400)
**GOVERNMENT:** Multiparty republic
**ETHNIC GROUPS:** Kazak 40%, Russian 38%, German 6%, Ukrainian 5%, Uzbek, Tatar
**LANGUAGES:** Kazak (official); Russian, the former official language, is widely spoken
**RELIGIONS:** Mainly Islam, with a Christian minority
**CURRENCY:** Tenge

Kazakstan is a vast flat country in W central Asia. It stretches over 2,000mi (3,000km) from the VOLGA and CASPIAN SEA lowlands in the W to the ALTAI and TIAN SHAN mountains in the E. The Caspian Sea lowlands extend E through the ARAL SEA region and include the Karagiye depression at 433ft (132m) below sea level. Eastern Kazakstan contains several freshwater lakes, the largest of which is Lake BALKHASH. Kazakstan's rivers have been used extensively for irrigation, causing ecological problems: the ARAL SEA has shrunk from 25,830sq mi (66,900sq km) in 1960 to 12,989sq mi (33,642sq km) in 1993. Whole fishing villages are now barren desert.

### CLIMATE

Kazakstan has a continental dry climate. Winters are cold. At ALMATY, snow covers the ground for an average of 100 days each year.

### VEGETATION

Kazakstan has very little woodland. Grassy steppe covers much of the N, while the S is desert or semidesert. However, large dry areas between the Aral Sea and Lake Balkhash are irrigated farmland.

### HISTORY

Little is known of the early history of Kazakstan, except that it was the home of nomadic peoples. In 1218 the Mongol emperor GENGHIS KHAN conquered the region. Following his death the empire was divided into khanates. Feudal trading towns emerged beside the oases. In the late 15th century the towns formed a Kazak state, which fought for its independence from the neighboring khanates. In 1731 Kazakstan appealed to Russia for protection and voluntarily acceded to the Russian empire. In the early 19th century, Russia abolished the khanates, and encouraged Russian settlement throughout Kazakstan.

The conscription of Kazaks during World War I aroused much resentment, and after the Russian Revolution (1917) demands for independence grew. In 1920 Kazakstan became an autonomous Soviet republic, and a full constituent republic in 1936. During the 1920s and 1930s the process of Russification increased. Stalin's forced collectivization of agriculture and rapid industrialization led to great famine. Soviet minorities were transported to Kazakstan. In the 1950s, the "Virgin Lands" project sought to turn vast areas of grassland into cultivated land to feed the Soviet Union. The Soviets placed many of their nuclear missile sites in Kazakstan and also built their first fast-breeder nuclear reactor at Mangyshlak. In 1986 nationalist riots were prompted by the imposition of a Russian to lead the republic. Following the dissolution of the Soviet Union, Kazakstan declared independence (December 1991) and joined the COMMONWEALTH OF INDEPENDENT STATES (CIS).

### POLITICS

A former Communist Party leader, Nursultan Nazarbayev, was Kazakstan's first elected president. He introduced free-market reforms and a multiparty constitution. Multiparty elections were held in 1994. In a 1995 referendum Nazarbayev was confirmed as president until 2000. In 1996 the government announced plans to move the capital to AQMOLA by 2000. Aqmola is nearer to the main industrial areas and mineral resources in the N.

### ECONOMY

Kazakstan is a developing country (1995 GDP per capita, US$3,010). The break-up of the Soviet Union hit Kazak exports. In 1994 it entered into a single-market agreement with other Central Asian states. Its post-independence free-market reforms have encouraged much inward investment. Industry accounts for 41% of earnings. Kazakstan is rich in minerals. It is the world's ninth largest producer of bituminous coal. Its gas, oil, and gold reserves are being increasingly exploited. In 1996 construction started on a pipeline to Russia. Agriculture is highly developed. Grain is the principal crop. Cotton and wool are also produced.

determine the nature of rebirth. Buddhism rejects this continuity of the "soul" through REINCARNATION. The intention behind an action determines the fate of an individual. Release from rebirth into NIRVANA depends on knowledge of the Real, which in turn enables neutral action. *See also* YOGA

**Karnak** *See* LUXOR

**Kashmir** Region in N India and NE Pakistan; former Indian princely state. When the Indian subcontinent was partitioned in 1947, the maharaja of Kashmir acceded to India, precipitating war between India and Pakistan. A ceasefire agreement left it divided between the Indian-controlled state of JAMMU AND KASHMIR and the Pakistan-controlled areas in the N and W of the region. The N area of Kashmir is ruled directly by the Pakistan government; the W area, Azad Kashmir, is partly autonomous. The Aksai Chin area of Kashmir, on the border with Tibet, is occupied by China. Indian Jammu, and Kashmir has remained in a state of unrest. Kashmir includes parts of the Himalayas and the KARAKORAM RANGE. The Vale of Kashmir, in the valley of the Jhelum River, is the most populated area, and wheat and rice are grown. Total area: 85,806sq mi (222,236sq km).

**Kasparov, Gary** (1963– ) Azerbaijani chess player, b. Gary Weinstein. In 1985 he defeated Anatoly KARPOV to become the youngest-ever chess world champion. Kasparov successfully defended his title against Karpov in 1986, 1987 and 1990. In 1996 he defeated the IBM Deep Blue chess computer.

**Katmandu** (Kathmandu) Capital of Nepal, situated *c.*4,500ft (1,370m) above sea level in a valley of the Himalayas. It was founded in AD 723. It was an independent city from the 15th century until 1768, when it was captured by Gurkhas. Katmandu is Nepal's administrative, commercial, and religious center. Pop. (1991) 419,073.

**Katowice** City in S Poland. Founded in the 16th century and chartered in 1865, it was occupied by Germany throughout World War II. It is one of Poland's foremost industrial centers, producing coal, iron and steel, heavy machinery, and chemicals. Pop. (1993) 366,900.

**Katz, Sir Bernard** (1911– ) British biophysicist. He shared the 1970 Nobel Prize for physiology or medicine with Ulf von Euler and Julius Axlrod. Katz discovered how the NEUROTRANSMITTER acetylcholine is released by neural impulses, causing muscles to contract.

**Kaufman, George Simon** (1889–1961) US dramatist. He collaborated on more than 40 plays. Kaufman won the Pulitzer Prize for the musical *Of Thee I Sing* (1931). He won a second Pulitzer Prize for *You Can't Take It With You* (1936), written in collaboration with Moss HART. Kaufman and Hart also produced *The Man Who Came To Dinner* (1939). He worked with Edna Ferber on *Stage Door* (1936). Kaufman directed *Guys and Dolls* (1950).

**Kaunas** City and port in S Lithuania. Founded in the 11th century, it became part of Russia in 1795. It was capital of independent Lithuania (1918–40). Industries: iron and steel, electrical machinery, chemicals, textiles. Pop. (1990) 592,500.

**Kaunda, Kenneth David** (1924– ) Zambian statesman, president (1964–91). He led Northern Rhodesia to independence as Zambia, becoming its first president. In 1972 Kaunda imposed single-party rule. He was a staunch opponent of APARTHEID and played a leading role in establishing an independent Namibia (1990). In 1991 severe economic problems and political unrest forced him to concede multiparty elections in which he was defeated by Frederick Chiluba. In 1997, following a failed military coup, Kaunda was imprisoned. He was released in 1998.

**Kawabata, Yasunari** (1899–1972) Japanese novelist. His best-known works are *Snow Country* (1948), *Thousand Cranes* (1952), and *The Sound of the Mountain* (1952). He was awarded the 1968 Nobel Prize for literature.

**Kawasaki** City in SE Honshu Island, on Tokyo Bay, Japan. The city suffered extensive damage from bombing during World War II. Industries: iron and steel mills, machinery, motor vehicles, petrochemicals, shipbuilding. Pop. (1993) 1,168,000.

**Kazak** Turkic-speaking Muslim people who inhabit the Republic of KAZAKSTAN and the adjacent Sinkiang province of China. Traditionally nomadic, in the 20th century they settled within the collective farm system of the former Soviet Union.

**Kazakstan** Republic in central Asia. *See* country feature

**Kazan, Elia** (1909–99) US film director and novelist, b. Turkey. Kazan was one of the founders of the ACTORS' STUDIO. His work in the cinema includes *A Tree Grows in Brooklyn* (1945), *Gentleman's Agreement* (1947), and *On the Waterfront* (1954). He wrote two best-selling novels: *America, America* (1962), and *The Arrangement* (1967).

**Kazan** City and port on the Volga River, E European Russia; capital of TATAR REPUBLIC. Founded in the 13th century, Kazan became the capital of the Tatar khanate (1438). Conquered by Ivan IV, it served as the E outpost of Russian colonization. Industries: electrical equipment, engineering, oil refining, chemicals, fur. Pop. (1992) 1,104,000.

**Kazantzakis, Nikos** (1885–1957) Greek writer. His epic poem *The Odyssey* (1938) is an ambitious modern sequel to Homer's work. Kazantakis is best-known for religious and philosophical novels, such as *Zorba the Greek* (1946) and *The Last Temptation of Christ* (1951).

**Kearny, Stephen Watts** (1794–1848) US general. He participated in the War of 1812 and in numerous wars on the Western frontier. In 1846 he took possession of New Mexico, promising full citizenship to the Native Americans. He also led a successful march to California, taking San Diego (1846) and Los Angeles (1847).

**Keaton, Buster (Joseph Francis)** (1895–1966) US movie actor and director. Keaton's acrobatic stunts and deadpan features made him one of the biggest comedy stars of the silent-film era. His ten full-length movies include the classics *The Navigator* (1924), and *The General* (1926). The advent of the "talkies" hearlded a decline in his career.

▲ **Keaton** A family music-hall background provided the US comic actor and director Buster Keaton with many of the ideas for his sophisticated and completely visual slapstick style. Many of his films, including *The Navigator* (1924) and *The General* (1926) are becoming increasingly recognized for their comic inventiveness.

**Keats, John** (1795–1821) English poet, one of the major figures of ROMANTICISM. His first volume, *Poems* (1817), included "On First Looking into Chapman's Homer". Keats was savagely criticized for the four-volume romance *Endymion* (1818). *Lamia, Isabella, The Eve of St Agnes and Other Poems* (1820) included the ballad "La Belle Dame sans Merci" and the magnificent lyrics "Ode on a Grecian Urn", "Ode to a Nightingale" and "Ode to Autumn". Keats died of tuberculosis in Rome, leaving unfinished the epic *Hyperion*. Percy SHELLEY mourned his passing in his elegy *Adonais* (1821)

**Keelung** (Chilung) City on the East China Sea, N Taiwan. Occupied by the Spanish in the early 17th century, it was later briefly in Dutch hands. Under Japanese occupation (1895–1945) the city developed rapidly. An important commercial center, it is the country's principal naval base. Industries: fishing, chemicals, shipbuilding. Pop. (1992) 355,894.

**Keillor, Garrison Edward** (1942– ) US author and humorist. His bittersweet stories about the fictional community of Lake Wobegon feature in *Happy To Be Here* (1981), *Leaving Home* (1987), and *We Are Still Married* (1989).

**Keller, Helen Adams** (1880–1968) US social worker, writer, and lecturer. With the help of her teacher Anne Sullivan, she overcame the loss of sight, hearing, and speech, caused by an early illness, to master several languages and lecture throughout the world. Her books include *The Story of My Life* (1902), *The World I Live In* (1908), and *The Open Door* (1957).

**Kellogg-Briand Pact** (1928) International peace agreement negotiated by US secretary of state Frank B. Kellogg and French foreign minister Aristide BRIAND. It renounced war as a means of settling international disputes and was subsequently signed by most of the world's governments.

**Kelly, Gene** (1912–96) US dancer, choreographer, movie star, and director. His greatest films, codirected with Stanley Donen, were *On the Town* (1949), *An American in Paris* (1951) and the hugely popular *Singin' in the Rain* (1951).

**Kelly, Grace Patricia** (1929–82) US movie actress. She appeared in *High Noon* (1952) and *Mogambo* (1953), and won an Academy Award for her leading role in *The Country Girl* (1954). She retired from the screen after marrying Prince Rainier of Monaco in 1956. Kelly died in a car accident.

**kelp** Any of several brown SEAWEEDS commonly found on Atlantic and Pacific coasts, a type of brown ALGAE. A source of iodine and potassium compounds, kelps are now used in a number of industrial processes. Giant kelp (*Macrocystis*) exceeds 150ft (46m) in length. Phylum Phaeophyta.

K

▶ **Kennedy** US president John F. Kennedy's youth, charm, and good looks helped him to become one of the most popular US presidents. His liberal policies and support of civil rights, while making him many friends within minority groups, alienated more conservative elements. There has been much mystery surrounding his assassination in Dallas in 1963. The exhaustive but hotly debated Warren Report upheld the official theory that it was the work of a lone gunman, Lee Harvey Oswald. Other theories suggest that the assassination was the work of a number of coconspirators.

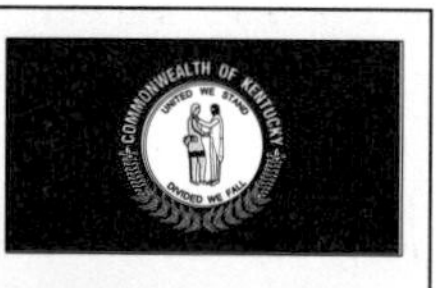


**KENTUCKY**
**Statehood :**
June 1, 1792
**Nickname :**
Bluegrass state
**State bird :**
Kentucky cardinal
**State flower :**
Goldenrod
**State tree :**
Kentucky coffee tree
**State motto :**
United we stand; divided we fall

**Kelvin, William Thomson, 1st Baron** (1824–1907) British physicist and mathematician after whom the absolute scale of temperature is named. The Kelvin temperature scale has its zero point at absolute zero and degree intervals the same size as the degree Celsius. The freezing point of water occurs at 273K (32°F or 0°C) and the boiling point at 373K (212°F or 100°C). In THERMODYNAMICS he resolved conflicting interpretations of the first and second laws.

**Kemal Atatürk** *See* ATATÜRK, KEMAL

**Kempis, Thomas à** (1380–1471) German Augustinian monk and spiritual writer. Ordained in 1413, he remained in the monastery of the Brethren of the Common Life, near Zwolle, for most of his life. He wrote or edited numerous treatises on the life of the soul. The most famous work often attributed to him is *Imitation of Christ (c.*1415–24*)*. Other works include *Soliloquium Animae* and *De Tribus Tabernaculis*.

**Kendall, Edward Calvin** (1886–1972) US chemist who worked on the biological effects of the HORMONES of the ADRENAL GLANDS, in particular CORTISONE, which he isolated. He shared the 1950 Nobel Prize for physiology or medicine.

**Keneally, Thomas Michael** (1935– ) Australian novelist. His best-known work, *Schindler's Ark* (1982), won the British Booker Prize, and formed the basis of Steven SPIELBERG's film *Schindler's List* (1993).

**Kennedy, Anthony McLeod** (1936– ) US Supreme Court justice. The third choice to fill the Supreme Court vacancy left by the retirement of Associate Justice Lewis Powell in 1987, Kennedy is considered a moderate conservative who is both flexible and pragmatic. A lawyer, lobbyist, and appellate judge before his selection for the Supreme Court, he developed working ties with then-California governor Ronald REAGAN as well as with future attorney general Edwin Meese.

**Kennedy, John Fitzgerald** (1917–63) 35th US President (1961–63). He was elected to Congress as a Democrat from Massachusetts in 1946, serving in the Senate from 1953 to 1960. Kennedy gained the presidential nomination in 1960 and narrowly defeated Richard NIXON. He adopted an ambitious and liberal program, under the title of the "New Frontier," and embraced the cause of CIVIL RIGHTS, but his planned legislation was frequently blocked by Congress. In foreign policy, Kennedy founded the "Alliance for Progress," the aim of which was to improve the image of the US abroad. Adopting a strong anticommunist line, he was behind the BAY OF PIGS disaster (1961) and outfaced KHRUSHCHEV in the ensuing CUBAN MISSILE CRISIS, which was followed by a US-Soviet treaty banning nuclear tests. He increased military aid to South Vietnam. John F. Kennedy was assassinated in Dallas, Texas, on November 22, 1963.

**Kennedy, Joseph Patrick** (1888–1969) US businessman and politician. He was chairman of the Securities and Exchange Commission (1934–35) and ambassador to Great Britain (1937–40). He was involved in many philanthropic endeavors, especially the Joseph P. Kennedy Memorial Foundation, founded for his son killed in World War II. He was determined that his sons, Joseph P. Kennedy Jr., John F. KENNEDY, Robert KENNEDY, and Edward KENNEDY, should enter politics.

**Kennedy, Robert Francis** (1925–68) US lawyer and politician. He served on the Senate Select Committee on Improper Activities in Labor or Mangement Field (1957–59), where he clashed with the Teamsters' Union president Jimmy HOFFA. In 1960 he managed the successful presidential campaign of his brother John F. KENNEDY. He became US attorney general (1961–64), vigorously enforcing CIVIL RIGHTS laws and promoting the Civil Rights Act of 1964. After his brother's assassination, he left the cabinet and was elected (1964) senator for New York. While a candidate for the Democratic presidential nomination, he was assassinated (June 4) in Los Angeles.

**Kennedy Space Center** *See* CAPE CANAVERAL

**Kent, Rockwell** (1882–1971) US painter, author, and illustrator whose pictorial works won great popularity for their vivid portrayal of the wilderness. He wrote and illustrated several books, notably *Wilderness* (1920), *Voyaging Southward* (1924), and *Greenland Journal* (1962).

**Kentucky** State in SE central US; the capital is FRANKFORT. Other major cities include Lexington and Louisville. Ceded to Britain by France in 1763, Kentucky became the 15th state. Its loyalties were divided at the outbreak of the CIVIL WAR, and the state was invaded by both sides. Most of the area consists of rolling plains. In the SE the Cumberland Mountains dominate a rugged plateau region. The state is drained chiefly by the Ohio and Tennessee rivers. Tobacco is the chief crop, followed by hay, corn, and soybeans. The state is noted for breeding thoroughbred racehorses. Industries: electrical equipment, machinery, chemicals, primary metals. Kentucky is also a major producer of coal. Area: 40,395sq mi (104,623sq km). Pop. (1990) 3,685,296.

**Kentucky and Virginia Resolutions** (1798 and 1799) Declarations of states' rights. Drafted by Thomas JEFFERSON (Kentucky Resolutions) and James MADISON (Virginia), they expressed opposition to the ALIEN AND SEDITION ACTS. They denied the right of the federal government to exercise powers not granted it by the constitution and declared that states had the right to judge the constitutionality of federal acts.

**Kenya** Republic on the coast of E Africa. *See* country feature

**Kenya, Mount** Extinct volcanic mountain in central Kenya. The second-highest mountain in Africa, it was first climbed in 1899. It consists of three peaks, the highest of which is Batian, rising to 17,058ft (5,200m).

**Kenyatta, Jomo** (1893–1978) Kenyan statesman, president of Kenya (1964–78). A KIKUYU, he led the struggle for Kenyan independence from 1946. Kenyatta was imprisoned (1952–61) by the British colonial authorities for alleged involvement in the MAU MAU uprising. As leader of the Kenya African National Union (KANU), he became the first president of an independent Kenya. Although Kenyatta suppressed domestic opposition, he presided over a prosperous economy and generally followed pro-Western policies. He was succeeded by Daniel arap MOI.

**Kepler, Johannes** (1571–1630) German mathematician and astronomer. He supported the heliocentric theory put forward by COPERNICUS. Kepler succeeded Tycho BRAHE as imperial mathematician to Emperor Rudolf II. From Brahe's observations, he concluded that Mars moves in an elliptical orbit, and he went on to establish his three laws of planetary motion: **law one** states that the orbit of a planet is an ellipse with the Sun at one of the foci; **law two** (law of areas) states that the line joining the planet to the Sun (radius vector) sweeps out equal areas in equal times; **law three** states that the square of the period of revolution (P) is directly proportional to the cube of the mean distance of the planet from the Sun. The *Rudolphine Tables* (1627), based on Brahe's observations and Kepler's laws, remained the most accurate until the 18th century.

**Kerala** State on the Arabian Sea, SW India; the capital is Trivandrum. One of India's smallest states, it is the most densely populated. Fishing is important. Products: rubber, tea, coffee, coconuts, cashews, ivory, textiles, teak, chemicals, minerals. Area: 15,005sq mi (38,864sq km). Pop. (1991) 29,098,518.

**keratin** Fibrous PROTEIN present in large amounts in SKIN cells, where it serves as a protective layer. Hair and fingernails are made up of cells filled with keratin, which is also the basis of claws, horns, and feathers.

**Kerensky, Alexander Feodorovich** (1881–1970) Russian politician. In July 1917 he became prime minister of the provisional government, after the overthrow of the Czar. Deposed by the BOLSHEVIKS in the RUSSIAN REVOLUTION, he fled into exile.

**Kern, Jerome David** (1885–1945) US songwriter. His outstanding musical is *Showboat* (staged 1927; filmed 1936, 1959), containing the song "Ol' Man River." He influenced Richard RODGERS and George GERSHWIN.

**kerosene** (paraffin) Distilled PETROLEUM product that is heavier than gasoline but lighter than diesel fuel. Kerosene is used in camping stoves, tractor fuels, and fuels for aircraft.

**Kerouac, Jack** (1922–69) US novelist and poet. His first novel was *The Town and the City* (1950). *On the Road* (1957) established Kerouac as the leading novelist of the BEAT MOVEMENT. Later works include *The Dharma Bums* (1958), *Desolation Angels* (1965), and the posthumously published *Visions of Cody* (1972).

**Kerry** County in Munster province, SW Republic of Ireland; the county town is Tralee. It is a mountainous region with an indented coastline and many lakes. Oats and potatoes are grown, and sheep and cattle raised. Industries: tourism, fishing. Area: 1,815sq mi (4,701sq km). Pop. (1991) 121,894.

**kestrel** (windhover) Small FALCON that lives mainly in Europe, and hovers over its prey before attacking. It feeds mainly on rodents, insects, and small birds. Length: 12in (30cm). Species *Falco tinnunculus*.

**kettledrum** *See* TIMPANI

**Key, Francis Scott** (1779–1843) US poet. He wrote the US national anthem, "The Star Spangled Banner," while watching the shelling of Fort McHenry (1814) as a prisoner on a British ship in Chesapeake Bay. The anthem first appeared anonymously as a poem, "In Defense of Fort M'Henry." It was adopted as the national anthem by Congress in 1931.

**key** In music, term used to indicate TONALITY in a composition, based on one of the major or minor scales. The key of a piece of music is indicated by the key signature at the left hand end of the stave. The key of a passage may, however, change by the addition of accidentals before prescribed notes; a change of key is known as a modulation.

**keyboard instrument** Large group of musical instruments played by pressing keys on a keyboard. Notes are sounded by hitting or plucking a string (as in the PIANO or HARPSICHORD), passing air through a pipe or reed (as in the ORGAN or ACCORDION), or electronically (as in the SYNTHESIZER).

**Keynes, John Maynard** (1883–1946) British economist. In *The General Theory of Employment, Interest, and Money* (1936), which was strongly influenced by the GREAT DEPRESSION, Keynes established the foundation of modern MACROECO-

## KENYA

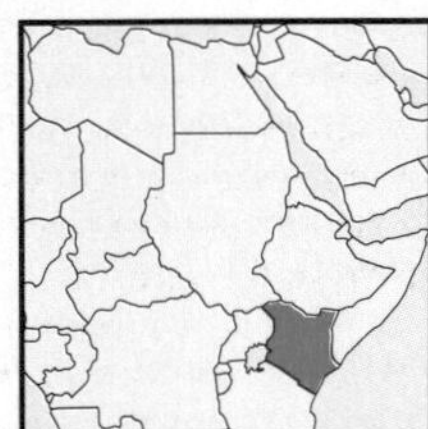

Kenya's flag dates from 1963, when the country became independent. It is based on the flag of KANU (Kenya African National Union), the political party that led the nationalist struggle. The Masai warrior's shield and crossed spears represent the defense of freedom.

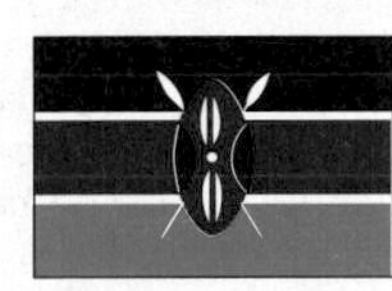

**AREA:** 224,081sq mi (580,370sq km)
**POPULATION:** 26,985,000
**CAPITAL (POPULATION):** Nairobi (1,346,000)
**GOVERNMENT:** Multiparty republic
**ETHNIC GROUPS:** Kikuyu 21%, Luhya 14%, Luo 13%, Kamba 11%, Kalenjin 11%
**LANGUAGES:** Swahili and English (both official)
**RELIGIONS:** Christianity (Roman Catholic 27%, Protestant 19%, others 27%), traditional beliefs 19%, Islam 6%
**CURRENCY:** Kenya shilling = 100 cents

The Republic of Kenya straddles the Equator in East Africa. MOMBASA lies on the narrow coastal plain. Most of Kenya comprises high plains. In the NW is an area of high scrubland around Lake Turkana. In the SW are the Kenyan highlands, including Mount KENYA, the country's highest peak at 17,057ft (5,199m), and the capital, NAIROBI. The Great RIFT VALLEY cuts through W Kenya.

### CLIMATE

Mombasa is hot and humid. Inland the climate is moderated by elevation: Nairobi has summer temperatures 18°F (10°C) lower than Mombasa.

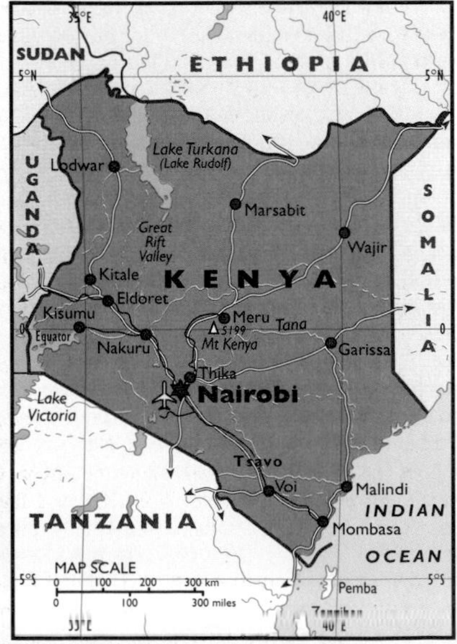


### VEGETATION

The coast is lined with mangrove swamps. The Inland plains are bushlands. Much of the N is semidesert. Forests and grasslands are found in the densely populated SW highlands.

### HISTORY AND POLITICS

Some of the earliest hominid fossils have been found in S Kenya. Kenya's coast has been a trading center for more than 2,000 years. In the 8th century, the Arabs founded settlements. Vasco da Gama landed in 1498, and Portuguese traders controlled the area in the 16th century. In 1729 Arab dynasties regained control. Britain gained rights to the coast in 1895. Colonization began in 1903, and land was acquired from the KIKUYU for plantations and farms. The territory was divided into the inland Kenya Colony and the coastal Protectorate of Kenya. European settlement intensified. The employment of Africans as plantation and farm laborers led to social unrest. MAU MAU waged an armed struggle (1952–56) for land rights and independence. Britain declared a state of emergency. In 1963 Kenya achieved independence, and became a republic in 1964. Jomo KENYATTA was the first president. Many Europeans emigrated. Kenyatta's authoritarian regime tried to establish unity. Territorial disputes with Uganda and Tanzania and drought created civil unrest. In 1978 Kenyatta died and was succeeded by Daniel Arap MOI. Moi rejected calls for democracy and cracked down on dissent. In 1982 the Kenya African National Union (KANU) became the sole legal party. In 1988, after nationwide riots the government agreed to electoral reform. Moi was re-elected in 1992 and 1997, but independent observers claimed both polls were rigged.

### ECONOMY

Kenya is a developing country (1995 GDP per capita, US$1,380). Agriculture employs *c*.80% of the people and accounts for *c*.50% of exports. Kenya is the world's fourth largest tea producer. Coffee is also an important cash crop. Many Kenyans are subsistence farmers. The chief food crop is maize. Kenya's wildlife parks and reserves attract many tourists.

**The Citrus Swallowtail** is an example of the fascinating wildlife found in Kenya.

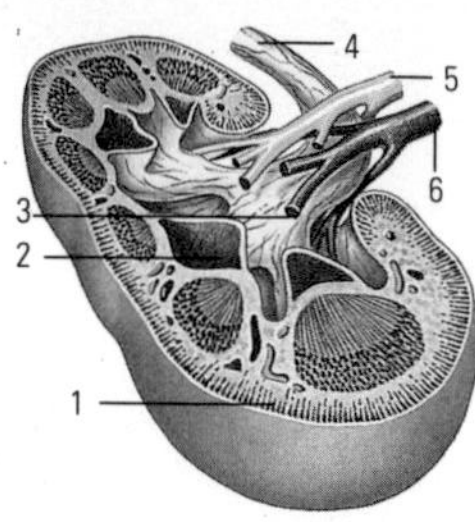


▲ **kidney** The human kidney is enclosed in a fibrous capsule, and consists of an outer cortex region (1), a medulla region (2) with pyramidal-shaped areas, and an inner pelvis region (3) which leads into the ureter (4). The renal artery (5) conducts blood into the kidney to be filtered, which is then carried away by the renal vein (6).

NOMICS. He advocated the active intervention of government in the economy to stimulate employment and prosperity. He was highly influential as an economic adviser in World War II, and took a leading role in the BRETTON WOODS CONFERENCE (1944).

**KGB** (*Komitet Gosudarstvennoye Bezhopaznosti*, Rus. Committee for State Security) Soviet secret police. In the 1980s, it employed an estimated 500,000 people and controlled all police, security, and intelligence operations in the Soviet Union. It also gathered military and political information about other countries. The KGB opposed liberalization under GORBACHEV, and its chief was a leader of the attempted coup against him in 1991. After the collapse of communism and the break-up of the Soviet Union, it underwent extensive reform.

**Khachaturian, Aram Ilyich** (1903–78) Armenian composer. He wrote a piano concerto (1936) and a violin concerto (1940), but his best-known works are probably the ballets *Gayane* (1942) and *Spartacus* (1953).

**Khafre, Great Sphinx of** Monumental statue of the SPHINX at GIZA, Egypt. Its name derives from the pharaoh whose pyramid it sits in front of and whose portrait is said to be represented by the sphinx's face. The strange and compelling symbolism of its part human, part animal body continues to baffle archaeologists.

**Kharkov** (Kharkiv) City in NE Ukraine. It was founded in the 17th century to serve as a stronghold for the Ukrainian Cossacks defending Russia's S border. During the 19th century it developed industrially, stimulated by nearby coalfields. From 1919–34 it was capital of the Ukrainian Soviet Socialist Republic. Industries: mining machinery, ballbearings, chemicals, electrical goods. Pop. (1991) 1,623,000.

**Khartoum** Capital of Sudan, at the junction of the Blue NILE and White Nile rivers. Khartoum was founded in the 1820s by MUHAMMAD ALI. In 1885 it was besieged by Mahdists, and General GORDON was killed. In 1898 it became the seat of government of the Anglo-Egyptian Sudan, and from 1956 the capital of independent Sudan. Industries: cement, gum arabic, chemicals, glass, cotton textiles, printing. Pop. (1983) 476,218.

**Khayyám, Omar** *See* OMAR KHAYYÁM

**Khazars** Turkic people who first appeared in the lower Volga region *c.*2nd century AD. Between the 8th and 10th centuries their empire prospered and extended from N of the Black Sea to the Volga River and from W of the Caspian Sea to the Dnieper River. They conquered the Volga Bulgars and fought the Arabs, Russians, and Pechenegs. In the 8th century, their ruling class was converted to JUDAISM. Their empire was destroyed in 965 by the army of Sviatoslav, Duke of Kiev.

**Khmer** Language of up to 85% of the inhabitants of Cambodia. It belongs to the Mon-Khmer language group and has given its name to the people who speak it. A Khmer empire was set up between the 9th and 15th centuries AD. Cambodia was renamed the Khmer Republic in 1970. When the Republic fell to the KHMER ROUGE in 1975, the country was renamed Kampuchea; the name Cambodia was restored in 1989.

**Khmer Rouge** Cambodian communist guerrilla organization. It gained control of Cambodia in 1975. Led by POL POT and Khieu Samphan, it embarked on a forced communist transformation of Cambodian society, during which an estimated 2 to 3 million people died. The regime lost power to the Vietnamese after a period of intense conflict in 1977–78. The Kampuchean National United Front for National Salvation, supported by the Vietnamese, founded a People's Republic in 1979. In 1982 the Khmer Rouge joined a coalition with Prince SIHANOUK (the former Cambodian leader) and the Khmer Peoples National Liberation Front. From 1988 attempts were made to settle the political situation by peaceful means. In 1991 each faction signed a ceasefire agreement, which was to be monitored by UNITED NATIONS (UN) troops. After an election in 1993, in which the Khmer Rouge refused to take part, Prince Sihanouk's parliamentary monarchy was reestablished. The Khmer Rouge continued hostilities and have been officially banned since 1994.

**Khoisan** Group of South African languages. The Khoikhoi and SAN are the two largest groups of native speakers of these languages. The Khoisan languages also include Sandawe and Hadza, spoken by small tribal groups in Tanzania. *See also* CLICK LANGUAGE

**Khomeini, Ruhollah** (1900–89) Iranian ayatollah (religious leader). An Islamic scholar with great influence over his SHIITE students, he was an active opponent of Muhammad Reza Shah PAHLAVI. Exiled in 1964, he returned to Iran in triumph after the fall of the Shah in 1979. His rule was characterized by strict religious orthodoxy, elimination of political opposition and economic turmoil. In 1989 Khomeini issued a *fatwa* (death order) against author Salman RUSHDIE. He was succeeded by Hojatoleslam RAFSANJANI. *See also* IRAN-IRAQ WAR

**Khrushchev, Nikita Sergeyevich** (1894–1971) Soviet statesman, first secretary of the Communist Party (1953–64) and prime minister (1958–64). Noted for economic success and ruthless suppression of opposition in the Ukraine, he was elected to the Politburo in 1939. After STALIN died, Khrushchev made a speech denouncing him and expelled his backers from the central committee. Favouring detente with the West, he yielded to the US in the CUBAN MISSILE CRISIS. Economic setbacks and trouble with China led to his replacement by Leonid BREZHNEV and Aleksei KOSYGIN in 1964.

**Khyber Pass** Mountain pass in the Safid Kuh range, on the frontier between Afghanistan and Pakistan, linking the Kabul valley in Afghanistan (W) with Peshawar in Pakistan (E). Height: 3,520ft (1,073m). Length: 30mi (50km).

**kibbutz** Collective settlement in Israel that is owned by its members. The idea developed fromthe pioneering communities established by the Jewish settlers in a part of ancient Palestine that became Israel in 1948.

**Kickapoo** Major tribe of Algonquian-speaking Native North Americans, originally occupying south-central Wisconsin. In 1852 part of the tribe went to Texas, and then to Mexico, where many of their descendants still inhabit a reservation area in Chihuahua. Eventually most of the Kickapoo moved to Oklahoma, where some 1,500 now live.

**Kidd, William** (1645–1701) Scottish pirate, commonly known as Captain Kidd. After a successful career as a privateer, he turned to piracy on an expedition to East Africa in 1696. In 1699 he was arrested in Boston, Massachusetts, and sent to England where he was tried and hanged for piracy.

**Kiddush** Blessing recited before a meal on the eve of the Jewish Sabbath or of a festival. The head of the household says the prayer over a cup of wine, which is then passed around to each member to sip.

**kidney** In vertebrates, one of a pair of organs responsible for regulating blood composition and the EXCRETION of waste products. The kidneys are at the back of the abdomen, one on each side of the backbone. The human kidney consists of an outer cortex and an inner medulla with about one million tubules (NEPHRONS). Nephrons contain numerous CAPILLARIES, which filter the blood entering from the renal ARTERY. Some substances, including water, are reabsorbed into the blood. URINE remains, which is passed to the URETER and on to the BLADDER. *See also* HOMEOSTASIS

**kidney machine** (artificial kidney) Equipment designed to remove toxic wastes from the blood in kidney failure. Plastic tubing is used to pipe blood from the body into the machine, where waste products are filtered out by DIALYSIS.

**Kiel** City and seaport in N Germany, at the head of the Kiel Canal linking the North Sea and the Baltic Sea; capital of SCHLESWIG-HOLSTEIN state. Today Kiel is a yachting center. Industries: shipbuilding, textiles, precision instruments, printed matter. Pop. (1990) 248,000.

**Kierkegaard, Søren (Aaby)** (1813–55) Danish philosopher and theologian, regarded as the founder of modern EXISTENTIALISM. He believed that the individual must exercise FREE WILL, making deliberate decisions about the direction of his/her life. Critical of HEGEL's speculative philosophy, he considered that religious faith was, at its best, blind obedience to an irrational God. His books include *Either/Or* (1843) and *Philosophical Fragments* (1844).

**Kiesinger, Kurt Georg** (1904–88) German statesman, chancellor of West Germany (1966–69). He was elected to the Bundestag as a Christian Democrat in 1949. As federal chancellor, Kiesinger maintained the conservative policy of his predecessors, ADENAUER and ERHARD.

**Kiev** (Kiyev) Capital of Ukraine and a seaport on the

Dnieper River. Founded in the 6th or 7th century, Kiev was the capital of Kievan Russia. It later came under Lithuanian, then Polish rule before being absorbed into Russia. It became the capital of the Ukrainian Soviet Socialist Republic in 1934, and of independent Ukraine in 1991. Industries: shipbuilding, machine tools, footwear, furniture. Pop. (1993) 2,600,000.

**Kigali** Capital of Rwanda, central Africa. It was a trade center during the period of German and Belgian colonial administration, becoming the capital when Rwanda achieved independence in 1962. Industries: tin mining, cotton, tanning, textiles, coffee. Pop. (1993) 234,500.

**Kikuyu** Bantu-speaking people of the highlands of Kenya, E Africa. British conquest strained their political and agricultural system; the result was an outbreak of terrorism during the 1950s by a group known as MAU MAU. After Kenya gained independence in 1963, they were the country's most important tribe, forming 20% of the population.

**Kilauea** Volcanic crater in Hawaii, on SE Hawaii Island. It last erupted in 1968 and is the largest active crater in the world. Height: 4,090ft (1,247m). Depth: 500ft (152m).

**Kildare** County in Leinster province, E Republic of Ireland; the county town is Naas. A low-lying region, the chief rivers are the Liffey, Boyne, and Barrow. Primarily agricultural, Kildare is noted for its breeding of racehorses. Area: 654sq mi (1,694sq km). Pop. (1991) 122,656.

**Kilimanjaro** Mountain in NE Tanzania, near the border with Kenya. The highest mountain in Africa, it is an extinct volcano with twin peaks joined by a broad saddle. Coffee is grown on the intensely cultivated S slopes. Height: Kibo 19,340ft (5,895m); Mawenzi 16,896ft (5,150m).

**Kilkenny** County in Leinster province, SE Republic of Ireland; the county town is Kilkenny. Part of the central plain of Ireland, it is drained by the Suir, Barrow, and Nore rivers. Farmers grow cereal crops and vegetables, and cattle are reared. The chief industries are brewing and coal mining. Area: 796sq mi (2,062sq km). Pop. (1991) 73,635.

**killdeer** Noisy bird of North American meadows, known for its alarm call and distraction displays. Its plumage is white with a double black breast band and chestnut rump and tail. Family Charadriidae; species *Charadrius vociferus*.

**killer whale** Toothed marine mammal of the DOLPHIN family that lives in the world's oceans, especially colder regions. A fierce predator, it is black above and white below, with a white patch above each eye. Length: 30ft (9m). Species: *Orcinus orca*.

**kilogram** (symbol kg) SI unit of mass defined as the mass of the international prototype cylinder of platinum-iridium kept at the International Bureau of Weights and Measures near Paris. One kilogram is equal to 1,000g (2.2lb).

**Kimberley** City in South Africa; capital of Northern Cape province. It was founded in 1871 after the discovery of diamonds nearby. Today it is one of the world's largest diamond centers. Other industries are the processing of gypsum, iron, and manganese. Pop. (1991) 167,060.

**Kim Il Sung** (1912–94) Korean statesman, first premier of North Korea (1948–72) and president (1972–94). He joined the Korean Communist Party in 1931 and led a Korean unit in the Soviet army during World War II. In 1950 Kim led a North Korean invasion of South Korea, precipitating the KOREAN WAR (1950–53). Chairman of the Korean Workers' Party from 1948, his government suppressed all opposition and pursued strictly orthodox communist policies. He was succeeded by his son, KIM JONG IL.

**Kim Jong Il** (1941– ) North Korean statesman, president (1994– ), son of KIM IL SUNG. In 1980 he was officially named as his father's successor, assuming a more important role in government and being included in the personality cult that surrounded his father.

**Kim Young Sam** (1927– ) South Korean statesman, president (1992–97). He was president of the New Democratic Party (NDP) from 1974. In 1979 he was banned from politics for his opposition to President Park. The ban was lifted in 1985. As leader of the Democratic Liberal Party (DLP), Kim Young Sam became president of South Korea.

**kinetic energy** Energy that an object possesses because it is in motion. It is the energy (symbol K) given to an object to set it in motion; it depends on the mass ($m$) of the object and its velocity ($v$), according to the equation $K = \frac{1}{2}mv^2$. On impact, it is converted into other forms of energy such as heat, sound, and light. *See also* POTENTIAL ENERGY

▲ **killer whale** The large triangular dorsal fin and the black and white body are the two obvious features of the killer whale (*Orcinus orca*). It is found mostly in polar seas and is generally considered to be the most ferocious of whales. Almost any creature in the sea is considered as food by the 30ft (9m) killers.

**kinetics** In physics, one of the branches of DYNAMICS. In chemistry, a branch of physical chemistry that deals with the rates of chemical reactions.

**kinetic theory** Theory in physics dealing with matter in terms of the forces between particles and the energies they possess. There are five principles to the kinetic theory: matter is composed of tiny particles; these are in constant motion; they do not lose energy in collision with each other or the walls of their container; there are no attractive forces between the particles or their container; and at any time the particles in a sample may not all have the same energy.

**King, B.B. (Riley B.)** (1925– ) US blues guitarist and singer-songwriter. His albums include *Blues is King* (1967) and *Lucille Talks Back* (1975).

**King, Billie Jean** (1943– ) US tennis player. King won the US Open women's singles four times (1967, 1971–72, 1974); a record of 20 of Wimbledon titles, including six singles titles (1966–68, 1972–73, 1975); the Australian Open (1968); and the French Open (1972). She also dominated women's singles and advocated parity in the prize money for men's and women's competitions.

**King, Martin Luther, Jr.** (1929–68) US Baptist minister and CIVIL RIGHTS leader. In 1956 he led the boycott of segregated public transport in Montgomery, Alabama. As founder (1960) and president of the Southern Christian Leadership Council (SCLC), he became a national figure. King opposed the Vietnam War and demanded measures to relieve poverty, organizing a huge march on Washington (1963) where he made his famous ("I have a dream...") speech. In 1964 he became the youngest person to be awarded the Nobel Peace Prize. He was assassinated (April 4, 1968) in Memphis, Tennessee, where he had gone to support striking workers. His wife, **Coretta Scott King** (1927– ), became a civil rights leader after his death. In 1998 his son, **Martin Luther King III**, became leader of the SCLC.

**King, Rufus** (1755–1827) US statesman. As a member of the CONTINENTAL CONGRESS (1784–87), he introduced legislation calling for a constitution and prohibiting slavery in the Northwest Territory. He then helped to draft and pass the federal Constitution. He moved to New York in 1788. He served as a US Senator (1789–96, 1813–25) and as ambassador to Great Britain (1796–1803, 1825–26). He was an unsuccessful presidential candidate (1816).

**King, Stephen** (1947– ) US novelist and short-story writer. King is a master of the modern horror novel. Many of his books, such as *The Shining* (1977) and *Misery* (1987), have been made into successful films.

**King, William Lyon Mackenzie** (1874–1950) Canadian politician, prime minister (1921–30, 1935–48). His career was marked by the drive for national unity, culminating in the Statute of WESTMINSTER (1931). He made concessions to the Progressives, and he was conciliatory toward French-Canadian demands. In foreign policy his basic sympathies were isolationist and anti-British, but he cooperated closely with Britain and the US during World War II.

**kingbird** (tyrant flycatcher) New World flycatcher whose habitat is mainly in tropical America. It dives at intruders and snaps up insects. It grows to 6.8in (17cm).

**kingdom** Most widely adopted TAXONOMY for living organ-

▲ **King** US civil rights leader Martin Luther King was an inspiring orator of impressive moral impact. Often criticized by more militant activists, his policy of passive resistance was based on Gandhi's activities in India. During the latter part of his life he became increasingly concerned with economics as well as racial discrimination.

K

▲ **kingfisher** The kingfisher (*Alcedo atthis*) is widespread throughout Europe, Asia, N Africa, and eastward to the Solomon Islands. The birds live on the banks of freshwater streams and lakes feeding on small minnows and sometimes reptiles and crustaceans.

isms is the Five Kingdoms system, in which the kingdom is the topmost level (taxon). The Five Kingdoms are Animalia (ANIMAL), Plantae (PLANT), Fungi (FUNGUS), PROKARYOTAE, and PROTISTA. Two subkingdoms are often recognized within Prokaryotae, ARCHAEBACTERIA and EUBACTERIA, but the bacteria are so diverse that many taxonomists think they comprise more than one kingdom. Some believe that they merit the status of a new, even higher category, DOMAINS. *See also* EUKARYOTE; PLANT CLASSIFICATION

**kingfisher** Compact, brightly colored bird with a straight, sharp bill, which dives for fish along rivers, streams, and lakes. It nests in a horizontal hole in an earth bank. Length: 5–17in (13–43cm). Family Alcedinidae.

**King George's War** (1744–48) Inconclusive struggle between France and Britain for control over North America. Both sides enlisted Native-American allies in fighting over disputed boundaries in Nova Scotia, New England, and the Ohio Valley. By the Peace of Aix-la-Chapelle (1748), conquered territory was restored by mutual agreement.

**King Philip's War** (1675–76) War between English settlers and Native Americans in New England. The Wampanoags, under their chief Philip (Metacomet), rebelled against increasing white aggression. Colonial forces eventually gained the upper hand and wreaked still greater destruction on native settlements. King Philip was killed in 1676.

**Kings I and II** Two books in the OLD TESTAMENT, called Third and Fourth Kingdoms in the Greek SEPTUAGINT. These books recount the history of the kingdom of ISRAEL from the end of the reign of DAVID (*c*.970 BC) to the fall of Judah and the destruction of Jerusalem by the Babylonians in 586 BC.

**Kingsley, Charles** (1819–75) British writer. He was one of the first clergymen to support Charles DARWIN, whose ideas he partly incorporated into *The Water Babies* (1863). His immensely popular historical novels include *Hypatia* (1843) and *Hereward the Wake* (1866).

**king snake** Nonpoisonous SNAKE that lives in the US. It is generally black with white or yellow markings. Length: to 4.2ft (1.3m). Family Colubridae, genus *Lampropeltis*.

**Kingston** Capital and largest city of Jamaica. It was founded in 1693. It rapidly developed into Jamaica's commercial center, based on the export of raw cane sugar, bananas, and rum. In 1872 it became the island's capital. Kingston is the cultural heart of Jamaica. In recent years Kingston has been plagued by urban disturbances and armed drug gangs. Pop. (1991) 643,800.

**Kingstown** Capital and chief port of St. Vincent and the Grenadines, on the SW coast. Exports: cotton, sugarcane, molasses, cacao, fruit. Pop. (1991) 26,223.

**King William's War** (1689–97) North American part of the war between England and France. Frontenac, the French governor of Canada, sent expeditions against the New York, New Hampshire, and Maine frontiers. The English, under Sir William Phipps (of Massachusetts), sailed up the St. Lawrence River to take Quebec, but failed (1690). Bloody border conflicts with the Indians also occurred. Port Royal, Nova Scotia, was captured and then lost by the English (1690–91).

**kinkajou** Nocturnal foraging mammal of the RACOON family that lives in forests of Central and South America. Primarily a fruit and insect eater, it lives almost entirely in trees. Length: to 22.7in (57.5cm); weight: to 6lb (2.7kg). Family Procyonidae; species *Potos flavus*.

► **Kirov Ballet** *The Nutcracker* by Tchaikovsky was just one of many ballets which ensured the reputation over the years of the Kirov Ballet. However, in recent years the company has been accused by some of falling standards and a desire to increase commerciality at the cost of its art.

**Kinsey, Alfred Charles** (1894–1956) US zoologist, noted for his studies on human sexual behavior. He was director of the Institute for Sex Research, Indiana University, and is best known for *Sexual Behavior in the Human Male* (1948) and *Sexual Behavior in the Human Female* (1953).

**Kinshasa** (formerly Léopoldville) Capital of Zaire, a port on the Zaire River, on the Zaire-Congo border. It replaced Boma as the capital of the Belgian Congo in 1923. When Zaire gained independence in 1960, it continued as the capital, changing its name in 1966. Industries: tanning, chemicals, brewing, textiles. Pop. (1991 est.) 3,804,000.

**kinship** Relationship by blood or marriage, sometimes extended to cover relations of affinity. It also refers to a complex of rules in society governing descent, succession, inheritance, residence, marriage, and sexual relations. *See also* INCEST

**Kiowa** Major tribe of Tanoan-speaking Native North Americans who moved from their earlier Yellowstone–Missouri River homeland into the S Plains region, where they eventually allied with the Comanche and Arapaho. Today the descendants of the Kiowa live mostly in Oklahoma.

**Kipling, Joseph Rudyard** (1865–1936) British author, b. India. His *Barrack Room Ballads and Other Verses* (1892), which include the poem *If*, established his reputation. His novels include *The Light That Failed* (1890) and *Kim* (1901). He also wrote many children's stories, including *The Jungle Book* (1894) and *Just So Stories* (1902). Kipling was the first English writer to be awarded the Nobel Prize for literature (1907).

**Kirchhoff, Gustav Robert** (1824–87) German physicist. With Robert BUNSEN, he developed the spectroscope, with which they discovered CESIUM and RUBIDIUM in 1860. He is famous for two laws that apply to multiple-loop electric circuits. Kirchhoff's laws state that (1) at any junction the sum of the currents flowing is zero, and (2) the sum of the ELECTROMOTIVE FORCES (EMF) around any closed path equals the sum of the products of the currents and impedances (resistances).

**Kirchner, Ernst Ludwig** (1880–1938) German painter and printmaker, a leader of the expressionist artists known as Die BRÜCKE. Kirchner characteristically portrayed urban scenes. His art was condemned by the Nazis as degenerate and he committed suicide. *See also* EXPRESSIONISM

**Kiribati** (formerly Gilbert Islands) Independent nation in the W Pacific Ocean, comprising about 33 islands, including the Gilbert, Phoenix, and Line Islands, and straddling the Equator over a vast area; the capital is Bairiki (on Tarawa). British navigators first visited the islands during the late 18th century. They became a British protectorate in 1892. Full independence within the Commonwealth of Nations was granted in 1979. The mining of phosphates dominated the economy until 1980, when production ended because of diminishing resources. Agriculture is now the major economic activity. Land area: 277sq mi (717sq km). Pop. (1995 est.) 80,000

**Kiritimati** (Christmas Island) Largest atoll in the world, one of the Line Islands, forming part of KIRIBATI. It was the site of nuclear tests by Britain (1956–62) and the US (1962). Area: 222sq mi (575sq km). Pop. (1990) 2,537.

**Kirov, Sergei Mironovich** (1888–1934) Soviet politician. An effective speaker, he was elected to the Communist Party Politburo in 1930. His murder, probably on Stalin's orders, served as a pretext for the Stalin purges (1934–38).

**Kirov** Former name (1934–92) for VYATKA

**Kirov Ballet** Ballet company founded in 1735 at St. Petersburg. Under the direction of PETIPA (1862–1903), the Kirov Ballet was the world's top company, with principal dancers such as PAVLOVA and NIJINSKY. The **Kirov Opera** has also made a distinguished contribution to Russian culture.

**Kisangani** (formerly Stanleyville) City and port on the Congo River, N central Zaire. Kisangani was founded in 1883 by the English explorer Henry M. STANLEY. During the 1950s it was the headquarters of the Congolese National Movement led by Patrice LUMUMBA. During the 1960s it was the focus for a series of unsuccessful rebellions. In 1996 it was at the center of the Hutu refugee crisis in Zaire. Pop. (1984) 282,650.

**Kissinger, Henry Alfred** (1923– ) US statesman and political scientist, secretary of state (1973–77), b. Germany. In 1969 he became President NIXON's assistant for national security and chief adviser on foreign policy, helping to establish the STRATEGIC ARMS LIMITATION TALKS (SALT) with the Soviet Union. As secretary of state, Kissinger shared the Nobel Peace Prize (1973) with Le Duc Tho for his part in negotiating an end to the VIETNAM WAR. His "shuttle diplomacy" brought a ceasefire agreement between Egypt and Israel in the 1973 Yom Kippur War. After the fall of Nixon, Kissinger continued as secretary of state for President FORD.

**Kitchener, Horatio Herbert, 1st Earl** (1850–1916) British field marshal and statesman. He took part in the unsuccessful relief of General GORDON at Khartoum (1883–85), but reconquered Sudan in 1898 and became its governor-general. Kitchener served as chief of staff in the second of the SOUTH AFRICAN WARS (1900–02). He was appointed secretary of state for war at the outbreak of World War I.

**kite** Common name for several diurnal birds of prey, especially the red kite, *Milvus milvus*, which frequents wooded slopes in Europe. It has a hooked bill, long wings, and a long forked tail. Length: 24in (60cm). Family Accipitridae.

**kiwi** Any of three species of flightless, fast-running, forest and scrubland birds of New Zealand; especially the common brown kiwi, *Apteryx australis*. It has a long, flexible bill with which it probes for food in the ground. Family Apterygidae.

**Klee, Paul** (1879–1940) Swiss painter and graphic artist. Klee evolved his own pictorial language based on correspondences between line, color, and plane. Some of his images are entirely ABSTRACT, but some are recognizable figures. He taught at the BAUHAUS (1920–31) and at Düsseldorf Academy (1931–33) but returned to Switzerland in 1933 after the Nazis had condemned his work as degenerate. Characteristic works include *Graduated Shades of Red-Green* (1921) and *Revolutions of the Viaducts* (1937).

**Klemperer, Otto** (1885–1973) German conductor. He was celebrated for his interpretations of Beethoven, Brahms, and Mahler. In 1933, with the rise of Nazism in Germany, he went to the US and became conductor of the Los Angeles Philharmonic. In 1946 he returned to Europe as director of the Budapest Opera (1947– 50).

**Klimt, Gustav** (1862–1918) Austrian painter and designer, a founder of the Vienna SEZESSION group and the foremost ART NOUVEAU painter in Vienna. His style considerably influenced the decorative arts in Austria and the work of the painters Egon SCHIELE and Oskar KOKOSCHKA.

**Kline, Franz** (1910–62) US abstract expressionist painter. In the 1950s he began to paint large, stark, grid-like compositions, generally in black and white. He reintroduced color in his late works.

**Klondike Gold Rush** (1896–1904) Mass migration of gold prospectors to the Klondike region, YUKON TERRITORY, NW Canada. The rich gold deposits discovered in the Klondike River in 1896 brought more than 30,000 prospectors to the territory. Within a decade more than $100 million worth of gold had been extracted. The easily accessible lodes were exhausted, *c*.1910, but mining continues.

**Klopstock, Friedrich Gottlieb** (1724–1803) German poet. He anticipated the STURM UND DRANG movement and influenced other poets such as GOETHE, RILKE, and Hölderlin. While still a student he began writing the epic *The Messiah*.

**knight** In medieval Europe, a mounted warrior of intermediate rank. The knight began as a squire and was knighted with a sword touch on the shoulder after a period of trial. Knights were often landholders, owing military service to their overlord. Honorary orders of knighthood, such as the Knights of the Garter (1349), were founded toward the end of the Middle Ages, a tradition that continued into the modern era.

**Knights Hospitallers** Military Christian order founded in the 12th century. They adopted a military role to defend JERUSALEM. After the fall of Jerusalem (1187), they moved to Acre, then Cyprus, then Rhodes (1310), from where they were expelled by the Ottoman Turks (1522). The pope then gave them Malta, where they remained until driven out by Napoleon in 1798. The order still exists as an international, humanitarian charity.

**Knights of Labor** Workers' group formed in Philadelphia (1869). It was organized by Uriah S. Stephens, and became a

◀ **Klimt** *Hygieia* (1900–07) clearly shows the influence of the pre-Raphaelites on the Austrian painter Gustav Klimt. Much of his art, often erotic, features a bejeweled effect reminiscent of mosaics, a format in which he worked later in his life.

national organization in 1878. Skilled and unskilled workers, regardless of race, sex, or color, were eligible to join the local assemblies, which together formed one union. It reached peak membership of more than 700,000 in 1886. The union declined after the Haymarket Square riot in May 1886, and several strike failures. The organization was dissolved in 1913.

**Knights Templar** Military religious order established in 1118, with headquarters in the supposed Temple of Solomon in Jerusalem. With the KNIGHTS HOSPITALLERS, the Templars protected routes to Jerusalem for Christians during the CRUSADES. The possessions of the Templars in France attracted the envious attention of King PHILIP IV, who urged Pope Clement V to abolish the order in 1312.

**knitting** Hand-weaving of a textile by using rodlike needles to interlace loops of spun yarn. Knitting was apparently unknown in Europe before the 15th century, when the practice began in Spain and Italy, having arrived there probably from the Arab world. The first knitting machine was invented in England in 1589.

**Knossos** Ancient palace complex in N central Crete, 4mi (6.4km) SE of modern Iráklion. In 1900 Sir Arthur Evans began excavations that revealed that the site had been inhabited before 3000 BC. His main discovery was a palace from the MINOAN CIVILIZATION (built *c*.2000 BC and rebuilt *c*.1700 BC). Close to the palace were the houses of Cretan nobles. The complex also contains many frescoes. Knossos dominated Crete *c*.1500 BC but the palace was occupied *c*.1400 BC by invaders from MYCENAE.

**knot** Unit of measurement equal to one nautical mile per hour – one knot equals 1.15mph (1.852km/h). The speeds of ships and aircraft are generally expressed in knots, as are those of winds and currents.

**Know-Nothing movement** US political party active in the 1850s. Officially the American Party, it arose from secret, anti-immigrant societies and derived its nickname from its members' standard answer to inquiries. Its presidential candidate, Millard Fillmore, gained 20% of the popular vote in 1856 but, split over slavery, the party then disintegrated.

**Knox, Henry** (1750–1806) American Revolutionary War military officer. As commander of the Continental Army artillery, he hauled the guns captured at Fort Ticonderoga to Boston. He took part in every major battle of the war and was close adviser to George Washington, becoming a brigadier general in 1776. He was the first secretary of war (1785–94).

**Knox, John** (1514–72) Leader of the Protestant REFORMATION in Scotland. Ordained a Catholic priest, he was later converted to Protestantism and took up the cause of the Reformation. Captured by French soldiers in Scotland, he was imprisoned in France (1547), then lived in exile in England and Switzerland. In 1559 Knox returned to Scotland, where he continued to promote the Protestant cause. In 1560, the Scottish Parliament, under Knox's leadership, made PRESBYTERIANISM the state religion. In 1563 he was tried for treason but acquitted.

**Knoxville** City on the Tennessee River, E Tennessee, 105mi (169km) NE of Chattanooga. It is the seat of Knox county. Settled in 1786, the city was a supply center for westward-bound wagon trains (1792), and became Tennessee's first capital (1797–1812, 1817–19). In 1861 it was the headquarters of the Confederate armies in E Tennessee, and was taken by Union troops at the Battle of Fort Sanders (1863). Industries: livestock, farming, tobacco, marble quarrying, ore processing, textiles, furniture, cement, steel products, glass, chemicals, plastics, railroad shops, tourism, lumber. Pop. (1990) 165,039.

**koala** Small marsupial that lives in eucalyptus trees of Australia, eating their leaves. A single immature young is born, nurtured in its mother's pouch until fully formed, then carried on her back for a further six months. Length: 33in (85cm). Species *Phascolarctos cinereus*.

**Kobe** City and seaport on the N shore of Osaka Bay, SW Honshu Island, Japan. It is Japan's leading port and a major industrial center. In January 1995 more than 5,000 people were killed and 27,000 injured in an earthquake. Industries: shipbuilding, iron and steel, electronics, chemicals. Pop. (1993) 1,468,000.

**Kodály, Zoltán** (1882–1967) Hungarian composer. With BARTÓK he collected and systematized Hungarian folk music, which was the principal influence in his work. Among his best-known compositions are the *Psalmus Hungaricus* (1923) and the comic opera *Háry János* (1927).

**Koestler, Arthur** (1905–83) British novelist and philosopher, b. Hungary. *Darkness at Noon* (1940), his best-known novel, is a biting indictment of Stalinist totalitarianism. His other novels also embody political themes. He died in a suicide pact with his wife.

**Koffka, Kurt** (1886–1941) US psychologist, b. Germany. With Wolfgang KÖHLER and Max Wertheimer, he was a founder of GESTALT PSYCHOLOGY. He wrote *The Growth of the Mind* (1921), and *Principles of Gestalt Psychology* (1935).

**Kohl, Helmut** (1930– ) German statesman, chancellor (1982–98). Between 1976 and 1982 he led the Christian Democratic Union (CDU) Party opposition to Helmut SCHMIDT. Kohl succeeded Schmidt as chancellor. His conservative approach advocated strong support for NATO and a return to the traditional values of the West German state. Kohl strongly supported closer integration in the European Union (EU) and the establishment of the EURO. In 1990 he presided over the reunification of East and West Germany and was elected as the first chancellor of the new unified Germany. Re-elected in 1994 and 1996, Kohl lost the 1998 election to Gerhard Schröder.

**Köhler, Wolfgang** (1887–1967) US psychologist, b. Estonia. With Kurt KOFFKA and Max Wertheimer, he was a key figure in GESTALT PSYCHOLOGY. His work on animal learning and problem solving is summarized in *The Mentality of Apes* (1917).

**Kokoschka, Oskar** (1886–1980) Austrian painter. He was influenced by the elegance of KLIMT but soon developed his own type of EXPRESSIONISM. His work is characterized by forceful, energetic draftsmanship and restless brushwork.

**kolanut** (colanut) Fruit of an African tree that bears the same name, from which is extracted an ingredient of cola soft drinks. Family Sterculiaceae; species *Cola acuminata*.

## KOREA, NORTH

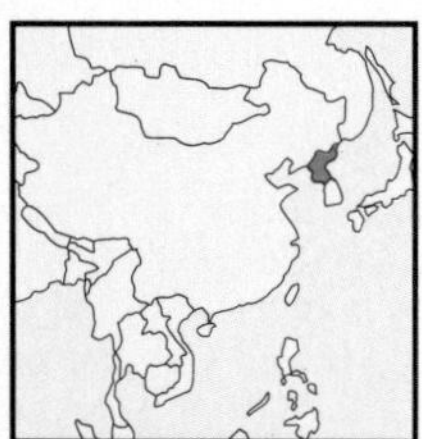

The flag of the Democratic People's Republic of Korea (North Korea) has been flown since Korea was split into two states in 1948. The colors are traditional ones in Korea. The design, with the red star, indicates that North Korea is a communist country.

**AREA:** 46,540sq mi (120,540sq km)
**POPULATION:** 22,618,000
**CAPITAL (POPULATION):** Pyongyang (2,639,448)
**GOVERNMENT:** Single-party people's republic
**ETHNIC GROUPS:** Korean 99%
**LANGUAGES:** Korean (official)
**RELIGIONS:** Traditional beliefs 16%, Chondogyo 14%, Buddhism 2%, Christianity 1%
**CURRENCY:** North Korean won = 100 chon

The Democratic People's Republic of Korea occupies the N part of the Korean peninsula. North Korea is largely mountainous. The capital, PYONGYANG, lies on the W coastal plain. North Korea's border with South Korea is based on the 38th parallel. (For land, climate, and pre-1953 history, *see* KOREA and KOREAN WAR)

### HISTORY

In 1948 North Korea established a communist government led (1948–94) by KIM IL SUNG. Kim Il Sung's Stalinist regime exploited North Korea's rich mineral resources. Industry was nationalized. Heavy industry and arms production greatly increased. Agriculture was collectivized and mechanized.

After the Korean War several million Koreans fled Kim Il Sung's dictatorial regime. North Korea remained largely closed to outside interests. Alliances were formed with China and the Soviet Union, but the collapse of the latter had adverse effects on North Korea's economy. Its emphasis on military industry had a destabilizing effect on regional politics and internal economic planning. Since 1991 Korea's economy has slumped. In 1991 North and South Korea signed a non-aggression pact and agreed on a series of meetings on reunification. The process was halted in 1994 with the death of Kim Il Sung. He was succeeded by his son, KIM JONG IL.

### POLITICS

During the early 1990s North Korea's nuclear weapons building program gathered momentum. In 1994 North Korea briefly withdrew from the Nuclear Non-Proliferation Treaty. They rejoined after agreeing to halt the reprocessing of plutonium, in return for guarantees on energy supplies and the establishment of economic and diplomatic relations with the US. In 1995 severe flooding caused more than $15 billion of damage and devastated agricultural production. In 1996 the United Nations sent emergency food aid to relieve famine. In 1998 North Korea launched a ballistic missile over Japanese airspace.

### ECONOMY

North Korea has considerable mineral resources, including coal, copper, iron ore, lead, tin, tungsten, and zinc. Yet it is a net consumer of energy and reliant on oil imports (1992 GDP per capita, US$3,026). Industries include chemicals, iron and steel, machinery, processed food, and textiles. Agriculture employs more than 40% of the workforce. Rice is the leading crop.

**Kollwitz, Käthe** (1867–1945) German graphic artist and sculptor. She was influenced by experiences of the poverty-stricken districts of N Berlin. Her best-known works depict suffering, especially of women and children. She made her name with the series of etchings, *The Weavers' Revolt* (1897–98) and *Peasants' War* (1902–08).

**Kommunizma Pik** (Communism Peak) Mountain in central Asia, in SE Tajikistan, in the Pamirs region. Known as Mount Garmo until 1933 and Stalin Peak until 1962, it was the highest peak in the former Soviet Union. Height: 24,590ft (7,495m).

**komodo dragon** Giant monitor lizard that lives on four islands to the E of Java, Indonesia; it is the largest lizard in the world. Length: 10ft (3m). Family Varanidae; species *Varanus komodoensis.*

**Königsberg** *See* KALININGRAD

**Konya** City in S central Turkey. Known in ancient times as Iconium, it was first settled in the 8th century BC. The capital of the SELJUK sultanate of Rum from 1099, it was annexed by the Ottoman sultan in 1472. It is the religious center of the whirling DERVISHES. Industries: cotton, carpets. Pop. (1990) 543,460.

**kookaburra** (laughing jackass) Large KINGFISHER of Australia, known for its call resembling fiendish laughter. Groups often scream in unison at dawn, midday, and dusk. They feed on animals. Species *Dacelo gigas.*

**Koran** (Quran) Sacred book of ISLAM. According to Muslim belief, the Koran contains the actual word of God (Allah) as revealed by the angel GABRIEL to the Prophet MUHAMMAD. Muhammad is said to have received these revelations over two decades beginning *c.* AD 610 and ending in 632, the year of his death. The 114 *suras* (chapters) of the Koran are the source of Islamic belief and a guide for the whole life of the community. The central teachings of the Koran are that there is no God but Allah and all must submit to Him, that Muhammad is the last of His many messengers (which have included Abraham, Moses, and Jesus), and that there will come a day of judgment. In addition to these teachings, the Koran contains rules that a Muslim must follow in everyday life.

**Korea** Peninsula in E Asia, separating the Yellow Sea from the Sea of Japan. The Yalu and Tumen rivers form most of its N border with China. **Land and climate** The E seaboard is mountainous, rising in the NE to 9,003ft (2,744m) at Mount Paektu. The mountains descend in the W to coastal lowlands. The traditional capital, SEOUL, lies close to the 38th parallel border between North Korea and South Korea. The Korean Archipelago lies off the S coast, and includes the province of Cheju-do. North Korea experiences long and severe winters: lakes and rivers can remain frozen for up to four months a year. Summers are warm. South Korea has a more tropical climate with occasional typhoons in the rainy months (July–August). **History** Korea's calendar starts in 2333 BC. China was a dominant influence. The first native Korean state was established in the 1st century AD, and Korea was unified under the Silla dynasty in the 7th century. Korea was invaded by Mongols in 1231 and eventually surrendered. The Yi dynasty ruled Korea from 1392–1910. Early in the Yi period, Seoul was made the new capital and CONFUCIANISM became the official religion. In the 17th century Korea was a semiindependent state, dominated by the Manchu dynasty. A long period of isolationism followed. In the late 19th century Korea became more active in foreign affairs, due to the growing power of Japan. After the RUSSO-JAPANESE WAR (1904–05) Korea was effectively a Japanese protectorate and was formally annexed in 1910. Japan's enforced industrialization of Korea caused widespread resentment. Following Japan's defeat in World War II, Korea was divided into two zones of occupation: Soviet forces N of the 38th parallel, and US forces S of the line. Attempts at reunification failed, and in 1948 two separate regimes were established: the Republic of Korea in the S and the Democratic People's Republic in the N. In June 1950 North Korea invaded South Korea. The ensuing KOREAN WAR (1950–53) resulted in millions of deaths and devastated the peninsula. An uneasy truce has prevailed ever since. Attempts at reunification continue.

**Korea, North** Republic in E Asia. *See* country feature

**Korea, South** Republic in E Asia. *See* country feature, page 378

**Korean** National language of North and South Korea. Some scholars class it as one of the ALTAIC LANGUAGES. It is spoken by more than 50 million people. The Korean alphabet developed in the 15th century.

**Korean War** (1950–53) Conflict between North Korea, supported by China, and South Korea, supported by UN forces dominated by the US. South Korea was invaded by forces of the North in June 1950. The UNITED NATIONS Security Council, during a boycott by the Soviet Union, voted to aid South Korea. Major US forces, plus token forces from its allies, landed under the overall command of General Douglas MACARTHUR. The invaders were driven out, but when the UN forces advanced into North Korea, China intervened and drove them back, recapturing Seoul. After more heavy fighting, UN forces slowly advanced until virtual stalemate ensued near the 38th Parallel, the border between North and South Korea. Negotiations continued for two years before a truce was agreed in July 1953. Total casualties are estimated at 4 million.

**Korematsu v. United States** (1944) US Supreme Court decision that upheld the constitutionality of the Japanese evacuation and encampment program ordered by President Franklin D. ROOSEVELT early in World War II to combat a "potentially grave danger to public safety." The court justified the incarceration of US citizens without the rudiments of due process protections as "an emergency war measure," but many criticized the court's position. The decision was repealed in 1983.

**Kornberg, Arthur** (1918– ) US biochemist. In 1959 he shared (with Severo Ochoa) the Nobel Prize for physiology or medicine for work on the synthesis of RNA and DNA, an important contribution to the study of genetics.

K

**Kosciusko, Mount** Mountain in SE Australia, in the Great Dividing Range, in SE New South Wales. The highest mountain in Australia, it lies inside a national park and is a winter sports resort. Height: 7,310ft (2,228m).

**Kościuszko, Thadeus** (1746–1817) Polish politician and soldier. After the second partition of Poland in 1793, he led a revolutionary movement to regain Polish independence. It was initially successful, but the invading armies of Russia and Prussia proved too strong, and Kościuszko was imprisoned (1794–96) and then exiled.

**Kosovo** Autonomous province in S Serbia; the capital is Pristina. Ottoman victory in the Battle of Kosovo Field (1389) broke the power of Serbia. In 1913 it was reclaimed by Serbia and was incorporated into Yugoslavia in 1929. After World War II it became an autonomous province of Serbia. In 1974 Kosovo was granted a degree of autonomy. In 1990 the majority Albanian population demanded greater autonomy. Serbia responded by imposing direct rule. In 1999 an intensive campaign of "ethnic cleansing" by the Yugoslav army led NATO to launch sustained air-strikes on Serbia. Area: 4,205sq mi (10,887sq km). Pop. (1991) 1,956,200.

**Kossuth, Lajos** (1802–94) Hungarian statesman. In 1848 Kossuth led the Hungarian Revolution against Habsburg rule and was appointed provisional governor of the independent republic. In 1849 the Russians crushed the uprising, forcing him to flee. He continued to champion Hungarian independence from exile but the Compromise of 1867, which created the AUSTRO-HUNGARIAN EMPIRE, put an end to his hopes.

**Kosygin, Aleksei Nikolayevich** (1904–80) Soviet statesman, premier (1964–80). He was elected to the Communist Party Central Committee in 1939 and the Politburo in 1948. Kosygin served as an economics expert to Joseph STALIN. He was removed on the accession of Nikolai KHRUSHCHEV, but returned to share power with Leonid BREZHNEV.

**Koussevitzky, Sergei Aleksandrovich** (1874–1951) US conductor and musician, b. Russia. A virtuoso double-bass player, he is chiefly remembered as conductor of the Boston Symphony Orchestra (1924–49).

**Kowloon** Peninsula on the SE coast of China, part of HONG KONG. One of the most densely populated areas of the world, it was ceded to Britain by China in 1860. Industries: shipbuilding. Area: 3.5sq mi (9sq km). Pop. (1986) 2,301,691.

**Krakatoa** Small volcanic island in W Indonesia, in the Sunda Strait between Java and Sumatra. In 1883 one of the world's largest volcanic eruptions destroyed most of the island. The resulting tidal waves caused 50,000 deaths and great destruction. Height: 2,667ft (813m).

**Kraków** (Cracow) City in S Poland. Founded in the 8th century, it was made a residence of the Polish kings in the 12th century and subsequently capital of Poland. In 1795 it was ceded to Austria. After a period of independence (from 1815) it was restored to Austria in 1846. The city became part of Poland after World War I. Historic buildings include the Wawel Cathedral. The Jagiellonian University (1364) is one of the oldest in Europe. Today Kraków is a manufacturing center. Industries: chemicals, metals, machinery. Pop. (1993) 751,300.

**Krasnodar** City and port on the E bank of Kuban River, SW European Russia; capital of Krasnodar Kray. Founded in 1794 by CATHERINE II as a frontier outpost, it was known as Yekaterinodar until 1920. Industries: oil refining, machine tools, textiles, metalworking. Pop. (1992) 635,000.

**Krasnoyarsk** City and port on the W bank of the upper Yenisei River, W Siberian Russia; capital of Krasnoyarsk Kray. Founded in 1628 by the COSSACKS, it was attacked in the later 17th century by Tatars and other tribes. It underwent rapid development after the discovery of gold in the area. Industries: shipbuilding, heavy machinery, electrical goods, cement, timber, flour milling. Pop. (1992) 925,000.

**Krebs, Sir Hans Adolf** (1900–81) British biochemist, b. Germany. In 1953 he shared (with F.A. Lipmann) the Nobel Prize for physiology or medicine for his discovery of the CITRIC ACID cycle, the process that results in the production of energy in living organisms (RESPIRATION).

**Kremlin** (Rus. citadel) Historic center of Moscow. It is a roughly triangular fortress covering *c.*90 acres (36.5ha). The Kremlin walls were built of timber in the 12th century and its first stone walls were built in 1367. Within the walls several cathedrals face on to a central square; the Great Kremlin Palace was the czar's Moscow residence until the revolution. In March 1918 the Supreme Soviet established the Kremlin complex as the location of all government offices. Today, the Kremlin is the home of the Russian presidential offices.

**Křenek, Ernst** (1900–91) US composer, b. Austria, who emigrated to the US in 1938. From 1920 in Berlin he experimented with atonal music, and after 1930 in Vienna he adopted the TWELVE-TONE MUSIC technique of SCHOENBERG. He created a sensation with the jazz opera *Jonny spielt auf* (1925–26).

## KOREA, SOUTH

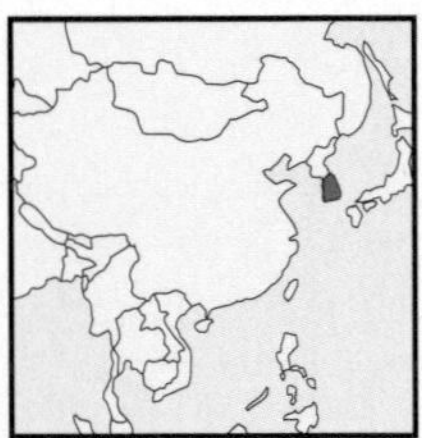

South Korea's flag, adopted in 1950, is white, the traditional symbol for peace. The central yin-yang symbol signifies the opposing forces of nature. The four black symbols stand for the four seasons, the points of the compass, and the Sun, Moon, Earth, and Heaven.

**AREA:** 38,232sq mi (99,020sq km)
**POPULATION:** 43,663,000
**CAPITAL (POPULATION):** Seoul (10,799,000)
**GOVERNMENT:** Multiparty republic
**ETHNIC GROUPS:** Korean 99%
**LANGUAGES:** Korean (official)
**RELIGIONS:** Buddhism 28%, Christianity (Protestant 19%, Roman Catholic 6%)
**CURRENCY:** South Korean won = 100 chon

The Republic of Korea occupies the S part of the Korean peninsula. South Korea is mountainous. The capital, SEOUL, lies on the W coastal lowlands. Other major cities include INCHON, TAEGU, and the port of PUSAŃ, on the SE coast. Cheju-do, the largest island, includes Mount Halla, South Korea's highest peak, at 6,398ft (1,950m). (For land, climate, and pre-1953 history, *see* KOREA and KOREAN WAR)

### HISTORY AND POLITICS

South Korea's first government, led (1948–60) by Syngman RHEE, was beset by economic problems. South Korea was a predominantly agricultural economy, heavily dependent on the N for energy and resources. South Korea's infrastructure was devastated by the Korean War. Rhee's corrupt and repressive regime became increasingly unpopular. The massacre of student protestors in 1960 sparked nationwide disturbances and a military junta, led by General PARK Chung Hee, seized power in 1961. Park's presidency (1963–79) brought rapid economic growth. Helped by US aid, South Korea became a major manufacturer and exporter. In 1972 Park introduced martial law and passed a new constitution which gave him almost unlimited powers. In the social and political sphere his regime pursued increasingly authoritarian policies. Park was assassinated in 1979, but the military still dominated the government. Opposition to the political climate continued to grow. In 1987 a new constitution ensured the popular election of the president and reduced the presidential term to five years. In 1988 Seoul hosted the summer Olympic Games. Relations with North Korea continued to improve, and in 1991 the two countries signed a nonaggression pact and established a series of summit meetings on reunification. In 1992 the long-standing opposition leader, KIM YOUNG SAM, became president. His administration was South Korea's first full civilian government in 32 years. The death of North Korean president Kim Il Sung stalled reunification talks. The wealth gap between the two Koreas is one of the greatest potential challenges facing any unification. In 1998 Kim Dae Jung succeeded Kim Young Sam as president.

### ECONOMY

South Korea is an upper-middle-income developing country (1992 GDP per capita, US$9,250). For much of the late 20th century it was one of the world's fastest growing industrial economies. US aid of more than $6 billion (1945–78) played a major part in the economic success story. South Korea's industrial conglomerates (*chaebols*) have benefited from a highly-educated workforce and import controls. Major *chaebols* include Hyundai, Daewoo, and Samsung. South Korea's protectionist policies are slowly giving way to free market reforms. The largest sector of the economy is services, employing 50% of the work force. Manufactured goods, machinery, and transport equipment make up 66% of South Korea's exports. South Korea is the world's fifth largest car producer. It is also a major producer of iron and steel, cement, electrical and electronic products. It is reliant on the importation of raw materials. Agriculture employs 17% of the workforce. South Korea is the world's eighth largest producer of rice. It also has the world's tenth largest fish catch. In 1997 several major *chaebols* collapsed. Overlending by banks and the crisis in the rest of Southeast Asia devastated South Korea's economy. The International Monetary Fund (IMF) agreed to a record US$21 billion rescue package. Labor reform laws led to redundancies and rising unemployment.

**krill** Collective term for the large variety of marine crustaceans found in all oceans. They are strained and used as food by various species of baleen WHALE.

**Krishna** Most celebrated hero of Hindu mythology. He was the eighth AVATAR (incarnation) of VISHNU and primarily a god of joyfulness and fertility. Many devotional cults grew up around him, as well as legends and poems. Krishna is the hero of the MAHABHARATA and the deliverer of the BHAGAVAD GITA. He is commonly depicted as a youth with a blue face. *See also* HARE KRISHNA

**Krishnamurti, Jiddu** (1895–1986) Hindu religious leader. He founded the World Order of Star with Annie BESANT, the theosophist leader, dissolving it in 1929, and in 1969 founded the Krishnamurti Foundation in Ojai, California.

**Kroeber, Alfred Louis** (1876–1960) US anthropologist, one of the most important cultural anthropologists of the early 20th century. He helped to advance the study of Native North American ethnology, linguistics, and folklore.

**Kropotkin, Peter Alexeievich** (1842–1921) Russian anarchist leader. He was jailed for seditious propaganda in 1874, but escaped into exile in 1876. Living mostly in Britain, he became one of the most important theorists of anarchist socialism, criticizing the centralizing tendencies of Marxism. He argued in *Mutual Aid* (1902) that cooperation rather than competition is the natural order of things. *See also* ANARCHISM

**Kruger, Paul (Stephanus Johannes Paulus)** (1825–1904) South African statesman and soldier, president (1883–1902) of the South African Republic. In the 1830s he took part in the GREAT TREK. In 1877 Britain annexed Transvaal and Kruger led the fight for independence. He fought in the first of the SOUTH AFRICAN WARS and became the first president of the South African Republic. Kruger was reelected in 1888, 1893, and 1898. His refusal to grant equal status to non-BOER settlers precipitated the second South African War. Kruger was forced into exile, where he sought support for the Boer cause. He died in Switzerland.

**krypton** Gaseous nonmetallic element (symbol Kr), a NOBLE GAS. Discovered in 1898, krypton makes up about 0.0001% of the Earth's atmosphere by volume and is obtained by the fractional distillation of liquid air. It is used in fluorescent lamps, lasers, and in electronic heart valves. Properties: at.no. 36; at.wt. 83.80; density 3.73; m.p. −249.9°F; (−156.6°C); b.p. −242.1°F; (−152.3°C); most common isotope $^{84}Kr$ (56.9%).

**Kuala Lumpur** Capital of Malaysia, in the S Malay peninsula. Founded in 1857, it was made the capital of the Federated Malay States in 1895, of the Federation of Malaya in 1957 and of Malaysia in 1963. It has two universities and many striking modern buildings. It is a commercial center whose industries include tin and rubber. Pop. (1990) 1,231,500.

**Kubelík** Name of two Czech musicians. **Jan** (1880–1940) was a violinist and composer, highly regarded for his technical mastery. **Rafael** (1914– ), his son, was an eminent conductor as well as a composer. He was musical director of the Metropolitan Opera Company, New York (1973–74).

**Kublai Khan** (1215–94) Mongol Emperor (1260–94). Grandson of GENGHIS KHAN, he completed the conquest of China in 1279, establishing the YÜAN dynasty, which ruled until 1368. He conquered the Southern SUNG dynasty and extended operations into SE Asia, although his attempt to invade Japan was thwarted by storms. He conducted correspondence with European rulers and apparently employed Marco POLO.

**Kubrick, Stanley** (1928–99) US film director. An ambitious, fiercely independent AUTEUR, his films include *Dr Strangelove* (1963), *2001: A Space Odyssey* (1968), *A Clockwork Orange* (1971), *The Shining* (1980) and *Full Metal Jacket* (1987). His final film was *Eyes Wide Shut* (1999).

**kudu** Large African ANTELOPE found S of the Sahara. The body is gray-brown with vertical white stripes and the male bears long, spiral horns. Genus *Tragelaphus*.

**Kuiper, Gerard Peter** (1905–73) US astronomer, b. Netherlands. He discovered the satellites Miranda (of Uranus) in 1948 and Nereid (of Neptune) in 1949. He found methane in the atmospheres of Uranus, Neptune, and Titan, and carbon dioxide in the atmosphere of Mars.

**Ku Klux Klan (KKK)** Name of two secret, white, racist groups in the US. The first Ku Klux Klan was organized in the South in 1866. Opposed to RECONSTRUCTION, it attempted to enforce labor discipline in plantation districts and to maintain white supremacy by preventing blacks from voting. Klansmen dressed in white robes and hoods terrorized black communities. By 1872 the Klan had been suppressed by Federal authorities. A second Ku Klux Klan was founded in 1915, embracing broader-based racism directed also against Catholics, Jews, and communists. By the mid-1920s its membership was estimated at four million. It declined thereafter, but there was a minor resurgence in the 1960s and in some Southern states in the 1990s.

**Kumasi** City in central Ghana; capital of ASHANTI region. The second-largest city in Ghana, it was the capital of the Ashanti kingdom in the 17th and 18th centuries, before being annexed by the British in 1901. It is a commercial center for a cocoa-growing region. Industries: food processing, handicrafts, timber. Pop. (1984) 376,246.

**Kun, Béla** (1886–1937) Hungarian political leader. With the support of LENIN, Kun led communist agitation against the new republic of Hungary and led a communist regime for a few months in 1919. His attempt to turn Hungary into a Soviet-style republic was defeated by Romanian troops. He probably died in Stalin's purges.

**Küng, Hans** (1928– ) Swiss Roman Catholic theologian. He became the first important Roman Catholic theologian to question the doctrine of papal infallibility and the dogma of the Virgin Mary, for which he was censured by the Vatican (1979) and forbidden to teach Catholic theology.

**kung fu** Ancient Chinese martial art based on the idea that the best form of defense against violence utilizes actions that combine attack and defense.

**Kuomintang** Nationalist Party in China, which was the major political force during and after the creation of a republic in 1911. It was first led by SUN YAT-SEN. It cooperated with the Communist Party until 1927 when Sun's successor, CHIANG KAI-SHEK, turned against the communists, initiating a civil war. Cooperation was renewed in order to repel the Japanese from 1937–45, after which the civil war was resumed. With the communists victorious, Chiang set up a rump state on the island of Taiwan, where the Kuomintang survives.

**Kupka, František** (1871–1957) Czech painter, etcher, and illustrator active mainly in Paris. He was among the first painters to develop purely abstract painting. His works include *Fugue in Red and Blue* (1912). *See also* ABSTRACT ART

**Kurdistan** Extensive mountainous and plateau region in SW Asia, inhabited by the KURDS and including parts of E Turkey, NE Iran, N Iraq, NE Syria, S Armenia, and E Azerbaijan. Plans for the creation of a separate Kurdish state were put forward after World War I but subsequently abandoned. Area: *c.*74,000sq mi (192,000sq km).

**Kurds** Predominantly rural, Islamic population numbering some 18 million, who live in a disputed frontier area of SW Asia that they call KURDISTAN. Traditionally nomadic herdsmen, they are mainly SUNNI Muslims who speak an Iranian dialect. For 3,000 years they have maintained a unique cultural tradition, although internal division and constant external invasion have prevented them from uniting into one nation. In recent times, their main conflicts have been with Iran and Iraq. After the Iran-Iraq War (1988), Iraq destroyed many Kurdish villages and their inhabitants. The Iraqi response to a Kurdish revolt after the Gulf War caused 1.5 million Kurds to flee to Iran and Turkey. In 1996 Iraqi troops invaded the region and captured the Kurdish city of Irbil. The US responded by launching cruise missiles at Iraqi military installations. Today, *c.*8 million Kurds live in E Turkey, *c.*4 million in N Iraq, *c.*500,000 in Syria, and *c.*100,000 in Azerbaijan and Armenia.

**Kuril Islands** (Kurilskiye Ostrova) Chain of 30 large and 26 smaller islands in SAKHALIN region, Russia, extending 750mi (1,200km) from the S Kamchatka Peninsula to NE Hokkaido, Japan, and separating the Sea of Okhotsk from the Pacific Ocean. The N islands were settled by Russians, the S islands by Japanese. In 1875 Russia gave the islands to Japan in exchange for full control of Sakhalin Island. After World War II the islands were ceded to the Soviet Union. Industries: sulfur mining and whaling. Area: 6,023sq mi (15,600sq km).

▲ **krill** The shrimplike krill, some of the most important animals of the plankton, are about 2in (5cm) long when fully grown. They belong to a group of crustaceans (found in all oceans) characterized by luminescent organs along their sides, on their undersides and heads. *Euphausia superba* (shown) is the most important species of the Antarctic seas, for it supports much of the warm-blooded life of the southern oceans.

K

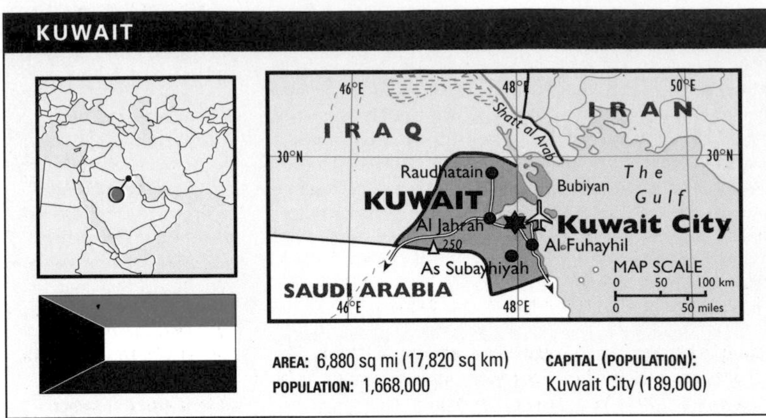


**Kurosawa, Akira** (1910–98) Japanese film director. In *Rashomon* (1950) he introduced the world of the SAMURAI warriors to Western audiences. The popularity of this genre was confirmed with *The Seven Samurai* (1954). *Dursu Uzala* (1975) and *Ran* (1985) both won Academy awards for best foreign language film.

**Kursk** City in W Russia, at the confluence of the Tuskoc and Seim rivers. Founded in 1095, it was destroyed by the TATARS in 1240 and rebuilt as a frontier post in 1586. Industries: iron and steel, chemicals, synthetic fibers, shoes, electrical equipment. Pop. (1992) 435,000.

**Kush** Kingdom and former state in NUBIA. Lasting from *c.*1000 BC to *c.*AD 350, it conquered Egypt in the 7th–8th centuries BC. It was later defeated by the Assyrians and moved its capital to Meroë in the Sudan. After Roman and Arab attacks in the N, Meroë was captured by the Axumites in *c.*AD 350.

**Kutusov, Mikhail Illarionovich** (1745–1813) Russian general. He was the supreme commander during the Napoleonic Wars. After the French abandoned Moscow in 1812, he forced them to retreat in winter, harrying them by guerrilla warfare.

**Kuwait** (Al Kuwayt) Small state in the NE Arabian Peninsula, N of the Persian Gulf. The capital is Kuwait City. Kuwait was founded in the early 18th century. In 1899 it became a British protectorate, becoming fully independent in 1961. In 1990 it was invaded by IRAQ. Many thousands of Kuwaitis were killed, kidnapped or taken hostage. In the GULF WAR (1991) allied coalition forces, led by the USA, liberated Kuwait. Iraqi troops set light to oil wells as they retreated, causing widespread environmental damage. The cost of post-war reconstruction was estimated at US$100 billion. In 1992 Kuwait held its first parliamentary elections. The Amir, Shaikh Jabir al-Sabah, holds executive power. Oil was discovered in 1938 and Kuwait's huge oil reserves have made it one of the world's richest countries (1995 GDP per capita, US$23,790).

**Kuznetsov, Alexander** (1929–79) Ukrainian writer. His writings include the novels *Continuation of a Legend* (1957) and *Babi Yar* (1966). *See also* BABI YAR

**Kwakiutl** Tribe of Native North Americans. They speak the Wakashan language, and are closely related to the Bella Bella. They number *c.*2,000 and occupy N Vancouver Island in British Columbia, Canada.

**Kwa languages** Group of languages making up a branch of the Niger-Congo family of African languages. Kwa languages include Yoruba and Ibo of S Nigeria; Ewe of Ghana, Togo, and Benin; Akan of Ivory Coast and Ghana; Gã of Accra city; and Bini of Benin.

**KwaZulu-Natal** Province in E South Africa, bordered by the Indian Ocean and the Drakensberg Mountains; the capital is Pietermaritzburg. It was created in 1994 from the Zulu homeland, KwaZulu, and the former province of Natal. Industries: sugar, textiles, tanning, and oil refining. Area: 33,578sq mi (92,180sq km). Pop. (1995 est.) 8,713,100.

**Kyd, Thomas** (1558–94) English dramatist who achieved popular success with *The Spanish Tragedy* (*c.*1589). Kyd was a member of the literary circles of his day, associating with MARLOWE. In 1593 he was arrested for treasonable activities.

**Kyoto** City on W central Honshu Island, Japan; capital of Kyoto prefecture. Founded in the 6th century, it was the capital of Japan for more than 1,000 years. Industries: porcelain, lacquerware, textiles, precision tools. Pop. (1993) 1,395,000.

**Kyrgyz** Turko-Mongolian people who inhabit the Republic of KYRGYZSTAN in central Asia. Muslim nomadic pastoralists, they began to settle in the TIAN SHAN region of KYRGYZSTAN in the 7th century. They were colonized by the Russians during the 19th century. After fighting the BOLSHEVIKS in the civil war (1917–21), many Kyrgyz perished in the ensuing famine.

**Kyrgyzstan** (Kirghizia) Landlocked republic between China, Tajikistan, Uzbekistan, and Kazakstan. **Land and climate** A mountainous country, the highest mountain, Pik Pobedy, reaches 24,406ft (7,439m) above sea level. The largest of the country's many lakes is Ozero (Lake) Issyk-Kul in the NE. The lowlands of Kyrgyzstan have warm summers and cold winters, but in the mountains, January temperatures plummet to −18°F (−28°C). Much of Kyrgyzstan has a low annual rainfall. Mountain grassland is the dominant vegetation. Less than a tenth of the land is under plow. **History** The area that is now Kyrgyzstan was populated in ancient times by nomadic herders. MONGOL armies conquered the region in the early 13th century. Islam was introduced in the 17th century. China gained control of the area in the mid-18th century, but, in 1876 Kyrgyzstan became a province of Russia. In 1916 Russia put down a rebellion and many local people fled to China. In 1922, when the Soviet Union was formed, Kyrgyzstan became an autonomous region. In 1936 it became a Soviet Socialist Republic. Under communism, nomads were forced to live on government-run farms. **Politics** In August 1991 Kyrgyzstan declared independence. The Communist Party was dissolved. President Askar Akayev began to introduce free-market reforms. In 1994 a new constitution was adopted. There are tensions between the rural nomadic Kirghiz and the urban Russians and Uzbeks. **Economics** Agriculture, especially livestock raising, is the chief activity (1995 GDP per capita, US$1,800). The chief products include cotton, eggs, fruits, grain, tobacco, vegetables, and wool. Industries are concentrated around the capital, BISHKEK. Exports include wool, chemicals, cotton, and metals.

**Kyushu** Island in S Japan; the southernmost of the four principal Japanese islands. The terrain is mountainous, and the irregular coastline has many natural harbors. It is the most densely populated of the Japanese islands. The chief port is NAGASAKI. Products: rice, tea, tobacco, fruit, soybeans. Industries: mining, fishing, timber, textiles, porcelain, metals, machinery. Area: 16,274sq mi (42,149sq km). Pop. (1992 est.) 13,314,000.

**Kyzyl Kum** (Kizil Kum) Desert of central Asia, in Uzbekistan and S Kazakstan, between the rivers Amudarya and Syrdarya. Cotton and rice are grown in the irrigated river valleys, and Karakul sheep are raised by tribespeople. Area: *c.*89,000sq mi (230,000sq km).

**Laban, Rudolph von (1879–1958)** German modern dance theorist. He was an inspiration behind the German school of modern dance. *See also* MODERN DANCE.
**labor** In childbirth, stages in the delivery of the FETUS at the end of pregnancy. In the first stage, contractions of the UTERUS begin and the sac containing the amniotic fluid ruptures. In the second stage, the contractions strengthen and the baby is propelled through the birth canal. The third stage is the expulsion of the PLACENTA and fetal membranes, together known as the afterbirth.
**labor force** All members of the population who are working or looking for work. The absolute size of the labor force varies with the time of year and with economic conditions. Normally the labor force expandes in the summer as schools close and contracts in the fall as schools open. In recessions, when employment opportunities are limited, many people leave the labor force (that is, they stop looking for work) and return to it when jobs are available. The size of the labor force relative to total population is a measure of the health of the economy.
**Labor, US Department of** US government department. It administers and enforces statutes benefiting wage earners, improving working conditions, and providing opportunities for employment. In 1903 it was part of the Department of Commerce and Labor, becoming a separate department in 1913.
**Labour Party** Social democratic political party, traditionally closely linked with the trade-union movement. There are Labour Parties in many countries, including Australia, Britain, Canada, Israel, and New Zealand. The first British socialist parties, founded in the 1880s, united in the Independent Labour Party (ILP) in 1893. The ILP created the Labour Representation Committee in 1900, which was renamed the Labour Party in 1906. Labour formed a brief minority government in 1924 under Ramsay MACDONALD and again in 1929–31. Labour joined the wartime coalition of World War II and its leader, Clement ATTLEE, was deputy prime minister from 1942. After a landslide Labour victory in 1945, the Attlee government introduced a series of social reforms. Labour won the general election of 1964 under Harold WILSON and continued in power until 1970. From 1974–79 it was in office mostly as a minority administration. Tony BLAIR, under the slogan of "New Labour," moved the party to the right, which contributed to a general election victory for the party in May 1997. Blair became prime minister in the new Labour government.
**Labrador** Mainland part of NEWFOUNDLAND province, E Canada, bordered W and S by Quebec and E by the Atlantic Ocean. The coast was visited by John CABOT in 1498. It passed to Britain under the Treaty of Paris (1736). Between 1809 and 1827 the boundaries between Newfoundland and Quebec were under dispute. In 1949 Labrador became part of Canada. It is mountainous with an indented coastline. Industries: timber, fishing, iron ore mining. Area: 112,826sq mi (292,220sq km).
**La Bruyère, Jean de** (1645–96) French satirist. He ridiculed French life in his best-known work, *The Characters of Theophrastus, Translated from the Greek, with the Characters and Mores of This Age* (1688).
**laburnum** Several Eurasian shrubs and small trees of the genus *Laburnum*, especially the common Laburnum, *L. anagyroides*, which has drooping clusters of yellow flowers. It bears pods with poisonous seeds. Family Fabaceae/Leguminosae.
**labyrinth** Intricate structure of chambers and passages, generally constructed to confuse anyone within it. In Greek mythology, MINOS had a labyrinth built by DAEDALUS to confine the MINOTAUR.
**lac** Name of an insect and the sticky substance it secretes onto twigs; the deposit is harvested in Asia for use in shellac and red lac dye. Species *Laccifer lacca*.
**Lacaille, Nicolas Louis de** (1713–62) French astronomer. From 1751–53 he surveyed the Southern-Hemisphere skies, introducing 14 new S constellations. In 1761 he made an accurate measurement of the Moon's distance; this made possible a more accurate method of determining terrestrial longitude.
**lacemaking** Manufacture of lace, an openwork ornamental fabric made from fine threads of linen, cotton, silk, wool, or artificial fibers. Needlepoint lace was made with needle and thread, using embroidery stitches on a linen backing. Bobbin lace (pillow lace) was made using bobbins of thread. The threads were crossed, braided, twisted, or woven around pins stuck into a pillow. Most lace is now made by machine.

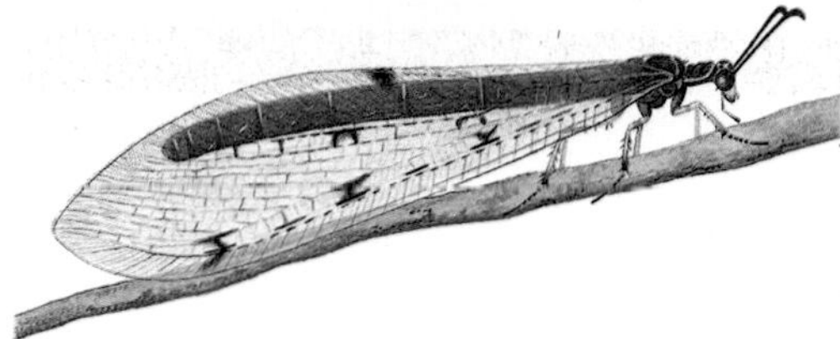

▲ **lacewing** The European lacewing (*Eurolean europaeus*), also known as the ant lion grows to 2cm (0.8in). A member of the Neuroptera order, lacewings are found throughout the world. The larva of the lacewing is a fierce predator of certain small insects, particularly aphids.

**lacewing** Any of numerous species of neuropteran insects, especially members of the families Chrysopidae and Hemerobiidae, which are found worldwide. Common green lacewings have a slender greenish body, long antennae, and two pairs of delicate, lacy, veined wings. Length: to 2.8in (7cm).
**lachrymal gland** Organ that produces tears. It is located in the orbital cavity, and is controlled by autonomic nerves. It produces slightly germicidal tears that flow through ducts to the surface of the eye to lubricate it.
**Laclos, Pierre (Ambroise François) Choderlos de** (1741–1803) French general and novelist. His *Les Liaisons Dangereuses* (1782) caused a sensation and was only belatedly recognized as a great work.
**lacquer** Varnish used for ornamental or protective coatings; it forms a film by loss of solvent through evaporation. Lacquer is usually composed of a cellulose derivative in combination with a resin.
**lacrosse** Ball game that originated among the Iroquois Native Americans of Canada and the US. It is played by teams of 10 male or 12 female players. They carry sticks that have a thonged meshwork head like a flexible scoop. The ball may be conveyed, passed, or hit with the stick, or kicked, but only the goalkeepers are allowed to handle it. Lacrosse became Canada's national game in 1867.
**lactation** Secretion of milk to feed the young. In pregnant women, HORMONES induce the breasts to enlarge, and prolactin (a pituitary hormone) stimulates breast cells to begin secreting milk. The milk appears in the breast immediately after the birth of the baby. Its flow is stimulated by suckling.
**lactic acid** Colorless organic acid (2-hydroxypropanoic acid, $CH_3CHOHCOOH$) formed from LACTOSE by the action of bacteria. It is also produced in muscles, when ANEROBIC respiration occurs due to insufficient oxygen, and causes muscle fatigue. Lactic acid is used in foods and beverages, in tanning, dyeing, and adhesive manufacture. Properties: sp.gr. 1.206; m.p. 64.4°F (18°C); b.p. 251.6°F (122°C).
**lactose** (milk sugar) Disaccharide present in milk, made up of a molecule of GLUCOSE linked to a molecule of galactose. It is important in cheesemaking.
**Ladoga** (Rus. *Ladozhskoye Ozero*, Finnish, *Laatokka*) Europe's largest lake, in NW Russia (near the Finnish border). It is drained by the Neva River. Formerly divided between Finland and the Soviet Union, it has been entirely within the Russian border since the Soviet invasion of Finland in 1940. Area: 6,826sq mi (17,678sq km).
**ladybug** (ladybird) Any of a large number of small, brightly colored beetles; most common species are red with conspicuous black spots and a black and white head. Ladybugs and their larvae are regarded as useful by farmers because their diet consists primarily of aphids. Family Coccinellidae.
**La Farge, John** (1835–1910) US artist and writer. His first major work, the decoration of Trinity Church, Boston, established his reputation for mural painting and designing stained glass. He did much of his best work for churches. La Farge was also known for his watercolors.
**Lafayette, Marie Joseph Gilbert de Motier, Marquis de** (1757–1834) French general who fought for the colonists in the AMERICAN REVOLUTION. He distinguished himself in the

***L/l, 12th letter of the alphabet, can be traced to the Semitic letter* lamedh, *which passed into Greek as* lambda. *It became slightly modified in the Roman alphabet and in this form has passed into English.***



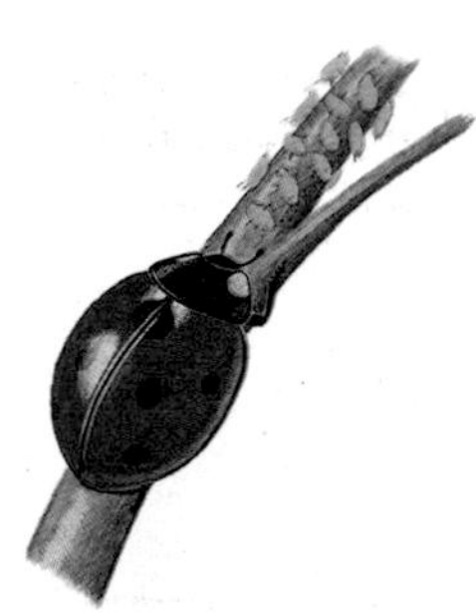

▲ **ladybug** The seven-spot ladybug (or ladybird) (*Coccinealla septempunctata*) is found throughout Europe. It is the largest of the European ladybugs, growing to 0.4in (8mm). Both the adults and larvae feed on aphids, making them popular with gardeners. During the winter large numbers hibernate together.

▲ **Lamarck** French naturalist Jean-Baptiste Lamarck's theories of evolution were highly influential in the 19th century, but were proved false by the work of Charles Darwin. Lamarck believed that adaptations were caused by behavior and were then passed on to offspring; for example the giraffe developed a long neck over generations because its ancestors were always reaching to feed on higher branches.

L

Yorktown campaign (1781). Returning to France, he became a member of the National Assembly during the FRENCH REVOLUTION. In 1791 he lost popular support by ordering his troops to fire on a riotous crowd; he deserted to the Austrians in 1792. He lived in retirement during Napoleon I's reign.

**Lafitte, Jean** (1780–*c*.1826) US pirate and smuggler. The leader of a large pirate band on the Gulf of Mexico, he preyed on Spanish commerce. He received a pardon from US president James Madison for leading his men against the British in the War of 1812. After the war, he and his pirates lived on an island that is present-day Galveston. Some members of his colony raided American property in 1820, and the US government dispatched a naval force against him; Lafitte and his closest associates escaped and were not heard of again.

**La Follette, Robert Marion** (1855–1925) US political leader. He was a Republican congressman (1885–91) and governor of Wisconsin (1900–06). As a senator (1906–25), he fought for workers and farmers against Republican-supported business. He was chosen as Progressive presidential candidate before being replaced by Theodore ROOSEVELT in 1912. He ran again in 1924.

**La Fontaine, Jean de** (1621–95) French poet noted for his fables, considered among the masterpieces of French literature. His *Fables choisies, mises en vers* (1668–94) consists of some 240 fables. He was elected to the Académie Française in 1683.

**Lagerkvist, Pär Fabian** (1891–1974) Swedish author. One of the major Scandinavian writers of the 20th century, his key works include *Anguish* (1916) and *The Hangman* (1933). International recognition came with *The Dwarf* (1944) and *Barabbas* (1950); in 1951 he was awarded the Noble Prize for literature.

**Lagerlöf, Selma** (1858–1940) Swedish novelist. Her greatest novel, *Jerusalem* (1901), was inspired by a visit to Palestine. In 1909 she became the first Swedish writer to be awarded the Noble Prize for literature.

**lagoon** Shallow stretch of seawater protected from waves and tides by a strip of land or coral.

**Lagos** Largest city and chief port of Nigeria, in the S of the country, on the Gulf of Guinea. Lagos grew as a YORUBA settlement from the 17th –19th centuries, coming under British control in 1861 after years of Portuguese exploitation through the slave trade. It became the capital of independent Nigeria in 1960, but was replaced by ABUJA in 1982. Industries: brewing, ship repairing, textiles, crafts. Pop. (1992) 1,347,000.

**Lagrange, Joseph Louis** (1736–1813) French mathematician. He created the calculus of variations, devised a mathematical analysis of perturbations in gravity, and made contributions in many other areas, including the mathematics of sound and mechanics.

**Lagrangian points** One of the five points at which a celestial body can remain in equilibrium with respect to two much more massive bodies orbiting each other.

**LaGuardia, Fiorello Henry** (1882–1947) US lawyer and political leader. He entered New York state politics and was deputy attorney general (1915–17). He served as a Republican US representative (1917–21). After World War I, he returned to the House (1923–33). As New York City mayor (1934–45), he fought corruption, strengthened the police and fire departments, and generally promoted public works projects. During World War II, he directed the Office of Civilian Defense (1941–42). In 1946 he was appointed to head the UN Relief and Rehabilitation Administration.

**Lahore** City on the Ravi River, NE Pakistan; capital of Punjab province and Pakistan's second-largest city. It was used as a royal residence under the MOGUL EMPIRE. It was part of the Sikh kingdom from 1767 and passed to the British in 1849. From 1955–70 it was capital of West Pakistan. It is an important commercial and industrial center. Industries: iron, steel, textiles. Pop. 2,953,000.

**Laing, R.D. (Ronald David)** (1927–1989) Scottish psychiatrist. He was an exponent of existential psychology and produced radical work on the nature of schizophrenia. He believed that the mentally ill are not necessarily maladapted: a psychotic disorder may be a reasonable reaction to the stresses of the world.

**laissez-faire** 19th-century economic doctrine. In reaction to MERCANTILISM, the proponents of laissez-faire adopted Adam SMITH's argument that trade and industry would best serve the interests of all if government interference was reduced to a minimum, so that market forces would be allowed to determine production, prices, and wages.

**lake** Inland body of water, generally of considerable size and too deep to have rooted vegetation completely covering the surface. The expanded part of a river and a reservoir behind a dam are also termed lakes.

**Lake District** Region of Cumbria, NW England, containing the principal English lakes. Its spectacular mountain and lakeland scenery and its literary associations make it a major tourist attraction. Among its 15 lakes are Derwent Water, Grasmere, Buttermere, and Windermere. The highest point is Scafell Pike at 3,210ft (978m). The Lake District National Park was established in 1951. Area: 866sq mi (2,243sq km).

**lake dwelling** Prehistoric settlement built on piles within the margins of lakes. Cattle and sheep were raised on lakeside pasture. Lake dwellings in Europe have been found in Germany, Switzerland, Italy, and Britain. Most are of the Bronze Age.

**Lake Erie, Battle of** (1813) WAR OF 1812 battle in which the US fleet under Commander Oliver H. Perry defeated British Captain Robert Barclay's fleet near Put-in-Bay, Ohio. The victory gave the US control of Lake Erie. Perry's report, "We have met the enemy and they are ours," made him a national hero.

**Lake Poets** Three English poets who lived in the Lake District of N England *c*.1800: William WORDSWORTH (1770–1850), Samuel Taylor COLERIDGE (1772–1834), and Robert SOUTHEY (1774–1843).

**Lakshmi** (Padma or Sita) In Hindu mythology, the lotus goddess, wife of VISHNU, who existed at the beginning of creation rising from the ocean borne by a lotus. Lakshmi was the goddess of beauty and youth, and was also worshiped as goddess of wealth and good fortune. She is often depicted with or as a lotus.

**Lalande, Joseph Jérôme Le Français de** (1732–1807) French astronomer whose main achievement was a catalog of over 47,000 stars. Lalande became professor of astronomy at the Collège de France in 1762, a post he held for 46 years. He was made director of the Paris Observatory in 1768.

**Lalique, René** (1860–1945) French jewelry designer whose work significantly contributed to the ART NOUVEAU movement. In 1920 he began to produce Lalique glass, which immediately became popular.

**Lamaism** *See* TIBETAN BUDDHISM

**Lamarck, Jean-Baptiste Pierre Antoine de Monet, Chevalier de** (1744–1829) French biologist. His theories of EVOLUTION (Lamarckism), according to which ACQUIRED CHARACTERISTICS are inheritable, influenced evolutionary thought throughout most of the 19th century, but were disproved by Charles DARWIN.

**Lamb, Charles** (1775–1834) British writer. He is best known for his essays, most famously collected as *The Essays of Elia* (1820–23; 1833). He is also remembered for his children's books, which include the perennially popular *Tales from Shakespeare* (1807), on which he collaborated with his sister, Mary (1764–1847).

**Lamb, Willis Eugene Jr** (1913– ) US physicist who applied new techniques to measure the lines of the hydrogen SPECTRUM. He found that the actual positions (wavelengths) varied from the positions predicted by DIRAC's theory. For this research, he shared the 1955 Noble Prize for physics.

**Lamentations** Old Testament book bewailing the destruction of JERUSALEM and the great TEMPLE there in 587 or 586 BC; it is commonly attributed to the author of the Book of JEREMIAH.

**Lammas** Christian festival of thanksgiving for the harvest celebrated on August 1 in medieval England. It was originally one of the QUARTER DAYS.

**lamp** Form of artificial lighting. Early lamps burned fuels, such as animal fat, wax, and oil. Coal gas was used from the early 1800s. The ELECTRIC LIGHT became popular in the early 1900s. Most modern lamps are electrically powered and are of three main types: incandescent, discharge (or vapor), and fluorescent.

**lamprey** Eel-like, jawless vertebrate found in marine and fresh waters on both sides of the Atlantic and in the Great Lakes. It feeds by attaching its mouth to fish and sucking their blood. Length: to 3ft (91cm). Family Petromyzondiae.

**Lancashire** County in NW England, bordered by Cumbria (N), North and West Yorkshire (E), Greater Manchester, and Merseyside (S), and the Irish Sea (W); the county town is Preston. Other major towns include Lancaster (the administrative center), Blackpool, and Blackburn. It was occupied in Roman times and later formed part of an Anglo-Saxon kingdom. From the 16th century, textile manufacturing became increasingly important, and by the early 19th century cotton goods were vital to the county's economy. In the 20th century, cotton and its other traditional industry, coal, sharply declined. It is drained by the rivers Lune and Ribble, and its lowland regions are predominantly agricultural. Area: 1,183sq mi (3,064sq km). Pop. (1994) 1,424,000.

**Lancaster, Burt** (1913–94) US movie actor and producer. A former circus acrobat, he made his first film, *The Killers*, in 1946. Other films include *Elmer Gantry* (1960), *Bird Man of Alcatraz* (1962), *The Leopard* (1963), and *Atlantic City* (1980).

**Lancaster, House of** English royal dynasty. The first earl of Lancaster was Edmund "Crouchback" (1245–96), son of HENRY III. In 1361 the title and lands passed to JOHN OF GAUNT via his wife. Their son became HENRY IV in 1399. During the Wars of the ROSES in the 15th century, the royal houses of Lancaster and York, both PLANTAGENETS, contended for the crown.

**Lancelot of the Lake** In Arthurian legend, the father of Galahad and one of the most famous knights; he is portrayed as the lover of GUINEVERE, wife of King ARTHUR.

**Lanchow** *See* LANZHOU

**Landau, Lev Davidovich** (1908–68) Soviet physicist. His many contributions included the basic theories describing ferromagnetism and liquid HELIUM. In 1927 he proposed a concept for energy called the density matrix which was later used in QUANTUM MECHANICS. He received the 1962 Nobel Prize for physics for his research into condensed matter, especially helium.

**Landis, Kenesaw Mountain** (1866–1944) US jurist and sports administrator. Baseball's first commissioner (1920–44), he was a US district judge before taking control of baseball following the 1919 "Black Sox" scandal. He restored the game's integrity and was elected to the Baseball Hall of Fame in 1944.

**Landon, Alfred Mossman** (1887–1987) US political leader. After making a fortune as an independent oil operator, he was elected governor of Kansas in 1932 and nominated as the Republican presidential candidate in 1936, losing to Franklin D. Roosevelt. A progressive, Landon was a successful reform governor who fought the Ku Klux Klan and oil and utility monopolies.

**Landor, Walter Savage** (1775–1864) British poet and writer. His works include *Gebir: a Poem in Seven Books* (1798), but it is for his prose dialogues, *Imaginary Conversations of Literary Men and Statesmen* (1824–29), that he is chiefly remembered.

**Landowska, Wanda** (1877–1959) Polish harpsichordist and pianist who lived in Paris from 1919 and in the US from 1941. An authority on early music, she founded the Ecole de Musique Ancienne (1925) in Paris.

**landscape gardening** Arranging gardens to produce certain effects. Two main traditions are the Sino-English, with its retention of the informality of nature; and the Franco-Italian, with its geometric patterns. The second tradition arose in Italy during the RENAISSANCE. It is best exemplified in the parterres of VERSAILLES, designed by André LE NÔTRE. In England the naturalist style developed in the 18th century, with William KENT, Humphrey Repton, and "Capability" BROWN.

**landscape painting** Art of portraying natural scenery. While landscape painting was central to the art of the East, especially China, the West did not recognize it as a separate genre until the 16th century. Landscape painting came into full flower in 17th-century Holland; Jacob van Ruisdael is regarded as the greatest Dutch landscape painter. In Italy Annibale Carracci invented the "ideal landscape." CLAUDE LORRAIN and Nicholas POUSSIN arranged natural elements into artificial compositions. In the 19th century, mystical and romantic landscapes were created by painters such as FRIEDRICH in Germany and TURNER in Britain, as well as a number of North American artists. COROT and CONSTABLE introduced a more naturalistic approach, which led to the enormous popularity which landscape achieved through IMPRESSIONISM. The 20th-century abstract and surrealist painters have also reinvented the genre.

**Landsteiner, Karl** (1868–1943) US pathologist, b. Austria. He discovered the four different BLOOD GROUPS (A, B, AB, and O) and demonstrated that certain blood groups are incompatible with others. He won the 1930 Noble Prize for physiology or medicine. In 1940, with A. S. Wiener, he identified the rhesus (Rh) factor.

**Lanfranc** (c.1005–89) Italian theologian. He was a BENEDICTINE monk whose priory at Bec in Normandy became a center for European scholars in the 1040s. As a counselor of William of Normandy, he became Archbishop of Canterbury (1070–89).

**Lang, Fritz** (1890–1976) Austrian film director and writer. His best-known works include *Metropolis* (1927) and *M* (1931). He later moved to Hollywood, where he directed *Fury* (1936).

**Lange, Dorothea** (1895–1965) US photographer. Her portraits of urban poor and migrant laborers in California during the GREAT DEPRESSION, and her images of rural America taken for the Farm Security Administration (1935–42), are classics of documentary photography.

**Langland, William** (1331–99) English poet. His poem *Piers Plowman*, a late flowering of the alliterative tradition in English verse, is considered one of the most important works of medieval literature.

**Langley, Samuel Pierpont** (1834–1906) US astronomer who showed that mechanical flight was possible. He did this by building large steam-powered model aircraft in 1896, which achieved the most successful flights up to that time.

**Langmuir, Irving** (1881–1957) US physical chemist who invented a gas-filled tungsten lamp. He also devised the atomic-hydrogen welding process and techniques to produce rain by cloud seeding. In 1932 he received the Nobel Prize for chemistry for his work in surface chemistry.

**Langton, Stephen** (*c*.1150–1228) English cardinal and scholar who was one of England's most controversial archbishops of Canterbury. His appointment by Pope INNOCENT III (1207) was bitterly opposed by King JOHN, and he was prevented from entering England and occupying his post until 1213. Langton supported the barons concerning the MAGNA CARTA (1215).

**language** System of human communication. Although there are more than 4,000 different languages, they have many characteristics in common. Almost every human language uses a fundamentally similar grammatical structure, or syntax. Families of languages have been constructed, such as the INDO-

◀ **Lang** The work of Austrian film director Fritz Lang has been widely acclaimed for its dramatic composition and exacting detail. *Metropolis* (1927) is considered the greatest of all his films. An intense silent film, it portrays a stylized and fantastic vision of the future of society.

L

EUROPEAN family, but their composition and origins are the subject of continuing debate. Historical studies of language are undertaken by the disciplines of ETYMOLOGY and PHILOLOGY. LINGUISTICS usually involves contemporary language.

**Languedoc-Roussillon** Region of S France, extending from the Rhône valley to the foothills of the Pyrenees; the capital is MONTPELLIER. Languedoc was originally settled by the Romans. It later became part of the CAROLINGIAN empire, before passing to the French crown in 1271. Languedoc-Roussillon is one of the world's major wine-producing regions. The industry is based on the fertile soils along the Garonne River and the alluvial Mediterranean coastal plain. Area: 10,706sq mi (27,736sq km). Pop. (1990) 1,926,514.

**langur** Any of about 15 species of medium to large MONKEYS of SE Asia and the East Indies. They are slender, with long hands and tails. Tree dwellers, they are found from sea level to snowy Himalayan slopes up to an elevation of 13,000ft (4,000m). Length: 17–31in (43–78cm). Family Cercopithecidae; genus *Presbytis*.

**Lansing** Capital city of Michigan, on the Grand River, S Michigan. First settled in the 1840s, it was made the state capital in 1847. Industries: motor vehicles, metal goods, machinery. Pop. (1991) 127,321.

**lantern fish** Any of numerous species of marine fish in Atlantic and Mediterranean waters, especially *Diaphus rafinesquiei*. It is identified by light organs along its sides. Length: 3in (7.5cm). Family Myctophidae.

**lanthanide series** (lanthanide elements, rare-earth metals) Series of 15 rare metallic elements with atomic numbers from 57–71. They are, in order of increasing atomic numbers: lanthanum (sometimes not considered a member), cerium, praseodymium, neodymium, promethium, samarium, europium, gadolinium, terbium, dysprosium, holmium, erbium, thulium, ytterbium, and lutetium. Their properties are similar. They occur in monazite and other rare minerals and are placed in Group III of the periodic table.

**lanthanum** Silvery-white metallic element (symbol La) of the LANTHANIDE SERIES, first identified in 1839. Its chief ores are monazite and bastnasite. Soft, malleable, and ductile, lanthanum is used as a catalyst in cracking crude oil, in alloys, and to manufacture optical glasses. Properties: at. no.57; at.wt. 138.9055; sp.gr. 6.17; m.p. 1,688°F (920°C); b.p. 6,249°F (3,454°C); most common isotope $^{139}$La (99.91%).

**Lanzhou** (Lanchow) City on the HUANG HE river, W China; capital of Gansu province. An old walled city dating from the 6th century BC, it is now a major transportion center. The principal industry is oil refining. Since 1960 it has been the base for the Chinese nuclear industry. Pop. (1993) 1,340,000.

**Laocoön** Priest of Apollo or Poseidon during the Trojan War, described in Virgil's *Aeneid*. Speaking of the wooden Trojan Horse,he exhorted the Trojans to fear the Greeks even when they offered gifts. For this, and because he had broken his oath of celibacy, he and his sons were strangled by two sea-serpents sent by Apollo.

**Laos** Landlocked republic in Southeast Asia; the capital is VIENTIANE. **Land and climate** Mountains and high plateaus cover most of Laos. The highest point is Mount Bia, at 9,242ft (2,817m), in central Laos. Most people live on the plains bordering the MEKONG River and its tributaries. The Mekong is one of Asia's longest rivers and forms much of Laos's NW and SW borders. The Annam Cordillera mountains form the E border with Vietnam. Laos has a tropical monsoon climate, with dry, sunny winters. Temperatures rise until April, when moist SW winds herald the monsoon season. Forests cover about 60% of the land. Common trees in the N include laurel, oak, and pine, while the S forests contain trees such as bamboo, ebony, rosewood, and teak. **Economy** Laos is one the world's poorest countries (1992 GDP per capita, US$1,760). Agriculture employs *c*.76% of the workforce and accounts for 60% of GDP. Rice is the main crop; timber and coffee are also exported. Hydroelectricity is produced at power stations along the Mekong. The "Golden Triangle," on the border with Cambodia and Burma, is the center for the illegal production of opium. Laos is thought to be the world's third-largest producer of opium. In 1986 Laos began to introduce liberal economic reforms, including the encouragement of private enterprise. Inflation has rapidly reduced and in 1995 the economy grew by 8%. **History** In 1353 Fa Ngoun founded the kingdom of Lan Xang (land of a million elephants). Theravada Buddhism was adopted as the official religion. In 1707 the kingdom divided into the N kingdom of Luang Prabang and the S kingdom of Vientiane. In the early 19th century the kingdoms were controlled by Siam. In 1893 Siam deferred to French power and Laos was ruled as part of French INDOCHINA. In 1945 Laos was occupied by Japan. In the aftermath of World War II, Laos in 1947 became a semi-autonomous constitutional monarchy. In 1953 Laos achieved independence, but was plunged into civil war. The communist Patriotic Front (Pathet Lao) controlled most of N Laos, and royalist forces controlled Vientiane. For most of the next 22 years Laos was riven by sectarian conflict. The North Vietnamese use of the Ho Chi Minh Trail through Laos as a military supply line saw US bombardment of E Laos, and US military and financial support to the Laotian government against the Pathet Lao. By 1974 the Pathet Lao had secured most of Laos. The victory of the Viet Cong in the VIETNAM WAR (1957–75) enabled the final victory of Pathet Lao. The king abdicated and a democratic republic was proclaimed. Vietnam remained a powerful influence on Laos. **Politics** The 1991 constitution confirmed the Lao People's Revolutionary Party (LPRP) as the only legal political party. President Nouhak Phoumsavan was elected in 1992.

**Lao Tzu** (Laozi) (604–531 BC) Chinese philosopher, credited as the founder of TAOISM. Tradition says that he lived in the 6th century BC and developed Taoism as a mystical reaction to CONFUCIANISM. He is said to have written *Tao Te Ching*, the sacred book of Taoism.

**La Paz** Administrative capital and largest city of Bolivia, in the W of the country. Founded by the Spanish in 1548 on the site of an Inca village, it was one of the centers of revolt in the War of Independence (1809–24). Located at 12,000ft (3,600m) in the Andes, it is the world's highest capital city. Industries: chemicals, tanning, flour-milling. Pop. (1992) 1,126,000.

**Laplace, Pierre Simon, Marquis de** (1749–1827) French astronomer and mathematician. Laplace made significant advances in PROBABILITY theory. His study and application of Newton's theory of gravitation to the Solar System

**LAOS**

**AREA:** 91,428sq mi (236,800sq km)
**POPULATION:** 4,469,000
**CAPITAL (POPULATION):** Vientiane (449,000)
**GOVERNMENT:** Single-party republic
**ETHNIC GROUPS:** Lao 67%, Mon-Khmer 17%, Tai 8%
**LANGUAGES:** Lao (official)
**RELIGIONS:** Buddhism 58%, traditional beliefs 34%, Christianity 2%, Islam 1%
**CURRENCY:** Kip = 100 at

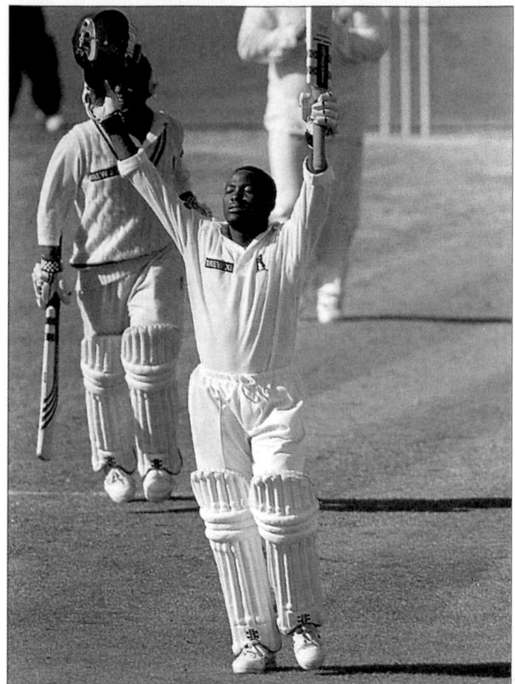

◀ **Lara** West Indian cricketer Brian Lara. A prodigious left-handed batsman, he beat Gary Sober's world record of runs made in a single test-match innings in 1994 when he scored 375 against England in Antigua. His total of 501 against Durham, England, is the highest number of runs scored in a first-class match.

was summarized in his book *Celestial Mechanics* (1798–1827). He also did fundamental work in the study of heat, magnetism and electricity.

**Lapland** Region in N Europe, lying almost entirely within the Arctic Circle and including N Norway, the northernmost parts of Sweden and Finland, and the W part of the Kola Peninsula of Russia. Mountains are in Norway and Sweden, but TUNDRA predominates in the NE. The S regions are forested. The harsh climate has restricted settlement. Industries: hydroelectricity, fishing, mining for iron ore, copper, and nickel. Tourism is important. Area: *c*.150,000sq mi (388,500sq km).

**La Plata** City in E Argentina, 35 mi (56km) SE of Buenos Aires. Founded in 1882, the city was called Eva PERÓN from 1946-55. La Plata functions as Argentina's largest oil refining center. Its port, Ensenada, is a major exporter of oil, cereals, and frozen meat. Pop. (1991) 640,000.

**La Plata, Río de** *See* PLATA, RÍO DE LA

**Lapps** People inhabiting LAPLAND. The mountain Lapps are nomadic herders of reindeer, while those of the forest and coast are seminomadic and live by hunting, trapping, and fishing. Their racial origins are uncertain.

**lapwing** (peewit) Any of several species of birds, especially the Eurasian lapwing, *Vanellus vanellus*, a wading bird with a conspicuous crest. It commonly nests in open agricultural land and defends its young by luring predators away, feigning a broken wing. Length: 12in (30cm). Family Charadriidae.

**Lara, Brian Charles** (1969– ) West Indian cricketer, b. Trinidad. He was captain of Trinidad at the age of 20. In 1994, as a member of the Warwickshire English county team, he achieved a world first-class record score of 501 (not out) against Durham.

**larch** Any CONIFER tree of the genus *Larix*, native to cool and temperate regions of the Northern Hemisphere. Larches bear cones and needlelike leaves that, unusually for a conifer, are shed annually. Family Pinaceae.

**Lardner, Ring (Ringgold Wilmer)** (1885–1933) US short-story writer and humorist. In 1916 he published *You Know Me, Al*, a collection of racy short stories about baseball players. Among his best-known stories are "Haircut," "Champion," and "The Love Nest."

**Largo Caballero, Francisco** (1869–1946) Spanish political leader. he was prime minister of the Popular Front government (1936) and continued in power into the Spanish CIVIL WAR until May 1937. He fled to France on Franco's victory, was imprisoned under the German occupation, and died in Paris.

**lark** Any of several small birds, known for their melodious songs. Most common in Europe are the woodlark (*Lullula arborea*), skylark (*Alauda arvensis*), and shorelark (*Eremophila alpestris*). All are mottled brown. They feed on insects, larvae, crustaceans, or berries. Length: to 7in (18cm). Family Alaudidae.

**Larkin, Philip Arthur** (1922–85) British poet. He found his characteristic voice with *The Less Deceived* (1955). Other works include *The Whitsun Weddings* (1964) and *High Windows* (1974). He edited the *Oxford Book of Twentieth Century Verse* (1973). His *Collected Poems* were published in 1988.

**larkspur** *See* DELPHINIUM

**La Rochefoucauld, François, Duc de** (1613–80) French writer of maxims and epigrams. In 1635 he was involved in an intrigue against Cardinal RICHELIEU and took part in the FRONDES revolts (1648–53). He wrote *Réflexions ou Sentences et Maximes Morales* (1665).

**La Rochelle** Seaport on the Bay of Biscay, W France; capital of Charente-Maritime department. An English possession during the 12th–13th centuries, it changed hands several times during the HUNDRED YEARS WAR (1337–1453). In the 16th century it became a HUGUENOT stronghold, but capitulated to the forces of Cardinal RICHELIEU in 1628. Industries: shipbuilding, oil refining, sawmilling. Pop. (1990) 71,094.

**Larousse, Pierre** (1817–75) French lexicographer. He founded the publishing firm Larousse, which produced *The Great Universal Dictionary of the 19th Century* (1866–76), the first of a famous series of dictionaries and encyclopedias.

**larva** Developmental stage in the life cycle of many invertebrates and some other animals. A common life cycle, typified by the BUTTERFLY, is egg, larva, PUPA, adult. The larva metamorphoses (or pupates) to become an adult. Names for it in different organisms include MAGGOT, CATERPILLAR, and TADPOLE.

**laryngitis** Inflammation of the LARYNX and vocal cords. Symptoms include a sore throat, hoarseness, coughing, and breathing difficulties. It is usually due to a respiratory tract infection.

**larynx** (voice box) Triangular cavity located between the TRACHEA (windpipe) and the root of the tongue. Inside it are the vocal cords. These are thin bands of elastic tissue, which vibrate when outgoing air passes over them, setting up resonant waves that are changed into sound by the action of throat muscles and the shape of the mouth.

▲ **lark** Found in many regions of Africa, Europe, and Asia, and some parts of North America and Australasia, larks (family *Alaudidae*) are notable for their songs. The crested lark (*Galerida cristata*) (shown) has a sandy coloration suited for camouflage in the dry, dusty grassland habitats in which it is found.

## LARYNX

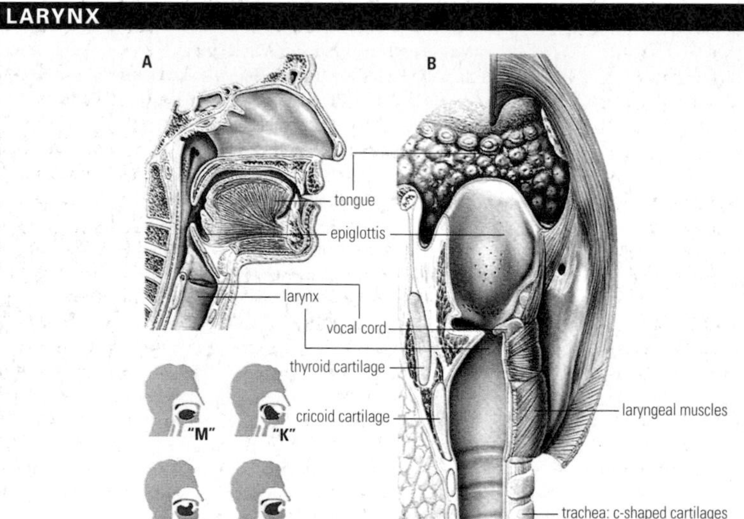


The larynx, together with the epiglottis, tongue, and mouth and lips are the principal organs of speech. A side view (A) and back view (B) of these organs are shown. Air pushed out from the lungs through the larynx causes the vocal cords to vibrate, producing a continuous singing tone, the "voice." This tone can be altered in "pitch" by varying the arrangement of the cartilages of the larynx (thyroid and cricoid) by action of the associated muscles. As air passes through the mouth, the voice is modulated and broken up by changing the position and shape of the other organs to produce speech. The different vowels are produced by altering the shape of the mouth. Consonants (four shown) are formed when the stream of air is suddenly emitted or cut off.

**▶ laser surgery** Used for a number of surgical operations today, lasers were initially used in surgery for operations involving the eye, notably to correct detached retinas. The ultrafine beam of light is a much more delicate instrument than a scalpel, and the energy of the laser cauterizes an incision as soon as it is made.

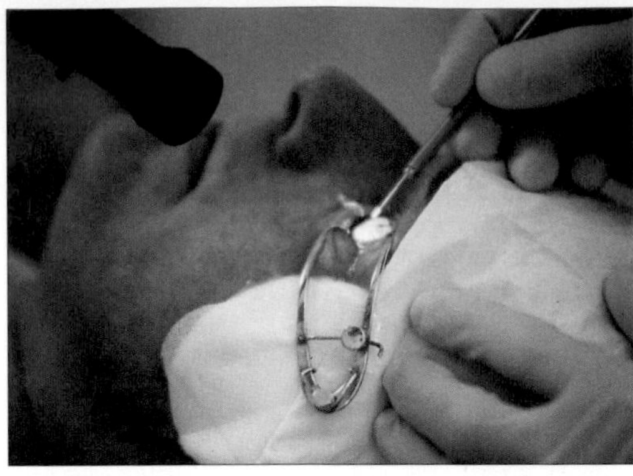

**La Salle, René Robert Cavelier, Sieur de** (1643–87) French explorer of North America. In 1668 he sailed for Canada to make his fortune in the fur trade. He explored the Great Lakes area and was governor of Fort Frontenac on Lake Ontario (1675). On his greatest journey, he followed the Mississippi to its mouth (1682), naming the land Louisiana and claiming it for France.

**La Scala** (Teatro alla Scala) One of the world's greatest opera houses, in Milan, Italy. Designed by Giuseppe Piermarini, it opened in 1776 and has been the scene of many famous premieres, among them Bellini's *Norma*, Verdi's *Otello*, and Puccini's *Madame Butterfly*.

**Las Casas, Bartolomé de** (1474–1566) Spanish missionary, known as the Apostle of the Indies. He went to Hispaniola in 1502 and spent his life trying to help the Native Americans; his *History of the Indies* documents their persecution by Spanish colonists.

**Lascaux** Complex of caves in the French Pyrenees, discovered in 1940. They contain examples of 13 different styles of PALEOLITHIC wall paintings, depicting horses, ibex, stags, and a reindeer. The caves were closed in 1963 in order to halt the deterioration of the paintings. *See also* CAVE PAINTING

**laser** (acronym for **l**ight **a**mplification by **s**timulated **e**mission of **r**adiation) Optical MASER, a source of a narrow beam of intense **coherent light** or ultraviolet or infrared radiation. It was first developed in 1960 by the US physicist Theodore H. Maiman. The source can be a solid, liquid, or gas. A large number of its atoms are excited to a higher energy state. One PHOTON of radiation emitted from an excited atom then stimulates the emission of another photon, of the same frequency and direction of travel, which in turn stimulates the emission of more photons. The photon number multiplies rapidly to produce a laser beam of very high energy content. It has applications in medicine, research, engineering, telecommunications, holography, and other fields.

**laser printer** Computer printer with a laser diode to control image formation. The laser beam scans lines across an electrically charged drum. The beam flashes on and off according to whether each point is to be light or dark. Exposed areas become discharged. the charged areas attract toner power, thus forming an image. Charged plain paper picks up the powder image from the drum. A heated roller fuses the powder onto the paper to make the image permanent.

**laser surgery** Surgical treatment carried out using a LASER beam. The high energy in an extremely narrow laser beam can burn through body tissues to make a fine "cut." The heat also seals blood vessels, so there is much less bleeding than when a knife is used. Some forms of skin cancer are treated in this way.

**Laski, Harold Joseph** (1893–1950) British political scientist and teacher. A prominent figure in the socialist FABIAN SOCIETY, he served on the national executive of the Labour Party (1937–49) and as party chairman (1945–46).

**Las Palmas** (Las Palmas de Gran Canaria) Spanish city, in NE Grand Canary Island; capital of Las Palmas province. Founded in 1478, the city expanded considerably after the building of the port in 1883. It is now a tourist resort. Its port, Puerto de la Luz, is the chief port in the Canary Islands, exporting bananas, sugar, tomatoes, and almonds. Pop. (1994) 372,000.

**Lassa fever** Acute viral disease, classified as a hemorrhagic fever. The virus, first detected in 1969, is spread by a species of rat found only in W Africa. It causes internal bleeding, fever, headache, and muscle pain.

**Lasso, Orlando di** (1532–94) Flemish composer. Employed by Albert V of Bavaria after 1556, he became famous throughout Europe and is ranked as one of the greatest composers of the late 16th century. He was known for his madrigals, masses, and motets.

**Last Supper** (Lord's Supper) Final meal shared by JESUS CHRIST and his disciples in Jerusalem during or just before the Passover, in the course of which Jesus instituted the Christian EUCHARIST.

**Las Vegas** Largest city in Nevada, in the S of the state. It is a world-famous gambling and entertainment center. With more than 13 million visitors per year, it is one of the US's major tourist destinations. The Mormons established a colony on the site in 1855–57. Nevada legalized gambling in 1931 and the city grew rapidly. Its first big gambling casino opened in 1946. Las Vegas is also the commercial center for a mining and ranching area. Pop. (1990) 258,295.

**La Tène** Archeological site in Switzerland, discovered in the 19th century. It gives its name to the second phase of Celtic culture, from c.500 BC to c.50 BC. The origin of the culture, which replaced the HALLSTATT culture, was contact with Greek and Etruscan influences. It was a highly warlike culture, hierarchically organized with kings, a priestly class (the DRUIDS), warriors, farmers, and slaves. La Tène weaponry was late IRON AGE. The La Tène Celts conquered central Europe in the fourth and third centuries, but by 50 BC they had submitted to German invaders from the N and Roman from the S.

**latent heat** Heat absorbed or given out by a substance as it changes its phase at constant temperature. When ice melts, its temperature remains the same until it has been completely transformed into water; the heat necessary to do this is called the latent heat of fusion.

**Lateran Councils** Five ECUMENICAL COUNCILS of the Western Church, held in the Lateran Palace in Rome. The first, held in 1123, confirmed the Concordat of WORMS of 1122. The second, in 1139, condemned simony and the marriage of the clergy. The third, in 1179, decreed that the pope was to be elected by a two-thirds majority of the College of Cardinals. The fourth in 1215, defined the doctrine of the EUCHARIST, officially using the term "TRANSUBSTANTIATION." The fifth, in 1512–17, introduced minor reforms in the wake of the REFORMATION.

**Lateran Treaty** (1929) Agreement between Italy and the VATICAN. The Italian government recognized the Vatican as an independent sovereign state with the pope as its temporal head, and the Vatican surrendered the Papal States and Rome. Roman Catholicism was affirmed as Italy's state religion.

**latex** Milky fluid produced by certain plants, the most important being the RUBBER TREE. Rubber latex is gum resins and fats in a watery medium. It is used in paints, special papers, and adhesives, and to make sponge rubbers. Synthetic rubber latexes are also produced.

**Latimer, Hugh** (1485–1555) English clergyman and Protestant martyr. He defended King HENRY VIII's divorce from Catherine of Aragon. In 1535 he was made bishop of Worcester, but resigned his see in 1539 as a protest against the temporary reaction in favor of Catholicism. With the accession of EDWARD VI (1547), he resumed preaching. When the Roman Catholic MARY I came to the throne (1553), he was charged with heresy and, refusing to recant, was burned at the stake.

**Latin** Language of ancient Rome, the Roman empire and of educated medieval European society. It belongs to the family of INDO-EUROPEAN LANGUAGES. Its earliest written records are inscriptions and legal formulas of the late 6th century BC. As Rome extended its rule throughout Italy, Latin gained supremacy. By the 3rd century BC, a literary form of Latin was evolving, which achieved its richest form between 70 BC and AD 18. The prose of CICERO, Julius CAESAR, and LIVY and the poetry of CATULLUS, VIRGIL, HORACE, and OVID are among the greatest works in the language. Spoken Latin was used throughout the Roman empire. It eventually broke up into numerous dialects, which formed the basis of the ROMANCE LANGUAGES. Latin remained the language of the church, science, medicine, and law, and of education and most written transactions in Europe throughout the Middle Ages. It was still used in some scholarly and diplomatic circles in the 19th century, and the Roman Catholic mass was in Latin until the 1960s.

**Latin America** Those parts of the Western Hemisphere (excluding French-speaking Canada) where the official or chief language is a ROMANCE LANGUAGE. Commonly it refers to the 18 Spanish-speaking republics and Brazil (Portuguese) and Haiti (French). Occasionally it includes some islands of the WEST INDIES.

**Latin literature** Literature of ancient Rome. The earliest works date from the 3rd century BC, and were imitations of Greek plays and epic poetry by Livius Andronicus and Naevius. One of Rome's greatest dramatists, PLAUTUS wrote in a similar style in the early 2nd century BC. Latin literature reached its stylistic peak in the 1st century BC. This so-called Golden Age ended soon after the death of AUGUSTUS in AD 14. The following century was noted for the writings of Seneca the Elder, TACITUS, PLINY THE ELDER, and PETRONIUS. After *c.*100 AD, Latin literature went into a decline from which it was revived by Christian authors such as AUGUSTINE OF HIPPO.

**latitude** Distance N or S of the Equator, measured at an angle from the Earth's center. All lines of latitude are parallel to the Equator, which is the zero line of latitude.

**La Tour, Georges de** (1593–1652) French painter of religious and genre scenes. He is famous for his nocturnal scenes lit by a single candle. Many art historians consider him to be one of the most important representatives of 17th-century French CLASSICISM. His work includes *Christ and St. Joseph in the Carpenter's Shop* (*c.*1645) and the *Lamentation over St. Sebastian* (1645).

**Latrobe, Benjamin Henry** (1766–1820) US architect, b. England. His monumental public buildings include some of the earliest examples of Greek revival and Gothic revival in the US, including the Bank of Pennsylvania, Philadelphia (1789). He also worked on the rebuilding of the Capitol in Washington, D.C. (1815–17).

**Latter Day Saints, Church of** *See* MORMONS

**Latter Day Saints, Reorganized Church of Jesus Christ of** *See* MORMONS

**Latvia** Baltic republic in NW Europe; the capital is RIGA. **Land and climate** Latvia consists mainly of flat plains separated by low hills. Small lakes and peat bogs are common and its highest point is only 1,020ft (311m) above sea level. Latvia's main river is the Daugava (Western Dvina). Riga has warm summers, but the winter months (December to March) are subzero and the sea often freezes. Moderate rainfall occurs throughout the year, with light snow in winter. Forests cover about 40% of the county. About 27% of the land is under crops. **Economy** Latvia is a lower-middle-income country (1992 GDP per capita, US$6,060). It faced many problems in transforming its government-run economy into a free-market one. The country lacks natural resources and has to import many of the materials needed for its most valuable activity, manufacturing. Products include electronic goods, farm machinery, fertilizers, and processed food. Latvia produces only about 10% of the electricity it needs and the rest has to be imported from Belarus, Russia, and Ukraine. Farm products include barley, dairy products, beef, oats, potatoes, and rye. **History** The ancestors of most modern Latvians settled in the area about 2,000 years ago. Between the 9th and 11th centuries, the region was attacked by Vikings from the W and Russians from the E. In the 13th century, German invaders took over. From 1561 the area was partitioned between various groups, including Poles, Lithuanians, and Swedes. In 1710 Peter the Great took Riga and, by the end of the 18th century, Latvia was under Russian rule. Just after the end of World War I, Latvia declared itself independent. In 1939 Germany and the Soviet Union made a secret agreement to divide up parts of E Europe and, in 1940, Soviet troops invaded Latvia, which became part of the Soviet Union. German forces seized Latvia in 1941, but Soviet troops returned in 1944. **Politics** Under Soviet rule, many Russian immigrants settled in Latvia. In the late 1980s, when reforms were being introduced in the Soviet Union, Latvia's government relaxed communist laws, allowed press and religious freedom, and made Latvian the official language. In 1990 it declared the country to be independent, an act that was finally recognized by the Soviet Union in September 1991. Latvia held its first free elections in 1993. In 1994 Latvia adopted a law restricting the naturalization of non-Latvians, including many Russian settlers. In 1995 Latvia joined the Council of Europe and formally applied to join the European Union.

**Laud, William** (1573–1645) English cleric, Archbishop of Canterbury (1633–45) and religious adviser to CHARLES I. Working closely with Charles I, he imposed press censorship, enforced a policy regulating wages and prices, and sought to remove PURITANS from important positions in the church. His attempt to impose the English prayer book upon the Scots was one of the causes of the CIVIL WAR. Laud was impeached (1640) by the LONG PARLIAMENT.

**Lauda, Niki (Nikolas)** (1949– ) Austrian motor racing driver who, driving for Ferrari, won the world drivers' championship in 1975, 1977, and 1984. In 1976 he suffered near-fatal injuries.

**Laue, Max Theodor Felix von** (1879–1960) German physicist. He was director of the Institute for Theoretical Physics in Berlin. Using IONS in a crystal as a grating, he produced X-RAY interference patterns, showing that X-rays are waves. For the discovery of X-ray diffraction in crystals, Laue received the 1914 Nobel Prize for physics.

**lauraceae** Large family of flowering plants, mostly evergreen shrubs and trees, including LAUREL, CINNAMON, and SASSAFRAS; it is found in warm and temperate regions worldwide. The flowers are generally green and are followed by berries.

**laurel** Evergreen shrubs and trees native to S Europe and cultivated in the US. Included is the noble or bay laurel (*Laurus nobilis*) with leathery, oval leaves, tiny yellowish flowers and purple berries. Height: 60–70ft (18–21m). Family LAURACEAE

**Laurel and Hardy** US comedy team who starred in more than 200 films. Stan Laurel (1890–1965), b. Britain, played the thin, bumbling oaf. His US partner Oliver Hardy (1892–1957) played the fat, would-be charmer. Their films include *Leave 'em Laughing* (1928), *The Music Box* (1932), and *Way Out West* (1937).

**Laurier, Sir Wilfrid** (1841–1919) Canadian statesman. The first French-Canadian to lead a federal party (the Liberals,

## LATVIA

**AREA:** 24,938sq mi (64,589sq km)
**POPULATION:** 2,632,000
**CAPITAL (POPULATION):** Riga (910,200)
**GOVERNMENT:** Multiparty republic
**ETHNIC GROUPS:** Latvian 53%, Russian 34%, Belorussian 4%, Ukrainian 3%, Polish 2%, Lithuanian, Jewish
**LANGUAGES:** Latvian (official)
**RELIGIONS:** Christianity (including Lutheran, Russian Orthodox, and Roman Catholic)
**CURRENCY:** Lats = 10 santimi

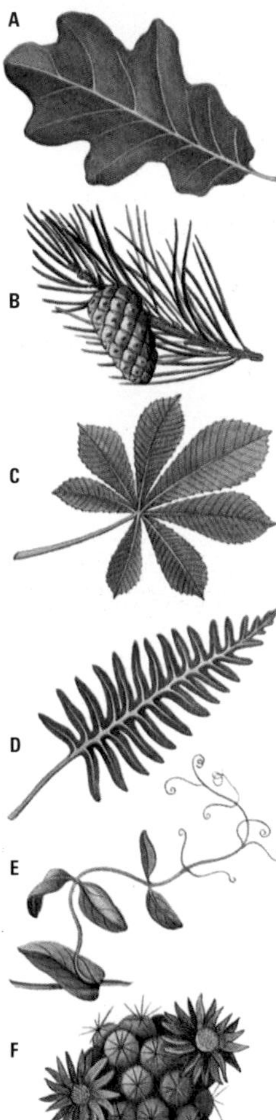


▲ **leaf** Leaves exhibit a wide variety of shapes. The penduncculate oak (*Quercus rober*) (A) and the Scots pine (Pinus sylvestris) (B) have simple leaves, with a single leaf blade, while the horse chestnut (*Aesculus hippocastrum*) (C) and ferns, such as Polypodium (D) have compound leaves. The leaflets of compound leaves either radiate from one point (palmate) as in the case of the horse chestnut, or are arranged in opposite pairs down the main stalk (pinnate) as is the case with ferns. The primary function of leaves is photosynthesis, but in addition leaflets may be modified into climbing tendrils (E), or protective spines, as in the cactus *Mammillaria zeilmannia* (F).

1887–1919), he was prime minister of Canada in 1896–1911. He created a separate Canadian navy in 1909 and signed a reciprocal tariff agreement with the US in 1911.

**Lausanne** City on the N shore of Lake Geneva, SW Switzerland; capital of Vaud canton. Originally a Celtic settlement, it became an episcopal see in the 6th century. In 1536, it was conquered by BERN and accepted the Reformation. Industries: leather, brewing, chemicals. Pop. (1991) 265,000.

**Lautrec, Henri Toulouse** *See* TOULOUSE-LAUTREC, HENRI MARIE RAYMOND DE

**lava** Molten rock or MAGMA that reaches the Earth's surface and flows out through a volcanic vent in streams or sheets. There are three main types of lava: vesicular, such as pumice; glassy, such as obsidian; and even-grained. Chemically, lavas range from acidic to ultrabasic.

**Laval, Pierre** (1883–1945) French statesman. He was prime minister (1931–32, 1935–36), but his government fell as a result of the unpopularity of the Hoare-Laval Pact, which approved Italy's conquest of Ethiopia. In 1940 he joined the VICHY GOVERNMENT, becoming its head under Marshal PÉTAIN. This was seen as treason by the FREE FRENCH and he was executed after the war.

**Laver, Rod (Rodney George)** (1938– ) Australian tennis player. He won the US (1962, 1969), British (1961, 1962, 1968, 1969), Australian (1960, 1962, 1969), and French (1962, 1969) singles championships, becoming the first man to win the "Grand Slam" twice (1962, 1969).

**Lavoisier, Antoine Laurent** (1743–94) French chemist who founded modern chemistry. He demolished the PHLOGISTON theory (which said that phlogiston was lost during combustion) by demonstrating the function of oxygen in combustion. He named oxygen and hydrogen and showed how they combined to form water. In collaboration with Claude Berthollet, he published *Methods of Chemical Nomenclature* (1787), which laid down the modern method of naming substances.

**Law, (Andrew) Bonar** (1858–1923) British politician, b. Canada. In 1911 he became the first leader of the Conservative Party from a manufacturing background. He was chancellor of the exchequer (1916–19) and prime minister (1922–23).

**Law, John** (1671–1729) French financier, b. Scotland. His banking and stock-market schemes created a boom in France, where he founded a state bank, later named the Banque Générale, in 1716. His "Mississippi Scheme" (1717) attracted huge investment in French Louisiana. A dip in public confidence caused heavy selling and the whole scheme collapsed. Law died in exile, a bankrupt.

**law** System of rules governing society, enforced by punishments specified by society. The major systems are COMMON LAW, ROMAN LAW, and EQUITY.

**Law and the Prophets** Two major divisions of the OLD TESTAMENT. The Law or the Law of Moses, is the first five books of the Old Testament, known as the TORAH in Hebrew and the PENTATEUCH in Greek. The Prophets consists of several books grouped differently according to Jewish or Christian tradition. The groupings include: (a) Joshua, Judges, I and II Samuel, and I and II Kings; (b) Isaiah, Jeremiah, and Ezekiel; and (c) Hosea, Joel, Amos, Obadiah, Jonah, Micah, Nahum, Habakkuk, Zephaniah, Haggai, Zechariah, and Malachi.

**Lawrence, D.H. (David Herbert)** (1885–1930) British novelist, short-story writer, and poet. His novels include *Sons and Lovers* (1913), *Women in Love* (1920), and *Lady Chatterley's Lover* (privately published 1928). He also wrote numerous short stories, plays, essays, and miscellaneous non-fiction

**Lawrence, Ernest Orlando** (1901–58) US physicist. In 1930, as professor at the University of California at Berkeley, he built the first cyclotron, a subatomic particle ACCELERATOR. He received the 1939 Nobel Prize for physics. LAWRENCIUM was named for him.

**Lawrence, T.E. (Thomas Edward)** (1888–1935) (Lawrence of Arabia) British soldier. He joined the army in World War I and in 1916 led the Arab revolt against the Turks. He was a successful guerrilla commander, leading Arab forces into Damascus, Syria, in October 1918. He published his account of the Arab revolt, *The Seven Pillars of Wisdom*, privately in 1926.

**Lawrence, Sir Thomas** (1769–1830) One of the most brilliant British portrait painters of his age. His portrait of *Queen Charlotte* (1789) won immediate acclaim. He became Painter in Ordinary to the King and was sent to Europe to paint the allied leaders involved in the defeat of NAPOLEON.

**Lawrence of Arabia** *See* LAWRENCE, T.E. (THOMAS EDWARD)

**lawrencium** Radioactive metallic element (symbol Lr), one of the ACTINIDE SERIES. It was first made in 1961 at the University of California at Berkeley by bombarding CALIFORNIUM with boron nuclei. Properties: at.no. 103; at.wt. 262; most stable isotope $^{256}$Lr (half-life 27 seconds).

**laxative** Any agent used to counteract constipation. They include bulk-forming drugs, stimulant laxatives, fecal softeners, and saline purgatives.

**Laxness, Halldór Kiljan** (1902– 98) Icelandic novelist. He was awarded the 1955 Noble Prize for literature. His fiction includes *Independent People* (1934–35), *The Atom Station* (1948), *Paradise Reclaimed* (1960), and the trilogy *Iceland's Bell* (1943–46).

**Lazarus** Either of two men mentioned in the New Testament. In John 11 Lazarus was the brother of Mary and Martha of Bethany. Four days after his death, Jesus miraculously restored him to life. In Luke 16 Lazarus is the poor man in Christ's parable about a beggar and a rich man.

**L-dopa** (levodopa) Naturally occurring amino acid used to relieve some symptoms of PARKINSON'S DISEASE. It sometimes suppresses the trembling, unsteadiness, and slowness of movement that characterize the condition.

**Leaching** In geology, process by which chemicals and nutrients are removed from a soil. Rainwater, especially in warm climatic regions, will dissolve anything anything soluble and wash it away. Once removed, these solubles can only be replaced slowly. as a result, leached soils become coarse and infertile. Saline soils can, however, be reclamed for agriculture by leaching out salts.

**Leacock, Stephen Butler** (1869–1944) Canadian humorist, b. Britain. His *Literary Lapses* (1910) proved popular for their gentle satire and love of the absurd. He also wrote *Sunshine Sketches of a Little Town* (1912).

**lead** Metallic element (symbol Pb) of Group IV of the periodic table. Its chief ore is GALENA (lead sulfide), from which lead is obtained by roasting. Exposure to lead from paints, pipes, gasoline, and other sources can lead to lead poisoning. Soft and malleable, it is used as a shield for X-rays and nuclear radiation, and in batteries, cable sheaths, and alloys such as pewter and solder. Chemically lead is unreactive and a poor conductor of electricity. Properties: at.no. 82; at.wt. 207.19; sp.gr. 11.35; m.p. 621.5°F (327.5°C); b.p. 3,164°F (1,740°C); most common isotope $^{208}$Pb (52.3%).

**Leadbelly** (1888–1949) Popular name of US composer and blues singer Huddie LEDBETTER.

**leaf** Part of a plant, an organ that contains the green pigment CHLOROPHYLL and is involved in PHOTOSYNTHESIS and TRANSPIRATION. It usually consists of a blade and a stalk (petiole), which attaches it to a stem or twig. Most leaves are simple (undivided), but some are compound.

**leafhopper** Any of numerous species of small, slender insects of the family Cicadellidae. Leaf hoppers feed by sucking the sap of plants and may, in large numbers, do a great deal of damage. Many species are brightly colored.

**leaf insect** Any of several species of flat, green insects that resemble leaves and are found throughout tropical Asia. The female has large leathery forewings with markings like leaf veins. Order Phasmida; family Phylliidae. *See also* STICK INSECT

**League of Nations** International organization, forerunner of the UNITED NATIONS (UN). Created by the Treaty of VERSAILLES (1919) ending World War I, it was impaired by the refusal of the US to join. The threats to peace from Germany, Italy, and Japan caused the League to collapse in 1939. It was dissolved in 1946.

**League of Women Voters** US political organization. It was founded in 1920. A nonpartisan organization, it is comprised of women citizens who distribute information on issues and candidates and campaign to encourage registration and voting.

**Leakey, Louis Seymour Bazett** (1903–72) English archeologist and anthropologist. He discovered fossils in East Africa that proved humans to be older than had been thought. In 1931 he began to research Olduvai Gorge in Tanzania with his wife Mary (1913–96). She continued working in East Africa, often with their son RICHARD (1944– ), who became director of the National Museums of Kenya.

**Leakey, Richard Erskine Frere** (1944– ) Kenyan paleoanthropologist and archeologist, son of Mary and Louis LEAKEY. At Lake Turkana, Kenya, Leakey discovered (1972) a 1.9 million year-old skull of *Homo habilis*. Other discoveries include a *Homo erectus* skeleton *c*.1.6 million years old. Leakey became director (1988–94) of the Kenyan Wildlife Service. His campaign against the ivory trade brought him into the political arena, and in 1995 he co-founded the Safina Party. See also HUMAN EVOLUTION

**Lean, Sir David** (1908–91) British film director. Lean's early films, such as *Brief Encounter* (1945), were collaborative projects with Noel COWARD. He is known for meticulously crafted spectaculars, such as *The Bridge on the River Kwai* (1957) and *Lawrence of Arabia* (1962), for which he won Best Director Academy Awards. Other films include *Doctor Zhivago* (1965) and *Ryan's Daughter* (1970). In 1984 he made his final film, *A Passage to India*, and was knighted.

**Lear, Edward** (1812–88) British poet, painter, and draftsman. He is famous for his tragicomic nonsense verse for children. He invented such characters as the *Owl and the Pussycat*. Books include *The Book of Nonsense* (1846) and *Laughable Lyrics* (1877).

**learning** Acquisition of skills and concepts by a variety of processes. The oldest theories held learning to be an associative process by which ideas, images, and events become linked in the mind. Behaviorists believed that learning was related to conditioning. GESTALT PSYCHOLOGY dealt with such learning potentials as problem solving; modern COGNITIVE PSYCHOLOGY concentrates on mental processes such as concept formation.

**leather** Animal hide, treated to make it hard-wearing and resistant to decay. Most leather is made from cattle hide, but many other kinds of skin are used too. The skin is first cured, via a drying process or the application of salt. It is then washed and prepared for tanning, a process that usually consists of treating the skin with a solution of chromium salts or plant extract (TANNIN).

**Leavis, F.R. (Frank Raymond)** (1895–1978) British literary critic. His works of criticism include *The Great Tradition* (1948), *The Common Pursuit* (1952), and *D.H. Lawrence, Novelist* (1955).

**Lebanon** Republic in sw Asia. See country feature, page 391

**Lebed, Aleksander Ivanovich** (1950– ) Russian general and politician. As commander of the Tula Airborne Troops Division, he stood guard at the Supreme Soviet building during the attempted coup of August 1991. Running against YELTSIN in the 1996 presidential elections, Lebed's support was such that Yeltsin offered him a government position to win his votes. He was appointed national security adviser but dismissed later that year.

**Leblanc, Nicolas** (1742–1806) French chemist. In 1790 he devised a process for producing soda ash (sodium carbonate, $Na_2CO_3$) from salt (sodium chloride, NaCl) by treating it with sulfuric acid.

**LeBrun, Charles** (1619–90) French painter. As chief painter to LOUIS XIV, he created the Galerie d'Apollon at the Louvre (1661) and much of the interior of VERSAILLES, including the Hall of Mirrors (1679–84). He became director of the ACADÉMIE FRANÇAISE in 1663.

**Le Carré, John** (1931– ) British writer. His first novel was *Call for the Dead* (1961), in which he introduces George Smiley, his best-known character. Among his popular stories of espionage are *The Spy Who Came in from the Cold* (1963), *A Small Town in Germany* (1968), *Tinker, Tailor, Soldier, Spy* (1974), *The Russia House* (1989), and *The Tailor of Panama* (1996).

**Le Châtelier's principle** Principle announced by the French chemist Henry Louis Le Châtelier (1850–1936) in 1888. It states that if a system in a state of equilibrium is disturbed, it tends to restore the equilibrium.

**Leclanché cell** Electric cell invented by Georges Leclanché, *c*.1865. Its ANODE was a zinc rod and its CATHODE a carbon plate surrounded by packed manganese dioxide. These electrodes were dipped into a solution of ammonium and zinc chlorides. It is the basis of the dry cell or BATTERY.

**Leconte de Lisle, Charles Marie René** (1818–94) French poet. He was the leader of the antiromantic Parnassian school, and his work includes *Poèmes antiques* (1852) and *Poèmes barbares* (1862). He was elected to the Académie Française in 1866.

**Le Corbusier** (1887–1963) French architect, b. Switzerland as Charles Édouard Jeanneret. His early work exploited the qualities of reinforced concrete in cubelike forms. His Unité d'Habitation, Marseilles (1946–52) was a design widely adopted for modern mass housing. Later, Le Corbusier evolved a more poetic style, of which the highly sculptural chapel of Notre-Dame-du-Haut at Ronchamp (1955) is the

▲ **leaf insect** Masters of disguise, leaf insects such as *Phyllium crurufolium* (shown here), have legs and wings adapted to resemble leaves. In their tropical Asian habitats their predators find them difficult to spot. Some species have taken this adaptation a stage further, by laying eggs that resemble the seeds of various plants.

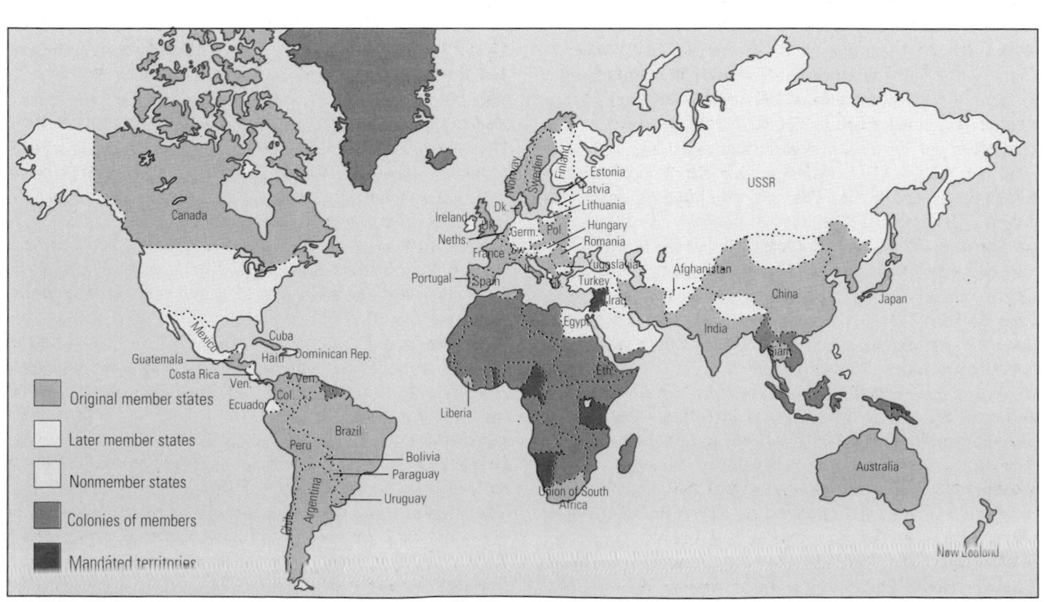


◀ **League of Nations** Set up following World War I to arbitrate over international disputes, the original members of the League of Nations were the 32 states that signed the Covenant and ratified it (although the US did not ratify), and those states that joined by invitation. Other states were admitted at later dates by a two-thirds vote of the Assembly. The lack of US support weakened the League to the point that it was largely ineffectual as a forum for world peace.

► **Le Corbusier** The pilgrimage chapel of Notre-Dame-du-Haut, Ronchamp, France, was built by Le Corbusier in 1955. The flowing, highly sculptural concrete structure deliberately resembles a nun's headdress in both form and coloration. A combination of the southern wall of the chapel, which contains numerous stained glass windows, and structures of the northern wall, which break through the roof, suffuse the interior with light.

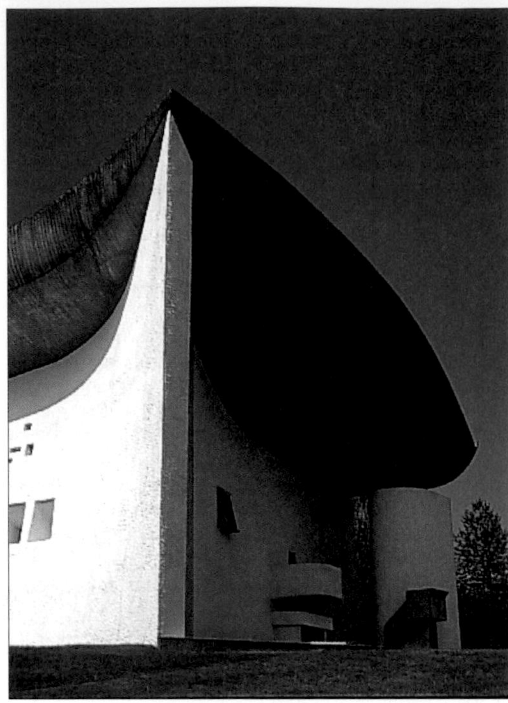

finest example. In the 1950s he laid out the town of Chandigarh, India, and built its majestic supreme courts. His last major work was the Visual Arts Center at Harvard (Cambridge, Massachusetts, 1963).

**Leda** In Greek mythology, Queen of Sparta, wife of Tyndareus, and mother of CLYTEMNESTRA. She was also the mother of CASTOR AND POLLUX and HELEN by ZEUS. The myth reveals that Zeus came to her in the form of a swan.

**Ledbetter, Huddie** (1888–1949) US composer and blues singer, better known as Leadbelly. Folklorist John A. Lomax discovered him in prison and used his songs in the book *Negro Folk Songs as Sung by Lead Belly* (1936). He composed many classic blues songs including "Goodnight Irene," and "Rock Island Line."

**Lee, Ann** (1736–84) British mystic, member of the United Society of Believers in Christ's Second Appearing, popularly called the SHAKERS. The Shaker sect was persecuted in Britain, and in 1774 Lee and eight others fled to the American colonies. In 1776 she founded a colony near Albany, New York.

**Lee, Charles** (1731–82) US Revolutionary soldier, b. England. Serving in the Seven Years War, he took part in the capture of Montreal (1760). At the beginning of the American Revolution, he became a major general in the Continental army. Captured by the British in 1778, he passed information to them. He rejoined the revolutionary soldiers but was dismissed for incompetence.

**Lee, Henry** (1756–1818) US Revolutionary soldier and father of Robert E. LEE. His excellent service during the American Revolution earned him the nickname "Light-Horse Harry." He served as governor of Virginia (1792–95) and as a Federalist congressman (1799–1801). On the occasion of George Washington's death (1799), Lee described him as being "first in war, first in peace, and first in the hearts of his countrymen."

**Lee, Laurie** (1914-97) British author and poet. His collections of poetry include and *My Many-Coated Man* (1955). He is best known for his autobiography *The Edge of Day* (UK: *Cider with Rosie*) (1959), and his accounts of travels in Spain during the Spanish Civil War. He has also written short stories.

**Lee, Richard Henry** (1732–94) US political leader. As a delegate to the CONTINENTAL CONGRESS, he proposed the resolution on which the Declaration of Independence was based (1776). He opposed the Constitution on the grounds that it diminished the power of the states. He was president of Congress (1784–86) and one of the first senators from Virginia (1789–92).

**Lee, Robert E. (Edward)** (1807–70) Commander of the Confederate forces in the CIVIL WAR. In 1862 he was appointed commander of the main Confederate force, the Army of Virginia. He won the Second Battle of BULL RUN and defeated the Union forces at FREDERICKSBURG and CHANCELLORSVILLE. His invasion of the North ended in decisive defeat at GETTYSBURG in July 1863. He was finally trapped by Ulysses S. GRANT, who accepted his surrender in April 1865.

**Lee, Spike** (1957– ) US movie director, writer, and actor. His first feature, *She's Gotta Have It* (1986), was shot in black-and-white, and revealed a promising talent. Other films include *Malcolm X* (1992) and *Crooklyn* (1994).

**Lee, Tsung-Dao** (1926– ) US physicist, b. China. He and his colleague Chen Ning YANG showed that among the weak interactions of subatomic particles, the law of conservation of parity (that nature, in effect, makes no distinction between right- and left-handedness) does not always hold. For this, Lee and Yang were awarded the 1957 Nobel Prize for physics.

**leech** Any of numerous species of freshwater, marine, and terrestrial annelids found in tropical and temperate regions. Its tapered, ringed body has a sucking disk at each end. Many species live on the blood of animals. Length: 0.5–2in (13–51mm). Class Hirudinea.

**Leeds** City and county district on the Aire River, West Yorkshire, N England. Its woolen industry dates from the 14th century, but it was in the 18th–19th centuries that the city became famous for its cloth manufacture; it remains the center of England's wholesale clothing trade. Other industries: aircraft components, textile machinery, engineering. Pop. (1994) 529,000.

**leek** Biennial plant related to the onion; it originated in the Mediterranean region and is cultivated widely for culinary purposes. Family Liliaceae, species *Allium porrum*.

**Lee Teng-hui** (1923– ) Chinese politician, president of Taiwan (1988– ). A member of the ruling Nationalist Party (Kuomintang), he became vice president of the party (and of Taiwan) in 1984. On the death of Chiang Ching-kuo in 1988, Lee Teng-hui became president and was subsequently elected. He was largely responsible for the rapid liberalization of Taiwan.

**Leeuwenhoek, Anton van** (1632–1723) Dutch scientist. He built simple microscopes with a single lens, which were so accurate that they had better magnifying powers than the compound microscopes of his day. He investigated and described many microorganisms.

**Leeward Islands** Group of islands in the West Indies, comprising the N section of the Lesser Antilles; it includes the US and British VIRGIN ISLANDS, GUADELOUPE, ANGUILLA, ANTIGUA AND BARBUDA, MONTSERRAT, ST. KITTS-NEVIS, and St. Martin. Colonization began in the early 17th century. For the next 200 years control of the islands fluctuated between Britain and France. The economy is based on agriculture and tourism. Major crops include fruits and sugar.

**left wing** In politics, used to describe socialist parties, people, or opinions. It originated in France after the French Revolution, and comes from the seating arrangement of the National Assembly in 1789, where the nobles sat on the president's right and the commons on his left. The terms left, right, and center are also used to describe views within a party. *See also* RIGHT WING

**legacy** Personal property – usually a sum of money – bequeathed (to a legatee) in a WILL. One will may include a number of legatees.

**Léger, Fernand** (1881–1955) French painter. An influential member of the School of Paris, he evolved a form of CUBISM jokingly called "tubism" because of its emphasis on cylindrical, mechanical forms.

**legion** Basic organizational unit of the Roman army until the fall of the empire in the West in the 5th century AD. During the great period of Rome's expansion, a legion was about 6,000 men strong, consisting mainly of heavy infantrymen (legionaries), with some light troops and cavalry in support. The legion was subdivided into cohorts (420 men each), maniples (120 men each), and centuries (100 men each).

**legionnaire's disease** Pneumonia-like lung disease caused by the bacterium *Legionella pneumophila*. It takes its name from the serious outbreak that occurred during a convention of the American Legion held in Philadelphia in 1976.

**Legion of Honor** (Légion d'Honneur) French award, created by Napoleon I in 1802 to reward civil and military service. The highest class of award is the great cross (*grand-croix*). The usual award is Knight of the Legion (*Chevalier de la Légion*), marked by a distinctive red ribbon.

**legislation** *See* LAW

**legislature** Representative assembly whose primary function is the enactment of laws. Legislatures can be either unicameral or bicameral (composed of one or two chambers). In the US, the SENATE is constitutionally more powerful than the HOUSE OF REPRESENTATIVES, and both houses are elected. In most democracies, including Britain, the "lower" or more directly elected chamber is the more powerful, and the "upper" chamber filled by government appointees or hereditary members.

**legumes** Members of the pea family of flowering plants, including many trees, shrubs, vines, and herbs whose roots bear nodules that contain nitrogen-fixing bacteria. The fruit is typically a pod (legume) containing a row of seeds. Food species include the PEA, runner BEAN, SOYBEAN, LENTIL, broad bean, and kidney bean. *See also* NITROGEN FIXATION; NITROGEN CYCLE; ROOT NODULE

**Lehár, Franz** (1870–1948) Austrian composer, b. Hungary. From 1890 he traveled as a bandmaster in Austria. He composed more than 30 operettas, of which *The Merry Widow* (1905) is the most popular today.

**Le Havre** City and seaport at the mouth of the Seine River, on the English Channel, N France. Founded in the 16th century on the site of a fishing village, it was enlarged and fortified, and is now France's second-largest port. It is the principal export point for Paris and a transatlantic and cross-Channel passenger port. Industries: chemicals, fertilizers, timber, food processing, oil-refining. Pop. (1990) 195,854.

**Lehmann, Lotte** (1888–1976) US soprano, b. Germany. She was the most illustrious singer of operatic roles and Lieder of her time. She sang with the Vienna State Opera (1914–38) and the METROPOLITAN OPERA COMPANY, New York, from 1934 until her retirement in 1961.

**Leibniz, Gottfried Wilhelm** (1646–1716) German philosopher and mathematician. Leibniz made many practical inventions, including a calculating machine (1671). He published his

## LEBANON

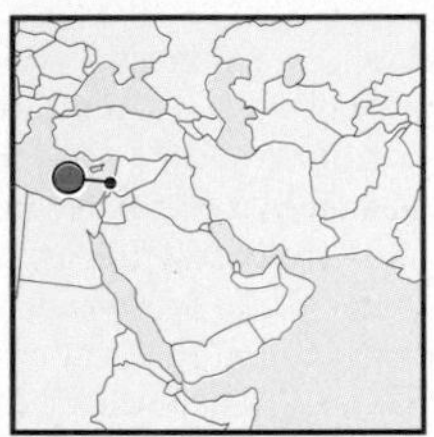

Lebanon's flag was adopted in 1943. It uses the colors of Lebanese nationalists in World War I (1914–18). The cedar tree on the white stripe has been a Lebanese symbol since Biblical times. Because of deforestation, only a few of Lebanon's giant cedars survive.

**AREA:** 4,015sq mi (10,400sq km)
**POPULATION:** 2,838,000
**CAPITAL (POPULATION):** Beirut (1,500,000)
**GOVERNMENT:** Multiparty republic
**ETHNIC GROUPS:** Arab (Lebanese 80%, Palestinian 12%), Armenian 5%, Syrian, Kurdish
**LANGUAGES:** Arabic (official)
**RELIGIONS:** Islam 58%, Christianity 27%, Druse
**CURRENCY:** Lebanese pound = 100 piastres

The Republic of Lebanon lies on the E shores of the Mediterranean Sea. A narrow coastal plain contains the capital BEIRUT, and the second-largest city of TRIPOLI. Behind the plain are the rugged Lebanese Mountains, which rise to 10,131ft (3,088m). The Anti-Lebanon Mountains form the E border with Syria. Between the two ranges is the Bekaa Valley, a fertile farming area and site of the ancient city of BAALBEK.

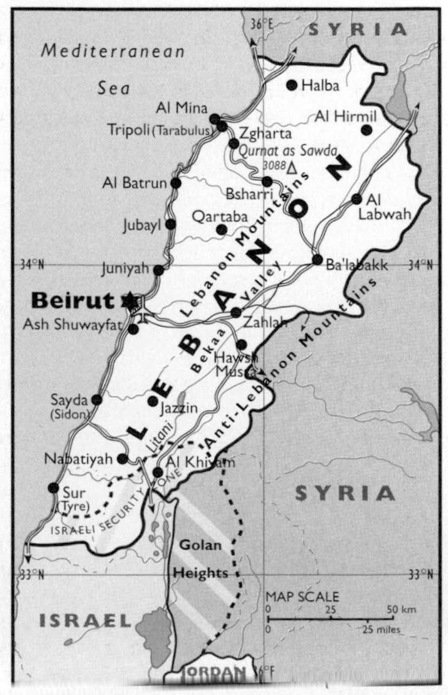


### CLIMATE

Coastal regions have a typical Mediterranean climate, with hot, dry summers and mild, wet winters. Onshore winds bring heavy winter rain to the W slopes of the mountains.

### VEGETATION

Lebanon was famous in ancient times for its cedar forests, but these have largely disappeared. Forests now cover only 8% of the land.

### HISTORY

In *c*.3000 BC Canaanites founded the city of TYRE and established what became known as PHOENICIA. In 332 Alexander the Great conquered the territory. In 64 BC the region fell to the Romans. Christianity was introduced in AD 325. Arab conquest in the 7th century saw the introduction of Islam, but Christian MARONITES predominated. Lebanon was one of the principal battlefields of the CRUSADES (1100–1300). In 1516, Lebanon became part of the Ottoman empire, and Turkish rule continued until World War I. After the war Lebanon and Syria were mandated to France. In 1926 Lebanon gained a republican constitution. In 1945 Lebanon became fully independent. During the 1950s Lebanon's economy grew rapidly and it pursued a pro-Western foreign policy. This infuriated the Arab population and US troops were called in to crush a 1958 rebellion. Lebanon did not participate in the 1967 or 1973 ARAB-ISRAELI WARS. In the late-1960s Lebanon came under increasing military pressure from Israel to act against Palestinian guerillas operating in S Lebanon. In 1975 civil war broke out between Maronite, SUNNI, SHIITE, and DRUSE militias. About 50,000 Lebanese died and the economy was devastated. In 1976 Syrian troops imposed a fragile ceasefire. In 1978 Israel moved into S Lebanon to destroy Palestinian bases. UN peacekeeping forces were called in to separate the factions. In 1982 Israel launched a full-scale attack on Palestinian bases in Lebanon. The 1983 deployment of US and European troops in Beirut was met by a terrorist bombing campaign. Multinational forces left in 1984, and Israeli troops withdrew to a buffer zone in S Lebanon. In 1987 Syrian troops occupied Beirut. In 1990 an uneasy truce was called and the government began to disarm the militias. Syria maintained troops in West Beirut and the Bekaa Valley. The Syrian-backed HEZBOLLAH and Israeli-backed South Lebanon Army (SLA) continued to operate in S Lebanon.

### POLITICS

In 1996 Israel attacked Hizbullah guerrilla bases in S Lebanon in retaliation for terrorist strikes in Israel. Elias Hrawi presidency (1989–98) saw the beginnings of reconstruction in Beirut. In 1998 General Emile Lahoud was appointed president. Fighting continues in Israeli-occupied S Lebanon.

### ECONOMY

The civil war devastated Lebanon's valuable tourism, trade and financial sectors (1992 GDP per capita, $2,500). Manufacturing was also badly damaged. Manufactures include chemicals, electrical goods and textiles. Farm products include fruits, vegetables, and sugar beet.

► **Leigh** Although she epitomized in looks and manner an English lady, the English actress Vivien Leigh in fact will be most remembered for her two Academy-Award winning roles as American heroines, Scarlet O'Hara in *Gone with the Wind*, and Blanche du Bois in *A Streetcar Named Desire*. Suffering from tuberculosis for much of her career, she was often exhausted while working on set.

discovery of differential and integral CALCULUS, made independently of Sir Isaac NEWTON. He believed the universe comprises a hierarchy of constituents (monads) with God at the top asserting a divine plan. His major works include *New Essays Concerning Human Understanding* (1765).

**Leicester, Robert Dudley, Earl of** (1532–88) English courtier. He was a favorite of Queen ELIZABETH I, who ennobled him. Marriage to Elizabeth seemed possible, but instead, Elizabeth proposed his marriage to MARY, QUEEN OF SCOTS, who rejected him.

**Leicester** City in central England; county town of Leicestershire. It was founded in the 1st century AD as a Roman town (Ratae Coritanorum) and was conquered by the Danes in the 9th century. The city became famous for its hosiery and footwear. Pop. (1994) 297,000.

**Leicestershire** County in E central England; the county town is LEICESTER. The area is drained chiefly by the Soar and Wreak rivers. The uplands of the E are devoted to farming, and the W has more industry. Wheat, barley, sheep, and dairy cattle are important, and the region is famous for its hosiery and Stilton cheese. Area: 986sq mi (2,553sq km). Pop. (1994) 916,900.

**Leiden** (Leyden) City on the Oude Rijn River, W Netherlands, 9mi (15km) NE of The Hague. Leiden received its city charter in the 13th century and developed a textile industry. The Pilgrim Fathers lived there before setting out for America in 1620. Industries: textiles, printing, and publishing. Pop. (1993) 192,000.

**Leif Ericsson** (c.970–1020) Norse adventurer and explorer. Son of ERIC THE RED, he sailed from Greenland in 1003 to investigate land in the west. Among the places he visited were Helluland (probably Baffin Island), Markland (Labrador), and VINLAND.

**Leigh, Mike** (1943– ) Innovative English film director, playwright, and screenwriter. His debut feature, *Bleak Moments* (1971), established his reputation for social realism. After a long break, he made the acclaimed *High Hopes* (1988), *Naked* (1993) and *Secrets and Lies* (1995) gained Leigh international recognition.

**Leigh, Vivien** (1913–67) British film and stage actress. She received Academy Awards for her performances as Scarlett O'Hara in *Gone With The Wind* (1939) and for her moving portrayal of Blanche du Bois in *A Streetcar Named Desire* (1951). She was married to Laurence OLIVIER from 1937 to 1960.

**Leinster** Province in E Republic of Ireland, comprising the counties of Carlow, Dublin, Kildare, Kilkenny, Laois, Longford, Louth, Meath, Offaly, Westmeath, Wexford, and Wicklow. It is the most populous of Ireland's four provinces and includes the most fertile farmland in the whole of the country. The province's major city is DUBLIN. Area: 7,581sq mi (19,635sq km). Pop. (1991) 1,860,949.

**Leipzig** City in E central Germany, at the confluence of the Pleisse, White Elster, and Parthe rivers. Founded as a Slavic settlement in the 10th century, it became a commercial center. It was the scene of the Battle of the Nations in 1813. The birthplace of Richard Wagner, it was also home to J.S. Bach for 27 years. The printing industry (founded in 1480) is important. Industries: textiles, machinery. Pop. (1993 est.) 494,200.

**Leisler's Rebellion** (1689–91) Popular insurrection in colonial New York, led by Jacob Leisler (1640–91), a Protestant champion of King William III. The rebellion ended with Leisler's hanging, although he was posthumously pardoned by Parliament (1695).

**leitmotiv** German word for a guiding theme in musical compositions. It is a theme that recurs throughout a work, usually an OPERA or a piece of PROGRAM MUSIC.

**Leitrim** County in Connacht province, N Republic of Ireland, narrowly bounded on the NW by Donegal Bay; the capital is Carrick-on-Shannon. Hilly in the N, undulating in the S, it is drained by the Shannon River and its tributaries. Farming is the main occupation. Area 589sq mi (1,525sq km). Pop. (1991) 25,301.

**Lely, Sir Peter van der Faes** (1618–80) Dutch portrait painter, active in England. Principal Painter to CHARLES II, he is associated with the Restoration court. He established the tradition of the society portrait. His best-known paintings include two series, *The Windsor Beauties* and the famous *Admirals*.

**Lemaître, Abbé Georges Édouard** (1894–1966) Belgian astrophysicist who formulated the BIG BANG theory for the origin of the Universe. He saw the Universe as originally analogous to a radioactive atom, with all the energy and matter concentrated into a kernel, which Lemaître called the "primeval atom." He argued that an EXPANDING UNIVERSE would have originated in the explosion of that primeval atom.

**Le Mans** City in NW France; capital of Sarthe department. It is world-famous as the venue of the Le Mans 24-hour race for sports cars. Pop. (1990) 145,502.

**lemming** Any of several species of RODENTS, native to Arctic regions. They have brown fur, small ears, and a short tail. They occasionally migrate in large numbers, and some species in Norway have suffered great losses by drowning while doing so. Family Cricetidae.

**Lemmon, Jack** (1925– ) US film actor. He won an Academy Award as best supporting actor in *Mister Roberts* (1955). Lemmon won the best acotr Oscar forhis performance in *Save the Tiger* (1973). A versatile player, he has starred in Billy Wilder comedies such as *Some Like It Hot* (1959), *The Apartment* (1960), and *The Front Page* (1975), as well as in serius dramas like *The China Syndrome* (1979) and *Missing* (1982).

**lemon** Evergreen tree and its sour, yellow citrus fruit. Grown primarily in the US and subtropical regions, it is mostly used in cooking and in drinks. Height of tree: to 20ft (6m). Family Rutaceae; species *Citrus limon*.

**lemur** Any of several small primitive, mainly arboreal (tree-dwelling) and nocturnal, herbivorous PRIMATES that live in Madagascar. It resembles a squirrel, but has grasping monkey-like hands. Lemurs have changed little in 50 million years, closely resembling the ancestors of man and other primates. Family Lemuridae.

**Lena** River in E central Russia. It rises in the Baikal Mountains, flows generally N through the central Siberian uplands and empties through a wide delta into the Laptev Sea (part

► **lemur** The ring-tailed lemur (*Lemur catta*), like the 16 or so other species of lemur, is found only in Madagascar and small neighboring islands. The various species range in size, the smallest being no larger than a rat, while the largest reaches a similar size to a cat. All species are arboreal and omnivorous, feeding on fruit, insects, and small mammals.

of the Arctic Ocean). Though navigable for 2,135mi (3,437km) of its 2,730mi (4,400km) route, it is frozen from early fall to late spring.

**Lenard, Philipp Eduard Anton** (1862–1947) German physicist, b. Hungary. He was awarded the 1905 Noble Prize for physics for his studies of CATHODE RAYS. His work was important in the development of ELECTRONICS and NUCLEAR PHYSICS.

**Lendl, Ivan** (1960– ) Czech tennis player. Lendl led the world rankings for a record 270 weeks, winning seven Grand Slam singles titles, but never Wimbledon.

**lend-lease** US program of assistance during World War II. The Lend-Lease Act was passed in March 1941, before the US became a combatant. It empowered President Franklin ROOSEVELT to transfer military equipment to other countries in the US national interest. The first beneficiaries were Britain and China. The program was later extended to other allies, notably the Soviet Union.

**L'Enfant, Pierre Charles** (1754–1825) US architect and engineer, b. France. he went to America (1777) and served in the Continental army. At George Washington's invitation he planned the national capital (1791), but the high cost caused his dismissal. More than a century later the development of Washington, D.C., was pursued according to his plans.

**Lenin, Vladimir Ilyich** (1870–1924) Russian revolutionary. He evolved a revolutionary doctrine, based mainly on MARXISM, in which he emphasized the need for a vanguard party to lead the revolution. In 1900 Lenin went into exile, founding what became the BOLSHEVIKS (1903). After the first part of the RUSSIAN REVOLUTION of 1917, he returned to Russia. Lenin denounced the liberal republican government of KERENSKY and demanded armed revolt. After the Bolshevik revolution (November 1917), he became leader of the first Soviet government. He withdrew Russia from World War I and totally reorganized government and economy. In 1919 he founded the third COMMUNIST INTERNATIONAL.

**Leningrad** Former name for ST. PETERSBURG

**Lennon, John** (1940–80) English singer and songwriter, a member of the BEATLES. Lennon cowrote the vast majority of the Beatles' songs with Paul MCCARTNEY and appeared in the band's films and in *How I Won the War* (1967). He published *In His Own Write* (1964) and *A Spaniard in the Works* (1965). A major figure in the peace movement, he married Yoko Ono in 1969. He was shot dead by Mark Chapman in New York.

**LENS**

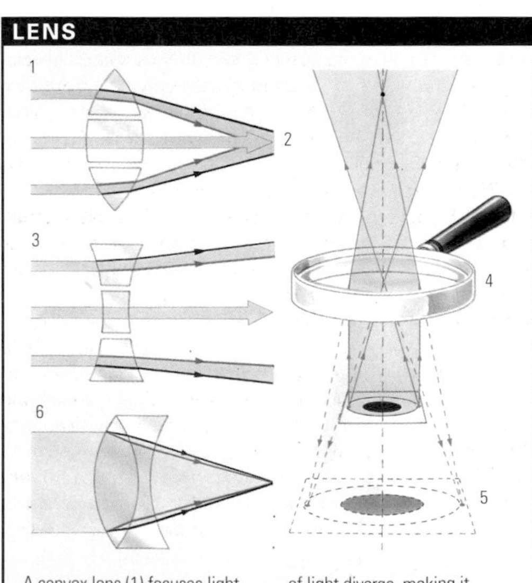


A convex lens (1) focuses light on a single point (2) by diffracting the beams of light toward each other. A concave lens (3) diffracts parallel rays of light, making them diverge. A magnifying glass (4) is a convex lens. The glass makes the rays of light diverge, making it appear that they come from a larger image (5) than is the actual case. Cameras use a combination of convex and concave lenses (6) to focus light on the film without separation of the colors of the spectrum.

◀ **Lenin** "Lenin Lived, Lenin Lives, Lenin will always Live!" Founder of the Bolsheviks and the first leader of the Soviet Union, Vladimir Ilyich Lenin retained absolute authority from November 1917 to 1922. His desire for a workers' revolution did not stop with Russia, and he worked unceasingly for a worldwide revolution. His interpretation of Marxism (Marxism-Leninism) stressed the leading role of the Communist Party in establishing communism.

**Le Nôtre, André** (1613–1700) French landscape gardener. His grandiose, geometric style established the French garden as the leading style in contemporary Europe. Le Nôtre became royal gardener in 1637 and created such farmous gardens as VERSAILLES, Chantilly, and the Tuileries in Paris.

**lens** Piece of transparent glass, plastic, quartz, or organic matter, bounded by two surfaces, usually both spherical, that changes the direction of a light beam by REFRACTION. A convex lens bends light rays toward the lens axis. A concave lens bends rays away from the axis. The optical IMAGE may be right side-up or inverted, real or virtual, and magnified or reduced in size.

**Lent** Period in the Christian year that precedes Easter. In the Western Churches it begins on Ash Wednesday and is 40 days long (Sundays are not included); in the Eastern Church it lasts 80 days (neither Saturdays nor Sundays are counted). Lent is a time of fasting, abstinence, and penitence to prepare for the remembrance of the crucifixion and resurrection of JESUS CHRIST.

**lentil** Annual plant of the pea family that grows in the Mediterranean region, SW Asia and N Africa. It is cultivated for its nutritious seeds. Height: to 20in (51cm). Family Fabaceae/Leguminosae; species *Lens culinaris*.

**Lenya, Lotte** (*c.*1898–1981) Austrian singer and actress. She became famous in two notable BRECHT plays with musical scores by her husband Kurt WEILL, namely *The Threepenny Opera* (1928) and *The Rise and Fall of the City of Mahagonny* (1930). She immigrated to the US in 1935.

**Leo I, Saint** (390–461) (Leo the Great) Pope (440–61). He established important points of doctrine, including the dual nature of Christ, which he propounded at the Council of CHALCEDON (449). By personal meetings, he saved Rome from ATTILA (452) and the Vandal leader Gaiseric (455).

**Leo III** (*c.*750–816) Pope (795–816). With the help of CHARLEMAGNE, Leo imposed his rule on Rome, and crowned Charlemagne emperor on Christmas Day, 800. This strengthened papal authority in Rome and led to recognition of the pope and emperor as religious and secular leaders of Western Christendom.

**Leo X** (1475–1521) Pope (1513–21), b. Giovanni de' Medici, son of Lorenzo de' MEDICI. He presided over the Fifth Lateran Council, which failed to enact church reforms. In 1517 Martin LUTHER published his theses at Wittenberg and was excommunicated by Leo in 1521.

**León** City in W Nicaragua, Nicaragua's second-largest city. It was founded near Lake Managua in 1524. In 1610 a severe earthquake forced the city's reconstruction on its present

▲ **leopard** The leopard (*Panthera pardus*) and the "black panther," a member of the same species but with different coloration, are found in tropical rain forests of Africa and Asia. Powerful, agile hunters, they feed on any animal they can overpower. If they are unable to consume their prey at one sitting, leopards will drag the carcass into a tree out of the reach of scavengers.

L

site.For 300 years it served as the nation's capital. In 1821, when Nicaragua gained independence from Spain, a bitter rivalry between León and Granada led to civil war. In 1858 MANAGUA was proclaimed the new capital. León was the scene of bitter fighting between SANDINISTA guerrillas and government forces in the late 1970s. Industries: food processing, leather goods, cigars, cotton. Pop. (1994 est.) 158,577.

**León** City in NW Spain; capital of León province. A military camp in Roman times, it was occupied by the Moors in the 8th century. Recaptured in 882 by Alfonso III of Asturias, it was capital of the medieval kingdom of Asturias and León until 1230. Industries: leather, cotton, textiles, iron, glass, pottery, tourism. Pop. (1991) 144,137.

**Leonardo da Vinci** (1452–1519) Florentine painter, sculptor, architect, engineer, and scientist. He was the founder of the High RENAISSANCE style. By the 1470s he had developed his characteristic style of painting figures who seem rapt in sweet melancholy. In *c.*1482 he moved to Milan where he worked mainly for Duke Ludovico Sforza. He painted the *Last Supper* (1495–98) using a new mural technique, which proved unstable. When the French invaded Milan in 1499, he left for Florence. From 1500–06 he created his finest paintings, including the *Mona Lisa*.

**Leoncavallo, Ruggiero** (1858–1919) Italian composer. He traveled all over Europe working as an accompanist and composer of music-hall songs. Of his operas, *I Pagliacci* (1892) alone has withstood the test of time.

**Leone, Sergio** (1921–89) Italian film director, creator of the "spaghetti western." The "Man With No Name" trilogy of *A Fistful of Dollars* (1964), *For a Few Dollars More* (1965), and *The Good The Bad and The Ugly* (1966) revived Clint EASTWOOD's career. The epics *Once Upon a Time in the West* (1968) and *Once Upon a Time in America* (1984) were commercially unsuccessful but later reappraised as his masterworks.

**leopard** Solitary big CAT found throughout Africa and S Asia, sometimes called a panther. It has a round head with a short nose, and a long, thin tail. The coat may be yellow and white with dark spots, or almost completely black. It feeds on birds, monkeys, antelopes, and cattle. Length: to 8ft (2.45m) including the tail; weight: to 200lb (90.6kg). Family Felidae; species *Panthera pardus*.

**Leopold I** (1640–1705) Holy Roman emperor (1658–1705). Throughout his long reign, he defended the extensive HAPSBURG dominions against foreign aggression. Leopold joined the European defensive alliances against the France of LOUIS XIV in 1686, 1689, and 1701.

**Leopold II** (1747–92) Grand Duke of Tuscany as Leopold I (1765–90); Holy Roman emperor (1790–92). The third son of MARIA THERESA, he succeededhis father, FRANCIS I, as ruler in Tuscany and his brother JOSEPH II as Holy Roman emperor. By reversing many of Joseph's reforms, Leopold pacified much of the empire. He was involved in the Declaration of Pillnitz which aimed to restore Louis SVI. It was one of the main causes of the FRENCH REVOLUTIONARY WARS.

**Leopold I** (1790–1865) First king of independent Belgium (1831–65). Son of the duke of Saxe-Coburg-Saalfield, he became a British subject after marrying the daughter of the future King George IV (1816). He was an important influence on Queen VICTORIA, his niece, and was largely responsible for her marriage to Prince Albert.

**Leopold II** (1835–1909) King of Belgium (1865–1909). He initiated colonial expansion and sponsored the expedition of Henry STANLEY to the Congo (1879–84). In 1885 he established the Congo Free State (Zaire), under his own personal rule. He was forced to cede the Congo to the Belgian state (1908).

**Leopold III** (1901–83) King of Belgium (1934–51). When the Germans invaded Belgium (1940) during World War II, he declined to accompany the government into exile and surrendered. He remained in Belgium during the war, until removed to Germany in 1944. On his return, he encountered such fierce opposition that he abdicated in favor of his son, Baudouin.

**Lepanto, Battle of** (1571) Naval engagement in the Gulf of Patras, off Lepanto, Greece. The last great battle between fleets of war galleys, it was the first major victory of the Christians over the Ottoman Turks.

**lepidoptera** Order of insects that includes MOTHS and BUTTERFLIES; they are found in every continent except Antarctica.

**leprosy** (Hansen's disease) Chronic, progressive condition affecting the skin and nerves, caused by infection with the microorganism *Mycobacterium leprae*. Lepromatous leprosy is a contagious form in which raised nodules appear on the skin and there is thickening of the skin and peripheral nerves. In tuberculoid leprosy there is loss of sensation in parts of the skin, sometimes with loss of pigmentation and hair. Now confined almost entirely to the tropics, leprosy is treated with a combination of drugs, but the nerve damage is irreversible.

**lepton** One of a class of ELEMENTARY PARTICLES. There are 12 types, including the ELECTRON and electron-NEUTRINO, muon and muon-neutrino, tau and tau-neutrino, together with their antiparticles (antileptons). Leptons are governed by the WEAK NUCLEAR FORCE. They have no QUARK substructure.

**Lermontov, Mikhail Urevich** (1814–41) Russian poet and novelist. The novel *A Hero of Our Time* (1840) and the final version of *The Demon* (1841) were written in exile.

**Le Sage, Alain René** (1668–1747) French novelist and dramatist. The best known of his 100 or so comedies is *Crispin, Rival of his Master* (1707). His novel *Histoire de Gil Blas de Santillane* (1715–35) is the first masterpiece of PICARESQUE fiction.

**lesbianism** Term that describes female HOMOSEXUALITY.

**Lesbos** (Lesvos or Mylini) Third-largest Greek island, 6mi (10km) off the NW coast of Turkey in the Aegean Sea; the capital is Mitilíni. It was settled by the Aeolians *c.*1000 BC. In the 7th and 6th centuries BC it was a cultural center. It was held at various times by Persia, Greek city-states, Macedonia, Rome, and Byzantium. The Ottomans occupied the island from 1462–1913, when it passed to Greece. Products: olives, wheat, grapes, and citrus fruits. Industries: fishing and tourism. Area: *c.*630sq mi (1,630sq km). Pop. (1991) 103,700.

**lesion** Any abnormality in a body tissue due to injury or disease. Examples are ulcers and tumors.

**Lesotho** (formerly Basutoland) Enclave kingdom within the Republic of South Africa; the capital is MASERU. **Land and climate** The scenic Drakensberg Range forms Lesotho's NE border with KWAZULU-NATAL, and includes its highest peak, Thabana Ntlenyana, at 11,424ft (3,482m). Most people live in the W lowlands, site of Maseru, or in the S valley of the Orange River, which rises in NE Lesotho and flows through South Africa to the Atlantic Ocean. All land in Lesotho is held by the king in trust for the SOTHO nation. Lesotho's climate is greatly affected by altitude; 66% of the land lies above 4,921 ft (1,500m). Maseru has warm summers and cold winters. Rainfall averages *c.*28in (700mm). Grassland covers much of Lesotho. Trees and shrubs grow only in sheltered valleys. **Economy** Lesotho is a "low-income," less-developed country. It lacks natural resources. Agriculture, mainly at subsistence level, is the main activity. Major farm products include beans, cattle, hides and skins, corn, wool, and wheat. Manufactured products include processed food, handicrafts, and textiles. Tourism is developing. **History** The early 19th-century tribal wars dispersed the Sotho. In the 1820s a Sotho kingdom was formed by Moshoeshoe I in present-day Lesotho. Moshoeshoe I was forced to yield to the British, and in 1868 the area became a protectorate. In 1871 it became part of the British Cape Colony, but after British failure to disarm the Sotho, the area fell under direct rule. Sotho opposition to incorporation into the Union of South Africa saw the creation of the independent kingdom of Lesotho in 1966. Moshoeshoe II, great-grandson of Moshoeshoe I, became king. In 1970 Leabua Jonathan suspended the constitution and banned opposition parties. The next 16 years were characterized by civil conflict between government and Basuto Congress Party (BCP) forces. In 1986 a military coup led to the reinstatement of Moshoeshoe II. In 1990 he was deposed and replaced by his son, Letsie III. The BCP won the 1992 multiparty elections and the military council was dissolved. **Recent events** In 1994 Letsie III attempted to overthrow the government. In January 1995 Moshoeshoe II was restored to the throne. His death in 1996 saw the restoration of Letsie III. In 1997 a majority of BCP politicians joined a new party, the Lesotho Congress for Democracy (LCD), thus turning the BCP into the opposition.

**less developed countries (LDCs)** Those countries, primarily of Africa, Asia, and Latin America, that have little or no industrial base. Characteristically, they have high rates of population growth, high infant mortality, short life expectancy, low levels of literacy, and poor distribution of wealth.

**Lesseps, Ferdinand Marie, Vicomte de** (1805–94) French diplomat and engineer. He conceived the idea of a canal through the isthmus of Suez, linking the Red Sea with the Mediterranean. He formed the Suez Canal Company, securing finance from the French government. Digging began in 1859 and the canal was opened in November 1869. His scheme to construct the PANAMA CANAL began in 1879, but was abandoned seven years later when his company failed.

**Lesser Antilles** *See* ANTILLES

**Lessing, Doris May** (1919– ) British novelist, b. Persia, who was brought up in Rhodesia. Her first novel, *The Grass Is Singing* (1950), is a story of racial hatred. Her *Children of Violence* quintet (1952–69)explores the social position of women; *The Golden Notebook* (1962) is a key feminist text. Lessing also wrote science fiction novels, such as *The Making of the Representative for Planet 8* (1982). Other works include *The Good Terrorist* (1985).

**Lessing, Gotthold Ephraim** (1729–81) German philosopher, writer, and critic. He portrayed his commitment to the German enlightenment in the verse play *Nathan der Weise* (1779).

**Le Tellier, Michel** (1603–85) French statesman, minister of war (1643–66) and chancellor (1677–85). As war minister, he was partly responsible for the reorganization of the French army, creating a strong, permanent, centrally controlled force. Strongly anti-Huguenot, Le Tellier signed the Revocation of the Edict of Nantes (1685).

**Lethe** In Greek mythology, the river of forgetfulness in HADES. All who drank from it lost their memories.

**lettuce** Annual plant widely cultivated in salads. Most varieties of *Lactuca sativa* are cool-weather crops. The leaves form a compact head or loose rosette.

**leucite** Gray or white feldspar mineral, a potassium aluminum silicate, $KAl(SiO_3)_2$. Unstable at high pressures, it can be found in potassium-rich lava flows and volcanic plugs. Hardness 5.5–6; sp.gr. 2.5.

**leukemia** Any of a group of cancers in which the bone marrow and other blood-forming tissues produce abnormal numbers of immature or defective LEUKOCYTES. This over-production suppresses output of normal blood cells and PLATELETS, leaving the person vulnerable to infection, anemia, and bleeding. Acute lymphoblastic leukemia (ALL) is predominantly a disease of childhood; acute myelogenous leukemia (AML) is mainly seen in older adults. Both forms are potentially curable.

**leukocyte** White blood cell, a colorless structure containing a nucleus and CYTOPLASM. There are two types of leukocytes – LYMPHOCYTES and PHAGOCYTES. Normal blood contains 5,000–10,000 leukocytes per cu in of blood. Excessive numbers of leukocytes are seen in such diseases as LEUKEMIA.

**LESOTHO**

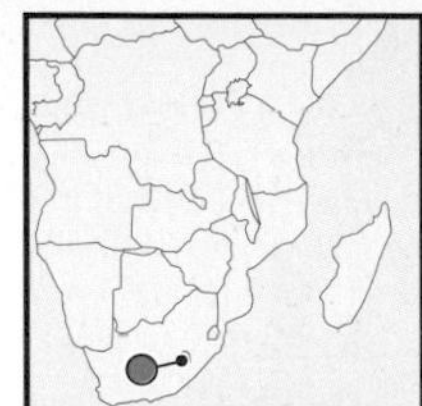

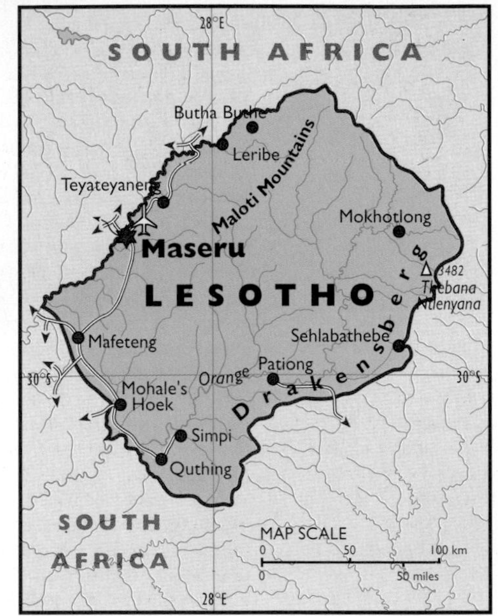


**AREA:** 11,718sq mi (30.350sq km)
**POPULATION:** 1,836,000
**CAPITAL (POPULATION):** Maseru (367,000)
**GOVERNMENT:** Constitutional monarchy
**ETHNIC GROUPS:** Sotho 99%
**LANGUAGES:** Sesotho and English (both official)
**RELIGIONS:** Christianity 93% (Roman Catholic 44%), traditional beliefs 6%
**CURRENCY:** Loti = 100 lisente

**Le Vau, Louis** (1612–70) French architect. Inspired by contemporary Italian BAROQUE buildings, he evolved a classic 17th-century French style, seen in his designs for the Palace of VERSAILLES (1669–85).

**levee** Natural embankment formed alongside a river by the deposition of silt when the river is in flood. Levees can help to prevent flooding and are sometimes built up and strengthened artificially.

**Levellers** (1645–49) Members of a radical movement in England in the COMMONWEALTH period (*c.*1645–57). They wanted sweeping parliamentary reform, religious toleration, and a fairer, more egalitarian society. In 1647 their leaders, including John LILBURNE, presented a constitution to Oliver CROMWELL. When their demands were not met, several mutinies broke out in the army, resulting in their suppression.

**lever** Simple machine used to multiply the force applied to an object, usually to raise a heavy load. A lever consists of a rod and a point (fulcrum) about which the rod pivots. An example is the crowbar.

**Leverrier, Urbain-Jean-Joseph** (1811–77) French astronomer. He successfully predicted that an unknown planet (Neptune) was responsible for discrepancies between the calculated and observed orbital motion of Uranus.

**Levi, Primo** (1919–87) Italian writer. A Jew, he joined a guerrilla movement in World War II. He was captured and

◀ **Lessing** British novelist Doris Lessing drew heavily on her childhood experiences in Rhodesia (now Zimbabwe) to create her best-known work, *The Grass is Singing* (1950). The novel's exploration of racial and sexual themes made her unpopular with the Rhodesian authorities.

L

sent to Auschwitz. Levi survived, but was haunted by the HOLOCAUST. His books, such as *If This is a Man* (1947), *The Truce* (1963), and *The Periodic Table* (1984), are attempts to deal with his experiences.

**leviathan** In Hebrew mythology, an immense serpent living in the depths of the ocean that embodied everything evil.

**Levine, James** (1943– ) US pianist and conductor. In 1964 he became assistant conductor of the Cleveland Orchestra. He was later principal conductor (1973) and then musical director (1975) of the New York METROPOLITAN OPERA. In 1982 he debuted at Bayreuth and is acknowledged as a leading interpreter of Wagner.

**Lévi-Strauss, Claude** (1908–90) French anthropologist. In *The Elementary Structures of Kinship* (1949) and *Structural Anthropology* (1958), Lévi-Strauss outlined the science of STRUCTURALISM. In 1959 he became professor of anthropology at the College of France. In 1973 he was elected to the Académie Française.

**Levites** Clan of religious officials in ancient Israel. It is possible that they once were one of the 12 tribes of Israel mentioned in the Old Testament, descended from Levi, the third son of JACOB. By the time of JESUS CHRIST, the Levites ran the entire Temple organization with the exception of the priesthood.

**Leviticus** Third book of the PENTATEUCH or TORAH. It is primarily a manual for the instruction of priests.

**Lewis, (Frederick) Carl (Carlton)** (1961– ) US track and field athlete. In a glittering career, Lewis won nine Olympic gold medals: 100m, 200m, 4×100m relay and long jump (1984, Los Angeles), equalling Jesse OWENS' feat; 100m and long jump (Seoul, 1988); long jump and 4×100m relay (Barcelona, 1992); and long jump (Atlanta, 1996). Lewis set 100m world records at the Seoul Olympics (9.97sec) and the 1991 World Championships (9.86sec).

L

**Lewis, C.S. (Clive Staples)** (1898–1963) English scholar, critic, and writer. He is best known for his religious and moral books written after his conversion to Christianity, particularly *The Screwtape Letters* (1942) and his autobiography *Surprised by Joy* (1955). Lewis wrote a number of highly acclaimed children's books, including *The Lion, the Witch and the Wardrobe* (1950).

**Lewis, John Llewellyn** (1880–1969) US labor leader. He served as president of the United Mine Workers (UMW) from 1920 to 1960. After splitting with the American Federation of Labor (AFL) over the unionization of mass-production industries, he formed the CONGRESS OF INDUSTRIAL ORGANIZATIONS (CIO) and was its president from 1935 to 1940. His strikes during World War II led to the restrictive legislation.

**Lewis, Meriwether** (1774–1809) US explorer. An army officer, he was secretary to Thomas JEFFERSON, who chose him to lead the expedition to the Pacific (1804). In 1808 he was appointed governor of Louisiana Territory. He died of a gunshot wound, either by suicide or murder. *See also* LEWIS AND CLARK EXPEDITION

**Lewis, (Harry) Sinclair** (1885–1951) US writer. His first novel, *Main Street* (1920), set out his central theme – the hypocrisy and parochialism of small town, Midwestern society. *Babbitt* (1922), often cited as his greatest work, is the story of a businessman who refuses to conform. Lewis refused the Pulitzer Prize for *Arrowsmith* (1925). In 1930 he became the first US writer to be awarded the Nobel Prize for literature.

**Lewis, (Percy) Wyndham** (1884–1957) British painter, critic, and novelist. He was the central figure of the VORTICISM movement. His work was greatly influenced by FUTURISM and NIETZSCHE. After World War I he produced a series of novels and essays.

**Lewis and Clark Expedition** (1804–06) US expedition to seek a route by water from the Mississippi to the Pacific Ocean. Instigated by President JEFFERSON, it was led by army officers Meriwether LEWIS and William Clark, with the assistance of a Shoshone woman, SÁCAJAWEA. It reached the Pacific at the mouth of the Columbia River and produced valuable information about the country and peoples of the Northwest.

**Lexington** City in the bluegrass region of NE central Kentucky. The city is a famous breeding ground for thoroughbred horses. It also has the world's largest tobacco market. Other industries: automobile parts, electrical machinery, distilling. Pop. (1992) 232,252.

**Lexington and Concord, Battles of** (April 1775) First battles of the AMERICAN REVOLUTION. British troops marching from Boston to Concord, Massachusetts, were intercepted by MINUTEMEN (militiamen) at Lexington Green. Several minutemen were killed, and the British advanced to Concord and destroyed military supplies. Returning to Boston the British were involved in several skirmishes and suffered nearly 300 casualties.

**Leyden jar** Earliest and simplest device for storing static electricity, developed *c.*1745 in Leyden, Holland. The original electrical condenser (capacitor), it consists of a foil-lined glass jar partly filled with water and closed with a cork through which protrudes a brass rod wired to the foil. To charge the jar, friction is applied to the tip of the rod.

**Leyte Gulf, Battle of** Air and naval engagement between Japanese and US forces in the Philippines in October 1944. In the battle, the largest naval battle in history, the Japanese navy suffered severe losses.

**Lhasa** Capital of Tibet (Xizang Zizhiqu) Autonomous Region, in SW China, on a tributary of the Brahmaputra, at 11,800ft (3,600m) in the N Himalayas. An ancient religious center, it was occupied by the Chinese in 1951. After the Tibetan revolt against the occupation (1959–60), many of Lhasa's temples and monasteries were closed. The 17th-century Potala Palace was the home of the DALAI LAMA. Today the city is an important trading center, also manufacturing chemicals and processing gold and copper. Pop. (1992) 124,000.

**liana** Any ground-rooting woody vine that twines and creeps extensively over other plants for support; it is common in tropical forests. Some species may reach a diameter of 24in (60cm) and a length of 330ft (100m).

**Liaoning** Coastal province in NE China, bordering North Korea; the capital is Shenyang. Japan conquered the Liaotung peninsula during the RUSSO-JAPANESE WAR (1904–05) and developed the province's industries and railroads. It later formed part of the Japanese puppet state MANCHUKUO (1932–45). After World War II it fell under the joint control of Russia and China. Since 1955 it has been a Chinese province. Liaoning is the chief site of China's heavy industry. The province has rich coal and iron ore reserves and supplies 20% of China's electrical power. It includes the cities of Anshan, Fushun, and Dalian (China's major port). The principal river is the Liao. Area: 58,300sq mi (151,000sq km). Pop. (1990) 39,980,000.

**Libby, Willard Frank** (1908–80) US chemist. From 1941–45 he worked on the separation of isotopes for the atom bomb. This led to his development of radioactive carbon-14 dating, for which he was awarded the 1960 Noble Prize for chemistry.

**libel** Permanent, false statement to a third person containing an imputation against the reputation of another. Any defamatory publications in permanent form (such as an article, picture, film, or broadcast statement) are treated as libel. Although usually a civil offense, libel may be considered criminal in certain circumstances. In the US, libel against public figures must be proven factually incorrect and made with malicious intent.

**Liberal Democrats** (officially, Social and Liberal Democrats) British political party, formed in March 1988 by the merger of the LIBERAL PARTY and the Social Democratic Party (SDP). Since 1988 it has been led by Paddy ASHDOWN. The smallest of the main political parties, it has vigorously campaigned for PROPORTIONAL REPRESENTATION (PR).

**liberalism** Political and intellectual belief that advocates the right of the individual to make decisions, usually political or religious, according to the dictates of conscience. Its modern origins lie in the 18th-century ENLIGHTENMENT. In politics it opposes arbitrary power and discrimination against minorities.

**Liberal Party** British political party. It grew out of the early 19th-century WHIG PARTY. The first official use of the name was the National Liberal Federation (1877), founded by Joseph CHAMBERLAIN. Its predominant interests were free trade, religious and individual liberty, financial retrenchment, and constitutional reform. Its greatest leader was William

GLADSTONE, who led four governments (1868–74, 1880–85, 1885–86, and 1892–94). The 1906 government of Campbell-Bannerman legalized TRADE UNIONS, reformed the House of Lords and introduced progressive SOCIAL SECURITY measures. In 1908 Herbert ASQUITH became leader and prime minister. In 1916 LLOYD GEORGE formed a coalition government with the CONSERVATIVE PARTY. Since that administration, it has never formed a government. After the formation of the Social Democratic Party (SDP) in 1980, the Liberal Party entered into an alliance, and then merged with it in 1987. In 1988 the Liberal members and most of the SDP formed the LIBERAL DEMOCRATS. A small Liberal Party still exists.

**Liberal Party** Canadian political party. Holding principles similar to the British Liberal Party, it was formed in 1854. Its first administration (1873–78), under Alexander Mackenzie, was anti-railroad and advocated free trade. Under Wilfrid LAURIER (1896–1911), the Liberals supported ethnic conciliation, independence, and immigration. Later, it held power under Lester PEARSON (1963–68), Pierre TRUDEAU (1968–79, 1980–84), John Turner (1984), and Jean CHRÉTIEN (1993– ).

**Liberal Republican Party** US political party organized in the late 1860s by Republican leaders to protest the conservative policies and scandals of Ulysses S. GRANT's first administration. Liberal Republicans favored leniency to the South, civil service reform, and a lower tariff. Leaders of the party included Carl Schurz, Charles Francis ADAMS, and Horace GREELEY. Greeley, the party's presidential candidate in the 1872 campaign, was defeated, and the movement died out.

**Liberia** Republic in w Africa on the Atlantic coast. **Land and climate** Liberia's Atlantic coast stretches over 311mi (500km), and is the site of the capital and chief port, MONROVIA. A narrow coastal plain rises to a plateau region, with the highest land on the border with Guinea. The most important rivers are the Cavally, which forms the border with Ivory Coast, and the St. Paul. Liberia has a tropical climate with high annual temperatures and humidity. There are two rainy seasons. Mangrove swamps and lagoons line the coast, while inland, forests cover nearly 40% of the land. Liberia also has areas of tropical savanna. Only 5% of the land is cultivated. **Economy** Civil war has devastated Liberia's economy. Until the 1950s Liberia was a plantation economy. Agriculture still employs 75% of the work force, mainly at subsistence level. Chief food crops include cassava, rice, and sugar cane. Rubber, cocoa, and coffee are grown for export. Timber is also exported. Crude materials, principally iron ore, account for over 90% of Liberia's exports. **History** Liberia was founded in 1821 by the AMERICAN COLONIZATION SOCIETY. In 1822 the Society landed African-American former slaves at a coastal settlement, which they named Monrovia. In 1847 Liberia became a fully independent republic. For many years Americo-Liberians controlled Liberia's government, and the US Firestone Company's rubber plantations covered over 1 million acres (400,000ha). Under the leadership (1944–71) of William Tubman, Liberia's economy grew and social reforms were adopted. Tubman's successor, William R. Tolbert, was assassinated in a military coup in 1980, and Master-Sergeant Samuel Doe led the new military government. Doe's brutal and corrupt regime won a fraudulent election in 1985. In 1990 civil war broke out, and the Economic Community of West African States (ECOWAS) sent a five-nation peacekeeping force. Doe was assassinated and an interim government, led by Amos Sawyer, was formed. **Recent events** Civil war raged on, and by mid-1993, an estimated 150,000 people had died and hundreds of thousands were homeless. In 1995 a ceasefire was agreed and a council of state, composed of formerly warring leaders, was established. Conflict resumed when one faction's leader, Roosevelt Johnson, was dismissed from the council. A further ceasefire was agreed in July 1996. In 1997 elections, former warlord Charles Taylor and his National Patriotic Council secured a resounding victory.

**Liberty Bell** Historic US monument in front of Independence Hall, Philadelphia. According to legend, it was rung in July 1776 to celebrate the signing of the American Declaration of Independence.

**libido** In psychoanalysis, term used by Sigmund FREUD to describe instinctive sexual energy. Freud later enlarged its meaning to include all mental energy (or life energy) that accompanies strong desires.

**library, US public** US tax-supported institution open t all citizens in the community where it is located. The first free public tax-supported local library in the US was probably at Peterborough, NewHampshire (1833); the first in a city was at Boston (1854). Andrew CARNEGIE endowed more than 1,400 libraries from 1897 to 1917.

**Library of Congress** US national library located in Washington, D.C. It is supported mainly by congressional appropriations. The library was originally established (1800) to serve as a research facility for members of Congress. Its responsibilities have been expanded to include copyrighting, inter-library loans, and the publication of cumulative catalogs. Its collection includes more than 60,000,000 items. Its librarian is appointed by the president and confirmed by Congress.

**libretto** Text of an opera or operetta. From 1597 libretti were printed to commemorate performances; by the mid-18th century, public audiences used them to follow the opera's story. A number of composers have written their own libretti, notably Wagner.

**Libreville** Capital and largest city of Gabon, w central Africa, at the mouth of the Gabon River, on the Gulf of Guinea. Founded by the French in 1843 and named Libreville (Fr. Freetown) in 1849, it was initially a refuge for escaped slaves. The city has expanded with the development of the country's minerals and is now also an administrative center. Other industries: timber (hardwoods), palm oil, and rubber. Pop. (1993) 418,000.

**Libya** Republic in n Africa. See country feature, page 398

**lice** *See* LOUSE

**lichen** Plant consisting of a FUNGUS in which microscopic (usually single-celled) ALGAE are embedded. The fungus and its algae form a symbiotic association in which the fungus contributes support, water, and minerals, while the algae contribute food produced by PHOTOSYNTHESIS. *See also* SYMBIOSIS

**Lichtenstein, Roy** (1923–97) US painter, sculptor, and graphic artist. He is regarded as a leading exponent of POP ART. Among his best-known paintings are *Whaam!* (1963) and *Good Morning, Darling* (1964).

**licorice** *See* LIQUORICE

## LIBERIA

**AREA:** 43,000sq mi (111,370sq km)
**POPULATION:** 2,580,000
**CAPITAL (POPULATION):** Monrovia (425,000)
**GOVERNMENT:** Multiparty republic
**ETHNIC GROUPS:** Kpelle 19%, Bassa 14%, Grebo 9%, Gio 8%, Kru 7%, Mano 7%
**LANGUAGES:** English (official)
**RELIGIONS:** Christianity 68%, Islam 14%, traditional beliefs and others 18%,
**CURRENCY:** Liberian dollar = 100 cents

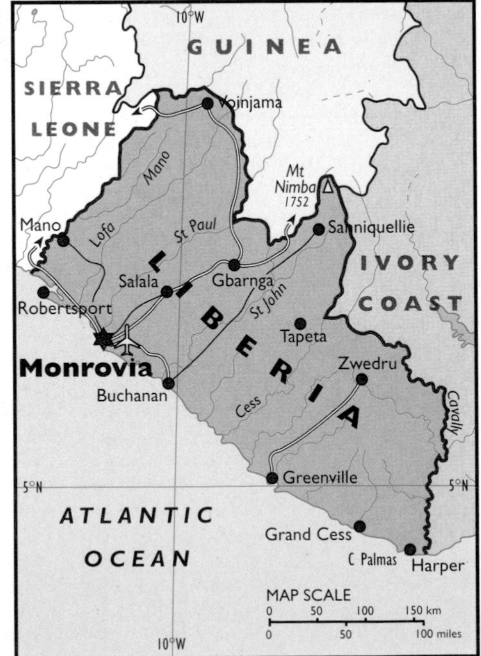

**Lie, Trygve Halvdan** (1896–1968) Norwegian statesman, first secretary-general of the UNITED NATIONS (UN) (1946–52). He blamed both sides for the COLD WAR, but antagonized the Soviet Union by his support for UN intervention in the Korean War (1950).

**Liebig, Baron Justus von** (1803–73) German chemist. He was the first to realize that animals use oxygen to get energy from food. Liebig also showed that plants derive their minerals from the soil, and introduced synthetic fertilizers into agriculture.

**Liebknecht, Karl** (1871–1919) German communist revolutionary. With Rosa LUXEMBURG, he was a leader of the communist group known as the SPARTACISTS. After the failure of the Spartacist rising (1919), they were murdered while in police custody.

**Liebknecht, Wilhelm** (1826–1900) German revolutionary. After taking part in the REVOLUTION OF 1848, he was exiled to England where he became an associate of Karl Marx. In 1863 he was a founder of the Marxist German Socialist Party. He was elected to the Reichstag (parliament) in 1874.

**Liechtenstein** Independent principality in W central Europe at the E end of the Alps, between Austria (E) and Switzerland (W); the capitalof the principality is Vaduz. The principality was formed in 1719 through the merging of Vaduz and Schellenberg. It remained part of the Holy Roman Empire until 1806. A member of the German Confederation from 1815, it gained independent status in 1866. In 1921 Liechtenstein entered into a currency union with Switzerland and, in 1923, a customs union. Until 1990 Switzerland also handled its foreign policy. In 1990 the principality joined the UN. Liechtenstein has a constitutional and hereditary monarchy, the ruling family is the Austrian house of Liechtenstein. Women could not vote until 1984. Liechtenstein is the fourth-smallest country in the world and one of the richest (1992 GDP per capita, $34,000). Since 1945 it has rapidly developed a specialized manufacturing base. The major part of state revenue is derived from international companies attracted by the low taxation rates. Tourism is increasingly important. It is also world-famous for its postage stamps. Area: 61sq mi (157sq km). Pop. (1990) 28,777.

**lied** (Ger. song) It has a more specific connotation in current usage as the art song of German Romantic composers – especially Franz Schubert, Hugo Wolf, Johannes Brahms, and Robert Schumann.

**lie detector** (polygraph) Electronic device that may be capable of detecting lies. The lie detector monitors such fac-

## LIBYA

Libya's flag was adopted in 1977. It replaced the flag of the Federation of Arab Republics, which Libya left in that year. Libya's flag is the simplest of all world flags. It represents the country's quest for a green revolution in agriculture.

**AREA:** 679,358SQ MI (1,759,540SQ KM)
**POPULATION:** 4,875,000
**CAPITAL (POPULATION):** Tripoli (990,697)
**GOVERNMENT:** Single-party socialist state
**ETHNIC GROUPS:** Libyan Arab and Berber 89%, others 11%
**LANGUAGES:** Arabic (official)
**RELIGIONS:** Islam
**CURRENCY:** Libyan dinar = 1,000 dirhams

The North African state of Libya consists of three geographical areas: the NW and NE Mediterranean coastal plains are home to the majority of Libya's population. The NE plain includes Libya's capital, TRIPOLI; the NW plain its second-largest city, BENGHAZI. The SAHARA occupies 95% of Libya, inhabited only at scattered oases. The desert rises to 7,500ft (2,286m) at Bette Peak, on the S border with Chad.

### CLIMATE

The coastal plains have a Mediterranean climate, with hot, dry summers and mild, moist winters. Inland, the average annual rainfall drops to 4in (100mm) or less.

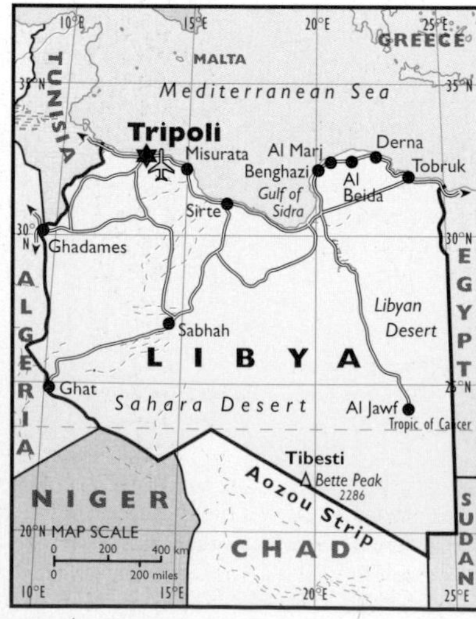


### VEGETATION

Shrubs and grasses grow on the N coasts, with some trees in wetter areas. At the desert oases date palms provide shade from the sun.

### HISTORY

The earliest known inhabitants of Libya were the BERBERS. Between the 7th century BC and the 5th century AD, the region came under the rule of Greeks, Carthaginians, Romans, and Vandals. Magnificent Roman ruins survive. Arabs invaded Libya in AD 642 and Islam remains the dominant religion. From 1551 Libya was part of the Turkish Ottoman empire, power resided with local rulers or JANISSARIES. During the 17th century Barbary pirates used bases on the Libyan coast to attack shipping. In the 19th century US, British, and French forces attempted to curb their power. Italy invaded Libya in 1911, and by 1914 had conquered the whole territory. Attempts at colonization were made in the 1930s and in 1939 Libya was formally incorporated into Italy. During World War II the country was a battleground for many of the North Africa Campaigns. Following the Allied victory Libya was placed under UN mandate until 1951, when it became an independent monarchy. In 1953 Libya joined the Arab League, and in 1955 became a member of the UN. In 1969 the king was overthrown in a military coup led by Colonel Muammar al-QADDAFI. A Revolutionary Command Council set about the nationalization of industry, the establishment of an Islamic state, and the reduction of foreign interference. In 1970 the British closed all their military bases. In 1971 Libya entered a Federation with Egypt and Syria. Libya maintained an anti-Israel foreign policy and Qaddafi aided Palestinian guerrilla movements. During the 1980s Libyan and US relations deteriorated further. Following an attack on US forces, the US placed an oil embargo on Libya. In 1986, following evidence of Libyan support of international terrorism, the US bombed Tripoli and Benghazi. In 1992 Libya was accused of sheltering the terrorists responsible for the bombing of a domestic airliner over Lockerbie, and economic sanctions were imposed. Libya has a long-standing territorial dispute with Chad, and sent troops to intervene in the civil war. In 1994 the International Court of Justice dismissed Libya's claim to the Aozou Strip in N Chad.

### POLITICS

Qaddafi has attracted worldwide criticism for his support for revolutionary movements. In 1995 all Palestinians were deported from Libya in protest against the PLO-Israeli peace agreement.

### ECONOMY

The discovery of oil in 1958 transformed Libya's economy. Oil revenue was used to finance welfare services and development projects. Formerly one of the world's poorest countries, it has become Africa's richest in terms of its GDP per capita (1992, $9,782). Oil accounts for over 95% of exports, and Libya remains a developing country because of this structural imbalance. Libya has oil refineries and petrochemical plants. Agriculture is important, but it is dependent on food imports.

tors as heart rate, breathing rate, and perspiration, all of which may be affected when a person lies.

**Liège** (Flemish, Luik) City and river port in E Belgium, at the confluence of the Meuse and Ourthe rivers; capital of Liège province. Settled in Roman times, it became part of Belgium in 1830. During the 19th century it was one of the first steel-making and coal-mining centers. It was occupied by the Germans in both World Wars and severely damaged in the Battle of the Bulge (1944–45). After World War II the city's steel industry drastically declined. Liège is a commercial center. Industries: chemicals, electronics. Pop. (1991) 195,201.

**life** Feature of organisms that sets them apart from inorganic matter. Life can be regarded as the ability to obtain energy from the Sun or from food and to use this for growth and reproduction. The current theory on life's origin is that giant molecules, similar to proteins and nucleic acids, reacted together in the watery surface environment of the young Earth that is now commonly called the primordial soup.

**life expectancy** Potential length of individual human life based on the average for any given group. It is affected by such things as teh economy, modernization, health standards, and infant mortality rates.

**lift** In AERODYNAMICS, force that acts upward on the undersurface of an AIRFOIL, or wing. The lift force is a result of the upward pressure underneath the airfoil being greater than the downward pressure on the top.

**ligament** Bands of tough fibrous CONNECTIVE TISSUE that join bone to bone at the joints.

**Ligeti, György** (1923– ) Hungarian composer whose avant-garde works involve shifting patterns of tone colors. After 1956, Ligeti's work on electronic sound influenced his compositions, especially *Atmosphères* (1961) and *Lux Aeterna* (1966).

**light** Part of the total electromagnetic spectrum that can be detected by the human eye. Visible light is in the wavelength range from about 400nm (violet) to 770nm (red). Light exhibits typical phenomena of wave motion, such as REFLECTION, REFRACTION, DIFFRACTION, light polarization, and INTERFERENCE. In the 17th century Isaac NEWTON believed in a particle theory of light. The wave theory was well-established by the second decade of the 19th century after the work of Thomas Young. At the beginning of the 20th century, experiments on the PHOTOELECTRIC EFFECT and the work of Max PLANCK revived the idea that light can behave like a stream of particles. This dilemma was resolved by the QUANTUM THEORY, according to which light consists of elementary particles called PHOTONS. When light interacts with matter, as in the photoelectric effect, energy is exchanged in the form of photons and so light seems to be particles. Otherwise, it behaves as a wave.

**lighthouse** Building, often in the form of a tower, with a light at the top to guide vessels at night. Lighthouses are built on land and at sea. Some mark ports and harbors, while others warn of shallow waters or dangerous rocks. Originally, a lighthouse keeper was always in attendence, but modern lighthouses are often unmanned and operated by remote control. The light system may produce a steady beam, a rotating beam, or a pattern of flashes. Today, lighthouses are becoming less important as many vessels are equipped with highly accurate satellite-aided navigation equipment called GPS (Global Positioning System).

**lightning** Visible flash of light accompanying an electrical discharge between clouds or between clouds and the surface, most commonly produced in a THUNDERSTORM.

**light-year** Unit of astronomical distance equal to the distance traveled in free space or a vacuum by light in one tropical year. One light-year is equal to $5.88 \times 10^{12}$ mi ($9.4607 \times 10^{12}$ km).

**lignin** Complex noncarbohydrate substance in woody tissues (especially XYLEM of plants), often in combination with cellulose. It is lignin that gives wood its strength. To obtain pure cellulose for the paper and rayon industries, the lignin has to be removed.

**lilac** Any of 20 species of evergreen ornamental shrubs and small trees of the genus *Syringa*, which bear pointed clusters of tiny fragrant white to purple flowers. Height: to 20ft (6m). Family Oleaceae.

**Lilburne, John** (1614–57) English republican, leader of the LEVELERS. Imprisoned (1638–40) under CHARLES I, he fought for Parliament during the CIVIL WAR (1642–45). Captured, he escaped execution when Parliament arranged an exchange of prisoners. Demanding greater equality and religious freedom, he led protests against the government of CROMWELL. Often imprisoned, he spent his last years among Quakers.

**Lilienthal, Otto** (1849–96) German engineer and pioneer of glider design. In 1891 Lilienthal became the first person to control a glider in flight. He made about 2,500 more flights before his death in a crash.

**Lille** (Flemish, Lisle) City in NW France, near the Belgian border; capital of Nord department. A fortified town in the 11th century, it changed hands several times in its history. It flourished in the 16th century under the dukes of Burgundy. In the late 17th century Lille became capital of French Flanders, and the building of its stock exchange established its commercial reputation. Lille is a major industrial, commercial, and cultural city. Industries: textiles, engineering. Pop. (1990) 172,142.

**lily** Any of species of perennial, BULB-producing plants of the genus *Lilium*, from temperate and subtropical regions. They have erect stems and various leaf arrangements. The showy flowers may be almost any color.

**lily of the valley** Perennial woodland plant native to Europe, Asia, and E US. It has broad, elongated leaves and bears stalks of tiny, white, bell-shaped fragrant flowers. Family Liliaceae; species *Convallaria majalis*.

**Lima** Capital and largest city of Peru, on the Rímac River at the foot of the Cerro San Cristóbal. Lima was founded in 1535 by Francisco PIZARRO. It functioned as the capital of the Spanish New World colonies until the 19th century. During the War of the Pacific, Lima was occupied by Chilean forces (1881–83). It is the commercial and cultural center of Peru. With the oil-refining port of Callao, the Lima metropolitan area is the third-largest city of South America, and handles over 75% of Peru's manufacturing. Pop. (1993) 6,386,308.

**limb** Jointed extension of the vertebrate body, used for locomotion and manipulation of the environment.

**limbic system** Collection of structures in the middle of the brain. Looped around the HYPOTHALAMUS, the limbic system is thought to be involved in emotional responses, such as fear and aggression, the production of mood changes, and the laying down of memories.

**limbo** In Roman Catholic theology, the abode of souls excluded from HEAVEN but not condemned to any other punishment. This concept, which never became doctrine, said unbaptized infants go to limbo after death.

**Limbourg, Pol de** (active 1380–1416) Franco-Flemish manuscript illustrator. Pol and his brothers, Jan and Hermann, became court painters to Jean, duc de Berry in 1411. Their masterpiece is a Book of Hours known as *Les Très Riches Heures du Duc de Berry* (1413–15). *See also* ILLUMINATION

**lime** Name for any of the deciduous linden trees that grow in the N temperate zone. It has serrated, heart-shaped leaves with small, fragrant, yellowish flowers. The American lime, *T. americana*, is also called basswood. Family Tiliaceae.The common British linden, *Tilia vulgaris*, is one of the three British species.

**lime** Small tropical tree (*Citrus aurantifolia*) of the rue family (Rutaceae). The trees grow to 8–15ft (2.4–4.6m) and yield small, green, acid fruits. The juice was valuable in the 18th and 19th centuries on long sea voyages; the vitamin C helped to ward off SCURVY.

**Limerick** City on the Shannon estuary, SW Republic of Ireland; capital of Limerick county, Munster province. In the 9th century it was sacked by Norse invaders. At the beginning of the 11th century, Brian Boru made Limerick the capital of Munster. In the 12th century the city was occupied by English forces who built a castle. During the

▲ **lily** Grown mainly in temperate and tropical regions, the showy displays of color make lilies a common sight in gardens in many regions of the world. Most lilies thrive in well-drained, moist soil and a sunny location.

L

▲ **lime** The American lime or linden (*Tilia americana*), also known as American basswood, has some of the largest leaves found on deciduous trees, with examples reaching 12in (30cm) long. In the past the wood was widely used in carving, because it was firm but workable.

▲ **limpet** The conical shell of limpets (*Patella sp* shown) differs from most other gastropods, which have coiled shells. Found in rocky, coastal regions of the Pacific and Atlantic, limpets remain attached to the rock by a muscular "foot," occasionally leaving their position to feed on seaweed.

▲ **Lincoln** US president Abraham Lincoln was born into a frontier family and received little formal education as a boy. After reading law, he was elected to the House of Representatives in 1847. The highly publicized Lincoln-Douglas debates over the pro-slavery Kansas-Nebraska Act won Lincoln national fame. He went on to win the presidential election of 1860, and his dogged determination to retain the Union and refuse Southern secession brought about the start of the Civil War.

► **ling** A member of the cod family, the various species of ling (Molva molva shown) are a commercially important fish. They are long-bodied fish, growing to 7ft (2m) and weighing up to 45lb (20kg).

17th century the city was besieged by both the armies of Oliver Cromwell and William III. Industries: lacemaking, salmon fishing. Pop. (1993 est.) 75,436.

**limestone** SEDIMENTARY ROCK composed primarily of carbonates. Generally formed from deposits of the skeletons of marine invertebrates, it is used to make cement and lime and as a building material.

**Limoges** City on the Vienne river, W central France; capital of the department of Haute-Vienne. A Roman settlement, it was later a tribal capital of the Gauls. Its enamel industry culminated in the 16th-century craftsmanship of Léonard Limousin, but was devastated during the Thirty Years' War. In the late 18th century, the city flourished once more with the establishment of manufacturing porcelain. Since 1945 economic expansion has been led by the exploitation of uranium mines near Ambazac. Pop. (1990) 133,464

**limpet** Primitive gastropod MOLLUSK commonly found fixed to rocks along marine shores. It has a caplike shell and a large muscular foot. Length: to 5in (13cm). Families: Patellacea, Acmaeidae, and Fissurellidae.

**Limpopo** (Crocodile) River in S Africa. It rises in NE South Africa, in the former Transvaal province. It forms part of the border between South Africa and Botswana, then the border of South Africa and Zimbabwe before crossing Mozambique to enter the Indian Ocean NE of Maputo. Length: *c.*1,100mi (1,770km).

**Lin Biao** (1907–71) Chinese communist general and political leader. He defeated CHIANG KAI-SHEK in Manchuria (1948), helping to secure the victory of the communists in 1949. Lin was a leader of the CULTURAL REVOLUTION (1966–69) and compiled the book of quotations from MAO ZEDONG known as the *Little Red Book.*

**Lincoln, Abraham** (1809–65) 16th US President (1861–65). Elected to the Illinois legislature for the WHIG PARTY in 1834, he studied to become a lawyer. He served in the House of Representatives (1847–49) and unsuccessfully ran for the Senate for the new REPUBLICAN PARTY against Stephen A. DOUGLAS in 1858. He was Republican candidate for president in 1860. Lincoln's victory made the secession of the Southern, slave-owning states inevitable, and his determination to defend FORT SUMTER began the CIVIL WAR. A strong commander-in-chief, he played a leading role in military planning. In September 1862 he issued the EMANCIPATION PROCLAMATION, and in November 1863 delivered his famous GETTYSBURG ADDRESS. Lincoln was reelected in 1864 and saw the war to a successful conclusion. On April 14, 1865, five days after the surrender of Robert E. LEE, he was shot by John Wilkes BOOTH, a Southern sympathizer. He died the next day.

**Lincoln** City in E England; the county town of LINCOLNSHIRE. Founded by the Romans as Lindum Colonia, it thrived on its wool trade until the 14th century. The castle was begun in the reign of William I. Lincoln Cathedral (begun *c.*1073) has one of the original copies of the Magna Carta. Industries: agricultural and automobile parts. Pop. (1991) 81,900.

**Lincoln** State capital and second-largest city of Nebraska. Founded in 1856 as Lancaster, its name was changed in honor of Abraham LINCOLN. The city was made state capital when Nebraska was admitted to the Union in 1867. Lincoln is a center for livestock and grain, and more recently for insurance. Industries: rubber products, pharmaceuticals. Pop. (1990) 191,972.

**Lincoln-Douglas Debates** Series of seven 1858 debates between Senator Stephen DOUGLAS and Abraham LINCOLN. Douglas was the incumbent Democrat running for the US Senate seat from Illinois. Lincoln was the Republican candidate. Although Lincoln lost the election, his view of slavery as a "moral, social, and political wrong" enhanced his national standing.

**Lincolnshire** County in E England, bordering the North Sea; the county town is LINCOLN. The area was settled by the Romans and an Anglo-Saxon kingdom was later established in Lindsey. In the Middle Ages it was a prosperous farming region. In 1974 part of N Lincolnshire was incorporated into the new authority of Humberside. Apart from the undulating Wolds, the region is flat, drained by the Trent, Welland, and Witham rivers. Agriculture is the mainstay of the economy, mainly cereals, sugar beets, and sheep. Area 2,273sq mi (5,886sq km). Pop. (1994) 605,800.

**Lind, Jenny** (1820–87) ("Swedish nightingale") Sweden's most famous operatic soprano. She made her debut in 1838, and after world success in coloratura roles she settled in London (*c.*1852).

**Lindbergh, Charles Augustus** (1902–74) US aviator. He became an international hero when, in *The Spirit of St. Louis*, he made the first nonstop transatlantic solo flight, from New York to Paris (1927) in 33 hours 30 minutes. In 1932 his baby son was kidnapped and murdered.

**Lindisfarne Gospels** Manuscript illuminated in the Hiberno-Saxon style in the late 7th or 8th century. It may have been executed for Eadfrith, Bishop of Lindisfarne (698–721).

**Lindsay, (Nicholas) Vachel** (1879–1931) US author who styled himself "the vagabond poet." He traveled throughout the US holding poetic revival meetings to stimulate a popular taste for poetry through what he called the "higher vaudeville." *The Congo and Other Poems* (1914) and *General William Booth Enters into Heaven* (1913) contain much of his best work.

**linear script** Early form of writing, found on clay tablets in Crete and Greece. Linear A was in extensive use during the middle period of the MINOAN CIVILIZATION (*c.*2100–*c.*1450 BC). Linear B was an adaptation of Linear A, used by the MYCENAEAN CIVILIZATION of mainland Greece to write their early form of Greek. Linear B was used from *c.*1450 BC to the end of the Mycenaean period, *c.*1150 BC. In 1952 Michael Ventris deciphered Linear B; Linear A still defies analysis.

**linen** Yarn and fabric made of fibers from the FLAX plant. The fibers are released from the substance that binds them by retting (soaking) the long stems in water. The fibers are spun to form yarn, which is then woven.

**ling** Food fish related to the COD found in the Atlantic Ocean. It is brown and silver and has long dorsal and ventral fins. Length: to 7ft (2m); weight: 8lb (3.6kg). Family Gadidae; species *Molva molva.*

**lingua franca** Language that serves as a medium of communication between people who otherwise lack a common tongue. PIDGIN English is an example.

**linguistics** Systematic study of LANGUAGE, its nature, structure, constituent elements, and changes. As a discipline, linguistics embraces PHONETICS, phonology (the study of sound systems within languages), GRAMMAR (including SYNTAX), SEMANTICS, and pragmatics (the study of language use).

**Linnaeus, Carolus** (1707–78) (Carl von Linné) Swedish botanist and taxonomist. His *Systema Naturae*, published in 1735, laid the foundation of the modern science of TAXONOMY by including all known organisms in a single classification system. He devised the system of BINOMIAL NOMENCLATURE, which gave standardized Latin names to every organism.

**linseed** *See* FLAX

**linseed oil** Oil pressed from seeds of cultivated FLAX *(Linum usitatissimum)*. Because of its drying qualities, it is an important ingredient of oil paints and printing inks and is used to make VARNISH and linoleum.

**Linz** City in NW Austria and a major port on the Danube River; capital of Upper Austria. Founded in Roman times as Lentia, it became a provincial capital of the Holy Roman Empire in the late 15th century. Austria's third-largest city, Linz is a commercial and industrial center. Manufactured goods include iron and steel, chemicals, and fertilizers. Pop. (1991) 203,044.

◀ **lion** Prides of lions (Panthera leo) are commonly seen lazing in the shade of a tree. Lionesses, which lack manes, do most of the killing, often working as a team to stalk prey. Lions themselves have no natural enemies except humans.

**lion** Large CAT that lives on African savannas south of the Sahara and in SW Asia. It is golden yellow with light spots under the eyes. The male has a deep neck mane. The female does most of the hunting and preys on antelopes, zebras, and bush pigs. Length: to 8.5ft (2.5m) overall. Family Felidae; species *Panthera leo*.

**Lipchitz, Jacques** (1891–1973) French sculptor, b. Lithuania. He created one of the first cubist sculptures, *Man with Guitar* (1914). After moving to the US in 1941 his work became more spiritual and more solid in structure. His works include *Sailor with a Guitar* (1914) and *Prayer* (1943). *See also* CUBISM

**Li Peng** (1928– ) Chinese political leader. He studied in Moscow, returning to China in 1955. He became deputy premier (1983) and a member of the politburo in 1985, then premier in 1987. During the pro-democracy demonstrations of 1989 he declared martial law, leading to the military intervention against students demonstrating in TIANANMEN SQUARE, Beijing.

**lipid** One of a large group of fatty organic compounds in living organisms. They include animal fats, vegetable oils, and natural waxes. Lipids form an important food store and energy source in plant and animal cells.

**Lipmann, Fritz Albert** (1899–1986) US biochemist, b. Germany. He isolated and partially explained the molecular structure of COENZYME A, derived from the B vitamin pantothenic acid. For this and other work on metabolism, he shared the 1953 Nobel Prize for physiology or medicine with the biochemist Hans KREBS.

**Li Po** (701–62) Chinese poet of the T'ANG dynasty. He was a Taoist, and the influence of TAOISM can be seen in the sensual and spiritual aspects of his work. He is said to have drowned while drunk.

**Lippi, Filippino** (1457–1504) Florentine painter. The son of Fra Filippo LIPPI, he studied with BOTTICELLI. He completed the frescos of MASACCIO in Santa Maria del Carmine (1484). His fresco cycles are in the Caraffa Chapel, Santa Maria sopra Minerva, Rome (1488–93) and the Strozzi Chapel, Santa Maria Novella, Florence. He also painted altarpieces.

**Lippi, Fra Filippo** (1406–69) Florentine painter. His early work shows the influence of MASACCIO, but from *c.*1440 he developed his own style. His most characteristic subject was the Virgin and Child. His finest fresco cycle depicts the lives of St. Stephen and St. John in Prato Cathedral. Lippi was a major influence on the 19th century British artists of the PRE-RAPHAELITE BROTHERHOOD.

**Lippmann, Gabriel** (1845–1921) French physicist who won the Nobel Prize for physics in 1908. The first person to produce a color photograph of the visible spectrum, he also invented the direct color process of photography. His work was important in the development of holograms. *See also* HOLOGRAPHY

**Lippmann, Walter** (1889–1974) US journalist and author. He was an influential columnist on the New York *Herald Tribune*, combining a realistic view of politics with a strong moral sense. his books include *A Preface to Morals* (1929) and *The Public Philosophy* (1955).

**liquid** State of MATTER intermediate between a GAS and a SOLID. A liquid substance has a relatively fixed volume but flows to take the shape of its container. A liquid at room temperature, such as water, can be changed into a vapor (its gaseous state, steam) by heating, or into a solid (ice) by cooling.

**liquid crystal** Substance that can exist halfway between the liquid and solid states with its molecules partly ordered. By applying a carefully controlled electric current, liquid crystals turn dark. They are used in liquid crystal displays (LCDs) in pocket calculators.

**liquorice** (licorice) Perennial plant of the pea family, native to the Mediterranean region and cultivated in temperate and subtropical areas. It bears spikes of blue flowers. The dried roots are used to flavor confectionery, tobacco, and medicines. Height: to 3ft (90cm). Family Fabaceae/Leguminosae; species *Glycyrrhiza glabra*.

**Lisbon** (Lisboa) Capital, largest city, and chief port of Portugal, at the mouth of the TAGUS River, on the Atlantic Ocean. An ancient Phoenician settlement, the city was conquered by the Romans in 205 BC and, after waves of Teutonic invasions in the 5th century AD, fell to the Moors in 716. In 1147 the Portuguese reclaimed the city, and in 1260 it became the nation's capital. It declined under Spanish occupation from 1580–1640. The city was devastated by an earthquake in 1755. Lisbon is an international port and tourist center. Industries: steel, shipbuilding, chemicals. Pop. (1991) 2,561,000.

**Lissitzky, El (Eliezor Markovich)** (1890–1941) Innovative Russian painter. MALEVICH inspired him to create a series of paintings that simulate 3-D architectonic constructs. In 1921 he arranged an important exhibition in Berlin of contemporary Russian abstract art. *See also* CONSTRUCTIVISM

**Lister, Joseph, 1st Baron** (1827–1912) British surgeon who introduced the principle of antisepsis. Using carbolic acid (phenol) as the antiseptic agent, in conjunction with heat sterilization of instruments, he brought about a dramatic decrease in post-operative fatalities.

**Liszt, Franz** (1811–86) Hungarian composer and pianist. His music influenced composers including WAGNER (who married Liszt's daughter Cosima), Richard STRAUSS, and

**LIQUID CRYSTAL**

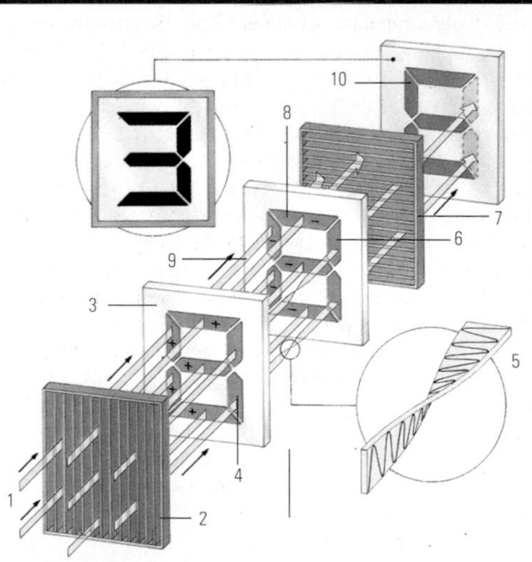

Liquid-crystal displays use the property of liquid crystals to twist the polarization of light to produce numbers or symbols. Incoming light (1) is first regimented in one plane by a polarizer (2) before it passes through the first of two plates of glass (3) on which are fixed electrodes (4). Seven electrodes are needed to represent Arabic numerals. The liquid crystal is between the two plates of glass and twists light (5) passing through uncharged electrodes (6). This light can pass through the second polarizer (7) and can be seen. The light passing through the charged electrodes (8) is not twisted (9), is blocked by the polarizer, and cannot be seen forming the components of the number (10).

L

Maurice RAVEL. Among his compositions are two popular piano concertos, Hungarian rhapsodies, and a mass of piano, orchestral, and choral music.

**litany** Prayer taking the form of a series of petitions and responses. A member of the clergy intones or speaks the petitions, to each of which the congregation replies with the same response, such as "pray for us." In the Anglican Church, a general supplication entitled "the Litany" is included in the BOOK OF COMMON PRAYER.

**liter** Metric unit (symbol l or L) equal to a cubic decimeter, one thousandth of a cubic meter. Another definition, used from 1901–68, was that 1 liter equaled the volume of 1kg of pure water at 39°F (4°C). A liter is equivalent to 0.264 gallons or 0.22 imperial gallons.

**literary criticism** Discipline concerned with literary theory and the evaluation of literary works. It effectively began with PLATO's comments on the role of poets in his *Republic*; ARISTOTLE's response to this, the *Poetics*, represents the first systematic attempt to establish principles of literary procedure. Notable later contributions to the debate include Sir Philip SIDNEY's *The Defense of Poesie* (1595); DRYDEN's *Of Dramatick Poesie* (1668); WORDSWORTH's preface to *Lyrical Ballads* (1798); SHELLEY's *A Defense of Poetry* (1820), and the critical works of Matthew ARNOLD, in particular, *Culture and Anarchy* (1869). The 20th century has seen an explosion of literary critical effort, such as the writings of T.S ELIOT, I.A. Richards, William Empson, and F.R. LEAVIS; also important are the writings of STRUCTURALISM and post-structuralism, notably Roland BARTHES, Michel FOUCAULT, and Jacques Derrida. The late 20th century saw new critical approaches such as DECONSTRUCTION and FEMINISM.

**literature** Collections of writings, usually grouped according to language, period, and country of origin. Within such groupings, literature may be further divided into forms, such as poetry and prose, and within these again into categories, such as verse drama, nonfiction prose, novels, epic poems, tragedies, satires, and so on. *See also* LITERARY CRITICISM; POETRY; PROSE

**lithium** Common silvery metallic element (symbol Li), one of the ALKALI METALS, first isolated in 1817. Ores include lepidolite and spodumene. Chemically it is similar to sodium. The element, which is the lightest of all metals, is used in alloys, and in glasses and glazes; its salts are used in medicine. Properties at.no. 3; at.wt. 6.941; sp.gr. 0.534; m.p.356.9°F (180.5°C); b.p. 2,456.6°F (1,347°C); most stable isotope $^{7}$Li (92.58%).

**lithography** In art, method of printing from a flat inked surface. In traditional lithography, invented in the 1790s, the design is made on a prepared plate or stone with a greasy pencil, crayon, or liquid. Water applied to the surface is absorbed where there is no design. Oil-based printing ink, rolled over the surface, sticks to the design, but not to the moist areas. Pressing paper onto the surface produces a print.

**lithosphere** The upper layer of the solid Earth; it includes the CRUST and the uppermost MANTLE. Its thickness varies but is *c*.40mi (60km); it extends to a depth of *c*.125mi (200km). It is made up of tectonic plates that move independently, giving rise to PLATE TECTONICS.

**Lithuania** Baltic republic in NW Europe; the capital is VILNIUS. **Land and climate** Lithuania is a mostly lowland country, with SE highlands. Ice Age MORAINE covers most of Lithuania and includes over 2,800 lakes. The longest river is the Neman, which rises in Belarus and flows through Lithuania to the Baltic Sea. Winters are cold: average January temperature, 23°F (–5°C). Summers are warm: average July temperature 63°F (17°C). Average rainfall is c.25in (630mm). Farmland covers *c*.75% of Lithuania, and forests only 16%. Pine is predominant in the W and S, oak and birch in the center, and spruce in the E. **Economy** As a Russian republic, Lithuania rapidly industrialized. Since independence it has experienced many problems of transition from a command economy into a more market-oriented one. Lithuania is a developing country. It lacks natural resources and is dependent on Russian raw materials. Manufacturing is the most valuable export sector: major products include chemicals, electronic goods, and machine tools. Dairy and meat farming and fishing are also important activities. **History** The first independent, unified Lithuanian state emerged in 1251, and by the 14th century had expanded E as far as Moscow. In 1386 Lithuania entered into a dynastic union with Poland. The two countries were unified as a Commonwealth in 1569. The final partition of Poland saw Lithuania become part of the Russian empire (1795). In February 1918 Lithuania declared its independence. In 1920 it signed a peace treaty with the Soviet Union, and Poland captured Vilnius. In 1926 a military coup established a dictatorial government. In 1940 the Soviet Union annexed Lithuania as a Soviet republic. In 1941 German troops occupied Lithuania and many Lithuanian Jews were murdered. Soviet troops recaptured the territory in 1944. Nationalist demands forced the Lithuanian Communist Party to agree to multiparty elections in 1989. The 1990 elections were won by the nationalists, and Lithuania proclaimed its independence. In January 1991 Soviet troops and nationalist forces fought on the streets of Vilnius. A referendum voted overwhelmingly in favor of independence, and the Soviet Union recognized Lithuania as an independent republic in September 1991. **Politics** The Democratic Labor Party, containing many ex-communists, won 1992 elections. In 1993 Algirdas Brazauskas, a former Communist Party chairman, became president and Soviet troops completed their withdrawal. In 1996 Lithuania signed a treaty of association with the European Union (EU). In 1997 Valdas Adamkus was elected president.

**litmus** Dye that is purple in neutral aqueous solutions; it is used to indicate acidity (turning red) or alkalinity (turning blue). It is most familiar in the form of litmus paper used as an acid-base indicator. *See also* PH

**Little America** Region in Antarctica, S of the Bay of Whales. It was explored from 1928 to 1930 by Admiral R. E. BYRD, and used as the headquarters for his second expedition. it was also the base fot he US Antarctic Service Expedition (1939–41) and the US Naval Operation High Jump expedition (1946–47).

**Little Bighorn, Battle of** Victory of SIOUX and CHEYENNE Native Americans against the US cavalry led by Colonel George CUSTER in June 1876. Sometimes known as "Custer's Last Stand," it was the last major victory of Native Americans against the US army. The cavalry regiment of 225 men was annihilated by the Sioux, led by SITTING BULL and CRAZY HORSE, near the Little Bighorn River in Montana.

**Little Entente** (1920–38) Alliance between Romania, Yugoslavia, and Czechoslovakia after World War I to main-

**LITHUANIA**

**AREA:** 25,200sq mi (65,200sq km)
**POPULATION:** 3,759,000
**CAPITAL (POPULATION):** Vilnius (578,000)
**GOVERNMENT:** Multiparty republic
**ETHNIC GROUPS:** Lithuanian 80%, Russian 9%, Polish 7%, Belarussian 2%
**LANGUAGES:** Lithuanian (official)
**RELIGIONS:** Christianity (mainly Roman Catholic)
**CURRENCY:** Litas = 100 centai

tain post-war boundaries. It helped to prevent ANSCHLUSS (uniting of Germany and Austria) until 1938.

**Little Richard** (1935– ) US singer-songwriter and pianist, b. Richard Penniman. He achieved fame in the late 1950s with songs such as *Tutti Frutti* (1956) and *Good Golly Miss Molly* (1958). After a near-fatal plane accident, he was ordained a minister in the Church of the Seventh Day Adventists and has oscillated between music and ministry ever since.

**Little Rock** Capital and largest city of Arkansas, on the Arkansas River. Founded in 1814, it became the state capital in 1821. In 1957 federal troops enforced a US Supreme Court ruling against racial segregation in schools. Industries: electronics, textiles. Pop. (1992) 176,870.

**Little Turtle** Chief of the Miami Native Americans. Known for his rhetorical skills, intelligence, and military talent, he and his army defeated General Josiah Harmar in 1790 and General Arther St. Clair in 1791. After several defeats, however, he signed the Treaty of Greenville (Ohio) in 1795 and lost much land to the settlers. He was a peacemaker later in his life.

**liturgy** Established order of the rituals of public ceremonies and worship of an organized religion. In Christianity, the term also refers to the Divine Office or to the rites proper to specific days, such as GOOD FRIDAY, or to particular sacraments, such as BAPTISM. In the Eastern Orthodox Church, the Divine Liturgy refers specifically to the celebration of the Eucharist.

**Liu Shao-ch'i** (1898–1974) Chinese communist leader. He became one of the chief theorists of the Chinese Communist Party, ranking second to Mao Zedong. Liu was made official head of state in 1959, but was purged in 1968 during the CULTURAL REVOLUTION and died in prison.

**liver** Large organ located in the upper right abdomen of VERTEBRATES. Weighing up to 4.5lbs (2kg) in an adult human, it is divided into four lobes and has many functions. It is extremely important in the control of the body's internal environment (HOMEOSTASIS). It receives nutrients from the intestine and is a site of metabolism of proteins, carbohydrates, and fats. It synthesizes BILE and some vitamins, regulates the blood-glucose level, produces blood-clotting factors, breaks down worn-out ERYTHROCYTES, and removes toxins from the blood. Its many metabolic reactions are the body's main source of heat, distributed by the blood. *See also* INSULIN

**Liverpool** City and seaport on the N side of the Mersey River estuary, Merseyside, NW England. Liverpool was founded in the 10th century and became a free borough in 1207. The first wet dock was completed in 1715, and the city expanded rapidly to become Britain's largest port. In the early 20th century it was the major embarkation port for emigration to the New World. In the 1980s, inner-city regeneration included the Albert Dock refurbishment. Liverpool Free Port (Britain's largest) was opened in 1984. The sixth-largest city in England and the principal Atlantic port, Liverpool has over 2,000 acres (800ha) of dockland. Pop. (1991) 452,450.

**liverwort** Any of about 9,000 species of tiny nonflowering green plants, which, like the related mosses, lack specialized tissues to transport water, food, and minerals. Liverworts belong to the plant phylum Bryophyta.

**Livingston, Robert R.** (1746–1813) US Revolutionary war patriot and diplomat. He served in the Continental Congress (1775–76, 1779–81, 1784–85) and helped draw up the Declaration of Independence. He and James MONROE went to France and successfully negotiated the LOUISIANA PURCHASE (1803) for $15 million.

**Livingstone, David** (1813–73) British explorer of Africa. He went to South Africa as a missionary in 1841 and became famous through his account of his journey across the continent from Angola to Mozambique (1853–56). He set off in 1866 to find the source of the Nile. He disappeared and was found in 1871 by Henry Morton STANLEY on Lake Tanganyika.

**Livy** (59–17 BC) (Titus Livius). One of the greatest Roman historians. He began his *History of Rome* c.28 BC. Of the original 142 books, 35 have survived in full.

**lizard** Reptile found on every continent; there are 20 families, *c*.3,000 species. It has a scaly cylindrical body with four

▲ **lizard** The smooth-scaled agamid (*Leiolepis belliana*) is a lizard of SE Asia. Its body is flattened from top to bottom, an adaptation suited to its habit of burrowing up to 40in (1m) into the soil.

legs, a long tail, and moveable eyelids. Most are terrestrial, and many live in deserts. There are also semiaquatic and arboreal (tree-dwelling) forms, including the flying dragon. Length: 2in–10ft (5cm–3m). Order Squamata; suborder Sauria.

**Ljubljana** (Laibach) Capital and largest city of Slovenia, at the confluence of the Sava and Ljubljanica rivers. Ljubljana was founded as Emona by the Roman emperor Augustus in 34 BC. From 1244 it was the capital of Carniola, an Austrian province of the Hapsburg empire. During the 19th century it was the center of the Slovene nationalist movement. The city became part of Yugoslavia in 1918. When Slovenia became independent (1991), Ljubljana became capital. Industries: textiles, paper and printing. Pop. (1991) 268,000.

**llama** Domesticated South American even-toed, ruminant mammal. It has been used as a beast of burden by Native Americans for more than 1,000 years. It has a long, woolly coat and slender limbs and neck. The smaller alpaca is bred for its wool. Family Camelidae; genus *Lama*.

**Llewelyn ap Gruffydd** (d.1282) (Llewelyn the Last) Prince of Wales. Allied with the rebellious English barons, he gained control of as much territory as his grandfather, LLEWELYN AP IORWERTH. He was recognized as prince of Wales by the Treaty of Montgomery (1267). The accession of Edward III brought his ruin. He renewed his rebellion in 1282 and was killed in battle.

**Llewelyn ap Iorwerth** (1173–1240) (Llewelyn the Great) Welsh prince of Gwynedd. He captured Mold from the English (1199) and established his suzerainty in Gwynedd, then gained control of Powys. He allied himself with the English barons against John and was recognized as suzerain by all the Welsh princes.

**Lloyd, Harold** (1893–1971) US movie comic whose screen career spanned the silent and sound years. An expert stunt man, Lloyd did cliff-hanging, death-defying escapades in his films. His early work includes *Grandma's Boy* (1922) and *The Freshman* (1925).

**Lloyd George, David** (1863–1945) British statesman, prime minister (1916–22). A Welsh Liberal, he sat in the House of Commons from 1890. As chancellor of the exchequer (1908–15), he increased taxation to pay for social measures such as old-age pensions. His "People's Budget" (1909)

◀ **Llama** Domesticated for over a thousand years, llamas (*Lama peruana*, shown) are used primarily as pack animals in S and W South America, from sea level to elevations of 16,500ft (5,000m). They thrive in a semidesert habitat feeding on mountain grass. They grow to 4ft (1.2m) long and to a height at the shoulder of 4ft (1.2m).

provoked a constitutional crisis, which led to a reduction of the powers of the House of Lords. In 1916 he joined with Conservatives to dislodge the prime minister, ASQUITH, whom he replaced. He won an easy victory for his coalition government in 1918 and was a leading figure at the peace conference at VERSAILLES. He ended the Irish crisis by the treaty creating the Irish Free State (1921).

**Lloyd's** Insurance market in London, dealing especially in marine insurance. Lloyd's began in the 17th century as a coffee house, where businessmen willing to insure shipping gathered. Between 1988 and 1993, losses led to changes in the regulations.

**Lloyd Webber, Andrew** (1948– ) British composer. He composed *Joseph and the Amazing Technicolor Dreamcoat* (1967) while still a student. The lyricist, Tim Rice, was also his collaborator on the rock opera *Jesus Christ Superstar* (1971) and *Evita* (1978). *Cats* (1981) was a long-running hit, as were *The Phantom of the Opera* (1986) and *Sunset Boulevard* (1993). His brother **Julian** (1951– ) is a highly respected cellist.

**loach** Small freshwater fish in mountain streams of Asia and Europe; there are more than 200 species. British loaches are the stone loach (*Nemachilus barbatula*) and the spined loach (*Cobitis taenia*).

**Lobachevsky, Nikolai Ivanovich** (1793–1856) russian mathematician. he was educated at Kazan University and appointed professor there in 1816. He announced in 1826 the creation of one of the first comprehensive systems of NON-EUCLIDIAN GEOMETRY.

**lobby** A group or individual representing special interests and attempting to influence legislation and government decisions. Lobbyists in the US are required to register annually with the House and Senate and to submit quarterly reports of their activities.

**lobelia** Genus of 365 species of flowering plants found worldwide, mainly trailing or bedding plants. The flowers may be blue, red, or white and irregularly shaped, and the leaves are simple. Family Lobeliaceae.

**lobster** Large, long-tailed, marine decapod crustacean. Some species are prized edible shellfish. True lobsters possess enlarged bulbous chelae (claws) and a segmented body

**lobotomy** *see* LEUCOTOMY

**local color** Literary form emphasizing customs, dialect, and other characteristics that have escaped standardizing cultural influences. The American form, influenced by English and French traditions, was popular in the late 19th century and had its greatest impact on the short story. Bret Harte's *The Luck of Roaring Camp* (1868) is often considered the first US example. Other local colorists include George Washington Cable, Joel Chandler HARRIS, E. W. Howe, and Sarah Orne Jewett.

**local government** System of regional administration differing in each country. Local government in England developed from the Municipal Reform Act (1835), which first established elected councils in cities. The system follows the general principles of the British system. The county is the usual political subdivision, but there is considerable variation between the organizations in different states, and the relationships between the states themselves and central government are complex, often involving shared responsibilities.



▶ **lobster** The Norway lobster (Nephrops norvegicus), a small burrowing form up to 8in (20cm) long found off NE Atlantic coasts, is a typical crustacean. With the crabs, crayfish, prawns, and shrimps, it is classified in a subgroup of the order Decapoda ("10 legs") called the Reptantia ("walking," although they are able to swim short distances). The legs are borne in pairs (1–5), the first of which is enlarged to form nipping claws (chelae) (6). Of the two pairs of antennae (7, 8), the second may be far longer than the body. With the eyes (9), the antennae are the principal sense organs. The body segments are visible only on the abdomen (10) for the thorax is covered by a hard shell (the carapace) (11). The tail (12) is a characteristic fan shape.

**Locarno Pact** (1925) Group of international agreements that attempted to solve problems of European security outstanding since the Treaty of VERSAILLES of 1919. The pact established Germany's w borders and enabled Germany to enter the LEAGUE OF NATIONS. The general peace established at Locarno was soon disturbed by HITLER.

**loch** Scottish word for "lake." For individual lochs *see* place names.

**lock** Structure built into a stretch of inland waterway to raise or lower water levels. Each lock consists of two sets of lock gates. A vessel enters the lock, the gates are closed, and sluices are opened to admit or release enough water to bring the vessel to the same level as the water beyond the second pair of gates.

**Locke, John** (1632–1704) English philosopher and exponent of EMPIRICISM. In 1679 his friendship with the Earl of Shaftesbury, accused of conspiracy against Charles II, made him a target of suspicion and he went into exile in the Netherlands (1683–89). He returned to England only after the Glorious Revolution. Locke rejected the concept of "innate ideas" and held that all ideas are placed in the mind by experience.

**lockjaw** *See* TETANUS

**locomotive** Engine that moves under its own power, usually on rails. In 1804 Richard TREVITHICK in England built the first locomotive, which was steam powered. The first on a passenger railroad was George STEPHENSON's *Locomotion*, built in 1825. Electric locomotives arrived in the late 19th century. Diesel, diesel-electric, and gas-turbine ones were introduced in the 20th century.

**locus** In geometry, the path of a specified point when it moves to satisfy certain conditions. A circle is the locus of a point in a plane moving in such a way that its distance from a fixed point (the center) is constant.

**locust** Insect (a type of GRASSHOPPER) that migrates in huge swarms. They may contain up to 40 billion insects, and cover an area of *c*.385sq mi (1,000sq km). Length: 0.5–4in (12.5–100mm). Order Orthoptera; species *Schistocerca gregaria*.

**Lodge, Henry Cabot** (1850–1924) US political leader and historian. He represented Massachusetts in the House of Representatives (1887–93) and the Senate (1893–1924). He was a conservative Republican. As Senate majority leader and chairman of the Foreign Relations Committee (1918–24), he led the successful opposition to US membership in the LEAGUE OF NATIONS.

**Lódź** Second-largest city in Poland, c.75mi (120km) sw of Warsaw. A small market town intil the 19th century, Lódź grew under Russian occupation after 1820 to become the center of the Polish textile industry. Taken by the Russians in 1815, the town was returned to Poland in 1918. Industries: textiles, machinery. Pop. (1991) 847,000.

**loess** Light-colored fine silt or clay deposited by the wind, generally unstratified. The loess in the Mississippi River Valley is believed to have been produced by glacial action and then transported by wind.

**Logan, Mount** Peak in the St. Elias Mountains, sw Yukon, Canada. At 19,849ft (6,050m), it is the highest in Canada and second-highest in North America.

**loganberry** Biennial, hybrid, red-berried bramble. A cross between the BLACKBERRY and RASPBERRY, it is disease-prone and is grown only in sheltered areas. Family Rosaceae; species *Rubus ursinus loganbaccus*.

**logarithm** Aid to calculation devised by John NAPIER in 1614 and developed by the English mathematician Henry Briggs. A number's logarithm is the power to which a base must be raised to equal the number, i.e. if $b^x = n$, then $\log_b n = x$, where $n$ is the number, b the base, and $x$ the logarithm. Common logarithms have base 10, and so-called natural logarithms have base e (2.71828...). Logarithms to the base 2 are used in computer science and information theory.

**logic** Branch of philosophy that deals with the processes of valid reasoning and argument. Logic defines the way in which one thing may be said to follow from, or be consequent upon, another. This is known as deductive logic. Inductive logic, in which a general conclusion is drawn from a particular fact or facts, is the preserve of science. Although logical systems were devised in China and India, the history of logic in the West began in the 4th century BC with the Greek philosopher ARISTOTLE. In the Middle Ages, Pierre ABÉLARD used logic in the synthesis of ideas that was the goal of SCHOLASTICISM. Various post-Renaissance scholars, including LEIBNIZ, developed the foundations of modern logic. Symbolic, or mathematical, logic was outlined in the 19th century by George BOOLE and developed by Gottlob FREGE. Modern formal logic or symbolic logic utilizes symbols to represent precisely defined classes of proposition connected to each other by such operators as "and," "or," "if... then."

**logical positivism** Early 20th-century school of philosophy whose adherents consider that only empirically verifiable scientific propositions are meaningful. Its roots were in the logic of Gottlob FREGE and Bertrand RUSSELL, the positivism of Ernst Mach and, above all, the claim of Ludwig WITTGENSTEIN that philosophy was the clarification of thought.

**logos** In philosophy, intellect or reason; in a larger sense the rational principle that orders the universe. As used in the New Testament Gospel of St. John, the Greek word *logos* was in the Authorized Version translated as "the Word." The Word can be tierh the intention of God (His rational principle) or the outward expression of that intention – both describing JESUS CHRIST.

**Loire** Longest river in France. The Loire rises in the Cévennes range, on the SE edge of the MASSIF CENTRAL, and flows N and NW to Orléans. It then turns SW into a wide, fertile basin. The cities of TOURS and Angers lie on its banks. It then flows through the Pays de la Loire to NANTES, emptying into the Bay of BISCAY at St-Nazaire. It is connected by a series of canals to the RHÔNE and SEINE rivers. Length: 635mi (1,020km).

**Lollards** Followers of the 14th-century English religious reformer John WYCLIFFE. They helped to pave the way for the REFORMATION and challenged many doctrines and practices of the medieval church, including TRANSUBSTANTIATION, clerical celibacy, and the authority of the PAPACY. They went among the people as "poor preachers," teaching that the Bible was the sole authority in religion. After 1401 many Lollards were burned as heretics, and in 1414 they had an unsuccessful uprising in London and then went underground.

**Lombard League** Defensive alliance of the cities of Lombardy in N Italy (1167). Its purpose was to resist the reestablishment of imperial authority by FREDERICK I. Led by Pope ALEXANDER III, the league defeated the emperor at Legnano (1176). By the Peace of Constance in 1183 the cities retained independence. The league was active again in 1226 against FREDERICK II.

**Lombards** Germanic peoples who inhabited the area E of the lower Elbe River until driven W by the Romans in AD 9. In 568 they invaded N Italy under Alboin and conquered much of the country, adopting Catholicism and Latin customs. The Lombard kingdom reached its peak under Liutprand (d.744). It went into decline after defeat by the Franks under CHARLEMAGNE (775).

**Lombardy** (Lombardia) Region in N Italy, bordering Switzerland in the N; the capital is MILAN. Lombardy is Italy's most populous and industrial region. It is divided into the provinces of Bergamo, Brescia, Como, Cremona, Mantova, Milano, Pavia, Sondrio, and Varese. North Lombardy is an Alpine region with many lakes. South Lombardy is dominated by the fertile plain of the Po River. The plains have been a major European battleground. Area: 9,202sq mi (23,834sq km). Pop. (1991) 8,856,074.

**Lomé** Capital and largest city of the Republic of Togo, W Africa, on the Gulf of Guinea. Made capital of German Togoland in 1897, it later became an important commercial

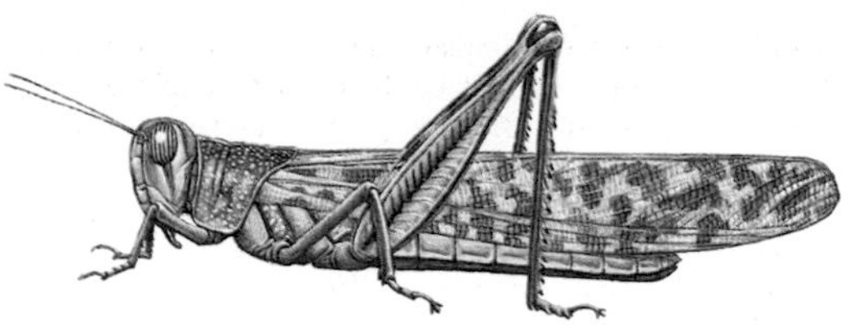

◀ **locust** Types of grasshoppers that respond to overcrowding by migrating in huge swarms, locusts occur in two forms. The solitary form (shown) is relatively inactive. The gregarious form is distinguished by the darker color of the immature insects, or nymphs.

center. It was the site of conferences in 1975 and 1979 that produced a trade agreement (known as the Lomé Convention) between the European Community and 46 African, Caribbean, and Pacific states. Its main exports are coffee and cocoa. Pop. (1991) 590,000.

**Lomond, Loch** Long, narrow lake in Strathclyde and Central regions, W central Scotland. It is drained by the Leven River into the Firth of Clyde. The largest Scottish loch, it is 21mi (37km) long and 625ft (190m) deep at its deepest part. It is dominated at the N end by Ben Lomond (height: 3,192ft/973m). Area: 27.5sq mi (70sq km).

**London, Jack** (1876–1916) US novelist and short-story writer. He is best known for his Alaskan novels, such as *Call of the Wild* (1903) and *White Fang* (1906).

**London** Capital of the United Kingdom, and (after Moscow) the second-largest city in Europe, located on both banks of the THAMES River, 40mi (65km) from its mouth in the North Sea, SE England. Since 1965 it has been officially called Greater London: comprising the square mile of the City of London and 13 inner and 19 outer boroughs, covering a total of 610sq mi (1,580sq km). Little is known of London before the Romans set up camp in the 1st century AD. Called Londinium, it was their most important town in Britain, developing as a port and commercial center. By the 3rd century the population numbered *c*.40,000. After the Romans left Britain, London declined until the 9th century, when ALFRED THE GREAT made it the seat of government. The prosperity of England during the Tudor period firmly established London's wealth and importance. In the reign of Elizabeth I the population increased from fewer than 100,000 to almost 250,000. The plague of 1665 killed 75,000 Londoners and the FIRE OF LONDON the next year destroyed many buildings. Sir Christopher WREN played an important role in the reconstruction of the city, designing many churches, including ST. PAUL'S. During the 19th century the population reached 4 million. By the end of the century London was the world's biggest city. Much of E London was rebuilt after bomb damage during World War II, and in the late 1980s the largely derelict docklands were rapidly developed. London remains one of the world's most important administrative, financial, commercial, and industrial cities. Industries: tourism, entertainment, engineering, chemicals, paper, printing and publishing, clothing, brewing. Pop. (1994) 6,966,800.

**London, University of** University founded in 1836, originally comprising King's College and University College. The university now comprises 14 colleges, 6 medical schools, and 11 postgraduate medical institutions, as well as various other academic institutes.

**Londonderry** *See* DERRY

**Long, Huey Pierce** (1893–1935) US political leader. A formidable populist and opponent of big business, he was Democratic governor of Louisiana (1928–32). As a senator (1932–35), he attracted wide support with an ambitious plan for redistribution of wealth. He was assassinated.

**Long Beach** City in S California, 20mi (32km) S of Los Angeles. Oil was discovered in 1921 and there are artificial oil islands in its harbor. The *Queen Mary* is berthed here as a tourist center, museum, and hotel. Industries: oil, automobile parts. Pop. (1990) 429,321.

**Longfellow, Henry Wadsworth** (1807–82) US poet. He is chiefly remembered for his narrative poems, such as *Evangeline* (1847) and *The Song of Hiawatha* (1855). *Ballads and Other Poems* (1842) contains two of his most popular shorter poems, "The Wreck of the Hesperus" and "The Village Blacksmith."

▲ **Lorenz** Austrian scientist Konrad Lorenz studied the behavior of animals for much of his life. Unlike animal psychologists, who studied animal behavior in laboratories, Lorenz studied animals in their natural environments and arrived at radically different conclusions as to why animals behave in certain ways.

**Longhi, Pietro** (1702–85) Italian painter. He devoted himself chiefly to small-scale genre pictures, especially scenes of the domestic manners of the Venetian middle classes, such as *The Exhibition of the Rhinoceros at Venice*.

**longhorn** Almost extinct breed of beef cattle, originally from Mexico, descended from European cattle introduced by Spanish conquistadors. They are now used only as rodeo and show animals.

**Long Island** Island in SE New York State, bounded on the S by the Atlantic Ocean and separated from Manhattan by the East River and from Connecticut by Long Island Sound. Originally inhabited by the Delaware Native Americans, it was settled by the Dutch West India Company and the Massachusetts Bay Colony in the 17th century. About 120mi (190km) long, it has commuter towns, light industry, fishing, and holiday resorts. Area: 1,723sq mi (4,463sq km). Pop. (1990) 6,861,454.

**Long Island, Battle of** (August 27, 1776) American Revolution battle. George WASHINGTON's army, divided by the East River, was defeated on Long Island by British General William HOWE. The American army retreated to Manhattan avoiding capture.

**longitude** Angular measurement around the Earth, usually in degrees E or W of an imaginary N–S line through the prime MERIDIAN. All N–S lines are called either meridians or lines of longitude.

**long jump** Field event in which competitors run up to a take-off board and try to leap the farthest.

**Long March** Enforced march of the Chinese RED ARMY in 1934–35, during the war against the Nationalist (Kuomintang) forces. Led by Chu Teh and MAO ZEDONG, 90,000 communist troops, accompanied by *c*.15,000 civilians, broke through a Nationalist encirclement of their headquarters and marched some 6,000mi (10,000km) from Jiangxi province, SE China, to Shanxi province in the NW. Under frequent attack, they suffered 45,000 casualties. The march prevented the extermination of the Communist Party.

**Long Parliament** English Parliament initially summoned by CHARLES I in November 1640. It followed the SHORT PARLIAMENT, which lasted only weeks. Antagonism between Charles and Parliament resulted in the outbreak of the English CIVIL WAR. The Long Parliament sat, with intervals, for 20 years. Oliver CROMWELL expelled hostile members in PRIDE'S PURGE (1648), and thereafter it was known as the RUMP PARLIAMENT.

**Longstreet, James** (1821–1904) Confederate CIVIL WAR general. He served prominently at the First Battle of Bull Run, Antietam, Fredericksburg, Gettysburg, Chickamauga, the Wilderness, and Richmond.

**loon** (diver) Diving bird of the Northern Hemisphere, known for its harsh call. It has black, white, and gray plumage. An excellent swimmer, it often stays submerged while fishing. Length: 35in (88cm). Family Gaviidae.

**Loos, Adolf** (1870–1933) Czech architect who pioneered modern building design. His most important projects were houses built between 1904–10; Steiner House (Vienna, 1910) was one of the first to use concrete. *See also* MODERNISM

**loran (long range navigation)** Radio navigational system for guiding ships and aircraft. Pairs of transmitters emit signal pulses that are picked up by a receiver. By measuring the difference in time between the signals reaching the receiver, the vessel's position can be plotted.

**Lorca, Federico García** (1898–1936) Spanish poet and dramatist. His poetry, ranging from *Gypsy Ballads* (1928) to *The Poet in New York* (1940), was internationally acclaimed. In the theater, his early farces gave way to tragedies, such as the trilogy *Blood Wedding* (1933), *Yerma* (1935), and *The House of Bernarda Alba* (1936). He was killed in the Spanish CIVIL WAR.

**Lord Chancellor** Head of the British legal system, an office of cabinet rank. His duties include acting as head of the judiciary and as speaker of the House of Lords.

**Lord Dunmore's War** (1774) Dispute involving colonial settlers and Native Americans. Virginia's royal governor, John Murray, Earl of Dunmore, took control of W Pennsylvania. Settlers then began moving into Kentucky. These two infringements into lands that the Native Americans considered theirs provoked the Shawnee and Ottawa tribes into war. Colonel Andrew Lewis led his troops to victory over Chief Cornstalk at the Battle of Point Pleasant.

**Lord's Prayer** Prayer JESUS CHRIST taught his disciples. It is found in Matthew 6:9–13, and slightly differently in Luke 11:2–4. It is also called *Pater Noster* (Lat. Our Father).

**Lorelei** Large rock in the Rhine River near Sankt Goarshausen, W Germany. According to legend, a beautiful maiden called Lorelei drowned herself in despair over her faithless lover, only to rise as a siren to lure fishermen to their doom on the rock.

**Loren, Sophia** (1934– ) Italian movie actress. Her films include *The Black Orchid* (1959), *Two Women* (1960) – for which she won an Academy Award in 1961 – and *Marriage Italian Style* (1964).

**Lorentz, Hendrik Antoon** (1853–1928) Dutch physicist. His early work was concerned with the theory of electromagnetic radiation devised by James Clerk MAXWELL. This led him to the Lorentz transformation (connecting the space and time coordinates of an event as observed from two frames of reference) and the prediction of the Lorentz-Fitzgerald contraction (objects change length due to their movement relative to the observer), both of which helped Albert EINSTEIN to develop his special theory of RELATIVITY. Lorentz also worked on the ZEEMAN EFFECT, for which he and Pieter Zeeman were awarded the 1902 Noble Prize for physics.

**Lorenz, Konrad** (1903–89) Austrian pioneer ethologist. He observed that instinct played a major role in animal behavior, as for example in IMPRINTING. In 1973 he shared, with N. TINBERGEN and K. von FRISCH, the Noble Prize for physiology or medicine. *See also* ETHOLOGY

**loris** Any of several species of primitive, tailless, tree-dwelling, nocturnal PRIMATES of S Asia and the East Indies. They have soft, thick fur, and large eyes, and feed mainly on insects. Length: 7–15in (18–38cm). Family Lorisidae; genera *Loris* and *Nycticebus*.

**Lorrain, Claude** *See* CLAUDE LORRAIN

**Lorraine** (Ger. Lothringen) Region of NE France, bounded N by Belgium, Germany, and Luxembourg, E by ALSACE, S by Franche-Comté, and E by CHAMPAGNE. The capital is Nancy. Lorraine is divided into four départements. In the 10th century it was divided into two duchies, Upper and Lower Lorraine. In 1766 it became a French province. In 1871 E Lorraine was joined to form the German territory of Alsace-Lorraine. Industries: brewing and winemaking. It also has rich iron ore deposits. Area: 9,089sq mi (23,547sq km). Pop. (1990) 2,305,700.

**Los Alamos** Town in New Mexico, site of a large scientific laboratory. During World War II the laboratory was one of the centers for the MANHATTAN PROJECT, which produced the atom bomb. After the war, the laboratory developed the HYDROGEN BOMB.

**Los Angeles** (City of Angels) City in SW California, on the Pacific coast; the second-largest US city (after New York) and the nation's leading manufacturing base. The city was founded in 1781 by Mexican settlers. At the conclusion of the MEXICAN WAR (1848) the US acquired Los Angeles. The city grew with the completion of the Southern Pacific (1876) and Santa Fe (1885) railroads. The discovery of oil (1894) and the development of the HOLLYWOOD film and television industry encouraged further growth. During World War II the city's industry boomed with the need for aircraft and munitions, and many African Americans migrated to the city. In 1965 five days of riots in the Watts district left 34 dead and $200 million damages. In 1992 the acquittal of four policemen on a charge of beating an African-American suspect sparked off further race riots, which left 58 dead and $1 billion damages. Air pollution is also a major problem. A 1994 earthquake killed 57 people and caused $15–30 billion of damage. Greater Los Angeles sprawls over 465sq mi (1,204sq km) joined by a freeway network. Over 600,000 Mexican-Americans live here, more than in any other US city, the majority in the overcrowded barrio of E Los Angeles. The city also has one of the largest black communities in the US (over 500,000 African Americans), especially in the S central district of Watts. Central Los Angeles consists mainly of Hollywood, the heart of the US film industry. Greater Los Angeles includes Anaheim (home of Disneyland) and Santa Monica. Aerospace is the city's principal industry. Industries: film and television, oil refining, electronic equipment. It is a major tourist center. Pop. (1990) 3,489,779.

**Lost Generation** Designation for disillusioned American intellectuals, writers, and artists after World War I. The term is attributed to a remark ("You are all of a lost generation") made by Gertrude STEIN to Ernest HEMINGWAY. Other Lost Generation writers include F. Scott FITZGERALD, Ezra POUND, and John Dos Passos.

**Lot** Biblical character who was living in SODOM at the time when God decided to destroy it (Genesis 11:31–14:16. 19). Lot survived, but his wife looked back at the city and was turned into a pillar of salt.

**Lothair I** (795–855) Frankish emperor (840–55). Eldest son of LOUIS I, he was co-emperor with his father from 817. War broke out on the death of Louis (840) between Lothair and his two brothers. Lothair was defeated at Fontenoy (841) and in 843 the Frankish empire was divided in three by the Treaty of Verdun. Lothair retained the title of emperor and ruled the Middle Kingdom, consisting of the Low Countries, N France, Switzerland, and N Italy.

**Lothair II** (826–69) King of Lotharingia (855–69). He inherited LOTHARINGIA (Lorraine) from his father, the Frankish Emperor LOTHAIR I, and in 863 he inherited the kingdom of Provence from his brother.

**Lothair II** (1070–1137) King of the Germans and Holy Roman emperor (1125–37), sometimes called Lothair III, "the Saxon." He secured the throne by successful war against the HOHENSTAUFEN (1125–35). He encouraged German eastward expansion and supported Pope Innocent II, invading Italy in 1136–37.

**Lotharingia** Part of CHARLEMAGNE's empire inherited by his descendant LOTHAIR II, after whom it is named. Roughly, Lotharingia included modern Lorraine (whose name is itself a corruption of Lotharingia), Alsace, NW Germany, Luxembourg, Belgium, and The Netherlands.

**Lotto, Lorenzo** (1480–1556) Italian painter. Lotto's painting was very inconsistent but the best examples, such as *The Annunciation* altarpiece in Santa Maria sopra Mercanti in Recanati, show great freshness of observation and psychological insight.

**lotus** Common name for WATER LILIES of the genus *Nelumbo* and several tropical species of the genus *Nymphaea*. The circular leaves and flowers of some species may be 2ft (60cm) across. Family Nymphaeaceae. The genus *Lotus* is made up of the trefoils of the unrelated Fabaceae/Leguminosae family.

**Lotze, Rudolf Hermann** (1817–81) Germany philosopher who developd a form of personalistic and teleological idealism. According to his philosophy, which is expounded in his book Metaphysik (1841), all entities ultimately find unity in the "world ground," a synthesis of physical and evolutionary processes involving an infinite spirit, or God. it fell into disrepute shrtly after Lotze's death. His influence on later 19th- and early 20th-century idealist philosophers was significant.

**loudspeaker** Device for converting changing electric currents into sound. The most common type has a moving coil attached to a stiff paper cone suspended in a strong magnetic field. By ELECTROMAGNETIC INDUCTION, the changing currents in the coil cause the cone to vibrate, thus creating sound waves.

**Louis I** (778–840) Emperor of the Franks (814–840), called "the Pious." He succeeded his father, CHARLEMAGNE. He struggled to maintain Charlemagne's empire. Louis's attempts to provide an inheritance for his four sons provoked civil war.

**Louis VI** (1081–1137) King of France (1108–37). He was the effective ruler for several years before he succeeded his father, Philip I. He reestablished control of the royal domain, increasing the authority of the royal courts and enjoying the strong support of the church.

**Louis VII** (*c.*1120–80) King of France (1137–80). His marriage to Eleanor of Aquitaine extended the French crown's lands to the Pyrenees. As king, he consolidated royal power. Returning from the Second Crusade, he divorced Eleanor for alleged infidelity. She married HENRY II of England, whose French territories then became greater than those of Louis. Louis retaliated by supporting the rebellions of Henry's sons.

**Louis IX** (1214–70) King of France (1226–70), later known as St. Louis. His mother, Blanche of Castile, was regent from 1226–36 and during his first absence from France (1248–52). Louis defeated the English at Taillebourg (1242) and led the Sixth Crusade in 1248. He was taken prisoner and did not return until 1254.

**Louis XII** (1462–1515) King of France (1498–1515). On becoming king, he had his first marriage annulled to wed Anne of Britanny, resulting in the incorporation of Britanny in France. He succeeded his cousin, CHARLES VIII, and was involved throughout his reign in the dynastic wars arising from Charles's invasion of Italy in 1494. Louis continued this policy, invading Italy in 1499. He was defeated by the HOLY LEAGUE and forced to surrender all his Italian acquisitions (1513).

**Louis XIII** (1601–43) King of France (1601–43). Son of Henry IV and MARIE DE MÉDICIS, he forcibly ended his mother's regency in 1617 and exiled her. He increasingly relied on Cardinal RICHELIEU, who exercised total authority from 1624. Louis approved crushing the Huguenots (Protestants) at home while making alliances with Protestant powers abroad, in opposition to the Hapsburgs, during the THIRTY YEARS' WAR.

**Louis XIV** (1638–1715) King of France (1643–1715). The first part of his reign was dominated by Cardinal MAZARIN. From 1661, Louis ruled personally as the epitome of absolute monarchy and became known as the "Sun King" for the luxury of his court. As ministers, he chose men of low rank or the junior nobility, such as the able COLBERT. Louis's wars of aggrandizement in the Low Countries and elsewhere drained the treasury. His revocation of the Edict of NANTES drove Huguenots abroad, weakening the economy. In the War of the SPANISH SUCCESSION, the French armies were at last defeated.

**Louis XV** (1710–74) King of France (1715–74). Grandson and successor of LOUIS XIV, he failed to arrest the slow decline. Disastrous wars, especially the War of the AUSTRIAN SUCCESSION and the SEVEN YEARS' WAR, resulted in financial crisis and the loss of most of the French empire. The monarchy became deeply unpopular.

**Louis XVI** (1754–93) King of France (1774–92). Grandson and successor of LOUIS XV, he married the Austrian archduchess MARIE ANTOINETTE in 1770. Louis' lack of leadership qualities allowed the *parlements* (supreme courts) and aristocracy to defeat the efforts of government ministers, such as Jacques NECKER, to carry out vital economic reforms. The massive public debt forced Louis to convoke the STATES GENERAL to raise taxation. His indecisiveness on the composition of the States General led the third (popular) estate to proclaim itself a National Assembly, signaling the start of the FRENCH REVOLUTION. The dismissal of Necker and rumors that Louis intended to forcibly suppress the assembly led to the storming of the BASTILLE (14 July 1789). In October 1789 the royal family were confined to the Tuileries palace. Early French defeats in the war against Austria and Prussia led to the declaration of a republic. Louis was tried for treason by the Convention and found guilty. He was guillotined on 21 January 1793.

**Louis XVII** (1785–95) Son of LOUIS XVI, proclaimed king of France by royalists in 1793. He was placed in the care of a shoemaker by the Republican government after the execution of his father, and probably died of neglect.

**Louis XVIII** (1755–1824) King of France (1814–24). Brother of LOUIS XVI, he fled from the Revolution to England. He was restored to the throne in 1814, but was forced to flee again during the HUNDRED DAYS until Napoleon's final defeat at Waterloo (1815). He agreed to a constitution providing for parliamentary government and a relatively free society.

**Louis, Joe** (1914–81) (Joseph Louis Barrow) US boxer. He won the world heavyweight title from James J. Braddock in Chicago in 1937, and retired undefeated in 1949. He fought 25 successful defenses and scored 21 knockouts, including the historic 1938 defeat of Max Schmeling. He returned to the ring, lost on points to Ezzard Charles (1950) and was knocked out by Rocky Marciano (1951). Louis held the title longer than any other heavyweight.

▲ **loris** The slow loris (*Nycticebus coucang*) is found in the forests of SE Asia. Their tailless bodies grow to 12in (30cm). A nocturnal primate, the slow loris clings so closely to the branches of its arboreal habitat that it is able to climb upside down.

L

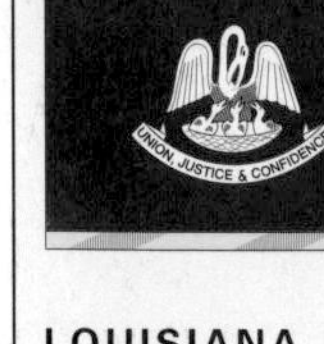


**LOUISIANA**
**Statehood:**
April 30, 1812
**Nickname:**
Pelican State
**State bird:**
Brown pelican
**State flower:**
Magnolia
**State tree:**
Bald cypress
**State motto:**
Union, Justice and Confidence

**Louisiana** State on the Gulf of Mexico, S central US; the capital is BATON ROUGE. In 1699 the French colony of Louisiana was founded. It was later ceded to Spain but regained by France in 1800. In the LOUISIANA PURCHASE (1803) Napoleon sold it to the US. In 1861 it joined the Confederacy, being readmitted to the Union in 1868. The discovery of oil and natural gas in the early 20th century provided a great boost to the economy. Racial discrimination left the large African-American community (30% of the population) politically powerless until the 1960s. Louisiana consists of the MISSISSIPPI alluvial plain and the Gulf coastal plain. The Mississippi Delta in the SE of the state was formed by silt. It covers *c.* 13,000sq mi (33,700sq km), about 25% of the state's total area. The tidal shoreline is 7,721mi (12,426km) long. Nearly 15% of the state is marshland. N of the marshes, rolling prairies stretch to the Texas border. Almost half the state is forested. It has a mainly subtropical climate. Low-lying land and heavy rainfall make it prone to flooding. It is a leading producer of soybeans, sweet potatoes, rice, and sugar cane. Fishing is a major industry, particularly shrimps and crayfish. Louisiana is second only to Texas in US mineral production. Petroleum and coal account for more than 95% of mining income. Area: 48,523sq mi (125,674sq km). Pop. (1992) 4,278,889.

**Louisiana Purchase** (1803) Transaction involving a large area of land purchased from France by the United States. The 825,000sq mi (2,136,000sq km) of territory, from the Mississippi River to the Rocky Mountains, was bought for $15,000,000.

**Louis Philippe** (1773–1850) King of France (1830–48). He returned to France from exile in 1814. He gained the throne after the JULY REVOLUTION in 1830. Although known as the "Citizen King," he retained much power himself. He abdicated when revolution broke out again and the Second Republic was declared in February 1848. He died in exile in England.

**Louisville** City in NW Kentucky, a port on the Ohio River; largest city in Kentucky. Established as a military base in 1778 by George Rogers Clark, it was named for LOUIS XVI of France. It developed into a coal-shipping center by the mid-19th century. Host to the famous Kentucky Derby, the city has many stud stables. Industries: bourbon whiskey, tobacco. Pop. (1990) 269,063.

**Lourdes** Town in SW France, in Hautes-Pyrénées department; a center of religious pilgrimage. In 1858 a 14-year-old peasant girl called Bernadette Soubirous claimed to have had visions of the Virgin Mary in the nearby grotto of Massabielle, where there is an underground spring. In 1862 the Roman Catholic Church declared the visions to be authentic. The waters of the spring, believed to have healing powers, are the focus of pilgrimages by up to 5 million visitors a year.

**louse** Common name for various small, wingless insects, parasitic on birds and mammals. There are two main groups in different sub-orders of Phthiraptera. The chewing lice (Mallophaga) feed mainly on the feathers of birds. The biting or sucking lice (Anoplura) feed only on the blood of mammals. Both are small, pale, and flattened, with leathery or hairy skins.

**Louth** County in the NE Republic of Ireland, in Leinster province, bordering Northern Ireland (N) and the Irish Sea (E); the capital is Dundalk. It is a low-lying region, except in the hilly NW and the mountainous N, drained by the Fane, Dee, and Castletown rivers. Industries: textiles, footwear, processed food. Area: 317sq mi (821sq km). Pop. (1991) 90,724.

**Louvre** France's national museum and art gallery in Paris. It holds a collection of more than 100,000 works, including paintings, drawings, prints, and sculpture. Originally a royal palace, the Louvre became a museum in the 18th century and opened as the first national public gallery in 1793, after the Revolution.

**lovebird** Any of nine species of small parrots that live mainly in Africa and Madagascar. Both sexes are brightly colored and are often kept as cage birds. The largest species is the rosy-faced lovebird (*Agapornis roseicollis*) of South Africa.

**Lovelace, Richard** (1618–58) English CAVALIER poet. A flamboyant and ardent royalist, he was imprisoned in 1642 and 1648, during which time he wrote *To Althea, from Prison* and *To Lucasta, Going to the Wars*.

**Low Countries** Region of NW Europe now occupied by the NETHERLANDS, BELGIUM, and LUXEMBOURG. It was the most advanced and prosperous region of N Europe during the Middle Ages and Renaissance, under the dukes of BURGUNDY from 1384 and the HAPSBURGS from 1477. The Dutch gained independence as the United Provinces in 1609. The southern Netherlands (Belgium) became an independent kingdom in 1830. Luxembourg was ruled by the Dutch house of Orange until 1890, when it passed to another branch.

**Lowell, Amy** (1874–1925) US poet and critic, sister of Percival LOWELL. Her work embraced such avant-garde movements as IMAGISM and introduced what she called "polyphonic prose," although her later collections reverted to more conventional forms. Her first book, *A Dome of Many-colored Glass*, appeared in 1912.

**Lowell, James Russell** (1819–91) US poet, author and editor involved in the abolitionist movement. *A Fable for Critics*, the first series of the satirical *The Biglow Papers*, which were influential in the abolitionist cause, and *The Vision of Sir Launfal*, all appeared in 1848. He succeeded to LONGFELLOW'S Harvard professorship in 1855, founded *Atlantic Monthly* (1857–61) and served as US ambassador to Britain (1880–85).

**Lowell, Percival** (1855–1916) American astronomer, brother of Amy LOWELL. In 1894 he built an observatory at Flagstaff, Arizona. He observed Mars, producing intricate maps of the so-called canals, which he ascribed to the activities of intelligent beings. He studied the orbits of Uranus and Neptune, and calculated that their orbital irregularities were caused by an undiscovered Planet X. This led to the discovery of the planet Pluto in 1930.

**Lowell, Robert** (1917–77) US poet. Lowell was perhaps the most important voice in American poetry to emerge after World War II. His early work, such as the Pulitzer Prize-winning *Lord Weary's Castle* (1946), is rich in Catholic symbolism. He is best known for his later, more intimate "confessional" style, best represented by the autobiographical *Life Studies* (1959). He won a second Pulitzer Prize for *The Dolphin* (1973).

**Lower Saxony** Region of N Germany, formed in 1946 by the merging of the provinces of Hanover, Brunswick, Oldenberg, and Schaumberg–Lippe. Agriculture focuses on cereal crops. Industries: machine construction, electrical engineering. Area 18,376sq mi (47,606sq km), pop. (1993 est.) 7,648,004.

**Lowry, L.S. (Lawrence Stephen)** (1887–1976) British painter. He is best known for the highly personal way in which he portrayed cityscapes of his native Salford (Greater MANCHESTER).

**Loyalists** In US history, North American colonists who refused to renounce their loyalty to the British crown after the DECLARATION OF INDEPENDENCE (July 1776). Active loyalists, or Tories, comprised *c.*20% of the population. Some fought in the British army or Loyalist units. Many were eventually forced into exile, especially in Canada. The term also applies to those people of Northern Ireland who oppose a united Ireland, preferring rather to remain part of the UK.

**LSD** (lysergic acid diethylamide) Hallucinogenic drug, causing changes in mental state, sensory confusion, and behavioral changes, resulting from the drug blocking the action of serotonin in the brain. First synthesized in the 1940s, LSD was made illegal in the US in the mid-1960s.

**Luanda** Capital, chief port, and largest city of Angola, on the Atlantic coast of SW Africa. First settled by the Portuguese in 1575, its economy was based on the shipment of more than 3 million slaves to Brazil until the abolition of slavery in the 19th century. Today it exports crops from the province of Luanda. Industries: oil refining, metalworking. Pop. (1990) 1,544,000.

**Lübeck** Baltic port in NE Germany, in Schleswig-Holstein state, at the mouth of the Trave River. A Slavonic city in the

11th century, in 1138 it was destroyed by fire. In 1143 it was refounded as part of Holstein. In 1226 it was made a free imperial city and later rose to a preeminent position in the Hanseatic League. During the 16th century the city began to decline. In 1937 it was incorporated into Schleswig-Holstein. The city was badly damaged by Allied bombing during World War II. The port is the principal employer. Industries: shipbuilding, aeronautical equipment. Pop. (1990) 216,500.

**Lublin** City in SE Poland. Founded in the late 9th century as a fortified settlement, Lublin developed as a trade center, acquiring municipal rights in 1317. The city has twice produced national governments: Poland's first Council of Workers' Delegates (a temporary authority) was formed in 1918; and in 1944, following the retreat of the German army, the provisional government was convened in Lublin. Today it is the focus for a fertile, mixed farming region and a transportation and industrial center, producing heavy machinery, textiles, and electrical goods. Pop. (1991) 352,000.

**lubricant** Oil, grease, or other substances placed between moving parts to redue friction and dissipate heat. Most lubricants are now derived from petroleum.

**Lucas, George** (1944– ) US film director, writer, and producer. He achieved fame as the creator of *Star Wars* (1977) and its sequels. His other films include *American Graffiti* (1973) and *Raiders of the Lost Ark* (1981).

**Lucas van Leyden** (1494–1533) Dutch painter and engraver. His engravings include *Ecco Homo* and *Dance of the Magdalene* (1519). Among his paintings are *Chess Players* (*c*.1508) and *Last Judgment* (1526).

**Lucerne** (Luzern) City on Lake Lucerne, central Switzerland, 25mi (40km) SSW of Zurich. It joined the Swiss Confederation in 1332. Lucerne became the capital of the French-inspired Helvetic Republic in 1803, but rejoined the Confederation in 1848. It is an important summer resort and the center of the cereal-growing canton of Lucerne. Industries: engineering, metal goods, chemicals, textiles. It is also host to a summer music festival. Pop. (1994 est.) 61,656.

**Lucifer** Name given in ancient Roman times to the planet VENUS. In classical mythology, Lucifer's Greek counterpart was Phosphorus. In Christian mythology, Lucifer was an epithet of SATAN and a symbol of overbearing pride.

**Lucknow** City in N India, on the Gomati River; capital and largest city of Uttar Pradesh. The first Mogul emperor of India conquered the city in 1528. It was the capital of the kingdom of Oudh (1775–1856), then of Oudh province (1856–77) and of the United Provinces (1887). Lucknow was later the center of the MUSLIM LEAGUE in its campaign (1942–47) for an independent Pakistan. Industries: papermaking, distilling, chemicals, printing, handicrafts. Pop. (1991) 1,642,000.

**Lucretia** In Roman legend, the beautiful and pure wife of Lucius Tarqauinius Collatinus. After being raped by Sextus Targinius, the son of the Etruscan king of Rome, she demanded that her father and husband should avenge her and then stabbed herself to death. Lucius Junius Brutus then led the populace in a rebellion and the Roman Republic was established.

**Lucretius** (c.95–55bc) (Titus Lucretius Carus) Latin poet and philosopher. His long poem, *De rerum natura* (*On the Nature of Things*) is based on the philosophy of EPICURUS.

**Luddites** Unemployed workers in early 19th-century England who vandalized the machines that had put them out of work. They were chiefly hand-loom weavers who had been replaced by mechanical looms. The riots started in the Nottingham area in 1811 and spread to Lancashire and Yorkshire before dying out after 1815.

**Ludendorff, Erich** (1865–1937) German general. He played a major part in revising the SCHLIEFFEN PLAN before World War I. In 1914 he masterminded the victory over the Russians at Tannenberg. In 1916 he and Hindenburg were given supreme control of Germany's war effort. In the 1920s he was a member of the Nazi Party.

**Ludlow, Roger** (1590–1664) English colonist in North America. He helped found Dorchester, Massachusetts, and became deputy governor of Massachusetts in 1634. He evolved the state's first codified laws, known as Ludlow's Code. He returned to England in 1654.

**lugworm** Marine WORM that lives in the sand of the seabed. With the aid of bristles, it burrows a U-shaped tunnel in sand or mud, from which it rarely emerges. Length: up to 12in (30cm). Genus *Arenicola*.

**Lukacs, György** (1885–1971) Hungarian literary critic and philosopher. He was a key figure in the 1956 rising. His writings include *History and Class Consciousness* (1923) and *The Historical Novel* (1955).

**Luke, Saint** Author, according to Christian tradition, of the gospel that bears his name and of the ACTS OF THE APOSTLES in the New Testament. He is said to have been a physician, to have been able to speak and write Greek, and may have been a non-Jew born in Antioch, Syria (modern-day Antakiyah, Turkey). Luke is the patron saint of painters. His feast day is October 18.

**Luke, Gospel according to Saint** Third book of the New Testament and one of the three SYNOPTIC GOSPELS. It is traditionally attributed to St. LUKE. One of its sources is the Gospel according to St. MARK.

**Lully, Jean-Baptiste** (1632–87) French composer, b. Italy, who was an early influence on the development of French opera. He joined the court musicians to Louis XIV in 1652. After a series of comedy-ballets (1658–64) came *Cadmus and Hermione* (1673), which has been termed the first French lyrical tragedy. Other operas include *Alceste* (1674) and *Proserpine* (1680).

**lumbago** Pain in the lower region of the back. It is due to strain or poor posture. When associated with SCIATICA, it may be due to a slipped disk. *See also* RHEUMATISM

**lumen** SI unit (symbol lm) measuring the amount of light in a certain area for one second. The light is emitted in a unit solid angle (one steradian) from a source of unit intensity (one CANDELA).

**Lumière, Louis Jean and Auguste** Two brothers, Louis Jean (1864–1948) and Auguste (1862–1954), who were pioneers of CINEMATOGRAPHY. They invented an early combination of motion-picture camera and projector called the Cinématographe. Their film *Lunch Break at the Lumière Factory* (1895) is generally considered to be the first motion picture. By 1895 the brothers had made improvements in color photography.

**luminescence** *See* FLUORESCENCE; PHOSPHORESCENCE

**luminism** Art style followed by a group of 19th-century US painters. The Luminists were concerned with the depiction of light and atmospheric effects. The leading figures were George Caleb BINGHAM, Asher Durand, and members of the HUDSON RIVER SCHOOL.

**luminosity** Absolute brightness of a star, given by the amount of energy radiated from its entire surface per second. It is expressed in watts (joules per second), or in terms of the Sun's luminosity. Bolometric luminosity is a measure of the star's total energy output, at all wavelengths. Absolute magnitude is an indication of luminosity at visual wavelengths.

**lumpfish** (lumpsucker) Marine fish of the North Atlantic coasts, the pectoral fins of which join to form a sucker, with which it attaches itself to rocks. Length: up to 2ft (61cm); weight 13lb (6kg). Family Cyclopteridae.

**Lumumba, Patrice Emergy** (1925–61) African political leader, first prime minister of the Republic of the Congo. He was a leader of the independence movement against Belgian rule and became prime minister in 1960. Refusing to accept dismissal after three months, he was captured by government troops and killed.

**lunar eclipse** *See* ECLIPSE

**lungfish** Elongated fish found in shallow freshwater and swamps in Africa, South America, and Australia from which the first AMPHIBIANS developed. It has primitive lungs, and during a dry season the various species can breath air or survive total dehydration by burrowing into the mud. Order Dipnoi.

**lungs** Organs of the RESPIRATORY SYSTEM of vertebrates, in which the exchange of gases between air and blood takes

▲ **Lumière** On March 22, 1895 Louis Lumière (pictured) and his brother, Auguste, projected their first motion picture. On December 28, 1895 they projected several short pictures to a paying audience for the first time. This date is now considered by many to be the birthday of cinema. Lumière initially shot his pictures himself, but later employed photographers, who were sent all over the world to record important events.

place. They are located in the pleural cavity within the ribcage. This cavity is lined by two sheets of TISSUE (the pleura), one coating the lungs and the other lining the walls of the thorax. Between the pleura is a fluid that cushions the lungs and prevents friction. Light and spongy, lung tissue is composed of tiny air sacs, called ALVEOLI, which are served by networks of fine CAPILLARIES. *See also* GAS EXCHANGE; VENTILATION

**lupin** Any ANNUAL and PERENNIAL plants of the genus *Lupinus*, in the pea family. They have star-shaped compound leaves and tall showy spikes of flowers. Height: to 8ft (2.4m). Family Fabaceae/Leguminosae.

**lupus erythematosus** Autoimmune disease affecting the skin and connective tissue. The discoid form causes red patches covered with scales, often on the cheeks and nose. The systemic or disseminated form varies in severity. Nine times more common in women than in men, the disease is treated mainly with corticosteroids.

**lupus vulgaris** Tuberculous infection of the skin. Often starting in childhood, it causes the formation of brownish nodules, leading to ulceration and scarring. Treatment is with antituberculous drugs.

**Lusaka** Capital and largest city of Zambia, in the S central part of the country, at an altitude of 4,200ft (1,280m). Founded by Europeans in 1905 to service the local lead mining, it replaced Livingstone as the capital of Northern Rhodesia (later Zambia) in 1935. Lusaka is the center of a fertile agricultural region and is a major financial and commercial city. Industries: textiles, shoe manufacture. Pop. (1990) 982,000.

**lute** Plucked stringed instrument popular in 16th- and 17th-century Europe. It has an almond-shaped body and fretted neck and originally had 11 gut strings. It was played to accompany songs and stylized dances and has been revived in recent years as a concert instrument.

**Lutetium** (Lutecium) Metallic element (symbol Lu) of the Lanthanide group, first isolated in 1907 from element ytterbium. Chief ore is monazite (phosphate). The element has no commercial uses. Properties: at.no. 71; at.wt. 174.97; sp.gr. 9.835; m.p. 3,013°F (1,656°C); b.p. 5,999°F (3,315°C); most common isotope $^{175}$Lu (97.41%).

**Luther, Martin** (1483–1546) German Christian reformer who was a founder of PROTESTANTISM and leader of the REFORMATION. He was concerned about the problem of salvation, deciding that it could not be attained by good works but was a free gift of God's grace. In 1517 he affixed his 95 Theses to the door of the Schlosskirche in Wittenberg. This was a document that included, among other things, statements challenging the sale of INDULGENCES. This action led to a quarrel between Luther and church leaders, including the pope. Luther decided that the Bible was the true source of authority and renounced obedience to Rome. He was excommunicated, but gained followers among churchmen as well as the laity. *See also* LUTHERANISM

**Lutheranism** Doctrines and Church structure that grew out of the teaching of Martin LUTHER. The principal Lutheran doctrine is that of justification by faith alone (*sola fide*). Luther held that grace cannot be conferred by the Church but is the free gift of God's love. He objected to the Catholic doctrine of TRANSUBSTANTIATION. Instead, Luther believed in the real presence of Christ "in, with, and under" the bread and wine (Consubstantiation). These and other essentials of Lutheran doctrine were set down by Philip MELANCHTHON in 1530 in the AUGSBURG CONFESSION, which has been the basic document of the Lutherans ever since. In 1947 the Lutheran World Federation was formed.

**Luthuli, Albert John Mvumbi** (1898–1967) South African civil-rights leader. Elected chief of a Zulu community, he became president of the AFRICAN NATIONAL CONGRESS (ANC) in 1952 during a period of increasing militancy that led to the banning of the ANC in 1960. He was the first African awarded the Nobel Peace Prize (1960). Thereafter his movements were closely restricted, and in 1962 his publications were banned.

**Lutoslawski, Witold** (1913–94) Polish composer. He gained international recognition with his Concerto for Orchestra (1954). He later experimented with serialism, notably in *Funeral Music* (1958), and aleatory techniques, as in *Venetian Games* (1961).

**Lutyens, (Agnes) Elisabeth** (1906–83) British composer, dauther of Sir Edwin LUTYENS. she worked mainly within the TWELVE-TONE MUSIC SYSTEM. her works include various symphonies as well as *Quincunx for Orchestra* (1959–60) and the operas *The Numbered* and *Isis and Osiris* (both 1973).

**Lutyens, Sir Edwin Landseer** (1869–1944) British architect. He built a reputation on original designs for houses. He developed a talent for more majestic commissions in his World War I memorials, notably the Cenotaph (1922) in Whitehall, London. His most ambitious project was his plan for the imperial capital of New Delhi (1913–30).

**lux** SI unit (symbol lx) of illumination, equal to one LUMEN per square meter.

**Luxembourg** Independent grand duchy in W Europe, bordered by Belgium, France, and Germany; the capital is LUXEMBOURG. **Land and climate** Luxembourg is divided geographically into the forested ARDENNES plateau and the fertile Bon Pays in the S. In the E, the Moselle and Sauer river valleys provide fertile farmland. Luxembourg has a temperate climate. Forests cover *c*.20% of Luxembourg, farms 25%, and pasture another 20%. **Economy** There are rich deposits of iron ore, and Luxembourg is a major producer of iron and steel. Other industries include chemicals, textiles, tourism, banking, and electronics. Farmers raise cattle and pigs. Major crops include cereals, fruits, and grapes for winemaking. The city of Luxembourg is a major center of European administration and finance. **History** In the 11th century the county of

**LUNGS**

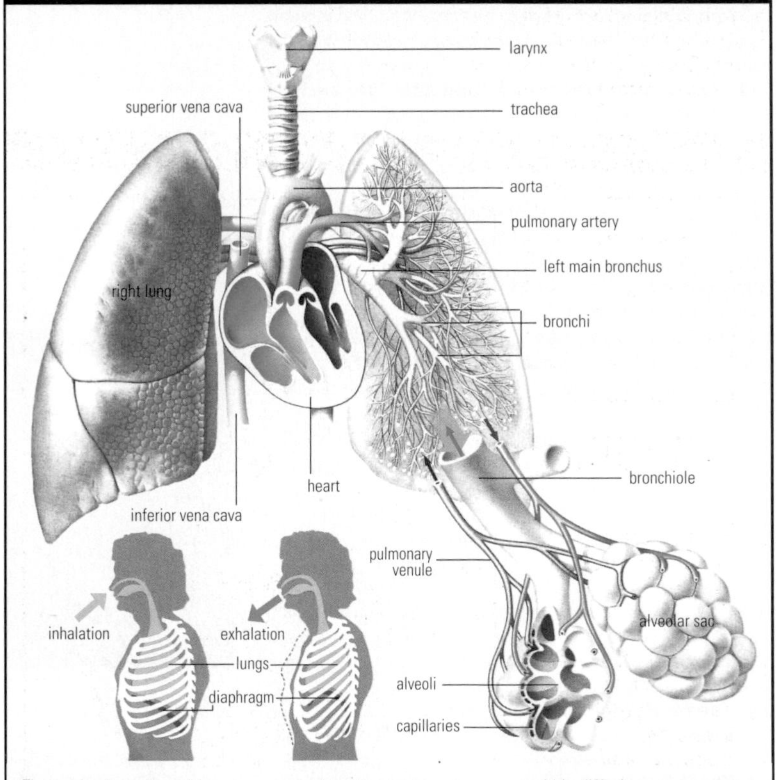

The mechanism of breathing introduces air into the lungs for the exchange of oxygen and carbon dioxide. Air is funneled into the trachea, the flexible windpipe is ringed with cartilage. The trachea forks into the left and right bronchi, which enter their respective lungs. Each bronchus branches into several small segments, or bronchi, terminating ultimately in more than 250,000 respiratory bronchioles, each about 0.02in (0.5mm) in diameter. Beyond lie the alveolar ducts leading into hollow alveoli. Here in the alveoli, networked with capillaries only one cell in width, diffusion occurs across a fine membrane. Stale blood is re-oxygenated and makes its way back to the heart to be pumped to each living cell in the body. Carbon dioxide is eliminated from the lungs in expired air. The inset diagram shows the position of the diaphragm during breathing.

Luxembourg formed one of the largest fiefs of the Holy Roman Empire. In 1354 Luxembourg became a duchy. In 1482 it passed to the HAPSBURG dynasty, and in the 16th century it was incorporated in the Spanish Netherlands. In 1714 it passed to Austria. It was occupied by France during the Napoleonic Wars and was made a Grand Duchy at the CONGRESS OF VIENNA (1815). In 1839 Belgium acquired a large part of the duchy. In 1867 Luxembourg was recognized as an independent state and its neutrality was guaranteed by the European powers. Luxembourg was occupied by Germany in World War I and in 1940 Germany invaded again. In 1948 it joined NATO. In 1960 Belgium, Netherlands, and Luxembourg formed the economic union of Benelux. Luxembourg was one of the six founders of the European Community (EC). In 1964 Prince Jean became Grand Duke. **Politics** Following 1994 elections, the Christian Social People's Party (CD) and the Luxembourg Socialist Workers' Party (SOC) formed a coalition government. Jean-Claude Juncker (CD) became prime minister.

**Luxembourg** Capital of the Grand Duchy of Luxembourg, at the confluence of the Alzette and Pétrusse rivers. Luxembourg was a stronghold in Roman times. The walled town developed around a 10th-century fortress. The Treaty of London (1867) dismantled the fortress. It is the seat of the European Court of Justice, the Secretariat of the Parliament of the European Union, the European Monetary Fund, the European Investment Bank, and the European Coal and Steel Union. Industries include iron and steel, chemicals, textiles, and tourism. Pop. (1995) 76,446.

**Luxemburg, Rosa** (1871–1919) German socialist leader, b. Poland. She was an active revolutionary and anti-nationalist in Russian Poland. She founded the radical left-wing Spartacist League in 1916 with Karl LIEBKNECHT. Both she and Liebknecht are thought to have been murdered while under arrest in 1919.

**Luxor** (El Uqsur) City in E central Egypt, on the E bank of the Nile River; known to the ancient Egyptians as Weset and to the ancient Greeks as Thebes. After the PYRAMIDS, Luxor's temples and tombs constitute Egypt's greatest pharaonic monuments. There are remains of many temples and tombs, dating back nearly 4,000 years. Luxor Temple lies on the banks of the Nile in the heart of the city where, until the 19th century, it remained half buried. It was linked to the Karnak temple, 1mi (2.5km) N of Luxor, by an avenue of sphinxes. Karnak's temple complex covers 100 acres (40ha) and was built over 1,300 years. The site has three separate temples, the greatest of which is the Temple of Amon. The Valley of the Kings, on the Nile's W bank, contains the tombs of many pharaohs. The 1922 discovery of Tutankhamen's tomb revealed the lavish treasure buried with kings. In 1997 58 tourists were massacred by Muslim fundamentalists. Pop. (1992) 146,000.

**Luzon** Largest island of the PHILIPPINES, occupying the N part of the group; the main cities are QUEZON CITY and the nation's capital, MANILA. Luzon accounts for about one-third of the land mass of the Philippines and over 50% of its population. The coastal areas are generally mountainous, the highest peak being Mount Pulog at 9,606ft (2,928m). The fertile central plain is a major rice-producing region. The indigenous Igorots also farm rice on the steep mountain terraces. The Bicol peninsula in the SE has many coconut plantations. Luzon also has gold, chromite, and copper. Manila Bay is one of the world's finest natural harbors. Luzon led revolts first against Spanish rule in 1896 and then against US rule in 1899. In 1941 the island was invaded by the Japanese. US forces staged a last desperate stand on BATAAN peninsula in 1942. In 1945 the Japanese were finally expelled. Several US bases have remained on the island since World War II. Area: 40,420sq mi (104,688sq km). Pop. (1992 est.) 30,500,000.

**Lvov, Prince Georgi Yevgenevich** (1861–1925) Russian political leader. A Constitutional Democrat, he was elected by the Duma (parliament) to form a provisional government on the abdication of Nicholas II in March 1917. His government was feeble and grought in a number of socialists whose first loyalty was to the soviets. Lvov resigned in July in favor of Kerensky. He was imprisoned by the Bolshviks after the November revolution, but escaped to France.

**Lvov** (Lemberg) City in W Ukraine, on a tributary of the Bug River, close to the Polish border. Founded in 1256 by a Ukrainian prince, it was captured by Poland in 1340. Lvov became part of Austria in 1772, and in 1918 was briefly the capital of the Ukrainian Republic, before reverting to Poland. It was annexed by the Soviet Union (1945–91). Industries: heavy machinery, chemicals, oil refining. Pop. (1992) 807,000.

**Lycopodophyta** Taxonomic group (phylum) of about 1,000 species of VASCULAR PLANTS related to ferns, which includes the CLUB MOSSES, selaginellas, and quillworts. They have branching underground stems (RHIZOMES) and upright shoots supported by roots. Some species are EPIPHYTES.

**Lycurgus** (active *c.*625 BC) Semimythical lawgiver of ancient Sparta. He was the author of the political and social system in Sparta, who probably lived at the time of the slave revolt in the mid-7th century BC.

**Lydia** Ancient kingdom of W Asia Minor. Under the Mermnad dynasty (*c.*700–547 BC), it was a powerful and prosperous state, the first to issue a coinage, with its capital at Sardis. Its last king was CROESUS, famous for his wealth, who was defeated by the Persians under CYRUS THE GREAT in 547 BC.

**lye** Concentrated solution of CAUSTIC SODA.

**Lyell, Sir Charles** (1797–1875) British geologist. He was influential in shaping 19th-century ideas about science and wrote the popular three-volume *Principles of Geology* (1830–33), *Elements of Geology* (1838), and *The Geological Evidence of the Antiquity of Man* (1863).

**Lyly, John** (1553–1606) English poet, dramatist, and writer of prose romances. His prose comedies and pastoral romances include *Sappho and Phao* (1584) and *Midas* (1592), but he is best known for the elaborate prose style that he evolved in *Euphues* (1578).

**lyme disease** Condition caused by a spirochete transmitted by the bite of a TICK that lives on deer. It usually begins with a red rash, often accompanied by fever, headache, and pain in the

▲ **lute** Capable of great expressiveness, the lute requires a high degree of skill on the part of the player, or lutenist. The instrument was once played throughout w Europe, particularly in Middle Eastern countries, from where, it is assumed, it originated.

L

## LUXEMBOURG

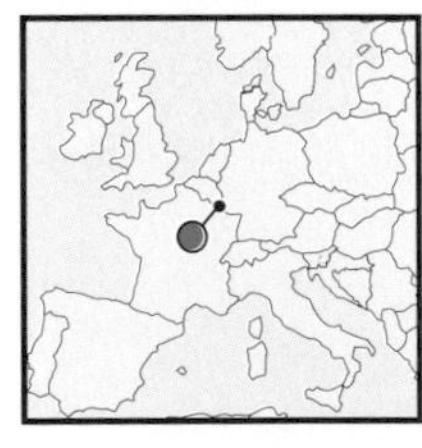

**AREA:** 1,000sq mi (2,590sq km)
**POPULATION:** 390,000
**CAPITAL (POPULATION):** Luxembourg (76,446)
**GOVERNMENT:** Constitutional monarchy (Grand Duchy)
**ETHNIC GROUPS:** Luxembourger 71%, Portuguese 10%, Italian 5%, French 3%, Belgian 3%, German 2%
**LANGUAGES:** Letzeburgish (Luxembourgian-official), French, German
**RELIGIONS:** Christianity (Roman Catholic 95%, Protestant 1%)
**CURRENCY:** Luxembourg franc = 100 centimes

▲ **lynx** The S European lynx (*Felis lynx*) is found only in inaccessible mountain sierras in S Spain and Portugal. It is the same species as the common lynx, which is found in North America and Asia as well as Europe, but has more clearly defined markings. The red lynx, or bobcat (*Felix rufus*) ranges throughout North America as far S as Mexico. It has adapted to living in a variety of habitats, and is among the most common wildcats in the US.

muscles and joints. Untreated, the disease can lead to chronic arthritis, and there may also be involvement of the nervous system, heart, liver, or kidneys. It is treated with ANTIBIOTICS.

**lymph** Clear, slightly yellowish fluid derived from the BLOOD and similar in composition to plasma. Circulating in the LYMPHATIC SYSTEM, it conveys LEUKOCYTES (white blood cells) and some nutrients to the tissues.

**lymphatic system** System of connecting vessels and organs in vertebrates that transport LYMPH through the body. Lymph flows into lymph capillaries and from them into lymph vessels, or lymphatics. These extend throughout the body, leading to lymph glands that collect lymph, storing some of the LEUKOCYTES (white blood cells). Lymph nodes empty into large vessels, linking up into lymph ducts that empty back into the CIRCULATORY SYSTEM. The lymphatic system plays a major role in the body's defense against disease.

**lymph node** (lymph gland) Massof tissue occurring along the major vessels of the LYMPHATIC SYSTEM. Lymph nodes are filters and reservoirs that collect harmful material, notably bacteria and other disease organisms, and often become swollen when the body is infected.

**lymphocyte** Type of LEUKOCYTE (white blood cell) found in vertebrates. Produced in the bone marrow, they are mostly found in the LYMPH and blood and around infected sites. In human beings lymphocytes form about 25% of white blood cells and play an important role in combating disease. B-lymphocytes produce antibodies and T-lymphocytes maintain immunity.

**Lynch, David** (1946– ) US film and television director and screenwriter. His penchant for the grotesque and surreal was evident in Eraserhead (1977). Lynch gained widespread recognition and oscar nominations for The Elephant Man (1980). In 1990 he released Wild at Heart, winning the Palm d'Or at Cannes.

**lynx** Any of several small CATS in forests of central and N Europe, along the French-Spanish border, and in the US. It may be yellow-gray or reddish-brown. It has long legs, tufted ears, and characteristic beardlike hair on its cheeks. Length: to 46in (116cm). Family Felidae.

**Lyon** (Eng. Lyons) City and river port in SE France, at the confluence of the Rhône and Saône rivers; capital of Rhône department. Lyon was founded by the Romans as Lugdunum in 43 BC and became the capital of Roman GAUL. Its historic association with silk began in the 15th century. It was also one of the first printing centers. In 1793 Lyon was devastated by French Revolutionary troops. During World War II it was a stronghold of the French resistance movement. Lyon is the third-largest city in France and Europe's biggest producer of silk and rayon fabrics. Pop. (1990) 415,487.

## LYMPH NODE

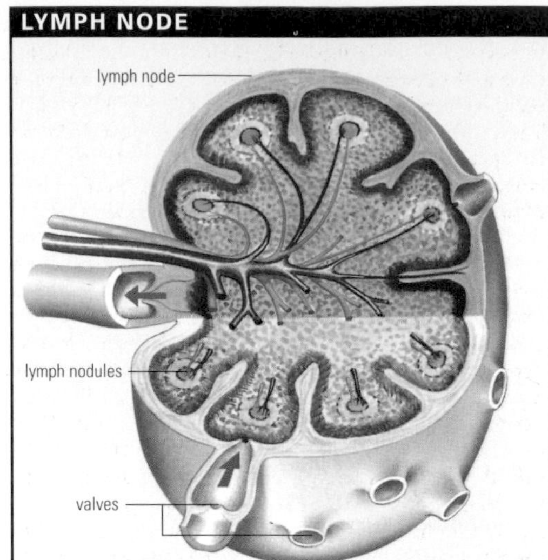


The lymph system is a network of lymphatic vessels which collects tissue fluid (the lymph) and conducts it back to the bloodstream. In the process it transports nutrients from blood to cells and cell wastes back into capillaries. Lymph drains through the system but the lymphatics possess valves to prevent backflow. Lymphatic nodes are scattered along the lymph vessels but particularly in the neck, armpits, and groin. In the tissue around the nodes microorganisms are destroyed by macrophage cells, while antibody-synthesizing white blood cells, the lymphocytes, are produced by the lymph nodules.

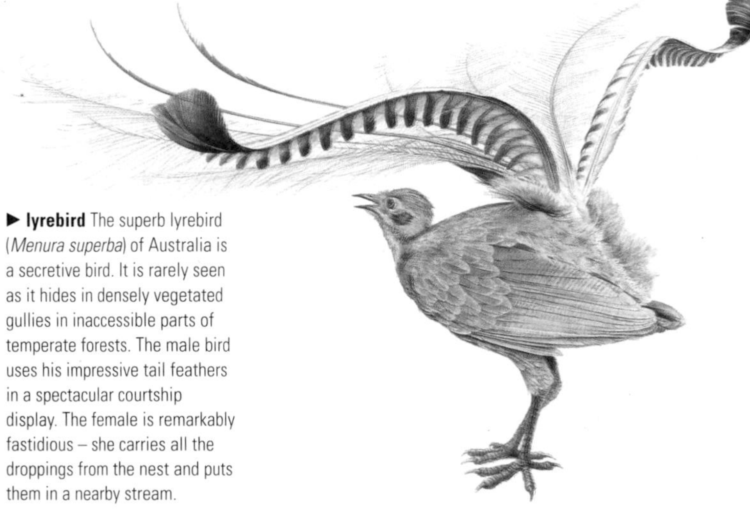

► **lyrebird** The superb lyrebird (*Menura superba*) of Australia is a secretive bird. It is rarely seen as it hides in densely vegetated gullies in inaccessible parts of temperate forests. The male bird uses his impressive tail feathers in a spectacular courtship display. The female is remarkably fastidious – she carries all the droppings from the nest and puts them in a nearby stream.

**lyre** Ancient stringed musical instrument. Used originally by the Sumerians, it was introduced into Egypt and Assyria in the second millennium BC. In classical Greek times it usually had seven strings supported by a wooden frame and attached to a sound box at the base; the strings were plucked using a bulky plectrum. In Europe since the Middle Ages they have more commonly been played with a bow.

**lyrebird** Either of two shy Australian songbirds; the superb lyrebird (*Menura superba*) and Albert's lyrebird (*M. alberti*). These large, perching birds have lyre-shaped tails displayed during courtship performances.

**Lysander** (d.395 BC) Spartan general. He was responsible for the victory over Athens during the PELOPONNESIAN WAR (429–404 BC), defeating the Athenian fleet in 406 and 405 and obtaining Persian support for Sparta. He lost influence in Sparta after the accession of King Agesilaus II in 399 BC.

Lysenko, Trofim Denisovich (1898–1976) Russian agronomist and geneticist. he expanded the theory of Lamarck with his own ideas of plant genetics (Lysenkoism). He promised the Soviet government vast increases in crop yields through the application of his theories.

*M/m, 13th letter of the alphabet, derived from the Semitic letter* **mem** *(meaning* **water***). The corresponding Greek letter was* **mu,** *which went via the Etruscan alphabet to Latin as* **m.**

**Maastricht** Capital city of Limburg province, on the Maas (Meuse) River, SE Netherlands. The city's strategic location close to the Belgian and German borders has meant frequent occupation by foreign armies. In 1992 the MAASTRICHT TREATY was signed here. The city is the commercial, industrial, and transportation center for a wide region. Industries: dairy products, paper, leather goods, glass. Pop. (1994) 118,102.

**Maastricht Treaty** (February 7, 1992) Agreement on EUROPEAN UNION (EU) signed by the leaders of 12 European nations at MAASTRICHT, SE Netherlands. It included a timetable for the introduction of a single currency (the EURO) and a common European citizenship for nationals of all member states. The treaty introduced the principle of subsidiarity, whereby decisions are taken at the most appropriate level: local, regional, or national. It extended qualified majority voting in the EUROPEAN COUNCIL OF MINISTERS and increased the powers of the EUROPEAN PARLIAMENT over the budget and the EUROPEAN COMMISSION. A separate protocol on social policy (the social chapter) was adopted by 11 states with the UK opting-out. The UK signed up to the social chapter in the Amsterdam Treaty (1997).

**Mabuse** (1478–1536) (Jan Gossaert) Netherlandish painter. He began his career in the tradition of Gerard DAVID and Hugo van der Goes, but changed his style dramatically after a visit to Italy as an assistant to Philip of Burgundy in 1508–09. Italianate features appeared within his Netherlandish style, as seen in his *Neptune and Amphitrite* (1516).

**McAdam, John Loudon** (1756–1836) Scottish engineer who invented the macadam road surface. He proposed that roads should be raised above the surrounding ground, with a base of large stones covered with smaller stones and bound together with fine gravel.

**macadamia** Genus of Australian trees of the family Proteaceae. Most species have stiff, oblong, lance-like leaves. The edible seeds are round, hard-shelled nuts, covered by thick husks that split when ripe. Height: to 60ft (18m).

**Macao** (Macau) Portuguese overseas province in SE China, 40mi (64km) W of Hong Kong, on the Pearl River estuary; it consists of the 2sq mi (6sq km) Macao Peninsula and the nearby islands of Taipa and Colôane. The city of Santa Nome de Deus de Macao (coextensive with the peninsula) is connected by a narrow isthmus to the Chinese province of GUANGZHOU. The first European discovery was by Vasco da Gama in 1497. The Portuguese colonized the island in 1557. In 1849 Portugal declared it a free port. In 1887 the Chinese government recognized Portugal's right of "perpetual occupation." Competition from Hong Kong and the increased silting of Macao's harbor led to the port's decline toward the end of the 19th century. In 1974 Macao became a Chinese province under Portuguese administration. It is scheduled to be returned to China in 1999. Macao's economy is based on gambling and tourism. Other industries: textiles, electronics, plastics. Pop. (1991) 339,464.

**macaque** Diverse group of omnivorous, medium-sized to large Old World MONKEYS found from NW Africa to Japan and Korea. Most are yellowish brown and are forest dwellers and good swimmers. Weight: to 29lb (13kg). Genus *Macaca. See also* BARBARY APE; RHESUS

**MacArthur, Douglas** (1880–1964) US general. A division commander in World War I, he became army chief of staff in 1930 and military adviser to the Philippines in 1935, retiring from the US army in 1937. He was recalled in 1941 and conducted the defense of the Philippines until ordered out to Australia. As supreme Allied commander in the SW Pacific (1942), he directed the campaigns that led to Japanese defeat. He was appointed commander of UN forces on the outbreak of the KOREAN WAR in 1950. Autocratic and controversial, he was relieved of his command by President TRUMAN in April 1951.

**Macaulay, Thomas Babington** (1800–59) English historian and statesman. He upheld liberal causes in Parliament (1830–38) and served on the British governor's council in India (1834–38), where he introduced a Western education system. He re-entered Parliament but spent his later years mainly in writing his *History of England* (1849–61).

**Macbeth** (d.1057) King of Scotland (1040–57). In 1040 he killed Duncan I, his cousin, in battle and seized the throne. English intervention on behalf of Duncan's son (later Malcolm III Canmore) resulted in his defeat by Siward, earl of Northumbria, at Dunsinane Hill, near Scone (1054). Macbeth fled north, and was eventually killed by Malcolm at Lumphanan. Shakespeare based his eponymous tragedy on Holinshed's inaccurate 16th-century *Chronicle*.

**Maccabees, Books of** Four historical books, the first two of which are included in the Roman Catholic Deuterocanonical books of the Bible and the Protestant APOCRYPHA. These two are modeled on the Old Testament books of CHRONICLES and are a valuable historical source for the period they describe. The other two books of Maccabees are PSEUDEPIGRAPHA.

**McCarthy, Joseph Raymond** (1908–57) US Republican senator, leader of a crusade against alleged communists in the US government. Taking advantage of anti-communist sentiment in the COLD WAR, he widened his attack to other sectors of public life including the film industry. During the period of "McCarthyism" many of those accused of communism were blacklisted. McCarthy polarised US society; many regarded his hearings as show trials or witch-hunts, while others considered him a hero. In 1954 his HOUSE UN-AMERICAN ACTIVITIES COMMITTEE (HUAC) turned its attention to the army. The hearings were televised, and McCarthy's accusations were shown to be baseless.

**McCarthy, Mary** (1912–89) US writer and drama critic. She wrote several novels, including *A Charmed Life* (1955) and *The Group* (1963). Among her non-fiction works are *Venice Observed* (1956) and *Memories of a Catholic Girlhood* (1957).

**McCartney, Sir Paul** (1942– ) English singer-songwriter. He was the bass player in The BEATLES and co-wrote most of the band's hit songs with John LENNON. The release of his solo album, *McCartney* (1970), marked the breakup of The Beatles. McCartney formed his own group, Wings (1971–81), with his wife Linda (1942–98). In 1977 "Mull of Kintyre" became the UK's bestselling single. In 1995 he was involved in a brief reformation of The Beatles. During the 1990s McCartney turned to more classically inspired work, such as *Liverpool Oratorio* (1991) and *Standing Stone* (1997). He was knighted in 1997.

**McClellan, George Brinton** (1826–85) US general and political leader. He served in the MEXICAN WAR and was appointed commander of Union forces early in the CIVIL WAR (November 1861). He directed major campaigns in 1862 but his conservative tactics irked President LINCOLN and he was replaced. He ran unsuccessfully as Democratic candidate for president against Lincoln in 1864 and was governor of New Jersey (1878–81).

**McCormick, Cyrus Hall** (1809–84) US inventor. He invented the reaper in 1831. A large scale manufacturing operation and widespread advertising, together with his inventions of the twine binder and side-rake, brought him financial success and revolutionized harvesting.

**McCullers, Carson** (1917–67) US writer. McCullers' remarkable first novel, *The Heart is a Lonely Hunter* (1940), showed her to be a sensitive exponent of the "southern gothic" style epitomized by Tennessee WILLIAMS and William FAULKNER. Other works include *Reflections in a Golden Eye* (1941) and the novella *The Ballad of the Sad Cafe* (1951), dramatized by Edward ALBEE in 1963.

**McCullough v. Maryland** (1819) Landmark US Supreme Court case in which the court reinforced the federal government's supremacy over the states by denying an individual state the right to tax a US bank.

**MacDiarmid, Hugh** (1892–1978) Scottish poet, b. Christopher Murray Grieve. A nationalist and communist, MacDiarmid was the dominant poetic voice in Scotland from the early 1920s. His revival of Scots as a medium for poetry was influential in the 20th-century Scottish renaissance. MacDiarmid's masterpiece is *A Drunk Man Looks at the Thistle* (1926).

**Macdonald, Sir John Alexander** (1815–91) Canadian statesman, first prime minister of the Dominion of Canada (1867–73, 1878–91). He strengthened the Dominion by introducing protective tariffs, encouragement of western settlement, and the acquisition of HUDSON'S BAY COMPANY lands (1869). His efforts to organize a transcontinental railroad led to the Pacific Scandal and electoral defeat (1873).

**MacDonald, (James) Ramsay** (1866–1937) British statesman, prime minister (1924, 1929–31, 1931–35), b. Scotland. He entered Parliament in 1906 and became leader of the LABOUR PARTY in 1911. His opposition to Britain's participation in World War I lost him the leadership in 1914. Re-elected in 1922, he regained the party leadership and became Britain's first Labour prime minister. His minority government fell within months. In 1929 he became prime minister again, but the Great Depression led to the collapse of the Labour government (1931). MacDonald remained as prime minister at the head of a Conservative-dominated national government. He was succeeded as prime minister by Stanley BALDWIN.

**MacDowell, Irvin** (1818–85) Union Civil War general. He commanded the Union troops at the First Battle of BULL RUN and later commanded a corps in the Army of the Potomac. Blamed for the defeat at the Second Battle of Bull Run, he was removed from command but later reinstated.

**Macedon** Ancient country in SE Europe, roughly corresponding to present-day MACEDONIA, Greek Macedonia, and Bulgarian Macedonia. The Macedonian king Alexander I (d. 420 BC) initiated a process of Hellenization. PHILIP II founded the city of Thessaloníki (348 BC) and was acknowledged as king of Greece in 338 BC. His son, ALEXANDER THE GREAT, built a world empire, but this rapidly fragmented after his death (323 BC). Macedon was eventually defeated by the Romans in the Macedonian Wars and the empire was restricted to Macedonia proper. In 146 BC Thessaloníki became capital of the first Roman province. In AD 395 Macedonia became part of the Eastern Roman (Byzantine) empire. Slavs settled in the 6th century, and from the 9th to the 14th century control of the area was contested mainly by Bulgaria and the Byzantine empire. A brief period of Serbian hegemony was followed by Ottoman rule from the 14th to 19th century. In the late 19th century Macedonia was claimed by Greece, Serbia, and Bulgaria. In the first of the BALKAN WARS, Bulgaria gained much of historic Macedonia, but it was decisively defeated in the Second Balkan War and the present-day boundaries were established.

**Macedonia** Greek region, bordering the Former Yugoslav Republic of MACEDONIA; the capital is THESSALONÍKI. A mountainous region, it includes many ancient sites, such as the former capital, Pella.

**Macedonia** Republic in SE Europe. *See* country feature

**McEnroe, John Patrick, Jr** (1959– ) US tennis player, b. Germany. He was an exquisite stroke-maker whose fiery temperament often led to conflict with officials. McEnroe won the US Open singles four times (1979–81, 1984) and Wimbledon three times (1981, 1983–84). He and Peter Fleming also captured 10 Grand Slam doubles titles.

**McGovern, George Stanley** (1922– ) US senator (1963–81) and presidential candidate. A Democrat, he was a US representative from South Dakota (1957–61). An outspoken opponent of the Vietnam War, he ran for president against Republican incumbent Richard Nixon in 1972 but carried only the state of Massachusetts. He lost his Senate seat in 1980.

## MACEDONIA

At the center of Macedonia's flag, introduced in August 1992, was an emblem found on the war-chest of Philip II of Macedon. The Greeks claimed this symbol as their own, and, in 1995, Macedonia agreed to redesign its flag, as shown here.

**AREA:** 9,600sq mi (24,900sq km)
**POPULATION:** 2,174,000
**CAPITAL (POPULATION):** Skopje (440,577)
**GOVERNMENT:** Multiparty republic
**ETHNIC GROUPS:** Macedonian 65%, Albanian 21%, Turkish 5%, Romanian 3%, Serb 2%
**LANGUAGES:** Macedonian
**RELIGIONS:** Christianity (mainly Eastern Orthodox, with Macedonian Orthodox and Roman Catholic communities), Islam
**CURRENCY:** Denar = 100 paras

The landlocked Former Yugoslav Republic of Macedonia is a largely mountainous country in SE Europe. The land rises to Mount Korab, at 9,068ft (2,764m), on the border with Albania. Most of Macedonia is drained by the Vardar River, and the capital, SKOPJE, lies on its banks. In the SW, Macedonia shares the large lakes of Ohrid and Prespa with Albania and Greece.

### CLIMATE

The climate of Macedonia is mainly continental, with hot summers and cold winters with often heavy snowfall. Rainfall is slightly heavier in early summer and fall.

### VEGETATION

Mountain forests of beech and oak are common, but farmland covers *c*.30% of Macedonia.

### HISTORY

For history pre-1913, *See* MACEDON

The BALKAN WARS (1912–13) ended with the flight of thousands of Macedonians into Bulgaria, and the division of Macedonia into Greek Macedonia, Bulgarian Macedonia, and Serbian Macedonia (the largest portion, in the N and center). At the end of World War I, Serbian Macedonia became part of the Kingdom of the Serbs, Croats, and Slovenes (later YUGOSLAVIA). Macedonian nationalists waged an armed struggle against Serbian domination. Between 1941 and 1944, Bulgaria occupied all Macedonia, but a peace treaty restored the 1913 settlement. In 1946 President TITO created a federal Yugoslavia, and Macedonia became one of its constituent republics. Regional tension among Greece, Bulgaria, and Yugoslavia remained strong. Multiparty elections in 1990 produced the first postwar noncommunist regional government. In September 1991 the breakup of the Yugoslav Federation led to Macedonia's declaration of independence. It renounced all territorial claims to Greek and Bulgarian Macedonia, but under pressure from Greece the EU refused to recognize its sovereignty, on the grounds that its name, flag, and currency were signs of its territorial intentions.

### POLITICS

In 1993 the UN accepted the new republic as a member and all the EU members, except Greece, established diplomatic relations with the FYRM. In 1994 Greece banned Macedonian trade through Greece. The ban was lifted in 1995, when Macedonia agreed to redesign its flag and remove any claims to Greek Macedonia from its constitution. Internal tensions exist between Macedonians and the Albanian minority. In 1998 elections a right-wing coalition formed a new government.

### ECONOMY

Macedonia is a developing country (1995 GDP per capita, US$1,550). The poorest of the six former republics of Yugoslavia, its economy was devastated by UN trade sanctions against the rump Yugoslav federation and by the Greek embargo. In 1995 unemployment was running at 45% and inflation at 57%. Manufactures, especially metals, dominate its exports. Macedonia mines coal, but imports oil and natural gas. Agriculture employs nearly 17% of the work force, and Macedonia is nearly self-sufficient in food. Crops include cotton, corn, tobacco, and wheat.

**McGuffey, William Holmes** (1800–73) US educator. A professor of languages, he was president of Cincinnati College (1836–39) and Ohio University (1839–43). As the creator and author of the McGuffey readers, spellers, and primers, he was a major influence on the education of 19th-century Americans.

**Machaut, Guillaume de** (*c*.1300–77) French poet, musician, and diplomat. His best-known poetry, which influenced CHAUCER and anticipated the ballade and the rondeau, is to be found in *Le livre de Voir-dit* (1361–65). A leading figure of the *ars nova*, he was among the first to compose polyphonic settings of poetry and the Mass.

**Machiavelli, Niccolò** (1469–1527) Florentine statesman and political theorist. He served from 1498 to 1512 as an official in the republican government of Florence, but lost his post when the Medici family returned to power. His most famous work, *The Prince* (1513), offered advice on how the ruler of a small state might best preserve his power, including judicious use of force. The term Machiavellian, to describe immoral and deceitful political behavior, arose from a simplification of Machiavelli's ideas.

**machine** Device that modifies or transmits a force in order to do useful work. In a basic, or simple, machine, a force (**effort**) overcomes a larger force (**load**). The ratio of the load (output force) to the effort (input force) is the machine's **force ratio** (formerly MECHANICAL ADVANTAGE). The ratio of the distance moved by the load to the distance moved by the effort is the **distance ratio** (formerly velocity ratio). The ratio of the work done by the machine to that put in it is the EFFICIENCY, usually expressed as a percentage. The three primary machines are the inclined plane (which includes the screw and the wedge), the LEVER, and the wheel (which includes the PULLEY, and the WHEEL AND AXLE).

**machine gun** Weapon that loads and fires automatically and is capable of sustained rapid fire. The firing mechanism is operated by recoil, or by gas from fired ammunition. The gun may be water- or air-cooled. The first widely used machine gun was invented (1883) by Hiram MAXIM. *See also* GATLING GUN

**machine tools** Power-driven machines for cutting and shaping metal and other materials. Shaping may be accomplished in several ways, including shearing, pressing, rolling, and cutting away excess material using lathes, shapers, planers, drills, milling machines, grinders, and saws. Other techniques include the use of machines that use electrical or chemical processes to shape the material. Advanced machine-tool processes include cutting by means of LASER beams, high-pressure water jets, streams of PLASMA (ionized gas), and ULTRASONICS. Today, computers control many cutting and shaping processes carried out by machine tools and ROBOTS.

**Mach number** Ratio of the speed of a body or fluid to the local speed of sound. Mach 1 therefore refers to the local speed of sound. An aircraft flying at below Mach 1 is said to be subsonic. SUPERSONIC FLIGHT means flying at speeds above Mach 1. Mach numbers are named for the Austrian physicist Ernst Mach (1838–1916).

**Machu Picchu** Ancient fortified town, 50mi (80km) NW of Cuzco, Peru. The best-preserved of the INCA settlements, it is situated on an Andean mountain saddle, 6,750ft (2,057m) above sea level. A complex of terraces extends over 5sq mi (13sq km), linked by more than 3,000 steps. Machu Picchu was discovered in 1911 by US explorer Hiram BINGHAM, who dubbed it the "lost city of the Incas."

**Macke, August** (1887–1914) German painter. He was a prominent member of the BLAUE REITER group and specialized in sensitive watercolors. During visits to Paris (1907–12), he was influenced by Robert DELAUNAY and by experimental groups, notably FAUVISM and ORPHISM. His own work remained basically in the style of EXPRESSIONISM.

**Mackenzie, Sir Alexander** (1764–1820) Canadian fur trader and explorer, b. Scotland. In 1778 he moved to Montreal. In 1787 Mackenzie became a partner in the fur-trading North West Company. In 1793 his journey to the Pacific via the Peace and Fraser rivers proved the impossibility of a sea passage to the west, although it was the first crossing of the continent N of Mexico. He wrote *Voyages...to the Frozen and Pacific Oceans* (1801).

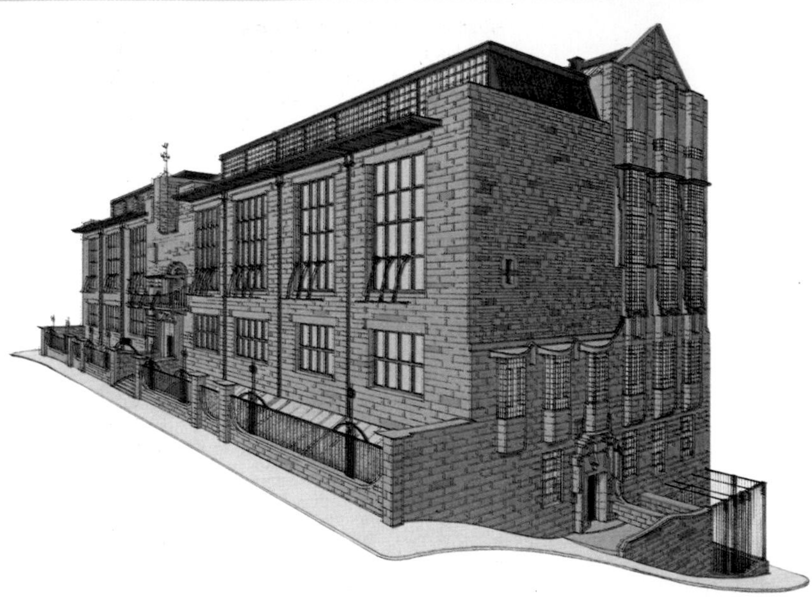

▲ **Mackintosh** Glasgow School of Art (1909). Scottish architect Charles Rennie Mackintosh based his work upon the tradition of Scottish baronial architecture, arriving at a simplified style stripped of all formal ornamentation. The clarity of line of the Glasgow School of Art shows art nouveau influences.

**Mackenzie** River in NW Canada. The longest river in Canada, it flows *c*.1,120mi (1,800km) NW from the Great Slave Lake to the Arctic Ocean. Between the Great Slave and Athabasca lakes, the Mackenzie is called the Slave River. Minerals are the principal economic resource of the basin.

**mackerel** Fast-swimming, agile, marine food fish related to the TUNA and found in shoals in the N Atlantic, N Pacific, and Indian oceans. The mackerel has a streamlined body and powerful tail. The body color is silvery blue with dark side bars. It has a voracious appetite and lives on smaller fish and plankton. Length: 2ft (61cm). Family Scombridae.

**McKinley, William** (1843–1901) 25th US president (1897–1901). McKinley sat in the House of Representatives as a Republican (1876–90) and was elected governor of Ohio in 1891. He defeated William Jennings Bryan in the presidential election of 1896. A strong and effective president, he was largely preoccupied by foreign affairs. McKinley gained the support of Congress for the SPANISH-AMERICAN WAR (1898) and sanctioned US participation in suppression of the BOXER REBELLION in China (1900). McKinley declared that ISOLATIONISM was "no longer possible or desirable." Re-elected in 1900, he was shot dead by an anarchist on September 6, 1901. McKinley was succeeded by Theodore ROOSEVELT.

**McKinley, Mount** Peak in S central Alaska, in the Alaska Range, and the highest peak in North America. Permanent snowfields cover more than half the mountain. Wildlife is abundant on the lower slopes, in particular the caribou and white Alaskan mountain sheep. It is included in Mount McKinley National Park (since 1980 known by the Aleutian name of Denali). Height: 20,321ft (6,194m).

**Mackintosh, Charles Rennie** (1868–1928) Scottish architect, artist, and designer. He was one of the most successful and gifted exponents of ART NOUVEAU. His buildings, such as the Glasgow School of Art (1898–1909), were notable for their simplicity of line and skillful use of materials. Mackintosh's ideas had an enormous influence on early 20th-century European architecture, especially in Germany and Austria.

**MacLeish, Archibald** (1892–1982) US poet and playwright. One of the "LOST GENERATION" of US artists in Paris during the 1920s, he was strongly influenced by Ezra POUND and T.S. ELIOT. His works include the epic poem *Conquistador* (1932) and *Collected Poems* (1952), both of which won Pulitzer prizes, as did his verse play *J.B.* (1958). Other verse plays include *Nobodaddy* (1926), and *The Trojan Horse* (1952).

**McLuhan, (Herbert) Marshall** (1911–80) Canadian academic and expert on communications. His view that the forms in which people receive information (such as television, radio, and computers) are more important than the messages themselves was presented in his books *The Mechanical Bride: Folklore of Industrial Man* (1951), *Understanding Media* (1964), and *The Medium is the Message* (1967).

**McMillan, Edwin Mattison** (1907–91) US physicist. In 1951 he shared the Nobel Prize for chemistry with Glenn Seaborg for the discovery of NEPTUNIUM and other TRANSURANIC ELEMENTS. McMillan worked on the atomic bomb at Los Alamos, New Mexico, then on the cyclotron with Ernest LAWRENCE at the University of California at Berkeley. He developed the synchrocyclotron that led to modern nuclear ACCELERATORS. He shared the 1973 Atoms for Peace prize.

**Macmillan, (Maurice) Harold** (1894–1986) British statesman, prime minister (1957–63). He entered Parliament in 1924. Macmillan held a succession of Conservative cabinet posts, including minister of defense (1954–55) and chancellor of the exchequer (1955–57), before succeeding Anthony EDEN as prime minister. Macmillan improved Anglo-American relations and sought a *rapprochement* between Moscow and Washington. His attempt to lead Britain into the European Economic Community (EEC) faltered in the face of French premier Charles DE GAULLE's opposition. Macmillan's campaign on the theme of domestic prosperity ("you've never had it so good") won him a landslide victory in the 1959 general election. His second term was beset by recession and the Profumo scandal. Macmillan resigned on grounds of ill health and was succeeded by Alec DOUGLAS-HOME. In 1984 he was made Earl of Stockton.

**MacNeice, Louis** (1907–63) Northern Irish poet. MacNeice was a leading member of a left-wing group of writers of the 1930s, later dubbed the "Auden circle". MacNeice and W.H. AUDEN collaborated on *Letters from Iceland* (1937). Other volumes include *Autumn Journal* (1939) and *Solstices* (1961). Other works include the verse play *The Dark Tower* (1947).

**McPherson, Aimee Semple** (1890–1944) US evangelist. In 1926 she founded the International Church of the Foursquare Gospel. Claiming to be guided by God, she professed faith healing and the gift of tongues, and her flamboyant methods were phenomenally successful. In May 1926 she disappeared while swimming and reappeared a month later claiming to have been kidnapped. She was tried for fraud and, although acquitted, never regained her former influence.

**macroeconomics** Study of the economic system as a whole, rather than the study of individual markets as in MICROECONOMICS. It involves the determination of items such as GROSS NATIONAL PRODUCT (GNP) and the analysis of unemployment, INFLATION, growth, and the balance of payments. *See also* ECONOMICS; KEYNES, JOHN MAYNARD

## MADAGASCAR

The colors on this flag are those used on historic flags in Southeast Asia, because it was from there that the ancestors of many Madagascans came around 2,000 years ago. The flag was adopted in 1958, when Madagascar became a self-governing republic under French rule.

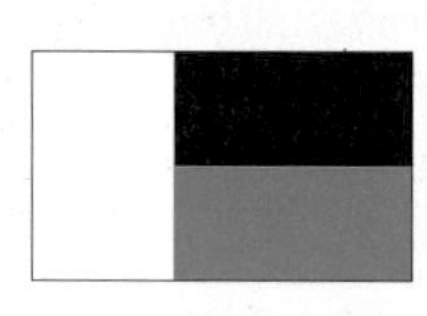

**AREA:** 226,656sq mi (587,040sq km)
**POPULATION:** 12,827,000
**CAPITAL (POPULATION):** Antananarivo (802,000)
**GOVERNMENT:** Republic
**ETHNIC GROUPS:** Merina 27%, Betsimisaraka 15%, Betsileo 11%, Tsimihety 7%, Sakalava 6%
**LANGUAGES:** Malagasy (official), French, English
**RELIGIONS:** Christianity 51%, traditional beliefs 47%, Islam 2%
**CURRENCY:** Malagasy franc = 100 centimes

The Republic of Madagascar lies 240mi (385km) off the SE coast of Africa and is the world's fourth-largest island. In the W, a wide coastal plain gives way to a central highland region, mostly between 2,000ft (600m) to 4,000ft (1,200m). This is the most densely populated region and home of the capital, ANTANANARIVO. The land rises in the N to the volcanic peak of Tsaratanana, at 9,436ft (2,876m). The land slopes off in the E to a narrow coastal strip.

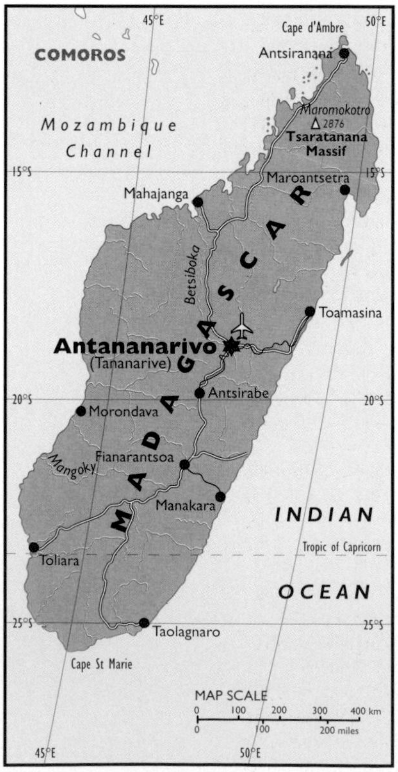

### CLIMATE

Antananarivo lies in the tropics, but temperatures are moderated by altitude. Winters (April to September) are dry, but heavy rain falls in summer. The E coastlands are warm and humid, while the W is drier.

### VEGETATION

Grass and scrub grow in the S. Forest and tropical savanna once covered much of the country, but large areas have been cleared for farming, destroying natural habitats and seriously threatening Madagascar's unique and diverse wildlife.

### HISTORY

Africans and Indonesians arrived over 1,400 years ago, and Muslims arrived in the 9th century. In the early 17th century Portuguese missionaries tried to convert the native population. The 17th century saw the creation of small kingdoms. In the early 19th century the Merina began to subdue smaller tribes, and by the 1880s they controlled nearly all the island. In 1896 the French defeated the Merina, the monarchy was abolished, and Malagasy became a French colony. In 1942 Vichy colonial rule was overthrown by the British, and the Free French reasserted control. During 1946–48 a rebellion against French power was brutally dispatched; perhaps as many as 80,000 islanders died. Republican status was adopted in 1958 and full independence achieved in 1960. President Tsiranana's autocratic government adopted many unpopular policies, such as the advocacy of economic relationships with South Africa's apartheid regime. In 1972 the military took control of government. In 1975 Malagasy was renamed Madagascar and Lieutenant Commander Didier Ratsiraka proclaimed martial law and banned opposition parties. During the 1980s Madagascar was beset by civil strife and numerous failed coups. In 1991 the opposition forces formed a rival government, led by Albert Zafy. In 1993 multiparty elections Zafy became president. In 1995 he was granted the right of prime ministerial appointment. In 1996 Zafy was impeached. In 1997 elections Ratsiraka regained the presidency.

### ECONOMY

Madagascar is one of the world's poorest countries (1995 GDP per capita, US$640). The land has been badly eroded by deforestation and overgrazing. Farming, fishing, and forestry employ about 80% of the work force. Food and live animals form 66% of all exports. The major cash crop is coffee. Madagascar produces about 66% of the world's natural vanilla. Other exports include cloves, sisal, and sugar. Madagascar's food crops include bananas, cassava, rice, and sweet potatoes. It is hoped that Madasgacar's 150,000 unique species of plants and animals will encourage ecotourism.

**macromolecule** Molecule up to 1,000 times greater in diameter than the molecules of most substances. Many proteins, nucleic acids, plastics, resins, rubbers, and natural and synthetic fibers are made up of such giant units.

**macrophage** Large white blood cell (LEUKOCYTE) found mainly in the liver, spleen, and lymph nodes. It engulfs foreign particles and microorganisms by phagocytosis. Working together with other LYMPHOCYTES, it forms part of the body's IMMUNE SYSTEM.

**Madagascar** Republic in the Indian Ocean. *See* country feature

**mad cow disease** *See* BOVINE SPONGIFORM ENCEPHALOPATHY

**Madeira Islands** Archipelago and autonomous Portuguese region, off the NW African coast, *c*.260mi (420km) N of the Canary Islands, in the Atlantic Ocean; the capital and chief port is FUNCHAL (on Madeira). Madeira, the largest, and Porto Santo are the only inhabited islands. The region's warm and stable climate makes it a popular European tourist destination. Industries include the production of Madeira (a fortified wine), sugarcane, fruit, and embroidery. Area: 307sq mi (794sq km). Pop. (1991) 253,400.

**Maderna, Bruno** (1920–73) Italian composer, conductor, and leader of the Italian avant-garde. In 1955 he founded, with BERIO, the electronic music studio of Italian Radio. His use of electronic media was often combined with live performance.

**Madero, Francisco Indalecio** (1873–1913) Mexican statesman, president (1911–13). He was imprisoned (1910) for his opposition to the dictatorship of Porfirio DÍAZ and was forced to flee to Texas, where he called for a MEXICAN REVOLUTION. With the aid of "Pancho" VILLA and Emiliano ZAPATA, Madero overthrew Díaz. Madero was a weak president and the revolutionary movement rapidly and violently fragmented. He was murdered during a military coup led by his former general Victoriano HUERTA.

**Madhya Pradesh** State in central India; the capital is BHOPAL. Other major cities include Gwalior and Indore. During the 16th and 17th centuries the region was ruled by the indigenous Gonds. In the 18th century the MARATHAS assumed control. In 1820 it was occupied by the British and from 1903 to 1950 it was known as the Central Provinces and Berar. In 1956 Madhya Bharat, Vindhya Pradesh, and Bhopal were incorporated into the new state of Madhya Pradesh. Lying between the Deccan and Gangetic plains, it is the largest state in India. The economy is dominated by agriculture. Major crops include wheat, rice, and cotton. Madhya Pradesh is also rich in mineral resources, such as bauxite, iron ore, and manganese. Bhopal has many chemical and electrical industries. Area: 171,261sq mi (443,446sq km). Pop. (1991) 66,181,170.

**Madison, James** (1751–1836) Fourth US President (1809–17). He was a close adviser to George WASHINGTON until, dismayed by the growing power of the executive, he broke with the Federalist Party, his former allies. He became associated with Thomas JEFFERSON and the Democratic-Republican Party. Jefferson, as president, made him secretary of state in 1801, and he succeeded Jefferson in the presidency, winning the election easily in spite of his association with the unsuccessful EMBARGO ACT of 1807. As president he was unable to avoid the WAR OF 1812 with Britain, which provoked threats of secession in New England. The successful conclusion of the war restored national prosperity, and Madison, the "Father of the Constitution," retired to his Virginia plantation as an admired elder statesman. His wife, Dolley (1768–1849), was known as a talented, gracious hostess.

**Madison** State capital and second-largest city of Wisconsin; on an isthmus between lakes Mendota and Monona. Founded as the state capital in 1836, it was incorporated as a city in 1856. It is an educational and manufacturing center in a dairy-farming region. Industries: agricultural machinery, meat and dairy products, medical equipment. Pop. (1990) 191,262.

**Madonna** (1958– ) US popular singer and actress, b. Madonna Louise Veronica Ciccone. Her first hit was "Like A Virgin" (1984). After a promising acting debut in *Desperately Seeking Susan* (1985), Madonna's film career was less consistent and she turned to other media. The documentary *Madonna: Truth or Dare* (1991) was followed by the dance album *Erotica* (1992) and the book *Sex* (1992). Other films include Evita (1996).

◀ **Madonna** US singer and actress Madonna is among the most successful pop artists of all time. A string of hit singles in the 1980s launched her career, which was notable for her raunchy and spectacularly staged live concerts. She subsequently turned to acting, appearing in films including *Desperately Seeking Susan* (1985), *A League of their Own* (1992). She won critical acclaim for her portrayl of Eva Perón in the musical movie *Evita* (1996). The dance album *Ray of Light* (1998) marked another shift in style.

**Madonna** Representation in painting or sculpture of the Virgin MARY, usually with the infant Jesus. The early Christians painted the Madonna in their catacombs, and she was a feature of many outstanding Byzantine ICONS. The advent of the Renaissance brought less stylized representations, and portraits of her during that period were produced by almost every great painter and sculptor.

**Madras** Former name for CHENNAI

**Madrid** Capital and largest city of Spain, lying on a high plain in the center of the country on the Manzanares River. It is Europe's highest capital city, at an altitude of 2,149ft (655m). Madrid was founded in the 10th century as a Moorish fortress. It was captured by Alfonso VI of Castile in 1083. In 1561 Philip II moved the capital from Valladolid to Madrid. The French occupied the city during the PENINSULAR WAR (1808–14). The city expanded considerably in the 19th century. During the Spanish CIVIL WAR Madrid remained loyal to the Republican cause and was under siege for almost three years. Its capitulation in March 1939 brought the war to an end. Modern Madrid is a thriving cosmopolitan center of commerce and industry. Sights include the Prado art gallery. Industries: tourism, banking, publishing. Pop. (1991) 2,909,792.

**madrigal** Form of unaccompanied vocal music orginating in Italy in the 14th century. Early madrigals feature two or three parts and a highly ornamented upper part. During the 16th and early 17th centuries the number of voices was increased and the style became more contrapuntal. The middle period of madrigal composition (*c*.1540–80) was dominated by Italian masters (Andrea GABRIELI; PALESTRINA) and Flemish composers such as Orlando di LASSO. The late period (*c*.1580–1620) was dominated by Italians such as Carlo GESUALDO and MONTEVERDI and English composers such as William BYRD, Orlando GIBBONS, and Thomas Weelkes.

**Madurai** City on the Vaigai River, in Tamil Nadu state, S India. It served as the capital of the Pandya dynasty (5th century BC–11th century AD) and the Nayaka kingdom (*c*.1550–1736) before passing to the British in 1801. Industries: weaving, brassware, woodcarving, tourism. Pop. (1991) 1,094,000.

**Maeterlinck, Maurice** (1862–1949) Belgian dramtist. His plays include *The Princess Maleine* (1889), *Pelléas and Mélisande* (1892), and *The Blue Bird* (1908), first produced in Moscow by STANISLAVSKY. Maeterlinck won the 1911 Nobel Prize for literature.

**Mafia** Name given to organized groups of Sicilian bandits. Originating in feudal times, the Mafia spread to the US in the early 20th century, and became involved in organized crime.

**Magdalene, Mary** *See* MARY MAGDALENE, SAINT

**Magdeburg** City on the Elbe River, central Germany; capital of Saxony-Anhalt state. In the 13th century the city was granted a charter, and Magdeburg prospered as a leading member of the HANSEATIC LEAGUE. During the 16th century it was one of the centers of the Protestant REFORMATION. In 1631, during the

M

▲ **magnolia** The flowers of the magnolia tree or shrub reveal it to be a relatively primitive plant. Like the earliest known flowering plants, its sepals resemble its petals. Native to E Asia and North America, they are popular in temperate gardens for their early white/pink flowers.

THIRTY YEARS WAR, Magdeburg was sacked and destroyed by fire. The city also suffered heavy bomb damage in World War II. A major inland port, it is linked to the Rhine and the Ruhr by the Mittelland Canal. Industries: iron and steel, scientific instruments, chemicals. Pop. (1990) 274,000.

**Magellan, Ferdinand** (1480–1521) Portuguese explorer, leader of the first expedition to circumnavigate the globe. He sailed to the East Indies and may have visited the Spice Islands (Moluccas) in 1511. Subsequently he took service with Spain, promising to find a route to the Moluccas via the New World and the Pacific. Magellan set out with five ships and nearly 300 men in 1519. He found the waterway near the S tip of South America that is now named Magellan's Strait. After severe hardships, the expedition reached the Philippines, where Magellan was killed in a local conflict. Only one ship, the *Victoria*, completed the round-the-world voyage.

**Magellanic Clouds** Two small satellite GALAXIES of the MILKY WAY galaxy, visible in skies around the South Pole as misty stellar concentrations. The Small Cloud (**Nubecula Minor**), located in the constellation of Tucana, is irregular; the Large Cloud (**Nubecula Major**), mostly in the constellation of Dorado, is vaguely spiral. Their distance is *c.*150,000 light-years away.

**maggot** Name commonly given to the legless LARVA of a fly. It is primarily used to describe those larvae that infest food and waste material; others are generally called grubs or caterpillars.

**Maghreb** Arabic term for NW Africa, generally applied to Morocco, Algeria, Tunisia, and sometimes Libya.

**Magi** (sing. Magus) Members of a hereditary priestly class of ancient Persia (Iran), responsible for certain religious ceremonies and cultic observances. By the time of Christ, the term Magi applied to astrologers, soothsayers, and practitioners of the occult. The coming of the Magi to Jesus is marked in the Western Church by the feast of Epiphany. In the East it is celebrated at Christmas.

**magic** Use or apparent use of natural or spirit forces to produce results that seem logically impossible. Belief in magic is associated mainly with primitive societies, although traces can still be found (such as superstitions) in highly developed countries. There are two main types of magic: **black** magic (which makes use of evil spirits and delights in evil for evil's sake) and **white** magic (used to good purpose and to counteract the evil effects of black magic). *See also* WITCHCRAFT

**magic realism** 20th-century school of fiction. Particularly associated with post-1945 Latin American novelists (such as Gabriel GARCÍA MÁRQUEZ), magic realism is characterized by the interweaving of realistic and fantastical or supernatural elements. García Márquez's *One Hundred Years of Solitude* (1967) is the greatest example of the genre.

**MAGNETIC DISK**

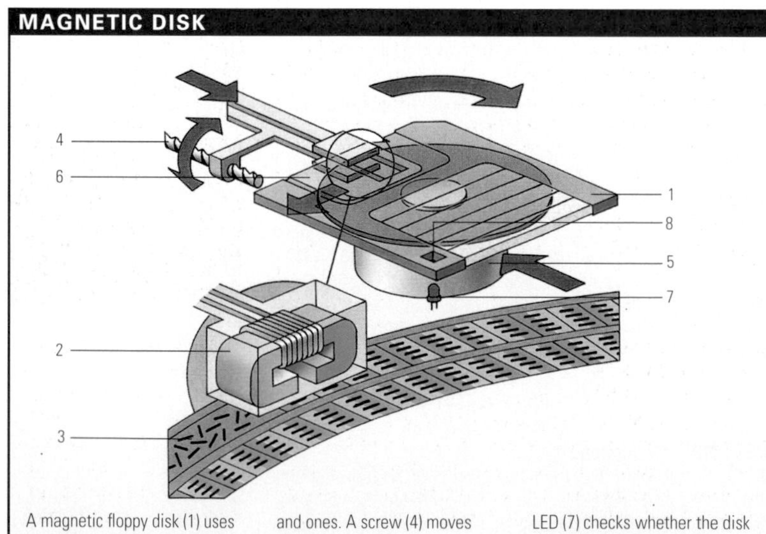


A magnetic floppy disk (1) uses a magnetic head, a tiny electromagnet (2), to polarize magnetic particles in the surface of the disk (3). The polarization represents zeros and ones. A screw (4) moves the head across the disk which is spun by a motor (5). When the disk is inserted, a lever moves aside the protective window over the disk (6). An LED (7) checks whether the disk is write-protected. If the light can pass through a window on the disk (8) it is protected, and no new data can be stored on the disk or old data removed.

**magistrate** Civil official invested by the government, usually local, with authority to administer the law. A magistrate is a judicial officer, inferior to a judge, and is often a justice of the peace or similar official.

**magma** Molten material that is the source of all IGNEOUS ROCKS. The term refers to this material while it is still under the Earth's crust. In addition to its complex silicate composition, magma contains gases and water vapor.

**Magna Carta** "Great Charter" issued by King JOHN of England in June 1215. He was forced to sign the charter by his rebellious barons at Runnymede, an island in the Thames River. The 63 clauses of the Magna Carta were mainly concerned with defining, and therefore limiting, the feudal rights of the king and protecting the privileges of the church.

**magnesia** Magnesium oxide (MgO), a white, neutral, stable powder formed when magnesium is burned in oxygen. It is used industrially in firebrick and medicinally in stomach powders. Magnesium carbonate, found as magnesite and also used as an antacid, is often called magnesia.

**magnesium** Silvery-white metallic element (symbol Mg), one of the ALKALINE-EARTH METALS. Magnesium's chief sources are magnesite and DOLOMITE. Magnesium burns in air with an intense white flame and is used in flashbulbs, fireworks, flares, and incendiaries. Magnesium alloys are light and used in aircraft fuselages, jet engines, missiles, and rockets. Chemically the element is similar to CALCIUM. Hydrated magnesium sulfate is called Epsom salts. Properties: at.no. 12; at. wt. 24.312; sp.gr. 1.738; m.p. 1,200°F (648.8°C); b.p. 1,994°F (1,090°C); most common isotope $^{24}$Mg (78.7%).

**magnet** Object that produces a MAGNETIC FIELD, an area around the magnet in which other magnetizable objects experience a force. Lodestones, which are naturally magnetic, were used as early magnets, and strong magnetic materials were later recognized as containing either iron, cobalt, nickel, or their mixtures. A typical permanent magnet is a straight or horseshoe-shaped magnetized iron bar. The Earth is a giant magnet, its magnetic lines of force being detectable at all latitudes. An ELECTROMAGNET is much stronger than a permanent one and is used for raising heavy steel weights and scrap. A superconducting magnet, the strongest of all, has special alloys cooled to very low temperatures. *See also* MAGNETISM.

**magnetic disk** Plastic disk coated with magnetic material and used for storing computer PROGRAMS and DATA (information) as a series of magnetic spots. Most computers contain a HARD DISK unit for general storage. There is also a unit for inserting portable, lower-capacity **floppy disks**. Data is stored magnetically on both sides of a floppy disk, and is read by magnetic heads in the computer as the disk rotates at *c.*300rpm. *See also* CD-ROM

**magnetic field** Region surrounding a magnet, or a conductor through which a current is flowing, in which magnetic effects, such as the deflection of a compass needle, can be detected. A magnetic field can be represented by a set of lines of force (flux lines) spreading out from the poles of a magnet or running around a current-carrying conductor. The direction of a magnetic field is the direction a tiny magnet takes when placed in the field. **Magnetic poles** are the field regions in which MAGNETISM appears to be concentrated. If a bar magnet is suspended to swing freely in the horizontal plane, one pole will point north; this is called the north-seeking or **north pole**. The other pole, the south-seeking or **south pole**, will point south. Unlike poles attract each other; like poles repel each other. The Earth's magnetic poles are the ends of the huge "magnet" that is Earth.

**magnetic flux** Lines of force or of magnetic induction in a MAGNETIC FIELD. These lines can be seen as the closed curves followed by iron filings placed near a magnet. The direction of the flux at any point is the direction of the magnetic field, and the closeness of the flux (number of flux lines in a given area) is a measure of the magnetic field strength.

**magnetic recording** Formation of a record of electrical signals on a wire or tape by means of a pattern of magnetization. In an audio tape recorder, plastic tape coated with iron oxide is fed past an electromagnet that is energized by the amplified currents produced by a MICROPHONE. By ELECTROMAGNETIC INDUCTION, variations in magnetization (from the oscillating current produced by the sound) are induced in the particles of iron oxide on the tape. When played back, the tape is fed past a similar electromagnet, which converts the patterns into sound, which is in turn fed to an AMPLIFIER and LOUDSPEAKER.

**magnetic resonance** Absorption or emission of electromagnetic radiation by atoms placed in a magnetic field. Spectrometers for nuclear magnetic resonance (NMR) use radio frequencies for chemical analysis and research in nuclear physics, and medically to analyze body tissues. Magnetic resonance imaging (MRI) is a medical scanning system for the brain, spinal cord, and other tissues of the body.

**magnetism** Properties of matter and of electric currents associated with a field of force (MAGNETIC FIELD) and with a north–south polarity (magnetic poles). All substances possess these properties to some degree because orbiting electrons in their atoms produce a magnetic field; similarly, an external magnetic field will affect the electron orbits. All substances possess weak magnetic (**diamagnetic**) properties and will tend to align themselves with the field, but in some cases this diamagnetism is masked by the stronger forms of magnetism: paramagnetism and ferromagnetism. **Paramagnetism** is caused by electron spin and occurs in substances having unpaired electrons in their atoms or molecules. The most important form of magnetism, **ferromagnetism**, is shown by substances such as iron and nickel, which can be magnetized by even a weak field due to the formation of tiny regions, called domains, that behave like miniature magnets and align themselves with an external field. In 1864 James Clerk MAXWELL produced a unified mathematical theory of ELECTRICITY and magnetism (ELECTROMAGNETISM).

**magnetite** Iron oxide mineral ($Fe_3O_4$). It is a valuable iron ore, found in igneous and metamorphic rocks. It is black, metallic, and brittle. Permanently magnetized deposits are called lodestone. Hardness 6; s.g. 5.2.

**magnification** Measure of the enlarging power of a MICROSCOPE or TELESCOPE. It is the size of an object's image produced by the instrument compared with the size of the object viewed with the unaided eye. In an astronomical telescope, magnification is equal to the ratio of the FOCAL LENGTH of the objective (the lens or lenses nearest the object) to the focal length of the eyepiece.

**magnitude** In astronomy, numerical value expressing the brightness of a celestial object on a logarithmic scale. **Apparent** magnitude is the magnitude as seen from Earth, determined by either eye, photographically, or photometrically. It ranges from positive through zero to negative values, the brightness increasing rapidly as the magnitude decreases. **Absolute** magnitude indicates intrinsic luminosity and is defined as the apparent magnitude of an object at a distance of 10 parsecs (32.6 light-years) from the object.

**magnolia** Any of *c*.40 species of trees and shrubs of the genus *Magnolia*, native to North and Central America and E Asia. They are valued for their white, yellow, purple, or pink flowers. Height: to 100ft (30m). Family Magnoliaceae.

**magpie** Bird of the CROW family, closely related to the JAY, found mostly in the Northern Hemisphere. The common magpie (*Pica pica*) has a chattering cry, a long greenish-black tail and short wings. It has a clearly defined white underside with black above. Length: 18in (46cm). Family Corvidae.

**Magritte, René** (1898–1967) Belgian painter. Influenced by DADA, Magritte's *The Menaced Assassin* (1926) is a landmark in the development of SURREALISM. He concentrated on the analysis of pictorial language, placing familiar objects in incongruous surroundings, and disturbing the link between word and image. Other works that explore paradox and ambiguity include *The Key of Dreams* (1930).

**Magyars** People who founded the kingdom of HUNGARY in the late 9th century. From their homeland in NE Europe, they moved gradually south over the centuries and occupied the Carpathian basin in 895. Excellent horsemen, they raided the German lands to the west until checked by Otto I in 955. They adopted Christianity and established a powerful state that included much of the N Balkans, but lost territory to the Ottoman Turks after the battle of Mohács (1526). The remainder of the kingdom subsequently fell to the HAPSBURG empire.

**Mahabharata** (Sanskrit, Great Epic of the Bharata Dynasty) Poem of almost 100,000 couplets, written between *c*.400 BC and *c*.AD 200. It is considered one of India's two major Sanskrit epics, the other being the RAMAYANA. The verse is important both as literature and as Hindu religious instruction and incorporates the BHAGAVAD GITA (Song of the Lord). Its central theme is the dynastic feud between the Kauravas and the Pandavas.

**Maharashtra** State in W India, bordering on the Arabian Sea; the capital is MUMBAI. From the 14th–17th centuries the area was under Muslim rule. In the 17th century it came under the control of the local Maratha tribe. Britain incorporated Maharashtra into its Indian empire in the early 19th century. India's third-largest state in both area and population, it was formed in 1960 and is composed of five subregions: Konkan, Deccan, Khandesh, Marathwada, and Vidarbha. Most of the land lies on the dry, W Deccan plateau where farming is poor. Rice is grown along the coast. The area has rich mineral deposits, including manganese and coal. Industries, such as textiles and chemicals, are concentrated in the major cities, especially Mumbai. Area: 118,827sq mi (307,762sq km). Pop. (1991) 78,707,000.

**Mahatma** (Sanskrit, Great Soul) Person of special holiness. The term is used by Hindus, but has no specific place in organized Hindu religion. The most famous Mahatma of modern times was Mohandas K. GANDHI.

**Mahayana** (greater vehicle) One of the two main schools of Buddhism, the other being the THERAVADA, also known as *Hinayana*. *Mahayana* Buddhism was dominant in India from the 1st to the 12th century and is now prevalent in Tibet, China, Korea, and Japan. Unlike the *Hinayana* (smaller vehicle) school, it conceives of the Buddha as divine, the embodiment of the absolute and eternal truth.

**Mahdi** Messianic Islamic leader. The title usually refers to Muhammad Ahmad (1844–85) of Sudan, who declared himself to be the Mahdi (the Rightly Guided One) in 1881 and led the attack on KHARTOUM (1885). He set up a great Islamic empire with its capital at Omdurman. His reign lasted only about six months before he died in June 1885. His followers were defeated at Omdurman (1898).

**Mahfouz, Naguib** (1911– ) Egyptian novelist. He is celebrated mainly for the "Cairo Trilogy" (1956–57) of realist novels (*Palace Walk*, *Palace of Desire*, *Sugar Street*), which examine the fate of a middle-class family in Cairo between 1917 and the birth of the republic in 1952. In 1988 Mahfouz became the first writer in Arabic to be awarded the Nobel Prize for literature.

**Mahler, Gustav** (1860–1911) Austrian composer and conductor. Mahler conducted the Vienna State Opera (1897–1907) and Metropolitan Opera (1908–10). He completed nine symphonies (the unfinished tenth was left as a full-length sketch), which incorporated folk elements and expanded the size of the orchestra. His second, fourth and eighth symphonies feature choral parts. Other works include the song cycles *Das Lied von der Erde* (1908) and *Kindertotenlieder* (1902).

**Mahmud II** (1785–1839) Sultan of the OTTOMAN EMPIRE (1808–39). His reign saw conflict with Greece, Russia, and Egypt. He was initially successful against Greece in the Greek War of Independence, but Russian and British intervention forced him to capitulate (1829) and started the Russo-Turkish war (1828–29). Mahmud then lost the support of the viceroy of Egypt, Muhammad ALI, which led to the invasion of Turkey, precipitating Egyptian independence.

**mahogany** Any of numerous species of tropical American deciduous trees and their wood, valued for furniture making. Mahogany has composite leaves, large clusters of flowers, and winged seeds. Height: to 60ft (18m). Family Meliaceae.

**Mailer, Norman** (1923– ) US novelist. Mailer's debut novel, *The Naked and the Dead* (1948), was one of the major works on World War II. His combative political journalism, such as *Why are we in Vietnam?* (1967) and *The Prisoner of Sex* (1971), have courted controversy. *Armies of the Night* (1968) and *The Executioner's Song* (1979) both won Pulitzer prizes.

▲ **magpie** Found in temperate regions of Europe, Asia, North Africa, and NW North America, magpies are members of the crow family. The common magpie (*Pica pica*) of Europe and North America, which grows to 18in (46cm), has gained an unfavorable reputation primarily due to its aggressive behavior toward other birds, and its tendency to kill distressed lambs or sickly calves.

M

▲ **Mailer** US novelist Norman Mailer was often critical of American social values. His first novel, *The Naked and the Dead* (1948), drew heavily on his own experiences of war in the Pacific. The antiwar theme was repeated in other writings, most notably in *Why Are We in Vietnam?* (1967) and *Armies of the Night* (1968). Often shocking with his radical sexual attitudes, Mailer attacked early feminist movements in his work *The Prisoner of Sex* (1971).

**MAINE**
**Statehood:**
March 15, 1820
**Nickname:**
Pine Tree State
**State bird:**
Chickadee
**State flower:**
White pine cone and tassel
**State tree:**
White pine
**State motto:**
I direct

Mailer has experimented with a variety of genres, from thrillers such as *Tough Guy's Don't Dance* (1984), to historical novels such as *Ancient Evenings* (1983). *The Gospel According to the Son* (1997) was a political reworking of the life of Jesus.

**Maillol, Aristide** (1861–1944) French sculptor. Initially a painter and tapestry designer, he concentrated on sculpture after 1900 and his work was almost exclusively of the female nude. He turned away from the fluid forms and emotive romanticism of RODIN toward the ideals of Classical Greek sculpture.

**Maimonides, Moses** (1135–1204) Jewish philosopher, Hebrew scholar, and physician, b. Spain. As a youth he was attracted to Aristotelian philosophy, which influenced his well-known *Guide of the Perplexed*, a plea for a more rational philosophy of Judaism. He emigrated to Egypt in 1159 after a tyrannical Muslim sect took over his native Córdoba. In Cairo he became court physician to SALADIN and was the recognized leader of Egyptian Jewry. His *Mishneh Torah* is a systematic compilation of Jewish oral law. Other works on Jewish law and philosophy and on medicine confirmed him as one of the most influential thinkers of the Middle Ages.

**Maine** State in the extreme NE US, in NEW ENGLAND; the capital is AUGUSTA. The largest city is PORTLAND. Inhabited by the Abenaki Native Americans, Maine was explored by John Cabot in 1498. The first British settlement, Fort St. George, was established in 1607 but quickly abandoned. Firm colonization began in the 1620s. Further British settlements were hindered by French and Native American resistance. In 1652 it fell under the administration of the MASSACHUSETTS BAY COMPANY and then of MASSACHUSETTS proper in 1691. In 1820 Maine achieved statehood and became the 23rd state of the Union. Economic development was rapid, based on the trading ports and Maine's lumber resources for shipbuilding. The land is generally rolling country with mountains in the W and more than 2,000 lakes. The chief rivers are the St. John, Penobscot, Kennebec, and St. Croix. Three-quarters of Maine is forested. The major economic sector is the manufacture of paper and wood products. Economic development has been hampered by poor soil, a short growing season, geographic remoteness, and a lack of coal and steel. Broiler chickens and blueberries are the major agricultural products. Lobsters are the economic mainstay of the modern fishing industry. Tourism is an increasingly important sector. Sites of interest include the Acadia National Park and the start of the Appalachian Trail in Baxter State Park. Area: 33,215sq mi (86,026sq km). Pop. (1990) 1,127,928.

**Maine, USS** US battleship mysteriously blown up and sunk in the harbor of Havana, Cuba, in February 1898. The *Maine* disaster became an important precipitating event in the SPANISH-AMERICAN WAR. With Cubans revolting against Spain, the ship had been sent to protect US citizens, and the bombing was attributed to foreign enemies. The cry "Remember the *Maine*," incited war fever, and in April the Spanish-American War began.

**Mainz** City in W Germany, at the confluence of the Rhine and Main rivers; capital of Rhineland-Palatinate. It was founded in 1 BC as a Roman camp. In AD 1118 it was made a free city. In the 15th century, Mainz flourished as a major European center of learning. Today Mainz is an important transport and commercial center. Pop. (1990) 183,300.

**Major, John** (1943– ) British statesman, prime minister (1990–97). He entered parliament in 1979. In 1989 Margaret THATCHER unexpectedly made him foreign secretary then chancellor of the exchequer. Following Mrs Thatcher's resignation, Major emerged as her compromise successor. He moderated the excesses of Thatcherism, such as scrapping the unpopular POLL TAX. Major lent full military support to the US in the GULF WAR (1991). He led the CONSERVATIVE PARTY to a surprise victory in the 1992 general election. The catastrophic events of "Black Wednesday" (16 September 1992) forced Britain to withdraw from the EUROPEAN MONETARY SYSTEM (EMS) and devalue the pound. The issue of Europe haunted the rest of his term and fractured the Conservative Party. Political scandals and sleaze contributed to Tony BLAIR's landslide victory at the 1997 general election. Major resigned as party leader and was succeeded by William Hague.

▲ **Major** Conservative politician and British prime minister, John Major succeeded Margaret Thatcher as leader of the Conservative Party and prime minister in 1990. His consensual approach to government contrasted strongly with Margaret Thatcher's more autocratic style, and helped guide the Conservatives to a fourth consecutive election victory in 1992. Despite an improving economy, the combination of accusations of government incompetence and a party divided over Europe meant that his administration in 1997 suffered electoral defeat at the hands of a rejuvenated Labour Party.

**MALARIA**

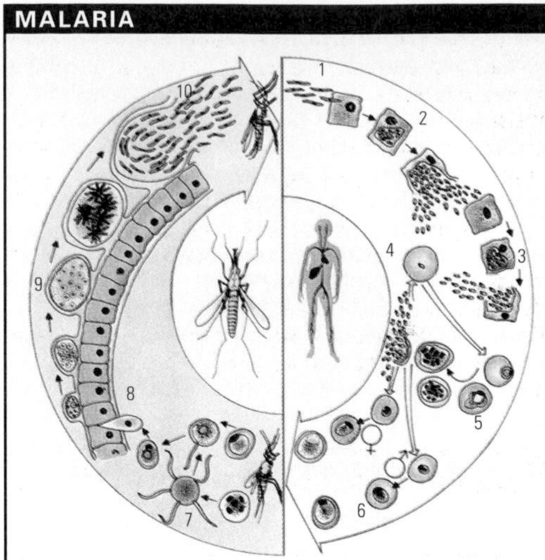



The life cycle of the malaria parasite *Plasmodium* requires two hosts, the *Anopheles* mosquito and a human host, with adverse effects of infection only appearing in the human host. An infected mosquito injects thousands of *Plasmodium* organisms into the bloodstream when it bites a human (1). These penetrate liver cells, multiply, and cause cell rupture (2). Released organisms may reinfect liver cells (3) but usually progress to infect red blood cells (4, 5). Male and female parasites shortly appear in the red blood cells (6). At this stage another mosquito bites the human and takes infected blood from him (7). Fertilization occurs within the mosquito, the "embryo" penetrating the stomach wall (8). Within the cyst formed (9) thousands or organisms develop. The cyst ruptures, organisms released travel to the salivary glands, and from here they are injected into a second human host (10).

**Majorca** (Mallorca) Largest of the BALEARIC ISLANDS, in the W Mediterranean, *c.*145mi (233km) off the Spanish coast; the capital is PALMA. The island is administered by Spain as part of the Baleares autonomous region. In 1229 James I of Aragon captured the island from the Moors and founded the kingdom of Majorca. During the Spanish Civil War it served as a base for Italian forces supporting General Franco. Excluding the mountainous NW, the island is chiefly fertile, with rolling hills and a mild climate. Agricultural products include olives, figs, and citrus fruits. Tourism is the island's economic mainstay. Area: 1,405sq mi (3,639sq km). Pop. (1987 est.) 605,512.

**Makarios III** (1913–77) Greek-Cypriot leader. Appointed Greek Orthodox archbishop of Cyprus in 1950, he led the movement for ENOSIS (union with Greece), and was deported by the British in 1956. He was elected president when Cyprus became independent in 1959, but was briefly overthrown (1974) by Greek Cypriots still demanding *enosis*. The coup provoked unrest among Turkish Cypriots and led to a Turkish invasion and the subsequent partition of Cyprus into Greek and Turkish sections, which Makarios was unable to prevent.

**Malabo** Seaport capital of Equatorial Guinea, on BIOKO island, in the Gulf of Guinea, W central Africa. Founded in 1827 as a British base to suppress the slave trade, it was known as Santa Isabel until 1973. The city stands on the edge of a volcanic crater that was breached by the Atlantic to create a natural harbor. Industries: fish processing, hardwoods, cocoa, coffee. Pop. (1992) 35,000.

**Malacca** (Melaka) State in Malaysia, in SW Malay Peninsula, on the Strait of Malacca; the capital is Malacca. The city was founded in 1403 and prospered as the leading trade center for E Asia. The Muslim sultanate of Malacca became the region's most powerful empire and the center for the spread of Islam throughout Malaya. In 1511 Malacca was conquered by the Portuguese, passed to the Dutch in 1641, and in 1824 it was ceded to Britain. In 1957 it became a state of independent Malaya and, in 1963, of Malaysia. Area: 640sq mi (1,658sq km). Pop. (1993 est.) 583,400.

**Malachi** Last of the books of the 12 minor prophets and last book of all of the Old Testament in the Authorized Version. Probably written *c.*460 BC, it addresses the Jews who had returned to Judaea after the Babylonian Captivity but were disillusioned by the continuing harshness of their existence.

**Málaga** City and seaport in S Spain, on the coast of Andalusia, at the mouth of the Guadalmedina River; capital of Málaga province. It was founded in the 12th century BC by the Phoenicians. Modern tourism has swollen the city's population and spilled over into the nearby resorts of Torremolinos, Marbella, and Fuengirola. Industries: wine, beer, textiles, food processing. Pop. (1991) 512,136.

**Malagasy** *See* MADAGASCAR

**Malamud, Bernard** (1914–86) US novelist and short-story writer. His central theme is the nature of Jewish identity. His novels include *The Assistant* (1957), and *A New Life* (1961). Malamud won a Pulitzer Prize for his novel *The Fixer* (1966). His short-story collections include *Rembrandt's Hat* (1973).

**malaria** Parasitic disease resulting from infection with one of four species of *Plasmodium* PROTOZOA. Transmitted by the *Anopheles* mosquito, it is characterized by fever and enlargement of the spleen. Attacks of fever, chills, and sweating typify the disease and recur as new generations of parasites develop in the blood. The original antimalarial drug, QUININE, has given way to synthetics such as chloroquine. With 270 million people infected, malaria is one of the most widespread diseases, claiming two million lives a year.

**Malawi** Republic in E central Africa. *See* country feature

**Malawi, Lake** (formerly Lake Nyasa) Lake in E central Africa, in the Great RIFT VALLEY, bordered by Tanzania (N), Mozambique (E), and Malawi (S and W). First sighted by the

## MALAWI

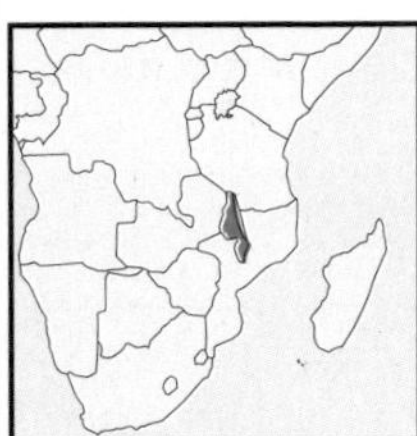

The colors in Malawi's flag come from the flag of the Malawi Congress Party, which was adopted in 1953. The symbol of the rising sun was added when Malawi became independent from Britain in 1964. It represents the beginning of a new era for Malawi and Africa.

**AREA:** 45,745sq mi (118,480sq km)
**POPULATION:** 8,823,000
**CAPITAL (POPULATION):** Lilongwe (268,000)
**GOVERNMENT:** Multiparty republic
**ETHNIC GROUPS:** Maravi (Chewa, Nyanja, Tonga, Tumbuka) 58%, Lomwe 18%, Yao 13%, Ngoni 7%
**LANGUAGES:** Chichewa and English (both official)
**RELIGIONS:** Christianity (Protestant 34%, Roman Catholic 28%), traditional beliefs 21%, Islam 16%
**CURRENCY:** Kwacha = 100 tambala

The landlocked republic of Malawi in SE Africa is dominated by Lake MALAWI, which constitutes 50% of its area. The lake forms most of Malawi's E border with Tanzania and Mozambique, and is drained in the S by the Shire River (a tributary of the ZAMBEZI). The capital, LILONGWE, lies in a valley of the central plateau. Mountains fringe the W edge of Lake Malawi, rising in the S to 9,843ft (3,000m) at Mlange.

### CLIMATE

The lowlands are hot and humid throughout the year, but the uplands have a pleasant climate. Lilongwe has a warm, sunny climate, though frosts sometimes occur in July and August.

### VEGETATION

Grassland and tropical savanna cover much of Malawi, with woodland growing in wet areas.

### HISTORY AND POLITICS

The SAN were gradually displaced by Bantu-speakers, who formed the Maravi kingdom (15th–18th century). In the early 19th century, the area was a center of the slave trade. In 1891 it became a British protectorate. Slavery was abolished and coffee plantations established. In 1907 it became known as Nyasaland. A 1915 rebellion against British domination was suppressed. In 1953 Britain made Nyasaland part of the Federation of Rhodesia (now Zimbabwe) and Nyasaland (the Federation also included present-day Zambia). The Congress Party, led by Dr. Hastings BANDA, strongly opposed the Federation. In 1959 a state of emergency was declared. The Federation was dissolved in 1963, and in 1964 Nyasaland achieved independence as Malawi. Banda was the first postcolonial prime minister, and when Malawi became a republic in 1966 he was made president. Malawi became a one-party state and Banda's autocratic government established diplomatic relations with South Africa's apartheid government in 1967. In 1971, as the newly appointed president-for-life, Banda became the first postcolonial black African head of state to visit South Africa. Malawi became a shelter for rebels and refugees from the civil war in Mozambique; more than 600,000 were accomodated in the late 1980s. Banda's repression of opposition became more brutal. International aid for the 1992 famine was tied to improvements in human rights and the establishment of multiparty democracy. In 1994 elections Banda and his Malawi Congress Party were defeated. Bakili Muluzi of the United Democratic Front became president. In 1995 Banda and his political associates were acquitted of murder.

### ECONOMY

Malawi is one of the world's poorest countries (1995 GDP per capita, US$750). More than 80% of the work force are farmers, most at subsistence level. Major food crops include cassava, corn, and rice. Chief export crops include tobacco, tea, sugar, and cotton. Malawi lacks mineral resources and has few manufacturing industries. Lake fishing is an important activity.

**Malawi's rich flora is revealed in this 1967 stamp showing wild flowers (*Ochna macrocalyx*).**

explorer Caspar Boccaro in 1616, the lake was visited by David Livingstone in 1859. The third-largest lake in Africa, it is fed chiefly by the Ruhuhu River and drained by the Shire.

**Malayalam** Language spoken on the w coast of extreme s India, principally in the state of Kerala. It belongs to the Dravidian family of languages and there are *c.*20 million speakers. It is one of the 15 constitutional languages of India.

**Malayo-Polynesian languages** Alternative term for Austronesian languages

**Malay Peninsula** Promontory of se Asia, stretching for *c.*700mi (1,100km) between the Strait of Malacca and the South China Sea. The n part of the peninsula is now s Thailand and the s part forms Malaya (w Malaysia). Singapore lies off its s tip. A mountain range is the backbone of the peninsula, rising to 7,186ft (2,190m) at Mount Gunong Tahang. Most of the vegetation is dense tropical rain forest. The peninsula is one of the world's largest producers of tin and rubber. Today the peninsula is populated equally by Malays and Chinese. The region was controlled almost continuously from the 8th to the 13th centuries by the Buddhist Sailendra dynasty from Sumatra. In the 15th century the Malaccan empire held sway. For the next three centuries the region came under the control of the various European imperial powers. In 1909 Britain assumed control of a majority of the states and reached a border agreement with Siam (Thailand). Area: *c.*70,000sq mi (180,000sq km).

**Malaysia** Federation of se Asian states. *See* country feature

**Malcolm X** (1925–65) (Malcolm Little) US African-American nationalist leader. While in prison, Malcolm joined the Black Muslims and, after his release in 1953, became their leading spokesman. Following an ideological split with the founder of the movement, Elijah Muhammad, he made a pilgrimage to Mecca, became an orthodox Muslim, and formed a rival group. His assassination may have been authorized by the Black Muslims.

**Maldives** Republic in the Indian Ocean, *c.*400mi (640km) sw of Sri Lanka, consisting of *c.*1,200 low-lying coral islands grouped into 26 atolls; the largest island and capital is Male. The islands (of which 200 are inhabited) are prone to flooding. The climate is tropical, and the monsoon season lasts from April to October. Coconuts and copra are the primary crop. Fishing is traditionally the major industry, and the leading export-earner is the bonito (Maldives tuna). Since 1972 tourism has been encouraged to boost foreign reserves. The

## MALAYSIA

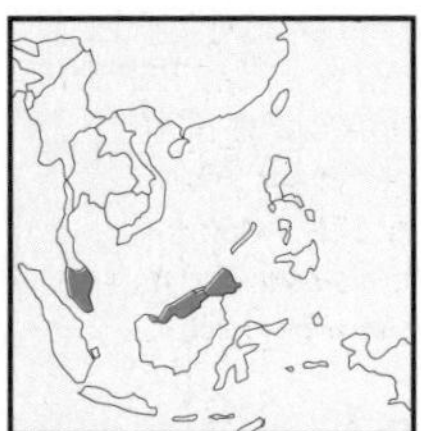

This flag was adopted when the Federation of Malaysia was set up in 1963. The red and white bands date back to a revolt in the 13th century. The star and crescent are symbols of Islam. The blue represents Malaysia's place in the Commonwealth.

**AREA:** 127,316sq mi (329,750sq km)
**POPULATION:** 18,181,000
**CAPITAL (POPULATION):** Kuala Lumpur (1,231,500)
**GOVERNMENT:** Federal constitutional monarchy
**ETHNIC GROUPS:** Malay and other indigenous groups 62%, Chinese 30%, Indian 8%
**LANGUAGES:** Malay (official)
**RELIGIONS:** Islam 53%, Buddhism 17%, Chinese folk religions 12%, Hinduism 7%, Christianity 6%
**CURRENCY:** Ringgit (Malaysian dollar) = 100 cents

The Federation of Malaysia consists of two main parts: **West Malaysia** is on the Malay Peninsula between the Strait of Malacca and the South China Sea. It is home to *c.*80% of the population and includes the capital, Kuala Lumpur. **East Malaysia** consists of the states of Sabah and Sarawak, in n Borneo. Within Sarawak is the independent nation of Brunei. East and West Malaysia consist of coastal lowlands with mountainous interiors. The highest peak is Kinabalu (Sabah), at 13,455ft (4,101m).

### Climate and Vegetation

Malaysia has a hot and rainy climate. There are sw and nw monsoon seasons. Kuala Lumpur has an annual average of 200 days of rain. Dense rain forest covers *c.*60% of Malaysia; only 13% of the land is farmed.

### History and Politics

(For early history, *See* Malay Peninsula; Sabah and Sarawak)

In 1641 the Dutch captured Malacca and controlled much of the trade through the narrow strait. In 1795 Britain conquered Malacca. In 1819 Britain founded Singapore, and in 1826 formed the Straits Settlement, consisting of Penang, Malacca, and Singapore. In 1867 the Straits Settlement became a British colony. Sabah and Sarawak became a British protectorate in 1888. In 1896 the states of Perak, Selangor, Pahang, and Negeri Semblian were federated. In 1909 the states of Johor, Kedah, Kelantan, Perlis, and Terengganu formed the Unfederated Malay States. Japan occupied Malaysia during World War II. After Japan's defeat, the British expanded the Federation of Malaya (1948) to include the unfederated states, and Malacca and Pinang. Communists (largely from the Chinese population) began a protracted guerrilla war, and many Chinese were forcibly resettled. In 1957 the Federation of Malaya became an independent state within the Commonwealth of Nations. In 1963 Singapore, Sabah, and Sarawak joined the Federation, which became known as Malaysia. Tension over Chinese representation led to the secession of Singapore in 1965. The New Economic Policy (1970–90) was largely successful in reducing ethnic tension caused by economic inequality. The United Malays National Organization (UMNO) has held power since independence. In 1997 choking pollution from smog and the economic crisis in se Asia led to criticism of Dr. Mahathir Muhammad's premiership (1979– ). In 1998, after publicly calling for Mahathir's resignation, deputy prime minister Anwar Ibrahim was arrested on charges of corruption and sodomy.

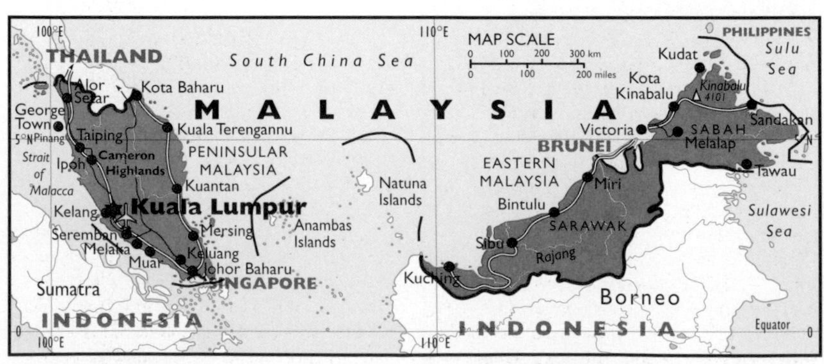


### Economy

Malaysia is an upper-middle-income developing country (1995 GDP per capita, US$9,020). The National Development Policy (1990–2000) was the second stage in its rapid industrialization. In the early 1990s growth averaged 8% per annum. In 1997 Malaysia's stock market lost 60% of its value. In 1998 the ringgit was withdrawn from international foreign exchange markets. Manufactured goods account for 78% of exports. Malaysia is the world's largest producer of palm oil, second-largest producer of tin, and third-largest producer of natural rubber. Agriculture is an important activity. Rice is the chief food crop.

chief religion is Sunni Muslim. From the 14th century the country was ruled by the ad-Din dynasty. In 1518 the islands were claimed by the Portuguese. From 1665 to 1886 they were a dependency of Ceylon (Sri Lanka). In 1887 they became a British protectorate. In 1965 they achieved independence as a sultanate. In 1968 the sultan was deposed and a republic was declared. In 1982 Maldives joined the Commonwealth. An attempted coup in 1988 was suppressed with the aid of Indian troops. Area: 115sq mi (298sq km). Pop. (1990) 213,215.

**Male** Largest of the Maldive Islands, in the Indian Ocean. The island atoll forms the only urban area in the group, trading in bonito (Maldives tuna), breadfruit, copra, and other coconut products. The extension of the airport to facilitate long-haul flights has boosted tourism. Pop. (1990) 55,000.

**Malenkov, Georgi Maksimilianovich** (1902–88) Soviet statesman, prime minister (1953–55). On STALIN's death (1953), Malenkov succeeded him as prime minister and leader of the Communist Party. He was soon superseded by KHRUSHCHEV as party leader and in 1955 lost the premiership also. Implicated in an unsuccessful coup against Khrushchev in 1957, Malenkov was dispatched to manage a power station in Siberia. In 1961 he was expelled from the party.

**Malevich, Kasimir** (1878–1935) Russian painter, an important pioneer of geometric ABSTRACT ART. He absorbed ideas from CUBISM (LÉGER in particular) and FUTURISM and experimented with the fragmentation and multiplication of images, as in *The Knife Grinder* (1912). He founded the SUPREMATISM movement (1913) and later concentrated on developing CONSTRUCTIVISM.

**Mali** Largest country in W Africa. *See* country feature

**Malinowski, Bronislaw** (1884–1942) British anthropologist, b. Poland, considered by many to be one of the pioneers of social anthropology. His work with primitive peoples led him to believe that every aspect or norm of a society is a function vital to its existence.

**mallard** Common freshwater duck. The male is black, white, brown, and gray with a green head, whereas the female is mottled brown with blue wing markings. It dabbles or feeds from the surface. Length: 28in (63cm). Species *Anas platyrhynchos*.

**Mallarmé, Stephane** (1842–98) French poet and leading exponent of SYMBOLISM. He published relatively few poems as *Poésies* in 1899. His most notable compositions include *Hérodiade* (1869) and *L'Après-Midi d'un faune* (1876).

**Malle, Louis** (1932–95) French movie director. His first

## MALI

**The colors on Mali's flag are those used on the flag of Ethiopia, Africa's oldest independent nation. They symbolize African unity. This flag was used by Mali's African Democratic Rally prior to the country becoming independent from France in 1960.**

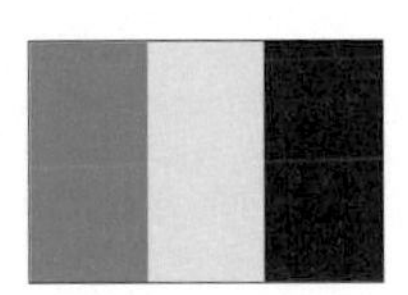

**AREA:** 478,837sq mi (1,240,190sq km)
**POPULATION:** 9,818,000
**CAPITAL (POPULATION):** Bamako (646,000)
**GOVERNMENT:** Multiparty republic
**ETHNIC GROUPS:** Bambara 32%, Fulani (or Peul) 14%, Senufo 12%, Soninke 9%, Tuareg 7%, Songhai 7%, Malinke (Mandingo or Mandinke) 7%
**LANGUAGES:** French (official)
**RELIGIONS:** Islam 90%, traditional beliefs 9%, Christianity 1%
**CURRENCY:** CFA franc = 100 centimes

The landlocked N African republic of Mali is generally flat. Northern Mali is part of the SAHARA, which rises to the border with Algeria. This region contains many wadis (dry river valleys). The old trading city of TIMBUKTU lies on the edge of the desert. The main rivers, the Sénégal and the Niger, are both in S Mali. The capital, BAMAKO, lies on the banks of the Niger.

### CLIMATE

Northern Mali has a hot, arid climate. The S has enough rain for cultivation. Dry and dusty harmattan winds blow from the Sahara.

### VEGETATION

Over 70% of Mali is desert or semidesert with sparse vegetation. Central and SE Mali is a dry grassland region known as the SAHEL. In prolonged droughts, the N Sahel dries up and becomes part of the Sahara. Southern Mali, the most densely populated region, is covered by fertile farmland and tropical savanna.

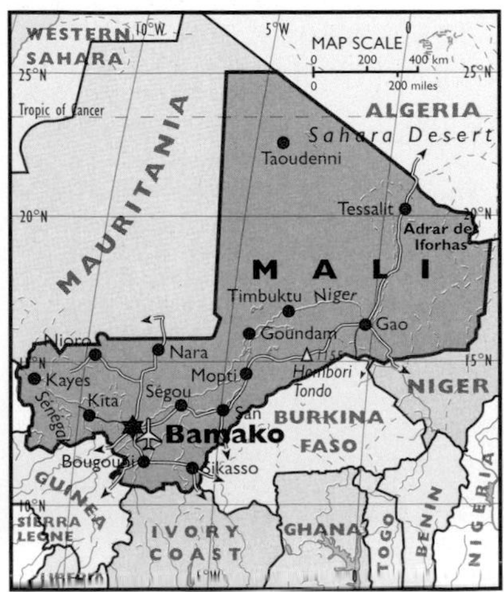


### HISTORY

The region of Mali has lain at the heart of many of Africa's historic empires. From the 4th to the 11th centuries, the region was part of the ancient Ghana empire. The medieval empire of Mali was one of the world's most powerful and prosperous powers; its gold riches were legendary. The 14th-century reign of Emperor Mansa Musa saw the introduction of Islam, and the development of Timbuktu as a great center of learning and the trans-Saharan trade. The SONGHAI empire dominated the region during the 15th century. In the 19th century France gradually gained control. In 1893 the region became known as French Sudan, and in 1898 was incorporated into the Federation of West Africa. Nationalist movements grew more vocal in their opposition to colonialism. In 1958 French Sudan voted to join the French Community as an autonomous republic. In 1959 it joined with SENEGAL to form the Federation of Mali. Shortly after gaining independence, Senegal seceded, and in 1960 Mali became a one-party republic. Its first president, Modibo Keita, was committed to nationalization and pan-Africanism. In 1962 Mali adopted its own currency. In 1963 Mali joined the ORGANIZATION OF AFRICAN STATES (OAS). Economic crisis forced Keita to revert to the franc zone and permit France greater economic influence. Opposition led to Keita's overthrow in a military coup in 1968. The army group formed a National Liberation Committee, and appointed Moussa Traoré as prime minister. During the 1970s the Sahel suffered a series of droughts, which contributed to a devastating famine that claimed thousands of lives. In 1979 a new constitution was adopted, and Traoré was elected president. In 1991 he was overthrown in a military coup. In 1992 a new constitution provided for a multiparty democracy.

### POLITICS

The Alliance for Democracy in Mali (ADEMA) won the 1992 elections and Alpha Oumar Konaré became president. A settlement provided a special administration for the N TUAREGS. In 1997 Konaré was re-elected and Traoré was sentenced to life imprisonment.

### ECONOMY

Mali is one of the world's poorest countries (1995 GDP per capita, US$550). Agriculture, including nomadic pastoralism, employs 85% of the work force. Farming is hampered by water shortages, and only 2% of the land is cultivated. Another 25% is used for grazing animals. Food crops include millet, rice, and sorghum. The chief cash crops are cotton, peanuts, and sugarcane. Fishing is an important economic activity. Mali has vital mineral deposits of gold and salt. In 1984 Mali rejoined the franc zone, and is a major recipient of international aid to support its free market reforms.

M

## MALTA

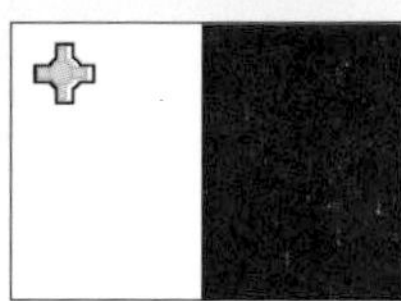

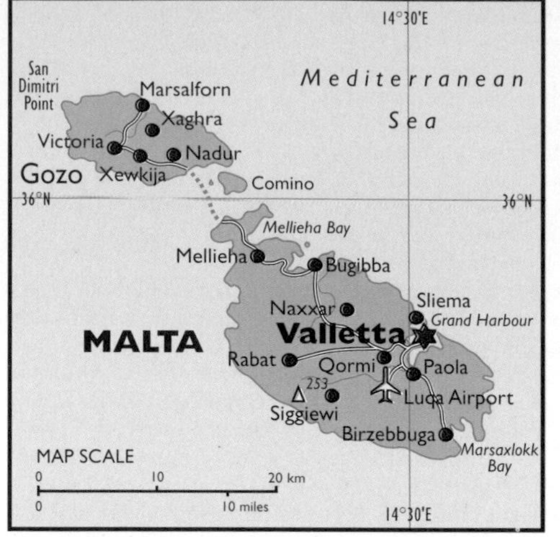


**AREA:** 122sq mi (316sq km )
**POPULATION:** 359,000
**CAPITAL (POPULATION):** Valletta (102,571)
**GOVERNMENT:** Multiparty republic
**ETHNIC GROUPS:** Maltese 96%, British 2%
**LANGUAGES:** Maltese and English (both official)
**RELIGIONS:** Christianity (Roman Catholicism 99%)
**CURRENCY:** Maltese lira = 100 cents

feature, *Ascenseur pour l'Echaufaud* (1957) was a landmark in the French NOUVELLE VAGUE. Other movies from this period include *Les Amants* (1958), and *Le Feu Follet* (1963). Malle's first English language film was *Pretty Baby* (1978). Other US movies include *Atlantic City* (1981). His best-known work was *Au Revoir Les Enfants* (1987). Malle's final film was *Vanya on 42nd Street* (1995).

**mallow** Annual and perennial plants occurring in tropical and temperate regions of the world. The flowers are pink and white. The mallow family includes more than 900 species of plants, of which cotton, okra, hollyhock, and hibiscus are among the best known. Family Malvaceae; especially genus *Malva*.

**malnutrition** Condition resulting from a diet that is deficient in necessary components such as PROTEINS, FATS, or CARBOHYDRATES. It can lead to deficiency diseases, increased vulnerability to infection, and death.

**Malory, Sir Thomas** (active 1460–70) English author. He wrote *Le Morte d'Arthur*, which recounts the legend of King ARTHUR. The book was apparently written in prison and completed in 1469, but Malory's identity is obscure.

**Malraux, André** (1901–76) French intellectual, novelist, politician, and war hero. His novels, *The Conquerors* (1928), *Man's Estate* (1933), and *Days of Hope* (1937), are based on his experiences in China (1925–27), in the Spanish Civil War (1936–39), and in the French resistance during World War II.

**malt** Germinated grain, usually BARLEY, used in beverages, beer, and foods. The grain is softened in water and allowed to germinate. This activates ENZYMES, which convert the starch to malt sugar (maltose). The grain is then kiln-dried.

**Malta** Archipelago republic in the Mediterranean Sea, *c.*60mi (100km) S of Sicily; the capital is VALLETTA (on Malta). **Land and climate** Malta consists of two main islands, Malta (area: 95sq mi/246sq km) and Gozo (26sq mi/67sq km); the small island of Comino, located between the two large islands; and two tiny islets. The islands are low-lying. Malta island is composed mostly of limestone. Gozo is largely covered by clay, and as a result, its landscapes are less arid. The climate is typically Mediterranean, with hot, dry summers and mild, wet winters. In spring, the SIROCCO may raise temperatures and damage crops. Malta has no forests, and 38% of the land is arable. **History** Malta has evidence of Stone Age settlement dating back *c.*4,000 years. The Phoenicians colonized Malta in about 850 BC. They were followed by the Carthaginians, Greeks, and Romans. In AD 395 Malta became part of the E Roman (Byzantine) empire. Arab invasion in 870 introduced Islam, but Christian rule was restored in 1091 by Roger I, Norman king of Sicily. A succession of feudal lords ruled Malta until the early 16th century. In 1530 the Holy Roman Emperor gave Malta to the KNIGHTS HOSPITALLERS. The Knights, who had fought in the CRUSADES, held Malta against a Turkish siege in 1565. The French under NAPOLEON I took Malta in 1798, but, with help from Britain, they were driven out in 1800, and in 1814 Malta became a British colony. Malta became a strategic British base. In World War II, Italian and German aircraft bombed the islands. In recognition of the bravery of Maltese resistance, the British king George VI awarded the George Cross to Malta in 1942. In 1953 Malta became a NATO base. Malta became independent in 1964, and in 1974 it became a republic. In 1979 British forces withdrew from Malta. In the 1980s Malta declared itself a neutral country. **Politics** In 1990 Malta applied to join the European Community. In 1997 the newly-elected Malta Labour Party pledged to rescind the application. The Nationalist Party, led by the pro-European Edward Adami, regained power in 1998 elections. **Economy** Malta is an upper-middle-income developing country (1992 GDP per capita, US$8,281). It lacks natural resources. Machinery and transportation equipment account for more than 50% of exports. Malta's historic naval dockyards are now used for commercial shipbuilding and repair. The state-owned Malta Drydocks is Malta's leading industry. Manufactures include chemicals, electronic equipment, and textiles. The largest economic sector is services, especially tourism. The rocky soil makes farming difficult, and Malta produces only 20% of its food. Malta has a small fishing industry.

**Malthus, Thomas Robert** (1766–1834) British economist and minister famous for his *Essay on Population* (1798). According to Malthusian theory, population increases geometrically but the food supply can increase only arithmetically so that population must eventually overtake it, with famine, war, and disease as consequences.

**maltose** (malt sugar) Disaccharide ($C_{12}H_{22}O_{11}$) that contains two molecules of the simple sugar GLUCOSE. It is produced by the hydrolysis of STARCH by the enzyme AMYLASE and by the breakdown of starches and GLYCOGEN during digestion.

**mamba** Any of several large, poisonous African tree snakes of the cobra family, Elapidae. The deadly black mamba (*Dendroaspis polylepsis*) is the largest species. It is gray, greenish-brown, or black and is notoriously aggressive; its bite is almost always fatal. Length: to 14ft (4.3m).

▲ **mammoth** The mammoth was a hairy elephantlike mammal that inhabited the steppes and tundra of North America, Europe, and Asia during the ice ages of the Pleistocene period. Complete specimens have been found preserved in ice formations in Russia and are reddish brown in color. The mammoth was a herbivore, and while its body was of a similar size to modern elephants it possessed a larger head and tusks, and a thick coat of hair to protect it from the cold.

## MAMMALIAN FEET

The feet of mammals have evolved in many different ways from the basic mammalian foot (A), possessed by the earliest shrewlike mammal. Seals (B) have developed evenly graduated toes for a webbed paddle. Moles (C) have truncated toes for leverage when digging. The camel's two toes (D) are padded for walking on sand. Horses have a hoof (E) instead of claws, and elongated feet for speed, as has the cheetah (F). Bats (G) have enormously elongated digits to support wings. Kangaroos' toes (H) are for hopping. Lemurs (I) and sloths (J) have forelimbs for grasping trees.

**Mameluke** Military elite in Egypt and other Arab countries. The Mamelukes of Egypt overthrew the Ayyubid dynasty in 1250. They halted the MONGOLS, defeated the Crusaders, and crushed the ASSASSINS. Though conquered by the Ottoman Turks in 1517, they continued to control Egypt until supressed by MUHAMMAD ALI (Mehemet Ali) in 1811.

**Mamet, David** (1947– ) US dramatist and film director. He is noted for his sharp, perceptive dialogue. Mamet won a Pulitzer Prize for *Glengarry Glen Ross* (1983). Other plays include *American Buffalo* (1975) and *Oleanna* (1992). Screenplays include *The Postman Always Rings Twice* (1981) and *The Untouchables* (1987). He made his directorial debut with *House of Games* (1987).

**mammal** Class (Mammalia) of VERTEBRATE animals characterized by mammary glands in the female and full, partial, or vestigial hair covering. Mammals are warm-blooded. They have a four-chambered heart with circulation to the lungs separate from the rest of the body. As a group, mammals are active, alert, and intelligent. They usually bear fewer young than other animals and give them longer and better parental care. Most mammals before birth grow inside the mother's body and are nourished from her by means of a placenta. When born, they continue to feed on milk from the mother's mammary glands. There is a wide range of features, shapes, and sizes among mammals. Mammals include 17 orders of placentals, one MARSUPIAL order – all live-bearing – and an order of egg-laying MONOTREMES. They probably evolved about 180 million years ago from a group of warm-blooded reptiles. Today, mammals range in size from shrews weighing a few grams to the blue whale, which can weigh up to 150 tons.

**mammary gland** *See* BREAST

**mammoth** Extinct PLEISTOCENE ancestor of the elephant. Many were covered with long red or brown hair. The prominent tusks were long and curved, sometimes crossing in adult males. In summer months the permafrost of Siberia has been known to yield whole specimens that have been frozen for as long as 30,000 years. Genus *Mammuthus*.

**Mammoth Cave National Park** National park in W Kentucky. One of the largest cave systems in the world, it contains extensive passages, many still unexplored, and spectacular limestone formations.

**man** Zoological term for a HUMAN BEING

**Man, Isle of** Island off the NW coast of England, in the Irish Sea; the capital is Douglas. In the Middle Ages it was a Norwegian dependency, subsequently coming under Scottish, then English rule. It has been a British crown possession since 1828 and has its own government (the Tynwald). The basis of the economy is tourism although agriculture is important, the chief products being oats, fruit, and vegetables. Area: 221sq mi (572sq km). Pop. (1991) 69,788.

**Managua** Capital of Nicaragua, in the W central part, on the S shore of Lake Managua. It became the capital in 1855. The city suffered damage from earthquakes in 1931 and 1962. It is the economic, industrial, and commercial hub of Nicaragua. Industries: textiles, tobacco, cement. Pop. (1985) 682,111.

**Manama** (Al-Manamah) Capital of Bahrain, on the N coast of Bahrain Island, in the Persian Gulf. It was made a free port in 1958, and a deepwater harbor was built in 1962. It is the country's principal port and commercial center. Industries: oil refining, banking, boatbuilding. Pop. (1988) 151,500.

**manatee** Any of three species of large, plant-eating, sub-ungulate, aquatic mammals found primarily in shallow coastal waters of the Atlantic Ocean. It has a tapered body ending in a large rounded flipper; there are no hindlimbs. Length: to 14.7ft (4.5m); weight: 1,500lb (680kg). Family Trichechidae; genus *Trichechus*.

**Manchester** City on the Irwell River, NW England. In AD 79 the Celtic town was occupied by the Romans, who named it Mancunium. The textile industry (now in decline) dates back to the 14th century. In 1830 the world's first passenger railroad was constructed between LIVERPOOL and Manchester. In 1894 the Manchester Ship Canal opened, providing the city with its own access to the sea. Modern Manchester has a diverse manufacturing base, including chemicals, pharmaceuticals, printing, and publishing. Pop. (1991) 404,861.

◀ **manatee** The Florida, or West Indian, manatee (*Trichechus manatus*) like all manatees is related to the elephant. Manatees live in fresh or brackish estuarine waters in family groups consisting of parents and offspring. Peaceful, herbivorous animals, they feed on plants growing on the sea floor or riverbed.

**Manchu** Nomadic peoples of MANCHURIA. They established the QING dynasty.

**Manchukuo** Japanese puppet state in MANCHURIA (1932–45). It was under the nominal rule of the pretender to the QING throne, Henry PU YI. The state of Manchukuo was not recognized by most foreign governments and, after the defeat of Japan in 1945, Manchuria was returned to China.

**Manchuria** Region of NE China, now included in the provinces of Heilongjiang, Jilin, and Liaoning. Manchuria is rich in mineral deposits and has become one of China's leading sites for heavy industry. It is a major agricultural area, whose chief product is soybeans. Dalian is the principal port. The Manchus conquered China in the 17th century, and at the end of the 19th century the Chinese constructed the railroads and the Russians developed the naval facilities at Port Arthur. In the 1904–05 RUSSO-JAPANESE WAR Japan seized control of S Manchuria and Port Arthur. In 1931 Japan occupied the whole of Manchuria and established the puppet state of MANCHUKUO. During World War II the region's industry supplied the Japanese war effort. In 1945 Manchuria was occupied by Soviet forces, who destroyed many factories. In 1948 the Chinese communists defeated the Manchurian nationalists and reconstruction began. From 1960 to 1990 the region was at the forefront of Sino-Soviet hostilities. Area: *c*.600,000sq mi (1,500,000sq km).

**Manchurian Incident** Japanese seizure of Manchuria (1931). The Japanese seized Mukden in September and rapidly overran the province, setting up the puppet state of MANCHUKUO. The ensuing Sino–Japanese War later merged into World War II. After the defeat of Japan (1945), Manchuria was returned to China.

**Mandalay** City in central Burma (Myanmar), on the Irrawaddy River; capital of Mandalay division. Founded in 1857, Mandalay was the last capital (1860–85) of the Burmese kingdom before it was annexed to Britain. The city was occupied by the Japanese during World War II and suffered severe damage. Pop. (1983) 532,985.

**Mandan** Dakota name for a Siouan tribe of Native North Americans inhabiting the upper Missouri River area between the Heart and Missouri rivers. From an early population of 3,600, epidemics introduced by European travelers decimated the tribe; today, about 350 live on the Fort Berthold Reservation in North Dakota.

**mandarin** (mandarine) Type of orange with a sweet flavor. The **tangerine** is a flattish, loose-skinned species of mandarin orange. Family Rutaceae; species *Citrus reticulata*.

**Mandarin** Major dialect of CHINESE, the spoken language of *c*.70% of the population of China. It was originally the language of the imperial court. Mandarin is the basis of modern standard Chinese. *See also* CANTONESE

**Mandela, Nelson Rolihlahla** (1918– ) South African statesman, president (1994– ). He joined the AFRICAN NATIONAL CONGRESS (ANC) in 1944, and for the next 20 years led the campaign of civil disobedience against South Africa's apartheid government. Following the SHARPEVILLE Massacre (1960), Mandela formed *Umkhonte We Sizwe* (Spear of the Nation), a paramilitary wing of the ANC. In 1961 the ANC

▲ **Mandela** South African president Nelson Mandela struggled for a democratic South Africa for much of his life, and spent 27 years in prison charged with attempting to overthrow the government. He was primarily responsible for the far-reaching revolution that turned South Africa into a "rainbow republic," and his charismatic personality and benevolence made him a national and international figure of great moral stature.

► **mandrill** A species of baboon, the mandrill (*Mandrillus sphinx*) is found in Equatorial West Africa. The extraordinary colors of the mandrill's face intensify if the animal becomes annoyed or excited. Zoologists believe that this visual display has replaced the baring of teeth to express anger common to most other baboons.

was banned. In 1964 Mandela was sentenced to life imprisonment for political offences. He spent the next 27 years in prison on Robben Island, becoming a symbol of resistance to apartheid. International sanctions forced F.W. DE KLERK to begin the dismantling of apartheid. In February 1990 Mandela was released and resumed his leadership of the newly legalized ANC. In 1993 Mandela and de Klerk shared the Nobel Peace Prize. In 1994 Mandela gained two-thirds of the popular vote in South Africa's first multiracial democratic elections. A strong advocate of the need for reconciliation, he made de Klerk deputy president (1994–96) in his government of national unity. In 1996 he divorced his wife, **Winnie** (1934– ), who was convicted of kidnapping and of being an accessory to assault. In 1997 Mandela was replaced as president of the ANC by Thabo Mbeki.

**Mandelbrot, Benoit B.** (1942– ) US mathematician, b. Poland. He has made major contributions to CHAOS THEORY and is best known for coining the term FRACTAL. His book *The Fractal Geometry of Nature* contains many examples of natural fractals. The Mandelbrot set, a fractal object, is named for him.

**mandolin** Stringed musical instrument related to the LUTE and associated with 18th-century Italy. It has four or six paired wire strings, which are played with a plectrum. It is most often used today as an accompaniment to folk songs and dances.

**mandrake** Plant of the potato family, native to the Mediterranean region and used since ancient times as a medicine. It contains the ALKALOIDS hyoscyamine, scopolamin, and mandragorine. Leaves are borne at the base of the stem, and the large greenish-yellow or purple flowers produce a many-seeded berry. Height: 16in (40cm); family Solanaceae; species *Mandragora officinarum*.

**mandrill** Large BABOON that lives in dense rain forests of central W Africa. Mandrills roam in small troops and forage for their food on the forest floor. The male has a red-tipped, pale blue nose, yellow-bearded cheeks, and a reddish rump. Height: 30in (75cm) at the shoulder; weight: to 119lb (54kg). Species *Mandrillus sphinx*.

**Manet, Édouard** (1832–83) French painter. Although his name is usually linked with the IMPRESSIONISM movement, he did not consider himself an impressionist. The famed *Le Déjeuner sur l'Herbe* was violently attacked by critics when exhibited (1863), as was *Olympia*, a portrait of a well-known courtesan. However, he finally achieved recognition with later works, such as *Le Bar aux Folies-Bergère* (1881).

**manganese** (symbol Mn) Gray-white metallic element that resembles iron and was first isolated in 1774. Its chief ores are pyrolusite, manganite, and hausmannite. The metal is used in alloy steels, ferromagnetic alloys, fertilizers, and paints, and as a gasoline additive. Properties: at.no. 25; at. wt. 54.938; sp.gr. 7.20; m.p. 2,271°F (1,244°C); b.p. 3,564°F (1,962°C); most common isotope $^{55}$Mn (100%). *See also* TRANSITION ELEMENTS

**mango** Evergreen tree native to SE Asia and grown widely in the tropics for its fruit. It has lanceolate leaves, pinkish-white clustered flowers, and yellow-red fruit, which is eaten ripe or preserved when green. Height: to 60ft (18m). Family Anacardiaceae; species *Mangifera indica*.

**mangrove** Common name for any one of 120 species of tropical trees or shrubs found in marine swampy areas. Its stiltlike aerial roots, which arise from the branches and hang down into the water, produce a thick undergrowth, useful in the reclaiming of land along tropical coasts. Some species also have roots that rise up out of the water. Height: to 70ft (20m). Chief family: Rhizophoraceae.

**Manhattan** Borough of NEW YORK CITY, in SE New York state; lying mainly on Manhattan Island and bounded W by the HUDSON River. In 1625 the Manhattan Indians sold the island to the Dutch West India Company and the town of New Amsterdam was built. The British captured the Dutch colony in 1664 and renamed it New York. In 1898 Manhattan became one of five boroughs established by the Greater New York Charter. Industries: electrical goods, chemicals, fabricated metals, finance, tourism, entertainment, broadcasting, publishing. Pop. (1990) 1,487,536.

**Manhattan Project** Code name given to the development of the US atom bomb during WORLD WAR II. Work on the bomb was carried out in great secrecy by a team including Enrico FERMI and J. Robert OPPENHEIMER. The first test took place on July 16, 1945, near Alamogordo, New Mexico, and the following month bombs were dropped on Japan.

**mania** Mental illness marked by feelings of intense elation and excitement. Speech is rapid and physical activity frenetic. In extreme cases mania is accompanied by violent behavior.

**manic depression** (bipolar disorder) Mental illness featuring recurrent bouts of DEPRESSION, possibly alternating with periods of MANIA. Depressive and manic symptoms may alternate in a cyclical pattern, be mixed, or be separated by periods of remission and disturbances of thought and judgment.

**Manichaeism** Religious teaching of the Persian prophet Mani based on a supposed primeval conflict between light and darkness. The Manichaean sect, which was influenced by ZOROASTRIANISM and CHRISTIANITY, spread rapidly to Egypt and Rome, where it was considered a Christian heresy, and eastward to Chinese Turkistan, where it survived probably until the 13th century.

**Manifest Destiny** Slogan to justify the US westward and southward expansion movement in the 19th century. Coined by a Democratic editor, John L. O'Sullivan (1845), it was exploited by President James K. POLK when the US annexed Texas and won lands from Mexico. Later the theory of manifest destiny contributed to the acquisition of Alaska, Hawaii, and territory taken in the Spanish-American War.

**Manila** Capital of the Philippines, on Manila Bay, SW Luzon island. Manila is the industrial, commercial, and administrative heart of the Philippines. The Pasig River bisects the city. On the S bank stands the old walled city (Intramuros), built by the Spanish in the 16th century on the site of a Muslim settlement. It became a trading center for the Pacific area. On the N bank lies Ermita, the administrative and tourist center. In 1942 Manila was occupied by the Japanese. In 1945 the old city was destroyed in a battle between Japanese and Allied forces. Pop. (1990) 1,587,000.

**Manila Bay, Battle of** (May 1, 1898) Battle in the SPANISH-AMERICAN WAR in which US Admiral George DEWEY defeated the Spanish fleet in a seven-hour battle. Spanish losses were heavy, with 381 men killed and all the Spanish craft destroyed. US casualties included eight wounded; no ships were damaged.

**Manitoba** Province in S central Canada, the easternmost of the prairie provinces, bordered by Hudson Bay (NE) and the US (S); the capital and largest city is WINNIPEG. In 1670 Charles II granted the land to the HUDSON'S BAY COMPANY. In 1869 the company sold it to the newly created confederation of Canada. Manitoba was created a province in 1870. The terrain varies from the prairie country and lake district of the S to the rugged upland of the Canadian Shield of the NE and the tundra of the far N. Manitoba is famous for wheat fields. Dairy farming and the rearing of poulty are also important. Manufacturing includes food products, clothing, electrical products, machinery, metals, and transportation equipment. Mineral deposits include nickel, copper, and zinc. There are large oil fields in the

SW of the province and extensive timber reserves. Area: 250,946sq mi (649,947sq km). Pop. (1994 est.) 1,131,100.

**Mann, Horace** (1796–1859) US educational reformer. As secretary of the Massachusetts board of education (1837–48), he established teacher-training schools, increased teachers' salaries, and improved teaching practices. He served in Congress (1848–53) as an anti-slavery Whig.

**Mann, Thomas** (1875–1955) German novelist and essayist. An outstanding figure of 20th-century German literature, Mann linked individual psychological problems to the decline in European culture. His first novel, *Buddenbrooks* (1901), a family saga, was an immediate success. It was followed by other works, including the novella *Death in Venice* (1912), the treatise *Reflections of a Non-political man* (1918), and *The Magic Mountain* (1924). In 1930 he published *Mario and the Magician*, an attack on the vulgarity of dictatorship. Other important works are *Joseph and His Brothers* (1933–43), *Doctor Faustus* (1947), and *Felix Krull* (1953). He was awarded the 1929 Nobel Prize for literature.

**Mannerheim, Carl Gustav Emil, Baron von** (1867–1951) Finnish field marshal and statesman, president (1944–46). He served in the Russian army and was a general in World War I. In 1918 Mannerheim led the anti-Bolshevik forces to victory in the Finnish Civil War and became regent of an independent Finland. In 1919 he retired. In 1931 he planned the Mannerheim Line across Karelia. Mannerheim commanded Finnish forces in the Finnish-Russian War (1939–40, 1941–44), and led the first post-war Finnish administration.

**mannerism** In art history, loose term generally applied to the art and architecture of Italy between the High RENAISSANCE and the BAROQUE (*c*.1520–1600). A self-conscious style, it aimed to exceed the Renaissance in terms of emotional impact. In architecture, mannerism is best represented by GIULIO ROMANO's Palazzo del Tè, Mantua (1526). Mannerist painting is characterized by elongated figures in distorted poses, often using a lurid palette of colours. Leading painters included VASARI, PARMIGIANO, PONTORMO, and Giovanni LANFRANCO. Theorists are still debating the scope of mannerism: it has been extended to include MICHELANGELO, RAPHAEL, El GRECO, the FONTAINEBLEAU SCHOOL, and the Romanist painters of the Netherlands. *See also* CELLINI, BENVENUTO

**Mannheim** City and river port in central Germany, in Baden-Württemberg state, on the E bank of the Rhine River, at the mouth of the Neckar River. Originally a fishing village, it was fortified in 1606 and destroyed by the French in 1689. It was rebuilt in 1697, became the seat of the Rhine Palatinate (1719–77), and passed to Baden in 1803. Industries: chemicals, oil refining, engineering, paper, textiles. Pop. (1990) 316,900.

**Mansfield, Katherine** (1888–1923) British short-story writer, b. New Zealand. Her first volume, *In a German Pension* (1911), shows the influence of CHEKHOV. Mansfield's delicate humour and deceptively simple style are best represented by *The Garden Party* (1922) and *The Dove's Nest* (1923). She led a troubled life and died of tuberculosis.

**manslaughter** Crime of killing another person accidentally or for humane motives. Manslaughter usually merits less punishment than MURDER.

**Manson, Charles** (1934– ) US cult leader. In 1967 he established a commune based on free love and complete subservience to him. In 1969 members of the cult committed a series of brutal murders, including that of Roman POLANSKI's wife Sharon Tate (1943–69). Manson and his accomplices were sentenced to death, later commuted to life imprisonment.

**Mantegna, Andrea** (1431–1506) Italian painter and engraver. In 1460 he became court painter to the Gonzaga family in Mantua and decorated the Camera degli Sposi in the Duke's Palace. This room contains the first example of illusionistic architecture to have been created since antiquity. Mantegna's other great work for the Gonzagas was his series of oil paintings, *The Triumph of Caesar* (*c*.1480–95).

**mantis** (praying mantis) Any of several species of mantids, insects found throughout the world. They have powerful front legs used to catch and hold their insect prey. Colors range from brown and green to bright pink. Length: 1–6in (25–150mm). Family Mantidae.

**mantissa** Decimal part of a LOGARITHM

**Mantle, Mickey Charles** (1931–96) US baseball player. A home-run hitting (536) center fielder, he played with the New York Yankees (1951–68). He was a three time Most Valuable Player (1956–57, 1962) and won the triple crown (home runs, runs batted in, batting average) in 1956. He was elected to the Baseball Hall of Fame in 1974.

**mantle** Layer of the Earth between the CRUST and the CORE, which extends to a depth of 1,795mi (2,890km). The mantle forms the greatest bulk of the Earth: 82% of its volume and 68% of its mass. The uppermost part is rigid, solid, and brittle and together with the Earth's crust forms the **lithosphere**. From a depth of about 40mi (60km) down to 125mi (200km) the mantle has a soft zone, which is called the **asthenosphere**. Temperature and pressure are in balance so that much of the mantle material is near melting point or partly melted and capable of flowing. The remainder of the mantle is thought to be more solid but still capable of creeping flow. In the lower mantle several changes in seismic velocity can be detected. The chemical constitution of the mantle is uncertain, but it is thought to be made up of iron-magnesian silicates.

**mantra** Sacred word, verse, or formula recited during prayers or meditation in HINDUISM and BUDDHISM. Mantras include such chantings as the symbolic sound *Aum* (or *Om*).

**Manu** In Hindu mythology, the hero of the deluge. Manu caught a fish that offered to save him in exchange for its life. The fish had Manu build a ship, which it towed to the Himalayas when the floods came. There it was tied to a tree until the waters receded. Manu is the generic name for each of the 14 consecutive rulers of the Earth. The present ruler is the seventh, the son of the Vedic Sun god Vivasvan.

**Manx** Language formerly spoken in the Isle of Man. Closely related to Scottish GAELIC, it was spoken by most of the native inhabitants until *c*.1700, when English was introduced. By 1900 there were only a few thousand speakers left.

**Manzoni, Alessandro** (1785–1873) Italian novelist and poet. His poetry expressed his religious faith, but his masterpiece is an historical novel, *The Betrothed* (1827), regarded as one of the most outstanding works of Italian literature.

**Maori** Polynesian population, the original inhabitants of New Zealand. Traditionally, Maoris lived by agriculture, hunting, and fishing. They retain strong attachments to their language, culture, and customs. In Maori society, tattooing, carving, and weaving were developed arts, and their war chants (*haka*) are still kept alive. Since the 1970s the Maoris have been increasingly politically active, and some of their land has been returned to them. *See also* MAORI WARS

**Maori Wars** (1843–48, 1860–72) Series of conflicts in which the indigenous MAORIS resisted the British colonization of New Zealand. They arose when the settlers broke the terms of the Treaty of Waitangi (1840). The rebellions of the 1840s were led by the Maori chiefs Hone Heke and Te Rauparaha. The second phase (the Taranaki Wars) was led by the Kingitanga unity movement. In 1865 a native land court was established. In 1867 a Maori school system was formed and the Maoris allowed representation in the New Zealand legislature.

**Mao Zedong** (1893–1976) Chinese statesman, founder and chairman (1949–76) of the People's Republic of China. In 1921 Mao helped found the Chinese COMMUNIST PARTY. After the nationalist KUOMINTANG, led by CHIANG KAI-SHEK, dissolved the alliance with the communists in 1927, Mao helped established rural soviets. In 1931 he was elected chairman of the Soviet Republic of China. The advance of nationalist forces forced Mao to lead the Red Army on the LONG MARCH (1934–35). In 1937 the civil war was suspended as communists and nationalists combined to fight the second SINO-JAPANESE WAR. Civil war resumed in 1945. By 1949 the nationalists had been driven out of mainland China. Mao became chairman of the People's Republic. He was re-elected in 1954. In 1958 Mao attempted to distinguish Chinese COMMUNISM from its Soviet counterpart by launching the GREAT LEAP FORWARD. The programme ended in mass starvation, and the withdrawal of Soviet aid. The CULTURAL REVOLUTION was an attempt by Mao and his wife, JIANG QING, to reassert Maoist ideology. Mao became supreme commander of the nation and army (1970). Mao's

▲ **mango** The fruit of the mango tree has a delicate fragrance. Its juicy flesh surrounds a single flat seed. The tree itself is grown as a garden plant throughout the tropical region.

death created a power vacuum. A struggle developed between the GANG OF FOUR, HUA GUOFENG, and DENG XIAOPING. *Quotations from Chairman Mao Zedong* (1967), popularly known as "The Little Red Book," is a worldwide bestseller.

**maple** Genus of deciduous trees native to temperate and cool regions of Europe, Asia, and North America. They have yellowish or greenish flowers and winged seeds. They are grown for ornament, shade, or timber, depending on the species; the sugar maple is also tapped for maple syrup. Height: 15–120ft (4.6–36m). Family Aceraceae; genus *Acer*.

**Maputo** (Lourenço Marques) Capital and chief port of Mozambique, on Maputo Bay, in the S of the country. It was visited by the Portuguese in 1502 and was made the capital of Portuguese East Africa in 1907, being known as Lourenço Marques until 1976. It is linked by rail to South Africa, Swaziland, and Zimbabwe, and is a popular resort area. Industries: footwear, textiles, rubber. Pop. (1992 est.) 2,000,000.

**Maracaibo** City and port in NW Venezuela, between Lake Maracaibo and the Gulf of Venezuela. Founded in 1529, it was sacked in 1669. It expanded after the discovery of oil in 1917 and is now the country's second-largest city. Industries: oil processing, coffee, cacao, sugar. Pop. (1990) 1,207,513.

**Marat, Jean Paul** (1743–93) French revolutionary. A physician, he founded *L'Ami du Peuple* (Friend of the People), a journal that supported the JACOBINS. His murder by Charlotte CORDAY, a member of the GIRONDINS, was exploited for propaganda by the Jacobins and contributed to the REIGN OF TERROR.

**marathon** Long-distance race. The standard marathon is 26.2mi (42.2km), which was the distance run by the ancient Greek soldier who brought news of the victory over the Persians at Marathon to Athens in 490 BC.

**Marathon, Battle of** (490 BC) Victory of the Greeks, mainly Athenians, during the PERSIAN WARS. The defeat of a much larger Persian army on the Marathon plain NE of Athens secured Attica from the invasion of CYRUS THE GREAT.

**marble** Metamorphic rock composed largely of recrystallized limestones and dolomites. The color is normally white, but when tinted by serpentine, iron oxide, or carbon can vary to shades of yellow, green, red, brown, or black. It has long been a favorite building and sculpting material.

**Marbury v. Madison** (1803) US Supreme Court decision that established the supremacy of the Constitution over congressional legislation and the court's role as interpreter of the Constitution. It also established the court's power to overturn unconstitutional legislation.

**Marceau, Marcel** (1923– ) French mime artist. His best known creation was Bip, a sad, white-faced clown with a tall, battered hat. Marceau made several films, and made a memorable appearance in *Silent Movie* (1976).

**Marche** Region in E central Italy, between the Apennines and the Adriatic Sea; the capital is Ancona. Except for a narrow coastal plain, Marche is mountainous. Farming is the principal economic activity; major crops include cereals, olives, and grapes. Area: 3,743sq mi (9,692sq km). Pop. (1990) 1,435,570.

**Marciano, Rocky** (1923–69) US boxer, b. Rocco Francis Marchegiano. In 1951 he became only the second boxer to knock out Joe LOUIS. In 1952 Marciano won the world heavyweight title by knocking out Joe Walcott. In 1956 Marciano retired undefeated.

**Marconi, Guglielmo** (1874–1937) Italian physicist who developed RADIO. By 1897 he was able to demonstrate radio telegraphy over 12mi (19km) and established radio communication between France and England in 1899. By 1901 radio transmissions were being received across the Atlantic Ocean. He was awarded the Nobel Prize for physics in 1909.

**Marco Polo** *See* POLO, MARCO

**Marcos, Ferdinand Edralin** (1917–89) Philippine statesman, president (1965–86). He was elected to the Philippine Congress in 1949. As president, Marcos received support from the US for his military campaigns (1969) against communist guerrillas and secessionists on MINDANAO. Continued civil unrest led to the imposition of martial law in 1972. His regime acquired a reputation for corruption and repression, symbolized by the extravagance of his wife, **Imelda** (1930– ). In 1983 his main rival, Benigno Aquino, was assassinated and political opposition coalesced behind Benigno's widow, Cory AQUINO. Marcos appeared to win the 1986 general election, but allegations of vote-rigging forced him into exile. In 1988 US authorities indicted both him and Imelda for fraud. Ferdinand was too ill to stand trial and died in Hawaii. Imelda was subsequently acquitted. In 1992 Imelda unsuccessfully ran for president.

**Marcus Aurelius (Antoninus)** (121–180) Roman emperor (161–180) and philosopher of the STOIC school. He was born Marcus Annius Verus. For eight years (161–169) he ruled as co-emperor with his adoptive younger brother Lucius Aurelius Verus (d.169). His much-admired *Meditations*, his one surviving work, is a collection of philosophical thoughts and ideas that occurred to him during his campaigns, on the last of which he died.

**Marcuse, Herbert** (1898–1979) US political philosopher, b. Germany. He is noted for his critical reinterpretations of MARXISM and for his Freudian analysis of 20th-century industrial society. Marcuse's advocacy of civil resistance found favor with student activists in the 1960s. His works include *Eros and Civilization* (1955) and *One-Dimensional Man* (1964).

**Mardi Gras** Community festival or carnival held on Shrove Tuesday, the day before the beginning of Lent, in many Roman Catholic countries, particularly France. In the US, most notably New Orleans, it includes street parades, concerts, and dances.

**Mare, Walter de la** *See* DE LA MARE, WALTER

**Margaret of Anjou** (1430–82) Wife of HENRY VI of England from 1445. During the Wars of the ROSES she, rather than Henry, led the cause of Lancaster, raising troops in France. After her only son, Edward, was killed at Tewkesbury (1471) she was taken prisoner. Ransomed by Louis XI of France in 1476, she left England for good.

**margarine** Butterlike substance made from vegetable fats blended with aqueous milk products, salt, flavoring, food coloring, emulsifier, and vitamins A and D.

**marguerite** PERENNIAL plant of the daisy family native to the Canary Islands. It has white-rayed, yellow-centered flower heads about 2in (5cm) across. Height: to 3ft (91cm). Family Asteraceae/COMPOSITAE; species *Argyranthemum frutescens*.

**Mariana Islands** Volcanic island chain in the W Pacific Ocean, stretching over 500mi (800km) of the Marianas Trench, *c*.1,500mi (2,400km) E of the Philippines. The group comprises GUAM and the islands of the Northern Marianas: Saipan, Tinian, Rota, Pagan, and 11 smaller islands. Discovered by Ferdinand MAGELLAN in 1521 and named Islands of Thieves, the islands were renamed the Marianas in 1668. The Northern Marianas came under German control in 1898, subsequently passing to Japan. They were taken by US forces in 1944, and in 1947 became part of the US Trust Territory of the Pacific Islands. In 1978 the Commonwealth of the Northern Mariana Islands was formed in association with the US, and in 1986 the islanders acquired US citizenship. Trusteeship status was ended in 1990. Exports include sugarcane, coconuts, and coffee. Tourism is important. Area (excluding Guam): 179sq mi (464sq km). Pop. (1990) 43,345.

**Maria Theresa** (1717–80) Archduchess of Austria, ruler of the Austrian HAPSBURG empire (1740–80). She succeeded her father, Emperor CHARLES VI, but was challenged by neighboring powers in the War of the AUSTRIAN SUCCESSION (1741–48), losing Silesia to Prussia but securing the imperial title for her husband, FRANCIS I. She formed an alliance with France, but failed to regain Silesia in the SEVEN YEARS WAR (1756–63). From 1765 she ruled jointly with her son, Emperor JOSEPH II.

**Marie Antoinette** (1755–93) Queen of France. Daughter of the Emperor FRANCIS I and MARIA THERESA of Austria, she married the future LOUIS XVI in 1770. Her life of pleasure and extravagance contributed to the outbreak of the FRENCH REVOLUTION in 1789. She initiated the royal family's attempt to escape in 1791, was held prisoner, and was finally guillotined.

**Marie de Médicis** (1573–1642) Queen of France. A member of the Medici family, daughter of the Grand Duke of Tuscany, she married HENRY IV of France (1600). He was assassinated the day after she was crowned queen in 1610, possibly with her connivance. As regent for her son, LOUIS XIII, she relied on Italian advisers and reversed Henry's anti-Hapsburg policy. She was constantly at odds with Louis after 1614 and antagonized Cardinal Richelieu. Failing to have him dismissed in 1630, she was forced to leave France, settling in Brussels (1631).

**Marie Louise** (1791–1847) French Empress, daughter of Emperor Francis II. In 1810 she married Napoleon I. In 1811 she gave birth to a son, the future Napoleon II. Marie Louise acted briefly as regent during Napoleon's absences on campaign. Alienated from him by 1814, she was made duchess of Parma.

**marigold** Any of several mostly golden-flowered plants, mainly of the genera *Chrysanthemum*, *Tagetes*, and *Calendula*, all of the daisy family (Asteraceae/Compositae). Those most commonly cultivated are the French marigold (*Tagetes patula*) and the African marigold (*T. erecta*).

**marijuana** Narcotic drug prepared from the dried leaves of the Indian hemp plant (*Cannabis sativa*); it is different from hashish, which is prepared from resin obtained from the flowering tops of the plant. Possession of the drug is illegal in many countries. *See also* cannabis

**Marine Corps, US** Branch of the armed forces that is a service within the department of the Navy. It consists of approximately 196,000 personnel and conducts the land operations connected with naval operations. The operational forces consist of three divisions, three aircraft wings, and supporting troops, and are organized into task forces to conduct amphibious operations. *See also* Joint Chiefs of Staff; Navy, United States.

**Mariner program** Series of US space probes to the planets. **Mariner 2** flew past Venus in 1962, and **Mariner 4** flew past Mars in July 1965, photographing craters on its surface. **Mariner 5** passed Venus in October 1967, making measurements of the planet's atmosphere. **Mariners 6 and 7** obtained further photographs of Mars in 1969. **Mariner 9** went into orbit around Mars in November 1971. It made a year-long photographic reconnaissance of the planet's surface and obtained close views of the two moons, Phobos and Deimos. **Mariner 10**, the last of the series, was the first two-planet mission, passing Venus in February 1974 and then encountering Mercury three times, in March and September 1974 and March 1975.

**Marinetti, Filippo Tommaso** (1876–1944) Italian poet, novelist, dramatist, and founder of futurism. In such works as *Futurismo e Fascismo* (1924), he embraced fascism and advocated the glorification of machinery, speed, and war. One of his earliest collections of poetry was entitled simply *Destruction*; another was called *War: the Only Hygiene of the World* (1915).

**Marion, Francis** (1732–95) American Revolutionary officer, know as the "Swamp Fox." He commanded the South Carolina militia in guerrilla-type raids on the British. He participated in the defense of Charleston.

**Maris, Roger Eugene** (1934–85) US baseball player. Playing for the New York Yankees, Maris set a season home-run record (61) in 1961, eclipsing Babe Ruth's mark (60) of 1927. Maris hit a total of 275 home runs during his major-league career from 1957 to 1968.

**Marius, Gaius** (157–86 BC) Roman political and military leader. His policy of recruiting poor men without property contributed to the bond between Roman troops and their commanders. He also revised standard army training and equipment. His rivalry with Sulla forced him out of Rome, but he raised an army and recaptured the city (87 BC).

**marjoram** Perennial herb of the mint family (Lamiaceae/Labiatae) *c.*24in (60cm) tall with purplish flowers. It is native to the Mediterranean region and w Asia and is cultivated as an annual in northern climates. Species *Origanum vulgare*.

**Mark, Saint** (active 1st century AD) Apostle and possibly one of the four evangelists of the New Testament. He is identified with John Mark (Acts 12:12. 15:37), the cousin of the apostle St. Barnabas. He accompanied both Barnabas and St. Paul on several missionary journeys until a disagreement with Paul caused him to detach himself. Christian tradition says that he went off to become secretary to St. Peter and to write the first gospel. His feast day is April 25.

**Mark, Gospel according to Saint** Second gospel in the New Testament, but the earliest in composition. It was written about AD 55–65 and is believed to be one of two reference works (the other being "Q") used by St. Matthew and St. Luke in compiling their gospels. It is traditionally attributed to St. Mark and is one of the three Synoptic gospels – those presenting a common view of Jesus Christ's life.

**Mark Antony** *See* Antony, Mark

**market economy** Economy in which resources are controlled by the operation of free-markets (in which the forces of supply and demand operate without interference). The opposite is a controlled economy, in which market forces are under governmental control; in a mixed economy, there is partial governmental control.

**Markova, Dame Alicia** (1910– ) English ballerina, b. Lilian Alicia Marks. In 1931 she joined the Vic-Wells Ballet and was its first prima ballerina. Classical ballets in which she excelled include *Giselle*, *Les Sylphides*, and *Swan Lake*. In 1935 she founded the Markova-Dolin Ballet with Anton Dolin.

**Marlborough, John Churchill, 1st duke of** (1650–1722) English general. In 1685 he helped James II defeat Monmouth, but switched allegiance in support of the Protestant Glorious Revolution (1688). Due partly to his wife's friendship with Queen Anne, Marlborough was appointed captain-general of the Allied armies in the War of the Spanish Succession. His strategic skill gained a famous victory at Blenheim. Churchill was rewarded with a dukedom and Blenheim Palace. When the Tories regained power, Marlborough was dismissed (1711) and went into exile.

**Marley, Bob (Robert Nesta)** (1945–81) Jamaican singer-songwriter. Marley and his band, The Wailers, transformed reggae into an internationally popular music form with hit singles such as "Get Up, Stand Up" (1973) and "No Woman No Cry" (1974). He combined faith in Rastafarianism with political statement. Marley's albums include *Natty Dread* (1975), *Exodus* (1977), and *Uprising* (1980).

**Marlowe, Christopher** (1564–93) English poet and playwright. He played a part in making blank verse the vehicle of Elizabethan drama. Much of Marlowe's success derives from his ability to humanize his overreaching heroes, as in *Tamburlaine the Great* (1590), *The Tragical History of Doctor Faustus* (1604), and *The Jew of Malta* (1633). His masterpiece is *Edward II* (1592). His greatest poems are *Hero and Leander* (1598) and *The Passionate Shepherd* (1599). He served as a spy in Francis Walsingham's intelligence service and was killed in a tavern brawl.

**marmoset** Small diurnal, arboreal monkey of tropical America. Among the smallest of the monkeys, marmosets are the size of small squirrels. They have soft, dense fur and pointed, sickle-shaped nails. Family Callitrichidae; typical genus *Callithrix*.

**marmot** Stocky ground squirrel, native to North America, Europe, and Asia. Most marmots have brown to gray fur, short, powerful legs, and furry tails. Length, excluding tail: 12–24in (30–60cm); weight: 6.6–16.5lb (3–8kg). Family Sciuridae. *See also* woodchuck

**Marne, battles of** Two battles on the Marne River, N France, during World War I. The first (**September 1914**) was a counterattack directed by General Joffre, which checked the German drive on Paris. The second (**July 1918**) was another Allied counterstroke, which stopped the last German advance and preceded the final Allied offensive.

**Maronite** Member of a Christian community of Arabs in Lebanon and Syria, who have spread by emigration to Egypt, Cyprus, s Europe, and North and South America. The Maronite Church claims origins both from St. Maron (d.407), a Syrian hermit, and St. John Maro, patriarch of Antioch (685–707). In 680 the Maronites were condemned as Monotheletic heretics by the Third Council of Constantinople. In 1182 they returned to communion with the pope. They are an Eastern Othodox Church in union with Rome but retaining their own rite and canon law. The 19th-century massacre of Maronites by the Druse led to French intervention in Lebanon and Syria. Today, Maronites number more than 1 million.

**Marquesas Islands** Volcanic island group in the Pacific Ocean, s of the Equator and N of Tuamotu, including Fatu Hiva, Hiva Oa, and Nuku Hiva, and forming part of French Polynesia; the capital is Taiohae (on Nuku Hiva). The islands were first discovered by a Spanish navigator in 1595. The French took possession in 1842. The islands are mountainous, with fertile val-

▲ **marjoram** Wild marjoram (*Origanum vulgare*) is a pungent-flavored herb much used in Mediterranean cooking to season meat, poultry, soups, and omelettes. It is known in its dried form as oregano.

M

## MARROW

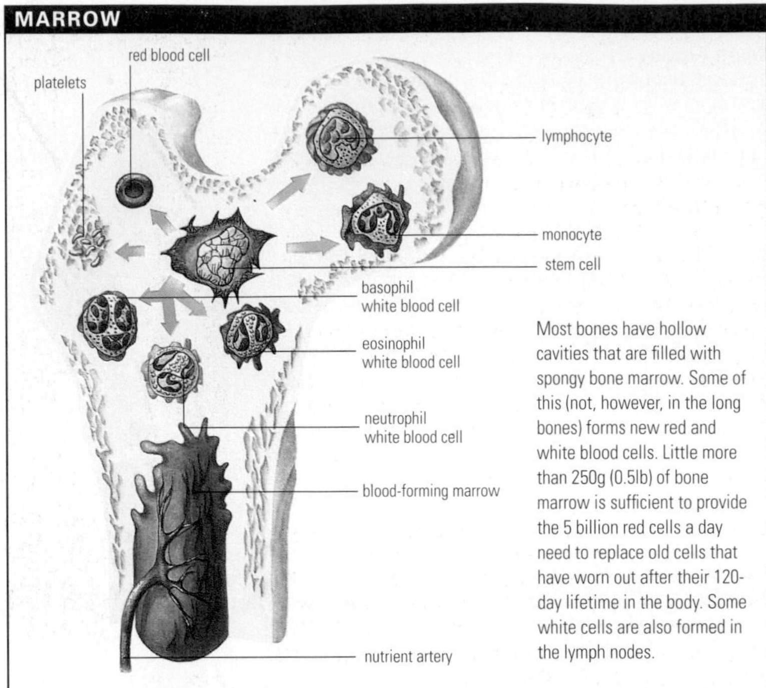


Most bones have hollow cavities that are filled with spongy bone marrow. Some of this (not, however, in the long bones) forms new red and white blood cells. Little more than 250g (0.5lb) of bone marrow is sufficient to provide the 5 billion red cells a day need to replace old cells that have worn out after their 120-day lifetime in the body. Some white cells are also formed in the lymph nodes.

leys and several good harbors. Exports include tobacco, vanilla, and copra. Area: 405sq mi (1,049sq km). Pop. (1988) 7,538.

**Marquette, Father Jacques** (1637–75) French Jesuit missionary and explorer in North America. In 1666 he arrived in Quebec as a missionary priest. In 1673 Marquette and Louis JOLLIET led the first European expedition along the upper Mississippi, exploring it as far as the mouth of the Arkansas River.

**Márquez, Gabriel García** *See* GARCÍA MÁRQUEZ, GABRIEL

**Marrakech** (Marrakesh) City in W central Morocco, at the NW foot of the Atlas Mountains. Founded in 1062 by the ALMORAVIDS, it was the country's capital until 1147 and subsequently served as the sultan's residence. The second-largest city in Morocco, sights include the Koutoubia mosque and the Medina. Industries: tourism, leather. Pop. (1983) 439,728.

**marriage** In the modern Western sense, legal status of a man and a woman joined by ceremony as husband and wife. This is known as MONOGAMY, but some societies practise polyandry and POLYGAMY. The modern stress on the importance of individual choice of partner is historically and culturally very unusual. Arranged marriages, for instance, are the norm in Hindu and Muslim communities. *See also* FAMILY; KINSHIP

**marrow** Soft tissue containing blood vessels, found in the hollow cavities of BONE. The marrow found in many adult bones is somewhat yellowish and functions as a store of fat. The marrow in the flattish bones is reddish and contains cells that give rise eventually to ERYTHROCYTES (red blood cells) as well as to most of the LEUKOCYTES (white blood cells), but not LYMPHOCYTES and platelets.

**Mars** Fourth major planet from the Sun. Mars appears red to the naked eye because of the high iron content of its surface crust, and is also known as the Red Planet. The atmosphere consists mainly of 95% carbon dioxide, 2.5% nitrogen, and 1.5% argon, with smaller quantities of oxygen, carbon monoxide, and water vapor. Its axial tilt is similar to the Earth's, so it passes through a similar cycle of SEASONS. The surface temperature on Mars varies between extremes of 130K and 290K. The surface of Mars reveals a long and complex history of geological activity. The major difference in terrain is between the largely smooth, lowland volcanic plains of the northern hemisphere and the heavily cratered uplands of the south. The biggest volcanic structure on Mars is Olympus Mons, which is hundreds of kilometers across and 17mi (27km) high. Other geographical features, such as some giant canyons, are channels in which rivers once flowed. The variable polar icecaps appear to be composed of solid carbon dioxide with underlying caps of water ice. Mars has two tiny SATELLITES in very close orbits, Phobos and Deimos. In 1996 scientists investigating a meteorite, thought to have originated on Mars, found fossilized microorganisms that some believe indicate the presence of primitive life on the planet.

### MARS: DATA

Diameter (equatorial): 4,217mi (6,787km)
Mass (Earth = 1): 0.11
Volume (Earth = 1): 0.15
Density (water = 1): 3.94
Orbital period: 687.0 days
Rotation period: 24h 37m 23s
Average surface temperature: −9°F (−23°C)

**Mars** Ancient Roman god of war, often depicted as an armed warrior; one of the three protector-deities of the city of Rome itself (with JUPITER and Quirinus). He was originally associated with agriculture but later took on his dominant military aspects; the wolf and woodpecker were sacred to him.

**Marsalis, Wynton** (1961– ) US musician. Before forming his own group, he was a member (1980–82) of Art Blakey's Jazz Messengers. Marsalis is one of the few jazz musicians to successfully crossover into classical music. His albums include *Black Codes (From the Underground)* (1984) and the Grammy Award-winning *Blood on the Fields* (1996).

**Marseilles** (Marseille) City and seaport in SE France, on the Gulf of Lyon and connected to the Rhône River by an underground canal; capital of Bouches-du-Rhône department. The oldest city in France, it was founded in 600 BC by Phocaean Greeks. During the Crusades, Marseilles was a commercial center and shipping port for the Holy Land. The 19th-century French conquest of Algeria and the opening of the Suez Canal (1869) brought great prosperity to the city. Industries: chemicals, engineering. Pop. (1990) 800,550.

**marsh** Flat wetland area, devoid of peat, saturated by moisture during one or more seasons. Typical vegetation includes grasses, sedges, reeds, and rushes. Marshes are valuable wetlands and maintain water tables in adjacent ecosystems. Unlike BOGS, they have alkaline, not acidic soil, *See also* SWAMP

**Marshall, George Catlett** (1880–1959) US general and statesman, secretary of state (1947–49) and defense secretary (1950–51). He served as US chief of staff (1939–45) during World War II. He initiated the MARSHALL PLAN of economic assistance for post-war Europe. In 1953 Marshall was awarded the Nobel Peace Prize.

**Marshall, John** (1755–1835) Chief justice of the US Supreme Court (1801–35). He gained national prominence as a member of the Virginia constitutional ratification convention (1788), when he argued successfully for the CONSTITUTION against Patrick HENRY. Marshall raised the Supreme Court to great prestige and established basic precepts for constitutional interpretation. Important cases he presided over include MARBURY V. MADISON (1803), FLETCHER V. PECK (1810), DARTMOUTH COLLEGE V. WOODWARD (1819), and GIBBONS V. OGDEN (1824).

**Marshall, Thurgood** (1908–93) US lawyer and Supreme Court justice. As counsel (1938–62) for the NATIONAL ASSOCIATION FOR THE ADVANCEMENT OF COLORED PEOPLE (NAACP), he played a key role in obtaining US Supreme Court judgments against racial segregation in schools. He was appointed solicitor general (1965) and became the first African-American associate justice of the US Supreme Court (1967–91).

**Marshall Islands** Republic in the W Pacific Ocean, E of the Caroline Islands, consisting of a group of atolls and coral reefs; the capital is Dalap-Uliga-Darrit (on Majuro Atoll). The islands were first explored by Spain in the early 16th century. Annexed to Germany in 1885, the group was occupied by Japan in 1914 and by US forces in World War II. In 1947 the islands became part of the US-administered Trust Territory of the Pacific Islands. The Trusteeship ended in 1990 and in 1991 the islands joined the UN as a full member state. Products: copra, coconuts, tropical fruits, vegetables, fish. Area: *c.*70sq mi (180sq km). Pop. (1994 est.) 54,000.

**Marshall Plan** US program of economic aid to European countries after World War II. Promoted by the secretary of state, General MARSHALL, its purpose was to repair war damage and promote trade within Europe, while securing political stability. The Soviet Union and E European countries declined to participate. Between 1948 and 1951, 16 countries received a total of US$12 billion.

**marsupial** Mammal of which the female usually has a pouch (marsupium), within which the young are suckled and protected. At birth, the young are in a very early stage of development. Most marsupials are Australasian, and include such varied types as the KANGAROO, KOALA, WOMBAT, TAS-

MANIAN DEVIL, BANDICOOT, and marsupial MOLE. The only marsupials to live outside Australasia are the OPOSSUMS and similar species found in the Americas. *See also* MONOTREME

**marten** Any of several species of carnivorous mammals of the WEASEL family that live in forests of Europe, Asia, and North and South America. Martens have a long body and short legs and are hunted for their fur. The dark brown skins of the SABLE, *Martes zibellina*, are the most valuable. Family Mustelidae.

**Martí, José** (1853–95) Cuban poet and essayist. His verse reflected his belief that poetry and politics were inseparable. He was forced into exile and lived in New York before returning to Cuba, where he died fighting the Spanish. Many Latin American writers have been influenced by his works. *Ismaelillo* (1882) and *Versos sencillos* (1891) contain his best poems.

**Martin, Saint** (*c*.315–*c*.397) Patron saint of France, bishop of Tours (371–97). As a Roman soldier, he is reputed to have torn his cloak to share it with a beggar. In *c*.360 Martin founded the first monastery in Gaul, at Poitiers. He was an evangelical bishop. His feast day (November 11) is known as Martinmas.

**martin** Fast-flying bird closely related to the SWALLOW and native to Europe and North America. It has long, pointed wings and short legs. Species include the house martin (*Delichon urbica*), purple martin (*Progne subis*), and sand martin (*Riparia riparia*). Family Hirundinidae.

**Martin du Gard, Roger** (1881–1958) French novelist. His major works, such as *Jean Barois* (1913) and the eight-novel series *Les Thibault* (1922–40), deal with moral and intellectual dilemmas. He was awarded the 1937 Nobel Prize for literature.

**Martini, Simone** (1284–1344) Italian painter. His imposing fresco, the *Maestà*, combines elements of BYZANTINE ART and GOTHIC ART and presages the RENAISSANCE. The *Annunciation* (1333) is often considered to be his most accomplished work.

**Martinique** Island in the Caribbean, in the Windward group of the Lesser Antilles, forming an overseas département of France; the capital is Fort-de-France. Discovered in 1502 by Christopher COLUMBUS, Martinique was inhabited by Carib Indians until they were displaced by French settlers after 1635. Attacked in the 17th century by the Dutch and the British, the island became a permanent French possession after the Napoleonic Wars. Of volcanic origin, it is the largest of the Lesser Antilles. The original capital, St. Pierre, was completely destroyed by a volcanic eruption in 1902. Industries: tourism, sugar, rum, fruits, cocoa, tobacco, vanilla, vegetables. Area: 417sq mi (1,079sq km). Pop. (1990) 359,579.

**Martins, Peter** (1946– ) Danish dancer, choreographer and ballet director. His partnership with Suzanne Farrell was one of the greatest in the history of ballet. Martins was principal dancer with the New York City Ballet (1969–83), before becoming its joint ballet master (with Jerome ROBBINS), then director (1990– ). His choreographed works include *Les Gentilhommes* (1987), and *A Musical Offering* (1991).

**Martinů, Bohuslav** (1890–1959) Czech composer. Much of his music is based on Bohemian folk rhythms and Czech dances. He composed many operas and ballets, including *The Butterfly that Stamped* (1929) and *Comedy on a Bridge* (*c*.1950), as well as orchestral and chamber works.

**Martin v. Hunter's Lessee** (1816) Landmark US Supreme Court case in which Chief Justice MARSHALL upheld the court's right to reverse state court decisions that conflicted with rights granted under the Constitution.

**Marvell, Andrew** (1621–78) English metaphysical poet and satirist. He is chiefly remembered today for his lyric poetry, first collected in 1681 in a volume that included "The Garden," "Bermudas," and his best-known poem, "To His Coy Mistress."

**Marx, Karl Heinrich** (1818–83) German social philosopher, political theorist, and founder (with Friedrich ENGELS) of international COMMUNISM. He produced his own philosophical approach of DIALECTICAL MATERIALISM. He proclaimed that religion was "the opium of the people" and in *The German Ideology* (1845–46), written with Engels, described the inevitable laws of history. In Brussels he joined the Communist League and wrote with Engels the epoch-making *Communist Manifesto* (1848). Marx took part in the REVOLUTIONS OF 1848 in France and Germany, then went to London (1849), where he lived until his death. His work at the British Museum produced a stream of writings, including *Das Kapital* (3 vols., 1867, 1885, 1894, the last two edited by Engels), which became the "Bible of the working class." In 1864 the International Workingmen's Association (the First International) was formed and Marx became its leading spirit. His expulsion of BAKUNIN from the Association in 1872 led to its collapse. Marx was one of the most important political theorists of modern times. *See also* MARXISM

**Marx Brothers** US team of vaudeville and film comedians. The Marx Brothers consisted of Chico (Leonard) (1891–1961), Harpo (Arthur) (1893–1964), Groucho (Julius) (1895–1977), Gummo (Milton) (1894–1977), and Zeppo (Herbert) (1901–79), the latter two both withdrew from the group by 1935. Their films include *Animal Crackers* (1930), *Duck Soup* (1933), and *A Night at the Opera* (1935).

**Marxism** School of SOCIALISM that arose in 19th-century Europe as a response to the growth of industrial CAPITALISM. It is named for Karl MARX. According to Marxism, a communist society was historically inevitable. Capitalism, because of its emphasis on profits, would eventually so reduce the condition of workers that they would rebel, overthrow the capitalists, and establish a classless society in which the means of production were collectively owned. *The Communist Manifesto* (1848) and *Das Kapital* (1867, 1885, 1894) both contain ideas central to Marxism, which forms the basis of COMMUNISM and strongly influenced the related ideology, socialism. *See also* CLASS; DIALECTICAL MATERIALISM; LENIN, VLADIMIR ILYICH; MAO ZEDONG

**Mary** (Blessed Virgin Mary) (active 1st century AD) Mother of JESUS CHRIST. She figures prominently in the first two chapters of the Gospels according to St. MATTHEW and St. LUKE, which record Christ's birth. Mary has always been held in high regard in Christendom. In the early church, the principal Marian feast was called the Commemoration of St. Mary, from which developed the later feast of the ASSUMPTION (August 15). Other Marian feasts are: the Nativity (September 8), the ANNUNCIATION or Lady Day (March 25), the Purification or Candlemas (February 2), the Visitation (July 2), and (for Roman Catholics) the IMMACULATE CONCEPTION (December 8).

**Mary I** (1516–58) (Mary Tudor) Queen of England (1553–58), daughter of HENRY VIII and CATHERINE OF ARAGON. During the reign of her half-brother, EDWARD VI, she remained a devout Catholic. On Edward's death, the duke of NORTHUMBERLAND arranged the brief usurpation of Lady Jane GREY but Mary acceded with popular support. In 1554 a Spanish alliance was secured by her marriage to the future King PHILIP II of Spain. The marriage provoked a rebellion, led by Sir Thomas WYATT, and hostility intensified after England lost Calais to France in 1558. Mary's determination to re-establish papal authority saw the restoration of heresy laws. The resultant execution of *c*.300 Protestants, including CRANMER, LATIMER, and RIDLEY, earned her the epithet "Bloody Mary." She was succeeded by ELIZABETH I.

**Mary II** (1662–94) Queen of England, Scotland, and Ireland, eldest daughter of JAMES II. Despite her father's conversion to Catholicism, Mary was brought up a Protestant. In 1677 she married her cousin, William of Orange, and moved to Holland. The GLORIOUS REVOLUTION (1688–89) resulted in the exile of James II, and she and her husband were invited to assume the English throne as Mary II and WILLIAM III (OF ORANGE).

**Mary, Queen of Scots** (1542–87) Daughter of JAMES V, she succeeded him as queen when one week old. She was sent to France aged six and married the future FRANCIS II of France in 1558. On his death in 1560 she returned to Scotland, where, as a Catholic, she came into conflict with Protestant reformers. Her marriage to Lord Henry Stuart (Lord Darnley) was also resented and soon broke down. After Darnley's murder (1567), she married Lord Bothwell, possibly her husband's murderer. Following a rebellion of Scottish nobles, she was forced to abdicate in favor of her infant son, James VI (later JAMES I of England). Although she raised an army, it was defeated (1568) and Mary fled to England. Kept in captivity, she became involved in plots against ELIZABETH I and was eventually executed.

**Maryland** State in E US, on the Atlantic Ocean; the capital is

▲ **Marx Brothers** From top, Chico, Harpo, Groucho, and Zeppo, the Marx Brothers, were born in New York City. They were encouraged toward vaudeville by their ambitious mother, Minna. After many unsuccessful years, they finally made it to Broadway with *I'll Say She Is* (1924). Zeppo left the team early but the remaining brothers each developed a distinctive style: Chico was the piano player with the broad Italian accent; Harpo was the harp player who never spoke a word; and Groucho was the mustached wisecracker. Their humor is seen at its best in *Duck Soup* (1933).

M

**MARYLAND**
**Statehood :**
April 28, 1788
**Nickname :**
Old Line State, Free State
**State bird :**
Baltimore oriole
**State flower :**
Black-eyed Susan
**State tree :**
White oak
**State motto :**
Manly deeds, womanly words

ANNAPOLIS. The largest city is BALTIMORE. The first settlements were founded in 1634. Maryland (which was one of the 13 original states) was active in the move toward American independence. In 1791 the state ceded an area of land on the Potomac River to create the District of Columbia, the site of the national capital. During the CIVIL WAR, Maryland was one of the border states that did not secede from the Union, but its citizens served in both armies. The western half of the state is part of the Piedmont plateau region. Maryland is dominated by Chesapeake Bay and its coastal marshlands. The rearing of cattle and chickens is the most important farming activity. Corn, hay, tobacco, and soybeans are the chief crops. Industries: iron and steel, shipbuilding, primary metals, transportation equipment, chemicals, electrical machinery, fishing. Area: 9,775sq mi (25,316sq km). Pop. (1990) 4,781,468.

**Mary Magdalene, Saint** (active 1st century AD) Early follower of Jesus Christ, from the village of Magdala on the W shore of the Sea of Galilee. According to the gospels, Christ freed her of seven demons. She accompanied Christ on his preaching tours in Galilee, saw his crucifixion and burial, and was the first person to see him after his resurrection. She is often identified as a repentant prostitute. Her feast day is July 22.

**Masaccio** (1401–28?) Florentine painter of the early RENAISSANCE, b. Tommaso Giovanni di Mone. His three most important surviving works are: a polyptych (1426) for the Carmelite Church, Pisa; a fresco cycle that he created with Masolino portraying the life of St Peter, in the Brancacci Chapel, Santa Maria del Carmine, Florence (*c.*1425–28); and the *Trinity* fresco in Santa Maria Novella, Florence (*c.*1428).

**Masada** Fortified hill near the Dead Sea, SE Israel. It was the scene of the final defense of the Jewish ZEALOTS against the Romans during the Jewish revolt that began in AD 66. The defenders, *c.*1,000 in strength, committed mass suicide rather than surrender (AD 73).

**Masai** African people of Kenya and Tanzania, consisting of several subgroups who speak a Nilotic language. They are characteristically tall and slender. Their patrilineal, egalitarian society is based on nomadic pastoralism, cattle being equated with wealth. The traditional Masai *kraal* is a group of mud houses surrounded by a thorn fence.

**Masaryk, Tomáš** (1850–1937) Czechoslovak statesman and philosopher, first president of CZECHOSLOVAKIA (1918–35). In 1900 he founded the Czech Peoples Party to represent Czech interests in the AUSTRO-HUNGARIAN EMPIRE. Masaryk fled at the outbreak of World War I and (with Eduard BENEŠ) formed the Czechoslovak national council. In 1918 he returned as president. Revered as the "father" of the nation, Masaryk enacted land reforms and pursued a liberal path on minority rights. He was succeeded by Beneš.

**Masefield, John Edward** (1878–1967) English poet and novelist. His first volume *Salt-Water Ballads* (1902) includes "Sea Fever". He was poet laureate from 1930. Masefield is best-known for his long narrative poems such as *The Everlasting Mercy* (1911) and *Reynard the Fox* (1919).

**maser** (acronym for **m**icrowave **a**mplification by **s**timulated **e**mission of **r**adiation) Device using atoms artificially kept in states of higher energy than normal to provide amplification of high-frequency radio signals. They are used to measure signals from outer space. In 1953 the first maser was built by Charles TOWNES, for which he shared the 1964 Nobel Prize for physics with Nikolai BASOV and Alexander PROKHOROV. It used electrostatic plates to separate high-energy ammonia atoms from low-energy ones. Radiation of a certain frequency would then stimulate the high-energy ammonium atoms to emit similar radiation and strengthen the signal. *See also* LASER

**Maseru** Capital of Lesotho, on the Caledon River, near the W border with South Africa. Originally a trading town, it was capital of the British Basutoland protectorate (1869–71, 1884–1966) and remained the capital when the kingdom of Lesotho achieved independence in 1966. It is a commercial, transportation, and administrative center. Pop. (1992 est.) 367,000.

**Mashhad** (Arabic, shrine of martyrdom) City in NE Iran, close to the border with Turkmenistan; capital of Khorasan province. It is an Islamic holy city and a place of pilgrimage for SHI'A Muslims. In 809 the Abbasid Caliph HARUN AL-RASHID was buried here and in 818 the Imam Ali Riza died while visiting Harun's grave. An ornate shrine was built over both their tombs. In the 18th-century Mashhad became the capital of Persia. Today Mashhad is Iran's second-largest city and a major trade center. It is famous for its carpet and textile manufacture. Pop. (1986) 1,463,508.

**Mason, George** (1725–92) US political leader. A wealthy Virginian, he was a principal author of the Virginia constitution and Declaration of Rights (1776), which influenced the US BILL OF RIGHTS and DECLARATION OF INDEPENDENCE.

**Mason-Dixon Line** Border of Pennsylvania with Maryland and West Virginia. It is named for the men who surveyed it in the 1760s. It was regarded as the dividing line between slave and free states at the time of the MISSOURI COMPROMISE (1820–21), and became the popular name for the boundary between North and South in the US.

**masque** Dramatic presentation that originated in Italy but became popular in the English court and the great houses of the nobility during the late 16th and early 17th centuries. The masque consisted of verse, comedy, and, as an essential feature, a dance for a group of masked revelers. The earliest masque text is *Proteus and the Adamantine Rock* (1594).

**mass** Celebration of the EUCHARIST in the Roman Catholic Church and among some High Church Anglicans. The Catholic rite comprises the Liturgy of the Word and the Liturgy of the Eucharist, which includes the Offertory, the sacrifice of Christ's body and blood under the guise of bread and wine. In the late 20th century, the mass underwent a number of changes following the Second VATICAN COUNCIL (1962–65).

**mass** In music, a setting of the Roman Catholic religious service in Latin. Composers from all eras have written masses. One of the most famous is J.S. BACH's Mass in B minor. In the 19th century mass settings increased in scale until they were more likely to be performed in concert halls than in church services.

**mass** (symbol *m*) Measure of the quantity of matter in an object. Scientists recognize two types of mass. The **gravitational** mass of a body is determined by its mutual attraction to another, reference body, such as the Earth, as expressed in NEWTON'S LAW OF GRAVITATION. Spring balances and platform balances proved a measure of gravitational mass. The **inertial** mass of a body is determined by its resistance to a change in state of motion, as expressed in the second law of motion. INERTIA balances provide a measure of inertial mass. According to EINSTEIN's principle of equivalence, upon which his general theory of RELATIVITY is based, the inertial mass and the gravitational mass of a given body are equivalent. *See also* WEIGHT

**Massachusetts** State in NE US, in NEW ENGLAND, on the Atlantic Ocean; the capital and largest city is BOSTON. Other major cities are Worcester, Springfield, Cambridge, and New Bedford. The first settlement was made in 1620 at Plymouth on Massachusetts Bay by the PILGRIMS. Boston was founded by English Puritans in 1630 and it became the center of the MASSACHUSETTS BAY COLONY. The state played a leading role in events leading up to the American Revolution and was the scene of the first battle. After achieving statehood in 1788 Massachusetts prospered. In the E of the state is a low-lying coastal plain. The uplands of the interior are divided by the Connecticut River valley and the Berkshire valley. The principal rivers are the Housatonic, Merrimack, and Connecticut. A highly industrialized region, Massachusetts is one of the most densely populated states in the nation. Agricultural produce includes cranberries, tobacco, hay, vegetables, and market garden and dairy products. Industries: electronic equipment, plastics, paper, machinery, printing and publishing, fishing. Area: 7,838sq mi (20,300sq km). Pop. (1990) 6,016,425.

**Massachusetts Bay Company** English company chartered in 1629. Its purpose was trade and colonization of the land between the Charles and Merrimack rivers in North America. A group of Puritans, led by John WINTHROP, gained control of the company and founded the Massachusetts Bay Colony in 1630. They took the company's charter with them to Massachussetts and thus enjoyed considerable autonomy. Within a decade, *c.*20,000 people, mainly English Puritans, settled in the colony.

**MASSACHUSETTS**
**Statehood:** February 6, 1788
**Nickname:** Bay State
**State bird:** Chickadee
**State flower:** Mayflower
**State tree:** American elm
**State motto:** By the sword we seek peace, but peace only under liberty

**Massachusetts Institute of Technology (MIT)** University in Cambridge, Massachusetts. It is recognized as a leading technical college, with facilities that include a large nuclear reactor, a high-energy particle ACCELERATOR, and a nuclear science laboratory. There are more than 70 special laboratories either directly associated with or affiliated with MIT.

**Massenet, Jules Émile-Frédéric** (1842–1912) French Romantic composer who dominated 19th-century French lyric opera. He composed many operas, including *Le Cid* (1885), *Werther* (1892), and *Thérèse* (1909). His two masterpieces are considered to be *Manon* (1884) and *Thaïs* (1894).

**Massif Central** Extensive mountainous plateau in SE central France. The volcanic AUVERGNE Mountains form the core of the region, which also includes the Cévennes (SE) and the Causses (SW). Sheep and goats are grazed on the slopes. Hydroelectric power is generated there, and coal and kaolin are mined. The highest peak is Puy de Sancy, rising to 6,186ft (1,886m). Area: *c*.32,800sq mi (85,000sq km).

**Massine, Léonide** (1896–1979) US choreographer and ballet dancer, b. Russia. His choreography includes *Le Soleil de Nuit* (1915), *La Boutique Fantasque* (1919), and *Three Cornered Hat* (1919). He influenced the development of choreography when he created his first symphonic ballet, *Les Présages* (1933). He also performed in the films *The Red Shoes* (1948) and *Tales of Hoffmann* (1951).

**Massinger, Philip** (1583–1640) English dramatist. He wrote more than 40 plays, often in collaboration, many of which are now lost. He is best known for his realistic yet highly symbolic satires of domestic life, such as *A New Way to Pay Old Debts* (1621–22) and *The City Madam* (*c*.1632).

**mass production** Manufacture of goods in large quantities by standardizing parts, techniques, and machinery. American inventor Eli WHITNEY introduced mass production in 1798 to produce weapons. The assembly line, a conveyor belt carrying work through a series of assembly areas, was introduced in 1913 by Henry FORD. Many mass-production processes depend on computer control of machines, including ROBOTS.

**mass spectrograph** (mass spectrometer) Instrument for separating ions according to their masses (or more precisely, according to their charge-to-mass ratio), used in chemical analysis. In the simplest types, the ions are first accelerated by an electric field and then deflected by a strong magnetic field; the lighter the ions the greater the deflection. By varying the field, ions of different masses can be focused in sequence onto a photographic plate or detector and a record of charge-to-mass ratios obtained.

**mastectomy** In surgery, removal of all or part of the female breast. It is performed to treat cancer. Simple mastectomy involves the breast alone; or, when the cancer has spread, radical mastectomy may be undertaken, removing also the lymphatic tissue from the armpit.

**Masters, Edgar Lee** (1868–1950) US poet and novelist. Although he wrote several volumes, he never repeated the early success of his *Spoon River Anthology* (1915), a series of free verse monologs spoken by the dead of a small Midwest town.

**Masters, William Howell** (1915– ) US physician who, with his psychologist wife Virginia (née Johnson) (1925– ), became noted for studies of the physiology and anatomy of human sexual activity. Their works include *Human Sexual Response* (1966) and *Human Sexual Inadequacy* (1970).

**mastiff** (Old English mastiff) Large fighting dog first bred in England over 2,000 years ago. It has a broad, rounded head with a dark-colored, square muzzle and small V-shaped ears. The wide deep-chested body is set on strong legs with large feet. The short, coarse coat may be brown, gray, or brindle. Height: to 33in (84cm) at shoulder; weight: to 210lb (95kg).

**mastodon** Any of several species of extinct elephantine mammals, all of which existed mainly in the PLEISTOCENE epoch. Mastodons had a long coat of red hair; the grinding teeth were notably smaller and less complex than those of modern elephants, and the males had small tusks on the lower as well as the upper jaw. Genus *Mastodon*.

**Mata Hari** (1876–1917) Dutch courtesan, b. Margaretha Geertruida Zelle. In 1917 she was arrested in Paris as a German agent and subsequently executed. Although her conduct was suspicious, few people now believe she was the mysterious secret agent that the French authorities alleged.

**materialism** System of philosophical thought that explains the nature of the world as dependent on MATTER. The doctrine was formulated as early as the 4th century BC by DEMOCRITUS. PLATO developed the contrasting philosophy of IDEALISM. The early followers of BUDDHISM were materialists. DIALECTICAL MATERIALISM as formulated by Karl MARX is a modern development of the theory. *See also* EPICURUS; MONISM; STOICISM

**mathematical induction** Method of proving that a mathematical statement is true for any positive integer $n$ by proving (1) that it is true for a base value, for example 1, and (2) that if it is true for a value $k$ then it is also true for $k + 1$. If (1) and (2) hold, then it follows in a finite number of steps that the statement is true for any positive integer $n$.

**mathematics** Study concerned originally with the properties of numbers and space; now more generally concerned with deductions made from assumptions about abstract entities. Mathematics is often divided into pure mathematics, which is purely abstract reasoning based on axioms, and applied mathematics, which involves the use of mathematical reasoning in other fields, such as engineering, physics, chemistry, and economics. The main divisions of pure mathematics are GEOMETRY, ALGEBRA, and analysis. This last deals with the concept of limits and includes differential and integral CALCULUS. *See also* ARITHMETIC; TRIGONOMETRY

**Mather, Cotton** (1663–1728) Puritan minister in colonial Massachusetts. His father, **Increase** Mather (1639–1723) doubted the reliability of testimony at the SALEM witch trials, and his *Cases of Conscience* (1693) helped to stop the executions. In 1723 Cotton succeeded his father at the Boston ministry. He supported the SALEM witch trials, though not the subsequent executions, yet was sympathetic to scientific and philosophical ideas. He was one of the founders of Yale University, and a member of the Royal Society, London.

**Mathewson, "Christy" (Christopher)** (1880–1925) US baseball player. A right-hand pitcher, he played for the New York Giants (1900–16) and the Cincinnati Reds (1916), whom he also managed (1916–18). He won 373 games, recorded 77 shutouts, and was elected to the Baseball Hall of Fame in 1936.

**Matisse, Henri Emile Benoît** (1869–1954) French painter, sculptor, graphic artist, and designer. Having experimented with NEO-IMPRESSIONISM in paintings such as *Luxe, calme et volupte* (1905), he developed the style of painting that became known as FAUVISM. After a relatively brief flirtation with CUBISM, Matisse turned back to the luminous and sensual calmness that typified his art. He became ill in later life, but produced one of his greatest works, the design of the Chapel of the Rosary at Vence (1949–51). He also started making colored paper cutouts, such as *L'Escargot* (1953). Matisse's most famous sculptures include a series of four bronzes called *The Back* (1909–29).

**Mato Grosso** State in W central Brazil, bordered S by MATO GROSSO DO SUL, and W and SW by Bolivia; the capital is Cuiabà. First settled in the early 18th century by miners seeking gold and diamonds, it became a state in 1889. Much of the area lies on the central plateau of Brazil, and there is rain forest in the N and marshland in the SW. The W has good grazing land, and cattle rearing is the chief occupation. Rice, corn, and sugarcane are grown. There are extensive mineral deposits but most of them are unexploited. Area: 340,156sq mi (881,000sq km). Pop. (1991) 2,020,581.

**Mato Grosso do Sul** State in SW Brazil, bordered N by MATO GROSSO, W by Bolivia, and W and S by Paraguay; the capital is Campo Grande. Early pioneers exploited the area's gold and diamonds but there was little permanent settlement until the late 20th century. In 1979 it was created a separate state from the S part of Mato Grosso. Most of Mato Grosso do Sul lies on an extension of the central plateau of Brazil. There are vast mineral resources, including iron ore and manganese. Agriculture and livestock are important. Area: 135,347sq mi (350,548sq km). Pop. (1991) 1,778,494.

**matriarchy** Any society or group that is ruled by women. Matriarchal societies exist among some primitive peoples in South America. *See also* PATRIARCHY

**matrix** Rectangular array of numbers in rows and columns. The number of rows need not equal the number of columns. Matrices can be combined (added and multiplied) according to certain rules. They are useful in the study of transformations of coordinate systems and in solving sets of simultaneous equations.

**matter** Any material that takes up space. Ordinary matter is made up of ATOMS, which are combinations of ELECTRONS, PROTONS, and NEUTRONS. Atoms, in turn, make up ELEMENTS, an ordered series of substances that have atoms with from one proton in their nuclei (hydrogen) to a hundred or more. All matter exerts an attractive force on other matter, called GRAVITATION. Charged particles exert an attractive or repulsive ELECTROMAGNETIC FORCE that accounts for nearly all everyday phenomena. The strong interaction force is responsible for binding the protons and neutrons in an atomic NUCLEUS, and the weak interaction is responsible for beta decay. *See also* ANTIMATTER; FUNDAMENTAL FORCES; MATTER, STATES OF; MOLECULE

**matter, states of** Classification of MATTER according to its structural characteristics. Four states of matter are generally recognized: solid, liquid, gas, and plasma. Any one ELEMENT or compound may exist sequentially or simultaneously in two or more of these states. SOLIDS may be crystalline, as in salt and metals; or amorphous, as in tar or glass. LIQUIDS have molecules that can flow past one another but that remain almost as close as in a solid. In a GAS, molecules are so far from one another that they travel in relatively straight lines until they collide. In a PLASMA atoms are torn apart into electrons and nuclei by extremely high temperatures, such as those in stars.

**Matterhorn** (Monte Cervino) Mountain peak in Switzerland, in the Pennine Alps, on the Swiss–Italian border. It has a distinctive pyramidal peak formed from several cirques and was first climbed in 1865 by the British mountaineer Edward Whymper. Height: 14,691ft (4,478m).

**Matthew, Saint** (active 1st century AD) Apostle and probably one of the four evangelists of the New Testament. In the lists of the disciples given in the SYNOPTIC GOSPELS, Matthew is sometimes called Levi. Before his calling he was a tax collector working in Capernaum, a village on the Sea of Galilee, in the service of King Herod Antipas. Feast day: September 21 in the West, November 16 in the East.

**Matthew, Gospel according to Saint** Gospel usually placed first in the New Testament but probably written after those of St. MARK and St. LUKE. Written about AD 70–75, it is traditionally ascribed to St. MATTHEW, the tax gatherer who became one of the 12 disciples. The Gospel according to St. Matthew contains more of the teachings, parables, and sayings of Jesus than any other gospel. It is also the only SYNOPTIC GOSPEL written in a Jewish, rather than a Hellenistic, style and emphasizes links between the Old and New Testaments.

**Maugham, (William) Somerset** (1874–1965) British novelist, short-story writer, and dramatist, b. France. He achieved fame initially as a dramatist with plays such as *Lady Frederick* (1912) and *The Circle* (1921). Maugham's first successful novel was *Of Human Bondage* (1915). Other novels include *The Moon and Sixpence* (1919), and *Cakes and Ale* (1930). Maugham's experiences in World War I inform the short-story collection *Ashenden* (1928).

**Mau Mau** Anti-colonial terrorist group of the KIKUYU tribe of Kenya. Members were bound by secret oath to expel European settlers from Kenya. In 1952 a state of emergency was declared following a series of attacks on white settlers. The violence escalated and *c*.11,000 black Africans opposed to the Mau Mau were slaughtered in reprisals. Jomo KENYATTA was imprisoned (1953–60) on suspicion of leading the ampaign. By 1957 British soldiers had captured more than 20,000 Kikuyu, but the human and financial cost of the effort made decolonization inevitable. In 1963 Kenya achieved independence and Jomo Kenyatta was elected prime minister.

**Mauna Kea** (White Mountain) Dormant shield volcano in central Hawaii. Mauna Kea is the highest island mountain in the world at 13,796ft (4,205m). At the snowcapped peak of the volcano stands **Mauna Kea Observatory**, the world's biggest astronomical site with many large telescopes, such as the W.M. Keck 33-ft (10-m) telescope.

**Mauna Loa** Active volcano in central Hawaii, S of Mauna Kea. The second highest active volcano in the world, Mauna Loa has many craters. Kilauea is the largest. Mokuaweoweo is the summit crater. The greatest eruption was in 1881. Major eruptions also took place in 1942, 1949, 1975, and 1984. Height: 13,678ft (4,169m).

**Maundy Thursday** In the Christian liturgical calendar, the day before GOOD FRIDAY, commemorating the institution of the EUCHARIST and the washing of the disciples' feet by Jesus, described in St. JOHN's Gospel.

**Maupassant, Guy de** (1850–93) French short-story writer and novelist. He produced one of his greatest short stories, "Boule de suif", for the collection *Les Soirées de Médan* (1880). Maupassant wrote more than 300 short stories; a number are collected in *La Maison Tellier* (1881), *Contes de la Bécasse* (1883), and *L'Inutile Beauté* (1890). His novels include *Une Vie* (1883), *Bel-Ami* (1885), and *Pierre et Jean* (1887).

**Mauriac, François** (1885–1970) French novelist and playwright. His novels, *A Kiss for the Leper* (1922), *Genitrix* (1923), and *The Desert of Love* (1925), portray the futility of pursuing fulfillment through material comfort and secular love. He also wrote poetry and volumes of memoirs and autobiography. He was awarded the 1952 Nobel Prize for literature.

**Mauritania** Republic in NW Africa; the capital is NOUAKCHOTT. **Land and climate** The low-lying Sahara desert covers most of Mauritania. A sandstone plateau runs N to S through the center of Mauritania. In the SE lies the Hodh basin. The majority of Mauritanians live in the semiarid SW region of SAHEL. Tropical savanna covers much of the rainier S. **History and Politics** Berbers migrated to the region in the first millennium AD. The Hodh basin lay at the heart of the ancient Ghana empire (700–1200), and towns grew up along the trans-Saharan caravan routes. In the 14th and 15th century the region formed part of the ancient Mali empire. Portuguese mariners explored the coast in the 1440s, but European colonialism did not begin until the 17th century, when trade in gum arabic became important. Britain, France, and the Netherlands were all interested in this trade, and France set up a protectorate in 1903. In 1920 the region became a separate colony within French West Africa. In 1958 Mauritania became a self-governing territory in the French Union, before achieving full independence in 1960. Mokhtar Ould Daddah was elected president, and reelected in 1966 and 1971. Mauritania became a one-party state. Devastating drought increased dissatisfaction with Ould Daddah's regime. In 1973 Mauritania withdrew

## MAURITANIA

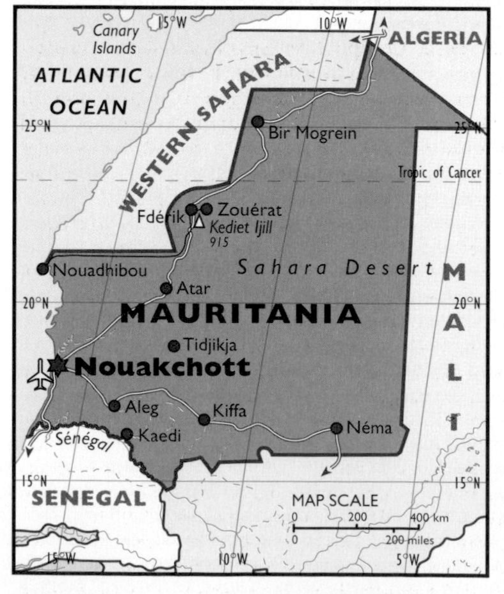


**AREA:** 395,953sq mi (1,025,520sq km)
**POPULATION:** 2,143,000
**CAPITAL (POPULATION):** Nouakchott (393,325)
**GOVERNMENT:** Multiparty Islamic republic
**ETHNIC GROUPS:** Moor (Arab-Berber) 70%, Wolof 7%, Tukulor 5%, Soninke 3%, Fulani 1%
**LANGUAGES:** Arabic (official)
**RELIGIONS:** Islam 99%
**CURRENCY:** Ouguiya = 5 khoums

from the franc zone and joined the Arab League. In 1976 Spain withdrew from Spanish Sahara: Morocco occupied the N 66% of the territory, while Mauritania took the rest. Nationalists, led by the guerrillas of the Popular Front for the Liberation of Saharan Territories (POLISARIO) began an armed struggle for independence, which drained Mauritania's resources. In 1978 Ould Daddah was overthrown in a military coup, and a military committee assumed control. In 1979 Mauritania withdrew from Western Sahara, and Morocco assumed sole authority (for political developments, *see* WESTERN SAHARA). In 1984 recognition of Western Sahara's independence provoked civil unrest, and Ould Taya came to power. In 1991 Mauritania adopted a new constitution. In 1992 multiparty elections Ould Taya was elected president. He was re-elected in 1997. Tension continues between the black African minority in S Mauritania and Arabs and Berbers in the N. **Economy** Mauritania is a low-income developing country (1995 GDP per capita, $1,540). The chief resource and leading export is iron ore. Agriculture employs 69% of the work force. Recent droughts have forced many nomads to migrate to urban areas. Farmers in the SE grow crops such as dates, millet, rice, and sorghum.

**Mauritius** Republic in the SW Indian Ocean, *c*.500mi (800km) E of Madagascar; the capital is Port Louis (on Mauritius). The country consists of the main island of Mauritius, 20 nearby islets, and the dependency islands of Rodrigues, Agalega, and Cargados Carajos. The climate is subtropical, with up to 200in (5,000mm) of rain a year. Its vast plantations produce sugarcane; sugar and molasses are the major exports. The increase in tourism and textile production have partly compensated for the decline in the sugar market. Ethnic and class divisions, combined with economic austerity, created a divided society in the 1980s. The Dutch began to colonize the island in 1598, and named it after Prince Maurice of Nassau. In 1715 it came under the control of France. The French established the sugarcane plantations and imported African slave labor. In 1810 Britain seized Mauritius, and it was formally recognized as a British colony in 1814. In 1833 slavery was abolished and Indian forced labor was used. In 1968 Mauritius achieved independence as a member of the Commonwealth. It became a republic in 1992. Area: 790sq mi (2,046sq km). Pop. (1990) 1,058,942.

**Maurya empire** (321–185 BC) Ancient Indian dynasty and state founded by CHANDRAGUPTA (r. *c*.321–*c*.291 BC). His son, Bindusara (r. *c*.291–*c*.268 BC), conquered the Deccan, and all N India was united under ASHOKA (r. *c*.264–*c*.238 BC), Chandragupta's grandson. After Ashoka's death the empire broke up, the last emperor being assassinated *c*.185 BC.

**mausoleum** Impressive tomb. The widow of Mausolus (from whom the term derives), ruler of Caria, raised a great tomb to his memory at HALICARNASSUS (*c*.350 BC). It became one of the SEVEN WONDERS OF THE WORLD. The best-known mausoleum is the TAJ MAHAL in India.

**Maxim, Sir Hiram Stevens** (1840–1916) US inventor of the Maxim MACHINE GUN (1883). His other inventions include a smokeless powder and a delayed-action fuse.

**Maximilian I** (1459–1519) Holy Roman emperor (1493–1519), son and successor of FREDERICK III. Maximilian was one of the most successful members of the HAPSBURG dynasty. He gained Burgundy and the Netherlands by marriage, and defended them against France. He was less successful in asserting control over the German princes and involvement in the Italian Wars led to his defeat by the Swiss (1499). Maximilian strengthened the Hapsburg heartland in Austria and through marriage diplomacy ensured that his grandson and successor, CHARLES V, inherited a vast European empire.

**Maximilian, Ferdinand Joseph** (1832–67) Emperor of Mexico (1864–67), brother of the Emperor FRANZ JOSEPH. An Austrian archduke, he was offered the throne of Mexico after the French invasion (1862). When the French withdrew in 1867, Maximilian was overthrown by the liberal forces of Benito JUÁREZ and executed.

**Maxwell, James Clerk** (1831–79) Scottish mathematician and physicist, first director of the Cavendish Laboratory at Cambridge, England. His outstanding theoretical work revealed the existence of ELECTROMAGNETIC RADIATION. Maxwell used the theory of the electromagnetic field for **Maxwell's equations**, which provided a unified mathematical theory of LIGHT, ELECTRICITY and MAGNETISM. He also established the nature of Saturn's rings and completed vital work in thermodynamics and statistical mechanics. The former unit of magnetic flux, the maxwell (symbol Mx), was named after him (it has been replaced by the SI unit, the weber). *See also* BOLTZMANN, LUDWIG

**Maya** Outstanding culture of classic American civilization. Occupying S Mexico and N Central America, it was at its height from the 3rd to 9th centuries. They built great temple-cities, with buildings surmounting stepped PYRAMIDS. They were skillful potters and weavers, and productive farmers. They worshiped gods and ancestors, and blood sacrifice was an important element of religion. Maya civilization declined after *c*.900, and much was destroyed after the Spanish conquest in the 16th century. The modern Maya, numbering *c*.4 million, live in the same area and speak a variety of languages related to that of their ancestors. *See also* CENTRAL AND SOUTH AMERICAN MYTHOLOGY

**Mayakovsky, Vladimir** (1893–1930) Russian poet and dramatist. He was the leader of the Russian FUTURISM movement and founded the journal *Left Arts Front*. Mayakovsky is often referred to as the voice of the RUSSIAN REVOLUTION. His poem *150,000,000* (1920) and the play *Mystery Bouffe* (1918) were propaganda pieces for the new Soviet Union. Mayakovsky's late work, such as the plays *Bedbug* (1928) and *Bath-House* (1930), display his disillusionment with the bureaucracy of the regime. He committed suicide.

**Mayan** Family of languages spoken on the Yucatán Peninsula of Mexico, and in Guatemala and part of Belize by the MAYA. There are several dozen of these languages, the most important being Yucatec, of Mexico, and Quiché, Cakchiquel, Mam, and Kekchi, of Guatemala.

**May beetle** (June bug) Medium-sized, stout, brownish SCARAB BEETLE that feeds on tree foliage. The white grubs that eat roots of various crops are one of the most destructive soil pests facing farmers. Genus *Phyllophaga*.

**May Day** First day of May, traditionally celebrated as a festival, the origin of which may lie in the spring fertility rites of pagan times. The Roman festival of Flora, goddess of spring, was held from April 28 to May 3. In some countries May Day is a holiday in honor of workers, and may be accompanied by a military display.

**Mayflower** Ship that carried the PILGRIMS from Plymouth, England to Massachusetts in September, 1620. It carried 120 English Puritans, some from a congregation that had settled in the Netherlands, who established the PLYMOUTH COLONY in December that year.

**Mayflower Compact** Agreement to establish a preliminary government for the PILGRIMS. It was signed by the 41 adult male passengers of the *Mayflower* on November 21, 1620, at sea off the New England coast. The compact bound signers to majority-rule government in the Pilgrim colony, pending receipt of a royal charter. The compact is significant as a first step in the development of democracy in America.

**mayfly** Soft-bodied insect found worldwide. The adult does not eat and lives only a few days, but the aquatic larvae (NYMPH) may live several years. Adults have triangular front wings, characteristic threadlike tails, and vestigial mouthparts; they often emerge from streams and rivers in swarms. Length: 0.4–1in (10–25mm). Order Ephemeroptera.

**Mayo** County in NW Republic of Ireland, in Connaught province, bounded to the N and W by the Atlantic Ocean; the county town is Castlebar. A largely mountainous region, it has numerous lakes and is drained by the rivers Errif and Moy. Oats and potatoes are the chief crops. Cattle, sheep, pigs, and poultry are reared. Industries: woolen goods, toys. Area: 2,084sq mi (5,397sq km). Pop. (1991) 110,713.

**Mayotte** (Mahore) French-administered archipelago in the Indian Ocean, E of the COMOROS. The two major islands are Grande Terre and Petite Terre (Pamanzi). Grande Terre includes the new capital, Mamoudzou. Mayotte was a French colony from 1843 to 1914, when it was attached to the Comoro group. In 1974 the rest of the Comoros became independent, while Mayotte voted to remain a French dependency. In 1976 it became an overseas collectivity of France. The economy is primarily agricultural; the chief products are bananas and mangoes. Area: 144sq mi (373sq km). Pop. (1991) 94,410.

**Mays, Willie Howard, Jr.** (1931– ) US baseball player. A right-handed hitter with 660 home runs and an outstanding center fielder, he played with the New York and San Francisco Giants (1951–52, 1954–72) and the New York Mets (1972–73). He was elected to the Baseball Hall of Fame in 1979.

**Mazarin, Jules** (1602–61) French statesman and Roman Catholic cardinal, b. Italy. He was the protégé of Cardinal RICHELIEU and chief minister under ANNE OF AUSTRIA from 1643. During the FRONDE (1648–52), Mazarin played off the various factions and, though twice exiled from France, emerged in control. As a former papal diplomat, he was a skilful negotiator of the treaties that ended the THIRTY YEARS WAR.

**Mazzini, Giuseppe** (1805–72) Italian patriot and theorist of the RISORGIMENTO. A member of the *Carbonari* (Italian republican underground) from 1830, he founded the "Young Italy" movement in 1831, dedicated to the unification of Italy. He fought in the REVOLUTIONS OF 1848 and ruled in Rome in 1849, but was then exiled. Unlike GARIBALDI or CAVOUR, Mazzini remained committed to popular republicanism.

**Mbabane** Capital of Swaziland, in the NW of the country, in the high veld region of S Africa. It is both an administrative and commercial center, serving the surrounding agricultural region. Tin and iron ore are mined nearby. Pop. (1986) 38,290.

**Mboya, Thomas Joseph** (1930–69) Kenyan political leader. In the forefront of the struggle for independence, he was a founder of the Kenya African National Union (KANU). He served in the government of Jomo KENYATTA (1963–69). Mboya's assassination provoked rioting against the KIKUYU.

**ME** (abbreviation of **m**yalgic **e**ncephalomyelitis) Also known as chronic fatigue syndrome and postviral fatigue syndrome, it is a condition defined as extreme fatigue that persists for six months or more and is not relieved by rest. It ranges in severity from chronic weariness to total physical collapse. The cause of the condition is unknown.

**Mead, George Herbert** (1863–1931) US philosopher and social psychologist. A founder of PRAGMATISM, influenced by John DEWEY, Mead studied the mind, the self, and society. His studies of the behavior of individuals and small groups led to the sociological theories of symbolic interactionism.

**Mead, Margaret** (1901–78) US cultural anthropologist, curator of ethnology (1926–69) at the American Museum of Natural History. Her fieldwork n the SW Pacific formed the basis of her first and most famous work, *Coming of Age in Samoa* (1928). She helped develop the national-character approach to anthropology. Some of her early conclusions about Samoan society have been criticized for shortcomings in perspective and sampling technique.

**Meade, George Gordon** (1852–72) Union Civil War general, b. Spain. Originally an engineer, he led infantry in the war and rose to command the Army of the Potomac. His first and most successful battle was GETTYSBURG (July 1–3, 1863), where he defeated Robert E. LEE.

**mean** (arithmetic mean) Mathematical average. It is found by adding a group of numbers and dividing by the number of items in the group. Thus, for numbers $a$, $b$, $c$, and $d$, the mean is $(a + b + c + d)/4$.

**measles** (rubeola) Extremely infectious viral disease of children. The symptoms (fever, catarrh, skin rash, and spots inside the mouth) appear about two weeks after exposure. Hypersensitivity to light is characteristic. Complications such as pneumonia occasionally occur, and middle-ear infection is also a hazard. Vaccination produces lifelong IMMUNITY.

**Mecca** (Makkah) City in W Saudi Arabia and the holiest city of ISLAM. The birthplace of the prophet MUHAMMAD, only Muslims are allowed in the city. Mecca was originally home to an Arab population of merchants. When Muhammad began his ministry here the Meccans rejected him. The flight or HEJIRA of Muhammad from Mecca to MEDINA in 622 marked the beginning of the Muslim era. In 630 Muhammad's followers captured Mecca and made it the center of the first Islamic empire. The OTTOMAN Turks held the city from 1517 to 1916, finally losing their control after Arabian independence. Mecca fell in 1924 to the forces of Ibn SAUD, who later founded the Saudi Arabian kingdom. Much of Mecca's commerce depends on Muslim pilgrims undertaking the HAJJ to the Great Mosque enclosing the KAABA. Pop. (1991 est.) 630,000.

**mechanical advantage** (force ratio) Factor by which any machine multiplies an applied force. It may be calculated from the ratio of the forces involved or from the ratio of the distances through which they move, as with simple machines such as the LEVER and PULLEY. *See also* EFFICIENCY

**mechanical engineering** Field of ENGINEERING concerned with the design, construction, and operation of machinery. Mechanical engineers work in many branches of industry, including transportation, power generation, and tool manufacture. Achievements in mechanical engineering include the development of wind and water TURBINES, STEAM ENGINES, and INTERNAL COMBUSTION ENGINES.

**mechanics** Branch of physics concerned with the behavior of MATTER under the influence of FORCES. It may be divided into solid mechanics and fluid mechanics. Another classification is as STATICS – the study of matter at rest – and DYNAMICS – the study of matter in motion. In **statics**, the forces on an object are balanced and the object is said to be in equilibrium; static equilibrium may be stable, unstable, or neutral. **Dynamics** may be further divided into kinematics – the description of motion without regard to cause – and KINETICS – the study of motion and force. Classical dynamics rests primarily on Isaac NEWTON'S LAWS of motion. Modern physics has shown these laws to be special cases approximating to more general laws. Relativistic mechanics deals with the behaviour of matter at high speeds, approaching that of light, whereas QUANTUM MECHANICS deals with the behaviour of matter at the level of atoms and molecules. *See also* QUANTUM THEORY; RELATIVITY

**Mecklenburg-Vorpommern** State in NE Germany, on the Baltic coast; the capital is Schwerin. In 1621 the region was divided into the duchies of Mecklenburg-Schwerin and Mecklenburg-Güstrow, which became part of the German empire (1817) and then free states of the Weimar Republic. In 1934 the two states were unified. In 1946 they were joined with Pomerania to form a region of East Germany. In 1990, as part of German reunification, Mecklenburg-West Pomerania was reconstituted as one of the five new states of the Federal Republic. It is mainly a low-lying agricultural state. On the coast are the Baltic ports of Rostock, Wismar, and Straslund. Area: 8,944sq mi (23,170sq km). Pop. (1993) 1,843,455

**Medawar, Sir Peter Brian** (1915–87) British zoologist, b. Brazil. He shared the 1960 Nobel Prize for physiology or medicine with Sir Frank Macfarlane Burnet for their discovery of acquired immune tolerance. Medawar confirmed that if foreign tissue is introduced in the embryonic stages of development it may be reintroduced later without inducing a negative response from the IMMUNE SYSTEM.

**Medea** Daughter of Aeëtes, King of Colchis, whom she defied to help Jason retrieve the Golden Fleece. Renowned as a sorceress, she lived with JASON for many years in Corinth but fled to Athens after his desertion of her caused her to murder their children, and his new wife, in a jealous rage.

**Medellín** City in NW central Colombia; capital of Antioquia department and the second-largest city in Colombia. It was founded in the early 17th century. In recent years it has become the focal point of the country's illegal cocaine trade. Gold and silver are mined nearby. Industries: food processing, coffee, chemicals, steel. Pop. (1992) 1,581,364.

**media** General term for the modern channels of public information. Traditionally, they are RADIO, TELEVISION, NEWSPAPERS, and CINEMA, but the INTERNET is increasingly accepted as a form of the media. These media disseminate information and entertainment on a wide scale and their powers of manipulating people are the subject of much discussion and research.

**median** In statistics, the middle item in a group found by ranking the items from smallest to largest. In the series, 2, 3, 7, 9, 10, for example, the median is 7. With an even number of items the MEAN of the two middle items is taken as the median. Thus in the series 2, 3, 7, 9, the median is 5.

**Medici, Catherine de'** *See* CATHERINE DE' MEDICI

**Medici, Cosimo de' (the Elder)** (1389–1464) Ruler of Florence (1434–64). With the Medici banking fortune he led the oligarchy that was expelled from Florence in 1433 but returned to rule permanently the next year. He increased the Medici fortune, strengthened Florence by alliance with Milan and Naples, and was a great patron of the scholars and artists of the early Renaissance.

**Medici, Cosimo I de' (the Great)** (1519–74) Duke of Florence (1537–74), grand duke of Tuscany (1569–74). Under Cosimo's authoritarian rule, Florence flourished and its territory swelled with the acquisition of Siena. He was given the title of grand duke by the pope.

**Medici, Lorenzo de'** (1449–92) Ruler of Florence, grandson of Cosimo (the Elder). Lorenzo succeeded his father, Piero, in 1469. His grip on power worried Pope Sixtus IV who instigated a coup led by the rival Pazzi family. Lorenzo survived an assassination attempt and ruthlessly clamped down on his enemies. His patronage of RENAISSANCE artists drained the Medici coffers so Lorenzo gained control of public funds. A notable poet, he also encouraged writers. His autocratic rule was attacked by Girolamo SAVONAROLA.

**medicine** Practice of the prevention, diagnosis, and treatment of disease or injury; the term is also applied to any agent used in the treatment of disease. Medicine has been practiced since ancient times, but the dawn of modern Western medicine coincided with accurate anatomical and physiological observations first made in the 17th century. By the 19th century practical diagnostic procedures had been developed for many diseases; BACTERIA had been discovered and research undertaken for the production of immunizing serums in attempts to eradicate disease. The great developments of the 20th century include the discovery of PENICILLIN and INSULIN, CHEMOTHERAPY (the treatment of various diseases with specific chemical agents), new surgical procedures including organ transplants, and sophisticated diagnostic devices such as radioactive tracers and various scanners. Alternative medicine, such as osteopathy, homeopathy, or acupuncture, some of which have existed for hundreds of years, is becoming increasingly popular, and some alternative therapies are being accepted within conventional medicine.

**medieval music** Music produced in Europe during the later Middle Ages, *c.*1100–1400. It was dominated by Christian liturgical vocal choruses called CHANTS, which were sung in polyphonic style. Secular songs were transmitted orally by traveling Saxon, French, and German troubadours or Minnesingers. In the 14th and 15th centuries, guilds of professional musicians were formed, and musical notation began to become more sophisticated, enabling composers to transmit whole works to later generations. *See also* MOTET; MUSICAL NOTATION; POLYPHONY

**Medina** City in Saudi Arabia, N of Mecca. Originally called Yathrib, the city was renamed Medinat an-Nabi (Prophet's city) after MUHAMMAD fled Mecca and settled here in 622. Medina became his capital. In 661 the UMAYYAD caliphs moved their capital to DAMASCUS, and Medina's importance declined. It came under Turkish rule (1517–1916), after which it briefly formed part of the independent Arab kingdom of the Hejaz. In 1932 it became part of Saudi Arabia. Pop. (1991 est.) 400,000.

**Mediterranean Sea** Largest inland sea in the world, lying between Europe and Africa and extending from the Strait of Gibraltar in the W to the coast of SW Asia in the E. The Mediterranean was once a trade route for Phoenicians and Greeks, later controlled by Rome and Byzantium. In the Middle Ages Venice and Genoa were the dominant maritime powers until the rise of the Ottoman Turks. The opening of the Suez Canal in 1869 made the Mediterranean one of the world's busiest shipping routes and the development of the Middle Eastern oil fields further increased its importance. The Mediterranean is connected to the Black Sea via the Dardanelles, the Sea of Marmara and the Bosporus, and to the Red Sea by the Suez Canal. It includes the Tyrrhenian, Adriatic, Ionian, and Aegean seas. It receives the waters of several major rivers, including the Nile, Rhône, Ebro, Tiber, and Po. There are *c.*400 species of fish, and tuna, sardines, and anchovies are among those caught commercially. In recent years pollution has become a major issue. Area: 969,100sq mi (2,509,972km).

**Meegeren, Hans van** (1889–1947) Dutch painter and celebrated forger, especially of VERMEER paintings, such as *Christ at Emmaus* (1937). He deceived art experts for years and was discovered only after his own confession in 1945.

**meerkat** (suricate) Any of a number of small carnivorous mammals closely related to the MONGOOSE, native to the bush country of southern Africa. It is similar in appearance to the mongoose but without the bushy tail. Length: 19in (47cm). Typical species *Suricata suricatta*.

**megalith** (lit. huge stone) Prehistoric stone monument. Historians usually apply the term to the gigantic slabs that form many stone circles, half circles, and rows in N Europe. These constructions date from the NEOLITHIC and early BRONZE AGE. One of the best-known and complex examples is the circle at STONEHENGE (*c.*2100–2000 BC). Megaliths existed long before the first stone buildings of Mycenean Crete. *See* DOLMEN; MENHIR

**Megiddo** Ancient city of CANAAN. Strategically located on the route from Egypt to Mesopotamia, it was the scene of many battles, notably between the Egyptians and the Syrians in 1486 BC. It was often rebuilt, notably under the kings of ancient Israel in the 10th–9th centuries BC and after the Assyrian conquest of *c.*734 BC.

**Mehta, Zubin** (1936– ) Indian conductor. He was musical director of the Montreal Symphony (1961–67), Los Angeles Philharmonic Orchestra (1961–77), and New York Philharmonic (1978–91). In 1977 Mehta was made artistic director for life of the Israel Philharmonic.

**Meiji, Mutsohito** (1852–1912) Emperor of Japan (1867–1912), whose reign saw the transformation of Japan into a modern, industrial state. Mutsuhito introduced sweeping reforms, including the abolition of feudalism, a western-style constitution, the establishment of state education, and encouragement of industrial growth.

**Meiji Restoration** (1868) Constitutional revolution in Japan. Opposition to the shogunate built up after Japan's policy of isolation was ended by US Commodore PERRY in 1854. Pressure for modernization resulted in a new imperial government, at first dominated by former samurai, with the young Emperor MEIJI as its symbolic leader.

**meiosis** In biology, the process of cell division that reduces the CHROMOSOME number from DIPLOID to HAPLOID. Meiosis involves two nuclear divisions. The first division halves the chromosome number in the cells; the second division then forms four haploid "daughter" cells, each containing a unique configuration of the parent cells' chromosomes. In most higher organisms, the resulting haploid cells are the GAMETES, or sex cells, the OVA and SPERM. In this way meiosis enables the genes from both parents to combine in a single cell without increasing the overall number of chromosomes. *See also* MITOSIS

**Meir, Golda** (1898–1978) Israeli stateswoman, prime minister (1969–74), b. Ukraine as Golda Mabovitch. In 1906 her family emigrated to the US, and she became active in ZIONISM. In 1921 Meir emigrated to Palestine. In 1936 she became head of the Jewish labor movement. After Israeli independence, Meir became minister of labor (1949–56) and foreign minister (1956–66). She succeeded Levi ESHKOL as prime minister.

◀ **Medici** Detail from *The Journey of the Magi* (1459–61) by Benozzo Gozzoli in the Palazzo Medici-Riccardo, portraying Lorenzo de' Medici as one of the three Magi. Lorenzo the Magnificent, as he was also known, was a great patron of the Renaissance. A fine humanist poet and an astute politician, he was a generous supporter of many notable artists, among them Ghirlandaio, Botticelli, Leonardo da Vinci, and Michelangelo. His main collecting interest, however, was in antique coins and gems.

M

Meir managed to maintain a fragile domestic coalition while negotiating with Israel's Arab neighbours. She was forced to resign following criticism of the government's lack of preparedness for the 1973 ARAB–ISRAELI WAR.

**Meistersinger** German poet-musician of the 15th–16th centuries. They were organized in guilds, which held competitions and awarded prizes. Generally, the songs were religous and followed strict conventions. A famous meistersinger, the cobbler Hans Sachs (1494–1576), was immortalized in the opera *Die Meistersinger von Nürnberg* (1868) by Richard Wagner.

**Melanchthon, Philip** (1497–1560) German theologian and educator, considered with Martin LUTHER as a founder of PROTESTANTISM. Melanchthon wrote the *Confessions of Augsburg* (1530), a statement of Protestant beliefs. He also helped Luther with his German translation of the New Testament.

**Melanesia** Collective term for a number of island groups in the W Pacific Ocean, generally S of the equator, W of the International Date Line, N and E of Australia. It includes the Bismarck Archipelago, SOLOMON ISLANDS, New Hebrides, and the TONGA group. Melanesia is one of the subdivisions of OCEANIA. The others are POLYNESIA and MICRONESIA.

**melanin** Dark pigment found in the skin, hair, and parts of the eye. The amount of melanin determines skin color. Absence of melanin results in an ALBINO.

**Melba, Dame Nellie** (1861–1931) Australian soprano, b. Helen Porter Mitchell. Initially a high coloratura soprano, she was famous in the roles of Lucia (Donizetti's *Lucia di Lammermoor*) and Gilda (Verdi's *Rigoletto*) and later for such lyric roles as Mimí (Puccini's *La Bohème*).

**Melbourne, William Lamb, 2nd Viscount** (1779–1848) British statesman, prime minister (1834, 1835–41). He entered Parliament as a Whig in 1805. As home secretary (1830–34) in Earl GREY's administration, Melbourne was responsible for the suppression of the TOLPUDDLE MARTYRS. As prime minister, he oversaw reform of the POOR LAW (1834) but resisted changes to the CORN LAWS. Melbourne gave Lord PALMERSTON control of foreign affairs and tutored Queen VICTORIA in statecraft. He was succeeded by Sir Robert PEEL.

**Melbourne** City and port on the River Yarra at the N end of Port Phillip Bay, SE Australia; capital of Victoria state. Founded in 1835 by settlers from Tasmania, it became the state capital in 1851 and served as the seat of the Australian federal government from 1901 to 1927. Melbourne is Australia's second largest city. A major centre of finance, commerce, communications and transport, and Australia's largest cargo-handling port, it exports wool, flour, meat, fruit and dairy produce. Manufacturing is also important. Industries: aircraft, automobiles, shipbuilding, textiles, chemicals. Pop. (1993 est.) 3,189,200.

**Mellon, Andrew William** (1855–1937) US financier. He inherited a fortune, which he increased through industrial investment and banking. Later, Mellon was secretary of the treasury under three presidents (1921–32). A generous patron of the arts, he was ambassador to Britain (1932–33). He donated the funding for the National Gallery of Art, Washington, D.C.

**melodrama** Theatrical form originating in late 18th-century France and achieving its greatest popularity during the following century. It relied on simple, violent plots in which virtue was finally rewarded.

► **melon** Melons belong to the cucumber and marrow family, and many different types have been cultivated. Cantaloupe melons (right) are true melons while watermelons (left) belong to the same family but a different genus. Melons grow successfully only in warm climates or under glass if temperatures are cooler.

**melody** In music, a sequence of notes that makes a recognizable musical pattern. The term is most commonly used of the dominant part or voice (the "tune") in Romantic and light music, in which harmonic accompaniment is nearly always subordinate. Music featuring several melodies simultaneously is termed "contrapuntal" or POLYPHONY, and is characteristic of the late BAROQUE period. *See also* COUNTERPOINT; HARMONY

**melon** Annual vine and its large, fleshy, edible fruit. Melons grow in warm temperate and subtropical climates. The cantaloupe melon, with its rough skin, probably originated in Armenia; the smoother yellow rind honeydew, in SE Asia. The large, dark green watermelon, with its red watery flesh, is believed to have come from Africa. Family Cucurbitaceae.

**melting point** Temperature at which a substance changes from solid to liquid. The melting point of the solid has the same value as the freezing point of the liquid, so the melting point of ice, 0°C (32°F), is the same as the freezing point of water.

**Melville, Herman** (1819–91) US novelist. He became a sailor in 1839 and joined a whaling ship in 1841. His first novel, *Typee* (1846), recounts his experiences among remote island natives. *Moby Dick*, an allegorical story of the search for a great whale, was written in 1851. *Billy Budd* was published in 1924 and was the inspiration for BRITTEN's opera of the same name. Melville's work was neglected during his lifetime, but *Moby Dick* is now regarded as a classic of US literature.

**membrane** In biology, boundary layer or layers inside or around a living CELL or TISSUE. Cell membranes include the plasma membrane surrounding the cell, the network of membranes inside the cell (endoplasmic reticulum) and the double membrane surrounding the nucleus. The multicellular membranes of the body comprise: the mucous membranes of the respiratory, digestive, and urinogenital passages; the synovial membranes of the joints; and the membranes that coat the inner walls of the abdomen and thorax, and the surfaces of organs. *See also* EPITHELIUM

**Memling, Hans** (1440–94) (Hans Memlinc) Flemish painter, b. Germany. Memling had a flourishing workshop from which he produced a large number of portraits and religious works. His patrons included the Italians Tommaso Portinari and his wife, whom he painted in *c*.1468.

**memory** Capacity to retain information and experience and to recall or reconstruct them in the future. Modern psychologists often divide memory into two types, short-term and long-term. An item in short-term memory lasts for *c*.10–15 seconds after an experience, but is lost if not used again. An item enters long-term memory if the item is of sufficient importance or if the information is required frequently.

**Memphis** Ancient city of Egypt, S of Cairo, part of which is now occupied by the village of Mit Ra-hina. Founded in *c*.3100 BC by MENES, the city was formerly the royal residence and capital of Egypt. Material from its ruins was used by the Arabs for building Cairo.

**Memphis** City and river port in SW Tennessee, on the Mississippi River; largest city in Tennessee. Strategically located on Chickasaw Bluff above the Mississippi, the site of Memphis was used as a French (1682), Spanish (1794), and US (1797) fort before the first permanent settlement was made in 1819. Today it is a major transportation center and livestock market. Industries: lumber, farm machinery, cotton, food processing, pharmaceuticals. Pop. (1990) 610,337.

**Menander** (*c*.342–*c*.292 BC) Greek playwright. He wrote more than 100 comedies, of which only one survives in full. As the outstanding exponent of the New Comedy of Hellenistic times, he is regarded as the founder of the comedy of manners, his plays being concerned with domestic problems.

**Mencius** (*c*.372–289 BC) (Mengzi) Chinese philosopher of the Confucian school. He held that human beings are basically good but require cultivation to bring out the goodness. His teachings were recorded in the *Book of Mencius*, one of the Four Books in the canonical writings of CONFUCIANISM.

**Mencken, H.L. (Henry Louis)** (1880–1956) US social critic. He was a witty and ferociously savage critic of US middle-class culture. His influence was at its height while he was editor of the *American Mercury* (1924–33). He also wrote a multi-volume study of *The American Language* (1919–48).

**Mendel, Gregor Johann** (1822–84) Austrian naturalist. He discovered the laws of HEREDITY and laid the foundation for the modern science of GENETICS. His study of the inheritance of characteristics such as flower color, height of plants, and texture of the seeds of garden peas was published in *Experiments with Plant Hybrids* (1866). It was rediscovered in 1900.

**mendelevium** (symbol Md) Radioactive, metallic element that is the ninth of the TRANSURANIC ELEMENTS in the ACTINIDE SERIES. A. Ghiorso and colleagues at the University of California first synthesized it in 1955 by the alpha-particle bombardment of einsteinium-253. Properties: at.no. 101; at. wt. 258; most stable isotope $^{258}$Md (half-life 2 months).

**Mendeleyev, Dmitri Ivanovich** (1834–1907) Russian chemist who devised the PERIODIC TABLE. Mendeleyev demonstrated that chemically similar elements appear at regular intervals if the elements are arranged in order by atomic weights. He classified the then known 60 elements and left gaps in the table, predicting the existence and properties of several unknown elements later discovered. The radioactive element MENDELEVIUM is named for him.

**Mendelsohn, Erich** (1887–1953) German architect. He designed the Einstein Observatory at Potsdam (1920), E Germany, the most famous example of EXPRESSIONISM.

**Mendelssohn (-Bartholdy), (Jakob Ludwig) Felix** (1809–47) German composer and conductor. A child prodigy, at 16 he composed an octet and at 17 he wrote his overture to *A Midsummer Night's Dream*. His orchestral works include a famous violin concerto (1845) and five symphonies. He also wrote much piano and chamber music. His two oratorios, *St. Paul* (1836) and *Elijah* (1846), are considered to be among the greatest of the 19th century.

**Mendès-France, Pierre** (1907–82) French statesman, prime minister (1955–56). During World War II he was imprisoned by the Vichy regime but escaped to London in 1941. There he enlisted in the Free French air force, later joining General de GAULLE's government in exile. He reentered parliament in 1946. After the defeat of the French army at Dien Bien Phu in 1954 he became prime minister, promising and achieving an end to France's involvement in Indochina. He also prepared the way for Tunisian independence. However, his harsh economic measures led to his downfall.

**Menem, Carlos Saúl** (1935– ) Argentinian statesman, president (1989– ). He was imprisoned (1976–81) by the military government. Menem invoked the name of Juan PERÓN in his campaign for president. He introduced privatization, released hundreds of political prisoners and improved relations with the UK over the fate of the FALKLAND ISLANDS. He was re-elected in 1995.

**Menes** Egyptian king (*c.*3100 BC), regarded as the first king of the First Dynasty. He unified upper and lower Egypt, establishing the Old Kingdom with its capital at Memphis.

**menhir** Archeological term given to single standing stones found in W Europe. Probably of NEOLITHIC origin, they are usually tall and square in section, tapering toward the top. They are thought to have been used to mark places of religious or ritual significance. *See also* DOLMEN; MEGALITH

**Menière's disease** Chronic condition of the inner EAR affecting hearing and balance. Symptoms are deafness, vertigo, and ringing in the ears (tinnitus). Caused by excessive fluid in the inner ear, it occurs in middle age or later. It is generally treated with ANTIHISTAMINE drugs.

**meningitis** Inflammation of the meninges (membranes) covering the brain and spinal cord, resulting from infection. Bacterial meningitis is more serious than the viral form. Symptoms include headache, fever, nausea, and stiffness of the neck. The disease can vary from mild to lethal.

**Mennonites** Christian sect founded by the Dutch reformer Menno Simons (1496–1561) and influenced by ANABAPTIST doctrines. They believe in the BAPTISM of adult believers and reject infant baptism as well as the doctrine of the real presence in the EUCHARIST.

**Menominee** (Menomini) Algonquian-speaking tribe of Native North Americans once occupying the Menominee River, Wisconsin, to the area around Michilimackinac. Today *c.*3,500 inhabit the Menomini Reservation in NE Wisconsin.

**menopause** Stage in a woman's life marking the end of the reproductive years, when the MENSTRUAL CYCLE becomes irregular and finally ceases, generally around the age of 50. Popularly known as the "change of life," it may be accompanied by unpleasant effects such as hot flashes, excessive bleeding, and emotional upset. HORMONE REPLACEMENT THERAPY (HRT) is designed to relieve menopausal symptoms.

**menorah** Sacred seven-branched candelabra that has become a symbol of Judaism throughout the world. It is rich in symbolic meaning. Some interpret it in terms of the seven planets, the tree of life, or the six-day creation of the universe with the center shaft representing the Sabbath. An eight-branched menorah is used during the HANUKKAH festival.

**Menshevik** Moderate faction of the Russian Social Democratic Labor Party. The Mensheviks ("the minority") split from the more radical BOLSHEVIKS ("the majority") in 1903. They believed in "scientific socialism" and favored a gradual transformation of society, whereas the Bolsheviks wanted total revolution organized by a small, central group of disciplined revolutionaries. The Mensheviks were suppressed in 1922.

**menstrual cycle** (menarce) In humans and some higher primates of reproductive age, the stage during which the body prepares for pregnancy. In humans the average cycle is 28 days. At the beginning of the cycle, HORMONES from the PITUITARY GLAND stimulate the growth of an ovum (egg cell) contained in a follicle in one of the two OVARIES. At approximately mid-cycle the follicle bursts, the egg is released (ovulation) and travels down the FALLOPIAN TUBE to the UTERUS. The follicle (now called the corpus luteum) secretes two hormones, PROGESTERONE and ESTROGEN, during this secretory phase of the cycle, and the ENDOMETRIUM thickens, ready to receive

▲ **Mendelssohn** A highly respected conductor, Felix Mendelssohn's concert tours took him to Italy, France, England, and Scotland, the latter inspiring his popular orchestral overture *The Hebrides* (also known as "Fingal's Cave") and the Scottish Symphony. Typical of German romanticism, his compositions often have extramusical associations, with inspiration coming from literature, historical events, or beautiful scenery.

**MENSTRUAL CYCLE**

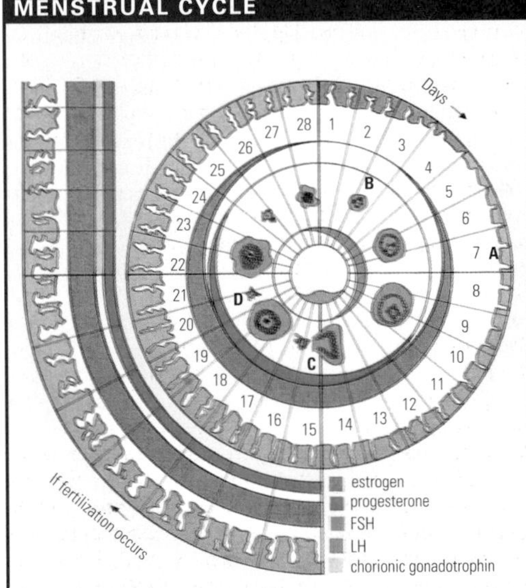


The changes occurring during the menstrual cycle are controlled by the balance of the follicle stimulating hormone (FSH) and luteinizing hormone (LH) secreted by the pituitary. The diagram shows the changing levels of these, and of estrogen and progesterone induction from the ovarian follicle, together with changes in the structure of the uterine wall (A) and development of the follicle (B), in a circular form through a normal 28-day cycle. The sharp increase in LH at about mid-cycle causes ovulation (C) and, if fertilization does not occur, the corpus luteum (D) formed degenerates around day 26 as pituitary hormone levels fall. The consequent withdrawal of estrogen and progesterone causes the uterine wall to shed itself in the menstrual flow. This then proliferates again under the influence of estrogen from a new follicle. If fetilization and egg implantation do occur the placenta produces chorionic gonadotrophin possibly as early as day 21, which allows the corpus luteum to continue to produce estrogen and progesterone until the placenta takes over.

M

► **Messerschmitt** Founder of a successful aircraft manufacturing company, Messerschmitt designed the aircraft used by the Luftwaffe in World War II and joined Hitler's War Council in 1937. His Me-262, a swept-wing jet fighter, was used by the Russians as a model for their MiG fighter aircraft.

the fertilized egg. Should fertilization (conception) not occur, the corpus luteum degenerates, hormone secretion ceases, the endometrium breaks down, and menstruation occurs in the form of a loss of blood. In the event of conception, the corpus luteum remains and maintains the endometrium with hormones until the PLACENTA is formed. In humans, the onset of the menstrual cycle (menarche) occurs at PUBERTY; it ceases with the MENOPAUSE (around 50 years).

**mental handicap** Intellectual functioning that is below the average, irrespective of cause. It is usually related to congenital conditions but can arise later in life through brain damage. Assuming a normal intelligence quotient or IQ of 90–110, impairment is often described as borderline (IQ 68–85), mild (IQ 52–67), moderate (IQ 36–51), severe (IQ 20–35), and profound (IQ under 20).

**mental disorder** Any failure of mental health that is severe enough for psychiatric treatment to be appropriate. Some mental disorders can be attributed to injury or organic disease of the BRAIN. Mental disorder may also be the result of a hereditary predisposition. Other disorders are psychogenic, without any clear evidence of any physiological cause. SCHIZOPHRENIA, severe DEPRESSION, and MANIC DEPRESSION are the most widespread of mental disorders. Neurotic disorders, which can be severe but do not often warrant prolonged stays in hospital, include persistent anxiety, PHOBIAS, obsessions, and HYSTERIA.

**menthol** ($C_{10}H_{19}OH$) White, waxy crystalline compound having a strong odor of peppermint. Its main source is oil of peppermint from the plant *Mentha arvensis*. It is an ingredient of decongestant ointments and nasal sprays, and is used to flavor toothpaste and cigarettes.

**Menuhin, Yehudi, Baron** (1916–99) British violinist, b. USA. A child prodigy, he gave his first concert aged seven. In 1932 Menuhin recorded Elgar's violin concerto, the composer conducting. In 1942 Bela Bartók wrote his solo violin sonata for him. Menuhin was director (1959–68) of the Bath Festival and in 1963 founded the Yehudi Menuhin School for young, gifted musicians. He was knighted in 1965. He was often accompanied on the piano by his sister **Hephzibah** Menuhin (1920–81).

**Menzies, Sir Robert Gordon** (1894–1978) Australian statesman, the country's longest-serving prime minister (1939–41, 1949–65). In the immediate aftermath of World War 2, he encouraged British and US commitment to the security of Southeast Asia and supported the ANZUS PACT and the SOUTHEAST ASIA TREATY ORGANIZATION (SEATO). Menzies supported the USA in the Vietnam War.

**mercantilism** Seventeenth-century trade policy advocating state intervention in economic affairs, primarily to maximize exports. Foreign trade was publicly controlled to produce the maximum possible surplus in the nation's trade balance, thus increasing the country's store of silver and gold, which constitute the "nation's wealth." Trade was controlled through tariffs on imported goods. Mercantilism was criticized by the proponents of LAISSEZ-FAIRE and FREE TRADE.

**Mercator, Gerardus** (1512–94) Flemish cartographer. His huge world map of 1569 employed the system of projection now named for him, in which lines of longitude, as well as latitude, appear as straight, parallel lines.

**Mercury** Smallest of the four inner planets and the planet closest to the Sun. It has no known satellite. Very little was known about Mercury's surface until the Mariner 10 probe made three close approaches to the planet in 1974 and 1975, and returned pictures of nearly half the surface. These showed a heavily cratered, lunarlike world marked by valleys and ridges. Radar mapping of Mercury's polar regions in 1991 and 1992 revealed what may be water ice on the floors of craters permanently in shadow. There is a very tenuous atmosphere, mainly of helium and sodium, and a weak magnetic field.

**MERCURY: DATA**

Diameter (equatorial): 3,031mi (4,878km)
Mass (Earth = 1): 0.055
Volume (Earth = 1): 0.056
Density (water = 1): 5.44
Orbital period: 89.97 days
Rotation period: 68.646 days
Average surface temperature: 800°F (427°C)

**mercury** (quicksilver, symbol Hg) Liquid metallic element, known from earliest times. The chief ore is cinnabar (a sulfide), from which it is extracted by roasting. The silvery element is poisonous and the only metal that is liquid at normal temperatures. Mercury is used in barometers, thermometers, laboratory apparatus, mercury-vapor lamps, and mercury cells. Mercury compounds are used in pharmaceuticals. Properties: at.no. 80; at. wt. 200.59: sp.gr. 13.6; m.p. −37.97°F (−38.87°C); b.p. 673.84°F (356.58°C); most common isotope $^{202}$Hg (29.8%).

**Meredith, George** (1828–1909) British novelist and poet. Most modern critics regard *The Egoist* (1879) as his masterpiece, followed by *Diana of the Crossways* (1885). In his last years, he wrote mainly poetry.

**merganser** Any of several species of slender freshwater or marine DUCKS that dive for food, especially the red-breasted merganser (*Mergus serrator*), which has a hooked bill. The goosander (*M. merganser*) differs mainly in coloration. Family Anatidae.

**meridian** Circle that runs through the North and South Poles, at right angles to the equator. *See also* LONGITUDE

**Mérimée, Prosper** (1803–70) French dramatist and short-story writer. He wrote a large body of dramatic work in the 1820s, but is best remembered for his historical novellas and short stories. These include the collection of short stories *Mosaïque* (1833), and the novellas *Colomba* (1841) and *Carmen* (1845), on which Georges BIZET based his opera.

**meristem** In plants, a layer of cells that divides repeatedly to generate new tissues. It is present at the growing tips of shoots and roots, and at certain sites in leaves. In monocotyledons the leaf meristem is at the base, explaining why grasses continue to grow when the leaf tips are removed by grazing or mowing. *See also* CAMBIUM

**merlin** Small European FALCON found in hills and open moorland. Feeding on small birds, it may hover, but not as commonly as the KESTREL. Length: to 13in (33cm). Species *Falco columbarius*.

**Merovingian** (476–750) Frankish dynasty. It was named for Merovech, a leader of the Salian Franks, whose grandson CLOVIS (r. *c*.481–511) ruled over most of France and, converting to Christianity, established the common interests of the Frankish rulers and the already Christian population of his new kingdom. The last Merovingian king was overthrown by PEPIN, founder of the Carolingian dynasty.

**Merseyside** Metropolitan county in NW England, formed in 1974. It lies on both banks of the estuary of the Mersey River. The major town is LIVERPOOL. In the 19th century shipbuilding and ship repair grew in importance, and Liverpool became one of Britain's leading ports. Today, the main industries are motor vehicles, chemicals, and electrical goods. Area: 253sq mi (655sq km). Pop. (1991) 1,403,642.

**mesa** Large, broad, flat-topped hill or mountain of moderate height and with steep, clifflike sides. A mesa is capped with layers of resistant horizontal rocks which may then erode to form narrower buttes.

**mescaline** Psychedelic drug obtained from the dried tops of the peyote cactus, *Lophophora williamsii*. In North America, mescaline is used in some Native American religious rites.

**Mesmer, Franz (Friedrich Anton)** (1734–1815) Austrian physician. Mesmer's interest in "animal magnetism" led to his development of mesmerism (HYPNOSIS) as a therapeutic treatment. Ridiculed by fellow scientists, Mesmer died in obscurity.

**Mesolithic** (Middle Stone Age) In NW Europe the period in human cultural development following the PALEOLITHIC and preceding the NEOLITHIC. It followed an ice age (*c*.8000 BC). As the environment changed, scrub gave way to forest and small game proliferated. A nomadic form of life became unnecessary and human settlement was a feature of this period, as were flint tools.

**meson** Subatomic particle, member of a subgroup of

HADRONS, all of which have either zero or integral spin. They include the pions, kaons, and eta mesons.

**mesophyll** Soft tissue located between the two layers of epidermis in a plant leaf. In most plants, mesophyll cells contain chlorophyll-producing structures called CHLOROPLASTS, which are essential to PHOTOSYNTHESIS.

**Mesopotamia** Ancient region between the TIGRIS and EUPHRATES rivers in SW Asia, roughly corresponding to modern Iraq. It was the setting of one of the earliest human civilizations, resulting from the development of irrigation in the 6th millennium BC and the extreme fertility of the irrigated land. The first cities were established by the Sumerians *c*.2500 BC. The first empire builders on a large scale were the people of Akkadia under SARGON, who conquered the Sumerian cities *c*.2300 BC. BABYLONIA gained supremacy in the 18th century BC and was followed by others, notably the Assyrians. Later ruled by foreigners, such as Persians, Greeks, and Romans, Mesopotamia gradually lost its distinctive cultural traditions. *See also* SUMERIA

**Mesozoic** Third era of geologic time, extending from *c*.248–65 million years ago. It is divided into three periods: the TRIASSIC, JURASSIC, and CRETACEOUS. For most of the era the continents are believed to have been joined into one huge landmass called PANGAEA. The period was also characterized by the variety and size of its reptiles.

**Messerschmitt, Willy (Wilhelm)** (1898–1978) German aircraft designer, famous for the Messerschmitt Bf-109 fighter used by the LUFTWAFFE during World War II. Messerschmitt also designed the ME-262, the first jet-propelled aircraft to be used in combat (1944).

**Messiaen, Olivier** (1908–92) French composer and organist. His organ works, including *L'Ascension* (1933) and *La Nativité du Seigneur* (1935), are important contributions to the repertoire of that instrument. Among other compositions is the monumental ten-movement *Turangalîla-symphonie* (1949) and an opera on the life of Francis of Assisi.

**Messiah** Savior or redeemer. Specifically, the Messiah was the descendant of King DAVID expected by the Jews of ancient times to become their king, free them from foreign bondage, and rule over them in a golden age of glory, peace, and righteousness. The word is Hebrew in origin, meaning "anointed," and refers to the "idealized" king as having been anointed by God or his representative in the way that David and his successors were. The title "Christ," derived from the Greek version of the term Messiah, was applied to Jesus by his followers.

**Messina** Seaport city in Italy, in NE Sicily, on the Strait of Messina; capital of Messina province. It was founded by the Greeks in *c*.730 BC. The city was conquered by mercenaries, whose backing from Rome led directly to the first of the PUNIC WARS. From 241 BC Messina was free city of Rome. In the 9th century it was conquered by the Muslim Saracen army and then by the Normans in 1061. In 1190 Messina was taken by the Crusaders and was ruled by Spain from 1282 to 1714. In 1860 it was liberated by Giuseppe Garibaldi. In 1908 an earthquake killed more than 80,000 people and destroyed most of the city. Exports: wine, citrus fruit, olive oil, chemicals. Industries: chemicals, pharmaceuticals, processed foods. Pop. (1991) 231,693.

**metabolism** Chemical and physical processes and changes continuously occurring in a living organism. They include the breakdown of organic matter (catabolism), resulting in energy release, and the synthesis of organic components (anabolism) to store energy and build and repair TISSUES.

**metal** Element that is a good conductor of heat and electricity – the atoms of which are bonded together within crystals in a unique way. Mixtures of such elements (ALLOYS) are also metals. About three-quarters of known elements are metals. Most are hard, shiny materials that form oxides. Malleability and ductility are further metallic characteristics. Some metals have very high melting points and various high-temperature applications: TUNGSTEN, with the highest melting point of all at 6,170°F (3,410°C), is employed for incandescent-lamp filaments. ALUMINUM, followed by IRON, are the two most abundant and useful of metals. TITANIUM, although rarely seen as a metal, is more commonly distributed than the more familiar COPPER, ZINC, and LEAD. Other metals of economic importance, because they can undergo nuclear FISSION, are URANIUM and PLUTONIUM.

**metalloid** ELEMENT having some properties typical of metals and some normally associated with nonmetals. Metalloids are sometimes called semimetals or semimetallic elements. Examples are SILICON, GERMANIUM, and ARSENIC. Some metalloids are SEMICONDUCTORS.

**metallurgy** Science and technology concerned with metals. Metallurgy includes the study of: methods of extraction of metals from their ores; physical and chemical properties of metals; ALLOY production; and the hardening, strengthening, corrosion-proofing, and ELECTROPLATING of metals. *See also* ANODIZING; GALVANIZING

**metamorphic rock** Broad class of rocks that have been changed by heat or pressure from their original nature – SEDIMENTARY, IGNEOUS, or older metamorphic. The changes characteristically involve new crystalline structure, the creation of new minerals, or a radical change of texture. For example, the metamorphic rock slate is made from sedimentary shale.

**metamorphosis** Change of form during the development of various organisms, such as the changing of a caterpillar into a moth, or a tadpole into a frog. Sometimes the change is gradual, as with a grasshopper, and is known as incomplete metamorphosis. Complete metamorphosis usually involves the more distinct stages of LARVA, PUPA, and IMAGO.

**metaphor** Figure of speech that draws a comparison. It differs from ordinary comparisons in its inventiveness, and from a simile in the complexity of the idea expressed. "Fleece as white as snow," is a simile, whereas "His political life was a constant swimming against the tide," is a metaphor.

**metaphysical poetry** English literary form of the 17th century, characterized by the combination of unlike ideas or images to create new representations of experience, and a reliance on wit and subtle argument. Although this method was by no means new, in the hands of such writers as George

**▼ metamorphosis** When common frogs mate, fertilization and egg laying occur in water (1). Within an hour, the jelly around the egg swells to produce frogspawn (2). The eggs develop (3) and produce embryos (4) that hatch as long-tailed tadpoles with external feathery gills six days after fertilization (5). Mouths and eyes develop later and the tails become powerful means of propulsion. Hind legs are well formed by week eight (6), meanwhile, the tadpole has changed from a herbivore to a carnivore. Via an intermediary gill and lung stage, the tadpole changes from gill- to lung-breathing, its internal lungs growing as its external gills are absorbed; the process is complete when the gills fully disappear at month three, by which time the forelegs are well developed (7). Metamorphosis is complete when the young frog (8) loses its tail.

HERBERT, Andrew MARVELL, and John DONNE it infused new life into English poetry.

**metaphysics** Branch of philosophy that deals with the first principles of reality and with the nature of the universe. Metaphysics is divided into ONTOLOGY, the study of the essence of being, and COSMOLOGY, the study of the structure and laws of the universe. Leading metaphysical thinkers have included PLATO, ARISTOTLE, DESCARTES, LEIBNIZ, KANT, and A.N. WHITEHEAD.

**meteor** (shooting star) Brief streak of light in the night sky caused by a METEOROID entering the Earth's upper atmosphere at high speed from space. A typical meteor lasts from a few tenths of a second to a few seconds, depending on the meteoroid's impact speed, which can vary from about 7–45mi/s (11–70km/s). At certain times of the year there are meteor showers, when meteors are more numerous than usual.

**meteorite** That part of a large meteoroid (a small particle or body following an Earth-crossing orbit) that survives passage through the Earth's atmosphere and reaches the ground. Most of a meteoroid burns up in the atmosphere to produce METEORS, but about 10% reaches the surface as meteorites and micrometeorites. Meteorites generally have a pitted surface and a fused charred crust. There are three main types: iron meteorites (siderites); stony meteorites (aerolites); and mixed iron and stone meteorites. Some are tiny particles, but others weigh up to 200 tons.

**meteorology** Study of weather conditions, a branch of CLIMATOLOGY. Meteorologists study and analyze data from weather ships, aircraft, and satellites in order to compile maps showing the state of the high- and low-pressure regions in the Earth's atmosphere. They also anticipate changes in the distribution of the regions and forecast the future weather.

**meter** In poetry, a regular rhythmic pattern. It imposes a regular recurrence of stresses, typically dividing a line into equal units called metrical feet. The most commonly used metrical feet are anapaest, dactyl, iamb, and trochee. The meter of a poem is described according to the kind and number of metrical feet per line: for example, iambic pentameters have five iambs per line.

**meter** Instrument that measures a particular quantity. For example, a gas meter measures the amount of gas that has flowed in a certain time, and a voltmeter measures the voltage between two points in an electrical circuit.

**meter** (symbol m) SI unit of distance. Conceived as being one ten millionth of the surface distance between the North Pole and the equator, it was formerly defined by two marks on a platinum bar kept in Paris. It is now defined as the length of the path traveled by light in a vacuum during 1/299,792,458 of a second. 1 meter equals 39.3701 inches.

**methanal** (formaldehyde) Colorless, inflammable, poisonous gas, HCHO, with a penetrating odor. It is the simplest aldehyde and is produced by the oxidation of METHANOL by air. It was discovered by August von HOFMANN in 1867. Most methanal is in the form of formalin. Methanal is used in the manufacture of dyes and plastics. Chief properties: sp.gr. 0.82; m.p. −133.6°F (−92°C); b.p. −2.2°F (−19°C).

**methane** ($CH_4$) Colorless, odorless HYDROCARBON, the simplest ALKANE (paraffin). It is the chief constituent of NATURAL GAS, from which it is obtained. It is produced by decomposing organic matter, such as in marshes, which led to its original name of marsh gas. In the air, it contributes to the GREENHOUSE EFFECT and an increase in global temperature. Methane is used in the form of natural gas as a fuel. Properties: m.p. −296.5°F (−182.5°C); b.p. −263.2°F (−164°C).

**methanoic acid** (formic acid, HCOOH) Colorless, corrosive, pungent, liquid carboxylic acid. It is used to produce insecticides and for dyeing, tanning, and electroplating. It occurs naturally in a variety of sources – stinging ants, nettles, pine needles, and sweat. The simplest of the carboxylic acids, it can be produced by the action of concentrated sulfuric acid on sodium methanoate. Properties: sp.gr. 1.22; m.p. 46.9°F (8.3°C); b.p. 213.4°F (100.8°C).

**methanol** (methyl alcohol) Colorless, poisonous, flammable liquid ($CH_3OH$), the simplest of the ALCOHOLS. It is obtained synthetically either from carbon monoxide and hydrogen, by the oxidation of natural gas, or by the destructive distillation of wood. It is used as a solvent and a gasoline additive and to produce rocket fuel and gasoline. Properties: m.p. −137°F (−93.9°C); b.p. 148.8°F (64.9°C).

**Methodism** Worldwide religious movement that began in England in the 18th century. It was originally an evangelical movement within the CHURCH OF ENGLAND, started in 1729 by John and Charles WESLEY. John Wesley stayed within the Anglican Church until his death in 1791. In 1795 the Wesleyan Methodists became a separate body and divided into other sects, which were reunited with the United Methodist Church in the 20th century. In the US, the Methodist Episcopal Church was founded in 1784. Today there are more than 50 million Methodists worldwide.

**Methuselah** In the Old Testament (Genesis 5:25–27), the longest-lived of all human beings; son of ENOCH and eighth in descent from ADAM and EVE. He is said to have died at the age of 969 and was the father of many children, including Lamech, the father of NOAH.

**methylated spirit** Industrial form of ETHANOL (ethyl alcohol). It contains 5% METHANOL (methyl alcohol), which is extremely poisonous, and enough pyridine to give it a foul taste. It is dyed purple and used as a solvent and fuel.

**metric system** Decimal system of WEIGHTS AND MEASURES based on the METER (m) and the KILOGRAM (kg). Larger and smaller metric units are related by powers of 10. Devised in 1791, the metric system is used internationally by scientists (particularly as SI UNITS) and has been adopted for general use by most Western countries, although the IMPERIAL SYSTEM is still commonly used in the US and for certain measurements in Britain.

**Metropolitan Museum of Art** Art museum in New York City. Founded in 1870, the museum has a large and diverse permanent art collection, including numerous Egyptian, Greek, and Roman works. Much of the medieval collection is housed in a separate complex, The Cloisters. In addition to European sculpture, there are more than 4,600 European paintings ranging from the 15th century to the present, as well as many US paintings and sculptures. The Oriental art collection numbers 30,000 pieces.

**Metropolitan Opera Company** New York City company famous for the high standard of its productions. Operas premiered at "the Met" include *Gianni Schicchi* (1918) and *The Girl of the Golden West* (1910), both by Puccini. The Metropolitan Opera House was opened in 1883; it moved to the Lincoln Center for the Performing Arts in 1966.

**Metternich, Klemens Wenzel Lothar, Prince von** (1773–1859) Austrian statesman. As foreign minister (1809–48) and chancellor (1821–48), he was the leading European statesman of the post-Napoleonic era. Following Austria's defeat in the NAPOLEONIC WARS (1809), he adopted a conciliatory policy toward France. After Napoleon's retreat from Moscow (1812), he formed the QUADRUPLE ALLIANCE (1813), which led to Napoleon's defeat. He was the dominant figure at the Congress of VIENNA (1814–15) and at subsequent conferences held under the CONGRESS SYSTEM. In 1815 he secured peace in Europe and thereafter became increasingly autocratic, pressing for the intervention of the great powers against any revolutionary outbreak. He was driven from power by the REVOLUTION OF 1848.

**Metz** City on the Moselle River, NE France; capital of Moselle department. One of Roman Gaul's chief cities, it was burned by Vandals in 406 and by Huns in 451. After the 8th century the bishops of Metz ruled a vast empire. Made a free imperial city in 12th century, Metz enjoyed considerable prosperity. It was taken by France in 1552 but became part of Germany in 1871 after the Franco–Prussian War. The Treaty of Versailles (1919) restored it to France. Industries: metals, machinery, tobacco, wine, tanning, clothing. Pop. (1990) 119,594.

**Mexican Border Campaign** (1916–17) Punitive US military expedition. Mexican revolutionary Pancho VILLA's raids in New Mexico had resulted in the loss of US lives. In retaliation, a US force of 15,000 men under General John J. PERSHING entered Mexico on March 15, 1916. The expedition's forces grew and penetrated 300mi (480km) into Mexico, arousing anti-American feeling. US withdrawal (January 27, 1917) averted war. Mexican General Venustiano CARRANZA was soon able to establish a constitutional government.

**Mexican Revolution** (1910–40) Extended political revolution that improved the welfare of the Mexican underprivileged. The Mexican Revolution was prompted by the dictatorial, elitist presidency of Porfirio DÍAZ. In 1910 Díaz, who had agreed not to run for reelection following the threat of armed revolt led by Francisco MADERO, reneged on his agreement and was reelected. He was forced to resign in 1911 by Madero, who was subsequently elected. Madero intended to make land ownership more egalitarian, to strengthen labor organizations, and to lessen the influence of the Catholic Church. He was assassinated in 1913, however, by his former general Victoriano HUERTA. The repressive regime of Huerta caused massive unrest in the peasant community, who found leaders in Venustiano CARRANZA, Francisco "Pancho" VILLA, and Emiliano ZAPATA. Huerta resigned and Carranza became president (1914). Although some agrarian, educational, and political reforms continued, it was Lázaro CÁRDENAS (inaugurated 1934) who finally introduced sweeping measures involving land distribution, support of the labor movement, and improving health and education.

**Mexican War** (1846–48) War between Mexico and the US. It broke out following US annexation of TEXAS (1845). The Mexicans were swiftly overwhelmed, and a series of US expeditions effected the conquest of the southwest. The war ended when General Winfield Scott, having landed at Vera Cruz in March 1847, defeated the army of SANTA ANNA and entered Mexico City on September 8. In the Treaty of GUADALUPE-HIDALGO (1848), Mexico ceded sovereignty over California and New Mexico, as well as Texas north of the Rio Grande.

**Mexico** Republic in S North America. *See* country feature, page 444

**Mexico, Gulf of** Gulf on SE coast of the US and E coast of Mexico; Cuba is at the Gulf's entrance. It connects with the Atlantic Ocean through the straits of Florida, and with the Caribbean Sea through the strait of Yucatan. The Mississippi and Rio Grande rivers empty into the gulf. It is a source of shrimp and petroleum. Depth (max.): 12,714ft (3,878m). Area: 700,000sq mi (1,813,000sp km).

**Mexico City** Capital of Mexico, largest city in the world, situated in a volcanic basin at an altitude of 7,800ft (2,380m), in the center of the country. Mexico City is the nation's political, economic, and cultural center. It suffers from overcrowding and high levels of pollution and is vulnerable to earthquakes. The former AZTEC capital, known as Tenochtitlán, was destroyed by Hernán Cortés in 1521. A new city was constructed, which acted as the capital of Spain's New World colonies for the next 300 years. During the MEXICAN WAR, the city was occupied by US troops (1847). In 1863 French troops conquered the city and established MAXIMILIAN as emperor. It was recaptured in 1867 by Benito JUÁREZ's republican forces. In 1914–15, the city was captured and lost three times by the revolutionary forces of Emiliano ZAPATA and Francisco VILLA. The city is a major tourist center. Pop. (1990) 15,047,685.

**Meyerbeer, Giacomo** (1791–1864) German composer, b. Jakob Liebmann Beer. His early operas were in the Italian tradition, influenced by Gioacchino Rossini. His greatest acclaim, however, came in Paris, where his works laid the foundations of French grand opera. With libretti by Eugene Scribe, these operas included *Robert le Diable* (1831), *Les Huguenots* (1836), and *Le Prophète* (1849).

**mezzo-soprano** (middle soprano) Range of the human voice falling between SOPRANO and CONTRALTO. It grew popular with opera composers in the 19th century, when the CASTRATO voice (which had a similar range) became less usual.

**Miami** City and port on Biscayne Bay in SE Florida. Originally a small agricultural community, it developed quickly after 1895 when the railroad was extended and the harbor dredged. Modern Miami is a popular tourist resort, with luxury hotels and many sporting facilities. Industries: clothing, concrete, metal products, fishing, printing and publishing. Pop. (1990) 358,548.

**mica** Group of common rock-forming minerals characterized by a platy or flaky appearance. All contain aluminum, potassium, and water; other metals, such as iron and magnesium, may be present. Micas have perfect basal cleavage. Common micas are muscovite and the biotite group. Muscovite is commonly found in coarse-grained acidic rocks, schists, and gneisses, and in sedimentary rocks. The biotite micas are found in a wide range of igneous and metamorphic rocks, but more rarely in sedimentary rocks.

**Michael, Saint** One of the four archangels mentioned in the Bible, the others being GABRIEL, RAPHAEL, and Uriel. In the Old Testament, Michael is the guardian of Israel and the highest of the archangels. In the New Testament book of Revelation, he is said to have thrown down the Dragon (Satan). His feast day is September 29 (Michaelmas). He is given prominence also in ISLAM.

**Michael** (1921– ) King of Romania (1927–30, 1940–47). He succeeded his grandfather as a child, surrendered the throne to his father in 1930, and regained it when his father abdicated (1940). He backed the overthrow of the fascist rule of Ion Antonescu in 1944, whereupon Romania joined the Allies in World War II. Michael was forced to abdicate when the communists gained power (1947).

**Michelangelo Buonarroti** (1475–1564) Florentine sculptor, painter, architect, and poet. He was one of the outstanding figures of the High RENAISSANCE and a creator of MANNERISM. He spent five years in Rome where he made his name with a statue of *Bacchus* (1497) and the *Pietà* (1499, now in St Peter's). In 1501 he returned to Florence where he carved the gigantic *David*, which symbolizes the new-found confidence of the Florentine Republic. In 1505 Pope JULIUS II called him to Rome to carry out two substantial commissions. The first, a magnificent tomb for Julius I, ended in disaster due to lack of funds from the Pope's heirs. The other, a vast painting for the Sistine Chapel ceiling (1508–12), was Michelangelo's most sublime achievement. He added *The Last Judgment* later (1536–41). Among Michelangelo's other great (unfinished) works are the Medici Chapel and the Biblioteca Laurenziana, both for the Church of San Lorenzo in Florence. For the last 30 years of his life, Michelangelo concentrated on architecture. He created the magnificent cathedral of ST PETER'S, Rome, but died before completing it.

**Michelson, Albert Abraham** (1852–1931) US physicist, b. Germany. In 1887 he conducted an experiment with Edward Morley to determine the velocity of the Earth through the ETHER, using an INTERFEROMETER of his own design. The negative result of the Michelson-Morley experiment prompted G.F.

▼ **Michelangelo** Detail of the Sistine Chapel ceiling, Vatican Palace, Rome showing *Creation of Adam* (1510) by Michelangelo. Although he preferred sculpture to painting, Michelangelo worked almost singlehandedly on the ceiling between 1508 and 1512. He learned the fresco technique from Ghirlandaio in Florence, although his most important lessons came from copying figures by Giotto and Masaccio.

M

Mexico's flag dates from 1821. The stripes were inspired by the French tricolor. The emblem in the center contains an eagle, a snake, and a cactus. It is based on an ancient Aztec legend about the founding of the capital, Tenochtitlán (now Mexico City).

**AREA:** 756,061sq mi (1,958,200sq km)
**POPULATION:** 89,538,000
**CAPITAL (POPULATION):** Mexico City (15,047,685)
**GOVERNMENT:** Federal republic
**ETHNIC GROUPS:** Mestizo 60%, Native American 30%, European 9%
**LANGUAGES:** Spanish (official)
**RELIGIONS:** Christianity (Roman Catholic 90%, Protestant 5%)
**CURRENCY:** New peso = 100 centavos.

The North American nation of Mexico is the world's largest Spanish-speaking country. Mexico is largely mountainous. The SIERRA MADRE Occidental begins in the NW state of CHIHUAHUA, and runs parallel to Mexico's W coast and the Sierra Madre Oriental. MONTERREY lies in the foothills of the latter. Between the two ranges lies the Mexican Plateau. The S part of the plateau contains a series of extinct volcanoes, rising to Citlaltépetl, at 18,701ft (5,700m). This region includes many of Mexico's largest cities, including the capital (and world's largest city), MEXICO CITY, and GUADALAJARA. The S highlands of the Sierra Madre del Sur include the archaeological sites in OAXACA. Mexico contains two large peninsulas: the mountainous and arid BAJA CALIFORNIA in the NW; and the lowland YUCATÁN peninsula in the SE. CIUDAD JUÁREZ and NUEVO LAREDO are important cities on the border with the United States.

## CLIMATE

Mexico's climate varies greatly according to altitude. Most rain occurs between June and September, and rainfall decreases N of Mexico City. Over 70% of Mexico has a desert or semidesert climate. Irrigation is essential for agriculture.

## VEGETATION

The N deserts are abundant in plants such as cactus, mesquite, and yucca. Luxuriant rain forests exist in the S, and Mexico also has areas of tropical grassland.

## HISTORY

One of the earliest NATIVE AMERICAN civilizations was the OLMEC (800–400 BC). The MAYA flourished between AD 300 and 900. The TOLTEC empire was dominant between 900 and *c.*1200. But it was the AZTEC who dominated the central plateau from their capital at Tenochtitlán (modern Mexico City). Many splendid PYRAMIDS and temples remain from these civilizations. Fernández de Córdoba was the first European to explore Mexico, in 1517. During 1519–21 Spanish *conquistadors*, led by Hernán CORTÉS, captured the capital and the Aztec emperor MONTEZUMA. In 1535 the territory became the viceroyalty of New Spain. Christianity was introduced. Spanish rule was harsh and unpopular. HIDALGO Y COSTILLO's revolt (1810) failed to win the support of creoles. In 1821 Mexico gained independence and General Augustín de ITURBIDE became emperor. In 1823 republicans seized power and, in 1824, Mexico became a republic. In 1832 SANTA ANNA became president. War with Texas escalated into the MEXICAN WAR (1846–48) with the United States. Under the terms of the Treaty of GUADALUPE-HIDALGO (1848), Mexico lost 50% of its territory. A revolution led to the overthrow of Santa Anna in 1855, and civil war broke out. Liberal forces, led by Benito JUÁREZ, triumphed in the War of Reform (1858–61), but conservatives with support from France installed MAXIMILIAN of Austria as emperor in 1864. In 1867 republican rule was restored and Juárez became president. In 1876 an armed revolt gave Porfiro DÍAZ the presidency. Beside the period 1880–84, the Díaz dictatorship lasted until 1910. Following an armed insurrection, Francisco MADERO became president in 1911, but was toppled by General Victoriano HUERTA in 1913. Huerta's dictatorial regime prolonged the MEXICAN REVOLUTION (1910–40) and led to US intervention. The US-backed forces of CARRANZA battled with the peasant armies of VILLA and ZAPATA. During the 1920s and 1930s Mexico introduced land and social reforms. After World War II, Mexico's economy developed with the introduction of liberal reforms. Relations with the US improved greatly, though problems remain over Mexican economic migration and drug trafficking.

## POLITICS

The Institutional Revolutionary Party (PRI) has ruled Mexico continuously since its formation in 1929. In 1994 the Zapatista National Liberation Army (ZNLA) staged a revolt in the S state of Chiapas, principally calling for land reforms and recognition of Native American rights. In 1994 Ernesto ZEDILLO of the PRI was elected president. In 1997 congressional elections, the PRI lost its majority for the first time since 1929.

## ECONOMY

Mexico is an upper-middle-income developing country (1995 GDP per capita, US$6,400), faced with problems of unemployment, inflation, inequality, and illegal emigration to the United States. Mexico's heavy borrowing on the strength of its oil reserves in the 1970s led to economic depression in the 1980s with the drop in oil prices. In June 1993 Mexico joined the Organization for Economic Cooperation and Development (OECD). In 1994 Mexico, the US, and Canada formed the North American Free Trade Association (NAFTA), the world's single largest trading bloc. In 1994 Mexico was plunged into economic crisis. Only a $50 billion loan from the US prevented Mexico defaulting on its foreign debts. An austerity package of wage freezes, interest rate rises, and tax increases was introduced. Remarkably, the loan was repaid in 1997. In 1997 the economic crisis in SE Asia led to a stock market crash and a devaluation of the peso. Mexico is the world's fifth largest producer of crude oil. Machinery and transport equipment account for 32% of exports, minerals and fuels 30%. Other manufactures include chemicals, clothing, steel, and textiles. Many factories near the US border assemble goods (such as automobile parts and electrical products) for US companies. Agriculture is important, contributing *c.*8% of GDP and employing 28% of the work force. Mexico is the world's fifth largest producer of coffee. Beef and dairy cattle and other livestock are raised. Fishing is also an important activity. The largest sector of the economy is services. Other growing industries include forestry and tourism.

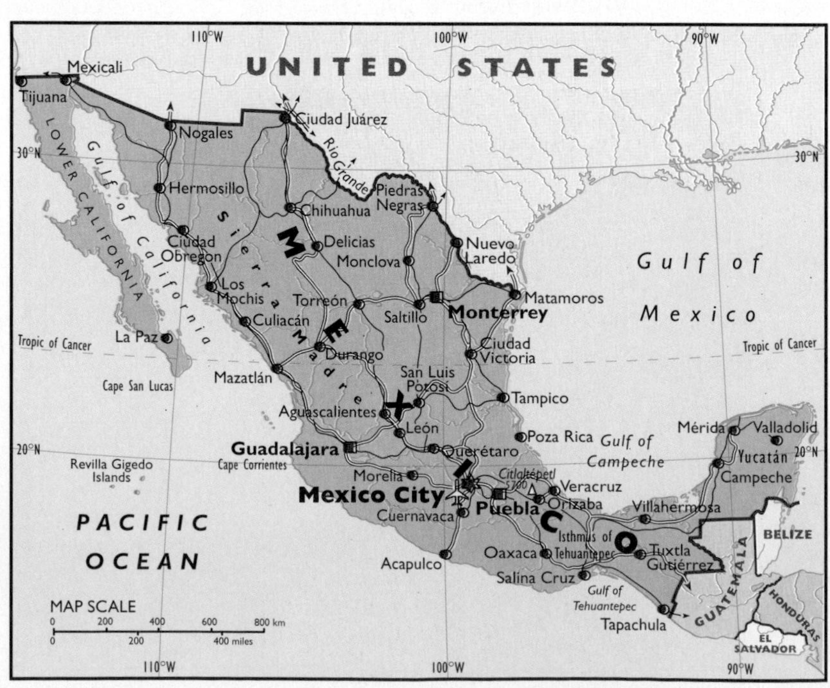

FITZGERALD to suggest that the length of objects change due to this sort of motion and led to the theory of RELATIVITY. In 1907 Michelson became the first US scientist to win a Nobel Prize.

**Michener, James** (1907–97) US writer. He won a Pulitzer Prize (1948) for his first collection of short stories, *Tales of the South Pacific* (1947). With *Hawaii* (1959), Michener established a pattern of panoramic novels, which he continued in later works such as *Chesapeake* (1978), *Texas* (1985), and *Caribbean* (1989).

**Michigan** State in N central US, bordered by four of the GREAT LAKES; the capital is LANSING. The largest city is DETROIT. First settled by the French in the 17th century, the region was ceded to Britain after the SEVEN YEARS WAR. The British finally left the area in 1796 and Michigan became a US territory in 1805, achieving full statehood in 1837. The opening of the Erie Canal in 1825 aided its growth, but the real industrial boom came with the development of the motor vehicle industry in the early 20th century. Michigan is made up of two peninsulas separated by the Straits of Mackinac, which connect lakes Michigan and Huron. The Upper Peninsula has swampland on the NE lake shore and mountains in the W. Copper and iron ore are mined and timber is a valuable resource. The Lower Peninsula is also forested and mineral deposits include oil, gypsum, sandstone, and limestone. In the S cereal crops are cultivated and livestock rearing is important. The Lower Peninsula has most of Michigan's population and industries, which include motor vehicles, primary and fabricated metals, chemicals, and food products. Area: 58,110sq mi (150,544sq km). Pop. (1990) 9,295,297.

**Michigan, Lake** Third-largest of the five GREAT LAKES of North America, and the only one entirely within the US. Discovered by the French in 1634, it is connected to Lake Huron by the Straits of Mackinac. The St. Lawrence Seaway opened up the lake to international trade. Chicago is on the SW shore. Area: 22,300sq mi (57,757sq km).

**Micmac** Algonquian-speaking tribe of Native North Americans, once inhabiting Nova Scotia, Cape Breton Island, Prince Edward Island, and Newfoundland. They were probably the first Native Americans to meet the early European explorers. About 4,000 still live in the northeastern area.

**microbiology** Study of microorganisms, their structure, function and significance. Mainly concerned with single-cell forms such as VIRUSES, BACTERIA, PROTOZOA, and FUNGI, it has immense applications in medicine and the food industry. Microbiology began in the 17th century with the invention of the microscope, which enabled scholars to view microorganisms for the first time. Pioneers include Robert HOOKE, Anton van LEEUWENHOEK, and Louis PASTEUR. *See also* BIOTECHNOLOGY

**microcomputer** Small COMPUTER that has its CENTRAL PROCESSING UNIT (CPU) on an integrated circuit (SILICON CHIP) called a MICROPROCESSOR.

**microeconomics** Study of individual components of the economic system. It analyzes individual consumers and producers, the market conditions, and the law of SUPPLY AND DEMAND. It is one of the two major subdivisions of ECONOMICS; the other is MACROECONOMICS.

**microelectronics** In ELECTRONICS, systems designed and produced without wiring or other bulky components. They allow a high packing density, greatly reducing the size of component assemblies. Following World War II, the application of such newly developed devices as the TRANSISTOR saw the beginnings of the microelectronics industry. This accelerated with the development of the PRINTED CIRCUIT. Even further reduction in size, or microminiaturization, was achieved with INTEGRATED CIRCUITS. Molecular electronics is a new development that promises to be the ultimate in size reduction.

**Micronesia** Group of islands located in the W Pacific Ocean, N of Polynesia. Micronesia includes BELAU, KIRIBATI, the MARIANA ISLANDS, the FEDERATED STATES OF MICRONESIA, NAURU, and TUVALU.

**Micronesia, Federated States of** Republic in the W Pacific Ocean, consisting of all the CAROLINE ISLANDS except BELAU. The 607 islands of the republic are divided into four states: Kosrae, Pohnpei, Truk, and Yap. The capital, Palikir, is on the main island of Pohnpei. The islands are widely dispersed. The economy is heavily dependent on US aid. Land use is limited to subsistence agriculture. The islands were formally annexed by Spain in 1874. In 1899 they were sold to Germany. Japan occupied the archipelago in 1914 and in 1920 was given a mandate to govern by the League of Nations. In 1944 US naval forces captured the islands, and in 1947 they came under formal US administration as part of the UN Trust Territory of the Pacific Islands. In 1979 the Federated States of Micronesia came into being, with Belau remaining a US trust territory. In 1986 a compact of free association with the US was signed. In 1990 UN trust status was annulled, and in 1991 Micronesia became a full member of the UN. Area: 272sq mi (705sq km). Pop. (1991) 107,662.

**microphone** Device for converting sound into varying electric currents of the same frequency. Live music performers often use a moving coil microphone, in which a coil attached to a diaphragm vibrates in a stationary magnetic field. The recording industry prefers the condenser microphone, which employs a CAPACITOR. Crystal microphones use the PIEZOELECTRIC EFFECT.

**microprocessor** Complex INTEGRATED CIRCUIT used to control the operation of a COMPUTER or other equipment.

**microscope** Optical device for producing an enlarged image of a minute object. The first simple microscope was made in 1668 by Anton van LEEUWENHOEK. The modern compound microscope has two converging lens systems, the objective and the eyepiece, both of short focal length. The **objective** produces a magnified image, which is further magnified by the **eyepiece** to give the image seen by the observer. Because of the nature of the visible spectrum of LIGHT, an optical microscope can magnify objects only up to 2,000 times. For extremely small objects, an ELECTRON MICROSCOPE is used.

## MICROSCOPE

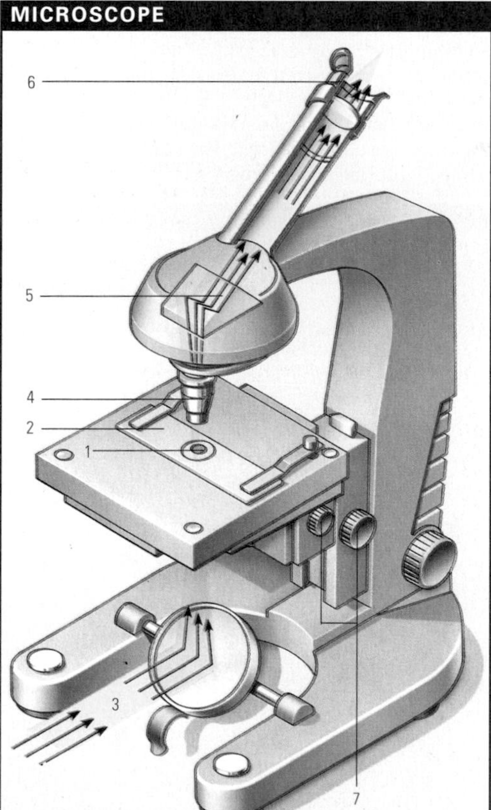


An optical microscope magnifies a sample (1) held on a slide (2). Light from below (3) illuminates the sample, which is magnified by a lens (4) that can be changed. A prism arrangement (5) direct the image onto an eyepiece (6). The position of the sample can be altered physically by turning knobs (7) that bring the image into position and focus.

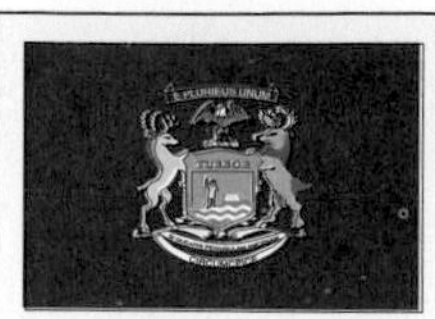

**MICHIGAN**
**Statehood:** January 26, 1837
**Nickname:** Wolverine State
**State bird:** Robin
**State flower:** Apple blossom
**State tree:** White pine
**State motto:** If you seek a pleasant peninsula, look around you

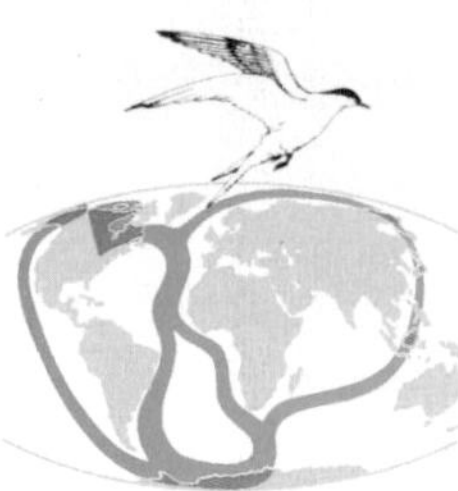

▲ **migration** Remarkable annual migrations are made by birds of northern temperate regions flying south in fall to new breeding grounds, and returning north in spring to breed. The arctic tern nests in polar regions and flies south along one of the various routes shown to the islands of Antarctica, the round trip often totaling 20,000mi (32,000km).

**microsurgery** Delicate surgery performed under a binocular microscope using specialized instruments, such as microneedles as small as 0.08in (2mm) long, sutures 20 micrometers in diameter, ENDOSCOPES, and LASERS. It is used in a number of specialized areas, including the repair of nerves and blood vessels, eye, ear, and brain surgery, and the reattachment of severed parts.

**microwave** Form of ELECTROMAGNETIC RADIATION with a wavelength between 0.04in (1mm) and 3.3ft (1m) and a frequency range of *c*.255 to 300,000MHz. Microwaves are used for RADAR, RADIO, and TELEVISION broadcasting, high-speed microwave heating (in ovens), and cellular telephones.

**Midas** Name of several historical Phrygian rulers and one legendary foolish king in Classical mythology. As a reward for rendering a service to a god, King Midas asked that everything he touched should become gold. Midas found he was unable to eat or drink because his food, too, was transformed. His story was told by OVID.

**Mid-Atlantic Ridge** Underwater topographic feature along the margin between the diverging American crustal plate on one side and the European and African plates on the other. It runs for 8,700mi (14,000km) along the middle of the Atlantic Ocean. Iceland is located on the ridge itself and was formed by the outpourings of volcanic lava.

**Middle Ages** Period in European history covering roughly 1,000 years between the disintegration of the Roman empire in the 5th century and the period of the RENAISSANCE, in about the 15th century. The Middle Ages are sometimes divided into Early (up to the 10th century), High (10th–14th centuries), and Late Middle Ages. The Middle Ages were, above all, the age of the Christian church, whose doctrine was widely accepted in Europe, and of the social-political structure known as the FEUDAL SYSTEM. In the arts, the Middle Ages encompassed the GOTHIC period (from the 11th century), and in science and learning, the predominance of ISLAM.

**Middle East** Geographical term loosely applied to the region that comprises the predominantly Islamic countries of the E Mediterranean, NE Africa, and SW Asia. It is usually taken to include Bahrain, Cyprus, Egypt, Iran, Iraq, Israel, Jordan, Kuwait, Lebanon, Libya, Oman, Qatar, Saudi Arabia, Sudan, Syria, United Arab Emirates, and Yemen.

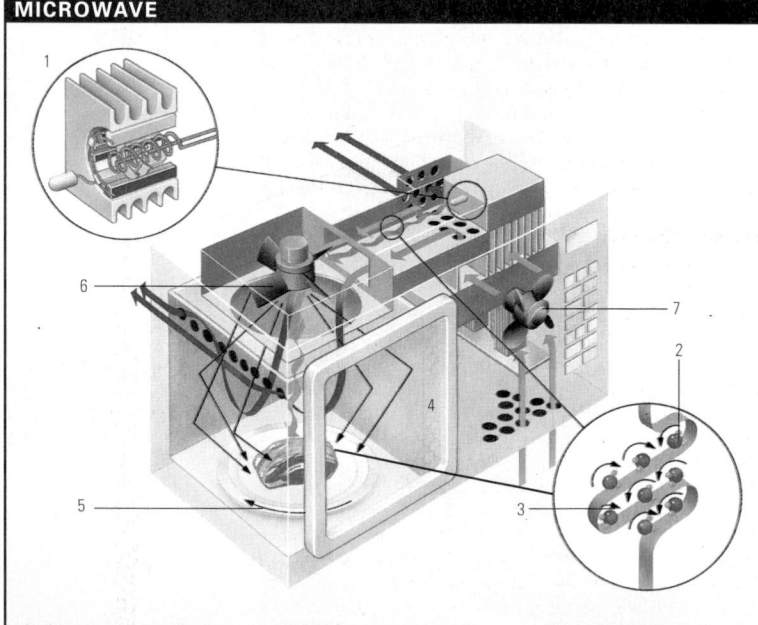

**MICROWAVE**

A microwave oven exploits the presence of water in food to cook things from the inside. An oven generates microwaves in a magnatron (1) and when the microwaves penetrate the food they cause water molecules (2), which have a postive side and a negative side, to rotate (3) generating heat through friction with the food. The oven is heavily insulated (4) to prevent leakage of microwaves. A rotating plate (5) and paddles (6), which ensure an even distribution of microwaves, make sure the food cooks evenly. To dissipate the hot air, generated by the cooking and by the magnatron, a fan (7) pushes cold air around the oven.

**Middle English** Form of the English language in use from *c*.1100 until *c*.1450. This period saw the borrowing of many words from Norman French. Grammatical gender was superseded by natural gender, and the use of an Anglo-Norman writing system caused radical changes in spellings.

**Middlesex** Former county of SE England, adjoining LONDON. The area was settled by Saxon tribes in the 5th century. Throughout its history it was overshadowed by London. In 1888 it became an administrative county, losing much of its area to the county of London. In 1965 most of the county was absorbed into Greater London, the remainder going to SURREY and HERTFORDSHIRE.

**Midway Islands** Coral atoll in the central Pacific Ocean, *c*.1,250mi (2,000km) WNW of Honolulu, consisting of two small islands, Easter and Sand. The islands were annexed to the US in 1867 and were made an air base in 1935. They were the scene of the World War II Battle of Midway (1942). The islands are now administered by the US Department of the Interior. Area: 2sq mi (5sq km). Pop. (1995 est.) 2,000.

**Midwest** (Middle West) Imprecise term referring to the interior plains of the US around the W GREAT LAKES and the upper Mississippi River valley. It usually refers to the states of INDIANA, ILLINOIS, IOWA, KANSAS, MICHIGAN, MINNESOTA, MISSOURI, NEBRASKA, OHIO, and WISCONSIN. Traditionally, the Midwest has been the manufacturing heartland of the US. The national shift to the service sector has contributed to the decline of its heavy industrial base. The Midwest is also one of the world's richest agricultural regions; the major crop is wheat.

**Mies van der Rohe, Ludwig** (1886–1969) US architect , b. Germany. A pioneer of MODERNISM, he first attracted attention in the 1920s with his unexecuted designs for glass and steel skyscrapers. Mies was the last director (1930–33) of the BAUHAUS, moving the school to Berlin before it was closed by the Nazis. In 1938 he emigrated to the USA. Mies planned (1942–58) the new campus of the Illinois Institute of Technology, Chicago. His technological aesthetic exerted a profound influence on architects such as Gordon BUNSHAFT, Eero SAARINEN, and Philip JOHNSON. Other buildings include Lake Shore Drive, Chicago (1948–51), and the Seagram Building, New York (1958).

**migraine** Recurrent attacks of throbbing headache, mostly on one side only, often accompanied by nausea, vomiting, and visual disturbances. It results from changes in diameter of the arteries serving the brain. More common in women, it is seen usually in young adults and often runs in families. Attacks, which may last anything from two to 72 hours, are often associated with trigger factors, such as certain foods (especially chocolate), missed meals, consumption of alcohol, fatigue, exposure to glare, or use of the contraceptive pill. It can be treated, or in some cases prevented, with various drugs.

**migration** Any periodic movement of animals or humans, usually in groups, from one area to another, in order to find food, breeding areas, or better conditions. Animal migration involves the eventual return of the migrant to its place of departure. Fish migrate between fresh and salt water or from one part of an ocean to another. Birds usually migrate along established routes. Mammals migrate usually in search of food. For thousands of years the deserts of central Asia widened inexorably and this phenomenon resulted in the human migration of pre-historic tribes to China, the Middle East, and Europe. Another type of migration occurred in the 14th century when the Maoris of New Zealand left their overpopulated homes in the islands of central Polynesia.

**Milan** (Milano) City in NW Italy; capital of Lombardy region. It was conquered by Rome in 222 BC. It was a free commune by the 12th century and was a powerful Italian state under the Sforza family from 1447 to 1535, when it was taken by the Spanish. It was ruled by Napoleon (1796–1814) and subsequently by the Austrian Hapsburgs, before becoming part of Italy in 1860. It is Italy's leading commercial, financial, and industrial center. Industries: motor vehicles, machinery, electrical goods, textiles, clothing, publishing. Pop. (1991) 1,369,231.

**mildew** External filaments and fruiting structures of numerous moldlike FUNGI. Mildews are PARASITES of plants and cause substantial damage to growing crops.

**Milhaud, Darius** (1892–1974) French composer. In the incidental music to Claudel's translation of Aeschylus' *Orestes* (1913–22), he experimented with polytonality. He also included jazz elements in his compositions, notably *La Création du Monde* (1923). His most ambitious work was the opera *Christophe Colombe* (1930).

**military draft** *See* CONSCRIPTION

**milk** Liquid food secreted from mammary glands by the females of nearly all mammals to feed their young. The milk of domesticated cattle, sheep, goats, horses, camels, and reindeer has been used as food by humans since prehistoric times, both directly and to make BUTTER, CHEESE, and yogurt. Milk is a suspension of fat and protein in water, sweetened with lactose sugar.

**Milky Way** Faint band of light visible on clear dark nights encircling the sky along the line of the galactic equator. It is the combined light of an enormous number of stars, in places obscured by clouds of interstellar gas and dust. It is in fact the disk of our GALAXY, viewed from our vantage point within it.

**Mill, James** (1773–1836) Scottish philosopher, father of John Stuart MILL. He became a friend of Jeremy BENTHAM, and together they evolved the doctrine of UTILITARIANISM. Mill wrote an *Analysis of the Phenomena of the Human Mind* (1829) and, among other works, a multi-volume history of the British East India Company, for which he worked.

**Mill, John Stuart** (1806–73) Scottish philosopher, son of James MILL. He defended EMPIRICISM and inductive LOGIC in *System of Logic* (1843). Mill is chiefly remembered for *On Liberty* (1859), a classic exposition of LIBERALISM. In *Utilitarianism* (1861) he developed Jeremy BENTHAM's theory, outlining a more humanist version of UTILITARIANISM. Mill also championed women's rights in *The Subjection of Women* (1869).

**Millais, Sir John Everett** (1829–96) English painter and illustrator, a founder member of the PRE-RAPHAELITE BROTHERHOOD. His pre-Raphaelite works, such as *Christ in the House of his Parents* (1850), show the Brotherhood's liking for righteous subjects. He later started to paint more sentimental subjects such as *Bubbles* (1886), which the Pears Soap Company used as an advertisement.

**Millay, Edna St Vincent** (1892–1950) US poet. She first attracted attention for *A Few Figs from Thistles* (1920). Millay won a Pulitzer Prize for *The Harp Weaver and Other Poems* (1923). Other works include the sonnet sequence *Fatal Interview* (1931).

**millenarianism** Belief, widespread in Christianity until the 4th century, that Christ's second coming will bring a thousand years of peace on Earth. It has its origins in the Judaic notion of the MESSIAH and a literal translation of the Book of REVELATIONS (20). It was supplanted by St AUGUSTINE's allegorical interpretation of the kingdom of God. It was revived during the REFORMATION by sects such as the ANABAPTISTS and the MORAVIAN CHURCH. Since the 19th century, MORMONS and ADVENTISTS have professed millenarian beliefs. Some sects, such as JEHOVAH'S WITNESSES, have forecast the imminence of the second coming.

**millennium** Period of one thousand years. The Christian CALENDAR takes the birth of JESUS CHRIST as year 0. MILLENARIANISM holds that Christ will return to Earth to reign for 1,000 years. In computing, the so-called "**millennium bug**" is found in computer programs that are unable to compute the year 2000 as following 1999.

**Miller, Arthur** (1915– ) US dramatist. His Pulitzer Prize-winning play *Death of a Salesman* (1949) is a masterpiece of 20th-century theatre. *The Crucible* (1953) is both a dramatic reconstruction of the SALEM witch trials and a parable of the MCCARTHY era. Miller won a second Pulitzer Prize for *A View From the Bridge* (1955). He was married (1955–61) to Marilyn MONROE, and wrote the screenplay for her film *The Misfits* (1961). *After the Fall* (1964) is a fictionalized account of their relationship. Other plays include *All My Sons* (1947) and *Playing for Time* (1981).

**Miller, (Alton) Glenn** (1904–44) US jazz trombonist and bandleader. He led the most popular dance band of all time, featuring *Moonlight Serenade* and *In the Mood* (1939), which Miller composed. His band played to servicemen all over the world during World War II. He died in an air accident while flying from England to France.

**Miller, Henry** (1891–1980) US author. Most of his novels were first published in Paris and were banned as obscene in the US and Britain until the 1960s. They include *Tropic of Cancer* (1934) and *Tropic of Capricorn* (1939). He is also remembered for the trilogy, *Sexus*, *Plexus*, and *Nexus* (1949–60).

**Millet, Jean-François** (1814–75) French painter. Millet is best known for solemn, gritty scenes of rural life and labour, such as *Sower* (1850) and *The Angelus* (1859). His strengths as an artist show in his drawings, which stress the dignity of his figures without any trivializing detail.

**millet** CEREAL grass that produces small, edible seeds. The stalks have flower spikes and the hulled seeds are white. In Russia, W Africa, and Asia it is a staple food. In W Europe it is used mainly for pasture or hay. Pearl millet (*Pennisetum glaucum*) grows in poor soils and is used as food in India and Africa. Height: 39in (1m). Family Poaceae/Gramineae.

**Millikan, Robert Andrews** (1868–1953) US physicist. His oil drop experiment enabled him to determine the ELECTRIC CHARGE of an ELECTRON. Millikan went on to study the PHOTOELECTRIC EFFECT, verifying the equation of Albert EINSTEIN and gaining a precise value for PLANCK's constant. In 1923 he was awarded the Nobel Prize for physics.

**millipede** Any of numerous species of elongated, invertebrate, arthropod animals with large numbers of legs. Found throughout the world, it has a segmented body, one pair of antennae, and two pairs of legs per segment, and can be orange, brown, or black. All species avoid light and feed on plant tissues. Length: 0.2–11in (2–280mm). Class Diplopoda.

**Milne, A.A. (Alan Alexander)** (1882–1956) English writer of stories and poems for children. Milne wrote the verses in *When We Were Very Young* (1924) and *Now We Are Six* (1927), and the stories in *Winnie-the-Pooh* (1926) and *The House at Pooh Corner* (1928).

**Milošević, Slobodan** (1941– ) Serbian statesman, president of SERBIA (1989–97), president of YUGOSLAVIA (1997– ). In 1986 he became head of the Serbian Communist Party. As Serbian president, Milošević was confronted with the breakup of the federation of Yugoslavia. After his re-election in 1992, he gave support to Serbs in CROATIA and BOSNIA-HERZEGOVINA. Milošević gradually distanced himself from the brutal activities of the Bosnian Serb leaders MLADIĆ and KARADZIĆ. In November 1995 he signed the Dayton Peace Accord with the Bosnian president IZETBEGOVIC and the Croatian president TUDJMAN to end the civil war in the former Yugoslavia. In 1997 he was forced to concede some opposition victories in municipal elections after mass demonstrations in Belgrade. In 1998 Milošević ordered Serbian forces to crush a rebellion in the province of KOSOVO. In 1999 his refusal to grant autonomy to the majority Albanian population in Kosovo led to NATO air strikes.

**Milosz, Czeslaw** (1911– ) Polish poet and novelist, b. Lithuania. His novels *The Valley of the Issa* (1955) and *The Usurpers* (1955) demonstrate an acute critical self-awareness. His celebrated volume of essays, *The Captive Mind* (1953) analyzes the effects of communism on writers. His poetry is collected in *Selected Poems* (1973). He was awarded the 1980 Nobel Prize for literature.

**Milstein, César** (1927– ) British molecular biologist and immunologist, b. Argentina. He shared the 1984 Nobel Prize for physiology or medicine for helping to develop antibodies that can be commercially produced for drugs and diagnostic tests. In 1975 he and the German immunochemist Georges Köhler developed a technique for cloning monoclonal antibodies (MABs) that combat diseases by targeting their sites.

**Milton, John** (1608–74) English poet. His first major pieces are the masque *Comus* (1634), and the pastoral elergy *Lycidas* (1637). Milton was a champion of Parliament in the English CIVIL WARS (1642–51). His *Areopagitica* (1644) is a classic argument for freedom of the press. His defense of regicides in *The Tenure of Kings and Magistrates* (1649) earned him a position in Oliver CROMWELL's government. Blind from 1652, Milton was forced into hiding after the RESTORATION (1660). *Paradise Lost*, perhaps the greatest epic poem in English, was first published in ten books (1667). In 1674 he produced a revised

▲ **millipede** The pill millipedes (*Glomeris marginata*) have the peculiar ability to roll up when disturbed, tucking their heads in. The shell-like cuticle covering the segments of a millipede's body provides excellent protection against prying predators.

M

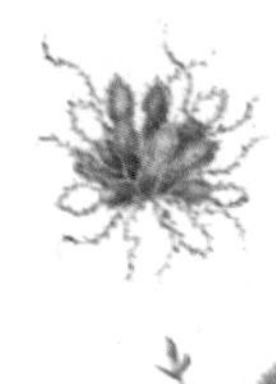

▲ **mimosa** Native to tropical and subtropical regions of Brazil, the leaves of the mimosa (*Mimosa pudica*) are sensitive. The plant will shrink when touched.

**MINNESOTA**
**Statehood:**
May 11, 1858
**Nickname:**
Gopher State
**State bird:**
Common loon
**State flower:**
Pink and white lady-slipper
**State tree:**
Norway pine
**State motto:**
Star of the North

edition in 12 books. Written in blank-verse, it relates the theological stories of Satan's rebellion against God, and Adam and Eve in the Garden of Eden. Its sequel, *Paradise Regained* (1671), describes Christ's temptation. His poetic drama *Samson Agonistes* (1671) forms the libretto of Handel's oratorio.

**Milwaukee** City and port of entry on the W shore of Lake Michigan, in SE Wisconsin. It was founded in 1836, and during the second half of the 19th century received many German settlers. Industries: brewing, diesel and gasoline engines, construction, electrical equipment. Pop. (1990) 628,088.

**mime** In drama, communication of mood, story, and idea through the use of gestures, movements, and facial expressions, with no verbal interaction. It derives from Greek and Roman theatrical traditions. Modern mime artists include Marcel MARCEAU.

**mimosa** Genus of plants, shrubs, and small trees native to tropical North and South America. They have showy, feather-like leaves and heads or spikes of white, pink, or yellow flowers. Family Mimosaceae.

**mina** (myna or mynah) Any of several species of tropical birds of SE Asia, S Africa, Australasia, and the Pacific Islands; it is related to the STARLING. A natural mimic, especially the species *Gracula religiosa*, it imitates other birds. It feeds mainly on fruit. Length: to 13in (33 cm). Family Sturnidae.

**minaret** Tower of a MOSQUE from which the MUEZZIN calls a Muslim to prayer. A mosque may have several minarets and they vary enormously in shape and height. The earliest minarets were built in Egypt *c.*673 as low square towers; later Persian developments included covered balconies and extensive tiling.

**mind** Hypothetical faculty postulated to account for the ability of conscious beings to think, feel, will, or behave. The mind is considered to control, or consist of, so-called mental processes. Dualist philosophers, such as René DESCARTES, have distinguished between mind and matter as two totally independent entities. IDEALISM suggests that the world is a product of the mind and dependent on experience. MATERIALISM begins within a concept of a material world independent of experience; the mind is not separate from the physical but derives from it.

**Mindanao** Second-largest island of the Philippines, in the S of the archipelago; Davao is the major port and city. The island is forested and mountainous, rising to the active volcano of Mount Apo, at 9,690ft (2,954m) the highest peak in the Philippines. Islam arrived in the 14th century, and the disparate Muslim groups united to resist foreign intervention, such as Spain in the 16th century and the US in the 20th century. In the 1960s the government encouraged Philippine colonization of the island, and the dispossessed Moros began to advocate secession from the Philippines. In 1969 the Philippine army began a military campaign that resulted in thousands of deaths. The island's economy is primarily agricultural, although tin-mining takes place around Mindanas. Area: 36,537sq mi (94,631sq km). Pop. (1990) 14,297,000.

**mine** Excavation from which minerals (mainly coal and metal ores) are extracted. Underground mines are of two main types: shaft mines and drift mines. **Shafts** are sunk vertically in the Earth's crust until they reach the depth of the seams to be exploited, which are then reached by tunnels or galleries. **Drift** mines are generally shallower, the seams being reached by a drift, or gradually sloping shaft, which leads on to a gallery system. In **strip** (opencast) mining, the seams are near or on the surface and are exposed by dragline machines that dig away the topsoil.

**mine** Concealed explosive device detonated through contact with individuals or vehicles. Underwater mines are used either to protect or to blockade coastal areas.

**mineralogy** Investigation of naturally occurring inorganic substances found on Earth and elsewhere in the Solar System. *See* GEOCHEMISTRY; MINERALS; PETROLOGY

**mineral** Natural, homogeneous and, with a few exceptions, solid and crystalline material that forms the Earth and make up its ROCKS. Most are formed through inorganic processes, and more than 3,000 minerals have been identified. They are classified on the basis of chemical makeup, crystal structure, and physical properties such as hardness, specific gravity, cleavage, color, and luster. Some minerals are economically important as ORES from which metals are extracted. *See* individual articles

**Minerva** Roman goddess of the arts, professions, and handicrafts, whose cult is believed to have originated in Etruria. Later She was identified with the Greek goddess ATHENA.

**Ming** Imperial Chinese dynasty (1368–1644). It was founded by a Buddhist monk and peasant leader, Chu Yüan-chang (r.1328–98), who expelled the Mongol YÜAN dynasty and unified China by 1382. Under the despotic rule of the early Ming emperors, China experienced a period of great artistic and intellectual distinction and economic expansion. Decline began in the late 16th century, and in 1644 a rebel leader took Peking (Beijing). A Ming general summoned aid from the MANCHU, who overthrew the dynasty and established their own.

**Mingus, Charles** (1922–79) US jazz bass player, composer, and bandleader. His large-scale compositions and use of over-dubbing inspired a generation of modern jazz musicians. *The Black Saint and the Sinner Lady* (1963) is his masterpiece.

**miniature painting** Term that originally meant the art of manuscript ILLUMINATION but was later applied to very small paintings, usually portraits. In Europe, the earliest miniatures were produced in the late 15th century and executed in the same materials as illuminated manuscripts. During the 18th century miniaturists usually painted in watercolor on ivory and sometimes worked in oils on metal. After the mid-19th century the art of miniature painting declined in the West because of competition from PHOTOGRAPHY, but the tradition remained strong in several Islamic countries and in India.

**minimal access surgery** Term used to encompass operations that do not involve cutting open the body in the traditional way. Minimal access (keyhole) procedures are performed either by means of an ENDOSCOPE or by passing miniature instruments through a fine catheter into a large blood vessel. The surgical LASER is also used.

**minimal art** Movement in 20th-century painting and sculpture that used only the most fundamental geometric forms. It originated in the 1950s as a reaction against the chaotic emotions provoked by ABSTRACT EXPRESSIONISM.

**minimalism** Trend in musical composition, beginning in the 1960s, in which short melodic or rhythmic fragments are repeated in gradually changing patterns, usually in a simple harmonic context. Many minimalist composers, such as Steve REICH and Philip GLASS, were influenced by the repetitive patterns of Indian and other non-Western music.

**mink** Small, semiaquatic mammal of the WEASEL family, with soft, durable, water-repellent hair of high commercial value. They have slender bodies, short legs, and bushy tails. Wild mink have dark brown fur with long black outer hair. Ranch mink have been bred to produce fur of various colors. They eat fish, rodents, and birds. Escaped ranch mink can be a serious threat to indigenous wildlife. Length to: 29in (73cm) including the tail; weight: 3.5lb (1.6kg). Family Mustelidae.

**Minneapolis** City and port on the Mississippi River, next to SAINT PAUL, in SE Minnesota; the largest city in Minnesota. First settled in the 1840s, it developed timber and flour milling industries and is now an important processing and distribution center for grain and cattle. Industries: farm machinery, food processing, electronic equipment, computers, printing, and publishing. Pop. (1990) 368,383.

**minnesingers** Medieval German poets or singers of courtly love (or *minne*), similar in style to the Provençal TROUBADOURS whom they originally copied. An individual German style developed in the 14th century, and several of the poems are considered among the best of Middle High German lyric verse.

**Minnesota** State in N central US, on the Canadian border; the capital is ST. PAUL. Other major cities include MINNEAPOLIS and Duluth. French fur traders arrived in the 17th century. The area E of the Mississippi passed to Britain after the SEVEN YEARS WAR, then to the US after the AMERICAN REVOLUTION. The lands W of the Mississippi were acquired from France in the LOUISIANA PURCHASE of 1803. Minnesota was organized as a territory in 1849, acquiring statehood in 1858. Europeans settled the area during the 1880s. The terrain varies from the prairies of the S to the forests of the N. There are mountains in the E. The state is drained chiefly by the Minnesota, St. Croix,

M

and Mississippi rivers. Wheat and corn are the major crops, and many farms raise dairy cattle. There are rich deposits of iron ore in the Mesabi Range in the E. Since the 1950s manufacturing has replaced agriculture as the main economic activity. Industries: food processing, electronic equipment, machinery, paper products, chemicals, printing, and publishing. Area: 79,617sq mi (206,207sq km). Pop. (1990) 4,375,099.

**minnow** Subfamily of freshwater fish found in temperate and tropical regions. It includes shiners, dace, chub, tench, and bream. More specifically, the term includes small fish of the genera *Phoxinus* and *Leuciscus*. Length: 1.5–18in (4–46cm). Family Cyprinidae.

**Minoan civilization** (*c*.3000–*c*.1100 BC) Ancient AEGEAN CIVILIZATION that flourished on the island of Crete, named for the legendary King MINOS. The Minoan period is divided into three parts: Early (*c*.3000–*c*.2100 BC), Middle (*c*.2100–*c*.1550 BC), and Late (*c*.1550–*c*.1100 BC). In terms of artistic achievement, and perhaps power, Minoan civilization reached its height in the Late period. The prosperity of Bronze Age Crete is evident from the works of art and palaces excavated at KNOSSOS, Phaistos, and other sites. It was based on trade and seafaring.

**minor** In law, a person under a certain age, who is forbidden certain activities. In the US, the age of majority varies from state to state but is 18 for voting purposes throughout the country.

**Minos** In Greek mythology, the son of EUROPA and ZEUS, king of Crete. He was consigned at his death to HADES to judge human souls. He angered POSEIDON who, in revenge, caused the king's wife Pasiphaë to give birth to the monstrous MINOTAUR.

**Minotaur** In Greek mythology, beast with the head of a bull and the body of a man, the issue of Pasiphaë, wife of MINOS, and a bull. He was confined by Minos in the LABYRINTH built by DAEDALUS. The Minotaur was killed by THESEUS.

**Minsk** Capital of Belarus, on the Svisloc River. Founded *c*.1060, it was under Lithuanian and Polish rule before becoming part of Russia in 1793. During World War II the city's large Jewish population was exterminated by the occupying Germans. In 1991 it became the capital of the newly independent Belarus. Industries: textiles, machinery, motor vehicles, electronic goods. Pop. (1991) 1,633,600.

**minstrel** Itinerant musician and professional entertainer; more specifically, a secular musician, usually an instrumentalist. Minstrels were popular from the 12th to 17th centuries, and some were attached to courts. In the 14th and 15th centuries, their social importance was reflected in the number of minstrel guilds that were formed throughout Europe.

**mint** In botany, any species of aromatic herbs, with a characteristic flavor, of the genus *Mentha*. It is commonly used as a flavoring in cooking, confectionery, and medicines. Most species have oval leaves and spikes of purple or pink flowers. Family Lamiaceae/Labiatae. *See also* PEPPERMINT

**minuet** French dance fashionable at the court of Louis XIV from 1650. Graceful and precise, it is danced by couples and played in triple time. It became popular as a dance in the 18th century and was a familiar movement in the SUITES of composers such as HANDEL and MOZART.

**Minuit, Peter** (1580–1638) First governor of New Netherland, b. Netherlands. He bought Manhattan Island (1620) for Dutch West India Company from Native Americans for $24 worth of trinkets. He was recalled as governor (1631). He returned (1638) as leader of New Sweden on the Delaware River, founding colonies at Trenton, New Jersey, and Wilmington, Delaware.

**minutemen** Local militia units in the AMERICAN REVOLUTION. The first such units were formed in Massachusetts in 1774, and minutemen took part in the opening battles of LEXINGTON AND CONCORD in 1775. The name was adopted by certain extreme right-wing groups in the US in the 1960s, and was given to a class of ballistic missiles.

**Miocene** Geological epoch beginning about 25 million and ending about 5 million years ago. It falls in the middle of the TERTIARY period and is marked by an increase in grasslands over the globe at the expense of forests, and the development of most of the modern mammal groups.

**miracle** Event or occurrence that is contrary to the laws of nature and is assumed to be the result of supernatural or divine intervention. Most religions include a belief in miracles. The mythologies of ancient India, the Middle East, Greece, and Rome abound with wonders brought about by the gods, but in both Christianity and Judaism, a human agent is generally involved.

**mirage** Type of optical illusion sometimes seen near the Earth's surface when light is refracted (bent) as it passes between cool dense air to warmer, less dense air. Mirages are most commonly seen shimmering on hot, dry roads; the shimmer is a refracted image of the sky.

**Miranda v. Arizona** (1966) Landmark US Supreme Court decision during the term of Chief Justice Earl WARREN. Expanding the doctrine of Escobedo v. Illinois, the court set out a stiff code of police conduct that required that an accused be fully informed of his rights and be allowed to contact counsel before questioning.

**Miró, Joan** (1893–1983) Spanish painter and graphic artist. Early works reveal experimentation with FAUVISM, CUBISM and DADA. His *Catalan Landscape* (1923) heralds his more mature work and a close affinity with ABSTRACT ART and PRIMITIVISM. In 1924 Miró became a member of the SURREALISM movement, producing works such as *Dog barking at the moon* (1926). His work is often playful, but the Spanish Civil War provoked him into creating darker, more savage images.

**miscarriage** Popular term for a spontaneous ABORTION, the loss of a FETUS from the UTERUS before it is sufficiently developed to survive.

**misdemeanor** Criminal offense that is too slight to be considered a FELONY. In the US misdemeanors incur such punishments on conviction as fines, community service, or short custodial sentences in local jails.

**Mishima, Yukio** (1925–70) Japanese writer. An early novel, *Confessions of a Mask* (1949), is a partially autobiographical study of homosexuality. His final work, the four-volume *The Sea of Fertility* (1965), is an epic of modern Japan. He committed ritual suicide in 1970 at Tokyo's military headquarters, which he had occupied with his small private army.

**Mishna** Collection of Jewish legal traditions and moral precepts that form the basis of the TALMUD. The Mishna was compiled in *c*.AD 200 under Rabbi Judah ha-Nasi. It is divided into six parts: laws pertaining to agriculture; laws concerning the sabbath, fasts, and festivals; family laws; civil and criminal laws; laws regarding sacrifices; and laws concerning ceremonial regulations.

**missile** Unmanned and self-propelled flying weapon. Ballistic missiles travel in the outer atmosphere and can be powered only by rockets. Cruise missiles travel in the lower atmosphere and can be powered by jet engines. GUIDED MISSILES carry self-contained guidance systems or can be controlled by radio from the ground.

**Missionary Societies** Organizations for the promotion of Christianity among non-Christians. The first such society was established in New England in 1649. The 19th century saw the emergence of interdenominational and geographically specialized societies. Today governments or agencies, such as Christian Aid, have taken over much of the Societies' work.

**Mississippi** State in the S central US, on the Gulf of Mexico; the capital and largest city is JACKSON. Other major cities are Meridian, Biloxi, Vicksburg, and Laurel. The French claimed the region in 1682, but it passed to Britain after the SEVEN YEARS WAR. The Territory of Mississippi was organized in 1798. The state seceded from the Union in 1861. It was a battleground during the American CIVIL WAR. Racial segregation remained in force until the 1960s when the state became a focus of the civil rights movement. The land slopes W from the hills of the NE to the Delta, a fertile plain between the Mississippi and Yazoo rivers. Pine forests cover most of the S of the state as far as the coastal plain. Primarily an agricultural state, Mississippi is the leading producer of cotton in the US; hay and soybeans are also grown. Dairy farming is of great importance. There are valuable reserves of oil and natural gas. Other industries: clothing, wood products, chemicals. Area: 47,689sq mi (123,515sq km). Pop. (1990) 2,573,216.

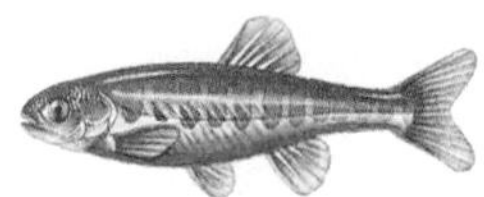

▲ **minnow** Found in freshwater habitats all over the world, the minnow (*Phoxinus* sp.) will swim in shoals to reduce the chance of individuals being preyed upon.

▲ **mint** Long been used as a food flavoring, many species of mint (*Mentha* sp.) are known, and they show subtle differences in the aroma they discharge. Crosses between water mint (*Mentha aquatica*) and spearmint (*Mentha spicata*) are the basis of cultivated peppermint (*Mentha* x *piperita*), which is commercially grown on a wide scale in the USA, and used to flavor gums, toothpaste, and a variety of drugs.

M

**MISSISSIPPI**
**Statehood:** December 10, 1817
**Nickname:** Magnolia State
**State bird:** Mockingbird
**State flower:** Magnolia
**State tree:** Magnolia
**State motto:** By valor and arms

**MISSOURI**
**Statehood:**
August 10, 1821
**Nickname:**
"Show me" State
**State bird:**
Eastern bluebird
**State flower:**
Hawthorn
**State tree:**
Flowering dogwood
**State motto:**
The welfare of the people shall be the supreme law

**Mississippi** Principal river of the US, second-longest national river (after the MISSOURI), *c.*2,350mi (3,780km) long. It rises in NW Minnesota and flows SE (forming many state boundaries along its course), emptying into the Gulf of Mexico via its huge marshland delta in SE Louisiana. Its chief tributaries include the Missouri, Ohio, Arkansas, and Tennessee rivers. A major transport route, it is connected to the GREAT LAKES and the ST. LAWRENCE SEAWAY (N) and the Intracoastal Waterway (E). Major ports on the river include MINNEAPOLIS, ST. LOUIS, MEMPHIS, and NEW ORLEANS. In 1541 Hernando DE SOTO became the first European to discover the river. In 1682 La Salle sailed down the Mississippi to the Gulf of Mexico and gained control of the region. In 1803 it was acquired by the US as part of the LOUISIANA PURCHASE. The Mississippi was used as a major transport route by Union forces during the Civil War. Since the 1950s improvements have been made to the river's channels, enabling bulkier freight to be transported.

**Mississippian Period** In the US, name given to the earlier part of the CARBONIFEROUS period.

**Missouri** State in central US, W of the Mississippi River; the capital is JEFFERSON CITY. The largest cities are ST. LOUIS, KANSAS CITY, and SPRINGFIELD. The French were the first to settle the area, in the mid-18th century. The US acquired the region as part of the LOUISIANA PURCHASE of 1803. The Missouri Territory was organized in 1812 and became a main corridor of westward migration. Missouri was admitted to the Union in 1821 without restrictions on slavery, but when the American CIVIL WAR began sympathies were bitterly divided and there was much violence. The state remained in the Union. Geographically it is divided into two parts. To the N of the Missouri River is prairie country, where farmers grow corn and raise livestock; S of the river are the foothills and plateaus of the Ozark Mountains. In the SW is a small wheat-growing area, and in the SE are the cotton fields of the Mississippi floodplain. The chief mineral resources are coal, lead, zinc, and iron ore. Missouri's economy is based on manufacturing. Industries: transportation equipment, food processing, chemicals, printing and publishing, fabricated metals, electrical machinery. Area: 68,898sq mi (178,446sq km). Pop. (1990) 5,117,073.

**Missouri** ("Big Muddy") Longest river of the US at *c.*2,560mi (4,120km) long; the major tributary of the MISSISSIPPI. It rises at the confluence of the Jefferson, Madison, and Gallatin rivers in the Rocky Mountains, Montana. It then flows E through Great Falls cataracts and Fort Peck reservoir. In North Dakota it turns SE across the Great Plains, passing through Sioux City, OMAHA, and KANSAS CITY. It joins the Mississippi River 17mi (27km) N of St. Louis, Missouri. Sioux City, Iowa, is the head of navigation. Seasonal fluctuation in flow is a major problem and the Missouri has seven major dams along its route. Its major tributaries are the Yellowstone and Platte rivers. The river was used as a trade route by the Native Americans for centuries before its discovery by the French explorers Marquette and Jolliet in 1683. Mapped by the LEWIS AND CLARK EXPEDITION (1804–06), the river was used by traders, gold seekers, and pioneers as a route to the NW.

**Missouri Compromise** Effort to end the dispute between slave and free states in the US in 1820–21. Pushed through Congress by Henry CLAY, it permitted Missouri to join the union as a slave state at the same time as Maine was admitted as a free state, preserving an equal balance between slave and free.

**mistletoe** Any of numerous species of evergreen plants that are semiparasitic on tree branches. It has small, spatula-shaped, yellowish-green leaves and generally forms a large dense ball of foliage. The mistletoe taps into the branch of its host to sap its food supply, avoiding the necessity of growing roots itself. Families: Loranthaceae/Viscaceae.

**mistral** Wind prevalent in the NW Mediterranean during the winter. It sweeps from the MASSIF CENTRAL, down the Rhône valley, reaching the Rhône delta as a strong, dry wind.

**Mitchell, Billy (William)** (1879–1936) US air force general. He commanded the US army air forces in World War I. His immoderate advocacy of air power led to his being court-martialed for insubordination (1925). Developments during World War II largely confirmed his ideas.

**MOBILE TELEPHONE**

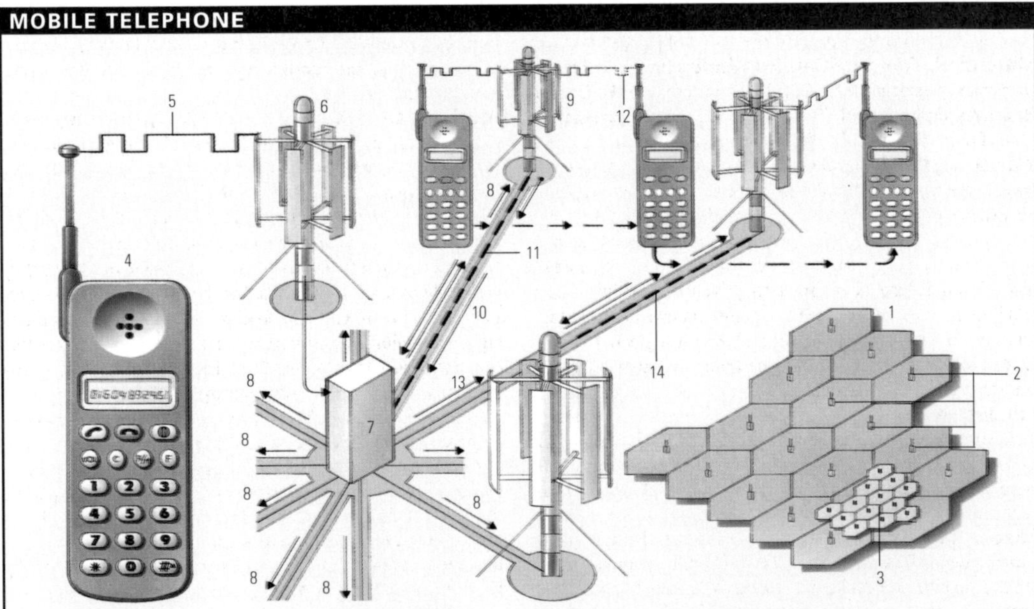

Mobile phone networks use a system of cells (1). By having a transmitter (2) in each cell the same frequencies can be used in each cell allowing an enormous capacity for calls. Where there are many users, such as the heart of a city (3), the cells are much smaller – further multiplying the number of frequencies available. A digital mobile phone (4) sends digital information (5) to a transmitter tower (6). Digital phones are better than analog versions because they reduce background noise and interference and are more difficult to bug. The transmitter passes the message to the systems' central exchange (7). If the call is for another mobile phone the exchange sends a message (8) to the other transmitters, which in turn send out a message to locate the receiving phone. The transmitter locating the required phone (9) sends a confirmation message to the exchange (10) which then connects the conversation (11 - dotted line). When a phone moves out of range of a transmitter (12) a complicated procedure ensures the conversation can continue seamlessly. When the phone's signal to the transmitter becomes weaker the exchange sends a message (13) to the transmitters in the surrounding cells to see which is receiving the strongest signal. It then transfers the conversation to that transmitter (14 - dotted line).

M

**mite** Minute ARACHNID found worldwide, many as parasites on plants and animals. The adult has four pairs of legs with claws at the tip, and a fused head and abdomen. Length: 0.02–0.1in (0.5–3mm). Class Arachnida; order Acarina. *See also* CHIGGER; TICK

**Mitford** Name of six British sisters, the daughters of Lord and Lady Redesdale (family name Mitford). The most famous, **Nancy** Freeman Mitford (1904–73), was a novelist and biographer. Her first successful novel was *The Pursuit of Love* (1945), which was followed by *Love in a Cold Climate* (1949) and *The Blessing* (1951). Her sister **Jessica** Mitford (1917–96) also wrote, protesting about snobbery, as in *The American Way of Death* (1963) and *Kind and Usual Punishment* (1973). The other two notable sisters, **Unity** Valkyrie (1914–48) and **Diana** (1910–96), turned to fascism, the former traveling to Germany and becoming a disciple of Adolf HITLER and the latter marrying Sir Oswald MOSLEY.

**Mithridates VI** (132–63 BC) King of Pontus (120–63 BC). He attempted to extend his rule southward but was repeatedly defeated by the Romans. He was overwhelmed by the forces of SULLA in the war of 88–85 BC and lost his kingdom in a second campaign in 83–82. He reconquered it in 74 but was defeated by POMPEY in 66 and fled to the Bosporus. He was planning an invasion of Italy when his troops mutinied, and he committed suicide.

**mitochondrion** Structure (organelle) inside a CELL containing ENZYMES necessary for energy production. Mitochondria are found in the cytoplasm of most types of cell (but not in bacteria). *See also* RESPIRATION

**mitosis** Nuclear division of a CELL resulting in two genetically identical "daughter" cells with the same number of chromosomes as the parent cell. Mitosis is the normal process of TISSUE growth, and is also involved in ASEXUAL REPRODUCTION. *See also* MEIOSIS

**Mitra** (Mithra or Mithras) God who in different forms was worshiped in India, Persia, and then the Roman empire, and whose cult was the basis of Mithraism. In Vedic mythology, Mitra was the spirit of the day, of the rain, and of the sun, linked closely with VARUNA. The Persian Mitra was a popular deity of the ACHAEMENID empire, revered as the god of light and power.

**Mitterrand, François Maurice Marie** (1916–96) French statesman, president (1981–96). He was active in the French Resistance during World War II, and served in the government of the Fourth Republic. In 1965 he united the parties of the left and narrowly lost the presidential election in 1974. In 1981 elections Mitterrand defeated the incumbent GISCARD D'ESTAING. He was re-elected in 1988. Mitterrand introduced reforms, including the abolition of capital punishment, and favoured state intervention in managing the economy. In the 1980s some nationalized industries returned to private ownership. After 1986, he had to cooperate with Gaullist (conservative) prime minister Jacques CHIRAC. Mitterrand was a supporter of the EUROPEAN UNION (EU) and of close Franco-German relations. He was succeeded by Jacques Chirac.

**mixture** In chemistry, two or more substances that retain their specific identities when mixed (such as air containing oxygen, nitrogen, and other gases). The identities remain separate no matter in what proportion or how closely the components are mixed. *See also* COMPOUND; SOLUTION

**Mladić, Ratko** (1943– ) Bosnian Serb general and military commander. Mladić came to international prominence in 1992, after civil war broke out in Bosnia-Herzegovina. As the aggressive and ruthless commander of the Bosnian Serb army, he earned the sobriquet "Butcher of the Balkans" and was formally indicted in 1996 as a war criminal.

**Mobile** City and seaport at the mouth of Mobile River, sw Alabama, USA. Settled in 1711 by the French, it was ceded to Britain in 1763 and seized by the USA in 1813. During the Civil War it was the scene of a battle between Federal and Confederate naval forces. Industries: textiles, paper, timber, aluminium, chemicals, oil refining, shipbuilding. Pop. (1990) 196,278.

**mobile telephone** (cellular TELEPHONE) Portable radio that connects users to the public telephone system. They operate within a network of radio cells. The first generation operated with analog signals, the second generation with digital signals.

**MODEM**

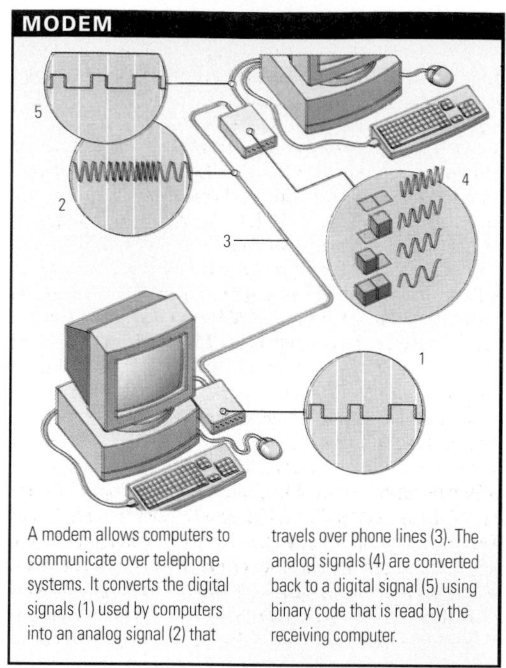


A modem allows computers to communicate over telephone systems. It converts the digital signals (1) used by computers into an analog signal (2) that travels over phone lines (3). The analog signals (4) are converted back to a digital signal (5) using binary code that is read by the receiving computer.

**Mobutu Sese Seko** (1930–97) Zairean political leader, b. Joseph-Désiré Mobutu. He was defense minister under Patrice LUMUMBA. Having control of the army, he deposed Lumumba in 1960. In 1965 he led a coup against Joseph Kasavubu, becoming prime minister in 1966 and president in 1967. His corrupt, autocratic rule became increasingly unpopular, but he maintained his discredited regime, often from France, with the support of the security forces. In 1997 he was forced into exile by a Tutsi-dominated revolt led by Laurent Kabila.

**mockingbird** Any of a group of New World birds, known for imitating other birds. The common mockingbird (*Mimus polyglottos*) of the US is typical; it is about 11in (27cm) long, ashy above with brownish wings and tail marked with white. Family Mimidae.

**mock orange** (Philadelphus or sweet syringa) Ornamental deciduous shrub native to the Western Hemisphere and Asia. It has solitary, white or yellowish, fragrant flowers. Family Hydrangeaceae; genus *Philadelphus*.

**mode** Classified scheme developed during the 4th to 16th centuries AD to systematize music. From the scale worked out scientifically by PYTHAGORAS, St. Ambrose in the 4th century is thought to have devised four "authentic" modes, the Dorian, Phrygian, Lydian, and Mixolydian. All the modes comprised eight notes within the compass of an octave. Pope Gregory (6th century) added four "plagal" modes, which were essentially new forms of the Ambrosian modes (Hypodorian, Hypophrygian etc.). Glareanus (16th century) added the Aeolian and Ionian modes, the basis of the minor and major scales respectively.

**mode** In statistics, a measure of central tendency. It is computed by determining the item that occurs most frequently in a data set. It is a quick measure of central tendency, but is not as commonly used as the MEDIAN or MEAN.

**Model Parliament** English parliament summoned by EDWARD I in 1295. For the first time, knights of the shire and burgesses (representatives of the Commons) dealt with the affairs of the nation with the king and magnates. This enlargement of the Commons' function was held to be the model for the future. They had previously merely agreed to what the king and the magnates had already decided.

**modem** (modulator-demodulator) Electronic device for sending and receiving COMPUTER signals through a telephone system. The electrical pulses produced by a computer are fed into a modem, which uses the pulses to modulate a continuous tone (carrier) by a process called FREQUENCY MODULATION (FM). At the other end, another modem extracts the pulses (demodulation), so that they can be fed into a receiving computer. *See also* COMPUTER NETWORK; INTERNET

M

▶ **Modigliani** *Girl with Pigtails* (1901) The Italian painter and sculptor Modigliani spent most of his life in Paris, but his studies of Renaissance masters in Italy had a strong influence on his work. Influenced by Brancuși, Modigliani's achievements may have been limited, but his legendary bohemian lifestyle, his passion for his work, and his tragic early death from tuberculosis have ensured him a lasting reputation.

**modern dance** Dance style that began to develop during the late 19th century as a protest against classical ballet. It is often said to have been pioneered by Isadora DUNCAN. In Europe and the US, such innovators as Rudolph von Laban, Ruth St. Denis, and Ted Shawn attempted to make dance a viable contemporary art form.

**modernism** Twentieth-century movement in art, architecture, design, and literature that, in general, concentrates on space and form, rather than content or ornamentation. In **architecture** and design, early influences were BAUHAUS (1919–33) and individuals such as Walter GROPIUS and MIES VAN DER ROHE. Modernism developed the use of new building materials, such as glass, steel, and concrete. While difficult to define and date precisely, the echoes of **literary** modernism can still be heard in late-20th-century fiction. The most recognizably distinct form is the STREAM OF CONSCIOUSNESS narrative, as evidenced in the work of Virginia WOOLF and James JOYCE's seminal novel, *Ulysses* (1922). The outstanding example of modernist poetry is the fragmentary *The Wasteland* (1922) by T.S. ELIOT. Literary modernism exhibits an increasing concern with psychological states and the subconscious. **Artists** such as PICASSO and Marcel DUCHAMP adopted new techniques of representation and worked in previously unexploited media. The movements of DADA and SURREALISM were vital to this new experimentation. In **music**, composers such as STRAVINSKY and SCHOENBERG challenged previously held notions of tonality. *See also* POSTMODERNISM

**Modigliani, Amedeo** (1884–1920) Italian painter, sculptor, and draftsman. Many of his sculptures portray elongated heads, inspired by the primitive strength of African masks and caryatids. During World War I he returned to painting, focusing mainly on erotic female nudes and portraits.

**modulation** In physics, process of varying the characteristics of one wave system in accordance with those of another. It is basic to RADIO broadcasting. In AMPLITUDE MODULATION (AM), the amplitude of a high-frequency radio carrier wave is varied in accordance with the frequency of a current generated by a sound wave. For static-free, short-range broadcasting FREQUENCY MODULATION (FM) is used, in which the frequency of the carrier wave is modulated.

**Mogadishu** Capital and chief port of Somalia, on the Indian Ocean. Mogadishu was founded by Arabs in the 10th century. In the 16th century it was captured by the Portuguese and became a cornerstone of their trade with Africa. In 1871 control passed to the sultan of Zanzibar, who first leased (1892) and then sold (1905) the port to the Italians. Mogadishu was made the capital of Italian Somaliland. During World War II the city was occupied by the British from 1941. In 1960 Mogadishu became the capital of independent Somalia. During the 1980s the city was devastated by civil war, its population swollen by refugees escaping famine and drought. In 1992 UN troops were flown into Mogadishu to control aid distribution but withdrew in 1995 after little success. Pop. (1990 est.) 1,200,000.

**Mogul empire** (1526–1857) Muslim empire in India. It was founded by BABUR, who conquered Delhi and Agra (1526). The Mogul empire reached its height under Akbar (r.1556–1605), Babur's grandson, when it extended from Afghanistan to the Bay of Bengal and as far south as the Deccan. Religious tolerance encouraged by Akbar was reduced under his successors, JAHANGIR (r.1605–27), SHAH JAHAN (1627–58), and AURANGZEB (1658–1707). Mogul art and architecture reached a peak under Shah Jahan, builder of the TAJ MAHAL. By the death of Aurangzeb, the Mogul dynasty was in decline. The last Mogul emperor was deposed by the British in 1858 after the rising known as the Indian Mutiny.

**Mohammed** Alternative spelling of MUHAMMAD

**Mohawk** Iroquoian-speaking Native North American tribe of the IROQUOIS CONFEDERACY, formerly inhabiting central New York State. Today there are about 2,000 Mohawks. Most are farmers on two reservations in Ontario, Canada, but some are migrant workers in the US and Canadian steel industries.

**Mohican** (Mahican) Algonquian-speaking tribe of Native North Americans, formerly inhabiting the upper Hudson valley in New York, and the area E of the Housatonic River in Connecticut. They once numbered about 3,000. Today 525 Mohicans occupy the Stockbridge-Munsee Reservation in Wisconsin.

**Moho** (Mohorovičić discontinuity) Boundary between the Earth's CRUST and MANTLE. It is identified by a sharp increase in the velocity of seismic waves passing through the Earth, and is named for the Croatian geophysicist Andrija Mohorovičić, who first recognized it in 1909. The velocity increase is explained by a change to more dense rocks in the mantle. The depth of the Moho varies from *c.*3mi (5km) to 37mi (60km) below the Earth's surface.

## MOLDOVA

**AREA:** 13,010 sq mi (33,700 sq km)
**POPULATION:** 4,458,000
**CAPITAL (POPULATION):** Chisinau, 700,000
**GOVERNMENT:** Multiparty republic
**ETHNIC GROUPS:** Moldovan 65%, Ukrainian 14%, Russian 13%, Gagauz 4%, Jewish 2%, Bulgarian
**LANGUAGES:** Moldovan (Romanian) (official)
**RELIGIONS:** Christianity (Eastern Orthodox)
**CURRENCY:** Leu

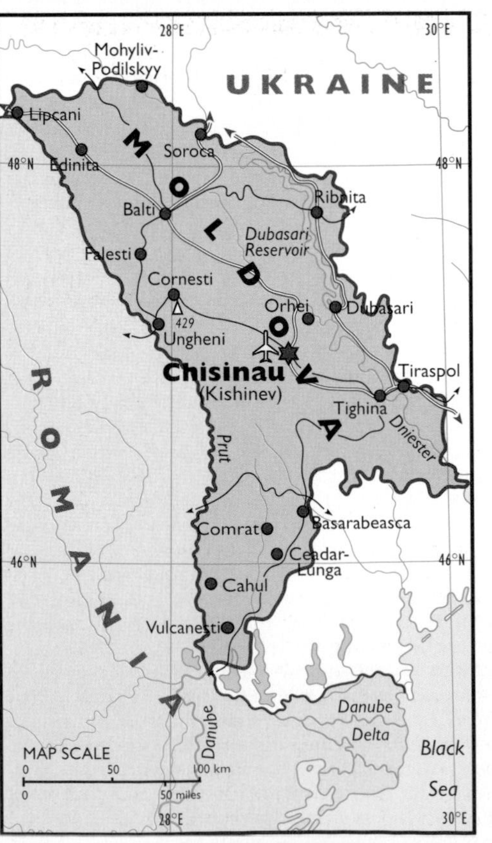

**Moholy-Nagy, László** (1895–1946) Hungarian designer, painter, and sculptor. He was one of the founders of CONSTRUCTIVISM. He taught at the BAUHAUS (1923–28) before working in Berlin as a stage designer and filmmaker. He then moved to Paris, Amsterdam, and London. In 1937 he emigrated to the US and became director of the New Bauhaus.

**Moi, Daniel (Torotich) Arap** (1924– ) Kenyan political leader, president (1978– ). He was the British-appointed representative to the Kenya Legislative Council from 1958 until independence (1964). He was elected president in 1978, succeeding KENYATTA. He continued his predecessor's liberal economic policies but came under increasing international criticism for his repressive rule. He was reelected in 1992 and 1997.

**Mojave Desert** Arid region with low, barren mountains in S California, surrounded by mountain ranges on the N and W, and the Colorado Desert on the SE. It was formed by volcanic eruptions and deposits from the Colorado River. Area: *c.*15,000sq mi (38,850sq km).

**mold** Mass composed of the spore-bearing mycelia (vegetative filaments) and fruiting bodies produced by numerous fungi. Many molds live off fruits, vegetables, cheese, butter, jelly, silage, and almost any dead organic material. Roquefort, camembert, and stilton cheeses involve the use of mold. Although many species are pathogenic (disease-causing), PENICILLIN and a few other ANTIBIOTICS are obtained from molds. *See also* FUNGICIDE; FUNGUS; SLIME MOLD

**Moldavia** Historic Balkan region, between the CARPATHIAN MOUNTAINS in Romania and the DNIEPER River in MOLDOVA. Major cities in the Romanian portion include Galaţi and Suceava. Moldavia is primarily an agricultural region. Under Roman rule it formed the major part of the province of DACIA and today's population is Romanian-speaking. In the 14th century it became an independent principality ruled by the Vlachs; its lands included Bessarabia and Bukovina. In 1504 Moldavia was conquered by the Turks and remained part of the Ottoman empire until the 19th century. In 1775 Bukovina was lost to the Austrians, and in 1815 Bessarabia was taken by Russia. After the Russo–Turkish War (1828–29) Russia became the dominant power. In 1856 the twin principalities of Moldavia and WALLACHIA were given considerable autonomy. Three years later they were united under one crown to form ROMANIA, but Russia reoccupied S Bessarabia in 1878. In 1920 Bessarabia and Bukovina were incorporated into the Romanian state. In 1924 the Soviet republic of Moldavia was formed, which in 1947 was enlarged to include Bessarabia and N Bukovina. In 1989 the Moldovans asserted their independence by making Romanian the official language, and in 1991, following the dissolution of the Soviet Union, Moldavia became the independent republic of MOLDOVA.

**Moldova** Republic in E Europe; the capital is CHISINAU. **Land and climate** Moldova is a mostly hilly country. A large plain covers the S. The main river is the Dniester, which flows through E Moldova. The climate is moderately continental, with warm summers and fairly cold winters. Most rainfall occurs during the warmer months. Forests of hornbeam, oak, and other trees grow in N and central Moldova. In the drier S, most of the region is now used for farming, with rich pasture along the rivers. **History and Politics** In the 14th century, the Moldovans formed the state of Moldavia. (for history pre-1991, *see* MOLDAVIA) Following independence in 1991, the majority Moldovan population wished to rejoin Romania, but this alienated the Ukrainian and Russian populations E of the Dniester, who declared their independence from Moldova as the Transdniester republic. War raged between the two, with Transdniester supported by the Russian 14th Army. In August 1992 a ceasefire was declared. In 1994 multiparty elections were won by the former communists of the Agrarian Democratic Party. A referendum rejected reunification with Romania. Parliament voted to join the COMMONWEALTH OF INDEPENDENT STATES (CIS). A new constitution (1994) established a presidential parliamentary republic. In 1995 Transdniester voted in favour of independence in a referendum. In 1996 Russian troops began to withdraw. In 1996 Petru Lucinschi was elected president. **Economy** Moldova is a lower-middle-income developing economy (1992 GDP per capita, US$3,670). developing economy. Agriculture is important and major products include fruits, grapes for winemaking, corn, sugar beets, sunflower seeds, tobacco, vegetables, and wheat. Farmers also raise livestock, including dairy cattle and pigs. Moldova has no major natural resources and has to import materials and fuels for its industries. Major manufactures include agricultural machinery, refrigerators, washing machines, and television sets, while the leading exports include food, wine, tobacco, textiles, and footwear.

**mole** (symbol mol) SI unit of amount of substance. This is the amount of substance that contains as many elementary units, such as atoms and molecules, as there are atoms in 0.012kg of carbon-12. A mass of one mole of a compound is its relative molecular mass (molecular weight) in grams.

**mole** Any of several species of small, burrowing, mainly insectivorous mammals that live in various habitats worldwide. The European mole, *Talpa europaea*, has short brown or black fur, a short tail, and wide clawed forefeet for digging tunnels. Its eyes are sensitive only to bright light. Length: to 7in (18cm). Family Talpidae.

▲ **mole** Grant's desert mole (*Eremitalpa granti*) is found in South Africa. It is a golden mole, and although it resembles true moles, it is not closely related.

**molecular biology** Biological study of the makeup and function of molecules found in living organisms. Major areas of study include the chemical and physical properties of proteins and of nucleic acids such as DNA. *See also* BIOCHEMISTRY

**molecular weight** *See* RELATIVE MOLECULAR MASS

**molecule** Smallest particle of a substance (such as a compound) that exhibits the properties of that substance. Molecules consist of two or more ATOMS held together by CHEMICAL BONDS. For example, water molecules consist of two atoms of hydrogen bonded to one atom of oxygen ($H_2O$). A molecule (unlike an ION) has no electrical charge. *See also* MACROMOLECULE

**Molière** (1622–73) French playwright, b. Jean-Baptiste Poquelin. An accurate observer of contemporary modern manners, he is regarded as the founder of modern French comedy. His best-known comedies include *Tartuffe* (1661), *The Misanthrope* (1667), and *The Miser* (1669). His work found favor with Louis XIV but was unpopular with church leaders. His last play was *The Imaginary Invalid*, during a performance of which he collapsed and died.

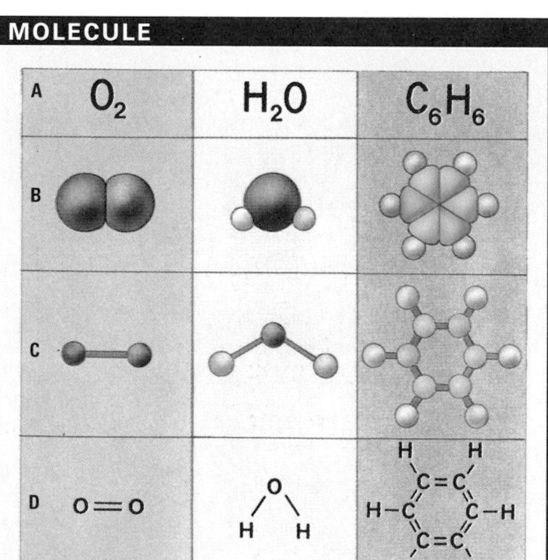


Molecules are groups of bonded atoms. They can be groups of the same atoms as in oxygen ($O_2$) or combinations of different elements, such as water ($H_2O$) and benzene ($C_6H_6$). Molecules can be illustrated in four ways. Line one (A), the chemical formula, lists the type and number of atoms in a molecule but does not show their structure. Line two (B) is the closest representation of the actual shape of the molecule but does not detail the bonds between the atoms. Line three (C) is less realistic but does show the bonding. Line four (D) combines the chemical formula, using the abbreviations of the periodic table, and symbolic representation of the bonding structure.

M

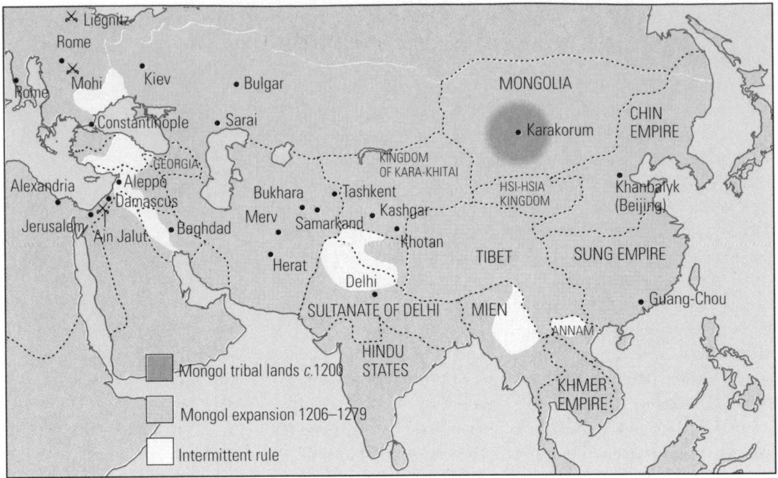


▲ **Mongol** In 1206, under the leadership of Genghis Khan, the Mongols extended the territory under their rule, until by 1279 it stretched from China to the Euphrates.

**mollusk** Any of more than 80,000 species of invertebrate animals in the phylum Molluska. They include the snails, clams, and squids, and a host of less well-known forms. Originally marine, members of the group are now found in the oceans, in fresh water, and on land. There are six classes: the GASTROPODS, CHITONS, univalves (slugs and snails), BIVALVES, tusk shells, and CEPHALOPODA. The mollusk body is divided into three: the head, the foot, and the visceral mass. Associated with the body is a fold of skin (the mantle) that secretes the limy shell typical of most mollusks. The head is well developed only in snails and in the cephalopods. The visceral mass contains the internal organs. The sexes are usually separate but there are many hermaphroditic species.

**Molotov, Vyacheslav Mikhailovich** (1890–1986) Soviet statesman, premier (1930–41), and foreign minister (1939–49, 1953–56). A loyal ally of STALIN, Molotov became a full member of the Politburo in 1926. As foreign minister, one of his first acts was to sign the Nazi-Soviet Pact (1939). He lost favor under KHRUSHCHEV, and was demoted and expelled from the Communist Party in 1962. He was readmitted in 1984.

**Moluccas** (Maluku) Island group and province in E Indonesia, between Sulawesi (W) and New Guinea (E); the capital is Ambon. The fabled Spice Islands were originally explored by Magellan in the early 16th century, and later settled by the Portuguese. The Dutch took the islands in the 17th century and monopolized the spice trade. After Indonesian independence the S Moluccas became the focus of a movement for secession. The group includes the larger islands of Halmahera, Ceram, and Buru, and the island groups of Sula, Batjan, Obi, Kai, Aru, Tanimbar, Banda, Babar, and Leti. Products: spices, copra, timber, sago. Area: 28,759sq mi (74,505sq km). Pop. (1990) 1,857,790.

**molybdenum** (symbol Mo) Silvery-white metallic element; one of the TRANSITION ELEMENTS. It was first isolated in 1782. Its chief ore is molybdenite. Hard but malleable and ductile, it is used in alloy steels, x-ray tubes, and missile parts; molybdenum compounds are used as catalysts and lubricants. It is one of the essential TRACE ELEMENTS for plant growth. Properties: at.no. 42; at. wt. 95.94; sp. gr. 10.22; m.p. 4,730°F (2,610°C); b.p. 10,040°F (5,560°C); most stable isotope $^{98}$Mo (23.78%).

**Mombasa** City and seaport on the Indian Ocean, SW Kenya, partly on Mombasa Island and partly on the mainland (to which it is connected by causeway). From the 11th to 16th centuries Mombasa was a center of the Arab slave and ivory trades. From 1529 to 1648 it was held by the Portuguese. Taken by Zanzibar in the mid-19th century, the city passed to Britain in 1887, when it was made capital of the British East Africa Protectorate. Kenya's chief port, Mombasa exports coffee, fruit, and grain. Industries: tourism, food processing, glass, oil refining, aluminum products. Pop. (1989) 465,000.

**moment of a force** *See* TORQUE

**moment of inertia** For a rotating object, the sum of the products formed by multiplying the point masses of the rotating object by the squares of their distances from the axis of the rotation.

**momentum** Product of the mass and linear velocity of an object. One of the fundamental laws of physics is the principle that the total momentum of any system of objects is conserved at all times, even during and after collisions.

**Monaco** Principality in S Europe, on the Mediterranean coast, forming an enclave in French territory near the border with Italy; the capital is Monaco-Ville. Ruled by the Grimaldi family from the end of the 13th century, it came under French protection in 1860. The chief source of income is tourism, attracted by the casinos of MONTE CARLO. There is some light industry, including printing, textiles, and postage stamps. Area: 0.7sq mi (1.9sq km). Pop. (1990) 29,972.

**Monaghan** County in Ulster province, NE Republic of Ireland, on the boundary with Northern Ireland; the county town is Monaghan. The S and E are hilly, but the rest of the county is a fertile plain. The Blackwater and the Finn are the chief rivers. It is primarily an agricultural county and the main crops are potatoes, oats, and flax. Beef and dairy cattle are raised. Industries: linen milling, footwear, furniture. Area: 498sq mi (1,290sq km). Pop. (1991) 51,293.

**monasticism** Ascetic mode of life followed by men and women who have taken religious vows and belong to a recognized Roman Catholic or Orthodox religious order. Christian monasticism is said to have its origins in the late-3rd-century asceticism of the desert hermits of Egypt, St. ANTHONY and St. Pachomius. In time, this solitary life was replaced by a communal approach, in which community members followed a strict rule. The earliest such rule in Europe was that laid down by St. BENEDICT OF NURSIA in the 6th century. Monasticism still embraces community life of enclosed Christian orders, such as the CISTERCIANS and the reformed CARMELITES. There are, however, many more orders that combine asceticism with social welfare work and spiritual guidance to society at large. Spiritual leadership for a society provided through monasticism is also found in HINDUISM, BUDDHISM, JAINISM, and TAOISM.

**Monck, George, 1st duke of Albemarle** (1608–70) English soldier and diplomat. In the English CIVIL WAR, Monck fought for CHARLES I (1643–44). After his capture and imprisonment (1644–46), Monck changed sides and helped Oliver CROMWELL to quell an Irish rebellion. He was rewarded with command of the forces in Scotland (1651). Monck was a general in the DUTCH WARS. After the collapse of the PROTECTORATE, he supported the return of the RUMP PARLIAMENT. Monck led the campaign for the RESTORATION of CHARLES II.

**Mondale, Walter Frederick** (1928– ) US statesman, vice president (1977–81). A lawyer and Democrat, he served (1960–64) as attorney general for Minnesota and then was appointed to complete Hubert HUMPHREY's term in the US Senate. Mondale was elected to a full term in 1966 and again in 1972. He was Jimmy CARTER's running mate in the successful

## MONGOLIA

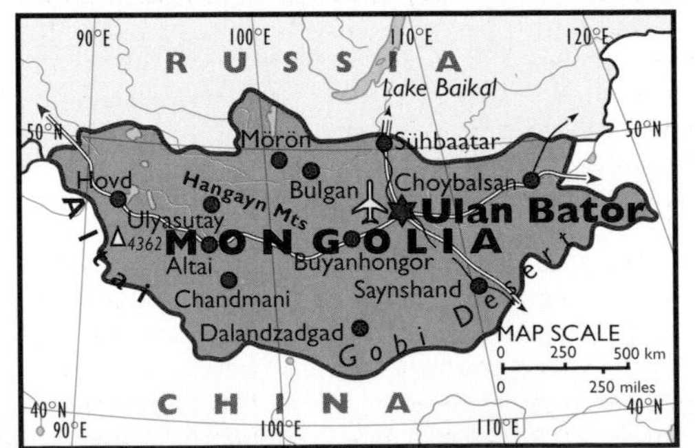

**AREA:** 604,826sq mi (1,566,500sq km)
**POPULATION:** 2,130,000
**CAPITAL (POPULATION):** Ulan Bator (601,000)
**GOVERNMENT:** Multiparty republic
**ETHNIC GROUPS:** Khalkha Mongol 79%, Kazakh 6%
**LANGUAGES:** Khalkha Mongolian (official)
**RELIGIONS:** Tibetan Buddhism was once the main religion; reliable recent information is unavailable
**CURRENCY:** Tugrik = 100 möngö

campaign of 1976. After defeat in the 1980 election, he went into private law practice but emerged in 1984 to run for the presidency, choosing Geraldine FERRARO as his running mate. Mondale was defeated overwhelmingly by Ronald REAGAN. He later served effectively as ambassador to Japan.

**Mondrian, Piet** (1872–1944) Dutch painter, cofounder (with Theo van Doesburg) of De STIJL and a pioneer of ABSTRACT ART, b. Pieter Mondriaan. Influenced by CUBISM, Mondrian developed a distinctive, geometric style, which he dubbed "neo-plasticism." In 1917 he founded the art magazine *De Stijl*. Mondrian's art, such as *Composition in Yellow and Blue* (1925), informed the BAUHAUS movement and the INTERNATIONAL STYLE in architecture. In 1940 he moved to the USA where his pieces, such as *Broadway Boogie-Woogie* (1942–43), became more colourful, reflecting his interest in jazz and dance rhythms.

**Monera** *See* PROKARYOTAE

**Monet, Claude** (1840–1926) French painter. A founder of IMPRESSIONISM, Monet's piece *Impression, Sunrise* (1872) gave the movement its name. During the 1860s he studied in Paris with RENOIR, Sisley and Bazille. The group painted from nature, recording the transient effects of light. Monet often painted the same scene several times, such as the *Gare St-Lazare* (1876–78) and *Rouen Cathedral* (1892–94). In 1870 he stayed with PISSARRO in London, and made studies of the Thames River. In 1883 he settled in Giverny. Despite failing sight, Monet's last series, *Water Lilies* (1906–26), is his most vibrant.

**monetarism** Economic and monetary theory that argues that changes in monetary stability are the principal causes of changes in the economy. It asserts the importance of controlling the money supply as the means of achieving a noninflationary, stable economy capable of supporting high employment and economic growth. This theory is associated particularly with the views of Milton FRIEDMAN, whose early work in the 1950s and 1960s stimulated the initial debate. Interest in monetarism revived in the 1970s, and was extremely influential in the US and the UK in the 1980s.

**money** Any type of payment that is generally accepted within an economy as a medium of exchange for goods and services. It may take many forms besides currency or cash (coins and banknotes). A large portion of the money supply may be in the form of deposits within a banking system.

**Mongol** Nomadic people of E central Asia who overran a vast region in the 13th–14th centuries. The different tribes in the area were united by GENGHIS KHAN in the early 13th century and conquered an empire that stretched from the Black Sea to the Pacific Ocean and from Siberia to Tibet. Genghis Khan's possessions were divided among his sons and developed into four khanates, one of which was the empire of the Great Khan (KUBLAI KHAN), which included China. In the 14th century TAMERLANE, allegedly a descendant of Genghis, conquered the Persian and Turkish khanates, and broke up the GOLDEN HORDE. By the end of the century the true Mongol khanates had practically disappeared.

**Mongolia** Republic in central Asia; the capital is ULAN BATOR. **Land and climate** Sandwiched between China and Russia, Mongolia is the world's largest landlocked country. High plateaus cover most of Mongolia, with the highest plateau in the W between the ALTAI Mountains and Hangai Mountains. The Altai Mountains contain Mongolia's highest peaks, rising to 14,311ft (4,362m). The land descends toward the E and S, where part of the GOBI Desert is situated. Ulan Bator lies on the N edge of a desert plateau in the heart of Asia. It has bitterly cold winters, dropping to −58°F (−50°C). Summer temperatures are moderated by altitude. Mountain forests contain birch, cedar, larch, pine, and spruce. Mongolia has large areas of steppe grassland. Plants become increasingly sparse to the S. **History and Politics** In the 13th century, GENGHIS KHAN united the Mongolian peoples and built up a great empire. Under his grandson, KUBLAI KHAN, the Mongol empire extended from Korea and China to E Europe and Mesopotamia. The empire broke up in the late 14th century, and in the early 17th century, Inner Mongolia came under Chinese control. By the late 17th century, Outer Mongolia also became a Chinese province. In 1911, the Mongolians drove the Chinese out of Outer Mongolia and established a short-lived Buddhist kingdom. In 1919 China reestablished control. In 1924 the Mongolian People's Republic was established (Inner Mongolia remained a Chinese province). The Mongolian Peoples's Revolutionary Party (MPRP) became the sole political party. The revolution in ownership prompted the Lama Rebellion (1932), which saw the migration of thousands of peoples and millions of livestock into Inner Mongolia. From the 1950s, Mongolia supported Soviet policies, especially in relation to Sino–Soviet disputes. In 1961 Mongolia was accepted into the United Nations. Popular demonstrations led to multiparty elections in 1990, which were won by the MPRP. In 1992 a new constitution confirmed the process of liberalization. In 1993 President Ochirbat was re-elected, despite the MPRP refusing to endorse him as a candidate. In 1996 the Democratic Union Coalition formed the first non-communist government for more than 70 years. In 1997 Ochirbat was ousted by Natsagyn Bagabandi, leader of the MPRP. **Economy** Mongolia is a lower-middle-income developing country (1995 GDP per capita, US$1,950). Traditional nomadic life was disrupted by communism, and under forced collectivization many were placed in permanent settlements, but nomads still exist, especially in the Gobi Desert. In the mid-20th century, Mongolia rapidly industrialized, especially the mining of coal, copper, gold, and molybdenum. Minerals and fuels now account for *c.*50% of Mongolia's exports. Livestock and animal products remain important. Economic development is hampered by lack of labor and poor infrastructure.

▲ **mongoose** The banded mongoose (*Mungos mungo*) is a formidable snake killer of Africa and India. Lithe and swift, it relies on speed and agility to evade the poisonous fangs of its prey. The banded mongoose will also feed on small ground game.

**mongoose** Small, agile, carnivorous mammal of the CIVET family, native to Africa, S Europe, and Asia. It has a slender, thickly furred body and a long, bushy tail. Mongooses eat rodents, insects, eggs, birds, and snakes. Some may be domesticated, but most are highly destructive. Length: 18–45in (46–115cm). Family Viverridae.

**monism** In METAPHYSICS, doctrine that reality consists of a single unifying substance, or that the mental and physical are indivisible. SPINOZA saw this substance as God, while HEGEL believed it was the Spirit. The term was coined by the German philosopher Christian Wolf (1679–1734). Monism contrasts with DUALISM. *See also* PLURALISM

**monitor** Any of several species of powerful lizards that live in Africa, S Asia, Indonesia, and Australia, including the KOMODO DRAGON (*Varanus komodoensis*). Most species are dull-colored with yellow markings; many are semiaquatic. Length: to 10ft (3m). Family Varanidae.

**Monitor and Merrimack** Ironclad warships that fought an indecisive battle (1862) in Hampton Roads, Virginia, during the CIVIL WAR. This was the first battle between ironclad ships. The *Merrimack*, which had been scuttled by the US navy, was raised by the Confederates and given armor plating. Renamed the *Virginia*, it was designed to break the Union blockade of Southern ports. The *Monitor*, a new ironclad, was designed to destroy it. The *Virginia* was subsequently destroyed by the Confederates while retreating.

**Monk, Thelonious Sphere** (1917–82) US jazz pianist. He helped to develop the BEBOP jazz style in the 1940s and had a style featuring dissonances and distinctive chord structures. His best-known work is "'Round Midnight."

**monk** Member of a monastic community living under vows of religious observance such as poverty, chastity, and obedience. *See* MONASTICISM

**monkey** Any of a wide variety of mostly tree-dwelling, diur-

▲ **monkey** The howler monkey (*Allouata caraya*) is named for its very loud and persistent roaring calls. It inhabits the forests of tropical South America, feeding mainly on fruit and nuts, but also eating a variety of small animals. It can grow to 3ft (1m) in length, with its tail reaching a similar length.

M

► **Monroe** US actress Marilyn Monroe has attained legendary status. A talented comedy actress, she will always be remembered as a vivacious sex symbol. Her career and private life were a constant source of public interest, particularly her marriages to such high profile men as Joe DiMaggio and Arthur Miller, and her alleged relationships with President Kennedy and his brother Bobby Kennedy.

nal, omnivorous PRIMATES that live in the tropics and subtropics. Most monkeys have flat, humanlike faces, relatively large brains, and grasping hands. They fall into two broad groups – Old World monkeys (family Cercopithecidae) and New World monkeys (Cebidae). The 60 **Old World** species include MACAQUES, BABOONS, BARBARY APES, and LANGUR monkeys. They all have non-prehensile (unable to grasp) tails. They range in distribution from Japan and N China through S Asia and Africa. The 70 species of **New World** monkeys include CAPUCHIN monkeys, SPIDER MONKEYS, and MARMOSETS. They are all tree dwellers, and most have grasping (prehensile) tails. They live in tropical forests of Central and South America.

**monkey puzzle** (Chilean pine) Evergreen tree native to the South American Andes mountains. It has tangled branches, with spirally arranged, sharp, flat leaves. The female seeds are edible. Height to 150ft (45m). Family Araucariaceae; species *Araucaria araucana.*

**Monmouth, James Scott, duke of** (1649–85) English nobleman, illegitimate son of CHARLES II. As captain general, Monmouth defeated the Scots at Bothwell Bridge (1679). Allied with the Earl of SHAFTESBURY, he became leader of the Protestant opposition to the succession of the Duke of York (later JAMES II). The discovery of a plot (1683) forced Monmouth into exile in Holland. Upon James' accession (1685), he launched a rebellion. Despite initial success, Monmouth lacked the support of the nobility and was defeated by the Duke of MARLBOROUGH at the Battle of Sedgemoor. He was executed.

**monocotyledon** Subclass of flowering plants (ANGIOSPERMS) characterized by one seed leaf (COTYLEDON) in the seed embryo; the leaves are usually parallel-veined. Examples include lilies, onions, orchids, palms, and grasses. The larger subclass of plants is DICOTYLEDON.

**monogamy** Principle that a relationship or MARRIAGE is an exclusive union between two people. It is commonly supported by legal institutions. *See also* POLYGAMY

**monomer** Chemical compound composed of single molecules, as opposed to a POLYMER, which is built up from repeated monomer units. For example, propene (propylene) is the monomer from which polypropene (polypropylene) is made.

**mononucleosis** Acute disease, usually of young people, caused by the EPSTEIN-BARR VIRUS. There are an increased number of white cells (monocytes) in the blood and symptoms include fever, painful enlargement of the LYMPH nodes, and pronounced lassitude. There may be a sore throat, skin rash, and digestive disorder.

**monopoly** Sole supplier or producer of a product or service. A monopolist industry has complete power over the market for its product and is able to determine levels of output and prices. In many countries there are regulations to limit or prevent monopolies.

**monotheism** Belief in the existence of a single God. Judaism, Christianity, and Islam are the three major monotheistic religions.

**monotreme** One of an order of primitive mammals that lay eggs. The only monotremes are the PLATYPUS and two species of ECHIDNA, all native to Australasia. The eggs are temporarily transferred to a pouch beneath the female's abdomen where they eventually hatch and are nourished by rudimentary mammary glands. *See also* MARSUPIAL

**Monroe, James** (1758–1831) Fifth US President (1817–25). A Virginian, he fought in the American Revolution, studied law under JEFFERSON, and served in a succession of offices, including governor of Virginia. He helped to negotiate the LOUISIANA PURCHASE (1803) and was secretary of state under MADISON. He was elected president in 1816 and reelected, unopposed, in 1820. His administration is noted for achievements in foreign policy. They included agreement on the US–Canadian border, the acquisition of Florida, and the MONROE DOCTRINE.

**Monroe, Marilyn** (1926–62) US film star, b. Norma Jean Baker. Her films include *Gentlemen Prefer Blondes* (1953), *The Seven Year Itch* (1955), *Bus Stop* (1956), *Some Like It Hot* (1959), and *The Misfits* (1961). She attended Lee STRASBERG'S ACTORS' STUDIO and married playwright Arthur MILLER in 1956. She has lived on as an icon of beauty and has consistently inspired both analysis of and tributes to her life.

**Monroe Doctrine** Foreign policy statement made by President James MONROE to Congress in 1823. It asserted US authority over the American continent and declared that European interference in the western hemisphere would be regarded as "dangerous to peace and safety;" also, that the US would not become involved in the internal conflicts of Europe.

**Monrovia** Capital and chief port of Liberia, West Africa, on the estuary of the St. Paul River. It was settled in 1822 by freed US slaves on a site chosen by the American Colonization Society. Monrovia exports latex and iron ore; it also has warehouses and facilities for ship repairing. Its own manufactures include bricks and cement. Pop. (1984) 425,000.

**monsoon** Seasonal reversal of winds, and their associated abrupt weather changes, that blow inshore in summer and offshore over nearby oceans in winter. The monsoon occurs annually in S Africa and E Asia and is centered on the Indian subcontinent where it occurs as a distinct rainy season.

**monstera** Genus of tropical American, climbing or trailing plants with large glossy leaves that are commonly holed or deeply incised. *Monstera deliciosa* is a popular houseplant; it is often called a Swiss-cheese plant. Family Araceae.

**montage** (Fr. *monter*, to mount) Cinematic film-editing technique. A series of shots are cut and spliced in a particular way in order to obtain a desired narrative, structural, or purely aesthetic effect. The Odessa Steps sequence in Sergei EISENSTEIN'S *The Battleship Potemkin* (1925) is a classic example of montage.

**Montale, Eugenio** (1896–1981) Italian poet, journalist, critic, and translator. In 1922 he helped to found the literary magazine *Primo Tempo* and from 1948 was the literary editor of *Corriere della Sera.* His poetry is characteristically pessimistic in tone, especially in *Cuttlefish Bones* (1925). He was awarded the 1975 Nobel Prize for literature.

**Montana** State in NW US, on the Canadian border; the capital is HELENA. Other major cities include Billings and Great Falls. Until the US acquired the area in the LOUISIANA PURCHASE of 1803, it was relatively unexplored. The discovery of gold in 1852 brought a rush of immigrants and the Territory of Montana was organized in 1864. The opening of the Northern Pacific Railroad in 1883 provided a stimulus to growth and development. The W section of Montana is dominated by the ROCKY MOUNTAINS. The E is part of the GREAT PLAINS, drained by the Missouri and Yellowstone rivers. Sheep and cattle are raised on the plains. The principal crops (grown by means of irrigation) are wheat, hay, barley, and sugar beets. The Rockies have large mineral deposits including copper, silver, gold, zinc, lead, and manganese. Oil, natural gas, and coal are found in the SE. Industries: lumber, petroleum products, tourism. Area: 147,137sq mi (381,086sq km). Pop. (1990) 799,065.

**Mont Blanc** Highest peak in the Alps and the second-highest peak in Europe, lying on the border between France and Italy. It was first climbed in 1786. The 7-mi (11-km) tunnel through the base of Mont Blanc (1958–62) is the longest road tunnel in the world. Height: 15,781ft (4,810m).

**MONTANA**
**Statehood:** November 8, 1889
**Nickname:** Treasure State
**State bird:** Western meadowlark
**State flower:** Bitterroot
**State tree:** Ponderosa pine
**State motto:** Gold and silver

**Montcalm, Louis-Joseph de Montcalm-Gozon, marquis de** (1712–59) French general in North America. Commander in chief of the French army in Canada (1756–59), he won several victories against the British, including the Battle of Fort Ticonderoga (1758). In 1759 he held Quebec against a British siege for several months, but when the British, under James WOLFE, climbed the cliffs from the St. Lawrence River to the Plains of Abraham, he was taken by surprise. Both he and Wolfe were killed in the battle.

**Monte Carlo** Town in N MONACO, on the Mediterranean coast. It was founded in 1858 by Prince Charles III of Monaco. Today it is a popular resort noted for its scenery and mild climate. The Casino is a great tourist attraction. Pop. (1982) 13,154.

**Montenegro** (Crna Gora) Constituent republic of YUGOSLAVIA; the capital is Podgorica (formerly Titograd). The region was part of the Serbian empire until the Turkish invasion of 1355. SERBIA was decisively defeated by Turkey in 1389, while Montenegro successfully resisted the sultan's rule. By 1500 most of the territory had been surrendered to the Ottomans. In 1799 Turkey recognized Montenegro's independence. In 1851 a monarchy was established, and in 1878 the sovereignty of the state was formally recognized. In 1910 Nicholas I assumed the title of king and sought to expel the Turks. In 1914 he declared war on Austria, and Montenegro was quickly overrun by the Austro-German armies. He was deposed in 1918 and Montenegro was united with Serbia. In 1946 Montenegro became a republic of Yugoslavia. In 1989 the local communist leadership resigned. In the 1990 elections the communists were returned to power in Montenegro, but four of the former six Yugoslav republics voted to secede from the union. Montenegro supported Serbia in the establishment of a new, Serb-dominated federation. In a 1992 referendum Montenegro voted to remain part of the rump Yugoslav federation with Serbia. It is a mountainous region that remains industrially underdeveloped. Much of the land is barren, and agriculture is mainly centered on the Zeta Valley. Industries: tobacco, grain, stock raising, bauxite mining. Area: 5,331sq mi (13,812sq km). Pop. (1991) 615,035.

**Montessori, Maria** (1870–1952) Italian educator who believed that preschool children, given an environment rich in manipulative materials and free from restraint, would develop their creative and academic potential. Her method was adapted for use in many of the school systems in the US and Britain.

**Monteverdi, Claudio** (1567–1643) Italian composer. He was the last and greatest master of the MADRIGAL. Monteverdi introduced greater dramatic power and characterization to the opera form. Many of his operas were lost: the surviving ones include *Orfeo* (1607) and *The Coronation of Poppea* (1642). He is also remembered for his *Vespers* (1610).

**Montevideo** Capital of Uruguay, in the S part of the country, on the Río de la Plata. Originally a Portuguese fort (1717), it was captured by the Spanish in 1726 and became the capital of Uruguay in 1828. One of South America's major ports, it is the base of a large fishing fleet and handles most of the country's exports. Products include textiles, dairy goods, wine, and packaged meat. Pop. (1992 est.) 1,383,660.

**Montezuma** Name of two AZTEC emperors. **Montezuma I** (r.1440–69) increased the empire by conquest. **Montezuma II** (r.1502–20) allowed the Spaniards under CORTÉS to enter his capital, Tenochtitlán, unopposed, in 1519, and subsequently became their captive.

**Montgolfier, Joseph Michel** (1740–1810) and **Jacques Étienne** (1745–99) French inventors of the hot-air balloon. In 1782 the brothers experimented with paper and linen balloons filled with hot gases collected over a fire. In November 1783, the brothers launched the first balloon to carry humans.

**Montgomery, Bernard Law, 1st Viscount Montgomery of Alamein** (1887–1976) British general. As commander of the British Eighth Army in World War II, he defeated ROMMEL and the AFRIKA KORPS at EL ALAMEIN and pursued them across North Africa. He led the invasion of Sicily and Italy. He helped to plan the Normandy landings (1944), and, under the overall command of General EISENHOWER, led the Allied forces in the initial stages. He was Deputy Supreme Allied Commander, Europe (1951–58).

**Montgomery** State capital of Alabama, in SE central Alabama. Made state capital in 1847, in 1861 it became the first capital of the Confederate States of America. It subsequently grew in importance. In the 1950s it was the scene of the beginnings of the civil rights movement. Industries: textiles, fertilizers, machinery. Pop. (1990) 187,106.

**month** Time taken for the Moon to travel completely around the Earth. The sidereal month is the time of one revolution with respect to the stars and is equal to 27.32 days. Since the Earth is in motion around the Sun, the synodic month – from full moon to full moon – is longer than the sidereal month and is equal to 29.53 days.

**Montpelier** State capital of Vermont, in the N central part of the state, at the confluence of Winooski and North Branch rivers. First settled in the 1780s, it was made the state capital in 1805. Industries: tourism, machinery, granite quarrying, timber products, maple sugar and syrup, plastics. Pop. (1990) 8,247.

**Montpellier** City in S France, 6mi (10km) N of the Mediterranean coast; capital of Hérault département. Founded in the 8th century, it was a possession of the counts of Toulouse until the 13th century. In the 1960s the population grew rapidly with an influx of refugees from Algeria. Industries: textiles, metal goods, wine, printing, chemicals. Pop. (1990) 207,996.

**Montreal** City in Canada, in S Quebec province, on Montreal Island and the N bank of the St. Lawrence River; second-largest city in Canada and the country's chief port. The site was settled by the French in 1642. It remained under French control until 1760 when it was taken by the British. The city's growth accelerated with the opening of the Lachine Canal in 1825, connecting it to the Great Lakes. Montreal served as the seat of the Canadian government from 1844 to 1849. Industries: aircraft, electrical equipment, rolling-stock, textiles, oil refining, metallurgy, chemicals. Pop. (1990) 1,017,666.

**Montserrat** British dependent territory in the West Indies, a volcanic island in the Leeward Islands, in the Lesser Antilles group; the capital and chief port is Plymouth. Discovered in 1493 by Christopher COLUMBUS, it was colonized in 1632 by the British. It formed part of the Leeward Island colony from 1871 to 1956, when it became a Dependent Territory. The shipping of agricultural produce, especially cotton, is the chief economic activity. There is also light industry. Area: 40sq mi (102sq km). Pop. (1991) 11,597.

**Moon** Natural satellite of a planet; in particular the natural satellite of the planet Earth. Apart from the Sun it is the brightest object in the sky as seen from the Earth because of its proximity, being at a mean distance of only 239,000mi (384,000km). Its diameter is 2,160mi (3,476km). The Earth and Moon revolve around a common center of gravity. As the Moon orbits the Earth, it is seen to go through a sequence of PHASES as the proportion of the illuminated hemisphere visible to us changes. An observer on Earth always sees the same side of the Moon because its orbital period around the Earth is the same as its axial rotation period. The surface features may be broadly divided into the darker maria, which are low-lying volcanic plains, and the brighter highland regions (sometimes called terrae), which are found predominantly in the southern part of the Moon's near side and over the entire far side. The origin of the Moon is uncertain. A current theory is that a Mars-sized body collided with the newly formed Earth, and debris from the impact formed the Moon. The chemical composition of material brought back from the Moon has been found to consist mainly of silica, iron oxide, aluminum oxide, calcium oxide, titanium dioxide, and magnesium oxide. Lunar rocks are IGNEOUS ROCKS. The Moon has only the most tenuous of atmospheres; Apollo instruments detected traces of gases, such as helium, neon, and argon. The surface temperature variation is extreme, from 100 to 400K. In 1998 it was confirmed that there was water-ice near the Moon's poles.

**Moore, Brian** (1921– ) Canadian novelist, b. Northern Ireland. His books examine the nature of religious and sexual guilt, and the plight of the individual when transplanted from a familiar environment. Moore's novels include *The Lonely Passion of Miss Judith Hearne* (1955), *I Am Mary Dunne* (1968), *Black Robe* (1985), and *The Colour of Blood* (1987).

**Moore, Henry** (1898–1986) English sculptor and graphic

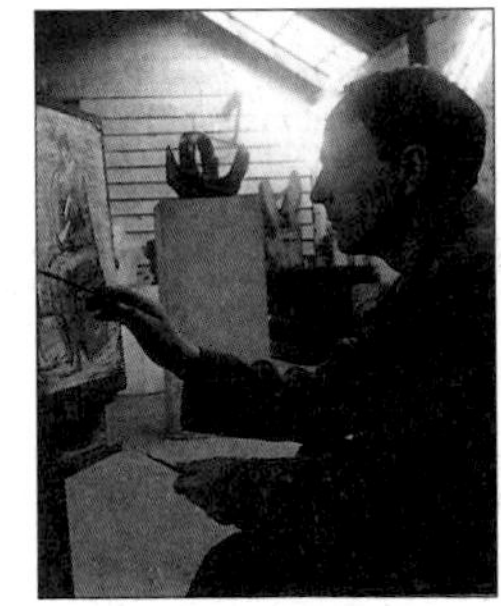

▲ **Moore** British sculptor Henry Moore was influenced more by ancient Mexican and Sumerian carving than the classical ideals of the Renaissance. He rejected academic techniques in favor of a method called "truth to materials," which allowed the shape and texture of stone or wood to be an integral part of the work.

M

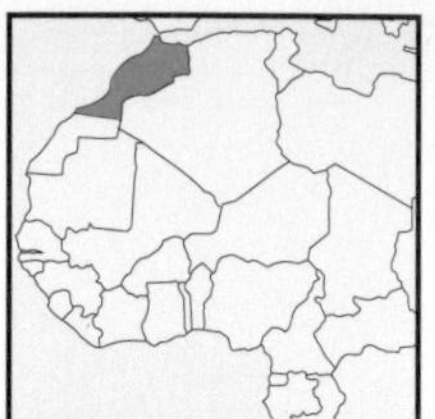

Morocco has flown a red flag since the 16th century. The green pentagram (five-pointed star), called the Seal of Solomon, was added in 1915. This design was retained when Morocco gained its independence from French and Spanish rule in 1956.

**AREA:** 172,413sq mi (446,550sq km)
**POPULATION:** 26,318,000
**CAPITAL (POPULATION):** Rabat (518,616)
**GOVERNMENT:** Constitutional monarchy
**ETHNIC GROUPS:** Arab 70%, Berber 30%
**LANGUAGES:** Arabic (official)
**RELIGIONS:** Islam 99%, Christianity 1%
**CURRENCY:** Moroccan dirham = 100 centimes

The NW African kingdom of Morocco is separated from Europe by the narrow Strait of Gibraltar. The majority of the population live on the narrow W coastal plain, which includes the capital RABAT, the largest city and port CASABLANCA, and the cities of TANGIER and AGADIR. The ATLAS mountains dominate central Morocco, and Djebel Toubkal (in the Haut Atlas) is the highest peak in North Africa, at 13,665ft (4,165m). The Rif Atlas lie in the far N. Between the Atlas mountains and the coastal plain lies a broad plateau, which includes the cities of FEZ and MARRAKECH. Southern Morocco forms part of the SAHARA, which continues into the disputed territory of WESTERN SAHARA.

## CLIMATE

The Atlantic coast of Morocco is cooled by the Canaries Current. Inland, summers are hot and dry. During the mild winters (October to April) SW winds from the Atlantic bring moderate rainfall, and snow on the Haut Atlas.

## VEGETATION

The Sahara is barren. Forests of cedar, fir, and juniper swathe the mountain slopes. The coastal plain is a fertile region.

## HISTORY

BERBERS settled in the area *c.*3,000 years ago. Jewish colonies were established under Roman rule. In *c.*AD 685 Morocco was invaded by Arab armies, who introduced Islam and Arabic. In 711 Moroccan Muslims (Moors) invaded Spain. In 788 Berbers and Arabs were united in an independent Moroccan state. Fez became a major religious and cultural center. In the mid-11th century the ALMORAVIDS conquered Morocco, and established a vast Muslim empire. They were succeeded by the ALMOHAD dynasty. In the 15th century the Moors were expelled from Spain, and Spain and Portugal made advances into Morocco. In 1660 the present ruling dynasty, the Alawite, came to power. Most of the European-held territory was reclaimed.

In the mid-19th century Morocco's strategic and economic potential began to attract European imperial interest, especially that of France and Spain. In 1912 Morocco was divided into French Morocco and the smaller protectorate of Spanish Morocco. Nationalist resistance was strong. Abd al-Krim led a revolt (1921–26) against European rule. In 1942 Allied forces invaded Morocco and removed the pro-Vichy colonial government. In 1947 the sultan, Sidi Muhammad, called for the reunification of the French and Spanish Morocco, but France refused and exiled the Sultan in 1953. Continuing civil unrest forced the French to accede to the return of the sultan in 1955.

In 1956 Morocco gained independence, although Spain retained control of two small enclaves, Ceuta and Melilla. In 1957 Morocco became an independent monarchy when Sidi Muhammad changed his title to King Muhammad V. In 1961 Muhammad was succeeded by his son, King HASSAN II. During the 1960s Morocco was faced with external territorial disputes, especially with Algeria, and internal political dissent. In 1965 Hassan II declared a state of emergency and assumed extraordinary powers. While the 1972 constitution reduced royal influence, Morocco remains only nominally a constitutional monarchy, and in effect the king wields all political power. In 1976 Spain finally relinquished its claim to Spanish Sahara, and the region became known as Western Sahara. Western Sahara was divided between Morocco and Mauritania.

In 1979 Mauritania withdrew and Morocco assumed full control of the phosphate-rich region, but met with fierce resistance from independence movements. *(See* WESTERN SAHARA for political developments)

## POLITICS

In 1993 the collapse of several coalition governments led to Hassan II's appointment of an administration. In 1994 Morocco restored diplomatic links with Israel. In 1995 Hassan II formed a new government of technocrats and members of the Entente National. In 1996 a referendum approved the establishment of a bicameral legislature, with a directly elected lower chamber. In 1997 elections a new coalition government was formed.

## ECONOMY

The postindependence exodus of Europeans and Jews from Morocco created an economic vacuum. The cost of war in Western Sahara further strained Morocco's scant resources. Morocco is a lower-middle-income, developing country (1995 GDP per capita, US$3,340). Its main resource is phosphate rock, which is used to make fertilizers. Morocco is the world's fourth largest phosphate producer, and processes 75% of the world's reserves of phosphates. The principal mines are located near Khouribga.

Agriculture employs 46% of the work force. In the mountains, most agriculture is undertaken by peasant farmers or nomadic pastoralists. The chief commercial farming areas are the Atlantic coastal plains and the inland plateaus, where farming is made possible by extensive irrigation. The main crops include barley, beans, citrus fruits, grapes, corn, olives, sugar beets, and wheat. Fishing is another important activity.

Casablanca, the chief manufacturing city and largest port, is also a thriving tourist center. Morocco, in general, is an important tourist destination; the annual number of visitors exceeds three million and contributes more than US$1.36 billion annual receipts. Tourism is centered on the Atlantic Coast resorts, the Atlas Mountains, and the historic cities of Marrakech, Fez, and Rabat.

In 1996, as part of a rapidly improving infrastructure, Morocco and Spain agreed to build a tunnel linking the two countries.

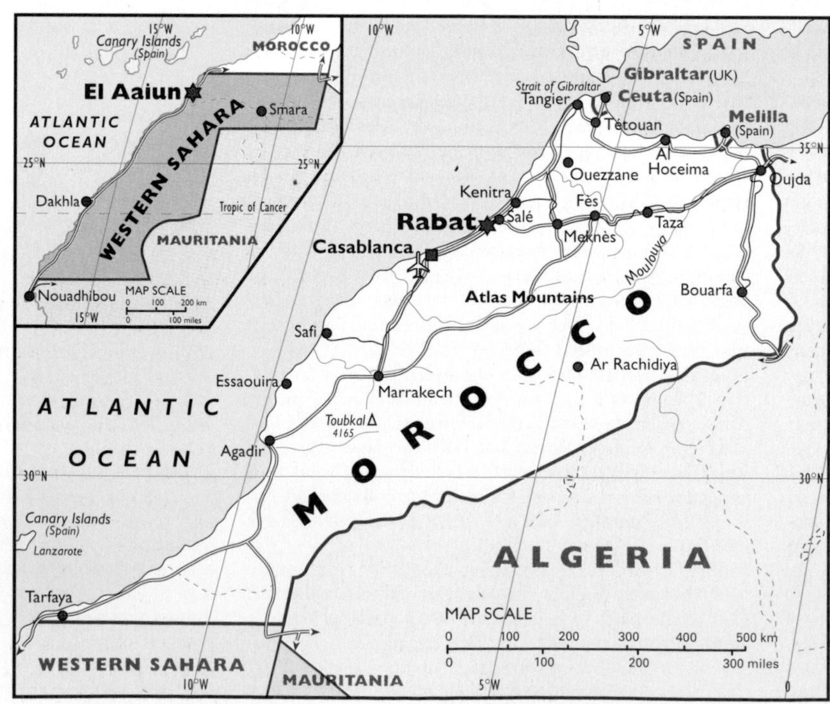

artist. Moore is acknowledged as one of the greatest sculptors of the 20th century. The most characteristic features of his art are hollowed-out or pierced spaces, such as *Reclining Figure* (1938). He based most of his work on natural forms, and one of his favourite themes was the mother and child. Many of his sculptures are placed in parks rather than galleries.

**Moore, Marianne** (1887–1972) US poet. Her poetry is considered among the most distinguished US verse of the 20th century, with its wit, irony, and wide-ranging subject matter and its highly accomplished technical discipline. *Collected Poems* (1951) was awarded a Pulitzer Prize.

**moorhen** (waterhen) Common Old World aquatic bird of the RAIL family. It has black plumage and a yellow bill, and its long toes lack the webs or lobes typical of other water birds. Length: to 13in (32.5cm). Species *Gallinula chloropus*.

**Moors** Name given to the predominantly Berber people of NW Africa. In Europe the name is applied particularly to the North African Muslims who invaded Spain in 711 and established a distinctive civilization that lasted nearly 800 years. It was at its height under the Cordoba CALIPHS in the 10th–11th centuries. The Christian rulers of N Spain gradually reconquered the country, and after the ALMOHAD empire broke up in the 13th century, Granada alone survived until it fell in 1492.

**moose** Species of DEER found in North America and N Eurasia (when it is sometimes known as the European elk). It is the largest of all deer. Height at the shoulder: to 6ft (1.9m); weight: 1,800lb (820kg). Family Cervidae; Species *Alces alces*.

**moraine** General term indicating a mound, ridge, or other visible accumulation of unsorted glacial drift, predominantly TILL. **End** moraines are formed when a GLACIER is either advancing or retreating and the rock material is dumped at the glacier's edge. **Ground** moraines are sheets of debris left after a steady retreat of the glacier.

**Moravia, Alberto** (1907–90) Italian novelist. His early novels, including *The Time of Indifference* (1929) and *The Fancy Dress Party* (1940), were critical of fascism, and he was forced into hiding until 1944. Later works include *The Woman of Rome* (1947), *The Conformist* (1951), and *Two Women* (1957).

**Moravia** Region of the CZECH REPUBLIC, bordered N by the Sudetes Mountains, E by the Carpathian Mountains, and W by Bohemia. Cities include BRNO and Ostrava. A fertile agricultural region, Moravia also has mineral resources, especially coal and iron. These helped the region's rapid industrialization in the 20th century. In the 9th century Moravia established a large empire and adopted Christianity. In the 10th century the empire fell and Moravia was first conquered by the MAGYARS, then subsumed into the HOLY ROMAN EMPIRE. From the 11th to 16th centuries it was part of the kingdom of BOHEMIA. In 1526 it became Austrian HAPSBURG territory and a process of Germanification was begun. A failed revolution in 1849 led to Moravia becoming Austrian crown land. In 1918 when the Hapsburgs were deposed, Moravia became a part of Czechoslovakia. In 1938 S Moravia was annexed by Germany, and in 1939 Moravia became a German protectorate. Following World War II, Moravia was restored to Czechoslovakia, and the German population expelled. In 1960 Moravia was divided into S Moravia and N Moravia.

**Moravian Church** Protestant church that originated in Bohemia and Moravia in the 15th century among followers of Jan HUS. In the 18th century, Moravians began extensive missionary work. Several groups migrated to North America, where they founded settlements in Bethlehem, Pennsylvania, and Winston-Salem, North Carolina. Today, there are Moravian communities in Europe, North and South America, Africa, and N India.

**More, Sir Thomas** (1478–1535) English scholar and statesman. He was a leading exponent of HUMANISM. His most famous work, *Utopia* (1516), portrays an ideal state founded on reason. More succeeded Cardinal WOLSEY as lord chancellor (1529) but, unhappy at HENRY VIII's break with the pope, resigned in 1532. He enraged the king by refusing to subscribe to the Act of Supremacy, making the king head of the English Church, and he was executed for treason.

**Morgan, Sir Henry** (1635–88) Welsh adventurer in the Caribbean. He led a band of buccaneers against Spanish colonies and ships, capturing and looting Panama (1671). In 1672 he was sent back to England charged with piracy, but was greeted as a hero and returned to the West Indies with a knighthood as lieutenant governor of Jamaica.

**Morgan, J.P. (John Pierpont)** (1837–1913) US financier. Son of a rich banker, he formed what became the influential banking house of J.P. Morgan in 1871. He built a vast financial and industrial empire, financing and consolidating US industries, including the giant US Steel Corporation (1901).

**Morgan, Thomas Hunt** (1866–1945) US biologist who was awarded the 1933 Nobel Prize for physiology or medicine for the establishment of the CHROMOSOME theory of HEREDITY. His discovery of the function of chromosomes through experiments with the fruit fly (*Drosophila*) is related in his book *The Theory of the Gene* (1926).

**Mörike, Eduard Friedrich** (1804–75) German poet. He wrote several volumes of subtle lyric poetry, including *Gedichte* (1938), a collection he added to in 1848, 1856, and 1867. It ranks among the finest examples of late German ROMANTICISM. Other works include the novel *Maler Nolten* (1832).

**Mormons** ADVENTIST sect, the full name of which is the Church of Jesus Christ of Latter-day Saints. It was established in Manchester, New York, in 1830 by Joseph SMITH. Believing that they were to found Zion, or a New Jerusalem, Smith and his followers moved west. They tried to settle in Ohio, Missouri, and Illinois, but were driven out. Joseph Smith was murdered in Illinois in 1844. Brigham YOUNG then rose to leadership and in 1846–47 took the Mormons to UTAH.

**Morocco** Country in NW Africa. *See* country feature

**Moroni** Capital of the COMOROS Islands, on SW Grande Comore. Founded by Arab settlers, it replaced Mayotte as capital in 1958. Chief exports are coffee, vanilla, cacao, and timber and metal products. Pop. (1988 est.) 22,000.

**morphine** White crystalline ALKALOID derived from OPIUM. It depresses the CENTRAL NERVOUS SYSTEM and is used as an ANALGESIC for severe pain. An addictive drug, its use is associated with a number of side-effects, including nausea. Morphine was first isolated in 1806. *See also* HEROIN

**Morricone, Ennio** (1928– ) Italian film composer. He wrote the scores for Sergio LEONE's "spaghetti westerns" *A Fistful of Dollars* (1964), *The Good, the Bad, and the Ugly* (1966), and *Once Upon a Time in the West* (1968). Other scores include *The Untouchables* (1987) and *The Mission* (1986).

**Morris, Gouverneur** (1752–1816) US political leader and diplomat. He served in the CONTINENTAL CONGRESS and, after moving to Philadelphia, represented Pennsylvania in the CONSTITUTIONAL CONVENTION (1787). He was minister to France and England (1789–94) and represented New York in the US Senate (1800–03).

**Morris, Robert** (1734–1806) US politician. He emigrated from England in 1747 and became a wealthy merchant in Philadelphia. As a member of the CONTINENTAL CONGRESS he signed the Declaration of Independence. Appointed superintendent of finance (1781–84), he regulated military purchasing and organized the first bank, the Bank of North America (1781). In 1798 he went bankrupt and was imprisoned.

**Morris, William** (1834–96) English artist, craftsman,

◀ **Morris** The Red House, Bexley Heath, near London, was designed in 1859–60 by the architect Philip Webb for (and in collaboration with) William Morris. The illustration shows the north and east of the house. It became one of the basic buildings of modern architecture. Morris and Webb created a simple brick building with echoes of traditional architecture in its high-pitched roof, Gothic arches, and Queen Anne windows. Among the house's more revolutionary features is the raising of the kitchen to the ground floor from its customary position in the basement, and the provision of windows to allow servants to overlook the gardens.

M

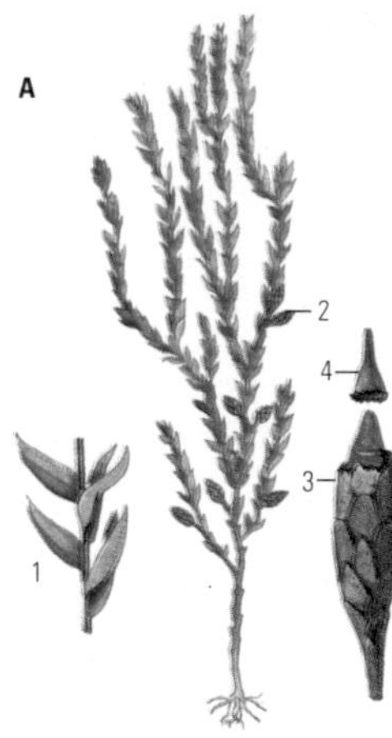


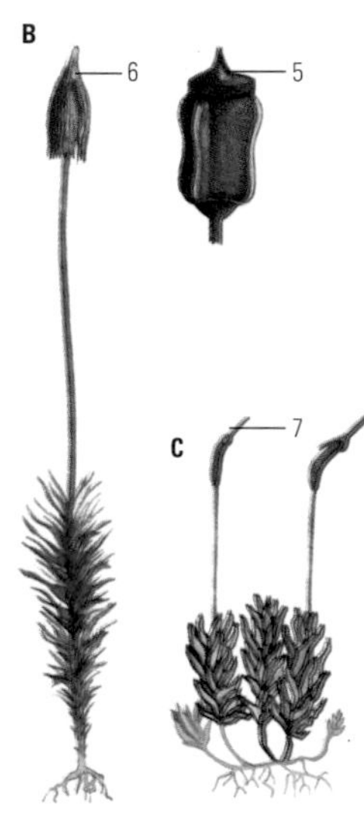

▲ **moss** Mosses vary in growth and color according to species. *Fontinalis anti pyretica* (A) is an aquatic moss, whose boat-shaped leaves have a sharp keel (1); the capsules are oblong or cylindrical (2, 3) and there is a pointed cap (4). *Polytrichum commune* (B) is extremely common and has a capsule (5) that looks like a four-sided box. It bears a long, golden brown cap (6) which is released before the spores are dispersed. *Atrichum undulatum* (C) is common on heaths and in woods, and has a capsule (7) with a long, pointed cap. *Schistostega pennata* (D), has flattened, translucent leaves.

M

writer, social reformer, and printer. Associated with the PRE-RAPHAELITE BROTHERHOOD (PRB), he founded (1861) the ARTS AND CRAFTS MOVEMENT, a collection of decorators and designers influenced by medieval craftsmanship. Morris is perhaps best remembered for his wallpaper designs, which anticipated ART NOUVEAU in their use of the S-curve. In the 1880s he became interested in socialism, writing *News from Nowhere* (1890). In 1890 Morris founded Kelmscott Press.

**Morrison, Toni** (1931– ) US writer, b. Chloe Anthony Wofford. Her first novel, *The Bluest Eye* (1970), established her as a major voice in AMERICAN LITERATURE. Her chronicles of African-American experience in the rural South include *Song of Solomon* (1977) and *Tar Baby* (1981). *Beloved* (1987), a powerful indictment of slavery, won a Pulitzer Prize. Other works include *Jazz* (1992). Morrison was awarded the 1993 Nobel Prize for Literature.

**Morse, Samuel Finley Breese** (1791–1872) US inventor of the **Morse code**. A successful artist, he became interested in developing a practical electric TELEGRAPH *c.*1832. His receiver was based on an electromagnet. Using a simple system of dots and dashes, now known as the Morse code, he set up the first US telegraph from Washington to Baltimore in 1844.

**Morton, "Jelly Roll"** (1885–1941) US jazz pianist, bandleader, and composer, b. Ferdinand Joseph La Menthe. Morton played in the brothels of Storyville in New Orleans, before making some of the first jazz recordings (1923). Morton and his band, the Red Hot Peppers, combined blues, ragtime, and "stomp" music on classics such as *Wolverine Blues* (1923).

**mosaic** Technique of surface decoration using small pieces of colored material set tightly together in an adhesive to form patterns or pictures. The technique was employed for floor and wall decorations in ancient Mesopotamia and Greece. Roman mosaics commonly featured a central design or a portrait, surrounded by a decorative geometric border. The art developed rapidly in early Christian times especially during the 4th–6th centuries and continues to be used for floors, church interiors, and wall decorations.

**Moscow** (Moskva) Capital of Russia and largest city in Europe, on the Moskva River. The site has been inhabited since Neolithic times, but Russian records do not mention it until 1147. It had become a principality by the end of the 13th century, and in 1367 the first stone walls of the KREMLIN were constructed. By the end of the 14th century the city had emerged as the focus of Russian opposition to the Mongols. Polish troops occupied the city in 1610, but were driven out two years later. Moscow was the capital of the Grand Duchy of Russia from 1547 to 1712, when the capital was moved to ST. PETERSBURG. In 1812 Napoleon and his army occupied Moscow but were forced to flee when the city burned to the ground. In 1918, following the Bolshevik Revolution, it became the capital of the SOVIET UNION. The failure of the German army to seize the city in 1941 was the Nazis' first major setback in World War II. The KREMLIN is the center of the city and the administrative heart of the country. Adjoining it are Red Square, the Lenin Mausoleum, and the 16th-century cathedral of Basil the Beatified. Industries: metalworking, oil-refining, motor vehicles, filmmaking, precision instruments, chemicals, publishing, wood and paper products, tourism. Pop. (1993) 8,881,000.

**Moscow, Grand Duchy of** Historic Russian state. Centered on the trading center of MOSCOW, it emerged from Mongol and Tatar rule in the late 15th century as the center of a unified Russian state, defeating the principality of NOVGOROD and absorbing part of Lithuania.

**Moscow Art Theater** Russian theater, famous for its contribution to naturalistic theater. It was founded in 1898 by STANISLAVSKY and Nemirovich-Danchenko. The original company was composed of amateur actors from the Society of Art and Literature who were committed to adopting a more rigorous, serious, and professional approach to staging as well as acting. It was at the Moscow Art Theater that Stanislavsky developed his influential method principle.

**Moses** (active *c.*13th century BC) Biblical hero who as a prophet and leader of the ancient Hebrew people was the central figure in their liberation from bondage in Egypt and a formative influence in the founding of their nation-state, Israel. His story is recounted in the Old Testament books of Exodus and Numbers. He was an abandoned Hebrew child brought up in the pharaoh's court. As a man, Moses sought to lead the Hebrews out of Egypt, and eventually was permitted to lead the EXODUS. God revealed himself to Moses on Mount Sinai, but made the Israelites wander in the desert for a further 40 years before they entered the promised land of CANAAN.

**Moses, Grandma (Anna Mary Robertson)** (1860–1961) US primitive painter. She only began painting when she was in her late seventies. Her scenes of country life, based on recollections from her youth, became world-famous through prints and greeting cards. Well-known examples are *Out for the Christmas Trees* and *Thanksgiving Turkey*.

**Moslem** *See* MUSLIM

**Mosley, Sir Oswald Ernald** (1896–1980) British fascist. In 1931 he formed the leftist New Party but in 1932 swung to the right and founded the virulently anti-Semitic British Union of Fascists, modeled on German and Italian FASCISM. His outspoken support for HITLER led to his internment during World War 2. Following the defeat of Nazi Germany in World War 2, Mosley's pernicious influence declined.

**mosque** Islamic place of worship. Mosques are usually decorated with abstract and geometric designs, because ISLAM prohibits the imitation of God's creation. The building's parts include a DOME, a *mihrab* (prayer niche), which shows the direction of MECCA; a MINARET, from which the MUEZZIN calls the faithful to prayer; and a *sahn* (courtyard) often with a central fountain for ritual ablution. The complex often includes a *madressa* (school). *See also* ISLAMIC ART AND ARCHITECTURE

**mosquito** Long-legged, slender-winged insect, found throughout the world. The female sucks blood from warm-blooded animals. Some species carry the parasites of diseases, including MALARIA, YELLOW FEVER, DENGUE, viral ENCEPHALITIS, and FILARIASIS. The larvae are aquatic. Adult length: 0.12– 0.36in (3–9mm) Family Culicidae.

**Mosquito Coast** (Mosquitia) Coastal region bordering on the Caribbean Sea, *c.*40mi (65km) wide, now divided between Nicaragua and Honduras. A British protectorate from 1740, it was returned to its original inhabitants (the Miskito) in 1860. In 1894 it became part of Nicaragua. International arbitration awarded the N part to Honduras in 1960. The region, which consists mainly of tropical forest, swamp, and lagoons, is only thinly populated.

**moss** Any of *c.*14,000 species of small, simple non-flowering green plants that typically grow in colonies, often forming dense carpets. They do not have specialized tissues for transporting water, food, and minerals, although they do have parts resembling the stems, leaves, and roots of the higher (flowering) plants. They reproduce by means of SPORES produced in a capsule on a long stalk. The spores germinate into branching filaments, from which buds arise that grow into moss plants. Mosses grow on soil, rocks, and tree trunks in a wide variety of habitats, especially in shady damp places. *See also* ALTERNATION OF GENERATIONS; BRYOPHYTE

**Mossi** People inhabiting Burkina Faso and who are found in

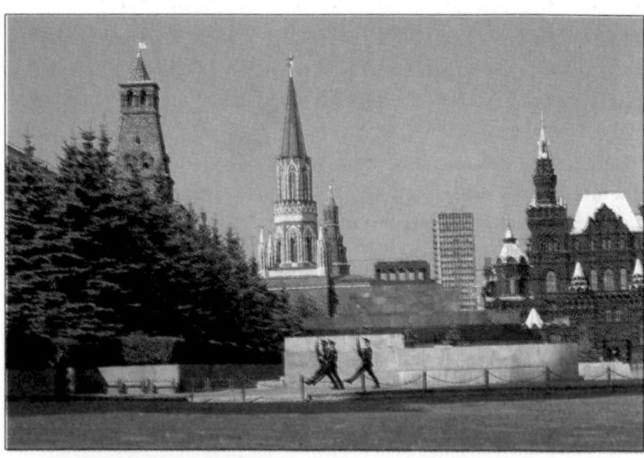

▲ **Moscow** The Lenin Mausoleum is situated on the W side of Red Square, Moscow. Now the largest city in Europe, Moscow is attracting greater foreign business interests and tourists since many economic and social restrictions were lifted.

small numbers elsewhere in West Africa. Their traditional livelihood involves growing staple crops, including millet and sorghum.

**motet** Musical form prominent in all choral church music from *c.*1200 to 1600. In the 13th and 14th centuries it consisted of three unaccompanied voice parts. The Renaissance motet of the 15th century, usually in four or five parts, was contrapuntal in style. PALESTRINA composed some of the purest examples of the form. After 1600 there were new developments in the form, including occasional instrumental parts and texts in vernacular languages.

**moth** Insect of the order LEPIDOPTERA, found in almost all parts of the world. It is distinguished from a BUTTERFLY mainly by its nonclubbed antennae, although there are a few exceptions. Most moths are nocturnal. Like a butterfly, a moth undergoes METAMORPHOSIS. It has a long, coiled proboscis for sipping liquid food, particularly the nectar of flowers.

**Motherwell, Robert** (1915–91) US painter and writer. He was a pioneer of ABSTRACT EXPRESSIONISM. Perhaps his best-known work is the series *Elegies to the Spanish Republic*. He was the editor of the influential *The Documents of Modern Art* series (1944–57).

**motor** Mechanism that converts energy (such as heat or electricity) into useful work. The term is sometimes applied to the internal combustion ENGINE but is more often applied to the ELECTRIC MOTOR. ROCKET engines are motors that can leave the Earth's atmosphere because they carry both fuel and oxidizer. Ion motors are in development, intended for spacecraft propulsion: a stream of ions, possibly from a nuclear reactor, is accelerated in a strong electrostatic field to produce a reaction that drives the spacecraft.

**motorcycle** Powered vehicle, usually with two wheels. The German Gottlieb DAIMLER is credited with building the first practical motorcycle (1885). Motorcycles are classified in terms of engine capacity, usually 50cc to 1200cc. Transmission of power to the rear wheel is by chain, shaft, or belt. The clutch, accelerator, and front brake controls are on the handlebars. Foot pedals control the gear change and rear brake.

**motorcycle racing** Sport in which motorcyclists compete on road circuits, cross country (scrambling and trials), on grass tracks, and on cinder tracks (speedway). The first organized race took place in France in 1906, from Paris to Nantes. The world championship started in 1949. The championship is organized by engine capacity: the 500cc is the premier title.

**motor nerve** NERVE carrying messages to the muscles from the BRAIN via the SPINAL CORD. The cell bodies of some motor NERVES form part of the spinal cord. Motor nerves are involved in both reflex action and voluntary muscular control.

**Motown** Highly successful record company, whose artists made a major contribution to popular music of the 1960s. Founded in Detroit in 1959 by Berry Gordy, Jr., the company had artists including Smokey Robinson, Marvin GAYE, and Stevie WONDER on its books during its long and influential life. Berry sold Motown to the MCA company in 1988.

**Mott, Lucretia Coffin** (1793–1880) US social reformer. An outspoken opponent of slavery, she was one of the founders of the American Anti-Slavery Society (1833). She turned some of her attention to feminism after she was refused a seat as delegate to the World's Anti-Slavery Convention in London (1840). With Elizabeth Cady STANTON, she organized the first women's rights convention at Seneca Falls, New York (1848).

**mound builders** Name given to the Native North Americans responsible for groups of ancient earth mounds found in the Ohio and Mississippi river valleys. The mounds contain skeletons or ashes with buried ceremonial objects. Some are simple shapes, others more intricate representing birds or snakes. The largest, the Cahokia Mound in Illinois, is *c.*1,000ft (300m) long and 100ft (30m) high.

**mountain** Part of the Earth's surface that rises steeply to at least 2,000ft (610m). They are identified geologically by their most characteristic features, and are classified as FOLD, volcanic, or fault-block mountains. Mountains may occur as single isolated masses, as ranges, or in systems or chains.

**mountaineering** Sport and leisure activity of climbing mountains that gained popularity in Europe in the 18th and 19th centuries. The MATTERHORN was first scaled in 1865. In 1953 the world's highest mountain, EVEREST, was climbed by Edmund HILLARY and Tenzing Norgay. By the mid-1990s Everest had been scaled by thousands of people – although the mountain continued to claim an average of three lives per year.

**mountain lion** *See* PUMA

**Mountbatten, Louis, 1st Earl Mountbatten of Burma** (1900–79) British admiral, great-grandson of Queen Victoria, uncle of Prince Philip. During World War II, Mountbatten directed (1942–43) commando raids upon Norway and France. In 1943 he was appointed Allied commander-in-chief in SE Asia, and led operations against the Japanese in Burma. He accepted the Japanese surrender. Mountbatten was the last viceroy (1947–48) of British India, overseeing the transition to independence. He was murdered by an IRA bomb.

**mouse** Any of numerous species of small, common RODENTS found in a variety of habitats throughout the world; especially the omnivorous, brown-gray house mouse (*Mus musculus*) of the family Muridae. This prolific nest builder, often associated with human habitation, is considered a destructive pest and is believed to carry disease-producing organisms. It may grow as long as 8in (20cm) overall, and has been bred for use in laboratories and as a pet. Many species within the family Cricetidae are also called mice, as are pocket mice (Heteromydiae), jumping mice (Zapodidae), and marsupial mice (Dasyuridae).

**mouth** In animals, the anterior (front) end of the ALIMENTARY CANAL, where it opens to the outside. In humans and other higher animals, it is the cavity within the jaws, containing the teeth and tongue.

**Moynihan, Daniel Patrick** (1927– ) US social scientist and public official. He was active in the administrations of Kennedy, Johnson, and Nixon and has been a Democratic senator from New York since 1977. His best-known books include *Beyond the Melting Pot* (1963) and *Counting Our Blessings* (1980).

**Mozambique** Republic in SE Africa. *See* country feature, page 462

**Mozart, Wolfgang Amadeus** (1756–91) Austrian composer. A child prodigy on the piano, Mozart was taken by his father, Leopold, on performing tours in Europe (1762–65), during which he composed his first symphonies. In the 1770s he worked at the prince archbishop's court in Salzburg. Masses, symphonies and his first major piano concerto date from this time. Opera was his primary concern, and in 1780 he composed *Idomeneo*, which is impressive for its rich orchestral writing and depth of expression. In the 1780s he moved to Vienna, where he was to spend most of the rest of his life, becoming court composer to the Austrian emperor in 1787. In this decade, he composed and performed his greatest piano concertos, the last eight of his 41 symphonies and the brilliant comic operas *Le Nozze di Figaro* (1786), *Don Giovanni* (1787) and *Così fan tutti* (1790). In the last year of his life, Mozart wrote the operas *Die Zauberflöte* and *La Clemenza di Tito*, the clarinet concerto and the *Requiem* (completed by a pupil). In all, he composed more than 600 works, perfecting the CLASSICAL style and foreshadowing ROMANTICISM.

**Muckrakers** Name given to US journalists and other writers who exposed corruption in politics and business in the early 20th century. The term was first used by Theodore ROOSEVELT in 1906.

**mucous membrane** Sheet of TISSUE (or EPITHELIUM) lining all body channels that communicate with the air, such as the mouth and respiratory tract, the digestive and urogenital tracts, and the various glands that secrete mucus, which lubricates and protects tissues.

**muezzin** Person who calls MUSLIMS to prayer. In small MOSQUES, the call is given by the IMAM. In larger ones, a muezzin is specially appointed for that purpose.

**Mugabe, Robert Gabriel** (1925– ) Zimbabwean statesman, prime minister (1980– ), president (1987– ). In 1961 he became deputy secretary-general of Joshua NKOMO's Zimbabwe African People's Union (ZAPU). In 1963 Mugabe was forced into exile and co-founded the Zimbabwe African National Union (ZANU). He was imprisoned by Ian SMITH's white minority Rhodesian regime, and spent the next decade

▲ **moth** The male Madagascan moon moth (*Argema mittrei*) has a wingspan of 4in (10cm). It has feather antennae that are able to detect the scent given off by a female when she is ready to mate. The pheremone scent can be detected many miles away.

▲ **mouse** The house mouse (*Mus musculus*) is found throughout the world. Due to its close association with people, the house mouse can .be a transmitter of diseases. On average it has a body length of up to 4in (10cm) and a similar length tail.

(1964–74) in detention. In 1976 ZAPU and ZANU merged to form the Patriotic Front, which became the first black majority government. During the 1980s Mugabe shifted away from communism. He succeeded Canaan Banana as president. Mugabe won Zimbabwe's first multi-party elections (1990). He was a leading opponent of APARTHEID.

**mugwumps** US political faction. A group of independent, or liberal, Republicans, they deserted their party's candidate, James G. Blaine, in the 1884 presidential election. They considered him corrupt, and supported the Democratic candidate, Grover CLEVELAND, who won.

**Muhammad** (*c*.570–632) Arab prophet and inspirational religious leader who founded ISLAM. He was born in the Arabian city of MECCA. He was orphaned at the age of six and went to live first with his grandfather and then with his uncle. At the age of 25, he began working as a trading agent for Khadijah, a wealthy widow of 40, whom he married. For 25 years, she was his closest companion and gave birth to several children. Only one brought him descendants – his daughter FATIMA, who became the wife of his cousin ALI. In *c*.610, Muhammad had a vision while meditating alone in a cave on Mount Hira, outside Mecca. A voice three times commanded him to "recite," and he felt his body compressed until he could hardly breathe. Then he heard the words of the first of many revelations that came to him in several similar visions over the next two decades. The revelations came from Allah, or God, and Muhammad's followers believe that they were passed to Muhammad through the angel GABRIEL. At the core of his new religion was the doctrine that there is no God but Allah and His followers must submit to Him – the word *islam* means "submission." Muhammad gained followers but also many enemies among the Meccans. In 622 he fled to MEDINA. Muslims, the followers of Islam, later took this HEGIRA as initiating the first year in their calendar. Thereafter, Muhammad won more followers. He organized rules for the proper worship of Allah and for Islamic society. He also made war against his enemies. He conquered Mecca in 630. Most of the Arab tribes allied with him. In Medina, he married the woman who became his favorite wife, Aishah, the daughter of ABU BAKR, one of his strongest supporters. Muhammad is considered an ideal man, but he never claimed supernatural powers, and he is not held to be divine. His tomb is in the Holy Mosque of the Prophet, in Medina.

**Muhammad, Elijah** (1897–1975) Leader of the BLACK MUSLIMS (1934–75), b. Elijah Poole. He became leader in

## MOZAMBIQUE

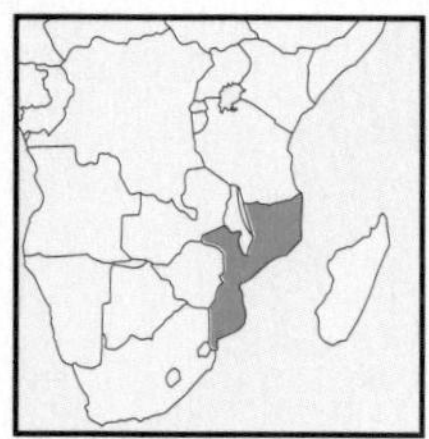

Mozambique's flag was adopted when the country became independent from Portugal in 1975. The green stripe represents fertile land, the black stands for Africa and the yellow for mineral wealth. The badge on the red triangle contains a rifle, a hoe, a cogwheel, and a book.

**AREA:** 309,494sq mi (801,590sq km)
**POPULATION:** 14,872,000
**CAPITAL (POPULATION):** Maputo (2,000,000)
**GOVERNMENT:** Multiparty republic
**ETHNIC GROUPS:** Makua 47%, Tsonga 23%, Malawi 12%, Shona 11%, Yao 4%, Swahili 1%, Makonde 1%
**LANGUAGES:** Portuguese (official)
**RELIGIONS:** Traditional beliefs 48%, Christianity (Roman Catholic 31%, others 9%), Islam 13%
**CURRENCY:** Metical = 100 centavos

The SE African republic of Mozambique faces the Indian Ocean. The coastline is dotted with the mouths of many rivers, including the LIMPOPO and the ZAMBEZI. The coast is fringed by swamps and offshore coral reefs. The only natural harbor is the capital, MAPUTO. The coastal plains make up 50% of Mozambique's land area. To the N of the Zambezi, the plain is narrow, while to the S it is much broader. Inland, a savanna plateau rises to highlands at the frontiers with Zimbabwe, Zambia, Malawi, and Tanzania.

### Climate

Mozambique has a tropical climate. The warm, south-flowing Mozambique Current gives Maputo hot and humid summers, though winters are mild and fairly dry.

### Vegetation

Tropical savanna is the most widespread vegetation. Palm trees are found along the coast, and there are rain forests of ebony and ironwood.

### History and Politics

Bantu-speakers arrived in the first century AD. Arab traders in gold and ivory settled in coastal regions from the 10th century AD. Vasco da GAMA was the first European to discover Mozambique, in 1498, and in 1505 Portugal established its first settlement. During the 16th century Portuguese adventurers built huge, semi-autonomous plantations. In the 18th and 19th centuries, Mozambique was a major center of the slave trade. In 1910 Mozambique formally became a Portuguese colony. Nationalist opposition increased with unfair land rights, forced labor, and social inequity. In 1961 the Front for the Liberation of Mozambique (FRELIMO) was founded to oppose Portuguese rule. In 1964 FRELIMO launched a guerrilla war. In 1975 Mozambique gained independence, and Samora Machel became president. Many Europeans fled the country, taking vital capital and resources. The new FRELIMO government established a one-party Marxist state. FRELIMO's assistance to liberation movements in Rhodesia (now Zimbabwe) and South Africa was countered by these white-minority regimes' support of the Mozambique National Resistance Movement (RENAMO) opposition. Civil war raged for 16 years, claiming tens of thousands of lives. In 1986 Samora Machel died and was succeeded by Joachim Chissano. In 1989 FRELIMO dropped its communist policies and agreed to end one-party rule. In 1992, faced with severe drought and famine, a peace agreement was signed between FRELIMO and RENAMO. In 1994 Chissano was elected president. In 1995 Mozambique became the 53rd member of the Commonwealth of Nations.

### Economy

Mozambique is one of the world's poorest countries (1995 GDP per capita, US$810). Agriculture employs 85% of the workforce, mainly at subsistence level. Crops include cassava, cotton, cashew nuts, fruits, corn, rice, sugarcane, and tea. Fishing is also important. Shrimps, sugar, and copra are exported. Despite its large hydroelectric plant at Cahora Bassa dam on the Zambezi River, manufacturing is on a comparatively small scale. Electricity is exported to South Africa.

1934, following the disappearance of the movement's founder, Wallace D. Fard. During World War II he was imprisoned for encouraging draft-dodging. The rhetorical skills of MALCOLM X gained the movement national attention, and tensions grew until Malcolm was suspended from the movement. Under Muhammad's leadership, the Muslim doctrines were codified and membership increased.

**Muhammad II** (1429–81) Ottoman sultan (1451–81), considered to be the true founder of the OTTOMAN EMPIRE. He captured Constantinople (1453) and made it the capital of the Ottoman empire.

**Muhammad Ali** (1769–1849) Albanian soldier who founded an Egyptian dynasty. In 1798 he took part in an OTTOMAN expeditionary force sent to Egypt to drive out the French. He was unsuccessful, but after the departure of the French quickly rose to power. In 1805 he was proclaimed the Ottoman sultan's viceroy. In 1811 he defeated the MAMELUKES, who had ruled Egypt since the 13th century. He put down a rebellion in Greece in 1821 but his fleet was later destroyed by the European powers at the Battle of NAVARINO in 1827. Muhammad challenged the sultan and began the conquest of Syria in 1831. The European powers again intervened and he was compelled to withdraw.

**Muhammad Ali** *See* ALI, MUHAMMAD

**Muhammad Reza Pahlavi** *See* PAHLAVI, MUHAMMAD REZA

**Mujaheddin** Muslim militants dedicated to waging a holy war. The term is most used of the guerrilla fighters of Iran in the 1970s–80s, and of Afghanistan in the 1980s–90s.

**mulberry** Any member of the genus *Morus*, trees and shrubs that grow in tropical and temperate regions. They have simple leaves, and the male flowers are catkins, while the female flowers are borne in spikes. Several species are cultivated for their fleshy, edible fruits.

**mule** HYBRID offspring of a female HORSE and a male ASS; it is different from the smaller hinny, which is the result of a cross between a male horse and a female ass. Brown or gray, it has a uniform coat and a body similar to a horse, but has the long ears, heavy head, and thin limbs of an ass. Known since ancient times, the hardy mule is commonly used as a draft or pack animal. It is usually sterile. Height: 5.8ft (1.8m).

**mule deer** Game animal that inhabits the w US from Alaska to Mexico. It is red-brown with a black-tipped white tail; the male bears antlers. It is generally solitary, but often gathers in herds in winter. Height: to 3.5ft (1.1m) at the shoulder. Family Cervidae; species *Odocoileus hemionus*.

**mulla** Muslim cleric well-versed in the Sharia (Islamic law). There are no formal qualifications for a man to become a mulla, but he will usually have attended a *madressa* (religious school).

**Muller, Hermann Joseph** (1890–1967) US geneticist. He found that he could artificially increase the rate of mutations in the fruit fly (Drosophila) by the use of X-rays. He thus highlighted the human risk in exposure to radioactive material. He was awarded he 1946 Nobel Prize for physiology or medicine.

**mullet** (gray mullet) Marine food fish found in shoals in shallow tropical and temperate waters throughout the world. Its torpedo-shaped body is green or blue and silver. Size: to about 3ft (90cm); weight: 15lb (6.8kg). Family Mugilidae.

**Mulroney, Brian** (1939– ) Canadian statesman, prime minister (1984–93). In 1983 Mulroney became an MP and leader of the Progressive Conservative Party. In his first term, he signed the Meech Lake Accord (1985), which constitutionally made Quebec a "distinct society." In 1987 he negotiated a free trade treaty with the US, which led to the 1992 NORTH AMERICAN FREE TRADE AGREEMENT (NAFTA). The status of Quebec contined to vex his administration and, following defeat in a national referendum, Mulroney resigned. He was succeeded as prime minister and party leader by Kim Campbell.

**multiple sclerosis (MS)** Incurable disorder of unknown cause in which there is degeneration of the myelin sheath that surrounds nerves in the brain and spinal cord. Striking mostly young adults (more women than men), it is mainly a disease of the world's temperate zones. Symptoms may include unsteadiness, loss of coordination, and speech and visual disturbances. Affected people typically have relapses and remissions over many years.

**Mumbai** (Bombay) Largest city in India, situated on an island off the w coast; capital of Maharashtra state. In 1534 it was ceded to the Portuguese. In 1661 the British gained control of Bombay as part of Catherine of Braganza's dowry to Charles II. It was the headquarters of the British EAST INDIA COMPANY until 1858. Bombay's "Gateway to India" was the first sight many colonists had of India. Bombay has the largest population of PARSIS in India. The city has some fine Victorian public architecture. Bombay is a cultural, educational, trade, and financial centre, and the site of the world's largest film industry. It is India's second-largest port (after CALCUTTA). The city is home to the University of Bombay (1857) and the Indian Institute of Technology (1958). Industries: chemicals, textiles, oil refining, motor vehicles. Pop. (1991) 9,925,891.

**Mumford, Lewis** (1895–1990) US writer and critic, best known for his essays on town planning and architecture, which include *The City in History* (1961) and *Roots of Contemporary Architecture* (1972). He also published works on a variety of subjects, including *Herman Melville* (1929) and *Renewal of Life* (1934, 1938, 1944, 1951).

**mummy** Human body embalmed and usually wrapped in bandages before burial. The practice was common in ancient Egypt, where religion decreed that the dead would require the use of their bodies in the afterlife. Certain other peoples, including the Incas of South America, had similar practices.

**mumps** Viral disease, most common in children, characterized by fever, pain, and swelling of one or both parotid salivary glands (located just in front of the ears). The symptoms are more serious in adults, and in men inflammation of the testes (orchitis) may occur, with the risk of sterility. Children over 18 months of age can be vaccinated against the disease. One attack of mumps generally confers lifelong immunity.

**Munch, Edvard** (1863–1944) Norwegian painter and printmaker. He was one of the most influential of modern artists, inspiring EXPRESSIONISM. His tortured, isolated figures and violent coloring caused a scandal when he exhibited his work in Berlin in 1892, but his paintings inspired progressive artists to form the SEZESSION. He compiled a series of studies of love and death entitled a *Frieze of Life*, which included *The Scream* (1893). Other important works are *Ashes* (1894) and *Virginia Creeper* (1898).

**Munich** (München) City in s Germany, on the Isar River; capital of BAVARIA. Founded in 1158, the city became the residence of the dukes of Bavaria in 1255. Occupied by the Swedes in 1632 and the French in 1800, Munich developed rapidly in the 19th century, when its population grew to more than 100,000. From the early 1920s Munich was the center of the Nazi Party. It sustained heavy bombing damage in World War II. Industries: chemicals, brewing, pharmaceuticals, motor vehicles, tobacco, tourism. Pop. (1990) 1,241,300.

**Munich Agreement** Pact agreed in September 1938 by Britain, France, Italy, and Germany to settle German claims

▲ **mule** Traditionally common in regions where there is low mechanization, mules have been used as pack animals for many thousands of years. They need very little food, though they are strong and can endure hard conditions. Normally they cannot breed, but occasionally a female will produce a foal; the male is always sterile.

M

◄ **Munch** *Girls on the Bridge* (1901). Norwegian painter Edvard Munch is famous for his portrayals of mental anguish, which expressed a deep sense of disillusionment with contemporary life. In 1908 Munch suffered a severe mental breakdown; his gradual recovery is reflected in the more optimistic tone of his later work.

on Czechoslovakia. Hoping to preserve European peace, Britain and France compelled Czechoslovakia, not represented at Munich, to surrender the predominantly German-speaking SUDETENLAND to Nazi Germany on certain conditions. HITLER ignored the conditions and six months later his troops took over the rest of the country, an action that finally ended the Anglo-French policy of APPEASEMENT.

**Munich Putsch** (Beer hall Putsch) Attempted coup in 1923 by Adolf HITLER and the Nazi Party to overthrow the republican government of Bavaria, which began in a beer hall. The coup proved abortive and Hitler was arrested and sentenced to five years in the Landsberg fortress, of which he served only nine months.

**Munro, H.H. (Hector Hugh)** *See* SAKI

**muntjac** Small primitive form of Asian DEER. It is brown with cream markings and has tusklike canine teeth and short, two-pronged antlers. There are two well-known species, the Indian muntjac or barking deer (*Muntiacus muntjak*) and the Chinese muntjac *(M. reevesi)*. Height: to 24in (60cm) at the shoulder; weight: to 40lb (18kg). Family Cervidae.

**mural** Painting or other design medium applied directly to a wall; a FRESCO is a type of mural. The Egyptians, Greeks, and Romans produced murals in TEMPERA as well as fresco. In the Renaissance, mural painting was allied with architecture in efforts to create illusions of space. The 20th century has accorded more significance to the exterior mural as exemplified by the works of the Mexicans José Clemente OROZCO and Diego RIVERA. Porcelain and liquid silicate enamels are among the media used in modern murals.

**Murasaki, Shikibu** (978–1014) Japanese diarist and novelist. She is best known for her novel *The Tale of Genji*, which she is thought to have written *c.*1000. It is one of the first works of fiction written in Japanese.

**Murcia** Autonomous region in SE Spain; the capital is Murcia. It was settled in *c.*225 BC by the Carthaginians, who founded the port of Cartagena and the city of Murcia. The Moors captured the region in the 8th century. In the 11th century Murcia became an independent kingdom, but in the 13th century it fell under the control of Castile. Murcia is an arid, rugged province with desert vegetation. Historically, the region has been associated with the production of silk, concentrated around the city of Murcia. Area: 4,368sq mi (11,317sq km). Pop. (1991) 1,045,601.

**murder** Unlawful killing of a person, performed with malice or forethought. Committed accidentally, under sufficient provocation, or in self-defense, a killing may not constitute murder. *See also* MANSLAUGHTER

**Murdoch, Dame (Jean) Iris** (1919–99) British novelist and moral philosopher, b. Ireland. She created her own genre, the philosophical love story. Murdoch's early novels, culminating in *The Bell* (1958), are short and concise. Her later novels, such as *The Black Prince* (1973), the Booker Prize-winning *The Sea, the Sea* (1978), *The Good Apprentice* (1985), and *The Book and the Brotherhood* (1987), are longer and more elaborate. Recurrent themes include the difference between sacred and profane love, and the nature of chance.

**Murdoch, (Keith) Rupert** (1931– ) US media tycoon, b. Australia. In 1952 he assumed control of his late father's newspaper, *The Adelaide News*. Murdoch transferred his successful recipe of sensationalist journalism to British tabloid newspapers. In 1973 he moved into the US newspaper market, acquiring the *Boston Herald* and *The Star*. In Britain, he bought *The Times* and the *Sunday Times*. In 1985 Murdoch became a US citizen. He began to diversify into other media industries, acquiring 50% of 20th Century Fox. In 1989 Murdoch launched his own satellite television network, Sky Television. He was also involved in the development of digital, cable television.

**Murillo, Bartolomé Estebán** (1617–82) Spanish painter. He made his name with a series of 11 pictures showing the lives of the Franciscan saints (1645–46). His mature style is characterized by soft, idealized figures.

**Murray** Longest river in Australia. It flows 1,610mi (2,590km) from the Australian Alps in SE New South Wales through Lake Alexandrina, and empties into the Indian Ocean at Encounter Bay, SE of Adelaide. It forms a large part of the border between New South Wales and Victoria. Its main tributary is the Darling. The Murray valley contains almost all the irrigated land in Australia.

**Murrow, Ed (Edward Roscoe)** (1908–65) US journalist. He joined the Columbia Broadcasting System (CBS) in 1935 and during World War II gained fame for his vivid descriptions of the Battle of Britain. After the war he became a CBS vice president and then a news analyst. Murrow also produced many programs for television, including the popular *See It Now* and *Person to Person*. He was director of the US Information Agency (1961–64).

**Muscat** (Masqat, Maskat) Capital of Oman, on the Gulf of Oman, in the SE Arabian Peninsula. The city was held by the Portuguese from 1508–1650, when it passed to Persia. After 1741 it became capital of Oman. In the 20th century its rulers developed treaty relations with Britain. Industries: fish and dates, natural gas, chemicals. Pop. (1990 est.) 380,000.

**muscle** Tissue that has the ability to contract, enabling movement. There are three basic types: SKELETAL MUSCLE, smooth muscle, and cardiac muscle. Skeletal muscle, or striped muscle, is the largest tissue component of the human body, comprising about 40% by weight. It is attached by TENDONS to the BONES of the SKELETON and is characterized by cross-markings known as striations. Smooth muscle lines the digestive tract, blood vessels, and many other organs. It is not striated. Cardiac muscle is found only in the heart and differs

**MUSCLE**

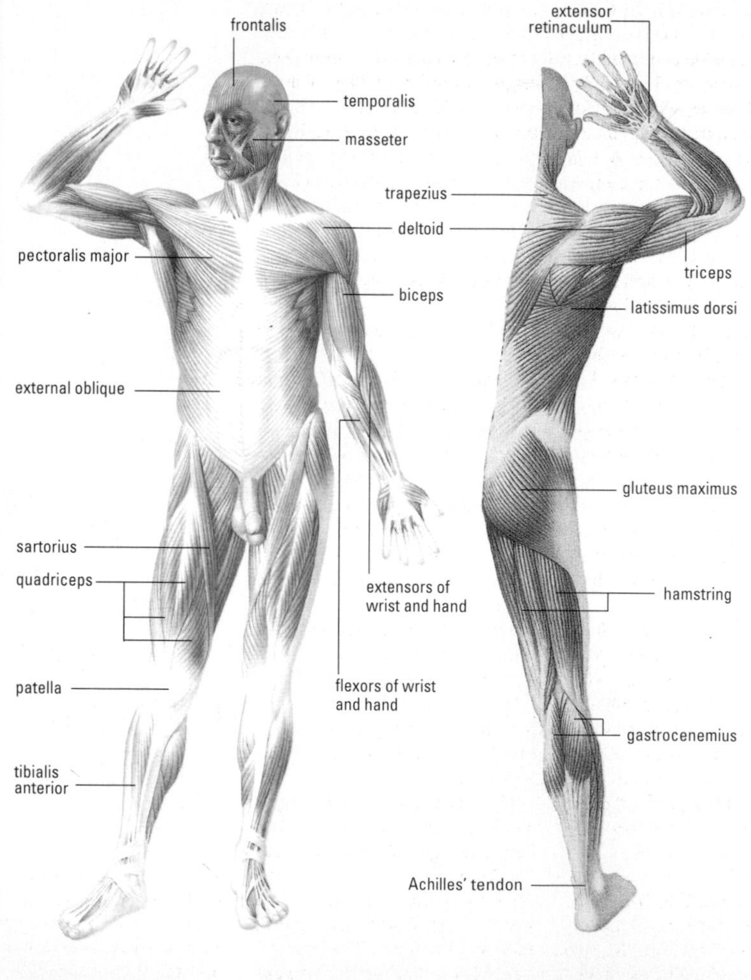

Muscles are contractile tissue, which can initiate or maintain movement in the body. Muscles comprise 35–40% of the total body weight and there are over 650 human skeletal muscles (some of those directly under the skin are shown) controlled by the nervous system. Skeletal muscles may be massive, like the gluteus maximus in the buttock, or minute, like the stapedius muscle inside the middle ear. Most skeletal muscles join one bone to another, and have their "origin" on one immobile bone, and their "insertion" on the more mobile bone.

from the other types of muscle in that it beats rhythmically and does not need stimulation by a nerve impulse to contract. *See also* INVOLUNTARY MUSCLE; VOLUNTARY MUSCLE

**muscular dystrophy** Any of a group of hereditary disorders in which the characteristic feature is progressive weakening and ATROPHY of the muscles. The commonest type, Duchenne muscular dystrophy, affects boys, usually before the age of four. Muscle fibers degenerate, to be replaced by fatty tissue.

**muses** In Classical mythology, nine daughters of the Titan Mnemosyne (memory) and ZEUS. Calliope was the muse of epic poetry, Clio of history, Erato of love poetry, Euterpe of lyric poetry, Polyhymnia of song, Melpomene of tragedy, Terpsichore of choral dance, Thalia of comedy, and Urania of astronomy.

**mushroom** Any of numerous relatively large fleshy fungi, many of which are gathered for food. A typical mushroom consists of two parts: an extensive underground cobwebby network of fine filaments (hyphae), called the mycelium, which is the main body of the fungus, and a short-lived fruiting body (the visible mushroom).

**Musial, Stan (Stanley Frank)** (1920– ) US baseball player. Nicknamed "Stan the Man," he played for the St. Louis Cardinals (1941–44, 1946–63) and compiled a league record 3,630 hits (broken in 1981 by Pete Rose). Musial hit a total of 475 home runs and had a .331 lifetime batting average. He was named the National League's "Most Valuable Player" three times (1943, 1946, 1948) and was elected to the Baseball Hall of Fame in 1969.

**music** Sound arranged for instruments or voices, for many purposes, exhibiting a great variety of forms and styles. It can be split into categories, including ROCK, JAZZ, BLUES, FOLK MUSIC, SOUL MUSIC, RAP, HOUSE MUSIC, and COUNTRY AND WESTERN. Within classical music, there are distinct historical periods – MEDIEVAL MUSIC (1100–1400), RENAISSANCE MUSIC (1400–1600), BAROQUE (1600–1750), CLASSICAL MUSIC (1750–*c.*1800), and Romantic (*c.*1800–1900) (*see* ROMANTICISM). In the 20th century, various techniques developed, notably SERIAL MUSIC, TWELVE-TONE MUSIC, and IMPRESSIONISM. Composers also experimented with ELECTRONIC MUSIC.

**musical** Genre of popular dramatic light entertainment exemplified by firm plot, strong songs, and vivacious dance numbers. It developed at the end of the 19th century from elements of light opera, revue, and burlesque. The most popular musicals originated in the US with the work of George GERSHWIN, Jerome KERN, Richard RODGERS, Oscar HAMMERSTEIN, and Stephen SONDHEIM. Audiences in the 1970s responded to the works of Tim Rice and Andrew LLOYD WEBBER, including *Jesus Christ Superstar* (1971) and *Evita* (1978). Lloyd Webber was extremely successful in the 1980s with *Cats* (1981) and *The Phantom of the Opera* (1986). Successful film musicals, such as *West Side Story* (1961), *My Fair Lady* (1964), and *The Sound of Music* (1965), are generally based on stage originals. Original film musicals include *Forty-Second Street* (1933), *Meet Me in St. Louis* (1944), and *Singin' in the Rain* (1952).

**musical form** Structural scheme that gives shape and artistic unity to a composition. The standard forms are binary, ternary, rondo, and sonata. Each consists of a number of musical sections or subsections. **Binary** form consists of two sections, which may be contrasted in idea, key, or tempo but which complement each other within the musical entity. **Ternary** form consists of a restatement of the first section after a middle section of contrasted material; an example is the MINUET and trio. In **rondo** form, the number of sections varies, but there is at least one restatement of the first section. **Sonata** form, as its name suggests, evolved with the sonata and is used most often for the first movement of a sonata or SYMPHONY. The exposition states (usually) two subjects, which are developed musically in the middle section, before being stated in the recapitulation.

**musical notation** Method of writing down music – the language of music. Staff notation defines the absolute and relative pitches of notes; half notes, quarter notes, and so on indicate their time values.

**music hall** Stage for popular variety shows, originally tavern annexes, devoted to comic song, acrobatics, magic shows, juggling, and dancing. The popularity of the music hall was at its height in late Victorian and Edwardian England but declined with the advent of radio and motion pictures in the 1930s. In the US, it was often known as VAUDEVILLE.

◄ **muskrat** The scent of the muskrat (*Ondatra zebithicus*) from which it gets its name, comes from special glands. The animal was originally a native of North America but it has been introduced into other parts of the world for its fur.

**musicology** Academic study of music. The term embraces various disciplines, including the study of music history, the analysis of compositions, acoustics, and ethnomusicology. The study of music history began in the 18th century. Musicological research in the 20th century is responsible for the increased interest in and performance of early music.

**muskellunge** Freshwater fish found in the Great Lakes. A type of PIKE, it has a shovel-like bill, sharp teeth, and elongated body. It eats fish, amphibians, birds, and small mammals. Length: to 5.5ft (167.6cm); weight: 110lb (50kg). Family Esocidae; species *Esox masquinongy*.

**musk ox** Large, wild, shaggy RUMINANT, related to oxen and GOATS, native to N Canada and Greenland. Its brown fur reaches almost to the ground, and its down-pointing, recurved horns form a helmet over the forehead. When threatened, the herd forms a defensive circle round the calves. Length: to 7.5ft (2.3m); weight: to 903lb (410kg). Family Bovidae; species *Ovibos moschatus*. *See also* OX

**muskrat** Large aquatic RODENT (a type of VOLE) native to North America. It is a good swimmer, with partly webbed hind feet and a long, scaly tail. Its commercially valuable fur (musquash) is glossy brown and durable. Length, including tail: to 21in (53.5cm); weight: to 4lb (1.8kg). Family Cricetidae; species *Ondatra obscura* and *O. zibethica*.

**Muslim** (Arabic, one who submits) Follower or believer in ISLAM. A Muslim is one who worships ALLAH alone and holds MUHAMMAD to be the only true prophet. Today, there are *c.*935 million Muslims worldwide.

**Muslim League** Political organization (founded 1906) to protect the rights of Muslims in British India. The League cooperated with the predominantly Hindu National Congress until the 1930s when, fearing Hindu domination, it turned to independent action under the leadership of Muhammed Ali JINNAH. Although pro-British, in 1940 it called for a separate Muslim state, which was achieved when the country was partitioned at independence (1947). At first the League dominated politics in Pakistan but subsequently split into rival factions.

**mussel** Any of several species of bivalve MOLLUSKS with thin oval shells. Marine species of the family Mytilidae are found throughout the world in dense colonies on sea walls and rocky shores, where they attach themselves by means of strands called byssus threads. The edible mussel, *Mytilus edulis*, is sometimes cultivated on ropes hanging from rafts. Freshwater mussels of the family Unionidae, found in northern continents only, produce PEARLS.

**Musset, Alfred de** (1810–57) French poet and playwright. He is best remembered for his poems which, after 1834, appeared in the periodical *Revue des Deux Mondes*. His four lyrics *Les Nuits* (1835–37) are the most famous of his poems.

**Mussolini, Benito** (1883–1945) Italian fascist dictator. He turned to revolutionary nationalism in World War I and in 1919 founded the Italian Fascist movement. The Fascists' march on Rome in 1922 secured Mussolini's appointment as prime minister. He imposed one-party government with himself as *Il Duce* ("the leader"), or dictator. His movement was a model for HITLER in Germany, with whom Mussolini formed an alliance in 1936. Imperial ambitions led to the conquest of Ethiopia (1935–36) and the invasion of Albania (1939). Mussolini delayed entering World War II until a German victory seemed probable in 1940. A succession of

▲ **mussel** The common mussel (*Mytilus edulis*) is edible and cultivated on ropes hanging from stakes or similar structures driven into seabeds, or on ropes suspended from floating rafts. Both methods first involve the collection by settlement of mussel "seed" or "spat." The seed may then be transferred to farming areas free from predators or pollution.

defeats led to his fall from power in 1943. He was briefly restored as head of a puppet government in N Italy by the Germans, but in April 1945, fleeing Allied forces, he was captured and killed by Italian partisans.

**Mussorgsky, Modest Petrovich** (1839–81) Russian composer, one of the "Russian Five" who promoted nationalism in Russian music. His finest work is the opera *Boris Godunov* (1868–69). Other important works include the piano work *Pictures at an Exhibition* (1874, later orchestrated by several composers) and *A Night on the Bare Mountain* (1867). After his death much of his work was edited and revised, mostly by Nikolai RIMSKY-KORSAKOV.

**Mustafa Kemal** *See* ATATÜRK, KEMAL

**mustang** Feral HORSE of the Great Plains, descended from horses that were imported from Spain. The mustang has short ears, a low-set tail, and round leg bones. During the 17th century there were 2–4 million mustangs, whereas today only *c*.20,000 survive in the SW US.

**mustard** Any of various species of annual and perennial plants, native to the temperate zone. These plants have pungent-flavored leaves, cross-shaped, four-petaled flowers, and carry pods. The seeds of some species are ground to produce the condiment mustard. Family Brassicaceae/Cruciferae.

**mutation** Sudden change in an inherited characteristic of an organism. This change occurs in the DNA of the GENES. Natural mutations during reproduction are rare, occur randomly, and usually produce an organism unable to survive in its environment. Occasionally the change results in the organism being better adapted to its environment and, through NATURAL SELECTION, the altered gene may pass on to the next generation. Natural mutation is therefore one of the key means by which organisms evolve. The mutation rate can be increased by exposing genetic material to ionizing radiation, such as X-rays or UV light, or mutagenic chemicals. *See also* EVOLUTION

**Muti, Riccardo** (1941– ) Italian conductor. In 1968 he made his debut with the Italian Radio Symphony Orchestra. In 1973 Muti became chief conductor of the Philharmonia Orchestra. He was principal conductor of the Philadelphia Orchestra (1981–92) and musical director of La Scala (1986– ).

**Mutter, Anne-Sophie** (1963– ) German violinist. She made her concerto début with the Berlin Philharmonic in 1977, having come to the notice of Herbert von KARAJAN, with whom she later recorded all the major violin concertos.

**mutual fund** (unit trust) Pooled investment vehicle. A mutual fund invests the combined assets of a number of investors. This allows smaller investors to diversify their holdings, reducing risk.

**mutualism** Relationship with mutual benefits for the two or more organisms involved. An alternative term for SYMBIOSIS, it usually refers to two organisms of different species.

**Muybridge, Eadweard** (1830–1904) US photographer, b. Britain. After immigrating to the US in 1852, he became a pioneer of motion PHOTOGRAPHY. From 1878 he recorded the movements of animals and people by using a series of still cameras. In 1881 he invented the Zoopraxiscope, a forerunner of motion pictures, which projected animated pictures on a screen. *See also* CINEMA

**Myanmar** Official name of BURMA since 1989

**Mycenae** Ancient city in Greece, 7mi (11km) N of modern Argos, which gave its name to the MYCENAEAN CIVILIZATION. Dating from the third millennium BC, Mycenae was at its cultural peak *c*.1580–1120 BC. It was destroyed in the 5th century BC. Later restored, by the 2nd century AD it was in ruins. The ruins of the city were discovered by Heinrich SCHLIEMANN in 1874–76.

**Mycenaean art** Greek art of the Late Bronze Age. The name comes from the fortress-city of MYCENAE and refers to the work of the late Helladic period (*c*.1500–1100 BC). Its greatest achievements came in the fields of architecture, which included both grand fortifications and beehive tombs, and in pottery, precious metalwork, and fresco.

**Mycenaean civilization** (*c*.1580–1120 BC) Ancient Bronze age civilization centered around MYCENAE, S Greece. The Mycenaeans entered Greece from the N, bringing with them advanced techniques, particularly in architecture and metallurgy. By 1400 BC, having invaded Crete and incorporated much of MINOAN CIVILIZATION, the Mycenaeans became the dominant power in the Aegean, trading as far as Syria, Palestine, and Egypt, and importing luxurious goods for their wealthy and cultured citadel palaces. It is uncertain as to why the Mycenaean civilization collapsed, but it was most likely due to invasion by the Dorians.

**mycology** Science and study of FUNGUS

**mycorrhiza** (fungus root) Association between certain fungi and the root cells of some VASCULAR PLANTS. The fungus may penetrate the root cells or form a mesh around them. Water and minerals enter the roots via these threads. Sometimes the fungus digests organic material for the plant. *See also* SYMBIOSIS

**My Lai** Vietnamese village, scene of a massacre (March 16, 1968) of Vietnamese civilians by US soldiers. Believing they were infiltrating a Viet Cong stronghold, US soldiers massacred more than 300 unarmed civilians, including women and children. The incident was at first covered up; when it came to public attention, it contributed to the US public's disillusion with the VIETNAM WAR.

**mynah** *See* MINA

**myopia** (short-sightedness) Common disorder of vision in which near objects are seen sharply, but distant objects are hazy. It is caused either by the eyeball being too long or the eye's LENS being too powerful, so that light rays entering the EYE focus in front of the retina. It is easily corrected with concave lenses in spectacles or CONTACT LENSES.

**myrrh** Aromatic, resinous, oily gum obtained from thorny, flowering trees such as *Commiphora myrrha* (family Burseraceae). Known and prized since ancient times, myrrh has commonly been used as an ingredient in incense, perfumes, and medicines.

**myrtle** Any of numerous species of evergreen shrubs and trees that grow in tropical and subtropical regions, especially the aromatic shrub, *Myrtus communis*, of the Mediterranean region. Its leaves are simple and glossy; the purple-black berries that follow the white flowers were once dried and used like pepper. Family Myrtaceae.

**mystery play** (miracle play) Medieval English drama based on a religious theme. Mystery plays were originally used by the clergy to teach their illiterate congregation the principal stories of the Bible. By the 14th century, they had become a popular entertainment. Each year, the plays were performed by the various craft guilds in a town. In England the mystery plays from four towns have survived: Chester, York, Wakefield, and Coventry.

**mysticism** Belief in, or experience of, a perception of reality that is elevated above normal human understanding. It may involve some form of spiritual search for unity of self with God or the universe. It is found in most major religions, and the exponents of mysticism – called mystics – may experience trances, dreams, or visions. In India, mysticism has long been important in HINDUISM and is based on YOGA. Mysticism in Judaism is apparent in HASIDISM and the CABBALA. Mystics in the Far East have mostly been followers of TAOISM or BUDDHISM.

**mythology** Literally, telling of stories, but usually collectively defined as the myths of a particular culture. A myth occurs in a timeless past, contains supernatural elements and seeks to dramatize or explain such issues as the creation of the world (CREATION MYTH) and human beings, the institutions of political power, the cycle of seasons, birth, death, and fate. Most mythologies have an established pantheon, or hierarchy, of gods who are more or less anthropomorphic. *See also* AFRICAN MYTHOLOGY; CELTIC MYTHOLOGY; CENTRAL AND SOUTH AMERICAN MYTHOLOGY; CHINESE MYTHOLOGY; EGYPTIAN MYTHOLOGY; GREEK MYTHOLOGY; NORTH AMERICAN MYTHOLOGY; OCEANIC MYTHOLOGY; PERSIAN MYTHOLOGY, ANCIENT; TEUTONIC MYTHOLOGY

**myxedema** Disease caused by deficient function of the THYROID GLAND, resulting in fatigue, constipation, dry skin, a tendency toward weight gain and, in the later stages, mental dullness. It mostly affects middle-aged women. Treatment involves administration of the thyroid hormone thyroxine.

*N/n, 14th letter of the alphabet, is derived from the Semitic letter* **nun,** *which was the pictorial representation of a fish. It was adopted by the Greeks as the letter* **nu** *and subsequently by the Romans.*

**Nabokov, Vladimir** (1899–1977) US novelist, b. Russia. He left Russia in 1919 and settled in Germany. He immigrated to the US in 1940, but left for Switzerland in 1959. He wrote novels, first in Russian and later in English, that extended the scope of language by exploring the precise connotations of words. These include *Bend Sinister* (1947), *Lolita* (1955) – the highly controversial story of an older man's sexual obsession with a young girl – and *Ada* (1969).

**Nader, Ralph** (1934– ) US consumer affairs activist and lobbyist. His book *Unsafe at any Speed* (1965) called for improved automobile design. He subsequently examined issues concerned with mining, nuclear power, meat processing, and airlines. He heads a public interest law firm staffed with specialists in consumer affairs.

**nadir** Point on the CELESTIAL SPHERE vertically below the observer. It is diametrically opposite the ZENITH.

**Nadir Shah** (1688–1747) Ruler of Persia (1736–47). After seizing the throne he embarked upon a series of wars against neighboring states. He invaded India, sacking Delhi, and conducted campaigns against Russia and Turkey. His ceaseless warring ruined the country's economy and his cruelty aroused hostility from his subjects. He was assassinated by his own soldiers.

**Nagasaki** Port in SW Japan, on W Kyūshū island. In the 16th century it was the first Japanese port to receive Western ships and became a center of Christian influence. During Japanese isolation (1639–1859) it was the only port open to foreign trade. In August 1945 the inner city was destroyed by a US atomic bomb, and more than 70,000 people were killed. Sites include the Chinese Temple (1629) and Peace Park. Industries: shipbuilding and heavy engineering. Pop. (1993) 439,000.

**Nagorno-Karabakh** Autonomous region of Azerbaijan, between the Caucasus and Karabakh mountains. The capital is Stepanakert. During the 19th century the region was absorbed into the Russian empire. In 1921 it was annexed to the Azerbaijan republic. In 1991 the region declared its independence and Azerbaijan responded by imposing direct rule. The ensuing civil war claimed thousands of lives. In 1993 Armenian troops occupied the enclave and a peacc agreement was reached in 1994. The main activities are farming and silk production. Area: 1,700sq mi (4,400sq km). Pop. (1990) 192,400

**Nagoya** City and port in central Japan, on Honshū island, on the Pacific Ocean. The city grew up around the 17th-century castle. Industries: iron and steel, textiles, motor vehicles, aircraft. Pop. (1993) 2,095,000.

**Nagpur** City in W central India, in Maharashtra state. Founded in the 18th century as the capital of the kingdom of Nagpur, it became the capital of Berar state (from 1903) and of Madhya Pradesh state (1947–56). Industries: metal goods, transportation equipment, cigarettes, textiles, pottery, glass, leather, pharmaceuticals, brassware. Pop. (1991) 1,624,572.

**Nagy, Imre** (1896–1958) Hungarian communist leader. As prime minister (from 1953), he antagonized the Soviet government with nationalistic and liberal policies and was forced from power, but was recalled during the Hungarian revolution (1956). He demanded the withdrawal of Soviet troops and the abolition of dictatorship. Moscow promised concessions, but Soviet tanks moved in and Nagy was executed.

**Nahuatl** Native American language of the UTO-AZTECAN linguistic family of the S US and Central America. It is spoken today by about a million people, mostly in Mexico.

**nail** In anatomy, tough KERATIN outgrowth from the fingers and toes of primates.

**naiad** In Greek mythology, female figure or NYMPH, identified with streams, rivers and lakes.

**Naipaul, V.S. (Vidiadhar Surajprasad)** (1932– ) West Indian novelist and short-story writer. He was educated in his native Trinidad and at Oxford, but later settled in London. His novels include *A House for Mr. Biswas* (1961), the Booker Prize-winning *In a Free State* (1971), and *A Bend in the River* (1979). His travelogues include *Among the Believers: An Islamic Journey* (1981) and *A Turn in the South* (1989).

**Nairobi** Capital and largest city of Kenya, in the S central part of the country. Founded in 1899, Nairobi replaced Mombasa as the capital of the British East Africa Protectorate in 1905. Nairobi has a national park (1946), a university (1970), and several institutions of higher education. It is an administrative and commercial center. Industries: cigarettes, textiles, chemicals, food processing, furniture, glass. Pop. (1989) 1,346,000.

**Naismith, James** (1861–1939) US sportsman and inventor of basketball, b. Canada. Many of his rules are still in use today.

**Nakhichevan** Autonomous republic of Azerbaijan, bounded N and E by Armenia, S and W by Iran, and W by Turkey; the capital is Nakhichevan. It became part of Russia in 1828, an autonomous republic within the Soviet Union in 1924, and in 1991 became part of the independent republic of Azerbaijan, but was subsequently disputed between Armenia and Azerbaijan. Crops: grains, cotton, tobacco, fruit, grapes. Industries include mining, silk textiles, and food processing. Area: 2,120sq mi (5,500sq km). Pop. (1994) 315,000.

**Namath, Joe (Joseph William)** (1943– ) ("Broadway Joe") US football player. Joining the New York Jets in 1965 as quarterback, he had a hugely successful career over 13 seasons. In 1967 he passed for a record 4,007 yards.

**Namib Desert** Coastal desert region of Namibia, between the Atlantic Ocean and the interior plateau. It has less than 0.4in (1cm) of rain a year and is almost completely barren. Diamonds are mined. Length: *c.*1,200mi (1,900km).

**Namibia** (formerly South West Africa) Republic in SW Africa. **Land and climate** Namibia can be divided into four geographical regions. The arid NAMIB DESERT runs along the entire Atlantic coast. Inland, a central plateau, mostly between 2,950 and 6,560ft (900–2,000m), includes the capital, WINDHOEK. The highest point is Brandberg Mountain, at 8,550ft (2,606m). In the N lies an alluvial plain, which includes the marshlands of the Caprivi Strip. To the E is the W fringe of the KALAHARI. The ORANGE River forms Namibia's S border. Namibia is a warm, arid country. Windhoek has an average annual rainfall of 15in (370mm). The N is the wettest part of Namibia, with *c.*20in (500mm) of annual rain. Grassland and shrub cover much of the interior. The Etosha National Park is a magnificent wildlife reserve. **History** The nomadic SAN inhabited the region *c.*2,000 years ago. They were gradually displaced by Bantu-speakers, such as the Ovambo, Kavango, and Herero. Portuguese navigators arrived in the early 15th century. Colonization began in earnest in the 19th century. In 1884 Germany claimed the region as a protectorate, and subsumed it into the territory of South West Africa. Local rebellions were brutally suppressed.

**NAMIBIA**

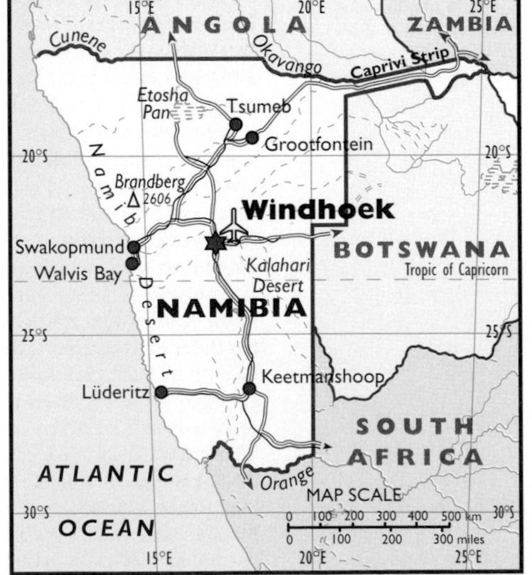


**AREA:** 318,694 sq mi (825,414sq km)
**POPULATION:** 1,562,000
**CAPITAL (POPULATION):** Windhoek (126,000)
**GOVERNMENT:** Multiparty republic
**ETHNIC GROUPS:** Ovambo 50%, Kavango 9%, Herero 7%, Damara 7%, whites 6%, Nama 5%
**LANGUAGES:** English (official)
**RELIGIONS:** Christianity 9)% (Lutheran 51%)
**CURRENCY:** Namibian dollar = 100 cents

▲ **Napoleon I** Emperor of the French, Napoleon Bonaparte was a military and organizational genius. After various military victories, he established order at home with his Napoleonic Code. He achieved his greatest military victory at Austerlitz over Russia and Austria in 1805. He soon controlled much of continental Europe but his invasion of Russia (1812) was a disaster. He was eventually defeated at the Battle of Waterloo in 1815.

The discovery of diamonds in 1908 increased European settlement. During World War I it was occupied (1915) by South African troops. In 1920 South Africa was granted a mandate. After World War II South Africa refused to relinquish control. In 1966 the SOUTH WEST AFRICA PEOPLE'S ORGANIZATION (SWAPO) began a guerrilla war against South Africa. In 1968 the UN called on South Africa to withdraw. In 1971 the International Court of Justice declared that South African rule over Namibia was illegal. South Africa refused to comply and divided Namibia into bantustans. International pressure forced South Africa to promise Namibia independence, but then qualified the terms. Civil war raged from 1977. A UN security council peace settlement was finally implemented in 1989. SWAPO won multiparty elections in November 1989. In March 1990 Namibia became an independent republic within the British Commonwealth. Sam Nujoma became its president, and was reelected in 1994. In 1994 South Africa renounced its claim to Walvis Bay and it was incorporated into Namibia. **Economy** Namibia is the world's seventh largest producer of diamonds, and ninth largest producer of uranium (1995 GDP per capita, US$4,150). Minerals make up 90% of exports. Farming employs *c*.40% of the workforce. The main activity is cattle and sheep farming. The chief food products are corn, millet, and vegetables. Atlantic fishing is also important.

**Nanak** (1469–1539) Indian spiritual teacher, and founder and first guru of SIKHISM. Nanak preached a monotheistic religion that combined elements from both HINDUISM and ISLAM. In 1519 he founded the town of Kartarpur in Punjab, where he attracted many followers.

**Nan-ch'ang** (Nan-ch'ang-hsien) City in SE China; capital of Jiangxi province. It was founded as a walled city in the 3rd century BC. A failed communist coup here in 1927 is commemorated on Army Day (August 1). Industries: rice, tea, cotton textiles, machinery. Pop. (1993) 1,420,000.

**Nanking** (Nanjing) City on the Yangtze River, E China; capital of Jiangsu province. Founded in the 8th century BC, it served as the capital of China at various times. The Treaty of Nanking (1842) ended the OPIUM WAR with Britain and opened five Chinese ports to foreign trade. It was the seat of SUN YAT-SEN's presidency in 1912. In 1937, during the SINO-JAPANESE WAR, Nanking was captured by the Japanese, who massacred over 100,000 of the population. Notable sites include the city wall and tombs of Ming emperors. Industries: iron and steel, oil refining, chemicals. Pop. (1993) 2,430,000.

**nanotechnology** Micromechanics used to develop working devices the size of a few nanometers. (A nanometer is one billionth of a meter.) US scientists have etched an electric motor from silicon that is smaller than 0.1 mm wide, and have made workable gears with a diameter less than a human hair.

**Nansen, Fridtjof** (1861–1930) Norwegian explorer and statesman. After a pioneering crossing of Greenland (1888), he designed a ship to withstand being frozen in ice so that currents would carry her to the North Pole. She did not reach the Pole, but crossed the Arctic Ocean undamaged (1893–96). Nansen and one companion failed in an attempt to reach the Pole with skis and kayaks. After 1918 Nansen was involved in humanitarian work. He was awarded the Nobel Peace Prize in 1922.

**Nantes** City at the mouth of the Loire River, W France; capital of Loire-Atlantique department. France's seventh-largest city has been an important trading center since Roman times. In the 10th century it was captured from Norse invaders by the duke of Brittany. Nantes remained a residence of the dukes until 1524, and their tombs lie in the city's 15th-century Gothic cathedral. Nantes developed around its port. By the 18th century it had become France's largest port. During World War II it was a center of the French resistance movement. Industries: shipbuilding, sugar refining, food products. Pop. (1990) 244,995.

**Nantes, Edict of** (1598) French royal decree establishing toleration for HUGUENOTS (Protestants). It granted freedom of worship and legal equality for Huguenots within limits, and ended the Wars of RELIGION. The Edict was revoked by Louis XIV in 1685, causing many Huguenots to emigrate.

**naphtha** Any of several volatile liquid-hydrocarbon mixtures. In the 1st century AD, "naphtha" was mentioned by Pliny the Elder. Alchemists used the word for various liquids of low boiling point. Several types of products are now called naphtha, including coal-tar naphtha and petroleum naphtha.

**naphthalene** Important hydrocarbon ($C_{10}H_8$) composed of two benzene rings sharing two adjacent carbon atoms. A white, waxy solid, naphthalene is soluble in ether and hot alcohol and is highly volatile. It is used in mothballs, dyes, and synthetic resins. It occurs in coal tar. Properties m.p. 176°F (80°C); b.p. 424°F (218°C).

**Napier, John** (1550–1617) Scottish mathematician. He developed "Napier's Bones," a calculating apparatus that he used to invent logarithms (1614) and the present form of decimal notation.

**Naples** (Napoli) City in S central Italy, on the Bay of Naples; capital of the province of Campania. Founded *c*.600 BC as a Greek colony, Naples was conquered by Rome in the 4th century BC. Successively ruled by the Byzantines, Normans, Spanish, and Austrians, it became the capital of the Kingdom of the Two Sicilies in 1734, eventually joining the Kingdom of Italy in 1860. Notable buildings include the 13th-century Gothic cathedral, the Church of the Holy Apostles, the University (1224), and the Music Conservatory (1537). The city contains areas of great economic deprivation. Industries: textiles, leather, steel, shipbuilding, aircraft, telecommunications, tourism. Pop. (1991) 1,067,365.

**Napoleon I** (1769–1821) (Napoléon Bonaparte) Emperor of the French (1804–15), b. Corsica. The greatest military leader of modern times, he became a brigadier (1793) after driving the British out of Toulon. He was given command in Italy (1796) where he defeated the Austrians and Sardinians. In 1798 he launched an invasion of Egypt. French defeats in Europe prompted his return to Paris (1799), where his coup of 18 Brumaire (November 9) overthrew the Directory and set up the Consulate, headed by himself. He enacted sweeping administrative and legal reforms with the *Code Napoléon*, while defeating the Austrians at Marengo (1800) and making peace with the British at Amiens (1802). In 1804 he crowned himself emperor. Efforts to extend French power provoked renewal of war in 1803. Napoleon's Grand Army shattered his continental opponents but, after TRAFALGAR (1805), Britain controlled the seas. Napoleon tried to defeat Britain by a commercial blockade, which led indirectly to the PENINSULAR WAR in Portugal and Spain. By 1812 he controlled most of continental Europe. His invasion of Russia (1812) ended in the destruction of the Grand Army, encouraging a new coalition against France, which captured Paris in March 1814. Napoleon was exiled to ELBA, but in March 1815 he returned to France. The HUNDRED DAYS of his renewed reign ended with defeat at WATERLOO in June. Napoleon was exiled to St. Helena, where he died.

**Napoleon III** (1808–73) (Louis Napoleon) Emperor of the French (1852–70). The nephew of NAPOLEON I, he twice attempted a coup in France (1836 and 1840). Returning from exile after the FEBRUARY REVOLUTION (1848), he was elected president of the Second Republic. In 1851 he assumed autocratic powers and established the Second Empire (1852), taking the title Napoleon III. His attempt to establish a Mexican empire under the Archduke MAXIMILIAN ended in disaster, and in 1870 he was provoked by BISMARCK into declaring war on Prussia. Defeat at Sedan was followed by a republican rising that ended his reign.

**Napoleonic Wars** (1803–15) Campaigns by a series of European coalitions against French expansion under NAPOLEON I. Britain declared war in 1803 and formed the Third Coalition with Austria, Russia, and Sweden in 1804. Napoleon defeated the Austrians at Ulm and the Russians and Austrians at AUSTERLITZ (1806), but the British won a decisive naval victory at TRAFALGAR (1805). Prussia joined the Fourth Coalition (1806) but was defeated at Jena. Resistance to the French occupation of Portugal (1807) began the PENINSULAR WAR. The Fifth Coalition (1809) collapsed with the defeat of Austria at Wagram. In 1812 Napoleon invaded Russia. Bitter weather forced his retreat, and much of his army perished. Against the Sixth Coalition, Napoleon was defeated at Leipzig. Allied forces entered Paris in 1814. War was renewed during the HUNDRED DAYS, but ended in the final defeat of Napoleon by WELLINGTON and Blücher at WATERLOO (1815).

**Nara** City on S Honshu island, Japan, ; capital of Nara prefecture. A center of Japanese Buddhism, Nara was founded in 706. From 710 to 784 it acted as Japan's first imperial capital. Todai-ji (East Great Temple) houses a 72ft (22m) tall bronze statue of Buddha. The 7th-century Horyuji temple is reputedly Japan's oldest building. The tomb of Jimmu, Japan's first emperor, is here. The main industry is textiles. Pop. (1993) 353,000.

**Narcissus** In Greek mythology, a beautiful youth who rejected the love of the nymph ECHO and was punished by being made to fall in love with his own reflection in a pond. He pined away and was turned into a flower. The NARCISSUS is named for him, as is the term "narcissism" in psychology, which refers to an exaggerated regard for oneself.

**narcissus** Genus of Old World, bulb-forming, garden flowers, including daffodils and jonquils. The long, pointed leaves surround yellow, orange, or white trumpet-like flowers. Family Amaryllidaceae.

**narcotic** Any drug that induces sleep or relieves pain, especially opium and its derivatives, such as HEROIN and MORPHINE. These drugs have largely been replaced as sedatives because of their addictive properties, but they are still used for severe pain, notably in terminal illness. Other narcotics include alcohols (such as ETHANOL) and BARBITURATES.

**Narragansett** Algonquian-speaking tribe of Native Americans who occupied part of Rhode Island. Once the most powerful New England group, they were almost entirely wiped out during KING PHILIP'S WAR (1675–76).

**narwhal** Small, toothed Arctic WHALE. The male has a twisted horn, half as long as its body, which develops from a tooth and protrudes horizontally through one side of the upper lip. Length: up to 16ft (5m). Species *Monodon monoceros*.

**NASA** Acronym for NATIONAL AERONAUTICS AND SPACE ADMINISTRATION

**Naseby, Battle of** Final battle of the first English CIVIL WAR, fought in June 1645. Royalist troops under Prince RUPERT were defeated by the Parliamentarians under CROMWELL and FAIRFAX.

**Nash, Ogden** (1902–71) US poet. Among his many volumes of humorous and satirical poetry are *Free Wheeling* (1931), *I'm a Stranger Here Myself* (1938), and *Everyone But Me and Thee* (1962). He also wrote the lyrics for *One Touch of Venus* (1943), a musical comedy in collaboration with S.J. Perelman.

**Nashville** Capital of Tennessee, a port on the Cumberland River. Settled in 1779, it became state capital in 1843. During the Civil War, it was the scene of a decisive Union victory. Nashville merged with Davidson County in 1963. It is a country music center and the home of the Country Music Hall of Fame, and the Grand Old Opry. Nashville has many neoclassical buildings, two universities, and a technical institute. Industries: music, publishing, machinery. Pop. (1990) 510,784.

**Nassau** Capital of the Bahama Islands, West Indies, a port on the NE coast of New Providence Island. Founded in the 1660s by the British, during the 18th century it was a pirate stronghold. It is a commercial center and popular winter tourist resort. Exports include sisal, citrus fruit, and vegetables. Pop. (1990) 172,000.

**Nasser, Gamal Abdel** (1918–70) Egyptian soldier and statesman, prime minister (1954–56) and first president of the republic of Egypt (1956–70). In 1942 he founded the Society of Free Officers, which secretly campaigned against British imperialism and domestic corruption. Nasser led the 1952 army coup against King FAROUK. He quickly ousted the nominal prime minister General Muhammad Neguib and assumed presidential powers. Nasser's nationalization of the SUEZ CANAL (1956) prompted an abortive Anglo-French and Israeli invasion. He emerged as champion of the Arab world. Nasser formed the short-lived United Arab Republic (1958–61) with Syria. Nasser briefly resigned after Israel won the SIX DAY WAR (1967). The crowning achievement of his brand of Arab socialism was the ASWAN dam (1970).

**Natal** Former name (1910–94) of KWAZULU-NATAL province, E South Africa.

**Natchez** Tribe of Muskogean-speaking Native Americans

▲ **narwhal** Generally found only in the male, the distinctive tusk of the narwhal (*Monodon monoceros*) develops from the left tooth of a pair in the upper jaw. The function of the tusk remains unknown. Narwhals feed on fish and squid.

of the southern Mississippi region. Today only a handful of Natchez people survive in Oklahoma.

**Nation, Carry Amelia Moore** (1846–1911) US social reformer and temperance leader. Her alcoholic first husband turned her against liquor. Wielding a hatchet, which became her symbol, Nation began her anti-saloon campaign in the 1890s in Kansas, where saloons were illegal, and carried her crusade into several other states.

**National Academy of Sciences** US organization made up of elected members (based on original research in several fields of science). It was founded in 1863. The academy acts as an official advisor to the federal government on science and technology matters.

**National Aeronautics and Space Administration (NASA)** US government agency that organizes civilian aeronautical and space research programs. NASA was established in 1958 and was the agency behind the many US successes in SPACE EXPLORATION, including the landing of the first people on the Moon and the SPACE SHUTTLE. It has various departments located throughout the US. The Lyndon B. Johnson Space Center in Houston, Texas, is responsible for manned space flights. Space rockets, both manned and unmanned, are launched from the John F. Kennedy Space Center at CAPE CANAVERAL, Florida.

**National American Woman Suffrage Association (NAWSA)** Organization formed by merger of the National and the American Woman Suffrage associations. With two million members in 1917, it was one of the most active groups supporting women's political freedom. Prominent leaders of the association included Elizabeth Cady Stanton, who was president (1892–1900).

**National Association for the Advancement of Colored People (NAACP)** US CIVIL RIGHTS organization. Founded in 1909, its objectives are "to achieve through peaceful and lawful means, equal citizenship rights for all American citizens by eliminating segregation and discrimination in housing, employment, voting, schools, the courts, transportation, and recreation." Early leaders included W.E.B. DU BOIS. The NAACP set up the successful Legal Defense and Educational Fund to finance court battles over discriminatory practices, of which *Brown v Board of Education of Topeka, Kansas* (1954) argued by Thurgood MARSHALL, was a major victory. It also cooperates with other minority protection groups. Its publications include *Crisis*.

**national debt** *See* DEBT, NATIONAL

**National Guard** Volunteer citizen militia in the US. Units are under state jurisdiction in peacetime and in times of national emergency may be activated for federal duty. Units are also activated during disasters and civil unrest. In 1824 the 7th Regiment of the New York State Militia took the title "National Guards," and the term came into general use for state militias after the National Guard Association was formed in 1878. Units are located in all states, and members are trained in the regular armed services. Thereafter, they attend regular meetings and field exercises.

**National Industrial Recovery Act (NIRA)** Federal legislation passed in 1933 to help business overcome the effects of the DEPRESSION. NIRA permitted the firms in a given industry to cooperate rather than compete. The act was to be administered by the National Recovery Agency (NRA), which was to enforce the industry codes. In 1935 the Supreme Court declared the NIRA unconstitutional.

**nationalism** Ideology according to which all people owe a supreme loyalty to their nation and which holds that each nation should be embodied in a separate state. Nationalist sentiment, drawing upon and extolling a common culture, language, and history, can be a powerful unifying force. With

▲ **Nasser** First president of the republic of Egypt, Gamal Abdel Nasser was a British-trained soldier. In 1952 he led the army coup that ousted King Farouk. Becoming president in 1956, he provoked an international crisis by nationalizing the Suez Canal. Having fought in the 1948 Arab–Israeli War, he brought on the 1967 Arab–Israeli War by blocking the Israeli port of Elat.

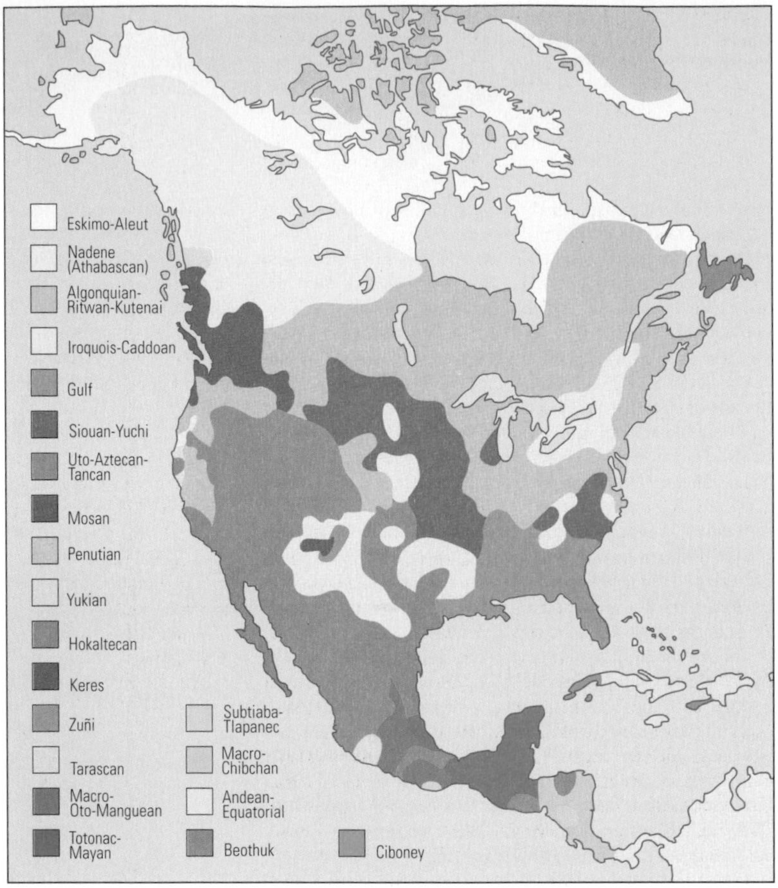

▲ **Native American** A map of the main language groups of North America including the Carribean area and Mexico.

the exception of national independence movements, nationalism is essentially conservative and dwells on a nation's past.

**nationalization** Policy of acquiring for public ownership enterprises that were formerly privately owned. Advocates of nationalization maintain that bringing essential industries under government control enhances social and economic equality. The communist states of E Europe nationalized large parts of their industry and agriculture following World War II, and many other European states nationalized some of their major industries, such as coal, steel, and transportation. In the 1980s the trend was toward PRIVATIZATION. *See also* SOCIALISM

**National Labor Relations Board** Independent federal agency established in 1935. Its principal functions are to prevent and remedy unfair labor practices by employers and labor organizations and to conduct secret elections among employees to determine whether they wish to be represented by a labor organization.

**National Organization for Women (NOW)** US feminist group founded in 1966 by Betty FRIEDAN and other feminists. A politically oriented organization, NOW aims to establish full equality for women.

**national parks** Protected areas where restraint on the killing of wildlife is enforced, and forests, waters, and other natural environments are preserved from commercial use. The US was the first country to set aside large reserves for preservation and recreation, and Yellowstone National Park was the first of these to be established (1872). The degree of protection varies greatly from country to country. The main purpose of the famous African national parks is game preservation.

**National Security Council (NSC)** US federal agency within the executive branch of government. Founded in 1947, it considers policies on matters concerning national security and makes recommendations to the president. It comprises the president, vice president, secretary of state, secretary of defense, other advisers, and staff.

**national service** *See* CONSCRIPTION

**National Socialism** (Nazism) Doctrine of the National Socialist German Workers' (Nazi) Party, 1921–45. It was biologically racist (believing that the so-called Aryan race was superior to others), anti-Semitic, nationalistic, anticommunist, antidemocratic, and antiintellectual. It placed power before justice and the interests of the state before the individual. These beliefs were stated by the party's leader, Adolf HITLER, in his book *Mein Kampf* (1925). *See also* FASCISM

**Native Americans** Indigenous peoples of the American continent. **North America** Native North Americans are believed to be descended from Asian peoples who crossed via the Bering Strait or the Aleutian Islands about 20,000 BC or earlier. These people spread throughout North, Central, and South America and developed many distinct regional cultures with hundreds of different languages. Native North Americans may be divided into eight cultural and geographic groups: the Arctic area; the Northeastern-Mackenzie area; the Northwest Coast area; the Southwestern area; the Plains area; the California-Intermountain area; the Southwestern area; and the Mesoamerican area. *See* separate articles for individual tribes. **South America** Native South Americans derived from North American groups who migrated S. Three main culture groups inhabiting distinct geographic areas are recognized: (1) Native Americans of the Andean area developed the highest cultures of the continent. After AD 1300 the QUECHUA culture dominated almost the entire region. (2) Native Americans of the Amazon Basin are mainly isolated, primitive, agricultural communities of many localized tribes. (3) Native Americans of the pampas successfully resisted Inca and Spaniard alike. In the southernmost portion of the continent live the Tierra del Fuegans, who are now few in number.

**Native Australians** Indigenous peoples of Australia. Originally from SE Asia, Native Australians are thought to have colonized Australia 40,000–45,000 years ago. Before the arrival of Europeans (*c.*1788) they probably numbered more than 400,000, but many thousands died from European diseases when they were placed in reserves. All the 500 tribal groups led a nomadic life, hunting and gathering. They believe that the land is a religious phenomenon inhabited by spirits of their ancestors, which may take either human or animal form, and these beliefs are celebrated in legends, song, mime, carving, and painting. They were granted the right to full Australian citizenship in 1967 and were first included in the census in 1971, when their estimated numbers were 140,000. The Aboriginal Land Rights Act (1976) and the Aboriginal and Torres Islander Heritage Protect Act (1984) have resulted in an increased population approaching 300,000 by the mid-1990s.

**Native North American art** Traditional art produced by the indigenous peoples of North America. The INUIT of the Arctic area have been producing ivory carvings since prehistoric times and are also noted for their ceremonial masks (made from driftwood or whalebone). The NW region is best known for its TOTEM POLES, while in California, basketweaving and pottery were specialties. Similar crafts were practiced by the PUEBLO people of the SW, who also created remarkable prehistoric wall paintings. The painted decoration of animal hides was popular in the Great Plains, while in the Eastern Woodlands, there was a preference for copper ornaments and stone carvings.

**Native North American languages** Any of more than 100 languages spoken in N and Central America by descendants of the various indigenous peoples. The languages fall into many families. In the US and Canada, they include ALGONQUIAN, ATHABASCAN, and SIOUX. In the US and Mexico, UTO-AZTECAN languages are most common, with NAHUATL the most widely spoken of these. Other language groups are Oto-Mangean in Mexico, and MAYAN in Mexico and Guatemala.

**Native South American languages** Any of more than 1,000 languages spoken in South America by between 10 and 12 million people. Among the more important linguistic families are CHIBCHA, ARAWAK, and Tupian. Widely spoken languages are QUECHUA and Aymará, found in Peru and Bolivia. Another important language is GUARANÍ, of Paraguay.

**nativity** Birth of a New Testament figure as marked by a Christian feast. In general, the term refers to the birth of JESUS CHRIST, as described in the GOSPELS. These accounts relate that Jesus' birth in a stable in BETHLEHEM was attended by wonders – the sudden appearance of a bright star, angels rejoicing, and the arrival of shepherds and the MAGI to pay homage to the infant. Christians celebrate Jesus' Nativity at the festival of CHRISTMAS on December 25. Other Nativity festivals are also held during the Church year.

**NATO** Acronym for NORTH ATLANTIC TREATY ORGANIZATION

**Nat Turner Insurrection** (1831) Slave revolt in Virginia. It was led by Nat TURNER, a preacher who believed he was inspired by God to seek vengeance for African Americans. With *c.*70 men, he killed 57 whites in four days before the revolt was crushed. Many African Americans died in revenge killings, while Turner and 19 others were hanged.

**natural** In musical notation, an accidental sign placed before a note; it cancels a SHARP or FLAT.

**natural gas** Fossil fuel associated geologically with PETROLEUM. The fossil history of the two fuels is the same, since they were both formed by the decomposition of ancient marine plankton. The main constituent of natural gas is methane, $CH_4$.

**naturalism** Late 19th-century literary movement that began in France and was led by Emile ZOLA. An extension of REALISM, it emphasized the importance of documentation. Writers sought to represent unselective reality with all its emotional and social ramifications. A major exponent of naturalistic drama was August STRINDBERG. The movement declined by the beginning of the 20th century but influenced the development of the modern US novel and social realist art.

**natural rights** Concept that human beings possess certain fundamental and inalienable rights, as described by John LOCKE. Among these rights were life, property ownership, and political equality. *See* HUMAN RIGHTS

**natural selection** In EVOLUTION, theory that advantageous change in an organism tends to be passed on to successive generations. Changes arise out of natural genetic VARIATION, especially MUTATION. Those that give an individual organism a greater capacity for survival and reproduction in a particular environment help it produce more offspring bearing the same beneficial characteristic or trait. This theory was proposed by Charles DARWIN in his book *The Origin of Species* (1859). It is still regarded as the key mechanism of evolution.

**nature-nurture controversy** Debate over whether people's INTELLIGENCE, behavior, and other characteristics are influenced more by heredity or environment. The controversy has raised strong feelings, particularly over the question of whether intelligence is genetically fixed or the result of the way children are brought up and educated. Most psychologists now believe that behavioral and intellectual traits result from a complex mix of many factors.

**naturopathy** System of medical therapy that relies exclusively on the use of natural treatments, such as exposure to sunlight, fresh air, and a healthy diet of organically grown foods. Herbal remedies are preferred to manufactured drugs.

**Nauru** Island republic in the W Pacific Ocean, a coral atoll located halfway between Australia and Hawaii, and the world's smallest independent state. Nauru has rich deposits of high-grade phosphate rock, the sale of which accounts for 98% of its exports. Nauru was explored by a British navigator, John Hunter, in 1798. In 1888 the atoll was annexed to Germany. During World War I Nauru was occupied by Australian forces. During World War II the Japanese occupied Nauru. In 1968 it became an independent republic within the British Commonwealth. Area: 8sq mi (21sq km). Pop. (1990) 8,100.

**nautilus** (chambered nautilus) Cephalopod mollusk found in W Pacific and E Indian oceans at depths down to 660ft (200m). Its large coiled shell is divided into numerous, gas-filled chambers, which give it buoyancy, with the body located in the foremost chamber. Its head has 60–90 retractable, thin tentacles without suckers, and it moves by squirting water from a funnel. Shell size *c.*10in (25cm). Family Nautilidae; genus *Nautilus*. *See also* CEPHALOPODA; MOLLUSK.

**Navajo** Athabascan speaking tribe, the largest group of NATIVE AMERICANS in the US. Their reservation in Arizona and New Mexico is the biggest in the country. In the early 1990s the growing population numbered *c.*150,000.

**Navarino, Battle of** (1827) Naval battle off the port of Navarino (Pylos), Greece. The British, French, and Russian fleets destroyed the Turkish-Egyptian fleet of Ibrahim Pasha. The battle helped to ensure Greek independence (1829).

**Navarre** Autonomous region and ancient kingdom in N Spain, stretching from the Ebro River to the W Pyrenees border; the capital is Pamplona. For 400 years Navarre defended against invasions by the Visigoths, Arabs, and Franks. In the 11th century, Sancho III of Navarre ruled over most of Christian Spain. In 1512 S Navarre was annexed by Ferdinand II of Aragon. The N part was incorporated as French crown land in 1589. The Spanish region has historically maintained semiautonomous status. It is a mountainous, mainly agricultural region, producing cattle, grapes, timber, cereals, vegetables, and sugar beets. Area: 4,023sq mi (10,421sq km). Pop. (1991) 519,227.

**nave** (Lat. *navis*, ship) Central and main area of a church or cathedral. It extends from the main entrance to the transepts and includes the main aisle. It is the area for the congregation.

**navigation** Determining the position of a vehicle and its course. Five main techniques are used: dead reckoning, piloting, celestial navigation, inertial guidance, and radio navigation. The last includes the use of radio beacons, LORAN, radar navigation, and satellite navigation systems. Instruments and charts enable the navigator to determine position, expressed in terms of LATITUDE and LONGITUDE, direction in degrees of arc from true north, speed, and distance traveled.

**Navigation Acts** English 17th-century statutes placing restrictions on foreign trade and shipping. The first Navigation Act (1651) declared that English trade should be carried only in English ships, and was the main cause of the first Anglo-Dutch War. Later acts placed restrictions on the trade of the colonies.

**Navratilova, Martina** (1956– ) US tennis player, b. Czechoslovakia. She employed a left-handed serve-volley attacking style of tennis and is considered one of the greatest tennis players ever. She won 167 singles tournaments, including Wimbledon on 9 occasions.

**Navy, US** Naval service of the US armed forces. It consists of more than 500,000 personnel under the president, who is commander in chief of the armed forces, and the general supervision of the secretary of the Navy and his adviser, the chief of naval operations (CNO), who is the Navy's highest ranking officer. Currently the Navy operates cruisers, destroyers, and patrol ships, aircraft carriers, amphibious warfare ships, conventional and missile submarines, and aircraft. The Navy was established by Congress in 1798, although naval activities had begun during the American Revolution. The

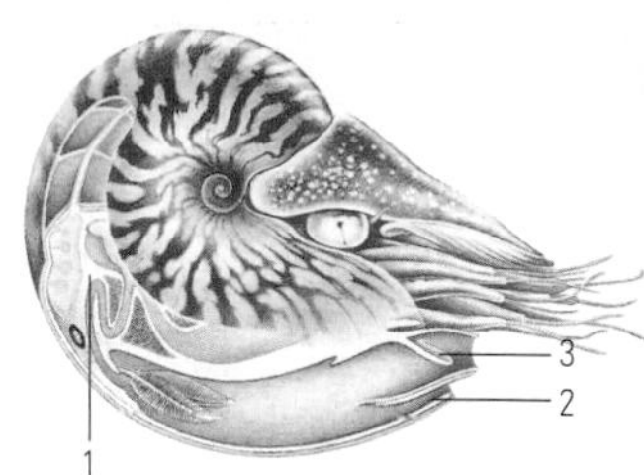


▲ **nautilus** The shell is divided into about 30 compartments, but the body of the nautilus only occupies the first, and largest, chamber (1). All other chambers are self-contained buoyancy tanks filled with gas. The nautilus nevertheless is a poor shape for swimming. Water passes into the mantle (2) around its whole edge. It is expelled from the funnel (3) by the funnel muscles themselves, and by the animal expanding its body in the shell. Unlike its relatives squids, octopuses, and cuttlefish, the nautilus cannot contract its mantle, which is attached to its shell.

**NAVIGATION**

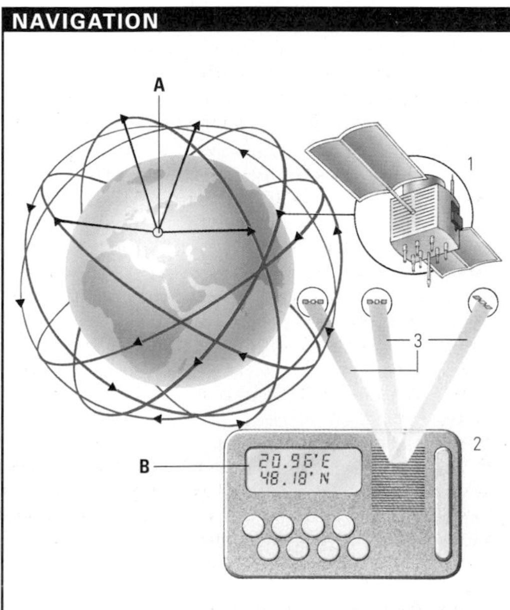


The world is ringed by 24 global positioning satellites (1) launched by the US. At any time four are above the horizon wherever you are on Earth (A). With a handheld receiver (2) that compares the time signals (3) from the satellite, your position can be fixed to a remarkable degree of accuracy. The receivers are now small enough to fit in the hand, and display either longitude or latitude (B) or a grid reference. Each satellite carries an atomic clock and transmits time signals to Earth. The receiver knows exactly where each satellite should be at any given time, and by simultaneously analyzing the time the signals from three satellites take to reach the receiver, it can compute its own position to within 33ft (10m). Aircraft and military users use a fourth satellite signal for even greater accuracy.

**NEBRASKA**
**Statehood:**
March 1, 1867
**Nickname:**
The Cornhusker State
**State bird:**
Western meadowlark
**State flower:**
Goldenrod
**State tree:**
Cottonwood
**State motto:**
Equality before the law

Navy has taken an active part in US military operations from the Barbary coast wars in the early 19th century to the Vietnam conflict in the late 20th. *See also* DEFENSE, DEPARTMENT OF; JOINT CHIEFS OF STAFF; MARINE CORPS, US

**Nazism** *See* NATIONAL SOCIALISM

**Neagh, Lough** Lake in Northern Ireland, the largest freshwater lake in the British Isles. It has many feeder channels, the largest of which is the Bann River. The lake is noted for its fishing (especially trout and eels). Area: 153sq mi (396sq km).

**Neanderthal** Middle PALEOLITHIC variety of human, known from fossils in Europe and Asia. Neanderthals were discovered when a skeleton was unearthed in the Neander Valley in W Germany in 1856. The bones were thick and powerfully built and the skull had a pronounced brow ridge. Neanderthals are now considered a separate species of human, and not thought to be ancestral to modern humans. Neanderthals predated modern humans in Europe, but were superseded by them *c*.35,000 years ago. *See also* HUMAN EVOLUTION

**near sight** Common disorder of vision in which near objects are seen sharply but distant objects are hazy. It is caused either by the eyeball being too long or the eye's lens being too powerful, so that light rays entering the eye focus in front of the RETINA. It is easily corrected with concave lenses in spectacles or contact lenses.

**Nebraska** State in W central US, in the Great Plains; the capital is LINCOLN. OMAHA is the largest city. The region was acquired under the LOUISIANA PURCHASE of 1803 and was unexplored until the LEWIS AND CLARK EXPEDITION the following year. The territory of Nebraska was created in 1854. Nebraska was admitted to the union in 1867. The land rises gradually from the E to the foothills of the Rocky Mountains in the W, and is drained chiefly by the Platte River, a tributary of the MISSOURI. The E half of the state is farmland where farmers grow grains and raise cattle and pigs. Nebraska's economy is overwhelmingly agricultural. Industries: food processing, oil, and sand, gravel, stone quarrying. Area: 76,878sq mi (199,113sq km). Pop. (1990) 1,578,385.

**Nebuchadnezzar** (*c*.630–562BC) Second and greatest king of the Chaldaean (New Babylonian) empire (605 BC–562 BC) who had a profound effect on the lands of the ancient Middle East. He subjugated Syria and Palestine but was himself defeated by Egyptian forces in 601 BC. He occupied JUDAH, capturing JERUSALEM in 597 BC and installing the puppet king Zedekiah on the throne of Judah. Following Zedekiah's rebellion, Nebuchadnezzar destroyed the city and Temple of Jerusalem and deported its population into exile in BABYLON. A brilliant military leader, Nebuchadnezzar continued to follow an expansionist strategy. He was responsible for many buildings in Babylon and according to legend built for his Median wife the famous hanging gardens, which became one of the SEVEN WONDERS OF THE WORLD. Biblical accounts of Nebuchadnezzar's involvement with Judah and the Jews appear principally in II Kings, Jeremiah, and Daniel.

**nebula** (Lat. cloud) Region of interstellar gas and dust. There are three types. **Emission** nebulae are bright diffuse nebulae that emit light and other radiation as a result of ionization and excitation of the gas atoms by ultraviolet radiation. In contrast, the brightness of **reflection** nebulae results from the scattering by dust particles of light from nearby stars. **Dark** nebulae are not luminous: interstellar gas and dust absorb light from background stars, producing apparently dark patches in the sky.

**neck** In vertebrates, the part of the body that connects the head and the trunk. In human beings it contains the seven cervical vertebrae of the spinal column and, to the front, the throat or pharynx, leading to the TRACHEA and ESOPHAGUS.

**Necker, Jacques** (1732–1804) French financier and statesman, b. Switzerland. A Protestant banker, he was finance minister (1776–81) under LOUIS XVI. Dismissed, he was recalled to deal with a financial crisis in 1788 and advised calling the STATES GENERAL. The political demands of the Third Estate caused Necker's second dismissal, but the consequent riots, leading to the storming of the BASTILLE, forced Louis XVI to reappoint him.

**necrosis** Death of plant or animal tissue. It can be caused by disease, injury, or interference with the blood supply.

▲ **Nelson** English naval commander, Nelson was one of the greatest of all naval heroes. At the outbreak of war with France (1793), he served with distinction under Admiral Hood, losing his right eye and right arm. He blockaded Toulon for two years until the French fleet finally eluded him. He was killed at the ensuing Battle of Trafalgar, in which the French fleet was destroyed.

**nectarine** Variety of PEACH tree and its sweet, smooth-skinned, fleshy fruit. The tree and stone are identical to those of the peach. Family Rosaceae; species *Prunus persica nectarina*.

**Nefertiti** (active 14th century BC) Queen of Egypt as wife of AKHNATEN. Exceptionally beautiful, she supported her husband's innovative religious ideas. Her best surviving representation is a bust in the Berlin Museum.

**Negev** Desert region in S Israel that extends from Beersheba to the border with Egypt at Elat, and accounts for over half of Israeli land. An irrigation network has greatly increased cultivation in the region. The area has good mineral resources including copper, phosphates, natural gas, gypsum, ceramic clay, and magnesium ore. Area: *c*.5,130sq mi (13,300sq km).

**negligence** In law, failure to exercise reasonable care toward material goods, other people, or oneself, resulting in unintentional harm. Most cases involving negligence are decided by a jury.

**Nehru, Jawaharlal** (1889–1964) Indian statesman, first prime minister of independent India. Son of a prominent Indian nationalist, and educated in England, he belonged to the more radical wing of the Indian National Congress and was its president in 1929 and later. Conflicts with the British resulted in frequent spells in prison, but he took a leading part in the negotiations leading to the independence of India and Pakistan and headed the Indian government from 1947 until his death. Internationally, he followed a policy of nonalignment, and became a respected leader of the Third World. *See* CONGRESS PARTY

**Nelson, Horatio, Viscount** (1758–1805) Britain's most famous naval commander. Joining the navy aged 12, he was a captain at 20. Nelson lost an eye in action in 1794 and his right arm in 1797. Having played a notable part in the victory at Cape St. Vincent (1797), he again used unorthodox tactics in the Battle of the Nile (Abukir Bay) in 1798. Nelson was killed at the moment of his greatest victory, when he destroyed the combined French and Spanish fleets at TRAFALGAR (1805). He is remembered for his courage and ability and for a longstanding love affair with Emma Hamilton.

**nematode** *See* ROUNDWORM

**Nemesis** In Greek mythology, personification of the gods' disapproval, jealousy, and retribution.

**neoclassicism** Movement in late 18th- and early 19th-century European art and architecture. Neoclassicism grew out of the Age of ENLIGHTENMENT, whose exponents admired the order and clarity of ancient Greek and Roman art. The archeological discoveries at Herculaneum and Pompeii, Italy, in the 1740s helped to stimulate interest in these ancient civilizations. Many of the movement's pioneers congregated in Rome, notably Johann Winckelmann, CANOVA, John Flaxman, Gavin Hamilton, and Bertel Thorvaldsen. The most powerful neoclassical painter was Jacques Louis DAVID, whose work expressed great severity and grandeur. The concurrent GREEK REVIVAL had more superficial aims, which, in architecture, involved imitating the simplicity of ancient Greek buildings.

**neo-Darwinism** Development of Darwinism that incorporates the modern ideas of genetic HEREDITY, with DARWIN's ideas of EVOLUTION through NATURAL SELECTION.

**neodymium** Silver-yellow, metallic element (symbol Nd) of the LANTHANIDE SERIES. It is used to manufacture lasers, and neodymium salts are used to color glass. Properties: at.no. 60; at.wt. 144.24; sp.gr. 7.004; m.p. 1,850°F (1,010°C); b.p. 5,554°F (3,068°C); most common isotope $^{142}$Nd (27.11%).

**neofascism** Revival of the principles of FASCISM. Neofascism surfaced in Germany in the 1980s, feeding on muted social discontent and the presence of many foreign workers. In France some Jewish graves were desecrated and Italian neofascism has had moderate electoral success. Neofascist elements are visible in the US in certain white supremacist groups.

**neo-Impressionism** Late 19th-century painting style, originating in France and involving the use of POINTILLISM. The style is seen at its purest in the works of SEURAT.

**Neolithic** (New Stone Age) Period in human cultural development following the PALEOLITHIC. The Neolithic began about 8000 BC in W Asia, and about 4000 BC in Britain. It was during this period that people first lived in settled villages, domesticated and bred animals, cultivated cereal crops, and practiced stonegrinding and flint mining.

**neon** Gaseous, nonmetallic element (symbol Ne), a NOBLE GAS. Colorless and odorless, it is present in the atmosphere (0.0018% by volume) and is obtained by the fractional distillation of liquid air. Its main use is in discharge tubes for advertising signs (emitting a bright red glow while conducting electricity) and in gas lasers, geiger counters, and particle detectors. The element forms no compounds. Properties: at.no. 10; at.wt. 20.179; m.p. −415.6°F (−248.67°C); b.p. −410.89°F (−246.05°C); most common isotope $^{20}$Ne (90.92%).

**Neoplatonism** School of philosophy that dominated intellectual thought between about AD 250 and 550. It combined the ideas of PYTHAGORAS, the STOICS, PLATO, and ARISTOTLE with strains from JUDAISM, oriental religions, and Christianity. Fundamental to Neoplatonism was the concept of the One, something that transcends knowledge or existence but from which are derived intelligence and the Soul. Neoplatonism's influence persisted throughout the Middle Ages and even during the Renaissance.

**neorealism** Italian film movement (1945–50) that dealt with the harshness of life and death. Roberto ROSSELLINI directed the first such film, called *Open City* (1945), using nonprofessionals and real locations.

**Nepal** Independent kingdom in central Asia, between India (S) and China (N); the capital is KATMANDU. **Land and climate** Nepal comprises three distinct regions. A S lowland area (terai) of grassland, forests, and national park is the location for much of Nepal's agriculture and timber industry. The central Siwalik mountains and valleys are divided between the basins of the Ghaghara, Gandak, and Kosi rivers. Between the Gandak and Kosi lies Katmandu valley, the country's most populous area and center for Nepal's main source of currency: tourism. The last region is the main section of the Himalayas and includes Mount EVEREST. **History** In 1768 Nepal was united under GURKHA rule. Gurkha expansion into N India ended in conflict with Britain. British victory led Nepal to ratify its present boundaries and accept permanent British representation in Katmandu. From 1846 to 1951 Nepal was ruled by hereditary prime ministers from the Rana family. In 1923 Britain recognized Nepal as a sovereign state. Gurkha soldiers fought with distinction in the British army during both world wars. In 1951 the Rana government was overthrown and the monarchy restored. In 1959 the first national constitution was adopted and free elections took place. In 1960 King Mahendra dissolved parliament, and the democratic constitution was replaced by village councils (*panchayat*). In 1972 King Birendra succeeded. Mass demonstrations in 1990 led to the establishment of a new democratic constitution, with the king retaining joint executive powers. Multiparty elections in 1991 were won by the Nepali Congress Party. **Politics** The United Marxist Leninist Party formed a short-lived minority government in 1994. In 1995 a coalition government was formed, but the prime minister was replaced in 1997. **Economy** The most important economic activity in the Himalayas is livestock farming (especially yaks) and the growing of medicinal herbs. Nepal is an undeveloped rural country, heavily reliant on Indian trade and cooperation.(1995 GDP per capita, US$1,170)

**nephritis** (Bright's disease) Inflammation of the KIDNEY. It is a general term, used to describe a condition rather than any specific disease. It may be acute or chronic, often progressing to kidney failure.

**nephron** Basic functional unit of the mammalian KIDNEY. There are more than one million nephrons in a human kidney. Each consists of a cluster of tiny blood capillaries, cupped in a structure with an attached long, narrow tubule. Blood enters the kidney under pressure, and water and wastes are forced into the tubule. Some water and essential molecules are reabsorbed into the bloodstream; the remaining filtrate, URINE, is passed to the BLADDER for voiding.

**Neptune** Roman god, originally associated with fresh water but later identified with the Greek god POSEIDON and hence the sea. He was often depicted carrying a trident and riding a dolphin. His festival was in July.

**Neptune** Eighth planet from the Sun. The mass, orbit, and position of an unseen planet had been calculated by LEVERRIER and, independently, by British astronomer John Couch Adams (1819–92). Neptune was first observed in 1846 and is invisible to the naked eye. Through a telescope it appears as a small, greenish-blue disk with very few details. The upper atmosphere is about 85% molecular hydrogen and 15% helium. Its predominant blue color is due to a trace of methane, which strongly absorbs red light. Several different atmospheric features were visible at the time of the fly-by of the Voyager 2 probe in 1989. There were faint bands parallel to the equator, and spots, the most prominent of which was the oval Great Dark Spot (GDS), about 8,000mi (12,500km) long and 4,500mi (7,500km) wide, which is a giant anticyclone. White, cirrus-type clouds of methane crystals cast shadows on the main cloud deck some 30mi (50km) below. There are also the highest wind speeds recorded on any planet, at over 1,250mi/h (2,000km/h) in places.

**neptunium** Radioactive, metallic element (symbol Np), the first of the TRANSURANIC ELEMENTS of the ACTINIDE SERIES. The silvery element is found in small amounts in uranium ores. Properties: at.no. 93; at.wt. 237.0482; sp.gr. 20.25; m.p. 1,184°F (640°C); b.p. 7,056°F (3,902°C); most stable isotope $^{237}$Np (half-life 2.2 million years).

**Nero** (37–68) Roman emperor (54–68). One of the most

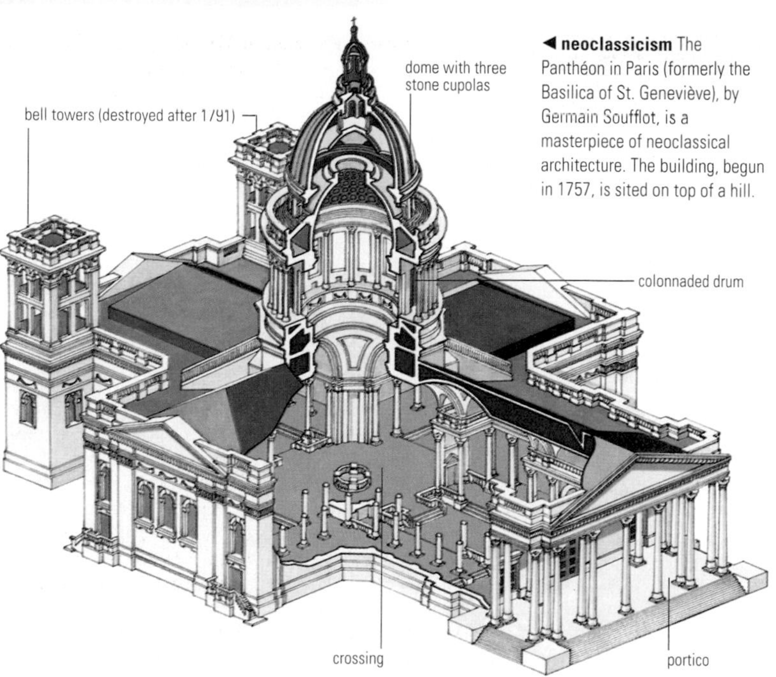


◄ **neoclassicism** The Panthéon in Paris (formerly the Basilica of St. Geneviève), by Germain Soufflot, is a masterpiece of neoclassical architecture. The building, begun in 1757, is sited on top of a hill.

**NEPTUNE: DATA**

Diameter (equatorial): 30,707mi (49,528km)
Mass (Earth = 1): 17.2
Volume (Earth = 1): 57
Density (water = 1): 2.06
Orbital period: 164.8 years
Rotation period: 16h 7m 0s
Average surface temperature: −364°F (−220°C)
Surface gravity (Earth = 1): 0.98

**NEPAL**

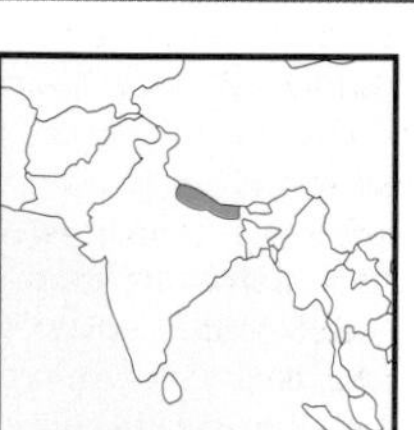

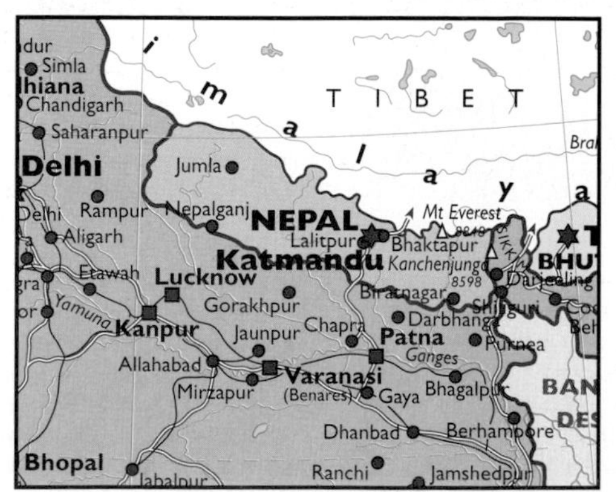


**AREA:** 54,363sq mi (140,800sq km)
**POPULATION:** 21,953,000
**CAPITAL (POPULATION):** Katmandu (419,073)
**LANGUAGES:** Nepali
**CURRENCY:** Nepalese rupee = 100 paisa

## NERVOUS SYSTEM

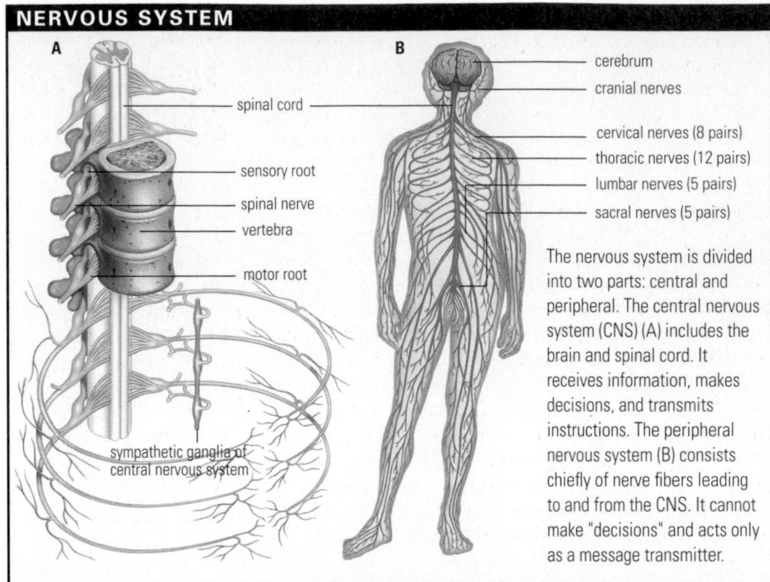


The nervous system is divided into two parts: central and peripheral. The central nervous system (CNS) (A) includes the brain and spinal cord. It receives information, makes decisions, and transmits instructions. The peripheral nervous system (B) consists chiefly of nerve fibers leading to and from the CNS. It cannot make "decisions" and acts only as a message transmitter.

notorious of rulers, he was responsible for the murders of his half-brother, his mother, and his first wife. Rome was burned (64), according to rumor, at Nero's instigation. He blamed the Christians and began their persecution. Faced with widespread rebellion, Nero committed suicide.

**Neruda, Pablo** (1904–73) Chilean poet, b. Neftalí Ricardo Reyes. He identified with the impoverished masses and was active in politics. His poetry presents the tragedy of the human condition through surreal imagery. His best-known work is the epic *Canto General* (*General Song*, 1950). He was awarded the 1971 Nobel Prize for literature.

**nerve** Collection of NEURONS providing a communications link between the vertebrate NERVOUS SYSTEM and other parts of the body. Afferent or sensory nerves transmit nervous impulses to the CENTRAL NERVOUS SYSTEM; efferent or MOTOR NERVES carry impulses away from the central nervous system to muscles.

**nerve cell** *See* NEURON

**Nervi, Pier Luigi** (1891–1979) Italian architect. He is noted for his innovative use of concrete. He established himself as a major creative force with his designs for the Giovanni Berta stadium at Florence (1932). He co-designed the UNESCO building, Paris (1954–58) and the Pirelli skyscraper, Milan (1958).

**nervous breakdown** Popular term for a mental and emotional crisis in which the person either is unable or feels unable to function normally. It is an imprecise term and may refer to any of a range of conditions. *See also* MENTAL ILLNESS

**nervous system** Communications system consisting of interconnecting nerve cells or NEURONS that coordinate all life, growth, and physical and mental activity. The mammalian nervous system consists of the CENTRAL NERVOUS SYSTEM (CNS) and the PERIPHERAL NERVOUS SYSTEM.

**Ness, Loch** Freshwater lake in N Scotland, running SW to NE along the geological fault of Glen More. It is 24mi (38km) long and 754ft (230m) deep and forms part of the Caledonian Canal. Accounts of a Loch Ness monster date back to the 15th century, but the veracity of the legend has never been established.

**Nestorianism** Christian heresy according to which JESUS CHRIST, the incarnate God, possesses two separate natures, the one divine and the other human, as opposed to the orthodox belief that Christ is one person who is at once both God and man. The heresy was associated with Nestorius, Bishop of Constantinople, who died *c*.451. It was condemned by the Councils of EPHESUS (431) and CHALCEDON (451). Nestorius was deposed and banished. His supporters, however, gradually organized themselves into a separate Church, which had its center in Persia (Iran). Nestorians have survived as a small community.

**Netanyahu, Benjamin** (1949– ) Israeli statesman, prime minister (1996– ). He served as a permanent representative to the UN (1984–88) and became leader of the right-wing Likud Party in 1993. After the assasination of Yitzhak RABIN, Netanyahu was elected prime minister in 1996. His uncompromising leadership and Likud's opposition to the ISRAELI-PALESTINIAN ACCORD threatened to disrupt the peace process.

**netball** Seven-member ball game played by women. It is a variant of BASKETBALL. Only two players of each team are allowed in the shooting circle at goal, which is the same size and height as basketball but without a backboard. The game is played chiefly in the English-speaking countries and the British Commonwealth.

**Netherlands** Country in NW Europe. *See* country feature

**Netherlands Antilles** Group of five main islands (and part of a sixth) in the West Indies, in the Caribbean Sea, forming an autonomous region of the Netherlands; the capital is Willemstadt (on CURAÇAO). The islands were settled by the Spanish in 1527 and captured by the Dutch in 1634. They were granted internal self-government in 1954. The group includes Aruba, Bonaire, Curaçao (the largest island), Saba, Saint Eustatius, and the S half of Saint Maarten. Industries: oil refining, petrochemicals, phosphates, tourism. Area: 383sq mi (993sq km). Pop. (1992) 189,474.

**nettle** Any of numerous species of flowering plants of the genus *Urtica*, especially the stinging nettle (*U. dioica*), which is typical of the genus in that it has stinging hairs along the leaves and stem. It has heart-shaped serrated leaves, small green flowers, and is sometimes used for medicinal or culinary purposes. The stinging agent is formic acid. Family Urticaceae.

**network** *See* COMPUTER NETWORK

**neuralgia** Intense pain from a damaged nerve, possibly tracking along its course. Forms include trigeminal neuralgia, which features attacks of stabbing pain in the mouth area, and post-herpetic neuralgia following an attack of SHINGLES.

**neurology** Branch of medicine dealing with the diagnosis and treatment of diseases of the NERVOUS SYSTEM.

**neuron** (nerve cell) Basic structural unit of the NERVOUS SYSTEM that enables rapid transmission of impulses between different parts of the body. It is composed of a cell body, containing a nucleus, and a number of trailing processes. The largest of these is the axon, which carries outgoing impulses; the rest are dendrites, which receive incoming impulses.

**neurosis** Emotional disorder such as anxiety, depression, or various phobias. It is a form of mental illness in which the main disorder is of mood, but the person does not lose contact with reality as happens in PSYCHOSIS.

**neurotransmitter** Any one of several dozen chemicals involved in communication between nerve cells or between a nerve and muscle cells. When an electrical impulse arrives at a nerve ending, a neurotransmitter is released to carry the signal across the specialized junction (synapse) between the nerve cell and its neighbor. Some drugs work by disrupting neurotransmission. *See also* NERVOUS SYSTEM

**neutrality** Policy of non-involvement in hostilities between states. It is recognized by international law, mainly in the Declaration of Paris of 1856 and the Hague Conventions V and XIII of 1907. A state proclaiming its neutrality must be wholly impartial and refrain from helping or hindering any side.

**neutralization** In chemistry, the mixing, or TITRATION, of equivalent amounts of an acid and a base in an aqueous medium until the mixture is neither acidic nor basic (pH of 7).

**neutrino** (symbol v) Uncharged ELEMENTARY PARTICLE with no mass or a very low mass, spin 1/2, and traveling at the speed of light. Classified as a LEPTON, it has little reaction with matter and is difficult to detect. Neutrinos are created and destroyed by particle decays with weak interaction. There are three types. The ELECTRON neutrino is closely associated with the electron and is produced when protons and electrons react to form NEUTRONS, as in the Sun. The muon neutrino is associated with the muon and occurs in high-energy reactions. The tau neutrino is associated with the tau particle.

**neutron** (symbol n) Uncharged ELEMENTARY PARTICLE that occurs in the atomic nuclei of all chemical elements except the lightest isotope of HYDROGEN. Outside the nucleus, it is unstable, decaying with a half-life of 11.6

▲ **nettle** Bearing both male and female flowers, the stinging nettle (*Urtica dioica*) has bristle-like stinging hairs, which are long, hollow cells. The tips of these are toughened with silica and they are easily broken off. When the plant is touched, the hairs penetrate the skin like surgical needles, the tips are lost, and the poison contained in the cells is released.

minutes into a PROTON, ELECTRON, and antineutrino. Its neutrality allows it to penetrate and be absorbed in nuclei and thus to induce nuclear transmutation and FISSION.

**neutron bomb** Nuclear weapon that produces a small blast but a very intense burst of high-speed neutrons. The lack of blast means that buildings are not heavily damaged. The neutrons, however, produce intense RADIATION SICKNESS in people located within a certain range of the explosion.

**neutron star** Extremely small, dense star that consists mostly of NEUTRONS. Neutron stars are formed when a massive star explodes as a SUPERNOVA, blasting off its outer layers and compressing the core so that its component protons and electrons merge into neutrons. They are observed as PULSARS. They have masses comparable to that of the Sun, but diameters of only about 12mi (20km) and average densities of about $10^{15}$g/cm$^3$.

**Nevada** State in W US; the capital is CARSON CITY. The US acquired the region in 1848 at the end of the MEXICAN WAR. When gold and silver were found in 1859, settlers flocked to Nevada. Much of the state lies in the Great Basin, but the SIERRA NEVADA rise steeply from its W edge. Nevada's dry climate and steep slopes have hindered the development of an agricultural economy. Hay and alfalfa are the chief crops; sheep and cattle grazing is much more important. Most of Nevada's economic wealth comes from its mineral deposits, which include copper, lead, silver, gold, zinc, and tungsten. Industries include chemicals, timber, electrical machinery, and glass products. It is a tourist area and, in cities such as LAS VEGAS and Reno, gambling provides an important source of state revenue. Area: 110,539sq mi (286,297sq km). Pop. (1990) 1,201,833.

**Nevelson, Louise** (1900–88) US sculptor and painter, b. Russia. In the 1950s she began constructing her famous painted collection of boxes, wooden objects, and cast-offs from old houses. Her "sculptural walls" include *Sky Cathedral* (1958) and *Dawn's Wedding Feast* (1959). Her later pieces are free-standing, including bins and barrels filled with long flexible poles. She was elected to the American Academy and Institute of Arts and Letters in 1979.

**New Age** System of philosophy and religion that came to prominence during the late 1980s and traces its origins to a variety of sources, including oriental mysticism and new scientific ideas. The New Age movement embraces diverse issues, including feminism, astrology, ecology, spiritualism, and pagan ritual, and takes a holistic approach to healing.

**NEVADA**
**Statehood:**
October 31, 1864
**Nickname:**
The Silver State
**State bird:**
Mountain bluebird
**State flower:**
Sagebrush
**State tree:**
Pinon pine
**State motto:**
All for our country

## NETHERLANDS

The flag of the Netherlands, one of Europe's oldest, dates from 1630, during the long struggle for independence from Spain, which began in 1568. The tricolor became a symbol of liberty that inspired many other revolutionary flags around the world.

**AREA:** 16,033sq mi (41,526sq km)
**POPULATION:** 15,178,000
**CAPITAL (POPULATION):** Amsterdam (724,096)
**GOVERNMENT:** Constitutional monarchy
**ETHNIC GROUPS:** Netherlander 95%, Indonesian, Turkish, Moroccan, German
**LANGUAGES:** Dutch (official)
**RELIGIONS:** Christianity (Roman Catholic 34%, Dutch Reformed Church 17%, Calvinist 8%), Islam 3%
**CURRENCY:** Guilder = 100 cents

The kingdom of the Netherlands is popularly known as HOLLAND, and with Belgium and Luxembourg forms the LOW COUNTRIES. Except in the far SE, the Netherlands is flat and *c.*40% lies below sea level. Large areas (*polders*) have been reclaimed from the sea. Dykes prevent flooding and have created IJSSELMEER. The maritime provinces include the constitutional capital AMSTERDAM, the administrative capital THE HAGUE, and the cities of ROTTERDAM, DELFT, HAARLEM, LEIDEN, GRONINGEN, and UTRECHT.

### CLIMATE

The Netherlands has a temperate maritime climate, with mild winters and abundant rainfall.

### VEGETATION

The Netherlands is very densely populated. About 66% of the land is arable or grazing land. The country is irrigated by a series of canals.

### HISTORY AND POLITICS

During the 4th to 8th centuries the region was ruled by the Franks, and in the 10th century became part of the Holy Roman Empire. In the 14th and 15th centuries trade flourished through the HANSEATIC LEAGUE. In 1477 the region passed to the Habsburgs. PHILIP II's attempt to impose the Inquisition met with fierce resistance. The N Protestant provinces, led by WILLIAM I (THE SILENT), declared independence in 1581. The foundation of the Dutch EAST INDIA COMPANY in 1602 marked the beginnings of empire. The mercantile class became the patrons of DUTCH ART. Following the THIRTY YEARS WAR, the Peace of WESTPHALIA (1648) recognized the independence of the N and S provinces as the United Provinces. In 1652 Jan de WITT established a republic. Trading rivalry with England led to the DUTCH WARS. The Treaty of BREDA (1667) confirmed Dutch imperial possessions. In 1672 France invaded and De Witt was murdered. The House of ORANGE reestablished control under WILLIAM III (OF ORANGE). France controlled the Netherlands from 1795 to 1813. In 1815 the former United Provinces, Belgium, and Luxembourg united to form the kingdom of the Netherlands under WILLIAM I. Belgium broke away in 1830. In 1890 Luxembourg also seceded, and WILHELMINA began her long reign. The Netherlands was neutral in World War I. Germany invaded in May 1940; most Dutch Jews were deported to Poland and murdered. Queen Wilhelmina was exiled during World War II. ARNHEM was a vital bridgehead in the Allied liberation. In 1948 Wilhelmina abdicated in favor of her daughter, Juliana. In 1949 the Netherlands joined NATO, and Indonesia gained its independence. In 1957 it was a founder member of the European Community, and in 1958 formed the Benelux customs union. It gave Netherlands New Guinea and Suriname independence in 1962 and 1975 respectively. It retains the islands of the NETHERLANDS ANTILLES. In 1980 Queen Juliana abdicated in favor of her daughter, Beatrix. Post-1945, the Netherlands has been ruled by a succession of coalition governments. In 1994 Wim Kok was elected prime minister, and again in 19998 as head of a center-left coalition.

### ECONOMY

The Netherlands has prospered through its European ties (1995 GDP per capita, US$19,950). Private enterprise has combined with progressive social policies. Services account for 65% of GDP and industry 30%. Highly industrialized, products include aircraft, chemicals, electronics, machinery. Natural resources include natural gas, but it imports raw materials. Agriculture is intensive, employing only 5% of the workforce. Dairy farming is the leading agricultural activity. Other products: cheese, barley, flowers, bulbs.

**NEW HAMPSHIRE**
**Statehood:**
June 21, 1788
**Nickname:**
The Granite State
**State bird:**
Purple finch
**State flower:**
Purple lilac
**State tree:**
White birch
**State motto:**
Live free or die

**Newark** City in NE New Jersey, on the Passaic River and Newark Bay, connected to nearby New York City by tunnel. Founded in 1666 by the Puritans, Newark began its industrial growth after the American Revolution. It is an important commercial and financial center. Industries: electrical equipment, paints, chemicals. Pop. (1990) 275,221.

**New Brunswick** Maritime province in E Canada, on the US–Canadian border; the capital is Fredericton. The region was first explored by Jacques CARTIER in 1534. It was ceded to Britain in 1713, but settlement was slow. Many loyalists entered the region from the American colonies during the AMERICAN REVOLUTION. The province of New Brunswick was established in 1784. In 1867 New Brunswick joined NOVA SCOTIA, QUEBEC, and ONTARIO to form the Dominion of CANADA. The land rises gradually from E to W and is drained chiefly by the St. John and Miramichi rivers. More than three quarters of the province is forested. The chief crops are hay, clover, oats, potatoes, and fruit. Industries: timber, leather goods, pharmaceuticals, machinery. There are also valuable mineral deposits. The largest towns are St. John and Moncton. Area: 28,354sq mi (73,437sq km). Pop. (1991) 723,900.

**New Caledonia** (Nouvelle Calédonie) French overseas territory in the SW Pacific Ocean, *c*.750mi (1,210km) E of Australia, consisting of New Caledonia, Loyalty Islands, Isle des Pins, Isle Bélep, and Chesterfield and Huon Islands; the capital is NOUMÉA (on New Caledonia). Discovered in 1774 by Captain COOK, the islands were annexed by France in 1853. The group became a French overseas territory in 1946. In the 1980s there was a growing separatist movement. Direct French rule was imposed in 1988. Products: copra, coffee, cotton, nickel, iron, manganese, cobalt, chromium. Area: 7,170sq mi (18,575sq km). Pop. (1989) 164,182.

**Newcastle upon Tyne** City in NE England, a major port on the Tyne River; administrative center of Tyne and Wear. The site of a fort in Roman times, Newcastle acquired a Norman castle in the 11th century. It was a major wool-exporting port in the 13th century and later a coal-shipping center. Its shipbuilding industry is in decline, but heavy engineering is still important. Other industries: pharmaceuticals, engineering, aircraft. Pop. (1991) 259,541.

**New Deal** Program for social and economic reconstruction in the US launched by President Franklin D. ROOSEVELT (1933–39) and designed to restore prosperity after the GREAT DEPRESSION. It was based on massive and unprecedented federal intervention in the economy. Early measures, including extensive public works, were mainly concerned with relief. The New Deal encountered bitter resistance from conservatives and did not avert recession in 1937–38. Industrial expansion, full employment, and agricultural prosperity were achieved less by the New Deal than by World War II. However, the program laid the basis for future federal management of the economy and provision of social welfare.

**New Delhi** Capital of India, in the N of the country, on the Yamuna River in Delhi Union Territory. Planned by the British architects Sir Edwin LUTYENS and Herbert Baker, it was constructed during 1912–29 to replace Calcutta as the capital of British India. Whereas the old city of DELHI (to the SW) is primarily a commercial center, New Delhi has an administrative function. Industries include textile production, chemicals, machine tools, plastics, food processing, electrical appliances, traditional crafts. Pop. (1991) 301,800.

**New England** Region in NE US, made up of the states of MAINE, NEW HAMPSHIRE, VERMONT, CONNECTICUT, MASSACHUSETTS, and RHODE ISLAND. In 1643 the New England Confederation was set up by some of the colonies for the purposes of defense and to establish a common policy toward the Native Americans. New England was the center of events leading up to the AMERICAN REVOLUTION. The region became highly industrialized after the War of 1812 and developed as a center of literature and learning. It was home to writers such as EMERSON, HAWTHORNE, and THOREAU and the literary movement TRANSCENDENTALISM.

**New Forest** Region of forest and heathland in S England, in S Hampshire. It was established as a royal hunting ground in 1079 by William I. The forest includes many species of trees. Pigs, cattle, and ponies are reared. It is a popular tourist resort. Area: *c*.148sq mi (383sq km).

**Newfoundland** Rescue and working dog originally bred by fisherman in Newfoundland. It has a massive head with a square, short muzzle, and small, triangular ears set close to the head. The full-chested, broad-backed body is set on short, strong legs and the tail is broad and long. Height: 28in (71cm) at the shoulder; weight: 150lb (68kg).

**Newfoundland and Labrador** Province in E Canada, on the Atlantic Ocean, consisting of the mainland region of LABRADOR and the island of Newfoundland plus adjacent islands; the capital is ST. JOHN'S (in Newfoundland). Norsemen are believed to have landed on the coast of Labrador *c*.AD 1000. John CABOT reached the island in 1497. The region became a British colony in 1824. It remained apart from the rest of Canada until 1949, when it became the country's tenth province. The island of Newfoundland is a plateau with many lakes and marshes. Labrador has tundra in the N and the cold climate and lack of transport facilities have hindered economic development. There are, however, valuable mineral resources. Timber is an important industry, and the Grand Banks is one of the world's best cod-fishing areas. Area 156,185sq mi (404,420sq km). Pop. (1991) 568,474.

**New France** Area of North America claimed by France in the 16th–18th centuries. It included the St. Lawrence valley, the Great Lakes region, and the Mississippi valley. Parts were lost during the Anglo–French wars of the 18th century, and the whole of New France passed to Britain in 1763.

**New Frontier** Term describing the legislative program of President John F. KENNEDY (1961–63). It included massive expenditure on social reforms and welfare as well as ambitious new projects such as the PEACE CORPS and manned space flight.

**New Guinea** Second-largest island in the world, part of the E Malay archipelago, in the W Pacific Ocean. Discovered in the early 16th century, New Guinea was colonized by the Dutch, the Germans, and the British during the next two centuries. In 1904 the British-administered part was transferred to Australia and during World War I Australian forces seized German New Guinea. The E half eventually achieved independence as PAPUA NEW GUINEA in 1975. The W half, IRIAN JAYA, became a province of Indonesia in 1969. The island has a tropical climate and is mountainous. Produce includes copra, cocoa, coffee, rubber, coconuts, and tobacco. Area: 342,000sq mi (885,780sq km).

**New Hampshire** State in NE US, on the Canadian border; the capital is CONCORD. The first settlement was made in 1623. Much of the land is mountainous and forested. The principal rivers are the Connecticut and the Merrimack, and there are more than 1,000 lakes. Farming is restricted by poor, stony soil and is mostly concentrated in the Connecticut Valley. Dairy and truck-farm produce, hay, apples, and potatoes are the chief products. New Hampshire is highly industrialized. There is abundant hydroelectricity. Industries: electrical machinery, paper and wood products, printing and publishing, leather goods, textiles. Area: 9,304sq mi (24,097sq km). Pop. (1990) 1,109,253.

**New Haven** City and port in S Connecticut, on Long Island Sound. Founded by Puritans in 1638, it shared the role of capital of Connecticut with HARTFORD from 1701 to 1875. The presence of YALE UNIVERSITY (founded 1701) has made the city a cultural center. Pop. (1990) 130,474.

**Ne Win, U** (1911– ) Burmese military and political leader. On Burma's independence from Britain (1948), he commanded the army, and in 1958–60 was prime minister. In 1962 he returned to power, imposing autocratic rule with his Burma Socialist Program Party. He was president (1974–81) under a new constitution.

**New Jersey** State in E US, on the Atlantic coast, S of New York; the capital is TRENTON. Other major cities include NEWARK, ATLANTIC CITY, and Paterson. Settlement began in the 1620s, when the Dutch founded the colony of New Netherland (later New York). When the British took the colony in 1664 the land between the Hudson and Delaware rivers was separated and named New Jersey. The N of the state is in the Appalachian highland region; SE of this area are

**NEW JERSEY**
**Statehood:**
December 18, 1787
**Nickname:**
The Garden State
**State bird:**
Eastern goldfinch
**State flower:**
Purple violet
**State tree:**
Red oak
**State motto:**
Liberty and prosperity

the Piedmont plains, and more than half the state is coastal plain. A variety of crops are grown, and dairy cattle and poultry are also important. New Jersey is, however, industrial and densely populated. Major industries are chemicals, pharmaceuticals, rubber goods, textiles, electronic equipment, copper smelting, and oil refining. Area: 7,836sq mi (20,295sq km). Pop. (1990) 7,730,188.

**Newman, Barnett** (1905–70) US painter. He was closely associated with ABSTRACT EXPRESSIONISM but he developed a distinctive kind of mystical abstraction, expressed in its earliest complete form in *Onement* (1948). Along with Mark ROTHKO, Newman pioneered monochromatic color field painting and the use of huge canvases.

**Newman, Cardinal John Henry** (1801–90) British theologian. As leader of the OXFORD MOVEMENT (1833–45), he had a powerful effect on the Church of England, equaled only by the shock of his conversion to Roman Catholicism (1845). A great literary stylist, he is remembered especially for his autobiography, *Apologia pro vita sua* (1864).

**Newman, Paul** (1925– ) US film actor, director, and producer. He is known for his portrayals of independent and wryly humorous antiheroes in such films as *The Hustler* (1961), *Hud* (1963), *Cool Hand Luke* (1967), *Butch Cassidy and the Sundance Kid* (1969), and *The Sting* (1973). *The Color of Money* (1986; Academy Award) and *The Hudsucker Proxy* (1994) rank highly among his more recent films.

**New Mexico** State in SW US, on the Mexican border; the capital is SANTA FE. The largest city is ALBUQUERQUE. The first permanent Spanish settlement was established at Santa Fe in 1610. The US acquired the region in 1848 at the end of the MEXICAN WAR. It entered the Union in 1912 as the 47th state. The first atomic bomb was exploded at Alamogordo in 1945. The Sangre de Cristo Mountains in the N flank the Rio Grande, which runs N to S through the state. The terrain includes desert, forested mountains, and stark mesa. In the S and SW are semiarid plains. The S Pecos and Rio Grande rivers are used to irrigate cotton crops; hay, wheat, dairy produce, and chili peppers are also important. Much of the land is pasture. A large proportion of the state's wealth comes from mineral deposits, including uranium, manganese, copper, silver, turquoise, oil, coal, and natural gas. Area: 121,335sq mi (314,334sq km). Pop. (1990) 1,515,069.

**New Netherland** Dutch colonial territory in North America, stretching from the Hudson to the Delaware River. The Dutch claim was based on the explorations of Henry Hudson. Under charter to the Dutch West India Company., settlers founded Fort Nassau (Albany) and New Amsterdam (New York City). The latter was settled by Peter Minuit (1626). The last and most able governor, Peter Stuyvesant, annexed New Sweden (1655). The area was taken over by England in 1664.

**New Orleans** City and river port in SE Louisiana, between Lake Pontchartrain and the Mississippi River. Founded by the French in 1718, it was ceded to Spain in 1763 and acquired by the US under the LOUISIANA PURCHASE of 1803. Its industries expanded rapidly in the 20th century after the discovery of oil and natural gas. New Orleans made an important contribution to the development of JAZZ. It is also the home of the annual MARDI GRAS festival. Industries include food processing, petroleum, natural gas, oil and sugar refining, shipbuilding, tourism, aluminum, and petrochemicals. Pop. (1990) 496,938.

**New Orleans, Battle of** Engagement fought on January 8, 1815; the last battle in the WAR OF 1812. It took place two weeks after the Treaty of Ghent was signed because news of the treaty had not reached New Orleans. The Americans under General Andrew Jackson won the battle with only 71 killed, while the British suffered 2,500 casualties.

**Newport** City and port in Narragansett Bay, SE Rhode Island. Founded in 1639, it served as joint state capital with Providence until 1900. It is home to music festivals and for many years hosted the America's Cup yachting races. Tourism is the chief industry. Other industries include shipbuilding and electronic instruments. Pop. (1990) 28,227.

**Newport News** City in SE Virginia, on the James River, 11mi (18km) NNW of NORFOLK; it comprises the Port of Hampton Roads, together with Norfolk and PORTSMOUTH. It was the scene of the CIVIL WAR naval battle between the MONITOR AND MERRIMACK (1862). It later grew in importance as a coal-shipping port. Newport News is one of world's largest shipbuilding and repair centers. Industries: food processing, metal products, building materials, textiles, paper, oil refining. Pop. (1990) 170,045.

**New South Wales** State in SE Australia, on the Tasman Sea; the capital is SYDNEY. Captain James COOK first visited the area in 1770, claiming the E coast of Australia for Britain and naming it New South Wales. It achieved responsible government in 1855, becoming a state of the Commonwealth of Australia in 1901. The Great Dividing Range separates the narrow coastal lowlands from the W plains that occupy two-thirds of the state. The MURRAY River and its tributaries are used extensively for irrigation. Wheat, wool, dairy produce, and beef are the principal agricultural products. The state has valuable mineral deposits. New South Wales is the most populous and most industrialized state in Australia. Steel is the chief product. Area: 309,180sq mi (801,430sq km). Pop. (1991) 5,730,947.

**newspaper** Periodical publication, usually daily or weekly, conveying news and comment on current events. Handwritten news sheets were posted in public places in ancient Rome under such titles as *Acta Diurna* (Daily Events). In Europe, the invention and spread of printing in the 15th century facilitated the growth of newspapers. The earliest examples were printed in German cities, soon followed by Venice, the Low Countries, and other states in the 16th century.

**newt** Any of numerous species of tailed AMPHIBIANS of Europe, Asia, and North America. The common European newt, *Triturus vulgaris*, is terrestrial, except during the breeding season when it is aquatic and the male develops ornamental fins. Its body is long and slender and the tail is laterally flattened. Length: to 7in (17cm). Family Salamandridae.

**New Testament** Second part of the Bible, consisting of 27 books all originally written in Greek after AD 45 and concerning the life and teachings of JESUS CHRIST. It begins with three SYNOPTIC GOSPELS (MATTHEW, MARK, and LUKE), which present a common narrative of Christ's life and ministry, and a fourth gospel (JOHN), which is more of a theological meditation. The ACTS OF THE APOSTLES records the early development and spread of Christianity. Next are 21 letters (EPISTLES) addressed to specific early Church communities; the New Testament ends with the REVELATION of St. John the Divine (otherwise known as the Apocalypse), which is an interpretation of history designed to demonstrate the sovereignty of God.

**Newton, Sir Isaac** (1642–1727) English scientist. He studied at CAMBRIDGE and became professor of mathematics there (1669–1701). His main works were *Philosophiae Naturalis Principia Mathematica* (1687) and *Opticks* (1704). In the former, he outlined his laws of motion and proposed the principle of universal GRAVITATION; in the latter he showed that white light is made up of colors of the SPECTRUM and proposed his particle theory of light. He also created the first system of CALCULUS in the 1660s, but did not publish it until the German mathematician Gottfried LEIBNIZ had published his own system in 1684. He built a reflecting telescope in *c.*1671.

**newton** SI unit (symbol N) of FORCE. One newton is the force that gives a mass of 1kg an acceleration of one meter per second per second.

**Newton's laws** Three physical laws of motion, formulated by the English scientist Isaac NEWTON. The **first** law states that an object remains at rest or moves in a straight line at constant speed unless acted upon by a FORCE. The **second** law, which enables force to be calculated, states that force is proportional to the rate of change of MOMENTUM.

**NEW MEXICO**
**Statehood:**
January 16, 1912
**Nickname:**
The Land of Enchantment
**State bird:**
Roadrunner
**State flower:**
Yucca flower
**State tree:**
Pinon pine
**State motto:**
It grows as it goes

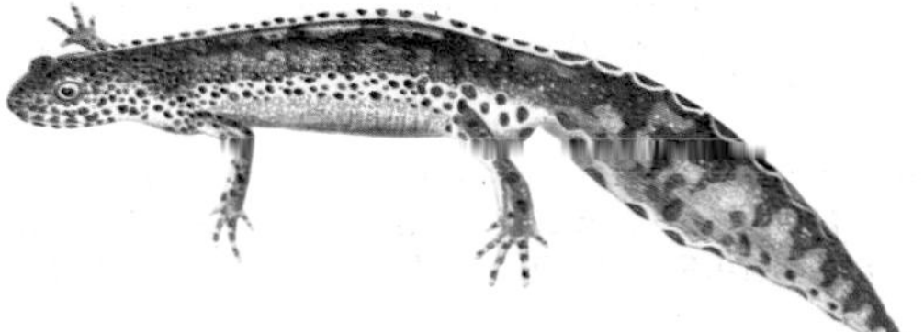

◀ **newt** An amphibian from mountainous regions of central Europe, the alpine newt (*Triturus alpestris*) feeds on worms and insects. Normally dull brown or black, the male develops bright colors in the breeding season.

**NEW YORK**
**Statehood :**
July 26, 1788
**Nickname :**
The Empire State
**State bird :**
Bluebird
**State flower :**
Rose
**State tree :**
Sugar maple
**State motto :**
Ever upward

The **third** law states that every force has associated with it an equal and opposite force. *See also* MECHANICS

**new town** Satellite town in the UK designed to rehouse residents from a nearby large city and to create local employment. The construction of some 37 new towns began in 1946 and continued until 1975.

**New Wave** Term used to describe the musical successor to PUNK, following its decline in the late 1970s. Groups such as Blondie, Police, Depeche Mode, Devo and Talking Heads epitomized this more tuneful and refined style.

**New York** State in NE US, bounded by the Canadian border, the Great Lakes, the Atlantic Ocean, and three New England states; the capital is ALBANY. NEW YORK CITY is by far the largest city in the state. Henry HUDSON discovered New York Bay in 1609 and sailed up the river that now bears his name. The NEW NETHERLAND colony was established in the Hudson valley. In 1664 it was seized by the British and renamed New York. It was one of the 13 original states of the Union. The opening of the ERIE CANAL in 1825 was an enormous stimulus to New York's growth. Throughout US history its economic strength and large population have given it great influence in national affairs. Much of the state is mountainous, the ADIRONDACK MOUNTAINS (NE) and Catskills (SE) being the principal ranges. The W consists of a rolling plateau sloping down to Lake Ontario and the St. Lawrence valley. The HUDSON and its tributary, the Mohawk, are the chief rivers. Agricultural produce is varied. New York is the leading manufacturing and commercial state in the US. Industries: clothing, machinery, chemicals, electrical equipment, paper, optical instruments. Area: 49,108sq mi (127,190sq km). Pop. (1993 est.) 18,197,154.

**New York City** City and port in SE New York State, at the mouth of the HUDSON River; largest city (by population) in the US. Manhattan Island was settled in 1624 and was bought from the Native Americans in 1626 by the Dutch West India Company. New Amsterdam was founded at the S end of the island. In 1664 the British took the colony and renamed it New York. The founding of the Bank of New York by Alexander HAMILTON and the opening of the ERIE CANAL in 1825 made New York the principal US commercial and financial center. From the CIVIL WAR, the city received a great influx of immigrants. It is made up of five boroughs: MANHATTAN, the BRONX, BROOKLYN, QUEENS, and STATEN ISLAND. Monuments and buildings of interest include the STATUE OF

## NEW ZEALAND

New Zealand's flag was designed in 1869 and adopted as the national flag in 1907 when New Zealand became an independent dominion. The flag includes the British Blue Ensign and four of the five stars in the Southern Cross constellation.

**AREA:** 104,629sq mi (270,990sq km)
**POPULATION:** 3,414,000
**CAPITAL (POPULATION):** Wellington (329,000)
**GOVERNMENT:** Constitutional monarchy
**ETHNIC GROUPS:** New Zealand European 74%, New Zealand Maori 10%, Polynesian 4%
**LANGUAGES:** English and Maori (both official)
**RELIGIONS:** Christianity (Anglican 21%, Presbyterian 16%, Roman Catholic 15%, Methodist 4%)
**CURRENCY:** New Zealand dollar = 100 cents

New Zealand consists of two mountainous main islands and several smaller ones, *c.* 1,000mi (1,600km) SE of Australia. Much of NORTH ISLAND is volcanic; Ngauruhoe and Ruapehu are active. It is noted for its hot springs and geysers. The N has fertile peninsulas and river basins. New Zealand's largest river (Waikato) and largest lake (Taupo) are both on North Island. North Island cities include the capital, WELLINGTON, and the largest port, AUCKLAND. The Southern Alps extend for almost the entire length of SOUTH ISLAND, rising to Mount COOK at 12,313ft (3,753m). South Island is famed for its glaciers and fjords. The major South Island cities are CHRISTCHURCH and DUNEDIN. Territories include the ROSS DEPENDENCY in Antarctica. COOK ISLANDS and NIUE are associated states.

### CLIMATE

The climate varies from N to S. Auckland has a warm, humid climate throughout the year. Wellington has cooler summers, while in Dunedin, temperatures can dip below freezing in winter. Rainfall is heaviest on the W highlands.

### VEGETATION

Only small areas of original *kauri* forests survive, mainly in the N and S extremities of South Island. Beech forests grow in the highlands, and large plantations are grown for timber. Abundant sunshine is ideal for E coast vineyards.

### HISTORY AND POLITICS

MAORI settlers arrived in New Zealand more than 1,000 years ago. The first European discovery was by the Dutch navigator Abel TASMAN in 1642. The British explorer James COOK landed in 1769. Trade in fur and whaling brought British settlers in the early 19th century. A series of intertribal wars (1815–40) killed tens of thousands of Maoris. In 1840 the first British settlement at Wellington was established. The Treaty of WAITANGI (1840) promised to honor Maori land rights in return for recognition of British sovereignty. In 1841 New Zealand became a separate colony. Increasing colonization led to the Maori Wars (1845–48, 1860–72). In 1893 New Zealand was the first country to extend the franchise to women. In 1907 New Zealand became a self-governing dominion in the British Commonwealth. New Zealand troops fought on the side of the Allies in both World Wars. In 1973 Britain joined the European Community, and New Zealand's exports shrank. Since the 1980s, it has pursued a more independent economic and foreign policy. In 1985 *Rainbow Warrior*, was blown up in Auckland harbor, prompting the adoption of antinuclear policies. Maori rights and the preservation of Maori culture remain a political issue. A 1992 referendum voted in favor of the introduction of proportional representation. After 1996 elections the National Party (NP) and New Zealand First (NZF) formed a coalition government. In 1997 Jenny Shipley became New Zealand's first woman prime minister. In 1998 the NZF withdrew from the coalition.

### ECONOMY

During the 1980s New Zealand shifted from a state-controlled economy, with a large welfare state, to a more market-oriented one (1995 GDP per capita, US$16,360). The economy was badly affected by the financial crisis in SE Asia. It has traditionally depended on agriculture, particularly sheep- and cattle-rearing. Manufacturing now employs twice as many people as agriculture. Tourism is the fastest growing economic sector.

LIBERTY, the EMPIRE STATE BUILDING, Rockefeller Center, the METROPOLITAN MUSEUM OF ART, the Museum of Modern Art, the Guggenheim Museum, Lincoln Center, and Carnegie Hall. It is one of the world's leading ports and financial centers. Industries: clothing, chemicals, metal products, scientific instruments, shipbuilding, food processing, broadcasting, entertainment, tourism, publishing. Pop. (1990) 7,322,564.

**New Zealand** Archipelago state in the S Pacific. *See* country feature

**Ney, Michel** (1769–1815) French general, one of the most brilliant of NAPOLEON's commanders. He fought in the FRENCH REVOLUTIONARY and NAPOLEONIC WARS, notably at Friedland (1807) and in the retreat from Moscow (1812). He urged Napoleon to abdicate in 1814 and accepted the BOURBON restoration, but rejoined Napoleon during the HUNDRED DAYS and fought gallantly in the WATERLOO campaign. He was subsequently executed as a traitor.

**Nez Percé** (Fr. pierced nose) Tribe of Native North Americans living in central Idaho, SW Washington, and NE Oregon.

**Ngo Dinh Diem** *See* DIEM, NGO DINH

**Niagara Falls** Waterfalls on the Niagara River on the border of the US (W New York state) and Canada (SE Ontario); divided into the Horseshoe, or Canadian, Falls and the American Falls. The Canadian Falls are 158ft (48m) high and 2,600ft (792m), wide; the American Falls are 167ft (51m) high and 1,000ft (305m) wide.

**Niamey** Capital of Niger, W Africa, in the SW part of the country, on the Niger River. It became capital of the French colony of Niger in 1926. It grew rapidly after World War II and is now the country's largest city and its commercial and administrative center. Manufactures include textiles, ceramics, plastics, and chemicals. Pop. (1988) 392,169.

**Nicaea, Councils of** Two important ecumenical councils of the Christian church held in Nicaea (modern Iznik, Turkey). The first was convoked in AD 325 to resolve the problems caused by the emergence of ARIANISM. It promulgated a creed, affirming belief in the divinity of Christ. The Second Council of Nicaea, held in 787, was summoned by the patriarch Tarasius to deal with the problem of the worship of icons.

**Nicaragua** Republic in Central America. *See* country feature, page 480

**Nice** City in SE France, on the Mediterranean coast; capital of Alpes-Maritimes département. Founded by Phocaean Greeks in the 4th century BC, Nice was conquered by Rome in the 1st century AD. In the 10th century it passed to the counts of Provence. In 1388 it became a possession of the House of Savoy. Nice was under French rule from 1792 to 1814, when it was returned to Savoy, becoming permanently part of France in 1860. It is a major center of the French Riviera. Industries: tourism, olive oil, perfumes, textiles, electronics. Pop. (1990) 342,349.

**Nicene Creed** Statement of Christian faith named for the First Council of NICAEA (325). Its exact origin is, however, uncertain. The Nicene Creed defends the orthodox Christian doctrine of the TRINITY against the ARIAN heresy. It is subscribed to by all the major Christian Churches and is widely used by them in their celebrations of the EUCHARIST. *See also* APOSTLES' CREED; ATHANASIAN CREED

**Nicholas, Saint** Patron saint of children and sailors. Traditionally he was Bishop of Myra in Asia Minor in the 4th century and is the subject of many legends. In one he secretly gave gold to three poor girls as their dowry. From this came the custom of giving presents on his feast day, December 6, a habit later transferred to Christmas in most countries. His name in one Dutch dialect, *Sinter Claes*, became Santa Claus.

**Nicholas I** (1796–1855) Czar of Russia (1825–55). Ascending the throne in 1825, he was immediately confronted by the Decembrist revolt, during which a secret society of officers and aristocrats assembled some 3,000 troops in St. Petersburg, demanding a representative democracy. Having crushed the rebels, he ruthlessly suppressed rebellion in Poland and assisted Austria against the Hungarian revolution of 1848. His pressure on Turkey led to the CRIMEAN WAR (1853–56).

**Nicholas II** (1868–1918) Last czar of Russia (1894–1917). Torn between the autocracy of his father, ALEXANDER III, and the reformist policies of ministers such as Count Sergei Witte, he lacked the capacity for firm leadership. Defeat in the RUSSO-JAPANESE WAR was followed by the RUSSIAN REVOLUTION OF 1905. Nicholas agreed to constitutional government but, as danger receded, removed most of the powers of the Duma (parliament). In World War I he took military command (1915), but defeat in war again provoked revolution (1917). Nicholas was forced to abdicate, and in July 1918 he and his family were executed by BOLSHEVIKS.

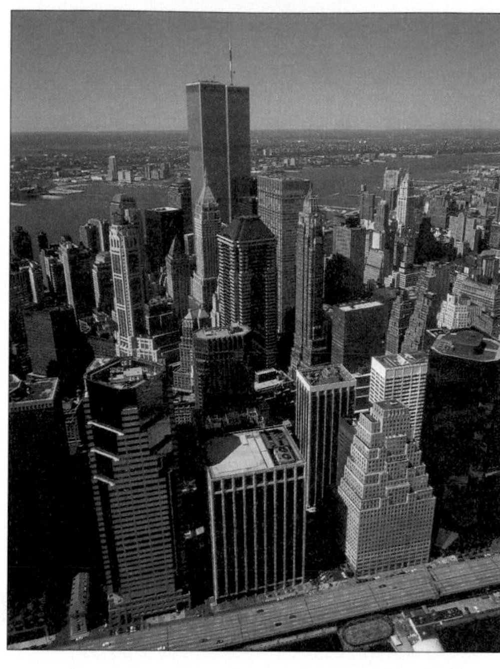

◄ **New York City** The famous skyline of New York City is that of the island of Manhattan, one of the five boroughs of the city. The tallest buildings in the photograph are the World Trade Center. Its two skyscrapers were the tallest in the world on their completion in 1973.

**Nicholson, Ben** (1894–1982) British painter, one of the champions of ABSTRACT ART in Britain. Influenced by CUBISM and Piet MONDRIAN, he developed a geometric abstract style, which he expressed in austere carved and painted reliefs, such as *White Relief* (1935). He later produced a series of freely abstracted still-lifes and landscapes, before returning to reliefs in the 1960s.

**Nicholson, Jack** (1937– ) US film actor. He first attracted attention in a small part in *Easy Rider* (1969). Oscar-nominated several times for films such as *Five Easy Pieces* (1970) and *Chinatown* (1974), he eventually won Academy Awards for *One Flew Over The Cuckoo's Nest* (1975) and *Terms of Endearment* (1983). He has consistently demonstrated his versatility, from films such as *The Shining* (1980), *The Postman Always Rings Twice* (1981), and *Prizzi's Honor* (1985) to *Batman* (1989) and *Mars Attacks!* (1996).

▲ **Nicholson** One of the most versatile film actors, Jack Nicholson received Academy Awards for his memorable performances in *One Flew over the Cuckoo's Nest* (1975) and *Terms of Endearment* (1983). His role is often that of an outsider.

**nickel** Silvery-white, metallic element (symbol Ni), one of the TRANSITION ELEMENTS. Its chief ores are pentlandite and niccolite. Hard, malleable, and ductile, nickel is used in stainless steels, other special alloys, coinage, cutlery, storage batteries, and as a hydrogenation catalyst. Properties: at.no. 28; at.wt. 58.71; sp.gr. 8.90; m.p. 2,647°F (1,453°C); b.p. 4,950°F (2,732°C); most common isotope $^{58}$Ni (67.84%).

**Nicklaus, Jack William** (1940– ) US golfer. He has secured 20 major championship wins. His record in the

◄ **Niagara Falls** Two spectacular waterfalls on the Niagara River are known as the Niagara Falls. They lie on the border between the US and Canada. Goat Island separates the Canadian Falls from the American. The Niagara Falls provide hydroelectric power as well as attracting vast numbers of tourists.

▲ **Nietzsche** The influential German philosopher Friedrich Nietzsche's work was distorted by the Nazis and used to defend their idea of an Aryan super-race.

British Open is unparalleled, with three victories and a top six place in 15 consecutive years. He won the Masters six times, the last victory being in 1986.

**Nicosia** (Levkosía) Capital of Cyprus, in the central part of the island. Known to the ancient world as Ledra, the city was later successively held by the Byzantines, French crusaders, and Venetians. The Ottoman Turks occupied the city from 1571 to 1878, when it passed to Britain. It is now divided into Greek and Turkish sectors. Manufactures include cigarettes, textiles, and footwear. Pop. (1992 est.) 177,451.

**nicotine** Poisonous ALKALOID obtained from the leaves of TOBACCO, used in agriculture as a pesticide and in veterinary medicine to kill external parasites. Nicotine is the principal addictive agent in smoking tobacco. *See also* CIGARETTE

**Nielsen, Carl** (1865–1931) Danish composer, known internationally for his six symphonies. He also composed concertos for violin, flute, and clarinet, two operas, a woodwind quintet, and four string quartets.

**Niemeyer, Oscar** (1907– ) Brazilian architect. An early advocate of modern architecture, he worked with LE CORBUSIER on the Ministry of Education and Health Building in Rio (1936–45). He subsequently developed an original approach: elegant, subtropical luxury expressed through curving, sculptural forms. In the late 1950s Niemeyer began designing the main public buildings at Brasilia.

**Niemöller, Martin** (1892–1984) German Protestant minister and theologian. He opposed Hitler's creation of a "German Christian Church" and was arrested in 1938 because of his opposition to the Nazi Party. In 1961 he became a President of the World Council of Churches.

**Nietzsche, Friedrich Wilhelm** (1844–1900) German philosopher who rejected Christianity and the prevailing morality of his time and emphasized people's freedom to create their own values. He studied classical philology and taught Greek. In 1879 he abandoned philology for philosophy, and worked out his view of the freedom of the individual over the next decade. He presented his notion of the *Übermensch* (superman), the idealized man, strong, positive, and able to impose his wishes upon the weak and worthless, in *Thus Spake Zarathustra* (1883–85). Other works include *Beyond Good and Evil* (1886) and *On the Genealogy of Morals* (1887).

**Niger** Nation in N central Africa. *See* country feature

**Niger** Major river of W Africa. It rises in the Fouta Djallon plateau in the SW Republic of Guinea and flows NE through

## NICARAGUA

Nicaragua's flag was adopted in 1908. It was the flag of the Central American Federation (1823–39), which included Costa Rica, El Salvador, Guatemala, Honduras, and Nicaragua. It resembles the flag of El Salvador except for the shading of the blue and the central motif.

**AREA:** 50,000sq mi (130,000sq km)
**POPULATION:** 4,130,000
**CAPITAL (POPULATION):** Managua (682,111)
**GOVERNMENT:** Multiparty republic
**ETHNIC GROUPS:** Mestizo 77%, White 10%, Black 9%, Native American 4%
**LANGUAGES:** Spanish (official)
**RELIGIONS:** Christianity (Roman Catholic 91%, others 9%)
**CURRENCY:** Córdoba oro (gold córdoba) = 100 centavos

The Republic of Nicaragua is the largest country in Central America. The Central Highlands rise in the NW Cordillera Isabella to over 8,000 ft (2,400m) and are the source for many of the rivers that drain the E plain. The Caribbean coast forms part of the MOSQUITO COAST. Lakes Managua and Nicaragua lie on the edge of a narrow volcanic region, which contains Nicaragua's major urban areas, including the capital, MANAGUA, and the second-largest city of LEÓN. This region is highly unstable with many active volcanoes, and is prone to earthquakes.

### CLIMATE

Nicaragua has a tropical climate, with a rainy season from June to October. The Central Highlands are cooler, and the wettest part is the Mosquito Coast, with *c.*165in (4,200mm) of annual rain.

### VEGETATION

Rain forests cover large areas in the E, with trees such as cedar, mahogany, and walnut. Tropical savanna is common in the drier W.

### HISTORY AND POLITICS

Christopher Columbus reached Nicaragua in 1502 and claimed the land for Spain. By 1518 Spanish forces had subdued the indigenous population, and Nicaragua was ruled as part of the Spanish Captaincy-General of Guatemala. In the 17th century Britain secured control of the Caribbean coast. In 1821 Nicaragua gained independence, and formed part of the Central American Federation (1825–38). In the mid-19th century Nicaragua was ravaged by civil war, and US and British interference. The US was interested in the construction of a trans-isthmian canal through Nicaragua. In 1855 William WALKER invaded and established himself as the short-lived president of Nicaragua. José Santos Zemalya's dictatorial regime gained control of Mosquito Coast, and formed close links with the British. Following his downfall, civil war raged once more. In 1912 US marines landed to protect a pro-US regime, and in 1916 the US gained exclusive rights to the canal. Liberal opposition to US occupation resulted in guerrilla war, led by Augusto César Sandino. In 1933, the US marines withdrew, but set up the National Guard to help defeat the rebels. In 1934 Sandino was assassinated by Anastasio SOMOZA, director of the National Guard and official president from 1937.

Somoza's dictatorial regime led to political isolation. He was succeeded by his sons Luis (1956) and Anastasio (1967). Anastasio's diversion of international relief aid following the devastating 1972 Managua earthquake cemented opposition. In 1979 the SANDINISTA National Liberation Front (FSLN) overthrew the Somoza regime. The Sandinista government, led by Daniel Ortega, instigated wide-ranging socialist reforms. The US, concerned over the Sandinistas' relations with Cuba and the Soviet Union, sought to destabilize the government by organizing and funding the CONTRA rebels. A ten-year civil war destroyed the economy, and created dissatisfaction with the Sandinistas.

In 1990 elections, the Sandinistas lost power to the National Opposition Union coalition of opposition parties. Violeta CHAMORRO became president. Many of Chamorro's reforms were blocked by her coalition partners and the Sandinista-controlled trade unions. In 1996 elections, Chamorro was defeated by the Liberal leader, Arnoldo Aleman.

### ECONOMY

Nicaragua faces many problems in rebuilding its shattered economy and introducing free-market reforms. Agriculture is the main activity, employing *c.*50% of the work force and accounting for 70% of exports. Major cash crops include coffee, cotton, sugar, and bananas. Rice is the main food crop. It has some copper, gold, and, silver, but mining is underdeveloped. Most manufacturing is based in and around Managua.

Guinea into the Mali Republic, where it forms an extensive inland delta. It then flows in a great curve across the border into Nigeria and S into another vast delta before emptying into the Gulf of Guinea. Length: 2,600mi (4,180km).

**Niger-Congo languages** Group of nearly a thousand languages spoken by more than 300 million people in sub-Saharan Africa. The main ones are BANTU (spoken in S Africa), FULANI (Guinea, Senegal, and other W African countries), SWAHILI (E coast), YORUBA (primarily Nigeria), and Malinke (Mali).

**Nigeria** Republic in W Africa. *See* country feature, page 482

**Nightingale, Florence** (1820–1910) British nurse, b. Italy. She founded modern NURSING and is best known for her activities in the CRIMEAN WAR. In 1854 she took a unit of 38 nurses to care for wounded British soldiers. In 1860 she founded the Nightingale School and Home for nurse training at St. Thomas's Hospital, London.

**nightingale** Migratory Old World songbird of the THRUSH family (Turdidae). The common nightingale of England and W Europe (*Luscinia megarhynchos*) is ruddy-brown with light gray underparts. Length: *c*.6.5in (16.5cm).

**nightjar** Insect-eating, nocturnal bird found worldwide. It has a whirring cry. Length: 10.5in (27cm). Family Caprimulgidae.

**nightshade** Name given to various species of poisonous flowering plants, but especially to the DEADLY NIGHTSHADE (*Atropa belladonna*) and its close relatives.

**nihilism** Doctrine of certain Russian revolutionaries in the late 19th century. It condemned contemporary society as hostile to nature and rejected nonrational beliefs. Nihilists demanded radical reform of government and society by violent means.

**Nijinsky, Vaslav** (1890–1950) Russian dancer, often regarded as the greatest male ballet dancer of the 20th century. Dancing with the BALLETS RUSSES, his most noted roles were in *Petrushka*, *Les Sylphides*, and *Scheherazade*. From 1912 he choreographed such ballets as *L'Après-midi d'un faune*, *Jeux*, and *Le Sacre du printemps* for DIAGHILEV.

**Nile** Longest river in the world, flowing *c*.4,160mi (6,700km) from the Kagera headstream, E Burundi, to its Mediterranean delta in NE Egypt. The Kagera flows generally N before emptying into Lake VICTORIA. The Victoria Nile flows from Lake Victoria to Lake ALBERT in Uganda. From Lake Albert to the Sudanese border, it is called the Albert Nile. It continues to flow N through the S Sudanese swamps as the Bahr el Jebel. From Malakâl to KHARTOUM the river is called the White Nile. At Khartoum it converges with the

## NIGER

This flag was adopted shortly before Niger became independent from France in 1960. The orange stripe represents the Sahara in the north, and the green the grasslands in the south. Between them, the white stripe represents the Niger River, with a circle for the sun.

**AREA:** 489,189sq mi (1,267,000sq km)
**POPULATION:** 8,252,000
**CAPITAL POPULATION:** Niamey (392,169)
**GOVERNMENT:** Multiparty republic
**ETHNIC GROUPS:** Hausa 53%, Zerma-Songhai 21%, Tuareg 11%, Fulani (or Peul) 10%
**LANGUAGES:** French (official)
**RELIGIONS:** Islam 98%
**CURRENCY:** CFA franc = 100 centimes

The Republic of Niger is a landlocked nation in N central Africa. The N plateaus lie in the SAHARA. Central Niger contains the rugged, partly volcanic Aïr Mountains, which reach a height of 6,634ft (2,022m) near Agadez. The S consists of broad plains, including the Lake CHAD basin in SE Niger, on the borders with Chad and Nigeria. The only major river is the NIGER in the SW. The narrow Niger valley is the country's most fertile and densely populated region, and includes the capital, NIAMEY.

### CLIMATE

Niger is one of the world's hottest countries. The hottest months are March to May, when the HARMATTAN wind blows from the Sahara. Niamey has a tropical climate, with a rainy season from June to September. Rainfall decreases from S to N. Northern Niger is practically rainless.

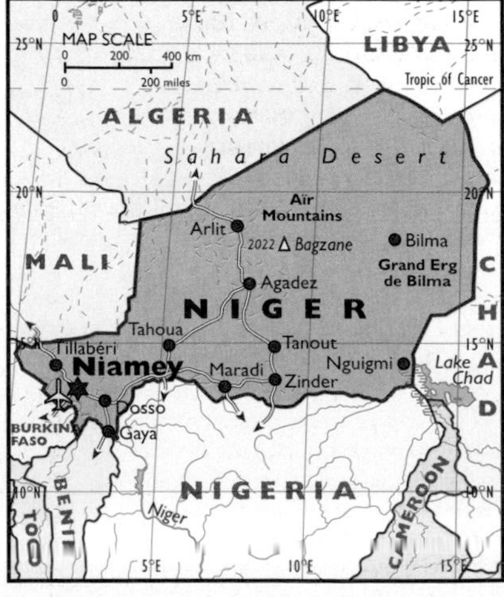


### VEGETATION

The far S consists of tropical savanna. Animals, such as buffaloes, elephants, giraffes, and lions, are found in the "W" National Park, which Niger shares with Benin and Burkina Faso. Most of S Niger lies in the SAHEL region of dry grassland. The Aïr Mountains support grass and scrub. The N deserts are generally barren.

### HISTORY AND POLITICS

Neolithic remains have been found in the N desert. Nomadic TUAREG settled in the Aïr Mountains in the 11th century AD, and by the 13th century had established a state based on Agadez and the trans-Saharan trade. In the 14th century, the HAUSA settled in S Niger. In the early 16th century the SONGHAI empire controlled much of Niger, but were defeated by the Moroccans at the end of the century. In the early 19th century the FULANI gained control of much of S Niger. The first French expedition arrived in 1891, but Tuareg resistance prevented full occupation until 1914. In 1922 Niger became a colony within French West Africa. In 1958 Niger voted to remain an autonomous republic within the French Community. Full independence was achieved in 1960. Hamani Diori became Niger's first president, and maintained close ties with France. Drought in the Sahel began in 1968 and killed many livestock and destroyed crops. In 1974, a group of army officers, led by Lieutenant-Colonel Seyni Kountché, overthrew Hamani Diori, and suspended the constitution. Kountché died in 1987, and was succeeded by his cousin General Ali Saibou. In 1991 Tuaregs in N Niger began an armed campaign for greater autonomy. A national conference removed Saibou, and established a transitional government. In 1993 multiparty elections, Mahamane Ousmane of the Alliance of Forces for Change (AFC) coalition became president. The collapse of the coalition led to further elections in 1995, which were won by the National Movement for a Development Society (MNSD), but a military coup, led by Colonel Ibrahim Bare Mainassara, seized power. A peace accord was signed between the government and the Tuaregs. In 1996 elections, Brigadier General Mainassara became president.

### ECONOMY

Niger has been badly hit by droughts, which have caused great suffering and food shortages, and the destruction of the traditional nomadic lifestyle. Niger's chief resource is uranium, and it is the world's second largest producer. Uranium accounts for over 80% of exports; most of it is exploited by the French Atomic Energy Authority. Some tin and tungsten are also mined. Other mineral resources are largely unexploited. Despite its resources, Niger is one of the world's poorest countries (1995 GDP per capita, $750). Farming employs 85% of the workforce, though only 3% of the land is arable and 7% is used for grazing. Food crops include beans, cassava, millet, rice, and sorghum. Cotton and peanuts are leading cash crops.

Nigeria's flag was adopted in 1960 when Nigeria became independent from Britain. It was selected after a competition to find a suitable design. The green represents Nigeria's forests. The white in the center stands for peace.

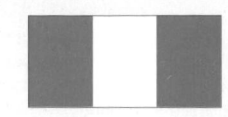

**AREA:** 356,668sq mi (923,770sq km)
**POPULATION:** 88,515,000
**CAPITAL (POPULATION):** Abuja (305,900)
**GOVERNMENT:** Federal republic
**ETHNIC GROUPS:** Hausa 21%, Yoruba 21%, Ibo (or Igbo) 19%, Fulani 11%, Ibibio 6%
**LANGUAGES:** English (official)
**RELIGIONS:** Christianity (Protestant 26%, Roman Catholic 12%, others 11%), Islam 45%
**CURENCY:** Naira = 100 kobo

The Federal Republic of Nigeria is the most populous nation in Africa. Nigeria has a sandy coastline, fringed by a belt of mangrove swamps and lagoons, which includes the former capital, LAGOS. The NIGER and Benue rivers meet in central Nigeria, and run S into the Niger Delta, where BENIN CITY is situated. North of the coastal lowlands is a hilly region of rain forest and savanna. At the foot of the great plateau of Nigeria lies the city of IBADAN. The plateau is a region of high wooded and savanna plains, and includes the capital, ABUJA. In the extreme NE lies the Lake CHAD basin. In the NW lies the Sokoto plains. The Adamawa Highlands extend along the SE border with Cameroon, and contain Nigeria's highest point at 6,699ft (2,042m).

### CLIMATE

Lagos has a tropical climate, with high temperatures and rain throughout the year. The N is drier and often hotter than the S, though the highlands are cooler. KANO in N central Nigeria has a marked dry season from October to April.

### VEGETATION

Behind the coastal swamps are rain forests, though large areas have been cleared by farmers. The plateau contains large areas of tropical savanna with forested river valleys. Open grassland and semiarid scrub occur in drier areas. To the N lie the dry grasslands of the SAHEL.

### HISTORY AND POLITICS

Excavations around the Nigerian village of Nok have uncovered some of the oldest and most beautiful examples of African sculpture. The Nok civilization flourished between 500 BC and AD 200. In the 11th century, the Kanem-Bornu kingdom extended S from Lake Chad into Nigeria, and the HAUSA established several city-states. In SW Nigeria, the state of BENIN and the YORUBA kingdom of Oyo flourished in the 15th century. They were renowned for their brass, bronze, and ivory sculptures. The SONGHAI empire dominated N Nigeria in the early 16th century. The Portuguese were the first Europeans to reach the Nigerian coast, and they established trading links with Benin in the late 15th century. Nigeria became a center of the slave trade, with major European powers competing for control. The IGBO established city-states built on the wealth of the trade. In the early 19th century, the FULANI captured many of the Hausa city-states. Sokoto retained its independence. The SW began a protracted civil war. In 1807 Britain renounced the slave trade, but other countries continued the practice. In 1861 Britain seized Lagos, ostensibly to stop the trade. By 1885 Britain controlled all of S Nigeria, and gradually extended northward. By 1906 Britain had conquered all of Nigeria, and divided the country into the Colony (Lagos) and Protectorate of Southern Nigeria and the Protectorate of Northern Nigeria. In 1914 the two were combined. Britain ruled indirectly through colonial officials and local rulers. Cities, infrastructure, and industries developed. In 1954 Nigeria was federated into three regions (N, E, and W) plus the territory of Lagos. In 1960 Nigeria gained independence, and became a republic in 1963. In 1966 Igbo army officers staged a successful coup, but the regime was rapidly topped by a Hausa-led coup. In 1967, the Igbo, increasingly concerned for their safety within the federation, formed the independent republic of BIAFRA. For the next three years civil war raged in Nigeria, until Biafra capitulated.

The division of Nigeria into 30 states reflects the fact that it contains more than 250 ethnic and language groups, and several religious ones. The early 1970s were more peaceful, as Nigeria expanded its oil industry. Nigeria joined OPEC in 1971. Oil revenue created widespread government corruption, and widened the wealth gap. Drought in the SAHEL killed much livestock and led to mass migration to the S. After several military coups, civilian rule was briefly restored in 1979. Following 1983 elections, the military seized power again. Between 1960 and 1996 Nigeria enjoyed only nine years of civilian government. In 1993, presidential elections, won by Chief Moshood Abiola, were declared invalid by the military government. The army commander-in-chief, General Sanni Abacha, gained power. In 1994 nationwide demonstrations prompted Abiola to form a rival government, but he was swiftly arrested. In 1995 General Abacha was given an open-ended term in office, vowing to restore civilian rule by 1998. His regime was criticized for human rights abuses and the suppression of opposition. In November 1995, after the execution of nine activists, Nigeria was suspended from the British Commonwealth. In 1998 General Abacha died and was succeeded by General Abubakar. The death in prison of Abiola (July 1998) prompted widespread rioting. In 1999 elections General Olusegun Obasanjo, a former military ruler (1976–79) of Nigeria, became president.

### ECONOMY

Nigeria is a low income developing country, with great economic potential (1995 GDP per capita, US$1,220). It is the world's eleventh-largest producer of crude oil, which accounts for 95% of its exports. Agriculture employs 43% of the workforce. Nigeria is the world's third-largest producer of palm oil and palm kernels, fourth-largest producer of groundnuts, sixth-largest producer of cocoa, and seventh-largest producer of rubber. Cattle rearing is important in the N grasslands, while fishing is a major activity in the S. Manufacturing is diversifying. Products include chemicals and clothing. Nigeria has petroleum refineries, vehicle assembly plants, and steel mills.

Blue Nile. As simply the Nile, the river continues to flow N to the Egyptian border. There it flows into the man-made Lake Nasser, created by the damming of the river at ASWAN. From Aswan the river flows through LUXOR to CAIRO. N of Cairo is the Nile Delta, Egypt's largest agricultural area. The Nile empties into the Mediterranean at Damietta and Rosetta. As well as supporting the agriculture of Egypt and Sudan, the Nile is used for transportation, hydroelectricity, and tourism.

**Nimitz, Chester William** (1885–1966) US admiral. He served in submarines during World War I and commanded the Pacific fleet during World War II, directing operations against the Japanese at Midway and subsequent battles.

**Nineveh** Capital of ancient ASSYRIA, on the Tigris River (opposite modern Mosul, Iraq). The site was first occupied in the 6th millennium BC. It became the Assyrian capital under SENNACHERIB (r.704–681 BC). The city walls were more than 7.5mi (12km) long and contained gardens irrigated by canals. Nineveh was sacked by the Medes in 612 BC, but continued to be occupied until the Middle Ages.

**niobium** Shiny, gray-white TRANSITION ELEMENT (symbol Nb) of the second transition series. Its chief ore is pyrochlore. Soft and ductile, niobium is used in special stainless steels and in alloys for rockets and jet engines. Properties: at.no. 41; at.wt. 92.9064; sp.gr. 8.57; m.p. 4,474°F (2,468°C); b.p. 8,568°F (4,742°C); most common isotope $^{93}Nb$ (100%).

**Nirvana** Conception of salvation and liberation from rebirth in the religions of ancient India – HINDUISM, BUDDHISM, and JAINISM. To Hindus, *nirvana* is extinction in the supreme being, brought about by internal happiness, internal satisfaction, and internal illumination. To Buddhists, it is the attainment of a transcendent state of enlightenment through the extinction of all desires. To Jainists, it is a state of eternal blissful repose.

**nitrate** Salt of NITRIC ACID ($HNO_3$). Nitrate salts contain the nitrate ion ($NO_3^-$), and some are important naturally occurring compounds, such as saltpeter (potassium nitrate, $KNO_3$) and Chile saltpeter (sodium nitrate, $NaNO_3$). Nitrates are used as food preservers, fertilizers, explosives, and as a source of nitric acid. They can be an environmental hazzard.

**nitric acid** Colorless liquid ($HNO_3$) that is one of the strongest mineral acids. Nitric acid attacks most metals, resulting in the formation of NITRATES, and is a strong oxidizing agent. It is used in the manufacture of agricultural chemicals, explosives, plastics, dyes, and rocket propellants.

**nitrogen** Common, gaseous, nonmetallic element (symbol N) of Group V of the periodic table. Colorless and odorless, it is the major component of the atmosphere (78% by volume), from which it is extracted by fractional distillation of liquid air. It is present in all plants and animals. The main industrial use is in the HABER PROCESS. Nitrogen compounds are used in fertilizers, explosives, dyes, foods, and drugs. The element is chemically inert. Properties: at. no. 7; at.wt. 14.0067; sp.gr. 1.2506; m.p. −345.75°F (−209.86°C); b.p. −320.4°F (−195.8°C); most common isotope $^{14}N$ (99.76%).

**nitrogen cycle** Circulation of NITROGEN through plants and animals in the BIOSPHERE. Plants obtain nitrogen compounds for producing essential proteins through assimilation. Nitrogen-fixing bacteria in the soil or plant root nodules take free nitrogen from the soil and air to form the nitrogen compounds used by plants to grow. The nitrogen is returned to the soil and air by decay or denitrification.

**nitrogen fixation** Incorporation of atmospheric NITROGEN into chemicals for use by organisms. Nitrogen-fixing microorganisms (mainly BACTERIA and CYANOBACTERIA) absorb nitrogen gas from the air, from air spaces in the soil, or from water, and build it up into compounds of AMMONIA. Other bacteria can then change these compounds into NITRATES, which can be taken up by plants. *See also* NITROGEN CYCLE

**nitroglycerine** Oily liquid used in the manufacture of explosives. It is also used in medicine (as glyceryl trinitrate) to relieve the symptoms of ANGINA.

**nitrous oxide** (dinitrogen oxide) Colorless gas ($N_2O$) that is used as an anesthetic or analgesic during surgical or dental operations. It is known as "laughing gas" since it produces exhilaration. It is also used in making pressurized foods.

**Niue** Island territory in the S Pacific Ocean, 1,340mi (2,160km) NE of New Zealand; the capital is Alofi. The largest coral island in the world, Niue was first visited by Europeans in 1774. In 1901 it was annexed to New Zealand. In 1974 it achieved self-government in free association with New Zealand. The island is prone to hurricanes and tropical rainstorms. Its economy is mainly agricultural. The major export is coconut. Area: 100sq mi (260sq km). Pop. (1991) 2,239.

**Nixon, Richard Milhous** (1913–94) 37th US President (1969–74). He was elected as a Republican to the House of Representatives in 1946 and the Senate in 1950. He came to prominence as a member of the House Un-American Activities Committee (HUAC). He was vice-president under EISENHOWER (1953–61), but lost the presidential election of 1960 to John F. KENNEDY. He was nominated as presidential candidate again in 1968, narrowly defeating the Democrat, Hubert Humphrey. As president (1969–74), he adopted the policy of détente with the Soviet Union and opened US relations with communist China. Overwhelmingly reelected in 1972, he withdrew US troops from the VIETNAM WAR (1973). The WATERGATE affair revealed that he was personally implicated in the obstruction of justice, and he resigned to avoid impeachment.

**Nkrumah, Kwame** (1909–72) First President of Ghana (1960–66). He formed the Convention People's Party in the Gold Coast in 1949. Imprisoned by the British in 1950, he was released to become prime minister (1952) after his party won the elections. In 1957 the Gold Coast became independent as Ghana and Nkrumah became the first postcolonial prime minister. In 1964 he made Ghana a one-party state. Economic failures, inefficiency, and corruption brought his regime into disrepute, and he was deposed in a military coup.

**Noah** Old Testament patriarch who was the only person righteous enough to be chosen by God to survive (with his family) the destruction of the FLOOD. In Genesis 6–9, Noah built an ARK, in accordance with God's strict instructions, to carry and shelter himself, all his family, and selected animals and birds. Noah and his sons and their wives were the ancestors of the human race after the Flood.

**Nobel, Alfred Bernhard** (1833–96) Swedish chemist, engineer, and industrialist. He invented DYNAMITE in 1866, and patented a more powerful explosive, gelignite, in 1876. With the fortune he made from the manufacture of explosives, he founded the NOBEL PRIZES.

**nobelium** Radioactive, metallic element (symbol No), one of the ACTINIDE SERIES of elements (atomic numbers from 89 to 103). Seven isotopes are known. Properties: at.no. 102, most stable isotope $^{255}No$ (half-life 3 minutes). *See also* TRANSURANIC ELEMENTS

**Nobel Prize** Awards given each year for outstanding contributions in the fields of physics, chemistry, physiology or medicine, literature, and economics and to world peace. Established in 1901 by the will of Swedish scientist Alfred NOBEL, the prizes are awarded annually on December 10. The winners are selected by committees based in Sweden and Norway.

**Nobili, Leopoldo** (1784–1835) Italian physicist who was a pioneer in electrochemistry. He generated electricity using platinum ELECTRODES in an alkaline nitrate ELECTROLYTE and devised the astatic galvanometer to measure the current.

**noble gas** (inert gas) Helium, neon, argon, krypton, xenon, and radon – the elements (in order of increasing atomic number) forming group 0 of the PERIODIC TABLE. They are colorless, odorless, and very unreactive. They have low reactivity because their outer electron shells are complete (two electrons for helium and eight each for the rest), thus offering no VALENCE "hooks."

**nocturne** In music, a quiet piece trying to reflect the atmosphere and mood of night-time. First used by John Field for some of his piano pieces, the title was later used by Frédéric CHOPIN. Claude DEBUSSY composed three orchestral nocturnes.

**No drama** Form of Japanese symbolic drama that developed between the 12th or 13th and the 15th centuries. It was influenced by ZEN, and the actors were originally Buddhist priests. The plots were taken chiefly from Japanese mythology and poetry. With little character or plot development, the No play seeks to convey a moment of experience or insight. It is highly stylized and uses masks, music, dance, and song. No was central to the development of KABUKI THEATER.

**Nolan, Sidney** (1917–92) Australian painter. He is famed for a series of paintings (begun in 1946) based on the life of a notorious outlaw, Ned Kelly. He continued painting subjects that portrayed events from Australian history, notably the *Eureka Stockade* series (1949). His almost surreal landscapes express the hard, scorched majesty of the outback.

**Nolde, Emil** (1867–1956) German painter and graphic artist who exemplified EXPRESSIONISM. He trained as a woodcarver before turning to painting relatively late. He painted his subjects (often flowers or landscapes) with deep, glowing colors and simplified outlines, bringing the works to the borders of ABSTRACT ART. Although he was a member of Die BRÜCKE (1905–07), he was essentially a solitary figure.

**nomad** Member of a wandering group of people who live mainly by hunting or herding. Nomadism has been regarded as an intermediate state between hunter-gatherer and farming societies. Today, nomadic groups survive only in the more remote parts of Africa, Asia, and the Arctic.

**nominalism** Philosophical theory, opposed to REALISM, that denies the reality of universal concepts. Whereas realists claim that there are universal concepts, such as *roundness* or *dog,* that are referred to by the use of these terms, nominalists argue that such generalized concepts cannot be known, and that the terms refer only to specific qualities common to particular circles or dogs that have been encountered up to now. Nominalism was much discussed by the scholastic philosophers of the Middle Ages.

**nonalignment** *See* NEUTRALITY

**nonconformism** Dissent from or lack of conformity with the religious doctrines or discipline of an established church, especially the CHURCH OF ENGLAND. The term Nonconformist applies to all the sects of British Protestantism that do not subscribe to the principles of the established Anglican Church or the established CHURCH OF SCOTLAND. It arose in England in reaction to the Act of Uniformity (1662). Movements such as CONGREGATIONALISM and PRESBYTERIANISM, BAPTISTS, and QUAKERS proliferated. Nonconformist Churches were eventually granted freedom of worship in 1689 and civil and political rights in 1828. Other Nonconformist movements, METHODISM and UNITARIANISM, were added to their ranks during the 18th century.

**nonfigurative** (nonobjective) Art that makes no attempt to represent objects from the physical world. The term comprises all ABSTRACT ART that does not rely on the appearance of the visual world for the source of its ideas.

**nonjurors** Clergy in England and Scotland who refused to take the oath of allegiance to WILLIAM III and MARY II in 1689. Anglo-Catholic in sympathy, they included several bishops and about 400 priests in England and most of the Scottish episcopal clergy.

**Nono, Luigi** (1924–90) Italian composer. An early follower of Anton WEBERN, he gained international recognition with the *Canonic Variations* (1950), an orchestral work based on a note series of Arnold SCHOENBERG. He composed several political works, including the antifascist opera *Intolerance* (1960).

► **Nolde** *Flowers in a Garden.* Flowers were a favorite subject of the expressionist painter Nolde, who was fascinated by the expressive potential of color. Declared degenerate by the Nazis and forbidden to paint, his later works were small watercolors that he painted in secret.

**Nootka** Tribe of Native Americans living along the W coast of Vancouver Island, British Columbia. They were once expert fishermen and were the only Native Americans on Canada's Pacific coast to hunt whales.

**Nordenskjöld, Nils Adolf Erik, Baron** (1832–1901) Swedish explorer and scientist. A geologist by training, he explored the Greenland icecap and the Arctic Ocean. In 1878 he led the Swedish expedition in the *Vega*, which was the first ship to sail through the NORTHEAST PASSAGE.

**norepinephrine** Hormone secreted by nerves in the autonomic nervous system and by the ADRENAL GLANDS. It slows the heart rate and constricts small arteries, thus raising the blood pressure. It is used therapeutically to combat the fall in blood pressure that accompanies shock.

**Norfolk** County of E England; the county town is NORWICH. The region was home to the ICENI tribe in the 3rd century BC. After the departure of the Romans it became part of the ANGLO-SAXON kingdom of East Anglia, but was later subjugated by the Danes. In the Middle Ages, Norfolk was a center of the wool industry. The land is generally low-lying and is used mainly for agriculture. The region is drained by the Waveney, Yare, Bure, and Ouse rivers, and by the BROADS. Today Norfolk produces cereals and root vegetables; poultry farming and fishing are also important. Area: 2,073sq mi (5,372sq km). Pop. (1991) 745,613.

**Norfolk** City-port on Elizabeth River, SE Virginia. Norfolk was founded in 1682; it forms the port of Hampton Roads, together with NEWPORT NEWS and PORTSMOUTH. Norfolk was almost completely destroyed by fire during the American Revolution (1776). In the Civil War it acted as a Confederate naval base. It is now the largest US naval complex. Exports: coal, grain, tobacco. Industries: shipbuilding, motor vehicles, chemicals, textiles. Pop. (1990) 261,229.

**Norfolk Broads** *See* BROADS, NORFOLK

**Norfolk Island** Territory of Australia in the SW Pacific Ocean, *c*.900mi (1,450km) E of Australia. Visited in 1774 by Captain James Cook, it was a British penal colony (1788–1814, 1825–55). Many people living on Pitcairn Island, descendants of the *Bounty* mutineers, were resettled here in 1856. The chief economic activities are agriculture and tourism. Area: 13sq mi (34sq km). Pop. (1991) 1,912.

**Noriega, Manuel (Antonio Morena)** (1934– ) Panamanian general. In 1963 Noriega became head of Panama's National Defense Forces and was made chief of military intelligence in 1969. Recruited as a CIA operative by the US, Noriega became an important backstage powerbroker. During 1983–89 he was effectively Panama's paramount leader, ruling behind puppet presidents. In 1987 evidence emerged of Noriega's criminal activities, and the US withdrew its support. In 1988 he was indicted by a US court on drug-connected charges and accused of murder. In December 1989 US troops invaded Panama and installed a civilian government. Noriega surrendered to US forces and was taken to the US for trial on corruption, drug trafficking, and money laundering. In April 1992 he was sentenced to 40 years in prison.

**Norman architecture** ROMANESQUE architectural style of the Normans in England, N France, and S Italy. Characteristic buildings include the cathedrals at St. Étienne and Caen in France, and Durham in England (begun 1093). The style was marked by massive proportions, square towers, round arches, and little decoration.

**Norman Conquest** Invasion of England in 1066 by WILLIAM I (the Conqueror), duke of Normandy. William claimed that EDWARD THE CONFESSOR (d.1066) had recognized him as heir to the throne of England, and he disputed the right of HAROLD II to be Edward's successor. William's army defeated and killed Harold at the battle of HASTINGS, then advanced on London, where William was accepted as king. The ruling class, lay and ecclesiastical, was gradually replaced by Normans, and Norman institutions were imposed.

**Normandy** Region and former province of NW France, coextensive with the départements of Manche, Calvados, Orne, Eure, and Seine-Maritime. Part of the Roman province of Gaul, it was absorbed into the Frankish kingdom of Neustria in the 6th century. In the mid-9th century it was invaded by

Vikings. It was the seat of William, Duke of Normandy (later WILLIAM I), who invaded England in 1066. Normandy was recovered by the French in 1204. It was the site of the NORMANDY CAMPAIGN of June 1944. It is characterized by forests, flat farmlands, and rolling hills. The economy is based on livestock rearing, dairy products, fruit, cider, and fishing.

**Normandy Campaign** Allied invasion of German-occupied France, launched on June 6, 1944 (D-Day). Commanded by EISENHOWER, the invasion was the largest amphibious operation in history. The successful landings were the start of the final campaign of WORLD WAR II in W Europe.

**Norman French** Dialect of Old French spoken by the Normans at the time of the conquest of England (1066). In Normandy, it was the general language, but it was also used by the Normans in England where it coexisted with contemporary MIDDLE ENGLISH for about three centuries.

**Normans** Descendants of Vikings who settled in NW France in the 9th–10th centuries. They created a powerful state, with a strongly centralized feudal society and warlike aristocracy. In the 11th century, under Robert GUISCARD and ROBERT II, they defeated the Muslims to create a kingdom in Sicily. In 1066 Duke William conquered England and became WILLIAM I.

**Norns** In Germanic mythology, three maidens who spun or wove the fate of both mortals and gods. Their names were Urth (Past), Verthandi (Present), and Skuld (Future).

**Norodom Sihanouk** (1922– ) Cambodian political leader. As king (1941–55, 1993– ), prime minister (1955–60), and head of state (1960–70, 1975–76, 1991–93), he was the leading political figure in Cambodia. Following a coup in 1970, he established a government in exile in China. He returned to Cambodia with the KHMER ROUGE in 1975 and formed another government in exile after the Vietnamese invasion in 1979. He returned to Cambodia in 1991 after signing an agreement providing for the end of the civil war and was installed as king when UN peacekeepers left in 1993.

**Norris, Frank** (1870–1902) US novelist. Considered one of the most striking naturalistic writers, he first attracted attention with *McTeague* (1899). Norris is also noted for his trilogy about wheat: *The Octopus* (1901), *The Pit* (1903), and *The Wolf* (unfinished).

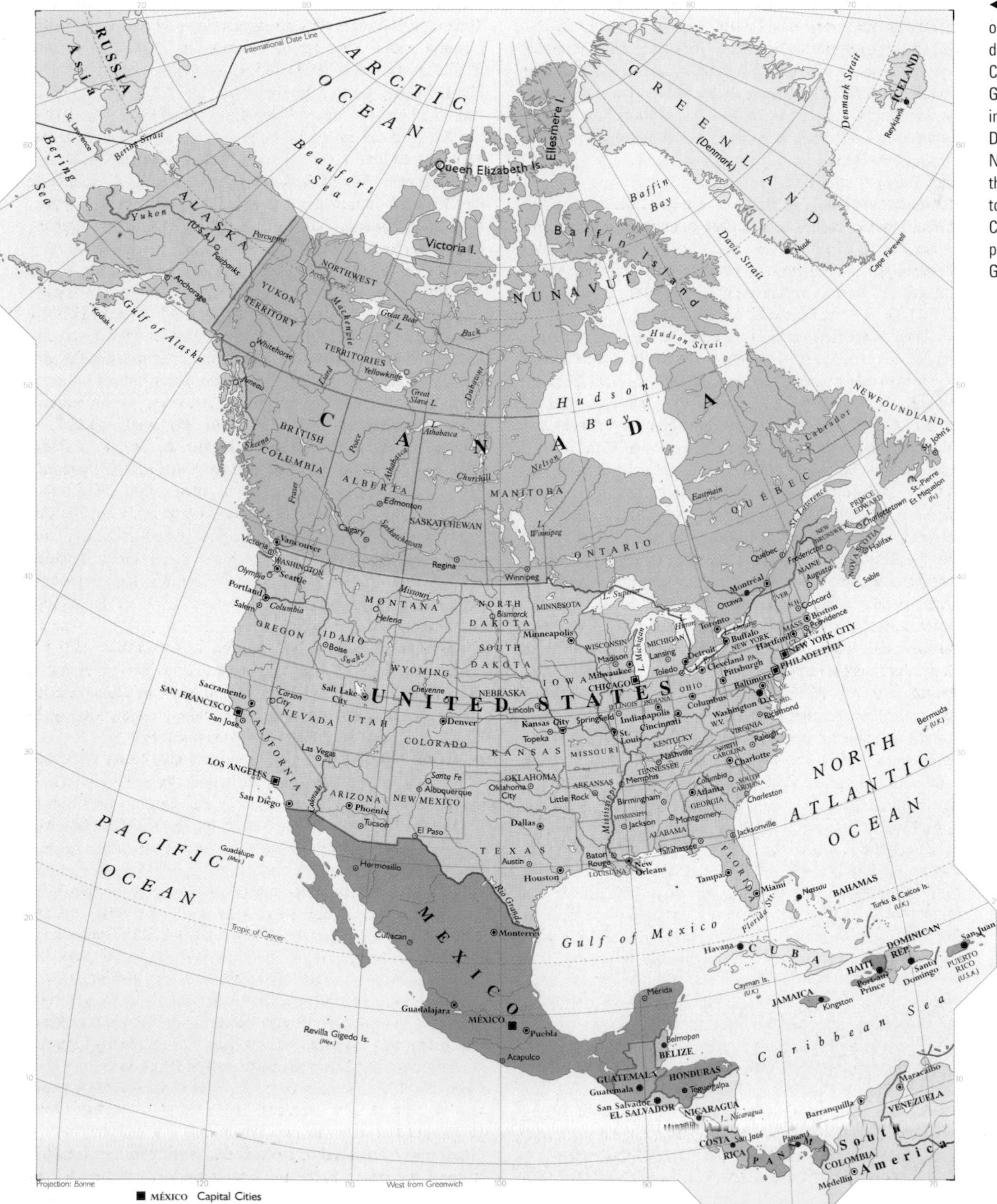


◀ **North America** The N part of the American continent is divided fairly evenly between Canada and the US. Greenland, the largest island in the world, is a part of Denmark. The climate of North America ranges from the tropical Caribbean islands to the arctic tundra of N Canada, Alaska, and the permanent icesheet covering Greenland.

**Norse literature** Literature of the Scandinavian Norsemen, written between the 9th and the 12th century. It consists mainly of mythological poetry and SAGAS. The works were set down in stone and wood, and survived orally to be recorded in the 12th–14th centuries.

**North, Frederick, Lord** (1732–92) British statesman, and prime minister (1770–82). He entered Parliament at the age of 22 and served in several governments, before becoming prime minister. North's repressive measures against unrest in the North American colonies, particularly the INTOLERABLE ACTS, have been blamed for their rebellion. He was forced to resign in 1783.

**North, Oliver Laurence** (1943– ) US marine lieutenant colonel. He was recruited as an aide to the National Security Council and was involved in several covert operations. The Congressional committee that investigated the notorious IRAN-CONTRA AFFAIR in 1987 revealed him as the central figure, and he was subsequently convicted of three criminal charges. He was pardoned in 1992.

**North America** Continent, including the mainland and offshore islands N of and including Panama. **Land** North America extends N of the Arctic Circle and S almost to the Equator. To the W it is bordered by the Bering Sea and the Pacific Ocean, and to the E by the Atlantic Ocean. There are many islands off both coasts, particularly to the N in the Arctic Ocean, and to the SE in the Caribbean Sea. There are two major mountain ranges: the APPALACHIANS in the E and the ROCKY MOUNTAINS in the W. Between these two ranges lie the fertile GREAT PLAINS and the Central Lowlands. In the E, a long coastal plain extends from New England to Mexico. The W coast is more mountainous. **Structure and Geology** Much of Canada is an old Precambrian shield area forming a saucer-shaped depression centered in HUDSON BAY. The Appalachians also have their origins in the Precambrian era. In the W, the complex fold mountains of the Rockies and the Pacific Margin are much younger and continue into South America as the ANDES. **Lakes and rivers** Lake SUPERIOR is the largest lake in North America, 31,820sq mi (82,413sq km), and together with MICHIGAN, HURON, ERIE, and ONTARIO, makes up the GREAT LAKES. The ST. LAWRENCE River forms a navigable link between the Great Lakes and the Atlantic Ocean. The longest river is the combined MISSISSIPPI-MISSOURI system. Other important rivers include the YUKON, MACKENZIE, COLORADO, COLUMBIA, DELAWARE, and RIO GRANDE. **Climate and vegetation** Its geographical range means that every climatic zone is represented. In the far N, there are areas of tundra and arctic conditions. In the interior, sheltered by high mountains, there are deserts. Tropical rain forest is found in the lower areas of Central America. On much of the continent the climate is temperate. The Great Plains region is temperate, and the natural vegetation is grass, bordered by mixed and coniferous forests in the mountains to the E, W, and N. **People** North America's first settlers probably arrived about 45,000 years ago from Asia by way of Alaska. By the time the Vikings arrived from Europe, around AD 1000, NATIVE AMERICANS occupied the entire continent. European settlement accelerated after Christopher Columbus's voyage in 1492. The Spaniards settled in Mexico and the WEST INDIES. The English and French settled farther N; Swedes, Germans, and Dutch also formed settlements. Europe's political and economic problems later drove larger numbers to the New World. Descendants of Spanish settlers are predominant in Mexico, Central America, and some Caribbean islands. French concentrations exist in Quebec province, Canada, and parts of the West Indies. In Central America and the Caribbean, European descendants are in the minority. **Economy** Much of North America benefits from fertile soil and a climate conducive to agriculture. The North American plains are one of the world's major grain and livestock-producing areas. The S area produces mainly cotton, tobacco, coffee, and sugarcane. There is also substantial industrial development. Mining is important, particularly in Canada and Mexico. **Recent history** The early 20th century saw mass immigration to the US and Canada. The US has been the dominant economic force on the continent throughout the 20th century. In the SPANISH AMERICAN WAR (1898) the US emerged as a world power. In 1903 Theodore ROOSEVELT enforced construction of the PANAMA CANAL, control of which is due to return to Panama in 1999. The US emerged from World War II as a world superpower. The ideological battle between CAPITALISM and COMMUNISM led to the COLD WAR and US involvement in the KOREAN WAR and VIETNAM WAR. Since 1994, Canada, the US, and Mexico have been linked through the NORTH AMERICAN FREE TRADE AGREEMENT (NAFTA). As the US and Canada have developed more service-based economies, some manufacturing has transferred to Mexico. Economic inequality and instability remain major issues in Mexico. Since World War II, many Caribbean islands have gained independence. A US trade embargo since CASTRO's revolution (1959) has crippled Cuba's economy. Central America has also been dominated by US interests and by repressive regimes and economic inequality. *Highest mountain* MOUNT MCKINLEY (Denali) 20,321ft (6,194m) *Longest river* Mississippi-Missouri 3,760mi (6,050km) *Population* 395,000,000 *Largest cities* MEXICO CITY (15,047,685); NEW YORK CITY (7,322,564); LOS ANGELES (3,489,779) *See also* individual country articles

**North American Free Trade Agreement (NAFTA)** Treaty designed to eliminate trade barriers between Canada, Mexico, and the US. The agreement was signed in 1992, and NAFTA came into effect on January 1, 1994. Some Latin American countries have also applied to join.

**North American mythology** Traditional beliefs of Native North Americans. The Native North Americans displayed a great diversity of languages and cultures, but their mythologies had many common features. Among these was the concept of heroes in the form of animal deities, such as Raven or Coyote, believed to have been the original inhabitants of the country. They brought order into the world by gaining possession of fire, wind, and rain and by establishing laws and institutions. They also created mountains and rivers and other natural features. Native Americans had numerous gods, including the Great Spirit and the Earth Mother of the Algonquians, and the gods of thunder and wind of the Iroquois. Belief in protective or harmful spirits remains universal, and the SHAMAN plays a central part in religious life, acting as an intermediary between humans and the spirit world.

**Northamptonshire** County in central England; the county town is Northampton. There are traces of pre-Celtic habitations as well as Roman and Anglo-Saxon settlement. The land is undulating and is drained by the Welland and Nene rivers. Much of the region is devoted to pasture, wheat growing, and forestry. Products include cereals, potatoes, and sugar beets. There are extensive iron ore deposits, and iron and steel industries remain important. Industries: footwear, engineering, food processing. Area: 914sq mi (2,367sq km). Pop. (1991) 578,807.

**North Atlantic Treaty Organization (NATO)** Intergovernmental organization, military alliance of the US, Canada, and 14 European countries. The original treaty was signed in Washington in 1949 by Belgium, Britain, Canada, Denmark, France, Iceland, Italy, Luxembourg, Norway, Portugal, Netherlands, and the US. Since then, Greece, Turkey, Spain, and Germany have joined. In July 1997, despite Russian opposition, the Czech Republic, Hungary, and Poland were invited to join. NATO's headquarters is in Brussels. During the COLD WAR, it was the focus of the West's defense against the Soviet Union.

**North Carolina** State in E US, on the Atlantic coast; the capital is RALEIGH. The first English colony in North America was founded in 1585 on Roanoke Island. Permanent settlers moved into the region from Virginia in the 1650s. It was the last state to secede from the Union. North Carolina's coastal plain is swampy near the shore and low-lying. Its W edge rises to rolling hills, and farther W are the Blue Ridge and Great Smoky Mountains. It is the leading producer of tobacco in the US. Important agricultural products are corn, soybeans, peanuts, pigs, chickens, and dairy produce. Industries: textiles, timber, fishing, tourism, electrical machinery, chemicals. Mineral resources: phosphate, feldspar, mica, kaolin. Area: 52,712sq mi (136,523sq km). Pop. (1990) 6,628,637.

**NORTH CAROLINA**
**Statehood:**
November 21, 1789
**Nickname:**
The Tar Heel State
**State bird:**
Cardinal
**State flower:**
Flowering dogwood
**State tree:**
Pine
**State motto:**
To be, rather than to seem

**Northcliffe, Alfred Charles William Harmsworth, Viscount** (1865–1922) British newspaper publisher, b. Ireland. He began his career as a freelance journalist but, with the help of his brother Harold, was soon publishing his own popular periodicals. In 1896 he launched the *Daily Mail*, whose concise, readable style of news presentation proved very successful. In 1905 he founded the *Daily Mirror*, the first picture paper, and in 1908 gained control of *The Times*.

**North Dakota** State in N central US, on the Canadian border; the capital is BISMARCK. French explorers first visited the region in 1738. The US acquired the W half of the area from France in the LOUISIANA PURCHASE (1803), and the rest from Britain in 1818 when the boundary with Canada was fixed. Dakota was divided into North and South Dakota in 1889. The region is generally low-lying and is drained by the Missouri and Red rivers. Wheat, barley, rye, oats, sunflowers, and flaxseed are the chief crops. Cattle rearing is the most important economic activity. Area: 70,665sq mi (183,022sq km). Pop. (1990) 638,800.

**Northeast Passage** Route from the Atlantic to the Pacific via the Arctic Ocean. Unsuccessful attempts were made to find the passage by Dutch and English mariners from the 16th century. The complete voyage was first made by Baron NORDENSKJÖLD in 1878–80.

**Northern Cape** Province in SW South Africa; the capital is Kimberley. Northern Cape was created in 1994 from the N part of the former CAPE PROVINCE. Area: 139,650sq mi (361,800sq km). Pop (1994) 737,360.

**Northern Ireland** *See* IRELAND, NORTHERN

**northern lights** Popular name for the AURORA borealis.

**Northern Province** Province in N South Africa; the capital is Pietersburg. In 1994 Northern Transvaal was formed from the N part of the former province of TRANSVAAL. In 1995 it was renamed Northern Province. Area: 46,970sq mi (123,280sq km). Pop. (1994 est.) 5,201,630.

**Northern Territory** Territory in N central Australia bounded by the Timor and Arafura seas (N), and the states of Western Australia (W), South Australia (S), and Queensland (E); the capital is DARWIN. In 1863 it was annexed to South Australia but in 1911 was brought under the control of the federal government. In 1978 it achieved internal self-government. The territory lies mostly within the tropics. The coastal areas are flat with many offshore islands, and the region rises inland to a high plateau, the Barkly Tableland. In the mainly arid south are the Macdonnell Ranges and AYERS ROCK. Today there is little farming but some government-aided stock-breeding. Manganese ore, bauxite, and iron are mined. Area: 520,280sq mi (1,347,525sq km). Pop. (1993) 169,298.

**Northern War** (1700–21) Conflict in N Europe between Sweden and its neighbors. It began with an attack on Sweden by Denmark, Saxony, Poland, and Russia. CHARLES XII of Sweden defeated all his opponents (1700–06), but war was renewed in 1707 when Charles invaded Russia. The Swedes were decisively defeated at Poltava (1709). Charles took refuge with the Ottoman Turks, encouraging their attack on Russia in 1710–11. At the ensuing peace treaties (1719–21), Sweden lost virtually all its northern empire.

**North Island** Smaller, more populated of the main islands of New Zealand; separated from SOUTH ISLAND by Cook Strait. The chief cities are WELLINGTON, AUCKLAND, and Hamilton. The island contains several mountain ranges, Lake Taupu (New Zealand's largest lake), fertile coastal plains, and numerous hot springs. Most of New Zealand's dairy produce comes from North Island. Industries; wood pulp, paper, mining, fishing. Area: 44,297sq mi (114,729sq km). Pop. (1991) 2,553,413.

**North Korea** *See* KOREA, NORTH

**North Pole** Most northerly point on Earth; the N end of the Earth's axis of rotation, 450mi (725km) N of Greenland. Geographic north lies at 90° latitude, 0° longitude. The Arctic Ocean covers the entire area.

**North Sea** Arm of the Atlantic Ocean, lying between the E coast of Britain and the European mainland and connected to the English Channel by the Straits of Dover. Generally shallow, it is *c*.600mi (960km) long, with a maximum width of 400mi (640km). It is a major fishing ground, shipping route, and, since 1970, an important source of oil and natural gas. Area: *c*.220,000sq mi (580,000sq km).

**Northumberland, John Dudley, Duke of** (1502–53) Effectively ruler of England (1549–53). He was one of the councillors named by HENRY VIII to govern during the minority of EDWARD VI. In 1553 he attempted to usurp the succession through his daughter-in-law, Lady Jane GREY, but was thwarted by popular support for the rightful queen, MARY I. He was subsequently executed for treason.

**Northumberland** County in NE England, on the border with Scotland; the county town is Morpeth. In the 2nd century AD HADRIAN'S WALL was built to defend Roman Britain from the N tribes. In the 7th century the region became part of the Saxon kingdom of Northumbria. The land slopes down from the Cheviot Hills in the NW, and the region is drained by the Tyne, Tweed, Blythe, and Coquet rivers. The county is largely rural, the chief farming activities being cattle and sheep rearing. Barley and oats are grown and forestry is important. Coal is mined in the S. Area: 1,943sq mi (5,033sq km). Pop. (1991) 304,694.

**Northumbria, Kingdom of** Largest kingdom in Anglo-Saxon England. Formed in the early 7th century, it included NE England and SE Scotland up to the Firth of Forth. In the age of the historian BEDE and the LINDISFARNE GOSPELS, Northumbria experienced a blossoming of scholarship and monastic culture. Its power declined in the 8th century.

**North-West Frontier Province (NWFP)** Province in NW Pakistan bounded by Afghanistan (N and W), located near Khyber Pass; the capital is Peshawar. Historically important during the time of Alexander the Great, in 1849 it became part of British India, and was annexed to Pakistan in 1947. It is largely agricultural. Area: 41,000sq mi (106,200sq km). Pop. 10,937,000.

**Northwest Ordinance** Decree of the CONTINENTAL CONGRESS (1787), establishing the Northwest Territory. Based on plans proposed by a committee chaired by JEFFERSON, it created a government for the territory, between the Ohio and Mississippi rivers, and laid down the policy for federal land sales.

**Northwest Passage** Western route from the Atlantic to the Pacific via N Canada. Many European explorers in the 16th–17th centuries tried to find a passage through North America to the Pacific. The effort was renewed in the 19th century. The expedition of Sir John FRANKLIN, which set out in 1845, was lost with all hands, but during the search for survivors, the route was established. First to make the passage in one ship was Roald AMUNDSEN in 1903–06.

**North-West Province** Province in NW South Africa; the capital is Mmabatho. North-West Province was created from the NW part of the former province of TRANSVAAL. Area: 44,489sq mi (116,190sq km). Pop. (1994 est.) 3,252,991.

**Northwest Territories** Region in N Canada, covering more than 33% of the country and consisting of mainland Canada N of latitude 60°N, and hundreds of islands in the Arctic Archipelago. The capital is Yellowknife. Much of the N and E of the province is tundra, inhabited by INUIT and other native peoples. The HUDSON'S BAY COMPANY acquired the area under a charter from CHARLES II in 1670. In 1869 the Canadian government bought the land from the company. The present boundaries were set in 1912. In 1999 part of the Northwest Territories will become the Inuit land of Nunavut. Most economic development has occurred in Mackenzie district, which has large tracts of softwoods and rich mineral deposits. Area: 1,320,000sq mi (3,426,000sq km). Pop. (1992) 57,649.

**North Yorkshire** County in N England; the administrative center is YORK. Other major towns include Scarborough, Whitby, and Harrogate. In the 9th century a thriving culture was destroyed by the Scandinavian invasions. In the Middle Ages the region became noted for its many monastic foundations. In the W of the county are the PENNINES. In the E are the North Yorkshire Moors. North Yorkshire is predominantly agricultural, with dairy farming, cereals, and hill sheep farming. There is some manufacturing industry. Area: 3,208sq mi (8,309sq km). Pop. (1991) 702,161

**Norway** Scandinavian kingdom in NW Europe. *See* country feature, page 488

**NORTH DAKOTA**

**Statehood:** November 2, 1889

**Nickname:** The Flickertail State

**State bird:** Western meadowlark

**State flower:** Wild prairie rose

**State tree:** American elm

**State motto:** Liberty and union, now and forever, one and inseparable

**Norwegian** Official language of Norway, spoken by nearly all the country's four million inhabitants. It belongs to the northern branch of the Germanic family of INDO-EUROPEAN LANGUAGES.

**Norwich** City and county town of NORFOLK, E England. It was already an important market town in the 11th century. There are many fine churches dating from the medieval period, including the Norman cathedral (1096). Industries: textiles, machinery, chemicals, electrical goods, foodstuffs, footwear. Pop. (1991) 120,895.

**nose** In human beings, other primates, and some vertebrates, the prominent structure between the eyes. It contains receptors sensitive to various chemicals (sense of SMELL) and serves as the opening to the respiratory tract, warming and moistening the air and trapping dust particles on the MUCOUS MEMBRANES.

**Nostradamus** (Michel de Nostredame) (1503–66) French seer and astrologer. After practicing as a doctor, he began making astrological predictions in 1547. These were published in rhyming quatrains in *Centuries* (1555) and represented one verse for every year from then till the end of the world (in the 1990s). To avoid prosecution as a magician, he completely changed the order of the verses so that no time sequence was discernible.

**notary** (notary public) Public official who authenticates documents such as deeds and contracts by witnessing them.

**notochord** In chordates and the early embryonic stages of vertebrates, the flexible, primitive backbone; in mature vertebrates it is replaced by the SPINE.

**Notre Dame** Early Gothic CATHEDRAL in Paris (1163–1250). One of the most daring constructions of its time, it has a wide nave and double ambulatory, and the W façade was imitated in many French churches.

**Nottingham** City and county town of NOTTINGHAMSHIRE, on the Trent River, N central England. Originally a 6th-century Anglo-Saxon settlement, it is the traditional birthplace of ROBIN HOOD. The city grew rapidly in the 19th century, becoming famous for the manufacture of fine lace, cotton, and hosiery. It is an important center of communications and transport. Industries: textiles, engineering, bicycles, electronic equipment, pharmaceuticals. Pop. (1991) 263,522.

**Nottinghamshire** County in central England; the county town is NOTTINGHAM. The land slopes down from the E ridges

## NORWAY

This flag became the national flag of Norway in 1898, although merchant ships had used it since 1821. The design is based on the Dannebrog, the flag of Denmark, the country that ruled Norway from the 14th century until the early 19th century.

**AREA:** 125,050SQ MI (323,900SQ KM)
**POPULATION:** 4,286,000
**CAPITAL (POPULATION):** Oslo (459,292)
**GOVERNMENT:** Constitutional monarchy
**ETHNIC GROUPS:** Norwegian 97%
**LANGUAGES:** Norwegian (official), Lappish, Finnish
**RELIGIONS:** Christianity (Lutheran 88%)
**CURENCY:** Krone = 100 ore

The Kingdom of Norway forms the W part of the Scandinavian peninsula. Norway's coast is fringed by many islands and long, deep fjords. The Arctic islands of SVALBARD and Jan Mayen are Norwegian possessions. Many of Norway's cities lie on or near fjords, including the capital, OSLO, BERGEN and TRONDHEIM. The land rises steeply from the coastal lowlands to a 5,000ft (1,500m) central plateau. Europe's largest glacier field, Josdtedalsbreen, lies W of Galdhøppigen, Norway's highest point at 8,100ft (2,469m). The plateau contains many deep valleys with lakes and fast-flowing rivers, such as the Glåma.

### CLIMATE

North Atlantic Drift gives Norway a mild climate. Most of Norway's seaports remain ice-free throughout the year. Snow covers the land for over three months every year. In Trømso, the sun does not set between November and January.

### VEGETATION

Large areas of the rugged mountains are bare rock. Forest and woods cover *c*.27% of Norway, with trees such as birch, pine, and spruce.

### HISTORY AND POLITICS

Norway's seafaring tradition dates back to the VIKINGS, who raided W Europe between the 9th and 11th centuries. OLAF II introduced Christianity in the early 11th century, but was deposed by King CANUTE II of Denmark. HAAKON IV re-established unity in the early 13th century. In 1319 Sweden and Norway were joined. In 1397 Norway, Sweden, and Denmark were united in the Kalmar Union. For the next four centuries Norway was subject to Danish rule. Lutheranism became the state religion in the mid-16th century. In 1814 Denmark ceded Norway to Sweden. Norway declared its independence, but Swedish troops forced Norway to accept union under the Swedish crown. An independent monarchy was established in 1905. Norway remained neutral in World War 1. In the 1920s it rapidly industrialized and in the 1930s adopted progressive social welfare provisions. In April 1940 German troops invaded. Over 50% of Norway's merchant fleet was destroyed in the resistance. Liberation was achieved in May 1945. Norway joined NATO in 1949 and was a co-founder (1960) of the European Free Trade Association (EFTA). In 1972 and 1994 referendums, Norway voted against joining the European Community. In 1977 Gro Harlem Brundtland became Norway's first woman prime minister and was reelected in 1993. In 1991 Olav V was succeeded by his son, Harald V. In 1996 Bruntland was replaced by Thorbjeorn Jagland. The 1997 general election produced a disappointing result for Jagland's Labor Party, and it was replaced by a centrist government under Kjell Magne Bondevik.

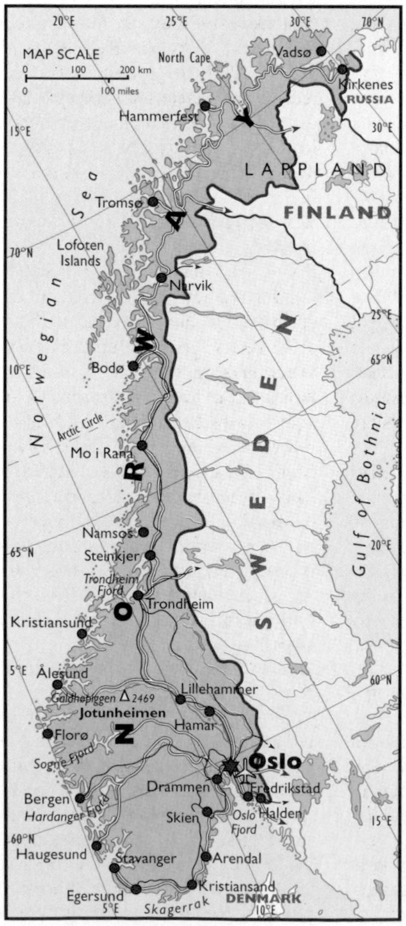

### ECONOMY

Norway has one of the world's best standards of living (1995 GDP per capita, $21,940). Its main exports are natural gas and oil, which was found in 1969. Norway is the world's eighth-largest producer of crude oil. Per capita, it is the world's largest producer of hydroelectricity. Manufactures include petroleum products, wood pulp, chemicals, aluminum, and paper. Farmland covers *c*.3% of the land. Dairy farming and meat production are the chief activities, but food must be imported. Fishing is also important.

of the PENNINES in the W to the lowlands of the E. The principal river is the Trent. Wheat, barley, and sugar beets are the chief crops; beef and dairy cattle are also important. There are rich deposits of coal in the county. Nottinghamshire has long been noted for its textile industries. Area: 836sq mi (2,164sq km). Pop. (1991) 993,872.

**Nouakchott** Capital of MAURITANIA, NW Africa, in the SW part of the country, *c.*5mi (8km) from the Atlantic Ocean. Originally a small fishing village, it was chosen as capital of Mauritania, when it became independent in 1960. Nouakchott now has an international airport and is the site of modern storage facilities for petroleum. Light industries have also been developed and handicrafts are important. Pop. (1988) 393,325.

**Nouméa** City and seaport in SW New Caledonia island, S Pacific Ocean; the capital of NEW CALEDONIA. Originally called Port-de-France, it was made capital of New Caledonia in 1854. Nouméa was used as a French penal colony during the later 19th century. Local mining products include nickel, chrome, and manganese. Pop. (1989) 65,110.

**noun** Member of a linguistic class or category consisting of words that serve to name a person, place, thing, or concept. In traditional grammar, nouns form one of the so-called parts of speech. Modern linguistics experts, however, tend to define them in terms of their grammatical function.

**nouveau roman** (Fr. new novel) Experimental fictional form. Pioneered by Alain ROBBE-GRILLET, Samuel BECKETT, and Nathalie Sarraute during the 1950s, it was influenced by the work of Franz KAFKA and James JOYCE and also by film technique. It is characterized by meticulously detailed description, the avoidance of value judgments, and a consciousness of the artificiality of time sequences.

**nova** Faint star that undergoes unpredictable increases in brightness by several magnitudes, apparently due to explosions in its outer regions, and then slowly fades back to normal. *See also* VARIABLE STAR

**Novalis** (1772–1801) German romantic poet and novelist, b. Friedrich Leopold, Baron von Hardenberg. He began his major work, the mythical romance *Heinrich von Ofterdingen*, in 1799, but had not completed it by the time of his early death. His work was a significant influence on the development of German ROMANTICISM.

**Nova Scotia** Maritime province in SE Canada, consisting of a mainland peninsula, the adjacent Cape Breton Island, and a few smaller islands; the capital is HALIFAX. The first settlement of Nova Scotia was made by the French at Port Royal in 1605. The mainland was awarded to Britain in 1713, and Cape Breton Island was seized from the French in 1758. Nova Scotia joined NEW BRUNSWICK, QUEBEC, and ONTARIO to form the Dominion of CANADA in 1867. The land is generally low-lying, rolling country, and there are extensive forests. The principal crops are hay, apples, grain, and vegetables. There are valuable coal deposits on Cape Breton Island. Fishing is very important, cod, lobster, and haddock being the largest catches. Industries: shipbuilding, pulp and paper, steelmaking, food processing. Area: 21,425sq mi (55,490sq km). Pop. (1991) 899,942.

**novel** Narrative fiction, usually in prose form, that is longer and more detailed than a SHORT STORY. The word is derived from the Latin word *novus* (new) and the Italian NOVELLA (a short tale with an element of surprise). The roots of the modern novel are generally traced to CERVANTES' *Don Quixote* (1605–15); its development as a major literary form can be seen in 18th-century Britain in Daniel DEFOE's *Robinson Crusoe* (1719) and Samuel RICHARDSON's *Pamela* (1740). The 20th century has seen considerable formal experimentation, with developments such as the STREAM OF CONSCIOUSNESS technique and the NOUVEAU ROMAN.

**novella** Short, highly structured prose narrative. The form was developed by Giovanni BOCCACCIO in the *Decameron* (1348–53), and has proved popular since the 18th century. In modern usage, the term broadly denotes a work of prose fiction that is longer than a short story but shorter than a NOVEL.

**Noverre, Jean-Georges** (1727–1810) French choreographer and ballet reformer. He abolished the conventional, meaningless gestures of ballet, and initiated the *ballet d'action* in which dance and story were united.

◀ **Notre-Dame** The Early Gothic cathedral of Notre-Dame is situated on the Ile de la Cité in Paris, France, seen here from the Seine River. A fine example of Gothic architecture, it is noted for its flying buttresses, which were a technical advance providing support, and for the rose window in the west façade.

**Novgorod** City in NW Russia, on the Volchov River. One of Russia's oldest cities, it was supposedly founded by the Varangian prince RURIK in the 9th century. Its inhabitants were forcibly converted to Christianity in 989. It subsequently became capital of a vast territory. After a long fight for supremacy, the city was forced to submit to Moscow in 1478. In 1570 IVAN IV (THE TERRIBLE) massacred the inhabitants. It declined in importance after the founding of ST. PETERSBURG. During World War II it suffered great destruction. Industries: distilling, foodstuffs, electrical engineering, furniture, chinaware. Pop. (1992) 235,000.

**Novi Sad** City in NE Serbia, a port on the Danube River; capital of the autonomous province of VOJVODINA. Industries include machinery, electrical goods, chemicals, textiles, and tobacco. Pop. (1991) 179,626

**Novosibirsk** City on the Ob River, S Siberia, Russia. Founded in 1896 after the construction of the Trans-Siberian Railroad, it grew quickly. During World War II it received complete industrial plants moved from war areas of the W Soviet Union. It is now a center for scientific research. Industries: agricultural and mining machinery, metallurgy, machine tools, chemicals, textiles, foodstuffs. Pop. (1992) 1,442,000.

**Nu, U** (1907–95) Burmese statesman, prime minister (1948–56, 1957–58, 1960–62). Active in the independence movement, he was independent BURMA's first prime minister. He returned to power in 1960, but in 1962 he was ousted in the military coup of U NE WIN. After years of exile, he returned to Burma in 1980 and was later placed under house arrest.

**Nuba** Name for a group of several unrelated peoples inhabiting a region of S Sudan. Most Nuba peoples are farmers and many tribes cultivate terraces on rugged granite hillsides. Animal husbandry is also practiced. The predominant religious rituals are closely linked to agricultural fertility rites.

**Nubia** Ancient state on the upper Nile in NE Africa. It was closely associated with Egypt. At its height, Nubia extended from Egypt to the Sudan. At first ruled by Egypt, it later controlled Egypt in the 8th and 7th centuries BC. It converted to Christianity in the 6th century AD and became part of Ethiopia in the 14th century.

**nuclear disarmament** *See* DISARMAMENT; STRATEGIC ARMS LIMITATION TALKS (SALT)

**nuclear energy** ENERGY released during a nuclear reaction as a result of the conversion of mass into energy according to Einstein's equation $E = mc^2$. Nuclear energy is released in two ways: by FISSION and by FUSION. Fission is the process responsibile for the atomic bomb and for NUCLEAR REACTORS now contributing to energy requirements throughout the world. Fusion provides the energy for the Sun and the stars and for the HYDROGEN BOMB. It also offers the prospect of cheap energy once a method has been perfected for controlling fusion reactions. *See also* NUCLEAR WEAPON

**nuclear family** In anthropology, term used to describe a family unit of two adults joined by conjugal link and their children. Ideally the nuclear family provides economic and emotional security to both the parents and children.

**nuclear fission** *See* FISSION, NUCLEAR

**nuclear fusion** *See* FUSION, NUCLEAR

**nuclear physics** Branch of physics concerned with the structure and properties of the atomic nucleus. The principal means of investigating the nucleus is the SCATTERING experiment, carried out in particle ACCELERATORS, in which a nucleus is bombarded with a beam of high-energy ELEMENTARY PARTICLES, and the resultant particles analyzed. Study of the nucleus has led to an understanding of the processes occurring inside stars, and has enabled the building of NUCLEAR REACTORS.

**nuclear reactor** Device in which nuclear FISSION reactions are used for power generation or for the production of radioactive materials. In nuclear power stations, NUCLEAR ENERGY is released as heat for use in electricity generation. In the reactor, the fuel is a radioactive heavy metal: uranium-235, uranium-233, or plutonium-239. In these metals, atoms break down spontaneously, undergoing a process called RADIOACTIVE DECAY. Some NEUTRONS released in this process strike the nuclei of fuel atoms, causing them to undergo fission and emit more neutrons. These cause more fissions to occur. In this way a CHAIN REACTION is set up, and heat is produced in the process. The heat is absorbed by a circulating coolant, often liquid sodium, and transferred to a boiler to raise steam to drive an electricity GENERATOR. Experiments are being undertaken with FUSION reactors.

**nuclear waste** Residues containing radioactive substances. After URANIUM, PLUTONIUM, and other useful fission products have been removed, some long-lived radioactive elements remain, such as cesium-137 and strontium-90. The storage of nuclear waste is a major environmental issue.

**nuclear weapon** Device whose enormous explosive force derives from nuclear FISSION or FUSION reactions. The first atom bombs were dropped by the US on the Japanese cities of HIROSHIMA and NAGASAKI in August 1945. The bombs consisted of two stable subcritical masses of URANIUM or PLUTONIUM which, when brought forcefully together, caused the CRITICAL MASS to be exceeded, thus initiating an uncontrolled nuclear fission reaction. In such detonations, huge amounts of energy and harmful radiation are released: the explosive force can be equivalent to 200,000 tons of TNT. The HYDROGEN BOMB (H-bomb or thermonuclear bomb), first tested in 1952, consists of an atom bomb that on explosion provides a temperature high enough to cause nuclear FUSION in a surrounding solid layer, usually lithium deuteride.

**NUCLEAR REACTOR**

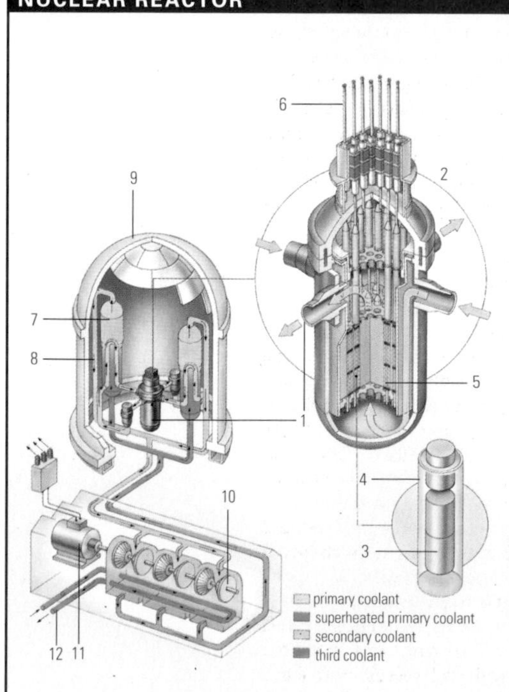


A pressurized water reactor (PWR) is so named because the primary coolant (1) that passes through the reactor core (2) is pressurized to prevent it from boiling. The uranium-235 fuel is loaded into the reactor in pellets (3) contained by the fuel rods (4). To prevent an uncontrolled chain reaction the fuel rods are separated by control rods of graphite (5). All the rods are loaded into the reactor from above (6). The primary coolant is heated by the fission reaction in the fuel rods and circulates into a steam generator (7) where it superheats the secondary coolant (8). The secondary coolant leaves the protective containment vessel (9) and drives turbines (10) which produce electricity through a generator (11). A third coolant loop (12) cools the secondary coolant, transferring the heat to a sea, river, or lake. Reducing the temperature of the secondary coolant increases the efficiency of the transfer from the primary to the secondary coolant.

**nucleic acid** Chemical molecules present in all living cells and in viruses. They are of two types, DNA (deoxyribonucleic acid) and RNA (ribonucleic acid), both of which play fundamental roles in heredity. *See also* GENE; CHROMOSOME

**nucleon** Any of the particles found within the nucleus of an ATOM: a NEUTRON or a PROTON.

**nucleosynthesis** Production of all the various chemical elements that exist in the universe from one or two simple atomic nuclei. It is believed to have occurred by way of large-scale nuclear reactions during cosmogenesis and is still in progress in the Sun and other stars.

**nucleus** In biogology, membrane-bound structure that contains the CHROMOSOMES in most cells. Exceptions include BACTERIA and mature red blood cells. Instead of chromosomes, bacteria have a naked molecule of DNA in the CYTOPLASM. As well as holding genetic material, the nucleus maintains cell processes. Nucleus is also the term for the central part of an ATOM.

**Nuevo Łaredo** City in NE Mexico, on the Rio Grande, opposite Laredo, Texas. Founded in 1755, it was separated from Laredo during the Mexican War (1848). It lies at the N end of the Inter-American Highway, and is a railroad terminus and international trade center. Industries: trade (cotton and livestock), natural gas, tourism. Pop. (1990) 218,413.

**Nuffield, William Richard Morris, 1st Viscount** (1877–1963) British automobile manufacturer and philanthropist. He developed low-price, mass-produced cars and revolutionized the British car industry. In 1952 he became chairman of the British Motor Corporation (BMC), which was an amalgamation of the Morris and Austin companies.

**Nujoma, Sam** (1929– ) Namibian politician, president of Namibia (1990– ). A founder and leader of the SOUTH WEST AFRICA PEOPLE'S ORGANIZATION (SWAPO) from 1959, Nujoma was exiled by the South African government to Tanzania in 1960. Forced to resort to a policy of armed struggle from 1966, Nujoma controlled an army of highly effective SWAPO guerrillas. After negotiating Namibia's independence through the United Nations, he returned in 1989, when the first free elections were held. He was re-elected in 1994.

**Nukualofa** Capital of Tonga, in the SW Pacific Ocean, on the N coast of Tongatabu Island. The chief industry is copra processing. Pop. (1986) 29,018.

**nullification** In US history, the idea that a state may choose not to enforce a law passed by the federal government. First advanced in the KENTUCKY AND VIRGINIA RESOLUTIONS (1798), it influenced Southern thinking on states' rights before the Civil War. It was tested in 1832, when the South Carolina legislature nullified the Tariff Law of 1828, declaring it unconstitutional. The crisis was defused when South Carolina accepted a compromise Tariff Act (1833).

**numbat** (banded anteater) Squirrel-like Australian marsupial that feeds on TERMITES. The female, unlike most marsupials, has no pouch. The numbat has a long snout and lateral white bands on its red-brown coat. Length: 18in (46cm). Species *Myrmecobius fasciatus*.

**number** Symbol representing a quantity used in counting or calculation. All ancient cultures devised their own number systems for the practical purposes of counting and measuring. From the basic process of counting we get the natural numbers. This concept can be extended to define the INTEGERS, the RATIONAL NUMBERS, the REAL NUMBERS, and the COMPLEX NUMBERS. *See also* BINARY SYSTEM; IRRATIONAL NUMBER

**Numbers** Fourth book of the Bible and of the PENTATEUCH. Its central theme is a relation of events that took place during the Israelites' 40 years of wandering in the desert of the Sinai Peninsula, in search of the Promised Land of CANAAN. Interwoven with their story is a collection of religious material, including laws concerning purification rituals and procedures for sacrificing to God.

**number theory** Branch of mathematics concerned with the properties of natural numbers (whole numbers) or special classes of natural numbers such as PRIME NUMBERS and perfect numbers. The 4th-century BC Greek mathematician EUCLID proved that the number of primes was infinite. One of the unresolved problems in number theory is to find formulae for the generation of the primes. Pierre de FERMAT in the 17th century and Leonhard EULER in the 18th century both explored aspects of number theory.

**numeral** Symbol used alone or in a group to denote a number. Arabic numerals are the 10 digits from 0 to 9. ROMAN NUMERALS consist of seven letters or marks.

**nun** Woman belonging to a female religious order who has taken monastic vows (*see* MONASTICISM). Nuns may belong to either an enclosed order or one that encourages its members to work in the world for the welfare of society at large. BUDDHISM, CHRISTIANITY, and TAOISM all have monastic orders of nuns. Nuns serve a preparatory period called a novitiate, after which they take their final vows. For centuries, Christian nuns lived in closed orders, but in 1633 St. VINCENT DE PAUL founded the Sisters of Charity, an order of nuns who work outside the convent serving the community.

**Nunn, Trevor** (1940– ) British stage director. He was appointed artistic director of the ROYAL SHAKESPEARE COMPANY (RSC) (1968). He directed the hit West End musicals *Cats* (1981) and *Starlight Express* (1984). In 1996 he was appointed artistic director of the National Theater of Great Britain.

**Nur-ad-Din** (1118–74) (Nureddin) Ruler of Syria. He united Muslim forces in Syria to resist the Christians of the CRUSADES. He recaptured Edessa from the Christians in 1146 and in 1154 took Damascus from the Seljuk Turks.

**Nuremberg** (Nürnburg) City in S Germany, in Bavaria, 92mi (151km) NW of Munich. It began as a settlement around an 11th-century castle, later becoming a free imperial city. It was a center of learning and artistic achievement in Germany during the 15th and 16th centuries. During the 1930s it was the location of the annual congress of the Nazi Party, and after World War II was the scene of the NUREMBERG TRIALS (1945–46). Today Nuremberg is an important commercial and industrial center. Industries: textiles, pharmaceuticals, electrical equipment, machinery, publishing and printing, motor vehicles, toys, brewing. Pop. (1990) 498,500.

**Nuremberg Trials** (1945–46) Trials of Germans accused of war crimes during World War II, held before a military tribunal. The tribunal was established by the US, Britain, France, and the Soviet Union. Several Nazi leaders were sentenced to death and others to terms of imprisonment.

**Nureyev, Rudolf** (1938–93) Soviet ballet dancer and choreographer. While on tour in Paris in 1961 he defected from the Soviet Union. He was noted for his spectacular technical virtuosity and dramatic character portrayal. Major ballets in which he had leading roles included *Sleeping Beauty*, *Giselle*, and *Swan Lake*, and he regularly partnered Margot FONTEYN.

**Nurhachi** (1559–1626) Organizer and creator of the MANCHU state in China. He welded related tribes into a powerful unit, creating the Manchu military banner organization for control and mobilization. Among other innovations, he introduced a writing system for administrative purposes.

**nursing** Profession that has as its general function the care of people who, through ill-health, disability, immaturity, or advanced age, are unable to care for themselves. Modern nursing is continually broadening its range of services. Caring for the sick was particularly emphasized by the early Christian Church; many religious orders and, later, chivalric orders, performed such "acts of mercy." In the 18th century the need for reform in nursing was revealed and, by the end of the 19th century, certain principles of Florence NIGHTINGALE's teaching had been adopted in England and the US. Today, in countries with advanced healthcare systems, there are many nursing specialties, with standards laid down by relevant professional bodies.

**nut** Dry, one-seeded fruit with a hard, woody or stony wall. It develops from a flower that has petals attached above the OVARY (inferior ovary). Examples include ACORNS and HAZEL nuts.

**nutation** Oscillating movement (period 18.6 years) superimposed on the steady precessional movement of the Earth's axis so that the precessional path of each celestial pole on the CELESTIAL SPHERE follows an irregular rather than a true circle. It results from the varying gravitational attraction of the Sun and Moon on the Earth. *See also* PRECESSION

◄ **nuclear weapon** The detonation of a large nuclear weapon above ground creates a huge mushroom cloud of radioactive dust and debris above the explosion that can reach several miles in height. The hazardous airbourne dust is then free to be carried in any direction by the prevailing winds. The devastation covers a wide area: a 15 megaton hydrogen bomb will cause all flammable material within 12mi (20km) to burst into flame.

**nutcracker** Crow-like bird of evergreen forests of the Northern Hemisphere. A projection inside the bill turns it into a highly efficient seed cracker or nutcracker. The European thick-billed nutcracker (*Nucifraga caryocatactes*) is a typical species. Family Corvidae. Length: 12in (30cm).

**nuthatch** Bird found mainly in the Northern Hemisphere and occasionally in Africa and Australia. It is bluish-gray above and white, gray, or chestnut underneath. It eats nuts, opening them with its sharp bill. It also feeds on insects, spiders, and seeds. Length: 3.5–7.5in (9–19cm). Family Sittidae.

**nutmeg** Evergreen tree native to tropical Asia, Africa, and America. Its seeds yield the spice nutmeg; the spice mace comes from the seed covering. Height: up to 60ft (18m). Family Myristicaceae.

**nutrition** Processes by which plants and animals take in and make use of food substances. The science of nutrition involves identifying the kinds and amounts of nutrients necessary for growth and health. Nutrients are generally divided into PROTEINS, CARBOHYDRATES, FATS, MINERALS, and VITAMINS.

**Nuuk** (Danish *Godthåb*) Capital and largest town of Greenland, at the mouth of a group of fjords on the SW coast. Founded in 1721, it is the oldest Danish settlement in Greenland. Industries: fishing and fish processing, scientific research. Pop. (1993) 12,181.

**Nyerere, Julius Kambarage** (1922– ) Tanzanian statesman, first president of Tanzania (1964–85). When the country became independent from Britain in 1962 he became president of Tanganyika and, after its union with Zanzibar in 1964, of Tanzania. He established a one-party state. A leading international spokesman for African affairs, he sent troops to help topple the regime of Idi AMIN in neighboring Uganda (1979). Under his autocratic but generally benign socialist government, Tanzania made striking progess in social welfare and education, but in the 1980s economic setbacks encouraged demands for greater democracy. Nyerere retired as president in 1985.

**nylon** Any of numerous synthetic materials consisting of polyamides (with protein-like structures) developed in the US in the 1930s. It can be formed into fibers, filaments, bristles, or sheets. Nylon is characterized by elasticity and strength and is used chiefly in yarn, cordage, and molded products.

**Nyman, Michael** (1944– ) English composer. In his early career, influenced by John CAGE, he explored experimental music. His works include operas, notably *The Man who Mistook his Wife for a Hat* (1986), but he is best known for his film scores. These include *The Draftsman's Contract* (1982), *Prospero's Books* (1991), and *The Piano* (1993). His accessible musical style is characterized by the repetition and variation of harmonic, melodic, and rhythmic patterns.

**nymph** In Greek mythology, female spirit said to be a guardian of natural objects. They were identified with specific locations, and commonly with trees and water.

**nymph** Young insect of primitive orders that do not undergo complete METAMORPHOSIS. The term is used to designate all immature stages after the egg. The nymph resembles the adult and does so more closely with each successive molting. Some examples are the aquatic nymphs of dragonflies, mayflies, and damsel flies.

*O/o, 15th letter of the alphabet, is derived from the Phoenician alphabet. It entered the Greek alphabet as* **omicron**, *"short o", and passed unchanged into the various languages in which it is used today.*

**oak** Common name of almost 600 species of the genus *Quercus*, which are found in temperate areas of the Northern Hemisphere and at high elevations in the tropics. Most species are hardwood trees that grow 60–100ft (18–30m) tall. Leaves are simple, often lobed, and sometimes serrated. The flowers are greenish and inconspicuous; male flowers hang in catkins. The fruit is an acorn, surrounded by a cup.

**Oakland** City in California, opposite Golden Gate Bridge; it is the seat of Alameda county. Founded in 1820, it is the site of the San Francisco-Oakland Bay Bridge (1936), and is also the center of the Bay Area Rapid Transit system (1972). It is the home of baseball's Oakland A's and football's Oakland Raiders. Industries: chemicals, food processing, shipping port, glass works. Pop. (1990) 372,242.

**Oakley, Annie** (1860–1926) US entertainer. She was an expert shot, eventually beating a noted marksman, Frank E. Butler, whom she married. She was the star of Buffalo Bill's Wild West Show for 17 years.

**oarfish** Any of several deepwater marine ribbonfish. Its long, thin body has a dorsal fin extending along its entire length. Two long oarlike pelvic fins protrude from beneath the head. Length: to 20ft (6m). Genus *Regalecus*.

**OAS** Abbreviation of the ORGANIZATION OF AMERICAN STATES

**oasis** Fertile location that has water in an arid landscape. Usually, ground water is brought to the surface in a well, but an oasis may occur where a river flowing from a wetter region crosses a desert.

**oat** Cereal plant native to W Europe and cultivated worldwide. The flower comprises numerous florets that produce one-seeded fruits. Mainly fed to livestock, oats are also eaten by humans. Family Poaceae/Gramineae; species *Avena sativa*.

**Oates, Joyce Carol** (1938– ) US novelist, short-story writer and poet. Oates' first book of short stories was *By the North Gate* (1963). Her works, such as the trilogy of novels *A Garden of Earthly Delights* (1967), *Expensive People* (1968) and *Them* (1969), are grim chronicles of violence and deprivation in modern America. Other novels include *The Assassins* (1975), *You Must Remember This* (1987), and *We Were the Mulvaneys* (1996).

**oath** Promise or pledge, especially a solemn one involving an appeal to God to witness the truth of the pledge. In a corporal oath, usually taken by a person before giving evidence in a court of law, a witness swears to the truth of a statement. Giving false evidence under oath is perjury.

**OAU** Abbreviation of the ORGANIZATION OF AFRICAN UNITY

**Oaxaca** (officially Oaxaca de Juárez) City in S Mexico; capital of Oaxaca state. Oaxaca is an agricultural state, and coffee is the principal crop. Tourists use the city as a base for exploring its archeological sites, such as Monte Albán. The city is renowned for its jewelry and handwoven textiles. Pop. (1990) 213,985.

**Ob** River in W Siberia, central Russia. It flows NW then NE through the lowlands of W Siberia, before continuing N and then E to enter the Gulf of Ob, an arm of the Kara Sea within the Arctic Ocean. Length: 2,300mi (3,680km). With its principal tributary, the Irtysh, it is the seventh-longest river in the world: 3,360mi (5,410km).

**obelisk** Stone monolith that usually has a tapering, square-based column with a pyramid-shaped point. Pairs of obelisks stood at the entrance to ancient Egyptian temples, such as Karnak (LUXOR). The two Cleopatra's needles in New York's Central Park and on London's Thames Embankment date from 1500 BC, long before CLEOPATRA's reign.

**Oberammergau** Village in upper Bavaria, S Germany, famous for its PASSION PLAY. The performance takes place once every 10 years, in fulfillment of a vow made by the inhabitants in 1634 during an outbreak of the plague.

**obesity** Condition of being overweight, generally defined as weighing 20% or more above the recommended norm for the person's sex, height, and build. Obese people are at increased risk of disease and have a shorter life expectancy than those of normal weight.

**oboe** WOODWIND musical instrument. It has a slightly flared bell and, like the BASSOON, is a double-reed instrument. The earliest true oboes were used in the mid-17th century and have been widely used since the 18th century.

**Obote, (Apollo) Milton** (1924– ) Ugandan political leader. He created the Uganda People's Congress in 1960, and became the first prime minister of independent Uganda (1962–66). In 1966 he became president of a more centralized state. He was ousted by his army chief, Idi AMIN, in 1971, but returned to power after Amin was overthrown in 1979. Obote was again overthrown by an army coup in 1985.

**Obregón, Álvaro** (1880–1928) Mexican statesman, president (1920–24). Obregón supported Francisco MADERO's revolution against Porfirio DÍAZ. When Madero was overthrown by Victoriano HUERTA, Obregón joined forces with Venustiano CARRANZA, "Pancho" VILLA and Emiliano ZAPATA to defeat Huerta. Obregón became president in 1920. Widely regarded as a capable leader, he enacted some notable reforms, especially in education. Reelected in 1928, he was assassinated before he could take office. *See also* MEXICAN REVOLUTION

**observatory** Location of TELESCOPES and other equipment for astronomical observations. Large optical telescopes are housed in domed buildings usually sited well away from the smoke of cities. Radio observatories are open sites containing one or more large radio telescopes. The largest radio-telescope dishes have been built in natural mountain hollows: the Arecibo Observatory in Puerto Rico is 975ft (300m) across.

**obsidian** Rare, gray to black, glassy volcanic rock. It is the uncrystallized equivalent of rhyolite and GRANITE. It makes an attractive semiprecious stone. Hardness 5.5; s.g. 2.4.

**obstetrics** Branch of medicine that deals with pregnancy, childbirth, and the care of women following delivery.

**O'Casey, Sean** (1880–1964) Irish playwright. His first play, *The Shadow of a Gunman* (1923), immediately made him famous. *Juno and the Paycock* (1924) was followed by *The Plow and the Stars* (1926). His later works, such as *The Silver Tassie* (1929), are in an expressionistic style, very different from the realism of his early plays. He also wrote a multi-volume autobiography.

**Occam's razor** *See* WILLIAM OF OCCAM

**occupational therapy** Development of practical skills to assist patients recovering from illness or injury. Therapists oversee a variety of pursuits, from the activities of daily living (ADLs), such as washing and dressing, to hobbies and crafts.

**ocean** Continuous body of saltwater that surrounds the continents and fills the Earth's great depressions. There are five main oceans, the ATLANTIC, PACIFIC, INDIAN, ARCTIC, and Antarctic, and they cover 71% of the Earth's surface. The oceans may be divided by region (littoral, pelagic, and ABYSSAL) or by depth (CONTINENTAL MARGIN, deep sea plain, and deep trenches). The SEAFLOOR has a varied topography, with vast mountain chains, valleys, and plains. Ocean water consists of about 3.5% dissolved minerals.

**Oceania** Collective term applied to the islands in the central and S Pacific Ocean. It includes the islands of MELANESIA, MICRONESIA, and POLYNESIA and, sometimes, Australasia (Australia and New Zealand) and the Malay Archipelago.

**Oceanic art** Art of OCEANIA. Much of it involves objects used in religious rites. Among the most notable examples are the giant, stone, ancestor-cult figures of EASTER ISLAND, MAORI wood carvings, and the carved drums, masks, stools, and shields of NEW GUINEA.

**oceanic basin** One of two major provinces of the deep ocean floor, lying at more than 1.2mi (2km) in depth. The mid-ocean ridges form the other province. Together they constitute 56% of the Earth's surface. The deep ocean basin is underlain by a thin basaltic crust, *c*.4.3mi (7km) thick, and is covered by thin sediment and dotted by low abyssal hills.

**oceanic current** Movement of sea water between layers of varying temperature and density. Ocean circulation is produced by CONVECTION, with warm currents traveling away from the equator, cooler water moving from the poles. In the Southern Hemisphere the oceanic currents move in a counterclockwise system, whereas in the Northern the system is clockwise, an effect caused by the Earth's rotation. There are about 50 major currents, including the GULF STREAM of the N

Atlantic and the Humboldt (Peru) current off the W coast of South America. *See also* CORIOLIS EFFECT; EL NIÑO

**Oceanic mythology** Traditional beliefs of the native inhabitants of OCEANIA. Among the Polynesians, there are various accounts of the creation of the world by the celestial deity Tangaroa (Ta'aroa). **Maui**, the most famous of the Polynesian mythic heroes, often thought of as half god and half human, is known for his cunning deeds. In Melanesian creation myths, the beginning of the world is seen as a movement that brings order out of chaos. In the daily life of the Melanesians, there are a vast number of unseen forces – benevolent spirits, demons, ghosts, and the souls of the departed – to be dealt with by means of elaborate rituals. Ancestor worship is an important part of social life. The supernatural force of **mana** plays a vital role in most Oceanic mythology.

**oceanography** Science of the marine environment. It studies oceans and seas past and present, shorelines, sediments, rocks, muds, plants, animals, temperatures, tides, winds, currents, formation and erosion of abyssal depths and heights, and the effect of neighboring land masses.

**ocelot** Small cat that lives in the S US, Central and South America. Its valuable fur is yellowish with elongated dark spots. It feeds on small birds, mammals, and reptiles. Length: to 5ft (1.5m). Family Felidae; species *Felis pardalis*.

**Ochs, Adolph** (1858–1935) US newspaper publisher under whose direction the *New York Times* became one of the world's most influential newspapers. He bought the failing newspaper in 1896 and gave it the slogan: "All the news that's fit to print."

**O'Connell, Daniel** (1775–1847) ("the Liberator") Irish nationalist leader. He led resistance to Britain's remaining anti-Catholic laws and founded the Catholic Association. In 1828 he was elected to the British Parliament; the Act of CATHOLIC EMANCIPATION (1829) was passed to enable him to take his seat. He tried unsuccessfully to extract reforms from the government.

**O'Connor, (Mary) Flannery** (1925–64) US writer. Her first novel was *Wise Blood* (1952). Other works include *The Violent Bear It Away* (1960), and the short-story collection *A Good Man is Hard to Find* (1955). O'Connor suffered from lupus, a terminal illness.

**O'Connor, Sandra Day** (1930– ) US Supreme Court justice. A Republican, she won election to two full terms in the Arizona Senate and was elected majority leader in 1973. She served on the Superior Court in Phoenix (1974–79), until her appointment to the Arizona Court of Appeals. In 1981 she was appointed associate justice of the US Supreme Court. The first woman to sit on the court, she is moderately conservative.

**octane number** Indication of the antiknock properties of a liquid motor fuel. The higher the number, the less likely the possibility of the fuel detonating.

**octave** In music, the interval between any given note and another one that is exactly twice (or half) the frequency of the first and thus, acoustically, a perfect consonance. In Western music it encompasses the eight notes of the diatonic SCALE.

**Octavian** *See* AUGUSTUS

**October Revolution** *See* RUSSIAN REVOLUTION

**octopus** Predatory cephalopod mollusk with no external shell. Its saclike body has eight powerful suckered tentacles. Many of the 150 species are small, but the common octopus (*Octopus vulgaris*) grows to 30ft (9m). Family Octopodidae.

**ode** Lyric poem of unspecific form but typically of heightened emotion or public address. The first great writer of odes was PINDAR, but more simple were the lyrical odes of HORACE and CATULLUS. In 17th-century England it was taken up by JONSON, HERRICK, and MARVELL. Representative of the more personal type are the 19th-century works of WORDSWORTH, SHELLEY, and KEATS.

**Oder** Second-longest river in the catchment basin of the Baltic Sea. It rises in the NE of the Czech Republic, flows N and W through SW Poland, before turning N, forming the Polish-German border and reaching the Baltic Sea. The Oder has many navigable tributaries, notably the Neisse and Warta rivers. Length: 550mi (886km).

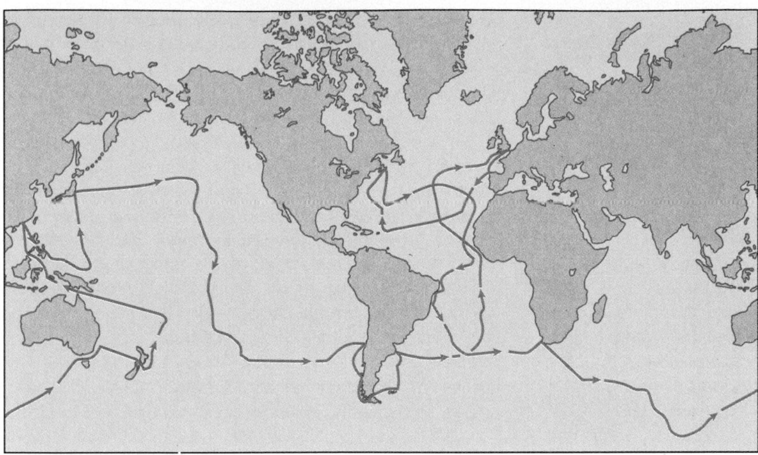

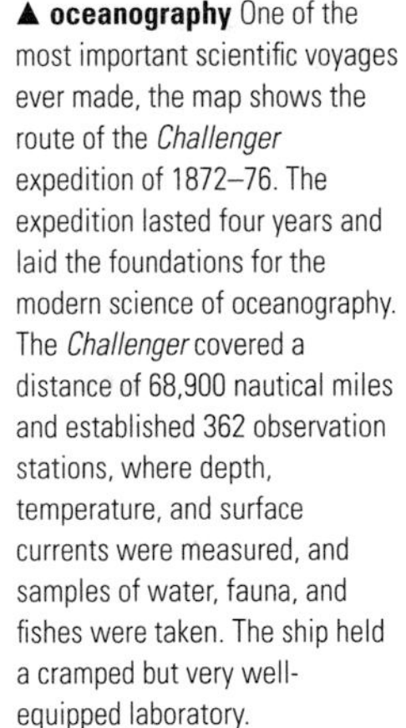

▲ **oceanography** One of the most important scientific voyages ever made, the map shows the route of the *Challenger* expedition of 1872–76. The expedition lasted four years and laid the foundations for the modern science of oceanography. The *Challenger* covered a distance of 68,900 nautical miles and established 362 observation stations, where depth, temperature, and surface currents were measured, and samples of water, fauna, and fishes were taken. The ship held a cramped but very well-equipped laboratory.

**Odessa** City and port on the Black Sea, S Ukraine. A Tatar fortress was established here in the 14th century. It later passed to Poland-Lithuania and then to Turkey (1764). Brought under Russian control in 1791, it was made a naval base. Odessa was the scene of the mutiny on the battleship *Potemkin* during the revolution of 1905. Industries: fishing, whaling, shipbuilding and repairing, oil refining, metalworking, chemicals, heavy machinery. Pop. (1991) 1,101,000.

**Odets, Clifford** (1906–63) US social protest dramatist. He helped to organize the Group Theater in 1931. His plays include *Awake and Sing* (1935), *Waiting for Lefty* (1935), and *Golden Boy* (1937). He later moved to Hollywood, where he wrote and directed films including *The Country Girl* (1950).

**Odin** Principal god in Norse mythology. Identified with the Teutonic god Woden, he is considered to be the god of wisdom, culture, war, and death. He lived with the Valkyries in VALHALLA, where he received the souls of dead warriors.

**Odoacer** (*c*.433–93) (Odovacar) Chief of the Germanic Heruli people and conqueror of the West ROMAN EMPIRE. The Heruli were Roman mercenaries until 476, when they declared Odoacer king of Italy. After the Ostrogoths invaded in 489, Odoacer was murdered.

**odontology** Study of the structure, development and diseases of the teeth. It is closely allied with DENTISTRY.

**Odysseus** (Ulysses) Greek hero of HOMER's epic poem, the ODYSSEY. King of the city-state of Ithaca, husband of the faithful PENELOPE, he was an astute and brave warrior. It was Odysseus who devised the stratagem of the wooden TROJAN HORSE in order to enter Troy.

**Odyssey, The** Epic poem of 24 books attributed to HOMER. The story of ODYSSEUS tells of his journey home from the Trojan Wars after 10 years of wandering.

**OECD** Abbreviation of the ORGANIZATION FOR ECONOMIC COOPERATION AND DEVELOPMENT(OECD)

**Oedipus** In Greek mythology and literature, son of Laius (king of Thebes) and Jocasta; father of Antigone, Ismene, Eteocles, and Polynices by his own mother. SOPHOCLES told how Oedipus was saved from death as an infant and raised in Corinth. He inadvertently killed his father, solved the riddle of the SPHINX, and became king of Thebes. There he married Queen Jocasta, unaware that she was his own widowed mother. On discovering the truth he made himself blind.

◀ **ocelot** A member of the flesh-eating mammal order (Carnivora), the ocelot (*Felis pardalis*) is found in Central and South America, and sometimes as far N as Texas. It measures from 31–58in (80–147cm) long and is grouped with all other cats in the family Felidae.

O

**OHIO**
**Statehood:**
March 1, 1803
**Nickname:**
The Buckeye State
**State bird:**
Cardinal
**State flower:**
Scarlet carnation
**State tree:**
Buckeye
**State motto:**
With God, all things are possible

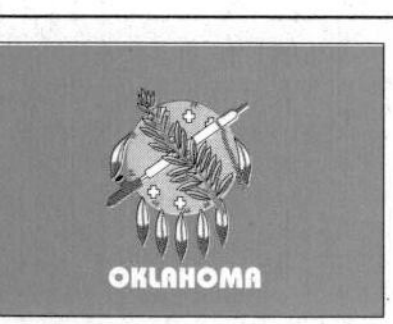


**OKLAHOMA**
**Statehood:**
November 16, 1907
**Nickname:**
The Sooner State
**State bird:**
Scissor-tailed flycatcher
**State flower:**
Mistletoe
**State tree:**
Redbud
**State motto:**
Labor conquers all things

**Oedipus complex** In psychoanalytic theory, a collection of unconscious wishes involving sexual desire for the parent of the opposite sex and jealous rivalry with the parent of the same sex. Sigmund FREUD held that children pass through this stage between the ages of three and five. The complex in females is sometimes known as the Electra complex, a term coined by C.G. JUNG. The theory has been considerably modified, if not totally rejected, by most modern practitioners.

**Oersted, Hans Christian** (1777–1851) Danish physicist. He took the first steps in explaining the relationship between ELECTRICITY and MAGNETISM, thus founding the science of ELECTROMAGNETISM.

**Offenbach, Jacques Levy** (1819–80) French composer. His reputation was founded on the brilliance of his numerous operettas, notably *Orpheus in the Underworld* (1858).

**Office of Strategic Services (OSS)** US World War II agency. Headed by Major General William ("Wild Bill") Donovan, it was formed in 1942 to gather and interpret data on the enemy and to give support to anti-Axis resistance groups. Disbanded in 1945, many of its members later became associated with the CENTRAL INTELLIGENCE AGENCY (CIA).

**offset** Method of PRINTING widely used for high-volume publications. A roller applies ink to the printing plate, which is mounted on a rotating cylinder. The image is then transferred (offset) to a cylinder with a rubber covering, called the blanket. This transfers the image to the paper. Usually, the plates are made by LITHOGRAPHY, and the process is called offset lithography. Separate plates are used for each color.

**O'Flaherty, Liam** (1897–1984) Irish novelist and short story writer. His novels, often dealing with social conditions in Ireland, include *The Informer* (1925), *The Puritan* (1931), *Famine* (1937), and *Insurrection* (1950). Other works include *The Short Stories of Liam O'Flaherty* (1956).

**Oglethorpe, James Edward** (1696–1785) English general and colonist. After military service, he became interested in social reform, particularly the problems of debtors. Taking a group to North America, he settled in Savannah and founded the colony of Georgia for imprisoned English debtors. It was chartered in 1732.

**O'Hara, John** (1905–70) US writer. His first novel was *Appointment in Samarra* (1934). O'Hara adapted his novel *Pal Joey* (1940) into a musical. Other works include *Butterfield 8* (1935), *A Rage to Live* (1949), and *Ten North Frederick* (1955).

**O'Higgins, Bernardo** (1778–1842) South American revolutionary leader and ruler of Chile. He commanded the Chilean army against the Spanish. Defeated in 1814, he joined José de SAN MARTÍN in Argentina to defeat the Spanish at Chacabuco (1817). Appointed "supreme director" of Chile, he declared independence in 1818 but resigned in 1823.

**Ohio** State in E central US, bounded by Lake Erie in the N; the capital is COLUMBUS. Other cities include Cincinnati, Toledo, and CLEVELAND. Britain acquired the land in 1763 at the end of the Seven Years' War. It was ceded to the US after the American Revolution, and in 1787 it became part of the Northwest Territory. Ohio was accepted into the Union in 1803. Mostly low-lying, the state is drained chiefly by the OHIO, Scioto, Miami, and Muskingum rivers. Ohio's large farms produce hay, corn, wheat, soybeans, and dairy foods, and cattle and pigs are raised. The state is highly industrialized. Ohio produces sandstone, oil, natural gas, clay, salt, lime, and gravel. Its lake ports handle large amounts of iron and copper ore, coal and oil. Industries: vehicle and aircraft manufacture, transportation equipment, primary and fabricated metals. Area: 41,222sq mi (106,764sq km). Pop. (1990) 10,847,115.

**Ohio** River in E central US, formed at the confluence of the Allegheny and Monongahela rivers at Pittsburgh in W Pennsylvania. It flows W and then SW to join the Mississippi River at Cairo, Illinois. The Ohio River valley is a highly industrialized region, and large quantities of raw materials and manufactured goods are shipped along the river. There are various engineering schemes to prevent spring flooding and improve navigability. Length: 976mi (1,571km).

**ohm** (symbol Ω) SI unit of electrical resistance, equal to the resistance between two points on a conductor when a constant potential difference of one VOLT between them produces a current of one AMPERE.

**Ohm's law** Statement that the amount of steady current through a material is proportional to the voltage across the material. Proposed in 1827 by the German physicist Georg Ohm (1787–1854), Ohm's law is expressed mathematically as $V = IR$ (where $V$ is the voltage in volts, $I$ is the current in amperes and $R$ is the resistance in ohms).

**oil** General term to describe a variety of substances, whose chief shared properties are viscosity at ordinary temperatures, a density less than that of water, inflammability, insolubility in water, and solubility in ether and alcohol. Mineral oils, most notably crude oil or petroleum oil, are used as fuels. Animal and vegetable oils (fatty oils or fats) are used as food, lubricants, and as a major ingredient of soap. In addition, there are essential oils from plants, which, unlike fatty oils, are volatile. Fatty oils can be classified into two groups: drying, such as linseed and poppyseed oil, and nondrying, such as olive and castor oil.

**oil painting** Method of painting that uses pigments saturated in a drying oil medium. Widely used in Europe since the 16th century, oil is still the most versatile paint medium because of its range of textures and colors.

**oil palm** Tree grown in humid tropical regions of Africa and Madagascar, source of oil for margarine and soap. The long, feather-shaped fronds rise from a short trunk. Height: 30–50ft (9–15m). Family Arecaceae/Palmae.

**Ojibwa** (Chippewa) Group of Algonquian-speaking Native North Americans. In the 17th century they were constantly at war with the SIOUX, eventually driving them across the Mississippi River. Since then they have lived on reservations in Michigan, Wisconsin, Minnesota, and North Dakota. Today, *c.*90,000 live in the US and Canada.

**okapi** Even-toed, hoofed ruminant of African equatorial rain forests. It is purplish in color with striped legs. Family Giraffidae; species *Okapia johnstoni*.

**Okeechobee** Large, freshwater lake in S central Florida, N of the Everglades. Fed by the Kissimmee River and drained by the Caloosahatchee River. Area: 700sq mi (1,813sq km).

**O'Keeffe, Georgia** (1887–1986) US painter. O'Keeffe's first exhibition was in 1916, and in 1924 she married Alfred STIEGLITZ. Her early works were stylized and associated with ABSTRACT ART. She is best known for her microscopically detailed paintings of flowers, such as *Black Iris* (1926). Her use of vibrant color was combined with strong overtones of sexual symbolism. Many other works were more abstract.

**Okefenokee Swamp** Swampland in SE Georgia and NE Florida; drained by the Suwanee and St. Mary's rivers. Area: 600sq mi (1,813sq km).

**Okhotsk, Sea of** Arm of the N Pacific Ocean off the E coast of Russia, bounded E by the Kamchatka Peninsula and SE by the Kuril Islands. It is connected with the Sea of Japan by the Tatar and La Pérouse straits, and with the Pacific Ocean by passages through the Kuril Islands. It is icebound from November to June. The chief ports are Magadan and Korsakov in Russia. Area: 590,000sq mi (1,528,000sq km).

**Okinawa** Largest island of the Okinawa archipelago, SW of mainland Japan, part of the RYUKYU ISLANDS group in the W Pacific Ocean; the major settlement is Naha. The N is mountainous, densely forested, and sparsely populated. Economic activity, such as agriculture and fishing, is concentrated in the S. In the last major amphibious offensive of the World War II, US troops landed there in April 1945 and met fierce Japanese resistance. Okinawa surrendered in June 1945 after nearly 50,000 US casualties. The island remained under US administration until 1971. The US still maintains some bases there. Area: 454sq mi (1,176sq km). Pop. (1990) 1,222,458.

**Oklahoma** State in central S US; the capital is OKLAHOMA CITY. Other important cities are TULSA and Lawton. Much of the area was acquired by the US from France in the LOUISIANA PURCHASE (1803). During Andrew Jackson's presidency, the US Congress created the Indian Territory in the region for NATIVE AMERICANS moved by the federal government from states in the E. Cattle farmers who had settled to the W of this area organized the Territory of Oklahoma in

1889. This was merged with the Indian Territory to form the state of Oklahoma in 1907. The W of the state is part of the GREAT PLAINS. The E is hilly. The area is drained chiefly by the Arkansas and Red rivers. Wheat and cotton are the leading crops, but livestock is more important. There are many minerals, but oil and natural gas form the basis of Oklahoma's economic wealth. Area: 69,918sq mi (181,089sq km). Pop. (1990) 3,189,456.

**Oklahoma City** Capital and largest city of Oklahoma, in the center of the state on the North Canadian River. The area was settled in 1889. The city was made the state capital in 1910, and prospered with the discovery of rich oil deposits in 1928. It was the site of a terrorist bomb in April 1995, which killed 168 people and injured 400 others. Industries: oil refining, grain milling, cotton processing, steel products, electronic equipment, aircraft. Pop. (1990) 404,014.

**okra** (gumbo) Annual tropical plant with red-centered yellow flowers. The green fruit pods are eaten as a vegetable. Height: 2–6ft (0.6–1.8m). Family Malvaceae; species *Hibiscus esculentus*

**Olaf II** (995–1030) Norwegian king and patron saint of Norway. Olaf became king in 1015. He introduced Christianity, but this was unpopular with a number of chiefs, who rebelled, backed by CANUTE II of Denmark. Olaf was exiled in 1029 and killed in battle the next year. Following reports of miracles at his grave, he was made patron saint of Norway in 1164.

**old age** Last period of a human being's life, often defined as after the age of 70. Old age is usually characterized by physical changes such as loss of hair, failing sight and a general slowing of the body's systems. This physical deterioration is most visible in those body tissues which do not regenerate easily because they are largely composed of non-living materials: the bones, joints, and connective tissue. Brain cells also do not regenerate but their progressive loss is not necessarily a major factor in ageing.

**Old Catholics** Religious movement rejecting the dogma of PAPAL INFALLIBILITY, which had been announced by the First Vatican Council of 1870. The Old Catholics set up churches in German- and Dutch-speaking Europe, which later united in the Union of Utrecht in 1889. Since then the Archbishop of Utrecht has been head of the International Old Catholic Congress. Old Catholics have much affinity with Anglicans.

**Oldenburg, Claes** (1929– ) US sculptor, a leading member of the POP ART movement. He is famous for his gigantic sculptures based on everyday objects, such as *Lipstick* (1969), and for his "soft sculptures" and pieces representing food.

**Olds, Ransom Eli** (1864–1950) US industrialist. He built his first gasoline-powered car in 1896, and in 1899 helped found the world's first automobile factory in Detroit, Michigan. Olds was the first person to mass-produce low-cost cars. The Oldsmobile company is named for him.

**Old Testament** First and older section of the BIBLE, originally written in Hebrew or Aramaic, and accepted as religiously inspired and sacred by both Jews and Christians. Among Jews it is known as the Hebrew Bible. It begins with the creation, but the main theme of the Old Testament is the history of the Hebrews. In addition, there are many examples of prophetic writing, poetry, and short narrative tales. It comprises the PENTATEUCH or TORAH (Genesis to Deuteronomy); the Historical Books (Joshua to I and II Kings); the Wisdom Books (Job, Proverbs, and Ecclesiastes); the Major Prophets (Isaiah, Jeremiah, and Ezekiel); the 12 Minor Prophets (Hosea to Malachi); and the miscellaneous collection of books known as the Writings (including Psalms and the Song of Songs). Sometimes included is a collection of books written in the final three centuries BC, known as the APOCRYPHA. The number, order, and names of the books of the Old Testament vary between the Jewish and Christian traditions; texts for both are based mainly on the SEPTUAGINT. Parts of the ancient Hebrew text were found among the DEAD SEA SCROLLS. *See also* LAW AND THE PROPHETS

**Olduvai Gorge** Site in N Tanzania, East Africa, where remains of primitive humans have been found. Louis LEAKEY uncovered four layers of remains dating from *c.*2 million years ago to *c.*15,000 years ago. The gorge, which is 25mi (40km) long and 320ft (100m) deep, runs through the Serengeti Plain.

**oleander** Evergreen shrubs of the genus *Nerium*, native to the Mediterranean region. They have milky poisonous sap, clusters of white, pink, or purple flowers and smooth leaves. The best-known is the rosebay (*N. oleander*). Family Apocynaceae.

**oligarchy** System of government in which power is concentrated in the hands of a few, who rule without the requirement of popular support and without external check on their authority.

**Oligocene** Extent of GEOLOGICAL TIME from about 38 to 25 million years ago. It is the third of five epochs of the TERTIARY period. During this time, the climate cooled, and many mammals evolved, including an ancestor of the modern horse.

**oligopoly** In economics, a situation of imperfect competition, which exists in an industry that contains a few firms producing similar products that are usually only differentiated by either brand or type. *See also* MONOPOLY

**olive** Tree, shrub, or vine and its fruit, especially the common olive tree, *Olea europaea*, native to the Mediterranean region. It has leathery, lance-shaped leaves, a gnarled and twisted trunk and may live for more than 1,000 years. The fruit is bitter and inedible before processing. Height: to 30ft (9m). Family Oleaceae. *See also* OLIVE OIL

**Olive Branch Petition** (1775) Final attempt at reconciliation with Britain by the Second CONTINENTAL CONGRESS. Written by John Dickinson, it was adopted on July 5, but ignored by King George III.

**olive oil** Yellowish liquid oil, containing oleic acid, obtained by pressing OLIVES. It is used for cooking, as a salad oil, in the manufacture of soap, and in medicine. It contains an extremely low proportion of fatty acids.

**Olivier, Laurence Kerr, Baron Olivier of Brighton** (1907–89) English actor and director. He was the outstanding Shakespearean interpreter of his generation. Olivier made his film debut in 1930, and established himself as a romantic lead in films such as *Wuthering Heights* (1939) and *Pride and Prejudice* (1940). In 1944 Olivier and Ralph Richardson became directors of the OLD VIC. He won a Special Academy Award for his directorial debut, *Henry V* (1944). Olivier's second film, *Hamlet* (1948), earned him Oscars for best actor and best picture. He was director (1963–73) of the National Theatre of Great Britain.

**olivine** Ferromagnesian mineral, $(MgFe)_2SiO_4$, found in basic and ultrabasic IGNEOUS ROCKS. Olivine has orthorhombic system crystals and is usually olive-green. It is glassy and brittle with no cleavage. Hardness 6.5–7; s.g. 3.3.

**Olmec** Early civilization of Central America, which flourished between the 12th and 4th centuries BC. Its heartland was the S coast of the Gulf of Mexico, but its influence spread more widely. From the 9th century BC the main Olmec center was La Venta. Olmec art included high-quality carving of jade and stone, notably giant human heads in basalt. The Olmec heritage can be traced through later civilizations, including the MAYA.

**Olmsted, Frederick Law** (1822–1903) US landscape artist. He designed Central Park in New York City (1857–61) and the Capitol grounds in Washington, D.C. (1844–92), among other projects. Olmsted helped acquire the Yosemite Valley for a national park, serving as commissioner of Yosemite (1863–65). He also laid out the grounds at the World's Fair in Chicago (1893).

**Olympia** Area in S Greece, the site of an ancient sanctuary and of the original OLYMPIC GAMES. Buried by earthquakes in the the 6th century AD, Olympia was not rediscovered until the 18th century. It contained some of the finest works of Classical art and architecture, including the huge temple of Zeus, which contained a giant statue of the god that was numbered among the SEVEN WONDERS OF THE WORLD.

**Olympia** State capital and port of entry in SW Washington, on S tip of Puget Sound. It was made capital of Washington Territory in 1853. Development was spurred with the coming of the railroad in the 1880s and its port was expanded during both World Wars. Industries: agriculture, food canning, beer, oysters, lumber. Pop. (1990) 27,447.

▲ **okra** Originating in Africa and now widely cultivated throughout the tropics, the okra plant (*Hibiscus esculentus*) is related to the cotton plant. Its sticky green pods are picked ten weeks after planting, and are eaten as a vegetable.

▲ **Olivier** Perhaps the greatest classical actor of his time, Laurence Olivier played all the great Shakespearean roles in the theater and also presented many of them on film. During his rich film career, he played a number of romantic leads, including that of Max de Winter in *Rebecca* (1940). His Shakespearean films were rapturously received, notably *Henry V* (1944) and *Hamlet* (1948), both of which he produced, directed, and starred in. His private life attracted a great deal of press attention, particularly his second marriage to actress Vivien Leigh.

**Olympic Games** World's major international athletic competition, held in two segments – the Summer Games and the Winter Games – from 1992 alternating so that there are two years between segments, but four years before a segment is repeated. The games were first celebrated in 776 BC in OLYMPIA, Greece, and were held every four years until AD 393, when they were abolished by the Roman emperor. The modern summer games were initiated by Baron Pierre de Coubertin, and were first held in Athens, Greece, in 1896. Women did not compete until 1912. The games were canceled during World War I and World War II. Summer events include archery, track and field events, basketball, boxing, canoeing, cycling, diving, equestrian sports, fencing, field hockey, gymnastics, handball, judo, rowing, shooting, soccer, swimming, volleyball, weightlifting, and yachting. Winter events include the biathlon, bobsledding, ice hockey, skating, and skiing. The control of the games is vested in the International Olympic Committee, which lays down the rules and chooses venues.

**Olympus** Mountain range in N Greece, on the border of Thessaly and Macedonia, *c.*25mi (40km) long. Its peak, Mount Olympus, is the highest point in Greece, at 9,570ft (2,917m). It was first climbed in 1913. In ancient Greek mythology it was considered to be the home of the gods, closed to mortal eyes.

**Om** (Aum) Sacred, mystical symbol representing a sound considered to have divine power by Hindus, Buddhists, and other religious groups. The sound is chanted at the beginning and end of prayers and is used as a mantra in meditation.

**Omaha** Siouan-speaking tribe of Native North Americans. In the 1880s they participated in a major political action against the US government concerning ownership of Native American lands. Today some 2,000 Omaha people reside in Nebraska and Oklahoma.

**Omaha** Port on the Missouri River, in E Nebraska. The area was ceded to the US government in 1854. It was the capital of Nebraska Territory from 1854 to 1867. It is a leading livestock market and meat processing center, and a major insurance center. Pop. (1990) 335,795.

**Oman** Sultanate on the SE corner of the Arabian peninsula, SW Asia; the capital is MUSCAT. **Land and climate** Oman is 95% desert. On the Gulf of Oman coast lies the fertile plain of Al Batinah, and the city of Muscat. The plain is backed by the Al Hajar mountains, which rise, at Jebel Sham, to 9,905ft (3,019m). In the S lies part of the barren and rocky Rub' al Khali desert ("Empty Quarter"). The sultanate also includes the tip of the Musandam Peninsula, overlooking the strategic Strait of Hormuz, and separated from the rest of Oman by the United Arab Emirates. Oman has a hot tropical climate. In Muscat, summer temperatures rise to 117°F (47°C). Parts of the N mountains have an average annual rainfall of 16in (400mm), but most of Oman has less than 5in (125mm). Date palms grow on the coastal plain and around desert oases. Grassy pasture occurs on the Al Hajar mountains and on the S coast. **History and Politics** In ancient times, Oman was an important trading area on the main route between The Gulf and the Indian Ocean. Islam was introduced in the 7th century AD, and Muslim culture remains a unifying force. In 1507 the Portuguese captured several seaports in Oman, including Muscat. Portugal controlled maritime trade until expelled by the Ottomans in 1659. Oman set up trading posts in East Africa, including Zanzibar in 1698 and, until the 1860s, was the dominant Arabian power. The Al Said family have ruled Oman since taking power in 1741. During the 20th century, the sultanate often has been in conflict with religious leaders (imams) of the Ibahdi sect, pressing for the establishment of a more theocratic society. British colonial interference and economic inequality led to popular rebellions in the 1950s and 1960s. Insurrectionist forces continued to control much of S Oman. In 1970 Sultan Said bin Taimur was deposed by his son, Qaboos bin Said. In 1971 Oman joined the UN and the Arab League. Qaboos bin Said initiated the modernization of health, education, and social welfare. In 1981 Oman was a founder member of the Gulf Cooperation Council (GCC). Ties with the UK and the US remain strong. In 1990 Oman allowed coalition forces to use its military bases during the Gulf War. **Economy** Oman is an upper-middle-income developing country (1995 GDP per capita, US$8,140). Its economy is based on oil production. Oil was first discovered in 1964, and now accounts for more than 90% of exports. The industry attracts many migrant workers. Oil refining and the processing of copper are among Oman's few manufacturing industries. Agriculture supports 50% of the workforce. Major crops include alfalfa, bananas, coconuts, dates, limes, tobacco, vegetables, and wheat. Some farmers raise camels and cattle. Fishing, especially for sardines, is also important, but Oman is reliant on food imports.

**OMAN**

**AREA:** 82,278sq mi (212,460sq km)
**POPULATION:** 1,631,000
**CAPITAL (POPULATION):** Muscat (250,000)
**GOVERNMENT:** Monarchy with a consultative council
**ETHNIC GROUPS:** Omani Arab 74%, Pakistani 21%
**LANGUAGES:** Arabic (official)
**RELIGIONS:** Islam 86%, Hinduism 13%

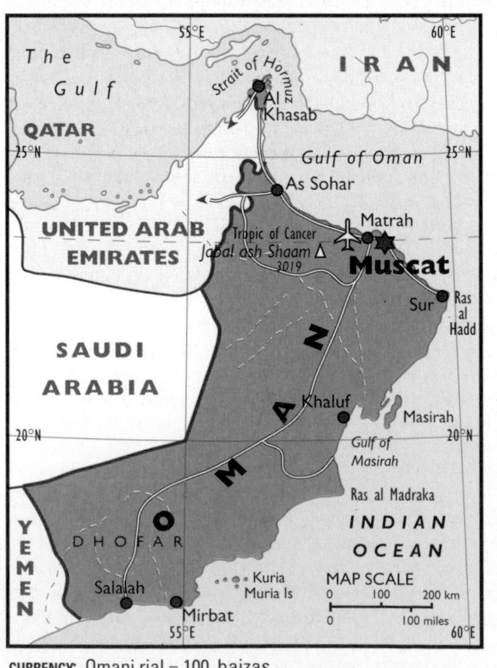


**CURRENCY:** Omani rial = 100 baizas

**Omar** (581–644) (Umar) Second CALIPH, or ruler of ISLAM. He was converted to Islam in 618 and became a counselor of MUHAMMAD. He chose the first caliph, ABU BAKR, in 632 and succeeded him two years later. Under his rule, Islam spread by conquest into Syria, Egypt, and Persia, and the foundations of an administrative empire were laid.

**Omar Khayyám** (1048–1131) Persian poet, mathematician, and astronomer. He so impressed the Sultan that he was asked to reform the calendar. His fame in the West is due to a collection of verses freely translated by Edward Fitzgerald as *The Rubáiyát of Omar Khayyám* (1859).

**Omayyads** *See* UMAYYADS

**ombudsman** Official appointed to safeguard citizens' rights by investigating complaints of injustice made against the government or its employes. The office was created in Sweden in 1809. A number of other countries adopted the office from the mid-1950s onwards. The first US state to appoint an ombudsman was Hawaii, in 1967.

**omen** Observed phenomenon that can be interpreted as a prediction of future events, either good or bad. Common omens in folk beliefs include weather changes and astronomical events, especially the sudden appearance of a comet.

**omnivore** Any creature that eats both animal and vegetable foods – examples are human beings and pigs. Omnivorous animals are characterized by having teeth adapted for cutting, tearing, and pulping food.

**Omsk** City on the Irtysh and Om rivers, W Siberia, Russia. Founded as a fortress town in 1716, from 1918–19 it was the headquarters of the anti-Bolshevik Kolchak government. It is now a major port. Industries: oil refining, chemicals, engineering, agricultural machinery, textiles. Pop. (1992) 1,169,000.

**onager** Fast-running animal related to the ASS, found in semidesert areas of Iran and India. The onager is dun-colored with a dorsal stripe that reaches the tip of the tail. Height at the shoulder: 2.9–4.9ft (0.9–1.5m). Family Equidae; species *Equus hemionus onager.*

**onchocerciasis** (river blindness) Tropical disease of the skin and connective tissue, caused by infection with filarial worms; it may also affect the eyes, causing blindness. It is transmitted by blood-sucking blackflies found in Central and South America and Africa.

**oncogene** Gene that, by inducing a cell to divide abnormally, contributes to the development of CANCER. Oncogenes arise from gene mutations (proto-oncogenes), which are present in all normal cells and in some viruses. *See also* GENETICS

**oncology** In medicine, specialty concerned with the diagnosis and treatment of CANCER.

**Onega, Lake** (Onezhskoye Ozero) Lake in NW Russia, near the border with Finland; second-largest lake in Europe. It drains SW through the Svir River to Lake Ladoga, and has numerous inlets and islands along its N shore. The chief port is Petrozavodsk. Area: 3,710sq mi (9,610sq km).

**O'Neill, Eugene Gladstone** (1888–1953) US dramatist. His first full-length play, *Beyond the Horizon* (1920), won the Pulitzer Prize, as did *Anna Christie* (1921). *The Emperor Jones* (1920) was an experiment with EXPRESSIONISM. O'Neill won a third Pulitzer Prize for *Strange Interlude* (1928). His interest in Greek tragedy is evident in *Mourning Becomes Electra* (1931). In 1936 O'Neill won the Nobel Prize for literature. Suffering from Parkinson's disease, he did not produce another play until *The Iceman Cometh* (1946). O'Neill won a posthumous Pultizer Prize for *Long Day's Journey into Night* (1956).

**O'Neill, Thomas P. (Philip), Jr. ("Tip")** (1912–94) US politician, speaker of the US House of Representatives (1977–86). In 1952 he was elected to Congress as a Democrat. O'Neill was noted for his behind-the-scenes manipulation of legislative programs. During the early 1980s he was a constant opponent of President Reagan's budget proposals. He wrote *Man of the House: The Life and Political Memoirs of Speaker Tip O'Neill* (1987).

**onion** Hardy, bulb-forming, biennial plant of the lily family, native to central Asia, and cultivated worldwide for its strong-smelling, edible bulb. It has hollow leaves and white or lilac flowers. Height: to 50in (130cm). Family Alliaceae/Liliaceae.

**on-line publishing** Distribution of information for public access using COMPUTER networks instead of physical media, such as paper or CD-ROMs. Access to on-line publications may be free or allowed in return for payment. The content of on-line publications may be enhanced by the use of such features as hypertext, search facilities, and multimedia. The majority of on-line publishing takes place over the INTERNET, particularly by means of the WORLD WIDE WEB (WWW).

**Onondaga** One of the members of the Six Nations of the IROQUOIS CONFEDERACY. A major group of Native North Americans, they lived around Onondaga County, New York, where some 1,400 still live.

**Ontario** Province in SE Canada, bounded to the S by four of the Great Lakes (Superior, Huron, Erie, and Ontario) and the US; the capital is TORONTO. Ontario is Canada's most populous province, and other major cities include OTTAWA, HAMILTON, Windsor, and London. Trading posts were established in the region during the 17th century by French explorers. The area became part of New France, but was ceded to Britain in 1763. Ontario was known as Upper Canada until 1841, when it joined with QUEBEC to form the province of Canada. In 1867 the Dominion of Canada was created, and the province of Ontario was established. In the N is the forested Canadian Shield, with its lowlands bordering on Hudson and James bays. To the E and S are the lowlands of the ST. LAWRENCE River and the Great Lakes, where agriculture and industry are concentrated. Cattle, dairy produce, and pigs are important. The chief crops are tobacco, corn, wheat, and vegetables. The Canadian Shield has many mineral deposits. Industries: motor vehicles, transportation equipment, metallurgy, chemicals, paper, machinery, electrical goods. Area: 412,582sq mi (1,068,587sq km). Pop. (1994 est.) 10,900,000.

**Ontario, Lake** Smallest of the GREAT LAKES, bounded by New York state (S and E) and Ontario province, Canada (S, W and N). Fed chiefly by the Niagara River, the lake is drained by the St. Lawrence River. Part of the St. Lawrence Seaway, it is a busy shipping route. The chief Canadian cities on the lake are TORONTO, HAMILTON, and Kingston; on the US shore are Rochester and Oswego. Area: 7,600sq mi (19,680sq km).

**ontogeny** Total biological development of an organism. It includes the embryonic stage, birth, growth, and death.

**ontology** Branch of METAPHYSICS that studies the basic nature of things; the essence of "being" itself.

**onyx** Semiprecious variety of the mineral CHALCEDONY, a form of AGATE. It has straight parallel bands. White and red forms are called carnelian onyx; white and brown, sardonyx. It is found mostly in India and South America.

**ooze** Fine-grained, deep-ocean deposit containing materials of more than 30% organic origin. Oozes are divided into two main types. CALCAREOUS ooze at depths of 6,562–12,792ft (2,000–3,900m) contains the skeletons of animals such as foraminifera and pteropods. SILICEOUS ooze at depths of more than 3,900m contains skeletons of radiolarians and diatoms.

**opal** Non-crystalline variety of QUARTZ, found in recent volcanoes, deposits from hot springs, and sediments. Usually colorless or white with a rainbow play of color in gem forms, it is the most valuable of quartz gems. Hardness 5.5–6.5; s.g. 2.0.

**op art** (optical art) US ABSTRACT ART movement, popular in the mid-1960s. It relies on optical phenomena to confuse the viewer's eye and to create a sense of movement on the surface of the picture. Leading exponents include Victor Vasarély, Kenneth Noland, and Bridget Riley.

**OPEC** Acronym for ORGANIZATION OF PETROLEUM EXPORTING COUNTRIES

**opencast mining** *See* STRIP MINING

**open cluster** (galactic cluster) Group of young stars in the spiral arms of our GALAXY, containing from a few tens of stars to a few thousand. They are usually several light-years across. One example is the PLEIADES.

**Open Door policy** US policy designed to preserve its commercial interests in China in the early 20th century. It originated in a pronouncement by the US secretary of state, John M. HAY, in 1899. At that time, China was divided into spheres of interest among European powers and Japan. The open door policy demanded that trade and traders from other countries should receive equal rights with other foreigners in China.

**open-hearth process** Method of producing STEEL in a furnace heated by overhead flames. The flames come from gas or oil burners, and oxygen may be blown through the furnace to increase its temperature. Pig iron, scrap steel, and limestone are heated together. Various impurities form slag, which is removed from the surface of the molten metal. Other materials are added to the metal to produce steel of the required type.

**opera** Stage drama that is sung. It combines acting, singing, orchestral music, set and costume design, making spectacular entertainment. The best-known opera houses include LA SCALA (Milan), the Opéra (Paris), the ROYAL OPERA (London), the State Opera (Vienna), the Festspiele (BAYREUTH), and the METROPOLITAN OPERA (New York). Opera began in Italy in *c*.1600. The classical style evolved in *c*.1750; its greatest exponent was MOZART. The 19th century was dominated by VERDI and WAGNER. Twentieth-century opera has been marked by a profusion of styles by composers such as PUCCINI, STRAUSS, BERG, and BRITTEN. *See also* OPERA BUFFA; OPÉRA COMIQUE; OPERA SERIA; OPERETTA

**opera buffa** Style of Italian comic opera that developed in mid-18th-century Naples. Light and simple in style, it introduced the elaborate finale that influenced the subsequent development of opera. An early example is *La Serva Padrona* (1733) by Giovanni Pergolesi.

**opéra comique** Style of French opera that began in the late 18th century. Its hallmarks are a witty plot involving some spoken dialogue, romantic subject matter, and simple engaging music. The genre can also include tragic works, such as Bizet's *Carmen* and Offenbach's *Tales of Hoffmann*.

O

## OPTICAL FIBERS

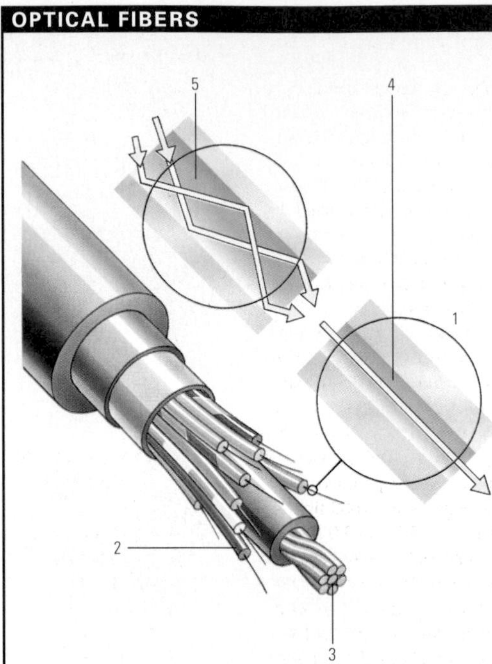


Optical fibers carry information as signals of light. The glass core (1) of a fiber optic cable is clad in glass of a different refractive index which confines the light pulses in the core. The light signal cannot leave the core because it always hits the edge of the core at too shallow an angle to escape. A sheath (2) provides physical protection and bundles of the sheathed cores are given strength by a central steel wire (3). Narrow cores (4) are now used because they allow signals to be sent over greater distances without blurring. In a wider cable (5) more reflections can occur, causing the pulse to spread out and merge with adjacent pulses. To prevent this more space must be left between pulses in wider cables and that limits the volume of data that can be transmitted.

▲ **orchid** The bee orchid (*Ophrys apifera*) of Europe tempts its pollinators with sex rather than nectar. Its elaborate flowers imitate the color, shape, texture, and scent of female bees of the genus *Eucera*. Male bees, which emerge before the females, alight on the flower's broad platform or labellum and attempt to mate with it. Structures containing thousands of pollen grains adhere to the bee's body, anchored by the sticky ends of their stalks. The bee transfers the pollen to other flowers, and cross-fertilization is followed by the formation of thousands of tiny seeds.

**opera seria** Style of Italian opera in the 17th and early 18th centuries. The plots were usually heroic or tragic. Priority was given to virtuoso vocal display in elaborate arias. The formalism and stylization of such operas prompted a reaction that gave rise to the development of OPERA BUFFA.

**operetta** Type of light OPERA involving songs, dialogue, sometimes dancing, and an engaging story. Operettas developed from attempts by composers to reach wider audiences. Among these composers were Johann STRAUSS, Arthur SULLIVAN (with W.S. GILBERT), and Jacques OFFENBACH.

**ophthalmology** Branch of medicine that specializes in the diagnosis and treatment of diseases of the eye.

**ophthalmoscope** Instrument for examining the interior of the eye, invented by Hermann von HELMHOLTZ in 1851.

**Ophüls, Max** (1902–57) German film director. His contribution was superbly realized in two masterpieces, *Letter from an Unknown Woman* (1948) and *Reckless Moment* (1949). His son, **Marcel** (1927– ), is a documentary-maker. He often presents controversial issues, such as the Nuremberg trials in *The Memory of Justice* (1975) and the Bosnian war in *Veillées d'Armes* (1994).

**opium** Drug derived from the unripe seed-pods of the opium POPPY. Its components and derivatives have been used as NARCOTICS and ANALGESICS for many centuries. It produces drowsiness and euphoria and reduces pain. MORPHINE and CODEINE are opium derivatives.

**Opium Wars** (1839–42) Conflict between Britain and China. It arose because Chinese officials prevented the importation of opium. After a British victory, the Treaty of Nanking gave Britain trading rights in certain ports and the grant of Hong Kong. A second, similar war (1856–60) was fought by the British and French against China. When China refused to ratify the Treaty of Tientsin (1858), Anglo-French forces occupied Peking (Beijing).

**Oporto** City and port on the Douro River, NW Portugal. A Roman settlement, it was occupied by the Visigoths (540–716) and the Moors (716–997) before being brought under Portuguese control in 1092. By the 17th century it was a famous wine center and its PORT is still exported. Portugal's second-largest city, Oporto lies in an industrialized region. Industries: textiles, fishing, fruit, olive oil. Pop. (1991) 310,640.

**opossum** (possum) New World MARSUPIAL animal. The only marsupial found outside Australasia. Omnivorous tree-dwellers, they have silky gray fur (except on the long prehensile tail), and feign death when in danger. The common opossum, *Didelphis marsupialis*, grows up to 20in (50cm) long, plus a 12in (30cm) tail. Family Didelphidae.

**Oppenheimer, (Julius) Robert** (1904–67) US theoretical physicist. He was appointed director (1943–45) of the Los Alamos laboratory in New Mexico, where he headed the MANHATTAN PROJECT to develop the atomic bomb. In 1949 he opposed the construction of the HYDROGEN BOMB and in 1953 was suspended by the Atomic Energy Commission. He was subsequently reinstated.

**opposition, leader of the** In parliamentary systems, the leader of the party that is runner-up in a general election. In the UK, official recognition was given to the leader of the opposition in 1937.

**optical disk** In computing, a high-density storage device consisting of a disk on which data is recorded and read by a laser. The most common type is a CD-ROM, although an audio compact disc is also a read-only device of this kind. A recording facility is provided by a WORM disk (write once, read many), on which a computer can save data once, and then read it repeatedly but not be able to change it.

**optical fiber** *See* FIBER OPTICS

**optical illusion** Effect in which visual information is misleading or misinterpreted. Natural optical illusions are often created by light REFRACTION such as a MIRAGE of water on a hot, dry road.

**optics** Branch of physics concerned with the study of LIGHT and its behavior. Fundamental aspects are the physical nature of light, both as a wave phenomenon and as particles (PHOTONS), and the REFLECTION, REFRACTION, and polarization of light. Optics also involves the study of mirrors and LENS systems and of optically active chemicals and crystals that polarize light. *See also* POLARIZED LIGHT

**optometry** Testing of vision in order to prescribe corrective eyewear, such as spectacles or contact lenses. It is distinct from OPHTHALMOLOGY.

**Opus Dei** International Roman Catholic organization of laymen and a few priests, known for its highly conservative political and religious influence. It was founded (1928) in Spain. Its members seek to put into practice Christian values through their chosen professions.

**oracle** In ancient Greece, a priest or priestess who gave the answer of a god to questions put by individuals. The most famous was the oracle of Apollo at DELPHI. The god spoke through a priestess (Pythia), whose words were, in turn, interpreted by priests. Answers tended to be ambiguous, so that the oracle could never be said to be wrong.

**Oran** City and seaport on the Gulf of Oran, NW Algeria. Founded in the 10th century, it was taken by Spain from its Arab rulers in 1509. Captured by Ottoman Turks in 1708, it was retaken by Spain in 1732. Under French rule from 1831 to 1962, it developed as a naval base. It is Algeria's second-largest city. Industries: iron ore, textiles, chemicals, cereals, wine, fruit. Pop. (1987) 609,823.

**Orange** Longest river of South Africa. It rises in the Drakensberg Mountains in N Lesotho and flows generally W, forming the boundary between FREE STATE and CAPE PROVINCE. It continues W through the Kalahari and Namib deserts, forming South Africa's border with Namibia. It empties into the Atlantic Ocean at Oranjemund. Length: *c*.1,300mi (2,100km).

**orange** Evergreen citrus tree and its fruit. There are two basic types. The sweet orange (*Citrus sinensis*) is native to Asia and widely grown in the US and Israel. The fruit develops without flower pollination and is often seedless. The sour orange (*C.aurantium*) is widely grown in Spain for the manufacture of marmalade. Related fruits include the mandarin, tangerine, and satsuma, all varieties of *C. reticulata*. Height: to 30ft (9m). Family Rutaceae; genus *Citrus*.

**Orange, House of** Royal dynasty of the Netherlands. Orange was a principality in S France, which was inherited by WILLIAM I (THE SILENT) in 1544. He led the successful Dutch revolt against Spain in the late 16th century. WILLIAM III became king of England in 1689. The son of William V became king of the Netherlands in 1815 as WILLIAM I.

**Orange Free State** Former name (1854–1995) of the FREE STATE province of South Africa.

**Orangemen** Members of the Orange Society, or Orange Order. It was founded (1795) in Ulster in response to the mainly Roman Catholic, nationalist United Irishmen, and was named for the Protestant hero, WILLIAM III, prince of Orange. His victory over the Catholic JAMES II at the Battle of the BOYNE (1690) is celebrated on its anniversary, July 12.

**orang-utan** Great APE native to forests of Sumatra and Borneo. It has a bulging belly and a shaggy, reddish-brown coat. It swings by its arms when traveling through trees, but proceeds on all fours on the ground. Height: 5ft (1.5m); weight: to 220 lb (100kg). Species *Pongo pygmaeus*. *See also* PRIMATES

**oratorio** Form of sacred musical composition for solo voices, chorus, and orchestra. The first of these compositions were presented in oratories (chapels) in 17th-century Italy. Outstanding examples are Handel's *Messiah* (1742) and Elgar's *Dream of Gerontius* (1900).

**orbit** Path of a celestial body in a gravitational field. The path is usually a closed one about the focus of the system to which it belongs, as with those of the planets around the Sun. Most celestial orbits are elliptical, although the ECCENTRICITY can vary greatly. It is rare for an orbit to be parabolic or hyperbolic.

**orchestra** Group of musicians who play together. During the 17th century string orchestras developed out of viol consorts; in the 18th century some wind instruments were added. The woodwind section was soon established, and by the end of the 19th century the brass section was too. Modern orchestras consist of between 80 and 120 players divided into sections: strings (violin, viola, cello, double bass, and harp), woodwind (flute, oboe, clarinet, and bassoon), brass (trumpet, trombone, French horn, and tuba), and percussion.

**orchid** Any plant of the family Orchidaceae, common in the tropics. There are *c*.35,000 species. All are perennials and grow in soil or as EPIPHYTES on other plants. Parasitic and saprophytic species are also known. All orchids have bilaterally symmetrical flower structures, each with three sepals. They range in diameter from *c*.0.1in (2mm) to 15in (38cm).

**order** In TAXONOMY (biological classification), a group of related plants or animals; order is one rank below CLASS and a rank above FAMILY. For example, the tiger is of the order Carnivora (CARNIVORES).

**orders, holy** In the Roman Catholic, Orthodox, and Anglican churches, the duties of the clergy, and the grades of hierarchical rank as outlined in the office of ORDINATION. A person is ordained as a subdeacon, deacon, priest, or bishop. These ranks are known as the major orders. The minor orders are those of porter, lector, exorcist, and acolyte.

**orders of architecture** In classical architecture, style and decoration of a column, its base, capital, and entablature. Of the five orders, the Greeks developed the Doric, Ionic, and Corinthian. The Tuscan and Composite orders were Roman adaptations. A typical **Doric** column has no base, a relatively short shaft with surface fluting meeting in a sharp edge and an unornamented capital. The **Ionic** order is characterized by slender columns with 24 flutes and prominent spiral scrolls on the capitals. The **Corinthian** is the most ornate of the Classical orders of architecture. A typical Corinthian column has a high base, a slim, fluted column, and a bell-shaped capital with acanthus-leaf ornament.

**ordination** Process of consecrating a person as a minister of religion. In Christian Churches organized along episcopal lines, ordination confirms the ordinand (the individual undergoing the process) as a priest or minister in holy ORDERS. In Roman Catholic and Orthodox Churches, the rite of ordination is a SACRAMENT. In Protestant Churches without episcopal organization, ordination is carried out by ministers, ruling elders, or specially selected lay persons.

**ordination of women** Official recognition of women as priests or ministers by a church. In Christianity, the ban on women as full members of the clergy has persisted in some churches, notably the Roman Catholic Church. During the 20th century, however, many Protestant churches began to admit women first as deacons and later as priests and ministers.

**Ordovician** Second-oldest period of the PALEOZOIC era, 505 to 438 million years ago. All animal life was restricted to the sea. Numerous invertebrates flourished and included trilobites, brachiopods, corals, graptolites, mollusks, and echinoderms. Remains of jawless fish from this period are the first record of the vertebrates.

**ore** Mineral or combination of minerals from which metals and nonmetals can be extracted. It occurs in veins, beds, or seams parallel to the enclosing rock or in irregular masses.

**oregano** (marjoram) Dried leaves and flowers of several perennial herbs of the genus *Oreganum*, native to Mediterranean lands and w Asia. It is a popular culinary herb. Family Lamiaceae/Labiatae; genus *Origanum*.

**Oregon** State of NW US, on the Pacific coast; the capital is SALEM. Other major cities include PORTLAND and Eugene. Trading posts were set up in the 1790s, mainly by the HUDSON'S BAY COMPANY. From 1842 the OREGON TRAIL brought more settlers. Oregon Territory was formed in 1848 and was admitted to the Union in 1859. It is dominated by the forested slopes of the CASCADE and the Coast ranges. Between the two lies the fertile Willamette Valley. The COLUMBIA and the Willamette are the major rivers. Agricultural products include cattle, dairy produce, wheat, and market garden products. Oregon produces more than 20% of the nation's softwood timber. Area: 96,981sq mi (251,180sq km). Pop. (1993 est.) 3,038,000.

**Oregon Trail** Main route of US pioneers to the West in the 1840s and 1850s. It ran 2,000mi (3,200km) from Independence, Missouri, to Fort Vancouver on the Columbia River in Oregon and crossed the Rocky Mountains via South Pass. The journey took about six months. It was heavily used from 1843, when "Oregon fever" attracted thousands of settlers. After 1848, when gold was discovered in California, the numbers began to decline.

**Orestes** In Greek legend, the son of AGAMEMNON and CLYTEMNESTRA, and brother of ELECTRA. He killed his mother and her lover Aegisthus to avenge their murder of his father.

**Orff, Carl** (1895–1982) German composer. He used deliberately primitive rhythms in his best-known works, *Carmina Burana* (1937) and *Catulli Carmina* (1943), and the opera *Trionfo di Afrodite* (1953).

**organ** In biology, group of TISSUES that form a functional and structural unit in a living organism. The major organs of the body include the brain, heart, lungs, skin, liver, and kidneys. Leaves, flowers, and roots are examples of plant organs.

**organ** KEYBOARD INSTRUMENT. The player sits at a console and regulates a flow of air to ranks of pipes, producing rich tones. The organ was in use in Christian churches in the 8th century. The modern organ dates from the BAROQUE period.

**organic chemistry** *See* CHEMISTRY

**Organization for Economic Cooperation and Development (OECD)** International consultative body set up in 1961 by the major Western trading nations. Its aims are to stimulate economic growth and world trade by raising the standard of living in member countries and by coordinating aid to less developed countries. Its headquarters are in Paris and it has 24 member nations including all the worlds major powers.

**Organization of African Unity (OAU)** Intergovernmental organization. Founded in 1963, the OAU brings together all African states. It aims to safeguard African interests and independence, encourage the continent's development, and settle disputes among member states. Its headquarters are in Addis Ababa, Ethiopia.

**Organization of American States (OAS)** Organization of 35 member states of the Americas that promotes peaceful settlements to disputes, regional cooperation in the limitation of weapons, and economic and cultural development. It was created in 1948 during an international meeting held in Colombia. The successor to the Pan American Union, the OAS is affiliated to the UNITED NATIONS (UN). Its headquarters are in Washington, D.C.

**Organization of Petroleum Exporting Countries (OPEC)** Intergovernmental organization established in 1960 by many of the world's major oil producing states to safeguard their interests. It was able to control oil prices in the 1970s, but its influence has waned since then, largely because of internal differences and the emergence of major oil-producing countries outside OPEC. Its headquarters are in Vienna, Austria.

Doric

Ionic

Corinthian

Composite

Tuscan

▲ **orders of architecture** The five main orders of architecture were first presented by Sebastiano Serlio (1475–1554) in Book IV of his treatise on architecture (1537).

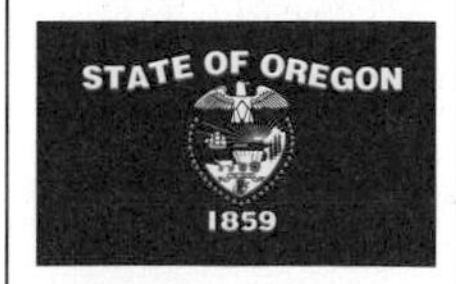


**OREGON**
**Statehood :**
February 14, 1859
**Nickname :**
The Beaver State
**State bird :**
Western meadowlark
**State flower :**
Oregon grape
**State tree :**
Douglas fir
**State motto :**
She flies with her own wings

O

## OSCILLOSCOPE

An oscilloscope displays an electronic signal on a display in analog form. Usually time is represented on the x axis (horizontal) with the y axis (vertical) recording the incoming voltage - here a heartbeat (1). The signal from the object being monitored is converted into an electrical voltage (2). That voltage is shown in visible form on the screen of a cathode ray tube (3) similar to a black and white television. Deflector magnets (4) direct the stream of electrons from the electron gun (5). The magnets sweep the electron beam from left to right over a set period, while variations in the voltage of the external signal cause the wave pattern. The control box (6) allows the period of the x axis and the strength of the signal displayed to be changed.

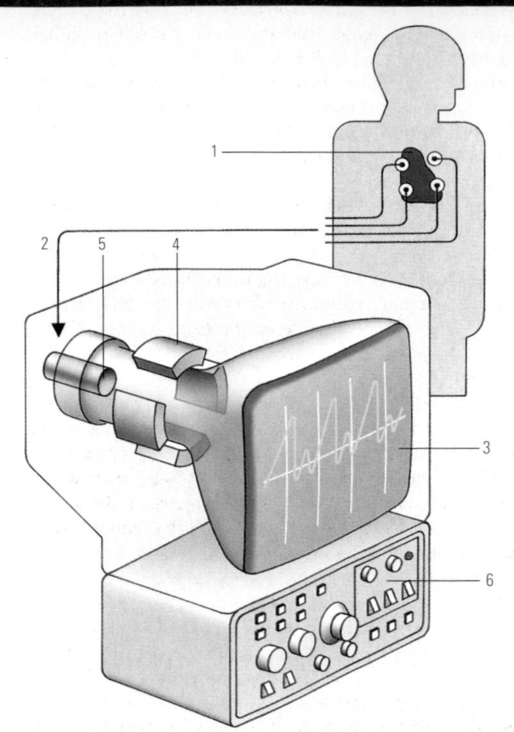


**orgasm** Physiological culmination of sexual stimulation, marked by general release of muscular tension and waves of contractions causing climactic spasms of vaginal muscles in the female and ejaculation (the release of SEMEN) in the male.
**original sin** Sin committed by ADAM and EVE for which they were expelled from the Garden of EDEN and were made mortal (Genesis 3). The sin was their eating from the tree of the knowledge of good and evil against God's strict instructions. Adam and Eve's guilt was deemed to have been passed down to their descendants through all the generations.
**Orinoco** River in Venezuela. Rising in the Sierra Parima Mts in S Venezuela, it flows NW to Colombia, then N, forming part of the Venezuela-Colombia border, and finally E into the Atlantic Ocean by a vast delta. Length: *c*.1,281mi (2,062km).
**oriole** Two unrelated types of songbirds. The New World oriole (family Icteridae) is brightly colored and builds hanging nests in trees. The Old World oriole (family Oriolidae) has similar coloring and lays eggs in a cup-shaped nest.
**Orion** Prominent constellation, representing a hunter. Four young stars form a conspicuous quadrilateral containing a row of three other stars representing his belt.
**Orion nebula** Emission nebula visible to the naked eye in the constellation ORION. It is a mass of gas surrounding a quadrilateral grouping of four hot O-type stars (the trapezium).
**Orissa** State in NE India, on the Bay of Bengal; the capital is Bhubaneswar. After being ruled by Hindus, Afghans, and Moguls, it was ceded to the Mahrattas in 1751. Occupied by the British in 1803, it was proclaimed a constituent state of India in 1950. Industries: mining, fishing, rice, wheat, sugarcane, oilseeds, forestry. Area: 60,147sq mi (155,782sq km). Pop. (1991) 31,659,736.
**Orkney Islands** Archipelago of more than 70 islands off the N coast of Scotland. Mainland (Pomona) is the largest; other principal islands include Hoy and South Ronaldsay. The land is a low-lying, fertile plain, and the climate is mild and wet. Scapa Flow (between Mainland and Hoy) was the major British naval base in both World Wars. The economy is predominantly agricultural. Area: 376sq mi (974sq km). Pop. (1991) 19,612.
**Orlando, Vittorio Emanuele** (1860–1952) Italian statesman, prime minister (1917–19). He became prime minister after a succession of Italian defeats in World War I. He represented Italy at the Treaty of Versailles. His early support for MUSSOLINI turned to opposition in 1925. After World War II he rejoined the Senate and ran for president (1948).
**Orlando** City in central Florida. Orlando is one of the world's most popular tourist destinations, with the Disney World and Magic Kingdom theme park. Established in 1827 as a trading post, Orlando was incorporated as a city in 1875 and expanded with the arrival of the railroad. Industries: citrus-growing, aerospace, electronics. Pop. (1990) 164,693.
**Orléans, Louis-Philippe, Duc d'** (1747–93) French Bourbon prince. A liberal, he was elected to the National Convention (1782) and voted for the king's execution. When his son, the future King LOUIS PHILIPPE, defected (1793), he was arrested and subsequently executed during the REIGN OF TERROR.
**Orléans** City on the Loire River, N central France; capital of Loiret department. Besieged by the English during the HUNDRED YEARS WAR, it was relieved by JOAN OF ARC in 1429. During the 16th-century Wars of RELIGION, the city was besieged by Catholic forces and held by them until the Edict of NANTES. Industries: tobacco, textiles, fruit and vegetables, chemicals. Pop. (1991) 105,111.
**Ormuzd** *See* AHURA MAZDAH
**ornithology** Study of birds. Included in general ornithological studies are classification, structure, function, evolution, distribution, migration, reproduction, ecology, and behavior.
**Orozco, José Clemente** (1883–1949) Mexican painter. In his wash drawings, *Mexico in Revolution* (1911–16), Orozco aimed to demonstrate the futility of war. His MURALS are grand in both scale and mood, none more so than *Katharsis* (1934). His later paintings, such as *Hidalgo and Castillo* (1949), are highly emotive.
**Orpheus** In Greek mythology, the son of Calliope by APOLLO, and the finest of all poets and musicians. Orpheus married Eurydice, who died after being bitten by a snake. He descended into the Underworld to rescue her and was allowed to regain her if he did not look back at her until they emerged into the sunlight. He could not resist, and Eurydice vanished forever.
**orphism** (orphic cubism) Term invented in 1912 by APOLLINAIRE to describe a new art form combining elements of CUBISM, FUTURISM, and FAUVISM. The style was first associated with the work of Robert and Sonia DELAUNAY and its other exponents exerted considerable influence in Germany through the works of KLEE and KANDINSKY. *See also* BLAUE REITER
**Orr, Robert Gordon (Bobby)** (1948– ) Canadian ice hockey player. He played in the NHL for the Boston Bruins (1966–76) and Chicago Black Hawks (1976–78). Orr is the only defenseman to lead the league scoring table and was the first defenseman to score more than 100 points in a season.
**Ortega Saavedra, Daniel** (1945– ) Nicaraguan statesman, president (1984–1990). He joined the SANDANISTAS (FSLN) in 1963, was imprisoned and tortured, and later exiled to Cuba. In 1979 Ortega returned to Nicaragua to lead the Nicaraguan Revolution that toppled the SOMOZA government. In February 1990, he lost the presidency to Violeta CHAMORRO. He remains the leader of the FSLN.
**orthoclase** ($KAlSi_3O_8$, potassium aluminum silicate) Essential mineral in acidic IGNEOUS rocks and common in METAMORPHIC rocks. It has a monoclinic system of crystals and is usually white. Hardness 6–6.5; sp.gr. 2.5–2.6.
**orthodontics** *See* DENTISTRY
**Orthodox Church** (Eastern Orthodox Church) Family of Christian national churches mostly of E Europe. The churches are independent but acknowledge the primacy of the Patriarch of Constantinople. They developed from the Church of the BYZANTINE EMPIRE, which separated from that of Rome in 1054. The Russian Orthodox Church is by far the largest. *See also* SCHISM
**orthography** System governing the presentation of the letters of words in handwriting or in printed type, according to accepted linguistic conventions. Orthography is essentially the spelling system used in a language and the principles underlying such a system.
**orthopedics** Branch of medicine that deals with the diagnosis and treatment of diseases, disorders, and injuries of bones, muscles, tendons, and ligaments.

**Orton, Joe (John Kingsley)** (1933–67) English playwright who specialized in black satirical comedies. *Entertaining Mr. Sloane* and *Loot* appeared in London in 1964 and 1965 respectively. *What the Butler Saw* was produced in 1969 after Orton's murder by his lover, Kenneth Halliwell.

**Orwell, George** (1903–50) British novelist and essayist, b. Eric Arthur Blair in India. His service (1922–27) with the Indian imperial police in Burma formed the basis of *Burmese Days* (1934). Other early autobiographical works include *Down and Out in Paris and London* (1933), *The Road to Wigan Pier* (1937), and *Homage to Catalonia* (1938), the latter on his experiences in the Spanish Civil War. Orwell, however, is best-known for his fictions on totalitarianism: the satirical fable *Animal Farm* (1945), and the dystopic novel *1984* (1949).

**oryx** (gemsbok) Any of four species of ANTELOPES. The male has a tuft of hair at the throat and both sexes carry long horns ringed at the base. Two species are almost extinct, but the other two survive in considerable numbers in Africa. Height: 4ft (1.2m). Family Bovidae.

**Osage** Tribe of Native North Americans. Hunters with a strong religious tradition, they settled at different times in Kansas, Missouri, and Oklahoma. Numbering *c.*7,000 today, they have prospered since the discovery of oil on their Oklahoma reservation.

**Osaka** City on Osaka Bay, S Honshū island, Japan; capital of Osaka prefecture. Japan's third-largest city and its principal industrial port, Osaka was intensively bombed during World War II. It is a major transportation hub. The city was the imperial capital during the 4th–8th centuries. During the Edo Period the city became the commercial center of Hideyoshi. Pop. (1993) 2,495,000.

**Osborne, John James** (1929–95) English dramatist whose play *Look Back in Anger* (1956) established his reputation as one of the ANGRY YOUNG MEN of English theater. His other successes included *The Entertainer* (1957) and *Luther* (1961) but later works such as *The Hotel in Amsterdam* (1968) provoked critical hostility.

**Oscar** (officially Academy Award) Prize awarded annually for services to the cinema by the US Academy of Motion Picture Arts and Sciences. The gold-plated bronze statuettes stand 10in (25cm) high.

**Osceola** (*c.*1800–38) Native American leader of the SEMINOLE Native Americans in Florida in the Second Seminole War (1835–37). President Jackson ordered the Seminoles removed to the West, but Osceola took his people into the Everglades to continue the fight.

**oscillating Universe theory** Variant of the BIG BANG theory in which it is suggested that the Universe passes through successive cycles of expansion and contraction (or collapse). At the end of the collapse phase, with the Universe packed into a small volume of great density, it is possible that a "bounce" would occur. The Universe would thus oscillate between Big Bang and "Big Crunch" episodes and so be infinite in age.

**oscillator** In physics, a device for producing sound waves, as in a SONAR or an ultrasonic generator. In electronics, an oscillator circuit converts direct current (DC) electricity into high-frequency alternating current (AC).

**oscilloscope** (cathode-ray oscilloscope) Electronic instrument in which a CATHODE-RAY TUBE (CRT) system displays how quantities, such as voltage or current, vary over a period of time. The electron beam that traces the pattern on the screen is moved by a time-base generator within the oscilloscope. The result is generally a curve or graph on the screen.

**osier** Any of various willows, especially *Salix viminalis* and *S. purpurea*, the flexible branches and stems of which are used for wickerwork.

**Osiris** In Egyptian mythology, the god of the dead. He is generally depicted wearing a feathered crown and bearing the crook and flail of a king. In the myths, Osiris was killed by his brother SETH. His sister and wife, ISIS, retrieved the corpse, and Osiris' son Horus avenged his death.

**Oslo** Capital of Norway, in the SE of the country, at the head of Oslo Fjord. The city was founded in the mid-11th century. Largely destroyed by fire in 1624, it was rebuilt by CHRISTIAN IV, who named it Christiania. In 1905 it became the capital of independent Norway, and was renamed Oslo in 1925. Industries: machinery, wood products, food processing, textiles, chemicals, shipbuilding. Pop. (1990) 459,292.

**Osman I** (1258–1326) Founder of the OTTOMAN EMPIRE. As ruler of the small Osmanli, or Ottoman, state in NW Anatolia (Turkey), he declared his independence of the SELJUK sultan *c.*1290. He expanded his territory in frequent wars against the BYZANTINE EMPIRE.

**osmium** (symbol Os) Bluish-white metallic element, one of the TRANSITION ELEMENTS. The densest of the elements, osmium is associated with platinum; the chief source is as a by-product from smelting nickel. Like IRIDIUM, osmium is used in producing hard alloys. It is also used to make electrical contacts and pen points. Properties: at.no.76; at.wt. 190.2; sp.gr. 22.57; m.p. 5,513°F (3,045°C); b.p. 9,081°F (5,027°C); most common isotope $^{192}$Os (41.0%).

**osmosis** Diffusion of a solvent (such as water) through a selectively permeable MEMBRANE (one which only allows the passage of certain dissolved substances) into a more concentrated solution. Because the more concentrated solution contains a lower concentration of solvent molecules, the solvent flows by diffusion to dilute it until concentrations of solvent are equal on both sides of the membrane. Osmosis is a vital cellular process. *See also* TURGOR PRESSURE

**osprey** HAWK that lives beside lakes and in coastal regions of all continents except Antarctica. It has a short hooked bill, broad ragged wings, and a white head; it has brownish-black plumage on its back and a cream breast. Length: 20–24in (51–61cm). Family Pandionidae, species *Pandion haliaetus*.

**Ossetia** Region of the central Caucasus. The region is divided along the Terek River. **North Ossetia** is an autonomous republic within the Russian Federation, whose capital is Vladikavkaz. **South Ossetia** is an autonomous region of GEORGIA, whose capital is Tshkinvali. Ossetia is a mountainous agricultural region, producing fruit, wine, and grain. North Ossetia has rich mineral deposits. Ossetia became part of the Russian empire in the early 19th century. Area: North Ossetia, 3,000sq mi (8,000sq km); South Ossetia, 1,500sq mi (3,900sq km). Pop. North Ossetia (1990), 638,000; South Ossetia (1990), 99,800.

**ossification** (osteogenesis) Process of BONE formation in vertebrates. Bone is formed through the action of special cells called osteoblasts, which secrete bone-forming minerals that combine with a network of COLLAGEN fibers.

**Ostend Manifesto** (October 1854) Document in US history, drawn up in Ostend, Belgium by Pierre Soulé, James Y. Mason, and James BUCHANAN. The document warned Spain that the US would take Cuba by force if Spain refused to sell the island. Protests arose both in the US and Europe and the manifesto was finally denounced by the US secretary of state, William Marcy.

**osteomyelitis** Infection of the BONE, sometimes spreading along the marrow cavity. Rare except in diabetics, it can arise from a compound fracture, where the bone breaks through the skin, or from infection elsewhere in the body. It is accompanied by fever, swelling, and pain. The condition may be treated with immobilization, ANTIBIOTICS, and surgical drainage.

**osteopathy** System of alternative medical treatment based on the use of physical manipulation to rectify damage caused by mechanical stresses. The concept was formulated (1874) by US physician Andrew Still.

**osteoporosis** Condition where there is loss of bone substance, resulting in brittle bones. It is common in older people, especially in women following the MENOPAUSE; it may also occur in Cushing's syndrome and as a side-effect of prolonged treatment with corticosteroid drugs. There is no cure, but it may be treated with calcium supplements and a drug called disodium etidronate. HORMONE REPLACEMENT THERAPY (HRT) may help to prevent its occurrence in post-menopausal women.

**ostrich** Largest living bird, found in central Africa. It is flightless and has a small head and long neck. Plumage is black and white in males, brown and white in females. Eggs are laid in holes in the sand. Height: to 8ft (2.5m); weight: to 345lb (155kg). Family Struthionidae; species *Struthio camelus*.

▲ **ostrich** Africa is the home of the ostrich, the largest living bird. It is the only member of the order Struthioniformes. Several large ground-dwelling birds, the ostrich, rhea, emu, and cassowary, all resemble each other quite closely, but are thought to have arisen independently, and as such are examples of a phenomenon called convergent evolution.

O

▲ **Oswald** Although he vehemently asserted his innocence, claiming that he had been framed, Lee Harvey Oswald was widely believed to be the assassin of US president John F. Kennedy in 1963. Oswald was shot and killed while in police custody before he came to trial. Rumors that Oswald was a double agent, and conspiracy theories that suggest more than one gunman carried out the assassination, persist.

**Ostrogoths** *See* Goth

**Ostrovsky, Alexsandr Nikolayevich** (1823–86) Russian dramatist. He is an important figure in 20th-century Russian realism. Many of his plays deal with the life of the Russian merchant class. His plays include *Poverty is no Crime* (1854), and *The Thunderstorm* (1859).

**Oswald, Lee Harvey** (1939–63) Alleged assassin of US president John F. Kennedy, on November 22, 1963, in Dallas, Texas. Before he could stand trial, he was shot and killed in police custody by Jack Ruby. *See also* Warren Commission

**Othman** (Uthman) (574–656) Third caliph (644–56) A son-in-law of Muhammad, he was a member of the Umayyad family of Mecca. He was blamed for widespread revolts and intrigues, culminating in his assassination.

**O'Toole, Peter** (1932– ) Irish stage and film actor. He exhilarated British theater audiences with his stage performances as Shylock in *The Merchant of Venice* (1960) and *Hamlet* (1963). O'Toole was nominated for an Academy Award for his first film role in *Lawrence of Arabia* (1962). Other Oscar nominations include *Becket* (1964), *The Lion in Winter* (1968), *Goodbye Mr Chips* (1969), and *The Ruling Class* (1972). Other films include *My Favorite Year* (1982), and *The Last Emperor* (1987).

**otosclerosis** Inherited condition in which overgrowth of bone in the middle ear causes deafness. It is gradual in onset and twice as common in women as in men. Surgery can rebuild the sound conduction mechanism.

**Ottawa** Group of Algonquian-speaking Native North Americans. Hunter-farmers, they originally lived north of the Great Lakes. They allied with the French and Hurons, but were broken into five groups by the Iroquois and Anglo-Americans and now live in the Great Lakes area, Kansas, and Oklahoma.

**Ottawa** Capital of Canada, in SE Ontario, on the Ottawa River and the Rideau Canal. Founded in 1826 as Bytown, it acquired its present name in 1854. Queen Victoria chose it as capital of the United Provinces in 1858, and in 1867 it became the national capital of the Dominion of Canada. Industries: glassmaking, printing, publishing, sawmilling, pulpmaking, clocks and watches. Pop. (1991) 313,987.

**otter** Semi-aquatic carnivore found everywhere except Australia. Otters have narrow, pointed heads with bristly whiskers, sleek furry bodies, short legs with webbed hind feet, and long tapering tails. The river otter (genus *Lutra*) is small to medium-sized and spends considerable time on land. Family Mustelidae.

**Otto I (the Great)** (912–73) King of the Germans (936–73) and first Holy Roman emperor (962–73). He succeeded his father, Henry I, in Germany and defeated rebellious princes and their ally, Louis IV of France. Royal power was further augmented by Otto's close control of the church. In 955 he crushed the Magyars at Lechfeld. He invaded Italy to aid Queen Adelaide of Lombardy, married Adelaide, and became king of Lombardy. In 962 he was crowned as Roman emperor (the "Holy," meaning "Christian," was added later).

**OVUM**

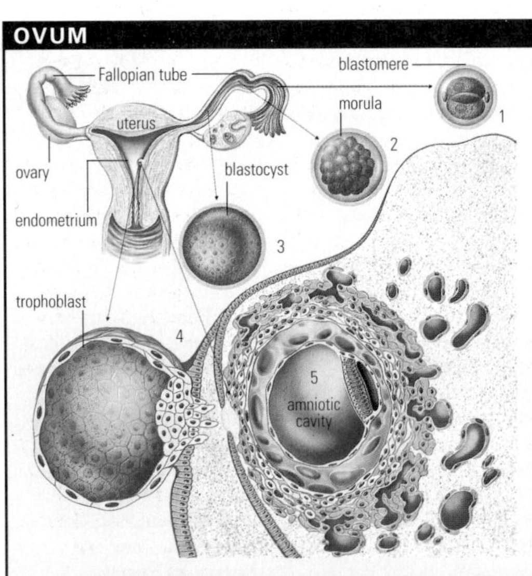


It takes about a week for the fertilized ovum to pass down the Fallopian tube and implant itself in the uterine lining, the endometrium. Within hours of conception mitosis begins with the development of a sphere of an increasing number of cells; the sphere starts as the blastomere (1), develops into the morula (2) of about 64 cells. At this stage it changes into a hollow, fluid-containing ball – blastocyst (3) – with the inner cell mass at one end. It can now begin implantation (4). By the ninth day after conception the blastocyst has sunk deep into the endometrium (5) and is already receiving nutrition from the mother.

**Otto IV** (1174–1218) (Otto of Brunswick) Holy Roman emperor (1198–1215). A member of the Guelph family, Otto antagonized the powerful Pope Innocent III by his invasion of Italy against the Hohenstaufen King Frederick I (later the Emperor Frederick II). With Innocent's support, Frederick was elected king by the German princes (1212) and supported by Philip II of France. Otto was defeated by Philip at Bouvines (1214) and forced to retire.

**Ottoman empire** Former Turkish state that controlled much of SE Europe, the Middle East, and North Africa between the 14th and 20th centuries. It was founded by Osman I (r.1290–1326). He ruled a small principality in Anatolia, which he greatly enlarged at the expense of the Byzantine empire. The contest with the Byzantines ended with the capture of Constantinople (now Istanbul), which became the Ottoman capital in 1453. Under Suleiman I (the Magnificent) (r.1520–66), the Ottoman empire included the Arab lands of the Middle East and North Africa, SE Europe, and the E Mediterranean. The decline of Ottoman power began before 1600, and thereafter, Ottoman territory was reduced in wars with its European neighbors, Austria and Russia. After World War I, when Ottoman territory was reduced to roughly the present Turkish borders, nationalists led by Atatürk deposed the last Ottoman sultan and created the modern Turkish republic (1923).

**Ouagadougou** Capital of Burkina Faso, West Africa. Founded in the late 11th century as capital of the Mossi empire, it remained the center of Mossi power until captured by the French in 1896. Industries: handicrafts, textiles, food processing, peanuts, vegetable oil. Pop. (1985) 442,223.

**ouzel** (ousel) Heavy-bodied bird found in the mountains of Asia, Europe, and the Western Hemisphere. The ring ouzel (*Turdus torquatus*) has black plumage, with a white chest collar. Family Turdidae.

**ovary** In biology, part of a multicellular animal or a flowering plant that produces egg cells (ova), the female reproductive cells; in vertebrates it also produces female sex hormones. In female humans there is an ovary on each side of the uterus. Controlled by the pituitary gland, each ovary produces estrogen and progesterone, which control the functioning of the female reproductive system. In flowering plants, the female sex cells are contained within structures called ovules inside the ovary. After fertilization the ovules develop into seeds, and the ovary develops into fruit. *See also* hormone; menstrual cycle

**overfishing** Practice of catching too many marine creatures for an ecological balance to be maintained, resulting in the severe reduction in, or even disappearance of, catches of food fishes, whales, and other marine animals. Overfishing has become a worldwide concern, with falling catches in most of the world's major fisheries. It remains an international problem largely because of the inability of marine law to regulate fishing and whaling. The term is also used of freshwater fishing, although reductions in freshwater fish stocks are more commonly the result of pollution.

**overture** Instrumental prelude to an opera or operetta; the term now also includes an orchestral composition in its own right, usually lively in character. Famous operatic overtures were composed by Mozart, Rossini, and Wagner.

**Ovid** (43 BC–AD 18) (Publius Ovidius Naso) Roman poet. He was a great success in Rome until, aged 50, he was exiled by Augustus. Ovid's poems, mainly elegaics, fall into three categories: love poetry, such as *Amores* and *Ars Amatoria*; poems of exile, such as *Tristia*; and mythological poetry, such as his masterpiece *Metamorphoses*, written in hexameters.

**ovule** In seed-bearing plants, part of the reproductive organ that contains an egg cell or ovum and develops into a seed after fertilization. In angiosperms, ovules develop inside an ovary. In gymnosperms, ovules are borne on the inner surface of the cone without any covering.

**ovum** (egg cell) Female gamete produced in an ovary. After fertilization by sperm it becomes a zygote, which is capable of developing into a new individual.

**Owen, Robert** (1771–1858) Welsh industrialist and social reformer. He believed that better conditions for workers would lead to greater productivity, and put these beliefs into practice at his textile mills in Scotland. Owen also attempted to establish a self-contained cooperative community in New Harmony, Indiana (1825–27). His ideas provided the basis for the COOPERATIVE MOVEMENT.

**Owen, Wilfred** (1893–1918) English poet. His World War I poems, which include "Strange Meeting", "Anthem for Doomed Youth", and "Dulce et Decorum Est", are a searing indictment of war. After Owen's death in action, Siegfried SASSOON handle their publication. They form the basis of Britten's *War Requiem* (1962).

**Owens, Jesse** (1913–80) African-American athlete. He broke several world records for jumping, hurdling, and running (1935–36). At the 1936 Olympic Games in Berlin Owens won four gold medals, angering HITLER, who was supremely confident in ARYAN superiority. His 200m and long-jump records remained unbroken for more than 20 years.

**owl** Bird that is found worldwide, except at extreme latitudes. Owls have round heads, hooked bills, large eyes, and long, curved talons. They are soundless in flight. Most are nocturnal, and feed on small birds and mammals. The order (Strigiformes) is divided into two families: barn owls (Tytonidae) and typical owls (Strigidae).

**ox** Domesticated cattle of the genus *Bos*. The term is specifically applied to castrated males used as draft animals. Many varieties of wild cattle are sometimes called wild oxen.

**oxalic acid** ($C_2H_2O_4$) Poisonous, colorless crystalline organic acid whose salts occur naturally in some plants, such as sorrel and rhubarb. It is used for metal and textile cleaning and in tanning. Properties: m.p. 214.7°F (101.5°C).

**oxbow** Crescent-shaped section of a river channel that no longer carries the main discharge of water. It is formed by contact at the neck of a MEANDER loop, leaving the loop abandoned as stagnant water and silty marsh.

**Oxford** City and county district in S central England, on the Thames River; the county town of Oxfordshire. Established as a trading center and fort, it was raided by the Danes in the 10th and 11th centuries. During the English Civil War the city was a Royalist stronghold. Industries: motor vehicles, steel products, electrical goods, printing, publishing. Pop. (1991) 110,113.

**Oxford, University of** Oldest university in Britain. It developed from a group of teachers and students who gathered in OXFORD in the 12th century. The first colleges, University, Balliol, and Merton, were founded between 1249 and 1264. Women were not admitted until 1878.

**Oxford Movement** Attempt by some members of the CHURCH OF ENGLAND to restore the ideals of the pre-REFORMATION Church. It lasted from *c.*1833 to the first decades of the 20th century. The main proponents were John Keble, Edward Pusey, and John NEWMAN.

▲ **Oxford** Dating from the mid-12th century, Oxford University is one of the most venerable institutions of higher learning in Europe. It is organized as a collection of self-contained, autonomous residential colleges, each employing its own teachers and enrolling its own students. The first three colleges were founded in the mid-13th century; Christ Church College, shown here, was established in 1546.

**Oxfordshire** County in S central England, bounded in the NW by the COTSWOLDS and in the SE by the Chilterns, and drained by the THAMES River. The county town is OXFORD. It lies mostly within the Thames basin. The economy is based on agriculture, mainly sheep and arable farming, dairying, and beef production. Industries: motor vehicles, pressed steel, light engineering. Area: 1,008sq mi (2,611sq km). Pop. (1991) 547,584.

**oxidation-reduction** (redox) Chemical reaction involving simultaneous OXIDATION (a loss of one or more electrons by an atom or molecule) and reduction (a gain of those electrons by another atom or molecule). Oxidation–reduction reactions are important in many biochemical systems.

**oxide** Any inorganic chemical compound in which OXYGEN is combined with another element. Oxides are often formed by burning the element in air or oxygen.

**oxygen** (symbol O) Common gaseous element that is necessary for the RESPIRATION of plants and animals and for combustion. Colorless and odorless, oxygen is the most abundant element in the Earth's crust (49.2% by weight) and is a constituent of water and many rocks. It is also present in the atmosphere (23.14% by weight). Oxygen can be obtained by the ELECTROLYSIS of water or fractional distillation of liquid air. It is used in apparatus for breathing (oxygen masks) and resuscitation (oxygen tents); liquid oxygen is used in rocket fuels. Oxygen is chemically reactive, and forms compounds with nearly all other elements (especially by OXIDATION). Properties: at.no. 8; at.wt. 15.9994; sp.gr. 1.429; m.p. −361.1°F (−218.4°C;); b.p. −297.3°F (−182.96°C;); most common isotope $^{16}O$ (99.759%). *See also* OXIDATION-REDUCTION; OZONE

**oxygen debt** Insufficient supply of oxygen in the muscles following vigorous exercise. This reduces the breakdown of food molecules that generate energy, causing the muscles to overproduce lactic acid creating a sensation of fatigue and sometimes muscular cramp. Automatic rapid breathing after exercise takes in extra oxygen.

**oxytocin** Hormone produced by the posterior PITUITARY GLAND in women during the final stage of pregnancy. It stimulates the muscles of the UTERUS, initiating the onset of labor and maintaining contractions during childbirth. It also stimulates lactation.

**oyster** Edible BIVALVE mollusk found worldwide in temperate and warm seas. The European flat, or edible, oyster *Ostrea edulis* occurs throughout coastal waters. The pearl oyster (*Pinctada fucats*) is used to produce cultured pearls.

**oystercatcher** Seashore bird with a strikingly marked black-and-white stocky body and bright orange legs and beak. Oystercatchers feed on mollusks, prying them open with their long beaks. Length: 17in (43cm). Family Haematopodidae; typical genus *Haematopus*.

**Ozark Plateau** Mountainous upland region in S central US, extending from SW Missouri across NW Arkansas into Oklahoma. The Boston Mountains contain the highest peaks, exceeding 2,000ft (610m). The Ozarks are a source of lead and zinc. Noted for their scenery, forests and numerous lakes, they are a popular tourist region. Area: *c.*50,000sq mi (129,500sq km).

**ozone** ($O_3$) Unstable, pale-blue, gaseous allotrope of OXYGEN. It has a characteristic pungent odor and decomposes into molecular oxygen. It is present in the atmosphere, mainly in the OZONE LAYER. Prepared commercially by passing a high-voltage discharge through oxygen, ozone is used as an oxidizing agent in bleaching, air-conditioning, and purifying water. *See also* ALLOTROPY

**ozone layer** Region of Earth's atmosphere in which OZONE ($O_3$) is concentrated. It is densest at altitudes of 13–16mi (21–26km). Produced by ultraviolet radiation in incoming sunlight, the ozone layer absorbs much of the ultraviolet, thereby shielding the Earth's surface. Aircraft, nuclear weapons, and some aerosol sprays and refrigerants yield chemical agents that can break down high altitude ozone, which could lead to an increase in the amount of harmful ultraviolet radiation reaching the Earth's surface. *See also* CHLOROFLUOROCARBON (CFC)

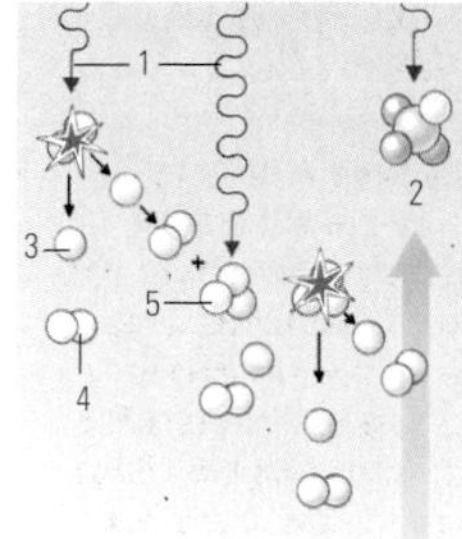


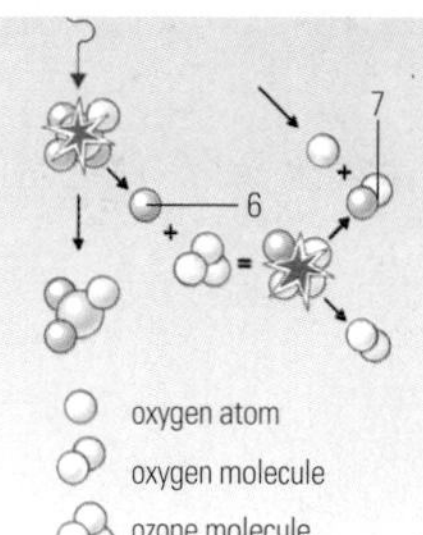


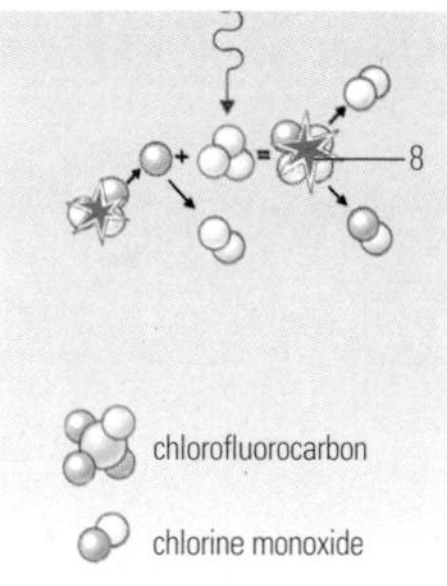


▲ **ozone** A naturally occurring substance, ozone acts as a sunscreen for the Earth because its molecules absorb the Sun's ultraviolet radiation (1). The presence of chlorofluorocarbon pollution (2) causes the ozone layer to break down, allowing ultraviolet rays through. Ozone is created when ultraviolet rays split oxygen molecules. The lone oxygen atoms (3) bond with oxygen molecules (4) to make ozone (5). When, however, chlorofluorocarbons are present, they are split by the ultraviolet rays. The released chlorine atom (6) in turn splits ozone molecules to form a chlorine monoxide molecule (7) and oxygen. The process is continued as the chlorine monoxide absorbs the lone oxygen atoms that previously formed ozone. This frees the chlorine atom, which splits another ozone molecule (8) creating another chlorine monoxide molecule and oxygen.

O

*P/p, 16th letter of the Roman alphabet, descends from the Semitic letter* **pe**, *a word meaning* **mouth**. *The letter was modified in shape by the Greeks and taken into their alphabet as* **pi**.

**paca** (spotted cavy) Shy, nocturnal, tailless RODENT of South America; it is brown with rows of white spots and has a relatively large head. A burrow dweller, it feeds mainly on leaves, roots, and fruit. Length: to 30in (76cm). Family Dasyproctidae; species *Cuniculus paca*.

**pacemaker** (sinoatrial node) Specialized group of cells in the vertebrate HEART that contract spontaneously, setting the pace for the heartbeat itself. If it fails it can be replaced by an artificial pacemaker, an electronic unit that stimulates the heart by means of tiny electrical impulses.

**Pacific Ocean** Largest and deepest OCEAN, covering *c*.33% of the Earth's surface and containing more than 50% of the Earth's sea water. The Pacific extends from the Arctic Circle to Antarctica, and from North and South America in the E to Asia and Australia in the W. The E Pacific region is connected with the Cordilleran mountain chain, and there is a narrow CONTINENTAL MARGIN. The ocean is ringed by numerous volcanoes, known as the Pacific Ring of Fire. There are a number of large islands in the Pacific, most of which are in the S and W. The major ones are New Zealand and the Japan and Malay archipelagos. The average depth of the Pacific is 14,000ft (4,300m). The greatest-known depth is that of the Challenger Deep (SW of Guam in the Mariana Trench), which has a depth of 36,198ft (11,033m). Most fishing in the Pacific Ocean is done on the continental margins. Crab, herring, cod, sardine, and tuna are the principal catch. Area: *c*.64,000,000sq mi (166,000,000sq km).

**Pacino, Al (Alberto)** (1940– ) US film actor. He studied method acting at Lee STRASBERG's Actors' Studio. He appeared three times (1972, 1974, and 1990) in his famed role as Michael Corleone (in *The Godfather* and its two sequels), for which he received two of his several Academy Award nominations. He finally won a Best Actor Academy Award for *Scent of a Woman* (1992). His other films include *Serpico* (1973), *Dog Day Afternoon* (1975), *Scarface* (1983), and *Heat* (1995).

**paddlefish** Primitive bony fish related to the sturgeon and found in the basins of the Mississippi and Yangtze rivers. Blue, green, or gray, it has a long paddle-like snout. Length: 6ft (1.8m). Family Polyodontidae.

**Paderewski, Ignacy Jan** (1860–1941) Polish pianist, composer, and statesman. He wrote a piano concerto (1888) and a symphony (1907), and his opera *Manru* was first produced in Dresden in 1901. He became prime minister and minister of foreign affairs of the newly created Polish state in 1919.

**Padua** (Padova) City in NE Italy, in Veneto region. The city is first mentioned (as Patavium) early in the 4th century BC. In the Middle Ages it was a flourishing artistic center. Ruled by the Carrara family from 1318, it came under Venetian control in 1405. In 1815 it passed to Austria, and took a leading part in the movement for Italian independence. The city is renowned for its art treasures. Industries: motor vehicles, textiles, machinery, electrical goods. Pop. (1991) 215,137.

**Paganini, Niccolò** (1782–1840) Italian violinist, the most famous virtuoso of his day. He enlarged the range of the violin by exploiting harmonics and mastered the art of playing double and triple stops.

**Paganism** In modern usage, religious beliefs other than JUDAISM, CHRISTIANITY, and ISLAM. First applied in Latin usage to those who did not accept Christianity, the term can be derogatory.

▶ **paca** Found in tropical America, the paca (*Cuniculus paca*) is a shy rodent that lives in forests near water. It can reach a length of up to 30in (76cm) and an adult can weigh up to 20lb (9kg).

**Pagnol, Marcel** (1894–1974) French author, playwright, and film director. He wrote *Topaze* (1928) and the trilogy *Marius* (1929), *Fanny* (1931), and *César* (1937), set in Marseilles. He directed a number of films. His popularity was revived with the films *Jean de Florette*, and *Manon des Sources* (both 1986).

**pagoda** Eastern TEMPLE in the form of a multistoried, tapering tower. The basic design is either square or polygonal, and each story is a smaller replica of the one beneath. The stories often have wide, overhanging roofs, and the buildings are usually made of wood, brick, or stone. Pagodas originated in India and spread with the diffusion of BUDDHISM to China, Korea, and Japan.

**Pahlavi, Muhammad Reza Shah** (1919–80) Shah of Iran (1941–79), son of Reza Shah PAHLAVI. He encouraged rapid economic development and social reforms. The westernization of Iran, combined with a repressive regime and worsening social inequalities, aroused strong discontent among religious fundamentalists and others. In 1979 a theocratic revolution, led by Ayatollah KHOMEINI, forced him into exile. He died in Egypt.

**Paige, "Satchel" (Leroy Robert)** (1906–82) US baseball player. A right-hand pitcher in the Negro leagues (1924–48), he did not get an opportunity to play major league baseball until he was 42, joining the Cleveland Indians in 1948. He switched to the St. Louis Browns in 1951 and retired two years later. During his career, he pitched 50 no-hit games and played in 1,500. He was elected to the Baseball Hall of Fame in 1971.

**pain** Unpleasant sensation signaling actual or threatened tissue damage as a result of illness or injury; it can be acute (severe but short-lived) or chronic (persisting for a long time). Pain is felt when specific nerve endings are stimulated. Pain is treated in a number of ways, most commonly by drugs known as ANALGESICS.

**Paine, Thomas** (1737–1809) Anglo-American revolutionary political writer. He emigrated from England to Pennsylvania in 1754. His pamphlet *Common Sense* (1776) demanded independence for the North American colonies. He returned to England in 1787 and published *The Rights of Man* (1791–92), a defense of the French Revolution. Accused of treason, he fled to France in 1792. He became a French citizen and was elected to the National Convention, but later imprisoned (1793–94). He returned to the US in 1802.

**paint** Coating applied to a surface for protective, decorative, or artistic purposes. Paint is composed of PIGMENT (color) and a liquid vehicle (binder or medium) that suspends the pigment, adheres to a surface, and hardens when dry. Pigments are made of metallic compounds, usually oxides, or synthetic materials. Vehicles may be oils, water mixed with a binding agent, organic compounds, or synthetic RESINS.

**Painted Desert** Barren high plateau region in N central Arizona, E of the Colorado and Little Colorado rivers. Erosion and heat have exposed bands of red and yellow sediment and bentonite clay. Area: *c*.7,500sq mi (19,400sq km).

**painting** Art of using one or more colors, generally mixed with a medium (such as oil or water) and applied to a surface with a brush, finger, or other tool to create pictures. Paintings are among the earliest of historical records. Painting in early civilizations, such as Egypt, was largely a matter of filling in with color areas outlined by drawing. Little Greek painting survives (apart from that on pottery). The Romans were greatly influenced by Greek art, as the fine FRESCO paintings at Pompeii and Herculaneum demonstrate. In the early Christian and Byzantine periods, traditions in mural painting and manuscript ILLUMINATION were established that were to last throughout the Middle Ages. When the humanist ideals of the RENAISSANCE took root in S Europe, the range of subjects and techniques available to the artist widened enormously. The period also saw the first use of oil paint on canvas, the beginnings of GENRE PAINTING and pure portraiture. It was also the age of PERSPECTIVE and of a more natural approach to form and composition. The great painters of the BAROQUE period added an unrivaled bravura brushwork and drama of vision. North of the Alps the Renaissance had spread more gradually than in Italy. The 17th-century Dutch painters' choice of intimate, everyday subjects was the antithesis of the grand manner characteristic of the Italian masters. By the 18th century British painters had become established in portraiture, animal, and landscape painting, although overshadowed by the great Venetian masters. The 19th century opened with the supremacy of NEOCLASSICISM challenged by the new ROMANTICISM. Both schools were superseded, first by IMPRESSIONISM and then by a succession of new movements in the late-19th and early 20th centuries. Most of these movements – Impressionism, POSTIMPRESSIONISM, SYMBOLISM, FAUVISM, CUBISM, and SURREALISM – originated with artists living in Paris. Germany was the cradle of EXPRESSIONISM and Russia contributed SUPREMATISM. In the latter half of the 20th century, the US has produced many original movements, such as ABSTRACT EXPRESSIONISM, POP ART, and OP ART.

**Paisiello, Giovanni** (1740–1816) Italian composer, principally of operas. As court composer (1776–84) to Catherine II (the Great) of Russia, he wrote *The Barber of Seville* (1782), which became popular throughout Europe until the version by Rossini superseded it.

**Paiute** Shoshonean-speaking tribe of Native North Americans. They are divided into two major groups: the Southern Paiute (or "Digger Indians" during the Gold Rush days) who occupied W Utah, N Arizona, SE Nevada, and California; and the Northern Paiute ("Snake Indians") who inhabited W Nevada, S Oregon, and E California. Today the Paiute number some 4,000.

**Pakistan** Republic in S Asia. *See* country feature, page 506

**palate** Roof of the mouth, comprising the bony front part known as the hard palate, and the softer fleshy part at the back, known as the soft palate.

**Palatinate** Historic state of the Holy Roman Empire, including the present German state of Rhineland-Palatinate and parts of adjacent states. It was ruled from 1156 by the counts palatine. It was a center of the German Reformation.

**Palau** Former name for BELAU

**paleobotany** Study of ancient plants and pollen that have been preserved by carbonization, waterlogging, or freezing. Some plants have been preserved almost intact in frozen soils and in AMBER.

**Paleocene** Geological epoch from about 65 to 55 million years ago. It is the first epoch of the TERTIARY period, when the majority of the DINOSAURS had disappeared and the small early mammals were flourishing.

**paleography** Study of early writing. Its broad sense includes all inscriptions; more narrowly it includes only inscribed wax, parchment, papyrus, or paper.

**Paleolithic** (Old Stone Age) Earliest stage of human history, from *c*.2 million years ago until between 40,000 and 10,000 years ago. It was marked by the use of stone tools and covers the evolution of humans from *Homo habilis* to *Homo sapiens*.

**Paleolithic art** Art from the PALEOLITHIC period. Typical works are realistic cave paintings of bison, deer, and hunting scenes. The best-known surviving examples are those at ALTAMIRA and LASCAUX. Other forms include portable art, such as carved animals and figurines.

**paleomagnetism** Study of changes in the direction and intensity of Earth's MAGNETIC FIELD through GEOLOGICAL TIME. This is important in the investigation of the theory of CONTINENTAL DRIFT. The EARTH'S polarity has reversed at least 20 times in the past 4–5 million years; earlier changes cannot at present be determined.

**paleontology** Study of the FOSSIL remains of plants and animals. Evidence from fossils is used in the reconstruction of ancient environments and in tracing the evolution of life.

**Paleozoic** Second era of geological time, after the PRECAMBRIAN era, lasting from 590 million to 248 million years ago. It is subdivided into six periods: CAMBRIAN, ORDOVICIAN, SILURIAN, DEVONIAN, CARBONIFEROUS, and PERMIAN. Invertebrate animals evolved hard skeletons in the Cambrian; fish-like vertebrates appeared in the Ordovician; amphibians emerged in the Devonian; and reptiles in the Carboniferous.

**Palermo** City and seaport in Italy, in NW Sicily, on the Tyrrhenian Sea; capital of Sicily. The city was founded by the Phoenicians in the 8th century BC. It passed to the Romans in 254 BC, and came under Byzantine control in the 6th century AD. From the 9th to 11th centuries it prospered under benevolent Arab rule. Captured by the Normans in 1072, it enjoyed a brief period of fame as the capital of the Kingdom of Sicily and again under the Holy Roman emperor Frederick II, who established his court here. Palermo subsequently came under Spanish, then Austrian rule. It was the scene of the outbreak of the 1848 revolution in Italy and was captured by Giuseppe GARIBALDI in 1860. Industries: shipbuilding, textiles. Pop. (1991) 698,556.

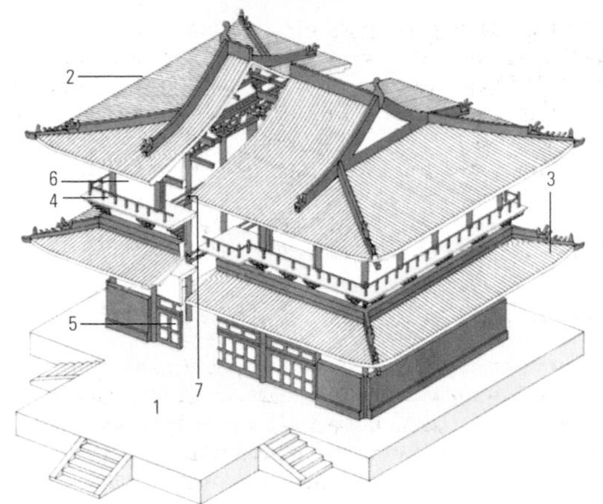


**◀ pagoda** A typical Chinese pagoda is built on a stone podium (1). The wooden hall has a two-story elevation covered by a single hipped roof (2). The first story is overhung by shallow eaves (3), which are supported by bracketing, as is the balcony (4). Divided into five bays, doors occupy the center three bays (5), which are left open on the upper story (6). The fabric of the roof is wood; it is insulated with mud and tiled. The interior has a gallery (7) on each story around the central wall that is the full height of the temple.

**Palestine** Territory in the Middle East, on the E shore of the Mediterranean Sea; considered a Holy Land by Jews, Christians, and Muslims. Palestine has been settled continuously since 4000 BC. The Jews moved into Palestine from Egypt *c*.2000 BC but were subjects of the Philistines until 1020 BC, when SAUL, DAVID, and SOLOMON established Hebrew kingdoms. The region was then under Assyrian and, later, Persian control before coming under Roman rule in 63 BC. In succeeding centuries Palestine became a focus of Christian pilgrimage. It was conquered by the Muslim Arabs in 640. In 1099 Palestine fell to the Crusaders, but in 1291 they in turn were routed by the MAMELUKES. The area was part of the OTTOMAN EMPIRE from 1516 to 1918, when British forces defeated the Turks at Megiddo. Jewish immigration was encouraged by the BALFOUR DECLARATION. After World War I the British held a League of Nations mandate over the land W of the JORDAN River (now once again called Palestine). Tension between Jews and the Arab majority led to an uprising in 1936. World War II and Nazi persecution brought many Jews to Palestine, and in 1947 Britain, unable to satisfy both Jewish and Arab aspirations, consigned the problem to the United Nations. The UN proposed a plan for separate Jewish and Arab states. This was rejected by the Arabs, and in 1948 (after the first of several ARAB-ISRAELI WARS) most of ancient Palestine became part of the new state of ISRAEL; the GAZA STRIP was controlled by Egypt and the WEST BANK of the Jordan River by JORDAN. These two areas were subsequently occupied by Israel in 1967. From the 1960s, the PALESTINE LIBERATION ORGANIZATION (PLO) led Palestinian opposition to Israeli rule, which included acts of terrorism and an uprising in the occupied territories. In 1993 Israel reached an agreement with the PLO, and in 1994 the Palestine National Authority took over nominal administration of the Gaza Strip and West Bank.

**Palestine Liberation Organization (PLO)** Organization of Palestinian parties and groups, widely recognized as the representative of the Palestinian people. It was founded in 1964 with the aim of dissolving the state of Israel and establishing a Palestinian state. Many of its component guerrilla groups were involved in political violence against Israel and, in the 1970s, in acts of international terrorism to further their cause. Dominated by the al-Fatah group led by Yasir ARAFAT, in 1974 the PLO was recognized as a government in exile by the Arab League and the United Nations. In the early 1990s, PLO representatives conducted secret negotiations with Israel, culminating in a peace agreement signed in 1993. *See also* PALESTINE; WEST BANK; GAZA STRIP

P

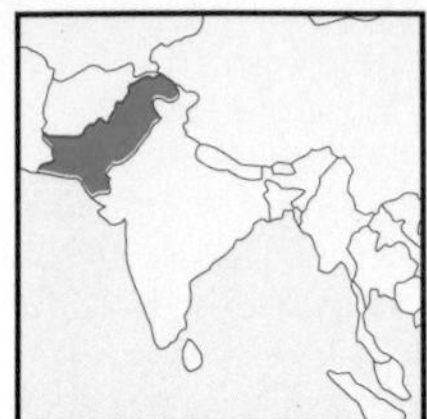

Pakistan's flag was adopted in 1947, when the country became independent from Britain. The color green, the crescent Moon, and the five-pointed star are all traditional symbols of Islam. The white stripe represents the other religions in Pakistan.

**AREA:** 307,374sq mi (796,100sq km)
**POPULATION:** 115,520,000
**CAPITAL (POPULATION):** Islamabad (201,000)
**GOVERNMENT:** Federal republic
**ETHNIC GROUPS:** Punjabi 60%, Sindhi 12%, Pushtun 13%, Baluch, Muhajir
**LANGUAGES:** Urdu (official)
**RELIGIONS:** Islam 97%, Christianity, Hinduism
**CURRENCY:** Pakistan rupee = 100 paisa

The Islamic Republic of Pakistan is divided into the four provinces of BALUCHISTAN, NORTH-WEST FRONTIER PROVINCE, PUNJAB, and SIND. The mountains of the HINDU KUSH extend along the NW border with Afghanistan. In N Pakistan lies the disputed territory of KASHMIR. This mountainous region is occupied by Pakistan but claimed by India. It contains the world's second highest peak, K2, at 28,251ft (8,611m), in the KARAKORAM range. At the foot of the mountains lies Pakistan's capital, ISLAMABAD, and the city of RAWALPINDI. The Punjab plains ("land of the five rivers") are drained by the River INDUS and its four main tributaries (Jhelum, Beas, Ravi, and Sutlej). Lahore lies on the border with India. The alluvial plain continues into Sind, which includes HYDERABAD and KARACHI (Pakistan's major port). Baluchistan is an arid plateau region.

## CLIMATE

Most of Pakistan has hot summers and cool winters. Rainfall is sparse, except in the monsoon season (June–October).

## VEGETATION

Forests grow on mountain slopes, but most of Pakistan is covered by dry grassland.

## HISTORY AND POLITICS

The Indus Valley civilization developed *c.*4,500 years ago. Waves of invaders later entered the area. The Kushans conquered the entire region in the 2nd century AD. Arabs conquered Sind in 712 and introduced Islam. In 1206 Pakistan became part of the Delhi Sultanate. In 1526 the Sultanate was replaced by the MOGUL EMPIRE, which introduced URDU. In the late 18th century Ranjit Singh conquered the Punjab, and introduced SIKHISM. The early 19th century saw the emergence of the British EAST INDIA COMPANY as a dominant force. The British conquered Sind (1843) and Punjab (1849). Much of Baluchistan was conquered in the 1850s. Pathans in the NW resisted subjection, and the British created a separate province in 1901. The dominance of Hindus in British India led to the formation of the MUSLIM LEAGUE (1906). In the 1940s the League's leader, Muhammad Ali JINNAH, gained popular support for the idea of a separate state of Pakistan (Urdu, land of the pure) in Muslim-majority areas. British India achieved independence in 1947, and was partitioned into India and Pakistan. The resulting mass migration and communal violence claimed over 500,000 lives. In 1947 the long-standing war with India over Kashmir began. Jinnah became Pakistan's first governor-general. Muslim Pakistan was divided into two parts: East Bengal and West Pakistan, more than 1,000mi (1,600km) apart. Pakistan was faced with enormous political and administrative problems. In 1955 East Bengal became East Pakistan, and in 1956 Pakistan became a republic within the Commonwealth of Nations. General Muhammad AYUB KHAN led a military coup in 1958, and in 1960 established presidential rule. His dictatorship brought constitutional changes, but failed to satisfy East Pakistan's claim for greater autonomy. The proindependence Awami League won a landslide victory in 1970 East Pakistan elections. In 1971 East Pakistan declared independence as BANGLADESH. West Pakistani troops invaded. The ensuing civil war killed hundreds of thousands of people, and millions fled to India. India sent troops to support Bangladesh. West Pakistan was forced to surrender and Zulfikar Ali BHUTTO assumed control. In 1977 a military coup, led by General Zia-ul-Haq, deposed Bhutto. In 1978 General Zia proclaimed himself president and Bhutto was hanged for murder. During the 1980s Pakistan received US aid for providing a safe haven for Mujaheddin fighters in the war in Afghanistan. In 1985 Zia ended martial law. In 1988 Zia dismissed parliament, but died shortly after in a mysterious plane crash. The Pakistan People's Party (PPP) won the ensuing elections and Benazir BHUTTO, daughter of Zulfikar, became president. Charged with nepotism and corruption, she was removed from office in 1990. The following election was won by the Islamic Democratic Alliance, led by Nawaz Sharif. In 1991 Islamic law was given precedence over civil law. Sharif also faced charges of corruption and lost the 1993 elections to Benazir Bhutto. In 1994 civil disorder flared in Sind, inspired by a militant campaign for an autonomous Karachi province. Bhutto was again dismissed on corruption charges in 1996. Political disenchantment saw a low turnout in 1997 elections and a landslide victory for Nawaz Sharif. In 1998 Pakistan became the world's seventh nuclear power.

## ECONOMY

Pakistan is a low-income developing country (1995 GDP per capita, US$2,230). Pakistan faces a foreign debt of US$42 billion. The economy is based on agriculture, which employs *c.*47% of the workforce. Pakistan has one of the world's largest irrigation systems. It is the world's third-largest producer of wheat. Other crops include cotton, fruit, rice, and sugar cane. Pakistan produces natural gas and coal, as well as iron ore, chromite, and stone. Major products include clothing and textiles. Small-scale craft industries, such as carpets, are also important.

**Palestrina, Giovanni Pierluigi da** (1525–94) Italian composer who spent most of his life in the service of the church. He wrote masses, magnificats, litanies, and about 600 motets in four to eight or twelve parts. He also composed almost 100 secular madrigals.

**Pali** Ancient Indian language in which the Buddhist canon of sacred writings was compiled in the 1st century BC. It comes from classical Sanskrit and is still the liturgical language of the THERAVADA branch of Hinayana Buddhism, the form of Buddhism prevailing in Sri Lanka, Burma, and Thailand.

**Palladianism** Architectural style especially popular in England, derived from the work of Andrea PALLADIO. Based on Roman Classicism, it emphasized symmetrical planning and harmonic proportions. Inigo JONES introduced it to England. There was a revival of interest in Palladianism in the early 18th century.

**Palladio, Andrea** (1508–80) Italian RENAISSANCE architect. He studied Roman architecture and published his own designs and drawings of Roman ruins in *Four Books of Architecture* (1570). *See also* PALLADIANISM

**palladium** (symbol Pd) Shiny silver-white metallic element of the TRANSITION ELEMENTS. It was discovered in 1803 by the English chemist William Wollaston. Malleable and ductile, palladium is found in nickel ores associated with platinum. It does not tarnish or corrode and is used for electroplating, surgical instruments, dentistry, jewelry, and for catalytic converters for automobiles. Properties: at.no. 46; at. wt. 106.4; sp. gr. 12.02; m.p. 2,826°F (1,552°C); b.p. 5,684°F (3,140°C); most common isotope $^{106}$Pd (27.3%).

**palm** Member of a family of trees found in tropical and subtropical regions. Palms have a woody, unbranched, trunk with a crown of large, stiff leaves. The leaves may be palmate (fan-like) or pinnate (feather-like). Palm trunks are covered with fibers. Palms are the source of wax, oil, fibers, sugar, and other foods. Height: 200ft (60m). Family Arecacae/Palmae.

**Palma** (Palma de Mallorca) City and seaport in Spain, in W Majorca (Mallorca) Island; capital of the BALEARIC ISLANDS. Under Roman rule from the 2nd century BC, Palma later became part of Byzantium before falling to the Arabs in the 8th century. Conquered by James I of Aragon in the 13th century, it was finally united with Spain in 1469. Industries: tourism, pottery, glasswork, leather goods. Pop. (1991) 296,754.

**Palmer, Arnold Daniel** (1929– ) US golfer. He won the US Open Championship in 1960, the British Open in 1961 and 1962, and the Masters tournament in 1958, 1960, 1962, and 1964.

**Palmer, Samuel** (1805–81) British Romantic landscape painter and graphic artist, the most important follower of William BLAKE. He enjoyed his most productive period at Shoreham, Kent (1826–35), where he was the focal point for a group of artists called the Ancients.

**Palmerston, Henry John Temple, 3rd Viscount** (1784–1865) British statesman. He was a dominant influence on foreign affairs, 1830–65. He vigorously upheld British interests abroad, initiating the OPIUM WAR to help British merchants.

**Palm Sunday** In the Christian year, the Sunday before Easter. Palm Sunday commemorates Jesus Christ's triumphal entry into Jerusalem, when the people spread palm branches before him. It also markes the beginning of HOLY WEEK, the period of days commemorating his betrayal, trial, and crucifixion.

**Palmyra** (Tadmur, City of Palms) Ancient oasis city, in the Syrian Desert. By the 1st century BC it had become a city-state by virtue of its control of the trade route between Mesopotamia and the Mediterranean. In *c.*AD 30 the city-state became a Roman dependency under local rule. By the 2nd century AD Palmyra's influence had spread to Armenia. In 267 ZENOBIA became queen, and severed the state's links with Rome. In 273 the Roman emperor Aurelian laid waste to the city. Today, visitors are attracted to its extensive ruins.

**Palo Alto, Battle of** (May 1846) First battle of the MEXICAN WAR, fought near Brownsville, Texas. US General Zachary TAYLOR defeated a Mexican force under Mariano Arista. US casualties were minimal, though the Mexicans lost several hundred men.

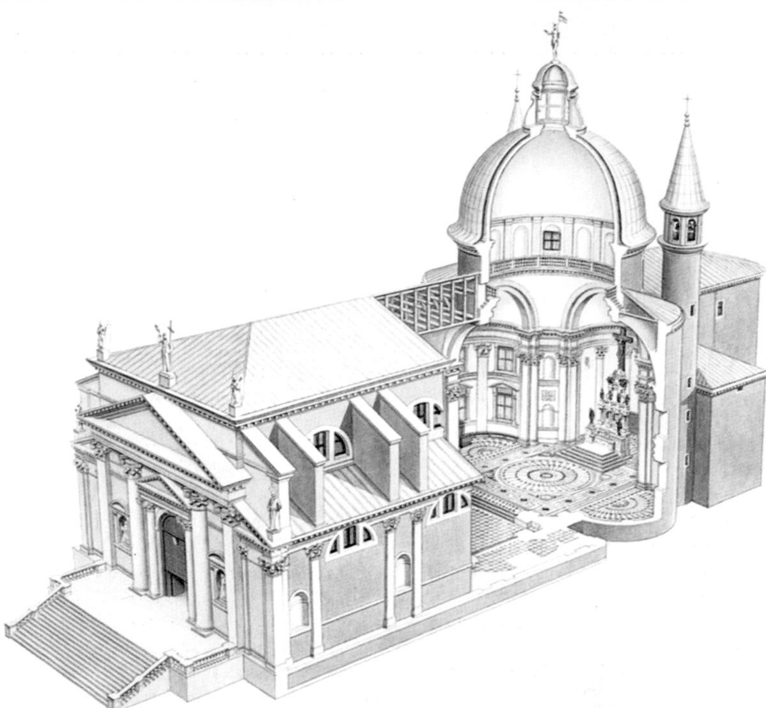

▲ **Palladio** The Redentore, Venice (1577–92) is a superb example of Italian architect Andrea Palladio's work. The whole church is raised on a podium, has a choir separated from the chancel (Palladio's innovation), an absolute minimum of nonarchitectural ornament, and a light, spacious interior. It was financed by the Venetian state, in fulfillment of a vow on deliverance of the city from the plague of 1575–76.

**Palomar, Mount** Peak in S California, 45mi (72km) NNE of San Diego. It is the site of the **Palomar Observatory**, which houses the 48-in (122-cm) Schmidt telescope and a 200-in (508-cm) reflecting telescope. Palomar is administered jointly with Mount Wilson Observatory as the Hale Observatories.

**palpitation** Condition where a person becomes aware of his or her (usually rapid) heartbeat. It is normal when experiencing strong emotion, such as excitement or fear, but otherwise may be a symptom of disease.

**Pamirs** Mountainous region in central Asia, lying mostly in Tajikistan and partly in Pakistan, Afghanistan, and China. The region forms a geological structural knot from which the TIAN SHAN, KARAKORAM, Kunlun, and HINDU KUSH mountain ranges radiate. The climate is cold during winter and cool in summer; the terrain includes grasslands and sparse trees. The main activity is sheep herding, and some coal is mined. The highest peak is KOMMUNIZMA PIK, at 24,590ft (7,495m).

**pampas grass** Species of tall, reedlike GRASS native to South America and widely cultivated as a lawn ornamental. Female plants bear flower clusters, 3ft (90cm) tall, which are silvery and plumelike. Family Poaceae/Gramineae; species *Cortaderia selloana*.

**Pamplona** Ancient city in N Spain; capital of Navarre province. In 68 BC it was rebuilt by POMPEY, and in AD 778 conquered by CHARLEMAGNE. In the 11th century it was made capital of the kingdom of Navarre. In 1512 control of Pamplona passed to Ferdinand of Aragon, who united Navarre with Castile. During the PENINSULAR WAR, Pamplona was captured from the French by the Duke of Wellington (1813). Industries: rope and pottery manufacture. Pop. (1991) 179,251.

**Pan** In Greek mythology, the god of woods and fields, shepherds, and their flocks. He is depicted with the horns, legs, and hooves of a goat. A forest dweller, he pursued and loved the DRYADS and led their dances while playing the syrinx, the reed pipes that were his invention.

**Pan-Africanism** Historical political movement for the unification and independence of African nations. It began at the Pan-African Congress of 1900 in London, organized by western black leaders. It met five times between 1900 and 1927, and worked to bring gradual self-government to African colonial states. In 1945 the Pan-African Federation convened the sixth congress. It demanded autonomy and independence for African states. As independence was gained, the movement broke up and was eventually replaced by the ORGANIZATION OF AFRICAN UNITY (OAU), formed in 1963.

▲ **pampas grass** Native to Argentina, pampas grass (*Cortaderia argentea*) was originally grown to provide food for grazing animals. More recently, it has been grown extensively as an ornamental plant in gardens.

P

## PANAMA

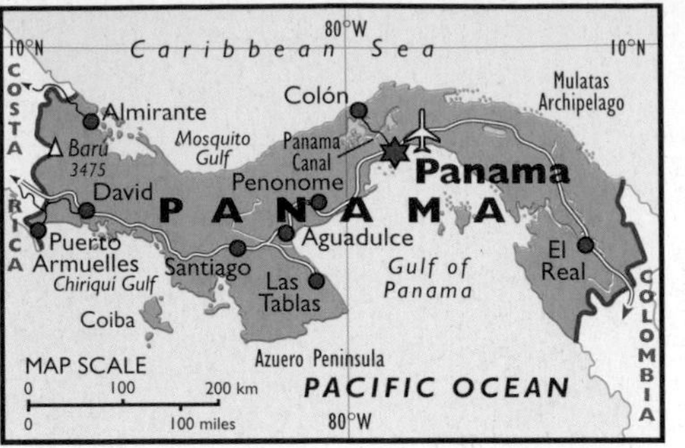


**AREA:** 29,761sq mi (77,080sq km)
**POPULATION:** 2,515,000
**CAPITAL (POPULATION):** Panama City (584,803)
**GOVERNMENT:** Multiparty republic
**ETHNIC GROUPS:** Mestizo 60%, Black and Mulatto 20%, White 10%, Amerindian 8%, Asian 2%
**LANGUAGES:** Spanish (official)
**RELIGIONS:** Christianity (Roman Catholic 84%, Protestant 5%), Islam 5%
**CURRENCY:** Balboa = 100 cents

**Panama** Republic on the Isthmus of Panama, connecting Central and South America; the capital is PANAMA CITY. **Land and climate** The narrowest part of Panama is less than 37mi (60km) wide. The PANAMA CANAL cuts across the isthmus. The Canal has given Panama great international importance, and most Panamanians live within 12mi (20km) of it. Most of the land between the Pacific and Caribbean coastal plains is mountainous, rising to 11,400ft (3,475m) at the volcano Barú; Panama has a tropical climate. The rainy season is between May and December. The Caribbean side of Panama has about twice as much rain as the Pacific side. Tropical forests cover *c*.50% of Panama. Mangrove swamps line the coast. Subtropical woodland grows on the mountains, while tropical savanna occurs along the Pacific coast. **History** Christopher COLUMBUS landed in Panama in 1502. In 1510 Vasco Núñez de Balboa became the first European to cross Panama and see the Pacific Ocean. The indigenous population were soon wiped out and Spain established control. In 1821 Panama became a province of Colombia. After a revolt in 1903, Panama declared independence from Colombia. In 1904 the US began construction of the Panama Canal and established the Panama Canal Zone. Since it was opened in 1914, the status of the Canal has been a feature of Panamanian politics. US forces intervened in 1908, 1912, and 1918 to protect US interests. Panama has been politically unstable throughout the 20th century, with a series of dictatorial regimes and military coups. Civil strife during the 1950s and 1960s led to negotiations with the US for the transfer of the Canal Zone. In 1977 a treaty confirmed Panama's sovereignty over the Canal, while providing for US bases in the Canal Zone. The US agreed to hand over control of the Canal on December 31, 1999. In 1983 General NORIEGA took control of the National Guard, and ruled Panama through a succession of puppet governments. In 1987 the US withdrew its support for Noriega after he was accused of murder, electoral fraud, and aiding drug smuggling. In December 1989 he made himself president and declared war on the US. On December 20, 1989, 25,000 US troops invaded Panama. Noriega was captured in January 1990 and taken to the US for trial. Pérez Balladares was elected president in 1994. **Economy** The Panama Canal is a major source of revenue, generating jobs in commerce, trade, manufacturing, and transport (1995 GDP per capita, US$5,980). After the Canal, the main activity is agriculture, which employs 27% of the workforce. Rice is the main food crop. Bananas, shrimps, sugar, and coffee are exported. Tourism is also important. Many ships are registered under Panama's flag, due to its low taxes.

**Panama Canal** Waterway connecting the Atlantic and Pacific oceans across the Isthmus of Panama. A canal, begun in 1882 by Ferdinand de LESSEPS, was subsequently abandoned because of bankruptcy. The US government decided to finance the project to provide a convenient route for its warships. The main construction took about ten years to complete, and the first ship passed through in 1914. The 51-mi (82-km) waterway reduces the sea voyage between San Francisco and New York by about 7,800mi (12,500km). Control of the canal passes from the US to Panama at the end of 1999.

**Panama City** Capital of Panama, near the Pacific end of the Panama Canal. It was founded by Pedro Arias de Avila in 1519, and was destroyed and rebuilt in the 17th century. It became the capital of Panama in 1903 and developed rapidly after the construction of the PANAMA CANAL in 1914. Industries: brewing, shoes, textiles, oil-refining, plastics. Pop. (1990) 584,803.

**Pan-American Games** Athletic competition for all countries in the Americas, similar to the OLYMPIC GAMES. The first games were held in 1951 in Buenos Aires, Argentina, and have since been held every four years.

**Pan-American Highway** Road system linking the s US, Mexico, Central America, and South America. Work on the Pan-American Highway started in the late 1920s, and the system is still being extended. By 1990 it included more than 29,000mi (47,000km) of roads.

**Panchen Lama** Tibetan Buddhist religious leader who is second in importance to the DALAI LAMA. In 1923 the ninth Panchen Lama fled to China because of disagreements with the Dalai Lama. In 1938 Bskal-bzang Tshe-brtan, a boy of Tibetan parentage, was born in China and later hailed by the Chinese government as the 10th Panchen Lama. When the Dalai Lama fled to India in 1959, the Chinese government officially recognized this Panchen Lama as the true leader of Tibet. However, in 1964 he was stripped of his power. He died in 1989. In December 1995 another Tibetan boy, Gyaincain Norbu, was selected by the Chinese government and enthroned in Beijing as the 11th Panchen Lama. He is not recognized as such by the Tibetan government-in-exile, nor by the majority of the international community. *See also* TIBETAN BUDDHISM

**pancreas** Elongated gland lying behind the stomach, to the left of the midline. It secretes pancreatic juice into the SMALL INTESTINE to aid digestion. Pancreatic juice contains the enzymes AMYLASE, TRYPSIN, and lipase. The pancreas also contains a group of cells known as the islets of Langerhans, which secrete the hormones INSULIN and glucagon, concerned in the regulation of blood-sugar level. *See also* DIABETES

**panda** Two mainly nocturnal mammals of the raccoon family. The lesser panda, *Ailurus fulgens*, ranges from the Himalayas to w China. It has soft, thick, reddish brown fur, a white face, and a bushy tail. It feeds mainly on fruit and leaves, but is also a carnivore. Length: 46in (115cm) overall. The rare giant panda, *Ailuropoda melanoleuca*, inhabits bamboo forests in China (mainly Tibet). It has a short tail and a dense white coat with characteristic black fur on shoulders, limbs, ears, and around the eyes. It eats mainly plant material, particularly bamboo shoots. Length: 5ft (1.5m); weight: 350lb (160kg).

**Pandora** In Greek mythology, the first woman. She was created on ZEUS' orders as his revenge on PROMETHEUS, who had

► **panda** The giant panda (*Ailuropoda melanoleuca*) is found in mountain forests in parts of Sichuan, central China, and on the slopes of the Tibetan plateau. It is a rare, solitary animal that usually lives on the ground, but will climb trees if pursued. They spend about 12 hours a day feeding, mainly on bamboo stems and shoots. It is an endangered species, and pairs have been encouraged to breed in captivity.

created men and stolen fire from heaven for them. When she opened a great jar she had been ordered by Zeus not to look into, all the evils of the human race flew out. Hope alone remained inside the jar. In later tradition the jar became a box.

**Pangaea** Name for the single supercontinent that formed about 240 million years ago, and which began to break up at the end of the Triassic period. *See also* GONDWANALAND

**pangolin** (scaly anteater) Any of several species of toothless insectivorous mammals, covered with horny overlapping plates, that live in Asia and Africa. It has short, powerful forelegs with which it climbs trees and tears open the nests of tree ants, on which it feeds. Length: to 70in (175cm). Family Manidae; genus *Manis*.

**Pankhurst, Emily (Emmeline Goulden)** (1858–1928) British leader of the militant movement for women's suffrage, the SUFFRAGETTE MOVEMENT. She set up the Women's Social and Political Union in 1903, supported by her daughters, Christabel (1880–1958) and Sylvia (1882–1960). Their militant tactics courted prosecution, and they gained further publicity in prison by hunger strikes.

**Panmunjom Talks** (1951–53) UN–North Korean truce discussions that ended the KOREAN WAR. It took two years to reach an agreement that gave South Korea slightly more territory than it had when the war began in 1950. A demilitarized zone was established between North and South Korea.

**pansy** Common name for a cultivated hybrid VIOLET. An annual or short-lived perennial, it has velvety flowers, usually in combinations of blue, yellow, and white, with five petals. Height: to about 6–12in (15–30cm). Family Violaceae; species *Viola tricolor.*

**pantheism** Religious system, contrasted with certain forms of DEISM, that is based on the belief that God (or gods) and the universe are identical. No distinction is recognized between the creator and creatures.

**pantheon** Ancient Greek and Roman temple for the worship of all the gods. The most famous example is the Pantheon in Rome, originally built by Agrippa (27 BC), rebuilt by Hadrian (*c.*AD 120), and converted into the church of Santa Maria Rotonda in the 7th century. The term was later extended to apply to a building honoring illustrious public figures.

**panther** *See* LEOPARD

**pantomime** Theatrical spectacle in Britain, with its modern origins in early-18th-century France. It has come to mean a Christmas extravaganza, with music and comic actors. Popular in England by the 19th century, the "dame" figure was traditionally played by a male actor and the principal boy by a female.

**Paolozzi, Sir Eduardo** (1924– ) Scottish sculptor and graphic artist. He created box-like, chromium-plated sculptures evocative of jazz-age amusement arcades and picture palaces. Since the 1950s, he has worked mainly on large-scale abstract sculptures.

**Papa** In Oceanic mythology, Papa is both a great mother of the gods and an earth goddess. The people of Hawaii consider her to be an ancestress of divine origins. In New Zealand she forms part of the creation myth of the Maoris, and is married to the sky god, Rangi.

**papacy** Office, status, or authority of the pope as head of both the ROMAN CATHOLIC CHURCH and the VATICAN CITY. The pope is nominated Bishop of Rome and Christ's spiritual representative on Earth. He is elected by the College of Cardinals. There have been more than 260 holders of the office of pope. *See also* PAPAL INFALLIBILITY

**Papago** Piman-speaking tribe of Native North Americans who inhabited the Gila and Santa Cruz river valleys of S Arizona, and N Sonora, Mexico. Today, *c.*11,000 Papago people live S of Tucson, Arizona.

**papal bull** Official letter from the pope, consisting of a formal announcement. Such a document usually contains a decree relating to doctrine, CANONIZATION, ecclesiastical discipline, promulgation of INDULGENCES, or some other matter of general importance.

**papal infallibility** Roman Catholic doctrine according to which the pope, under certain conditions, cannot make a mistake in formal statements on issues of faith or morals. It

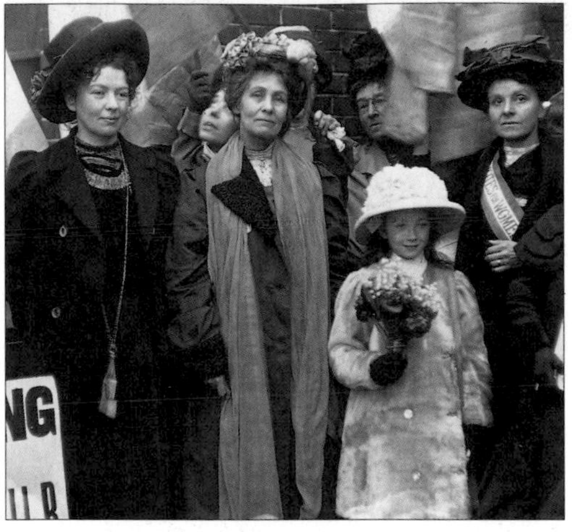

◄ **Pankhurst** The pioneers of the fight for women's suffrage in Britain, Emily Pankhurst and her daughter Christabel were frequently arrested because of their use of militant protest tactics. They interrupted meetings of the cabinet, political parties, and even the House of Commons. Later they turned to even more violent methods of protest, including arson. The law granting British women full voting rights was passed a few weeks after Emily's death.

was defined in its present form, amid great controversy, at the First VATICAN COUNCIL (1869–70).

**Papal States** Territories of central Italy under the rule of the popes (756–1870). In the 15th century the papal government displaced the feudal magnates who had ruled the Papal States in the Middle Ages and imposed direct control from Rome. The territory was temporarily lost during the Napoleonic period, restored to the papacy in 1815, and annexed by the Italian nationalists during the RISORGIMENTO. The LATERAN TREATY of 1929 restored the VATICAN in Rome to papal rule.

**Papandreou, Andreas** (1919–96) Greek statesman, prime minister (1981–89, 1993–96). In the mid-1970s he founded the Pan-Hellenic Socialist Movement (PASOK), becoming leader of the opposition in 1977. In 1981 Papandreou was elected as Greece's first socialist prime minister, and he was reelected in 1985. Implicated in a financial fraud, he was unable to form a government following the election of 1989 and resigned. Cleared of fraud, Papandreou was reelected in 1993.

**papaya** Palmlike tree widely cultivated in tropical America for its fleshy, melonlike, edible fruit. It also produces the ENZYME papain, which breaks down proteins. Height: to 20ft (6m). Family Caricaceae; species *Carica papaya.*

**Papeete** Capital and chief port of French Polynesia, in the S Pacific Ocean, on the NW coast of Tahiti. It is a trade center for the islands and a tourist resort. Its exports include copra, mother-of-pearl, and vanilla. Pop. (1988) 78,814.

**Papen, Franz von** (1879–1969) German politician. He was a member of the Prussian parliament (1921–32) and was Chancellor of Germany in 1932. He helped Adolf HITLER to become chancellor in 1933, acting briefly as his

▼ **papacy** Innocent III (1198–1216) extended the power of the medieval papacy at the expense of kings and princes by intervening throughout Europe to combat any challenge, temporal or spiritual, to the Roman Catholic Church's authority.

Papal States from 1213
Vassals of papacy
Intervention by papacy
New relations
Sphere of papal influence
Byzantine states
Under Muslim rule
Holy Roman Empire

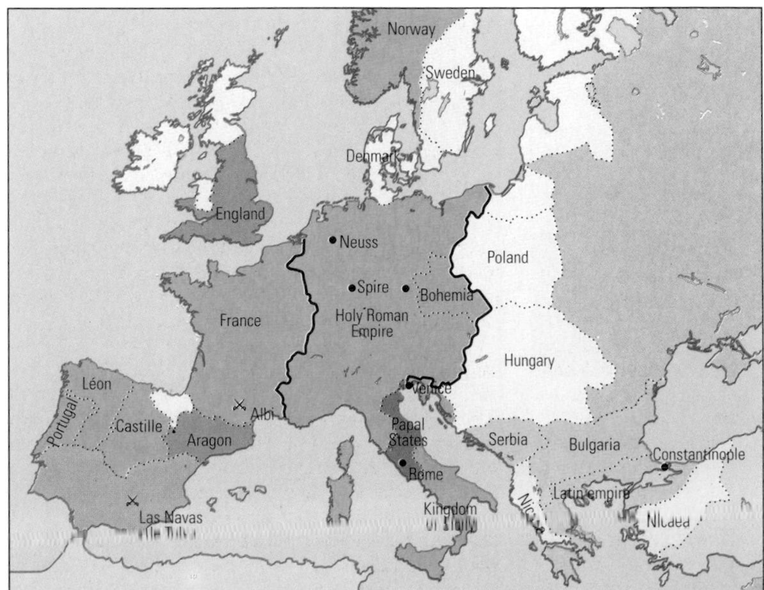

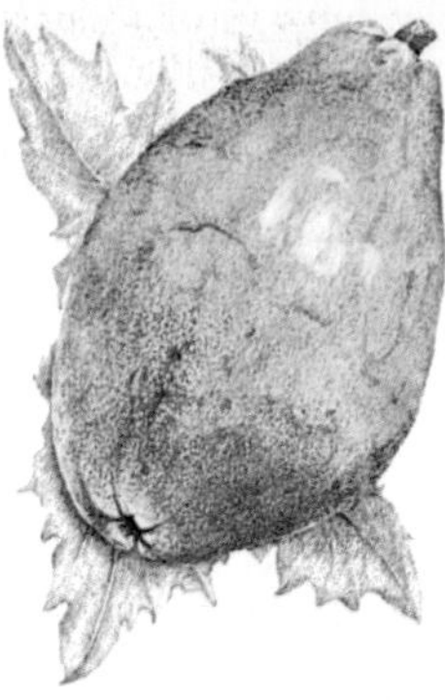

▲ **papaya** The skin of the papaya ripens from green to yellow or orange. Its succulent pulp encloses small, black/brown seeds in its center. Papain, an enzyme contained in the leaves and unripe fruit, is used to tenderize meat.

vice-chancellor. In 1946 he was acquitted by the war crimes tribunal at the NUREMBERG TRIALS.

**paper** Sheet or roll of compacted cellulose fibers with a wide range of uses. The word "paper" derives from PAPYRUS, the plant that the Egyptians used more than 5,500 years ago to make sheets of writing material. The modern process of manufacture originated *c.*2,000 years ago in China and consists of reducing wood fiber, straw, rags, or grasses to a pulp by the action of an ALKALI, such as CAUSTIC SODA (sodium hydroxide). The noncellulose material is then extracted and the residue is bleached. After washing and the addition of a filler to provide a smooth and flat surface, the pulp is made into thin sheets and dried.

**papier-mâché** (Fr. chewed paper) Method of molding forms using paper strips soaked in a starch. The technique originated in 18th-century France. The British adopted the technique to produce a thin paperboard to make trays and moldings which were popular in Victorian times. It is still widely used in the production of decorative objects.

**Papineau, Louis Joseph** (1786–1871) French-Canadian political leader. His quarrels with Britain, which rejected his plan for greater French-Canadian autonomy, incited his followers to rebellion (1837). He escaped arrest by fleeing to the US, then to France. Granted an amnesty (1847), he returned to Canada and was a member of the unified legislature (1848–54).

**Papp, Joseph** (1921–91) US stage director and producer. In 1954 he founded the New York Shakespeare Festival, which performed plays such as *Much Ado About Nothing* (1972) for free in Central Park.

**paprika** Popular, spicy condiment, a red powder ground from the fruit of a sweet PEPPER (capsicum) native to central Europe. Family Solanaceae.

**pap test** Sample of cells from the female genital tract, specially stained to detect malignant or premalignant disease. It is named for its discoverer, George Papanicolaou.

**Papua New Guinea** Independent Commonwealth island group in Melanesia, SW Pacific, 100mi (160km) NE of Australia; the capital is PORT MORESBY. **Land and climate** Papua New Guinea includes the E part of New Guinea, the Bismarck Archipelago, the N SOLOMON ISLANDS, the Trobriand and D'Entrecasteaux Islands, and the Louisiade Archipelago. The land is largely mountainous, rising to Mount Wilhelm at 14,790ft (4,508m), E New Guinea. In 1995 two volcanoes erupted in Eastern New Britain. East New Guinea also has extensive coastal lowlands. Papua New Guinea has a tropical climate. The monsoon season runs from December to April. Forests cover more than 70% of the land. The dominant vegetation is rain forest. Mangrove swamps line the coast. "Cloud" forest and tussock grass are found on the higher peaks. **History and politics** The first European sighting of the island was made by the Portuguese in 1526. In 1828 the Dutch took W New Guinea (now IRIAN JAYA in Indonesia). In 1884 Germany took NE New Guinea as German New Guinea and Britain formed the protectorate of British New Guinea in SE New Guinea. In 1906 British New Guinea passed to Australia as the Territory of Papua. In 1921 German New Guinea became the League of Nations mandate Territory of New Guinea under Australian administration. Japan captured the islands in 1942, and the Allies reconquered them in 1944. In 1949 Papua and New Guinea were combined to form the Territory of Papua and New Guinea. In 1973 the Territory achieved self-government as a prelude to full independence as Papua New Guinea in 1975. Since independence, the government of Papua New Guinea has worked to develop its mineral reserves. One of the most valuable reserves was a copper mine at Panguna on BOUGAINVILLE. Conflict developed when the people of Bougainville demanded a larger share in mining profits. Following an insurrection, the Bougainville Revolutionary Army proclaimed independence in 1990. In 1992 and 1996 Papua New Guinea launched offensives against the rebels. The use of highly paid mercenaries created unrest in the army. In 1997 troops and civilians surrounded parliament and forced the resignation of the prime minister, Sir Julius Chan. He was succeeded by Bill Skate. In April 1998 a permanent cease-fire was declared on Bougainville. In July 1998 a tidal wave hit N Papua New Guinea, killing more than 1,600 people. **Economy** Agriculture employs 75% of the workforce, many at subsistence level. Minerals, notably copper and gold, are the most valuable exports. Papua New Guinea is the world's ninth-largest producer of gold. Other exports include yams, coffee, timber, palm oil, cocoa and lobster. Manufacturing industries process farm, fish and forest products.

**PAPUA NEW GUINEA**

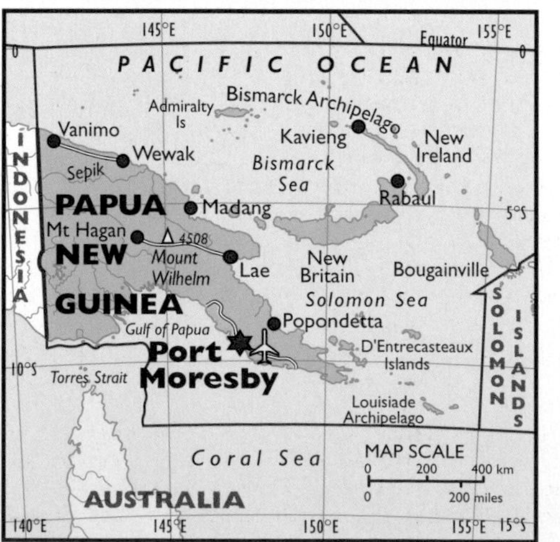


**AREA:** 178,073 sq mi (462,840sq km)
**POPULATION:** 4,056,000
**CAPITAL (POPULATION):** Port Moresby (193,242)
**GOVERNMENT:** Constitutional monarchy
**ETHNIC GROUPS:** Papuan 84%, Melanesian 1%
**LANGUAGES:** English (official)
**RELIGIONS:** Christianity (Protestant 58%, Roman Catholic 33%, Anglican 5%), traditional beliefs 3%
**CURRENCY:** Kina = 100 toea

**papyrus** Stout, perennial water plant, native to S Europe, N Africa, and the Middle East, and used by the ancient Egyptians to make writing material. Strips of the stem were arranged in layers, crushed, and hammered to form a loosely textured, porous kind of PAPER. Height: to 15ft (4.5m). Family Cyperaceae; species *Cyperus papyrus*.

**parable** Short, simple story intended to convey a moral or religious message. It differs from an ALLEGORY in that it deals with events that might reasonably happen in nature. The best-known parables are those attributed to Jesus Christ in the New Testament, including the Good Samaritan and the Prodigal Son.

**parabola** Mathematical curve, a CONIC section traced by a point that moves so that its distance from a fixed point, the focus, is equal to its distance from a fixed straight line, the directrix. It may be formed by cutting a cone parallel to one side. The general equation of a parabola is $y = ax^2 + bx + c$, where a, b, and c are constants.

**Paracelsus** (1493–1541) Swiss physician and alchemist, real name Philippus Aureolus Theophrastus Bombast von Hohenheim. According to Paracelsus, the human body is primarily composed of salt, sulfur, and mercury, and it is the separation of these elements that causes illness. He introduced mineral baths.

**parachute** Lightweight fabric device for slowing movement through the air. Parachutes allow people to descend safely from aircraft or are used to drop cargo and supplies. The most common use is for the sport of SKYDIVING.

**paradise** Place of perfect happiness and contentment. Most of the world's myths and religions mention such a realm of bliss, often as an abode of God or the gods or a region that has been lost to humanity or to which believers may aspire to go after death. Christianity also associates it with the Garden of EDEN before ADAM and EVE were cast out.

**paradox** Self-contradictory or absurd statement that conflicts with preconceived notions of what is reasonable or possible, but which is significant when considered from the appropriate viewpoint. A well-known paradox is that of ZENO OF ELEA, who reasoned that motion is impossible.

**Paraguay** Landlocked republic in central South America; the capital is ASUNCIÓN. **Land and climate** Paraguay is bisected by the Paraguay River. The majority of the population live between the E bank of the Paraguay River and the PARANÁ River, which forms the S border with Argentina. The S has extensive marshes. West of the Paraguay River is part of the GRAN CHACO, a flat grassy plain that extends into Bolivia and Argentina. The S is subtropical. Rainfall is heaviest in the SE Paraná plateau. The Chaco is the driest and hottest part of Paraguay. Paraguay is a country of coarse grass, shrub, and scrub forest, with some hardwood forests. **History** The earliest known inhabitants of Paraguay were the GUARANÍ. Spanish and Portuguese explorers reached the area in the early 16th century. In 1537 a Spanish expedition built a fort at Asunción, which became the capital of Spain's colonies in SE South America. From the late 16th century, Jesuit missionaries worked to protect the Guaraní from colonial exploitation and convert them to Christianity. In 1767 the Spanish king expelled the Jesuits. In 1776 Paraguay was subsumed into the colony of the viceroyalty of Río de la Plata. Paraguay declared independence in 1811. The disastrous War of the Triple Alliance (1865–70) against Brazil, Argentina, and Uruguay killed more than 50% of Paraguay's population and resulted in great loss of territory. Border disputes with Bolivia led to the Chaco War (1932–35) in which Paraguay regained some land. In 1954 General Alfredo Stroessner led a successful military coup. His dictatorial regime suppressed all political opposition. In 1989, shortly after reelection for an eighth successive term, Stroessner was overthrown by General Andrés Rodríguez. In 1993 multiparty elections, Juan Carlos Wasmosy was elected as Paraguay's first civilian president since 1954. An attempted military coup was foiled in 1996. In 1996 General Lino Oviedo was imprisoned for leading an attempted military coup. In 1999 Oviedo was released by President Raúl Cubas, who was later forced to resign. **Economy** Agriculture and forestry are the leading activities, employing 48% of the work force. Paraguay has large cattle ranches, and many crops are grown in the fertile soils of E Paraguay. Paraguay is the world's seventh-largest producer of soybeans. Other crops include cassava, cotton, and coffee. Major exports include timber, coffee, tannin, and meat products. In 1973 construction started on the Itaipú Dam on the Paraná River. It is one of the world's largest dams.

**PARAGUAY**

**AREA:** 157,046sq mi (406,750sq km)
**POPULATION:** 4,579,000
**CAPITAL (POPULATION):** Asunción (637,737)
**GOVERNMENT:** Multiparty republic
**ETHNIC GROUPS:** Mestizo 90%, Native American 3%
**LANGUAGES:** Spanish and Guaraní (both official)

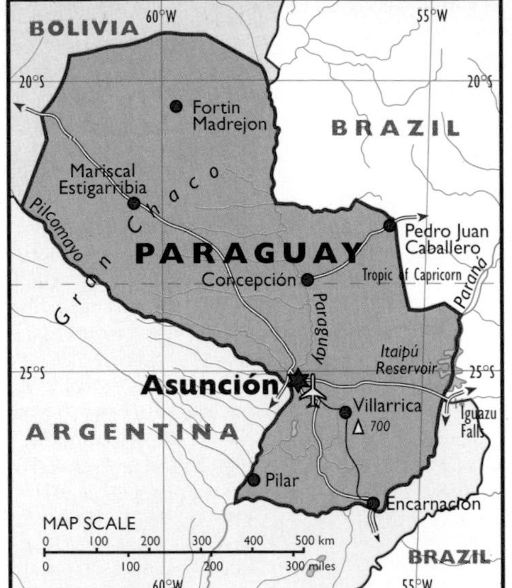


**RELIGIONS:** Christianity (Roman Catholic 96%, Protestant 2%)
**CURRENCY:** Guaranø = 100 céntimos

**parakeet** *See* PARROT

**parallax** Angular distance by which a celestial object appears to be displaced with respect to more distant objects, when viewed from opposite ends of a baseline. The parallax of a star (**annual** parallax) is the angle subtended at the star by the mean radius of the Earth's orbit (one astronomical unit); the smaller the angle, the more distant the star. *See also* PARSEC

**parallelogram** Quadrilateral (four-sided plane figure) having each pair of opposite sides parallel and equal. Both the opposite angles of a parallelogram are also equal. A parallelogram with all four sides equal is called a RHOMBUS.

**Paralympic Games** Sports meeting held every four years in conjunction with the OLYMPIC GAMES and in which all competitors are physically handicapped. Much of the full Olympic program of events is staged.

**paralysis** Weakness or loss of muscle power; it can vary from a mild condition to complete loss of function and sensation in the affected part. It can be associated with almost any disorder of the NERVOUS SYSTEM, including brain or spinal cord injury, infection, stroke, poisoning, or progressive conditions such as a tumor or motor neuron disease. Paralysis is very rarely total.

**Paramaribo** Capital of Surinam, a port on the Surinam River. It was founded in the early 17th century by the French and became a British colony in 1651. It was held intermittently by the British and the Dutch until 1816, when the latter finally took control until independence. Industries: bauxite, timber, sugarcane, rice, rum, coffee, cacao. Pop. (1993 est.) 200,970.

**Paraná** River in SE central South America. It rises in SE Brazil, flows S into Argentina, forming the SE and S border of Paraguay, and joins the Uruguay River to form the Río de la PLATA. It is an important route for inland communications. Combined length: Paraná/Plata c.2,490mi (4,000km).

**paranoia** Term in psychology for a psychotic disorder characterized by a systematically held, persistent delusion, usually of persecution or irrational jealousy. Paranoia can accompany SCHIZOPHRENIA, manic-depressive disorder, drug or alcohol abuse, or brain damage.

**paraplegia** PARALYSIS of both legs. It is usually due to spinal cord injury, and often accompanied by loss of sensation below the site of the damage.

**parapsychology** Branch of psychology concerned with research into phenomena that appear inexplicable by traditional science. It involves research into EXTRASENSORY PERCEPTION (ESP), such as TELEPATHY, and precognition (perceiving future events).

**parasite** Organism that lives on or in another organism (the host) upon which it depends for its survival; this arrangement may be harmful to the host. Parasites occur in many groups of plants and in virtually all major animal groups. A parasite that lives in the host is called an **endoparasite**; a parasite that survives on the host's exterior is an **ectoparasite**. Many parasites, such as PROTOZOA, FLEAS, and WORMS, carry disease or cause sores, which may become infected. The European CUCKOO and cowbird rely on other birds to rear their young, and are therefore considered "brood parasites." In **parasitoidism**, the relationship results in the death of the host.

**parathyroid glands** Four small endocrine glands, usually embedded in the back of the THYROID GLAND, that secrete a HORMONE to control the level of calcium and phosphorus in the blood. Overproduction of parathyroid hormone causes loss of calcium from the bones to the blood; a deficiency causes tetany (involuntary muscle spasm). *See also* ENDOCRINE SYSTEM

**Paré, Ambroise** (1517–90) French physician regarded by some as the founder of modern surgery. In 1537 he was employed as an army surgeon and in 1552 became surgeon to HENRY II. Paré introduced new methods of treating wounds and revived the practice of tying arteries during surgery instead of cauterizing them.

**Pareto, Vilfredo** (1848–1923) Italian economist and sociologist. He studied the application of mathematics to economic theory and wrote *Manual of Political Economy* (1906). As a sociological theorist, Pareto concentrated on ruling élites and wrote *Mind and Society* (1916).

**Paris** In Greek legend, the son of PRIAM and Hecuba. After he chose APHRODITE as the victor in a competition among goddesses, she helped him to abduct HELEN, wife of Menelaus, King of Sparta. This kidnapping sparked the TROJAN WAR, in which he slew ACHILLES.

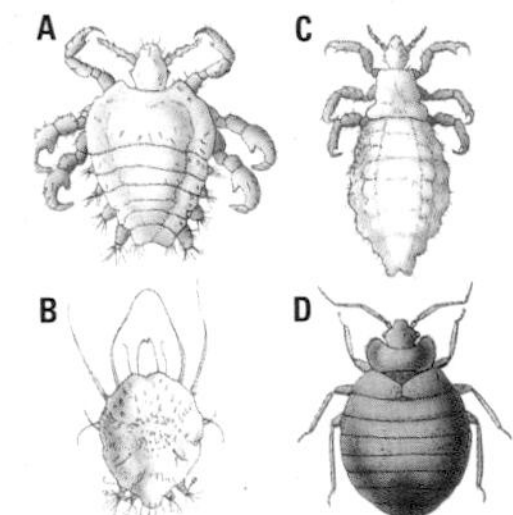


▲ **parasite** Some external parasites live either on, or nearby, humans. The crab louse (A) lives on areas of the body with widely spaced coarse hair. The acarus mite (B) is just about visible to the human eye, and is responsible for causing scabies. The body louse (C) is one of the more dangerous parasites. It is a carrier of epidemic typhus. The common bedbug (D) is found all over the world. During the day it is inactive, but at night it finds humans and sucks their blood.

P

**Paris** Capital of France, on the SEINE River. When the Romans took Paris in 52 BC, it was a small village on the Ile de la Cité on the Seine. Under their rule it became an important administrative center. Paris was the capital of the Merovingian Franks in the 5th century but subsequently declined. It was reestablished as the French capital by the Capetian kings in the 10th century. The city expanded rapidly in the 11th and 12th centuries. During the 14th century Paris rebelled against the Crown and declared itself an independent commune. It suffered further civil disorder during the Hundred Years War. In the 16th century it underwent fresh expansion, its architecture strongly influenced by the Italian Renaissance. In the reign of Louis XIII, Cardinal RICHELIEU established Paris as the cultural and political center of Europe. The FRENCH REVOLUTION began in Paris when the BASTILLE was stormed by crowds in 1789. Under Emperor NAPOLEON I the city began to assume its present-day form. The work of modernization was continued during the reign of NAPOLEON III, when Baron Haussmann was commissioned to plan the boulevards, bridges, and parks. Although occupied during the Franco–Prussian War (1870–71) and again in World War II, Paris was not badly damaged. The city proper consists of the Paris department, Ville de Paris. Its suburbs lie in the departments of the Ile-de-France region. It has many famous buildings and landmarks popular with tourists. Paris remains the hub of France despite attempts at decentralization, and retains its importance as a European cultural, commercial, and communications center. Paris is noted for its fashion industry and for the manufacture of luxury articles. Industries: motor vehicles, chemicals, textiles, clothing. Pop. (1990, city) 2,152,423; (metropolitan) 9,318,821.

**Paris, Treaties of** Name given to several international agreements made in Paris. The most notable include: the treaty of 1763, which ended the SEVEN YEARS WAR; the treaty of 1783, in which Britain recognized the independence of the US; the treaty of 1814, which settled the affairs of France after the first abdication of Napoleon; the treaty of 1815, after Napoleon's final defeat; the treaty of 1856, ending the CRIMEAN WAR; the treaty of 1898, ending the SPANISH–AMERICAN WAR and giving the Philippines to the US; and the main international settlement (1919) after World War I, more often called the Treaty of VERSAILLES. Also signed in Paris was the truce in the VIETNAM WAR (1973), in which the US agreed to withdraw its forces.

**Paris, Universities of** Collection of 13 autonomous universities, created in 1970 and known as Paris I–XIII, situated in and around Paris. Paris I–VIII replaces the original University of Paris. Each university specializes in a particular area of academic study. The original **Sorbonne**, which was founded in the 12th century, is the administrative center of the universities.

**Paris Commune** (March 18–May 28, 1871) Revolutionary government in Paris. Anger with the national government provoked Parisians into establishing an independent city government. Socialists and other radicals played an important part in the Commune. Besieged by the forces of the national government, the city fell and the Commune was violently suppressed. The slaughter of an estimated 30,000 people alienated many French workers and encouraged revolutionary doctrines.

**parish** In Louisiana, the equivalent of a county in other states.

**parity** In physics, term used to denote space-reflection symmetry. The principle of conservation of parity states that physical laws are the same in a left- and right-handed coordinate system. This was regarded as inviolable until 1956, when Chen Ning YANG and Tsung-Dao LEE showed that it was transgressed by certain interactions between elementary atomic particles. Parity is also used in information theory to denote a coding method employed in message transmission to detect errors.

**Park, Mungo** (1771–1806) British explorer. He was asked by the African Association (forerunner of the Royal Geographical Society) to investigate the course of the Niger River (1795). He explored *c.*280mi (450km) of the Upper Niger, a journey described in his *Travels...* (1799). On a second expedition (1805) he and his companions were ambushed and killed.

**Park Chung Hee** (1917–79) President of South Korea (1963–79). He seized power in a military coup in 1961, ruled for two years as a general, then resigned from the army. He was elected President in 1963, 1967, and 1971. Park was assassinated by the head of the South Korean Central Intelligence Agency.

**Parker, Alan** (1944– ) English film director. His debut feature, *Bugsy Malone* (1976), was followed by *Midnight Express* (1978), for which he received an Oscar nomination. *Mississippi Burning* (1988) earned him a second nomination. Other films include *Birdy* (1985), *The Commitments* (1991), and *Evita* (1997).

**Parker, Charlie (Charles Christopher)** (1920–55) US jazz alto saxophonist, nicknamed "Bird." He recorded with Dizzy GILLESPIE and Bud POWELL in the 1940s, and was the most important of the founders of the jazz style called BEBOP.

**Parker, Dorothy** (1893–1967) US poet, short-story writer, and critic. She wrote three volumes of poetry, the first of which, *Enough Rope* (1926), was a bestseller. Her gift for witty epigrams is evident throughout her work.

**Parkinson, Norman** (1913–90) British fashion and portrait photographer. He worked for *Harper's Bazaar* (1935–40) and *Vogue* (1945–60). Awarded the CBE in 1981, he had exhibitions in London, Paris, and Venice.

**Parkinson's disease** Degenerative BRAIN disease characterized by tremor, muscular rigidity, and poverty of movement and facial expression. It arises from a lack of the NEUROTRANSMITTER DOPAMINE. Slightly more common in men, it is rare before the age of 50. Foremost among the drugs used to control the disease is L-DOPA.

**Parkman, Francis** (1823–93) US historian. His masterpiece is *France and England in North America* (eight volumes, 1865–84), one of the greatest works on North American history.

**parliament** Legislative assembly that includes elected members and acts as a debating forum for political affairs. Many parliamentary systems are based on the British Parliament. It emerged in the late 13th century as an extension of the king's council, and has been housed at Westminster since that time. It is the supreme power in the country. Parliament comprises the monarch, in whose name members of the government act, and two Houses: the HOUSE OF LORDS, an upper chamber of hereditary and life peers, bishops, and law lords, and the HOUSE OF COMMONS. There are 659 members of the Commons (known as "members of Parliament" or MPs), elected in single-member constituencies by universal adult suffrage. The prime minister and cabinet members are almost always members of the Commons. There is a maximum of five years between elections.

**Parma** City in N Italy; capital of Parma province. Parma is famed for Parma ham and Parmesan cheese. It was founded by the Romans in 183 BC. In the 9th century AD it became a bishopric, and in 1513 was incorporated into the Papal States. In 1545 Pope Paul III established the duchy of Parma, and until 1731 it was controlled by the Farnese family. In 1802 Napoleon conquered Parma, and in 1815 handed control to his second consort, Marie Louise of Austria. Despite bombing in World War II, Parma retains many historic buildings. Pop. (1991) 170,520.

**Parmigiano** (1503–40) (Francesco Mazzola) Northern Italian painter and graphic artist, a master of MANNERISM. Among his best-known works are *Madonna with St. Zachary* (*c.*1530) and *Vision of St. Jerome* (*c.*1527).

**Parnassus** Mountain peak in central Greece. In ancient times it was considered sacred to APOLLO, DIONYSUS, and the MUSES, and was the site of the equally sacred Castalian spring, which lies just above DELPHI, at the S foot of the mountain. Height: 8,061ft (2,457m).

**Parnell, Charles Stewart** (1846–91) Irish political leader. He entered the British Parliament in 1875, vigorously supporting HOME RULE for Ireland. He was imprisoned (1881–82), but his power reached its peak in 1886, when the government introduced the Home Rule Bill. The bill was eventually defeated. His career collapsed when he was cited as corespondent in the divorce of William O'Shea, whose wife, Kitty, he later married.

P

**parody** Work in which the characteristics of artists or their works are imitated and exaggerated for comic effect. While parody exists in music and the arts, it is most commonly associated with literature and has its roots in ancient Greece. Among 20th-century writers who have made effective use of parody are Max BEERBOHM, James JOYCE, and Stephen LEACOCK.

**parole** Early release of prisoners before the expiration of their sentences. Parole is given under certain circumstances, usually as a reward for good behavior, and is subject to controls. The prisoner remains under sentence and may be recalled for violating any restrictions. Parole is supervised by a probation officer. The parole procedure is regulated by statute in the US.

**parotid gland** One of two SALIVARY GLANDS located one on either side of the mouth just in front of the ear. With ducts opening on the inside of the cheek, it is the gland that becomes swollen during an attack of MUMPS.

**parrot** Common name for many tropical and subtropical birds. Parrots are brightly colored and have thick, hooked bills. They include BUDGERIGARS, macaws, lories, lorikeets, parakeets, keas, kakapos, and others. In the wild they nest in tree holes, rock cracks, or on the ground. Length: 3in–3ft (7.5–90cm). Family Psittacidae.

**Parry, Sir (Charles) Hubert Hastings** (1848–1918) British composer. His mastery of choral music is best shown in *Blest Pair of Sirens* (1887). He is chiefly celebrated for *Jerusalem* (1916).

**parsec** (pc) Distance at which a star would have a PARALLAX of one second of arc; equivalent to 3.2616 light-years, 206,265 astronomical units, or $3.0857 \times 10^{13}$ km.

**Parsi** (Parsee) Modern descendant of a small number of ancient Persian Zoroastrians who emigrated to Gujarat in India from the 10th century onward. Modern Parsis, concentrated in Bombay, follow a mixture of ZOROASTRIANISM and some Indian beliefs and practices.

**parsley** Branching biennial herb, native to the Mediterranean region and cultivated for its aromatic leaves used for flavoring and as a garnish. It has heads of small, greenish-yellow flowers. Height: to 3ft (0.9m). Family Apiaceae/Umbelliferae; species *Petroselinum crispum.*

**parsnip** Biennial vegetable native to Eurasia, widely cultivated for its edible white taproot. The plant has many leaves. The roots develop slowly until cool weather sets in, and then they mature quickly. Family Apiaceae/Umbelliferae; species *Pastinaca sativa.*

**Pärt, Arvo** (1935– ) Estonian composer. His early works were written in a traditional "Soviet" style. In the 1970s, Pärt adopted a minimalist style that he called "tintinnabula." Among his most celebrated works are *Tabula Rasa* (1977), *Cantus in memoriam Benjamin Britten* (1980), and the *St. John Passion* (1981).

**parthenogenesis** Development of a female sex cell or GAMETE without fertilization. It leads to the production of offspring that are genetically identical to the mother. This process occurs naturally among some plants and invertebrates, such as APHIDS.

**Parthenon** Temple to the goddess ATHENA erected (447–432 BC) by PERICLES on the ACROPOLIS in Athens. The finest example of a DORIC ORDER temple, it was badly damaged by an explosion in 1687. Most of the surviving sculptures were removed by Lord Elgin in 1801–03. *See* ELGIN MARBLES

**Parthia** Region in ancient Persia, corresponding approximately to the modern Iranian province of Khurāsān, with part of S TURKMENISTAN. It was the seat of the Parthian empire, founded after a successful revolt against the SELEUCIDS (238 BC). Under the Arsacid dynasty, the Parthian empire extended, at its peak, from Armenia to Afghanistan. In AD 224 the Parthians were defeated by the rising power of the SASSANIDS and the empire rapidly crumbled.

**particle accelerator** *See* ACCELERATOR

**particle physics** Branch of physics that studies SUBATOMIC PARTICLES and interactions between them. Physicists now recognize more than 300 different subatomic particles. The indivisible, fundamental units of matter are known as ELEMENTARY PARTICLES. They are termed the gauge BOSON, LEPTON, and QUARK. Other subatomic particles, termed HADRONS, are made up of two or more elementary particles. For example, PROTONS and NEUTRONS are made up of three quarks, and MESONS are made up of two quarks. Most subatomic particles are unstable and decay into other particles.

◄ **Parthenon** The ceremonial centerpiece of the Acropolis, Athens's hilltop temple complex, the Parthenon was constructed in the fifth century BC in honor of Athena, the city's patron goddess. It was designed by Athens's foremost architects and ornamented by its most gifted sculptors. A carved frieze, a section of which is shown here, ran around the top of the inner wall. It depicted the Panathenaia, the annual festival in honor of Athena.

**partridge** Any of several species of game birds found worldwide. True partridges of Europe belong to the pheasant family (Phasianidae), and include the common partridge *Perdix perdix*, which has been introduced to North America. It lives on heathland, sandy scrub, and farmland and feeds on plants and insects.

**Parvati** In Hindu mythology, the wife of the god SHIVA in one of her more benevolent aspects as a mountain goddess. Parvati is also the mother of the elephant-headed god GANESH and his brother Skanda. She is generally depicted as a young woman.

**Pasadena** City in S California, 8mi (13km) NE of Los Angeles. It was founded in 1874 at the foot of the Sierra Madre mountains. It is the site of the California Institute of Technology (1891), the annual Tournament of Roses Parade (1890), and the Rose Bowl football game. Industries: electronic equipment, ceramics, plastics, aircraft components, cosmetics. Pop. (1980) 119,374.

**Pascal, Blaise** (1623–62) French scientist and mystic. With Pierre de FERMAT, Pascal laid the foundations of the mathematical theory of PROBABILITY. He also contributed to calculus and hydrodynamics, devising Pascal's law in 1647. It states that the pressure applied to an enclosed fluid (liquid or gas) is transmitted equally in all directions and to all parts of the enclosing vessel. The SI unit of pressure is named for him.

**Pashto** (Pushto) One of the two major languages of Afghanistan, the other being Persian. Pashto is spoken by about 12 million people in E Afghanistan and N Pakistan. It is historically the language of the PATHAN tribes and is written in an adapted Arabic alphabet. One of the Iranian languages, it forms part of the Indo-European family of languages.

**Pasolini, Pier Paolo** (1922–75) Italian poet, novelist, and film director. A Marxist, he wrote about urban poverty with great realism in novels such as *A Violent Life* (1959). Films he directed include *The Gospel According to St. Matthew* (1964), and *The Decameron* (1970).

**passion** In Christian theology, the suffering of JESUS CHRIST from the time of his praying in the garden of Gethsemane until his death on the cross. Passion Sunday is the fifth Sunday in Lent; PALM SUNDAY and EASTER follow.

**passion flower** Any plant of the genus *Passiflora*, climbing tropical plants that probably originated in tropical America, especially the widely cultivated blue passionflower, *P. caerulea*. Flowers are red, yellow, green, or purple; the outer petals ring a fringed center. The leaves are lobed and some species produce edible fruits, such as granadilla and calabash. Family Passifloraceae.

**passion play** Dramatic presentation of Christ's PASSION, death, and resurrection, originally developed in medieval Europe. The best-known example of this tradition is still held every ten years in OBERAMMERGAU, Germany.

**Passover** (Pesach) Jewish festival of eight days, commemorating the Exodus from Egypt and the redemption of the Israelites. Symbolic dishes are prepared, including bitter herbs (*maror*) and unleavened bread (*matzot*), to remind the Jews of the haste with which they fled Egypt. It is a family celebration,

▲ **passion flower** A climbing woody plant, the passion flower, makes its way by means of twining tendrils. Some species produce large, edible fruits.

at which the HAGGADAH is read. Christ's Last Supper, at which he instituted the EUCHARIST, was a Passover meal.

**passport** Government-issued document facilitating travel to and from different countries. Its use became widespread after World War I. A passport identifies its holder as a citizen or national of a specific country and under that country's protection.

**pasta** Food, high in carbohydrate, made from semonna derived from durum wheat. Associated with Italian cooking, it comes in a variety of shapes and sizes.

**Pasternak, Boris** (1890–1960) Soviet poet, novelist, and translator. After the death of Stalin he began work on *Dr. Zhivago* (1957), his best-known novel in the West. Its themes offended officials, and he was expelled from the Soviet Writers Union; the book was not published in the former Soviet Union until the 1980s. He was also compelled by official pressure to retract his acceptance of the 1958 Nobel Prize for literature.

**Pasteur, Louis** (1822–95) French chemist and one of the founders of microbiology. He discovered that microorganisms can be destroyed by heat, a technique now known as PASTEURIZATION. Pasteur also discovered that he could weaken certain disease-causing microorganisms and then use the weakened culture to vaccinate against the disease.

**pasteurization** Controlled heat treatment of food to kill bacteria and other microorganisms, discovered by Louis PASTEUR in the 1860s. Milk is pasteurized by heating it to 161.6°F (72°C) for 16 seconds. Ultrapasteurization is now used to produce UHT (ultra-heat-treated) milk; it is heated to 270°F (132°C) for one second to provide a shelf-life of several months.

**pastoral** In literature, work portraying rural life in an idealized manner, especially to contrast its supposed innocence with the corruption of the city or royal court. In classical times THEOCRITUS and VIRGIL wrote pastoral poems. The form was revived during the RENAISSANCE by such poets as DANTE, PETRARCH, BOCCACCIO, and SPENSER. MILTON and SHELLEY were noted for their pastoral elegies, and poets such as William WORDSWORTH and Robert FROST have been loosely referred to as pastoral poets.

**pastoralism** Form of subsistence agriculture that involves the herding of domesticated livestock. Societies practicing this are small, restricted by the large amount of grazing land needed for each animal. Indigenous pastoralism is widespread in N Africa and central Asia. *See also* NOMAD

▲ **Pavlov** During his study of the digestive process in dogs, the Russian physiologist Ivan Pavlov worked out his theory of conditioned reflexes. He established that dogs salivated when they were presented with food. This was a reflex action that the dog could not control. He then "conditioned" a dog, by ringing a bell every time he gave it food. Eventually the dog would salivate whenever it heard the bell. His work helped to establish the physiological basis of behavior.

**Patagonia** Region in Argentina, E of the Andes Mountains, extending to the Strait of Magellan; the term is sometimes used to include part of S Chile. The area was first visited by MAGELLAN in the early 16th century. It was colonized in the 1880s, many of the settlers being Welsh or Scottish. Most of Patagonia is located on arid, windswept plateau lands. Until recently sheep rearing was the main source of income. Oil production has now become important, and coal and iron ore are mined in the S. Area: 311,000sq mi (805,490sq km).

**patella** (kneecap) Large, flattened, roughly triangular bone just in front of the joint where the FEMUR and TIBIA are linked. It is surrounded by bursae (sacs of fluid) that cushion the joint.

**patent** (letters patent) Privilege granted to the inventor of a product or process. A patent excludes others from producing or making use of it for a limited period, unless licensed by the holder of the patent.

**Paternoster** Latin name (meaning "Our Father") for the LORD'S PRAYER.

**Pathans** (Pashtuns) MUSLIM tribes of SE Afghanistan and NW Pakistan. They speak various dialects of an E Iranian language, PASHTO, and are composed of about 60 tribes, numbering in total perhaps 10 million. Formerly, they were pastoralists inhabiting the mountainous border regions, but they are now mainly farmers and are more widely spread. In their clashes with the British in the 19th century, they gained a reputation as formidable warriors. Their way of life was disrupted during the Soviet occupation (1979–89) and the subsequent civil wars in Afghanistan.

**Pathé, Charles** (1863–1957) Pioneer French film producer. He produced many short films, and is credited with having made one of the first long films, *Les Misérables* (1909). Through the Pathé newsreels, he helped develop the film DOCUMENTARY.

**pathogen** Microorganism that causes disease in plants or animals. Animal pathogens are commonly BACTERIA and VIRUSES, while plant pathogens include FUNGI.

**pathology** Study of diseases, their causes, and the changes they produce in the cells, tissues, and organs of the body.

**Paton, Alan Stewart** (1903–88) South African novelist and reformer. Strongly opposed to APARTHEID, he helped to found the South African Liberal Party, of which he was president (1958–68). His two best-known novels were *Cry, the Beloved Country* (1948) and *Too Late the Phalarope* (1953).

**patriarch** Head of a family or tribe, invested in certain circumstances with the status or authority of a religious leader. In the Old Testament, the term referred either to the ancestors of the human race who lived on Earth before the Flood (as recorded in Genesis 1–11) or more commonly to the ancestors of the ancient Israelites, namely: ABRAHAM, ISAAC, JACOB, and Jacob's 12 sons (Genesis 12–50). Since about the 4th century AD, the word has also been used as an ecclesiastic title for a few exalted Eastern Christian bishops.

**patriarchy** Social organization based on the authority of a senior male, usually the father, over a family.

**patrician** Aristocratic class in the ancient Roman Republic, members of the SENATE. In the early years of the republic, the patricians controlled all aspects of government and society. Under the empire the division between patricians and PLEBIANS disappeared.

**Patrick, Saint** (active 5th century AD) Patron saint of Ireland. Facts about his life are confused by legend. What is known of him comes almost entirely from his autobiography, *Confessio*. He was born in Britain into a Romanized Christian family. Abducted by marauders at the age of 16, he was carried off to Ireland and sold to a local chief. After six years as a herdsman, during which period he became increasingly reliant on his Christian faith, he escaped back to Britain. He was sent to Ireland as a missionary by Pope Celestine I (432), and established an episcopal see at Armagh. His missionary work was so successful that Christianity was firmly established in Ireland before he died. By tradition he is also said to have banished snakes from Ireland. His feast day is March 17.

**Patton, George Smith, Jr.** (1885–1945) US general. In World War I he served with the American Expeditionary Force (AEF) in France. A controversial and highly successful officer, he commanded a tank corps in North Africa and the 7th Army in Sicily in World War II. After the Normandy invasion in 1944, he commanded the 3rd Army in its dash across France and into Germany. As military governor of Bavaria after the war, he was criticized for leniency to Nazis and was removed to command the US 15th Army.

**Paul, Saint** (active 1st century AD) Apostle of JESUS CHRIST, missionary, and early Christian theologian. His missionary journeys among the Gentiles form a large part of the ACTS OF THE APOSTLES. His many letters (epistles) to early Christian communities, recorded in the NEW TESTAMENT, represent the most important early formulations of Christian theology following the death of Jesus Christ. Named Saul at birth, he was both a Jew and a Roman citizen, brought up in the Roman colony of Tarsus, in what is now S Turkey. He saw the teachings of Jesus as a major threat to JUDAISM, and became a leading persecutor of early Christians. Traveling to Damascus to continue his persecution activities, he suddenly saw a bright light while on the road and heard the voice of Jesus addressing him. Having thus undergone his religious conversion, he adopted the name Paul and thereafter became a fluent and energetic evangelist and teacher of Christianity. In *c.*60 he was arrested after returning to Jerusalem and taken as a prisoner to Rome, where he died sometime between 62 and 68, probably suffering a martyr's execution.

**Paul III** (1468–1549) Pope (1534–49), b. Alessandro Farnese. As pope, he largely initiated the COUNTER REFORMATION. He sponsored reform, approved the JESUITS, and summoned the Council of TRENT (1545).

**Paul VI** (1897–1978) Pope (1963–78), b. Giovanni Battista Montini. He earned a reputation as a reformer as archbishop of Milan (1954–63). He continued the Second VATICAN COUNCIL, begun by John XXIII, but disappointed liberals by upholding the celibacy of priests, papal primacy, and condemning contraception.

**Paul I** (1754–1801) Emperor of Russia (1796–1801). He reestablished the principle of hereditary succession and instituted repressive measures to protect Russia from the influence of the French Revolution. Paul's erratic conduct and his hostility toward his son, Alexander, led to his murder by nobles and military officers.

**Paul I** (1901–64) King of the Hellenes (1947–64), brother and successor to George II. During his reign, he followed a pro-Western policy and received US aid to help Greece's economic recovery after World War II. Paul was succeeded by his son, CONSTANTINE II.

**Pauli, Wolfgang** (1900–58) US physicist, b. Austria. His work on QUANTUM THEORY led him to formulate (1925) the EXCLUSION PRINCIPLE, which explains the behavior of electrons in atoms. Pauli received the 1945 Nobel Prize for physics for the work. In 1931 he had predicted the existence of the NEUTRINO, and lived to see his prediction verified in 1956.

**Pauling, Linus Carl** (1901–94) US chemist. He applied QUANTUM THEORY to chemistry. His work on the application of WAVE MECHANICS to molecular structure led to the 1954 Nobel Prize for chemistry. In the 1950s Pauling worked on the structure of PROTEINS, and his suggestion DNA molecules were arranged in a helical structure anticipated the research of Francis CRICK and James WATSON. A leader in the campaign for nuclear disarmament, Pauling was awarded the 1962 Nobel Peace Prize.

**Pavarotti, Luciano** (1935– ) Italian tenor. He made his operatic debut, as Rodolfo in Puccini's *La Bohème*, in 1961. Pavarotti toured the world many times, making his US debut in 1968. He later formed part of the popular concert grouping called *The Three Tenors*, along with José CARRERAS and Plácido DOMINGO.

**Pavese, Cesare** (1908–50) Italian poet, novelist, and translator. His translations of English and American novels had considerable influence on Italian literature of the time. His work with the Resistance during World War II influenced his own creative writing, which includes the poem *The Political Prisoner* (1949) and the novel *The Moon and the Bonfire* (1950).

**Pavlov, Ivan Petrovich** (1849–1936) Russian neurophysiologist. His early work centered on the physiology and neurology of digestion, for which he received the 1904 Nobel Prize for physiology or medicine. Pavlov is best known for his studies of CONDITIONING of behavior in dogs. His works include *Conditioned Reflexes* (1927).

**Pavlova, Anna** (1881–1931) Russian ballerina who made her debut in 1899. She left Russia in 1913 to tour with her own company. She excelled in *Giselle*, *The Dragonfly*, *Autumn Leaves*, and the *Dying Swan*, choreographed for her by Michel FOKINE in 1905.

**Pawnee** Caddoan-speaking tribe of Native North Americans. They are related to the Arikara, who once occupied the Central Platte and Republican River areas in Nebraska. Today, *c*.1,500 Pawnee live on reservations in Oklahoma.

**Paxton, Sir Joseph** (1803–65) English architect and landscape gardener. Paxton designed the CRYSTAL PALACE for the Great Exhibition of 1851 in London.

**Paz, Octavio** (1914–98) Mexican poet and essayist. His work has gone from Marxism to SURREALISM and oriental philosophies. His poetry was collected in translation as *The Collected Poems of Octavio Paz, 1957–1987* (1987). He has also written essays and literary criticism, including *The Labyrinth of Solitude* (1950). Paz was awarded the 1990 Nobel Prize for literature.

**pea** Climbing annual plant (*Pisum sativum*), probably native to W Asia. It has small oval leaves and white flowers that give rise to pods containing wrinkled or smooth seeds, which are a popular vegetable. It grows to 6ft (1.8m). Family Fabaceae/Leguminosae

**Peace Corps** US government agency, organizing work by volunteers in developing countries. The Corps was established in 1961 by President John F. KENNEDY. Peace Corps volunteers usually spend two years overseas and are paid only a basic local wage.

**peach** Small fruit tree (*Prunus persica*) native to China and grown throughout temperate areas. The lance-shaped leaves appear after the pink flowers in spring. The fruit has a thin, downy skin and white or yellow flesh, with a hard "pit" in the middle. It is eaten fresh or preserved. Height: to 20ft (6.5m). Family Rosaceae.

**Peacock, Thomas Love** (1785–1866) English writer of satirical poetry and romances. Peacock is remembered for his idiosyncratic satirical novels, which include *Headlong Hall* (1816), *Nightmare Abbey* (1818), *Crotchet Castle* (1831), and *Gryll Grange* (1860–61).

**peacock** (peafowl) Any of several species of birds of Asia and Africa. The male is called a peacock and the female a peahen; peacock has become the common name for both sexes. The male has a 60in (150cm) tail, which it can spread vertically as a semicircular fan with a pattern of eyelike shapes. The body of the male may be metallic blue, green, or bronze, depending on the species. Hens lack the tail and head ornaments and are brown, red, or green. In the wild, peafowl inhabit open, lowland forests, roosting in trees. Eggs are laid in a ground nest. Length of body: 30in (75cm). Family Phasianidae; genera *Pavo* and *Afropavo*.

**peafowl** *See* PEACOCK

**Peak District** Plateau area at the S end of the PENNINES, Derbyshire, central England. The Peak District National Park was established in 1951. The highest point is Kinder Scout, at 2,088ft (636m). Area: 542sq mi (1,404sq km).

**Peale, Charles Willson** (1741–1827) US painter, inventor, naturalist, and father of a family of artists. In 1782 he opened the first US art gallery, in Philadelphia, where he exhibited his own portraits. He later expanded the gallery into the country's first natural history museum. In 1795 he painted his most celebrated picture, *The Staircase Group*, a portrait of two of his sons.

**peanut** (groundnut) Annual leguminous plant *Arachis hypogaea* of the PEA family. Native to South America, it is now grown in temperate regions of the world; the major producers are China and India. In the 19th century, US scientist George Washington CARVER researched more than 300 uses for it. The seeds (peanuts) are a valuable source of protein and yield an oil used both in food and in industry. Family: Fabaceae Leguminosae

**pear** Tree and its edible fruit, native to N Asia and S Europe and grown throughout the world in temperate regions. The tree has white flowers and glossy, green leaves. The greenish-yellow, brownish, or reddish fruit, picked unripe and allowed to mature, is eaten fresh or preserved. Height: 50–75ft (15–23m). Family Rosaceae; species *Pyrus communis*.

**pearl** Hard, smooth, iridescent concretion of calcium carbonate produced by certain marine and freshwater bivalve MOLLUSKS. It is composed of nacre, or mother-of-pearl, which forms the inner layer of mollusk shells. A pearl results from an abnormal growth of nacre around foreign matter, such as a grain of sand.

**Pearl Harbor** US naval base in Hawaii. On December 7, 1941, the base, headquarters of the US Pacific fleet, was attacked by aircraft from a Japanese naval task force, which had approached within range of the islands unobserved. About 300 aircraft and 18 ships were destroyed or severely damaged, and about 2,400 people killed. The attack provoked US entry into WORLD WAR II.

**Pears, Sir Peter** (1910–86) British tenor. A lifelong friend of Benjamin BRITTEN, he created many roles in Britten's operas, including the title roles of *Peter Grimes* (1945) and *Albert Herring* (1949), and Aschenbach in *Death in Venice* (1973).

**Pearse, Patrick Henry** (1879–1916) Irish author and political figure. He headed the revival of interest in Gaelic culture, writing poems, short stories, and plays. He led the insurgents in the EASTER RISING (1916) and was court-martialed and executed by British authorities.

**Pearson, Lester Bowles** (1897–1972) Canadian statesman, prime minister (1963–68). He entered parliament in 1948. His work in settling the Suez Crisis earned

▲ **peanut** The peanut (*Arachis hypogaea*), is the second most important source of vegetable oil after soybeans.

▲ **pear** A fruit from a plant of the rose family, pears thrive in warmer temperate regions. In Canada, Australia, and South Africa a large proportion of the crop is canned, whereas in Europe and the US, canning is less significant.

P

▲ **pecan** Mottled brown shells of the pecan burst apart to release the ripe nut. The pecan, a relative of the walnut, grows on large trees that are found in warm temperate parts of North America. Pecans make excellent dessert nuts.

him the 1957 Nobel Peace Prize. He became leader of the Liberal Party in 1958.

**Peary, Robert Edwin** (1856–1920) US Arctic explorer. He made several expeditions to Greenland (1886–92) and in 1893 led the first of five expeditions toward the North Pole. He was the first person to reach the pole (April 1909).

**Peasants' Revolt** (1381) Rebellion in England. The immediate provocation was a POLL TAX (1380). Fundamental causes were resentment at feudal restrictions and wages held down artificially, despite the shortage of labor caused by the BLACK DEATH. Led by Wat TYLER, the men of Kent marched into London, where they were pacified by RICHARD II. Promises to grant their demands were broken after they dispersed.

**Peasants' War** (1524–25) Rebellion of German peasants, the largest popular uprising in European history. Sparked by anger over increasing dues demanded by the princes, there was widespread pillaging in the countryside of s Germany. The peasants hoped for and needed the support of Martin LUTHER, but he rejected their charter of liberties and their rebellion was harshly suppressed.

**peat** Dark brown or black mass of partly decomposed plant material. It forms in bogs and areas of high rainfall, and contains a high proportion of water. Its high carbon content makes it suitable for use as a fuel.

**peat moss** Decomposed organic matter (HUMUS) obtained from disintegrated sphagnum MOSS (bog moss). The most widely obtainable source of humus, it is dug into soil and added to compost to retain moisture. Its continuing use poses an ecological threat to peat bogs.

**pecan** North American nut tree that bears a nut resembling a small, smooth-shelled WALNUT. Valued for its flavor, it consists of 70% fat and is used in many desserts. Family Juglandaceae; species *Carya illinoiensis*.

**peccary** Omnivorous, piglike mammal native to the SW US and Central and South America. It has coarse, bristly hair. Collared peccaries, or javelinas (*Tayassu taja*), have dark-gray hair with a whitish collar. White-lipped peccaries (*Tayassu pecari*) have brown hair. Weight: 50– 66lb (23–30kg). Family Tayassuidae.

**Peck, (Eldred) Gregory** (1916– ) US film star. His many appearances include leading roles in *Keys of the Kingdom* (1944), *Spellbound* (1945), *The Gunfighter* (1950), *Moby Dick* (1956), *To Kill a Mockingbird* (1962, Academy Award for Best Actor), *McKenna's Gold* (1968), *The Omen* (1976), and *MacArthur* (1977). He starred in two versions of *Cape Fear* (1962 and 1991).

**Peckinpah, (David) Sam (Samuel)** (1926–84) US director who worked in television, directing *Gunsmoke* and *The Westerner* series, before turning his attentions to film. Since *The Wild Bunch* (1969), he has been associated with violent action films. His other films include *Straw Dogs* (1971), *The Getaway* (1973), and *Bring Me the Head of Alfredo Garcia* (1975).

**pectin** Water-soluble POLYSACCHARIDE found in the cell walls and intercellular tissue of certain ripe fruits or vegetables. When fruit is cooked, pectin yields a gel that is the basis of jellies and jams.

**pediatrics** Medical specialty devoted to the diagnosis and treatment of disease and injury in children.

**pediment** Low-pitched gable formed by the sloping eaves of a pitched roof and a horizontal cornice. The classic triangular pediment appeared in Greek temples such as the PARTHENON. Later architects developed more extravagant forms, featuring curved, broken, and inverted styles over doors and windows.

**Pedro I** (1798–1834) Emperor of Brazil (1822–31). Son of the future JOHN VI of Portugal, he fled with the rest of the royal family to Brazil in 1807. When his father reclaimed the Portuguese Crown (1821), he became prince regent of Brazil and declared it an independent monarchy (1822). His reign was marked by military failure against Argentina (1825–28), and revolt in Rio de Janeiro (1831). He abdicated and returned to Portugal, where he secured the succession of his daughter, Maria II, to the Portuguese throne.

**Pedro II** (1825–91) Emperor of Brazil (1831–89). He reigned under a regency until 1840. His reign was marked by internal unrest and external threats from Argentina and Paraguay. Slavery was abolished in 1888, and Pedro's policy was generally reformist, antagonizing the military and the rich planters. He was forced to resign in 1889, retiring to Europe, while Brazil became a republic.

**Peel, Sir Robert** (1788–1850) British statesman, one of the founders of the CONSERVATIVE PARTY. As TORY PARTY home secretary, he created the first modern police force, the Metropolitan (London) Police, in 1829. He was chiefly responsible for passage of the CATHOLIC EMANCIPATION Act (1829), and was prime minister in 1834–35 and 1841–46. Peel became converted to the doctrine of FREE TRADE, and the Irish FAMINE convinced him of the need to repeal the CORN LAWS. The proposal split the Party, and he resigned (1845). He returned to power and carried through the repeal.

**peerage** British nobility holding any of the following titles: baron, viscount, earl, marquess, or duke. Although all titles were originally hereditary, these are now rare, and nonhereditary life peerages are more usually granted. Peers constitute the Lords Temporal section of the HOUSE OF LORDS, having the right to sit in the House and vote.

**peer group** Term used in SOCIOLOGY to mean a group whose members share certain characteristics. A peer group may be defined on the basis of income, mental ability, education, social status, occupation, age, or any other such category.

**Pegasus** (Winged Horse) Northern constellation between Andromeda and Cygnus. Three of its bright stars form the Giant Square in Pegasus with Alpha Andromedae; the brightest is Epsilon, with a magnitude of 2.30.

**Pegasus** In Greek mythology, winged horse. Born out of the blood of MEDUSA, it was tamed by BELLEROPHON and helped him in his battles. Later, it carried the thunderbolts of ZEUS.

**Pei, Ieoh Ming** (1917– ) US architect, b. China. Important buildings include the National Airlines Terminal at Kennedy International Airport, New York (1971), the East Building to the National Gallery of Art, Washington, D.C. (1978), and the John F. Kennedy Library, Boston (1979). He designed the pyramid in front of the Louvre, Paris (1989).

**Peirce, Charles Sanders** (1839–1914) US scientist, philosopher, and logician, a leading exponent of PRAGMATISM. He explained it in a series of six articles published between 1877 and 1878. He also helped to develop SEMIOTICS, the study of the use of signs and symbols.

**Peking** *See* BEIJING

**Pelagius** Monk and theologian, probably born in Britain, who preached the heresy of Pelagianism. In *c.*380 he went to Rome and became the spiritual guide of many clerics and lay persons. After 410 he preached in Africa, where his ideas were denounced by St. AUGUSTINE OF HIPPO, and later in Palestine. He maintained that man is master of his own salvation and denounced the idea of original sin. He was excommunicated by Pope Innocent I in 417.

**Pelé** (1940– ) (Edson Arantes do Nascimento) Brazilian soccer player. He led Brazil to three World Cup victories (1958, 1962, and 1970). Apart from 1975–77, when he played for the New York Cosmos, all his club games were played for Santos. He scored 1,281 goals.

**pelican** Any of several species of stout-bodied inland water birds, with a characteristic distensible pouch under its bill for scooping up fish from shallow water. It is generally white or brown and has a long hooked bill, long wings, short thick legs, and webbed feet. Length: to 6ft (1.8m). Family Pelecanidae; genus *Pelecanus*.

**pellagra** Disease caused by a deficiency of nicotinic acid, one of the B group of vitamins. Its symptoms are lesions of the skin and mucous membranes, diarrhea, and mental disturbance.

**Peloponnesian Wars** (431–404 BC) Conflict in ancient Greece between ATHENS and SPARTA. The underlying cause was Sparta's fear of Athenian hegemony, while Athenian hostility toward CORINTH, Sparta's chief ally, provoked the Spartan declaration of war. Having a stronger army, Sparta regularly invaded Attica, while Athens, under PERICLES, relied on its navy. The Peace of Nicias (420 BC) proved temporary. Neither side kept to the agreement, and in 415 BC Athens launched a disastrous attack on Syracuse, which

▲ **Peel** The Conservative politician Sir Robert Peel was known for his opposition to the Reform Act and the Corn Laws. He is perhaps best known for the establishment of the London police force (1828), hence the nickname Peelers or Bobbies.

P

encouraged Sparta to renew the war. With Persian help, Sparta built up a navy which, under LYSANDER, defeated Athens in 405 BC. Besieged and blockaded, Athens surrendered.

**Peloponnesos** (Pelopónnisos) Peninsula in S Greece, connected to the mainland by the Isthmus of CORINTH. The chief cities are Patras, Corinth, Pirgos, and SPARTA. A mountainous region, it also included the ancient cities of Argos and Megalopolis. The peninsula was involved in the Persian Wars (500–449 BC), and it was the site of many battles between Sparta and Athens during the PELOPONNESIAN WARS (431–404 BC). In 146 BC the region fell to the Romans. Held by the Venetians from 1699 to 1718, then by the Ottoman Turks, the peninsula passed to Greece after independence. Industries: silk, fish, manganese, chromium, fruits, tourism. Area: 8,400sq mi (21,800sq km). Pop. (1991) 1,077,002.

**pelota** Generic name given to a range of games in which a small, hard ball is hit with gloved or bare hand or with a scoop-shaped wicker racket known as a *cesta*. Enjoyed mostly in the Basque regions of Spain and France, and in South America, pelota games can be played across a net or against a wall in a two- or three-sided court known as a *fronto*. JAI ALAI, the fastest of all pelota games, is played by professionals.

**Peltier effect** Phenomenon of the temperature changes at a junction where an electric current passes from one kind of metal to another. When a current passes through a thermocouple (thermometer), the temperature at one junction increases while that at the other decreases. The effect was discovered in 1834 by the French physicist Jean Charles Peltier. It is the opposite of the SEEBECK EFFECT. *See also* THERMOELECTRICITY

**pelvis** Dish-shaped bony structure that supports the internal organs of the lower abdomen in vertebrates.

**penal colony** Settlement to which convicted criminals were transported for imprisonment and hard labor. British convicts were sent to North America until the AMERICAN REVOLUTION, then to Australia until the mid-19th century. French convicts were transported to New Caledonia and French Guiana. Political prisoners in the Soviet Union were transported to camps in Siberia.

**penance** Carrying out of a specified act as a mark of sincere regret following the commission of a sin or sins. The most common penance, prescribed by a priest after ABSOLUTION, is to say a prayer at a special time.

**Penang** (Pinang) Island of MALAYSIA, off the NW coast of the Malay Peninsula, which (together with a coastal strip on the mainland) comprises a state of Malaysia; the capital is Penang. The island was Britain's first possession in Malaya (1786). In 1826 it united with Singapore and MALACCA, and in 1867 the group became the Straits Settlements colony. Penang joined the Federation of Malaya in 1948. Its products include rice, rubber, and tin. The city of Penang is the principal port of Malaysia. Area: 400sq mi (1,000sq km). Pop. (1993 est.) 1,141,500.

**penates** Ancient Roman gods of the household, worshiped at home with the lares (spirits of ancestors). Originally penates were the spirits of the storeroom.

**Penderecki, Krzysztof** (1933– ) Polish composer. His reputation began in 1960 with his *Threnody for the Victims of Hiroshima* for string orchestra. Other pieces include a *Passion According to St. Luke* (1963–65), operas, and two symphonies (1973 and 1980).

**pendulum** Any object suspended at a point so it swings in an arc. A simple pendulum consists of a small heavy mass attached to a string or light rigid rod. A compound pendulum has a supporting rod whose mass is not negligible. The pendulum was first used to regulate clocks in 1673 by Christiaan HUYGENS. Foucault's pendulum, devised by Jean FOUCAULT, swings in all directions and was used to demonstrate the Earth's rotation.

**Penelope** In Greek mythology, wife of ODYSSEUS. As described in HOMER's *Odyssey*, she had been married for only a year when her husband left for ten years of war and ten of wandering. She remained faithful, putting off her many suitors with the promise that she would choose one when her weaving was done. By day she wove and by night she undid her work.

**penguin** Flightless sea bird that lives in the Southern Hemisphere and ranges from the Antarctic northward to the Galápagos Islands. Their wings have been adapted to flippers and their webbed feet help to propel their sleek bodies through the water. Although they are awkward on land, they are fast and powerful swimmers, easily able to catch the fish and squid that they feed on. Height: to 4ft (1.2m). Family Spheniscidae.

**penicillin** ANTIBIOTIC agent derived from molds of the genus *Penicillium*. The first antibiotic discovered (by Sir Alexander FLEMING in 1928), it can be produced synthetically. It can produce allergic reactions, and some microorganisms have become resistant.

**Peninsular Campaign** (April–July 1862) Series of battles in the CIVIL WAR resulting from the attempt by Union forces under George MCCLELLAN to take Richmond, Virginia, by advancing up the peninsula between the York and James rivers. The Confederates, under Joseph JOHNSTON and later General Robert E. LEE, checked the advance.

**Peninsular War** (1808–14) Campaign of the NAPOLEONIC WARS in Portugal and Spain. A British force commanded by the future Duke of WELLINGTON supported Portuguese and Spanish rebels against the French. Wellington's forces gradually drove the French out of the Iberian peninsula and, after the victory of Vitoria (1813), invaded S France. Napoleon's abdication (1814) brought the campaign to an end.

**penis** Male reproductive organ. It contains the URETHRA, the channel through which URINE and SEMEN pass to the exterior, and erectile tissue that, when engorged with blood, causes the penis to become erect.

**Penn, William** (1644–1718) English QUAKER leader and chief founder of what later became the US state of PENNSYLVANIA. Because of his advocacy of religious freedom, he was imprisoned four times. He persuaded King CHARLES II to honor an unpaid debt by granting him wilderness land in America to be settled by the Quakers and others seeking refuge from religious persecution. The colony was named the Commonwealth of Pennsylvania in his honor.

**Pennines** Range of hills in N England, extending from the Tyne Gap and Eden Valley on the border with Scotland to the valley of the Trent River. The hills are a series of highland blocks dissected by rivers such as the Tees and Ribble. The rearing of sheep is the chief occupation. The highest peak is Cross Fell, rising to 2,930ft (893m). Length: *c.*160mi (260km).

**Pennsylvania** State in E US; one of the Middle Atlantic states; the capital is HARRISBURG. The chief cities are PHILADELPHIA, PITTSBURGH, and Scranton. Swedish and Dutch settlements were made along the DELAWARE River in the mid-17th century. By 1664 the area was controlled by the English, and William PENN received a charter from Charles II in 1681 for what is now Pennsylvania. It was one of the 13 original states of the Union. The DECLARATION OF INDEPENDENCE was signed and the US Constitution was ratified in Philadelphia, the national capital from 1790 to 1800. The Union victory at the Battle of GETTYSBURG in July 1863 was a turning point in the CIVIL WAR. Apart from small low-lying areas in the NW and SE, the state is composed of a series of mountain ridges and rolling hills. Farming is concentrated in the SE; the principal crops are cereals, tobacco, potatoes, and fruit, and dairy products are important. Pennsylvania has rich deposits of coal and iron ore. The state has long been a leading producer of steel, which today accounts for about a quarter of the nation's output. Industries: chemicals, cement, electrical machinery, metal goods. Area: 45,333sq mi (117,412sq km). Pop. (1990) 11,881,643.

**Pennsylvanian Period** In the US, name given to the later part of the CARBONIFEROUS period.

**pension** Money paid regularly to a retired person. Pension plans may be funded by the government, such as social security, or by companies; both plans involve regular financial contributions by the individual for a qualifying period.

**Pentagon** Headquarters of the US Department of Defense, in Arlington, Virginia. The complex is made up of five concentric buildings in pentagonal form and covers 34 acres (14ha). It was completed in 1943. The Pentagon has come to signify the US military establishment.

▲ **pelican** The brown pelican (*Pelecanus occidentalis*) has a large bill with a distensible pouch that it uses to catch the fish on which it feeds. It lives on the coasts of tropical and subtropical America.

**PENNSYLVANIA**
**Statehood :**
December 12, 1787
**Nickname :**
The Keystone State
**State bird :**
Ruffed grouse
**State flower :**
Mountain laurel
**State tree :**
Hemlock
**State motto :**
Virtue, liberty, and independence

▲ **penguin** The royal penguin (*Eudyptes schlegeli*), like many other species of penguin, is a highly social bird. During the breeding season colonies of up to 2 million royal penguins amass on Macquarie Island, SW of New Zealand.

▲ **pepper** Green peppers are used to flavor food. The strong flavor of some varieties of pepper is due to the presence of capsaicin which is found in the walls of the fruit.

**pentagon** Five-sided plane figure. Its interior angles add up to 540°. For a regular pentagon (whose sides and interior angles are equal), each interior angle is 108°.

**Pentateuch** (Gk. Five scrolls) First five books of the Bible, traditionally attributed to MOSES and in JUDAISM referred to collectively as the *Torah*, or Law. The Pentateuch comprises the five OLD TESTAMENT books of GENESIS, EXODUS, LEVITICUS, NUMBERS, and DEUTERONOMY. Composed over a very long period (possibly 1,000 years or more), they were probably collected in their present form during the BABYLONIAN CAPTIVITY of the Jews.

**pentathlon** Athletic competition that originated in ancient Greece and consisting of five events. The modern pentathlon is an Olympic sport. Based on military training, it consists of cross-country running, cross-country riding, swimming, epée fencing, and pistol-shooting.

**Pentecost** Important religious festival celebrated in May or June. In Judaism, it is a festival held seven weeks after the second day of the PASSOVER, commemorating the giving of the Law to MOSES. In the Christian calendar it is also known as Whitsunday, falling seven weeks after Easter.

**Pentecostal Churches** Fellowship of revivalist Christian sects, inspired by the belief that all Christians should seek to be baptized with the Holy Spirit and experience events such as speaking in tongues. Pentecostalists believe in the literal truth of the Bible, and many abstain from alcohol and tobacco and disapprove of dancing, theater, and other such pleasures. The Pentecostal movement began in the US at Topeka, Kansas, in 1901. It became organized in Los Angeles in 1906 and spread rapidly to other countries. The Pentecostal Churches now have a collective world membership of *c.*10 million.

**Penzias, Arno Allan** (1933– ) US astrophysicist, b. Germany, who with Robert Wilson discovered the cosmic background radiation, which scientists agree supports the BIG BANG theory. They shared the 1978 Nobel Prize for physics with Russian physicist Peter Kapitza.

**peony** Perennial plant native to North America and Eurasia. It has glossy, divided leaves and large white, pink, or red flowers, and is frequently cultivated in gardens. Height: to 3ft (0.9m). Tree peonies grow in hot, dry areas and have brilliant blossoms of many colors. Height: to 6ft (1.8m). Family Paeoniaceae; genus *Paeonia*.

**Pepin III (the Short)** (*c.*714–68) First CAROLINGIAN king of the Franks (750–68). He and his brother Carloman inherited the office of "mayor of the palace" (de facto ruler) in 741. In 747 Carloman entered a monastery and in 750 Pepin deposed the last Merovingian king, Childeric III, and was anointed king of the Franks. He defeated the LOMBARDS in 754 and 756. He ceded the conquered territories (the future PAPAL STATES) to the papacy in what was known as the Donation of Pepin. Pepin was the father of CHARLEMAGNE.

**pepper** (capsicum) Perennial woody shrub native to tropical America. The fruit is a many-seeded, pungent berry whose size depends on the species. Included are bell, red, cayenne, and CHILI peppers. They all belong to the NIGHTSHADE family, Solanaceae; genus *Capsicum*.

**peppermint** Common name for *Mentha piperita*, a perennial herb of the MINT family (Lamiaceae/Labiatae) cultivated for its ESSENTIAL OIL, which is distilled and used in medicine and as a flavoring.

**pepsin** Digestive ENZYME secreted by GLANDS of the STOMACH wall as part of the GASTRIC JUICE. In the presence of hydrochloric acid it catalyzes the splitting of PROTEINS in food into polypeptides.

**peptide** Molecule consisting of two or more linked AMINO ACID molecules. Peptides containing several amino acids are called polypeptides. PROTEINS consist of polypeptide chains with up to several hundred amino acids cross-linked to each other in various ways.

**Pepys, Samuel** (1633–1703) English diarist. His *Diary* (1660–69) describes his private life and the English society of his time. It includes a vivid account of the RESTORATION, the PLAGUE, and the Great FIRE OF LONDON (1666). It was not published until 1815, and not in complete form until 1983.

**Pequot** Tribe of Algonquian-speaking Native North Americans who once lived in the Thames River valley region of Connecticut. They were almost entirely wiped out in the PEQUOT WAR. In the mid-1990s there were only about 500 people of Pequot ancestry.

**Pequot War** (1637) Conflict between the PEQUOTS and the Connecticut colonists. Reacting to an attack that killed 30 white settlers, the colonists destroyed the Pequot tribe. Captain John Mason killed over 600 Native American men, women, and children in a battle on the Mystic River. Survivors became slaves in the West Indies or to the Mohawk and Mohegan tribes.

**percentage** Quantity expressed as the number of parts in 100 (considered to be a whole). Fractions can be expressed as a percentage by multiplying by 100, for example, 3/4 becomes 75%.

**perception** Process by which the brain acquires and organizes incoming stimuli from the sensory nerves, translating them into meaningful information.

**perch** Freshwater food fish found in Europe and the US E of the Rocky Mountains. The North American yellow perch (*Perca flavescens*) is gold-colored with black side-bars. Weight: 2.2–6lb (1.0–2.7kg). Family Percidae.

**percussion** Term for any of several musical instruments that produce sound when struck. They are divided into two groups: ideophones, in which the whole object vibrates (such as CYMBALS, gongs, and XYLOPHONES); and membranophones, in which a stretched skin or membrane vibrates (this group includes all DRUMS).

**Percy, Sir Henry** (1364–1403) English nobleman, known as "Hotspur" for his zeal in guarding the Scottish-English border. Son of the Earl of Northumberland, he supported the deposition of RICHARD II in 1299, but later quarreled with the new king, HENRY IV. In 1403 he and his father, in alliance with Owain GLYN DŴR, launched a rebellion. They were defeated at Shrewsbury, where Percy was killed.

**peregrine falcon** Crow-sized, gray, black, and white BIRD OF PREY. It inhabits craggy open country or rocky coastlines and marshes or estuaries. The largest breeding FALCON in Britain, it flies swiftly with prolonged glides. Length: to 19in (48cm). Family Falconidae; species *Falco peregrinus*.

**perennial** Plant with a life cycle of more than two years. It is a common term for flowering herbaceous and woody plants. They include the LILY, DAISY, and IRIS, and all TREES. *See also* ANNUAL; BIENNIAL

**Peres, Shimon** (1923– ) Israeli statesman, b. Poland. He was one of the founders of the Labor Party (1968), becoming its leader in 1977. Peres was prime minister (1986–88)

## PERISTALSIS

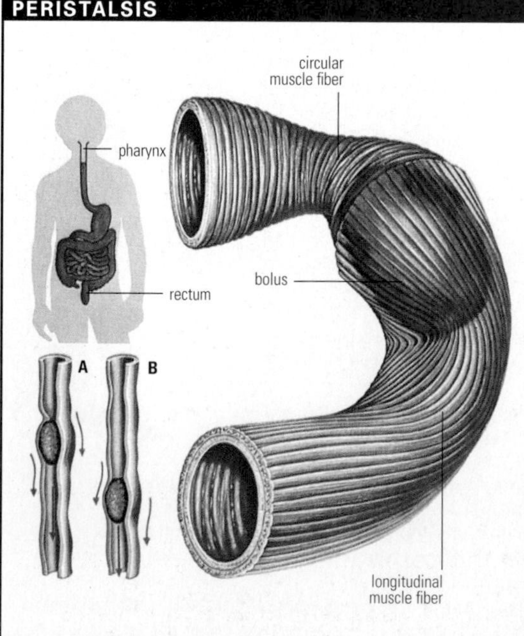


The digestive tract can be regarded as a long muscular tube extending from the pharynx to the rectum. The walls of the tube bear an inner, circular muscle fiber coat and an outer, longitudinal muscle fiber coat. As the ball of food (bolus) formed in the mouth enters the pharynx, a reflex action is initiated. The produces slow, wavelike contractions of the walls of the esophagus and later along the whole length of the tract. These peristaltic waves involve the contraction of the circular muscle fibers behind the bolus (A) and their relaxation in front of the bolus. Longitudinal muscles provide the wavelike action. The two functions together push the ball down the tract (B). The whole process of peristalsis is an involuntary response.

P

in the Labor-Likud coalition. In 1992, losing the party leadership to Rabin, he played an important part in the Palestine peace process. On Rabin's assassination (1995), he succeeded him as prime minister but lost the election of 1996 to Benjamin NETANYAHU.

**perestroika** (Rus. reconstruction) Adopted by Soviet prime minister, Mikhail GORBACHEV in 1986, *perestroika* was linked with GLASNOST. The restructuring included reform of government and the bureaucracy, decentralization, and abolition of the Communist Party monopoly. Liberalization of the economic system included the introduction of limited private enterprise.

**Pérez de Cuéllar, Javier** (1920– ) Peruvian diplomat, fifth secretary-general of the United Nations (1982–91). The initial crisis of the Falklands War (1982) was soon forgotten, and his two terms as secretary-general are considered highly successful.

**performance art** Events that take place before an audience, but which defy the traditional definitions of DRAMA and MUSIC. Arguably originating in the US in the 1960s, performance art is often visually oriented.

**perfume** Substance that produces a pleasing fragrance. The scents of such plants as rose, citrus, lavender, and sandalwood are obtained from their ESSENTIAL OILS. These are blended with a fixative of animal origin, such as musk, ambergris, or civet. Liquid perfumes are usually alcoholic solutions containing 10–25% of the perfume concentrate; colognes and toilet waters contain about 2–6% of the concentrate.

**Pergamum** Ancient city-state on the site of modern BERGAMA, W Turkey. It was founded by Greek colonists under license from the Persian emperors in the 4th century BC. At its peak in the 3rd–2nd centuries BC, it controlled much of W Asia Minor. In 133 BC it was bequeathed to Rome by Attalus III.

**Pergolesi, Giovanni Battista** (1710–36) Italian composer. His intermezzo *La Serva Padrona* (1733), became a model for Italian OPERA BUFFA. His *Stabat Mater* (1730) is one of the finest examples of Baroque religious music.

**Peri, Jacopo** (1561–1633) Italian composer. His musical drama *Dafne* (1597) is generally regarded as the first opera.

**perianth** Outer region of a flower. The perianth includes all the structures surrounding the reproductive organs and usually consists of an outer whorl of sepals (calyx) and an inner whorl of petals (corolla).

**pericarp** In seed plants, the wall of a ripened fruit that is derived from the ovary wall.

**Pericles** (490–429 BC) Athenian statesman. He dominated Athens from *c.*460 BC to his death, overseeing its golden age. He is associated with achievements in art and literature, including the building of the PARTHENON, while strengthening the Athenian empire and government. He initiated the PELOPONNESIAN WARS (431–404 BC) but died of plague at the outset.

**peridot** Gem variety of transparent green OLIVINE, a silicate mineral. Large crystals are found on St. John's Island in the Red Sea and in Burma.

**peridotite** Heavy IGNEOUS ROCK of coarse texture composed of olivine and pyroxene with small flecks of mica or hornblende. It alters readily into SERPENTINE.

**perigee** Point in the orbit about the Earth of the Moon, or of an artificial satellite, at which the body is nearest to the Earth.

**perihelion** Point in the orbit of a planet, asteroid, comet, or other body (such as a spacecraft) moving around the Sun at which the body is nearest the Sun.

**periodic table** Arrangement of the chemical elements in order of their ATOMIC NUMBERS in accordance with the periodic law first stated by the Russian chemist Dmitri MENDELEYEV in 1869. In the modern form of the table, the elements are arranged into 18 vertical columns and seven horizontal periods. The vertical columns containing groups are numbered I to VII (sometimes called IA to VIIA) with a final column numbered 0. The metallic TRANSITION ELEMENTS are arranged in the middle of the table between groups II and III. ALKALI METALS are in Group I and ALKALINE-EARTH METALS in Group II. Metalloids and nonmetals are found from groups III to VII, with the HALOGENS in Group VII and the NOBLE GASES (inert gases) collected into group 0. The elements in each group have the same number of VALENCE electrons and accordingly have similar chemical properties. Elements in the same horizontal period have the same number of electron shells.

**peripheral nervous system** All parts of the nervous system that lie outside the CENTRAL NERVOUS SYSTEM (brain and spinal cord). It comprises the 12 pairs of cranial nerves, which principally serve the head and neck region, and 31 pairs of spinal nerves with their fibers extending to the farthermost parts of the body.

**periscope** Optical instrument consisting of a series of mirrors or prisms that allows a person to view the surroundings from a concealed position by changing the direction of the observer's line of sight. It is most commonly associated with SUBMARINES.

▲ **Peres** One of the founders of the Israeli Labor Party and prime minister of Israel (1986–88), Shimon Peres left his post as foreign minister to become prime minister after the assassination of Yitzhak Rabin in 1995.

▼ **periodic table** The periodic table arranges chemical elements according to their atomic number. The vertical columns, called groups, contain elements with similar chemical properties. The horizontal rows, called periods, are arranged in order of increasing atomic number and all elements in a row have the same number of electron shells. Elements colored green in the table are nonmetals; those colored orange are metals; those colored yellow are metalloid; those colored blue, purple, or pink are transition metals; the purple ones are the rare-earth elements; and the pink ones the transactinide elements.

## PERIODIC TABLE

KEY: atomic number — 43; atomic symbol — **Tc**; name of element — Technetium; relative atomic mass — [97] (most stable isotope in brackets)

| GROUP I | II | | | | | | | | | | | III | IV | V | VI | VII | 0 |
|---|---|---|---|---|---|---|---|---|---|---|---|---|---|---|---|---|---|
| 1<br>**H**<br>Hydrogen<br>1.00794 | | | | | | | | | | | | | | | | | 2<br>**He**<br>Helium<br>4.0026 |
| 3<br>**Li**<br>Lithium<br>6.941 | 4<br>**Be**<br>Beryllium<br>9.0122 | | | | | | | | | | | 5<br>**B**<br>Boron<br>10.81 | 6<br>**C**<br>Carbon<br>12.011 | 7<br>**N**<br>Nitrogen<br>14.0067 | 8<br>**O**<br>Oxygen<br>15.9994 | 9<br>**F**<br>Fluorine<br>18.998 | 10<br>**Ne**<br>Neon<br>20.179 |
| 11<br>**Na**<br>Sodium<br>22.9898 | 12<br>**Mg**<br>Magnesium<br>24.305 | | | | | | | | | | | 13<br>**Al**<br>Aluminium<br>26.9815 | 14<br>**Si**<br>Silicon<br>28.086 | 15<br>**P**<br>Phosphorus<br>30.9738 | 16<br>**S**<br>Sulphur<br>32.06 | 17<br>**Cl**<br>Chlorine<br>35.453 | 18<br>**Ar**<br>Argon<br>39.948 |
| 19<br>**K**<br>Potassium<br>39.098 | 20<br>**Ca**<br>Calcium<br>40.06 | 21<br>**Sc**<br>Scandium<br>44.956 | 22<br>**Ti**<br>Titanium<br>47.90 | 23<br>**V**<br>Vanadium<br>50.941 | 24<br>**Cr**<br>Chromium<br>51.996 | 25<br>**Mn**<br>Manganese<br>54.9380 | 26<br>**Fe**<br>Iron<br>55.847 | 27<br>**Co**<br>Cobalt<br>58.9332 | 28<br>**Ni**<br>Nickel<br>58.70 | 29<br>**Cu**<br>Copper<br>63.546 | 30<br>**Zn**<br>Zinc<br>65.38 | 31<br>**Ga**<br>Gallium<br>69.72 | 32<br>**Ge**<br>Germanium<br>72.59 | 33<br>**As**<br>Arsenic<br>74.9216 | 34<br>**Se**<br>Selenium<br>78.96 | 35<br>**Br**<br>Bromine<br>79.904 | 36<br>**Kr**<br>Krypton<br>83.80 |
| 37<br>**Rb**<br>Rubidium<br>85.4678 | 38<br>**Sr**<br>Strontium<br>87.62 | 39<br>**Y**<br>Yttrium<br>88.906 | 40<br>**Zr**<br>Zirconium<br>91.22 | 41<br>**Nb**<br>Niobium<br>92.906 | 42<br>**Mo**<br>Molybdenum<br>95.94 | 43<br>**Tc**<br>Technetium<br>[97] | 44<br>**Ru**<br>Ruthenium<br>101.07 | 45<br>**Rh**<br>Rhodium<br>102.905 | 46<br>**Pd**<br>Palladium<br>106.4 | 47<br>**Ag**<br>Silver<br>107.868 | 48<br>**Cd**<br>Cadmium<br>112.40 | 49<br>**In**<br>Indium<br>114.82 | 50<br>**Sn**<br>Tin<br>118.69 | 51<br>**Sb**<br>Antimony<br>121.75 | 52<br>**Te**<br>Tellurium<br>127.75 | 53<br>**I**<br>Iodine<br>126.9045 | 54<br>**Xe**<br>Xenon<br>131.30 |
| 55<br>**Cs**<br>Caesium<br>132.905 | 56<br>**Ba**<br>Barium<br>137.34 | 57–71<br>Lanthanide Series | 72<br>**Hf**<br>Hafnium<br>178.49 | 73<br>**Ta**<br>Tantalum<br>180.948 | 74<br>**W**<br>Tungsten<br>183.85 | 75<br>**Re**<br>Rhenium<br>186.207 | 76<br>**Os**<br>Osmium<br>190.2 | 77<br>**Ir**<br>Iridium<br>192.22 | 78<br>**Pt**<br>Platinum<br>195.09 | 79<br>**Au**<br>Gold<br>196.9665 | 80<br>**Hg**<br>Mercury<br>200.59 | 81<br>**Tl**<br>Thallium<br>204.37 | 82<br>**Pb**<br>Lead<br>207.2 | 83<br>**Bi**<br>Bismuth<br>208.98 | 84<br>**Po**<br>Polonium<br>[209] | 85<br>**At**<br>Astatine<br>[210] | 86<br>**Rn**<br>Radon<br>[222] |
| 87<br>**Fr**<br>Francium<br>[223] | 88<br>**Ra**<br>Radium<br>[226] | 89–103<br>Actinide Series | 104<br>**Db**<br>Dubnium<br>[261] | 105<br>**Hn**§<br>Hahnium<br>[262] | 106<br>**Rf**<br>Rutherfordium<br>[263] | 107<br>**Uns**<br>Unnilseptium<br>[262] | 108<br>**Uno**<br>Unniloctium<br>[265] | 109<br>**Une**<br>Unnilenium<br>[266] | | | | | | | | | |
| LANTHANIDE SERIES (rare earth elements) | | 57<br>**La**<br>Lanthanum<br>138.9055 | 58<br>**Ce**<br>Cerium<br>140.12 | 59<br>**Pr**<br>Praeseodymium<br>140.9077 | 60<br>**Nd**<br>Neodymium<br>144.24 | 61<br>**Pm**<br>Promethium<br>[145] | 62<br>**Sm**<br>Samarium<br>150.36 | 63<br>**Eu**<br>Europium<br>151.96 | 64<br>**Gd**<br>Gadolinium<br>157.25 | 65<br>**Tb**<br>Terbium<br>158.9254 | 66<br>**Dy**<br>Dysprosium<br>162.50 | 67<br>**Ho**<br>Holmium<br>164.9308 | 68<br>**Er**<br>Erbium<br>167.26 | 69<br>**Tm**<br>Thulium<br>168.9342 | 70<br>**Yb**<br>Ytterbium<br>173.04 | 71<br>**Lu**<br>Lutetium<br>174.97 | |
| ACTINIDE SERIES (radioactive rare earth elements) | | 89<br>**Ac**<br>Actinium<br>[227] | 90<br>**Th**<br>Thorium<br>[illegible] | 91<br>**Pa**<br>Protactinium<br>[illegible] | 92<br>**U**<br>Uranium<br>238.029 | 93<br>**Np**<br>Neptunium<br>237.0482 | 94<br>**Pu**<br>Plutonium<br>[244] | 95<br>**Am**<br>Americium<br>[243] | 96<br>**Cm**<br>Curium<br>[247] | 97<br>**Bk**<br>Berkelium<br>[247] | 98<br>**Cf**<br>Californium<br>[251] | 99<br>**Es**<br>Einsteinium<br>[254] | 100<br>**Fm**<br>Fermium<br>[257] | 101<br>**Md**<br>Mendelevium<br>[256] | 102<br>**No**<br>Nobelium<br>[254] | 103<br>**Lr**<br>Lawrencium<br>[256] | |

§Another proposed name is unnilpentium

**peristalsis** Series of wavelike movements that propel food through the gut or digestive tract. It is caused by contractions of the smooth INVOLUNTARY MUSCLE of the gut wall.

**peritoneum** Strong membrane of CONNECTIVE TISSUE that lines the body's abdominal wall and covers the abdominal organs. *See also* PERITONITIS

**peritonitis** Inflammation of the PERITONEUM. It may be caused by bacterial infection or chemical irritation or it may arise spontaneously in certain diseases. Symptoms include fever, abdominal pain, distension, and shock. Treatment is directed at the underlying cause.

**periwinkle** Any of several species of trailing or erect evergreen plants that are cultivated as ground cover and for hanging baskets. Family Apocynaceae.

**periwinkle** (winkle) Any of several marine snails, gastropod mollusks that live in clusters along marine shores. A herbivore, it nestles in cracks among rocks. Many are edible. Length: to lin (2.5cm). Family Littorinidea; genus *Littorina*.

**perjury** Act of deliberately bearing false witness under oath or under affirmation in administrative or legislative proceedings. Perjury is a crime that may be punished by fine or imprisonment. Inducing another person to commit perjury is known as **subornation of perjury**; it is also a crime.

**Perkins, Frances** (1882–1965) US social worker and political figure. As governor of New York, Franklin D. ROOSEVELT named her state industrial commissioner (1929). When Roosevelt was elected president, he gave Perkins the responsibility for implementing the NEW DEAL labor legislation. As secretary of labor (1933–45), she was the first woman to be a US cabinet member.

**permafrost** Land that is permanently frozen, often to a considerable depth. The top few inches generally thaw in the summer, but the meltwater is not able to sink into the ground because of the frozen subsoil. *See also* TUNDRA

**Permian** Geological period of the PALEOZOIC era lasting from 286 to 248 million years ago. There was widespread geologic uplift and periods of glaciation in the southern continents. Many groups of marine invertebrate animals became extinct during the period.

**Perón, Eva Duarte de** (1919–52) Argentine political leader, first wife of Juan PERÓN. Known as "Evita," she administered Argentina's social welfare agencies and was the country's chief labor mediator. Eva's popularity contributed to the longevity of the Peronist regime.

**Perón, Juan Domingo** (1895–1974) Argentine statesman, president (1946–55, 1973–74). An army officer, he became the leading figure in the military junta (1943–46). Perón cultivated the trade unions and earned support from the poor by social reforms, greatly assisted by his wife, "Evita" PERÓN. He won the presidential election (1946) and was reelected in 1952. Changing economic circumstances and the death of his wife reduced Perón's popularity and he was overthrown in 1955. He retired to Spain, but returned to regain the presidency in 1973.

**Perot, (Henry) Ross** (1930– ) US businessman. A self-made billionaire, he was known for his antibureaucratic activism. In 1992 Perot's unsuccessful bid for the US presidency as a third-party candidate gained national attention as he mobilized a significant movement against the "gross inefficiencies" of American government.

**perpendicular style** Final period of English Gothic architecture, from *c*.1330 to the mid-16th century. Named for the strong vertical lines of its window tracery and paneling, it had fan vaulting and flattened arches.

**perpetual motion** Hypothetical machine that continues to work without any energy being supplied. It would require either the complete elimination of FRICTION, or would violate the laws of THERMODYNAMICS.

**Perry, Fred (Frederick John)** (1909–95) English table tennis and tennis player. World table tennis champion in 1929, Perry won three successive Wimbledon tennis singles titles (1934–36). He also won the US, French, and Australian titles.

**Perry, Matthew Calbraith** (1794–1858) US naval officer. In 1837 he commanded the first steam vessel in the US Navy, the *Fulton*. Perry also organized the first naval engineer corps. He was responsible for opening up Japan to the West (1853–54).

**Perry, Oliver Hazard** (1785–1819) US naval officer, brother of Matthew PERRY, he served in the Tripoli campaign (1801–05). In the WAR OF 1812, he built and manned a fleet in Lake Erie. In September 1813, his victory over the British fleet near Put-In-Bay, Ohio, gave the US control of the lake. His message after the battle, "We have met the enemy and they are ours," is often quoted.

**Perry, William** (1927– ) US statesman, secretary of defense (1994–96). Perry served in the US Army Corps of Engineers (1946–47) in Japan. After employment in high-technology industries, Perry joined the Department of Defense in 1977. He was deputy secretary of defense (1993–94) before becoming secretary of defense.

**Persephone** In Greek mythology, goddess of spring. She was the daughter of ZEUS and the Earth goddess DEMETER. When Persephone was abducted by HADES, famine spread over the Earth. To prevent catastrophe, Zeus commanded Hades to release her. He did so, and thus, each year, spring returns to the Earth. Persephone was known as Proserpine to the Romans.

**Persepolis** City of ancient Persia (Iran), *c*.35mi (60km) NE of SHIRAZ. It was the capital (539–330 BC) of the ACHAEMENID empire, and was renowned for its splendor. It was destroyed by the forces of ALEXANDER THE GREAT in 330 BC.

**Perseus** In Greek mythology, son of Danaë and ZEUS. Perseus beheaded the snake-haired gorgon MEDUSA, turned ATLAS to stone, and rescued the princess ANDROMEDA from being sacrificed to a sea monster.

**Pershing, John Joseph** (1860–1948) US general. He led a punitive expedition against Pancho VILLA in Mexico (1916) before being appointed to command the American Expeditionary Force (AEF) in World War I (1917–19). Returning a hero, he later served as army chief of staff (1921–24).

**Persia** Former name of IRAN, in SW Asia. The earliest empire in the region was that of Media (*c*.700–549 BC). It was overthrown by the Persian king, CYRUS THE GREAT, who established the much larger ACHAEMENID dynasty (*c*.550–330 BC), destroyed by ALEXANDER THE GREAT. Alexander's successors, comprising the SELEUCIDS, were replaced by people from PARTHIA in the 3rd century BC. The Persian SASSANID dynasty was established by Ardashir I in AD 224. Weakened by defeat by the Byzantines under HERACLIUS, it was overrun by the Arabs in the 7th century.

**Persian art** Earliest manifestations of art in Persia (Iran), prior to the 7th-century development of ISLAMIC ART AND ARCHITECTURE. The oldest pottery and engraved seals date back to *c*.3500 BC. The greatest achievements of Persian art occurred during the rule of the ACHAEMENID (*c*.550–330 BC) and SASSANID (AD 224–642) dynasties. The former is best represented by the low relief carvings and massive gateway figures executed for the palace of Darius at PERSEPOLIS. The Sassanians excelled at metalwork and sculpture.

**Persian Gulf** (Arabian Gulf) Arm of the Arabian Sea between Arabia and the Asian mainland, and connected to it by the Strait of Hormuz and the Gulf of Oman. Britain had achieved supremacy in the Gulf by the mid-19th century. The discovery of oil in the 1930s increased its importance, and (after British withdrawal in the 1960s) both the US and the Soviet Union sought to increase their influence. Tension was heightened by the IRAN-IRAQ WAR in the 1980s, and the GULF WAR against Iraq in 1991. The Gulf is a major shipping and oil supply route. Area: *c*.93,000sq mi (240,000sq km).

**Persian** (Farsi) Official language of IRAN. It is spoken by nearly all of Iran's population as a first or second language. It is also widely used in Afghanistan. Persian belongs to the Indo-Iranian family of INDO-EUROPEAN LANGUAGES. Persian has borrowed from ARABIC and is written in the Arabic script.

**Persian mythology, ancient** Beliefs of the Persian people *c*.500 BC. The oldest Persian deity was MITRA, who was identified with the sun. He was a god of courage and enlightenment, and led the chariot of the sun across the sky on its daily journey. In the Zoroastrian period MITRA became subordinate

P

to AHURA MAZDAH, who was worshiped by the ACHAEMENID kings of Persia as the creator and ruler of the world. Ahura Mazdah was engaged in an eternal conflict with Ahriman, the principle of evil. At a later period both Ahura Mazdah and Ahriman (or Angra Mainyu) were regarded as the twin offspring of Zurvan (Time). Their cosmic struggle would end ultimately with the victory of Ahura Mazdah.

**Persian Wars** (499–479 BC) Conflict between the ancient Greeks and Persians. In 499 BC the IONIAN cities of Asia Minor rebelled against Persian rule. Athens sent a fleet to aid them. Having crushed the rebellion, the Persian emperor, DARIUS I, invaded Greece but was defeated at MARATHON (490 BC). In 480 BC his successor, XERXES, burned Athens but withdrew after defeats at SALAMIS and PLATAEA (479 BC). Under Athenian leadership, the Greeks regained territory in Thrace and Anatolia, until the PELOPONNESIAN WARS (431 BC).

**persimmon** Any of several trees of the genus *Diospyros* that produce reddish-orange fruit which is sour and astringent until ripe. Species include the North American persimmon (*D. virginiana*) and the Japanese persimmon (*D. kaki*). Family Ebenaceae.

**personality** Emotional, attitudinal, and behavioral characteristics that distinguish an individual. Personality traits are assessed by a variety of methods, including personality tests and projective techniques. Influential theories of personality in psychology include Sigmund FREUD'S PSYCHOANALYSIS, JUNG'S theories of personality types, and social theories.

**perspective** Method of showing three-dimensional objects and spatial relationships in a two-dimensional image. The linear perspective system is based on the idea that parallel lines converge at a vanishing point as they recede into the distance.

**perspiration** *See* SWEATING

**Perth** City on the Swan River, sw Australia; capital of Western Australia. Founded in 1829, the city grew rapidly after the discovery of gold at Coolgardie in the 1890s, the development of the port at Fremantle, and the construction of railroads in the early 20th century. Industries: textiles, cement. Pop. (1993 est.) 1,221,200.

**Peru** Republic in w South America. See country feature

**Perugia** City on the Tiber River, central Italy; capital of Perugia province. A major Etruscan city, Perugia passed to Rome in 310 BC. In the 6th century AD it was captured by the Lom-

## PERU

Peru's flag was adopted in 1825. The colors are said to have been inspired by a flock of red and white flamingos which the Argentine patriot General José de San Martín saw flying over his marching army when he arrived in 1820 to liberate Peru from Spain.

**AREA:** 496,223SQ MI (1,285,220SQ KM)
**POPULATION:** 22,454,000
**CAPITAL (POPULATION):** Lima (6,386,308)
**GOVERNMENT:** Transitional republic
**ETHNIC GROUPS:** Quechua 47%, Mestizo 32%, White 12%, Aymara 5%
**LANGUAGES:** Spanish and Quechua (both official)
**RELIGIONS:** Christianity (Roman Catholic 93%, Protestant 6%)
**CURRENCY:** New sol = 100 centavos

The Republic of Peru, in w South America, is divided into three geographical areas. Along the Pacific coast lies a narrow strip of desert. Peru's major urban areas, such as the capital, LIMA, are sited beside oases. The center is dominated by three ranges of the ANDES Mountains. In the foothills of the Cordillera Occidental lies Peru's second-largest city, AREQUIPA. The range includes Peru's highest peak, Mount Huascarán, at 22,205ft (6,768m). The Cordillera Central merges into the Cordillera Oriental, site of CUZCO and the INCA ruins of MACHU PICCHU. Between the E and W ranges lies the Altiplano Plateau, site of many lakes, including Lake TITICACA. In the E lie forested highlands and the lowlands of the AMAZON basin.

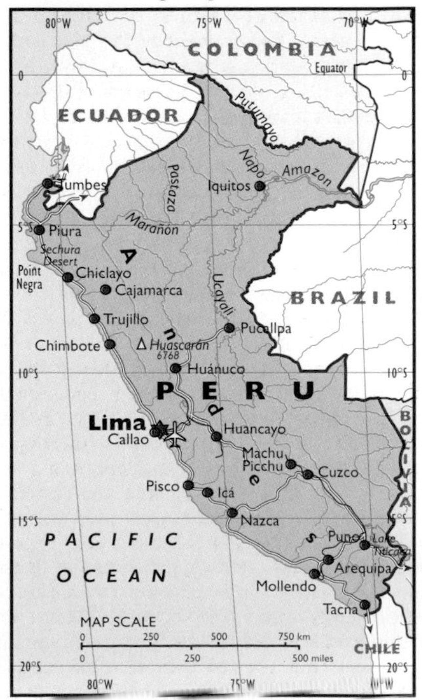


### CLIMATE

Lima has an arid climate. EL NIÑO brings infrequent violent storms. Inland, there is more frequent precipitation. The high Andes are permanently snowcapped. The E is hot and rainy.

### VEGETATION

The coastal desert oases form Peru's major growing region. Mountain grassland lies on the higher slopes of the Andes. The E is a region of *selva*, tropical rain forest with trees such as rosewood and rubber. Here the major crop is coca.

### HISTORY AND POLITICS

Native American civilizations developed over 10,000 years ago. By *c.*AD 1200, the Inca had established a capital at Cuzco. By 1500 their empire extended from Ecuador to Chile. In 1532 the Spanish conquistador Francisco PIZARRO captured the Inca ruler ATAHUALPA. By 1533 Pizarro had conquered most of Peru; he founded Lima in 1535. In 1544 Lima became capital of Spain's South American empire. Spain's rule caused frequent native revolts, such as that of TUPAC AMARU. In 1820 José de SAN MARTÍN captured coastal Peru. In 1821 Peru declared independence. Spain still held much of the interior, and Simón BOLÍVAR completed liberation in 1826. In 1836 Peru and Bolivia formed a short-lived confederation. In the War of the Pacific (1879–84) Peru lost some of its S provinces to Bolivia. The early 20th century was characterized by dictatorship and the growing gap between a wealthy oligarchy and the poverty of the native population. From 1968–80 a military junta failed to carry out democratic reforms. Austerity measures introduced by the civilian government during the 1980s caused civil unrest. *Sendero Luminoso* (Shining Path) and the Tupac Amaru Revolutionary Movement (MRTA) have waged an insurgency campaign that has claimed over 30,000 lives. Alberto Fujimori was elected in 1990, and began a series of anti-terrorist measures. In 1992 he suspended the constitution and dismissed parliament. The guerrilla movements leaders were captured. A new constitution was adopted in 1993. Fujimori was reelected in 1995. In December 1996 MRTA guerrillas captured the Japanese embassy in Lima. The four month-long siege ended when the army stormed the complex killing all the guerrillas. In 1998 Peru and Ecuador signed a peace agreement resolving a protracted border dispute.

### ECONOMY

Peru is a lower-middle-income developing country (1995 GDP per capita, US$3,770). Agriculture employs 35% of the workforce. Major crops include beans, maize, potatoes, and rice. Coffee, cotton, and sugar cane are major exports. Peru lands the world's third-largest fish catch and is the eighth-largest producer of copper ore. Since 1990 a number of free-market reforms have reduced inflation and foreign debt.

▲ **Pfeiffer** One of Hollywood's most popular leading actresses, Michelle Pfeiffer rose to stardom with her role in *The Witches of Eastwick* in 1987. Since then, she has received three Academy Award nominations. A versatile actress, she has played a wide range of roles, from a gangster's moll in *Married to the Mob* (1988), to the sheltered southerner who finds independence in *Love Field* (1992), and the seductive Catwoman in *Batman Returns* (1992).

bards and became a duchy. For centuries, Perugia was the scene of various power struggles, before being subdued by the papacy in 1540. In 1860 it was incorporated into a united Italy. Perugia has always been the artistic center of UMBRIA. The modern city's economy is based on tourism and commerce. It is also renowned for its chocolate. Pop. (1991) 144,732.

**Perugino, Pietro Vannucci** (1445–1523) Italian painter, an important figure in the art of the early Renaissance. He was a notable fresco painter. His *Christ Delivering the Keys to St. Peter*, painted for the Sistine Chapel in Rome, did much to establish his reputation.

**Peshawar** City in NW Pakistan, 9mi (16km) E of the KHYBER PASS. Brought under Muslim rule in the 10th century, it fell to the Afghans in the 16th century. Conquered by the Sikhs in 1834, it was annexed by Britain in 1849. In 1948 it became part of Pakistan. In the 1980s and 1990s it was a base for rebel groups operating in Afghanistan. The modern city is famous for handicrafts, carpets, and leather goods. Industries: textiles, chemicals, paper. Pop. (1981) 555,000.

**Pestalozzi, Johann Heinrich** (1746–1827) Swiss educational reformer whose theories formed the basis of modern elementary education. His books include *How Gertrude Teaches Her Children* (1801).

**pesticide** Chemical substance that is used to kill pests. A HERBICIDE is used for weeds, an insecticide for insects and a FUNGICIDE for fungal diseases.

**Pétain, Henri Philippe** (1856–1951) French general and political leader. In World War I his defense of VERDUN (1916) made him a national hero. He was appointed commander-in-chief in 1917 and held high positions between the wars. With the defeat of France in 1940, he was recalled as prime minister. He signed the surrender and became head of the collaborationist VICHY regime. He was charged with treason after the liberation of France in 1945 and died in prison.

**petal** Part of a flower. The petals of a flower are together known as the corolla. Surrounded by SEPALS, flower petals are often brightly colored and may secrete nectar and perfume to attract the insects and birds necessary for cross-pollination. Once fertilization occurs, the petals usually drop off.

**Peter, Saint** (d. *c.*64) APOSTLE of JESUS CHRIST. He was born Simon, son of Jonas, and was a fisherman from Bethsaida, on the Sea of Galilee. He and his brother ANDREW were called by Jesus to be disciples. Jesus gave Simon the name Peter (John 1:42). Peter was one of Jesus' closest and most loyal associates. While Jesus was on trial before the SANHEDRIN, Peter denied knowing him three times, just as Jesus had predicted. After Jesus' ascension, Peter was the first publicly to preach Christianity in Jerusalem. He took Christianity to Samaria. Imprisoned by King Herod, he was allegedly rescued by an angel of the Lord. In his final years, he seems to have left Jerusalem and undertaken a missionary journey. Roman Catholic theology accepts him as the first head of the Church and the first bishop of Rome, from whom the popes claim succession. His feast day is June 29.

**Peter I (the Great)** (1672–1725) Emperor of Russia (1682–1725), regarded as the founder of modern Russia. After ruling jointly with his half-brother Ivan (1682–89) he gained sole control in 1689. He employed foreign experts to modernize the army, transportation, and technology. He compelled the aristocracy and the church to serve the interests of the state, eliminating ancient tradition. In the NORTHERN WAR, Russia replaced Sweden as the dominant power in N Europe and gained lands on the Baltic, where Peter built his new capital, St. Petersburg. In the E, he warred against Turks and Persians and initiated the exploration of Siberia.

**Peter I** (1844–1921) King of Serbia (1903–21). He was brought up in exile and educated in France while the Obrenović dynasty ruled Serbia. He was elected king when his father, ALEXANDER Obrenović, was assassinated. He became the first king of the new kingdom of Serbs, Croats, and Slovenes (later known as Yugoslavia) in 1918.

**Peter II** (1923–70) Last king of Yugoslavia (1934–41). He succeeded to the throne at the age of 11. The actual ruler was his uncle, Prince Paul, who was deposed in 1941 by a military coup. Peter ruled for a month until the invasion of the AXIS POWERS, when he fled to London. After the monarchy was abolished in 1945 he settled in the US.

**Peterloo Massacre** (1819) Violent suppression of a political protest in Manchester, England. A large crowd demonstrating for reform of Parliament was dispersed by soldiers. Eleven people were killed and 500 injured.

**Petipa, Marius** (1819–1910) Russian dancer and choreographer. He rose to fame in 1847 as principal dancer at the Maryinski Theater, St. Petersburg, and was choreographer of the Imperial Russian Ballet (1862–1903). His *Don Quixote* (1869), *Sleeping Beauty* (1890), and *Raymonda* (1898) laid the foundations of classical ballet. *See also* KIROV BALLET

**petition of right** Means by which an English subject could sue the crown; in particular, the statement of grievances against the crown presented by Parliament to CHARLES I in 1628. It led to the dissolution of Parliament and Charles's period of untrammeled rule.

**Petőfi, Sándor** (1823–49) Hungarian poet and revolutionary. His writings include *Versek* (1844) and a novel *A Hóhér Kötele* (1845). His poetry inspired the patriots of the Hungarian revolution of 1848, in which he was killed.

**Petra** Ancient city in what is now SW Jordan. It was the capital of the Nabataean kingdom from the 4th century BC. It was captured by the Romans in the 2nd century AD. The city, which was rediscovered in 1812 and is the scene of extensive excavation, can be reached only through narrow gorges. Many of its remarkable ruined houses, temples, theaters, and tombs were cut from the high, pinkish sandstone cliffs that protected it.

**Petrarch, Francesco** (1304–74) Italian lyric poet and scholar. Most of his lyric poems, *Rime sparse*, have as their subject "Laura," a woman idealized in the style of earlier poets but in a more realistic light.

**petrel** Any of several small oceanic birds related to the ALBATROSS. Most of them nest in colonies and fly over open water, feeding on squid and small fish. They have webbed feet and tubular nostrils. Length: to 16in (42cm). Order Procellariifarmes.

**Petrie, Sir William Matthew Flinders** (1853–1942) British archeologist and Egyptologist. He helped to develop important excavation methods and techniques and founded the Egypt Research Account in 1894, later known as the British School of Archaeology in Egypt. His most important work was at Memphis.

**Petrified Forest National Park** Park in E Arizona, US. Established in 1906 as a national monument and in 1962 as a national park, it is an extensive natural exhibit of petrified wood. It also features Native American ruins and petroglyphs, as well as a portion of the PAINTED DESERT. Area: 147sq mi (381sq km).

**petrochemical** Chemical substance derived from PETROLEUM or NATURAL GAS. The refining of petroleum is undertaken on a large scale not only for fuels but also for a wide range of chemicals. These chemicals include ALKANES (paraffins) and ALKENES (olefins), BENZENE, TOLUENE, NAPHTHALENE, and their derivatives.

**petroleum** (crude oil) Fossil fuel that is a complex chemical mixture of HYDROCARBONS. It accumulates in underground deposits and probably originated from the remains of long-dead organisms, particularly marine plankton. Petroleum is rarely found at the original site of formation but migrates laterally and vertically until it is trapped. Most petroleum is extracted via oil wells from reservoirs in the Earth's crust sealed by upfolds of impermeable rock, or by salt domes that form traps. The most widespread form of petroleum is **gasoline**. A major HYDROCARBON fuel, it consists mainly of hexane, octane, and heptane. Often other fuels and substances are added to gasoline to alter its properties. *See also* NATURAL GAS

**petrology** Study of rocks, including their origin, chemical composition, and location. Formation of the three classes of rocks – IGNEOUS (of volcanic origin); SEDIMENTARY (deposited by water); METAMORPHIC (either of the other two changed by temperature and pressure) – is studied.

**Petronius** (d. *c.*AD 66) Roman writer, assumed author of the *Satyricon*, a humorous tale giving vivid glimpses of contemporary society. He committed suicide when accused of plotting against Emperor NERO.

**petunia** Genus of flowering plants of the nightshade family that originated in Argentina, and the common name for any of the varieties that are popular as bedding plants. Most varieties derive from the white flowered *P. axillaris* and the violet-red *P. integrifolia*; they may be erect, shrubby, or pendant. The bell-shaped flowers have five petals and may be almost any color. Family Solanaceae.

**Pétursson, Hallgrímur** (1614–74) Icelandic poet. He was a blacksmith and a fisherman, before becoming a priest in 1651. His reputation rests on a single extended work, the *Passiusálmar* or *The Passion Hymns of Iceland* (1666), written after he contracted leprosy.

**Pevsner, Antoine** (1886–1962) French sculptor, b. Russia. He was influenced by CUBISM, but became a leading exponent of CONSTRUCTIVISM, creating works in bronze and other materials. In the 1930s he concentrated on NON-FIGURATIVE structures. A later work is *Monument Symbolizing the Liberation of the Spirit* (1956).

**pewter** Any of several silver-colored, soft ALLOYS that consist mainly of tin and lead. The most common form has about four parts of tin to one of lead, combined with small amounts of antimony and copper.

**peyote** (mescal) Either of two species of cactus of the genus *Laphophora* that grow in the US. The soft-stemmed *L. williamsii* has pink or white flowers in summer and a blue-green stem. *L. diffusa* has white or yellow flowers. Peyote contains many ALKALOIDS, the principal one being MESCALINE, a hallucinogenic drug.

**Pfeiffer, Michelle** (1957– ) US film actress. After receiving an Oscar nomination for her supporting role in *Dangerous Liaisons* (1988), she gained further nominations for lead performances in *The Fabulous Baker Boys* (1989) and *Love Field* (1992). She also starred in *The Age of Innocence* (1993).

**pH** Numerical scale that indicates the acidity or alkalinity of a solution. The pH value measures the concentration of hydrogen ions. The scale runs from 0 to 14. A solution is acidic if the pH is less than 7 and alkaline if greater than 7.

**phaeophyta** Taxonomic division (phylum) of the kingdom Protoctista that consists of the brown ALGAE. Classified by some biologists as plants, the simple organisms belonging to this group are mostly marine, found mainly in the intertidal zone of rocky shores. They include familiar seaweeds such as *Fucus* (wracks) and *Ascophyllum* (bladder wrack). The largest, *Macrocystis*, grows to over 320ft (100m) at up to 18in (0.5m) per day. *Sargassum* forms vast floating masses in the Sargasso Sea in the mid-Atlantic.

**Phaëthon** In Greek mythology, son of HELIOS, the Sun god. He drove his father's Sun chariot across the sky but lost control of the horses, setting the Earth on fire as he approached too close. To save the world, Zeus struck him from the reins with a thunderbolt.

**phagocyte** Type of LEUKOCYTE (white blood cell) able to engulf other cells, such as bacteria. It digests them in the defense of the body against infection.

**phalanger** (possum) Any of about 45 species of mainly nocturnal arboreal marsupials of Australasia. It has opposable digits for grasping branches and the tail is long and prehensile. Family Phalargeridae.

**pharaoh** Title of the rulers of ancient EGYPT. Though loosely applied to all Egyptian kings, the title was only adopted during the New Kingdom. The pharaoh was considered divine, an incarnation of the god HORUS.

**Pharisees** Members of a conservative Jewish religious group, prominent in ancient Palestine from the 2nd century BC to the time of the destruction of the second Temple in Jerusalem (AD 70). They were a political party opposed to the pagan influences of their Greek and Roman conquerors, but by New Testament times were largely nonpolitical. They were the founders of orthodox JUDAISM and were often in conflict with the SADDUCEES.

**pharmacology** Study of the properties of drugs and their effects on the body.

**pharmacopoeia** Reference book listing drugs and other preparations in medical use. Included are details of their formulae, dosages, routes of administration, known side-effects, and precautions.

**Pharos** Island off N Egypt, in the Mediterranean, connected to the mainland by a causeway built by ALEXANDER THE GREAT. A lighthouse was completed by Ptolemy II in *c.*280 BC and was considered one of the SEVEN WONDERS OF THE WORLD. According to writers of the time, it was *c.*450ft (135m) tall and its light could be seen 40mi (65km) away. It was destroyed by an earthquake in 1346. Pharos is now part of the city of Alexandria.

**pharynx** Cavity at the back of the nose and mouth that extends down toward the ESOPHAGUS and TRACHEA. Inflammation of the pharynx, usually caused by viral or bacterial infection, is known as pharyngitis.

**phase** Proportion of the illuminated hemisphere of a body in the Solar System (in particular the Moon) as seen from Earth. The phase of a body changes as the Sun and the Earth change their relative positions. The phases of the Moon are new, crescent, half, gibbous, and full.

**phase** In physics, a stage or fraction in the cycle of an oscillation, such as the wave motion of light or sound waves. This is usually measured from an arbitrary starting point or compared with another motion of the same frequency. Two waves are said to be "in phase" when their maximum and minimum values happen at the same time. If not, there is a "phase difference," as seen in interference phenomenon. Phase can also refer to any one of the states of MATTER.

**pheasant** Game bird of the genus *Phasianus* native to Asia, introduced into Europe and North America. PEACOCKS and GUINEA FOWL belong to the same family. Males are showy, with brownish green, red, and yellow feathers; females are smaller and brownish. Length: up to 35in (89cm). Family Phasianidae.

**phenol** Aromatic compound group whose members each have an attachment of a hydroxyl group to a carbon atom forming part of a BENZENE ring. The simplest of the family is also called phenol or carbolic acid ($C_6H_5OH$). Phenols are colorless liquids or white solids at room temperature. They are used for such products as aspirin, dye, fungicide, explosive, and as a starting material for nylon and epoxy resin.

**phenomenalism** Philosophical proposition that human knowledge is restricted to the content of mental impressions.

**phenomenology** School of philosophy at the turn of the century from the work of Edmund HUSSERL. He moved away from causal explanations of experience toward direct description of experienced phenomena.

**phenotype** Physical characteristics of an organism resulting from HEREDITY. Phenotype is distinct from GENOTYPE, since not all aspects of genetic makeup manifest themselves.

**pheromone** Substance secreted externally by certain animals that influences the behavior of members of the same species. Common in mammals and insects, these substances are often sexual attractants. They may be part of urine, or secreted by specific glands.

**Phidias** (490–430 BC) Sculptor of ancient Greece. During his lifetime he was best known for two gigantic chryselephantine (gold and ivory) statues, one of Athena for the Parthenon and the other of Zeus for his temple at Olympia. The Zeus was one of the SEVEN WONDERS OF THE WORLD. He also worked on the Parthenon friezes.

**Philadelphia** City and port at the confluence of the Delaware and Schuylkill rivers, SE Pennsylvania. The site was first settled by Swedes in the early 17th century. The city was found-

◀ **pheasant** The golden pheasant (*Chrysolophus pictus*) is found in the highlands of central China. This pheasant is distinguished by its yellow head, rump, and lower back, and by its golden collar edged in blue-black with red underparts. The golden pheasant is a member of a very diverse order (Galliformes), but alll members have naked feet, no airsacs in the neck, and unfeathered nostrils.

P

ed by William PENN in 1681. By 1774 it was a major commercial, cultural, and industrial center of the American colonies and played an important part in their fight for independence. The CONTINENTAL CONGRESSES were held in the city and the DECLARATION OF INDEPENDENCE was signed here in 1776. The CONSTITUTIONAL CONVENTION met in Philadelphia and adopted the US Constitution in 1787. Philadelphia served as capital of the US from 1790 to 1800. Industries: shipbuilding, textiles, chemicals. Pop. (1990) 1,585,577.

**Philip, Saint** (active 1st century AD) One of the original 12 APOSTLES of JESUS CHRIST. Philip came from Bethsaida, on the Sea of Galilee. Christian tradition says he preached in Asia Minor and met a martyr's death. His feast day is May 3 (in the West) or November 14 (in the East). He appears to be a different person from Philip the Evangelist, one of the seven DEACONS who aided the apostles. According to tradition, he became bishop of Tralles, now in Turkey. His feast day is June 9.

**Philip II** (1165–1223) (Philip Augustus) King of France (1180–1223). Greatest of French medieval kings, he increased the royal domain. His main rival was HENRY II of England. Philip supported the rebellions of Henry's sons, fought a long war against RICHARD I and, during the reign of JOHN, occupied Normandy and Anjou. English efforts to regain them were defeated at Bouvines in 1214. Philip persecuted Jews and Christian heretics, joined the Third Crusade but swiftly withdrew, and opened the crusade against the Albigenses in s France.

**Philip IV (the Fair)** (1268–1314) King of France (1285–1314). Partly to pay for wars against Flanders and England, he expelled the Jews (1306), confiscating their property. Claiming the right to tax the clergy involved him in a long and bitter quarrel with Pope Boniface VIII. After the death of Boniface (1303), Philip secured the election of a French pope, Clement V, based at Avignon.

**Philip VI** (1293–1350) King of France (1328–50) First of the house of Valois, he was chosen to succeed his cousin, CHARLES IV, in preference to the rival claimant, EDWARD III of England. After the outbreak of the HUNDRED YEARS WAR (1337), many of his vassals supported Edward. Philip suffered serious defeats in the naval battle of Sluys (1340) and at CRÉCY (1346).

## PHILIPPINES

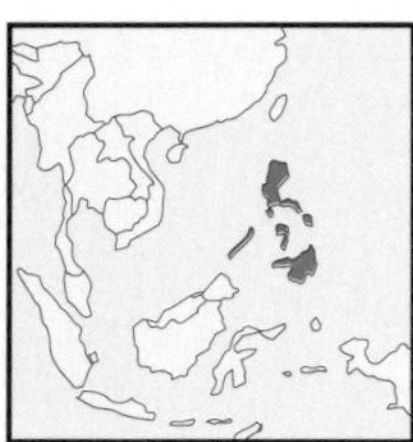

This flag was adopted in 1946, when the country won its independence from the United States. The eight rays of the large sun represent the eight provinces that led the revolt against Spanish rule in 1898. The three smaller stars stand for the three main island groups.

**AREA:** 115,300SQ MI (300,000SQ KM)
**POPULATION:** 64,259,000
**CAPITAL (POPULATION):** Manila (1,587,000)
**GOVERNMENT:** Multiparty republic
**ETHNIC GROUPS:** Tagalog 30%, Cebuano 24%, Ilocano 10%, Hiligaynon Ilongo 9%, Bicol 6%, Samar-Leyte 4%
**LANGUAGES:** Pilipino (Tagalog) and English (both official)
**RELIGIONS:** Christianity (Roman Catholic 84%, Philippine Independent Church or Aglipayan 6%, Protestant 4%), Islam 4%
**CURRENCY:** Philippine peso = 100 centavos

The Republic of the Philippines, in Southeast Asia, consists of over 7,000 islands, of which 1,000 are inhabited. LUZON and MINDANAO islands constitute over 66% of land area. Around Manila Bay (Luzon), lies the capital, MANILA, and the second-largest city, QUEZON CITY. The islands are mainly mountainous with several active volcanoes, one of which is the highest peak, Mount Apo, at 9,692ft (2,954m). Narrow coastal plains give way to forested plateaus. Earthquakes are common.

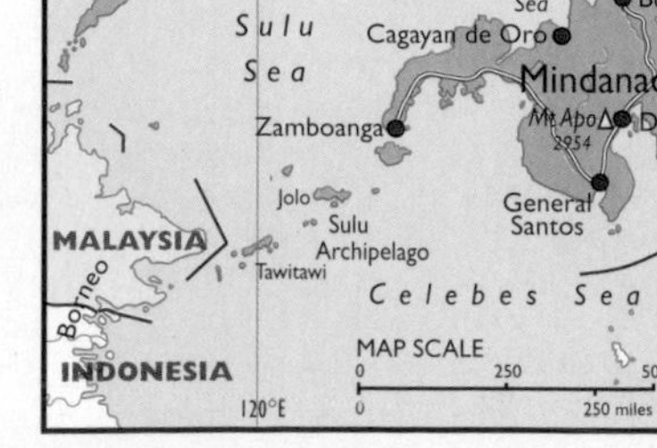


### CLIMATE

The Philippines has a tropical climate, with high annual temperatures. The dry season runs from December to April, but the rest of the year is wet. Much of the rainfall is due to typhoons.

### VEGETATION

Mangrove swamps line many coasts. Over 33% of the land is forested. Much of the land is fertile.

### HISTORY AND POLITICS

Islam was introduced in the late 14th century. In 1521 the Portuguese navigator Ferdinand MAGELLAN landed near Cebu. In 1565 Spain began its conquest of the islands. In 1571 the Spanish founded Manila, and named the archipelago *Filipinas*, after Philip II. It became a vital trading center, subject to frequent attack from pirates. In 1896 the Filipinos revolted against Spanish rule and declared independence. In the SPANISH-AMERICAN WAR (1898), the US defeated the Spanish navy in Manila Bay. Filipinos seized Luzon. Manila was captured with US help. In the Treaty of Paris (1898) the islands were ceded to the US. From 1899 to 1902 Filipinos fought against US control. The Commonwealth of the Philippines was established in 1935. Manuel Luis QUEZON became the first president. In 1941 the Japanese invaded, and captured Manila by 1942. General MACARTHUR was forced to withdraw and US forces were ousted from BATAAN. In 1944 the US began to reclaim the islands. In 1946 the Philippines became an independent republic. The US was granted a 99-year lease on military bases (subsequently reduced to 25 years from 1967). In 1965 Ferdinand MARCOS became president. Marcos's response to mounting civil unrest was brutal. In 1972 he declared martial law. In 1981 Marcos was reelected amid charges of electoral fraud. In 1983 the leader of the opposition, Benigno Aquino, was assassinated. His widow, Cory AQUINO, succeeded him. Marcos claimed victory in 1986 elections, but faced charges of electoral fraud. Cory Aquino launched a campaign of civil disobedience. The US withdrew its support for the regime and Marcos was forced into exile. Aquino's presidency was marred by attempted military coups. In 1992 Fidel Ramos succeeded Aquino as president. The US closed its military bases at the end of 1992. In 1996 an agreement was reached with the Moro National Liberation Front, ending 24 years of rebellion on Mindanao. It allowed the creation of a Muslim state. In 1998 the fragile cease-fire was broken. In May 1998 Ramos was succeeded by Joseph Estrada.

### ECONOMY

The Philippines is a lower-middle-income developing country (1995 GDP per capita, US$2,850). The economy was not as badly affected as others by the regional economic crisis in 1998. Agriculture employs 45% of the workforce. It is the world's second-largest producer of rice and fourth-largest producer of bananas. Rearing livestock, forestry, and fishing are important.

**Philip II** (382–336 BC) King of Macedonia (359–336 BC). He conquered neighboring tribes and extended his rule over the Greek states, defeating the Athenians at Chaeronea in 338 BC and gaining reluctant acknowledgment as king of Greece. He was preparing to attack the Persian empire when he was assassinated, leaving the task to his son, ALEXANDER THE GREAT.

**Philip II** (1527–98) King of Spain (1556–98), king of Portugal (1580–98). From his father, the Emperor CHARLES V, he inherited Milan, Naples, Sicily, the Netherlands, and Spain with its empire in the New World. War with France ended at Château-Cambrésis (1559), but the revolt of the Netherlands began in 1566. A defender of Roman Catholicism, Philip launched the unsuccessful ARMADA of 1588 to crush the English who, as fellow Protestants, aided the Dutch.

**Philip V** (1683–1746) King of Spain (1700–46). Because he was a grandson and a possible successor of LOUIS XIV of France, his accession to the Spanish throne provoked the War of the SPANISH SUCCESSION. By the Treaty of UTRECHT (1713), he kept the Spanish throne by exclusion from the succession in France and the loss of Spanish territories in Italy and the Netherlands.

**Philip, Prince, Duke of Edinburgh** (1921– ) Husband of Queen ELIZABETH II of Britain and Prince Consort. He was born in Corfu, the son of Prince Andrew of Greece, and educated in Britain. He became a naturalized British citizen and took the surname Mountbatten. In 1947 he married Elizabeth after becoming the Duke of Edinburgh. He was created a prince in 1957.

**Philippi** Ancient city of E Macedonia. It was the site of the victory of Mark ANTONY and Octavian (later the Emperor AUGUSTUS) over CASSIUS and BRUTUS, the assassins of Julius Caesar, in 42 BC. Philippi became the first European city to receive a Christian mission when visited by St. Paul.

**Philippines** Republic in the SW Pacific Ocean, SE Asia. *See* country feature

**Philistine** Member of a non-Semitic people who lived on the S coast of modern Israel, known as Philistia, from *c.*1200 BC. They clashed frequently with the Hebrews. Today the term philistine may be applied to a person indifferent to culture.

**Phillips, Wendell** (1811–84) US social reformer. He became a close associate of abolitionist William Lloyd GARRISON and was president of the Antislavery Society (1865–70). He also advocated women's and workers' rights and temperance.

**philodendron** Genus of house plants native to tropical America. Philodendrons have shiny, heart-shaped leaves, which are sometimes split. Height: 4in–6ft (10cm–1.8m). Family Araceae.

**philology** Study of both language and literature. In addition to phonetics, grammar, and the structure of language, philology also includes textual criticism, ETYMOLOGY, and the study of art, archeology, religion, and any system related to ancient or classical languages.

**philosophy** Study of the nature of reality, knowledge, ethics, and existence by means of rational inquiry. The oldest known philosophical system is the Vedic system of India, which dates back to the middle of the 2nd millennium BC or earlier. Like other Eastern philosophies, it is founded upon a largely mystical view of the universe and is integrated with India's main religion, HINDUISM. From the 6th century BC, Chinese philosophy was largely dominated by CONFUCIANISM and TAOISM. Also in the 6th century, Western philosophy began among the Greeks with the work of THALES of Miletus. Later Pre-Socratic philosophers included PYTHAGORAS, EMPEDOCLES, Anaxagoras, Parmenides, HERACLITUS, ZENO OF ELEA, and DEMOCRITUS. Greek philosophy reached its high point with SOCRATES, who laid the foundations of ethics, PLATO, who developed a system of universal ideas, and ARISTOTLE, who founded the study of LOGIC. ZENO OF CITIUM evolved the influential philosophy of stoicism, which contrasted with the system of EPICUREANISM, founded by EPICURUS. A dominant school of the early Christian era was NEOPLATONISM, founded by Plotinus in the 3rd century AD. The influence of Aristotle and other Greeks pervaded the thought of Muslim philosophers, such as AVICENNA and AVERRÖES, and the Spanish-born Jew, Moses MAIMONIDES. In the work of scholastic philosophers such as ABÉLARD, Albertus Magnus, Saint Thomas AQUINAS, and WILLIAM OF OCCAM, philosophy became a branch of Christian theology. Modern scientific philosophy began in the 17th century, with the work of DESCARTES. His faith in mathematics was taken up by LEIBNIZ. In England, HOBBES integrated his materialist world view with a social philosophy. The 18th-century empiricists included BERKELEY and HUME. The achievements of KANT in Germany and the French Encyclopedists were also grounded in science. In the 19th century, a number of diverging movements emerged, among them the classical idealism of HEGEL, the dialectical materialism of MARX and ENGELS, the POSITIVISM of COMTE, and the work of KIERKEGAARD and NIETZSCHE, which emphasized the freedom of the individual. In the 20th century, dominant movements included EXISTENTIALISM, LOGICAL POSITIVISM, PHENOMENOLOGY, and VITALISM. *See also* AESTHETICS; EPISTEMOLOGY; LOGIC; METAPHYSICS

**phlebitis** Inflammation of the wall of a vein. It may be caused by infection, trauma, underlying disease, or the presence of VARICOSE VEINS. Symptoms include localized swelling and redness. Treatment includes rest and anticoagulant therapy.

**phloem** Vascular tissue for distributing dissolved food materials in plants. Phloem tissue contains several types of cells. The most important are long, hollow cells called sieve-tube cells. Columns of sieve tubes are joined end to end, allowing passage of materials from cell to cell. The sieve tubes are closely associated with "companion cells," which have dense cytoplasm and many MITOCHONDRIA and are thought to produce the energy needed to transport the food substances (*see* ACTIVE TRANSPORT). Phloem may also contain fibers, which help to support the tissue. *See also* XYLEM

**phlogiston** Odorless, colorless, and weightless material believed by early scientists to be the source of all heat and fire. COMBUSTION was believed to involve the loss of phlogiston. The phlogiston theory was proved erroneous when the true nature of combustion was explained by Antoine LAVOISIER.

**Phnom Penh** (Phnum Pénh) Capital of Cambodia, in the S of the country, a port at the confluence of the Mekong and Tonle Sap rivers. Founded in the 14th century, the city was the capital of the Khmers after 1434. It became the capital of the country in 1865. Occupied by the Japanese during World War II, it was extensively damaged during the Cambodian civil war. After the communists took over in 1975 the population was drastically reduced when many of its inhabitants were forcibly removed to work in the countryside. Industries: rice milling, brewing, distilling. Pop. (1994 est.) 920,000.

**phobia** Irrational and uncontrollable fear that persists despite reassurance or contradictory evidence. Psychoanalytic theory suggests that phobias are actually symbolic subconscious fears and impulses.

**Phobos** Larger of the two SATELLITES of Mars, discovered in 1877 by Asaph Hall. It is a dark, irregular body, measuring 17 × 14 × 12 mi (27 × 22 × 19 km). It may well be a captured asteroid.

**Phoenicia** Greek name for an ancient region bordering the E Mediterranean coast. The Phoenicians were related to the Canaanites. Famous as merchants and sailors, they never formed a single political unit, and Phoenicia was dominated by Egypt before *c.*1200 BC and by successive Near Eastern empires from the 9th century BC. The Phoenician city-states such as Tyre, Sidon, and Byblos reached the peak of their prosperity in the intervening period, but the Phoenicians dominated trade in the Mediterranean throughout the Bronze Age. Expert navigators, they traded for tin in Britain and sailed as far as West Africa. The Phoenicians founded colonies in Spain and North Africa, notably CARTHAGE.

**Phoenician mythology** Beliefs in the Phoenician city-states of the E Mediterranean *c.*500 BC. The most ancient god was El, the father of all gods and the creator of man. Closely related to the Hebrew YAHWEH, he was a remote, benevolent deity, usually depicted as an old man, but also noted for his sexual powers. BAAL, the storm god and the god of fertility, occupied an important place in the divine hierarchy.

P

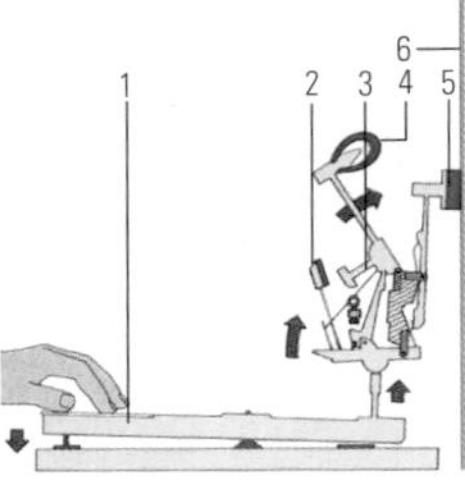


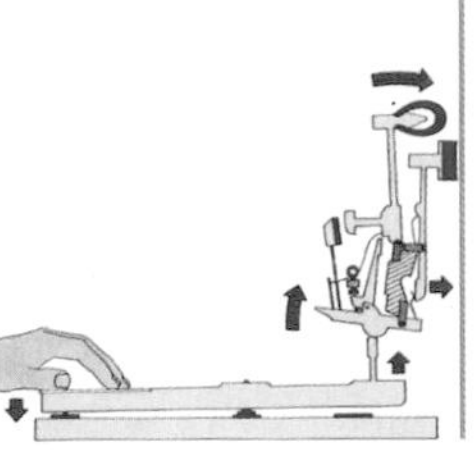

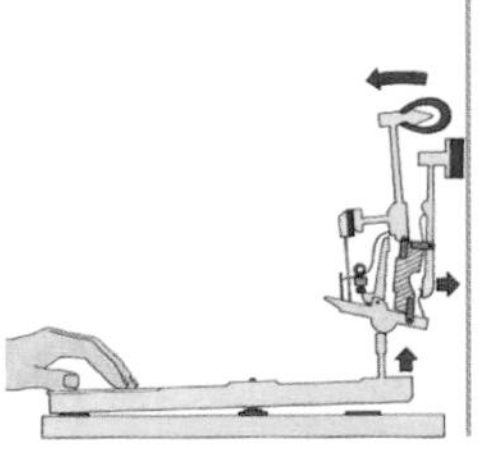

P

▲ **piano** Each key (1) of an upright piano controls a separate hammer (2), damper (3), string (4), an escapement (5), and a check (6). When a key is depressed, a felt covered hammer is thrown against the strings for that particular pitch. At the same time a felt covered damper is lifted allowing the strings to vibrate. The hammer quickly bounces away from the strings, allowing a maximum vibration. When the key is released the damper falls back onto the strings. The hammers are connected to the keys, via a series of levers, called the action, involving an escapement and a check which catches the hammer as it returns.

**Phoenix** Capital of Arizona, on the Salt River. Founded in 1870, the city expanded after agriculture in the area was made possible using the water of the Salt River for irrigation. It became the capital in 1889. Industries: computer parts, aircraft, fabricated metals. It is a popular winter resort. Pop. (1990) 983,403.

**phoenix** Mythological eagle-like bird linked with sun-worship, especially in ancient Egypt. Of gold and scarlet plumage, only one phoenix could exist at a time, usually with a life span of about 500 years. When death approached, the phoenix built a nest of aromatic plant material and was then consumed by fire. From the ashes of the pyre rose a new phoenix.

**pholidota** Small order of mammals, containing only one genus, *Manis*, in the family Manidae; its members are called PANGOLINS. Some species are entirely toothless and feed almost exclusively on ants and termites.

**phoneme** Minimum unit of significant sound; a speech sound distinguishing meaning. The phonemes /p/ and /b/ distinguish "tap" from "tab."

**phonetics** Study of the sounds of speech, divided into three main branches: articulatory phonetics (how the speech organs produce sounds); acoustic phonetics (the physical nature of sounds, mainly using instrumental techniques); and auditory phonetics (how sounds are received by the ear and processed). Linguists have devised notation systems for human speech. *See also* LINGUISTICS

**phosgene** Colorless, toxic gas, chemical name carbonyl chloride ($COCl_2$). It was used as a poison gas in World War I, but is now used in the manufacture of various dyestuffs and resins. Properties: b.p 46.8°F (8.2°C), m.p.–180.5°F (–118°C).

**phosphate** Chemical compounds derived from phosphoric acid ($H_3PO_4$). The use of phosphates as fertilizers can cause environmental damage.

**phosphor** Substance capable of luminescence (storing energy and later releasing it as light). They are used in coating inside cathode-ray tubes and in fluorescent lamps.

**phosphorescence** Form of luminescence in which a substance emits light of one wavelength. Unlike fluorescence, it may persist for some time after the initial excitation. In biology, phosphorescence is the production of light by an organism without associated heat, as with a firefly.

**phosphoric acid** Group of ACIDS, the chief forms of which are tetraoxophosphoric acid ($H_3PO_4$) (formerly orthophosphoric acid), metaphosphoric acid ($HPO_3$), and heptaoxodiphosphoric acid ($H_4P_2O_7$) (formerly pyrophosphoric acid). Tetraoxophosphoric acid is a colorless liquid obtained by the action of sulfuric acid on phosphate rock (calcium phosphate); it used in fertilizers, soaps, and detergents. Metaphosphoric acid is obtained by heating tetraoxophosphoric acid; it is used as a dehydrating agent. Heptaoxodiphosphoric acid is formed by moderately heating tetraoxophosphoric acid or by reacting phosphorus pentoxide ($P_2O_5$) with water; it is used as a catalyst and in metallurgy.

**Phosphoros** In Greek mythology, the light-bearer. The name is synonymous with Lucifer and the morning star, VENUS. Generally portrayed as a man bearing a torch, he was the herald and harbinger of the dawn.

**phosphorus** (symbol P) Common, nonmetallic element of Group V of the periodic table, discovered by Hennig Brand in 1669. It occurs, as PHOSPHATES, in many minerals; apatite is the chief source. The element is used in making PHOSPHORIC ACID for detergents and fertilizers. Small amounts are used in insecticides and in matches. Phosphorus exhibits ALLOTROPY. Properties: at.no. 15; at.wt. 30.9738; sp.gr. 1.82 (white), 2.34 (red); m.p. 111.38°F (44.1°C) (white); b.p. 536°F (280°C) (white); most common isotope $^{31}P$ (100%).

**photocell** *See* PHOTOELECTRIC CELL

**photocopying** Reproduction of words, drawings, or photographs by machine. In a photocopying machine, a light shines on the item to be copied, and an optical system forms an image of it. Various techniques may be used to reproduce this image on paper. In a modern plain-paper copier, the image is projected onto an electrically charged **drum**, coated with the light-sensitive element SELENIUM. Light makes the selenium conduct electricity, so bright areas of the drum lose their charge. The dark areas, which usually correspond to image detail, retain their charge, and this attracts particles of a fine powder called **toner**. Electrically charged paper in contact with the drum picks up the pattern of toner powder. A heated **roller** fuses the powder so that it sticks to the paper and forms a permanent image.

**photoelectric cell** (photocell) Device that produces electricity when light shines on it. It was formerly an electron tube with a photosensitive cathode, but nearly all modern photocells are made using two electrodes separated by light-sensitive semiconductor material. Photoelectric cells are used as switches (electric eyes), light detectors (burglar alarms), devices to measure light intensity (light meters), or power sources (solar cells).

**photoelectric effect** Liberation of electrons from the surface of a material when light, ultraviolet radiation, x-rays, or gamma rays fall on it. The effect can be explained only by the QUANTUM THEORY: PHOTONS in the radiation are absorbed by atoms in the substance and enable electrons to escape by transferring energy to them.

**photography** Process of obtaining a permanent image of an object, either in black and white or in color, on treated paper or film. A CAMERA is used to expose a film to an image of the object to be photographed, for a set time. In black and white photography, the film is covered on one side with an emulsion containing a SILVER halide (silver bromide or silver chloride). The silver compound is exposed, so that it reduces easily to metallic silver when treated with a **developer**. The action of the developer is to produce a black deposit of metallic silver particles on those parts of the film that were exposed to light, thus providing a "**negative**" image. After fixing in "**hypo**" (thiosulphate) and washing, the negative can be printed by placing it over a piece of sensitized paper and exposing it to light so that the silver salts in the paper are affected in the same way as those in the original film. The dark portions of the negative let through the least light, and the image on the paper is reversed back to a positive. Color photography works on a similar, but more complex, process. *See also* DAGUERRE, LOUIS JACQUES MANDE; TALBOT, WILLIAM FOX; individual artists

**photon** Quantum of ELECTROMAGNETIC RADIATION, such as light; a "particle" of LIGHT. The energy of a photon equals the frequency of the radiation multiplied by PLANCK's constant. Absorption of photons by atoms and molecules can cause excitation or ionization. A photon may be classified as a stable ELEMENTARY PARTICLE of zero rest mass, zero charge, and SPIN 1, traveling at the velocity of light. It is its own antiparticle. Virtual photons are thought to be continuously exchanged between charged particles and thus to be the carriers of ELECTROMAGNETIC FORCE. *See also* QUANTUM THEORY

**photoperiodism** Biological mechanism that governs the timing of certain activities in an organism by reacting to the duration of its daily exposure to light and dark. For example, the start of flowering in plants is determined by day length. *See also* BIOLOGICAL CLOCK

**photosphere** Visible surface of the SUN. It is a layer of highly luminous gas about 300mi (500km) thick and with a temperature of about 6,000K, falling to 4,000K at its upper level. The photosphere is the source of the Sun's visible spectrum. Sunspots and other visible features of the Sun are situated in the photosphere.

**photosynthesis** Chemical process occurring in green plants, algae, and many bacteria, by which water and carbon dioxide are converted into food and oxygen using energy absorbed from sunlight. The reactions take place in the CHLOROPLASTS. In the first part of the process, light is absorbed by CHLOROPHYLL and splits water into hydrogen and oxygen. The hydrogen attaches to a carrier molecule and the oxygen is set free. The hydrogen and light energy build a supply of cellular chemical energy, adenosine triphosphate (ATP). Hydrogen and ATP convert the carbon dioxide into sugars, including glucose and starch.

**phototropism** Growth of a plant in response to the stimulus of light, which increases cell growth on the shaded side of the plant, resulting in curvature toward the source of light.

**Phrygia** Historic region of W central Anatolia. A prosperous kingdom was established by the Phrygians, immigrants from SE Europe, early in the 1st millennium BC, with its capital at Gordion. MIDAS was a legendary Phrygian king. In the 6th century BC Phrygia was taken over by Lydia, then by Persia and later empires.

**phylacteries** (tefillin) Two leather boxes containing scriptural passages worn by adult Jewish males in Orthodox and Conservative Jewish religious services. These are ceremonially put on with leather straps for certain ritual prayers.

**phylloxera** Small, yellowish insect of the order Homoptera that is a pest on grape plants in Europe and the W US. It attaches itself to the leaves and roots and sucks the plant's fluids, resulting in the eventual rotting of the plant. It destroyed all of France's native root stock of *vitis vinifera*. Family Phylloxeridae; species: *Phylloxera vitifoliae*.

**phylogenetics** Study of the evolutionary relationships between organisms. In **molecular phylogeny**, the evolutionary distances between organisms are analyzed by comparing the DNA sequences of specific GENES. At the most fundamental level, molecular phylogeny has revealed that all known organisms evolved from a common ancestor and can be grouped into five KINGDOMS.

**phylum** In the systematic categorization of living organisms, a major group within the animal KINGDOM. It comprises a diverse group of organisms with a common fundamental characteristic. In plant classification, the analogous category is sometimes called division. *See also* TAXONOMY

**physical chemistry** Study of the physical changes associated with CHEMICAL REACTIONS and the relationship between physical properties and chemical composition. The main branches are THERMODYNAMICS, concerned with the changes of energy in physical systems; chemical kinetics, concerned with rates of reaction; and molecular and atomic structure. Other topics include ELECTROCHEMISTRY, SPECTROSCOPY, and some aspects of NUCLEAR PHYSICS.

**physical units** Units used in measuring physical quantities. For example, the KILOGRAM unit of mass is defined as the mass of a specified block of platinum. Other masses are measured by weighing them and comparing them, directly or indirectly, with this. Various systems of units exist, founded on certain base units. They include Imperial units (foot, pound, second), CGS units (centimeter, gram, second), and MKS units (meter, kilogram, second). For all scientific purposes, SI UNITS have been adopted.

**physics** Branch of science concerning MATTER and ENERGY. Physics seeks to identify and explain their many forms and relationships. Modern physics recognizes four FUNDAMENTAL FORCES in nature: GRAVITATION, which was first adequately described by Isaac NEWTON; ELECTROMAGNETIC FORCE, codified in the 19th century by MAXWELL's equations; WEAK NUCLEAR FORCE, which is responsible for the decay of some subatomic particles; and STRONG NUCLEAR FORCE, which binds together atomic nuclei. The latter is some $10^{12}$ times stronger than the weak force and is the least understood in physics. Branches of physics include PARTICLE PHYSICS, GEOPHYSICS, BIOPHYSICS, ASTROPHYSICS, and NUCLEAR PHYSICS. Physics may also be divided into six fundamental theories: Newtonian MECHANICS, THERMODYNAMICS, ELECTROMAGNETISM, STATISTICAL MECHANICS, RELATIVITY, and QUANTUM MECHANICS.

**physiology** Branch of biology concerned with the functions of living organisms, as opposed to their structure (anatomy).

**physiotherapy** (physical therapy) Use of various physical techniques to treat disease or injury. Its techniques include massage, manipulation, exercise, heat, hydrotherapy, and electrical stimulation.

**phytochrome** Blue-green pigment that occurs in plant leaves. One form of phytochrome ($P_R$) absorbs red light and is converted by it into another form ($P_{FR}$) that absorbs infrared light. Normal sunlight contains more red than infrared light, so the ratio of these two forms of phytochrome provides the means by which a plant detects the difference between day and night. It also regulates certain plant activities governed by light, such as the start of the flowering period and the greening of leaves. *See also* PHOTOPERIODISM.

**pi** (π) Symbol used for the ratio of the circumference of a CIRCLE to its diameter. It is an IRRATIONAL NUMBER, and an approximation to five decimal places is 3.14159. The ratio 22/7 has often been used as a rougher approximation.

**Piaf, Edith** (1915–63) French cabaret singer, real name Edith Giovanna Gassion. Her recording career spanned nearly 30 years, and the emotional impact of her voice in songs such as *Non, je ne regrette rien* won her an international reputation.

**Piaget, Jean** (1896–1980) Swiss psychologist, who developed a comprehensive theory of the intellectual growth of children in the 1920s and 1930s. He wrote several influential books, including *The Origin of Intelligence in Children* (1954).

**piano** (pianoforte) Musical instrument whose sound is made with strings struck by hammers that are moved from a keyboard. Its invention (*c.*1709) is attributed to Bartolomeo Cristofori. Its name, from the Italian *piano* (soft) and *forte* (strong or loud), was adopted because its range of volume (as of tonal quality) far exceeded that of earlier instruments. The modern grand piano, much larger, louder, and more resonant than the 18th-century piano, was developed in the early 19th century.

**Piatigorsky, Gregor** (1903–76) US cellist and teacher, b. Russia. He was first cellist of the Berlin Philharmonic (1924–28). In 1929 he moved to the US and appeared as a soloist with major orchestras.

**Picardy** Region and former province of N France, on the English Channel; it includes Somme, and parts of Pas-de-Calais, Oise, and Aisne departments. It was a French province from 1477 until the French Revolution, when it was replaced by a smaller department. Picardy was the scene of heavy fighting during WORLD WAR I. The area is made up of the plateau to the N of Paris where wheat and sugar beets are grown; the valley of the Somme, where industrial centers such as Amiens are located; and the coast, where fishing is important. Area: 7,488sq mi (19,399sq km) Pop. 1,810,700.

**picaresque** (Sp. *pícaro*, rogue or knave) Term first applied to an early genre of prose fiction, such as *Don Quixote* (1615), in which a roguish hero has a series of adventures, providing the author with a means for satirical comment. In a general sense, the term is often used to refer to fiction that is episodic in structure.

**Picasso, Pablo** (1881–1973) Spanish painter, sculptor, graphic artist, designer, and ceramicist. Art historians often divide his work into separate periods. During his "Blue" and "Rose" periods (1900–07), he turned from portrayals of poor and isolated people to representations of harlequins, acrobats, and dancers in warmer colors. In 1904 he settled in Paris and became the center of a group of progressive artists and writers. In 1906 he began analyzing and reducing forms. The result was his spectacular canvas *Les Demoiselles d'Avignon* (completed 1907), which is now seen as a watershed in the development of

◀ **Picasso** The most famous, prolific, and versatile artist of the 20th century, Pablo Picasso was the driving force behind most of the radical art movements that occurred in the first half of the century. No single artist of the period had a greater expressive and emotional range. He produced remarkable paintings, sculptures, collages, lithographs, and ceramics, and also designed stage sets and costumes for theater and ballet.

P

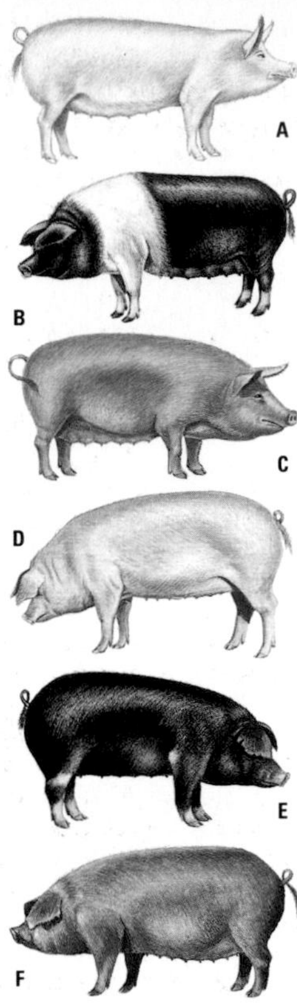


▲ **pig** Among nature's most efficient and omnivorous scavengers, there are a number of purebred pigs. The large white or Yorkshire (A) is the dominant breed in Britain. The saddlebacks (B) are popular free-range stocks in England, but are mainly used for cross breeding. The sandy-colored Tamworth (C), was traditionally a forest pig. The China (D) and Chester White (E) are popular in the US, along with the long red Duroc (F), but are uncommon in other countries.

▲ **pigeon** Homing pigeons can successfully navigate home over hundreds of miles, from sites never previously visited. It is thought they use the stars to navigate with at night, while during the day they rely on the position of the Sun. Experiments have also shown that homing pigeons have a navigational backup using the Earth's magnetic fields.

contemporary art. The fragmentary forms in the painting also heralded CUBISM. In the 1920s he produced solid classical figures but at the same time he was exploring SURREALISM. Picasso's sculpture ranks as highly as his painting. He was one of the first to use assembled rather than modeled or carved materials. The most famous example is his *Head of a Bull, Metamorphosis* (1943), which consists of a bicycle saddle and handlebars.

**Piccard, Auguste** (1884–1962) Swiss physicist who explored the STRATOSPHERE and deep seas. In 1931 a hydrogen balloon carried an airtight aluminum sphere, containing Piccard and an assistant, to an altitude of almost 51,800ft (15,800m). This was the first ascent into the stratosphere. From 1948 he experimented with designs for a diving vessel called a bathyscaphe. In 1953 Piccard and his son **Jacques** (1922– ) descended in the bathyscaphe *Trieste* to a depth of about 10,000ft (3,100m) in the Mediterranean Sea. In 1960 Piccard and a naval officer used the same craft in the Pacific Ocean to reach a record of 35,800ft (10,900m).

**piccolo** WOODWIND musical instrument of the FLUTE family. About half the size of the flute and pitched one octave higher, it is played in the same way.

**Pickford, Mary** (1893–1979) US film actress, b. Gladys Mary Smith, famous in silent films. These include *Poor Little Rich Girl* (1917), *Pollyanna* (1919), and *Little Lord Fauntleroy* (1921). In 1919 she established the United Artists Corporation with Charlie CHAPLIN, Douglas FAIRBANKS, and D.W. Griffith.

**Picts** Ancient inhabitants of E and N Scotland. By the 8th century they had a kingdom extending from Caithness to Fife, and had adopted Christianity. To the W and S of the Picts, invaders from Ireland had established the kingdom of Dalriada; in 843 its king, Kenneth I, also became king of the Picts, uniting the two kingdoms into the kingdom of Scotland.

**pidgin** Simplified form of a language, differing from other LINGUA FRANCAS by comprising a very limited vocabulary and being used for communication between people who do not speak the same language. Most pidgins in use today are based on English, French, Spanish, or Portuguese.

**Piedmont** (Piemonte) Region of NW Italy, bounded to the N, W, and S by mountains, and to the E by the Po Valley; it comprises the provinces of Alessandria, Asti, Cuneo, Novara, Torino, and Vercelli. Already an important region in Roman times, it was later subject to Lombard, then Frankish rule. Under the influence of Savoy from the early 15th century, it became part of the kingdom of Sardinia in 1720. In the early 19th century it was the focus of the movement for Italian independence, joining a united Italy in 1861. The Po Valley has some excellent farmland. Products: grain, vegetables, fruit, dairy. Industries: winemaking, motor vehicles. Area: 9,800sq mi (25,400sq km). Pop. (1991) 4,302,565.

**Pierce, Franklin** (1804–69) 14th US President (1853–57). He represented New Hampshire in the US House of Representatives (1833–37) and the Senate (1837–42). He gained the Democratic presidential nomination as a compromise candidate and was elected in 1852. The most notable feature of his presidency was his endorsement of the Kansas-Nebraska Act (1854), which resulted in near-civil war in Kansas between pro- and antislavery settlers.

**Piero della Francesca** (1415–92) (Piero dei Franceschi) Italian painter. He was familiar with the innovations made by MASACCIO, DONATELLO, Filippo LIPPI, and others. He drew their achievements together to create a monumental, deeply reflective style. His most important work is the FRESCO series depicting the *Legend of the True Cross* (finished *c.*1465) for the choir of San Francesco, Arezzo.

**Piero di Cosimo** (1462–1521) Italian painter. The pictures attributed to him are bizarre mythologies peopled by fauns, centaurs, and primitive men. These paintings are sometimes comic, but he could also create moving scenes, such as *Death of Procris* (*c.*1510).

**Pierre** Capital of South Dakota, on the Missouri River, opposite Fort Pierre. Originally the capital of the Arikara Native Americans, it was a trading settlement in the early 19th century before being established as a railroad terminus in 1880. It became the permanent state capital in 1904. Its economy is based on government services and agriculture (grain, cattle). Pop. (1990) 12,906.

**Pietism** Influential Christian spiritual movement within Protestantism, founded in the late 17th century by the German Lutheran minister, Philipp Spener (1635–1705). Its aim was to revitalize evangelical Christianity by emphasizing spiritual issues.

**piezoelectric effect** Creation of positive electric charge on one side of a nonconducting crystal and a negative charge on the other when the crystal is squeezed. The pressure results in an electric field that can be detected as voltage between the opposite crystal faces. The effect has been used in gramophone pickups, crystal microphones, and cigarette lighters.

**pig** Any of numerous species and varieties of domestic and wild swine of the family Suidae. The male is generally called a boar; the female, a sow. A castrated boar is usually known as a hog. It is generally a massive, short-legged omnivore with a thick skin. Wild pigs include the warthog, wild BOAR, bush pig, and babirusa.

**pigeon** (dove) Any of a large family of wild and domestic birds found throughout temperate and tropical parts of the world, but concentrated in S Asia and the Australian region. Pigeons have small heads, short necks, plump bodies, and scaly legs and feet. Plumage is loose but thick. Length: to 18in (46cm). Family Columbidae; typical genus, *Columba*.

**pigment** Colored, insoluble substance used to impart color to an object and added for this purpose to PAINTS, inks, and plastics. They generally function by absorbing and reflecting light.

**pigmentation** In biology, a natural chemical that gives color to TISSUES. In humans, the skin, hair, and iris are colored by the pigment MELANIN, together with the HEMOGLOBIN in ERYTHROCYTES (red blood cells), which also acts as a pigment.

**pika** Any of 12 species of short-haired relatives of the RABBIT. They live in cold regions of Europe, Asia, and the W US. Length: to 8in (20cm). Genus *Ochotona*.

**Pike, Zebulon Montgomery** (1779–1813) US explorer. An army officer, he was sent to explore the newly purchased Louisiana Territory. Pike discovered but failed to climb Pike's Peak, in SE Colorado. He was killed during the WAR OF 1812.

**pike** Predatory, freshwater fish found in E North America and parts of Europe and Asia. It has a shovel-shaped mouth and a mottled, elongated body. Length: to 54in (137cm); weight: to 46lb (21kg) Family Esocidae; genus *Esox*.

**pike perch** Freshwater food and game fish of Central Europe, where it includes the zander, and of North America, where it is related to the walleye and sauger. A dark olive, mottled fish, the pike perch has an elongated body and large head and mouth. Length: to 91.4cm (3ft); weight: to 25lb (11kg). Family Percidae; species *Stizostedion vitreum*.

**pilchard** Marine food fish resembling a herring, found in shoals along most coasts except those of Asia. They support a huge canning industry. The young are sometimes called SARDINES. Length: less than 18in (45.7cm). Family Clupeidae; species *Sardina pilchardus*.

**pilgrimage** Religiously motivated journey to a shrine or other holy place to gain spiritual help or guidance, or for the purpose of thanksgiving. Pilgrimages are common to many religions, particularly in the East.

**Pilgrims** Group of English PURITANS who immigrated to North America in 1620. After fleeing to Leiden, Netherlands, in 1608, seeking refuge from persecution in England, they decided to look for greater religious freedom by founding a religious society in America. They sailed from Plymouth, England, on the MAYFLOWER and founded the PLYMOUTH COLONY in present-day Massachusetts.

**pill, the** Popular term for oral contraceptives based on female reproductive HORMONES. They work by preventing ovulation. Two types of synthetic hormone, similar to ESTROGEN and PROGESTERONE, are generally used. Possible side-effects include headache, HYPERTENSION, weight gain, and a slightly increased risk of THROMBOSIS. *See also* CONTRACEPTION

**pilot fish** Marine fish that lives in warm seas, often found swimming close to sharks, ships and other large objects. A blue fish with five to seven dark bar markings on the sides and a white tail, it feeds on smaller fish. Length: to 2ft (60cm). Family Carangidae; species *Naucrates ductor*.

**Pilsen** *See* PLZEŇ

**Pilsudski, Józef** (1867–1935) Polish general and statesman, instrumental in securing Poland's independence. During World War I he led Polish forces against Russia, hoping to establish a Polish state. After independence, Pilsudski became head of state. His attempt to create a larger Polish state during the Polish–Soviet War failed, although he inflicted a remarkable defeat on the invading Russians in 1920. He retired in 1923, but seized power again in 1926 and established an authoritarian personal rule that lasted until his death.

**Pima** Tribe of Native North Americans speaking a Uto-Aztecan tongue, and closely related to the PAPAGO. They occupied the Gila and Salt river valleys in S Arizona, where some 8,000 still reside today. They are the descendants of the ancient Hohokam people.

**pimpernel** Small, trailing annual plant of the genus *Anagallis*, native to Britain and the US. The single, small, five petalled flowers are scarlet, white, or blue. The yellow pimpernel, a creeping European plant of shady areas, is *Lysimachia nemorum*. Family Primulaceae.

**Pinckney, Charles** (1757–1824) US politician. He was the youngest member of the CONTINENTAL CONGRESS (1784–87) and played a major role at the CONSTITUTIONAL CONVENTION (1785–87). As minister to Spain (1801–05), he secured Spanish acceptance of the LOUISIANA PURCHASE. He served as South Carolina's governor (1789–92, 1796–98, 1806–08).

**Pincus, Gregory Goodwin** (1903–67) US biologist who helped to develop the contraceptive PILL using synthetic HORMONES.

**Pindar** (522–438 BC) Greek poet known for his choric lyrics and triumphal ODES. Of the 17 volumes of Pindar's works known to his contemporaries, only 44 odes survive, written to celebrate victories in athletic games.

**pine** Any of various EVERGREEN, cone-bearing trees of the genus *Pinus*, most of which are native to cooler temperate regions of the world. Many have two types of shoots, some with needle-like leaves, and others with deciduous, scale-like leaves. The reproductive organs may be catkins or cones. Many species are valued for soft wood, wood pulp, oils, and resins. Family: Pinaceae.

**pineal body** Small gland attached to the undersurface of the vertebrate brain. In human beings, it has an endocrine function, secreting the hormone melatonin, which is involved in daily rhythms. *See also* ENDOCRINE SYSTEM

**pineapple** Tropical, herbaceous, perennial plant that is cultivated in the US, South America, Asia, Africa, and Australia; also the fruit of the plant. The fruit is formed from the flowers and bracts and grows on top of a short, stout stem bearing stiff, fleshy leaves. Height: to 4ft (1.2cm). Family Bromeliaceae; species *Ananas comosus*.

**pink** Common name for several genera of the pink family (Caryophyllaceae), especially the genus *Dianthus* of more than 300 species, most of which are native to the Mediterranean region. Short, herbaceous perennials, many are hardy evergreens with showy, fragrant flowers. Leaves are simple and usually opposite, and the symmetrical flowers are usually bisexual. *See also* CARNATION

**Pinkerton, Allan** (1819–84) US detective, b. Scotland. He moved to the US in 1842, and became a detective in the Chicago police force, resigning in 1850 to establish his own agency, Pinkerton's National Detective Agency. He organized and headed a federal intelligence service (1861).

**Pink Floyd** British rock group formed in 1964 with original members Syd Barrett, Roger Waters, Nick Mason, and Rick Wright. Barrett was replaced by David Gilmour in 1968. Their most acclaimed albums are *Dark Side of the Moon* (1973) and *The Wall* (1979).

**pinna** Flap of skin and cartilage that comprises the visible, external part of the EAR. It helps to collect sound waves and direct them into the ear canal.

**Pinochet Ugarte, Augusto** (1915– ) Ruler of Chile (1973–89). He led the military coup that overthrew Salvador Allende and headed a four-man junta, taking the title of president under a new constitution in 1981. His policies were pursued by ruthless means, including torture and murder. After a referendum (1988) in which a majority voted against extending his presidency, he permitted free elections but, until 1988, retained command of the armed forces.

**Pinter, Harold** (1930– ) British playwright. His successes include *The Birthday Party* (1958), *The Caretaker* (1960), *The Homecoming* (1965), *Old Times* (1971), and *No Man's Land* (1975). More recent plays include *Moonlighting* (1993). In most of his plays, ordinary characters and settings are presented in an atmosphere of mystery and fear.

**Pinyin** System of spelling used to transliterate ideographic Chinese characters into the Roman alphabet. It is a phonetic system and was officially adopted by the People's Republic of China in 1958.

**Pioneer program** Series of unmanned interplanetary probes launched by the US. In 1960 Pioneer 5 measured distances within the SOLAR SYSTEM and studied magnetism and the SOLAR WIND. Pioneer 10, launched in 1972, reached Jupiter in 1973. It investigated the planet's atmosphere and magnetic field and sent back more than 300 pictures of the planet. Pioneer 11, launched in 1973, reached Jupiter in 1974 and Saturn in 1979, discovering two moons there.

**pipefish** Any of numerous species of marine fish found in the shallow, warm, and temperate waters of the Atlantic and Pacific oceans. Related to the seahorse, it has a pencil-like body. Its mouth is at the end of a long snout. Length: to 23in (58cm). Family Syngnathidae.

**Piper, John** (1903–92) British watercolor painter and art critic. Some of his most striking works are the pictures of bomb-damaged buildings that he made during World War II. After 1950 he designed stage sets for operas and created stained glass windows.

**pipit** (fieldlark, titlark) Any of more than 50 small, brown, inconspicuous birds that resemble LARKS in habits and appearance. They are found worldwide. The plumage of both sexes is a similar streaked brown or grayish color, with a long, white-edged "wag" tail. Length: 6in (15cm). Family Motacillidae; genus *Anthus*.

**piracy** Robbery by force of arms on the high seas. Pirates usually attacked ships of all nations indiscriminately and were therefore distinguished from the crews of PRIVATEERS, who were in the service of a country and held a commission authorizing them to attack the shipping of certain belligerent powers. Piracy was prevalent until the 19th century.

**Piraeus** Seaport city in SE Greece, 5mi (8km) SW of Athens; largest Greek port. Piraeus was planned *c.*490 BC and rapidly developed into the major sea outlet. It was destroyed by the Roman general SULLA in 86 BC and fell into decline. In the 19th century, following Greek independence, a process of reconstruction led to the creation of the modern naval and commercial port. Industries: shipbuilding, oil refining, textiles, chemicals. Pop. (1991) 182,671.

**Pirandello, Luigi** (1867–1936) Italian dramatist, novelist, and short-story writer. Among his plays are *Six Characters in Search of an Author* (1921) and *As You Desire Me* (1930). His novels include *The Late Mattia Pascal* (1923). He won the 1934 Nobel Prize for literature.

▲ **pine** The lodgepole pine (*Pinus contorta*) grows in W North America, reaching a height of 60ft (18m). It is a small, vigorous mountain tree that is hardy to an altitude of 11,000ft (3,500m).

P

◀ **pineapple** An important cash crop in some tropical regions, pineapples bear fleshy fruit, which can be eaten fresh, but the majority is tinned or turned into pineapple juice.

▲ **piranha** The red piranha (*Rooseveltiella natterei*) of South America is notorious for its ferocity. Its powerful jaws have sharp teeth, and it makes up for its relatively small size – 14in (35cm) – by swimming in large shoals. These represent a threat to larger fish, land animals, and even humans. They feed in bouts, rather than continuously, and use their sense of smell to locate their prey.

**Piranesi, Giovanni Battista** (1720–78) Italian engraver and architect. He lived in Rome where he became famous for his *Vedute*, 137 etchings of the ancient and modern city (1745).

**piranha** (piraya) Tropical, bony, freshwater fish that lives in rivers in South America. It is a voracious predator, with formidable teeth and an aggressive temperament. Piranhas usually travel and attack in shoals and can pose a serious threat to much larger creatures. Length: to 24in (61cm). Family Characidae; genus *Serrasalmus*.

**Pisa** City on the Arno River, Tuscany, w central Italy. Already an important Etruscan town, Pisa prospered as a Roman colony from *c*.180 BC. In the Middle Ages it was a powerful maritime republic but later came under Florentine domination. Industries: tourism, textiles, glass, machine tools. Pop (1992 est.) 108,000.

**Pisanello** (*c*.1395–*c*.1455) (Antonio Pisano) Italian painter and medalist. Working in the International Gothic style, he drew detailed studies of birds, people, and costumes. His medals of important people of his time are of historic value.

**Pisano, Nicola** (1225–84) Italian sculptor. In Pisa he executed his first masterpiece, the pulpit for the Baptistry (1260). In his work on the cathedral pulpit in Siena (1265–68) he was aided by his son, **Giovanni** (*c*.1250– *c*.1320), whose taste in decoration was influenced by the French Gothic style.

**Piscator, Ervin Friedrich Max** (1893–1966) German stage director. He developed the concept of EPIC THEATER, which BRECHT incorporated into the work of the Berliner Ensemble. Piscator believed theater should be a political medium. *See also* EXPRESSIONISM

**Pisces** (the Fishes) Inconspicuous equatorial constellation situated on the ecliptic between Aquarius and Aries; it is the 12th sign of the Zodiac.

**Pisistratus** (605–527 BC) Athenian ruler. He became leader of the popular party in Athens. He seized control by force in 560 BC but was overthrown in 554 BC and driven into exile. With support from Thebes and Argos, he regained power in 541 BC and ruled as "tyrant" until his death.

**Pissarro, Camille** (1830–1903) French painter who adopted IMPRESSIONISM. In the 1880s he experimented with the pointillist theories of Georges SEURAT but abandoned them in the 1890s for a freer interpretation. His works include *Louvre from Pont Neuf* (1902).

**pistachio** Deciduous tree native to the Mediterranean region and E Asia. It is grown commercially for the edible greenish seed (the pistachio nut) of its wrinkled red fruit. Height: to 20ft (6m). Family Anacardiaceae; species *Pistacia vera*.

**pistil** Female organ located in the center of a flower. It consists of an OVARY, a slender STYLE, and a STIGMA, which receives POLLEN.

**pistol** FIREARM held and fired in one hand. The first were matchlocks, in which a glowing fuse ignited the charge; by the end of the 16th century, wheel locks and the cheaper flintlocks were also in use. The invention of the percussion cap in 1815 enabled pistol technology to advance rapidly, and Samuel Colt's revolver of 1835 was the first reliable repeating firearm. Since then pistols have become capable of automatic fire.

**Pitcairn Island** Volcanic island in the central S Pacific Ocean forming (together with the uninhabited islands of Henderson, Ducie, and Oeno) a British crown colony. First sighted in 1767, Pitcairn was settled in 1790 by mutineers from the British ship HMS *Bounty*. Some of their descendants still live on the island. The principal economic activity is the growing and exporting of fruit. Area: 1.7sq mi (4.6sq km). Pop. (1994) 56.

**pitch** Quality of sound that determines its position in a musical scale. It is measured in terms of the frequency of sound waves (measured in hertz) – the higher the frequency, the higher the pitch.

**pitchblende** *See* URANINITE

**pitcher plant** Any of several species of INSECTIVOROUS PLANT of the tropics and subtropics. Insects are trapped in the vase-shaped leaves, which are lined with bristles. Trapped insects decompose and are absorbed as nutrients by plant cells. The flower is usually red. Height: 8–24in (20–61cm). Family Sarraceniacea; genera *Sarracenia* and *Nepenthes*.

**Pitt, William, the Younger** (1759–1806) British statesman, prime minister (1783–1801, 1804–06). The second son of William PITT, earl of Chatham, he entered Parliament in 1781, became chancellor of the exchequer in 1782 and shortly after became Britain's youngest prime minister, aged 24. He resigned in the face of GEORGE III's refusal to consider CATHOLIC EMANCIPATION. He returned to power in 1804 and died in office. His reputation rests chiefly on his reforming financial and commercial policies in the 1780s, which restored British prosperity and prestige after the disaster of the AMERICAN REVOLUTION.

**Pittsburgh** City at the confluence of the Allegheny and Monongahela rivers (forming the Ohio river), SW Pennsylvania. Fort Duquesne was founded on the site by the French *c*.1750. Captured by the British in 1758, it was renamed Fort Pitt. Pittsburgh grew as a steel manufacturing center in the 19th century (the industry is now in decline). Industries: glass, machinery, petroleum products. Pop. (1990) 369,379.

**pituitary gland** Major gland of the ENDOCRINE SYSTEM, located at the base of the BRAIN. In human beings it is about the size of a pea and is connected to the HYPOTHALAMUS by a stalk. It produces many HORMONES, some of which regulate the activity of other endocrine glands, while others control growth.

**Pius V, Saint** (1504–72) Pope (1568–72), b. Antonio Ghislieri. He was an energetic reformer of the Church and enemy of Protestantism. He excommunicated Queen ELIZABETH I of England in 1570. During his reign, he succeeded in eliminating Protestantism from Italy. He was canonized in 1712.

**Pius VII** (1742–1823) Pope (1800–23), b. Barnaba Gregorio Chiaramonti. He secured the Concordat of 1801 with NAPOLEON I. After Napoleon took Rome in 1808 and annexed the PAPAL STATES in 1809, Pius excommunicated him and was removed and imprisoned until 1814. On his restoration he encouraged the reform of religious orders and education.

**Pius IX** (1792–1878) Pope (1846–78), b. Giovanni Maria Mastai-Ferrett. He was driven from Rome (1848–50), but restored by NAPOLEON III. He defended German Catholics from persecution by BISMARCK. In 1869 Pius convened the First VATICAN COUNCIL, which proclaimed the principle of PAPAL INFALLIBILITY.

**Pius X, Saint** (1835–1914) Pope (1903–14), b. Giuseppe Melchiorre Sarto. He opposed religious MODERNISM, placing several modernist books on the INDEX in 1907. He also condemned the separation of Church and state in France and recodified CANON LAW (a revision published posthumously in 1917). He was canonized in 1954.

**Pius XI** (1857–1939) Pope (1922–39), b. Achille Ratti. He denounced totalitarianism, both communist and fascist, though he was forced to make political compromises with fascist governments. In 1929 he signed the LATERAN TREATY with Mussolini, which recognized the sovereignty of the Vatican.

**Pius XII** (1876–1958) Pope (1939–58), b. Eugenio Pacelli. Fearing political reprisals, he failed to denounce the Nazis and the persecution of Jews during World War II. He was openly hostile to communism.

**Pizarro, Francisco** (1471–1541) Spanish *conquistador* of the INCA empire of Peru. He served under CORTÉS and led expeditions to South America (1522–28). Having gained royal support, he led 180 men to Peru in 1530. They captured and later murdered the Inca ATAHUALPA, and took Cuzco, the capital (1534). Pizarro acted as governor of the conquered territory, founding Lima in 1535.

**placebo** Harmless substance that has no active ingredient, given in place of actual medication. It may be psychologically effective and bring about improvement in a patient's condition. It is also used in drug trials: some subjects take placebos and others the drugs to be tested, and the reactions of the two groups are compared.

**placenta** Organ in mammals (except monotremes and marsupials) that connects the FETUS to the UTERUS of the mother. Part of the placenta contains tiny blood vessels through which oxygen and food are carried from the mother to the embryo via the umbilical cord and wastes are carried from the embryo to the mother's bloodstream to be excreted. The placenta secretes hormones that maintain pregnancy and is discharged from the mother's body as the afterbirth, immediately after delivery.

**plagioclase** Type of FELDSPAR. Plagioclase minerals occur in IGNEOUS and METAMORPHIC rocks. Off-white, or sometimes pink, green, or brown, they are composed of varying proportions of the silicates of sodium and calcium with aluminum. They show an oblique cleavage and have triclinic system crystals. Hardness 6–6.5; s.g. 2.6.

**plague** Acute infectious disease of humans and rodents caused by the bacillus *Yersinia pestis*. In humans it occurs in three forms: bubonic plague, most common and characterized by vomiting, fever, and swellings of the lymph nodes called "buboes"; pneumonic plague, in which the lungs are infected; and septicaemic plague, in which the bloodstream is invaded. Treatment is the administration of vaccines, bed rest, antibiotics, and sulfa drugs.

**plaice** Marine flatfish found along the w European coast. An important food fish, it is brown or gray with orange spots. Length: to 3ft (90cm); weight: to 26lb (11.8kg). Family Pleuronectidae; species *Pleuronectes platessa*.

**Plaid Cymru** (Party of Wales) Welsh nationalist political party, founded in 1925 as Plaid Genedlaethol Cymru. Its first member of the House of Commons was elected in 1966. It advocates Welsh independence (from the United Kingdom) within the European Union.

**plainsong** (plainchant) Collection of unharmonized liturgical melodies of the Western Church, traditionally performed unaccompanied. Plainsong goes back to the beginning of the Christian era. The melodies use free rhythms, and the musical "scales" they employ derive from the "modes" of ancient Greek music. In the 6th century, plainsong was reformed, supposedly at the behest of Pope GREGORY I ("the Great"). In this reformed state (known as Gregorian chant), the range of a melody is not more than five notes.

**Planck, Max Karl Ernst Ludwig** (1858–1947) German theoretical physicist whose revolutionary QUANTUM THEORY helped to establish modern physics. In 1900 he came to the conclusion that the frequency distribution of BLACK BODY radiation could only be accounted for if the radiation was emitted in separate "packets" called quanta, rather than continuously. Planck's constant (1900) links wave and particle behaviour on the atomic scale. His equation, relating the energy of a quantum to its frequency, is the basis of quantum theory. He was awarded the 1918 Nobel Prize for physics for his work.

**plane** In mathematics, a flat surface such that a straight line joining any two points on it lies entirely within the surface. Its general equation in the three-dimensional CARTESIAN COORDINATE SYSTEM is $ax + by + cz = d$, where a, b, c, and d are constants.

**planet** Large, nonstellar body in orbit around a star, shining only by reflecting the star's light. In our SOLAR SYSTEM there are nine major planets, as opposed to the thousands of small bodies known as ASTEROIDS or minor planets. *See also* MERCURY; VENUS; EARTH; MARS; JUPITER; SATURN; URANUS; NEPTUNE; PLUTO

**planetarium** Domed building in which a projector displays an artificial sky in order to demonstrate the positions and motions of the Sun, Moon, planets, and stars.

**plankton** All the floating or drifting life of the ocean, especially that near the surface. The organisms are very small and move with the currents. There are two main kinds: phytoplankton, floating plants; and zooplankton, floating animals. They are a vital part of the food chain.

**plant** Any member of the kingdom Plantae, a large kingdom of multicellular organism whose cells have cellulose cell walls and contain CHLOROPLASTS or similar structures (plastids). Plants develop from DIPLOID embryos and have a regular alternation of HAPLOID and diploid generations in their life cycles. Most plants are green and make their own food by PHOTOSYNTHESIS. A few are colorless PARASITES or SAPROPHYTES. Simple plants reproduce by means of SPORES, while more advanced plants produce SEEDS and FRUITS. Plants show a wide range of biochemistry; some produce chemicals such as ALKALOIDS, NARCOTICS, and even cyanide; others secrete substances into the soil to prevent other plants growing near them. Many of these chemicals form the bases for the development of DRUGS. Plants are classified on the basis of their morphology (shape and structure). The most important phyla are the Bryophyta (BRYOPHYTES), which includes the mosses and liverworts; LYCOPODOPHYTA (CLUB MOSSES); Sphenophyta (HORSETAILS); Filicinophyta (FERNS); Cycadophyta (CYCADS); Ginkgophyta (GINKGO); Coniferophyta (CONIFERS); and Angiospermophyta (ANGIOSPERMS). *See also* ALTERNATION OF GENERATIONS

**Plantagenet** English royal dynasty (1154–1485). The name encompasses the ANGEVINS (1154–1399) and the houses of LANCASTER and YORK. They are descended from Geoffrey of Anjou and Matilda, daughter of HENRY I. The name was adopted by Richard, duke of York and father of EDWARD IV, during the Wars of the ROSES.

**plantain** Plant with a rosette of basal leaves and spikes of tiny, greenish white flowers; it grows in temperate regions and was used for medicinal purposes. Family Plantaginaceae; genus *Plantago*. The name plantain is also given to a tropical banana plant believed to be native to SE Asia and now cultivated throughout the tropics. It has green fruit that is larger and starchier than a banana. It is eaten cooked. Height: to 33ft (10m). Family Musaceae; species *Musa paradisiaca*.

**plant classification** System devised to group PLANTS according to relationships among them. Plants are known by common names that often vary from area to area, but have only one correct scientific name. *See* TAXONOMY

**plant genetics** Science of heredity and variation in plants. Research in GENETICS since 1900 has supplied the principles of plant breeding, especially HYBRIDIZATION. Genetic engineers grow cell and TISSUE CULTURES by the replication or cloning of sterile plant types. They also concentrate on isolating individual GENES with the aim of producing new color varieties for traditional flowers, improving the flavor of food crops, breeding resistance to pests and herbicides, and lengthening the shelf life of harvested crops. *See also* GENETIC ENGINEERING

**plaque** Abnormal deposit building up on a body surface, especially the film of saliva and bacteria on TEETH. It leads to tooth decay and gum disease.

**plasma** In biology, liquid portion of the BLOOD in which the cells are suspended. It contains an immense number of ions, inorganic and organic molecules such as immunoglobulins, and hormones and their carriers. It clots upon standing.

**plasma** In physics, an ionized gas that contains about the same amount of positive and negative IONS. Plasma, often described as the fourth state of MATTER, occurs at enormous temperatures, as in the interiors of the Sun and other stars and in fusion reactors.

◄ **Pitt the Younger** The British statesman William Pitt became prime minister when he was only 24, the youngest man to achieve that position. An ambitious and determined politician, he led the country for 20 years, His great parliamentary rival was Charles James Fox.

P

**plastic** Synthetic material composed of organic molecules, often in long chains called POLYMERS, that can be shaped and then hardened. Plastics are synthesized from common materials, mostly from petroleum. CELLULOSE comes from cotton or wood pulp, CASEIN from skimmed milk, others from chemicals derived from plants. Thermoset plastics, such as BAKELITE, stay hard once set, while thermoplastics, such as polyethyene, can be resoftened by heat. Biodegradable plastics are environmentally friendly because they eventually decompose.

**plastic surgery** Branch of surgery that involves the reconstruction of deformed, damaged, or disfigured parts of the body. Cosmetic surgery, such as facelifts, is performed solely to improve appearance.

**plastid** Type of organelle found in the cells of plants and green algae. CHLOROPLASTS and leucoplasts are two examples of plastids, which have a double membrane and contain DNA.

**Plata, Río de la** Estuary in SE South America formed by the junction of the PARANÁ and URUGUAY rivers at the border between Argentina and Uruguay. It was first explored by Europeans in the early 16th century. The cities of BUENOS AIRES and MONTEVIDEO lie on its S and N shores respectively. It is 170mi (270km) long, and 120mi (190km) wide at its mouth. Area: *c.*13,500sq mi (35,000sq km).

**Plataea, Battle of** (479 BC) Decisive battle of the PERSIAN WARS. The Greeks under the Spartan Pausanias and the Athenian Aristides won a total victory. The Persian army was almost destroyed and its commander, Mardonius, killed. The battle ended the ambitions of XERXES to conquer Greece.

**plateau** Extensive, fairly flat, raised area of land. Mountains may stand up above the general level of a plateau, or it may be carved by deep river valleys or canyons to form a **dissected** plateau. An **intermontaine** plateau is completely surrounded by mountains.

**platelet** Colorless, usually spherical structures found in mammalian BLOOD. Chemical compounds in platelets, known as factors and cofactors, are essential to the mechanism of BLOOD CLOTTING. The normal platelet count is about 300,000 per cu mm of blood.

**plate tectonics** Theory or model to explain the distribution, evolution, and causes of the Earth's crustal features. It proposes that the Earth's CRUST and part of the upper MANTLE (the LITHOSPHERE) is made up of several separate, rigid slabs, termed plates, which move independently forming part of a cycle in the creation and destruction of crust. The plates collide or move apart at the margins, and these produce zones of earthquake and volcanic activity. Plate movement is thought to be driven by convection currents in the mantle. *See also* SEAFLOOR SPREADING

**PLATE TECTONICS**

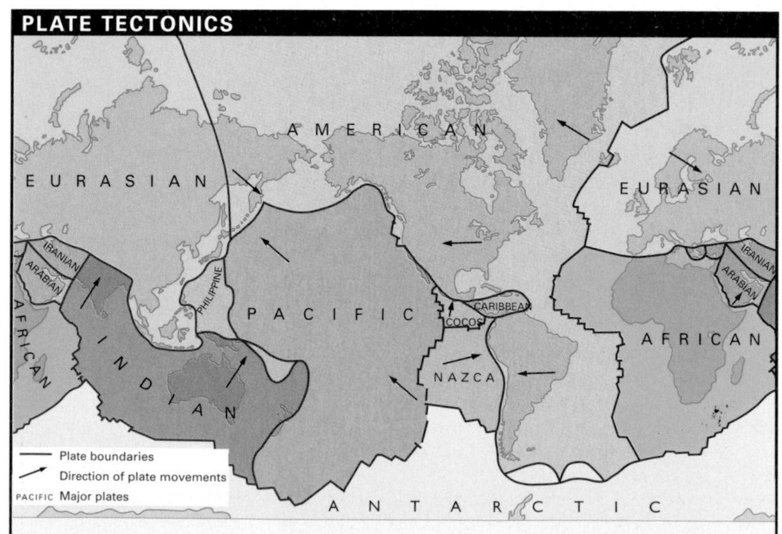


The discovery that the continents are carried along on the top of slowly moving crustal plates provided the mechanism for the drift theories to work. The plates converge and diverge along margins marked by seismic and volcanic activity. Plates diverge from mid-ocean ridges where molten lava pushes up and forces them apart at a rate of up to 1.5in (3.75cm) a year; converging plates form either a trench (where the oceanic plates sink below the lighter continental rock) or mountain ranges (where two continents collide).

**Plath, Sylvia** (1932–63) US poet. Her verse includes *The Colossus* (1960) and *Ariel* (1965). The latter was published after her suicide, as were *Crossing the Water* (1971), *Winter Trees* (1971), and *Collected Poems* (1981). She wrote one novel, *The Bell Jar* (1963). She was married to the British poet Ted HUGHES.

**platinum** (symbol Pt) Lustrous, silver-white metal, one of the TRANSITION ELEMENTS. Discovered in 1735, it is chiefly found in certain ores of nickel. Malleable and ductile, it is used in jewelry, dentistry, electrical-resistance wire, magnets, thermocouples, surgical tools, electrodes, and other laboratory apparatus, and as a CATALYST in catalytic converters for car exhausts. It is chemically unreactive and resists tarnishing and CORROSION. Properties: at.no. 78; at. wt. 195.09; sp. gr. 21.45; m.p. 3,222°F (1,772°C); b.p. 6,872°F (3,800°C); most common isotope $^{195}$Pt (33.8%).

**Plato** (427–347 BC) Ancient Greek philosopher and writer who formulated an ethical and metaphysical system based upon philosophical IDEALISM. From *c.*407 BC he was a disciple of SOCRATES, from whom he may have derived many of his ideas about ethics. Following the trial and execution of Socrates in 399 BC, Plato withdrew to Megara, after which he is believed to have traveled extensively in Egypt, Italy, and Sicily. He visited Syracuse in Sicily three times, in about 388, 367, and 361–360 BC, during the reigns of the tyrants Dionysius I and II. Plato sought to educate Dionysius II as a philosopher-king and set up an ideal political system under him, but the venture failed. Meanwhile, in Athens, Plato set up his famous ACADEMY (*c.*387 BC). In the Academy he taught several young people, including ARISTOTLE. In addition to being a philosopher of great influence, Plato wrote in the form of dialogues, in which SOCRATES genially interrogates another person, demolishing their arguments. All of Plato's 36 works survive. His most famous dialogues include the *Symposium* (a discussion on the nature of love). Plato's greatest work was the *Republic*, an extended dialogue on justice, in which he outlined his view of the ideal state.

**Platt Amendment** (1901) US legislation effectively making CUBA a US protectorate after the SPANISH–AMERICAN WAR. It was repealed in 1934, although the US retained the right to maintain its naval base on Guantánamo Bay.

**platypus** MONOTREME mammal of Australia and Tasmania. It is amphibious, lays eggs, and has webbed feet, a broad tail, and a soft, duck-like bill. The male has a poison spur on the hind foot. It is 24in (60cm) long and eats small invertebrates. Family Ornithorhynchidae; species *Ornithorhynchus anatinus*.

**Plautus, Titus Maccius** (254–184 BC) Roman comic playwright. His works, such as *Miles Gloriosus* (*c.*211 BC), were modeled on Greek originals. Shakespeare's *The Comedy of Errors* (1593) derives from Plautus' *Menaechmi*.

**plebeian** General body of Roman citizens, as distinct from the small PATRICIAN class. In the early years of the Republic they were barred from public office and from marrying a patrician. The gulf between the two classes gradually closed. By the 3rd century BC there was little legal distinction between them.

**plebiscite** (Lat. *plebis citum,* decree of the people) Proposal put before the people and enacted by the people by a direct vote of an entire district or country. Plebiscites are usually concerned with matters of a national importance such as the election of a leader or choice of government.

**Pléiade, La** Group of seven 16th-century French poets. They were Pierre de RONSARD, the leader of the group, Joachim du Bellay (1522–60), Jean-Antoine de Baïf (1532–89), Rémy Belleau (1528–77), Estienne Jodelle (1532–73), Pontus de Tyard (1522–1605) and Jean Dorat. Among the earliest writers of the French RENAISSANCE, they advocated French as a literary language.

**Pleiades** Young, OPEN CLUSTER in the constellation Taurus, popularly called the Seven Sisters. Although only six or seven stars are visible to the naked eye, there are in fact over a thousand embedded in a reflection NEBULA. The brightest member

P

is Alcyone, which is more than 300 times as luminous as the Sun. The cluster lies just over 400 light-years away.

**Pleistocene** Geological epoch that began about 2 million years ago, during which humans and most forms of familiar mammalian life evolved. Episodes of climatic cooling in this epoch led to the best-known ice age in the Earth's history. It ended around 8000 BC.

**Plekhanov, Georgy Valentinovich** (1857–1918) Russian revolutionary. After leading populist demonstrations, he was exiled in 1880 and adopted Marxism. He worked with LENIN until 1903 when, as leader of the MENSHEVIKS, he split with him. He returned to Russia in 1917 and died shortly after the RUSSIAN REVOLUTION.

**Plessy v. Ferguson** (1896) US Supreme Court decision following the Civil Rights Cases of 1883. Plessy held that a state law requiring separation of races on public transportation facilities did not violate the 14th Amendment. Thus, state-enforced segregation was acceptable until Plessy was overruled in BROWN V. BOARD OF EDUCATION OF TOPEKA in 1954.

**pleura** Double membrane that lines the space between the lungs and the walls of the chest. The fluid between the pleura lubricates the two surfaces to prevent friction during breathing movements.

**pleurisy** Inflammation of the PLEURA. It is nearly always due to infection, but may arise as a complication of other diseases.

**Pliny the Elder** (AD 23–79) (Gaius Plinius Secundus) Roman author of *Historia Naturalis* (*Natural History*). His one major surviving work covers a vast range of subjects, mixing fact and fiction.

**Pliny the Younger** (AD 62–114) (Gaius Plinius Caecilius Secundus) Roman administrator. The nephew and adopted son of PLINY THE ELDER, he became a senator and governor of Bythnia (*c.*112). He is best known for his correspondence with the Emperor TRAJAN, which provides a unique record of the life of a Roman gentleman.

**Pliocene** Last era of the TERTIARY period that lasted from 5 to 2 million years ago and preceded the PLEISTOCENE. Animal and plant life was similar to that of today.

**PLO** *See* PALESTINE LIBERATION ORGANIZATION

**Plotinus** (205–270) Ancient philosopher, who was the founder of NEOPLATONISM. He opened a school in Rome *c.*244. In essence, Plotinus conceived of the universe as a hierarchy proceeding from matter, through soul and reason, to God. His pupil and biographer, Porphyry, compiled and edited Plotinus' writings into six books of nine chapters each, known as the *Enneads*.

**plover** Any of several species of wading shorebirds, many of which migrate long distances over open seas from Arctic breeding grounds to Southern Hemisphere wintering areas. It has a large head, a plump gray, brown, or golden speckled body, and short legs. Length: to 11in (28cm). Family Charadriidae; genera include *Charadrius* and *Pluvialis*.

**plow** Agricultural implement used to cut furrows in soil for aeration and in preparation for sowing or planting. The first plow appeared in the NEOLITHIC period, and in the BRONZE AGE became metal-tipped wooden wedges fastened to a single handle and a beam, pulled by men or oxen. This form remained virtually unchanged until the 19th century when the moldboard was introduced in the US. This was a curved board that turned over the slice of earth cut by the plow's blade or share.

**Plowright, Joan Anne** (1929– ) English actress. She often appeared in classical productions with her husband Laurence OLIVIER; her modern works included the first performance of John OSBORNE's *The Entertainer* (1957).

**plum** Fruit tree, mostly native to Asia and naturalized in Europe and North America, widely cultivated for its fleshy, edible fruit, which has a hard "pit" at the center. The most common cultivated plum of Europe and Asia is *Prunus domsetica*; in North America, the Japanese plum (*Prunus salicina*) is crossed with European varieties to give several cultivated strains. Family Rosaceae.

**plumule** In botany, an embryonic shoot that develops during germination of a seed.

**pluralism** In politics, theory that state power is wielded by a number of groups with conflicting interests, none of which is able to establish absolute authority. In philosophy, pluralism is the name given to the theory that there are many ultimate substances, rather than one, as in MONISM. Pluralism can also mean the holding of more than one office at the same time, especially within the Church.

**Plutarch** (46–120) Greek biographer and essayist. His best known work is *The Parallel Lives*, which consists of biographies of soldiers and statesmen.

**Pluto** Roman god of the underworld, equivalent to the Greek god HADES. He ruled over the land of the dead and was also a god of wealth, since his realm contained all underground mineral riches.

**Pluto** Smallest and outermost planet of the Solar System. The last planet in our Solar System to be discovered. Independently, William H. Pickering and Percival LOWELL calculated the possible existence of Pluto. The planet was eventually located in 1930 by Clyde Tombaugh within 5° of Lowell's predicted position. Pluto seems to have a mottled surface with light and dark regions, and signs of polar caps. The surface is covered with icy deposits consisting of 98% nitrogen, with traces of methane, and also probably water, carbon dioxide, and carbon monoxide. Pluto has a single moon, Charon, which is so large that some astronomers consider Pluto/Charon as a double planet.

**plutonium** (symbol Pu) Silver-white, radioactive, metallic element of the ACTINIDE SERIES. It was first synthesized in 1940 by Glenn Seaborg and associates at the University of California at Berkeley by the deuteron (heavy hydrogen) bombardment of URANIUM. It is found naturally in small amounts in uranium ores. $^{239}$Pu (half-life 24,360 years) is made in large quantities in breeder reactors. It is a fissile element used in NUCLEAR REACTORS and nuclear weapons. The element is very toxic and absorbed by bone, making it a dangerous radiological hazard. Properties: at.no. 94; sp. gr. 19.84; m.p. 1,186°F (641°C); b.p. 5,850°F (3,232°C); most stable isotope $^{244}$Pu (half-life 25,000 years). *See also* TRANSURANIC ELEMENTS

**Plymouth** City and port on the Tamar estuary, Devon, SW England. In 1588 Sir Francis DRAKE set out from Plymouth to attack the Spanish ARMADA, and the MAYFLOWER sailed for America in 1620. It has a naval base, and ferry links with France and Spain. Industries: China clay, machine tools. Pop. (1991) 243,373.

**Plymouth Brethren** Strictly Puritan sect of evangelical Christians, founded in Ireland in the late 1820s by J.N. Darby, an ordained Anglican. Their name comes from their having established their first English center at Plymouth in 1831.

**Plymouth Colony** First colonial settlement in New England (founded 1620). The settlers were a group of about 100 Puritan Separatist PILGRIMS, who sailed on the MAYFLOWER and settled on what is now CAPE COD Bay, Massachusetts. They named the first town after their port of departure. Lacking a royal charter, government was established by the MAYFLOWER COMPACT. During the first winter nearly half the settlers died. Plymouth Colony became part of Massachusetts in 1691.

**Plzeň** (Pilsen) City in W Czech Republic. Founded in the 13th century by King Wenceslaus II, it was a focal point for Roman Catholic resistance during the HUSSITE Wars. It is a center for heavy industry, and is internationally famous for its beer. Pop. (1990) 175,000.

**pneumatic** Device powered by compressed air normally used to produce rotary or a reciprocating (back and forth) motion to speed up operations such as sawing, grinding, digging, hammering, and riveting. The pneumatic drill used in roadworks has a reciprocating, pounding motion at speeds of between 80–500 revs per minute.

**pneumoconiosis** Occupational disease principally of miners working in confined and dusty conditions. Caused by inhaling irritants, often only as minute specks, the disease inflames and can finally destroy lung tissue.

**pneumonia** Inflammation of the LUNG tissue, most often caused by bacterial infection. Most at risk are the very young, the aged, and those whose immune systems have been undermined by disease or certain medical treatments. The commonest form is pneumococcal pneumonia, caused by the bac-

▲ **plum** A hybrid of two other fruits, the cherry plum and the sloe, the plum tree (*Prunus domestica*) is a hardy tree that thrives in temperate regions worldwide.

**PLUTO: DATA**

Diameter (equatorial): 1,444mi (2,324km)
Mass (Earth = 1): 0.002
Volume (Earth = 1): 0.01
Density (water = 1): 2.03
Orbital period: 247.7 years
Rotation period: 6.375 days
Average surface termperature: –382°F (–230°C)

P

terium *Streptococcus pneumoniae*. Symptoms include fever, chest pain, coughing, and the production of rust-colored sputum. Treatment is with ANTIBIOTICS.

**pneumothorax** Presence of air in the pleural space between the lungs and the chest wall. It may arise spontaneously or be caused by injury or disease. The lung is liable to collapse.

**Po** Italy's longest river, in N Italy. It rises in the Cottian Alps near the French border, and flows E to empty into the Adriatic Sea. The Po valley is an important industrial and agricultural region, and water from the river is used extensively in irrigation schemes. Length: 405mi (650km).

**Pocahontas** (1595–1617) Native American princess and early colonial heroine. According to legend, she saved the life of John SMITH, leader of the JAMESTOWN colonists, when he was about to be killed by her father, POWHATAN. Captured by the colonists in 1613, she adopted their customs and in 1614 married John Rolfe. She died during a visit to England.

**Po Chü-i** (772–846) Chinese poet of the T'ANG period. He wrote poems of social protest in simple, everyday language.

**pod** Fruit of any leguminous plant, such as a pea or bean. A pod is an elongated, caselike structure filled with seeds. It develops from a single CARPEL, and when ripe splits down both sides to release the seeds. Family Papilionaceae/Leguminosae. *See also* LEGUME

**podiatry** Treatment and care of the foot. Podiatrists treat such conditions as corns and bunions and devise ways to accommodate foot deformities.

**Poe, Edgar Allan** (1809–49) US poet and short-story writer. Much of his finest poetry, such as *The Raven* (1845), deals with horror in the tradition of the GOTHIC NOVEL. Other works include the poem *Annabel Lee* (1849), and the stories *The Fall of the House of Usher* (1839) and *The Pit and the Pendulum* (1843).

**poet laureate** Title conferred by the British monarch on a poet whose duty is then to write commemorative verse on important occasions. The position has been held by, among others, Robert SOUTHEY (1813–43), WORDSWORTH (1843–50), TENNYSON (1850–92), and Sir John BETJEMAN (1972–84). Ted HUGHES has been poet laureate since 1984. The US appoints a poet laureate for a one-year term.

**poetry** Literary medium that employs the line as its formal unit, and in which the sound, rhythm, and meaning of words are all equally important. Until the modern introduction of the concept of FREE VERSE, poetry was characteristically written in regular lines with carefully structured METERS, often with RHYMES. *See also* LITERATURE; PROSE

**pogrom** Russian term for a destructive riot, generally applied to attacks on Jews in Russia in the late 19th and early 20th centuries. They were usually by anti-Semitic mobs and often instigated by local authorities.

**poikilothermic** (ectothermic) Describes an animal whose body temperature fluctuates with the temperature of its surroundings, often referred to as cold-blooded. Reptiles, amphibians, fish, and invertebrates are cold-blooded. They can control their body temperature only by their behavior – by moving in and out of the shade, or orientating themselves to absorb more or less sunlight. *See also* HOMOIOTHERMIC

**Poincaré, (Jules) Henri** (1854–1912) French mathematician. He worked on CELESTIAL MECHANICS, winning an award for his contribution to the theory of orbits. In 1906, independently of EINSTEIN, he obtained some of the results of the special theory of RELATIVITY.

**Poincaré, Raymond Nicolas Landry** (1860–1934) French statesman. He served in several government posts and was prime minister (1912–13) before becoming president (1913–20). An ardent nationalist and conservative, he accepted his opponent CLEMENCEAU as premier in 1917, in the cause of national unity. Poincaré was again prime minister in 1922–24 and 1926–29. He ordered the occupation of the RUHR in 1923 to force German payment of REPARATIONS.

**poinsettia** Showy house plant native to Mexico. It has tapering leaves and tiny yellow flowers centered in leaflike red, white, or pink bracts. In its natural environment, the tree grows to about 16ft (5m). Height: to 2ft (60cm) when potted. Family Euphorbiaceae; species *Euphorbia pulcherrima*.

**pointer** Smooth-coated sporting and gun dog that was developed in the 17th century for hunting. It can be trained to indicate the direction in which game lies by standing motionless, aligning its muzzle, body, and tail. It has a wide head and a strong, lean body. The short, dense coat can be white with black, or brown markings. Height: to 25in (63cm); weight: to 60lb (27kg).

**Point Four program** US plan to share its scientific and technological knowledge with less developed countries. The plan received its name after it was first proposed by President TRUMAN in his 1949 inaugural address. By 1950 the plan had been included in general US foreign policy.

**pointillism** (Fr. *pointiller*, to dot) Technique of painting in regular dots or small dashes of pure color, developed from NEO-IMPRESSIONISM by Georges SEURAT. From a distance, the dots create a vibrant effect.

**poisoning** Adverse effects of substances, either natural or synthetic, introduced into the body or produced as side-products of the organism itself. Some poisons are toxic in small doses; others work cumulatively, over longer periods. Levels of sensitivity and treatments vary.

**poison ivy** North American shrub that causes a severe, itchy rash on contact with human skin. It has greenish flowers and white berries. Species *Rhus radicans* and *R. toxicodendron*. Family Anarcardiaceae.

**Poitier, Sidney** (1924– ) US actor and director. His early films included *Porgy and Bess* (1959). He won an Academy Award for *Lilies of the Field* (1963). His later films include *Guess Who's Coming to Dinner* (1967) and *In the Heat of the Night* (1967). Directorial credits include *Stir Crazy* (1980) and *Sneakers* (1992).

**Poitiers** City on the Clain River, W central France; capital of Vienne department and chief town of Poitou-Charentes region. Poitiers was the ancient capital of the Pictones (a Gallic tribe), and an important center of early European monasticism. In the 5th century, the city fell to the Visigoths, who were in turn defeated by the Merovingian king Clovis I (507). In Poitiers, in 732, the Franks halted the advance of the Muslim Saracens. The Battle of Poitiers (1356) was an important English victory in the HUNDRED YEARS WAR. Industries: metallurgy, printing, chemicals. Pop. (1990) 107,625.

**poker** Card game believed to have originated in Europe in the 16th century. Basically a gambling game, the object is to win the pot (all the bets that are made after each card is dealt) by holding the best combination of cards (in same suit, in pairs or triples, or in numerical sequence), or by bluffing the other players into withdrawing.

**Poland** Republic in central Europe. *See* country feature

**Polanski, Roman** (1933– ) Polish actor and director. His first full-length film, *Knife in the Water* (1962), was followed by *Repulsion* (1965) and *Cul de-Sac* (1966). Later films include *Rosemary's Baby* (1968), *Chinatown* (1974), *Tess* (1980), and *Death and the Maiden* (1994).

**polar bear** Large white bear that lives on Arctic coasts and ice floes. It spends most of its time at sea on drifting ice, often swimming for many miles. It preys chiefly on seals and is hunted for fur and meat. Length: 7.5ft (2.3m); weight: to 900lb (405kg). Species *Thalarctos maritimus*.

**Polaris** *See* POLE STAR

**polarized light** Light waves that have electromagnetic vibrations in only one direction. Three types are plane-polarized, circularly polarized, and elliptical-polarized light, each depending on the net direction of the vibrations. Polarizing sunglasses use a POLAROID material to reduce the glare from light polarized by reflection from horizonal surfaces.

**Polaroid** Trade name for a refracting material invented by the US physicist Edwin Land (1909–91). It only transmits a certain type of POLARIZED LIGHT; all other light is absorbed. Polaroid material is used in sunglasses to reduce the glare. In 1947 Land developed a polaroid camera that produced a finished print within one minute.

**Pole, Reginald** (1500–58) English cardinal, the last Roman Catholic archbishop of Canterbury. A cousin of HENRY VIII, Pole opposed Henry's divorce of CATHERINE OF ARAGON and moved to Italy during the REFORMATION, returning to England

P

Poland's flag was adopted when the country became a republic in 1919. Its colors were taken from the 13th-century coat of arms of a white eagle on a red field. This coat of arms still appears on Poland's merchant flag.

**AREA:** 120,726SQ MI (312,680SQ KM)
**POPULATION:** 38,356,000
**CAPITAL (POPULATION):** Warsaw (1,653,300)
**GOVERNMENT:** Multiparty republic
**ETHNIC GROUPS:** Polish 98%, Ukrainian 1%
**LANGUAGES:** Polish (official)
**RELIGIONS:** Christianity (Roman Catholic 94%, Orthodox 2%)
**CURRENCY:** Zloty = 100 groszy

The Republic of Poland is mostly lowland, forming part of the great European plain. The N, lagoon-lined, Baltic Sea coast includes the ports of GDAŃSK and SZCZECIN, and the mouths of the VISTULA and ODER rivers. There are many lakes, especially in the NE. The central plains include Poland's capital, WARSAW, and the cities of POZNAŃ, ŁÓDZ, and LUBLIN. Poland's best farmland is in the SE Polish uplands. Beyond the cities of KATOWICE and KRAKOW, the land rises to Mount Rysy, at 8,199ft (2,499m), in the CARPATHIAN MOUNTAINS. In the SW lies the region of SILESIA, and its capital WROCLAW.

### CLIMATE

Poland has a continental climate, with warm summers and bitterly cold, snowy winters. The N coast is much milder than the S highlands.

### VEGETATION

Forests cover *c.*30% of Poland. Nearly 50% of the land is arable.

### HISTORY

In the 9th century AD Slavic tribes unified the region. The Piast dynasty came to power. Boleslav I became the first king of Poland (1025), but the kingdom disintegrated in the 12th century. Ladislas I reunified Poland in 1320, but the dynasty collapsed under the might of the TEUTONIC KNIGHTS. The 16th century rule of the Jagiello dynasty is regarded as Poland's "golden age." In 1569 Poland and Lithuania were united. In JOHN II's reign, Poland was plundered by Sweden, Russia, and Turkey. JOHN III SOBIESKI restored some prestige, but his death brought division. Following the War of Succession (1733–35) Russia dominated Polish affairs. In 1772 and 1793 Poland was partitioned among Austria, Prussia, and Russia. The defeat of a Polish revolt in 1795 led to further partition, and Poland ceased to exist. The Congress of Vienna (1814–15) established a small, semi-independent Polish state based on Kraków. Polish uprisings in 1848 and 1863 against Russian dominance led to more impositions. In World War I Poland initially fought with Germany against Russia, but Germany occupied Poland.

Poland regained its independence in 1918. In 1920 Poland recaptured Warsaw from Russia. In 1921 Poland became a republic. The 1920s and 1930s were a period of dictatorship and military rule. In September 1939, following a secret pact between Hitler and Stalin, Germany invaded and Poland was partitioned between the Soviet Union and Germany. Britain declared war. Following the German invasion of the Soviet Union, all of Poland fell under German rule. The Nazis established concentration camps, such as AUSCHWITZ. More than 6 million Poles perished. Only 100,000 Polish Jews, from a prewar community of over 3 million, survived the HOLOCAUST. Polish resistance intensified. In 1944 a provisional government was established. In August 1944 the Warsaw uprising began, but was ruthlessly crushed by the Germans. In 1945 Poland regained its independence. It lost land in the E to the Soviet Union, but gained sections of Prussia from Germany. In 1949 Poland joined the COUNCIL FOR MUTUAL ECONOMIC ASSISTANCE (COMECON). In 1952 Poland became a people's republic, modeled on the Soviet constitution. In 1955 it was a founder member of the WARSAW PACT. Uprisings in 1956 led to the formation of a more liberal administration led by Wladslaw Gomulka. The collectivization of agriculture was reversed, and restrictions on religious worship were relaxed. Inflation and recession during the 1970s led to further riots and political protests. In 1980 striking dockers in Gdańsk, led by Lech WALESA, formed a trade union called SOLIDARITY, which gained support. In 1981 Jaruzelski declared martial law, Solidarity was banned, and its leaders arrested. Continuing recession and civil unrest led to the lifting of martial law in 1983. Following reforms in the Soviet Union, Solidarity was legalized and won free elections in 1989. In 1990 the Communist Party was disbanded and Walesa became president.

### POLITICS

In 1995 elections, Walesa was defeated by the leader of the Democratic Left Alliance, Aleksander Kwaśniewski. Kwasniewski continued the policies of his predecessor, stating that he would lead Poland into NATO and the European Community. In 1996 Poland joined the Organization for Economic Cooperation and Development (OECD). Poland has faced huge problems in the transition to a market economy. In 1997 it was invited to join NATO. Parliamentary elections in 1997 were won by a center-right coalition.

### ECONOMY

Before World War II, Poland had a mainly agricultural economy. Under communism, industry expanded greatly. Today, 27% of the workforce is employed in agriculture and 37% in industry. Upper Silesia is the richest coal basin in Europe. Poland is the world's fifth-largest producer of lignite and seventh-largest producer of bituminous coal. Copper ore is also a vital mineral resource. Manufacturing accounts for *c.*24% of exports. Poland is the world's fifth-largest producer of ships. Agriculture remains important. Major crops include barley, potatoes, and wheat. The transition to a free-market economy has doubled unemployment and increased foreign debt. Economic growth, however, is slowly returning (1995 GDP per capita, US$5,400).

P

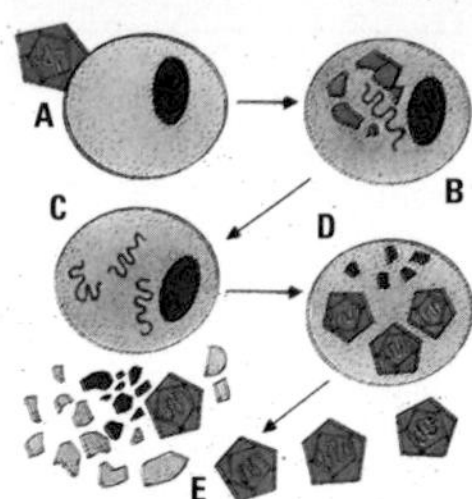


▲ **poliomyelitis** A viral disease that affects the human nervous system, poliomyelitis (polio) can often cause paralysis. Cells of the throat and intestines are the first to become infected. Virus absorption to the cell surface occurs (A), followed by penetration of the cell. Within the cell the virus protein coat is shed releasing a coiled nucleic acid stand (B). Nucleic acid replication occurs (C), each new strand becoming surrounded by a protein coat (D). As many as 500 new infectious viruses are released as the cell bursts and dies (E).

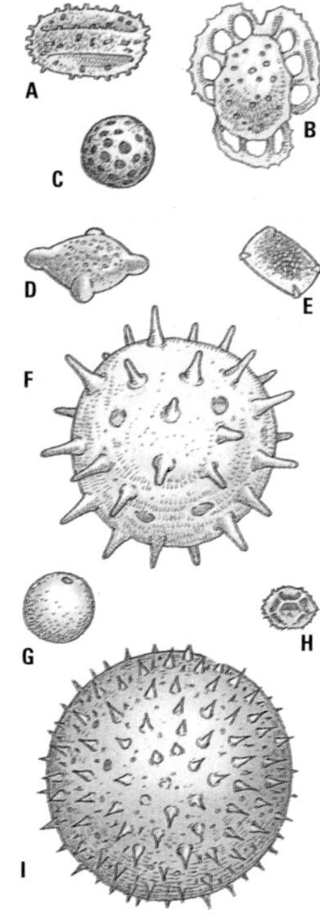


▲ **pollen** Pollen grains are found in pollen sacs, which are in the anthers (part of the stamens). Pollen grains are safe and effective storers of the male gametes (sex cells). They come in all shapes and sizes depending on the species of plant. The selection shows mistletoe (A), venus fly trap (B), spinach (C), honeysuckle (D), touch-me-not (E), cotton (F), rice (G), dandelion (H), and hollyhock (I).

in 1554 as papal legate to the Roman Catholic Queen MARY I. She made him archbishop of Canterbury in 1556.

**pole** Generally, either of the two points of intersection of the surface of a sphere and its axis of rotation. The Earth has four poles: the North and South geographic poles, where the Earth's imaginary axis meets its surface; and the north and south magnetic poles, where the Earth's MAGNETIC FIELD is most concentrated. A bar magnet has a north pole, where the magnetic flux leaves the magnet, and a south pole, where it enters. A pole is also one of the terminals (positive or negative) of a battery, electric machine, or circuit.

**polecat** Any of several species of small, carnivorous, nocturnal mammals that live in wooded areas of Eurasia and N Africa; especially *Mustela putorius*, the common polecat. It has a slender body, long bushy tail, and brown to black fur known as fitch. It eats small animals, birds, and eggs. Length: 18in (45.7cm). Family Mustelidae.

**Pole Star** (Polaris, North Star) Important navigational star, nearest to the N celestial star. It is in the constellation Ursa Minor and always marks due N.

**pole vault** Field event in athletics in which contestants use a pole to swing themselves up and over a horizontal bar suspended between two uprights. The bar is progressively raised; vaulters who fail to clear a height in three attempts are eliminated. The winner vaults the highest. Pole vaulting has been an Olympic sport since 1896.

**police** Body of people concerned with maintaining civil order and investigating breaches of the law. The first independent police force was established in Paris in 1667, becoming a uniformed force in 1829. Britain's first regular professional force was the Marine Police Establishment in 1800. The Metropolitan Police was created by Sir Robert PEEL in 1829. The New York City Police Department was formed in 1844.

**poliomyelitis** (polio) Acute viral infection of the nervous system affecting the nerves that activate muscles. Often a mild disease with effects limited to the throat and intestine, it is nonetheless potentially serious, with paralysis occurring in 1% of patients. It becomes life-threatening only if the breathing muscles are affected, in which case the person may need artificial ventilation. It has become rare in developed countries since the introduction of vaccination in the mid-1950s.

**Polish** National language of Poland, spoken by virtually all of the country's 39 million people. It belongs to the Slavonic family of INDO-EUROPEAN LANGUAGES. Polish is written in the Roman (Latin) alphabet, but with a large number of diacritical marks to represent the various Slavonic vowels and consonants.

**Polish Corridor** Strip of land along the River VISTULA, dividing East Prussia from the rest of Germany, and providing Poland with access to the Baltic Sea (1919–39). It was created by the Treaty of VERSAILLES after World War I, when Poland became independent. The arrangement caused disputes between Germany and Poland, exploited by HITLER to justify his invasion of Poland in 1939.

**Politburo** (political bureau) Administrative and policy-making body of the Soviet Communist Party. Formerly called the PRESIDIUM, it consisted of 11–12 full members and 6–9 candidate members chosen by the Party's central committee.

**political correctness (PC)** Ostentatiously moral attitude on contemporary issues. Political correctness in the 1990s means conspicuously avoiding the perceived moral evils of the age – notably discrimination.

**political party** Group organized for the purpose of electing candidates to office and for promoting a particular set of political principles. *See* articles on individual parties.

**politics** Sphere of action in human society in which power is sought in order to regulate the ways in which people shall live together. For a society to engage in politics, it must conceive of society as being in a state of perpetual change.

**Polk, James Knox** (1795–1849) 11th US President (1845–49). During his administration, California and New Mexico were acquired as a result of the US victory in the MEXICAN WAR (1846–48), which Polk's aggressive policy had largely provoked. He also gained Oregon through the Oregon Treaty (1846).

**polka** Lively Bohemian folk dance. It became fashionable in Paris in the 1940s, and thereafter in Europe and the Americas. It is often performed as a ballroom dance.

**pollen** Yellow, powderlike SPORES that give rise to the male sex cells in flowering plants. Pollen grains are produced in the anther chambers on the STAMEN. When the pollen lands on the STIGMA of a compatible plant, it germinates, sending a long pollen tube down through the STYLE to the OVARY. During this process, one of its nuclei divides, giving rise to two male nuclei (the equivalent of male sex cells or GAMETES), one of which fuses with a female sex cell in FERTILIZATION. The other sex cell fuses with two more of the female nuclei to form a special tissue, the endosperm. In many species, this tissue develops into a food store for the embryo in the seed. *See also* POLLINATION; ALTERNATION OF GENERATIONS

**pollination** Transfer of POLLEN from the STAMEN to the STIGMA of a flower. Self-pollination occurs on one flower and cross-pollination between two flowers on different plants. Pollination occurs mainly by wind and insects.

**Pollock, Jackson** (1912–56) US painter. A leading figure in abstract expressionism. He began experimenting with ABSTRACT ART in the 1940s. In 1947 he began pouring paint straight onto the canvas. Instead of brushes he used sticks or knives to create the surface patterns. This method has been called ACTION PAINTING. His works include *The Blue Unconscious* (1946).

**poll tax** Tax of a fixed sum imposed on all liable individuals. Such taxes were occasionally levied by medieval governments: one provoked the PEASANTS' REVOLT (1381) in England. Southern US states after the Civil War made the right to vote dependent on payment of a poll tax, a device to disenfranchise poor blacks. A poll tax called the Community Charge, introduced in Britain in 1989, was withdrawn after civil disobedience.

**pollution** Spoiling of the natural environment, generally by industrialized society. Pollution is usually a result of an accumulation of waste products, although excess of noise or heat that has adverse effects on the surrounding ecology is also considered as pollution.

**Pollux** *See* CASTOR AND POLLUX

**Pollux** (Beta Geminorum) Brightest star in the constellation Gemini; a red giant. Characteristics: apparent mag. 1.15; absolute mag. 0.7; spectral type KO; distance 35 light-years.

**Polo, Marco** (1254–1324) Venetian traveler in Asia. In 1274 he accompanied his father and uncle on a trading mission to the court of KUBLAI KHAN, the MONGOL emperor of China. According to his account, he remained in the Far East more than 20 years, becoming the confidant of Kublai Khan and traveling throughout China and beyond. His account, *The Description of the World*, became the chief source of European knowledge of China for centuries.

**polo** Field game played on horseback. Two teams of four players, on a field up to 600ft (182m) by 900ft (273m), each try to hit a small ball into a goal using flexible mallets. A game consists of four, six, or eight chukkas (periods), each 7.5 minutes long; additional chukkas may be played to decide a game if the scores are tied. Polo originated in Persia in ancient times, and spread throughout Asia. It was revived in India in the 19th century, and was taken up by British army officers there. It was first played in Britain in 1868, and is also played in the US.

**polonium** (symbol Po) Rare, radioactive, metallic element of Group VI of the PERIODIC TABLE, discovered in 1898 by Marie CURIE. It is found in trace amounts in uranium ores and may be synthesized. Properties: at.no. 84; sp.gr. 9.40; m.p. 489°F (254°C); b.p. 1,764°F (962°C); most stable isotope $^{209}$Po.

**Pol Pot** (1928–98) Cambodian ruler. He became leader of the communist KHMER ROUGE, which overthrew the US-backed government of Lon Nol in 1975. He instigated a reign of terror in Cambodia (renamed Kampuchea). Intellectuals were massacred, and the people in the cities driven into the countryside. Estimates suggest that 1–4 million died. Pol Pot's regime was overthrown by a Vietnamese invasion in 1979. He continued to lead the Khmer Rouge. In 1997 it was reported that Pol Pot had been sentenced to life imprisonment by a Khmer Rouge court for the murder of a Khmer Rouge comrade. The following year he died of heart failure.

**poltergeist** Noisy spirit or ghost, supposedly responsible for unexplained sounds and activity.

**polyanthus** Any of a group of spring-flowering, perennial primroses of the genus *Primula*. Occurring mainly in the N temperate zone, they may be almost any color. They have basal leaves and disc-shaped flowers, branching from a stalk to form a ball-like cluster. Height: to 6in (15cm). Family Primulaceae.

**Polybius** (200–120 BC) Greek historian. A leader in the Achaean Confederation, he was deported as an honored hostage to Rome in 168 BC. He became a friend of SCIPIO AFRICANUS MINOR and accompanied him to Spain and Africa. He was present at the destruction of Carthage in 146 BC, and later acted as intermediary between Rome and the Achaeans.

**polychlorinated biphenyl (PCB)** Any of several stable mixtures – liquid, resinous, or crystalline – of organic compounds. They are used as lubricants and heat-transfer fluids. The use of PCBs has been restricted since 1973 because they are toxic and their resistance to decomposition poses a threat to wildlife.

**polyester** Class of organic substance composed of large molecules arranged in a chain or a network and formed from many smaller molecules through the establishment of ester linkages. Polyester fibers are resistant to chemicals and are made into ropes and textiles.

**polyethene** (polyethylene) POLYMER of ETHENE. It is a partially crystalline, lightweight, thermoplastic RESIN, with high resistance to chemicals, low moisture absorption, and good insulating properties.

**polygamy** Marriage in which more than one spouse is permitted. More often it is used to denote **polygyny** (several wives) than **polyandry** (several husbands). Polygamy is legal and commonplace in many nations, notably many Muslim and African countries.

**polygon** Plane geometric figure having three or more sides intersecting at three or more points (vertices). They are named according to the number of sides or vertices: triangle (three-sided), quadrilateral (four-sided), hexagon (six-sided). A regular polygon is equilateral (has sides equal in length) and equiangular (has equal angles).

**polygraph** *See* LIE DETECTOR

**polyhedron** In geometry, three-dimensional solid figure whose surface is made up of POLYGONS. These are called the faces of the polyhedron, and the points at which they meet are the vertices.

**polymer** Substance formed by the union of from two to several thousand simple molecules (monomers) to form a large molecular structure. Some, such as cellulose, occur in nature; others form the basis of PLASTICS and synthetic RESINS. *See also* POLYMERIZATION

**polymerase chain reaction (PCR)** Chemical reaction, speeded up by an ENZYME, that is used to make large numbers of copies of a specific piece of DNA, starting from only one or few DNA molecules. It enables scientists to make large enough quantities of DNA to be able to analyze it or manipulate it. PCR is extremely important in GENETIC ENGINEERING and GENETIC FINGERPRINTING.

**polymerization** Chemical combination of several molecules to form straight-chain molecules, cross-linked giant molecules, or a combination of both, all called POLYMERS. It is the major industrial process in the manufacture of PLASTICS. In nature, large biochemical compounds (such as PROTEINS and NUCLEIC ACIDS) are formed by polymerization.

**Polynesia** One of the three divisions of OCEANIA, and the general term for the islands of the central Pacific Ocean; MICRONESIA and MELANESIA lie to the W. The principal islands in Polynesia are the Hawaiian Islands, Phoenix Islands, Tokelau Islands, the Samoa group, Easter Island, Cook Islands, and French Polynesia. Because of their Maori population, the two larger islands of New Zealand are also usually included. The islands are mostly coral or volcanic in origin. The inhabitants show physical similarities, and share common cultural and linguistic characteristics.

**polynomial** Sum of terms that are powers of a variable. For example, $8x^4 - 4x^3 + 7x^2 + x - 11$ is a polynomial of the fourth degree (the highest power four). In general a polynomial has the form $a_0x^n + a_1x^{n-1} + a_2x^{n-2} + \dots\dots\dots + a_{n-2}x^2 + a_{n-1}x + a_n$, although certain powers of $x$ and the constant term $a_n$ may be missing. The values $a_n$, $a_{n-1}$, etc., are the coefficients of the polynomial.

**polyp** Body type of various species of animals within the phylum Cnidaria. It has a mouth surrounded by extensible tentacles and a lower end that is adapted for attachment to a surface. It may be solitary, as in the SEA ANEMONE, but is more often an individual of a colonial organism such as CORAL.

**polyp** In medicine, swollen mass projecting from the wall of a cavity lined with mucous membrane, such as the nose. Some growths can be cancerous.

**polyphony** Vocal or instrumental part music in which the compositional interest centers on the "horizontal" aspect of each moving part rather than on the "vertical" structure of chords. The golden age of polyphonic music was the 16th century, and masters of that time included Giovanni PALESTRINA and William BYRD.

**polysaccharide** Any of a group of complex CARBOHYDRATES made up of long chains of monosaccharide (simple-sugar) molecules. GLUCOSE is a monosaccharide, and the polysaccharides STARCH and CELLULOSE are both polymers of glucose. Polysaccharides function both as food stores (starch in plants and GLYCOGEN in animals) and as structural materials (cellulose and PECTIN in the cell walls of plants, and CHITIN in the protective skeleton of insects).

**polystyrene** Synthetic organic POLYMER, composed of long chains of the aromatic compound styrene. It is a strong thermoplastic RESIN, acid- and alkali-resistant, nonabsorbent, and an excellent electrical insulator.

**polytheism** Belief in or worship of many gods and goddesses. The ancient Egyptian, Babylonian, Greek, and Roman religions were all poytheistic, as were the religions of the Americas before the European settlement. HINDUISM is a modern polytheistic religion. *See also* ANCESTOR WORSHIP; ANIMISM; MONOTHEISM

**polyunsaturate** Type of FAT or OIL that has molecules of long CARBON chains with many double bonds. Polyunsaturated fats exist in fish oils and most vegetable oils. At room temperature, unsaturated oils are liquids and SATURATED FATS are solids. Polyunsaturates, which have low or no CHOLESTEROL content, are widely used in margarines and cooking oils. They are considered healthier than saturated fats.

**polyvinyl chloride (PVC)** White, tough, solid thermoplastic that is a polymer of vinyl chloride. A PVC can be softened and made elastic with a plasticizer. Easily colored and resistant to weather and fire, PVC is used to produce a variety of products, including fibers, pipes, and coatings for raincoats and upholstery.

**Pombal, Sebastião José de Carvalho e Mello, Marquês de** (1699–1782) Portuguese statesman, minister for foreign affairs (1750–56). Pombal was virtual ruler of Portugal until the death of King Joseph in 1777. He increased royal power at the expense of the old nobility, the INQUISITION, and the JESUITS, whom he expelled in 1759. He reformed the administration, economy, education, and army, and encouraged trade with Brazil.

**pomegranate** Deciduous shrub or small tree native to W Asia. It has shiny, oval leaves and orange-red flowers. The round fruit has a red, leathery rind and numerous seeds that are coated with an edible pulp. Family Punicaceae; species *Punica granatum.*

**Pompadour, Jeanne-Antoinette Poisson, Marquise de** (1721–64) Influential mistress and confidante of LOUIS XV after 1745. A strong influence on the court, she was a great patron of the arts.

**Pompeii** Ancient Roman city in SE Italy, buried by volcanic eruption in AD 79. Pompeii was founded in the 8th century BC and ruled by Greeks, Etruscans, and others before it was conquered by Rome in 89 BC. The eruption of Mount VESUVIUS was so sudden and violent that about 2,000 died and the city was swiftly covered by volcanic ash, preserving ordinary houses intact until excavation began in the 18th century.

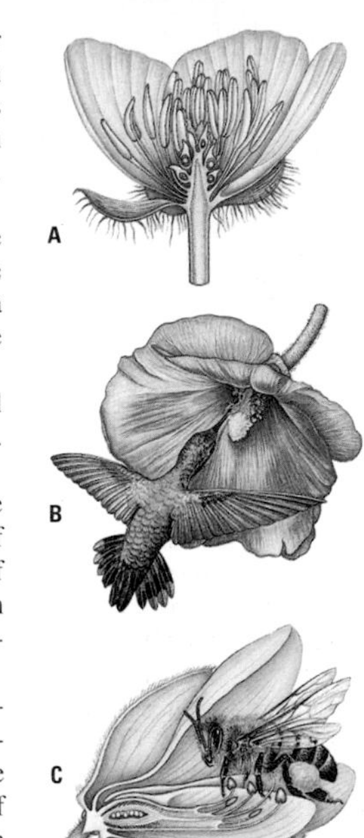

▲ **pollination** Flowers are adapted to different pollination methods. Nonspecialized simple flowers, such as the buttercup (A), can be pollinated by a variety of means. Other flowers can only be pollinated by one method. There are bird-pollinated flowers, such as the hummingbird-pollinated hibiscus (B); bee-specialized flowers, including the gorse (C); and wind-pollinated flowers, such as the catkins found on the hazel (D).

▲ **pomegranate** The flesh of the pomegranate (Punica granatum), a fruit about the size of an apple, is densely packed with seeds that scatter when the fruit is burst. The pale yellow seeds are surrounded by a bright red, fleshy coating, which has a refreshing, astringent flavor. Although native to W Asia, it is now cultivated in warm regions throughout the world.

P

▲ **pondweed** The weedy, aquatic plant pondweed (*Potamogeton* sp.) is among the first flowering plants to colonize wetland areas. Over time, they encourage sediment to build up around the wetland edges, creating areas of shallower water where other species can take root. The runoff of agricultural chemicals, such as fertilizers, encourages the rapid growth of pondweed, accelerating the rate of evolution of wetland areas, often to a degree that can damage the habitat for other species of plants and animals.

**Pompey** (106–48 BC) (Gnaeus Pompeius Magnus) Roman general. He fought for SULLA in 83 BC and campaigned in Sicily, Africa, and Spain. He was named consul with CRASSUS in 70 BC and fought a notable campaign against MITHRIDATES VI of Pontus in 66 BC. In 59 BC he formed the first triumvirate with Crassus and his great rival, Julius CAESAR. After the death of Crassus, Pompey joined Caesar's enemies, and civil war broke out in 49 BC. Driven out of Rome by Caesar's advance, Pompey was defeated at Pharsalus in 48 BC and fled to Egypt, where he was murdered.

**Pompidou, Georges Jean Raymond** (1911–74) French statesman. He served on DE GAULLE's staff from 1944 and was a member of the powerful council of state (1946–57), becoming premier in 1958. After De Gaulle's resignation, he succeeded him as president (1969–74). He died in office.

**Ponce de León, Juan** (1460–1521) Spanish explorer. A veteran of COLUMBUS's second voyage, he conquered Puerto Rico for Spain (1508–09) and in 1513 led an expedition to explore rumored islands north of Cuba. He reached land near what is now St. Augustine, Florida. He returned in 1521 with a colonizing expedition and received an arrow wound from which he later died.

**pondweed** Any of numerous species of a family of aquatic, perennial, flowering plants of the genus *Potamogeton*, found mostly in temperate regions in freshwater lakes, but also in brackish and salt water. Most pondweeds have spike-like flowers that stick out of the water, and submerged or floating leaves. Family Potamogetonaceae.

**Pontiac's Rebellion** (1763–66) Native American rising against the British. Pontiac (d.1769) was an OTTAWA chief who led a loose association of allies hostile to the British takeover of Quebec (1760). A number of outposts in the Great Lakes region were overrun. News of the French withdrawal from North America fatally weakened the campaign, which soon collapsed.

**pontifex** Priest of ancient Rome, a member of the college of priests who organized Rome's state religion. Since the 5th century AD, the title *Pontifex Maximus* has been in use in a Christian context as a designation for the pope.

**Pontius Pilate** (active 1st century AD) Roman prefect or procurator (governor) of Judaea at the time when JESUS CHRIST was crucified. Pilate was made procurator of Judaea in AD 26 and earned a reputation for arrogance and cruelty. He died after AD 36.

**Pontormo, Jacopo Carucci** (1494–1557) Italian painter. He is thought to have painted *Vertumnus and Pomona* (1520–21), which shows the neurotic qualities characteristic of the MANNERISM he practiced. Other paintings include *The Madonna* (1518), *The Visitation* (1516), and *Deposition* (*c*.1527).

**Pontus** Ancient kingdom of NE Anatolia (Turkey). The coastal cities were colonized by Greeks in the 6th–5th centuries BC and retained virtual autonomy under the Persian empire. The kingdom of Pontus reached the height of its power under MITHRIDATES VI, the Great, who conquered Asia Minor, gained control of the Crimea, and threatened Rome. After his defeat by Pompey (65 BC), the country was divided up under Roman rule but maintained its commercial prosperity.

**pony** Any of several breeds of small horses, usually solid and stocky. They are commonly used as a children's saddle horse, for show, and for draft. Types include the hardy Shetland pony; the Dartmoor and Exmoor ponies of Cornwall, Somerset, and Devon; the gray Highland pony; the Welsh pony; and the Welsh Cob. Height: 45–57in (115–45cm) at the shoulder.

**Pony Express** US relay mail service between Saint Joseph, Missouri, and Sacramento, California, in 1860–61. About 25 riders changed horses at 190 staging posts on the 1,800mi (3,200km) journey. The time for the journey was ten days, less than half the time taken by stagecoach. The service was gradually discontinued as the telegraph system was established.

**poodle** Breed of dog believed to have originated in Germany. Bred originally to retrieve from water, its intelligence has made it a popular pet. It has a rounded skull, a long straight body, and a high-set tail, often docked. The thick, wiry coat is commonly clipped into an ornate style. The main sizes are standard, miniature, and toy. Height: (standard) more than 15in (38cm) at the shoulder.

**pool** Type of billiards game of US origin. One version is played with eight single-color balls and seven striped balls (all numbered 1 to 15), plus a white cue ball, on a rectangular table with four corner pockets and two side pockets. The most popular version divides the striped balls and the single-color balls, except the black ball, between the two players (or two teams), so that the black ball (number 8) is the last to be potted.

**poor laws** English legislation designed to prevent begging and vagrancy. Introduced in the 16th century and consolidated in the Poor Law Act of 1601, they required individual parishes to provide for the local poor. Later, workhouses were established. The social reforms of the 20th century replaced the poor-law system.

**pop art** Movement inspired by consumerist images and popular culture that flourished in the US and Britain from the late 1950s to the early 1970s. It took its ideas from comic books, advertisements, packaging, television, and movies.

**Pope** *See* PAPACY

**Pope, Alexander** (1688–1744) British poet. He wrote lyric and elegiac poetry and published fine translations of HOMER (1720 and 1726) and *Imitations of Horace* (1733). Among his finest work are the satires, which include the mock epic *The Rape of the Lock* (1714), *The Dunciad* (1728), and *An Epistle to Dr. Arbuthnot* (1735).

**poplar** Any of a number of deciduous, softwood trees of the genus *Populus*, native to cool and temperate regions. The oval leaves grow on stalks, and flowers take the form of catkins. Some species are called cottonwoods because of the cottonlike fluff on their seeds. Height: to 200ft (60m). Family Salicaceae. The yellow poplar of the US, also called the tulip tree, bears orange-yellow, tuliplike flowers. Family Magnoliaceae; species *Liriodendron tulipifera*.

**Popocatépetl** Snow-capped, dormant volcano in central Mexico, 45mi (72km) SE of Mexico City. The crater contains sulfur deposits. Height: 17,887ft (5,452m).

**Popper, Sir Karl Raimund** (1902–94) British philosopher of natural and social sciences, b. Austria. He proposed his theory of falsification in *The Logic of Scientific Discovery* (1934), saying scientific "truth" cannot be absolutely confirmed.

**poppy** Any annual or perennial plant of the genus *Papaver*, family Papaveraceae, or any related plant. About 100 species of the genus exist. They have bright red, orange, or white flowers, often with dark centers, with four thin, overlapping petals and two thick sepals; all produce the milky sap, LATEX. The unripe capsules of the Asian opium poppy are used to produce the drug OPIUM. Plants closely related to the true poppy include the California poppy and the Welsh poppy.

▲ **poppy** Cultivated since the Middle Ages, the opium poppy (*Papaver somniferum*) is the natural source of the drug opium and its derivatives, morphine and heroin. These are extracted from the latex of the seed pods. The seeds themselves are used as cattle food and as a source of oil. The dramatic flower makes the plant a popular garden ornamental.

**popular front** Alliance of left-wing political parties. In Europe, such alliances were formed in the 1930s partly in reaction to threats from the extreme right and with the encouragement of the Soviet Union. A popular-front government came to power in France, under Léon BLUM (1936–37), and in Spain (1936), where it provoked a military revolt and civil war. In more recent times, revolutionary parties in many African and Asian contries have adopted the name.

**population** Estimated world total (1990), 5,300 million. United Nations prediction of population in the year 2000 is *c.* 6,200 million. The approximate percentage of the world's population in each main area of the world is Asia: 60%; Europe and North America: 20%; Africa and South America: 19%; Oceania, including Australia and Antartica: less than 1%.

**Populist Party** (officially People's Party) US political party active in the 1890s. It originated among farmers' alliances at a time of agrarian discontent. It won seats in local and state elections in 1890 and nominated a presidential candidate, James B. Weaver, in 1892, advocating free silver (unlimited minting of silver coins) and nationalization of transportation. In 1896 the party supported the Democratic candidate, William Jennings Bryan. After 1908 it gradually disintegrated.

**porcelain** White, glasslike, nonporous, hard, translucent ceramic material. Porcelain is widely used for tableware, decorative objects, laboratory equipment, and electrical insulators. It was developed by the Chinese in the 7th or 8th century. True or hard-paste porcelain is made of kaolin (white china clay) mixed with powdered petuntse (FELDSPAR). Soft-paste porcelain is composed of clay and powdered glass.

**porcupine** Short-legged, mostly nocturnal, herbivorous rodent with erectile, defensive quills in its back. Old World porcupines of the family Hystricidae have brown to black fur with white-banded quills and are terrestrial. New World porcupines of the family Erethizontidae are smaller with yellow to white quills and are arboreal. The largest European and African rodent, the African crested porcupine (*Hystrix cristata*) attains a length of about 31in (80cm).

◀ **porcupine** Protection for the porcupine (the Indian porcupine, *Hystrix indica*, is shown here) is provided by a coat of spines. It can erect these when danger threatens. The spines are loosely attached and may become embedded in predators.

**pornography** Visual or aural material presenting erotic behavior that is intended to be sexually stimulating, and is lacking in artistic or other forms of merit. It is often considered to be demeaning to both sexuality and to the body; many people, especially some feminists, have called for a total ban. Pornographic content, however, is difficult to assess, because the response of individuals varies. There is legal CENSORSHIP in most countries, but the interpretation of the law is subjective.

**porphyria** Group of rare genetic disorders in which there is defective METABOLISM of one or more porphyrins, the breakdown products of hemoglobin. It can produce a wide range of effects, including intestinal upset, HYPERTENSION, weakness, abnormal skin reactions to sunlight, and mental disturbance. A key diagnostic indicator is that the patient's urine turns reddish-brown if it is left to stand. There is no specific remedy and treatment tends to be supportive.

**porpoise** Small, toothed WHALE with a blunt snout. Found in most oceans, the best known is the common porpoise of the Northern Hemisphere. Its body is black above and white below. Length: to 5ft (1.5m). Family Delphinidae; species *Phocaena phocaena*.

**Porsche, Ferdinand** (1875–1951) German car manufacturer who designed the Volkswagen Beetle. In 1934 Porsche produced plans for an affordable car that the Nazis named *Volkswagen* ("people's car") and promised to mass produce. In fact, production did not start until 1945. Porsche also produced sports cars.

**port** Fortified wine produced in the Douro Valley in N Portugal. It may be white, tawny (translucent brown), or red, and contains 17–20% alcohol. A vintage port is aged in oak casks for 15 to 20 years.

**port** Place equipped for the loading and unloading of ships and boats. Many ports are built on the coast in natural or artificial harbors. Other ports are inland, linked to the sea by river or canal. Specially designed ports provide facilities for passenger services, naval vessels, fishing boats, oil tankers, and ships carrying general cargo.

**Port-au-Prince** Capital of Haiti, a port on the SE shore of the Gulf of Gonâve, on the W coast of Hispaniola. It was founded by the French in 1749, becoming the capital of Haiti in 1770. Industries: tobacco, textiles, cement, coffee, sugar. Pop. (1992) 1,255,078.

**Port Elizabeth** Seaport on Algoa Bay, Eastern Cape province, S Republic of South Africa. First settled in 1799 by the British, the city grew after the completion of the railway line to Kimberley in 1873. In 1977 the antiapartheid activist Steven BIKO was killed here. Exports: diamonds, fruit, wool. Industries: motor vehicles, chemicals. Pop. (1991) 853,204.

**Porter, Cole** (1891–1964) US composer and lyricist. The majority of his musicals for stage and film were vastly successful. They include *Anything Goes* (1934), *Kiss Me Kate* (1948), and *High Society* (1956). Among his most popular songs are "Night and Day," "Let's Do It," "Begin the Beguine," and "In the Still of the Night."

**Porter, Katherine Anne** (1890–1980) US author. Works include *Pale Horse, Pale Rider* (1939), *The Leaning Tower* (1944), and her best-known work, *Ship of Fools* (1962). Her collected short stories won a Pulitzer Prize in 1965.

**Portland** City and port on the Willamette River, NW Oregon. First settled in 1845, it developed as a major port for exporting timber and grain after 1850. It was a supply station for the California goldfields and the Alaska gold rush (1897–1900). Educational establishments include Lewis and Clark College (1867), the University of Portland (1901), Portland State University and Reed College. It is Oregon's largest city. Industries: shipbuilding, timber. Pop. (1990) 437,319.

**Portland** Largest city and port in Maine. Due to its deep natural harbor on Casco Bay, a settlement (Falmouth) was established here in 1632. In 1775 it was devastated by the British during the American Revolution. From 1820–32 it was state capital. The modern city is an oil terminus and shipping center. Pop. (1990) 64,538.

**Port Louis** Capital of Mauritius, a seaport in the NW of the island. It was founded by the French in 1735. It grew in importance as a trading port after the opening of the Suez Canal. The main export is sugar. Pop. (1993) 144,250.

**Port Moresby** Capital of Papua New Guinea, on the SE coast of New Guinea. Settled by the British in the 1880s, its sheltered harbor was the site of an important Allied base in World War II. It developed rapidly in the postwar period. Exports: gold, copper, rubber. Pop. (1990) 193,242.

**Port of Spain** Capital of Trinidad and Tobago, on the NW coast of Trinidad. The city was founded by the Spanish in the late 16th century and was seized by Britain in 1797. From 1958 to 1962 it was the capital of the Federation of the West Indies. The city has attractive botanical gardens and is a popular tourist resort. It is a major Caribbean shipping center. Pop. (1990) 58,400.

**Porto-Novo** Capital of Benin, West Africa, a port on the Gulf of Guinea near the border with Nigeria. Settled by 16th-century Portuguese traders, it later became a shipping point for slaves to America. It was made the country's capital at independence in 1960. Today it is a market for the surrounding agricultural region. Exports: palm oil, cotton, kapok. Pop. (1982) 208,258.

**portrait** Likeness of a real person. Portraits as a genre represent individual people, often emphasizing particular physical, psychological, or social attributes. Impressive portraits have been discovered in the art of ancient Greece, Egypt, and Rome, as well as in the antique art of many other cultures. In the West, the genre came into its own in the 18th century, when the fashion for formal portraits of famous people spread from France to England. In the 20th century photographic portraits have become popular. *See also* LANDSCAPE PAINTING

**Port Said** City and seaport in NE Egypt, at the entrance to the SUEZ CANAL. Founded in 1859, at the beginning of the construction of the Suez Canal, by the end of the 19th century, it was Egypt's chief port after ALEXANDRIA. Industries: fishing, tobacco, cotton, textiles. Pop. (1990) 461,000.

**Portsmouth** City and seaport in Hampshire, S England; Britain's principal naval base. The area was first settled in the late 12th century and was already a base for warships when the naval dockyard was laid down in 1496. Industries: engineering, ship repairing, electronics. Pop. (1991) 174,697.

**Portsmouth** Seaport city in SE New Hampshire, on the Atlantic Ocean at the mouth of Piscataqua River. The oldest city in the state, it was settled in 1624 and incorporated in 1653. The Treaty of Portsmouth was signed here in 1905, ending the Russo-Japanese War. Industries: tourism, plastics, machine tools. Pop. (1990) 25,925.

**Portsmouth** City on the Elizabeth River (opposite Norfolk), SE Virginia. Founded in 1752, it was the scene of heavy fighting in both the American Revolution and the Civil War. Portsmouth is part of one of the largest naval dockyard and shipyard complexes in the US. Industries: shipbuilding, chemicals. Pop. (1990) 103,907.

**Portugal** Republic on the W side of the IBERIAN PENINSULA, SW Europe. *See* country feature

**Portuguese** National language of both Portugal and Brazil, spoken by about 10 million people in the former and 100 million in the latter country. In addition, another 15 million people speak it in Angola, Mozambique, and other former Portuguese colonies. A ROMANCE LANGUAGE, it is closely related to Spanish.

**Portuguese man-of-war** Colonial COELENTERATE animal found in marine subtropical and tropical waters. It has a bright blue gas float and long, trailing tentacles with highly poisonous stinging cells. It is not a true jellyfish: the tentacles are actually a cluster of several kinds of modified medusae and POLYPS. Length: to 60ft (18m). Class Hydrozoa; genus *Physalia*.

**Poseidon** In Greek mythology, god of all waters, and brother of ZEUS and HADES, identified with the Roman god NEPTUNE. Poseidon controlled the monsters of the deep, created the horse (he was the father of PEGASUS) and sired Orion and Polyphemus. He is always represented holding a trident.

**positivism** Philosophical doctrine asserting that "positive" knowledge (definite or scientific facts) can be obtained through direct experience. Positivism was first proposed by Auguste COMTE and was a dominant system of 19th-century philosophy. Logical positivism was developed in the 20th century, initially by the philosophers of the Vienna Circle, as an attempt to link "positive knowledge" to the strict application of logic.

**positron** Particle that is identical to the ELECTRON, except that it is positively charged, making it the antiparticle of the electron. It was observed in 1932 in cosmic RADIATION by Carl ANDERSON. It is also emitted from certain radioactive nuclei. Electron-positron pairs can be produced when GAMMA RADIATION interacts with matter. *See also* ANTIMATTER; ELEMENTARY PARTICLE

**positron emission tomography (PET)** Medical imaging technique (used particularly on the brain) that produces three-dimensional images. Radioisotopes, injected into the bloodstream prior to imaging, are taken up by tissues where they emit POSITRONS that produce detectable photons.

**possum** Popular name for any of the PHALANGERS of Australasia. The term is also a US word for the OPOSSUM.

**Postal Service, US** US federal government agency, responsible for mail delivery. The Postal Service is directed by the

## PORTUGAL

Portugal's flag was adopted in 1910 when the country became a republic. The green represents Henry the Navigator (1394–1460), who sponsored many Portuguese explorers. The red symbolizes the monarchy. The shield reflects Portugal's leading role in world exploration.

**AREA:** 35,670SQ MI (92,390SQ KM)
**POPULATION:** 9,846,000
**CAPITAL (POPULATION):** Lisbon (2,561,000)
**GOVERNMENT:** Multiparty republic
**ETHNIC GROUPS:** Portuguese 99%, Cape Verdean, Brazilian, Spanish, British
**LANGUAGES:** Portuguese (official)
**RELIGIONS:** Christianity (Roman Catholic 95%, other Christians 2%)
**CURRENCY:** Escudo = 100 centavos

The Republic of Portugal lies on the W side of the IBERIAN PENINSULA. The Atlantic coastal plain includes the capital, LISBON, and OPORTO. In the S lies the ALGARVE. In central Portugal, the Serra da Estrela contains Portugal's highest peak, at 6,352ft (1,991m). The TAGUS and DOURO river valleys support most of Portugal's agriculture. Portugal also includes the autonomous islands of the AZORES and MADEIRA. The overseas territory of MACAO will return to China in 1999.

### CLIMATE

Portugal has a maritime climate. Compared to other Mediterranean lands, summers are cooler and winters are milder. Most rain falls in winter.

### VEGETATION

Forests cover *c*.36% of Portugal. It is the world's leading producer of cork, made from the bark of the cork oak. Olive trees are common. Almond, carob, and fig trees are found in the far S.

### HISTORY AND POLITICS

Visigoths conquered the region in the 5th century AD. In 711 they were ejected by the Moors. In 1139 Alfonso I defeated the Moors. Portugal's independence was recognized by Spain in 1143. The reconquest was completed in 1249, when the Moors were removed from the Algarve. JOHN I founded the Aviz dynasty in 1385 and launched Portugal's colonial and maritime expansion. His son, HENRY THE NAVIGATOR, captured the Azores and Madeira. The reign of Manuel I was Portugal's "golden age." By 1510 Portugal had established colonies in Africa, Asia, and South America. The fall of the Aviz dynasty brought PHILIP II of Spain to the throne. For the next 60 years, Portugal was subject to Spanish control. JOHN IV established the BRAGANZA dynasty (1640–1910). In the 18th century Marquês de POMBAL reformed Portugal's institutions and rebuilt Lisbon. JOHN VI was forced to flee to Brazil during the PENINSULA WAR (1808–14). His son, PEDRO I, declared Brazilian independence in 1722. In 1910 Portugal became a republic. In 1926 a military coup overthrew the government. Antonio de Oliveira SALAZAR became prime minister in 1932. The terms of the 1933 constitution enabled Salazar to become Western Europe's longest-ruling dictator. The *Estado Novo* (New State) was repressive and the economy stagnated. In 1968 Salazar was replaced by Marcello Caetano. Failure to liberalize the regime and the cost of fighting liberation movements in its African colonies led to a military coup in 1974. In 1975 many Portuguese colonies gained independence. In 1976 a new liberal constitution was adopted. In 1986 Portugal joined the European Community and Marco Soares became president. The Portuguese economy emerged from recession. In 1996 Soares was replaced by Jorge Sampaio.

### ECONOMY

In 1999 Portugal became one of the 11 states to adopt the EURO. Its commitment to the EUROPEAN UNION (EU) has seen the economy emerge from recession (1995 GDP per capita, US$12,670). Manufacturing accounts for 33% of exports. Textiles, footwear, and clothing are major exports. Portugal is the world's fifth-largest producer of tungsten and the world's eighth-largest producer of wine. Olives, potatoes, and wheat are also grown. Tourism is a rapidly growing sector.

postmaster general and the deputy postmaster general, both of whom are appointed by, and sit on, the Board of Governors. The nine governors are appointed by the president with the approval of the Senate.

**postimpressionism** Various movements in painting that developed (*c.*1880–*c.*1905), especially in France, as a result of or reaction to IMPRESSIONISM. Roger Fry, the British painter and theorist, invented the term when he organized the exhibition *Manet and the postimpressionists* at the Grafton Gallery, London, in 1910. The show revolved around the work of CÉZANNE, GAUGUIN, and VAN GOGH, who are still considered to be the dominant figures in this phase of modern art.

**postmodernism** Originally, an architectural movement that started in the 1970s in reaction to the monotony of international MODERNISM. Its exponents sought new ways to merge anthropomorphic details or traditional design elements (especially from classical buildings) with 20th-century technology. The term is no longer restricted to architecture. In literature, postmodernism is less antimodernism than a successor to it, and is characterized by works that refer to their own fictionality. In the early 1980s the concept of postmodernism exploded into popular culture. Postmodernism is often regarded as a general cultural phenomenon rather than a particular artistic movement. *See also* DECONSTRUCTION

**post-mortem** (autopsy) Dissection of a body to determine the cause of death. It is to confirm a diagnosis or to establish the cause of an unexpected death.

**postnatal depression** Mood disorder, characterized by intense sadness, which may develop in a mother within a few days of childbirth. It ranges from mild cases of the "baby blues," which are usually short-lived, to the severe depressive illness known as puerperal psychosis.

**post-traumatic stress disorder** Anxiety condition that may develop in people who have been involved in or witnessed some horrific event. It is commonly seen in survivors of battles or major disasters. The condition is characterized by repeated flashbacks to distressing events, hallucinations, nightmares, insomnia, edginess, and depression. As many as 10% of sufferers are left with permanent psychological disability.

**potash** Any of several potassium compounds, especially potassium oxide ($K_2O$), potassium carbonate ($K_2CO_3$), and potassium hydroxide (KOH). Potash is mined for use as fertilizer because potassium is an essential element for plant growth. Potassium carbonate is used for making soap and glass, and potassium hydroxide for soap and detergents.

**potassium** (symbol K) Common metallic element first isolated in 1807 by Sir Humphry DAVY. Its chief ores are sylvite, carnallite, and polyhalite. Chemically it resembles sodium. Potassium in the form of POTASH is used as a fertilizer. The natural element contains a radioisotope, $^{40}$K (half-life $1.3 \times 10^9$ yr), which is used in the radioactive dating of rocks. Properties: at. no. 19; at. wt. 39.102; sp.gr. 0.86; m.p. 146.6°F (63.7°C); b.p. 1,425°F (774°C); most common isotope $^{39}$K (93.1%). *See also* ALKALI METALS

**potato** Plant native to Central and South America and introduced into Europe by the Spaniards in the 16th century. Best grown in a moist, cool climate, it has oval leaves and violet, pink, or white flowers. The potato itself is an edible TUBER. The leaves and green potatoes contain the alkaloid solanine and are poisonous if eaten raw. Family Solanaceae; species *Solanum tuberosum.*

**Potawatomi** Algonquian-speaking Native Americans. Originally united with the OTTAWA and the OJIBWA, these hunter-farmers were driven by the Sioux SE from Wisconsin, migrating as far as Indiana before driven W by white settlers. They were eventually settled on reservations in Oklahoma, Kansas, Michigan, and Wisconsin, where they now number about 2,000.

**Potemkin, Grigori Aleksandrovich, Prince** (1739–91) Russian soldier and politician. Involved in the coup that brought Catherine the Great to power in 1762, he became her lover for a time and remained until his death the most powerful man in Russia.

**potential, electric** Energy required to transfer a unit positive electric charge from an infinite distance to a given point in an electric field. The unit of electric potential is the VOLT, and the Earth's potential is taken by convention to be zero. A battery's electric potential can make current flow in an external circuit. POTENTIAL DIFFERENCE is the difference in the values of electric potential between two points in an electric field or circuit.

**potential difference** Difference in electric potential between two points in a circuit or electric field, usually expressed in volts. It is equal to the work done to move a unit electric charge from one of the points to the other. *See also* ELECTROMOTIVE FORCE (EMF)

**potential energy** Type of ENERGY an object possesses because of its vertical position in the Earth's gravitational field; also the energy stored in a system such as a compressed spring or in an oscillating system such as a pendulum. An object on a shelf has potential energy given by $mgh$, where $m$ is its mass, g the acceleration due to gravity, and $h$ the height of the shelf.

**Potomac** River in the E US. It rises in West Virginia at the confluence of the North and South Branch rivers, and flows E and SE to Chesapeake Bay on the Atlantic coast, forming the boundaries of Maryland–West Virginia and Maryland–Virginia. The river is navigable for large ships as far as Washington, D.C. Length: 287mi (462km).

**Potsdam** City on the Havel River, E Germany; capital of Brandenburg state. During the 18th century it was a residence of the Prussian royal family. The 1805 Peace of Potsdam strengthened the alliance between Russia and Prussia against France. The POTSDAM CONFERENCE took place here in 1945. Industries: food processing, textiles. Pop. (1990) 138,700.

**Potsdam Conference** (July–August 1945) Summit meeting of Allied leaders in WORLD WAR II held in Potsdam, Germany. The main participants were US President TRUMAN, Soviet leader STALIN, and the British prime minister, at first CHURCHILL, later ATTLEE. It dealt with problems arising from Germany's defeat, including the arrangements for military occupation and the trial of war criminals, and issued an ultimatum to Japan demanding surrender.

**Potter, Beatrix** (1866–1943) British children's author who created the characters of Peter Rabbit, Jemima Puddleduck, Squirrel Nutkin, and others in her animal stories. Her first books were *The Tale of Peter Rabbit* (1901) and *The Tailor of Gloucester* (1902).

**Potter, Dennis** (1935–94) English playwright. He is best known for his television plays, notably *Pennies from Heaven* (1978), *Blue Remembered Hills* (1979), and *The Singing Detective* (1986).

**pottery** Objects shaped of clay and hardened by fire or dried in the sun. The making of pottery is dependent on the plasticity and durability of clay after firing. The finished object can be divided into three categories: earthenware, the ordinary pottery dating from primitive times, baked at 1,292°F (700°C) or lower; stoneware, fired at up to 2,102°F (1,150°C), less porous, and until modern times produced more commonly in the Far East than in Europe; and PORCELAIN, fired at 2,552°F (1,400°C). After a clay pot is formed and dried it is fired in a kiln; glaze is then applied, and the pot is refired.

**potto** Slow-moving African primate with large eyes and a pointed face; it is nocturnal and arboreal. The common potto has sturdy limbs, a short tail, and small spines. Its woolly fur is gray-red. Length: 15in (37cm), excluding the tail. Species *Perodicticus potto.*

**Poulenc, Francis** (1899–1963) French composer and a member of Les SIX. Spontaneity and melodiousness characterize his works, which include ballets, notably *Les Biches* (1923), orchestral works, chamber music, piano music, and songs. He also composed two operas.

**poultry** Collective term for domestic fowl reared as a source of meat and eggs. Chickens are the most important domesticated bird in the world. They are the major source of eggs and an important meat source. These light-skeletoned birds have short, weak wings, strong legs, chin wattles, and a head comb. Males are known as cocks; females as hens; and castrated males as capons. Some breeds, such as Rhode Island, Wyandotte, and Plymouth Rock, are raised for meat and eggs. Others, such as White Plymouth Rock, Cornish, and Rock Cor-

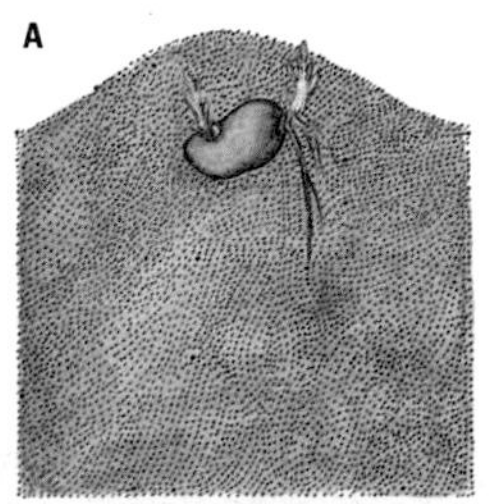

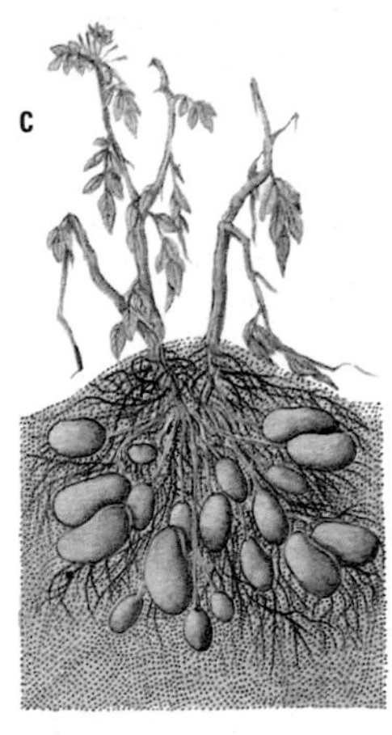


▲ **potato** The growth of the potato (*Solanum tuberosum*) takes three to seven months depending on variety. The tuber is covered with earth in fertile ground and shoots its stems through "eyes" in the skin surface (A). At six weeks a large canopy of leaf growth develops and tubers grow (B) on underground shoots. Leaf growth is dried chemically (C) to aid harvesting.

P

▲ **Pound** The US expatriate poet and critic Ezra Pound had a major influence on 20th-century Anglo-American literature, influencing writers such as Hemingway, Eliot, and Joyce.

nish, mainly supply meat. Species *Gallus domesticus*. Other forms of poultry are DUCK, GOOSE, GUINEA FOWL, and TURKEY.

**Pound, Ezra Loomis** (1885–1972) US poet and literary critic. He was a leading figure in literary MODERNISM and a founder of IMAGISM and VORTICISM. In 1907 Pound emigrated to England. His early experimental works *Exultations* and *Personae* (both 1909) established him as a leading member of the avant-garde. In 1924 Pound moved to Italy, and during World War 2 he made pro-fascist, anti-Semitic broadcasts to the USA. In 1945 he was escorted back to the USA and indicted for treason. Pound was judged mentally unfit to stand trial and confined to a mental hospital (1946–58). He spent the rest of his life in Italy. Pound's masterpiece is the epic *Cantos* (1925–60), a reconstruction of Western civilization in free verse.

**Pound, Roscoe** (1870–1964) US jurist and educator. He is noted for his belief that laws should be compatible with popular attitudes and adaptable to social and economic changes.

**pound** Imperial unit of weight equal to 0.453kg. It became a unit of currency when a pound (lb) weight of silver was divided into 240 penny units. The pound STERLING has been the main unit of English currency since the Middle Ages.

**Poussin, Nicolas** (1594–1665) French painter who worked mainly in Rome. At first inspired by MANNERISM, he later specialized in mythological subjects. In the late 1630s he turned to more elaborate Old Testament and historical themes, such as *The Eucharist* (1644–48) and *The Seven Sacraments* (1648).

**Powell, Anthony Dymoke** (1905– ) British novelist. He is best known for *A Dance to The Music of Time*, a series of 12 novels that portrays the snobbish world of the English upper classes after World War I, beginning with *A Question of Upbringing* (1951) and ending with *Hearing Secret Harmonies* (1975).

**Powell, "Bud" (Earl)** (1924–66) US jazz pianist and composer. A key figure in the development of BEBOP, he played with Charlie PARKER, Charlie MINGUS, Dizzy GILLESPIE and other modern jazz masters, although mental illness limited his activity.

**Powell, Cecil Frank** (1903–69) British physicist. He developed a technique to record SUBATOMIC PARTICLES directly onto film. In 1947 he used this method to investigate COSMIC RADIATION and discovered a new particle, the pion (pi MESON). This discovery supported the theory of nuclear structure proposed by Hideki YUKAWA. Powell subsequently discovered the antiparticle of the pion and the decay process of kaons (K mesons). He was awarded the 1950 Nobel Prize for physics.

**Powell, Colin Luther** (1937– ) US general. He fought in the Vietnam War and rose through the ranks to be national security adviser (1987–89) and the first African-American chairman of the JOINT CHIEFS OF STAFF (1989–93) during the Gulf War.

**power** In mathematics, number of times a number is multiplied or divided by itself. If 2 is raised to the power 3 (written $2^3$, called 2 cubed, or 2 to the 3rd power) it is $2 \times 2 \times 2$ or 8. A negative power indicates a fraction: eg $2^{-3}$ is $1/2^3$, or 1/8. A fractional power indicates a root – the power $^1/_2$ is a square root, and the power $^1/_3$ is a cube root: eg 8 to the power $^1/_3$ (written $8^{1/3}$) means a number (the cube root) which, when multiplied by itself three times, yields 8; the root is 2. Any number to the power 0 equals 1.

**power** In physics, rate of doing WORK or of producing or consuming energy. It is a measure of the output of an engine or other power source. James WATT was the first to measure power; he used the unit called HORSEPOWER. The modern unit of power is the WATT.

**power of attorney** Formal authority for one person to act on behalf of another in legal and financial matters.

**Powhatan** (1550–1618) Chief of the Powhatan Confederacy of Native North Americans, which controlled the region of America around Jamestown at the time of the first English setlement (1607). The confederacy included *c*.30 peoples. According to legend, the colonists' leader, John SMITH, was saved from execution only by the intercession of POCAHONTAS, Powhatan's daughter. Later, he approved her marriage to another colonist, John Rolfe, and thereafter maintained friendly relations with the colony until his death.

**Powys** County in E central Wales; the administrative center is Llandrindod Wells. Offa's Dyke and the later Norman castles were built as border defenses by the Welsh and English. During the Middle Ages, Powys was a powerful kingdom. It is drained by the Usk, Wye, and Taff rivers. Sheep and cattle are reared. Area: 1,960sq mi (5,077sq km). Pop. (1991) 117,647.

**Poznań** City on the Warta River, W Poland. One of the oldest Polish cities, it became the seat of the first Polish bishopric in 968. It was the center of Polish power in the 15th–17th centuries. In 1793 it passed to Prussia. The Grand Duchy of Poznań was created in 1815 as part of Prussia, but the area reverted to Poland in 1919. Industries: metallurgy, agricultural machinery, electrical equipment, chemicals, textiles. Pop. (1993) 589,700.

**praetor** Title of public official in ancient Rome, usually translated as "magistrate." From 242 BC two praetors were elected, serving a one-year term, usually followed by appointment as provincial governor. By the 1st century BC there were eight praetors. The office declined in importance under the emperors.

**pragmatism** Philosophical school holding the view that the truth of a proposition has no absolute standing but depends on its practical value or use. Primarily supported by US philosophers, it was first proposed by C. S. PEIRCE and was adopted by William JAMES and John DEWEY.

**Prague** (Praha) Capital of the Czech Republic, on the Vltava River. Founded in the 9th century, it grew rapidly after Wenceslaus I established a German settlement in 1232. In the 14th century it was the capital of BOHEMIA. It was the capital of the Czechoslovak republic (1918–93). It was occupied in World War II by the Germans and liberated by Soviet troops in 1945. Prague was the center of Czech resistance to the Soviet invasion of the country in 1968. It is an important commercial center. Industries: engineering, iron and steel. Pop. (1990) 1,215,000.

**Prague Spring** (1968) Short-lived political and social reorganization in Czechoslovakia. In January Alexander DUBČEK, a liberal communist, gained power and initiated reforms intended to create "socialism with a human face." In August Soviet tanks rolled into Prague, imposing a Soviet occupation.

**Praia** Capital of Cape Verde, a port on the S shore of São Tiago Island. It is the site of a meteorological station and is a key point in the Atlantic telegraph cable network. A trading center for the Cape Verde Islands, Praia exports castor oil, sugarcane, oranges, and coffee. Industries: fishing, straw hats. Pop. (1990) 61,707.

**prairie** Region of treeless plain. The prairies of North America extend from Ohio through Indiana, Illinois, and Iowa to the Great Plains, and N into Canada. Others include the pampas of S South America and the steppes of central Europe and Asia.

**prairie chicken** Chicken-sized, pale brown GROUSE of the W US. It has brown and black, pointed tail feathers and white neck feathers. During courtship displays, the male erects his neck feathers by inflating orange neck air sacs. Species *Tympanuchus cupido*.

**prairie dog** Squirrel-like rodent of W North America, named for its barking cry. It has a short tail and its fur is grizzled brown to buff. Active by day, it feeds on plants and insects and lives in communal burrows that are interconnected to form colonies. Length: 12in (30cm). Genus *Cynomys*. *See also* GROUND SQUIRREL

**praseodymium** (symbol Pr) Silver-yellow metallic element of the LANTHANIDE SERIES. It was first isolated in 1885 by Carl von Welsbach. Its chief ores are monazite and bastnasite. Soft, malleable, and ductile, praseodymium is used in carbon electrodes for arc lamps, and its green salts are used in colored glasses, ceramics, and enamels. Properties: at.no.59; at. wt. 140.9077; sp. gr. 6.77; m.p. 1,708°F (931°C); b.p. 6,354°F (3,512°C); only one isotope $^{141}$Pr (100%).

**prawn** Any of numerous species of edible crustaceans in the order Decapoda; it is generally larger than a SHRIMP. Typical genera include *Penaeus*, *Pandalus*, *Crangon*, and

P

*Nephrops*, which includes the Dublin bay prawn. Large prawns are called scampi.

**Praxiteles** (370–330 BC) Greek sculptor whose graceful style epitomized the 4th-century BC Greek ideal. In ancient times his most famous work was the *Aphrodite from Cnidus* (350 BC), of which there are several copies.

**prayer** Act of thanking, adoring, conferring with, or petitioning a divine power; also the form of words used for this purpose. Many religions have set forms for praying. Muslims recite prayers while facing in the direction of MECCA. In Christianity, the Roman Catholic missal contains regulated customary prayers. The Book of COMMON PRAYER plays the same role in the Anglican Communion. Prayer can also be the private devotional act of an individual using his or her own words.

**praying mantis** *See* MANTIS

**Precambrian** Oldest and longest era of Earth's history, lasting from the formation of the Earth about 4.6 billion years ago to the beginning of a good fossil record about 590 million years ago. Precambrian fossils are extremely rare, probably because the earliest life forms did not have hard parts suitable for preservation. Also, Precambrian rocks have been greatly deformed. Primitive bacteria and cyanobacteria have been identified in deposits that are more than 3 billion years old.

**precession** Wobble of the axis of a spinning object. It occurs as a result of the torque on the spin axis, which increases as the angle of precession increases. The Earth precesses about a line through its center and perpendicular to the plane of the ECLIPTIC extremely slowly (a complete revolution taking 25,800 years) at an angle of 23.5°. The motion of a GYROSCOPE shows precession, because the entire ring containing the spinning wheel and its axle precesses around the support pivot.

**precipitate** Formation of an insoluble solid in a liquid either by direct reaction or by varying the liquid composition to diminish the solubility of a dissolved compound.

**precipitation** In meteorology, all forms of water particles, whether liquid or solid, that fall from the atmosphere to the ground. Distinguished from cloud, fog, dew, and frost, precipitation includes rain, drizzle, snow, and hail. Measured by rain and snow gauges, the amount of precipitation is expressed in millimeters or inches of liquid water depth.

**pre-Columbian art and architecture** Arts of Mexico, Central America, and the Andean region of South America before colonization. In the MAYA Classical period, beginning *c.*200 AD, many cities or ceremonial centers were built in Central America. Their pyramid temples were paralleled by the TEOTIHUACÁN, ZAPOTEC, and Mixtec cultures, and were succeeded by TOLTEC and AZTEC civilizations in the post-Classical period (900–1300 AD). Monumental building was achieved without wheels or the use of the arch; surfaces were often decorated with dazzling patterns. In the Andean region, the early Chavin sculptures were succeeded by the Mochica, the Tiahuanaco, and finally, in the 14th century, by the rich temple architecture and sophisticated engineering of the INCA. Gold-working, weaving, and sculpture were other important pre-Columbian arts.

**predestination** Christian doctrine that a person's ultimate spiritual salvation or condemnation by God has been ordained in advance. According to this doctrine, people are at birth committed to the events of life, and their fate is mapped out for them. Most Christians qualify the premise by seeing God's prevision subject to possible revision depending on the will and spirituality of the individual. This last position is the solution to which most Christians adhere. The concept of predestination is also found in ISLAM.

**pregnancy** Period of time from conception until BIRTH, in humans normally about 40 weeks (280 days). It is generally divided into three 3-month periods called trimesters. In the first trimester, the EMBRYO grows from a small ball of cells to a FETUS *c.*3in (7.6cm) in length. At the beginning of the second trimester movements are first felt and the fetus grows to about 14in (36cm). In the third trimester the fetus attains its full body weight. *See also* LABOR

**prehistory** Term to describe the period of human cultural development before the invention of writing. *See* BRONZE AGE; IRON AGE; MESOLITHIC; NEOLITHIC; PALEOLITHIC; STONE AGE

**prelude** In music, a preliminary movement that serves to introduce a work of which it may or may not formally be a part. It was often used as the first movement of a SUITE. The popularity of CHOPIN's piano preludes led to its associations with a short piece of an imaginative nature.

**premature birth** Birth of a baby prior to 37 weeks' gestation or weighing less than 5.5lb (2.5kg). Premature babies are more at risk than those born at full term and often require special care.

**Preminger, Otto Ludwig** (1906–86) US film director and producer. *Laura* (1944) marked the beginning of his career, and *The Moon is Blue* (1953) was his first independent production. In 1960 he made the epic *Exodus*, using the wide screen for the first time. His later films include *Hurry Sundown* (1967).

**premolar** In the dentition of adult human beings and other mammals, the two crushing or cutting TEETH between the CANINES and MOLARS on both sides of the upper and lower jaws; there are usually eight in all.

**Prendergast, Maurice Brazil** (1859–1924) US painter. A European visit in 1898 fired his admiration for POST-IMPRESSIONISM. He was a member of a group of US painters known as The Eight, and exhibited with them in their famous show of 1908. His works include *Umbrellas in the Rain* (1899) and *Central Park* (1901).

**Preparedness Movement** (1915–16) Campaign for greater defense strength. Prominent people, including Theodore Roosevelt, urged that the US end its policy of unarmed neutrality. After the torpedo of the liner LUISITANIA by German submarines (1915), military interests helped force President Wilson to reverse his position.

**preposition** Linguistic category or part of speech that shows the relationship (such as position or direction) between its complement and some other word in the sentence. In the English phrase, "The book on the table," the word *on* specifies the relationship between the word *book* and the prepositional complement *table*.

**Pre-Raphaelite Brotherhood (PRB)** Name adopted in 1848 by a group of young English painters who joined forces to revitalize British art. The Pre-Raphaelites took their name from their source of inspiration: the simplicity of Italian painting before the time of Raphael. The most prominent members of the PRB were Dante Gabriel ROSSETTI, John Everett MILLAIS, and William Holman HUNT. They attracted fierce criticism for their rejection of RAPHAEL but were helped by the support of John RUSKIN. By 1853 the PRB had largely dissolved but Rossetti maintained the name, and under his influence a second wave of Pre-Raphaelite painting began in the 1860s. It lasted well into the 20th century and was characterized by sentimental and artificial scenes of medieval romance. *See also* MORRIS, WILLIAM

**Presbyterianism** Major form of Protestant Christianity that became the national CHURCH OF SCOTLAND in 1690. It arose in the mid-16th century from the teachings of John CALVIN in Switzerland, and was taken to Britain by the Scottish religious reformer John KNOX. Ministers, occasionally called pastors, are elected by their congregations and confirmed in their office by the Presbytery, a group of ministers from the local area. Members of the Presbytery are responsible for ordaining and installing (and removing) church ministers. Once ordained, the minister carries out his work assisted by elders and trustees. Annually each presbytery sends delegates to a synod and to a General Assembly. In 1972 the Presbyterian Church of England (formed 1876) united with the CONGREGATIONAL Church of England and Wales. There are Presbyterian Churches all over the world, particularly in North America, where the Presbyterian Church (US) was formed in 1983 through the merger of several older groups.

**Prescott, William Hickling** (1796–1859) US historian. An expert on the Spanish conquests in America, his most famous works are *A History of the Conquest of Mexico* (1843) and *A History of the Conquest of Peru* (1847).

**prescription** Order written by a doctor, dentist, or veterinary surgeon for drugs or other medication to be dispensed by a pharmacist. It should give details of the quantity to be dis-

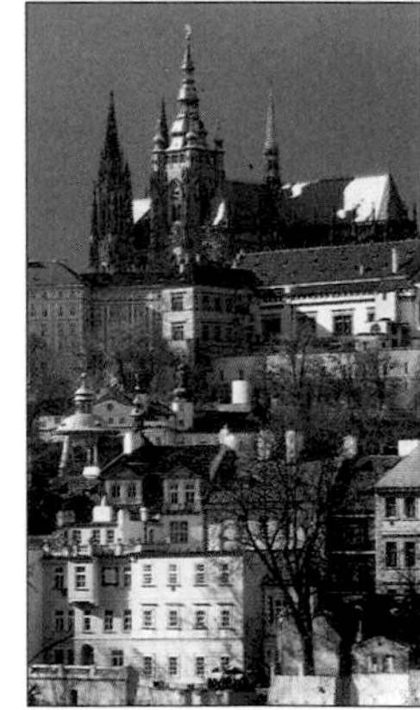

▲ **Prague** Hradčany Castle overlooks the beautiful old city and the River Vltava. A large complex, most of it dates from the reign of Holy Roman Emperor Charles IV. Within the complex is St. Vitus cathedral, which contains the tomb of Saint Wenceslas; the Royal Palace, which is the seat of the presidents; and many other important buildings.

**▶ primates** Because primates have large brains, they can learn complex skills and pass them down through the generations. Chimpanzees, for example, demonstrate high intelligence in their use of tools. They have been observed using sticks to "fish" for termites. Young chimpanzees learn this by observing their parents – aged between two and three years, they manipulate sticks as a form of play, and by the time they are four, they have mastered the use of the tool.

pensed, the dosage, the route of administration (such as by mouth), and any precautions.

**President of the United States** US chief executive officer, as defined in Article II of the Constitution; elected by eligible voters through the Electoral College for a term of four years. No president may serve more than two terms under the provisions of Amendment XXII. The president must be a natural-born citizen and at least 35 years of age. The Constitution specifies that presidential powers include those of commander-in-chief of the armed forces; the appointment of Supreme Court justices, ambassadors, and other officials; and the authority to grant pardons, make treaties with foreign countries with the advice and consent of two-thirds of the Senate; and veto legislation. The president is required to report to the Congress from time to time on the state of the union; to preserve, protect, and defend the constitution; and to "faithfully execute" the laws. Presidential power is limited by the system of checks and balances.

**Presley, Elvis** (1935–77) US singer who dominated rock and roll from his first recordings in 1953 until 1963. "Jailhouse Rock," "Hound Dog," "Heartbreak Hotel," and "Love Me Tender" are among his most successful songs. He also starred in films.

**press** *See* NEWSPAPER

**press, freedom of the** Noninterference in the media by government. The freedom of the press is a term accepted to mean the freedom of newspapers, or other media forms, to publish (usually political) news and opinions, independent of, and unhindered by, the preferred views of government. The freedom of the press is a cherished principle of democracy.

**pressure** (symbol Pa) In physics, the force on an object's surface divided by the area of the surface. The SI unit is the pascal; 1 pascal is equal to the pressure exerted by a force of 1 newton on an area of $1m^2$. In meteorology, the millibar (symbol mb), which equals 100 pascals, is commonly used.

**Prester John** Legendary ruler of a Christian kingdom in Asia or Africa in the Middle Ages. European Christians hoped to make an alliance with him against the Muslims in the age of the CRUSADES. The origin of the legend may have been Ethiopia, where the COPTIC CHURCH survived in the Middle Ages.

**Pretoria** City in Gauteng province, South Africa, 30mi (48km) NE of Johannesburg. It was founded in 1855 by Marthinus Pretorius. It became the capital of the Transvaal in 1860 and of the South African Republic in 1881. The Peace of Vereeniging, which ended the Boer War, was signed here in 1902. In 1910 it became the capital of the Union of South Africa. Pretoria is an important communications center. Industries: steel production, car assembly, diamond mining. Pop. (1990) 1,080,187.

**Previn, André George** (1929– ) US conductor, pianist, and composer, b. Germany. His early career was as a jazz pianist and musical director of Hollywood film scores, for which he won Academy Awards on four occasions. He was principal conductor of the London Symphony Orchestra (1968–79). He became music director of the Los Angeles Philharmonic Orchestra in 1986.

**Prévost d'Exiles, Antoine François** (1697–1763) (L'abbé Prévost) French novelist who lived as, alternately, a Jesuit novice, soldier, and forger. His most famous work is *Manon Lescaut* (1731).

**Priam** In Greek legend, the king of Troy at the time of the war with Greece. He had been installed as king in his youth by HERACLES, but by the time of the Ten Years' War was an old man. His sons HECTOR and PARIS were killed by the Greek forces. He was killed by Neoptolemus, the son of ACHILLES.

**Price, (Mary) Leontyne** (1927– ) US soprano. She made a triumphant debut at the Metropolitan Opera, New York, in 1961 in Verdi's *Il Trovatore*. She later appeared in many of the world's leading opera houses.

**prickly heat** Skin rash caused by blockage of the sweat glands in hot, humid weather. It occurs most often in infants and obese people. It disappears as the body cools.

**prickly pear** CACTUS with flat or cylindrical joints. It grows in North and South America and has been introduced into Europe, Africa, and Australia. The jointed pads have tufts of bristles, and the edible fruit is red and pulpy. Family Cactaceae; genus *Opuntia*.

**Pride's purge** (1648) Expulsion of *c.*140 members from the English LONG PARLIAMENT. It was carried out by Colonel Thomas Pride (d.1658) on the orders of the army council. The aim was to rid Parliament of members anxious to negotiate with CHARLES I. The remnant, known as the RUMP PARLIAMENT, voted to put Charles on trial.

**Priestley, J.B. (John Boynton)** (1894–1984) British author and literary critic. His novels include *The Good Companions* (1929), *Angel Pavement* (1930), and *Bright Day* (1946). Among his plays are *Time and the Conways* (1937) and *An Inspector Calls* (1945), both of which explore his theories of time.

**Priestley, Joseph** (1733–1804) British chemist and clergyman who discovered OXYGEN in 1774. He also discovered a number of other gases, including AMMONIA and oxides of NITROGEN. He studied the properties of CARBON DIOXIDE. Priestley was an advocate of the later discredited PHLOGISTON theory.

**primary** Method used in the US to select candidates for an election. In a direct primary, the commonest type, any number of party members may run and are voted for in a ballot of all the members. In an open primary, all the parties in an election are involved, and the voter votes for both the party and candidate of his or her choice. In a presidential election year, most US states select delegates to the national party convention in a presidential primary, the delegates having announced which presidential candidate they support.

**primary school** School that provides elementary education for children starting at compulsory school age. In the US, primary-school education starts either at kindergarten or first grade and continues through the sixth grade.

**primate** Regional head of an episcopally structured church. The term functions as a title. In the Church of England, it describes the Archbishop of Canterbury, who is "Primate of all England," and the Archbishop of York, who is "Primate of England."

**primates** Order of mammals that includes MONKEYS, APES, and HUMAN beings. Primates, native to most tropical and subtropical regions, are mostly herbivorous, diurnal (day-active), arboreal (tree-dwelling) animals. Their hands and feet, usually with flat nails instead of claws, are adapted for grasping. Most species have opposable thumbs, and all but humans have opposable big toes. They have a poor sense of smell, good hearing, and acute binocular vision. The outstanding feature of primates is a large complex brain and high intelligence. Primate characteristics are less pronounced in the relatively primitive prosimians (including tree shrews, BUSHBABIES, LORISES, and TARSIERS) and are most pronounced in the more numerous and advanced anthropoids (monkeys, apes, and human beings).

**prime minister** Chief executive and head of government in a country with a parliamentary system. He or she is usually the leader of the largest political party in PARLIAMENT. The office evolved in Britain in the 18th century, along with the CABINET system and the shift of power away from the crown toward the HOUSE OF COMMONS.

**prime number** Positive or negative integer, excluding one and zero, that has no FACTORS other than itself or one. Examples are 2, 3, 5, 7, 11, 13, and 17. The integers 4, 6, 8,... are not prime numbers since they can be expressed as the product of two or more primes.

**primitivism** Russian form of EXPRESSIONISM. It developed *c*.1905–20 and was influenced by Russian folk art, FAUVISM, and CUBISM. It was characterized by simplified forms and powerful color, used principally to depict scenes from working-class life. MALEVICH worked in the style early in his career.

**Primo de Rivera, Miguel** (1870–1930) Spanish dictator (1923–30). He staged a coup in 1923 with the support of King ALFONSO XIII. He dissolved parliament and established a military dictatorship modeled on the government of MUSSOLINI. He restored order and helped to end the revolt of Abd-el-Krim in Morocco (1926). He was forced from power shortly before his death.

**primrose** Any of numerous species of herbaceous, generally perennial plants of the genus *Primula*, which grow in the cooler climates of Europe, Asia, Ethiopia, Java, and North America. It has a tuft of leaves rising from the rootstock and clustered flowers of pale yellow to deep crimson. In Britain the name refers to *Primula vulgaris*. Family Primulaceae.

**Prince** (1960– ) US singer-songwriter and guitarist, b. Prince Rogers Nelson. He first achieved major success with the album *Purple Rain* (1984). Others include *Lovesexy* (1988) and *Diamonds and Pearls* (1990). In 1995 he became "the artist formerly known as Prince."

**prince** Royal title first used after the breakup of the CAROLINGIAN empire in the 9th century. In the UK, the heir to the English throne has customarily received the title Prince of Wales since 1301. Other sons of the monarch are also designated "prince."

**Prince Edward Island** Province in E Canada, an island in the Gulf of St. Lawrence off the coast of New Brunswick and Nova Scotia; the capital is Charlottetown. The island was discovered by Jacques CARTIER in 1534. In the early 18th century, it was colonized by French settlers as the Ile St. Jean. Ceded to Britain in 1763, it was renamed in 1799 and became a province of Canada in 1873. Fishing and agriculture are the most important economic activities. Area: 2,184sq mi (5,657sq km). Pop. (1993 est.) 131,600.

**Princeton** Borough in W central New Jersey; a leading academic and research center. Princeton was settled in the late 17th century and named in honor of William III, Prince of Orange-Nassau (1724). An important battle in the American Revolution took place in January 1777, when George Washington defeated the British forces. Princeton University, which is part of the Ivy League, was established in 1746. Pop. (1990) 12,016.

**printed circuit** Network of electrical conductors chemically etched from a layer of copper foil on a board of insulating material such as plastic, glass, or ceramic. It interconnects components such as capacitors, resistors, and integrated circuits (SILICON CHIPS). The printed circuit board (PCB) represents one stage in the miniaturization of electronic circuits. *See also* INTEGRATED CIRCUIT (IC)

**printing** Technique for multiple reproduction of images, such as text and pictures. In ancient China and Japan carved wooden blocks were inked to print pictures. From the 10th century, the Chinese used separate pieces of type, so that each page could be printed from arrangements of standard characters. Metal type made by casting first appeared in Korea around 1403. In Europe, GUTENBERG and CAXTON developed the use of letterpress in the 1400s. Printing expanded rapidly in the 1700s and 1800s. LITHOGRAPHY enabled printers to produce impressive color prints. For text, stereotype printing plates were cast from the pages of type, so that the type could be reused for setting other pages. TYPESETTING machines speeded up the process of setting up pages. The invention of photography in the 1820s led to the development of new techniques for reproducing photographs in print, such as the HALFTONE PROCESS. More recently, production speeds have greatly increased with the application of photosetting, in which the type is set photographically on sheet film, and OFFSET printing. Today, many publications are produced using a WORD PROCESSOR to enter the text. Desktop publishing programs allow images of the text and pictures to be arranged on screen.

**prion** Infective agent that appears to consist simply of a protein. Prions are thought to cause diseases such as CREUTZFELD-JAKOB DISEASE and kuru in humans, BOVINE SPONGIFORM ENCEPHALOPATHY (BSE) in cattle, and SCRAPIE in sheep. It is not yet understood how prions work; unlike viruses and bacteria, they do not contain DNA or RNA.

**prism** In mathematics, a solid geometrical figure whose ends are congruent (most commonly triangles) and perpendicular to the length, with the other faces rectangles. The volume of a prism is equal to the area of the end multiplied by the length of the prism. In physics, a prism is a piece of transparent material, such as glass, plastic, or quartz, in which a light beam is refracted and split into its component colors (spectrum) by dispersion.

**prison** Building for the confinement of criminals or people detained by the legal authorities. In most societies before the 18th century, criminals were subject to capital or corporal punishment or transportation, and prisons were places of temporary confinement only. Early prisons were usually squalid, badly organized, and often brutal. During the ENLIGHTENMENT, penalties grew less harsh, and prisons developed into penal institutions: imprisonment became the punishment. Conditions improved in the 19th century, with emphasis on rehabilitation rather than mere punishment.

**prisoner of war (POW)** In international law, military personnel captured by the enemy in an armed conflict between states. Their treatment is generally expected to be humane. The terms of the first international convention on prisoners of war, signed at the Hague peace conference of 1899, were widened by the 1907 Hague Convention and the GENEVA CONVENTION of 1949.

**privateer** Privately owned vessel with a government commission to capture enemy shipping. Their government licenses, called letters of marque, distinguished privateers from pirates. Crews were unpaid but were allowed to keep the booty. Privateering was at its height from the 16th to the 18th century. It was abolished by the Hague Conference of 1907.

**private sector** The part of a country's economy that is not under state control. In the private sector capital resources and enterprises are owned by companies. The private sector is sometimes taken to include the work of individuals. *See also* PUBLIC SECTOR

**PRISM**

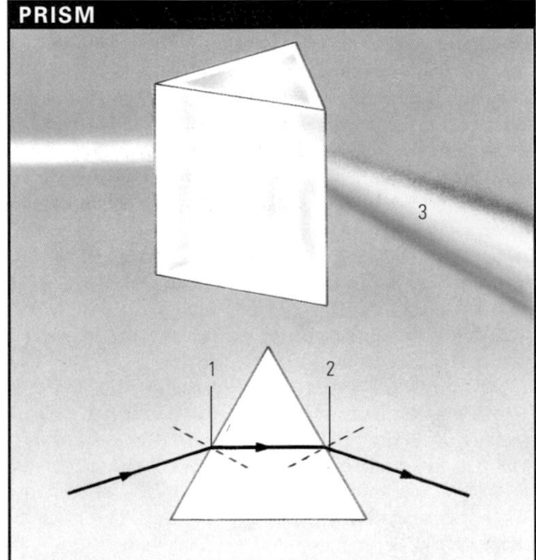


When light hits a prism it is refracted by the two surfaces it hits (1, 2). White light splits into the spectrum (3) because each of the colors of the spectrum have varying wavelengths. For example, the short wavelengths of blue and indigo are refracted more than the colors farther down the spectrum with longer wavelengths, such as orange and red.

P

**privatization** Transfer of state-run enterprises to private ownership. It is the opposite of NATIONALIZATION. In the 1980s policy-makers in some European countries, as well as Canada, Japan, and New Zealand, maintained that economic growth would best be encouraged by governments selling nationalized industries to independent enterprises, which were then free to respond to market forces and create a more efficient and competitive company. By the late 1980s and early 1990s the trend was taken up by former eastern bloc countries.

**Privy Council** Group of leading advisers to the British monarch. It developed in the Middle Ages out of the King's Council (Curia Regis). As the CABINET system of government developed, the Privy Council became increasingly restricted in its powers. Its Judicial Committee, established by legislation in 1833, is the final appeal court for most Commonwealth countries.

**probability** Number representing the likelihood of a given occurrence. The probability of a specified event is the number of ways that event may occur divided by the total possible number of outcomes, assuming that each possibility is equally likely. For instance, in one throw of a six-sided die, there are six possible outcomes, and three of these result in an even number: the probability of throwing an even number is thus 3/6, or 1/2.

**probate** Legal term for the certification by a court of law that a document purporting to be the WILL of a person who has died is valid. The term also applies to the official copy of a will, with the certificate of validity.

**probation** Sentence of a court of law on a young or first-time offender that allows the offender to remain at liberty subject to certain conditions and under the supervision of a probation officer. It is not regarded as a conviction. Breach of probation is an offense.

**Proclamation of 1763** British government edict designed to restrain encroachment on Native American lands by settlers following the FRENCH AND INDIAN WARS. It forbade settlement west of the line of the Appalachians.

**Procyon** (Alpha Canis Minoris) Brightest star in the constellation of Canis Minor and one of the stars nearest to the Sun. The star, known as Procyon A, has a faint white dwarf companion, Procyon B. Characteristics: apparent mag. 0.34 (A), 10.8 (B); absolute mag. 2.6 (A), 13.1 (B); spectral type F5 (A), wF (B); distance 11.4 light-years.

**production** In economics, methods by which wealth is produced. It is one of the basic principles of economics. The factors of production are land, labor, and CAPITAL.

**progesterone** Steroid HORMONE secreted mainly by the corpus luteum of the mammalian OVARY and by the PLACENTA during pregnancy. Its principal function is to prepare and maintain the inner lining (endometrium) of the UTERUS for pregnancy. Synthetic progesterone is one of the main components of the contraceptive PILL.

**prognosis** Doctor's prediction regarding the likely course and outcome of a patient's disorder. The prognosis is based on a doctor's knowledge of the disorder, the patient, and the probable effects of treatment.

**program** (SOFTWARE) Set of instructions that enables a COMPUTER to carry out a task. Programs can be written in a variety of COMPUTER LANGUAGES, and are stored on a magnetic DISK. To make a computer perform a particular task, a program is loaded into the computer's RAM.

**programming** Preparation of a COMPUTER so that it can perform a specific task. Before being given DATA, a computer must be given a set of instructions, or a PROGRAM, telling it how to deal with the data. Each instruction is a single step and all information must be in the form of binary numbers. For computer programmers, languages have been developed that make the task of programming increasingly intuitive.

**program music** (illustrative music) Music that aims to describe a scene or tell a story. Program music is an essential concept in the music of the romantic period; perhaps the earliest example from this time is BEETHOVEN's 6th Symphony (The Pastoral). Symphonic poems by Bedřich SMETANA and Jean SIBELIUS are later instances. *See also* ROMANTICISM

**Progressive Conservative Party** Major Canadian political party, known in French as *Parti Progressiste-Conservateur du Canada*. Formerly called the Liberal-Conservative Party (formed under John A. MACDONALD in 1854), the party adopted its present name in 1942. The Progressive Conservatives were in a minority for much of this century, with only 1958–63 under John DIEFENBAKER and a nine-month period in 1979–80 under Joe Clark seeing them in power. But with Brian MULRONEY as its leader, the Progressive Conservatives returned to government in 1984 with a record majority and were returned again with a smaller majority in 1988. Mulroney was succeeded by Kim Campbell in 1993, but the party lost disastrously to the Liberals in the general election later that year.

**progressive education** Movement that began in the late 19th century in Europe and the US, as a reaction to traditional education. In Europe FROEBEL, PESTALOZZI, and MONTESSORI were influential in the movement, which aimed to educate "the whole child." In the US, the movement owed much to the philosophy of John DEWEY. It led in some cases to what critics termed laxness, and produced a "back to basics" movement.

**Progressive Party** US political party. The original party (Bull Moose Party) was formed in 1912 by the supporters of Theodore ROOSEVELT after he had failed to regain the Republican nomination from William H. TAFT. By splitting the Republican vote, it ensured a Democratic victory. In 1916 the Progressives endorsed the Republican candidate. The name was also applied to the supporters of Robert M. LA FOLLETTE in 1924 and to the dissident Democrats who nominated Henry A. WALLACE in 1948. *See also* PROGRESSIVISM

**progressivism** US reform movement. In the early 20th century the Progressives favored governmental regulation of big business, child labor laws, female suffrage, and such political reforms as the direct primary, the referendum, and the power of recall. The movement, mostly middle class and urban in nature, reached its peak in 1912 with the formation of the PROGRESSIVE PARTY, which nominated Theodore ROOSEVELT for president and polled 30% of the popular vote. After 1916 the movement gradually went into decline.

**Prohibition** (1919–33) Period in US history when the manufacture, sale, and transport of alcoholic drinks were prohibited. It was instituted by the 18th amendment to the US Constitution, confirmed by the Volstead Act (1919). Smuggling, illicit manufacture, corruption of government officials and police, and the growth of organized crime financed by BOOTLEGGING made it a failure. Prohibition was repealed by the 21st amendment (1933).

**projector** Instrument with a lens system, used to cast images onto a screen from an illuminated flat object. An **episcope** is a projector for opaque objects such as a printed page; it uses light that is reflected from the object. A **diascope** is a projector for transparent objects such as photographic slides and films; it uses light transmitted through the object. An **epidiascope** can project images from both transparent and opaque objects. A motion-picture projector produces moving images from many frames (pictures) on a transparent film.

**Prokaryotae** (formerly Monera) Biological KINGDOM that includes BACTERIA and CYANOBACTERIA (formerly blue-green algae). They have more simple cells than other organisms. DNA is not contained in chromosomes in the NUCLEUS, but lies in a distinct part of the CYTOPLASM called the nucleoid. They have no distinct membrane-surrounded structures (organelles). Cell division is simple and in the rare cases where SEXUAL REPRODUCTION occurs, genetic material is simply transferred from one partner to another; there are no separate sex cells. In photosynthetic prokaryotes, PHOTOSYNTHESIS takes place on the cell membrane. At present two subkingdoms are recognized: ARCHAEBACTERIA and EUBACTERIA. *See also* ASEXUAL REPRODUCTION; EUKARYOTE; SYMBIOSIS

**Prokhorov, Alexandr Mikhaylovich** (1916– ) Soviet physicist who shared the 1964 Nobel Prize for physics with Nikolai BASOV and the US physicist Charles H. TOWNES. His research in quantum electronics resulted in the development of the MASER and LASER.

**Prokofiev, Sergei** (1891–1953) Russian composer, whose style is characterized by biting dissonances within rich harmony. His most popular works include the ballets

*Romeo and Juliet* (1935) and *Cinderella* (1944); the *Classical* (first) Symphony (1918); *Peter and the Wolf* (1936); and the comic opera *The Love for Three Oranges* (1921).

**prolapse** Displacement of an organ due to weakening of supporting tissues. It most often affects the rectum, due to bowel problems, or the UTERUS following repeated pregnancies.

**proletariat** Marxist term for those classes of an industrial society that have no source of income other than wages. According to MARX, the proletariat is the true creator of the objects produced by industry, and would become an irresistible force.

**promenade concerts** Annual concert series organized by the BBC in the Royal Albert Hall, London, where inexpensive standing room is available. Such concerts originated in Paris in 1833 and from 1838 were given at Drury Lane, Covent Garden, and elsewhere. "Proms" in their modern series began at the Queen's Hall, London, in 1895, under the baton of Sir Henry Wood.

**Prometheus** In Greek mythology, the fire-giver. He created the human race, provided them with reason, and stole fire from the gods. For this theft, ZEUS had him chained to a rock where an eagle consumed his liver for eternity. In some myths he was rescued by HERACLES.

**promethium** (symbol Pm) Radioactive metallic element of the LANTHANIDE SERIES. It was made in 1941 by particle bombardment of NEODYMIUM and PRASEODYMIUM. Promethium occurs in minute amounts in uranium ores. The isotope $^{147}Pm$ is used in phosphorescent paints, x-rays, and nuclear-powered batteries for space vehicles. Properties: at.no. 61; m.p. 1,976°F (1,080°C); b.p. 4,460°F (2,460°C); most stable isotope $^{145}Pm$ (half-life 17.7 years).

**pronghorn** Only extant member of the family Antilocapridae, related to the ANTELOPE. It is a horned, hoofed, herbivorous animal of the W US and N Mexico. The swiftest North American mammal, it is said to be capable of a speed of 50mph (80km/h) over short distances. Height: 3ft (90cm); weight: 100lb (45kg).

**pronoun** Linguistic category (part of speech) that has no complete independent meaning and that derives some aspect of meaning from elsewhere. Deictic pronouns take some of their meaning from context, such as *you*, whose meaning changes according to who is speaking and who is addressed. Anaphoric pronouns take some of their meaning from a previous part of what is said or written: in the sentence *The piano stood where everyone could see it, it* refers to the piano mentioned (its antecedent). Types of pronouns are personal, relative, intensive, reflexive, interrogative, and demonstrative.

**propaganda** Systematic manipulation of public opinion through the communications media. Many political, economic, and social organizations, and pressure groups of all kinds employ some kind of propaganda.

**propane** Colorless, flammable gas ($C_3H_8$), the third member of the ALKANE series of HYDROCARBONS. It occurs in natural gas, from which it is obtained; it is also obtained during petroleum refining. Propane is used (as bottled gas) as a fuel, as a solvent, and in the preparation of many chemicals. Properties: m.p. −310°F (−190°C); b.p. −43.6°F (−42°C).

**propanol** (propyl alcohol) Colorless ALCOHOL used as a solvent and in the manufacture of various chemicals. It exists as two ISOMERS. Normal propanol, $CH_3CH_2CH_2OH$, is a by-product of the synthesis of METHANOL (methyl alcohol). Isopropanol (isopropyl alcohol), $(CH_3)_2CHOH$, is a secondary alcohol that is easily oxidized into acetone.

**propanone** Colorless flammable liquid ($CH_3COCH_3$) made by oxidizing isopropanol. It is a raw material for the manufacture of many organic chemicals and is a widely used solvent. Properties: sp.gr. 0.79; m.p. –138.6°F (–94.8°C); b.p. 133.2°F (56.2°C).

**propeller** Device for producing thrust, usually mounted on a rotating shaft. The cross-section of an aircraft propeller reveals an aerofoil shape. This allows it to function as a rotating wing; it generates forward thrust by producing aerodynamic lift. A ship's propeller, or screw, "screws" the ship through the water.

**propene** (propylene) Colorless, aliphatic hydrocarbon, $C_3H_6$, manufactured by the thermal cracking of ETHENE. It is used in the manufacture of a wide range of chemicals including vinyl and acrylic resins. Properties: m.p. −301°F (−185°C); b.p. −54.4°F (−48°C).

**prophet** Individual who is thought to be a divinely inspired messenger from a god, or is believed to possess the power to foretell future events. The classic examples of prophets were the holy men and seers who preached by the authority of YAHWEH to the Jews of the Old Testament kingdoms of ISRAEL and JUDAH. Part of the Old Testament consists of books devoted to their preachings. The term *prophet* also applied to ABRAHAM, MOSES, and SAMUEL. JOHN THE BAPTIST fulfilled the role of a New Testament prophet, predicting the coming of the Messiah. In ancient Greece and Rome, divinely inspired prophetesses made oracular pronouncements to those who consulted them. Among Muslims, MUHAMMAD is held to be a prophet. In both Buddhist and Hindu literature predictions occur, and many prophetic reformers have occurred in HINDUISM.

**proportion** Mathematical relation of equality between two ratios, having the form a/b = c/d. A continued proportion is a group of three or more quantities, each bearing the same ratio to its successor, as in 1:3:9:27:81.

**proportional representation (PR)** System of electoral representation in which the allocation of seats reflects the proportion of the vote commanded by each candidate or party. The main contrast is with a system in which representatives are elected for each of numerous single constituencies. Proportional representation is found in almost all countries other than English-speaking ones and former British colonies.

**propylene** *See* PROPENE

**proscenium** In the theater the front part of the stage, especially the arch, first used in the 17th-century Italian theater to create a picture-frame effect.

**prose** In LITERATURE, a relatively unstructured form of language. Unlike the metrical discipline of POETRY, prose is more closely connected with the rhythms of everyday speech.

**Proserpine** Roman equivalent of PERSEPHONE.

**prospecting** Search for exploitable mineral deposits using methods based on geology and mineralogy. These methods involve extensive sampling – the analysis and examination of materials taken from holes drilled at regular intervals. Other techniques include the analysis of the velocity of waves resulting from underground explosions, the measurement of variations in the Earth's magnetic field, and the detection of gravity anomalies. For radioactive minerals, Geiger counters are used. Aerial photography is a versatile method.

**Prost, Alain** (1955– ) French racing driver. He was Formula 1 champion four times between 1985 and 1993. He is renowned for his technical competence.

**prostaglandin** Series of related FATTY ACIDS, with hormone-like action, present in SEMEN and liver, brain, and other tissues. Their biological effects include the lowering of blood pressure and the stimulation of contraction in a variety of smooth-muscle tissues, as in the UTERUS.

**prostate gland** Gland in the male reproductive tract surrounding the URETHRA. It secretes specific chemicals that mix with sperm cells and other secretions to make up SEMEN.

**prostitution** Provision of sexual services for reward, usually money. Most prostitutes are women. In Britain prostitution is not illegal, but soliciting, living off the earnings of prostitution, and brothel-keeping are.

**protactinium** (symbol Pa) Rare, radioactive, metallic element of the ACTINIDE SERIES, first identified in 1913. Its chief source is URANINITE. Properties: at.no. 91; at.wt. 231.0359; sp.gr. 15.4; m.p. 2,192°F (1,200°C); b.p. 7,232°F (4,000°C); most stable isotope $^{231}Pa$ (half-life 3.25 x $10^4$ yr).

**Protectorate** In English history, the period in which Oliver CROMWELL ruled as lord protector (1653–58), followed by his son Richard (1658–59). The term also describes a state that is controlled by a larger one, without necessarily being under direct colonial rule.

**protein** Organic compound containing many AMINO ACIDS linked together by PEPTIDE bonds. Living cells use about 20 amino acids, which are present in varying amounts. The order of amino acids in proteins is controlled by the cell's

P

▲ **Proust** Once a frequent visitor to the aristocratic salons of Paris at the turn of the century, the French novelist Marcel Proust became a recluse after the death of his mother when he was 34 years old. His 13-volume work, *Remembrance of Things Past*, is written in long, cascading sentences, and it is founded on the effects of involuntary memory, the moment when a chance impression obliterates the present and propels one into the past.

RNA. The most important proteins are ENZYMES, which determine all the chemical reactions in the cell, and ANTIBODIES, which combat infection.

**Protestantism** Branch of Christianity formed in protest against the practices and doctrines of the old ROMAN CATHOLIC CHURCH. Protestants sought a vernacular Bible to replace the Latin VULGATE, and to express individual nationalism. The movement is considered to have started when Martin LUTHER nailed his 95 theses to a Wittenberg church door. His predecessors included John WYCLIFFE and Jan HUS. Later supporters included Ulrich ZWINGLI and John CALVIN. The Protestants held the EUCHARIST to be a symbolic celebration, as opposed to the Roman Catholic dogma of TRANSUBSTANTIATION, and claimed that because Christ is the sole medium between God and man, his function cannot be displaced by priests. This led to an emphasis on individual contemplation of the scriptures. *See also* ANGLICANISM

**Proteus** In Greek mythology, a sea god, son of Oceanus and Tethys. He is depicted as a little old man of the sea. Proteus had the gift of prophecy and the ability to alter his form at will.

**proteus** Generic name given to both the cystitis-producing bacterium *(Proteus mirabilis)* and the amphibian the olm *(Proteus anguinus)*.

**prothrombin** Precursor of the blood ENZYME thrombin, which is formed from prothrombin. It plays an essential role in forming blood clots, which help to stop bleeding.

**Protista** *See* PROTOCTISTA

**Protoctista** (formerly Protista) Kingdom that includes such widely differing groups as ALGAE (including large seaweeds), AMOEBAS and other PROTOZOA, slime molds, and downy mildews.

**proton** (symbol p) Stable ELEMENTARY PARTICLE with a positive charge equal in magnitude to the negative charge of the ELECTRON. It forms the nucleus of the lightest isotope of HYDROGEN, and with the NEUTRON is a constituent of the nuclei of all other elements. It is made up of three QUARKS. The proton is a BARYON with a mass 1836.12 times that of the electron. The number of protons in the nucleus of an element is equal to its ATOMIC NUMBER. Protons also occur in primary cosmic rays. Beams of high-velocity protons, produced by particle ACCELERATORS, are used to study nuclear reactions.

**protoplasm** Term referring to the living contents of a plant or animal CELL. It includes both the NUCLEUS and the CYTOPLASM of cells.

**protozoa** Phylum of unicellular organisms found worldwide in marine or fresh water, free-living and as parasites. These microscopic animals have the ability to move (by CILIA or pseudopodia) and have a nucleus, cytoplasm, and cell wall; some contain CHLOROPHYLL. Reproduction is by FISSION or encystment. Length: 0.1in (0.3mm). The 30,000 species are divided into four classes: Flagellata, Cnidospora, Ciliophora, and Sporozoa.

**Proudhon, Pierre Joseph** (1809–65) French journalist and philosopher. His anarchist theories of liberty, equality, and justice conflicted with the communism of Karl MARX. He argued that "property is theft." His greatest work was *Système des contradictions économiques* (1846).

► **Przewalski's horse** Because it is not descended from domestic horses, Przewalski's horse (*Equus przewalski*) is the last truly wild horse. They still exist in their natural state in a small area of SW Mongolia, although the species thrives in zoos. Numbers have been reduced because they have to compete with livestock for grazing areas and water.

**Proust, Marcel** (1871–1922) French novelist whose *À la recherche du temps perdu* (1913–27) is regarded as one of the great works of world literature. Proust was actively involved in the DREYFUS AFFAIR (1897–99), but ill health caused him to withdraw from society.

**Provençal** Variety of the Occitan language, spoken in Provence, SE France. It is a ROMANCE LANGUAGE belonging to the family of INDO-EUROPEAN LANGUAGES. It enjoyed a great literary flowering as the language of the TROUBADOURS of the 12th and 13th centuries.

**Provence** Region and former province of SE France, roughly corresponding to the present departments of Var, Vaucluse, and Bouches-du-Rhône, and parts of Alpes-de-Haute-Provence and Alpes-Maritimes. The coastal area was settled *c.*600 BC by the Greeks, and the Romans established colonies in the 2nd century BC. The region came under Frankish control in the 6th century AD. It passed to the Holy Roman Empire in the 11th century. It retained its distinctive identity and language (PROVENÇAL), and was the focus of a revival of secular literature and music in the Middle Ages. It was finally united with France in 1481, and remained a province until the French Revolution. Fruit and vegetables are grown and tourism is the major industry.

**Proverbs** Book of the Old Testament, probably the oldest existing example of Hebrew WISDOM LITERATURE. The book's subtitle attributes its authorship to King SOLOMON, but in fact scholars consider that it contains material from various periods later than Solomon's time.

**Providence** Capital of Rhode Island, a port on Providence Bay in NE Rhode Island. The city was founded in 1636 as a refuge for religious dissenters from Massachusetts. It later enjoyed great prosperity through trade with the West Indies. The city played an active role in the American Revolution. Industries: jewelry, electrical equipment, silverware. Pop. (1990) 160,728.

**Proxima Centauri** Nearest star to the Sun, slightly closer than the nearby star ALPHA CENTAURI. It was long thought to be part of the Alpha Centauri system, but some astronomers now believe it to be an unrelated star.

**prozac** One of a small group of antidepressants, known as selective SEROTONIN re-uptake inhibitors (SSRIs). They work by increasing levels of serotonin in the brain. Serotonin, or 5-hydroxytryptamine (5-HT), is a NEUROTRANSMITTER involved in a range of functions. Low levels of serotonin are associated with DEPRESSION. *See also* DRUG

**Prud'hon, Pierre Paul** (1758–1823) French painter of portraits and historical themes. A favorite of two French empresses, Josephine and Marie-Louise, he bridged the gap between late 18th- and early 19th-century painting by creating work that was elegant and emotional.

**Prussia** Historic state of N Germany. The region was conquered by the TEUTONIC KNIGHTS in the 13th century. The duchy of Prussia, founded in the 15th century, passed to the electors of BRANDENBURG in 1618. They took the title of king of Prussia in 1701. Under FREDERICK WILLIAM I and FREDERICK II in the 18th century, Prussia became a strong military power, absorbing SILESIA and parts of Poland. After defeats in the NAPOLEONIC WARS, Prussia emerged again as a powerful state at the Congress of VIENNA (1815). In the 19th century Prussia displaced Austria as the leading German power and, under BISMARCK, led the movement for German unity, accomplished in 1871. Comprising 65% of the new German empire, it was the leading German state until World War I. It ceased to exist as a political unit in 1945.

**Przewalski's horse** (Mongolian wild horse) Only surviving species of the original wild HORSE, found only in Mongolia and Sinkiang. It is small and stocky with an erect black mane. Its red-brown coat is marked with a darker line on the back and shoulders and leg stripes. Height: to 4.8ft (1.5m) at the shoulder. Family Equidae; species *Equus caballus przewalskii*.

**psalm** Musical hymn or sacred poem. The most famous are contained in the Book of PSALMS, in the Old Testament.

**Psalms, Book of** Book of the Old Testament, consisting of 150 hymns, lyric poems, and prayers. The works were collected over a very long period, at least from the 10th to the 5th centuries BC, and probably achieved their final form before the 2nd century BC. Most carry titles added afterward, and 73 are stated to have been composed or collected by King DAVID.

**Pseudepigrapha** Jewish writings of the period 200 BC – AD 200 that have been falsely attributed to a biblical author. The term refers more widely to almost all ancient Jewish texts that have not been accepted as canonical by the Christian Church. *See also* APOCRYPHA

**pseudomorphism** In mineralogy, chemical or structural alteration of a mineral without change in shape. It is exemplified by petrified wood.

**psittacosis** (parrot fever) Disorder usually affecting the respiratory system of birds. Caused by a bacterium, it can be transmitted to human beings, producing pneumonia-like symptoms. Treatment is with ANTIBIOTICS.

**psoriasis** Chronic recurring skin disease featuring raised, red, scaly patches. The lesions frequently appear on the chest, knees, elbows, and scalp. Treatment is with tar preparations, steroids, and ultraviolet light. Psoriasis is sometimes associated with a form of ARTHRITIS.

**Psyche** In Greek mythology, a beautiful mortal woman loved by EROS. She was also the personification of the soul.

**psychiatry** Analysis, diagnosis, and treatment of mental illness and behavioral disorders. It includes research into the cause and prevention of mental disorders, and the administering of treatment, usually by physical means such as drugs and electroconvulsive therapy. Some psychiatrists also use psychotherapeutic techniques.

**psychoanalysis** Method of therapy devised by FREUD and BREUER in the 1890s for treating behavior disorders, particularly NEUROSIS. It is characterized by its emphasis on unconscious mental processes and on treatment by free association and the therapist's interpretation.

**psychology** Study of mental activity and behavior. It includes the study of perception, thought, problem solving, personality, emotion, mental disorders, and the adaptation of the individual to society. It overlaps with many other disciplines, including PHYSIOLOGY, PHILOSOPHY, ARTIFICIAL INTELLIGENCE, and social ANTHROPOLOGY. Central areas of psychology include neuropsychology, which relates experience and behavior to brain functioning; COGNITIVE PSYCHOLOGY, which studies thought processes; SOCIAL PSYCHOLOGY, in which behavior is studied in its social context; and DEVELOPMENTAL PSYCHOLOGY, which studies the way in which children's cognitive and emotional development takes place. Applied psychology aims to use the discipline's insights into human behavior in practical fields such as education and industry.

**psychopathic personality** (antisocial personality) Personality disorder that leads to antisocial, often aggressive, behavior. There appears to be little anxiety, guilt, or neurosis, and psychoanalytic theory regards this disorder as stemming from an incompletely developed SUPEREGO.

**psychopharmacology** Study of how DRUGS affect behavior. Drugs are classified according to their effect: sedative hypnotics, such as BARBITURATES; stimulants, such as AMPHETAMINES; opiate narcotics, such as HEROIN; and psychedelics and hallucinogens, such as LSD.

**psychosis** Serious mental illness in which the patient loses contact with reality, in contrast to NEUROSIS. It may feature extreme mood swings, delusions, or hallucinations, distorted judgment, and inappropriate emotional responses. Organic psychoses may spring from brain damage, advanced SYPHILIS, senile DEMENTIA, or advanced EPILEPSY. Functional psychoses, for which there is no known organic cause, include SCHIZOPHRENIA and manic-depressive psychosis.

**psychosomatic** Describing a physical complaint thought to be rooted, at least in part, in psychological factors. The term has been applied to many complaints, including asthma, migraine, ulcers, and hypertension.

**psychotherapy** Treatment of a psychological disorder by nonphysical methods. It is carried out either with individuals or groups and usually involves some sort of "talking cure" and the development of a rapport between patient and therapist. Psychotherapy is often based on PSYCHOANALYSIS,

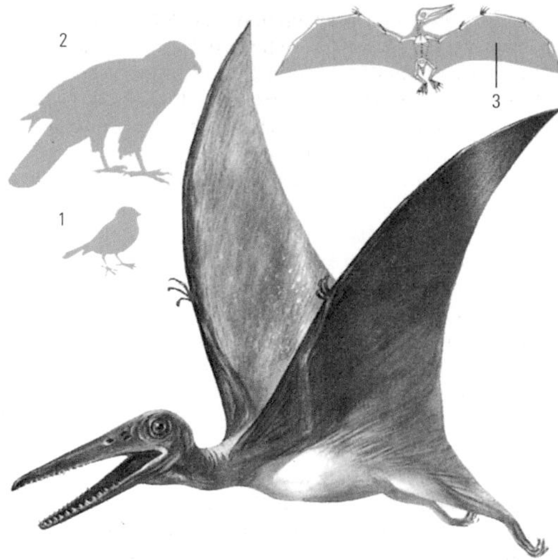


◄ **pterodactyl** living during the late Jurassic and early Cretaceous periods, the flying reptiles known as pterodactyls varied in size. The smallest specimen was the size of a sparrow (1) and the largest was the size of a hawk (2). Like the bats of today, it had a wing membrane (3) attached to an elongated fourth finger, and hind limbs and tail.

**ptarmigan** Any of three species of northern or alpine grouse, all of which have feathered legs; especially the Eurasian ptarmigan, *Lagopus mutus*. The wings and breast are white in colder months, but in the spring they become a mottled gray-brown. It inhabits high barren regions, feeding on leaves and lichens. Length: to 14in (36cm). Family Tetraonidae.

**pteridophyte** Commonly used name for any of a group of spore-bearing VASCULAR PLANTS. *See also* TRACHEOPHYTE

**pterodactyl** Any of several species of small PTEROSAURS. Almost tail-less, it had a large toothed beak and flimsy membranous wings. Fossil remains show a lack of muscular development and the absence of a breast keel. It is therefore believed that pterodactyls were gliders, incapable of sustained flapping flight.

**pterosaur** Extinct flying reptile with wing membranes supported by a single, elongated finger on each side. Distributed throughout the world during Jurassic and Cretaceous times, early forms had teeth and tails; later forms were tailless and had toothless beaks.

**polytetrafluorethylene (PTFE)** Chemically inert, solid plastic, known also by the trade names Teflon and Fluon. PTFE is used as a heat-resistant material for heat-shields on spacecraft, as a nonstick coating on cooking utensils, and as a lubricant. PTFE is stable up to about 572°F (300°C).

**Ptolemy I** (367–283 BC) (Ptolemy Soter) King of ancient Egypt, first ruler of the Ptolemaic dynasty, which ruled Egypt for *c.*300 years (323–30 BC). A leading Macedonian general of ALEXANDER THE GREAT, Ptolemy I was granted Egypt in the division of Alexander's empire upon the latter's death in 323 BC. After many struggles for control, he assumed the title of king in 305 BC. He prospered largely from trade, controlling much of E Mediterranean region by the time of his death, and from his control of land and taxes. He established his former soldiers as settlers in Egypt, and endeavored to unite the country through the cult of Serapis, although he also supported traditional Egyptian religion. He made his capital at ALEXANDRIA, where he created the famous library. He abdicated in 284 BC in favor of his son, PTOLEMY II.

**Ptolemy II** (*c.*308–246 BC) (Ptolemy Philadelphus) King of ancient Egypt (284–246 BC), son of PTOLEMY I. He built Alexandria into the cultural and commercial center of the Greek world, attracting poets such as Callimachus and Theocritus, and greatly expanding the collection of books in the Library of Alexandria.

**Ptolemy** (90–168) (Claudius Ptolemaeus) Greek astronomer and geographer. He worked at the library of Alexandria, Egypt. His main works were *Almagest*, which described an Earth-centered universe, and *Geography*, which provided the basis for a world map. Ptolemy was regarded as the most reliable authority by Muslim and Christian scholars until the Renaissance.

**puberty** Time in human development when sexual maturity is reached. The reproductive organs take on their adult form, and secondary sexual characteristics, such as the growth of pubic hair, start to become evident. Girls develop breasts and

P

▲ **Puccini** A performance of Verdi's Aida inspired the young Giacomo Puccini to enter a music conservatory and train as a composer. The combination of dramatic libretti and magnificent music have ensured his operas a permanent place in the world's opera houses. His best-known works are passionate love stories with tragic endings.

begin to menstruate; in boys there is deepening of the voice and the growth of facial hair. Puberty may begin at any time from about the age of ten, usually occurring earlier in girls than in boys. The process is regulated by HORMONES.

**public sector borrowing requirement (PSBR)** Amount a government needs to borrow to cover its expenditure. A government principally raises its money by taxes and excise duties. If it has to spend more than the amount covered by these sources, it must raise the rest by borrowing. To do this, it issues short-term and long-term STOCKS and BONDS, on which it pays INTEREST. These loans form part of the national DEBT.

**Puccini, Giacomo** (1858–1924) Italian composer of operas. Among his works, which all combine dramatic libretti with magnificent music, are *La Bohème* (1896), *Tosca* (1900), and *Madam Butterfly* (1904).

**Pueblo** Generic name for Native American tribes inhabiting the Mesa and Rio Grande regions of Arizona and New Mexico. They belong to several language families, including Tewa, Hopi, and Zuni. The multistory buildings of the Zuni gave rise to the legendary "Seven Cities of Cíbola" eagerly sought by the Spaniards.

**Puerto Rico** Self-governing island commonwealth (in union with the US) in the West Indies, the most E island of the Greater Antilles. The capital is San Juan. Believed to have been first visited by Columbus in 1493, the island was a Spanish colony until 1898, when it was ceded to the US. In 1952 it was proclaimed a semi-autonomous commonwealth. The decline in the sugar industry in the 1940s created considerable unemployment. Many Puerto Ricans immigrated to the US. The island is of volcanic origin, and much of the land is mountainous and unsuitable for agriculture. The main crops are sugar, tobacco, coffee. Industries: tourism, textiles. Area: 3,425sq mi (8,870sq km). Pop. (1993 est.) 3,552,039.

**puff adder** Widely distributed African VIPER. Its skin usually has yellow markings on brown. It hunts large rodents and its poisonous bite can be fatal to humans. Up to 80 young are born at one time. Length: to 4ft (1.2m). Family Viperidae; species *Bitis arietans*.

**puffball** Any of a large order of MUSHROOMS (Lycoperdiales) whose SPORE masses become powdery at maturity and are expelled in "puffs" when pressed. Puffballs are stemless, and some are edible.

**puffin** Small diving bird of the AUK family (Alcidae), found in large colonies in the Northern Hemisphere. The Atlantic puffin (*Fratercula arctica*) has a short neck, a triangular bill with red, yellow, and blue stripes, and reddish legs and feet. The puffin lays a single egg in a burrow about 3.3–6.6ft (1–2m) deep on a cliff. Length: about 12in (30cm)

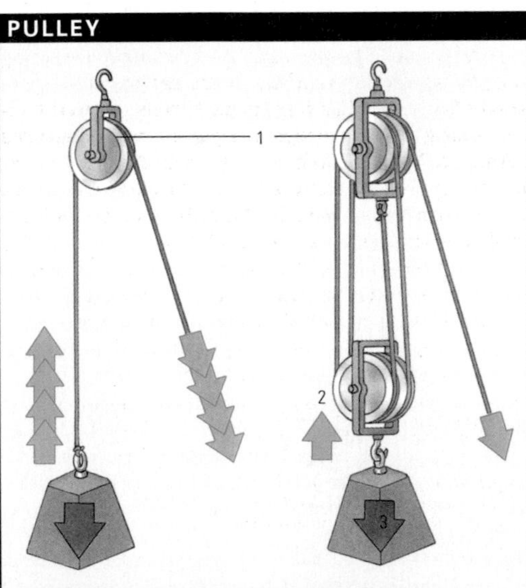


Pulleys (1) multiply the effect of a force applied. By passing the rope through four pulleys the upward pulling force (2) is multiplied four times, allowing a person to lift a weight (3) not normally liftable.

With four pulleys, however, the rope has to be pulled four times as far to move the weight the same distance. To move the weight up 3.3ft (1m) the rope must be pulled down 13ft (4m).

▲ **puffin** Feeding entirely on prey that they find underwater, puffins (*Fratercula arctica*, shown here) can catch small or slow moving fish for themselves or for their unfledged chicks and can carry as many as ten small fish at a time in their colorful beaks. They nest in large colonies on cliffs by the sea.

▲ **puma** A wild cat found in a variety of habitat types of the New World, the puma (*Felis concolor*), gives birth to between one and six cubs.

**pug** Small dog that probably originated in China. It has a large head, a blunt muzzle, and facial wrinkles. The wide-chested, short body is set on strong legs. The short coat may be gray, light brown, or black with a characteristic black face. Height: to 11in (28cm) at the shoulder; weight: to 18lb (8kg).

**Puglia** (Apulia) Region in SE Italy, consisting of the provinces of Bari, Brindisi, Foggia, Lecce, and Taranto; the capital is Bari. Colonized by the Greeks, it was taken by the Romans in the 3rd century BC. Conquered in turn by Goths, Lombards, and Byzantines, it later formed part of the Holy Roman Empire. The region became part of Italy in 1861. Products: wheat, almonds, figs, tobacco. Industries: iron and steel. Area: 7,472sq mi (19,357sq km). Pop. (1992 est.) 4,049,972.

**Pulitzer, Joseph** (1847–1911) US newspaper publisher, b. Hungary, who founded the PULITZER PRIZE. He made the *New York World* America's largest circulation daily newspaper. He crusaded for oppressed workers and against alleged big business and government corruption.

**Pulitzer Prize** Annual US awards for outstanding achievement in journalism, letters, and music. The cost is met by a trust fund left by Joseph PULITZER to the trustees of Columbia University. The first prize was awarded in 1917. There are prizes for fiction, drama, US history, biography, poetry, and musical composition.

**pulley** Simple machine used to multiply force or to change the direction of the force's application. A simple pulley consists of a wheel, often with a groove, attached to a fixed structure. Compound pulleys consist of two or more such wheels, some movable, that allow a person to raise objects much heavier than he or she could lift unaided.

**Pullman, George Mortimer** (1831–97) US industrialist and developer of the railroad sleeping car. The first modern sleeping car went into service in 1865.

**Pullman Strike** (June–July 1894) US labor struggle. When the manufacturers of Pullman railroad cars in Chicago cut wages, the frustrated workers were joined by the American Railway Union led by Eugene V. DEBS. A strike and a boycott of Pullman cars were called. It crippled railroad traffic in 27 states. For the first time in US labor history a court injunction against strikers was issued. There was violence. Federal troops, sent by President Grover Cleveland, arrived on July 4. Debs was arrested and jailed on July 17, and the strike ended.

**pulsar** Object emitting radio waves in pulses of great regularity. They were first noticed in 1967 by the British radio astronomer Jocelyn Bell. Pulsars are believed to be rapidly rotating NEUTRON STARS. More than 500 pulsars are now known, flashing at rates from about 4 seconds to 1 millisecond.

**pulse** Regular wave of raised pressure in arteries that results from the flow of blood pumped into them at each beat of the HEART. The pulse is usually taken at the wrist. The average pulse rate is about 70 per minute in adults.

**pulse** Any leguminous plant of the pea family with edible seeds, such as the bean, lentil, pea, peanut, and soybean. The term may also refer to the seed alone. Pulses are also used for oil production. Family Fabaceae/Leguminosae. *See also* LEGUME

**puma** (mountain lion, cougar) Large cat found in mountains, forests, swamps, and jungles of the Americas. It has a small, round head, erect ears, and a heavy tail. The coat is tawny with dark brown on the ears, nose, and tail; the underparts are white. It preys mainly on deer and small animals. Length: to 7.5ft (2.3m), including the tail; height: to 30in (75cm) at the shoulder. Family Felidae; species *Felis concolor.*

**pumice** Light rock formed when molten LAVA is blown to a rock froth by the sudden discharge of gases during a volcanic action. It is used as a light abrasive.

**pump** Device for raising, compressing, propelling, or transferring fluids. The lift pump, for raising water from a well, and the bicycle pump are reciprocating (to-and-fro) pumps. In many modern pumps, a rotating impeller (set of blades) causes the fluid to flow. Jet pumps move fluids by forcing a jet of liquid or gas through them.

**pumpkin** Orange, hard-rinded, edible garden fruit of a trailing annual VINE found in warm regions of the Old World and the US; a variety of *Cucurbita pepo*. In the US the pumpkin is also called a squash, especially the winter pumpkin *Cucurbita maxima* and *C. moschata*. Family Cucurbitaceae.

**punctuated equilibrium** Theory, expounded by Stephen Jay Gould and Niles Eldridge in 1972, that is strongly skeptical of the notion of gradual change in the EVOLUTION, as advocated by Charles DARWIN. They held that each species is in a steady state (equilibrium), which is punctuated by brief but intense periods of sudden change that give rise to new species.

**Punic Wars** (264–146 BC) Series of wars between Rome and Carthage. In the First Punic War (264–241 BC), Carthage was forced to surrender Sicily and other territory. In the Second (218–201 BC), the Carthaginians under HANNIBAL invaded Italy and won a series of victories. They were eventually forced to withdraw, whereupon the Romans invaded North Africa and defeated Hannibal. The Third Punic War (149–146 BC) ended in the destruction of Carthage.

**Punjab** State in N India, bounded W and NW by Pakistan; the capital is CHANDIGARH. In the 18th century Sikhs wrested part of the region from Mogul rule and established a kingdom. In 1849 it was annexed by the British. In 1947 the Punjab was split between the new countries of India and Pakistan, the smaller E part going to India. In 1966 this was further reorganized into two states, HARYANA and Punjab, which is now the only Indian state with a Sikh majority. Apart from Chandigarh, other major cities include AMRITSAR and Jullundur. Punjab is mainly a flat plain. Much of the land is irrigated and agriculture is important. Industries: textiles, woolens, electrical goods. Area: 19,450sq mi (50,376sq km). Pop. (1991) 20,281,969.

**Punjab** Province in NE Pakistan, bounded E and S by India; the capital is LAHORE. It was subject to a succession of foreign conquerors, including Aryans, Greeks, and the British. The province was formed in 1947, acquiring its present boundaries in 1970. The area lies on an alluvial plain and most of the land under cultivation is irrigated. Agriculture is the chief source of income, with wheat and cotton the major crops. Industries: textiles, machinery, electrical appliances. It is Pakistan's most heavily populated province. Area: 79,703sq mi (206,432sq km). Pop. (1985 est.) 53,840,000.

**Punjabi** (Panjabi) Language spoken by 50 million people in the PUNJAB. It belongs to the Indo-Iranian family of INDO-EUROPEAN LANGUAGES and is one of the 15 languages recognized by the Indian Constitution. It has similarities to HINDI.

**punk** Term used to describe music and fashion of the mid-1970s, characterized by raw energy and iconoclasm. Heavily influenced by US bands, such as the New York Dolls, punk was pioneered in Britain by the Sex Pistols and the Clash. Often antiestablishment, the associated fashions in dress, hair, and makeup were also designed to shock.

**pupa** Nonfeeding, developmental stage during which an insect undergoes complete METAMORPHOSIS. It generally occurs as part of a four-stage life cycle from the egg, through LARVA, to pupa, then adult. Most pupae consist of a protective outer casing inside which the tissues of the insect undergo a drastic reorganization to form the adult body. Insects that undergo pupation include the many different kinds of BUTTERFLY and BEETLE and many kinds of FLY. The pupa is often called a CHRYSALIS in butterflies and moths.

**pupil** In the structure of the EYE, circular aperture through which light falls onto the LENS; it is located in the center of the IRIS. Its diameter changes by reflex action of the iris to control the amount of light entering the eye.

**Pupin, Michael Idvorsky** (1858–1935) US physicist and inventor, b. Yugoslavia. He devised a means of extending the range of long-distance telephone communications by placing loading coils at intervals along the transmitting wire.

**puppet theater** Miniature stage for shows of glove puppets, marionettes, rod puppets, and flat and shadow figures. Such theaters existed in ancient Egypt and in Greece in the 5th century BC, in China, Java, and elsewhere in Asia, and reached their peak of popularity in 18th-century Europe.

**Purcell, Henry** (1659–95) English composer and organist of the Baroque period. It is his church music for which he is most famous; much of it is still frequently performed. His only opera, *Dido and Aeneas* (1689), is regarded as an early masterpiece of the form.

**purgatory** Place or state intermediate between HEAVEN and HELL where a soul that has died in a state of grace is purged of its sins before entering heaven. In the teachings of the Roman Catholic Church, souls that die with unforgiven venial and forgiven mortal sins go to purgatory.

**Purim** Ancient Jewish celebration of thanksgiving, held on the 14th day of the Jewish month of Adar (in February or March). It commemorates the deliverance of the Jews of Persia from a plot to destroy them. The story, which appears in the Old Testament Book of ESTHER, is read on this festival in all synagogue services. The gift of alms to the poor is obligatory, and the festival is associated with a carnival atmosphere.

**Puritans** British Protestants who were particularly influential during the 16th and 17th centuries. They originated in the reign of ELIZABETH I as a faction within the CHURCH OF ENGLAND; their chief aim was to make it a truly Protestant Church, rather than an Anglo-Catholic one. Following the ideas of CALVIN, they were initially opposed to Anglicanism because of its preoccupation with what they considered to be "popish" practice. However, they later demanded the setting up of PRESBYTERIANISM. Many of the parliamentary opponents of JAMES I and CHARLES I in the 17th century were Puritans. Among them were religious separatists who immigrated to America. The English CIVIL WAR (1642–49) resulted from attempts by Puritan parliamentarians to block Charles I's policies on religious grounds. After the war, the Puritans' zenith was reached when Oliver CROMWELL assumed full executive power in 1653. The authority of the Church of England as an Anglican institution was reestablished in 1660, although 30 years later Presbyterianism was accepted as the state-supported form of Christianity in Scotland. In England, the Puritans lived on as Dissenters and Nonconformists.

▲ **pumpkin** Related to cucumbers, pumpkins are soft-fleshed with a high water content. As food, the rind is removed and the flesh is pulped. As well as serving as food for humans, pumpkins are also cultivated as livestock feed.

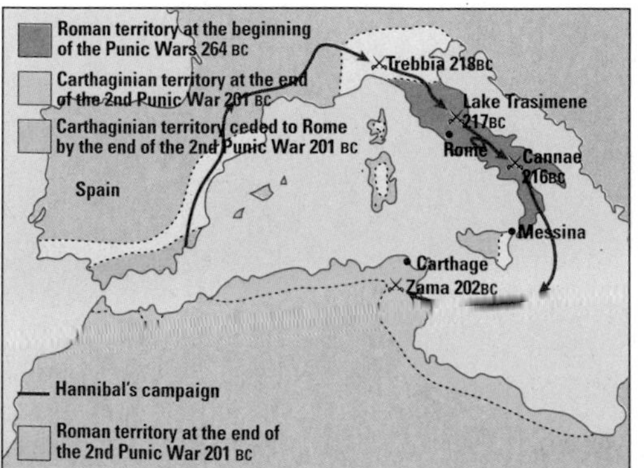


◀ **Punic Wars** To make an effective challenge to Carthage's domination of the w Mediterranean, Rome had to become a naval power. A large fleet was constructed and equipped with boarding devices to allow for hand-to-hand fighting at which the Romans excelled. As a result, after initial reverses they inflicted naval defeat on Carthage in the First Punic War.

▲ **Pushkin** Often called the father of modern Russian literature, Alexander Pushkin demonstrated his talent for poetry while he was a still a student in St. Petersburg. Influenced by Byron, his romantic masterpiece was *Eugene Onegin*, a tale of unrequited love.

**purpura** Purplish patches on the skin due to seepage of blood from underlying vessels. Physical injury, vitamin deficiencies, some allergies, and certain drugs are among the causes.

**pus** Yellowish fluid forming as a result of bacterial infection. It comprises blood serum, LEUKOCYTES, dead tissue, and living and dead BACTERIA. An ABSCESS is a pus-filled cavity.

**Pusan** City on the Korea Strait, SE South Korea. It has thrived through its trading links with Japan. The Japanese modernized the city's harbor facilities during their occupation of Korea (1905–45). In the Korean War Pusan acted as the United Nations' supply port. Pusan is the nation's leading port and second-largest city. It is an industrial and commercial center. Industries: iron and steel, shipbuilding. Pop. (1990) 3,798,000.

**Pushkin, Alexander Sergeievich** (1799–1837) Russian poet and novelist. He was exiled for his political beliefs in 1820, the year in which his folk poem *Ruslan and Lyudmila* was published. *The Prisoner of the Caucasus* (1822) is his response to the beauty of the Crimea and the Caucasus. Pushkin's masterpiece was the verse novel *Eugene Onegin* (1833). He died in a fight fought over his wife, Natalia.

**Pu Yi, Henry** (1906–67) Last Emperor of China (1908–11). His reign name was Hsuan Tung. Deposed after the formation of the Chinese republic, he was temporarily rescued from obscurity to become president, later "emperor," of the Japanese puppet state of MANCHUKUO in 1932. Captured by Soviet forces (1945), he was delivered to MAO ZEDONG and imprisoned (1949–59). He later worked as a gardener in Beijing.

**PVC** *See* POLYVINYL CHLORIDE (PVC)

**pyelitis** Inflammation of the pelvis of the KIDNEY, where urine collects before draining into the URETER. More common in women, it is usually caused by bacterial infection. Treatment is with ANTIBIOTICS and copious fluids.

**pygmy** Member of a group of people who average less than 4.6ft (1.5m) in height. African Pygmies inhabit parts of central Africa and Zaire; Asian Pygmies, often called Negritos, are found mainly in the Philippines and Malaysia. Most Pygmies are hunters and gatherers, with few crafts. Their numbers are declining rapidly.

**Pym, John** (1584–1643) English leader of the parliamentary opposition to CHARLES I. In the LONG PARLIAMENT (1640) he took part in drafting the GRAND REMONSTRANCE (1641). He was one of the five members whom Charles tried to arrest in the House of Commons (1642).

**Pynchon, Thomas** (1937– ) US novelist whose works are noted for their offbeat humor and inventiveness. They include *V* (1963), *Vineland* (1990), and *Mason and Dixon* (1997). His best-known work, *Gravity's Rainbow* (1973), won the National Book Award.

**Pyongyang** Capital of North Korea, in the W of the country, on the Taedong River. An ancient city, it was the capital of the Choson, Koguryo, and Koryo kingdoms. In the 16th and 17th centuries it came under both Japanese and Chinese rule. Pyongyang's industry developed during the Japanese occupation from 1910–45. It became the capital of North Korea in 1948. During the KOREAN WAR it suffered considerable damage. Industries: cement, iron and steel. Pop. (1984) 2,639,448.

**pyramid** In geometry, solid figure having a polygon as one of its faces (the base), the other faces being triangles with a common vertex. Its volume is one third of the base area times the vertical height.

► **pyramids** The three Egyptian pyramids at Giza are one of the Seven Wonders of the World, and the only to have survived virtually intact into the modern age. The largest was built for the pharaoh Khufu, and vast pyramids were constructed at Giza for Kahfre and Mankaure, also during the fourth dynasty. Although these are the best known of the Egyptian pyramids, many others were also constructed in the Nile Valley and elsewhere in the country, but they have not been as well preserved.

**Pyramids** Monuments on a square base with sloping sides rising to a point. They are associated particularly with ancient EGYPT, where some of the largest have survived almost intact. They served as burial chambers for pharaohs. The earliest Egyptian pyramid was a step pyramid (ZIGGURAT), built *c*.2700 BC for Zoser. Pyramid building in Egypt reached its peak during the 4th dynasty, the time of the Great Pyramid at GIZA. The largest pyramid in the world, it was built for Khufu *c*.2500 BC, and stands 480ft (146m) high with sides 758ft (231m) long at the base. The largest New World ziggurat pyramid was built in TEOTIHUACÁN, Mexico, in the 1st century AD; it was 216ft (66m) high with a surface area of 547,200sq ft (50,600sq m).

**Pyrenees** Range of mountains in S France and N Spain, extending in an almost straight line E to W from the Mediterranean Sea to the Bay of Biscay. They were formed in the Tertiary era. The Pyrenees contain deposits of marble, gypsum, and oil, and there are extensive forests. Sheep and goat grazing is the chief farming activity. The highest point is Pico de Aneto, 11,168ft (3,406m). Length: 270mi (435km).

**Pyrenees, Peace of the** (1659) Treaty between France and Spain after the THIRTY YEARS WAR. France gained territory in Artois and Flanders, and Philip IV of Spain reluctantly agreed to his daughter's marriage to LOUIS XIV. She was to renounce her claim to the Spanish throne in exchange for a subsidy. Because Spain could not pay the subsidy, the renunciation became void, resulting in the War of Devolution.

**pyridoxine** VITAMIN $B_6$, a coenzyme in the metabolism of AMINO ACIDS in the body. Pyridoxine is found in lean meat, egg yolks, milk, and fish. A deficiency can lead to anemia, and it is also taken as a vitamin supplement by those who believe it helps ease depression.

**pyrite** (fool's gold) Widespread sulfide mineral, iron sulfide ($FeS_2$), occurring in all types of rocks and veins. It is a brass-yellow color. It crystallizes as cubes and octahedra, and also as granules and globular masses. It is opaque, metallic, and brittle. Hardness 6.5; s.g. 5.0.

**pyrometer** THERMOMETER for use at extremely high temperatures. An optical pyrometer consists essentially of a small telescope, a RHEOSTAT (a type of variable RESISTOR), and a filament. When the telescope is aimed at a furnace or other hot object, the filament appears dark against the background. As the electric current flowing through the filament is increased slowly, using the rheostat, it grows brighter until it matches the intensity of the furnace. The amount of current is a measure of the temperature.

**pyroxene** Important group of rock-forming, silicate minerals. They are usually dark greens, browns, and blacks. Crystals are usually short prisms with good cleavages. Hardness 2.3–4; s.g. 5.5–6.

**Pyrrho** (*c*.360– *c*.270 BC) Greek philosopher, considered the founder of SKEPTICISM. His doctrine was that nothing can be known because every statement can be plausibly contradicted; therefore wisdom is in reserved judgment.

**Pyrrhus** (*c*.319–272 BC) King of Epirus (307–302, 295–272 BC). An able general, he fought several battles against Rome. Although he won, the cost was so heavy that victory was useless, hence the term "pyrrhic victory."

**Pythagoras** (*c*.580–500 BC) Greek philosopher and founder of the Pythagorean school. The Pythagoreans were bound to their teacher by rigid vows and were ascetic in their way of life. They believed in the TRANSMIGRATION OF SOULS and that numbers and their interrelationships constitute the true nature of things in the universe. Pythagoras is credited with many advances in mathematics and geometry, medicine, and philosophy. The famous **theorem** that the square of the hypotenuse of a right-angled triangle equals the sum of the squares of the other two sides is named for him, but was already known to the Egyptians and Babylonians. His brotherhood was suppressed at the end of the 6th century, but its doctrines were revived by the Romans *c*.500 years later.

**python** Name of more than 20 species of nonpoisonous snakes of the BOA family (Boidae), found in tropical regions. Like boas, pythons kill their prey (birds and mammals) by squeezing them in their coils. Unlike boas, pythons lay eggs. Subfamily Pythoninae.

**Qaddafi, Muammar al-** (1942– ) Libyan commander in chief and chairman of the Revolutionary Command Council. In 1969 he led the coup that toppled King Idris I. As head of state, Qaddafi sought to remove all vestiges of Libya's colonial past. He shut down US and British bases, nationalized all petroleum assets, and encouraged a return to Islamic law. In 1983 Libya bombed the neighboring state of Chad. Qaddafi has supported a number of unsuccessful attempts to bring Libya into union with other Arab countries. He has also lent assistance to various international terrorist groups. In 1986 the US bombed Libya in an attempt to stop this aid. Qaddafi survived, but one of his children was killed. He has been accused of protecting the Lockerbie bombers.

**Qatar** Sheikhdom on the Qatar peninsula in the Persian Gulf; the capital is DOHA. The low-lying land is mostly stony desert, with some salt flats. Qatar's territory includes several offshore coral islands, the most important being Habal, an oil storage and export terminal. The climate is hot and humid, and a scant water supply is supplemented by desalination schemes. Forty percent of Qatar's population are Sunni Muslims, although only 25% are native Qataris, who are descended from three BEDOUIN tribes. Once a part of the Ottoman empire, Qatar was a British protectorate from 1916 to 1971, when it achieved independence. It is an absolute monarchy. Sheikh Khalifa bin Hamad Al-Thani became Emir after a coup in 1972. During the 1980s, Qatar's status was threatened by the regional dominance of Iran and Iraq and a territorial dispute with BAHRAIN. In the GULF WAR (1991), Allied coalition forces were deployed on Qatar's territory and Palestinian migrant workers expelled because of the pro-Iraqi stance of the Palestine Liberation Organization (PLO). In 1995 the Emir was overthrown and replaced by his son, Sheikh Hamad bin Khalifa Al-Thani. A coup attempt failed in 1996. Qatar is heavily dependent on food imports. Its high standard of living (1995 GDP per capita, $17,690) is derived from oil and gas reserves. Oil was discovered in 1939, and today it accounts for *c.*90% of exports and 80% of income. Oil revenue has been used to diversify its industrial base and develop agriculture. The economy is heavily dependent on an immigrant work force, many from India and Pakistan. Area: 4,415sq mi (11,437sq km). Pop. (1986) 369,079.

**Qin** (formerly Ch'in) Imperial dynasty of China (221–206 BC). Originating in NW China, the Qin emerged after the collapse of the ZHOU dynasty; its founder was QIN SHIHUANGDI. The first centralized imperial administration was established, with the country divided into provinces, each under a governor. Uniformity was encouraged in every sphere, including law, language, coinage, weights, and measures. The GREAT WALL took permanent shape during this period.

**Qing** (formerly Ch'ing) Imperial Manchurian dynasty of China (1644–1911). It was established (1636) by NURHACHI following the collapse of the MING dynasty, but it was not until the fall of Peking that the Qing became the official ruling dynasty. The Qing emperors extended their influence. By 1800 they exercised control over an area stretching from Siam (Thailand) and Tibet to Mongolia and the Amur River. The dynasty weakened in the 19th century, following internal struggles, such as the TAIPING REBELLION, and with the increase of foreign influence, particularly after the OPIUM WARS. It ended with the abdication of PU YI in 1911 and the establishment of the Chinese republic.

**Qinghai** (Tsinghai) Province in NW China; the capital is Xining (Sining). Although parts of the region have long been under Chinese control, until recent times it was occupied mainly by Tibetan and Mongol nomads. It became a province of China in 1928. A mountainous region, it is the source of some of Asia's greatest rivers, including the HUANG HE, YANGTZE, and Mekong. There is farming of wheat, barley, and potatoes, and stock rearing. The province is famous for its horses. Iron ore, coal, oil, salt, and potash are extracted. Area: 278,486sq mi (721,280sq km). Pop. (1990) 4,430,000.

**Qin Shihuangdi** (259–210 BC) Emperor of China (221–210 BC). The first emperor of the QIN dynasty, he reformed the bureaucracy and consolidated the GREAT WALL. In the 1970s excavations of his tomb on Mount Li (near XIAN) revealed, among other treasures, an "army" of *c.*7,500 life-size terra-cotta guardians.

**Qom** City in W central Iran. The burial place of FATIMA, her shrine is a place of pilgrimage for SHI'A Muslims. Industries: textiles, rugs, pottery, glass, shoes. Pop. (1986) 543,139.

**quadrant** In plane geometry, a quarter of a circle, bounded by radii at right angles to each other and by the arc of the circle. In analytic geometry it is one of the four sections of a plane divided by an $x$ axis and a $y$ axis. A quadrant is also a device for measuring angles, based on a 90° scale.

**quadratic equation** Algebraic equation in which the highest exponent of the variable is 2; an equation of the second degree. A quadratic equation has the general form $ax^2 + bx + c = 0$, where $a$, $b$, and $c$ are constants. It has, at most, two solutions (roots), given by the formula $x = [-b \pm \sqrt{(b^2 - 4ac)}]/2a$.

**Quadruple Alliance** Alliance among four states, in particular three alliances in Europe in the 18th and 19th centuries. The first was formed (1718) by Britain, France, the Holy Roman emperor, and the Netherlands against PHILIP V of Spain, after he seized Sicily and Sardinia. The second was formed (1814) by Austria, Britain, Prussia, and Russia against NAPOLEON I. After Napoleon's defeat the four partners created the CONGRESS SYSTEM. The third Quadruple Alliance (1834) consisted of Britain and France in support of Portugal and Spain, where liberal monarchies were threatened by reactionary claimants.

**quail** Any of a group of Old World gamebirds. The European quail (*Coturnix coturnix*), a small, short-tailed bird with a white throat and mottled brownish plumage, is found throughout Europe, Asia, and Africa. The Australian quail (*Turnix velox*) is a stocky, brownish bird. They scrape for fruits and seeds and nest on the ground. The Japanese quail (*C. coturnix japonica*) is used as a source of meat and eggs in Europe and the US.

**Quakers** (officially Society of Friends) Christian sect that arose in England in the 1650s, founded by George FOX. The name derived from the injunction given by early Quaker leaders that their followers tremble at the word of the Lord. Quakers rejected the episcopal organization of the CHURCH OF ENGLAND, believing in the priesthood of all believers and the direct relationship between man and the spiritual light of God. Quakers originally worshiped God in meditative silence unless someone was moved by the Holy Spirit to speak. Since the mid-19th century, their meetings have included hymns and readings. The largest national Quaker Church is in the US, where it began with the founding of a settlement by William PENN in Pennsylvania (1681). Today, there are *c.*200,000 Quakers worldwide.

**qualitative analysis** Identification of the chemical elements or ions in a substance or mixture. *See also* QUANTITATIVE ANALYSIS

**Quant, Mary** (1934– ) English fashion designer. In 1955 she opened her first boutique, in Chelsea, London. Quant appealed to the growing youth market. Her designs, such as the miniskirt and her extensive use of vinyl, have become synonymous with "swinging London" in the 1960s.

**quantitative analysis** Identification of the amount of chemical constituents in a substance or mixture. Chemical methods use reactions such as precipitation (the suspension of small particles in a liquid), NEUTRALIZATION, and OXIDATION, and measure volume (volumetric analysis) or weight (gravimetric analysis). Physical methods

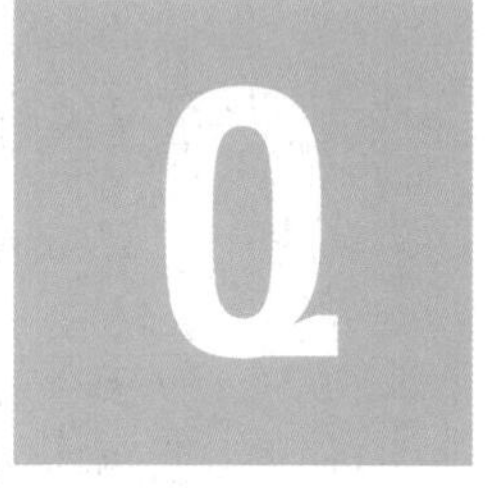


***Q/q, 17th letter of the Roman alphabet, derived from the Semitic* qoph, *meaning* monkey. *It was taken into the Greek alphabet as* koppa. *It entered the Roman alphabet in c.AD 114 and assumed its current form c.1500.***

Q

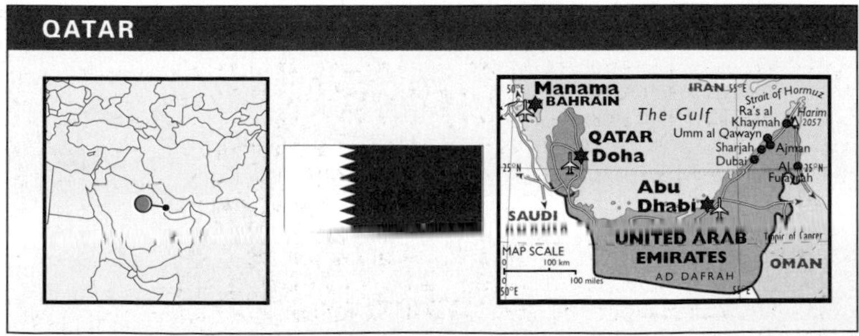

measure qualities such as density and refractive index (how much light is refracted by a medium).

**Quantrill, William Clarke** (1837–65) Confederate guerrilla leader during the Civil War. His guerrilla army terrorized and murdered Union sympathizers in Missouri and Kansas. In 1862 Quantrill was made a captain in the Confederate Army. In 1863 he was responsible for the murder of some 150 citizens of Lawrence, Kansas. He was killed by federal forces in Kentucky.

**quantum chromodynamics** Study of the properties of QUARKS in which, to explain permissible combinations of quarks to form various ELEMENTARY PARTICLES, each is assigned a color. Quarks are given one of the three primary colors: red, green, and blue. When three quarks combine to form BARYONS, the resulting color is always white. Antiquarks are given one of the three complementary colors: cyan, magenta, and yellow. When a quark combines with an antiquark to form a MESON, the resulting color is also white.

**quantum electrodynamics (QED)** Use of QUANTUM MECHANICS to study the properties of ELECTROMAGNETIC RADIATION and how it interacts with charged particles. For example, the theory predicts that a collision between an ELECTRON and a PROTON should result in the production of a PHOTON of electromagnetic radiation, which is exchanged between the colliding particles.

**quantum mechanics** Use of QUANTUM THEORY to explain the behavior of ELEMENTARY PARTICLES. In the quantum world, waves and particles are interchangeable concepts. In 1924 Louis de BROGLIE suggested that particles have wave properties, the converse having been postulated (1905) by Albert EINSTEIN. In 1926 Erwin SCHRÖDINGER used this hypothesis to predict particle behavior on the basis of wave properties, but a year earlier Werner HEISENBERG had produced a mathematical equivalent to Schrödinger's theory without using wave concepts at all. In 1928 Paul DIRAC unified these approaches while incorporating RELATIVITY into quantum mechanics. The complete modern theory of quantum mechanics was derived by Richard FEYNMAN in the 1940s. *See also* QUANTUM NUMBERS

**quantum numbers** In physics, a set of four numbers used to classify electrons and their atomic states. The **principal** quantum number (symbol $n$) gives the electron's energy level; the **orbital** quantum number (symbol $l$) describes its angular momentum; the **magnetic** quantum number (symbol $m$) describes the energies of electrons in a magnetic field; and the SPIN quantum number (symbol $m_s$) gives the spin of the individual electrons. *See also* QUANTUM THEORY

**quantum theory** Together with the theory of RELATIVITY, the foundation of 20th-century physics. It is concerned with the relationship between MATTER and ENERGY at the elementary or subatomic level and with the behavior of ELEMENTARY PARTICLES. According to the theory, all radiant energy is emitted and absorbed in multiples of tiny "packets" or quanta. The idea that energy is radiated and absorbed in quanta was proposed (1900) by Max PLANCK. Using Planck's work, Albert EINSTEIN quantized light radiation and explained (1905) the PHOTOELECTRIC EFFECT. In 1913 Niels BOHR used quantum theory to explain atomic structure and the relationship between the energy levels of an atom's electrons and the frequencies of radiation emitted or absorbed by the atom. *See also* QUANTUM MECHANICS; QUANTUM NUMBERS

**quarantine** Originally a 40-day waiting period during which ships were forbidden to discharge passengers or freight, to prevent transmission of plague or other diseases. Today, the term refers to any period of isolation legally imposed on people, animals, plants, or goods in order to prevent the spread of contagious disease.

**quark** Any one of six ELEMENTARY PARTICLES and their antiparticles (antiquarks); the constituents of the HADRON group of SUBATOMIC PARTICLES. They occur in one of six "flavors": up, down, top, bottom, charmed, and strange. Antiquarks have similar flavors, but their charge is opposite to that of their corresponding quark. Quarks always exist in combination; free quarks cannot exist.

**quarrying** Method of excavating rock from open-pit mines. Quarried rock is called stone. **Explosives** are generally used in industrial quarrying. The rock, such as limestone, is shattered by detonating explosives placed in strategically drilled holes. A **channeling** method is used for softer rock, such as sandstone. In this process a line of holes is drilled perpendicular to the cleavage lines in the rock; wedges (plugs) are inserted into the holes and hammered until the rock is split.

**quartz** ($SiO_2$) Rock-forming mineral, the natural form of silicon dioxide (silica). It is widely distributed, occurring in igneous and metamorphic rocks (notably granite and gneiss), and in clastic sediments. It is also found in mineral veins. It forms six-sided crystals. Pure quartz is clear and colorless, but the mineral may be colored by impurities. The most common varieties are colorless quartz (rock crystal), rose, yellow, milky, and smoky. The most usual cryptocrystalline varieties, whose crystals can be seen only under a microscope, are CHALCEDONY and FLINT. Quartz crystals exhibit the PIEZOELECTRIC EFFECT and are used in electronic clocks and watches to keep accurate time. Hardness 7; s.g. 2.65.

**quartzite** METAMORPHIC ROCK usually produced from sandstone, in which the quartz grains have recrystallized. Quartzite is a hard and massive rock. It is usually white, light gray, yellow, or buff, but it can be colored green, blue, purple, or black by various minerals.

**quasar** (quasi-stellar object) In astronomy, an object that appears to be a massive, highly compressed, extremely powerful source of radio and light waves, characterized by a large RED SHIFT. If such red shifts are due to the DOPPLER EFFECT, it can be deduced that quasars are more remote than any other objects previously identified; many are receding at velocities greater than half the speed of light. Their energy may result from the gravitational collapse of a GALAXY or from many SUPERNOVAS exploding in quick succession, although there seems to be no reason why such events should be occurring.

**Quasimodo, Salvatore** (1901–68) Italian poet. His first volume, *Waters and Land* (1930), established him as the leading Italian "hermetic" poet. Quasimodo was imprisoned for anti-fascist conduct in World War II. His later poetry, such as *Day after Day* (1947), marks a shift to a poetry of social engagement. He was also a prodigious translator. Quasimodo was awarded the 1959 Nobel Prize for literature.

**Quaternary period** Most recent period of the CENOZOIC era, beginning about 2 million years ago and extending to the present. It is divided into the PLEISTOCENE epoch, characterized by a periodic succession of great ice ages, and the HOLOCENE epoch, which started some 10,000 years ago.

**quattrocento** (It. fourteen hundred) Art history term applied to the 15th-century period of the Italian RENAISSANCE. Venice was its cultural center and leading figures included the painters Fra ANGELICO, Fra Filippo LIPPI, MASACCIO, and UCCELLO; the architects BRUNELLESCHI and ALBERTI; and the sculptors DONATELLO and GHIBERTI.

**Quayle, (James) Dan (Danforth)** (1947– ) US statesman, vice president (1989–93). In 1976 he was elected to the US House of Representatives as a conservative Republican. Quayle served as US senator for Illinois (1981–89). In 1988 he was a controversial choice as George BUSH's vice-presidential running mate. As vice president, he was a focus of criticism throughout the Bush administration.

**Quebec** (Québec) Province in E Canada; the largest province in area and second-largest in population; the capital is QUEBEC and the largest city is MONTREAL. Most of the province, however, is on the Canadian Shield and is relatively uninhabited. In 1535 Jacques CARTIER landed on the Gaspé peninsula of E Canada and in 1536 he sailed up the ST. LAWRENCE RIVER. In 1608 Samuel de CHAMPLAIN established the first settlement on the present-day site of Quebec city. It served as a headquarters for the fur-traders' exploration of the interior. Following the FRENCH AND INDIAN WARS (1754–63), French Canada was ceded to Britain by the Treaty of Paris (1763). Quebec retained its distinctive French culture. The Constitution Act of 1791 separated off the area W of the Ottawa River as the colony of Upper Canada (now ONTARIO). Quebec became the British colony of Lower Canada. The revolt (1837) led by Louis PAP-

INEAU saw the appointment of the Earl of DURHAM. With the establishment of the Dominion of Canada in 1867, Quebec became a province. In the later 20th century the French-speaking inhabitants of the province intensified their demands for recognition of their cultural heritage, including complete independence. In a 1995 referendum a tiny majority of the population voted against independencec. The lowlands by the St. Lawrence River are the center of industry and agriculture; the province's small farms provide vegetables, tobacco, and dairy produce. Quebec produces much hydroelectric power and timber. Copper, iron, zinc, asbestos, and gold are mined. Area: 594,860sq mi (1,540,687sq km). Pop. (1991) 6,895,963.

**Quebec** (Québec) City and port at the confluence of the the St. Lawrence and St. Charles rivers, S QUEBEC province, Canada. It is the capital of Quebec province. Samuel de Champlain established a French trading post on the site of Quebec in 1608. Captured by the British in 1629, the city was returned to France and became the capital of New France in 1663. It was ceded to Britain in 1763. The city served as the capital of Lower Canada (1791–1841) and of the United Provinces of Canada (1851–55, 1859–65), before becoming capital of Quebec province in 1867. In recent years, Quebec has become a focal point for Canada's French-speaking separatists. Industries: shipbuilding, paper, leather, textiles, machinery, canning, tobacco, chemicals. Pop. (1991) 167,517.

**Quebec Act** (1774) Act of British Parliament creating a government for Quebec. It set up a council to assist the governor and recognized the Roman Catholic Church and the French legal and landholding systems in the former French colony. Quebec's boundary was extended south to the Ohio River, a cause of resentment among the 13 North American colonies.

**Quechua** Most widely spoken of all Native South American languages, with *c*.5 million speakers in Peru, 1.5 million in Bolivia and 500,000 in Ecuador. Originally the language of the great INCA empire, it is related to Aymará, the two forming the Quechumaran family.

**Queen Anne style** Art history term applied to a British style of decorative arts (especially furniture) popular during the reign (1702–14) of Queen ANNE. The style is characterized by elegance and simplicity. Curved cabriole legs are a distinctive feature, as are inlay, veneering, and lacquerwork.

**Queen Anne's War** *See* FRENCH AND INDIAN WARS

**Queens** Largest borough of NEW YORK CITY, on the W end of Long Island, SE New York state. First settled by the Dutch in the early 17th century, the area came under English control in 1664. It was created a borough of Greater New York in 1898. Queens has La Guardia and John F. Kennedy International airports and St. John's University (1870). It is a residential and industrial area and its manufacturing industries produce consumer goods for New York City. Area: 108sq mi (280sq km). Pop. (1990) 1,951,598.

**Queensberry, John Sholto Douglas, Marquess of** (1844–1900) British nobleman who sponsored the Queensberry rules – the basis of the rules for modern BOXING. Drafted mainly by John G. Chambers of the British Amateur Athletic Club, the Queensberry rules were standardized in 1889. In 1895 Queensberry publicly insulted Oscar WILDE because of the latter's association with his son, Lord Alfred Douglas. Wilde unsuccessfully sued Queensberry for libel and was convicted of homosexual practices.

**Queensland** State in NE Australia; the capital is BRISBANE. Queensland was originally part of New South Wales and served as a penal colony from 1824 to 1840. In 1859 it became a separate colony and a state of the Commonwealth of Australia in 1901. Nearly 50% of Queensland lies N of the Tropic of Capricorn and there are rain forests in the N. The GREAT DIVIDING RANGE separates the fertile coastal strip from the interior plains. Its chief crops are sugarcane, wheat, cotton, and tropical fruits. Beef cattle are important. The main industry is mining, and there are are valuable mineral deposits (copper, lead, zinc, bauxite, oil, and natural gas). Area: 667,000sq mi (1,727,530sq km). Pop. (1993 est.) 3,155,400.

**quetzal** Forest bird of Central America. The male is bright green above and crimson below with iridescent green tail plumes forming a 2ft (60cm) train. The female nests in a hole, often in a tree, and lays two eggs, which are incubated by both parents. Family Trogonidae; species *Pharomachrus mocinno*.

**Quetzalcóatl** God of CENTRAL AND SOUTH AMERICAN MYTHOLOGY, a principal deity of the TOLTECS, MAYA, and AZTECS. He took the form of a feathered serpent, who created humans by fertilizing bones with his own blood. He was associated with agriculture and the arts. A legend telling of his exile from his homeland is probably based on a ruler who took his name. In 1519 CORTÉS landed in Mexico on the god's birthday, and since Quetzalcóatl was expected to return in man's form, the Aztecs associated Cortés with the god.

**Quezon, Manuel Luis** (1878–1944) Philippine statesman, first president of the Commonwealth of the Philippines (1935–44). In 1901 he was imprisoned for his part in the revolt against US rule. After his release, Quezon became leader of the Nationalist Party and, as commissioner to the US (1909–16), secured the passage of the Tydings-McDuffie Bill (1934) that paved the way for independence. An autocratic president, Quezon instigated administrative reforms. His strengthening of Philippine defences failed to prevent Japan's invasion.

**Quezon City** City on LUZON island, adjacent to MANILA, N Philippines. Second-largest city in the Philippines, it was named for Manuel Luis QUEZON and was capital of the Philippines from 1948 to 1976. It is mainly a residential area. Industries: textiles. Pop. (1990) 1,632,000.

**Quiché** Mayan group of Native South Americans located in the highlands of W Guatemala. Archeological remains show large pre-conquest population centers and an advanced civilization. Today, they are the largest Native American group in Guatemala.

**quietism** Mystical Christian movement begun by the Spanish priest Miguel de Molinos in the 17th century. It achieved great influence in 17th-century France and in the Wesleyan movement of 18th-century Britain. Its adherents believed that only in a state of absolute surrender to God was the mind able to receive the saving infusion of grace.

**quince** Shrub native to the Middle East and central Asia. Its greenish-yellow fruit is used in preserves. Height: to 20ft (6m). Family Rosaceae; species *Cydonia oblonga*

**Quine, Willard Van Orman** (1908– ) US philosopher. He was professor of philosophy at Harvard (1948–78). Quine was committed to philosophy as a branch of natural science. In *Two Dogmas of Empiricism* (1951), he argued for a holistic approach to empiricism, abandoning the analytic-synthetic distinction made by Immanuel KANT. In *Word and Object* (1960), Quine put forward the notion of the indeterminancy of translation. Other works include *From a Logical Point of View* (1953) and *Pursuit of Truth* (1990). *See also* LOGICAL POSITIVISM

**quinine** White, crystalline substance isolated in 1820 from the bark of the cinchona tree. It was once widely used in the treatment of MALARIA, but has been largely replaced by drugs that are less toxic and more effective.

**quinsy** Inflammation of the tonsils, caused by an abscess, often a complication of TONSILLITIS. It is generally treated with antibiotics.

**Quisling, Vidkun** (1887–1945) Norwegian fascist leader. A former minister of defense (1931–33), he founded the National Union Party (1933), based on the German Nazi Party. In 1940 he collaborated with the invading Germans, and they set him up as a puppet ruler during their occupation of Norway. After World War II he was shot as a traitor.

**Quito** Capital of Ecuador, in the N central part of the country; it lies almost on the Equator and at 9,260ft (2,850m) above sea-level. The site was originally settled by Native Americans, and was captured (1487) by the INCAS. In 1534 it was taken by Spain, and liberated (1822) by Antonio José de SUCRE. A cultural and political center, it is the site of the Central University of Ecuador (1787) and has a notable observatory. The 17th-century cathedral is the burial place of de Sucre. Products include textiles and handicrafts. Pop, (1990) 1,100,847

**Qumran** Ancient village on the NW shore of the Dead Sea, in the Israeli-occupied West Bank. In 1947 the DEAD SEA SCROLLS (writings of a Jewish sect that settled in Qumran *c*.100 BC –AD 68) were found in nearby caves.

Q

*R/r, 18th letter of the English alphabet, used in the alphabets of other W European languages, It is a consonant and is descended from the Semitic letter* **resh**, *meaning* **head**. *It passed almost unchanged into the Greek alphabet as* **rho** *and from there to the Roman alphabet.*

**Ra** (Re) In Egyptian mythology, Sun god of Heliopolis and lord of the dead. He sailed his sun boat across the sky by day and through the underworld by night. He is most often depicted as falcon-headed, with a solar disk on his head.

**Rabat** Capital of Morocco, in the N of the country, on the Atlantic coast. Rabat dates from Phoenician times, but the fortified city was founded in the 12th century by the ALMOHAD ruler, Abd al-Mumin. In later years it became a refuge for Moors expelled from Spain. Under French rule (from 1912) it was made the capital of the protectorate of Morocco. Industries: rugs, textiles, food processing. Pop. (1982) 518,616.

**rabbi** Person qualified through study of the Hebrew Bible and the Talmud to be the chief religious leader of a Jewish congregation and the person responsible for its education and spiritual guidance. Modern Israel has a rabbinic council with two chief rabbis, one representing the Sephardic tradition, the other representing the Ashkenazi.

**rabbit** Long-eared, herbivorous mammal of the family Leporidae, including the European common rabbit and the American cottontail. The common rabbit is *Oryctolagus cuniculus* and has thick, soft, grayish-brown fur. The wide variety of domesticated rabbits are also of this species. Length: 14–18in (35–45cm); weight: 3–5lb (1.4–2.3kg). *See also* HARE

**Rabelais, François** (1494–1553) French humanist and satirist. He is famed for his classic series of satires, now known collectively as *Gargantua and Pantagruel*. The series itself consists of *Pantagruel* (1532), *Gargantua* (1534), *Le Tiers Livre* (1546), *Le Quart Livre* (1552), and *Le Cinquième Livre* (1564). Although condemned as obscene by theologians and the Sorbonne, Paris, his books became widely popular.

**rabies** (hydrophobia) Viral disease of the central nervous system. It can occur in all warm-blooded animals but is especially feared in dogs due to the risk of transmission to human beings. The incubation period varies from a week or two to more than a year. It is characterized by severe thirst, although attempting to drink causes painful spasms of the larynx; other symptoms include fever, muscle spasms, and delirium. Once the symptoms have appeared, death usually follows within a few days. Anyone bitten by a rabid animal may be saved by prompt injections of rabies vaccine and antiserum.

**Rabin, Yitzhak** (1922–95) Israeli statesman. As chief of staff (1964–68), he directed Israeli operations in the SIX DAY WAR (1967). He was ambassador to the US (1968–73) and prime minister (1974–77). As minister of defense (1984–90), he directed operations against the Palestinian INTIFADA and, having regained leadership of the Labor Party from his colleague and rival, Shimon PERES, became prime minister again in 1992. In 1993 he reached an agreement with the PALESTINE LIBERATION ORGANIZATION (PLO), promising progress toward Palestinian autonomy in the occupied territories. In November 1995 he was assassinated by an Israeli extremist.

▲ **Rabin** Because of his willingness to compromise with the Palestinians in the quest for peace in the Middle East, Israeli prime minister Yitzhak Rabin was assassinated by an Israeli extremist in 1995. He rose to prominence as a member of the military establishment and entered politics in the 1970s as a member of the Labor Party. He served several terms as prime minister.

**raccoon** (racoon) Stout-bodied, omnivorous, mostly nocturnal mammal of North and Central American wooded areas. Raccoons have a black, mask-like marking across their eyes and a long, black-banded tail. They have agile and sensitive front paws and typically dip for food in water. The seven species include the North American *Procyon lotor*. Length: 16–24in (40–61cm); weight: 22–48lb (10–22kg). Family Procyonidae.

**race** Informal classification of the human species according to hereditary (genetic) differences. Different racial characteristics arose among geographically separated populations partly through environmental adaptation across many generations. However, because there is no evidence of genetic racial distinctions, anthropologists reject the term.

**Rachmaninov, Sergei** (1873–1943) Russian composer and pianist. Piano Concerto No. 2 (1901), *Rhapsody on a Theme of Paganini* (1934), and Symphony No. 2 (1907) are among his most popular works. Composing in the Russian romantic tradition, his works include songs, four piano concertos, and three symphonies.

**Racine, Jean Baptiste** (1639–99) French dramatist. His early plays, such as *La Thebaïde* (1664) and *Alexandre le Grand* (1665), were influenced by contemporaries, such as CORNEILLE. Racine is regarded as the greatest tragedian of the French classical period. His major verse tragedies are *Andromaque* (1667), *Britannicus* (1669), *Bérénice* (1673), *Bajazet* (1672), and *Phèdre* (1677).

**racism** Doctrine advocating the superiority of one human RACE. Racism has been the avowed policy of certain regimes, which, as a result, sanctioned slavery and discriminatory practices. In 1967 racism was defined by UNESCO as "antisocial beliefs and acts which are based on a fallacy that discriminatory inter-group relations are justifiable on biological grounds."

**Rackham, Arthur** (1867–1937) British illustrator and watercolorist, whose work was inspired by the goblins, fairies, and weird beasts of Nordic folk tales. Among his best-known illustrations are the ones he created for Charles LAMB's *Tales from Shakespeare* (1899).

**racquets** Game played by two or four people in an enclosed 60 × 30ft (18.3 × 9.1m) court. Each player uses a gut-strung racket with a circular head. A service line is painted on the front wall at a height of 9.6ft (2.9m) and a fixed wooden board, also on the front wall, extends 27in (68.6cm) up from the floor. The serve must be above the service line and must land behind a short line 24ft (7.3m) from the back wall. Games are played to 15 points.

**radar** (acronym for **ra**dio **d**etecting **a**nd **r**anging) Electronic system for determining the direction and distance of objects. Developed during World War II, it works by the transmission of pulses of RADIO waves to an object. The object reflects the pulses, which are detected by an antenna. By measuring the time it takes for the reflected waves to return, the object's distance may be calculated, and its direction ascertained from the alignment of the receiving radar antenna.

**radar astronomy** Branch of astronomy in which radar pulses, reflected back to Earth from celestial bodies in the solar system, are studied for information concerning their distance from Earth, their orbital motion, and large surface features. Techniques developed for radar mapping of planetary surfaces have proved particularly important for cloud-covered VENUS.

**radian** Angle formed by the intersection of two radii at the center of a CIRCLE, when the length of the arc cut off by the radii is equal to one radius in length. Thus, the radian is a unit of angle equal to *c*.57.295°, and there are $2\pi$ radians in 360°.

**radiation** Transmission of energy by SUBATOMIC PARTICLES or ELECTROMAGNETIC RADIATION.

**radiation, cosmic** (cosmic rays) Streams of SUBATOMIC PARTICLES from space that constantly bombard the Earth at velocities approaching the speed of light. Primary cosmic rays are high-energy RADIATION that comes from the Sun and other sources in outer space. They consist mainly of atomic nuclei and PROTONS. When primary cosmic rays strike gas molecules in the upper atmosphere, they yield showers of secondary cosmic rays, which consist of energetic protons, NEUTRONS, and pions. Further collisions yield muons, ALPHA PARTICLES, POSITRONS, ELECTRONS, GAMMA RADIATION, and PHOTONS.

**radiation, heat** Energy given off from all solids, liquids, or gases as a result of their temperature. The energy comes from the vibrations of atoms in an object and is emitted as ELECTROMAGNETIC RADIATION, often in the form of INFRARED WAVES.

**radiation, nuclear** Particles or ELECTROMAGNETIC RADIATION emitted spontaneously and at high energies from atomic nuclei. Possible causes include RADIOACTIVE DECAY, which yields ALPHA PARTICLES, BETA PARTICLES, GAMMA RADIATION and, more rarely, POSITRONS. It can also result from spontaneous FISSION of a nucleus, with the ejection of neutrons or gamma rays.

**radio** Method of communication between a transmitter and a receiver of radio waves (*see* ELECTROMAGNETIC RADIATION). The term is most often used for a receiver of a sound broadcast. A radio signal of fixed FREQUENCY (the carrier wave) is generated at the transmitter. The sound to be broadcast is converted by a MICROPHONE into a varying electrical signal that is combined with the carrier by means of MODULATION. This is passed to an AERIAL from which it is transmitted into the atmosphere. At the receiver, an aerial intercepts the signal, and it undergoes "detection," the reverse of modulation, to retrieve the sound signal. It is amplified through a loudspeaker that reproduces the sound. TELEVISION uses radio waves to send sound and picture signals. RADAR transmits pulses of radio waves. New technology enables DIGITAL SIGNALS to be carried via radio waves. *See also* AMPLITUDE MODULATION (AM); BROADCASTING; FREQUENCY MODULATION (FM)

**radioactive decay** Process by which a radioactive ISOTOPE (radioisotope) loses SUBATOMIC PARTICLES from its nucleus and so becomes a different element. The disintegration of the nuclei occurs with the emission of ALPHA PARTICLES (helium nuclei) or BETA PARTICLES (electrons), often accompanied by GAMMA RADIATION. The two processes of alpha or beta decay cause the radioisotope to be transformed into a different atom. **Alpha** decay results in the nucleus losing two protons and two neutrons; **beta** decay occurs when a NEUTRON changes into a PROTON, with an ELECTRON (beta particle) being emitted in the process. Thus, the ATOMIC NUMBER changes in both types of decay, and an isotope of another element is produced, which might also be radioactive. In a large collection of atoms there is a characteristic time (the HALF-LIFE) after which one-half of the total number of nuclei would have decayed. This time varies from millionths of a second to millions of years, depending on the isotope concerned. The activity of any radioactive sample decreases exponentially with time. *See also* CARBON DATING

**radioactivity** Spontaneous emission of RADIATION from an atomic nucleus. The process by which a radioactive nucleus disintegrates is known as RADIOACTIVE DECAY.

**radio astronomy** Study of radio waves (ELECTROMAGNETIC RADIATION with wavelengths from about 1mm to many meters) that reach the Earth from objects in space. Observations can be made using a RADIO TELESCOPE. Radio noise from the Milky Way was discovered in 1931 by Karl JANSKY and the subject grew rapidly after World War II. The number of radio sources increases with distance, showing that the Universe has been evolving with time. This, combined with the discovery at radio wavelengths of the cosmic microwave background, is evidence in favor of the BIG BANG theory of the origin of the Universe.

**radio galaxy** GALAXY that emits strong ELECTROMAGNETIC RADIATION of radio frequency. These emissions seem to be produced by the high-speed motion of ELEMENTARY PARTICLES in strong magnetic fields.

**radiography** Use of X-RAYS to record the interiors of opaque bodies as photographs. Industrial X-ray photographs can show assembly faults and defects in metals. In medicine and dentistry, radiography is invaluable for diagnosing bone damage, tooth decay, and internal disease. Using modern scanning techniques, cross-sectional outlines of the body can be obtained showing organs, blood vessels, and diseased parts.

**radiology** Medical specialty concerned with the use of RADIATION and radioactive materials in the diagnosis and treatment of disease. *See also* RADIOGRAPHY; RADIOTHERAPY

**radio telescope** Instrument used to collect and record radio waves from space. The basic design is the large single dish or parabolic reflector, up to 330ft (100m) in diameter. Radio waves are reflected by the dish via a secondary reflector to a focus, where they are converted into electrical signals. The signals are amplified and sent to the main control room, where there is further amplification before analysis and recording. *See also* RADIO ASTRONOMY; TELESCOPE

**radiotherapy** In medicine, the use of RADIATION to treat tumors or other pathological conditions. It may be done either by implanting a pellet of a radioactive source in the part to be treated, or by dosing the patient with a radioactive isotope or by exposing the patient to precisely focused beams of radiation from a machine such as an x-ray machine or a particle accelerator. Synthesized radioisotopes are the most effective; cobalt-60 is often used as it produces highly penetrating gamma radiation. In the treatment of various types of CANCER, the radiation slows down the proliferation of the cancerous cells.

**radish** Annual garden vegetable developed from a wild plant native to cooler regions of Asia. Its leaves are long and deeply lobed; the fleshy root, which may be red, white, or black, is eaten raw. Family Brassicaceae; species *Raphanus sativus*.

**Radisson, Pierre Esprit** (1636–1710) French fur trader and explorer in Canada. He spent two years as a captive of the Iroquois, and later traveled W of Lake Superior. After disagreeing with the French authorities, he helped the English in establish posts on Hudson Bay.

**RADAR**

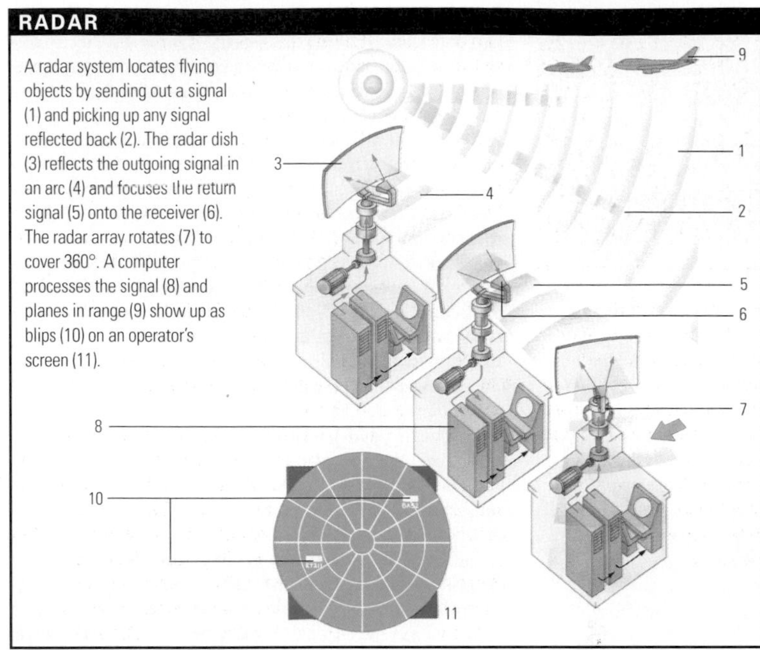


A radar system locates flying objects by sending out a signal (1) and picking up any signal reflected back (2). The radar dish (3) reflects the outgoing signal in an arc (4) and focuses the return signal (5) onto the receiver (6). The radar array rotates (7) to cover 360°. A computer processes the signal (8) and planes in range (9) show up as blips (10) on an operator's screen (11).

**radium** (symbol Ra) White, radioactive, metallic element of the ALKALINE-EARTH METALS, first discovered in pitchblende in 1898 by Pierre and Marie CURIE; the metal is present in uranium ores. It is used in RADIOTHERAPY. Radium has 16 isotopes, which emit alpha, beta, and gamma radiation, as well as heat. RADON gas is a decay product. Properties: at.no. 88; at.wt. 226.025; sp.gr. 5.0; m.p. 1,292°F (700°C); b.p. 2,084°F (1,140°C); most stable isotope $^{226}$Ra (half-life 1,622 years).

**radius** In anatomy, one of the two forearm bones, extending from the elbow to the wrist. The radius rotates around the ULNA, permitting the hand to rotate and be flexible.

**radon** (symbol Rn) Radioactive, gaseous element, a NOBLE GAS. It was first discovered in 1899 by Ernest RUTHERFORD. The 20 known isotopes, which are alpha particle emitters, are present in the Earth's atmosphere in trace amounts. Radon is mainly used in medical RADIOTHERAPY. Chemically, it is mostly inert but does form fluoride compounds. Properties: at.no. 86; sp.gr. 9.73; m.p. −95.8°F (−71°C); b.p. −79.24°F (−61.8°C); most stable isotope $^{222}$Rn (half-life 3.8 days).

**RAF** *See* AIR FORCE, ROYAL

**Raffles, Sir Thomas Stamford** (1781–1826) British colonial administrator, founder of Singapore. When Java returned to Dutch rule (1816), he bought the island of Singapore for the British East India Company (1819). Under his guidance it developed rapidly into a prosperous free port.

**rafflesia** Parasitic plant native to Sumatra and Java. It grows as a PARASITE on the roots of jungle vines and has no stem or leaves. The foul-smelling, reddish-brown flowers are 3.25ft (1m) in diameter, the world's largest flowers. Family Rafflesiaceae; species *Rafflesia arnoldii*.

**Rafsanjani, Hojatoleslam Ali Akbar Hashemi** (1934– ) Iranian cleric and statesman, president of Iran (1989–97). In 1979, after KHOMEINI's triumphant return from exile, he became speaker of the Iranian parliament. A leading figure in the new theocracy, Rafsanjani was acting commander of the armed forces in the final stages of the IRAN-IRAQ WAR. Following Khomeini's death, Rafsanjani became president. His presidency witnessed a slight easing of tension in relations with the West.

**raga** (Sanskrit, color) In Indian music, a sequence of five to seven notes that is used exclusively for the duration of a performance as a basis for improvisation. Its basic structure can be written in the form of a scale. Mood or atmosphere are created by emphasizing certain parts.

**Ragnarök** In Scandinavian mythology, the doom of the Gods. Heralded by bitter cold and moral decline, it signalled the end of the world and the defeat of the gods and heroes of VALHALLA by the forces of fiery destruction – giants, demons and an all-devouring wolf.

▲ **Rafsanjani** The former Iranian president Hojatoleslam Ali Akbar Hashemi Rafsanjani trained as a Shiite mullah with Ayatollah Khomeini at Qom before Khomeini went into exile. Following the overthrow of Shah Pahlevi, Rafsanjani served in Khomeini's revolutionary government. His presidency saw a slight thawing in relations with the West.

R

▲ **ragwort** There are *c.*1,200 species of ragwort (also known as groundsel) around the world. Some are cultivated specially as garden plants; others grow wild. Many species, including the common ragwort (*Senecio jacobaea*) are poisonous to livestock, but others have medicinal uses, helping to heal wounds and to bring on or increase menstrual flow.

**ragtime** Name given to an early style of JAZZ, particularly associated with piano playing. Its essential ingredient is the constant syncopation, or "ragging", of a straightforward tune. Rags were a theme and a set of written variations. Scott JOPLIN was the most popular ragtime composer.

**ragwort** Any of several plants with daisylike flowers, including the common ragwort (*Senecio jacobaea*), which bears flat-topped clusters of yellow flower heads. A similar US plant is golden ragwort, or golden groundsel (*Packera aurea*). Height: to 4ft (1.3m). Family Asteraceae/Compositae.

**rail** Slender, long-legged marsh bird. Rails are shy, generally nocturnal and often emit melodious calls. They lay 8–15 eggs in a reed-and-grass ground nest. Length: 4–18in (10–45cm). Family Rallidae. Typical genus *Rallus*.

**railroad** (railway) Form of transport in which cars (carriages) run on a fixed track, usually steel rails. Railroads date from the 1500s, when wagons used in mines were drawn by horses along tracks. English engineer Richard TREVITHICK built the first steam LOCOMOTIVE in 1804. In 1825 George Stephenson's *Locomotion* became the first steam locomotive to pull a passenger train. The first full passenger-carrying railroad, the Liverpool and Manchester Railroad, was opened in 1830. In 1830 in the US, *Tom Thumb* was the first domestically produced steam locomotive. The first transcontinental railroad was completed in 1869, when the Union Pacific Railroad from Nebraska met the Central Pacific Railroad from California in Utah. The world's first underground railroad to carry passengers was the City and South London Railroad in 1890. Steam locomotives are still used in India, but most countries use electric, diesel, or diesel-electric locomotives. Modern developments include high-speed trains such as the Japanese "Bullet" train or the French TGV (Train à Grande Vitesse) that travel at an average speed of *c.*185mph (300km/h). **Maglev** (magnetic levitation) trains use magnetism to hold them above a guide rail. **Air** trains hover above the track by an air cushion.

**rain** Water drops that fall from the Earth's atmosphere to its surface, as opposed to fog or dew which drift as suspensions, and snow or hail which fall as ice particles. Warm air passing over the sea absorbs water vapor and rises in thermal currents, or on reaching a mountain range. The water vapor condenses and forms clouds, accounting for the usually heavier annual rainfall on windward, compared to leeward, mountain slopes. *See also* PRECIPITATION; HYDROLOGICAL CYCLE

**rainbow** Multicolored band, usually seen as an arc opposite to the Sun or other light source. The primary bow is the one usually seen; in it the colors are arranged from red at the top to violet at the bottom. A secondary bow, in which the order of the colors is reversed, is sometimes seen beyond the primary bow. The colors are caused by reflection of light within spherical drops of falling rain, which cause white light to be dispersed into its constituent wavelengths. The colors usually seen are those of the visible SPECTRUM: red, orange, yellow, green, blue, indigo, and violet.

**rain forest** Dense forest of tall trees that grows in hot, wet regions near the equator. The main rain forests are in Africa, Central and S America, and SE Asia. They comprise 50% of the timber growing on Earth and house 40% of the world's animal and plant species. They also, through PHOTOSYNTHESIS, supply most of the world's oxygen. This is why the present rapid destruction of the rain forests (up to 50 million acres are destroyed annually to provide timber and land for agriculture) is a cause of great concern. Also, clearing rain forests contributes to the GREENHOUSE EFFECT and may lead to GLOBAL WARMING. There are many species of broad-leaved evergreen trees in rain forests, which grow up to 180ft (60m) tall. The crowns of other trees, up to 135ft (45m) tall, form the upper canopy of the forest. Smaller trees form the lower canopy. Climbing vines interconnect the various levels, providing habitats for many kinds of birds, mammals, and reptiles. Very little light penetrates to the forest floor, which consequently has few plants. Rain forest trees provide many kinds of food and other useful materials, such as Brazil nuts, cashews, figs, and mangosteens, as well as fibrous kapok and the drugs quinine and curare.

► **rail** Native to marshes all around the world, rails are poor fliers that rely on their dull coloration for protective camouflage. Their strong legs allow them to run through dense undergrowth. The Ypecaha wood rail (*Aramides ypecaha*) shown here is found in Brazil, Paraguay, Uruguay, and Argentina.

**Rainier III** (1923– ) Ruler of MONACO. He succeeded his grandfather Louis II in 1949 and married actress Grace KELLY in 1956. They had three children.

**Rainier, Mount** Peak in W central Washington; the highest point in the Cascade Range. The summit of this ancient volcano is the center of the greatest single-peak glacier system in the US. Height: 14,410ft (4,395m).

**raisin** Dried, sweet, seedless GRAPE. Special varieties are grown, particularly in Australia and the W US.

**Rajasthan** State in NW India, on the border with Pakistan; the capital is JAIPUR. Other major cities include UDAIPUR, JODHPUR, and Jaisalmer. Rajasthan was the homeland of the RAJPUTS. Rajasthan state was formed in 1950 and enlarged in 1966. The THAR DESERT in the W is inhabited by pastoral nomads. The E is part of the DECCAN plateau and wheat, millet, and cotton are grown with the aid of irrigation. Coal, marble, mica, and gypsum are mined. Industries: handicrafts, cotton milling. Area: 132,149sq mi (342,266sq km). Pop. (1991) 44,005,990.

**Rajneesh, Shree** (1931–1990) (Chandra Mohan Jain) Indian religious leader who founded a religious movement in India in the 1970s based on what he called "loving meditation." The movement soon spread to Europe, and later to the US.

**Rajput** Predominantly Hindi, warrior caste from NW India. They became powerful in the 7th century AD, gaining control of an historic region named Rajputana. After the Muslim conquests in the 12th century they retained their independence, but by the early 17th century had submitted to the MOGUL EMPIRE. In the early 18th century they extended their control. In the 19th century most of their territorial gains were lost to the Marathas, Sikhs, and the British empire. During the colonial period much of Rajputana retained its independence under local princely rule. After Indian independence in 1947 most of the princes lost their powers. *See also* RAJASTHAN

**Raleigh, Sir Walter** (1552–1618) English soldier, explorer, and writer. A favorite courtier of ELIZABETH I, he organized expeditions to North America, including a failed attempt to found a colony. He fought in France and against Spain and sat in Parliament. On JAMES I's ascension to the throne, he was imprisoned for treason (1603–1616), during which time he wrote his *History of the World*. He gained release in order to lead an expedition to Guiana in search of the gold of EL DORADO but was betrayed to the Spanish authorities and returned to prison and later executed for treason.

**Raleigh** Capital of North Carolina, in the E central part of the state. Founded in 1792 as state capital, it was named for Sir Walter Raleigh. It is a market center for the cotton and tobacco trade. Industries: food processing, textiles, electronic equipment. Pop. (1990) 207,951.

**RAM** (**r**andom **a**ccess **m**emory) INTEGRATED CIRCUITS (chips) that act as a temporary store for computer PROGRAMS and DATA (information). To run a program on a computer, the program is first transferred from a MAGNETIC DISK, or other storage device, to the RAM. The RAM also holds documents produced when the program is used. Another part of the RAM stores the images to be displayed on the screen. The contents of the RAM are lost when the computer is switched off.

**Rama** Hero of the RAMAYANA. A chivalrous husband, obedient to sacred law, he was considered to be the seventh incarnation of VISHNU. His name became synonymous with God.

**Ramadan** Ninth month of the Islamic year, set aside for fasting. Throughout Ramadan, the faithful must abstain from food, drink, and sexual intercourse between sunrise and sunset. They are also encouraged to read the whole of the KORAN in remembrance of the "Night of Power," when MUHAMMAD is said to have received his first revelation from ALLAH via the angel GABRIEL.

**Ramakrishna** (1836–86) (Gadadhar Chatterji) Hindu spiritual teacher who taught that all religions were basically united in a common goal of union with the same God. His chief disciple, Swami Vivekananda, founded the Ramakrishna Mission in India (1897).

**Raman, Sir Chandrasekhara Venkata** (1888–1970) Indian physicist. He greatly influenced the growth of science in his country and founded the Raman Institute (1946). Raman received the 1930 Nobel Prize for physics for his research on the diffusion of light and his discovery of the **Raman effect**. This states that there is a slight change in the frequency of monochromatic (single-wavelength) light that has been scattered by passing through a transparent material. This effect appears as secondary spectral lines on each side of the primary spectral line. *See also* SCATTERING

**Ramayana** (Romance of Rama) Great epic poem of SANSKRIT LITERATURE. Written in *c.*300 BC along with the MAHABHARATA, it is ascribed to the poet Valmiki and comprises 24,000 couplets in seven books. It concerns the adventures of RAMA, his wife Sita and others.

**Rambert, Dame Marie** (1888–1982) British ballet dancer, teacher, and choreographer, b. Poland. Rambert was a member of DIAGHILEV'S BALLETS RUSSES (1912–13). In 1920 she founded her own school, which became known as the Ballet Rambert in 1935.

**Rameau, Jean Philippe** (1683–1764) French composer and musical theorist. His most famous opera is *Castor et Pollux* (1737). His other works include the dramatic ballet *Les Indes Galantes* (1735).

**Ramsay, Sir William** (1852–1916) British chemist. Working with Lord RAYLEIGH, he discovered ARGON in air. Later he discovered HELIUM, NEON, and KRYPTON. He was knighted in 1902 and awarded the 1904 Nobel Prize for chemistry.

**Ramses II** Egyptian king of the 19th dynasty (r.1290–1224 BC). He reigned during a period of unprecedented prosperity and power. His efforts to confirm Egypt's dominant position in Palestine led to a major clash with the HITTITES at Kadesh in 1285 BC. A truce was agreed in 1269, and Ramses later married a Hittite princess. He built many splendid monuments, including the temple at ABU SIMBEL.

**Ramses III** Egyptian king of the 20th dynasty (r. *c.*1194–1163 BC). He defended Egypt from attacks by Libya and the Sea Peoples. Later in his reign, however, Egypt withdrew into political and cultural isolation.

**Rand** *See* WITWATERSRAND

**Rand, Ayn** (1905–82) US author, b. Russia. She immigrated to the US in 1926. Her first novel was *We the Living* (1936). Other works include *Anthem* (1938), *The Fountainhead* (1943), and *Atlas Shrugged* (1957). The last two serve as vehicles for her philosophy of objectivism, which espouses individual self-fulfillment in a capitalist society. Rand scorned weakness and altruism and regarded selfishness as a virtue.

**Randolph, Asa Philip** (1889–1979) US labor leader and civil rights activist. He founded the Brotherhood of Sleeping Car Porters (1925) and became a leading spokesman for the employment rights of blacks. He influenced President Roosevelt's executive order (1941) on fair employment practices and led the 1963 march on Washington for jobs and freedom.

**Randolph, Edmund** (1753–1813) US lawyer and political leader. He was aide to George Washington during the AMERICAN REVOLUTION. As a delegate to the CONSTITUTIONAL CONVENTION of 1787, he proposed the Virginia Plan, which favored the large states. He was the first US attorney general (1789–94) and was secretary of state (1794–95). He was also senior counsel for Aaron Burr (1807).

**Rangi** In the creation myth of the Maoris, the Sky god who forms such a close embrace with the Earth goddess Papa that their unborn children cannot emerge. When they are finally separated, Light and Darkness make their first appearance in the world. Rangi also figures in other Oceanic myths.

**Rangoon** (Yangon) Capital of Burma (Myanmar), a seaport on the Rangoon River *c.*21mi (34km) N of the Andaman Sea.

**RAILROAD**

Modern railroads feature trains, such as the Eurostar, with bogies that use an articulated air suspension system. This has great weight savings. The bogies (1) link the carriages, which are attached to a metal frame (2) through a ball joint (3). Instead of each carriage having a bogie at either end, there is a single suspension unit between two carriages. Dampers (4) modify articulation to improve passenger comfort. The black rings between the frame and the wheel unit are the air suspension units.

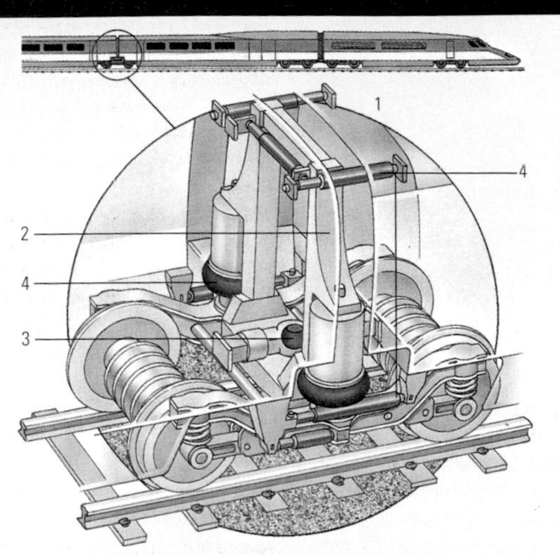


The site of an ancient Buddhist shrine, Rangoon was made capital of Burma in 1886 when the British annexed the country. The scene of fighting between British and Japanese forces in World War II, it is the country's chief trade center. Industries: oil refining, timber, rice, iron ores. Pop. (1983) 2,458,712.

**Ranjit Singh** (1780–1835) Indian maharaja, founder of the Sikh kingdom of the Punjab. At the age of 12, he became the ruler of a small territory in NW India. He absorbed neighboring states, and in 1799 established his capital at Lahore. In 1803 he took possession of the Sikh holy city of Amritsar. He established the E boundary of his kingdom on the Sutlej River. Turning his attention to the W and N, he captured Peshawar and Kashmir. His kingdom collapsed after his death.

**Rank, J. (Joseph) Arthur** (1888–1972) British industrialist and film magnate, chairman of many film companies. He promoted the British film industry when Hollywood and US film companies had a virtual monopoly.

**ransom** Money demanded in return for the release of a hostage. In medieval times, the demanding of ransoms was legally sanctioned, and it was a feudal right of a lord captured in battle to have a ransom paid by his tenants. Today, ransom demands are associated with hijacking and kidnapping and are a criminal offense.

**rap** Form of music that became popular during the early 1980s with bands such as Grandmaster Flash. Rap had its roots in the improvised street poetry of African-American and Hispanic teenagers in New York. The music places an emphasis on DJs who mix different tracks together, sometimes "scratching" for increased effect.

**rape** Plant grown for animal fodder and for its small, black seeds, which yield rape oil, used industrially as a lubricant. It has curly, blue-green leaves, small, yellow flowers, and slender seed pods. Family Brassicaceae; genus *Brassica*.

**rape** Crime of sexual intercourse without the victim's consent, often involving the use of force, implied or actual. If the victim is considered incapable of giving consent (for example because s/he is below the age of consent), this is known as statutory rape, and evidence of lack of consent is not required. Marital rape is now considered a crime in many states.

**Raphael** Biblical archangel who, with MICHAEL, GABRIEL, and Uriel, serves as a messenger of God. According to passages in the apocryphal Book of Tobit and the pseudepigraphal Second Book of Enoch, he is one of the seven holy angels who present the prayers of the saints to God.

**Raphael** (1483–1520) (Raphael Sanzio or Raphael Santi) Italian painter, one of the finest artists of the High RENAISSANCE. Born in Urbino, Raphael absorbed HUMANISM as a child. One of his most important commissions was the decoration (1509) of the four *stanze* (rooms) in the Vatican. He only completed two of these but the first, the *Stanza della Segnatura*, gave him the chance to exercise his skills to the full. The room contains two large FRESCOS, the *School of Athens* and the *Disputà*, both of which show Raphael's mas-

▲ **rape** Widely cultivated throughout China, India, and Europe, rape (*Brassica napus*) produces seeds that have an oil content of 40–50%. Once it is extracted, the oil is used for cooking, lubrication, fuel, and the manufacture of soap and rubber. The seed residue is used for animal feed and fertilizer. Rape fields are easily identified by the bright yellow color of the flowers.

R

▲ **raspberry** Popular as a wild fruit from ancient times, raspberries (*Rubus* sp.) have been cultivated since the early 17th century. The fruits grow on usually thorny bushes, although thornless varieties also exist. There are more than 200 varieties of raspberry in Asia, where the fruit is thought to have originated.

tery of PERSPECTIVE. After BRAMANTE's death he became architect to St. Peter's, Rome.

**rare earth** *See* LANTHANIDE SERIES

**raspberry** Fruit grown in polar and temperate regions of Europe, North America, and Asia. The black, purple, or red fruit is eaten fresh or preserved. Canes, rising from perennial roots, bear fruit the second year. Family Rosaceae; species *Rubus idaeus*.

**Rasputin, Grigori Yefimovich** (1872–1916) Russian peasant mystic. He exercised great influence at the court of NICHOLAS II because of his apparent ability to cure the crown prince Alexis's hemophilia. He attracted suspicion because of his advocacy of sexual ecstasy as a means of religious salvation. He was poisoned by a group of nobles in 1916, and when this failed, he was shot and drowned.

**Rastafarianism** West Indian religion focusing on veneration of Ras Tafari (HAILE SELASSIE I). The movement was started in Jamaica in the 1920s by Marcus GARVEY. He advocated a return to Africa to overcome black oppression. Rastafarians follow a strict diet.

**rat** Any of numerous small RODENTS found worldwide. Most species are herbivorous. The best known are the black rat (*Rattus rattus*) and brown rat (*R. norvegicus*), both of the family Muridae. They carry diseases and destroy or contaminate property and food. Both live everywhere that humans live.

**ratio** Number relating two numbers or two quantities of the same kind, such as two prices or two lengths, that indicates their relative magnitude. Ratios, as of the numbers 3 and 4, can be written as a fraction 3/4, or with a colon (3:4).

**rationalism** Philosophical theory that knowledge about the nature of the world can be obtained solely by reason, without recourse to experience. Rationalist philosophers, such as DESCARTES, LEIBNIZ, and SPINOZA, argued that reality could be logically deduced from "self-evident" *a priori* premises. It is usually contrasted with EMPIRICISM. In theology, rationalism holds that faith be explicable by human reason rather than divine revelation.

**rational number** Number representing the ratio of two integers, the second of which is not zero. Thus, 1/2, 18/11, 0, −2/3, and 12 are all rational numbers. Any rational number can be represented as a terminating decimal (such as 1.35) or a recurring decimal (such as 18/11 = 1.636363....). *See also* IRRATIONAL NUMBERS

**ratite** Group of large, usually flightless birds with flat breastbones instead of the keel-like prominences found in most flying birds. Ratites include the OSTRICH, RHEA, CASSOWARY, EMU, KIWI, and the unusual flying tinamou.

**rattlesnake** Any of about 30 species of venomous New World pit vipers characterized by a tail rattle of loosely connected segments of unshed skin. It ranges from Canada to South America, usually in arid regions. Most are blotched with dark diamonds, hexagons, or spots on a lighter background. They feed mostly on rodents. Length: 1–8ft (30cm–2.5m). Family Viperidae. *See also* SNAKE

**Rauschenberg, Robert** (1925– ) US painter and graphic artist, who gained recognition in the 1950s with his collages and assemblages. His works combined techniques, including dripped paint and collage, as in *The Bed* (1955). From 1955 his works juxtaposed SURREALISM with ABSTRACT EXPRESSIONISM, as in *Monogram* (1959).

**Ravel, (Joseph) Maurice** (1875–1937) French composer, a leading exponent of IMPRESSIONISM. His piano compositions include *Jeux d'eau* (1901), *Gaspard de la nuit* (1908), and *Le Tombeau de Couperin* (1917). Among his orchestral works are *Rhapsodie espagnole* (1907) and *Bolero* (1927). Ravel also composed the ballet *Daphnis and Chloë* (1912) and the song cycle *Shéhérazade* (1903).

► **rattlesnake** Not normally aggressive, rattlesnakes try to avoid confrontation by warning of their presence. Their unmistakable and menacing rattle is produced by "bells" of hard skin on the end of the tail. The amount of venom they produce far exceeds that needed to kill the rodents that form their usual prey. They can also use it to protect themselves against large predators.

**raven** Large bird of the CROW family found in deserts, forests, and mountainous areas of the Northern Hemisphere. It has a long, conical bill, shaggy throat feathers, a wedge-shaped tail, and black plumage with a purple sheen. It eats carrion or any other animal food. Length: to 27in (68cm). Family Corvidae.

**Ravenna** City in Emilia-Romagna, NE Italy. It was the capital of the Western Roman Empire in the 5th century AD. It was briefly capital of the Ostrogothic kingdom and then the seat of the Byzantine government in Italy. An independent republic in the 13th century, it was under papal rule from the 16th–19th centuries, becoming part of the kingdom of Italy in 1860. Industries: petroleum, natural gas, furniture, cement, fertilizers, sugar refining. Pop. (1991) 135,834.

**Ray, Man** (1890–1976) US photographer, painter, sculptor, and filmmaker, the founder of the New York DADA movement with Marcel DUCHAMP and Francis Picabia. He is best known for photographs produced without a camera by placing objects on light-sensitive paper and exposing them to light.

**Ray, Satyajit** (1921–92) Indian film director with a worldwide following. His trilogy of films about life in modern India, *Pather Panchali* (1955), *The Unvanquished* (1956), and *The World of Apu* (1959), are regarded as classics.

**ray** Any of several species of cartilaginous, mostly marine fish related to the SKATE, SHARK, and CHIMAERA. The ray is flattened dorso-ventrally; its body extends sideways into large, winglike pectoral fins that are "flapped" while swimming. The tail is narrow and may be whiplike or bear poisonous spines. Electric (torpedo) rays stun their prey with electrical charges of up to 200 volts. Length: 5ft (1.5m).

**Rayburn, Samuel Taliaferro** (1882–1961) US political leader. Beginning his political career in the Texas state legislature (1907–12), he was elected to the House of Representatives (1913) and served until his death. He helped Franklin D. ROOSEVELT get his NEW DEAL laws passed in the House (1931–37). He was elected Speaker of the House (1940), and held that position twice as long as any predecessor.

**Rayleigh, John William Strutt, Lord** (1842–1919) British physicist. His work was chiefly concerned with various forms of wave motion. He was awarded the 1904 Nobel Prize for physics for his discovery (with William Ramsay) of the noble gas ARGON and for work on gas densities.

**rayon** Fine, smooth fiber made from solutions of CELLULOSE. It was the first synthetic textile. Viscose rayon, the most common, is spun-dried and has a strength approaching NYLON. Acetate rayon is made of filaments of cellulose ACETATE.

**razor-billed auk** (razorbill) Stocky, penguin-like seabird that lives along coastlines in the cold parts of the Northern Hemisphere. It is black and white with a white-ringed, narrow bill. Length: 16in (41cm). Species *Alca torda*.

**razor clam** Bivalve MOLLUSK. With a long, thin, narrow, hinged shells, this mollusk is common on beaches of the Northern Hemisphere. Family Solenidae.

**reading** Ability to comprehend visual symbols representing language, usually in the form of written or printed characters. Opinions differ over the precise physical nature of this process and over whether the language involved – phonetic, non-phonetic, or ideographic – is influential in the speed of learning and the retention of vocabulary.

**Reagan, Ronald Wilson** (1911– ) 40th US President (1981–89). A well-known film actor, he joined the Republican Party (1962) and won a landslide victory to become governor of California (1966–74). Nominated as presidential candidate at his third attempt in 1980, he defeated CARTER. Surviving an assassination attempt (1981), he introduced large tax cuts and reduced public spending, except on defense. By the end of his second term, budget and trade deficits had reached record heights. Fiercely anticommunist, he adopted strong measures against opponents abroad, invading Grenada (1983) and undermining the SANDINISTA regime in Nicaragua. While pur-

◀ **ray** Found in all oceans, the various species of electric ray (*Dasyatis* sp.) use the electric charge they can generate both for stunning prey and warding off predators – the shock of between 35 and 60 volts may be strong enough to stun humans. They feed on smaller animals and have specially adapted teeth for crushing shells.

suing his Strategic Defense Initiative (SDI, or "Star Wars"), he reached an arms control agreement with GORBACHEV (1987) and welcomed improved relations with the Soviet Union. The last year of his presidency was overshadowed by the IRAN-CONTRA AFFAIR. Reagan was succeeded by his vice-president George BUSH.

**realism** Broad term in art history, often interchangeable with NATURALISM. Critics and historians use it to define art that tries to represent objects accurately and without emotional bias. It is also used to denote a movement in 19th-century French art, led by COURBET, against conventional subjects, focusing instead on unidealized scenes of modern life. **Superrealism** is a 20th-century movement, in which real objects are depicted in very fine detail so that the overall effect appears unreal. *See also* SOCIALIST REALISM

**realism** Philosophical doctrine according to which universal concepts, as well as tangible things, exist in their own right, outside the human mind that recognizes or perceives them. The idea developed from a medieval view that "universals" are real entities rather than simply names for things. Realism was thus opposed to NOMINALISM. Some philosophers rejected this view in favor of moderate realism, which held that "universals" exist only in the mind of God. *See also* IDEALISM

**real number** Any number that is a RATIONAL NUMBER or an IRRATIONAL NUMBER. Real numbers exclude imaginary numbers (the square roots of negative quantities). *See also* COMPLEX NUMBER

**real tennis** Medieval game played with racket and ball on a rectangular indoor court surrounded by walls, three out of four of which are surmounted by a sloping roof; there are other hazards at each end. The game was first played during the 12th century in French monastic cloisters. In Australia it is called "royal tennis" and in the US it is "court tennis."

**Rebellion of 1837** Risings in favor of self-rule in Upper and Lower Canada (ONTARIO and QUEBEC). In Upper Canada, the rising was led by William Lyon Mackenzie and soon fizzled out. The revolt in Lower Canada, led by Louis PAPINEAU, was more serious, and was severely suppressed. The outbreaks led to the DURHAM report and the union of Upper and Lower Canada (1841).

**receptacle** Biological structure that serves as a container for reproductive cells or organs in plants. In flowering plants, the receptacle is the enlarged end of a stalk to which the flower is attached. In ferns, it is the mass of tissue that forms the sporangium (the spore-bearing organ). In some seaweeds, it is the part that seasonally becomes swollen and carries the reproductive organs.

**recession** In economics, phase of the business cycle associated with a declining economy. Its manifestations are rising unemployment, contracting business activity, and decreasing purchasing power of consumers. Government policy, such as cuts in government spending or taxes, may be used to stimulate and expand the economy during a recession. If a recession is not checked, it can degenerate into a DEPRESSION.

**Recife** City and port on the Atlantic coast, NE Brazil; the capital of Pernambuco state. Originally settled by Portuguese in the 1530s, it was under Dutch occupation in the 17th century. It is now a major port and shipping center, exporting sugar, cotton, and coffee. Pop. (1991) 1,290,149.

**reciprocal** Quantity equal to the number 1 divided by a specified number. The reciprocal of 2 is $\frac{1}{2}$, and the reciprocal of $\frac{1}{2}$ is 2.

**recombinant DNA research** Branch of GENETIC ENGINEERING involving the transferral of a segment of DNA from a source organism into a host organism (typically a microbe). The transferred segment is spliced into the host's overall DNA structure, thus altering the information contained in its GENETIC CODE. When the host undergoes asexual cell division, each product cell carries a replica of the new DNA. In this way numerous clones of the new cell can be made. *See* RESTRICTION ENZYME

**Reconstruction** In US history, the process of restoring the former Confederate states to the Union after the CIVIL WAR. It was the cause of fierce controversy within Congress. The relatively pro-Southern approach of President Andrew JOHNSON led to his impeachment. The Republicans were determined to establish the political and CIVIL RIGHTS of African Americans, and they succeeded in imposing the program known as Radical Reconstruction over presidential veto. It alienated many Southern whites, and growing violence in the 1870s required the presence of federal troops. When Rutherford B. HAYES became president (1877), he withdrew the troops, Southern Republican governments collapsed, and Reconstruction was abandoned.

**recorder** Simple WOODWIND musical instrument, popular in Europe since the 15th century. It comprises an end-blown straight tube with eight finger holes. Modern recorders include soprano, descant, tenor, and bass instruments.

**recording** Storing of signals that represent sound or images, on a medium such as a plastic disk or magnetic tape. In disk recording, the sounds or images being recorded are electronically modified and converted into movements of a stylus. The stylus cuts an original lacquer disk, which is then electroplated to make a master negative. In magnetic recording, sound is recorded on tape with a TAPE RECORDER; a VIDEO RECORDING machine records sound and vision. Recent advancements in recording techniques include digital methods of recording, and the development of laser technology for the revolutionizing invention of the COMPACT DISC (CD). *See also* DIGITAL AUDIO TAPE (DAT)

**rectangle** Four-sided geometric figure (quadrilateral), the interior angles of which are right angles and each pair of opposite sides is of equal length and is parallel. It is a special case of a PARALLELOGRAM.

**rectifier** Component of an electric CIRCUIT that converts alternating current (AC) into direct current (DC). The rectifier is usually a semiconductor DIODE. *See also* ELECTRIC CURRENT

**rectum** In humans and many other vertebrates, last part of the large INTESTINE, where the feces are stored prior to evacuation.

**recycling** Natural and manufactured processes by which substances are broken down and reconstituted. In nature, elemental cycles include the CARBON CYCLE, NITROGEN CYCLE, and HYDROLOGICAL CYCLE. Natural cyclic chemical processes include the metabolic cycles in the bodies of living organisms. Manufactured recycling includes the use of bacteria to break down organic wastes to harmless, or even beneficial, substances. Large quantities of inorganic waste, such as metal scrap, glass bottles, and building spoil, are recycled.

**red admiral** European butterfly with red bars on the wings and black wing tips spotted with white..The caterpillar is dark with light sidestripes and branching spikes. Family Nymphalidae; species *Vanessa atalanta*.

**red algae** Taxonomic group (PHYLUM) of reddish ALGAE, the Rhodophyta. They are numerous in tropical and subtropical seas. Most are slender, branching seaweeds that form shrub-like masses. Some become encrusted with calcium carbonate and are important in reef formation. Rhodophytes have red and purplish pigments, which help to absorb light for photosynthesis. They also have CHLOROPHYLL. They have complex life cycles with two or three distinct stages, involving ALTERNATION OF GENERATIONS.

**Red Army** Army of the former Soviet Union. It was characterized by a high degree of political control, and was institutionalized at all levels with a system of commissars. During World War II the Red Army grew to more than 20 million men. It was renamed the Soviet Army in 1946. The Red Army was also the name of the Chinese revolutionary guard before it was formally renamed the People's Liberation Army.

**red blood cell** *See* ERYTHROCYTE

▲ **Reagan** Appearing in more than 50 films from the time of his Hollywood debut in the 1930s, Ronald Reagan was a celebrity in the US before he entered politics in the mid-1960s. Genial and optimistic, and highly skilled in televisual presentation, he was very popular, particularly with the right wing of the Republican party. A few years after leaving office, he admitted that he was suffering from Alzheimer's Disease and received a great deal of public sympathy.

R

▲ **Redford** Best known for his starring roles in films from *Butch Cassidy and the Sundance Kid* (1969) to *Indecent Proposal* (1993), Robert Redford began his acting career on the Broadway stage, where he starred in the 1963 production of *Barefoot in the Park*, in which he later played the male lead on film. Always highly selective in choosing his film roles, he began to direct in the 1980s. He also established the Sundance Institute in Utah, a training center for young independent filmmakers and the home of an important annual US Film Festival.

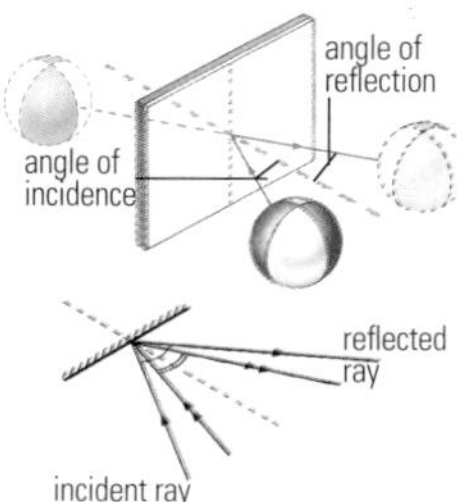


▲ **reflection** The top diagram shows the reflection of an image in a mirror. The image reflects back with an angle of reflection the same as the angle of incidence. The image, however, appears to the eye to be behind the mirror on an extension of the angle of reflection. The bottom line drawing illustrates that the angle of reflection is always the same as the angle of incidence, whether the angle is acute or oblique.

**Red Cloud** (1822–1909) Native American chief of the Oglala SIOUX. He fought tenaciously against settlers and the US army trying to establish the Bozeman Trail, a path west to the Montana gold fields. The government was forced to abandon the trail (1868) and signed a peace treaty with Red Cloud.

**Red Cross** International organization that seeks to alleviate human suffering, particularly through disaster relief and aid to war victims. It is composed of more than 150 independent national societies in most countries, with central headquarters in Geneva, Switzerland. It is staffed largely by volunteers. The name comes from its symbol: a red cross on a white background. The organization is known as the Red Crescent in Muslim countries.

**redcurrant** Widely cultivated shrub and its small, round, red, edible fruit; it is closely related to the blackcurrant. Family Grossulariaceae; species *Ribes silvestre*.

**red dwarf** Star at the lower end of the main sequence. Red dwarfs have masses of between 0.8 and 0.08 of a solar mass. They are of small diameter, relatively low surface temperature (2,500–5,000K) and low absolute magnitude.

**Redford, Robert** (1937– ) US film actor, director, and producer. He shot to fame in 1969 opposite Paul NEWMAN in *Butch Cassidy and the Sundance Kid*. His popularity increased with *The Great Gatsby* (1974) and *All the President's Men* (1976). He won an Academy Award for his directorial debut, *Ordinary People* (1980), and received considerable acclaim for *A River Runs Through It* (1992) and *Quiz Show* (1994).

**Redgrave** Name of a family of British actors and actresses. **Sir Michael** (1908–85), also a director and writer, made major stage appearances in Shakespeare's *Hamlet*, *Macbeth*, and *As You Like It*. He appeared in many films, including *The Way to the Stars* (1945) and *The Browning Version* (1951). His children are actors. **Vanessa** (1937– ) frequently appears on the London stage. She won an Academy Award as Best Supporting Actress in *Julia* (1977) and played in other films including *Prick Up Your Ears* (1987) and *Howard's End* (1992). **Corin** (1939– ) has acted on stage and television, and **Lynn** (1943– ) received an Oscar nomination for *Georgy Girl* (1966).

**Red Guards** Chinese youth movement active in the CULTURAL REVOLUTION (1966–68). They were named for the groups of armed workers who took part in the Bolshevik revolution in Russia (1917). The Chinese Red Guards attacked revisionists, westerners, and alleged bourgeois influences. Originally encouraged by Mao, they caused severe social disorder and were suppressed after 1968.

**Red Jacket** (1758–1830) (Otetiani) Native American chief of the SENECA. He was called Red Jacket from his association with the British colonial army during the AMERICAN REVOLUTION. He astutely exploited the differences between rival groups, and in the War of 1812 supported the US against the British. During his chieftainship he was a powerful advocate of the preservation of Iroquois traditions.

**Redon, Odilon** (1840–1916) French painter and graphic artist. He was an exponent of SYMBOLISM. He worked mainly in black and white, creating a fantasy world of weird amorphous creatures. In the 1890s he began painting mythological scenes and flower paintings in radiant colors.

**Red Sea** Narrow arm of the Indian Ocean between NE Africa and the Arabian Peninsula, connected to the Mediterranean Sea by the Gulf of Suez and the Suez Canal. With the building of vessels too large for the canal and the construction of pipelines, the Red Sea's importance as a trade route has diminished. Its maximum width is about 200mi (320km). Area: 169,000sq mi (438,000sq km).

**redshank** Eurasian wading bird of the SANDPIPER family. It has a long slender bill, mottled gray, brown, and white plumage, and characteristic slender red legs. Length: to 11in (28cm). Family Scolopacidae; species *Tringa totanus*.

**red shift** ($z$) Lengthening of the wavelength of light or other ELECTROMAGNETIC RADIATION from a source, caused either by the source moving away (the DOPPLER EFFECT) or by the expansion of the Universe (cosmological red shifts). It is defined as the change in the wavelength of a particular spectral line, divided by the rest wavelength of that line. The Doppler effect results from motion through space; cosmological red shifts are caused by the expansion of space itself stretching the wavelengths of light traveling toward Earth.

**reduction** *See* OXIDATION-REDUCTION

**redwood** *See* SEQUOIA

**Reed, Lou** (1944– ) US rock singer-songwriter and guitarist, b. Louis Firbank. He was a member (1965–73, 1993) of the New York avant-garde band, The Velvet Underground. The group's first album, *The Velvet Underground and Nico* (1967), was co-produced by Andy WARHOL. Reed's first solo album, *Transformer* (1972), featured the songs "Walk on the Wild Side" and "Perfect Day".

**reed** Aquatic GRASS native to wetlands throughout the world. The common reed (*Phragmites communis*) has broad leaves, feathery flower clusters, and stiff smooth stems. Dry reed stems are used for thatching, construction, and musical pipes. Height: to 10ft (3m). Family Poaceae/Gramineae.

**reed instrument** Musical instrument that produces sound when an air current vibrates a fiber or metal tongue. In a CLARINET or reed organ pipe, a beating reed vibrates against a hole at the end of the tube. The OBOE and BASSOON have double-reed mouthpieces, the two tongues vibrating against each other when blown.

**reef** Rocky outcrop lying in shallow water, especially one built up by CORALS or other organisms.

**referendum** Political process in which legislation or constitutional proposals are put before all voters for approval or rejection. This direct form of voting was known in Greece and other early democracies and is used today in some countries.

**reflection** Change in direction of part or all of a WAVE. When a wave, such as a light or sound wave, encounters a surface separating two different media, it is bounced back into the original medium. The incident wave (striking the surface), reflected wave, and the normal (line perpendicular to the surface) all lie in the same plane; the incident wave and reflected wave make equal angles with the normal.

**reflex action** Rapid involuntary response to a particular stimulus – for example, the "knee-jerk" reflex that occurs when the bent knee is tapped. It is controlled by the nervous system.

**reflex camera** CAMERA that allows the user to view and focus through the lens of the camera. A plane mirror and prism reflect the scene through the lens on to a ground glass screen. When the photographer presses the shutter on a **single-lens reflex (SLR)** camera, the mirror flips back and light reaches the film. A **twin-lens reflex** (TLR) camera has two sets of lenses, one for viewfinding, the other for passing light directly onto the film. *See also* PHOTOGRAPHY

**reflexor** *See* MUSCLE

**Reform Acts** British acts of Parliament extending the right to vote. The Great Reform Bill (1832) redistributed seats in the House of Commons to include large cities that were previously unrepresented. The second Reform Act (1867) extended the FRANCHISE to include better-off members of the working class. The acts of 1884 and 1885 gave the vote to most adult males. Women over 30 gained the vote in 1918, and the Representation of the People Act (1928) introduced universal adult suffrage.

**Reformation** Sixteenth-century European movement that sought reform of the universal CATHOLIC CHURCH and resulted in the development of PROTESTANTISM. More than a revolt against the ecclesiastical and doctrinal authority of the church, it also represented a protest against the interference of the church in secular matters and the questionable activities of the contemporary clergy, notably the sale of INDULGENCES and holy relics. In the 14th and 15th centuries the Catholic Church had been tested by the LOLLARDS, the HUSSITES, and HUMANISM. The year 1517 is often given as the starting date for the Reformation, when Martin LUTHER nailed his 95 theses to the Schlosskirche in Wittenburg, Germany. Luther's attack on the corruption of the church and the doctrines of papal supremacy, TRANSUBSTANTIATION, and clerical celibacy won the support of several German princes. In Zurich, Switzerland, the Reformation was led first by Ulrich ZWINGLI and then by John CALVIN. CALVINISM was adopted in France (*see* HUGUENOTS), the Netherlands, and Scandinavia. In England, the Reformation was at first more political than religious. In 1534 Thomas CROMWELL drafted the

Act of Supremacy that rejected papal authority and made King HENRY VIII the head of the English Church. Under EDWARD VI Protestantism was established by the Book of COMMON PRAYER (1552). In 1559, in the reign of Elizabeth I, the CHURCH OF ENGLAND was formally established. In Scotland, the Reformation was led by John KNOX and PRESBYTERIANISM was established as the state religion in 1560. *See also* COUNTER-REFORMATION

**Reformed church** Any Christian denomination that came into being during the REFORMATION by separating, as a congregation, from the old universal Catholic Church (the Western Church). More specifically, Reformed churches are those churches that adopted CALVINISM in preference to LUTHERANISM. In the US, the largest Reformed churches, such as the Dutch Reformed Church and the Evangelical and Reformed Church, originated from N European countries.

**refraction** Bending of a WAVE, such as a light or sound wave, when it crosses the boundary between two media, such as air and glass, and undergoes a change in velocity. The incident wave (striking the surface), refracted wave, and the normal (line perpendicular to the surface) all lie in the same plane. The incident wave and refracted wave make an angle of incidence, *i*, and an angle of refraction, *r*, with the normal. The index of refraction for a transparent medium is the ratio of the speed of light in a vacuum to its speed in the medium. It is also equal to sin *i*/sin *r*. **Snell's law** states that this ratio is constant for a given interface.

**refrigeration** Process by which the temperature in a refrigerator is lowered. In a domestic refrigerator, a refrigerant gas such as AMMONIA or Freon is first compressed by a pump and cooled in a condenser where it liquefies. It is then passed into an evaporator where it expands and boils, absorbing heat from its surroundings and thus cooling the refrigerator. It is then passed through the pump again to be compressed. Refrigeration is also used for air conditioners.

**refugee** Person who leaves his or her native land because of expulsion or to avoid persecution and seeks asylum in another country. The United Nations High Commission for Refugees (UNHCR) is responsible for the welfare of refugees.

**Regency style** In England, style of art and architecture fashionable when the future George IV was Prince Regent (1811–20) and during his reign. A period of great variety, it generally denotes designs that are elegant and refined.

**regeneration** Biological term for the ability of an organism to replace one of its parts if it is lost. Regeneration also refers to a form of ASEXUAL REPRODUCTION in which a new individual grows grows from a detached portion of a parent organism.

**Regensburg** (Fr. *Ratisbon*) City and port at the confluence of the Danube and Regen rivers, Bavaria, S Germany. Founded by the Romans as Castra Regina, it was captured by Charlemagne in 788. During the 13th century Regensburg flourished on the commercial trade with the Middle East and India and became an imperial free city. From 1663–1806 it was the seat of the Imperial Diet. In 1810 Regensburg was annexed to Bavaria, and in 1853 was made a free port. Pop. (1990) 123,700.

**reggae** Form of West Indian popular music. It came into prominence in the mid-1960s, growing out of rock-steady and ska. It is characterized by a hypnotically repetitive back beat. Modern variations on the form include RAGGA and lover's rock. Bob MARLEY was largely responsible for bringing reggae to a worldwide audience.

**Rehnquist, William Hubbs** (1924– ) US jurist and lawyer, chief justice (1986– ) of the Supreme Court. A political conservative, he was chosen by President Nixon to direct the Office of Legal Counsel of the Department of Justice (1968–71). In 1971 Nixon appointed him an associate justice of the Supreme Court.

**Reich, Steve** (1936– ) US composer. His works are characterized by transforming musical patterns. Many of his compositions were written for his percussion ensemble, Steve Reich and Musicians, who achieved fame with *Drumming* (1971).

**Reich, Wilhelm** (1897–1957) Austrian psychoanalyst and clinical assistant to FREUD from 1922 to 1928. In the US from 1939, he claimed to have discovered "orgone" energy, a primal force in the atmosphere. The function of the sexual orgasm was to discharge orgone energy. In 1950 he was imprisoned for fraud and died in jail.

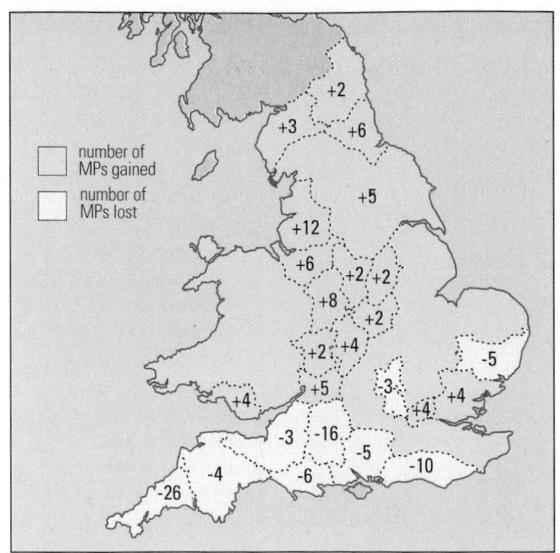


◀ **Reform Acts** In early 19th-century Britain, many of the agricultural boroughs whose population had steadily declined still returned members to Parliament, whereas the new, densely populated industrial areas were severely underrepresented. Some of the seats taken away from the underpopulated boroughs by the Reform Bill were redistributed among these industrial centers, while others were used to increase county representation.

**Reichenbach, Hans** (1891–1953) US philosopher, b. Germany. Associated with the development of LOGICAL POSITIVISM, he also contributed to the study of PROBABILITY and INDUCTIVE LOGIC. His works include *Elements of Symbolic Logic* (1947) and *The Rise of Scientific Philosophy* (1951).

**Reichstag** German parliament building. Erected 1884–94, the Reichstag is where the lower legislative assembly of Germany – also called the Reichstag – met until 1933, when it was severely damaged in a fire. After the reunification of Germany in 1990, it once again served as the meeting place of Germany's parliament.

**Reign of Terror** (June 1793–July 1794) Phase of the FRENCH REVOLUTION. It began with the overthrow of the GIRONDINS and the ascendancy of the JACOBINS under ROBESPIERRE. Against a background of foreign invasion and civil war, opponents were ruthlessly persecuted and *c.*1,400 executed by the GUILLOTINE. The Terror ended with a coup on July 27, 1794 in the National Convention, when Robespierre and leading Jacobins were arrested and executed.

**Reims** City on the Vesle River, NE France; a port on the Aisne-Marne Canal. CLOVIS I was baptized and crowned here in 496, and it was the coronation place of later French kings. Reims is the center of the champagne industry. Other industries: woolen goods, metallurgy, chemicals, glass. Pop. (1990) 180,620.

**reincarnation** Passage of the soul through successive bodies, causing the rebirth of an individual and the prolonging of his or her existence on Earth. In HINDUISM and BUDDHISM, an individual's KARMA (earthly conduct) determines the condition into which one is born in the next life.

**reindeer** (caribou) Large DEER of N latitudes, which ranges from Scandinavia across Siberia to North America. It has thick fur and broad hoofs, which help to spread the animal's weight on snow. It stands up to 4.6ft (1.4m) tall at the shoulders, and feeds on grasses and saplings in the summer and lichens it finds beneath the snow in the winter. It is domesticated for meat and as a pack animal by the Lapps. Both sexes have antlers. Species *Rangifer tarandus*.

◀ **reindeer** Always found in herds, reindeer (*Rangifer tarandus*) migrate vast distances between summer and winter feeding grounds. They are adapted to two different environments: tundra and woodland. Their large hooves can spread when they walk on snow or soft ground.

REMOTE SENSING

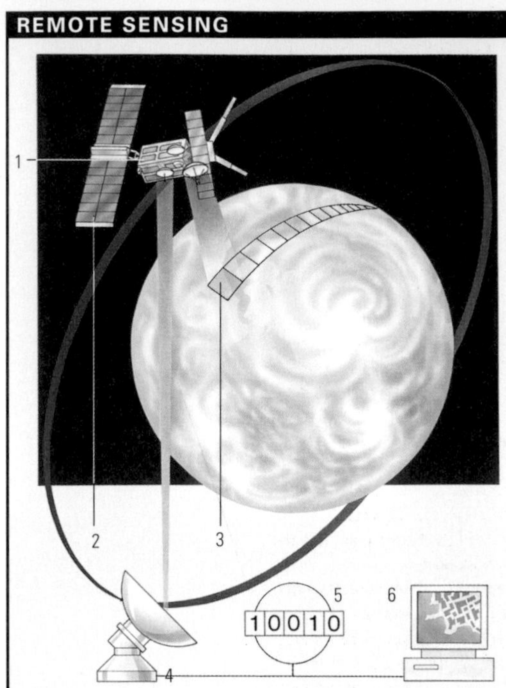


Remote sensing satellites (1) view the Earth from space using various sensors and cameras. The ways of looking at the Earth are divided between active and passive. Active devices, such as optical cameras and infrared scanners, pick up reflected radiation. Active instruments send out radio pulses and record the return signal. One of the strengths of active scanning is the ability to see through cloud. The satellites, powered by a solar sail (2), use orbits which take them over the whole of the Earth over a series of days (3). Images of the Earth's surfaces are beamed down to ground stations (4) in digital form (5), and are converted into pictures by computers (6).

**Reinhardt, "Django" (Jean-Baptiste)** (1910–53) Belgian jazz guitarist. He blended folk music with jazz and swing styles and is noted for his improvisations. In 1934 he formed a quintet with the violinist Stéphane Grappelli and they played as the "Hot Club." He also played in the US with Duke ELLINGTON.

**relative atomic mass (r.a.m.)** (atomic weight) Mass of an atom of the naturally occurring form of an element divided by $\frac{1}{12}$ of the mass of an atom of carbon-12. The naturally occurring form may consist of two or more isotopes, and the calculation of the r.a.m. must take this into account.

**relative density** (specific gravity) Ratio of the DENSITY of a substance to the density of water. Thus, the relative density of gold is 19.3: it is *c.*19 times denser than an equal volume of water.

**relative molecular mass** (molecular weight) Mass of a molecule, the sum of the relative atomic masses of all its atoms. It is the ratio of the average mass per molecule of an element or compound to one-twelfth of the mass of an atom of carbon-12. The molecular masses of reactants (elements or compounds) must be known in order to make calculations about yields in a chemical reaction.

**relativity** Theory, proposed by Albert EINSTEIN, based on the postulate that the motion of one body can be defined only with respect to that of a second body. This led to the concept of a four-dimensional space-time continuum in which the three space dimensions and time are treated on an equal footing. The **special theory**, put forward in 1905, is limited to the description of events as they appear to observers in a state of uniform relative motion. The more important consequences of the theory are: (1) that the velocity of light is absolute, that is, not relative to the velocity of the observer; (2) that the mass of a body increases with its velocity, although appreciably only at velocities approaching that of light; (3) that mass ($m$) and energy ($E$) are equivalent, that is, $E = mc^2$, where $c$ is the velocity of light (this shows that when mass is converted to energy, a small mass gives rise to large energy); (4) the Lorentz-Fitzgerald contraction, that is, bodies contract as their velocity increases, again only appreciably near the velocity of light; and (5) an object's sense of elapsed time expands, "time dilation." The **general theory** of relativity, completed in 1915, is applicable to observers not in uniform relative motion. This showed the relation of space and GRAVITATION. The presence of matter in space causes space to "curve," forming gravitational fields; thus gravitation becomes a property of space itself. This leads to such observable phenomena as the curvature of light from distant stars. The existence of BLACK HOLES is postulated as a consequence of general relativity.

**relief** (It. *rilievo*, projection) Three-dimensional sculpture projecting from a flat background. In *alto-relievo* (high relief) the protrusion is great, *basso-relievo* (low relief) protrudes only slightly, and *mezzo-relievo* is between the two.

**religion** Code of beliefs and practices formulated in response to a spiritual awareness of existence. It may involve either faith in a state of existence after earthly death, or a desire for union with an omnipotent spiritual being, or a combination of the two. Polytheistic religions, such as those of ancient Egypt, Greece, and Rome, entailed the worship of many distinct gods or personifications of nature. Many cultures classified their deities into hierarchies known as pantheons; some religions, such as HINDUISM, still have such pantheons. Other ancient religions, some of which incorporated belief in a state of existence after death, were more of a system of ethical philosophy concentrating on metaphysical contemplation (for example, BUDDHISM and TAOISM). The ancient Hebrews were among the first people to worship a single omniscient and omnipotent being, YAHWEH. The basis of their religion was a covenant or agreement that they believed had been made between Yahweh and themselves. He gave them his protection in return for their total faith and obedience. Common to all religions dominated by a single omnipotent force (such as JUDAISM, CHRISTIANITY, and ISLAM) is the idea that the power is omnipresent or all places at once, and that it is beyond the physical plane occupied by humans. In many religions, both monotheistic and polytheistic, sacrifice to an individual god or to God is an important element, either in propitiation, or to redeem the faithful from some wrongdoing, or in thanksgiving.

**Religion, Wars of** (1562–98) Series of religious conflicts in France. At stake was freedom of worship for HUGUENOTS, but it was also a struggle between crown and nobility. The Huguenot leaders were, successively, Louis I de CONDÉ, Caspard de Coligny, and Henry of Navarre (later HENRY IV). The Catholic party was led by the House of GUISE. The crown, represented by CATHERINE DE' MEDICI and her sons, CHARLES IX and HENRY III, attempted to pursue a moderate Catholic line. The first three civil wars (1562–63, 1567–68, 1568–70) ended in the Treaty of St Germain (1570), which granted concessions to the Protestants. Hostilities recommenced with the SAINT BARTHOLOMEW'S DAY MASSACRE (1572). The fifth civil war (1574–76) resulted in the Edict of Beaulieu that granted freedom of worship to Huguenots. The Catholic party formed a Holy League and the edict was revoked, prompting renewed conflict. Henry III's naming of Henry of Navarre as his heir led to the War of the Three Henrys (1585–89). Henry IV emerged victorious and the Edict of NANTES (1598) extended toleration to the Huguenots.

**Remarque, Erich Maria** (1898–1970) German novelist, b. Erich Paul Remark. A World War I veteran, his best-known novel, *All Quiet on the Western Front* (1929), is a savage indictment of war. The sequel *The Road Back* (1931) concerns Germany's post-war collapse and readjustment.

**Rembrandt Harmenszoon van Rijn** (1606–69) Dutch painter and graphic artist. Between 1625 and 1631 he painted many self-portraits. He settled in Amsterdam (1631–32), becoming highly regarded as a painter of group portraits such as the *Anatomy Lesson of Dr. Tulp* (1632). By 1636 he was painting in the richly detailed BAROQUE style typified by the *Sacrifice of Abraham* (1636). In 1642 he finished his famous group portrait, *The Corporalship of Captain Frans Banning Cocq's Civic Guards* (or *The Night Watch*). By 1656 he was so deeply in debt that he withdrew from society. During these later years he produced some of his greatest works, such as *Jacob Blessing the Sons of Joseph* (1656) and *The Jewish Bride* (late 1660s). His works total more than 300 paintings, some 300 etchings, and 1,000 drawings.

**Remington, Frederic** (1861–1909) US painter and sculptor. His romantic depictions of cowboys and Native Americans became immensely popular. His works include *The Scout, Friends or Enemies* (1908), and the bronze *Bronco Buster*. His style is detailed and realistic.

**remote sensing** Any method of obtaining and recording information from a distance. The most common sensor is the CAMERA used in aircraft, satellites, and space probes to collect and transmit information back to Earth (often by radio). The resulting photographs provide a variety of information, including archeological evidence and weather data. MICROWAVE sensors use radar signals that can penetrate cloud. Infrared sensors can measure temperature differences over an area.

**Remus** *See* ROMULUS AND REMUS

**Renaissance** (Fr. rebirth) Period of European history lasting roughly from the mid-15th century to the end of the 16th century. The word was used by late 15th-century Italian scholars to describe the revival of interest in classical learning. It was helped by the fall of Constantinople to the Ottoman Turks in 1453, which resulted in the moving of classical texts to Italy. In Germany, the invention of a printing press with movable type assisted the diffusion of the new scholarship. In religion, the spirit of questioning led to the REFORMATION. In politics, the Renaissance saw the rise of assertive sovereign states – Spain, Portugal, France, and England – and the expansion of Europe beyond its own shores, with the building of trading empires in Africa, the East Indies, and America. The growth of a wealthy urban merchant class led to a tremendous flowering of the arts. *See also* RENAISSANCE ARCHITECTURE; RENAISSANCE ART; RENAISSANCE MUSIC

**Renaissance architecture** Architectural style that began in Italy in the 15th century and spread throughout Europe until the advent of MANNERISM and the BAROQUE in the 16th and 17th centuries. Revolting against GOTHIC ARCHITECTURE, it used Roman motifs. In Italy, BRUNELLESCHI and ALBERTI studied the Roman ruins. In France, the style was first employed by Lescot, who was commissioned by Francis I to work on the Louvre (1546).

**Renaissance art** Style that emerged in Italy in the 15th century, heavily influenced by classical Greek or Roman models and by the new HUMANISM. In painting, the decisive differences between Gothic and Renaissance painting emerged in Florence in the early 15th century. These differences included: the development of PERSPECTIVE; a new interest in composition and color harmonies; the increasing use of secular or pagan subject matter; the rise of portraiture; constant experimentation to develop new skills; and a growing concern for the expression of the individual artist. The creators of High Renaissance painting were LEONARDO DA VINCI, MICHELANGELO, and RAPHAEL. The ideas of the Italian artists were taken to France and N Europe and emulated with national variations. **Renaissance literature** found an early exponent in PETRARCH; other Italian Renaissance literary figures include DANTE and MACHIAVELLI. By the 16th century the Renaissance literary movement had reached N Europe, where it inspired much poetry and history writing and culminated, in England, in the dramas of Shakespeare.

**Renaissance music** Music composed in Europe from *c.*1400–1600. It was mainly religious vocal POLYPHONY, usually MASSES and MOTETS. Nonreligious music at this time was mainly in the form of songs – Italian and English MADRIGALS, French *chansons*, German *Lieder* – and some instrumental music for organ, clavier, lute, or for small ensembles. Composers of this period include PALESTRINA, LASSO, BYRD, and GABRIELI.

**renewable energy** (alternative energy) ENERGY from a source that can be replenished or that replenishes itself, and is more environmentally safe than traditional energy forms such as COAL, GAS, or NUCLEAR ENERGY. SOLAR ENERGY harnesses the rays of the Sun. TIDAL POWER stations use the gravitational force of the Sun and Moon on the ocean. Wave power harnesses the natural movement of the sea. The power of rivers and lakes can be tapped by damming the flow and using turbines to generate HYDROELECTRICITY. WIND POWER schemes have existed for centuries in the form of WINDMILLS. Another, less well-known, renewable source is the GEOTHERMAL ENERGY produced in the Earth's crust.

**Reni, Guido** (1575–1642) Italian painter who became the leading master of Bolognese art. His most celebrated works include *Massacre of the Innocents* (1611), *Aurora* (1613), and *Atlanta and Hippoinenes* (*c.*1625).

**Rennes** City at the confluence of the Ille and Vilaine rivers, NW France; capital of Ille-et-Vilaine department. During the Middle Ages, Rennes served as capital of Brittany under the Angevin dukes. In the 16th century it became the seat of the Parliament of Brittany. The city suffered heavy bombing in World War II. Industries: leather goods, printing, textiles, electronic equipment, motor vehicles. Pop. (1990) 199,396.

**rennet** Substance used to curdle milk in cheesemaking. It is obtained as an extract from the inner lining of the fourth stomach of calves and other young ruminants, and is rich in rennin, an ENZYME that coagulates the casein (protein) of milk.

**Renoir, (Pierre) Auguste** (1841–1919) French impressionist painter. In 1874 he contributed to the first exhibition of IMPRESSIONISM and masterpieces of this period include *La Loge* (1874) and *Le Moulin de la Galette* (1876). In the early 1880s Renoir became interested in the human figure with such works as *Bathers* (1884–87) and *After the Bath* (*c.*1895).

**Renoir, Jean** (1894–1979) French film director and actor, son of Pierre Auguste RENOIR. His best-known films are *La Grande Ilusion* (1937) and *La Règle du Jeu* (1939). His work is noted for its lyric response to nature and humanity and for subtlety of style. Other films include *Nana* (1926), *Madame Bovary* (1934), *French Cancan* (1955), and *C'est la Revolution* (1967).

**reparations** War damage payments, especially those demanded by the victorious Allies from the defeated Central Powers at the Treaty of VERSAILLES (1919). The US did not ratify the treaty and waived all reparation claims.

**Representatives, House of** *See* HOUSE OF REPRESENTATIVES

**repression** Process by which unacceptable thoughts or memories are kept in the UNCONSCIOUS so that they cannot cause guilt or distress. In Freudian psychology, it is part of the function of the ego, whereby it controls the primal and instinctual urges of the id. Repressed desires find an outlet in dreams, and are believed to be at the root of various neurotic disorders.

**reproduction** Process by which living organisms create new organisms similar to themselves. Reproduction may be sexual or asexual, the first being the fusion of two special reproductive cells from different parents, and the second being the generation of new organisms from a single organism. ASEXUAL REPRODUCTION is the more limited, found mainly in PROTOZOA, some INVERTEBRATES, and in many plants. By contrast, almost all living organisms have the capacity for SEXUAL REPRODUCTION. In the majority of cases the species has two kinds of individuals – male and female – with different sex functions. Male and female sex cells (in animals, sperm and egg) fuse to produce a new cell, the ZYGOTE, which contains genetic information from both parents, and from which a new individual develops. Alternatively, organisms may be HERMAPHRODITES, each individual of the species having male and female functions, so that when two of them mate each individual fertilizes the other's eggs. Sexually reproducing plants (or generations) are called GAMETOPHYTE; ones which reproduce asexually, SPOROPHYTE. *See also* ALTERNATION OF GENERATIONS; POLLEN

**reptile** Any one of about 6,000 species of VERTEBRATES distributed worldwide. Reptiles are cold-blooded. Most lay

▼ **Renoir** *Bal du Moulin de la Gallete, Montmartre* (1876). The impressionist painter Auguste Renoir delighted in painting the human figure, particularly women. This example clearly shows how he explored the effects of light and shadow on faces and bodies, which was typical of his early work. From the 1880s, influenced by a trip to Italy and study of the Old Masters, his style became more linear, moving away from the free brushwork of the 1870s.

R

yolky eggs on land. Some species – particularly snakes – carry eggs in the body and bear live young. The skin is dry and covered with scales or embedded with bony plates. Their limbs are poorly developed or nonexistent. Those with limbs usually have five clawed toes on each foot. There are four living orders: Chelonia (TURTLES); Rhynchocephalia (TUATARA); Squamata (scaly reptiles such as SNAKES and LIZARDS); and Crocodilia (ALLIGATORS and CROCODILES).

**republic** State in which sovereignty is vested in the people or their elected or nominated representatives. A republic may also be understood to be a state in which all segments of society are enfranchised and the power of the state is limited.

**Republican Party** US political party. It was organized in 1854 as an amalgamation of the WHIG PARTY and Free-Soilers, with workers and professional people who had formerly been known as Independent Democrats, Know-Nothings, Barnburners, or Abolitionists. Its first successful presidential candidate was Abraham LINCOLN (elected 1860). During the early 20th century, the Republicans were generally the minority party to the DEMOCRATIC PARTY in Congress, especially in the House of Representatives. Later there was a reversal. There was a Republic president for all but four years between 1969 and 1993. Under presidents REAGAN and BUSH, the Republican Party seemed to have captured the popular vote until CLINTON's charismatic campaign restored Democratic fortunes. In 1994 the Republicans regained control of The Senate and House of Representative, and retained majorities in the 1998 elections. Today, the Republican Party is considered to be more conservative than the DEMOCRATIC PARTY.

**requiem** Solemn choral service for the dead sung in Roman Catholic Churches. Mozart, Verdi, Fauré, and Berlioz, among others, have composed requiems.

**resin** (rosin) Artificial or natural POLYMER that is generally viscous and sticky. Artificial resins include polyesters and epoxies and are used as adhesives and binders. Natural resins are secreted by various plants. Oleoresin, secreted by conifers, is distilled to produce turpentine; resin remains after the oil of turpentine has been distilled off.

**resistance** (symbol $R$) Property of an electric conductor, calculated as the ratio of the voltage applied to the conductor to the current passing through it. The SI unit of resistance is the OHM. It represents the opposition to the flow of electric current. *See also* RESISTOR

**resistance movement** Underground organizations that worked against German rule in occupied countries of Europe during World War II. In some countries, such as Poland and Yugoslavia, they were strong enough to mount armed resistance. Elsewhere, as in France, the Low Countries, and Scandinavia, their role was confined to sabotage and intelligence.

**resistivity** (symbol $\rho$) Electrical property of materials. Its value is given by $\rho = AR/l$, where $A$ is the cross-sectional area of a conductor, $l$ is its length and $R$ is its RESISTANCE. Resistivity is generally expressed in units of ohm-meters and is a measure of the resistance of a piece of material of given size.

**resistor** Electrical CIRCUIT component with a specified RESISTANCE. Resistors limit the size of the current flowing. Those for electronic circuits usually consist of carbon particles mixed with a ceramic material and enclosed in an insulated tube. Resistors for carrying larger currents are coils of insulated wire.

**resonance** Increase in the amplitude of vibration of a mechanical or acoustic system when it is forced to vibrate by an external source. It occurs when the FREQUENCY of the applied force is equal to the natural vibrational frequency of the system. Large vibrations can cause damage to the system.

**resources** In economics, a country's collective means of support. Economists divide resources into four categories: land, labor, capital, and raw materials.

**Respighi, Ottorino** (1879–1936) Italian composer who was influenced by Nikolai Rimsky-Korsakov. He is best known for the symphonic poems *Fountains of Rome* (1917) and *Pines of Rome* (1924). He also composed songs, chamber music, and operas.

**respiration** Series of chemical reactions by which complex molecules (food molecules) are broken down to release energy in living organisms. These reactions are controlled by ENZYMES, and are an essential part of METABOLISM. There are two main types of respiration: AEROBIC and ANAEROBIC. In **aerobic** respiration, oxygen combines with the breakdown products and is necessary for the reactions to take place. **Anaerobic** respiration takes place in the absence of oxygen. In most living organisms, the energy released by respiration is used to convert ADENOSINE DIPHOSPHATE (ADP) to ADENOSINE TRIPHOSPHATE (ATP), which transports energy around the cell. At the site where the energy is needed, ATP is converted back to ADP, with the aid of a special enzyme, and energy is released. The first stages of respiration take place in the cytoplasm and the later stages in the MITOCHONDRIA. *See also* KREBS, SIR HANS ADOLF; TRANSPIRATION

**respiratory system** System in air-breathing animals concerned with GAS EXCHANGE. The respiratory tract begins with the nose and mouth, through which air enters the body. The air then passes through the LARYNX and into the TRACHEA. The trachea at its lower end branches into two bronchi, each BRONCHUS leads to a LUNG. The bronchi divide into many bronchioles, which lead in turn to bunches of tiny air sacs (ALVEOLI), where the exchange of gases between air and blood takes place. Exhaled air leaves along the same pathway.

**response, conditioned** Learned pairing of a response to an artificial stimulus. In the classic experiments of PAVLOV, dogs were taught to associate the ringing of a bell with their being given food, and they began to salivate just at the sound of the bell. The dog's salivation in these experiments was the conditioned response.

**Restoration** In English history, the reestablishment of the monarchy in 1660. After the death of Oliver CROMWELL, his son and successor, Richard, was unable to prevent growing conflict. He resigned (1659), and the crisis was resolved by the march of General MONCK from Scotland. Army leaders backed down and a new Parliament was elected. From exile, CHARLES II issued the Declaration of Breda (1660), promising an amnesty to most opponents, payment of the arrears in the army's wages, and religious toleration. He was invited by a new Parliament to resume the throne. The term Restoration is often extended to the period following 1660, and is especially associated with a flowering of English literature, notably in RESTORATION DRAMA. In French history, it refers to the restoration of the BOURBONS (1814–30) after the defeat of Napoleon.

**Restoration drama** In England, plays and performances in the period following the restoration of CHARLES II, when the theaters were reopened. The drama reflected the laxity of court morals through broad satire, farce, wit, and bawdy comedy. Major dramatists included DRYDEN and CONGREVE.

**restriction enzyme** ENZYME used in GENETIC ENGINEERING to cut a molecule of DNA at specific points, in order to insert or remove a piece of DNA. There are many different restriction enzymes; each cuts the DNA at a specific sequence of bases, allowing great precision in genetic engineering.

**resurrection** Rising of the dead to new life, either in heaven or on Earth. JUDAISM, CHRISTIANITY, and ISLAM all hold that at the end of the world there will come a Day of Judgment on which those worthy of eternal joy will be allowed to draw near to God, while those unworthy will be cast out into darkness. The term also applies to the rising of JESUS CHRIST from the dead on the third day after his crucifixion.

**resuscitation** Measures taken to revive a person who is on the brink of death. The most successful technique available to the layman is mouth-to-mouth resuscitation. Medical staff receive instruction in cardiopulmonary resuscitation (CPR), which involves the use of specialized equipment and drugs to save patients whose breathing and/or heartbeat suddenly stop.

**retina** Inner layer of the EYE, composed mainly of different kinds of NEURONS, some of which are the visual receptors of the eye. Receptor cells, known as cones and rods, are sensitive to light. Cones respond to the spectrum of visible colors; rods respond to shades of gray and to movement. The rods and cones connect with sensory neurons, which in turn connect with the optic nerve, which carries the visual stimuli to the brain.

**retriever** Sporting dog originally used to kill or cripple downed game and return it to the hunter; today it is also used to locate game and is a popular pet. The main breeds include the golden retriever and the Labrador retriever.

**retrovirus** Any of a large family of VIRUSES (Retroviridae) that, unlike other living organisms, contain the genetic material RNA (ribonucleic acid) rather than the customary DNA (deoxyribonucleic acid). In order to multiply, retroviruses make use of a special enzyme to convert their RNA into DNA, which then becomes integrated with the DNA in the cells of their hosts. Diseases caused by retroviruses include the HUMAN IMMUNODEFICIENCY VIRUS (HIV) that causes AIDS.

**Réunion** Volcanic island in the Indian Ocean, in the Mascarene group, *c.*435mi (700km) E of Madagascar, an overseas département of France; the capital is St. Denis. Discovered in 1513 by the Portuguese, it was claimed by France in 1638. The island became an overseas département in 1948 and part of an administrative region in 1973. Exports: sugar, rum, corn, tobacco. Area: 969sq mi (2,510sq km). Pop. (1994 est.) 645,000.

**Reuters** News agency that transmits international news between major cities worldwide. It originated as a service between Britain and continental Europe, using the telegraph. It is jointly owned by Australian, New Zealand, and British newspapers.

**Revelation** (Apocalypse) Last book of the NEW TESTAMENT. It was written perhaps as late as AD 95 by St. John the Divine. In highly allegorical and prophetic terms, it concentrates on depicting the end of Creation, the war between good and evil, the Day of Judgment, and the ultimate triumph of good.

**Revere, Paul** (1735–1818) American silversmith and patriot, famous for his ride from Charlestown to Lexington, Massachusetts. Revere made his ride on April 18, 1775 to warn the colonists of Massachusetts of the approach of British troops at the start of the AMERICAN REVOLUTION. It was commemorated in LONGFELLOW's poem, "Paul Revere's Ride" (1863).

**reversible reaction** Chemical reaction in which the products can change back into the reactants. Thus nitrogen and hydrogen can be combined to give ammonia (as in the HABER PROCESS) and ammonia may be decomposed to nitrogen and hydrogen. Such processes yield an equilibrium mixture of reactants and products. *See also* CHEMICAL EQUILIBRIUM

**revisionism** Political theory derived from MARXISM. Eduard Bernstein, the first Marxist revisionist, asserted in 1890 that capitalism was not in crisis, and that the move to socialism would be a matter of peaceful evolution. This conflicted directly with orthodox Marxist belief in the inevitable collapse of capitalism. After 1945 the term was used by communist regimes to condemn political movements that threatened official party policy.

**revolution** Movement of a planet or other celestial object around its orbit, as distinct from ROTATION of the object on its axis. A single revolution is the planet's or satellite's "year."

**revolution** In a political sense, fundamental change in values, political institutions, social structure, and leadership brought about by a large-scale, successful revolt. The totality of change distinguishes it from coups, rebellions, and wars of independence, which seek and achieve only particular changes. The term is also used to indicate great economic and technical changes, such as the INDUSTRIAL REVOLUTION.

**Revolutions of 1848** Series of revolutions in European countries which broke out within a few months of each other. The general cause was the frustration of liberals and nationalists with the governing authorities, and a background of economic depression. The risings began with the FEBRUARY REVOLUTION against LOUIS PHILIPPE in France, which resulted in the foundation of the Second Republic. It inspired revolts in Vienna (forcing the resignation of METTERNICH), and among the national minorities under Austrian rule. In Germany, liberals forced FREDERICK WILLIAM IV to summon a constitutional assembly, while advocates of German unification hoped to achieve their aim in the Frankfurt Parliament. *See also* RISORGIMENTO

**Revolutions of 1989** Popular risings in East European states against communist governments. Long-suppressed opposition to Soviet-dominated rule erupted spontaneously in most of the Soviet satellite states. Within months, the communists were driven from power and a democratic system installed. They were followed by the withdrawal of the constituent republics of the Soviet Union which, though unwelcome to Moscow, also encountered little serious resistance.

**revue** Theatrical entertainment purporting to give a review, usually satirical, of current fashions, events, and personalities.

**Reykjavík** Capital of Iceland, a port on the SW coast. Founded *c.*870, it was the island's first permanent settlement. It expanded during the 18th century and became the capital in 1918. During World War II it served as a British and US air base. Industries: food processing, fishing, textiles, metallurgy, printing and publishing, shipbuilding. Pop. (1993) 101,824.

**Reynolds, Albert** (1933– ) Irish statesman, taoiseach (1992–94). Reynolds entered the Dáil in 1977 and quickly joined the FIANNA FÁIL cabinet. He was dismissed in 1991 after trying to displace the prime minister, Charles HAUGHEY. Reynolds eventually succeeded Haughey. In 1992 elections Fianna Fáil lost their majority and he was forced into coalition with the Labour Party. Reynolds and the British prime minister, John MAJOR, issued the DOWNING STREET DECLARATION (1993). In 1994 the Labour Party withdrew its support and Reynolds was forced to resign. He was succeeded by John BRUTON.

**Reynolds, Sir Joshua** (1723–92) English portrait painter and writer on art. In 1768 he became the first president of the Royal Academy (RA) and espoused the principles of the "Grand Manner" style in his annual *Discourses* (1768–90) to the Academy. These describe how painting, through allusions to classical, heroic figures, can be a scholarly activity. His masterpiece portraits are remarkable for their individuality and sensitivity to the sitter's mood, many of whom are painted in classical poses, such as *Mrs Siddons as the Tragic Muse* (1784).

**rhapsody** Musical term applied in the 19th and 20th centuries to orchestral works, usually in one continuous movement and most often inspired by a nationalist or romantic theme.

**rhea** Either of two species of large, brownish, flightless, fast-running South American birds resembling a small OSTRICH. They feed mostly on vegetation and insects. Height: to 5ft (1.5m). Family Rheidae.

**Rhee, Syngman** (1875–1965) Korean statesman, first president (1948–60) of South Korea. He was imprisoned (1898–1904) for his opposition to Japanese rule before living (1912–45) in exile in the USA. In 1919 Rhee became leader of a government-in-exile. After World War 2 he was leader of US-occupied South Korea. His presidency was marked by the KOREAN WAR. Rhee's regime became increasingly authoritarian and corrupt. After his reelection for a fourth time, accusations of vote-rigging sparked riots, and Rhee was forced to resign.

**rhenium** (symbol Re) Silver-white metallic element, one of the TRANSITION ELEMENTS, which have incomplete inner electron shells. Discovered in 1925, rhenium is found in molybdenite and PLATINUM ores from which it is obtained as a by-product. It is heavy and used in alloys in thermocouples, camera flashlights, and electronic filaments, and is also a useful catalyst. Properties: at.no. 75; at.wt. 186.2; sp.gr. 21.0; m.p. 5,756°F (3,180°C); b.p. 10,160°F (5,627°C); most common isotope $^{187}$Re (62.93%).

**rheostat** Variable RESISTOR for regulating an electric current. The resistance element may be a metal wire, carbon, or a conducting liquid. Rheostats are used to adjust generators, to dim lights, and to control the speed of electric motors.

**rhesus** Medium-sized, yellow-brown MACAQUE monkey of India. Short-tailed, it has a large head with a bare face, large ears, and closely spaced, deep-set eyes. Height: 2ft (60cm). Species *Macaca mulatta.*

**rhetoric** Art of discourse and persuasive speaking; language, written or spoken, designed to impress or persuade. Rhetoric is valued in public speaking, but the sophistication of many of its modern techniques may have led to increased suspicion of rhetoricians – such as politicians – on the part of a better-informed public.

**rheumatic fever** Inflammatory disorder characterized by fever and painful swelling of the joints. Rare in the modern developed world, it mostly affects children and young adults. An important complication is possible damage to the heart valves, leading to rheumatic heart disease in later life.

**rheumatism** General term for a group of disorders whose symptoms are pain, inflammation, and stiffness in the bones, joints, and surrounding tissues. Usually some form of ARTHRITIS is involved.

R

▲ **rhea** Living in open country, the flightless rhea roams the pampas of South America in flocks of up to 30. Standing tall, it can detect approaching danger even in high grass. When threatened, it can run faster than a horse.

► **rhinoceros** The yellow-billed oxpecker (*Buphagus africanus*) and the African White Rhino (*Cerato therium simum*) have a symbiotic relationship. The oxpecker, a type of African starling, feeds by pulling ticks from the animal's hide and sipping blood that oozes from tick wounds. The rhino benefits from the removal of the parasites.

**Rhine** (Rhein, Rhin, or Rijn) River in W Europe. It rises in SE Switzerland in the Swiss Alps and flows N, bordering on or passing through Switzerland, Austria, Liechtenstein, Germany, France, and the Netherlands to enter the North Sea at Rotterdam. The Rhine is navigable to oceangoing vessels as far as Basel, Switzerland, and is a major transport route for some of W Europe's most industrialized areas. Length: *c.*820mi (1,320km).

**Rhineland** Region in W Germany along the W bank of the Rhine River. It includes Saarland and Rhineland-Palatinate, and parts of Baden-Württemberg, Hesse, and North Rhine-Westphalia.

**rhinitis** Inflammation of the mucous membrane of the nose. It may be an allergic reaction (such as HAY FEVER) or a symptom of a viral infection, such as the common cold.

**rhinoceros** (rhino) Massive, herbivorous mammal native to Africa and Asia. Rhinos are the second largest land mammals (after HIPPOPOTAMUSES). The largest of the five species, the central African white rhino *Ceratotherium simum*, reaches a height of 2m (1.5ft) at the shoulder. Rhinos have thick skin and poor eyesight and are solitary grazers or browsers. In the heat of the day they like to wallow in muddy pools. Now rare except in protected areas, rhinos are illegally hunted for their horns (believed to have aphrodisiac properties). Weight: 1–3.5 tonnes. Family Rhinocerotidae.

**rhizoid** Fine, hairlike growth used for attachment to a solid surface by some simple organisms, such as certain fungi and mosses. The rhizoid lacks the conducting TISSUES of a root.

**rhizome** Root-like underground stem of certain plants. It usually grows horizontally, is rich in accumulated starch, and can produce new roots and stems asexually. Rhizomes differ from roots in producing buds and leaves. *See also* TUBER

**Rhode Island** State in NE US, on the Atlantic coast in New England; the smallest state in the US; the capital is PROVIDENCE. Other major cities include Warwick, Pawtucket, and Cranston. The region was first settled in 1636 by people from Massachusetts seeking religious freedom. It was granted a royal charter in 1663. It was occupied by British troops during the American Revolution. Much of the land is forested, but there is some dairy farming. Potatoes, hay, apples, oats, and corn are the chief crops, and fishing is significant. Other industries: textiles, fabricated metals, silverware, machinery, electrical equipment, and tourism. Area: 1,214sq mi (3,144sq km). Pop. (1993 est.) 1,000,012.

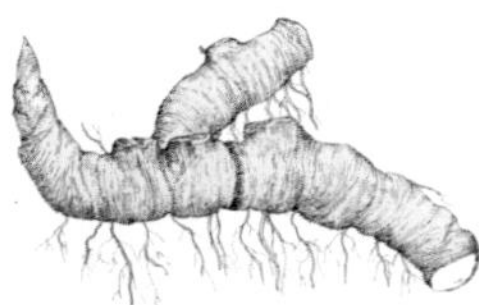

▲ **rhizome** Unlike other plant storage organs, rhizomes are not replaced annually. They grow continually, branching as they do so, and each growing tip produces aerial shoots. The oldest parts slowly die off. Shown here is the rhizome of Solomon's seal (*Polygonatum multiflorum*).

**Rhodes, Cecil John** (1853–1902) South African statesman, b. Britain. In 1870 Rhodes emigrated to Natal and made a fortune in the Kimberley diamond mines. In 1880 he founded the De Beers Mining Company. Rhodes dreamed of building a BRITISH EMPIRE in Africa that stretched from the Cape to Cairo. In 1885 he persuaded the British government to form a protectorate over Bechuanaland. In 1889 he founded the British South Africa Company, which occupied Mashonaland and Matabeleland, thus forming RHODESIA (now Zambia and Zimbabwe). Rhodes was prime minister (1890–96) of Cape Colony. The discovery of his role in Leander JAMESON's attempt to overthrow Paul KRUGER in the TRANSVAAL led to his resignation.

**Rhodes** (Ródhos) Greek island in the SE Aegean Sea; the largest of the Dodecanese archipelago. It was colonized by the Dorians *c.*1000 BC and later conquered at different times by Persia, Sparta, Athens, Macedon, Rome, and the Byzantine empire. The island was captured in 1310 by the Knights Hospitallers, who defended it against the Turks for more than 200 years. It was taken by the Ottoman Turks in 1522. Ceded to Italy in 1912, it was awarded to Greece in 1947. The chief city is Rhodes. Products: wheat, tobacco, cotton, olives, fruits, vegetables. Area: 540sq mi (1,400sq km). Pop. (1981) 88,000.

**Rhodesia** Former name of a territory in S central Africa. The area was developed by Cecil RHODES. In 1923 Southern Rhodesia became a self-governing British colony, and in 1924 Northern Rhodesia was made a British protectorate. In 1953 the two Rhodesias were united with Nyasaland (now MALAWI) in the Central African Federation. When the federation was dissolved in 1963, Northern Rhodesia gained independence as ZAMBIA. The name Rhodesia was used by Southern Rhodesia until the country achieved independence as ZIMBABWE in 1980.

**rhodium** (symbol Rh) Silver-white metallic element, one of the TRANSITION ELEMENTS. Discovered in 1803, it is associated with PLATINUM and its chief source is as a by-product of NICKEL smelting. It resists tarnish and corrosion and is used in hard platinum alloys and jewelry. Properties: at.no. 45; at.wt. 102.906; sp.gr. 12.4; m.p. 3,571°F (1,966°C); b.p. 6,741°F (3,727°C); most common isotope $^{103}$Rh (100%).

**rhododendron** Large genus of shrubs and small trees that grow in the acid soils of cool temperate regions in North America, Europe, and Asia. Primarily evergreen, they have leathery leaves and bell-shaped white, pink, or purple flowers. Family Ericaceae. *See also* AZALEA

**rhodophyta** *See* RED ALGAE

**rhombus** Plane figure with all of its sides equal in length but no right angles. A rhombus is a type of PARALLELOGRAM with diagonals that bisect each other at right angles.

**Rhône** River in W Europe. It rises in the Rhône Glacier in S Switzerland, runs through the Bernese Oberland, flows W to Lake Geneva and then crosses the French border. It continues S through LYON and AVIGNON to Arles, where it branches into the Grand Rhône and the Petit Rhône, which both enter the Mediterranean W of Marseilles. Length: 505mi (813km).

**rhubarb** Perennial herbaceous plant native to Asia and cultivated in cool climates throughout the world for its edible leaf stalks. It has large, poisonous leaves and small white or red flowers. Height: to 4ft (1.2m). Genus *Rheum.*

**rhyme** Identity or similarity of final sounds in two or more words, such as keep/deep, baking/shaking. Rhyme is used in poetry to reinforce METER. End rhymes establish verse lines, while internal rhymes emphasize rhythmic structures.

**rhythm and blues** Form of popular music. It developed as an urban form of the BLUES and was also influenced by JAZZ. An energetic and relatively simple music, it was the basis of ROCK AND ROLL.

**rib** Long, curved bones that are arranged in pairs, extending sideways from the backbone of vertebrates. In fish and some reptiles they extend the length of the spine; in mammals they form the framework of the chest, and protect the lungs and heart. There are 12 pairs of ribs in humans.

**Ribbentrop, Joachim von** (1893–1946) German diplomat and politician. In 1932 he joined the Nazi Party and became foreign affairs adviser to Adolf HITLER in 1933. Ribbentrop negotiated the secret Nazi-Soviet Pact (1939) with MOLOTOV but steadily lost influence during World War 2. At the NUREMBERG TRIALS (1946), he was convicted of war crimes and hanged.

**Ribera, José** (1591–1652) Spanish painter and graphic artist. His early work used dark shadows, but Ribera was also capable of expressing tenderness. His late paintings, such as *The Club-footed Boy* (1642), are often richly colored and softly modeled. Until the Napoleonic Wars, he and Batholomé MURILLO were the only Spanish painters of international repute.

**riboflavin** VITAMIN $B_2$ of the B complex, lack of which impairs growth and causes skin disorders. It is a coenzyme important in transferring energy within cells. Soluble in water, riboflavin is found in milk, eggs, liver, and green vegetables.

**ribonucleic acid** *See* RNA

**ribosome** Tiny structure in the CYTOPLASM of EUKARYOTE

cells, involved in synthesizing PROTEIN molecules. Proteins are made up of specific sequences of AMINO ACIDS, and segments of DNA, called GENES, contain the instructions for individual proteins. The DNA molecule is too large to escape from the CELL nucleus into the cytoplasm, but a "copy" is made in the form of messenger RNA (mRNA), and this travels to the ribosomes. Ribosomes attach themselves to the mRNA, then assemble the amino acids in the correct sequence to form a particular protein. Ribosomes are made up of proteins and ribosomal RNA. *See also* GENETIC CODE

**Ricardo, David** (1772–1823) English political economist. He advocated FREE TRADE and the repeal of the CORN LAWS. Ricardo's LABOR theory of value (that the price of commodities reflects the labour involved in their production), advanced in *Principles of Political Economy and Taxation* (1817), had a profound influence on Karl MARX.

**rice** Plant native to SE Asia and Indonesia, cultivated in many warm humid regions, and the main grain food for Middle and Far East countries. It provides a staple diet for half the world's population. It is an annual grass; the seed and husk is the edible portion. It is usually grown in flooded, terraced paddies with hard subsoil to prevent seepage. Species *Oryza sativa*.

**Richard I** (1157–99) King of England (1189–99), known as Richard the Lion-heart or *Coeur de Lion*. He was involved in rebellions against his father, HENRY II, before succeeding him. A leader of the Third CRUSADE (1189–92), Richard won several victories but failed to retake Jerusalem. Between 1192 and 1194 he was held prisoner by Emperor HENRY VI. Meanwhile, his brother JOHN conspired against him in England, while in France PHILIP II invaded Richard's territories. The English revolt was contained, and from 1194 Richard endeavoured to restore the ANGEVIN empire in France.

**Richard II** (1367–1400) King of England (1377–99), son of EDWARD THE BLACK PRINCE. Richard succeeded his grandfather, EDWARD III, and soon was faced with the PEASANTS' REVOLT (1381). His reign was marked by conflict with the barons. Richard's uncle, JOHN OF GAUNT, led a council of regency until 1381. On the orders of the "lords appellant", the "Merciless Parliament" (1388) executed many of Richard's supporters. Richard reasserted control and reigned ably until he began to assume authoritarian powers. In 1397–98 he exacted his revenge on the lords appellant by having the duke of Gloucester murdered and the duke of Hereford (son of John of Gaunt) banished. In 1399 Richard confiscated Gaunt's estates. Hereford led a successful revolt and was crowned HENRY IV. Richard was imprisoned and died in mysterious circumstances.

**Richard III** (1452–85) King of England (1483–85). As Duke of Gloucester, he ably supported his brother, EDWARD IV, in N England. When Edward died, Richard became protector and had the young King EDWARD V declared illegitimate and took the crown himself. Edward and his younger brother, the "Princes in the Tower", subsequently disappeared. Richard's numerous enemies supported the invasion of Henry Tudor (HENRY VII) in 1485. Richard's death at the battle of BOSWORTH ended the Wars of the ROSES.

**Richards, Viv (Isaac Vivian Alexander)** (1952– ) West Indian cricketer, b. Antigua. He made his test debut in 1974, and was West Indies captain (1985–91). Richards played English county cricket for Somerset (1974–86) and Glamorgan (1990–93). In 1991 he retired from test cricket. Richards made 24 centuries in a total of 121 test matches.

**Richardson, Sir Ralph David** (1902–83) British actor. His distinguished career included fine Shakespearean and modern performances. He appeared in numerous films, including *The Heiress* (1949) and *Greystoke: The Legend of Tarzan, Lord of the Apes* (1984), receiving Oscar nominations for both. Other films include *Dr Zhivago* (1965).

**Richardson, Samuel** (1689–1761) English novelist and printer. He wrote his first work of fiction, the novel *Pamela* (1740–41), after the age of 50. It was followed by two more novels of letters, *Clarissa* (1747–48) and *Sir Charles Grandison* (1753–54). His work prompted Henry FIELDING's parodies *An Apology for the Life of Shamela Andrews* (1741) and *Joseph Andrews* (1742).

**Richelieu, Armand Jean du Plessis, duc de** (1585–1642) French cardinal and statesman. A protégé of MARIE DE MÉDICIS and a cardinal from 1622, he became chief of the royal council in 1624. He suppressed the military and political power of the HUGUENOTS, but tolerated Protestant religious practices. He alienated many powerful Catholics by his policy of placing the interests of the state above all else. He survived several aristocratic plots against him. In the THIRTY YEARS' WAR, he formed alliances with Protestant powers against the HAPSBURGS. His more scholarly interests resulted in the foundation of the ACADÉMIE FRANÇAISE (1635).

**Richler, Mordecai** (1931– ) Canadian novelist. His satirical novels, such as *The Apprenticeship of Duddy Kravitz* (1959), explore the Jewish ghetto of his native Montreal, while the experience of North Americans in the UK is wryly observed in *Cocksure* (1968) and *St. Urbain's Horseman* (1971). Later novels include *Joshua Then and Now* (1980) and *Solomon Gursky Was Here* (1989).

**Richmond** Capital of Virginia, in E Virginia, and a port on the James River. Settled in 1637, the city was made state capital in 1779. During the CIVIL WAR it was the capital of the CONFEDERATE STATES (1861) until it fell to Union forces in 1865. Industries: metal products, tobacco processing, textiles, clothing, chemicals, publishing. Pop. (1990) 203,056.

**Richter, Burton** (1931– ) US physicist. Working with a very powerful particle ACCELERATOR, he discovered (1974) a new subatomic particle (which he named psi); it is a type of MESON. For this work Richter shared the 1976 Nobel Prize for physics with fellow American Samuel Ting, who had discovered the same particle during independent experiments.

**Richter scale** Classification of EARTHQUAKE magnitude set up in 1935 by the American geologist Charles Richter. The scale is logarithmic – each point on the scale increases by a factor of ten – and is based on the total energy released by an earthquake, as opposed to a scale of intensity that measures the damage done at a particular place.

**rickets** Disorder in which there is defective growth of bone in children; the bones fail to harden sufficiently and become bent. Due either to a lack of VITAMIN D in the diet or to insufficient sunlight to allow its synthesis in the skin, it results from the inability of the bones to calcify properly.

**Rickover, Hyman George** (1900–86) US naval officer, b. Russia. He is called the "father of the nuclear submarine" for his work on the first such vessel, *The Nautilus*, launched in 1954. In 1947 Rickover joined the Atomic Energy Commission and was director of the Navy's nuclear propulsion program until 1982. He was also known as an outspoken critic of US education standards. Rickover became a full admiral in 1973.

**Ride, Sally** (1951– ) US astronaut. As a mission specialist aboard the SPACE SHUTTLE *Challenger*, she was the first US woman to fly in space (1983). Ride resigned from the space program in 1987.

**Ridgway, Mathew Bunker** (1895–1993) US military officer. He served in the War Department (1939–42) before he became commander of the 82nd Airborne Division in World War II. He was given command of the 8th Army in Korea, and in 1951 he replaced MACARTHUR as commander of the UN forces there. In 1952 Ridgway was made US commander in Europe and he was army chief of staff (1953–55) until his retirement.

**Ridley, Nicholas** (1500–55) English bishop and Protestant martyr. As chaplain to Thomas CRANMER he helped to compile the BOOK OF COMMON PRAYER (1549). In 1553 he supported the Protestant Lady Jane GREY against the Catholic MARY I (MARY TUDOR). Convicted of heresy under Mary, he was burned at the stake.

**Riefenstahl, Leni** (1902– ) German film director who was employed by Adolf Hitler to make propaganda films. Her films include *The Blue Light* (1932), *Triumph of the Will* (1934), and *Olympische Spiele* (1936).

**Riel, Louis** (1844–85) French-Canadian revolutionary, leader of the *métis* (people of mixed French and native descent) in the Red River rebellion in Manitoba (1869–70). When it collapsed, he fled to the US. In 1884 he led resistance to Canada's western policies in Saskatchewan and set up a rebel government in 1885. He was captured and subsequently executed for treason.

**RHODE ISLAND**
**Statehood:**
May 29, 1790
**Nickname:**
Ocean State
**State bird:**
Rhode Island Red
**State flower:**
Violet
**State tree:**
Red maple
**State motto:**
Hope

R

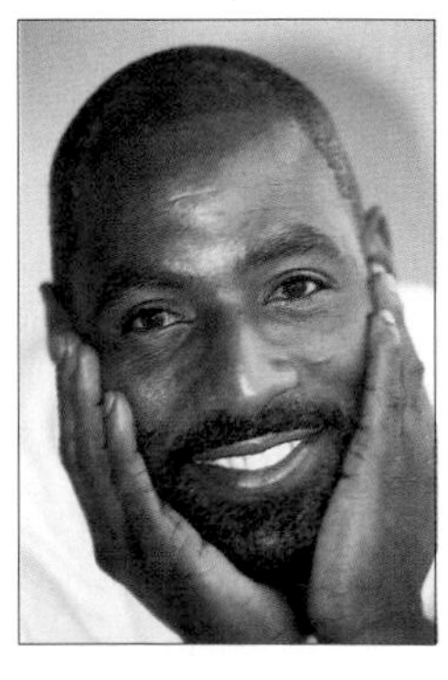

▲ **Richards** The greatest attacking batsman of his generation, in 1980 Viv Richards became the first West Indies player to make 100 centuries (100 runs) in first-class cricket. He scored more test runs than any other West Indies player in history – 8,540 runs.

## RIFT VALLEY

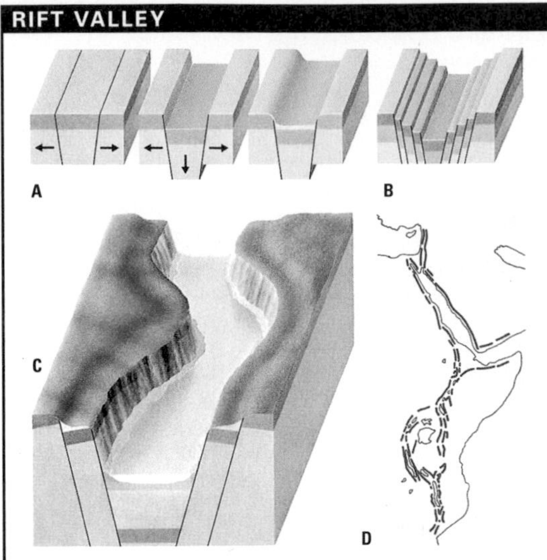


Rift valleys are formed by tension between two roughly parallel faults (A), causing downward earth movement resulting in the formation of a *graben* (trough of land between two faults). Sometimes a number of parallel faults results in land sinking in steps (B). A typical example of a step-faulted rift valley is shown (C). A series of block faults can occur on either side of a graben, sometimes tilting in the process of creating the block-faulted rift valley. The East African Rift Valley (D) is perhaps the world's best example of this geological formation.

**Riemann, Georg Friedrich Bernhard** (1826–66) German mathematician who laid the foundations for much of modern mathematics and physics. He worked on integration, functions of a complex variable, and differential and non-Euclidean GEOMETRY, which was later used in the general theory of RELATIVITY.

**rifle** FIREARM with spiral grooves (rifling) along the inside of the barrel to make the bullet spin in flight, thereby greatly increasing range and accuracy over that of a smoothbore weapon. Not until the Minié rifle of 1849 were rifled weapons widely used. During the 19th century, breech-loading and magazine rifles were developed, and since World War II, assault rifles, capable of automatic fire, have come into general use.

**rift valley** Depression formed by the subsidence of land between two parallel faults. Rift valleys are believed to be formed by thermal currents within the Earth's MANTLE that break up the CRUST into large slabs or blocks of rock, which then become fractured.

**Rift Valley** (Great Rift Valley) Steep-sided, flat-floored valley in SW Asia and E Africa. It runs from N Syria, through the Jordan Valley and the Dead Sea, and then continues as the trough of the Red Sea through E Africa to the lower valley of the Zambezi River in Mozambique. Dotted along its course are a number of significant lakes, including TANGANYIKA and Turkana. Length: *c*.4,000mi (6,400km).

**Riga** Capital of Latvia, on the Daugava River, on the Gulf of Riga. Founded at the start of the 13th century, in 1282 it joined the Hanseatic League, becoming a major Baltic port. In 1710 Latvia was captured by Peter the Great. In 1918 it became the capital of independent Latvia. In 1940, when Latvia was incorporated into the Soviet Union, thousands of its citizens were deported or executed. Under German occupation from 1941, the city reverted to Soviet rule in 1944 and subsequently suffered further deportations and an influx of Russian emigrants. In 1991 it reassumed its status as capital of an independent Latvia. Industries: shipbuilding, engineering, electronic equipment, chemicals, textiles. Pop (1991) 910,200.

**rigor mortis** Stiffening of the body after death brought about by chemical changes in muscle tissue. Onset is gradual from minutes to hours, and it disappears within about 24 hours.

▶ **Rio de Janeiro** Famous for its carnival, held annually before Lent, Rio de Janeiro is the second-largest city in Brazil. it has many remarkable buildings and monuments, ranging from 17- and 18th-century churches to striking examples of modern architecture. Its Copacabana beach is world-famous.

**Rilke, Rainer Maria** (1875–1926) German lyric poet, b. Prague. His first volume, *The Book of Hours* (1899–1903), was inspired by visits to Russia. During a 12-year stay in Paris he developed the "object poem," used in *New Poems* (1907–08); thereafter he published little until 1922, when *Sonnets to Orpheus* and his masterpiece *Duino Elegies* both appeared.

**Rimbaud, Arthur** (1854–91) French anarchic poet who influenced SYMBOLISM. He had a stormy relationship with VERLAINE, under whose tutelage he wrote *The Drunken Boat* (1871). In 1873 they separated and *A Season in Hell* appeared. Rimbaud abandoned poetry to travel, returning to Paris shortly before his death. In 1886 *Les Illuminations* was mischievously published by Verlaine as the work of the late Arthur Rimbaud.

**Rimsky-Korsakov, Nikolai Andreievich** (1844–1908) Russian composer, one of the RUSSIAN FIVE. His operas include *The Snow Maiden* (1881) and *The Golden Cockerel* (1907), and among his most popular orchestral works are *Sheherazade* (1888), *Capriccio espagnole* (1887), and *The Flight of the Bumblebee* from the opera *Czar Saltan* (1900).

**ringworm** Fungus infection of the skin, scalp, or nails. The commonest type of ringworm is athlete's foot (*tinea pedis*). It is treated with antifungal preparations.

**Rio de Janeiro** City on Guanabara Bay, SE Brazil. Discovered by Europeans in 1502, it was later colonized by the French, then the Portuguese. By the 18th century it was a major outlet for gold mined in the hinterland. In 1763 it became the seat of the viceroy and from 1834–1960 it was Brazil's capital. The second-largest city in Brazil, it is its commercial and industrial center. Its warm climate and beaches make it a popular tourist resort. There are large shanty towns surrounding the city. Industries: coffee, sugar refining, shipbuilding, pharmaceuticals, publishing and printing. Pop. (1991) 5,336,179.

**Rio Grande** River in North America. It rises in the San Juan Mountains of SW Colorado, and flows generally S through New Mexico. It forms the border between Texas and Mexico and empties into the Gulf of Mexico just E of Brownsville, Texas, and Matamoros, Mexico. The river is largely unnavigable and is used for irrigation and hydroelectricity. Length: *c*.1,885mi (3,035km).

**riot** Uncontrolled crowd violence, usually resulting in indiscriminate destruction. Most modern police forces include special riot squads. Methods of crowd control include water cannon, CS gas (tear gas), plastic bullets and, in some countries, electronic stun guns.

**Ripley, George** (1802–80) US social reformer. In 1841 he established an experimental community, Brook Farm, in Massachusetts. It was based on a farming and handicraft economy, with communal ownership of property. After it failed (1847), he continued his advocacy of social reform as a writer and editor in *The Harbinger* and other publications.

**Risorgimento** (It. resurgence) Nationalist movement resulting in the unification of Italy in 1859–70. With the restoration of Austrian and Bourbon rule in 1815, revolutionary groups formed, notably the Young Italy movement of MAZZINI, whose aim was a single, democratic republic. His influence was at its peak in the REVOLUTIONS OF 1848. In Sardinia-Piedmont (the only independent Italian state), the aim of the chief minister, CAVOUR, was a parliamentary monarchy under the royal house of Savoy. Securing the support of France under Napoleon III in a war against Austria, he acquired much of Austrian-dominated N Italy in 1859. In 1860 GARIBALDI conquered Sicily and Naples. Although Garibaldi belonged to the republican tradition of Mazzini, he cooperated with Cavour, and the kingdom of Italy was proclaimed in 1861 under VICTOR EMMANUEL II of Savoy. Other regions were acquired later. Rome, the future capital, was seized when the French garrison withdrew in 1870.

**river** Large natural channel containing water which flows downhill under gravity. A river system is a network of connecting channels. It can be divided into tributaries which collect water and sediment, the main trunk river, and the dispersing system at the river's mouth where much of the sediment is deposited. The discharge of a river is the volume of water flowing past a point in a given time. The velocity of a river is controlled by the slope, its depth, and the roughness of the riverbed. Rivers carry sediment as they flow, by the processes of traction (rolling), saltation (jumping), suspension (carrying), and solution. Most river sediment is carried during flood conditions, but as a river returns to normal flow it deposits sediment. This can result in the EROSION of a river channel or in the building up of floodplains, sand, and gravel banks. All rivers tend to flow in a twisting pattern, even if the slope is relatively steep, because water flow is naturally turbulent. Over time, on shallow slopes, small bends grow into large MEANDERS. The current flows faster on the outside of bends eroding the bank while sedimentation occurs on the inside of bends where the current is slowest. This causes the curves to exaggerate forming loops. Rivers flood when their channels cannot contain the discharge. Flood risk can be reduced by straightening the channel, dredging sediment, or making the channel deeper by raising the banks. *See also* DELTA; LEVÉE; OXBOW

**Rivera, Diego** (1886–1957) Mexican painter, married to fellow artist Frida KAHLO. He is one of Mexico's three great 20th-century muralists (the others being OROZCO and Siqueiros). He often used symbolism and allegory to depict events in Mexico's history, and to express his hope for a Marxist future. His work adorns a number of public buildings in Mexico City.

**Riviera** Region of SE France and NW Italy, on the Mediterranean Sea, extending 230mi (370km) from Cannes, France, to La Spezia, Italy. Its spectacular scenery and mild climate make it a leading tourist center. Resorts include NICE and CANNES in France and MONTE CARLO in Monaco.

**Riyadh** Capital of Saudi Arabia, in the E central part of the country, *c.*235mi (378km) inland from the Persian Gulf. In the early 19th century it was the domain of the Saudi dynasty, becoming capital of Saudi Arabia in 1932. The chief industry is oil refining. Pop. (1994 est.) 1,500,000.

**RNA** (ribonucleic acid) Chemical (NUCLEIC ACID) that controls the synthesis of PROTEIN in a cell and is the genetic material in some viruses. The molecules of RNA in a cell are copied from DNA and consist of a single strand of nucleotides, each containing the sugar ribose, phosphoric acid, and one of four bases: adenine, guanine, cytosine, or uracil. Messenger RNA (mRNA) carries the information for protein synthesis from DNA in the cell NUCLEUS to the RIBOSOMES in the CYTOPLASM. Transfer RNA (tRNA) brings AMINO ACIDS to their correct position on the mRNA. Each AMINO ACID is specified by a sequence of three bases in mRNA.

**Roach, Hal** (1892–1992) US film producer. He is best remembered for his silent comedy shorts. Cofounder of The Rolin Film Company in 1915, he encouraged Harold LLOYD, LAUREL AND HARDY, and Will ROGERS.

**roach** European freshwater carp found in muddy and brackish waters. Colors include silver, white, and green. Length: to 16in (40cm). Family Cyprinidae; species *Rutilus rutilus*.

**road runner** Fast-running, desert cuckoo that lives in SW US. It has a crested head, streaked brownish plumage, long, strong legs, and long tail. It feeds on ground animals including snakes, which it kills with its long, pointed beak. Family Cuculidae; species *Geococcyx californianus*.

**Robbe-Grillet, Alain** (1922– ) French novelist and theoretician, one of the originators of the NOUVEAU ROMAN in the 1950s. He later worked in films, writing the screenplay for *Last Year at Marienbad* (1961). His books include the novels *The Erasers* (1953), *Topology of a Phantom City* (1976), and *Djinn* (1981), and the critical work, *Toward a New Novel* (1963).

**Robbins, Jerome** (1918–98) US ballet choreographer and dancer. In 1940 he joined the American Ballet Theater. Robbins is celebrated for his choreography of Broadway musicals, including *The King and I* (1951, filmed 1956), *West Side Story* (1957, filmed 1961), and *Fiddler on the Roof* (1964, filmed 1971). From 1983 to 1990 he was joint ballet master of the New York City Ballet with Peter MARTINS.

**Robert I (the Bruce)** (1274–1329) King of Scotland (1306–29). Descended from a prominent Anglo-Norman family, he swore fealty to EDWARD I of England (1296) but joined the Scottish revolt against the English in 1297. After killing a rival, he had himself crowned king of Scotland (1306) but, defeated at Methven (1306) by the English, he fled the kingdom. Returning on Edward's death (1307), the Bruce renewed the struggle, and in 1314 he defeated the English at BANNOCKBURN, securing Scottish independence.

**Robert II** (1054–1134) (Robert Curthose) Duke of Normandy (1087–1106), eldest son of WILLIAM I (THE CONQUEROR). He disputed Normandy and England with his younger brothers, WILLIAM II and HENRY I, and played a prominent part in the First CRUSADE (1096–99). In 1106 he was defeated and captured by Henry and imprisoned for life.

**Robeson, Paul** (1898–1976) US actor and singer. He played the title role in Eugene O'Neill's *Emperor Jones* and Othello in Shakespeare's tragedy. Robeson is best known for his bass renditions of Negro spirituals and "Ol' Man River" in the musical, *Show Boat* (1927). In 1952 Robeson was awarded the Stalin Peace Prize, and his association with communism led to ostracism in the USA. He lived abroad from 1958 to 1963.

**RIVER**

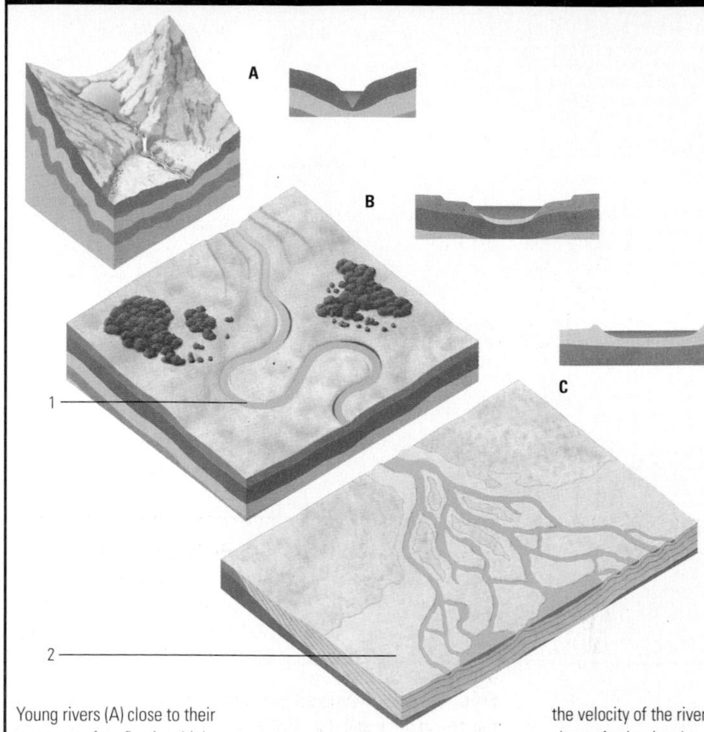


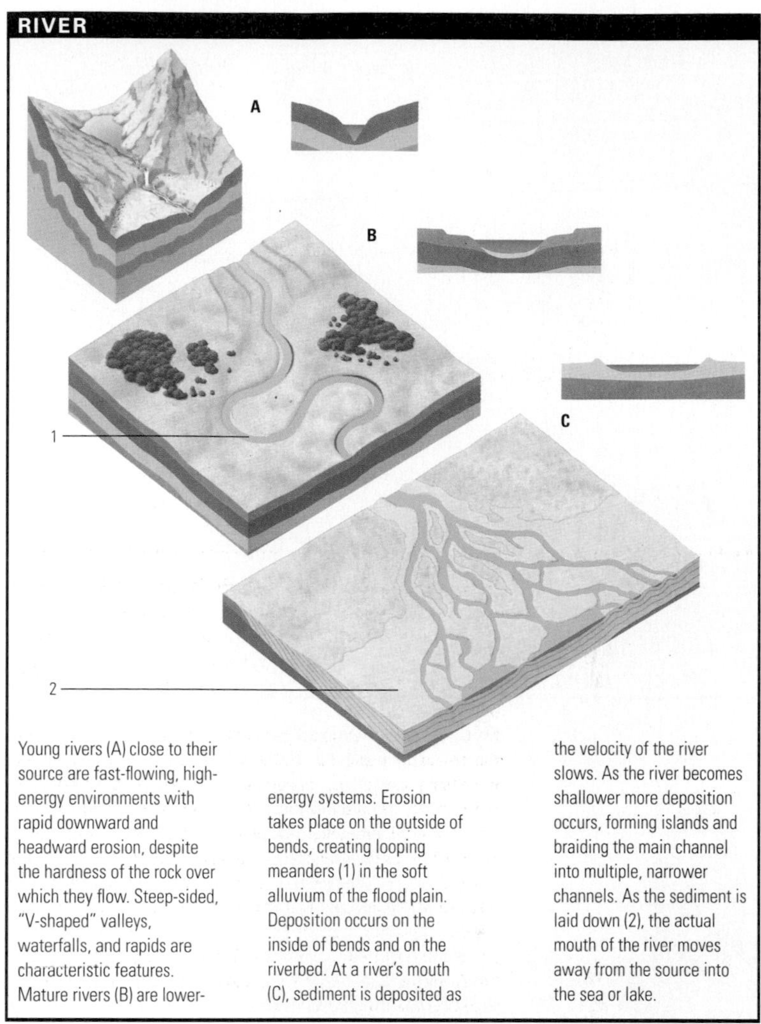

Young rivers (A) close to their source are fast-flowing, high-energy environments with rapid downward and headward erosion, despite the hardness of the rock over which they flow. Steep-sided, "V-shaped" valleys, waterfalls, and rapids are characteristic features. Mature rivers (B) are lower-energy systems. Erosion takes place on the outside of bends, creating looping meanders (1) in the soft alluvium of the flood plain. Deposition occurs on the inside of bends and on the riverbed. At a river's mouth (C), sediment is deposited as the velocity of the river slows. As the river becomes shallower more deposition occurs, forming islands and braiding the main channel into multiple, narrower channels. As the sediment is laid down (2), the actual mouth of the river moves away from the source into the sea or lake.

◀ **Rivera** *La Civilisation Tarasque: Dyeing Material.* Despite being interested in cubism and influenced by the work of Henri Rousseau, Diego Rivera's work is rooted in the Mexican tradition. Characteristic of his style are simplified, flat geometric forms in expressive colors.

R

ROBOT

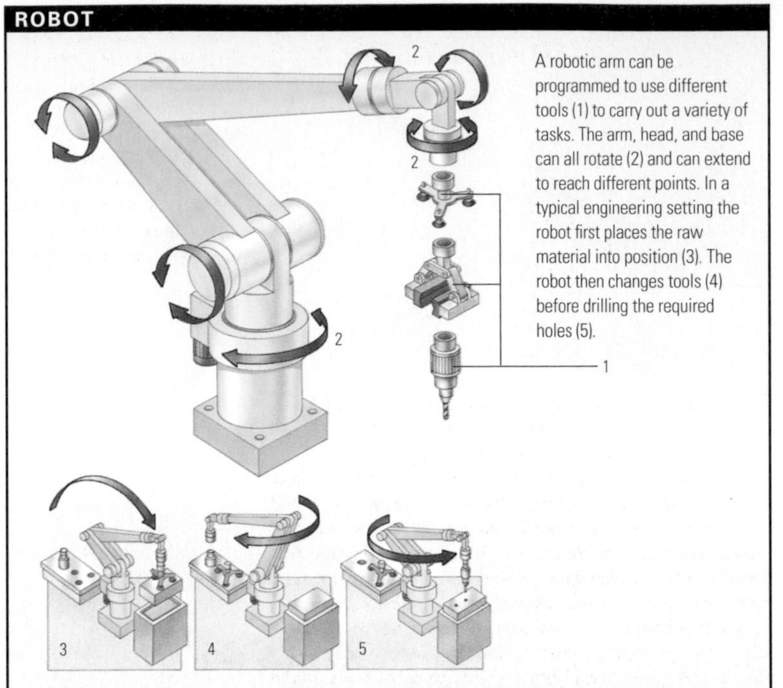

A robotic arm can be programmed to use different tools (1) to carry out a variety of tasks. The arm, head, and base can all rotate (2) and can extend to reach different points. In a typical engineering setting the robot first places the raw material into position (3). The robot then changes tools (4) before drilling the required holes (5).
1
2
3
4
5


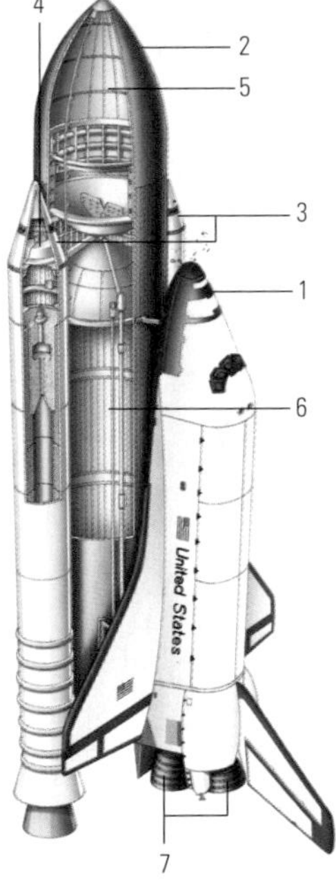


▲ **rocket** The space shuttle has three main components when it is launched. The orbiter (1) is attached to an external fuel tank (2), which is bracketed by booster rockets (3). The booster rockets are filled with solid fuel, and once the fuel has been burned, the boosters are jettisoned and return to Earth by parachute (4). The solid fuel is a mixture of an iron oxide catalyst, an oxidizer, and powdered aluminum. The liquid oxygen (5) and liquid hydrogen (6), contained in the external fuel tank, feed the shuttle's three main engines (7).

**Robespierre, Maximilien François Marie Isidore de** (1758–94) French revolutionary leader. Elected to the National Assembly in 1789, he advocated democracy and liberal reform. In 1791 he became leader of the JACOBINS, and gained credit when his opposition to war with Austria was justified by French defeats. With the king and the GIRONDINS discredited, Robespierre led the republican revolution of 1792 and was elected to the National Convention. His election to the Committee of Public Safety (June 1793) heralded the REIGN OF TERROR. Ruthless methods seemed less urgent after French victories in war, and Robespierre was arrested in the coup of 9th Thermidor (July 27) 1794 and executed.

**robin** Small Eurasian bird, with a characteristic red-orange breast. Length: to 5.5in (14cm). Family Turdidae; species *Erithacus rubecula*. The much larger American robin (*Turdus migratorius*) is a member of the thrush family and is *c*.10in (25cm) long.

**Robin Hood** Legendary English outlaw. Medieval tradition describes him as a displaced nobleman living with his outlaw band in Sherwood Forest, near Nottingham. Robin robbed the rich and gave to the poor, fighting a running battle with the sheriff of Nottingham and the corrupt administration of King JOHN.

**Robinson, Edward G.** (1893–1973) US movie actor, b. Emanuel Goldenberg. His most famous role was that of the gangster in *Little Caesar* (1930). Other films include *Double Indemnity* (1944) and *The Night has a Thousand Eyes* (1948).

**Robinson, Edwin Arlington** (1869–1935) US poet. His first volume of poems, *The Torrent and The Night Before* (1896), was followed by *The Town down the River* (1910), *The Man against the Sky* (1916), and *The Three Taverns* (1920). He was awarded the Pulitzer Prize in 1921, 1924, and 1927.

**Robinson, Jackie (Jack Roosevelt)** (1919–72) US baseball player, the first African-American player in the major leagues. Signed by the Brooklyn Dodgers in 1947, he compiled a lifetime batting average of .311 before retiring in 1956. He helped the Dodgers to six World Series.

**Robinson, Mary** (1944– ) Irish stateswoman, president (1990–97). In 1969 she entered politics as a senator. Robinson became the Republic of Ireland's first woman president. Her stand on human rights and support for the campaign to liberalize laws on abortion and divorce gave the office a high profile. In 1997 Robinson became UN Commissioner for Human Rights.

**Robinson, Sugar Ray** (1920–89) US boxer, b. Walker Smith. He was world welterweight champion (1946–50) and won the middleweight title five times (twice in 1951, 1955, 1957, 1958–60). Robinson lost only 19 of his 202 professional bouts.

**robot** Automated machine used to carry out various tasks. Robots are often computer-controlled, the most common type having a single arm that can move in any direction. Such robots are used to carry out various tasks in car manufacturing.

**Rob Roy** (1671–1734) Scottish outlaw, b. Robert MacGregor. He took to banditry after his lands were confiscated by the Duke of Montrose. Rob Roy took part in the JACOBITE rising of 1715. His exploits were romanticized in Sir Walter SCOTT's novel *Rob Roy* (1817).

**Rochester** City and port of entry in W New York, 70mi (113km) ENE of Buffalo, on Lake Ontario. The first permanent settlement was made in 1812 and industrial growth was spurred by Erie Canal. Specialized industries developed from 1850, including Eastman Kodak. Industries: cameras, photographic supplies, office equipment. Pop. (1990) 230,356.

**rock** Solid material that makes up the Earth's crust. Rocks are classified by origin into three major groups: IGNEOUS ROCKS, SEDIMENTARY ROCKS, and METAMORPHIC ROCKS.

**rock** (rock and roll) Form of popular music characterized by amplified guitars and singing, often with repetitive lyrics and driving rhythms. Rock music appealed largely to a white audience who found its forerunner, RHYTHM AND BLUES, inaccessible. It developed out of rural US BLUES and FOLK MUSIC to become a major form of cultural expression in the 1960s. Rock and roll was popularized by Bill HALEY and the film *Rock Around the Clock* (1956). Its modern offshoots include heavy metal, grunge, and PUNK.

**Rockefeller, John Davison** (1839–1937) US industrialist and philanthropist. In 1863 Rockefeller built an oil refinery in Cleveland, which was incorporated in 1870 into the Standard Oil Company of Ohio. On retirement, he devoted his attention to charitable corporations, donating *c*.US$550 million. In 1913 he founded the Rockefeller Foundation.

**Rockefeller, Nelson Aldrich** (1908–79) US vice president (1974–77) and New York governor, nephew of John D. ROCKEFELLER. He was elected governor in 1958 as a Republican. Rockefeller was re-elected three times before resigning in 1973. In 1974 President Gerald FORD picked him to fill the vacant office of vice president.

**rocket** Slender, tapering MISSILE or craft powered by a rocket ENGINE. Most of its volume contains fuel; the remainder is the payload (such as an explosive, scientific instruments, or a spacecraft). **Liquid-fueled** rockets use a fuel (such as liquid hydrogen) and an oxidizer (usually liquid oxygen), which are burned together in the engine. **Solid-fueled** rockets have both fuel and oxidizer in a solid mixture. Rockets can be single-stage or multistage. They gain THRUST from the reaction (referred to in the third of NEWTON'S LAWS of motion) produced by rapid, continuous output of exhaust gases. The walls of a rocket's combustion chamber and the exit nozzle must be cooled to protect them against the heat of the escaping gases, whose temperature may be as high as 3,000°C. Today, payloads are put into orbit by the SPACE SHUTTLE. Konstantin TSIOLKOVSKY is regarded as the "father of astronautics." In 1926 Robert H. GODDARD launched the first liquid-fueled rocket. During World War II Wernher VON BRAUN developed the first long-range GUIDED MISSILES. Saturn V, the largest rocket ever built, delivered 7.5 million lb (3.4 million kg) of thrust.

**Rockwell, Norman** (1894–1978) US illustrator, an immensely popular painter of rural and small-town life. He was best known for the covers he created for *The Saturday Evening Post* (1916–63).

**Rocky Mountains** Major mountain system in W North America. Extending from Mexico to the Bering Strait, N of the Arctic Circle, the mountains form the CONTINENTAL DIVIDE. The highest point is Mount Elbert.

**rococo** Playful, light style of art, architecture, and decoration that developed in early 18th-century France. It soon spread to Germany, Austria, Italy, and Britain. Rococo brought to interior decoration swirls, scrolls, shells, and arabesques. It was also applied to furniture, porcelain, and silverware. Rococo painters include WATTEAU, FRAGONARD, and BOUCHER. It was superseded by the more somber style of NEOCLASSICISM.

**rodent** Any member of the vast order Rodentia, the most numerous and widespread of all mammals, characterized by a pair of gnawing incisor teeth in both the upper and lower jaws. Numbering close to 2,000 species, including the rat, MOUSE, SQUIRREL, BEAVER, DORMOUSE, PORCUPINE, and GUINEA PIG, rodents live throughout the world. Most are small and light.

**rodeo** Sport with origins in the practical work of a COWBOY. A major entertainment in North America, its seven main events are saddle bronco (unbroken horse) riding, bareback bronco riding, bull riding, calf roping, single-steer roping and team roping, and steer wrestling.

**Rodgers, Richard Charles** (1902–79) US composer of BROADWAY musicals. He worked first with Lorenz Hart and then with Oscar HAMMERSTEIN on successful musicals, including *Oklahoma!* (1943), *Carousel* (1945), *South Pacific* (1949), *The King and I* (1951), and *The Sound of Music* (1959).

**Rodin, Auguste** (1840–1917) French sculptor. His first major work, *The Age of Bronze* (exhibited in 1878), caused a scandal because the naked figure was so naturalistic. His next great project was *The Gates of Hell*, unfinished studies for a bronze door for the Musée des arts décoratifs, Paris. It provided him with the subjects for further great sculptures, including *The Thinker* (1880), *The Kiss* (1886), and *Fugit Amor* (1897). Perhaps his most extraordinary work is the full-length bronze of BALZAC, completed in 1897.

**Rodrigo, Joaquin** (1901– ) Spanish composer. He made his name with the *Concierto de Aranjuez* (1939), for guitar and orchestra. He also wrote concertos for violin, cello, piano, harp, and flute as well as other pieces for guitar and orchestra.

**Roebling, John Augustus** (1806–69) US engineer and industrialist, b. Germany. In 1831 he emigrated to the US and became a civil engineer. Roebling directed the construction of suspension bridges across the Allegheny and Niagara rivers. In 1869 he was appointed chief engineer of the Brooklyn Bridge, but was killed in an accident during an early survey. His son **Washington Augustus** Roebling (1837–1926) succeeded his father as chief engineer on the Brooklyn Bridge, overseeing its completion in 1883.

**Roethke, Theodore** (1908–63) US poet. His first volume was *Opera House* (1941). Other collections include *The Waking: Poems 1933–53* (1953), which won both a Pulitzer Prize and the National Book Award.

**Rogers, Ginger** (1911–95) US actress and dancer. Rogers is chiefly remembered for her dancing partnership with Fred ASTAIRE in film musicals, such as *Flying Down To Rio* (1933), *Top Hat* (1934) and *Swing Time* (1936). She won an Oscar for best actress in *Kitty Foyle* (1940).

**Rogers, Will (William Penn Adair)** (1879–1935) US comedian. He appeared in VAUDEVILLE as a cowboy and joined the Ziegfeld Follies in 1914. Through Rogers' contributions to film, radio, and a syndicated newspaper column, he became known as the "cowboy philosopher."

**role** In social science, a person's perception of how to act in a given situation. For children, learning roles is central to the process of social development. Formal roles, such as teachers, doctors, and police officers, help to define our behavior in impersonal situations, while informal roles, such as husband and mother, are founded on personal relationships. *See also* STATUS

**roller** Any of several species of Eurasian birds that roll over in flight. An occasional visitor to Britain, *Coracius garrulus*, has blue-green plumage and flies as far north as Sweden; it usually winters in Africa. Family Coraciidae.

**Rolling Stones, The** British rock group, formed in 1962 around vocalist Mick Jagger (1943– ), guitarist Keith Richards (1943– ), bassist Bill Wyman (1941– ) and drummer Charlie Watts (1942– ). Their rebellious posturing courted great controversy and publicity and a founder member, Brian Jones (1942–69), died after a drugs overdose. Early hit singles included "Satisfaction" (1965), "Paint it Black" (1966) and "Jumpin' Jack Flash" (1968). Million-selling records include *Beggar's Banquet* (1968), and *Exile on Main Street* (1972).

**ROM** (acronym for **R**ead-**O**nly **M**emory) INTEGRATED CIRCUITS (chips) that act as a permanent store for DATA (information) required by a COMPUTER. The contents of ordinary ROM chips are set by the manufacturer and cannot be altered by the user. The stored data is available to a computer's MICROPROCESSOR whenever it is switched on.

◀ **Rolling Stones** Formed in the 1960s, the Rolling Stones remain one of the most successful rock and roll bands. With their aggressive music and overtly sexual and political lyrics, they contrasted with the Beatles in the 1960s. In the 1970s, their extravagantly staged worldwide tours increased their popularity. They continue to tour and record.

**Roman art and architecture** Classical art and architecture of ancient ROME. Prior to 400 BC, Roman art was largely ETRUSCAN art in the form of tomb decorations, after which Greek influence became dominant. Few examples of later Roman painting have survived: the best examples are found in the Italian towns of POMPEII and HERCULANEUM. Another common art form was the MOSAIC. Floors and walls were decorated mostly in elaborate geometric patterns, but mosaics were also created to depict everyday scenes, or gods and goddesses. In sculpture the Romans excelled in portrait busts and reliefs. In architecture, notable features include their adoption of the ARCH, VAULT, and DOME. Fine examples include the Pantheon and COLOSSEUM in Rome.

**Roman Britain** Period of British history from the Roman invasion in the reign of CLAUDIUS I (AD 43) until *c*.410. The occupation included Wales but not Ireland nor most of Caledonia (Scotland). Its northern frontier was marked by HADRIAN'S WALL from *c*.130. Only the English lowlands were thoroughly Romanized, but in that region Roman rule brought a period of prosperity not matched for more than 1,000 years. Roman power disintegrated in the 3rd century. By 400, attacks from Ireland, Scotland, and the continental mainland were increasing, but Roman troops were withdrawn to deal with enemies nearer home. In 410 the Emperor Honorius warned the Britons to expect no further help. Local Romano-British kings held out for more than 100 years before lowland Britain was overrun by the ANGLO-SAXONS.

**Roman Catholic Church** Christian denomination that acknowledges the supremacy of the pope (*see* PAPACY; PAPAL INFALLIBILITY). An important aspect of the doctrine is the primacy given to the Virgin MARY, whom Roman Catholics believe to be the only human born without sin (IMMACULATE CONCEPTION). Before the REFORMATION in the 16th century, the word "Catholic" applied to the Western Church as a whole, as distinguished from the EASTERN ORTHODOX CHURCH based at Constantinople. The Reformation led to a tendency for the Roman Catholic Church to be characterized by rigid adherence to doctrinal tradition from the 16th to the early 20th century. The desire for a reunited Christendom led to a more liberal attitude in the mid-20th century. There are some 600 million Roman Catholics worldwide, with large numbers in S Europe, Latin America, and the Philippines. The government of the Church is episcopal, with archbishops and bishops responsible for provinces and dioceses. The center of the Roman Catholic liturgical ritual is the MASS or EUCHARIST. Since the second VATICAN COUNCIL (1962–65), the Roman Catholic Church has undergone marked changes, notably the replacement of Latin by the vernacular as the language of the liturgy. There are *c*.600 million Roman Catholics worldwide.

**romance** (Old French *romanz*, vulgar tongue) Literary form, typically a heroic tale or ballad usually in verse. The form derives from the medieval narratives of TROUBADOURS. The romance spread throughout Europe during the 12th century, was used in English by CHAUCER, remaining popular through the 16th century

**Romance languages** Indo-European Languages that evolved from LATIN. They include Italian, French, Spanish, Portuguese, Romanian, Catalan, Provençal, and Romansh (a language spoken in parts of Switzerland).

▲ **Roman art and architecture** During the imperial period of Roman art, from the 1st to the 3rd century AD, jewelry-making reached a level not to be surpassed until the Renaissance in the 16th century. Early on, the snake motif was very popular, along with other decorative styles borrowed from Greek and Etruscan culture. Soon, however, Roman jewelry began to make greater use of gemstones and intricate, pierced decoration.

R

**Roman empire** Mediterranean empire formed (*c*.27 BC) by AUGUSTUS after the assassination (*c*.44 BC) of Julius CAESAR. Its power centre was ancient ROME. The Romans adopted the culture of ancient Greece, but their empire was based on military power and ROMAN LAW. In terms of technology and arguably culture, Roman civilization was not surpassed in Europe until the Renaissance. By the death of AUGUSTUS (AD 14), the empire included most of Asia Minor, Syria, Egypt, and the whole North African coast. In the 1st and 2nd centuries AD Britain was conquered; in the E, Roman rule extended to the Caspian Sea and the Persian Gulf, and further territory, including DACIA (Transylvania), was added in SE Europe. The empire was at its greatest extent at the death of TRAJAN (AD 117), when it included all the lands around the Mediterranean and extended to N Britain, the Black Sea, and Mesopotamia. HADRIAN (r.117–138) called a halt to further expansion. Rome reached the height of its power during the first 150 years of imperial rule, becoming a city of grand, monumental buildings with perhaps 1 million inhabitants. In the 3rd century AD pressure from Germanic tribes and the Persians, plus economic difficulties, contributed to the breakdown of government. Armies in the provinces broke away from Rome. DIOCLETIAN restored order, and from his time the empire tended to be split into E and W divisions. CONSTANTINE founded an E capital at CONSTANTINOPLE (330). Rome was increasingly challenged by different peoples, such as the GOTHS who sacked the city in 410. By 500 the Roman empire in the west had ceased to exist. The Eastern or BYZANTINE EMPIRE survived until 1453.

**Romanesque** Architectural and artistic style that spread throughout W Europe during the 11th and 12th centuries. English Romanesque architecture includes ANGLO-SAXON and NORMAN styles. *See also* ARCH; RIB; VAULT

**Romania** Balkan republic of SE Europe. *See* country feature

**Romanian** Official language of Romania, spoken by up to 25 million people in Romania, Macedonia, Albania, and N Greece. It belongs to the Romance branch of the Indo-European family. Originally written in CYRILLIC characters, Romanian has used the Roman alphabet since 1860.

**Roman law** System of CIVIL LAW developed between 753 BC and the 5th century AD, which forms the basis of civil law in many parts of the world. Roman law was enacted originally by the PATRICIANS, then, after 287 BC, by the PLEBEIAN assemblies. From 367 BC magistrates (*praetors*) proclaimed the legal principles (*edicta*) which became an important source of law known as *jus honorium*. The emperor could also enact laws and by the mid-2nd century AD became the sole creator of laws. Roman law can be divided into two parts: *jus civile* (civil law), which applied only to Roman citizens and was codified in the TWELVE TABLES of 450 BC; and *jus gentium*, originally applying to foreigners in Rome and to others within Roman lands who were not citizens, which gradually merged into *jus civile*. Roman law was codified by the Emperor JUSTINIAN I (r.527–64) and was adapted by many later invaders.

**Roman numeral** Letter used by the ancient Romans and succeeding European civilizations to represent numbers before the adoption of Arabic numerals. There were seven individual letters: I (1), V (5), X (10), L (50), C (100), D (500), and M (1,000). Combinations were used to represent the numbers. From 1 to 10 they ran: I, II, III, IV, V, VI, VII, VIII, IX, and X. The tens ran: X, XX, XXX, XL, L, and so on up to XC, which represented 90.

**Romanov** Russian imperial dynasty (1613–1917). Michael, the first Romanov czar, was elected in 1613. His descendants, especially PETER I (THE GREAT) and CATHERINE II (THE GREAT), a Romanov by marriage, transformed Russia into the world's largest empire. The last Romanov emperor, NICHOLAS II, abdicated in 1917 and was later murdered by the BOLSHEVIKS.

**Romans** In the New Testament, a letter by St. PAUL to the Christians of Rome, written *c*.57, probably while Paul was in Corinth. In it, he declares the universality of the saving power of God realized in the life, death, and resurrection of Jesus.

**romanticism** Late 18th- and early 19th-century cultural movement. Its exponents valued individual experience and intuition, rather than the orderly, concrete universe of CLASSICAL artists. For this reason, romantics and classicists are often seen as opposites, but in fact they shared a belief in IDEALISM, as opposed to the exponents of REALISM and RATIONALISM. An emphasis on nature rather than science was also a characteristic. Leading European literary romantics include GOETHE, SHELLEY, BYRON, KEATS, and SCHILLER. In the US, POE, LONGFELLOW, WHITMAN, COOPER, HAWTHORNE, and MELVILLE typified the style. William BLAKE was both a romantic poet and artist. Other artists include DELACROIX, Caspar David FRIEDRICH, GÉRICAULT, and TURNER, and the US artists of the HUDSON RIVER SCHOOL.

**romanticism** Period of music history lasting from *c*.1800 to 1910. It is characterized by the primacy of emotional expression and imagination, in contrast to the restrained and strict forms of the CLASSICAL era. Orchestras expanded as composers experimented with unusual and colorful orchestration to express extra-musical influences. Leading romantic composers include WAGNER, BERLIOZ, MENDELSSOHN, SCHUMANN, CHOPIN, and LISZT.

**Romany** (Gypsy) Nomadic people and their language. Romanies are believed to have originated in N India, and now inhabit Europe, Asia, America, Africa, and Australia. They first appeared in Europe in the 15th century. Their nomadic lifestyle has aroused prejudice, often resulting in persecution. Their folklore is part of popular tradition. The Romany language originated in N India, and like HINDI and SANSKRIT to which it is related, it belongs to the Indo-Iranian branch of the family of INDO-EUROPEAN LANGUAGES. Many Romanies today speak it as a second language, but there is little written Romany.

**Rome** (Roma) Capital of Italy, on the Tiber River, W central Italy. Founded in the 8th century BC, it was probably an Etruscan city-kingdom in the 6th century BC. The Roman Republic was founded *c*.500 BC. By the 3rd century BC, Rome ruled most of Italy and began to expand overseas. In the 1st century AD the city was transformed as successive emperors built temples, palaces, public baths, arches, and columns. It remained the capital of the Roman empire until 330 AD. It was sacked in the 5th century during Barbarian invasions and its population (already in decline) fell rapidly. In the Middle Ages Rome became the seat of the PAPACY. It was sacked again in 1527 by the army of the emperor Charles V. Rome flourished again in the 16th and 17th centuries. Italian troops occupied it in 1870, and in 1871 it became the capital of unified Italy. MUSSOLINI did much to transform Rome into a modern capital. It is home to the VATICAN CITY. Industries: tourism, pharmaceuticals, chemicals, oil refining, engineering, textiles. Pop. (1991) 2,775,250.

**Rome, ancient** Capital of the Roman republic. According to tradition, Rome was founded in 753 BC by ROMULUS AND REMUS. By 509 BC the Latin-speaking Romans had thrown off the rule of ETRUSCAN kings and established an independent republic dominated by an aristocratic elite. Its history was one of continual expansion, and by 340 BC Rome controlled Italy S of the Po River. By the 3rd century BC the PLEBEIAN class had largely gained political equality. The PUNIC WARS gave it dominance of the Mediterranean in the 2nd century BC, when major eastward expansion began with the conquest of the Greek Aegean. The republican constitution was strained by social

▶ **Romanesque** The enduring monuments of Romanesque architecture are the churches and cathedrals of the period. Many regional differences in style existed. Dating from the 11th century, Monza Cathedral in Lombardy, shown here, is a prime example of a central Italian Romanesque building. The dominant feature of its facade is the striped pattern of facing material, a common motif of the Italian Romanesque – surface ornamentation was very important. The entrance is elaborated with columns, another popular design feature, with a rose window above.

division and military dictatorship. SPARTACUS' slave revolt was crushed by POMPEY, who emerged as SULLA's successor. Pompey and Julius CAESAR formed the First Triumverate (60 BC). Caesar emerged as leader and greatly extended Rome's territory and influence. His assassination led to the formation of the ROMAN EMPIRE under AUGUSTUS (27 BC).

**Rome, Treaties of** (1957) Two agreements establishing the European Economic Community, now the EUROPEAN UNION (EU) and the EUROPEAN ATOMIC ENERGY COMMISSION (EURATOM). The 1957 treaty was extensively amended by the Single European Act (1986) and the MAASTRICHT TREATY (1992), but still forms the basis of the EU.

**Rommel, Erwin** (1891–1944) German general. He commanded tanks in France in 1940 and later led the AFRIKA KORPS in a victorious campaign in North Africa, until defeated by the British at EL ALAMEIN (1942). Transferred to France in 1943, he was unable to repel the invasion of NORMANDY and was wounded. Implicated in the plot against Hitler in July 1944, he committed suicide.

**Romulus and Remus** In Roman mythology, founders of ROME. Twin bothers, they were said to be sons of Mars. Amulius, who had usurped the throne, ordered the babies to be drowned in the Tiber. They survived and were suckled by a wolf before being found by a shepherd, Faustulus. They built a city on the site of their rescue. Romulus killed Remus during a quarrel.

**Ronsard, Pierre de** (1524–85) French poet and leader of the PLÉIADE. His *Odes* (1550) and *Les Amours* (1552) brought him fame and royal patronage. Other works include the incomplete national epic *La Franciade* and *Sonnets pour Hélène* (1578), some of his finest love poems.

**Röntgen, Wilhelm Konrad** (1845–1923) German physicist. In 1895 Röntgen discovered X-RAYS. He also did important work on electricity, the specific heats of gases, and the heat CONDUCTIVITY of crystals. In 1901 Röntgen was awarded the first Nobel Prize for physics.

**röntgen** (symbol R) Former unit used to measure X-RAY or GAMMA RADIATION. One röntgen causes sufficient ionization to produce a total electric charge of $2.58 \times 10^{-4}$ coulombs on all the positive (or negative) ions in one kilogram of air. The unit has been replaced by the SI unit, the GRAY (symbol Gy).

**rook** Large European bird of the CROW family. It has glossy black plumage, but commonly loses the feathers from about its face. It feeds on grain and insects, and has a characteristic raucous cry. Family Corvidae; species *Corvus frugilegus*.

## ROMANIA

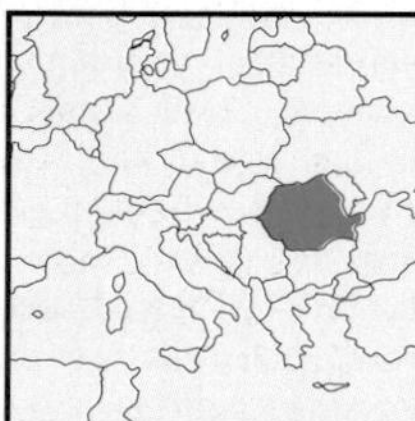

Romania's flag, adopted in 1948, uses colors from the arms of the provinces, which united in 1861 to form Romania. A central coat of arms, added in 1965, was deleted in 1990 after the fall of the Communist regime under the dictator Nicolae Ceauşescu.

**AREA:** 91,699sq mi (237,500sq km)
**POPULATION:** 23,185,000
**CAPITAL (POPULATION):** Bucharest (2,350,984)
**GOVERNMENT:** Multiparty republic
**ETHNIC GROUPS:** Romanian 89%, Hungarian 7%, Romany (Gypsy) 2%
**LANGUAGES:** Romanian (official)
**RELIGIONS:** Romanian Orthodox 87%, Roman Catholic 5%, Greek Orthodox 4%)
**CURRENCY:** Romanian leu = 100 bani

The Balkan republic of Romania is dominated by a central plateau. The CARPATHIAN MOUNTAINS run in a horseshoe shape from N to SW, and frame the region of TRANSYLVANIA. Eastern and S Romania form part of the DANUBE river basin; the site of the capital, BUCHAREST. The Danube's delta, near the Black Sea, is one of Europe's most important wetlands. The port of CONSTANŢA lies on the Black Sea coast. The extreme W lowlands include the city of TIMIŞOARA.

### CLIMATE

Romania has hot, dry summers and cold winters. It is one of the sunniest places in Europe, with more than 2,000 hours of sunshine every year.

### VEGETATION

Arable land accounts for *c*.66% of Romania. Forests cover 28%; oak predominates at lower levels, beech and conifer on the higher slopes, and mountain pastures near the summits.

### HISTORY

Modern Romania roughly corresponds to ancient DACIA, which was conquered by the Romans in AD 106. The Dacians assimilated Roman culture and language, and the region became known as Romania. In the 14th century, the principalities of WALLACHIA (S) and MOLDAVIA (E) were formed. Initially, the princes retained local autonomy, but in the 18th century the Ottoman empire dominated Romania. In the late 18th century, the Turkish empire began to break up. Russia captured Moldavia and Wallachia in the Russo-Turkish War (1828–29). Romanian nationalism intensified, and the two provinces were united in 1861. The Congress of Berlin (1878) ratified Romania as an independent state, and in 1881 CAROL I became king. Neutral at the start of World War I, Romania joined the Allies in 1916, but was occupied by German forces in 1917. The Allied victory led to Romania acquiring large regions, such as Transylvania. In 1927 MICHAEL became king, but surrendered the throne to his father, CAROL II, in 1930. Political instability and economic inequality led to the growth of fascism and anti-semitism. At the start of World War II, Romania lost territory to Bulgaria, Hungary, and the Soviet Union. In 1940 Michael was restored. Ion Antonescu became dictator and, in June 1941, Romania joined the German invasion of the Soviet Union. During World War II more than 50% of Romanian Jews were murdered. In 1944 Soviet troops occupied Romania, Antonescu was overthrown, and Romania surrendered. In 1945 a communist-dominated coalition assumed power, led by Gheorghe Gheorghiu-Dej. In 1947 Romania became a people's republic. In 1952 Romania adopted a Soviet-style constitution. Industry was nationalized and agriculture collectivized. In 1949 Romania joined the Council of Mutual Economic Assistance (COMECON), and in 1955 became a member of the Warsaw Pact. In 1965 Gheorghiu-Dej was succeeded by Nicolae CEAUŞESCU. Rapid industrialization and political repression continued. In December 1989 Ceauşescu and his wife were executed. Ion ILIESCU, a former Communist official, formed a provisional government. In May 1990 elections, the National Salvation Front, led by Ion Iliescu, won a large majority. In 1991 a new constitution was approved. In 1992 Ion Iliescu was reelected. In 1995 Romania applied to join the European Union. In 1996 elections Iliescu was defeated by Emil Constantinescu and his centre-right coalition. In 1998 disputes within the coalition led to the resignation of the prime minister.

### ECONOMY

Communism's over-concentration on heavy industry devastated Romania's economy (1995 GDP per capita, US$4,360). Today, industry accounts for 40% of GDP. Oil, natural gas, and antimony are the main mineral resources. Agriculture employs 29% of the workforce and constitutes 20% of GDP. Romania is the world's second-largest producer of plums (after China). It is the world's ninth largest producer of wine. Other major crops include corn and cabbages. Economic reform is slow. Unemployment and foreign debt remain high.

▲ **rosemary** A strongly flavored culinary herb, rosemary (*Rosmarius officinalis*) leaves are used as a seasoning for meat and fish. Its aromatic oil is used in perfumes and medicines. Since the earliest times, the plant has symbolized remembrance and faithfulness.

**Roosevelt, (Anna) Eleanor** (1884–1962). US reformer and humanitarian, wife of Franklin ROOSEVELT. She was a supporter of social causes, including civil rights. She served as US delegate to the United Nations, (1945–52, 1961–62) and chairman of the UN Commission on Human Rights (1946–51).

**Roosevelt, Franklin Delano** (1882–1945) 32nd US President (1933–45). He served in the New York State Senate as a Democrat, as assistant secretary of the navy under Woodrow WILSON (1913–20), and was vice-presidential candidate in 1920. In 1921 Roosevelt lost the use of his legs as a result of polio. He was governor of New York (1928–32) and won the Democratic candidacy for president. He was elected in 1932. To deal with the GREAT DEPRESSION, he embarked upon his NEW DEAL. He was reelected in 1936 and won an unprecedented third term in 1940 and a fourth in 1944. When World War II broke out in Europe, he gave as much support to Britain as a neutral government could, until the Japanese attack on PEARL HARBOR ended US neutrality. He died in office and was succeeded by Harry S. TRUMAN.

**Roosevelt, Theodore** (1858–1919) 26th US President (1901–09). He was popularly known as "Teddy" and was the fifth cousin of Franklin D. ROOSEVELT and uncle of Eleanor ROOSEVELT. Roosevelt gained national fame as the organizer of the Rough Riders in the SPANISH-AMERICAN WAR (1898). In 1899 he became Republican governor of New York, and vice president in 1901. The assassination of President MCKINLEY (1901) made him president, and he was reelected in 1904. A vigorous progressive, Roosevelt moved to regulate monopolies through antitrust legislation. Other radical reforms were increasingly blocked by Congress. Abroad, he expanded US power and prestige, gaining the PANAMA CANAL and taking an increasing role in world affairs. Roosevelt's mediation after the RUSSO-JAPANESE WAR won him the Nobel Peace Prize (1905). After retiring in 1909, he challenged his successor, President TAFT, for the presidency in 1912 as leader of his National PROGRESSIVE PARTY (Bull Moose Party). The Republican split resulted in a Democratic victory.

**Root, Elihu** (1845–1937) US lawyer and statesman. A leading lawyer, Root became secretary of war immediately following the SPANISH-AMERICAN WAR (1898); he supervised the affairs of Cuba and of the new territories of the Philippines and Puerto Rico. In 1905 Root was appointed secretary of state and was awarded the Nobel Peace Prize in 1912. He also served in the Senate (1909–15) and as president of Andrew CARNEGIE's philanthropic trusts.

**root** Underground portion of a VASCULAR PLANT that serves as an anchor and absorbs water and minerals from the soil. Some plants, such as the dandelion, have taproots with smaller lateral branches. Other plants, such as the grasses, develop fibrous roots with lateral branches.

**root** In mathematics, fractional POWER of a number. The SQUARE ROOT of a number, $x$, is written as either $\sqrt{x}$ or $x^{\frac{1}{2}}$. The fourth root of $x$ may be written in radical form as $\sqrt[4]{x}$ or in power form as $x^{\frac{1}{4}}$. The fourth root of 16, for example, is 2 since $2 \times 2 \times 2 \times 2 = 16$.

**root nodule** Small swelling in the roots of various plants, such as LEGUMES, that contain nitrogen-fixing bacteria. *See also* NITROGEN CYCLE; NITROGEN FIXATION

**Rorschach test** (ink-blot test) In psychology, test used to analyze a person's motives and attitudes when these are projected into ambiguous situations. The individual is presented with 10 standardized ink blots and interpretation is based on the description of them.

**rosary** Form of meditational prayer that contemplates the life of Jesus and the Blessed Virgin Mary within the Catholic and Orthodox churches. A rosary is also the string of beads on which a count may be kept of the number of prayers said.

**Rose, Pete** (1942– ) US baseball player. Known as "Charlie Hustle," he played, primarily as an infielder, for the Cincinnati Reds (1963–78), Philadelphia Phillies (1979–83), and Montreal Expos (1984). Rose was then player-manager (1984–86) and manager (1986–89) of the Cincinnati Reds. In 1989 he was barred from baseball for insider gambling. Rose holds records for his total career hits (4,256) and games played (3,562).

**rose** Wild or cultivated flowering shrub of the genus *Rosa*. Most roses are native to Asia, several to America, and a few to Europe and NW Africa. The stems are usually thorny, and flowers range in color from white to yellow, pink, crimson, and maroon; many are fragrant. There are *c.*150 species. Family Rosaceae.

**Roseau** Capital of Dominica, in the Windward Islands, a port on the SW coast at the mouth of the Roseau River. The city was burnt by the French in 1805, and virtually destroyed by a hurricane in 1979. Tropical vegetables, oils, spices, limes, and lime juice are exported. Pop. (1991) 15,853.

**rosemary** Perennial evergreen herb of the mint family. It has small, needle-like leaf clusters of small pale-blue flowers. Sprigs of rosemary are commonly used as a flavoring. Family Lamiaceae/Labiatae; species *Rosmarinus officinalis*.

**Rosenberg, Alfred** (1893–1946) German Nazi leader, b. Estonia. He edited the newspaper of the National Socialist Party. Rosenberg's book *The Myth of the 20th Century* (1930) formed the basis of the ANTI-SEMITISM of NATIONAL SOCIALISM. In 1941 he became minister for the occupied E regions. Rosenberg was convicted of war crimes at the NUREMBERG TRIALS and executed.

**Rosenberg Case** (1951–53) US espionage case. A New York couple, Julius and Ethel Rosenberg, were found guilty of passing atom bomb secrets to Soviet agents. The trial gained international attention because many felt the couple were the victims of COLD WAR hysteria. They were the first US civilians executed for espionage.

**Roses, Wars of the** (1455–85) English dynastic civil wars. They are named for the badges of the rival royal houses of York (white rose) and Lancaster (red rose). Both houses were descended from Edward III. The Lancastrian king, HENRY VI, was challenged by Richard, Duke of York, who gained brief ascendancy after the battle of St. Albans (1455). The Lancastrians recovered control, but in 1460 Richard, supported by the powerful Earl of WARWICK, forced Henry to recognize him as his heir. Richard was killed months later, but the Yorkist victory at Towton (1461) put his son on the throne as EDWARD IV. In 1469 Warwick changed sides and Edward was deposed, but returned to win the decisive victory of Tewkesbury (1471). A final phase of the wars began with the seizure of the throne by RICHARD III in 1483. He was defeated and killed at BOSWORTH, when Henry Tudor (HENRY VII) won the crown with support from both houses.

**Rosetta Stone** Slab of black basalt inscribed with the same text in Egyptian HIEROGLYPHS, demotic (a simplified form of Egyptian hieroglyphs), and Greek script. By comparing the three versions, first Thomas Young (1818) and later Jean-François Champollion (1822) deciphered the hieroglyphs, leading to a full understanding of hieroglyphic writing.

**rosewood** Any of several kinds of ornamental hardwoods derived from various tropical trees. The most important are Honduras rosewood, *Dalbergia stevensoni*, and Brazilian rosewood, *D. nigra*. It varies from a deep, ruddy brown to purplish and has a black grain. Family Fabiaceae/Leguminose

**Rosh Hashanah** Jewish New Year and first day of the month of Tishri (generally in September). It is the day on which a ceremonial ram's horn, the *shophar* or *shofar*, is blown to call sinners to repentance – the Day of Judgment or of Remembrance – and the day which begins the Ten Days of Penitence that end with the Day of Atonement, YOM KIPPUR.

**Rosicrucians** Esoteric, secret, worldwide society, using supposedly magical knowledge drawn from ALCHEMY. The name comes from pamphlets published by Christian Rosenkreutz *c.*1615, of whom there is no other record. The modern movement has splintered into several factions.

**Ross, Betsy** (1752–1836) US seamstress, said to have made the first American "stars and stripes" flag.

**Ross, Diana** (1944– ) US singer. She began her career with the vocal trio, The Supremes, whose MOTOWN hits included "Where Did Our Love Go" (1964) and "Baby Love" (1964). In 1970 Ross went solo. She was nominated for an Academy Award for her portrayal of the jazz singer Billie HOLIDAY in the film *Lady Sings the Blues* (1972).

**Ross Dependency** Region of Antarctica which includes Ross Island, the coast along the Ross Sea and nearby islands.

It has been under the jurisdiction of New Zealand since 1923. Area: land mass, *c.*160,000sq mi (415,000sq km); ice shelf, *c.*174,000sq mi (450,000sq km).

**Rossellini, Roberto** (1906–77) Italian film director and producer. His post-war films, such as *Open City* (1945), were landmarks in Italian NEO-REALISM. Rossellini made a series of films with his wife, Ingrid BERGMAN, such as *Stromboli* (1949).

**Rossetti, Christina Georgina** (1830–94) English poet, sister of Dante Gabriel ROSSETTI. Her most enduring work, mainly religious in content, is contained in *Goblin Market and Other Poems* (1862) and *The Prince's Progress and Other Poems* (1866).

**Rossetti, Dante Gabriel** (1828–82) English poet and painter. A founder member of the PRE-RAPHAELITE BROTHERHOOD, he developed a distinctive style of medieval romanticism after the group dispersed. Rossetti's lush style is evident in idealized portraits of women. His portraits were often modeled on his wife, Elizabeth Siddal. Rossetti's poetry includes *Ballads and Sonnets* (1881). He died of drug addiction.

**Rossini, Gioacchino Antonio** (1792–1868) Italian opera composer. His comic operas, including *The Barber of Seville* (1816) and *La Cenerentola* ("Cinderella," 1817), demonstrate his wit and sense of melody. His serious operas include *William Tell* (1829).

**Rosso, Il** (1495–1540) (Giovanni Battista Rosso) Italian painter and decorative artist. He collaborated with Primaticcio in decorating the royal palace at FONTAINEBLEAU and helped to found the FONTAINEBLEAU SCHOOL.

**Rostand, Edmond** (1868–1918) French poet and dramatist. His major verse plays include *Cyrano de Bergerac* (1897), *L'Aiglon* (1900), and *Chantecler* (1910).

**Rostropovich, Mstislav Leopoldovich** (1927– ) Azerbaijani cellist and conductor. In 1960 he gave the first London performance of Shostakovich's First Cello Concerto. His friend Benjamin BRITTEN composed several works for him. In 1975 Rostropovich defected from the Soviet Union. He was musical director (1977–94) of the National Symphony Orchestra, Washington, D.C.

**rotation** Turning of a celestial body about its axis. In the Solar System, the Sun and all the planets, with the exception of Uranus and Venus, rotate from W to E.

**Roth, Philip** (1933– ) US novelist and short-story writer. His works often draw on his Jewish background. Roth established his name with the short-story collection *Goodbye Columbus* (1959). His best-known novel is *Portnoy's Complaint* (1969). Other works include *Zuckerman Bound* (1985), *Operation Shylock* (1993) and *American Pastoral* (1997).

**Rothko, Mark** (1903–70) US painter, b. Russia. A leader of the New York School, he developed a highly individual style featuring large, rectangular areas of thinly layered, pale colors arranged parallel to each other. Toward the end of his life, Rothko introduced darker colors, notably maroon and black. Examples of this phase can be seen in his nine paintings entitled *Black on Maroon* and *Red on Maroon* from the late 1950s.

**Rothschild, Meyer Amschel** (1744–1812) German financier, founder of a banking dynasty. He made his fortune in Frankfurt during the Napoleonic Wars. His five sons established branches in the financial centers of Europe. The Rothschilds were one of the chief financial powers in the 19th century, but developments in state financing reduced their influence. The family continues to be active in banking and as winemakers.

**rotifer** (wheel animacule) Microscopic metazoan found mainly in freshwater. Although it resembles ciliate PROTOZOA, it is many-celled with a general body structure similar to that of a simple WORM. Rotifers may be elongated or round, and are identified by a crown of cilia around the mouth. Class Rotifera.

**Rotterdam** City at the junction of the Rotte and the New Meuse rivers, W Netherlands; chief port and second-largest city in the Netherlands. Founded in the 14th century, it expanded with the construction of the New Waterway (1866–72), making it accessible to oceangoing vessels. In 19[illegible] the opening of the Europort harbor made Rotterdam one of the largest ports in the world. It has a large transit trade with industrial areas of Europe, in particular the RUHR in Germany. Industries: shipbuilding, petrochemicals, electronic goods. Pop. (1994) 598,521.

**rottweiler** German cattle dog. The short-backed, strong body is set on muscular, medium-length legs and the tail is commonly docked. The short, coarse, flat coat is black with brown markings. Height: to 27in (68.5cm) at the shoulder.

**Rouault, Georges** (1871–1958) French painter, printmaker, and designer. Studying under Gustave MOREAU with MATISSE, he became acquainted with FAUVISM. A mental crisis turned him toward more painful subjects. By the 1930s, he had designed book illustrations, ceramics, and tapestries as well as the sets for Diaghilev's ballet, *The Prodigal Son* (1929). From the 1930s Rouault concentrated on religious art.

**Rouen** City and port on the Seine River, NW France; capital of Seine-Maritime department. Already important in Roman times, by the 10th century Rouen was one of Europe's leading cities. Under English rule (1066–1204, 1419–49), it was the scene of JOAN OF ARC's trial and burning in 1431. Badly damaged in World War II, it was later rebuilt. Industries: textiles, iron, petrochemicals, perfume, leather. Pop. (1990) 102,723.

**roulette** Game of chance in which people gamble on which of 37 numbered slots (38 in the US) in a spinning wheel a small white ball will end up in when the wheel stops. Gamblers place their bets on a table marked out with the numbers. The bank wins all stakes if the ball stops on 0 (and 00 in the US).

**Roundheads** Name given to Puritans and other supporters of Parliament during the English CIVIL WAR. It was originally a derogatory nickname for Puritans who cut their hair short, in contrast to the ringlets of the CAVALIERS (Royalists).

**roundworm** Parasite of the class Nematoda, which inhabits the intestine of mammals. It breeds in the intestine. The larva bores through the intestinal wall, is carried to the lungs in the bloodstream and crawls to the mouth where it is swallowed. Length: 6–12in (15–30cm).

**Rousseau, Henri** (1844–1910) French painter, greatest of all naive painters. Rousseau is best known for his scenes from an imaginary tropical jungle, such as *Surprised! (Tropical Storm with Tiger)* (1891) and *The Dream* (1910).

**Rousseau, Jean Jacques** (1712–78) French philosopher of the Age of Reason, whose ideas about society helped to shape the political events that resulted in the French Revolution. He was born a Protestant in Geneva, Switzerland, and became a Roman Catholic in the 1730s. Later in his life he reconverted to Protestantism in order to regain his citizenship rights in Geneva. In 1740 Rousseau moved to Paris and devoted himself to a career as a writer and composer. In the 1740s he contributed articles on music to the Encyclopédie of DIDEROT, and won fame for his essay *Discourses on Science and the Arts* (1750). In *The Social Contract* (1762), he argued that man had

◄ **Rossetti** *Beata Beatrix* (*c.*1864–70). One of the founders of the Pre-Raphaelite Brotherhood, the artist and poet Dante Gabriel Rossetti had a lush and romantic painting style. Although his poetry was first published when he was 18, he remained virtually unknown as a poet until late in life. His paintings had a great influence on other artists, particularly the symbolists.

R

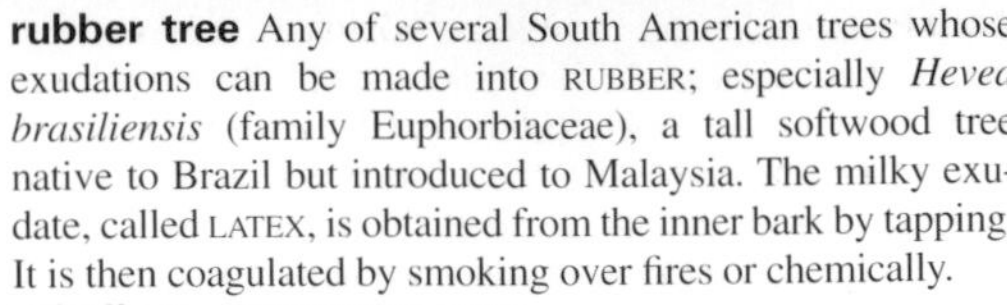

been corrupted by civilization. His ideas on individual liberation from the constraints of society were developed in the novel *Émile* (1762). He described his early, wandering life in an autobiography, *Confessions*, published posthumously in 1782.

**Rousseau, Théodore** (1812–67) French painter, leading member of the BARBIZON SCHOOL. He was at the forefront of the open-air movement in landscape painting, and from 1836 he worked in the forest of Fontainebleau near Paris.

**rowing** Using oars to propel a boat; a leisure activity and a sport. It was unofficially included in the Olympic Games in 1900 and has been a full Olympic event since 1904. Modern racing boats hold crews of two (pairs), four (fours), or eight (eights), each crew member using both hands to pull one oar (to use two oars is **sculling**). A coxswain steers for eights and directs the crew; pairs and fours may or may not have a coxswain. *See also* BOAT RACE

**Royal Academy of Arts (RA)** British national academy of the arts, founded by George III in 1768 and based in London. Members aimed to raise the status of the arts by establishing high standards of training and organizing annual exhibitions.

**Royal Canadian Mounted Police** Federal police of Canada, popularly known as the Mounties. They were organized in 1873 and opened their first post at Emerson (1874). Active in the RIEL rebellion, the Yukon gold rush, and both World Wars, today they provide police manpower in most provinces.

**Royal Greenwich Observatory** UK national astronomical observatory, founded at Greenwich, London, in 1675. After World War II the observatory moved to Herstmonceux in Sussex and, in 1990, it moved to Cambridge. The decision to close it down was taken in 1998.

**Royal Marines** British soldiers who serve at sea. The marines are also a mobile force which can be put ashore at any time to operate as conventional soldiers. Their first great success was the capture of Gibraltar in 1704. They played significant roles in both world wars.

**Royal Navy** Fighting force that defends Britain's coastal waters and its merchant shipping. The first naval fleet in Britain was built by ALFRED THE GREAT in 878 to fight off the Viking raids. In the 16th century Henry VII built the first specialist naval ships and established the first dockyards. The following centuries saw a struggle for naval supremacy between Britain, France, and the Netherlands, culminating in the Battle of TRAFALGAR. The British victory heralded the supremacy of the Royal Navy that lasted into the 20th century. Since World War II the role of the Royal Navy has diminished.

**Royal Opera House** (originally Covent Garden Theatre) Home of The Royal Opera and, from 1946, of Sadler's Wells Ballet (now The Royal Ballet), London, England. The theater was first opened in 1732 and the present building was completed in 1858. The Royal Opera traditionally performs works in the language in which they were written.

**Royal Shakespeare Company (RSC)** State-subsidized British theatrical repertory company, based in Stratford-upon-Avon. Originally known as the Shakespeare Memorial Company, it received a royal charter in 1961. In 1960 it established a second base in London and presented Shakespearean plays alongside other classical and contemporary pieces.

**Royal Society** British society founded in 1660 and incorporated two years later. Its aim was to accumulate experimental evidence on a wide range of scientific subjects, including medicine and botany as well as the physical sciences. In the 20th century, the Royal Society became an independent body of scientists encouraging research.

**rubber** Elastic solid obtained from the latex of the RUBBER TREE. **Natural** rubber consists of a POLYMER of cis-isoprene and is widely used for vehicle tires and other applications, especially after VULCANIZATION. **Synthetic** rubbers are polymers tailored for specific purposes.

**rubber plant** Evergreen FIG native to India and Malaysia. Tree-sized in the tropics, juvenile specimens are grown as house plants in temperate regions. Once cultivated for its white LATEX to make India rubber, it has large, glossy, leathery leaves and a stout, buttressed trunk. Height: to 100ft (30m). Family Moraceae; species *Ficus elastica*.

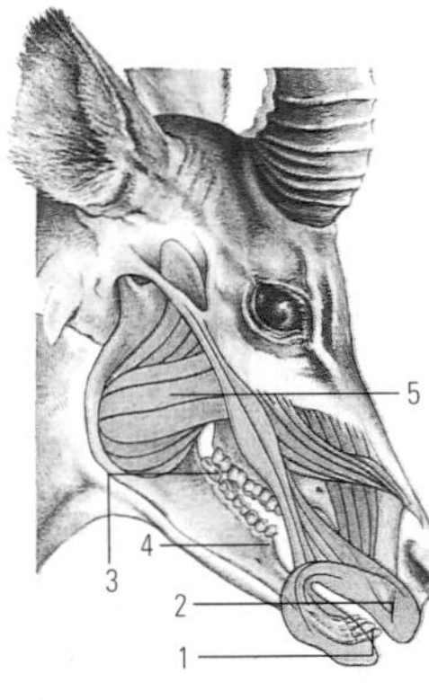


▲ **ruminant** Impalas are found in the grasslands of central and eastern Africa. Like other ruminants, they can regurgitate food in small amounts once it has been partly digested, for chewing again, reswallowing, and further digestion. This enables them to obtain a lot of food in a short time, then retreat to a safe, sheltered place to digest it. When grazing, an impala grasps vegetation between its spade-like incisors (1) and a hard upper pad (2) and pulls it up rather than biting it off. The molars (3) are ideal for chewing. The gap between incisors and molars (4) allows the tongue to mix food with saliva. The powerful masseter muscle (5) moves the jaw up and down, while other facial muscles move it laterally for grinding.

**rubber tree** Any of several South American trees whose exudations can be made into RUBBER; especially *Hevea brasiliensis* (family Euphorbiaceae), a tall softwood tree native to Brazil but introduced to Malaysia. The milky exudate, called LATEX, is obtained from the inner bark by tapping. It is then coagulated by smoking over fires or chemically.

**rubella** *See* GERMAN MEASLES

**Rubens, Peter Paul** (1577–1640) Flemish painter, engraver, and designer, most influential BAROQUE artist of N Europe. He began to gain an international reputation with his huge, vigorous TRIPTYCHS, *Raising of the Cross* (1610–11) and *Descent from the Cross* (1611–14). He worked for many of the royal families of Europe and his most notable commissions included 25 gigantic paintings of Marie de' Medicis; and a group of more than 100 mythological paintings for Philip IV of Spain.

**Rubicon** Ancient name for the Fiumicino River in N central Italy. It formed the border between Italy and Cisalpine Gaul. In 49 BC Julius CAESAR precipitated civil war by "crossing the Rubicon" into Italy with his army, hence the modern phrase meaning to take an irrevocable step.

**rubidium** (symbol Rb) Silver-white, metallic element of the ALKALI METALS. It was discovered in 1861 by Robert BUNSEN and Gustav KIRCHHOFF. The element has few commercial uses; small amounts are used in photoelectric cells. It chemically resembles SODIUM but is more reactive. Properties: at.no. 37; at.wt. 85.4678; sp.gr. 1.53; m.p. 102°F (38.89°C); b.p. 1,270°F (688°C); most common isotope $^{85}$Rb (72.15%).

**Rubinstein, Artur** (1887–1982) US pianist, b. Poland. He made his debut with the Berlin Symphony Orchestra at the age of 12. Rubeinstein is celebrated for his interpretations of CHOPIN and Spanish composers.

**ruby** Gem variety of the mineral CORUNDUM (aluminum oxide), whose characteristic red color is due to impurities of chromium and iron oxides. The traditional source of rubies is Burma. Today, synthetic rubies are widely used in industry.

**Rudolf I** (1218–91) German king (1273–91), founder of the HAPSBURG dynasty. His election as king ended a period of anarchy (1250–73). Rudolf set out to restore the position of the monarchy, and won the duchies of Austria, Styria, and Carniola from Ottokar II of Bohemia (1278). He was never crowned emperor, and failed to persuade the electors to confirm his son, Albert I, as his successor, though in 1298 Albert eventually succeeded to the German throne.

**Rudolf II** (1552–1612) Holy Roman emperor (1576–1612), son and successor of the Emperor Maximilian II. He moved the imperial capital to Prague, which became a center of the RENAISSANCE. His opposition to Protestantism caused conflict in Bohemia and Hungary. A Hungarian revolt was suppressed by his brother and successor, Matthias, to whom he ceded Hungary, Austria, Moravia (1608), and Bohemia (1611).

**ruff** Bird of the SANDPIPER family (Scolopacidae). The male is noted for a collar of long feathers about its neck, and for its antic courtship performances. The female is called a reeve. The ruff migrates across N Europe and N Asia to Africa and India. Species *Philomachus pugnax*.

**Ruffin, Edmund** (1974–1865) US agronomist and slavery apologist. He pioneered the use of fertilizers, crop rotation, drainage, and improved methods of plowing to eliminate soil depletion. Ruffin is chiefly remebered, however, for the articles he wrote in defense of slavery and secession. In 1861 he fired the first shot on Fort Sumter, which began the Civil War. When the Confederacy collapsed, Ruffin committed suicide.

**rugby** Ball game for two teams in which an oval ball may be handled as well as kicked. The purpose is to touch the ball down in the opposition in-goal area for a **try**, which allows a kick at the H-shaped goal (a **conversion**). Players may not pass the ball forward or knock it forward when attempting to catch it. The field of play is rectangular, 330ft (100m) long and 180–225ft (55–68m) wide, and play consists of two 40-minute halves. **Rugby union** is a 15-a-side game, which used to be restricted to amateurs. It is most popular in Britain, France, South Africa, New Zealand, and Australia. Rugby league is a 13-a-side game for professionals and amateurs, played mostly in England, Australia, New Zealand, and France. Rugby enjoys some popularity as a US college sport.

**Ruhr** River in Germany; its valley is Germany's manufacturing heartland. The Ruhr River rises in the Rothaargebirge Mountains, and flows W for 146mi (235km) to join the RHINE River at DUISBURG. Major cities on its banks include ESSEN, DORTMUND, and Mülheim. In the 19th century, the Krupp and Thyssen families intensively mined the region's high-quality coking coal and developed massive steelworks. Between 1923 and 1925 France and Belgium occupied the Ruhr in order to compel Germany to pay the agreed war reparations. During World War II its many armaments factories marked it out as a major Allied target and more than 75% of the region was destroyed. The postwar decline in demand for coal led to a shift to light industry, and the region regained prosperity.

**rum** Alcoholic spirit made by the fermentation of molasses and other sugarcane products, which are then distilled. When distilled, rum is colorless, but storage in wooden casks and the addition of caramel give it a brown color.

**Rumi** (1207–73) Persian poet, b. Jalal ad-Dinar-Rumi. A theologian and teacher whose huge body of work – some 30,000 couplets and numerous *rubaiyat* or quatrains – was inspired by SUFISM. He is generally regarded as Persia's finest poet. His main work is the epic *Mathnawi* (or *Masnavī*).

**ruminant** Cud-chewing, even-toed, hoofed mammal. They include the OKAPI, DEER, GIRAFFE, ANTELOPE, CATTLE, SHEEP, and GOAT. All except the chevrotain have four-chambered stomachs, and they are known for re-chewing food previously swallowed and stored in one of the chambers.

**Rump Parliament** (1648–53) Name given to the LONG PARLIAMENT in England after 140 members were expelled. Unrepresentative and quarrelsome, it was dissolved by CROMWELL in 1653. It was recalled after the collapse of the PROTECTORATE in 1659, and expelled members were reinstated.

**Runcie, Robert Alexander Kennedy** (1921– ) British Anglican clergyman, archbishop of Canterbury (1980–91). He was ordained in 1951 and became bishop of St. Albans in 1970. In 1982 Runcie signed a pledge to move toward unity with the Roman Catholic Church during Pope John Paul II's historic trip to the UK. He was succeeded by George CAREY.

**rune** Angular character or letter of an alphabet formerly used by Germanic peoples in early medieval times. Also called futhark after its first six letters (*f*, *u*, *th*, *a*, *r*, and *k*), the runic alphabet may have been developed by an unknown Germanic people from a N Italian alphabet.

**runner** In botany, a long, thin stem that extends along the surface of the soil from the axil of a plant's leaf, and serves to propagate the plant. At points (nodes) along its length, a runner has small leaves with buds that develop shoots and roots and turn into small independent plants as the runner dies. Runners are produced by such plants as strawberries and creeping buttercups. *See also* ASEXUAL REPRODUCTION

**Rupert, Prince** (1619–82) British military commander, b. Bohemia and raised in the Netherlands. His uncle, CHARLES I, made him commander of the cavalry in the English CIVIL WARS. Rupert was undefeated until MARSTON MOOR (1644). He was dismissed after the Royalist defeat at NASEBY (1645) and his surrender at Bristol. He led raids against English shipping during the PROTECTORATE period, and, after the Stuart RESTORATION, he served as an admiral in the DUTCH WARS.

**rupture** *See* HERNIA

**Rurik** (d. *c*.879) Semi-legendary leader of the Varangians (VIKINGS) in Russia and first Prince of Novgorod. In *c*.862 he established his rule, a date usually taken as marking the beginning of the first Russian state. The capital was moved to KIEV under Rurik's successor, Oleg, and members of his dynasty ruled there, and later in Moscow, until the 16th century, eventually being replaced by the ROMANOVS.

**Rush, Benjamin** (*c*.1745–1813) US physician and reformer. He practiced medicine in Philadelphia and in 1789 became professor of medicine in the University of Pennsylvania. As a member of the Continental Congress (1776–77), he signed the Declaration of Independence. An avid reformer, Rush established the first US free medical dispensary (1786), worked for the abolition of slavery, and advocated a modern prison system and education for women. He was treasurer of the US Mint (1797–1813).

**rush** Any of *c*.700 species of perennial, tufted bog plants found in temperate regions. It has long, narrow leaves and small flowers crowded into dense clusters. The most familiar rush is *Juncus effusus*, found in Europe, Asia, North America, Australia, and New Zealand. It has brown flowers and ridged stems. Height: 1–5ft (30–152cm). Family Juncaceae.

**Rush-Bagot Convention** (1817) British-US agreement providing for disarmament of the US-Canadian border. Besides ensuring an unfortified frontier, it agreed limits for ships of the two countries in the Great Lakes.

**Rushdie, (Ahmed) Salman** (1947– ) British novelist, b. India. His early works, including the Booker Prize-winning *Midnight's Children* (1981), were eclipsed by *Satanic Verses* (1988). This novel incited the condemnation of Islamic extremists who perceived the book as BLASPHEMY, and he was sentenced to death by the Iranian leader, Ayatollah KHOMEINI. In hiding, Rushdie wrote a number of works, including a children's book, *Haroun and the Sea of Stories* (1990), and the novel *The Moor's Last Sigh* (1995). Other works include *The Ground Beneath Her Feet* (1999).

**Ruskin, John** (1819–1900) British author, artist, and social reformer. A strong religious conviction was the basis for his advocacy of Gothic naturalism as the best style through which to praise God. Ruskin's ideas on architecture are outlined forcefully in his books: *The Seven Lamps of Architecture* (1849) and *The Stones of Venice* (three vols., 1851–53). His five-volume work *Modern Painters* (1834–60) championed the paintings of J.M.W. TURNER. After 1851 Ruskin supported the PRE-RAPHAELITE BROTHERHOOD.

**Russell, Bertrand Arthur William, 3rd Earl** (1872–1970) Welsh philosopher, mathematician, and social reformer. A fellow at Trinity College, Cambridge, his pupils included Ludwig WITTGENSTEIN. Russell's most influential work, the monumental *Principia Mathematica* (1910–13), written in collaboration with A.N. WHITEHEAD, set out to show how mathematics was grounded in LOGIC. In *Our Knowledge of the External World* (1914), he developed a novel approach to problems in EPISTEMOLOGY. Russell's commitment to pacifism led to his imprisonment in 1918. He supported, however, the antifascist aims of World War II. Russell's *History of Western Philosophy* (1946) was a popular bestseller. In 1950 he was awarded the Nobel Prize for literature.

**Russell, Charles Taze** *See* JEHOVAH'S WITNESSES

**Russell, George William** (1867–1935) Irish poet, essayist, journalist, and painter, who wrote under the pen name A.E. A leading figure of the Irish literary renaissance, he published many collections of romantic and often mystical poetry, among them *The Divine Vision* (1904) and *Midsummer Eve* (1928).

**Russell, John, 1st Earl** (1792–1878) British statesman, prime minister (1846–52, 1865–66). He entered Parliament in 1813. He was one of the founders of the LIBERAL PARTY. Russell succeed Sir Robert PEEL as prime minister. His first administration collapsed following the resignation of his foreign secretary, Viscount PALMERSTON. Russell returned as foreign secretary (1852–55), but retired after accusations of incompetence during the CRIMEAN WAR. He returned as foreign secretary (1859–65) under Palmerston and became prime minister again on Palmerston's death. His second term was curtailed by the defeat of a new Reform Bill (1866). *See also* REFORM ACTS

**Russell, Ken** (1927– ) English film director. His adaptation of D.H. Lawrence's *Women in Love* (1969) gained an Academy nomination. Russell's reputation as the *enfant terrible* of British cinema was reinforced by *The Music Lovers* and *The Devils* (both 1971). Other films include *Mahler* (1973), *Tommy* (1975), *Valentino* (1977), *Altered States* (1980), and *Gothic* (1987).

**Russia** Federation in E Europe and N Asia. *See* country feature, page 580

**Russian** Official language of the Russian Federation and several other republics. It is the primary language of around 170 million people and is a second language for millions more. It is the most important of the Slavic languages, which form a subdivision of the family of INDO-EUROPEAN LANGUAGES. It is written in the CYRILLIC alphabet.

**Russian architecture** Architectural style that began as a

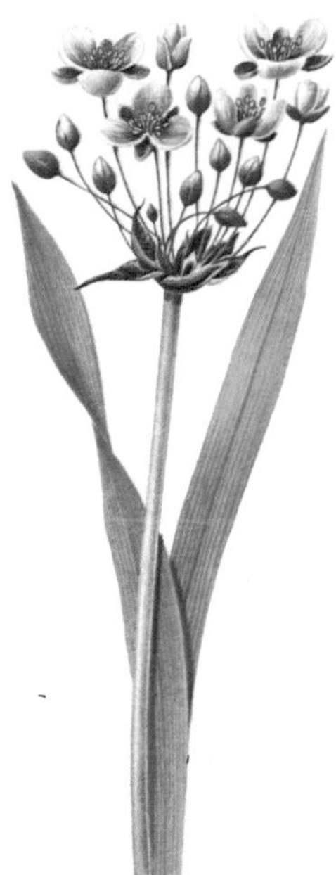

▲ **rush** A decorative aquatic plant, the flowering rush (*Butomus umbellatus*) has an attractive, three-petaled flower that grows above the surface of the water. The long leaves have parallel veins without a central vein or midrib.

▲ **Rushdie** After the publication of *Satanic Verses* (1988), Ayatollah Khomeini imposed a *fatwa* (death penalty) on Salman Rushdie. The death threats against him (and his publishers and translators) were serious enough to drive him into hiding under police protection. He has continued to publish both works of fiction and essays. In 1998 the Iranian government revoked the death sentence and Rushdie returned to public life.

R

In August 1991, Russia's traditional flag, first used in 1699, was restored as Russia's national flag. When Russia formed part of the Soviet Union, this flag was replaced by the hammer and sickle.

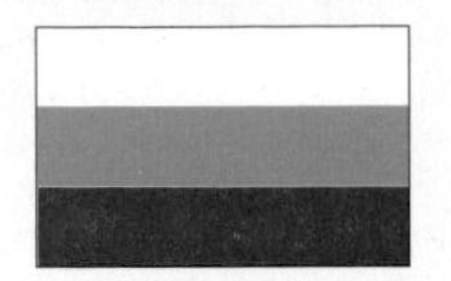

**AREA:** 6,592,800sq mi (17,075,000sq km)
**POPULATION:** 149,527,000
**CAPITAL (POPULATION):** Moscow (8,881,000)
**GOVERNMENT:** Federal multiparty republic
**ETHNIC GROUPS:** Russian 82%, Tatar 4%, Ukrainian 3%, Chuvash 1%, more than 100 other nationalities
**LANGUAGES:** Russian (official)
**RELIGIONS:** Christianity (mainly Russian Orthodox, with Roman Catholic and Protestant minorities), Islam, Judaism
**CURRENCY:** Russian ruble = 100 kopecks

The Russian Federation is the world's largest country. The URALS form a natural border between European and Asian Russia (SIBERIA). About 25% of Russia lies in Europe, W of the Urals. European Russia contains about 80% of Russia's population, including the capital, MOSCOW. It is predominantly a vast plain. The CAUCASUS Mountains form Russia's SW border with Georgia and Azerbaijan, and include Europe's highest peak, Mount ELBRUS, at 18,481ft (5,633m). GROZNYY, capital of CHECHENIA, lies close to the Georgian border. The port of ASTRAKHAN lies on the shore of the CASPIAN SEA, the world's largest inland body of water. ST. PETERSBURG, Russia's second-largest city, is a Baltic seaport. ARCHANGEL is the major White Sea port. European Russia's major rivers are the DON and the VOLGA (Europe's longest river). VOLGOGRAD lies on its banks. SIBERIA is a land of plains and plateaus, with mountains in the E and S. It is drained by the OB, YENISEI, and LENA rivers. The industrial center of NOVOSIBIRSK lies on the Ob River. Close to the Mongolian border lies Lake BAIKAL (the world's deepest lake). On its shores lies IRKUTSK. VLADIVOSTOCK is the major port on the Sea of Japan. SAKHALIN and the KURIL ISLANDS have often been a source of conflict with Japan. The KAMCHATKA PENINSULA contains many active volcanoes.

### CLIMATE

The climate varies from N to S and also from W to E. Moscow has a continental climate with cold, snowy winters and warm summers. Siberia has a much harsher and drier climate. In Northern Siberia winter temperatures often fall below −51°F (−46°C).

### VEGETATION

The far N is tundra. Mosses and lichens grow during the short summer, but the subsoil is permafrost. To the S is the taiga, a vast region of coniferous forest. In the W and E are mixed forests of conifer, oak, and beech. South-central Russia contains large areas of former steppe, most of which is now under the plow; its dark chernozem soils are among the world's most fertile. The semidesert lowlands around the Caspian Sea are hardy grassland. The Caucasus Mountains have lush forests of oak and beech.

### HISTORY AND POLITICS

Traditionally, the Varangian king, RURIK, established the first Russian state in *c.*AD 862. His successor, Oleg, made KIEV, his capital and the state became known as Kievan Rus. VLADIMIR I adopted Greek Orthodox Christianity as the state religion in 988. VLADIMIR and Kiev vied for political supremacy. In 1237–40, the Mongol TATARS conquered Russia and established the GOLDEN HORDE. Saint ALEXANDER NEVSKI became Great Khan of Kiev. In the 14th century Moscow gradually grew in importance and the Grand Duchy of MOSCOW was established in 1380. IVAN III (THE GREAT) greatly extended the power of Moscow, began the construction of the KREMLIN, and completed the conquest of the Golden Horde in 1480. In 1547 IVAN IV (THE TERRIBLE) was crowned czar of all Russia. Ivan the Terrible conquered the Tatar khanates of KAZAN (1552) and Astrakhan (1556), gaining control of the Volga River, and began the conquest of Siberia. Following the death of Boris GODUNOV (1605), Russia was subject to foreign incursions and ruled by a series of usurpers. In 1613 Michael founded the ROMANOV czarist dynasty that ruled Russia until 1917. The reign (1696–1725) of PETER I (THE GREAT) marked the start of the westernization and modernization of Russia: central governmental institutions were founded, and the Church was subordinated to the Crown. Centralization was achieved at the expense of increasing the number of serfs. Russia expanded W to the Baltic Sea, and St. Petersburg was founded in 1703. Peter made it his capital in 1712. In 1762, CATHERINE II (THE GREAT) became empress. Under her authoritarian government, Russia became the greatest power in continental Europe, acquiring much of Poland, Belarus, and Ukraine. Alexander I's territorial gains led him into direct conflict with the imperial ambitions of Napoleon I. Napoleon captured Moscow in 1812, but his army was devastated by the harsh Russian winter. The Decembrist Conspiracy (1825) unsuccessfully tried to prevent the accession of

Nicholas I. Nicholas' reign was characterized by the battle against liberalization. At the end of his reign, Russia became embroiled in the disastrous Crimean War (1853–56). Alexander II undertook much-needed reforms, such as the emancipation of the serfs. Alexander III's rule was more reactionary, but continued Russia's industrialization, helped by the construction of the Trans-Siberian Railroad. Alexander was succeeded by the last Romanov czar, Nicholas II. In the 1890s, drought caused famine in rural areas and there was much discontent in the cities. Defeat in the Russo-Japanese War (1904–05) precipitated the Russian Revolution of 1905. Nicholas II was forced to adopt a new constitution and establish an elected duma (parliament). The democratic reforms were soon reversed, revolutionary groups were brutally suppressed, and pogroms were encouraged. The Russian Social Democratic Labor Party was secretly founded in 1898, supported primarily by industrial workers. In 1912 the Party split into Bolshevik and Menshevik factions. Russia's support of a Greater Slavic state contributed to the outbreak of World War I. Russia was ill-prepared for war, and suffered great hardship. The Russian Revolution (1917) had two main phases. In March, Nicholas II was forced to abdicate (he and his family were executed in July 1918), and a provisional government was formed. In July, Kerensky became prime minister, but failed to satisfy the radical hunger of the soviets. In November 1917, the Bolsheviks, led by Lenin, seized power and proclaimed Russia a Soviet Federated Socialist Republic. In 1918, the capital was transferred to Moscow. Under the terms of the Treaty of Brest-Litovsk (1918), Russia withdrew from World War I, but was forced to cede much territory to the Central Powers. For the next five years, civil war raged between the Reds and Whites (monarchists and anticommunists), complicated by foreign intervention. The Bolsheviks emerged victorious, but Russia was left devastated. In 1922 Russia was united with Ukraine, Belarus, and Transcaucasia (Armenia, Azerbaijan, and Georgia) to form the Union of Soviet Socialist Republics (USSR).

(for history 1922–91, *See* Soviet Union)

In June 1991 Boris Yeltsin was elected President of the Russian Republic. In August 1991 communist hardliners arrested the Soviet president Gorbachev and attempted to capture the Russian parliament in Moscow. Democratic forces rallied behind Yeltsin, and the coup was defeated. Yeltsin emerged as the major power-broker. On 25 December 1991, Gorbachev resigned as president of the USSR, and on 31 December the Soviet Union was dissolved. The Russian Federation became a co-founder of the Commonwealth of Independent States (CIS), composed of former Soviet Republics. In March 1992 a new Federal Treaty was signed between the central government in Moscow and the autonomous republics within the Russian Federation. Chechenia refused to sign, and declared independence. Yeltsin's reforms were frustrated by institutional forces, forcing him to dissolve parliament in September 1993. Parliamentary leaders formed a rival government, but the coup failed. In December 1993 a new democratic constitution was adopted. Progress in democratization and economic reform was slow. Many ethnic groups demanded greater autonomy within the Federation. In 1992 direct rule was imposed in Ingush and North Ossetia. From 1994 to 1996, Russia was embroiled in a costly civil war in the secessionist state of Chechenia. In May 1996, despite concern about his ill-health, Yeltsin was re-elected. In 1998 the Russian economy was devastated by the financial crisis in Southeast Asia. In March 1998 Yeltsin dismissed the entire cabinet, including the prime minister Viktor Chernomyrdin. In August 1998 the stock market collapsed and the rouble was devalued by 50%. Yeltsin again dismissed the entire cabinet and was forced to appoint Yevgeni Primakov as prime minister. In 1999 Russia condemned NATO's bombing of Yugoslavia and Chernomyrdin acted as a mediator between Serbia and NATO.

## Economy

Under Soviet rule, Russia was transformed from an essentially agrarian economy into the world's second greatest industrial power (after the United States). By the 1970s, concentration on the military-industrial complex and the creation of a bloated bureaucracy had caused the economy to stagnate. Gorbachev's policy of perestroika was an attempt to correct this structural weakness. Yeltsin sped up the pace of reform. In 1993 the command economy was abolished, private ownership was reintroduced and mass privatization began. By 1996, 80% of the Russian economy was in private hands. A major problem remains the size of Russia's foreign debt (1996, US$125 billion). Industry employs 46% of the workforce and contributes 48% of GDP (1995 GDP per capita, US$4,480). Mining is the most valuable activity. Russia is rich in resources; it is the world's leading producer of natural gas and nickel and the world's third largest producer of crude oil, lignite, and brown coal. It is the world's second largest manufacturer of aluminum and phosphates. Light industries, producing consumer goods, are growing in importance. Most farmland is still government-owned or run as collectives. Russia is the world's largest producer of barley, oats, rye, and potatoes. It is the world's second-largest producer of beef and veal.

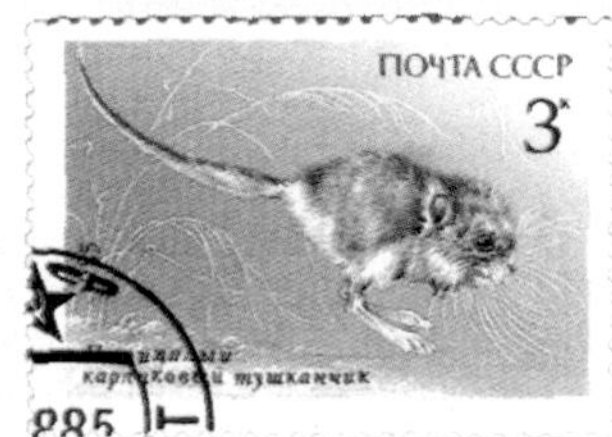


**This stamp**, one of a set of five entitled "Protected Animals," was issued in 1985 by the USSR (CCCP in the Cyrillic alphabet). It shows the hopping rodent, Satunin's jerboa.

R

▲ **Ruth** Nicknamed "the Bambino," Babe Ruth was one of the greatest baseball players of all time. A talented pitcher, his batting skills led him to achieve a career home-run record that lasted more than 25 years after his death. He spent the bulk of his career with the New York Yankees, and their stadium, built while he was on the team, was known as "the house that Ruth built". His colorful personality was as big as his talent, and he was a major US celebrity of the 1920s and 1930s. In 1936, the year after he retired, he was elected to the Baseball Hall of Fame.

regional variety of Byzantine architecture in the 10th century with the Christianization of Russia. Important centers of architectural activity developed at Kiev, Novgorod, and Pskov. Early churches were built of wood. The Cathedral of Sancta Sophia, Kiev (1018–37) was the first stone construction. The distinctive onion-shaped dome was introduced in the 12th century at the Cathedral of Sancta Sophia, Novgorod. During the 15th century Russia was subject to a series of western European trends, and Italian architects built the KREMLIN in a Renaissance style. Peter the Great and Catherine brought ROCOCO and neoclassical principles to St. Petersburg. In the 19th century there was a revival of medieval Russian architecture.

**Russian art** Paintings and sculpture produced in Russia after *c.*1000 AD, as distinct from the earlier SCYTHIAN art. In the Middle Ages, Russian art carried on BYZANTINE ART traditions, and was primarily religious. After the fall of Constantinople (1453), Russia regarded itself as the spiritual heir of Byzantium but its finest artworks were largely produced by foreigners. This began to change in the latter part of the 19th century, when Ilya REPIN and the Wanderers breathed new life into Russian art. This led to a fruitful period in the early 20th century, when Russia was at the heart of new developments in MODERNISM, SUPREMATISM, and CONSTRUCTIVISM.

**Russian Five** Group of Russian composers, active during the 1860s and 1870s, who hoped to create a truly Russian style of music. They were BALAKIREV, César Cui, BORODIN, MUSSORGSKY, and RIMSKY-KORSAKOV.

**Russian literature** Literary works of Russia until 1917, then of the Soviet Union until 1991. Thereafter the literature properly belongs to the individual republics. Russian literature has its origins in religious works dating from *c.*1000 AD. They include biographies of saints, chronicles, hymns, and sermons. After the 1600s, Western influences are found. ROMANTICISM beginning in the late 1700s – dominated by Nikolai Karamzin (*Letters of a Russian Traveler*, 1790) and Alexander PUSHKIN (*Boris Godunov*, 1825) – gave way to the realism of Leo TOLSTOY (*War and Peace*, 1869), Fyodor DOSTOEVSKY (*The Brothers Karamazov*), Anton CHEKHOV (*Uncle Vanya*, 1899), and Maxim GORKY (*The Lower Depths*, 1902). The revolutionary feelings that dominated the early part of the 20th century witnessed a literary revival. Major figures included the symbolist poet Alexander Blok (*The Twelve*, 1918) and the post-symbolists such as Vladimir MAYAKOVSKY. After the Russian Revolution (1917), many writers fled overseas to escape censorship. The authors who remained had to depict only favorable images of the Soviet Union. The major authors of this period were Boris PASTERNAK and Alexei Tolstoy (*Road to Calvary*, 1941). Criticism of the regime was published, however, in works by novelists Alexander SOLZHENITSYN (*One Day in the Life of Ivan Denisovich*, 1962) and Yuri Trifonov (*Another Life*, 1975), and by poet Alexander Tvardovsky. *See also* SOCIALIST REALISM

**Russian Orthodox Church** *See* EASTERN ORTHODOX CHURCH

**Russian Revolution** (1917) Events in Russia that resulted, first, in the founding of a republic (March) and, second, in the seizure of power by the BOLSHEVIKS (November). (In the calendar in use at the time, the two stages took place in February and October.) Widespread discontent, a strong revolutionary movement, and the hardships of World War I forced Czar NICHOLAS II to abdicate in March. A provisional government was formed by liberals in the Duma (parliament), which represented only the middle classes. Its aim was to make Russia into a liberal democracy and to defeat Germany. Workers and peasants had a different agenda: greater social and economic equality and an end to the war. The provisional government faced a challenge from the powerful socialist SOVIET in Petrograd (St. Petersburg), which in May formed a coalition government that included Alexander KERENSKY, prime minister from July, and other socialists. The launching of a new military offensive, combined with disappointing reforms, discredited the government and the socialist parties associated with it. Meanwhile, soviets sprang up in many cities; in the countryside, peasants seized land from the gentry; at the front, soldiers deserted. In the cities, the Bolsheviks secured growing support in the soviets. In November, at the order of LENIN, they carried out a successful coup in Petrograd. The Kerensky government folded, but a long civil war ensued before Lenin and his followers established their authority throughout Russia.

**Russian Revolution of 1905** Series of violent strikes and protests against czarist rule in Russia. It was provoked mainly by defeat in the RUSSO-JAPANESE WAR (1904–05). It began on Bloody Sunday (January 22), when a peaceful demonstration in St. Petersburg was fired on by troops. Strikes and peasant risings spread, culminating in a general strike in October, which forced the czar to institute a democratically elected duma (parliament). By the time it met in 1906, the government had regained control. Severe repression followed.

**Russo-Japanese War** (1904–05) Conflict arising from the rivalry of Russia and Japan for control of Manchuria and Korea. The war began with a Japanese attack on Port Arthur. Russia suffered a series of defeats on land and at sea, culminating in the Battle of Mukden (February–March 1905) and the annihilation of the Baltic fleet at Tsushima (May). Russia was forced to surrender Korea, the Liaotung Peninsula, and s Sakhalin to Japan.

**rust** In botany, group of FUNGI that live as PARASITES on many kinds of higher plants. Rusts damage cereal crops and several fruits and vegetables. They have complex life cycles that involve growth on more than one host plant.

**rust** Corrosion of iron or its alloys by a combination of air and water. Carbon dioxide from the air dissolves in water to form an acid solution that attacks the iron to form iron(II) oxide. This is then oxidized by oxygen in the air to reddish-brown iron (III) oxide. Rusting may be prevented by GALVANIZING.

**Ruth** Eighth book of the Old Testament recounting the story of Ruth, a young Moabite widow. It tells of Ruth's decision to settle in Israelite territory and her eventual marriage to the wealthy Boaz, whereby she becomes the great-grandmother of Israel's greatest leader, King DAVID.

**Ruth, "Babe" (George Herman)** (1895–1948) US baseball player. He held the career home-run record (714) until 1974, surpassed by Hank AARON. Ruth's record of 60 home runs in one season (154 games) was not topped until the season was extended to 162 games. He played for the Boston Red Sox (1914–19), New York Yankees (1920–34), and Boston Braves (1935). Ruth began his career as a pitcher and established a World Series record of 29 2/3 consecutive scoreless innings that lasted until 1961. He was elected to the Baseball Hall of Fame in 1936.

**ruthenium** (symbol Ru) Silver-white, metallic element, one of the TRANSITION ELEMENTS. It was discovered in 1827 and first isolated in 1844. Ruthenium is found in PLATINUM ores. It is used as a catalyst, and its alloys are used in electrical contacts and to color glass and ceramics. Properties: at.no. 44; at.wt. 101.07; sp.gr. 12.41; m.p. 4,190°F (2,310°C); b.p. 7,052°F (3,900°C); most common isotope $^{102}$Ru (31.61%).

**Rutherford, Ernest, Lord** (1871–1937) British physicist, b. New Zealand, who pioneered NUCLEAR PHYSICS. He discovered and named alpha and beta radiation, named the NUCLEUS, and proposed a theory of the radioactive transformation of ATOMS for which he received the 1908 Nobel Prize for chemistry. In Cambridge, under J.J. THOMSON, he discovered the URANIUM radiations. At McGill University, Canada, Rutherford formed the theory of atomic disintegration with Frederick SODDY. At Manchester (1907), he devised the nuclear theory of the atom and, with Niels BOHR, the idea of orbital electrons. In 1919, at the Cavendish Laboratory, his research team became the first to split an atom's nucleus. Rutherford predicted the existence of the NEUTRON, later discovered by James CHADWICK.

**rutile** Black to red-brown oxide mineral, titanium dioxide ($TiO_2$), found in igneous and metamorphic rocks and quartz veins. It occurs as long, prismatic crystals in the tetragonal system and as granular masses. It has a metallic luster, is brittle, and is used as a gemstone. Hardness 6–6.5; sp.gr. 4.2.

**Rutledge, John** (1739–1800) US politician. He was a delegate to the Stamp Act Congress (1765) and two Continental Congresses (1774–76, 1782–83). Rutledge played a key role at the federal Constitutional Convention (1787) and was an associate justice on the Supreme Court (1778–91). He

R

resigned to become chief justice of the South Carolina supreme court (1791–95).

**Ruwenzori** Mountain range in central Africa on the Uganda-Zaire border, between lakes Albert and Edward. The range peaks at Mount Margherita, 16,763ft (5,109m). Length: 75mi (121km).

**Ruyter, Michiel de** (1607–76) Dutch naval commanders. During the first of the DUTCH WARS (1652–54) he reached the rank of vice admiral. In the second Dutch War (1665–67), Ruyter commanded the fleet that defeated the English off Dunkirk (1666). In 1667 he sailed up the Medway, destroying much of the English fleet. In the third Dutch War (1672–74), Ruyter was again victorious.

**Rwanda** Nation in E central Africa. *See* country feature

**Ryder, Albert Pinkham** (1847–1917) US painter. Born at the fishing port of New Bedford, Massachusetts, many of his works depict the sea. His paintings, which have a strange brooding quality, were well known in his lifetime and have been much imitated.

**Ryder Cup** Biennial competition in which a team of professional male golfers from the US plays a team from Europe. The event consists of eight 18-hole foursomes, eight 18-hole four-balls, and 16 18-hole singles.

**rye** Hardy cereal grass originating in SW Asia and naturalized throughout the world. It grows in poorer soils and colder climates than most other cereals can stand. It has flower spikelets that develop one-seeded grains. It is used for flour, as a forage crop, and for making alcoholic drinks. Height: to 3ft (0.9m). Family Poaceae/Gramineae; species *Secale cereale*.

**Ryle, Sir Martin** (1918–84) British physicist and radio astronomer. After studying radar during World War II, he pioneered RADIO ASTRONOMY. He also cataloged radio sources, which led to his discovery of QUASARS.

**Ryukyu Islands** Japanese archipelago in the W Pacific Ocean, extending *c.*600mi (965km) between Kyushu in S Japan and Taiwan; it separates the East China Sea (W) from the Philippine Sea (E). Inhabited since early times, the islands were invaded by China in the 14th century and by Japan in the 17th century, and were relinquished by China to Japan in 1879. After World War II they were administered by the US, being restored to Japan in 1972. The group includes OKINAWA, Amami, and Sakishima. Agriculture and fishing are the chief occupations. Area: *c.*850sq mi (2,200sq km). Pop. (1984 est.) 1,161,000.

## RWANDA

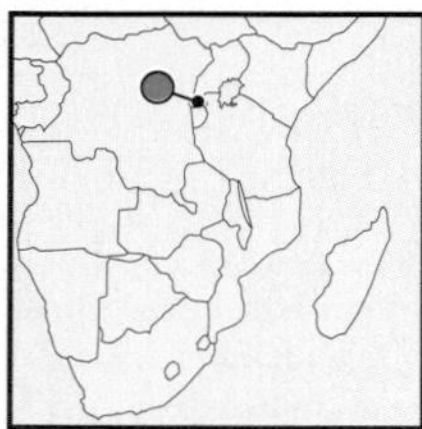

Rwanda's flag has the red, yellow, and green colors used on the flag of Ethiopia, Africa's oldest independent nation. These three colors symbolize African unity. The 'R' distinguishes Rwanda's flag from the flag of Guinea. Rwanda adopted this flag in 1961.

**AREA:** 10,170sq mi (26,340sq km)
**POPULATION:** 7,526,000
**CAPITAL (POPULATION):** Kigali (234,500)
**GOVERNMENT:** Republic
**ETHNIC GROUPS:** Hutu 90%, Tutsi 9%, Twa 1%
**LANGUAGES:** French and Kinyarwanda (both official)
**RELIGIONS:** Christianity 74% (Roman Catholic 65%), traditional beliefs 17%, Islam 9%
**CURRENCY:** Rwanda franc = 100 centimes

The Republic of Rwanda is Africa's most densely populated country. It is a small state in the heart of Africa, bordered by Uganda (N), Tanzania (E), Burundi (S), and Zaire (W). The W border is formed by Lake Kivu and the Ruzizi River. Rwanda has a rugged landscape, dominated by high, volcanic mountains, rising to Mount Karisimbi, at 14,787ft (4,507m). The capital, KIGALI, stands on the central plateau. East Burundi consists of stepped plateaus, which descend to the lakes and marshland of the Kagera National Park on the Tanzania border.

### CLIMATE

Rwanda's climate is moderated by altitude. Rainfall is abundant. The dry season is June–August.

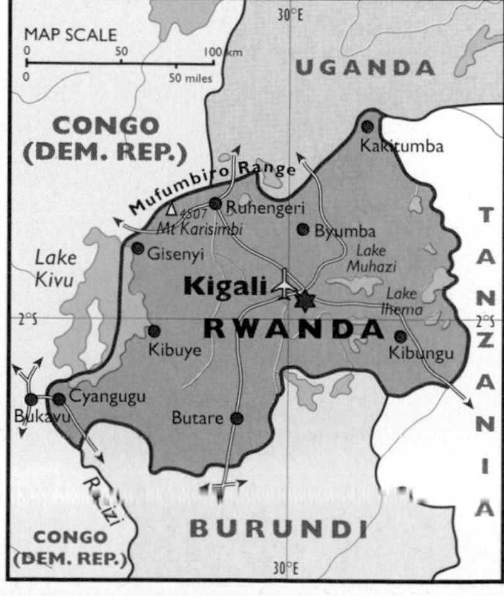


### VEGETATION

The lush rain forests in the W are one of the last refuges for the mountain gorilla. Many of Rwanda's forests have been cleared, 35% of the land is now arable. The steep mountain slopes are intensively cultivated. Despite contour plowing, heavy rain has caused severe soil erosion.

### HISTORY AND POLITICS

Twa pygmies were the original inhabitants of Rwanda, but *c.*1,000 AD, Hutu farmers began to settle, gradually displacing the Twa. In the 15th century, Tutsi cattle herders migrated from the N, and began to dominate the Hutu. By the late 18th century, Rwanda and Burundi formed a single Tutsi-dominated state, ruled by a king (*mwami*). In 1890, Germany conquered the area and subsumed it into German East Africa. During World War I, Belgian forces occupied (1916) both Rwanda and Burundi. In 1919 it became part of the Belgian League of Nations mandate territory of Ruanda-Urundi (which in 1946 became a UN trust territory). The Hutu majority became more vociferous in their demands for political representation. In 1959 the Tutsi *mwami* died. The ensuing civil war between Hutus and Tutsis claimed more than 150,000 lives. Hutu victory led to a mass exodus of Tutsis. The 1960 elections were won by the Hutu Emancipation Movement, led by Grégoire Kayibanda. In 1961 Rwanda declared itself a republic. Belgium recognized independence in 1962. Kayibanda became president. Rwanda was subject to continual Tutsi incursions from Burundi and Uganda. In 1973 Kayibanda was overthrown in a military coup, led by Major General Habyarimana. In 1978 Habyarimana became president. During the 1980s, Rwanda was devastated by drought. More than 50,000 refugees fled to Burundi. In 1990 Rwanda was invaded by the Tutsi-dominated Rwandan Patriotic Front (RPF), who forced Habyarimana to agree to a multiparty constitution. UN forces were drafted in to oversee the transition. In April 1994 Habyarimana and the Burundi president were killed in a rocket attack on their aircraft. The Hutu army and militia launched a premediated act of genocide against the Tutsi minority, killing between 500,000 and 1 million Tutsis within three months. In July 1994 an RPF offensive toppled the government and created 2 million Hutu refugees. A government of national unit was formed. More than 50,000 people died in the refugee camps in E Zaire, before international aid arrived. Hutu militia remained in control of the camps, their leaders facing prosecution for genocide. The sheer number of refugees (1995, one million refugees in Zaire and 500,000 in Tanzania) destabilized regional politics. In 1996 UN troops left Rwanda. In 1998 former prime minister Jean Kambanda was sentenced to life imprisonment for genocide by the UN International Criminal Tribunal.

### ECONOMY

Rwanda is a low-income developing country (1995 GDP per capita, US$540). Most people are subsistence farmers. Crops include bananas, beans, cassava, and sorghum. Some cattle are raised, mainly by Tutsis. Rwanda's most valuable crop is coffee, accounting for more than 70% of exports.

*S/s, 19th letter of the Roman alphabet. It is descended from the Semitic letter* **sin** *or* **shin,** *meaning* **tooth.** *It passed into the Greek alphabet primarily as the Greek letter* **sigma.**

**Saarinen, Eero** (1910–61) US architect, b. Finland. His work linked with EXPRESSIONISM and the INTERNATIONAL STYLE. One of his most exciting buildings was the TWA terminal at New York's Kennedy Airport (1956–62). Other notable designs include the General Motors Technical Center in Warren, Michigan (1948–56) and the US Embassy in London (1955–61).

**Saarland** State in SW Germany on the borders with France (S) and Luxembourg (W); the capital is Saarbrücken. Belonging intermittently to France, the Saar was finally ceded to Prussia after the defeat of Napoleon I in 1815. France administered the region after World War I, but in a 1935 plebiscite 90% of the people voted to return to Germany. French forces again occupied the Saar after World War II. Saarland finally gained the status of a West German state in 1967. The forested valley of the Saar River is contains blast furnaces and steel works, exploiting local coal and nearby iron ore. There is some agriculture. Area: 992sq mi (2,570sq km). Pop. (1989 est.) 1,054,000.

**Sabah, Sheikh Jabir al Ahmad al-** (1928– ) (Jabir III) Emir of Kuwait (1977– ). A member of the ruling family of Al-Sabah, a dynasty founded by Sheikh Sabah al-Awal (r.1756–72), he succeded Sabah III al Salim. When Iraq invaded Kuwait (1990), Jabir took refuge in Saudia Arabia and set up a government in exile. He returned to Kuwait in 1991.

**Sabah** (North BORNEO) State of MALAYSIA and one of the four political subdivisions of the island of Borneo. Ceded to the British in 1877, it remained the British Protectorate of North Borneo until 1963, when it became an independent state of the Malaysian Federation. The terrain is mountainous and forested. The capital is Kota Kinabalu (1990 pop. 208,484). The main products include oil, timber, rubber, coconuts, and rice. Area: 29,545sq mi (76,522sq km). Pop. (1990) 1,736,902.

**Sabbath** Seventh day of the week, set aside as a sacred day of rest. For Jews, the Sabbath runs from sunset on Friday to sunset on Saturday. Christians set aside Sunday for their Sabbath.

**saber-toothed tiger** Popular name for a prehistoric member of the CAT family (Felidae) that existed from the OLIGOCENE period to the PLEISTOCENE period. It had extremely long canine teeth adapted to killing large herbivores. Subfamily Machairodontinae, genus *Smilodon.*

**Sabin, Albert Bruce** (1906–93) US virologist, b. Russia. In 1957 he developed a live virus oral VACCINE against POLIOMYELITIS. It replaced Jonas SALK's inactivate VIRUS vaccine.

**Sabines** Ancient people of central Italy. They inhabited the Sabine Hills NE of Rome. After sporadic fighting, the Sabines were conquered in 290 BC and Romanized.

**sable** MARTEN native to Siberia. It has been hunted almost to extinction for its soft fur, which is dark brown, sometimes flecked with white. Length: to 24in (60cm). Family Mustelidae; species *Martes zibellina.*

**Sacagawea** (*c.*1787–*c.*1812) Native American interpreter for the LEWIS AND CLARK EXPEDITION (1804–06). A member of the Shoshone band, she was a vital guide and interpreter for the expedition to the Pacific Ocean, obtaining food and horses from the Native Americans. Monuments to her are found in Oregon, Montana, Idaho, and North Dakota.

**saccharide** Organic compound based on SUGAR molecules. Monosaccharides include GLUCOSE and FRUCTOSE. Two sugar molecules join together to make a disaccharide, such as LACTOSE or SUCROSE. POLYSACCHARIDES have more than two sugar molecules. *See also* CARBOHYDRATE

**saccharin** ($C_7H_5NO_3S$) Synthetic substance used as a substitute for SUGAR. It is derived from TOLUENE. In 1977 it was tenuously linked with some forms of cancer in humans, and is no longer widely used.

**Sacco and Vanzetti Case** Controversial robbery-murder trial taken up as a cause by intellectuals, radicals, and liberals in the 1920s. At the height of the Red Scare (April 1920), two men robbed and killed a paymaster and his guard in South Braintree, Massachusetts. Italian immigrant anarchists Nicola Sacco and Bartolomeo Vanzetti were convicted (1921) and executed (1927) for the crime. Their supporters claimed the verdict was a reflection of anti-Italian, anti-radical bigotry. There is continued belief in Vanzetti's innocence, although a 1961 ballistics test suggested the fatal bullet came from Sacco's gun.

▲ **saber-toothed tiger** A fierce, carnivorous mammal, the saber-toothed tiger (*Smilodon* sp.) lived in North and South America during the Pleistocene period. It possessed two long fangs and a wide-opening jaw structure that enabled it to kill its prey by stabbing and slashing at its throat. *Smilodon* was more powerfully built than a modern tiger, but is not thought to have been a fast runner, and probably ambushed its prey at waterholes.

**Sackville-West, Vita (Victoria Mary)** (1892–1962) English poet and novelist. A member of the BLOOMSBURY GROUP, her best-known works include *The Edwardians* (1930), *All Passion Spent* (1931), and the long poem *The Land* (1926).

**sacrament** Symbolic action in which the central mysteries of a religious faith are enacted and which, on some accounts, confers divine grace upon those to whom it is given or administered. For Protestants there are two sacraments: BAPTISM and the Lord's Supper (*see* LAST SUPPER). In the Roman Catholic and Eastern Orthodox Churches, the sacraments are baptism, CONFIRMATION, the EUCHARIST, holy ORDERS, matrimony, PENANCE, and the anointing of the sick.

**Sacramento** State capital of California at the confluence of the Sacramento and American rivers; seat of Sacramento County. The first settlement was established (1839) by John A. Sutter and the California gold rush of 1848 spurred development. In 1854 Sacramento became state capital. In 1963, a 43mi (69km) deepwater channel was completed that links the inland port to San Francisco Bay. It is the distribution center for the fertile Sacramento valley. Government agencies and military installations, such as the McClellan Air Force base, have contributed to the local economy. Other industries: missile development, transportation equipment, food processing. Pop. (1992) 382,816.

**sacrifice** Offering or destruction of precious objects – food and drink, flowers and incense, animals and human beings – for religious purposes. Sacrifices are made in order to maintain a relationship with a god or in the hope of winning divine favor or to atone for guilt.

**Sadat, (Muhammad) Anwar (al-)** (1918–81) Egyptian statesman, president (1970–81). A close associate of NASSER, he was vice president (1964–66, 1969–70), and succeeded Nasser as president. After the ARAB-ISRAELI WARS of 1973, he signed an historic Egypt-Israel peace treaty in 1979. Sadat was assassinated by Islamic fundamentalists.

**Sadducees** Jewish sect active in Judaea from *c.*200 BC until the fall of Jerusalem in AD 70. By the time of Jesus, the main difference between them and the PHARISEES was their refusal to recognize the oral traditions surrounding the Scriptures as part of the Hebrew Law.

**Sade, Donatien Alphonse François, Marquis de** (1740–1814) French novelist and playwright, and a founder of the modern French prose style. Imprisoned for sexual offenses, De Sade wrote many licentious novels, among them *Justine* (1791) and *Juliette* (1797).

**Safavid** Persian dynasty (1501–1722) that established the territorial and Shiite theocratic principles of modern Iran. The dynastic founder, Shah ISMAIL, claimed descent from a Shiite SUFISM order, and the state adopted Shiism as the state religion. His successor, ABBAS I, accepted the Ottoman occupation of W Iran and concentrated on subduing the threat to Iran's E borders. His death created a power vacuum and Iran's borders contracted. Shah Husayn's concentration on the capture of Bahrain enabled Afghan troops to overrun the country. His forced abdication in 1722 marked the end of Safavid rule.

**saffron** (fall CROCUS) Perennial crocus, native to Asia Minor. It has purple or white flowers. The golden, dried stigmas of the plant are used as a flavoring or dye. Family Iridaceae; species *Crocus sativus.*

**saga** In old NORSE LITERATURE (especially Icelandic), prose narrative that relates the lives of historical figures. The sagas were written between the 7th and 14th centuries. Notable examples include the *Gísla saga*, the *Njáls saga*, and the *Heimskringla* by SNORRI STURLUSON.

**Sagan, Carl Edward** (1934–96) US astronomer and author. He taught at Harvard University and Smithsonian Astrophysical Observatory before joining (1968) the astronomy faculty of Cornell University. Sagan hosted the popular television series *Cosmos* (1980). His works include *The Dragons of Eden* (1977), *Broca's Brain* (1979), and *Contact* (1985).

**sage** Common name for a number of plants of the MINT family (Lamiaceae/Labiatae) native to the Mediterranean region. The best known is *Salvia officinalis*, an aromatic perennial herb used widely for seasoning. Height: 6–15in (15–38cm).

**sagebrush** Aromatic shrub common in arid areas of W

North America. The common sagebrush has small, silvery-green leaves and bears clusters of tiny white flower heads. Height: to 6.5ft (2m). Family Asteraceae/Compositae; species *Artemisia tridentata*.

**Sagittarius** Southern constellation between Scorpio and Capricorn. It is rich in stellar CLUSTERS and interstellar matter. The brightest star is Epsilon Sagittarii (*Kaus Australis*), magnitude 1.8. In astrology, it is the ninth sign of the zodiac, represented by an archer.

**sago palm** (fern palm) Feather-leaved PALM tree native to swampy areas of Malaysia and Polynesia. Its thick trunk contains sago, a type of starch. Height: 4–30ft (1.2–9.1m). Family Arecaceae/Palmae; species *Metroxylon sagu*.

**saguaro** Large CACTUS native to SW North America. White, night-blooming flowers appear when the plant is 50 to 75 years old. Its red fruit is edible. Height: to 40ft (12m). Family Cactaceae; species *Carnegiea gigantea*.

**Sahara** World's largest desert, with an area of *c*.3,500,000sq mi (9,000,000sq km), covering nearly a third of Africa's total land area. It consists of Algeria, Niger, Libya, Egypt, and Mauritania, the S parts of Morocco and Tunisia, and the N parts of Senegal, Mali, Chad, and Sudan. It extends *c*.3,000mi (4,800km) W to E from the Atlantic Ocean to the Red Sea, and stretches *c*.1,200mi (1,900km) N to S from the ATLAS Mountains to the SAHEL. The annual rainfall is usually less than 4in (10cm) and there is very little natural vegetation. Two-thirds of the Sahara is stony desert, and the topography ranges from the Tibesti Massif (N Chad) at 11,000ft (3,400m) to the QATTARA DEPRESSION (Egypt) at 436ft (133m) below sea-level. Oases act as vital centers for water, crop farming, and transportation, and the Sahara's two million inhabitants are concentrated around them. The two main ethnic groups are the TUAREG and the Tibu. Nomads continue to herd sheep and goats. Transportation is still primarily by camel and horse. Mineral deposits include salt, iron ore, phosphates, oil, and gas.

**Sahel** Band of semiarid scrub and savanna grassland in Africa, S of the SAHARA. It extends through Senegal, S Mauritania, Mali, Burkina Faso, N Benin, S Niger, N Nigeria, and S central Chad. Over the past 30 years the Sahara has encroached on the N Sahel in the world's most notorious example of DESERTIFICATION.

**Saigon** *See* HO CHI MINH CITY

**sailing** *See* YACHT

**saint** Man or woman who has manifested exceptional holiness and love of God during his or her life. In the New Testament, all believers are called saints, but since the 2nd century the title has usually been reserved for men and women of the most outstanding merit. In the Roman Catholic and Eastern Orthodox churches, individual saints are regarded as having a special relationship with God and are therefore venerated for their perceived role as intercessors. The Protestant reformers of the 16th century abolished the veneration of saints, saying that all believers have access to God through Christ. *See also* CANONIZATION; individual saints

**Saint Bartholomew's Day Massacre** (August 24, 1572) Mass murder of HUGUENOTS (French Protestants) on St. Bartholomew's feast day. Huguenot leaders had gathered in Paris for the marriage of Henry of Navarre (later HENRY IV). Acting on the orders of CATHERINE DE' MEDICI, the massacre began when soldiers killed Huguenot leaders and continued in the provinces until October 3, leaving *c*.70,000 dead.

**St. Bernard** Swiss mountain dog with excellent scenting abilities used to find people lost in deep snow. It has a massive head, and a dense white and red coat. Height: to 29in (74cm) at the shoulder; weight: to 170lb (77kg).

**St. Croix** (Santa Cruz) Largest of the US VIRGIN ISLANDS, West Indies. Christiansted, on NE coast, is the chief town. St. Croix was ruled by several nations until it was sold by Denmark to the US (1917). Industries: rum, sugar, livestock. Area: 84sq mi (218sq km). Pop. (1990) 50,139.

**Saint-Exupéry, Antoine de** (1900–44) French novelist and aviator. His experiences as a pilot provided the material for his novels, which include *Southern Mail* (1928), *Night Flight* (1931), and *Flight to Arras* (1942). He is best known for his classic fable *The Little Prince* (1943). He was killed in World War II.

**St. George's** Capital and port on the SW coast of GRENADA, West Indies. Founded in 1650 as a French settlement, it was capital of the British WINDWARD ISLANDS (1885–1958). Industries: rum distilling, sugar processing, tourism. Pop. (1989) 35,742.

**St. Germain, Treaty of** (1919) Part of the peace settlement after World War I. It established the new republic of Austria from the old AUSTRO-HUNGARIAN EMPIRE.

**St. Helena** Rocky island in the S Atlantic, *c*.1,200mi (1,900km) from the coast of W Africa; its capital is Jamestown (1992 pop. 1,500). It became a British crown colony in 1834 and is chiefly known as the place of Napoleon I's exile. It is now a UK dependent territory and administrative center for the islands of ASCENSION and TRISTAN DA CUNHA. Area: 47sq mi (122sq km). Pop. (1992) 5,700.

**St. Helens, Mount** Volcanic peak in the Cascade Range, SW Washington. Dormant since 1857, it erupted on May 18, 1980, killing 60 people. The 9,580ft (2,950m) summit was reduced to 8,312ft (2,560m), with a deep horseshoe crater. Two more eruptions occurred in the following two weeks, and it is predicted to erupt again in the early 21st century.

**St. John** Largest city and industrial center of New Brunswick, E Canada. A major year-round port, St. John lies on the Bay of Fundy at the mouth of the St. John River. The first settlement was established (1783) by a band of Loyalists fleeing the American Revolution. St. John became the first Canadian city to be incorporated (1785). Industries: oil and sugar refining, paper.

**St. John of Jerusalem, Knights Hospitallers of** *See* KNIGHTS HOSPITALLERS

**St. John's** Port and capital of Antigua, in the Leeward Islands, West Indies. Industries: tourism, rum, sugar, cotton. Pop. (1992) 38,000.

**St. John's** Capital and major port of Newfoundland, Canada, on the SE coast of Newfoundland Island. Founded in 1583, it is one of the oldest settlements in North America. Industries: fishing and fish processing, iron, shipbuilding, textiles, paper. Pop. (1991) 171,859.

**St. Kitts-Nevis** Self-governing state in the Leeward Islands, West Indies. The state includes the islands of Saint Kitts (Saint Christopher), Nevis, and Somberro. Basseterre (on Saint Kitts) is the capital (1992 pop. 12,605). The islands were discovered in 1493 by COLUMBUS, and settled by the English (1623) and the French (1624). Disputes over possession were settled in Britain's favor in 1783, and the islands achieved self-government in 1967. Industries: tourism, sugar, cotton, salt, coconuts. Area: 120sq mi (310sq km). Pop. (1991) 40,618.

▲ **sage** Many culinary herbs, such as sage (*Salvia* sp.), are members of the Labiatae (mint) family. Sage has had a variety of medicinal uses for thousands of years. The word "sage" (meaning wise) derives from the ancient belief that the herb enhanced people's memories.

◀ **sago palm** Flourishing in SE Asian freshwater swamps, the sago palm (*Metroxylon sagu*) is a primary source of carbohydrate in tropical regions. Just before flowering, the palm is cut, and the pith of the trunk ground to make sago flour.

S

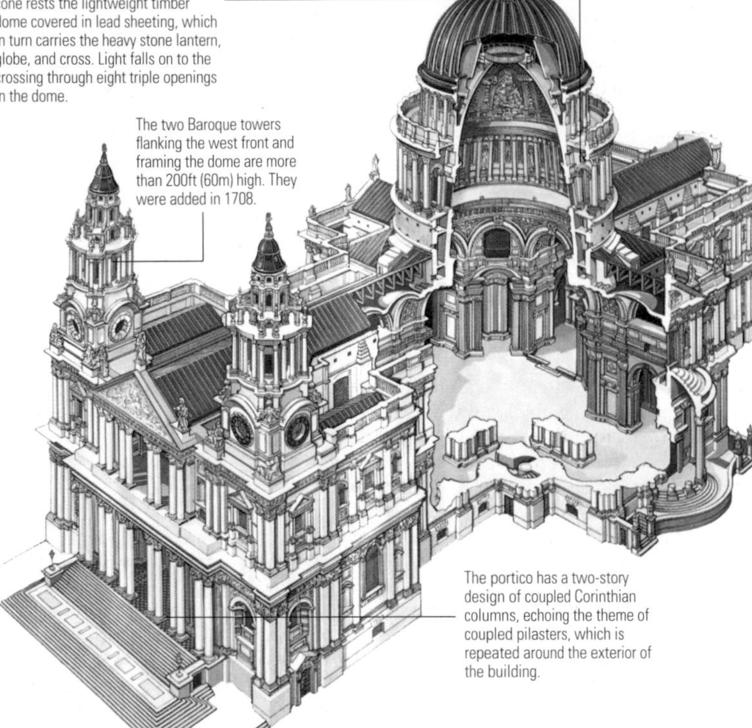

The drum of St. Paul's is an extremely complex structure. The huge outer dome was skillfully constructed above an inner, lower dome. Between the two, Wren placed a tall cone of bricks, reinforced by two iron chains; on this cone rests the lightweight timber dome covered in lead sheeting, which in turn carries the heavy stone lantern, globe, and cross. Light falls on to the crossing through eight triple openings in the dome.
Thirty-two buttresses surround the drum, finishing in columns to create a classical effect.
The two Baroque towers flanking the west front and framing the dome are more than 200ft (60m) high. They were added in 1708.
The portico has a two-story design of coupled Corinthian columns, echoing the theme of coupled pilasters, which is repeated around the exterior of the building.


▲ **St. Paul's** Old St. Paul's, a Gothic cathedral the portico of which was added by Inigo Jones, had to be pulled down following the Great Fire of London in 1666. It was rebuilt by Christopher Wren (1675–1710). The plan is a Latin cross, 460ft (140m) long by 100ft (30m) wide. At the crossing, eight piers carry the dome, one of London's most famous landmarks. The wooden model for Wren's earlier design has been preserved.

**Saint Laurent, Louis Stephen** (1882–1973) Canadian statesman, prime minister (1948–57). A distinguished lawyer, he was justice minister and attorney-general (1941–46). Saint Laurent succeeded W.L. MACKENZIE KING as prime minister and leader of the Liberal Party.

**St. Lawrence** Second-longest river in Canada, flowing from the NE end of Lake Ontario to the Gulf of St. Lawrence, Quebec. The river forms the boundary between the US and Canada for *c*.110mi (180km) of its total length of 750mi (1,200km). Since the completion of the ST. LAWRENCE SEAWAY in 1959, the river has been navigable to all but the very largest vessels. It is the major freight-carrying river in Canada. The St. Lawrence system of canals, locks, and dams generates much of the hydroelectric power used in Ontario and New York.

**St. Lawrence Seaway** Waterway in Canada and the US. Built in the 1950s, it connects the GREAT LAKES with the Atlantic Ocean. The St. Lawrence Seaway extends *c*.470mi (750km) from N of Montreal down to the N shore of Lake Erie using canals and locks that bypass the rapids along the ST. LAWRENCE River. The waterway also includes the Welland Canal, which bypasses Niagara Falls. The St. Lawrence Seaway allows oceangoing vessels to reach industrial lakeside ports of central North America, such as Detroit, Chicago, and Toronto.

**St. Louis** City and port in E Missouri, on the Mississippi River near its confluence with the Missouri. The second-largest city in Missouri, it was founded in 1763 by the French. It was held by Spain from 1770 to 1800, returned briefly to France, and then ceded to the US in the Louisiana Purchase (1803). Industries: mineral processing, brewing, chemicals, transport equipment. Pop. (1992) 383,733.

**St. Lucia** Volcanic island in the Windward group, West Indies; the capital is Castries. The island changed hands 14 times between France and Britain before being ceded to Britain in 1814. It achieved self-government in 1979. Industries: tourism, bananas. Area: 238sq mi (616sq km). Pop. (1991) 133,308.

**St. Mark's** BASILICA in Venice. Begun in 829 to enshrine the remains of the city's patron saint, St. Mark, it was restored after a fire in 976. It was later demolished and rebuilt in the 11th century in the BYZANTINE style.

**St. Moritz** Winter-sports center and tourist resort, on Lake St. Moritz, E Switzerland, at an altitude of 5,980ft (1,822m). The site of the 1928 and 1948 Winter Olympics, it is the home of the Cresta Run. St. Moritz is also noted for its mineral springs. Pop. (1991) 8,700.

**St. Paul** State capital and port of entry, on the E bank of the Mississippi River, in E MINNESOTA, just E of MINNEAPOLIS, its twin city. In 1849 St. Paul became capital of Minnesota territory, and developed rapidly as a river port and transportation center. Today, it is a major manufacturing and distribution center. Industries: computers, electronics, printing, automobiles. Pop. (1992) 268,266.

**St. Paul's** Anglican cathedral in London, built (1675–1710) on the site of a medieval cathedral destroyed in the Great Fire of London (1666). It was designed in a classical style by Sir Christopher WREN.

**St. Peter's** Great Christian BASILICA in the VATICAN CITY. In 1506 Pope Julius II laid the foundation stone on the site of an earlier structure over the grave of St. Peter. The church was completed in 1615 during the reign of Pope Paul V, under the architectural supervision of Carlo Maderno (1556–1629).

**St. Petersburg** (formerly Petrograd and Leningrad) Second-largest city in Russia and a major Baltic seaport at the E end of the Gulf of Finland, on the delta of the Neva River. Founded in 1703 by PETER I (THE GREAT), the city was the capital of Russia from 1712 to 1918. It was the scene of the Decembrist revolt of 1825 and the Bloody Sunday incident in the Russian Revolution of 1905. Renamed Petrograd in 1914, it was a center of the political unrest that culminated in the RUSSIAN REVOLUTION. The workers of Petrograd were the spearhead of the 1917 revolution, and the city was renamed Leningrad (1924). It suffered extensive damage during World War II and has been massively rebuilt. Renamed St. Petersburg (1991) following the breakup of the Soviet Union, it enjoys federal status within the Russian Republic. Industries: shipbuilding, heavy engineering, brewing, publishing, electronics, chemicals. Pop. (1994) 4,883,000.

**St. Petersburg** Residential city on Tampa Bay, W central Florida. Known as "Sunshine City," St. Petersburg was first settled in 1888, and incorporated in 1892. It is a yachting and fishing resort and the site of the 15mi (24km) long Sunshine Skyway Bridge. Industries: concrete, aluminum products. Pop. (1990) 240,318.

**St. Pierre and Miquelon** Group of eight small islands in the Gulf of St. Lawrence, SW of Newfoundland, Canada. The capital is St. Pierre (pop. 5,000) on the island of the same name; Miquelon is the largest island. The group was claimed for France in 1535 and since 1985 has been a "territorial collectivity," sending delegates to the French parliament. Fishing is the most important activity, and has led to disputes with Canada. Area: 93sq mi (242sq km). Pop. (1990) 6,392.

**Saint-Saëns, Charles Camille** (1835–1921) French composer, pianist, and organist. He is best remembered for the opera *Samson and Delilah* (1877), the Third Symphony (1886), the *Carnival of the Animals* (1886), and the *Danse Macabre* (1874).

**St. Sophia** *See* HAGIA SOPHIA

**St. Thomas** Second-largest island of the US VIRGIN ISLANDS, West Indies. Charlotte Amalie, capital of US Virgin Islands, is on the S coast. The first European to discover the island was Christopher Columbus in 1493. It was first settled by the Dutch. Industries: rum, tourism. Area: 28sq mi (72sq km). Pop. 48,166.

**St. Valentine's Day Massacre** (February 14, 1929) Gangland killings in Chicago, Illinois. The perpetrators were gunmen of Al CAPONE, disguised as policemen, and the seven victims were members of a rival gang of bootleggers during the PROHIBITION era.

**St. Vincent and the Grenadines** Island state between St. Lucia and Grenada, Windward Islands, West Indies. The capital is Kingstown (1991 pop. 26,233). It comprises the volcanic island of St. Vincent and five islands of the Grenadine group, including Mustique. St. Vincent remained uncolonized until British settlement in 1762. St. Vincent was part of the British Windward Islands colony from 1880 to 1958. Self-government was granted in 1969, followed by full independence within the Commonwealth of Nations in 1979.

Agriculture dominates the economy; major crops include arrowroot, bananas, and coconuts. Area: 150sq mi (388sq km). Pop. (1991) 106,499.

**Sakhalin** (Jap. *Karafuto*) Island off the E coast of Russia, between the seas of Okhotsk and Japan. The capital is Yuzhno-Sakhalinsk (1992 pop. 174,000). Settled by Russians and Japanese in the 18th and 19th centuries, it came under Russian control in 1875. In 1905 Japan regained the S, but was forced to cede it again in 1945. The island is mountainous and forested, with a harsh climate. Sakhalin has large deposits of coal and iron ore; oil extracted in the NE is piped to the Russian mainland. Industries: timber, fishing, canning. Area: 29,500sq mi (76,400sq km). Pop. (1989) 709,000.

**Sakharov, Andrei Dimitrievich** (1921–89) Soviet physicist and social critic. His work in nuclear FUSION was instrumental in the development of the Soviet HYDROGEN BOMB. An outspoken defender of civil liberties, Sakharov created the Human Rights Committee in 1970 and received the 1975 Nobel Prize for Peace.

**Saladin** (1138–93) (Salah ad-din) Muslim general and founder of the Ayyubid dynasty. From 1152 he was a soldier and administrator in Egypt. Appointed grand vizier in 1169, Saladin overthrew the FATIMIDS in 1171 and made himself sultan. After conquering most of Syria, he gathered widespread support for a JIHAD to drive the Christians from Palestine (1187). Saladin reconquered Jerusalem, provoking the Third Crusade (1189). His rule restored Egypt as a major power and introduced a period of stability and growth.

**Salam, Abdus** (1926– ) Pakistani physicist who in 1967 proposed a theory that unifies the electromagnetic and weak nuclear forces (*see* FUNDAMENTAL FORCES) within the nucleus of an atom. Salam, Steven WEINBERG, and Sheldon GLASHOW worked independently on the theory (now known as the Weinberg-Salam theory) and shared the 1979 Nobel Prize for physics.

**salamander** Any of 320 species of amphibians found worldwide, except in Australia and polar regions. It has an elongated body, a long tail, and short legs. Most species lay eggs, but some give birth to live young. The largest European species, the fire salamander (*Salamandra salamandra*), may attain a length of 11in (28cm). Order Urodela.

**Salazar, António de Oliveira** (1889–1970) Dictator of Portugal (1932–68). He became prime minister and assumed dictatorial powers (1932). Imposing a semi-fascist constitution (1933), Salazar held power with a powerful army and secret police, enforcing law and order at the cost of economic progress. He was sympathetic to FRANCO in Spain, remained neutral in World War II, and subsequently sought good relations with the West.

**Salem** State capital of Oregon, on the Willamette River. Founded in 1840 by Methodist missionaries, it was made territorial capital in 1851 and state capital in 1859. Industries: timber, paper, textiles, food canning, meat packing, high-technology equipment. Pop. (1990) 112,050.

**Salem** City on Massachusetts Bay, NE Massachusetts, 14mi (22km) NE of Boston. First settled in 1626, Salem achieved notoriety for its witchcraft trials (1692), when 19 people were hanged. Industries: electrical products, leather goods, textiles, tourism. Pop. (1990) 38,090.

**salicylic acid** Colorless, crystalline solid ($C_7H_6O_3$), derivatives of which are used as analgesics (including ASPIRIN, acetylsalicylic acid), antiseptics, dyes, and liniments. It occurs naturally in plants, including willow bark and oil of wintergreen.

**Salieri, Antonio** (1750–1825) Italian composer. As court composer in Vienna, he composed many operas, much sacred music, and vocal and orchestral works.

**Salinger, J.D. (Jerome David)** (1919– ) US novelist. Well-known as a reclusive writer who shuns publicity, he achieved fame with his first book and only novel, *Catcher in the Rye* (1951). The story of a tortured teenager, it is recounted in modern speech, and its style influenced a generation of new US writers. His other works are collections of short stories, including *Franny and Zooey* (1961), *Raise High the Roof Beam, Carpenters*, and *Seymour: An Introduction* (both 1963).

**Salish** Band of Native North Americans formerly the principal inhabitants of parts of present-day Idaho, Montana, Oregon, and Washington in the US and British Columbia in Canada. There are two major groupings: Coast Salish and Interior Salish. **Coast Salish** were mainly a fishing community. In the winter, they built long houses. European settlers tried to suppress their potlatch rituals. Today, *c.*12,000 Coast Salish live on reservations in the US and Canada. The **Interior Salish** lived on the plateau E of the US Coast Mountains and the Canadian Coast Range. Their culture was more akin to the Plains Native Americans. They roamed widely, living in tepees, and hunted of buffalo. Today, *c.*20,000 Interior Salish remain on reservations in Canada and the US.

**saliva** Fluid secreted into the mouth by the SALIVARY GLANDS. In vertebrates, saliva is composed of about 99% water with dissolved traces of sodium, potassium, calcium, and the ENZYME amylase. Saliva softens and lubricates food to aid swallowing, and amylase starts the digestion of starches.

**salivary glands** Three pairs of GLANDS located on each side of the mouth that form and secrete SALIVA. The parotid gland, just below and in front of each ear, is the largest; the submaxiallary gland is near the angle of the lower jaw; and the sublingual gland is under the side of the tongue.

**Salk, Jonas Edward** (1914–95) US medical researcher. Salk developed the first VACCINE against POLIOMYELITIS in 1952. It used an inactivate poliomyelitis VIRUS.

**salmon** Marine and freshwater fish of the Northern Hemisphere. The Pacific salmon (*Oncorhynchus*) hatches, spawns, and dies in freshwater, but spends its adult life in the ocean. The Atlantic salmon (*Salmo salar*) is a marine trout that spawns in rivers on each side of the Atlantic Ocean and then returns to the sea. Weight: to 80lb (36kg). Family Salmonidae.

**salmonella** Several species of rod-shaped bacteria that cause intestinal infections in human beings and animals. *Salmonella typhi* causes TYPHOID FEVER; other species cause GASTROENTERITIS. The bacteria are transmitted by carriers, particularly flies, and in food and water.

**Salome** (active 1st century AD) Daughter of Herodias and stepdaughter of Herod Antipas. She conspired with her mother to have JOHN THE BAPTIST executed.

**salsa** Term first used in the early 1970s for the Cuban-inspired music being produced in New York. Salsa is a percussive and brass-led big band music. It embraces dance forms, including rumba, mambo, and guaracha.

**salt** Ionic compound formed, along with water, when an ACID is neutralized by a BASE. The hydrogen of the acid is replaced by a metal or ammonium ion. The most familiar is SODIUM CHLORIDE. Salts are typically crystalline compounds. They usually dissolve in water to form a solution that can conduct electricity.

**Salt Lake City** State capital in N central Utah, 13mi (21km) E of GREAT SALT LAKE. Founded in 1847 by the MORMONS under Brigham YOUNG, it grew rapidly to become capital of the Territory of Utah (1856) and the State of Utah (1896). Salt Lake City is the world headquarters of the Mormon Church. Zinc, gold, silver, lead, and copper are mined nearby. Other industries: missiles, rocket engines, oil refining, tourism, printing and publishing. Pop. (1992) 165,835.

**Salvador** (Bahia) Seaport city in E central Brazil; capital of BAHIA state. Founded by the Portuguese in 1549 as Bahia, it was the capital of Brazil until 1763. Portuguese colonizers built vast sugar plantations using African slave labor, and the city is noted for its African culture. Industries: oil refining, petrochemicals, tobacco, sugar, coffee, industrial diamonds. Pop. (1991) 2,056,000.

**Salvador, El** *See* EL SALVADOR

**Salvation Army** International Christian society devoted to the propagation of the gospel among the working classes. Its origin was the Christian Revival Association, founded (1865) in London by William BOOTH. In 1878 it became the Salvation Army and the members, led by "General" Booth, were given ranks. Under the leadership of Booth's son, Bramwell, its work spread to other parts of the world.

**Salween** River in Southeast Asia. It rises in the Tibetan Plateau, E Tibet, and flows S through Yunnan province, cutting deep gorges through the terrain. It empties into the Andaman

▲ **salamander** The fire salamander (*Salamandra salamandra*, top) is found in central, S, and W Europe, NW Africa, and SW Asia. Its bright coloration acts as a warning to potential predators. Within the skin of the fire salamander are many glands that secrete a sticky, irritant fluid that wards off larger predators and can be fatal to smaller animals. Although the fire salamander obtains oxygen mainly through gas exchange on the surface of its body, it has a set of primitive lungs. The dusky salamander (*Desmognathus* sp., bottom) on the other hand has no lungs. Respiration is carried out entirely through surface gas exchange. This is only possible if the surface is kept moist by secretions from mucous glands.

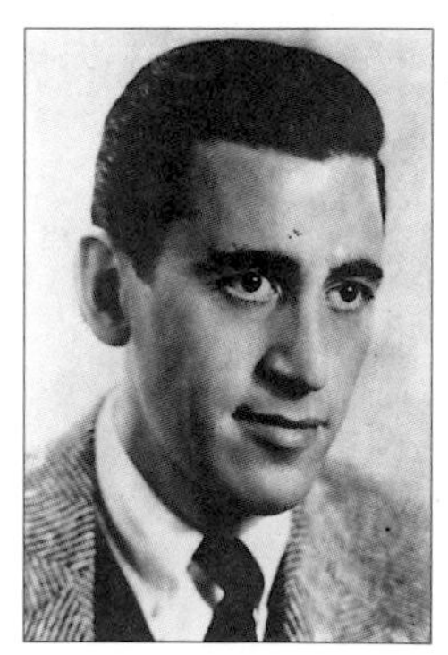

▲ **Salinger** US author J.D. Salinger is famous for his depictions of lonely characters frustrated by a boring and conformist world. His only novel, *The Catcher in the Rye* (1951), is an enduringly popular tale of disaffected youth. He has been twice married and divorced. He now lives in rural seclusion while continuing to write and study Zen philosophy.

S

Sea. It forms many rapids along its course and despite its length of *c*.1,740mi (2,800km) is navigable for only 75mi (120km) upstream.

**Salzburg** City on the Salzach River, NW Austria, capital of the Alpine Salzburg state. It grew around a 7th-century monastery and became part of Bavaria in 1809, but was returned to Austria by the Congress of Vienna. Mozart's birthplace and the home of several music festivals, its most important industry is tourism. Pop. (1991) 144,000.

**Samaria** Ancient region and town of central Palestine. It was built as the capital of the N kingdom of Israel in the 9th century BC. Conquered by Shalmaneser *c*.722 BC and SARGON, Samaria was later destroyed by John Hyrcanus I and rebuilt by HEROD THE GREAT. *See also* SAMARITANS

**Samaritans** Descendants of those citizens of SAMARIA who escaped deportation after their kingdom was overrun by the Assyrians in 722 BC. The Jews to the south rejected them. The Samaritans call themselves "Children of Israel" (Bene-Yisreal) and their sole religious scripture is the TORAH.

**samarium** (symbol Sm) Gray-white, metallic element of the LANTHANIDE SERIES. First identified spectroscopically in 1879, its chief ores are monazite and bastnasite. Samarium is used in carbon-arc lamps, as a neutron absorber in NUCLEAR REACTORS, and as a catalyst. Some samarium alloys are used in making powerful permanent magnets. Properties: at.no. 62; at. wt. 150.35; sp. gr. 7.52; m.p. 1,962°F (1,072°C); b.p. 3,256°F (1,791°C); most common isotope $^{152}$Sm (26.72%).

**Samarkand** City in the fertile Zeravshan valley, SE Uzbekistan. One of the oldest cities in Asia, it was conquered by ALEXANDER THE GREAT in 329 BC. A vital trading center on the SILK ROAD, it flourished under the Arab UMAYYAD empire of the 8th century. In 1220 it was destroyed by GENGHIS KHAN, but in 1370 was made the capital of the Mongol empire of TAMERLANE. Ruled by the Uzbeks from the 16th century, it was taken by the Russians in 1868, though it remained largely a center of Muslim culture. Products: cotton, silk, leather goods, wine, tea, carpets, canned fruit, motor vehicle parts. It is a major scientific research center. Pop. (1990) 370,000.

**Samoa** Volcanic island group in the S Pacific, comprising the independent state of WESTERN SAMOA and the US-administered AMERICAN SAMOA. Extending *c*.350mi (560km), the islands are fringed by coral reefs.The majority of the population are indigenous Polynesians. The first European discovery of the islands was in 1722.

**Sampras, Pete** (1971– ) US tennis player. In 1990 he became the youngest-ever winner of the US Open and also won the first Grand Slam Cup. He went to win a further three US Opens (1993, 1995–96), five Wimbledon titles (1993–95, 1997, 1998), and the Australian Open (1994, 1997).

**Samson** Israelite judge and Old Testament hero renowned for his great physical strength. Samson was a Nazarite, whose strength lay in his long hair. When his mistress DELILAH discovered this, she had his hair cut off while he slept and handed him over to the PHILISTINES. Samson regained his strength as his hair regrew, and when called upon to display his strength in the Philistine Temple of Dagon, he pulled down its central pillars and roof, killing himself and thousands of his captors.

► **Sampras** US tennis player Pete Sampras celebrates his 1995 Wimbledon singles title. Born in Washington D.C., Sampras dominated men's singles in the mid to late 1990s. With a futher Wimbledon title in 1998, he equaled Borg's modern-day record of five titles. He is renowned for his fast and devastatingly accurate serve and strong volleys.

**Samuel** Ninth and tenth books of the OLD TESTAMENT. Through the stories of Samuel, the prophet and judge, and of SAUL and DAVID, Israel's first two kings, they describe the transition of ISRAEL from a collection of tribes under separate chiefs to a single nation ruled through a monarchy. Historically the events belong roughly to the 11th century BC.

**Samuelson, Paul Anthony** (1915– ) US economist. He was noted for his work in macroeconomics and mathematical economics. His best-known work is *Economics: An Introductory Analysis* (1948). Samuelson also wrote *Foundations of Economic Analysis* (1947). In 1970 he received the Nobel Prize for economics.

**Samurai** Member of the elite warrior class of feudal Japan. Beginning as military retainers in the 10th century, the samurai came to form an aristocratic ruling class. They conformed to a strict code of conduct, known as BUSHIDO ("the way of the warrior").

**San** (Bushmen) Khoisan-speaking people of S Africa. They have lived in the region for thousands of years and until recently had a hunting and gathering culture. About half still follow the traditional ways, mostly in the Kalahari region of Botswana and Namibia.

**Sana'a** (San'a) Capital and largest city of Yemen, 40mi (65km) NE of the Red Sea port of Hodeida. Situated on a high plateau at 7,500ft (2,280m), it claims to be the world's oldest city, founded by Shem, eldest son of Noah. During the 17th century and from 1872 to 1918 it was part of the Ottoman empire. In 1918 it became capital of an independent Yemen Arab Republic, and in 1990 capital of the new, unified Yemen. It is noted for its handicrafts. Agriculture (grapes) and industry (iron) are also important. Pop. (1988) 427,502.

**San Andreas fault** Geological FAULT line extending more than 600mi (950km) through California. It lies on the boundary between the North American and the eastern Pacific plates of the Earth's crust. PLATE TECTONIC movement causes several thousand EARTHQUAKES each year, although only a few are significant. The most destructive occurred in 1906: it horizontally displaced land around the fault by up to 21ft (6.4m) and killed 503 people. Notable tremors occurred in 1989 and 1994.

**San Antonio** City on the San Antonio River, S central Texas. In 1718 Martín de Alarcón founded the mission-fort of San Antonio de Valero (the ALAMO). San Antonio became the major Spanish settlement in Texas. In 1821 the town became part of an independent Mexico. In 1835 Texas settlers revolted against Mexican rule. The Battle of the Alamo (1836) saw 187 settlers defend the fort for 13 days against 5,000 Mexican troops. The fort was captured (March 6) and all the defenders killed. In April the Republic of Texas gained independence. In 1845 Texas became a state. The city flourished with the arrival of the railroad (1877). Industries: military, aerospace, electronics, health care, oil refining, chemicals, financial services, tourism. Pop. (1992) 966,437.

**sanctions** Punitive action taken by one or more states against another stopping short of direct military intervention. Sanctions can include the cessation of trade, severing of diplomatic relations, the use of a blockade, and the breaking of cultural and sporting contacts.

**sanctuary** Holy or reserved part of any religious building. In a Roman temple the sanctuary was called the *adytum* or *cella*. In a Christian church, the chancel or presbytery is the sanctuary. The term also applied to a church precinct or other sacred place where a fugitive from justice could claim immunity from arrest.

**Sand, George** (1804–76) French novelist, b. Amandine Aurore Lucie Dupin, also remembered for her relationships with Musset and Chopin. Romantic novels such as *Lélia* (1833) and *Mauprat* (1837) advocate women's right to independence. Her later work includes *The Haunted Pool* (1846) and *The*

*Master Bellringers* (1853), masterpieces of rural life. Her autobiographical works include *A Winter in Majorca* (1842).

**sand** Mineral particles worn away from rocks by EROSION, individually large enough to be distinguished with the naked eye. Sand is composed mostly of QUARTZ, but black sand (containing volcanic rock) and coral sand also occur. *See also* SANDSTONE

**sandalwood** Any of several species of Asian trees of the genus *Santalum*, many of which are PARASITES on the roots of other plants. The fragrant wood is used in carving and joss sticks. The distilled oil is used in perfumes and medicines. Height: to 33ft (10m). Family Santalaceae.

**Sandburg, Carl** (1878–1967) US poet and biographer. Strongly influenced by Walt Whitman, his first volume of poetry was *Chicago Poems* (1916). Other collections include *Cornhuskers* (Pulitzer Prize, 1918), *Smoke and Steel* (1920), *Good Morning, America* (1928), and *The People, Yes* (1936). Sandburg also won Pulitzer prizes for his *Complete Poems* (1950) and for his biography *Abraham Lincoln: The War Years* (1939).

**San Diego** City in S California, almost adjoining Tijuana on the Mexican border. In 1542 Juan Rodríguez Cabrillo sailed into San Diego Bay and in 1769 the first Spanish fort in California was founded on the site. Located on a fine natural Pacific harbor, San Diego has a huge naval base and is an important center for scientific research (especially oceanography). Other industries: aerospace, health care, electronics, shipbuilding, tourism, fishing, fish canning. Pop. (1992) 1,148,851.

**Sandinistas** (Sandinista National Liberation Front) Revolutionary group in Nicaragua. They took their name from Augusto Cesar Sandino (1895–1934), who was killed for his opposition to the dominant SOMOZA family. The Sandinistas overthrew the Somoza regime in 1979, and formed a government led by Daniel ORTEGA. In power, they were opposed by right-wing guerrillas, the CONTRAS, supported by the US. The conflict ended when the Sandinista agreed to free elections. They lost, but the Contras were disbanded and the Sandinistas remain an influential political force.

**sandpiper** Wading bird that breeds in cold regions and migrates long distances to winter in warm areas, settling in grass or low bushes near water. It feeds on invertebrates and nests in a grass-lined hole in the ground. Length: 6–24in (15–60cm). Family Scolopacidae.

**sandstone** SEDIMENTARY ROCK composed of sand grains cemented in such materials as SILICA or calcium carbonate.

**San Francisco** City and port in W California, on a peninsula bounded by the Pacific Ocean (W) and SAN FRANCISCO BAY (E), which are connected by the Golden Gate Strait. Founded by the Spanish in 1776, it was captured (1846) by the US in the Mexican War. A gold rush (1848) swelled the town's population. Devastated by an earthquake and fire in 1906, San Francisco was quickly rebuilt and prospered with the opening of the Panama Canal. Industry developed rapidly and it became the leading commercial city on the West Coast. Today, it comprises (with OAKLAND and SAN JOSE) the fourth-largest metropolitan area in the US. Its mild climate and cosmopolitan feel make it a major tourist center. Sites include Golden Gate Bridge and Fisherman's Wharf. Other industries: shipbuilding, oil refining, aircraft, fishing, printing and publishing. Pop. (1992) 728,921.

**San Francisco Conference on International Organization** (1945) Meeting that drafted the charter forming the UNITED NATIONS (UN). Delegates representing 50 nations met in San Francisco from April 25. With World War II ending, the Allies wanted to safeguard future peace. The UN charter was signed on June 26.

**Sanger, Frederick** (1918– ) English biochemist who became the first person to win two Nobel Prizes for chemistry. Sanger was awarded his first prize in 1958 for finding the structure of INSULIN. His second came in 1980 (shared with the US molecular biologists Walter GILBERT and Paul Berg) after work on the chemical structure of NUCLEIC ACID.

**Sanger, Margaret Higgins** (1883–1966) US social reformer, founder of the first birth control clinic in North America. She advocated birth control to prevent dangerous, illegal abortions and to alleviate poverty. Sanger founded the National Birth Control League in 1914 and opened a clinic in Brooklyn in 1916.

**Sanhedrin** Ancient Jewish religious council, prominent in Jerusalem during the period of Roman rule in Palestine. The Great Sanhedrin is believed to have served as a legislative and judicial body on both religious and political issues. JESUS CHRIST appeared before the Sanhedrin after his arrest.

**San José** Capital and largest city of Costa Rica, capital of San José province in central Costa Rica. Founded *c.*1736, it succeeded Cartago as capital of Costa Rica in 1823 and became the center of a prosperous coffee trade. Products: coffee, sugarcane, cacao, vegetables, fruit, tobacco. Pop. (1992) 303,000.

**San Jose** City in W California, 40mi (64km) SE of San Francisco. Founded in 1777, it was California's capital from 1849 to 1851. It is the center of a rich fruit-growing region, but is now best known as the focal point of "Silicon Valley," the hub of the US computer industry. Pop. (1992) 801,331.

**San Jose scale** Scale insect introduced into California in *c.*1880 from E Asia. Now spread across the US, these insects suck juices from trees and shrubs, often destroying the plants. Length: 0.1in (2.5mm). Family Diaspididae; species *Quadraspidiotus perniciosus*.

**San Juan** Capital, largest city, and major port of PUERTO RICO, on the NE coast of the island. It has one of the finest harbors in the West Indies. Founded in 1508, the port prospered during the 18th and 19th centuries, and in 1898 was captured by the US during the Spanish-American War. San Juan is the commercial and financial center of Puerto Rico. Exports: coffee, tobacco, fruit, sugar. Industries: cigars, sugar refining, rum distilling, metal products, pharmaceuticals, tourism. Pop. (1990) 437,745.

**San Juan Hill, Battle of** *See* SPANISH-AMERICAN WAR

**San Marino** World's smallest republic and perhaps Europe's oldest state, in the Apennines, near the Adriatic Sea, NE Italy. According to legend, it was founded in the early 4th century AD. Its mountainous terrain has enabled it to retain a separate status, becoming an independent commune in the 13th century. The economy is largely agricultural. Tourism is vital to the state's income. While San Marino has its own currency and stamps, Italian and Vatican City equivalents are widely used. There are two towns: Serraville (1991 pop. 7,264), and the capital San Marino (1993 pop. 4,335). Area: 24sq mi (61sq km). Pop. (1993) 24,003.

**San Martín, José de** (1778–1850) South American revolutionary. He led revolutionary forces in Argentina, Peru, and Chile, gaining a reputation as a bold commander and imaginative strategist. After defeating the Spaniards in Argentina, San Martín gained the element of surprise in Chile (1817–18) by crossing the Andes. He captured Peru (1821) after an unexpected naval attack. In 1822 San Martín surrendered his effective rule of Peru to Simón BOLÍVAR and retired to Europe.

**San Salvador** Capital and largest city of El Salvador, central El Salvador. Founded in 1524 near the volcano of San Salvador, which rises to 6,184ft (1,885m) and last erupted in 1917, the city has been frequently damaged by earthquakes. The main industry is the processing of coffee grown on the rich volcanic soils. Other industries: beer, textiles, tobacco. Pop. (1992) 422,570.

**Sanskrit** Classical language of India, the literary and sacred language of HINDUISM, and a forerunner of the modern Indo-Iranian languages spoken in N India, Pakistan, Nepal, and Bangladesh. Sanskrit was brought to India (*c.*1500 BC) by immigrants from the NW. The old form of the language (Vedic Sanskrit) gradually became simplified, achieving its classical form *c.*500. Sanskrit is one of the INDO-EUROPEAN LANGUAGES. Although only *c.*3,000 Indians are able to speak Sanskrit today, it has been designated one of India's national languages.

**Sanskrit literature** Classical literature of India. The two main periods in Sanskrit literature are the Vedic (*c.*1500–*c.*200 BC) and the overlapping Classical (*c.*500 BC–*c.*AD 1000). The Vedic period produced the VEDAS, the earliest works in Sanskrit literature and among the most important. Later Vedic literature included the UPANISHADS. The early classical period contributed the MAHABHARATA and the RAMAYANA. They are significant both as literature and as Hindu sacred works.

S

**Santa Anna, Antonio López de** (1794–1876) Mexican general and dictator. He was the dominant political figure in Mexico from 1823 to 1855, sometimes as president, sometimes unofficially as the result of a coup. In 1836 he failed to subdue the rebellion in TEXAS, but regained power after gallant action against a French raid on Vera Cruz (1838). After his failure in the MEXICAN WAR (1846–48), he went into exile. He returned to power in 1853, but was overthrown in 1855.

**Santa Barbara** City in s California; seat of Santa Barbara County. The Spanish built a fort here in 1782 and the Spanish mission (1786) is a major tourist site. Santa Barbara was incorporated in 1850. Pop. (1990) 85,571.

**Santa Cruz de Tenerife** Capital of the CANARY ISLANDS and largest city in TENERIFE. Founded in 1494, it has a fine harbor and exports fruit, vegetables, and sugar. Industries: oil refining, tourism. Pop. (1991) 189,317.

**Santa Fe** (formerly Santa Fé de Vera Cruz) City in N Argentina, capital of Sante Fé province. Founded in 1573, it was the center of Jesuit missions and a fortification against the Native Americans. Its main exports are grain, cotton, timber, wool, and cattle. Pop. (1991) 406,388.

**Santa Fe** State capital of New Mexico, at the foot of the Sangre de Cristo Mountains. The oldest US capital city, it was founded *c.*1609 by the Spanish and acted as a center of Spanish–Native American trade for more than 200 years. Mexico's independence in 1821 opened trade with the US. Santa Fe functioned as the w terminus of the Santa Fe Trail. In 1846 US troops captured the city, and in 1850 the region became US territory, achieving statehood in 1912. Today, it is primarily an administrative, tourist, and resort center. Pop. (1992) 59,004.

**Santayana, George** (1863–1952) US philosopher and poet, b. Spain. After 1939 Santayana withdrew from the world, a seclusion reflected in the moral detachment of his writing. He stressed both the biological nature of the mind and its creative and rational powers. His works include *The Sense of Beauty* (1896), *The Life of Reason* (1905), and the popular novel *The Last Puritan* (1935).

**Santiago** Capital of Chile, on the Mapocho River, central Chile. Founded in 1541, it was destroyed by an earthquake in 1647. Most of the city's architecture is post-1850. It is Chile's administrative, commercial, and cultural center, accounting for nearly a third of the population. Industries: textiles, pharmaceuticals, food processing, clothing. Pop. (1992) 4,385,381.

**Santo Domingo** (formerly Cuidad Trujillo, 1936–61) Capital and chief port of the Dominican Republic, on the s coast of the island, on the Ozama River. Founded in 1496, the city is the oldest continuous European settlement in the Americas. It was the base for the Spaniards' conquering expeditions until it was devastated by an earthquake in 1562. It houses more than a third of the country's population, many of whom work in the sugar industry. Pop. (1991) 2,055,000.

**São Paulo** City on the Tietê River, SE Brazil, capital of São Paulo state, located almost exactly on the Tropic of Capricorn. Founded by the Jesuits in 1554, it grew as the base for expeditions into the interior in search of minerals. It expanded in the 17th century as a trading center for a large coffee region. While its large quantities of agricultural produce are now shipped through its port of Santos, São Paulo has become a major and diverse industrial center attracting migrants from the interior. It is the world's fastest-growing metropolis. Pop. (1991) 9,646,185 (metropolitan area 16,567,317). São Paulo state houses up to 60% of Brazil's industry and most of its sugar production. Pop. (1991) 31,588,925.

**São Tomé and Príncipe** Republic in the Gulf of Guinea, 190mi (300km) off the w coast of Africa. The capital is São Tomé. The country consists of two main islands, São Tome (the largest) and Príncipe. The islands are volcanic and mountainous, the vegetation predominantly tropical rain forest. The islands were discovered (uninhabited) in 1471 and, in 1483, a settlement was established at São Tomé. In 1522 the islands became a Portuguese colony. The Dutch controlled the islands from 1641 to 1740, but the Portuguese regained control and established plantations in the latter half of the 18th century. The official language is Portuguese and the major religion is Roman Catholicism. The islands became independent when the Portuguese pulled out in 1975, ushering in 16 years of Marxist rule. Cocoa, coffee, bananas, and coconuts are grown on plantations, and their export provides the republic's only serious source of income. Area: 387sq mi (1,001sq km). Pop. (1995) 131,100.

**sap** Fluid that circulates water and nutrients through plants. Water is absorbed by the roots and carried, along with minerals, through the XYLEM to the leaves. Sap from the leaves is distributed throughout the plant.

**sapphire** Transparent to translucent gemstone variety of CORUNDUM. It has various colors produced by impurities of iron and titanium, the most valuable being deep blue.

**Sappho** Greek poet of the early 6th century BC. Her passionate love poetry, written on the island of Lesbos – from which the word lesbian derives – was regarded by PLATO as the expression of "the tenth Muse."

**saprophyte** Plant that obtains its food from dead or decaying plant or animal tissue. Generally it has no CHLOROPHYLL. Saphrophytes include most FUNGI and some flowering plants.

**Saracens** Name applied by the ancient Greeks and Romans to the Arab tribes who threatened their borders. The name later included all Arabs and eventually all Muslims. As a term similar to "Moors" it was used by medieval Christians to denote their Muslim enemies.

**Sarajevo** Capital of Bosnia-Herzegovina, on the Miljacka River. It fell to the Turks in 1429 and became a flourishing commercial center in the Ottoman empire. Passing to the Austro-Hungarian empire in 1878, the city was a center of Serb and Bosnian resistance to Austrian rule. On June 28, 1914 the Austrian Archduke Franz Ferdinand and his wife were assassinated here by a Serbian nationalist (an act that helped to precipitate World War I). In 1991 Bosnia-Herzegovina declared its independence from Yugoslavia, and a bloody civil war ensued among Croatian, Bosnian, and Serbian forces. Sarajevo became the focal point of the war between Bosnian Serb troops and Bosnian government forces. The city lay under prolonged siege, often without water, electricity, or basic medical supplies. After the 1995 peace agreement (the Dayton Accord), it in effect became a Bosnian city, with the 1991 population figure of 526,000 drastically reduced as many Serbs fled.

**Sarasvati** In Hindu mythology, goddess of the arts, sciences, and eloquent speech. Depicted as a beautiful young woman, she is credited with the invention of Sanskrit. She later became the consort of BRAHMA.

**Saratoga, Battle of** (October 1777) First American victory in the AMERICAN REVOLUTION, fought in upper New York. In the series of battles, the British were prevented from linking up with other forces at Albany and winning the Hudson valley. Surrounded, the British were forced to surrender to the Americans under Horatio GATES. The US victory persuaded the French to intervene against Britain.

**Sarawak** Largest state of Malaysia, in NW Borneo, comprising a highland interior and swampy coastal plain; the capital is Kuching City. Ruled as an independent state by Britain after 1841, it was made a British protectorate in 1888 and a crown colony in 1946. Sarawak became part of Malaysia in 1963, triggering a three-year dispute with Indonesia. Products: oil, coconuts, rice, rubber, sago. Area: 48,050sq mi (124,449sq km). Pop. (1990) 1,648,217.

**sarcoidosis** Disorder of unknown cause characterized by enlargement of the lymph nodes and the formation of scar-like tissue in the lungs and possibly elsewhere in the body.

**sarcoma** Cancerous growth or TUMOR arising from muscle, fat, bone, blood or lymph vessels, or connective tissue. *See also* CANCER

**sardine** Small, marine food fish found throughout the world. It has a laterally compressed body, a large toothless mouth, and oily flesh. Length: to 1ft (30cm). Species include the California *Sardinops caerulea*, South American *Sardinops sagax*, and the European sardine, or PILCHARD, *Sardina pilchardus*. Family Clupeidae.

**Sardinia** Mountainous island of Italy, 130mi (208km) w of the Italian mainland, separated by the Tyrrhenian Sea. The

S

only large city is Cágliari, the capital. A trading center for the Phoenicians, Greeks, Carthaginians, and Romans, Sardinia became a kingdom in 1720, and in 1861 its king, Victor Emmanuel II, became the first king of Italy. Wheat, barley, grapes, olives, and tobacco are grown, and sheep and goats are reared. Salt extraction is important, and other minerals include coal, lead, magnesium, manganese, and zinc. Area: 9,302sq mi (24,090sq km). Pop. (1992) 1,651,902.

**Sargasso Sea** Area of calm, barely moving water in the N Atlantic between the West Indies and the Azores. It takes its name from the large quantities of floating seaweed (*Sargassum*) covering its surface.

**Sargent, John Singer** (1856–1925) US painter. Greatly influenced by Velázquez and Hals, he is best known for his glamorous and elegant portraits.

**Sargent, Sir (Harold) Malcolm (Watts)** (1895–1967) English conductor. He conducted the Royal Choral Society from 1928 and the BBC Symphony Orchestra from 1950–57.

**Sargon** (*c*.2334–*c*.2279 BC) King of Akkadia (*c*.2316–*c*.2279 BC). One of the first of the great Mesopotamian conquerors, he was a usurper who founded his capital at Agade (Akkad), from which his kingdom took its name. Sargon conquered Sumeria and upper Mesopotamia and extracted tribute from lands as far W as the Mediterranean.

**Sargon** (d. 705 BC) King of ASSYRIA (721–705 BC). He conquered SAMARIA in 721 BC and, according to tradition, dispersed those Israelites who became the "lost tribes" of Israel. Sargon established an imperial administration and defeated his enemies before being killed in battle against the Cimmarians.

**Sark** One of the CHANNEL ISLANDS of the United Kingdom, divided into Great Sark and Little Sark. Sark is part of the bailiwick of GUERNSEY, with a feudal organization dating from the late 17th century. There are no automobiles and the residents pay no income tax. The population swells with summer tourists. Area: 2.1sq mi (5.5sq km). Pop. (1991) 575.

**Sarnoff, David** (1891–1971) US communications executive. As director of the Radio Corporation of America (RCA), Sarnoff recognized the potential of commercial television and helped to develop color TV.

**Saroyan, William** (1908–81) US novelist, short-story writer, and dramatist. Saroyan followed the success of his first play, *My Heart's in the Highlands* (1939), with the Pulitzer Prize-winning *The Time of Your Life* (1939) and the autobiographical *My Name is Aram* (1940). His subsequent works were less successful, although *The Cave Dwellers* (1957) received some critical acclaim.

**sarsaparilla** Tropical, perennial vine of the genus *Smilax*, native to Central and S America. Its roots are used to impart an aromatic flavor to medicines and drinks. The main species used are *S. aristolochiaefolia*, *S. regelii*, and *S. febrifuga*. Family Liliaceae.

**Sartre, Jean-Paul** (1905–80) French philosopher and writer. Sartre was the leading advocate of EXISTENTIALISM. His debut novel, *Nausea* (1939), depicted man adrift in a godless universe, hostage to his own angst-ridden freedom. Sartre was a fighter in the French Resistance during World War II. During the war he began to write plays, such as *Huis Clos* (*No Exit*) (1944). His major philosophical work is *Being and Nothingness* (1943). After the war Sartre wrote a trilogy of novels, *The Roads to Freedom* (1945–49), and founded (1945) the philosophy periodical *Modern Times*. His complex relationship with Marxism is explored in *Critique of Dialectical Reason* (1960). Sartre refused the 1964 Nobel Prize for literature on "personal" grounds, but is later said to have accepted it. He had a long-term relationship with Simone de BEAUVOIR.

**Saskatchewan** Province in W central Canada, the southern half on the fertile Great Plains and the northern half in the lake-strewn Canadian Shield. The principal cities are Saskatoon (1991 pop. 186,058), Regina (the capital, pop. 179,178), Prince Albert (34,181), and Moose Jaw (33,593). The first permanent white settlement was in 1774, but development was slow until the construction of the transcontinental Canadian Pacific Railroad in 1885. Saskatchewan was admitted to the Dominion of Canada in 1905. Wheat, oats, barley, rye, flax, and rapeseed are also grown. The province's rich mineral deposits include uranium, copper, zinc, gold, coal, oil, natural gas, and the world's largest fields of potash. Most industries process raw materials, and steel is also manufactured. Area: 251,700sq mi (570,110sq km). Pop. (1991) 988,928.

**Saskatchewan** River in S central Canada, formed by the confluence of the North and South Saskatchewan rivers. It flows E to empty into Lake Winnipeg. With its tributaries, the Saskatchewan drains most of Canada's prairie provinces. Length: *c*.340 mi (550km).

**sassafras** Small E North American tree with furrowed bark, green twigs, yellow flowers, and blue berries. Oil from the roots is used to flavor root beer. Family Lauraceae; species *Sassafras albidum*.

**Sassanid** (Sassanian) Royal dynasty of Persia (Iran) (AD 224–651). Founded by Ardashir I (r.224–241), the Sassanids revived the native Persian traditions of the ACHAEMENIDS, confirming ZOROASTRIANISM as the state religion. There were about 30 Sassanid rulers, the most important after Ardashir being Shapur II (309–379), Khoshru I (531–579), and Khoshru II (590–628), whose conquest of Syria, Palestine, and Egypt marked the height of the dynasty's power. The Sassanids were finally overthrown by the Arabs.

**Sassoon, Siegfried** (1886–1967) English poet and author. His disillusionment with military service in World War I inspired some memorable war poetry. The semiautobiographical trilogy *The Complete Memoirs of George Sherston* (1937) includes Sassoon's most famous novel, *Memoirs of a Fox-hunting Man* (1928).

**Satan** Name for the DEVIL. Satan first appeared in the Old Testament as an individual angel, subordinate to God. Gradually, however, Satan took on a more sinister role. In the New Testament, he was the devil who tempted JESUS CHRIST. Satan emerged in medieval Christian theology as the chief devil, ruler of hell, and source of all evil.

**satellite** Celestial body orbiting a planet or star. In the Solar System, planets with satellites are Earth (1), Mars (2), Jupiter (16), Saturn (18), Uranus (15), Neptune (8) and Pluto (1). There are probably more satellites of the giant planets awaiting discovery. They vary enormously in their size, orbit, surface features, and supposed origin.

**satellite, artificial** Spacecraft placed in orbit around the Earth or other celestial body. Satellites can perform many tasks and send back data or pictures to the Earth. **Communications** satellites relay microwave signals from one part of the Earth to another. **Navigation** satellites transmit radio signals that enable navigators to determine their positions. *Sputnik 1* was the first artificial satellite, launched on October 4, 1957.

**satellite television** Television services transmitted to viewers via communications SATELLITES in orbit around the Earth. Signals beamed are retransmitted to the satellites from ground stations back to viewers' dish-shaped receiving aerials.

**Satie, Erik** (1866–1925) French composer. He developed a deceptively simple style in piano pieces such as *Trois Gymnopédies* (1888). Satie also composed the ballets *Parade* (1917) and *Relâche* (1924), and a choral work, *Socrate* (1918).

**satire** Literary work in which human foibles and institutions are mocked, ridiculed, and parodied. In Roman times a satire was a poem in hexameters, a form established through the work of Lucilius, HORACE, and JUVENAL. In the Middle Ages it often took the form of *fabliaux* or bestiaries, using animal characters to illustrate typical human failings. Since Thomas MORE's *Utopia* (1516), utopian or dystopian fiction, such as ZAMYATIN'S *We* (1924) and SWIFT's *Gulliver's Travels* (1726), has frequently been used as a medium for satire. Dramatists have often employed the form, as in the plays of ARISTOPHANES, Ben JONSON, MOLIÈRE, Oscar WILDE, and Bertolt BRECHT.

**Sato, Eisaku** (1901–75) Japanese statesman, prime minister (1964–72). Sato held a number of cabinet posts (1948–64) before becoming prime minister. His term in office is notable for its foreign policy successes, such as the restoration of rela-

▲ **Sartre** French philosopher, playwright, and novelist Jean-Paul Sartre studied at the Sorbonne in Paris with Simone de Beauvoir, who remained his close associate. He was influenced by German philosophers including Heidegger and Marx, and has written several studies of literary figures. Outspoken against US policies in Vietnam, he encouraged student rebellion in the US in 1968.

**SATURN: DATA**

Diameter (equatorial): 74,901mi (120,536km)
Mass (Earth = 1): 95.2
Volume (Earth = 1): 744
Density (water = 1): 0.71
Orbital period: 29.46 years
Rotation period: 10h 13m 59s
Average surface temperature: –356°F (–180°C)

tions with South Korea (1965). Sato negotiated the return (1972) of OKINAWA from the USA. A provision that US forces were allowed to remain on the island, however, inflamed public opinion. In 1974 he was awarded the Nobel Peace Prize.

**saturated compound** In organic chemistry, compounds in which the carbon atoms are bonded to one another by single COVALENT BONDS, not by the more reactive double or triple bonds. For this reason, they tend to be unreactive.

**saturated fat** Organic fatty compounds, the molecules of which contain only saturated FATTY ACIDS combined with GLYCEROL. These acids have long chains of carbon atoms that are bound together by single bonds only. *See also* SATURATED COMPOUND

**saturated solution** In chemistry, a SOLUTION containing so much of a dissolved compound (SOLUTE) that no more will dissolve at the same temperature.

**Saturn** Sixth planet from the Sun and second-largest in the SOLAR SYSTEM. Its famous rings are made up of particles ranging from dust to objects a few meters in size, all in individual orbits. The main rings are only about half a mile thick. **Voyager** space probes revealed the ring system to be made up of thousands of separate ringlets. Saturn has an internal heat source, which probably drives its weather systems. It is assumed to be composed predominantly of hydrogen, with an iron–silicate core about five times the Earth's mass, surrounded by an ice mantle of perhaps 20 Earth masses. The upper atmosphere contains 97% hydrogen and 3% helium, with traces of other gases.

**satyr** In Greek mythology, god of the woods and attendant of DIONYSUS. Sensual and lascivious, satyrs were later depicted by the Romans as goat-legged, goat-bearded men with budding horns. Satyr is also the common name for any butterfly of the Satyridae family.

**Saud, Abdul Aziz ibn** (1880–1953) Founder and first king of Saudi Arabia (1932–53). As leader of the Saudi dynasty, he was forced into exile in 1891 by the rival Rashid dynasty. He returned in 1902 and extended his authority, driving out the Turks and the Hashemites and founding the modern Saudi state in 1932.

**Saudi Arabia** Arabic kingdom on the Arabian Peninsula, SW Asia. *See* country feature

**Saul** First king of the Hebrew state of ancient ISRAEL (r.*c*.1020–*c*.1000 BC). He was the son of Kish, a member of the tribe of Benjamin. He was anointed by the prophet SAMUEL and acclaimed by all Israel. Through much of his reign he waged war against Israel's threatening neighbors, notably the PHILISTINES, the AMMONITES, and the Amalekites. He and his sons eventually died in battle against the Philistines on Mount Gilboa. The story of Saul is contained in the First Book of Samuel, the ninth book of the Old Testament.

**SATELLITE**

Four artificial satellite orbits around the globe are illustrated. Two are equatorial: one, a geostationary satellite, orbits at 21,500mi (35,900km) (1); another has a lower orbit (2). A polar orbit, as used by remote sensing satellites, is shown running vertically around the Earth (3) and the last is an angled elliptical orbit used by communications satellites for the high latitudes of the Earth (4). The diagrams above the orbital diagram show the launching of an Intelsat communication satellite by a NASA shuttle (5) and the two main types of satellites. To prevent them being knocked off course by the fluctuations in the Earth's magnetic field, satellites are given centrifugal stability in one of two ways. The first is to rotate the whole satellite, as is the case in "spinners" such as the Intelsat satellite (6). The other method is to have gyroscopes within the satellite (7).

**sauna** Wood-lined room in which a wood-fired stove (or an electric heater) raises the temperature to between 140 and 203°F (60 and 95°C). The sauna was originally a semi-religious exercise of the Finns.

**Saussure, Ferdinand de** (1857–1913) Swiss linguist, founder of modern linguistics. Saussure delivered a series of lectures at the University of Geneva between 1907 and 1911, which were published posthumously (1916) as *Course in General Linguistics*. For Saussure, language was a system of signs whose meaning is defined by their relations to each other. His work laid the foundation for STRUCTURALISM and SEMIOTICS.

**savanna** Plain with coarse grass and scattered tree growth, particularly the wide plains of tropical and subtropical regions. An extensive example is the savanna of the East African tableland.

**Savannah** City and port on the Savannah River, E Georgia. The oldest city in Georgia, it was founded in 1733 and became the seat of the colonial government in 1754. During the American Revolution, Savannah was captured (1778) by the British and resisted all attempts at invasion until 1782. The city prospered on the tobacco and cotton trade. During the Civil War, Savannah remained a Confederate stronghold until December 1864. Today, it is still a major port exporting tobacco, cotton, and sugar. Industries: chemicals, petroleum, paper products, rubber, tourism. Pop. (1992) 138,908.

**Savimbi, Jonas** (1934– ) Angolan political leader. Prominent in the struggle for independence from Portugal, he formed the National Union for the Total Independence of Angola (UNITA) in 1966. After independence (1975), the rival Popular Movement for the Liberation of Angola (MPLA) emerged as the major power and banned all other political parties. Savimbi mounted a guerrilla war against the MPLA. In 1991 President DOS SANTOS and Savimbi signed a peace agreement. Savimbi refused to recognize the 1992 reelection of Dos Santos, and civil war resumed. UNITA's dwindling support led to the Lusaka Protocol (1994). Savimbi refused the vice-presidency and fighting resumed as UNITA retained control of *c*.50% of Angola.

**savings and loan association** US financial institution that is organized as a mutual, issuing shares or ownership certificates to its depositors. Savings and loan associations (S&Ls) take deposits, on which the shares are based, and provide mortgage loans, as well as real estate and business loans. High-risk loan policies in the early 1980s led to many bankruptcies, and the federal government was forced to bail them out, at a high price.

**Savonarola, Girolamo** (1452–98) Italian religious reformer. His sermons attacked the corruption and decadence of the papacy and the state of Florence. After the death of Lorenzo de' MEDICI (1494), Savonarola became spiritual and political leader of the city. His support for the invasion of CHARLES VIII of France infuriated Pope Alexander VI, and he was excommunicated in 1497. Public hostility to his austere regime intensified. Savonarola was arrested and hanged for heresy.

**Savoy** Area of SE France, bounded by Lake Geneva (N), the Rhône River (W), the Dauphiné (S), and the Alps of Italy and Switzerland (E); it includes the departments of Haute Savoie and Savoie. It was part of the first Burgundian kingdom, the kingdom of Arles and, in the 11th century, the Holy Roman Empire (as a county). In 1416 it became a duchy and its area was enlarged, incorporating parts of France, Switzerland, and Italy. An Italian state in the 16th century, it was part of the kingdom of SARDINIA after 1713. Savoy was annexed by France in 1792, returned to Sardinia in 1815, and finally ceded to France by the Treaty of Turin in 1860.

**sawfish** Any of several species of sharklike, flat-bodied RAYS that live in tropical marine and brackish waters. It has a gray or black-brown body with an elongated, saw-toothed snout resembling a flat blade. Length: to 16ft (5m). Family Pristidae; genus *Pristis*.

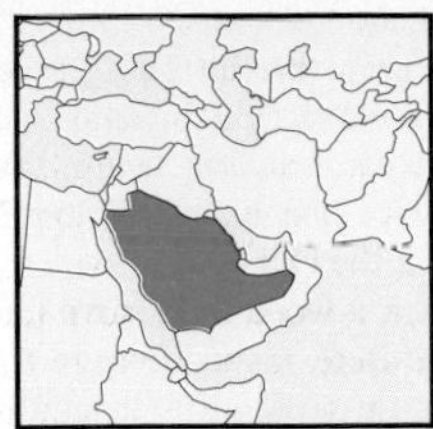

Saudi Arabia's flag was adopted in 1938. It is the only national flag with an inscription as its main feature. The Arabic inscription above the sword means "There is no God but Allah, and Muhammad is the Prophet of Allah."

**AREA:** 829,995sq mi (2,149,690sq km)
**POPULATION:** 15,922,000
**CAPITAL (POPULATION):** Riyadh (1,500,000)
**GOVERNMENT:** Absolute monarchy
**ETHNIC GROUPS:** Arab (Saudi 82%, Yemeni 10%, other Arab 3%)
**LANGUAGES:** Arabic (official)
**RELIGIONS:** Islam 99% (almost exclusively Sunni), Christianity 1%
**CURRENCY:** Saudi riyal = 100 halalah

The Kingdom of Saudi Arabia occupies about 75% of the Arabian peninsula in SW Asia. Desert constitutes over 95% of the land. The Gulf of AQABA and the RED SEA lie off the W coast. The W coastal lands are divided into two main regions. The *Hejaz* (boundary) plain in the NW includes the holy cities of MECCA and MEDINA, and Saudi Arabia's main port, JIDDAH. In the SW is the *Asir* (inaccessible) highland region, which contains the country's highest point, Sawda, at 10,279ft (3,133m). The Tihama is a narrow, fertile SW coastal plain. In the center lies the *Najd* (plateau), which contains Saudi Arabia's capital, RIYADH. The plateau descends E to the Al Hasa lowlands. This region is the center of the Saudi oil industry, and contains Saudi Arabia's largest oasis. In the N is the Nafud Desert. The S of Saudi Arabia is dominated by the bleak Rub' al Khali (Empty Quarter), the world's largest expanse of sand.

## CLIMATE

Saudi Arabia has a hot, dry climate. Summer temperatures in Riyadh often exceed 104°F (40°C). The Asir highlands have an average rainfall of 12in–20in (300–500mm). The rest of the country has less than 4in (100mm).

## VEGETATION

Grass and shrub provide pasture on the W highlands and parts of the central plateau. The deserts contain few plants, except around oases.

## HISTORY

Mecca is the holiest place in Islam. It was the birthplace of the Prophet Muhammad in AD 570, and is the site of the KAABA. In the 18th century, the Wahhabi (a strict Islamic sect) gained the allegiance of the Saud family, who formed an independent state in Nejd. With the support of the Bedouin, the Wahhabi rapidly conquered most of the Arabian peninsula. In the 1810s the region was conquered by Turkey. Abdul Aziz ibn SAUD laid the foundations of the modern state of Saudi Arabia. In 1902 Ibn Saud captured Riyadh, and by 1906 had taken the whole of the Nejd. In 1913 the Turkish province of Al Hasa also fell. In 1920 Ibn Saud captured the Asir, and by 1925 he had conquered the Hejaz. In 1932 the territories were combined to form the kingdom of Saudi Arabia. Ibn Saud became king, ruling in accordance with the sharia of Wahhabi Islam. Oil was discovered in 1936 by the US company Arabian Standard Oil, which later became the Arabian American Oil Company (Aramco). In 1945 Saudi Arabia joined the Arab League. In 1953 Ibn Saud died, and was succeeded by his eldest son, King Saud, who ruled with the aid of Crown Prince Faisal. Saud's concern at the growing power of Nasser's Egypt was heightened by the overthrow of the Yemen royal family by pro-Nasser republican forces. Saud sent troops to Yemen to aid the monarchists. In 1964 Saud was overthrown, and Faisal became king. In 1970 Saudi troops were withdrawn from Yemen. In 1971 British troops withdrew from the Gulf. Faisal supported the creation of the United Arab Emirates and sought to increase national ownership of Saudi's oil wealth. In 1974 Saudi Arabia agreed to a 60% share in Aramco. In 1975 King Faisal was assassinated, and Crown Prince Khalid became king. Khalid's conservativism was challenged by the growth of Islamic fundamentalism, especially in Iran. In 1979 Shiite fundamentalists captured the Great Mosque in Mecca. The rebellion was brutally suppressed. Saudi Arabia's support for Iraq in the IRAN-IRAQ WAR (1980–88) led to Iranian attacks on Saudi shipping. In 1982 Khalid died and was succeeded by Prince Fahd. In 1990 over 1,400 pilgrims died in a stampede during the HAJJ. When Iraq invaded Kuwait in 1990, King Fahd invited coalition forces to protect it against possible Iraqi aggression. Saudi air and land forces played a significant role in the Allied victory in the GULF WAR (1991).

## POLITICS

The king retains supreme authority, though a 60-man Consultative Council of royal nominees has been in existence since 1963. In 1996 the council's president ruled out elections on Islamic grounds. Saudi Arabia has no formal constitution. It attracts much international criticism for human rights abuses, especially for its state executions and treatment of women and minorities.

## ECONOMY

Saudi Arabia is the world's largest producer and exporter of crude oil. It has *c.*25% of the world's known oil reserves and in 1994 supplied over 13% of world demand. Oil and oil products make up 85% of its exports. Oil revenue has been used to develop education, services, light industry, farming, and purchasing of military hardware. The construction of desalination plants has played an important part in improving the supply of fresh water. In the mid-1980s, world oil prices slumped dramatically and many infrastructure projects were abandoned. Agriculture employs 48% of the workforce, although only 1% of the land is fertile. Crops grown in Asir and at oases include dates and other fruits, vegetables, and wheat. Some nomadic livestock herders remain. Mecca is visited by more than 1.5 million pilgrims a year, making this a vital addition to state revenue.

▲ **saxifrage** The rue-leaved saxifrage (*Saxifrage tridactylites*) thrives in dry conditions and is capable of growing on rocks and walls. It is a member of the widespread family Saxifragaceae, whose name in Latin means "breaker of rocks."

**sawfly** Any of 400 species of primitive, plant-feeding WASPS that lack a narrow waist between thorax and abdomen. Most sawflies are in the family Tenthredinidae. Length: to 0.8in (20mm). Order Hymenoptera.

**Saxe-Coburg-Gotha** Duchy in Saxony, Germany, whose ruling dynasty intermarried with many royal families. After Prince Albert married the English Queen VICTORIA, Saxe-Coburg-Gotha became the name of the English royal house until it was changed to Windsor in 1917.

**saxifrage** Perennial plant of the genus *Saxifraga* native to temperate and mountainous regions of Europe and North America. The leaves are massed at the base and the branched clusters of small flowers are white, pink, purple or yellow. Height: to 2ft (60cm). Family Saxifragaceae.

**Saxons** Ancient Germanic people. By the 5th century they had settled in NW Germany, N Gaul, and S Britain. In Germany they were subdued by CHARLEMAGNE. In Britain, along with other Germanic tribes, known collectively as ANGLO-SAXONS, they evolved into the English.

**Saxony** Federal state and historic region in E central Germany; the capital is DRESDEN. Initially, it referred to the homeland of the SAXONS in NW Germany. It eventually (1815–71) comprised the Prussian province of Saxony and the kingdom of Saxony. After 1945 the province of Saxony was united with Anhalt to form the state of SAXONY-ANHALT, with MAGDEBURG as its capital. From 1871 to 1918 the kingdom of Saxony was part of the German empire. In the aftermath of World War I, the kingdom was made a state of the Weimar Republic, with Dresden as its capital. After World War II, it joined the German Democratic Republic (East Germany). Following German reunification in 1991, it became a state in the Federal Republic of Germany. Area: 7,106 sq mi (18,409 sq km). Pop: (1993 est.) 4,608,000.

**Saxony-Anhalt** Federal state in S Germany, with Lower Saxony to the NW and Saxony to the SE; the capital is MAGDEBURG. Other major cities include Halle and Dessau. The history of the region coincides with that of SAXONY until 1871, when it became a state of the German empire. After World War II, the Red Army briefly occupied the region and the district was abolished in 1952..Following German reunification in 1991, Saxony-Anhalt was re-formed as a federal state of Germany. The region is mainly plains with the Harz Mountains rising in the SW of the state. Predominantly an industrial region, its major manufactures are machine and transportation equipment. Area: 7,892sq mi (20,445sq km). Pop: (1994) 2,759,213.

**saxophone** Musical instrument with single reed, conical metal tube, and finger keys. It was invented by Adolphe Sax in the 1840s. Four members of the saxophone family are commonly used today; these are the soprano (in B flat), the alto (in E flat), the tenor (in B flat) and the baritone (in E flat). They are used mostly in jazz.



► **Saxons** In the course of the 6th and 7th centuries the once-unified Roman province of Britain was split into a collection of petty kingdoms, barbarian Saxon in the S and E, Celtic in the W and N. Organized by family and clan, the Saxon kingdoms developed into seven more stable entities. The frontiers, however, were not constant, kingship was personal rather than hereditary, and the balance of power was constantly changing.

**Sayers, Dorothy L. (Leigh)** (1893–1957) English novelist and playwright, best known for her detective fiction. Lord Peter Wimsey appeared in 10 books including *Whose Body?* (1923) and *Gaudy Night* (1935). She also wrote religious dramas and translated Dante.

**scabies** Contagious infection caused by a female mite, *Sarcoptes scabiei*, which burrows into the skin to lay eggs. It can be seen as a dark wavy line on the skin and is treated with antiparasitic creams.

**scabious** Annual or perennial plant of the genus *Scabiosa* of the TEASEL family (Dipsacaceae), native to temperate parts of Europe and Asia, and the mountains of E Africa.

**scalar** Mathematical quantity that has only a magnitude, as opposed to a VECTOR, which also has direction. Mass, energy, and speed are scalars.

**scale** In biology, small hard plate that forms part of the external skin of an animal. It is usually a development of the SKIN layers. In most fish, scales are composed of bone in the dermal skin layer. The scales of reptiles are horny growths of the epidermal skin layer and are composed mostly of the fibrous protein KERATIN.

**scale** In music, term for the ordered arrangement of intervals that forms the basis of musical composition. There are many types of scale. In Western music the most important has been the seven-note diatonic scale, both in its major and minor forms. The 12-note CHROMATIC scale has a regular progression of semitones.

**Scalia, Antonin** (1936– ) US Supreme Court justice. In 1986 Ronald REAGAN nominated him for the US Supreme Court vacancy caused by William REHNQUIST's elevation to chief justice. An advocate of judicial restraint, Scalia earned a reputation for his conservative decisions.

**scallop** Edible, BIVALVE mollusk. One shell, or valve, is usually convex and the other almost flat. The shell's surface is ribbed (scalloped). Most scallops have a row of eyes that fringe the fleshy mantle. Width: 1–8in (2.5–20cm). Family Pectinidae.

**Scandinavia** In physicial geography, the N European peninsular countries of SWEDEN and NORWAY. In a broader, cultural sense it also includes DENMARK, FINLAND, ICELAND, and the FARÖE ISLANDS. The climate ranges from subarctic in the N to humid continental in the center and marine in the W and SW. The terrain is mountainous in the W with swift-flowing streams. In the E the land slopes more gently and there are thousands of lakes, notably in Finland. Part of the region lies within the Arctic Circle, where tundra predominates. Denmark and S Sweden have the best farmland. A large proportion of the land is forested, there are rich mineral deposits, particularly of iron ore and copper, and fishing is still important. The largest cities are STOCKHOLM and GOTHENBURG in Sweden; OSLO in Norway; COPENHAGEN in Denmark; and HELSINKI in Finland. Area: *c*.485,000sq mi (1,258,000sq km).

**Scandinavian art** Art in the Nordic countries dates back to the end of the Ice Age, when the first rock carvings were made. There was a tendency to use intricate interlacing patterns, which reached a peak in the stonework and woodcarving of the Viking period (*c*.800–*c*.1050). It was only at the end of the 18th century that artists of international standing emerged. Chief among these was Edvard MUNCH. Scandinavia has also made great contributions to the applied arts, most notably to the development of ART NOUVEAU and FUNCTIONALISM.

**scandium** (symbol Sc) Silver-white, metallic element of Group III of the periodic table, discovered in 1897. It is found in thortveitite and, in small amounts, in other minerals. Scandium is a soft metal used as a radioactive tracer and in nickel alkaline storage batteries. Chemically it resembles the rare-earth metals of the LANTHANIDE SERIES. Properties: at.no. 21; at. wt. 44.956; sp. gr. 2.99; m.p. 2,802°F (1,539°C); b.p. 5,130°F (2,832°C); most common isotope $^{45}$Sc (100%).

**scanning** In medicine, use of a non-invasive system to detect abnormalities in the body. Detectable waves (x-rays, gamma rays, ultrasound) are passed through the part of the body to be investigated and the computer-analyzed results are displayed as images on a screen.

**scar** Fibrous connective tissue that forms at the site of a wound or disease in any tissue of the body. Most scars develop after an injury to the DERMIS. A new EPIDERMIS is formed without oil glands, hair follicles, or elastic tissue.

**scarab beetle** Any of several different species of broad beetles distributed worldwide. Most, including the June bug, Japanese beetle, and rhinoceros beetle, are leaf chafers. A smaller group, including the DUNG BEETLE, are scavengers. Family Scarabaeidae.

**Scarlatti, Alessandro** (1660–1725) Italian BAROQUE composer who laid the foundations of the musical idioms that shaped music to the time of Beethoven. Scarlatti was the founder of Neopolitan opera, establishing the OPERA SERIA style. He wrote more than 100 operas, including *Mitridate Eupatore* (1707) and *Il Tigrane* (1715), and nearly 700 chamber cantatas.

**Scarlatti, (Giuseppe) Domenico** (1685–1757) Italian composer, son of Alessandro SCARLATTI. A harpsichord virtuoso, he settled in Spain and is primarily known for his harpsichord sonatas, of which he composed more than 500. He is considered the founder of modern keyboard technique and the greatest Italian composer of keyboard music of the BAROQUE period.

**scarlet fever** (scarlatina) Acute infectious disease, usually affecting children, caused by BACTERIA in the *Streptococcus pyogenes* group. There is a red body rash, fever, vomiting, and a sore throat. It is treated with ANTIBIOTICS.

**scattering** In physics, deflection of the path of SUBATOMIC PARTICLES by ATOMS. It is the means by which the structure of atoms was discovered. Ernest RUTHERFORD, Hans GEIGER, and Ernest Marsden fired ALPHA PARTICLES through thin metal films and noted their scattering. Rutherford then predicted the existence of the atomic nucleus. Most knowledge of ELEMENTARY PARTICLES has been obtained by scattering experiments carried out in particle ACCELERATORS.

**Schechter Poultry Corporation v. United States** (1935) US Supreme Court decision invalidating President Franklin ROOSEVELT's National Recovery Administration (NRA). The court declared that the NRA codes could not be applied to a firm not engaged in interstate commerce. This limited view of the commerce clause was short lived, and NLRB v. Jones and Laughlin subsequently insured success for Roosevelt's New Deal programs.

**Scheele, Karl Wilhelm** (1742–86) Swedish chemist. In 1771 Scheele discovered OXYGEN, but publication of his find was delayed and the credit went to Joseph PRIESTLEY. He made other important discoveries, including CHLORINE, GLYCEROL, and a number of organic acids.

**Schelling, Friedrich Wilhelm Joseph von** (1775–1854) German philosopher. His early work, *System of Transcendental Idealism* (1800), attempted to develop J.G. FICHTE's science of knowledge alongside a philosophy of nature. His philosophy of IDEALISM, with its stress on the perfection of the Absolute, became the blueprint for ROMANTICISM.

**Schenck v. United States** (1919) Landmark US Supreme Court case in which Oliver Wendell HOLMES stated the "clear and present danger" test defining the limits of 1st Amendment protection. The court ruled that no speech was protected if illegal action was the likely result of such speech.

**Schiele, Egon** (1890–1918) Austrian painter, one of the greatest exponents of EXPRESSIONISM. His characteristic paintings portray anguished or isolated naked figures whose distorted bodies reflect their mental pain. Schiele also produced landscapes and semiallegorical pictures.

**Schiller, Johann Christoph Friedrich von** (1759–1805) German dramatist, historian, and philosopher. His early, blank verse plays, such as *The Robbers* (1781) and *Don Carlos* (1787), are classics of the STURM UND DRANG period. Schiller's aesthetic and philosophical ideas were influenced by the IDEALISM of Kant. His masterpiece is the trilogy *Wallenstein* (1800). Other historical plays include *Mary Stuart* (1801), *Maid of Orleans* (1801), and *William Tell* (1804). Schiller's "Ode to Joy" forms the finale of Beethoven's Ninth Symphony.

**schism** Split or division within a church, sect, or other religious organization, or a breakaway from a church. Before the Protestant REFORMATION, there were two other important schisms within Christianity. The first was the split between the Eastern (ORTHODOX) Church and the Western (ROMAN CATHOLIC) Church brought about by the two churches drifting apart over centuries and by an escalating series of disputes culminated in a complete break in 1054. The so-called GREAT SCHISM occurred in the 14th and 15th centuries and involved a split within the Roman Catholic Church itself. Various reasons, including civil war in Italy, led to the papacy transferring to AVIGNON, France, from 1309 to 1377. Rivalry grew between Avignon and Rome, with rival popes elected from 1378 to 1417. The schism was eventually resolved by the Council of CONSTANCE (1417).

◀ **saxophone** Named for its 19th-century inventor, Adolphe Sax, the saxophone is a single reed instrument which combines features of the oboe and the clarinet and is usually keyed in E flat and B flat. It is shown here complete (top right) and with its mouthpiece (A) and neckpiece (B) separate.

**schist** Large group of METAMORPHIC ROCKS that have been made cleavable, causing the rocks to split into thin plates leaving a wavy, uneven surface.

**schizophrenia** Severe mental disorder marked by disturbances of cognitive functioning, particularly thinking. As well as the characteristic loss of contact with reality, symptoms can include HALLUCINATIONS and DELUSIONS, and muffled or inappropriate emotions. The disorder was first identified (1808) by Eugen BLEULER. Biochemical research suggests that schizophrenia may be caused by high levels of DOPAMINE, a NEUROTRANSMITTER.

**Schlegel, August Wilhelm von** (1767–1845) German poet, critic, and scholar. The founder and editor of the *Athenaeum*, Schlegel was one of the leading propagandists of German ROMANTICISM. His major work was *On the Language and Wisdom of India* (1808).

**Schlesinger, Arthur Meier, Jr.** (1917– ) US historian. Schlesinger achieved prominence with *The Age of Jackson* (1945). He served as special assistant to President John F. KENNEDY (1961–63). His *A Thousand Days* (1965), an account of the Kennedy administration, was followed by *Robert Kennedy and His Times* (1978).

**Schleswig-Holstein** Federal state and historic region in NW Germany; the capital is KIEL. It occupies the S of the Jutland peninsula and extends from the Elbe River to the border with Denmark. The Kiel Canal links the North Sea with the Baltic. The Eider River forms the historic border between Schleswig and Holstein. In the early 12th century, the duchy of Holstein was created as part of the Holy Roman Empire, while Schleswig was made a fiefdom independent of Danish control. They were twice united under the Danish crown, but not incorporated into the Danish state. In 1848 Frederick VII proclaimed the complete union of Schleswig with Denmark, the predominantly German population of both duchies rebelled, and the German Confederation occupied the two duchies. The Treaty of London (1852) re-established the duchies' personal union with Denmark. In 1863 Denmark once more tried to incorporate Schleswig into the state proper. Prussia and Austria declared war. In 1865 Schleswig was administered by Prussia, and Holstein by Austria. The result-

▲ **scallop** The various scallops (*Pecten* sp.) are found in offshore waters in many parts of the world. The shell of the scallop has been used as decorative embellishment since Roman times, and was also used as an emblem by the pilgrims who traveled to Santiago de Compostela, Spain.

▲ **scarab beetle** The fierce-looking Hercules beetle (*Dynastes hercules*) is a type of scarab beetle. The male (shown here) can grow up to 8in (20cm) and possesses a large horn that grows up to 4in (10cm) from its head. Unlike the male, the female does not possess a horn, and its wing cases are covered in a layer of red hairs.

S

ing tension led to the AUSTRO-PRUSSIAN WAR (1866), and the Prussian victory created the state of Schleswig-Holstein. In 1920, following a plebiscite, the N part of Schleswig was returned to Denmark. In 1937 the city of Lübeck was incorporated into the German state of Schleswig-Holstein. The land is mainly flat and fertile. The region's principal economic activities are shipping and fishing, concentrated along the Baltic coast. Area: 6,075sq mi (15,738sq km). Pop. (1993 est.) 2,695,000

**Schliemann, Heinrich** (1822–90) German archeologist. In 1871 his excavations in Hisarlik, Turkey, proved to be the site of the Homeric city of TROY.

**Schmidt, Helmut** (1918– ) Chancellor of West Germany (1974–82). He became chairman of the Social Democratic Party (SDP) in 1967, and was minister of defense (1969–72) and finance (1972–74) before succeeding Willy BRANDT as chancellor. He was reelected in 1976 and 1980, but was forced to resign.

**Schnabel, Artur** (1882–1951) Austrian pianist and composer who lived in the US after 1939. Schnabel was best known as an interpreter of the classical repertoire, notably Mozart and Beethoven, whose 32 piano sonatas he edited and recorded.

**Schnitzler, Arthur** (1862–1931) Austrian dramatist and novelist. His plays, such as *Anatol* (1893) and *La Ronde* (1900), explore the morality of *fin de siècle* Vienna.

**Schoenberg, Arnold Franz Walter** (1874–1951) Austrian composer. In early works, such as *Verklärte Nacht* (1899), he extended the chromaticism of ROMANTICISM. The song cycle *Das Buch der hängenden Gärten* (1908) and the expressionist opera *Erwartung* (1909) revolutionized modern music by abandoning traditional TONALITY. Schoenberg's form of SERIAL MUSIC, known as TWELVE-TONE MUSIC, was first employed in Suite for Piano (1923). His operatic masterpiece, *Moses und Aron*, remained unfinished at his death.

**scholasticism** Medieval philosophy that attempted to join faith to reason by combining theology with classical Greek and Roman thought. Scholasticism was first explored by John Scotus Erigena in the 9th century and by ANSELM OF CANTERBURY in the 11th century. Its greatest thinkers were Albertus Magnus and Thomas AQUINAS in the 13th century and DUNS SCOTUS at the turn of the 14th century.

**Schongauer, Martin** (1450–91) German painter and engraver. He was influenced by Netherlandish art, particularly the work of Rogier van der WEYDEN, but his style is highly individual.

**school** Place of EDUCATION, usually at primary or secondary level. In Western countries there are usually several parallel school systems: one provided by the state and financed by taxpayers; one financed partly by churches in conjunction with the state or parents; and the third privately financed by parents. In the US, the term "public school" refers to schools subsidized by public taxes.

**Schopenhauer, Arthur** (1788–1860) German philosopher whose exposition of the doctrine of the will opposed the IDEALISM of HEGEL and influenced NIETZSCHE, WAGNER, and others. Schopenhauer's system, described in his main work, *The World as Will and Idea* (1819), was an intensely pessimistic one.

**Schrödinger, Erwin** (1887–1961) Austrian physicist. He founded the science of quantum WAVE MECHANICS and shared the 1933 Nobel Prize for physics with Paul DIRAC. *See also* QUANTUM MECHANICS

**Schubert, Franz Peter** (1797–1828) Austrian composer whose symphonies represent the final extension of the classical SONATA form, and whose LIEDER (songs) are the height of ROMANTICISM in lyricism. Among his more popular works are symphonies such as the Eighth ("Unfinished," 1822) and the Ninth in C major (1825). Schubert wrote more than 600 songs to the lyrics of such poets as Heine and Schiller; these include the cycles *Die schöne Müllerin* (1823) and *Winterreise* (1827). In his tragically short lifetime he also composed much chamber music; and his String Quintet (1828) is a masterpiece.

**Schulz, Charles M. (Monroe)** (1922– ) US cartoonist. His comic strip "Peanuts" became a popular newspaper feature in more than 65 countries. Schulz's simply drawn characters, such as Charlie Brown and Snoopy the Dog, became household names.

**Schumacher, Michael** (1969– ) German racing driver. He began Formula 1 racing in 1991 and soon joined the Benetton team. He won his first Grand Prix (Belgium) in 1992. Schumacher won the world drivers' championship in 1994 and 1995. He switched to race for Ferrari in 1996. A gifted driver, Schumacher narrowly failed to win the 1997 and 1998 titles.

**Schuman, William** (1910–92) US composer. In 1943 his cantata, *A Free Song* (1942), won the first Pulitzer Prize for music. In 1962 Schuman became president of the Lincoln Center, New York. Notable works include the Third Symphony (1941) and an opera, *The Mighty Casey* (1953).

**Schumann, Clara Josephine Wieck** (1819–96) German pianist and composer, wife of Robert SCHUMANN. She was an outstanding interpreter of the works of her husband and of their friend BRAHMS. She composed chamber works, piano pieces, and songs.

**Schumann, Robert Alexander** (1810–56) German composer and leading figure of ROMANTICISM. Schumann's piano compositions include *Kinderszenen* (1838), *Carnaval* (1834–35), and *Waldscenen* (1848–49). Among his best song cycles is *Frauenliebe und Leben* (1840). His "Spring" Symphony (1841) and Piano Concerto (1841–45) are among his best-known orchestral works.

**Schwarzenegger, Arnold** (1947– ) US actor, b. Austria. He won the Mr. Universe bodybuilding title five times before turning to acting. His first major film was *Conan the Barbarian* (1982). Schwarzenegger's expressionless, almost nonverbal acting perfectly suited the robot role in the cult hit *The Terminator* (1984). Comedies such as *Twins* (1988) revealed a talent for self-parody. Other films include *True Lies* (1994).

**Schwarzkopf, Dame Elisabeth** (1915– ) German soprano known for her versatility in recitals, oratorios, and opera. She sang with the Berlin State Opera from 1938 to 1942 and became principal soprano of the Vienna State Opera in 1944. She made many fine recordings.

**Schwarzkopf, H. Norman** (1934– ) US general. He served in the Vietnam War and in 1983 was deputy commander of the US forces that invaded Grenada. As supreme commander of the Allied forces in the GULF WAR (1991), he liberated Kuwait from Iraqi occupation. After retiring from the army, he published his memoirs, *It Doesn't Take a Hero* (1992).

**Schweitzer, Albert** (1875–1965) Theologian, musician, medical missionary, and philosopher. He was born in Alsace and spent most of his life in Gabon (then French Equatorial Africa), where he founded the Lambaréné Hospital in 1913. He was honored as a scientist and humanitarian, and as an organist and an expert on J.S. Bach. He was awarded the 1952 Nobel Peace Prize.

**sciatica** Severe pain in the back and radiating down the leg. It is usually caused by inflammation of the sciatic nerve or by pressure on the spinal nerve roots.

**science fiction** Literary genre in which reality is subject to certain transformations in order to explore man's potential and his relation to his environment; these transformations are usually technological and the stories set in the future or in imaginary worlds. The birth of the modern genre is generally dated to the US comic strip *Amazing Stories* (1926). Until the 1960s most science fiction involved adventure stories set in space.

► **Schumacher** German Formula 1 racing driver Michael Schumacher is widely regarded as one of the most talented drivers of recent times. Following his success with Benetton, Schumacher moved to Ferrari, where the car's unreliability has not enabled him to repeat the success he enjoyed with Benetton. Well known for his ability to work with mechanics in order to obtain the optimum "set-up" for his car, he is renowned for fast, pre-race (qualifying) lap-times that enable him to gain pole-position.

Some writers, such as Isaac ASIMOV, explored the paradoxes contained in purely scientific ideas; others, including Ray BRADBURY, stressed the moral implications of their stories.

**scientology** "Applied religious philosophy" based on a form of psychotherapy called **dianetics**, which was founded in California (1954) by L. Ron HUBBARD. It advocates confrontation with, and assimilation of, painful experiences from the past to achieve true mental health. The movement is officially known as the Church of Scientology. It has aroused controversy over its methods of recruiting and keeping members.

**Scilly, Isles of** Archipelago of more than 140 isles and islets in the Atlantic Ocean off the coast of Cornwall, SW England. The terrain is mostly rocky. The capital, Hugh Town, is on St. Mary's. Total pop. (1991) 2,900.

**Scipio Africanus Major** (236–183 BC) (Publius Cornelius Scipio) Roman general in the second of the PUNIC WARS. He defeated the Carthaginian forces in Spain (209 BC). Elected consul in 205, he invaded North Africa and defeated HANNIBAL at Zama (202 BC), earning the honorary surname Africanus.

**Scipio Africanus Minor** (185–129 BC) (Publius Cornelius Scipio Aemilianus) Roman general of the third PUNIC WAR. He took his grandfather-by-adoption's name, SCIPIO AFRICANUS MAJOR. He destroyed Carthage in 146 BC, ending the Punic Wars, and in 133 ended a long war in Spain by destroying the city of Numantia.

**sclerosis** Degenerative hardening of tissue, usually due to scarring following inflammation or as a result of aging. It can affect the brain and spinal cord, causing neurological symptoms, or the walls of the arteries.

**Scopes trial** (1925) Court case that culminated the long anti-evolution campaign spearheaded by Fundamentalists. It upheld the constitutionality of a Tennessee law forbidding the teaching of evolutionary theory. The trial involved John Thomas Scopes, a high school biology teacher, and was a forensic battle between defense attorney Clarence DARROW and William Jennings BRYAN, who assisted the prosecution. It turned into a national circus and a public humiliation of Bryan.

**Scorpio** Eighth astrological sign of the ZODIAC. It is identified with the scorpion that caused the death of the hunter Orion and stung the horses of Phaëthon.

**scorpion** Any of numerous species of ARACHNIDS that live in warmer regions worldwide. It has two main body sections, two eyes, a pair of pedipalps (pincers), and a long tail ending in a curved, poisonous sting. Length: to 7in (17cm). Class Arachnida; order Scorpionida.

**Scorsese, Martin** (1942– ) US film director. His first major success was *Alice Doesn't Live Here Anymore* (1975). Scorsese often cast Robert DE NIRO in leading roles, such as in *Taxi Driver* (1976), *Raging Bull* (1980), and *The King of Comedy* (1983). Other films include *Goodfellas* (1990), *Cape Fear* (1991), *The Age of Innocence* (1993), and *Kundun* (1997).

**Scotland** Northern part of the main island of Great Britain, and a constituent of the United Kingdom of Great Britain and Northern Ireland; the capital is EDINBURGH. The largest city is GLASGOW. Scotland is administratively divided into nine regions and three island authorities. Its jagged coastline features many islands (including the ORKNEY and SHETLAND ISLANDS), lochs (including LOMOND and NESS) and firths. Major Scottish rivers include the TAY and CLYDE. Scotland can be broadly divided into three geographical regions: the Southern Uplands, immediately N of the English border, which are sparsely populated, hilly moorland; the Central Lowlands, where the majority of the population live; and the HIGHLANDS, including BEN NEVIS. In prehistory Scotland was inhabited by the PICTS. Kenneth I united the lands of the Picts and the SCOTS in AD 843. In 1174, with the development of feudalism, Scotland was made a fiefdom of England. In 1189 Richard I granted Scottish freedom, but the enmity between England and Scotland (in alliance with France) continued. EDWARD I forced the Scots to submit, only for William WALLACE to lead a Scottish revolt. ROBERT I (THE BRUCE) recaptured much Scottish land and defeated the English at the Battle of BANNOCKBURN (1314); this led to England's recognition of Scottish independence in 1328. The 15th century was characterized by internal factionalism and weak government. JAMES IV and many Scottish nobles were killed at the Battle of Flodden (1513). The Protestant REFORMATION quickly took root in Scotland via the preaching of John KNOX. In 1513 JAMES V cemented the French alliance by marrying Mary of Guise, a French Catholic. When her daughter, MARY, QUEEN OF SCOTS, assumed the throne in 1561, England supported the Scottish Protestants, and France backed the Catholics. In 1567 the Protestant faction forced Mary to relinquish the throne. Her son, James VI, assumed the Scottish crown, and in 1601 he was also crowned JAMES I of England, thereby uniting the English and Scottish thrones. The Scots opposed Charles I in the English CIVIL WAR, but the king's concessions to PRESBYTERIANISM won the support of the COVENANTERS. The GLORIOUS REVOLUTION reestablished Presbyterianism as the Scottish national church. The massacre of the Macdonald clan by WILLIAM III at Glencoe in 1692 tarnished enthusiasm for his rule, and the JACOBITE agitation prompted the constitutional union of the two crowns in the Act of UNION (1707). At CULLODEN Moor (1746) the Jacobite insurgency was finally suppressed with the defeat of the Highlanders led by Prince Charles Edward STUART. (*See* UNITED KINGDOM for subsequent history) A 1979 referendum for a separate Scottish assembly was defeated, but in 1997 a referendum voted in favor of devolution. Scotland retains its own church, education, and legal system. The principal agricultural activity is the rearing of livestock; oats and potatoes are the chief crops. Coal mining and heavy industry dominated the economy of the central lowlands by the late 19th century, but declined in the 1980s. The discovery of North Sea oil and natural gas in the 1970s benefited the Scottish economy. Other industries: textiles, whisky, beer, fishing. Area: 29,797sq mi (77,167sq km). Pop. (1991) 4,998,567.

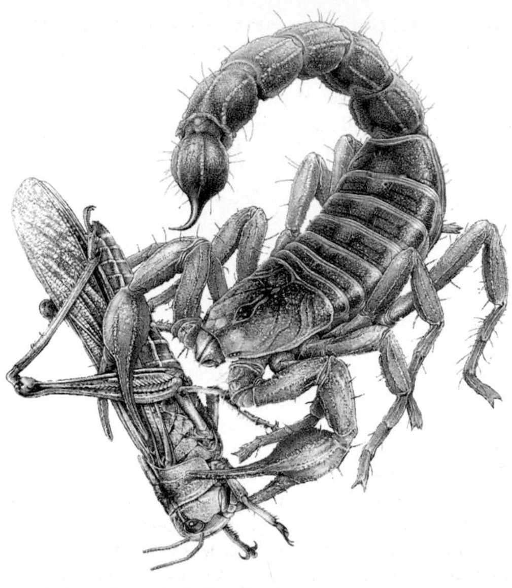

◀ **scorpion** The sting of the scorpion is worked by opposing muscles fixed to the base of the sting, which contract and relax, forcing the sharp tip into its prey's tissue. The poison, stored in the poison gland, is forced down and out of the tip of the sting by muscles located around the gland.

**Scotland Yard** Name given to the headquarters in London of the Metropolitan Police, and synonymous with the Criminal Investigation Department (CID).

**Scots** Originally a Celtic people from N Ireland. They were Gaelic speaking. Their raids on the W coast of Roman Britain from the 3rd to the 5th century failed to establish independent settlements in Wales or NW England. In the 5th century, however, they were able to establish the kingdom of Dalriada in Pictish territory. From the 11th century the term has been applied to those people living in Scotland.

**Scott, Sir George Gilbert** (1811–78) English architect, prominent figure in the GOTHIC REVIVAL. He achieved a reputation with his design for the church of St. Nicholas, Hamburg. Scott was involved in the restoration of Westminster and Ely Cathedrals. He designed the Albert Memorial (1862–70), and St. Pancras Station, London. His son, **Giles Gilbert Scott** (1880–1960), designed the new Anglican Cathedral in Liverpool, the last major example of the Gothic revival.

S

▲ **Scott** British Antarctic explorer Robert Scott and his four companions pulled heavy sledges by hand across the high polar plateau in their trek to the South Pole in 1910–12. All five died, and their bodies were later recovered along with Scott's diaries, scientific collections, and letters to the widows of his companions. The story of their tragic journey has entered into British folklore.

**Scott, Robert Falcon** (1868–1912) Scottish Antarctic explorer. Scott's first expedition (1901–04), in the *Discovery*, to the South Pole ended in failure. His second expedition (1910–12) reached the Pole, but found that Roald AMUNDSEN had got there first. Beset by blizzards on their return journey, Scott and his party perished within 11mi (18km) of safety.

**Scott, Sir Walter** (1771–1832) Scottish novelist and poet. He began his career with a collection of old Scottish ballads, *Minstrelsy of the Scottish Border* (1802–03). The wider fame brought by *The Lay of the Last Minstrel* (1805) was consolidated by the poems *Marmion* (1808) and *The Lady of the Lake* (1810). In 1814 he turned to historical fiction. His first novel, *Waverley* (1814), was an immediate success and was followed by a series of Scottish novels, including *Rob Roy* (1817) and *The Heart of Midlothian* (1818). Among his later novels are *Ivanhoe* (1819), *Kenilworth* (1821), and *Quentin Durward* (1823).

**Scott, Winfield** (1786–1866) US general. His bravery in the WAR OF 1812 made him a national hero. Further success in the AROOSTOOK WAR led to his appointment (1841) as supreme commander of the US army. In the MEXICAN WAR (1846–48), Scott led the triumphant march from Vera Cruz to Mexico City. In 1852 he was the Whig presidential candidate but lost to Franklin PIERCE. Scott retired at the outbreak of the Civil War.

**Scottish** (Scots) Dialect of English traditionally spoken in Scotland and regarded by some experts as a distinct GERMANIC language. It is also called Lowland Scots (or Lallans), to distinguish it from the Scots GAELIC spoken in the Scottish Highlands, or broad Scots, to differentiate it from the English of Scotland's middle class. It developed from the Northumbrian dialect of EARLY ENGLISH before AD 700. Before the union of the English and Scottish crowns in 1603, the Scottish language was both a national language and an official court language. It continues as a spoken dialect in many areas and has continued to be a vehicle for a lively and vibrant literature.

▲ **seahorse** Related to the pipe fishes – family Syngnathidae - (back), the seahorse (*Hippocampus* sp) is the only fish with a prehensile tail, which it uses to cling to seaweed. The seahorse swims weakly with an upright stance, and is carried along by ocean currents.

**scrapie** Fatal disease of sheep and goats that affects the central nervous system, causing staggering and itching. It is caused by a PRION, a slow-acting, viruslike, microscopic particle. The animal usually dies within six months of exhibiting symptoms.

**scree** (talus) Heap of rock waste lying at the bottom of a cliff. It is made up of particles that have been loosened from the cliff rock by WEATHERING.

**Scriabin, Alexander Nicolas** (1872–1915) Russian composer and pianist. He wrote highly original piano music in which he used chords built in fourths instead of the usual major and minor triads. His most significant works include ten piano sonatas, *The Poem of Ecstasy* (1908), three symphonies, and many piano pieces.

**scribe** Court secretary in ancient times; in JUDAISM, member of a class of scholars expert in Jewish law. From the late 6th century, the Scribes functioned as teachers and interpreters of the TORAH.

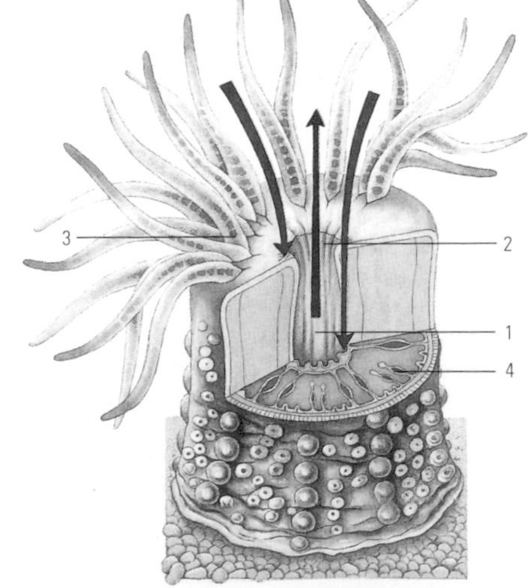


► **sea anemone** Having no rigid structures, the sea anemone supports itself by circulating water around its central cavity (1). Water is drawn in down siphonoglyphs (grooves) (2) at the side of the cavity, and is expelled up the center. The tentacles (3) can be withdrawn by individual retractor muscles (4).

**scriptures** Sacred writings of a RELIGION. In Christianity, they are the books of the OLD TESTAMENT and NEW TESTAMENT, with or without those of the APOCRYPHA. It is also possible to speak of the KORAN as the scripture of ISLAM or the VEDAS as the scriptures of HINDUISM.

**scuba diving** Diving with the use of **s**elf-**c**ontained **u**nderwater **b**reathing **a**pparatus, or scuba. The equipment usually consists of tanks of compressed air connected to a demand regulator.

**sculpin** Any of 300 species of bottom-dwelling, usually marine, fish found in temperate and cold waters of the N Atlantic Ocean. Grayish and mottled with yellow, it has a large bony head covered with prickles. Length: to 2ft (60cm). Family Cottidae.

**sculpture** Art of creating forms in three dimensions, either in the round or in relief. Techniques employed include carving (in wood, stone, marble, ivory, etc.), modeling (in clay, wax, etc.), or casting (in bronze and other metals). The history of sculpture parallels that of PAINTING. The early civilizations of Egypt, Mesopotamia, India, and the Far East were rich in sculpture. The Greeks developed a style of relief and free-standing sculpture. Roman sculptors were influenced by the Greeks, but forsook the Greek ideal in portraiture, which they enriched with individual characterization. Medieval European sculpture was frequently a feature of ROMANESQUE and GOTHIC churches, many of which were covered with carvings. Highly stylized in the Romanesque period, this architectural sculpture became more realistic in the Gothic era. Prior to the RENAISSANCE, individual sculptors rarely achieved fame. The Florentine Renaissance was enriched by the works of such masters as GHIBERTI, DONATELLO, and MICHELANGELO. High BAROQUE sculpture is exemplified in the works of the architect-sculptor BERNINI in Rome. Pierre Puget was the movement's leading exponent in France where, in the 18th century, it was superseded by NEOCLASSICISM. This extended into the 19th century, when it was rivaled and replaced by a movement of realist sculpture, such as that of RODIN. African, Aztec, and other ethnic and ancient sculpture have stimulated great modern sculptors such as PICASSO, MODIGLIANI, BRANCUSI, and MOORE.

**scurvy** Disease caused by a deficiency of VITAMIN C (ascorbic acid). It is characterized by weakness, painful joints, and bleeding gums.

**Scylla** In Greek mythology, a female sea monster. Once a beautiful nymph beloved of POSEIDON, she was changed by CIRCE into a long-necked, six-headed beast. She lived with CHARYBDIS beside the Straits of Messina between Sicily and Italy and devoured sailors.

**Scythians** Nomadic people who inhabited the steppes N of the Black Sea in the 1st millennium BC. In the 7th century BC their territory extended into Mesopotamia, the Balkans, and Greece. Powerful warriors, their elaborate tombs contain evidence of great wealth. Pressure from the Sarmatians confined them to the Crimea (*c*.300 BC) and their culture eventually disappeared.

**sea anemone** Sessile, polyp-type COELENTERATE found in marine pools and along rocky shores. It has a cylindrical body with tentacles around its mouth; the color varies according to species. Height: to 8in (20cm). Class Anthozoa; genera include *Tealia*, *Anemonia*, and *Metridium*.

**Seaborg, Glenn Theodore** (1912– ) US physicist. During World War II he worked on the development of the atom bomb. In 1940 Seaborg and Edwin M. MCMILLAN discovered PLUTONIUM. They went on to isolate the entire ACTINIDE SERIES. Seaborg and McMillan shared the 1951 Nobel Prize for chemistry for their work on the TRANSURANIC ELEMENTS.

**sea cow** *See* DUGONG

**sea cucumber** Marine ECHINODERM found in rocky areas. It is a cylindrical animal with a fleshy body in five parts around a central axis; it has branched tentacles around the mouth. Species include the cotton-spinners (*Holothuria* spp). Class Holothuroidea.

**seafloor** Floor of the oceans, which includes a variety of different landforms. The major features of the seafloor are the continental shelf, the continental rise, the abyssal floor,

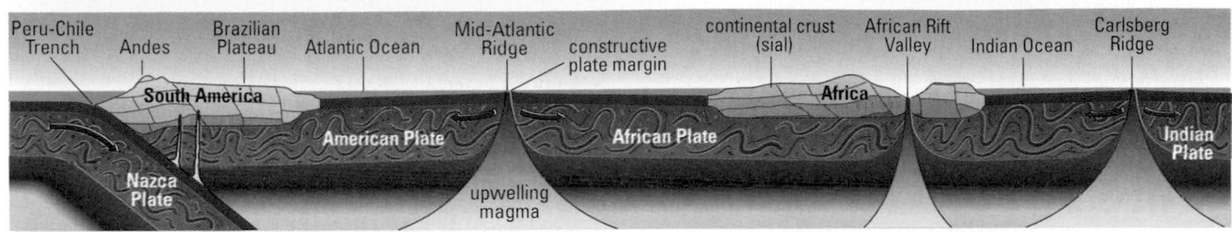

Seafloor spreading in the Atlantic Ocean


Seafloor spreading in the Indian Ocean and continental plate collision

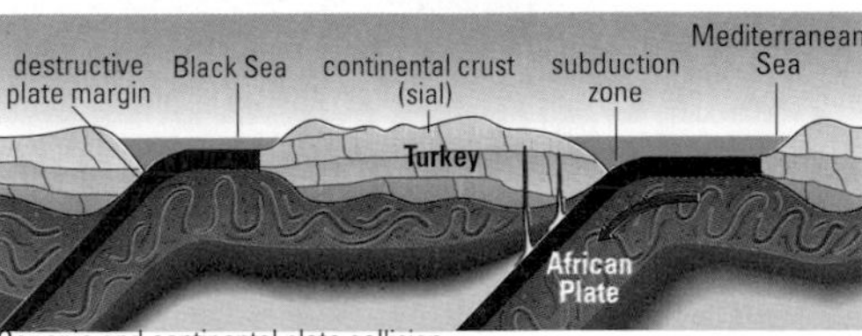

Oceanic and continental plate collision

◀ **seafloor spreading** The vast ridges that divide the Earth's crust beneath each of the world's oceans mark the boundaries between tectonic plates that are gradually moving in opposite directions. As the plates shift apart, molten magma rises from the mantle to seal the rift and the seafloor slowly spreads toward the continental landmasses. The rate of spreading has been calculated by magnetic analysis of the rock at about 1.5in (3.7cm) a year in the North Atlantic Ocean. Underwater volcanoes mark the line where the continental rise begins. As the plates meet, much of the denser ocean crust dips beneath the continental plate and melts back into the magma.

seamounts, oceanic trenches, and oceanic ridges. The ABYSSAL floor is *c*.1.8mi (3km) deep and is mostly made of basaltic rock covered with fine-grained (pelagic) sediment consisting of dust and the shells of marine organisms. Oceanic trenches are up to 7mi (11km) deep, typically 30–60mi (50–100km) wide, and may be thousands of miles long. Oceanic ridges are long, linear, volcanic structures that tend to occupy the middle of seafloors; they are the sites of crustal spreading. *See also* OCEAN; CONTINENTAL MARGIN; SEAFLOOR SPREADING

**seafloor spreading** Theory that explains how CONTINENTAL DRIFT occurs. It proposes that the sea floor is moved laterally as new basalt rock is injected along mid-ocean ridges and so the floor becomes older with increasing distance from the ridge. *See also* PLATE TECTONICS

**seahorse** Marine fish found in shallow tropical and temperate waters. It swims in an upright position and has an outer bony skeleton of platelike rings, a mouth at the end of a long snout, and a curled, prehensile tail with which it clings to seaweed. The male incubates the young in a brood pouch. Length: 1.5–12in (3.8–30.5cm). Family Syngnathidae.

**seal** Any of several species of carnivorous, primarily marine, aquatic mammals. It feeds on fish, crustaceans, and other marine animals; various species are hunted for meat, hides, oil, and fur. Species of true, earless seals such as the leopard seal (*Hydrurga leptonyx*), hooded seal (*Cystophora cristata*), and bearded seal (*Erignathus barbatus*) are included in the family Phocidae. They swim with powerful strokes of their hind flippers and sinuous movements of the whole trunk. Members of the eared family Otariidae have longer fore flippers, used for propulsion, and use all four limbs when moving on land. They include fur seals (genera *Callorhinus* and *Arctocephalus*) and species of SEA LION. Order Pinnepedia.

**sea lily** Crinoid ECHINODERM found in deep marine waters. Seldom seen, it has many branched arms with ciliated grooves for food collecting radiating from a tiny body disk. Spineless, it attaches itself to the ocean bottom with a stalk. Class Crinoidea.

**sea lion** Any of five species of SEALS that live in coastal waters of the Pacific and feed primarily on fish and squid. They have streamlined bodies and long fore flippers for propulsion. The males of all species, except the California sea lion (*Zalophus californianus*), have manes. The largest species is the Steller sea lion (*Eumetopias jubata*); it may reach 11ft (3.3m) in length. Order Pinnepedia; family Otariidae.

**seaplane** Aircraft that can land on and take off from water. The first practical seaplane was built in the US by Glenn H. Curtiss and flown in 1911. There are two main types of seaplane. **Floatplanes** have large floats that support the fuselage above the water. **Flying boats** float on their boat-shaped hulls, with small floats supporting the wings.

**sea slug** (nudibranch) Any of numerous species of marine gastropod mollusks, related to snails and found throughout the world. They have no shells, quills or mantle cavities, frequent shallow water, and feed primarily on sea anemones. Order Nudibranchia.

**seasons** Four periods of the year based on differential solar heating of the Earth as it makes its annual revolution of the Sun. The Northern Hemisphere receives more solar radiation when its pole is aimed toward the Sun in summer and less in winter when it is aimed away, whereas the opposite holds for the Southern Hemisphere. The seasons begin at the vernal (spring) and autumnal EQUINOXES and the winter and summer SOLSTICES.

**sea squirt** Any of numerous species of small, sac-like, marine animals, with no true backbone. A sedentary creature, it constantly draws in and discharges water for food and oxygen, and can shoot out water when disturbed. Class Ascidiacea.

**SEATO** Acronym for SOUTHEAST ASIA TREATY ORGANIZATION (SEATO)

**Seattle** City and seaport in W Washington, on Elliott Bay between Lake Washington and Puget Sound. Settled in 1851, it developed rapidly after the arrival of the railroad (1893). Seattle served as the gateway for the Alaska Gold Rush (1897). Seattle has been an aerospace center since William Boeing opened his first factory here in 1916. Seattle's economy has diversified in recent years. The computer company Microsoft has its headquarters here. Industries: shipbuilding, precision instruments, chemicals, lumber, fishing, tourism. Pop. (1992) 519,598.

**sea urchin** Spiny ECHINODERM animal found in marine tidal pools along rocky shores. Round with long, radiating (often poisonous) moveable spines, its skeletal plates fuse to form a perforated shell. Class Echinoidae.

**seaweed** Any of numerous and varied species of brown, green, or red ALGAE, found in greatest profusion in shallow waters on rocky coasts. KELPS are the largest forms. Many species are important for the manufacture of fertilizers or food, or as a valuable source of chemicals such as iodine. Kingdom Protoctista.

**sebaceous gland** Gland in the skin producing the oily substance sebum, which is secreted onto the skin and hair, making them water-repellent and supple.

**Sebastian, Saint** (d. *c*.AD 288) Roman Christian martyr. Legend says that he was a favorite of the emperor DIOCLETIAN who, on learning that Sebastian was a Christian, condemned him to be killed by arrows. He survived and later voluntarily appeared before Diocletian, who this time had him beaten to death. His feast day is January 20.

**Sebastiano del Piombo** (1485–1547) (Sebastiano Luciani) Italian painter of the VENETIAN SCHOOL. He went to Rome in 1511 to create a series of mythological FRESCOS at the Villa Farnese. Some of his best works are his portraits.

**seborrhea** Disorder of the SEBACEOUS GLANDS characterized by overproduction of sebum, resulting in red, scaly patches on the skin and dandruff.

**secant** In TRIGONOMETRY, ratio of the length of the hypotenuse to the length of the side adjacent to an acute angle in a right-angled triangle. The secant of angle $A$ (sec $A$) is equal to the reciprocal of its COSINE.

**secession** Formal separation from an organized body. The term is usually applied to the withdrawal of a political unit from the state of which it formed a part. One example is the secession of 11 Southern states from the US to form the Confederate States of America (1861).

▲ **seal** The harp seal (*Phoca groenlandica*, top) is a true seal, and breeds in North Atlantic and Arctic oceans and migrates s in winter. They feed on large plankton and fish, and grow to a length of nearly 6.5ft (2m), and can weigh up to 400lb (180kg). The northern fur seal (*Callorhinus ursinus*, bottom), unlike the harp seal, is an eared seal. It migrates in winter from the Bering Sea to California and Japan. It feeds on squid, fish, and crustaceans. They too grow to 6.5ft (2m) and an adult male can weigh between 400 and 650lb (180–300kg).

S

► **secretary bird** Found in sub-Saharan Africa, the secretary bird (*Sagittarius serpentarius*) gets its name from the feathers that protrude behind its head, resembling quill pens. It is a well-known snake killer and runs after its prey on foot in a zigzag fashion. The snake is killed by a blow from the foot, followed by battering from the wings. The secretary bird is so unlike other members in the same order that it is placed in a separate family.

**second** (symbol s) SI unit of time defined as the time taken for 9,192,631,770 periods of vibrations of the electromagnetic radiation emitted by a cesium-133 atom. It is commonly defined as 1/60 of a minute. *See also* PHYSICAL UNITS

**Second World War** *See* WORLD WAR II

**secretary bird** BIRD OF PREY found in Africa S of the Sahara. It is pale gray with black markings and has quill-like feathers behind its ears, large wings, and long legs and tail. It feeds on reptiles, eggs, and insects. Height: 4ft (1.2m). Species *Sagittarius serpentarius*.

**secretion** Production and discharge of a substance, usually a fluid, by a cell or a GLAND. The substance so discharged is also known as a secretion. Secretions include ENZYMES, HORMONES, SALIVA, and sweat.

**Secret Service, US** Law enforcement agency within the Treasury Department. It is charged with stopping all counterfeiting and forging of US money, and with the protection of the president, vice president, president-elect, and presidential candidates and their families.

**Securities and Exchange Commission (SEC)** US federal agency established in 1934. Its general objective is to protect the interests of the public and investors against malpractice in the markets.

**sedative** Drug used for its calming effect, to reduce anxiety and tension; in high doses it induces sleep. *See also* BARBITURATE; BENZODIAZEPINE; NARCOTIC

**sedge** Any of numerous species of grasslike perennial plants, especially those of the genus *Carex*, widely distributed in temperate, cold, and tropical mountain regions, usually in wet conditions. Cultivated as ornamentals, they have narrow leaves and spikes of brown, green, or greenish yellow flowers. Family Cyperaceae.

**sediment** In geology, a general term used to describe any material that is transported and deposited by water, ice, wind, or gravity. It includes material, such as lime, that is transported in solution and later precipitated, and organic deposits such as coal and coral reefs.

**sedimentary rock** Type of rock formed of mineral or organic particles that have been moved by the action of water, wind, or glacial ice (or have been chemically precipitated from solution) to a new location. Following a process of compaction and cementation, the particles usually form layers of sedimentary rock.

**Seebeck effect** Thermoelectric effect important in the thermocouple for temperature measurement. If wires of two different metals are joined at their ends to form a circuit, a current flows if the junctions are kept at different temperatures. It is the reverse of the PELTIER EFFECT.

**seed** Part of a flowering plant that contains the embryo and food store. It is formed in the ovary by FERTILIZATION of the female GAMETE (*see* POLLEN). Food may be stored in a special tissue called the **endosperm**, or it may be concentrated in the swollen seed leaves (COTYLEDONS). Seeds are the unit of dispersal of ANGIOSPERMS and CONIFERS. *See also* FRUIT; GERMINATION

**Seeger, Pete** (1919– ) US folk singer. Influenced by the social protest lyrics of Woody GUTHRIE, Seeger composed many US folk standards, such as "If I Had A Hammer" (1949) and "Where Have All the Flowers Gone?" (1956).

**Segovia, Andrés** (1893–1987) Spanish guitarist who established the guitar as a concert instrument. He adapted the instrument to the complex music of modern composers and transcribed early contrapuntal music.

**Segrè, Emilio Gino** (1905–89) US physicist, b. Italy, who shared the 1959 Nobel Prize for physics with Owen Chamberlain for the discovery of the antiproton. In 1937 Segrè discovered TECHNETIUM, the first element to be artificially produced, and in 1940 he helped to discover ASTATINE and plutonium-239. *See also* ANTIMATTER

**segregation** Separation of a specific group from the rest of society on such grounds as race, religion, or sex. Such separation might be enshrined in law, as in the Southern states of the US before the CIVIL RIGHTS movement, or in South Africa in the era of APARTHEID.

**Seine** River in N central France. It rises in Langres Plateau near Dijon and flows NW through PARIS to enter the English Channel near Le Havre. It is connected to the Loire, Rhône, Meuse, Schelde, Saône, and Somme rivers by a network of canals. With its main tributaries (Aube, Marne, Oise, Yonne, Loing, and Eure), the Seine drains the entire Paris Basin and is the most important river of N France.

**seismology** Study of seismic waves, the shock waves produced by EARTHQUAKES. The velocity of seismic waves varies according to the material through which they pass. Primary (P) and secondary (S) waves are transmitted by the solid earth. Only P waves are transmitted through fluid zones. The movement of seismic waves is detected and recorded by seismographs.

**Selassie, Haile** *See* HAILE SELASSIE

**Selene** In Greek mythology, goddess of the Moon, daughter of Hyperion, and sister of Helios (the Sun) and Eos (the Dawn). Each night she drove her chariot across the sky, as her brother Helios, had done during the day.

**selenium** (symbol se) Gray METALLOID element of Group VI of the periodic table, discovered (1817) by J.J. BERZELIUS. Its chief source is as a by-product in the electrolytic refining of copper. It is extensively used in photoelectric cells, solar cells, xerography, and red pigments. Properties: at.no. 34; at. wt. 78.96; sp. gr. 4.79; m.p. 422.6°F (217°C); b.p. 1,265°F (684.9°C); most common isotope $^{80}$Se (49.82%).

**Seles, Monica** (1973– ) US tennis player, b. Yugoslavia. At the age of 16, she won her first Grand Slam title (French Open, 1990). She repeated this success in 1991 and 1992. Seles has won the Australian Open four times (1991–93, 1996), and the US Open twice (1991–92). In 1993 her career was halted when she was stabbed by a fan of her arch rival Steffi GRAF. In 1995 she resumed competitive tennis.

**Seleucids** Hellenistic dynasty founded (*c.*300 BC) by SELEUCUS I, a former general of ALEXANDER THE GREAT. Centered on Syria, it included most of the Asian provinces of Alexander's empire, extending from the E Mediterranean to India. War with the Ptolemies of Egypt and, later, the Romans steadily reduced its territory. In 63 BC it became the Roman province of Syria.

**Seleucus** Name of two kings of Syria. **Seleucus I** (*c.*355–281 BC) was a trusted general of ALEXANDER THE GREAT and founder of the SELEUCID dynasty. By 281 BC he had secured control of Babylonia, Syria, and all of Asia Minor, founding a western capital at Antioch to balance the eastern capital of Seleucia, in Babylon. He appeared to be on the brink of restoring the whole of Alexander's empire under his rule when he was murdered. **Seleucus II** (r.247–226 BC) spent his reign fighting Ptolemy III of Egypt and Antiochus Hierax, his brother and rival, losing territory to both.

**Selim III** (1761–1808) Ottoman sultan (1789–1807) After ending a war against Russia and Austria *c.*1791, he began a program to westernize the state's finances and armed forces.

He was assassinated during a revolt of JANISSARIES and conservatives who opposed his reforms.

**Seljuk** Nomadic tribesmen from central Asia who adopted Islam in the 7th century and founded the Baghdad sultanate in 1055. Their empire included Mesopotamia, Syria, and Persia. Under Alp Arslan, they defeated the Byzantines at Manzikert in 1071, which led to their occupation of Anatolia. They revived Sunni administration and religious institutions, checking the spread of Shi'a Islam and laying the organizational basis for the future Ottoman administration. In the early 12th century the Seljuk empire began to disintegrate, and the Seljuk states were conquered by the MONGOLS in the 13th century.

**Selkirk, Thomas Douglas, 5th earl of** (1771–1820) Scottish colonizer. In 1803 he established settlements in Prince Edward Island and Ontario. In 1811 he gained a controlling share of the HUDSON'S BAY COMPANY and founded the Red River Settlement in Manitoba.

**semantics** Branch of LINGUISTICS and PHILOSOPHY concerned with the study of meaning. In historical linguistics, it generally refers to the analysis of how the meanings of words change over time. In modern linguistics and philosophy, semantics seeks to assess the contribution of word-meaning to the meanings of phrases and sentences, and to comprehend the relationship among and between words and the things they refer to or stand for.

**semaphore** Device or technique that communicates messages visually; a type of optical telegraph. A railroad semaphore signal consists of a vertical post on which a single projecting arm is mounted, whose angle indicates "all clear" or "danger." In flag semaphore, a signaler indicates letters and numerals by the position of his outstretched arms, emphasized with flags.

**semen** Fluid in a male that contains SPERM from the TESTES and the secretions of various accessory sexual glands. In humans each ejaculate is normally *c*.3–6ml by volume and contains about 200 to 300 million sperm.

**semiconductor** Substance with electrical CONDUCTIVITY between that of a CONDUCTOR and an INSULATOR. The conductivity increases as temperature increases. A semiconductor consists of elements, such as GERMANIUM and SILICON, or compounds, such as aluminum phosphide, with a crystalline structure. At normal temperatures, some electrons break free and give rise to *n*-type (negative) conductivity with the electrons as the main carriers of the electric current. The holes (electron deficiencies) left by these electrons give rise to *p*-type (positive) conductivity with the holes as the main carriers. Impurities are usually added to the semiconductor material in controlled amounts to add more free electrons or create more holes. A semiconductor junction is formed where there is an abrupt change along the length of the crystal from one type of impurity to the other. Such a *p-n* junction acts as a very efficient RECTIFIER and is the basis of the semiconductor DIODE.

**Seminole** Native North American band that separated from the main CREEK group in the late 18th century and fled S into Florida under pressure of wars with white settlers. Seminole involvement in wars against the US led to the First Seminole War (1717–18). In 1832 some Seminole leaders signed a treaty agreeing to move to Oklahoma. Others opposed the move and the Second Seminole War (1835–42) began. The war claimed 1,500 US troops and cost more than $20 million before the Seminoles were forced to surrender and move west. Today, *c*.12,000 Seminole live in Florida and Oklahoma.

**semiotics** (semiology) Study of signs and symbols, both visual and linguistic, and their function in communication. Pioneers of semiotics include Charles Sanders PEIRCE and Ferdinand de SAUSSURE. Roland BARTHES and Claude LÉVI-STRAUSS developed the principles of semiotics further, into STRUCTURALISM.

**Semiramis** In Assyrian mythology, a queen and goddess, wife of Ninus, founder of NINEVEH. Daughter of a fish goddess and the god of wisdom, she was reared by doves. After the death of Ninus she ruled alone, founded the city of Babylon, and led victorious armies against numerous enemies until, opposed by her son, she took the form of a dove and flew away.

**Semites** Peoples whose native tongue belongs to the SEMITIC LANGUAGES group. They originally inhabited an area in Arabia and spoke a common language, Proto-Semitic. Among the modern Semites are Arabs, native Israelis, and many Ethiopians.

**Semitic languages** Group of languages spoken by peoples native to N Africa and the Middle East and forming one of the five branches of the Afro-Asiatic language family. The Semitic languages are divided into three sub-branches: **North West Semitic** (including HEBREW, ARAMAIC, and Eblaite); **North East Semitic** (consisting of Akkadian); and **Central and Southern Semitic** (including ARABIC, South Arabian, and Ethiopic). Only Hebrew and Arabic have survived to develop modern forms.

**Semmelweiss, Ignaz Philipp** (1818–65) Hungarian physician, probably the first to recognize the importance of ANTISEPTIC in preventing infection. In 1847, during a outbreak of puerperal fever, he ordered doctors at the Vienna General Hospital to wash their hands before treating a patient. His ideas were ridiculed until confirmed by Joseph LISTER.

**Senate** Upper house of the US legislature, which together with the HOUSE OF REPRESENTATIVES forms the CONGRESS. It is composed of two senators from each state, who are elected for six-year terms. Elections are held every other year, with about one third of the Senate elected at a time. There are usually 16 standing committees, and committee chairs retain their positions for as long as their party has a majority of the votes. The approval of a simple majority of the Senate is necessary for major presidential appointments, and a two-thirds majority for treaties. The Senate can initiate legislation except on fiscal matters. Officially, the presiding officer of the Senate is the vice president, but the position is often delegated.

**Senate, Roman** Chief governing body of the Roman republic. It originated as a royal council under the early kings. By the 2nd century BC it controlled all matters of policy. Senators were chosen for life by the CENSORS and at first were mainly former CONSULS. They numbered 300, raised to 600 under SULLA, to 900 by CAESAR, and reduced to 600 under AUGUSTUS. PLEBEIANS gained entry in the 4th century BC. Under the empire, the emperor's control of military and civil officials gradually restricted the senate to judicial matters and to the city government in Rome. Under the late empire, senatorial status was extended to the landowning elite.

**Sendak, Maurice** (1928– ) US author and illustrator of imaginative books for children. Sendak's *Where the Wild Things Are* was awarded the Caldecott Medal in 1964.

◀ **Seles** US tennis player Monica Seles is renowned for her ruthless competitiveness, fast court speed, and ferocious groundstrokes. Her long rivalry with Steffi Graf was interrupted when Seles was stabbed by one of Graf's fans. Seles tried to bring a case for damages against the German Tennis Federation, claiming that she was not provided with sufficient protection, but was unsuccessful.

S

**Seneca, Lucius Annaeus** (AD 4–65) Roman STOIC philosopher, b. Spain. Based on Greek models, Seneca's nine tragedies, such as *Phaedra, Medea*, and *Oedipus*, have had a lasting impact on European literature. His other works include 12 books of *Moral Essays* and many philosophical letters.

**Seneca** Most populous division of the IROQUOIS CONFEDERACY; a tribe of Native North Americans who inhabited N New York. Today, *c*.7,000 Seneca live on reservations in W New York. In 1848 the Seneca Nation was formed by the peoples of the Allegany and Cattaraugus reservations. Other Seneca live in Oklahoma, Pennsylvania, and Ontario.

**Seneca Falls Convention** (1848) Women's rights convention held at Seneca Falls, New York. Elizabeth Cady STANTON and Lucretia MOTT organized the convention, the first demanding equal rights for women.

**Senegal** Republic on the NW coast of Africa. *See* country feature

**Senghor, Léopold Sédar** (1906– ) Senegalese statesman and poet. He was the first president (1960–80) of the republic of Senegal. As president, he led (1974) Senegal into the West African Economic Community. His poetry, such as *Songs of the Shade* (1945), is intended for voice with musical accompaniment. Senghor was the first African to be elected to the Académie Française (1984).

**Senna, Ayrton** (1960–94) Brazilian racing driver. In 1984 he began racing in Formula 1. In 1985 Senna won his first grand prix. He went on to win 41 Grands Prix but died in a crash at the San Marino Grand Prix.

**senna** Plants, shrubs, and trees of the genus *Senna* native to warm and tropical regions; some species grow in temperate areas. They have rectangular, feathery leaves and yellow flowers. Family Fabaceae/Leguminosae.

**Sennacherib** (d. 681 BC) King of ASSYRIA (704–681 BC). Son and successor of SARGON, he led expeditions to subdue Phoenicia and Palestine (701 BC), and defeated the Elamite-Chaldean alliance (691 BC). In 689 BC he destroyed Babylon and devoted himself to rebuilding his capital, NINEVEH. *See also* ASHURBANIPAL

**Sennett, Mack** (1884–1960) US film director, producer, and actor. Films made by his Keystone company brought fame to Charlie CHAPLIN, Mabel Normand, Fatty Arbuckle, and the Keystone Kops.

**senses** Means by which animals gain information about their environment and physiological condition. The five senses, SIGHT, HEARING, TASTE, SMELL, and TOUCH, all rely on specialized receptors on or near the external surface of the body.

**Seoul** (Kyongsong) Capital of South Korea, on the Han River. The political, commercial, industrial, and cultural center of South Korea, it was founded (1392) as the capital of the Yi dynasty. From 1910 to 1945 it developed rapidly under Japanese governorship. After World War II, Seoul was the headquarters of the US army of occupation. Following the 1948 partition, it became the capital of South Korea. Seoul's capture by North Korean troops precipitated the start of the KOREAN WAR, and the following months witnessed the city's virtual destruction. In March 1951 Seoul became the headquarters of the UN command in Korea. In 1996 Seoul was the scene of violent student demonstrations for reunification with North Korea. Pop. (1994) 10,799,000.

**sepal** Modified leaf that makes up the outermost portion of a flower bud. Although usually green and inconspicuous once the flower is open, in some species the sepals look like the PETALS.

**separation of powers** US political principle that aims to prevent despotic rule by a system of checks and balances among the different branches of government. It was a guiding principle of the founders of the US CONSTITUTION. The three branches of government (executive, legislative, and judicial) act as checks on each other.

**Sephardim** Descendants of the Jews of medieval Spain and Portugal. Iberian Jews followed the Babylonian rather than the Palestinian Jewish tradition, and developed their own language, Ladino. After the expulsion of the Jews from Spain (1492), many settled in Ottoman parts of the Middle East and North Africa. Continuing persecution led many of them to form colonies in Amsterdam and other cities in NW Europe. Many Sephardic Jews were killed in the HOLOCAUST. *See also* ASKENAZIM

**Sepoy Rebellion** *See* INDIAN MUTINY

**sepsis** Destruction of body tissue by disease-causing (pathogenic) bacteria or their toxins. Local or widespread inflammation may occur, possibly followed by NECROSIS, the death of tissue. Treatment is with ANTIBIOTICS.

**septicemia** Term for severe SEPSIS or BLOOD POISONING

**Septuagint** Earliest surviving Greek translation of the Hebrew Bible (the OLD TESTAMENT), made for the Greek-speaking Jewish community in Egypt in the 3rd and 2nd centuries BC. It contains the entire Jewish CANON plus the APOCRYPHA. The Septuagint is divided into four sections: the law, history, poetry, and prophets. It is still used by the Greek Orthodox Church.

**sequoia** Two species of giant evergreen conifer trees native to California and S Oregon: the giant sequoia (*Sequoiadendron giganteum*) and the Californian redwood (*Sequoia sempervirens*). They grow to 330ft (100m). Family Taxodiaceae.

**Sequoia National Park** Park in the SIERRA NEVADA, E California. Established in 1890, it features groves of giant SEQUOIA and Mount WHITNEY, the highest US mountain outside Alaska. Area: 386,862acres (156,679ha).

**Serbia** Balkan republic that, combined with the smaller republic of MONTENEGRO, forms the rump federal state of YUGOSLAVIA. The republic is bounded N by Hungary, E by Romania and Bulgaria, S by Macedonia, SW by Albania and Montenegro, W by BOSNIA-HERZEGOVINA and NW by CROATIA. It includes the provinces of Vojvodina (N) and Kosovo (S), formerly autonomous under the Yugoslav federation. The capital is BELGRADE, other major cities include Nǐs(Serbia), Novi Sad (Vojvodina), and Pr̆istina (Kosovo). The republic can be geographically divided between the mountainous S and the fertile N plain drained by the DANUBE, Sava, Tisza, and Morava rivers. Vojvodina is the principal agricultural area, producing fruit and grain. Serbia is the principal industrial area, with mining and steel manufacture. Kosovo is a poor region with large coal deposits. The area was settled by Serbs in the 7th century AD, and they adopted Orthodox Christianity under BYZANTINE rule. Serbia became the leading Balkan power until, in 1389, it was defeated by the Ottoman Turks. The Ottomans divided the territory and installed a puppet regime. In 1459 Serbia became a province of the OTTOMAN EMPIRE. The 18th-century decline of the Ottoman empire encouraged Serbian nationalism. In 1829 Serbia gained autonomy under Russian protection. In 1867 Milan Obrenović began a war in support of a rebellion against Turkish rule in Bosnia and Herzegovina. Russia intervened to aid Serbia and, in 1878, Turkey finally granted Serbia complete independence. In 1903 King Alexander Obrenović was assassinated, and PETER I became king. In 1908, when Austro-Hungary annexed Bosnia and Herzegovina, Serbia responded by forming the Serbian League. In 1912 the alliance defeated the Turks, but disintegrated into factional feuding. In 1913 Serbia defeated Bulgaria in the second Balkan War. The expansion of Serbian territory in the BALKAN WARS antagonized Austria, and the assassination of the Austrian Archduke FRANZ FERDINAND led to the outbreak of World War I. In 1918 Serbia became the leading force in the kingdom of the Serbs, Croats, and Slovenes, renamed YUGOSLAVIA in 1929. During World War II, Yugoslavia was occupied and divided by the German army. Resistance was twofold: TITO led the Yugoslav communist partisans, and Mihajović led the Serbian nationalists (Chetniks). In 1946 Serbia became an autonomous republic within Tito's neocommunist Yugoslavia. In 1987 President Slobodan MILOŠEVIĆ restated nationalist claims for a Greater Serbia, including Vojvodina, Kosovo, and Serb-populated areas in Croatia, Bosnia-Herzegovina, and Macedonia. In 1989 Serbian troops were sent to suppress Albanian nationalism in Kosovo. In 1991 Serbia prevented Croatia from assuming presidency of the federation. Croatia and SLOVENIA responded by declaring

S

independence, and the Serbian-controlled Yugoslav army invaded. In 1991 the army withdrew from Slovenia. In 1992 a UN-brokered ceasefire was agreed between Serbia and Croatia, allowing Serbia to keep the territory it had captured. Serbian troops quickly seized nearly 75% of the newly recognized republic of Bosnia-Herzegovina and pursued a policy of "ethnic cleansing," forcibly resettling, incarcerating, or killing Muslims and repopulating villages with Serbs. The UN imposed sanctions on the Serbian regime, but atrocities continued on both sides. In 1995 Bosnian Serb troops captured UN protected areas, and Western governments and NATO launched air strikes against Serb targets. Bosnia-Herzegovina and Croatia began a new offensive against Serbia and reclaimed much lost territory. The US-brokered Dayton Peace Accord (November 1995) divided Bosnia-Herzegovina into provinces. In September 1996 democratic elections were held in Serbia, but Milŏsević refused to recognize opposition victories. Following peaceful, mass demonstrations in Belgrade, Milŏsević conceded some of the Zajedno coalition victories. In 1997 Milŏsević resigned the Serbian presidency in order to become president of Yugoslavia. In 1998 Montenegro sought greater independence from Serbia and fighting recommenced in KOSOVO.

**Serbs** Slavic people who settled in the Balkans in the 7th century and who became Christians in the 9th century. They were distinguished from Croats and Slovenes by their use of the Cyrillic, not the Roman, alphabet. Most of them now live in Serbia, but there are Serb minorities in BOSNIA and CROATIA.

**serf** Person legally bound to a lord. In Europe, under the FEUDAL SYSTEM serfs had to provide labor and other services and were usually bound to the land, holding a portion for their own use. Gone from W Europe by the end of the Middle Ages, serfdom persisted in Russia and parts of E Europe into the mid-19th century.

**serial music** Technique of musical composition in which a work is structured on a fixed series of notes; the series is repeated in various permutations for the duration of the work. The TWELVE-TONE MUSIC of Arnold SCHOENBERG is a form of serial music.

**series** Mathematical expression obtained by adding the terms of a sequence. Thus, the series 1 + 4 + 9 + 16 +... is formed from the sequence 1, 4, 9, 16,.... Series may be finite or infinite, and infinite series may converge. An infinite

## SENEGAL

This flag was adopted in 1960 when Senegal became independent from France. It uses the three colors that symbolize African unity. It is identical to the flag of Mali, except for the five-pointed green star. This star symbolizes the Muslim faith of most of its people.

**AREA:** 75,954sq mi (196,720sq km)
**POPULATION:** 7,736,000
**CAPITAL (POPULATION):** Dakar (1,729,823)
**GOVERNMENT:** Multiparty republic
**ETHNIC GROUPS:** Wolof 44%, Fulani-Tukulor 24%, Serer 15%
**LANGUAGES:** French (official)
**RELIGIONS:** Islam 94%, Christianity (mainly Roman Catholic) 5%, traditional beliefs and others 1%
**CURRENCY:** CFA franc = 100 centimes

The Republic of Senegal, on the NW coast of Africa, contains the continent's most westerly point, the volcanic Cape Verde, on which the capital, DAKAR, stands. It entirely surrounds The Gambia. The Atlantic coastline from St. Louis to Dakar is sandy. Plains cover most of Senegal, though the land rises gently in the SE. The N forms part of the SAHEL. The main rivers are the Sénégal, which forms the N border, and the Casamance in the S. The Gambia River flows from Senegal into The Gambia.

### CLIMATE

Dakar has a tropical climate, with a rainy season between June and September. Temperatures are higher inland. Rainfall is greatest in the S.

### VEGETATION

Desert and semidesert cover NE Senegal. In central Senegal, dry grasslands and scrub predominate. Mangrove swamps border parts of the S coast. The far S is a region of tropical savanna, though large areas have been cleared for farming. Senegal has several protected parks; the largest is the Niokolo-Kobo Wildlife Park.

### HISTORY AND POLITICS

During the 6th–10th centuries Senegal formed part of the empire of ancient Ghana. Between the 10th to the 14th centuries the Tukolor state of Tekrur dominated the Sénégal valley. The ALMORAVID dynasty of Zenega Berbers introduced Islam, and it is from the Zenega that Senegal got its name. In the 14th century the Mali empire conquered Tekrur. In the early 15th century, the WOLOF established the Jolof empire. The SONGHAI empire began to dominate the region. In 1444 Portuguese sailors became the first Europeans to reach Cape Verde. Trading stations were rapidly established in the area. In the 17th century, Portugal's influence was replaced by France and the Netherlands. France gradually gained control of the valuable slave trade, and founded St. Louis in 1658. By 1763 Britain had expelled the French from Senegal and, in 1765, set up Senegambia, the first British colony in Africa. France had regained control of the region by 1783. In the mid-19th century France battled for control of the interior. Dakar was founded in 1857. In 1895 Senegal became a French colony within the federation of French West Africa. In 1902 the capital of this huge empire was transferred from St. Louis to Dakar. Dakar became a major trading center. In 1946 Senegal joined the French Union. In 1959 Senegal joined French Sudan (now Mali) to form the Federation of Mali. Senegal withdrew in 1960, and became an independent republic within the French community.

Léopold Sédar SENGHOR became Senegal's first postcolonial president. Following an unsuccessful coup (1962), Senghor gradually assumed wider powers. During the 1960s, Senegal's economy deteriorated, and a succession of droughts caused starvation and widespread civil unrest. During the 1970s, S Senegal acted as a base for guerrilla movements in Guinea and Portuguese Guinea (modern Guinea-Bissau). In 1974 Senegal was a founding member of the West African Economic Community. In 1981 Senghor was succeeded by Abdou Diouf, and Senegalese troops put down an attempted coup in The Gambia. In 1982 the two countries were joined in the Confederation of Senegambia, but the union was dissolved in 1989. In 1989–90 Senegal was at war with Mauritania. Internal conflict continued, particularly in the S Casamance region, where a secessionist movement had gathered strength.

### ECONOMY

Senegal is a lower-middle-income developing country (1995 GDP per capita, $1,780). Agriculture employs 81% of the work force, mainly at subsistence level. Food crops include cassava, millet, and rice. Senegal is the world's sixth-largest producer of peanuts, its major cash crop and export. France is the major market. Phosphates are Senegal's chief mineral resource, but it also refines oil. Dakar is a busy port with many industries. Fishing is an important activity.

S

series that fails to converge is said to diverge. A series formed from increasing powers of a variable is a power series; convergent power series are used for representing many functions.

**Sermon on the Mount** Address given by JESUS CHRIST to his disciples and a huge crowd of other listeners on one of the hills above GALILEE. It presents many of the now familiar Christian teachings. *See also* BEATITUDES

**serotonin** Chemical found in cells of the gastrointestinal tract, blood platelets, and brain tissue, concentrated in the midbrain and HYPOTHALAMUS. It is a VASOCONSTRICTOR and has an important role in the functioning of the nervous system and in the stimulation of smooth muscles.

**serpentine** ($Mg_3Si_2O_5(OH)_4$) Group of sheet silicate minerals, hydrated magnesium silicate. Serpentine minerals are usually green. They have monoclinic system crystals. They are commonly used in decorative carving; fibrous varieties are used in asbestos cloth. Hardness 2.5–4; s.g. 2.5–2.6.

**Serra, Saint Junípero** (1713–84) Spanish Franciscan missionary. In 1769 Serra founded the first mission in California near San Diego. In 1770 another mission was founded at Monterrey and he remained president of Alta California missions. In 1988 Serra was beatified.

**serum** Clear fluid that separates out if BLOOD is left to clot. It is essentially of the same composition as PLASMA, but without fibrinogen and clotting factors.

**serval** (bush cat) Orange and black spotted cat found in grassy areas of sub-Saharan Africa. It has a narrow head and long legs, neck, and ears. Length: body 30–40in (70–100cm); tail 14–16in (35–40cm); weight: 15–25lb (6.8–11.3kg). Family Felidae; species *Felis serval.*

**Servetus, Michael** (1511–53) Spanish physician and theologian. Servetus published (1531–32) his unorthodox opinions concerning the TRINITY. In medicine, he discovered that blood circulates through the lungs. Forced to flee from the INQUISITION, Servetus was unwelcome among Reformation and Catholic theologians alike. Under the orders of John CALVIN, he was arrested and tried in Geneva and burned as a heretic.

**servomechanism** Device that provides remote control to activate a mechanism. An input signal, such as a radio impulse or mechanical movement, is converted into a mechanical output, such as a lever or amplified hydraulic force. Some servomechanisms, such as the automatic pilot of an aircraft, incorporate a feedback mechanism that makes them independent of human control.

**sesame** Tropical plant native to Asia and Africa, cultivated for its oil and seeds. It has oval leaves, pink or white flowers, and seed capsules along the stem. Height: 2ft (60cm). Family Pedaliaceae; species *Sesamum indicum.*

**sessile** In zoology, describing an animal that remains fixed in one place. Sedentary animals, such as sea anemones, barnacles, limpets, and mussels, are usually permanently attached to a surface. The term sessile is also used to describe the eyes of crustaceans that lack stalks and sit directly on the animal's head. In botany, sessile describes any structure that has no stalk (in cases where one might be expected) and grows directly from a STEM. Examples include the acorns and leaves of some oak trees.

**Sessions, Roger** (1896–1985) US composer whose complex and highly individual works include a violin concerto (1935), eight symphonies, a concertino for chamber orchestra (1972), and piano and organ works.

**set** In mathematics, a defined collection of objects. The objects are called the elements or members of the set. The number of members can be finite or infinite, or even be zero (the **null set**). Various relations can exist between two sets, $A$ and $B$: $A$ equals $B$ if both sets contain exactly the same members; $A$ is included in or is a subset of $B$ if all members of $A$ are members of $B$; disjoint sets have no members in common; overlapping sets have one or more common members. Operations on sets produce new sets: the union of $A$ and $B$ contains the members of both $A$ and $B$; the intersection of $A$ and $B$ contains only those members common to both sets.

**Seth** Egyptian god. Although a beneficent god in pre-dynastic Egypt, Seth became linked with darkness and was later seen as a god of evil and the rival of HORUS.

**Seton, Saint Elizabeth Ann** (1774–1821) US teacher and charity organizer. In 1805 she joined the Roman Catholic Church. Seton founded (1808) the first Catholic elementary school in the US. In 1809 she founded the American Sisters of Charity. Her sainthood was proclaimed in 1975. Her feast day is January 4.

**setter** Long-haired, hunting dog used to find game and stand on point until the hunter arrives; it also retrieves. Modern types include English, Irish, and Gordon.

**set theory** Branch of mathematics developed by Georg CANTOR in the late 19th century. Based on George BOOLE's work on mathematical logic, it manipulates SETS of abstract or real objects rather than logical propositions. It is concerned with the properties of sets.

**Settlement, Act of** (1701) English parliamentary statute regulating the succession to the throne. The purpose of the act was to prevent the restoration of the Catholic STUART monarchy. It settled the succession on SOPHIA of Hanover, granddaughter of JAMES I, and her heirs, providing they were Protestants. The crown was inherited (1714) by Sophia's son, who became GEORGE I.

**settlement house** (neigborhood center) Welfare institution to improve living conditions in urban areas. In 1884 the first settlement house, Toynbee Hall, was founded in London. In 1886 Stanton Colt established the first US center in New York City.

**Seurat, Georges Pierre** (1859–91) French painter and founder of NEO-IMPRESSIONISM. From 1876 to 1884 he developed his theory of color vision known as POINTILLISM, which was based on the juxtaposition of pure color dots. His paintings include *Bathing at Asnières* (1883–84) and *Sunday in Summer on the Island of La Grande-Jatte* (1886).

**Seuss, Dr.** (1904–91) (Theodor Seuss Geisel) US children's writer and illustrator. His first book, *And to Think That I Saw It on Mulberry Street* (1937), established his style of combining doggerel verse with zany artwork. In 1957 he published *The Cat in the Hat*, the first in a series of more than 50 "Beginner" books designed to help children to learn to read.

**Sevastopol** (Sebastopol) Black Sea port on the sw of the Crimean Peninsula, Ukraine. Founded in 1783 by Catherine II, the city became home to the Russian Black Sea fleet and was the major strategic objective of the CRIMEAN WAR, besieged from October 1854 to September 1855. The Russians sank their own fleet to block the harbor entrance, and inflicted heavy Allied casualties before evacuating. The fortifications were destroyed, only to be rebuilt after 1871, and by 1890 the city was again a working naval base. In 1995 Ukraine agreed to allow the Russian fleet to maintain its base here in return for Ukrainian ownership of 19% of the fleet. Pop. (1993) 366,000.

**Seven Days' Battles** (1862) Engagement of the CIVIL WAR that ended the PENINSULAR CAMPAIGN. In the final, ferocious battle at Malvern Hill, near Richmond, Virginia, the Union forces of General George MCCLELLAN won a tactical victory. Subsequently, however, McClellan withdrew, leaving the field to the Confederates under Robert E. LEE.

**Seventh-day Adventists** Christian denomination whose members expect Jesus Christ to return to Earth in person. They hold the SABBATH on Saturday and accept the BIBLE literally as their guide for living. The sect was organized formally in the US in 1863 and today it is the largest worldwide ADVENTIST denomination.

**Seven Weeks War** *See* AUSTRO-PRUSSIAN WAR

**Seven Wonders of the World** Group of fabled sights that evolved from various ancient Greek lists. They were, in chronological order: the PYRAMIDS of EGYPT; the HANGING GARDENS OF BABYLON; the statue of ZEUS by PHIDIAS at OLYMPIA; the temple of ARTEMIS at EPHESUS; the MAUSOLEUM at HALICARNASSUS; the COLOSSUS OF RHODES; and the PHAROS at ALEXANDRIA.

**Seven Years War** (1756–63) Major European conflict that established Britain as the foremost maritime and colonial power and ensured the survival of Prussia as a major

S

power in central Europe. The war was a continuation of the rivalries involved in the War of the AUSTRIAN SUCCESSION (1740–48). Britain and Prussia were allied, with Prussia undertaking nearly all the fighting in Europe, against Austria, Russia, France, and Sweden. FREDERICK II (THE GREAT) of Prussia fought a defensive war against superior forces. Only his brilliant generalship, and the withdrawal of Russia from the war in 1762, saved Prussia from being overrun. Overseas, Britain and France fought in North America (FRENCH AND INDIAN WARS), India, and West Africa, with the British gaining major victories. At the end of the war, the Treaty of PARIS (1763) confirmed British supremacy in North America and India, while the Treaty of Hubertusberg left Prussia in control of Silesia.

**Severn** Longest river in the UK, flowing 180mi (290km) through Wales and W England. It rises on Mount Plynlimon in W Wales, flows NE to Shrewsbury, turns SE and then SW to enter the Bristol Channel through a wide estuary. The Severn is connected by canal to the THAMES, Mersey, and Trent rivers.

**Severus, Lucius Septimius** (146–211) Roman emperor (193–211). He was proclaimed emperor by his troops, who marched on Rome and persuaded the Senate to confirm him. To secure his position, Severus dissolved the Praetorian Guard, replacing it with his own men, and proclaimed himself posthumously adopted by the Emperor MARCUS AURELIUS (d.180). He divided (208) Britain into two provinces and launched a campaign to conquer Scotland. Repulsed, he died at York.

**Sevier, John** (1745–1815) US politician, soldier, and frontiersman. In the AMERICAN REVOLUTION he led the force that defeated the British at Kings Mountain, North Carolina (1780). After the war, Tennessee settlers formed the state of Franklin, and Sevier served (1785–88) as governor. Indicted for treason, he later became the first governor of Tennessee (1796–1801, 1803–09). Sevier also served in Congress (1789–91, 1811–15).

**Seville** Port on the Guadalquivir River, SW Spain, capital of Seville province. Ruled by the Romans from the 2nd century BC to the 5th century AD, it was taken by the Moors in 712 and served as the center of the Moorish kingdom until conquered (1248) by Ferdinand III. Sites include a 15th-century Gothic Cathedral that includes remnants of a mosque. The port exports fruit (notably oranges) and wine. Industries: agricultural machinery, shipbuilding, chemicals, textiles, porcelain, shipping, tourism. Pop. (1991) 659,126.

**Sèvres** In ceramics, high-quality PORCELAIN made from 1765 to the present day at a factory in the Paris suburb of Sèvres. Pieces are either of soft-paste (a porcellaneous substance) or hard-paste (true porcelain).

**Sèvres, Treaty of** (1920) Peace treaty between Turkey and its European opponents in World War I that imposed harsh terms on the Ottoman sultan. The treaty, never ratified, was replaced by the Treaty of LAUSANNE (1923).

**Sewall, Samuel** (1652–1730) American colonial jurist, b. England. In 1661 his family immigrated to New England. In 1683 Sewall was elected to the general court. As one of the judges at the SALEM withcraft trials, he was responsible for the condemnation of 19 persons. In 1697 Sewall made a public confession of error.

**Seward, William Henry** (1801–72) US statesman. He lost the Republican nomination for president (1860) to Abraham LINCOLN, who appointed him secretary of state. Seward succeeded in maintaining good relations with Europe during the CIVIL WAR and his handling of the TRENT AFFAIR averted British recognition of the Confederacy. He was wounded in the shooting that killed Lincoln but continued in office under Andrew JOHNSON, negotiating (1867) the purchase of Alaska.

**sewing machine** Machine that uses a needle to stitch material together with thread. The first basic sewing machine was invented (1846) in the US by Elias Howe. In 1851 Isaac Merrit SINGER invented a machine for continuous stitching. There are two basic types: lockstitch and chain-stitch. The **chain-stitch** machine uses a single thread, holding a loop of thread under the seam. **Lockstitch** machines run on the same principle, but use a second thread run underneath the steel plate.

**sex** Classification of an organism into male or female, denoting the reproductive function of the individual. In mammals the presence of sex organs, OVARIES in the female, TESTES in the male, are **primary** sexual characteristics. **Secondary** sexual characteristics such as size, coloration, and hair growth are governed by the secretion of SEX HORMONES. In flowering plants, the female sex organs are the CARPEL, including the OVARY, STYLE, and STIGMA, and the male organs the STAMENS. Male and female organs may occur in the same flower or on separate flowers or plants. *See also* SEXUAL REPRODUCTION

**sex discrimination** Unequal treatment of people because of gender. This usually involves involves denial of economic or social opportunities and may result from prejudice, stereotyping, or social pressure. Efforts to elimininate sex discrimination include legislation, WOMEN'S RIGHTS MOVEMENTS, and consciousness raising groups.

**sex hormones** Chemical "messengers" secreted by the gonads (TESTES and OVARIES). They regulate sexual development and reproductive activity and influence sexual behavior. In males they include TESTOSTERONE, made by the testes; in females, the sex hormones ESTROGEN and PROGESTERONE are produced by the ovaries.

**sextant** Optical instrument for finding LATITUDE (angular distance N or S of the Equator). The sextant consists of a frame with a curved scale marked in degrees, a movable arm with an ordinary mirror at the pivot, a half-silvered glass, and a telescope. The instrument measures the angle of a heavenly body above the horizon, which depends on the observer's latitude. A set of tables gives the corresponding latitude for various angles measured.

**Sexton, Anne** (1928–74) US poet. She studied at Boston University under Robert LOWELL. Her first poetry collection, *To Bedlam and Part Way Back* (1960), set out her confessional style. Sexton won a Pulitzer Prize for *Live or Die* (1966). She committed suicide.

**sexual intercourse** Term used to describe sexual relations between people. It is most commonly used to describe the insertion of the male penis into the female vagina. *See also* CONTRACEPTION; ORGASM; SEXUAL REPRODUCTION

**sexually transmitted disease (STD)** Any disease that is transmitted by sexual activity involving the transfer of body fluids. It encompasses a range of conditions that are spread primarily by sexual contact, although they may also be transmitted in other ways. These include ACQUIRED IMMUNE DEFICIENCY SYNDROME (AIDS), pelvic inflammatory disease, and viral HEPATITIS. Older STDs, such as SYPHILIS and GONORRHEA, remain significant public health problems.

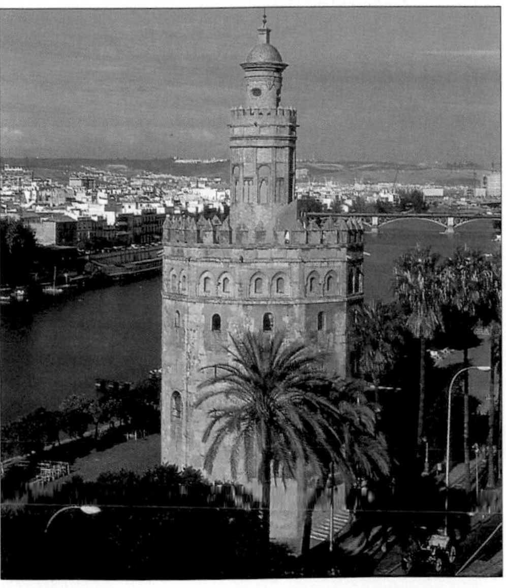

◄ **Seville** A Moorish watchtower, in Seville, S Spain. Seville was the center of the Moorish kingdom in Spain from 712 to 1248, and was also the major port in Spanish colonial history. Its cathedral, built around a mosque, is the world's largest Gothic church. Seville's April fair is famous for its flamenco dancing.

S

**sexual reproduction** Biological process of reproduction involving the combination of genetic material from two parents. It occurs in different forms throughout the plant and animal kingdoms. This process gives rise to variations of the GENOTYPE and PHENOTYPE within a species. GAMETES, HAPLOID sex cells produced by MEIOSIS, contain only half the number of CHROMOSOMES of their parent cells (which are DIPLOID). At FERTILIZATION, the gametes, generally one from each parent, fuse to form a ZYGOTE with the diploid number of chromosomes. The zygote divides repeatedly and the cells differentiate to produce an EMBRYO and, finally, a fully formed organism.

**Seychelles** Republic consisting of more than 100 islands in the Indian Ocean, *c.*600mi (970km) N of Madagascar. Seychelles comprises two geologically distinct island groups: the volcanic, **Granitic** group are to the NE, and include the three principal, inhabited islands of Mahé, Praslin, and La Digue. Mahé is home to more than 80% of the republic's people; Seychelles' capital, Victoria, lies on its NE coast. To the SW lie the **Outer** group of coral islands. In 1502 Vasco da Gama explored the islands and named them the "Seven Sisters." The islands were colonized in 1756 by the French, who established spice plantations worked by slaves from Mauritius. In 1794 the archipelago was captured by the British during the Napoleonic Wars and, in 1814, became a dependency of Mauritius. In 1903 the Seychelles became a separate crown colony. In 1976 they achieved full independence within the Commonwealth of Nations. In 1977 a coup established Albert René as president. In 1981 South African mercenaries attempted to overthrow the government. Continued civil unrest, and another failed coup in 1987, led to the first multiparty elections (1991). In 1993 Albert René was elected for a fourth term. Creole is the most widely spoken language. Tourism is the largest industry; exports include coconuts and tuna. Area: 175sq mi (453sq km). Pop. (1993 est.) 72,250

**Seyfert galaxy** Class of galaxies that have extremely bright, compact nuclei and whose spectra show strong emission lines. About 1% of all galaxies are Seyferts. They emit strongly at ultraviolet and infrared wavelengths, and exhibit a degree of short-term variability.

**Sezession** Radical movement (formed 1897) of young Austrian artists who organized their own exhibitions and aligned themselves with progressive European contemporaries. The first president was Gustav KLIMT; other members included Oskar KOKOSCHKA and Egon SCHIELE.

**Shackleton, Sir Ernest Henry** (1874–1922) Irish Antarctic explorer. He led an expedition (1907–09) that reached to within 97mi (155km) of the South Pole. On his second expedition (1914–16), his ship was crushed by ice and his men marooned on a small island. Shackleton's successful rescue mission, which he described in *South* (1919), is one of the epics of polar exploration.

**shad** Saltwater fish of the HERRING family that swims upriver to spawn. Shads are prized for their roe. Deep-bodied, they have a notch in the upper jaw for the tip of the lower jaw. Length: to 30in (75cm). Family Clupeidae.

**Shaffer, Peter** (1926– ) English dramatist. Following the success of *Five Finger Exercise* (1960), he wrote *The Private Ear and The Public Eye* (1962). Schaffer's plays *Equus* (1973), and *Amadeus* (1979) were both filmed.

**Shaftesbury, Anthony Ashley Cooper, 1st Earl of** (1621–83) English statesman. He was a member of the COMMONWEALTH council of state under Oliver CROMWELL. Dismayed by the autocracy of the PROTECTORATE, he supported the RESTORATION of CHARLES II (1660) and was rewarded with the chancellorship. Opposed to the earl of CLARENDON, Shaftesbury became lord chancellor (1672) but was soon dismissed. His determination to prevent the succession of the Catholic JAMES II drove him to found (1673) the WHIG PARTY in opposition to DANBY. Shaftesbury's support for the duke of MONMOUTH led to his exile (1682) in Holland.

**Shaftesbury, Anthony Ashley Cooper, 7th earl of** (1801–85) British social reformer. He was the chief driving force behind the acts that prohibited employment of women

## SEXUAL REPRODUCTION

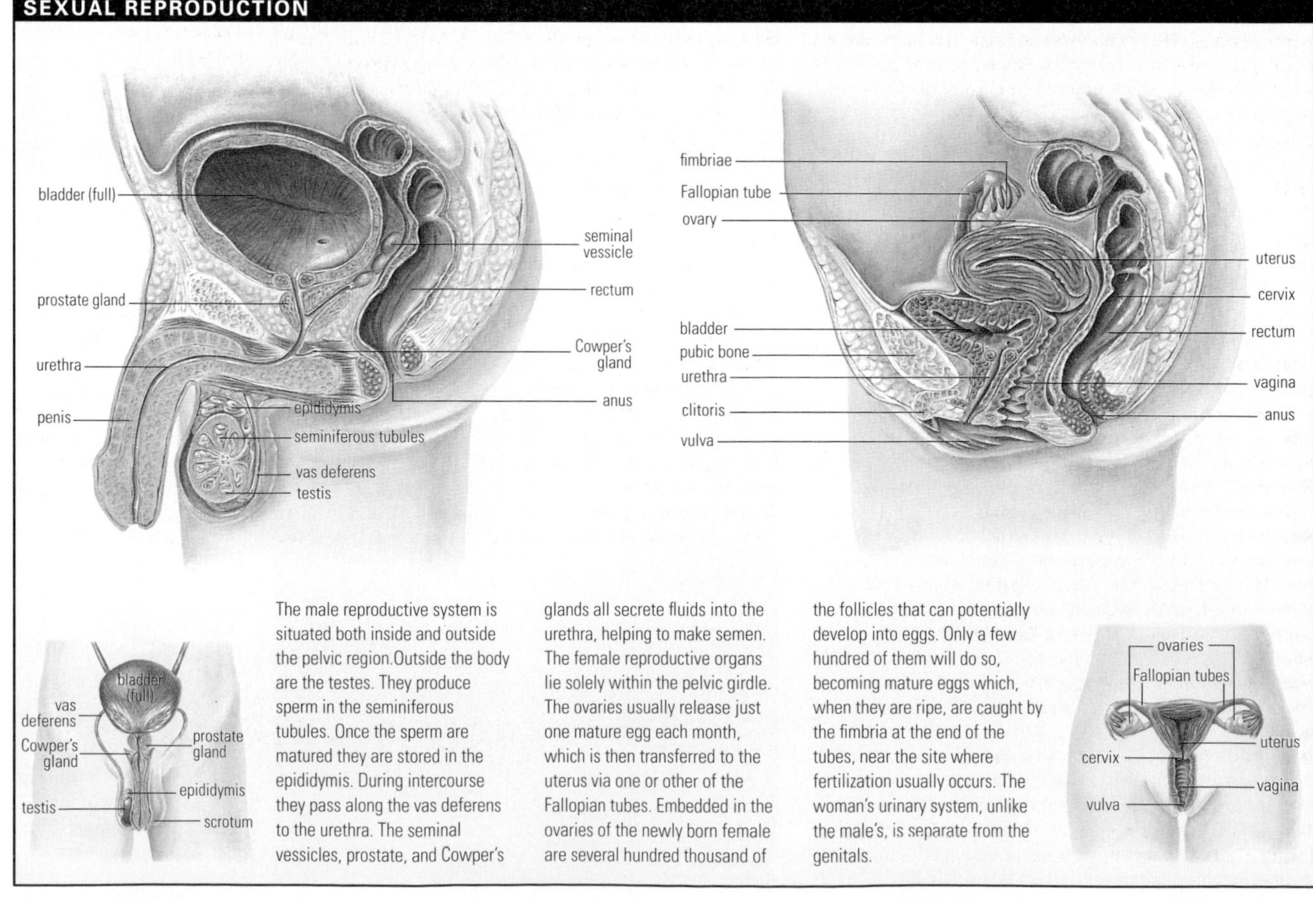


The male reproductive system is situated both inside and outside the pelvic region.Outside the body are the testes. They produce sperm in the seminiferous tubules. Once the sperm are matured they are stored in the epididymis. During intercourse they pass along the vas deferens to the urethra. The seminal vessicles, prostate, and Cowper's glands all secrete fluids into the urethra, helping to make semen. The female reproductive organs lie solely within the pelvic girdle. The ovaries usually release just one mature egg each month, which is then transferred to the uterus via one or other of the Fallopian tubes. Embedded in the ovaries of the newly born female are several hundred thousand of the follicles that can potentially develop into eggs. Only a few hundred of them will do so, becoming mature eggs which, when they are ripe, are caught by the fimbria at the end of the tubes, near the site where fertilization usually occurs. The woman's urinary system, unlike the male's, is separate from the genitals.

and young children in mines (1842) and restricted the working day to ten hours (1847).

**Shah Jahan** (1592–1666) MOGUL emperor of India (1628–58). Third son of JAHANGIR, he secured his succession by killing most of his male relatives. His campaigns expanded the MOGUL EMPIRE and accumulated great treasure. Though relatively tolerant of Hinduism, he made Islam the state religion. Shah Jahan was responsible for building the TAJ MAHAL, and the vast ornamental chambers of the Red Fort at DELHI, which he made his capital.

**Shahn, Ben** (1898–1969) US painter, lithographer, and photographer, b. Lithuania. His work reflected his concern with social and political injustices, notably the SACCO AND VANZETTI CASE. In the 1930s he worked with Diego RIVERA on murals for the Rockefeller Center, New York. He was involved with the Farm Security Administration, painting and photographing rural poverty.

**Shaka** (1787–1828) King of the ZULU. In *c.*1816 he claimed the throne, forming a powerful Zulu army and extending his control over all of what is now ZwaZulu-Natal. Shaka maintained good relations with the white government in the Cape, but his harsh rule provoked domestic opposition and he was killed by his half brother.

**Shakers** (officially United Society of Believers in Christ's Second Appearing) US religious sect. Originally an offshoot of the English QUAKERS, the nickname derived from the fervor of their religious ceremonies. In 1774 Ann LEE and eight of her followers immigrated to New York. "Mother Ann" believed she was the female reincarnation of Jesus Christ. After her death (1784), the movement spread and by *c.*1850 they numbered *c.*6,000 in more than 18 communes. One of the central beliefs of Shakers is the dual (male and female) nature of the Deity. Other tenets include celibacy, sexual equality, pacifism, and the sanctity of labor. They are noted for their crafts.

**Shakespeare, William** (1564–1616) English poet and dramatist. By 1592 he was established in London, having already written the three parts of *Henry VI*. By 1594 Shakespeare was a member of the Lord Chamberlain's Men and in 1599 a partner in the GLOBE THEATRE, where many of his plays were presented. He retired to STRATFORD-UPON-AVON around 1613. His 154 *Sonnets*, which were first published in 1609, stand among the finest works in ENGLISH LITERATURE. The plays are usually divided into four groups – historical plays, comedies, tragedies, and late romances. Shakespeare's plots are generally drawn from existing sources, such as Holinshed.

**shale** Common SEDIMENTARY ROCK formed from mud or clay. Characterized by very fine layering, it may contain material such as FOSSILS, carbonaceous matter, and oil.

**shallot** Perennial plant native to W Asia and widely cultivated in temperate climates. It has thin, small leaves and clustered bulbs, which have a mild, onionlike flavor. Family Liliaceae; species *Allium cepa*.

**shaman** Tribal witch doctor or medicine man believed to be in contact with spirits or the supernatural worlds. Shamanism is found among the ESKIMOS and NATIVE AMERICANS and in Siberia, where the term originated. African equivalents also exist. *See also* ANIMISM

**Shamir, Yitzhak** (1915– ) Israeli statesman, prime minister (1983–84, 1986–92). He was the leader (1940–48) of the Stern Gang of Zionist guerrillas against the British mandate in Palestine. Shamir became head (1955–65) of Mossad, Israel's secret service. He was foreign minister (1980–83) under Menachim BEGIN and succeeded him as prime minister and head of the right-wing Likud Party. In 1986 he succeeded Shimon PERES as head of a coalition government. Shamir oversaw the Jewish settlement of the WEST BANK and GAZA STRIP. In 1992 he was defeated by Yitzhak RABIN, and Benjamin NETANYAHU succeeded him as leader of Likud.

**shamrock** Plant with three-part leaves, usually taken to be *Trifolium repens* or *T. dubium*, the national emblem of Ireland. Legend tells that St. Patrick used it to symbolize the Trinity. Family Leguminosae. Black medic (*Medicago lupulina*) and Wood sorrel (*Oxalis acetosella*) are sold often as shamrock.

**Shang** (Yin) Early Chinese dynasty (*c.*1523–*c.*1027 BC). Successors to the Hsia (Xia) dynasty, the Shang was based in the valley of the Huang He (Yellow River). During the Shang period, the Chinese written language was perfected, techniques of flood control and irrigation were practiced, and artifacts were made in cast bronze.

**Shanghai** Largest city and port in China, 13mi (22km) from the Yangtze (Changjiang) delta, SE China. By the Treaty of Nanking (1842), the city was opened to foreign trade, which stimulated economic growth. The US, Britain, France, and Japan all held areas of the city. Occupied by the Japanese in 1937, Shanghai was restored to China at the end of World War II and fell to the communists in 1949. Industries: textiles, steel, chemicals, publishing, rubber, farm machinery, shipbuilding, pharmaceuticals, financial services. Pop. (1993) 8,760,000.

**Shankar, Ravi** (1920– ) Indian musician. He was responsible for popularizing the SITAR and Indian music in general in the West. Shankar founded the National Orchestra of India and was music director of All-India Radio (1948–56). He toured Europe and the US extensively during the 1960s and 1970s.

**Shannon** Longest river in the Republic of Ireland and the British Isles. It rises on Cuilcagh Mountain, NW County Cavan, and flows S through loughs Allen, Ree, and Derg, S across the central plain of Ireland to Limerick, and then W to enter the Atlantic Ocean. The Shannon separates Connacht from the provinces of Leinster and Munster. Length: 230mi (370km).

**Shapley, Harlow** (1885–1972) US astronomer who provided the first accurate model of the MILKY WAY. By observing CEPHEID VARIABLE stars in globular clusters, he calculated the distance to each cluster in the galaxy, obtaining a picture of its shape and size.

**share** *See* STOCK

**sharia** Traditional law of ISLAM, believed by Muslims to be the result of divine revelation. It is drawn from a number of sources, including the KORAN and a collection of teachings and legends about the life of MUHAMMAD known as the *Hadith*.

**Sharjah** Capital of the Sheikdom of Sharjah, third-largest of the seven UNITED ARAB EMIRATES, on the Persian Gulf, E Arabia. A British protectorate until 1971, the sheikdom is part of a prosperous oil- and gas-producing area. Pop. (1984) 125,000.

**shark** Torpedo-shaped, cartilaginous fish found in subpolar to tropical marine waters. They have well-developed jaws, bony teeth, usually 5 gill slits on each side of the head, and a characteristic lobe-shaped tail with a longer top lobe. Sharks are carnivorous and at least 10 species are known to attack humans. There are about 250 living species. Order Selachii. *See also* DOGFISH; HAMMERHEAD; WHALE SHARK; WHITE SHARK

**Sharpeville** Black township, N of Vereeniging, South Africa, scene of a massacre (March 1960) by South African security forces. When a large crowd failed to disperse, the police opened fire, killing 67 people and wounding 186. The massacre led to greater militancy in the struggle against APARTHEID.

**Shatt al Arab** Channel formed by the confluence of the TIGRIS and EUPHRATES rivers, SE Iraq. It flows SE to the Persian

**SHAKESPEARE'S PLAYS**

**Histories: (date written)**
*Henry VI (part I)* (1589–90)
*Henry VI (part II)* (1590–91)
*Henry VI (part III)* (1590–91)
*Titus Andronicus* (1590–94)
*Richard III* (1592–93)
*King John* (1595–97)
*Richard II* (1595)
*Henry IV (part I)* (1596)
*Henry IV (part II)* (1597)
*Henry V* (1599)
*Julius Caesar* (1599)
*Troilus and Cressida* (1601–02)
*Timon of Athens* (1605–09)
*Antony and Cleopatra* (1606–07)
*Coriolanus* (1607–08)
*Henry VIII* (1613)

**Comedies:**
*The Comedy of Errors* (1590–94)
*Love's Labour's Lost* (1590–94)
*The Two Gentlemen of Verona* (1592–93)
*The Taming of the Shrew* (1592)
*A Midsummer Night's Dream* (1595)
*The Merchant of Venice* (1596–98)
*The Merry Wives of Windsor* (1597)
*Much Ado About Nothing* (1598)
*As You Like It* (1599)
*Twelfth Night* (1600–02)
*All's Well That Ends Well* (1602–03)
*Measure for Measure* (1604–05)

**Tragedies:**
*Romeo and Juliet* (1595–96)
*Hamlet* (1600–01)
*Othello* (1604)
*King Lear* (1605–06)
*Macbeth* (1605–06)

**Late Romances:**
*Pericles* (1607–08)
*Cymbeline* (1609–10)
*The Winter's Tale* (1611)
*The Tempest* (1613)

▼ **shark** The mako shark (*Isurus oxyrhyncus*) belongs to the mackerel shark family, the same family to which the great white belongs. A ferocious predator, the mako's streamlined body enables it to swim at speeds of over 40mph (65km/h). Makos are found in the Atlantic, Pacific, and Indian oceans, and like the great white, have been known to attack humans. Adults reach over 12ft (3.7m) and weigh up to 880lb (400kg).

Gulf through a wide delta. Forming the border between Iraq and Iran, its lower course was the scene of bitter fighting during the IRAN-IRAQ WAR (1980–88).

**Shaw, George Bernard** (1856–1950) Irish dramatist, critic, and member of the FABIAN SOCIETY. Shaw transformed Victorian theatre, rejecting melodrama in favor of socially conscious drama. His first play to be publicly performed was *Arms and the Man* (1894). Later plays include *Candida* (1897), *Man and Superman* (1904), *Major Barbara* (1905), *Pygmalion* (1913), and *Saint Joan* (1923). Although many of his plays were comedies, they expressed his radical political and philosophical ideas. Shaw received the 1925 Nobel Prize for literature.

**Shawnee** Algonquian-speaking tribe of NATIVE AMERICANS. Their early home was along the Cumberland River in Tennessee, but today most of the 5,000 Shawnee descendants live in Oklahoma. This number includes many DELAWARE, who are closely related to them.

**Shays' Rebellion** (1786–87) Revolt by debt-ridden farmers against the state government in W Massachusetts. It was prompted by the failure of the state senate to take preventive action against farm foreclosures caused by high taxation. Daniel Shays, a destitute farmer, led 1,200 insurgents against the state supreme court, sitting in Springfield. Several marches by the rebels were repulsed by government troops, although eventually tax laws were enacted to help the farmers. Shays was pardoned.

**Shearer, Alan** (1970– ) English soccer player. He began his professional career in 1988 with Southampton. A powerful striker, in 1992 he joined Blackburn Rovers. In 1997 he moved to the Newcastle team for a world record transfer fee of 15 million pounds (*c.*$25 million).

**shearwater** Seabird related to the ALBATROSS and PETREL. Most species are brown or black with pale underparts. Shearwaters live mainly on the ocean; they feed on fish and squid, and burrow nests in coastal cliffs. Length: 7.5–22in (19–56cm). Family Procellariidae.

**Sheba** (Saba) Ancient kingdom of S Arabia celebrated for its trade in gold, spices, and precious stones. According to the Bible, the Queen of Sheba visited Jerusalem to hear the wisdom of SOLOMON in the 10th century BC.

**sheep** Ruminants of the genus *Ovis*, and those of the less numerous genera *Pseudois* and *Ammotragus*. Domestic sheep, *O. aries*, are now bred for WOOL, fur (karakul), and meat. Wild species are found in the mountains of Europe, Asia, Africa, and North America. Family Bovidae.

**sheepdog** Any of several breeds of dog that were originally bred to herd and guard sheep. The term includes such breeds as the Old English sheepdog, Shetland sheepdog, COLLIE, border collie, and GERMAN SHEPHERD.

**Sheffield** City and county district in South Yorkshire, N England. A hilly city, it lies at the confluence of the Don River and its tributaries, the Sheaf, Rivelin, and Lordey. It is a major industrial center, noted for steel and steel products. Pop. (1991) 501,202.

**shell** In zoology, hard protective case of various MOLLUSKS. The case is secreted by the epidermis of the mollusk and consists of a protein matrix strengthened by calcium carbonate.

**Shelley, Mary Wollstonecraft** (1797–1851) English novelist, daughter of Mary WOLLSTONECRAFT. She eloped with Percy SHELLEY in 1814 and married him in 1816. Her later works of fiction, which include *The Last Man* (1826) and *Lodore* (1835), have been eclipsed by her first novel, *Frankenstein* (1818).

**Shelley, Percy Bysshe** (1792–1822) English poet. A committed atheist, he was expelled (1811) from Oxford University. His poems include *Queen Mab* (1813), which reflected his political idealism, "Ode to the West Wind" (1819), "To a Skylark" (1820) ,and *Adonais* (1821). *Prometheus Unbound* (1820), a four-act lyrical drama, is often regarded as his masterpiece. From 1818 he lived in Italy with his secondwife Mary, and it was here that he met BYRON. He drowned in a boating accident.

**shellfish** Common name for edible shelled MOLLUSKS and CRUSTACEA. Shelled mollusks include CLAMS, MUSSELS, OYSTERS, and SCALLOPS; crustaceans include SHRIMPS, LOBSTERS, and CRABS.

**Shenyang** (formerly Mukden) Capital of Liaoning province, on the Hun River, NE China. Once capital of the Qing dynasty, it was the site of the MANCHURIAN INCIDENT (1931), which served as the pretext for the Japanese invasion of Manchuria. The Japanese were responsible for the development of the city's industrial base. Today, Shenyang is China's fourth, largest city and an industrial powerhouse. Industries: aircraft, machine tools, heavy machinery, cables, cement. Pop. (1993) 3,860,000.

**Shepard, Alan Bartlett, Jr.** (1923–98) US astronaut. In 1961 he became the first American to be launched into space. In 1971 Shepard commanded *Apollo 14* and became the fifth man to walk on the lunar surface.

**Shepard, Sam** (1943– ) US playwright and actor. A leader of US avant-garde theater, he often focuses on the disjunction between contemporary US society and the American dream. Shepard won a Pulitzer Prize for *Buried Child* (1978). *True West* (1983) is a trilogy on the myth of the West. His screenplays include *Paris, Texas* (1984). He acted in and wrote the screenplays for *Fool for Love* (1985) and *Crimes of the Heart* (1986).

**Sheridan, Philip Henry** (1831–88) Union general in the CIVIL WAR. In 1864 Sheridan was appointed commander of the cavalry corps of the Army of the Potomac and led an attack on General LEE's communications. The success of General Jubal A. EARLY in the Shenandoah Valley prompted General Ulysses S. GRANT to give Sheridan command of all Union forces in the area. Sheridan devastated the valley and General CUSTER completed the defeat of Confederate forces. Sheridan cut off Lee's retreat and forced his surrender at APPOMATTOX (1865). In 1884 he succeeded William T. SHERMAN as commanding general of the US army.

**Sheridan, Richard Brinsley** (1751–1816) English dramatist and politician. He excelled in comedies of manners, such as *The Rivals* (1775) and *The School for Scandal* (1777). Entering Parliament (1780) as a member of the Whig Party, Sheridan became one of the most brilliant orators of his generation.

**Sherman, John** (1823–1900) US statesman, brother of William T. SHERMAN. He served in the House of Representatives (1855–61) and Congress (1861–77, 1881–97). In 1867 Sherman was appointed chairman of the Senate finance committee and oversaw the financial reforms of the RECONSTRUCTION period. As secretary of the treasury (1877–81), he guided the implementation of the Resumption Act. In his second term in Congress, Sherman was reponsible for the passage of the SHERMAN ANTI-TRUST ACT and the Sherman Silver Purchase Act (both 1890).

**Sherman, William Tecumseh** (1820–91) Union general in the CIVIL WAR. In 1861 he served as a colonel in the First Battle of BULL RUN. Sherman fought under General Ulysses S. GRANT in the Battle of SHILOH (1862) and was promoted to major general. He led the 15th Corps in the Siege of VICKSBURG (1863) and commanded the Army of the Tennessee in the Chattanooga Campaign. In 1864 Sherman became supreme commander in the West. Following his capture of ATLANTA (September 1864), Sherman led his army on the famous "march to the sea." Sherman's advance through the Carolinas was even more destructive. In April 1865 he accepted General Joseph E. JOHNSTON's surrender. Sherman succeeded Grant as commanding general of the US army (1869–83).

**Sherman Anti-Trust Act** (1890) US legislation to regulate trusts. It prohibited any industrial combination in restraint of trade or commerce. A critical weakness of the act was its obscure definitions of "trust," "combination," and "restraint," hence it was not vigorously enforced.

**Sherrington, Sir Charles Scott** (1857–1952) English physiologist. He established physiological psychology with his book *The Integrative Action of the Nervous System* (1906). Sherrington shared the 1932 Nobel Prize for physiology or medicine.

**sherry** Fortified wine. It has a characteristic raisiny flavor produced by a special method of vinification and blending. True sherry comes from Jerez, Spain.

**Sherwood, Robert Emmet** (1896–1955) US dramatist.

▲ **Shaw** One of the best-known and most prolific 20th-century dramatists, George Bernard Shaw was an ardent socialist, and much of his work is subtly critical of capitalist society. Shaw, here pictured aged 90, was also an acutely perceptive music and drama critic and social and economic commentator, producing a vast amount of material in various forms throughout his life.

His first play was *The Road to Rome* (1927). Sherwood won four Pulitzer Prizes: *Idiot's Delight* (1936), *Abe Lincoln in Illinois* (1938), *There Shall be No Night* (1940), and his memoir *Roosevelt and Hopkins* (1948). He was a speechwriter for President Franklin D. Roosevelt. Sherwood won an Oscar for Best Screenplay for *The Best Years of Our Lives* (1946).

**Shetland Islands** Group of *c*.100 islands NE of the Orkneys, 130mi (210km) off the N coast of Scotland, constituting an administrative region. Settled by Norse invaders in the 9th century, the islands were seized by Scotland in 1472. The principal islands are Mainland (which has the main town of Lerwick), Yell, Unst, Whalsay, and Bressay. The islands are rocky with thin soils, but oats and barley are grown in places. Fishing and livestock are important, and the islands are famous for SHETLAND PONIES. The region is also noted for its woolen clothing. More recently, oil and tourism have become major industries. Area: 553sq mi (1,433sq km) Pop. (1991) 22,522.

**Shetland pony** One of the smallest types of light horse. Originating in the SHETLAND ISLANDS, it makes an ideal child's mount. Height: typically 28in (71cm) at the shoulder; weight: 350lb (169kg).

**Shevardnadze, Eduard Ambrosievich** (1928– ) Georgian statesman, president (1992– ). A close ally of Mikhail GORBACHEV, Shevardnadze was Soviet foreign minister (1985–90). He oversaw the Soviet withdrawal from Afghanistan and worked on détente with the West. In 1990 Shevardnadze resigned and formed the Democratic Reform Movement. As president of Georgia, he sought Russian help to overcome supporters of the deposed leader, Zviad Gamsakhurdia. Shevardnadze escaped assassination attempts in 1995 and 1998.

**Shi'a** Second-largest branch of ISLAM. Shiites believe that the true successor of MUHAMMAD was ALI, whose claim to be CALIPH was not recognized by SUNNI Muslims. It rejects the *Sunna* (the collection of teachings outside the KORAN) and relies instead on the pronouncements of a succession of holy men called IMAMS. The SAFAVID dynasty in Iran were the first to adopt Shi'a as a state religion. One of the principal causes of the Iranian revolution was Shah PAHLAVI's attempt to reduce clerical influence on government. Ayatollah KHOMEINI's Shiite theocracy stressed the role of Islamic activism in liberation struggles. The largest Shi'a group is the Twelve-Imaam Shiites; the other major group is the ISMAILIS.

**Shikoku** Smallest of the four main islands of Japan, S of Honshū and E of Kyūshū. The interior is mountainous and extensively forested, and most settlements are on the coast. The principal cities are Matsuyama, Takamatsu, and Tokushima. Products: rice, tea, wheat, timber, fish, tobacco, fruit, soybeans, camphor, copper. Area: 7,258sq mi (18,798sq km). Pop. (1995) 4,183,000.

**Shiloh, Battle of** (April 6–7, 1862) Major battle in the CIVIL WAR, fought in the vicinity of Shiloh Church, Hardin County, Tennessee. Confederate generals Albert S. Johnston and P.G.T. BEAUREGARD planned to defeat the Union Army of the Tennessee under General Ulysses S. GRANT before the arrival of further Union troops. The Confederate attack caught the Union by surprise but reinforcements enabled Grant to force Beauregard to withdraw. The battle cost more than 13,000 Union and 10,000 Confederate lives.

**shingles** (herpes zoster) Acute viral infection of sensory nerves. Groups of small blisters appear along the course of the affected nerves. The condition can be very painful.

**Shinto** (Jap. way to the gods) Indigenous religion of Japan. Originating as a primitive cult of nature worship, it was shaped by the influence of CONFUCIUS and, from the 5th century, BUDDHISM. A revival of the ancient Shinto rites in the 17th century contributed to the rise of Japanese nationalism in the late 19th century. Shinto has many deities in the form of spirits, souls, and forces of nature.

**ship** Vessel for conveying passengers and freight by sea. The earliest seagoing ships were probably Egyptian, making voyages to the E coast of Africa in *c*.1500 BC. In *c*.AD 200 extensive sea voyages were being made by Chinese ships that carried more than one mast and featured a rudder, some 1,200 years before such ships appeared in Europe. In the Mediterranean region, the galleys of the Greek, Phoenician, and Roman navies combined rows of oars with a single square sail, as did the Viking longboats, which were capable of withstanding violent seas. By the 14th and 15th centuries, carracks and galleons were being developed to fulfill the EXPLORATION of the New World. Fighting ships of the 17th and 18th centuries included frigates of various designs. Sailing freighters culminated in the great clippers of the late 19th century. Early in the century, the first steamships had been built. They were powered by wood, or coal-burning STEAM ENGINES that drove large paddle wheels. In 1819 the first Atlantic crossing was made by "steam-assisted sail," and this crossing soon became a regular service. By the mid-19th century steamships were driven by propellers, or screws. Marine steam TURBINES were developed at the turn of the 19th century and gradually replaced reciprocating (back-and-forth cranking) steam ENGINES for large vessels, early examples being the ocean liners of the 1900s. Oil, rather than coal, soon became the favored fuel for large marine engines. Diesel engines were developed in the early 1900s, but were considered unreliable and did not replace steam turbines until the 1970s. Some of the newest military ships and icebreakers are fitted with nuclear engines in which heat from a NUCLEAR REACTOR drives steam turbines. *See also* AIRCRAFT CARRIER; BOAT; SUBMARINE

**Shiraz** Capital of Fars province, in the Zagros Mountains, SW Iran. An ancient city established near PERSEPOLIS, it was an artistic center from the 4th century. From the 7th century it was a trade center, and in the 9th century it developed into a place of Muslim pilgrimage. From 1750 to 1794 Shiraz was the capital of Persia. Still noted for its carpets, its other products include metalwork, textiles, cement, and sugar. Pop. (1991) 965,117.

**Shiva** (Siva) Major god of HINDUISM. A complex god who

◀ **Shearer** English striker Alan Shearer became England captain for the 1996 European Championship. He later moved from Blackburn Rovers to Newcastle United but was plagued by injury in the 1996–97 season.

◀ **ship** Worldwide expansion of Europe's trading empire during the 18th century was made possible by ships, such as the heavily armed East Indiaman shown here.

transcends the concepts of good and evil, Shiva represents both reproduction and destruction. He periodically destroys the world in order to create it once more. He takes little part in the human affairs, although his wife, KALI, is actively involved in them.

**shock** Acute circulatory failure, possibly with collapse. Caused by disease, injury, or emotional trauma, it is characterized by weakness, pallor, sweating, and a shallow, rapid pulse. In shock, blood pressure drops to a level below that needed to oxygenate the tissues.

**Shockley, William Bradford** (1910–89) US physicist who, with his colleagues, John BARDEEN and Walter BRATTAIN, invented the TRANSISTOR. In 1947 they produced a point-contact transistor and a junction transistor. They shared the 1956 Nobel Prize for physics.

**shock therapy** *See* ELECTROCONVULSIVE THERAPY

**shoebill stork** (whale-headed stork) Tall wading bird found in papyrus marshes of tropical NE Africa. It has a shoe-shaped bill with a sharp hook, a short neck, darkish plumage, and long legs. It feeds at night on small animals. Height: to 4.6ft (1.4m). Family Balaenicipitidae; species *Balaeniceps rex.*

**shōgun** Title of the military ruler of Japan, first conferred upon Yoritomo in 1192. The Minamoto (1192–1333), Ashikaga (1338–1568), and TOKUGAWA (1603–1868) shōgunates ruled feudal Japan, although an emperor retained ceremonial and religious duties. The shōgunate ended with the MEIJI RESTORATION (1868).

**Sholes, Christopher Latham** (1819–90) US journalist and politician who helped to develop the first commercially successful typewriter in 1867. The Remington Arms Company later purchased all rights in it.

**Sholokhov, Mikhail Alexandrovich** (1905–84) Soviet novelist, famous for his novel about his native land, *Tikhy Don* (1928–40), which was translated as *And Quiet Flows the Don* (1934) and *The Don Flows Home to the Sea* (1940). Sholokhov was awarded the 1965 Nobel Prize for literature.

**shooting** Competitive sport involving FIREARMS, in which a competitor, or team of competitors, fires at stationary or moving targets. The three main types of shooting are rifle, pistol, and clay-pigeon shooting. Within **rifle** shooting, the three basic classes of competition are for air rifle, small-bore, and large-bore rifle; all but air rifle shooting are Olympic sports. The two main forms of **pistol** shooting, rapid-fire (or silhouette) and free shooting, are both Olympic sports. There are three disciplines of **clay-pigeon** shooting – Olympic trench, skeet, and down-the-line shooting. The first two types are Olympic sports.

**shorthand** System of writing, used to record speech quickly. Phonetic shorthand systems first appeared during the 18th century, and the most famous system, **Pitman's** shorthand, was published in 1837. All the sounds of the English language are represented by 49 signs for consonants and 16 signs to indicate vowels. The **Gregg** system of phonetic shorthand, widely taught in the US, has a script based on ordinary writing.

**Short Parliament** (1640) English Parliament that ended 11 years of personal rule by CHARLES I. Charles was forced to summon Parliament to raise revenue through taxation for war against Scotland. When it refused his demands, he dissolved it, but had to summon the LONG PARLIAMENT a few months later.

**Shoshone** (Shoshoni) Native North Americans of the UTO-AZTECAN LANGUAGE group. They occupy reservations in California, Idaho, Nevada, Utah, and Wyoming. They were divided into the COMANCHE, the Northern, the Western, and the Wind River Shoshone. Today, there are *c.*9,500 Shoshone.

**Shostakovich, Dmitri Dmitrievich** (1906–75) Russian composer. Shostakovich's use of contemporary western musical developments in his compositions did not conform with Soviet SOCIALIST REALISM. His opera *The Lady Macbeth of the Mtsenk District* (1934) received international acclaim, but was later criticized in *Pravda*. Other works were deliberately more conventional. He composed 15 symphonies, 13 string quartets, ballets, concertos, piano music, film music, and vocal works.

**shot put** Field event in which a competitor throws a heavy metal ball from a position close to the neck by means of a swift extension of the arm. Throughout the put, the athlete must remain inside the throwing circle. Men throw a 16lb (7.3kg) shot; women an 8lb 13oz (4kg) shot. The shot put has been an Olympic event since 1909.

**shoulder** In human anatomy, mobile joint at the top of the arm. It consists of the ball-and-socket joint between the upper arm bone (HUMERUS) and the SHOULDER BLADE (scapula).

**shoulder blade** (scapula) In vertebrates, either of two large, roughly triangular, flat bones found one on either side of the upper back. They provide for the attachment of muscles that move the forelimbs. *See also* SHOULDER

**Shreveport** City on Red River, NW Louisiana. Founded in 1835 and incorporated as a city in 1871, it developed after the discovery (1906) of oil at Caddo Lake. It is the site of the annual Louisiana State Fair, and the Centenary College (1825). Industries; cotton, oil, natural gas, clothing, food products, lumber. Pop. (1990) 198,518.

**shrew** Smallest mammal, found throughout the world. It is an active, voracious insectivore that eats more than its own weight daily. Family Soricidae.

**shrike** (butcherbird) Small, perching bird found worldwide, except in South America and Australia. It dives at its prey – insects, small birds, mice – hitting them with its strong, hooked bill and then impaling them on a sharp fence post, twig or thorn. Family Laniidae

**shrimp** Mostly marine, swimming crustacean. Its compressed body has long antennae, stalked eyes, a beaklike prolongation, a segmented abdomen with five pairs of swimming legs, and a terminal spine. There are true, sand, and pistol shrimps. Large, edible shrimps are often called PRAWNS or scampi. Length: 2–3in (5–7.5cm).

**Shropshire** (Salop) County in W England; the county town is Shrewsbury. To the N of the SEVERN River, the land is generally low-lying, and to the S it rises to the Welsh hills. Part of Mercia in Anglo-Saxon history, after the Norman Conquest it became part of the Welsh Marches. The economy is primarily agricultural. Area: 1,347sq mi (3,490sq km). Pop. (1991) 406,387.

**Shrove Tuesday** Day before Ash Wednesday, which is the first day of LENT. *See also* CARNIVAL; MARDI GRAS

**shrub** (bush) Woody, perennial plant that is smaller than a TREE. Instead of having a main stem, a shrub branches at or slightly above ground level into several stems. Its hard stem distinguishes it from an HERB. Shrubs such as rhododendrons and azaleas are popular ornamentals.

**sial** In geology, uppermost of the two main rock classes in the Earth's crust. Sial rocks are so called because their main constituents are silicon and aluminum. They make up the material of the continents and overlay the SIMA.

**Siam** *See* THAILAND

**Siamese twins** Identical TWINS who are born physically joined together, sometimes with sharing of organs. Surgical separation can be a complex procedure.

**Sian** *See* XIAN

**Sibelius, Jean Julius Christian** (1865–1957) Finnish composer whose work represents the culmination of nationalism in Finnish music. He is best known for his orchestral works, including seven symphonies, a violin concerto (1903–05), and the tone poems *En Saga* (1892) and *Finlandia* (1899).

**Siberia** (Sibir) Extensive region of Asian Russia, extending E to W from the Ural Mountains to the Pacific Ocean, and N to S from the Arctic Ocean to the steppes of Kazakstan and the border with Mongolia. The region includes areas of tundra, taiga, and steppe, almost half of it forested. Drained chiefly by the vast north-flowing OB, YENISEI, and LENA rivers and their tributaries, Siberia can be divided into five geographical areas: (1) the W Siberian plain, between the URALS and the Central Plateau, favors dairy farming, but wheat, oats, flax, potatoes, rye, and sugar beets are grown. Two thirds of the population live in the SW, where industry is concentrated in cities such as NOVOSIBIRSK and OMSK, and in the Kuznetz Basin, which has large coal deposits; (2) the Central Siberian plateau, between the Yenisei and Lena rivers. KRASNOYARSK lies on the Yenisei and the city of Yakutsk on the Lena. The region is Russia's chief producer of gold, mica, diamonds, and aluminum, and forestry

▲ **shoebill stork** Although it displays some behavioral similarities to pelicans and herons, the shoebill stork (*Balaeniceps rex*) is the sole member of a separate bird family, Balaenicipidae. It uses its distinctive, shovel-like bill to dig in the mud to find the fish and aquatic animals on which it feeds. Despite its large size and clumsy, sluggish appearance on land, it is a graceful flyer with broad wings. Silent and solitary birds, shoebills have unwebbed feet that are specially adapted to walking on marshy land.

is an important industry; (3) the NE Siberian mountains lie to the E of the Lena. The region is sparsely populated due to the Arctic climate. Verkhoyansk is the world's coldest permanent settlement. The breeding of reindeer, fishing, and seal hunting are the chief occupations; (4) the mountains of the S Trans-Baikal region form the watershed between the Pacific and the Arctic. The major city is IRKUTSK, close to Lake BAIKAL; (5) the volcanic and mountainous KAMCHATKA peninsula. The Cossacks conquered Siberia between 1581 and 1644, although the Far Eastern territory was held by the Chinese until 1860. Mining developed in the 19th century, and Siberia was used as a penal colony for political prisoners by the Russian empire and its Soviet successor. Large-scale settlement began after the construction (1881–1905) of the TRANS-SIBERIAN RAILROAD; Siberia's population doubled between 1914 and 1946. The economic development of the region was rapid. The importance of Siberian grain was emphasized during World War II, and in the 1950s Khrushchev encouraged the cultivation of land in the SW. The 1960s saw the development of vast hydroelectric schemes in the Trans-Baikal region. Area: 5,331,000sq mi (13,807,000sq km). Pop. (1994) 35,605,000.

**Sibyl** Prophetess of Greek and Roman mythology. The Sibyl of Cumae offered nine books of her prophecies to Tarquinius Superbus of Rome. He refused her price so she began burning the books until he bought the remaining three for the price she had asked for all nine. They were consulted in times of national emergency.

**Sichuan** (Szechwan) Province in SW China, almost completely surrounded by mountains, and the most populous in the country; the capital is Chengdu. The E part of the region comprises the large, heavily populated Red Basin, the most prosperous area of China. Sichuan is China's leading producer of rice, corn, and sweet potatoes, while soybeans, barley, and fruit are also grown. Livestock, including cattle, pigs, horses, and oxen, are reared, particularly in the W. Salt, coal, and iron are mined; other products include rapeseed oil and silk, for which Sichuan was once world famous. Area: 219,774sq mi (569,215sq km). Pop. (1990) 106,370,000.

**Sicily** Largest and most populous island in the Mediterranean Sea, off the SW tip of the Italian peninsula, comprising (with nearby islands) an autonomous region of Italy. The capital is PALERMO; other major cities include MESSINA. It is separated from Italy by the narrow Strait of Messina. Mostly mountainous, Sicily's Mount ETNA, at 10,958ft (3,340m), is the highest volcano in Europe. Strategically situated between Europe and Africa, from the 5th–3rd centuries BC it was a battleground for the rival Roman and Carthaginian empires and, following the first PUNIC WAR in 241 BC, became a Roman province. At the end of the 11th century, the island and S Italy were conquered by the Normans. In 1266 the throne passed to Charles of Anjou, whose unpopular government caused the Sicilian Vespers revolt (1282) and the election of an Aragónese king. In 1302 peace terms led to Aragón keeping Sicily, while S Italy became the Angevin kingdom of Naples. In 1735 the two regions were reunified under the rule of the Bourbon Don Carlos (Charles III of Spain). Centuries of centralization under Spanish imperial rule led to the crowning of Ferdinand I as King of Two Sicilies in 1816. Sicilian independence revolts of 1820 and 1848–49 were ruthlessly suppressed. In 1860 Garibaldi liberated the island and it was incorporated into the new, unified state of Italy. Agriculture is Sicily's economic mainstay. Grain, olives, wine, and citrus fruits are the principal products; tourism is also important. Sicily is one of the poorest local economies in Europe. Area: 9,925sq mi (25,706sq km). Pop. (1992) 4,997,705.

**Sickert, Walter Richard** (1860–1942) English painter. He inspired a circle of progressive painters to form the Camden Town Group and later the London Group. He was a precursor of the 1950s "kitchen sink" school of drama in his rejection of "nice" subjects in favor of drab domestic interiors, sordid bedroom scenes, and a spirit of desperate boredom, as in *Ennui* (*c*.1914).

**sickle-cell anemia** Inherited blood disorder, mainly affecting black people, featuring an abnormality of HEMOGLOBIN. The hemoglobin is sensitive to a deficiency of oxygen and it distorts erythrocytes, causing them to become rigid and sickle shaped. Sickle cells are rapidly lost from the circulation, leading to anemia and jaundice.

◀ **shrew** Among the smallest of the mammals, shrews inhabit forests all around the world: two examples are tree shrews *(Tupaia glis*, top), which live in SE Asia, and forest elephant shrews (*Petrodromus tetradactylus*, bottom), found in Kenya and SW Africa. Because they are extremely active with very high metabolic rates, shrews must eat constantly just to stay alive: they will die of starvation if they are deprived of food for even a few hours. Although they have poor vision, they have keen senses of smell and hearing, and loud noises can cause them to faint or even to drop dead. They produce a foul-smelling secretion from special glands on their backs, which protects them from most mammalian predators, but this does not deter many birds of prey, including hawks and owls.

**sidereal period** Orbital period of a planet or other celestial body with respect to a background star. It is the true orbital period. **Sidereal time** is local time reckoned according to the rotation of the Earth with respect to the stars. The sidereal day is 23 hours, 56 minutes, and 4 seconds of mean solar time, nearly 4 minutes shorter than the mean solar day. The sidereal year is equal to 365.25636 mean solar days.

**sidewinder** (horned rattlesnake) Nocturnal RATTLESNAKE found in deserts of the SW US and Mexico. It has hornlike scales over the eyes and is usually tan with a light pattern. It loops obliquely across the sand, leaving a J-shaped trail. Length: to 30in (75cm). Family Viperidae; species *Crotalus cerastes*. The term also describes desert-dwelling snakes of the Old World.

**Sidney, Sir Philip** (1554–86) English poet, diplomat, and courtier. His intricate romance *Arcadia* (1590) is the earliest example of PASTORAL in English. *Astrophel and Stella* (1591), the first English SONNET sequence, was inspired by his love for Penelope Devereux. *An Apology for Poetry* (1595) is the most important critical work of the Elizabethan era. Sidney died at the Battle of Zutphen.

**Siegfried** In ancient Germanic literature, hero figure who corresponds with Sigurd in Norse mythology, although accounts vary. In the story of Brunhild he is slain, but elsewhere he is generally victorious in his adventures. He plays a major part in the Germanic epic tale of the *Nibelungenlied* and in WAGNER's operatic adaptation of that tale, *The Ring of the Nibelung*.

**Siemens** German brothers associated with the electrical engineering industry. **Ernst Werner** von Siemens (1816–92) developed an electric telegraph system in 1849. With **Karl** (1829–1906), he set up subsidiaries of the family firm in London, Vienna, and Paris. **Friedrich** (1826–1904) and **Karl Wilhelm** (later William) (1823–83) developed a regenerative furnace that was used extensively in industry.

**Siena** Capital of Siena province, Tuscany, central Italy. It is one of Italy's foremost tourist attractions. The town lends its name to the yellow-brown pigment sienna, present in the region's soil, and the area is famous for its orange marble. Founded by the Etruscans, Siena became a commune in the 12th century. During the 13th century, it rapidly expanded to rival Florence, and was the center of the Ghibelline faction. In the mid-16th century, it fell under the control of the Medici. In art history, it is especially famed for the Sienese School of painting (13th–14th centuries). Pop. (1990) 58,278

**Sienkiewicz, Henryk** (1846–1916) Polish novelist and short-story writer. He glorified Poland's struggle for nationhood in the trilogy *With Fire and Sword* (1884), *The Deluge* (1886), and *Pan Michael* (1887–88). He gained international recognition with *Quo Vadis?* (1896). He was awarded the 1905 Nobel Prize for literature.

**Sierra Leone** Republic on the W coast of Africa; the capital is FREETOWN. **Land and climate** The coast contains several deep estuaries in the N, with lagoons in the S, but the most prominent feature is the mountainous Freetown (or Sierra Leone) peninsula. North of the peninsula is the Rokel River estuary, W Africa's

S

best natural harbor. Behind the coastal plain, the land rises to mountains, with the highest peak, Loma Mansa, reaching 6,391ft (1,948m). Sierra Leone has a wet, tropical climate, with the heaviest rainfall between April and October. Swamps cover much of the coastal areas. Inland, much of the original rain forest has been destroyed and replaced by low bush and coarse grassland. The N is covered largely by tropical savanna. **History and politics** Portuguese sailors reached the coast in 1460; in the 16th century the area became a source of slaves. In 1787 Freetown was founded as a home for freed slaves. In 1808 the settlement became a British crown colony. In 1896 the interior was made a protectorate. In 1951 the protectorate and colony were united. In 1961 Sierra Leone gained independence within the Commonwealth of Nations. In 1971 it became a republic. In 1978 the All People's Congress became the sole political party. A 1991 referendum favored the restoration of multiparty democracy, but in 1992 a military group seized power. A civil war began between the government and the Revolutionary United Front (RUF). The RUF fought to end foreign interference and to nationalize the diamond mines. Following multiparty elections in 1996, a civilian government was installed, led by Ahmad Tejan Kabbah. In November 1996 Kabbah and the RUF signed a peace agreement ending a war that had claimed more than 10,000 lives. In May 1997 a military group, led by Major Johnny Paul Koroma, seized power. The Economic Community of West African States (ECOWAS) imposed sanctions and Nigeria led an intervention force that restored Kabbah in 1998. **Economy** Sierra Leone has a low-income economy (1995 GDP per capita, US$580). Agriculture employs 70% of the work force, many at subsistence level. Chief food crops include rice, cassava, and corn, and export crops include cocoa and coffee. The most valuable exports are minerals, including diamonds, bauxite, and rutile (titanium ore).

**Sierra Madre** Principal mountain range in Mexico, from the US border to SE Mexico and extending S into Guatemala. It comprises the Sierra Madre Occidental, Sierra Madre Oriental, Sierra Madre del Sur, and the subrange Sierra Madre del Guatemala. The ranges enclose the central Mexican plateau and have long been a barrier to E–W travel. The main range is 1,500mi (2,400km) long and *c.*10–300mi (16–480km) wide. The highest peak is Orizaba (Giltaltepetl) in the Sierra Madre Oriental, at 18,700ft (5,700m).

**Sierra Nevada** Mountain system in E California. In the E it rises steeply from the Great Basin, while the W edge slopes more gently down to the Central Valley of California. The snow-fed rivers are used to irrigate the Central Valley and also to provide hydroelectric power. Mount WHITNEY, 14,495ft (4,418m), is the highest peak. The range is 400mi (650km) long.

**sight** Sense by which form, color, size, movement, and distance of objects are perceived. It is the detection of light by the EYE, enabling visual images to form.

**Sigismund** (1368–1437) Holy Roman emperor (1411–37), and king of Germany (1410–37), Hungary (1387–1437), and Bohemia (1419–37). As king of Hungary, he was defeated by the OTTOMAN Turks in 1396 and 1427. In Bohemia he was challenged by the HUSSITE revolt. As emperor (crowned 1433), he was partly responsible for ending the GREAT SCHISM (1415). Sigismund secured the succession on Albert II, his son-in-law, the first ruler of the HAPSBURG dynasty.

**Signac, Paul** (1863–1935)·French painter. Signac was the main writer of NEO-IMPRESSIONISM, especially in *D'Eugène Delacroix au néo-impressionisme* (1899). His painting later became much freer and his color more brilliant, such as *View of the Port of Marseille* (1905).

**sign language** Non-phonetic means of personal communication, using hand symbols, movements, and gestures. It is used as a primary means of communication among deaf people or people with impaired hearing.

**Sikhism** Indian religion founded in the 16th century by NANAK, the first Sikh GURU. Combining HINDU and MUSLIM teachings, it is a MONOTHEISTIC religion whose adherents believe that their God is the immortal creator of the universe. All human beings are equal, and Sikhs oppose any CASTE system. The path to God is through prayer and meditation, but nearness to God is only achievable through divine grace. Sikhs believe in REINCARNATION and spiritual guidance from their guru or leader. Begun in Punjab as a pacifist religion, Sikhism became an activist military brotherhood and a political force. All Sikh men came to adopt the surname Singh ("lion"). Since Indian independence, Sikh extremists have periodically agitated for an independent Sikh state, called Khalistan. In 1984 the leader of a Sikh fundamentalist revival was killed by government forces at the Golden Temple of AMRITSAR, and in retaliation Indira GANDHI was assassinated by her Sikh bodyguard. More than 1,000 Sikhs died in the ensuing riots.

**Sikh Wars** (1845–46, 1848–49) Two wars between the Sikhs and the British in NW India. After the death of RANJIT SINGH in 1839, disorder affected the Sikh state in the PUNJAB. When Sikh forces, including many non-Sikhs, crossed the frontier on the Sutlej River, the British declared war. After several battles involving heavy casualties on both sides, the British advanced to Lahore, where peace was agreed (1846). The conflict was renewed two years later, but superior British artillery led to a Sikh defeat at Gujrat (1849). The Sikhs surrendered and the Punjab was annexed to British India.

**Sikkim** State in N India, bounded by Tibet, China (N and NE), Bhutan (SE), India (S), and Nepal (W), with its capital at Gangtok (1991 pop. 25,024). The terrain is generally mountainous, rising to Mount KANCHENJUNGA, at 28,185ft (8,591m) the world's third-highest peak. After the 17th century Sikkim was ruled by the rajas of Tibet. It had come under British influence by 1816, and after British withdrawal from India in 1947, Sikkim became independent. Political unrest led to the country becoming a protectorate (1950), and then an associate state (1975) of India. Agriculture is the main source of income; major crops include corn, rice, barley, fruits, tea, and cardamom. Tourism is a growing industry. Area: 2,734sq mi (7,096sq km). Pop. (1991) 406,457.

**Sikorsky, Igor Ivanovich** (1889–1972) US aeronautical engineer, b. Russia. In 1913 he built and piloted the world's first multimotored airplane. In 1919 Sikorsky immigrated to the US. He is best known for his development of the HELICOPTER.

**Silesia** Historic region in E central Europe, now mostly lying in SW Poland, with the remainder in the N Czech Republic and SE Germany. A former Polish province, it passed from Poland to Bohemia in the 14th century, became part of the Hapsburg empire, and was seized by

## SIERRA LEONE

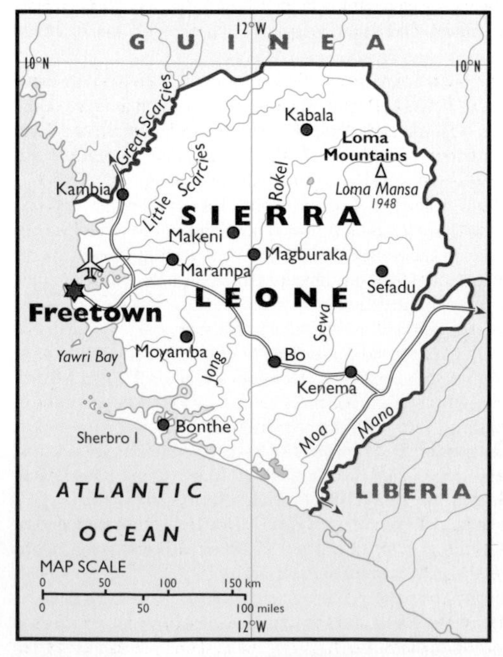


**AREA:** 27,699sq mi (71,740sq km)
**POPULATION:** 4,376,000
**CAPITAL (POPULATION):** Freetown (469,776)
**GOVERNMENT:** Transitional
**ETHNIC GROUPS:** Mende 35%, Temne 37%, Limba 8%,
**LANGUAGES:** English (official)
**RELIGIONS:** Traditional beliefs 51%, Islam 39%, Christianity 9%
**CURRENCY:** Leone = 100 cents

Prussia from Austria in 1742. In World War II it was invaded by the Soviet Union, but in 1945 a greater part of the land was returned to Poland by the terms of the POTSDAM CONFERENCE. Upper Silesia is primarily an industrial region of mining and metals, centering on KATOWICE; Lower Silesia, with a milder climate, is more agricultural.

**silica** (silicon dioxide, $SiO_2$) Compound of SILICON and oxygen. It occurs naturally as QUARTZ and chert (which includes FLINT). Silica is used in the manufacture of glass, ceramics, and SILICONE.

**silicate** Any of a large group of rock-forming minerals made up of SILICON and oxygen in $SiO_4$ units bonded to various metals. Silicate minerals, such as FELDSPAR, GARNET, and MICA, form more than 90% of the material of the Earth's crust. Glass is a mixture of silicates with small amounts of other substances. Sodium silicates are used as adhesives and in the production of detergents.

**silicon** (symbol Si) Common, gray, nonmetallic element of Group IV of the periodic table. Silicon is found only in combinations such as SILICA and SILICATE. It is the second most abundant element in the Earth's crust (27.7% by weight). Silicon "chips" are extensively used in microprocessors. Properties: at.no. 14; at. wt. 28.086; sp. gr. 2.33; m.p. 2,570°F (1,410°C); b.p. 4,271°F (2,355°C); most common isotope $^{28}Si$ (98.21%).

**silicon chip** Small piece of SILICON etched to carry many tiny ELECTRIC CIRCUITS. Silicon chips are at the heart of most electronic equipment. Chips are etched, layer by layer, onto slivers of pure silicon. Each layer is "doped" to give it particular electrical properties, and the combination of different layers form components such as TRANSISTORS and DIODES. *See also* CHARGE-COUPLED DEVICE (CCD); INTEGRATED CIRCUIT (IC); PRINTED CIRCUIT; SEMICONDUCTOR

**silicone** Odorless and colorless polymer based on SILICON. Silicones are inert and stable at high temperatures, and are used in lubricants, varnishes, adhesives, water repellents, hydraulic fluids, and artificial heart valves.

**Silicon Valley** High-technology manufacturing complex in Santa Clara county, California, centring on the city of SAN JOSE. It has the greatest concentration of electronics and computing industries in the US.

**silicosis** Chronic, occupational lung disease, caused by prolonged inhalation of SILICA dust in occupations such as mining and stone grinding.

**silk** Natural fiber produced by many creatures, notably the SILKWORM. The many kinds of silk cloth include crépe, satin, taffeta, and velvet. Almost all silk is obtained from silkworms reared commercially; a single cocoon can provide between 2,000–3,000ft (600–900m) of filament. When the cocoons have been spun, the silk farmer heats them to kill the insects inside. The cocoons are then soaked to unstick the fibers, and the strands from several cocoons are unwound together to form a single thread of yarn. The Chinese were the first to use silk. Sicily was one of the first European production centers and the industry spread to Italy, Spain, and France. Silk manufacturing developed in England in the 17th century. China is still the largest producer of raw silk.

**Silk Road** (Silk Route) Ancient trade route linking China with Europe, the major artery of all Asian land exploration before AD 1500. For 3,000 years the manufacture of SILK was a secret closely guarded by the Chinese. Silk fetched extravagant prices in Greece and Rome, and the trade became the major source of income for the Chinese ruling dynasties. By 100 BC 12 caravan trains were making the perilous annual journey along the Silk Road, and the tax on the trade provided a third of all the HAN dynasty's revenue. The silk trade began to decline in the 6th century, when the SILKWORM's eggs were smuggled to Constantinople and the secret was exposed. During the 13th century, European merchants (including Marco POLO in 1271) traveled along the Silk Road when it was controlled by the Mongols. In the 14th century trade became possible via a sea route to the Far East.

**silk-screen printing** (serigraphy) In PRINTING, a means of producing a print, generally on paper. A screen composed of a mesh of silk or artificial fibers is stretched over a wooden frame; a design is "stopped out" (painted) on the mesh, using glue, varnish, gelatin, or a paper stencil. To make the print, ink is taken across the screen with a squeegee; the pressure of this pushes the ink through the unstopped areas of the mesh. Several screens may be used to build up a multicolored print.

## SILICON CHIP

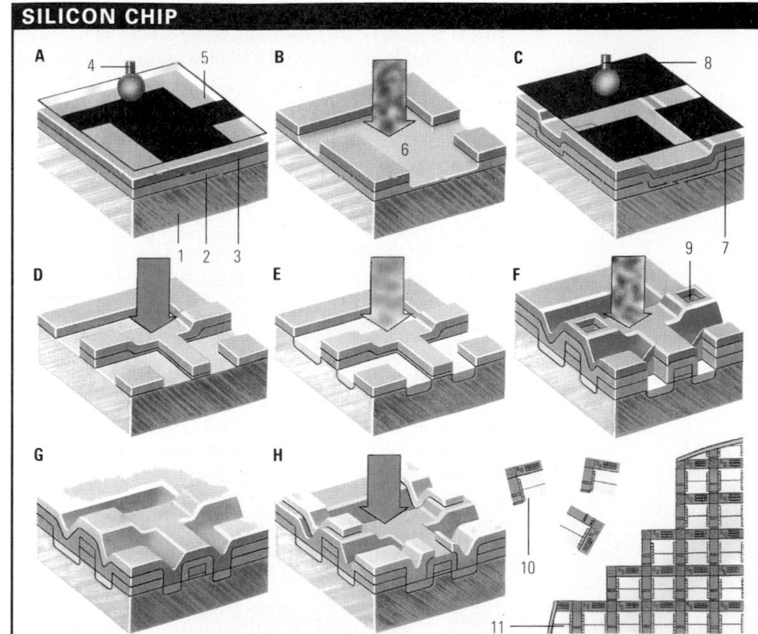


A silicon chip is manufactured by building up layers on top of a wafer of silicon (1). (A) First a layer of silicon dioxide (2), an insulator, is laid down followed by photo-sensitive photoresist (3). Photoresist hardens when hit by ultraviolet light (4). By using a mask (5) the area to be hardened can be controled. (B) The unhardened area shielded by the mask can then be rinsed out with a solvent (6). The photoresist is then removed by hot gases. (C) The same process is used to apply a conducting polysilicon (7). Again ultraviolet light fixes the photoresist (8) in the unmasked area. (D) A solvent removes the photoresist. (E) N-type silicon, which only carries a negative charge, is then created by doping of the silicon base. (F) A third masking process creates shafts (9) to the n-type silicon. (G) An aluminum layer is then applied. (H) A fourth masking forms electrical contacts connecting the layers of silicon.Hundreds of chips are simultaneously made on a single wafer of silicon (10) before they are eventually separated (11) and mounted individually for use.

**silkworm** Moth CATERPILLAR that feeds chiefly on MULBERRY leaves. The common domesticated *Bombyx mori* is raised commercially for its SILK cocoon. Length: 3in (7.5 cm). Family Bombycidae.

**silt** Mineral particles produced by the WEATHERING of rock. These particles are carried along in streams and rivers, to be deposited in the gently flowing lower reaches of rivers. When the river overflows its bank, the silt deposit forms fertile land.

**Silurian** Third-oldest period of the PALEOZOIC era, 438 to 408 million years ago. Marine invertebrates resembled those of ORDOVICIAN times, and jawless fish began to evolve. The earliest land plants (psilopsids) and first land animals (archaic mites and millipedes) developed. Mountains formed in NW Europe and Greenland.

**silver** (symbol Ag) White, metallic element in the second series of TRANSITION ELEMENTS. It occurs in argentite (a sulfide) and horn silver (a chloride), and is also obtained as a by-product in the refining of copper and lead. Silver ores are scattered worldwide, Mexico being the major producer. Silver is used for some electrical contacts and on some PRINTED CIRCUITS. Other uses include jewelry, ornaments, coinage, mirrors, and silver salts for light-sensitive materials used in photography. The metal does not oxidize in air, but tarnishes if sulfur compounds are present. Properties: at.no. 47; at.wt. 107.868; sp.gr. 10.5; m.p. 1,763°F (961.93°C), b.p. 4,104°F (2,212°C); most common isotope $^{107}Ag$ (51.82%).

**silverfish** (bristletail) Primitive, gray, wingless insect found throughout the world. It lives in cool, damp places feeding on starchy materials such as food scraps and paper. It gets its name from the silvery scales that cover its body. Length: 0.5in

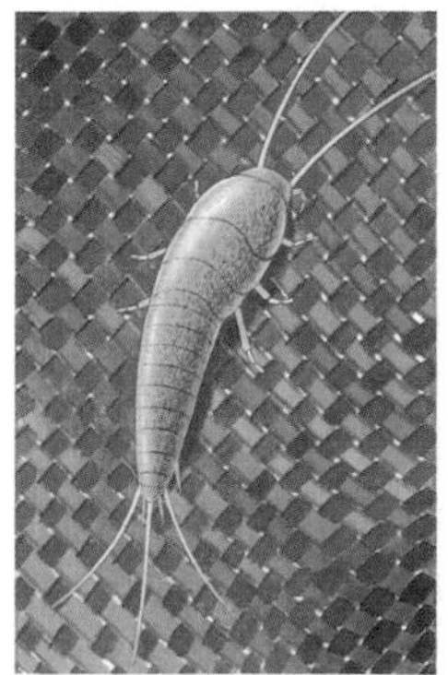

▲ **silverfish** Because they feed on starchy materials, including paste, paper, fabric, and wallpaper, silverfish *(Lepisma saccharina)* can be highly destructive in cool, damp, dark interiors such as basements, archives, and other storage facilities. However, they can be controlled with the use of insecticides or poisonous baits.

S

(13mm). Family Lepismatidae; species *Lepisma saccharina.*

**sima** In geology, undermost of the two main rock-classes that make up the Earth's crust, so called because its main constituents are silicon and magnesium. It underlies the SIAL of the continents.

**Simenon, Georges** (1903–89) Prolific French novelist. His character Maigret, a Parisian police inspector, is one of the best-known creations in 20th-century DETECTIVE FICTION.

**simile** Figure of speech comparing two things. It differs from ordinary comparisons in that it compares, for effect, things usually considered dissimilar and sharing only one common characteristic, as, for example, in the phrase "his fleece was white as snow."

**Simon, Neil** (1927– ) US playwright. His first play was the comedy *Come Blow Your Horn* (1961). Simon has had more Broadway hits than any other US playwright and many of his plays have been turned into films. His major successes include *Barefoot in the Park* (1963), *The Odd Couple* (1965), *Plaza Suite (1968), The Prisoner of Second Avenue* (1971), *California Suite* (1976), *Brighton Beach Memoirs* (1983), and *Biloxi Blues* (1984).

**Simon, Paul** (1942– ) US singer-songwriter. With Art Garfunkel (1941– ), he formed the pop duo **Simon and Garfunkel**, whose album *Sound of Silence* (1966) sold more than a million copies. Other recordings include *Scarborough Fair* (1966), *Bookends* (1968), and *Bridge over Troubled Water* (1970), soon after which the duo split up. Simon's successful solo records include *Still Crazy After All These Years* (1975) and *Graceland* (1986).

**Simpson, O.J. (Orenthal James)** (1947– ) US football player. "O.J." was a running back for the Buffalo Bills (1969–77), and the San Francisco 49ers (1978–79). In 1973 he set a record for most yards gained rushing in a single season (2,003). In 1975 Simpson scored a record 23 touchdowns in a season. His career record of 11,236 yards gained is second in the all-time list. In 1979 he retired from football to pursue a career as a sports commentator and actor. In 1994 he was arrested on a charge of murdering his wife and her male friend. The jury found him not guilty, but in 1997 a civil jury found him liable for wrongful death, and he was fined $30 million.

**Simpson, Wallis Warfield Spencer, Duchess of Windsor** (1896–1986) Wife of the Duke of Windsor, the former King EDWARD VIII of England. A US divorcee, she began her association with Edward when he was Prince of Wales. Their relationship caused controversy and resulted in Edward's abdication in December 1936. Having divorced her second hus-

## SINGAPORE

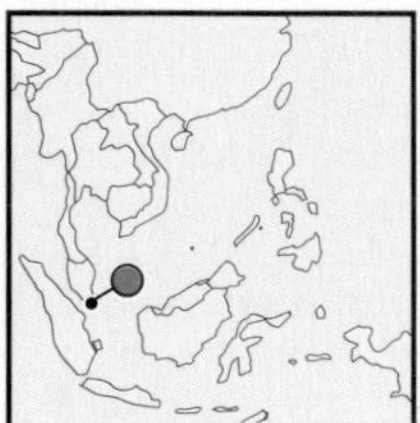

Singapore's flag was adopted in 1959 and it was retained when Singapore broke away from the Federation of Malaysia in 1963. The crescent stands for the nation's ascent. The stars stand for Singapore's aims of democracy, peace, progress, justice, and equality.

**AREA:** 239 sq mi (618sq km)
**POPULATION:** 3,003,000
**CAPITAL (POPULATION):** Singapore City (2,812,000)
**GOVERNMENT:** Multiparty republic
**ETHNIC GROUPS:** Chinese 78%, Malay 14%, Indian 7%
**LANGUAGES:** Chinese, Malay, Tamil, and English (all official)
**RELIGIONS:** Buddhism, Taoism, and other traditional beliefs 54%, Islam 15%, Christianity 13%, Hinduism 4%
**CURRENCY:** Singapore dollar = 100 cents

Singapore is a small republic at the s tip of the MALAY PENINSULA. It consists of the large Singapore Island, and 59 small islets, 20 of which are inhabited. Singapore Island is *c.*26mi (42km) wide and 14mi (23km) across. It is linked to the peninsula by a 3,465ft- (1,056m-) long causeway. The land is mostly low-lying; the highest point, Bukit Timah, is only 577ft (176m) above sea level. Its strategic position, at the convergence of some of the world's most vital shipping lanes, has ensured its success.

### CLIMATE

Singapore has a hot, humid equatorial climate, with temperatures averaging 86°F (30°C). Total average annual rainfall, 95in (2,413mm). Rain occurs (on average) 180 days each year.

### VEGETATION

Rain forest once covered Singapore, but forests now cover only 5% of the land. Today, most of Singapore is urban land. The distinction between island and city has all but disappeared. Farmland covers 4% of the land and plantations of permanent crops make up 7%.

### HISTORY

According to legend, Singapore was founded in 1299. It was first called Temasak (sea town), but was renamed Singapura (city of the lion). Singapore soon became a busy trading center within the Sumatran Srivijaya kingdom. Javanese raiders destroyed it in 1377. Subsumed into Johor, Singapore became part of the powerful MALACCA sultanate. In 1819 Sir Thomas Stamford RAFFLES of the British EAST INDIA COMPANY leased the island from Johor, and the Company founded the city of Singapore. In 1826 Singapore, Pinang, and Malacca formed the Straits Settlement. Singapore soon became the most important British trading center in Southeast Asia, and the Straits Settlement became a Crown Colony in 1867. Despite British defensive reinforcements in the early 20th century, Japanese forces seized the island in 1942. British rule was restored in 1945. In 1946 the Straits Settlement was dissolved and Singapore became a separate colony. In 1959 Singapore achieved self-government. Following a referendum, Singapore merged with Malaya, SARAWAK, and SABAH to form the Federation of MALAYSIA (1963). In 1965 Singapore broke away from the Federation to become an independent republic within the Commonwealth of Nations.

### POLITICS

The People's Action Party (PAP) has ruled Singapore since 1959. Lee Kuan Yew. served as prime minister from 1959 until 1990, when he resigned and was succeeded by GOH CHOK TONG. The economy has expanded rapidly. The PAP has been criticized by human rights groups for its authoritarian social policies and suppression of political dissent. In 1997 Goh Chok Tong and the PAP were reelected.

### ECONOMY

Singapore is a high-income economy (1992 GDP per capita, $18,330). It is one of the world's fastest growing (tiger) economies. Historically, Singapore's economy has been based on transshipment, and this remains a vital component. It is one of the world's busiest ports, annually handling more than 320 million tons of cargo (1994). The postwar economy has diversified. Singapore has a highly skilled and productive work force. The service sector employs 65% of the work force; banking and insurance provide many jobs. Manufacturing is the largest export sector. Industries include computers and electronics, telecommunications, chemicals, machinery, scientific instruments, ships, and textiles. It has a large oil refinery. Farming is relatively unimportant. Most farming is highly intensive, and farmers use the latest technology and scientific methods.

band, Ernest Simpson, she married Edward in 1937.

**simultaneous equations** Two or more equations that can be manipulated to give common solutions. In the simultaneous equations $x + 10y = 25$ and $x + y = 7$, the problem is to find values of $x$ and $y$, such that those values are solutions of both the equations simultaneously. This can be done by subtracting the two equations to give a single equation in $y$, which can then be solved. Substituting the value of $y$ in either equation gives the value of $x$.

**sin** State or instance of being or acting in a way that is contrary to the ideals of righteousness propounded by a religion. In Christianity, the seven deadly sins are anger, avarice, envy, gluttony, lust, pride, and sloth. In Islam, the only sin is to deny that Allah is the only God. *See also* ORIGINAL SIN

**Sinai** Peninsula constituting a protectorate of Egypt, bounded by the Gulf of Suez and the Suez Canal (W), the Gulf of Aqaba and the Negev Desert of Israel (E), the Mediterranean Sea (N), and the Red Sea (S). It is a barren plateau region, sandy in the N, rising to granite ridges in the S, and still inhabited chiefly by nomads. The peninsula is the site of Jabal Musa (Mount Sinai). It was the scene of fierce fighting in the ARAB-ISRAELI WARS (1956, 1967, 1973). After being occupied by the Israelis in 1967, it was returned to Egypt in 1982. The region is divided into two Egyptian governorates of North and South Sinai; Total area: 22,671sq mi (58,714sq km). Pop. (1991 est.) 264,000, all but 41,000 in North Sinai.

**Sinatra, Frank (Francis Albert)** (1915–98) US popular singer and actor. Sinatra began his career in the jazz bands of Harry James and Tommy Dorsey. His interpretations of standards, on records such as *Songs for Swinging Lovers* (1956) and *Come Fly with Me* (1958) are definitive. Sinatra won an Academy Award for his role in *From Here to Eternity* (1953). Other films include *Guys and Dolls*, *The Man With The Golden Arm* (both 1955), and *The Manchurian Candidate* (1962). He married Ava Gardner and later Mia Farrow.

**Sinclair, Upton Beall** (1878–1968) US novelist and social reformer. One of the MUCKRAKERS, Sinclair's first novel, *The Jungle* (1906), exposed conditions in the Chicago meat-packing industry. Other novels include *The Money Changers* (1908), *King Coal* (1917), and *Dragon's Teeth* (1942; part of an 11-volume *roman-fleuve* entitled *World's End*), for which he won a Pulitzer Prize.

**Sind** Province in S Pakistan, bounded by India (E and S) and the Arabian Sea (SW). KARACHI is the national and provincial capital. HYDERABAD is the next largest city. Sind largely consists of the alluvial plain and delta of the INDUS River. The region is hot and arid. Under Arab rule from the 7th to 11th centuries, it then came under Turkish Muslim control. Sind was part of British India (1843–1937). An autonomous province from 1937 until partition in 1947, it received many Muslim refugees from India after the creation of Pakistan. The economy is agricultural. Grain, cotton, sugarcane, fruits, and tobacco are grown. Sind is famous for its handicrafts. Area: 54,428sq mi (140,914sq km). Pop. (1985 est.) 21,682,000.

**Sindhi** Language of Pakistan and India, spoken by *c*.15 million people in the province of Sind, S Pakistan, and across the border in India. It belongs to the Indic branch of the INDO-EUROPEAN LANGUAGES.

**sine** In a right-triangle, ratio of the length of the side opposite an acute angle to the length of the hypotenuse. The sine of angle $A$ is usually abbreviated to $\sin A$.

**Singapore** Archipelago republic at the S end of the Malay Peninsula, SE Asia. *See* country feature

**Singer, Isaac Bashevis** (1904–91) US novelist and short-story writer, b. Poland. His novels of Jewish life, written in Yiddish, include *The Family Moskat* (1950), *The Magician of Lublin* (1960), *The Slave* (1962), *Shosha* (1978), and *The Penitent* (1983). He was awarded the 1978 Nobel Prize for literature.

**Singer, Isaac Merrit** (1811–75) US manufacturer, inventor of a rock drill (1839) and of a single-thread SEWING MACHINE ([illegible]). Singer's machine allowed continuous and curved stitching.

**Sinn Féin** (Gaelic, Ourselves Alone) Irish republican, nationalist party founded in 1905 by Arthur GRIFFITH. It seeks to bring about a united IRELAND. Sinn Féin became a mass party after the EASTER RISING (1916). It won 75% of the vote in the last all-Ireland election (1918) and formed an Irish assembly (the Dáil Éircann) led by Éamon DE VALERA. A two-year war of independence was fought between Britain and the IRISH REPUBLICAN ARMY (IRA), led by Michael COLLINS. The Anglo-Irish Treaty (1921) partitioned Ireland into the Irish Free State and Northern Ireland. Sinn Féin was split and the country plunged into civil war. The pro-treaty wing (FINE GAEL), led by William Cosgrave, formed a government. De Valera, leader of the anti-treaty wing, withdrew from Sinn Féin and formed FIANNA FÁIL (1926). In 1938 the remaining republican intransigents joined the outlawed IRA. In 1969 two groups emerged that mirrored the factions of the Provisional and Official IRA. "Official" Sinn Féin became the Workers Party. The Provisionals refused to recognize the authority of Dublin or Westminster. The president of Sinn Féin, Gerry Adams, has been elected to Westminster three times (1983, 1987, 1997).

**Sino-Japanese Wars** Two wars between China and Japan, marking the beginning and the end of Japanese imperial expansion on the Asian mainland. The first (1894–95) arose from rivalry for control of Korea. In 1894 Japanese influence helped to provoke a rebellion in Korea. Both states intervened, and the Japanese forces swiftly defeated the Chinese. China was forced to accept Korean independence and ceded territory including Taiwan and the Liaotung peninsula. The latter was returned after European pressure. The second war (1937–45) developed from Japan's seizure of Manchuria (1931), where it set up the puppet state of MANCHUKUO. Further Japanese aggression led to war, in which the Japanese swiftly conquered E China, driving the government out of Peking (Beijing). US and British aid was dispatched to China (1938) and the conflict merged into World War II, ending with the final defeat of Japan in 1945.

**Sino-Tibetan languages** Large family of tonal, monosyllabic languages. It includes CHINESE; the Tibeto-Burman languages; the Thai languages; and possibly Miao (Meo) and Yao, spoken in S China and SE Asia.

**sinus** Hollow space or cavity, usually in bone. Most often the term refers to the paranasal sinuses, any of the four sets of air-filled cavities in the skull near the nose.

**Sioux** (Dakota) Group of seven NATIVE AMERICAN tribes inhabiting Minnesota, Nebraska, North and South Dakota, and Montana. In the 18th century they numbered *c*.30,000. The largest of the tribes was the Teton. The Sioux hunted buffalo and held sun dances. They opposed US forces in the American Revolution and the War of 1812. The tribes concluded several treaties with the US government (1815, 1825, 1851), and finally agreed in 1867 to settle on a reservation in SW Dakota. The discovery of gold in the Black Hills and the rush of prospectors brought resistance from Sioux chiefs such as SITTING BULL and CRAZY HORSE. In 1876 they defeated General CUSTER at the Battle of LITTLE BIGHORN. The last confrontation was the Massacre at WOUNDED KNEE (1890), which resulted in the massacre of more than 200 Sioux. Today, the Sioux number more than 50,000.

**siren** Aquatic, tailed AMPHIBIAN of North America. The adult

◄ **sitar** Originally developed in India in the 14th century, the sitar is either played solo or in an ensemble, with tabla (small kettle-drums) and a tambura (a lutelike instrument that produces a droning sound). Popularized by Ravi Shankar, it has also been used in Western music since the 1960s.

S

is neotenic (reaches sexual maturity while retaining the larval physical form). These eel-like animals have external gills, tiny forelegs, and minute eyes. They have no hind legs. Length: to 36in (92cm). Family Sirenidae. *See also* SALAMANDER

**Sirens** In Greek mythology, three sea nymphs with women's heads and bird's bodies. They lived on a rocky island near the straits of Messina, home to SCYLLA and CHARYBDIS, and their beautiful singing was believed to attract sailors on to the rocks.

**Sirius** (Alpha Canis Majoris, Dog Star) Brightest star visible from Earth, in the northern constellation of Canis Major. Its luminosity is 23 times that of the Sun.

**sirocco** Hot, dry, sand-laden wind that blows N from the Sahara Desert, picking up moisture from the Mediterranean, and bringing oppressive weather to that region.

**Sistine Chapel** Private chapel of the popes in the VATICAN, painted by some of the greatest artists of RENAISSANCE Italy. It was built between 1473 and 1481 for Pope Sixtus IV. The side walls were decorated with FRESCOS by PERUGINO, Pinturicchio, BOTTICELLI, GHIRLANDAIO, and Signorelli. Its most celebrated features are the ceiling, window lunettes, and altar wall painted by MICHELANGELO between 1508 and 1541.

**Sisulu, Walter** (1912– ) South African civil rights activist, a fierce opponent of APARTHEID. Sisulu became secretary general of the AFRICAN NATIONAL CONGRESS (ANC) in 1949. The ANC was declared illegal in 1961 and Sisulu, Nelson MANDELA, and six others were sentenced (1964) to life imprisonment. In 1989 Sisulu was released (1989) by F.W. DE KLERK and, after the legalization of the ANC, became its deputy president (1991–94).

**Sisyphus** In Greek mythology, founder and king of Corinth. He was punished for trying to trick Thanatos (Death) by being condemned to the underworld to work for eternity, pushing a rock to the top of a steep hill. The rock rolled back to the base of the hill as soon as Sisyphus reached the summit.

**SKELETON**

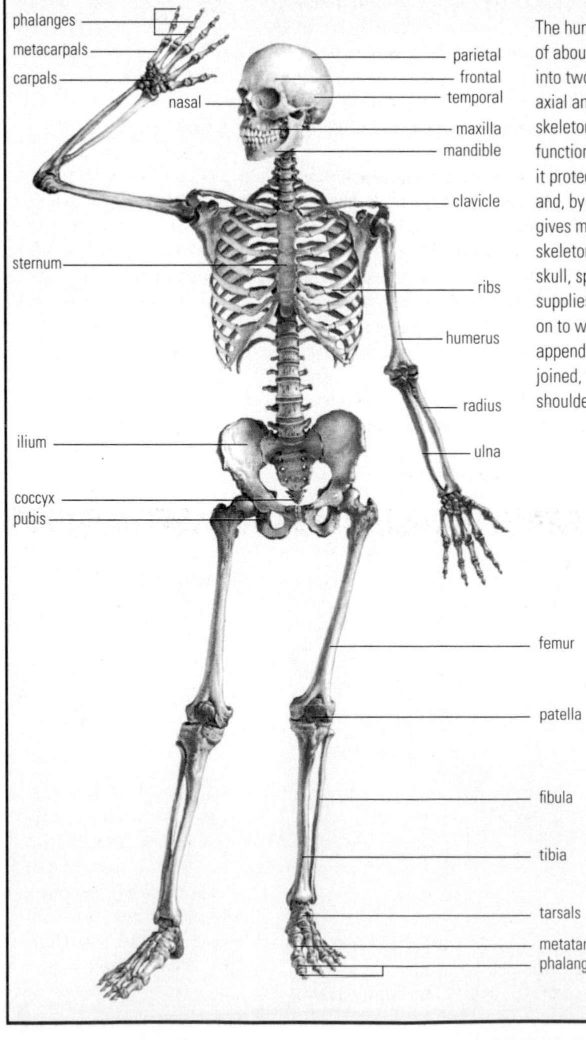

The human skeleton consists of about 206 bones divided into two broad groups, the axial and appendicular skeletons. It has three functions: it supplies support; it protects the internal organs; and, by using muscles, it gives movement. The axial skeleton, consisting of the skull, spine, and rib cage, supplies the basic structure on to which the limbs, the appendicular skeleton, are joined, via the pelvic and shoulder girdles.

**sitar** Indian stringed musical instrument with a gourdlike body and long neck. It has three to seven strings, tuned in fourths or fifths, and a lower course of 12 strings. Ravi SHANKAR is one of its greatest players. *See* illustration on page 615

**Sitting Bull** (1831–90) Native American leader, chief of the SIOUX. With others, he led the attack on General CUSTER's cavalry at the Battle of LITTLE BIGHORN (1876). In 1881 Sitting Bull was captured and imprisoned for two years. Later, he joined the Wild West Show of Buffalo Bill. In 1890 Sitting Bull initiated a new Ghost Dance to protect Sioux braves. He was killed resisting arrest.

**Sitwell, Dame Edith** (1887–1964) English poet. Her anthology *Wheels* (1916) encouraged experimentalism in British verse. Sitwell contributed the words to WALTON's *Façade* (1922). She also wrote a biography of Alexander POPE (1930) and the *English Eccentrics* (1933).

**Sitwell, Sir Osbert** (1892–1969) English writer, brother of Dame Edith SITWELL. He wrote the words for WALTON's *Belshazzar's Feast* (1931). Sitwell is best known for his five volumes of family history, including *Left Hand, Right Hand* (1945) and *Noble Essences* (1950).

**SI units** (Système International d'Unites) Internationally agreed system of units, derived from the mks (meter, kilogram, and second) system. SI units are now used for many scientific purposes and have replaced the fps (foot, pound, and second) and cgs (centimeter, gram, and second) systems. The seven basic units are: the METER (m), KILOGRAM (kg), SECOND (s), AMPERE (A), KELVIN (K), MOLE (mol), and CANDELA (cd).

**Six, Les** Collective name for six French composers who were organized as a group by Jean COCTEAU in 1917. The members were Georges Auric, Louis Durey, Arthur HONEGGER, Darius MILHAUD, Francis POULENC, and Germaine Tailleferre.

**Six Day War** (1967) Episode of the ARAB-ISRAELI WARS. Israeli forces rapidly defeated the four Arab states (Egypt, Jordan, Syria, and Iraq). Israel gained control of the old city of Jerusalem, Jordanian territory on the WEST BANK (of the Jordan River), the GOLAN HEIGHTS, and the SINAI PENINSULA, including the GAZA STRIP.

**Six Nations** *See* IROQUOIS CONFEDERACY

**skating** *See* ICE SKATING; ROLLER SKATING

**skeet** *See* SHOOTING

**skeletal muscle** In human beings and other mammals, the most plentiful of the three types of MUSCLE comprising the bulk of the body. It is also known as **voluntary muscle** because it is under conscious control, or as striated muscle because of its characteristic striped appearance under the microscope. *See also* INVOLUNTARY MUSCLE

**skeleton** Bony framework of the body of a VERTEBRATE. It supports and protects the internal organs, provides sites of attachment for muscles, and a system of levers to aid locomotion. *See also* EXOSKELETON

**Skelton, John** (1460–1529) English poet. He was tutor to the young Henry VIII, and took holy orders in 1498. Skelton wrote satires on the court, the clergy, and Cardinal WOLSEY. His work includes *Speak, Parrot*, *Colin Clout*, *Why Came Ye Not to Court*, and the long secular morality play *Magnyficence* (c.1516).

**skepticism** Philosophical attitude that asserts the limited nature of knowledge and questions the validity of SUBJECTIVE perception. The SOPHISTS were the first group of skeptics. PYRRHO's extreme skepticism argued that definite knowledge is impossible and that reality is inaccessible. *See also* HUME, David ; KANT, Immanuel

**skiing** Method of "skating" on snow using flat runners (skis) made of various materials, attached to ski boots; the skier may also use hand-held poles to assist balance. The principal forms of competitive skiing are Alpine skiing, ski jumping, cross-country skiing, and freestyle skiing. Freestyle skiing was added to the Winter Olympic schedule in 1994; the other disciplines have been Olympic sports since 1924.

**skin** Tough, elastic outer covering of invertebrates. In mammals, it is the largest organ of the body and serves many functions. It protects the body from injury and from the entry of some microorganisms, and prevents dehydration. Nerve endings in the skin provide the sensations of touch, warmth, cold, and pain. It helps to regulate body temperature through sweating, regulates moisture loss, and keeps itself smooth and pliable with an oily secretion from the SEBACEOUS GLANDS. Structurally, the skin consists of two main layers: an outer layer (EPIDERMIS) and an inner layer (DERMIS). The top layer of epidermis is made of closely packed dead cells constantly shed as microscopic scales. Below this is a layer of living cells that contain pigment and nerve fibers; they divide to replace outer layers. The dermis contains dense networks of connective tissue, blood vessels, nerves, glands, and hair follicles.

**skin diving** *See* SCUBA DIVING

**skink** Common name for more than 600 species of LIZARDS found in mild and tropical regions. They have cylindrical bodies covered with shiny scales, cone-shaped heads, and tapering tails. They eat small insects, plants, or other lizards. Length: to 26in (66cm). Family Scincidae.

**Skinner, Burrhus Fredric** (1904–90) US psychologist. He developed the concept of operant conditioning (control of behavior by its consequences or reinforcements). His books include *Science and Human Behavior* (1953), *Beyond Freedom and Dignity* (1971), and a controversial novel about social engineering, *Walden II* (1948).

**Skopje** Capital of Macedonia, on the Vardar River. Founded by the Romans, it became the capital of the Serbian empire in the 14th century, fell to the Turks in 1392, and was incorporated into Yugoslavia in 1918. It became capital of Macedonia in 1945. Much of Skopje was destroyed in a 1963 earthquake. Industries: metals, textiles, chemicals. Pop. (1994) 440,577.

**skull** (cranium) In vertebrates, brain case that supports and protects the brain, eyes, ears, nose, and mouth.

**skunk** Nocturnal, omnivorous mammal that lives in the US and Central and South America. It has powerful anal scent glands, which eject a foul-smelling liquid, used in defense. It has a small head, and a slender, thickly furred body with short legs and a large, bushy tail. The coat is black with bold white warning markings along the back. The most common species is the striped skunk, *Mephitis mephitis*. Length: to 15in (38cm); weight: 10lb (4.5kg). Family Mustelidae.

**Skye** Largest island in the Inner Hebrides, off the NW coast of Scotland. The chief town is Portree. Its spectacular scenery makes it a popular vacation attraction. A bridge to the mainland was opened in 1996. Occupations include rearing livestock, weaving, and fishing. Area: 670sq mi (1,735sq km). Pop. (1991) 8,139.

**slander** In law, oral defamation of a person's character made in the presence of one or more witnesses. *See also* LIBEL

**slate** Gray to blue, fine-grained, homogeneous METAMORPHIC ROCK, which splits into smooth, thin layers. It is formed by the metamorphosis of SHALE, and is valuable as a roofing material.

**Slav** Largest ethnic and linguistic group of peoples in Europe. Slavs are generally classified in three main divisions: the East Slavs, the largest division, include the Ukrainians, Russians, and Belorussians; the South Slavs include the Serbs, Croats, Macedonians, and Slovenes (and frequently also the Bulgarians); the West Slavs comprise chiefly the Poles, Czechs, Slovaks, and Wends.

**slavery** Social system in which people are the property of their owner, and are compelled to work without pay. Slavery of some kind was common to practically all ancient societies and to most modern societies until the 19th century. Common in ancient Egyptian, Roman, and Greek societies, an extreme form of slavery also existed in the Americas from the 16th century, where the need for cheap labor in European colonies was not satisfied by enslaving Native Americans or by acquiring poor Europeans as servants. This situation gave rise to the highly organized and profitable **Atlantic triangle slave trade**. Ships sailed from ports such as LIVERPOOL with guns and other goods, which were exchanged for slaves in states on West African coasts. The slaves were sold in markets in the Caribbean, Brazil, and North America, mainly to work on farms and plantations. On the return journey, the ships carried colonial produce from the Americas to Europe. An estimated 15 million Africans were sold into slavery. Millions more died on the voyage

## SKIN

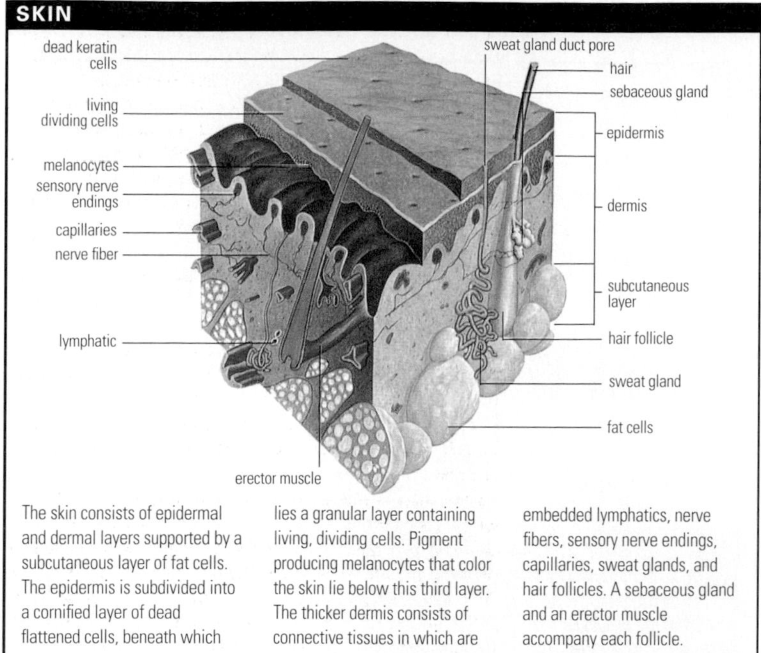


The skin consists of epidermal and dermal layers supported by a subcutaneous layer of fat cells. The epidermis is subdivided into a cornified layer of dead flattened cells, beneath which lies a granular layer containing living, dividing cells. Pigment producing melanocytes that color the skin lie below this third layer. The thicker dermis consists of connective tissues in which are embedded lymphatics, nerve fibers, sensory nerve endings, capillaries, sweat glands, and hair follicles. A sebaceous gland and an erector muscle accompany each follicle.

**Slavic languages** (Slavonic languages) Group of languages spoken in E Europe and the former Soviet Union, constituting a major subdivision of the family of INDO-EUROPEAN LANGUAGES. The main ones in use today are Russian, Ukrainian, and Belorussian (East Slavic); Polish, Czech, Slovak, and Sorbian or Lusatian, a language spoken in E Germany (West Slavic); and Bulgarian, Serbo-Croat, Slovenian, and Macedonian (South Slavic). Some Slavic languages are written in the Cyrillic alphabet, others in the Roman.

**sleep** Periodic state of unconsciousness from which a person or animal can be roused. During an ordinary night's sleep there are intervals of deep sleep associated with rapid eye movement (REM) sleep. It is during this REM sleep that dreaming occurs. *See also* DREAM

**slime mold** Any of a small group of strange, basically single-celled organisms that are intermediate between the plant and animal kingdoms. During their complex life cycle they pass through several stages. These include a flagellated swimming stage, an amoebalike stage, a stage consisting of a slimy mass of protoplasm with many nuclei, and a flowering sporangium stage.

**slipped disc** (prolapsed intervertebral disk) Protrusion of

▲ **sloth** Like only a few other herbivores, sloths survive on a particularly poor diet of tough leaves by means of a lifestyle that involves very little expenditure of energy. They sleep a lot and move extremely slowly. In fact, they have only half the musculature of most mammals, and their food may take a whole week to pass through the digestive system. The two-toed sloth (*Choleopus*), shown here, has two toes on its front legs and three on its back legs.

## SLIME MOLD

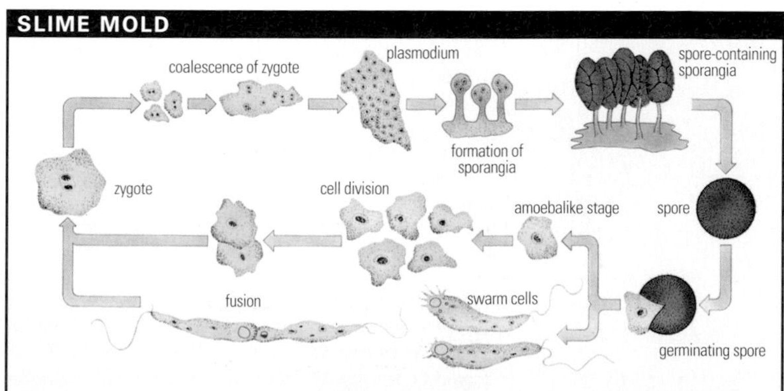


The slime molds (Myxomycetales) are a primitive group of organisms that although sometimes classed as a fungi, have certain characteristics, particularly those associated with nutrition, which are more protozoan. During one stage of their life-cycle they form aggregates of cells that resemble and move like *amoebas*. However, the slime molds are also like lower plants in spore formation.

## SLOVENIA

**AREA:** 7,817sq mi (20,251sq km)
**POPULATION:** 1,996,000
**CAPITAL (POPULATION):** Ljubljana (268,000)
**GOVERNMENT:** Multiparty republic
**ETHNIC GROUPS:** Slovene 88%, Croat 3%, Serb 2%, Bosnian 1%
**LANGUAGES:** Slovene
**RELIGIONS:** Christianity (mainly Roman Catholic)
**CURRENCY:** Tolar = 100 stotin

the soft, inner core of an intervertebral disc through its covering, causing pressure on the spinal nerve roots. It is caused by a sudden mechanical force on the spine. It leads to stiffness and SCIATICA.

**sloe** *See* BLACKTHORN

**sloth** Any of several species of slow-moving, herbivorous mammals of Central and South America. It has long limbs with long claws and spends most of its life in trees, where it generally hangs upside down. Length: to 2ft (60cm); weight: to 12lb (5.5kg). Family Brachipodidae.

**Slovak** Official language of the Slovak Republic, spoken by *c.*5 million people. It is closely related to Czech.

**Slovak Republic** (Slovakia) Republic in central Europe. *See* country feature

**Slovenia** Mountainous republic in SE Europe; the capital is LJUBLJANA. The Republic of Slovenia was one of the six republics that made up the former YUGOSLAVIA. Much of the land is mountainous, rising to 9,393ft (2,863m) at Mount Triglav in the Julian Alps in the NW. Central and E Slovenia contain hills and plains drained by the Drava and Sava rivers, while W Slovenia contains the Karst region, an area of limestone landscapes. Here, surface water flows downward through swallow holes into deep caves, including the Postojna caves near Ljubljana, which are the largest in Europe. **Climate** The short coast has a mild Mediterranean climate, but inland the climate is more continental. The mountains are snowcapped in winter and most of Slovenia has cold winters and hot summers. Rain occurs in every month in Ljubljana and late summer is the rainiest season. **Vegetation** Farmland covers about 35% of the land and forests another 50%. **History and Politics** The ancestors of the Slovenes, the W branch of the South Slavs, settled in the area around 1,400 years ago. For most of the time from the 13th century until 1918, Slovenia was ruled by the Austrian HAPSBURGS. In 1918 Slovenia became part of the Kingdom of the Serbs, Croats, and Slovenes, which was renamed Yugoslavia in 1929. During World War II, Slovenia was invaded and partitioned between Italy, Germany, and Hungary, but after the war, Slovenia again became part of Yugoslavia. From the late 1960s, some Slovenes demanded independence, but the central Yugoslav government opposed the breakup of the federation. In 1990 elections were held and a noncommunist coalition government was established. Slovenia declared itself independent, which led to brief fighting between Slovenes and the federal army. Slovenia did not, however, become a battlefield like other parts of the former Yugoslavia. In 1992 the European Community recognized Slovenia's independence and further elections were held. In 1993 a coalition government, led by the Liberal Democrats, was set up. In 1996 Slovenia applied to join the European Union (EU). **Economy** Slovenia is an upper-middle-income developing country (1992 GDP per capita US$6,500). The transformation of a centrally planned economy, and the fighting in other parts of former Yugoslavia, have caused problems for Slovenia. Manufacturing is the leading activity. Major manufactures include chemicals, machinery, transportation equipment, metal goods, and textiles. Major crops include corn, fuit, potatoes, and wheat.

**slowworm** (blindworm) European snakelike, legless lizard of grassy areas and woodlands. It is generally brownish; the female has a black underside. It has pointed teeth and feeds primarily on slugs and snails. Length: to 12in (30cm). Family Anguidae; species *Anguis fragilis*.

**slug** Mostly terrestrial, gastropod MOLLUSK, identified by the lack of shell and uncoiled viscera. It secretes a protective slime, which is also used to aid locomotion. Length: to 8in (20cm). Class Gastropoda; subclass Pulmonata; genera *Arion, Limax. See also* SEA SLUG

**small intestine** Part of the DIGESTIVE SYSTEM that, in humans, extends – about 20ft (6m) coiled and looped – from the STOMACH to the large INTESTINE, or colon. Its function is the digestion and absorption of food. *See also* DUODENUM; ILEUM

**smallpox** Formerly a highly contagious viral disease characterized by fever, vomiting, and skin eruption. It remained endemic until the World Health Organization (WHO) vaccination campaign, launched in the late 1960s. Global eradication was achieved by 1980.

**smell** (olfaction) Sense that responds to airborne molecules. The olfactory receptors in the nose can detect even a few molecules per million parts of air.

**smelt** Small, silvery food fish related to SALMON and TROUT. It lives in the N Atlantic and Pacific oceans and in North American inland waters. Family Osmeridae.

**smelting** Heat treatment for separating metals from their ORES. The ore, often with other ingredients, is heated in a furnace to remove nonmetallic constituents. The metal produced is later purified.

**Smetana, Bedřich** (1824–84) Czech composer. His masterpiece, *The Bartered Bride* (1866), is one of the greatest folk operas. Among other popular works by Smetana is the cycle of symphonic poems *Má Vlast* (My Country, 1874–79), which includes the *Vltava*.

**Smirke, Robert** (1781–1867) English neoclassical architect, one of the chief promoters of the CLASSICAL REVIVAL in British architecture. Smirke's most famous building is the Brtish Museum, begun in 1823.

**Smith, Adam** (1723–90) Scottish philosopher, regarded as the founder of modern economics. His book *The Wealth of Nations* (1776) was enormously influential in the development of Western CAPITALISM. It outlined the theory of the DIVISION OF LABOR. In place of MERCANTILISM, Smith proposed the doctrine of LAISSEZ–FAIRE: that governments should not interfere in economic affairs and that FREE TRADE increases wealth.

**Smith, Alfred Emanuel** (1873–1944) US politician. He was governor of New York (1919–20, 1923–28), supporting social welfare legislation and public works projects. A candidate for the presidential nomination in 1924, he ran in 1928 but lost the election to Herbert HOOVER.

**Smith, Bessie** (1895–1937) US singer, known as the "Empress of the BLUES." In 1923 Smith made her recording debut and sold more than two million records. Her powerful voice and poignant phrasing accompanied early jazz greats, such as Louis ARMSTRONG. Her popularity plummeted during the Depression. Smith died after being refused treatment at a whites-only hospital following a serious car accident.

**Smith, David** (1906–65) US sculptor. He is perhaps the most important US sculptor of the 20th century. Influenced by CUBISM and PICASSO in particular, in 1933 Smith began to work in metal. His welded sculptures often incorporated machinery parts. Smith's works are non-representational, but evoke suggestions of landscape or still life. From the 1950s he worked on the *Cubi* series. These are mostly vertical constructions built up from cylinders of polished stainless steel.

**Smith, Ian Douglas** (1919– ) Rhodesian statesman, prime minister (1964–78). He founded (1961) the Rhodesia Front Party, and sought independence from Britain. In 1965

Smith's white minority regime issued a unilateral declaration of independence (UDI). Persistent international sanctions and guerrilla warfare forced his government to accept free elections (1980). Smith was defeated by Robert MUGABE's Zimbabwe African National Union (ZANU). He continued to lead white opposition.

**Smith, John** (1580–1631) English soldier and colonist. He was instrumental in establishing the first English colony in North America, at JAMESTOWN (1607). Exploring Chesapeake Bay, Smith was captured by POWHATAN and possibly saved from death by Powhatan's daughter, POCAHONTAS. In 1608, by obtaining corn from the local people, Smith saved the colony from starvation. In 1609 he returned to England.

**Smith, Joseph** (1805–44) US religious leader and founder of the MORMON Church of Jesus Christ of the Latter Day Saints (1830). His *Book of Mormon* (1830) was based on writings he claimed were given to him on golden plates by a heavenly messenger named Moroni. In 1830 Smith led his followers to found the New Zion. In 1844 he was jailed on a charge of treason at Carthage, Illinois, where he was murdered by a mob.

**Smith, Stevie** (1902–71) English poet, b. Florence Margaret Smith. She first came to public notice with *Novel on Yellow Paper* (1936). Smith's witty and often pathetic poetry was collected in 1975 and includes the title poem of her 1957 volume *Not Waving But Drowning*.

**Smithsonian Institution** US independent trust, based in Washington, D.C. Created in 1846, the Institution funds research, publishes the results of explorations and investigations, and preserves for reference more than 65 million items of scientific, cultural, and historical interest. These are housed in the nation's largest group of museums, which include the National Gallery of Art and the National Air and Space Museum.

**smog** Dense atmospheric mixture of smoke and fog or chemical fumes, commonly occurring in urban or industrial areas. It is most dense during temperature inversions.

**Smolensk** City on the upper reaches of the Dnieper River, E Russia, near the Belarus border, capital of Smolensk oblast. It was an important medieval commercial center on the routes from Byzantium to the Baltic, and from Moscow to Warsaw. The capital of Belorussia in the 12th century, it was sacked (1238–1240) by the Mongols. During the 15th and 16th centuries it was a battleground for Polish and Russian forces. In 1812 Napoleon I seized the city and burned it in retreat from the Russian army. Occupied by Germans from 1941 to 1943, it

## SLOVAK REPUBLIC

This flag, using the typical red, white, and blue Slavonic colors, dates back to 1848. The Slovak Republic adopted it in September 1992, prior to independence on January 1, 1994. The three blue mounds in the shield represent three mountain ranges.

**AREA:** 18,932sq mi (49,035sq km)
**POPULATION:** 5,297,000
**CAPITAL (POPULATION):** Bratislava (440,421)
**GOVERNMENT:** Multiparty republic
**ETHNIC GROUPS:** Slovak, Hungarian, with small groups of Czechs, Germans, Gypsies, Poles, Russians, and Ukrainians
**LANGUAGES:** Slovak (official)
**RELIGIONS:** Christianity (Roman Catholic 60%, Protestant 6%, Orthodox 3%)
**CURRENCY:** Slovak koruna

The Slovak Republic (Slovakia) in central Europe is dominated by the CARPATHIAN MOUNTAINS. The Tatra range on the N border include the republic's highest peak, Gerlachovka, at 8,711ft (2,655m). To the S is a fertile lowland, drained by the DANUBE River, on whose banks stands the capital, BRATISLAVA.

### CLIMATE

The Slovak Republic has a continental climate, with cold, dry winters and warm, wet summers. Bratislava has average temperatures ranging from −3°C (27°F) in January to 68°F (20°C) in July, and an average annual rainfall of 24in (600mm). The highlands are much colder and wetter.

### VEGETATION

Forests cover 41% of the Slovak republic. Evergreen trees predominate in the mountains. Beech, birch, linden, and oak are more characterstic of lowland areas. Arable land accounts for another 31% of land use.

### HISTORY

Slavic peoples settled in the region in the 5th and 6th centuries AD. In the 9th century the area formed part of the empire of MORAVIA. In the 10th century it was conquered by the MAGYARS, and for nearly 900 years the region was dominated by Hungary. At the end of the 11th century, it was subsumed into the kingdom of Hungary. In the 16th century, the Ottoman empire conquered much of Hungary, and Slovakia was divided between the Turks and the Austrians. From 1541–1784 Bratislava served as the Hapsburg capital. The joint rule of MARIA THERESA and JOSEPH II pursued a policy of Magyarization, which increased nationalist sentiment. The AUSTRO-HUNGARIAN EMPIRE was formed in 1867, and continued the suppression of native culture. Many Slovaks fled to the US. During World War I, Slovak patriots fought on the side of the Allies. After the defeat of Austro-Hungary (1918), Slovakia was incorporated into Czechoslovakia as an autonomous region (for 1918–93 history, *see also* CZECHOSLOVAKIA)

The Czechs dominated the union, and many Slovaks became dissatisfied. Following the MUNICH PACT (1938), part of Slovakia became an independent state, while much of S Slovenia (including Kosice) was ceded to Hungary. In March 1939 Slovakia gained nominal independence as a German protectorate. In August 1939 Hitler invaded Czechoslovakia, and Slovakia became a Nazi puppet state. In 1944 Soviet troops liberated Slovakia, and in 1945 it returned to Czechoslovakia. The Prague Spring (1968) saw the introduction of a federal structure, which survived the Soviet invasion. The dramatic collapse of Czech communism in 1989 spurred calls for independence. Elections in 1992 were won by the Movement for a Democratic Slovakia, led by Vladimir Mečiar. The federation was dissolved on January 1, 1993, and the Slovak Republic became a sovereign state, with Mečiar as prime minister.

### POLITICS

The Slovak Republic has maintained close relations with the Czech Republic. In 1996 the Slovak Republic and Hungary ratified a treaty enshrining their respective borders and stipulating basic rights for the 560,000 Hungarians in the Slovak Republic. Following elections in 1998, a coalition government was formed, led by Mikulas Dzurinda of the Slovak Democratic Coalition.

### ECONOMY

Before 1948 the economy was primarily agrarian. Communism developed industry. Post-independence governments have attempted to diversify industrial ownership and production. The transition was painful: industrial output fell, unemployment and inflation rose (1995 GDP per capita, US$3,610). In 1995 the privatization programme was suspended. Manufacturing employs 33% of the workforce. Bratislava and Kosice are the chief industrial cities. Major products include ceramics, machinery and steel. Farming employs 12% of the workforce. Crops include barley and grapes. Tourism is growing.

S

saw some of World War II's fiercest fighting. It is an important transportation and distribution center. Industries: linen, textile machines, timber, electrical goods, flour milling, distilling, brewing. Pop. (1994) 353,000.

**Smollett, Tobias George** (1721–71) Scottish novelist and surgeon. *The Adventures of Peregrine Pickle* (1751) was in a typically bawdy, PICARESQUE vein. His masterpiece is *The Expedition of Humphrey Clinker* (1771), a comic, epistolary novel. Smollett also translated Voltaire and Cervantes.

**smooth muscle** *See* INVOLUNTARY MUSCLE

**smut** Group of plant diseases caused by parasitic fungi, also called smuts, that attack many cereals. The diseases are named for the sooty black masses of reproductive spores produced by the fungi. *See also* PARASITE

**Smuts, Jan Christiaan** (1870–1950) South African statesman, prime minister (1919–24, 1939–48). He was a guerrilla commander during the SOUTH AFRICAN WARS (1899–1902), but afterwards worked with Louis BOTHA to establish the Union of South Africa (1910). During World War I, Smuts suppressed a pro-German revolt, commanded British forces in East Africa, and became a member of the British war cabinet. Upon Botha's death, he succeeded as prime minister. Smuts formed a second administration after James HERTZOG opposed entry into World War II. After the war, he was defeated by the APARTHEID policies of the Nationalist Party.

**Smyrna** *See* IZMIR

**snail** Terrestrial, marine, or freshwater gastropod mollusk. It has a large fleshy foot, antennae on its head, and a coiled protective shell encasing an asymmetric visceral mass. It may breathe through gills (aquatic species) or through a kind of air-breathing lung (terrestrial species), and has a radula – a rasping organ in its mouth. Some species, such as the Roman snail (*Helix pomatia*), are edible. Length: to 14in (35cm). Class Gastropoda.

**snake** Any of *c*.2,700 species of legless, elongated REPTILES forming the suborder Serpentes of the order Squamata (which also includes LIZARDS). There are 11 families. They range in length from *c*.4in (10cm) to more than 30ft (9m). There are terrestrial, arboreal, semiaquatic, and aquatic species; one group is entirely marine; many are poisonous. They have no external ear openings, eardrums, or middle ears; sound vibrations are detected through the ground. Their eyelids are immovable and their eyes are covered by a transparent protective cover. The long, forked, protractile tongue is used to detect odors. Their bodies are covered with scales. Poisonous snakes have hollow or grooved fangs, through which they inject venom into their prey. *See* individual species

**snakebite** Result of an injection of potentially lethal SNAKE venom into the bloodstream. There are three types of venomous snake: the **Viperidae**, subdivided into true VIPERS and pit vipers, whose venom causes internal hemorrhage; the **Elapidae** (including COBRAS, MAMBAS, kraits), whose venom paralyzes the nervous system; and the **Hydrophidae**, Pacific sea snakes with venom that disables the muscles. Treatment is with antivenoms.

**snapdragon** Any of several species of perennial plants of the genus *Antirrhinum*, with saclike, two-lipped, purple, red, yellow, or white flowers. The common snapdragon (*A. majus*) is a popular garden plant. Height: 0.5–3ft (15–91cm). Family Scrophulariaceae.

**snapper** Marine food fish found in tropical waters of the Indo-Pacific and Atlantic oceans. Length: to 3ft (90cm); weight: 110lb (50kg). Family Lutjanidae.

**snipe** Any of several species of migratory, long-billed shorebirds found in swamps and coastal areas worldwide. It is generally mottled brown and buff. Length: 12in (30cm). Family Scolopacidae; genus *Gallinago*.

► **snail** Remarkably adept at exploring new habitats, snails originated in the sea, but over the course of time some 22,000 species adapted to life on dry land, losing their gills and evolving air-breathing lungs. Most species of land snail of the genus *Helix*, shown here, live on the ground and are dull in coloration. A few species are arboreal: these tend to be brightly colored. Others have returned to aquatic environments and must surface periodically to breathe.

**Snorri Sturluson** (1179–1241) Icelandic poet and historian. His *Prose Edda* is a collection of Norse mythology and a discussion of the art of poetry. *Heimskringla*, SAGAS of the Norwegian kings to 1184, mingles NORSE LITERATURE, history, and legend.

**Snow, C.P. (Charles Percy), Baron** (1905–80) English novelist, scientist, and civil servant. He is especially remembered for his lecture *The Two Cultures and the Scientific Revolution* (1959), which diagnosed a radical divide between scientists and literary intellectuals. Snow also wrote an 11-volume novel sequence, known collectively as *Strangers and Brothers* (1940–70); it includes *The Corridors of Power* (1963).

**snow** Flakes of frozen water that fall from clouds to the Earth's surface. Snowflakes are symmetric (usually hexagonal) crystalline structures. *See also* PRECIPITATION

**snowdrop** Low-growing, perennial plant of the Mediterranean region, widely cultivated as a garden ornamental. The drooping, green and white, fragrant flowers appear early in spring. The common snowdrop (*Galanthus nivalis*) has narrow leaves; height: to 6in (15cm). Family Amaryllidaceae.

**Soane, Sir John** (1753–1837) British architect. One of the most original of all British architects, he developed his own personal style of CLASSICISM. He designed the Bank of England (1795–1827).

**Sobers, Sir Gary (Garfield St Aubrun)** (1936– ) Barbadian cricketer, perhaps the game's greatest all-rounder. Sobers played 93 test matches for West Indies (39 as captain), scoring 8,032 runs and taking 235 wickets. He played county cricket for Nottinghamshire and, against Glamorgan (1968), became the first player to score six sixes in an over in first-class cricket.

**soap** Cleansing agent made of salts of fatty acids, used to remove dirt and grease. Common soaps are produced by heating fats and oils with an alkali, such as sodium hydroxide or potassium hydroxide. Soap consists of long-chain molecules; one end of the chain attaches to grease while the other end dissolves in the water, causing the grease to loosen and form a floating scum. *See also* DETERGENT

**soccer** (association football) Arguably the most popular worldwide ball game. It involves 2 teams of 11 players who attempt to force a round ball into their opponents' goal. It is played on a rectangular field of maximum size 390 × 300ft (120 × 90m), minimum 300 × 150ft (90 × 45m). The goals are 24ft (7.32m) wide by 8ft (2.44m) high. Only the goalkeeper may handle the ball, and then only in the penalty area of the goal he is defending. The other players may play the ball in any direction with any other part of the body; essentially it is kicked or headed. The game is played over two 45-minute periods. Modern soccer rules were formulated in 19th-century England, and the Football Association (FA) was founded in 1863. Soccer soon spread beyond Britain, and in 1904 FIFA (*Fédération internationale de football association*) was formed to control the sport at world level. Soccer has been played at the Olympic Games since 1908. The first of the quadrennial World Cup competitions was held in 1930.

**social contract** Concept that society is based on the surrender of natural freedoms by the individual to the organized group or state in exchange for personal security. The concept can be traced back to the ancient Greeks. It was developed by Thomas HOBBES and John LOCKE, and by Jean Jacques ROUSSEAU in *The Social Contract* (1762).

**social democracy** Political ideology concerning the introduction of socialist ideals without an immediate overhaul of the prevailing political system. Before 1914 MARXIST parties of central and E Europe termed themselves social democrats. Contemporary social democracy, however, has been invoked by those wishing to distinguish their socialist beliefs from the dogmas of Marxist parties. *See also* CHRISTIAN DEMOCRATS; SOCIAL DEMOCRATIC LABOUR PARTY (SDLP)

**Social Democratic Labour Party (SDLP)** Political party in Northern Ireland that leans toward SOCIALISM. It favors eventual unification of the province with the Republic of Ireland. Founded in 1970, its leader from 1983 was civil rights activist John HUME. The party seeks to use nonviolent, constitutional methods to attain its goals.

**social history** Branch of HISTORY focusing on the ordinary lifestyle of people in communities of all types and sizes at specific times and places. *See also* ETHNOLOGY

**socialism** System of social and economic organization in which the means of production are owned not by private individuals but by the community, in order that all may share more fairly in the wealth produced. Modern socialism dates from the late 18th and early 19th centuries. Many forms of socialism exist both in theory and in practice, differing over such questions as the degree of state control and the rights of individuals. With the REVOLUTIONS OF 1848, socialism became a significant political doctrine in Europe. Karl MARX, whose *Communist Manifesto* was published in that year, believed that socialism was to be achieved only through the CLASS struggle. Thereafter, a division appeared between the revolutionary socialism of Marx and his followers, later called COMMUNISM or Marxism-Leninism, and more moderate doctrines that held that socialism could be achieved through education and the democratic process. In Russia, the revolutionary tradition culminated in the RUSSIAN REVOLUTION of 1917. From the moderate wing, social-democratic parties, such as the British LABOUR PARTY, emerged. They were largely instrumental in mitigating the effects of the market economy in w Europe through political measures and by securing social justice and welfare. *See also* LENIN, VLADIMIR ILYICH

**Socialist Party** US political party. It was formed in 1901 by the unification of the Social Democratic Party and the Socialist Labor Party. Dedicated to the state ownership of all public utilities and important industries, its best-known leaders were Eugene V. DEBS and Norman Thomas.

**socialist realism** State policy on the arts, promoted by the Soviet Union from the 1930s to the 1980s. It asserted that all the arts should appeal to ordinary workers and should be inspiring and optimistic in spirit. Art that did not fulfill these precepts was effectively banned, and most serious writers, artists, and composers were forced underground or into exile.

**social psychology** Field that studies individuals interacting with others in groups and with society. Topics include attitudes and how they change, prejudice, rumors, aggression, altruism, group behavior, conformity, and social conflict. There is some overlap with SOCIOLOGY.

**social security** Public provision of economic aid to help alleviate poverty and deprivation. In 1883 Germany became the first country to adopt social security legislation. By the end of the 1920s, public social security provisions had been adopted throughout Europe. In 1909 the UK adopted an old-age pension scheme, and in 1911 LLOYD GEORGE drafted the National Insurance Act to provide health and unemployment insurance. In the US, as part of the NEW DEAL, the Social Security Act (1935) was adopted. It provided unemployment compensation, old-age pensions, and federal grants for state welfare programs, but covered only those in commercial and industrial occupations. This was expanded in 1939. In 1965 Congress enacted the Medicare program, which provided medical benefits for persons over 65 and the Medicaid program for the poor. Such programs have proved costly, and many governments are seeking to encourage private provision.

**Social Security Administration** Division of the US Department of Health and Social Services that is responsible for administering Federal Social Security programs. *See also* SOCIAL SECURITY

**social work** Community assistance and/or care. Social workers monitor the well-being of families known to have problems, and sometimes have the power to remove children from parents deemed to be dangerously violent or abusive. They may be asked to assist the police in dealing with juvenile suspects. They also help various handicapped, homeless, or unemployed people.

**Society Islands** South Pacific archipelago, part of FRENCH POLYNESIA; the capital is PAPEETE on TAHITI. The archipelago is divided into two groups of mountainous, volcanic, and coral islands. Only eight are inhabited. The larger **Windward** group includes the islands of Tahiti, Moorea, Maio, and the smaller Mehetia and Tetiaroa. The **Leeward** group includes Raiatéa (the largest and site of the chief town, Uturoa), Tahaa, Huahine, Bora-Bora, and Maupiti. Tourism is the most important industry, with 148,000 people visiting the islands in 1993. The economy is primarily agricultural, and the major crop is copra, with coconut trees dominating the coastal plains. The islands were first sighted by Europeans in 1607. The French claimed the islands in 1768. In 1769 the islands were visited by James COOK, who named them after the Royal Society. In 1843 they were made a French protectorate and in 1880 became a French colony. In 1946 they became a French overseas territory. The principal language is Tahitian. Area: 558sq mi (1,446sq km). Pop. (1992) 165,000.

**Society of Friends** *See* QUAKERS

**Society of Jesus** *See* JESUITS

**sociobiology** Study of how GENES can influence social behavior. A basic tenet of biology is that physical characteristics, such as structure and physiology, evolve through NATURAL SELECTION of those traits that are most likely to guarantee an organism's survival. Sociobiologists hold the controversial view that this selection process applies to social behaviors.

**sociology** Scientific study of society, its institutions, and processes. It examines areas such as social change and mobility, and underlying cultural and economic factors. Auguste COMTE invented the term "sociology" in 1843, and since the 19th century numerous complex and sophisticated theories have been expounded by Herbert SPENCER, Karl MARX, Emile DURKHEIM, Max WEBER, and others.

**Socotra** Island territory in the Indian Ocean, s of the Arabian Peninsula; the capital is at Tamridah. Strategically placed at the entrance to the Red Sea, it was taken as a protectorate by the British in 1866. In 1967 it chose to join South Yemen and is now administered by Yemen. The mountainous terrain includes peaks rising to *c.*5,000ft (1,500m). The economy is based on stock-rearing, but exports include tobacco, ghee, dates, myrrh. Area: 1,200sq mi (3,100sq km). Pop. 12,000.

**Socrates** (*c.*469–*c.*399 BC) Greek philosopher. He laid the foundation for an ethical philosophy based on the analysis of human character and motives. The son of a sculptor, he fought in the PELOPONNESIAN WARS. Information about his life and philosophy is found in the writings of PLATO, his most gifted pupil, and the historian and military leader XENOPHON, who knew him. According to these accounts, Socrates believed that moral excellence is attained through self-knowledge. For Socrates, knowledge and virtue were synonymous; immorality was founded on ignorance. His criticism of tyranny attracted powerful enemies and he was charged with impiety and corrupting the young. Condemned to death, he drank the poisonous draft of hemlock required by law.

**soda** Any of several sodium compounds, especially sodium carbonate ($Na_2CO_3$), usually manufactured from common salt (sodium chloride, NaCl) and ammonia by the Solvay process. The anhydrous (lacking water) form is known as soda ash; washing soda is hydrated sodium carbonate ($Na_2CO_3.10H_2O$).

**Soddy, Frederick** (1877–1956) British chemist who was awarded the 1921 Nobel Prize for chemistry for his studies of radioactive ISOTOPES. In 1920 he revealed the value of isotopes in computing geological age. With Ernest RUTHERFORD, he worked out an explanation of RADIOACTIVE DECAY and later, with William RAMSAY, found HELIUM to be a product of URANIUM decay.

**sodium** (symbol Na) Common, silvery-white metallic element, one of the ALKALI METALS, first isolated in 1807 by Sir Humphry DAVY. It occurs in the sea as salt (sodium chloride) and in many minerals. Its chief source is sodium chloride, from which it is extracted by electrolysis. The soft, reactive metal is used in gasoline additives and as a heat-transfer medium in nuclear reactors. Properties: at.no. 11; at.wt. 22.9898; sp.gr. 0.97; m.p. 208.05°F (97.81°C); b.p. 1,620°F (882°C).

**sodium bicarbonate** (sodium hydrogen carbonate, $NaHCO_3$, popularly known as bicarbonate of soda) White, crystalline salt that decomposes in acid or on heating to release carbon dioxide gas. It has a slightly alkaline reaction and is an ingredient of indigestion medicines.

**sodium carbonate** *See* SODA

**sodium chloride** Common salt (NaCl). It is the major mineral component of seawater, making up 80% of its dissolved material. Sodium chloride is also the major ELECTROLYTE of liv-

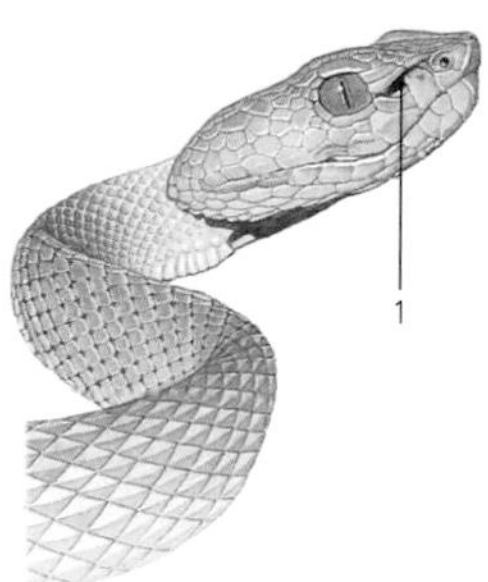


▲ **snake** Many snakes feed on small nocturnal mammals, and must find their prey in the semi-darkness. They do so with the aid of heat-sensitive organs located in pits on the upper jaw (1). The heat sensors feed the information to the same part of the brain as the eyes. In this way snakes can "see" a thermal image of the animal superimposed on its visual image.

▲ **Sobers** West Indian cricketer Sir Gary Sobers was one of the most talented players of all time and the only person to score over 8,000 test runs and take over 200 test wickets. He could bowl fast, medium, and spin deliveries and held the world record for the highest test innings (365 not out) from 1958 to 1994. He was knighted on his retirement in 1975.

S

ing cells, and the loss of too much salt, through evaporation from the skin or through illness, is dangerous. It is used as a seasoning, to cure and preserve foods, and in the chemical industry.

**sodium hydroxide** *See* CAUSTIC SODA

**Sodom and Gomorrah** In the Old Testament, two cities S of the DEAD SEA, notorious for their carnality and vice. God could not find even ten good men within Sodom, and so destroyed both it and Gomorrah with fire and brimstone. LOT and his family were allowed to escape, but Lot's wife lagged behind, was turned to a pillar of salt, and died.

**Sofia** (Sofija) Capital of Bulgaria and Sofia province, in W central Bulgaria, at the foot of the Vitosha Mountains. The city was founded by the Romans (as Serdica) in the 2nd century AD for its hot mineral springs. It was ruled by the Byzantine empire (as Triaditsa) from 1018 to 1185. Sofia passed to the second Bulgarian empire (1186–1382), and then to the Ottoman empire (1382–1878). The city was taken by Russia in 1877 and chosen as the capital of Bulgaria by the Congress of Berlin. Industries: steel, machinery, textiles, rubber, chemicals, metallurgy, leather goods. Pop. (1990) 1,141,142.

**softball** Game similar to BASEBALL in which a lighter bat, a larger and softer ball, and a smaller field are used. It is played by two teams of nine or ten people. The rules are close to those of baseball except for the pitching delivery (underhand) and the number of innings (seven instead of nine). Softball was originally invented as an indoor game in Chicago in 1888 and increased in popularity when moved outdoors in 1930. The sport is governed by the Amateur Softball Association, founded in 1934. The International Softball Federation coordinates competition in more than 20 nations.

**software** COMPUTER PROGRAM and any associated data file. The term software is used to distinguish these coded instructions and data from computer HARDWARE, or equipment. *See also* CD-ROM; MAGNETIC DISK

**soil** Surface layer of the Earth, capable of supporting plant life. It consists of undissolved minerals produced by the weathering and breakdown of surface rocks, organic matter, water, and gases. Many different types of soil exist and are characterized by a series of distinct horizons (layers).

**solar cell** Device that converts sunlight directly to electricity. It normally consists of a *p*-type (positive) silicon crystal and an *n*-type (negative) one. Light radiation causes electrons to be released and creates a POTENTIAL DIFFERENCE so that current can flow between electrodes connected to the two crystals. The cells are *c*.10% efficient. Solar cells are often used to power small electronic devices such as pocket calculators. Several thousand cells may be used in panels to provide power of a few hundred watts. *See also* SOLAR ENERGY

**solar constant** Steady rate at which energy from the SUN is received from just outside the Earth's atmosphere. Its value is *c*.1.353 kilowatts per square meter (perpendicular to the Sun's rays).

**SOLAR CELL**

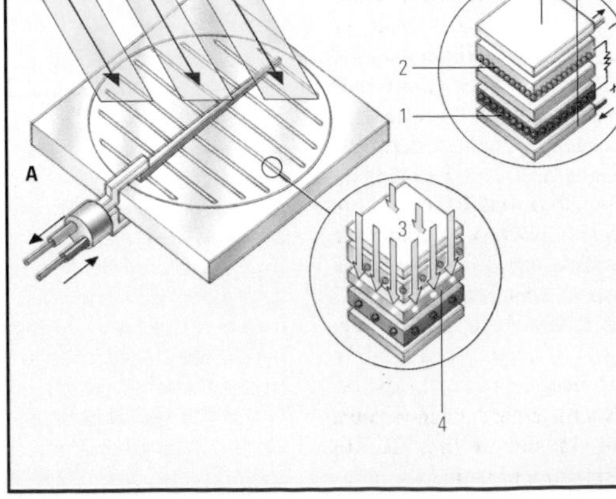

A solar (photovoltaic) cell (A) is made up of two silicon semiconductors between metal contacts. One of the silicon semiconductors tends to collect positive charge (1), the other negative (2), creating a potential difference. As light photons (3) hit the *p-n* semiconductor junction between the semiconductors (4) they displace electrons which are attracted to the positive semiconductor. There is thus a potential difference (voltage) generated between the metal contacts (5)

**solar energy** Heat and light from the Sun consisting of ELECTROMAGNETIC RADIATION, including heat (infrared rays), light, and radio waves. About 35% of the energy reaching the Earth is absorbed; most is spent evaporating moisture into clouds, and some is converted into organic chemical energy by PHOTOSYNTHESIS in plants. All forms of energy (except NUCLEAR ENERGY) on Earth come ultimately from the Sun. SOLAR CELLS are used to power instruments on spacecraft, and experiments are being done to store solar energy in liquids from which electricity can be generated.

**solar flare** Sudden and violent release of matter and energy from the Sun's surface, usually from the region of an active group of SUNSPOTS. Flares emit radiation across the electromagnetic spectrum. Particles are emitted, mostly electrons and protons and smaller numbers of neutrons and atomic nuclei. A flare can cause material to be ejected in bulk in the form of prominences. When energetic particles from flares reach the Earth, they may cause radio interference, magnetic storms, and more intense auroras.

**Solar System** The SUN and all the celestial bodies that revolve around it: the nine PLANETS, together with their SATELLITES and ring systems, the thousands of ASTEROIDS and COMETS, meteoroids, and other interplanetary material. The boundaries of the Solar System lie beyond the orbit of Pluto to include the Kuiper Belt and the Oort Cloud of comets. The Solar System came into being nearly 5 billion years ago, probably as the end-product of a contracting cloud of interstellar gas and dust. *See also* BIG BANG

**solar wind** Particles accelerated by high temperatures of the solar CORONA to velocities great enough to allow them to escape from the Sun's gravity. The solar wind deflects the tail of the Earth's magnetosphere and the tails of comets away from the Sun.

**sole** Marine flatfish found in the Atlantic Ocean from NW Africa to Norway, especially *Solea solea*. A food fish, it is green-gray or black-brown with dark spots. Length: to 24in (60cm). Family Soleidae.

**Solemn League and Covenant** (September 1643) Agreement between the LONG PARLIAMENT and the Scots during the English CIVIL WAR. In return for Parliament's promise to reorganize the established church on a PRESBYTERIAN basis, the Scots agreed to raise an army in the North of England against CHARLES I. The Scottish help led directly to the Parliamentary victory over the Royalists at MARSTON MOOR.

**solid** State of matter in which a substance has a relatively fixed shape and size. The forces between atoms or molecules are strong enough to hold them in definite locations (about which they can vibrate) and to resist compression. *See also* CRYSTAL; GAS; LIQUID

**Solidarity** Polish organization that provided the chief opposition to the communist regime during the 1980s. The National Committee of Solidarity was founded in 1980 among shipyard workers in GDAŃSK led by Lech WALESA. Solidarity organized strikes and demanded economic improvements, but soon acquired a political, revolutionary character. Banned from 1981, it reemerged as a national party, winning the free elections of 1989 and forming the core of the new democratic government.

**solid-state physics** Physics of SOLID materials. From the study of the structure, binding forces, electrical, magnetic, and thermal properties of solids has come the development of the SEMICONDUCTOR, MASER, LASER, and SOLAR CELL.

**Solomon** (d.922 BC) King of Israel (*c*.972–922 BC), son of DAVID and Bathsheba. His kingdom prospered, thanks partly to economic relations with the Egyptians and Phoenicians, enabling Solomon to build the TEMPLE in Jerusalem. His reputation for wisdom reflected his interest in literature, although the works attributed to him, including the SONG OF SOLOMON, were probably written by others.

**Solomon Islands** Melanesian archipelago and nation in the SW Pacific Ocean, SE of New Guinea. The capital is Honiara (on Guadalcanal). Solomon Islands include several hundred islands spread over 900mi (1,400km) of the Pacific Ocean. The principal islands are volcanic, mountainous, and covered by equatorial rain forest. The N Solomons have a tropical oceanic climate, but further S there is a longer cool season. The largest island is Guadalcanal, and other inhabited islands include Choiseul, Malaita, New Georgia, San Cristobal (Makira), Santa Isabel (Ysabel), and the Shortland islands. The vast majority of the population are indigenous Melanesians. The first European discovery of the islands was by the Spanish in 1568. The islands resisted colonization until the late 19th century. In 1893 the S islands became a British protectorate and the N was controlled by the Germans from 1895. In 1900 Germany ceded its territory to Britain. During World War I BOUGAINVILLE and Buka (now in Papua New Guinea) were occupied by Australian troops, and were mandated to Australia in 1920. In 1942 the S islands were occupied by Japanese troops. After heavy fighting, particularly on Guadalcanal, the islands were liberated by US troops in 1944. In 1976 the Solomons became self-governing and, in 1978, achieved full independence within the Commonwealth of Nations. The coastal plains are used for subsistence farming, which supports 90% of the population. Coconuts are the major products, tuna is the biggest export earner, and lumber is the main industry. Area: *c.*10,770sq mi (27,900sq km). Pop. (1993) 349,500.

**solstice** Either of the two days each year when the Sun is at its greatest angular distance from the celestial equator, leading to the longest day and shortest night (summer solstice) in one hemisphere of the Earth, and the shortest day and longest night (winter solstice) in the other hemisphere. In the Northern Hemisphere the summer solstice occurs on or about June 21 and the winter solstice on or about December 22.

**Solti, Sir Georg** (1912–97) British conductor, b. Hungary. He was music director of Covent Garden Opera (now ROYAL OPERA), London (1961–71); Orchestre de Paris (1971–75); and the Chicago Symphony Orchestra (1969–91). An outstanding operatic music director, he was the first conductor to record (1965) Wagner's entire *Ring* cycle.

**solubility** Mass (grams) of a SOLUTE that will saturate 100 grams of SOLVENT under given conditions to give a SATURATED SOLUTION. Solubility generally rises with temperature, but for a few solutes, such as calcium sulfate, increasing temperature decreases solubility in water.

**solute** Gaseous, liquid, or solid substance that is dissolved in a SOLVENT to form a SOLUTION.

**solution** Liquid (the SOLVENT) into which another substance (the SOLUTE) is dissolved, or a liquid consisting of two or more chemically distinct compounds, inseparable by filtering. The amount of a solute dissolved in a solvent is called the concentration. *See also* MIXTURE

**solvent** Liquid that dissolves a substance (the SOLUTE) without changing its composition. Water is the most universal solvent, and many inorganic compounds dissolve in it. Ethanol, ether, acetone, and carbon tetrachloride are common solvents for organic substances. *See also* SOLUTION

**Solzhenitsyn, Alexander** (1918– ) Russian novelist. Sentenced to a forced labor camp in 1945 for criticizing Stalin, he was subsequently exiled to Ryazan, but was officially rehabilitated in 1956. His novels include *One Day in the Life of Ivan Denisovich* (1962), *The First Circle* (1968), *Cancer Ward* (1968), and *August 1914* (1971). He was awarded the 1970 Nobel Prize for literature. Criticism of the Soviet regime in *The Gulag Archipelago* (1974) led to his forced exile to the West, from which he returned to Russia only in 1994.

**Somalia** Republic in extreme E Africa. *See* country feature, page 624

**Somerset** County on the Bristol Channel, SW England. The county is divided into five districts, with the administrative center at Taunton (1991 pop. 93,969). Other major towns include Yeovil and Bridgewater. The region is generally low-lying in the center and is drained chiefly by the Avon, Exe, and Parrett rivers. Much of the land is given over to agriculture. Dairy farming and fruit growing are the most important economic activities and the region is noted for Cheddar cheese and cider. Limestone is mined. Area: 1,332sq mi (3,452sq km). Pop. (1991) 460,368.

**Somme, Battle of the** Major WORLD WAR I engagement in N France along the Somme River. It was launched by Douglas HAIG on July 1, 1916. On the first day the British suffered 60,000 casualties in an attempt to break through the German lines. A trench war of attrition continued until the offensive was abandoned on November 19, 1916. Total casualities were over one million, and the British had advanced only 10mi (16km). A second battle around St. Quentin (March–April 1918) is sometimes referred to as the Second Battle of the Somme. A German offensive designed to secure victory before the arrival of US troops was halted by Anglo-French forces.

**Somoza García, Anastasio** (1896–1956) Central figure in Nicaraguan politics from 1936, when he ousted President Sacasa. Somoza created both a dictatorial government and a political dynasty; he was succeeded in office by his two sons, Luis and Anastasio. The Somoza dynasty was overthrown by the SANDINISTAS in 1979.

**sonar** (acronym for **so**und **n**avigation **a**nd **r**anging) Underwater detection and navigation system. The system emits high-frequency sound that is reflected by underwater objects and detected on its return.

**sonata** Musical composition in several movements. In the BAROQUE era, sonatas were usually written for two melodic parts and a continuo. In the CLASSICAL period, the sonata became a more clearly defined form for one or two instruments. The movements, usually three or four in number, are in closely related keys. The first movement of a sonata is usually in sonata form, a widely used MUSICAL FORM. The second movement is generally slow in tempo and the third and perhaps fourth movements are faster.

**Sondheim, Stephen** (1930– ) US composer and lyricist. Sondheim made his mark on Broadway in 1957 with the lyrics for *West Side Story*. His first success as a lyricist-composer was *A Funny Thing Happened on the Way to the Forum* (1962). His reputation was enhanced with works such as *A Little Night Music* (1972), *Sunday in the Park with George* (1984), and *Assassins* (1991).

**Songhai** West African empire, founded *c.*AD 700. In 1468 Sonni Ali captured the market city of TIMBUKTU and the Songhai empire acquired control of most of the trade in W Africa. Sonni was succeeded by Askia Muhammad I, who further increased the Songhai stranglehold on trade routes. The empire began to disintegrate because of factional infighting. The Songhai peoples still control much of the trans-Saharan trade.

**sonic boom** Sudden noise produced by shock waves from an aircraft flying at SUPERSONIC SPEED. The shock waves are formed by the buildup of sound waves at the front and back of the aircraft. These waves spread out and sweep across the ground behind the aircraft, often causing a double bang.

**sonnet** Poem of 14 lines, most often in iambic pentameter and usually employing Petrarchan or Shakespearean rhyme schemes. The Petrarchan consists of an octet and a sestet, usually with an *abbaabbacdecde* rhyme scheme. The Shakespearean, having a final rhyming couplet, is *ababcdcdefefgg*.

**Sons of Liberty** American colonial group. This secret organization was founded, principally in Connecticut and New York, to protest against the STAMP ACT (1765). It sought freedom and liberty in the 13 British colonies.

**Sontag, Susan** (1933– ) US writer, critic, and essayist. Perhaps best known as a critic on popular culture, as in *Against Interpretation* (1966), she has also written novels and short stories, including *The Benefactor* (1963) and *Death Kit* (1967). In more recent years, she has experimented with STRUCTURALISM, particularly evident in her *Illness as Metaphor* (1978) and *Aids and its Metaphors* (1986).

**Sophia** (1630–1714) Electress of Hanover. A granddaughter of JAMES I and the widow of the elector of Hanover, she was recognized as heir to the English throne by the Act of SETTLEMENT (1701), to ensure a Protestant succession and prevent the return of the Catholic STUARTS. When she died, her son, the current elector, became king as GEORGE I.

**Sophists** Professional Greek teachers of the 5th–4th centuries BC. Although not a formal school, they emphasized the intellectual and rhetorical skills needed to succeed in ancient Greek society, and regarded law and ethics as convenient human inventions with no basis in natural law. Serious philosophers, such as PLATO, disapproved of them.

▲ **Solzhenitsyn** Russian writer Alexander Solzhenitsyn served with distinction in the Red Army in World War II, but his criticism of strict censorship in Russia led to all except his first novel being banned. His works are mostly semiautobiographical and expose corruption in Russian society while supporting socialism.

S

**Sophocles** (*c.*496–*c.*406 BC) Greek playwright. Of his 100 plays, only seven tragedies and part of a Satyr play remain. These include *Ajax*, *Antigone* (*c.*442–441 BC), *Electra* (409 BC), *Oedipus Rex* (*c.*429 BC), and *Oedipus at Colonus* (produced posthumously). His works introduced a third speaking actor and increased the members of the chorus from 12 to 15.
**soprano** Highest singing range of the female human voice. The normal range may be given as two octaves upward from middle C, although exceptional voices may reach notes higher. Sopranos have always been important in opera, with various types of soprano (dramatic, lyric, or coloratura) taking different types of roles.
**Sorbonne** College of the University of PARIS, founded in 1253 by Robert de Sorbon (1201–74) and located in what is now the Latin Quarter of Paris. Established for the education of students of theology, it was for centuries an intellectual center of Roman Catholic religious thought, but toward the end of the 19th century, it became purely secular.
**sorghum** Tropical cereal grass native to Africa and cultivated throughout the world. Types raised for grain are varieties of *Sorghum vulgare,* which have leaves coated with white waxy blooms and flower heads that bear up to 3,000 seeds. It yields meal, oil, starch, and dextrose (a sugar). Height: 2–8ft (0.5–2.5m). Family Poaceae/Gramineae.
**sorrel** (dock) Herbaceous, perennial plant native to temperate regions. It has large leaves that can be cooked as a vegetable and small green or brown flowers. Height: to 6ft (2m). Family Polygonaceae; genus *Rumex*, especially *Rumex acetosa*.
**Sosnowiec** *See* KATOWICE
**Sotho** Major cultural and linguistic group of S Africa. It includes the Northern Sotho of TRANSVAAL, South Africa, the Western Sotho (better known as the Tswana) of BOTSWANA, and the Southern Sotho (Basotho or Basuto) of LESOTHO. Although dominating the rural territories they inhabit, the four million or so Sotho share those areas with people of other Bantu-speaking tribes. Many work and live in the urban areas and surrounding townships.
**Soto, Hernando de** *See* DE SOTO, HERNANDO
**soul** Nonmaterial or nontangible part of a person that is the central location of his or her personality, intellect, emotions, and will; the human spirit. Most religions teach that the soul lives on after the death of the body.
**soul music** Form of popular music. The term designates

## SOMALIA

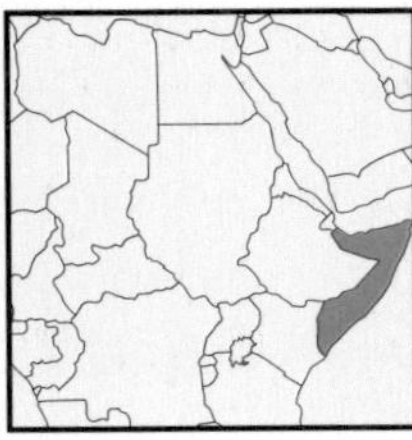

This flag was adopted in 1960, when Italian Somaliland in the south united with British Somaliland in the north to form Somalia. The colors are based on the United Nations flag and the points of the star represent the five regions of East Africa where Somalis live.

**AREA:** 246,201sq mi (637,660sq km)
**POPULATION:** 9,204,000
**CAPITAL (POPULATION):** Mogadishu (1,200,000)
**GOVERNMENT:** Single-party republic, military dominated
**ETHNIC GROUPS:** Somali 98%, Arab 1%
**LANGUAGES:** Somali and Arabic (both official), English, Italian
**RELIGIONS:** Islam 99%
**CURRENCY:** Somali shilling = 100 cents

The Somali Democratic Republic occupies part of the E Horn of Africa. A narrow, mostly barren, coastal plain borders the Indian Ocean and the Gulf of Aden. The capital, MOGADISHU, is also Somalia's major port. In the interior, the land rises to a plateau, nearly 3,300ft (1,000m) high. In the N is a highland region. The S contains the only rivers: the Scebeli and the Giuba.

### CLIMATE

Rainfall is light throughout Somalia; the wettest regions are in the far S and N highlands. Drought is a persistent problem. Temperatures on the plateaus and plains regularly reach 90°F (32°C).

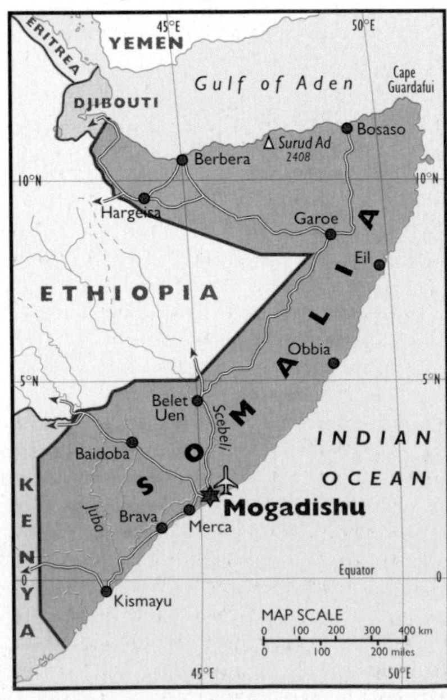


### VEGETATION

Much of Somalia is dry grassland or semi-desert. There are areas of wooded grassland, with trees such as acacia and baobab. Plants are most abundant in the the lower Giuba valley.

### HISTORY AND POLITICS

In the 7th century, Arab traders established coastal settlements and introduced Islam. Mogadishu was founded in *c.*900 as a trading center. The interest of European imperial powers increased after the opening of the Suez Canal (1869). In 1887 Britain established a protectorate in what is now N Somalia. In 1889 Italy formed a protectorate in the central region, and extended its power to the S by 1905. In 1896 France established a colony in modern-day Djibouti. In 1936 Italian Somaliland was united with the Somali regions of Ethiopia to form Italian East Africa. During World War II, Italy invaded (1940) British Somaliland. British forces reconquered the region in 1941 and captured Italian Somaliland. In 1950 Italian Somaliland returned to Italy as a UN trust territory. In 1960 both Somalilands gained independence and joined to become the United Republic of Somalia. Somalia was faced with pan-Somali irredentists, calling for the creation of a "Greater Somalia" to include the Somali-majority areas in Ethiopia, Kenya, and Djibouti. The failure of reunification forced a successful military coup, led by Major General Siad Barre. The country became the Somali Democratic Republic. During the 1970s, Somalia and Ethiopia fought for control of the Ogaden Desert, inhabited mainly by Somali nomads. Ethiopia forced Somalia to withdraw in 1978, but internal resistance continued. Drought and civil war led to nearly a million refugees fleeing to Somalia. In 1991 Barre was overthrown and the United Somali Congress (USC) seized power. Somalia disintegrated into civil war between rival clans. The Somali National Movement gained control of NW Somalia, and declared a separate state of Somaliland Republic. The new state has not gained international recognition. Mogadishu was devastated by an attack from the Somali National Alliance (SNA). Civil war and drought combined to create a devastating famine, which claimed thousands of lives. The UN was slow to provide relief, and when aid arrived was unable to secure distribution. US marines led a task force to secure food distribution, but became embroiled in conflict with Somali warlords. Following the deaths of UN troops, US marines withdrew in 1994. The lack of a central government contributed to the deaths of thousands of Somalis in flooding (1997). The Cairo Declaration (December 1997) held out hope of an end to factional feuding and the installation of a transitional government.

### ECONOMY

Somalia is a low income developing country, shattered by drought and civil war (1992 GDP, $1,100). Many Somalis are nomadic herdsmen. Live animals, hides, and skins are the major exports. Bananas are grown in the S.

S

black music that developed in the US in the 1960s from RHYTHM AND BLUES. Soul is also used generically to describe music that possesses a certain "soulful" quality. Its influence has extended into many popular musical styles.

**sound** Physiological sensation perceived by the brain via the EAR, caused by an oscillating source, and transmitted through a material medium as a sound wave. The velocity at which a sound wave travels through a medium depends on the ELASTICITY of the medium and its DENSITY. If the medium is a gas, the sound wave is longitudinal and its velocity depends on the gas temperature. The velocity of sound in dry air at standard temperature and pressure (STP) is 741mph (331m/s) and depends on the height above sea level. Pure sounds are characterized by PITCH, TIMBRE, and intensity (the rate of flow of sound energy).

**sound barrier** Name for the cause of an aircraft's difficulties in accelerating to a speed faster than that of sound. When approaching the speed of sound, an aircraft experiences a sudden increase in drag and loss of lift. These are caused by the build-up of sound waves to form shock waves at the front and back of the aircraft. The problems were solved by designing aircraft with smaller surface area, swept-back wings, and more powerful engines. *See also* SONIC BOOM

**sound recording** Conversion of sound waves into a form that can be stored and reproduced. Thomas EDISON's phonograph (1877) recorded sound vibrations as indentations made by a stylus on a revolving cylinder wrapped in tinfoil. Emile Berliner's gramophone improved the process by using a zinc disk instead of a cylinder. The volume was amplified by the addition of acoustical horns, which were replaced before World War I by valve amplifiers. Molded thermoplastic records were introduced in 1901. In 1927 and 1928 patents were issued in the US and Germany for MAGNETIC RECORDING processes. Later innovations include high-fidelity (hi-fi), stereophonic, and quadrophonic reproduction. Modern recordings on COMPACT DISC (CD) usually employ laser-scanned digital signals.

**Sousa, John Philip** (1854–1932) US composer and bandmaster. He composed about 100 marches, including *Semper Fidelis* (1888) and *The Stars and Stripes Forever* (1896). He also composed numerous operettas, of which the most famous is *El Capitan* (1896).

**sousaphone** Largest BRASS musical instrument of the TUBA family. It was introduced by John Philip SOUSA to fortify the bass section of US military bands.

**South Africa** Republic in S Africa. *See* country feature, page 626

**South African Wars** Two wars between the AFRIKANERS (Boers) and the British in South Africa. The **first** (1880–81) arose from the British annexation of the Transvaal in 1877. Under Paul KRUGER, the Transvaal regained autonomy, but further disputes, arising largely from the discovery of gold and diamonds, provoked the **second**, greater conflict (1899–1902), known to Afrikaners as the Second War of Freedom and to the British as the Boer War. It was also a civil war between whites; black Africans played little part on either side. In 1900 the British gained the upper hand, defeating the Boer armies and capturing Bloemfontein and Pretoria. Boer commandos fought a determined guerrilla campaign but were forced to accept British rule in the peace treaty signed at Vereeniging (1902).

**South America** Fourth-largest continent, the S of the two continents of America, in the Western Hemisphere, connected to North America by the isthmus of PANAMA. **Land** Off the N coast lies the Caribbean Sea, off the E the Atlantic Ocean, and the W the Pacific Ocean. It is politically divided into 12 independent nations: BRAZIL and ARGENTINA (the two largest), BOLIVIA, CHILE, COLOMBIA, ECUADOR, GUYANA, PARAGUAY, PERU, SURINAM, URUGUAY, and VENEZUELA, plus the French overseas département of FRENCH GUIANA. It is *c.*4,750mi (7,640km) long (Punta Gallinas, Colombia to Cape Horn, Chile), and at its widest (near the Equator) *c.*3,000mi (5,300km). **Structure and geology** South America's W edge towers above the rest of the continent, which slopes downward toward the Atlantic Ocean, except for the Guiana and Brazilian Highlands. These form the continental shield. The middle of the continent is marked by a series of lowlands. The ANDES, which stretch from Colombia to Chile, contain the highest peaks of the Americas, and ACONCAGUA (Argentina) is the tallest mountain outside Asia, at 22,834ft (6,960m). The ATACAMA DESERT, a coastal strip in N Chile, is the driest place on Earth. PATAGONIA is a semi-arid plateau, composed of rocky terraces to the E of the Andes. Major islands include the FALKLAND ISLANDS (a British crown colony) and the GALÁPAGOS (a territory of Ecuador). **Lakes and rivers.** Excluding Lake MARACAIBO (5,217sq mi/13,512sq km) as an extension of the Gulf of Venezuela, the largest lake in South America is Lake TITICACA, on the Peru-Bolivia border, covering 3,200sq mi (8,300sq km). Lengthy rivers combine to form three major systems that reach the Atlantic. At 3,990mi (6,430km) the AMAZON is the world's second-longest river (after the Nile). With its many substantial tributaries, it drains by far the biggest of the world's river basins. Flowing S is the PARAGUAY-PARANÁ system and NE is the ORINOCO. **Climate and vegetation** Except in the mountains and the S, the climate remains generally warm and humid. Much of the N supports tropical RAIN FOREST, while lowlands in the extreme N and the central region have a cover of tropical grass. The Pampas, S of the Tropic of CAPRICORN, produce temperate grasslands, but vegetation is scarce to the far SE of the mountains. In the S, pine and other temperate forests grow along the W coast. **People** Some Incas (QUECHUAS) still remain in the Andes, as do some Mapucho (Araucanians) of Chile. But the majority of the population is mestizo (of dual Indian and European descent), except in Argentina, S Brazil, Chile, and Uruguay, whose population is primarily European. Since the early 19th century many Europeans (especially Italians) and Asians (particularly Japanese) have migrated to Argentina and Brazil. Sizable black populations exist in Brazil, Colombia, French Guiana, and Venezuela, descendants of slaves brought from Africa to work in the sugarcane, coffee, rubber, and cotton plantations. The majority of the continent's people live in urban areas close to the coast, SÃO PAULO being by far the largest example. Latin American Spanish and Portuguese are the dominant continental languages and Roman Catholicism is the major religion. **Recent history** The early 1900s saw a number of conflicts within and between countries of the region. Notable among these were the territorial Chaco Wars (1928–30, 1932–35) between Bolivia and Paraguay. South American republics failed to become world powers until the end of World War II, helped by the formation of the United Nations in 1945 and the ORGANIZATION OF AMERICAN STATES (OAS) in 1948, which gave them influence in international affairs. Many countries of South America have swung between military dictatorships and democratic governments, mainly caused by wildly fluctuating economic fortunes, which in turn have brought about extremes of wealth and poverty, leading to unrest and instability. The periodic repressive regimes have often been the focus of international condemnation of human rights abuses. During the 1980s and 1990s, international pressure, particularly from the US, has also been brought to bear on those governments, notably Bolivia and Colombia, who are either unwilling or unable to control the production and export of vast quantities of cocaine. **Economy** About 30% of the workforce is employed in subsistence farming, working 15% of the land, most of which is owned by Europeans. Chief exports include cash crops such as coffee, bananas, sugarcane, and tobacco. The drug industry is also important: Peru and Colombia are major cultivators of coca leaves, and Colombia supplies over 50% of the world's illegal trade in cocaine. Industrial development and mineral exploitation have been dominated by Europe and the US. Since 1945 South American countries have sought greater economic independence, yet reliance on banking finance has often led to a burden of debt. Another drawback has been the scarcity of continental coal reserves and the dependence on petroleum, especially in Venezuela's MARACAIBO region. The Guiana and Brazilian Highlands have large deposits of iron ore and the Andes range has many copper reserves. Bolivia has large tin mines, and Brazil reserves of manganese. However, despite the industrialization of some countries, particuarly Brazil, Venezuela, and Argentina, most

▲ **sorghum** The most widely cultivated grain in Africa, sorghum is also commonly grown in Asia and the US. It is more tolerant of a hot climate than corn and many other grains, and is extremely resistant to drought. High in carbohydrates, it is usually eaten after being ground into a paste and made into bread, cakes, or porridges. It is also used extensively in the manufacture of beer.

S

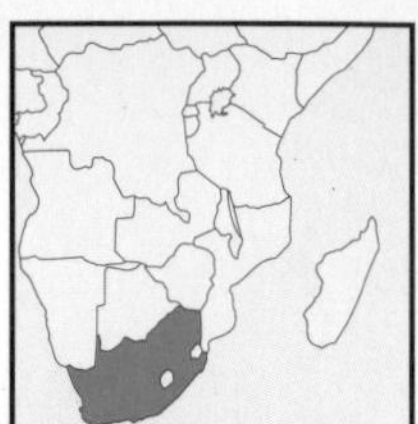

South Africa's flag was first flown in 1994 when the country adopted a new, nonracial constitution. It incorporates the red, white, and blue of former colonial powers, Britain and the Netherlands, together with the green, black, and gold of black organizations.

**AREA:** 470,566sq mi (1,219,916sq km)
**POPULATION:** 39,790,000
**CAPITAL (POPULATION):** Cape Town (legislative, 2,350,157); Pretoria (administrative, 1,080,187); Bloemfontein (judicial, 300,150)
**GOVERNMENT:** Multiparty republic
**ETHNIC GROUPS:** Black 76%, White 13%, Colored 9%, Asian 2%
**LANGUAGES:** Afrikaans, English, Ndebele, North Sotho, South Sotho, Swazi, Tsonga, Tswana, Venda, Xhosa, Zulu (all official)
**RELIGIONS:** Christianity 68%, Hinduism 1%, Islam 1%
**CURRENCY:** Rand = 100 cents

The Republic of South Africa is the southernmost African country. A narrow coastal margin includes: the Indian Ocean port of Durban; the dry s tablelands, Little and Great Karoo; Cape Town on the Cape of Good Hope; and part of the Namib Desert. The interior forms part of the African plateau. The plateau rises in the E to an escarpment over 6,000ft (2,000m) high, on the fringe of which lies Bloemfontein. Soweto, Johannesburg, and Pretoria all lie on the N of the escarpment. The highest peaks are in the Drakensberg range, on the E border of Lesotho. In the N lies part of the Kalahari Desert. In the NE are the Witwatersrand goldfields. Kimberley has the largest diamond mines. The Kruger National Park lies on the border with Mozambique. The longest river is the Orange.

## Climate

Most of South Africa is subtropical. The SW has a Mediterranean climate. Much of the plateau is arid, and the Namib Desert is almost rainless.

## Vegetation

Grassland covers much of the high interior, with tropical savanna in lower areas. Forest and woodland cover only 3% of the land, and *fynbos* (scrub vegetation) is found in the Cape region.

## History

The indigenous people of South Africa are the San. The first European settlement was not until 1652, when the Dutch East India Company founded a colony at Table Bay. Dutch Afrikaners (*Boers*) established farms, employing slaves. From the late 18th century, conflict with the Xhosa intensified, as the Boers trekked inland. In the early 19th century, Britain gained control of the Cape. Following Britain's abolition of slavery in 1833, the Boers began the Great Trek. They met with fierce resistance, particularly from the Zulu kingdom. The Boer republics of Transvaal and Orange Free State were established in 1852 and 1854. The discovery of diamonds and gold in the 1870s and 1880s increased the pace of colonization, and Britain sought to gain control of Boer- and Zulu-held areas. The British defeated the Zulu in the Zulu War (1879), and Zululand was annexed to Natal (1897). In 1890 Cecil Rhodes became governor of Cape Colony. Britain defeated the Boers in the South African Wars (1880–81, 1899–1902). The Union of South Africa was formed in 1910, with Louis Botha as prime minister. In 1912 the African National Congress (ANC) was founded. During World War I, South Africa captured Namibia (1915), and after the war it was mandated to the Union. In 1919 Jan Smuts succeeded Botha as prime minister.

In 1931 Smuts's successor and Nationalist Party founder (1914), James Hertzog, realized Afrikaner ambitions as South Africa achieved full independence within the Commonwealth of Nations. Smuts regained power in 1939, and South Africa joined the Allies in World War II. The Nationalist Party won the 1948 election, advocating a policy of apartheid. Apartheid placed economic, social, and political restrictions on nonwhites. The ANC began a campaign of nonviolent resistance, but after the Sharpeville massacre (1960), Nelson Mandela formed a military wing. In 1961, faced by international condemnation, Nationalist prime minister Verwoerd established South Africa as a republic. In 1964 Mandela was jailed. Verwoerd was assassinated in 1966, and was succeeded by Vorster. Vorster involved South African forces in attempts to prevent black majority rule in South Africa's neighboring states. The crushing of the 1976 Soweto uprising marked a new wave of opposition. In 1977 Steve Biko died in police custody. In 1978 P.W. Botha was elected prime minister. During the 1970s, four bantustans (homelands) gained nominal independence. External economic sanctions forced Botha into reform. In 1984 a new constitution gave Indian and Colored minorities some parliamentary representation; black Africans were still excluded. From 1985 to 1990, South Africa was in a state of emergency. Archbishop Desmond Tutu called for further sanctions. In 1989 President F. W. de Klerk began the process of dismantling apartheid. In 1990 Mandela was released and reassumed leadership of a newly legalized ANC. Clashes continued between the ANC and Chief Buthelezi's Zulu Inkatha movement. In 1994 the ANC won South Africa's first multi-racial elections, and Mandela became president. De Klerk remained as vice president in a coalition government until 1996. In 1997 Thabo Mbeki replaced Mandela as president of the ANC.

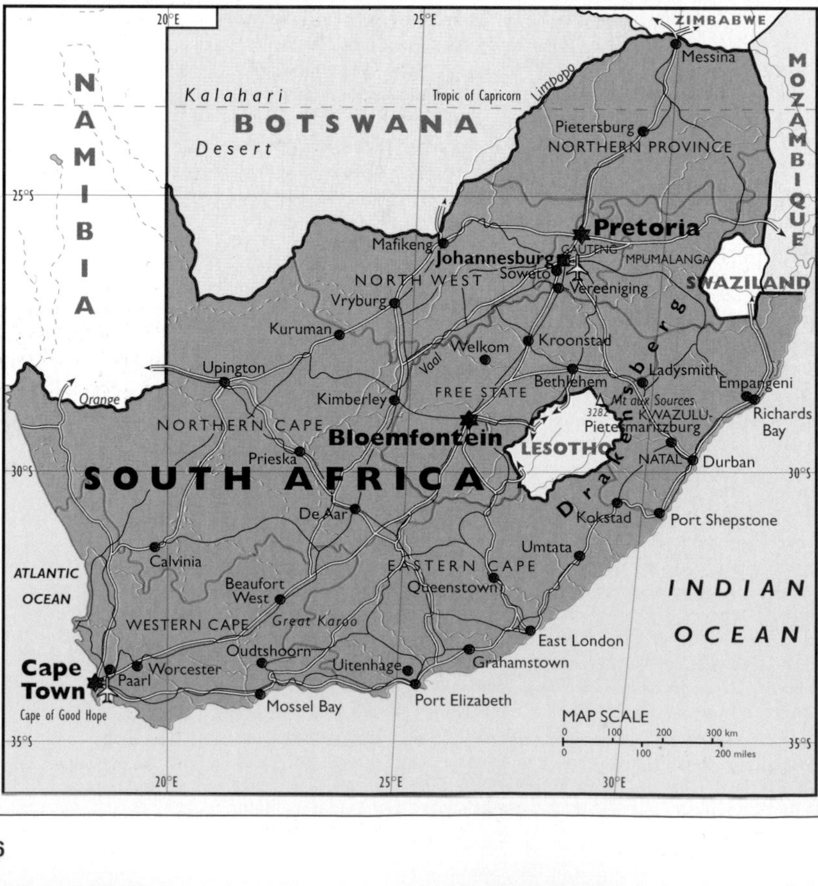

## Economy

Mining forms the base of Africa's most industrialized economy (1995 GDP per capita, US$5,030). South Africa is the world's leading producer of gold and fifth-largest producer of diamonds. Chromite, coal, copper, iron ore, manganese, platinum, silver, and uranium are also mined. Sanctions, falling gold price, and civil and industrial strife created prolonged recession. Unemployment stood at 45% (1995). Major manufactures include chemicals, iron and steel. Agriculture employs more than 33% of the workforce. Major products include fruits, grapes for wine-making, maize, meat and sugar cane.

countries remain industrially underdeveloped. During the 1970s and 1980s, the rush for economic growth and industrialization was often at the expense of the continent's rain forests. Worldwide treaties in the 1990s have attempted to slow down the deforestation, but with little success. Industrialization has also often been seen to exacerbate the continent's high inflation and huge debt crises. Total area: *c.*6,868,000sq mi (17,793,000sq km); *Highest mountain* Aconcagua 22,834ft (6,960m) *Longest river* Amazon 3,990mi (6,430km) *Population* 299,000.000 *Largest cities* São Paulo 16,567,317; Buenos Aries 11,652,050; Rio de Janeiro 5,336,179.

**Southampton** Port and county district in Hampshire, S England. At the head of Southampton Water and a port since Roman times, the city is Britain's principal passenger port and a major commercial port. Industries: shipbuilding, engineering, oil refining. Pop. (1994) 214,000.

**South Australia** State in S central Australia, on the Great Australian Bight. The capital is ADELAIDE, home to 60% of the state's population. Other major cities include Salisbury and Elizabeth. The S coast of Australia was visited by the Dutch in 1627, the first English colonists arrived in 1836, and the region was federated as a state in 1901. The area is hilly in the E (Flinders Ranges) and the N (Musgrave Ranges), and in the W are the E parts of the Great Victoria Desert and the Nullarbor Plain. The MURRAY in the SE is the only important river, and farming is mainly confined to this area. Barley, oats, wheat, rye, and grapes are the chief crops, and livestock are grazed in the N. Mineral deposits include iron ore, uranium, silver, lead, salt, gypsum, opals, coal, and natural gas. Industries: heavy metals, mining, transport equipment. Whyalla has the largest shipyards in Australia. Area: 379,760sq mi (984,380sq km). Pop. (1994) 1,471,000.

**South Carolina** State on the Atlantic Ocean, in the SE US; the capital and largest city is COLUMBIA. The main port is CHARLESTON. The land rises from the coastal plain to the rolling hills of the Piedmont plateau to the BLUE RIDGE MOUNTAINS in the NW. The region is drained by many rivers including the SAVANNAH, which forms most of the Georgia border. From 1633 the English were the first to settle the

◄ **South America** In the N of South America is the Amazonian rainforest, the world's largest area of tropical rainforest. Its rapid deforestation is a major cause of environmental concern. The Atacama Desert, in N Chile, is the driest place on Earth. The imposing Andes ranges run parallel to the W, Pacific coast. In the far S of the continent lies Cape Horn, a cold, isolated region notorious for its violent storms. Spanish and Portuguese colonization of South America began in the 16th century. Native cultures, such as the Inca, were conquered or converted to Roman Catholicism. In the early 19th century much of the continent gained independence. The descendants of European settlers, however, continued to dominate South American politics and economics. The inequitable distribution of land and power has been a major cause of political instability.

Projection: Lambert's Azimuthal Equal Area

■ LIMA Capital Cities

**SOUTH CAROLINA**
**Statehood :**
May 23, 1788
**Nickname :**
The Palmetto State
**State bird :**
Carolina wren
**State flower :**
Carolina jessamine
**State tree :**
Palmetto
**State motto :**
Prepared in mind and resources

**SOUTH DAKOTA**
**Statehood:**
November 2, 1889
**Nickname:**
The Sunshine State
**State bird:**
Ring-necked pheasant
**State flower:**
American pasqueflower
**State tree:**
Black Hills spruce
**State motto:**
Under God the people rule

area permanently. South Carolina became a royal province in 1729, and a plantation society evolved based on rice, indigo, and cotton. One of the original thirteen US states (1789), it was the first to secede from the Union and the first shots of the CIVIL WAR were fired at FORT SUMTER. The state was devastated in 1865 by Union troops. Major crops include tobacco, soybeans, corn, sweet potatoes, and peanuts. Tourism is the state's second-biggest source of income after textiles and clothing. Area: 31,055sq mi (80,432sq km). Pop. (1992) 3,602,854.

**South China Sea** Part of the Pacific Ocean, surrounded by SE China, Indochina, the MALAY PENINSULA, Borneo, the Philippines, and Taiwan; connected to the East China Sea by the Formosa Strait. The world's largest "sea," its chief arms are the Gulf of Tonkin and Gulf of Thailand. The Si, Red, Mekong, and Chao Phraya rivers flow into it. Area: 848,000sq mi (2,300,000sq km). Average depth: 3,740ft (1,140m).

**South Dakota** State in the N central US, on the GREAT PLAINS. The capital is PIERRE; the largest cities are SIOUX FALLS and Rapid City. The land rises gradually from the E to the Black Hills (featuring Mount RUSHMORE) in the W and the Badlands in the SW, with the Missouri River bisecting the state. One fifth of the area W of the river is semiarid plain, inhabited mainly by Native Americans, and the rest is divided into large cattle and sheep ranches. East of the Missouri, livestock rearing is important and wheat, corn, oats, soybeans, and flax are also grown. Meat packing and food processing are by far the most important industries. South Dakota is the largest producer of gold in the US, but tin, beryllium, stone, sand, and gravel are also mined. French trappers claimed the region for France in the 1740s, and the US acquired part of the land in the LOUISIANA PURCHASE of 1803. Trading and military posts were the only settlements until the 1850s. Dakota Territory was formed in 1861. The discovery of gold in the Black Hills in 1874 led to an increase in population, and the territory was divided into the states of North and South Dakota, both of which joined the Union in 1889. Area: 77,047sq mi (199,551sq km). Pop. (1992) 708,411.

**Southeast Asia** Region bounded by India, China, and the Pacific Ocean, and comprising BURMA, THAILAND, MALAYSIA, CAMBODIA, LAOS, VIETNAM, PHILIPPINES, SINGAPORE, and INDONESIA. Area: *c*.1,740,000sq mi (4,506,600sq km).

**Southeast Asia Treaty Organization (SEATO)** Regional defense agreement signed by Australia, New Zealand, France, Pakistan, the Philippines, Thailand, Britain, and the US in Manila in 1954. It was formed in response to communist expansion in Southeast Asia. With administrative headquarters in Bangkok, SEATO had no standing forces. Some members were unwilling to support the US in the VIETNAM WAR, and SEATO was abandoned in 1977. The nonmilitary aspects of the treaty were replaced by the ASSOCIATION OF SOUTHEAST ASIAN NATIONS (ASEAN).

**South Georgia** Island in the S Atlantic Ocean, *c*.1,100mi (1,750km) E of TIERRA DEL FUEGO. Mountainous and arid, it rises to 9,626ft (2,934m). A British dependency administered from the Falklands, it has a research station and garrison but no permanent population.

**South Glamorgan** County on the Bristol Channel, S WALES. The capital is CARDIFF. The county is divided into two districts, Cardiff and the Vale of Glamorgan. The Vale of Glamorgan is fertile agricultural land. The major economic activity is dairy farming. Cardiff is an industrial district. Industries: engineering, steel. Area: 161sq mi (416sq km). Pop. (1991) 383,000.

**South Island** Larger of the two principal islands that comprise NEW ZEALAND. Its chief cities are CHRISTCHURCH, DUNEDIN, and Invercarguill. The Southern Alps extend the length of the island and separate the thickly forested W coast from the Canterbury Plains in the E. Cereal growing, sheep and cattle rearing, and dairying are important on the Plains, and tourism is a valuable source of income in most parts. Area: 58,093sq mi (150,461sq km). Pop. (1991) 881,540.

**South Pole** Southernmost geographical point on the Earth's surface. The magnetic south pole is located *c*.1,500mi (2,400km) from the geographical South Pole. The South Pole lies 9,816ft (2,992m) above sea level, *c*.300mi (480km) S of the Ross Ice Shelf.

**South Sea Bubble** (1720) Speculation in the shares of the English South Sea Company ending in financial collapse. The South Sea Company was founded in 1711 for trade in the Pacific. Shares sold so well and interest was so high that in 1720 the company volunteered to finance the national debt. The result was intensive speculation with a 900% rise in the price of shares, until the bubble burst in September 1720, bankrupting investors and closing banks. Credit for saving the company and the government was given to Robert WALPOLE.

**South West Africa** *See* NAMIBIA

**South West Africa People's Organization (SWAPO)** Political organization, formed in 1960 in South West Africa (now NAMIBIA). Swapo's aim was to achieve independence for Namibia and to this end declared itself at war with South Africa. Soon after ANGOLA gained independence in 1975, SWAPO established guerrilla bases there. In 1978 these bases were attacked by South Africa. Truce talks in Geneva in 1981 failed, and in 1984 SWAPO refused to cooperate with the rival Multi-Party Conference (MCP) in drawing up a timetable for independence. When independence was achieved, SWAPO fought a general election in 1989 and gained 57% of the votes and 75% of the seats in the constituent assembly. In 1990 SWAPO leader Sam NUJOMA became president of Namibia. He was reelected in 1994.

**South Yorkshire** Metropolitan county in N central England. The county is divided into four districts, with Barnsley its administrative center. South Yorkshire's only city is SHEFFIELD. The area includes the PEAK DISTRICT National Forest and the W Pennine moors. The Don River flows E across the county. Industries: iron, steel, coal mining. Area: 603sq mi (1,561sq km). Pop. (1991) 1,249,300.

**soviet** Russian revolutionary workers' council. Soviets appeared briefly in the 1905 revolution and again in 1917. The Petrograd (St. Petersburg) Soviet, led by TROTSKY, was the leading organization in the BOLSHEVIK revolution of November 1917. In the Soviet Union, soviets were organized at every level from village upward. At the top was the Supreme Soviet, the chief legislative body.

**Soviet Union** (officially Union of Soviet Socialist Republics) Former federal republic, successor to the Russian empire and the world's first communist state. The Soviet Union was formed on December 30, 1922 and, when dissolved on December 31, 1991, was the largest country in the world. The BOLSHEVIK regime led by LENIN, came to power in the 1917 RUSSIAN REVOLUTION. Lenin's government survived civil war and famine (1918–22) by instituting a centralized command economy. In 1921 the New Economic Policy (NEP) marked a return to a mixed economy. In 1922 a treaty of union was signed by the republics of RUSSIA, UKRAINE, Belorussia (now BELARUS), and TRANSCAUCASIA. In 1923 a new constitution was adopted establishing the supremacy of the COMMUNIST PARTY OF THE SOVIET UNION (CPSU) and the Supreme Soviet as the highest legislative body. Lenin died in January 1924 and a power struggle ensued between TROTSKY and STALIN. Stalin emerged the victor and Trotsky was expelled in 1927. In 1928 the first Five-Year Plan was adopted. It transformed Soviet agriculture and industry. Collective and state farms were imposed on the peasantry, and industrialization was accelerated. The urban population rapidly doubled. The collectivization schemes directly led to the 1932–34 Ukraine famine, which claimed over seven million lives. State control infiltrated all areas of society, and was sometimes brutally imposed by the secret police. The systems of state control led to the creation of a massive bureaucratic administration. The murder of KIROV in 1934 led to the Stalinist purges and the wave of terror in 1936–38. The purges targeted supposed dissidents, Soviet Jews, and ethnic groups. In 1936 Transcaucasia was divided into the republics of GEORGIA, ARMENIA, and AZERBAIJAN. In August 1939 Stalin concluded a nonaggression pact with Hitler. Germany and the USSR invaded Poland and divided up the country. In 1940 Soviet expansion incorporated the Baltic states of LITHUANIA, LATVIA, and ESTONIA

S

into the Union. A costly war with Finland led to the formation of the Karelo-Finnish republic. On June 22, 1941 Germany invaded Russia. The 1943 failure of the siege of STALINGRAD led to the surrender of 330,000 Axis troops, and was a turning-point in WORLD WAR II. The RED ARMY launched a counteroffensive that liberated much of E Europe. World War II devastated the Soviet Union. It is estimated that 25 million Soviet lives were lost. The Soviet Union and the US emerged as the two postwar superpowers. Their antagonistic ideologies and ambitions led to the COLD WAR. The Soviet sphere of influence extended into Albania, Bulgaria, Czechoslovakia, East Germany, Hungary, Poland, and Romania. The importance of the military-industrial sector in Soviet politics was greatly enhanced. In 1948 the Soviet army attempted to blockade the W sectors of BERLIN. In 1949, when NATO was formed, the Soviet Union exploded its first atom bomb. In March 1953 Stalin died and a collective leadership was installed. In 1955 the WARSAW PACT was established as the Communist counterpart to NATO. In 1956, at the 20th CPSU Congress, KHRUSHCHEV made his famous secret speech denouncing Stalin as a dictator. In October 1956 a Hungarian uprising against Moscow domination was crushed by Soviet troops. In 1958 Khrushchev won the battle for succession. He began a policy of liberalization. Economic decentralization entailed a reduction in the bloated bureaucracy. Huge areas of "virgin land" were opened to grain cultivation in order to prevent further famine. New alliances were formed with worldwide anti-colonial movements, and Khrushchev formulated a policy of peaceful coexistence with the West. The Cold War shifted into a technological battle to produce more powerful weapons of mass destruction and a Space Race. In 1957 the Soviet Union launched *Sputnik 1*, the world's first artificial satellite, and in 1961, Yuri GAGARIN became the first man in space. Also in 1961 the Berlin Wall was built to divide East from West Berlin. In 1962 the CUBAN MISSILE CRISIS shattered the Cold War standoff and the world stood at the brink of nuclear war. Khrushchev agreed to remove Soviet missiles and catastrophe was avoided. In October 1964 Khrushchev was removed from office by a conservative collective leadership headed by BREZHNEV and KOSYGIN. They were determined to reverse his liberal reforms and improve the Soviet economy. Brezhnev ruled by consensus and brought close political associates such as ANDROPOV (KGB chief) and GROMYKO (Foreign Minister) into his politburo. He instituted cautious economic reforms and agricultural production increased dramatically. In foreign affairs, the "Brezhnev doctrine" preserved the right of the Soviet Union to intervene in Communist states to preserve international communism. On August 21, 1968 the doctrine was invoked to stem the liberalization of Czechoslovakia, and Warsaw Pact troops invaded to crush the "Prague Spring." Leading dissident scientists and intellectuals, such as SOLZHENITSYN and SAKHAROV, were sent to prison or forced into exile. Many Soviet Jews emigrated in the early 1970s. In 1969 an era of superpower détente began with a series of STRATEGIC ARMS LIMITATION TALKS (SALT) resulting in the signing of SALT I by Brezhnev and NIXON in 1972. In 1975 the Helsinki Accords recognized the postwar European borders. In 1977 Brezhnev was elected president and a new constitution was formed. In 1979 SALT II was signed, but the Soviet invasion of Afghanistan ended the period of détente and the treaty was never ratified by the US. In 1980 the US led a boycott of the Moscow Olympics and placed new, intermediate range Pershing II missiles on European soil. The Soviet economy stagnated with the stabilization of oil prices and its outdated manufacturing technology. Brezhnev died in 1982 and Andropov was elected leader. He began a series of far-reaching economic reforms targeting centralization, corruption, inefficiency, and alcoholism. He promoted a series of advisers, including GORBACHEV, to implement the reforms. His term was short; he died after a mere 15 months in office. He was replaced by a hardline Brezhnevite, Konstantin Chernenko. Chernenko died 13 months later and, in March 1985, Gorbachev became CPSU General Secretary and began a process of economic restructuring (PERESTROIKA) and political openness (GLASNOST). The 1986 CHERNOBYL disaster provided the first test of glasnost. Dissidents were released and restraints on emigration were lifted. Gorbachev began a new détente initiative, focusing on nuclear DISARMAMENT. A series of meetings with REAGAN led to the Intermediate Nuclear Forces (INF) Treaty, which agreed to scrap intermediate-range nuclear missiles. The Soviet Union agreed to halt the disastrous war in Afghanistan and all its troops withdrew by February 1989. Perestroika continued the process begun by Andropov by reducing bureaucracy and allowing a more mixed economy. The restructuring was hampered by opposition from conservatives (anxious to prevent change) and radicals led by Boris YELTSIN, urging more far-reaching policies. In March 1989 the first pluralist elections since 1917 were held, and Gorbachev was elected state president. The tide of reform swept over Eastern Europe; by the close of 1989 every communist leader in the Warsaw Pact had been overthrown. The constituent republics of the Soviet Union began to clamor for secession. In 1989 Gorbachev and BUSH declared an end to the Cold War and the West promised economic support to the Soviet Union. In 1990 the political and economic situation worsened. The Baltic republics, KAZAKSTAN and GEORGIA demanded independence and ARMENIA and AZERBAIJAN fought for control of NAGORNO-KARABAKH. In March 1990, the newly elected Soviet parliament authorized the private ownership of the means of production. The central economic principle of Marxism was removed and the CPSU fractured. Boris Yeltsin resigned his membership. Amid the breakdown in federal government structures, the economy declined by 4%. In December 1990 Gorbachev gained emergency presidential powers and the conservatives demanded action to prevent the disintegration of the Union of Soviets. Paratroopers were sent to LATVIA and LITHUANIA to prevent secession. Miners went on strike, calling for Gorbachev's resignation. SHEVARDNADZE resigned and went on to form the Democratic Reform Movement. In June 1991 a new Union Treaty was drafted which devolved power to the republics and reconstituted the federal government. It was approved by nine republics, but Armenia, the Baltic states, Georgia, and MOLDOVA refused to cooperate. Also in June 1991, Boris Yeltsin was elected president of the Russian republic. In July 1991 Gorbachev attended the Group of Seven (G7) summit and signed the Strategic Arms Reduction Treaty (START), reducing the number of long-range missiles. On August 18, 1991 a coup was launched against Gorbachev by hardliners. Gorbachev was kept under house arrest, while the coup leaders assumed control of the media and sent tanks into Moscow to capture the Russian parliament and Boris Yeltsin. The coup failed and Gorbachev was reinstated on August 22, 1991. The republics seized the opportunity to declare independence from federal control. Yeltsin emerged as the new political power broker. He banned the CPSU and seized its assets, took control of the Russian armed forces and forced Gorbachev to suspend the Russian Communist Party. Gorbachev resigned as General Secretary of the CPSU. In September 1991 the Baltic States of ESTONIA, Latvia, and Lithuania were granted independence. On December 8, 1991 Russia, UKRAINE, and Belarus formed the COMMONWEALTH OF INDEPENDENT STATES (CIS). By the end of December, the republics of Armenia, Azerbaijan, Kazakstan, KYRGYZSTAN, Moldova, TAJIKISTAN, TURKMENISTAN, and UZBEKISTAN had all joined the CIS. On December 25, 1991 Gorbachev resigned as president and, on December 31, the Soviet Union was officially dissolved.

**Soweto** (South-West Township) Group of black townships of more than a million people on the outskirts of JOHANNESBURG, South Africa. Soweto attracted international attention in June 1976, when a student demonstation against the compulsory teaching of Afrikaans in Bantu schools sparked a series of riots against the APARTHEID regime. The police brutally suppressed the disturbances, killing 618 people. Comprising mostly substandard government housing, it remained a focus of protest. Pop. (1991 official) 597,000.

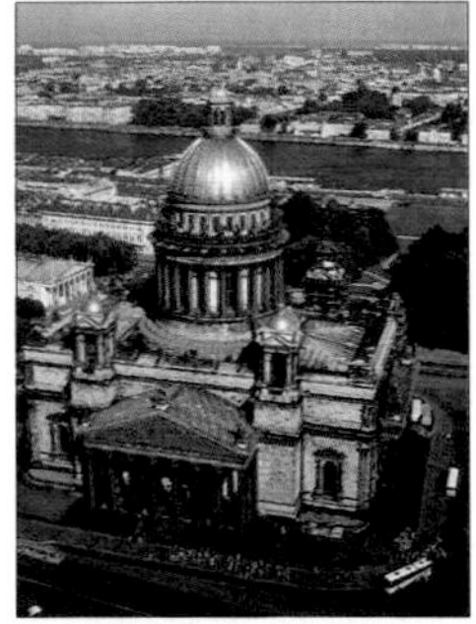

▲ **Soviet Union** St. Isaac's Cathedral, St. Petersburg. In the early years of the Soviet era, religious bodies were persecuted. Many priests and bishops were killed during the unrest following the Russian Revolution of 1917 and churches were plundered of their valuable relics. It was not until Gorbachev came to power that relations with the Russian Orthodox Church really improved. Relics were returned, it was granted legal status, and restrictions on worship were lifted.

S

▲ **soybean** Now grown extensively throughout the world, soybeans are native to China, where they were first cultivated some 4,000 years ago. They were introduced into North America in 1880. Their flowers vary from pure white to light purple. The beans themselves are yellow, brown, or black, depending on the variety. Cultivation has spread in response to the increasing world demand for protein. The main areas are the US, with more than half of world production, and the Far East, notably China, Japan, and Korea. The crop is also spreading into parts of South America, especially Brazil, and into developing African states.

**soybean** Annual plant native to China and Japan. It has oval, three-part leaves and small, lac flowers. Grown worldwide for food, forage, and oil, its seed is an important source of PROTEIN. Height 24in (60cm). Family Fabaceae/Leguminosae; species *Glycine max*.

**Soyer brothers** Raphael (1899–1987) and Moses (1899–1974) US painters, b. Russia. Twin brothers, they emigrated to the US in 1912, settling in New York City. They were known both for their street scenes and their portraits. Their brother, Isaac (1902–1981), also painted urban themes.

**Soyinka, Wole** (1934– ) Nigerian playwright, novelist, and poet. His plays include *The Lion and the Jewel* (1963), *Madmen and Specialists* (1970), *Jero's Metamorphosis* (1972), and *A Play of Giants* (1984). *The Road* (1965), *Season of Anomy* (1973), and *Death and the King's Horseman* (1975) are among his most powerful novels. He was detained without trial in 1967 during the Nigerian civil war and was not released until 1969. He was awarded the 1986 Nobel Prize for literature.

**Spaak, Paul-Henri** (1899–1972) Belgian statesman. He was prime minister or foreign minister of Belgium for most of the period 1936–66, and in 1946 was the first president of the UNITED NATIONS (UN) general assembly. A strong advocate of European unity, he was a founder of the Benelux (Belgium, Netherlands, and Luxemburg) union (1948), and the European Economic Community (1957). He was secretary-general of NATO (1957–61).

**space** Open expanse between matter. RELATIVITY states that space and time are aspects of one thing. More usually, space is taken to mean the Universe beyond the Earth's atmosphere, the vast region in which the density of matter is low.

**space exploration** Use of spacecraft to investigate outer space and heavenly bodies. *Sputnik 1*, launched into Earth orbit by the Soviet Union on October 4, 1957, was the first artificial satellite. Soviet cosmonauts, and their American equivalents, astronauts, orbited the Earth soon after. Unmanned space probes crash-landed on the Moon, sending back pictures to Earth during the descent. Then came soft landings, and probes made to orbit the Moon showed its hidden side for the first time. By 1968 Soviet space scientists had developed techniques for returning a Moon orbiter safely to the Earth. The Americans, in 1969, were first to land men on the Moon and return them safely to the Earth. By that time, probes had already been to Venus and Mars. **Chronology**: first space probe (Explorer 1, launched January 31, 1958); first probe to hit Moon (Lunik 2, launched September 12, 1959); first manned spaceflight (Yuri GAGARIN, on April 12, 1961); first close-up pictures of Mars (Mariner 4, received July 14, 1965); first person on the Moon (Neil ARMSTRONG, on July 21, 1969); first pictures from surface of another planet (Venera 9, received from Venus on October 22, 1975); first probes land on Mars (Viking 1 and 2, July 1976); Jupiter (1979), Saturn (1981), Uranus (1986), and Neptune (1989) were bypassed by Voyager 2; Giotto (1985) flew within 375mi (600km) of Halley's Comet, sending back photographs and composition data; the SPACE SHUTTLE Columbia was launched (1981); Galileo (launched 1989) dropped a sub-probe into Venus's atmosphere; Clementine probe (1994) thought to have discovered water-ice deposits in craters of the Moon; SOHO (launched 1995) to probe Sun's interior; Mars Pathfinder (launched 1996) deployed a "microrover," *Sojourner*, to explore and collect rock samples from Mars's surface. Cassini space probe (launched 1997) started on a seven-year journey towards Saturn.

**space research** Scientific and technological investigations that gather knowledge through SPACE EXPLORATION. The makeups and behaviors of stars, planets, and other cosmic materials were first determined by telescopes and more recently by the HUBBLE SPACE TELESCOPE launched in 1990 by NASA. Research projects have been carried into space by artificial SATELLITES, the SPACE SHUTTLE, space stations, and manned and unmanned space probes. The information gathered has been used in various fields.

**space shuttle** Reusable, rocket-powered US spacecraft. The main part of the shuttle, called the **orbiter** (of which four were built, *Columbia*, *Challenger*, *Discovery*, and *Atlantis*), looks like a bulky jet aircraft with swept-back wings. It ferries people and equipment between the ground and Earth orbit. It takes off attached to a large fuel tank, using its own three rocket engines, assisted by two booster rockets. The boosters are jettisoned about two minutes after launch and are later recovered for reuse. Six minutes later, the orbiter's main engines cut off and the external fuel tank is dumped. Maneuvering engines then put the craft into the required orbit. When it is time to return to Earth, these engines are used to provide reverse thrust. As a result, the craft slows down and descends into the atmosphere. It glides down and lands on a runway. The first space shuttle, *Columbia*, was launched into orbit on April 12, 1981. On mission 25 in January 1986, the shuttle *Challenger* exploded soon after launch, killing all seven on board. A leak had allowed burning gases from a booster rocket to ignite the fuel in the main tank.

**space station** Orbiting structure in space for use by astronauts and scientists. Space laboratories, such as *Skylab* and *Mir*, are space stations built for scientists to carry out a variety of experiments, study the Solar System, and observe distant parts of the Universe. They are capable of supporting astronauts for many months.

**spacesuit** Sealed garment enabling an astronaut to function in space. It is made from several layers of material and has a helmet with a plastic visor. The suit provides insulation from extremes of temperature, and protection from harmful radiation from the Sun and bombardment by tiny particles called micrometeoroids. Inside the suit, a breathing gas (oxygen) must be supplied. A built-in cooling system prevents the astronaut from overheating.

**space-time** In the RELATIVITY theory, central concept that unifies the three space dimensions with time to form a four-dimensional frame of reference. In 1907 the German mathematician Hermann Minkowski explained relativity theory by extending three-dimensional geometry to four dimensions. A line drawn in this space represents a particle's path both in space and time.

**spadix** In some flowering plants, a spike of small flowers; it is generally enclosed in a sheath called a SPATHE. A familiar example is the CUCKOOPINT (*Arum maculatum*).

**Spain** Kingdom on the Iberian peninsula. *See* country feature, page 632

**spaniel** Any of several breeds of sporting dogs that may be trained to locate and flush game, to drop for the hunter's shot and sometimes to retrieve on command. Land spaniels include the springer, cocker, and toy breeds. Water spaniels are usually RETRIEVERS.

**Spanish** Major world language, spoken as an official language in Spain, most of South America (except Brazil, French Guiana, Guyana, and Surinam), all of Central America, Mexico, Cuba, the Dominican Republic, and Puerto Rico. It is also spoken in a number of other countries, notably the US and former Spanish dependencies such as the Philippines. Its total number of speakers is more than 200 million. Spanish is a member of the Romance group of INDO-EUROPEAN LANGUAGES but its vocabulary contains a large number of words of Arabic origin, the result of Moorish domination of Spain for many centuries.

**Spanish-American War** (1898) Conflict fought in the Caribbean and the Pacific, between Spain and the US. The immediate cause was the explosion of the US battleship *Maine* at Havana. Fighting lasted ten weeks (April–July). The Spanish fleets in the Philippines and Cuba were destroyed. Spanish troops in Cuba surrendered after defeat at SAN JUAN HILL. The US also seized Guam and Wake Island, annexed Hawaii and the Philippines, and, at the Treaty of Paris, forced Spain to cede PUERTO RICO.

**Spanish Armada** *See* ARMADA, SPANISH

**Spanish art** Artistic tradition beginning with the Paleolithic cave paintings at Altamira. Successively occupied by the Romans, Visigoths, and Moors, Spain's earliest native traditions were the Mozarabic and Mudéjar styles, which blended Moorish and Christian elements. As the country was reconquered from the Moors, Spain drew closer to artistic developments in the rest of Europe. By the 16th century, it was the most powerful force on the continent, and this period coincided with the career of its first true genius, El GRECO. The most glittering era in Spanish art was the following century. The leading figures from this epoch are Diego VELÁZQUEZ, José RIBERA, and Francisco de Zurbarán. In later years, Francisco GOYA was one of the greatest of the ROMANTICISM movement and Pablo PICASSO was the dominant figure in 20th-century art.

**Spanish literature** One of the major early works is the epic poem *Cantar de M'o Cid* (*c*.1140). Major figures of the 14th and 15th centuries include the poet Juan Ruiz (*c*.1283–1350), the Marqués de Santilla, and Juan de Mena. The most important work of fiction of the 15th century was the novel *La Celestina* (1499). French and Italian influences predominated until the 16th century. The late 16th and 17th centuries are known as the Golden Age, with the work of Miguel de CERVANTES, whose *Don Quixote de la Mancha* (1605–15) is still seen as an influential masterpiece of European literature, the poet Luis de GÓNGORA Y ARGOTE, Lope de VEGA CARPIO, and the dramatist Pedro CALDERÓN DE LA BARCA. The 18th century witnessed a decline in Spanish writings, saved by the rise of ROMANTICISM. *Costumbrismo* (sketches of Spanish life and customs) flourished in the 19th century. In the early 20th century the writers of the Generation of '98 reexamined Spanish traditions. The Spanish CIVIL WAR (1936–39) drove many Spanish writers into hiding, and its reverberations can be seen in the grim realism of much of the work that followed. The theories of MODERNISM exerted an influence on formal technique and narrative style; the Generation of 1927 group of poets were also inspired by SURREALISM. Probably the most important Spanish writer of the 20th century, however, was Federico GARCÍA LORCA.

**Spanish Sahara** See WESTERN SAHARA

**Spanish Succession, War of the** (1701–14) Last of the series of wars fought by European coalitions to contain the expansion of France under LOUIS XIV. It was precipitated by the death of the Spanish king, Charles II, without an heir. He willed his kingdom to the French Philip of Anjou, Louis's grandson. England and the Netherlands supported the Austrian claimant to the Spanish throne, the Archduke (later Emperor) Charles. The ensuing war marked the emergence of Britain as a maritime and colonial power. The Spanish succession was settled by a compromise in the Peace of UTRECHT, with Philip attaining the Spanish throne on condition that he renounced any claim to France, and Britain and Austria receiving substantial territorial gains. Exhaustion of the participants, especially France, helped ensure general peace in Europe until the outbreak of the War of the AUSTRIAN SUCCESSION in 1740.

**Spark, Dame Muriel** (1918– ) British novelist, short-story writer, and poet. Her collected poems and short stories were published in 1967, but she is best known for her novels, including *Memento Mori* (1959), *Girls of Slender Means* (1963), *The Mandelbaum Gate* (1965), and *Symposium* (1990). *The Prime of Miss Jean Brodie* (1961) is a portrait of a charismatic schoolmistress.

**sparrow** Any of a number of small FINCH-like birds that live in or around human settlements. Typical is the house sparrow. The male has a chestnut mantle, gray crown and rump, and black bib. The female is duller and lacks the bib and gray rump. Sparrows feed, roost, and dust-bathe in noisy, twittering flocks. Basically seed eaters, with a preference for grain, they are widely regarded as pests. They also eat fruit, worms, and household scraps. Length: 5.75in (14.5cm). Family Ploceidae; species *Passer domesticus*.

**Sparta** City-state of ancient Greece, near the modern city of Spárti. Founded by DORIANS after *c*.1100 BC, Sparta conquered Laconia (SE Peloponnese) by the 8th century BC and headed the Peloponnesian League against Persia in 480 BC. In the PELOPONNESIAN WARS (431–404 BC) it defeated its great rival, ATHENS, but was defeated by THEBES in 371 BC and failed to withstand the invasion of PHILIP II of Macedon. In the 3rd century BC Sparta struggled against the ACHAEAN LEAGUE, subsequently joining it but coming under Roman dominance after 146 BC. The ancient city was destroyed by ALARIC and the GOTHS in AD 395. Sparta was famous for its remarkable social and military organization.

**Spartacists** Members of the German political party called the **Spartacus League**, which broke away from the Social Democrats during World War I. Led by Karl LIEBKNECHT and Rosa LUXEMBURG, the Spartacists refused to support the war effort and rejected participation in the post-Versailles republican government. They instigated a number of uprisings, including one in Berlin in 1919, after which they were brutally repressed and their leaders murdered.

**Spartacus** (d.71 BC) Thracian gladiator in Rome who led a slave revolt known as the Third Servile (Gladiatorial) War (73–71 BC). His soldiers devastated the land and then moved

▲ **spaniel** Although now very popular as pets, spaniels were originally bred to frighten game birds from undergrowth, much as beaters are employed to do now. Others can be trained to retrieve downed fowl. Originating in Spain, they were developed extensively in Britain.

**SPACE SHUTTLE**

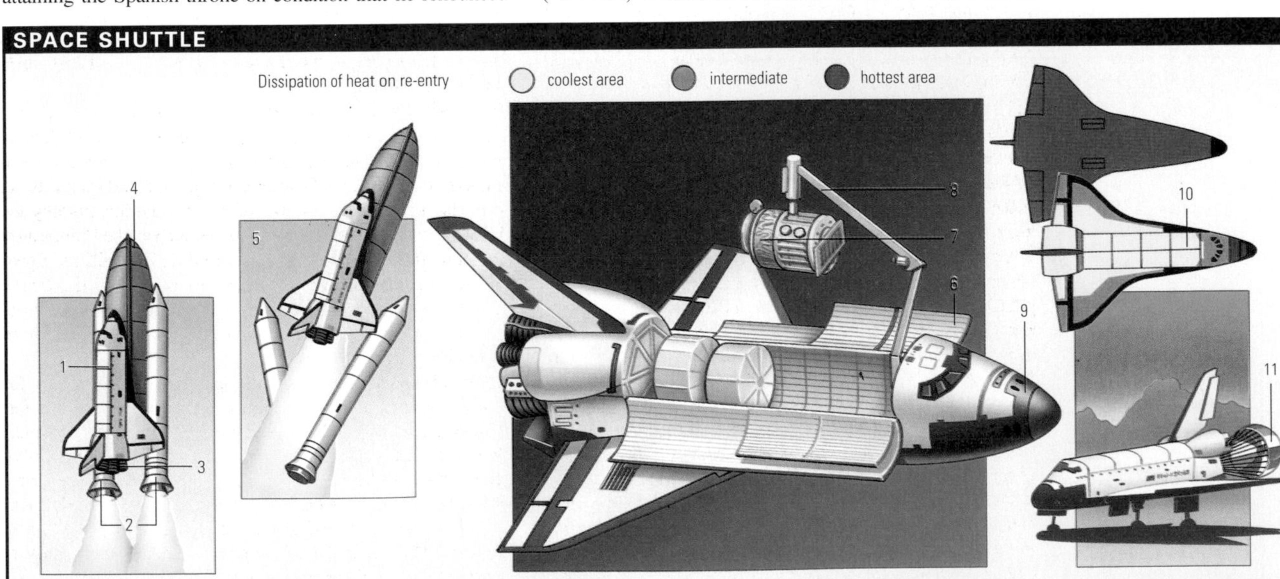


A space shuttle flight has three distinct parts. The first is reaching orbit. The orbiter (1) is propelled upward from the launch platform by two solid fuel boosters (2) and the shuttle's three engines (3) fed with liquid oxygen and liquid hydrogen fuel from the external tank (4). After the boosters have burned out they detach (5) and float to the surface of the Earth by parachute. The external tank detaches later and burns up in the Earth's upper atmosphere. Once in orbit the shuttle floats upside down above the Earth with its cargo bay doors (6) open to help dispel heat. Satellites (7) are launched from the cargo bay and can be retrieved with the use of an arm (8). While in orbit the shuttle maneuvers using helium-fueled thrusters in the nose (9). Finally, the space shuttle returns to land unpowered. The orbiter is shielded from the enormous heat that is generated on reentering the atmosphere by ceramic tiles (10) on its outer surface. A parachute (11) slows the vehicle on the runway.

S

The colors on the Spanish flag date back to those used by the old kingdom of Aragón in the 12th century. The present design, in which the central yellow stripe is twice as wide as each of the red stripes, was adopted in 1938, during the Spanish Civil War.

**AREA:** 194,896sq mi (504,780sq km)
**POPULATION:** 39,085,000
**CAPITAL (POPULATION):** Madrid (3,121,000)
**GOVERNMENT:** Constitutional monarchy
**ETHNIC GROUPS:** Castilian Spanish 72%, Catalan 16%, Galician 8%, Basque 2%
**LANGUAGES:** Castilian Spanish (official), Catalan, Galician, Basque
**RELIGIONS:** Christianity (Roman Catholic 97%)
**CURRENCY:** Peseta = 100 céntimos

The Kingdom of Spain occupies 80% of the Iberian peninsula. The central Spanish regions of ARAGÓN, CASTILE-LA MANCHA, and CASTILE-LEÓN form part of a vast plateau (the *Meseta*), in the center of which lies the capital, MADRID. The plateau is drained by the EBRO and TAGUS rivers. ZARAGOZA lies on the Ebro, and TOLEDO on the Tagus. The Cantabrian Mountains lie between LEÓN and the N coastal regions of GALICIA and ASTURIAS. BILBAO and PAMPLONA are the major cities in BASQUE COUNTRY. The PYRENEES form a natural border with France, and extend S into NAVARRE and CATALONIA. BARCELONA lies on the Costa Brava. On the E Mediterranean side lie the ports of VALENCIA and CARTAGENA, and the BALEARIC ISLANDS. ANDALUSIA includes the cities of SEVILLE and CÓRDOBA, and Spain's highest peak, Mulhacén, at 11,411ft (3,478m), in the Sierra Nevada, close to the city of GRANADA. Many Spanish resorts, such as MÁLAGA, lie on the Costa del Sol. The status of GIBRALTAR is disputed with Britain.

### CLIMATE

The *Meseta* has hot summers and cold winters. The S coast has Europe's mildest winters. Winter snowfall is heavy on the high mountains.

### VEGETATION

Forests cover 32% of Spain, mostly in the mountainous regions. Grassland and scrub cover much of the *Meseta*, but 30% of land is arable.

### HISTORY

Iberians and BASQUES were Spain's early inhabitants. In the 9th century BC, the Phoenicians established trading posts on the S coast. In *c.*600 BC Greek merchants set up colonies. In *c.*237 BC the Carthaginian general HAMILCAR BARCA conquered most of the peninsula. By the 1st century AD, most of Spain had fallen to the Romans; it became a prosperous province. From *c.*AD 400, Germanic tribes swept into Spain. During the 5th–8th centuries, Visigoths controlled S Spain. In 711 the MOORS defeated the Visigoths. Spain was rapidly conquered (except Asturias and the Basque Country) and an independent Muslim state founded (756). The ALHAMBRA is testimony to the splendor of MOORISH architecture. The Basques established an independent kingdom of Navarre. Asturias acted as the base for the Christian reconquest. While the Christian lands were unifying, the Muslim state was fracturing. In 1479 Castile and Aragón were united by the marriage of FERDINAND and ISABELLA. The reconquest of Granada (1492) saw Ferdinand and Isabella become rulers of all Spain. The INQUISITION was used to ensure Catholic supremacy through persecution and conversion. Columbus's discovery of America (1492) led to Spain becoming the leading imperial power. The Americas brought vast wealth. The 16th century was Spain's golden age. In 1519 Charles I became CHARLES V, Holy Roman emperor. The supremacy of the HAPSBURGS was established. The extension and centralization of power was continued by PHILIP II, who gained Portugal (1580). Spanish naval power was dented by the defeat of the Spanish ARMADA (1588). During the 17th century, Spain's political and economic power declined. The War of the SPANISH SUCCESSION (1701–14) resulted in the accession of PHILIP V, and the establishment of the BOURBON dynasty. CHARLES III brought the church under state control. CHARLES IV's reign ended in French occupation, and the appointment of Joseph BONAPARTE as king. Spanish resistance led to the restoration of the Bourbons in 1813. Many of Spain's New World colonies gained independence. The accession of ISABELLA II resulted in prolonged civil war with the CARLISTS. A short-lived constitutional monarchy and republic was followed by a further Bourbon restoration under ALFONSO XII and XIII. Spain remained neutral during World War I. From 1923 to 1930, Spain was ruled by the dictator PRIMO DE RIVERA. He was forced to resign and a second republic was proclaimed. The Popular Front won 1936 elections, and conflict between republicans and nationalists, such as the FALANGE, intensified. With the backing of the Axis powers, the nationalists led by General FRANCO emerged victorious from the Spanish CIVIL WAR (1936–39), and Franco established a dictatorship. Spain did not participate in World War II. Spain joined the UN in 1955. During the 1960s most of Spain's remaining colonies gained independence. In 1975 Franco died, and a constitutional monarchy was established under Juan Carlos. Spain began a process of democratization and decentralization of power. Spain joined NATO (1982) and the European Community (1986).

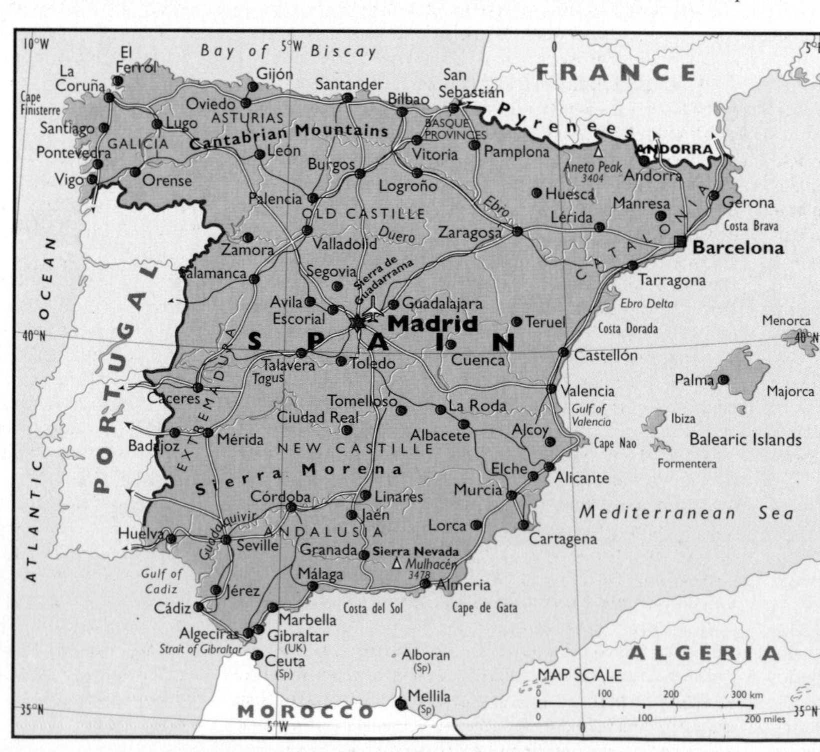


### POLITICS

Through much of its history there has been tension between government and the regions. Basque independence has been a constant issue. Since 1959 the militant Basque organization ETA has waged a campaign of terror. In 1977 the Basque Country (*Pais Vasco*), Catalonia, and Galicia gained limited autonomy. In 1996 José María AZNAR formed minority administration.

### ECONOMY

Spanish economic revival began in the 1950s, based on tourism and manufacturing. It has rapidly transformed from a largely poor, agrarian society into a prosperous industrial nation (1995 GDP per capita, US$14,520). Agriculture now employs only 10% of the work force. Spain is the world's third-largest wine producer. Other crops include citrus fruits, tomatoes, and olives. Sheep are the main livestock. Spain is the world's sixth-largest car producer. Other manufactures include ships, chemicals, electronics, metal goods, steel, and textiles. It lacks mineral resources. Unemployment remains high (1996, 22%).

s toward Sicily, where they were eventually defeated by CRASSUS with POMPEY's aid. Spartacus died in battle.

**spasm** Sustained involuntary muscle contraction. It may occur in response to pain, or as part of a generalized condition, such as spastic paralysis or TETANUS.

**spathe** Broad leaflike organ that spreads from the base of, or enfolds, the SPADIX of certain flowering plants.

**Speaker** Presiding officer who ensures procedures are adhered to in the legislatures of various countries. In the US House of Representatives, the speaker is elected from the majority party by the House. Powers include the recognition of members for debate, the appointment of select and conference committees, the referral of bills to committees, and the signing of documents on behalf of the House. The speaker follows the vice president in presidential succession. In the UK the Speaker of the House of Commons presides over debates but has no other formal powers.

**spearmint** Common name of *Mentha spicata*, a hardy perennial herb of the MINT family (Lamiaceae/Labiatae). Its leaves are used for flavoring, especially in sweets. Oil distilled from spearmint is used as a medicine. The plant has pink or lilac flowers that grow in spikes.

**Special Branch** Department within every British police force that is technically affiliated to MI5, the intelligence bureau within the Home Office. Its duties are to investigate and deter all activities against the nation, to protect visiting foreign rulers and dignitaries, and to monitor immigration.

**species** Group of physically and genetically similar individuals that interbreed to produce fertile offspring under natural conditions. Each species has a unique two-part Latin name, the first part being the GENUS name. So far, more than 1.5 million plant and animal species have been identified. *See also* TAXONOMY, BINOMIAL NOMENCLATURE

**specific gravity** *See* RELATIVE DENSITY

**specific heat capacity** Heat necessary to raise the temperature of 1kg of a substance by 1K (KELVIN) (1°C). It is measured in J/kgK (J equals joule).

**spectroscopy** Branch of OPTICS dealing with the measurement of the wavelength and intensity of lines in a SPECTRUM. The main tool in this study is the spectroscope. It produces a spectrum and a spectrograph photographs it. An analysis of the spectrogram can reveal the substances causing the spectrum by the position of emission and absorption lines and bands. A spectrometer is a calibrated spectroscope capable of precise measurements.

**spectrum** Arrangement of ELECTROMAGNETIC RADIATIONS ordered by wavelength or frequency. The visible light spectrum is a series of colors: red, orange, yellow, green, blue, indigo, and violet. Each color corresponds to a different wavelength of light. A spectrum is seen in a rainbow or when white light passes through a PRISM. This effect, also seen when visible light passes through a DIFFRACTION grating, produces a continuous spectrum in which all wavelengths (between certain limits) are present. Spectra formed from objects emitting radiations are called **emission** spectra. These occur when a substance is strongly heated or bombarded by electrons. An **absorption** spectrum, consisting of dark regions on a bright background, is obtained when white light passes through a semitransparent medium that absorbs certain frequencies. A line spectrum is one in which only certain wavelengths or "lines" appear. *See* SPECTROSCOPY

**speedwell** Common name applied to herbaceous plants of many species of the genus *Veronica* found throughout the world.

**Speke, John Hanning** (1827–64) British explorer of E Africa. After service in India he joined Richard BURTON in an expedition to Somalia (1854) and to the E African lakes (1856). In Burton's absence he reached Lake Victoria, which he identified as the source of the Nile.

**speleology** Study of CAVES and cave systems. Included also are the hydrological and geological studies concerned with the formation of STALAGMITES and STALACTITES and the influence of GROUNDWATER conditions on cave formation.

**Spencer, Sir Stanley** (1891–1959) British painter. During World War II he was a war artist and painted a series of large pictures showing shipbuilding on the Clyde. Spencer is also known for his nude paintings, such as the so-called *Leg of Mutton Nude* (1937).

**Spender, Stephen Harold** (1909–95) British poet. His best verse includes the often anthologized *I Think Continually of Those Who Were Truly Great*. His autobiography *World Within World* (1951) is a powerful evocation of his time. His *Collected Poems 1928–1985* appeared in 1985.

**Spengler, Oswald** (1880–1936) German philosophical historian. In *The Decline of the West* (1918–22), he expounded his theory that all civilizations are subject to an inevitable process of growth and decay, concluding that Western civilization was ending. His theory had some appeal in Germany in the 1930s.

**Spenser, Edmund** (1552–99) English poet. His poetry includes the pastoral *The Sheapheardes Calender* (1579); the sonnet sequence *Amoretti*, published with *Epithalamion* in 1595; *Four Hymns* and *Prothalamion* (both 1596). His life's work, however, was *The Faerie Queene* (1589–96).

**sperm** (spermatozoon) Motile male sex cell (GAMETE) in sexually reproducing organisms. It corresponds to the female OVUM (eggs). The head of the sperm contains the genetic material of the male parent, while its tail or other motile structure provides the means of moving to the ovum to carry out FERTILIZATION.

**spermatophyte** Seed-bearing plant, including most trees, shrubs, and herbaceous plants. It has a stem, leaves, roots, and a well-developed vascular system. The dominant generation is the SPOROPHYTE. The widely accepted Five Kingdoms classification classifies seed plants as several distinct phyla: the Angiospermophyta (flowering plants), Coniferophyta (conifers), Ginkgophyta (ginkgo or maidenhair tree), Cycadophyta (cycads), and Gnetophyta (a group of cone-bearing desert plants).

**sperm whale** Largest of the toothed WHALES. It has a squarish head and feeds on squid and cuttlefish. Species *Physeter catodon*.

**sphalerite** (blende) Sulfide mineral composed of zinc sulfide (ZnS), an important source of zinc. It has cubic system tetrahedral crystals or granular masses. It is white when pure, but more commonly yellow, black, or brown with a resinous luster. Hardness 3.5–4; s.g. 4.

**sphere** 3-D geometric figure formed by the locus in space of points equidistant from a given point (the center). The distance from the center to the surface is the radius, *r*. The volume is $(4/3)\pi r^3$ and the surface area is calculated at $4\pi r^2$.

**spherical trigonometry** Branch of mathematics that deals with the sides, angles, and areas of spherical triangles, that is, portions of the surface of a sphere bounded by three arcs or great circles. *See also* TRIGONOMETRY

**sphincter** Ring of muscle surrounding a body orifice which can open it or seal it off. Important sphincters include the pyloric sphincter in the stomach and the anal sphincter.

**sphinx** Mythical beast of the ancient world, usually represented with the head of a man or woman and the body of a lion. In Greek mythology, the riddle of the Sphinx of Thebes was solved by OEDIPUS, so destroying her evil power. Although found throughout the Middle East, images of sphinxes were especially popular in Egypt, where thousands were built.

**sphygmomanometer** Instrument used to measure BLOOD PRESSURE. The device incorporates an inflatable rubber cuff connected to a column of mercury with a graduated scale. The cuff is wrapped around the upper arm and inflated to apply pressure to a major artery. When the air is slowly released, the pressure readings can be ascertained from the scale.

**spice** Food flavoring consisting of the dried form of various plants. Spices were used in medieval times to disguise the taste of food that was decaying, and as preservatives. They also had medicinal and religious functions.

**spider** Any of numerous species of terrestrial, invertebrate, ARACHNID arthropods found throughout the world in a wide variety of habitats. Spiders have an unsegmented **abdomen** attached to a **cephalothorax** by a slender **pedicel**. There are no antennae; sensory hairs are found on the appendages (four pairs of walking legs). Most species have spinnerets on the abdomen for spinning silk to make egg cases and webs.

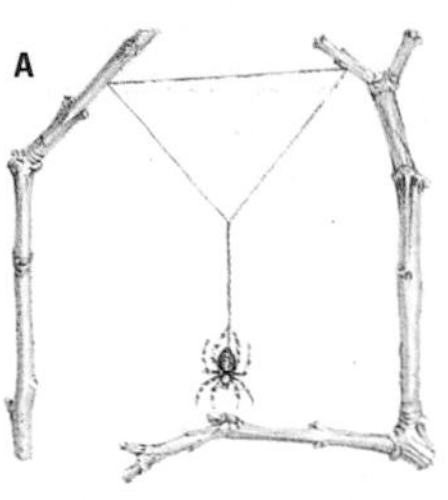


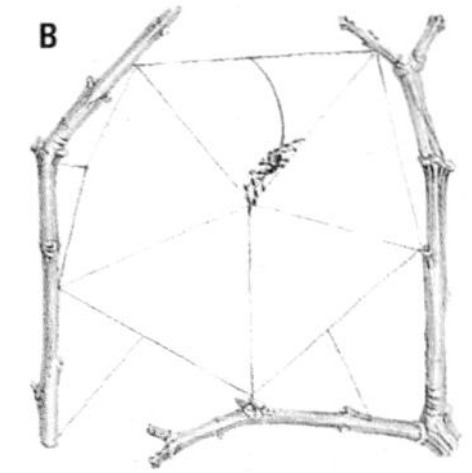


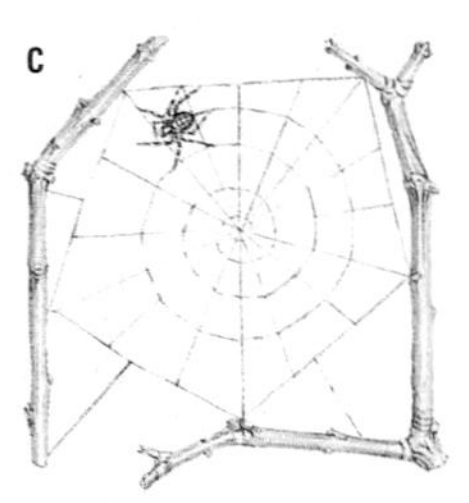


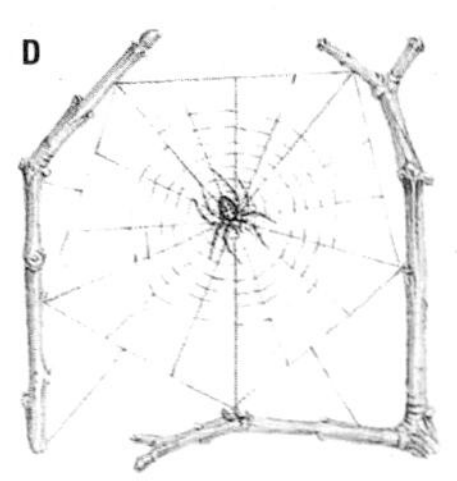


▲ **spider** When spinning its web for catching prey, the spider first casts out a thread of silk to form a horizontal strut. A second, drooping thread is trailed across below the bridge-line. Halfway along the second thread, the spider drops down on a vertical thread until it reaches a fixed object (A). It pulls the silk taut and anchors it, forming a "Y" shape, the center of which forms the hub of the web. The spider then spins the framework threads and the radials, which are linked together at the hub (B). After spinning the remainder of the radials, a wide temporary spiral of dry silk is laid down, working from the inside of the web outward (C). This holds the web together while the spider lays down the sticky spiral. This is laid down starting from the outside and is attached successively to each radial thread (D). The spider eats the remains of the dry spiral as it proceeds. The central dry spirals are left as a platform for the spider, which will often lie in wait there during the night but will retreat to a nearby silk shelter during the day.

S

▲ **Spielberg** The most commercially successful film director of all time, Steven Spielberg began his career in television. He went on to direct a series of hit films that included thrillers, action adventures, and science fiction. His production company, Amblin', has worked on many other films including *Back to the Future* (1985) and *Who Framed Roger Rabbit* (1988). Famous for his ability to convey a magical sense of childlike wonder in his films, Spielberg has also worked on more serious literary adaptations such as *The Color Purple* (1985), an epic story of slavery and freedom, and *Schindler's List* (1993), a harrowing document of the violence of the Holocaust.

**spider monkey** Medium-sized, arboreal (tree-dwelling), MONKEY found from S Mexico to SE Brazil. It has long, spidery legs, and a fully prehensile tail and is an agile climber, using the tail as a fifth limb. It eats mainly fruit and nuts. Genera *Ateles* and *Brachyteles*.

**Spielberg, Steven** (1947– ) US film director and producer. The success of *Jaws* (1975) established his reputation. *Close Encounters of the Third Kind* (1977) earned him an Academy Award nomination. The "Indiana Jones" trilogy began with *Raiders of the Lost Ark* (1981). Spielberg's mastery of special effects was confirmed by *E.T. The Extra-Terrestrial* (1982). In 1984, he founded an independent production company. *Jurassic Park* (1993) is one of the highest grossing films of all time. Its sequel was *The Lost World* (1997). Spielberg won two Academy Awards for best director: *Schindler's List* (1993) and the World War II epic *Saving Private Ryan* (1998).

**spin** (symbol *s*) In QUANTUM MECHANICS, intrinsic angular momentum possessed by some SUBATOMIC PARTICLES, atoms, and nuclei. This may be regarded by analogy as the spinning of the particle about an axis within itself. Spin is one of the quantum numbers by which a particle is specified.

**spina bifida** Congenital disorder in which the bones of the SPINE do not develop properly to enclose the SPINAL CORD. Surgery to close the defect is usually performed soon after birth but this may not cure the disabilities caused by the condition.

**spinach** Herbaceous, annual plant cultivated in areas with cool summers. Spinach is used as a culinary herb and as a vegetable. Family Chenopodiaceae; species *Spinacia oleracea.*

**spinal cord** Tubular, central nerve cord, lying within the SPINE. With the brain, it makes up the CENTRAL NERVOUS SYSTEM. It gives rise to the 31 pairs of spinal nerves, each of which has sensory and motor fibers.

**spinal tap** (lumbar puncture) Procedure for withdrawing CEREBROSPINAL FLUID from the lumbar (lower back) portion of the SPINAL CORD for laboratory examination to aid diagnosis.

**spine** (vertebral column) Backbone of VERTEBRATES, extending from the SKULL to the tip of the tail (if present) and enclosing the SPINAL CORD. The human spine consists of 26 vertebrae interspersed with disks of CARTILAGE. It articulates with the skull, ribs, and hip bones and provides points of attachment for the back muscles.

**spinet** Early musical instrument of the harpsichord family with one keyboard and one string to each note. The strings were plucked with a quill or leather plectrum.

**spinning** Process of making thread or yarn by twisting fibers together. The fibers may be of animal, vegetable, or synthetic origin. Machines developed for mechanizing the spinning process include the spinning wheel, spinning frame (invented by Richard ARKWRIGHT), spinning jenny (invented by James HARGREAVES), and spinning mule (invented by Samuel CROMPTON). Today, large machines carry out the same basic process, but at much increased speeds.

**Spinoza, Baruch** (1632–77) Dutch-Jewish rationalist philosopher, also known as Benedict de Spinoza. He was the son of Portuguese Jews who had been forced by the INQUISITION to adopt Christianity and had eventually fled to the relative religious freedom of the Netherlands. Spinoza argued that all mind and matter were modes of the one key substance, which he called either God or Nature. In *Ethics* (1677), he held that FREE WILL was an illusion that would be dispelled by man's recognition that every event has a cause.

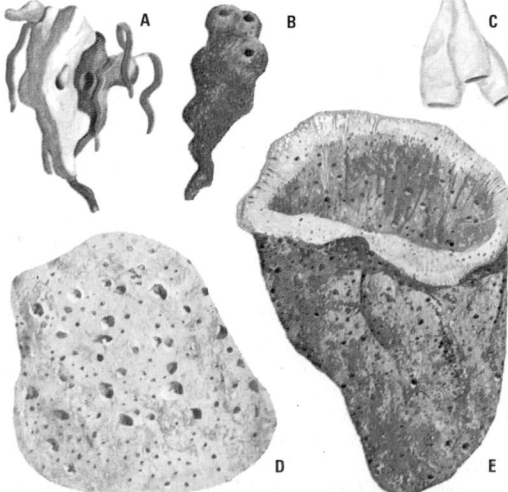

**spiny anteater** *See* ECHIDNA

**spirea** Genus of flowering, PERENNIAL shrubs native to the Northern Hemisphere. They have small flat leaves and clusters of white, pink, or red flowers. Many of the 100 species are grown as ornamentals. Height: 5ft (1.5m). Family Rosaceae.

**spiritual** Religious folk music, especially that associated with African-American culture. The words are generally adaptions of passages from the Bible, and the music is often in four-part harmony with certain specific features such as five-note melodies. Spirituals have influenced the development of other musical forms, such as the BLUES. *See also* GOSPEL MUSIC

**spiritualism** Belief that, at death, the personality of an individual is transferred to another plane of existence, with which communication from the world of the living is possible. The channel of such communication is a receptive living person called a **medium**. Spiritualism as a movement began in the US in 1848.

**spleen** Dark red organ located on the left side of the abdomen, behind and slightly below the stomach. It is important in both the lymphatic and blood systems, helping to process LYMPHOCYTES, destroying worn out or damaged ERYTHROCYTES, and storing iron. Removal of the spleen (splenectomy) is sometimes necessary following trauma or in the treatment of some blood disorders.

**Split** Major port on the Dalmatian coast of the Adriatic Sea, Croatia. Split was held by Venice from 1420 to 1797, when it passed to Austria. It became part of Yugoslavia in 1918. Croatia's second-largest city, Split's industries include shipbuilding, textiles, chemicals, cement, and tourism, which was severely disrupted by the wars following the breakup of Yugoslavia. Pop. (1991) 189,388.

**Spock, Dr. Benjamin McLane** (1903–98) US pediatrician and writer whose *The Common Sense Book of Baby and Child Care* (1946) reversed the trend in child-rearing by calling for parental warmth and understanding.

**Spode, Josiah** (1754–1827) British potter. He gave his name to Spode PORCELAIN, which became the standard English bone china. For this hybrid porcelain he used bone ash and feldspar in the paste as well as china clay and china stone.

**spoils system** Form of US political patronage. The practice of appointing loyal members of the party in power to public offices was first referred to as the spoils system under Andrew JACKSON. It reached its height *c.*1860–80 but declined after the Civil Service Act of 1883.

**Spokane** City and port of entry in E WASHINGTON, on the falls of the Spokane River. Originally inhabited by the Spokane tribe, a trading post was established in 1810. Settlement began *c.*1871 and industry was spurred by the arrival of the Northern Pacific Railroad (1881). It was incorporated as a city in 1891. Industries: lumber, food processing, metal refining, mining, cement. Pop. (1990) 177,165.

**sponge** Primitive, multicellular aquatic animal. Its extremely simple structure is supported by a skeleton of lime, silica, or spongin. There is no mouth, nervous system, or cellular coordination, nor are there any internal organs. Sponges reproduce sexually and by asexual budding. There are about 5,000 species, including the simple sponge genus *Leucosolenia*. Length: 0.4in–6ft (1mm–2m). Phylum: Porifera.

**spontaneous generation** Belief, now discredited, that living organisms arise from nonliving matter. It supposedly explained the presence of maggots on decaying meat.

**spoonbill** Any of several species of wading birds, each with a long bill that is flat and rounded at the tip; species are found in tropical climates throughout the world. It has large wings, long legs, a short tail, and white or pinkish plumage; it feeds on small plant and animal matter. Length: 3ft (90cm). Family: Threskiornithidae.

► **sponge** Classified according to the substance that makes up the supporting skeleton, the sponges include the breadcrumb sponge *Halichondria panica* (A), with a skeleton (B) composed of spicules of silicon. The purse sponge (*Grantia compressa*) (C) has a skeleton of calcium carbonate spicules and is placed in a group called calareous sponges. Two commercial sponges *Hippospongia equina* (D) and *Euspongia officinalis* (E) have skeletons of a horny, elastic substance called spongin. After harvesting from the seabed, they are dried, beaten, and washed to remove hard debris so that the only part remaining is the skeleton.

**spore** Small reproductive body that detaches from the parent organism to produce new offspring. Mostly microscopic, spores may consist of one or several cells (but do not contain an embryo) and are produced in large numbers. Some germinate rapidly, others "rest," surviving unfavorable environmental conditions. Spores are formed by FERNS, HORSETAILS, MOSSES, FUNGI, and BACTERIA.

**sporophyte** DIPLOID stage in the life cycle of a plant or alga. Usually, the sporophyte gives rise to HAPLOID SPORES which germinate to produce a haploid generation (the GAMETOPHYTE stage), which will produce the GAMETES. In FERNS, HORSETAILS, CONIFERS, and ANGIOSPERMS the diploid sporophyte is the dominant phase of the life cycle, the plant body we usually see. In mosses and liverworts, the main plant body is the gametophyte. *See also* ALTERNATION OF GENERATIONS

**sprain** Injury to one or more ligaments of a joint, caused by sudden over-stretching. Symptoms include pain, stiffness, bruising, and swelling. Treatment includes resting and supporting the affected part before gentle mobilization.

**sprat** (brisling) Small herring-like commercial fish found in the N Atlantic Ocean. It is slender and silvery. Length: to 5in (12.5cm). Family Clupeidae; species *Clupea sprattus*.

**spring** Mechanical device designed to be elastically compressed, extended, or deflected. It may be used to store energy, absorb shock, or maintain contact between two surfaces.

**springbok** (springbuck) Small, horned ANTELOPE native to S Africa; the national emblem of South Africa. The reddish-brown color on the back shades into a dark horizontal band just above the white underside. Height: to 3ft (90cm) at the shoulder. Family Bovidae; species *Antidorcas marsupialis*.

**Springfield** State capital of Illinois, 185mi (298km) SW of Chicago. Founded in 1818, it became state capital in 1837. It is the center of a fertile farming area. Industries: machinery, electronics, fertilizers. Pop. (1992) 106,429.

**spruce** Various evergreen trees, related to firs, native to mountainous or cooler temperate regions of the Northern Hemisphere. Pyramid-shaped and dense, they have angular rather than flattened needles, and pendulous cones. The timber is used in cabinet-making, and some species yield turpentine. Height: to 170ft (50m). Family Pinaceae; genus *Picea*.

**Sputnik** World's first artificial SATELLITE, launched by the Soviet Union on October 4, 1957. Weighing 184lb (83.5kg) and with a radio transmitter, *Sputnik 1* circled the Earth for several months.

**square** In geometry, rectangle with four sides of the same length. In arithmetic or algebra, a square is the result of multiplying a quantity by itself: the square of 3 is 9, and the square of $x$ is $x^2$.

**square root** (symbol $\sqrt{}$) Number or quantity that must be multiplied by itself to give a specified number or quantity. The square root of 4 is 2, often written as. $\sqrt{4} = 2$. A negative number has imaginary square roots.

**squash** Any of several species of vine fruits of various shapes, all of which belong to the genus *Cucurbita*. Squashes are native to the Americas, and are cultivated as vegetables. Family Cucurbitaceae.

**squash** Ball game played with small, round-headed rackets by two (or occasionally four) people on a rectangular, four-walled court. The wall at the front of the court is marked with three horizontal lines at different heights. The ball from the serve must land above the middle line (the cut line). Balls hitting the wall above the third line are out. The rubber ball may bounce off front, side, and back walls, but may bounce only once on the floor before it is struck. The object of each point is to make it impossible for the opponent to return the ball. The first player to score 15 points wins the game. It is played by both amateurs and professionals.

**squid** Any of numerous species of marine, cephalopod MOLLUSKS that have a cylindrical body with an internal horny plate (the pen) that serves as a skeleton. It has eight short, suckered tentacles surrounding the mouth, in addition to which there are two longer, armlike tentacles that can be shot out to seize moving prey. Several species of giant squid (genus *Architeuthis*) may reach 65ft (20m) in length. Class Cephalopoda; order Teuthoidea.

**squint** *See* STRABISMUS

**squirrel** Any of numerous species of primarily arboreal, diurnal rodents found throughout the world. Species of Eurasia, the US, and South America, such as the common gray squirrel, red squirrel, and flying squirrels, are the best known. Most species feed on nuts, seeds, fruit, insects, and some eat eggs and young birds. Most have short fur and characteristically bushy tails. Family Sciuridae.

**squirrel monkey** Either of at least two species of small, diurnal, arboreal MONKEYS of tropical South America; it has thick, dark fur and a long, heavy tail. *Saimiri sciureus* has a cap of grayish fur; *S. oerstedi* has a black cap and reddish fur on its back. Both are gregarious and live primarily on fruit. Length: to 16in (40cm); tail: 19in (47cm). Family Cebidae.

**Sri Lanka** State in the Indian Ocean. *See* country feature, page 636

**SS** (*Schutzstaffeln*, guards unit) Chief paramilitary force of Nazi Germany. It was originally Hitler's bodyguard but expanded under HIMMLER after 1928 to become the Nazi Party militia and internal police force. With its distinctive black uniform, the SS controlled the GESTAPO and the SD (security organization). It ran the CONCENTRATION CAMPS and, from 1936, controlled the police. After the outbreak of war it formed its own fighting units, notorious for their ferocity, known as the Waffen SS.

**Staël, (Anne-Louise-Germaine), Madame de** (1766–1817) French writer. One of the most influential intellectual figures of her time, she published two protofeminist novels, *Delphine* (1802) and *Corinne* (1807), but is best known for her works of social and esthetic philosophy. They include *A Treatise on the Influence of the Passions upon the Happiness of Individuals and of Nations* (1796), a key text of ROMANTICISM.

**Staffordshire** County in W central England. The terrain is composed of rolling hills with moorlands in the N. The region is drained chiefly by the Trent River. The county is primarily industrial. It includes the Potteries around Stoke-on-Trent and the Black Country, one of the great industrial hubs of England. Stafford (1991 pop. 117,800) is the county town. Area: 1,049sq mi (2,716sq km). Pop. (1991) 1,031,035.

**stag beetle** Large, brown or black BEETLE of Eurasian oak forests; the male bears large antler-like mandibles. The larvae feed on rotten wood. Length: to 3in (8cm). Family Lucanidae; species *Lucanus cervus*.

**stained glass** Colored glass used for decorative, often pictorial effect in windows. In its purest form, stained glass is made by adding metal-oxide coloring agents during the manufacture of glass. Shapes cut from the resulting sheets are then arranged to form patterns or images. These shapes are joined and supported by flexible strips of lead that form dark, emphatic contors. Details are painted onto the glass surfaces in liquid enamel and fused on by heat.

**stainless steel** Group of iron alloys that resist corrosion. Besides carbon, contained in all steels, stainless steels contain from 12% to 25% chromium. This makes the steel stainless by forming a thin, protective oxide coating on the surface. Most also contain nickel. Other metals and non-metals may be added to give the steel particular properties.

**stalactite** Icicle-like formation of CALCIUM CARBONATE found hanging from the roofs of CAVES. It is made by the precipitation of LIMESTONE out of water that has seeped into limestone caves.

**stalagmite** Deposit of crystalline CALCIUM CARBONATE rising from the floor of a cavern, and formed by dripping water that has seeped into limestone CAVES.

**Stalin, Joseph** (1879–1953) (Iosif Vissarionovich Dzhugashvili) Leader of the Soviet Union (1924–53). He supported LENIN and the BOLSHEVIKS from 1903, adopting the name Stalin ("man of steel") while editing *Pravda*, the party newspaper. Exiled to Siberia (1913–17), he returned to join the RUSSIAN REVOLUTION (1917) and became secretary of the central committee of the party in 1922. On Lenin's death in 1924, he achieved supreme power through his control of the party organization. He outmaneuvered rivals such as TROTSKY and BUKHARIN and drove them from power. From 1929 he was virtually dictator. He enforced collectivization of agriculture and intensive industrialization, brutally suppressing all opposition,

▲ **squash** Cultivated since prehistoric times, the many varieties of edible squash include the winter squash (*Cucurbita maxima*) shown here. Squash grow in a wide range of colors and shapes. There are also several varieties of inedible squash, which can be dried and put to different uses, serving, for example, as bowls or cups.

▲ **squirrel monkey** Found in many forested areas of South America, common squirrel monkeys (*Saimiri sciureus*) spend most of their time in the treetops, feeding on fruit and nuts as well as insects, eggs, and young birds. However, they are also known to feed on the ground and to make bold raids on areas of cultivated fruit. Lively and friendly, they commonly live in groups of up to 30 individuals who sleep huddled together on large tree branches. Sometimes they join into large bands numbering several hundred.

and, in the 1930s, he exterminated all opponents in a series of purges of political and military leaders. During World War II Stalin controlled the armed forces and negotiated skillfully during the YALTA CONFERENCE with CHURCHILL and ROOSEVELT. After the war he reimposed severe repression and forced puppet communist governments on the states of Eastern Europe.

**Stalingrad** *See* VOLGOGRAD

**Stalingrad, Battle of** (1942–43) Decisive conflict marking the failure of the German invasion of the Soviet Union during World War II. The city (now Volgograd) withstood a German siege from August 1942 to February 1943. Total casualties at Stalingrad exceeded 1.5 million.

**Stallone, Sylvester** (1946– ) US film actor and director. His screenplay and starring role in *Rocky* (1976) reflected his own story. Four sequels followed, three directed by Stallone. The *Rambo* trilogy developed his macho image. The mid-90s saw a comeback with *Demolition Man* (1993) and *The Specialist* (1994).

**stamen** Pollen-producing male organ of a FLOWER. It consists of an ANTHER, in which POLLEN is produced, on the end of a stalklike **filament**. The arrangement and number of stamens is important in the classification of flowering plants.

**Stamp Act** (1765) First direct tax levied on the American colonies by the British government. Introduced to raise revenue for the defense of the colonies, it required a special stamp on all printed material, including newspapers and legal documents. It roused widespread opposition, and led to the Stamp Act Congress (1765), at which representatives of nine colonies met in New York City and resolved that only the colonies could tax themselves. It was repealed in 1766.

**standard deviation** (symbol ø or *s*) In statistics, a measure of dispersion or deviation of scores from the average or mean of the scores. In a list of numbers, the deviation is found by calculating the difference from the MEAN of each score in the list. The value of each differing score is then squared, and the mean calculated. The deviation of the resultant mean is the SQUARE ROOT of that number.

**standard temperature and pressure (STP)** (normal temperature and pressure) In chemistry and physics, standard conditions for measurements, especially when comparing the volumes of gases. It is a temperature of 273K – 32°F (0°C) – and a pressure of 1 standard atmosphere (101,325 pascals).

**standing wave** In physics, a wave in which the points of maximum vibration (the **antinodes**) and the points of no

## SRI LANKA

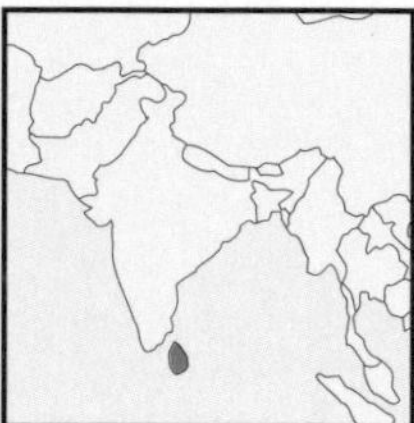

Sri Lanka's flag was adopted in 1951, three years after the country, then called Ceylon, became independent from Britain. The lion banner represents the ancient Buddhist kingdom. The stripes symbolize the minorities – Muslims (green) and Hindus (orange).

**AREA:** 25,332sq mi (65,610sq km)
**POPULATION:** 17,405,000
**CAPITAL (POPULATION):** Colombo (684,000)
**GOVERNMENT:** Multiparty republic
**ETHNIC GROUPS:** Sinhalese 74%, Tamil 18%, Sri Lankan Moor 7%
**LANGUAGES:** Sinhala and Tamil (both official)
**RELIGIONS:** Buddhism 69%, Hinduism 16%, Islam 8%, Christianity 7%
**CURRENCY:** Sri Lankan rupee = 100 cents

The Democratic Socialist Republic of Sri Lanka (formerly Ceylon) is a pear-shaped island, separated from SE India by the Palk Strait. A chain of coral islands (Adam's Bridge) almost joins the two countries. Most of Sri Lanka is low-lying. A coastal plain is fringed by cliffs and lagoons. On the SW coast lies the capital, COLOMBO. The S central core of Sri Lanka is a highland region. The highest peak is Pidurutalagala, at 8,281ft (2,524m). Nearby, Adam's Peak, at 7,359ft (2,243m), is a pilgrimage center. The major highland city is KANDY.

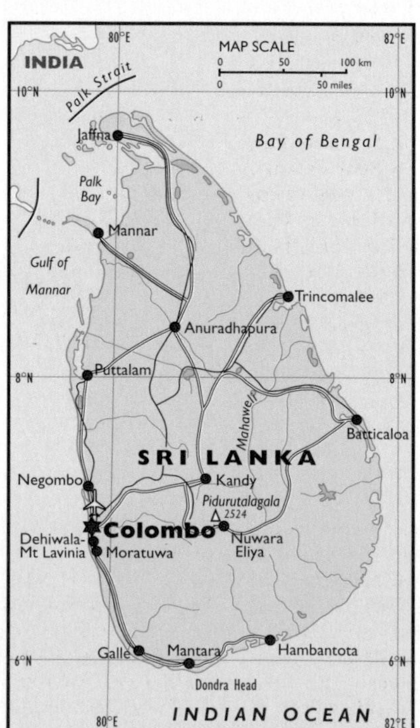


### CLIMATE

Western Sri Lanka has high temperatures and heavy rainfall. The monsoon season is between May and October. The N and E are drier.

### VEGETATION

Over 30% of Sri Lanka is tropical rain forest or woodland. The highlands are more open grassland. Over 14% of land is cultivated for tea and spice gardens, rice fields, and sugar plantations.

### HISTORY AND POLITICS

The native Veddahs were forced into the mountains *c.*2,400 years ago by SINHALESE settlers from N India. Some Veddahs remain in remote regions. The Sinhalese founded Anuradhapura in 437 BC, which acted as their capital and a center of THERAVADA Buddhism, until the arrival of the Tamils in the 8th century AD. The CHOLA dynasty conquered the island in the 11th century. The Sinhalese were gradually forced S. The Portuguese landed in 1505 and formed coastal settlements. In 1658 Portuguese lands passed to the Dutch EAST INDIA COMPANY. In 1796 the British captured the Dutch colonies, and in 1802 Ceylon became a crown colony. In 1815 Britain captured Kandy. Colonialism developed the plantations. In 1948 Ceylon achieved self-government within the Commonwealth of Nations. In the late 1950s, following the declaration of Sinhalese as the official language, communal violence flared between Tamils and Sinhalese. In 1958 Prime Minister Solomon BANDARANAIKE was assassinated. His widow, Sirimavo BANDARANAIKE, became the world's first woman prime minister (1960). Following a brief period in opposition, she was reelected in 1970. In 1972 Ceylon became the independent republic of Sri Lanka (resplendent island). The new republic was faced with resurgent demands for a separate Tamil state (Tamil Eelam) in N and E Sri Lanka. In 1983 secessionist demands spiraled into civil war between government forces and the TAMIL TIGERS. In 1987 the Sri Lankan government called for Indian military assistance. Unable to enforce a peace settlement, Indian troops withdrew in 1989. In 1993 President Ranasinghe Premadasa was assassinated. In 1994 Prime Minister Chandrika Bandaranaike Kumaratunga was elected president, and her mother, Sirimavo Bandaranaike, became prime minister for the third time. Military offensives against the Tamil Tigers led to the recapture of Jaffna in 1995. The Tamil Tigers refused to accept devolution and the war, which has claimed over 40,000 lives, continued.

### ECONOMY

Sri Lanka is a low-income developing country (1995 GDP per capita, $3,250). Agriculture employs 50% of the work force. Sri Lanka is the world's third-largest producer of tea It is also a leading producer of coconuts and rubber. Manufacturing has increased rapidly and contributes 67% of exports. Products include ceramics, textiles, and clothes. Tourism is also important.

vibration (the **nodes**) do not move. A standing wave is formed by the interference of waves of equal frequency and intensity traveling in opposite directions.

**Stanford, Leland** (1824–93) US railroad builder and politician. During the Civil War he was Republican governor of California (1861) and kept it in the Union. He was a founder of the Central Pacific Railroad and president of the Southern Pacific lines. While in the US Senate (1885–93) he secured financial aid for the railroads from state and municipal governments. He founded Stanford University in 1885 and named it for his son Leland.

**Stanford-Binet scale** Most commonly used English-language intelligence test for measuring a child's IQ. It was formulated at Stanford University, California, in 1916, as an adaptation of the Binet Scale. *See also* APTITUDE TEST

**Stanislavsky, Konstantin** (1863–1938) (Konstantin Sergeyevich Alekseyev) Russian actor, director, and teacher. His theory of drama, described in *My Life In Art* (1924), stressed a naturalistic approach and the value of the ensemble, with actors making emotional contact with their characters.

**Stanley, Sir Henry Morton** (1841–1904) British-US explorer of Africa, b. Wales. He emigrated to the US aged 16. He became a journalist and was commissioned by the *New York Herald* to lead an expedition in search of David LIVINGSTONE in E Africa. They met in 1871. On a second expedition, Stanley led a large party from the E African lakes down the Congo River to the W coast. He returned to the area (1880) as an agent for King LEOPOLD II and in 1887–89 led an expedition supposedly to rescue Emin Pasha from the Sudan, and pressed on, with heavy losses, to the Indian Ocean.

**Stanley** (Port Stanley) Capital and chief port of the FALKLAND ISLANDS, on East Falkland. Pop. (1991) 2,121.

**Stanton, Edwin McMasters** (1814–69) US statesman. Attorney general under President BUCHANAN and associated with S Democrats, he was a firm unionist and was appointed (1862) secretary of war by Abraham LINCOLN. Stanton retained his office under Andrew JOHNSON and attempted to mediate between the president and the Republican Congress over RECONSTRUCTION. Johnson's efforts to dismiss Stanton led to his own impeachment. Stanton was forced to resign after Johnson was acquitted in 1868.

**Stanton, Elizabeth Cady** (1815–1902) US social reformer. She was a lifelong worker for women's rights. She organized the SENECA FALLS CONVENTION (1848), the first public assembly in the US for female suffrage, and was later president of the National Woman Suffrage Association.

**staphylococcus** Spherical bacterium that grows in grape-like clusters and is found on the skin and mucous membranes of human beings and other animals. Pathogenic staphylococci cause a range of local or generalized infections, including PNEUMONIA and SEPTICEMIA. They may be destroyed by ANTIBIOTICS, although some strains have become resistant.

**star** Self-luminous ball of gas whose radiant energy is produced by FUSION reactions, mainly the conversion of hydrogen into helium. The temperatures and luminosities of stars are prescribed by their masses. The most massive stars are about 100 solar masses (a mass a hundred times greater than the Sun). Large stars are luminous and hot, and therefore appear blue. Medium-sized stars are yellow, while small stars are a dull red. The smallest stars contain less than one-twentieth of a solar mass. *See also* BINARY STAR, STELLAR EVOLUTION

**starch** CARBOHYDRATE stored in many plants and providing about 70% of human food in such forms as rice, potatoes, and cereals. Animals and plants convert it to GLUCOSE for energy (RESPIRATION). Consisting of linked glucose units, starch exists in two forms: **amylose**, in which the glucose chains are unbranched; and **amylopectin**, in which they are branched. It is made commercially from cereals, corn, potatoes, and other plants, and used in the manufacture of adhesives and foods.

**starfish** Any of numerous species of marine ECHINODERMS, with a central disk body and a five-rayed symmetry resulting in five to 40 radiating arms. The mouth is on the underside of the disk and the stomach can be extruded to take in other echinoderms and shellfish. Calcareous spines are embedded in the skin. Starfish move by means of tube feet,

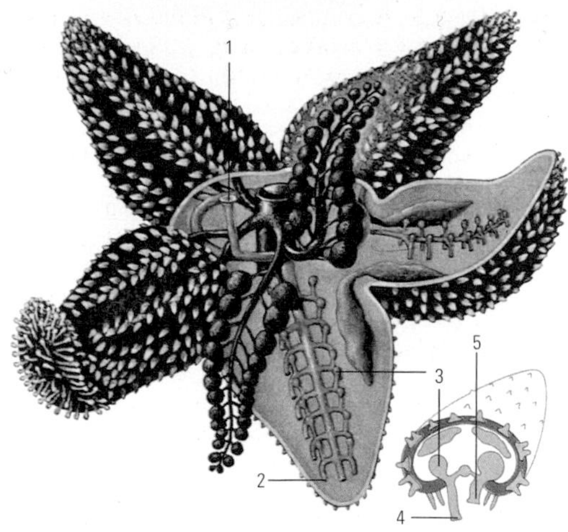


◀ **starfish** A starfish feeds by surrounding prey, pushing out its stomach through its mouth, and partially digesting the food, which is then taken back into the stomach extensions (red). It moves by means of a water-vascular system (blue) unique to echinoderms. Water enters through the sieve plate (1) and is drawn by tiny hairs through the five radial canals into the many pairs of tube feet (2) armed with suckers. When the ampulla (3) of each tube foot contracts, water is forced into the foot (illustrated in cross-section), which extends (4) and allows attachment to the hard rock. Muscles in the foot then shorten it (5) forcing water back into the ampulla and drawing the animal forward.

which they may also use for pulling open the bivalve mollusks on which they feed. Class Asteroidea.

**Stark, Johannes** (1874–1957) German physicist. He was awarded the 1919 Nobel Prize for physics for his discovery (1913) of the **Stark effect** (that a strong electric field can split lines in the spectra of atoms), and for his work demonstrating the DOPPLER EFFECT. In the 1920s, Stark rejected the theory of RELATIVITY and the QUANTUM THEORY.

**starling** Any of several species of small, aggressive birds found throughout the world. The common Eurasian starling, *Sturnus vulgaris*, is mottled black and brown. It feeds on the ground on insects and fruit, often damaging crops. Length: to 14in (36cm). Family Sturnidae.

**Star of David** (Shield of David) Six-pointed device formed by opposing two equilateral triangles. Known in Hebrew as *Magen David* or *Mogen David*, it was used as an emblem or magic sign by pagans, Christians, and Muslims, and gradually found its way into JUDAISM as a kabbalistic sign. It appears on the flag of the modern state of ISRAEL.

**Star-Spangled Banner, The** US national anthem. The words were written by a young lawyer, Francis Scott KEY, while he was detained by the British during the WAR OF 1812 and forced to witness the bombardment of Fort McHenry in 1814. The tune was taken from "To Anacreon in Heaven" a popular English song. Although long sung by the US Army and Navy, "The Star-Spangled Banner" became the NATIONAL ANTHEM when so designated by President WILSON in 1916.

**State, US Department of** US government department that conducts foreign policy. It is the oldest federal government department, created in 1789, and the secretary of state is a senior member of the cabinet.

**Staten Island** Island in SE New York, in New York Bay, coextensive with Richmond county of NEW YORK CITY and connected with Brooklyn by Verrazano-Narrows bridge (1964) and with New York City and Brooklyn by ferries. First settled in 1661, it was incorporated with New York City in 1898. Industries: shipbuilding, printing, publishing, oil refining, soap. Area: 64sq mi (166sq km). Pop. (1990) 378,977.

**states' rights** Doctrine that the states have authority in matters not delegated to the federal government. The controversy between federal and state jurisdiction peaked with John C. CALHOUN's interpretation that a state could refuse to obey a federal law it deemed unconstitutional. This led to the Nullification Crisis (1832) and contributed to the CIVIL WAR. More recently, it was an issue during the civil-rights movement of the 1950s and 1960s.

**static electricity** ELECTRIC CHARGES at rest. Electrically charged objects have either too many or too few ELECTRONS. COULOMB's law describes the forces that charged objects have on each other and relates the force to their charge and the distance between them. Static electricity can be produced by friction. Electrons may then jump off as a spark, shocking anyone touching the object. Lightning is a larger result of static electricity. This form of electricity is studied in **electrostatics**.

**statics** Branch of MECHANICS that deals with the action of forces on objects at rest. Its topics include finding the resul-

▲ **starling** With the brightest plumage of its family, the superb starling (*Spreo superbus*) lives in East Africa. Like the other starlings, it is noisy and bold and lives in large colonies, often near villages and towns. In general the starling family (Sturnidae) is highly adaptable – the common starling spread throughout North America within 80 years of its first introduction in 1890.

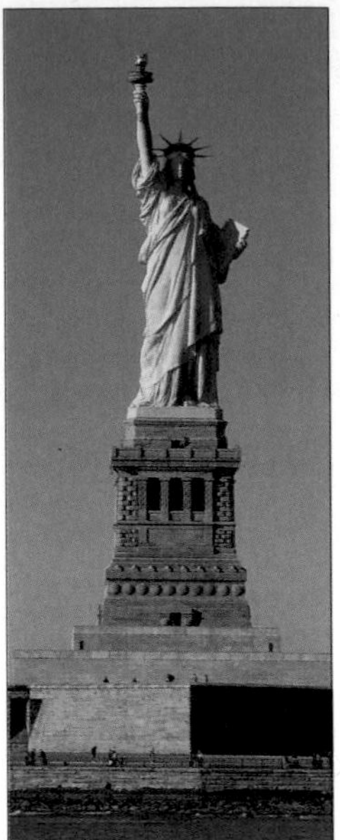

▲ **Statue of Liberty** One of the most famous structures in the world, the Statue of Liberty is an inspiring symbol of hope and freedom. Built on Liberty Island, the site of a former quarantine station and harbor fortification, the base of the statue is 150ft (45m) high, faced with granite. It is inscribed with a sonnet by Emma Lazarus titled *The New Colossus*, which welcomes immigrants to the US.

tant (net) of two or more forces; centers of gravity; moments; and stresses and strains. *See also* DYNAMICS

**statistical mechanics** Branch of physics that studies large-scale properties of MATTER based on the statistical laws of large numbers. The large number of molecules in such a system allows the use of statistics to predict the probability of finding the system in any state. The ENTROPY (disorder or randomness) of the system is related to its number of possible states; a system left to itself will tend to approach the most probable distribution of energy states. *See also* THERMODYNAMICS

**statistics** Science of collecting and classifying numerical data. Statistics can be **descriptive** (summarizing the data obtained) or **inferential** (leading to conclusions or inferences about larger numbers of which the data obtained are a sample). Inferential statistics are used to give a greater degree of confidence to conclusions, since statistics make it possible to calculate the probability that a conclusion is in error.

**Statue of Liberty** Large, copper statue of a woman, standing on Liberty Island in New York Harbor. A symbol of US democracy, it was a gift from France and built to commemorate the 1876 centenary of US independence. It was designed by BARTHOLDI on an iron framework designed and built by Gustave Eiffel. The statue's correct name is *Liberty Enlightening the World*. It stands 150ft (45m) tall to the top of the torch in the goddess's raised right hand. *See also* ELLIS ISLAND

**status** In western sociology, a person's social position in a hierarchically arranged society, based on factors including lifestyle, prestige, income, and education. Status can be inherited (**ascribed** status) or achieved by the acquisition of socially enviable possessions (**status symbols**). Such status is termed **achieved** status.

**steady-state theory** Cosmological theory put forward by Hermann Bondi and Thomas Gold in 1948, and further developed by Fred HOYLE and others. According to this theory, the Universe has always existed; it had no beginning and will continue forever. Although the Universe is expanding, it maintains its average density (steady-state) through the continuous creation of new matter. Most cosmologists now reject the theory because it cannot explain the cosmic microwave background or the observation that the appearance of the Universe has changed with time.

**stealth technology** Methods used to render an aircraft nearly invisible, primarily to radar and heat detection. To achieve "invisibility," a stealth aircraft must have sympathetic airframe design (all radar-reflecting "hard" edges smoothed away), engine exhaust dampers that mask and disperse jet efflux, and radar absorbent material that "holds" electronic emissions rather than reflecting them. The US Lockheed F-117A was the first stealth aircraft to enter frontline service(1983). It was followed a decade later by the Northrop B-2.

**steam engine** Engine powered by steam. In some engines, the steam forces pistons to move along cylinders. This results in a reciprocating (back-and-forth) motion. A mechanism usually changes this into rotary motion. Steam TURBINES are engines that produce rotary motion directly by using the steam to turn sets of fanlike wheels. The first steam engine, a form of pump used to remove water from mines, was built in 1689 by English inventor Thomas Savery. In 1712 Thomas Newcomen invented a steam-operated pump with pistons in Britain. From the 1760s, Scottish engineer James WATT produced more efficient steam engines. This led to the use of steam engines to power machinery in factories. In 1884 English engineer Charles Parsons invented the first practical steam turbine. His machines were so efficient that turbines soon started to replace reciprocating steam engines in power stations.

► **stealth technology** The Lockheed F-117A employs stealth technology to render itself practically invisible to radar. The aircraft's materials and design are such that its radar cross section (RCS) (the imaginary size of a perfectly reflecting object that would reflect the same amount of energy) is reduced to within the levels of background noise. To achieve this, compromises are required in terms of the aircraft's performance and operating and maintenance costs.

**stearic acid** (octadecanoic acid) Common saturated fatty acid ($C_{18}H_{36}O_2$), often found as glyceride in animal and vegetable fats. It is used in ointments, lubricants, creams, candles, and soap. Properties: sp.gr. 0.85; m.p. 158°F (70°C).

**steel** Group of iron alloys containing a little CARBON. The great strength of steel makes it an extremely important material in construction and manufacturing. The most common type is called **plain carbon** steel, because carbon is the main alloying material. This kind of steel usually contains less than 1% of carbon by weight. **Alloy** steels contain some carbon, but owe their special properties to the presence of manganese, nickel, chromium, vanadium, or molybdenum. **Low-alloy** steels, with less than 5% of alloying metals, are exceptionally strong and are used in buildings, bridges, and machine parts. *See also* STAINLESS STEEL

**Steele, Sir Richard** (1672–1729) British essayist and dramatist. He helped set the tone of public debate in his various publications, including most notably *The Tatler* (1709–11) and *The Spectator* (1711–12), which he co-founded with Joseph ADDISON. Of his plays, only *The Conscious Lovers* (1722) has won lasting acclaim.

**Steen, Jan** (1626–79) Dutch painter. He excelled as a painter of children and his work includes many fine historical, mythological, and religious themes. Many of his compositions depict taverns and celebrations.

**Steichen, Edward** (1897–1973) US photographer. First a portraitist and fashion photographer, he pioneered aerial photography during World War I and commanded naval combat photography during World War II. He was also director of the photography department of the Museum of Modern Art, New York (1947–62).

**Stein, Gertrude** (1874–1946) US author and critic. She was influential in the US expatriate community in Paris. Her prodigious output includes the novel *Three Lives* (1909) and *The Autobiography of Alice B. Toklas* (1933), a fictionalized account of her life.

**Steinbeck, John** (1902–68) US novelist. He first came to notice with *Tortilla Flat* (1935), the success of which was consolidated by the novella *Of Mice and Men* (1937). Later novels include *Cannery Row* (1945), *East of Eden* (1952), and his masterpiece, *The Grapes of Wrath* (1939), which earned him a Pulitzer Prize and a National Book Award. He was awarded the 1962 Nobel Prize for literature.

**Steiner, Rudolf** (1861–1925) Austrian philosopher and educator who helped to found the German THEOSOPHY movement. He later developed a philosophy of his own, called **anthroposophy**, which sought to explain the world in terms of people's spiritual nature or thinking independent of the senses.

**stem** Main, upward-growing part of a plant that bears leaves, buds, and flowers or other reproductive structures. In VASCULAR PLANTS the stem contains conducting tissues (XYLEM and PHLOEM). In flowering plants this vascular tissue is arranged in a ring (in DICOTYLEDONS) or scattered (in MONOCOTYLEDONS). They may be modified into underground structures (RHIZOMES, TUBERS, CORMS, BULBS). Stems vary in shape and size from the threadlike stalks of aquatic plants to tree trunks.

**Stendhal** (1783–1842) (Marie Henri Beyle) French novelist. His first novel, *Armance*, appeared to critical scorn in 1827. In 1830 he published the first of his two great novels *The Red and the Black*, whose ironic tones satirized Parisian contemporary society. *The Charterhouse of Parma* came out in 1839.

**Stephen, Saint** (977–1038) Stephen I of Hungary (r.1000–38), the first king of the Árpád dynasty. His chief work was to continue the Christianization of Hungary begun by his father, by endowing abbeys, inviting in foreign prelates, and suppressing paganism. He was canonized in 1083.

**Stephen** (1097–1154) King of England (1135–54). A nephew of HENRY I, he usurped the throne on Henry's death in spite of an earlier oath of loyalty to Henry's daughter, Matilda. A long civil war (1139–48) began when Matilda's forces invaded. Stephen received support from most of the English barons. He was captured in 1141 but exchanged for the Duke of Gloucester, Matilda's half-brother. After the death of his son, Eustace, in 1153, Stephen accepted Matilda's son, the future HENRY II, as heir to the throne.

**Stephens, Alexander Hamilton** (1812–83) US politician, vice president of the Confederacy (1861–65). A former governor of Georgia, he opposed secession while upholding the right of a state to secede. As Confederate vice president, he quarreled with Jefferson DAVIS over military conscription and other matters, damaging confidence in the government.

**Stephenson, George** (1781–1848) English engineer, regarded as the father of the LOCOMOTIVE. He built his first locomotive, *Blucher*, in 1814. His most famous locomotive, *Rocket*, was built in 1829. It ran on the Liverpool to Manchester line, one of the many railroad lines that he engineered.

**stereoscope** Optical device that produces an apparently three-dimensional image by presenting two slightly different plane images, usually photographs, to each eye. Some modern ones use POLARIZED LIGHT to project images that are viewed through polarized filters.

**sterility** Inability to reproduce. It may be due to INFERTILITY or, in humans and other animals, to surgical intervention.

**sterilization** Surgical intervention that terminates the ability of a human or other animal to reproduce. In women, the usual procedure is tubal ligation: sealing or tying off the FALLOPIAN TUBES so that fertilization can no longer occur. In men, a VASECTOMY is performed to block the release of sperm. The term is also applied to the practice of destroying microorganisms in order to prevent the spread of infection. Techniques include heat treatment, irradiation, and the use of disinfecting agents.

**sterling** Term for British currency. It is used to distinguish the UK pound from those of other currencies and can also be used to describe the quality and standard weight of coins. The sterling silver mark on silver (the stamp of a lion *passant*) represents a purity of more than 90%.

**Sterne, Laurence** (1713–68) British novelist, b. Ireland. He achieved immediate fame for the first two volumes of the novel *Tristram Shandy* (1760–67). Sterne's playful, anarchic experiments with form foreshadowed MODERNISM. He adopted the persona of the parson in Tristram Shandy for *The Sermons of Mr. Yorick* (1760–69) and *A Sentimental Journey* (1768).

**sternum** (breastbone) Flat, narrow bone extending from the base of the front of the neck to just below the diaphragm in the center of the chest. The top is attached by ligaments to the collarbones and the center part is joined to the ribs by seven pairs of costal cartilages.

**steroid** Class of organic compounds with a basic molecular structure of 17 carbon atoms arranged in four rings. Steroids are widely distributed in animals and plants, the most abundant being the sterols, such as cholesterol. Another important group are the steroid HORMONES, including the corticosteroids, secreted by the adrenal cortex, and the sex hormones (ESTROGEN, PROGESTERONE, and TESTOSTERONE). Synthetic steroids are widely used in medicine. Athletes sometimes abuse steroids to increase their muscle mass, strength, and stamina, but there are harmful side effects. Taking steroids is illegal in sports.

**stethoscope** Instrument that enables an examiner to listen to the action of various parts of the body, principally the heart and lungs. It consists of two earpieces attached to flexible rubber tubes that lead to either a disk or a cone.

**Stevens, John Paul** (1920– ) US jurist, associate justice of the Supreme Court. In private practice, he specialized in antitrust law. In 1975 FORD nominated him to the Supreme Court where he replaced William O. Douglas.

**Stevens, Thaddeus** (1792–1868) US political leader. As representative from Pennsylvania (1849–53, 1859–68), he was one of the fiercest opponents of slavery in Congress. Stevens successfully opposed the lenient policy of Andrew JOHNSON on RECONSTRUCTION and managed the impeachement of the president.

**Stevens, Wallace** (1879–1955) US poet. A lawyer and insurance company executive, his first collection of poems, *Harmonium*, appeared in 1923. His work is rich in metaphors, and in it he contemplates nature and society. His early poems are often set in the tropics and reflect the lushness of their location. His *Collected Poems* (1954) won a Pulitzer Prize.

**Stevenson, Adlai Ewing** (1835–1914) US statesman, vice president (1893–97). A Democratic Congressman from Illinois (1875–77, 1879–81), he headed the Illinois delegation to the 1892 convention. Stevenson's efforts to gain the renomination of Grover CLEVELAND were rewarded by his appointment as vice president.

**Stevenson, Robert Louis** (1850–94) Scottish novelist, essayist, and poet. He is celebrated for his classic children's adventure stories, such as *Treasure Island* (1883) and *Kidnapped* (1886). His later work includes historical novels, such as *The Black Arrow* (1888) and *The Master of Ballantrae* (1889), as well as the psychological novel *The Strange Case of Dr. Jekyll and Mr. Hyde* (1886). Stevenson spent the last years of his life in Samoa, where he wrote *The Ebb-Tide* (1894).

**Stewart, Jackie (John Young)** (1939– ) Scottish Formula 1 motor racing driver. He retired from racing in 1973 after winning what was then a record 27 Grand Prix. In 1997 he established his own Formula 1 racing team.

**Stewart, James Maitland** (1908–97) US film actor famed for his slow drawl. Stewart's roles in the Frank CAPRA comedies, *You Can't Take It With You* (1938) and *Mr. Smith Goes to Washington* (1939), gained plaudits and awards. Stewart won a Best Actor Oscar for *The Philadelphia Story* (1940). He starred in three Alfred HITCHCOCK films: *Rope* (1948), *Rear Window*, and *Vertigo* (1958). Other credits include *Anatomy of A Murder* (1959), *The Man Who Shot Liberty Valence* (1962), *Shenandoah* (1965), and *The Shootist* (1976).

**stick insect** (walking stick) Numerous species of herbivorous insects of the order Phasmida, which resemble the twigs upon which they rest. Some lay eggs that resemble seeds. Length: to 11in (32cm). *See also* LEAF INSECT

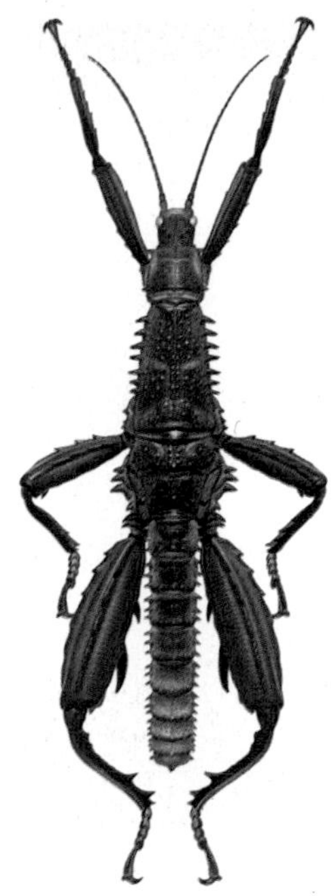

▲ **stick insect** Highly modified for the purposes of camouflage, the stick insects of New Guinea, such as *Euryacantha horrida*, shown here, mimic the plants on which they live. Because they look like twigs, which are inedible, they are protected from predators. Their spindly legs are barely noticeable at rest. Some stick insects may remain motionless for hours; others sway backward and forward as if moving with a breeze.

**stickleback** Small fish found in fresh, brackish, and salt water. It is usually brown and green, and may be identified by the number of spines along its sides and back. The male builds a nest of water plants and drives the female into it. He then watches the eggs and cares for the young. Length: 3–4.5in (8–11cm). Species include the three-spined *Gasterosteus aculeatus*. Family Gasterosteidae.

**Stieglitz, Alfred** (1864–1946) US photographer, editor, and promoter of modern art. In 1902 he founded the Photo-Secession Group. His photographs include classic portraits of his wife, Georgia O'KEEFFE, studies of Manhattan, and the cloud images known as "equivalents."

**stigma** In botany, the free upper part of the STYLE of the female organs of a flower, to which pollen grains adhere before FERTILIZATION.

**stigmata** Marks or wounds replicating those received by JESUS at the time of his trial and crucifixion. Saint Francis of Assisi is believed to have received stigmata miraculously in 1224. Stigmata have allegedly appeared on a further 330 people between the 14th and 20th centuries.

**Stijl, De** (Dutch, The Style) Group of modern artists that originated in Holland in 1917. They were associated with the eponymous art periodical founded by Piet MONDRIAN and Theo van Doesburg. De Stijl's aesthetic was an austere use of bold, vertical and horizontal lines, often breaking up primary colours. It was especially influential in architecture, informing the work of Gerrit RIETVELD.

**Stimson, Henry Lewis** (1867–1950) US statesman. He was secretary of war under President TAFT (1911–13). As secretary of state under President HOOVER (1929–33), he tried to secure international disarmament and formulated the "Stimson doctrine": that the US would not recognize territorial changes brought about by force. He was Franklin D. ROOSEVELT's secretary of war throughout World War II.

**stimulant** Substance that increases mental alertness and activity. There are a number of stimulants that act on the CENTRAL NERVOUS SYSTEM, notably drugs in the AMPHETAMINE

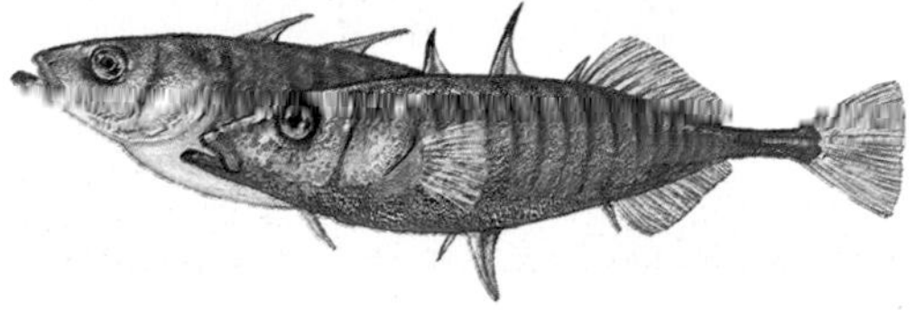

◀ **stickleback** Often found in estuaries, the males of the three-spined stickleback (*Gasterosteus aculeatus*) lure females by adopting a bright red belly coloring and performing a complex mating dance. They also use their coloring to defend territory against other males: they adopt a threatening head-down position that displays the red belly and the iridescent blue head at the same time.

## STOMACH

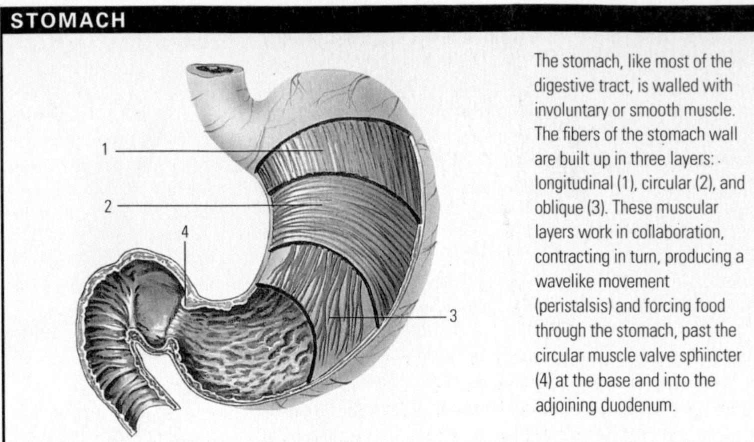


The stomach, like most of the digestive tract, is walled with involuntary or smooth muscle. The fibers of the stomach wall are built up in three layers: longitudinal (1), circular (2), and oblique (3). These muscular layers work in collaboration, contracting in turn, producing a wavelike movement (peristalsis) and forcing food through the stomach, past the circular muscle valve sphincter (4) at the base and into the adjoining duodenum.

group. Many common beverages, including tea and coffee, contain small quantities of the stimulant caffeine.

**stingray** Any of several species of bottom-dwelling elasmobranch fish that live in marine waters and in some rivers in South America. It has a flattened body, with winglike fins around the head. It has a long, slender tail. Its venomous sting is used to stun prey, but can cause injury to humans. Width: to 7ft (2m). Family Dasyatidae.

**stinkhorn** Any of several species of foul-smelling Basidiomycete fungi. At first, it resembles a small, whitish "egg," which contains the unripe fruit body. When ripe, the receptacle elongates, rupturing the egg. It carries with it a glutinous brownish spore mass that attracts the flies that disperse the spores. Genus *Phallus*.

**stoat** (ermine) Carnivorous mammal of the WEASEL family. Its slim body is about 12in (30cm) long, including the tail, and it has short legs and moves sinuously. It preys upon rabbits and smaller animals in many temperate and N parts of the world. In the latter regions its fur turns from red-brown and white to white in winter, when it is known as ermine. Family Mustelidae; species *Mustela ermina*.

**stock** (gilliflower) Annual plant native to S Europe, South Africa, and parts of Asia, cultivated as a garden flower. It has oblong leaves and pink, purple, or white flower clusters. Height: to 30in (80cm). Family Brassicaceae/Cruciferae; species *Matthiola bicornis*.

**stock** (share) Document representing money invested in a company in return for membership rights in the ownership of that company. Stockholders regularly receive payment of dividends that depend on the net profit of the company.

**stock exchange** (stock market, securities exchange) Organized market for the buying and selling of stocks issued by corporations. There are exchanges in major cities throughout the world, the largest are in New York and London.

**Stockhausen, Karlheinz** (1928– ) German composer and theorist, the most successful exponent of ELECTRONIC MUSIC. An example of his work is *Kontakte* (1960), which uses instruments with tape. His seven-part opera *Licht* was begun in 1977; four parts have been completed.

**Stockholm** Port and capital of Sweden, on Lake Mälar's outlet to the Baltic Sea. Founded in the mid-13th century, it became a trade center dominated by the HANSEATIC LEAGUE. GUSTAVUS I (VASA) made it the center of his kingdom and ended the privileges of Hanseatic merchants. The city became the capital of Sweden in 1436 and developed as an intellectual center in the 17th century. Industrial development dates from the mid-19th century. Industries: textiles, clothing, paper and printing, food processing, rubber, chemicals, shipbuilding, beer, electronics, metal, machine manufacturing. Pop. (1994) 1,708,502.

► **stonefly** An important source of food for freshwater fish, stoneflies (*Plecoptera* sp.) are hatched in the water and spend most of their lives there. Their nymph stage, during which they are aquatic, lasts from one to four years, while their adult phase, after they have left the water, is only of a few weeks' duration. As adults, they do not fly well and hover over the surface of streams, lakes, and rivers. Fishermen often use lures that resemble them.

**Stockton, Robert Field** (1795–1866) US naval officer. He served in the WAR OF 1812. In 1821 he played a major role in negotiating rights to what became LIBERIA. He commanded land and sea forces in the MEXICAN WAR (1846–48), proclaiming California a US territory, and was US senator from New Jersey (1851–53).

**Stoics** Followers of the school of philosophy founded by ZENO OF CITIUM in *c*.300 BC. Founded on the premise that virtue is attainable only by living in harmony with nature, stoicism stressed the importance of self-sufficiency and of equanimity in adversity. The philosophy was first expressed by Chrysippus in the 3rd century BC. It was introduced into Rome in the 2nd century BC, where it found its greatest adherents, SENECA in the 1st century AD, Epictetus in the 1st and 2nd centuries, and the 2nd-century emperor MARCUS AURELIUS.

**Stoker, Bram (Abraham)** (1847–1912) Irish novelist. He wrote several novels and a memoir of the actor Henry Irving (1906), but he is best remembered for the classic horror novel *Dracula* (1897).

**Stokowski, Leopold (Antoni Stanislaw)** (1882–1977) US conductor, b. Britain. He was director of the Cincinnati Symphony (1909–12) and conductor of the Philadelphia Orchestra (1912–36). He became known for his individual interpretations and flexibility of approach.

**stolon** Modified horizontal underground or aerial stem growing from the basal node of a plant. Aerial stolons, also called runners, may be slender, as in strawberry, or stiff and arching, as in bramble. The stolon produces a new plant at its tip, which puts out adventitious roots to anchor itself. *See also* VEGETATIVE REPRODUCTION; TUBER

**stomach** J-shaped organ, lying to the left and slightly below the DIAPHRAGM in human beings; one of the organs of the DIGESTIVE SYSTEM. It is connected at its upper end to the gullet (ESOPHAGUS) and at the lower end to the SMALL INTESTINE. The stomach itself is lined by three layers of muscle and a folded mucous layer that contains gastric glands. These GLANDS secrete hydrochloric acid that destroys some food bacteria and makes possible the action of pepsin, the ENZYME that digests PROTEINS. Gastric gland secretion is controlled by the sight, smell, and taste of food, and by hormonal stimuli, chiefly the HORMONE gastrin. As the food is digested, it is churned by muscular action into a thick liquid state called chyme, at which point it passes into the small intestine.

**stomata** In botany, pores found mostly on the undersides of leaves that allow atmospheric gases to pass in and out for RESPIRATION and PHOTOSYNTHESIS. Surrounding each stoma are two guard cells that can close to prevent excessive loss of water vapor. *See also* GAS EXCHANGE; TRANSPIRATION

**Stone, Harlan Fiske** (1872–1946) Chief justice of the US Supreme Court (1941–46). US attorney general under President Coolidge (1924–25), he was an associate justice of the Supreme Court from 1925 and was appointed Chief Justice by President Franklin D. Roosevelt (1941). He generally supported NEW DEAL legislation and the protection of individual civil liberties.

**Stone, Lucy** (1818–93) US feminist. With others, she organized the first US women's rights convention (1850). She set up several organizations for women's suffrage and founded the *Woman's Journal* in 1870.

**Stone Age** Period of human evolution defined by the use of stone tools. The Stone Age dates from the earliest identifiable broken-pebble tools made by human ancestors about 2.5 million years ago. The period is generally considered to have ended when metal tools first became widespread during the BRONZE AGE. The Stone Age is usually subdivided into the PALEOLITHIC, MESOLITHIC, and NEOLITHIC.

**stonecrop** Any plant of the genus *Sedum* of the family Crassulaceae, especially creeping sedum (*S. acre*), a succulent, low-growing plant of European origin with pungent, fleshy leaves and yellow flowers, found in rocky areas.

**stonefish** Bottom-dwelling, marine fish that lives in tropical waters of the Indo-Pacific Ocean. It has a warty, slime-covered body and sharp dorsal spines with which it can inflict a painful, sometimes deadly, sting to humans. Length: to 13in (33cm). Family Synancejidae; species *Synanceja verrucosa*.

**stonefly** (salmon fly) Soft-bodied insect with long, narrow front wings and chewing mouthparts, found throughout the world. The aquatic nymphs have branched gills, and the adults, used as bait by anglers, are brown to black. Length: 0.2–2.5in (5–60mm). Order Plecoptera.

**Stonehenge** Circular group of prehistoric standing stones within a circular earthwork on Salisbury Plain, S England, 8mi (13km) N of Salisbury. The largest and most precisely constructed MEGALITH in Europe, Stonehenge dates from the early 3rd millennium BC, although the main stones were erected *c*.2000–1500 BC. The large standing bluestones were brought from SW Wales *c*.2100 BC. The significance of the structure is unknown.

**Stoppard, Tom** (1937– ) English dramatist, b. Thomas Straussler. Plays such as *Rosencrantz and Guildenstern are Dead* (1966), *The Real Inspector Hound* (1968), and *Jumpers* (1972), confirmed his ability to combine philosophical speculation with humor. Other works include *Professional Foul* (1977) and *Arcadia* (1993). Stoppard wrote the screenplay for the movie *Shakespeare in Love* (1998).

**stork** Long-legged, wading bird that lives along rivers, lakes, and marshes in temperate and tropical regions, often nesting in colonies in trees. Usually black, white, and gray, storks have straight bills, long necks, robust bodies, and long broad wings. They are diurnal and feed on small animals. Length: 2.5–5ft (0.8–1.5m). Family Ciconiidae.

**Story, Joseph** (1779–1845) US jurist, Supreme Court justice (1811–45). He was only 32 years old when appointed to the Supreme Court. Story helped to strengthen the power of the Supreme Court and was an outspoken critic of slavery. He wrote legal textbooks and the classic *Commentaries on the Constitution* (1833).

**STP** *See* STANDARD TEMPERATURE AND PRESSURE (STP)

**strabismus** (squint) Condition in which the EYES do not look in the same direction. It may result from either disease of or damage to the eye muscles or their nerve supply, or an error of refraction within the eye.

**Strachey, (Giles) Lytton** (1880–1932) English biographer and essayist. His works included *Eminent Victorians* (1918), *Queen Victoria* (1921), and *Elizabeth and Essex* (1928). He introduced a psychological dimension to modern BIOGRAPHY.

**Stradivari, Antonio** (1644–1737) Italian violin maker. Originally an apprentice to Nicolo AMATI, Stradivari perfected violin design.

**Strafford, Thomas Wentworth, 1st earl of** (1593–1641) English minister of CHARLES I. He became chief adviser after the death of the Duke of Buckingham and proved an extremely capable administrator as lord president of the North (1628–33) and lord deputy of Ireland (1633–39). Charles made him an earl in 1640, but he attracted the wrath of Parliament and was executed.

**Strasberg, Lee** (1901–82) US theatrical director. One of the founders of the Group Theater (1931), he began teaching a "method" approach based on STANISLAVSKY's teachings. In 1947 Strasberg and Elia KAZAN founded the ACTORS' STUDIO. As the Studio's artistic director, he was influential in shaping the careers of many leading actors, such as Marilyn MONROE and Al PACINO.

**Strasbourg** City in E France, on the Ill River, capital of Bas-Rhin department and the commercial capital of the ALSACE region. Known in Roman times as Argentoratum, the city was destroyed by the Huns in the 5th century. It became part of the HOLY ROMAN EMPIRE in 923 and developed into an important commercial center, becoming a free imperial city in 1262. Strasbourg was a center of medieval German literature and of 16th-century Protestantism. It was seized by France in 1681, regained by Germany after the FRANCO-PRUSSIAN WAR, but recovered by France at the end of World War I. German troops occupied the city during World War II. Its river port on the Rhine, with its good canal connections, is

France's chief grain outlet. Industries: metallurgy, oil and gas refining, machinery, food processing. Pop. (1990) 252,338.

**Strategic Arms Limitation Talks (SALT)** Talks between the US and the Soviet Union to limit the expansion of NUCLEAR WEAPONS. The talks began in 1969 between Lyndon JOHNSON and Leonid BREZHNEV. In 1972 Richard NIXON and Brezhnev signed SALT I. This agreement limited antiballistic missile systems and produced an interim accord on intercontinental ballistic missiles (ICBMs). In 1973 a second phase began with meetings between Gerald FORD and Brezhnev, and in 1974 they agreed to limit ballistic missile launchers. SALT II, signed in Vienna between Jimmy CARTER and Brezhnev, banned new ICBMs and limited other launchers. The Soviet invasion of Afghanistan meant that the treaty was never ratified by the US Senate. Nevertheless, the superpowers observed its terms until Ronald REAGAN began to increase the US nuclear arsenal. In 1986 SALT was superseded by **Strategic Arms Reduction Talks (START)** between Mikhail GORBACHEV and Ronald REAGAN.

**Stratford upon Avon** Town in Warwickshire, central England, famous as the birthplace of William SHAKESPEARE and home of the ROYAL SHAKESPEARE COMPANY (RSC). Industries: tourism, engineering, boatbuilding, textiles. Pop. (1992) 22,800.

**Strathclyde** Region in W Scotland, bounded N by the Highlands, S by the Southern Uplands, and W by the Atlantic Ocean. Strathclyde is divided into 19 districts. The capital is GLASGOW; other major towns include Paisley, Kilmarnock, Clydebank, and Motherwell. The industrial heartland of Scotland, it contains half of Scotland's population. Sites include Loch LOMOND, Glencoe, and the islands of Mull, Arran, and Bute. In the late 9th century it was devastated by Norse raiders. It was incorporated into the Scottish kingdom in the 11th century. Industries: shipbuilding, engineering. Area: 5,222sq mi (13,529sq km) Pop: (1991) 2,248,700

**stratigraphy** Branch of geology concerned with stratified or layered rocks. It deals with the correlation of rocks from different localities using fossils and distinct rock types.

**Strauss, Johann (the Younger)** (1825–99) Austrian composer and conductor, son of Johann Strauss (1804–49), who was also a conductor and composer. He became extremely popular for his waltzes, such as *The Blue Danube*, *Tales from the Vienna Woods*, and *Wine, Women and Song*. Strauss also composed two popular operettas, *Die Fledermaus* (1874), and *The Gypsy Baron* (1885).

**Strauss, Richard** (1864–1949) German composer and conductor. His SYMPHONIC POEMS, such as *Don Juan* (1888), *Till Eulenspiegel* (1895), and *Also sprach Zarathustra* (1896), use brilliantly colored orchestration for characterization. His early operas, *Salome* (1905) and *Elektra* (1908), dealt with female obsession. *Der Rosenkavalier* (1911) also used the dramatic range of the human voice, but in a comic setting.

**Stravinsky, Igor Feodorovich** (1882–1971) Russian composer who revolutionized 20th-century music. His early ballets, *The Firebird* (1910) and *Petrushka* (1911), were commissioned by DIAGHILEV for his BALLETS RUSSES. The première of the ballet *The Rite of Spring* (1913) caused a riot because of its dissonance and unfamiliar rhythms. Stravinsky turned to Russian folk themes for *The Wedding* (1923) and neoclassicism in *Pulcinella* (1920). In 1939 he moved to the US, collaborating with George BALANCHINE on the abstract ballet *Agon* (1957). He also experimented with TWELVE-TONE MUSIC.

◀ **Stonehenge** Surrounded by a circular ditch and bank, the stones at Stonehenge, SW England, were arranged in three concentric series: The outermost is a circle of 30 upright stones linked at the top by lintel stones; the second is a circle of singular menhirs; the third is a horseshoe formed by five trilithons (two upright stones joined by a lintel) with a single upright stone (the altar stone) at the open end, facing the rising sun. It has been proposed that Stonehenge was a druid temple, or a huge astronomical observatory, or served various other forms of religious function, but its use remains uncertain.

▲ **Strauss** The son of a celebrated horn player in the Munich court opera, Richard Strauss began composing at the age of six, and had work published by the time he was eleven. He was influenced by Brahms, and later Wagner and Liszt, and was a prolific and progressive composer. A master of instrumental characterization, he developed German romanticism by exploring the limits of tonality.

▲ **strawberry** Intensively cultivated since the 15th century, strawberries (*Fragaria* sp.) have remained popular soft fruits. The fruiting season is short and the fruit is easily perishable once it is picked, but they can be grown in temperate regions throughout the world.

**strawberry** Fruit-bearing plant of the rose family, common in Europe and Asia. It has three-lobed leaves and clusters of white or reddish flowers. The large fleshy fruit is dotted with seeds (pips). Family Rosaceae; genus *Fragaria*.

**stream of consciousness** Literary style in which the thought processes of characters are presented in the disconnected, illogical, chaotic, or seemingly random way they might come to them, without the usual literary regard for narrative continuity or linear sequence. Edouard Dujardin's novel *Les Lauriers Sont Coupes* (1888) is generally regarded as the first example of the style in literature.

**Streep, Meryl** (1949– ) US film actress. She is renowned for her attention to realistic characterization. After an Academy Award nomination for *The Deer Hunter* (1978), Streep won a Best Supporting Actress Oscar for *Kramer vs. Kramer* (1979). Her performance as a Holocaust victim, in *Sophie's Choice* (1982), earned her an Academy Award for Best Actress. Other credits include *The French Lieutenant's Woman* (1991), *Silkwood* (1983), and *Out of Africa* (1985).

**Streisand, Barbra** (1942– ) US singer and actress. She achieved fame with her Broadway performance in *Funny Girl* (1964, filmed 1968). Streisand has made numerous recordings and starred in films such as *Hello Dolly* (1969) and *A Star is Born* (1976). She directed, produced, and starred in *Yentl* (1983) and the *Prince of Tides* (1993).

**streptococcus** Genus of gram-positive spherical or oval BACTERIA that grow in pairs or beadlike chains. They live mainly as parasites in the mouth, respiratory tract, and intestine. Some are harmless but others are pathogenic, causing SCARLET FEVER and other infections. Treatment is with ANTIBIOTICS.

**Stresemann, Gustav** (1878–1929) German statesman. He was the outstanding statesman of the WEIMAR REPUBLIC. Stresemann concluded the LOCARNO PACT (1925) and worked for a practicable postwar settlement with Germany's former enemies under the harsh terms imposed by the Treaty of VERSAILLES. He negotiated Germany's entry into the LEAGUE OF NATIONS (1926) and shared the 1926 Nobel Peace Prize with Aristide BRIAND.

**stress** In medicine and psychology, mental or physical strain brought on by pressures from the environment. Stress caused by frustrating and difficult work; family or social situations may be a factor in many mental and physical disorders.

**stress** In physics, internal tension in a material. **Tensile** stress stretches an object, **compressive** stress squeezes it, and **shearing** stress twists it. Fluid stresses are called PRESSURE.

**Strindberg, Johan August** (1849–1912) Swedish dramatist and novelist. His major dramatic theme was subjective, psychological experience. Drawing on the insights of Henrik IBSEN and the NATURALISM of Emile ZOLA, plays such as *The Father* (1887) and *Miss Julie* (1888) take a characteristically pessimistic view of gender relations. After suffering a mental breakdown, he produced *A Dream Play* (1902) and The Ghost Sonata (1907), both of which prefigure the Theatre of the ABSURD and German EXPRESSIONISM.

**stringed instrument** Musical instrument sounded by the vibration of strings. Instruments fall into different classes, according to the action used to set the strings in motion: bowed, chiefly those of the VIOLIN family; plucked, chiefly the HARP, LUTE, and GUITAR; and plucked and struck, such as the cittern and DULCIMER.

**strip mining** Stripping surface layers from the Earth's crust to obtain coal, ores, or other valuable minerals. Dragline excavators strip away surface layers and mechanical shovels distribute minerals and spoil. The minerals are carried away for grading and processing. Owners of opencast MINES in some countries are required to restore the environmental quality of the land after MINING has ceased.

**stroboscope** (strobe) Device that emits regular flashes of light. Stroboscopes usually have a calibrated scale from which the number of flashes per minute can be read. They are used in photography to make multiple exposures of moving subjects and in engineering to "slow down" or "stop" moving objects for observation.

**stroke** (apoplexy) Interruption of the flow of blood to the brain. It is caused by blockage or rupture of an artery and may produce a range of effects from mild impairment to death. Conditions that predispose to stroke include ATHEROSCLEROSIS and HYPERTENSION. Many major strokes are prevented by treatment of risk factors, including surgery and the use of anticoagulant drugs. Transient ischaemic attacks (TIAs), or "mini-strokes," which last less than 24 hours, are investigated to try to prevent the occurrence of a more damaging stroke.

**strong nuclear force** One of the four FUNDAMENTAL FORCES in nature. The strongest of the four forces, it binds together protons and neutrons within the NUCLEUS of an atom. Like the WEAK NUCLEAR FORCE it operates at very short distances (a millionth of a millionth of an inch) and therefore occurs only within the nucleus. *See also* GRAND UNIFIED THEORY (GUT)

**strontianite** Carbonate mineral, strontium carbonate ($SrCO_3$). It has an orthorhombic system, massive or columnar aggregates or hexagonal twinned crystals. It can be pale green, white, gray, yellow, or brown. It is found in veins, often in limestone. Hardness 3.5–4; sp.gr. 3.7.

**strontium** (symbol Sr) Silvery-white, metallic element of the alkaline-earth metals in Group II of the periodic table. Resembling CALCIUM physically and chemically, it occurs naturally in strontianite and celestite and is extracted by ELECTROLYSIS. Strontium salts are used to give a red color to flares and fireworks. The isotope $^{90}Sr$ (half-life 28 years) is a radioactive element present in fallout, from which it is absorbed into milk and bones; it is used in NUCLEAR REACTORS. Properties: at.no. 38; at.wt. 87.62; sp. gr. 2.554; m.p. 1,416°F (769°C); b.p. 2,523°F (1,384°C).

**structuralism** Twentieth-century school of critical thought. Ferdinand de SAUSSURE argued that underlying the everyday use of language is a language system (*langue*), based on relationships of difference. He stressed the arbitrary nature of the relationship between the **signifier** (sound or image) and the **signified** (concept). Initially a linguistic theory, structuralism was developed by Claude LÉVI-STRAUSS and Roland BARTHES into a mode of critical analysis of cultural institutions and products. It is associated especially with the notion of a literary text as a system of signs. *See also* DECONSTRUCTION; SEMIOTICS

**strychnine** Poisonous ALKALOID obtained from the plant *Strychnos nux-vomica*. In the past it was believed to have therapeutic value in small doses as a tonic. Strychnine poisoning causes symptoms similar to those of TETANUS, with death occurring due to SPASM of the breathing muscles.

**Stuart, Charles Edward** (1720–88) Scottish prince, known as "Bonnie Prince Charlie" or the "Young Pretender." A grandson of the deposed JAMES II, he led the JACOBITES in the rebellion of 1745 ("the '45") on behalf of his father, James, the "Old Pretender." Landing in the Scottish Highlands without the hoped-for backing of France, he gained the support of many clan chiefs, defeated government troops at Prestonpans, E central Scotland, and marched on London. Lacking widespread support in England, he turned back at Derby. The following year his largely Highland force was decimated in the Battle of CULLODEN. He escaped to the continent and lived in exile until his death.

**Stuart, Gilbert Charles** (1755–1828) US painter. One of the foremost US portraitists of the late 18th and early 19th century, he is celebrated for three portraits of George WASHINGTON. These paintings are known as the "Vaughan" type (1795), the "Lansdowne" types (1796), and the "Athenaeum" type (1796). The last is the model for Washington's face on the one-dollar bill.

**Stuart, "Jeb" (James Ewell Brown)** (1833–64) Confederate general in the CIVIL WAR. A graduate of West Point, Stuart was a cavalry commander and one of the most able subordinates of Robert E. LEE. His reputation was damaged at GETTYSBURG, when he undertook an independent operation that prevented him supporting Lee when needed. He died of wounds sustained at Yellow Tavern, Virginia.

**Stuart, James Francis Edward** (1688–1766) British claimant to the throne, called the "Old Pretender." He was the only son of JAMES II, and was proclaimed king of England by the JACOBITES on the death of his father (1701). He made two attempts to regain the throne (1708 and 1715), landing in Scotland, where support for the Stuart dynasty was greatest. On both occasions the cause was lost before James arrived. His son was Charles STUART.

**Stuart, Mary** *See* MARY II

**Stuarts** (Stewarts) Scottish royal house, which inherited the Scottish crown in 1371 and the English crown in 1603. The Stuarts descended from Alan, whose descendants held the hereditary office of steward in the royal household. Walter (d.1326), the sixth steward, married a daughter of King Robert I, and their son, Robert II, became the first Stuart king (1371). The crown descended in the direct male line until the death of James V (1542), who was succeeded by his infant daughter, MARY, QUEEN OF SCOTS. In 1603 her son, James VI, succeeded ELIZABETH I of England as JAMES I. In 1649 James's son, CHARLES I, was executed following the CIVIL WAR, but the dynasty was restored with the RESTORATION of CHARLES II in 1660. His brother, JAMES II, lost the throne in the GLORIOUS REVOLUTION (1685) and was replaced by the joint monarchy of WILLIAM III and MARY II, James's daughter. On the death (1714) of ANNE, James's second daughter, without an heir, the House of HANOVER succeeded. The male descendants of James II made several unsuccessful attempts to regain the throne, culminating in the JACOBITE rebellion of 1745.

**Stubbs, George** (1724–1806) English painter and engraver. Stubbs is celebrated chiefly for his book *The Anatomy of the Horse*, illustrated with his own engravings. *Horses attacked by a lion* (1770) reveals a more romantic approach.

**sturgeon** Large, primitive, bony fish found in temperate fresh and marine waters of the Northern Hemisphere. The ovaries of the female are the source of CAVIAR. It has five series of sharp-pointed scales along its sides, fleshy whiskers, and a tapering, snoutlike head. Family Acipenseridae; species Atlantic sturgeon (*Acipenser sturio*) length: to 11ft (3m), weight: to 600lb (270kg). The Eurasian freshwater sturgeon is also called beluga.

**Sturm und Drang** (Ger. Storm and Stress) German literary movement that takes its name from a play (1776) by F.M. von Klinger. Sturm and Drang rejected the prevailing NEOCLASSICISM in favour of subjectivity, artistic creativity and the beauty of nature. Associated principally with the early works of Johann Wolfgang von GOETHE, Friedrich SCHILLER and Johann Gottfried von HERDER, it is seen as a precursor of ROMANTICISM. Sturm und Drang influenced HAYDN's group of minor-key symphonies.

**Stuttgart** Capital of Baden Württemberg, SW Germany, on the Neckar River. Now the eighth largest city in Germany, Stuttgart was founded in *c.*950. The capital of the kingdom of Württemberg from 1495 to 1806, its industrial base expanded rapidly during the 19th century. Historically, it is associated with motor vehicle construction. Stuttgart was intensively bombed during World War II, but much of its famous architecture has survived. Industries: electronics, photographic equipment, publishing, wine, and beer. Pop. (1993) 598,000.

**Stuyvesant, Peter** (1610–72) Dutch colonial administrator. He became governor of the Caribbean islands of Curaçao, Bonaire, and Aruba in 1643, and in 1647 he became director-general of all the Dutch territories, including New Amsterdam (later New York City). In 1655 he ended Swedish influence in Delaware, and ruled the colny until it was taken over by the English in 1664 and renamed New York.

**style** In botany, part of a FLOWER – the tube that connects the pollen-receiving STIGMA at its tip to the OVARY at its base.

**Styx** In Greek mythology, the river across which the souls of the dead were ferried by Charon on their journey from the world of the living to the underworld.

**subatomic particles** Particles that are smaller than ATOMS or are of the types that make up atoms. They can be divided into two groups: the HADRONS, such as PROTONS and NEUTRONS, which can be further subdivided, and ELEMENTARY PARTICLES, such as QUARKS and ELECTRONS, which cannot be further divided.

**sublimation** Direct change from solid to gas, without an intervening liquid phase. Most substances can sublimate at certain pressures, but usually not at atmospheric pressure. *See also* CONDENSATION; EVAPORATION

**submarine** Seagoing warship capable of traveling both on and under the water. Experimental submarines were used in warfare from the late 18th century. Technical advances in the late 19th century led to the general spread of underwater craft in the world's navies. Early submarines were essentially surface ships with a limited ability to remain submerged. Once underwater, they depended on battery-powered electric motors for propulsion and, with a limited air supply, were soon forced to surface. Submerging is accomplished by letting air out of internal ballast tanks; trimming underwater is done by regulating the amount of water in the ballast tanks with pumps; and surfacing is accomplished by pumping water out of the tanks. Most modern submarines use nuclear power, which eliminates the need to surface while on operations.

**submersible** Small craft for underwater exploration, research, or engineering. Modern submersibles have evolved from simple divices. Diving bells were open-bottomed craft in which people were lowered into the water. A device called the bathysphere, invented in the 1930s, was a spherical observation chamber. The bathyscaphe, invented in the 1940s by Auguste PICCARD, had a spherical chamber attached to a much larger hull, which was used as a buoyancy control device. A new generation of submersibles evolved since the late 1950s. A typical craft has a spherical passenger capsule capable of withstanding water pressure down to *c.*12,000ft (3,600m). Attached to this is a structure containing batteries, an electric motor with propeller, lighting, a mechanical arm for gathering samples, and other equipment. A support ship launches and retrieves the submersible. Some submersibles are operated by remote control from the surface. *See also* COUSTEAU, JACQUES YVES

**subpoena** (Lat. under penalty) In law, an order that commands a person to appear before a court or judicial officer to give evidence at a specific time and place. Failure to obey a subpoena is a criminal offense.

**subsidiary** A company that is controlled to some extent by another corporation that holds a majority of the shares.

**subsidies** Government assistance to individuals or organizations to benefit the public. Subsidies are usually intended to promote growth or stability, generating higher outputs of certain products, or maintaining or reducing prices. They can be **direct** (for example, cash payments) or **indirect** (for example, when the government buys goods at artificially high prices or grants tax concessions). They are often used to protect industries by enabling them to offer more competitive prices. Commonly subsidized enterprises include agriculture, business expansion, housing, and regional development.

**substitution reaction** Chemical reaction in which one atom or group of atoms replaces (usually in the same structural position) another group in a molecule or ion.

**succession** Orderly change in plant and animal life in a biotic community over a long time period. It is the result of modifications in the community environment. The process ends in establishment of a stable ECOSYSTEM (climax community).

**succulent** Plant that stores water in its tissues to resist periods of drought. Usually PERENNIAL and EVERGREEN, they have bodies mostly made up of water storage cells, which give them a fleshy appearance. A well-developed CUTICLE and low rate of daytime TRANSPIRATION also conserve water. Succulent plants include CACTUS, LILY, and STONECROP.

◀ **Stubbs** *Joseph Smith, Lt. of Whittlebury Forest, Northamptonshire, on a dapple grey horse.* (c. 1762-64) A self-taught painter and etcher, George Stubbs used his interest in comparative anatomy to inform his portraits of horses and other animals. He was the most famous animal painter of his time, and his work is still admired for its accuracy and elegance.

S

cations in the community environment. The process ends in establishment of a stable ECOSYSTEM (climax community).

**succulent** Plant that stores water in its tissues to resist periods of drought. Usually PERENNIAL and EVERGREEN, they have bodies mostly made up of water storage cells, which give them a fleshy appearance. A well-developed CUTICLE and low rate of daytime TRANSPIRATION also conserve water. Succulent plants include CACTUS, LILY, and STONECROP.

**sucker** Any of several species of freshwater fish found mainly from N Canada to the Gulf of Mexico. A bottom-feeder similar to minnows, it has a thick-lipped mouth for feeding by suction. Length: to 26in (66cm); weight: to 12lb (5.4kg). Family Catostomidae.

**Sucre, Antonio José de** (1795–1830) South American revolutionary leader and first president of Bolivia (1826–28). He joined the fight for independence in 1811 and played a key role in the liberation of Ecuador, Peru, and Bolivia, winning the final, decisive battle at Ayacucho (1824). With Simón BOLÍVAR's support, Sucre became the first elected president of Bolivia, but local opposition forced his resignation. He was assassinated while trying to preserve the unity of Colombia.

**Sucre** City in S central BOLIVIA and the legal capital of Bolivia, the seat of government being La Paz. Known successively as La Plata, Chuguisaca, and Charcas, Sucre was renamed in 1839 after the revolutionary leader and first president of Bolivia, Antonio José de SUCRE. It is a commercial and distribution center for the surrounding farming region. Industries: cement, oil refining. Pop. (1992) 103,952.

**sucrose** Common white crystalline sugar, a disaccharide SUGAR ($C_{12}H_{22}O_{11}$) consisting of linked GLUCOSE and FRUCTOSE molecules. It occurs in many plants, but its principal commercial sources are SUGARCANE and SUGAR BEET. It is widely used for food sweetening and making preserves.

**Sudan** Republic and Africa's largest country, in NE Africa. *See* country feature

**sudden infant death syndrome (SIDS)** (crib death) Unexpected death of an apparently healthy baby, usually during sleep. The peak period seems to be around two months of age, although it can occur up to a year or more after birth. Claiming more boys than girls, it is more common in winter. The cause is unknown, but a number of risk factors have been identified, including prematurity and respiratory infection.

**Sudetenland** Border region of N Bohemia (Czech Republic), including part of the Sudeten Mountains. Largely popu-

## SUDAN

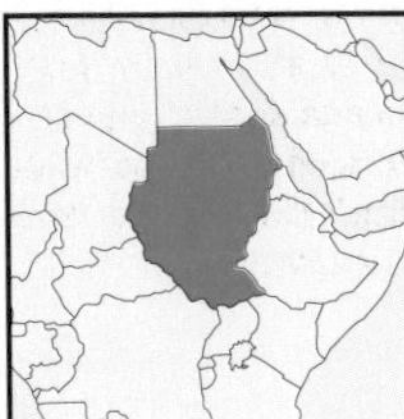

**Adopted in 1969, Sudan's flag uses colors associated with the Pan-Arab movement. The Islamic green triangle symbolizes prosperity and spiritual wealth. The flag is based on the one used in the Arab revolt against Turkish rule in World War I (1914–18).**

**AREA:** 967,493 sq mi (2,505,810sq km)
**POPULATION:** 26,656,000
**CAPITAL (POPULATION):** Khartoum (476,218)
**GOVERNMENT:** Military regime
**ETHNIC GROUPS:** Sudanese Arab 49%, Dinka 12%, Nuba 8%, Beja 6%, Nuer 5%, Azande 3%
**LANGUAGES:** Arabic (official)
**RELIGIONS:** Islam 73%, traditional beliefs 17%, Christianity (Roman Catholic 4%, Protestant 2%)
**CURRENCY:** Dinar = 10 Sudanese pounds

The Republic of Sudan is Africa's largest country. It extends from the arid SAHARA in the N to an equatorial swamp region (the *Sudd)* in the S. Much of the land is flat, but there are mountains in the NE and SE; the highest point is Kinyeti, at 10,456ft (3,187m). The NILE River (*Bahr el Jebel*) runs S–N, entering Sudan as the White Nile, converging with the Blue Nile at KHARTOUM, and flowing N to Egypt.

### CLIMATE

The climate ranges from the virtually rainless N deserts to the swamplands in the S. Khartoum is prone to summer dust storms (*haboobs*).

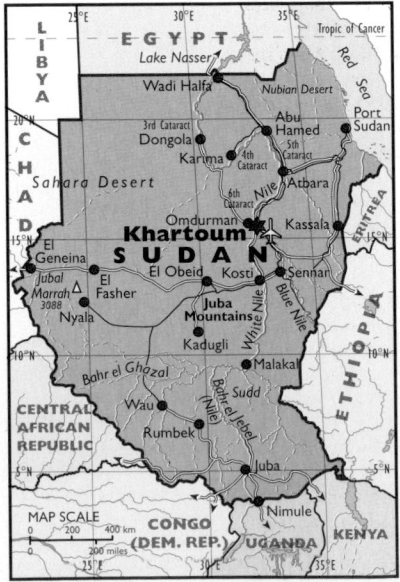

### VEGETATION

From the bare deserts of the N, the land merges into dry grasslands and savanna. Dense rain forests grow in the S.

### HISTORY AND POLITICS

The ancient state of NUBIA extended into N Sudan. In *c.*2,000 BC it became a colony of EGYPT. From the 8th century BC to *c.*350 AD, it was part of the KUSH kingdom. Christianity was introduced in the 6th century. From the 13th to 15th centuries, N Sudan came under Muslim control and Islam became its dominant religion. In 1821 MUHAMMAD ALI's forces occupied Sudan. Anglo-Egyptian forces, led by Charles George GORDON, attempted to extend Egypt's influence into the S. Muhammad Ahmad led a MAHDI uprising, which briefly freed Sudan from Anglo-Egyptian influence. In 1898 KITCHENER's forces defeated the Mahdists, and in 1899 Sudan became Anglo-Egyptian Sudan, governed jointly by Britain and Egypt. Opposition to colonial rule continued until independence in 1956. The S Sudanese, who are predominantly Christians or followers of traditional beliefs, revolted against the dominance of the Muslim N, and civil war broke out. In 1958 the civilian government was overthrown in a coup; re-established in 1964, it was overthrown again in 1969, when Gaafar Muhammad Nimeri seized control. In 1972 S Sudan was given considerable autonomy but unrest continued. The imposition of strict Islamic law in 1983 sparked further conflict with the Sudan People's Liberation Army (SPLA) in the S. Nimeri was deposed in 1985, and a civilian government came to power in 1986. In 1989 it was overthrown by Omar Hassan Ahmed al Bashir, who established a Revolutionary Command Council. In 1996 Bashir was reelected, though there had been no serious rival. The National Islamic Front (NIF) dominates the government and is believed to have strong links with Iranian terrorist groups. In 1996 the UN imposed sanctions on Sudan. Civil war between various SPLA factions and government forces continues in the S. By 1994 much of the area was government-controlled, but in 1995 and 1996 the SPLA gained ground. In 1996 a peace treaty, which involved the relinquishment of the fight for southern independence, was signed by the government and by some SPLA factions. Rejected by other factions, SPLA guerrilla activities continue. Food shortages and the displacement of people from areas of unrest have added to Sudan's economic difficulties.

### ECONOMY

Sudan is a low-income economy. Agriculture employs 62% of the people. The leading crops are cotton, millet, wheat, and sesame. Nomadic herders raise livestock. Mineral resources include chromium, gold, gypsum, and oil. Manufacturing industries produce cement, fertilizers, and textiles. The main exports are cotton, gum arabic, and sesame seeds.

1859–69 by the Suez Canal Company under the supervision of French canal builder Ferdinand de LESSEPS. In 1875 the British government became the major shareholder in the company. After Egypt nationalized the canal in 1956, Israeli and British forces attacked Egypt, and the canal was closed from 1956 to 1957 while repairs were carried out. It was again closed during the ARAB-ISRAELI WAR of 1967. The canal reopened in 1975. In the intervening period many new ships, especially oil tankers, became too large to pass through the canal. Loss of revenue forced Egypt to clear and widen the waterway.

**Suffolk** County in E England, on the North Sea coast; the county town is IPSWICH. The land is mainly low-lying and flat, rising in the SW. The principal rivers are the Orwell, Stour, and Waveney. The economy is mainly agricultural, growing cereal crops and sugar beets and rearing sheep, pigs, and poultry. Fishing is in decline. Industries: food processing, farm machinery, fertilizers, finance. Area: 1,470sq mi (3,807sq km). Pop. (1991) 632,266.

**suffrage** *See* FRANCHISE

**suffragette movement** Women's campaign in Britain in the late 19th and early 20th centuries to win the right to vote. It began in the 1860s, and developed until the founding of the National Union of Women's Suffrage Societies in 1897. Emmeline PANKHURST founded the Women's Social and Political Union in 1903. By 1910 the movement had split into several factions, including the Women's Freedom League (founded in 1908). In 1913 Sylvia Pankhurst founded the East London Federation, which organized marches in London. Women of the age of 30 and over were given the vote in 1918.

**Sufism** Mystic philosophical movement within ISLAM that developed among the SHI'A communities in the 10th and 11th centuries. Sufis stress the capability of the soul to attain personal union with God. *See also* DERVISH

**sugar** Sweet-tasting, soluble, crystalline monosaccharide or disaccharide CARBOHYDRATE. The common sugar in food and beverages is SUCROSE. This is also the main sugar transported in plant tissues. The main sugar transported around the bodies of animals to provide energy is GLUCOSE. *See also* SACCHARIDE

**sugar beet** Variety of BEET grown commercially for its high SUGAR content, which is stored in its thick, white roots. Family Chenopdiaceae; species *Beta vulgaris*.

**sugarcane** Perennial GRASS cultivated in tropical and subtropical regions throughout the world. After harvesting, the stems are processed in factories, and are the main source of SUGAR. Most cultivated canes are *Saccharum officinarum*. Height: to 15ft (4.5m). Family Poaceae/Gramineae.

**Suharto, Raden** (1921– ) Indonesian general and statesman, president (1967–98). Suharto seized power from President SUKARNO, averting an alleged communist coup, in 1966. He was formally elected president in 1968 and was reelected (unopposed) five times. Suharto ordered the invasion (1975) of East Timor. Under Suharto, Indonesia experienced rapid economic development, but his autocratic rule was criticized for frequent abuses of human rights. In 1997 economic collapse destabilized Suharto's government. In 1998 he was forced to resign after widespread student rioting.

**Suhrawardi, as-** (1155–91) Islamic philosopher and theologian, b. Persia (Iran). He was the founder of the Ishraqi (Illuminationist) school of thought, which embraced elements from many sources, including ORPHISM, Hellenism, ZOROASTRIANISM, SUFISM, and SHI'A Islam. His thinking is still in evidence in Iran today among mystical sects, such as the Nuyah. His principal work is *Kitab Hikmat al-ishraq* (*The Wisdom of Illumination*). He was put to death by Malikaz-Zahir, the son of SALADIN.

**suite** Musical form popular in the BAROQUE period, comprising a number of instrumental dances, which differ in meter, tempo, and rhythm but are generally all in the same key. The earliest suites date from the 16th century and usually involved only two dances, the pavane and galliard. By the 18th century the dances had become standardized: a prelude, allemande, courante, saraband, and gigue. There was some flexibility, and the minuet, gavotte, bourrée, and rondeau were often added.

**Sukarno, Achmad** (1901–70) First president of independent Indonesia. Founder of the Indonesian Nationalist Party (1927), he led opposition to Dutch rule and was frequently imprisoned or exiled (1933–42). At the end of World War II he declared Indonesian independence and became president of the new republic (1947–67). In the 1950s his rule became increasingly dictatorial. He dissolved the parliament, declared himself president for life (1963), and aligned himself with the communists. The failure of a communist coup against the leaders of the army in 1965 weakened Sukarno's position. He was forced out of power by the generals, led by SUHARTO, who eventually replaced him as president.

**Sukkoth** (Sukkat) Jewish Feast of Tabernacles, or Feast of Booths, a fall festival that lasts for seven days. It commemorates the wandering of the Jews in the desert and their salvation through God. A *sukkat*, or simple tent of branches, is raised in the synagogue. *See* TABERNACLE

**Sukkur** City in W Pakistan, on the Indus River, in Sind province. It is the site of the Sukkur Barrage across the Indus, controlling one of the largest irrigation schemes in the world with canals watering more than 5 million acres (12 million hectares) of the Indus valley. Completed in 1932, the dam is 190ft (58m) high and *c.*5,000ft (1,500m) long. Industries: textiles, foodstuffs. Pop. (1991) 350,000.

**Sulawesi** (formerly Celebes) Large island in E Indonesia, separated from Borneo by the Makasar Strait, with Ujung Pandang (formerly Makasar, 1990 pop. 913,196) the main port and largest city. A largely mountainous and volcanic island, the highest peak is Mount Rantekombola at 11,335ft (3,455m). The first European discovery was by the Portuguese in 1512. The Dutch assumed control in the early 17th century and successfully waged war against the native population in the 1666–69 Makasar War. In 1950 it became a province of the Indonesian republic, and it is made up of four separate provinces: Utara, Tengah, Selatan, and Tenggara. The population is primarily Malayan. Industries: fishing, agriculture. Area: 73,031sq mi (189,216sq km). Pop. (1990) 12,520,711

**Suleiman I (the Magnificent)** (1494–1566) Ottoman sultan (1520–66). He succeeded his father, Selim I. He captured Rhodes from the KNIGHTS HOSPITALLERS and launched a series of campaigns against the Austrian HAPSBURGS, defeating the Hungarians at Mohács (1526) and subsequently controlling most of the country. His troops besieged Vienna (1529), and his admiral, BARBAROSSA, created a navy that dominated the Mediterranean and ensured Ottoman control of much of the North African coastal region. In the east he won victories against the Safavids of Persia, and conquered Mesopotamia.

**sulfate** Salt of SULFURIC ACID ($H_2SO_4$). Examples include copper(II) sulfate ($CuSO_4$) and iron(II) sulfate ($FeSO_4$).

**sulfonamide drug** Any of a group of DRUGS derived from sulfanilamide, a red textile dye, that prevent the growth of bacteria. Introduced in the 1930s, they were the first antibacterials, prescribed to treat a range of infections. They were replaced by less toxic and more effective ANTIBIOTICS.

**sulfur** (symbol S) Nonmetallic element in Group VI of the periodic table, known since prehistory (the biblical brimstone). It may occur naturally as a free element or in sulfide minerals such as GALENA and iron pyrites, or in sulfate minerals such as GYPSUM. The main commercial source is native (free) sulfur, extracted by the Frasch process. It is used in the VULCANIZATION of rubber and in the manufacture of drugs, matches, dyes, fungicides, insecticides, and fertilizers. Properties: at.no. 16; at. wt. 32.064; sp. gr. 2.07; m.p. 235.0°F (112.8°C); b.p. 832.5°F (444.7°C). Most common isotope $^{32}S$ (95.1%).

**sulfuric acid** ($H_2SO_4$) Colorless, odorless liquid, one of the strongest acids known. It is produced by the oxidation of sulfur dioxide ($SO_2$). Sulfuric acid is a major industrial chemical, used in the manufacture of many acids, fertilizers, detergents, drugs, and a wide range of chemicals. Properties: sp.gr. 1.84; m.p. 50.5°F (10.3°C); b.p. 626°F (330°C).

**Sulla, Lucius Cornelius** (138–78 BC) Roman dictator (82–81 BC). Elected consul in 88 BC, he defeated MITHRIDATES VI in spite of the opposition of MARIUS, Cinna, and their supporters in Rome. Invading Italy, he captured Rome in 82 BC and massacred his antipatrician enemies.

**Sullivan, Sir Arthur Seymour** (1842–1900) British composer famous for a series of operettas written with the librettist

▲ **sugar** Sugar beets (left) and sugarcane (right) produce the same sugar – sucrose – but require completely different climatic conditions. Cane is grown as a single crop in tropical regions, while sugar beets form part of regular crop rotation in Europe, and North and South America. Although sugar is extracted by the same method from both sources, the yield of sugarcane is higher.

S

**SULFUR (FRASCH PROCESS)**

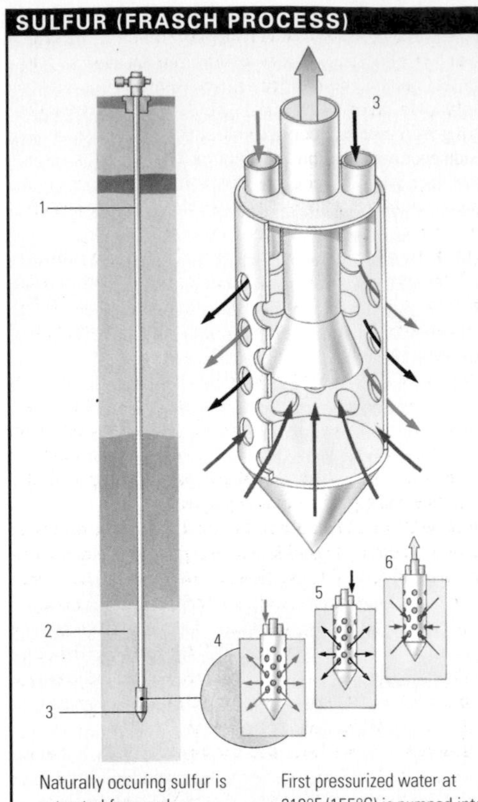


Naturally occuring sulfur is extracted from rock formations by a method known as the Frasch process. Bore holes (1) are dug to the sulfur-rich areas (2). A specialized head (3) is dropped down the bore hole. First pressurized water at 310°F (155°C) is pumped into the rock (4) melting the sulfur. The water is followed by compressed air (5) which forces the liquid containing the sulfur to the surface (6).

W.S. GILBERT. They included *H.M.S. Pinafore* (1878), *The Pirates of Penzance* (1879), and *The Mikado* (1885). Sullivan also composed one opera, *Ivanhoe* (1881), and oratorios, cantatas, and hymns, such as "Onward, Christian Soldiers".

**Sullivan, Louis Henry** (1856–1924) US architect and founder of the Chicago School of architecture. The Wainwright Building in St. Louis (1890) and the Transportation Building at the 1893 World's Exhibition in Chicago are counted among his best-known works.

**Sumatra** (Sumatera) Island in W Indonesia – the world's sixth-largest island. The W coast is rugged and mountainous, the Barisan Mountains rising to 12,500ft (3,800m), and nearly 60% of the lowland area is jungle. By the 7th century, India had established two states in Sumatra – Melayu and Srivijaya. The Portuguese landed on the island in the 16th century and the Dutch followed a century later. Britain held certain parts of the island briefly in the 18th and 19th centuries, and Sumatra became part of newly independent Indonesia in 1950. The principal cities (1990 figures) are Medan (1,685,972), Palembang (1,084,483), and Padang (477,344). The main products are oil (the largest earner), timber, rubber, tin, tobacco, palm oil, tea, coffee, sisal, and rice. Mining and farming were the chief occupations, but the N is being rapidly industrialized. Sumatra now accounts for around 75% of Indonesia's total income. Area: 164,000sq mi (425,000sq km). Pop. (1990) 36,505,703.

**Sumeria** World's first civilization, dating from before 3000 BC, in S MESOPOTAMIA. The Sumerians are credited with inventing cuneiform writing, many familiar sociopolitical institutions, and a money-based economy. Major cities were UR, Kish, and Lagash. During the third millennium it built up a large empire. In *c.*2340 BC, the Semitic peoples of AKKADIA conquered Mesopotamia, and by *c.*1950 BC the civilization had disintegrated.

**Sumner, Charles** (1811–74) US political leader. A passionate abolitionist, he was senator from Massachusetts (1851–74) and a leading Radical Republican during RECONSTRUCTION, supporting the impeachment of President Andrew JOHNSON.

**sumo wrestling** Traditional and popular sport of Japan. Pairs of wrestlers, who usually weigh more than 350lb (159kg), attempt to force each other out of a ring. The technique employs holds, trips, pushes, and falls. A referee monitors the brief bout and keeps score.

**Sun** Star at the center of the SOLAR SYSTEM, around which all other Solar System bodies revolve in their orbits. The Sun is a typical, average star. It consists of about 70% hydrogen (by weight) and 28% helium, with the remainder mostly oxygen and carbon. Its temperature, pressure, and density increase toward the center. Like all stars, the Sun's energy is generated by nuclear FUSION reactions taking place under the extreme conditions in the core. This core is about 250,000mi (400,000km) across. Energy released from the core passes up through the radiative zone, which is nearly 200,000mi (about 300,000km) thick, then passes through the 125,000 (200,000km) thick convective zone to the surface, the PHOTOSPHERE, from where it is radiated into space. Most of the Sun's visible activity takes place in the 300mi (500km) thick photosphere. Above the photosphere lies the chromosphere, which consists of hot gases and extends for thousands of kilometers. Extending outwards from the chromosphere for millions of miles is the CORONA, which emits the SOLAR WIND. The solar wind and the Sun's magnetic field dominate a region of space called the heliosphere, which extends to the boundaries of the Solar System.

**sunbird** Tropical, nectar-feeding songbird of the Old World, often considered a counterpart of the New World hummingbird. The males are usually brightly colored. Length: 3.5–6in (9–15cm). Family Nectariniidae.

**sunburn** Damage to skin caused by prolonged or unaccustomed exposure to sunlight. It varies in severity from redness and soreness to the formation of large blisters, which may be accompanied by shock. Excessive exposure to sunlight is associated with the skin cancer known as melanoma.

**sun dance** Important religious rite of the North American "Plains Indians." It was usually held annually in early summer and was performed around a TOTEM POLE. The sun dance was part of elaborate ceremonies held to reaffirm a tribe's affinity with nature and the universe.

**Sunday, Billy (William Ashley)** (1862–1935) US Presbyterian revivalist. After three years in professional baseball, he became a famous preacher at huge evangelical meetings across the country. He preached against alcohol, gaining a reputation as a temperance leader.

**Sunderland** County district in SE TYNE AND WEAR, NE England at the mouth of the Wear River. Once renowned for coal-mining and the biggest shipbuilding center in the world, it now has chemicals, vehicles, and furniture among its many industries. Pop. (1991) 289,040.

**sundew** Any INSECTIVOROUS PLANT of the genus *Drosera*, native to temperate swamps and bogs. Sundews have hairy basal leaves that glisten with a sticky dewlike substance that attracts and traps insects. The leaves then fold over the insect, and secrete ENZYMES to digest it. Family Droseraceae.

**sunfish** North American freshwater fish. A popular angler's fish, similar in appearance to PERCH, it has a continuous dorsal fin containing spiny and soft rays. The 30 species range in size from the blue spotted *Enneacanthus gloriosus* (length: 3.5in/8.9cm) to the large-mouth bass *Micropterus salmoides* (length: 32in/81cm; weight: 22lb/10kg). Family Centrarchidae.

**sunflower** Any of several annual and perennial plants of the genus *Helianthus*, native to North and South America. The flower heads resemble huge daisies with yellow ray flowers and a center disk of yellow, brown, or purple. The seeds yield a useful oil. The common sunflower (*H. annuus*) has 12-in (30-cm) leaves and flower heads more than 30cm across; height: to 12ft (3.5m). Family Asteraceae/Compositae.

**Sunni** Traditionalist orthodox branch of ISLAM, whose followers are called *Ahl as-Sunnah* ("People of the Path"). It is followed by 90% of Muslims. Sunnis accept the *Hadith*, the body of orthodox teachings based on Muhammad's spoken words outside the KORAN. The Sunni differ from the SHI'A sect in that they accept the first four caliphs (religious leaders) as the true successors of MUHAMMAD.

**sunspot** Region in the Sun's PHOTOSPHERE that is cooler than its surroundings and appears darker. Sunspots vary in size from *c.*600–30,000mi (1,000–50,000km), and occasionally up to *c.*125,000mi (200,000km). Their duration varies from a few hours to a few weeks, or months for the very biggest. Sunspots occur where there is a local strengthening of the Sun's magnetic field.

**sunstroke** Potentially fatal condition caused by over-exposure to direct sunlight, in which the body temperature rises to 105°F (40.5°C) or more. Symptoms include hot, dry skin, exhaustion, delirium, and coma. Urgent medical treatment is required, possibly in an intensive care unit. Recovery is usual within a day or two.

**Sun Yat-sen** (1866–1925) Chinese nationalist leader, first president of the Chinese Republic (1911–12). In exile (1895–1911), he adopted his "three principles of the people": nationalism, democracy, and prosperity. After the revolution of 1911 he became provisional president, but soon resigned in favor of the militarily powerful Yüan Shih-k'ai. When Yüan turned autocratic, Sun gave his support to the KUOMINTANG, or Nationalist Party, formed to oppose Yüan.

**supercluster** *See* GALAXY CLUSTER

**superconductivity** Electrical behavior in metals and alloys that are cooled to very low temperatures. In a superconducting circuit, an electric current flows indefinitely because there is no electrical resistance. Research continues to develop superconductors that function at higher temperatures.

**superego** In PSYCHOANALYSIS, level of personality that acts as a conscience or censor. It develops as a child internalizes the standards of behavior defined by the rewards and punishments of parents and society. *See also* ID; EGO

**superfluidity** Property of a liquid that has no viscosity and therefore no resistance to flow. Helium II – liquid helium at temperatures less than 2K, or –456°F (–271°C) – was the first known superfluid. Helium II apparently defies gravity by flowing up slopes. It also appears to contravene the laws of THERMODYNAMICS, by flowing from a cool region to a warmer one. *See also* CRYOGENICS; HELIUM

**Superior, Lake** Lake in the US and Canada, the largest freshwater lake in the world, bordered on the W by Minnesota, on the N and E by Ontario, and on the S by Michigan and Wisconsin. The most W of the five GREAT LAKES, it is connected to Lake HURON and the ST. LAWRENCE SEAWAY by the St. Mary's River and the Soo (Sault Ste. Marie) canals. A center for commercial and recreational fishing, the lake is also a major commercial transportation route, particularly for grain and iron ore from Duluth, Michigan, and Thunder Bay, Ontario. Area: 31,820sq mi (82,413sq km). Maximum depth: *c.*1,300ft (400m).

**supernova** Stellar explosion in which virtually an entire STAR is disrupted. For a week or so, a supernova may outshine all the other stars in its galaxy. After a couple of years the supernova has expanded so much that it becomes thin and transparent. For hundreds or thousands of years the ejected material remains visible as a supernova remnant. A supernova is about 1,000 times brighter than a NOVA.

**superposition, law of** In geology, law that states that in undisturbed layers of sedimentary deposits, younger beds overlie older ones.

**supersonic velocity** Velocity greater than that of the local speed of sound. In dry air at 32°F (0°C), this speed is about 1,080ft/s (330m/s) or 736mph (1,188km/h). Its magnitude is usually expressed as a MACH NUMBER. This is the ratio of the speed of a body to the speed of sound in a medium such as air. Any object traveling at supersonic velocity leaves behind a shock wave that a ground observer hears as a SONIC BOOM.

**supply and demand, law of** Economic balance between goods required and produced. The law of supply indicates that, other things being equal, as the price of an item increases, suppliers are willing to produce more, and as the price decreases producers are willing to produce less. Thus, price and quantity supplied are directly related. The law of demand states the reverse: as prices increase, consumers demand less, and as prices decrease, consumers demand more. Thus, prices and quantity demanded are inversely related.

**supply-side economics** Policies designed to reduce the role of governments in economic matters. The theory of supply-side economics is that production of goods and services can be stimulated by reducing taxes, thereby increasing the supply of money for investment. It also promotes governmental expenditure that generates industrial activity.

**suprematism** Abstract art movement launched in Russia in 1915 by Kasimir MALEVICH. Epitomized by the stark geometrical forms of Malevich's painting *White on White* (1919), suprematism had a profound influence on the development of geometrical ABSTRACT ART and CONSTRUCTIVISM.

**Supreme Court, Canadian** Highest court of appeal in Canada, established in 1875. Its judgment became final when appeals to the Judicial Committee of the Privy Council in London, England, were ended: for criminal cases in 1933, for civil cases in 1949. It sits in Ottawa and is composed of a chief justice and eight associated judges.

**Supreme Court, US** US court of final appeal, the highest in the nation. Its duty is to decide and interpret the constitutionality of state and federal legislation and of executive acts. Once the Supreme Court has arrived at a decision, all lower courts must follow it in similar cases. Cases are decided by majority vote. Created by the Constitution of 1787, the Supreme Court is made up of nine justices appointed for life by the president with the advice and consent of the Senate. *See also* biographies of individual justices; landmark cases

**Surabaja** Port in NE Java, second-largest city in Indonesia and capital of East Java province. An important naval base occupied by Japan in World War II, the city remains Indonesia's primary naval center. A fishing and industrial port, it has shipyards, textile mills, automobile assembly plants, and oil refining. Pop. (1990) 2,421,016.

**surfing** Water sport in which a person lies or stands on a specially designed wooden or fiberglass board, usually 4–6ft (1.2–1.8m) long, and is propelled by the crest of a wave toward the shore.

**surgery** Branch of medical practice concerned with treatment by operation. Traditionally it has mainly involved open surgery: gaining access to the operative site by way of an incision. However, the practice of using ENDOSCOPES has enabled the development of MINIMAL ACCESS SURGERY using minimally invasive techniques. Surgery is carried out under sterile conditions, using local or general ANESTHESIA.

**Surinam** (Suriname) Independent nation in NE South America, on the Atlantic Ocean, bordered by Brazil (S), French Guiana (E), and Guyana (W). Its capital is PARAMARIBO. Surinam is made up of the Guiana Highlands plateau, a flat coastal plain, and a forested inland region. Its many rivers serve as a source of hydroelectric power. **History** The region was discovered in 1499 by Spanish explorer Alfonso de Ojeda, but it was the British who founded the first colony (1651). In 1667 it was ceded to Holland in exchange for New Amsterdam (later New York), and in 1815 the Congress of Vienna gave the Guyana region to Britain and reaffirmed Dutch control of "Dutch Guiana." It became officially autonomous in 1954, and in 1975, as Surinam, gained full independence from the Netherlands and membership of the United Nations. In 1980 the military seized control, imposing martial law and banning political parties. Guerrilla warfare disrupted the economy. In 1987 a new constitution provided for a 51-member National Assembly, with powers to elect the president. Rameswak Shankar was elected president in 1988, but was overthrown by another military coup in 1990. In 1991 the New Front for Democracy and Development won the majority of seats in the National Assembly and their leader, Ronald Venetiaan, became president. The constitution was amended in 1992 to limit the power of the military. The 1996 general election resulted in a coalition government, led by Jules Wijdenbosch of the National Democratic Party. **Economy** Surinam's economy depends greatly on the export of bauxite, of which it is one of the

▲ **Sumeria** This Sumerian vessel dates from *c.*3500 BC. Clay was one of the few raw materials available to the Sumerians. The quality of their glazes and decorations were very advanced. The Sumerians were also renowned for their architecture, notably the stepped-pyramid ziggurats.

▲ **sunflower** Widely cultivated throughout Europe and North America, the common sunflower (*Helianthus annus*) produces seeds from which a light, high-quality oil is yielded. This oil is used in cooking, margarine, shortening, and confectionery. The nutritious seeds can also be eaten whole or used in breads and cereals for human consumption, or in poultry feed.

S

## SURINAM

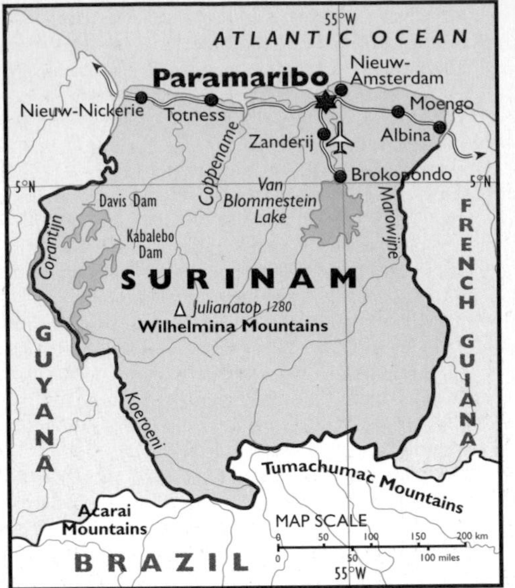


**AREA:** 63,069 sq mi (163,270sq km)
**POPULATION:** 438,000
**CAPITAL (POPULATION):** Paramaribo (200,970)
**GOVERNMENT:** Multiparty republic
**ETHNIC GROUPS:** Indian 37%, Creole, 31%, Indonesian 14%, Black 9%, Native American 3%, Chinese 3%, Dutch 1%
**LANGUAGES:** Dutch (official)
**RELIGIONS:** Christianity (Roman Catholic 23%, Protestant 19%), Hinduism 27%, Islam 20%
**CURRENCY:** Surinam guilder = 100 cents

world's largest producers. The chief agricultural products are rice, bananas, sugarcane, coffee, coconuts, lumber, and citrus fruits.

**surrealism** Influential movement in 20th-century art and literature; it evolved in the mid-1920s from Dadaism. Taking inspiration from Freudian theories of the subconcious, the surrealists used bizarre imagery and strange juxtapositions to surprise and shock viewers. Important surrealist writers include Louis Aragon, Georges Bataille, Paul ÉLUARD, and Benjamin Peret, while painters include Jean ARP, Max ERNST, René MAGRITTE, Salvador DALI, Joan MIRÓ, and Paul KLEE. *See also* DADA

**Surrey, Henry Howard, earl of** (1517–47) English poet. Like his cousin Catherine HOWARD, he died on the scaffold, a victim of the bloody power politics of HENRY VIII's court. He wrote some of the earliest English SONNETS and, with his translation of two books of the *Aeneid* by VIRGIL, introduced BLANK VERSE into English poetry.

**Surrey** County in SE England, bordering Greater London. From E to W are the North Downs, which slope down to the Thames Valley. The Wey and the Mole are the principal rivers. Much of the land in the W is devoted to farming, with dairy and market-garden produce, wheat and oats the chief products. Guildford (1991 pop. 122,378) is the county town. Area: 648sq mi (1,679sq km). Pop. (1991) 1,018,003.

**surveying** Accurate measurement of the Earth's surface. It is used in establishing land boundaries and the topography of landforms and for major construction and civil engineering work. For smaller areas, the land is treated as a horizontal plane. Large areas involve considerations of the Earth's curved shape and are referred to a geodetic surveys.

**suspension** Liquid (or gas) medium in which small solid (or liquid) particles are uniformly dispersed. The particles are larger than those found in a COLLOID and will settle if the suspension stands undisturbed.

**Sussex** Former county in SE England, on the English Channel, since 1974 divided into the counties EAST SUSSEX and WEST SUSSEX. Area: 1,457sq mi (3,773sq km).

**Sussex** Kingdom of Anglo-Saxon England, settled by the South Saxons under Aelle (*c.* AD 477). It was allegedly the last Anglo-Saxon kingdom to adopt Christianity (*c.*680). A number of kings of Sussex are known from the 7th–8th centuries, but at various times they were under the dominance of Mercia. Sussex was absorbed by WESSEX in the early 9th century.

**Sutherland, Graham** (1903–80) English painter, draftsman, and printmaker. During World War II he was employed as an official artist to record the effects of bomb damage. After the war he concentrated on religious themes and created the celebrated tapestry *Christ in Glory* (1962) for Coventry Cathedral.

**Sutherland, Dame Joan** (1926– ) Australian coloratura soprano. She joined the ROYAL OPERA, London, in 1952, and her performance in the title role of Donizetti's *Lucia di Lammermoor* in 1959 earned her worldwide acclaim. She went on to perform in all the world's major opera houses before her retirement in 1990.

**Sutra** Sacred or authoritative text in Indian philosophy or religion. In HINDUISM, it is a concise work for use within an oral tradition. Most philosophical traditions had their own sutras, which were written down in the first few centuries of the Christian era. In Buddhism, a sutra was a sometimes lengthy sacred text dealing with a specific point of doctrine.

**suttee** Former Indian custom of a widow throwing herself alive on to her husband's funeral pyre. Originally confined to royalty, it was forbidden under British Rule in 1829.

**Sutton Hoo** Archeological site in Suffolk, SE England. The 1939 excavation of the cenotaph of Raedwald, a Saxon King of East Anglia (d.625), was Britain's richest archeological find. The digs revealed a Saxon rowing boat 90ft (27m) long. In the center of the boat lay a wooden funeral chamber, containing silver plate, gold jewelry and coins, and bronze armor.

**Suva** Seaport on the SE coast of Viti Levu Island, in the SW Pacific Ocean, capital of the Fiji Islands. It is the manufacturing and trade center, with an excellent harbor. Exports include tropical fruits, copra, and gold. Pop. (1992) 73,500.

**Suzhou** (Soochow, Su-chow) City on the Grand Canal, Jiangsu province, E central China. Capital of Wu kingdom in the 5th century BC, its famous silk industry developed under the SUNG dynasty in the 12th century. It has been noted since 100 BC for its many gardens, temples, and canals. Industries: silk, cotton, embroidery, chemicals. Pop. (1991) 706,000.

**Suzman, Helen** (1917– ) South African politician. Suzman was an outspoken opponent of the APARTHEID regime in South Africa for 40 years. Elected to parliament in 1953, she formed the Progressive Party in 1959, and for the next 12 years was the only member. She retired from parliament shortly after the election of Nelson MANDELA.

▲ **Suzman** After studying economics at Witwatersrand University, Helen Suzman became a member of the South African parliament in 1953. As a strong opponent of apartheid, she gradually gained the respect of the black community and of the then ANC leader Nelson Mandela. She was a key figure in the South African Institute of Race Relations, and received the UN Human Rights Award in 1978.

**Svalbard** Archipelago in the Arctic Ocean, *c.*400 mi (640km) N of Norway, to which it has officially belonged since 1925. There are nine main islands, of which by far the largest is Spitsbergen. The administrative center and largest settlement is Longyearbyen on Spitsbergen. Ice fields and glaciers cover more than half the land mass, although the W edge of the islands is ice-free for most of the year. The islands are an important wildlife refuge, and protective measures have saved certain mammals from extinction. Animals include polar bear, walrus, and whale. Though Svalbard was discovered by the Vikings in 1194, the islands remained neglected until Willem Barents rediscovered them in 1596. During the 17th century, they were an important whaling center, and in the 18th century the lands were hunted by Russian and Scandinavian fur traders. Large coal deposits were found on Spitsbergen at the end of the 19th century, and the area was mined by Norway, Russia, and Sweden. In 1925 the islands became a sovereign territory of Norway (although over half the population is Russian), in return for allowing mining concessions to other nations. Area: 24,000sq mi (62,000sq km). Pop. (1994) 2,906.

**Svevo, Italo** (1861–1928) Italian novelist and businessman, b. Ettore Schmitz. Discouraged by the failure of his first two novels, he abandoned writing to pursue a career as a lawyer until his English tutor, the young James JOYCE, read his work and urged him to persevere. Largely psychological and introspective, his novels include *A Life* (1892) and his best-known work, *The Confessions of Zeno* (1923).

**Swahili** BANTU language of the Niger-Congo family of African languages. It developed as a LINGUA FRANCA and trading language in most of E Africa, becoming the official language of Tanzania in 1967 and of Kenya in 1973. It is also in use in parts of central Africa. Swahili is notable for its large number of Arabic loan words and its use of the Arabic alphabet. It has a large body of literature.

**swallow** Any of 75 species of graceful and agile birds with long, tapering wings and a long, forked tail. The common swallow (*Hirundo rustica*), known as the barn swallow in North America, is gray-blue with a light brown underside and red throat markings; it feeds primarily on insects, which it catches in flight. Length: 8in (20cm). Family Hirundinidae.

**swamp** Low-lying wetland area, found near large bodies of open water. Swamps are characterized by numerous plants and animals, including rushes and sedge in N regions, and species of trees, such as the swamp cypress, in warmer S areas. Swamps can prevent flooding by absorbing flood waters from rivers and coastal regions. *See also* BOG; MARSH

**swan** Any of several species of graceful, white or black waterfowl that nest in N Northern Hemisphere and migrate S for winter. Three species, including the Australian Black swan, live in the Southern Hemisphere. Most have broad, flat bills, long necks, plump bodies, and dense plumage. They dip their heads under water to feed on plant matter. Length: to 6.5ft (2m). Family Anatidae; genus *Cygnus*.

**Swansea** (Abertawe) City and county district on Swansea Bay at the mouth of the Tawe River, West Glamorgan, S Wales. The second-largest Welsh city, it is the administrative center of West Glamorgan and an industrial city that grew with the export of coal in the 19th century. Formerly noted for its production of steel, it is now dominated by light industry. Pop. (1991) 181,906.

**SWAPO** Acronym for SOUTH WEST AFRICA PEOPLE'S ORGANIZATION

**Swaziland** Small, landlocked, and mountainous kingdom in S Africa, bounded by South Africa (N, W, S) and Mozambique (E); its capital is MBABANE. **Land and climate** There are four land regions. In the W, the Highveld, with an average height of 3,950ft (1,200m), makes up 30% of Swaziland. The Middleveld, between 1,150 and 3,300ft (350–1,000m), covers 28% of the country, while the Lowveld, with an average height of 890ft (270m), covers another 33%. The Lebombo Mountains, the fourth region, reach 2,600 ft (800m) along the E border. The Lowveld is almost tropical, with an average temperature of 72°F (22°C) and a low rainfall of about 20in (500mm) a year. The altitude moderates the climate in the W and Mbabane has a climate typical of the Highveld, with warm summers and cool winters. **Vegetation** Meadows and pasture cover about 65% of Swaziland. Arable land covers 8% of the land and forests only 6%. **History** According to tradition, a group of Bantu-speaking people, under the Swazi chief Ngwane II, crossed the Lebombo range and united with local African groups to form the Swazi nation in the 18th century. Under attack from Zulu armies, the Swazi people were forced to seek British protection in the 1840s. Gold was discovered in the 1880s and many Europeans sought land concessions from the king, who did not realize that in doing this he was losing control of the land. In 1894 Britain and the Boers of South Africa agreed to put Swaziland under the control of the South African Republic (the Transvaal). At the end of the second SOUTH AFRICAN WAR (1899–1902), Britain took control of the country. In 1968 Swaziland became fully independent as a constitutional monarchy, with King Sobhuza II as head of state. In 1973 Sobhuza suspended the constitution and assumed supreme power. All political parties were banned in 1978. When Sobhuza died in 1982, his son, Makhosetive, was named as heir. In 1986 he was installed as king, taking the name Mswati III. In 1993 Swaziland held its first ever multiparty elections. Pro-democracy demonstrations forced Mswati to reconsider the ban on political parties. **Economy** Swaziland is a lower-middle-income developing country (1992 GDP per capita, $1,700). Agriculture employs 74% of the work force. Farm products and processed foods, including sugar, wood pulp, citrus fruits, and canned fruit, are the leading exports, though many farmers live at subsistence level. Mining has declined in importance in recent years. Swaziland's high-grade iron ore reserves were used up in 1978, while the world demand for its asbestos has fallen. Swaziland is heavily dependent on South Africa and the two countries are linked through a customs union.

**sweating** (perspiring) Loss of water, salts, and urea from the body surface of many mammals as a result of the action of certain glands (sweat glands). Sweat glands are situated in the dermis of the skin, and open onto the surface through tiny pores. In humans, they are found all over the body, but in some mammals they are found only on the soles of the feet. Sweating is controlled by the nervous system and forms an important part of the body's temperature control mechanism. The evaporation of sweat cools the skin and the blood passing through capillaries close to the skin surface. Excessive sweating must be compensated for by increased intake of water and salt.

**Sweden** Kingdom on the E half of the SCANDINAVIAN peninsula, N Europe. *See* country feature, page 650

**Swedenborg, Emanuel** (1688–1772) Swedish scientist, philosopher, theologian, and mystic. After a glittering scientific career, during which he wrote many books (notably on metallurgy and metaphysics), he turned to theological teaching after a spiritual crisis in the mid-1740s. In 1745 he gave up worldly learning to concentrate on religious affairs. His religious writings include *Heavenly Arcana* (1749–56), *The New Jerusalem* (1758), and *True Christian Religion* (1771).

**Swedish** National language of Sweden, spoken by virtually all the country's 8.7 million people. It is also spoken by many people in Finland. Closely related to Norwegian and Danish, it is a member of the northern branch of the Germanic family of INDO-EUROPEAN LANGUAGES.

**sweet pea** Climbing, annual plant native to Italy. Widely cultivated as an ornamental, it has fragrant, butterfly-shaped flowers of white, pink, rose, lavender, purple, red, or orange. Height: to 6ft (1.8m). Family Fabaceae/Leguminosae; species *Lathyrus odoratus*.

▲ **swallow** Extremely agile flyers, swallows spend most of their time in the air and feed on the wing. They often migrate extremely long distances: In North America, the common, or barn, swallow (*Hirundo rustica*, above) may summer in Canada and winter in South America. On the other side of the Atlantic, those that summer in Europe migrate to Africa or to the Indian subcontinent in the winter.

## SWAZILAND

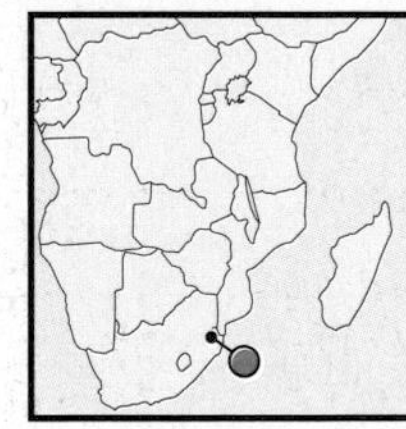

**AREA:** 6,703 sq mi (17,360sq km)
**POPULATION:** 792,000
**CAPITAL (POPULATION):** Mbabane (38,290)
**GOVERNMENT:** Monarchy
**ETHNIC GROUPS:** Swazi 84%, Zulu 10%, Tsonga 2%
**LANGUAGES:** Siswati and English (both official)
**LANGUAGES:** Christianity (Protestant 37%, indigenous African churches 29%, Roman Catholic 11%), traditional beliefs 21%
**CURRENCY:** Lilangeni = 100 cents

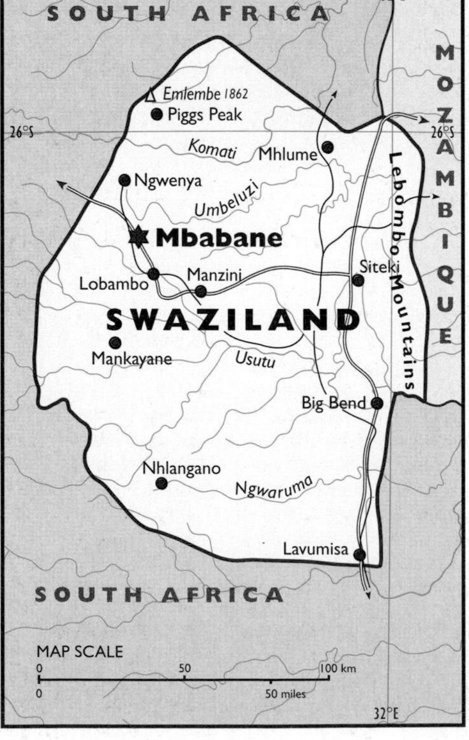

**sweet potato** Trailing plant native to South America and cultivated as a vegetable in Japan, Russia, and the Pacific. Its funnel-shaped flowers are pink or violet. The orange or yellow, tuberlike root is edible. Family Convolvulaceae; species *Ipomoea batatas*. *See also* YAM

**Swift, Jonathan** (1667–1745) Irish satirist and poet. He was ordained an Anglican priest in 1694 and became dean of St. Patrick's Cathedral in 1713. His early works include *The Battle of the Books* (1704) and *A Tale of a Tub* (1704). His best-known work, *Gulliver's Travels* (1726), is a satire on human follies. He wrote numerous works criticizing England's treatment of Ireland, including *A Modest Proposal* (1729). His poetry includes *Verses on the Death of Dr. Swift* (1739).

**swift** Any of several species of fast-flying, widely distributed birds. They have hooked bills, wide mouths, long narrow wings, and darkish plumage. They typically feed on insects, which they catch in flight, and build nests of plant matter held together with saliva. Length: to 9in (23cm). Family Apodidae.

**swimming** Self-propulsion of the body through water, a leisure activity or a competitive sport. Formal competition was first introduced in 1603 in Japan. The National Swimming Association was formed in England in 1837; the Fédération Internationale de Natation Amateur (FINA), the world governing body, was formed by 1908. There are four main strokes – breaststroke, crawl (freestyle), backstroke, and butterfly. Recognized race distances for men and women, established by the Fédération in 1968, range from 100m to 1,500m; there are also relay and medley races. Synchronized swimming also features at the Olympic Games and at the four-yearly world championships, as does DIVING. Swimming is one of the disciplines of the triathlon and the modern PENTATHLON.

**Swinburne, Algernon Charles** (1837–1909) British poet and critic. *Atalanta in Calydon* (1865) brought him fame, and his *Poems and Ballads* (1866) also won praise.

## SWEDEN

Sweden's flag was adopted in 1906. It had been in use since the time of King Gustavus Vasa (r.1523–60), who won many victories for Sweden and laid the foundations of the modern nation. The colors on the flag come from a coat of arms dating from 1364.

**AREA:** 173,730sq mi (449,960sq km)
**POPULATION:** 8,678,000
**CAPITAL (POPULATION):** Stockholm (692,594)
**GOVERNMENT:** Constitutional monarchy
**ETHNIC GROUPS:** Swedish 91%, Finnish 3%
**LANGUAGES:** Swedish (official), Finnish
**RELIGIONS:** Christianity (Lutheran 89%, Roman Catholic 2%)
**CURRENCY:** Swedish krona = 100 ore

The Kingdom of Sweden is the largest of the SCANDINAVIAN countries in both area and population. Most of N Sweden is mountainous; its highest point is Kebnekaise in LAPPLAND, at 6,946ft (2,117m). The S lowlands contain Sweden's largest cities, STOCKHOLM and GOTHENBURG, and two of Europe's largest lakes, Vänern and Vättern.

### CLIMATE

The climate of S Sweden is moderated by the Gulf Stream. Farther N the climate becomes more severe: at the Arctic Circle, the average number of days per year below freezing is 180.

### VEGETATION

Forest and woodland cover *c*.68% of Sweden. Arable land makes up 7% and grass only 1%.

### HISTORY AND POLITICS

The earliest inhabitants of the area were the Svear, who merged with the Goths in the 6th century AD. Christianity was introduced in the 9th century. Swedes are thought to have been among the VIKINGS who plundered areas to the S and E between the 9th and 11th centuries. Swedes (Varangians), led by RURIK, also penetrated Russia as far as the Black Sea. In 1319 Sweden and Norway were united under Magnus VII. In 1397 Sweden, Denmark, and Norway were united by the Danish Queen Margaret in the Kalmar Union. Her successors failed to control Sweden, and in 1520 Gustavus Vasa led a successful rebellion. He was crowned king, as GUSTAVUS I, of an independent Sweden in 1523. (Southern Sweden remained under Danish control until 1660.) Known as the founder of modern Sweden, Gustavus made the monarchy hereditary within the Vasa dynasty and made Lutheranism the state religion. Sweden's power was strengthened by John III's marriage to the king of Poland's sister. Their son, Sigismund III, a Roman Catholic, came to the throne in 1592 but was deposed (because of his religion) by CHARLES IX in 1599. Charles's son, GUSTAVUS II, won territory in Russia and Poland; further victories in the THIRTY YEARS WAR established Sweden as a great European power. CHARLES XII fought brilliant campaigns in Denmark, Poland, Saxony, and Russia, but his eventual defeat in Russia (1709) seriously weakened Sweden. The 18th century was marked by internal friction. Gustavus IV (r.1792–1809) brought Sweden into the NAPOLEONIC WARS. Charles XIII (r.1809–18) lost Finland to Russia in 1809, but the Congress of VIENNA granted Norway to Sweden as compensation. Industry grew during the late 19th century. In 1905 the union between Sweden and Norway was dissolved. Under Gustavus V (r.1907–50), Sweden was neutral in both World Wars. In 1946 it joined the United Nations. The current king, Carl XVI Gustaf, succeeded in 1973. In 1995 Sweden joined the European Union. The Social Democrats have been in government almost continuously since 1932. In 1994 they formed a minority government, led by Ingvar Carlsson. In 1996 Carlsson was replaced by Göran Persson. The cost of maintaining Sweden's extensive welfare services has become a major political issue.

### ECONOMY

Sweden is a developed industrial country (1995 GDP per capita, US$18,540). It has rich iron ore deposits, but other industrial materials are imported. Steel is a major product, and is used to manufacture aircraft, cars, and ships. Forestry and fishing are important. Farmland covers 10% of the land. Livestock and dairy farming are valuable activities; crops include barley and oats.

S

Some of the poems in the collection, including "The Garden of Proserpine," are among his finest. Two further series of *Poems and Ballads* appeared in 1876 and 1889.

**swing** Form of JAZZ, prevalent in the US during the 1930s and 1940s. It originated in the music of small groups who played a rhythm of four even beats to the bar, as opposed to the two beats to the bar of the New Orleans style. The groups also made more use of soloists, particularly saxophonists. Larger groups, such as those of Duke ELLINGTON and especially Count Basie, made great use of the new possibilities. Their innovations were taken up by white musicians such as Benny GOODMAN, the DORSEY brothers, and Glenn MILLER.

**Swithin, Saint** (d.862) Anglo-Saxon bishop of WINCHESTER from 852. Little is known about his life for certain. He was an adviser to the West Saxon kings Egbert and Ethelwulf. His feast day is July 15. According to superstition, the weather on St. Swithin's Day will remain for the next 40 days.

**Switzerland** Small, landlocked republic in central Europe. *See* country feature, page 652

**swordfish** (broadbill) Marine fish found worldwide in temperate and tropical seas. A popular food fish, it is silvery-black, dark purple, or blue. Its long flattened upper jaw, in the shape of a sword, is one-third of its length and is used to strike at prey. Length: to 15ft (4.50m); weight: 1,180lb (530kg). Family Xiphiidae; species *Xiphias gladius*.

**sycamore** Deciduous tree of the MAPLE family, native to central Europe and W Asia but widely naturalized. Also known as the great maple or false plane, it has deeply toothed, five-lobed leaves, greenish yellow flowers, and winged brown fruit. Height: to 110ft (33m). Family Aceraceae; species *Acer pseudoplatanus*. In the US the name Sycamore is given to *Platanus occidentalis* (family Platanaceae), an unrelated species.

**Sydenham, Thomas** (1624–89) English physician, often called the English Hippocrates. He initiated the cooling method of treating SMALLPOX, made a thorough study of epidemics, and wrote descriptions of MALARIA and GOUT.

**Sydney** State capital of New South Wales, SE Australia, on Port Jackson, an inlet on the Pacific Ocean. Sydney is the oldest and largest city, the most important financial, industrial, and cultural center, and the principal port in Australia. The city was founded in 1788 as the first British penal colony in Australia. Industries: shipbuilding, textiles, motor vehicles, oil refining, building materials, chemicals, brewing, tourism, clothing, paper, electronics. The city will host the summer Olympic Games in the year 2000. Pop. (1994) 3,738,500.

**syllogism** Logical argument consisting of three categorical propositions: two premises and a conclusion. It was devised by ARISTOTLE to establish the conditions under which the conclusion of a deductive inference is valid or not valid. A valid conclusion can only come from premises that are logically related to each other. Examples of syllogisms are as follows: All men are mortal; John is a man; therefore John is mortal (valid); All trees have leaves; a daffodil has leaves; therefore a daffodil is a tree (invalid).

**symbiosis** Relationship between two or more different organisms that is generally mutually advantageous to them. It is more accurately referred to as MUTUALISM. *See also* PARASITE

**symbolism** European art and literary movement. Symbolism had its origins in France in the 1880s when it arose as a reaction against the pragmatic REALISM of COURBET and IMPRESSIONISM. Its exponents wanted to express ideas or abstractions rather than simply imitate the visible world. The most powerful tendency in the movement stemmed from GAUGUIN and Émile Bernard (*c.*1888). Another less dynamic trend introduced formal innovations into traditional painting. Its chief exponents were Gustave MOREAU, Odilon REDON, and Puvis de Chavannes. Outside France, BURNE-JONES and MUNCH are considered to be symbolists. In literature, the movement included a group of poets active in the 19th century who were followers of VERLAINE and BAUDELAIRE, such as the SYMBOLISTS in France and writers in English such as Edgar Allen POE and Algernon SWINBURNE.

**symmetry** In biology, anatomical description of body form or geometrical pattern of a plant or animal. It is used in the classification of living things (TAXONOMY), and to clarify relationships. In mathematics a symmetrical figure is one that has an exact correspondence of shape about a point, line, or plane.

**symphonic poem** (tone poem) Orchestral piece of the late-Romantic period that describes in music a poem, story, or other extra-musical program. The term was first used by LISZT. *Till Eulenspiegel* and *Also sprach Zarathustra* by Richard STRAUSS are the best-known examples of the genre. *See also* PROGRAM MUSIC

**symphony** Large-scale musical work for orchestra. It has evolved steadily since the 18th century, when it received its first classical definition in the works of HAYDN and MOZART. A symphony usually has four movements and, in the classical tradition, has its first movement in SONATA form. The first symphonies were scored almost exclusively for stringed instruments of the violin family, but in the early 19th century the use of brass and woodwind sections had become general. Later composers of symphonies include BEETHOVEN, SCHUBERT, BRAHMS, BRUCKNER, MAHLER, SIBELIUS, and SHOSTAKOVICH.

**synagogue** Place of assembly for Jewish worship, education, and cultural development. Synagogues serve as communal centers, under the leadership of a RABBI, and house the ARK OF THE COVENANT. The first synagogue buildings date from the 3rd century BC, but may go back to the destruction of Solomon's TEMPLE in Jerusalem in 586 BC.

**synapse** Connection between the nerve ending of one NEURON and the next or between a nerve cell and a muscle. It is the site at which nerve impulses are transmitted using NEUROTRANSMITTERS.

**syncline** Downward FOLD in rocks. When rock layers fold down into a troughlike form, it is called a syncline. (An upward arch-shaped fold is called an anticline.)

**syncope** *See* FAINTING

**syndicalism** Early 20th-century form of socialism originating in France but also influential in Spain and Italy. It proposed public ownership of the means of production by small worker groups and called for the elimination of central government.

**Synge, John Millington** (1871–1909) Irish dramatist and poet who was important in the Irish Literary Renaissance. He was one of the organizers of the ABBEY THEATRE in 1904 and his works include *Riders to the Sea* (1904), *The Well of the Saints* (1905), and *The Playboy of the Western World* (1907). *See also* IRISH LITERATURE

**synodic period** Interval between two successive conjunc-

▲ **Swift** Irish author, poet, and national hero Jonathan Swift produced a wealth of material ranging from poetry to political pamphlets. His satirical masterpiece, *Gulliver's Travels* (1726), describes the travels of Lemuel Gulliver in four different imaginary lands and skillfully lampoons politicians and religious dissenters as well as philosophers, scientists, and eventually humans in general. Swift was paralyzed in his later years, and suffered from a brain disorder which, by 1742, had caused him to be pronounced insane.

**SYMBIOSIS**

*Iridomyrmex* ants and the *Myrmecodia* (ant plant) benefit mutually from a symbiotic relationship. The ants feed on the sugary nectar of the plant. This is produced in nectaries (1) which develop at the base of the flower (2) after the petals and sepals have fallen off. The plant benefits from the vital minerals in the ants' feces and waste materials (3), absorbed through the warty inner surface of the chambers (4). The ant plant is epiphytic, growing suspended from trees in upland rain forests, where the soils are often lacking in nutrients. The mineral nutrients provided by the ants supplement the plant's poor diet. As the plant grows, its stem enlarges and develops cavities that are invaded by the ants (5). These chambers do not interconnect but have separate passages to the outside (6). A complete ant colony soon becomes established in the plant.

S

tions or oppositions with the sun of a planet or the Moon as seen from the Earth. For the Moon, the synodic period is the time taken for a complete cycle of phases, equalling 29.53 days.

**Synoptic Gospels** Three of the GOSPELS of the New Testament, those of St. MATTHEW, St. MARK, and St. LUKE, which present a common account of the life of JESUS CHRIST. St. Mark's Gospel is generally held to have been the model for St. Matthew's and St. Luke's, although most scholars believe that the latter two have gathered some material from a common source known as "Q," which no longer exists.

**synovial fluid** Viscous, colorless fluid that lubricates the movable joints between bones. It is secreted by the synovial membrane. Synovial fluid is also found in the **bursae**, membranous sacs that help to reduce friction in major joints such as the shoulder, hip, or knee.

**syntax** Branch of grammar that encompasses the body of rules governing the ways in which words are put together to form phrases, clauses, and sentences in a language. The word syntax also describes the structure of a sentence or of an utterance produced by a writer or speaker.

**synthesizer** In music, an electronic instrument capable of producing a wide variety of different sounds, pitches, and timbres. The modern instrument was invented by Robert Moog in 1964. Computer technology is now used to control the instrument's different functions, enabling synthesizers to replicate non-electronic sounds.

**syphilis** Sexually transmitted disease caused by the bacterium *Treponema pallidum*. Untreated, it runs in three stages. The first symptom is often a hard, painless sore on the genitals, appearing usually within a month of infection. Months later, the second stage features a skin rash and fever. The third stage, often many years later, brings the formation of growths and serious involvement of the heart, brain, and spinal cord, leading eventually to blindness, insanity, and death. The disease is treated successfully with ANTIBIOTICS.

**Syracuse** (Siracusa) Italian seaport city in Sicily, on the Ionian Sea, capital of Syracuse province. Founded by Corinthian Greek colonists in 734 BC, it prospered and established its own colonies, triumphing over the Carthaginians in 480 BC. It grew to become the most important Hellenic city outside Greece. Industries: tourism, petrochemicals, food processing. Pop. (1992) 127,000.

**Syracuse** City in central New York, at S end of Onondaga

## SWITZERLAND

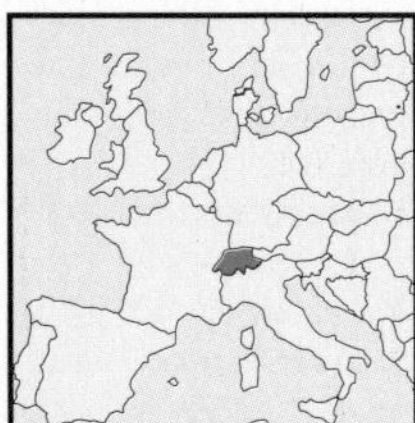

Switzerland has used this square flag since 1848, though the white cross on the red shield has been Switzerland's emblem since the 14th century. The flag of the International Red Cross, which is based in Geneva, was derived from this flag.

**AREA:** 15,942sq mi (41,290sq km)
**POPULATION:** 6,905,000
**CAPITAL (POPULATION):** Bern (135,600)
**GOVERNMENT:** Federal republic
**ETHNIC GROUPS:** German 64%, French 19%, Italian 8%, Yugoslav 3%, Spanish 2%, Romansch 1%
**LANGUAGES:** French, German, Italian, and Romansch (all official)
**RELIGIONS:** Christianity (Roman Catholic 46%, Protestant 40%)
**CURRENCY:** Swiss franc = 100 centimes

The Swiss Confederation is a mountainous, landlocked country in central Europe. The Jura Mountains lie on the W border with France. The Swiss Alps make up about 60% of the country. Switzerland's highest peak is Monte Rosa, at 15,217ft (4,634m). The plateau contains the cities of ZÜRICH, BASEL, LAUSANNE, and BERN, and Lakes GENEVA and Constance.

### Climate

The climate varies with altitude. The plateau has warm summers and cold, snowy winters.

### Vegetation

Grassland covers *c*.30% of the land and arable land *c*.10%. Forests cover *c*.32% and help to reduce the destructiveness of avalanches.

### History and Politics

Originally occupied by Celtic Helvetii people, the region was taken by Romans in 58 BC. Ruled by FRANKS in the 6th century AD, it was later divided between Swabia and Burgundy. United within the HOLY ROMAN EMPIRE, it came under HAPSBURG rule in the 13th century. In 1291 the CANTONS, Schwyz, Uri, and Unterwalden, united against the Hapsburgs. Traditionally led by William TELL, the Swiss League expanded and defeated the Hapsburgs (1386, 1388). The defeat of Emperor MAXIMILIAN in 1499 brought partial independence. Defeated by the French in 1515, the Swiss adopted neutrality. The REFORMATION caused religious divisions in Switzerland, but the confederation survived to achieve formal independence in 1648. The French Revolutionary Wars led to the overthrow of the oligarchy and the establishment of the Helvetic Republic (1798–1803). In 1815 the federation was fully reestablished. The Congress of VIENNA expanded it to 22 cantons and guaranteed its neutrality. A brief civil war led to the constitution of 1848, turning Switzerland into one federal state. Jura, the 23rd canton, was created in 1979. A referendum (1986) rejected Swiss membership of the UN to avoid compromising its neutrality. EC membership was also rejected (1992). In 1995 the ruling coalition, led by the Christian Democrats, was re-elected. In 1999 Ruth Dreifuss became Switzerland's first woman president.

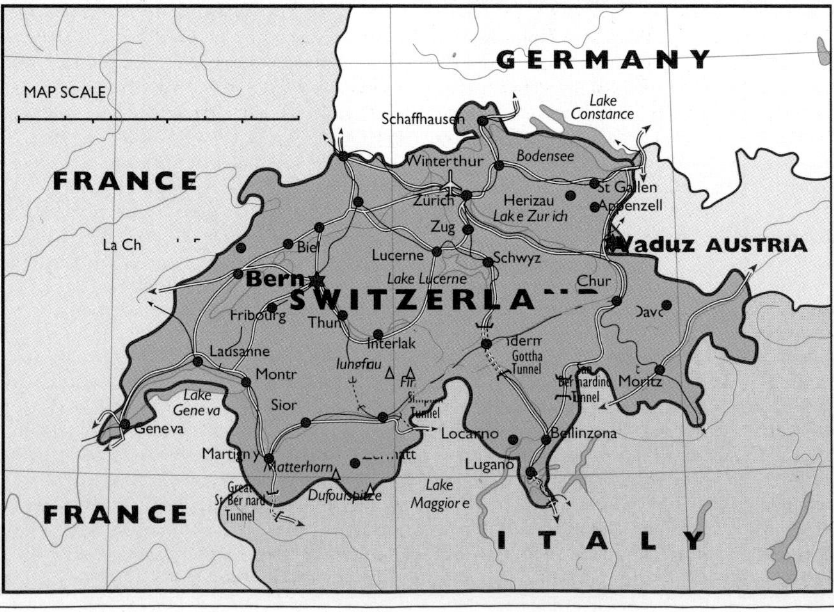

### Economy

Switzerland is wealthy and industrialized (1995 GDP per capita, US$25,860). Manufactures include chemicals, electrical equipment, machinery, precision instruments, watches, and textiles. Livestock, notably dairy farming, is the chief agricultural activity. Tourism is important, and Swiss banks attract worldwide investment.

S

Lake. Salt springs were discovered here 1654 by Father Simon LeMoyne, a French missionary. Settled in 1788, and incorporated as a city in 1847, it is the site of Syracuse University (1870), Maria Regina College (1934), Le Moyne College (1946), Onondaga Community College (1962), Everson Museum of Art (designed by I. M. Pei). Industries: roller bearings, electrical equipment, candles, soda ash, caskets, air-conditioning equipment. Pop. (1990) 164,860.

**Syria** Arab Republic in the Middle East. *See* country feature

**Syriac** Semitic language belonging to the eastern ARAMAIC group. In ancient times it was spoken in Edessa, now Urfa in SE Turkey. Because of the importance of Edessa as a center of Christianity in the 2nd century, Syriac was adopted by the neighboring Aramaic Christians and has been used ever since as a liturgical language by Oriental Christians of the Syrian rite. Syriac literature preserves many translations of Greek Christian texts that have not survived in the original Greek.

**Szechwan** *See* SICHUAN

**Szell, George** (1897–1970) US conductor and pianist, b. Hungary. He assisted Richard STRAUSS at the Berlin State Opera, and became its director (1924–30). In 1939 Szell moved to the US and became conductor (1942–46) of the METROPOLITAN OPERA, New York.

**Szent-Györgyi, Albert von** (1893–86) US biochemist, b. Hungary. He was awarded the 1937 Nobel Prize for physiology or medicine for his work on biological OXIDATION processes and the isolation of vitamin C. He also studied the biochemistry of MUSCLE, discovering the muscle protein actin.

**Szilard, Leo** (1898–1964) US physicist, b. Hungary. His early work established the relationship between information transfer and ENTROPY. Szilard devised a means of separating radioactive ISOTOPES, and suggested theories of aging, recall, and memory. He first proposed the nuclear bomb, which was developed during World War II. In 1942 his research work with Enrico FERMI at the University of Chicago produced the first sustained nuclear CHAIN REACTION based on uranium FISSION.

**Szymanowski, Karol** (1882–1937) Polish postromantic composer, who did much to promote the nationalist cause in his country. His early works were in the Germanic tradition, but he later composed in a nationalist style. Szymanowski's works include two violin concertos (1917, 1933) and the opera *King Roger* (1926).

## SYRIA

Syria has used this flag since 1980. It is the flag that was used by the United Arab Republic between 1958 and 1961, when Syria was linked with Egypt and North Yemen. The colors are those used by the Pan-Arab movement.

**AREA:** 71,498sq mi (185,180sq km)
**POPULATION:** 12,958,000
**CAPITAL (POPULATION):** Damascus (1,497,000)
**GOVERNMENT:** Multiparty republic
**ETHNIC GROUPS:** Arab 89%, Kurd 6%
**LANGUAGES:** Arabic (official)
**RELIGIONS:** Islam 90%, Christianity 9%
**CURRENCY:** Syrian pound = 100 piastres

The Syrian Arab Republic lies in the N MIDDLE EAST. It is divided into two regions. The smaller, densely populated W region comprises a narrow coastal plain and several mountain ranges. The Jabal an Nusayriyah range drops sharply to the Great RIFT VALLEY in the E. In the SW, the Anti-Lebanon range contains Syria's highest peak, Mount Hermon, at 9,232ft (2,184m). DAMASCUS (the capital) and ALEPPO lie in fertile valleys. Eastern Syria is mainly grassy plain and contains the valley of the EUPHRATES River. In the SE is the Syrian desert.

### CLIMATE

The coast has a Mediterranean climate, with warm, dry summers and mild, wet winters. To the E, the land becomes drier.

### VEGETATION

Only 4% of Syria is forested. Farmland covers *c.*30% of Syria, grassland makes up 44%.

### HISTORY

Syria's location on the trade routes between Europe, Africa, and Asia has made it a desired possession of many rulers. The area, including what is now Lebanon and some of modern-day Jordan, Israel, Saudi Arabia, and Iraq, was ruled by the HITTITES and by EGYPT during the 15th–13th centuries BC. Under the PHOENICIANS (13th–10th centuries BC), trading cities on the Mediterranean coast flourished. From the 10th century BC, Syria suffered invasions by ASSYRIANS and Egyptians. The ACHAEMENID empire provided stability. From the 3rd century BC, the SELEUCIDS controlled Syria, often challenged by Egypt. PALMYRA flourished as a city-state. The Romans conquered the region in AD 63. Christianity was introduced via Palestine. When the ROMAN EMPIRE divided in the 4th century, Syria came under BYZANTINE rule. Arabs invaded in AD 637, and most of the population converted to Islam. The UMAYYADS and ABBASID dynasties followed. In the 11th century, Syria was a target of the CRUSADES, but at the end of the 12th century SALADIN triumphed. MONGOL and MAMELUKE rule followed Saladin's death. In 1516 the area became part of the OTTOMAN EMPIRE. European interest in the region grew in the 19th century. During World War I, Syrian nationalists revolted and helped Britain defeat the Turks. After the war, Syria, now roughly its present size, became a French mandate territory. It achieved independence in 1941.

Syria has supported the Arab cause in the Middle East and has been involved in the ARAB-ISRAELI WARS. In 1967 it lost the GOLAN HEIGHTS to Israel, and in 1973 tried unsuccessfully to reclaim them. A UN-patrolled buffer zone was established in the area. It continues to be a source of considerable tension. Since independence, Syria has suffered from political instability, with many coups. In 1958 Syria joined the United Arab Republic with Egypt and North Yemen. Egypt's increasing power led to Syrian withdrawal from the UAR and the formation of a Syrian Arab Republic in 1961. The BA'ATH PARTY has been the ruling party since 1963. In 1970 Hafez al-ASSAD took power through a coup, and was reelected in 1971. A new constitution was adopted in 1973, declaring Syria to be a democratic, popular socialist state. Assad's stable but repressive regime has attracted international criticism. In the 1991 GULF WAR, Syria supported the coalition against Iraq. In 1994 Syria and Israel held talks over the Golan Heights. These talks, part of an attempt to establish a peace settlement for the entire region, received a setback when a right-wing coalition won the 1996 Israeli elections.

### ECONOMY

Syria is a lower-middle-income developing country (1995 GDP per capita, US$5,320). Its main resources are oil, hydroelectricity, and its fertile agricultural land. In 1990 crude oil accounted for 45% of exports, but Syria also exports farm products, textiles, and phosphates. Agriculture employs 23% of the workforce. The chief crops are cotton and wheat. Syria is rapidly diversifying its industrial base

S

# T

***T/t, 20th letter of the alphabet, is derived from the Semitic letter* taw *(meaning* mark*) and the Greek letter* tau*. The Roman letter had the same form as the modern* T.**

**Tabernacle** Portable shrine used by the Hebrews for worship during their wanderings in Sinai. It was a rectangular tent covered with a curtain of goat's hair and a layer of animal skins and roofed with a ceiling of linen tapestry decorated with cherubs. Inside the Tabernacle, the space was divided into two rooms: the **outer** room was the Holy Place, and the **inner** was the Holy of Holies, where God was believed to be present. The Holy of Holies contained the ARK OF THE COVENANT, above which was a slab of gold believed to be the throne of God. After the Hebrews settled CANAAN, there was no further need for the Tabernacle. Eventually, its relics were transferred to the TEMPLE built by Solomon in Jerusalem. In the Christian church, a tabernacle is a receptacle in which the Blessed Sacrament is reserved for the EUCHARIST, or a recess used for spiritual contemplation.

**table tennis** (Ping Pong™) Table sport played by two or four people, who use a rubber-covered, wooden paddle to hit a small, celluloid ball back and forth across a net 6in (15cm) high. The table is 9ft (2.7m) long and 5ft (1.5m) wide. After the serve, the ball must bounce only on the far side of the net. If the ball misses the table or fails to clear the net, the opponent scores a point. The winner is the first player to score 21 points, while leading by at least two points.

**taboo** (tabu) Prohibition of a form of behavior, object, or word. A thing may be regarded as taboo if it is unclean or if it is sacred. Breaking a taboo is believed to bring supernatural retribution and often brings social ostracism or other punishment. The term originates in Tonga.

**Tabriz** (formerly Tauris) Capital of East Azerbaijan province, NW Iran, in the foothills of Mount Sahand, and Iran's fourth-largest city. From 1295 the chief administrative center for the Persian empire, it was occupied by the Ottoman Turks and later held by the Russians. Tabriz's proximity to Turkey and the Commonwealth of Independent States makes it an important trading center. Manufactured goods: carpets, shoes, soap, textiles. Pop. (1986) 971,482.

**tachycardia** Increase in heart rate beyond the normal. It may occur after exertion or because of excitement or illness, particularly during fever; or it may result from a heart condition.

**Tacitus, Cornelius** (AD 55–120) Roman historian. His crisp style and reliability make him one of the greatest of Roman historians. His works include a eulogy for his father-in-law, Agricola, governor of Britain. His major works, the *Annals* and *Histories*, exist only in fragmentary form.

**Tacoma** Seaport city in W Washington, on Commencement Bay and Puget Sound, 25mi (42km) S of Seattle. Tacoma is beautifully situated between the Pacific Ocean and the Olympic Mountains (NW). Settled in 1852 and incorporated in 1884, the city's growth was spurred by the coming of the North Pacific Railway (1887). Industries: food and forest products, chemicals, metals, explosives, paints, shipbuilding. Pop. (1990) 176,664.

## TAIWAN

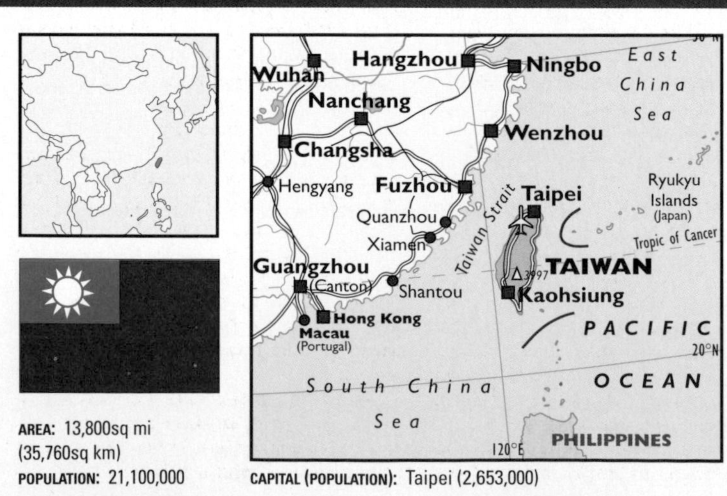


**AREA:** 13,800sq mi (35,760sq km)
**POPULATION:** 21,100,000

**CAPITAL (POPULATION):** Taipei (2,653,000)

**tadpole** Aquatic larva of a TOAD or FROG; it has a finned tail and gills, and lacks lungs and legs. Tadpoles of most species are herbivores, feeding on algae and other aquatic plants. During METAMORPHOSIS legs are grown, the tail is reabsorbed, and internal lungs take the place of gills.

**Taegu** City in S central South Korea; capital of North Kyŏngsang province and the country's third-largest city. Successfully defended by UN troops during the KOREAN WAR, it is the trading center for a large apple-growing area. The main industries are textiles, including silk and synthetic fabrics. Pop. (1990) 2,228,834.

**tae kwon do** Korean martial art. A form of unarmed combat developed over 2,000 years in Korea, it is characterized by high, standing, and jump kicks as well as punches. It is practiced both for sport and for spiritual development.

**Taft, Robert Alphonso** (1889–1953) US politician, son of President William Howard TAFT. He served in the Ohio state legislature before becoming US senator (1938–53). A conservative Republican, he sponsored the Taft-Hartley Act (1947), which restricted labor unions.

**Taft, William Howard** (1857–1930) 27th US President (1909–13) and 10th chief justice of the Supreme Court (1921–30). After a distinguished legal career, he gained great credit as governor of the Philippines (1901–04) and entered the cabinet of Theodore ROOSEVELT. Taft won the Republican nomination for president and was elected in 1908. His lack of political experience, and his tendency to side with the conservatives in the Republican Party against the progressives, caused increasing dissension. In 1912 Roosevelt, having failed to regain the presidential nomination, set up his own PROGRESSIVE PARTY. With the split in the Republican vote, the Democrat, Woodrow WILSON, won the election. Taft taught at Yale Law School until 1921, when he was appointed chief justice of the Supreme Court. While chief justice, he greatly streamlined the operations of the federal judiciary.

**Tagore, Rabindranath** (1861–1941) Indian poet and philosopher. Immensely gifted in many artistic fields, he wrote novels, essays, plays, and poetic works such as *Gitanjali*, for which he was awarded the Nobel Prize for literature in 1913. Greatly influential in the West as well as in India, he combined the traditions of both cultures.

**Tagus** (Tajo, Tejo) Longest river on the Iberian peninsula, flowing *c.*620mi (1,000km). It rises in the Sierra de Albarracin in Teruel, E central Spain, flowing generally SW for 488mi (785km), passing through Toledo, to the Spain-Portugal border. It then winds S to drain into the Atlantic at Lisbon. The Tagus estuary is one of the world's finest natural harbors.

**Tahiti** Island in the S Pacific Ocean, in the Windward group of the SOCIETY ISLANDS, the largest in FRENCH POLYNESIA and accounting for over half its population. Charted in 1767 by the British navigator Samuel Wallis and explored by Captain COOK, it was colonized by France in 1880. Tahiti is mountainous, rising to 7,339ft (2,237m), but also fertile, producing tropical fruits, copra, sugar cane, and vanilla. Industries: tourism, pearl fishing, phosphates. Paul GAUGUIN lived and painted here (1891–93, 1895–1901). Area: 408sq mi (1,058sq km). Pop. (1988) 115,820.

**Tai Chi** Neo-Confucian concept of the Supreme Ultimate, the intrinsic energy of the universe (*Chi*). A philosophic system was developed in the work of Chou Tun-i (1017–73) and Chu Hsi (1130–1200). *Tai Chi* also refers to the most popular form of exercise in China – a martial arts-based series of slow, flowing movements designed to enhance the effective flow of *Chi* around the body.

**Taipei** Capital and largest city of Taiwan, at the N end of the island. A major trade center for tea in the 19th century, the city was enlarged under Japanese rule (1895–1945) and became the seat of the Chinese Nationalist government in 1949. Industries: textiles, chemicals, fertilizers, metals, machinery. The city expanded from 335,000 people in 1945 to 2,653,000 in 1993.

**Taiping Rebellion** (1851–64) Revolt in China against the Manchurian QING dynasty. The fighting laid waste to 17 provinces and resulted in more than 20 million casualties. The Manchus never recovered their full ability to govern China.

**Taiwan** (officially the Republic of China) Pacific island, separated from the SE coast of the Chinese mainland by the 100mi (160km) Taiwan Strait. The republic comprises the main island of Taiwan, several islets, and the Pescadores group. The terrain is mostly mountainous and forested, and the highest peak is Yu Shan at 13,113ft (3,997m). The climate is semitropical and subject to typhoons. In 1590 the Portuguese visited the island, and named it Formosa ("beautiful"), but in 1641 the Dutch assumed full control of the island. They, in turn, were forced to relinquish control to the MING dynasty. In 1683 the ruling Chinese QING dynasty captured Taiwan and immigration increased. In 1895 it was ceded to Japan after the first SINO-JAPANESE WAR. Following the 1949 mainland victory of the Chinese Communist Party, the vanquished Nationalist KUOMINTANG government (led by CHIANG KAI-SHEK) and 500,000 troops fled to Taiwan. The new Chinese regime claimed sovereignty over the island, and in 1950 a Chinese invasion was prevented by the US Navy. The Nationalists, with continued US military and financial support, remained resolute. By 1965 the economic success of Taiwan had removed the need for US aid. In 1975 Chiang Kai-shek died and a gradual process of liberalization began. In 1979 the US switched diplomatic recognition from TAIPEI to Beijing. In 1987 martial law was lifted. In 1988 Lee Teng-hui became president. He accelerated the pace of liberalization. In 1996 China dispatched missiles close to the Taiwanese coast, reminding the world community of its territorial claims. In March 1996 Lee won the first democratic presidential elections. Agriculture, fishing, and forestry are important economic activities, and rice the principal crop. Spectacular economic growth from the mid-1950s was achieved primarily through low-cost, export-led manufacture of textiles, electrical goods, and machinery (1992 GDP per capita, US$12,000).

**Taiyuan** City in NE China; capital of Shanxi province. The region has rich coal and iron ore deposits, and Taiyuan is a major industrial city with iron and steel, chemical, engineering, and textile industries. Pop. (1990) 1,680,000.

**Tajiki** Iranian language spoken in Tajikistan and (with some TURKIC elements) in Afghanistan, S Russia, and much of central Asia. Tajiks, the native speakers of the language, constitute a minority of 30% within Tajikistan.

**Tajikistan** Republic in SE Central Asia. *See* country feature

**Taj Mahal** Muslim MAUSOLEUM near AGRA, India, built (1632–54) by the Mogul emperor SHAH JAHAN for his favorite wife, Mumtaz Mahal. The largest Islamic tomb for a woman, it stands in a Persian water garden representing Paradise.

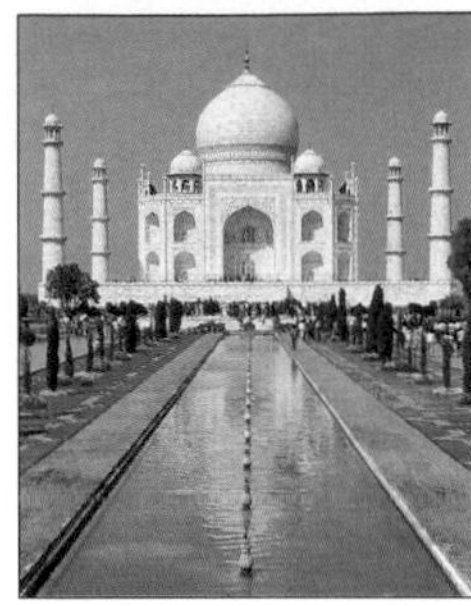

▲ **Taj Mahal** It took more than 20,000 skilled workmen drawn from all over India and Asia more than ten years to complete the mausoleum of the Taj Mahal. The building is intended to symbolize the throne of God.

## TAJIKISTAN

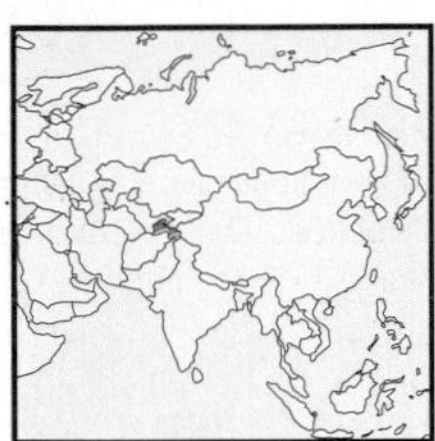

Tajikistan's flag was adopted in 1993. It replaced the flag, showing a hammer and sickle, that had been used during the Communist period. The new flag shows a gold crown under an arc of seven stars on the central white band.

**AREA:** 55,520 sq mi (143,100sq km)
**POPULATION:** 5,465,000
**CAPITAL POPULATION:** Dushanbe (592,000)
**GOVERNMENT:** Transitional democracy
**ETHNIC GROUPS:** Tajik 62%, Uzbek 24%, Russian 8%, Tatar, Kyrgyz, Ukrainian, German
**LANGUAGES:** Tajik (official)
**RELIGIONS:** Islam
**CURRENCY:** ruble = 100 kopecks

The mountainous Republic of Tajikistan, lies in SE Central Asia. In the N is the westernmost part of the TIAN SHAN range. In the E lie the snowcapped PAMIRS, including KOMMUNIZMA PIK at 24,590ft (7,495m). The capital, DUSHANBE, lies at the foot of the central Gissar-ALTAI range. In the NW lies part of the Fergana valley on the ancient route to SAMARKAND. In the SW, a plain extends from Dushanabe to the Amudarya River border with Afghanistan and Uzbekistan. Tajikistan is prone to earthquakes.

### CLIMATE

Tajikistan has a continental climate. Summers are hot and dry in the lowlands, but winters are long and cold in the mountains. Much of the country is arid, but the SE has heavy snowfalls.

### VEGETATION

Vegetation varies greatly according to altitude.

Much of Tajikistan consists of desert or rocky mountain landscapes capped by snow and ice.

### HISTORY AND POLITICS

The Tajiks are descendants of Persians who settled in the area *c.*2,500 years ago. Alexander the Great conquered the region in the 4th century BC. In the 7th century AD Tajikistan was conquered by Arabs, who introduced Islam. In the 9th century it fell to the Persian empire. The Tajik cities of BUKHARA and Samarkand were vital centers of trade and Islamic learning. In the 13th century Tajikistan was overrun by the Mongol hordes. From the 16th to the 19th centuries, Uzbeks ruled the area as the khanate of Bukhara. The fragmentation of the region aided Russian conquest from 1868. Following the RUSSIAN REVOLUTION (1917), Tajikistan rebelled against Russian rule. Though Soviet troops annexed N Tajikistan into Turkestan in 1918, the Bukhara emirate held out against the Red Army until 1921. In 1924 Tajikistan became an autonomous part of the republic of Uzbekistan. In 1929 Tajikistan achieved full republican status, but Bukhara and Samarkand remained in the republic of Uzbekistan. During the 1930s, vast irrigation schemes greatly increased agricultural land. Many Russians and Uzbeks were settled in Tajikistan. As the pace of reform accelerated in Russia, many Tajiks began to demand independence. In 1989 Tajik replaced Russian as the official language, and in 1990 the Tajik parliament declared itself the supreme sovereign body. In 1991 Tajikistan became an independent republic within the COMMONWEALTH OF INDEPENDENT STATES (CIS). In 1992 tension between the new government (consisting mainly of former communists) and an alliance of Islamic and democratic groups spiraled into full civil war. The government called for Russian military assistance, and by 1993 the Islamic-Democratic rebels had retreated into Afghanistan. Imamali Rakhmonov was elected president by the Supreme Soviet. Fighting continued along the Afghan border, and the rebels made frequent incursions into Tajikistan. In 1994 a brief cease-fire enabled elections to take place. Rakhmonov was elected president amid an opposition boycott. In 1995 the civil war resumed, and the Russian air force launched attacks on rebel bases in Afghanistan. Further elections in 1995 saw the return of the former communist People's Party of Tajikistan, amid charges of electoral corruption and another opposition boycott. In 1997 a peace agreement was signed formally ending the five-year civil war.

### ECONOMY

The poorest of the former Soviet republics, Tajikistan is a low-income developing country (1995 GDP per capita, US$1,920). It has faced enormous problems in the transition to a market economy. The cost of civil war devastated an already fragile economy. In 1994 Tajikistan ceded much of its economic sovereignty to Russia in return for financial and military assistance. Agriculture is the main activity. Cotton is the chief product. Livestock-rearing is also important. Tajikistan is rich in resources, such as hydroelectricity, oil, uranium, and gold. Aluminum is the major manufactured export. Textiles are also an important industry.

**takahe** Rare, flightless New Zealand bird, related to the RAIL and gallinule. Turkey-sized, it has a heavy, curved bill, a reddish shield on the forehead, and blue-green plumage. Family Rallidae; species *Notornis mantelli*.

**talc** Sheet silicate mineral, hydrous magnesium silicate, $Mg_3Si_4O_{10}(OH)_2$. It occurs as rare tabulate crystals in a monoclinic system and as masses. It is used as base for talcum powder and in ceramics. Hardness 1; sp.gr. 2.6.

**Taliban** Radical SUNNI political movement in Afghanistan. In 1996, from their headquarters in KANDAHAR, SW Afghanistan, Taliban militia launched themselves on Afghan society, vowing to spread SHARIA (Islamic law) throughout the country. They soon captured Kabul. Taliban's philosophy is drawn from extremist theologians in Pakistan and other Arab countries.

**Tallahassee** State capital of Florida. First discovered by Europeans in 1539, it was the site of a Spanish mission. Tallahassee became the capital of Florida Territory in 1824. Industries: chemicals, timber, paper, food processing, tourism. Pop. (1992) 130,357.

**Talleyrand-Périgord, Charles Maurice de** (1754–1838) French statesman, whose ability enabled him to serve in five very different French governments. Foreign minister under NAPOLEON I, he turned against him in 1807 and negotiated the restoration of the Bourbon monarchy in 1814. Under LOUIS PHILIPPE, he was ambassador to Britain. Perhaps his greatest service to France was his skillful diplomacy at the Congress of VIENNA.

**Tallinn** (Talin) Capital and largest city of Estonia, on the Gulf of Finland, opposite Helsinki. Founded in 1219 by the Danes, it became a member of the Hanseatic League (1285). It passed to Sweden in 1561 and was ceded to Russia in 1721. Developed in the 19th century for Russia's Baltic Fleet, it remains a major port and industrial center. Though it was badly damaged in World War II, the impressive Vyshgorod Castle remains. Industries: machinery, cables, paper, textiles, oil-field equipment. Pop. (1994) 490,000.

**Tallis, Thomas** English composer of church music. In 1575 Elizabeth I granted him and William BYRD a license to print and publish music; in that year they published the *Cantiones Sacrae*, a set of motets. His church music includes a setting of Lamentations, two masses, and a number of anthems. His contrapuntal skill shows in his 40-part motet, *Spem in alium*, probably written in 1573.

## TANZANIA

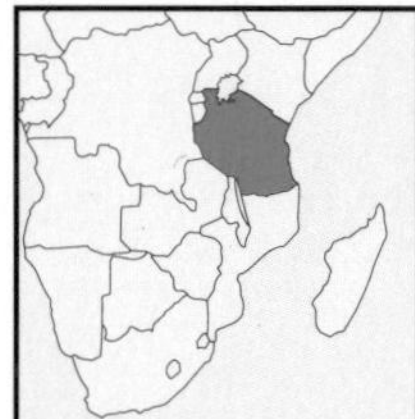

Tanzania's flag was adopted in 1964 when mainland Tanganyika joined with the island nation of Zanzibar to form the United Republic of Tanzania. The green represents agriculture and the yellow minerals. The black represents the people, while the blue symbolizes Zanzibar.

**AREA:** 364,899sq mi (945,090sq km)
**POPULATION:** 27,829,000
**CAPITAL POPULATION:** Dodoma (203,833)
**GOVERNMENT:** Multiparty republic
**ETHNIC GROUPS:** Nyamwezi and Sukuma 21%, Swahili 9%, Hehet and Bena 7%, Makonde 6%, Haya 6%
**LANGUAGES:** Swahili and English (both official)
**RELIGIONS:** Christianity (mostly Roman Catholic) 34%, Islam 33% (99% in Zanzibar), traditional beliefs and others 33%
**CURRENCY:** Tanzanian shilling = 100 cents

The United Republic of Tanzania consists of the mainland republic of Tanganyika and the island republic of ZANZIBAR. A narrow plain borders the Indian Ocean, and includes the largest city, DAR ES SALAAM. The interior is dominated by a plateau between 2,950ft to 4,900ft (900 to 1,500m). The capital, DODOMA, lies in the center of Tanzania. The plateau is broken by the Great RIFT VALLEY, the W arm of which contains Lake TANGANYIKA. The E arm runs through central Tanzania to meet the W arm near Lake MALAWI (Nyasa). The Serengeti Plain lies on the E shore of Lake VICTORIA. In the NE lies Africa's highest peak, Mount KILIMANJARO, at 19,344ft (5,896m).

### CLIMATE

The coastal region is hot and humid, with heavy rainfall in April and May. The plateau and mountains are much less humid. Mount Kilimanjaro is permanently snow-covered.

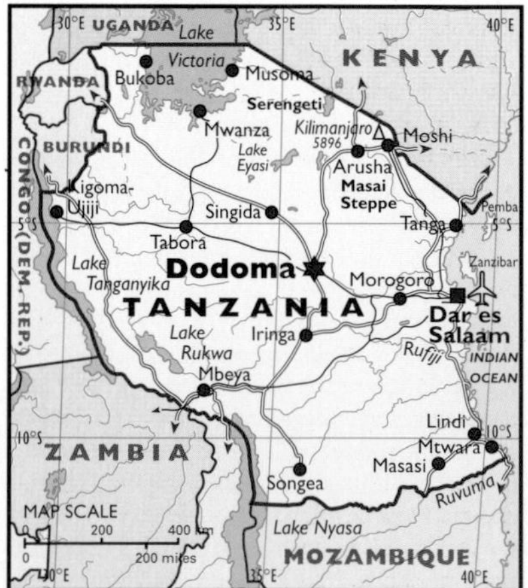


### VEGETATION

Mangrove swamps and palm groves line the coast. The plateau is vast, open savanna grass or woodland (*miombo*). Tanzania's rich wildlife is protected in national parks, which cover over 12% of the land. Only 5% of land is cultivated.

### HISTORY AND POLITICS

Dr. Louis LEAKEY discovered 1.75 million year-old fossils of *Homo habilis* in OLDUVAI GORGE. Around 2,000 years ago, Arabs, Persians, and Chinese probably traded with coastal settlements. In 1498 Vasco da Gama became the first European to land on the Tanzanian coast. For the next 200 years, the Portuguese controlled coastal trade. In 1698 the Portuguese were expelled with the help of Omani Arabs. During the 18th century, ZANZIBAR was the principal center of the E African ivory and slave trade. In 1841 the sultan moved his capital to Zanzibar. The interior of Tanganyika was opened up by new caravan routes bringing slaves and ivory to the coast for transshipment. In the European scramble for Africa, Tanganyika was subsumed into German East Africa (1887), and the sultanate of Zanzibar became a British protectorate (1890). Resistance to German colonial rule was fierce. The Germans established plantations and built railroads, and missionaries encouraged the spread of Christianity. During World War I, British and Belgian troops occupied German East Africa (1916), and in 1919 Tanganyika became a British mandate. The British ruled indirectly, via local leaders. In 1961 Tanganyika became the first East African state to gain independence. Julius NYERERE became the first post-colonial president. In 1963 Zanzibar gained independence, and in 1964 Tanganyika and Zanzibar merged to form Tanzania, though Zanzibar retained economic sovereignity. In 1967 Nyerere issued the Arusha Declaration, an outline of his self-help (*ujamaa*) form of socialism and egalitarianism. Despite promises of decentralization, Tanzania became a one-party state. In 1977 Tanganyika and Zanzibar's ruling parties merged to form the Party of the Revolution (CCM). In 1978 Uganda occupied N Tanzania. In 1979 Tanzania and Ugandan rebels staged a counterattack and overthrew the Ugandan president Idi AMIN. In 1985 Nyerere retired and was succeeded by Ali Hassan Mwinyi. In 1992 Mwinyi endorsed the principle of multiparty elections. In 1995 Benjamin Mkapa became the first president to be elected in a multiparty system. In 1997, after a prolonged drought, he declared a state of famine.

### ECONOMY

Tanzania is one of the world's poorest countries (1995 GDP per capita, US$640). Agriculture employs 85% of the workforce, mainly at subsistence level. Tanganyika's main export crops are coffee, cotton, tea, and tobacco. Zanzibar is the world's largest producer of cloves. Diamonds are the principal mineral resource. Manufacturing is mostly small-scale.

T

**Talmud** Body of Jewish religious and civil laws and learned interpretations of their meanings. Study of the Talmud is central to orthodox Jewish faith. It consists of two elements: the *Mishna* and the *Gemara*. The MISHNA is the written version, completed by *c*.AD 200, of a set of oral laws that were handed down from the time of MOSES (*c*.1200 BC). The **Gemara**, the interpretation and commentary on the Mishna, was completed by *c*.500. The Talmud consists of short passages from the Mishna followed by the relevant and extensive part of the Gemara.

**tamarind** Tropical tree native to Asia and Africa. It has divided, featherlike leaves and pale yellow flowers, streaked with red. The fruit pulp is used in beverages, food, and medicines. Height: 40–80ft (12–24m). Family Fabaceae/Leguminosae; species *Tamarindus indica*.

**tamarisk** Any of a group of shrubs usually found in semi-arid areas. They are DECIDUOUS and have slender branches covered with blue-green, scale-like leaves and clusters of small, white, or pink flowers. Height: to 30ft (9.1m). Family Tamaricaceae; genus *Tamarix*.

**tambourine** PERCUSSION musical instrument much used by wandering musicians in Europe in the Middle Ages. It comprises a narrow circular frame, made of wood, with a single parchment drumhead and metal jangles attached to the sides.

**Tamerlane** (1336–1405) (Turkish *Timur Leng*, Timur the Lame) Mongol conqueror, b. Uzbekistan. He claimed descent from GENGHIS KHAN. By 1369 Tamerlane had conquered present-day Turkistan and established SAMARKAND as his capital. He extended his conquests to the region of the GOLDEN HORDE between the Caspian and Black seas. In 1398 he invaded NW India and defeated the DELHI SULTANATE. He then turned toward the MAMELUKE empire, capturing Syria and Damascus. In 1402 he captured the Ottoman sultan Beyazid I at Angora. His death, at the head of a 200,000-strong invasion force of China, enabled the reopening of the SILK ROAD. His vast empire was divided among the Timurid dynasty.

**Tamil** Language spoken in S India, chiefly in the state of Tamil Nadu on the E coast, by up to 50 million people. In addition, there are about 3 million speakers in N SRI LANKA and about 1 million distributed throughout Malaysia, Singapore, Fiji, Mauritius, and Guyana.

**Tamil Tigers** Militant TAMIL group in SRI LANKA that seeks independence from the SINHALESE majority. Located mainly in the N and E of the island, the 3 million Tamils are Hindus, unlike the Buddhist Sinhalese. In the 1980s the Tamil Tigers embarked on a campaign of civil disobedience and terrorism. In 1986 autonomy for the Tamils was agreed by India and Sri Lanka, but no date fixed. The Indian army was sent in 1987 but withdrew in 1990, having failed to stop the violence.

**Tammany Hall** Democratic Party organization in New York City. It evolved from the fraternal and patriotic order of St. Tammany, founded in 1789, and rapidly became the focal point of resistance to the Federal Party. By 1865 Tammany Hall, under William "Boss" Tweed, had become the most important voice of the Democratic Party in the city and was synonymous with the organized corruption of urban politics. Not until the 1930s did its power begin to crumble.

**tanager** Small, brightly colored, American forest bird with a cone-shaped bill. It feeds on insects and fruit. The scarlet tanager (*Piranga olivacea*) of E North America has black on its wings and tail. Family Emberizidae.

**Taney, Roger Brooke** (1777–1864) US lawyer, chief justice of the Supreme Court (1836–64). As attorney-general (1831), he aided President JACKSON in a struggle with the Bank of the United States. He was appointed associate justice (1835) but was not confirmed by the Senate. In 1836 a Senate Democratic majority confirmed his appointment as chief justice. An advocate of states' rights, he nonetheless extended the scope and power of the Supreme Court. He was associated with *Dred Scott* v. *Sandford* (1857), which refused African-Americans the right of citizenship and denied Congress power to forbid slavery in the territories.

**T'ang** Chinese imperial dynasty (618–907). The early period was a golden age of China, when it was by far the largest, richest, and culturally most accomplished society in the world. T'ang armies carried Chinese authority to Afghanistan, Tibet, and Korea. Towns grew as trade expanded, new ideas and foreign influences were freely admitted, and the arts flourished. During the 8th century the dynasty was submerged in civil conflict.

**Tanganyika, Lake** Second-largest lake in Africa and the second-deepest freshwater lake in the world. It lies in E central Africa on the borders of Tanzania, Zaire, Zambia, and Burundi, in the RIFT VALLEY. Area: 12,700sq mi (32,893sq km), depth 4,715ft (1,437m).

**tangent** In TRIGONOMETRY, the ratio between the length of the sides opposite and adjacent to an acute angle within a right-angle triangle.

**Tangier** (Tanger) Port on the Strait of Gibraltar, N Morocco. An ancient Greek, Phoenician, and then Roman port, later occupied by Moors, it was taken by the Portuguese in 1471. It was passed to England (1662), but the English abandoned it to the Sultan of Morocco in 1684. Under international control from 1904 to 1956 (except during World War II), the city then became part of Morocco. Industries: rugs, pottery, shipping, fishing, tourism. Pop. (1990) 420,000.

**tango** Ballroom dance originating in Buenos Aires, Argentina, in the late 19th century. Developed from Argentinian *milonga*, it was a ballroom favorite in Europe and the US by 1915. It is characterized by quick, long strides and rapid reversals of direction on the balls of the feet.

**Tanizaki, Junichiro** (1886–1965) Japanese novelist and dramatist. He was influenced by classical Japanese literature and by BAUDELAIRE. His works include *Some Prefer Nettles* (1928–29) and *The Makioka Sisters* (1943–48).

**tank** Tracked, armored vehicle mounting a single primary weapon, usually an artillery piece, and one or more machine guns. Modern tanks have an enclosed, fully revolving turret and are heavily armored; main battle tanks weigh from 35 to 50 tons and usually have a crew of four. Developed in great secrecy by the British during World War I, tanks were first employed at the Battle of the Somme in 1916.

**tannin** (tannic acid) Any of a group of complex organic compounds derived from tree bark, roots, and galls, fruit, tea, and coffee. Tannin is used in tanning to cure hides and make leather, in inks and dyes, and as an astringent in medicine.

**tansy** Any of several mostly perennial plants characterized by fern-like, aromatic leaves and clusters of yellow, button-like flower heads. *Tanacetum vulgare*, native to Eurasia, is a common weed in North America. Height: to 3ft (90cm). Family Asteraceae/Compositae.

**tantalum** (symbol Ta) Rare, lustrous, blue-gray metallic element. Its chief ore is columbite-tantalite. Hard but malleable, tantalum is used as a wire and in electrical components, chemical equipment, and medical instruments. Properties: at.no. 73; at.wt. 180.948; sp.gr. 16.6; m.p. 5,425°F (2,996°C); b.p. 9,797°F (5,425°C); most common isotope $^{181}$Ta (99.988%).

**tantrism** Collective term for religious systems within BUDDHISM, JAINISM, and HINDUISM that are based on esoteric practices recorded in sacred texts called Tantras. For Hindus and Jains, the Tantras are post-Vedic (VEDAS) texts that give instruction on how to fulfill worldly (sexual) desires and attain spiritual experiences. The texts contain magic spells and MANTRAS, and give instructions on YOGA and meditative techniques for purifying and controlling the body and mind. For Buddhists, the Tantras are a set of writings attributed to BUDDHA explaining how the believer may attain enlightenment.

**Tanzania** Republic in E Africa. *See* country feature

**Tao Ch'ien** (365–427) Chinese poet, one of the greatest of the Chinese tradition. His simple style distinguished his work from the ornateness of his contemporaries'. His verse, which has a predominantly Taoist outlook, often extols the pleasures of nature and wine. *See also* TAOISM

**Taoiseach** Gaelic term for the PRIME MINISTER of the Republic of IRELAND.

**Taoism** Chinese philosophy and religion considered as being next to CONFUCIANISM in importance. Taoist philosophy is traced to a 6th-century BC classic of LAO TZU, the *Tao Te Ching*. The work's recurrent theme is the *Tao* (way or path). To follow the *Tao* is to follow the path leading to self-realization.

T

► **tapestry** By the Middle Ages one of the most common ways of creating tapestries was by using a low-warp loom (A). It had a back roller (1) to carry the unused warp threads, and a front roller (2) to carry the woven tapestry. These, and the drawing board (3), to which the design (4) is pinned, are supported by sturdy side beams (5). A slide block (6) enables the back roller to be moved to tighten the warp threads (7). The treadles (8) connected to heddle bars, are used to cross even and uneven warp threads. The weaver's tools are the bobbins, which carry the color threads (9), a boxwood comb and scrapper (10) to pack down the threads, and a mirror (11) to check the underside (the side that will be seen) of the tapestry during weaving.

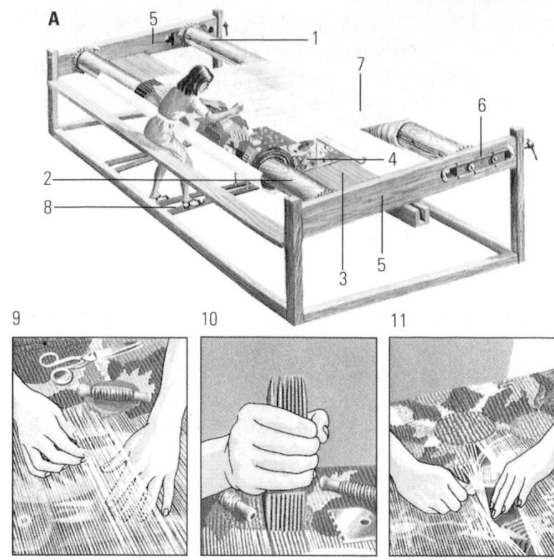

▲ **tarantula** The bite of the tarantula (*Aphonopelma* sp.) is not, in fact, dangerous to humans, though it is powerful enough to kill small birds, amphibians, or mice. Found in SW US and Central America, the body can be up to 3in (7.5cm) long and, including the legs, up to 10in (25cm) across.

► **tapir** The Brazilian tapir (*Tapirus terrestris*) is found in South America, from Venezuela to Paraguay. It inhabits wooded or grassy habitats near water and feeds on grass, small shrubs, and aquatic plants. Its dark brown color identifies it as a New World tapir, in contrast to the black-and-white Malayan Tapir.

Taoist ethics emphasize patience, simplicity, and the harmony of nature, achieved through the proper balance of the *yin*, or female principle, and *yang*, or male principle. As a religion, Taoism dates from the time of Chang Tao-ling, who organized a group of followers in AD 142. *See also* YIN AND YANG

**tap dancing** Dancing in which the toes and heels rapidly tap the floor to emphasize the rhythm of the accompanying music. This type of dance used to be performed in clogs, but now light shoes are worn, which have metal plates (known as taps) on the toes and the heels.

**tape, magnetic** Thin strip of plastic, coated on one side with a layer of iron or chromium oxide, used in audio and video tape recorders and computers. During recording, the oxide layer is magnetized by the recording head in a pattern corresponding to the input signal. During playback, the magnetized oxide particles induce an electric current almost identical to the one that produced them.

**tape recorder** Device which records and plays back sound on magnetically treated tape. Sound is transformed into electric current and fed to a TRANSDUCER, which converts it into the magnetic variations that magnetize the particles on the treated tape. *See also* TAPE, MAGNETIC; DIGITAL AUDIO TAPE (DAT)

**tapestry** Handwoven, plain weave fabric. Used for wall decoration and hangings, tapestry design is an ancient craft and a few fragments survive from 15th-century BC Egypt. The first great French woolen tapestry came from Arras in the 14th century AD. The most famous designs originated from the GOBELINS factory, Paris.

**tapeworm** Parasite of the genus *Taenia* that colonizes the intestines of vertebrates, including human beings. Caught from eating raw or under-cooked meat, it may cause serious disease.

**tapioca** *See* CASSAVA

**tapir** Any of several species of nocturnal, plant-eating, hoofed mammals native to forests of tropical South America and Malaysia. The tapir has a large head, a long, flexible snout, a heavy body, short legs, and a tiny tail. Length: to 7.5ft (2.5m). Family Tapiridae; genus *Tapirus*.

**tar** Black or dark brown, complex liquid mixture of HYDROCARBON compounds, derived from wood, coal, and other organic materials. Tar, from PETROLEUM oil, is a major source of hydrocarbons for the synthesis of pharmaceuticals, pesticides, and plastics; cruder tar compounds such as pitch are used for road surfacing and protecting lumber against rot and pests. Wood tar yields creosote and paraffin.

**Tarantino, Quentin** (1963– ) US film director and screenwriter. His controversial debut feature, *Reservoir Dogs* (1991), established his reputation for violent, discursive films. After writing the script for *True Romance* (1993), Tarantino made *Pulp Fiction* (1994), a cult hit which carried references to pop culture and film classics. Other films include *Jackie Brown* (1997).

**tarantula** Large, hairy wolf spider of S Europe, once thought to inflict a deadly bite that would cause madness. It spins no web, but chases and pounces on its prey. Length of body: to 1in (2.5cm). Family Lycosidae; species *Lycosa tarentula*. The name is also applied to the sluggish, dark, hairy spiders of SW US, Mexico, and South America. Many species burrow and feed on insects. Length of body: to 3in (7.5cm). Family Theraphosidae; genera *Aphonopelma* and *Eurypelma*.

**Tarawa** Town on an atoll of the same name in the W Pacific Ocean, capital of KIRIBATI. Located in the N central part of the group, it is the main trade center for the islands. Copra, fish, and fish products are its principal exports. Pop. (1990) 29,000.

**tariff** Tax placed on imports, calculated either as a percentage of the value of the item (ad valorem tariff) or per unit (specific duty). Tariffs may be used to discourage the import of certain types of goods or to adjust for price differentials in order to allow the home country's products to be competitive.

**Tarim Basin** Basin in XINJIANG region, NW CHINA, between the TIAN SHAN and Kunlun mountain ranges. Taklamakan Shamo, a desert, covers most of the region, and Turfan depression, China's lowest point, at 505ft (154m), is in the extreme E. The Tarim River is 1,260 mi (2,027km) long; formed by the confluence of the Kashgar and Yarkand rivers, it flows E then SE into the basin.

**taro** Large, tropical plant native to the Pacific Islands and SE Asia and cultivated in other parts of the world for its edible tuberous root. Family Araceae; species *Colocasia esculenta*. *See also* LILY

**tarot** Pack of 78 cards originating in their present form in 14th-century Italy. The cards are in two groups: the major arcana and the minor arcana. All 22 cards of the major arcana are pictorial, numbered, and captioned, and are most used today by astrologers and fortune-tellers. The minor arcana's 56 cards are in four suits, each numbered ace to ten plus four captioned court cards.

**tarpon** Tropical, marine game fish. Blue and bright silver, it has a long, forked tail. Length: to 6ft (180cm); weight: to 300lb (150kg). Species include the small Pacific *Megalops cyprinoides* and the large Atlantic *M. atlanticus*.

**tarragon** Perennial plant with liquorice-flavored leaves used fresh or dried in salads, pickles, and other food. Family Asteraceae/Compositae; species *Artemisia dracunculus*.

**tarsier** Any of several species of nocturnal PRIMATES of Indonesia. They are small, squat animals with large eyes, long tails, and monkey-like hands and feet. Family Tarsiidae; genus *Tarsius*.

**tartan** Cloth, usually woolen, with a pattern of stripes crossing at right angles. The crossbars are of different colors and widths, often on a red or green background. Tartan is associated mainly with the Highlands of Scotland. Most Scottish clans have their own, unique tartan patterns.

**Tartars** *See* TATARS

**Tasaday** Small group of isolated aboriginal people of the rain forests of S Mindanao in the Philippines. They are food-gathering cave dwellers with a STONE AGE culture.

**Tashkent** Largest city and capital of Uzbekistan, in the Tashkent oasis in the foothills of the TIAN SHAN mountains, watered by the Chirchik River. Ruled by the Arabs between the 8th and 11th centuries, the city was captured by TAMERLANE (1361) and by the Russians in 1865. The modern city is a terminus for road, rail, and air routes and is the region's economic center. Industries: textiles, chemicals, food processing, mining machinery, paper, porcelain, clothing, leather, furniture. Pop. (1990) 2,094,000.

**Tasman, Abel Janszoon** (1603–59) Dutch maritime explorer who made many discoveries in the Pacific. On his voyage of 1642–43 he discovered Tasmania. He reached New Zealand, but was attacked by Maoris in Golden Bay. He landed on Tonga and Fiji and sailed along the N coast of New Ireland. Although he circumnavigated Australia, he never sighted the mainland coast.

**Tasmania** Island state of Australia, separated from Victoria by the Bass Strait. The chief cities are HOBART, the state capital in the S, and Launceston in the N. Tasmania is mountainous and forested, with a temperate maritime climate. The first European discovery was made by Abel TASMAN in 1642 and it was named Van Diemen's Land. In 1777 Captain COOK visited it and claimed it for the British, who established a penal colony there. In 1825 Tasmania became a separate colony, and it was federated as a state of the Commonwealth of Australia in 1901. Mineral deposits include copper, tin, and zinc. The development of hydroelectric power has stimulated the growth of manufacturing, with metallurgy and textiles the main industries. Area 26,383sq mi (68,332sq km). Pop. (1991) 452,837.

**Tasmanian devil** Carnivorous marsupial with a bearlike appearance, found only in the forest and scrub of Tasmania. It feeds mainly on a wide variety of animal food, including carrion. Length: to 31in (80cm). Species *Sarcophilus harrisii*.

**Tasmanian wolf** (thylacine) Largest carnivorous marsupial. It probably became extinct on the mainland of Australia because of relentless hunting, although a few specimens are believed to have survived in forested areas of Tasmania. It has a wolflike appearance, but its coat is marked with transverse dark stripes on the back, hindquarters, and tail. Species *Thylacinus cynocephalus*.

**TASS** (acronym for **T**elegrafnoye **A**gentsvo **S**ovyetskovo **S**oyuza) News agency of the former Soviet Union. Affiliated with press agencies around the world, it was one of the major news services used by the Western press.

**Tasso, Torquato** (1544–95) Italian poet and prose writer. A member of the court at Ferrara from 1565, his masterpiece, *Jerusalem Delivered* (1575), an epic of the First Crusade, became a model for later writers.

**taste** One of the five SENSES responding to the chemical constituents of anything placed in the mouth. In human beings the taste buds of the tongue differentiate four qualities: sweetness, saltiness, bitterness, and sourness.

**Tatar Republic** Autonomous region in the Russian Federation populated mainly by the TATARS. Tatar nationalism has its origins in the Crimean Autonomous Socialist Republic, founded in 1921. The Republic was dissolved and the entire population deported by Stalin in 1945. After the breakup of the Soviet Union in 1991, many of the 300–400,000 exiled Tatars began to return to the Crimea.

**Tatars** (Tartars) Turkic-speaking people of central Asia. In medieval Europe the name Tatar was given to many different Asiatic invaders. True Tatars originated in E Siberia. They were converted to Islam in the 14th century, and became divided into two groups, one in S Siberia, who came under Russian rule, the other in the Crimea, which was part of the Ottoman empire until annexed by Russia in 1783.

**Tati, Jacques** (1908–82) French film actor and former music-hall artist, b. Jacques Tatischeff. After acting in several short comedy films in the 1930s, he directed his own *L'École des facteurs* (1947) and *Jour de Fête* (1949). His distinctive style of visual humor was developed in *Les Vacances de Monsieur Hulot* (1953), *Mon Oncle* (1958), *Playtime* (1968), and *Traffic* (1971).

**Tatlin, Vladimir Evgrafovitch** (1885–1953) Russian sculptor. In 1913, influenced by CUBISM and FUTURISM, he instigated the ABSTRACT ART style CONSTRUCTIVISM. He started to use industrial materials such as metal, tin, and glass in his work. Tatlin is celebrated for his *Reliefs*. These were innovative, three-dimensional constructions that removed pictorial illusion.

**Tatum, Art (Arthur)** (1910–56) US jazz pianist. Almost blind since birth, he established a standard for solo jazz piano technique. He made his first recording in 1932. His reputation for technical virtuosity has endured.

◀ **Tasmanian devil** The Tasmanian devil (*Sarcophilus harrisii*) was once found on the mainland of S Australia but is now confined to remote parts of the island of Tasmania. A nocturnal marsupial, it preys on a variety of animals as well as scavenging. Very strong for its size, its prey is sometimes larger than itself.

**Taurus** (the Bull) In astronomy, northern constellation on the ecliptic between Aries and Gemini. It contains the Pleiades and Hyades stellar clusters and the Crab Nebula. The brightest star is the 1st-magnitude Alpha Tauri (Aldebaran).

**Tavener, John Kenneth** (1944– ) English composer. His works are religious in character and inspiration, and simple in structure. He achieved early success with his biblical cantata, *The Whale* (1966). His conversion to the Eastern Orthodox Church (1977) was accompanied by a move towards a more austere musical style. *The Protecting Veil* (1987), for cello and orchestra, was inspired by a feast of the Orthodox Church.

**Taverner, John** (*c*.1490–1545) English composer. He composed mostly church music, notably masses and motets. His six-voice masses are complex contrapuntal structures; the smaller-scale masses are in a simpler, more restrained style.

**taxation** Compulsory money payments of various kinds made by members of a civil society to supply the expenditure of public authorities. Taxes are levied both on individuals and on corporations and are of two chief kinds, direct and indirect. **Direct** taxes are levied on income. **Indirect** taxes are levied on commodities and services. The fundamental purpose of taxation is to defray government expenditure on defense, social services, administration, and the repayment of public debts. Taxation may also be used to reduce the inequality of income and wealth in a community; changing the rate of income tax can either reduce or increase the purchasing power of consumers by altering the level of disposable income. Indirect taxes can check the flow of imports or exports in order to alter the balance of trade.

**taxonomy** Organization of plants, animals, and other organisms into categories based on similarities of genetic sequences, appearance, structure, or evolution. The categories, ranging from the most inclusive to the exclusive, are: KINGDOM, PHYLUM, class, ORDER, FAMILY, GENUS, SPECIES, and sometimes variety. There are also subphyla, subfamilies, and so on, in some categories. Ancient and extinct animals and plants are included in detailed classifications. *See also* PHYLOGENETICS; PLANT CLASSIFICATION

**Tay** River in central Scotland, rising in the Grampians and flowing SE to enter the North Sea through the Firth of Tay near Dundee. At 120mi (193km) it is the longest river in Scotland and has the largest drainage basin, 2,400sq mi (6,200sq km) in area. The Tay Bridge (1883–88) crosses the firth at Dundee.

**Taylor, Elizabeth** (1932– ) US film actress, b. England. She began her career as a child, attracting attention as the heroine of *National Velvet* (1944). An enduring box-office favorite, she appeared in such films as *A Place in the Sun* (1951), *Cat on a Hot Tin Roof* (1958), and *Who's Afraid of Virginia Woolf?* (1966). Married a total of eight times, she remains a celebrity. She is an active campaigner for AIDS charities.

**Taylor, Frederick Winslow** (1856–1915) US industrial engineer who was known as the father of scientific management. Taylor developed management methods for many industries, especially steel mills.

**Taylor, Zachary** (1784–1850) 12th US President (1849–50). A soldier with little formal education, he fought in the WAR OF 1812. In 1845 Taylor was ordered to occupy Texas, recently annexed, which set off the MEXICAN WAR. He emerged from the war as a popular hero. Taylor won the Whig nomination for president and the subsequent election (1848), but died suddenly after only 16 months in office.

**Tayside** Region in E Scotland, bounded N and W by the Grampians and E by the North Sea. The capital is DUNDEE, and other major cities include Perth. The N of the region is moun-

▲ **Taylor** Discovered by Los Angeles talent scouts when she was only a child, Elizabeth Taylor signed a contract with Metro-Goldwyn-Mayer that lasted until the 1960s. After her film debut in 1942 when she was only ten years old, she played juvenile roles throughout the 1940s and graduated to playing romantic leads within ten years. Famous for her violet eyes, she has had a tempestuous personal life, with multiple marriages (two of which were to the actor Richard Burton), treatment for drug and alcohol abuse, and surgery for a brain tumor.

T

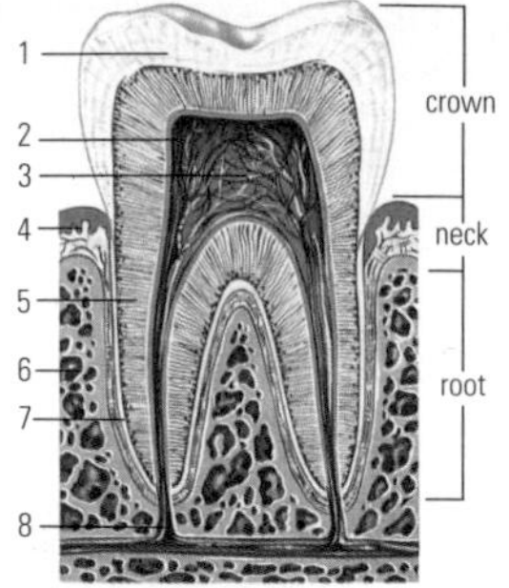


**Key:**
1 enamel
2 capillaries, nerves, lymphatics
3 pulp
4 gum
5 dentine
6 jaw
7 cementum
8 root canal

▲ **teeth** A human tooth consists of three parts – the crown, neck, and root. The crown is made up of a dense mineral, enamel, surrounding the hard dentine, which has a soft center – the pulp; the pulp is filled with blood vessels, lymphatics, and the nerve, which reach it through the root canal. The neck adheres to the gum, and the root penetrates the bone, where it is held in place by a ligament and cementum.

tainous and the S is low-lying farmland. It is drained by the Tay, Isla, Earn, South Esk, and Ericht rivers. The economy is primarily agricultural, the major products being beef and dairy products. Area: 2,896sq mi (7,502sq km). Pop. (1991) 383,848.

**Tbilisi** (Tiflis) Largest city and capital of Georgia, on the upper Kura River. Founded in the 5th century AD, it was ruled successively by the Persians, Byzantines, Arabs, Mongols, and Turks, before coming under Russian rule in 1801. Its importance lies in its location on the trade route between the Black Sea and Caspian Sea. It is now the administrative and economic focus of modern Transcaucasia. Industries: chemicals, petroleum products, locomotives, electrical equipment, beer, wine, whiskey. Pop. (1991) 1,279,000.

**Tchaikovsky, Peter Ilyich** (1840–93) Russian composer. His gift for melody and expressiveness is apparent in all his works, which include nine operas, four concertos, six symphonies, three ballets, and overtures. His ballets, among the most famous and popular of all time, are *Swan Lake* (1876), *The Sleeping Beauty* (1889), and *The Nutcracker* (1892); his operas include *Eugene Onegin* (1879) and *The Queen of Spades* (1890).

**tea** Family of trees and shrubs with leathery, undivided leaves and five-petalled blossoms. Among 500 species is *Camellia sinensis*, the commercial source of tea. Cultivated in moist, tropical regions, tea plants can reach 30ft (9m) in height, but are kept low by frequent picking of the young shoots for tea leaves. The leaves are dried immediately to produce green tea and are fermented before drying for black tea. Family Theaceae.

**teak** Tree, native to S India, Burma, and Indonesia, valued for its hard, yellowish-brown wood. Teak wood is water-resistant and takes a high polish; it is widely used for furniture and in shipbuilding. Height: 150ft (45m). Family Verbenaceae; species *Tectona grandis*.

**teal** Small, widely distributed river duck; many species have bright plumage. Teal dabble for food from the surface of the water. Family Anatidae, genus *Anas*.

**TELEPHONE**

Local telephone exchanges (1) connect local calls (2), which are analog signals (3). Long-distance calls are routed to the long-distance exchange (4) where they are converted from analog to digital. Digital snapshots are taken of the analog signal 8,000 times a second (every 125 microseconds) – enough information to recreate the analog signal accurately enough for the human ear. This whole process is called pulse-code modulation. Each eight-bit sample (5) is only 4 microseconds long which leaves 121 microseconds between each one on the telephone line. To increase capacity multiplexing combines the samples of up to 25 calls going to the same destination on the same line (6). This is done by feeding all the calls into a memory buffer (7) and then feeding them onto the long distance line in turn. At the receiving end, the process is reversed and the combined call is again fed into a memory buffer (8), separated (9), passed to the long-distance exchange (10) where it is turned back into an analog signal (11), and sent to the local exchange (12). From there it is routed to its final destination (13). The process happens so fast that the human ear hears a continuous voice.

**Teapot Dome Scandal** (1924) Corruption scandal involving President HARDING's administration over the fraudulent leasing of oil reserves. Secretary of the Interior, Albert Fall, was convicted of accepting bribes, and served one year in prison.

**tear gas** Chemical compound known as a lachrymator, a gas or aerosol that causes an excessive flow of tears. It blinds and incapacitates temporarily without causing permanent injury.

**tears** Salty fluid secreted by glands that moistens the surface of the eye. It cleanses and disinfects the surface of the eye and also brings nutrients to the CORNEA.

**teasel** Any of several species of plants that grow in Europe, the Middle East, and the US. They are prickly plants, with cup-like leaf bases that trap water. Species include fuller's teasel, whose purple flowers heads were used for carding wool. Family Dipsacaceae.

**technetium** (symbol Tc) Silver-gray, radioactive, metallic element, one of the TRANSITION ELEMENTS. Technetium is found in the fission products of uranium and is present in some stars. It is used in radioactive tracer studies. There are 16 known isotopes. Properties: at.no. 43; at.wt. 98.9062; sp.gr. 11.5; m.p. 3,942°F (2,172°C); b.p. 8,811°F (4,877°C); most stable isotope $^{99}$Tc (half-life $2.6 \times 10^6$ years).

**Technicolor** Trade name of the color film process, still used in the majority of motion pictures. A primitive Technicolor was first seen in 1917, and in 1933 Walt DISNEY used three-color Technicolor for the animated film *Flowers and Trees*.

**technocracy** Theory that engineers and scientists should have effective power in economic and social life. The term was coined in the US in 1919.

**technology** Systematic study of the methods and techniques employed in industry, research, agriculture, and commerce. More often the term is used to describe the practical application of scientific discoveries to industry.

**tectonics** Deformation within the Earth's CRUST and the geological structures produced by deformation including folds, faults, and the development of mountain chains. *See also* PLATE TECTONICS

**Tecumseh** (1768–1813) Native American leader. A SHAWNEE chief, he worked with his brother, known as the Prophet, to unite the Native Americans of the West and resist white expansion. After the Prophet's defeat, Tecumseh joined the British in the WAR OF 1812. He led 2,000 warriors in several battles and was killed fighting in Upper Canada.

**teeth** Hard, bone-like structures embedded in the jaws of vertebrates, used for chewing food, defense, or other purposes. Mammalian teeth have an outer layer of hard enamel. A middle layer consists of dentine, a bone-like substance capable of regeneration. A tooth's core contains pulp, which is softer and has a blood supply and nerves. *See also* DENTITION

**Teflon** Trade name for the plastic polytetrafluorethylene, also known as Fluon. *See* PTFE

**Tegucigalpa** Largest city and capital of HONDURAS, located in the central Cordilleras. Founded in the 16th century as a mining town, it became national capital in 1880. Industries: sugar, textiles, chemicals, cigarettes. Pop. (1991) 670,100.

**Tehran** Capital of Iran, 65mi (105km) S of the Caspian Sea, in a strategic position on the edge of the plains and in the foothills of the country's highest mountains. It replaced ISFAHAN as the capital of Persia in 1788. Reza Shah (r.1926–41) demolished the old fortifications and established a planned city. Tehran is now the industrial, commercial, administrative, and cultural center of the country. Its manufactures include cement, textiles, chemicals, and, most famously, carpets. Pop. (1991) 6,475,527.

**Tehran Conference** (1943) Meeting, in Tehran, of the British, Soviet, and US leaders (Winston CHURCHILL, Joseph STALIN, and Franklin D. ROOSEVELT) during World War II. It was the first meeting of the "Big Three."

**Teilhard de Chardin, Pierre** (1881–1955) French JESUIT philosopher and paleontologist. He worked in China (1923–1946) and shared in the discovery of Peking Man (a fossilized, Stone Age human). His efforts to reconcile scientific views of evolution with Christian faith led to his being asked by his religious superiors not to publish his philosophical works. His best-known work, *The Phenomenon of Man*, was finished in 1938 but published posthumously.

**Te Kanawa, Dame Kiri** (1948– ) New Zealand opera singer of Maori origin. She first attracted attention in the role of the Countess in Mozart's *The Marriage of Figaro* at the Royal Opera House, London (1970). She was made a dame in 1982.

**tektite** Dark, glassy objects, ranging in diameter from 0.0008in (20 micrometers) to 0.08in (2mm) (microtektites) and larger (to 4in/10cm), believed to be of either lunar origin or formed from liquefied rock during meteorite impact on Earth. They occur in limited areas, called strewn-fields, on continents and ocean floors.

**Tel Aviv** (Tel Aviv-Jaffa) City and port in Israel, on the Mediterranean Sea, *c.*30mi (50km) W of Jerusalem. The business, cultural, communications, and tourist center of Israel, it was founded in 1909 as a suburb of the port of Jaffa. During the British administration of Palestine (1923–48), the town grew rapidly as Jews fled persecution in Europe. It served as the seat of the transitional government and legislature of the new state of Israel (1948–49), until the capital was moved to JERUSALEM. In 1950 it was merged with Jaffa. Industries: construction, textiles, clothing. Pop. (1994) 355,200.

**telecommunications** Technology involved in the sending of information over a distance. The information comes in a variety of forms, such as digital signals, sounds, printed words, or images. The sending is achieved through TELEGRAPH, TELEPHONE, or RADIO, and the medium may be wires or electromagnetic (radio) waves, or a combination of the two. There are two basic types of message: digital, in which the message is converted into simple, coded pulses and then sent (as in MORSE code); and analog, in which the message – for example, a voice speaking – is converted into a series of electrical pulses that are similar in waveform to the modulations of the original message.

**telegraph** Any communications system that transmits and receives visible or audible coded signals over a distance. The first, optical, telegraphs were forms of semaphore. Credit for the electric telegraph and its code is generally given to Samuel MORSE, who in 1844 inaugurated the first public line between Washington and Baltimore. In 1866 the first permanently successful telegraph cable was laid across the Atlantic, and in 1875 Thomas EDISON invented a method of transmitting several messages simultaneously over the same wire.

**Telemann, Georg Philipp** (1681–1767) German composer. He wrote more than 40 operas, 600 overtures, and 44 settings of the Passion. His church music, of more historical importance than his operas, shows his technical mastery.

**teleology** Explanation of the universe, of natural phenomena, or of biological behavior, including human conduct, by reference to an end or purpose achieved or thought to be achieved by the thing being explained. Since the advent of modern science in the 17th century, things tend to be explained as having been caused by earlier events. This cause-and-effect approach is known as **efficient causation**. In teleology, this way of thinking is reversed in an approach called **final causation**, which explains that things have developed the way they have in order to achieve the effect we now perceive or experience. In the later 18th century, William Paley (1743–1805) applied a form of teleology to biological process, including human behavior, explaining biological organisms as complex and ingenious machines devised by an intelligent being specifically to act in the way that they do. As a theory of morality, teleological ethics derives the concept of moral duty or obligation from what is good as a goal or aim to be achieved.

**telepathy** Form of extrasensory perception involving the transmission and reception of thoughts without using the usual sensory channels. Such transference has never been conclusively proved although claims to telepathy have been extensively investigated.

**telephone** Instrument that communicates speech sounds over a distance by means of wires or micro-waves. In 1876 Alexander Graham BELL invented the prototype, which employed a diaphragm of soft iron that vibrated to sound waves. These vibrations caused disturbances in the magnetic field of a nearby bar magnet, causing an electric current of fluctuating intensity in the copper wire wrapped around the magnet. This current could be transmitted along wires to a distant identical device that reversed the process to reproduce audible sound. Later improvements separated the transmitter from the receiver, and replaced the bar magnet with batteries.

**telephoto lens** Camera lens with a long focal length. A true telephoto lens has a focal length longer than the physical length of the lens, as opposed to a long-focus lens, in which the focal length is equal to the physical length. For a 35mm

## TELESCOPE

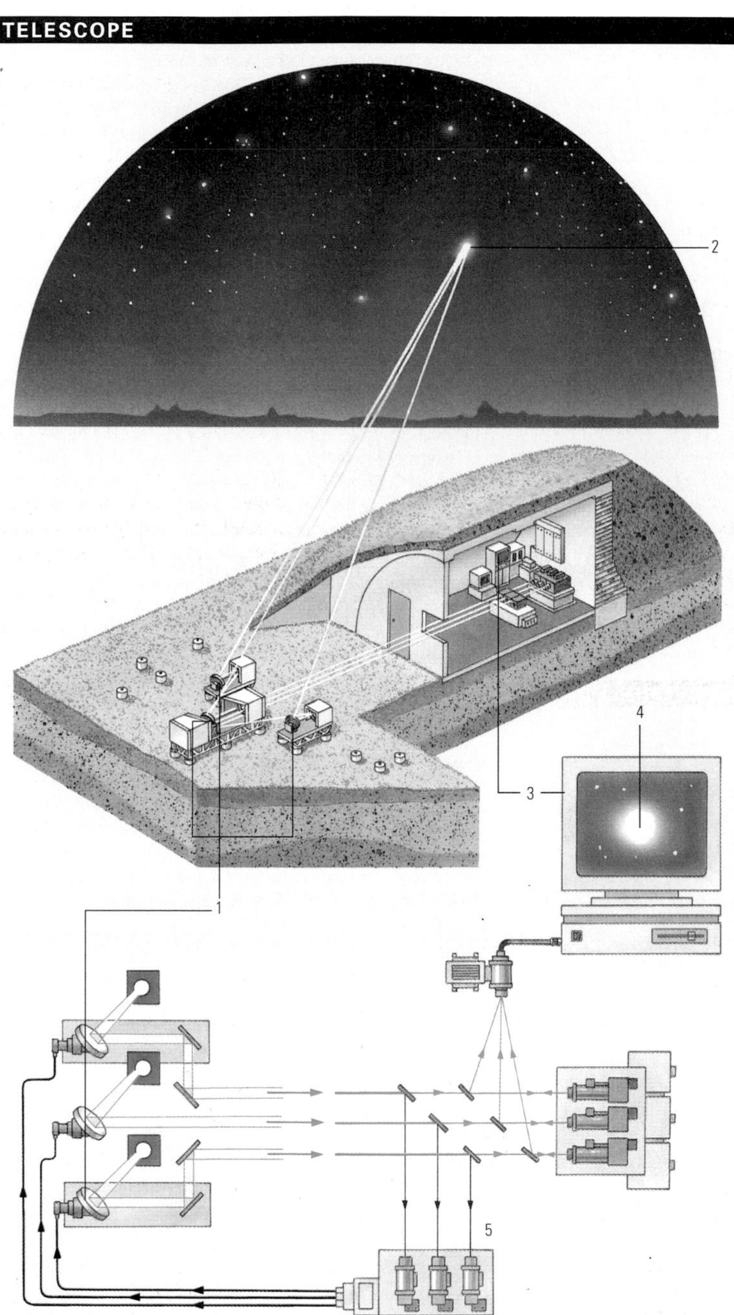


The COAST (**C**ambridge **O**ptical **A**perture **S**ynthesis **T**elescope) telescope, designed and built in Cambridge, England, is the most powerful optical telescope ever built. Instead of a single enormous reflective surface the Cambridge telescope uses the images collected by three small and relatively inexpensive optical telescopes, and combines them to form an extremely detailed image. The three telescopes (1) are focused on a single point (2), each one producing a fractionally different picture. As the Earth rotates the position of the telescopes alters in relation to the target star or planet. These pictures from different angles are blended together by computer equipment (3) to provide a single, highly detailed image (4). A small portion of light reflected by the telescopes is bled off (5) and used to confirm the targeting of the star as the Earth moves.

camera, any lens with a focal length of more than about 80mm may be regarded as a telephoto lens. For larger-format cameras the focal length may be as much as 1,000mm.

**telescope** Instrument for enlarging a distant object or studying electromagnetic radiation from a distant source. **Optical** telescopes can use lenses (refracting telescopes) or mirrors (reflecting telescopes); **catadioptric** telescopes use both in combination. The lens or mirror is the telescope's main light-gathering part (objective), and its diameter, known as the APERTURE of the telescope, determines its magnifying power. The point at which the objective concentrates the light from the source is its focus, and the distance from the focus to the objective is its FOCAL LENGTH. **Refracting** telescopes were extensively used after versions were invented by Hans Lippershey (1608) and GALILEO (1609). The problem caused by lens aberration was solved by combining lenses so their aberrations cancel each other out. **Reflecting** telescopes accomplished this. Sir Isaac NEWTON built an early astronomical reflector in 1668. Earth-bound telescopes have limitations because the incoming radiation has to pass through the Earth's atmosphere. This ceases to be a problem with telescopes in Earth orbit, such as the HUBBLE SPACE TELESCOPE. Orbiting telescopes can also detect other types of ELECTROMAGNETIC RADIATION more easily, such as infrared rays, ultraviolet rays, x-rays, and gamma rays. RADIO TELESCOPES are complex electronic systems that detect and analyze radio waves from beyond the Earth. The first radio telescope was built (1937) by the US radio engineer Grote Reber. Radio interferometers are arrays of smaller dishes that permit the investigation of even more distant radio sources. *See ilustration on page 661*

**teletext** System for transmitting text so that it can be displayed on TELEVISION receivers. Television companies transmit the text in coded form along with the sound and vision signals. Sets are equipped to receive teletext separately and decode the text signals so that they can be displayed on the screen.

**television** System that transmits and receives visual images by RADIO waves or cable. A television camera converts the images from light rays into electrical signals. The basis of most television cameras is an image orthicon tube. The electrical signals are amplified and transmitted as VERY HIGH FREQUENCY (VHF) or ULTRA HIGH FREQUENCY (UHF) radio waves. Typically, a television channel has a bandwidth of 5MHz (5 million cycles per second). The receiver (TV set) operates in reverse to the camera. On reception, the signals are amplified and converted to light again in a CATHODE-RAY TUBE. Color television has three synchronized image orthicon tubes in the camera, one for each of the three primary colors – red, blue, and green. The tube of the receiver has three electron guns and the face of the tube is covered with a mosaic of fine phosphors in groups of three, each emitting only red, blue, or green light when struck by a beam. These primary colors merge on the face of the screen to reconstitute the originally transmitted image.

**TENDON**

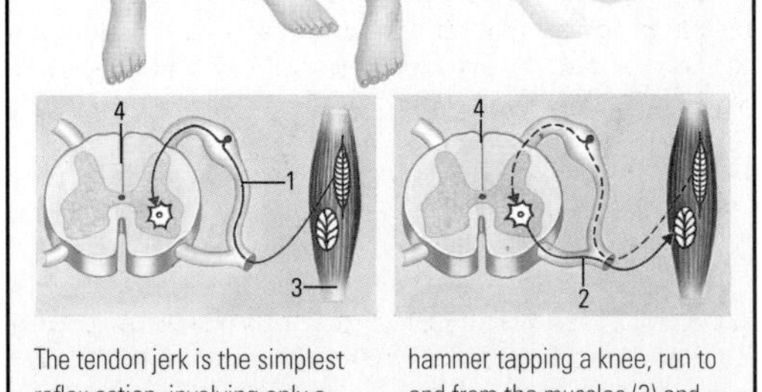

The tendon jerk is the simplest reflex action, involving only a sensory receptor neuron (1) and a motor neuron (2). Impulses, such those created by a hammer tapping a knee, run to and from the muscles (3) and traverse only one segment of the spinal cord (4). This reflex is independent of the brain.

**Telford, Thomas** (1757–1834) Scottish civil engineer who built roads, bridges, canals, docks, and harbors. His most notable achievements were the Caledonian Canal in Scotland, and the 580ft (177m) Menai Strait suspension bridge, connecting Anglesey with mainland Wales.

**Tell, William** Legendary Swiss hero, leader in the 14th-century war of liberation against Austria. For refusing to salute the cap of Albert I's steward, Gessler, he was made to shoot an arrow through an apple placed on his son's head.

**Teller, Edward** (1908– ) US physicist, b. Hungary, who has been called the father of the HYDROGEN BOMB. In 1935 he left Europe and settled in the US, where he did research on solar energy. During World War II, Teller contributed to atom bomb research with Enrico FERMI and was then involved in the MANHATTAN PROJECT at Los Alamos to produce the bomb. He was central in developing and testing (1952) the hydrogen bomb.

**tellurium** (symbol Te) Silver-white, metalloid element. It occurs naturally combined with gold in sylvanite, and its chief source is as a by-product of the electrolytic refining of copper. The brittle element is used in semiconductor devices, as a catalyst in petroleum cracking, and as an additive to increase the ductility of steel. Properties: at.no. 52; at.wt. 127.60; sp.gr. 6.24; m.p. 841.1°F (449.5°C); b.p. 1,814°F (989.8°C).

**Telstar** First active communications SATELLITE, launched by the US on July 10, 1962. It contained a microwave radio receiver, amplifier, and transmitter for relaying telephone and television signals. It operated for about 18 weeks, failed for five weeks, and then worked again for a further seven weeks before failing for good.

**tempera** Painting medium used extensively during the Middle Ages, made of powdered pigments mixed with an organic gum or glue, usually of egg yolk or egg white. Tempera dries quickly and is applied with a sable brush, one thin layer on another, so that the finished effect is semiopaque and luminous. During the 15th century the more flexible medium of oil painting began to replace tempera.

**temperance movement** Campaign in the US to wipe out the consumption of alcoholic beverages. Beginning in the late 18th century, the temperance crusade reached its peak with the ratification of the 18th Amendment (1919), which brought in the PROHIBITION Era. The amendment was later repealed (1933) after enforcement proved impossible. Prominent in the movement were Benjamin RUSH, Lyman BEECHER, Carry NATION, and Frances Willard.

**temperature** In biology, intensity of heat. In warm-blooded (HOMEOTHERMAL) animals, body temperature is maintained within narrow limits regardless of the temperature of their surroundings. This is accomplished by muscular activity, the operation of cooling mechanisms, such as vasodilation, vasoconstriction, and sweating, and metabolic activity. In humans, the normal body temperature is about 98.4°F (36.9°C), but this may vary with degree of activity. In so-called cold-blooded (POIKILOTHERMAL) animals, body temperature varies between wider limits, depending on the temperature of the surroundings.

**temperature** In physics, measure of the hotness or coldness of an object. Strictly, it describes the number of ENERGY states available to a substance or system. Two objects placed in thermal contact exchange HEAT energy initially but eventually arrive at thermal EQUILIBRIUM. At equilibrium, the most probable distribution of energy states among the atoms and molecules composing the objects has been attained. At high temperatures, the number of energy states available to the atoms and molecules of a system is large; at lower temperatures, fewer states are available. At a sufficiently low temperature, all parts of the system are at their lowest energy levels, the ABSOLUTE ZERO of temperature.

**tempering** Heat treatment to alter the hardness of an ALLOY. The effect produced depends on the composition of the alloy, the temperature to which it is heated, and the rate at which it is cooled. Usually, the metal is heated slowly to a specific temperature, then cooled rapidly.

**Temple, Shirley** (1928– ) US film actress. She became a child star in films such as *Rebecca of Sunnybrook Farm* (1938) and *The Blue Bird* (1940). Temple continued to make films as a young adult but could never recapture her early success. As Shirley Temple Black, she went into politics, serving as a US delegate to the UN (1969–70), then as US ambassador to Ghana (1974–76) and to Czechoslovakia (1989–93).

**temple** Place of worship for Jews and members of many other religions. Temples were a grand architectural focal point in the religion and culture of ancient Egypt and the Near East. In Mesopotamia, they took the form of elaborate towers called ZIGGURATS. Greek and Roman temples, with beautifully carved statues and columns, were houses fit for the gods. In Judaism, the term refers specifically to the first and second temples built in Jerusalem. Today, Jews worship in a local SYNAGOGUE or temple. Temples also exist as places of worship for Muslims, Hindus, Buddhists, and Sikhs.

**Temple, Jerusalem** Most significant shrine of the Jews, originally located on a hilltop known as Temple Mount in what is now East JERUSALEM. There have been three temples on the site. The first was built in the 10th century BC by order of SOLOMON as a repository for the ARK OF THE COVENANT. It was destroyed by Nebuchadnezzar, king of Babylon, in 587 BC. A second temple was completed in 515 BC by the Jewish exiles who had returned from Babylon in 537 BC. Between 19 and 9 BC, this second temple was replaced by a more elaborate structure; it was destroyed by the Romans in AD 70. Some of its ruins remain as a place of pilgrimage and prayer, known as the WESTERN WALL. Part of the ancient temple site is occupied by the Muslim DOME OF THE ROCK and al-Aqsa Mosque, both built in the late 7th century.

**tempo** Speed at which a piece of music should be performed, usually indicated on a score, in Western music, by Italian words, such as *allegro* (fast) and *adagio* (slow).

**Ten Commandments** (Decalogue) Code of ethical conduct held in Judeo-Christian tradition to have been revealed by God to MOSES on Mount Sinai during the Hebrew exodus from Egypt (*c.*1200 BC). They represent the moral basis of the Covenant made by YAHWEH (God) with Israel.

**tendon** Strong, flexible band of CONNECTIVE TISSUE that joins muscle to bone.

**tendril** Coiling part of stem or leaf, a slender, threadlike structure used by climbing plants for support.

**Tenerife** Largest of the Canary Islands, Spain, in the Atlantic Ocean, 40mi (64km) WNW of Grand Canary Island. It is a mountainous island with Pico de Teide, 12,198ft (3,718m), its highest peak. Products include dates, sugarcane, palms, and cotton. Tourism is the mainstay of the economy. The main town is SANTA CRUZ DE TENERIFE. Area 795sq mi (2,059sq km). Pop. (1991) 725,815.

**Tennent, Gilbert** (1703–64) American religious leader, b. Ireland. A Presbyterian minister and evangelist, he toured the colonies with English revivalist George Whitefield (1739–40) and became prominent in the GREAT AWAKENING. When the Presbyterian Church split (1741), he became leader of the evangelistic New Side. In 1758 he helped to reunite the New and Old sides.

**Tennessee** State in SE central US, between the Appalachian Mountains and the Mississippi River. The capital is NASHVILLE. Other cities include MEMPHIS, CHATTANOOGA, and Knoxville. The first European discovery was by Hernando DE SOTO in 1540. The French followed a century later, but their claim was ceded to Britain in 1763 and the first permanent settlement was established in 1769. In 1796 Tennessee became the 16th state of the Union. Tennessee's enthusiastic response to the request for volunteers during the Mexican War (1846–48) earned it the nickname of the Volunteer State. During the CIVIL WAR, the state was the site of some of the bloodiest battles, including Shiloh (1862) and Chattanooga (1863). In 1866 it became the first southern state to be readmitted to the Union. Christian fundamentalism has exerted a powerful influence, and the teaching of evolution was banned from 1925 to 1967. In the E are the GREAT SMOKY MOUNTAINS and the Cumberland Plateau. Beyond, the land slopes to the Mississippi River on the W border. West Tennessee has fertile floodplains, drained by the TENNESSEE RIVER, that produce cotton, tobacco, and soybeans. Mineral deposits include zinc and coal. Industries: chemicals, electrical equipment, foods, tourism. Area 42,244sq mi (109,411sq km). Pop. (1992) 5,025,621.

**Tennessee** River in Tennessee, N Alabama and W Kentucky. Formed by the confluence of the Holston and French Broad rivers, it joins the Ohio at Paducah, Kentucky, and forms part of the Alabama–Mississippi border. The US government's TENNESSEE VALLEY AUTHORITY (TVA, 1933) developed the river's hydroelectric potential (nine major dams) and transport facilities, along with irrigation and flood control. Length 652mi (1,050km).

**Tennessee Valley Authority (TVA)** NEW DEAL agency established as part of a long-range regional planning project (1933). An independent public corporation, it was authorized to build dams and power plants to control the Tennessee River. The success of TVA contributed greatly to the Tennessee River Valley's wealth.

**tennis** Racket and ball game played by either two (singles) or four (doubles) players. It is sometimes known as lawn tennis, despite being played on clay, concrete, shale, and wood, as well as grass. The game is played on a court 78ft (23.8m) by 27ft (8.2m) for singles. For doubles play the court is widened to 36ft (11m). It is bisected by a net 3ft (0.9m) high at the center. On each side of the net there are two service areas marked by rectangular lines. The ball is put into play by the server, who is allowed two attempts to hit it into the opposite service court. One player serves for a complete game. If the opponent returns the ball safely, play continues until one player fails to hit the ball, hits it into the net or hits it outside the confines of the court; the opponent then wins the point. A minimum of four points is required to win a game, which must be won by two clear points. A minimum of six games must be won to win a set, which is won by either two clear games or by winning the tiebreak game, played at six games all. Modern tennis evolved from REAL TENNIS in England in the 1860s.

**Tennyson, Alfred, 1st Baron** (1809–92) (Alfred Lord Tennyson) British poet. He became poet laureate in 1850. His body of work includes "The Charge of the Light Brigade" (1855). He also wrote deeply personal utterances, such as "Crossing the Bar" and the extended elegy for his friend Arthur Henry Hallam, *In Memoriam* (1850).

**tenor** Range of the human voice, falling below CONTRALTO and above BARITONE. It is the highest natural male voice apart from the COUNTERTENOR. In the 16th and early 17th centuries the tenor was the most important solo voice.

**tension** Molecular forces associated with the boundary layer of a liquid. It makes a liquid behave as if there were a "skin" on the surface. Attractive forces in this skin tend to resist disruption, so that a needle or razor blade placed carefully on the surface floats even though its density is many times that of the liquid.

**Teotihuacán** Ancient AZTEC city of Mexico, about 30mi (48km) N of Mexico City. It flourished between *c.*100 BC and *c.*AD 700. It contained huge and impressive buildings, notably the Pyramid of the Sun. At its greatest, *c.*AD 600, the city housed at least 100,000 people and was the center of a considerable empire.

**terbium** (symbol Tb) Silver-gray, metallic element of the LANTHANIDE SERIES. It is found in such minerals as monazite, gladolinite, and apatite. The soft element is used in semiconductors; sodium terbium borate is used in lasers. Properties: at.no. 65; at.wt. 158.9254; sp.gr. 8.234; m.p. 2,480°F (1,360°C); b.p. 5,506°F (3,041°C). Single isotope $^{159}$Tb.

**Teresa, Mother** (1910–97) (Agnes Gonxha Bojaxhiu) Macedonian Roman Catholic missionary. She began her missionary work as a teacher in Calcutta, India. In 1948 she left her convent in order to tend the homeless, starving, and sick in Calcutta's slums. Her Order of the Missionaries of Charity was established in 1950 and subsequently extended to other countries. She won the first Pope John XXIII Peace Prize in 1971 and the Nobel Peace Prize in 1979.

**Teresa of Avila, Saint** (1515–82) (Teresa de Cepeda y Ahumada) Spanish CARMELITE nun and mystic. In 1529 she entered the Convent of the Incarnation at Ávila. From 1558

**TENNESSEE**
**Statehood:**
June 1, 1796
**Nickname:**
The Volunteer State
**State bird:**
Mockingbird
**State flower:**
Iris
**State tree:**
Tulip poplar
**State motto:**
Agriculture and commerce

▲ **Mother Teresa** Recognized throughout the world for her charitable work in the slums of Calcutta, Mother Teresa worked not only with orphaned and handicapped children but also with lepers and other people with disfiguring diseases. There are more than 2,000 nuns in the order she founded, the Missionaries of Charity, who care for the ill and the dying throughout the world.

T

**▶ termite** Built of saliva and soil particles, termite mounds (A) dominate the African savanna. Most termites prefer to eat dead plant material that has been partly softened by fungus. This food supply is limited in dry conditions because fungi need moisture. For this reason *Macrotermes* termites create fungus chambers (1). These are combs of carton (a mixture of saliva and fecal pellets) which provide a large surface area on which the fungus grows. The fungus flourishes in the humid atmosphere of the nest as it breaks down the feces in the carton walls. Some termite species dig deep tunnels (2) to find underground water to make sure that the nest is moist enough for the fungus to thrive. The peaks of the mound (3) act as lungs. Air seeps into the main nest from an air cellar below (4). As the fungus breaks down the fecal comb heat is generated. The hot air rises, via a large central air space (5), into the chimneys (6). The walls of the nest are porous, so carbon dioxide diffuses into the chimneys. The newly oxygenated air loses heat to the air outside and cools, sinking back to the cellar. The royal cell (7) is located in the center of the nest, where the king (8) and the queen (9) can be protected. The workers, as well as feeding the royal couple, also remove the eggs to the brood chambers (10). There the workers lick the eggs to keep them clean. Most termite species have a variety of castes (B) or types. There are the temporarily winged reproductives (male and female) called alates (1), repsonsible for setting up colonies, the queen (2), the enlarged abdomen of which produces thousands of eggs, the soldier termites (3), which protect the colony, and the workers (4), which collect food, care for the queen, and serve as builders.

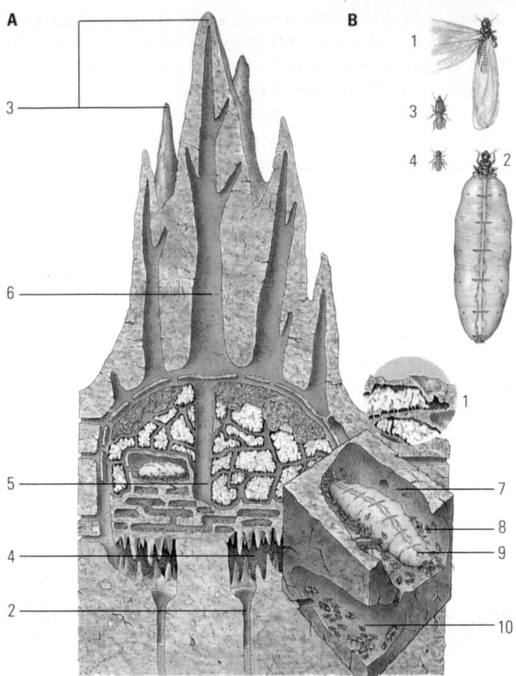


she set about reforming the Carmelite order for women, whose rules had become weakened. Under her influence, St. JOHN OF THE CROSS introduced a similarly restored Carmelite order for men. Her literary works, including an autobiography and the meditative *Interior Castle* (1577), as well as her monastic reforms, led to her canonization in 1622.

**terminal velocity** Maximum velocity attainable by a falling body or powered aircraft. It is dependent upon the shape of the body, the resistance of the air through which it is moving, and (in the case of aircraft) the thrust of the engines.

**termite** Social insect found worldwide in subterranean nests and above-ground mounds. They have a caste system, with a king and queen guarded and tended by soldiers, workers, and nymphs. Wood is a common component of their diet, which is digested with the help of symbiotic protozoa or bacteria that live in the termites' intestines. Length: 0.08–0.9in (0.2–2.25mm); queens: to 4in (10cm). Order Isoptera.

**tern** (sea swallow) Any of several species of graceful seabirds that live throughout the world. The tern is usually white and gray, and has a pointed bill, long pointed wings, a forked tail, and webbed feet; it dives for fish and crustaceans. Length: to 22in (55cm). Family Laridae; genus *Sterna*.

**terracotta** Hard, porous, usually unglazed, yellow, brown, or red earthenware (fired CLAY). Terracotta is used in building, sculpture, and pottery.

**terrapin** Any of several species of aquatic TURTLES that live in fresh or brackish water in the US and South America, especially the diamondback terrapin (*Malaclemys terrapin*). Length: to 9in (23cm). Family Emydidae.

**terrier** Any of several breeds of DOG. Originally trained to dig out game, they have been used to hunt badgers, foxes, and rats. When the quarry is located, the terrier or terriers are sent down to dig it out of its burrow. Separate breeds include the Sealyham terrier, fox terrier, and Manchester terrier. Larger breeds such as the Airedale terrier and Irish terrier are often used as guard and police dogs.

**territory** In animal behavior, the restricted life space of an organism. An area selected for mating, nesting, roosting, hunting, or feeding, it may be occupied by one or more organisms and defended against others of the same, or a different, species.

**terrorism** Use of violence, sometimes indiscrimin-ately, against persons and property for the nominal purpose of making a political statement. Intending to in-spire terror, terrorists act principally in the name of empowering political minorities, and to publicize perceived political grievances.

**Tertiary** Earlier period of the CENOZOIC era, lasting from 65 million to about 2 million years ago. It is divided into five epochs, starting with the PALEOCENE, followed by the EOCENE, OLIGOCENE, MIOCENE, and PLIOCENE. Early Tertiary times were marked by great mountain-building activity. Both marsupial and placental mammals diversified greatly. Archaic forms of carnivores and herbivores flourished, along with primitive primates, bats, rodents, and early whales.

**Tesla, Nikola** (1856–1943) US electrical engineer and inventor, b. Croatia, who pioneered the applications of high-voltage electricity. He developed arc lighting, the first generator of alternating current (AC), and the high-frequency Tesla coil.

**Test Ban Treaty** (1963) Agreement signed in Moscow by the Soviet Union, the US, and Britain to cease most tests of nuclear weapons. Nearly 100 other states eventually signed the treaty, although France and China continued to conduct tests in the atmosphere and underwater.

**testis** (plural testes) Male sex GLAND, found as a pair located in a pouch, the scrotum, external to the body. The testes are made up of seminiferous tubules in which SPERM are formed and mature, after which they drain into ducts and are stored in the epididymis prior to being discharged.

**testosterone** Steroid HORMONE secreted mainly by the mammalian TESTIS. It is responsible for the growth and development of male sex organs and male secondary sexual characteristics, such as voice change and facial hair.

**tetanus** (lockjaw) Life-threatening disease caused by the toxin secreted by the anaerobic bacterium *Clostridium tetani*. The symptoms are muscular spasms and rigidity of the jaw, which then spreads to other parts of the body, culminating in convulsions and death. The disease is treated with antitetanus toxin and ANTIBIOTICS.

**Tet Offensive** (1968) Campaign in the VIETNAM WAR. North Vietnamese and VIET CONG troops launched attacks on numerous towns and cities of South Vietnam during the Tet festival (lunar new year celebrations). Although of little strategic effect, the offensive discredited current US military reports that victory over North Vietnam was imminent.

**tetracyclines** Group of broad-spectrum ANTIBIOTICS effective against a wide range of bacterial infections.

**Teutonic Knights** German military and religious order, founded in 1190. Its members, of aristocratic class, took monastic vows of poverty and chastity. During the 13th century the knights waged war on non-Christian peoples, particularly those of Prussia, whom they defeated, annexing their land. They were defeated in 1242 by ALEXANDER NEVSKI and, in 1410, by the Poles and Lithuanians at Tannenberg.

**Teutonic mythology** Traditional beliefs of the Germanic peoples. Much of the mythology of pre-Christian Germany and Scandinavia is preserved in two Icelandic works, the Eddas. According to the Eddas, before the creation of the world there was a land of ice and shadows called Niflheim and a land of fire known as Muspellsheim. The two lands together created the first giant, Ymir. ODIN and his brothers killed Ymir and founded the race of gods. They then created the world from parts of Ymir's body, and made the first man and woman from pieces of trees. At the center of the worlds of gods and men stood a giant ash tree, Yggdrasil. Odin, the head of the AESIR (heroic gods), was the god of poetry and of battle. VALHALLA, a great hall in Asgard, was the resting place of warriors slain in battle. Next in line to Odin was THOR, the god of thunder, rain, and fertility. Others of the pantheon included the handsome Balder, and Loki, the son of a giant. The Vanir gods, regarded as less important than the Aesir, included Njörd, the sea god, his son Frey, a god of fertility, his daughter Freya, the goddess of love and magic, and Hel, the goddess of death and the underworld.

**Texas** State in central S US, bounded by the Gulf of Mexico (SE), separated from Mexico by the Rio Grande. Major cities are HOUSTON, DALLAS, SAN ANTONIO, AUSTIN (the state capital), and FORT WORTH. The Spaniards explored the region in the early 16th century, and it became part of the Spanish colony of Mexico. By the time Mexico attained independence in 1821, many Americans had begun to settle in Texas. They revolted against Mexican rule and in 1836, after defeating the Mexican army, established the Republic of Texas, recognized by the US in 1837. Eight years later Texas was admitted to the Union.

T

Eastern Texas has pine-covered hills and cypress swamps; cotton and rice are the main crops and the lumber industry is important. Cattle are raised on the plains of the Rio Grande valley, from where the land rises to the Guadalupe Mountains of W Texas and the Great Plains area of the Texas Panhandle in the N. Rich oil fields are a mainstay of the state's economy. Industries: oil refining, food processing, aircraft, electronics. Area 267,338sq mi (692,405sq km). Pop. (1992) 17,682,538.

**Texas Rangers** Mounted law officers organized in 1835 during the Texas Revolution against Mexico. They became a division of the Texas Department of Public Safety in 1935. Instrumental in the defense of early Texas, they were organized into two battalions in 1874, one to control frontier range wars, and one to stop banditry and cattle rustling along the Rio Grande. This was their period of greatest renown.

**Texas v. White** (1869) US Supreme Court decision affirming Abraham Lincoln's position that the Union was indissoluble and upholding Congress' authority to reconstruct the states. It ruled that, despite secession, Texas had remained a state and that Congress, not the executive, would recognize state governments.

**textiles** Fabrics, especially those produced by WEAVING yarn. The yarn is made by SPINNING natural or artificial FIBERS. Textiles are used to make clothing, curtains, carpets, sheets, blankets, towels, and many other products. Powered machines for spinning and weaving were introduced in the 18th century.

**Thackeray, William Makepeace** (1811–63) British novelist and satirist, b. India. *Vanity Fair* (1847–48), a satirical novel on upper-class London society at the start of the 19th century, is his best-known work. His other novels include *Pendennis* (1848–50), *Henry Esmond* (1852), and *The Virginians* (1857–59). Thackeray was a contributor to numerous publications, including *Punch*.

**Thai** National language of Thailand, spoken by most of the population. It is closely related to Lao, spoken across the border in Laos. It belongs to the Tai family, possibly a sub-family of the SINO-TIBETAN LANGUAGES group.

**Thailand** Kingdom in SE Asia. *See* country feature

**thalamus** One of two ovoid masses of gray matter located deep on each side of the forebrain. Sometimes called the sensory-motor receiving areas, they fulfill relay and integration functions in respect of sensory messages reaching the BRAIN.

**thalassemia** (Cooley's anemia) Group of hereditary disorders characterized by abnormal bone marrow and erythrocytes (red blood cells). The predominant symptom is ANEMIA, requiring frequent blood transfusions.

**TEXAS**
**Statehood:** December 29, 1845
**Nickname:** The Lone Star State
**State bird:** Mockingbird
**State flower:** Bluebonnet
**State tree:** Pecan
**State motto:** Friendship

## THAILAND

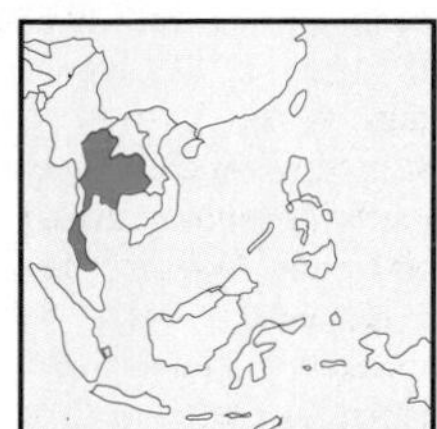

Thailand's flag was adopted in 1917. In the late 19th century, it featured a white elephant on a plain red flag. In 1916, white stripes were introduced above and below the elephant, but in 1917 the elephant was dropped and a central blue band was added.

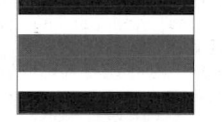

**AREA:** 198,116sq mi (513,120sq km)
**POPULATION:** 57,760,000
**CAPITAL POPULATION:** Bangkok (5,572,712)
**GOVERNMENT:** Constitutional monarchy
**ETHNIC GROUPS:** Thai 80%, Chinese 12%, Malay 4%, Khmer 3%
**LANGUAGES:** Thai (official)
**RELIGIONS:** Buddhism 94%, Islam 4%, Christianity 1%
**CURRENCY:** Thai Baht = 100 stangs

The Kingdom of Thailand is one of ten nations in Southeast Asia. Central Thailand is a fertile plain, drained mainly by the Chao Phraya. A densely populated region, it includes the capital, BANGKOK. To the NE lies the Khorat plateau, which extends to the MEKONG River border with Laos. The NW is mountainous, and includes the second-largest city, CHIANGMAI. The S forms part of the MALAY PENINSULA.

### CLIMATE

Thailand has a tropical climate. The monsoon season lasts from May to October. The central plains are much drier than other regions.

### VEGETATION

The N includes many hardwood trees, which are being rapidly exploited. The S has rubber plantations. Grass, shrub, and swamp make up 20% of land. Arable land, mainly rice fields, covers 33%.

### HISTORY AND POLITICS

The Mongol capture (1253) of a Thai kingdom in SW China, forced the Thai people S. A new kingdom was established around Sukhothai. In the 14th century, the kingdom expanded and the capital moved to Ayutthara. The first European contact was in the early 16th century. In the late 17th century, the kingdom was briefly held by the Burmese. European desire to acquire the brilliance of the Thai court, resulted in their expulssion for over a century, and Thailand remained the only Southeast Asian nation to resist colonization. In 1782 a Thai General became King Rama I, establishing the Chakkri dynasty which has ruled ever since. The country became known as Siam, and Bangkok acted as its capital. From the mid-19th century, Siam began a gradual process of westernization. In World War I, Siam supported the Allies. In 1932 Thailand became a constitutional monarchy. In 1938 Pibul Songgram became premier and changed the country's name to Thailand. In 1941 Pibul, despite opposition, invited Japanese forces into Thailand. In 1950 Bhumibol Adulyadej acceded to the throne as Rama IX. In 1957 Pibul was overthrown in a military coup. In 1992 public pressure forced elections, which saw a return to civilian rule. In 1997 the prime minister resigned amid criticism of his handling of the economic crisis. A new coalition government, led by Chuan Leekpai, was formed.

### ECONOMY

Thailand is a rapidly industrializing, developing nation (1995 GDP per capita, US$7,540). It was a founder of the ASSOCIATION OF SOUTHEAST ASIAN NATIONS (ASEAN). Manufacturing and services have grown rapidly. Agriculture employs 66% of the workforce. Thailand is the world's largest producer of pineapples and natural rubber. It is also the fourth-largest producer of rice, buffalo, and cassava. Thai silk is among the world's finest. Tourism is a vital source of revenue. In 1997 the economic crisis in Southeast Asia led to the collapse of its financial sector and a 20% devaluation of the baht. The International Monetary Fund (IMF) agreed to a US$17 billion rescue package.

T

▲ **Thatcher** Trained as a research chemist and as a lawyer specializing in tax law, Margaret Thatcher was first elected a Conservative member of Parliament in 1959. She quickly rose to prominence, joining the shadow cabinet in 1967, becoming leader of the party in 1975 and prime minister in 1979. Her forceful personality and determination to reform the British economy and society created considerable worldwide impact. The Russians called her the "Iron Lady." She was also known for her close relationship with US president Ronald Reagan. After her resignation as prime minister in 1990, she traveled and lectured internationally.

**Thales** (636–546 BC) First Greek scientist and philosopher of whom we have any knowledge. He made discoveries in geometry, such as that the angles at the base of an isosceles triangle are equal. He predicted the eclipse of the Sun that took place in 585 BC.

**thalidomide** Drug originally developed as a mild hypnotic, but whose use by women in early pregnancy until the early 1960s caused serious birth deformities. It is still manufactured for occasional use in the treatment of LEPROSY.

**thallium** (symbol Tl) Shiny, metallic element of Group III of the periodic table. Soft and malleable, it is obtained as a by-product of processing zinc or lead sulfide ores. It is used in electronic components, infrared detectors, and optical and infrared glasses. Thallium is a toxic compound, and thallium sulfide is used as a rodent and ant poison. Properties: at.no. 81; at.wt. 204.37; sp.gr. 11.85; m.p. 578.3°F (303.5°C); b.p. 2,655°F (1,457°C); most common isotope $^{205}$Tl (70.5%).

**Thames** Longest river in England. It rises in in the Cotswold Hills, E Gloucestershire, then flows E across S England and through London to enter the North Sea at The Nore. The river is tidal up to Teddington. Above London it is used mainly for recreational purposes. The river is navigable for ocean-going vessels below Tilbury. Length: 210mi (338km).

**Thanksgiving Day** National holiday in the US and Canada. Originating with the PILGRIMS in 1621, who celebrated the first harvest of the PLYMOUTH COLONY, it became an official holiday in 1863. In the US it is celebrated on the fourth Thursday in November; in Canada on the second Monday in October.

**Thant, U** (1909–74) Burmese diplomat, third secretary-general of the United Nations (UN) (1962–72). He was acting secretary-general from 1961 before being elected in his own right. He helped to settle major disputes including the civil wars in the Congo (Zaire) in 1963 and Cyprus in 1964.

**Thar Desert** (Great Indian Desert) Region in NW India and SE Pakistan, between the Aravalli Mountains (E) and the Indus River (W). The region covers parts of RAJASTHAN, GUJARAT, PUNJAB, and SIND. The desert areas of Rajasthan now benefit from the Indira Gandhi Canal, 400mi (650km) long, bringing water from HIMACHAL PRADESH. Area c.77,000sq mi (200,000sq km).

**Thatcher, Margaret Hilda, Baroness** (1925– ) British stateswoman, prime minister (1979–90). Perhaps the most influential British political leader since Winston CHURCHILL, she was secretary of state for education and science (1970–74) under Edward HEATH, whom she defeated for the party leadership in 1975. She beat James CALLAGHAN to become Britain's first woman prime minister. Her government embarked on a free-market program, which became known as THATCHERISM. Her monetarist policies, especially public spending cuts, provoked criticism and contributed to a recession, but her popularity was restored by victory in the FALKLANDS WAR (1982). Thatcher's determination to curb trade unions provoked a bitter miners' strike (1983–84). Controversial PRIVATIZATION of national utilities boosted revenue in a period of rapidly rising incomes, except among the poor. In 1987 Thatcher won a third term, but clashed with cabinet colleagues over economic and social policy and her hostile attitude to the EUROPEAN COMMUNITY (EC). A poll tax (1989) was widely seen as unfair and she was forced to resign. Thatcher was succeeded by John MAJOR.

**theater** Building where DRAMA is staged. Its architecture has evolved gradually from early times, when ritual was most often performed in the open air. In medieval Europe, churches were used as dramatic venues. Renaissance architects such as PALLADIO were commissioned to design private theaters with acoustics and perspective in mind. Popular, open stages evolved in Shakespearean England. By the Restoration, the PROSCENIUM arch stage had become established as the only viable form of theater. Since World War II, theatrical architecture has again stressed adaptability. *See also* DRAMA

**theater-in-the-round** Form of theatrical presentation derived from the ancient arena stage. The audience is seated on all sides of the players, thus creating a sense of informality between the actors and the audience.

**Thebes** City-state of ancient Greece, the dominant power in Boeotia. It was allied with Persia during the PERSIAN WARS, and during the 5th century BC was continually in conflict with Athens. It reached the peak of its power under Epaminondas in the 4th century BC, defeating the Spartans at Leuctra in 371 BC and invading the Peloponnese. The city was largely destroyed after a rising against ALEXANDER THE GREAT in 336 BC.

**Thebes** Greek name for the ancient capital of Upper Egypt, roughly corresponding to the present-day town of LUXOR.

**theft** (larceny) Dishonest appropriation of the property of another. A person is guilty of theft if depriving another of their rightful property with the intention of doing so.

**theism** Any of various philosophical and theological systems that profess belief in the existence of one Supreme Being, who is the creator of the universe. In most theistic systems, human beings have FREE WILL, and religious doctrines are usually based on divine revelation. *See also* MONOTHEISM; POLYTHEISM

**theocracy** Government by religious leaders in accordance with divine law. Theocracies were common in nonliterate societies and existed in ancient Egypt and the Orient.

**Theocritus** (310–250 BC) Greek poet, regarded as the father of pastoral poetry. His work, which influenced generations of later writers from VIRGIL to Matthew ARNOLD, is noted for its vivid expression and perceptive portrayal of rural life.

**Theodora** Name of three empresses of the BYZANTINE EMPIRE. The most famous Theodora (*c*.500–548) was the wife of JUSTINIAN I. A courtesan before her marriage, she had such influence that she almost ruled jointly. The second Theodora (d.867) ruled as regent (842–856) for her son Michael III. She expelled the iconoclasts and restored the worship of images. The third Theodora (980–1056) was co-ruler from 1042 and was briefly sole empress after the death of Constantine IX Monomachus (1055).

**Theodoric the Great** (454–526) King of the Ostrogoths and ruler of Italy. He drove ODOACER from Italy (488) and attempted to recreate the Western Roman Empire with himself as emperor. Religious differences and political rivalries frustrated his empire-building, and his kingdom was destroyed by JUSTINIAN after his death.

**Theodosius II** (401–450) Eastern Roman (Byzantine) emperor (408–50). An unassertive personality, he was dominated by ministers. His armies repelled Persian invasions, and the fortifications of Constantinople were strengthened. He promulgated the Theodosian Code of laws (438).

**theology** Systematic study of God or gods. In its narrowest sense, it is the investigation or expression of the beliefs and precepts of a religion. In a much broader sense, theology is intricately related to philosophical and historical studies and strives to achieve an understanding of various beliefs. Such preoccupations exercise the minds of theologians of Islam, Hinduism, and most other religions, as well as Christianity.

**theosophy** Religious philosophy that originated in the ancient world but was given impetus in 1875 when the Theosophical Society was founded in New York by the mystic Helen Blavatsky (b. Russia) and her followers. Modern theosophy continues a mystical tradition in Western thought represented by such thinkers as PYTHAGORAS and PLOTINUS, but is most significant in Indian thought. The main aims of the Theosophical Society are to promote a spiritual brotherhood of all humanity; to encourage the comparative study of religions, philosophy, and science; and to develop latent spiritual powers. Belief in the TRANSMIGRATION OF SOULS or REINCARNATION also occupies an important place in theosophical doctrine.

**Theravada** ("Doctrine of the Elders") Older of the two major schools of BUDDHISM. The doctrine originated early in the history of Buddhism as a contrast to MAHAYANA ("greater vehicle"). Theravada Buddhism stresses that sorrow and suffering can be conquered only by the suppression of desire. Desire can be suppressed only if the individual realizes that everything is always in a state of flux and the only stable condition is NIRVANA, an undefinable state of rest. This type of Buddhism is widespread in Sri Lanka and SE Asia.

**Thérèse of Lisieux, Saint** (1873–97) (Marie Françoise Thérèse Martin) French Carmelite nun. She entered the Carmelite convent at Lisieux at the age of 15. Later she suffered from depression and religious doubts, which she mastered by prayer. She died of tuberculosis. She chronicled her own spiritual struggle in a series of letters published in 1898 as *Story of a Soul*. She was canonized in 1925. Her feast day is October 1.

**thermal** Small-scale, rising current of air produced by local heating of the Earth's surface. Thermals are often used by gliding birds and human-built gliders. *See also* GLIDING

**thermionics** Study of the emission of electrons or ions from a heated conductor. This is the principle on which electron tubes (valves) work. The heated conductor is the CATHODE and the emitted electrons are attracted to the ANODE. A more modern aim for thermionics is the design and construction of thermionic power generators.

**thermodynamics** Branch of physics that studies heat and how it is transformed to and from other forms of ENERGY. The original laws of thermodynamics were developed by observing large-scale properties of systems, with no understanding of the underlying atomic structure. The three existing laws are now calculated from statistical and quantum mechanical principles. The **first law** states that the change in a system's internal energy is equal to zero, because heat and mechanical work are mutually convertible. The **second law** says that if a system is left alone, its ENTROPY tends to increase. This rules out the possibility of perpetual motion. The **third law** states that a system at ABSOLUTE ZERO would have an entropy of zero.

**thermometer** Instrument for measuring TEMPERATURE. A MERCURY thermometer depends on the expansion of the metal mercury, which is held in a glass bulb connected to a narrow, graduated tube. Temperatures can also be measured by a gas thermometer and by a resistance thermometer that measures resistance of a conductor. Common scales are the CELSIUS, FAHRENHEIT, and KELVIN.

**Thermopylae** Strategic mountain pass in E central Greece, site of several battles in ancient times. The most famous was the defense of the pass by Leonidas of SPARTA against the Persian invasion of XERXES I in 480 BC.

**thermosphere** Shell of light gases between the mesosphere and the exosphere, between 60mi (100km) and 280mi (450km) above the Earth's surface. The temperature steadily rises with height in the thermosphere.

**thermostat** Device for maintaining a constant temperature. A common type contains a strip of two metals, one of which expands and contracts more than the other. At a set temperature, the strip bends and breaks the circuit. As it cools, the strip straightens, makes contact, and the heating begins again once the circuit is complete.

**Theroux, Paul** (1941– ) US novelist and travel writer, resident in Britain. He has written short stories and a number of urbane and often funny novels, including *The Family Arsenal* (1976), *The Mosquito Coast* (1981), and *My Other Life* (1996). His fiction has been overshadowed by his travel writing, which includes *The Great Railroad Bazaar* (1975) and *Riding the Iron Rooster* (1988).

**Theseus** In Greek mythology, a great hero of many adventures, the son of Aethra by Aegeus, King of Athens, or by the sea god POSEIDON. His most famous exploit was the vanquishing of the MINOTAUR of Crete.

**Thespis** (6th century BC) Greek writer, according to tradition, the inventor of tragedy. He is also said to have introduced a character separate from the chorus, who provided dialogue by responding to the chorus' comments.

**Thessalonians, Epistles to the** Two of St. PAUL's earliest letters, forming the 13th and 14th books of the NEW TESTAMENT. The first letter was written *c.*AD 50, and the second followed shortly afterward. The letters contained encouragement and pastoral guidance for the Thessalonians and neighboring Christian communities.

**Thessaloníki** (Salonica) Port on the Gulf of Thessaloníki, Greece, the country's second-largest city and capital of Greek MACEDONIA. Founded *c.*315 BC, it flourished under the Romans after 148 BC as the capital of Macedonia. It was part of the Ottoman empire until 1913, when it was conquered by Greece. Industries: oil refining, textiles, metals, engineering, chemicals, cement, soap, wine, cigarettes. Pop. (1991) 383,967.

**thiamine** VITAMIN $B_1$ of the B complex, required for carbohydrate metabolism. Its deficiency causes BERIBERI. Thiamine is found in grains and seeds, nuts, liver, yeast, and legumes.

**Third Reich** Official name of Nazi Germany (1933–45). The first *Reich* (empire) was the Holy Roman Empire, the second the German empire of 1871–1918.

**Third World** Former term for LESS DEVELOPED COUNTRIES. "First" and "Second" world countries were those of the Western and Eastern blocs respectively.

**Thirteen Colonies** English colonies in North America that jointly declared independence from Britain (1776) and became the US. They were: Connecticut, Delaware, Georgia, Maryland, Massachusetts, New Hampshire, New Jersey, New York, North Carolina, Pennsylvania, Rhode Island, South Carolina, and Virginia. *See also* AMERICAN REVOLUTION

**Thirty Years War** (1618–48) Conflict fought mainly in Germany, arising out of religious differences and developing into a struggle for power in Europe. It began with a Protestant revolt in Bohemia against the HAPSBURG emperor, FERDINAND II. Both sides sought allies and the war spread to much of Europe. The Hapsburg generals Tilly and WALLENSTEIN registered early victories and drove the Protestant champion, CHRISTIAN IV of Denmark, out of the war (1629). A greater champion appeared in GUSTAVUS II (ADOLPHUS) of Sweden, who waged a series of victorious campaigns before being killed in 1632. In 1635 France, fearing Hapsburg dominance, declared war on Hapsburg Spain. Peace negotiations were not successful until the Peace of WESTPHALIA was concluded in 1648. War between France and Spain continued until the Peace of the PYRENEES (1659), and other associated conflicts continued for several years. The chief loser in the war, apart from German peasants, was the emperor, FERDINAND III, who lost control of Germany. Sweden was established as the dominant state in N Europe, while France replaced Spain as the greatest European power.

**thistle** Any of numerous species of plants with thorny leaves and yellow, white, pink, or purple flower heads with prickly bracts. The field thistle, *Cirsium discolor*, resembles the heraldic thistle, which is the national emblem of Scotland. Family Asteraceae/Compositae.

**Thomas, Saint** One of the original 12 APOSTLES or disciples of JESUS CHRIST. He has been called "Doubting Thomas" because, after the RESURRECTION of Christ, he refused to believe that the risen Lord had appeared to the other disciples (John 20). Only when Jesus appeared to him and allowed him to touch his wounds did he lay aside his doubts. According to Christian tradition, he took Christianity to India. His feast day is July 3.

**Thomas, Dylan Marlais** (1914–53) Welsh poet and short-story writer. A self-styled *enfant terrible*, his flamboyant alcoholic lifestyle led to his early death in New York. His public persona contributed to the popularity of his powerful, meticulously crafted but often willfully obscure verse. His first collection appeared when he was 19 years old; his *Collected Poems* was published in 1953. Many of his best short stories appear in *Portrait of the Artist as a Young Dog* (1940) and *Adventures in the Skin Trade* (1955). The "play for voices" *Under Milk Wood*, written in 1952, is perhaps his best-known work.

**Thomas, Norman Mattoon** (1884–1968) US politician. In 1926 he became leader of the Socialist Party and was its unsuccessful candidate for president six times between 1928 and 1948. A strong anticommunist, he campaigned for social welfare measures, civil rights, free speech, and world peace.

**Thomas à Kempis** *See* KEMPIS, THOMAS À

**Thomas Aquinas, Saint** *See* AQUINAS, SAINT THOMAS

**Thomism** Philosophy of Saint Thomas AQUINAS, one of the major systems in SCHOLASTICISM. Aquinas blended the philosophy of ARISTOTLE with Christian theology. Using Aristotle's concept of matter and form, he conceived a hierarchy in which spirit is higher than matter, soul higher than body, and theology above philosophy.

**Thompson, Emma** (1959– ) English actress and screenwriter. Thompson won an Academy Award for best actress in *Howard's End* (1991). She won a further Oscar for best screenplay for *Sense and Sensibility* (1995). Other films include *Remains of the Day* (1993) and *Carrington* (1995).

**Thomson, Sir George Paget** (1892–1975) British physicist, the son of Sir Joseph John THOMSON. He shared the 1937 Nobel Prize for physics with Clinton Davisson for

▲ **thistle** The creeping thistle is a weed, which is common on waste and cultivated land. Like the dandelion, it is a composite. There are about 150 species of *Cirsium* whose flowers may be violet, mauve, pink, yellow, or white.

T

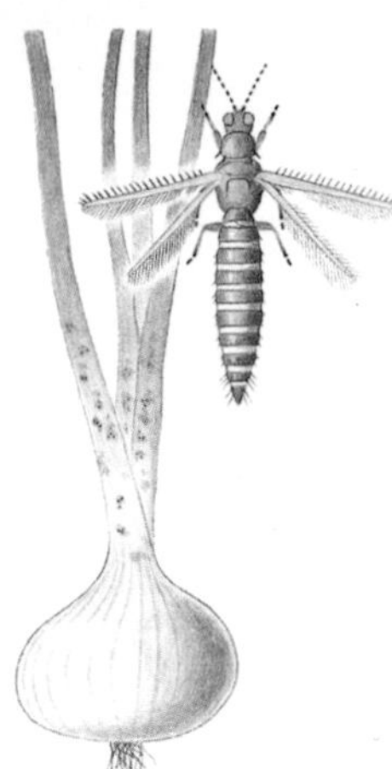

▲ **thrip** A tiny pest, thrips (order Thysanoptera) are significant for the damage they do to crops and for carrying disease. They have simple, fringed wings – or none at all – and unusual mouthparts with which they suck up plant juices. The onion thrips in both adult and nymphal stages infest a number of hosts to which they may transmit the tomato spotted wilt virus.

their independent work in diffracting ELECTRONS (1927). This work confirmed the wave nature of particles first predicted in 1923 by Louis de BROGLIE.

**Thomson, James** (1700–48) Scottish poet. His most famous poem, *The Seasons*, was published in four parts: *Winter* (1726), *Summer* (1727), *Spring* (1728), and *Autumn* (1730). Later poems include the patriotic *Liberty* (1734–36). Thomson's sensitivity to nature makes him a forerunner of ROMANTICISM.

**Thomson, Sir Joseph John** (1856–1940) British physicist. Thomson's discovery (1897) of the ELECTRON is regarded as the birth of PARTICLE PHYSICS. He was awarded the 1906 Nobel Prize for physics for his investigations into the electrical conductivity of gases. Thomson and Francis Aston produced evidence of ISOTOPES of neon. He transformed the Cavendish Laboratory into a major center for atomic research. He was the father of George THOMSON.

**Thomson, Virgil** (1896–1989) US critic and composer. He was music critic for the New York *Herald Tribune* (1940–54). Much influenced by Erik SATIE, his works include the operas *Four Saints in Three Acts* (1928, first production 1934) and *The Mother of Us All* (1947).

**Thor** In TEUTONIC MYTHOLOGY, god of thunder and lightning, corresponding to JUPITER. The eldest and strongest of ODIN's sons, he was represented as a handsome, red-bearded warrior, benevolent toward humans but a mighty foe of evil.

**thorax** In animal anatomy, part between the neck and abdomen. In mammals it is formed by the rib cage and contains the lungs, heart, and esophagus. In insects it consists of several segments to which legs and other appendages are attached.

**Thoreau, Henry David** (1817–62) US writer and naturalist. He was a friend of the transcendentalist Ralph Waldo EMERSON, who encouraged him to keep the journals from which he quarried much of his later work. An ardent individualist, he experimented in living a near-solitary life, rejecting materialism and finding fulfillment in observing plant and animal life. His essay *Civil Disobedience* (1849) has influenced many passive resistance movements.

**thorium** (symbol Th) Radioactive metallic element of the ACTINIDE ELEMENTS, first discovered in 1828. The chief ore is monazite (phosphate). The metal is used in photoelectric and thermionic emitters. One decay product is radon-220. Thorium is sometimes used in radiotherapy, and is increasingly used for conversion into uranium-233 for nuclear fission. Chemically reactive, it burns in air but reacts slowly in water. Properties: at.no. 90; at.wt. 232.0381; sp.gr. 11.72; m.p. 3,182°F (1,750°C); b.p. 8,654°F (4,790°C); most stable isotope $^{232}$Th ($1.41 \times 10^{10}$ yrs).

**thorn apple** Plant of the genus *Datura*, especially Jimson weed (*D. stramonium*), a poisonous, annual weed of tropical American origin. It has foul-smelling leaves and large white or violet trumpet-shaped flowers that are succeeded by round prickly fruits. Family Solanaceae.

**Thorpe, James Francis ("Jim")** (1888–1953) US athlete. A member of the Sac tribe, he won both the pentathlon and decathlon in the 1912 Olympics. In 1913 he was forced to give up his medals when it was discovered he had played semi-professional baseball. He played professional football with several teams (1915–26) and baseball with three different National League teams (1913–19). Recognized as the greatest American athlete for 1900–50, he was elected to the Football Hall of Fame in 1963. In 1973 the Amateur Athletic Union restored his Olympic records and medals.

**Thoth** In Egyptian mythology, scribe of the gods. He appears as the record keeper of the dead, patron of the arts and learning, inventor of writing, and as creator of the universe. Thoth is depicted as a man with the head of an ibis or as a baboon.

**Thrace** (Thráki) Ancient SE European country, now divided between Bulgaria, Greece, and European Turkey. From 1300–600 BC the Thracian lands extended W to the Adriatic and N to the Danube. By *c.*600 BC Thrace had lost much of its E lands to the Illyrians and Macedonians, and the Greeks established the colony of Byzantium. In 342 BC Philip II of Macedon conquered the country. After 100 BC it became part of the Roman empire. In the 7th century AD the N of the region was conquered by the Bulgarians, and by 1300 they controlled all Thrace. From 1361–1453 the region was disputed between the Bulgarians and the emerging Ottoman empire, eventually falling to the Turks. In 1885 N Thrace was annexed to Bulgaria. The regions either side of the Maritsa River became known as Eastern Thrace (Bulgaria) and Western Thrace (Turkey). After World War I, Bulgaria ceded S and most of E Thrace to Greece. The Treaty of LAUSANNE (1923) restored E Thrace to Turkey, and the region retains these boundaries. A fertile region, its main economic activity is agriculture.

**threadworm** Small ROUNDWORM of the phylum Aschelminthes. It is commonest in moist tropical regions and resembles a short length of hair or thread. It may inhabit the intestines of human beings and other animals, but can live and breed freely in soil. Species *Oxyurus vermicularis*.

**Three Mile Island** Island on the Susquehanna River near Harrisburg, Pennyslvania. It is the site of a nuclear power-generating plant where a near-disastrous accident took place in March 1979. The accident involved the failure of the feed-water system, which picks up heat from the system that has circulated through the reactor core, producing steam to power the turbines. Radioactive water and gases were released into the environment.

**thrip** Any of numerous species of slender, sucking insects found throughout the world. Species vary in color, but most feed on plants and some carry plant diseases. Length: to 0.3in (8mm). Order Thysanoptera.

**throat** *See* PHARYNX

**thrombophlebitis** Inflammation of the walls of veins associated with THROMBOSIS. It can occur in the legs during pregnancy.

**thrombosis** Formation of a blood clot in an artery or vein. Besides causing loss of circulation to the area supplied by the blocked vessel, it carries the risk of EMBOLISM.

**thrush** Any of numerous species of small songbirds of the family Turdidae. The European song thrush (*Turdus philomelos*) is mottled brown with a lighter, speckled breast. North American species include the (North American) robin, bluebird, and bluethroat. Length: to 12in (30cm).

**thrush** (candidiasis) Fungal infection of the mucous membranes, usually of the mouth but also of the vagina. Caused by the fungus *Candida albicans*, it is sometimes seen in people taking broad-spectrum ANTIBIOTICS.

**thrust** Driving force resulting from operation of a propeller, jet engine, or rocket engine. An aircraft propeller forces air backward, and jet and rocket engines expel gases backward. Thrust is produced in the forward direction in accordance with the third of NEWTON'S LAWS of motion.

**Thucydides** (460–400 BC) Ancient Greek historian. A commander in the PELOPONNESIAN WARS, his *History of the Peloponnesian War* is a determined attempt to write objective history, and it displays a profound understanding of human motives.

**thugs** Murderous gangs in India who preyed on travelers. They were members of a secret society, who killed their victims by ritual strangulation (*thuggee*) in honor of KALI, the Hindu goddess of destruction. They were eliminated by the British *c.*1830–50.

**thulium** (symbol Tm) Lustrous, silver-white, metallic element of the LANTHANIDE SERIES. Its chief ore is monazite but thulium is as rare as gold. Soft, malleable, and ductile, it combines with OXYGEN and the HALOGENS. It is used in arc lighting and portable x-ray units. Properties: at.no. 69; at.wt. 168.9342; sp.gr. 9.31; 2,813°F (1,545°C); b.p. 3,537°F (1,947°C); most stable isotope $^{169}$Tm (100%).

**thunderstorm** Electrical storm caused by the separation of electrical charges in clouds. Water drops are carried by updrafts to the top of a cloud, where they become ionized and accumulate into positive charges – the base of the cloud being negatively charged. An electrical discharge (a spark) between clouds, or between a cloud and the ground, is accompanied by light (seen as a LIGHTNING stroke) and heat. The heat expands the air explosively and causes it to reverberate and produce sounds and echoes called thunder.

**Thurber, James Grover** (1894–1961) US humorist and cartoonist. In 1927 he became a regular contributor of essays, short stories, and cartoons to the *New Yorker*. Collections of his essays and stories include *My Life and Hard Times* (1933)

T

and *My World and Welcome to It* (1942), which includes his best-known short story, *The Secret Life of Walter Mitty* (1932).

**Thuringia** Historic region of central Germany. Its rulers became powerful princes with the HOLY ROMAN EMPIRE in the 11th century. Thuringia was reconstituted as a state (*Land*) in 1920 under the WEIMAR REPUBLIC, but it lost its separate identity in 1952. The main economic activities are manufacturing and cereal cropping. Area: 6,244sq mi (16,176sq km). Pop. (1992) 2,545,808.

**Thutmose** Name of four kings of the 18th dynasty in ancient EGYPT. **Thutmose I** (r. *c*.1525–*c*.1512 BC) extended his kingdom southward into NUBIA, and campaigned successfully in the Near East. He was succeeded by his son, **Thutmose II** (r. *c*.1512–*c*.1504 BC), who married his half-sister, HATSHEPSUT. She ruled as regent for his son, **Thutmose III** (r. *c*.1504–1450 BC). Thutmose III expanded the kingdom to its greatest extent, defeating the Mitanni kingdom on the Euphrates River and pushing the southern frontier beyond the fourth cataract of the Nile. His grandson, **Thutmose IV** (r. *c*.1425–*c*.1416 BC), continued an expansive policy but also sought to strengthen the empire by peaceful means, marrying a Mitanni princess.

**thyme** Aromatic garden herb of the MINT family (Lamiaceae/Labiatae), used as an ornamental plant and in cooking. Purple-flowered, it yields an oil from which the drug thymol is prepared. Height: 6–8in (15–20cm). Genus *Thymus*.

**thymus gland** One of the endocrine GLANDS, located in the upper chest in mammals. In childhood it controls the development of lymphoid tissue and the immune response to infection. Disorder of the thymus may be associated with autoimmune diseases (those caused by the body's own antibodies). *See also* ENDOCRINE SYSTEM

**thyroid gland** H-shaped gland of the ENDOCRINE SYSTEM. It lies in the base of the neck, straddling the trachea below the Adam's apple. It secretes hormones, principally THYROXINE.

**thyroxine** Hormone secreted by the THYROID GLAND. It contains iodine and helps regulate the rate of metabolism; it is essential for normal growth and development.

**Tiananmen Square** World's largest public square, covering 98 acres (40ha) in Beijing, China. On the S side, a marble monument is dedicated to the heroes of the revolution. A huge portrait of Mao adorns the side of the Mao Zedong Memorial Hall. On May 4, 1919, China's first mass public rally was held in the square, where on October 1, 1949, MAO ZEDONG proclaimed the establishment of the People's Republic of China. In 1966 Mao made his pronouncements on the CULTURAL REVOLUTION to more than a million Red Guards assembled there. In April 1989 a series of nationwide pro-democracy demonstrations culminated in the occupation of the square by protesters. Hundreds of thousands of citizens joined in the demonstrations and student leaders organized hunger-strikes. On June 4, tanks and troops stormed the square. Official casualties were put at over 200 demonstrators and dozens of soldiers. Eyewitness reports suggest thousands of deaths. The government imposed a year-long martial law and executed several student leaders.

**Tianjin** (Tientsin) Port and industrial city on the Hai River, NE China. The country's third-largest city, it is also N China's most important international port. Founded in *c*.300 BC, it became prominent in the late 18th century due to its strategic position en route to Manchuria. In 1860, the British and French obtained the right to use Tianjin as a treaty port. In 1900 the city came under European occupation. Because of its excellent transport links, it remains the trading center for N China. Industries: iron, steel, heavy machinery, transport equipment, textiles, carpets. The city is administered as a special economic zone to encourage inward investment. Pop. (1993) 4,970,000.

**Tian Shan** (Tien Shan) Mountain range in central Asia, 1,500mi (2,400km) long, forming the border between Kyrgyzstan and Xinjiang, NW China. At their W edge, the Tian Shan ("Celestial Mountains") divide the Tarim and Junggar Basins. The range then rises to 24,406ft (7,439m) at Peak Pobeda, on the Chinese border with Kazakstan and Kyrgyzstan. The Issyk Kul in Kyrgyzstan is one of the world's biggest mountain lakes.

**Tiber** (Tevere) River in central Italy. Rising in the Etruscan Apennines, it flows S then SW through Rome and empties into the Tyrrhenian Sea at Ostia. The silting of the river has closed Fiumara, one of its two mouths, and its delta continues to expand; the ancient coastal port of Ostia Antica now lies 4mi (6km) inland. Length: 251 mi (404km).

**Tiberius** (42 BC–AD 37) (Tiberius Julius Caesar Augustus) Roman emperor (AD 14–37). He was the stepson of AUGUSTUS, who adopted him as his heir (AD 4). Initially, his administration was just and moderate, but he became increasingly fearful of conspiracy and had many people executed for alleged treason. He left Rome and spent his last years in seclusion on Capri.

**Tibet** (Xizang) Autonomous region in SW China. The capital and largest city is LHASA. Tibet is the highest region on earth, with an average altitude of 16,000ft (4,875m). An historically inaccessible area, Tibet is surrounded by mountains on three sides. The Tibetan HIMALAYAS include the world's highest mountain, EVEREST. Nam Co is the world's largest natural salt lake. Many of Asia's greatest rivers, including the YANGTZE, MEKONG, HUANG HE, INDUS, and GANGES have their source in Tibet, though its major river is the BRAHMAPUTRA. The area has scant rainfall, and the Brahmaputra valley is the only agricultural area and the location of the major cities. Many of the people remain nomadic pastoralists. Tibet is rich in mineral resources, such as gold, copper, and uranium. The Chinese government have built internal highways and links to the Chinese provinces. The principal religion is TIBETAN BUDDHISM. Until 1959, a large percentage of the urban male population were Buddhist monks (Lamas). From the 7th century, the spiritual leaders of Lamaism (the DALAI LAMA and the PANCHEN LAMA) also acted as the country's temporal rulers. Tibet flourished as an independent kingdom in the 7th century, and in the 8th century Padmasambhava developed the principles of MAHAYANA Buddhism and founded Lamaism. In 1206 Genghis Khan conquered the region, and it remained under nominal Mongol rule until 1720, when the Chinese QING dynasty claimed sovereignty. At the close of the 19th century the Tibetan areas of Ladakh and Sikkim were incorporated into British India, and in 1906 Britain recognized Chinese sovereignty over Tibet. In 1912 the fall of the QING dynasty prompted the Tibetans to reassert their independence. China, however, maintained its right to govern, and in 1950 the new communist regime sent its forces to invade. In 1951 Tibet was declared an autonomous region of China, nominally governed by the Dalai Lama. The Chinese government began a series of repressive measures principally targeting the Buddhist monasteries. In March 1959 a full-scale revolt against Chinese rule was suppressed by the Chinese People's Liberation Army. The Dalai Lama managed to flee to N India (December 25, 1959), and he established a government-in-exile at Dharamsala. In 1965 China formally annexed Tibet as an autonomous region. The CULTURAL REVOLUTION banned religious practice and 4,000 monasteries were destroyed. Many thousands of Tibetans were forced into exile by the brutality of the communist regime. Despite the restoration of some of the desecrated monasteries and the reinstatement of Tibetan as an official language, human rights violations continued. Pro-independence rallies in 1987–89 were violently suppressed by the Chinese army. Area: 471,841sq mi (1,222,070sq km). Pop. (1993) 2,290,000.

**Tibetan art** Virtually all art in Tibet is religious in character, designed to serve the elaborate rituals of TIBETAN BUDDHISM. All artworks are anonymous and most are undated. Paintings come in two forms – wall paintings and *thangkas*, which are banners, usually displayed in temples or carried in processions. *Thangkas* generally depict scenes from the life of a deity or *mandalas* (patterns used for meditation).

**Tibetan Buddhism** Distinctive blend of Mahayana BUDDHISM and Bonism (a pre-Buddhist shamanism). It mixes meditative monasticism with indigenous folk religion and involves a system of reincarnating lamas (monks). Both spiritual and temporal authority reside in the person and office of the DALAI LAMA. King Srong-tsan-gampo (b.617 or 629) sought to bring Buddhist teachers from China and India to Tibet. The Bon priests opposed the new Buddhist ways, and Buddhism was not thoroughly introduced into Tibet until the 8th century. Following reforms initiated by the 11th-century Indian master Atisha, four major sects emerged in Tibetan

▲ **thyme** Thyme (*Thymus vulgaris*) is a favorite herb for Mediterranean cooking and is an essential ingredient of a bouquet garni. It has a pungent aroma and retains much of its flavor when dried.

Buddhism. Of these, the Gelugpa order, to which the Dalai and PANCHEN LAMAS belong, was politically dominant from the 17th century. There are now two Gelugpa sects, the Red and Yellow monks. The Dalai Lama, a member of the latter, became revered as the "Living Buddha" and the spiritual and temporal ruler of Tibet. Each new Dalai Lama is believed to be a reincarnation of his predecessor. The Panchen Lama heads the Red monks.

**tibia** (shinbone) Inner and larger of the two lower leg bones. It articulates with the FEMUR, or upper leg bone, at the knee and extends to the ankle, where its lower end forms the projecting ankle bone on the inside of the leg. *See also* FIBULA

**tic** Sudden and rapidly repeated muscular contraction, limited to one part of the body, especially the face.

**tick** Any of numerous species of wingless, bloodsucking ARACHNIDS, the most notable of which are ectoparasites of vertebrates and invertebrates. Many species carry diseases (some fatal) in wild and domesticated animals and in humans Length: to 0.1in (3mm). Class Arachnida; order Acarina.

**tidal power** Energy harnessed from tidal movement of the Earth's oceans and used by humans. It is economic only where the tidal range is greater than about 15ft (4.6m). Modern schemes involve the use of turbogenerators driven by the passage of water through a tidal barrage.

## TIDAL POWER

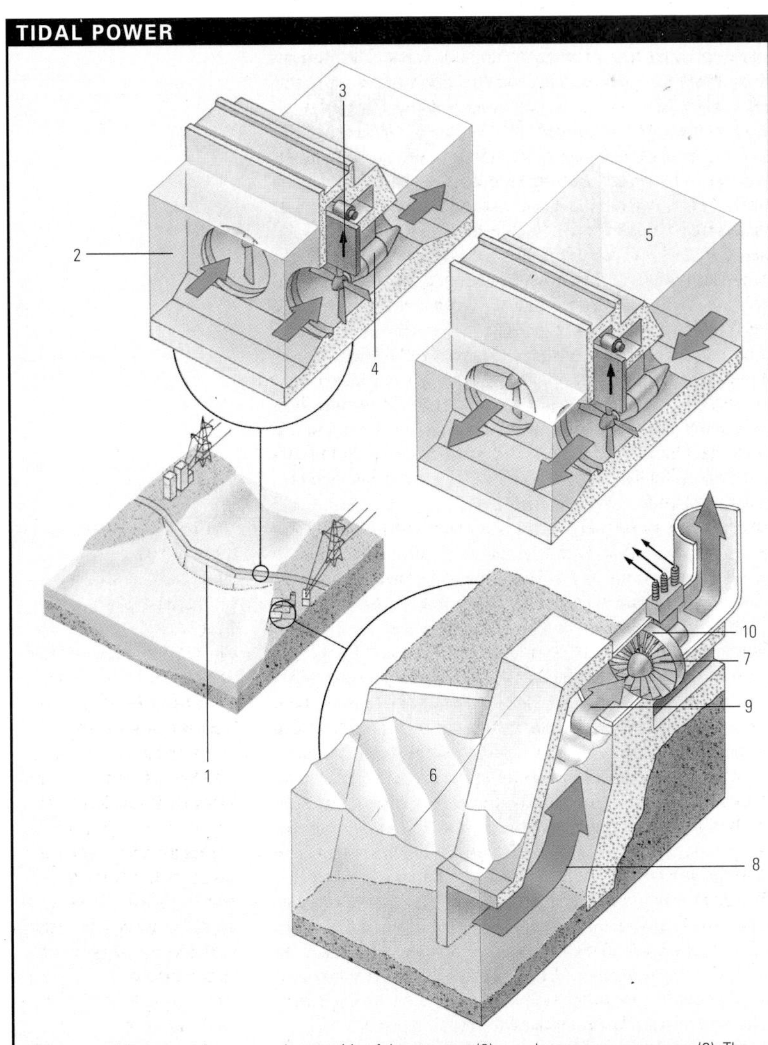


The power of the sea can be harnessed to generate electricity. Tidal power uses a barrage (1) across an estuary or bay. The barrage contains turbines which can spin with a flow of water in either direction. As the tide comes in gates on the barrage remain closed until a head of water has built up on the sea side of the structure (2). The gates are then opened (3) and the incoming tide flows through the barrage driving the turbines (4). As the tide falls the process is reversed with the gates closed until the sea has fallen below the level of water retained in the estuary (5). The second form of utilizing the sea harnesses wave power (6). The key difference is that the turbine (7) is air-driven not turned by water. As a wave hits the shore the force of the water (8) drives air (9) through the turbine blades (10). When the water level drops air is sucked back down through the turbine, spinning it again.

**tide** Periodic rise and fall of the surface level of the oceans caused by the gravitational attraction of the Moon and Sun. Tides follow the Moon's 28-day cycle, so they arrive at a given spot 50 minutes later each day. When the Sun and Moon are in conjunction or opposition, the greatest tidal range occurs, called spring tides. When they are in quadrature, when the Moon is half-full, tidal ranges are lowest and are called neap tides.

**Tiepolo, Giovanni Battista** (1696–1770) Italian painter. His pictures are full of action, using light, sunny colors, with figures and objects seen in a deep, theatrical PERSPECTIVE. The peak of his career came in the 1750s when he decorated the Kaisersaal and the grand staircase of the Prince Archbishop's Palace in Würzburg.

**Tierra del Fuego** (Sp. Land of Fire) Archipelago separated from mainland S South America by the Magellan Strait. It consists of one large island and other smaller islands. At the S extremity of the islands lies Cape Horn. The main island is politically divided between Argentina and Chile. The islands remained undiscovered by Europeans until Ferdinand MAGELLAN's landing in 1520. They were not settled until the 1880s, when the discovery of gold and later oil attracted many Europeans, Argentinians, and Chileans to the area. The indigenous population was killed by diseases brought by settlers. The mountainous terrain and harsh climate limit economic activity to sheep rearing and oil exploration. Area: 28,473sq mi (73,746sq km). Pop. (1991) 69,450.

**Tiffany, Louis Comfort** (1848–1933) US painter, designer, and a leader of the ART NOUVEAU style in the US. In 1878 he formed an interior decorating firm, which by 1900 was known as Tiffany Studios. It specialized in what he termed "favrile" glass: freely shaped iridescent glasswork, sometimes combined with various metals.

**tiger** Large, powerful cat found (in decreasing numbers) throughout Asia, mainly in forested areas. It has a characteristic striped coat of yellow, orange, white, and black, with the chin and underparts white. Relying on keen hearing, it hunts for birds, deer, cattle, and reptiles. The largest tiger is the Siberian race. Length to 13ft (4m) overall; weight: to 500lb (230kg). Family Felidae; species *Panthera tigris*.

**Tigris** River in SW Asia. Rising in the Taurus Mountains of E Turkey, it flows SE through Iraq, joining the Eu-phrates River to form the Shatt Al Arab waterway. The river is liable to sudden flooding, but there are flood-control schemes and the river irrigates more than 750,000 acres (300,000ha). It is navigable for shallow-draft vessels as far as BAGHDAD. Length: *c.*1,180mi (1,900km).

**till** In geology, sediment consisting of an unsorted mixture of clay, sand, gravel, and boulders that is deposited directly by the ice of GLACIERS.

**timber** *See* WOOD

**timbre** Characteristic of a musical sound determined by the number and intensity of the overtones (HARMONICS) produced as well as the principal (fundamental) note. Musical instruments of different types make characteristic sounds because of the different harmonics produced.

**Timbuktu** Town in N Mali, W Africa. It was founded by the Tuareg people in the 11th century and soon became a center of Muslim learning. The southern terminus of a Saharan caravan route, it later became famous throughout Europe as a market for slaves and gold. Sacked by the Moroccans in 1591 and seized by the French in 1893, its most important trading commodity today is salt. Pop. (1992 est.) 26,000.

**time** Perception of a sequential order in all experience; also the interval perceived between two events. A consideration of time falls within the disciplines of physics, psychology, philosophy, and biology. Until the theory of RELATIVITY was devised by Albert EINSTEIN, time was conceived of as absolute – a constant one-direction (past to future) flow. Since then the concept of time linked with distance in space ("space-time") has connected time with the relative velocities of those perceiving it. For clocks at velocities approaching that of light, time expands from the point of view of a stationary observer, but it still flows in the same direction.

**time scale** *See* GEOLOGICAL TIME

**time zone** One of 24 divisions of the Earth's surface, each 15° of LONGITUDE wide, within which the time of day is reckoned to be the same. At a conference held in Washington, D.C. in 1884, the meridian of Greenwich was adopted as the zero of longitude, and zones of longitude were established. Standard time in each successive zone westward is one hour behind that in the preceding zone. *See also* GREENWICH MEAN TIME (GMT)

**Timişoara** City in W Romania, on the Bega River and Canal. An ancient Roman settlement, it was ruled by the MAGYARS from 896, annexed to Hungary in 1010 and ruled by the Turks from 1552 to 1716, when it returned to Austria-Hungary. It passed to Romania in 1920. Events here in 1989 triggered the fall of the CEAUŞESCU regime. Industries: engineering, food processing, tobacco, chemicals, textiles, machinery. Pop. (1993) 325,359.

**Timor** Largest of the Lesser Sunda Islands in the Malay archipelago; part of INDONESIA. The chief towns are Kupang in the W and Dili in the E. From *c.*1520 Portuguese spice traders began to settle on Timor. When the Dutch landed in 1620 they settled on the W. During World War II the island was occupied by the Japanese. In 1950 West Timor became part of the Nusa Tenggara Timur province of the newly created Republic of Indonesia. In 1975 the Portuguese abandoned East Timor, and the colony declared its independence. Indonesia invaded, and in 1976 annexed East Timor. The East Timor independence movement FRETILIN has maintained resistance to Indonesian rule amid widespread reports of human rights violations. A mountainous island, its main products are rice, coconuts, coffee, and tobacco. Area: 13,074sq mi (33,857sq km). Pop. (both provinces) (1990) 4,015,394.

**timpani** (kettledrums) Principal percussion instruments in a symphony orchestra. They are hemispherical vessels of copper or brass with single skins, tuned by pedals or screws, and struck with sticks with hard felt heads. Military kettledrums were introduced to Europe by the Crusaders in *c.*1100.

**Timur** *See* TAMERLANE

**tin** (symbol Sn) Metallic element of Group IV of the periodic table, known from ancient times. Its chief ore is cassiterite (an oxide). Soft, malleable, and resistant to corrosion, tin is used as a protective coating for iron, steel, copper, and other metals, and in such alloys as solder, pewter, and bronze. Properties: at.no. 50; at.wt. 118.69; sp.gr. 7.29; m.p. 449.6°F (232°C); b.p. 4,118°F (2,270°C); most common isotope $^{118}$Sn (24.03%).

**Tinbergen, Nikolaas** (1907–88) Dutch ethologist. He shared with Konrad LORENZ and Karl von FRISCH the 1973 Nobel Prize for physiology or medicine for his pioneering work in ETHOLOGY. Tinbergen studied how certain stimuli evoke specific responses in animals.

**Tintoretto** (1518–94) (Jacopo Robusti) Italian painter. Among his notable works are *The Finding of the Body of St. Mark* (1562) and *The Last Supper* (1592–94). Some of his finest paintings are in the series of the life of Christ (1565–87).

**Tippecanoe, Battle of** (1811) Battle on the Tippecanoe River in Illinois in which US forces, under William Henry HARRISON, governor of Indiana Territory, were attacked by the Shawnee under SHAWNEE PROPHET, who opposed Harrison's land-grabbing actions. The battle was inconclusive, but it made a hero of Harrison.

**Tipperary** County in central S Republic of Ireland, in Munster province. The region is part of the central plain of Ireland, but there are hills in the S; the Suir and Shannon are the principal rivers. The soil is fertile, and Tipperary is one of the country's best farming regions. The county town is Clonmel. Area 1,643sq mi (4,255sq km). Pop. (1991) 132,772.

**Tippett, Sir Michael Kemp** (1905–98) English composer. His music incorporates apparently disparate musical forms and social themes of justice, pacifism, and humanism. Tippett's oratorio *A Child of Our Time* (1941) was a response to the Kristallnacht (1938) in Nazi Germany. His work includes four symphonies, other orchestral pieces, such as *Fantasia on a Theme of Corelli* (1953), piano and chamber music, and operas, including *The Midsummer Marriage* (1952), *King Priam* (1962), and *New Year* (1989).

◀ **tiger** Once common throughout Asia, the tiger has suffered much from the reduction of its habitat. Its greatest threat, however, comes directly from humans due to the increased availability of firearms. Reserves have been established in India for the protection of the tiger.

**Tirana** (Tiranë) Capital of Albania, on the Ishm River. It was founded in the early 17th century by the Ottoman Turks and became Albania's capital in 1920. In 1946 the communists came to power and the industrial sector of the city was developed. Industries: metal goods, agricultural machinery, textiles. Pop. (1991) 251,000.

**tire** Air-filled rubber and fabric cushion that fits over the wheels of vehicles to grip the road and absorb shock. The pneumatic tire was invented in 1845 but was not commonly used until the end of the century. It consists of a layer of fabric surrounded by a thick layer of rubber treated with chemicals to harden it and decrease wear and tear.

**Tirol** (Tyrol) Federal state in W Austria, bordered N by Germany and S by Italy. The capital is INNSBRUCK. The Romans conquered the region in 15 BC, and the Franks held it during the 8th century. In 1363 the province was taken by the Hapsburgs. In 1805 Napoleon I awarded Tirol to Bavaria in return for its support. In 1810 Napoleon gave S Tirol to the Italians, but the Congress of Vienna (1815) reunited Tirol with Austria. After World War I, when S Tirol was awarded to Italy, a process of Italianization was resisted by the German-speaking inhabitants. After World War II, S Tirol was made an autonomous Italian region. An Alpine region, its economy is now dominated by tourism, with visitors attracted by the Tyrolean Alps and the skiing conditions. Other economic activities are agricultural. Area: 4,882sq mi (12,647sq km). Pop. (1994) 654,753.

**tissue** Material of a living body consisting of a group of similar and often interconnected cells, usually supporting a similar function. Tissues vary greatly in structure and complexity. In animals they may be loosely classified according to function into epithelial, connective, skeletal, muscular, nervous, and glandular tissues.

**tissue culture** In biology, artificial cultivation of living TISSUE in sterile conditions. Tissue culture in laboratories is used for biological research or to help in the diagnosis of diseases. It is also used a means of propagating plant CLONES. *See also* GENETIC ENGINEERING

**Titan** Largest SATELLITE of Saturn, and the second largest in the Solar System, discovered by Christiaan Huygens in 1655. It is unique among planetary satellites in having a substantial atmosphere, consisting mostly of nitrogen, with some methane and other hydrocarbon compounds. It is composed of rock and water-ice. The surface temperature is 95K.

**Titania** In folklore, queen of the fairies and wife of OBERON. In OVID's writing she represents DIANA at the head of her nymphs. In Shakespeare's *A Midsummer Night's Dream* she quarrels with her husband over a changeling boy.

**Titanic** British passenger liner that sank on her maiden voyage (April 14–15, 1912). The largest vessel of her time, she was sailing from Southampton to New York when she struck an iceberg in the N Atlantic. About 1,500 people were drowned. The disaster led to international agreements on safety precautions at sea. In 1985 the wreck of the *Titanic* was located.

▼ **tides** The daily rise and fall of the ocean's tides are the result of the gravitational pull of the Moon and that of the Sun, though the effect of the latter is only 46.6% as strong as that of the Moon. The effect is greatest on the hemisphere facing the Moon and causes a tidal "bulge." When the Sun, Earth, and Moon are in line, tide-raising forces are at a maximum and spring tides occur; high tide reaches the highest values, and low tide falls to low levels. When lunar and solar forces are least coincidental with the Sun and Moon at an angle (near the Moon's first and third quarters), neap tides occur, which have a small tidal range.

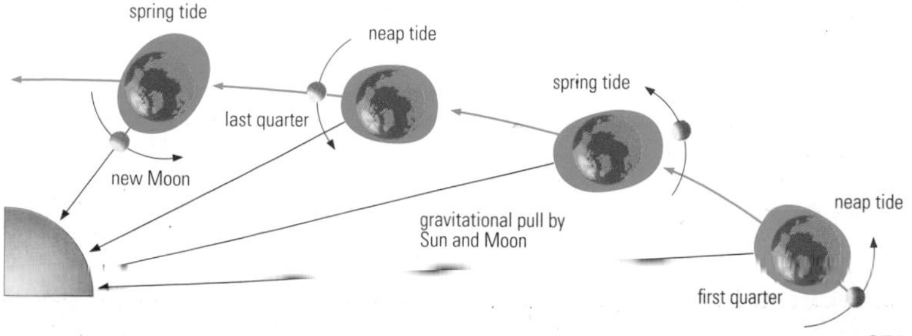

▶ **toad** The Surinam toad (*Pipa pipa*) lays 3–10 eggs, which the male fertilizes and presses into the back of the female; her skin swells up, enveloping the eggs within cysts. After carrying her offspring for about 80 days of development, the female molts and the young, miniature toads are released into the water.

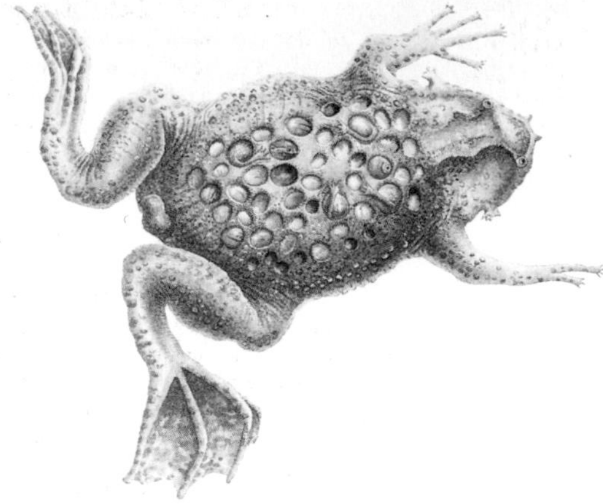

**titanium** (symbol Ti) Lustrous, silver-gray, metallic element of the TRANSITION ELEMENTS. A common element, it is found in many minerals, chief sources being ilmenite and RUTILE. Resistant to corrosion and heat, it is used in steels and other alloys, especially in aircraft, spacecraft, and guided missiles where strength must be combined with lightness. Properties: at.no. 22; at.wt. 47.90; sp.gr. 4.54; m.p. 3,020°F (1,660°C); b.p. 5,949°F (3,287°C); most common isotope $^{48}$Ti (73.94%).

**Titans** In Greek mythology, 12 gods and goddesses who were the sons and daughters of URANUS and GAIA. They were overthrown by the Olympians, led by Zeus.

**tithe** Tax of one-tenth of income levied to support a religious institution. Tithes were prescribed in the Old Testament and were a major source of church income in medieval Europe. They were generally abandoned in favor of other sources of income in the 19th century.

**Titian** (1485–1576) (Tiziano Vecellio) Venetian painter. He trained first with Giovanni BELLINI and then GIORGIONE. Titian evolved a brilliant, worldly style demonstrated in three magnificent altarpieces, *The Assumption*, *Pesaro*, and *St. Peter Martyr*. He combined the balance of High RENAISSANCE composition with a new dynam-ism, which heralded the BAROQUE. He favored vivid, simple colors, and often silhouetted dark forms against a light background. Between 1518 and 1523 he produced some of his finest mythological paintings, the *Worship of Venus*, *Bacchanal*, and *Bacchus and Ariadne*. In the 1540s his paintings were in a vigorous type of MANNERISM. His last work was the astonishingly powerful *Pietà*, which he designed for his own tomb. Titian's oil technique was freer and more expressive than any earlier style, and he had a revolutionary influence on later artists.

**Titicaca** Lake in the Andes on the Peru-Bolivia border, draining S through the Desaguader River into Lake Poo-pó. At an altitude of 12,500ft (3,810m), it is the highest navigable body of water in the world. The constant water supply has enabled the region to grow crops since ancient times. The lake is home to giant edible frogs and is also famed for its totora reeds, from which the Uru make their floating island homes and fishing rafts. Area: 3,200sq mi (8,290sq km); max. depth 920ft (280m).

**titles** Formerly hereditary designations corresponding to rank within a well-defined social hierarchy under an emperor or monarch. Modern-day hereditary titles may still be passed on, but most titles are conferred by a head of state for the lifetime of the recipient only. In the English-speaking world, formal hereditary titles for males are (in descending order of consequence): king, prince, duke, earl, viscount, baron.

**titmouse** (tit, chickadee) Small, stubby-bodied, and large-headed bird of open woodlands and wooded parks of the Northern Hemisphere and Africa. Most true titmice nest in self-drilled holes or abandoned woodpecker holes. Family Paridae; genus *Parus*. The long-tailed titmice and bush tits of Eurasia and W North America are larger and build closed, often hanging, nests. Subfamily Aegithalinae.

**Tito, Josip Broz** (1892–1980) Yugoslav statesman. As a Croatian soldier in the Austro-Hungarian army, he was captured by the Russians (1915) but released by the Bolsheviks in 1917. He helped to organize the Yugoslav Communist Party and adopted the name Tito in 1934. He led the Partisans' campaign against the Germans in Yugoslavia during World War II. In 1945 he established a communist government, and was prime minister (1945–53) and thereafter president, although virtually a dictator. Soviet efforts to control Yugoslavia led to a split between the two countries in 1948. At home, Tito sought to balance the deep ethnic and religious divisions in Yugoslavia and to develop an economic model of communist "self-management." Abroad, he became an influential leader of the Non-Aligned Movement. As later events confirmed, his greatest achievement was to hold the Yugoslavian federation together.

▲ **Tito** A forceful and charismatic personality, Tito ruled Yugoslavia from 1945 until his death in 1980. By maintaining tight, dictatorial control domestically, he was able to hold the country's various nationalist groups in check. He encouraged decentralization and worker participation in the economy, liberal policies for a Communist country. Internationally, he pursued an independent foreign policy, keeping his distance from the Soviet Union.

**titration** Method used in analytical chemistry to determine the concentration of a compound in a solution by measuring the amount needed to complete a reaction with another compound. A solution of known concentration is added in measured amounts to a liquid of unknown concentration until the reaction is complete. The volume added enables the unknown concentration to be calculated.

**Titus** (AD 39–81) Roman emperor (r.79–81). Elder son of VESPASIAN, he campaigned in Britain and Germany and captured and destroyed Jerusalem in 70 after a Jewish revolt. As emperor, he stopped persecutions for treason, built lavish baths, and gained great popularity. He was succeeded by DOMITIAN.

**Tlingit** NATIVE AMERICAN people of the SE coast of Alaska. Famous for their totem poles (featuring stylized forms of local wildlife), they rely economically on fishing, tourism, and government aid.

**TNT** (2,4,6–trinitrotoluene) Explosive organic compound ($C_7H_5N_3O_6$) made from TOLUENE by using sulfuric and nitric acids. Its resistance to shock (requiring a detonator to set it off) makes it one of the safest high explosives.

**toad** Any of many species of tail-less amphibians found worldwide, except Australasia. Most are short and rotund, moving with a crawling or hopping gait. Toads are differentiated from frogs by their rougher, bumpier skin and rounder body with shorter legs. Length: 1–10in (2–25cm). Order Anura; family Bu-fonidae. *See also* TADPOLE

**toadstool** Popular name for the fruiting body of a FUNGUS of the class Basidiomycetae. It usually refers to inedible species and describes the stool-like appearance of the reproductive organ. It consists of a stem and a cap, on which the spores are borne on gills or in tubes.

## TOGO

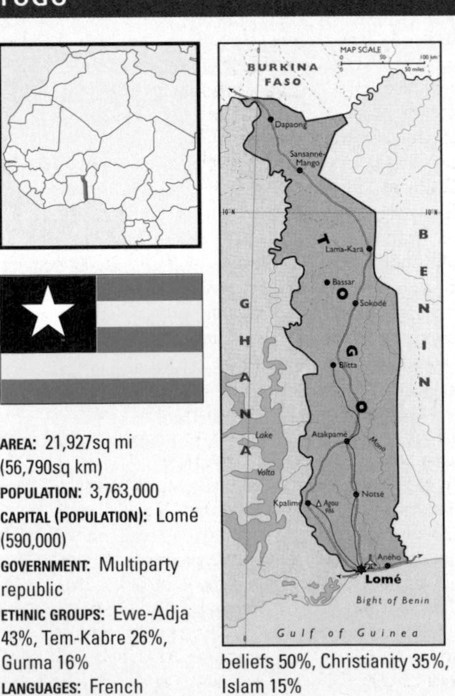


**AREA:** 21,927sq mi (56,790sq km)
**POPULATION:** 3,763,000
**CAPITAL (POPULATION):** Lomé (590,000)
**GOVERNMENT:** Multiparty republic
**ETHNIC GROUPS:** Ewe-Adja 43%, Tem-Kabre 26%, Gurma 16%
**LANGUAGES:** French (official), Ewe, Kabiye
**RELIGIONS:** Traditional beliefs 50%, Christianity 35%, Islam 15%
**CURRENCY:** CFA franc = 100 centimes

**tobacco** Herb native to the Americas cultivated worldwide for its leaves. It has large leaves with no stalk, and white, pink, or red star-shaped flowers. *Nicotiana tabacum* is the principal cultivated species. Seeds were brought to Europe in *c*.1520–30. Settlers in Virginia obtained seeds from the Spanish colonies (1612) and soon tobacco was the major crop of the Virginia colony and America's first export. Leaves are prepared for smoking by curing (drying) and then aging. Family Solanaceae (NIGHTSHADE family). Height: 2–6ft (0.6–2m).

**Tobago** *See* TRINIDAD AND TOBAGO

**Tocqueville, Alexis de** (1805–59) French historian. Sent on a fact-finding tour to the US by the French government, he produced *Of Democracy in America* (1835), the first in-depth study of the US political system. His later work includes *L'Ancien Régime et la Révolution* (1856).

**Togo** Small republic in W Africa; the capital is LOMÉ. It is divided geographically into four regions. The coastal plain is sandy; N of the coast is an area of fertile, clay soil. North again is the Mono Tableland, which reaches an altitude of *c*.1,500ft (450m), and is drained by the Mono River. The Atakora Mountains are the fourth region; N of the mountains is a plateau region. The vegetation is mainly open grassland. The historic region of Togoland comprised what is now the Republic of Togo and W Ghana. From the 17th–19th centuries, the Ashantis raided Togoland, seizing the indigenous inhabitants, the Ewe, and selling them to Europeans as slaves. As a German protectorate from 1884, it developed economically and Lomé was built. At the start of World War I, Britain and France captured Togoland from Germany. In 1922 it was divided into two mandates, which, in 1942, became UN trust territories. In 1957 British Togoland became part of Ghana. In 1960 French Togoland became independent as the Republic of Togo. In 1961 Slyvanus Olympio became the first president, but was assassinated in 1963. Nicolas Grunitzky became president, but in 1967 he was overthrown in a coup. Ghansimgbe Eyadéma, leader of the military coup, became president in 1972. The constitution of 1979 confirmed Togo as a single-party state, the sole legal party being the Rassemblement du peuple togolais (RPT). Reelected in 1972 and 1986, Eyadéma was forced to resign in 1991 after pro-democracy riots. Kokou Koffigoh was elected prime minister. Unrest continued with troops loyal to Eyadéma attempting to overthrow Koffigoh. In 1992 a new multi-party constitution was introduced and Eyadéma regained some power. In 1993 a rigged election, boycotted by opposition parties, was won by Eyadéma. In 1994 elections were won by an opposition alliance, but Eyadéma formed a coalition government. In 1998 Eyadéma was reelected in suspect elections. The majority of the population are engaged in subsistence agriculture (1995 GDP per capita, US$1,130). Cocoa, coffee, and cotton are the chief cash crops. Palm oil and phosphates are the principal exports.

**Tokugawa** Japanese hereditary dynasty which controlled Japan through the SHŌGUN (1603–1867). The Tokugawa shōgunate was established by Ieyasu Tokugawa (1543–1616) who completed the unification of Japan. The Tokugawa ruled through the provincial nobility (the Daimyo) and controlled much of the country's wealth and farmland as well as the emperor and priests. They banned Christianity and Western trade, reviving Confucianism, and isolated Japan from the rest of the world. The regime declined during the 19th century as their isolationist policy began to crack under Western pressure, and the last Tokugawa shōgun was overthrown before the MEIJI RESTORATION (1867).

**Tokyo** (Jap. eastern capital) Capital of Japan, on E central Honshū, at the head of Tokyo Bay. The modern city is divided into distinct districts: Kasumigaseki, Japan's administrative center; Marunouchi, its commercial center; Ginza, its shopping and cultural center; the W shore of Tokyo Bay (including Kawasaki and Yokohama seaport), its industrial center. Modern Tokyo also serves as the country's educational center with over 100 universities. Founded in the 12th century as Edo, it became capital of the TOKUGAWA shōgunate in 1603. In 1868 the Japanese Reformation reestablished imperial power, and the last shōgun surrendered Edo Castle. Emperor Meiji renamed the city Tokyo and it replaced Kyōto as the capital of Japan. The 1923 earthquake and subsequent fire claimed over 150,000 lives and necessitated the city's reconstruction, but in 1944–45 intensive US bombing destroyed over half the city, and another modernization and restoration program began. Industries: electronic equipment, cameras, automobile manufacture, metals, chemicals, textiles. Pop. (1994) 7,894,000.

**Toledo** Capital of Toledo province, in Castilla-La Mancha, on the Tagus River, central Spain. In the 6th century, Toledo was the capital of the Visigoths. In 1031 the Moors made it the capital of an independent kingdom. The city was fortified and acquired its enduring reputation for quality sword making. Toledo flourished as a multi-denominational city, with Mudéjar-style synagogues, mosques, and churches. In the 16th century, it became the spiritual capital of Catholic Spain and the headquarters of the Spanish Inquisition; Jews and Muslims suffered persecution and the synagogues were converted to churches. Pop. (1991) 59,563.

**Toledo** Industrial city and Great Lakes port on Lake Erie, NW Ohio, US, at the mouth of the Maumee River. The city was founded in 1794 as Fort Industry, settled as Port Lawrence in 1817, and renamed Toledo in 1833. Ohio and Michigan fought for control of the town in the so-called Toledo War (1835–36). It has been a center for glass manufacture since 1888. Industries: coal, glass, oil, transport equipment. Pop. (1992) 329,325.

**Tolkien, J.R.R. (John Ronald Reuel)** (1892–1973) English scholar and novelist. A respected academic, Tolkien is now remembered chiefly for his imaginative epic trilogy, *The Lord of the Rings* (1954–55). Both his prose style and the world of fantasy he created are reminiscent of the Norse SAGAS and Anglo-Saxon poetry that he taught at Oxford University.

**Tolpuddle Martyrs** Name given to six British farm laborers in Dorset, S England, who were convicted of a crime for forming a trade union (1834). The government was worried by the growth of organized labor, but as unions were not illegal, the Dorset men were charged with taking a seditious oath. After a public outcry, they were pardoned in 1836.

**Tolstoy, Leo Nikolaievich, Count** (1828–1910) Russian novelist and philosopher. While serving in the army, he took part in the defense of Sebastopol during the CRIMEAN WAR (1853–56); his descriptions of this appeared in the journal *Contemporary* and were noted for their unvarnished picture of the conflict. Having left the army, he wrote his masterpieces *War and Peace* (1865–69) and *Anna Karenina* (1875–77). Tolstoy is regarded as one of the world's greatest novelists.

**Toltec** (Nuhuatl, master builder) Ancient Native American civilization, whose capital was Tollán (Tula), Mexico. The Toltec were the dominant people in the region from AD 900 to 1200. Their architecture is characterized by PYRAMID building. Although theirs was considered a polytheistic culture, images of QUETZALCÓATL predominate. In the 12th century the civilization was gradually supplanted by the AZTEC.

**toluene** (methylbenzene) Aromatic hydrocarbon ($C_6H_5CH_3$) derived from coal tar and petroleum. It is a colorless, flammable liquid widely used as an industrial solvent and in motor fuels. Toluene is used in the manufacture of TNT. Properties: sp.gr. 0.87; m.p. −138.1°F (−94.5°C); b.p. 231.3°F (110.7°C).

**tomato** Fruit plant native to the Americas. It was cultivated in Europe as early as 1544, but was not eaten until the 16th century because it was believed to be poisonous. Species *Lycopersicum esculentum*. The small cherry to-mato is a variety (*L.e. cerasiforme*). Family Solanaceae.

**tomography** Technique of X-RAY photography in which details of only a single slice or plane of body tissue are shown.

**tonality** Harmonic system that underpins most Western music from the 17th century to the 20th, using the twelve major and twelve minor scales. The notes of the scale, and their corresponding chords and harmonies, have their own hierarchy around the central KEY note.

**tone poem** (symphonic poem) Orchestral piece of the late-romantic period that describes in music a poem, story, or other extra-musical program. *Till Eulenspiegel* and *Also sprach Zarathustra* by Richard STRAUSS are perhaps the best-known examples of the genre. *See also* PROGRAM MUSIC

**Tonga** (Friendly Islands) South Pacific island kingdom, *c*.1,370mi (2,200km) NE of New Zealand. The archipelago

▲ **Tolstoy** Born into a noble family, as a young man Tolstoy lived a dissolute life in Moscow before joining the army. He did much of his most renowned work before 1879, when he underwent a spiritual crisis culminating in his conversion to a rationalist Christian doctrine. He insisted on living by his new religious principles and renounced his fortune to live as a poor peasant (although remaining in his family home).

▲ **tobacco** Tobacco is produced mainly from the plant *Nicotiana tabacum*, which is cultivated worldwide. The leaves are removed from the plant and dried. Native Americans smoked tobacco leaves and used them medicinally, long before the arrival of Europeans in the New World.

T

▲ **tortoise** The North American box tortoise (*Terrapene carolina*) spends most of its time on land. As with other tortoises, it has a massive bony shell made of plates of keratin that are fused to the backbone and ribs. It can pull back its head under the shell when danger threatens.

consists of nearly 170 islands in five administrative groups, only 36 of which are inhabited. They are mainly coral atolls, but the W group are volcanic, with some active craters. The largest island is Tongatapu, the seat of the capital, Nukualofa, and home to 66% of the population. The N islands were discovered by Europeans in 1616, and the rest by Abel Tasman in 1643. During the 19th century, British missionaries converted the indigenous population to Christianity. In 1900 Tonga became a British protectorate. In 1970 the country achieved independence. The economy is dominated by agriculture, the chief crops are yams, tapioca, and fish. Area: 289sq mi (748sq km). Pop. (1991) 103,000.

**tongue** Muscular organ usually rooted to the floor of the mouth. The tongue contains the TASTE buds and helps to move food around the mouth for chewing and swallowing; animals also use it for lapping fluids and for grooming. In humans the tongue is vital for the production of speech. *See also* SENSES

**Tonkin** (Tongking) Historical region of N Vietnam. It was ruled by the Chinese from 111 BC to AD 939, later becoming independent. In 1801 it was united with Annam, and became part of the French protectorate of Indochina in 1883. After World War II it was again occupied by the Chinese. They withdrew under French pressure, but France never fully re-established control.

**Tonkin Gulf Resolution** (1964) Resolution of the US Congress authorizing the president to take military action in Vietnam in response to attacks on US forces. It was passed at the urging of President Lyndon B. Johnson after US destroyers were allegedly attacked by North Vietnamese torpedo boats in the Gulf of Tonkin. *See also* Vietnam War

**tonsillitis** Acute or chronic inflammation of the tonsils caused by bacterial or viral infection. It is signaled by fever, sore throat, and difficulty in swallowing. Chronic tonsillitis is often treated by surgical removal of the TONSILS (tonsillectomy).

**tonsils** Two masses of LYMPH tissue located at the back of the throat. They have a pitted surface that easily becomes infected (TONSILLITIS).

**tools** In archeology, objects used by early people to assist them to shape their environment. The first tools were probably unshaped stones, sticks, or bones. The techniques used for sharpening flints, in particular, are used to distinguish early cultures. Metal was originally introduced for ornament, with native copper the first metal to be worked, *c.*6000 BC.

**tooth** *See* TEETH

**topaz** Transparent, glassy mineral, aluminum fluosilicate, $Al_2SiO_4(F,OH)_2$, found in pegmatites. Its crystals are orthorhombic system. Topaz is colorless, white, blue, or yellow; some crystals are of gem quality. Hardness 8; sp.gr. 3.5.

**tope** Small SHARK that lives in British waters. It has a gray-brown body and is often found in schools, or near the bottom where it feeds on small fish. Length: to 6.5ft (2m). Family Carcharinidae; species *Galeorhinus galeus*.

**Topeka** State capital of Kansas, on the Kansas River, 55mi (90km) W of Kansas City. It was founded in 1854 by settlers from New England and became state capital in 1861. Topeka is a major transportation center for cattle and wheat. The Menninger Clinic, world-famous for its treatment of mental illness, is located here. Industries: food processing, printing, rubber goods, steel products, footwear. Pop. (1992) 120,257.

► **toucan** The New World counterparts of the hornbills, there are some 35 species of toucans in the forest of tropical America. The large, bright bill of the Toco toucan (*Ramphastos toco*) is typical of the family and is used to reach fruit.

**topiary** Practice of trimming densely leaved evergreen shrubs and trees into decorative artificial shapes.

**topology** Branch of mathematics concerned with those properties of geometric figures that are unchanged after a continuous deformation process such as squeezing, stretching, or twisting. The number of boundaries of a surface is such a property. Any plane closed shape (i.e. any line that eventually comes back to its beginning, all on a single plane) is topologically equivalent to a circle; a cube, a solid cone, and a solid cylinder are topologically equivalent to a sphere.

**Torah** (Hebrew, law) Hebrew name for the Pentateuch, the first five books of the Old Testament. The Torah is the body of written Jewish laws contained within these five books. It also describes the complete Jewish Bible.

**tornado** Funnel-shaped, violently rotating storm extending downward from the cumulonimbus cloud in which it forms. At the ground its diameter may be only about 310ft (100m). Rotational wind speeds range from 100–300mph (160–480km/h). Tornadoes occur in deep low pressure areas, associated with FRONTS or other instabilities. They occur particularly in E US.

**Toronto** Capital of Ontario province and Canada's largest city, on the N shore of Lake Ontario. An inland port at the mouth of the Don River, it is Canada's main banking, financial, and manufacturing center. The site was first visited in 1615 by the French explorer Étienne Brulé. In 1787 the British bought the site from Native Americans and the settlement of York was founded in 1793. During the War of 1812 the city was twice captured by US troops. In 1834 it was renamed Toronto (meeting place) and it became the capital of Ontario province in 1867. Its development as a distribution center was spurred by the 1959 opening of the St. Lawrence Seaway. Toronto produces over half of all Canada's manufacturing products. Industries: electrical equipment, brewing, printing and publishing, iron and steel, meat packing, aircraft and motor vehicle manufacture. Pop. (1991) 635,395 (metropolitan area 3,893,046).

**torpedo** Self-propelled underwater missile used by submarines, small surface warships, and aircraft to destroy enemy vessels. Modern torpedoes may be launched by rocket boosters and often have internal electronic equipment for guiding the missile to the target.

**torpedo ray** *See* RAY

**torque** Turning effect of a force. An example is a TURBINE that produces a torque on its rotating shaft to turn a generator. The output of a rotary engine, such as the familiar four-stroke engine or an electric motor, is rated by the torque it can develop. The unit of measurement is Nm (newton meter).

**Torquemada, Tomás de** (1420–98) Spanish churchman and grand inquisitor. A Dominican priest and confessor to King Ferdinand V and Queen Isabella I, he was appointed head of the Spanish Inquisition (1483). He was noted for the severity of his judgments and the harshness of his punishments.

**Torricelli, Evangelista** (1608–47) Italian physicist. Assistant and secretary to Galileo, he is credited with the first manufactured VACUUM (the Torricellian vacuum) and the invention of the mercury BAROMETER (1643).

**tort** In law, wrongful act or omission that can give rise to a civil action at law, other than concerning breach of contract. The law of tort includes negligence, libel, slander, trespass, false imprisonment, and nuisance.

**Tortelier, Paul** (1914–90) French cellist and composer. His career as one of the world's leading solo cellists began in 1947. His son Yan Pascal Tortelier (b.1947) is a noted conductor.

**tortoise** Terrestrial or freshwater reptile of the order Chelonia. All tortoises are heavily armored and enclosed within a high, domed, bony, box-like structure called a carapace (commonly shell). When disturbed, tortoises pull their scaly legs, head, and tail into the shelter of the shell. They live in tropical and subtropical regions, and hibernate in temperate countries. They are slow movers, feed almost entirely on plants and live to a great age. Length: usually to 1ft (30cm). A giant species, up to 5ft (1.9m) long, lives in the Galápagos Islands.

**torture** Infliction of pain on a person to extract information, a confession, or to indulge sadistic inclinations. It has been practiced in many cultures. Until the 18th century in Europe, it was considered a legitimate means of extracting a legal confession to a crime. The 1949 Geneva Convention included a clause against torture, but the use of torture has continued. There has been increasing recognition of "psychological torture," in which disorientation, fear, and loss of sleep and self-respect are used instead of or as well as the application of physical pain.

**Tory Party** Alternative name for the British CONSERVATIVE PARTY. The name Tory, originally meaning an Irish bandit, was applied insultingly in the 1680s to those who did not oppose a Catholic monarchy. It became the name of the political party that represented the interests of landowners and the Anglican Church in the 18th century. The Tories opposed the WHIGS.

**Toscanini, Arturo** (1867–1957) Italian conductor who became music director at LA SCALA, Milan, in 1898. He conducted the New York Philharmonic Orchestra (1928–36) and founded the NBC Symphony Orchestra in New York in 1937. He instilled remarkable energy into his orchestras, and his interpretations were marked by intense emotionalism and musical subtlety.

**totalitarianism** Form of government in which the state tries to acquire total control of every aspect of social and individual activity or thought, by means of controlling the mass media, suppression of opposition, and the often violent use of the police or army. The term arose in the 1920s to describe Italian FASCISM and has since been applied to Nazi Germany, the Soviet Union under communism, and many other states.

**totemism** Complex collection of ideas held by certain primitive societies about the relationships between human beings and the animals or plants around them. The natural objects or people with which many tribal societies believe they have a kinship or mystical relationship are called totems. Members of a totem group are prohibited from marrying others of the same group and from killing or eating their totem. Elaborate, often secret, rituals form an important part of totemistic behavior.

**totem pole** Carved, painted, wooden column erected by the Native Americans of the Pacific Coast of the US and Canada. Carved with stylized representations of real and mythical animals and men, its function is closer to that of an heraldic crest than a religious symbol. They are usually erected as roof supports, as doorways, as symbols of greeting, or as mortuary poles or grave markers.

**toucan** Any of 35 species of colorful, gregarious birds of the forests of tropical America, characterized by a large, colorful bill. The plumage is generally red, yellow, blue, black, or orange. It feeds on fruit and berries, which may be regurgitated to feed the young. Length: 2ft (60cm). Family Ramphastidae.

**touch** One of the five SENSES, functioning by means of specialized nerve receptors in the skin.

**Toulon** Capital of Var department, on the Mediterranean coast, SE France. Toulon is France's leading naval base and its largest Mediterranean port after Marseilles. Originally known as Telo Martius, the city was a Roman naval base and an important port of embarkation for the Crusaders. In 1942 the French navy was scuttled here to prevent German capture. Industries: shipbuilding and naval repairs. Pop. (1990) 167,619.

**Toulouse** City on the Garonne River, S France, capital of Haute-Garonne department. Canals connect the city, the fourth-biggest in France, to both the Mediterranean Sea and the Atlantic Ocean. The capital of the Visigoths in the 5th century, it became part of the French crown lands in 1271. The city is the center of the country's aviation industry. Other industries: paper, textiles, chemicals, fertilizers, armaments. Pop. (1990) 358,688.

**Toulouse-Lautrec, Henri Marie Raymond de** (1864–1901) French painter and lithographer. He chose a career in painting after a childhood accident left his legs permanently deformed. In *c.*1888 he began to illustrate the theatres, cabarets, music halls, cafés, and brothels of the Montmartre district of Paris, such as the *Moulin Rouge* series (1894). He was profoundly influenced by DEGAS and drew inspiration from GAUGUIN and Japanese wood-block prints. His prints depict powerfully simplified forms, and their impact helped to establish the poster as a respected art form.

**Tour de France** Premier professional road cycling race in Europe. Raced over three weeks from the end of June, it travels over all types of terrain in a series of timed stages. It mostly circles France, but ventures into other countries, and ends in Paris.

▲ **Tower Bridge** Like other moveable bridges, Tower Bridge in London has two cantilevered arms, each weighing more than 1,100 tons. Despite their weight, they can be entirely raised in less than one minute. Famous throughout the world, it is one of the city's most popular tourist attractions. There is a museum dedicated to the Bridge in the top gallery.

**Tourette's syndrome** (Gilles de la Tourette's syndrome) Rare disorder of movement. It is a lifelong affliction that starts in childhood with tics and involuntary grimaces. Involuntary sounds also frequently occur. Its cause is unknown.

**tourmaline** Silicate mineral, sodium or calcium aluminum borosilicate, found in IGNEOUS and METAMORPHIC rocks. Its crystals are hexagonal system and glassy, either opaque or transparent. Some are prized as gems. Hardness 7.5; sp.gr. 3.1.

**Tours** City between the Loire and Cher rivers, W central France, capital of Indre-et-Loire department. It was the seat of the French government in 1870 during the siege of Paris. A large wine market, Tours has food processing, electronic, and pharmaceutical industries. Pop. (1990) 129,509.

**Toussaint L'Ouverture, Pierre Dominique** (1744–1803) Haitian revolutionary leader. He took part in the slave revolt in Haiti in 1790, joined the Spaniards when they attacked the French in 1793, but fought for the French (1794) when they promised to abolish slavery. He virtually controlled the whole island of HISPANIOLA by 1801. In 1802 Napoleon sought to restore French control. Toussaint was forced to surrender and died a prisoner in France. In 1804 Haiti achieved independence.

**Tower Bridge** Cantilever bridge over the Thames River in London, built (1886–1894) by Sir Horace Jones. The bridge has a pseudo-Gothic tower at each side of the river and a double-leaf mechanism that opens to provide a 250ft (76m) gap.

**Tower of London** English royal castle. It was begun by William the Conqueror in 1078 and was extended by later monarchs. It served various functions throughout the centuries, as residence, arsenal, prison, and museum.

**Townes, Charles Hard** (1915–95) US physicist who invented (1953) the first operational MASER. He shared the 1964 Nobel Prize for physics with Alexsandr Prokhorov and Nikolai Basov.

**Townshend, Charles, 2nd Viscount** (1674–1738) English politician, known as "Turnip Townshend." Robert WALPOLE's brother-in-law, he helped to arrange George I's accession to the throne in 1714 and, as Secretary for the Northern Department, suppressed the Jacobite rebellion of 1715. He was forced to resign in 1730, and devoted his retirement to agricultural improvements.

**Townshend Acts** (1767) Series of taxes levied on the American colonies by Britain's Parliament. Proposed by the chancellor of the exchequer, Charles Townshend, they were to provide revenue to defray the cost of colonial government. They taxed such imports as glass, paper, lead, tea, and paint. The adverse colonial reaction ("Taxation without representation is tyranny") caused the repeal (1770) of all duties except that on tea.

**toxicology** Study of poisonous substances and their effects on living things.

**toxic shock syndrome** Potentially fatal condition in which there is a dangerous drop in blood pressure and rapid onset of fever, diarrhea, vomiting, and muscular pains. It is

T

caused by SEPTICEMIA (blood poisoning) arising from toxins put out by bacteria that normally reside in the body without causing harm. The syndrome is most often seen in young women using tampons during menstruation.

**toxin** Poisonous substance produced by a living organism. The unpleasant symptoms of many bacterial diseases are due to the release of toxins into the body by the BACTERIA. Many MOLDS, some larger FUNGI, and seeds of some higher plants produce toxins. The venom of many snakes contain powerful toxins.

**toxoplasmosis** Disease caused by the protozoan *Toxoplasma gondii*, which is transmitted from animals to human beings. It produces symptoms that are mild and flu-like in adults, but it can damage the nervous system, eyes, and internal organs.

**trace elements** Chemical elements that are essential to life but normally obtainable from the diet only in small quantities. They are essential to the reactions of ENZYMES and HORMONES.

**tracer, radioactive** Radioactive substance introduced into the body so that its progress can be tracked by special diagnostic equipment. This technique may help in the diagnosis of conditions such as thyroid disease.

**trachea** (windpipe) Airway that extends from the LARYNX to about the middle of the STERNUM (breastbone). Reinforced with rings of CARTILAGE, it is lined with hairlike CILIA that prevent dirt and other substances from entering the lungs.

**tracheophyte** In certain classification systems, any VASCULAR PLANT of the phylum Tracheophyta. Within this phylum are: psilopsids (leafless, rootless primitive forms, such as whisk fern); sphenopsids (such as HORSETAIL); lycopsids (such as CLUB MOSS); pteropsids (such as FERN); GYMNOSPERMS; and ANGIOSPERMS.

**tracheotomy** (tracheostomy) Surgical procedure in which an incision is made through the skin into the TRACHEA to allow insertion of a tube to facilitate breathing. It is done either to bypass any disease or damage in the trachea or to safeguard the airway if a patient has to spend a long time on a mechanical ventilator.

**trachoma** Chronic eye infection caused by the microorganism *Chlamydia trachomatis*, characterized by inflammation of the cornea with the formation of pus. A disease of dry, tropical regions, it is the major cause of blindness in the developing world.

**track and field** General name for various athletic events, including competition in foot racing, jumping, hurdling, throwing, and vaulting. Generally, at a track and field meet, the field events (throwing and vaulting) are held within the infield area of an oval track. The field events include the running hop-step-and-jump, the broad jump, the pole vault, the shot put, the discus throw, the hammer throw, the javelin throw, and the high jump. The track events include running races from 60 yards (54.6m) to 10,000 meters, hurdle races from 120 yards (109.2m) to 440 yards (400m), relay races from 400 meters to 4 miles (6.4km), and walking races of 20,000 and 50,000 meters. A combination of track and field events includes the decathlon (10 events held over two days), heptathlon (seven events held over two days), and the pentathlon (five events in the same day). Scoring for team events is on a point basis. When two teams compete, the scoring is five points for first place, three points for second place, and one point for third place. With more than two teams, the points may range from 10 for first place to one for sixth place. **History** Track and field events were held at the original OLYMPIC GAMES in Greece in 776 BC. The competition was revived in England in the 12th century, and in 1864, Oxford defeated Cambridge in the first college meet. In the US, the first organized meet was held in 1876. The sport played a major role in the successful resumption of the Olympic Games at Athens in 1896.

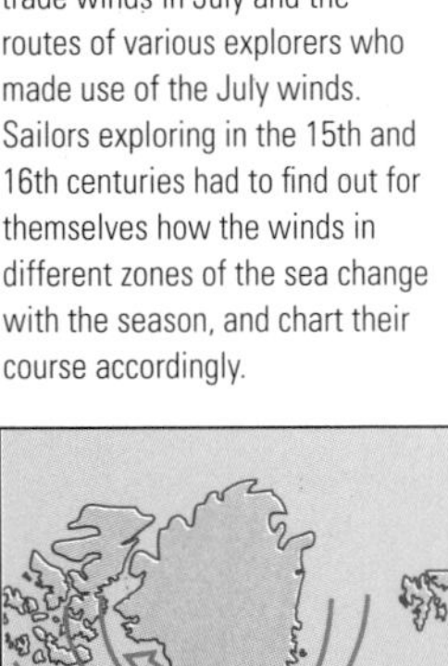

▼ **trade winds** The map shows the direction of the prevailing trade winds in July and the routes of various explorers who made use of the July winds. Sailors exploring in the 15th and 16th centuries had to find out for themselves how the winds in different zones of the sea change with the season, and chart their course accordingly.

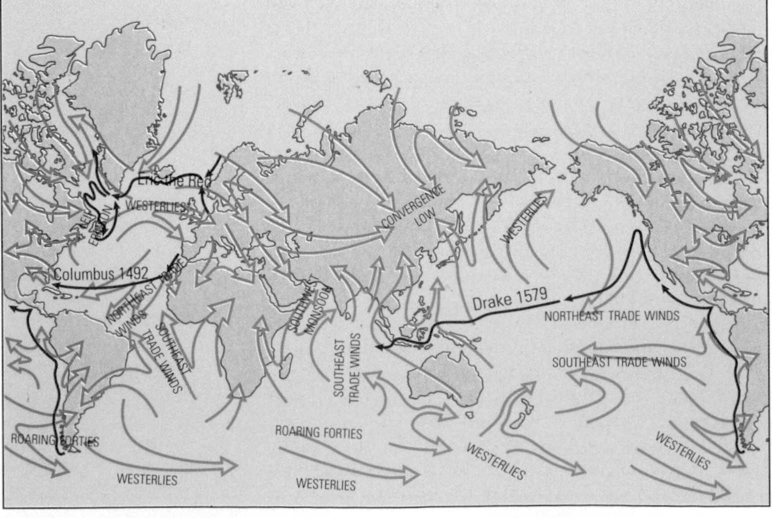


**Tractarianism** *See* OXFORD MOVEMENT

**tractor** Four-wheeled or tracked vehicle for moving and operating heavy implements, used mostly in farming and construction. The first tractors were built in the 1870s. Modern tractors have gasoline or diesel engines and can haul and power a wide range of implements, including hay balers, crop sprayers, and mowing machines.

**Tracy, Spencer** (1900–67) US film actor, renowned for his intelligent, sincere character portrayals. Following his debut in 1930, he became a leading Hollywood actor, appearing in nearly 80 films, of which nine, including *Adam's Rib* (1949), *Pat and Mike* (1957), and his last film, *Guess Who's Coming to Dinner* (1967), were with his on- and off-screen partner, Katharine HEPBURN. He won Academy Awards for *Captains Courageous* (1937) and *Boys Town* (1938).

**trademark** Distinguishing mark, such as a name, symbol, or word, attached to goods, which identifies them as made or sold by a particular manufacturer. A trademark must be registered at the patent office to establish an exclusive right to it.

**trade union** (labor union) Group of workers organized for the purpose of improving wages and conditions of work. The first trade unions were founded in Britain around the time of the INDUSTRIAL REVOLUTION. In the US, the labor unions and their members have generally accepted the capitalist system. The movement had become firmly established by 1886 with the founding of the American Federation of Labor. The AFL primarily represented skilled workers, and it was not until the creation of the CONGRESS OF INDUSTRIAL ORGANIZATIONS (CIO) in 1930 that unskilled labor gained some form of representation. The two organizations merged in 1955 to form the AMERICAN FEDERATION OF LABOR AND CONGRESS OF INDUSTRIAL ORGANIZATIONS (AFL-CIO).

**trade winds** Steady winds that blow westward toward the Equator from subtropical high pressure zones be-tween latitudes 30° and 40° N and S.

**Trafalgar, Battle of** (1805) British naval victory over the French and Spanish fleets off Cape Trafalgar, Spain. It ended NAPOLEON I's plans for an invasion of England. The victory was secured by the skillful tactics of the British commander, Lord NELSON, who was killed in the battle.

**tragedy** Form of drama in which a noble hero (the protagonist) meets a fate inherent in the drama's action. *Oedipus Rex* by SOPHOCLES is an early example, which was unmatched until the tragedies of Christopher MARLOWE. ARISTOTLE's *Poetics* systematized tragedy and introduced such ideas as *anagnorisis* (recognition) and *catharsis* (the purging of pity and terror in the spectator). *See also* AESCHYLUS; EURIPIDES; GREEK DRAMA

**Trail of Tears** Forced migration of Native Americans (1829–43) to new reservations W of the Mississippi and Missouri rivers. It involved bands of Shawnee, Dela-ware, Wyandot, Cherokee, Seminole, and others; thousands died en route from disease, lack of food, or abuse.

**Trajan** (53–117) Roman emperor (98–117), b. Spain. He distinguished himself as a general and administrator and was made junior co-emperor by Nerva in 97. With army support, he became emperor on Nerva's death. He conducted major campaigns in DACIA (101–102, 105–106) and against the people of PARTHIA (113–117), enlarging the Roman empire to its greatest extent.

**trampolining** Leisure pursuit and competitive sport in which acrobatic maneuvers are performed while bouncing on a canvas sheet stretched across a tightly sprung rigid frame.

**tranquilizer** Drug prescribed to reduce anxiety or tension and generally for its calming effect. Tranquilizers are used to control the symptoms of severe mental disturbance, such as schizophrenia or manic depression. They are also prescribed to relieve depression. Prolonged use of tranquilizers can produce a range of unwanted side effects.

**Transcaucasia** Former Soviet Republic, corresponding to the three constituent republics ARMENIA, AZERBAIJAN, and GEORGIA. Created in 1918 after the RUSSIAN REVOLUTION, it was re-formed in 1922 and granted full republic status in 1924. Georgia, Azerbaijan, and Armenia were reestablished as separate republics in 1936 and became independent nations on the break-up of the SOVIET UNION in 1990.

**transcendentalism** School of philosophy that traced its origin to the idealism of Immanuel KANT. It was concerned not with objects, but with our mode of knowing objects. It spread from Germany to England, where Samuel COLERIDGE and Thomas CARLYLE came under its influence. In the mid-19th century it spread to the US, where it was propagated by a literary circle based in Concord, Massachusetts. In general, it emphasized individual (as opposed to collective) moral and spiritual responsibilities and rejected materialism, returning to nature for spiritual guidance.

**transcendental meditation (TM)** Meditation technique based partly on Hindu practice and rediscovered in the 20th century by an Indian spiritual teacher, Guru Dev (d.1958). After his death, his pupil the Maharishi Mahesh Yogi introduced the technique to the West. Those who practice TM concentrate on and repeat a MANTRA over and over in order to become relaxed and achieve self-understanding. In physiological terms, TM decreases oxygen consumption and heart rate and increases skin resistance and alpha brain waves, yielding a relaxed mental state differing from sleep or hypnosis.

**transducer** Device for converting any nonelectrical signal, such as sound or light, into an electrical signal, and vice versa. Examples include MICROPHONES, LOUDSPEAKERS, and measuring instruments used in ACOUSTICS.

**transformer** Device for converting alternating current at one voltage to another voltage at the same frequency. It consists of two coils of wire coupled together magnetic-ally. The input current is fed to one coil (the primary), the output being taken from the other coil (the secondary).

**transform fault** Special class of strike-slip FAULT characteristic of mid-ocean ridges. Because of the transform faults, which are at right-angles to the ridge itself, the MID-ATLANTIC RIDGE does not run in a straight line.

**transfusion, blood** *See* BLOOD TRANSFUSION

**transhumance** Seasonal moving of livestock from one region to another. It occurs in societies living in zones with extensive climatic changes, such as in the mountainous terrain of the Arctic regions or the deserts of Central Africa.

**transistor** Electronic device made of SEMICONDUCTOR material that can amplify electrical signals. Transistors were first developed in 1948 by John BARDEEN, Walter BRATTAIN, and William SHOCKLEY, making possible many advances in technology, especially in computers, portable radios and televisions, satellites, industrial control systems, and navigation.

**transition elements** Metallic elements that have incomplete inner electron shells. They are characterized by variable valencies (combining power) and the formation of colored ions. *See also* PERIODIC TABLE

**translocation** In VASCULAR PLANTS, the movement of food materials in solution through the tissues from one part of the plant to another.

**transmigration of souls** Belief that the soul is reborn in one or more successive mortal bodies; a form of REINCARNATION. A tenet of Asian religions such as BUDDHISM, it was also accepted by the followers of PYTHAGORAS and Orphism in Greece during the 6th century BC. It is still common today in tribal religions such as that of the South African Venda.

**transpiration** In plants, the loss of moisture as water vapor from leaf surfaces or other plant parts. Most of the water entering plant roots is lost by transpiration. The process is speeded up in light, warm, and dry conditions. The flow of water from the roots to the STOMATA is called the transpiration stream.

**transplant** Surgical operation to introduce organ or tissue from one person (the donor) to another (the recipient); it may also refer to the transfer of tissues from one part of the body to another, as in grafting of skin or bone. Major transplants are performed to save the lives of patients facing death from end-stage organ disease. Organs routinely transplanted include the kidneys, heart, lungs, liver, and pancreas. Experimental work continues on some other procedures, including small bowel grafting. Many other tissues are commonly grafted, including heart valves, bone, and bone marrow. The oldest transplant procedure is corneal grafting, undertaken to restore the sight of one or both eyes. Most transplant material is acquired from dead people, although kidneys, part of the liver, bone marrow, and corneas may be taken from living donors.

**Transportation, US Department of** Cabinet-level department within the executive branch. The DOT was established in 1966 to administer transportation programs of the federal government. It also works to develop fast, safe, efficient, low-cost, and convenient transportation. DOT is directed by the secretary, who is a cabinet member and appointed by the president.

**transsexual** Person who permanently changes gender, or who desires to do so. It may be achieved partly through hormone treatment or through surgery, and in some countries the change can be accompanied by a legal change of status.

**Trans-Siberian Railroad** Russian railroad from Moscow to Vladivostok. The world's longest railroad, the major part, E from Chelyabinsk, was built in 1891–1905, giving Russia access to the Pacific via a link with the Chinese Eastern Railroad in Manchuria. The total length is *c*.5,750mi (9,000km).

**transubstantiation** Belief accepted by the Roman Catholic Church that, during the prayer of consecration at the MASS (the EUCHARIST), the "substance" of the bread and wine is changed into the "substance" of the body and blood of JESUS CHRIST, while the "accidents" (the outward forms of the bread and wine) remain unchanged. The doctrine was defined at the LATERAN COUNCIL of 1215. The definition involving "substance" and "accidents" was rejected by the architects of the REFORMATION.

**transuranic elements** (transuranium elements) Those elements with atomic numbers higher than that of URANIUM (92), the best known of which are members of the ACTINIDE SERIES (atomic numbers 89 to 103). All transuranic elements are radioactive. Only NEPTUNIUM and PLUTONIUM occur naturally in minute amounts but all can be synthesized. The only commercially important element in the group is plutonium, which is used in NUCLEAR WEAPONS and as a fuel for nuclear reactors.

**Transvaal** Former province of South Africa. In 1994–95 Transvaal was divided into NORTHERN PROVINCE, MPUMALANGA, GAUTENG, and NORTHWEST PROVINCE. The indigenous population are the Bantu-speaking Venda and Sotho peoples. In the 1836 GREAT TREK, the BOERS crossed the Vaal River to settle the region. In 1857 the South African Republic was formed. In 1877 the British annexed the republic. After a Boer revolt, the Transvaal was again granted internal self-government in 1881, under President Paul KRUGER. The 1886 discovery of gold in Witwatersrand attracted vast numbers of Britons and Germans, who were denied political rights. In 1902, following the SOUTH AFRICAN WARS, Transvaal became a British crown colony, and in 1910 it became a founding province in the Union of South Africa. In 1995 Transvaal ceased to exist as a political entity and was split into four of South Africa's nine new provinces.

**Transylvania** (Rom. Beyond the Forest) High plateau region in central and NW Romania, separated from the rest of Romania by the CARPATHIAN MOUNTAINS and the Transylvanian Alps. Its major cities are Cluj-Napoca, Brașov, and Sibiu. It was conquered by Hungary at the beginning of the 11th century, and occupied by the Turks in 1540. For the next 200 years it kept a semi-independent status as it played off the competing claims of Turkey and Austria. In 1765 it became an Austrian province. Hungarian supremacy was reestablished in 1867. After World War I, Hungary ceded the territory to Romania, which embarked on a whole-sale process of land redistribution and forced assimilation of other nationalities. Hungary annexed part of Transylvania in World War II, but was forced to return it in 1947. Transylvania is the legendary home of vampires.

T

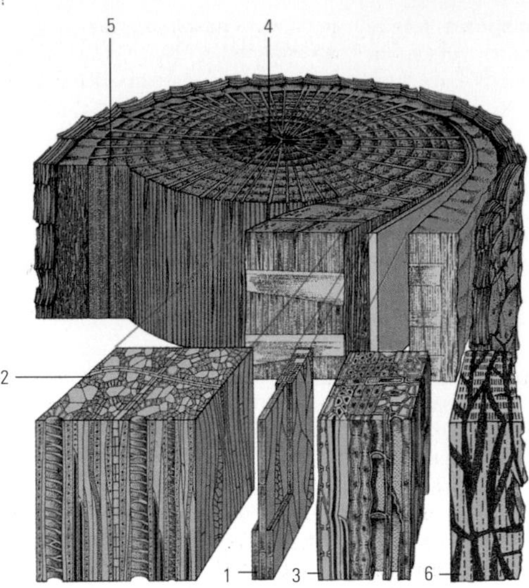


▶ **tree** Trees increase in girth by wings of new wood produced annually in temperate zones but less often in the tropics. The cambium (1) produces xylem (2) and phloem (3). They are alive but the heartwood (4) is dead. The medullary rays (5) allow the transport of food across the trunk. Bark (6) is a protective outer coating.

**Trappists** Popular name for the Cistercians of the Strict Observance, a religious order of monks and nuns that. originated in La Trappe Abbey, France, in 1664. They maintain complete silence and practice vegetarianism.

**trauma** Any injury or physical damage caused by some external event such as an accident or assault. In psychiatry, the term is applied to an emotional shock or harrowing experience.

**treason** Any act that intends to overthrow the recognized government or harm the head of state. Treason is an extremely serious criminal offense and is punishable by death in many countries. In the US, treason is defined by article 3 of the Constitution as levying war against the government or giving assistance to the enemy.

**treasury** Government department in most countries that is responsible for national finance and monetary policy.

**Treasury, US Department of the** US federal government department. It is composed of many bureaus and divisions that have four basic functions: formulating and recommending financial, tax, and fiscal policies; serving as financial agent for the government; enforcing financial and tax law; and manufacturing coins and currency. The department is directed by the secretary, who is a cabinet member and a major adviser to the president concerning domestic and international financial policy and tax policy. The department was established in 1789.

**tree** Woody, Perennial plant with one main stem or trunk and smaller branches. The trunk increases in dia-meter each year; the leaves are evergreen or Deciduous. The largest trees, Sequoias, can grow to more than 420ft (110m); the bristlecone pine can live for over 5,000 years.

**tree creeper** Brownish, agile bird that scurries up and down trees in cooler areas of the Northern Hemisphere. It uses its long, slightly down-curved bill to probe for insects under the bark. Length: 5in (13cm). Species *Certhia familiaris.*

**tree fern** Tree-like Fern of the family Cyatheaceae. Tree ferns grow in tropical and subtropical regions, particularly moist, mountainous areas. Height: 10–80ft (3–25m). There are 600 species. Phylum Filicinophyta; genus *Cyathea.*

**trefoil** Any of numerous plants, such as Clover, with leaves divided into three parts. Bird's-foot trefoil (*Lotus corniculatus*) is a perennial, used as forage. Family Fabaceae/Leguminosae.

**Trent, Council of** (1545–63) 19th ecumenical council of the Roman Catholic Church, which provided the main impetus of the Counter-Reformation in Europe. It met at Trent, N Italy, in three sessions under three popes (Paul III, Julius III, Pius IV). It clarified Catholic doctrine and refused concessions to the Protestants, while instituting reform of many of the abuses that had provoked the Reformation.

**Trent Affair** (1861) Diplomatic incident between the UK and the US during the Civil War. Union officers seized two Confederate commissioners from the British ship *Trent.* Britain claimed its neutrality had been violated. President Lincoln, wishing to avoid war with Britain, released the men.

**Trenton** State capital of New Jersey, on the Delaware River. It was settled by English Quakers in the 1670s. A city monument commemorates the 1776 battle in which George Washington crossed the frozen Delaware River to defeat Hessian troops during the American Revolution. Industries: ceramics, motor vehicle components, plastics, metal products, rubber goods, steel cables, textiles. Pop. (1992) 87,807.

**Trevithick, Richard** (1771–1833) British engineer and designer of steam engines. In 1801 he built a steam-powered road vehicle. In 1802 he patented a high-pressure steam engine, his most important invention. He built the first steam railroad Locomotive in 1803. In 1816 he went to Peru to install his steam engines in mines.

**triad** Chinese secret society. It existed in S China from the earliest days of the Qing empire in the 17th century until the 19th century, when the triads lent their support to the Taiping Rebellion. Today it is said to control Chinese organized crime throughout the world, with its chief center in Hong Kong.

**trial** In law, judicial examination or hearing of the facts and passing of sentence in a civil or criminal case. A Jury is usually present, though not always.

**trial by jury** Trial by a number of people (usually 12), who are sworn to deliver a verdict in a court of law on the evidence presented. As a method of trial, it developed from an Anglo-Saxon judicial custom. It is now the main method of trying criminal and some civil cases at common law in the Western world. *See also* Jury

**Triangle Trade** System of trade between American colonies, the West Indies, and African ports. The trade, partly in evasion of British laws, dealt in molasses, rum, and slaves. Imported molasses was made into rum in the colonies; rum was traded for slaves in Africa; slaves were traded for molasses in the West Indies.

**Triassic** First period of the Mesozoic era, lasting from 248 to 13 million years ago. Many new kinds of animals developed. On land, the first Dinosaurs roamed. Mammal-like reptiles were common, and by the end of the period the first true Mammals existed. In the seas lived the first ichthyosaurs, placodonts, and nothosaurs. The first frogs, turtles, crocodilians, and lizards also appeared. Plant life consisted mainly of primitive gymnosperms.

**tribune** Official of ancient Rome. Of the various kinds of tribune, some had military functions, some political. The tribunes of the Plebeians, generally ten in number and elected annually, gained an important role under the Republic. In the 2nd century BC, the Gracchi brothers used the office of tribune to pursue radical social reforms. *See also* Gracchus

**triceratops** Large, horned, ornithischian Dinosaur of the late Cretaceous period of W North America. The 8-ft (2.4-m) skull carried two 40-in (102-cm) horns above its eyes and a smaller horn at tip of its snout. Length: 20–25ft (6.1–7.6m); height: 8ft (2.4m); weight: 10 tons.

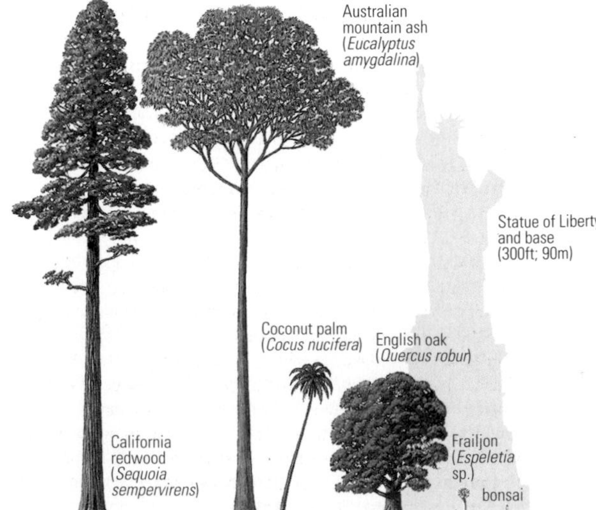


▶ **tree** Trees grow taller than any other living thing but can still survive in miniature form. If the roots are restricted either artificially, as in bonsai perfected in Japan, or by natural means, as when a seed germinates in very thin soil on a mountain, a fully formed tree only a few centimeters high will result. The California redwood, the tallest tree, is closely rivaled by a eucalyptus, such as the mountain ash of Australia. The coconut palm reaches its height of 90ft (27m) in a few short years. The English oak is one of 450 species of oak that grow as trees, bushes, and shrubs. It enlarges slowly – about 15ft (4.5m) – in ten years, but produces wood of prodigious strength. Espeletia grows on snowy ledges over 1,300ft (400m) up in the Sierra Nevada.

**Trieste** City on the Gulf of Trieste, at the head of the Adriatic Sea, NE Italy. It was an imperial free port from 1719 to 1891, becoming an Austrian crown land in 1867. It was ceded to Italy in 1919, occupied by Yugoslavia in 1945, but returned to Italy in 1954. It is an important industrial and commercial center with large shipyards. Industries: steel, textiles, petroleum. Pop. (1992) 228,398.

**triggerfish** Any of several tropical marine fish found in warm shallow Pacific waters, identified by a dorsal fin spine that can be erected to lodge the fish in a coral cavity, as a protection against predators. Length: to 24in (60cm). Family Balistidae; typical genus *Balistoides*.

**triglyceride** *See* LIPID

**trigonometric function** Six ratios of the sides of a right-angled triangle containing a given acute angle. They are the SINE, COSINE, TANGENT, COTANGENT, SECANT, and COSECANT of the angle. These functions can be extended to cover angles of any size by the use of a system of rectangular coordinates.

**trigonometry** Use of ratios of the sides of a right-angled triangle to calculate lengths and angles in geometrical figures. If three sides, or two sides and the included angle, or one side and two angles of a triangle are known, then all the other sides and angles may be found.

**trilobite** Any of an extinct group of ARTHROPODS found as fossils in marine deposits, ranging in age from CAMBRIAN through PERMIAN times. The body was mostly oval, tapering toward the rear and was covered by a chitinous skeleton. Transverse divisions show segmentation and bear pairs of jointed limbs. Most species were bottom-crawling, shallow-water forms and ranged in size from 0.25in (6mm) to 30in (75cm).

**Trinidad and Tobago** Republic composed of the two southernmost islands of the Lesser ANTILLES, in the SE Caribbean; the capital is PORT OF SPAIN on Trinidad. The larger island of **Trinidad** lies only 7mi (11km) off the Venezuelan coast. It is mainly low plains with coastal mangrove swamps. In SW Trinidad lies Pitch Lake, the world's largest natural source of asphalt. The Spanish colonized the island in the 16th century, but it was ceded to Britain in 1802. **Tobago** lies 19mi (30km) NE of Trinidad. The island, dominated by a mountain ridge, is heavily forested. Scarborough is the principal town. Tobago was initially settled by the British in 1616. After Spanish, Dutch, and French rule, in 1803 it became a British possession. Trinidad and Tobago were integrated into a single crown colony in 1883, becoming an independent state in 1962 and a republic in 1976. In 1990 the prime minister, Arthur Robinson, was captured and later released in an attempted coup. After 1995 elections, a coalition government of the United National Congress and the Alliance for Reconstruction came to power, with Basdeo Panday as prime minister. The economy is dominated by oil and gas production, asphalt, and tourism. Area: 1,980sq mi (5,128sq km). Pop. (1990) 1,169,600.

**Trinity** Central doctrine of Christianity, according to which God is three persons: the Father, the Son, and the HOLY SPIRIT or Holy Ghost. There is only one God, but he exists as "three in one and one in three." The nature of the Trinity is held to be a mystery that cannot be fully comprehended. The doctrine of the Trinity was stated in early Christian creeds to counter heresies such as GNOSTICISM. *See also* APOSTLES' CREED; ATHANASIAN CREED; JESUS CHRIST; NICENE CREED

**Triple Alliance** Name given to several international alliances involving three states. They included the anti-French alliance of Britain, the Netherlands, and Sweden of 1668, and the alliance of Britain, France, and the Netherlands of 1717, directed against Spanish ambitions in Italy. The most recent was the Triple Alliance of 1882, when Italy joined the Dual Alliance of Austria-Hungary and Germany. In South America, Argentina, Brazil, and Uruguay formed a triple alliance in the war against Paraguay (1865–70).

**Triple Entente** Name given to the alliance of Britain, France, and Russia before World War I. It developed from the Franco-Russian Alliance (1894), a counterbalance to the threat posed by the TRIPLE ALLIANCE of Germany, Austria, and Italy. Britain became allied with France in the ENTENTE CORDIALE (1904), and the Anglo-Russian Convention of 1907 completed the Triple Entente.

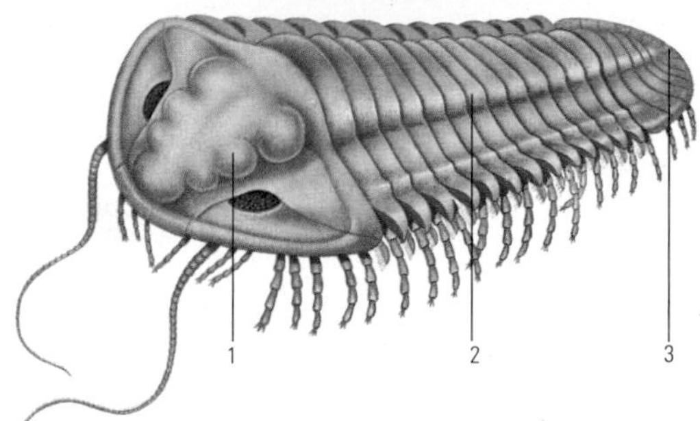


◄ **trilobite** The trilobite looked rather like today's woodlouse, being covered by a chitinous skeleton. This was divided into (1) the cephalon or headshield, which carried sensory organs and the glabella, a bump that housed the stomach; (2) the thorax, a region of articulated segments below each of which was a pair of legs; and (3) the pygidium or tail shield. Each limb consisted of a jointed organ for walking, a swimming and breathing organ, and a paddle that swept food particles toward the mouth.

**triple jump** In track and field, similar to the LONG JUMP with the exception that from the takeoff line a contestant takes two extended leaps on alternate legs to launch into the final jump.

**Tripoli** Capital and chief port of LIBYA, on the Mediterranean Sea. The city was founded in the 7th century BC by the Phoenicians and developed by the Romans. From the 7th century AD the Arabs developed Tripoli as a market center for the trans-Saharan caravans. In 1551 it was captured by the Ottoman Turks. It was made the capital of the Italian colony of Libya in 1911, and during World War II it functioned as an important base for Axis forces, before capture by the British in 1943. In 1986 Tripoli was bombed by the US Air Force in retaliation for Libya's support of terrorism. The city is the commercial, industrial, transport, and communications center of Libya. The oases comprise the most fertile agricultural area in N Africa. Pop. (1984) 990,697.

**Tripoli** Mediterranean port and second-largest city in LEBANON. It was an important city of the Seleucid and Roman empires. Captured in AD 638 by the Arabs, in 1109 Tripoli was conquered by the Crusaders, who developed the city's fortifications. In 1289 it returned to Islamic rule under the Egyptian MAMELUKES. The Turks held the city until the arrival of the British in 1918, and in 1920 it became a Lebanese city. It suffered severe damage during the 1975–76 Lebanese civil war. The city remains an important center for trade between Syria and Lebanon, and is the terminus of the oil pipeline from Iraq. Industries: oil refining, textiles, food processing. Pop. (1991) 203,000.

**Tripolitan War** (1801–05) Conflict between Tripoli and the US. For several years Tripoli and other Barbary states on the N coast of Africa had interfered with US commerce in the Mediterranean, capturing ships and demanding tribute. In 1801 Tripoli declared war on the US. After several land and sea battles, Tripoli agreed to leave US ships alone and the US ransomed all prisoners.

**triptych** Painting or carving consisting of three panels, traditionally used as an altarpiece. The panels may form one picture, or the outer panels may be separate and subordinate to the central picture.

**Tristan** (Tristram) Hero of many medieval romances, most commonly as a knight of the Round Table in the Arthurian legends. His fatal love for the Irish princess Isolde (or Iseult) is the subject of Richard Wagner's opera *Tristan and Isolde*.

**Tristan da Cunha** Group of four islands in the S Atlantic Ocean, located midway between S Africa and South America. The group was discovered in 1506 by the Portuguese and annexed by Britain in 1816. In 1961 Tristan, the only inhabitable island, suffered a volcanic eruption that caused a temporary evacuation. A British dependency, it is administered from ST. HELENA. Area of Tristan: 38sq mi (98sq km). Pop. (1988) 313, all of whom live in the settlement of Edinburgh.

**Triton** In Greek mythology, a sea god, son of Poseidon and Amphitrite. Half man, half fish, he had a scaled body, sharp teeth and claws, and a forked fish tail. He had power over the waves and possessed the gift of prophecy.

**triumphal arch** Massive masonry structure, containing one, two, or three arches covered with a flat, oblong attic. Triumphal arches were originally built by the Romans to commemorate specific victories, and in Imperial times only emperors could pass through them. They were decorated with bronze statuary and carved [illegible] the victories. *See also* ARC DE TRIOMPHE

T

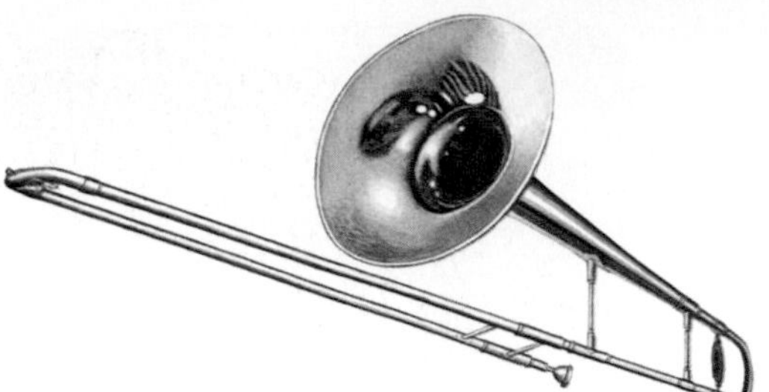

► **trombone** The modern trombone developed from the sackbut, which was well established by the 16th century. It quickly became associated with sacred and operatic music, soon becoming a standard member of the orchestra. It is also used in military and brass bands, and in jazz, where its glissando effect is often utilized.

**Trivandrum** (Triruvananthapuram) Seaport and resort city on the Malabar Coast, SW India, the largest city and capital of Kerala state. It served as capital of Travancore kingdom from 1745 and has an 18th-century fort, housing palaces and fine Hindu temples. Industries: tires, tiles, plywood, titanium products, textiles, soap, wood, and ivory products. Pop. (1991) 524,000.

**trogon** Brilliantly colored bird of dark tropical forests in America, Africa, and Asia. Trogons nest in holes in trees and feed on fruit and some insect larvae. Length: about 12in (30cm). Family Trogonidae; typical genus *Trogon*.

**Trojan horse** *See* TROJAN WAR.

**Trojan War** War between the Greeks and Trojans, lasting 10 years. Paris, son of King Priam of Troy, kidnapped Helen, wife of King Menelaus of Sparta. When the Trojans refused to return her, the Greeks formed an army. After nine years of fighting the Greeks pretended to sail for home, leaving behind a large, hollow, wooden horse in which they concealed warriors. Sinon persuaded the Trojans to bring the horse within the city walls, despite the warnings of Cassandra and Laocoön. That night the Greeks returned, the concealed warriors opened the city gates, and they destroyed the city. Homer wrote about the events of the war in his epic, the *Iliad*. Evidence from excavations carried out at Troy leads historians to believe that the legend reflects a real war (*c*.1200 BC) between the Greeks and the people of Troas, possibly over the control of the Dardanelles and Black Sea trade.

**Trollope, Anthony** (1815–82) British novelist. Most of his career was in the service of the Post Office. His large body of fiction, published from 1847, is often seen as epitomizing Victorian society. Best known among his enduringly popular novels are the Barsetshire chronicles, including *The Warden* (1855), *Barchester Towers* (1857), and *Doctor Thorne* (1858), and his novels of the Palliser family, including *Can You Forgive Her?* (1864–65) and *The Way We Live Now* (1874–75). His modest and workmanlike approach to his craft is documented in his posthumously published *Autobiography* (1883)

**trombone** BRASS musical instrument with a cylindrical bore, cupped mouthpiece, and flaring bell. It is usually played with a slide, except for a variant which has three or four valves. The tenor and bass trombones have a range of three and a half octaves.

**Trondheim** City on the S shore of Trondheim fjord, central Norway, the third-largest city in Norway. Founded as Nidaros in 997, the city was the political and religious capital of medieval Norway. Until 1906 the kings of Norway were crowned in the much-restored 12th-century cathedral. The city exports wood and metal products, and has fish canning, brewing, food processing, electronics, shipbuilding, clothing, soap, and hardware industries. Pop. (1990) 137,846.

**tropical diseases** Strictly speaking, all diseases predominantly associated with tropical climates. Major ones are MALARIA, KALA-AZAR, trypanosomiasis (SLEEPING SICKNESS), lymphatic FILARIASIS, and SCHISTOSOMIASIS (bilharzia). The infectious agents of tropical diseases include viruses, bacteria, protozoa, fungi, and worms of various kinds. Many of these disease microbes are spread by insect vectors, such as mosquitoes.

**tropics** *See* CANCER, TROPIC OF; CAPRICORN, TROPIC OF

**tropism** (tropic response) Response in growth and orientation of a plant or a part of it in relation to a directional, external stimulus, such as light or water.

**Trotsky, Leon** (1879–1940) (Lev Davidovich Bronstein) Russian revolutionary leader and theoretician. A Marxist revolutionary from 1897, he headed the workers' soviet in St. Petersburg in the RUSSIAN REVOLUTION OF 1905. Arrested, he escaped abroad and embarked on the work that made him, with LENIN, the leading architect of the RUSSIAN REVOLUTION. Trotsky returned to Russia after the March revolution (1917), and joined the BOLSHEVIKS. As chairman of the Petrograd (St. Petersburg) soviet, he set up the Military Revolutionary Committee to seize power, ostensibly for the Soviet, actually for the Bolsheviks. After the Bolshevik success, he negotiated the peace of BREST-LITOVSK, withdrawing Russia from World War I. As commissar of war (1918–25), he created the Red Army, which won the civil war and made the Bolshevik revolution safe. He criticized the growth of bureaucracy in the party, the lack of democracy, and failure to expand industrialization. He disapproved of Lenin's dictatorial tendencies in power. He fiercely objected to Stalin's adoption of a policy of "socialism in one country," rather than the world revolution in which Trotsky believed. He was driven from power, from the party, and eventually from the country. In exile he continued to write prolifically on many subjects. His ideas, though rejected in the Soviet Union, were extremely influential internationally, especially in Third World countries. In 1936 he settled in Mexico, where he was assassinated by a Stalinist agent.

**troubadour** Poet in the S of France from the 11th to the 14th century who wrote about love and chivalry. Troubadours' poems were sung by wandering minstrels called jongleurs. They wrote in the Provençal tongue, the *langue d'oc,* and much of their work, which was highly influential in the development of European lyric poetry, survives in songbooks.

**trough** In meteorology, area of low atmospheric pressure, usually an extension to a DEPRESSION. The opposite are ridges of high pressure.

**trout** Freshwater sport fish of North America and Europe. Also a good food fish, it is commonly propagated in hatcheries. Trout move upstream to spawn. Those that migrate to ocean between spawnings are called steelheads. Length: to 40.5in (103cm); weight: 37lb (17kg). Types include: the high mountain golden *Salvelinus aquakonita* of W North America, marked by vertical side bars; rainbow trout *Salmo gairdneri* marked by a longitudinal red stripe; brook trout, or char, *Salvelinus fontinalis* of E North America; large European brown trout *Salmo trutta*; and cutthroat *Salmo clarki* of W North America. Family Salmonidae.

**Troy** (Ilium) Ancient city at what is now Hissarlik, Turkey, familiar chiefly through HOMER's *Iliad*. Archeological excavation, begun by Heinrich SCHLIEMANN in the 1870s, suggests that the legend of the TROJAN WAR may be based on an actual episode. Nine cities have been detected in the archeological strata, dating from *c*.3000 BC and reaching a peak in Troy VI (*c*.1800–1300 BC). Troy VI was ruined by an earthquake. Its successor, Troy VIIA, was destroyed, apparently by enemy attack, in *c*.1200 BC, close to the legendary date of the fall of Troy.

**Troyes, Chrétien de** (active 1170) French poet, the author of the earliest extant Arthurian romances. Troyes' work includes translations of OVID and the romances *Erec* (after 1155), *Cligès* (*c*.1176), and the unfinished *Perceval (Le Conte du Graal)*, which contains the earliest known reference to the legend of the Holy Grail.

**Trudeau, Pierre Elliott** (1919– ) Canadian prime minister (1968–79, 1980–84). He was minister of justice before succeeding Lester PEARSON as prime minister. He promoted the economic and diplomatic independence of Canada, reducing US influence. Aided by his French-Canadian origins, he resisted QUEBEC separatism, imposing martial law to combat separatist terrorism in 1970. Defeated in the elections of 1979, he returned to power in 1980. Autonomy for Quebec was rejected in a referendum (1980), and Trudeau succeeded in winning agreement for a revised constitution (1981).

**Truffaut, François** (1932–84) French film director. His first feature film was *The 400 Blows* (1959). Other films include *Shoot the Pianist* (1960), *Jules and Jim* (1961), and *Pocket Money* (1976). Truffaut won an Academy Award for Best Foreign Language Film for *Day for Night* (1973). Deeply influenced by Alfred HITCHCOCK and Jean RENOIR, and a leading member of the NOUVELLE VAGUE, Truffaut scripted or coscripted all of his films.

**truffle** Any of several species of ascomycete FUNGI that grow underground, mostly among tree roots. Most are edible and are highly prized delicacies. Found in Europe, particularly France, and in parts of the US, they are hunted with trained pigs and dogs that can scent them out. Family Tuberaceae.

**Truman, Harry S.** (1884–1972) 33rd US President (1945–53). From a farming and small-business background in Missouri, he entered politics in the 1920s and won election to the Senate in 1934. In 1944 he was Franklin ROOSEVELT's running mate. Truman became president on Roosevelt's death, and was faced with many difficulties abroad. He approved the use of the atom bomb to force Japanese surrender (1945), ending WORLD WAR II, and adopted a robust policy toward the Soviet Union during the COLD WAR. Truman approved the MARSHALL PLAN (1947) and the creation (1949) of the NORTH ATLANTIC TREATY ORGANIZATION (NATO). Lacking Roosevelt's charisma, he was expected to lose the election of 1948, but won narrowly. In the KOREAN WAR, he was forced to dismiss the US commander, General MACARTHUR. In 1952 Truman declined renomination. He was succeeded by Dwight D. EISENHOWER.

**Truman Doctrine** Principle of US foreign policy under President TRUMAN. It promised support for any democratic country threatened by foreign domination. In practice, application of the principle was limited. The US did not act against communist takeovers in Eastern Europe, although it did resist the invasion of South Korea.

**trumpet** BRASS instrument of ancient origin. It has a cylindrical bore in the shape of a flattened loop and three piston valves. It became an important ceremonial instrument in the 15th century and by the late 17th century had become standard in the orchestra.

**trunkfish** (boxfish) Marine fish that lives in temperate and tropical waters. Its body is almost triangular when seen from the front, with a broad flat ventral region tapering to a narrow dorsal region. Length: to 20in (50cm). Family Ostraciontidae; genus *Lactophrys*.

**trust** In law, situation in which one person (the trustee) holds property for the benefit of another (the bene-ficiary). Trusts are generally created by a legal instrument such as a deed or a WILL.

**Truth, Sojourner** (1797–1883) US abolitionist. Born a slave in New York State, and unable to read or write, she was freed by the New York Emancipation Act (1827). Inspired by a religious calling, she became a leading propagandist for votes for women and abolition of SLAVERY.

**truth** State or condition of being true. A truth is something deemed to be genuine, an accurate representation of reality, or a statement that accords with proven, provable, or observable facts. Defining the distinction between truth and falsity has long been a major preoccupation of philosophers and logicians. Two famous theories for determining the meaning of truth are the **correspondence** theory, which defines it as "that which corresponds with facts," and the **coherence** theory, which defines it as "that which conforms with what we have come to accept." Other theories, espoused by pragmatists, take a utilitarian view of truth, defining it as "that which it is good, useful, or helpful to believe." This evaluative concept is also important in LOGIC, where either of two truth-values can be assigned to a statement, describing it as either true or false. *See also* EPISTEMOLOGY; ONTOLOGY; PRAGMATISM

**trypsin** Digestive enzyme secreted by the pancreas. It is secreted in an inactive form that is converted into active trypsin by an enzyme in the small intestine. It breaks down peptide bonds on the amino acids lysine and arginine. *See also* ALIMENTARY CANAL; DIGESTIVE SYSTEM

**tsetse fly** Any of several species of blood-sucking flies that live in Africa. Larger than a housefly, it has a gray thorax and a yellow to brown abdomen. Females transmit a cattle disease. Almost 80% of flies that bite humans are males, which carry SLEEPING SICKNESS. Length: to 0.6in (16mm). Order Diptera; family Muscidae; genus *Glossina*.

**Tsimshian** Native American tribe resident in coastal NW British Columbia, Canada, and SE Alaska. Some groups retain elements of animist totemic religion, but the original matrilineal social organization has all but disappeared. *See also* TOTEMISM

▲ **trout** The brown trout (*Salmo trutta fario*) is found throughout Asia Minor, Europe, and Iceland. Brown trout show great variety in shape, color, and markings and these are dictated by the nature and quality of the water and not, as in some flatfish and Perciformes, in response to visual stimuli.

**Tsiolkovsky, Konstantin Eduardovich** (1857–1935) Russian scientist who provided the theoretical basis for space travel. In 1898 he became the first person to stress the importance of liquid propellants in ROCKETS. He also proposed the idea of using multistage rockets to overcome GRAVITATION.

**tsunami** (seismic sea wave) Ocean wave caused by a submarine EARTHQUAKE, subsidence, or volcanic eruption. Erroneously termed a tidal wave, tsunamis spread radially from their source in ever-widening circles. Tsunamis can travel across oceans at speeds up to 250mph (400km/h) and reach heights of 33ft (10m). The eruption of KRAKATOA (1883) caused a tsunami that drowned over 30,000 people in Java and Sumatra.

**Tuareg** Fiercely independent BERBERS of Islamic faith, who inhabit the desert regions of N Africa. Their matrilineal, feudal society is based on nomadic pastoralism; it traditionally maintained a class of black, non-Tuareg servants. Tuareg males wear blue veils, while the women are unveiled. About half the population is no longer nomadic, and there have been demands for the Tuareg to have thier own homeland.

**tuatara** Nocturnal, lizard-like reptile of New Zealand; remarkable for being active at quite low temperatures and for being the sole surviving member of the primitive order Rhynchocephalia. It is brownish in color and has an exceptionally well-developed PINEAL BODY on its head. Length: to 2.3ft (70cm). Species *Sphenodon punctatus*.

**tuber** In plants, the short, swollen, sometimes edible underground stem, modified for the storage of food, as in the potato, or as a swollen root (for example dahlia). They enable the plant to survive an adverse season (winter or dry season), providing food for the later development of new shoots and roots.

**tuberculosis** (TB) Infectious disease caused by the bacillus *Mycobacterium tuberculosis*. It most often affects the lungs (pulmonary tuberculosis), but may involve the bones, joints, skin, lymph nodes, intestines, and kidneys. One-third of the world's population is infected, and up to 5% of those infected eventually develop TB. Poor urban living conditions mean that the disease is making a comeback in areas such as the US and Europe, where previously it had been in decline. The BCG vaccine against tuberculosis was developed in the 1920s and the first effective treatment drug, streptomycin, became available in 1944. However, the bacillus is showing increasing resistance to drugs and some strains are multi-resistant.

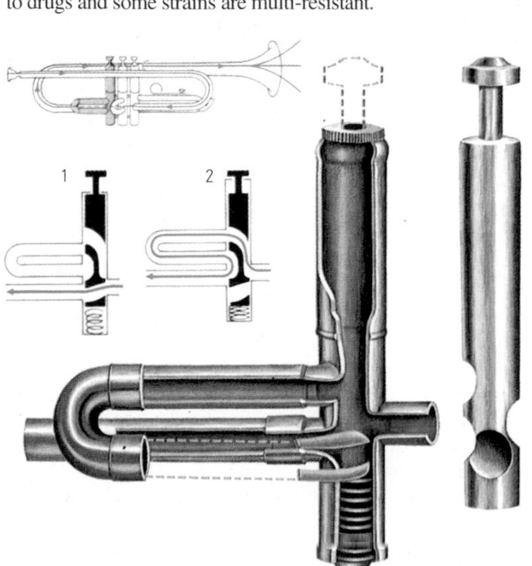


◀ **trumpet** A modern trumpet is fitted with three valves, which lower the pitch of the instrument by increasing its length; this is done by means of "crooks," which are brought into play when the valves are depressed. Valve no.1, nearest the mouthpiece, lowers the pitch by two semitones; the middle valve, no.2, lowers it by one semitone; and the furthest valve, no.3, by three semitones. A raised valve lets the air pass directly through (1); when the valve is depressed the air flows through the crook (2).

**TURBOCHARGER**

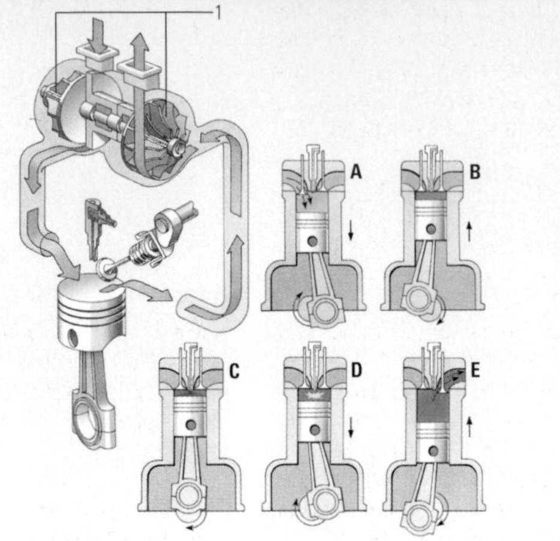

The diesel turbocharger uses the energy of the exhaust gases to force air into the cylinder via linked impellers (1). First air is sucked into the engine (A). The air is compressed into a space 22 times smaller (B). The compression heats the air. Diesel fuel is then injected in a swirling manner to maximize mixing, accentuated by the shape of the piston head (C). Combustion occurs spontaneously, without the need of a spark plug, pushing the piston down (D). The rotation of the crankshaft pushes the piston up, expelling the waste gases (E).

**Tubman, Harriet** (1820–1913) US abolitionist. Born a slave, she escaped to the North by following the UNDERGROUND RAILROAD. She then led *c.*300 fugitive slaves, including her parents, to freedom during the 1850s and became a prominent spokesperson for abolition.

**Tubman, William Vacanarat Shadrach** (1895–1971) President of Liberia (1944–71). A descendant of US freed slaves who settled the country during the 19th century, he was elected in 1944 and ruled unchallenged until his death. He preserved Liberia's close connections with the US, maintained prosperity, and showed consideration for the customs of the non-Westernized people of the interior.

**Tucana** (Toucan) Far southern constellation representing a toucan. Its overall faintness is redeemed by the presence of the small MAGELLANIC CLOUD and a superb globular cluster. It lies 15,000 light-years away.

**Tucson** City on the Santa Cruz River, S Arizona. The presidio fort of Tucson was built by the Spanish in 1776 and the city was state capital from 1867 to 1877. Today it is better known as a foothills resort with a dry, sunny climate. It services traditional economic activities including shipping cotton and cattle, textiles, meat-packing, and copper smelting, but its industries are increasingly high-tech, notably aircraft parts, electronics, and optical instruments. Pop. (1992) 415,079.

**Tudjman, Franjo** (1922– ) Croatian statesman, president of Croatia (1990– ). Tudjman was a professor of history in Zagreb during the 1960s. He was twice imprisoned by the Yugoslavian government for nationalist activities. In 1989 he founded the Croatian Democratic Union (HDZ) party, which helped form the coalition government of Bosnia-Herzegovina in 1990. He was elected president of Croatia, and retained this position during the civil war. Tudjman was reelected in 1997.

**Tudors** English royal dynasty (1485–1603). Of Welsh origin, they were descended from Owen Tudor (d.1461), who married the widow of HENRY V. Owen Tudor's grandson defeated RICHARD III at Bosworth in 1485 to win the English throne as HENRY VII.

**Tu Fu** (712–70) Chinese poet of the T'ANG dynasty who wrote about such topics as war, corruption, and patriotism. His poetry reflects his troubled personal life and laments the corruption and cruelty that prevailed at court.

**tulip** Hardy, bulb-forming plant of the genus *Tulipa*, native to Europe, Asia, and North Africa. Tulips have long, pointed leaves growing from the base and elongated, cup-shaped flowers that can be almost any color or combination of colors. Family Liliaceae; genus *Tulipa*.

**Tull, Jethro** (1674–1741) British agriculturalist. He influenced agricultural methods through his innovations and writing. He invented a mechanical drill for sowing in 1701 and advocated the use of manure and tilling in the growing period.

**Tulsa** Port on the Arkansas River, NE Oklahoma, the state's second-largest city. It developed with the arrival in 1882 of the Atlantic and Pacific Railroad; the 1901 discovery of oil further accelerated development. Industries: oil refining and research, oil field equipment, mining, metal goods, aerospace. Pop. (1992) 453,995.

**tumbleweed** Plant that characteristically breaks off near the ground in fall and is rolled along by the wind. Height: to 20in (51cm). Family Amaranthaceae; genus *Amaranthus*.

**tumor** Any uncontrolled, abnormal proliferation of cells, often leading to the formation of a lump. Tumors are classified as either benign (non-cancerous) or malignant.

**tuna** (tunny) Marine fish related to MACKEREL, found in tropical and temperate seas. An important commercial fish, it has a blue-black and silvery streamlined body with a large, deeply divided tail. Length: to 14ft (4.3m); weight: to 1,800lb (810kg).

**tundra** Treeless, level, or gently undulating plain characteristic of arctic and subarctic regions. It is marshy with dark soil that supports mosses, lichens, and low shrubs, but not trees. It has a permanently frozen subsoil known as PERMAFROST.

**tungsten** (wolfram, symbol W) Silvery-gray, hard, metallic element, one of the TRANSITION ELEMENTS. Tungsten has the highest melting point of all metals and is used for lamp filaments and in special alloys. Tungsten carbide is used in high-speed cutting tools. Chemically tungsten is fairly unreactive; it oxidizes only at high temperatures. Properties: at.no. 74; at.wt. 183.85; sp.gr. 19.3; m.p. 6,170°F (3,410°C); b.p. 10,220°F (5,660°C); most common isotope $^{184}$W (30.64%).

**Tunis** Capital and largest city of Tunisia, N Africa. It became the capital in the 13th century under the Hafsid dynasty. Seized by BARBAROSSA in 1534 and controlled by Turkey, it attained infamy as a haven for pirates. The French assumed control in 1881. Tunis' port facilities were greatly improved after independence in 1956. Products include olive oil, carpets, textiles, and handicrafts. The ruins of CARTHAGE are nearby. Pop. (1994) 674,100.

**Tunisia** Small republic in N Africa. *See* country feature

**tunny** *See* TUNA

**Tupí-Guaraní** Combination of two major tribes that now represents the major native cultural population in rural Brazil, Paraguay, and parts of Argentina. The Tupí traditionally inhabit the banks of the lower Amazon and much of coastal Brazil south to Uruguay. The Guaraní, a more scattered grouping, once lived mainly in what is now Paraguay, but migrated into Brazil and Argentina.

**turbidity current** Dense current in air, water, or other fluid caused by different amounts of matter in suspension. In the ocean, when sediment along the continental shelves breaks off and rushes downslope, the resulting turbidity current carves out submarine canyons, and deposits distinctively bedded layers on the ocean floor.

**turbine** Rotary device turned by a moving fluid (liquid or gas). The modern form of water turbine is like a many-bladed propeller and is used to generate HYDROELECTRICITY. In power stations that burn fuels to produce electricity, the energy released by the burning is harnessed by the blades of jet engine-like steam turbines. As they spin, the turbines turn GENERATORS that produce ELECTRICITY. Modern wind generators produce electricity when the wind turns their rotors. In gas turbines, hot gases from burning fuel turn turbines that can operate generators or other machinery.

**turbocharger** Device that boosts the performance of an INTERNAL COMBUSTION ENGINE. A TURBINE driven by exhaust gases compresses the fuel/air mixture before it passes through the inlet valve.

**turbot** Scaleless, bottom-dwelling, European marine FLATFISH. It has a broad flat body with both eyes on its gray-brown, mottled upper surface, which may also be covered in bony knobs. Length: to 3.3ft (1m). Family Scophthalmidae; species *Scophthalmus maximus*.

**Turgenev, Ivan Sergeievich** (1818–83) Russian novelist, playwright, and short-story writer. His novels often opposed social and political evils and attracted official disapproval. The play *A Month in the Country* (1855) can be considered the first psychological drama of the Russian Theater. After the appearance of his masterpiece *Fathers and Sons* (1862), he left Russia permanently.

**turgor pressure** Hydrostatic pressure generated in cells of plants and bacteria as a result of the uptake of water by OSMO-

SIS. Water diffuses through the semipermeable membrane of the cell, causing the cell to swell; the increase in volume is resisted by the limited elasticity of the cell wall. When water is lost, a plant's cells collapse and it wilts.

**Turin** (Torino) City on the Po River, NW Italy, the country's fourth-largest city and capital of Piedmont (Piemonte) region. A Roman town under Augustus, Turin became a Lombard duchy from 590 to 636. From 1720 to 1861 it was capital of the Kingdom of Sardinia and a center of the RISORGIMENTO. Damaged during World War II, Turin remains an important industrial center. Industries: electronic equipment, chemicals, machinery, rubber, paper, leather goods, pharmaceuticals, wines. In 1997 its Romanesque cathedral was badly damaged in a fire, but the TURIN SHROUD was saved. Pop. (1992) 952,736.

**Turing, Alan Mathison** (1912–54) English mathematician. In 1937 he invented the **Turing machine**, a hypothetical machine that could modify a set of input instructions. It was the forerunner of the modern COMPUTER. During World War 2 Turing played a major role in deciphering the German "Enigma" code. In 1950 he devised the **Turing test**, which paved the way for the foundation of ARTIFICIAL INTELLIGENCE (AI).

**Turin shroud** Sheet of very old linen kept in Turin Cathedral, by tradition the cloth in which the body of Christ was wrapped after the Crucifixion. It was photographed in 1898 when negatives were seen to show the shape of a human figure. In 1988 results of carbon dating tests revealed that the shroud had in fact been made sometime between AD 1260 and 1390, well over a millennium after the death of Christ.

**Turkey** Republic in SE Europe and Asia. *See* country feature, page 684

**turkey** North American game bird now widely domesticated throughout the world. The common wild turkey (*Meleagris gallopavo*), once abundant in North America, was overhunted and is now protected. The male, or gobbler, is often bearded. Length: 50in (125cm). Family Meleagrididae.

**Turkic languages** Divided into six or seven separate subclasses, languages that together form a branch of the ALTAIC family; Turkish is the most important. The languages are remarkable for their grammatical uniformity, structural interresemblances, and lack of linguistic change over the centuries.

**Turkistan** (Turkestan) Historic region of central Asia, inhabited by Turkic-speaking peoples. Western (Russian) Turkistan now consists of the republics of TURKMENISTAN, UZBEKISTAN, TAJIKISTAN, KYRGYZSTAN, and S KAZAKSTAN. It mainly comprises the deserts of KYZYL KUM and Kara Kum. Eastern (Chinese) Turkistan comprises the Chinese region of XINJIANG and

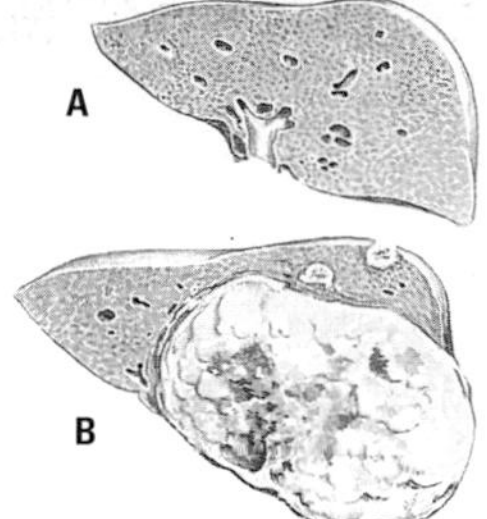


▲ **tumor** A tumor is a swelling composed of cells that have become independent of the body's control mechanism, so that they rapidly divide, and invade and kill surrounding tissue. Cross-sections of a healthy (A) and a diseased liver (B) are shown. The tumor shows a loss of cellular and structural differentiation and is unlike the tissue of origin.

## TUNISIA

Tunisia's flag originated in about 1835 when the country was officially under Turkish rule. It became the national flag in 1956, when Tunisia became independent from France. The flag contains two traditional symbols of Islam, the crescent and the star.

**AREA:** 63,170sq mi (163,610sq km)
**POPULATION:** 8,410,000
**CAPITAL POPULATION:** Tunis (674,100)
**GOVERNMENT:** Multiparty republic
**ETHNIC GROUPS:** Arab 98%, Berber 1%, French and other
**LANGUAGES:** Arabic (official)
**RELIGIONS:** Islam 99%
**CURRENCY:** Dinar = 1,000 millimes

The Republic of Tunisia is the smallest country in North Africa. The NW mountain ranges are a comparatively low extension of the ATLAS Mountains. In the center is a depression, containing the Chott Djerid salt lake. In the S lies part of the SAHARA desert. The fertile coastal lowlands include many fine Mediterranean ports, such as BIZERTE and the capital, TUNIS. Kairouan is the fourth most holy city in Islam.

### CLIMATE

Coastal regions have a Mediterranean climate, with dry, sunny summers and mild winters with moderate rainfall. Rainfall decreases and temperatures increase to the S.

### VEGETATION

Some cork oak forests grow in the N mountains. The S plateaus are covered by steppe with coarse grasses. The Sahara region is barren, except around oases.

### HISTORY AND POLITICS

In tradition, the Phoenician Queen DIDO founded CARTHAGE in 814 BC. The Romans destroyed the city in 146 BC, and the region was subsumed into the Roman Empire. The Arabs invaded in AD 640. The BERBERS slowly converted to Islam and Arabic became the principal language. In 1159 the ALMOHAD dynasty conquered Tunisia. From 1230 to 1574 Tunisia was ruled by the Hafsids. Spain's capture of much of Tunisia's coast led to the intervention of the Ottoman Empire, and the rule of Turkish governors (*beys*) continued into the 20th century. In the 16th century Tunisia's harbors were a refuge for Barbary pirates. France invaded in 1881 and Tunisia became a French protectorate (1883). French rule aroused strong nationalist sentiment, and Habib BOURGUIBA formed the Destour Socialist Party (PSD) in 1934.

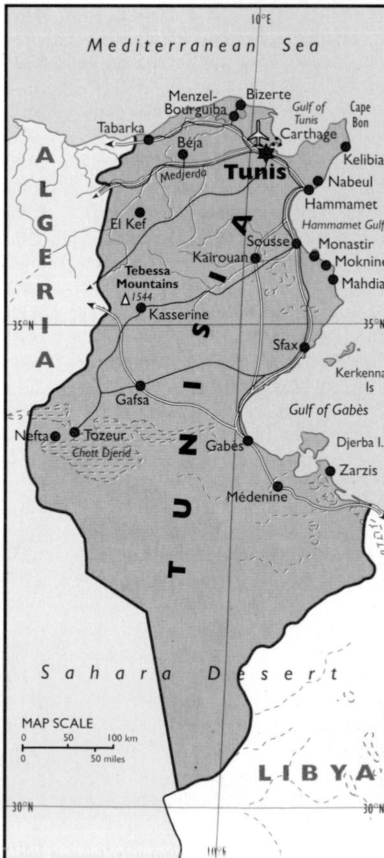


Tunisia was a major battleground of the North Africa campaigns in World War II. In 1956 it gained independence. In 1957 the *bey* was deposed and Tunisia became a republic, with Bourguiba as president. In 1975 Bourguiba was proclaimed president for life. Bourguiba pursued a moderate foreign policy and modernizing domestic policies. The first multiparty elections were held in 1981. Bourguiba's failing health created a succession crisis in the 1980s, and in 1987 he was deposed by Zine el Abidine Ben Ali. The PSD became the Constitutional Democratic Rally (RCD), and Ben Ali won a landslide victory in 1989 elections. He was reelected in 1994. The hegemony of the RCD remains a problem for its emerging democracy.

### ECONOMY

Tunisia is a middle-income developing country (1995 GDP per capita, US$5,000). It is the world's sixth-largest producer of phosphates. It also exports crude oil. Agriculture employs 26% of the workforce. Tunisia is the world's fourth-largest producer of olives. Other major crops include barley, dates, grapes for wine making, and wheat. Fishing and livestock-raising is also important. Tourism is a vital source of foreign exchange (1992 receipts, US$1,074 million). It has been an associate of the EC since 1969.

T

includes the TIAN SHAN mountains. Southern Turkistan consisted of part of N Afghanistan. For nearly two centuries Turkistan was the geographical bridge for trade between East and West. The first imperial power to control the region was PERSIA in 500 BC, but in *c*.330 BC ALEXANDER THE GREAT defeated the Persians and for the next few centuries, the region was disputed between Bactria, PARTHIA, and China. Market towns developed around the oases, centers for trade and religion. In the 8th century the Arabs conquered the region and the local population were converted to Islam. During the 13th century, the region was controlled by the Mongols, but then fractured into small, independent khanates. In 1867 the Russian empire imposed military rule over the area, and in 1918 Turkistan became an autonomous region within the SOVIET UNION. In 1924 the S part of Turkistan was divided into the republics of Uzbekistan and Turkmenistan; in 1929, Tajikistan became a republic and Kyrgyzstan followed in 1936. The N part of Russian Turkistan was incorporated into the Kazak republic, and Russian Turkistan became known as **Soviet Central Asia**.

**Turkmenistan** Republic in central Asia. The capital is ASHGABAT. Originally part of the Persian empire, it was overrun by Arabs in the 8th century AD. GENGHIS KHAN invaded in the 13th century, and it subsequently became part of TAMERLANE's vast empire. With the breakup of the Timurid dynasty, Turkmenistan came under Uzbek control. In the 19th century, Russia became increasingly dominant, and in 1899, despite resistance, Turkmenistan became part of Russian TURKISTAN. In 1925, as part of the Turkistan Autonomous Soviet Socialist Republic, it was absorbed into the SOVIET UNION. In 1991 it achieved independence and became a full member of the Commonwealth of Independent States (CIS) in 1993. In 1990 President Niyazov was elected head of state; his autocratic government prevents any political opposition to the ruling Democratic Party (formerly Communist Party). In a 1994 referendum Niyazov's term of presidency was extended to 2002. Almost 90% of Turkmenistan is covered by the KARA-KUM desert, parts of which are irrigated by the Kara-Kum canal. The chief crop is cotton and there are large reserves of natural gas and oil.

**Turks and Caicos Islands** Two island groups of the British West Indies, including more than 40 islands, eight of them inhabited. Discovered in 1512 by PONCE DE LEÓN, the islands were British from 1766, administered via Jamaica from 1873 to 1959, and a separate crown colony from 1973. Exports include salt, sponges, and shellfish, but the islands'

## TURKEY

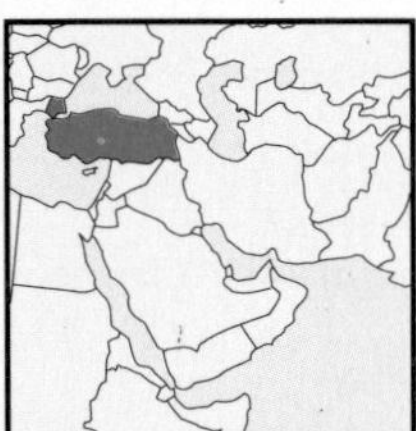

Turkey's flag was adopted when the Republic of Turkey was established in 1923. The crescent moon and the five-pointed star are traditional symbols of Islam. They featured on earlier Turkish flags used by the Turkish Ottoman empire.

**AREA:** 300,946sq mi (779,450sq km)
**POPULATION:** 58,775,000
**CAPITAL POPULATION:** Ankara (2,541,899)
**GOVERNMENT:** Multiparty republic
**ETHNIC GROUPS:** Turkish 86%, Kurdish 11%, Arab 2%
**LANGUAGES:** Turkish (official)
**RELIGIONS:** Islam 99%
**CURRENCY:** Turkish lira = 100 kurus

The Republic of Turkey straddles Europe and Asia. European Turkey (THRACE) is a small, fertile region, separated from Asia by the DARDANELLES, the BOSPORUS, and the Sea of Marmara. The major city is EDIRNE. ISTANBUL lies on both continents. Anatolia (ASIA MINOR) is a mainly mountainous region, rising in the E to 16,945ft (5,165m) at Mount ARARAT. The plateau region of Central Anatolia includes the capital, ANKARA. The Mediterranean coast is a popular tourist destination.

### CLIMATE

Central Turkey has hot, dry summers and cold winters. Western Turkey has a Mediterranean climate. The Black Sea coast has cooler summers.

### VEGETATION

Maquis is common in Mediterranean areas. Deciduous forests grow inland, with conifers on the mountains. The plateau is mainly dry steppe.

### HISTORY AND POLITICS

EPHESUS is one of the many ruins of the ancient Anatolian kingdoms of IONIA and PONTUS. In AD 330 Byzantium (Constantinople) became capital of the Roman empire; thence capital of the BYZANTINE EMPIRE (398). In the 11th century, the SELJUKS introduced Islam, and the capital moved to KONYA. In 1435 Constantinople was captured by MUHAMMAD II, and it served as capital of the OTTOMAN EMPIRE. Defeat in World War 1 led to the sultan signing the punitive Treaty of SÈVRES (1920). Nationalists, led by Mustafa Kemal (ATATÜRK), launched a war of independence. In 1923 Turkey became a republic, with Kemal as its president. ATATÜRK's 14-year dictatorship created a secular, Westernized state. In 1938 Atatürk died and was succeeded by Ismet INÖNÜ. Turkey was neutral throughout most of World War 2. In 1950 the first multiparty elections were held. A major post-war recipient of US aid, Turkey joined NATO in 1952. In 1960 a military coup led to the creation of a second republic. In 1965 Süleyman DEMIREL became prime minister. In 1974 Turkey invaded Northern CYPRUS; tension with Greece increased. In 1980 a military coup led to martial law. In 1987 martial law was lifted. In 1993 Demirel was elected president. In 1995 Necmettin Erbakan of the Islamist Welfare Party became prime minister. In 1997 tension between the pro-Islamic government and the military led to Erbakan's resignation. In 1998 prime minister Mesut Yilmaz resigned amid charges of corruption. Yalim Erez was appointed prime-minister designate. Since 1984 Turkey has fought the Kurdish Workers Party (PKK) in SE Turkey, Syria, and N Iraq. It has been accused of violating the human rights of KURDS. In 1999 Turkey captured the PKK leader, Abdullah Öcalan.

### ECONOMY

Turkey is a lower-middle income developing country (1995 GDP per capita, US$5,580). Agriculture employs 47% of the workforce. Turkey is a leading producer of citrus fruits, barley, cotton, wheat, tobacco, and tea. It is a major producer of chromium and phosphate fertilizers. Tourism is a vital source of foreign exchange.

main sources of income are now tourism and offshore banking. The capital is Cockburn Town on Grand Turk Island. Area: 166sq mi (430sq km). Pop (1990) 12,350.

**Turku** (Åbo) Finland's largest port, at the mouth of the Aurajoki River on the Baltic Sea. A Swedish settlement was established in 1157 and in 1220 it became the seat of the first Finnish diocese. It was the national capital until 1812. Fires in 1641 and 1827 destroyed much of the city. Industries: steel, shipbuilding, engineering, textiles, clothing. Pop. (1994) 162,370.

**turmeric** Herbaceous, perennial plant originally native to India and cultivated in SE Asia. The dried RHIZOME is powdered for use as seasoning, a yellow dye, and in medicines. Family Zingiberaceae; species *Curcuma longa*.

**Turner, Joseph Mallord William** (1775–1851) British landscape painter. He had become an associate of the Royal Academy by the age of 24 and was professor of perspective (1807–38). Turner's paintings were revolutionary in their representation of light, especially on water. His style changed dramatically in his late works, such as *The Slave Ship* (1840) and *Rain, Steam and Speed* (1844), in which the original subjects are almost obscured in a hazy interplay of light and color. His work had a profound influence on IMPRESSIONISM.

**Turner, Nat** (1800–31) US revolutionary. A slave in Southampton County, Virginia, he believed that he was called by God to take violent revenge on whites and win freedom for blacks. With *c*.70 followers, he was responsible for the death of more than 50 whites before the revolt was crushed. Turner was captured and hanged.

**Turner's syndrome** Hereditary condition in females, in which there is only one X-CHROMOSOME instead of two. It results in short stature, infertility, and developmental defects.

**turnip** Garden vegetable best grown in cool climates. The edible leaves are large and toothed with thick midribs. A biennial, it has a large, bulbous, white or yellow, fleshy root, which is cooked and eaten. Diameter: 3–6in (8–15cm). Height: to 20in (55cm). Family Brassicaceae/Cruciferae; species *Brassica rapa*.

**turnpike** Originally, a tollgate, a barrier across a road to prevent the passage of travelers or goods until a toll had been paid. The money raised was meant to be used to keep main roads in repair. The term is also used for some modern highways on which tolls are charged at intervals along the road.

**turnstone** Either of two species of migratory shore birds that use their curved bills to turn over pebbles in search of food; they nest on the Arctic TUNDRA. The vividly marked ruddy turnstone (*Arenaria interpres*) ranges widely in winter. Family Scolopacidae.

**Turpin, Dick** (1706–39) English highwayman. He engaged in many forms of robbery and was hanged for murder. He became a largely fictional hero.

**turquoise** Blue mineral, hydrated basic copper aluminum phosphate, found in aluminum-rich rocks in deserts. Its crystal system is triclinic and it occurs as tiny crystals and dense masses. Its color ranges from sky-blue and blue-green to a greenish gray and it is a popular gemstone. Hardness 6; sp.gr. 2.7.

**turtle** REPTILE found on land or in marine and fresh waters. Turtles have the most ancient lineage of all reptiles, preceding even the dinosaurs. They have a bony, horn-covered, boxlike shell (carapace) that encloses shoulder and hip girdles and all internal organs. All lay eggs on land. Terrestrial turtles are usually called TORTOISES, and some edible species found in brackish waters are called TERRAPINS. Marine turtles usually have smaller, lighter shells. Length: 4in–7ft (10cm–2m). Order Chelonia.

**Tuscany** Region in central Italy between the Mediterranean coast and the Apennine Mountains; the capital is FLORENCE. Other cities include SIENA and PISA. Tuscany is mostly mountainous with fertile valleys. Agriculture is the most important activity, with cereals, olives, and grapes among the main products. Carrara marble is quarried in the NW, and lead, zinc, antimony, and copper are mined in the SW. Industries: tourism, woolens, chemicals, steel, motor scooters, artisan industries. Area: 8,877sq mi (22,992sq km). Pop (1990) 3,528,735.

**Tuscarora War** (1711–13) Series of expeditions by colonists from North Carolina, South Carolina, and Virginia against the Tuscarora, who had attacked North Carolina settlers because of encroachments on Native-American lands. Defeated in 1713, the Tuscaroras moved to W Pennsylvania and became the sixth nation of the IROQUOIS CONFEDERACY.

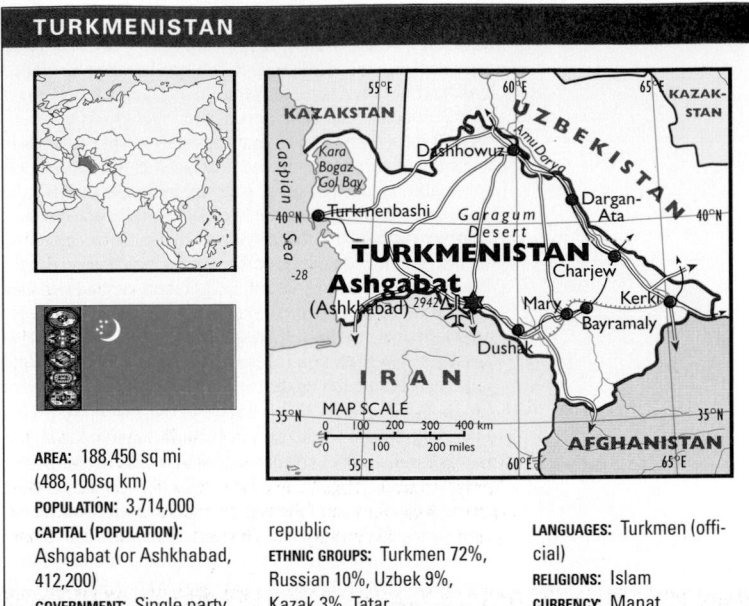

**TURKMENISTAN**

**AREA:** 188,450 sq mi (488,100sq km)
**POPULATION:** 3,714,000
**CAPITAL (POPULATION):** Ashgabat (or Ashkhabad, 412,200)
**GOVERNMENT:** Single party republic
**ETHNIC GROUPS:** Turkmen 72%, Russian 10%, Uzbek 9%, Kazak 3%, Tatar
**LANGUAGES:** Turkmen (official)
**RELIGIONS:** Islam
**CURRENCY:** Manat

**Tussaud, Madame Marie** (1761–1850) (Marie Grosholtz) Founder of the waxworks exhibition. She modeled wax figures in Paris, and in 1802 went to London with her collection. The present site of the exhibition, in Marylebone Road, London, has been its home since 1884.

**Tutankhamen** Egyptian pharaoh (active *c*.1350 BC) of the New Kingdom's 18th dynasty (1550–1307 BC). The revolutionary changes made by his predecessor, AKHNATEN, were reversed during his reign. The capital was reestablished at Thebes (LUXOR) and worship of AMON reinstated. Tutankhamen's fame is due to the discovery of his tomb by Howard Carter in 1922. The only royal tomb of ancient Egypt not completely stripped by robbers, it contained magnificent treasures.

**Tutu, Desmond Mpilo** (1931– ) South African Anglican clergyman. A prominent anti-APARTHEID campaigner, he trained as a teacher before becoming an Anglican priest in 1960. Tutu was Archbishop of Cape Town (1986–96). In 1984 he was awarded the Nobel Peace Prize. Since 1995 Tutu has chaired the Truth and Reconciliation Committee.

**Tuvalu** (formerly Ellice Islands) Independent republic in W Pacific Ocean, S of the equator and W of the International Date Line. None of the cluster of nine low-lying coral islands rises more than 15ft (4.6m) out of the Pacific, making them vulnerable to the rising sea levels that have been predicted. Poor soils restrict vegetation to coconut palms, breadfruit, and bush. The population survive by subsistence farming, raising pigs and poultry, and by fishing. Copra is the only significant export crop, but more foreign exchange is derived from the sale of elaborate postage stamps. The first European to discover the islands (1568) was the Spanish navigator Alvaro de Mendaña. The population was reduced from about 20,000 to just 3,000 in the three decades after 1850 by Europeans abducting workers for other Pacific plantations. The British assumed control in 1892, and it was subsequently administered with the nearby Gilbert Islands (now KIRIBATI). Tuvalu became a separate self-governing colony, achieving full independence within the Commonwealth in 1978. Area: 9.5sq mi (24sq km). Pop. (1991) 10,090.

**Twain, Mark** (1835–1910) (Samuel Langhorne Clemens) US writer, journalist, and lecturer. He took his pseudonym from the sounding calls of steamboatmen on the Mississippi, on the banks of which he was brought up. He was among the first to write novels in the American vernacular, such as *The*

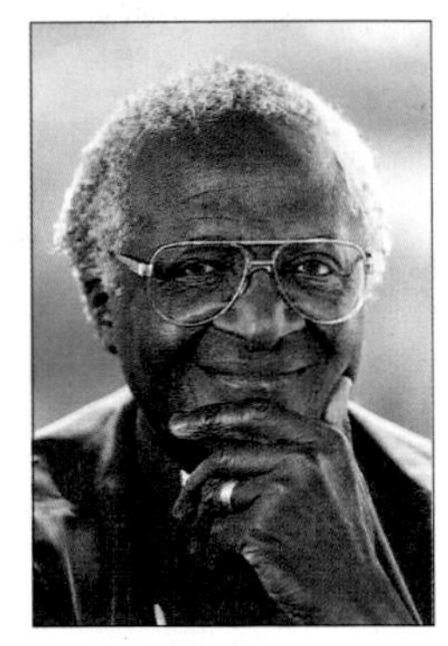

▲ **Tutu** The son of a school headmaster, Desmond Tutu studied theology at the University of South Africa and at the University of London before his ordination. An outspoken critic of the apartheid system, Tutu advocated the use of international economic sanctions to force the South African government toward reform. He also abhorred the use of violence, even by opponents of apartheid, always working for a peaceful settlement of the country's problems.

*Adventures of Tom Sawyer* (1876) and *The Adventures of Huckleberry Finn* (1884), which is seen as one of the great works of US fiction. Although he tends to be categorized as a humorist, his later books, such as *The Mysterious Stranger* (1916), are often bitter and pessimistic.

**tweed** Rough-textured cloth, usually all wool, from which warm clothes are made. Tweed originated in Scotland, but is now made in many countries. After spinning, the yarn is dyed with local LICHENS, giving the cloth its characteristic smell.

**Twelve Tables** Laws engraved on wooden tables representing the earliest codification of Roman law, traditionally dated 451–450 BC. Written by *decemviri* (a committee of 10), they codified the existing laws and customs of ancient Rome.

**twelve-tone music** (twelve-note music) SERIAL MUSIC in which the series contains all twelve notes of the CHROMATIC scale. Its introduction, in the early 20th century, is credited to Arnold SCHOENBERG. This method of composition relies not on the principle of TONALITY, in which the tonic or keynote is the focal center, but on the relationship between the twelve notes of the chromatic scale. The composer selects the order in which the notes are to be played and the resultant sequence is manipulated throughout the composition. Many composers have experimented with twelve-tone music; these include Anton WEBERN, Alban BERG, and Hans Werner HENZE.

**two-stroke engine** Engine in which the operation of each piston is in two stages. In the two-stroke cycle, a piston moves up a cylinder to compress a fuel-air mixture in the top. At the same time, more of the mixture is sucked in below the piston. A spark ignites the compressed mixture, causing an explosion. This sends the piston back down the cylinder. The piston forces the fresh fuel-air mixture out from beneath it and along a transfer port leading to the top part of the cylinder. The mixture forces the exhaust gases out from the top of the cylinder. The process then repeats.

**Tyler, John** (1790–1862) Tenth US President (1841–45). An aristocratic Virginian, he served in Congress and as governor of Virginia. He was a determined supporter of states' rights. The Whigs chose him as vice-presidential candidate with William H. HARRISON and he suceeded to the presidency on Harrison's death (1841). He came into conflict with the nationalistic Whigs in Congress, repeatedly vetoing legislation to create a national bank. His determination to annex TEXAS bore fruit after he had left office.

**Tyler, Wat** (d.1381) English leader of the PEASANTS' REVOLT. He was chosen as leader of the rebels in Kent, SE England, and led their march on London. He was eventually killed by the lord mayor of London while parleying with RICHARD II.

**Tyndale, William** (*c*.1494–1536) Religious reformer and Bible translator. He started printing an English version of the New Testament in Cologne, Germany, in 1525. After this, Tyndale began translating the Old Testament. He also wrote numerous Protestant tracts. He was eventually captured by the church authorities and burned at the stake as a heretic. His translation later provided a basis for the Authorized Version of the English Bible.

**Tyndall, John** (1820–93) Irish physicist who correctly suggested that the blue color of the sky is due to the scattering of light by particles of dust and other colloidal particles. By 1881 he had helped disprove the theory of SPONTANEOUS GENERATION by showing that food does not decay in germ-free air.

**Tyne** River in NE England. Formed at the confluence of the North Tyne (which rises in the S Cheviot Hills) and the South Tyne (which rises in Cumbria), it flows E for 30mi (48km) through Newcastle to enter the North Sea near Tynemouth. It was made fully navigable at the end of the 19th century.

**Tyne and Wear** Metropolitan council in NE England, formed in 1974 from parts of the former counties of NORTHUMBERLAND and DURHAM; it included the former county borough of NEWCASTLE-UPON-TYNE, its administrative center. A highly industrialized area, its staple industries of coal mining, iron and steel production, and shipbuilding declined after the 1920s. There were signs of a recovery in the 1990s based on various light industries. Area: 207sq mi (537sq km). Pop. (1991) 1,095,152.

**typesetting** Part of the PRINTING process. In early printing, wooden or metal type was set by hand. In hot-metal type processes, the linotype machine casts a complete line of molten type metal into a mold, and the monotype machine casts individual letters and spaces and arranges these in lines. Most type is now set using photographic or computerized processes.

**typhoid fever** Acute, sometimes epidemic communicable disease of the digestive system. Caused by *Salmonella typhi*, which is transmitted in contaminated water or food, it is characterized by bleeding from the bowel and enlargment of the spleen. Symptoms include fever, headache, constipation, sore throat, cough, and skin rash.

**typhoon** Name given in the Pacific Ocean to a HURRICANE, a violent tropical cyclonic storm.

**typhus** Any of a group of infectious diseases caused by RICKETTSIAE (small bacteria) and spread by parasites of the human body such as lice, fleas, ticks, and mites. Epidemic typhus, the result of infection by *Rickettsia prowazekii*, is the most serious manifestation. Associated with dirty, overcrowded conditions, it is mainly seen during times of war or famine.

**typography** Practice of designing typefaces and type styles mainly for use in printed texts. Typography is widely used in experimental, progressive art and design as well as conventional publishing. Movements that have revolutionized typography include FUTURISM, Dadaism, and SURREALISM. Individuals include Eric GILL and MOHOLY-NAGY. The term also refers to the art of fine PRINTING itself. *See also* DADA; TYPESETTING

**typology** System of groupings that aid understanding of the things being studied by distinguishing certain attributes or qualities among them that serve to link them together into a closed set of items.

**Tyr** (Tiw) In Germanic mythology, powerful sky god. He was also associated with war, government, and justice. The word Tuesday derives from Tyr's day.

**tyrannosaurus** Any of several species of large, bipedal, carnivorous, theropod DINOSAURS that lived during late CRETACEOUS times. Its head, 4ft (1.2m) long, was armed with a series of dagger-like teeth. The hind legs were stout and well developed, but the forelegs may have been useless except for grasping at close range. The best-known species is *T. rex*. Length: 47ft (14m); height: 20ft (6.5m).

**Tyre** Historic city on the coast of modern Lebanon. Built on an island, it was a major commercial port of ancient PHOENICIA. It supplied craftsmen and raw materials, especially cedarwood, for the building of the temple in Jerusalem in the 10th century BC, and established colonies, including CARTHAGE, around the E Mediterranean. Tyre was never successfully besieged until ALEXANDER THE GREAT built a causeway linking the island to the mainland (332 BC). Ruled by successive empires, including the Romans, it was captured by the Arabs in AD 638 and destroyed by the Mamelukes in 1291. Pop. (1991) 70,000.

**Tyrol** *See* TIROL

**Tyrone** Largest of the six counties of Northern Ireland, in the SW of the province. The county town is Omagh. Mainly hilly with the Sperrin Mountains in the N and Bessy Bell and Mary Gray in the S, the region is drained by the Blackwater and Mourne rivers. Cereals and root crops are grown and dairy cattle are raised. Industries: linen, whiskey, processed food. Area 1,260sq mi (3,263sq km). Pop. (1990) 153,000.

**Tyson, Mike** (1966– ) US boxer. In 1986 he became the youngest heavyweight champion in boxing history. Known for his devastating punching power, in 1987 he became the first undisputed heavyweight champion since 1978. In 1992 he was convicted of rape and sentenced to prison. Released in 1995, he regained his WBC heavyweight championship in 1996 by stopping Frank Bruno. Later in the year he was defeated by Evander Holyfield. In a 1997 rematch, Tyson was disqualifed for biting off part of Holyfield's ear. He was fined and banned from boxing for a year. In 1999 Tyson was convicted of assault and returned to prison.

**Tz'u Hsi** *See* CIXI

**U-2 incident** (1960) COLD WAR confrontation between the US and the Soviet Union, following the shooting-down of a US spy plane, while on a photographic reconnaissance mission over the Soviet Union. Nikita KHRUSHCHEV responded by cancelling a scheduled summit between the Soviet Union, US, UK, and France. President Dwight D. EISENHOWER denied the existence of such spy missions, but the U-2 pilot, Francis Gary Powers, was produced by the Soviet authorities and confessed to being a spy. Powers was released (1962) in a spy exchange.

**Uccello, Paolo** (1397–1475) Florentine painter. Celebrated as an early master of PERSPECTIVE, Uccello's works include *The Flood* (*c.*1450) and *The Rout of San Romano* (1454–57).

**Udaipur** City on Lake Pichola, Rajasthan, India. In 1586 it was made capital of the princely state of Udaipur by Udai Singh. The walled city has three palaces. It is an agricultural market and a center for textiles. Pop. (1991) 309,000.

**Uffizi** (It. offices) Chief public gallery in Florence, Italy, housing one of the greatest collections of Italian paintings. The palace was built in the 16th century by Giorgio VASARI for the Grand Duke Cosimo I de' MEDICI and once housed government offices. Painters of the Florentine and other Italian schools are represented with works by Piero della Francesca, Botticelli, Leonardo da Vinci, Michelangelo, Raphael, Titian, and many others, as well as Dutch and Flemish masters.

**UFO** Abbreviation of UNIDENTIFIED FLYING OBJECT

**Uganda** Republic in E central Africa. *See* country feature

**Ugarit** Ancient city in NW Syria. Inhabited as early as the 7th millennium BC, it was a great commercial power, trading with Mesopotamia and Egypt. Excavations have revealed a vast palace from the 14th century BC, and many large houses filled with treasures and artifacts.

**UHF** Abbreviation of ULTRA HIGH FREQUENCY

**Ujjain** City on the Sipra River, Madhya Pradesh, W central India. It is one of the seven holy cities of India, and a Hindu pilgrimage center. Nearby are the ruins of a city dating from the 2nd millennium BC. Pop. (1991) 362,000.

**ukiyo-e** Japanese paintings and woodblock prints that were prevalent in the Edo period (1615–1867). Their subject matter included people engaged in everyday activities as well as Kabuki actors. Moronobu (*c.*1625–95) is generally considered the originator of the true ukiyo-e print and he gained renown for his woodcut illustrations for popular literature. Other famous printmakers include HIROSHIGE, HOKUSAI, and UTAMARO.

**Ukraine** Independent state in E Europe. *See* country feature, page 688

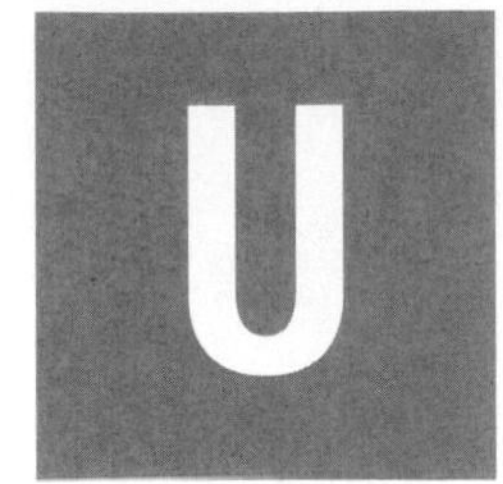


***U/u, 21st letter of the Roman alphabet. Like some other letters in the alphabet it is derived from the Semitic letter* vaw, *meaning* hook. *It was adopted by the Greeks before moving into the Roman alphabet.***

## UGANDA

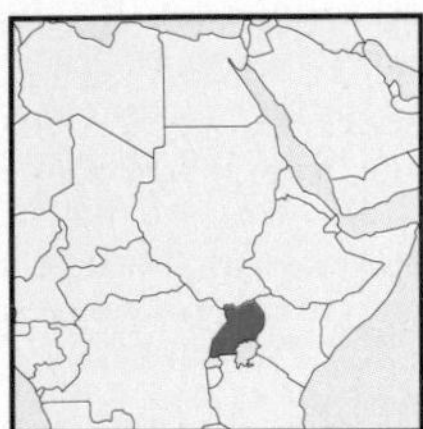

The flag used by the party that won the first national election was adopted as the national flag when Uganda became independent from Britain in 1962. The black represents the people, the yellow the sun, and the red brotherhood. The crested crane is the country's emblem.

**AREA:** 91,073sq mi (235,880sq km)
**POPULATION:** 18,592,000
**CAPITAL POPULATION:** Kampala (773,463)
**GOVERNMENT:** Republic in transition
**ETHNIC GROUPS:** Ganda 18%, Banyoro 14%, Teso 9%, Banyan 8%, Basoga 8%, Bagisu 7%, Bachiga 7%, Lango 6%, Acholi 5%
**LANGUAGES:** English and Swahili (both official)
**RELIGIONS:** Christianity (Roman Catholic 40%, Protestant 29%), traditional beliefs 18%, Islam 7%
**CURRENCY:** Uganda shilling = 100 cents

The Republic of Uganda is a landlocked country in E Africa. Most of Uganda consists of part of the African plateau, which slopes down from *c.*4,900ft (1,500m) in the S to 3,000ft (900m) in the N. In the W lies an arm of the Great RIFT VALLEY, which contains Lake ALBERT and the Albert NILE. Highland pockets lie in the SW and E. Much of S Uganda is made up of Lake VICTORIA, Africa's largest lake. The capital, KAMPALA, and ENTEBBE lie on the lakeside.

### CLIMATE

Uganda's equatorial climate is moderated by altitude. The wettest regions are the W mountains, especially the high Ruwenzori range.

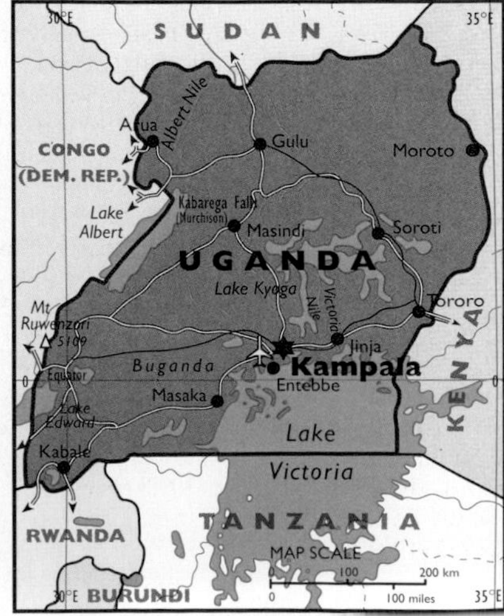


### VEGETATION

Nearly 20% of Uganda is covered by lakes or swamps. Some rain forest remains in the S. Wooded savanna covers central and N Uganda.

### HISTORY AND POLITICS

In *c.*1500 the Nilotic-speaking Lwo people formed various kingdoms in SW Uganda, including Buganda (kingdom of the Ganda) and Bunyoro. During the 18th century, the Buganda kingdom expanded and trade flourished. In 1862 a British explorer, John Speke, became the first European to reach Buganda. He was closely followed (1875) by Sir Henry STANLEY. The conversion activities of Christian missionaries led to conflict with Muslims. The *kabaka* (king) came to depend on Christian support. In 1892 Britain dispatched troops to Buganda, and in 1894 Uganda became a British protectorate. Unlike much of Africa, Uganda attracted Asian, rather than European, settlers. African political representation remained minimal until after World War II. In 1962 Uganda gained independence, with Buganda's *kabaka*, Mutesa II, as president and Milton OBOTE as prime minister. In 1966 Mutesa II was forced into exile. In 1967 Buganda's traditional autonomy was restricted, and Obote became executive president. In 1971 Obote was deposed in a military coup, led by Major General Idi AMIN. Amin quickly established a personal dictatorship, and launched a war against foreign interference, which resulted in the mass expulsion of Asians. It is estimated that Amin's regime was responsible for the murder of more than 250,000 Ugandans. Obote loyalists resisted the regime from neighboring Tanzania. In 1976 Amin declared himself president for life, and Israel launched a successful raid on Entebbe airport to end the hijack of one of its passenger planes. In 1978 Uganda annexed the Kagera region of NW Tanzania. In 1979 Tanzanian troops helped the Uganda National Liberation Front (UNLF) to overthrow Amin and capture Kampala. In 1980 elections Obote was swept back into office. Amid charges of electoral fraud, the National Resistance Army (NRA) began a guerrilla war. More than 200,000 Ugandas sought refuge in Rwanda and Zaire. In 1985 Obote was deposed in another military coup. In 1986 the NRA captured Kampala, and Yoweri Museveni became president. Museveni began to rebuild the domestic economy and improve foreign relations. In 1993 the *kabaka* of Buganda was re-instated as monarch. In 1996 Museveni won Uganda's first direct presidential elections. AIDS is one of the greatest issues facing Uganda; it has the highest number of reported cases in Africa.

### ECONOMY

Civil strife greatly damaged Uganda's economy (1995 GDP per capita, US$1,470). In 1997 it received money from the World Bank as part of a strategy to ease the debt burden of the world's poorest countries. Agriculture employs 86% of the workforce. Uganda is the world's seventh-largest producer of coffee. Cotton, sugar cane, and tea are also exported.

U

Ukraine's flag was first used between 1918 and 1922. It was readopted in September 1991. The colors were first used in 1848. They are heraldic in origin and were first used on the coat of arms of one of the Ukrainian kingdoms in the Middle Ages.

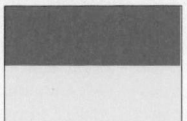

**AREA:** 233,100sq mi (603,700sq km)
**POPULATION:** 52,140,000
**CAPITAL POPULATION:** Kiev (2,600,000)
**GOVERNMENT:** Multiparty republic
**ETHNIC GROUPS:** Ukrainian 73%, Russian 22%, Jewish 1%, Belarussian 1%, Moldovan, Bulgarian, Polish
**LANGUAGES:** Ukrainian (official)
**RELIGIONS:** Christianity (mostly Ukrainian Orthodox)
**CURRENCY:** Hryvna

Ukraine (borderland) is the second-largest country in Europe (after Russia). The coastal lowlands include the Black Sea port of ODESSA. CRIMEA is a peninsula region, and contains the vital port of SEVASTOPOL. The DNIEPER River divides Ukraine into E and W. The capital, KIEV, lies on its banks. In the W, the CARPATHIAN MOUNTAINS rise to 6,762ft (2,061m), close to the Romanian border. The fertile central plateau is among the world's greatest producers of wheat and barley. In the E, the DONETS BASIN is one of the world's greatest industrial powerhouses. The cities of KHARKOV and DONETSK are major industrial centers.

## CLIMATE

Ukraine's continental climate is moderated by proximity to the Black Sea. Winters are most severe in the NE and the highlands. Rainfall is heaviest in summer.

## VEGETATION

The once-grassy central steppe is now mostly under the plow. The S black, chernozem soil is especially fertile. In the N, around the Pripet marshes, are large woodlands, with trees such as ash and oak. Pine forests swathe the slopes of the Carpathian and Crimean mountains.

## HISTORY

In ancient history the area was successively inhabited by Scythians and Sarmatians, before invasions by the Goths, Huns, Avars, and Khazars. The first Ukrainian Slavic community originates from this period. In the 9th century, the N regions were united by the Varangians as Kievan Rus. The empire disintegrated under the onslaught of the Mongol hordes. In the late 14th-century, Ukraine became part of Lithuania. In 1478 the Black Sea region was absorbed into the Ottoman empire. In 1569 the Lithuanian sector passed to Poland following the Poland-Lithuania union.

Polish rule was marked by the enserfment of the peasantry and persecution of the Ukrainian Orthodox Church. In 1648 refugees from Polish rule (COSSACKS) completed Ukraine's liberation. Independence was short-lived due to the emerging power of Russia. A succession of wars resulted (1775) in the division of Ukraine into three Russian provinces. The nationalist movement was barely suppressed, and found an outlet in Galicia. Ukraine's industry was developed from the 1860s.

In 1918 (following the Russian Revolution) Ukraine declared independence and was invaded by the Red Army, who were repulsed with the support of the Central Powers. The World War I armistice prompted the withdrawal of the Central Powers. A unified, independent Ukraine was once more proclaimed. The Red Army invaded again, this time with greater success. In 1921 W Ukraine was ceded to Poland, and in 1922 E Ukraine became a constituent republic of the Soviet Union. In the 1930s, Lenin's policy of appeasement was replaced by Stalin's autocratic, agricultural collectivization. It caused 7.5 million Ukrainians to die of famine. The 1939 Nazi-Soviet partition of Poland reunified the Ukraine. In 1940 it also acquired Northern Bukovina and part of Bessarabia from Romania. In 1945 it gained Ruthenia from Hungary and E Galicia from Poland.

After 1945 all Ukrainian land was unified into a single Soviet republic. In 1954 the Crimea was annexed to the Ukraine. Ukraine became one of the most powerful republics in the Soviet Union, contributing 30% of total Soviet industrial output. In 1986 the CHERNOBYL disaster contaminated large areas of Ukraine. After a unilateral declaration of sovereignty in 1990, Ukraine proclaimed its independence in August 1991. In December 1991 the former Communist leader Leonard Kravchuk was elected president and Ukraine joined the COMMONWEALTH OF INDEPENDENT STATES (CIS). Tensions with Russia over the Crimea, the Black Sea fleet, the control of nuclear weapons, and oil and gas reserves were eased by a 1992 treaty. Crimean independence was refused.

## POLITICS

In the 1994 presidential election Leonid Kuchma defeated Kravchuk. Kuchna continued the policy of establishing closer ties with the West, and sped up the pace of privatization. In 1995 direct rule was imposed on Crimea for four months. Subsequent elections saw reduced support for pro-Russian parties. Disputes continue over the extent of the powers of the Crimean legislature

## ECONOMY

Ukraine was plunged into economic crisis by the rapid dismantling of its command economy. It is a lower-middle income economy (1995 GDP per capita, US$2,400). Agriculture is important, and Ukraine has been called the breadbasket of Europe. It is the world's leading producer of sugar beet and the second-largest producer of barley. It is also a major producer of wheat. Other crops include corn, potatoes, sunflowers, and tobacco. Livestock rearing and fishing are other important activities.

Ukraine has extensive raw materials. The Donets Basin is the world's eighth-largest producer of bituminous coal. Krivoy Rog mines are the world's fourth-largest producer of iron ore, and Nikopol is the world's leading manganese ore producer. Many of the coal mines are exhausted, and in 1995 the government closed 19 coal mines. Antiquated technology contributes to the highest mining fatality rate in the world. Despite its hydroelectric and nuclear power stations, Ukraine is reliant on oil and natural gas imports. Ukraine's debt to Russia (1995, US$500 million) has been offset partly by allowing Russian firms majority shares in many Ukrainian industries.

**Ukrainian** Language spoken by *c*.40–45 million people in Ukraine. Significant Ukrainian-speaking communities are to be found in Kazakstan, Poland, Romania, the Slovak Republic, and Siberian Russia. Like Russian and Belorussian, Ukrainian belongs to the E branch of the Slavic family of INDO-EUROPEAN LANGUAGES.

**ukulele** (ukelele) Small guitar, which was developed in Hawaii from the Portuguese guitar. It is shaped like a classical guitar with a wooden body, round sound hole, and fretted fingerboard.

**Ulan Bator** (Ulaanbaatar, formerly Urga) Capital of Mongolia, on the Tola River. It dates back to the founding of the Lamaistic Temple of the Living Buddha in 1639, and it grew as a stop for caravans between Russia and China. It was later a focus for the Mongolian autonomy movement. It became the capital in 1921. Noted for its harsh climate and bleak, planned streets, it is the political, social, and economic center of Mongolia. Industries: textiles, building materials, leather, paper, alcohol, food products, carpets, glass. Pop. (1992) 601,000.

**Ulanova, Galina** (1910–98) Russian ballerina. In 1944 she became the prima ballerina of the BOLSHOI BALLET. Ulanova's skill in lyrical-dramatic interpretation and the purity and lightness of her classical style earned her international recognition. Her major roles include Leonid Lavrovsky's productions of *The Red Poppy*, *Giselle*, and *Romeo and Juliet*. In 1962 Ulanova retired and became a coach for the new generation of Bolshoi ballerinas.

**Ulbricht, Walter** (1893–1973) East German statesman, leader of East GERMANY (1950–71). A founder of the German Communist Party, Ulbricht was forced into exile by the rise of fascism, and he spent World War II in the Soviet Union. In 1949 he became deputy premier of the newly created German Democratic Republic (East Germany). In 1950 he became general secretary of the Communist Party. Ulbricht established close links with the Soviet Union. The repressive nature of his regime led to a rebellion in 1953 and the BERLIN WALL was built (1961) to prevent further defections to the West. In 1971 he was replaced as general secretary by Erich HONECKER.

**ulcer** Any persistent sore or lesion on the skin or on a mucous membrane, often associated with inflammation. Ulcers may be caused by infection, pressure, or chemical irritation.

**Ulm** Industrial city on the Danube River, Baden-Württemberg, S Germany. Founded before 800, it was an important political and commercial center of medieval Europe. The major landmark is the Gothic minster (1377), with the tallest spire in the world, at 528ft (161m). Industries: car manufacture, electrical goods, textiles, food products. Pop. (1993) 114,700.

**ulna** Long bone of the inner side of the forearm. At its upper end it articulates with the HUMERUS and the RADIUS.

**Ulster** Most northerly of Ireland's four ancient provinces, consisting of nine counties. Since 1922 six of these counties have been in Northern IRELAND, while Cavan, Donegal, and Monaghan form Ulster province in the Republic of IRELAND. Area: 3,094sq mi (8,012sq km). Pop. (1991) 232,000.

**Ulster Unionist Party** Largest Loyalist party in Northern IRELAND. It developed in the late 19th century to defend the six northern provinces of ULSTER from Irish home rule and to maintain the union with Britain. Almost exclusively Protestant, it was the ruling party in Northern Ireland from 1922 until the imposition of direct rule from Westminster in 1972. In 1998 the Ulster Unionist Party leader, David Trimble, became first minister of Northern Ireland.

**ultra high frequency (UHF)** Radio waves in the frequency band 300–3,000MHz. UHF waves have a wavelength of about 3ft (1m) or less and are used for TELEVISION broadcasting.

**ultrasonics** Study of sound waves with frequencies beyond the upper limit of human hearing (above 20,000Hz). In medicine, ultrasonics are used to locate tumors, produce fetal images, and to treat certain neurological disorders. Other applications of ultrasonics include the agitation of liquids to form emulsions and the detection of flaws in metals.

**ultraviolet radiation** Type of ELECTROMAGNETIC RADIATION of shorter wavelength and higher frequency than visible LIGHT. Wavelengths range from 4 to 400nm (nanometers). Sunlight contains ultraviolet (uv) rays, most of which are filtered by the OZONE LAYER. If the ozone layer is weakened, enough ultraviolet can reach the ground to harm living things. Excessive exposure to sunlight can cause sunburn and skin cancer in people with fair skin. Ultraviolet is used medically to sterilize equipment. *See also* RADIATION

**Ulysses** *See* ODYSSEUS

**Umayyads** (Omayyads) Dynasty of Arabian Muslim caliphs (661–750). From their capital at DAMASCUS, the Umayyads ruled a basically Arab empire, which stretched from Spain to India. They made little effort to convert conquered peoples to Islam, but there was great cultural exchange, and Arabic became established as the language of Islam. They were overthrown by the ABBASIDS.

**umbelliferae** Family of flowering plants, all of which have many small flowers borne in umbrella-like clusters (umbels) at the ends of stalks. Umbellifers are mainly herbs and shrubs. Many species are edible, including CARROT, PARSLEY, CELERY, PARSNIP, FENNEL, and DILL.

**umbilical cord** Long cord that connects a developing FETUS with the PLACENTA. At birth, the cord is cut from the placenta, leaving a scar on the baby's abdomen known as the navel.

**umbrella bird** Any of three species of large tropical American birds, each with a retractile, black, umbrellalike crest, and a long, often tubular-shaped, feathered lappet (tuft) on the throat. The ornate umbrella bird (*Cephalopterus ornatus*) lives in trees and feeds on fruits. Family Cotingidae.

**Umbria** Region in central Italy comprising the provinces of Perugia and Terni; the capital is PERUGIA. The only landlocked region of Italy, it is traversed by the APENNINES and drained by the TIBER River. Cereal crops, grapes, and olives are grown, and cattle and pigs are reared. The medieval hill towns scattered over the countryside attract tourists. Industries: iron and steel, chemicals, textiles, confectionery. Area: 3,265sq mi (8,456sq km). Pop. (1992) 814,796.

**UN** Abbreviation of UNITED NATIONS

## ULTRASONICS

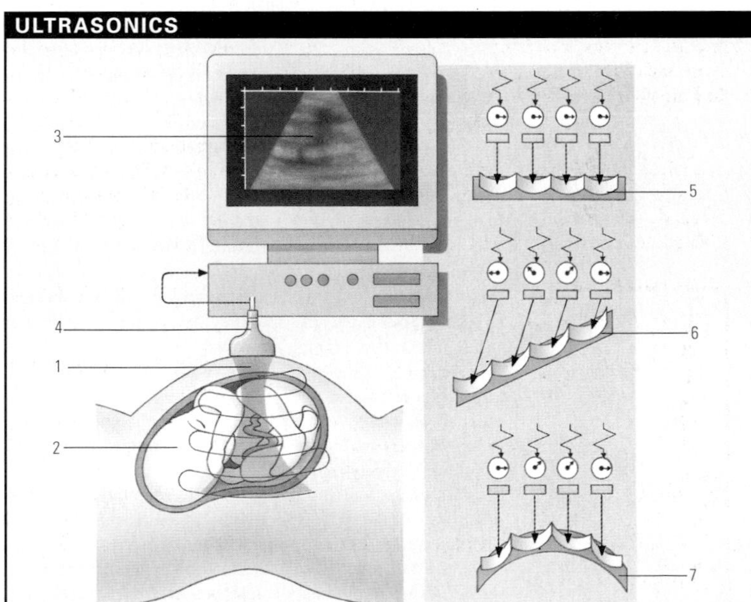


Ultrasonic, or ultrasound, scanners send out beams of sound (1) and read the returning echoes to build up a picture of structures below the surface (2). They are commonly used to view fetuses in the womb with the picture displayed on a real-time monitor (3). The sound waves used are above the range of human hearing and are created by piezoelectric crystals in the handset (4). These crystals change shape when the voltage is switched off. An ultrasonic scanner uses an oscillating voltage to make the crystals vibrate, producing sound of the right frequency. The process is reversed when an echo hits the tranducer and the sound wave is converted back into a voltage, which the monitor reads to build up an image. Each handset has dozens of the piezoelectric crystals on its face and by altering the timing of the oscillations of the voltage, the beam can be steered. When the voltage hits all the crystals at the same time a flat beam is issued (5). By sending the voltage to one end of the row of crystals before the other the beam can be steered (6). The beam of sound can also be focused by hitting the end crystals before the ones on the center (7).

**Un-American Activities Committee, House (HUAC)** Committee of the House of Representatives, established in 1938 to investigate political subversion. Created to combat Nazi propaganda, it began investigating extremist political organizations. After World War II, encouraged by Senator MCCARTHY, it attacked alleged communists in Hollywood and in the federal government. It was abolished in 1975.

**uncertainty principle** In physics, principle stating that it is not possible to know both the position and the momentum of a SUBATOMIC PARTICLE at the same time, because the act of measuring would disturb the system. It was established (1927) by Werner HEISENBERG.

**Uncle Sam** Symbolic figure personalizing the US. The name was first used during the WAR OF 1812. The appearance of Uncle Sam, tall, thin, and frock-coated, was developed by 19th-century cartoonists.

**unconformity** In geology, break in the time sequence of rocks layered one above the other. The gap may be caused by interruptions in the deposition of sediment, ancient erosion, earth movements, or other activity.

**unconscious** Term in psychology for that part of mental life believed to operate without the individual's immediate awareness or control. It includes memories that the person is not actually thinking about, and the organizing processes underlying speech and reading. In Sigmund FREUD's system, it is the area containing the desires and conflicts of the ID. C.G. JUNG believed that part of the unconscious (the collective unconscious) contains inherited concepts, shared by all other human beings.

**Underground Railroad** Secret network organized by free blacks and other ABOLITIONISTS before the CIVIL WAR to assist slaves escaping from the South. Though Quakers were prominent assistants (conductors), most escapees reached the North by their own efforts. One of the most prominent black conductors was Harriet TUBMAN. The major routes ran through Ohio, Indiana, and w Pennsylvania. In the North escaped slaves were guided through a series of safe houses (stations) to a place of safety, often Canada. The efforts of the railroad were exaggerated for propaganda purposes by both abolitionists and supporters of SLAVERY. In reality, probably no more than a few thousand slaves escaped in this manner.

**unemployment** Inability of workers who are ready, able, and willing to work to find employment. Unemployment is usually expressed as a percentage of the labor force. **Cyclical** unemployment exists when the level of aggregate demand in the economy is less than that required to maintain full employment. People are laid off, and their jobs simply disappear. **Structural** unemployment exists when jobs are available and workers are seeking jobs, but they cannot fill vacancies for some reason (for example, they lack proper training, or live too far away). **Technological** unemployment exists when workers are replaced by machines faster than they can find alternative employment. **Seasonal** unemployment occurs when workers are unable to find jobs at certain seasons of the year. Such workers are usually engaged in construction, agriculture, or the tourist industry. **Underemployment** is inefficient use of labor. For example, an employer may keep unneeded workers on the payroll when demand falls in order to have experienced help available when demand increases.

**UNESCO** Acronym for UNITED NATIONS EDUCATIONAL, SCIENTIFIC AND CULTURAL ORGANIZATION

**ungulate** MAMMAL with hoofed feet. Most ungulates, including cattle, sheep, pigs, and deer, are members of the order Artiodactyla (with an even number of toes). The order Perissodactyla (ungulates with an odd number of toes) consists of horses, tapirs, and rhinoceroses. The orders Proboscidea and Hyracoidea, collectively known as subungulates, contain elephants and hyraxs.

**UNICEF** Acronym for UNITED NATIONS CHILDREN'S FUND

**unicorn** In mythology and heraldry, a magical animal resembling a graceful horse or a young goat with one thin, conical or helical horn on its forehead.

**unidentified flying object (UFO)** Any flying object that cannot readily be explained as either a manmade craft or a natural phenomenon. Reports of UFOs have been documented since ancient times. With the development of aeronautics and astronautics, the number of sightings has increased enormously. The majority of supposed UFO sightings have various rational explanations, including optical floaters (in the observer's eye), weather balloons, and artificial satellites.

**Unification Church** International religious movement founded in South Korea in 1954 by Sun Myung Moon. Its adherents are popularly known as Moonies. The movement aims to reestablish God's rule on Earth through the restoration of the family. The Unification Church is noted for its mass weddings and has been accused of cultlike practices, such as brainwashing. *See also* CULT

**unified field theory** Attempt to extend the general theory of RELATIVITY to give a simultaneous representation of both gravitational and electromagnetic fields. A more comprehensive theory would also include the strong and weak nuclear forces. Although some success has been achieved in unifying the electromagnetic and weak nuclear forces, the general problem is still unsolved. *See also* GRAND UNIFIED THEORY (GUT)

**Union, Acts of** Series of acts uniting England with WALES (1536) and SCOTLAND (1707), and Britain with IRELAND (1800). In addition, the 1841 Act of Union united French-speaking Lower Canada and English-speaking Upper Canada. The Canadian act led to the establishment of a parliament for the province.

**Union of Soviet Socialist Republics** Official name for the SOVIET UNION

**Unitarianism** Version of Christianity that denies the TRINITY, accepts God as the father, and rejects the divinity of JESUS CHRIST. Originally considered a heresy, it flourished in Poland in the 16th century. Unitarianism in the 20th century has been identified with liberal politics and the movement for world peace and has taken an increasingly humanist point of view.

**United Arab Emirates** (UAE) Federation of the seven independent sheikhdoms of ABU DHABI, DUBAI, Ajman, Ras al-Khaimah, Fujairah, SHARJA and Umm al-Qaiwain. It is bordered by the Persian Gulf (N), Oman (E), Saudi Arabia (W and S), and Qatar (NW). The terrain is flat, consisting mainly of desert. Abu Dhabi is more than six times the size of the other states put together, has the largest population, is the biggest oil producer and provides the federal capital, the city of Abu Dhabi. The other significant populations are Dubai and Sharjah. The population is almost exclusively Muslim (mostly SUNNI), though the great majority of inhabitants are expatriate workers. Formerly known as the Trucial States, the area was a British protectorate from 1892. After World War II the sheikhdoms were granted internal autonomy. In 1971 British troops withdrew from the Persian Gulf and the United Arab Emirates was formed. The UAE was part of the coalition against Iraq in the GULF WAR (1991). The economy is dominated by crude oil and natural gas production, accounting for about half of its GDP. Oil was first discovered in Abu Dhabi in the early 1960s, and the 1973 increase in oil prices transformed a relatively impoverished region into one of the world's wealthiest (1995 GDP per capita, US$16.470). Area: 32,280sq mi (83,600sq km). Pop. (1993 est.) 2,083,000.

**United Kingdom** (UK) Kingdom on the British Isles, W Europe. *See* country feature, page 692

**United Nations (UN)** International organization set up to enable countries to work together for peace and mutual development. It was established (June 1945) in a charter signed in San Francisco by 50 countries. In 1995 the UN had 185 members, essentially all the world's sovereign states except for North and South Korea and Switzerland.

**United Nations agencies** Executive bodies operating on behalf of and responsible to the UNITED NATIONS (UN). They include: the FOOD AND AGRICULTURE ORGANIZATION (FAO, Rome); INTERNATIONAL ATOMIC ENERGY AGENCY (IAEA, Vienna); International Civil Aviation Organization (ICAO, Montreal); INTERNATIONAL LABOR ORGANIZATION (ILO, Geneva); International Maritime Organization (IMO, London); INTERNATIONAL MONETARY FUND (IMF, Washington, DC); International Telecommunication Union (ITU, Geneva); United Nations Conference on Trade and Development (UNCTAD, Geneva); UNITED NATIONS EDUCATIONAL, SCIENTIFIC

AND CULTURAL ORGANIZATION (UNESCO, Paris); United Nations High Commission for Refugees (UNHCR, Geneva); UNITED NATIONS CHILDREN'S FUND (UNICEF, New York); Universal Postal Union (UPU, Bern); WORLD BANK (International Bank for Reconstruction and Development or IBRD, New York); and its own agencies, the International Development Association (IDA) and International Finance Corporation (IFC); World Food Council (WFC, Rome); World Food Program (WFP, Rome); WORLD HEALTH ORGANIZATION (WHO, Geneva), and World Trade Organization (WTO, Geneva). For administration in its headquarters in New York, the UN has a Secretariat staffed by international personnel.

**United Nations Children's Fund (UNICEF)** Intergovernmental organization, agency of the United Nations. Founded in 1946 (as the United Nations International Children's Emergency Fund), its aim is to assist children and adolescents worldwide, particularly in war-devastated areas and developing countries.

**United Nations Educational, Scientific and Cultural Organization (UNESCO)** Intergovernmental organization, agency of the United Nations. Founded in 1945, it aims to promote peace by improving the world's standard of education and by bringing together nations in cultural and scientific projects. It also gives aid to developing countries.

**United Nations peacekeeping force** Military personnel and their equipment placed at United Nations' disposal by member states. The function of the force is to keep the peace between warring factions anywhere in the world, as requested by the UNITED NATIONS SECURITY COUNCIL. The first UN peacekeeping forces were deployed (June 1948) in the Sinai Peninsula and Beirut. The greatest number of US troops deployed was in Bosnia during the mid-1990s.

**United Nations Security Council** Council responsible for taking action against any nation or faction considered to represent a threat to the security or continued wellbeing of a member state. Such action can be political, economic or, as a last resort, military. The Council also has the power to hold a formal investigation into matters of common concern. There are five permanent member states: the US, UK, France, Russia, and China.

**United States Air Force Academy** US educational institution. It offers a four-year curriculum for air force cadets that includes a baccalaureate level education in airmanship, related sciences, and the humanities. It was founded in 1955 and established (1958) in Colorado Springs, Colorado. Graduates normally enter the air force as second lieutenants.

**United States Military Academy** US educational institution. Formally opened in 1802 and located in WEST POINT, New York, the academy is a four-year institution in which army cadets receive a general education, and theoretical and practical training as junior officers. Upon course completion, the cadets normally receive a commission as a second lieutenant in the army.

**United States Naval Academy** US educational institution. It offers a four-year program of academic, military, and professional instruction for the training and education of young people for the naval service. Completion of the program normally leads to a commission in the US navy or the US marine corps. It was established in 1845 at Annapolis, Maryland.

**United States of America** (USA) Federal republic in North America. *See* country feature, page 694

**units** *See* WEIGHTS AND MEASURES

**universal product code** *See* BAR CODE

**universal time** System of time reckoning based on the mean solar day, the average interval between two successive transits of the Sun across the GREENWICH meridian.

**Universe** Aggregate of all MATTER, ENERGY, and SPACE. On a large scale, the Universe is considered uniform: it is identical in every part. It is believed to be expanding at a uniform rate, the galaxies all receding from one other. The origin, evolution, and future characteristics of the Universe are considered in several cosmological theories. Recent developments in astronomy imply a finite Universe, as postulated in the BIG BANG theory. See also COSMOLOGY; STEADY-STATE THEORY

**university** Institution of higher learning. Universities grew from the *studia generalia* of the 12th century, which provided education for priests and monks and were attended by students from all parts of Europe. Bologna became an important center of legal studies in the 11th century. Other great *studia generalia* were founded in the mid-12th century at Paris, OXFORD, and CAMBRIDGE. The first Scottish university was founded at St. Andrews *c.*1412, the first Irish university at Dublin (Trinity College) in 1591. The oldest US university is HARVARD, which was founded in 1636.

**unnilquadium** *See* ELEMENT 104

**unsaturated compound** In organic chemistry, compound in which two or more carbon atoms are linked, or bonded together, with double or triple bonds. Simple examples are ETHENE and ETHYNE.

**untouchables** Fifth and lowest *varna* (class) of the Indian CASTE system, making up *c.*20% of India's population. The term arises from the belief among higher castes, such as BRAHMIN, that to touch *panchamas* amounts to ritual pollution or defilement. Although their pariah status and the resultant social injustice were legally abolished in India (1949) and Pakistan (1953), much discrimination remains. *See also* HINDUISM

**Upanishads** (Sanskrit, session) Texts of HINDUISM, constituting the final stage of Vedic literature. Written in prose and verse, they take the form of dialogues between teacher and pupil. They are of uncertain authorship and date from *c.*650 BC or earlier. Often referred to as the VEDANTA, the *Upanishads* speculate on reality and man's salvation. *See also* BRAHMANISM

**Updike, John Hoyer** (1932– ) US writer. Updike is best known for his lyrical chronicles of Rabbit Angstrom, whose relationship crises often reflect contemporary social pressures. The tetralogy began with *Rabbit Run* (1960) and *Rabbit Redux* (1971). *Rabbit is Rich* (1981) won a Pulitzer Prize. The series was completed by *Rabbit at Rest* (1990). Other novels, which explore sexuality and morality, include *Couples* (1968) and *The Witches of Eastwick* (1984, filmed 1987). A regular contributor to *New Yorker* magazine since 1955, Updike is a master of shorter prose, such as the essay collection *Hugging the Shore* (1984) and the collection *Forty Stories* (1987).

**Upper Volta** Former name (until 1984) of BURKINA FASO

**Uppsala** Medieval city in E Sweden. Its university was founded in 1477. King GUSTAVUS I (VASA) is buried in the 15th-century cathedral. Industries: machinery, building materials, pharmaceuticals, printing, metal goods. Pop. (1994) 181,000.

**Ur** (Ur of the Chaldees) Ancient city of SUMERIA, S MESOPOTAMIA. Ur flourished in the 3rd millennium BC, but in *c.*2340 BC it was conquered by SARGON I. The Akkadian period witnessed the integration of Semitic and Sumerian cultures. In *c.*2060 BC the great ZIGGURAT was built by King Ur-Nammu. In *c.*2000 BC much of the city was detroyed by the invading Elamites. In the 6th century BC NEBUCHADNEZZAR briefly restored Ur as a center of Mesopotamian civilization, but by the 5th century BC it had fallen into terminal decline.

**Urals** Range of mountains in Russia, traditionally marking the boundary between Europe and Asia. The range extends 1,500mi (2,400km) from the Arctic in the N to the Ural River and the Kazakstan frontier in the S. The mountains are exten-

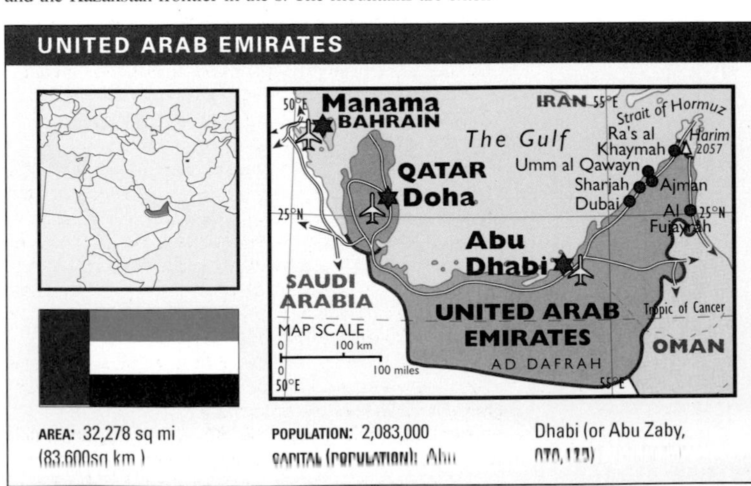

The flag of the United Kingdom was officially adopted in 1801. The first Union flag, combining the cross of St. George (England) and the cross of St. Andrew (Scotland), dates from 1603. In 1801 the cross of St. Patrick, Ireland's emblem, was added to form the present flag.

**AREA:** 94,202sq mi (243,368sq km)
**POPULATION:** 58,780,000
**CAPITAL POPULATION:** London (6,966,800)
**GOVERNMENT:** Constitutional monarchy
**ETHNIC GROUPS:** White 94%, Indian 1%, Pakistani 1%, West Indian 1%
**LANGUAGES:** English (official)
**RELIGIONS:** Christianity (Anglican 57%, Roman Catholic 13%, Presbyterian 7%, Methodist 4%, Baptist 1%), Islam 1%, Judaism, Hinduism, Sikhism
**CURRENCY:** Pound sterling = 100 pence

The United Kingdom of Great Britain and Northern IRELAND, is a union of four countries in the British Isles. Great Britain is composed of ENGLAND, SCOTLAND, and WALES. The Isle of MAN and the CHANNEL ISLANDS are self-governing UK dependencies. In 1536 England and Wales were formally united. Scotland and England were unified in the 1707 Act of Union. (For land, climate, vegetation, and separate history, *see* individual country articles.)

### HISTORY

In the 17th century England's development of empire was combined with a financial revolution which included the founding of the BANK OF ENGLAND (1694). Sir Robert WALPOLE's prime ministership (1721–42) marked the beginnings of CABINET government. Great Britain emerged from the SEVEN YEARS WAR (1756–63) as the world's leading imperial power. GEORGE III's conception of absolute monarchy and resistance to colonial reform led to conflict with parliament and contributed to the AMERICAN REVOLUTION (1776–83). William PITT (THE YOUNGER) oversaw the creation of the United Kingdom of Great Britain and Ireland (1801). The AGRICULTURAL REVOLUTION was both a cause and effect of the doubling of the population from 1801 to 1861. The INDUSTRIAL REVOLUTION brought profound socioeconomic changes. The 1820s and 1830s was an era of reform legislation including: the Act of CATHOLIC EMANCIPATION (1829); the abolition of SLAVERY (1833); harsh new POOR LAWS (1834), and the extension of the franchise to the middle class in the REFORM ACTS. Sir Robert PEEL's repeal of the CORN LAWS (1846) marked the beginnings of FREE TRADE and the emergence of the CONSERVATIVE PARTY from the old TORY PARTY. The LIBERAL PARTY similarly evolved out of the WHIG PARTY. The reign of VICTORIA saw the development of the second British Empire, spurred on by the imperial ambitions of Lord PALMERSTON. The importance of trade to the UK economy was firmly established. Between 1868 and 1880, UK politics was dominated by DISRAELI and GLADSTONE. The defeat of Gladstone's Home Rule Bill for Ireland (1886) split the Liberal Party. Between 1908 and 1916 Herbert ASQUITH and David LLOYD-GEORGE enacted a range of progressive social welfare policies, such as NATIONAL INSURANCE and state pensions. The growing power of Germany led to WORLD WAR I. GEORGE V changed the name of the British royal family from Saxe-Coburg to Windsor. The Allied victory cost the UK more than 750,000 lives. The UK was faced by rebellion in Ireland. The Anglo-Irish Treaty (1921) confirmed the partition of Ireland. The Irish Free State was formed in 1922, and the UK officially became known as the United Kingdom of Great Britain and Northern Ireland. In 1924 Ramsay MACDONALD formed the first LABOUR PARTY government. The COMMONWEALTH OF NATIONS was founded in 1931. In 1936 EDWARD VIII abdicated in favor of GEORGE VI. Neville CHAMBERLAIN's policy of APPEASEMENT toward Nazi Germany's growing imperial ambitions ended in failure. On September 3, 1939, following the German invasion of Poland, Britain declared war. From May 1940 Winston CHURCHILL led a coalition government which lasted throughout WORLD WAR II. Many UK cities were devastated in the Battle of BRITAIN (1940), but Britain remained unbowed. In 1941 the US and the Soviet Union joined the battle against Hitler. Germany surrendered in May 1945 and Japan in September 1945. Britain had lost more than 420,000 lives, and its economy was devastated. In 1945 elections, the Labour Party was swept back into power, with Clement ATLEE as prime minister. Atlee began a radical program of nationalization and increased welfare provision. The MARSHALL PLAN aided reconstruction. In 1948 the NATIONAL HEALTH SERVICE (NHS) was created. The British Empire was gradually dis-

Channel Is see page 117

## UNITED KINGDOM

mantled beginning with India in 1947. Most newly independent joined the Commonwealth. In 1949 the UK joined NATO. In 1951 Churchill returned to power. In 1952 ELIZABETH II succeeded George VI. Sir Anthony EDEN led Britain into the disastrous SUEZ CRISIS (1956). Sir Harold MACMILLAN realized the importance of Europe to UK trade. In 1959 the UK was a founder member of the European Free Trade Agreement (EFTA). In 1964 Harold WILSON narrowly defeated Sir Alec DOUGLAS-HOME. In 1968 the British Army was deployed in Northern Ireland to prevent the violent sectarian conflict that had followed civil rights marches. In 1971, under Edward HEATH, the UK adopted a decimal currency. In 1972 the British parliament assumed direct control of Northern Ireland. In 1973 the UK joined the EUROPEAN ECONOMIC COMMUNITY (EEC). Deep recession led to the introduction of a three-day working week. A miners' strike forced Heath to resign, and Wilson resumed office. The discovery of North Sea oil and natural gas decreased Britain's dependence on coal and fuel imports. James CALLAGHAN's inability to control labor unrest led to his defeat in 1979 elections. Margaret THATCHER became Britain's first woman prime minister. Thatcher introduced MONETARISM and PRIVATIZATION. Unemployment grew as Britain attempted to switch to a more service-centered economy. The FALKLANDS WAR (1982) contributed to Thatcher's reelection in 1983. A miners' strike (1984–85) was followed by further trade union restrictions. In 1987 Thatcher won a third general election. Urban decay, economic inequality, and an unpopular POLL TAX forced Thatcher to resign in 1990. John MAJOR signed the MAASTRICHT TREATY and won a surprise victory in the 1992 general election. He was soon forced to remove the pound from the EUROPEAN MONETARY SYSTEM (EMS). His administration was dogged by division over Europe. In the 1997 general election, Tony BLAIR's modernized Labour party won a landslide election to form the first Labour government for 18 years. In September 1997 referenda on devolution saw Scotland and Wales gain their own legislative assemblies. The Scottish assembly was given tax-varying power. The Good Friday Agreement (1998) offered the best chance of peace in Northern Ireland for a generation. In 1999 the UK contributed to NATO's military campaign in KOSOVO.

### ECONOMY

The UK is a major industrial and trading nation (1995 GDP per capita, US$19,260). Despite being a major producer of oil, petroleum products, natural gas, potash, salt, and lead, the UK lacks natural resources and has to import raw materials. In the early 20th century, the UK was a major exporter of ships, steel, and textiles. Automobiles remain a major product, but the economy has become more service-oriented, and high-technology industries have grown in importance. The UK produces only 66% of the food it needs. Agriculture employs only 2% of the workforce. Scientific and mass production methods ensure high productivity. Major crops include hops for beer, potatoes, carrots, sugar beet, strawberries, rapeseed, and linseed. Sheep are the leading livestock and wool is a leading product. Cheese and milk are major products. Fishing is another major activity. Financial services bring in much-needed revenue. Historic and cultural attractions make tourism a vital income source.

sively forested and the timber industry is important. The Urals' chief importance lies in their mineral deposits, which include iron ore, oil, coal, copper, nickel, gold, silver, zinc, and many precious stones. These resources have given rise to the Urals industrial region. Industrialism was increased under the first two Soviet five-year plans (1929–39) and during World War II, when many industries were moved from w Soviet Union. The highest peak is Mount Narodnaya, rising to 6,214ft (1,894m).

**uraninite** (pitchblende, $UO_2$) Dense, radioactive mineral form of uranium oxide. Uraninite is the chief ore of uranium and the most important source for uranium and radium. The blackish, lustrous ore occurs as a constituent of quartz veins. Hardness 5–6; sp.gr. 6.5–8.5.

**uranium** (symbol U) Radioactive, metallic element, one of the ACTINIDE SERIES. It was discovered in 1789 and is now used in NUCLEAR REACTORS and bombs. The ISOTOPE $^{238}U$ makes up more than 99% of natural uranium. Chemically, uranium is a reactive metal; it oxidizes in air and reacts with cold water. $^{235}U$ is fissionable and will sustain a neutron chain reaction as a fuel for reactors. Uranium is used to synthesize the TRANSURANIC ELEMENTS. Properties: at.no. 92; at. wt. 238.029; sp. gr. 19.05; m.p. 2,070°F (1,132°C); b.p. 6,904°F (3,818°C); most stable isotope $^{238}U$ (half-life $4.51 \times 10^9$ years).

**Uranus** Seventh planet from the Sun, discovered (1781) by Sir William HERSCHEL. Uranus is visible to the naked eye under good conditions. Like all the giant planets, it possesses a ring system and a retinue of SATELLITES. Like Pluto, Uranus' axis of rotation is steeply inclined, and its poles spend 42 years in sunlight, followed by 42 years in darkness. Exaggerated seasonal variations are, therefore, experienced by both the planet and its satellites. The fly-by of the Voyager 2 probe in 1986 provided most current knowledge of the planet. The upper atmosphere is about 83% molecular hydrogen, 15% helium, and the other 2% mostly methane. Uranus' 17 satellites are darkish bodies composed of ice and rock. The main components of Uranus' ring system were discovered in 1977 and others were imaged by Voyager.

**Uranus** In Greek mythology, the original god of the sky, and the husband and son of GAIA, with whom he was father to the TITANS and the CYCLOPES.

**Urban II** (*c.*1035–99) Pope (1088–99), b. Odo of Châtillon-sur-Marne. Urban carried on the reforms begun by Pope GREGORY VII. In 1095, at the Council of Clermont, he launched the idea of the First CRUSADE. His work as a reformer encouraged the development of the CURIA ROMANA.

**Urban V** (*c.*1310–70) Pope (1362–70), b. Guillaume de Grimoard. Crowned at AVIGNON, he tried in 1367 to return the papacy from Avignon to Rome. Insurrections at Rome and the Papal States forced him back to Avignon in 1370. As pope, he made a fruitless attempt to unite the Roman and Orthodox Churches.

**Urban VI** (1318–89) Pope (1378–89), b. Bartolomeo Prignano. The College of Cardinals declared his election invalid and appointed an ANTIPOPE, CLEMENT VII, beginning the GREAT SCHISM. Urban VI's papacy was marked by confusion and financial losses in the Papal States.

**Urdu** Language belonging to the Indic group of the Indo-Iranian subfamily of INDO-EUROPEAN LANGUAGES. It is the official language of Pakistan but is used as a first language by less than 10% of the population. It is also spoken by most Muslims in India. Urdu has virtually the same grammar as HINDI, the chief difference being that Urdu is written in the Arabic script. Both derive from SANSKRIT.

**urea** ($CO(NH_2)_2$) Organic compound, a white, crystalline solid excreted in URINE. Most vertebrates excrete their nitrogen wastes as urea; human urine contains about 25 grams of urea to a liter. Because it is so high in nitrogen, urea is a good fertilizer.

**ureter** In vertebrates, the long, narrow duct that connects the KIDNEY to the urinary BLADDER. It transports URINE from the kidney to the bladder.

**urethra** Duct through which URINE is discharged from the bladder in mammals. In males, the urethra is also the tube through which SEMEN is ejaculated.

**urethritis** Inflammation of the URETHRA. It is usually due to a SEXUALLY TRANSMITTED DISEASE, but may also arise from infection.

**Urey, Harold Clayton** (1893–1981) US chemist. He was awarded the 1934 Nobel Prize for chemistry for his isolation of DEUTERIUM, an isotope of hydrogen. Urey later isolated isotopes of oxygen, nitrogen, carbon, and sulfur. During World War II he helped in the research that led to the production of the atomic bomb. Urey then turned to GEOPHYSICS and worked on recreating the atmospheric conditions of the primeval Earth to elucidate the origin of life.

**urine** Fluid filtered out from the bloodstream by the KIDNEY. It consists mainly of water, salts, and waste products such as UREA. From the kidneys it passes through the URETERS to the BLADDER for voiding by way of the URETHRA.

**urogenital system** Organs comprising the body's urinary and reproductive systems. The urinary system consists of the

### URANUS: DATA

Diameter (equatorial): 31,765mi (51,118km)
Mass (Earth = 1): 14.6
Volume (Earth = 1): 67
Density (water = 1): 1.27
Orbital period: 84.01 years
Rotation period: 17h 14m 0s
Average surface temperature: −417°F (−214°C)
Surface gravity (Earth = 1): 0.79

U

The "Stars and Stripes" has had the same basic design since 1777, during the American Revolution. The 13 stripes represent the 13 original colonies in the Eastern United States. The 50 stars represent the 50 states of the Union.

**AREA:** 3,618,765sq mi (9,372,610sq km)
**POPULATION:** 259,681,000
**CAPITAL (POPULATION):** Washington, D.C. (585,221)
**GOVERNMENT:** Federal republic
**ETHNIC GROUPS:** White 80%, African-American 12%, other races 8%
**LANGUAGES:** English (official), Spanish, more than 30 others
**RELIGIONS:** Christianity (Protestant 53%, Roman Catholic 26%, other Christian 8%), Islam 2%, Judaism 2%
**CURRENCY:** US dollar = 100 cents

The United States of America is made up of a federal district (the capital Washington, D.C.) and 50 states (48 of which form a large block of land between Canada and Mexico). The other two states are Alaska in NW North America, which contains the country's highest peak, Mount McKinley at 20,322ft (6,194m), and the North Pacific archipelago of Hawaii. On the NE border with Canada are the Great Lakes. Chicago lies on the shore of Lake Michigan. The densely populated E seaboard includes the major cities of Boston, New York, Philadelphia, and Baltimore. The major rivers of the E are the Hudson, Delaware, and Potomac. Florida lies on a peninsula between the Atlantic and the Gulf of Mexico, and includes the city of Miami. The coastal plain is backed by the Appalachians, including the Blue Ridge Mountains. The central lowlands are drained by the Mississippi-Missouri river system, which forms an enormous delta near New Orleans. The Great Plains gently rise to the Rocky Mountains which form the continental divide. Mount Elbert is the highest peak in the Rockies. The Columbia and Colorado rivers flow into the Pacific Ocean. Between the Rockies and the Pacific coast lie plateaus, basins, and ranges. The Grand Canyon was carved out from the Colorado plateau by the Colorado River. The Great Basin includes Salt Lake City and desert regions including Las Vegas and Death Valley, the lowest point in the western hemisphere, 282ft (86m) below sea level. The Pacific seaboard, including the cities of San Francisco, Los Angeles, and San Diego, is fringed by mountain ranges such as the Sierra Nevada, which includes Mount Whitney (the highest peak outside Alaska). The NW Cascade Range contains active volcanoes, such as Mount St. Helens. Seattle lies in the foothills of the range. (*See also* individual gazetteer articles)

### Climate

Temperatures vary from the Arctic cold of Alaska to the intense heat of Death Valley. Of the 48 states, winters are cold and snowy in the N, but mild in the S. The S states have long, hot summers. Rainfall is heaviest in the NW, lightest in the SW.

### Vegetation

Alaska contains forests of conifers. In the N states are extensive forests, with huge redwoods along the Pacific coast, such as Sequoia National Park. In the E, the original deciduous forests only remain in protected areas, such as Great Smoky Mountains National Park. The dry, central prairies merge into the high steppe of the Great Plains. Large areas of the SW are desert.

### History and Politics

Native Americans arrived perhaps 40,000 years ago from Asia. Vikings, led by Leif Ericsson, probably reached North America 1,000 years ago, but did not settle. European exploration did not begin until the discovery of the New World by Christopher Columbus in 1492. The first permanent European settlement was founded by Spain in 1565 at St. Augustine, Florida. The French also formed settlements in Louisiana, but the first major colonists were the British, who founded Jamestown, Virginia, in 1607. In 1620 Puritans landed at Cape Cod, Massachusetts and founded the Plymouth Colony. The economic success of Massachusetts encouraged further colonization along the E coast. In 1681 William Penn founded Pennsylvania. In the southern colonies, slavery was used to develop plantations. During the 18th century, British mercantilism (especially the Navigation Acts) restricted commercial growth. The Great Awakening and the development of higher education promoted greater cultural self-consciousness. The defeat of the French in the French and Indian Wars (1754–63) encouraged independence movements. Benjamin Franklin's failure to win concessions from the British led to the American Revolution (1775–83), which

The highest mountain in the USA is Mount McKinley (6194m) in Alaska.

MAP SCALE
0 250 500 km
0 250 miles

ended British rule in the Thirteen Colonies. George Washington, commander-in-chief of the Continental Army, became the first president. The Articles of Confederation (1777) produced weak central government, and were superseded by the Constitution of the United States (1787). The Bank of the United States was created in 1791. US politics became divided between the Federalist Party and the Democratic Republican Party. In 1796 the Federalist president John Adams passed the Alien and Sedition Acts (1798). The XYZ Affair saw armed confrontation with France. In 1801 the Democratic-Republican Thomas Jefferson became president. Jefferson negotiated the Louisiana Purchase (1803), which nearly doubled the size of the US. James Madison led the US into the War of 1812, which cemented the nation's independence and culminated in the Monroe Doctrine (1823), which sought to protect the western hemisphere from European interference. The Missouri Compromise (1820) papered over the growing conflict between the commercial, industrial North and the cotton plantations of the proslavery South. The Democratic-Republican Party became simply the Democratic Party. Andrew Jackson's presidency furthered the westward expansion of the frontier. The march to the Pacific became the "manifest destiny" of the US. In 1841 William Harrison became the first Whig president. Texas was acquired (1845) and Oregon Territory (1846). The Mexican War (1846–48) confirmed US acquisitions. The 1848 discovery of gold in California prompted a rush of settlers. Territorial expansion was achieved at the expense of Native Americans, who were forced onto reservations. The addition of states to the Union intensified the conflict between free and slave states. The repeal of the Missouri Compromise led to the founding of the antislavery Republican Party (1854). In 1861 Abraham Lincoln became the first Republican president. The southern states seceded as the Confederate States of America. The Civil War (1861–65) claimed more than 600,000 lives and devastated the country. The Union victory resulted in the abolition of slavery. The enforced Reconstruction of the South was highly unpopular. Ulysses S. Grant's administration was plagued by corruption. In 1867 the US bought Alaska from Russia. The late 19th century was the era of the railroad, which sped industrialization and urban development. The gleaming, steel skyscrapers symbolized opportunity and millions of European immigrants were attracted to the US. In 1886 the American Federation of Labor was founded. The Spanish-American War (1898) heralded the emergence of the US as a major world power. Hawaii was annexed. Construction of the Panama Canal began in 1902. In 1917 Woodrow Wilson led the US into World War I. The economic boom and prohibition of the 1920s was followed by the the Great Depression of the 1930s. Franklin D. Roosevelt's New Deal attempted to restore prosperity. The Japanese bombing of Pearl Harbor (December 7, 1941) prompted US entry into World War II. Rearmament fueled economic recovery. Harry S. Truman became president on Roosevelt's death in 1945. The use of atomic bombs led to Japan's surrender. The US was a founder member of NATO. Postwar tension with the Soviet Union led to the Cold War and spurred the space race. In order to stem the spread of communism, US forces fought in the Korean War (1950–53). In 1955 Martin Luther King launched the civil rights movement. The start of John F. Kennedy's presidency was marred by the Cuban Missile Crisis (1962). Kennedy's assassination (November 22, 1963) shocked the nation. Lyndon Johnson led the US into the Vietnam War (1965–73). Anti-Vietnam protests were coupled with civil unrest. On July 20, 1969 Neil Armstrong became the first man on the Moon. In 1974 Richard Nixon was forced to resign by the Watergate scandal. The Camp David Agreement crowned Jimmy Carter's foreign policy initiatives. The start of Ronald Reagan's presidency (1981–89) marked the deepest recession since the Great Depression. Economic recovery brought increases in defense spending. Reagan's loosening grip on power was highlighted by the Iran-Contra affair (1987–88). Following the collapse of Soviet communism in 1991, George Bush proclaimed a New World Order. Despite the success of the Gulf War (1991), domestic recession led to Bush's defeat in 1992. Bill Clinton's reform program was largely blocked by a Republican-dominated Senate. Despite allegations of financial and personal scandal, economic recovery led to his reelection in 1996. In 1999 he survived impeachment charges and authorized the use of force against Iraq and Serbia.

### Economy

The US is the world's largest manufacturing nation (1992 GDP per capita, US$26,980). The 1992 North American Free Trade Agreement (NAFTA) with Canada and Mexico created the world's largest trading bloc. The US is the world's largest farm producer. Agriculture is highly mechanized, employing only 2% of the workforce. Major products include poultry, beef, and dairy cattle. Leading crops include cotton, hops for beer, fruits, peanuts, corn, potatoes, soybeans, tobacco, and wheat. Fishing is important. The US's chief natural resources include oil, natural gas, and coal. Timber and paper manufacture are important. Major industries include automobiles, chemicals, machinery, computers, and printing. California is the leading manufacturing state. Services form the largest sector, including finance and tourism (1992 receipts, US$53,361 million).

## URUGUAY

**AREA:** 68,498 sq mi (177,410sq km)
**POPULATION:** 3,116,802
**CAPITAL (POPULATION):** Montevideo (1,383,660)
**GOVERNMENT:** Multiparty republic
**ETHNIC GROUPS:** White 86%, Mestizo 8%, Mulatto or Black 6%
**LANGUAGES:** Spanish (official)
**RELIGIONS:** Christianity (Roman Catholic 66%, Protestant 2%), Judaism 1%
**CURRENCY:** Uruguay peso = 100 centésimos

▲ **Ustinov** Of French and Russian parentage, Peter Ustinov was born in London. A successful actor and playwright, in recent years he has become best known for his one-man shows, which provide him with the opportunity to portray a variety of characters.

KIDNEYS, URETERS, the BLADDER, and URETHRA. In males, the reproductive system consists of paired TESTES located in the scrotum; accessory glands; and the PENIS. In females, the reproductive system consists of: paired OVARIES; FALLOPIAN TUBES, which provide a passage from the ovaries to the UTERUS; the CERVIX; and the VAGINA.

**urology** Medical specialty concerned with the diagnosis and treatment of diseases of the urinary tract in women and of the urinary and reproductive systems in men.

**Ursa Major** (Great Bear) Northern constellation, whose main pattern, consisting of seven stars, is known as the **Big Dipper** or **Plow**. Five of the Plow stars make up a CLUSTER.

**Ursa Minor** Constellation that contains the north celestial pole. Its brightest star is Alpha, the POLE STAR. The constellation's seven main stars make a pattern resembling a faint and distorted plow.

**Ursula, Saint** (active 4th century AD) Legendary virgin and martyr, who according to some traditions was a British princess. She was especially honored at Cologne, where she is said to have been slain by the HUNS with her 11 (or in some reports 11,000) virgins on their return from a pilgrimage to Rome. She has become the patron of many educational establishments, including the Ursuline order.

**urticaria** *See* HIVES

**Uruguay** Republic in South America; the capital is MONTEVIDEO. **Land and climate** The land consists of low-lying plains and hills, rising to a highest point, Mirador Nacional, which is only 1,644ft (501m) above sea level. The main river in the interior is the Río Negro. The URUGUAY River, which forms the country's W border, flows into the Río de la PLATA, a large estuary leading into the South Atlantic Ocean. Uruguay has a mild climate, with rain throughout the year, though droughts sometimes occur. The summer months are pleasantly warm, especially near the coast. Grasslands cover 77% of Uruguay and arable land about 7%. Such trees as acacia, aloe, eucalyptus, and willow grow along the river valleys. Uruguay also has commercial tree plantations, including such trees as quebracho, whose wood and bark contain tannin, which is used in tanning and dyeing. **History** The original Native American inhabitants of Uruguay have largely disappeared. Many were killed by Europeans, others died of European diseases, while some fled into the interior. The first European to arrive in Uruguay was a Spanish navigator in 1516, but few Europeans settled there until the late 17th century. In 1726 Spanish settlers founded Montevideo in order to prevent the Portuguese gaining influence in the area. By the late 18th century, Spaniards had settled in most of the country, and Uruguay became part of a colony called the Viceroyalty of La Plata, which also included Argentina, Paraguay, and parts of Bolivia, Brazil, and Chile. In 1820 Brazil annexed Uruguay, ending Spanish rule. In 1825 Uruguayans, supported by Argentina, began a struggle for independence and finally, in 1828, Brazil and Argentina recognized Uruguay as an independent republic. Social and economic development were slow in the 19th century, with many revolutions and counterrevolutions. In 1903, following the election of Batlle y Ordóñez as president, Uruguay became a more democratic and stable country. From the 1950s, economic problems caused unrest. Terrorist groups, notably the Tupumaros, carried out murders and kidnappings. In 1972 the army crushed the Tupumaros, and then took over the government in 1973. Repressive military rule continued until 1984, when civilian rule was reestablished. However, economic difficulties and high foreign debts continued to threaten stability, provoking massive emigration. Julio María Sanguinetti, who had led Uruguay back to civilian rule in the 1980s, was reelected president in 1994. **Economy** Uruguay is an upper-middle-income developing country (1995 GDP per capita, US$6,630). Agriculture employs only 5% of the workforce, but farm products, notably hides and leather goods, beef and wool, are leading exports, while the main crops include corn, potatoes, sugar beet, and wheat. The leading manufacturing industries, situated mainly in and around Montevideo, are concerned with processing farm produce. Other manufactures include beer, cement, textiles, and tires. Tourism is important.

**Uruguay** River in SE South America. Rising in S Brazil and forming part of the boundary between Rio Grande do Sul and Santa Catarina states, it flows SW to form the boundary between Argentina and S Brazil, and then Argentina and Uruguay. It empties into the Río de la PLATA. Length: *c.*1,000mi (1,600km).

**USA** Abbreviation of UNITED STATES OF AMERICA

**USSR** Abbreviation of Union of Soviet Socialist Republics, *see* SOVIET UNION

**Ustinov, Peter Alexander** (1921– ) British actor and dramatist. His plays include *The Love of Four Colonels* (1951) and *Romanoff and Juliet* (1956). Ustinov has acted in many films, including *Billy Budd* (1962), which he also directed. In recent years he has won a reputation as an entertaining raconteur.

**usury** Lending of money at an excessive or unlawful rate of interest. Before the Middle Ages any payment for the use of money was regarded as usury by Christians. In the late Middle Ages reasonable interest on a loan became acceptable when the lender risked capital.

**Utah** State in the W US, in the Rocky Mountains. The state capital is SALT LAKE CITY, other cities include Provo and Ogden. Utah has two distinct geographical regions. To the E of the Wasatch are the Rockies. To the W is the GREAT BASIN, which includes GREAT SALT LAKE. Utah's major settlements lie in a fertile region between Great Salt Lake and the Wasatch range. In the Pleistocene epoch Western Utah was submerged beneath Lake Bonneville. Today, Bonneville Salt Flats are a site for land speed record attempts. In S Utah are spectacular canyons formed by the Colorado River. The first permanent settlement was made in 1847, when Brigham YOUNG led the MORMONS into the valley of Great Salt Lake. In 1848 the region was ceded to the US at the end of the MEXICAN WAR. Conflicts arose between federal authorities and the Church of the Latter-Day Saints, and in 1857–58 federal troops were sent to Utah. Settlement increased with the completion (1869) of the Union Pacific railroad and the land was made productive through irrigation schemes. Industry expanded rapidly during World War II, and the postwar development of hydoelectric plants continued this process. The terrain hinders agriculture, but hay, barley, wheat, beans, and sugar beet are grown. The chief farming activity is stock raising. Mining is also important: there are rich deposits of copper, petroleum, coal, molybdenum, silver, lead, and gold. Tourism is vital to the economy. Area: 84,915sq mi (219,931sq km). Pop. (1992) 1,811,215.

**Utamaro, Kitagawa** (1753–1806) Japanese master of the UKIYO-E woodblock color print, the first Japanese artist to become famous in the West. He excelled in depicting birds, flowers, and feminine beauty. His works were strongly erotic, precise, graceful, and immensely popular.

**Ute** Shoshonean-speaking tribe of Native North Americans. They were fierce, nomadic warriors, who engaged in warfare with other Native American tribes and hunted bison. Today, *c*.4,000 live on reservations in Colorado and Utah.

**uterus** (womb) Hollow, muscular organ located in the pelvis of female mammals. It protects and nourishes the growing FETUS until birth. The upper part is broad and branches out on each side into the FALLOPIAN TUBES. The lower uterus narrows into the CERVIX, which leads to the VAGINA. Its muscular walls are lined with mucous membrane (ENDOMETRIUM), to which the fertilized egg attaches itself. *See also* MENSTRUAL CYCLE

**utilitarianism** Branch of ethical philosophy. It holds that actions are to be judged good or bad according to their consequences. An action is deemed to be morally right if it produces good results. Utilitarianism was developed by the English philosophers Jeremy BENTHAM, James MILL, and J.S. MILL.

**Uto-Aztecan languages** Family of Native American languages spoken in SW US and Mexico. It includes COMANCHE of Oklahoma and SHOSHONE, spoken in some W states. In Mexico there are NAHUATL (the language of the Aztecs), Tarahumara, and Mayo.

**Utopianism** (Gk. no place) Projection of ideal states or alternative worlds, which are ordered for the benefit of all and where social ills have been eradicated. Sir Thomas MORE's *Utopia* (1516) outlines his notion of an ideal commonwealth based entirely on reason. It critically describes contemporary social existence, while prescribing a transcendent, imaginative vision of the best of all possible worlds. Enlightenment philosophers, such as Jean Jacques ROUSSEAU, portrayed a vision of a prefeudal European Golden Age. Writers such as SAINT-SIMON, Charles FOURIER, and Robert OWEN outlined ideal communities based on cooperation and economic self-sufficiency. Karl MARX and Friedrich ENGELS valued the social insights of utopianism, but rejected its unscientific analysis of political and economic realities. By the late 19th century, the utopian novel had become an established literary genre. Works such as *Erewhon* (1872) by Samuel Butler were influential. The spread of TOTALITARIANISM in Europe during the 1930s encouraged **dystopian** novels, such as *Brave New World* (1932) by Aldous Huxley and *1984* (1949) by George Orwell.

**Utrecht, Peace of** (1713–14) Series of treaties that ended the War of the SPANISH SUCCESSION. It confirmed the BOURBON King PHILIP V on the Spanish throne on condition that he renounced any claim to the throne of France. Austria received the Spanish Netherlands and extensive Italian territories; Britain gained Gibraltar, Minorca, and provinces of E Canada.

**Uttar Pradesh** State in N India, bordering Nepal and Tibet; its capital is LUCKNOW. The heartland of early Hindu civilization, it is the hub of India's Hindi-speaking region. It is by far the most populous Indian state. The region has the foothills of the Himalayas to the N and hills in the S, enclosing a low-lying plain drained by the GANGES and its tributaries. The economy is based on agriculture, mainly cereals, sugarcane, rice, and pulses, and the mining of coal, copper, bauxite, and limestone. Industries: cotton and sugar processing. Area: 113,673sq mi (294,413sq km). Pop. (1991) 139,112,287.

**Uzbekistan** Republic in central Asia; the capital is TASHKENT. **Land and climate** There are plains in the W and highlands in the E. The main rivers, the Amu Darya and Syr Darya, drain into the ARAL SEA. So much water has been diverted from these rivers to irrigate farmland that the Aral Sea has shrunk from 25,830sq mi (66,900sq km) in 1960 to 12,989sq mi (33,642sq km) in 1993. The dried-up lake area has become desert, like much of the rest of the country. Uzbekistan has a continental climate, with cold winters and hot summers. The W is extremely arid, with an average annual rainfall of *c*.8in (200mm), but parts of the highlands in the E have three times as much rain. Grassy steppe occurs in wetter areas, with forests on the mountain slopes. **History and politics** Turkic people first settled in the area that is now Uzbekistan *c*.1,500 years ago and Islam was introduced in the 7th century AD. MONGOLS invaded the land in the 13th century and, in the late 14th century, TAMERLANE ruled a great empire from SAMARKAND. Turkic Uzbek people invaded in the 16th century and gradually the area was divided into states (khanates). Russia controlled the area in the 19th century, and following the RUSSIAN REVOLUTION of 1917, the communists took over, establishing the Uzbek Soviet Socialist Republic in 1924. Under communism, all aspects of Uzbek life were controlled; religious worship was discouraged, but education, health, housing, and transportation services were improved. The communists also increased cotton production, but caused great environmental damage in doing so. In the 1980s, when reforms were being introduced in the Soviet Union, the Uzbeks demanded more freedom. In 1990 the government unilaterally declared independence from the Soviet Union. In 1991, following the break-up of the Soviet Union, Uzbekistan became a sovereign nation. It retained its links with Russia, however, through membership of the COMMONWEALTH OF INDEPENDENT STATES (CIS). On December 29, 1991, Islam Karimov, leader of the People's Democratic Party (formerly the Communist Party), was elected president. In 1992 and 1993 many opposition leaders were arrested. In order to avoid internal disruption, Karimov asserted that economic reform would be slow. Elections in 1994–95 resulted in a sweeping victory for the People's Democratic Party. A referendum in 1995 extended President Karimov's term in office until 2000. **Economy** Uzbekistan is a lower-middle-income developing country (1995 GDP per capita, US$2,370). The government controls most economic activity. The country produces coal, copper, gold, oil, and natural gas; manufactures include agricultural machinery, chemicals, and textiles. Agriculture is important, with cotton the main crop. Other crops include fruits, rice, and vegetables. Cattle, sheep, and goats are also reared. Uzbekistan's exports include cotton, gold, textiles, chemicals, and fertilizers.

**Uzbeks** Turkic-speaking people, originally from Persia, who form two thirds of the population of UZBEKISTAN. They took their name from Uzbeg Khan (d.1340), a chief of the GOLDEN HORDE . By the end of the 16th century, the Uzbeks had extended their rule to parts of Persia, Afghanistan, and Chinese TURKISTAN. Their empire was never united and in the 19th century its various states were absorbed by Russia.

**UTAH**
**Statehood :**
January 4, 1896
**Nickname :**
The Beehive State
**State bird :**
Sea gull
**State flower :**
Sego lily
**State tree :**
Blue spruce
**State motto :**
Industry

**UZBEKISTAN**

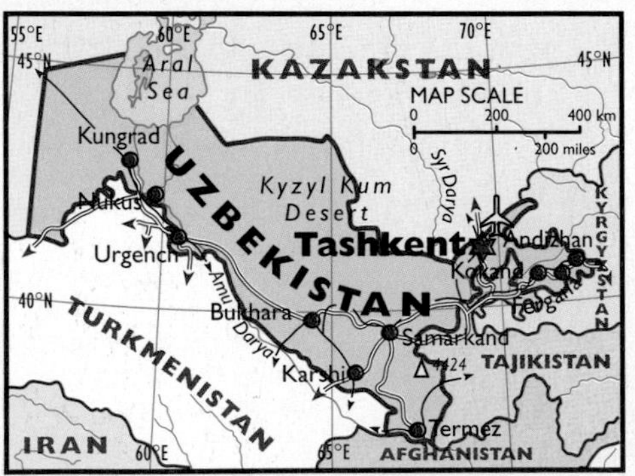


**AREA:** 172,740sq mi (447,400sq km)
**POPULATION:** 21,206,800
**POPULATION:** Tashkent (2,094,300)

**ETHNIC GROUPS:** Uzbek 71%, Russian 8%, Tajik 5%, Kazak 4%, Tatar 2%, Kara-Kalpak 2%, Crimean Tatar, Korean, Kyrgyz, Ukrainian, Turkmen

**LANGUAGES:** Uzbek (official)
**RELIGIONS:** Islam
**CURRENCY:** Som

U

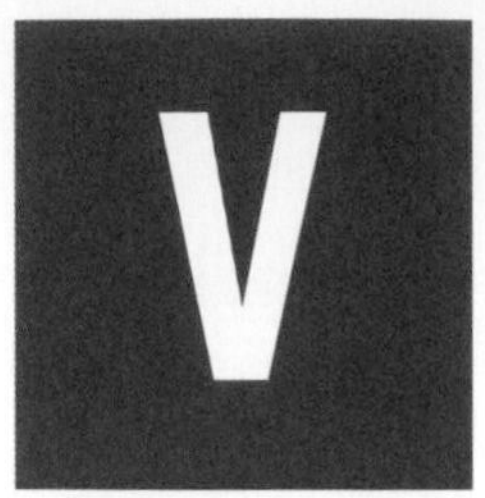

***V/v, 22nd letter of the Roman alphabet, derived (as were* f, u *and* y*) from the Semitic letter* vaw, *meaning* hook. *It was identical to* u *in the Greek and Roman alphabets, and was not differentiated from* u *in English until the Middle Ages.***

**V1, V2 rockets** (abbreviation for *Vergeltungswaffen*, Vengeance Weapons). The **V-1**s, popularly known as **doodlebugs**, **flying bombs**, or **buzz bombs,** were pilotless aircraft, powered by a pulse-jet engine, with a guidance system composed of a distance-measuring device, a GYROCOMPASS, and an altimeter. Launched by the LUFTWAFFE against SE England in June 1944, they carried about a ton of high explosive. Later the same year, England was attacked by the **V-2**, a long-range, ballistic missile carrying a 1-ton warhead to a range of 200mi (320km), with an altitude of 60–70mi (95–110km). It was powered by a mixture of liquid oxygen and ethyl alcohol, and was the precursor of postwar missiles.

**vaccination** Injection of a VACCINE in order to produce IMMUNITY against a disease. In many countries, children are vaccinated routinely against infectious diseases.

**vaccine** Agent used to give IMMUNITY against various diseases without producing symptoms. A vaccine consists of modified disease organisms, such as live, weakened VIRUSES, or dead ones that are still able to induce the production of specific ANTIBODIES within the blood. *See also* IMMUNE SYSTEM

**vacuole** Membrane-bound, fluid-filled cavity within the CYTOPLASM of a CELL. Vacuoles perform various functions including the discharge of wastes from cell metabolism.

**vacuum** Region of extremely low pressure. Interstellar space is a high vacuum, with an average density of less than 1 molecule per cubic centimeter; the highest man-made vacuums contain less than 100,000 molecules per cubic centimeter.

**vacuum flask** Container for keeping things (usually liquids) hot or cold. A vacuum flask is made with double, silvered, glass walls, separated by a near VACUUM. This vessel is held in an insulated metal or plastic case. The vacuum reduces heat transfer by conduction of convection between the contents and the surroundings. The silvering on the glass minimizes heat transfer by radiation.

**vagina** Portion of the female reproductive tract, running from the CERVIX of the UTERUS to the exterior of the body. Tubelike in shape, it receives the PENIS during sexual intercourse. Its muscular walls enable it to dilate during childbirth.

**valence** (valency) Measure of the "combining power" of a particular element, equal to the number of single CHEMICAL BONDS one atom can form or the number of electrons it gives up or accepts when forming a compound. Hydrogen has a valency of 1, carbon 4, and sulfur 2, as seen in compounds such as methane ($CH_4$), carbon disulfide ($CS_2$), and hydrogen sulfide ($H_2S$).

**Valencia** City in E Spain, capital of the province of Valencia, situated on the Turia River. The region of Valencia comprises the provinces of Alicante, Castellón, and Valencia. Originally settled by the Romans, the city was conquered by the MOORS in the 8th century, eventually becoming capital of the independent Moorish kingdom of Valencia. In the Spanish CIVIL WAR it was the last Republican stronghold to fall to Nationalist forces. It is an agricultural, industrial, and communications center. Industries: electrical equipment, chemicals, textiles, shipbuilding, machinery, fruit, wine. Tourists are drawn by the city's many fine buildings. Pop. (1991) 752,909.

**Valencia** City in N Venezuela, capital of Carabobo state. It was the capital of Venezuela in 1830, when the country was proclaimed independent of Greater Colombia. It is an industrial and transport center. Industries: textiles, paper, cement, glass, soap, furniture vehicles, brewing. Pop. (1990) 903,076.

**Valentine, Saint** Name traditionally associated with two legendary saints of the 3rd century: Valentine of Rome and Valentine of Interamna (modern Terni). The former was a Roman priest and physician, and the latter the Bishop of Terni. Little is known about either, and they may have been the same person. The martyrdom of both is commemorated on February 14. The custom of lovers exchanging cards on St. Valentine's Day possibly has its roots in the pagan Roman festival of Lupercalia, an ancient fertility rite celebrated in Rome on February 15.

**Valentino, Rudolph** (1895–1926) US silent-film star, b. Italy. He exemplified the Latin lover, and his films include *The Sheik* (1921), *The Eagle* (1925), and *Son of the Sheik* (1926). Valentino's early death from a ruptured ulcer caused widespread hysteria among his fans.

**valerian** (garden heliotrope) Plant native to Europe and N Asia and naturalized in the US. It has pinkish or pale purple flower clusters. Height: to 4ft (1.2m). Family Valerianaceae; species *Valeriana officinalis*.

**Valéry, Paul** (1871–1945) French poet and critic. He was influenced by MALLARMÉ, and his poems, which include *The Young Fate* (1917) and *Charmes* (1922), are characterized by lyricism and abstract thought. His *Notebooks* (1957–60) record his thoughts on a wide range of issues. He was elected to the Académie Française (1925).

**Valhalla** In Norse mythology, Hall of the Slain, where chosen warriors enjoyed feasts with the god ODIN. It is depicted as a glittering palace, with golden walls and a ceiling of burnished shields.

**Valium** Proprietary name for diazepam, a sedative drug in the BENZODIAZEPINE group. It is used in the treatment of anxiety, muscle spasms, and epilepsy.

**Valkyries** In Norse mythology, warlike handmaidens of the god ODIN, who selected and conducted to VALHALLA those slain heroes who merited a place with him.

**Valladolid** City on the Pisuerga River, NW central Spain, capital of Valladolid province. The city was liberated from the Moors by Castilian kings in the 10th century. There is a 12th-century Romanesque church and a monument to Christopher Columbus, who died in the city. Valladolid's university, founded in 1346, is one of the oldest in Spain. Industries: vehicles, railroad engineering, chemicals, flour milling, metalwork, textiles. The province produces fruit, wine, and cereals. Pop. (1991) 328,365.

**Valletta** Port and capital of Malta, on the NE coast of the island. It was founded in the 16th century and named for Jean Parisot de la Valette, Grand Master of the Order of the Knights of St. John, who organized the reconstruction of the city after repelling the Turks' Great Siege of 1565. Notable buildings include the Royal University of Malta (1592) and the Cathedral of San Giovanni (1576). Industries: shipbuilding and repairs, transshipment, tourism. Pop. (1995) 102,571.

**valley** Elongated, gently sloping depression of the Earth's surface. It often contains a stream or river that receives the drainage from the surrounding heights. A U-shaped valley was probably formed by a glacier, a V-shaped one by a stream. The term may also be applied to a broad, generally flat area that is drained by a large river.

**Valley Forge** Site of the winter camp of the army of George WASHINGTON in 1777–78, 21mi (34km) NW of Philadelphia, Pennsylvania. The men were short of food, proper housing, and clothes, and about 2,500 out of 11,000 died. Their ordeal became symbolic of the heroism of the colonial troops in the AMERICAN REVOLUTION.

**Valois, Dame Ninette de** (1898– ) Irish ballerina and choreographer, b. Edris Stannus. She danced with Diaghilev's BALLETS RUSSES (1923–26). In 1931 she founded the Sadler's Wells Ballet School, which later became the Royal Ballet.

**Valparaíso** Main port of Chile and capital of Valparaíso region, 60mi (100km) W of Santiago. Founded in 1536, the city has always been vulnerable to earthquakes. As well as Chile's chief port, it is also a cultural center, with two universities and museums of fine arts and natural history. Industries: chemicals, textiles, sugar refining, vegetable oils, paint. Pop. (1992) 276,736.

**value-added tax (VAT)** Indirect tax imposed in most European countries. Introduced in Britain in 1971, it consists of a series of taxes (calculated as a percentage) levied on goods (or services) in the various stages of their manufacture until the point of sale.

**valves** In anatomy, structures that prevent the backflow of blood in the HEART and VEINS. Heart valves separate and connect the two atria and ventricles, the right ventricle and the pulmonary artery, and the left ventricle and the aorta.

**vampire bat** Small, brown bat that lives in tropical and subtropical America. It uses its sharp teeth to slice the skin of resting animals (including human beings) and then laps up their blood. Length: 3in (7.6cm); wingspan 12in (30cm). Family Desmodontidae; species *Desmodus rotundus*.

**vanadium** (symbol V) Silver-white, metallic element, one of the TRANSITION ELEMENTS. Discovered in 1801, the malleable and ductile metal is found in iron, lead, and uranium ores, and in coal and petroleum. It is used in steel alloys to add strength and heat resistance. Chemically, vanadium reacts with oxygen and other nonmetals at high temperature. Properties: at.no. 23; at.wt. 50.9414; sp.gr. 6.1 at 65.6°F; m.p. 3,434°F (1,890°C); b.p. 6,116°F (3,380°C); most common isotope $^{51}$V (99.76%).

**Van Allen radiation belts** Two rings of radiation trapped by the Earth's magnetic field in the upper atmosphere. The belts contain high-energy, charged particles.

**Van Buren, Martin** (1782–1862) Eighth US President (1837–41). Van Buren served (1921–28) in the Senate. As Andrew JACKSON's secretary of state, his opposition to John C. CALHOUN's idea of NULLIFICATION earned him the vice-presidency (1832–36) and the Democratic nomination. As president, he supported STATES' RIGHTS on the slavery issue, embarked on the SEMINOLE Wars, and declined federal intervention in the economic depression (1837). He was defeated when he stood for reelection in 1840.

**Vancouver** City on the S shore of Burrard Inlet, S British Columbia, Canada. It is Canada's third-largest city and principal Pacific port. The area was first explored in 1792 by Captain George Vancouver. The building of the Canadian Pacific Railroad allowed it to grow into the largest city on the Canadian W coast. Its excellent sea and air links make it one of N America's leading centers for transportation and communication with countries of the Pacific Rim. Vancouver's beautiful harbor setting, pleasant climate, and position as the terminus of both trans-Canadian railroads make it a magnet for tourists. The city has two universities: British Columbia (1908) and Simon Fraser University (1963). Industries: tourism, timber, oil refining, shipbuilding, fish-processing. Pop. (1991) 471,844 (metropolitan 1,602,502).

**Vancouver Island** Island off the Pacific coast of British Columbia, Canada. Captain Cook visited it in 1778, it became a British Crown colony in 1849, and part of British Columbia in 1866. The largest island off the W coast of N America, the interior is rugged and forested. The main city, VICTORIA, is the province's capital. Industries: timber, fishing, copper, coal-mining, tourism. Area: 12,408sq mi (32,137sq km).

**Vandals** Germanic tribe who attacked the Roman empire in the 5th century AD. They looted Roman Gaul and invaded Spain in 409. Defeated by the GOTHS, they moved farther south and invaded North Africa (429), establishing a kingdom from which they controlled the W Mediterranean. They sacked Rome in 455. The Vandal kingdom was destroyed by the Byzantine general Belisarius in 533–34.

**Van de Graaff generator** Machine that generates high voltages by concentrating electrical charges on the outside of a hollow conductor. Positive or negative charges are sprayed onto a vertically moving belt that carries them up to a large hollow metal sphere where voltage builds up. An applied voltage of about 50,000 volts can generate up to 10 million volts.

**Vanderbilt, Cornelius** (1794–1877) US railroad owner and financier. He established a steamboat company (1829) and by 1846 was a millionaire. During the California gold rush (1849), he ran a shipping line between New York and San Francisco and then entered the transoceanic transportation business (1854). During the Civil War he built a railroad empire and in 1873 connected New York and Chicago by rail.

**Van der Waals, Johannes Diderik** (1837–1923) Dutch physicist. He was awarded the 1910 Nobel Prize for physics for his work on gases and the gas equation that he derived. The Van der Waals equation takes into account intermolecular attraction and repulsion, which were ignored by the KINETIC THEORY of gases.

**Van der Waals Forces** Weak forces of mutual attraction that contribute toward cohesion between neighboring ATOMS or MOLECULES. They are named for Johannes VAN DER WAALS.

**Van Diemen's Land** Original name of TASMANIA. It was discovered by Abel TASMAN in 1642 and named in honor of the Governor-General of the Dutch East Indies. It became part of New South Wales in 1803, was made a separate colony in 1825, given self-governing status in 1850, and named Tasmania in 1855.

**Van Dyck, Sir Anthony** (1599–1641) Flemish portrait and religious painter. He worked in RUBENS' studio before traveling abroad. He was invited to England in 1632 by Charles I, who made him court painter and a knight. His many depictions of English aristocrats greatly influenced future English portrait painting.

**Vane, Sir Henry** (1613–62) English parliamentary leader during the CIVIL WAR. A Puritan, he was governor of Massachusetts (1636–37) before returning to England to become a leader of parliamentary opposition to Charles I. A dominant figure in Parliament, he served in numerous posts under the COMMONWEALTH. Although not a regicide, Vane was executed after the RESTORATION (1660).

**Van Gogh, Vincent** (1853–90) Dutch painter, a leading exponent of EXPRESSIONISM and a formative influence on modern art. During his turbulent life, he sold only one painting. Virtually self-taught, his early works were often somber pictures of peasants. In 1886 he left Holland for Paris, where his work underwent a transformation. Two years later he went to Arles, in Provence, where he painted in a frenzy of prolific activity interspersed with bouts of mental illness and depression, which ended in suicide. During the last two years of his life, his paintings were executed with heavy brushwork in heightened, flamelike color, with passionate expression of light and emotion. To this period belong *Cypresses by Moonlight*, *The Bridge at Arles*, *Starry Night*, and his sunflower paintings.

**vanilla** Climbing orchid native to Mexico. The vines bear greenish-yellow flowers that produce seed pods 8in (20cm) long, which are the source of the flavoring vanilla. Family Orchidaceae; species *Vanilla planifolia*.

**Vanuatu** Volcanic island group in the SW Pacific Ocean, *c*.1,430mi (2,300km) E of Australia. The group consists of 13 large islands and 70 islets, the majority of them mountainous, which form a chain *c*.450mi (725km) in length. The main islands are Espiritu Santo, Efate (which has the capital Vila, 1992 pop. 19,750), Malekula, Pentecost, Malo, and Tanna. Discovered in 1606 by Pedro Fernandez de Queiros, the group was settled by the English and French in the early

◄ **Van Dyck** Portrait of King Charles 1 wearing the order of the garter, with a dog by his side. Born in Antwerp, the son of a cloth manufacturer, Sir Anthony Van Dyck was one of the great masters of 17th-century portraiture. After traveling and painting aristocratic portraits in Belgium and Italy, he was invited to England by Charles 1. His ability to capture the character of his subjects, often while presenting them in [illegible] poses, was highly influential.

V

1800s. Governed jointly by France and Britain as the New Hebrides from 1906, the islands became an independent parliamentary republic in 1980. The inhabitants live mainly by fishing, farming, and mining, with copra accounting for almost half of export earnings. Area: 4,707sq mi (12,190sq km). Pop. (1996 est.) 160,000.

**Van Vleck, John (Hasbrouck)** (1899–1980) US mathematician and physicist. He studied the behavior of electrons in noncrystalline, magnetic materials. In the 1930s, Van Vleck was the first scientist to use QUANTUM MECHANICS to explain the phenomenon of MAGNETISM. For this work, Van Vleck shared the 1977 Nobel Prize for physics.

**vaporization** (volatilization) Conversion of a liquid or solid into its vapor, such as water into steam. Some solids (such as ammonium chloride), when heated, pass directly into the vapor state, this is known as SUBLIMATION.

**vapor pressure** Pressure exerted by a vapor when it evaporates from a liquid or solid. When as many molecules leave to form vapor as return (in an enclosed space), this equilibrium is termed a saturated vapor pressure.

**Varanasi** (Benares, Banoras) City on the Ganges River, Uttar Pradesh state, N India. Varanasi is considered by Hindus to be their holy city. Each year it attracts millions of pilgrims who bathe in the river. BUDDHA is reputed to have preached his first sermon nearby. Silk brocade, brassware, and jewelry are among the city's specialist industries. Pop. (1991) 1,026,000.

**Varèse, Edgard** (1885–1965) French composer, a leading advocate of experimental music. He experimented with new rhythms and timbres and dissonant harmonies in his works, which include *Hyperprism* (1923) for wind instruments and percussion and *Déserts* (1954) for tape-recorded sound. He concentrated on ELECTRONIC MUSIC after the early 1950s.

**Vargas, Getúlio Dornelles** (1883–1954) Brazilian statesman, president (1930–45, 1951–54). Governor (1928–30) of Rio Grande do Sul, Vargas led a successful revolt after being defeated in presidential elections. His autocratic regime was bolstered by the army. Vargas established a corporative state, but there were few signs of economic improvement. His refusal to grant elections led to a military coup. Vargas' second term was tainted by scandal and and he was forced to resign.

**variable** In mathematics, symbol used to represent an unspecified quantity. Variables are used to express a range of possible values. For example, in the expression $x^2 + x + 1$, the quantity $x$ may be assigned the value of any real number; here $x$ is said to be an independent variable. If $y$ is defined by $y = x^2 + x + 1$, then $y$ is a dependent variable because its value depends on the value of $x$

**variable star** Star that varies in brightness over time. Intrinsic variables are stars that vary because of some inherent feature. In extrinsic variables, external factors, such as eclipses or obscuring dust, affect the amount of light reaching us from the star.

**variation** In biology, differences between members of the same SPECIES. Variation occurs naturally due to heredity and to differences in the environment during development. *See also* ADAPTATION; EVOLUTION

**variation** In music, a variety of treatments upon a single theme. Successive statements of the theme are altered by such means as simple elaboration, change of KEY, or change of time signature.

**varicose veins** Condition where the VEINS become swollen and distorted. They can occur anywhere in the body, but are commonly found in the legs.

**varnish** Solution of a RESIN or a PLASTIC that dries to form a hard, transparent, protective, and often decorative coating. Varnishes may have a matt or glossy finish. Pigments are often added to color the varnish.

**Varuna** In ancient Hindu mythology, the supreme ruler and possessor of universal power. He is worshiped as the upholder of moral order, and is closely identified with the Moon.

**Vasari, Giorgio** (1511–74) Italian painter, architect, and biographer. His fame now rests on his history of Italian art, *The Lives of the most excellent Painters, Sculptors, and Architects* (1550). This lively account is the single most important document of Italian RENAISSANCE art from GIOTTO to MICHELANGELO. In architecture he is noted for his design for the UFFIZI.

**Vasco da Gama** *See* GAMA, VASCO DA

**vascular bundle** Strand of conductive tissue that transports water and dissolved mineral salts and nutrients throughout a VASCULAR PLANT. They extend from the roots, through the stem, and out to the leaves. They consist of two types of tissue: XYLEM, which conducts water from the roots to the shoot and is located toward the center of the bundle; and PHLOEM, which conducts salts and nutrients and forms the outer regions of the bundle.

**vascular plant** Plant with vessels to carry water and nutrients within it. All higher plants – FERNS, CONIFERS, and ANGIOSPERMS – have a vascular system (XYLEM and PHLOEM).

**vasectomy** Operation to induce male sterility, in which the tube (vas deferens) carrying sperm from the testes to the PENIS is cut. A vasectomy is a form of permanent CONTRACEPTION, although in some cases the operation is reversible.

**vasoconstrictor** Any substance that causes constriction of blood vessels and, therefore, decreased blood flow. Examples include NOREPINEPHRINE, angiotensin, and the HORMONE vasopressin (also known as antidiuretic hormone).

**vasodilator** Any substance that causes widening of the blood vessels, permitting freer flow of blood. Vasodilator drugs are mostly used to treat HYPERTENSION and ANGINA.

**Västerås** Inland port at the mouth of the Svartan River on Lake Malaren, E Sweden. Founded in 1100, it was an important medieval city and was the scene of several diets, including the diet of Västerås Recess in 1527, which formed the Lutheran State Church, and the Diet of 1544, which made the Swedish throne hereditary. Industries: engineering, electronics, iron ore, timber, metal goods, textiles, glass. Pop. (1994) 122,988.

**VAT** *See* VALUE-ADDED TAX

**Vatican, The** Short name for the VATICAN CITY or the Vatican Palace. The **Vatican Palace** is the residence of the pope within the Vatican City. A building of more over 1,000 rooms clustered around a number of courtyards, it contains the papal apartments, the offices of the Vatican City state secretariat, state reception rooms, the Vatican Museums, the Vatican Archive, and the Vatican Library.

**Vatican City** Independent sovereign state, existing as a walled enclave on the W bank of the TIBER River, within the city of ROME. It is the official home of the PAPACY and an independent base for the Holy See (governing body of the ROMAN CATHOLIC CHURCH). The first papal residence was established here in the 5th century and it has been the papal home ever since, apart from a brief spell at AVIGNON in the 14th century. Vatican City did not achieve full independence until 1929. The world's smallest nation, its permanent population of *c.*1,000 (mostly unmarried males) includes the Pope's traditional SWISS GUARD of 100. The Commission, appointed to administer the Vatican's affairs, has its own radio service, police, and railroad station and issues its own stamps and coins. The treasures of the Vatican, notably MICHELANGELO's frescos in the SISTINE CHAPEL and ST. PETER'S, attract huge numbers of tourists and pilgrims. The Vat-

▼ **Varanasi** The holiest of Hindu cities, Varanasi is sited close to the confluence of two holy rivers, the Ganges and the Yamuna. The water of the Ganges is considered by Hindus to be purifying and multitudes of pilgrims descend the many Ghats (flights of steps) down to the river each day to bathe. The Ghats are also the site of open funeral pyres, where bodies are burned and the ashes washed into the river in the belief that the dead will be released from the earthly cycle of rebirths and enter heaven.

ican library contains a priceless collection of manuscripts. The official language is Latin. Area: 0.17sq mi (0.44sq km).

**Vatican Council, First** (1869–70) 20th ecumenical council of the Roman Catholic Church. Convened by Pope PIUS IX to rebut various contemporary ideas associated with the rise of liberalism and materialism, it is chiefly remembered for its declaration of PAPAL INFALLIBILITY.

**Vatican Council, Second** (1962–65) 21st ecumenical council of the Roman Catholic Church. It was convened by Pope JOHN XXIII to revive and renew Christian faith and to move the Church into closer touch with ordinary people. Among the most significant results were the introduction of the Mass in the vernacular, a greater role for lay people, and a greater tolerance for other sects and other religions.

**vaudeville** US variety entertainment. Its rise and fall followed the same pattern as its European counterpart, having its heyday in the late 19th century and eventually succumbing to the popularity of movies.

**Vaughan, Henry** (1622–95) Welsh poet. After studying law, he turned to medicine and became a doctor. His poetry belongs to the tradition of METAPHYSICS, and he was inspired by the work of George HERBERT. Vaughan's best work draws on his religious experience, most notably in *Silex Scintillans* (1650, revised 1655).

**Vaughan, Sarah** (1924–90) US singer. Her early work with Billy Eckstine led to the recording of "Lover Man" with Dizzy GILLESPIE. Often with full orchestral accompaniment, Vaughan sang with the bands of Duke Ellington and Count Basie. Albums include *After Hours* (1961).

**Vaughan Williams, Ralph** (1872–1958) British composer. His interest in English folk music is apparent in his three *Norfolk Rhapsodies* (1905–07) and his instrumental arrangement *Fantasia on Greensleeves*. He also used elements of English Tudor music in his *Mass in G Minor* (1923) for unaccompanied chorus. He wrote nine symphonies, the best known of which are the Sixth Symphony (1947) and the *Sinfonia Antarctica* (1952).

**vault** Curved roof or ceiling usually made of stone, brick, or concrete. The simple **barrel** vault is semicylindrical; the **groin** vault consists of two barrel vaults intersected at right-angles; the **ribbed groin** is the same as the ordinary groin vault except that it has ribs to give the edges extra support; the so-called Gothic vault has four pointed compartments; the **fan** vault has a delicate, fanlike appearance. English masons developed the fan vault in the 15th century using tracery to make it more elaborate, as in King's College Chapel, Cambridge.

**Veblen, Thorstein Bunde** (1857–1929) US sociologist and economist. He wrote *The Theory of the Leisure Class* (1899), in which he introduced the idea of conspicuous consumption. A perceptive critic of US capitalist society, he founded the institutionalist school, believing that economics must be studied in the context of social change.

**vector** In mathematics, a quantity that has both a magnitude and a direction, as contrasted with a SCALAR, which has magnitude only. For example, the VELOCITY of an object is specified by its speed and the direction in which it is moving; similarly, a FORCE has both magnitude and direction. Mass is a scalar quantity, but WEIGHT (the force of gravity on a body) is a vector.

**Vedanta** (Sanskrit, conclusion of the VEDAS) Best known and most popular form of Indian philosophy; it forms the foundation for most modern schools of thought in HINDUISM. One of the most influential Vedanta schools was that expounded by the 7th–8th-century philosopher Sankara. This school holds that the natural world is an illusion. There is only one self, Brahman-Atman; ignorance of the oneness of the self with BRAHMAN is the cause of rebirth. The system includes a belief in the TRANSMIGRATION OF SOULS and the desirability of release from the cycle of rebirth. *See also* UPANISHADS

**Vedas** Ancient and most sacred writings of HINDUISM. They consist of series of hymns and formulaic chants that constituted a Hindu LITURGY. There are four Vedas: *Rig Veda*, containing a priestly tradition originally brought to India by ARYANS; *Yajur Veda*, consisting of prayers and sacred formulas; *Sama Veda*, containing melodies and chants; and *Atharva Veda*, a collection of popular hymns, incantations, and magic spells. The Vedas were composed over a long period, between *c*.1500 and 1200 BC.

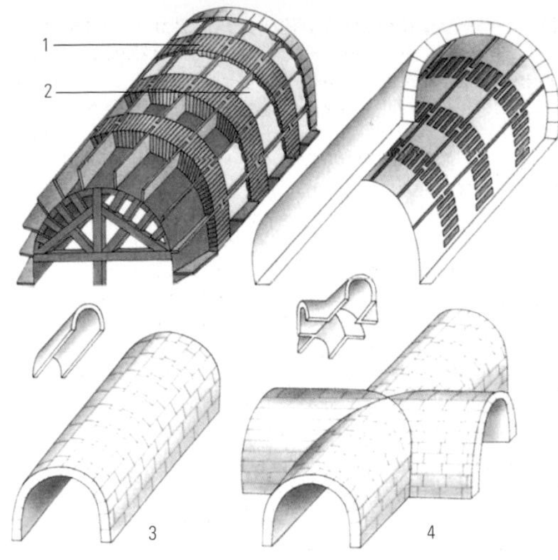


◀ **vault** Concrete enabled the Romans to build vaults of a size unequaled until the introduction of steel construction. Concrete vaults were supported on timber centering, which was removed after the concrete set. In some cases vaults were built of brick ribs (1), filled with concrete (2) to lighten the weight on the centering and avoid cracking. The simplest vault was the barrel, wagon, or tunnel (3) – basically a prolonged rounded arch – which was used for small spans and simple oblong structures with parallel sides. The cross-vault (4), formed by two barrels intersecting at right angles, was used over square apartments, or over long corridors divided by piers into square bays, each covered with a cross-vault.

**Vega** (Alpha Lyrae) White, main-sequence star in the constellation of Lyra; the fifth-brightest star in the sky. Its luminosity is 50 times that of the Sun.

**Vega Carpio, Félix, Lope de** (1562–1635) Spanish poet and Spain's first great dramatist. A prolific writer, he produced epics, pastorals, odes, sonnets, and novels. About 300 of his major works survive; the authentic oeuvre includes the plays *Peribáñez and the Commander of Ocaña* (*c*.1610) and *All Citizens Are Soldiers* (*c*.1613). Other works include a staggering amount of poems in a wide variety of forms and genres.

**vegetable** As opposed to ANIMAL, a form of life that builds up its tissues by means of growth using the energy of sunlight, carbon dioxide from the air, and the green pigment CHLOROPHYLL. This process is known as PHOTOSYNTHESIS. Vegetables, or green plants, need also to be supplied with water and mineral salts, which are usually present in the soil.

**vegetarianism** Practice of abstaining from eating meat and fish. A minority of vegetarian purists, known as vegans, further exclude from their diet all products of animal origin, such as butter, eggs, milk, and cheese. Vegetarianism has a religious basis in many cultures, particularly among various Jain, Hindu, and Buddhist sects.

**vegetative reproduction** Form of ASEXUAL REPRODUCTION in higher plants. It involves an offshoot or a piece of the original plant (from leaf, stem, or root) separating and giving rise to an entire new plant. It may occur naturally, as in strawberries reproducing by runners, or artificially, as in a house plant cutting yielding a new plant.

**vein** In mammals, vessel that carries deoxygenated blood to the heart. An exception is the pulmonary vein, which carries

**VEIN**

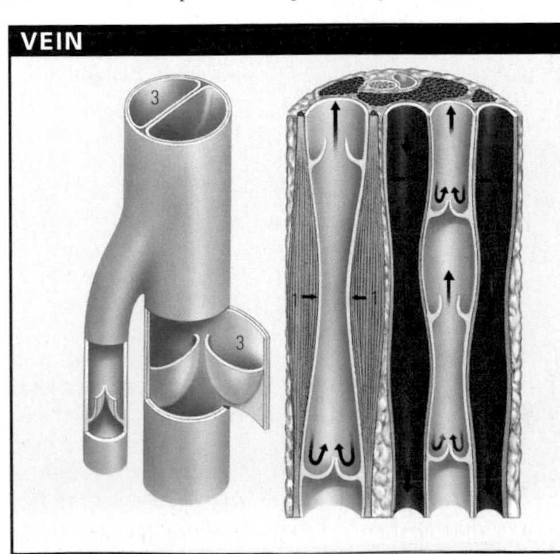


Veins carry blood to the heart. The returning venous blood moves slowly due to low pressure, and the veins can collapse or expand to accommodate variations in blood flow. Movement relies on the surrounding muscles, which contract (1) and compress the vein. Pulsation of adjacent arteries (2) has a regular pumping effect. Semilunar valves (3) are found at regular intervals throughout the larger veins and these allow the blood to move only in one direction.

oxygenated blood from the lungs to the left upper chamber of the heart. *See also* ARTERY; VENA CAVA

**Velázquez, Diego Rodriguez de Silva y** (1599–1660) Spanish painter. He was strongly influenced by Venetian art and the work of CARAVAGGIO, but he quickly developed a personal style that combined NATURALISM with a deep spirituality. He painted religious works and dignified GENRE PAINTINGS, notably *The Old Woman Cooking Eggs* (1618). In 1623 Velázquez became court painter to King Philip IV of Spain. During the 1630s and 1640s he produced a series of royal and equestrian portraits. A trip to Italy resulted in the portrait of *Pope Innocent X* (1650). Toward the end of his life, Velázquez continued to paint with dazzling brushwork, culminating in *The Maids of Honor* (*c*.1656). Unknown outside Spain until the early 19th century, he came to exercise a powerful influence on European artists, especially MANET.

**velocity** (symbol *v)* Rate of motion of a body in a certain direction. Velocity is a VECTOR (magnitude and direction), whereas speed, which does not specify direction, is a scalar.

**vena cava** Main VEIN of vertebrates. It supplies the HEART with deoxygenated blood, emptying into its right atrium.

**veneer** Extremely thin sheet of wood, or a thin sheet of a precious material such as ivory or tortoiseshell, which gives furniture or other objects the appearance of being more valuable than they are. Veneers may also be used as decorative shapes inlaid into a surface.

**venereal disease (VD)** Any of the diseases transmitted through sexual contact, chief of which are SYPHILIS, GONORRHEA, and chancroid. Syphilis is caused by the bacterium *Treponema pallidum*. PENICILLIN and its derivatives can still cure syphilis in its early stages. Gonorrhea is caused by the gonococcus bacterium and if diagnosed early may be treated with SULFONAMIDE DRUGS.

**Venetian School** School of Italian painting that flourished in the 15th, 16th, and 18th centuries. It was noted for the sumptuousness and radiance of its color. Early Venetian masters included the BELLINI and Vivarini families, who were followed by its greatest exponents, TITIAN and GIORGIONE. TINTORETTO and VERONESE represent the transition from RENAISSANCE to BAROQUE, while TIEPOLO, CANALETTO, and GUARDI revived Venetian painting in the 18th century.

**Venezuela** Republic in N South America. *See* country feature

## VENEZUELA

Venezuela's flag, adopted in 1954, has the same basic tricolor as the flags of Colombia and Ecuador. The colors were used by the Venezuelan patriot Francisco de Miranda. The seven stars represent the provinces in the Venezuelan Federation in 1811.

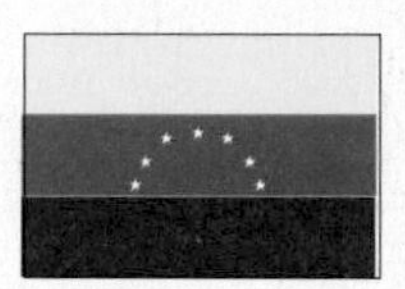

**AREA:** 352,143sq mi (912,050sq km)
**POPULATION:** 21,378,000
**CAPITAL (POPULATION):** Caracas (1,824,892)
**GOVERNMENT:** Federal republic
**ETHNIC GROUPS:** Mestizo 67%, White 21%, Black 10%, Native American 2%
**LANGUAGES:** Spanish (official)
**RELIGIONS:** Christianity (Roman Catholic 94%)
**CURRENCY:** Bolívar = 100 céntimos

The W part of the Republic of Venezuela contains the Maracaibo lowlands, which surround the the oil-rich Lake Maracaibo, and the city of MARACAIBO. Arms of the ANDES mountains extend across most of N Venezuela. Situated in this region are CARACAS and VALENCIA. A low-lying region, drained by the ORINOCO River, lies between the N mountains and the Guiana Highlands in the SE. The Guiana Highlands contain ANGEL FALLS, the world's highest waterfall, with a total drop of 3,212ft (980m).

### CLIMATE

Venezuela has a tropical climate. Lowland temperatures are always high, but the mountains are cooler and wetter. Much of the country has a marked dry season from December to April.

### VEGETATION

About 34% of Venezuela is forested, with dense rain forest in the Orinoco basin and in the Guiana Highlands. Tropical savanna covers the lowlands; mountain grassland occurs in the highlands. Only *c*.4% of the land is cultivated.

### HISTORY

The original inhabitants of Venezuela were the Arawak and Carib Native Americans. The first European to arrive was Christopher COLUMBUS, who sighted the area in 1498. In 1499 Amerigo VESPUCCI explored the coastline and nicknamed the country Venezuela (little Venice). Spanish settlements were soon established, and German explorers, notably Nikolaus Federmann, completed the conquest. Venezuela became part of the Spanish colonial administrative area of New Granada. In the late 18th century, uprisings against Spanish rule were led by Francisco de Miranda. Simón BOLÍVAR liberated Venezuela (1821), and it became part of Greater Colombia, a republic that also included Colombia, Ecuador, and Panama. In 1830 Venezuela became a separate state. The mid- to late-19th century was marked by political instability and civil war, with the country ruled by a series of dictators. Guzmán Blanco was followed by Joaquín Crespo and then Cipriano Castro, under whom financial corruption reached new heights. Juan Vicente GÓMEZ's long and autocratic rule (1908–35) provided the stability for Venezuela to pay off its debts, helped by international interest in its rich oilfields.

In 1945 a prodemocracy military junta, led by Rómulo Betancourt, gained control. In 1948 Rómulo Gallegos was elected president, but a military coup the same year reestablished a dictatorship. Popular uprisings in 1958 brought a return to democracy, with Betancourt elected president. Venezuela became increasingly prosperous, but left-wing uprisings, notably two communist revolts in 1962 (covertly supported by Fidel Castro), led to much violence.

### POLITICS

In 1976 Venezuela nationalized its oil industry, using the money to raise living standards. In 1989 Carlos Andrés Pérez became president. He introduced free-market economic reforms, but inflation and unemployment continued to rise. In 1992 there were two failed military coups. In 1993 Pérez resigned after charges of corruption. In 1994 Rafael Caldera became president. His austerity measures provoked civil unrest. In 1999 Hugo Chávez Frías of the Fifth Republic Movement (MVR), leader of one of the failed coups in 1992, became president.

### ECONOMY

Venezuela is an upper-middle-income developing country (1995 GDP per capita, US$7,900). Industry employs 17% of the work force, with the chief industry being petroleum refining, concentrated around Maracaibo; other industries include aluminum and steel production, centered around Ciudad Guayana. Oil accounts for 80% of the exports. Other exports include bauxite, aluminum, and iron ore. Agriculture employs 13% of the work force. Major crops include bananas and other fruits, coffee, corn, rice, and sugarcane.

**Venice** (Venezia) City on the Gulf of Venice, at the head of the Adriatic Sea, N Italy, capital of Venetia region. It is built on 118 islands, separated by narrow canals, in the Lagoon of Venice, and joined by causeway to the mainland. Settled in the 5th century, it became a vassal of the Byzantine empire until the 10th century. After defeating Genoa in 1381, Venice became the most important European sea-power, engaging in trade in the Mediterranean and Asia. Its importance declined in the 16th century, and it was ceded to Austria in 1797, becoming part of Italy in 1866. Venice is the site of many churches, palaces, and historic buildings, and it is one of Europe's foremost attractions, drawing more than two million tourists a year. Tourism imposes a massive strain on a city already suffering from erosion, subsidence, and pollution. Industries: glass-blowing, textiles, petrochemicals. Pop. (1992) 305,617.

**Venn diagram** In mathematics, diagrammatical representation of the relations between mathematical SETS or logical statements, named for the British logician John Venn (1834–1923). The sets are drawn as geometrical figures that overlap whenever different sets share some elements.

**ventilation** In biology, the process by which air or water is taken into and expelled from the body of an animal and passed over a surface across which GAS EXCHANGE takes place. Ventilation mechanisms include BREATHING, by which air is drawn into the LUNGS for gas exchange across the wall of the ALVEOLI, and the movements of the floor of a fish's mouth, coupled with those of its GILL covers, which draw water across the gills.

**ventricle** Either of the two lower chambers of the HEART.

**Ventris, Michael** (1922–56) British architect and linguist. In 1952 he deciphered MYCENEAN scripts, written in Linear B, found at Knossos, Crete, and other sites. His theory (now universally accepted) that Linear B was an archaic form of the Greek language was published, in collaboration with John Chadwick, in *Evidence for Greek Dialect in the Mycenean Archives* (1953).

**venture capital** Outside capital provided for a business. Venture capital is often needed to start up new businesses or to expand existing businesses. It is provided by investment banks and private investors.

**Venturi, Robert** (1925– ) US architect. Venturi argued that architectural MODERNISM was banal. His stress on the importance of "vernacular" or contextual architecture heralded POST-MODERNISM. His publications include *Complexity and Contradiction in Architecture* (1966) and *Learning from Las Vegas* (1972), in which consumer architecture is contrasted with the postmodern approach. His buildings include Chestnut Hill Villa (1962) and Gordon Wu Hall, Princeton University (1984).

**Venus** Second planet from the Sun, it is almost as large as the Earth. Visible around dawn or dusk as the so-called **morning star** or **evening star**, it is the most conspicuous celestial object after the Sun and Moon. A telescope shows the planet's dazzling, yellowish-white cloud cover, with faint markings. Venus' very high surface temperature was indicated by measurements at radio wavelengths in 1958. Space probes revealed more about the surface. A gently undulating plain covers two thirds of Venus. Highlands account for a further quarter, and depressions and chasms the remainder. Most of the surface features are volcanic in origin. The atmosphere consists of 96% carbon dioxide and 3.5% nitrogen, with traces of helium, argon, neon, and krypton. Venus has no satellites.

**Venus** Roman goddess originally associated with gardens and cultivation, but also with the ideas of charm, grace, and beauty. She became identified with the Greek goddess APHRODITE, and hence also personified love and fertility.

**verb** Linguistic category (part of speech) found in all languages, consisting of words typically denoting an action, an event, or a state (for example, in English, *to run, to snow, to depend*). Typical verbs are associated with one or more "arguments," such as subject and direct object. In English, verbs may be intransitive or transitive; intransitives have one argument *(she sneezed)* and transitives two, or rarely more (*she* played *tennis, she* taught *him Russian*). Verbs may carry grammatical information, including: person (as grammatical agreement with the subject); tense (relating to when the verb took place); aspect (whether what is meant is complete or incomplete at some reference time); number (whether any of the arguments are singular or plural); and voice (which argument serves as subject). In other languages, verbs may encode different information. A list of all forms of a verb is called its paradigm, and this may be regular (predictable by a rule) or irregular. The most irregular verbs in a language are often those in most frequent use and with the most general meaning.

**verbena** Genus of annual and perennial trees, shrubs, and herbs, native to the Western Hemisphere. Some species are popular garden plants and have pink, red, white, or purple flowers. Family Verbenaceae; there are about 250 species.

**Verdi, Giuseppe** (1813–1901) Italian composer, one of the supreme operatic masters of the 19th century. His early operas displayed an original and lively talent and a promising sense of the dramatic. Up to 1853 his masterpieces were *Rigoletto* (1851), *Il trovatore* (1853), and *La traviata* (1853). *Aïda* (1867) shows a development in style, with richer and more imaginative orchestration. With Verdi's last three operas, *Don Carlos* (1884), *Otello* (1887), and *Falstaff* (1893), Italian opera reached its greatest heights. Among other compositions are several sacred choral works, including the *Requiem* (1874).

**verdict** Conclusive pronouncement of a court of law. The verdict at most courts is either "guilty" or "not guilty" of the charge, although in some countries (including Scotland) there is the third alternative of "not proven." Whether the verdict is delivered by court authorities or by a panel of jurors depends on the type of court. Verdicts may be subject to appeal, if permission is granted, and may be overturned altogether if new and conclusive evidence appears at a later stage.

**Verdun, Battle of** (February–December 1916) Campaign of WORLD WAR I. A German offensive in the region of Verdun made initial advances, but was checked by the French under General PÉTAIN. After a series of renewed German assaults, the Allied offensive on the SOMME drew off German troops and the French regained the lost territory. Total casualties were estimated at one million.

**Verlaine, Paul** (1844–96) French poet. His early poetry, *Poèmes Saturniens* (1866) and *Fêtes Galantes* (1869), was influenced by BAUDELAIRE, with whom he is grouped as one of the *fin de siècle* decadents (an appellation amply fulfilled by his lifestyle). An intense relationship with RIMBAUD ended violently. While in jail (1874–75), he wrote *Songs Without Words* (1874), an early work of SYMBOLISM. Returning to Catholicism, his later poetry deals with the conflict between the spiritual and the carnal. His critical work includes the famous study *The Accursed Poets* (1884).

**Vermeer, Jan** (1632–75) Dutch painter, one of the most celebrated of all 17th-century Dutch painters. Early mythological and religious works gave way to a middle period featuring the serene and contemplative domestic scenes for which he is best known. The compositions are extremely simple and powerful, and the colors are usually muted blues, grays, and yellows. He treated light and color with enormous delicacy, as in the superb landscape, *View of Delft* (*c*.1660). Toward the end of his life, Vermeer began to paint in a heavier manner and his work lost some of its mysterious charm.

**Vermont** State in New England, NE US, on the Canadian border. The state capital is MONTPELIER; other major cities include Burlington. The Green Mountains range N–S and dominate the terrain; most of the W border of the state is formed by Lake Champlain. Samuel de CHAMPLAIN discovered the lake in 1609, but the region was not settled permanently until 1724. Land grant disputes with New Hampshire and New York persisted for many years. In 1777 Vermont declared its independence, retaining this unrecognized status until it was admitted to the Union in 1791. The region is heavily forested and arable land is limited. Dairy farming is by far the most important farming activity. Mineral resources include granite, slate, marble, and asbestos. Industries: pulp and paper, food processing, computer components, machine tools. Area: 9,609sq mi (24,887sq km). Pop. (1992) 571,334.

**Verne, Jules** (1828–1905) French author. He is chiefly remembered for his imaginative adventure stories, and he is often considered one of the founding fathers of science fic-

**VENUS: DATA**

Diameter (equatorial): 7521mi (12,104km)
Mass (Earth = 1): 0.815
Volume (Earth = 1): 0.86
Density (water = 1): 5.25
Orbital period: 224.7 days
Rotation period: 243.16 days
Average surface temperature: 896°F (480°C)
Surface gravity (Earth = 1) 0.90

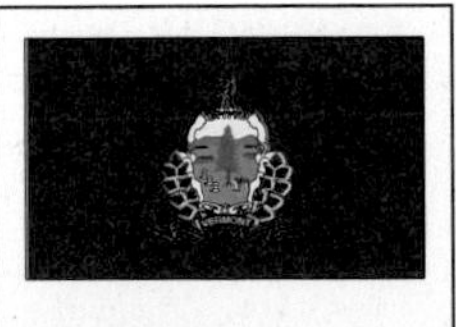

**VERMONT**
**Statehood:**
March 4, 1791
**Nickname:**
The Green Mountain State
**State bird:**
Hermit thrush
**State flower:**
Red clover
**State tree:**
Sugar maple
**State motto:**
Freedom and unity

V

▲ **vicuña** Native to the high Andes, the vicuña (*Vicugna vicugna*) is lives in small herds of six to twelve females with a single male. Prized for its expensive, fine fur, the vicuña was hunted to near extinction in the 1970s, until rerserves were established to protect the species. It is specially adapted to living at high altitudes, with an extremely high concentration of very efficient red blood cells that allow it to absorb oxygen quickly from the thin air.

tion. His popular novels include *Journey to the Center of the Earth* (1864), *Twenty Thousand Leagues Under the Sea* (1869), and *Around the World in Eighty Days* (1873).

**Verona** City on the Adige River, NE Italy, capital of Verona province. The city was captured by Rome in 89 BC and still has a Roman amphitheater. It prospered under the Della Scala family in the 13th and 14th centuries, and was held by Austria from 1797 to 1866, when it joined Italy. Industries: textiles, chemicals, paper, printing, wine. Pop. (1992) 255,492.

**Veronese, Paolo Caliari** (1528–88) Italian painter. A member of the VENETIAN SCHOOL, he excelled at painting large scenes featuring flamboyant pageants. He also painted religious and mythological themes. The Inquisition objected to his irreverent treatment of *The Last Supper* (1573) and he had to rename it *The Feast in the House of Levi*. Other celebrated works are his frescos for the Villa Barbaro near Treviso.

**veronica** (speedwell) Widely distributed genus of annual and perennial plants of the figwort family. The small flowers are white, blue, or pink. Height: 3–60in (7.5–153cm). Family Scrophulariaceae; the genus includes about 250 species.

**verruca** Form of WART on the sole of the foot, which is painful because it is forced to grow inward. It is due to infection with the human papillomavirus.

**Versailles** City in N France, 10mi (16km) SW of Paris, capital of Yvelines department. It is famous for its former royal palace, now visited by two million tourists a year. Louis XIII built his hunting lodge at Versailles. In 1682 Louis XIV made Versailles his royal seat and transformed the lodge into a palace. The architects Louis LE VAU, Jules HARDOUIN-MANSART, and Robert de Cotte built the monumental palace in a French classical style. The interior was designed by Charles LEBRUN, and includes the royal apartments and the Hall of Mirrors. The magnificent gardens were landscaped by André LE NÔTRE. The park also contains the Grand and Petit Trianon palaces. It was a royal residence until the French Revolution (1789). It was the scene of the signing of peace treaties after the Franco-Prussian War and World War I. Pop. (1990) 91,030.

**Versailles, Treaty of** (1919) Peace agreement concluding WORLD WAR I, signed at VERSAILLES. It represented a compromise between President Wilson's FOURTEEN POINTS and the demands of the European allies for heavy penalties against Germany. German territorial concessions included Alsace-Lorraine to France, and smaller areas to other neighboring states, as well as the loss of its colonies. The Rhineland was demilitarized, strict limits were placed on German armed forces, and extensive REPARATIONS for war damage were imposed. The treaty also established the LEAGUE OF NATIONS. It was never ratified by the US, which signed a separate treaty with Germany in 1921.

**vertebra** One of the bones making up the SPINE (vertebral column). Each vertebra is composed of a large solid body from the top of which winglike processes project to either side. The human backbone is composed of 26 vertebrae (the five of the sacrum and four of the coccyx fuse together to form two solid bones), which are held together by ligaments and intervertebral disks.

**vertebrate** Animal with individual disks of bone or cartilage called VERTEBRA, which surround or replace the embryonic NOTOCHORD to form a jointed backbone enclosing the spinal column. The principal division within vertebrates is between FISH and partly land-adapted forms (AMPHIBIANS), and the wholly land-adapted forms (REPTILES, BIRDS, and MAMMALS, although some mammals have adapted to a totally aquatic existence). Phylum CHORDATA; subphylum Vertebrata.

**vertigo** Dizziness, often accompanied by nausea. It is due to disruption of the sense of balance and may be produced by ear disorder, reduced flow of blood to the brain caused by altitude, emotional upset, or spinning rapidly.

**vervet monkey** *See* GUENON

**very high frequency (VHF)** Range or band of radio waves with frequencies between 30 and 300MHz and wavelengths between 3 and 33ft (1–10m). This band is used for TELEVISION and FREQUENCY MODULATION (FM) radio broadcasts to provide high-quality reception.

**Vesey, Denmark** (1767–1822) African-born slave who led a conspiracy among US slaves in the region of Charleston, South Carolina. Under cover of church meetings, Vesey, a preacher, and his followers planned an uprising, but they were betrayed and arrested. Vesey and about 35 others were hanged.

**Vespasian** (AD 9–79) (Titus Flavius Vespasianus) Roman emperor (69–79). A successful general and administrator, he was leading the campaign against the Jews in Palestine when he was proclaimed emperor by his soldiers. He proved a capable ruler, extending and strengthening the empire, rectifying the budget deficit, widening qualifications for Roman citizenship, and adding to the monumental buildings of Rome.

**Vespucci, Amerigo** (1454–1512) Italian maritime explorer. He was possibly the first to realize that the Americas constituted new continents, which were named for him by the German cartographer Martin Waldseemüller in 1507. Vespucci made at least two transatlantic voyages (1497–1504).

**Vesta** In Roman religion, goddess of fire and purity, supreme in the conduct of religious ceremonies. Vesta was guardian of the hearth and patron goddess of bakers.

**vestal virgins** In ancient Rome, priestesses of the cult of VESTA, who tended the sacred fire in the Temple of Vesta and officiated at ceremonies in the goddess' honor. The vestals remained in the service of the temple for up to 30 years under vows of absolute chastity, violation of which was punishable by burial alive.

**Vesuvius** (Vesuvio) Active volcano on the Bay of Naples, S Italy. The earliest recorded eruption was in AD 79, when POMPEII and HERCULANEUM were destroyed. The height of the volcano changes with each of the 30 or so eruptions recorded since Roman times.

**Veterans Affairs, US Department of** Cabinet-level department within the executive branch, established in 1989; formerly an independent federal agency, the Veterans Administration (established 1930). It administers a wide range of benefits for former members and dependents and beneficiaries of deceased former members of the US armed forces. It also provides benefits to members of the armed forces and to dependent children of seriously disabled veterans. Benefits include health care, insurance, pensions, rehabilitation, and education.

**Veterans' Day** National holiday on November 11th. It was originally called Armistice Day to commemorate the ceasefire of World War I in 1918. After the end of the Korean War in 1954, the name was changed so that US veterans of all wars could be honored.

**veterinary medicine** Medical science that deals with diseases of animals. It was practiced by the Babylonians and Egyptians some 4,000 years ago. In the late 18th century schools of veterinary medicine were established in Europe.

**VHF** Abbreviation of VERY HIGH FREQUENCY (VHF)

**vibraphone** PERCUSSION musical instrument with metal bars of different lengths that are struck with sticks or mallets to produce various notes. Tubes beneath the bars vibrate at the same frequency as the bar above and magnify the sound.

**viburnum** Genus of flowering shrubs and small trees, native to North America and Eurasia. All have small, fleshy fruits containing single, flat seeds. There are about 120 species. Family Caprifoliaceae.

**Vicenza** Industrial city in NE Italy, 40mi (64km) W of Venice. Founded as a Ligurian settlement, it was taken by Venice in 1404 and held by Austria from 1797 until 1866, when it was united with Italy. An important rail junction, its industries include steel, machinery, chemicals, textiles, printing, glass, and gold jewelry. Pop. (1992) 107,481.

**Vice President of the United States** Second-highest federal official. He is first in line to succeed to the presidency and does so in the event of death, resignation, physical disability, or removal by impeachment of the president. Although not a member, he presides over the Senate and may vote in the case of a tie, although he cannot participate in debates or committees. He participates in cabinet meetings and is a member of the National Security Council. He is elected on the same ticket as the president to serve a four-year term. He is dependent on the president for extraconstitutional responsibilities and, traditionally, is chosen to balance the

V

ticket and for party appeasement or reward. If the office becomes vacant, the president, with the consent of Congress, chooses another vice president.

**Vichy Government** During WORLD WAR II, regime of SE France after the defeat by Germany in June 1940. Its capital was the town of Vichy, and it held authority over French overseas possessions as well as the unoccupied part of France. After German forces occupied Vichy France in November 1942, it became little more than a puppet government.

**Vicksburg, Siege of** (1863) Offensive by Union forces under General GRANT during the CIVIL WAR. The capture of Vicksburg, Mississippi, on July 4 gave the Union control of the Mississippi River and split the Confederacy in two.

**Vico, Giambattista** (1668–1744) Italian philosophical historian. In his *New Science* (1725, revised 1730 and 1744), he advanced the arguments of historicism: that all aspects of society and culture are relevant to the study of history, and that the history of any period should be judged according to the standards and customs of that time and place.

**Victor Emmanuel II** (1820–78) King of Italy (1861–78). He succeeded his father, Charles Albert, as king of Piedmont-Sardinia in 1849. From 1852, guided by CAVOUR, he strengthened his kingdom, formed a French alliance, and defeated Austria (1859–61). In 1861 he assumed the title of king of Italy. Rome became his new capital after French troops withdrew (1870).

**Victor Emmanuel III** (1869–1947) King of Italy (1900–46). He appointed Benito MUSSOLINI prime minister in 1922. Although Mussolini established a dictatorship, the king retained the power to dismiss him, and eventually did so in 1943. He abdicated in 1946.

**Victoria** (1819–1901) Queen of Great Britain and Ireland (1837–1901) and empress of India (1876–1901). A granddaughter of GEORGE III, she succeeded her uncle, WILLIAM IV. In 1840 she married her first cousin, Prince Albert of SAXE-COBURG-GOTHA. During her reign, the longest in English history, the role of the monarchy was established as a ceremonial, symbolic institution, with virtually no power but much influence. She learned statecraft from her first prime minister, Lord MELBOURNE, and was greatly influenced by the hard-working Prince Albert. Among later prime ministers, she maintained excellent terms with DISRAELI (who astutely flattered her) but was on frosty terms with GLADSTONE (who lectured her). She reigned over an empire containing 25% of the world's people and 30% of its land. Britain's trade and industry made it the world's richest country. She was immensely popular.

**Victoria** State in SE Australia, bounded by the Indian Ocean, the Bass Strait, and the Tasman Sea. The capital is MELBOURNE (home to more than 65% of the state population); other major cities are Geelong, Ballarat, and Bendigo. The region was part of NEW SOUTH WALES until 1851, when it became a separate colony. The population increased rapidly after 1851, when gold was discovered at Ballarat and Bendigo. Victoria became part of the Commonwealth of Australia in 1901. The area is crossed by the Australian Alps and other ranges of the Eastern Highlands. Irrigation is used extensively to grow wheat, oats, barley, fruit, and vegetables, while sheep and dairy cattle are also important. Brown coal, natural gas, and oil are the chief mineral resources. Industries: motor vehicles, textiles, food processing. Area: 87,813sq mi (227,620sq km). Pop. (1991) 4,487,000.

**Victoria** Capital of the Seychelles, in the Indian Ocean. Situated on NE Mahé island, it has a deep-water harbor and is the only town of significant size in the group, acting as the administrative, commercial and tourist center of the country. Pop. (1992e) 30,000.

**Victoria** City on SE VANCOUVER ISLAND, capital of BRITISH COLUMBIA province, SW Canada. Founded in 1843, it developed during the gold rush of 1858. Industries: timber, paper, shipbuilding, fish processing, tourism. It also has a large naval base. Pop. (1991) 71,228.

**Victoria** (Victoria Nyanza) Lake in E central Africa, bordered by Uganda, Kenya, and Tanzania. The second-largest freshwater lake in the world, it is the chief reservoir of the Nile River. Its long coastline provides harbors for coastal towns, notably KAMPALA, Kisumu, and Mwanza. Area: 26,000sq mi (68,000sq km).

**Victoria Falls** Waterfalls on the Zambezi River, on the border of Zimbabwe and Zambia. Formed by water erosion along a fracture in the Earth's crust, they are divided by islets into five main sections. The first European discovery was in 1855 by David LIVINGSTONE. Maximum drop: 355ft (108m); width over 5,580ft (1,700m).

**vicuña** Graceful, even-toed, hoofed South American mammal. The smallest member of the CAMEL family, it is humpless and resembles the LLAMA. Its silky coat is tawny brown with a yellowish bib under the neck. Vicuña wool was used by the Inca kings and is still expensive and rare. Height: 34in (86cm) at the shoulder; weight: 100lb (45kg). Family Camelidae; species *Vicugna vicugna.*

**Vidal, Gore** (1925– ) US novelist, playwright, and essayist, b. Eugene Luther Vidal. His first novels draw on his experience of army life in World War II. Other works include the satirical *Myra Breckinridge* (1968) and its sequel *Myron* (1974). A number of his novels satirize the US political establishment, beginning with *Washington DC* (1967) and continuing with a series on US historical figures.

**video** Term used in television and computing to refer to electronic vision signals, and to equipment and software associated with visual displays. The picture component of a television signal is often referred to as the video. *See also* VIDEO RECORDING

**video disk** Vinyl disk coated with a reflective, metallic surfacing. On one side of the reflective surface is etched a spiral of microscopic pits corresponding to digital information that can be picked up by a laser scanner and converted electronically to video pictures and sound. Since the late 1980s video disks have been almost entirely superseded by the smaller, more comprehensive type of COMPACT DISK (CD) called a CD-ROM.

**video game** Game using electronically generated images displayed on a screen. Some video games test the skill of a single player, while other games allow two or more players to compete. *See also* VIRTUAL REALITY

**videotape recording** Recording and reproducing sound and moving pictures using magnetic tape. The video

**VIDEOTAPE RECORDING**

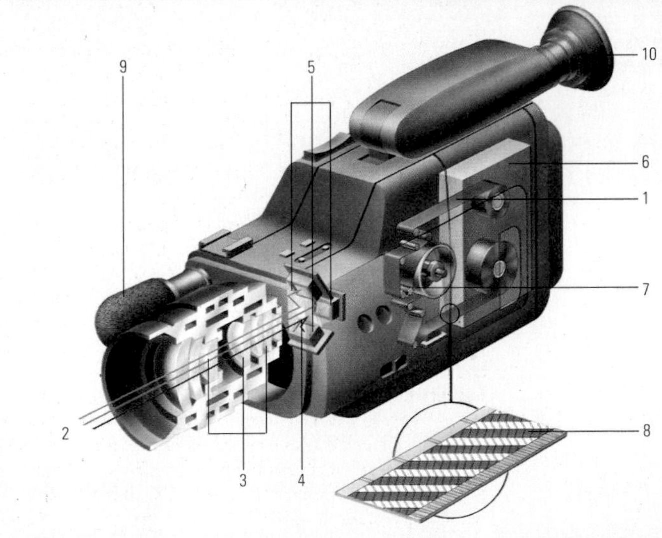

A videotape recorder (camcorder) converts an image into an electrical signal, which can then be stored on magnetic tape (1). Light from an image (2) is focused by a series of lenses (3) and then split into its component colors by a prism (4). The red, green, and blue light strike separate light-sensitive chips (5) that reproduce them in electronic form. The magnetic tape is housed in a protective case (6) that opens when inserted into the camcorder. The recording head (7) is angled and records information onto the tape in diagonal bands of magnetic particles (8). The helical scanning allows more information to be stored on a length of tape. A microphone (9) picks up sound, which is laid down in parallel to the visual information. Camcorders have a small television screen in the eyepiece (10) that allows the operator to play back and review the pictures taken. The camcorder can also be plugged directly into the television and the images played back

V

► **Vikings** The Vikings were those Scandinavians who left their homelands between *c.* AD800 and 1050, intent on trade, piracy, or settlement. Those of present-day Norway began their expansion by settling in the Orkneys and Shetland, fulfillling a need for land. It is believed that there may have been overpopulation and land shortage in Norway at this time; an additional reason may have been the tyrannical growth of royal power in Norway. From the Orkneys and Shetland, the Vikings moved to N England, Ireland, the Faröe Isles, and the Isle of Man, where the chiefs founded towns to further trade and act as bases for pirate attacks. In the Atlantic, the Norsemen discovered new lands – Iceland, Greenland, and North America. However, settlement of America was impossible due to overly long lines of communication. The Danes settled in the E lowlands of England and concentrated their activities along the coasts of the North Sea and Channel – in France and in Frisia. Some ventured further afield to Spain and the Mediterranean. The Swedes journeyed into Russia and acquired considerable wealth there. The Vikings were extremely fine seamen and skillful shipbuilders; they also developed fairly sophisticated means of land transportation. They were vitally important in Europe's trade and there is evidence that they had commercial connections with all the known world, especially in the E.

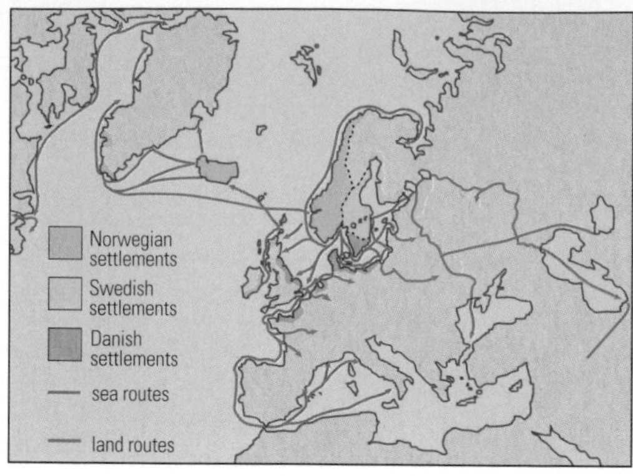


recorder developed from the audio magnetic tape recorder, from which it differs significantly in two respects: videotape is wider to accommodate the picture signals; and the relative speed at which the tape passes the magnetic head is greater in order to deal with the larger amount of information necessary for recording and reproducing pictures. *See also* MAGNETIC RECORDING

**videotext** General term for the different methods by which information can be brought to a television screen. Information that is transmitted by the broadcasting authority in parallel with the ordinary TV signals, and that may be screened simultaneously with or independently from other channels, is known as **teletext**. The system that brings information to the screen from a computer databank via a telephone landline is called **videotex**.

**Vienna** (Wien) Capital of Austria, on the DANUBE River. Vienna became an important town under the Romans, but after their withdrawal in the 5th century it fell to a succession of invaders from E Europe. The first HAPSBURG ruler was installed in 1276 and the city was the seat of the HOLY ROMAN EMPIRE from 1558 to 1806. Occupied by the French during the NAPOLEONIC WARS, it was later chosen as the site of the Congress of VIENNA. As the capital of the AUSTRO-HUNGARIAN EMPIRE, it was the cultural and social center of 19th-century Europe under the emperor FRANZ JOSEPH. It suffered an economic and political collapse following the defeat of the Central Powers in World War I. After World War II, it was occupied (1945–55) by joint Soviet-Western forces. Vienna's historical buildings include the 12th-century St. Stephen's Cathedral, the Schönbrunn (royal summer palace), and the Hofburg (a former residence of the Hapsburgs). Industries: chemicals, textiles, furniture, clothing. Vienna is the third-largest German-speaking city (after Berlin and Hamburg). Pop. (1993) 1,589,052.

**Vienna, Congress of** (1814–15) European conference that settled international affairs after the NAPOLEONIC WARS. It attempted, as far as possible, to restore the Europe of pre-1789, and it disappointed the hopes of nationalists and liberals. Among steps to prevent future European wars, it established the CONGRESS SYSTEM and the German Confederation, a loose association for purposes of defense.

**Vienna Boys' Choir** Austrian choir comprising 22 boys between the ages of eight and fourteen years. It was founded in 1498 as the choir of the court chapel. One of the world's best-known choirs, it tours regularly and makes recordings.

**Vientiane** (Viangchan) Capital and chief port of Laos, on the Mekong River, close to the Thai border, N central Laos. It was the capital of the Lao kingdom (1707–1828). The city became part of French INDOCHINA in 1893 and in 1899 became the capital of the French protectorate. Industries: textiles, brewing, cigarettes, hides, wood products. It is a major source of opium for world markets. Pop. (1992) 449,000.

**Viet Cong** Nickname for the Vietnamese communist guerrillas who fought against the US-supported regime in South Vietnam during the VIETNAM WAR. After earlier, isolated revolts against the government of Ngo Dinh DIEM, the movement was unified (1960) as the National Liberation Front (NLF), modeled on the VIET MINH.

**Viet Minh** Vietnamese organization that fought for independence from the French (1946–54). It resisted the Japanese occupation of French INDOCHINA during World War II. After the war, when the French refused to recognize it as a provisional government, it began operations against the colonial forces. The French were forced to withdraw after their defeat at DIEN BIEN PHU (1954).

**Vietnam** Republic in SE Asia. *See* country feature

**Vietnamese** National language of VIETNAM, spoken by about 70 million people. It is part of the Muong branch of the Mon-Khmer subfamily of Asiatic languages and derives some of its vocabulary from Mandarin Chinese.

**Vietnam War** (1954–75) Conflict between US-backed South Vietnam and insurgents known as the VIET CONG, who had the support of communist North Vietnam. It followed the partition of Vietnam in 1954 and was fueled by the US's fear of the spread of communism. The US received token support from its allies in the Pacific region, and North Vietnam was supplied by China and the Soviet Union. As fighting intensified, US troops were committed in increasing numbers: by 1968 there were more than 500,000. In spite of US technological superiority and command of the air, military stalemate ensued. The instability of the unrepresentative South Vietnamese government, heavy casualties, and daily TV coverage made the war highly unpopular in the US. A peace agreement, negotiated by Henry KISSINGER and Le Duc Tho, was signed in Paris in 1973; it provided for the withdrawal of US troops. In 1975 South Vietnam was overrun by North Vietnamese forces, and the country was united under communist rule.

**vigilante** Member of a street patrol of community residents organized with or without consent or assistance from the local police to prevent and deter such generally urban crimes as mugging, vandalism, joyriding, and burglary. In major cities such patrols may comprise semi-professional personnel who wear their own style of uniform and have their own hierarchy; such groups include the well-known Guardian Angels of the New York subway. Unless formally deputized by the police, however, a vigilante has no special law-enforcement powers.

**Vignola, Giacomo Barozzi da** (1507–73) Italian architect who succeeded MICHELANGELO as architect of ST. PETER'S (1567–73). His Gesú church, Rome (1568), with its revolutionary design uniting clergy and congregation more closely, has been widely copied. His other major works include the Palazzo Farnese, Caprarola (1559), and the Tempieto di San Andrea, Rome (1550).

**Vigny, Alfred de** (1797–1863) French poet, dramatist, and novelist. Pessimistic in tone, his work often emphasizes the lonely struggle of the individual in a hostile universe, as in the quintessential romantic drama *Chatterton* (1853). His best poems are found in *Poems Ancient and Modern* (1826), and his fiction includes the pioneering French historical novel *Cinq-Mars* (1826). *See also* ROMANTICISM

**Vigo, Jean** (1905–34) French film director. An original, lyrical filmmaker, he died tragically young of leukemia. His anarchic debut feature, *Zéro de Conduite* (1933), was banned in France until 1945. *Atalante* (1934), his second and last feature, is an elegant amalgam of social realism and poetic lyricism, set in a dreamlike Parisian landscape.

**Vigo** Seaport city on Vigo Bay, Galicia, NW Spain, near the Portuguese border. It was the scene of a naval battle in 1702, when an Anglo-Dutch fleet attacked Spanish galleons carrying a cargo of gold from the New World. Industries: fishing, fish processing and canning (mostly tuna and sardines), boatbuilding. Pop. (1991) 274,629.

**Vikings** Scandinavian, seaborne marauders, traders, and settlers, who spread throughout much of Europe and the North Atlantic region in the 9th–11th centuries. The remarkable Viking expansion seems to have been caused by rapid population growth and consequent scarcity of good farming land, as well as the desire for new sources of wealth. It was made possible by their advanced maritime technology, which enabled them to cross N European waters in a period when other sailors feared to venture out of sight of land. They were in many respects more advanced than other European peoples, notably in metalwork. Although they first appeared in their greatly feared "longships" as raiders on the coasts of NW Europe, later groups came to settle. Swedes, known as

Varangians, founded the first Russian state at Novgorod, and traded via the Volga River in Byzantium and Persia. Danes conquered much of N and E England. Norwegians created kingdoms in N Britain and Ireland, founding Dublin (*c*.840) and other cities; they also colonized Iceland and established settlements in Greenland. A short-lived settlement, VINLAND, was established in North America by LEIF ERICSSON in *c*.1003. In the early 10th century, the Vikings settled in Normandy. Anarchic conditions in 10th-century Scandinavia resulted in the formation of larger, more powerful kingdoms, and Viking expansion declined. It was renewed in a different form with the conquest of England by King Sweyn of Denmark in 1013 and the Norman Conquest of 1066.

**Viking space mission** US space project to investigate conditions on MARS (1976). Two spacecraft, Viking 1 and Viking 2, each attached to separate vehicles that orbited the planet, made the first successful landings on Mars. They transmitted much information to Earth, including dramatic photographs of the surface. *See also* SPACE EXPLORATION

**Villa, "Pancho" (Francisco)** (1877–1923) Mexican revolutionary leader. An outlaw, he later joined the forces of Francisco MADERO (1909) during the MEXICAN REVOLUTION. He sided with Venustiano CARRANZA for some time, but later supported Emiliano ZAPATA. Angered by US recognition of Carranza's government, Villa murdered US citizens in N Mexico and New Mexico. In 1920 he was pardoned in return for agreeing to retire from politics. He was assassinated three years later.

**villa** Large country house of the ROMAN EMPIRE and post-Roman period. In ancient Rome, they were the private residences of important citizens. They had spacious reception rooms, often with mosaic floors and sometimes even underfloor heating. Since then the term has been used to describe detached houses in a huge variety of sizes and styles.

**Villa-Lobos, Heitor** (1887–1959) Brazilian composer and conductor. He was influenced by Native South American folk music and the music of Claude Debussy. His range of works includes operas, ballets, symphonies, religious and chamber music. His nine *Bachianas Brasileiras* are a Brazilian transcription of the music of J.S. Bach.

**Villars, Claude Louis, duc de** (1653–1734) French general. In the War of the SPANISH SUCCESSION (1701–14) he won victories at Friedlingen (1702) and Hochstadt (1703).

**Villehardouin, Geoffroi de** (1150–1213) French historian. He was a leader of the Fourth CRUSADE, of which he wrote an

## VIETNAM

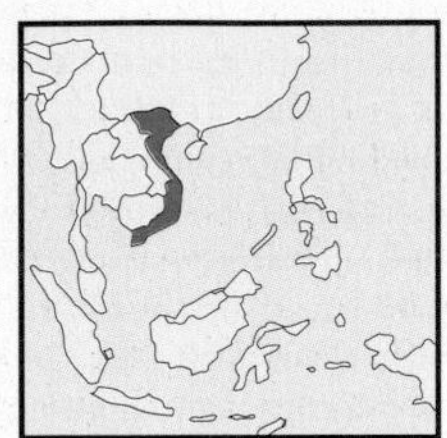

Vietnam's flag was first used by forces led by Ho Chi Minh during the liberation struggle against Japan in World War II (1939–45). It became the flag of North Vietnam in 1945. It was retained when North and South Vietnam were reunited in 1976.

**AREA:** 128,065sq mi (331,689sq km)
**POPULATION:** 72,500,000
**CAPITAL (POPULATION):** Hanoi (1,088,862)
**GOVERNMENT:** Socialist republic
**ETHNIC GROUPS:** Vietnamese 87%, Tho (Tay), Chinese (Hoa), Tai, Khmer, Muong, Nung
**LANGUAGES:** Vietnamese (official)
**RELIGIONS:** Buddhism 55%, Christianity (Roman Catholic 7%)
**CURRENCY:** Dong = 10 hao = 100 xu

The Socialist Republic of Vietnam occupies an S-shaped strip of land in Southeast Asia. The coastal plains include two densely populated river delta regions: in the N, the Red River delta is the site of HANOI and HAIPHONG; in the S, the MEKONG delta contains HO CHI MINH CITY. Inland, the Annam Cordillera forms much of the boundary with Cambodia. In the NW, the highlands extend into Laos and China.

### CLIMATE

Vietnam has a tropical climate. The summer months are hot and wet, with monsoon winds. The driest months, January to March, are cooler.

### VEGETATION

Forests cover *c*.30% of Vietnam and include teak and ebony trees. About 17% of the land is farmed. There are some mangrove swamps.

### HISTORY AND POLITICS

In 111 BC China seized Vietnam, naming it ANNAM. In 939 it became independent. In 1558 it split into two parts: TONKIN in the N, ruled from Hanoi; and Annam in the S, ruled from Hué. In 1802, with French support, Vietnam was united as the empire of Vietnam, under Nguyen Anh. The French took Saigon in 1859 and by 1887 had formed INDOCHINA from the union of Tonkin, Annam, and Cochin China.

Japan conquered Vietnam during World War II and established a Vietnamese state under Emperor Bao Dai. After the war, Bao Dai's government collapsed, and the nationalist VIET MINH, led by HO CHI MINH, set up a Vietnamese republic. In 1946 the French tried to reassert control and war broke out. Despite aid from the US, they were finally defeated at DIEN BIEN PHU. In

1954 Vietnam was divided along the 17th parallel, with North Vietnam under the communist government of Ho Chi Minh and South Vietnam under the French-supported Bao Dai. In 1955 Bao Dai was deposed and Ngo Dinh DIEM was elected president. Diem's rule was recognized as the legal government of Vietnam by many western countries, despite his authoritarian rule. North Vietnam, supported by China and the Soviet Union, extended its influence into South Vietnam, mainly through the VIET CONG. The US became increasingly involved in what they perceived to be the fight against communism. The conflict soon escalated into the VIETNAM WAR. After US forces were withdrawn in 1975, Ho Chi Minh's nationalist forces overran South Vietnam and it surrendered. In 1976 the reunited Vietnam became a Socialist Republic.In the late 1970s Vietnam invaded Cambodia, defeating the KHMER ROUGE government. It withdrew its troops in 1989. Vietnam's weak economy was improved in the late 1980s and 1990s with the introduction of free-market economic reforms, known as *Doi Moi*. In 1995 it became a member of ASEAN.

### ECONOMY

Vietnam is a low-income developing country (1992 GDP per capita, US$1,010). Agriculture employs 67% of the workforce. The main crop is rice, of which it is the world's fifth-largest producer. Other crops include bananas, coffee, groundnuts, and rubber. Vietnam also produces oil, phosphates, and coal; natural gas resources have been found.

▲ **violin** Late 17th-century violin. The violin was perfected in Italy by the Amati, Stradivari, and Guarneri families from 1650 to 1740. The great brilliance of violin tone soon overwhelmed the softer tones of the viols, which died out.

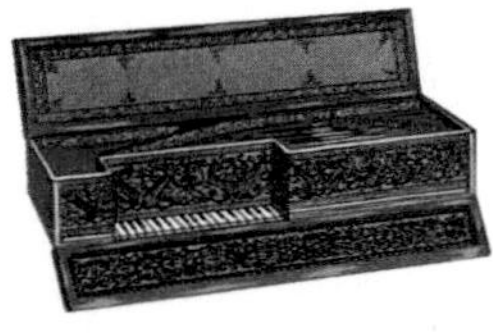

▲ **virginal** Related to the harpsichord, and producing a similar plucked sound, the virginal was a small keyboard instrument without legs. The best collection of virginal music is the Fitzwilliam Virginal Book (1606–16), consisting of pieces by English composers such as John Bull, William Byrd, and Giles Farnaby.

**VIRGINIA**
**Statehood:**
June 25, 1788
**Nickname:**
Old Dominion
**State bird:**
Cardinal
**State flower:**
Flowering dogwood
**State tree:**
Flowering dogwood
**State motto:**
Thus always to tyrants

incomplete account, *Conquest of Constantinople*, which was the first historical chronicle in French.

**villi** In anatomy, small, fingerlike projections of a MUCOUS MEMBRANE such as that which lines the inner walls of the SMALL INTESTINE. They increase the absorptive surface area of the gut. In digestion, intestinal villi absorb most of the products of food broken down in the STOMACH, DUODENUM, and ILEUM.

**Villon, François** (1430–1463) French lyric poet, b. François de Montcorbier or François des Loges. He led a troubled life after killing a priest in 1455. He wrote the famous *Ballad of a Hanged Man* while awaiting execution in 1462 (the sentence was later commuted to banishment). Among his other major works, which embrace a variety of forms, are *Le Petit Testament*, a satirical will in verse, and the more subtle *Le Grand Testament*, which is in part a lament for lost youth.

**Vilnius** Capital of Lithuania, on the Neris River. Founded in 1323 as the capital of the grand duchy of Lithuania, the city declined after the union of Lithuania-Poland. It has been the capital under many different rulers since that time. Despite World War II bombing, the old city retains many of its historic synagogues, churches, and civic buildings, as well as remnants of its 14th-century castle and fortifications. Industries: engineering, chemicals, textiles, food processing. Pop. (1994) 578,700.

**Vincent de Paul, Saint** (1581–1660) French priest. He founded the Congregation of the Mission (or Lazarists), and then in 1633 he helped to found the Sisters of Charity of St. Vincent de Paul to minister to the sick, the old, and orphans. He was canonized in 1737.

**vine** Plant with a long, thin stem that climbs rocks, plants, and supports. To aid their climb, vines develop modifications such as tendrils, disklike holdfasts, adventitious roots, and runners. Examples are tropical LIANA, wild GRAPE, and morning glory.

**vinegar** Any of various types of liquid condiment and preservative based on a weak solution of ETHANOIC ACID. It is produced commercially by the fermentation of alcohol. The major type of vinegar is known as malt vinegar, which, when distilled, becomes white (or clear) vinegar. Vinegar can also be processed from cider or wine.

**Vinland** Region of North America settled by VIKINGS from Greenland led by LEIF ERICSSON in *c.*1003. The existence of land W of Greenland had been reported a few years earlier. Leif stayed for one season only, but at least two other expeditions settled there briefly. Vinland was soon abandoned because of the hostility of local people.

**Vinson, Frederick Moore** (1890–1953) Chief justice of the US Supreme Court (1946–53). He served as congressman (1924–29, 1931–38), a federal judge (1938–42), and secretary of treasury (1945–46). Appointed chief justice of the Supreme Court (1946), he was a strong supporter of civil rights but believed in broad powers for the government. This was evident in his dissenting opinion in *Youngstown Sheet and Tube* v. *Sawyer* (1952).

**viol** Fretted STRINGED INSTRUMENT, played with a bow. It is held on or between the knees and, in its most usual shape, has sloping shoulders and a flat back. The six strings are tuned in fourths, in the same manner as the LUTE. A possible derivative is the modern DOUBLE BASS, which shows its ancestry by being tuned in fourths (unlike members of the violin family). Viols are still used today for the authentic performance of early music.

**viola** STRINGED INSTRUMENT of the VIOLIN family. It is slightly larger than the violin and its four strings are tuned a fifth lower. It is the tenor member of a string quartet.

**violet** Any of about 400 species of herbs and shrublets of the genus *Viola*, found worldwide. Violets may be annual or perennial, with five-petaled flowers that grow singly on stalks; usually blue, violet, lilac, yellow, or white. Family Violaceae.

**violin** STRINGED INSTRUMENT. It is thought to have derived from the *lira da braccio*, a Renaissance bowed instrument, and the rebec. It was perfected in Italy by the AMATI, STRADIVARI, and GUARNERI families between 1650 and 1740. The body is assembled from curved, wooden panels, the front pierced by two *f*-shaped soundholes. Four taut strings are played by drawing a bow across them, or sometimes by plucking them with the fingers (pizzicato).

**violoncello** *See* CELLO

**viper** Any of 150 species of poisonous SNAKES characterized by a pair of long, hollow, venom-injecting fangs in the front of the upper jaw. The fangs can be folded back when not in use. The common adder (*Vipera berus*) of Europe and E Asia has a dark, zigzag band along its back. Length: to 10ft (3m). Family Viperidae.

**Virgil** (70–19 BC) (Publius Vergilius Maro) Roman poet. He gained a high literary reputation in Rome with the *Eclogues* (42–37 BC) and the *Georgics* (37–30), a pastoral but instructive work on farming and country life. His greatest work was the *Aeneid*, which established him as an epic poet. It relates the adventures of the Trojan hero Aeneas, and echoes the themes of Homer's *Odyssey* and *Iliad*. Unfinished at his death, it was published at the command of Emperor AUGUSTUS.

**virginal** Musical instrument of the HARPSICHORD family. The strings, a single set running nearly parallel to the keyboard, are plucked by quills. Two keyboards, differing in size and pitch, were sometimes incorporated into the same case. Virginals were particularly popular in 16th- and 17th-century England.

**virgin birth** Christian doctrine teaching that JESUS CHRIST was conceived by the Blessed Virgin MARY through the power of the HOLY SPIRIT and without the involvement of a human male. That Jesus had no earthly father is a basic tenet of Roman Catholicism, all the Eastern Orthodox Churches, and most Protestant Churches.

**Virginia** State in E US, on the Atlantic coast, the most northerly of the "southern states"; the capital is RICHMOND. The coastal plain is low-lying. To the W the Piedmont Plateau rises to the BLUE RIDGE MOUNTAINS, and there are extensive forests. The first permanent British settlement in North America was at JAMESTOWN (1607). Virginia evolved an aristocratic plantation society based on vast tobacco holdings. Virginia's leaders were in the forefront of the American Revolution. During the CIVIL WAR, Richmond acted as the Confederate capital, and Virginia was the main battleground of the war. Virginia was readmitted to the Union in 1870. Farming is an important part of Virginia's economy, and the chief crops include tobacco, peanuts, grain, vegetables, and fruits. Dairying and poultry are also widespread. Industries: chemicals, shipbuilding, fishing, transportation equipment. Coal is the most important mineral deposit. Stone, sand, and gravel are quarried. Area: 40,814sq mi (105,710sq km). Pop. (1992) 6,394,481.

**Virginia Beach** City on the Atlantic Ocean, SE Virginia. Site of the Cape Henry memorial cross (commemorating the first landing of English colonists, 1607), and of the oldest brick house in the US, it is now a rapidly expanding tourist center with good beaches and recreational facilities. Its economy is helped by market gardening and nearby military complexes. The population increased by nearly 60% between 1980 and 1992, making it the state's largest city. Pop. (1992) 417,061.

**Virginia Plan** (1787) Program offered by the Virginia delegation at the Philadelphia CONSTITUTIONAL CONVENTION. It consisted of 15 resolutions concerning a structure of government for the Union. Among its features were: a bicameral national legislature in which the lower house would be elected by the people and the upper house by the lower chamber; an executive to be chosen by the legislature; and a judiciary with a Supreme Court and lower courts elected by the legislature. The plan favored the large states as representation was based on population and wealth. Some features were included in the Constitution.

**Virgin Islands, British** British colony in the West Indies. It is a group of 36 islands, which form part of the ANTILLES group; the capital is Road Town (on Tortola, the main island). First settled in the 17th century, the islands formed part of the LEEWARD ISLANDS colony until 1956. The chief economic activity is tourism. Area: 59sq mi (130sq km). Pop. (1993 est.) 17,000.

**Virgin Islands, US** Group of 68 islands in the Lesser ANTILLES, in the West Indies. They are administered by the US with the status of an "unincorporated territory." The chief islands are St. Croix and St. Thomas, which includes the capital Charlotte Amalie (1990 pop. 12,331). Spanish from 1553, the islands were Danish in 1917, when they were bought by the US for $25 million in order to protect the northern approaches to the newly completed PANAMA CANAL. Tourism is the biggest money earner. Industries: oil refining, aluminum, textiles, rum, pharmaceuticals, perfumes. Area 133sq mi (344sq km). Pop. (1990) 101,809.

**Virgin Mary** *See* MARY

**Virgo** (Virgin) Equatorial constellation on the ecliptic between Leo and Libra. It lies in a region of the sky that has many galaxies and galaxy clusters. The brightest star is the 1st-magnitude Alpha Virginis, or Spica.

**virology** Study of VIRUSES. The existence of viruses was established in 1892 by D. Ivanovski, a Russian botanist, who found that the causative agent of tobacco mosaic disease could pass through a porcelain filter impermeable to BACTERIA. The introduction of the electron microscope in the 1940s made it possible to view viruses.

**virtual reality** Use of computer graphics to simulate a three-dimensional environment that users can explore as if it were real. A virtual reality system can allow an architect to see what the inside of a building will look like before construction begins. The computer images are produced using the architect's drawings of the building. Some entertainment machines use virtual reality to simulate spaceflight adventures and various ball games.

**virus** Submicroscopic infectious organism. Viruses vary in size from 10 to 300 nanometers and contain only genetic material in the form of DNA or RNA. Viruses are incapable of independent existence: they can grow and reproduce only when they enter another cell, such as a bacterium or animal cell, because they lack energy-producing and protein-synthesizing functions. When they enter a cell, viruses subvert the host's metabolism so that viral reproduction is favored. Control of viruses is difficult because harsh measures are required to kill them. The animal body has, however, evolved some protective measures, such as production of INTERFERON and of ANTIBODIES directed against specific viruses. Where the specific agent can be isolated, VACCINES can be developed, but some viruses change so rapidly that vaccines become ineffective.

**Visconti, Luchino** (1906–76) Italian film director. He made his film debut in 1942 with *Ossessione*, which pioneered the Italian NEO-REALISM school. His other films include *Senso* (1953), *Rocco and His Brothers* (1960), *Death in Venice* (1971), and *Conversation Piece* (1975). An eminent and significant filmmaker, his later work was characterized by a more opulent style. He also received acclaim for his theater and opera work, and is seen as being responsible for the fame of Maria CALLAS.

**Visconti** Italian family that ruled Milan from the 13th century until 1447. Ottone Visconti (*c.*1207–95) was appointed archbishop of Milan in 1262 and used his position to become the first Visconti *signore* (lord) of Milan. Supporters of the GHIBELLINES, the Visconti established control over Lombardy in the 14th century, and in 1349 the title of *signore* became hereditary. Visconti lordship of Milan passed to the Sforza family in 1447.

**viscosity** Resistance to flow of a FLUID because of internal friction. The more viscous the fluid, the slower it flows. Viscosity is large for liquids and extremely small for gases.

**Vishnu** Major god of HINDUISM; one of the supreme triad of gods, along with BRAHMA and SHIVA. Vishnu was mentioned as a sun god in the VEDAS (*c.* 1500–*c.*1200 BC). Over the next 1,000 years or more, his importance grew and he became an amalgam of local cultic gods and heroes. In mythology, Vishnu is worshiped as a preserver and restorer. According to Hindu tradition, he reigns in heaven with his wife LAKSHMI, the goddess of wealth. From time to time, he comes into the world to fight evil, assuming a different incarnation each time. His incarnations have included RAMA and KRISHNA.

**Visigoths** *See* GOTH

**vision** *See* SIGHT

**Vistula** (Wisala) Longest river in Poland. It rises in the Carpathian Mountains of w Poland and flows NW through Warsaw, then NW through Torun to enter the Gulf of Danzig at Gdańsk. The major waterway of Poland, it serves a large area through a tributary system. Canals link it with other important rivers both E and W. Length: 675mi (1,090km).

## VIRTUAL REALITY

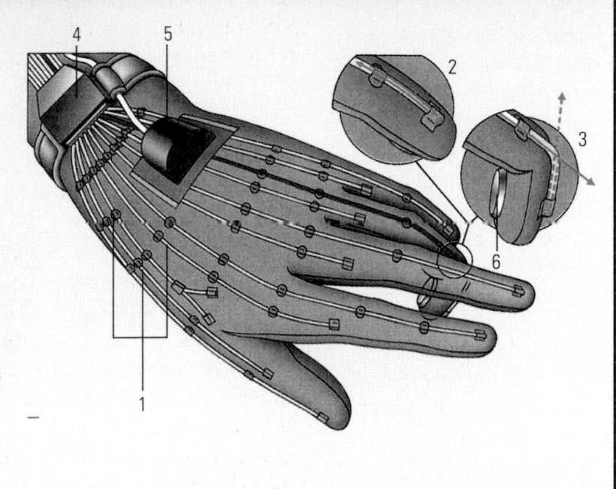


A data glove measures the movements of the wearer's hand and allows the user to manipulate objects in virtual reality. Fiber optic cables (1) on the glove detect the flexing of the hand. Light travels up and down the cables (2). When the cables are bent (3) they no longer reflect light back to the interface board (4). A position sensor (5) detects the movement of the glove in three dimensions. Fingertip padding (6) convinces the user they are touching an actual object.

**vitalism** Philosophical theory that all living organisms derive their characteristic qualities from a universal life force. Vitalists hold that the force operating on living matter is peculiar to such matter and is quite different from any forces outside animate things. In the late 20th century, few scientists give vitalism much credence, but it has influenced many forms of alternative medicine.

**vitamin** Organic compound that is essential in small amounts to the maintenance and healthy growth of all animals. Vitamins are classified as either water-soluble (B and C) or fat-soluble (A, D, E, and K). They are usually taken in the diet, but today most can be made synthetically. Some are synthesized in the body. Many vitamins act as coenzymes, helping ENZYMES in RESPIRATION and other metabolic processes. Lack of a particular vitamin can lead to a deficiency disease. **Vitamin E** is important in reproduction and many other biological processes. **Vitamin D** helps the body absorb phosphorus and calcium. It is essential for the normal growth of bone and teeth. Existing in human skin (activated by sunlight), vitamin D is also found in fish-liver oil, yeast, and egg yolk. **Vitamin C** (ascorbic acid) is commonly found in fruits and vegetables. It helps the body resist infection, and is essential to normal metabolism. **Vitamin B** is actually a group of 12 vitamins, important in assisting the process by which energy is produced in the body (RESPIRATION). Vitamin $B_1$ (THIAMINE) occurs in yeast and cereals. Another B vitamin is niacin (nicotinic acid) found in milk, meat, and green vegetables. Vitamin $B_{12}$ is needed for the formation of blood cells. It is found especially in meat, liver, and eggs. **Vitamin A** (retinol), found in fish-liver oil, is important for healthy eyes. *See also* RIBOFLAVIN

**Vitruvius** (active early 1st century AD) Roman architect and engineer. His encyclopedic *De Architectura* (before AD 27) covers almost every aspect of ancient architecture, including town planning, types of buildings, and materials. It is the only work of its type to survive from the ancient world.

**Vitus, Saint** (active 4th century) Italian martyr. Secretly raised as a Christian by his nurse, he was put to death during the persecutions of DIOCLETIAN. He is the patron saint of actors.

**Vivaldi, Antonio** (1675–1741) Italian composer. A master of the CONCERTO and a virtuoso violinist, he helped to standardize the three-movement concerto form and to develop the *concerto grosso* (a concerto for two or more solo instruments). His best-known work is *The Four Seasons* (1725). He also composed sacred vocal music and about 50 operas, of which 20 survive.

**viviparity** (vivipary) Process or trait among animals of giving birth to live young. Placental mammals show the highest development of viviparity, in which the offspring develops inside the body, within the mother's UTERUS.

**vivisection** Dissection of living bodies for experimental purposes. Work with laboratory animals in testing drugs,

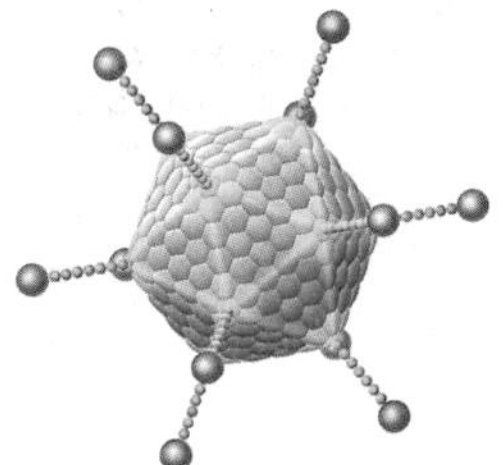

▲ **virus** The human adenovirus is of the type responsible for colds and sore throats. The virus is color coded for ease of identification. The casing consists of 252 protein molecules (capsomeres) arranged into a regular icosahedron (20 faces). This structure occurs in many viruses, representing the most economical packing arrangement around the DNA inside. Twelve of the capsomeres, located at the points of the icosahedron, are five-sided pentagon bases (yellow). The remaining 240 are six-sided hexons (green). Five of these (green-yellow) adjoin each penton base, from which extends a single fiber (red) tipped with a terminal structure (blue) that begins cell entry.

V

**►▼ volcano** Volcanoes (A) are formed when molten lava (1) from a magma chamber (2) in the Earth's crust forces its way to the surface (3). The classic cone-shaped volcano is formed of alternating layers of cooled lava and cinders (4) thrown out during an eruption. Side vents (5) can occur, and when offshoots of lava are trapped below the surface laccoliths (6) are formed. When a volcano's lava has a low silica content, the lava flows easily creating a low-angle, shield cone (B). Cinder cones (C) are created by volcanoes that produce ash and cinders not lava during eruptions. The layers of ash and cinders do not have the stability to create the classic cone-shaped volcano. When a magma chamber collapses, a caldera (D) is formed as the center of the volcanic cone follows suit. Lakes (1) often fill the resulting crater and subsequent upsurges of lava can create islands (2).

B

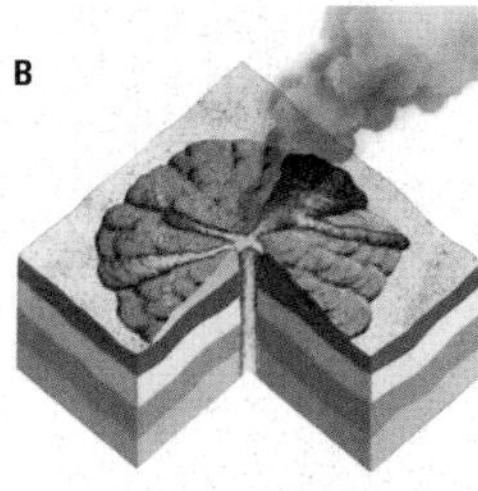

C

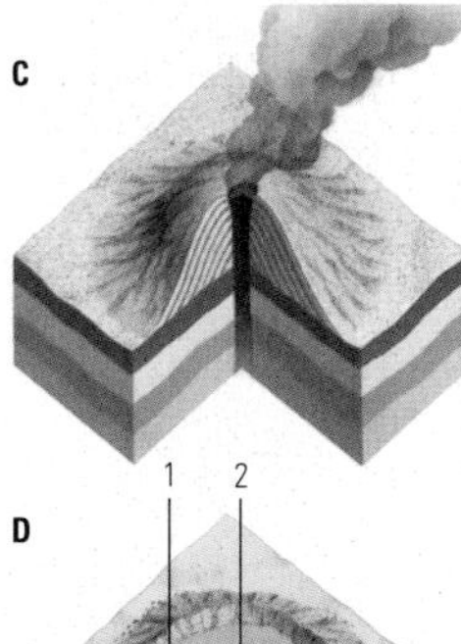

D

1 2

A

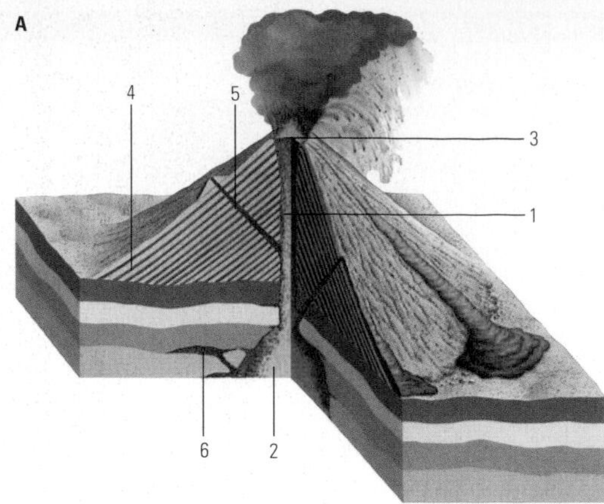


vaccines, and pharmaceuticals frequently involves such dissections. The ethical issue of experimenting on living animals is a matter of controversy.

**Vladimir** City on the N bank of the Klyazma River, Russia. Founded early in the 12th century by Vladimir II of Kiev, it is one of Russia's oldest cities. The grand dukes of Moscow were crowned here in the 14th century. Tourists are drawn partly by three 12th-century buildings – the two cathedrals and the Golden Gate (a fortified city gate). Industries: chemicals, cotton textiles, plastics, tractors, machine tools, electrical goods. Pop. (1994) 338,000.

**Vladimir I (the Great)** (956–1015) Grand Duke of Kiev and first Christian ruler of Russia (980–1015). Vladimir raised an army of VIKING mercenaries in 979 and conquered Polotsk and Kiev. Proclaimed prince of all Russia, he extended Russian territories, conquering parts of Poland and Lithuania. He became a Christian and married a Byzantine princess (988). St. Vladimir, as he is also called, established the Greek Orthodox faith in Russia.

**Vladivostock** Main port, naval base, and cultural center of SIBERIA, Russia, located around a sheltered harbor on the Pacific coast, 30mi (50km) from the Chinese border. Founded in 1860 as a military post, the city developed as a naval base after 1872. Vladivostock is the main E terminus of the TRANS-SIBERIAN RAILROAD. The harbor is kept open in winter by ice-breakers and is a major base for fishing fleets. Industries: ship repairing, oil refining, metal-working, timber products,. Pop. (1994) 637,000.

**Vlaminck, Maurice** (1876–1958) French painter, graphic artist, and writer. One of the leading exponents of FAUVISM, he painted with colors squirted straight from the tube, producing exuberant landscapes, which were partly inspired by the work of VAN GOGH. In 1908 he began using darker colors and studied CÉZANNE in an attempt to give his painting more weight.

**vocal cords** *See* LARYNX

**vocational education** Instruction in industrial or commercial skills. A range of levels of vocational training and qualification are available from schools and colleges, often in collaboration with organizations concerned to improve training and quality standards in particular areas of employment.

**Voice of America** (VOA) Radio station subsidized by the US government. It presents news, other generally factual information and cultural programs aimed primarily at US troops serving abroad. VOA was originally set up by the US Office of War Information in 1943–44 to broadcast war news and propaganda both to US troops and to English-speaking listeners in Europe and elsewhere.

**Vojvodina** Autonomous province in N Serbia, bordered by Croatia, Hungary, and Romania. The capital is NOVI SAD. From 1849–60 it was the independent crownland of Vojvodina, but it was ceded to Yugoslavia in 1920. Given nominal autonomy by Belgrade in 1946, it remains firmly part of Serbia. Only around 50% of the population are Serbs: the rest are Hungarian (19%), Croats, Slovaks, and Romanians. The province is densely populated with a fertile agricultural plain. Industries: fruit, cattle, food processing. Area: 8,301sq mi (21,500sq km). Pop. (1991) 2,013,889

**volcanism** (vulcanism) Volcanic activity. The term includes all aspects of the process: the eruption of molten and gaseous matter, the building up of cones and mountains, and the formation of LAVA flows, and GEYSERS.

**volcano** Vent from which molten rock or LAVA, solid rock debris, and gases issue. Volcanoes may be of the central vent type, where the material erupts from a single pipe, or of the fissure type, where material is extruded along an extensive fracture. Volcanoes are commonly classed as active, dormant, or extinct.

**vole** Short-tailed, small-eared, prolific RODENT that lives in the Northern Hemisphere. Most voles are grayish-brown, herbivorous ground-dwellers and are small. The semiaquatic water vole is the largest. Length: to 7in (18cm). Family Cricetidae.

**Volga** Europe's longest river, at 2,330mi (3,750km), in E European Russia. The river rises in the Valdai Hills, then flows E past Rzhev to Kazan, where it turns S. It continues SW to Volgograd, and then SE to enter the Caspian Sea below Astrakhan. The Volga is connected to the Baltic Sea by the Volga-Baltic Waterway, to Moscow by the Moscow Canal, and to the Sea of Azov (and the Black Sea) by the Volga-Don Canal. Many dams and hydroelectric power stations have been constructed along its course. Navigable for around 2,200mi (3,540km), it carries about two thirds of Russia's river freight traffic.

**Volgograd** Major Russian inland port on the VOLGA River, the E terminus of the Volga-Don Canal. During the Civil War that followed the Russian Revolution, it was defended by Bolshevik troops under Stalin (1918–20) and was renamed Stalingrad in his honor (1925). In the winter of 1942–43 it was almost completely destroyed in a fierce battle that halted the German advance. Rebuilt after World War II and renamed Volgograd in 1961, it is a major rail and industrial center. Industries: oil-refining, shipbuilding, chemicals, aluminum, steel, farm vehicles. Pop. (1992) 1,031,000.

**volleyball** Game in which a ball is volleyed by hand over a net across the center of a court by two six-a-side teams. The court is 59ft (18m) long by 29ft 6in (9m) wide; the top of the net is 8ft (2.4m) high. The object of the game is to get the ball to touch the ground within the opponents' half of the court, or to oblige an opponent to touch the ball before it goes directly out of court. Only the serving team can score, and failure to score loses service; 15 points wins a set, and a game is the best of five sets. Volleyball has been included in the Olympic Games since 1964.

**volt** (symbol V) SI unit of electric potential and ELECTROMOTIVE FORCE (EMF). It is the POTENTIAL DIFFERENCE between two points on a conducting wire carrying a current of one ampere when the power dissipated is 1 watt.

**Volta** West African river, *c.*290mi (470km) long, formed by the confluence of the Black Volta and White Volta rivers at New Tamale, central Ghana. The river flows S into the Gulf of Guinea at Ada. In 1965 it was dammed at Akosombo to form Lake Volta.

**Voltaire** (1694–1778) (François Marie Arouet) French philosopher, historian, playwright, and poet; the outstanding figure of the French ENLIGHTENMENT. Voltaire spent much of his life combating intolerance and injustice. He became a strong opponent of the Roman Catholic Church, and toward the end of his life made his home a refuge for victims of injustice and religious persecution. He spent three years in exile in England (1726–29) and was strongly influenced by English philosophers such as LOCKE. His eulogistic *Philosophical Letters* (1733) provoked official censure. A prolific writer, Voltaire wrote several tragedies and the philosophical novel *Candide* (1759), his best-known work. He contributed to the *Encyclopédie* of Diderot and outlined his view of morality in *Essay on Morals* (1756).

**voltmeter** Instrument for measuring the voltage (POTENTIAL DIFFERENCE) between two points in an electrical CIRCUIT. Voltmeters are always connected in parallel with the components whose voltages are being measured. A voltmeter has a high internal RESISTANCE compared with the resistance across which it is connected. *See also* AMMETER

**volume** Amount of space taken up by a body. Volume is measured in cubic units, such as $cm^3$ (cubic centimeters).
**voluntary muscle** *See* SKELETAL MUSCLE
**Volunteers in Service to America** (VISTA) Federal program under ACTION. It is comprised of volunteers working on projects to eliminate poverty and poverty-related human, social, and environmental problems in the US and its territories. Volunteers serve for up to two years providing such services as day care, health and legal aid, education, and city planning. It was established in 1964.
**vomiting** Act of bringing up the contents of the stomach by way of the mouth. Vomiting is a reflex mechanism that may be activated by any of a number of stimuli, including dizziness, pain, gastric irritation, or shock. It may also be a symptom of serious disease.
**Von Braun, Wernher** (1912–77) US aeonautical engineer, b. Germany. In World War II he was responsible for building the V-2 ROCKET. In 1945 he went to the US, where he developed the Jupiter ROCKET that took the first US satellite, Explorer 1, into space (1958). Von Braun joined the NATIONAL AERONAUTICS AND SPACE ADMINISTRATION (NASA) in 1960 and developed the Saturn rocket that took astronauts to the Moon.
**Vonnegut, Kurt, Jr.** (1922– ) US novelist. He often draws on the conventions of fantasy to satirize the horrors of the 20th century. His books, which regularly involve innovative experimentation with time sequences and narrative, include *Player Piano* (1952), *Slaughterhouse-Five* (1969), and *Hocus Pocus* (1991). He has published collections of short stories and volumes of essays. His recent fiction includes *Timequake* (1997).
**Von Neumann, John** (1903–57) US mathematician, b. Budapest. After leaving Hungary in 1919 he finally settling at Princeton University in 1930, where he became professor in 1933. His early contribution to quantum theory was followed by work on the atom bomb at LOS ALAMOS. He did important work on the foundations of mathematics and in the early development of computers. He was also responsible for the development of GAME THEORY.
**voodoo** Religious belief of African origin. It is prevalent in parts of Africa, but is better known as the national religion of Haiti. Adherents believe in the reincarnate qualities of **Loa**, which include deified ancestors, local gods, and Roman Catholic saints. Loa possesses the believers during dreams or ceremonies, which include dancing and hypnotic trances.
**Voronezh** Industrial port on the Voronezh River, W central Russia, capital of the Voronezh oblast. Founded as a fortress in 1586, it became a shipbuilding center under Peter I. During World War II the city was almost totally destroyed and most of it has been rebuilt. Industries: locomotives, machinery, synthetic rubber, oil, chemicals, food processing, cigarettes, television sets. Pop. (1992) 958,000.
**Voroshilov, Klimenty Yefremovich** (1881–1969) Soviet president (1953–60). A communist from 1903, he took a military rather than political role during the RUSSIAN REVOLUTION (1917). He was commissar for defense (1925–40), becoming president on Stalin's death. Implicated in a plot against Khruschev, he resigned.
**Vorster, Balthazar Johannes** (1915–83) Prime Minister of South Africa (1966–78). Imprisoned during World War 2 as a Nazi sympathizer, Vorster was a staunch advocate of APARTHEID under Hendrik Verwoerd and succeeded him as prime minister and Nationalist Party leader. He established Transkei as a "bantustan" and suppressed the SOWETO uprising (1976). Vorster invaded Angola to try to prevent Namibian independence. He became president in 1978, but corruption charges forced his resignation (1979).
**vortex** Eddy or whirlpool observed in FLUID motion. Vortices cannot occur in ideal (nonviscous) fluid motion, but they are important in the study of real fluids. In particular, the vortices occurring behind airfoils are of great interest in aerodynamic design.
**vorticism** British art movement. Derived from CUBISM and Italian FUTURISM, it was originated in 1913 by Wyndham LEWIS in an attempt to express the spirit of the time in harsh angular forms derived from machinery. David Bomberg, Henri GAUDIER-BRZESKA, and Jacob EPSTEIN were members of the movement.
**voting** Process employed to choose candidates for public office or to decide controversial issues. Early forms were by voice or sign, but the secret ballot became popular in order to eliminate the possibility of intimidation and corruption. Voters usually mark a piece of paper and deposit it in a ballot box, but in the US voting machines, operated by polling levers, are commonly in use.
**Voting Rights Act** (1965) US legislation authorizing federal authorities to check registration and voting procedures in order to protect rights of black voters in nine southern states. Within a year of its passage, the number of African-Americans registered in five Deep South states had increased by almost 50%.
**Voyager program** SPACE EXPLORATION program to study JUPITER, SATURN, URANUS, and NEPTUNE, using two unmanned craft launched 1977. The two Voyager probes were launched 16 days apart from Kennedy Space Center at CAPE CANAVERAL, Florida. They beamed back close-up pictures of Jupiter in 1979. The probes then passed Saturn, and showed the structure of the planet's rings. Voyager II went on to study Uranus in 1986 and Neptune in 1989. Both probes have now left the Solar System.
**Vulcan** (Volcanus) Roman god of fire and volcanoes, identified with the Greek god HEPHAESTUS. His temples were prudently sited outside city walls. Often invoked to avert fires, he was associated with thunderbolts and the Sun.
**vulcanization** Chemical process, discovered 1839, of heating SULFUR or its compounds with natural or synthetic RUBBER in order to improve the rubber's durability and resilience.
**Vulgate** Oldest surviving version of the complete BIBLE, compiled and translated, mostly from Greek, into Latin by St. JEROME from 382. The text was revised several times and was used universally in the Middle Ages. In 1546 it was promoted as the official Latin translation by the Council of TRENT.
**vulture** Large, keen-sighted, strong-flying bird that feeds on carrion. New World vultures, found throughout the Americas, include the CONDOR, turkey BUZZARD, and king vulture; family Cathartidae. Old World vultures, related to eagles, are found in Africa, Europe, and Asia, and include the Egyptian vulture and the griffon vulture; family Accipitridae.
**vulva** In human females, the external genitalia. Extending downward from the clitoris (a small, sensitive, elongated, erectile organ), a pair of fleshy lips (labia majora) surround the vulvar orifice. Within the labia majora, two smaller folds of skin (labia minora) surround a depression called the vestibule, within which are the urethral and vaginal openings.
**Vyatka** (formerly Kirov) City and river port on the W bank of the Vyatka River, W Russia; capital of Kirov region. Founded as Khlynov in 1174, it was annexed by Ivan III in 1489. The city was renamed Vyatka in 1780 and then known as Kirov from 1934 to 1992. It has a 17th-century cathedral. Industries: metal products, agricultural machinery, meat processing, timber, leather, furs. Pop. (1992) 493,000.

▲ **vulture** The red-headed turkey vulture (*Cathartes aura*) is a New World vulture, found from Canada to the Magellan Strait. It has a sharply hooked bill, with fleshy seres across the top, through which the nostrils open. Because it is not as strong as other birds of prey, it feeds chiefly on carrion or on helpless animals, which it can spot from a great distance.

V

*W/w, 23rd letter of the Roman alphabet, and like* **f, u, v** *and* **y,** *derived from the Semitic letter* **waw,** *meaning* **hook.** *The Greeks adopted* **waw** *into their alphabet as the letter* **upsilon.** *In Anglo-Saxon times, it appeared as* **VV.**

**Waco** City on the Brazos River, central Texas; settled as a ferry-crossing in 1849. In 1993 80 members of the BRANCH DAVIDIANS religious sect died during a confrontation with federal authorities. Industries: cotton, grain, tires, paper, furniture, clothing, cottonseed oil products, glass, aircraft parts. Pop. (1992) 103,997.

**Wagner, Richard** (1813–83) German composer. His works consist almost entirely of operas, for which he provided his own libretti. Early operas include *Der fliegende Holländer* (1843), *Tannhäuser* (1845), and *Lohengrin* (1850). With *Tristan and Isolde* (1865) and the four-part *Der Ring des Nibelungen* (1851–76) his genius is fully displayed. His rich, chromatic style lends emotional depth, and a web of LEITMOTIFS propel the drama. Other operas include *Die Meistersinger von Nürnberg* (1868) and the sacred stage drama *Parsifal* (1882).

**Wagner Act** (1935) First modern US labor law to be declared constitutional. It represented a positive change in government policy toward labor. The Wagner Act requires that the employer recognize the union, bargain collectively with it, and not interfere with employees' rights to join it. The Wagner Act was counterbalanced in 1947 by the Taft-Hartley Act.

**Waikato** Longest river in New Zealand, in central and NW North Island. It rises from Lake Taupo in the central highlands and flows NNW into the Tasman Sea. The river is navigable for 80mi (130km) of its 264-mi (425-km) course.

**Wailing Wall** *See* WESTERN WALL

**Waite, Morrison** (1816–88) Chief justice of the US Supreme Court (1874–88). He gained national prominence as US counsel in the ALABAMA CLAIMS case (1871–72). Appointed chief justice by Ulysses S. GRANT, Waite interpreted the constitutional amendments that were adopted after the Civil War. He also interpreted the "due process" clause of the 14th Amendment as a means to limit state power.

**Wake Island** Largest of three coral islands, known collectively as Wake Island, enclosing a lagoon in the W Pacific Ocean. The atoll was discovered by Spaniards (1568) and named by the British in 1796. It was annexed by the US (1898) and became a naval base, captured by Japan (1941) and recaptured in 1945.

**Waksman, Selman Abraham** (1888–1973) US microbiologist, b. Russia. He was awarded the 1952 Nobel Prize for physiology or medicine for his discovery (1943) of the antibiotic streptomycin. He developed techniques for extracting antibiotics from various microorganisms and discovered new ones, including neomycin.

**Walcott, Derek** (1930– ) Caribbean poet and dramatist. He has written many plays, including *Henri Christophe* (1950), *Drums and Colors* (1961), *O Babylon* (1978), and *Viva Detroit* (1992), but he is perhaps best known as a poet. His verse, the first volume of which was published in 1948, was collected in 1986. Other volumes include *Omeros* (1989). He was awarded the 1992 Nobel Prize for literature.

**Wald, George** (1906– ) US biologist. He shared the 1967 Nobel Prize for physiology and medicine for being "one of the world's greatest authorities on the biochemistry of perception." He studied visual pigments and the effect of light on these pigments. Wald was an outspoken critic of US policy in Vietnam. He later criticized DNA research and nuclear safety.

**Waldemar IV** (1320–75) (Waldemar Atterday) King of Denmark (1340–75). He restored the Danish kingdom after a century of disintegration by a mixture of force, diplomacy, and persuasion. In 1367 his enemies, including the HANSEATIC LEAGUE, united to drive him Denmark. He regained the throne at the Peace of Stralsund (1370).

► **wallaby** The pretty-faced wallaby (*wallabia pattyi*) inhabits the grassy hills and woodlands of Queensland and New South Wales. Its hopping gait is very efficient at high speeds, but at low speeds it is clumsy, using its forelegs and tail for support.

**Waldenses** Small Christian sect founded in the 12th century. It had its origins in the "Poor Men of Lyons," the followers of Peter Waldo of Lyons. The Waldenses renounced private property and led an ascetic life. They repudiated many Roman Catholic doctrines and practices, such as INDULGENCES, PURGATORY, and MASS for the dead, and denied the validity of SACRAMENTS administered by unworthy priests. The movement flourished briefly in the 13th century, but active persecution extinguished it except in the French and Italian Alps. Persecution continued until the Waldenses received full civil rights in 1848. In the later 19th century, many Waldenses emigrated to the Americas.

**Waldheim, Kurt** (1918– ) Austrian statesman and diplomat, fourth secretary-general of the United Nations (1972–81). He succeeded U THANT as secretary general, but proved to be a weak appeaser of the major powers. Waldheim's tenure was tainted by revelations of his Nazi war record and he was replaced by PÉREZ DE CUÉLLAR.

**Wales** Constituent member of the UNITED KINGDOM, occupying a broad peninsula in W Great Britain; the capital is CARDIFF. Another major city is SWANSEA. **Land and climate** In the N, lies Wales' highest peak, Snowdon, at 3,560ft (1,085m). ANGLESEY lies off the NW coast. The Black Mountains lie in the SE. The border regions and coastal plains are lowlands. The principal rivers are the SEVERN and Dee. On average, Cardiff experiences twice as much annual rainfall as London. **History** The Celtic-speaking Welsh stoutly resisted Roman invasion in the first centuries AD. St. DAVID introduced Christianity in the 5th century. In the 10th century political power was centralized. In the 11th century the English conquered the border counties and established the Welsh Marches. In 1282 Wales was conquered by the English Norman King Edward I, and in 1301 Prince Edward (later Edward II) became Prince of Wales. In the early 15th century, Owen Glendower led spirited resistance against English rule. The accession of the Welsh TUDOR dynasty to the English throne paved the way for the Act of Union (1536) of England and Wales. Wales supported the Royalist cause in the English Civil War. In the late 19th century Wales became the world's leading producer of coal. Rapid industrialization unemployment and poverty. From the 18th century Wales had been a center of nonconformism, and Calvinism injected new life into Welsh nationalism. In 1996 the Welsh Nationalist Party (Plaid Cymru) won its first seat in the Westminster Parliament and in 1997 a referendum voted for a devolved Welsh Assembly in Cardiff. The maintenance of a distinct Welsh culture has been strengthened by the teaching of Welsh in schools. **Economy** North Wales is predominantly agricultural, with the world's greatest density of sheep. Dairy farming is also important. Tourism is important in the coastal region of GWYNEDD. The S valleys and coastal plain are Wales' industrial heartland. The drastic late 20th-century decline of its traditional heavy industries of coal and steel (only one working mine remains), has been only partly offset by investment in light industries, such as electronics. Area: 8,016sq mi (20,761sq km). Pop. (1994) 2,913,000.

**Wales, Prince of** *See* CHARLES (PRINCE OF WALES)

**Walesa, Lech** (1943– ) Polish statesman and labor leader, president (1990–95). In August 1980 he organized SOLIDARITY, an independent, self-governing labor union. A general strike took place, and in December 1980 Polish administrators agreed to give workers the right to organize freely. In 1981 the government outlawed Solidarity, and Walesa was interned until late 1982 as part of the government's effort to silence opposition. In 1983 he was awarded the Nobel Peace Prize. Following reforms in the Soviet Union, Solidarity was legalized and won free elections in 1989. In 1990 the Communist Party was disbanded and Walesa became president.

**Walker, Alice** (1944– ) African-American writer. Her volumes of poetry include *Revolutionary Petunias and Other Poems* (1973). Walker won a Pulitzer Prize for her epistolary novel *The Color Purple* (1982). Other works include *In Search of My Mother's Garden* (1983).

**Walker, William** (1824–60) US adventurer in Central America. He led an armed band that attempted to seize land in Mexico in 1853. He made a similar invasion of Nicaragua in 1855, with US business support, and set himself up as president (1856), but was expelled in 1857. In 1860 he made a sortie into Honduras, but was captured and shot.

**walking stick** *See* STICK INSECT

**wallaby** Any of various medium-sized members of the kangaroo family of MARSUPIAL mammals, occurring chiefly in Australia. All species are herbivorous, feeding in open grassland at night. They move fast in a series of leaps, using both strong hind legs simultaneously, balanced by the tail. Length: head and body 18–41in (45–105cm); tail 13–30in (33–75cm). Family Macropodidae. *See also* KANGAROO

**Wallace, Alfred Russel** (1823–1913) English naturalist. He developed a theory of NATURAL SELECTION concurrently with but independent of Charles DARWIN. Wallace wrote *Contributions to the Theory of Natural Selection* (1870) outlining his theory of EVOLUTION.

**Wallace, George Corley** (1919– ) US governor of Alabama (1963–67, 1971–74, 1975–78, 1983–87). He attempted unsuccessfully to block federal efforts to end racial segregation in Alabama state schools (1962–66). Wallace was the leading spokesman against the civil rights movement. In 1972, while campaigning for the Democratic presidential nomination, he was shot and paralyzed from the waist down.

**Wallace, Henry Agard** (1888–1965) US statesman, vice president (1941–45). He was rewarded by President Franklin D. ROOSEVELT for his work on the NEW DEAL. As vice-president, Wallace worked to promote goodwill in Latin America. From 1945 to 1946 he was secretary of commerce under President TRUMAN. In 1948 he was an unsuccessful presidential candidate for the Progressive Party.

**Wallace, Sir William** (1270–1305) Scottish nationalist leader. He led resistance to the English king, EDWARD I. Wallace defeated an English army at Stirling Bridge (1297). The English were driven from Scotland, and Wallace pursued them over the border. He was confronted by Edward with a large army at Falkirk in 1298 and was defeated. He went into hiding, but was eventually captured (1305) and executed.

**Wallachia** (Walachia, Valahia) Historic region in Romania, formerly the principality between the Danube River and the Transylvanian Alps. It is said to have been established in 1290 by Ralph the Black, vassal of the king of Hungary, from whom the region secured temporary independence in 1330. It came gradually, however, under the domination of the Turks, whose suzerainty was acknowledged in 1417. Wallachia and MOLDAVIA became protectorates of Russia under the Treaty of Adrianople (1829) and by their union formed the state of ROMANIA in 1859. An important agricultural region, it has been developed industrially since World War II. Industries: oil, chemicals, heavy machinery. Area: 29,575sq mi (76,599sq km).

**Wallenstein, Albrecht Eusebius Wenzel von** (1583–1634) German general. During the THIRTY YEARS WAR (1618–48) he was commander of the armies of the Holy Roman Empire, winning a series of victories in the late 1620s but losing the Battle of Lützen (1632). Wallenstein was later convicted of treason, dismissed and then assassinated.

**Waller, Fats** (1904–43) US jazz pianist and composer, b. Thomas Waller. He wrote many successful tunes, including "Honeysuckle Rose" and "Ain't Misbehavin'."

**wallflower** Any of several species of PERENNIAL plants of the genera *Cheiranthus* and *Erysimum*, a few sweet-scented, that are commonly cultivated in Europe and the US. The European wallflower, *C. cheiri*, has lance-shaped leaves, and red, orange, yellow, or purple flowers. Height: to 36in (90cm). Family Brassicaceae/Cruciferae.

**Wallis, Sir Barnes Neville** (1887–1979) English aeronautical engineer and inventor, best known for his invention of the bouncing bomb during World War II. After the war, he designed the first swing-wing aircraft.

**Wallis and Futuna** French territory in the s Pacific Ocean, w of Samoa. The territory is made up of two small groups of volcanic islands, the Wallis Islands and the Hoorn Islands. The principal islands are Uvea, Futuna, and Alofi, with Uvea containing 60% of the population and the capital of Mata-Utu (1983 pop. 815). Timber is the main export. The French took the islands in 1842 and in 1959 they became an overseas territory. The islands' economy is based on subsistence agriculture of copra, cassava, yams, taro, and bananas. Pop. (1993 est.) 14,400.

**Walloons** French-speaking people of s Belgium, as opposed to the FLEMISH-speaking people of the N. They inhabit chiefly the provinces of Hainault, Liège, Namur, and s Brabant. Today, they number *c.*3,000,000.

**walnut** Deciduous tree native to North and South America, Europe, and Asia. It has smoother bark than HICKORY, to which it is related, and is grown for timber, ornament, and nuts. Height: to 165ft (50m). Family Juglandaceae; genus *Juglans*.

**Walpole, Horace, 4th Earl of Orford** (1717–97) English writer. His Gothic house near London represents a milestone in architectural taste; his bizarre novel *The Castle of Otranto* (1764) established a parallel fashion for the Gothic in literature. Walpole's reputation rests on his letters, which provide a portrait of Georgian England.

**Walpole, Sir Robert, 1st Earl of Orford** (1676–1745) British politician. Although he resigned as chancellor of the exchequer in 1717, after developing the first sinking fund, he restored order after the SOUTH SEA BUBBLE crisis in 1720. He returned as chancellor of the exchequer and first lord of the Treasury in 1721. He was forced to resign in 1742 because of opposition to his foreign policy.

**walrus** Arctic mammal; it has a massive body and a large head. Its tusks, developed from upper canine teeth, may reach 39in (1m) in length and are used to rake up the seafloor in search of mollusks and to climb on to ice floes. Length: to 12ft (3.7m). Family Odobenidae; species *Odobenus rosmarus*.

**Walter, Bruno** (1876–1962) German conductor. After a series of conducting posts in Europe, he went to the US in 1939. From 1947 to 1962 he was primarily associated with the METROPOLITAN OPERA COMPANY, New York.

**Walter, Thomas Ustick** (1804–87) US architect. He is known for his extensions to the CAPITOL at Washington, D.C. Walter also designed the interior of the Library of Congress.

**Walther von der Vogelweide** (1170–1230) German poet, considered the greatest MINNESINGER of the Middle Ages. He produced poems of enduring immediacy, such as the popular *Unter den Linden*.

**Walton, Ernest Thomas Sinton** (1903–95) Irish physicist. He shared the 1951 Nobel Prize for physics with John COCKCROFT for their development (1929) of the first nuclear particle ACCELERATOR. In 1931 they produced the first artificial nuclear reaction without radioactive isotopes, using high-energy protons to bombard lithium nuclei.

**Walton, Sir William Turner** (1902–83) English composer. His orchestral works include *Portsmouth Point* (1926) and the comedy overture *Scapino* (1941). He wrote *Crown Imperial* (1937), and *Orb and Scepter* (1953) as coronation marches for George VI and Elizabeth II. His most widely known works are the jazz-oriented *Façade* (1923), the oratorio *Belshazzar's Feast* (1931), and the opera *Troilus and Cressida* (1954).

**waltz** Dance performed by couples to music in triple time. A graceful ballroom dance, it became fashionable in the early 19th century, having developed from s German folk dances, such as the *Ländler*.

**Wang Mang** (33 BC–AD 23) Emperor of China. He overthrew the HAN dynasty and proclaimed the Hsin (New) dynasty in AD 8. Opposition from landowners and officials forced him to withdraw his reforms, and his one-emperor dynasty, which divides the Former Han from the Later Han, ended in his assassination.

▲ **walnut** Walnut trees are commercially valuable for their wood and nuts. Before the fruits harden into nuts they can be used for pickling, but once mature, they burst from their green casing and the edible nuts can be removed from the hard outer shell.

▼ **walrus** A unique relative of the seal, the walrus (*Odobenus rosmarus*) is assigned a family of its own. It is a gregarious animal, and has a tough hide and a thick fat layer, which helps protect against cold as well as the tusks of other walruses.

## WANKEL ROTARY ENGINE

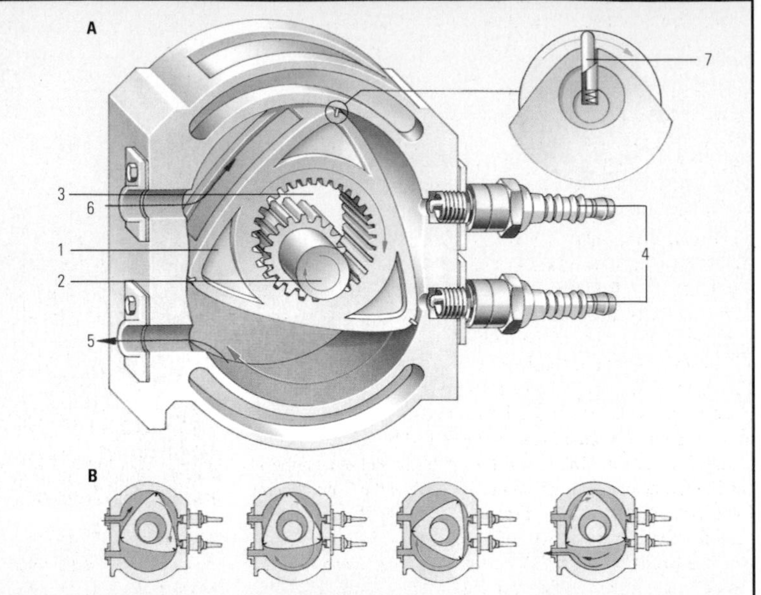

A rotary engine, such as the Wankel (A), compresses and ignites a gasoline/air mixture with a spark plug like a conventional combustion engine but does so with a rotating three-sided cylinder (1) not a straight-line action. The explosion of the fuel/air mixture drives further rotation continuing the process and driving a crankshaft (2) passing through the center of the cylinder. (3) The movement of the piston sucks air into the cylinder (so valves are not needed) and compresses the mixture as it continues to turn.The spark plugs (4) then ignite the mixture, which expands, rotating the piston and driving the crankshaft. The burned fuel is expelled through an outlet (5) as the piston turns, pulling in more air to repeat the process (6). The seals (7) at the edge of the piston's faces are important in creating the vacuum needed to pull in the fuel/air mixture and in compressing the mixture. A complete cycle is shown (B).

**Wankel rotary engine** Gasoline engine with rotors instead of pistons. German engineer Felix Wankel invented the engine in the 1950s. Each triangular rotor turns inside a casing. Gaps between the casing and rotor form three crescent-shaped combustion chambers. Each chamber goes through a sequence of events similar to those in a FOUR-STROKE ENGINE with pistons.

**wapiti** (elk) Large DEER of North America, closely related to the Old World red deer. It is gray-brown with a whitish rump and dark, brown-black legs, head, and neck; its antlers may span 5ft (1.5m). Height: to 5ft (1.5m); length: to 7.5ft (2.5m). Family Cervidae; species *Cervus canadensis*.

**war** Military combat between large communities, nations, and/or groups of nations. All-out (nuclear) war between major powers using modern weapons would undoubtedly result in what is known as "mutually assured destruction" (MAD). Other forms of war include civil war, in which factions within one state or community struggle between themselves for supremacy, and guerrilla war, in which partisan forces harass occupying or government troops by surprise attacks.

► **Warhol** Born in Pittsburgh, Andy Warhol was a successful commercial artist in New York before becoming a leading exponent of Pop art. In 1966 he collaborated with Lou Reed and his band the Velvet Underground on a pioneering tour of multimedia shows. He was shot and almost killed by Valerie Solanas, a radical feminist, in 1968. In the 1970s and '80s he remained active producing improvisational and experimental films as well as a magazine and portraits.

**warbler** Numerous birds of two families, one in the Old World (Sylviidae) and the other in the New World (Parulidae). Old World warblers include the hedge sparrow and tailorbird. Most New World warblers have brighter plumage.

**war crimes** Violations of international laws of WAR. The modern conception of war crimes followed the atrocities committed in World War II, resulting in the NUREMBERG TRIALS. *See also* GENEVA CONVENTION

**War Hawks** Name given to a group of Democratic-Republicans who urged expansionism and nationalism. Mainly from the western frontier, this group's continued outcry against British maritime practices helped start the WAR OF 1812 with Britain. Among its leaders were Henry CLAY and John C. CALHOUN.

**Warhol, Andy** (1928–87) US painter, printmaker, and filmmaker, innovator of POP ART. He achieved fame with his stencil pictures of Campbell's soup cans and his sculptures of Brillo soap pad boxes (1962). In 1965 Warhol gave up art to manage the rock group "The Velvet Underground." He continued to make controversial films, which often had a voyeuristic quality.

**warm-blooded** *See* HOMEOTHERMAL

**War of 1812** (1812–15) Conflict between the US and Britain. The main source of friction was British maritime policy during the NAPOLEONIC WARS, which included the impressment of sailors from US vessels and the interception of US merchant ships. Difficulties on the border with Canada also contributed. In 1811 President James MADISON reimposed the Nonintercourse Act on trade with the British. The US were ill-prepared for war and an invasion of Canada failed. Stephen DECATUR restored US pride. Victory on Lake Erie (September 1813) enabled US forces, led by William H. HARRISON, to force British troops back across the Canadian border. The possible secession of New England was raised by the HARTFORD CONVENTION and the end of the NAPOLEONIC WARS (1814) freed more British forces. They imposed a naval blockade and captured Washington, D.C., burning the White House. A US naval victory on Lake Champlain, however, ended the British threat to New York. With the war at stalemate, John Quincy ADAMS and Henry CLAY led US negotiations that resulted in the Treaty of Ghent (December 24, 1914). Andrew JACKSON's victory at New Orleans occurred after the signing of the treaty.

**war powers** In the US, constitutional powers given to the president as supreme military commander. They include the power to appoint armed forces officers, with the consent of the Senate. Congress alone is empowered to declare war, but presidents have carried out military actions without congressional approval or a formal declaration of war, such as in the Korean and Vietnam wars.

**Warren, Earl** (1891–1974) US politician and jurist. He was governor of California (1943–53) and an unsuccessful Republican candidate for vice president (1953). Appointed as chief justice (1953–69) of the US Supreme Court by President EISENHOWER, he began the "Warren Revolution" that lasted until his retirement. Some of his court's noteworthy cases include: BROWN V. BOARD OF EDUCATION OF TOPEKA (1954); *Engel* v. *Vitale* (1962), which prohibited prayers in public schools; and *Miranda* v. *Arizona* (1966), which made it obligatory that a suspect be informed of his rights, be provided with free state counsel, and has the right to remain silent. *See also* WARREN COMMISSION

**Warren, Robert Penn** (1905–89) US poet, novelist, and critic. A member of the Fugitives, a group of Southern agrarian poets, he coedited the *Southern Review* with Cleanth Brooks. Warren won Pulitzer prizes for his volumes of poetry *Brother to Dragons* (1953), *Promises* (1957), and *Now and Then* (1978). His most famous work is the Pulitzer Prize-winning novel *All the King's Men* (1946). In 1986 he became the first US poet laureate.

**Warren Commission** (1963–64) US presidential commission that investigated the assassination of President KENNEDY. It was headed by Earl WARREN. After taking evidence from 552 witnesses, it concluded that the act had been committed by Lee Harvey OSWALD, acting alone. Denial of conspiracy was not universally accepted.

**Warsaw** Capital and largest city of Poland, on the VISTULA River. Its first settlement dates from the 11th century. In 1596 it became Poland's capital and developed into the country's main trading center. From 1813 to 1915 it was controlled by Russia, and during World War I it was occupied by German troops. In 1918 it was liberated by Polish troops and was restored as capital of Poland. The 1939 German invasion and occupation of Warsaw marked the beginning of World War II. In 1940 the Germans isolated the Jewish ghetto, which contained 500,000 people, and when the Red Army liberated Warsaw, they found only 200 surviving Jews. After the war, the old town was reconstructed. Warsaw is a major transportation and industrial center. Industries: steel, automobiles, cement, machinery. Pop. (1993) 1,653,300.

**Warsaw Pact** Agreement creating the Warsaw Treaty Organization (1955), a defensive alliance of the Soviet Union and its communist allies in Eastern Europe. It was the equivalent of Western Europe's NORTH ATLANTIC TREATY ORGANIZATION (NATO). Its headquarters were in Moscow and it was controlled by the Soviet Union. Attempts to withdraw by Hungary (1956) and Czechoslovakia (1968) were crushed. It was dissolved after the collapse of the Soviet Union (1991).

**wart** Raised and well-defined small growth on the outermost surface of the skin, caused by the human papilloma virus. It is usually painless unless in a pressure area, as with a VERRUCA.

**wart hog** Wild, tusked PIG, native to Africa. It has brownish-black skin with a crest of hair along the back. Height: *c.*2.5ft (76cm) at shoulder; weight: 200lb (90kg). Family Suidae; species *Phacochoerus aethiopicus*.

**Warwick, Richard Neville, Earl of** (1428–71) English magnate, known as "the Kingmaker," who held the balance of power (1461–64) during the Wars of the ROSES. Breaking with EDWARD IV, Warwick changed sides and restored HENRY VI to the throne in 1470. Edward returned with fresh troops, and Warwick was defeated and killed at the Battle of Barnet.

**Warwickshire** County in central England. The land is gently rolling, rising to the Cotswold Hills in the S, and is drained by the Avon River. Cereals are the main crop, dairy cattle and sheep are raised. The county town is Warwick (1992 pop. 116,299). Area: 765sq mi (1,981sq km). Pop. (1991) 484,287.

**Washington, Booker T. (Taliaferro)** (1856–1915) US educator and black leader. Born a slave, he gained an education after the Civil War and became a teacher. He advocated self-help, education, and economic improvement as preliminaries to the achievement of equality for blacks, and he believed in compromise with white segregationists. He had considerable influence among whites as a spokesman for black causes.

**Washington, Denzel** (1954– ) US film actor. His first major role was in *Cry Freedom* (1987). He was chosen by Spike LEE to play the lead roles in *Mo' Better Blues* (1990) and *Malcolm X* (1992). Other credits include *Philadelphia* (1993), and *Devil in a Blue Dress* (1995).

**Washington, George** (1732–99) Commander in chief of the Continental army in the AMERICAN REVOLUTION and first president of the US (1789–97), b. Virginia. He fought with distinction in the FRENCH AND INDIAN WARS, and was a member (1759–74) of the house of burgesses. In 1775 Washington was chosen as commander in chief by the CONTINENTAL CONGRESS. With victory achieved, he resigned (1783) but was recalled from retirement to preside over the CONSTITUTIONAL CONVENTION at Philadelphia (1787). In 1789 Washington was elected, unopposed, as president of the new republic. He was unable to heal the divisions between his secretary of state, Thomas JEFFERSON, and his secretary of the treasury, Alexander HAMILTON. The FEDERALIST PARTY and the DEMOCRATIC REPUBLICAN PARTY emerged from this split. In 1793 Washington was reelected. His second administration was dominated by Federalists, and the Jeffersonians criticized John JAY's negotiation of peace terms with Britain. In 1796 Washington declined a third term as president. In his *Farewell Address* (September 17, 1796), Washington warned against the geographical divisions encouraged by the party system and advised the nation to steer clear of "permanent alliances" with foreign nations. He spent the rest of his life on the family estate at Mount Vernon.

**Washington** State in the extreme NW US, bounded on the N by British Columbia, Canada, E by Idaho, S by Oregon, and W by the Pacific Ocean. The state capital is OLYMPIA and the largest city is SEATTLE. In the NW is the navigable PUGET SOUND, along which lie Washington's major industrial and commercial cities. Its physiography and climate are dominated by the CASCADE RANGE, which crosses the state from N to S. Mount RAINIER and Mount ST. HELENS are notable peaks in the range. The coastal region to the W of the range is one of the wettest areas of the US and has some of the densest forest in the world; the region to the E of the Cascades is mostly treeless plain with low rainfall. An important wheat-producing area, the plateau is heavily dependent on various irrigation schemes. The COLUMBIA RIVER is one of the world's best sources of hydroelectricity, and is also used for irrigation. The Spanish discovered the mouth of the Columbia River in 1775, and in 1778 Captain COOK established the area's fur trading links with China. In 1792 George Vancouver mapped Puget Sound and Robert Gray sailed down the Sound to establish the US claim to the region. The claim was strengthened by the LEWIS AND CLARK EXPEDITION (1805), and the establishment of an American Fur Company trading post at the mouth of the Columbia by John Jacob ASTOR in 1811. From 1821 to 1846 the region was administered by the HUDSON'S BAY COMPANY. In 1846 a treaty with the British fixed the boundary with Canada, and in 1847 most of present-day Washington state became Oregon Territory. In 1853 Washington Territory was created. Exploitation of its forests and fisheries attracted settlement, and Washington was admitted to the Union in 1889. Washington is the leading producer of apples in the US. The largest mineral deposits are magnesium and aluminum ores. Industries: food processing, timber, aluminum, aerospace, computer technology. Area: 66,581sq mi (172,431sq km). Pop. (1992) 5,142,746.

**Washington, D.C.** Capital of the US, on the E bank of the POTOMAC River, coextensive with the District of Columbia and bordered by Maryland (NE and SE) and Virginia (W and S). The site was chosen as the seat of government in 1790, and the city was planned by the French army engineer Pierre Charles L'Enfant. Construction of the WHITE HOUSE began in 1793 and of the Capitol the following year. CONGRESS moved from Philadelphia in 1800. During the WAR OF 1812 the city was occupied by the British and many public buildings were burned (1814), including the White House and the Capitol. Washington is the legislative, judicial, and administrative center of the US, and the main governmental buildings comprise the Library of Congress, the SUPREME COURT OF THE UNITED STATES, the SENATE, the HOUSE OF REPRESENTATIVES, and various agency headquarters. Washington has severe social problems; many of its large black population live in slum housing. Pop. (1992) 585,221.

**Washington, Treaty of** (1871) Agreement settling a number of disputes involving the US, Britain, and Canada. The most serious was the question of the ALABAMA CLAIMS, which was submitted to international arbitration. US–Canadian disputes over fisheries and the border were also resolved.

**wasp** Any insect of the stinging Hymenoptera order that is neither a bee nor an ant. The common wasp (*Vespa vulgaris*) has a yellow body ringed with black. Adults feed on nectar, tree sap, and fruit. Length: to 1.2in (3cm). Family Vespidae.

**watch** *See* CLOCK

**water** ($H_2O$) Odorless, colorless liquid that covers about 70% of the Earth's surface and is the most widely used solvent. Essential to life, it makes up *c.*60–70% of the human body. It is a compound of hydrogen and oxygen with the two H–O links of the molecule forming an angle of 105°. This asymmetry results in polar properties and a force of attraction (hydrogen bond) between opposite ends of neighboring water molecules. These forces maintain the substance as a liquid, in spite of its low molecular weight, and account for its unusual property of having its maximum density at 39°F (4°C). Properties: sp.gr. 1.000; m.p. 32°F (0°C); b.p. 212°F (100°C). *See* DESALINATION

**water beetle** Aquatic BEETLE of several families. **Whirligig** beetles (family Gyrinidae) skim around the surface of water, feeding on small insects. **Water scavenger** beetles (family Hydrophilidae) feed on water plants. Their larvae are fierce

▲ **Washington** The first US president, George Washington was an outstanding military commander and statesman. He was highly influential in securing the adoption of the Constitution, and, after his election, strictly avoided overstepping the constitutional bounds of presidential power. Washington tried but failed to remain aloof from partisan struggles. The resignation of Thomas Jefferson lead to the creation of a two party system, and Washington aligned himself with the Federalists during his second term. In his famous farewell address he warned the USA against forming permanent alliances with foreign powers and being drawn into European conflicts.

**WASHINGTON**
**Statehood :**
November 11, 1889
**Nickname :**
The Evergreen State
**State bird :**
Willow goldfinch
**State flower :**
Coast rhododendron
**State tree :**
Western hemlock
**State motto :**
Alki (Native American for "by and by")

W

► **water buffalo** The asiatic water buffalo (*Bubalus bubalis*) feeds on river and lakeside vegetation. Both sexes carry large horns, but the males are generally larger and can weigh almost a ton. Wild water buffalo are extremely fierce and have been known to kill fully grown tigers. The domesticated animals are used to pull plows and carts, but produce little milk.

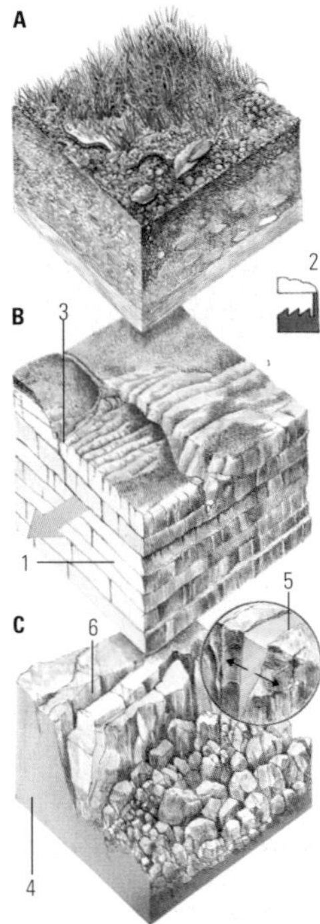


▲ **weathering** Weathering is the break down of rock in place. It occurs in two main ways: physical (A and C) and chemical (B), and usually in combination. At the surface plant roots and animals such as worms break down rock turning it into soil (A). In chemical weathering (B), soluble rocks such as limestone (1) are dissolved by ground water which is a very mild solution of carbonic acid. Acid rain caused by sulfate pollution (2) also attacks the rock. The water can create cave systems deep below the surface. Both heat and cold can cause physical weathering (C). When temperatures drop below freezing, freeze-thaw weathering can split even the hardest rocks such as granite (4). Water which settles in cracks and joints during the day expands as it freezes at night (5). That expansion cleaves the rock along the naturally occurring joints (6). In deserts, rock expands and contracts due to the extremes of cooling and heating resulting in layers of rock splitting off.

predators. **Predaceous diving beetles** are the most numerous water beetles. They are black, brown, or greenish and can stay underwater for long periods. They prey on snails and fish.

**water boatman** (water bug) Aquatic insect found worldwide. Its body is gray to black, oval and flat, with fringed, oar-like hind legs. Length: about 0.6in (15mm). Order Hemiptera; family Corixidae. The carnivorous "backswimmers" of the family Notonectidae are also sometimes called water boatmen.

**water buffalo** (caraboa) Large OX, widely domesticated in much of the tropical world; it is feral in some parts of India. Height: to 6ft (1.8m) at the shoulder. Family Bovidae; species *Bubalus bubalis*.

**watercolor** Paint that is made from a pigment ground up with a water-soluble gum, such as gum arabic; also, a PAINTING that is rendered in this medium.

**water cycle** *See* HYDROLOGICAL CYCLE

**Waterford** County in Munster province, S Republic of Ireland, on the Atlantic Ocean. It is a mountainous region, drained chiefly by the Blackwater and Suir rivers. The raising of beef and dairy cattle and sheep is the chief agricultural activity. Industries: fishing, food processing, tanning, glassware. The county town of Waterford (1991 pop. 40,300) is an important port for the whole of S Ireland. Area: 710sq mi (1,838sq km). Pop. (1991) 91,624.

**waterfowl** Aquatic birds, including species of DUCK, GOOSE, and SWAN, found throughout most of the world. Large flocks migrate from cool nesting grounds to warm winter homes. All have short bills, short legs, and dense plumage underlaid by down. Order Anseriformes.

**Watergate affair** (1972–74) US political scandal that led to the resignation of President NIXON. It arose from an attempted burglary of the Democratic Party's national headquarters in the Watergate building, organized by members of Nixon's reelection committee. Evidence of the involvement of the administration provoked investigations by the Senate and the Justice Department, which ultimately implicated Nixon. He was pardoned by his successor, Gerald FORD, but his closest advisers (Halderman, Erlichman, and Mitchell) were convicted.

**water lily** Any of about 90 species of freshwater plants, widely distributed in temperate and tropical regions. They have leaves that float at the surface, and showy flowers of white, pink, red, blue, or yellow. Family Nymphaeaceae; genera *Nymphaea*, *Nuphar*, *Nelumbo*, and *Victoria*. *See also* LOTUS

**Waterloo, Battle of** (1815) Final engagement of the NAPOLEONIC WARS, fought *c.*12mi (20km) from Brussels, Belgium. Allied forces were commanded by the Duke of WELLINGTON against Napoleon's slightly larger French forces. Fighting was even until the Prussians under Marshal Blücher arrived to overwhelm the French flank, whereupon Wellington broke through the center. The battle ended Napoleon's HUNDRED DAYS and resulted in his second, and final, abdication.

**watermelon** Trailing annual VINE, native to tropical Africa and Asia and cultivated in warm areas worldwide. Its edible fruit has a greenish rind, red flesh, and many seeds. Family Cucurbitaceae; species *Citrullus lanatus*. *See also* GOURD

**water moccasin** (cottonmouth) Venomous, semiaquatic SNAKE, native to the swamps of SE US. It is a pit VIPER, closely related to the COPPERHEAD. Adults have broad, brown bands along their bodies. When threatened, it bares its white mouth. They feed on warm-blooded animals. Length: to 5ft (1.5m). Family Viperidae; species *Agkistrodon piscivorus*.

**water pollution** Contamination of water by harmful wastes. In the US, the chief source of water POLLUTION is **industrial waste**. Toxic chemicals, such as POLYCHLORINATED BIPHENYL (PCB), are discharged as effluent and cannot be disinfected with CHLORINE. In addition, the burning of fossil fuels causes ACID RAIN. Untreated or partially treated **sewage** is another source of water pollution. Sewage treatment is unable to prevent the spread of viruses and some phosphorus-based detergents that cause EUTROPHICATION. Agricultural chemicals and wastes, such as PESTICIDES and FERTILIZERS, are another major cause of pollution. Once pollution has affected GROUND WATER it spreads more rapidly. Oil spills and ocean dumping are major causes of marine pollution. The Safe Drinking Water Act (1974) authorized the Environmental Protection Agency (EPA) to establish water quality standards.

**water polo** Game devised as an aquatic form of SOCCER. It is played by two teams of seven people in a pool. At each end of the pool is a net-enclosed goal defended by a goalkeeper. It has been an Olympic event since 1900.

**water power** *See* HYDROELECTRICITY

**water-skiing** Leisure activity and competitive sport in which a person skis across the surface of water while being towed by a motorboat. In **slalom**, skiers are towed several times through a series of staggered buoys. In **jumping**, each skier must ski up and over a wooden ramp. For the **tricks**, skiers devise their own 20-second routines of complex maneuvers.

**water table** In geology, level below which the ground is saturated. The height of the water table moves up or down depending on rainfall. Water located below the water table is called GROUND WATER.

**Watson, James Dewey** (1928– ) US geneticist and biophysicist. He is known for his role in the discovery of the molecular structure of deoxyribonucleic acid (DNA), and he shared the 1962 Nobel Prize for physiology or medicine with Francis CRICK and Maurice Wilkins. Watson later helped to break the GENETIC CODE of the DNA base sequences and found the ribonucleic acid (RNA) messenger that carries the DNA code to the cell's protein-forming structures.

**Watson, John Broadus** (1878–1958) US psychologist, founder of BEHAVIORISM. His work did much to make psychological research more objective and influenced B.F. SKINNER's theory of operant conditioning.

**Watt, James** (1736–1819) Scottish engineer. In 1765 he invented the condensing STEAM ENGINE. In 1782 Watt invented the double-acting engine, in which steam pressure acted alternately on each side of a piston. With Matthew Boulton, he coined the term "horsepower." The unit of power is called the WATT in his honor.

**watt** Unit of power in the SI system of units. A machine consuming one JOULE of energy per second has a power output of one watt. One horsepower corresponds to 746 watts. A watt is also a unit of electrical power, equal to the product of voltage and current.

**Watteau, Jean-Antoine** (1684–1721) French painter. His admiration for RUBENS' series *The Garden of Love* inspired his development of the category of *fêtes galantes*. These ROCOCO works, notably *The Embarkation for Cythera* (1717), combine elements of masquerade and COMMEDIA DELL' ARTE to create an aristocratic fantasy. They are pervaded by a sense of melancholy.

**Waugh, Evelyn Arthur St. John** (1903–66) English novelist. Waugh established his reputation with *Decline and Fall* (1928). *Vile Bodies* (1930), *A Handful of Dust* (1934), and *Put Out More Flags* (1942) reflect interwar, British, upper-class life, while *Brideshead Revisited* (1945) is informed by the Roman Catholicism to which he was converted in 1928. Among his other major works are the *Sword of Honor* trilogy: *Men at Arms* (1952), *Officers and Gentlemen* (1955), and *Unconditional Surrender* (1961).

**wave** In oceanography, moving disturbance traveling on or through water that does not move the water itself. Wind causes waves by frictional drag. Waves not under pressure from strong winds are called swells. Waves begin to break on shore or "feel bottom" when they reach a depth shallower than half the wave's length. When the water depth is *c.*1.3 times the wave height, the wave front is so steep that the top falls over and the wave breaks.

**wave** In physics, carrier of energy from place to place. Waves are caused by disturbances that result in oscillation. These oscillations then spread out (propagate) as waves. The velocity depends on the type of wave and on the medium. ELECTROMAGNETIC waves, such as light, consist of varying magnetic and electric fields vibrating at right angles to each other and to the direction of motion; they are **transverse** waves. Sound waves are transmitted by the vibrations of the particles of the medium itself, the vibrations being in the direction of wave motion; they are **longitudinal** waves. Sound waves, unlike electromagnetic waves, cannot travel through a vacuum and cannot undergo polarization. Both types of waves can undergo REFLECTION, REFRACTION, and give rise to INTERFERENCE phenomena. A wave is characterized by its WAVELENGTH and FREQUENCY, the VELOCITY of wave motion being the product of wavelength and frequency. *See also* POLARIZED LIGHT; WAVE AMPLITUDE; WAVE FREQUENCY

**wave amplitude** Peak value of a periodically varying quantity. This peak value may be either positive or negative, as the quantity varies either above or below zero.

**wave dispersion** Alteration of the refractive index of a medium with wavelength. It occurs with all ELECTROMAGNETIC waves but is most obvious at visible wavelengths, causing light to be separated into its component colors. Dispersion is when light passes through a refracting medium, such as a PRISM, and forms a SPECTRUM. Each color has a different wavelength, and so the prism bends each color by a different amount. *See also* REFRACTION

**wave frequency** Number of oscillations or wave cycles produced in 1 second, measured in HERTZ. It can be calculated from the wave VELOCITY divided by WAVELENGTH. By QUANTUM THEORY, the frequency of any ELECTROMAGNETIC RADIATION is proportional to the energy of the component photons.

**wavelength** (symbol $\lambda$) Distance between successive points of equal phase in a WAVE. The wavelength of water waves could be measured as the distance from crest to crest. The wavelength of a light wave determines its color. Wavelength is equal to the wave VELOCITY divided by the WAVE FREQUENCY.

**wave mechanics** Version of QUANTUM MECHANICS developed in 1926 by Erwin SCHRÖDINGER. It explains the behavior of electrons in terms of their wave properties. Although quickly superseded by a more complex formulation by Paul DIRAC, it is still widely used.

**wax** Solid, insoluble substance of low melting point. It is moldable and water-repellent. Animal and vegetable waxes are simple LIPIDS consisting of esters of fatty acids. Mineral waxes include PARAFFIN wax made from petroleum. Waxes are used in the manufacture of lubricants, polishes, cosmetics, and candles, and to waterproof leather and coat paper.

**Wayne, Anthony** (1745–96) American Revolutionary general. In 1777 he was made brigadier general and joined George WASHINGTON's army. He led a division at the Battle of Brandywine, fought at Germantown, and wintered with Washington at Valley Forge. In 1779 Wayne led the successful night attack on Stony Point, New York. He also fought in the Siege of YORKTOWN and occupied Charleston. Wayne briefly represented Georgia in Congress (1791). In 1792 he became commander in chief in the Northwest Territory and defeated the Ohio tribes in the Battle of Fallen Timbers (1794). Wayne secured the Treaty of Greenville (1795), the first to recognize Native American title to US lands.

**Wayne, John** (1907–79) US film actor, b. Marion Michael Morrison. His first major success was in the Western *Stagecoach* (1939), directed by John FORD. Wayne won a Best Actor Academy Award for *True Grit* (1969). Other films include *She Wore a Yellow Ribbon* (1949), *The Man Who Shot Liberty Valance* (1962), and *The Shootist* (1976).

**weak nuclear force** (weak interaction) One of the four FUNDAMENTAL FORCES in physics. It causes radioactive decay. The weak nuclear force can be observed only in the subatomic realm, being of very short range. It is weaker than the ELECTROMAGNETIC FORCE and the STRONG NUCLEAR FORCE (the strongest of the forces), but stronger than GRAVITATION.

**weasel** Any of several species of small, carnivorous, mostly terrestrial mammals of Eurasia, N Africa, and North and South America. Most species have small heads, long necks, slender bodies, short legs, and long tails. Reddish-brown with light colored underparts, some species turn completely white in winter. Weasels are fierce predators, eating eggs and rodents and often attacking much larger animals and domestic poultry. Length: 20in (50cm) overall. Family Mustelidae; Genus *Mustela.*

**weather** State of the atmosphere at a given locality or over a broad area, particularly as it affects human activity. Weather refers to short-term states (days or weeks) as opposed to long-term CLIMATE conditions.

**weather forecasting** *See* METEOROLOGY

**weathering** Breakdown and chemical disintegration of rocks and minerals at the Earth's surface by physical and chemical processes. In **physical** weathering in cold, wet climates, water seeping into cracks in the rock expands on freezing, so causing the rock to crack further and to crumble. Extreme temperature changes in drier regions, such as deserts, also cause rocks to fragment. **Chemical** weathering can lead to a weakening of the rock structure by altering the minerals of a rock and changing their size, volume, and ability to hold shape. Unlike EROSION, weathering does not involve transportation.

**Weaver, James Baird** (1833–1912) US politician. He represented Iowa in the House of Representatives (1879–81) and was the presidential candidate of the GREENBACK PARTY in 1880. Weaver returned to Congress (1885–89) and was a founder of the POPULIST PARTY, gaining more than one million votes as its presidential candidate in 1892.

**weaverbird** Any of several species of short-billed, often yellow-and-black, finch-like birds that weave complex nests from grass and leaves. Weaverbirds are gregarious insect-eaters of hot, dry areas. The African *Ploceus cucullatus* knots strands of grass together. Length: to 7.5in (22cm). Family Ploceidae.

**weaving** Process of making fabric by intertwining two sets of threads. A loom is threaded with a set of warp threads. The weft thread is wound round a shuttle and passed between the warp threads, which are separated according to the desired pattern. A reed keeps the woven rows tightly packed.

**Webb, Beatrice** (née Potter) (1858–1943) and **Sidney** (1859–1947) British social historians and politicians. Sidney Webb was one of the founders of the FABIAN SOCIETY. They founded the London School of Economics (1895), and the *New Statesman* magazine (1913).

**Weber, Carl Maria von** (1786–1826) German composer, conductor, and pianist. He helped establish a German national style in his operas *Der Freischütz* (1821) and *Euryanthe* (1823). He also composed piano and chamber music, concertos, and the popular *Invitation to the Dance* (1819).

**Weber, Max** (1864–1920) German sociologist. He advanced the concept of "ideal types," generalized models of social situations, as a method of analysis. In his book *The Protestant Ethic and the Spirit of Capitalism* (1904–05), Weber put forward the idea that CALVINISM was influential in the rise of capitalism.

**Webern, Anton von** (1883–1945) Austrian composer. His *Passacaglia* (1908) was written using late-romantic tonality. Influenced by his teacher, SCHOENBERG, he adopted atonality, as in the *Six Bagatelles* (1913), and then TWELVE-TONE MUSIC, such as his symphony (1928).

**Webster, Daniel** (1782–1852) US statesman. As a Federalist in the House of Representatives (1813–17), he defended the interests of New England and opposed the WAR OF 1812. Webster won fame as a lawyer in the DARTMOUTH COLLEGE V. WOODWARD case (1819). As US senator from Massachusetts (1827–41), he was one of the greatest orators of his generation. Webster supported the tariff of 1828, and opposed the proponents of STATES' RIGHTS and NULLIFICATION. In the **Webster-Hayne Debate** (1830) with Robert Y. Hayne, he defended the

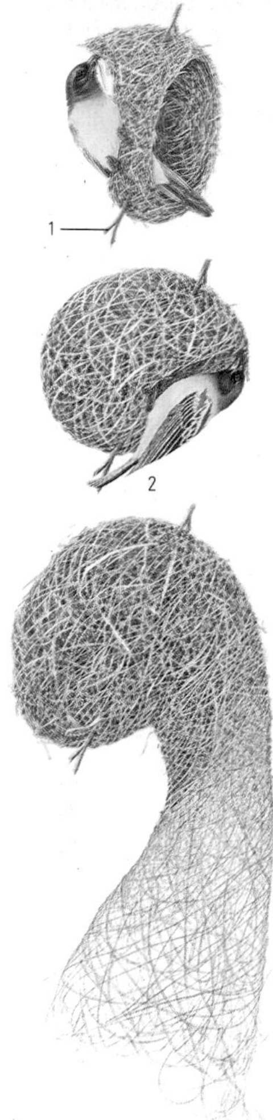


▲ **weaverbird** The weaverbird's nest is built by the male. Using no adhesive, he loops, twists, and knots leaf strips to make an enclosed hanging structure. Starting with a ring attached to a forked twig (1), he gradually adds a roof and entrance (2). When the finished nest is accepted by the female, she inserts soft, feathery grass tops or feathers to make a thick, soft lining around the egg chamber base. Young male birds' first nests are untidy; gradually, however, they learn how to make neater and better nests, using good vision and well-coordinated head movements to direct claws and beak to manipulate the nest material.

W

union, arguing, "Liberty and Union, now and forever, one and inseparable!" He opposed President JACKSON on the abolition of the BANK OF THE UNITED STATES and was a presidential candidate for the WHIG PARTY (1836). As secretary of state (1841–43) under presidents William Henry HARRISON and John TYLER, he negotiated the Webster-Ashburton Treaty (1843) that fixed the boundary between Maine and Canada. In his second term in the Senate (1845–50), Webster opposed the extension of SLAVERY but favored the COMPROMISE OF 1850. He also served as secretary of state (1850–52) to Millard FILLMORE.

**Webster, Noah** (1758–1843) US lexicographer and writer. His monumental, two-volume *American Dictionary of the English Language* (1828) contained 70,000 words. It helped standardize US pronunciation. A second edition appeared in 1840, and the work has continued to be revised regularly since then.

**wedge** In mechanics, an example of the inclined plane. It is used to multiply an applied FORCE while changing its direction of action. For example, if a metal or wooden wedge is driven into a block of wood, a force is exerted by the wedge at right angles to the applied force and greater than it.

**Wedgwood, Josiah** (1730–95) English potter. He pioneered the large-scale production of pottery at his Etruria works near Stoke-on-Trent and became famous for his creamware. Wedgewood is best known for his jasper ware, which gave expression to the contemporary interest in the revival of classical art.

**weed** Uncultivated or unwanted plant. Weeds are a threat to commercial crops because they compete for water and sunlight and harbor pests and diseases.

**weedkiller** *See* HERBICIDE

**weevil** Any of numerous species of beetles that are pests to crops, especially the numerous snout beetles (time weevils), with long, down-curved beaks for boring into plants. Family Curculionidae, the largest in the animal kingdom.

**Wegener, Alfred Lothar** (1880–1930) German geologist, meteorologist, and Arctic explorer. In *The Origin of Continents and Oceans* (1915), he first proposed the theory of CONTINENTAL DRIFT.

**weight** Force of attraction on a body due to GRAVITATION. An object's weight is the product of its MASS and the gravitational field strength at that point. Mass remains constant, but weight depends on the object's position on the Earth's surface, decreasing with increasing altitude.

**weightlessness** Condition experienced by an object when the force due to GRAVITATION is neutralized. Such an object is said to have zero gravity and no weight; it floats and cannot fall. Weightlessness can be experienced in space and during a free fall. The adverse effects on the human body of prolonged weightlessness (hydrogravics) include decreased circulation of blood, less water retention in tissues, and loss of muscle tone.

**weight lifting** Exercise or sport in which weights at the end of a bar are lifted over the head. Competitions are conducted according to weight classes that range from bantamweight to heavyweight. In a weight lifting competition, each participant uses three standard lifts known as two-hand press, clean-and-jerk, and snatch. The competitor who lifts the greatest combined total of weights wins. It has been an Olympic event since 1920.

**weights and measures** Agreed units for expressing the amount of some quantity, such as capacity, length, or weight. Early measurements were based on body measurements and on plant grains. In 1799 France introduced the metric system, in which the unit of length, the METER, was taken as one ten millionth of the distance from the equator to the North Pole. A LITER was the volume occupied by one KILOGRAM of water. *See also* SI UNITS

**Weil, Simone** (1909–1943) French philosopher and writer. In the late 1930s she had the first of several mystical experiences that drew her to the Roman Catholic Church. During World War II, Weil became an activist in the French Resistance. Most of her works were published after her death, and include *Gravity and Grace* (1947), and *Waiting for God* (1951).

**Weill, Kurt** (1900–50) German composer. He is best known for his satirical operas, which include *Der Protagonist* (1926) and the *Rise and Fall of the City of Mahagonny* (1927), the latter with a libretto by Bertolt BRECHT. *The Threepenny Opera* (1928) was a modern version of John Gay's *Beggar's Opera*, again with a libretto by Brecht. In 1935 Weill immigrated to the US and wrote several Broadway musicals, including *Street Scene* (1947) and *Lost in the Stars* (1949). His wife, Lotte LENYA, was a notable interpreter of his works.

**Weimar** City in the state of Thuringia, E central Germany. Founded in 975 and chartered in 1348, the city was capital of the Sax-Weimar duchy from 1547 to 1918. In the 18th century, Weimar was the literary capital of Europe. The 19th century witnessed a gradual artistic decline. In 1919 the German National Assembly convened here to establish the WEIMAR REPUBLIC and Walter GROPIUS founded the BAUHAUS. Pop. (1991) 59,100.

**Weimar Republic** (1919–33) Popular name for the republic of Germany created after World War I. It was named for the city of WEIMAR, where the constitution was drawn up (1919). It was hampered by severe economic difficulties. The Weimar constitution was suspended after Adolf HITLER became chancellor and the republic was superseded by the THIRD REICH.

**Weinberg, Steven** (1933– ) US physicist who in 1967, independently of Abdus Salam, proposed a theory that unifies the ELECTROMAGNETIC and WEAK NUCLEAR FORCES between subatomic particles – now known as the electroweak force. Later experiments proved the Salam-Weinberg hypothesis to be true. In 1979 they shared the Nobel Prize for physics with Sheldon Glashow. *See also* GRAND UNIFIED THEORY

**Weinberger, Caspar Willard** (1917– ) US statesman, secretary of defense (1981–87) under Ronald REAGAN. He served as secretary of health, education, and welfare (1973–75) for President Richard NIXON. As secretary of defense, Weinberger oversaw a large increase in the size of the armed forces and helped develop the strategic defense initiative (SDI).

**Weismann, August** (1834–1914) German biologist. His essay discussing the germ plasm theory, *The Continuity of the Germ Plasm* (1885), proposed the immortality of the germ line cells as opposed to body cells. It was influential in the development of modern GENETICS.

**Weiss, Peter** (1916–82) Swedish dramatist, b. Germany. His reputation was established with *Marat/Sade* (1934). Other plays include *The Investigation* (1965), and *Trotsky in Exile* (1970).

**Weizmann, Chaim** (1874–1952) Zionist leader and chemist, first president of Israel (1948–52). He was born in Russia and became a British subject in 1910. Weizmann was instrumental in securing the BALFOUR DECLARATION (1917). He served as president of the World Zionist Organization (1920–31, 1935–46).

**Weld, Theodore Dwight** (1803–95) US abolitionist. He and his wife, Angelina Grimké, were leading campaigners for the abolition of SLAVERY. Weld was editor (1836–40) of the *Emancipator*, the organ of the antislavery society. He wrote *American Slavery As It Is* (1839).

**welding** Technique for joining metal parts, usually by controlled melting. Several welding processes are used. In **fusion** welding, the parts to be joined are heated together until the metal starts to melt. On cooling, the molten metal solidifies to form a permanent bond between the parts. Such welds are usually strengthened with filler metal from a welding rod or wire. In **arc** welding, an electric arc heats the work and filler metal. In **oxyacetylene** welding, heat is provided by burning ethyne gas in oxygen. In resistance or **spot** welding, the heat is generated by passing an electric current through the joint. In brazing and soldering, the temperature used is sufficient to melt the filler metal, but not the parts that it joins.

**welfare state** Description of a state that takes responsibility for the health and subsistence of its citizens. Limited forms of welfare were introduced by Western governments in the late 19th century, such as Germany. Comprehensive policies were introduced after World War II, such as in the UK. *See also* SOCIAL SECURITY

**well** Shaft sunk in the Earth's CRUST through which water, oil, natural gas, brine, sulfur, or other mineral substances can be extracted. Artesian wells are sunk into water-bearing rock strata, the AQUIFERS, from which water rises under pressure in the wells to the surface.

**Welles, (George) Orson** (1915–85) US actor and director. His first film, *Citizen Kane* (1940), earned him a Best Screenplay Academy Award. As an actor, he starred in *The Third Man* (1949). Welles directed and acted in *The Lady of Shanghai* (1948), and *Touch of Evil* (1958). Disenchanted with Hollywood, he went into self-imposed exile in Europe, directing *The Trial* (1963), *Chimes at Midnight* (1966), and *The Immortal Story* (1968). Welles' vivid, radio dramatization (1938) of H.G. Wells' *War of the Worlds* caused mass panic and hysteria.

**Wellington, Arthur Wellesley, Duke of** (1769–1852) British general and statesman, prime minister (1828–30). He was knighted for his defeat of the Marathas in India (1803). In 1809 Wellesley became commander of allied forces in the PENINSULAR WAR. He gradually drove the French army back over the Pyrenees. Wellington's victory at the Battle of Toulouse (1814) precipitated NAPOLEON I's abdication. Wellesley was created the duke of Wellington. While representing Britain at the Congress of VIENNA (1814–15), he learned of Napoleon's escape from Elba. Wellington resumed command of allied troops and, with the Prussian General von Blücher, defeated Napoleon at the Battle of WATERLOO (1815). In 1819 he became a Tory cabinet minister. As prime minister, Wellington grudgingly accepted the passage of the Act of CATHOLIC EMANCIPATION (1829). He served as foreign secretary (1834–35) under Sir Robert PEEL.

**Wellington** Capital of New Zealand, in the extreme s of North Island, on Port Nicholson, an inlet of Cook Strait. First visited by Europeans in 1826, it was founded in 1840. In 1865 it replaced Auckland as capital. Wellington's excellent harbor furthered its development as a transportation and trading center. Much of the city's manufacturing industry (including textiles, clothing, transportation equipment, and machinery) is located in outlying suburbs. Pop. (1994) 329,000.

**Wells, H.G. (Herbert George)** (1866–1946) English writer. His reputation was established with the science fiction novels *The Time Machine* (1895), *The Invisible Man* (1897), and *The War of the Worlds* (1898). Later novels, including *Love and Mr. Lewisham* (1900), *Kipps* (1905), *Tono-Bungay* (1909), and *The History of Mr. Polly* (1910), draw on experiences more directly related in his *Experiment in Autobiography* (1934). *Ann Veronica* (1909), and *The New Machiavelli* (1911) reflect his interest in sociology and politics as a member of the FABIAN SOCIETY. Wells also wrote a number of short stories.

**Wells Fargo** American express company. It was established in 1852 by Henry Wells and William Fargo to serve the banking and shipping needs of California miners. The company took over the failing Pony Express, and by 1866 it operated the largest stagecoach network in America. By 1888 Wells Fargo had a transcontinental rail route. In 1918 it merged with the American Railway Express Company. Today, it operates an armored car service in the Eastern United States.

**Welsbach, Baron Carl Auer von** (1858–1929) Austro-Hungarian chemist who discovered the rare-earth elements neodymium and praseodymium. He is best known for his 1885 invention of the gas mantle, which produces a bright, incandescent light from a gas flame.

**Welsh** (*Cymraeg*) Language of Wales. It is spoken by less than 19% of the Welsh population, chiefly in the rural north and west. It belongs to the Brittonic sub-branch of the Celtic family of INDO-EUROPEAN LANGUAGES, and is closely related to BRETON and CORNISH. It survives more strongly than most other CELTIC LANGUAGES.

**Welsh pony** Light, saddle horse known in Wales since Saxon times. Usually a child's mount, it has the physique of a miniature coach horse. Height: to 48in (1.2m) at the shoulder; weight: to 500lb (225kg).

**Welty, Eudora** (1909– ) US short-story writer and novelist. Her works are set often in her native Mississippi. Welty's short story collections include *A Curtain of Green* (1941), and *The Golden Apples* (1949). Her novels, firmly in the Southern Gothic tradition, include the Pulitzer Prize-winning *The Optimist's Daughter* (1972). Her autobiography is *One Writer's Beginnings* (1984).

**Wenceslas, Saint** (907–29) Prince of Bohemia and patron saint of the Czechs. In *c.*925 he overthrew his mother who, as regent, persecuted Christians. He continued the Christianization of the country, which, together with his submission to the Germans, aroused opposition. He was killed by his brother and successor, Boleslav I.

**Wenceslaus** (1361–1419) King of the Germans (1378–1400) and king of Bohemia (1378–1419) as Wenceslaus IV. He succeeded his father, CHARLES IV, as emperor but was never crowned. Wenceslaus' neglect of German affairs angered the princes, who deposed him (1400) in favor of Rupert. He enabled his half-brother, SIGISMUND, to become (1387) king of Hungary. In Bohemia, Wensceslaus supported the reforms of Jan HUS.

**werewolf** In folklore, a person who changes into a wolf at night but reverts to human form by day. Some werewolves can change form at will; in others the change occurs involuntarily, under the influence of a full moon.

**Wergeland, Henrik Arnold** (1808–45) Norwegian poet and patriot. Much of his short life was devoted to working for Norwegian cultural independence from Denmark. Such works as *Creation, Man, and Messiah* (1830), and *The English Pilot* (1844) helped establish his reputation as Norway's national poet.

**Werner, Alfred** (1866–1919) Swiss chemist He was awarded the 1913 Nobel Prize for chemistry for his coordination theory of VALENCE in which he correctly suggested that metals have coordinate bonds which make ISOMERS possible in inorganic compounds.

**Wertheimer, Max** (1880–1943) German psychologist. Wertheimer was a founder of GESTALT PSYCHOLOGY. His early work concerned visual perception. Later, he attempted to apply Gestalt principles to cognitive and educational problems.

**Wesker, Arnold** (1932– ) English playwright. His childhood in the East End of London is recollected in the trilogy *Chicken Soup with Barley* (1958), *Roots* (1959), and *I'm Talking about Jerusalem* (1960). His experiences in World War II are the subject of *Chips with Everything* (1962). His later work includes *The Old Ones* (1972), and *The Wedding Feast* (1974).

**Wesley, Charles** (1707–88) English evangelist and hymnwriter, brother of John WESLEY. In 1735 he was ordained and in 1738 experienced an evangelical conversion. Wesley wrote nearly 6,000 hymns, including "Hark! the Herald Angels Sing" and "Love Divine, All Loves Excelling."

**Wesley, John** (1703–91) English theologian and evangelist, founder of METHODISM. With his brother Charles WESLEY, he founded (1729) the Holy Club at Oxford. In 1735 the brothers traveled as missionaries to the US, but John returned in 1737. In 1738, during a Moravian meeting, Wesley underwent a personal, religious experience that laid the foundation upon which he built the Methodist movement. Wesley's *Journal* (1735–90) records the extent of his itinerant preaching.

**Wessex** Anglo-Saxon kingdom established in Hampshire, SW England. Traditionally founded by Cerdic (r.519–534), by the beginning of the 9th century it had extended its territory to include much of s England. Egbert became overlord of all England, but his successors lost much of the kingdom to the Danes. ALFRED THE GREAT ensured that Wessex was the only English kingdom to escape Danish conquest.

**West, Benjamin** (1738–1820) US painter. He settled in Britain, where he became historical painter to George III and a leader of NEOCLASSICISM. Two of his best-known paintings are *Death of Wolfe* (1771), and *Penn's Treaty with the Indians* (1772).

**West, Mae** (1893–1980) US stage and film actress. She began her career in burlesque. Her first film was *Night After Night* (1932). Her overt sexuality and use of double entendre in *She Done Him Wrong*, and *I'm No Angel* (1933) led to a Production Code and censorship in the movie industry. Other films include *Go West Young Man* (1936), and *My Little Chickadee* (1940).

W

**West, Nathanael** (1903–40) US novelist, b. Nathan Wallenstein Weinstein. He wrote four novels: *The Dream Life of Balso Snell* (1931); *Miss Lonelyhearts* (1933), a grimly comic story about a columnist for the lovelorn; *A Cool Million* (1934); and *The Day of the Locust* (1939), a tale of false dreams and failed lives in Hollywood, where West spent his last years as a scriptwriter.

**West, Dame Rebecca** (1892–1983) English novelist and critic, b. Cicily Isabel Fairfield. She is best known for her first novel, *The Return of the Soldier* (1918), the story of a shell-shock victim. Her political works include *The Meaning of Treason* (1949) and a two-volume study of Yugoslavia, *Black Lamb and Grey Falcon* (1942). West also wrote psychological novels such as *The Thinking Reed* (1936) and *Birds Fall Down* (1966). Her last work was *1900* (1982).

**West Bank** Region W of the JORDAN River and NW of the Dead Sea. Under the United Nations plan for the partition of Palestine (1947), it was designated an Arab district. It was administered by Jordan after the first ARAB-ISRAELI WAR (1948) but captured by Israel in the SIX DAY WAR of 1967. In 1988 Jordan surrendered its claim to the Israeli-occupied West Bank to the PALESTINE LIBERATION ORGANIZATION (PLO). Under the terms of the ISRAELI-PALESTINIAN ACCORD (1993), limited autonomy in the West Bank was conceded to the newly formed Palestinian National Authority (PNA). Difficulties created by the growth of Israeli settlements, security disputes, and the accession (1996) of a Likud government in Israel threatened to disrupt progress toward total Israeli withdrawal.

**West Bengal** State in NE India bordering Nepal, Bhutan, and Sikkim (N), Bangladesh and Assam state (E), the Bay of Bengal (S), and Bihar and Orissa states (W). The state capital is CALCUTTA. It was formed in 1947 after the independence of India and Pakistan, and the partitioning of the former British province of BENGAL into Hindu West Bengal (India) and Muslim East Bengal (East Pakistan). In 1950 West Bengal absorbed the state of Cooch Bihar. In the 1970s political instability was caused by Muslim-Hindu disputes, large immigration from newly created BANGLADESH and Naxalite disturbances. The state is highly industrialized, its cities (notably Calcutta) attract male migrants from neighboring states. Industries: vehicles, steel, fertilizers, chemicals. Agricultural products include rice, fish, jute, oilseeds, tea, tobacco. Area: 34,258sq mi (88,752sq km). Pop. (1991) 68,077,965.

**Western** Type of popular fiction and film, native to the US, featuring "cowboys" and sometimes "Indians" in a Wild West setting. It first appeared in the form of short stories and novels in the "pulp" magazines of the late 19th century. Owen Wister's *The Virginian* (1902) is perhaps the defining influence on the form, and Zane GREY its most prolific exponent. *The Squaw Man* (1914), one of the first Hollywood Westerns, set a trend for a whole new breed of movie cowboy such as Tom Mix, Roy Rogers, Buck Jones, and "Hopalong Cassidy." More recent examples of the genre have reevaluated the treatment of Native Americans by settlers.

**Western Australia** State in Australia, bordered by the Timor Sea (N), the Indian Ocean (W and S), South Australia state, and the Northern Territory (E). The capital is PERTH, and other significant cities are Mandurah, Kalgoorlie, Bunbury, and Fremantle, Perth's ocean port. Though Western Australia was first visited by Dirck Hartog in 1616, settlement did not begin until 1826, when a penal colony was founded. The first free settlement was in 1829. By far the largest state in Australia, it was governed by New South Wales until 1831, becoming a state of the Commonwealth of Australia in 1901. The climate is mainly tropical or subtropical and more than 90% of the land is desert or semidesert. Only the SW, which enjoys a temperate climate, is permanently settled. Swan River is the state's only significant water source. The raising of sheep and cattle is the principal agricultural activity, but the production of cereals, fishing, and forestry are also important. Western Australia is the country's major gold-producing state, and there is also mining for iron ore, coal, nickel, uranium, bauxite, phosphates, oil, and natural gas. Industry is still expanding, and wine became a major earner during the 1980s. Area: 975,095sq mi (2,525,500sq km). Pop. (1991) 1,586,393.

**Western Cape** Province in SW South Africa, bounded by the Indian Ocean (S) and Atlantic Ocean (W). The capital is CAPE TOWN. Other major towns include Simonstown and Stellenbosch. Formerly part of CAPE PROVINCE, Western Cape was founded in 1994. Its chief physical features are Table Mountain (3,566ft high) and the rugged Swartberg Range (maximum height 7,627ft). Robben Island was the site of an offshore prison used to house political prisoners during the APARTHEID era. The main economic activity is agriculture, with fruit and tobacco growing, dairy farming and sheep rearing. There is also an important fishing industry, and an off-

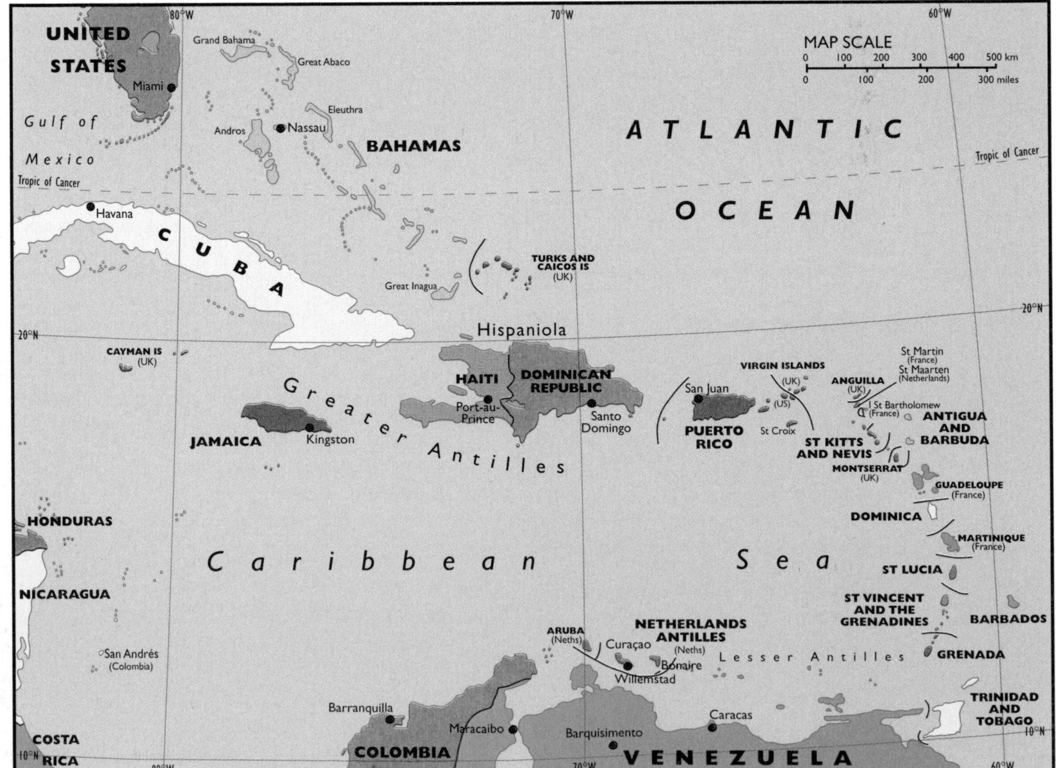


► **West Indies** Stretching for 2,000mi (3,200km), the island chain of the West Indies divides the Atlantic Ocean and the Caribbean. The region is famed for its great natural beauty, while its thousands of miles of sandy, secluded beaches make the West Indies a popular tourist destination.

shore gas field is exploited in Mossel Bay. Industries: chemicals, machinery, metal goods, textiles. Area: 50,500sq mi (129,390sq km). Pop. (1993) 3,620,200.

**Western Isles** *See* HEBRIDES

**Western Sahara** (formerly Spanish Sahara) Desert territory on the Atlantic coast of NW Africa, bordering Morocco (N), Algeria (NE), and Mauritania (E and S). The capital is El Aaiún. The territory comprises two districts; Saguia el Hamra in the N, and Río de Oro in the S. The population is composed of Arabs, BERBERS, and pastoral nomads, most of whom are SUNNI Muslims. The first European discovery was in 1434, but the area remained unexploited until the 19th century, and even then Spain controlled only the coastal area. In 1957 a nationalist movement overthrew the Spanish, but in 1958 the Spanish regained control of the region and merged Saguia el Hamra and Río de Oro to form the province of Spanish Sahara. In 1963 large phosphate deposits were discovered. In 1973 the Polisario Front began a guerrilla war that forced Spain to withdraw in 1976. Within a month, Morocco and Mauritania had partitioned the country. Polisario (backed by Algeria) continued to fight for independence, unilaterally renaming the country the Saharawi Arab Democratic Republic. In 1979 Mauritania withdrew, and Morocco assumed full control. In 1982 the Saharawi Republic was granted membership of the Organization of African Unity (OAU) and, by 1988, controlled most of the desert up to the Moroccan defensive line. Fragile ceasefires were agreed in 1988 and 1991. An estimated 200,000 Saharawis live in refugee camps, mostly in Algeria. Area: 102,680sq mi (266,769sq km). Pop. (1993 est.) 214,000.

**Western Samoa** Independent island republic in the S Pacific Ocean, encompassing the W half of the SAMOA island chain. It comprises the two large, volcanic, and mountainous islands of Savai'i and Upolu, the smaller islands of Manono and Apolima, and several uninhabited islets. The capital, Apia (on Upolu), has 66% of the total population. The cradle of Polynesian culture, the islands became a German protectorate under the terms of an 1899 treaty, but in 1914 New Zealand seized them and they were administered by New Zealand from 1920–61 under a League of Nations mandate and then a United Nations trusteeship. Resistance to New Zealand rule led to a plebiscite and, in 1962, Western Samoa became an independent state within the Commonwealth. Under a friendship treaty, New Zealand handles relations with governments outside the Pacific zone. The Polynesian population is employed mainly in subsistence agriculture, and the chief exports are coconut oil, taro, and copra. Area: 1,097sq mi (2,840sq km). Pop. (1991) 161,298.

**Western Wall** (Wailing Wall) Place in Jerusalem sacred to all Jews. It is a remnant of a wall of the great TEMPLE destroyed by the Romans in AD 70 and is the focus of many pilgrimages.

**West Glamorgan** County in S Wales on the Bristol Channel; the administrative center is SWANSEA. Tourists are attracted by the rugged Gower Peninsula. Area: 317sq mi (820sq km). Pop. (1991) 361,428.

**West Indies** Chain of islands encircling the Caribbean Sea and separating it from the Atlantic Ocean. They extend from Florida to Venezuela. Geographically they are divided into three main groups: the BAHAMAS, and the Greater and Lesser ANTILLES. Most islands are now independent, but were formerly British, Spanish, French, or Dutch possessions. The indigenous population was killed by the colonial powers, who fought for possession of the islands. The islands were transformed by the introduction of sugarcane in the 17th century, fueling the slave trade from Africa. *See* individual country articles

**Westinghouse, George** (1846–1914) US engineer and inventor. The best known of his hundreds of inventions was the air brake (1868), which made high-speed rail travel safe. In 1886 he formed the Westinghouse Electric Company for the transmission of electricity.

**Westmeath** County in Leinster province, N central Republic of Ireland. It is mainly low-lying, with many lakes or loughs, and is drained by the rivers SHANNON, Inny, and Brosna. The county town is Mullingar. Area: 681sq mi (1,763sq km). Pop. (1991) 61,880.

**West Midlands** Metropolitan county in central England. It is divided into seven council districts: BIRMINGHAM (the administrative center), COVENTRY, Dudley, Sandwell, Solihull, Walsall, and Wolverhampton. Area: 347sq mi (899sq km). Pop. (1991) 2,551,671.

**Westminster, City of** Part of the LONDON borough of Westminster since 1965. From 785 Westminster was the site of a monastery upon which EDWARD THE CONFESSOR built WESTMINSTER ABBEY. Parliament met in Westminster Palace until a fire in 1834 led to the building of the HOUSES OF PARLIAMENT (1840–68). Pop. (1991) 174,718.

**Westminster, Statutes of** English acts of the reign of EDWARD I. The first (1275) and second (1285) statutes enshrined Edward's overhaul of English law. A further statute of 1290 is sometimes called the third statute of Westminster. The Statute of Westminster of 1931 granted autonomy to the dominions in the British Empire.

**Westminster Abbey** Gothic church in London, originally the abbey church of a Benedictine monastery (closed 1539). In 1050 EDWARD THE CONFESSOR began to build a Norman church on the site. In 1245 Henry III began work on the present structure. The Lady Chapel, dedicated to Henry VII, is a fine example of the PERPENDICULAR STYLE. The two western towers were built (1722–45) by Sir Christopher WREN and Nicholas HAWKSMOOR. The 19th century restoration was managed by Sir George Gilbert SCOTT. It is cruciform in plan. Since William of Conqueror, most English monarchs have been crowned in the abbey. It is the burial place of 18 monarchs. Poets' Corner lies in the south transept.

**Weston, Edward** (1886–1958) US photographer. In 1932 he helped form the influential *64 group*. Weston's style of "straight photography" was sharp and direct, emphasizing the texture and forms of the natural world.

**Westphalia** Historic region of W Germany between the Rhine and Weser rivers. From 1180 it was a duchy under the archbishops of Cologne. Briefly a kingdom during the NAPOLEONIC WARS, it became a province of Prussia in 1816.

**Westphalia, Peace of** (1648) Series of treaties among the states involved in the THIRTY YEARS WAR. Peace negotiations began in 1642, and meetings were held in cities of Westphalia. In Germany, the peace established the virtual autonomy of the German states, and diminished the authority of the Holy Roman emperor. It also established the ascendancy of France, the power of Sweden in N Europe, and the decline of Spain.

**West Sussex** County in SE England; the county town is Chichester. Other towns include Crawley and Worthing. Area: 778sq mi (2,016sq km). Pop. (1991) 702,290.

**West Virginia** State in the Appalachian Mountain region, E central US. The capital is CHARLESTON. The land is mountainous and rugged. West Virginia has two narrow projections – the Northern Panhandle extends N between Ohio and Pennsylvania, and the Eastern Panhandle, which cuts E between Maryland and Virginia. Harpers Ferry lies on the bank of the Potomac River, which forms much of the state's E border. The Ohio River forms most of its W border. In 1727 Germans established the first settlement at New Mecklenburg (Shepherdstown). Settlers crossing the Appalachian and Allegheny mountains led to the last of the FRENCH AND INDIAN WARS (1754–63). The region was then part of Virginia, but political and economic disagreements, especially on slavery, arose between western Virginians and the dominant E. When Virginia seceded from the Union in May 1861 there was much opposition in the W, and it was admitted to the Union as West Virginia in 1863. Hay, tobacco, corn, and apples are the principal crops, but West Virginia also has rich mineral deposits and is the leading US producer of bituminous coal. Some 65% of the land is forested. Industries: glass, chemicals, steel, machinery, tourism. Area 24,181sq mi (62,629sq km). Pop. (1992) 1,808,860.

**West Yorkshire** County in N central England. It is divided into the districts of BRADFORD, Calderdale, Kirklees, LEEDS, and Wakefield (the county town). Area: 786sq mi (2,036sq km). Pop. (1991) 2,013,693.

**Wetland** Ecosystem where the water table lies close to the surface for much of the year. Wetlands include bogs, marshes,

**WEST VIRGINIA**
**Statehood :**
June 20, 1863
**Nickname :**
The Mountain State
**State bird :**
Cardinal
**State flower :**
Rhododendron
**State tree :**
Sugar maple
**State motto :**
Mountaineers are always free

W

▶ **whale** Among the largest and most intelligent animals that have ever lived, whales all belong to the order Cetacea. The beluga whale (*Delphinapterus leucas*, A) is an Arctic species, and travels in schools of many hundreds. It grows to 17ft (4.25m). The pilot whale (*Globicephala* sp., B) is found in most oceans except the polar seas. They migrate between cold and warm waters depending on the season. The Californian gray whale (*Eschrichtius glaucus*, C) is confined to the North Pacific. From the N seas they migrate S in winter to breed in the shallow, warmer seas off Baja California and South Korea. They feed on plankton, which they strain from the water by means of baleen plates (1).They grow to 30ft (9m).

swamps, and fens. There are both saltwater and freshwater wetlands. Coastal wetlands are said to contain a greater concentration of flora and fauna than any other ecosystem. They are also ecologically valuable as regulators of flooding and the water cycle. Many of the world's wetlands have been drained for farming or housing.

**Wexford** County in Leinster province, SE Republic of Ireland. The land is mostly low-lying. The chief river is the Slaney. Wexford is primarily an agricultural county. The county town is Wexford (1991 pop. 9,500). Area 908sq mi (2,351sq km). Pop. (1991) 102,069.

**Weyden, Rogier van der** (1400–64) Netherlandish painter. In 1436 he became official painter to the city of Brussels, where he lived for the rest of his life. His finest works include *Deposition* (before 1443), and he excelled at inventive compositions.

**whale** Any of several species of large aquatic mammals; it has a fishlike body with paddle-like flippers, and a tail flattened horizontally into flukes for locomotion. It spends its whole life in water. Two main groups exist: toothed whales and baleen whales. Toothed whales (Odontoceti) have simple teeth and feed primarily on fish and squid. They include the bottle-nosed whale, SPERM WHALE, and BELUGA. Baleen whales (Mysticeti), including the right whale, BLUE WHALE, and California gray whale, have no teeth but carry comblike plates of horny material (baleen or whalebone) in the roof of the mouth. These form a sieve, through which the whales strain krill on which they feed. Order Cetacea. The order also includes DOLPHINS and PORPOISES. *See also* WHALING

**whale shark** Largest species of SHARK; it lives in tropical waters throughout the world. Brownish to dark gray with white or yellow spots and stripes, this docile, egg-laying fish often travels near the surface. Length: 30ft (9m). Family Rhincodontidae; species *Rhincodon typus*.

**whaling** Industry involved in the pursuing and catching of WHALES for their oil and flesh. The modern whaling era began in the 1850s with the development of harpoons with explosive heads; after 1925 oceangoing factory ships were sent to the Antarctic. Since then most larger whale species, including the blue whale, have been hunted to near-extinction. In 1986 the International Whaling Commission (IWC) agreed a moratorium on commercial whaling. Whaling for "scientific purposes," by Japan, Iceland, and Norway, continued. In 1990 Norway claimed that whale numbers were high enough to sustain hunting; public opposition, however, remains strong.

**Wharton, Edith Newbold** (1862–1937) US novelist. She is best known for *Ethan Frome* (1911), a grim portrait of New England farm life, and her polished anatomies of New York society, *The House of Mirth* (1905) and *The Age of Innocence* (1920), for which she became the first woman to be awarded a Pulitzer Prize.

**wheat** CEREAL grass cultivated in the Middle East since 7000 BC; it is now grown worldwide. It is used for BREAD, PASTA, cake, and pastry flour. Wheat is also used in the preparation of MALT, dextrose, and ALCOHOL. Family Poaceae/Gramineae.

**Wheatstone, Sir Charles** (1802–75) English physicist and inventor. In 1843, with William Cooke, he improved the Wheatstone bridge, a device for measuring electrical resistance. In 1837 they patented an electric TELEGRAPH. Wheatstone also invented the harmonica.

▲ **wheat** Along with rice, wheat is the world's most important food crop.The kernels of the plant are ground into flour, which can then be used to make a variety of foods. Wheat remains green in color until it ripens, becoming golden-brown.

**wheel** Circular structure that revolves around a central axis. Before the wheel was invented, heavy loads were sometimes moved by rolling them on logs or on rounded stones. More than 5,000 years ago, sections of tree trunks were cut to form the first wheels for carts. Spoked wheels were introduced several hundred years later. Eventually, the wheel was used in simple machines, such as the waterwheel and potter's wheel.

**wheel and axle** Machine based on the principle that a small force applied to the rim of a wheel will exert a larger force on an object attached to the axle. The MECHANICAL ADVANTAGE, or force ratio, is the ratio of the radius of the wheel to that of the axle.

**whelk** Edible, marine GASTROPOD found on seashores. It has a coiled shell, with a smooth rim and a notch at the end. Family Buccinidae. Length: 5–7in (13–18cm).

**Whig** Semiformal parliamentary grouping in the UK from the late 17th to the mid-19th century. The Whigs were supporters of the GLORIOUS REVOLUTION (1688) and the succession of the House of HANOVER (1714). Between 1714 and the accession (1760) of GEORGE III, the TORIES were so discredited by association with the JACOBITES that most politicians became Hanoverian Whigs. In the reign of George III, Whiggism became the party of religious toleration, parliamentary reform, and opposition to slavery. From 1783 to 1830 the Whigs remained in opposition. They returned to office under Lord GREY, passing the Great Reform Act of 1832. By the 1850s they had been replaced by the LIBERAL PARTY.

**Whig Party** One of the two major US political parties from 1834 to 1854. In 1828 the supporters of John Quincy ADAMS and Henry CLAY formed the NATIONAL REPUBLICAN PARTY, a loose coalition of forces opposed to the presidency of Andrew JACKSON. Clay attempted to reconcile these diverse groups behind his "American System." His arguments for the tariff and the Bank of the United States drew the support of Eastern industrialists and businessmen. His support of STATES' RIGHTS attracted Southern plantation owners. In 1836 presidential elections the Whig Party fielded several candidates, including Daniel WEBSTER and William Henry HARRISON. This division helped secure the election of the Democrat Martin VAN BUREN. In 1840, with the support of Thurlow WEED and William H. SEWARD, William H. Harrison became the first Whig president. He died in office and was succeeded by his vice president, John TYLER. Tyler alienated the Whigs in Congress and his entire cabinet resigned. In 1844 Clay ran for president, but lost to James K. POLK. In 1848 Zachary TAYLOR became the second Whig president. He was succeeded by his vice president, Millard FILLMORE. The party, however, was being torn apart over the question of slavery. In 1848 several important party figures defected to the FREE SOIL PARTY. In 1852 elections the Whig candidate, Winfield SCOTT, was decisively defeated. Most Northern Whigs joined the new REPUBLICAN PARTY. Many Southern Whigs returned to the Democratic Party. Others, led by Millard Fillmore, formed the KNOW-NOTHING MOVEMENT.

**whiplash** Neck injury that results when the head is jerked rapidly backward and then forward. It occurs most often in car accidents, when the car is hit from behind. Neck muscles and ligaments are injured, causing pain and stiffness.

**whippet** Sporting dog that was originally bred in England for racing and hare coursing. It is capable of running at speeds of 35mph (56km/h). Height: to 22in (56cm) at the shoulder; weight: to 24lb (11kg).

**whippoorwill** *See* NIGHTJAR

**whirligig beetle** *See* WATER BEETLE

**whirlpool** Circular motion of a fluid. Whirlpools in rivers occur in regions where WATERFALLS or sharp breaks in topographic continuity make steady flow impossible. *See also* VORTEX

**whiskey** Alcoholic spirit made by distilling fermented cereal grains. Scotch whisky and Irish whiskey are both distilled from barley that has been allowed to sprout, then roasted, and finally "mashed" and distilled. In the US, corn and rye are used to produce bourbon whiskey (corn) and rye whiskey. After distillation, refined whiskey spirit is 70–85% alcohol by volume; all whiskeys are, therefore, heavily diluted. Almost all whiskeys are blended.

**Whiskey Rebellion** (1794) Revolt against the US government in W Pennsylvania. It was provoked by a tax on whiskey, and was the first serious challenge to federal authority. Collection of the tax met violent resistance, but when President Washington called out the militia, the rebellion collapsed.

**whist** Card game for four people. The aim is to accumulate "tricks" – sets of cards, one from each player, in which the player of the highest-value card "takes the trick." The object of ordinary whist is to amass more tricks than any other player. Other whist games include contract whist, in which players specify how many tricks they will make; and solo whist, in which one player contracts to make tricks. *See also* BRIDGE

**Whistler, James Abbott McNeill** (1834–1903) US painter and etcher, who lived and worked in England from 1859. He was a precursor of ABSTRACT ART. For Whistler, the artist's duty was to select elements from nature to create a harmonious composition that, like music, existed for its own sake. He sued John RUSKIN for stating that his *Nocturne in Black and Gold* (*c*.1874) flung "a pot of paint in the public's face." Whistler won the case, but the court costs left him bankrupt. His most famous painting is the portrait of his mother, entitled *Arrangement in Gray and Black* (1872). Other works include *Chelsea: Nocturne in Blue and Green* (*c*.1870). He also produced some 400 plates of etchings.

**Whitby** Coastal town in N Yorkshire, England. ST. HILDA founded an abbey here in 657, which was destroyed by the Danes in the 9th century. In *c*.663 the **Synod of Whitby** was held at the abbey. The subsequent break with the Celtic church placed the English church in line with mainstream European Christian theology.

**White, Byron Raymond** (1917– ) Associate Justice of the US Supreme Court (1962–93). He was appointed by President John F. KENNEDY. White supported the liberals on civil rights issues, such as affirmative action, but on issues of personal liberty usually voted conservative.

**White, E.B. (Elwyn Brooks)** (1899–1985) US essayist. Some of his articles for *The New Yorker* were collected in *The Wild Flag* (1946). White collaborated with James THURBER on the humorous book *Is Sex Necessary?* (1929). He also wrote three classics of children's literature: *Stuart Little* (1945), *Charlotte's Web* (1952), and *The Trumpet of the Swan* (1970).

**White, Edward Douglass** (1845–1921) Associate Justice of the US Supreme Court (1894–1910), ninth Chief Justice of the United States (1910–21). He was appointed chief justice by President TAFT. White is best known for his "rule of reason" antitrust decisions (1911) that resulted in the dissolution of Standard Oil and American Tobacco companies.

**White, Patrick** (1912–90) Australian novelist, b. Britain. His novels, concerned with Australian history and identity, include *The Tree of Man* (1955), *Voss* (1957), and *Riders in the Chariot* (1961). Later novels include *The Eye of the Storm* (1973), *A Fringe of Leaves* (1976), and *The Twyborn Affair* (1979). In 1973 White became the first Australian to win the Nobel Prize for literature. His autobiography is *Flaws in the Glass* (1981).

**White, Stanford** (1853–1906) US architect. He was a founding partner (1879) of the influential firm of McKim, Mead, and White. White designed Washington Arch (1895), and the Tiffany Building (1906). He was shot and killed by Harry K. Thaw.

**White, Walter Francis** (1893–1955) US civil rights leader. He was secretary (1931–55) of the NATIONAL ASSOCIATION FOR THE ADVANCEMENT OF COLORED PEOPLE (NAACP). White was a leading campaigner against racial prejudice and violence in the US. His autobiography is *A Man Called White* (1948).

**white ant** *See* TERMITE

**white blood cell** *See* LEUKOCYTE

**white dwarf** High-density type of star about the size of the Earth, but with a mass about that of the Sun. White dwarfs are of low luminosity and gradually cool down to become cold, dark objects.

**white-eye** Common name for a group of arboreal, songbirds found mainly in tropical forests in Africa, Asia, and Australasia. They are usually small and green, with a prominent ring of white feathers around the eyes. They have pointed bills and extensible tongues for feeding on fruits. Length: to 5in (12.5cm). Family Zosteropidae.

**Whitefield, George** (1714–70) English evangelical preacher, an important figure in early METHODISM. In 1738 he made his first visit to America. Whitefield's stirring, open-air sermons contributed to the GREAT AWAKENING. He broke away from John WESLEY to form the Calvinistic Methodist Church.

**whitefish** (cisco) Any of several species of freshwater food fish that live in Eurasia and the US. It is silvery, with large scales and a small mouth. Length: to 59in (150cm); weight: to 63lb (29kg). Family Salmonidae.

**Whitehead, A.N. (Alfred North)** (1861–1947) English philosopher and mathematician. In his "philosophy of organism" he attempted a synthesis of modern science and metaphysics. The system is presented in his *Process and Reality* (1929). His three-volume *Principia Mathematica* (1910–13), written in collaboration with Bertrand RUSSELL, is an important work in the study of LOGIC.

**Whitehorse** Capital of Yukon Territory, Canada. It lies on the Alaska Highway and the W bank of the Yukon River. The town developed during the Klondike gold rush (1897–98). Pop. (1991) 17,925.

**White House** Official residence of the US president, WASHINGTON, D.C. It was designed in the neoclassical style by James Hoban in 1792 and completed in 1800. After being burned down by the British in 1814, it was rebuilt, and the porticoes were added in the 1820s.

**White Mountains** Part of the Appalachian Mountain system, stretching from SW Maine to N New Hampshire. The mountains rise to Mount Washington, at 6,288ft (1,917m), in the Presidential Range. Much of this glaciated, granite region is included in a national forest.

**white shark** (great white shark) SHARK found in tropical and subtropical waters; it is the most aggressive of sharks. It has a crescent-shaped tail, and saw-edged triangular teeth; it is gray, blue, or brown with a white belly. Length: to 36ft (11m); weight: to 7,000lb (2,200kg). Family Isuridae; species *Carcharodon carcharias*.

**white whale** *See* BELUGA

**Whitgift, John** (1530–1604) English churchman. In 1583 he became archbishop of Canterbury. Whitgift tried to maintain a middle course in the REFORMATION, upholding the recently established doctrine of the CHURCH OF ENGLAND and strongly opposing the Puritans.

**whiting** Several unrelated food fish. The European whiting (*Merlangus merlangus*) is a haddock-like fish of the COD family, Gadidae. It is found primarily in the North Sea, where it feeds on invertebrates and small fish. It is silver with distinctive black markings at the base of the pectoral fin. Length: to 28in (70cm). Other fish commonly called whitings include the kingfish (*Menticirrhus saxatilis*) and the freshwater WHITEFISH (*Coregonus clupeaformis*).

**Whitman, Walt (Walter)** (1819–92) US poet. In 1855 he published at his own expense *Leaves of Grass*, a volume of 12 poems that included "Song of Myself." In 1856 and 1860 Whitman published enlarged editions of the work. *Drum Taps* (1865), which draws on his experience of medical service in the Civil War, and *Sequel to Drum-taps* (1866), which includes his famous elegies to Abraham Lincoln, "When Lilacs Last in the Dooryard Bloom'd" and "O Captain! My Captain!", were both incorporated into a much-expanded 1867 edition of *Leaves of Grass*. Whitman's use of free verse, symbolic association, and colloquial language represents a major transition in AMERICAN LITERATURE.

**Whitney, Eli** (1765–1825) US inventor and manufacturer. Whitney invented (1793) the COTTON GIN, which revolutionized cotton culture in the South and turned cotton into a prof-

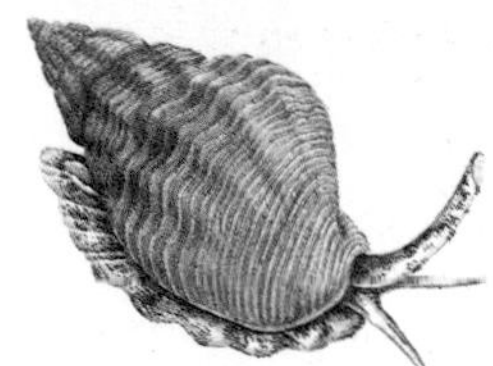

▲ **whelk** Found in temperate waters, the whelk (*Baccinum* sp.) can be eaten or used as bait. Whelks are scavengers and carnivores. They hold onto their victim, usually a crab or lobster, using their large muscular foot. They then bore a hole through the shell using an extensible proboscis tipped with an abrasive radula, through which they feed.

◀ **whiting** The European whiting (*Merlangus merlangus*) is found primarily in the North Sea, where it feeds on invertebrates and small fish. It is an important commercial fish and congregates in large shoals.

W

itable export. After 1798 he manufactured muskets at a factory in New Haven, Connecticut, which was one of the first to use mass-production methods.

**Whitney, Mount** Highest peak in the US (excluding Alaska), at 14,495ft (4,418m). Situated on the E edge of SEQUOIA NATIONAL PARK, it is part of the Sierra Nevada range in E California.

**Whittier, John Greenleaf** (1807–92) US Quaker poet. His first work was the pastoral *Legends of New England* (1831). He was a leader of the abolitionist movement and a founder of the Republican Party. His political poems include *Voices of Freedom* (1846), and *Songs of Labor* (1850). His most famous work is *Snow-Bound* (1866).

**Whittington, Dick (Richard)** (1358–1423) English merchant. He became wealthy dealing in fine cloth and was lord mayor of London on several occasions (1397–1420). Whittington is, however, best known as the subject of a legend about a poor boy who makes his fortune with the aid of his cat.

**Whittle, Sir Frank** (1907–96) English inventor. In 1930 he patented the first turbojet (gas turbine) engine for aircraft. Whittle developed the engine while a test pilot in the Royal Air Force (RAF), but he was refused government support until the outbreak of World War II. By 1941 his first jet plane was flying and the first jets entered service with the RAF in 1944. *See also* JET ENGINE

**whooping cough** (pertussis) Acute, highly contagious childhood respiratory disease. It is caused by the bacterium *Bordetella pertussis* and is marked by spasms of coughing, followed by a long-drawn intake of air, or "whoop." It is frequently associated with vomiting and severe nosebleeds. Immunization reduces the number and severity of attacks.

**Whorf, Benjamin Lee** (1897–1941) US linguist and anthropologist. Whorf and Edward SAPIR developed the Sapir-Whorf hypothesis, which states that "the structure of language influences thought processes and our perception of the world around us."

**whortleberry** *See* BILBERRY

**Wichita** City in S central Kansas, at the confluence of the Arkansas and Little Arkansas rivers. Established (1864) as a trading post by James Mead and Jesse Chisholm, it developed with the arrival of the Chisholm Trail and the railroad (1872). It was incorporated in 1886. A cattle town and later a wheat center, its growth was spurred by the discovery of oil (1915) and the development of the aircraft industry (1920). It is the largest city in the state. Industries: aviation, railroad workshops, oil refining, grain processing, meat-packing. Pop. (1992) 311,746.

**Wicklow** County in Leinster province, E Republic of Ireland; the county town is Wicklow. The terrain is dominated by the Wicklow Mountains. The Liffey, Slaney, and Avoca are the chief rivers. Sheep and cattle are reared and cereals grown. The scenery attracts many tourists. Area: 782sq mi (2,025sq km). Pop. (1991) 97,265.

**Wieland, Heinrich Otto** (1877–1957) German chemist who was awarded the 1927 Nobel Prize for chemistry for his research into BILE acids. He showed them to have a STEROID skeleton and thus found that they were structurally related to CHOLESTEROL.

**Wiener, Norbert** (1894–1964) US mathematician and originator of CYBERNETICS. He contributed to the development of the COMPUTER and to feedback systems that control the behavior of humans and machines.

**Wiesbaden** City on the Rhine River at the foot of the Taunus Mountains, W central Germany; the capital of Hessen lande. Founded in the 3rd century BC and later a Roman spa town, the city is still famous for its mineral springs. Wiesbaden was capital of the Duchy of Nassau from 1806 to 1866, when it passed to Prussia. Industries: metal goods, chemicals, cement, plastics, tourism, publishing. Pop. (1993) 269,600.

**Wiesel, Elie** (1928– ) US novelist, b. Romania. The sole family survivor from the Nazi concentration camp at Auschwitz, he became a US citizen in 1963. His work is an attempt to ensure that the HOLOCAUST is not forgotten. Wiesel won the 1986 Nobel Peace Prize. His first three accounts of concentration camp survivors, *Night* (1958), *Dawn* (1960) and *The Accident* (1961), are collected as *The Night Trilogy*. Other novels include *The Town Beyond the Wall* (1962), *A Beggar in Jerusalem* (1968), *The Fifth Son* (1985), and *The Forgotten* (1989).

**Wight, Isle of** Island and county off the S coast of England, separated from the mainland (Hampshire) by the Solent. Newport is the county town. The island's mild climate and coastal scenery make it a popular tourist destination. Cowes, the major port, is a famous yachting center. Area: 147sq mi (318sq km). Pop. (1991) 124,577.

**Wigner, Eugene Paul** (1902–95) US physicist, b. Hungary. During World War II, he worked on the MANHATTAN PROJECT. Wigner was the first physicist to apply group theory to QUANTUM MECHANICS. He discovered the law of conservation of parity. For his work on the structure of the atomic NUCLEUS, Wigner shared the 1963 Nobel Prize for physics.

**wigwam** Shelter used by Native North Americans of the E woodlands area. Wigwams were made from bark, reed mats, or thatch, spread over a pole frame, and should not be confused with the conical, skin-covered tepees of the Native Americans of the Plains.

**Wilbur, Richard** (1921– ) US poet. His first volume was *The Beautiful Changes* (1947). Wilbur won two Pulitzer prizes: *Things of This World* (1956), and *New and Collected Poems* (1988).

**Wilde, Oscar** (1854–1900) (Oscar Fingal O'Flahertie Wills) Irish dramatist, poet, prose writer, and wit. A leader of the AESTHETIC MOVEMENT, he wrote only one novel, *The Picture of Dorian Grey* (1891). His short-story collections include the *Happy Prince and Other Tales* (1888). Wilde is best known for his drama, which combines social criticism with epigrammatic wit. His plays include *Lady Windermere's Fan* (1892), *A Woman of No Importance* (1893), *An Ideal Husband* (1895), and his masterpiece *The Importance of Being Earnest* (1895). In 1895 Wilde was convicted of homosexual practices and sentenced to two years' hard labor. While in prison, he wrote *The Ballad of Reading Gaol* (1898).

**wildebeest** *See* GNU

**Wilder, Billy** (1906– ) US film director and screenwriter, b. Germany. His partnership with Charles Brackett began with comedy scripts, such as *Ninotchka* (1939). *Double Indemnity* (1944) is a classic FILM NOIR. Wilder won Academy Awards for best director, best picture, and shared the best screenplay prize with Brackett for *The Lost Weekend* (1945). Their last collaboration, *Sunset Boulevard* (1950), also earned them an Oscar for best screenplay. His solo career proved just as successful, with films such as *The Seven Year Itch* (1955) and

► **Wilde** A supporter of the Esthetic movement, Oscar Wilde shocked and enthrallled London society with his flamboyant style and caustic wit. He gave an acclaimed lecture tour in the USA, where, when asked on his arrival at customs if he had anything to declare, he reputedly replied "Only my genius." He married in 1884 and had two sons. He was financially ruined by bringing an unsuccessful court case for libel, and was himself then prosecuted and convicted for homosexuality. He spent his final years living in effective exile in France.

*Some Like it Hot* (1959). Wilder won further Academy Awards for best picture and best director for *The Apartment* (1960).

**Wilder, Laura Ingalls** (1867–1957) US writer of the "Little House" series of eight books for children. Starting with *The Little House in the Big Woods* (1932), the stories relate her own childhood, growing up, and marriage in pioneer America. The books formed the basis of a successful television series.

**Wilder, Thornton Niven** (1897–1975) US playwright and novelist. He received the Pulitzer Prize for his second novel, *The Bridge of San Luis Rey* (1927), which examines the role of destiny in the death of five travelers when a bridge collapses near Lima. Other novels include the *Woman of Andros* (1930), *Heaven's My Destination* (1934), and *The Eighth Day* (1967). He won further Pulitzer prizes for his plays *Our Town* (1938) and *The Skin of Our Teeth* (1942).

**Wilderness Campaign** (May–June 1864) Series of battles in the CIVIL WAR, fought in woodland 50mi (80km) NW of Richmond, Virginia. In the first battle (May 5–6), Ulysses S. GRANT's Army of the Potomac was surprised by the advance of the Confederate Army of Northern Virginia led by Robert E. LEE. In the second battle (May 8–19), Grant's assault on Confederate lines was repulsed with great loss of life. By the beginning of June, both armies were on the outskirts of Richmond. The Battle of Cold Harbor (June 3, 1864) was one of the bloodiest battles of the war. The campaign cost 60,000 Union lives and 20,000 Confederate lives.

**Wilhelmina** (1880–1962) Queen of the Netherlands (1890–1948). She helped keep the country neutral in World War I and often intervened in political affairs. During World War II, she led the government in exile in England and became a symbol of Dutch independence. In 1848 she abdicated in favor of her daughter, Juliania.

**Wilkins, Maurice Hugh Frederick** (1916– ) English biophysicist. He shared the 1962 Nobel Prize for physiology or medicine with James D. WATSON and Francis CRICK for his x-ray diffraction studies that helped to determine the molecular structure of DNA.

**Wilkinson, Sir Geoffrey** (1921– ) English chemist. He shared the 1973 Nobel Prize for chemistry with Ernst Fisher for their independent research on organometallic compounds of transition metals. In these compounds, the metallic atom is "sandwiched" between two carbon rings.

**Wilkinson, James** (1757–1825) American general. He served in the AMERICAN REVOLUTION, but was forced to resign (1778) because of his role in the CONWAY CABAL. In 1784 Wilkinson moved to Kentucky and joined a conspiracy with the Spanish governor of Louisiana to gain trade monopolies for himself and to give Kentucky to Spain. When war broke out with Native Americans in Ohio, Wilkinson returned to active service under Anthony WAYNE. As governor of Louisiana (1805–06), he conspired with Aaron BURR to take a large segment of the West to form Burr's own republic. When Burr was brought to trial, Wilkinson became the chief prosecution witness and avoided prosecution. Returning to the army, he was quickly dismissed after failing to capture Montreal in the WAR OF 1812.

**will** In law, a clear expression of intent by a person (the testator) concerning the disposal of his or her effects after death. The testator must be of sound mind and legal age, and the will must be witnessed by two competent people who are not beneficiaries. It may be altered or revoked by the testator at any time, with due legal process.

**Willemstadt** Capital of NETHERLANDS ANTILLES, on Curaçao Island, West Indies. The city is a free port, exporting oil from Venezuela and coffee. Oil refining and tourism are major industries. It has the largest dry dock in the Americas. Pop. (1986) 50,100.

**William I** (1797–1888) King of Prussia (1861–88) and emperor of Germany (1871–88). He was regent for his brother, FREDERICK WILLIAM IV, from 1858. His suppression of revolution in 1848–49 earned him a reputation as a reactionary, but as king he displayed sensible pragmatism and followed the advice of his chief minister, Otto von BISMARCK. William supported the unification of Germany, but accepted his proclamation as emperor reluctantly, fearing a reduction in Prussia's status.

**William II** (1859–1941) Emperor of Germany (1888–1918). He modeled himself on his grandfather, WILLIAM I, but lacked his good sense. In 1890 he dismissed BISMARCK and assumed leadership of the government. His aggressive foreign policy, including the construction of a navy, antagonized Britain, France, and Russia. Many regard his policies as largely responsible for the outbreak of World War I (1914). During the war, William was exclusively concerned with military matters. He abdicated after the armistice (November 1918).

**William I (the Conqueror)** (1027–87) King of England (1066–87) and Duke of Normandy (1035–87). Supported initially by Henry I of France, he consolidated his position in Normandy against hostile neighbors. On the death of EDWARD THE CONFESSOR, he claimed the English throne, having allegedly gained the agreement of King HAROLD in 1064. He defeated and killed Harold at the Battle of HASTINGS (1066) and subsequently enforced his rule over the whole kingdom. He rewarded his followers by grants of land, eventually replacing almost the entire feudal ruling class, and intimidated potential rebels by rapid construction of castles. He invaded Scotland (1072), extracting an oath of loyalty from Malcolm III Canmore, and Wales (1081), although he spent much of his reign in France. He ordered the famous survey known as the DOMESDAY BOOK (1086).

**William II (Rufus)** (1056–1100) King of England (1087–1100). He was the second surviving son of WILLIAM I (THE CONQUEROR). His elder brother, Robert Curthose (Robert II), was Duke of Normandy, and William had to crush revolts by Anglo-Norman lords in Robert's favor. He invaded the duchy twice, and in 1096 Robert mortgaged it to him to raise cash for the First Crusade. He invaded Scotland, later killing Malcolm III (1093), and subdued Wales (1097). He was killed hunting, allegedly, though improbably, by accident.

**William III (of Orange)** (1650–1702) King of England, Scotland, and Ireland (1689–1702). He was born after the death of his father, William II, Prince of Orange, and succeeded him as ruler in effect of the United Provinces (Netherlands) in 1572. In 1677 he married MARY, daughter of JAMES II of England, and, following the GLORIOUS REVOLUTION (1688), he and Mary, strong Protestants, replaced the Catholic James II. They ruled jointly until her death in 1694. In 1699 he organized the alliance that was to defeat the French in the War of the SPANISH SUCCESSION. Never popular in England, William approved the BILL OF RIGHTS (1689) and other measures that diminished the royal prerogative.

**William IV** (1765–1837) King of Great Britain and Ireland and elector of Hanover (1830–37). Third son of GEORGE III, he succeeded, unexpectedly, aged 65 after a long career in the navy. Nicknamed "Silly Billy," he was well-meaning though unkingly. He assisted the passage of the Great Reform Bill (1832), by creating new peers to give the government a majority in the House of Lords.

**William I** (1772–1843) First king of the Netherlands (1815–40) whose kingdom included Belgium and Luxembourg. He fought in the French Revolutionary and Napoleonic Wars. His forceful government offended liberals and Roman Catholics, and a revolution in Belgium (1830) was followed by Belgian independence (1839). Compelled to accept a constitution restricting his powers, he abdicated in favor of his son, William II.

**William I (the Lion)** (1143–1214) King of Scotland (1165–1214). He succeeded his brother Malcolm IV and forged what was later called the "Auld Alliance" with France. Captured by the English during an attempt to regain Northumbria, he was forced to swear fealty to HENRY II (1174). He regained Scotland's independence from RICHARD I in return for a cash payment toward the Third Crusade in 1189. William the Lion established the independence of the church, under the pope, and strengthened royal authority in the north.

**William I (the Silent)** (1533–84) Prince of Orange, leader of the revolt of the Netherlands against Spanish rule. In 1572 he became the leader of a broad coalition in the Low Countries that opposed Spanish rule on the principle of religious tolerance. It broke down in 1579, when the Catholic s

▲ **Wilson** US president Woodrow Wilson strove to keep the US neutral during World War I, but was forced to declare war by unrestricted German submarine attacks on US ships. In his war message to Congress, he stated that "the world must be made safe for democracy," and his subsequent public speeches did much to consolidate national support behind the war effort.

W

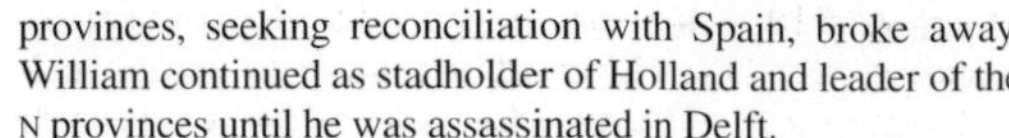

▲ **willow** The willows (family Salicaceae) are fairly small trees, the European willow growing to 35ft (10m). The seeds are light, wind dispersed, and contain little food. They often grow by water, where rapid germination is effected.

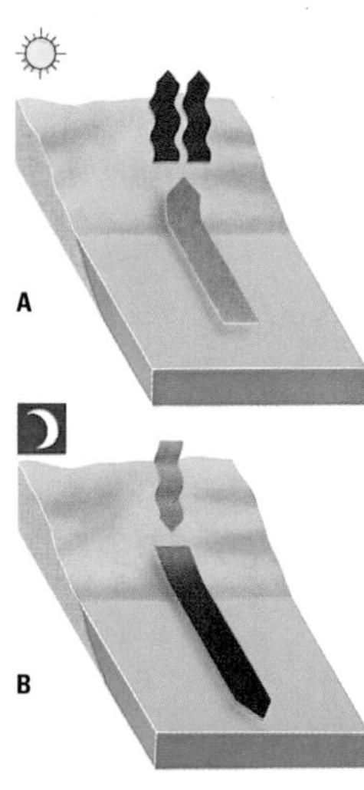


▲ **wind** Onshore winds (A) generally occur during the day. The land is heated by the Sun, causing the air over it to rise. As the warm air rises it is replaced by cooler air overlying the sea. At night, because the land loses heat more quickly than the sea, air flows down hillsides out to sea, where the air is relatively warmer, generating offshore breezes (B).



provinces, seeking reconciliation with Spain, broke away. William continued as stadholder of Holland and leader of the N provinces until he was assassinated in Delft.

**William of Occam** (1285–1349) English scholastic philosopher. Contributing to the development of formal LOGIC, he employed the principle of economy known as Occam's Razor; that is, a problem should be stated in its most basic terms. As a Franciscan monk, he upheld ideals of poverty against Pope John XXII and was excommunicated. In 1328 he was imprisoned in Avignon, France, but he escaped and fled to Munich, where he later died.

**Williams, Daniel Hale** (1858–1931) US surgeon. He organized the Provident Hospital, the first US hospital for blacks, and performed the first successful closure of a heart wound (1893).

**Williams, Ralph Vaughan** *See* VAUGHAN WILLIAMS, RALPH

**Williams, Roger** (1603–83) English Puritan minister. In 1631 he emigrated to the Massachusetts Bay colony. His radical politics and theology antagonized the Puritan authorities and he was expelled (1635). In 1636 Williams founded PROVIDENCE, the first settlement in RHODE ISLAND, on land purchased from the Narragansett. He returned to England and acquired a charter. Williams served (1654–57) as president of Rhode Island colony.

**Williams, Ted (Theodore Samuel)** (1918– ) US baseball player. He played as an outfielder for the Boston Red Sox for 19 seasons between 1939 and 1960. Williams won six American League batting titles and hit a total of 521 home runs at an average of .344. In 1941 he won the batting title with an average of .406, the last player to reach .400 in the major leagues.

**Williams, Tennessee (Thomas Lanier)** (1911–83) US playwright. His first Broadway play, *The Glass Menagerie* (1945), was awarded the New York Drama Critic's Circle Award. He received Pulitzer prizes for *A Streetcar Named Desire* (1947) and *Cat on a Hot Tin Roof* (1955). His other plays include *Suddenly Last Summer* (1958), *Sweet Bird of Youth* (1959), and *The Night of the Iguana* (1961). Many of his plays were set in the South, in a cloying and repressive environment that reflected the plight of the characters.

**Williams, William Carlos** (1883–1963) US poet. His deceptively simple style incorporates colloquial American. Williams' early work shows the influence of IMAGISM. His most monumental achievement was *Paterson* (1946–58), a five-volume epic of American life as seen in the microcosm of a New Jersey city. His *Pictures from Brueghel* (1962) won a posthumous Pulitzer Prize and his *Collected Poems* appeared in 1986–88.

**Williamsburg** Historic city in SE Virginia. It lies on a peninsula between the James and York rivers. Founded in 1633, Williamsburg was capital of Virginia from 1699 to 1779. The Virginia Resolution for American Independence was passed in the city in 1776. The Battle of Williamsburg (1862) was part of the PENINSULAR CAMPAIGN in the Civil War. In 1926 John D. Rockefeller Jr. provided for the restoration of the colonial city. Today, it is a major tourist site. Pop. (1990) 11,530.

**Willkie, Wendell Lewis** (1892–1944) US industrialist and politician. Although formerly a Democrat, he was a leader of business opposition to Franklin D. ROOSEVELT'S NEW DEAL. In 1940 he ran as the Republican candidate against Roosevelt. In his book *One World* (1943), he advocated the formation of a postwar world organization.

**will-o'-the-wisp** (Jack-o'-lantern) Mysterious light sometimes seen at night in marshy areas. It is thought to be due to the spontaneous combustion of METHANE.

**willow** DECIDUOUS shrub and tree native to cool or mountainous temperate regions. It has long, pointed leaves, and flowers borne on catkins. Familiar species include the weeping willow (*Salix babylonica*) with drooping branches, and pussy willow (*S. caprea*) with fuzzy catkins. Family Salicaceae.

**willow herb** *See* FIREWEED

**Wills, Helen Newington** (1906–98) (Helen Wills Moody) US tennis player. Wills won eight Wimbledon titles (1927–30, 1932–33, 1935, 1938), seven US Opens (1923–25, 1927–29, 1931) and four French Opens (1928–30, 1932). She also oversaw a change to more functional dress in women's tennis.

**Wilmington** City in N Delaware, at the junction of the Delaware and Christina rivers and Brandywine Creek. The first settlement in Delaware (1638), Wilmington was founded by Swedes. It was later enlarged by Dutch and British settlers and became the state's largest city. It is an important industrial center with shipyards, railroad shops, and chemical manufacturing plants. Pop. (1992) 72,411.

**Wilson, August** (1945– ) African-American playwright. He has written a series of plays which chronicle the black experience in the 20th century, including *Ma Rainey's Black Bottom* (1984). He has won two Pulitzer prizes for *Fences* (1987) and *The Piano Lesson* (1988).

**Wilson, Charles Thomson Rees** (1869–1959) English physicist who invented the Wilson cloud chamber used to study radioactivity, x-rays, and cosmic rays. It uses water droplets to track ions left by passing radiation. For this invention, he shared the 1927 Nobel Prize for physics with Arthur COMPTON.

**Wilson, Edmund** (1895–1972) US literary critic and writer. He was editor of *Vanity Fair* (1920–21), associate editor of *The New Republic* (1926–31), and regular critic for *The New Yorker* (1944–48). Wilson was married (1938–46) to Mary MCCARTHY. His highly influential critical work includes *Axel's Castle* (1931) on SYMBOLISM; *To the Finland Station* (1940) on the origins of the Russian Revolution; and *Patriotic Gore* (1962) on the literature of the Civil War

**Wilson, Sir (James) Harold** (1916–95) (Baron Wilson of Rievaulx) British statesman, prime minister (1964–70, 1974–76). Wilson entered Parliament in 1945. In 1951 he resigned from Clement ATTLEE'S cabinet. In 1963 Wilson succeeded Hugh GAITSKELL as Labour leader. In 1964 he won a narrow general election victory. His administration was faced with Rhodesia's unilateral declaration of independence and domestic recession. Wilson was forced to impose strict price and income controls and devalue sterling. In the 1970 general election he was defeated by Edward HEATH. Conflict between Labour's left- and right-wing over nationalization and membership of the European Economic Community (EUROPEAN COMMUNITY) threatened to divide the party. In 1974, however, Wilson returned to power at the head of a minority Labour government. In 1976 he unexpectedly resigned and was succeeded by Jim CALLAGHAN. In 1983 he was made a life peer.

**Wilson, (Thomas) Woodrow** (1856–1924) 28th US president (1913–21). As governor of New Jersey (1910–12), he gained a reputation as a progressive Democrat. In 1912 he unexpectedly gained the Democratic nomination. The split in the Republican vote between TAFT'S REPUBLICAN PARTY and Theodore ROOSEVELT'S PROGRESSIVE PARTY handed Wilson the presidency. His "New Freedom" reforms included the establishment of the FEDERAL RESERVE SYSTEM (1913). Several amendments to the US CONSTITUTION were introduced, including PROHIBITION (18th, 1919) and the extension of the FRANCHISE to women (19th, 1920). The MEXICAN REVOLUTION brought instability to the S border, and Wilson ordered John PERSHING'S intervention. Wilson's efforts to maintain US neutrality at the start of WORLD WAR I aided his reelection in 1916. The failure of diplomacy and continuing attacks on US shipping forced Wilson to declare war (April 1917) on Germany. His FOURTEEN POINTS (January 1918) represented US war aims and became the basis of the peace negotiations at the VERSAILLES peace conference (1919). Wilson was forced to compromise in the final settlement, but succeeded in securing the establishment of the LEAGUE OF NATIONS. Domestic opposition to the League was led by Henry Cabot LODGE, and the Republican-dominated Senate rejected it. In October 1919 Wilson suffered a stroke and became an increasingly marginal figure for the remainder of his term.

**Wiltshire** County in central S England. Trowbridge is the county town. Dominated by Salisbury Plain and the Marlborough Downs, much of this rural county is given over to agriculture. Tourists are attracted by the county's many historic sites: STONEHENGE and Avebury Hill are England's oldest monuments, built more than 4,000 years ago. Swindon, the main manufacturing center, is one of the fastest-growing cities in England. Industries: textiles, farm machinery, food processing, electrical goods. Area: 1,344sq mi (3,481sq km). Pop. (1991) 564,471.

**Wimbledon** Popular name for the All England Lawn Tennis Championships played annually at the All England Club, Wimbledon, SW London. It is the world's leading grass-court championship. It was first held in 1877 and was open only to amateurs until 1968. The championships have been held at the present site since 1922.

**winch** Drum that turns to pull or release a rope, cable, or chain. A winch is used to raise, lower, or pull heavy loads. The device may be motor-driven or operated by hand.

**Winchester** County town of Hampshire, S central England, on the Itchen River.. It became capital of the Anglo-Saxon kingdom of WESSEX in 519 AD. During the reign of ALFRED THE GREAT, it was capital of England. Despite the growth of London, Winchester retained its importance as a center of learning and religion throughout the medieval period. Much of the old city remains, including the ruins of a Norman castle. Pop. (1991) 96,386.

**wind** Air current that moves rapidly parallel to the Earth's surface. (Air currents in vertical motion are called updrafts or downdrafts.) Wind direction is indicated by wind or weather vanes, wind speed by ANEMOMETERS, and wind force by the BEAUFORT WIND SCALE. Steady winds in the tropics are called TRADE WINDS. MONSOONS are seasonal winds that bring predictable rains in Asia. Foehns (föhns) are warm, dry winds that are reproduced by compression accompanied by temperature rise as air descends the lee of mountainous areas in the Alps; a similar wind called CHINOOK exists in the Rockies. SIROCCOS are hot, humid Mediterranean winds.

**Windhoek** Capital and largest city of Namibia. In 1892 it was made the capital of the new German colony of South-West Africa. In 1990 Windhoek became capital of the independent Namibia. It is an important market for karakul sheepskins. Industries: diamonds, copper, meat packing. Pop. (1992) 126,000.

**wind instruments** Musical instruments that are sounded by blowing, which sets the air inside them vibrating. They may be classified into two types: WOODWIND and BRASS.

**windmill** Machine powered by the wind acting on sails or vanes. Windmills were built in the Middle East in the 7th century. The idea spread to Europe in the Middle Ages. Their use was widespread during the INDUSTRIAL REVOLUTION, but declined with the development of the STEAM ENGINE in the 19th century. *See also* RENEWABLE ENERGY; WIND POWER

**window** In computing, a rectangle visible on the screen of a computer that displays what is stored in part of the machine's memory or some other storage device. A window may show text, graphics, or other work in progress. The contents of a window are shown in text, often accompanied by symbols called icons.

**windpipe** *See* TRACHEA

**wind power** Harnessing of wind energy to produce power. Since the 1970s, advanced aerodynamic designs have been used to build wind turbines that generate electricity. The largest of these, on Hawaii, has two blades, each 160ft (50m) long, attached to a 20-story high tower. Individual turbines are often grouped in strategic locations (wind farms) to maximize the generating potential. Wind power is a cheap form of RENEWABLE ENERGY, but cannot as yet produce sufficiently large amounts of electricity to provide a realistic alternative to fossil fuel and nuclear power stations. *See also* WINDMILL

**Windsor, Duke of** *See* EDWARD VIII

**Windsor Castle** English royal residence, 20mi (32km) W of London. It was founded by WILLIAM I to defend the Thames valley. Much renovated, it retains the appearance of a medieval fortress.

**wind tunnel** Chamber in which scale models or full-size vehicles are tested in a controlled airflow. Some wind tunnels can reproduce extreme conditions of wind speed, temperature, and pressure. Structures are tested to check that winds cannot set up destructive vibrations.

**Windward Islands** Southern group of the Lesser ANTILLES islands, SE West Indies. They extend from the Leeward Islands to the NE coast of Venezuela. The principal islands are MARTINIQUE, GRENADA, DOMINICA, ST. LUCIA, ST. VINCENT AND THE GRENADINES group. The islands, volcanic in origin, are generally mountainous and forested. Crops include bananas, spices, limes, and cacao, but tourism is the leading industry. The islands were inhabited by the indigenous Carib until colonization began in the 17th century. The next two centuries witnessed a struggle for control between France and Britain. Britain came to control all the islands, except Martinique.

**wine** Alcoholic beverage made from the fermented juice (and some solid extracts) of fruits, herbs, and flowers – but classically from the juice and skins of grapes. The three standard grape wine colorations are white, red, and rosé, depending on the grape used and whether, and for how long, the grape skins are left on. For **white** wine, the grapes are fermented without the skin; for **red** wine, the whole grape is used; for **rosé** wine, the skins are removed after fermentation has begun. Dry wines are fermented until all the sugar has turned to alcohol; sweet wines are fermented for less time so that some sugar remains. Champagne is bottled while it is still fermenting. Table wines contain 7–15% alcohol by volume; fortified wines such as SHERRY contain added BRANDY, giving a 16–23% alcohol content.

**Winfrey, Oprah** (1954– ) US television talk-show host. She worked as a news reporter before anchoring the "A.M. Chicago Show" in 1984. Renamed "The Oprah Winfrey Show," it enjoyed great success. She also received an Academy Award nomination for Best Actress in the film *The Color Purple* (1985).

**wings** In biology, specialized organs for flight, which are possessed by most birds, many insects, and certain mammals and reptiles. The forelimbs of a bird have developed into such structures. Bats have membranous tissue supported by the digits ("fingers") of the forelimbs. Insects may have one or two pairs of veined or membranous wings.

**Winnebago** Native American band that in the 1820s and 1830s ceded its tribal lands in SW Wisconsin and NW Illinois to the US government. Linguistically part of the Siouan language group, the tribe's 3,000 members live mostly in reservations in Nebraska and Wisconsin.

**Winnipeg** Capital of Manitoba, Canada, at the confluence of the Assiniboine and Red rivers, in the far S of the province. Founded in 1812 by the HUDSON'S BAY COMPANY, the town grew after the completion of the Canadian Pacific Railroad (1882), and is now the major city of the Canadian

**WIND POWER**

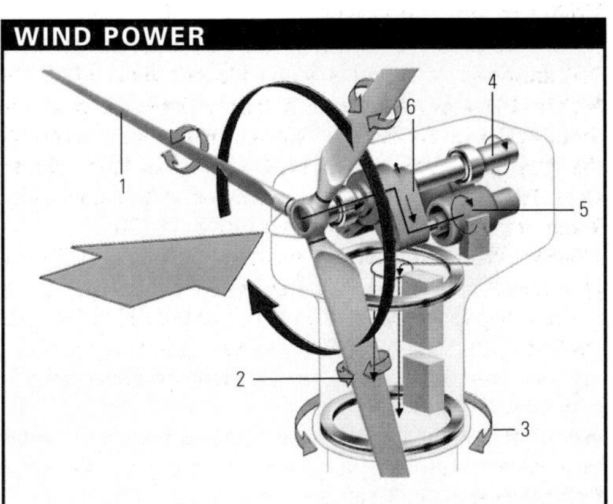


A wind generator converts the energy of the wind into electricity. Three-bladed variable pitch designs are the most efficient. Variable pitch means the attitude of the blades (1) can be changed. By altering the pitch (2) of the blades they can generate at maximum efficiency in varying wind conditions. The whole rotor assembly rotates (3) into the wind. The blades turn a prop shaft (4) that links to a generator (5) through gearing (6). The largest wind farms have thousands of linked turbines and can produce the same power as a fossil fuel power station.

W

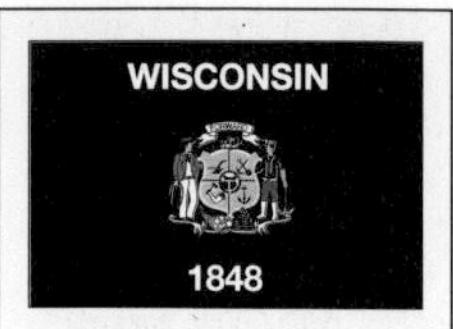


**WISCONSIN**
**Statehood:**
May 29, 1848
**Nickname:**
The Badger State
**State bird:**
Robin
**State flower:**
Wood violet
**State tree:**
Sugar maple
**State motto:**
Forward

prairies. It has one of the largest wheat markets in the world and vast flour mills, grain elevators, and food-processing plants. Pop. (1991) 616,790.

**Winnipeg, Lake** Lake in S central Manitoba province, the third-largest in Canada. It was used extensively by early fur traders and explorers in the 18th century. Fed by the Red, Saskatchewan, and Winnipeg rivers, and drained by the Nelson River to Hudson Bay, it is believed to be a remnant of the glacial Lake Agassiz. Area: 9,465sq mi (24,514sq km).

**Winston-Salem** City in central North Carolina. Salem was settled in 1766 by Moravians, and in 1849 land (later called Winston) was purchased from Moravians for the seat of the newly established Forsyth County; the two communities united in 1913. It is the chief tobacco manufacturing center in the US, and also produces furniture and textiles. Pop. (1992) 144,791.

**Winthrop, John** (1588–1649) Puritan colonist and theocratic governor of the MASSACHUSETTS BAY COLONY. As governor, he led 700 colonists to Salem (1630) and later to Charlestown and Boston. He was governor for 12 years (1630–34, 1637–40, 1642–44, 1646–49) and also served as president of the New England Confederation.

**wire** Strand of metal, made by drawing a rod through progressively smaller holes in metal dies. The drawing process toughens STEEL, so that a CABLE made from steel wire is much stronger than an undrawn steel rod of the same diameter. Copper and aluminum wires are used to make electric cables. If flexibility is important, each conductor is made of several fine strands of wire.

**wireworm** Long, cylindrical larva of the click beetle of N temperate woodlands. It is generally brown or yellow and is distinctly segmented. Most species live in the soil, and may cause serious damage to the roots of cultivated crops. Family Elateridae. *See also* MILLIPEDE

**Wisconsin** State in the N central US, SW of the GREAT LAKES and E of the Mississippi River. MADISON is the state capital and MILWAUKEE the largest city. The land is rolling plain that slopes gradually down from the N. There are numerous glacial lakes. The French claimed the region in 1634. Wisconsin was an important center in the fur trade and was ceded to Britain at the end of the FRENCH AND INDIAN WARS (1763). In 1783 it was ceded to the US. Settlement increased after the Black Hawk War (1832) ended Native American resistance. The Territory of Wisconsin was established in 1836 and admitted to the Union in 1848. Wisconsin is the leading US producer of milk, butter, and cheese, and the chief crops are hay, corn, oats, fruit, and vegetables. The state's most valuable resource, however, is timber: 45% of the land is forested. Mineral deposits include zinc, lead, copper, iron, sand, and gravel. Industries: farm machinery, brewing, tourism. Area: 56,154sq mi (145,438sq km). Pop. (1992) 4,992,664.

**wisdom literature** Collection of writings and sayings in the Hebrew Bible. From the Old Testament it includes the Books of Proverbs, Ecclesiastes, and Job, and the Song of Solomon, and from the Apocrypha it includes the Books of Ecclesiasticus and the Wisdom of Solomon.

**Wise, Stephen Samuel** (1874–1949) US rabbi of Reform Judaism and leader of the Zionist movement, b. Hungary. In 1907 he founded the Free Synagogue in New York to create a pulpit that was free from restraints. He was a founder of the Zionist Organization of America and of the American Jewish Congress. In 1922 he founded the Jewish Institute of Religion in New York.

**wisent** *See* BISON

**wisteria** Genus of hardy, woody vines, native to North America, Japan, and China. They have showy, fragrant, pendulous flower clusters of purplish-white, pink, or blue. Family Fabaceae/Leguminosae.

**witchcraft** Exercise of supernatural occult powers, usually due to some inherent power, rather than to an acquired skill such as sorcery. In Europe it originated in pagan cults and in mystical philosophies such as GNOSTICISM, which believed in the potency of both good and evil in the universe. In some societies, the belief in spirits is associated with attempts to control them through witchcraft for harmful or beneficial ends.

▲ **wolf** The shy, nocturnal maned wolf (*Chrysocyon brachyurus*) is found in deciduous forests and plains of South America. As with other plains predators, it feeds on almost anything from small animals to fruit. It is not a true wolf, however, but a member of the canine family.

**witch doctor** See SHAMAN

**Witt, Jan de** (1625–72) Dutch political leader. A republican and opponent of the House of Orange, he became grand pensionary and effectively head of government in 1653. He defeated the English in the second of the DUTCH WARS (1665–67). In 1672 he resigned after a French invasion and the accession of WILLIAM OF ORANGE as stadholder.

**Wittenberg** Town on the Elbe River, Sachsen-Anhalt state, E central Germany. Founded by Frederick III, its university became the cradle of the Protestant REFORMATION during the time Martin LUTHER and Philip MELANCHTHON were teaching there. Today, it is primarily a mining and industrial centre, producing chemicals, rubber goods, and machinery. Pop. (1993) 47,200.

**Wittgenstein, Ludwig** (1889–1951) Austrian philosopher. His masterwork, *Tractatus Logico-philosophicus* (1921), influenced LOGICAL POSITIVISM, positing the strict relationships between language and the physical world. After 1929 he criticized this hypothesis and these second thoughts were posthumously published in *Philosophical Investigations* (1953), in which he claimed that language was only a conventional "game," in which meaning was affected more by context than by formal relationships to reality.

**Witwatersrand** (Rand) Series of parallel mountain ranges more than 5,000ft (1,500m) high, forming a watershed between the Vaal and Olifant rivers, in S former TRANSVAAL, NE South Africa. The region extends *c.*62mi (100km) E and W of Johannesburg. Gold was first discovered in 1884. Witwatersrand produces about one third of the total world output of gold.

**Wodehouse, P.G. (Sir Pelham Grenville)** (1881–1975) English novelist and short-story writer. He began his career writing lyrics for musicals by, among others, Cole Porter and George Gershwin. Wodehouse wrote more than 100 humorous books, set in genteel Edwardian society. His most enduring creations are Bertie Wooster and his valet Jeeves, who first appeared in *The Man with Two Left Feet* (1917). During World War II, his ill-advised radio broadcasts from Berlin outraged British public opinion. In 1955 he became a US citizen.

**Woden** *See* ODIN

**Wöhler, Friedrich** (1800–82) German chemist who first isolated ALUMINUM and BERYLLIUM and discovered calcium carbide. In 1828 his synthesis of UREA (from the inorganic substance ammonium cyanate) was the first synthesis of an organic chemical compound from an inorganic one; it contributed to the foundation of modern organic chemistry.

**Wolf, Hugo** (1860–1903) Austrian composer, generally regarded as one of the finest composers of *Lieder*. He produced five "songbooks" setting poems by Mörike (1888), Eichendorff (1888–89), Goethe (1888–89), Spanish authors (1889–90), and Italian poets (1891, 1896), the last two in German translation.

**wolf** Doglike, carnivorous mammal, once widespread in the US and Eurasia, especially the gray wolf (*Canis lupus*), which is now restricted to the US and Asia. It is powerfully built with a wide head and neck, muscular limbs, large feet, and a deep-chested body; the tail is long and bushy. It has earned a reputation for savagery and cunning from attacks on livestock and human beings. Length: to 6.6ft (2m), including the tail. Family Canidae.

**Wolfe, James** (1727–59) British general. He commanded the force that captured Quebec by scaling the cliffs above the St. Lawrence River and defeating the French, under MONTCALM, on the Plains of Abraham (1759). This victory resulted in Britain's acquisition of Canada. Wolfe's death in action made him a hero.

**Wolfe, Thomas Clayton** (1900–38) US writer. His reputation rests on his sequence of four sprawling autobiographical novels, *Look Homeward, Angel* (1929), *Of Time and the River* (1935), *The Web and the Rock* (1939), and *You Can't Go Home Again* (1940).

**Wolfe, Tom (Thomas Kennerley)** (1931– ) US journalist and novelist. Wolfe established his reputation with his "New Journalism" essays on US counterculture, such as *The Electric Kool-Aid Acid-Test* (1968). His first novel,

*The Bonfire of the Vanities* (1987), was set in New York and was a biting satire on the materialist society.

**wolffish** Voracious fish that lives in the N waters of the Atlantic Ocean. It is brown or gray with long fins along its back and belly, and powerful jaws and teeth. It is valued as a food fish in Iceland, where its skin is made into leather. Length: 3ft (91cm). Family Anarhichadidae; species *Anarhichas lupus*.

**wolfram** *See* TUNGSTEN

**wolframite** ((FeMn)$WO_4$, iron-manganese tungstate) Black to brown mineral. It is the chief ore of the metal TUNGSTEN. It occurs as crystals in the monoclinic system, or as granular masses. It is found in quartz veins and pegmatites associated with granitic rocks, and also in hydrothermal veins. Hardness 5–5.5; sp.gr. 7–7.5

**Wolfram von Eschenbach** (1170–1220) German poet. His only complete work is the Middle High German epic *Parzival*. A masterpiece of medieval literature, it introduced the Grail legend into German.

**Wollongong** City and port in New South Wales, Australia, 40mi (65km) S of Sydney. The area was settled in 1815, and Wollongong became a major exporter of grain and coal and a large iron and steel center. Port Kembla has Australia's biggest steelworks. Other industries: chemicals, textiles, copper. Pop. (1994) 251,400

**Wollstonecraft, Mary** (1759–97) English author. Her *Vindication of the Rights of Women* (1792) was FEMINISM's first great work. She was the mother of Mary Wollstonecraft SHELLEY.

**Wolof** People of Senegal who speak a language belonging to the W Atlantic group of the NIGER-CONGO family. In the 15th century a Wolof empire dominated West Africa and traded in slaves with the Portuguese. They were converted to ISLAM in the 18th century.

**Wolsey, Thomas** (1475–1530) English cardinal and statesman, lord chancellor (1515–29). After the accession of HENRY VIII (1509), Wolsey became archbishop of York (1514) and then cardinal and lord chancellor. As chancellor, he controlled virtually all state business. Wolsey's attempts to place England at the centre of European diplomacy ended in failure. Despite becoming papal legate (1518), his ambition to become pope was never realized. Domestically, he made powerful enemies through his method of raising taxes through forced loans, his conspicuous wealth, and his pluralism. Wolsey gave HAMPTON COURT PALACE to Henry VIII, but his failure to obtain the king a divorce from CATHERINE OF ARAGON brought about his downfall. Thomas MORE replaced Wolsey as chancellor. Charged with high treason, he died before his trial.

**wolverine** Solitary, ferocious mammal, native to pine forests of the US and Eurasia, the largest member of the WEASEL family. Dark brown, with lighter bands along the sides and neck, it has a bushy tail and large feet. Length: 36in (91cm); weight: 66lb (30kg). Species *Gulo gulo*.

**WOODCUT**

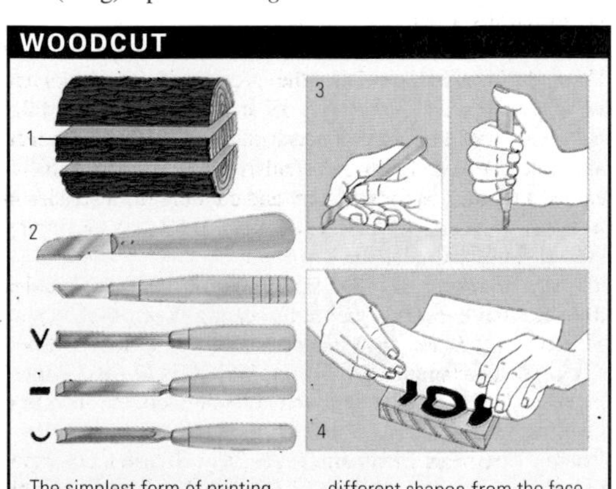


The simplest form of printing, woodcuts are produced by carving a design in relief on wood. A flat piece of wood is needed from the center of a log (1). Various different tools (2) are then used to cut different shapes from the face of the wood (3) and achieve the desired design. The wood is then rolled with ink, and pressed against paper (4). The resulting print appears as a negative image of the carving.

◄ **woodpecker** The ivory-billed woodpecker (*Campephilus principalis*) is the largest of the North American woodpeckers and is one of the rarest birds in the world. It is believed to be nearly extinct now; any that remain are thought to inhabit swamp forests in SE US and Cuba. Native American chiefs once adorned their belts with its bill and plumes, but tree felling has now removed most of the big trees in which it breeds.

**Woman's Christian Temperance Union (WCTU)** Organization formed to oppose the manufacture and use of alcoholic beverages. It was founded (1874) in Cleveland, Ohio. Its object is to educate the public against the abuses of liquor and it became an important woman's pressure group devoted to many types of social reform. Frances Willard, president of WCTU (1879–98), made it an international society in 1883.

**wombat** Either of two species of large, rodentlike marsupial mammals of SE Australia and Tasmania. Both species are herbivorous, primarily nocturnal, and live in extensive burrows. The common wombat (*Vombatus ursinus*) has coarse black hair and small ears. The hairy-nosed wombat (*Lasiorhinus latifrons*) has finer, gray fur, and large ears. Length: to 4ft (1.2m). Family Vombatidae.

**women's rights movement** Broad term for the international movement that began in the early 19th century, and which promotes and works for the equality of women. Originally concentrating on women's suffrage, the movement has since worked for equality of employment opportunity and pay, freedom from unjust social, political, and theological expectations, and an awakening of physical, intellectual, and emotional awareness for women. *See also* FEMINISM; SUFFRAGETTE MOVEMENT

**Wonder, Stevie** (1950– ) US SOUL singer and songwriter, b. Steveland Judkins Morris. Blind from birth, Wonder played the harmonica, keyboard, guitar and drums. In 1961 he joined MOTOWN Records. His first record was *Little Stevie Wonder* (1962). Other albums include *Talking Book* (1972), *Innervisions* (1973), *Songs in the Key of Life* (1976), and *Hotter Than July* (1980).

**Wood, Leonard** (1860–1927) US general and administrator. In the Spanish-American War, he led a volunteer cavalry unit, known as the Rough Riders. Wood was military governor (1899–1902) of Cuba. He called for military preparedness at the start of World War I. Wood served as governor general (1921–27) of the Philippines.

**wood** Hard substance that forms the trunks of trees; it is the XYLEM which comprises the bulk of the stems and roots, supporting the plant. Wood consists of fine, cellular tubes arranged vertically within the trunk, which accounts for its grain. The relatively soft, light-colored wood is called **sapwood**. The nonconducting, older, darker wood is called **heartwood**, and is generally filled with RESIN, gums, mineral salts, and TANNIN. The two chief types are softwoods, from CONIFERS such as PINE, and hardwoods from deciduous species such as OAK. Wood is commonly used as a building material, fuel, to make some types of PAPER, and as a source of CHARCOAL, CELLULOSE, ESSENTIAL OIL, LIGNIN, tannins, dyes, and SUGAR.

**woodchuck** (groundhog) MARMOT found from Alaska to the Gulf States, having grizzled black-brown hair. Using its sharp front teeth and short, strong legs, it digs burrows. It feeds heavily in autumn before hibernating. The woodchuck eats plants, often becoming a garden pest. Length: 2ft (61cm); Weight: to 14lb (6.3kg). Species *Marmota monax*.

**woodcock** Any of five species of reddish-brown shorebirds that nest in cool parts of the Northern Hemisphere and winter in warm areas. Both the Eurasian *Scolopax rusticola* and American *Philohela minor* insert their long, sensitive, flexible bills into swampy ground to find worms. Length: to 14in (34cm). Family Scolopacidae.

**woodcut** Oldest method of printing, using designs carved into wood. The carving produces a negative image, the carved areas representing blank spaces while the flat areas retain the

▲ **woodwind** The woodwind family of musical instruments is an important grouping in the modern orchestra. Shown above are the reed instruments: the bassoon (A), oboe (B), English horn (C), clarinet (D), and bass clarinet (E). The saxophone is sometimes included in this group. Sound is produced by the vibration of an air column, which is set in motion by the movement of the reed. Altering the length of the vibrating column, by closing or opening holes on the body of the instrument, produces different notes.

W

ink. Woodcuts were invented in China in the 5th century AD and became popular in Europe in the Middle Ages.

**wood engraving** Print made by incising a design on the flat, polished (cross-grain) transverse section of a block of hardwood. Textural and linear effects can be achieved by varying the pressure and direction of the cutting strokes. This technique developed from the less-sophisticated WOODCUT in 18th-century England.

**wood louse** (sowbug) Terrestrial, isopod crustacean found in damp conditions worldwide. It has an oval, segmented body, feeds mainly on vegetable matter, and retains its eggs in a brood pouch. Length: 0.75in (20mm). Order Isopoda; Genus *Oniscus*.

**woodpecker** Tree-climbing bird found nearly worldwide. Woodpeckers have strong pointed beaks and long, protrudable tongues, which in some species often have harpoonlike tips for extracting insect larvae. They have two toes pointing forward, and black, red, white, yellow, brown, or green plumage; some are crested. The tail is stiff and helps to support the bird's body when pressed against a tree trunk. Family Picidae.

**Woods, Tiger** (1975– ) US golfer. He won the US amateur championship three times (1994, 1995, 1996) before turning professional. In 1997 Woods became not only the youngest player to win a Masters, but also the first black man to do so. By 1998 he was ranked no.1 in the world.

**Woodstock** Name given to a music festival held between 15 and 17 August 1969 near Bethel, SW of Woodstock, New York. Forced to shift from the original location because of residents' protests, *c*.450,000 people arrived for the free outdoor concert. It was a celebration of both the music and aspirations of the hippie generation.

**Woodward, Robert Burns** (1917–79) US chemist. He was awarded the 1965 Nobel Prize for chemistry in recognition of his synthesis of a number of complex organic substances, including quinine, cholesterol, cortisone, strychnine, lysergic acid, reserpine, chlorophyll, and tetracycline.

**woodwind** Family of musical wind instruments that are traditionally made of wood but now often metal. They are played by means of a mouthpiece containing one or two reeds. The FLUTE and PICCOLO, however, are exceptional in that they are played by blowing across a hole. Other woodwind instruments include the CLARINET (single reed) and the OBOE, ENGLISH HORN, and BASSOON (all double reed). SAXOPHONES are also part of the woodwind family.

**woodworm** (furniture beetle) Larva of various species of beetles that burrow in wood. Woodworms can cause extensive damage. Their presence can be detected by holes in wood from which the adult beetles have emerged. Genera include *Anobium* and *Lyctus*.

**wool** Soft, generally white, brown, or black animal fiber that forms the fleece of sheep. Wool is also the name of the yarns and textiles made from the fibers after spinning, dyeing, and weaving. The fibers, composed chiefly of KERATIN, are treated to remove a fat called lanolin, which is used in some ointments.

**Woolf, Virginia** (1882–1941) English novelist and critic. Her novels, which often use the STREAM OF CONSCIOUSNESS style associated with MODERNISM, include *Mrs Dalloway* (1925), *To the Lighthouse* (1927), *Orlando* (1928), and *The Waves* (1931). *Between the Acts*, her last novel, was published posthumously. A member of the BLOOMSBURY GROUP, her long essay *A Room of One's Own* (1929) is a key text of feminist criticism. Her critical essays, including *Modern Novels* (1919) and *The Common Reader* (1925), are integral to modern literary theory.

**Woolworth, Frank Winfield** (1862–1919) US merchant. In 1879 he opened his first shop in Utica, New York. By the time of his death, he owned a chain of more than 1,000 stores. The Woolworth Building (1913), New York, was the world's tallest building, at 792ft (241m).

**Worcester** County town of Hereford and Worcester, on the Severn River, W central England. There is a cathedral dating from the 13th and 14th centuries. The Battle of Worcester (1651) was the last engagement of the English CIVIL WAR. Industries: Royal Worcester porcelain, Worcester sauce, shoes. Pop. (1991) 81,700.

**word processor** COMPUTER system used for compiling and printing text. The system may be designed just for this purpose, in which case it is called a dedicated word processor. More common is a general-purpose personal computer running a word-processing program. Text typed on the keyboard is displayed on the screen. Any errors are easily corrected before a "printout" is produced. The text can be stored on a magnetic disk for future use.

**Wordsworth, William** (1770–1850) English poet. He collaborated with Samuel Taylor COLERIDGE on *Lyrical Ballads* (1798). The collection concluded with his poem "Tintern Abbey." Wordsworth's preface to the second edition (1800) outlined the aims of English ROMANTICISM, which through the use of everyday language enabled "the spontaneous overflow of powerful feelings." Critics derided his style. In 1799 he and his sister Dorothy moved to the Lake District; his poetry always bound up with a love of nature. *The Prelude*, a long autobiographical poem, was completed in 1805 but only published posthumously in 1850. After *Poems in Two Volumes* (1807), which includes "Ode: Intimations of Immortality", it is generally recognized that his creativity declined. In 1843 he succeeded Robert SOUTHEY as poet laureate.

**work** In physics, energy transferred in moving a force. It equals the magnitude of the force multiplied by the distance moved in the direction of the force. If the force opposing movement is the object's weight $mg$ (where $m$ is the object's mass and g is the acceleration due to gravity), the work done in raising it a height $h$ is $mgh$. This work has been transferred in the form of POTENTIAL ENERGY; if the object falls a distance, the KINETIC ENERGY at the bottom of the fall equals the work done in raising it.

**Works Progress Administration (WPA)** Former US government agency, created (1935) under Franklin ROOSEVELT's NEW DEAL policy to stimulate national economic recovery. Billions of dollars were contributed to the scheme in which work programs provided jobs for the unemployed. About two million people were registered on WPA rolls at any one time between 1935 and 1941.

**World Bank** (International Bank for Reconstruction and Development (IBRD)) Intergovernmental organization based in Washington D.C. A specialized agency of the UNITED NATIONS since 1945, its role is to make long-term loans to member governments to aid their economic development. The major part of the Bank's resources are derived from the world's capital markets.

**World Council of Churches** International fellowship of Christian churches formed (1948) in Amsterdam, Netherlands. Its aim is to work for the reunion of all Christian churches and to establish a united Christian presence in the world. The headquarters of the council are in Geneva, Switzerland. Its membership consists of some 300 churches. The Roman Catholic Church is not a member, but has been sending observers to assemblies of the World Council of Churches since 1961.

**World Health Organization (WHO)** Intergovernmental, specialized agency of the UNITED NATIONS. Founded in 1948, it collects and shares medical and scientific information and promotes international standards for drugs and vaccines. WHO has made major contributions to the prevention of diseases such as malaria, polio, leprosy and tuberculosis, and the eradication of smallpox. Its headquarters are in Geneva, Switzerland.

W

► **World War I** The infantry of the British 15th Brigade on July 9th, 1918, under direct observation of the enemy near Morlancourt, Belgium, keep low down in the trenches. They are here seen at a bomb crater so close to the enemy lines that they could hear the Germans talking while the picture was being taken.

**World Trade Organization (WTO)** Body sponsored by the UNITED NATIONS to regulate international TRADE. The WTO was established on January 1, 1995 to replace the GENERAL AGREEMENT ON TARIFFS AND TRADE (GATT). The WTO took over GATT's rules with increased powers to regulate agriculture, clothing and textiles, intellectual property rights, and services.

**World War I** (1914–18) (Great War) International conflict precipitated by the assassination of the Austrian Archduke Francis FERDINAND by Serbs in Sarajevo (June 28, 1914). Austria declared war on Serbia (July 28), Russia mobilized in support of Serbia (from July 29), Germany declared war on Russia (August 1) and France (August 3), and Britain declared war on Germany (August 4). World War I resulted from growing tensions in Europe, exacerbated by the rise of the German empire since 1871 and the decline of Ottoman power in the Balkans. The chief contestants were the Central Powers (Germany and Austria) and the Triple Entente (Britain, France, and Russia). Many other countries were drawn in. Ottoman Turkey joined the Central Powers in 1914, Bulgaria in 1915. Italy joined the Western Allies in 1915, Romania in 1916 and, decisively, the US in 1917. Russia withdrew following the RUSSIAN REVOLUTION of 1917. In Europe fighting was largely static. After the initial German advance through Belgium was checked at the MARNE, the Western Front settled into a war of attrition, with huge casualties but little movement. On the Eastern Front, the initial Russian advance was checked by the Germans, who overran Poland before stagnation set in. An Anglo-French effort to relieve the Russians by attacking GALLIPOLI (1916) failed. Italy and Austria became bogged down on the Isonzo front. Campaigns were also fought outside Europe, against the Turks in the Middle East and the German colonies in Africa and the Pacific. At sea only one major battle was fought, at JUTLAND (1916). German submarines proved highly effective against Allied merchant ships in the Atlantic, but the naval blockade of Germany caused severe food shortages and helped end the war. An armistice was agreed in November 1918 and peace treaties were signed at VERSAILLES (1919). The war introduced new weapons, such as tanks, poison gas, airplanes, and depth charges. Casualties were high: *c.*10 million people were killed.

**World War II** (1939–45) International conflict arising from disputes provoked by the expansionist policies of Germany in Europe and Japan in the Far East. During the 1930s APPEASEMENT failed to check the ambitions of Adolf HITLER's regime in Germany. Having made a defensive pact with the Soviet Union (August 1939), Germany invaded Poland, whereupon Britain and France declared war (September 3). In 1940 German BLITZ tactics resulted in the rapid conquest of Denmark, Norway, the Low Countries, and France (June). Inability to gain command of the air prevented a German invasion of Britain (*see* BATTLE OF BRITAIN), although bombing devastated British cities and German submarines took a heavy toll of British merchant shipping. Italy, under MUSSOLINI, having annexed Albania (1939) and invaded Greece (1940), joined Germany in 1941. Germany invaded Greece, where the Italians had been checked, and Yugoslavia. In June 1941 the Germans, violating the pact of 1939, invaded the Soviet Union, advancing to the outskirts of Moscow and Leningrad (St. Petersburg). Italian defeats by the British in North Africa also drew in German troops, who threw back the British. In the Pacific, the Japanese attack on PEARL HARBOR (December 1941) drew the US into the war. Japan rapidly overran SE Asia and Burma, but the Battle of MIDWAY (June 1942) indicated growing US naval and air superiority. From 1942 the tide in Europe turned against Germany. Defeat at STALINGRAD (January 1943) was followed by a Soviet advance that drove the Germans out of the Soviet Union by August 1944. Defeats in North Africa in 1942–43 led to the Allied invasion of Italy, forcing the Italians to make peace (September 1943). German troops then occupied Italy, where they resisted the Allied advance until 1945. In June 1944 Allied forces invaded NORMANDY, liberated France, and advanced into Germany, linking up with the Soviets on the Elbe River (April 1945). Germany surrendered in May. Japan continued to resist, but surrendered in August after the US dropped atomic bombs on Hiroshima and Nagasaki. Estimates of the numbers killed in World War II exceed 50 million. The great majority of the dead were civilians, many murdered in the HOLOCAUST. Politically, two former allies, the US and the Soviet Union, emerged as the dominant world powers.

**Worldwide Fund for Nature (WWF)** International organization, established (1961) in Britain as the World Wildlife Fund. It raises voluntary funds for the conservation of endangered wild animals, plants, and places. Its headquarters are in Bland, Switzerland.

**worm** Any of a large variety of wriggling, limbless creatures with soft bodies. Most worms belong to one or other of four main groups: ANNELIDS, FLATWORMS, nematodes (ROUNDWORMS), and ribbon worms.

**Worms** Industrial town on the Rhine River, in Rhineland Palatinate, W Germany. In the 5th century it became the capital of the kingdom of Burgundy. It was made a free imperial city in 1156. Worms was annexed to France in 1797 but passed to Hesse-Darmstadt state in 1815. The French occupied the city from 1918 to 1930, and much of it was destroyed during World War II. Today, it is a center of the wine industry. Pop. (1991) 77,430.

**Worms, Concordat of** (1122) Agreement between the Holy Roman emperor Henry V and Pope Calixtus II settling the investiture conflict, a struggle over the control of church offices. The emperor agreed to the free election of bishops, and surrendered his claim to invest them. They were, however, to pay homage to him as feudal overlord for their temporal possessions.

**Worms, Diet of** (1521) Conference of the Holy Roman Empire presided over by Emperor CHARLES V. Martin LUTHER was summoned to appear before the Diet to retract his teachings. Luther refused to retract them, and the Edict of Worms (May 25, 1521) declared him an outlaw. The Diet was one of the most important confrontations of the early REFORMATION.

**wormwood** Genus (*Artemisia*) of aromatic bitter shrubs and herbs, including common wormwood (*A. absinthium*), a European shrub that yields a dark green oil used to make absinthe. Family Asteraceae/Compositae.

**Wounded Knee, Massacre at** (1890) Last engagement in the conflict between Native Americans and US forces. Fearing a rising by the Sioux, US troops arrested several leaders. Chief SITTING BULL was killed resisting arrest. Another group was arrested a few days later and brought to Wounded Knee, South Dakota. A shot was fired, and the troops opened fire. About 300 people, including women and children, were killed.

**Wren, Sir Christopher** (1632–1723) English architect, mathematician, and astronomer. He designed more than 50 new churches in the city of London based on syntheses of CLASSICAL, RENAISSANCE, and BAROQUE ideas; the greatest of these is ST. PAUL'S Cathedral. Among his many other works are Chelsea and Greenwich hospitals, London, and the Sheldonian Theater, Oxford.

**wren** Small, insect-eating songbird of temperate regions of Europe, Asia, and most of the New World. Many species have white facial lines. The typical winter wren (*Troglodytes troglodytes*) has a slender bill, rounded wings, upright tail, and dark brownish plumage; length: to 4in (10cm). Family Troglodytidae.

**wrestling** Sport in which two opponents try to throw each other to the ground or secure each other in an unbreakable hold, by means of body grips, strength, and adroitness. The two major competitive styles are **Greco-Roman** (most popular in continental Europe), which permits no tripping or holds below the waist, and **free-style** (most popular in the US and Britain), which permits tackling, leg holds, and tripping. A match consists of three periods of three minutes each; points are awarded for falls and other maneuvers. Wrestling originated in ancient Greece and has been part of the modern Olympics since 1904. *See also* SUMO WRESTLING

**Wright, Frank Lloyd** (1869–1959) US architect, regarded as the leading modernist designer of private housing. He worked as an assistant to Louis SULLIVAN in the Chicago School of

▲ **wren** Wrens are songbirds, and the winter wren (*Troglodytes troglodytes*) shown here is one of the best singers. It is the only species of wren native to the Old World, but is also found in N Asia and North America.

W

▲ **Wright brothers** On December 17, 1903 Wilbur and Orville Wright made the world's first flights in a power-driven, heavier-than-air machine. The aircraft cost less than $1,000 to construct. The first flight, by Orville, lasted only 12 seconds; the fourth flight, by Wilbur, lasted 59 seconds. In 1909, after further tests and improvements, the brothers established the Wright Company in New York City to manufacture aircraft.

**WYOMING**
**Statehood :** July 10, 1890
**Nickname :** The Equality State
**State bird :** Meadowlark
**State flower :** Indian paintbrush
**State tree :** Cottonwood
**State motto :** Equal rights

architecture, before his first independent design in 1893. His distinctive "organic" style of low-built, prairie-style houses was designed to blend in with natural contours and features. Influenced by JAPANESE ART AND ARCHITECTURE, Wright's open-plan approach to interiors was highly influential. His use of materials and mechanical construction techniques was radical. Notable buildings include Robie House, Chicago (1909), "Fallingwater", Bear Run, Pennsylvania (1936–37), and the Guggenheim Museum, New York (1946–59).

**Wright, Richard** (1908–60) US novelist. His novels include *Native Son* (1940), which describes the life of an African-American youth in white-dominated Chicago; and *Black Boy* (1945), an account of the author's boyhood in the South. He also wrote short stories.

**Wright brothers** US aviation pioneers. Wilbur Wright (1867–1912) and Orville Wright (1871–1948) assembled their first aircraft in their bicycle factory. In 1903 Orville made the first piloted flight in a power-driven plane at Kitty Hawk, North Carolina. This flight lasted just 12 seconds, and attracted little attention. In 1909 they established the Wright Company in New York.

**writing** Process or result of making a visual record for the purpose of communication by using symbols to represent the sounds or words of a language. Writing systems can be **ideographic** (using signs or symbols that represent concepts or ideas directly rather than the sound of words for them); **pictographic** (in which a picture or sign represents the meaning of a word or phrase); **syllabic** (in which signs represent groups of consonants and vowels); or **alphabetic** (in which symbols stand for individual speech sounds or certain combinations of sounds). The Chinese dialects have long made use of ideographic symbols. Ancient Egyptian HIEROGLYPHICS and CUNEIFORM scripts from Mesopotamia are originally pictographic. The LINEAR SCRIPTS of ancient Crete and Greece are syllabic, as is the modern Japanese Katakana. The Phoenicians were the first to use a phonetic system, with an ALPHABET of signs representing speech sounds. The Greek and Roman alphabets in use for most modern non-Asiatic languages are descended from the Phoenicians.

**Wroclaw** (Breslau) Industrial city and port on the Oder River, SW Poland. It is the capital of lower Silesia. Originally a Slavic settlement, it was destroyed by the Mongols in 1241, rebuilt by the Austrians from 1526, and ceded to Prussia in 1741. It developed as a trade center in the 19th century and became part of Poland with the Potsdam Conference. Wroclaw is Poland's fourth largest city. Industries: machinery, electrical equipment, textiles, paper, timber, chemicals. Pop. (1993) 643,600.

**Wuhan** City and river port in central China, at the confluence of the Han and Yangtze rivers. It is the capital of Hubei province and the fifth-largest city in China. The town developed as a treaty port following the 19th-century OPIUM WARS, and grew with the arrival of the railroad and China's first modern iron and steel plants in 1891. Wuhan itself was formed in 1950 after the merger of three cities (Hankow, Hanyang, and Wuchang), and is now the industrial and commercial hub of central China. Wuhan has China's largest cotton mill. Industries: textiles, iron, steel, heavy machinery, cement. Pop. (1993) 3,876,000.

**Wundt, Wilhelm** (1832–1920) German psychologist. He established the first laboratory for experimental psychology in 1879 at Leipzig, and did much to convince early psychologists that the mind could be studied with objective, scientific methods. His major publication is *Principles of Physiological Psychology* (1873–74).

**Wyatt, Sir Thomas** (1503–42) English poet and courtier, a pioneer of the English SONNET. He was popular at Henry VIII's court although, as an alleged former lover of Anne BOLEYN and friend of Thomas CROMWELL, he was briefly imprisoned in 1536 and 1541.

**Wycliffe, John** (1330–84) English religious reformer. Under the patronage of JOHN OF GAUNT, he attacked corrupt practices in the church and the authority of the pope, condemning in particular the church's landed wealth. His criticism became increasingly radical, questioning the authority of the pope and insisting on the primacy of scripture, but he escaped condemnation until after his death. His ideas were continued by the LOLLARDS in England and influenced Jan HUS in Bohemia.

**Wyeth, Andrew Newell** (1917– ) US painter. His best-known painting is *Christina's World* (1948). He was trained by his father, the illustrator N.C. Wyeth. His son, James (1946–) is also a noted artist.

**Wyler, William** (1902–81) US film director. Wyler won three best director and best picture Academy Awards: *Mrs Miniver* (1942), *The Best Years of Our Lives* (1946), and *Ben-Hur* (1959). Other credits include *Jezebel* (1938), *Wuthering Heights* (1939), *The Little Foxes* (1941), and *Roman Holiday* (1953).

**Wyndham, John** (1903–69) English novelist. He is remembered for his science-fiction "disaster" novels, such as *The Day of the Triffids* (1951). Other works include *The Kraken Wakes* (1953), *The Chrysalids* (1955), and *The Midwych Cuckoos* (1957).

**Wyoming** State in the NW US, rectangular and bounded by Montana (N), South Dakota (E), Colorado (S), Utah (SW), and Idaho (W). Wyoming has the nation's smallest state population. The state capital and largest city is CHEYENNE. Other important centers are Casper and Laramie. The landscape is dominated by mountains and 10 million acres (4 million hectares) of forest. The ROCKY MOUNTAINS cross the state from NW to SE. To the E of the Rockies lie the rolling grasslands of the Great Plains, and the center of the state is also high plains country. The N of the state is primarily tall grass plain, where bison roamed and were hunted by the CROW and then the SIOUX. The area is fertile farmland and cattle ranch country. YELLOWSTONE NATIONAL PARK is the nation's oldest and largest national park, occupying the entire NW corner of Wyoming. From the tops of the mountain ranges flow many rivers, including the North Platte and the Snake. Following the LOUISIANA PURCHASE (1803), by 1846 the US had acquired the entire territory through treaties. Later 19th-century development was linked to the fur trade and westward migration along the OREGON TRAIL. The 1860s marked the first dramatic arrival of new settlers: the Bozeman Trail was opened (1864); gold was discovered in S Wyoming (1867), and the railroad was completed (1868). By the end of the 1870s, the Native American population had been pacified and placed on reservations. The next 20 years were marked by a rise of vigilante groups to deal with cattle rustlers and outlaws, and in 1890 Wyoming became the 44th state of the Union. While cattle ranching and sheep and wheat farming remain important to the economy, Wyoming is primarily an oil-producing state. Oil was discovered in the 1860s, and in 1993 output totaled 87.7 million barrels. Other important mineral resources include coal and uranium. Area: 97,913sq mi (253,596sq km). Pop. (1992) 464,736.

**Wyszynski, Stefan** (1901–81) Polish Roman Catholic cardinal. As Primate of Poland from 1948, he protested against the communist attacks on the church during the trial of Bishop Kaczmarek of Kielce. In 1952 Pope Pius XII appointed him cardinal. Wyszynski was imprisoned from 1953 to 1956. In 1957 he was allowed to go to Rome to receive the honor of a cardinal's hat. In the early 1980s, he played an active mediating role between Solidarity and the government.

**Wythe, George** (1726–1806) US lawyer and judge. He held office in colonial Virginia and, as a delegate to the CONTINENTAL CONGRESS, signed the Declaration of Independence (1776). At the instigation of his former student, Thomas JEFFERSON, he was appointed the first professor of law in the US, at the College of William and Mary (1779–90).

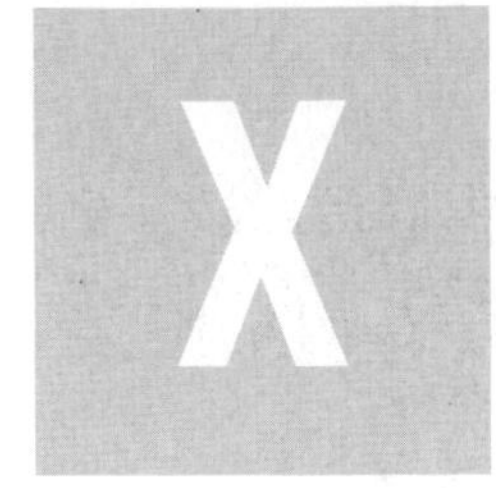

*X/x, 24th letter of the Roman alphabet. It is believed to have developed from the Semitic character,* **samekh.** *A letter resembling the modern* **X** *existed in the Greek alphabet,* **chi.**

**x-chromosome** One of the two kinds of sex-determining CHROMOSOME; the other is the Y-CHROMOSOME. In many organisms, including humans, females carry two x-chromosomes in their DIPLOID cell nuclei, whereas males carry one x- and one y-chromosome. Non-sexual characteristics are also carried on the x-chromosome, for example the genes for one form of colorblindness and for hemophilia. See also GENETICS; HEREDITY

**Xenakis, Yannis** (1922– ) Greek composer. He studied music under Arthur Honegger and Olivier Messiaen, and was also trained as an architect. Some of his work is TWELVE-TONE MUSIC and he has been a pioneer of the use of computers and mathematical models in the compositional process. His compositions include *Metastasis* (1954) and *Stratégie (1962).*

**xenon** (symbol Xe) Gaseous nonmetallic element, one of the NOBLE GASES. Discovered in 1898, xenon is present in the Earth's atmosphere (about one part in 20 million) and is obtained by fractionation of liquid air. Colorless and odorless, it is used in light bulbs, lasers, and arc lamps for cinema projection. The element, which has nine stable isotopes, forms some compounds, mostly with FLUORINE. Properties: at.no. 54; at.wt. 131.30; sp.gr. 5.88; m.p. −169.42°F (−111.9°C); b.p. −160.8°F (−107.1°C); most common isotope $^{132}Xe$ (26.89%).

**Xenophanes of Colophon** (560–478 BC) Traveling Greek poet and philosopher. He proposed a version of pantheism, holding that all living creatures have a common natural origin. His work survives only in fragmentary form.

**Xenophon** (430–354 BC) Greek historian. He studied with SOCRATES, whose teaching he described in *Memorabilia. Anabasis*, an account of his march with a Greek mercenary army across Asia Minor in 401–399 BC in support of a pretender to the Persian throne, is his best-known work. Other works include a history of Greece from 411 to 362 BC.

**xerography** Most common process used for PHOTOCOPYING.

**xerophyte** Any plant that is adapted to survive in dry conditions, in areas subject to drought, or in physiologically dry areas such as saltmarshes and acid bogs, where saline or acid conditions make the uptake of water difficult. Succulents such as cacti (see CACTUS) have thick fleshy leaves and stems for storing water. Other adaptations include the ability to reduce water loss by shedding leaves during drought, or having waxy or hairy leaf coatings, or reduced leaf area.

**Xerxes I** (519–465 BC) King of Persia (486–465 BC). Succeeding his father, DARIUS I, he regained Egypt and crushed a rebellion in Babylon before launching his invasion of Greece (480 BC). After his fleet was destroyed at the Battle of Salamis he retired. The defeat of the Persian army in Greece at the Battle of Plataea ended his plans for conquest. He was later assassinated by one of his own men. *See also* PERSIAN WARS

**Xhosa** (Xosa) Group of related BANTU tribes. The Xhosa moved from E Africa to the vicinity of the Great Fish River, S Africa, in the 17th–18th century. They were defeated by the Europeans in 1835, after which they came under European rule. In culture they are closely related to the ZULU. The 2.5 million Xhosa live in the Transkei and form an important part of South Africa's industrial and mining work force. Xhosa is the most widely spoken African language in South Africa.

**Xiamen** Seaport city in Fujian province, SE China. As Amoy, it flourished in the 19th century after being declared an open port by the Treaty of Nanking (1842). It gained extra strategic importance after the communists took control of the Chinese mainland (1949), and in 1981 it was granted the status of special economic zone, accelerating its role as the center of growing "unofficial" trade between China and Taiwan. Pop. (1993) 470,000.

**Xian** (Sian, formerly Changan) Capital of Shaanxi province at the confluence of the Wei and HUANG HE rivers, NW China. Inhabited since 6000 BC, from 255–206 BC it was the site of Xianyang, the capital of the QIN dynasty. The elaborate tomb of the dynastic founder, emperor QIN SHIHUANGDI, is a world heritage site and major tourist attraction. Xian was the focus for the introduction of Buddhism to China and in 652 the Big Wild Goose pagoda was built here. In the following centuries it became a major center for other religious missionaries. It is an important commercial center of a grain-growing region. Industries: cotton, textiles, steel, chemicals. Pop. (1993) 2,360,000.

**Xingu** Brazilian river, rising in central Mato Grosso state. It flows N for 1,230mi (1,980km) and empties into the Amazon River at its delta. It courses through rain forest and is navigable only in its lower reaches. The area focused international attention on the plight of Native Americans when a government proposal to dam the Xingu meant the flooding of tribal land. The dam and hydroelectric scheme was completed in December 1994 at a cost of $3.2 billion.

**Xinjiang** (Mandarin, new frontier; Sinkiang or Chinese Turkistan) Autonomous region in NW China, bordered by Tajikistan, Kyrgyzstan, and Kazakstan (N and W), Mongolia (E), and Kashmir and Tibet (S). The capital is Ürümqi. The region includes the Dzungarian Basin to the E and the Tarim Basin to the W. The ALTAI, TIAN SHAN, and Kunlun mountains frame the region to the N, W, and S respectively. First conquered by the Chinese in the 1st century BC, the region changed hands many times in the following centuries. From the 13th to 18th centuries it was loosely controlled by the Mongols. In 1756 the QING dynasty became the leading power in the region. It was made a Chinese province in 1881. It is a predominantly agricultural region growing wheat, cotton, corn, rice, millet, vegetables, and fruit; livestock rearing (particularly sheep) is also important. The area is rich in minerals, including oil, copper, zinc, gold, and silver. Industries: iron and steel, chemicals, textiles. Area: 636,075sq mi (1,647,435sq km). Pop. (1990) 15,370,000.

**x-ray astronomy** *See* ASTRONOMY

**x-ray crystallography** Use of X-RAYS to discover the molecular structure of CRYSTALS. It uses the phenomenon of x-ray diffraction, the scattering of an x-ray beam by the atomic structure of a crystal, and has been used to reveal the structure of crystalline DNA.

**x-rays** ELECTROMAGNETIC RADIATION of shorter wavelength, or higher frequency, than visible light, produced when a beam of electrons hits a solid target. X-rays were discovered in 1895 by the German physicist Wilhelm RÖNTGEN. They are normally produced for scientific use in x-ray tubes. Because they are able to penetrate matter that is opaque to light, x-rays are used to investigate inaccessible areas, especially of the body. *See also* RADIOGRAPHY

**xylem** Transport TISSUE of a plant, which conducts water and minerals from the roots to the rest of the plant and provides support. The most important cells are long, thin, tapering cells called **xylem vessels**. These cells are dead and have no cross-walls; they are arranged in columns to form long tubes, up which water is drawn. As water evaporates from the leaves (TRANSPIRATION), water is drawn across the leaf by OSMOSIS to replace it, drawing water out of the xylem. This suction creates a tension in the xylem vessels, and the side walls are reinforced with rings or spirals of LIGNIN, a rigid substance, to prevent them collapsing. Tiny holes in the walls of the xylem vessels, called pits, allow water to cross from one tube to another. In trees, the xylem becomes blocked with age, and new xylem forms toward the outside of the trunk to replace it. The core of dead, nonfunctioning xylem remains an essential part of the support system. *See also* PHLOEM; VASCULAR BUNDLE

**xylophone** Tuned PERCUSSION instrument. It is made of hardwood bars arranged as in a piano keyboard and played with mallets. The modern xylophone normally has a range of four octaves, extending from middle C upward.

**XYZ Affair** (1797–98) Diplomatic incident that strained US relations with France. President John ADAMS sent three representatives to renegotiate the French-US alliance of 1778, which had given way to hostility after the signing of JAY'S TREATY (1794). Three French agents, known as X, Y, and Z, demanded bribes and a loan before negotiations began, causing an uproar in the US and the recall of its commissioners.

*Y/y, 25th letter of the Roman alphabet. It was derived (as were* **f, u, v** *and* **w***) from the Semitic letter* **vaw.** *It was adopted by the Greeks as* **upsilon.** *The Romans made two letters out of upsilon – Y and V. They only employed Y when writing.*

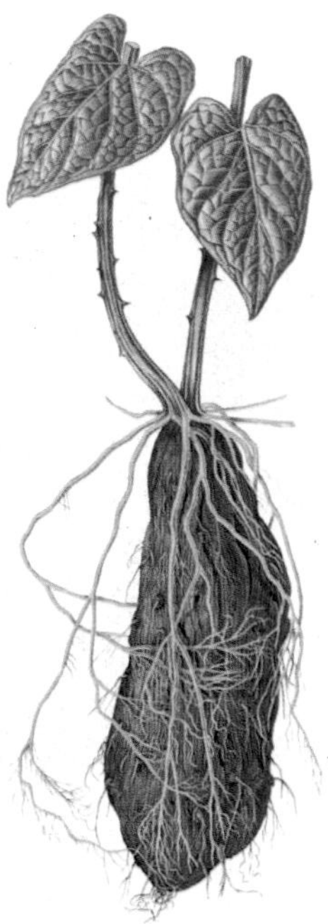

▲ **yam** Commercially important in E Asia and in tropical America, the yam (*Dioscorea* sp.) produces thick, starchy rhizomes, often weighing up to 30lb (13.6kg). These are a valuable food source and form part of the staple diet of many people worldwide, especially in Africa.

**yacht** Boat used for sport and recreation, powered by sail or motor. Sailing yachts, which are usually fore-and-aft rigged, vary from 20ft (6m) to over 100ft (30m) and include cutters, schooners, ketches, sloops, and yawls, as well as other types. Those fitted with diesel or gasoline engines are usually classified as cruising, or motor, yachts. Although most yachts are used for vacationing and cruising, yachting has been an international sport since 1851, when the Royal Yacht Squadron (formed at Cowes, England, in 1812) offered a silver cup as a prize for a race of 60mi (97km) around the Isle of Wight. The race was won by the schooner yacht, *America*, owned by the members of the New York Yacht Club (organized 1844); it has since been known as the AMERICA'S CUP. The Admiral's Cup is an international race held biennially since 1957 at Cowes, and The Observer Single-Handed Transatlantic Race has been held every four years since 1960. The Olympics have competition in seven yachting categories.

**Yahweh** Personal name of the God of the ancient Israelites of the Old Testament. God revealed His name to MOSES when He called to him out of the burning bush at Mount Horeb (Sinai) (Exodus 3:14). In Hebrew, it was made up of four consonants, YHWH, and was apparently related to the Hebrew verb "to be." Most English translations render it as "I am." *See also* JEHOVAH

**yak** Large, powerful, long-haired ox, native to Tibet, with domesticated varieties throughout central Asia; it inhabits barren heights up to 20,000ft (6,100m). Domesticated varieties are generally smaller and varied in color; they breed freely with domestic cattle. Wild yaks have coarse, black hair, except on the tail and flanks, where it hangs as a long fringe. The horns curve upward and outward. Height: to 6ft (1.8m) at the shoulder. Family Bovidae; species *Bos grunniens*.

**Yakutia** (officially Republic of Sakha) Constituent republic of the Russian Federation, NE Siberia. The capital is Yakutsk. The region is bounded by the Laptev and East Siberian seas (N) and the Stanovoy Range (S). It is the largest Russian republic and one of the coldest inhabited regions, with more than 40% of the territory within the Arctic Circle. The principal rivers are the LENA, Yana, Indirka, and Kolyma. A third of the population is Yakut, a Turkic-speaking people who settled in the Lena basin from the 13th–15th century. They are noted bone carvers, iron workers, and potters. The area was colonized by Russia during the 17th century, and many Yakuts were forcibly converted from shamanism to Christianity. A republic of the former Soviet Union (1922–91), Yakutia became a member of the new Russian Federation in 1992. Agriculture is only possible in the S. The major industry is diamond mining and processing. Other important minerals are gold, silver, lead, and coal. Timber is an important industry in the taiga regions. Area: 1,200,000sq mi (3,100,000sq km) Pop: (1994) 1,060,700

**Yale University** Institute of higher education in New Haven, Connecticut. Founded in 1701 in Branford, Connecticut, it operates several colleges for the study of arts, science, and social science, as well as professional schools and a graduate school. Its current charter dates from 1745. It is a member of the IVY LEAGUE.

**Yalow, Rosalyn** (1921– ) US biochemist. In the 1950s Yalow found that some people who received INSULIN injections developed ANTIBODIES against the hormone. She discovered that insulin, labeled with radioactive iodine, combined with the antibodies; from this she developed radioimmunological tests to detect and measure the amount of insulin present. She shared the 1977 Nobel Prize for physiology or medicine for her development of a method of detecting peptide HORMONES in the blood.

**Yalta Conference** (February 1945) Meeting of the chief Allied leaders of WORLD WAR II at Yalta in the Crimea, S Ukraine. With victory over Germany imminent, ROOSEVELT, CHURCHILL, and STALIN met to discuss the final campaigns of the war and the post-war settlement. Agreements were reached on the foundation of the UNITED NATIONS; the territorial division of Europe into "spheres of interest;" the occupation of Germany; and support for democracy in liberated countries. Concessions were made to Stalin in the Far East in order to gain Soviet support against Japan.

**yam** Any of several species of herbaceous vines that grow in warm and tropical regions; also the large, tuberous roots of several tropical species, which are edible. The plant is an annual with a long, climbing stem, lobed or unlobed leaves, and small clusters of greenish, bell-shaped flowers. The SWEET POTATO is also sometimes called a yam. Family Dioscoreaceae; genus *Dioscorea*.

**Yamoussoukro** Capital of IVORY COAST since 1983. Originally a small Baouké tribal village and birthplace of Ivory Coast's first president Félix HOUPHOUËT-BOIGNY, it has developed rapidly into the administrative and transport center of Ivory Coast. Yamoussoukro's Our Lady of Peace Cathedral (consecrated by Pope John Paul II in 1990) is the world's largest Christian church. Pop. (1988) 106,786.

**Yamuna** (Jumna) River in N central India. It rises in the Himalayas and flows S and SE. The Yamuna's confluence with the GANGES at ALLAHABAD is one of the most sacred Hindu sites. The TAJ MAHAL at AGRA lies on its bank. Navigable for almost its entire length, the Yamuna was once an important trade route and is now primarily used for irrigation. Length: *c*.860mi (1,380km).

**Yang, Chen Ning** (1922– ) US physicist, b. China. With Tsung-Dao LEE, he studied the decay of K mesons, which seemed to break down in two different ways, and in 1956 they concluded that in these weak interactions PARITY need not be conserved. In 1957 they shared the Nobel Prize for physics.

**Yangtze** (Chang Jiang) River in China, the longest in Asia and third longest in the world. Rising in the Kunlun Mountains in NE Tibet, it flows 3,900mi (6,300km) through the central Chinese provinces to the East China Sea near Shanghai. It was joined to the HUANG HE (Yellow River) by the Grand Canal in 610. Navigation becomes difficult at the spectacular Yangtze Gorges, between CHUNGKING and Yichang, but after Yichang (site of the huge Gezhouba Dam) it enters the fertile lowlands of Hubei province. The Yangtze and its main tributaries traverse one of the world's most populated areas, providing water for irrigation and hydroelectricity, and it is the country's most economically important waterway. The Chinese government's controversial Three Gorges dam scheme E of Fengjie, destined to take 15 years to complete, will create a reservoir about 375mi (600km) long, displacing some 1.2 million people.

**Yanomami** Native American tribal group living chiefly in the rain forests of N Brazil and S Venezuela. Traditionally seminomadic hunter-gatherers, during the 1980s and 1990s they lost much of their land to road builders, logging companies, and gold prospectors, causing the population to fall to around 18,000. Their plight raised international concern.

**Yaoundé** Capital of Cameroon, W Africa. Located in beautiful hills on the edge of dense jungle, it was founded by German traders in 1888. During World War I it was occupied by Belgian troops, and from 1921 to 1960 it acted as capital of French Cameroon. Since independence, it has grown rapidly as a financial and administrative center with strong Western influences. It is the site of the University of Cameroon (1962). The city also serves as a market for the surrounding region, notably in coffee, cacao, and sugar. Pop. (1991) 750,000.

**yard** Imperial unit of length equal to 3 feet. 1 yard (yd) equals 0.9144m.

**yarrow** *See* MILFOIL

**yaws** (framboesia) Contagious skin disease found in the humid tropics. It is caused by a spirochete (*Treponema pertenue*) related to the organism causing SYPHILIS. Yaws, however, is not a SEXUALLY TRANSMITTED DISEASE, but is transmitted by flies and by direct skin contact with the sores. It may cause disfiguring bone lesions.

**y-chromosome** One of the two kinds of sex-determining CHROMOSOME, the other is the X-CHROMOSOME. Many male organisms have one x- and one y-chromosome in their DIPLOID cell nuclei. SPERM cells contain either an x- or a y-chromosome, and since female ova (egg cells) always contain an x-chromosome, the resulting offspring is either XY (male) or XX (female). The y-chromosome is smaller than the x- and contains fewer GENES.

**year** Length of time taken by the Earth to circle once round the Sun in its orbit. It is defined in various ways, such as the sidereal year, which is timed with reference to the fixed stars.

**yeast** Any of a group of single-celled microscopic FUNGI found worldwide in the soil and in organic matter. Yeasts reproduce asexually by BUDDING or FISSION. Yeasts are also produced commercially for use in baking, brewing, and winemaking. They occur naturally as a bloom (white covering) on grapes and other fruit.

**Yeats, W.B. (William Butler)** (1865–1939) Irish poet and dramatist, often cited as the greatest English language poet of the 20th century. He and Lady Gregory founded (1904) the Abbey Theatre, Dublin, as an Irish national theatre. Yeats' plays *On Baile's Strand* (1905) and *Cathleen Ni Houlihan* (1902) were on the first bill, the latter often regarded as the beginning of the renaissance in IRISH LITERATURE. Yeats' early poetry, collected in *The Wanderings of Oisin, and Other Poems* (1889), betrays the influence of mysticism. *Responsibilities* (1914) was more direct, the poetry acting as contemporary commentary. Following the creation of the Irish Free State, Yeats served (1922–28) as a senator. His mature poetry includes *Michael Robartes and the Dancer* (1921, which contains "The Second Coming" and "Easter 1916") and *The Tower* (1928, which contains "Sailing to Byzantium"). Yeats received the 1923 Nobel Prize for literature.

**yellow fever** Acute infectious disease marked by sudden onset of headaches, fever, muscle and joint pain, jaundice, and vomiting; the kidneys and heart may also be affected. It is caused by a VIRUS transmitted by mosquitoes in tropical and subtropical regions. It may be prevented by vaccination.

**yellowlegs** Two species of American shore birds named for their long yellow legs. Both have black and white markings and white underparts. They nest in summer in N North America, laying four buf or brown eggs, and fly S as far as Chile in winter. Once overhunted, they are now protected species and their numbers have increased. Family Scolopacidae; species *Tringa melanoleuca* (greater yellowlegs), *Tringa flavipes* (lesser yellowlegs).

**Yellowstone National Park** Park in NW Wyoming, reaching into Montana and Idaho. Established in 1872, it is the oldest and one of the largest US NATIONAL PARKS. Formed by volcanic activity, the park contains almost 10,000 hot springs (including mammoth Hot Springs) and 200 geysers (the most famous of which is Old Faithful).. Other scenic attractions include the Yellowstone River and petrified forests. It is one of the world's greatest wildlife sanctuaries. In 1988 large-scale forest fires devastated much of the park. Area: 2.2 million acres (900,000 ha).

**Yeltsin, Boris Nikolayevich** (1931– ) Russian statesman, first democratically elected president of the Russian Federation (1991– ). He was Communist Party leader in Ekaterinburg (Sverdlovsk) before joining (1985) the reforming government of Mikhail GORBACHEV, becoming also party chief in Moscow. His blunt criticism of the slow pace of PERESTROIKA led to demotion in 1987, but his immense popularity gained him election as president of the Russian Republic in 1990. His prompt denunciation of the attempted coup against Gorbachev (August 1991) established his ascendancy. Elected president of the Russian Federation, he presided over the dissolution of the Soviet Union and the termination of Communist Party rule. Economic disintegration, rising crime, and internal conflicts, notably in Chechnya, damaged his popularity, and failing health reduced his effectiveness. Nevertheless, he was reelected in 1996.

**Yemen** Republic on the SE tip of the Arabian peninsula. *See* country feature, page 736

**Yenisei** (Yenesey) River in central Siberia, Russia. Formed by the confluence of the Bolshoi Yenisei and the Maly Yenisei at Kyzyl, it flows for 2,540mi (4,090km) W then N through the Sayan Mountains and across Siberia, forming the W border of the central Siberian plateau, emptying into the Yenisei Gulf on the Kara Sea. A large hydroelectric station has been built at Krasnoyarsk. The river is a source of sturgeon and salmon. A shipping route, some of its sections are frozen in winter. When the river is combined with the Angara (its major tributary), it is the world's fifth longest river, at 3,445mi (5,550km).

**Yerevan** Capital of Armenia, on the Razdan River, S Caucasus. One of the world's oldest cities, it was capital of Armenia as early as the 7th century (though under Persian control), and was a crucial crossroads for caravan routes between India and Transcaucasia. It is the site of a 16th-century Turkish fortress and a traditional winemaking center. Industries: chemicals, plastics, cables, tires, metals, vodka. Pop. (1994) 1,254,000.

**Yerkes Observatory** Observatory of the University of Chicago, at Williams Bay, Wisconsin. It was founded by George Ellery HALE. Its main instrument is a 40in (1m) refractor, opened in 1897 and still the largest in the world.

**Yersin, Alexandre Émile John** (1863–1943) French bacteriologist. In Hong Kong he discovered (1894) the plague bacillus and developed a serum against it in 1895. Yersin is also reputed to have introduced the rubber tree into Indochina.

**Yevtushenko, Yevgeny** (1933– ) Russian writer. During the 1960s, Yevtushenko headed a new wave of nonconformist, modern Soviet poetry. Rejecting SOCIALIST REALISM, Yevtushenko's rhetorical poetry anticipated GLASNOST in its examination of Soviet history. His most famous work, *Babi Yar* (1961), was a direct indictment of Soviet anti-Semitism. Other works include *Precocious Autobiography* (1963) and *The Bratsk Station* (1965).

**yew** Any of a number of evergreen shrubs and trees of the genus *Taxus*, native to temperate regions of the Northern Hemisphere. They have stiff, narrow, dark green needles, often with pale undersides, and poisonous red, berry-like fruits. Height: to 80ft (25m). Family Taxaceae.

**Yiddish** Language spoken by Jews living in central and E Europe and other countries (including the US) with Jewish communities. It first developed in W Europe in the 10th and 11th centuries and was taken E with migrating Jews. It is a variety of German, with many Hebrew, Aramaic, French, Italian, and Slavic words added. It is written using the Hebrew alphabet.

**Yin** Alternative transliteration of the SHANG dynasty

**yin and yang** Interaction of two complementary forces in the universe, as described in the Chinese philosophy of TAOISM. *Yin* and *yang* are two cosmic energy modes comprising the *Tao* or the eternal, dynamic way of the universe. Earth is *yin*, the passive, dark, female principle; heaven is *yang*, the active, bright, male principle. All the things of nature and society are composed of combinations of these two principles of polarity, which maintain the balance of all things. The hexagrams of the *I Ching* (*see* BOOK OF CHANGES) embody *yin* and *yang*.

**YMCA** Abbreviation of the YOUNG MEN'S CHRISTIAN ASSOCIATION

**yoga** (Sanskrit, union) Term used for a number of Hindu disciplines to aid the union of the soul with God. Based on the *Yoga-sutras* of Patañjali (written at about the time of Christ), the practice of yoga generally involves moral restraints, meditation, and the awakening of physical energy centers through specific postures (*asanas*) or exercises. Devoted to freeing the soul or self from earthly cares by isolating it from the body and the mind, these ancient practices became popular in the West during the second half of the 20th century as a means of relaxation, self-control, and enlightenment.

**yogurt** (yoghurt, yoghourt) Semisolid, cultured dairy food, fermented by bacteria. Pasteurized milk is inoculated with a culture of *Streptococcus acidophilus* and *Lactobacillus bulgaricus* and incubated to achieve a sourish acidity. Yogurt originated with nomadic tribes in Central Asia and became popular in the Balkans as a drink. It then spread throughout Europe and the US as a creamy, custard-like product, usually sweetened and often flavored with fruit.

**Yokohama** Port and major industrial city on the W shore of Tokyo Bay, SE Honshū, Japan. Japan's main port for many years, it is now the country's second largest city. It grew from a small fishing village to a major Japanese port after opening to foreign trade in 1859. It served as Tokyo's deep-water harbor and was a vital silk-exporting center. The city has been rebuilt twice: once, after the devastating earthquake in 1923, and again following intensive Allied bombing during World

▲ **Yeats** One of the greatest figures in 20th-century literature, W.B. Yeats was born in a suburb of Dublin, Ireland. At art school he developed an interest in mysticism, the occult, and Irish mythology, which provided the inspiration for much of his poetry. Yeats played a major role in the Irish cultural rennaissance and produced powerful, nationalist works, one of which, *Cathleen Ni Houlihan* (1902) is thought to have inspired the Easter Rising of 1916.

▲ **Yeltsin** Educated at Urals Polytechnic, Russian Federation president Boris Yeltsin began his career in the construction industry. He gained a reputation as an outspoken, hands-on reformer, and passed in and out of favor with the Politburo during the perestroika reforms of the 1980s. As president, he is a progressive advocate of price deregulation, privatization, and nuclear disarmament.

War II. Many of the modern port and industrial facilities have been built on land reclaimed from the sea. Industries: iron, steel, shipbuilding. Pop. (1994) 3,265,000.

**yolk** Rich substance found in the eggs or ova of most animals, except those of placental mammals. It consists of fats and proteins and serves as a store of food for the developing embryo.

**yolk sac** Membranous, saclike structure in the eggs (ova) of most animals. It is attached directly to the ventral surface or gut of the developing EMBRYO in the eggs of birds, reptiles, and some fish, and contains YOLK. The term also refers to an analogous saclike membrane that develops below the mammalian embryo. It contains no yolk but is connected to the umbilical cord.

**Yom Kippur** (Day of Atonement) Most solemn of Jewish holy days. It is the last of the Ten Days of Penitence that begin the New Year. On this day, set aside for prayer and fasting, humanity is called to account for its sins and to seek reconciliation with God. Yom Kippur is described as the SABBATH of Sabbaths, because the break from work is almost complete, and Jews must abstain from food, drink, and sex. *See also* ROSH HASHANAH

**Yonkers** City on the Hudson River, SE New York state. Land was originally purchased from Native Americans in 1639 by the Dutch West India Company. The acquittal of John Peter ZENGER here in 1735 helped set up freedom of the press in the US. The city has various museums (including the Hudson River Museum) and research institutions. Industries: elevators, chemicals, cables, telephone parts, art supplies. Pop. (1992) 186,063.

**York** City and county district in NORTH YORKSHIRE, N England. Located at the confluence of the Ouse and Foss rivers, it was an important Roman military post, an Anglo-Saxon capital, a Danish settlement, and then the ecclesiastical center of the North of England; York Minster cathedral dates from the 13th century. Its old buildings and museums make tourism important. Industries: engineering (including rail workshops), confectionery, precision instruments. Pop. (1991) 98,745.

**York, House of** English royal house, a branch of the PLANTAGENETS. During the Wars of the ROSES, rival claimants from the houses of York and LANCASTER contended for the crown. The Yorkist claimant, Richard, duke of York, was a great-grandson of EDWARD III. His son gained the crown as EDWARD IV. The defeat of Edward's brother, RICHARD III, by HENRY VII in 1485 brought the brief Yorkist line to a close.

**Yorkshire** *See* NORTH YORKSHIRE, SOUTH YORKSHIRE, and WEST YORKSHIRE

## YEMEN

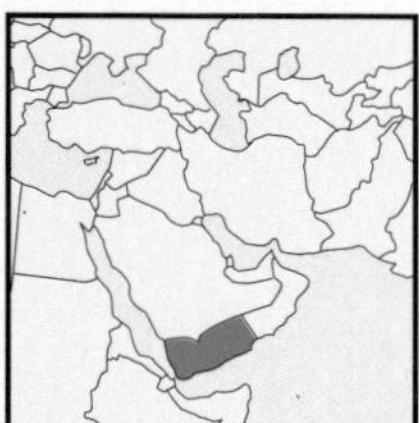

Yemen's flag was adopted in 1990 when the Yemen Arab Republic (North Yemen) united with the People's Democratic Republic of Yemen (South Yemen). This simple flag is a tricolor of red, white, and black; colors associated with the Pan-Arab movement.

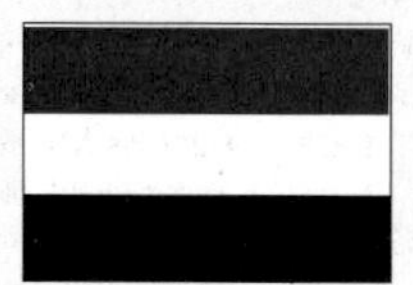

**AREA:** 203,849sq mi (527,970sq km)
**POPULATION:** 11,282,000
**CAPITAL (POPULATION):** Sana'a (427,502)
**GOVERNMENT:** Multiparty republic
**ETHNIC GROUPS:** Arab 96%, Somali 1%
**LANGUAGES:** Arabic (official)
**RELIGIONS:** Islam
**CURRENCY:** Yemen rial = 100 fils

The Republic of Yemen lies on the S tip of the Arabian peninsula. A narrow plain borders the Red Sea and the Arabian Sea coasts, and includes ADEN, the former capital of South Yemen. The W plain is backed by highlands, which rise to over 12,000ft (3,600m) near the capital SANA'A. The Arabian coastal plain includes the fertile Hadramaut valley, which runs through a lower mountain range. Much of Yemen's interior forms part of the Rub al Khali desert. The desert is bisected by a central plateau.

### CLIMATE

Most of Yemen is hot and rainless, except in the monsoon month of August. The highlands are the wettest part of Arabia and the temperature is moderated by altitude.

### VEGETATION

Palm trees grow along the coast. Plants such as acacia and eucalyptus flourish in the interior. Thorn shrubs and mountain pasture are found in the highlands. The Rub al Khali (Empty Quarter) is a barren desert.

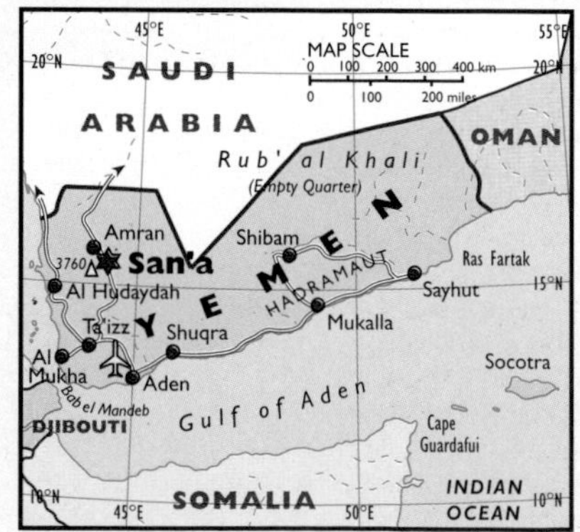


### HISTORY AND POLITICS

The ancient kingdom of SHEBA (Saba) flourished in present-day S Yemen between *c.*750 BC and 100 BC. The kingdom was renowned for its advanced technology and wealth, gained through its strategic location on important trade routes. The region was invaded by the Romans in the 1st century BC. Islam was introduced in 628 AD. The Rassite dynasty of the Zaidi sect established a theocratic state which lasted until 1962. The FATIMIDS conquered Yemen in *c.*1000. In 1517 the area became part of the Ottoman Empire, and largely remained under Turkish control until 1918. In the 19th century the Saudi Wahhabi sect ousted the Zaidi imams, but were in turn expelled by Ibrahim Pasha. In 1839 Aden was captured by the British. Following the defeat of the Ottomans in World War I, Yemen was ruled by Imam Yahya of the Hamid al-Din dynasty. In 1937 Britain formed the Aden Protectorate. In 1945 Yemen joined the Arab League. In 1948 Yahya was assassinated. Crown Prince Ahmed became imam. From 1958 to 1961 Yemen formed part of the United Arab Republic (with Egypt and Syria). A 1962 army revolution overthrew the monarchy and formed the Yemen Arab Republic. Civil war ensued between republicans (aided by Egypt) and royalists (aided by Saudi Arabia and Jordan). Meanwhile, the Aden Protectorate became part of the British Federation of South Arabia. In 1967 the National Liberation Front forced the British to withdraw from Aden and founded the People's Republic of South Yemen. Marxists won the ensuing civil war in South Yemen and renamed it the People's Democratic Republic of Yemen (1970). Border clashes between the two countries were frequent throughout the 1970s, and erupted into full-scale war (1979). Following lengthy negotiations, the two Yemens merged to form a single republic in 1990. Yemen's support for Iraq in the Gulf War (1991) led to the expulsion of 800,000 Yemeni workers from Saudi Arabia. A coalition government emerged from 1993 elections, but increasing economic and political tensions between North and South led to civil war in 1994. The South's brief secession from the union ended with victory for the Northern army. In 1995 agreement was reached with Saudi Arabia and Oman over disputed boundaries, but Yemen clashed with Eritrea over the Hanish Islands in the Red Sea. In 1999 several British citizens were arrested on terrorist charges.

### ECONOMY

Civil strife has devastated Yemen's economy, seriously damaging the country's infrastructure, such as the oil refinery at Aden. Yemen is a low income developing nation (1992 GDP per capita, $2,410). In 1995 inflation and unemployment stood at over 50%, forcing Yemen to borrow from the IMF. Agriculture employs 63% of the work force, mainly at subsistence level. The major economic activity is livestock-raising, principally sheep. Crops include sorghum, wheat, and barley. Oil extraction began in the NW in the 1980s. Natural gas is also exploited.

**Yorkshire terrier** Small, long-haired dog originally bred in Lancashire and Yorkshire, England, in the 19th century. It has a small head with a short muzzle and small, V-shaped, erect ears. The compact body has a short, straight back, and is set on short legs, which are hidden under the coat. The tail is commonly docked. The straight, fine, silky coat is generally blue and tan. Height: to 8in (20cm) at the shoulder; weight to 7lb (3kg).

**Yorktown, Siege of** (1781) Last major military campaign of the AMERICAN REVOLUTION. Trapped on the peninsula of Yorktown, Virginia, 7,000 British troops under Lord Cornwallis surrendered to superior US and French forces, after attempts to relieve them had failed.

**Yoruba** People of sw Nigeria of basically Christian or Islamic faith. Most are farmers, growing crops that include yams, corn, and cocoa. Many live in towns built around the palace of an *oba*, or chief, and travel daily to their outlying farms.

**Yosemite National Park** Spectacular NATIONAL PARK in the Sierra Nevada range of central California. Yosemite means "grizzly bear," and the park was named for the river that runs through it. Established in 1890, it is a mountainous area of glacial gorges and granite cliffs, rising to the 13,090ft (3,990m) of Mount Lyell. Yosemite Falls, the highest waterfall in North America, drops 2,425ft (739m) in two stages. Other features include Half Dome Mountain and the vertical rock-face of El Capitan. Area: 761,320acres (308,335ha).

**Young, Brigham** (1801–77) US religious leader, founder of Salt Lake City. An early convert to the Church of Jesus Christ of Latter-Day Saints (MORMONS), Young took over the leadership when Joseph SMITH, the founder, was killed by a mob in 1844. Young held the group together through persecutions and led their westward migration (1846–47) to Utah, where he organized the settlement that became Salt Lake City. He was governor of Utah Territory (1850–57).

**Young, "Cy" (Denton True)** (1867–1955) US baseball player. He became the game's top pitcher with 511 victories. Young played for five teams (1890–1911) and was elected to the Baseball Hall of Fame in 1937. His nickname "Cy" was short for "cyclone."

**Young, Lester Willis** (1909–59) US jazz saxophonist. A major jazz influence, with his cool and melodious improvisations, he made his name playing tenor saxophone with Count Basie's band. His abilities also extended to the alto saxophone and clarinet, and he made many guest appearances, including work with Benny Goodman and Dizzy Gillespie.

**Young, Neil** (1945– ) Canadian singer-songwriter and guitarist. Inspired by the diverse influences of folk, country, and rock, he has worked with Crosby Stills and Nash as well as solo. His recordings include *After the Goldrush* (1970), *Harvest* (1972), *Rust Never Sleeps* (1979), and *Arc-Weld* (1991).

**Young, Whitney, Jr.** (1921–71) US civil rights leader. He advocated improvement in economic opportunities, housing, and welfare for African-Americans. He served as the executive director of the National Urban League (1961–71). His books include *To Be Equal* (1964).

**Young Men's Christian Association (YMCA)** Christian association for young men established in London (1844) by George Williams. Its aim is to develop Christian morals and leadership qualities in young people. Clubs were soon formed in the US and Australia, and the world alliance of the YMCA was formed in Geneva in 1855. Women were accepted as members in 1971. *See also* YOUNG WOMEN'S CHRISTIAN ASSOCIATION

**Young Turks** Group of Turks who wished to remodel the OTTOMAN EMPIRE and make it a modern European state with a liberal constitution. Their movement began in the 1880s with unrest in the army and universities. In 1908 a Young Turk rising, led by ENVER PASHA and his chief of staff Kemal ATATÜRK, deposed Sultan Abdul Hamid II and replaced him with his brother, Muhammad V. Following a 1913 coup d'etat, Enver Pasha became a virtual dictator. Under Kemal Atatürk, the Young Turks merged into the Turkish Nationalist Party.

**Young Women's Christian Association (YWCA)** Christian association for young women, the counterpart of the YMCA. Two groups were founded simultaneously in 1855 in different parts of England, and the associations merged in 1877. The YWCA provides accommodation, education, recreation facilities, and welfare services to young women. It has local branches in more than 80 countries.

**Ysaÿe, Eugène** (1858–1931) Belgian violinist, conductor, teacher, and composer. He became professor of music at the Brussels Conservatory of Music in 1886 and later conductor of the Cincinnati Symphony Orchestra (1918–22). His compositions, mainly for the violin, are in a post-romantic style.

**ytterbium** (symbol Yb) Silver-white, metallic element of the LANTHANIDE SERIES. First isolated in 1828, ytterbium's chief ore is monazite. The shiny, soft element is malleable and ductile and is used to produce steel and other alloys. Properties: at.no. 70: at.wt. 173.04; sp.gr. 6.97; m.p. 1,515°F (824°C); b.p. 2,179°F (1,193°C); most common isotope $^{174}$Yb (31.84%).

**yttrium** (symbol Y) Silver-gray, metallic element of Group III of the periodic table. First isolated in 1828, it is found associated with lanthanide elements in monazite sand, bastnaesite, and gadolinite; it resembles the lanthanides in its chemistry. Yttrium was found in lunar rock samples collected by the Apollo 11 space mission. Its compounds are used in phosphors and communications devices, such as color televison picture tubes and superconducting ceramics. Properties: at.no. 39; at.wt. 88.9059; sp.gr. 4.47; m.p. 2,773°F (1,523°C); b.p. 6,039°F (3,337°C); most common isotope $^{89}$Y (100%).

**Yüan** (1246–1368) MONGOL dynasty in China. Continuing the conquests of GENGHIS KHAN, KUBLAI KHAN established his rule over China, eliminating the last SUNG claimant in 1279. He returned the capital to Beijing and promoted construction and commerce. Chinese literature took new forms during the Mongol period. Native Chinese were excluded from government, and foreign visitors, including merchants such as Marco POLO, were encouraged. Among the Chinese, resentment of alien rule was aggravated by economic problems, including runaway inflation. The less competent successors of Kublai were increasingly challenged by rebellion, culminating in the victory of the MING.

**Yucatán** State in the N part of the Yucatán Peninsula, SE Mexico. Its capital is Mérida. The terrain is low-lying, covered in places with scrub and cactus thickets. Once the center of the MAYA civilization, Yucatán was conquered by the Spanish in the 1540s. The region is a major producer of henequen (sisal hemp used for cordage). Other products: tobacco, sugar, cotton, tropical fruits. Fishing is important along the coast. Area: 14,868sq miles (38,508sq km). Pop. (1990) 1,362,940.

**yucca** Genus of *c.*40 species of succulent plants native to the S US, Mexico, and the West Indies. Most species are stemless, forming a rosette of leaves, or have a trunk. The flowers grow in clusters and are white, tinged with yellow or purple. The leaves are poisonous. Height: to 33ft (10m). Family Liliaceae.

**Yugoslavia** Balkan Federal Republic in se Europe. See country feature, page 738

**Yukawa, Hideki** (1907–81) Japanese physicist. In the 1930s he proposed that there was a nuclear force of very short range (less than $10^{-15}$ m) strong enough to overcome the repulsive force of protons and that diminished rapidly with distance. In 1949 he was awarded the Nobel Prize for physics for his prediction of the existence of the MESON.

**Yukon River** Fourth-longest river in North America, deriving its name from a Native American word meaning "great." It rises at Lake Tagish on the border of British Columbia, and flows N and NW through the Yukon Territory into Alaska. It then flows SW to enter the Bering Sea. It was a major transportation route during the KLONDIKE GOLD RUSH. Navigable for *c.*1,775mi (2,858km) of its 1,980mi (3,185km) course three months each year, it is ice-bound from October to June.

**Yukon Territory** Territory in the extreme NW of Canada, bounded by the Arctic Ocean (N), Northwest Territories (E), British Columbia (S), and Alaska (W). The capital and largest town is Whitehorse. In the N the region consists of Arctic waste and is virtually uninhabited. Further S there is spectacular mountain scenery with lakes and coniferous forests. The region is drained chiefly by the YUKON and MACKENZIE rivers. The climate is harsh, with freezing winters and short summers, though more temperate than Northwest Territories. In 1991 the Canadian government recognized the land claim of the indigenous Yukon (First Nation) Native Americans. The region, then part of Northwest Territories, was first explored by fur traders from the HUDSON'S BAY COMPANY after 1840. The KLONDIKE GOLD RUSH brought over 30,000 prospectors in the 1890s. Farming is extremely limited, but a few cereal crops and vegetables are grown in the valleys. The principal activity is mining, with major deposits including lead, zinc, and gold. There is also a healthy forestry industry. With a small manufacturing base, tourism plays an important part in the economy. Area: 186,675sq mi (483,450sq km). Pop. (1991) 27,797.

**Yunnan** (South of the Clouds) Province in S central China, bounded by Laos and Vietnam (S) and Burma (W); the capital is Kunming. Its remote, mountain location enabled Yunnan to retain an independent status until conquered by the Mongols in 1253. In 1659 it became a province of China, and it was captured by Chinese communist forces in 1950. Yunnan is divided, along ethnic lines, into eight autonomous districts that are home to many of China's minority nationalities. It is renowned for the rich diversity of its wildlife, particularly rare plant species. Agriculture is restricted to a few plains, with rice the major crop. Its valuable mineral resources include deposits of tin, tungsten, copper, gold, and silver. The province has road links with Vietnam and Burma. Mining and timber are the main industries. Area: 168,482sq mi (436,200sq km). Pop. (1990) 36,750,000.

**Yurok** Native American tribe formerly residing around the estuary of the Klamath River, California, and speaking an Algonquian language. Reduced in number to fewer than 1,000, the group is now mainly scattered along the N Californian coast.

**YWCA** Abbreviation of the YOUNG WOMEN'S CHRISTIAN ASSOCIATION

## YUGOSLAVIA

Yugoslavia's flag was adopted in 1992. Yugoslavia now consists of two republics (Serbia and Montenegro) which were formerly part of the socialist Federal People's Republic of Yugoslavia, which also included Bosnia-Herzegovina, Croatia, Macedonia, and Slovenia.

**AREA:** 39,449sq mi (102,173sq km)
**POPULATION:** 10,469,000
**CAPITAL (POPULATION):** Belgrade (1,168,454)
**GOVERNMENT:** Federal republic
**ETHNIC GROUPS:** Serb 62%, Albanian 17%, Montenegrin 5%, Hungarian, Muslim, Croat
**LANGUAGES:** Serbo-Croatian (official)
**RELIGIONS:** Christianity (mainly Serbian Orthodox, with Roman Catholic and Protestant minorities), Islam
**CURRENCY:** Yugoslav new dinar = 100 paras

The Federal Republic of Yugoslavia now consists of SERBIA and MONTENEGRO. The rump Yugoslav federation has not gained international recognition as the successor to the Socialist Federal Republic of Yugoslavia created by Josip TITO. In 1991 the federation began to disintegrate when SLOVENIA, CROATIA, and MACEDONIA declared independence. In 1992 BOSNIA-HERZEGOVINA followed suit. A narrow coastal strip on the Adriatic Sea includes Montenegro's capital, Podgorica. The interior of Montenegro consists largely of barren karst, including parts of the DINARIC ALPS and the BALKAN MOUNTAINS. Kosovo is a high plateau region. Serbia is dominated by the fertile lowland plains of the DANUBE, on whose banks lie the capital BELGRADE, and the N city of Novi Sad. (*see* individual country/republic articles for pre-1918 history and postindependence events)

### CLIMATE AND VEGETATION

The coastal Mediterranean climate gives way to the bitterly cold winters of the highlands. Belgrade has a continental climate. Forests cover about 25% of the republic, while farmland and pasture cover more than 50%.

### HISTORY AND POLITICS

Serbian-led demands for the unification of South Slavic lands were a major contributing factor to the outbreak of World War I. In 1918 the "Kingdom of Serbs, Croats, and Slovenes" was formed under the Serbian king, PETER I. He was succeeded by ALEXANDER I in 1921. In 1929 Alexander formed a dictatorship, and renamed the country Yugoslavia. PETER II's reign was abruptly halted by German occupation (1941) in World War II. Yugoslav resistance to the fascist puppet regime was stout. The main resistance groups were the communist partisans led by Tito and the royalist *chetniks*. In 1945 Tito formed the Federal People's Republic of Yugoslavia. In 1948 Yugoslavia was expelled from the Soviet-dominated Cominform. Tito adopted an independent foreign policy. In domestic affairs, agricultural collectivization was abandoned (1953), and new constitutions (1963, 1974) devolved power to the constituent republics in an effort to quell unrest. Following Tito's death in 1980, the country's underlying ethnic tensions began to resurface. In 1986 Slobodan MILǑSEVIĆ became leader of the Serbian Communist Party. In 1989 Milǒsević became president of Serbia and called for the creation of a "Greater Serbia." Federal troops were used to suppress demands for autonomy in Albanian-dominated Kosovo. In 1990 elections, noncommunist parties won majorities in every republic, except Serbia and Montenegro. Serbian attempts to dominate the federation led to the formal secession of Slovenia and Croatia in June 1991. The Serb-dominated Federal army launched a campaign against the Croats, whose territory included a large Serbian minority. A cease-fire was agreed in January 1992. The EC recognized Slovenia and Croatia as separate states. Bosnia-Herzegovina's declaration of independence in March 1992 led to a brutal civil war among Serbs, Croats, and Bosnian Muslims. In April 1992 Serbia and Montenegro announced the formation of a new Yugoslav federation, and invited Serbs in Croatia and Bosnia-Herzegovia to join. Serbian military and financial aid to the Bosnian Serb campaign of "ethnic cleansing" led the United Nations to impose economic sanctions on Serbia. The threat of further sanctions prompted Milošević to sever support for the Bosnian Serbs. In 1995 Milošević signed the Dayton Peace Accord, which ended the Bosnian war. In 1996 local elections, the Serbian Socialist (formerly Communist) Party was defeated in many areas. In 1997 massive and prolonged public demonstrations in Belgrade forced Milošević to acknowledge the poll results. Later in 1997 Milošević resigned the presidency of Serbia in order to become president of Yugoslavia. In Montenegro, tension remains high between pro- and anti-independence factions. In 1998 fighting erupted in Kosovo between Albanian nationalists and Serbian forces. In 1999, following the forced expulsion of Albanians from Kosovo, NATO launched an air war against Serbia and Montenegro in order to prevent a humanitarian crisis.

### ECONOMY

Yugoslavia's lower-middle income economy has been devastated by civil war and sanctions (1992 GDP per capita, $4,000). Hyperinflation is one of the greatest economic problems. The war has also seen a collapse in industrial production. Natural resources include bauxite, coal, and copper. Oil and natural gas are exploited from the N Pannonian plains and the Adriatic Sea. Manufactures include aluminum, cars, machinery, plastics, steel, and textiles. Agriculture remains important.

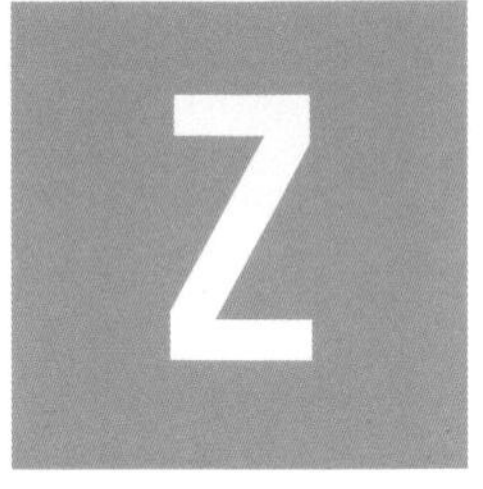

*Z/z, the 26th and last letter of the English alphabet and a letter also included in the alphabets of many other* W *European languages. It is derived from the Semitic letter* **zayin**, *which passed into Greek, where it was given its present form as* **zeta.**

**Zacharias, Saint** (d.752) (Zachary) Pope (741–52). He strengthened the Holy See and achieved a 20-year truce with the LOMBARDS. Along with St. BONIFACE, he established cordial relations with the FRANKS by supporting the accession of PEPIN III (THE SHORT) to the Frankish throne.

**Zacharias** Variant spelling of ZECHARIAH.

**Zagreb** Capital of Croatia, on the Sava River. Founded in the 11th century, it became capital of the Hungarian province of Croatia and Slavonia during the 14th century. The city was an important center of the 19th-century Croatian nationalist movement. In 1918 it was the meeting place of the Croatian diet, which broke all ties with Austria-Hungary. It later joined a new union with Serbia in what was to become Yugoslavia. In World War II, Zagreb was the capital of the Axis-controlled puppet Croatian state. Wrested from Axis control in 1945, it became capital of the Croatian Republic of Yugoslavia. Following the breakup of Yugoslavia in 1992, Zagreb remained capital of the newly independent state of Croatia. The old city has many places of historical interest, including a Gothic cathedral and a Baroque archiepiscopal palace. Zagreb is an academic center, containing a university (founded 1669) and an Academy of Arts and Sciences (1861). It is also the industrial and manufacturing heart of Croatia. Industries: steel, cement, machinery, chemicals. Pop. (1991) 726,770.

**zaibatsu** Large industrial conglomerates in Japan formed after the MEIJI RESTORATION (1868). Headed by powerful families such as Mitsui and Mitsubishi, they came to dominate the Japanese economy in the early 20th century. Though broken up during the US occupation after 1945, they subsequently reformed and reclaimed their dominant position.

**Zaire** Republic in W central Africa. *See* country feature, page 740

**Zaire River** *See* CONGO

**Zambezi** River in S Africa. Rising in NW Zambia, it flows in a rough "S" shape through E Angola and W Zambia. It turns E to form part of the Zambian border with Namibia and the entire border with Zimbabwe (including the VICTORIA FALLS). It crosses the widest part of Mozambique and turns SE to empty into the Indian Ocean. There is great potential for the generation of hydroelectricity along the river's course, and it has two of Africa's biggest dams: Kariba (Zambia-Zimbabwe) and Cabora Bassa (Mozambique). Length: 1,700mi (2,740km).

**Zambia** Landlocked republic in S central Africa. *See* country feature, page 741

**Zanzibar** Island region of TANZANIA, in the Indian Ocean, off the E coast of Africa; the capital is ZANZIBAR. The first European discovery was by Vasco da Gama in 1499, and the Portuguese quickly established colonial rule. In the late 17th century it came under the control of the Omani Arabs. It developed into the major center of the East African ivory and slave trade. The slave trade was halted in 1873, and in 1890 the sultanate of Zanzibar was made a British protectorate. In 1963 it became an independent state and a member of the British Commonwealth. Tension between the Arab ruling class and the indigenous Africans (who formed the majority of the population) led to the overthrow of the sultanate. In 1964 Zanzibar and Tanganyika merged to form the United Republic of Tanzania. Zanzibar retained control over domestic affairs. During the 1980s and 1990s, conflict developed between secessionist and mainland centralist forces. In 1993 a regional parliament for Zanzibar was established. The two largest population groups are the indigenous Hadimu and Tumbatu. The major religion is Sunni Muslim, and the main language is Swahili. The chief export is cloves and the biggest industry is fishing. Area: 641sq mi (1,660sq km). Pop. (1988) 375,539.

**Zapata, Emiliano** (1880–1919) Mexican revolutionary leader. Of peasant origin, he became leader of the growing peasant movement in 1910. His demands for radical agrarian reform, such as the return of *haciendas* (great estates) to native Mexican communal ownership, led to the MEXICAN REVOLUTION. In pursuit of "Land and Liberty," he opposed, successively, Porfiro DIAZ, Francisco MADERO, Victoriano HUERTA, and (with Pancho VILLA) Venustiano CARRANZA. His guerrilla campaign ended with his murder.

**Zaporizhzhya** City on the DNIEPER River, SE Ukraine. The area was settled in the 16th century by Zaporozhye Cossacks, leaders of the Ukrainian nationalist movement. In 1770 Zaporizhzhya was founded as a fortress, and in 1775 the Russian army of Catherine II forced the removal of the Cossacks. In the early 19th century, the fortress became a town, known as Aleksandrovsk until 1921. Zaporizhzhya consists of the old city and a new industrial area, development of which began in the 1930s with the construction of the Dneproges dam and a large hydroelectric plant. It is now one of the Ukraine's leading industrial complexes, producing aluminium, iron and steel, motor vehicles, and chemicals. Pop. (1991) 897,000.

**Zapotec** Native American group that inhabits part of the Mexican state of Oaxaca. The Zapotec built great pre-Columbian urban centres at Mitla and Monte Albán, and fought to preserve their independence from the rival Mixtecs and Aztecs until the arrival of the Spanish.

**Zaragoza** (Saragossa) City on the Ebro River, NE Spain; capital of Zaragoza province and Aragón region. The city was taken by the Romans in the 1st century BC and by Moors in the 8th century. In 1118 it was captured by Alfonso I of Aragón, who made it his capital. It was the scene of heroic resistance against the French in the Peninsular War (1808–09). Its main landmark is the Moorish palace of Aljafería. Other sites include the cathedrals of La Seo and El Pilar. The city is an important commercial and communications center. At the heart of an agricultural region, it acts as a distribution point for wine, olives, and cereals. Industries: heavy machinery, textiles. Pop. (1991) 586,219

**Zarathustra** *See* ZOROASTER

**Zealots** Jewish sect, active in opposition to Roman rule at the time of JESUS CHRIST and after. They refused to agree that Jews could be ruled by pagans, led resistance to the Roman census of AD 6, pursued a terrorist campaign, and played an important role in the rising of AD 66. Their activities continued into the 2nd century.

**zebra** Any of three species of strikingly patterned, striped, black-and-white, equine mammals of the grasslands of Africa; the stripes are arranged in various patterns, according to species. It has long ears, a tufted tail, and narrow hooves. Height: to 55in (140cm) at the shoulder. Family Equidae; genus *Equus*.

**zebu** (Brahman cattle) Numerous, domestic varieties of a single species of OX, native to India. Zebu have been used extensively in Asia and Africa, and have been introduced to the New World as livestock. Species *Bos indicus*.

**Zechariah** (Zachariah) Any of several biblical personalities. One of the most significant was a Jewish prophet of the late 6th century BC. He prophesied the rebuilding of the TEMPLE in JERUSALEM by the Jews who had returned from exile in BABYLON. In the Book of Zechariah, the 11th book of the 12 minor prophets of the OLD TESTAMENT, he described visions of four horsemen patrolling God's world, four horns symbolizing the destruction of Israel's enemies, and six other night visions prefiguring the coming of God in judgment. Many of Zechariah's images were taken up in the REVELATION of St. John the Divine. The other important Zechariah was the priest mentioned in the GOSPEL according to St. LUKE as the father of St. JOHN THE BAPTIST. According to the New Testament account (Luke 1), Zechariah was visited by the angel GABRIEL, who foretold the birth of John to Zechariah's wife Elizabeth. For doubting Gabriel's prophecy, Zechariah was struck dumb until the time of John's circumcision.

**Zedillo, Ernesto** (1951– ) President of Mexico (1994– ). Zedillo joined the Institutional Revolutionary Party (PRI) in 1971, and in 1994 ran for president after the PRI's candidate Luis Colosio was assassinated. He received just over 50% of the vote. He promised to combat unemployment and tackle the failing economy. Within a few months, however, he was forced to devalue the peso, despite his earlier successes in government finance.

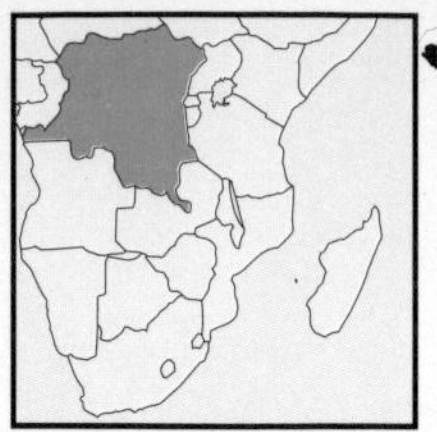

Congo (Zaïre) adopted a new flag in 1997 after Laurent Kabila rose to power. It is similar to the flag adopted immediately after independence was gained from Belgium in 1960. The blue represents the UN's role in securing independence for the country, and the six small stars stand for the original provinces of the independent state.

**AREA:** 905,365 sq mi (2,344,885sq km)
**POPULATION:** 42,552,000
**CAPITAL (POPULATION):** Kinshasa (3,804,000)
**GOVERNMENT:** Single-party republic
**ETHNIC GROUPS:** Luba 18%, Kongo 16%, Mongo 14%, Rwanda 10%, Azande 6%, Bandi and Ngale 6%, Rundi 4%, Teke, Boa, Chokwe, Lugbara, Banda
**LANGUAGES:** French (official)
**RELIGIONS:** Christianity (Roman Catholic 48%, Protestant 29%, indigenous Christian churches 17%), traditional beliefs 3%, Islam 1%
**CURRENCY:** Zaire = 100 makuta

The Republic of Zaire (renamed Democratic Republic of the Congo in May 1997) is dominated by the Congo River. The Congo basin is the world's second-largest drainage system. Behind a narrow Atlantic coastline, on the opposite bank of the Congo from Brazzaville, lies the capital, Kinshasa. North central Zaire consists of a high plateau, 3,300–4,600ft (1,000–1,400m) high, and includes the city of Kisangani. In the E, the plateau rises to 16,762ft (5,109m) in the Ruwenzori Mountains. Lakes Albert and Edward form much of the NE border with Uganda. Lake Kivu lies along its border with Rwanda. Lake Tanganyika forms the entire border with Tanzania. All the lakes lie in an arm of the Great Rift Valley. The S highland province of Shaba (Katanga) includes Zaire's second-largest city, Lubumbashi.

## Climate

Much of Zaire has an equatorial climate, which features high temperatures and heavy rainfall throughout the year. The S has a more subtropical climate.

## Vegetation

Dense equatorial rain forests grow in N Zaire. The S plateau is an area of savanna and swamps.

## History

By *c.*1000 AD, Bantu-speakers had largely displaced the native pygmy population. From the 14th century large Bantu kingdoms began to emerge. In 1482 a Portuguese navigator became the first European to reach the mouth of the Congo. In the 19th century slave and ivory traders formed powerful states. Henry Morton Stanley's explorations (1874–77) into the interior established the route of the Congo. In 1878 King Leopold II of Belgium employed Stanley to found colonies along the Congo. In 1885 Leopold proclaimed the foundation of the Congo Free State. Leopold's personal empire was gradually extended, and concessionaires were granted control of the lucrative rubber trade. Sir Roger Casement's denunciation of the inhuman exploitation of the native population resulted in international criticism. In 1908 Belgium responded by establishing direct control as the colony of Belgian Congo. European companies exploited African labor to develop the copper and diamond mines. Internal opposition to colonial rule was banned. In 1958 the French offered the Congo a free vote on independence. Nationalists in Belgium Congo demanded similar elections. In June 1960 independence was granted as the Republic of the Congo. Patrice Lumumba became prime minister. Belgium had not properly secured institutional changes and the state rapidly fractured. The mineral-rich province of Katanga demanded independence. Belgian troops, sent to protect its citizens and mining interests, were replaced by UN troops. In September 1960 Joseph Mobutu, commander-in-chief of the Congolese National Army, seized power. Lumumba was imprisoned and later murdered. In 1963 UN and government forces combined to force Katanga to drop its demands for secession. Following the withdrawal of UN troops in 1964, Belgian Congo was again plunged into civil war. Belgian troops once more intervened. In 1965 Mobutu proclaimed himself president. Mobutu began a campaign of "Africanization": Leopoldville became Kinshasa (1966); the country and river were renamed Zaire (1971); Katanga became Shaba (1972); and Mobutu adopted the name Mobutu Sese Seko. Zaire became a one-party state. Mobutu was reelected in uncontested elections in 1974 and 1977. Political repression and endemic corruption led to renewed civil war in Shaba (1977–78). Secessionist forces were again defeated with European aid. An ailing Mobutu, whose personal wealth was estimated at $5 billion, came under increasing pressure to reform. In 1990 he was forced to allow the formation of opposition parties, but national elections were repeatedly deferred. In 1995 millions of Hutus fled from Rwanda into E Zaire, to escape Tutsi reprisals. In 1996 rebel forces, led by Laurent Kabila, launched a successful offensive against Mobutu's regime. Mobutu was forced into exile. Zaire was renamed the country the Democratic Republic of the Congo. Kabila's presidency held out the hope of democratic reforms. In 1998 it was plunged into civil war between government forces and the Tutsi-dominated Congolese Rally for Democracy (RCD).

## Economy

Zaïre is a low-income developing country (1995 GDP per capita, US$490). It is the world's leading producer of cobalt and the second-largest producer of diamonds (after Australia). Copper is the major export. Zaïre has potential for hydroelectricity. A major economic problem is an inadequate infrastructure, especially the poor standard of the roads. Agriculture employs 71% of the workforce. Palm oil is the most vital cash crop. Other cash crops include cocoa, coffee, cotton, and tea. Food crops include bananas, cassava, maize, and rice. Corruption and hyperinflation are major obstacles to economic growth.

**Zeeman, Pieter** (1865–1943) Dutch physicist. He shared the 1902 Nobel Prize for physics with his teacher Hendrik LORENTZ for their 1896 discovery of the ZEEMAN EFFECT. He also detected the magnetic fields at the surface of the Sun.

**Zeeman effect** In physics, effect produced by a strong magnetic field on the light emitted by a radiant body; it is observed as a splitting of its spectral lines. It was first observed in 1896 by Pieter ZEEMAN. The effect has been useful in investigating the charge/mass ratio and magnetic moment of an ELECTRON.

**Zeffirelli, Franco** (1923– ) Italian theater, opera, and film director. He worked at London's Covent Garden on *Cavalleria rusticana*, at Stratford-upon-Avon on *Othello*, and on Broadway on *The Lady of the Camellias*. Renowned for their sumptuous and rich production, his films include *The Taming of the Shrew* (1966), *Romeo and Juliet* (1968), and *Brother Sun and Sister Moon* (1973). His major success, *Jesus of Nazareth* (1978), was originally made for television.

**Zeiss, Carl** (1816–88) German manufacturer of optical instruments. In 1846 he established a factory at Jena and made optical components, including lenses, binoculars, and microscopes.

**Zemin, Jiang** *See* JIANG ZEMIN

**Zen** Japanese school of BUDDHISM, initially developed in China, where it is known as Ch'an. Instead of doctrines and scriptures, Zen stresses mind-to-mind instruction from master to disciple in order to achieve *satori* (awakening of Buddha-nature). There are two major Zen sects. **Rinzai** (introduced to Japan from China in 1191) emphasizes sudden enlightenment and meditation on paradoxical statements. The **Soto** sect (also brought from China, in 1227) advocates quiet meditation. In its secondary emphasis on mental tranquillity, fearlessness, and spontaneity, Zen has had a great influence on Japanese culture. Zen priests inspired art, literature, the tea ceremony, and the NO DRAMA. In recent decades, a number of Zen groups have emerged in Europe and the US.

**Zend-Avesta** (AVESTA) Sacred book of ZOROASTRIANISM. The word *Zend* means tradition or commentary.

**Zenger, John Peter** (1697–1746) US printer and journalist, b. Germany. Editor of the *New York Weekly Journal* (1733), he attacked Governor William Cosby and was jailed for libel in 1734. He was later tried by a jury and acquitted. His case established truth as a defense for libel and made Zenger a symbol of the freedom of the press. He was public printer of New York (1737) and New Jersey (1738).

## ZAMBIA

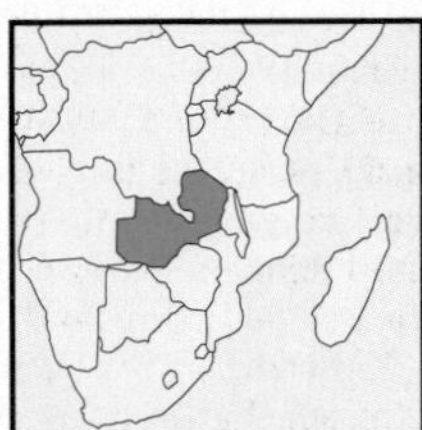

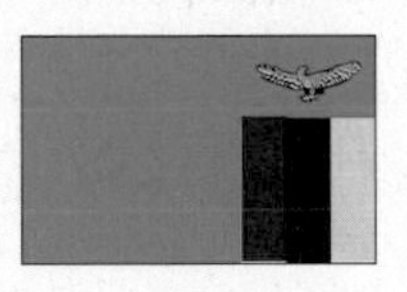

Zambia's flag was adopted when the country became independent from Britain in 1964. The colors are those of the United Nationalist Independence Party, which led the struggle against Britain and ruled until 1991. The flying eagle represents freedom.

**AREA:** 290,586 sq mi (752,614sq km)
**POPULATION:** 9,196,000
**CAPITAL (POPULATION):** Lusaka (982,000)
**GOVERNMENT:** Multiparty republic
**ETHNIC GROUPS:** Bemba 36%, Maravi (Nyanja) 18%, Tonga 15%
**LANGUAGES:** English (official)
**RELIGIONS:** Christianity (Protestant 34%, Roman Catholic 26%, African Christians 8%), traditional beliefs 27%
**CURRENCY:** Kwacha = 100 ngwee

The Republic of Zambia is a landlocked country in S Africa. Most of Zambia consists of a highland plateau between 3,000ft and 4,900ft (900m and 1,500m) high. The ZAMBEZI and Luangwa river valleys are the only low-lying areas. In the NE, the Muchinga Mountains rise above the flat plateau. The highest peak, 6,781ft (2,067m), lies close to the Lake TANGANYIKA border with Tanzania. Lake Mweru lies on the border with Zaire. Lake Bangweulu lies in the marshlands of Northern Province. The Zambezi forms Zambia's entire S border with Botswana and Zimbabwe. The spectacular VICTORIA FALLS and the man-made Lake Kariba lie on its banks.

### CLIMATE

Although Zambia lies in the tropics, temperatures and humidity are moderated greatly by altitude. The rainy season lasts from November to March. Rainfall is greatest in the N.

### VEGETATION

Grassland and wooded savanna cover much of Zambia. There are also several swamps. Evergreen forests exist in the drier SW.

### HISTORY AND POLITICS

In *c.*800 AD Bantu-speakers migrated to the area. By the late 18th century, Zambia was part of the copper and slave trade. The Scottish explorer David LIVINGSTONE made the first European discovery of Victoria Falls in 1855. In 1890 the British South Africa Company, managed by Cecil RHODES, made treaties with local chiefs. The area was administratively divided into NW and NE Rhodesia. Local rebellions were crushed. Intensive mining of copper and lead saw the development of the railroad in the early 1900s. In 1911 the two regions were joined to form Northern Rhodesia. In 1924 Northern Rhodesia became a British Crown Colony. The discovery of further copper deposits increased European settlement and the migration of African labor. In 1946 mineworkers formed the first national mass movement. In 1953 Britain formed the federation of Rhodesia (including present-day Zambia and Zimbabwe) and Nyasaland (now Malawi). In 1963, following a nationwide campaign of civil disobedience, the federation was dissolved. In 1964 Northern Rhodesia achieved independence within the Commonwealth of Nations as the republic of Zambia. Kenneth KAUNDA, leader of the United Nationalist Independence Party (UNIP), became Zambia's first president. Zambia was faced with problems of national unity, European economic dominance, and tension with the white-minority government in Rhodesia. Following his reelection in 1968, Kaunda established state majority holdings in Zambian companies. Zambia supported the imposition of economic sanctions on Rhodesia. In 1972 Kaunda banned all oppostion parties, and won the uncontested 1973 elections. In 1990 a new multiparty constitution was adopted. The Movement for Multiparty Democracy (MMD) won a landslide victory in 1991 elections. The MMD leader, Frederick Chiluba, became president. In 1993 Chiluba declared a state of emergency, following discovery of a UNIP coup attempt. Legislation excluded Kaunda from contesting the 1996 presidential elections. Chiluba was resoundingly reelected following a UNIP boycott. The government faced charges of electoral fraud. In 1997 a military coup was crushed. Kaunda was arrested and a state of emergency proclaimed. In 1998 Kaunda was freed and the state of emergency lifted.

### ECONOMY

Zambia is the world's fifth largest producer of copper ore, which accounts for 80% of exports (1995 GDP per capita, US$930). It is also the world's second largest producer of cobalt ore. The MMD's introduction of free market reforms has seen a large influx of aid and the reduction of national debt. Agriculture employs 38% of the workforce. Maize is the chief food crop. Cash crops include cassava, coffee, sugar cane, and tobacco.

**zenith** In astronomy, point on the CELESTIAL SPHERE that is directly overhead. The zenith distance of a heavenly body is the angle it makes with the zenith. It is diametrically opposite the NADIR.

**Zeno of Citium** (*c.*334–*c.*262 BC) Greek philosopher and founder of the STOICS. He attended lectures by various philosophers before formulating his own philosophy. Proceeding from the CYNIC concept of self-sufficiency, he stressed the unity of the universe and the brotherhood of men living in harmony with the cosmos. He claimed virtue to be the only good, and wealth, illness, and death to be of no human concern.

**Zeno of Elea** (495–430 BC) Greek philosopher. A disciple of Parmenides, he sought to reveal logical absurdities in theories of motion and change, using paradoxical arguments.

**zeolite** Group of aluminosilicates containing sodium, calcium, or barium, and loosely held water that can be continuously expelled on heating. Some zeolites occur as fibrous aggregates, whereas others form robust, non-fibrous crystals. Zeolites vary in hardness from 3 to 5 and in specific gravity from 2 to 2.4.

**Zephaniah** (active *c.*630 BC) OLD TESTAMENT prophet. He was named as the author of the Book of Zephaniah, the ninth of the 12 books of the Minor Prophets. He condemned Israel's religious and political corruption and stressed the certainty of God's judgment against Israel.

**Zeppelin, Ferdinand, Count von** (1838–1917) German army officer and inventor. He served in the armies of Württemburg and Prussia. While an observer with the Union army during the US Civil War, he made his first balloon ascent. In 1900 he invented the first rigid airship, which was called Zeppelin for him.

**Zernike, Frits** (1888–1966) Dutch physicist. In 1935 he developed the phase contrast microscope, in which objects being viewed (often living-cell biological specimens) take on a different color from their surroundings. For this work, he received the 1953 Nobel Prize for physics.

**Zeus** In Greek mythology, the sky god, lord of the wind, clouds, rain, and thunder. He is identified with the Roman god JUPITER. Zeus was the son of Rhea and Cronus, whom he deposed. Zeus was the supreme deity of the Olympians. He fathered huge numbers of children by his wives and others, often seducing goddesses, nymphs, and mortal women by taking the form of an animal.

**Zhao Ziyang** (1918– ) Chinese statesman who played a leading part in China's economic modernization. Zhao joined the Chinese COMMUNIST PARTY in 1938 and during the 1960s acted as party secretary of Guangdong province. He was dismissed by MAO ZEDONG during the CULTURAL REVOLUTION, but rehabilitated and restored to his post in 1971. In 1975 he was appointed party secretary of Sichuan province. Zhao introduced radical economic reforms, which vastly improved industrial and agricultural production. He was made premier in 1980. In 1987 LI PENG replaced him as premier and Zhao became general secretary. With the support of DENG XIAOPING, his liberal economic reforms moved China towards a market economy. In 1989 Zhao was dismissed from office and placed under house arrest for advocating negotiation with the pro-democracy demonstrators in TIANANMEN SQUARE.

**Zhejiang** (Chekiang) Province in SE China, S of the Yangtze River and on the East China Sea; the capital is Hangzhou. It was the center of the Sung dynasty in the 12th and 13th centuries. Many of Zhejiang's cities were razed during the Taiping Rebellion (1850–65). A mountainous region, it is one of China's most populous areas and includes the Zhoushan Archipelago. The province was designated a special economic zone to encourage inward capital investment. The major river is the Qiantang. Mount Tianmu is on the tourist and pilgrimage trails. Over a third of the region is pine or bamboo forest. The chief crops are rice and tea. Major industries include silk production and fishing. Area: 39,300sq mi (101,830sq km). Pop. (1990) 40,840,000.

**Zhengzhou** (Chengchow) City in E central China, 10mi (16km) S of the Huang He (Yellow) River; capital of Henan province. Capital of the Shang dynasty before 2000 BC, it has a walled city from that time. The present city grew with the railroad (1898) to become the main rail junction of E China. Industries: cotton, food processing, agricultural tools, thermal power. Pop. (1993) 1,690,000.

**Zhou** Chinese dynasty (1030–221 BC). After the nomadic Zhou overthrew the SHANG dynasty, Chinese civilization spread to most parts of modern China, although the dynasty never established effective control over the regions. The Late Zhou, from 772 BC, was a cultural golden age, marked by the writings of CONFUCIUS and LAO TZU. It was a period of rising prosperity. As the provincial states grew in power, the Zhou dynasty disintegrated.

**Zhou Enlai** (1898–1976) Chinese statesman. Zhou was a founder of the Chinese COMMUNIST PARTY. As a member of the Communist-KUOMINTANG alliance (1924–27), he directed the general strike (1927) in Shanghai. When CHIANG KAI-SHEK broke the alliance, Zhou joined the LONG MARCH (1934–35). He was the chief negotiator of a renewed peace (1936–46) with nationalist forces. After the establishment of a communist republic, Zhou became prime minister (1949–76) and foreign minister (1949–58). Although publicly supportive of the CULTURAL REVOLUTION, he protected many of its intended victims.

**Zhu De** (1886–1976) Chinese communist military leader. Zhu helped to overthrow (1912) the QING dynasty. In 1922 he met ZHOU ENLAI and joined the Chinese Communist Party. In 1928 Zhu joined forces with MAO ZEDONG, and led his section of the Fourth Red Army on the LONG MARCH (1934–35). Commander in chief during the Second Sino-Japanese War, he retained the post after the establishment of a communist republic (1949). Zhu held several important party posts before being denounced during the CULTURAL REVOLUTION.

**Zhukov, Georgi Konstantinovich** (1896–1974) Soviet military commander and politician. In World War II he led the defense of Moscow (1941) and defeated the German siege of Stalingrad and Leningrad (1943). In 1945 Zhukov led the final assault on Berlin. After STALIN's death, he became defence minister (1955). Although supportive of Nikita KHRUSCHEV's reforms, he was removed from office in 1957. He was rehabilitated in the 1960s, receiving the Order of Lenin in 1966.

**Ziegler, Karl** (1898–1973) German chemist. He shared the 1963 Nobel Prize for chemistry with Giulio Natta for research into POLYMERS. Ziegler discovered a technique that used a resin with metal ions attached as a catalyst in the production of POLYETHYLENE. He also researched aromatic compounds and organometallic compounds.

**ziggurat** Religious monument originating in BABYLON and ASSYRIA. It was constructed as a truncated, stepped PYRAMID, rising in diminishing tiers, usually square or rectangular. The shrine at the top was reached by a series of ramps. Ziggurats date from 3000–600 BC, and the one at UR still stands.

**Zimbabwe** Republic in S central Africa. *See* country feature

**zinc** (symbol Zn) Bluish-white, metallic element of Group II of the periodic table, known from early times. Chief ores are SPHALERITE, smithsonite, and calamine. Zinc is a vital trace element, found in erythrocytes (red blood cells). It is used in many alloys, including brass, bronze, and soft solder. It is corrosion-resistant and used in galvanizing iron. Zinc oxide is used in cosmetics, pharmaceuticals, paints, inks, pigments, and plastics. Zinc chloride is used in dentistry and to manufacture batteries and fungicides. Properties: at.no. 30; at. wt. 65.38; sp. gr. 7.133; m.p. 787.3°F (419.6°C); b.p. 1,665°F (907°C); most common isotope $^{64}$Zn (48.89%).

**Zinnemann, Fred** (1907–97) US film director, b. Austria. Zinnemann won his first Academy Award for the short film *That Mothers Might Live* (1938). He moved into commercial features, winning his second Oscar for the western *High Noon* (1952). Zinnemann won a third award for *A Man For All Seasons* (1966). Other films include *From Here to Eternity* (1953) and *Julia* (1978). His autobiography *A Life in the Movies* was published in 1992.

**Zion** Hill in E Jerusalem, Israel. Zion was originally the hill on which a Jebusite fortress was built. It now refers to the hill on which the TEMPLE was built. It is a center of Jewish spiritual life and symbolic of the Promised Land.

**Zionism** Jewish nationalist movement advocating the return of Jews to the land of Zion (Palestine). Though it represents a desire expressed since the Jewish DIASPORA began in the 6th century BC, the modern Zionist movement dates from 1897, when Theodor HERZL established the World Zionist Congress at Basel, Switzerland. In 1917 it secured British approval for its objective in the BALFOUR DECLARATION, and Jewish immigration to Palestine increased in the 1920s and 1930s. In 1947 the United Nations voted to partition Palestine between Jews and Arabs, leading to the foundation of the state of ISRAEL.

**zircon** Orthosilicate mineral, zirconium silicate ($ZrSiO_4$), found in IGNEOUS and METAMORPHIC rocks and in sand and gravel. It has prismatic crystals. It is usually light or reddish brown but can be colorless, gray, yellow, or green. It is used widely as a gemstone because of its hardness and high refractive index. Hardness 7.5; s.g. 4.6.

**zirconium** (symbol Zr) Grayish-white, metallic element, one of the TRANSITION ELEMENTS. Zirconium was discovered in 1789 by the German chemist Martin Klaproth. Its chief source is ZIRCON. Lunar rocks collected during the Apollo space missions show a higher content of zirconium than Earth ones, and zirconium exists in meteorites and stars, including the Sun. Chemically similar to titanium, it is used in ceramics and in alloys for wire and absorption of neutrons in nuclear reactors. Properties: at.no. 40; at.wt. 91.22; sp.gr. 6.51; m.p. 3,366°F (1,852°C); b.p. 7,911°F (4,377°C); most common isotope $^{90}Zr$ (51.46%).

**zither** STRINGED INSTRUMENT. It consists of a resonator in the form of a wooden box, with 30 to 45 strings stretched over it. A few of the strings are stretched over a fretted board for melody; the rest are used for accompaniment. The melody strings are plucked with the fingers or a plectrum.

**zodiac** (Gk. circle of animals) Belt on the CELESTIAL SPHERE that forms the background for the motions of the Sun, Moon, and planets (except Pluto). The zodiac is divided into twelve **signs**, which are named for the constellations they contained at the time of the ancient Greeks: Aries, Tau-

## ZIMBABWE

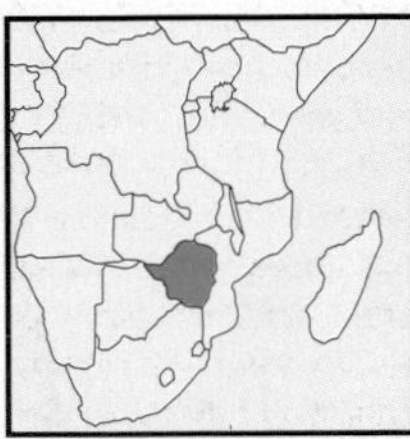

Zimbabwe's flag, adopted in 1980, is based on the colors used by the ruling Zimbabwe African National Union Patriotic Front (ZANU-PF). Within the white triangle is the Great Zimbabwe soapstone bird, the national emblem. In Bantu, Zimbabwe means stone house.

**AREA:** 150,873sq mi (390,579sq km)
**POPULATION:** 10,583,000
**CAPITAL (POPULATION):** Harare (1,184,169)
**GOVERNMENT:** Multiparty republic
**ETHNIC GROUPS:** Shona 71%, Ndebele 16%, other Bantu-speaking Africans 11%, Europeans 2%
**LANGUAGES:** English (official)
**RELIGIONS:** Christianity 45%, traditional beliefs 40%
**CURRENCY:** Zimbabwe dollar = 100 cents

The Republic of Zimbabwe is a landlocked country in S Africa. It mainly consists of a plateau 3,000–4,900ft (900–1,500m) high, between the ZAMBEZI and LIMPOPO rivers. The principal land feature is the High Veld, a ridge running from NE to SW. HARARE lies on the NE edge of the ridge. BULAWAYO lies on the SW edge. The Middle Veld is the site of many large ranches. Below 3,000ft (900m) is the Low Veld. Highlands lie on the E border with Mozambique.

### CLIMATE

The subtropical climate varies according to altitude. The Low Veld is much warmer and drier than the High Veld. November to March is mainly hot and wet. Winter in Harare is dry but cold.

### VEGETATION

Wooded savanna covers much of Zimbabwe. The Eastern Highlands and river valleys are forested. There are many tobacco plantations.

### HISTORY AND POLITICS

Bantu-speakers migrated to the region in AD 300. By 1200 the SHONA had established a kingdom in Mashonaland, E Zimbabwe. GREAT ZIMBABWE was the capital of this advanced culture. Portugal formed trading links in the early 16th century. In 1837 the Ndebele displaced the Shona from W Zimbabwe and formed Matabeleland. In 1855 David LIVINGSTONE made the first European discovery of VICTORIA FALLS. In 1888 Matabeleland became a British protectorate. In 1889 the British South Africa Company, under Cecil RHODES, was granted a charter to exploit the region's mineral wealth. Native revolts were crushed and the area became Southern Rhodesia (1896). In 1923 it became a British crown colony. European settlers excluded Africans from participation in the government and economy. In 1953 Southern Rhodesia, Northern Rhodesia (now Zambia), and Nyasaland (Malawi) became a federation. In 1961 Joshua NKOMO formed the Zimbabwe African People's Union (ZAPU). In 1963 the federation dissolved and African majority governments were formed in Zambia and Malawi. Southern Rhodesia became simply Rhodesia. Robert MUGABE formed the Zimbabwe African National Union (ZANU). In 1964 the white nationalist leader Ian SMITH became prime minister. Nkomo and Mugabe were imprisoned. In 1965 Smith made a unilateral declaration of independence (UDI) from Britain. The UN imposed economic sanctions. In 1969 Rhodesia became a republic. In 1974 Nkomo and Mugabe were released. Smith's refusal to implement democratic reforms intensified the guerrilla war between ZAPU and ZANU rebels and the Smith government aided by South Africa's apartheid regime. The 1979 Lancaster House Agreement established a timetable for full independence. ZANU won a decisive victory in February 1980 elections and Robert Mugabe became prime minister. In 1982 Nkomo was dismissed from the cabinet. Mugabe was decisively reelected in 1985. In 1987 ZANU and ZAPU merged. The post of prime minister was abolished as Mugabe became executive president. In 1988 Nkomo became vice president. Despite the formation of an opposition party, the Zimbabwe Unity Movement, Mugabe was easily reelected in 1990. In 1991 ZANU-PF abandoned Marxism. In 1996 Mugabe was elected for a fourth term.

### ECONOMY

Zimbabwe is a low income developing country (1995 GDP per capita US$2,030). The post-independence emigration of most of the white population removed vital capital. The government's redistribution of land to the African population via compulsory purchase schemes has been tainted by government corruption. Agriculture employs 70% of the work force. Zimbawe is the world's largest exporter of tobacco. Other cash crops include cotton, sugar, and beef. Corn is the main food crop. It has valuable mineral resources, especially around the Great Dyke, a low ridge that crosses the High Veld. Mining accounts for 20% of exports. Zimbabwe is a large producer of asbestos and fifth-largest producer of chromium ore. Gold and nickel are mined. In 1990 the government began to introduce free market reforms. The restructuring of the command economy has resulted in high unemployment. The servicing of national debt remains an economic problem.

▲ **Zola** Born in Paris the son of an Italian engineer, Émile Zola worked as a journalist before becoming a short-story writer and novelist. With Flaubert, the Goncourts, and Turgenev, he helped develop the "naturalistic school," which held that the novel should be strictly scientific. To this end he employed scientific techniques and observations in his novels, often describing professions and lifestyles in minute, and sometimes sordid, detail. He died by accidentally inhaling charcoal fumes from a blocked chimney.

rus, Gemini, Cancer, Leo, Virgo, Libra, Scorpio, Sagittarius, Capricorn, Aquarius, and Pisces. The constellations inside the Zodiac do not now correspond to those named by the ancients, because PRECESSION of the Earth's axis has meanwhile tilted the Earth in a different direction. To modern astronomers the zodiac has only historical significance. *See also* ASTROLOGY; ASTRONOMY

**Zola, Émile Edouard Charles Antoine** (1840–1902) French novelist. He became widely known following the publication of his third book, the novel *Thérèse Raquin* (1867). For the next quarter of a century he worked on what became the Rougon-Macquart sequence (1871–93), a 20-novel cycle telling the story of a family during the Second Empire; it established his reputation as the foremost exponent of the naturalistic school of fiction. The sequence includes his famous novels *The Drunkard* (1877), *Nana* (1880), *Germinal* (1885), and *The Human Animal* (1890). In 1898 he wrote a famous letter, beginning "*J'Accuse*," which denounced the punishment of Alfred Dreyfus. This led to a brief exile in England and, after the vindication of Dreyfus, a hero's return. *See also* DREYFUS AFFAIR

**Zollverein** German customs union formed in 1834 by 18 German states under Prussian leadership. By reducing tariffs and improving transport, it promoted economic prosperity. Nearly all other German states had joined the Zollverein by 1867, despite Austrian opposition. It represented the first major step toward the creation of the German empire (1871).

**zoo** (zoological gardens) Public or private institution in which living animals are kept and exhibited. Organized public zoos, sometimes called menageries or aquariums (for fish), have been operating for more than 500 years in Europe. Today nonprofit oganizations or zoological societies run most zoos in a scientific manner. They are organized for public recreation, as well as for scientific and educational purposes. The emphasis is on conservation of endangered species and exhibiting animals in natural settings.

**zoology** Study of animals; combined with BOTANY, it comprises the science of BIOLOGY. It is concerned with the structure of the animal and the way in which animals behave, reproduce, and function, their evolution, and their role in interactions with humankind and their environment. There are various subdivisions of the discipline, including ANATOMY, TAXONOMY, ECOLOGY, PALEONTOLOGY, and zoogeography (the distribution of animals). ANTHROPOLOGY is an extension of zoology. *See also* EMBRYOLOGY; GENETICS; MORPHOLOGY

**zoonosis** Any infection or infestation of VERTEBRATES that is transmissible to human beings.

**zooplankton** Animal portion of the PLANKTON. It consists of a wide variety of microorganisms, including COPEPOD and larval forms of higher animals. It is an important constituent of the ocean's food chain. There are few levels or areas of the ocean that have no zooplankton.

**Zoroaster** (*c*.628–*c*.551 BC) (Zarathustra) Ancient Persian (Iranian) religious reformer, founder of ZOROASTRIANISM. At the age of 30, he saw the divine being AHURA MAZDAH in the first of many visions. Unable to convert the petty chieftains of his native region, Zoroaster traveled to E Persia, where in Chorasmia (now in Khorasan province, NE Iran) he converted the royal family. By the time of Zoroaster's death (tradition says that he was murdered while at prayer), his new religion had spread to a large part of Persia. Parts of the AVESTA, the holy scripture of Zoroastrianism, are believed to have been written by Zoroaster himself.

**Zoroastrianism** Religion founded by ZOROASTER in the 6th century BC. It was the state religion of PERSIA from the middle of the 3rd century AD until the mid-7th century. Viewing the world as being divided between the spirits of good and evil, Zoroastrians worship AHURA MAZDAH as the supreme deity, who is forever in conflict with Ahriman, the spirit of evil. They also consider fire sacred. The rise of Islam in the 7th century led to the decline and near disappearance of Zoroastrianism in Persia. Today the PARSI comprise most of the adherents of Zoroastrianism, which has its main center in BOMBAY, India.

**Zulu** BANTU people of S Africa, most of whom live in KWAZULU-NATAL. They are closely related to the Swazi and the XHOSA. The Zulus have a patriarchal, polygamous society, with a strong militaristic tradition. Traditionally cereal farmers, they possessed large herds of cattle, considered to be status symbols. In the 19th century, under their leader SHAKA, they fiercely resisted colonialism. The predominant religion is now Christianity, although ethnic religions are still common. They are organized politically into the INKATHA movement under Chief Mangosutho BUTHELEZI.

**Zulu War** (1879) Conflict in South Africa between the British and the ZULU. Fearing a Zulu attack, the Afrikaners of Transvaal requested British protection. The British high commissioner demanded that the Zulu king, Cetewayo, disband his army. He refused, and the Zulu made a surprise attack at Isandhlwana, killing 800 British. Lacking modern weapons, the Zulu were checked at Rorke's Drift and decisively defeated at Ulundi.

**Zuni** PUEBLO Native Americans who live on the Zuni reservation in W New Mexico. The present pueblo is on the site of one of the seven Zuni villages discovered by Marcos de Niza in the early 16th century and identified as the mythical Seven Cities of Cibola. In 1540 CORONADO sacked the villages, and following a revolt in 1680 the Pueblo abandoned the site for fear of Spanish reprisal. Modern Zuni maintain their tradition and skills.

**Zurich** City on the Limmat River, at the NW end of Lake Zurich, in the foothills of the Alps, N Switzerland; the country's largest city. Conquered by the Romans in 58 BC, the city later came under Alemanni and then Frankish rule. It became a free imperial city in 1218 and joined the Swiss Confederation in 1351. In the 16th century it was a focal point of the Swiss REFORMATION. Ulrich ZWINGLI founded Swiss Protestantism at Zurich's cathedral in 1523. In the 18th and 19th centuries the city developed as a cultural and scientific center. It has the Swiss National Museum and many old churches. Zurich is the commercial hub of Switzerland and has numerous banking and financial institutions. Industries: motor vehicles, machinery, paper, textiles, electrical products, printing and publishing, tourism. Pop. (1991) 840,000.

**Zwingli, Ulrich** (1484–1531) Swiss Protestant theologian and reformer. He was ordained as a Roman Catholic priest in 1506, but his studies of the New Testament in ERASMUS's editions led him to become a reformer. By 1522 he was preaching reformed doctrine in Zurich, a center for the REFORMATION. More radical than LUTHER, he saw communion as mainly symbolic and commemorative. He died while serving as a military chaplain with the Zurich army during a battle against the Catholic cantons at Kappel.

**Zworykin, Vladimir Kosma** (1889–1982) US physicist and inventor, b. Russia, a pioneer of TELEVISION. In 1929 he joined the Radio Corporation of America (RCA), becoming its director of electronic development and (in 1947) a vice president. Zworykin and his colleagues developed the iconoscope, the forerunner of the modern television camera tube, and the kinescope, a CATHODE-RAY TUBE for TV sets. In 1928 he patented a color television system. He also invented the ELECTRON MICROSCOPE and developed a secondary emission multiplier for a sensitive radiation detector. In 1967 Zworykin received the National Medal of Science for his inventions and contributions to medical research.

**zygote** In sexual reproduction, a cell formed by fusion of a male and a female GAMETE. It contains a DIPLOID number of CHROMOSOMES, half contributed by the SPERM, half by the OVUM. Through successive cell divisions, the zygote develops into an EMBRYO.

**Zyuganov, Gennady** (1944– ) Russian politician. He moved up the Soviet Communist Party hierarchy in the 1970s and 80s, taking positions focused on ideology and propaganda. In 1993 he became chairman of the executive committee of the reconstituted Russian Communist Party and was elected to the State Duma (the lower house of the Russian parliament). In the 1995 parliamentary elections, the Communist Party gained the largest number of votes. Zyuganov mounted a strong challenge in the 1996 presidential elections, but was defeated by a coalition of Boris YELTSIN and Aleksander LEBED.

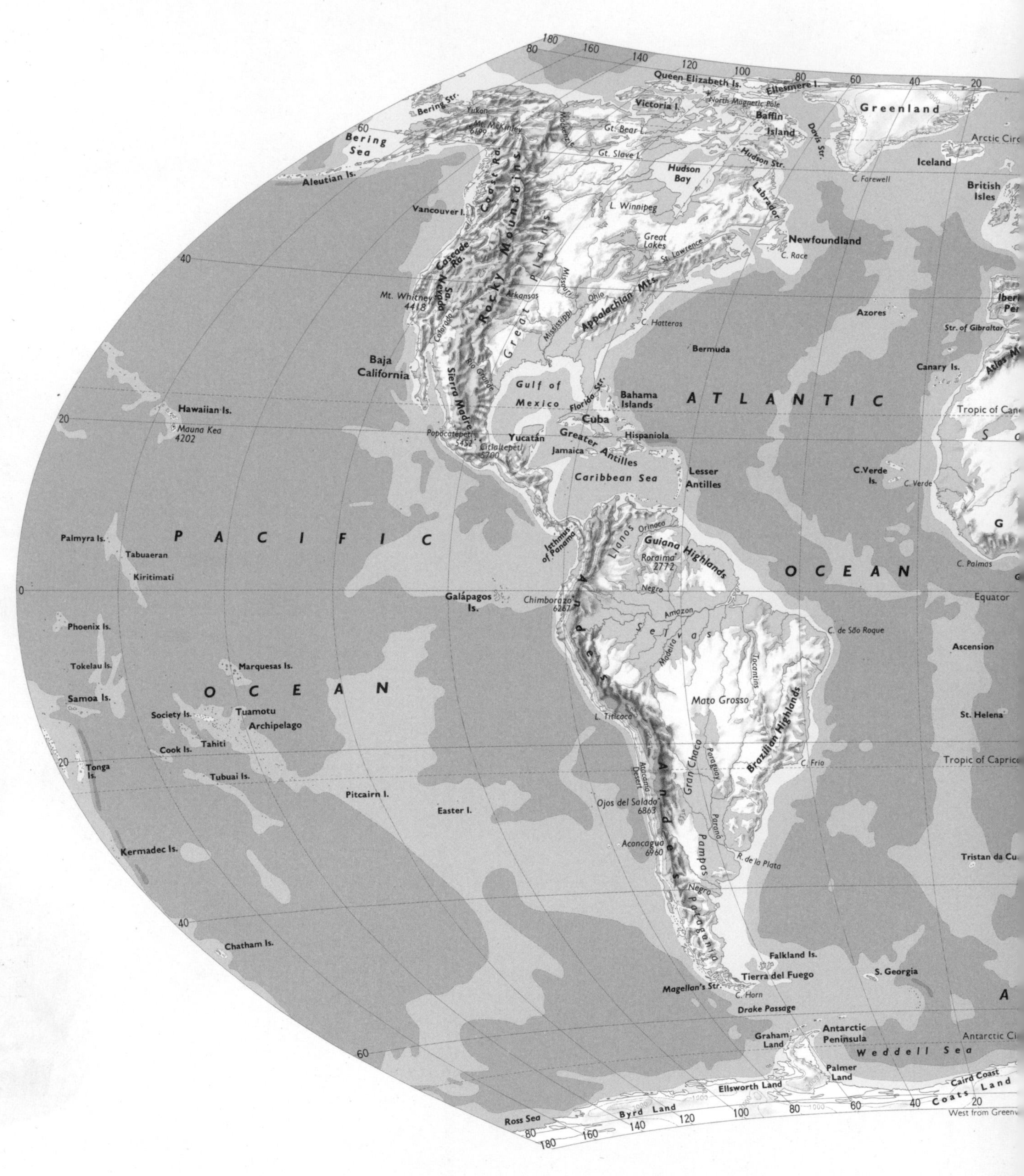

PACIFIC
OCEAN
ATLANTIC
OCEAN
Queen Elizabeth Is.
Ellesmere I.
Victoria I.
North Magnetic Pole
Greenland
Baffin Island
Davis Str.
Arctic Circle
Bering Str.
Bering Sea
Yukon
Mt. McKinley 6194
Gt. Bear L.
Gt. Slave L.
Hudson Bay
Hudson Str.
Iceland
Aleutian Is.
C. Farewell
British Isles
Vancouver I.
Coast Ra.
Rocky Mountains
L. Winnipeg
Labrador
Newfoundland
Great Lakes
St. Lawrence
C. Race
Cascade Ra.
Sa. Nevada
Mt. Whitney 4418
Great Plains
Missouri
Arkansas
Ohio
Appalachian Mts.
Mississippi
Colorado
C. Hatteras
Azores
Str. of Gibraltar
Bermuda
Baja California
Rio Grande
Sierra Madre
Gulf of Mexico
Florida Str.
Bahama Islands
Canary Is.
Atlas Mts.
Hawaiian Is.
Mauna Kea 4202
Cuba
Hispaniola
Tropic of Cancer
Popocatepetl 5452
Yucatán
Greater Antilles
Citlaltepetl 5700
Jamaica
Caribbean Sea
Lesser Antilles
C. Verde Is.
C. Verde
Palmyra Is.
Tabuaeran
Kiritimati
Isthmus of Panama
Llanos
Orinoco
Guiana Highlands
Roraima 2772
C. Palmas
Negro
Galápagos Is.
Chimborazo 6267
Equator
Amazon
Selvas
C. de São Roque
Phoenix Is.
Andes
Madeira
Tocantins
Ascension
Tokelau Is.
Marquesas Is.
Samoa Is.
Mato Grosso
Society Is.
Tuamotu Archipelago
Tahiti
L. Titicaca
St. Helena
Cook Is.
Brazilian Highlands
Gran Chaco
Paraguay
C. Frio
Tropic of Capricorn
Tonga Is.
Tubuai Is.
Atacama Desert
Pitcairn I.
Easter I.
Ojos del Salado 6863
Paraná
Kermadec Is.
Aconcagua 6960
Pampas
R. de la Plata
Tristan da Cunha
Negro
Patagonia
Chatham Is.
Falkland Is.
S. Georgia
Tierra del Fuego
Magellan's Str.
C. Horn
Drake Passage
Graham Land
Antarctic Peninsula
Antarctic Circle
Weddell Sea
Palmer Land
Caird Coast
Coats Land
Ellsworth Land
Ross Sea
Byrd Land
West from Greenwich